Oxford South African Concise Dictionary
SECOND EDITION

Oxford South African Concise Dictionary

SECOND EDITION

Edited by
The Dictionary Unit
for South African English

OXFORD
UNIVERSITY PRESS
SOUTHERN AFRICA

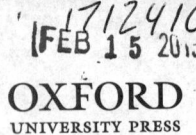

OXFORD
UNIVERSITY PRESS

SOUTHERN AFRICA

Oxford University Press Southern Africa (Pty) Ltd

Vasco Boulevard, Goodwood, Cape Town, Republic of South Africa
P O Box 12119, N1 City, 7463, Cape Town, Republic of South Africa

Oxford University Press Southern Africa (Pty) Ltd is a subsidiary of
Oxford University Press, Great Clarendon Street, Oxford OX2 6DP.

The Press, a department of the University of Oxford, furthers the University's objective of
excellence in research, scholarship, and education by publishing worldwide in

Oxford New York

Auckland Cape Town Dar es Salaam Hong Kong Karachi
Kuala Lumpur Madrid Melbourne Mexico City Nairobi
New Delhi Shanghai Taipei Toronto

With offices in

Argentina Austria Brazil Chile Czech Republic France Greece
Guatemala Hungary Italy Japan Poland Portugal Singapore South Korea
Switzerland Turkey Ukraine Vietnam

Oxford is a registered trademark of Oxford University Press
in the UK and in certain other countries

Published in South Africa
by Oxford University Press Southern Africa (Pty) Ltd, Cape Town

Oxford South African Concise Dictionary Second Edition
ISBN 978 0 19 598218 3

Based on the *Concise Oxford Dictionary* Tenth Edition © Oxford University Press 1964, 1976,
1982, 1990, 1995, 1999 with updates from the *Concise Oxford Dictionary* Eleventh Edition
© Oxford University Press 2006

© Oxford University Press Southern Africa (Pty) Ltd (text of the *Concise Oxford Dictionary*
Tenth and Eleventh Editions) 1999, 2006
© Dictionary Unit for South African English (additional South African entries and new entries
and meanings prepared for the *Oxford South African Concise Dictionary* First and Second
Editions) 2002, 2010

The moral rights of the author have been asserted
Database right in the *Concise Oxford Dictionary*, Oxford University Press
Database right in the additional South African entries and meanings and new entries and
meanings prepared for the *Oxford South African Concise Dictionary*, Dictionary Unit for South
African English

First published 2002 (*South African Concise Oxford Dictionary*)
Second edition 2010
Second impression 2011

All rights reserved. No part of this publication may be reproduced,
stored in a retrieval system, or transmitted, in any form or by any means,
without the prior permission in writing of Oxford University Press Southern Africa (Pty) Ltd,
or as expressly permitted by law, or under terms agreed with the appropriate
designated reprographics rights organization. Enquiries concerning reproduction
outside the scope of the above should be sent to the Rights Department,
Oxford University Press Southern Africa (Pty) Ltd, at the address above.

You must not circulate this book in any other binding or cover
and you must impose this same condition on any acquirer.

Publishing manager: Megan Hall
Managing editor: Phillip Louw, with assistance from Mary Reynolds
Editorial teams: see page vi
Editorial and cover assistance: Fred Pheiffer
Designers: Peter Burgess (A–Z), Sharna Sammy (extra matter and cover)
Dictionary development software: TshwaneLex
Computational assistance: TshwaneDJe HLT

Set in 7 pt on 7.1 pt Warnock by CBT Typesetting & Design cc (A–Z);
extra matter set by Baseline Publishing Services
Printed and bound by ABC Press, Cape Town
115571

Contents

Editorial Team	vi
Preface	vii
Guide to the Use of this Dictionary	ix
Abbreviations Used	xvi

The Oxford South African Concise Dictionary
A–L   1–700

Supplementary Pages
1	A History of English	SP 2
2	South African English	SP 6
3	English Uncovered	SP 8
4	Guide to Good English	SP 13
5	Countries of the World	SP 24
6	Prime Ministers and Presidents	SP 28
7	Kings and Queens	SP 30
8	Chemical Elements	SP 31
9	Greek Alphabet	SP 31
10	Metric Measures and Notation	SP 32
11	The Solar System	SP 34

M–Z   701–1388

Editorial Team

This dictionary was based on three important predecessors: the *Concise Oxford Dictionary Tenth Edition*, the *Concise Oxford Dictionary Eleventh Edition*, and the first edition of this dictionary under its original title, the *South African Concise Oxford Dictionary*. We are indebted to several teams for their work on those dictionaries and on this second edition of the South African dictionary.

Concise Oxford Dictionary Tenth Edition

Editor
Judy Pearsall

Chief science editor
Bill Trumble

Associate editors
Catherine Soanes
Angus Stevenson

Senior editors
Julia Elliot
Sara Hawker

Concise Oxford Dictionary Eleventh Edition

Editors
Catherine Soanes
Angus Stevenson
Sara Hawker

Corpus development and text processing
James McCracken

Word histories
Catherine Bailey
Julia Elliott

Pronunciations
Susan Wilkin

Science
Richard Lawrence
Liz Owen
David Shirt

Medicine
Jeremy Fairbank
Robin Ferner

Computing
Rowan Wilson

World English
Satarupa Chaudhuri
Tony Deverson
Heather Fitzgerald
Orin Hargraves
Bruce Moore

South African Concise Oxford Dictionary First Edition

Editor
Kathryn Kavanagh

Associate editors
Dorothea Mantzel
Tim van Niekerk

Jill Wolvaardt
Madeleine Wright

Oxford South African Concise Dictionary Second Edition

Editors
Tim van Niekerk
Jill Wolvaardt

Associate editor
Sheila Hicks

Contributing editors
Lorna Hiles
Dorothea Mantzel
Leela Pienaar
Mary Reynolds

Publishing manager
Megan Hall

Managing editor
Phillip Louw

Proofreaders
Annette de Villiers
Lorna Hiles
John Linnegar
Judy Norton
Elbert Visser

Preface

The second edition of this dictionary has been fully revised, updated, and redesigned, while keeping the features that made the first edition (published as the *South African Concise Oxford Dictionary*) so successful. The dictionary is intended for South Africans looking for a high-quality general English dictionary that also contains words and phrases that are mainly South African. Originally based on the tenth edition of the well known *Concise Oxford Dictionary*, it now includes updates from the eleventh edition of that dictionary. The team of lexicographers at the Dictionary Unit for South African English at Rhodes University has adapted the text of the *Concise Oxford Dictionary* for South African readers, amending or expanding definitions to make them relevant in the local context, and replacing items of peripheral usefulness with new words from general, as well as South African, English.

Features that are new to this edition of the *Oxford South African Concise Dictionary* include:

- many new words, for example *bucket list* and *social media*, and the South African *backyarder*, *leiwater*, and *mashonisa*
- supplementary material (in the middle of the dictionary) that includes a guide to good English, a history of the English language, a section on South African English, and useful tables of factual information
- an increased number of boxed notes to help users avoid many common mistakes in grammar, meaning, and usage
- word histories that trace the stories of some of our most interesting words and phrases.

In addition, a substantial guide to word formation is available as a supplement to this dictionary via Oxford's website. Its focus is words formed from suffixes such as *-archy* and *-graphy*, and it includes useful and fascinating tables of the many words formed from them (for example, *anarchy*, *matriarchy*, *biography*, *calligraphy*). The link is www.oxford.co.za/OSACD_word_formation

The hallmarks of the dictionary continue to be conciseness, clarity and accessibility, with ordinary, modern, unabbreviated English being used to explain technical and complex terms. Special attention has continued to be paid to technical and scientific vocabulary, and to keeping abreast of fast-moving fields such as computing and pharmacology. Rare, archaic and literary language is well represented.

Modern Oxford dictionaries are written and revised with the help of searchable databases containing hundreds of millions of English words in real contexts. The technology available now enables us to ensure that we have included all the words, phrases and meanings that form the central vocabulary of English in today's world. This makes current dictionaries much more likely to meet users' real needs – and to give space and attention to words that people actually want to look up. (See 'English Uncovered' on SP 8 in the middle pages to find out how dictionary writers keep track of developments in the language.)

Throughout its history, English has absorbed vocabulary from other languages. Many older words come from the Germanic languages (such as German and Dutch), French, Latin, and Greek. More recently, English has absorbed words from Arabic, Hindi, Italian, Spanish, Urdu, and Australian Aboriginal, Native American, and many other languages.

In the same way, South African English includes many words derived from the country's other languages. This dictionary includes words that have been fully assimilated into English, *and* words that might not be regarded as English, but which nonetheless are often found in local fiction, newspapers, and magazines, without any explanation of what they mean; it is simply assumed that South Africans will understand them. (See 'A History of English' and 'South African English' on SP 2–7 for a fuller account of this.)

The foundations for the research into South African English that underpins the *Oxford South African Concise Dictionary* were laid by the late Professor Bill Branford and his wife Dr Jean Branford. Their fascination for the special characteristics of English as it is used in South Africa and their scholarly work to record it set in motion the work of the Dictionary Unit for South African English (DSAE) at Rhodes University. In the forty years since it was established, the DSAE has continued the Branfords' work, firstly with Penny Silva, editor of *A Dictionary of South African English on Historical Principles* at the helm, and then under the experienced lexicographic hands of Kathryn Kavanagh, editor of the first edition of this dictionary. The current editorial team owes much to the work of these predecessors. Special mention should also go to Professor Rajend Mesthrie of the University of Cape Town, whose experience and knowledge of South African English in general, and of the Indian and township varieties within the language, have greatly assisted us.

To our host institution, Rhodes University, we owe a huge debt of gratitude. As an Associate Institute of the university, the DSAE continues to benefit from Rhodes's generous administrative support, as well as from the contributions of the many colleagues who willingly lend their technical expertise to help us with specialist terms. We are grateful too for the informed and enthusiastic support provided by the DSAE's Board of Directors, under the leadership of Professor Vivian de Klerk. Finally, the financial assistance the DSAE receives from the South African government, through the Pan South African Language Board, sustains the DSAE and enables it to continue its work of researching and documenting South Africa's own special variety of English.

Jill Wolvaardt and Tim van Niekerk

Guide to the Use of this Dictionary

This dictionary is designed to be as straightforward and self-explanatory as possible, and the use of special dictionary symbols and conventions has been kept to a minimum. Those that are used are explained in the following pages. The notes and the annotated sample entries that follow are designed to enable readers to understand the principles involved and the thinking behind the making of this dictionary.

Entry structure: core sense and subsenses

Within each part of speech, the first definition given is the core sense. This represents the typical, central, or core meaning of the word in modern standard English. The core meaning is not necessarily the oldest meaning, nor is it always the most frequent meaning, because figurative and extended senses are sometimes the most frequent. It is the meaning accepted by native speakers as the one which is most established as literal and central.

Each word has at least one core sense, which acts as a gateway to other, related subsenses. The relationship between core sense and subsense is indicated in the dictionary entry by placing the subsenses immediately after the core sense, and introducing each subsense with a solid arrow symbol. Many entries have more than one core sense. Each new core sense is introduced by a bold sense number, and each may have its own subsense or subsenses relating to it.

scorpion ■ n. **1** an arachnid with lobster-like pincers and a poisonous sting at the end of its tail. [Order Scorpiones.] ▸ used in names of similar arachnids and insects, e.g. false scorpion. **2** (**the Scorpions**) (in South Africa) the popular name for the Directorate of Special Operations, a special investigating unit focusing on organized crime and dissolved in 2009. ▸ used in names of governmental investigative units specializing in crime affecting specific sectors, e.g. the environment or water affairs: *Green Scorpions*, *Blue Scorpions*.
– ORIGIN Middle English: from Latin *scorpio(n-)*, based on Greek *skorpios* 'scorpion'.

The organization of core senses and subsenses is designed to show direct, logical relationships between the uses of a word. The aim is to help the user to navigate entries easily, find the relevant sense quickly, and build up an understanding of the ways in which different meanings of a word relate to each other.

Labels

Unless otherwise stated, the words and senses recorded in this dictionary are all part of standard English. Some words, however, are appropriate only to certain situations or are found only in certain contexts, and where this is the case, a label (or combination of labels) is used.

Register labels

Register labels refer to the particular level of use in the language – indicating whether a term is formal or informal, historical or archaic, and so on. The main register labels used follow.

formal: normally used only in writing, in contexts such as official documents
informal: normally used only by people when they are talking, or in informal writing
slang: informal language that is more common in speech than in writing, and is typically limited to a particular context or group
dated: no longer used by the majority of English speakers, but still encountered, especially among the older generation
archaic: old-fashioned language; not in ordinary use today, though sometimes used to give an old-fashioned effect and encountered in literature of the past
historical: still used today, but only to refer to some practice or artefact that is no longer part of the modern world, e.g. **cat-o'-nine-tails** or **rix-dollar**
poetic/literary: found only or mainly in poetry, or in literature written in a consciously 'literary' style
technical: normally used only in technical or specialist language, though not necessarily restricted to any specific subject field
rare: not in normal use
humorous: used with the intention of sounding funny or playful
euphemistic: used in place of a more direct or vulgar form
ironic: expressing meaning through language that means the opposite of what is being said, typically for humorous effect
dialect: not used in the standard language, but still widely used in certain local regions of the English-speaking world
offensive: likely to cause offence, especially racial offence, whether the speaker intends it or not
derogatory: intended to convey a low opinion or cause personal offence
vulgar slang: very informal language, especially that relating to sexual activity or bodily functions, which are widely regarded as taboo and may cause offence

Geographical labels

The main regional standards for the English language are British, US and Canadian, Australian and New Zealand, South African, Indian, and West Indian. The vast majority of words and senses listed in the dictionary are common to all the major regional standard varieties of English, but where important local differences exist, these are recorded.

The geographical label 'Brit.' implies that a word or sense is found typically in standard British English but not in standard American English nor South African English, though it may be found in other varieties. The label 'US' implies that the use is typically that of the USA, and is not standard in British English (nor, usually, in South African English), though it may be found in other varieties. But the 'S. African' label indicates that a word is used exclusively in South African English. Words like *trek* that were originally South African but have been assimilated into World English do not have a label.

Subject labels

Subject labels are used to indicate that a word or sense is associated with a particular subject field or specialist activity, such as Medicine, Aeronautics, or Cricket.

Grammar

Grammar is made explicit where it causes difficulty or is controversial, or is likely to be of special interest to the reader. The annotated entries on pages xii–xv include examples of the grammar support that the dictionary gives.

Spelling, inflections, and hyphenation

Spelling and inflections

This dictionary gives advice and information on spelling and inflections for words that are irregular or cause difficulty. The annotated entries on pages xii–xv illustrate this. More detailed notes on inflections are given in 'Guide to Good English' (SP 16 in the middle of the dictionary).

Hyphenation

Although standard spelling in English is usually fixed, hyphenation is not. In noun compounds, there are no firm rules to determine the use of one-word, two-word or hyphenated forms (except to show grammatical function). For example, **airstream**, **air-stream** and **air stream** are all found in standard texts. To save space, only one of the three forms is entered in this dictionary, but this does not imply that the others are incorrect. For guidance on the correct use of hyphens, see SP 22 in 'Guide to Good English' (in the middle of the dictionary).

Pronunciations

Pronunciations are given only when words are likely to cause problems for native or competent non-native speakers of English. The International Phonetic Alphabet (IPA) is used to represent the standard accent of English (generally considered to be the accent of people in the south of England). However, it is recognized that many variations of this are heard in standard speech in South Africa and elsewhere.

Easily-followed keys to the sounds that the symbols represent are given at the foot of each page.

Pronunciation of foreign words

Foreign words, or words borrowed from local languages, whether naturalized or not, are always given anglicized pronunciation, to represent the pronunciation used when mother tongue speakers of English use the words in an English context. For South African words that include click sounds, the anglicized pronunciation is given and is followed by an alternative with clicks.

Vowels

The short vowel sound in **gogga** is represented by this symbol: ɔ

Nasalized vowels are indicated with this sign: ~
ã au grat**in**   ɔ̃ cord**on** bleu
ɑ̃ arrondissem**ent**   ɔ̃ friss**on**

Clicks

Clicks in words from African languages are represented by the following symbols:

| (dental click) Mfecane   ! (post-alveolar click) mba**q**anga
‖ (lateral click) isi**X**hosa

xii

Find words quickly

Guide words show you the first and last entries on facing pages.

Letters on page-edges help you to find your way fast.

Find the right meaning

The core sense – the typical or central meaning – is given first, and is the gateway to related senses.

▶ introduces related subsenses, adding depth to your vocabulary.

Bold numbers introduce additional core senses.

■ clearly introduces each new part of speech.

Phrases and expressions enrich your range of fluent, idiomatic English.

Words derived from the root word extend your vocabulary.

Definitions of plants and animals are authoritatively backed up by their scientific names.

Hundreds of South African words and senses not found in most other dictionaries are defined.

Meanings of words belonging to particular subject-fields are labelled.

Numbers indicate separate entries for words with the same spelling but different meanings and origins. No confusion!

---

aardvark

A

aardvark /ˈɑːdfɑːk, ˈɑːdvɑːk/ ■ n. an African burrowing mammal, with long ears, a tubular snout, and a long extensible tongue, feeding on ants and termites. [*Orycteropus afer.*]
– ORIGIN C18: from S. African Dutch, from *aarde* 'earth' + *vark* 'pig'.

adaptor (also **adapter**) ■ n. **1** a device for connecting pieces of equipment. ▶ a device for connecting more than one plug at a time or plugs of a non-standard type to an electrical socket. **2** a person who adapts a text for filming, broadcasting, or the stage.

admit ■ v. (**admitted**, **admitting**) **1** confess to be true or to be the case. ▶ confess to or acknowledge (a crime, fault, or failure). **2** allow to enter. ▶ receive into a hospital for treatment. **3** accept as valid. **4** (**admit of**) allow the possibility of.
– DERIVATIVES **admitted** adj. **admittedly** adv.
– ORIGIN Middle English: from Latin, from *ad-* 'to' + *mittere* 'send'.

adopt ■ v. **1** legally take (another's child) and bring it up as one's own. **2** choose to take up or follow (an option or course of action). **3** Brit. choose as a candidate for office. ▶ formally approve or accept. **4** assume (an attitude or position).
– DERIVATIVES **adoptable** adj. **adoptee** n. **adopter** n. **adoption** n.
– ORIGIN C15 (*adoption* Middle English): from Latin, from *ad-* 'to' + *optare* 'choose'.

adult /ˈadʌlt, əˈdʌlt/ ■ n. a person who is fully grown and developed. ▶ Law a person who has reached the age of majority. ■ adj. fully grown and developed. ▶ of, for, or characteristic of adults.
– DERIVATIVES **adulthood** n. **adultly** adv.
– ORIGIN C16: from Latin *adolescere* (see ADOLESCENT).

ahead ■ adv. further forward in space or time. ▶ in advance. ▶ in the lead.
– PHRASES **ahead of 1** before: *we have a long drive ahead of us.* **2** earlier than planned or expected. **ahead of** (or **behind**) **the curve** (especially of a business or politician) ahead of (or lagging behind) current thinking or trends.

allocate ■ v. assign or distribute (resources or duties) to.
– DERIVATIVES **allocable** adj. **allocation** n. **allocative** adj. **allocator** n.
– ORIGIN C17 (*allocation* Middle English): from medieval Latin *allocare* 'allot'.

almond ■ n. **1** the oval edible nut-like kernel of the almond tree, growing in a woody shell. **2** the tree that produces this, related to the peach and plum. [*Prunus dulcis.*]
– ORIGIN Middle English: from Old French *alemande*, from medieval Latin *amandula*, from Greek *amugdalē*.

amakhosi /ˌamaˈkɔsi/ (also **amakosi**) ■ pl. n. S. African traditional leaders regarded collectively. See TRADITIONAL LEADER.
– ORIGIN pl. of isiXhosa and isiZulu *ink(h)osi* 'ruler, chief'.

askari /əˈskɑːri/ ■ n. (pl. same or **askaris**) **1** (in East Africa) a soldier or police officer. **2** (**Askari**) S. African historical an Umkhonto we Sizwe soldier who changed loyalties and joined the South African Police Force.
– ORIGIN C19: from Arabic *'askarī* 'soldier'.

asteroid /ˈastərɔɪd/ ■ n. **1** a small rocky body orbiting the sun. **2** Zoology an echinoderm of a class (Asteroidea) comprising the starfishes.
– DERIVATIVES **asteroidal** adj.
– ORIGIN C19: from Greek *asteroeidēs* 'starlike', from *astēr* 'star'.

bard¹ ■ n. **1** archaic or poetic/literary a poet, traditionally one reciting epics. ▶ (**the Bard**) Shakespeare. **2** (**Bard**) the winner of a prize for Welsh verse at an Eisteddfod.
– DERIVATIVES **bardic** adj.
– ORIGIN Middle English: from Scottish Gaelic *bàrd*, Irish *bard*, Welsh *bardd*.

bard² ■ n. a rasher of fat bacon placed on meat or game before roasting. ■ v. cover with bards.
– ORIGIN C18: from French *barde* in sense 'armour for the breast of a warhorse'.

CONSONANTS **b** but **d** dog **f** few **g** get **h** he

bastard /'bɑːstəd, 'bast-/ ■ n. **1** archaic or derogatory an illegitimate person. **2** informal an unpleasant or despicable person. ■ adj. **1** archaic or derogatory illegitimate. **2** no longer in its pure or original form.
— DERIVATIVES **bastardy** n.

battleaxe ■ n. **1** a large axe used in ancient warfare. **2** informal a formidably aggressive older woman.

blonde ■ adj. (also **blond**) (of hair) fair or pale yellow. ▸ having fair hair and a light complexion. ■ n. **1** a woman with blonde hair. ▸ informal, humorous a person, usually a woman, stereotypically perceived to be attractive but not intelligent. **2** the colour of blonde hair.
— DERIVATIVES **blondish** adj. **blondness** n.
— ORIGIN C17: from French, feminine of *blond*.

bokkie /'bɒki/ ■ n. S. African informal **1** an affectionate form of address, usually for a woman. **2** a girl. ▸ a girlfriend. **3** a small antelope or goat.
— ORIGIN Afrikaans: 'kid', diminutive of *bok* 'antelope, goat.'

boob¹ informal ■ n. **1** Brit. an embarrassing mistake. **2** N. Amer. a stupid person. ■ v. Brit. make an embarrassing mistake.
— ORIGIN C20: abbrev. of **BOOBY¹**.

boob² ■ n. informal a woman's breast.
— ORIGIN 1950s: abbrev. of **BOOBY²**, from dialect *bubby*; perhaps rel. to German *Bübbi* 'teat'.

bougainvillea /ˌbuːɡ(ə)n'vɪlɪə/ (also **bougainvillaea**) ■ n. an ornamental shrubby climbing plant widely cultivated in the tropics, with brightly coloured papery bracts surrounding the flowers. [Genus *Bougainvillea*.]
— ORIGIN named after the French explorer L. A. de *Bougainville*.

bouillabaisse /'buːjəˌbeɪs/ ■ n. a rich, spicy stew or soup made with fish, originally from Provence.
— ORIGIN French, from Provençal *bouiabaisso*.

carbonize (also **-ise**) ■ v. convert into carbon, by heating or burning.
— DERIVATIVES **carbonization** (also **-isation**) n.

catabolism /kə'tabəlɪz(ə)m/ (also **katabolism**) ■ n. Biology the breakdown of complex molecules in living organisms to form simpler ones, together with the release of energy; destructive metabolism.
— DERIVATIVES **catabolic** /katə'bɒlɪk/ adj.
— ORIGIN C19: from Greek *katabolē* 'throwing down'.

catalyse /'kat(ə)lʌɪz/ (US **catalyze**) ■ v. cause or accelerate (a reaction) by acting as a catalyst.
— DERIVATIVES **catalyser** n.
— ORIGIN C19: from **CATALYSIS**, on the pattern of *analyse*.

centilitre (US **centiliter**) (abbrev.: **cl**) ■ n. one hundredth of a litre.

centimetre (US **centimeter**) (abbrev.: **cm**) ■ n. one hundredth of a metre.

Cesarean (also **Cesarian**) ■ adj. & n. US spelling of **CAESAREAN**.

Esquimau ■ n. (pl. **Esquimaux**) archaic spelling of **ESKIMO**.

eunuch /'juːnək/ ■ n. a man who has been castrated.
— ORIGIN Old English: from Greek *eunoukhos* 'bedroom guard', from *eunē* 'bed' + a second element rel. to *ekhein* 'to hold'.

exacerbate /ɪɡ'zasəbeɪt, ɛk'sas-/ ■ v. make (something bad) worse.
— DERIVATIVES **exacerbation** n.
— ORIGIN C17 (*exacerbation* Middle English): from Latin *exacerbare* 'make harsh'.

extramural /ˌɛkstrə'mjʊər(ə)l/ ■ adj. (of a course of study) arranged for people who are not full-time members of a university or other educational establishment. ▸ additional to one's studies.
— DERIVATIVES **extramurally** adv.
— ORIGIN C19: from Latin *extra muros* 'outside the walls'.

fasciitis /ˌfasɪ'ʌɪtɪs, ˌfaʃɪ-/ ■ n. Medicine inflammation of the fascia of a muscle or organ.

faux pas /fəʊ 'pɑː/ ■ n. (pl. same) a social blunder.
— ORIGIN French, 'false step'.

fettuccine /ˌfɛtʊ'tʃiːneɪ, -ni/ (also **fettucini**) ■ pl. n. pasta made in ribbons.
— ORIGIN from Italian: pl. of *fettucina*, diminutive of *fetta* 'ribbon'.

xiii

Use appropriate language

Labels tell you if a word is formal, informal, offensive, etc. – vital for choosing words confidently. The labels are explained on page x.

Geographical labels enable you to distinguish local idiom from international English.

Check spelling

Every headword is an authoritative guide to modern spelling.

Acceptable variant spellings are given.

Spellings used in the US but not in formal British and SA English are labelled.

Variant spellings are cross-referred if they are alphabetically more than four entries away from the main entry.

Other variants, e.g. archaic or informal spellings are cross-referred to the main entry.

Pronounce words correctly

Selected words have easy pronunciation guides – excellent tools for fluency and confidence.

' before a syllable indicates where to place the primary stress, and ˌ shows where to place secondary stress.

Pronunciation guides use the International Phonetic Alphabet (IPA), the most accurate method for representing spoken sounds. The key to the phonetic symbols at the foot of every page makes it easy to interpret the guides. A guide to vowel sounds alternates with consonants.

See the guide to clicks and short and nasalized vowel sounds on page xi.

j yes **k** cat **l** leg **m** man **n** no **p** pen **r** red

xiv

Use the right inflections

Verbs with unusual or irregular tense forms have guides.

Verbs that inflect by doubling a consonant have guides.

Verbs ending in -y that inflect by changing -y to -i have guides.

Nouns with unusual plurals have guides.

Nouns ending in -y that form the plural with -ies have guides.

Adjectives that form the comparative and superlative forms by doubling a final consonant have guides.

Adjectives ending in -y and that take -ier and -iest have guides.

Where degrees of comparison often cause uncertainty, these are shown.

Use grammar and idiom well

Typical or compulsory language patterns are shown.

If a verb structure includes a direct object, this is shown in bold text.

Nouns that are plural in form but are normally used with a singular verb have a grammar note.

Nouns that you can use with a singular or a plural verb have a grammar note.

When an adjective is used postpositively (i.e. it comes after the noun it modifies) it has this label.

Noun senses in which the noun is normally placed before another noun to modify its meaning are indicated.

forgo

forgo (also **forego**) ■ v. (**-goes**; past **-went**; past part. **-gone**) go without (something desirable).
– ORIGIN Old English (see FOR-, GO¹).

forsake ■ v. (past **forsook**; past part. **forsaken**) chiefly poetic/literary abandon. ▶ renounce or give up.
– DERIVATIVES **forsakenness** n. **forsaker** n.
– ORIGIN Old English *forsacan* 'renounce, refuse', of West Germanic origin.

gad¹ ■ v. (**gadded, gadding**) (**gad about/around**) informal go around from one place to another in the pursuit of pleasure.
– ORIGIN Middle English: back-formation from obsolete *gadling* 'wanderer, vagabond', (earlier) 'companion', of Germanic origin.

gad² (also **by gad**) ■ exclam. archaic expressing surprise or emphatic assertion.
– ORIGIN C15: euphemistic alteration of GOD.

glorify ■ v. (**-ies, -ied**) 1 praise and worship (God). 2 describe or represent as admirable, especially unjustifiably or undeservedly. 3 [as adj. **glorified**] represented as or appearing more elevated or special than is the case: *the word processor is not merely a glorified typewriter*.
– DERIVATIVES **glorification** n. **glorifier** n.

gluteus /ˈɡluːtɪəs, ɡluːˈtiːəs/ ■ n. (pl. **glutei** /-tɪaɪ, -ˈtiːaɪ/) any of three muscles in each buttock which move the thigh, the largest of which is the gluteus maximus.
– DERIVATIVES **gluteal** adj.
– ORIGIN C17: modern Latin, from Greek *gloutos* 'buttock'.

goldfish ■ n. (pl. same or **-fishes**) a small reddish-golden carp popular in ponds and aquaria. [*Carassius auratus*.]

granary ■ n. (pl. **-ies**) 1 a storehouse for threshed grain. 2 a region supplying large quantities of corn: *Egypt was the granary of Rome*.
– ORIGIN C16: from Latin *granarium*.

grim ■ adj. (**grimmer, grimmest**) 1 very serious or gloomy; forbidding. ▶ (of humour) black or ironic. 2 unappealing, unattractive, or depressing.
– PHRASES **like** (or **for**) **grim death** with great determination.
– DERIVATIVES **grimly** adv. **grimness** n.
– ORIGIN Old English, of Germanic origin.

grumpy ■ adj. (**-ier, -iest**) bad-tempered and sulky.
– DERIVATIVES **grumpily** adv. **grumpiness** n.

handsome ■ adj. (**-er, -est**) 1 (of a man) good-looking. ▶ (of a woman) striking and imposing rather than conventionally pretty. 2 (of a thing) well made, imposing, and of obvious quality. 3 (of an amount) substantial; sizeable.
– DERIVATIVES **handsomely** adv. **handsomeness** n.
– ORIGIN Middle English: from HAND + -SOME¹; the original sense was 'easy to handle or use', hence 'apt, clever'.

holocaust /ˈhɒləkɔːst/ ■ n. 1 destruction or slaughter on a mass scale: *a nuclear holocaust*. ▶ (**the Holocaust**) the mass murder of Jews under the German Nazi regime in World War II. 2 historical a Jewish sacrificial offering burnt on an altar.
– ORIGIN Middle English: from Greek *holokauston*, from *holos* 'whole' + *kaustos* 'burnt'.

identify ■ v. (**-ies, -ied**) 1 establish the identity of. 2 recognize or select by analysis. 3 (**identify someone/thing with**) associate someone or something closely with. ▶ (**identify with**) regard oneself as sharing the same characteristics or thinking as (someone else).
– DERIVATIVES **identifiable** adj. **identifiably** adv.
– ORIGIN C17: from medieval Latin *identificare*, from late Latin *identitas* (see IDENTITY) + Latin *-ficare*, from *facere* 'make'.

linguistics /lɪŋˈɡwɪstɪks/ ■ **pl. n.** [treated as sing.] the scientific study of language and its structure.

links (also **golf links**) ■ **pl. n.** [treated as sing. or pl.] a golf course, especially one on sandy ground near the sea.
– ORIGIN Old English *hlinc* 'rising ground'.

manqué /ˈmɒŋkeɪ/ ■ adj. [postpos.] having failed to become what one might have been; unfulfilled: *an actor manqué*.
– ORIGIN C18: French, from *manquer* 'to lack'.

matchbox ■ n. 1 a small box in which matches are sold. 2 [as modifier] very small: *her matchbox apartment*.

| VOWELS | a cat | ɑː arm | ɛ bed | ɛː hair | ə ago |

peeping Tom ■ n. a furtive voyeur.
– ORIGIN from the name of the person said to have watched Lady Godiva ride naked through the English city of Coventry.

pelican ■ n. a large gregarious waterbird with a long bill and an extensible throat pouch for scooping up fish. [Genus *Pelecanus*: several species.]
– ORIGIN Old English *pellicane*, from Greek *pelekan*, prob. based on *pelekus* 'axe' (with ref. to its bill).

peninsula /pɪˈnɪnsjʊlə/ ■ n. a long, narrow piece of land projecting out into a sea or lake.
– DERIVATIVES **peninsular** adj.
– ORIGIN C16: from Latin *paeninsula*, from *paene* 'almost' + *insula* 'island'.

> **USAGE**
> Do not confuse the spellings **peninsula** and **peninsular**. **Peninsula** is a noun (*the end of the Cape Peninsula*), whereas **peninsular** is the adjectival form (*the peninsular part of Malaysia*).

pondok /ˈpɒndɒk/ (also **pondokkie** /pɒnˈdɒki/) ■ n. S. African a roughly built hut; a shack.
– ORIGIN Afrikaans, from Malay, 'hut, shed'.

quagga /ˈkwaxə/ ■ n. an extinct South African zebra with a yellowish-brown coat with darker stripes. [*Equus quagga*.]
– ORIGIN S. African Dutch, prob. from Khoikhoi, imitative of its braying.

ransack ■ v. **1** go hurriedly through (a place) stealing things and causing damage. **2** thoroughly search.
– DERIVATIVES **ransacker** n.
– ORIGIN Middle English: from Old Norse *rannsaka*, from *rann* 'house' + an element rel. to *sœkja* 'seek'.

safari ■ n. (pl. **safaris**) an expedition to observe or hunt animals in their natural habitat.
– ORIGIN C19: from Kiswahili, from Arabic *safara* 'to travel'.

thug ■ n. a violent and uncouth man, especially a criminal.
– DERIVATIVES **thuggery** n. **thuggish** adj. **thuggishly** adv. **thuggishness** n.

> **HISTORY**
> **Thug** comes from the Hindi word *ṭhag* 'swindler, thief', and beyond that goes back to ancient Sanskrit. The original Thugs were an organization of robbers and assassins in India, followers of the goddess Kali, who waylaid and strangled their victims in a ritually prescribed manner. The modern sense, denoting any violent man, was first recorded in 1839.

tik (also **tik-tik**) S. African ■ n. methamphetamine. ■ v. (**tikked**, **tikking**) informal use methamphetamine.
– DERIVATIVES **tikker** n.
– ORIGIN from Afrikaans *tik* 'click, tick', imitative of the sound emitted when smoked.

ventral ■ adj. Anatomy, Zoology, & Botany on or relating to the underside of an animal or plant; abdominal. Compare with **DORSAL**.
– DERIVATIVES **ventrally** adv.
– ORIGIN Middle English: from Latin *venter*, *ventr-* 'belly'.

vitamin C ■ n. another term for **ASCORBIC ACID**.

watt (abbrev.: **W**) ■ n. the SI unit of power, equivalent to one joule per second, corresponding to the rate of energy in an electric circuit where the potential difference is one volt and the current one ampere.
– ORIGIN C19: named after the Scottish engineer James Watt.

WHO ■ abbrev. World Health Organization.

who ■ pron. **1** [interrog. pron.] what or which person or people. **2** [rel. pron.] introducing a clause giving further information about a person or people previously mentioned. ▸ archaic the person that; whoever.
– ORIGIN Old English *hwā*, of Germanic origin.

> **USAGE**
> According to formal grammar, **who** forms the subjective case, while **whom** forms the objective case and so should be used in object position in a sentence. In modern English there are many speakers who rarely use **whom** at all, employing **who** in all contexts; today this use is broadly accepted in standard English.

ə: her ɪ sit i cosy iː see ɒ hot ɔː saw ʌ run

Abbreviations Used

Abbreviations in general use, such as 'etc.', 'i.e.', and 'p.m.', are listed and explained as entries in the dictionary itself.

abbrev.	abbreviation	neg.	negative
adj.	adjective	NZ	New Zealand
adv.	adverb	orig.	originally
Amer.	American	part.	participle
Austral.	Australian	phr.	phrase
Austral./NZ	Australian and New Zealand	phrs	phrases
		pl.	plural
aux.	auxiliary	possess.	possessive
b.	born	postpos.	postpositive
Brit.	British	predet.	predeterminer
C (as in C18 etc.)	century	prep.	preposition
cf.	compare with	prob.	probably
comb. form	combining form	pron.	pronoun
conj.	conjunction	pronunc.	pronunciation
contr.	contraction	ref.	reference
det.	determiner	rel.	related
E.	East	S.	South
eccles.	ecclesiastical	S. African	South African
exclam.	exclamation	sing.	singular
fem.	feminine	symb.	symbol
freq.	frequently	US	United States (of America)
imper.	imperative		
interrog.	interrogative	usu.	usually
masc.	masculine	v.	verb
n.	noun	var.	variant
N.	North	vars	variants
N. Amer.	North American	W.	West
N. English	Northern English	W. Indian	West Indian

Note on trademarks and proprietary status

This dictionary includes some words which have, or are asserted to have, proprietary status as trademarks or otherwise. Their inclusion does not imply that they have acquired for legal purposes a non-proprietary or general significance, nor any other judgement concerning their legal status. In cases where the editorial staff have some evidence that a word has proprietary status, this is indicated in the entry for that word by the label trademark, but no judgement concerning the legal status of such words is made or implied thereby.

Aa

Æ (also **æ**) ■ n. a letter used in Old English to represent a vowel intermediate between a and e (see **ASH**²).

A¹ (also **a**) ■ n. (pl. **As** or **A's**) **1** the first letter of the alphabet. **2** denoting the first, best, or most important in a set. **3** Music the sixth note of the diatonic scale of C major, having a standard frequency of 440 Hz. **4** the human blood type (in the ABO system) containing the A antigen and lacking the B.
– PHRASES **from A to B** from one's starting point to one's destination. **from A to Z** over the entire range.

A² ■ abbrev. **1** (in card games) ace. **2** (in showing goals or points conceded) against. **3** ampere(s). **4** (Å) ångstrom(s). **5** answer.

a¹ (**an** before a vowel sound) ■ det. **1** used when mentioning someone or something for the first time; the indefinite article. ▶ one single: *a hundred*. ▶ used when mentioning someone one does not know. ▶ someone like (the name specified). **2** per: *typing 60 words a minute*.
– ORIGIN Middle English: weak form of Old English *ān* 'one'.

a² ■ abbrev. **1** (in travel timetables) arrives. **2** atto- (10⁻¹⁸). **3** (with reference to sporting fixtures) away. **4** (used before a date) before. [from Latin *ante*.] ■ symb. (*a*) Physics acceleration.

-a¹ ■ suffix forming: **1** ancient or Latinized modern names of animals and plants: *primula*. **2** names of oxides: *baryta*. **3** geographical names: *Africa*. **4** ancient or Latinized modern feminine forenames: *Lydia*. **5** nouns from Italian, Portuguese, and Spanish: *stanza*.
– ORIGIN representing a Greek, Latin, or Romance feminine sing.

-a² ■ suffix forming plural nouns: **1** from Greek or Latin neuter plurals corresponding to a singular in *-um* or *-on* (such as *addenda*, *phenomena*). **2** in names (often from modern Latin) of zoological groups: *Insectivora*.

-a³ ■ suffix informal **1** of: *coupla*. **2** have: *mighta*. **3** to: *oughta*.
– ORIGIN representing a casual pronunciation.

a-¹ (often **an-** before a vowel) ■ prefix not; without: *atheistic*.
– ORIGIN from Greek.

a-² ■ prefix **1** to; towards: *aside*. **2** in the process of: *a-hunting*. ▶ in a specified state: *aflutter*.
– ORIGIN Old English, unstressed form of **ON**.

a-³ ■ prefix variant spelling of **AD-** before *sc*, *sp*, and *st* (as in *ascend*, *aspire* and *astringent*).

a-⁴ ■ prefix **1** of: *anew*. **2** utterly: *abash*.
– ORIGIN unstressed form of **OF** (sense 1); Anglo-Norman French *a-*, from Latin *ex*.

A1 ■ adj. informal excellent.

A3 ■ n. a standard size of paper, 420 × 297 mm.

A4 ■ n. a standard size of paper, 297 × 210 mm.

A5 ■ n. a standard size of paper, 210 × 148 mm.

AA ■ abbrev. **1** Alcoholics Anonymous. **2** anti-aircraft. **3** Automobile Association.

aa /ˈɑːɑː/ ■ n. Geology basaltic lava forming very rough, jagged masses with a light frothy texture. Often contrasted with **PAHOEHOE**.
– ORIGIN C19: from Hawaiian *'a-'a*.

AAM ■ abbrev. air-to-air missile.

aardvark /ˈɑːdfɑːk, ˈɑːdvɑːk/ ■ n. an African burrowing mammal, with long ears, a tubular snout, and a long extensible tongue, feeding on ants and termites. [*Orycteropus afer*.]
– ORIGIN C18: from S. African Dutch, from *aarde* 'earth' + *vark* 'pig'.

aardwolf /ˈɑːdwʊlf, ˈɑːdvʊlf/ ■ n. (pl. **aardwolves**) a black-striped African mammal of the hyena family, feeding mainly on termites. [*Proteles cristatus*.]
– ORIGIN C19: from S. African Dutch, from *aarde* 'earth' + *wolf* 'wolf'.

aargh /ɑː/ ■ exclam. an expression of anguish, horror, rage, or other strong emotion.

Aaron's beard /ˈɛːrən/ ■ n. a name given to the rose of Sharon and other plants.
– ORIGIN C19: alluding to the long beard of *Aaron* in the Bible, because of the hairy stamens of such plants.

Aaron's rod ■ n. the great mullein. [*Verbascum thapsus*.]
– ORIGIN C18: alluding to *Aaron* in the Bible, whose staff was said to have flowered (Numbers 17:8).

AB¹ ■ n. the human blood type (in the ABO system) containing both the A and B antigens.

AB² ■ abbrev. **1** able seaman. **2** US Bachelor of Arts. [from Latin *Artium Baccalaureus*.]

Ab ■ abbrev. Biology antibody.

ab ■ n. informal an abdominal muscle.

ab- (also **abs-**) ■ prefix away; from: *abdicate*.
– ORIGIN from Latin.

aback ■ adv. Nautical with the sail pressed back against the mast by a headwind.
– PHRASES **take someone aback** shock or surprise someone.
– ORIGIN Old English (see **a-²**, **BACK**).

abacus /ˈabəkəs/ ■ n. (pl. **abacuses**) **1** a frame with rows of wires or grooves along which beads are slid, used for calculating. **2** Architecture the flat slab on top of a capital, supporting the architrave.
– ORIGIN Middle English: from Greek *abax*, *abak-* 'slab, drawing board', of Semitic origin.

abaft /əˈbɑːft/ ■ adv. & prep. Nautical in or behind the stern of a ship.
– ORIGIN Middle English: from **a-²** + archaic *baft* 'in the rear'.

abakhwetha /ˌɑbəˈkwɛːtə, ˌɑbʌˈkwɛːtʌ/ (also **abakhethas**) ■ pl. n. (sing. **umkhwetha**) young Xhosa men who are being initiated into manhood at a circumcision school.
– ORIGIN from isiXhosa *umkhwetha* 'initiate', pl. *abakhwetha*.

abalone /ˌabəˈləʊni/ ■ n. an edible mollusc of warm seas, with a shallow ear-shaped shell lined with mother-of-pearl. [Genus *Haliotis*.]
– ORIGIN C19: from American Spanish *abulones*, pl. of *abulón*, from *aulón*, the name for California in an American Indian language.

abandon ■ v. **1** give up (an action or practice) completely. **2** desert or leave permanently. **3** (**abandon oneself to**) indulge in (a desire or impulse) without restraint. ▶ [as adj. **abandoned**] unrestrained; uninhibited: *a wild, abandoned dance*. ■ n. complete lack of inhibition or restraint.
– PHRASES **abandon ship** leave a ship because it is sinking.
– DERIVATIVES **abandonment** n.
– ORIGIN Middle English: from Old French *abandoner*, from *a-* 'to, at' + *bandon* 'control'.

abase /əˈbeɪs/ ■ v. belittle or degrade.
– DERIVATIVES **abasement** n.
– ORIGIN Middle English: from Old French *abaissier*, from *a-* 'to, at' + *baissier* 'to lower'.

abash ■ v. [usu. as adj. **abashed**] cause to feel embarrassed, disconcerted, or ashamed.
– ORIGIN Middle English: from Anglo-Norman French *abaiss-*, from Old French *esbair*, from *es-* 'utterly' + *bair* 'astound'.

abate /əˈbeɪt/ ■ v. **1** (of something bad) become less intense or widespread. **2** Law reduce or remove (a nuisance).
– DERIVATIVES **abatement** n.
– ORIGIN Middle English: from Old French *abatre* 'to fell', from Latin *battuere* 'to beat'.

abattoir /ˈabətwɑː/ ■ n. a slaughterhouse.
– ORIGIN C19: from French, from *abattre* 'to fell'.

abaxial

abaxial /ab'aksɪəl/ ■ adj. Botany facing away from the stem (in particular denoting the lower surface of a leaf). The opposite of ADAXIAL.

abaya /ə'beɪjə/ ■ n. a full-length, sleeveless outer garment worn by Arabs.
– ORIGIN C19: from Arabic *'abāya*.

Abba /'abə/ ■ n. **1** (in the New Testament) God as father. **2** (in the Syrian Orthodox and Coptic Churches) a title given to bishops and patriarchs.
– ORIGIN from Aramaic *'abbā* 'father'.

abba ■ v. (**abbaed**, **abbaing**) S. African carry (a child) on one's back.
– ORIGIN Afrikaans, from Khoikhoi *awa*.

abbacy /'abəsi/ ■ n. (pl. **-ies**) the office of an abbot or abbess.
– ORIGIN Middle English: from eccles. Latin *abbacia*, from *abbas* (see ABBOT).

abbé /'abeɪ/ ■ n. (in France) an abbot or other cleric.
– ORIGIN C16: French, from eccles. Latin *abbas* (see ABBOT).

abbess /'abɛs/ ■ n. a woman who is the head of an abbey of nuns.
– ORIGIN Middle English: from Old French *abbesse* 'female abbot'.

abbey ■ n. (pl. **-eys**) an establishment occupied by a community of monks or nuns.
– ORIGIN Middle English: from Old French *abbeie*, from medieval Latin *abbatia* 'abbacy'.

abbot ■ n. a man who is the head of an abbey of monks.
– DERIVATIVES **abbotship** n.
– ORIGIN Old English, from eccles. Latin *abbas*, from Aramaic *'abbā* (see ABBA).

abbreviate /ə'briːvɪeɪt/ ■ v. shorten (a word, phrase, or text).
– DERIVATIVES **abbreviation** n.
– ORIGIN Middle English: from late Latin *abbreviare* 'shorten', from Latin *brevis* 'short'.

ABC¹ ■ n. **1** the alphabet. **2** an alphabetical guide. ▶ the rudiments of a subject.

ABC² ■ abbrev. American (or Australian) Broadcasting Company.

abdabs ■ pl. n. Brit. informal (often in phr. **the screaming abdabs**) nervous anxiety or irritation.
– ORIGIN 1940s.

abdas /'abdas/ ■ n. S. African the ceremonial washing of a corpse, practised by Cape Muslims.
– ORIGIN from Persian *ābdast* 'ablution before prayer', from *āb* 'water' + *dast* 'hand'.

abdicate /'abdɪkeɪt/ ■ v. **1** (of a monarch) renounce the throne. **2** fail to fulfil or undertake (a duty).
– DERIVATIVES **abdication** n. **abdicator** n.
– ORIGIN C16: from Latin *abdicare* 'renounce', from *ab-* 'away, from' + *dicare* 'declare'.

abdomen /'abdəmən, ab'dəʊmən/ ■ n. the part of the body containing the digestive and reproductive organs; the belly. ▶ Zoology the hinder part of the body of an arthropod.
– ORIGIN C16: from Latin.

abdominal /ab'dɒmɪn(ə)l/ ■ adj. relating to the abdomen. ■ n. an abdominal muscle.
– DERIVATIVES **abdominally** adv.

abduct ■ v. **1** take (someone) away illegally by force or deception. **2** Physiology (of a muscle) move (a limb or part) away from the midline of the body or from another part. The opposite of ADDUCT¹.
– DERIVATIVES **abductee** n. **abduction** n. **abductor** n.
– ORIGIN C17: from Latin *abducere* 'lead away'.

abed ■ adv. archaic in bed.

abelia /ə'biːlɪə/ ■ n. an East Asian shrub of the honeysuckle family. [Genus *Abelia*.]
– ORIGIN named after the English botanist Clarke Abel (1780–1826).

Aberdeen Angus ■ n. a breed of hornless black beef cattle originating in Scotland.

aberrant /ə'bɛr(ə)nt/ ■ adj. departing from an accepted standard. ▶ chiefly Biology diverging from the normal type.
– DERIVATIVES **aberrance** n. **aberrancy** n. **aberrantly** adv.

aberration /ˌabə'reɪʃ(ə)n/ ■ n. an unwelcome or unacceptable deviation from what is normal. ▶ Biology a characteristic that deviates from the normal type. ▶ Optics the failure of rays to converge at one focus because of a defect in a lens or mirror. ▶ Astronomy the apparent displacement of a celestial object from its true position, caused by the relative motion of the observer and the object.
– DERIVATIVES **aberrational** adj.
– ORIGIN C16: from Latin, from *aberrare* 'to stray'.

ABET ■ abbrev. (in South Africa) Adult Basic Education and Training.

abet /ə'bɛt/ ■ v. (**abetted**, **abetting**) (usu. in phr. **aid and abet**) encourage or assist (someone) to do something wrong, in particular to commit a crime.
– DERIVATIVES **abetment** n. **abetter** (also **abettor**) n.
– ORIGIN Middle English: from Old French *abeter*, from *a-* 'to, at' + *beter* 'hound, urge on'.

abeyance /ə'beɪəns/ ■ n. a state of temporary disuse or suspension. ▶ Law the position of being without an owner or claimant.
– DERIVATIVES **abeyant** adj.
– ORIGIN C16: from Old French *abeance* 'aspiration to a title', from *abeer* 'aspire after'.

abhor /əb'hɔː/ ■ v. (**abhorred**, **abhorring**) detest; hate.
– DERIVATIVES **abhorrer** n.
– ORIGIN Middle English: from Latin *abhorrere*, from *ab-* 'away from' + *horrere* 'to shudder'.

abhorrent ■ adj. inspiring disgust and loathing.
– DERIVATIVES **abhorrence** n.

abide ■ v. **1** (**abide by**) accept or act in accordance with (a rule or decision). **2** (**can/could not abide**) informal be unable to tolerate. **3** [often as adj. **abiding**] (of a feeling or memory) endure. **4** archaic live; dwell.
– DERIVATIVES **abidingly** adv.
– ORIGIN Old English *ābīdan* 'wait'.

ability ■ n. (pl. **-ies**) **1** the capacity to do something. **2** skill or talent.
– ORIGIN Middle English: from Old French *ablete*, from Latin *habilitas*, from *habilis* 'able'.

-ability ■ suffix forming nouns of quality corresponding to adjectives ending in *-able* (such as *suitability* corresponding to *suitable*).
– ORIGIN from Latin *-abilitas*.

ab initio /ˌab ɪ'nɪtɪəʊ/ ■ adv. & adj. from the beginning.
– ORIGIN from Latin.

abiotic /ˌeɪbʌɪ'ɒtɪk/ ■ adj. not involving or derived from living organisms.

abject /'abdʒɛkt/ ■ adj. **1** extremely unpleasant and degrading: *living in abject poverty*. **2** completely without pride or dignity: *an abject apology*.
– DERIVATIVES **abjection** n. **abjectly** adv. **abjectness** n.
– ORIGIN Middle English ('rejected'): from Latin, from *ab-* 'away' + *jacere* 'to throw'.

abjure /əb'dʒʊə/ ■ v. formal solemnly renounce (a belief or claim).
– DERIVATIVES **abjuration** n.
– ORIGIN Middle English: from Latin, from *ab-* 'away' + *jurare* 'swear'.

ablation /ə'bleɪʃ(ə)n/ ■ n. **1** the loss of solid material (especially ice) by melting or evaporation. ▶ the erosion of rock by wind action. **2** the surgical removal of body tissue.
– ORIGIN Middle English: from Latin *ablat-*, *auferre* 'take away'.

ablative /'ablətɪv/ ■ adj. **1** Grammar denoting a case indicating an agent, instrument, or source, expressed by 'by', 'with', or 'from' in English. **2** involving ablation. ■ n. Grammar a word in the ablative case.
– ORIGIN Middle English: from Latin *ablativus*, from *auferre* (see ABLATION).

ablative absolute ■ n. a construction in Latin which consists of a noun and participle or adjective in the ablative case and which functions as a sentence adverb, for example *mirabile dictu* 'wonderful to relate'.

ablaze ■ adj. burning fiercely.

able ■ adj. (**-er**, **-est**) **1** having the power, skill, or means to do something. **2** having considerable proficiency or intelligence.
– DERIVATIVES **ably** adv.

abridge

−ORIGIN Middle English: from Old French *hable*, from Latin *habilis* 'handy', from *habere* 'to hold'.

-able ■ suffix forming adjectives meaning: **1** able to be: *calculable*. **2** subject to; relevant to: *taxable*. **3** having the quality to: *suitable*.
−DERIVATIVES **-ably** suffix forming corresponding adverbs.
−ORIGIN from Latin *-abilis*.

able-bodied ■ adj. not physically unfit or disabled.

able seaman ■ n. the lowest non-commissioned rank in the navy, below leading seaman.

abloom ■ adj. in bloom.

ablution /əˈbluːʃ(ə)n/ ■ n. **1** formal or humorous an act of washing. ▶ a ceremonial act of washing parts of the body or sacred containers. **2** (**ablutions**) Brit. (in army slang) a room with washing places and toilets.
−ORIGIN Middle English: from Latin, from *ab-* 'away' + *luere* 'wash'.

ABM ■ abbrev. anti-ballistic-missile.

Abnaki /abˈnɑːki/ (also **Abenaki** /abəˈnɑːki/) ■ n. (pl. same or **Abnakis**) **1** a member of an American Indian people of Maine and southern Quebec. **2** either or both of the two extinct Algonquian languages (Eastern Abnaki and Western Abnaki) of this people.
−ORIGIN from French *Abénaqui*, from Montagnais (an Algonquian language) *ouabanăkionek* 'people of the eastern land'.

abnegate /ˈabnɪɡeɪt/ ■ v. formal renounce or reject (something desired or valuable).
−DERIVATIVES **abnegation** n. **abnegator** n.
−ORIGIN C17: (*abnegation* Middle English): from Latin *abnegat-*, *abnegare* 'renounce', from *ab-* 'away, off' + *negare* 'deny'.

abnormal ■ adj. deviating from what is normal.
−DERIVATIVES **abnormality** n. **abnormally** adv.
−ORIGIN C19: from C16 *anormal*, from Greek *anōmalos* (see ANOMALY).

aboard ■ adv. & prep. **1** on or into (a ship, train, or other vehicle). **2** Baseball on base.
−ORIGIN Middle English: from a-² + BOARD.

abode¹ ■ n. formal or poetic/literary a house or home. ▶ residence: *their right of abode in Britain*.
−ORIGIN Middle English: from ABIDE.

abode² ■ v. archaic past of ABIDE.

abolish ■ v. formally put an end to (a practice or institution).
−DERIVATIVES **abolisher** n. **abolishment** n.
−ORIGIN Middle English: from Old French *abolir*, from Latin *abolere* 'destroy'.

abolition /abəˈlɪʃ(ə)n/ ■ n. the action of abolishing something.

abolitionist ■ n. a person who favours the abolition of something, especially capital punishment or (formerly) slavery.
−DERIVATIVES **abolitionism** n.

abomasum /ˌabəʊˈmeɪsəm/ ■ n. (pl. **abomasa** /-sə/) Zoology the fourth stomach of a ruminant, which receives food from the omasum and passes it to the small intestine.
−ORIGIN C17: from *ab-* 'away, from' + *omasum* (see OMASUM).

A-bomb ■ n. short for ATOM BOMB.

abominable ■ adj. causing moral revulsion. ▶ informal terrible.
−DERIVATIVES **abominably** adv.
−ORIGIN Middle English: from Latin *abominabilis*, from *abominari* 'deprecate', from *ab-* 'away, from' + *omen*, *omin-* 'omen'.

Abominable Snowman ■ n. (pl. **-men**) another term for YETI.

abominate /əˈbɒmɪneɪt/ ■ v. formal detest.
−DERIVATIVES **abominator** n.

abomination ■ n. a cause of disgust or hatred. ▶ a feeling of hatred.

aboral /abˈɔːr(ə)l/ ■ adj. Zoology furthest from or leading away from the mouth.
−DERIVATIVES **aborally** adv.

aboriginal ■ adj. inhabiting or existing in a land from the earliest times or from before the arrival of colonists; indigenous. ▶ (**Aboriginal**) of or relating to the Australian Aboriginals or their languages. ■ n. **1** an aboriginal inhabitant. ▶ (**Aboriginal**) a person belonging to one of the indigenous peoples of Australia. **2** (**Aboriginal**) any of the Australian Aboriginal languages.
−ORIGIN C17: from Latin *aborigines* (see ABORIGINE).

aborigine /abəˈrɪdʒɪniː/ ■ n. an aboriginal person, animal, or plant. ▶ (**Aborigine**) an Australian Aboriginal.
−ORIGIN C19: back-formation from C16 *aborigines* 'original inhabitants', from Latin *ab origine* 'from the beginning'.

abort ■ v. **1** carry out or undergo the abortion of (a fetus). **2** bring to a premature end because of a problem or fault. ■ n. informal an technical an act of aborting a flight or other enterprise.
−ORIGIN C16: from Latin *aboriri* 'miscarry', from *ab-* 'away, from' + *oriri* 'be born'.

abortifacient /əˌbɔːtɪˈfeɪʃ(ə)nt/ Medicine ■ adj. (of a drug) causing abortion. ■ n. an abortifacient drug.

abortion ■ n. **1** the deliberate termination of a human pregnancy. ▶ the natural expulsion of a fetus from the womb before it is able to survive independently. **2** informal, derogatory something imperfectly planned or made.
−DERIVATIVES **abortionist** n. (chiefly derogatory).

abortive ■ adj. **1** failing to produce the intended result. **2** Medicine (of a virus infection) failing to produce symptoms.
−DERIVATIVES **abortively** adv.

ABO system ■ n. a system of four basic types (A, AB, B, and O) into which human blood may be classified, based on the presence or absence of inherited antigens.

abound ■ v. exist in large numbers or amounts. ▶ (**abound in/with**) have in large numbers or amounts.
−ORIGIN Middle English: from Latin *abundare* 'overflow', from *ab-* 'from' + *undare* 'surge'.

about ■ prep. & adv. **1** [as prep.] on the subject of; concerning. **2** used to indicate movement within a particular area or location in a particular place. **3** [as adv.] approximately.
−PHRASES **be about to** be on the point of. **know what one is about** informal be sensible and self-possessed.
−ORIGIN Old English, from *on* 'in, on' + *būtan* 'outside of'.

about-face ■ n. chiefly N. Amer. another term for ABOUT-TURN.

about-turn ■ n. **1** Military a turn made so as to face the opposite direction. **2** a complete change of opinion or policy.

above ■ prep. & adv. **1** at a higher level than. **2** in preference to. **3** [as adv.] (in printed text) mentioned earlier.
−PHRASES **above all** (**else**) more so than anything else. **above board** legitimate and honest. **above oneself** conceited. **not be above** be capable of stooping to (an unworthy act).
−ORIGIN Old English, from *a-* 'on' + *bufan*, from *bi* 'by' + *ufan* 'above'.

ab ovo /ab ˈəʊvəʊ/ ■ adv. from the very beginning.
−ORIGIN Latin, 'from the egg'.

Abp ■ abbrev. Archbishop.

abracadabra ■ exclam. a word said by conjurors when performing a magic trick.
−ORIGIN C17: from Latin.

abrade /əˈbreɪd/ ■ v. scrape or wear away by friction or erosion.
−DERIVATIVES **abrader** n.
−ORIGIN C17: from Latin *abradere*, from *ab-* 'away, from' + *radere* 'to scrape'.

abrasion /əˈbreɪʒ(ə)n/ ■ n. the action or process of abrading or being abraded.

abrasive /əˈbreɪsɪv/ ■ adj. **1** (of a substance) capable of polishing or cleaning a hard surface by rubbing or grinding. **2** harsh or rough in manner. ■ n. a substance used for abrading.
−DERIVATIVES **abrasively** adv. **abrasiveness** n.
−ORIGIN C19: from Latin *abras-*, *abradere* (see ABRADE).

abreast ■ adv. **1** side by side and facing the same way. **2** alongside. **3** (**abreast of**) up to date with.

abridge ■ v. shorten (a text or film) without losing the

abroad

sense.
–DERIVATIVES **abridgeable** adj. **abridgement** (also **abridgment**) n. **abridger** n.
–ORIGIN Middle English: from Old French *abregier*, from late Latin *abbreviare* (see ABBREVIATE).

abroad ■ adv. **1** in or to a foreign country or countries. **2** in different directions; over a wide area. ▸ (of a feeling or rumour) widely current. **3** archaic out of doors. ■ n. foreign countries collectively.
–ORIGIN Middle English: from a-² + BROAD.

abrogate /ˈabrəɡeɪt/ ■ v. formal repeal or do away with (a law or agreement).
–DERIVATIVES **abrogation** n. **abrogator** n.
–ORIGIN C16: from Latin *abrogare* 'repeal', from *ab-* 'away, from' + *rogare* 'propose a law'.

abrupt ■ adj. **1** sudden and unexpected. **2** brief to the point of rudeness; curt. **3** steep.
–DERIVATIVES **abruptly** adv. **abruptness** n.
–ORIGIN C16: from Latin *abruptus* 'broken off, steep', from *ab-* 'away, from' + *rumpere* 'break'.

abruption ■ n. technical the sudden breaking away of a portion from a mass. ▸ Medicine premature separation of the placenta from the wall of the womb during pregnancy.

ABS ■ abbrev. **1** acrylonitrile-butadiene-styrene, a hard composite plastic. **2** anti-lock braking system.

abs- ■ prefix variant spelling of AB- before *c*, *q*, and *t* (as in *abscond*, *abstain*).

abscess ■ n. a swollen area within body tissue, containing an accumulation of pus.
–DERIVATIVES **abscessed** adj.
–ORIGIN C16: from Latin *abscessus*, from *ab-* 'away from' + *cedere* 'go'.

abscisic acid /abˈsɪsɪk/ ■ n. Biochemistry a plant hormone which promotes leaf detachment, induces seed and bud dormancy, and inhibits germination.
–ORIGIN 1960s: from ABSCISSION.

abscissa /abˈsɪsə/ ■ n. (pl. **abscissae** /-siː/ or **abscissas**) Mathematics the distance from a point on a graph to the vertical or *y*-axis; the *x*-coordinate. Compare with ORDINATE.
–ORIGIN C17: from *abscissa* (*linea*) 'cut-off (line)', from Latin *abscindere* (see ABSCISSION).

abscission /abˈsɪʃ(ə)n/ ■ n. Botany the process by which parts of a plant break off naturally, e.g. dead leaves.
–DERIVATIVES **abscise** /əbˈsʌɪz/ v.
–ORIGIN C17: from Latin *abscindere*, from *ab-* 'off' + *scindere* 'to cut'.

abscond /əbˈskɒnd, ab-/ ■ v. **1** leave hurriedly and secretly to escape from custody or avoid arrest. **2** (of bees) entirely abandon a hive.
–DERIVATIVES **absconder** n.
–ORIGIN C16: from Latin *abscondere* 'hide', from *ab-* 'away, from' + *condere* 'stow'.

abseil /ˈabseɪl, -zʌɪl/ ■ v. descend a near-vertical surface using a rope coiled round the body and fixed at a higher point.
–DERIVATIVES **abseiler** n. **abseiling** n.
–ORIGIN 1930s: from German *abseilen*, from *ab* 'down' + *Seil* 'rope'.

absence ■ n. **1** the state of being away from a place or person. **2** (**absence of**) the non-existence or lack of.

absent ■ adj. /ˈabs(ə)nt/ **1** not present. **2** showing a lack of attention. ■ v. /abˈsɛnt/ (**absent oneself**) stay or go away. ■ prep. /ˈabs(ə)nt/ N. Amer. without.
–DERIVATIVES **absently** adv.
–ORIGIN Middle English: from Latin *absens*, from *ab-* 'from, away' + *esse* 'to be'.

absentee ■ n. a person who is absent.

absenteeism ■ n. the practice of regularly staying away from work or school without good reason.

absent-minded ■ adj. forgetful.
–DERIVATIVES **absent-mindedly** adv. **absent-mindedness** n.

absinth /ˈabsɪnθ/ ■ n. **1** the shrub wormwood. **2** (usu. **absinthe**) a green aniseed-flavoured liqueur formerly made with wormwood.
–ORIGIN Middle English: from French *absinthe*, from Greek *apsinthion* 'wormwood'.

absolute /ˈabsəluːt/ ■ adj. **1** not qualified or diminished in any way; total. ▸ not subject to any limitation of power: *an absolute ruler.* **2** not relative or comparative. **3** Grammar (of a construction) syntactically independent of the rest of the sentence, as in *dinner being over, we left the table.* ▸ (of a transitive verb) used without an expressed object (e.g. *guns kill*). ▸ (of an adjective) used without an expressed noun (e.g. *the brave*). **4** Law (of a decree) final. See also DECREE ABSOLUTE. ■ n. Philosophy a value or principle regarded as universally valid or able to be viewed without relation to other things.
–DERIVATIVES **absoluteness** n.
–ORIGIN Middle English: from Latin *absolutus* 'freed, unrestricted', from *absolvere* (see ABSOLVE).

absolute advantage ■ n. Economics the ability of one individual or group to carry out an economic activity more efficiently than another individual or group.

absolute alcohol ■ n. ethanol containing less than one per cent of water by weight.

absolutely ■ adv. **1** with no qualification, restriction, or limitation. **2** used for emphasis or to express agreement. **3** not viewed in relation to other things or factors.

absolute majority ■ n. a majority over all rivals combined; more than half.

absolute music ■ n. instrumental music not intended to represent or illustrate anything. Compare with PROGRAMME MUSIC.

absolute temperature ■ n. a temperature measured from absolute zero in kelvins.

absolute title ■ n. Law the guarantee of title to the ownership of a property or lease.

absolute value ■ n. **1** Mathematics the magnitude of a real number without regard to its sign. **2** technical the actual magnitude of a numerical value or measurement, irrespective of its relation to other values.

absolute zero ■ n. the lowest temperature theoretically possible (zero kelvins, −273.15°C), at which the motion of particles which constitutes heat is minimal.

absolution ■ n. formal release from guilt, obligation, or punishment. ▸ ecclesiastical declaration of forgiveness of sins.
–PHRASES **absolution from the instance** S. African Law a judgement which permits proceedings to be reinstituted if new evidence can be produced.
–ORIGIN Middle English: from Latin *absolutio(n-)*, from *absolvere* (see ABSOLVE).

absolutism ■ n. belief in absolute principles in politics, philosophy, or theology.
–DERIVATIVES **absolutist** n. & adj.

absolve /əbˈzɒlv/ ■ v. declare free from guilt or responsibility. ▸ give absolution for (a sin).
–PHRASES **absolve from the instance** S. African Law grant a defendant an acquittal, pending possible reinstitution of proceedings if new evidence is produced.
–ORIGIN Middle English: from Latin *absolvere* 'set free, acquit', from *ab-* 'from' + *solvere* 'loosen'.

absorb /əbˈzɔːb, -ˈsɔːb/ ■ v. **1** soak up (liquid or another substance). **2** take in (information). **3** assimilate (a less powerful entity). **4** use up (time or resources). **5** reduce the effect or intensity of (sound or an impact). **6** [usu. as adj. **absorbed** or **absorbing**] engross the attention of.
–DERIVATIVES **absorbable** adj. **absorbedly** adv. **absorber** n. **absorbingly** adv.
–ORIGIN Middle English: from Latin, from *ab-* 'from' + *sorbere* 'suck in'.

absorbance ■ n. Physics a measure of the capacity of a substance to absorb light of a specified wavelength.

absorbent ■ adj. able to soak up liquid easily. ■ n. an absorbent substance or item.
–DERIVATIVES **absorbency** n.

absorption /əbˈzɔːpʃ(ə)n, -ˈsɔːp-/ ■ n. the process of absorbing or the action of being absorbed.
–DERIVATIVES **absorptive** adj.

absorption costing ■ n. a method of calculating the cost of a product or enterprise by taking into account overheads as well as direct costs.

abstain ■ v. **1** restrain oneself from doing something.

acanthamoeba

2 formally decline to vote.
- DERIVATIVES **abstainer** n.
- ORIGIN Middle English: from Latin *abstinere*, from *ab-* 'from' + *tenere* 'hold'.

abstemious /əbˈstiːmɪəs/ ■ adj. not self-indulgent, especially as regards eating and drinking.
- DERIVATIVES **abstemiously** adv. **abstemiousness** n.
- ORIGIN C17: from Latin *abstemius*, from *ab-* 'from' + *temetum* 'alcoholic liquor'.

abstention /əbˈstɛnʃ(ə)n/ ■ n. **1** an instance of abstaining from a vote. **2** abstinence.
- DERIVATIVES **abstentionism** n.
- ORIGIN C16: from late Latin *abstentio(n-)*, from *abstinere* (see ABSTAIN).

abstinence /ˈabstɪnəns/ ■ n. the fact or practice of abstaining, especially from drinking alcohol.
- DERIVATIVES **abstinent** adj. **abstinently** adv.
- ORIGIN Middle English: from Latin *abstinentia*, from *abstinere* (see ABSTAIN).

abstract ■ adj. /ˈabstrakt/ **1** theoretical rather than physical or concrete. **2** relating to or denoting art that does not attempt to represent external, recognizable reality. ■ v. /əbˈstrakt/ **1** consider theoretically or separately from something else. **2** extract or remove. ▶ (**abstract oneself**) withdraw. **3** [as adj. **abstracted**] not concentrating. **4** make a written summary of. ■ n. /ˈabstrakt/ **1** a summary of a book or article. **2** an abstract work of art.
- DERIVATIVES **abstractedly** adv. **abstractly** adv. **abstractor** n.
- ORIGIN Middle English: from Latin, from *ab-* 'from' + *trahere* 'draw off'.

abstract expressionism ■ n. a development of abstract art which aimed at subjective emotional expression with particular emphasis on spontaneous creativity (e.g. action painting).
- DERIVATIVES **abstract expressionist** n. & adj.

abstraction ■ n. **1** the quality or process of dealing with ideas rather than events. ▶ something which exists only as an idea. **2** a state of preoccupation. **3** abstract qualities in art. **4** the process of abstracting something.

abstractionism ■ n. **1** the principles and practice of abstract art. **2** the presentation of ideas in abstract terms.
- DERIVATIVES **abstractionist** n. & adj.

abstruse /əbˈstruːs/ ■ adj. difficult to understand; obscure.
- DERIVATIVES **abstrusely** adv. **abstruseness** n.
- ORIGIN C16: from Latin, from *abstrudere* 'conceal', from *ab-* 'from' + *trudere* 'to push'.

absurd ■ adj. wildly unreasonable, illogical, or inappropriate.
- DERIVATIVES **absurdity** n. **absurdly** adv.
- ORIGIN C16: from Latin *absurdus* 'out of tune', hence 'irrational'.

absurdism ■ n. the belief that human beings exist in a purposeless, chaotic universe.
- DERIVATIVES **absurdist** adj. & n.

abundance /əˈbʌnd(ə)ns/ ■ n. **1** a very large quantity of something. ▶ plentifulness; prosperity. **2** the amount of something present in a particular area or sample.
- ORIGIN Middle English: from Latin *abundantia*, from *abundare* (see ABOUND).

abundant ■ adj. plentiful. ▶ (**abundant in**) having plenty of.
- DERIVATIVES **abundantly** adv.

abuse ■ v. /əˈbjuːz/ **1** use to bad effect or for a bad purpose. **2** treat with cruelty or violence. ▶ assault sexually. **3** address in an insulting and offensive way. ■ n. /əˈbjuːs/ **1** the improper use of something. **2** cruel and violent treatment. ▶ sexual assault. **3** insulting and offensive language.
- DERIVATIVES **abuser** n.
- ORIGIN Middle English: from Latin *abuti* 'misuse', from *ab-* 'away' + *uti* 'to use'.

abusive ■ adj. **1** extremely offensive and insulting. **2** characterized by illegality or physical abuse.
- DERIVATIVES **abusively** adv. **abusiveness** n.

abut /əˈbʌt/ ■ v. (**abutted**, **abutting**) **1** (of land or a building) be next to or have a common boundary with. **2** touch or lean on.
- ORIGIN Middle English: from Anglo-Latin *abuttare*, from *a-* 'to' + Old French *but* 'end'; sense 2 is from Old French *abouter*, from *a-* + *bouter* (see BUTT¹).

abutilon /əˈbjuːtɪlɒn/ ■ n. a herbaceous plant or shrub of warm climates, with showy yellow, red, or mauve flowers. [Genus *Abutilon*.]
- ORIGIN from Arabic *ūbūṭīlūn* 'Indian mallow'.

abutment ■ n. **1** a structure supporting the lateral pressure of an arch or span. **2** a point at which something abuts something else.

abysm /əˈbɪz(ə)m/ ■ n. poetic/literary an abyss.
- ORIGIN Middle English: from Old French *abisme*, from late Latin *abyssus* 'bottomless pit'.

abysmal ■ adj. **1** informal extremely bad. **2** poetic/literary very deep.
- DERIVATIVES **abysmally** adv.

abyss /əˈbɪs/ ■ n. a very deep chasm. ▶ (**the abyss**) a catastrophic situation seen as likely to occur.
- ORIGIN Middle English: from Greek *abussos* 'bottomless', from *a-* 'without' + *bussos* 'depth'.

abyssal ■ adj. relating to or denoting the depths of the ocean.

Abyssinian ■ adj. historical of or relating to Abyssinia (the former name of Ethiopia). ■ n. **1** historical a native of Abyssinia. **2** a cat of a breed having long ears and short brown hair flecked with grey.

AC ■ abbrev. **1** (also **ac**) air conditioning. **2** (also **ac**) alternating current. **3** appellation contrôlée. **4** athletic club. **5** before Christ. [from Latin *ante Christum*.]

Ac ■ symb. the chemical element actinium.

-ac ■ suffix forming adjectives which are often also (or only) used as nouns, such as *maniac*. Compare with **-ACAL**.
- ORIGIN from Greek *-akos*.

a/c ■ abbrev. **1** account. **2** (also **A/C**) air conditioning.

ac- ■ prefix variant spelling of **AD-** assimilated before *c*, *k*, and *q* (as in *accept*, *acquit*, and *acquiesce*).

acacia /əˈkeɪʃə, -sɪə/ ■ n. a tree or shrub of warm climates which has yellow or white flowers and is typically thorny. [Genus *Acacia*: numerous species.]
- ORIGIN Middle English: from Greek *akakia*.

academe /ˈakədiːm/ ■ n. poetic/literary (often in phr. **the groves of academe**) academia.
- ORIGIN C16: from Latin *academia* (see ACADEMY).

academia /ˌakəˈdiːmɪə/ ■ n. the academic environment or community.
- ORIGIN 1950s: from Latin (see ACADEMY).

academic ■ adj. **1** of or relating to education and scholarship. ▶ scholarly rather than technical or practical. **2** (of an art form) conventional in an idealized or excessively formal way. **3** not of practical relevance. ■ n. a teacher or scholar in an institute of higher education.
- DERIVATIVES **academically** adv.
- ORIGIN C16: from medieval Latin *academicus*, from *academia* (see ACADEMY).

academical ■ adj. of or relating to a college or university.

academician /əˌkadəˈmɪʃ(ə)n/ ■ n. **1** a member of an academy. **2** N. Amer. an academic.

academy ■ n. (pl. **-ies**) **1** a place of study or training in a special field. ▶ [chiefly in names] US & Scottish a secondary school. **2** a society or institution of distinguished scholars, artists, or scientists.
- ORIGIN Middle English: from Greek *akadēmeia*, from *Akadēmos*, the hero after whom the garden where Plato taught was named.

Academy award ■ n. an award given by the Academy of Motion Picture Arts and Sciences for achievement in the film industry; an Oscar.

Acadian chiefly historical ■ adj. of or relating to the former French colony of Acadia (now Nova Scotia) in Canada. ■ n. a native or inhabitant of Acadia, or a descendant of the Acadians.

-acal ■ suffix forming adjectives such as *maniacal*, often making a distinction from nouns ending in *-ac* (as in *maniacal* compared with *maniac*).

acanthamoeba /əˌkanθəˈmiːbə/ ■ n. (pl. **acanthamoebae**

/-'miːbiː/) an amoeba of a genus which includes a number that can cause opportunistic infections in humans. [Genus *Acanthamoeba*.]

acanthus /əˈkanθəs/ ▪ n. 1 a herbaceous plant or shrub with bold flower spikes and spiny decorative leaves, found in warm regions of the Old World. [Genus *Acanthus*: many species.] 2 Architecture a representation of an acanthus leaf, used especially as a decoration for Corinthian column capitals.
– ORIGIN from Greek, from *akantha* 'thorn'.

a cappella /ˌa kəˈpɛlə, ˌaː/ ▪ adj. & adv. (of music) sung without instrumental accompaniment.
– ORIGIN Italian, 'in chapel style'.

Acari /əˈkɑːri/ ▪ pl. n. Zoology a large order of small arachnids which comprises the mites and ticks.
– DERIVATIVES **acarid** /ˈakərɪd/ n. & adj. **acarine** /ˈakərʌɪn/ n. & adj.
– ORIGIN from Greek *akari* 'mite, tick'.

acaricide /əˈkarɪsʌɪd/ ▪ n. a substance poisonous to mites or ticks.
– ORIGIN C19: from Greek *akari* 'mite, tick'.

acausal ▪ adj. not governed or operating by the laws of cause and effect.

accede /əkˈsiːd/ ▪ v. (usu. **accede to**) formal 1 assent or agree to. 2 assume (an office or position).
– ORIGIN Middle English: from Latin *accedere*, from *ad-* 'to' + *cedere* 'give way, yield'.

accelerant ▪ n. a substance used to aid the spread of fire. ▪ adj. technical accelerating or causing acceleration.

accelerate /əkˈsɛləreɪt/ ▪ v. begin to move more quickly. ▸ increase in rate, amount, or extent. ▸ Physics undergo a change in velocity.
– DERIVATIVES **acceleration** n. **accelerative** adj.
– ORIGIN C16 (*acceleration* C15): from Latin *accelerare* 'hasten', from *ad-* 'towards' + *celer* 'swift'.

accelerator ▪ n. 1 a foot pedal which controls the speed of a vehicle's engine. 2 Physics an apparatus for accelerating charged particles to high velocities. 3 a substance that speeds up a chemical process.

accent ▪ n. /ˈaks(ə)nt, -sɛnt/ 1 a particular way of pronouncing a language, associated with a country, area, or social class. 2 an emphasis given to a syllable, word, or note in speech or music. 3 a special or particular emphasis. 4 a mark on a letter or word indicating pitch, stress, or the quality of a vowel. ▪ v. /akˈsɛnt/ 1 [as adj. **accented**] spoken with a particular accent. 2 stress (a word, syllable, or note). 3 emphasize.
– DERIVATIVES **accentual** adj.
– ORIGIN Middle English: from Latin *accentus* 'tone, signal, or intensity'.

accentuate /əkˈsɛntʃʊeɪt, -tjʊ-/ ▪ v. make more noticeable or prominent.
– DERIVATIVES **accentuation** n.
– ORIGIN C18 (*accentuation* C15): from medieval Latin *accentuare*, from Latin *accentus* (see **ACCENT**).

accept ▪ v. 1 consent to receive (something offered). 2 regard favourably or with approval. 3 believe to be valid or correct. 4 take on (a responsibility or liability). ▸ tolerate or submit to.
– DERIVATIVES **acceptance** n. **acceptor** (also **-er**) n.
– ORIGIN Middle English: from Latin, from *ad-* 'to' + *capere* 'take'.

acceptable ▪ adj. 1 able to be accepted. 2 adequate.
– DERIVATIVES **acceptability** n. **acceptableness** n. **acceptably** adv.

access ▪ n. 1 the means or opportunity to approach or enter a place. ▸ the right or opportunity to use something or see someone. 2 retrieval of information stored in a computer's memory. 3 an attack or outburst of an emotion: *an access of rage*. ▪ v. 1 gain access to; make accessible. ▸ Computing obtain, examine, or retrieve (data). 2 approach or enter (a place).
– ORIGIN Middle English: from Latin *accessus*, from *accedere* (see **ACCEDE**).

access bond ▪ n. S. African a mortgage which permits borrowers to take out loans against extra capital paid into the account.

accessible ▪ adj. 1 able to be accessed. 2 friendly and easy to talk to; approachable. 3 easily understood or appreciated.
– DERIVATIVES **accessibility** n. **accessibly** adv.

accession ▪ n. 1 the attainment of a position of rank. 2 the formal acceptance of a treaty or joining of an association. 3 a new item added to a collection of books or artefacts. ▪ v. record the addition of (a new item) to a library or museum.

accessorize (also **-ise**) ▪ v. provide (a garment) with a fashion accessory.

accessory ▪ n. (pl. **-ies**) 1 a thing which can be added to something else in order to make it more useful, versatile, or attractive. ▸ a small article carried or worn to complement a garment. 2 Law a person who assists the perpetrator of a crime without taking part in it. ▪ adj. chiefly technical subsidiary or supplementary.
– DERIVATIVES **accessorial** adj. (chiefly Law).
– ORIGIN Middle English: from medieval Latin *accessorius* 'additional thing', from Latin *accedere* (see **ACCEDE**).

accessory nerves ▪ pl. n. Anatomy a pair of cranial nerves supplying certain muscles in the neck and shoulder.

acciaccatura /əˌtʃakəˈtjʊərə/ ▪ n. (pl. **acciaccaturas** or **acciaccature**) Music a grace note performed as quickly as possible before an essential note of a melody.
– ORIGIN Italian, from *acciaccare* 'to crush'.

accidence /ˈaksɪd(ə)ns/ ▪ n. dated the part of grammar concerned with the inflections of words.
– ORIGIN C16: from Latin *accidere* (see **ACCIDENT**).

accident ▪ n. 1 an unfortunate incident that happens unexpectedly and unintentionally. 2 something that happens by chance or without apparent cause. ▸ chance. 3 Philosophy a property of a thing which is not essential to its nature.
– ORIGIN Middle English: from Latin *accidere*, from *ad-* 'towards, to' + *cadere* 'to fall'.

accidental ▪ adj. 1 happening by accident. 2 incidental. 3 Philosophy relating to or denoting properties not essential to a thing's nature. ▪ n. 1 Music a sign indicating a momentary departure from the key signature by raising or lowering a note. 2 Ornithology another term for **VAGRANT**.
– DERIVATIVES **accidentally** adv.

accidie /ˈaksɪdi/ ▪ n. spiritual or mental sloth.
– ORIGIN Middle English: from medieval Latin *accidia*, from rare *acedia*, from Greek *akēdia* 'listlessness'.

accipiter /akˈsɪpɪtə/ ▪ n. Ornithology a hawk of a group distinguished by short, broad wings, such as the goshawk. [*Accipiter* and other genera.]
– DERIVATIVES **accipitrine** adj.
– ORIGIN from Latin, 'hawk, bird of prey'.

acclaim ▪ v. praise enthusiastically and publicly. ▪ n. enthusiastic public praise.
– DERIVATIVES **acclamation** n.
– ORIGIN C17: from Latin, from *ad-* 'to' + *clamare* 'to shout'.

acclimate /ˈaklɪmeɪt, əˈklʌɪmət/ ▪ v. chiefly N. Amer. acclimatize.
– DERIVATIVES **acclimation** n.
– ORIGIN C18: from French *acclimater*, from *a-* 'to, at' + *climat* 'climate'.

acclimatize (also **-ise**) ▪ v. 1 become accustomed to a new climate or new conditions. 2 Biology respond to changes in environmental factors. 3 Botany & Horticulture harden off (a plant).
– DERIVATIVES **acclimatization** (also **-isation**) n.
– ORIGIN C19: from French *acclimater* 'acclimatize'.

acclivity /əˈklɪvɪti/ ▪ n. (pl. **-ies**) an upward slope.
– ORIGIN C17: from Latin *acclivitas*, from *ad-* 'towards' + *clivus* 'a slope'.

accolade /ˈakəleɪd, ˌakəˈleɪd/ ▪ n. 1 something granted as a special honour or in recognition of merit. 2 a ceremonial touch on a person's shoulders with a sword at the bestowing of a knighthood.
– ORIGIN C17: from Provençal *acolada* 'embrace around the neck (when bestowing knighthood)', from Latin *ad-* 'at, to' + *collum* 'neck'.

accommodate ▪ v. 1 provide lodging or sufficient space for. 2 fit in with the wishes or needs of. ▸ [as adj. **accommodating**] fitting in helpfully with another's wishes or demands.

–DERIVATIVES **accommodatingly** adv.
–ORIGIN C16: from Latin *accommodare* 'make fitting', from *ad-* 'to' + *commodus* 'fitting'.

accommodation ■ n. **1** a room, building, or space in which someone may live or stay. ▶ (**accommodations**) chiefly N. Amer. lodgings. **2** a settlement or compromise. **3** adjustment to or reconciliation of changing circumstances. **4** the automatic adjustment of the focus of the eye by the lens.
–ORIGIN C17: from Latin, from *accommodare* (see **ACCOMMODATE**).

accommodationist ■ n. US a person who seeks compromise.

accommodation ladder ■ n. a ladder up the side of a ship allowing access from a small boat or a quayside.

accompaniment ■ n. **1** a musical part which supports or partners an instrument, voice, or group. **2** something that supplements or complements something else.
–ORIGIN C18: from French *accompagnement*, from *accompagner* 'accompany'.

accompanist ■ n. a person who provides a musical accompaniment.

accompany ■ v. (**-ies, -ied**) **1** go somewhere with. **2** be present or occur at the same time as. ▶ provide something as a complement to. **3** play a musical accompaniment for.
–ORIGIN Middle English: from Old French *accompagner*, from *compaignon* 'companion'.

accomplice /əˈkʌmplɪs, əˈkɒm-/ ■ n. a person who helps another commit a crime.
–ORIGIN C16: from Middle English *complice* 'an associate', from late Latin *complex, complic-* 'allied'.

accomplish ■ v. achieve or complete successfully.
–ORIGIN Middle English: from Old French *acomplir*, from Latin *ad-* 'to' + *complere* 'to complete'.

accomplished ■ adj. highly trained or skilled.

accomplishment ■ n. **1** something that has been achieved successfully. **2** an activity that one can do well.

accord ■ v. **1** give or grant someone (power or recognition). **2** (**accord with**) be harmonious or consistent with. ■ n. **1** an official agreement or treaty. **2** agreement or harmony.
–PHRASES **of one's own accord** voluntarily or without outside intervention. **with one accord** in a united way.
–ORIGIN Old English, from Old French *acorder* 'reconcile', from Latin *ad-* 'to' + *cor, cord-* 'heart'.

accordance ■ n. (in phr. **in accordance with**) in a manner conforming with.

accordant ■ adj. archaic agreeing or compatible.

according ■ adv. **1** (**according to**) as stated by or in. ▶ in a manner corresponding or in proportion to. **2** (**according as**) depending on whether.

accordingly ■ adv. **1** appropriately. **2** consequently.

accordion /əˈkɔːdɪən/ ■ n. a musical instrument played by stretching and squeezing with the hands to work a bellows that blows air over reeds, the melody and chords being sounded by buttons or keys.
–DERIVATIVES **accordionist** n.
–ORIGIN C19: from German *Akkordion*, from Italian *accordare* 'to tune'.

accost ■ v. approach and address boldly or aggressively.
–ORIGIN C16 ('lie or go alongside'): from French *accoster*, from Latin *ad-* 'to' + *costa* 'rib, side'.

accouchement /əˈkuːʃmɒ̃/ ■ n. archaic the action of giving birth.
–ORIGIN C18: French, from *accoucher* 'act as midwife', from *a-* + *coucher* (see **COUCH**[1]).

account ■ n. **1** a description of an event or experience. **2** a record of financial expenditure and receipts. ▶ a bill taking the form of such a record. **3** a service through a bank or similar organization by which funds are held on behalf of a client or goods or services are supplied on credit. **4** a facility allowing access to a computer or computational facility. **5** importance: *money was of no account to her*. ■ v. **1** consider or regard in a specified way. **2** (**account for**) supply or make up (a specified amount). **3** (**account for**) give a satisfactory record or explanation of. **4** (**account for**) succeed in killing or defeating.
–PHRASES **call** (or **bring**) **to account** require (someone) to explain a mistake or poor performance. **money of account** denominations of money used in reckoning but not current as coins. **on someone's account** for a specified person's benefit. **on account of** because of. **on no account** under no circumstances. **on one's own account** with one's own money or assets. **take account of** consider along with other factors before reaching a decision. **turn to** (**good**) **account** turn to one's advantage.
–ORIGIN Middle English: from Old French *aconter*, from *conter* 'to count'.

accountable ■ adj. **1** required or expected to justify actions or decisions. **2** explicable; understandable.
–DERIVATIVES **accountability** n. **accountably** adv.

accountancy ■ n. the profession or duties of an accountant.

accountant ■ n. a person who keeps or inspects financial accounts.
–ORIGIN Middle English: from Old French *aconter* (see **ACCOUNT**).

accounting ■ n. the action of keeping financial accounts.

accoutre /əˈkuːtə/ (US **accouter**) ■ v. (**accoutred**, **accoutring**; US **accoutered, accoutering**) (usu. **be accoutred**) clothe or equip, especially in something noticeable or impressive.
–ORIGIN C16: from French *accoutrer*, from Old French, from *a-* 'to, at' + *cousture* 'sewing'.

accoutrement /əˈkuːtəm(ə)nt, -trə-/ (US **accouterment**) ■ n. **1** an additional item of dress or equipment. **2** (**accoutrements**) a soldier's outfit other than weapons and garments.

accredit ■ v. (**accredited, accrediting**) **1** give credit to (someone) for something. ▶ (**accredit something to**) attribute something to. **2** [often as adj. **accredited**] give official authorization or sanction to. **3** send (a diplomat or journalist) to a particular place or post.
–DERIVATIVES **accreditation** n.
–ORIGIN C17: from French *accréditer*, from *a-* 'to, at' + *crédit* 'credit'.

accrete /əˈkriːt/ ■ v. grow or form by accumulation or coalescence.
–DERIVATIVES **accretion** n. **accretionary** adj. **accretive** adj.
–ORIGIN C18: from Latin, from *ad-* 'to' + *crescere* 'grow'.

accrual (also **accrual system**) ■ n. S. African Law a system whereby spouses retain individual assets brought into the marriage and share assets built up during the marriage. Compare with **COMMUNITY OF PROPERTY**.

accrue /əˈkruː/ ■ v. (**accrues, accrued, accruing**) **1** (of a benefit or sum of money) be received in regular or increasing amounts. **2** make provision for (a charge) at the end of a financial period.
–ORIGIN Middle English: from Old French *acreue*, from *acreistre* 'increase', from Latin *accrescere* (see **ACCRETE**).

acculturate /əˈkʌltʃəreɪt/ ■ v. assimilate or cause to assimilate a different culture.
–DERIVATIVES **acculturation** n.

accumulate /əˈkjuːmjʊleɪt/ ■ v. gather together a number or quantity of. ▶ build up.
–DERIVATIVES **accumulation** n. **accumulative** adj.
–ORIGIN C15: from Latin *accumulare* 'heap up', from *ad-* 'to' + *cumulus* 'a heap'.

accumulator ■ n. **1** a person or thing that accumulates. **2** a large rechargeable electric cell. **3** (S. African also **place accumulator**) a bet placed on a series of events, the winnings and stake from each being placed on the next.

accurate /ˈakjʊrət/ ■ adj. **1** correct in all details. **2** capable of or successful in reaching the intended target.
–DERIVATIVES **accuracy** n. **accurately** adv.
–ORIGIN C16: from Latin *accurare* 'do with care', from *ad-* 'towards' + *cura* 'care'.

accursed /əˈkəːsɪd, əˈkəːst/ ■ adj. **1** poetic/literary under a curse. **2** informal detestable.
–ORIGIN Middle English: from obsolete verb *accurse*, from *a-* (expressing intensity) + **CURSE**.

accusal ■ n. another term for **ACCUSATION**.

accusation ■ n. a charge or claim that someone has done something illegal or wrong.

accusative /əˈkjuːzətɪv/ Grammar ■ adj. denoting a case which expresses the object of an action or the goal of motion. ■ n. a word in the accusative case.
– ORIGIN Middle English: from Latin (casus) accusativus, translating Greek (ptōsis) aitiatikē '(the case) showing cause'.

accusatorial /əˌkjuːzəˈtɔːrɪəl/ ■ adj. Law involving accusation by a prosecutor and a verdict reached by an impartial judge or jury. Compare with ADVERSARIAL, INQUISITORIAL.

accuse ■ v. charge with an offence or crime. ▸ (**accuse someone of**) claim that someone has done something wrong.
– DERIVATIVES **accusatory** adj. **accuser** n. **accusing** adj. **accusingly** adv.
– ORIGIN Middle English: from Latin accusare 'call to account', from ad- 'towards' + causa 'reason, motive, lawsuit'.

accused ■ adj. charged with a crime. ■ n. (**the accused**) [treated as sing. or pl.] a person or group of people charged with a crime or on trial in a court.

accustom ■ v. **1** make used to. ▸ (**be accustomed to**) be used to. **2** [as adj. **accustomed**] customary.
– ORIGIN Middle English: from Old French acostumer, from a- 'to, at' + costume 'custom'.

AC/DC ■ adj. **1** alternating current/direct current. **2** informal bisexual.

ACDP ■ abbrev. African Christian Democratic Party.

ace ■ n. **1** a playing card with a single spot on it, the highest card in its suit in most games. **2** informal a person who excels at a particular activity. **3** Tennis a service that an opponent is unable to return. **4** Golf a hole in one. ■ adj. informal very good. ■ v. informal **1** (in tennis) serve an ace against. **2** Golf score an ace on. **3** get an A or its equivalent in (a test or exam).
– PHRASES **ace up one's sleeve** (or N. Amer. **in the hole**) a plan or piece of information kept secret until required. **hold all the aces** have all the advantages. **on one's ace** S. African informal on one's own. **within an ace of** very close to.
– ORIGIN Middle English: from Latin as 'unity, a unit'.

-acea ■ suffix Zoology forming the names of zoological groups: Crustacea. Compare with -ACEAN.
– ORIGIN from Latin, 'of the nature of'.

-aceae ■ suffix Botany forming the names of families of plants: Liliaceae.
– ORIGIN from Latin, 'of the nature of'.

-acean ■ suffix Zoology forming the singular of group names ending in -acea (such as crustacean from Crustacea).
– ORIGIN from Latin -aceus 'of the nature of'.

acellular ■ adj. Biology not divided into or containing cells. ▸ consisting of one cell only.

acentric ■ adj. **1** without a centre; not centralized. **2** Genetics (of a chromosome) having no centromere.

-aceous ■ suffix **1** Botany forming adjectives from family names: ericaceous. **2** chiefly Biology & Geology forming adjectives describing similarity: olivaceous.
– ORIGIN from Latin -aceus 'of the nature of'.

acephalous /eɪˈsɛf(ə)ləs, -ˈkɛf-/ ■ adj. without a head.
– ORIGIN C18: from Greek akephalos 'headless'.

acer /ˈeɪsə/ ■ n. a maple or related tree, with five-lobed leaves. [Genus Acer.]
– ORIGIN from Latin, 'maple'.

acerbic ■ adj. **1** sharp and forthright. **2** archaic or technical tasting sour or bitter.
– DERIVATIVES **acerbically** adv. **acerbity** n.
– ORIGIN C19: from Latin acerbus 'sour-tasting'.

acesulfame /ˌasɪˈsʌlfeɪm/ ■ n. a sulphur-containing compound used as a low-calorie artificial sweetener.
– ORIGIN 1980s.

acetabulum /ˌasɪˈtabjʊləm/ ■ n. (pl. **acetabula** /-lə/)
1 Anatomy the socket of the hip bone, into which the head of the femur fits. **2** Zoology a sucker or other cup-shaped structure.
– ORIGIN Middle English: from Latin, from acetum 'vinegar' + -abulum, denoting a container.

acetaldehyde /ˌasɪtˈaldɪhʌɪd/ ■ n. Chemistry a colourless volatile liquid aldehyde obtained by oxidizing ethanol.

acetamide /əˈsiːtəmaɪd, əˈsɛt-/ ■ n. Chemistry a crystalline solid with a characteristic musty odour, the amide of acetic acid.

acetaminophen /əˌsiːtəˈmɪnəfɛn, əˌsɛtə-, ˌasɪtə-/ ■ n. North American term for PARACETAMOL.
– ORIGIN 1960s: from para-acetylaminophenol.

acetate /ˈasɪteɪt/ ■ n. **1** Chemistry a salt or ester of acetic acid: lead acetate. **2** textile fibre or plastic made of cellulose acetate. ▸ a transparency made of cellulose acetate film. ▸ a direct-cut recording disc coated with cellulose acetate.

acetic acid /əˈsiːtɪk, əˈsɛt-/ ■ n. Chemistry the acid that gives vinegar its characteristic taste. [CH_3COOH.]
– ORIGIN C18: from French acétique, from Latin acetum 'vinegar'.

aceto- (also **acet-** before a vowel) ■ comb. form Chemistry representing ACETIC ACID or ACETYL.

acetogenic /əˌsiːtə(ʊ)ˈdʒɛnɪk, ˌasɪtəʊ-/ ■ adj. (of bacteria) forming acetic acid or acetates as a product of metabolism.

acetone /ˈasɪtəʊn/ ■ n. Chemistry a colourless volatile liquid ketone used as a solvent and synthetic reagent.
– ORIGIN C19: from ACETIC ACID.

acetous /əˈsiːtəs/ ■ adj. producing or resembling vinegar.
– ORIGIN Middle English: from late Latin acetosus 'sour', from Latin acetum 'vinegar'.

acetyl /ˈasɪtʌɪl, -tɪl/ ■ n. [as modifier] Chemistry of or denoting the acyl radical -$C(O)CH_3$, derived from acetic acid.

acetylate /əˈsɛtɪleɪt/ ■ v. Chemistry introduce an acetyl group into (a molecule).
– DERIVATIVES **acetylation** n.

acetylcholine /ˌasɪtʌɪlˈkəʊliːn, -tɪl-/ ■ n. Biochemistry a compound occurring in the nervous system, in which it functions as a neurotransmitter.

acetylene /əˈsɛtɪliːn/ ■ n. Chemistry a hydrocarbon gas which burns with a bright flame, used in welding and formerly in lighting. [C_2H_2.]
– ORIGIN C19: from ACETIC ACID.

Achaean ■ n. an inhabitant of Achaea in ancient Greece. ▸ poetic/literary a Greek. ■ adj. of or relating to Achaea or the Achaeans.

achalasia /ˌakəˈleɪzɪə/ ■ n. Medicine a condition in which the muscles of the lower part of the oesophagus fail to relax, preventing food from passing into the stomach.
– ORIGIN C20: from Greek a- 'without' + khalasis 'loosening'.

achar ■ n. variant spelling of ATJAR.

ache ■ n. a continuous or prolonged dull pain. ■ v. **1** suffer from an ache. **2** yearn.
– DERIVATIVES **aching** adj. **achingly** adv.
– ORIGIN Old English æce (n.), acan (v.); the modern spelling is due to a mistaken assumption that the word is derived from Greek akhos 'pain'.

achene /əˈkiːn/ ■ n. Botany a small, dry one-seeded fruit that does not open to release the seed.
– ORIGIN C19: from Greek a- 'not' + khainein 'to gape'.

Acheulian /əˈʃuːlɪən/ (also **Acheulean**) ■ adj. Archaeology relating to or denoting the main Lower Palaeolithic culture in Europe, dated to about 1 500 000–150 000 years ago.
– ORIGIN from St-Acheul in France, where objects from this culture were found.

achieve ■ v. bring about or accomplish by effort, skill, or courage.
– DERIVATIVES **achievable** adj. **achiever** n.
– ORIGIN Middle English: from Old French achever 'come or bring to a head', from a chief 'to a head'.

achievement ■ n. **1** a thing that is achieved. **2** the process or fact of achieving. **3** Heraldry a representation of a coat of arms with all the adjuncts to which a bearer of arms is entitled.

Achilles heel ■ n. a weakness or vulnerable point.
– ORIGIN C19: alluding to the mythological Greek hero Achilles, whose mother plunged him into the River Styx

---

VOWELS   a cat   ɑː arm   ɛ bed   ɛː hair   ə ago   əː her   ɪ sit   i cosy   iː see   ɒ hot   ɔː saw   ʌ run

when he was a baby, thus making his body invulnerable except for the heel by which she held him.

Achilles tendon ■ n. the tendon connecting calf muscles to the heel.

achiral /eɪˈkʌɪr(ə)l/ ■ adj. Chemistry (of a molecule) able to be superimposed on its mirror image; not chiral.

achlorhydria /ˌeɪklɔːˈhʌɪdrɪə, ˌaklɔː-/ ■ n. Medicine absence of hydrochloric acid in the gastric secretions.

Acholi /əˈtʃəʊli/ ■ n. (pl. same) 1 a member of a farming and pastoral people of northern Uganda and southern Sudan. 2 the Nilotic language of this people.
– ORIGIN the name in Acholi.

achondrite /əˈkɒndrʌɪt/ ■ n. a stony meteorite containing no small mineral granules (chondrules).

achondroplasia /əˌkɒndrə(ʊ)ˈpleɪzɪə, eɪ-/ ■ n. Medicine a hereditary condition in which the growth of long bones is retarded, resulting in short limbs.
– DERIVATIVES **achondroplasic** adj. **achondroplastic** adj.
– ORIGIN C19: from Greek *a*- 'without' + *khondros* 'cartilage' + *plasis* 'moulding'.

achromatic /ˌakrə(ʊ)ˈmatɪk/ ■ adj. 1 relating to or denoting lenses that transmit light without separating it into constituent colours. 2 without colour.
– DERIVATIVES **achromaticity** n. **achromatism** n.
– ORIGIN C18: from Greek *a*- 'without' + *khrōmatikos* (from *khrōma* 'colour').

achy ■ adj. (-ier, -est) suffering from an ache or aches.

acicular /əˈsɪkjʊlə/ ■ adj. technical needle-shaped.
– ORIGIN C18: from late Latin *acicula* 'small needle'.

acid ■ n. 1 a substance (typically, a corrosive or sour-tasting liquid) with particular chemical properties including turning litmus red, neutralizing alkalis, and dissolving some metals. ▶ Chemistry any molecule able to donate a proton or accept electrons in reactions. 2 informal the drug LSD. ■ adj. 1 containing or having the properties of an acid; having a pH of less than 7. 2 sharp-tasting or sour. 3 (of remarks) bitter or cutting.
– DERIVATIVES **acidic** adj. **acidification** n. **acidify** v. **acidity** n. **acidly** adv. **acidy** adj.
– ORIGIN C17: from Latin *acidus*, from *acere* 'be sour'.

acid drop ■ n. Brit. a boiled sweet with a sharp taste.

acid house ■ n. a kind of synthesized dance music with a fast repetitive beat, associated with the taking of drugs.

acid jazz ■ n. a kind of dance music incorporating elements of jazz, funk, soul, and hip hop.

acidophilic /ˌasɪdə(ʊ)ˈfɪlɪk, əˌsɪd-/ ■ adj. Biology 1 relating to or denoting cells readily stained with acid dyes. 2 growing best in acidic conditions.

acidophilus /ˌasɪˈdɒfɪləs/ ■ n. a bacterium used to make yogurt. [*Lactobacillus acidophilus*.]
– ORIGIN 1920s: modern Latin, 'acid-loving'.

acidosis /ˌasɪˈdəʊsɪs/ ■ n. Medicine an excessively acid condition of the body fluids or tissues.
– DERIVATIVES **acidotic** adj.

acid rain ■ n. rainfall made acidic by atmospheric sulphur and nitrogen oxides from the industrial burning of fossil fuels.

acid rock ■ n. a style of rock music popular in the late 1960s, associated with hallucinogenic drugs.

acid salt ■ n. Chemistry a salt formed by incomplete replacement of the hydrogen of an acid, e.g. potassium hydrogen sulphate (KHSO$_4$).

acid test ■ n. a conclusive test of success or value.
– ORIGIN from the original use denoting a test for gold using nitric acid.

acidulate /əˈsɪdjʊleɪt/ ■ v. make slightly acidic.
– DERIVATIVES **acidulated** adj. **acidulation** n.
– ORIGIN C18: from Latin *acidulus*, from *acidus* 'sour'.

acidulous /əˈsɪdjʊləs/ ■ adj. sharp-tasting; sour.
– ORIGIN C18: from Latin *acidulus*, from *acidus* 'sour'.

-acious ■ suffix (forming adjectives) inclined to; having as a capacity: *capacious*.
– ORIGIN from Latin *-ax, -ac-*.

-acity ■ suffix forming nouns of quality or state corresponding to adjectives ending in *-acious* (such as *audacity* corresponding to *audacious*).
– ORIGIN from Latin *-acitas*.

acquire

ack-ack ■ n. Military, informal anti-aircraft gunfire or guns.
– ORIGIN signallers' name for the letters *AA*; *ack* for *A* was replaced by *able* in 1942.

acknowledge ■ v. 1 accept or admit the existence or truth of. 2 confirm receipt of or gratitude for. 3 greet with words or gestures.
– ORIGIN C15: from obsolete Middle English verb *knowledge*, influenced by obsolete *acknow* 'acknowledge, confess'.

acknowledgement (also **acknowledgment**) ■ n. 1 the action or fact of acknowledging. 2 (**acknowledgements**) a statement printed at the beginning of a book expressing the author's gratitude to others.

ACLU ■ abbrev. American Civil Liberties Union.

acme /ˈakmi/ ■ n. the highest point of achievement or excellence.
– ORIGIN C16: from Greek *akmē* 'highest point'.

acne ■ n. a skin condition marked by numerous red pimples resulting from inflamed sebaceous glands.
– DERIVATIVES **acned** adj.
– ORIGIN C19: from Greek *aknas*, a misreading of *akmas*, from *akmē* 'highest point, peak, or facial eruption'.

Acol /ˈakɒl/ ■ n. Bridge a commonly used British system of bidding designed to enable partners with weaker hands to find suitable contracts.
– ORIGIN 1930s: from *Acol* Road in Hampstead, London, where the system was devised.

acolyte /ˈakəlʌɪt/ ■ n. 1 an assistant or follower. 2 a person assisting a priest in a religious service.
– ORIGIN Middle English: from eccles. Latin *acolytus*, from Greek *akolouthos* 'follower'.

aconite /ˈakənʌɪt/ ■ n. 1 a poisonous plant bearing spikes of hooded pink or purple flowers. [Genus *Aconitum*: many species, including monkshood.] 2 (also **winter aconite**) a small Eurasian plant bearing yellow flowers in early spring. [*Eranthis hyemalis*.]
– ORIGIN C16: from Greek *akoniton*.

acorn ■ n. the fruit of the oak, a smooth oval nut in a cup-like base.
– ORIGIN Old English, of Germanic origin; rel. to **ACRE**, later associated with **OAK** and **CORN**[1].

acorn squash ■ n. a winter squash of a variety with ridged dark green to orange rind and yellow flesh.

acoustic /əˈkuːstɪk/ ■ adj. 1 relating to sound or hearing. ▶ (of building materials) used for soundproofing or modifying sound. ▶ (of a device or system) utilizing sound energy. ▶ (of an explosive mine) set off by sound waves. 2 (of popular music or musical instruments) not having electrical amplification. ■ n. 1 the properties of a room or building that determine how sound is transmitted in it. 2 (**acoustics**) [treated as sing.] the branch of physics concerned with the properties of sound.
– DERIVATIVES **acoustical** adj. **acoustically** adv.
– ORIGIN C17: from Greek *akoustikos*, from *akouein* 'hear'.

acquaint ■ v. 1 (**acquaint someone with**) make someone aware of or familiar with. 2 (**be acquainted with**) know personally. ▶ (**be acquainted**) (of two or more people) know each other personally.
– ORIGIN Middle English: from Old French *acointier* 'make known', from Latin *accognoscere*, from *ad-* 'to' + *cognoscere* 'come to know'.

acquaintance ■ n. 1 the fact or state of being acquainted. 2 a person one knows slightly.
– DERIVATIVES **acquaintanceship** n.

acquiesce /ˌakwɪˈɛs/ ■ v. accept or consent to something without protest.
– DERIVATIVES **acquiescence** n. **acquiescent** adj.
– ORIGIN C17: from Latin, from *ad-* 'to, at' + *quiescere* 'to rest'.

acquire ■ v. come to possess. ▶ learn or develop (a skill, quality, etc.).
– PHRASES **acquired taste** a thing that one learns to like over time.
– DERIVATIVES **acquirement** n. **acquirer** n.
– ORIGIN Middle English, from Latin *acquirere* 'get in addition', from *ad-* 'to' + *quaerere* 'seek'.

acquired character (also **acquired characteristic**) ■ n. Biology a modification or change in an organ or tissue due to use, disuse, or environmental effects, and not inherited.

acquired immune deficiency syndrome ■ n. see AIDS.

acquisition /ˌakwɪˈzɪʃ(ə)n/ ■ n. **1** a recently acquired asset or object. **2** the act of acquiring.

acquisition accounting ■ n. a procedure in accounting in which the value of the assets of a company is changed from book to fair market level after a takeover.

acquisitive ■ adj. excessively interested in acquiring money or material things.
– DERIVATIVES **acquisitively** adv. **acquisitiveness** n.
– ORIGIN C19: from late Latin *acquisitivus*, from Latin *acquirere* (see ACQUIRE).

acquit ■ v. (**acquitted**, **acquitting**) **1** formally declare not guilty of a criminal charge. **2** (**acquit oneself**) conduct oneself or perform in a specified way. ▸ (**acquit oneself of**) archaic discharge (a duty or responsibility).
– DERIVATIVES **acquittal** n.
– ORIGIN Middle English: from medieval Latin *acquitare* 'pay a debt', from *ad-* 'to' + *quitare* 'set free'.

acre /ˈeɪkə/ ■ n. a unit of land area equal to 0.405 hectare (4 840 square yards).
– DERIVATIVES **acreage** n. **-acred** adj.
– ORIGIN Old English *æcer* (denoting the amount of land a yoke of oxen could plough in a day), of Germanic origin.

acrid /ˈakrɪd/ ■ adj. unpleasantly bitter or pungent.
– DERIVATIVES **acridity** n. **acridly** adv.
– ORIGIN C18: from Latin *acer, acri-* 'sharp, pungent'.

acriflavine /ˌakrɪˈfleɪvɪn, -iːn/ ■ n. a bright orange-red dye used as an antiseptic, derived from acridine, a chemical obtained from coal tar.
– ORIGIN C20: from **acridine** + Latin *flavus* 'yellow'.

acrimony /ˈakrɪməni/ ■ n. bitterness or ill feeling.
– DERIVATIVES **acrimonious** adj. **acrimoniously** adv.
– ORIGIN C16: from Latin *acrimonia*, from *acer, acri-* 'pungent, acrid'.

acrobat ■ n. an entertainer who performs acrobatics.
– DERIVATIVES **acrobatic** adj. **acrobatically** adv.
– ORIGIN C19: from Greek *akrobatos* 'walking on tiptoe', from *akron* 'tip' + *bainein* 'to walk'.

acrobatics ■ pl. n. [usu. treated as sing.] spectacular gymnastic feats.

acrolect /ˈakrə(ʊ)lɛkt/ ■ n. Linguistics the most prestigious dialect or variety of a language. Contrasted with BASILECT.
– DERIVATIVES **acrolectal** adj.
– ORIGIN 1960s: from Greek *akron* 'summit'.

acromegaly /ˌakrə(ʊ)ˈmɛɡəli/ ■ n. Medicine abnormal growth of the hands, feet, and face, caused by overproduction of growth hormone by the pituitary gland.
– DERIVATIVES **acromegalic** /-mɪˈɡalɪk/ adj.
– ORIGIN C19: from Greek *akron* 'tip, extremity' + *megas, megal-* 'great'.

acronym /ˈakrənɪm/ ■ n. a word formed from the initial letters of other words (e.g. *laser*, *Aids*).
– ORIGIN 1940s: from Greek *akron* 'end, tip' + *onoma* 'name'.

acropetal /əˈkrɒpɪt(ə)l/ ■ adj. Botany relating to or denoting growth upwards from the base or point of attachment. Often contrasted with BASIPETAL.
– DERIVATIVES **acropetally** adv.
– ORIGIN C19: from Greek *akron* 'tip' + Latin *petere* 'seek'.

acrophobia /ˌakrəˈfəʊbɪə/ ■ n. extreme or irrational fear of heights.
– DERIVATIVES **acrophobic** adj.
– ORIGIN C19: from Greek *akron* 'summit' + -PHOBIA.

acropolis /əˈkrɒpəlɪs/ ■ n. a citadel or fortified part of an ancient Greek city, built on high ground.
– ORIGIN Greek, from *akron* 'summit' + *polis* 'city'.

across ■ prep. & adv. from one side to the other of (something). ▸ expressing movement over a place or region. ▸ on or towards the other side of.
– PHRASES **across the board** applying to all.
– ORIGIN Middle English: from Old French *a croix*, *en croix* 'in or on a cross'.

acrostic /əˈkrɒstɪk/ ■ n. a poem or puzzle in which certain letters in each line form a word or words.
– ORIGIN C16: from Greek, from *akron* 'end' + *stikhos* 'row, line of verse'.

acrylic ■ adj. denoting a synthetic resin or textile fibre made from polymers of acrylic acid or acrylates.
– ORIGIN C19: from the liquid aldehyde *acrolein*, from Latin *acer* 'pungent' + *ol(eum)* 'oil'.

acrylic acid ■ n. Chemistry a pungent liquid organic acid which can be polymerized to make synthetic resins.
– DERIVATIVES **acrylate** n.

acrylonitrile /ˌakrɪlə(ʊ)ˈnʌɪtrʌɪl/ ■ n. Chemistry a pungent, toxic liquid used in making artificial fibres and other polymers.

ACT ■ abbrev. Australian Capital Territory.

act ■ v. **1** take action; do something. ▸ (**act up**) informal behave badly. **2** (**act for/on behalf of**) represent on a contractual or legal basis. ▸ [as adj. **acting**] temporarily doing the duties of another. **3** take effect or have a particular effect. **4** perform a fictional role in a play or film. ▸ behave so as to appear to be: *I acted dumb*. ▸ (**act something out**) perform a narrative as if it were a play. ■ n. **1** a thing done. **2** a simulation or pretence. ▸ a particular type of behaviour or routine: *he did his Sir Galahad act*. **3** Law a written ordinance of Parliament, Congress, etc. **4** dated a record of the decisions or proceedings of a committee or an academic body. **5** a main division of a play, ballet, or opera. **6** a set performance.
– PHRASES **act of God** an instance of uncontrollable natural forces in operation. **act of grace** a privilege or concession that cannot be claimed as a right. **get** (or **be**) **in on the act** informal become (or be) involved in a particular activity, in order to gain an advantage.
– DERIVATIVES **acting** n.
– ORIGIN Middle English: from Latin *actus* 'event, thing done', from *agere* 'do, act'.

actin /ˈaktɪn/ ■ n. Biochemistry a protein which forms (together with myosin) the contractile filaments of muscle cells.
– ORIGIN 1940: from Greek *aktis, aktin-* 'ray'.

actinian /akˈtɪnɪən/ ■ n. Zoology a sea anemone.
– ORIGIN C18: from the genus name *Actinia*, from Greek *aktis* 'ray'.

actinic /akˈtɪnɪk/ ■ adj. technical (of light or lighting) able to cause photochemical reactions, in photography, through having a significant short-wavelength or ultraviolet component.
– DERIVATIVES **actinism** n.
– ORIGIN C19: from Greek *aktis, aktin-* 'ray'.

actinide /ˈaktɪnʌɪd/ ■ n. Chemistry any of the series of fifteen radioactive metallic elements from actinium (atomic number 89) to lawrencium (atomic number 103) in the periodic table.
– ORIGIN 1940s: from ACTINIUM.

actinium /akˈtɪnɪəm/ ■ n. the chemical element of atomic number 89, a rare radioactive metallic element of the actinide series that occurs as an impurity in uranium ores. (Symbol: **Ac**)
– ORIGIN C20: from Greek *aktis, aktin-* 'ray'.

actinolite /akˈtɪnəlʌɪt/ ■ n. a green mineral of the amphibole group containing calcium, magnesium, and iron and occurring chiefly in metamorphic rocks and as a form of asbestos.
– ORIGIN C18: from Greek *aktis, aktin-* 'ray' + *lithos* 'stone' (because of the ray-like crystals).

actinomorphic /ˌaktɪnə(ʊ)ˈmɔːfɪk/ ■ adj. Biology characterized by radial symmetry, such as a starfish. Compare with ZYGOMORPHIC.
– DERIVATIVES **actinomorphy** n.
– ORIGIN C19: from Greek *aktis* 'ray' + *morphē* 'form'.

actinomycete /ˌaktɪnə(ʊ)ˈmʌɪsiːt/ ■ n. a filamentous bacterium of an order (Actinomycetales) including the streptomycetes.
– ORIGIN 1920s: from Greek *aktis* 'ray' + *mukētes*, pl. of *mukēs* 'fungus'.

action ■ n. **1** the process of doing something to achieve an aim. **2** a thing done. **3** the effect or influence of something such as a chemical. **4** a legal process; a lawsuit. **5** armed conflict. **6** the way in which something works or

moves. ■ v. take action on.
– PHRASES **in action** engaged in an activity; in operation. **out of action** not working.
– ORIGIN Middle English: from Latin *actio(n-)*, from *agere* 'do, act'.

actionable ■ adj. Law giving sufficient reason to take legal action.

action potential ■ n. Physiology the change in electrical potential associated with the passage of an impulse along the membrane of a muscle cell or nerve cell.

action replay ■ n. a playback of part of a television broadcast, especially one in slow motion.

action stations ■ pl. n. the positions taken up by military personnel in preparation for action.

activate ■ v. make active or operative. ▸ convert (a substance, molecule, etc.) into a reactive form.
– DERIVATIVES **activation** n. **activator** n.

activated carbon (also **activated charcoal**) ■ n. charcoal that has been heated or otherwise treated to increase its adsorptive power.

activated sludge ■ n. aerated sewage containing aerobic micro-organisms which help to break it down.

active ■ adj. **1** moving or tending to move about vigorously or frequently. ▸ (of a person's mind or imagination) alert and lively. **2** participating in a particular sphere or activity. **3** working. **4** (of an electric circuit) capable of modifying its state or characteristics automatically in response to input or feedback. **5** (of a volcano) erupting or having erupted in the historical times. **6** (of a disease) not in remission or latent. **7** having a chemical or biological effect on something. **8** Grammar denoting a voice of verbs in which the subject is typically the person or thing performing the action and which can take a direct object (e.g. *she loved him* as opposed to *he was loved*). The opposite of **PASSIVE**. ■ n. Grammar an active form of a verb.
– DERIVATIVES **actively** adv.
– ORIGIN Middle English: from Latin *activus*, from *agere* 'act, do'.

active immunity ■ n. Physiology immunity which results from the production of antibodies by the immune system.

active matrix ■ n. Electronics a display system in which each pixel is individually controlled.

active service ■ n. direct participation in military operations as a member of the armed forces.

active site ■ n. Biochemistry a region on an enzyme that binds to a protein or other substance during a reaction.

active transport ■ n. Biology the movement of ions or molecules across a cell membrane into a region of higher concentration, assisted by enzymes and requiring energy.

activism ■ n. the use of vigorous campaigning to bring about political or social change.
– DERIVATIVES **activist** n. & adj.

activity ■ n. (pl. **-ies**) **1** a condition in which things are happening or being done. ▸ busy or vigorous action or movement. **2** an action taken in pursuit of an objective. ▸ a recreational pursuit. **3** the degree to which something displays its characteristic property or behaviour.

act of contrition ■ n. (in the Roman Catholic Church) a penitential prayer.

actomyosin /ˌaktə(ʊ)ˈmaɪəsɪn/ ■ n. Biochemistry a complex of actin and myosin of which the contractile protein filaments of muscle tissue are composed.

actor ■ n. **1** a person whose profession is acting. **2** a participant in an action or process.

actress ■ n. a female actor.
– DERIVATIVES **actressy** adj.

actual /ˈaktʃʊəl, -tjʊəl/ ■ adj. **1** existing in fact. **2** current.
– DERIVATIVES **actuality** n. **actualization** (also **-isation**) n. **actualize** (also **-ise**) v.
– ORIGIN Middle English: from Old French *actuel* 'active, practical', from Latin *actus* (see ACT).

actually ■ adv. **1** as the truth or facts of a situation. **2** as a matter of fact; even.

actuary /ˈaktʃʊəri, -tjʊ-/ ■ n. (pl. **-ies**) **1** a person who compiles and analyses statistics in order to calculate insurance risks and premiums. **2** (also **actuarius**) S. African an officer of the Synod of the Dutch Reformed Church.

– DERIVATIVES **actuarial** adj. **actuarially** (also **actuarily**) adv.
– ORIGIN C16: from Latin *actuarius* 'bookkeeper', from *actus* (see ACT).

actuate /ˈaktʃʊeɪt, -tjʊ-/ ■ v. **1** cause to operate. **2** motivate to act in a particular way.
– DERIVATIVES **actuation** n. **actuator** n.
– ORIGIN C16: from medieval Latin *actuare*, from Latin *actus* (see ACT).

actus reus /ˌaktəs ˈreɪəs/ ■ n. Law action or conduct which is a constituent element of a crime, as opposed to the mental state of the accused. Compare with **MENS REA**.
– ORIGIN Latin, 'guilty act'.

acuity /əˈkjuːɪti/ ■ n. sharpness or keenness of thought, vision, or hearing.
– ORIGIN Middle English: from medieval Latin *acuitas*, from Latin *acuere* (see ACUTE).

aculeate /əˈkjuːlɪət/ ■ adj. Entomology denoting hymenopterous insects with stings, e.g. bees and wasps.
– ORIGIN C17: from Latin, from *aculeus* 'a sting', diminutive of *acus* 'needle'.

acumen /ˈakjʊmən, əˈkjuːmən/ ■ n. the ability to make good judgements and take quick decisions.
– ORIGIN C16: from Latin, 'sharpness, point', from *acuere* (see ACUTE).

acuminate /əˈkjuːmɪnət/ ■ adj. Biology (of a plant or animal structure) tapering to a point.
– ORIGIN C16: from late Latin *acuminare*, from *acuere* (see ACUTE).

acupoint /ˈakjʊpɔɪnt/ ■ n. any of the supposed energy points on the body where acupuncture needles are inserted or manual pressure is applied during acupressure.

acupressure /ˈakjʊˌprɛʃə/ ■ n. a system of complementary medicine in which manual pressure is applied to the body at specific points along supposed lines of energy.
– ORIGIN 1950s: blend of ACUPUNCTURE and PRESSURE.

acupuncture /ˈakjʊˌpʌŋ(k)tʃə/ ■ n. a system of complementary medicine in which fine needles are inserted in the skin at specific points along supposed lines of energy.
– DERIVATIVES **acupuncturist** n.
– ORIGIN C17: from Latin *acu* 'with a needle' + PUNCTURE.

acute ■ adj. **1** critical; serious. ▸ (of an illness) coming sharply to a crisis; severe. Often contrasted with **CHRONIC**. **2** perceptive; shrewd. ▸ (of a physical sense or faculty) highly developed. **3** (of an angle) less than 90°. **4** (of a sound) high; shrill. ■ n. short for **ACUTE ACCENT**.
– DERIVATIVES **acutely** adv. **acuteness** n.
– ORIGIN Middle English: from Latin *acuere* 'sharpen', from *acus* 'needle'.

acute accent ■ n. a mark (´) placed over certain letters in some languages to indicate a feature such as altered sound quality (e.g. in *fiancée*).

-acy ■ suffix forming nouns of state or quality: *celibacy*.
– ORIGIN from Latin *-atia*.

acyclic /eɪˈsʌɪklɪk, -ˈsɪk-/ ■ adj. **1** not displaying or forming part of a cycle. **2** Chemistry (of a compound or molecule) containing no rings of atoms.

acyclovir /eɪˈsʌɪkləʊˌvʌɪə/ ■ n. Medicine an antiviral drug used chiefly in the treatment of herpes and Aids.
– ORIGIN 1970s: from *acycl(ic)* + *vir(al DNA)*.

acyl /ˈeɪsʌɪl, ˈasɪl/ ■ n. [as modifier] Chemistry of or denoting a radical of general formula -C(O)R, where R is an alkyl group, derived from a carboxylic acid.
– ORIGIN C19: coined in German, from Latin *acidus* (see ACID).

acylate /ˈeɪsʌɪleɪt, ˈasɪl-/ ■ v. Chemistry introduce an acyl group into (a molecule or compound).
– DERIVATIVES **acylation** n.

AD ■ abbrev. Anno Domini (placed after a date, indicating that it comes the specified number of years after the traditional date of Christ's birth).
– ORIGIN Latin 'in the year of the Lord'.

A/D ■ abbrev. Electronics analogue to digital.

ad ■ n. informal **1** an advertisement. **2** Tennis advantage.

-ad

-ad¹ /ad, əd/ ■ suffix forming nouns: **1** in collective numerals: *myriad*. **2** in names of females in classical mythology: *dryad*. **3** in names of poems and similar compositions: *Iliad*. **4** forming names of members of some taxonomic groupings: *bromeliad*.
– ORIGIN from Greek *-as, -ad-*.

-ad² /əd/ ■ suffix forming nouns such as *ballad, salad*. Compare with **-ADE²**.
– ORIGIN from French *-ade*.

ad- (also **a-** before *sc, sp, st*; **ac-** before *c, k, q*; **af-** before *f*; **ag-** before *g*; **al-** before *l*; **an-** before *n*; **ap-** before *p*; **ar-** before *r*; **as-** before *s*; **at-** before *t*) ■ prefix **1** denoting motion or direction to: *advance*. **2** denoting reduction or change into: *adulterate*. **3** denoting addition or increase: *adjunct*.
– ORIGIN from Latin *ad* 'to'.

Ada /ˈeɪdə/ ■ n. a high-level computer programming language used chiefly in real-time computerized control systems, e.g. for aircraft navigation.
– ORIGIN 1980s: named after the C19 English mathematician *Ada* Lovelace.

adage /ˈadɪdʒ/ ■ n. a proverb or short statement expressing a general truth.
– ORIGIN C16: from Latin *adagium* 'saying', from form of *aio* 'I say'.

adamant ■ adj. refusing to be persuaded or to change one's mind.
– DERIVATIVES **adamance** n. **adamancy** n. **adamantly** adv.
– ORIGIN Old English, from Greek *adamas* 'untameable, invincible' (later used to denote the hardest metal or stone, hence diamond), from *a-* 'not' + *daman* 'to tame'.

adamantine /ˌadəˈmantʌɪn/ ■ adj. poetic/literary unbreakable.

Adam's apple ■ n. a projection at the front of the neck formed by the thyroid cartilage of the larynx, often prominent in men.
– ORIGIN C18: so named from the notion that a piece of the forbidden fruit became lodged in Adam's throat.

adapt ■ v. **1** make suitable for a new use or purpose. **2** become adjusted to new conditions.
– DERIVATIVES **adaptability** n. **adaptable** adj. **adaptably** adv. **adaptive** adj.
– ORIGIN Middle English: from Latin, from *ad-* 'to' + *aptare*, from *aptus* 'fit'.

adaptation ■ n. **1** the action or process of adapting or being adapted. **2** a film or play adapted from a written work. **3** Biology a change or the process of change by which an organism or species becomes better suited to its environment.

adaption ■ n. another term for ADAPTATION.

adaptive radiation ■ n. Biology the diversification of a group of organisms into forms filling different ecological niches.

adaptogen /əˈdaptədʒ(ə)n/ ■ n. (in herbal medicine) a natural substance considered to help the body adapt to stress.
– DERIVATIVES **adaptogenic** adj.

adaptor (also **adapter**) ■ n. **1** a device for connecting pieces of equipment. ▸ a device for connecting more than one plug at a time or plugs of a non-standard type to an electrical socket. **2** a person who adapts a text for filming, broadcasting, or the stage.

adaxial /adˈaksɪəl/ ■ adj. Botany facing toward the stem (in particular denoting the upper surface of a leaf). The opposite of ABAXIAL.

ADC ■ abbrev. **1** aide-de-camp. **2** analogue to digital converter.

add ■ v. **1** join to or put with something else. ▸ (**add up**) increase in amount, number, or degree. **2** put together (two or more numbers or amounts) to calculate their total value. ▸ (**add up to**) amount to. **3** (**add up**) informal make sense. **4** say as a further remark.
– ORIGIN Middle English: from Latin *addere*, from *ad-* 'to' + *dare* 'put'.

added value ■ n. another term for VALUE ADDED.

addendum /əˈdɛndəm/ ■ n. (pl. **addenda** /-də/) an extra item added at the end of a book or text.
– ORIGIN C17: Latin, 'that which is to be added', from *addere* (see ADD).

adder¹ ■ n. any of a group of highly venomous snakes with large hinged fangs, typically with a dark-patterned stocky body and a spade-shaped head, e.g. puff adder, berg adder. [Family Viperidae: many genera and species.] ▸ a small venomous Eurasian snake which has a dark zigzag pattern on its back. [*Vipera berus*.]
– ORIGIN Old English *nædre* 'serpent, adder', of Germanic origin; the initial *n* was later lost by wrong division of *a naddre*.

adder² ■ n. Electronics a unit which adds together two input variables.

adder's tongue ■ n. a fern with a single pointed oval frond and an unbranched spore-bearing stem. [Genus *Ophioglossum*.]

addict ■ n. a person who is addicted to something.
– ORIGIN C20: from the obsolete verb *addict*, from ADDICTED.

addicted ■ adj. **1** physically dependent on a particular substance. **2** devoted to a particular interest or activity.
– ORIGIN C16: from the obsolete adj. *addict* 'bound, devoted', from Latin *addicere* 'assign', from *ad-* 'to' + *dicere* 'say'.

addiction ■ n. the fact or condition of being addicted.

addictive ■ adj. causing or likely to cause addiction.

addition ■ n. **1** the action or process of adding. ▸ a person or thing added. **2** the process of adding numbers or amounts. ▸ Mathematics the process of combining matrices, vectors, or other quantities under specific rules to obtain their sum or resultant.

additional ■ adj. extra or supplementary to what is already present or available.
– DERIVATIVES **additionally** adv.

additional member system ■ n. a type of proportional representation in which each elector votes separately for a party and for a representative.

addition reaction ■ n. Chemistry a reaction in which one molecule combines with another to form a larger molecule with no other products.

additive ■ n. a substance added to improve or preserve something. ■ adj. characterized by, relating to, or produced by addition.

addle ■ v. [often as adj. **addled**] **1** confuse. **2** (of an egg) become rotten, producing no chick. ■ adj. **1** unsound; muddled: *the film is addle-brained*. **2** archaic (of an egg) rotten.
– ORIGIN Middle English: from Old English *adela* 'liquid filth', of Germanic origin.

address ■ n. **1** the particulars of the place where someone lives or an organization is situated. **2** Computing a binary number identifying a location in a data storage system or computer memory. **3** a formal speech. ▸ a person's manner of speaking. ▸ (**addresses**) archaic courteous or amorous approaches. ■ v. **1** write someone's name and address on (an envelope or parcel). **2** speak formally to. ▸ (**address something to**) direct one's remarks to. **3** think about and begin to deal with. **4** Golf prepare to hit (the ball).
– DERIVATIVES **addressee** n. **addresser** n.
– ORIGIN Middle English: from Latin *ad-* 'towards' + *directus* (see DIRECT).

addressable ■ adj. Computing relating to or denoting a memory unit in which all locations can be separately accessed by a particular program.

adduce /əˈdjuːs/ ■ v. cite as evidence.
– DERIVATIVES **adducible** adj.
– ORIGIN Middle English: from Latin *adducere*, from *ad-* 'towards' + *ducere* 'to lead'.

adduct¹ /əˈdʌkt/ ■ v. (of a muscle) move (a limb or other part) towards the midline of the body or towards another part. The opposite of ABDUCT.
– DERIVATIVES **adduction** n. **adductor** n.
– ORIGIN C19: from Middle English *adduction*, from *adducere* (see ADDUCE).

adduct² /ˈadʌkt/ ■ n. Chemistry the product of an addition reaction between two compounds.
– ORIGIN 1940s: from German *Addukt* (blend of *Addition* and *Produkt*).

-ade¹ ■ suffix forming nouns: **1** denoting an action that is completed: *blockade*. **2** denoting the body concerned in an action or process: *brigade*. **3** denoting the product or result of an action or process: *arcade*.
– ORIGIN from Spanish or Portuguese *ada*, from Latin *-atus*, past participial suffix.

-ade² ■ suffix forming nouns such as *decade*.
– ORIGIN from French *-ade*, from Greek *-as*, *-ad-*.

-ade³ ■ suffix forming nouns: **1** equivalent in sense to nouns ending in -ADE¹: *brocade*. **2** denoting a person: *renegade*.
– ORIGIN from Spanish or Portuguese *-ado*, masculine form of *-ada* (see -ADE¹).

adenine /ˈadɪniːn/ ■ n. Biochemistry a compound which is one of the four constituent bases of nucleic acids.
– ORIGIN C19: from Greek *adēn* 'gland'.

adeno- ■ comb. form relating to a gland or glands: *adenocarcinoma*.
– ORIGIN from Greek *adēn* 'gland'.

adenocarcinoma /ˌadɪnəʊˌkɑːsɪˈnəʊmə/ ■ n. (pl. **adenocarcinomas** or **adenocarcinomata** /-mətə/) Medicine a malignant tumour formed from glandular structures in epithelial tissue.

adenoids /ˈadɪnɔɪdz/ ■ pl. n. a mass of enlarged lymphatic tissue between the back of the nose and the throat.
– DERIVATIVES **adenoidal** adj.
– ORIGIN C19: from Greek *adēn* 'gland'.

adenoma /ˌadɪˈnəʊmə/ ■ n. (pl. **adenomas** or **adenomata** /-mətə/) Medicine a benign tumour formed from glandular structures in epithelial tissue.
– ORIGIN C19: from Greek *adēn* 'gland'.

adenosine /əˈdɛnə(ʊ)siːn/ ■ n. Biochemistry a nucleoside consisting of adenine combined with ribose.

adenosine monophosphate ■ n. another term for **ADENYLIC ACID**.

adenosine triphosphate ■ n. Biochemistry a compound which by its breakdown in the body (to adenosine diphosphate) provides energy for physiological processes such as muscular contraction.

adenovirus /ˌadɪnəʊˌvʌɪrəs/ ■ n. Medicine any of a group of DNA viruses first discovered in adenoid tissue, most of which cause respiratory diseases.

adenylic acid /ˌadɪˈnɪlɪk/ ■ n. Biochemistry a compound consisting of adenosine bonded to a single phosphate group, present in most DNA and RNA.
– DERIVATIVES **adenylate** n.

adept ■ adj. /ˈadɛpt, əˈdɛpt/ very skilled or proficient. ■ n. /ˈadɛpt/ a person who is adept at something.
– DERIVATIVES **adeptly** adv. **adeptness** n.
– ORIGIN C17: from Latin *adept-*, *adipisci* 'obtain, attain'.

adequate ■ adj. satisfactory or acceptable.
– DERIVATIVES **adequacy** n. **adequately** adv.
– ORIGIN C17: from Latin *adaequare* 'make equal to', from *ad-* 'to' + *aequus* 'equal'.

à deux /ɑːˈdəː/ ■ adv. for or involving two people.
– ORIGIN from French.

ADF ■ abbrev. automatic direction-finder.

ad fin. /adˈfɪn/ ■ adv. at or near the end of a piece of writing.
– ORIGIN from Latin *ad finem* 'at the end'.

ADHD ■ abbrev. attention deficit hyperactivity disorder.

adhere /ədˈhɪə/ ■ v. (**adhere to**) **1** stick fast to. **2** believe in and follow the practices of. **3** represent truthfully and in detail.
– DERIVATIVES **adherence** n.
– ORIGIN C15: from Latin, from *ad-* 'to' + *haerere* 'to stick'.

adherent /ədˈhɪər(ə)nt/ ■ n. someone who supports a particular party, person, or set of ideas. ■ adj. sticking fast to something.

adhesion /ədˈhiːʒ(ə)n/ ■ n. the action or process of adhering. ▸ Physics the sticking together of particles of different substances.

adhesive /ədˈhiːsɪv, -zɪv/ ■ adj. causing adherence; sticky. ■ n. an adhesive substance.
– DERIVATIVES **adhesively** adv. **adhesiveness** n.

ad hoc /adˈhɒk/ ■ adj. & adv. formed, arranged, or done for a particular purpose only.
– ORIGIN Latin, 'to this'.

adjudge

adhocracy /adˈhɒkrəsi/ ■ n. the replacement of a rigid bureaucracy with flexible and informal forms of organization.

ad hominem /adˈhɒmɪnɛm/ ■ adv. & adj. **1** associated with a particular person. **2** (of an argument) personal rather than objective.
– ORIGIN Latin, 'to the person'.

adiabatic /ˌeɪdʌɪəˈbatɪk, ˌadɪə-/ ■ adj. Physics **1** relating to or denoting a process or condition in which heat does not enter or leave the system concerned. **2** impassable to heat.
– DERIVATIVES **adiabatically** adv.
– ORIGIN C19: from Greek *adiabatos* 'impassable', from *a-* 'not' + *dia* 'through' + *batos* 'passable'.

adiate ■ v. S. African Law accept (an inheritance) as the beneficiary of a will. ▸ inherit.
– DERIVATIVES **adiation** n.
– ORIGIN from Latin *adire* 'to approach'.

adieu /əˈdjuː/ ■ exclam. chiefly poetic/literary goodbye.
– ORIGIN Middle English: from Old French, from *a* 'to' + *Dieu* 'God'.

ad infinitum /ˌad ɪnfɪˈnʌɪtəm/ ■ adv. endlessly; forever.
– ORIGIN Latin, 'to infinity'.

ad interim /ad ˈɪntərɪm/ ■ adv. for the meantime.
– ORIGIN Latin, from *ad* 'to' and *interim* 'meanwhile'.

adios /ˌadɪˈɒs/ ■ exclam. Spanish term for **GOODBYE**.
– ORIGIN Spanish *adiós*, from *a* 'to' + *Dios* 'God'.

adipocyte /ˈadɪpə(ʊ)sʌɪt/ ■ n. Biology a cell specialized for the storage of fat, found in connective tissue.
– ORIGIN 1930s: from ADIPOSE + -CYTE.

adipose /ˈadɪpəʊs, -z/ ■ adj. technical denoting body tissue used for the storage of fat.
– ORIGIN C18: from Latin *adeps, adip-* 'fat'.

adit /ˈadɪt/ ■ n. an access or drainage passage leading horizontally into a mine.
– ORIGIN C17: from Latin *aditus* 'approach, entrance'.

Adivasi /ˌɑːdɪˈvɑːsi/ ■ n. (pl. same or **Adivasis**) a member of an aboriginal tribal people of India.
– ORIGIN from modern Sanskrit *ādivāsī*, from *ādi* 'the beginning' + *vāsin* 'inhabitant'.

Adj. ■ abbrev. adjutant.

adjacent /əˈdʒeɪs(ə)nt/ ■ adj. **1** next to or adjoining something else. **2** Geometry (of a pair of angles) formed on the same side of a straight line when intersected by another line.
– DERIVATIVES **adjacency** n.
– ORIGIN Middle English: from Latin *adjacere* 'lie near to', from *ad-* 'to' + *jacere* 'lie down'.

adjective ■ n. Grammar a word naming an attribute of a noun, such as *sweet*, *red*, or *technical*.
– DERIVATIVES **adjectival** adj. **adjectivally** adv.
– ORIGIN Middle English: from Old French *adjectif*, from Latin *adicere* 'add'.

adjoin ■ v. [often as adj. **adjoining**] be next to and joined with.
– ORIGIN Middle English: from Old French *ajoindre*, from Latin *adjungere*, from *ad-* 'to' + *jungere* 'to join'.

adjoint ■ adj. Mathematics related to a given function, matrix, or quantity by a particular process of transposition.
– ORIGIN C19: from French, 'joined to', from *adjoindre* (see **ADJOIN**).

adjourn /əˈdʒəːn/ ■ v. **1** break off (a meeting) with the intention of resuming it later. **2** postpone (a resolution or sentence).
– DERIVATIVES **adjournment** n.
– ORIGIN Middle English ('summon to appear on a particular day'): from Old French *ajorner*, from *a jorn* (*nome*) 'to an (appointed) day'.

Adjt ■ abbrev. adjutant.

adjudge ■ v. **1** consider or declare to be true or the case. **2** (in legal use) award (compensation). **3** (in legal use) condemn to pay a penalty.
– DERIVATIVES **adjudgement** (also **adjudgment**) n.
– ORIGIN Middle English: from Old French *ajuger*, from Latin *adjudicare*, from *ad-* 'to' + *judicare*, from *judex* 'a judge'.

adjudicate

adjudicate /əˈdʒuːdɪkeɪt/ ■ v. make a formal judgement on a disputed matter. ▸ act as a judge in a competition.
— DERIVATIVES **adjudication** n. **adjudicative** adj. **adjudicator** n.
— ORIGIN C18: from Latin *adjudicare* (see ADJUDGE).

adjunct /ˈadʒʌŋ(k)t/ ■ n. **1** an additional and supplementary part. **2** an assistant. **3** Grammar a word or phrase in a sentence other than the verb or predicate. ■ adj. connected or added in an auxiliary way.
— DERIVATIVES **adjunctive** adj.
— ORIGIN C16: from Latin *adjungere* (see ADJOIN).

adjunction ■ n. Mathematics the joining of two sets to form a larger set.

adjure /əˈdʒʊə/ ■ v. formal solemnly urge to do something.
— DERIVATIVES **adjuration** n. **adjuratory** /-rət(ə)ri/ adj.
— ORIGIN Middle English: from Latin, from *ad-* 'to' + *jurare* 'swear'.

adjust ■ v. **1** alter slightly in order to achieve a correct or desired result. ▸ adapt or become used to a new situation. **2** assess (loss or damages) when settling an insurance claim.
— DERIVATIVES **adjustability** n. **adjustable** adj. **adjuster** n. **adjustment** n.
— ORIGIN C17: from obsolete French *adjuster*, from Latin *ad-* 'to' + *juxta* 'near'.

adjutant /ˈadʒʊt(ə)nt/ ■ n. a military officer acting as an administrative assistant to a senior officer.
— DERIVATIVES **adjutancy** n.
— ORIGIN C17: from Latin *adjutare*, from *adjuvare* (see ADJUVANT).

adjutant general ■ n. (pl. **adjutants general**) (in the British army) a high-ranking administrative officer. ▸ (in the US army) the chief administrative officer.

adjuvant /ˈadʒʊv(ə)nt/ Medicine ■ adj. (of therapy) applied after initial treatment for cancer to suppress secondary tumour formation. ■ n. a substance which enhances the body's immune response to an antigen.
— ORIGIN C16: from Latin *adjuvare*, from *ad-* 'towards' + *juvare* 'to help'.

ad-lib ■ v. (**ad-libbed**, **ad-libbing**) speak or perform in public without preparing in advance. ■ adv. & adj. **1** spoken without advance preparation. **2** as much and as often as desired. ■ n. an ad-lib remark or speech.
— ORIGIN C19: abbrev. of Latin *ad libitum* 'according to pleasure'.

ad litem /ad ˈlʌɪtɛm/ ■ adj. Law acting in a lawsuit on behalf of a child or an adult who cannot represent themself.
— ORIGIN Latin, 'for the lawsuit'.

Adm. ■ abbrev. Admiral.

adman ■ n. (pl. **-men**) informal a person who works in advertising.

admin ■ n. informal administration.

administer ■ v. **1** attend to the organization or implementation of. **2** dispense (a drug or remedy). ▸ deal out (punishment). **3** Christian Church (of a priest) perform the rites of (a sacrament). **4** archaic or Law direct the taking of (an oath).
— DERIVATIVES **administrable** adj.
— ORIGIN Middle English: from Latin, from *ad-* 'to' + *ministrare* (see MINISTER).

administrate ■ v. administer; carry out administration.
— DERIVATIVES **administrative** adj. **administratively** adv. **administrator** n.

administration ■ n. **1** the organization and running of a business or system. **2** the government in power. ▸ chiefly N. Amer. the term of office of a political leader or government. ▸ (in the US) a government agency. **3** Law the management and disposal of the property of a deceased person or debtor, or of an insolvent company, by a legally appointed administrator. **4** the action of administering.

administration board ■ n. S. African historical (under apartheid) a regional government body responsible for implementing laws and regulations which affected black people living outside the homelands.

administratrix /ədˌmɪnɪˈstreɪtrɪks/ ■ n. (pl. **administratrixes**, **administratrices** /-triːsiːz/) Law a female administrator of an estate.

admirable ■ adj. deserving respect and approval.
— DERIVATIVES **admirably** adv.

admiral ■ n. (**Admiral**) the highest commissioned rank in the navy, above vice admiral.
— DERIVATIVES **admiralship** n.
— ORIGIN Middle English: from Old French *amiral*, from Arabic *'amīr* 'commander'.

Admiral of the Fleet ■ n. the highest rank of admiral in the Royal Navy.

Admiralty ■ n. (pl. **-ies**) **1** (in the UK) the government department that formerly administered the Royal Navy, now used only in titles. **2** (**admiralty**) Law the jurisdiction of courts of law over cases concerning ships or the sea.

admire ■ v. regard with respect or warm approval. ▸ look at with pleasure.
— DERIVATIVES **admiration** n. **admirer** n. **admiring** adj. **admiringly** adv.
— ORIGIN C16 (*admiration* Middle English): from Latin, from *ad-* 'at' + *mirari* 'wonder'.

admissible ■ adj. **1** acceptable or valid. **2** having the right to be admitted to a place.
— DERIVATIVES **admissibility** n.

admission ■ n. **1** a confession. **2** the process or fact of being admitted to a place.

admit ■ v. (**admitted**, **admitting**) **1** confess to be true or to be the case. ▸ confess to or acknowledge (a crime, fault, or failure). **2** allow to enter. ▸ receive into a hospital for treatment. **3** accept as valid. **4** (**admit of**) allow the possibility of.
— DERIVATIVES **admitted** adj. **admittedly** adv.
— ORIGIN Middle English: from Latin, from *ad-* 'to' + *mittere* 'send'.

admittance ■ n. **1** the process or fact of entering or being allowed to enter. **2** Physics a measure of electrical conduction, numerically equal to the reciprocal of the impedance.

admix ■ v. chiefly technical mix with something else.
— DERIVATIVES **admixture** n.

admonish ■ v. reprimand firmly. ▸ earnestly urge or warn.
— DERIVATIVES **admonishment** n.
— ORIGIN Middle English: from Latin *admonere* 'urge by warning'.

admonitory /ədˈmɒnɪt(ə)ri/ ■ adj. giving or conveying a warning or reprimand.
— DERIVATIVES **admonition** n. **admonitor** n.

adnate /ˈadneɪt/ ■ adj. Botany joined by having grown together.
— ORIGIN C17: from Latin *adnatus*, variant of *agnatus* (see AGNATE).

ad nauseam /ad ˈnɔːzɪam, -sɪam/ ■ adv. to a tiresomely excessive degree.
— ORIGIN Latin, 'to sickness'.

ado ■ n. trouble; fuss.
— ORIGIN Middle English ('action, business'): from Old Norse *at* (used to mark an infinitive) + DO[1].

-ado /ˈeɪdəʊ, ˈɑː-/ ■ suffix forming nouns such as *bravado*, *desperado*.
— ORIGIN from Spanish and Portuguese *-ado*, from Latin *-atus*.

adobe /əˈdəʊbi, əˈdəʊb/ ■ n. a kind of clay used to make sun-dried bricks.
— ORIGIN C18: from Spanish, from *adobar* 'to plaster', from Arabic, from *al* 'the' + *ṭūb* 'bricks'.

adolescent ■ adj. in the process of developing from a child into an adult. ■ n. an adolescent boy or girl.
— DERIVATIVES **adolescence** n.
— ORIGIN Middle English: from Latin *adolescere*, from *ad-* 'to' + *alescere* 'grow, grow up'.

Adonai /ˌadɒˈnʌɪ, -ˈneɪʌɪ/ ■ n. a Hebrew name for God.
— ORIGIN from Hebrew *'ăḏōnāy*.

Adonis /əˈdəʊnɪs/ ■ n. an extremely handsome young man.
— ORIGIN from the name of a beautiful youth in Greek mythology.

| CONSONANTS | **b** but | **d** dog | **f** few | **g** get | **h** he | **j** yes | **k** cat | **l** leg | **m** man | **n** no | **p** pen | **r** red |

adopt ■ v. **1** legally take (another's child) and bring it up as one's own. **2** choose to take up or follow (an option or course of action). **3** Brit. choose as a candidate for office. ▸ formally approve or accept. **4** assume (an attitude or position).
– DERIVATIVES **adoptable** adj. **adoptee** n. **adopter** n. **adoption** n.
– ORIGIN C15 (*adoption* Middle English): from Latin, from *ad-* 'to' + *optare* 'choose'.

adoptive ■ adj. **1** (of a child or parent) in that relationship by adoption. **2** denoting a place chosen as one's permanent place of residence.
– DERIVATIVES **adoptively** adv.

adorable ■ adj. inspiring great affection.
– DERIVATIVES **adorability** n. **adorableness** n. **adorably** adv.

adoral /ad'ɔːr(ə)l/ ■ adj. Zoology relating to or denoting the side or end where the mouth is situated.
– DERIVATIVES **adorally** adv.
– ORIGIN C19: from Latin *ad* 'to, at' + ORAL.

adore ■ v. **1** love and respect deeply. **2** worship or venerate (a deity).
– DERIVATIVES **adoration** n. **adorer** n. **adoring** adj. **adoringly** adv.
– ORIGIN Middle English: from Latin *adorare* 'to worship', from *ad-* 'to' + *orare* 'speak, pray'.

adorn ■ v. decorate.
– DERIVATIVES **adorner** n. **adornment** n.
– ORIGIN Middle English: from Latin, from *ad-* 'to' + *ornare* 'deck, add lustre'.

adpressed ■ adj. Botany lying closely against an adjacent part or the ground.

adrenal /ə'driːn(ə)l/ ■ adj. relating to or denoting a pair of ductless glands situated above the kidneys which secrete adrenalin, noradrenaline, and corticosteroid hormones. ■ n. an adrenal gland.

adrenalin /ə'drɛn(ə)lɪn/ (also **adrenaline**) ■ n. a hormone secreted by the adrenal glands that increases rates of blood circulation, breathing, and carbohydrate metabolism.
– ORIGIN C20: from ADRENAL.

adrenergic /ˌadrɪ'nəːdʒɪk/ ■ adj. Physiology relating to or denoting nerve cells in which adrenalin, noradrenaline, or a similar substance acts as a neurotransmitter.
– ORIGIN 1930s: from ADRENALIN + Greek *ergon* 'work'.

adrenocorticotrophic hormone /əˌdriːnə(ʊ)ˌkɔːtɪkə(ʊ)'trəʊfɪk, -'trɒfɪk/ (also **adrenocorticotropic hormone** /-'trəʊpɪk, -'trɒpɪk/) ■ n. Biochemistry a hormone stimulating the adrenal cortex, secreted by the pituitary gland.

adret /'adreɪ/ ■ n. Geography a mountain slope which faces the sun. Compare with UBAC.
– ORIGIN from French, from *à* 'to' + *droit* 'straight'.

Adriatic /ˌeɪdrɪ'atɪk/ ■ adj. of or relating to the region comprising the Adriatic Sea and its coasts and islands. ■ n. (**the Adriatic**) this region.

adrift ■ adj. & adv. **1** (of a boat) drifting without control. **2** informal no longer fixed in position.

adroit /ə'drɔɪt/ ■ adj. skilful.
– DERIVATIVES **adroitly** adv. **adroitness** n.
– ORIGIN C17: from French, from *à droit* 'according to right, properly'.

ADSL ■ abbrev. asymmetric digital subscriber line, a technology for transmitting digital information over standard telephone lines.

adsorb /əd'zɔːb, -'sɔːb/ ■ v. (of a solid) hold (molecules of a gas, liquid, or solute) as a thin film on surfaces outside or within the material.
– DERIVATIVES **adsorbable** adj. **adsorption** n. **adsorptive** adj.
– ORIGIN C19: from Latin, from *ad-* (expressing adherence) + ABSORB.

aduki /ə'duːki/ ■ n. variant of ADZUKI.

adulation /ˌadjʊ'leɪʃ(ə)n/ ■ n. excessive admiration.
– DERIVATIVES **adulate** v. **adulator** n. **adulatory** adj.
– ORIGIN Middle English: from Latin, from *adulari* 'fawn on'.

adult /'adʌlt, ə'dʌlt/ ■ n. a person who is fully grown and developed. ▸ Law a person who has reached the age of majority. ■ adj. fully grown and developed. ▸ of, for, or characteristic of adults.
– DERIVATIVES **adulthood** n. **adultly** adv.
– ORIGIN C16: from Latin *adolescere* (see ADOLESCENT).

adulterant ■ adj. denoting a substance used to adulterate another.

adulterate /ə'dʌltəreɪt/ ■ v. render poorer in quality by adding another substance.
– DERIVATIVES **adulteration** n.
– ORIGIN C16: from Latin *adulterare* 'to corrupt'.

adulterer ■ n. (fem. **adulteress**) a person who has committed adultery.
– ORIGIN C16: from obsolete *adulter* 'commit adultery', from Latin *adulterare* 'debauch, corrupt'.

adultery ■ n. voluntary sexual intercourse between a married person and a person who is not their spouse.
– DERIVATIVES **adulterous** adj. **adulterously** adv.
– ORIGIN C15: from Latin *adulter* 'adulterer'.

adumbrate /'adʌmbreɪt/ ■ v. formal **1** give a faint or general idea of. ▸ foreshadow. **2** overshadow.
– DERIVATIVES **adumbration** n. **adumbrative** adj.
– ORIGIN C16: from Latin, from *ad-* 'to' (as an intensifier) + *umbrare* 'cast a shadow'.

Adv. ■ abbrev. S. African Advocate.

ad valorem /ˌad və'lɔːrɛm/ ■ adv. & adj. (of the levying of taxes or duties) in proportion to the value of the goods or transaction concerned.
– ORIGIN Latin, 'according to the value'.

advance ■ v. **1** move forwards. ▸ cause to occur at an earlier date than planned. **2** make or cause to make progress. **3** put forward (a theory or suggestion). **4** hand over (payment) to (someone) as a loan or before it is due. ■ n. **1** a forward movement. **2** a development or improvement. **3** an amount of money advanced. **4** an approach made with the aim of initiating a sexual or amorous relationship or encounter. ■ adj. done, sent, or supplied beforehand.
– PHRASES **in advance** ahead in time.
– ORIGIN Middle English: from Old French *avancer* (v.), from late Latin *abante* 'in front', from *ab* 'from' + *ante* 'before'.

advanced ■ adj. **1** far on in progress or life. **2** complex; not elementary. **3** very modern.

advanced gas-cooled reactor ■ n. a nuclear reactor in which the coolant is carbon dioxide, with uranium oxide fuel clad in steel and using graphite as a moderator.

advanced level ■ n. the higher of the two main levels of the GCE examination, taken at age 17 or 18. Compare with ORDINARY LEVEL.

advance guard ■ n. a body of soldiers preceding and making preparations for the main body of an army.

advancement ■ n. **1** the process of promoting a cause or plan. **2** the promotion of a person in rank or status. **3** a development or improvement.

advantage ■ n. **1** a condition or circumstance that puts one in a favourable position. ▸ benefit; profit. **2** Tennis a score marking a point interim between deuce and winning the game. ■ v. be of benefit to. ▸ [as adj. **advantaged**] prosperous.
– PHRASES **take advantage of 1** make unfair use of for one's own benefit. **2** dated seduce. **3** make good use of the opportunities offered. **to advantage** in a way which displays or uses the best aspects.
– DERIVATIVES **advantageous** /ˌadv(ə)n'teɪdʒəs/ adj. **advantageously** adv.
– ORIGIN Middle English: from Old French *avantage*, from *avant* 'in front', from late Latin *abante* (see ADVANCE).

advection /əd'vɛkʃ(ə)n/ ■ n. the transfer of heat or matter by the flow of a fluid, especially horizontally in the atmosphere or the sea.
– DERIVATIVES **advect** v. **advective** adj.
– ORIGIN C20: from Latin, from *ad-* 'to' + *vehere* 'carry'.

advent /'adv(ə)nt, -vɛnt/ ■ n. **1** the arrival of a notable person or thing. **2** (**Advent**) Christian Church the coming or second coming of Christ. ▸ the first season of the Church year, leading up to Christmas and including the four

Advent calendar

preceding Sundays.
– ORIGIN Old English, from Latin *adventus* 'arrival', from *ad-* 'to' + *venire* 'come'.

Advent calendar ■ n. a calendar containing small numbered flaps, one of which is opened on each day of Advent to reveal a picture appropriate to the season.

Adventist ■ n. a member of a Christian sect emphasizing belief in the imminent second coming of Christ.
– DERIVATIVES **Adventism** n.

adventitious /ˌadv(ə)nˈtɪʃəs/ ■ adj. **1** happening according to chance. **2** coming from outside; not native. **3** Biology formed accidentally or in an unusual position. **4** Botany (of a root) growing directly from the stem or other upper part of a plant.
– DERIVATIVES **adventitiously** adv.
– ORIGIN C17: from Latin *adventicius* 'coming to us from abroad'.

Advent Sunday ■ n. Christian Church the first Sunday in Advent.

adventure ■ n. **1** an unusual, exciting, and daring experience. ▸ excitement arising from this. **2** archaic a commercial speculation. ■ v. dated engage in an adventure.
– DERIVATIVES **adventurer** n. **adventuresome** adj. **adventuress** n.
– ORIGIN Middle English: from Old French *aventure* (n.), from Latin *adventurus* 'about to happen', from *advenire* 'arrive'.

adventurism ■ n. willingness to take risks in business or politics.
– DERIVATIVES **adventurist** n. & adj.

adventurous ■ adj. open to or involving new or daring methods or experiences.
– DERIVATIVES **adventurously** adv. **adventurousness** n.

adverb ■ n. Grammar a word or phrase that modifies the meaning of an adjective, verb, or other adverb, or of a sentence (e.g. *gently, very, fortunately*).
– ORIGIN Middle English: from Latin *adverbium*, from *ad-* 'to' + *verbum* 'word, verb'.

adverbial Grammar ■ n. a word or phrase functioning as a major clause constituent and typically expressing place (*in the garden*), time (*in May*), or manner (*in a strange way*). ■ adj. relating to or functioning as an adverb or adverbial.
– DERIVATIVES **adverbially** adv.

adversarial /ˌadvəˈsɛːrɪəl/ ■ adj. **1** involving or characterized by conflict or opposition. **2** Law (of a legal procedure) in which the parties in a dispute have the responsibility for finding and presenting evidence. Compare with ACCUSATORIAL, INQUISITORIAL.
– DERIVATIVES **adversarially** adv.

adversary ■ n. /ˈadvəs(ə)ri/ (pl. **-ies**) an opponent. ■ adj. /ˈadvəs(ə)ri, ədˈvəːsəri/ another term for ADVERSARIAL.
– ORIGIN Middle English: from Latin *adversarius* 'opposed, opponent', from *adversus* (see ADVERSE).

adverse /ˈadvəːs/ ■ adj. harmful; unfavourable.
– DERIVATIVES **adversely** adv.
– ORIGIN Middle English: from Latin *adversus* 'against, opposite', from *advertere*, from *ad-* 'to' + *vertere* 'to turn'.

USAGE
A common error is to use **adverse** instead of **averse**, as in *I am not adverse to helping out*, rather than the correct form *I am not averse to helping out*.

adversity ■ n. (pl. **-ies**) difficulty; misfortune.

advert /ˈadvəːt/ ■ n. informal an advertisement.

advertise ■ v. **1** promote or publicize. **2** archaic notify.
– DERIVATIVES **advertiser** n. **advertising** n.
– ORIGIN Middle English: from Old French *advertiss-*, *advertir*, from Latin *advertere* (see ADVERSE).

advertisement ■ n. **1** a notice or display advertising something. **2** archaic a notice to readers in a book.

advertorial /ˌadvəːˈtɔːrɪəl/ ■ n. an advertisement in the style of an editorial or objective journalistic article.

advice ■ n. **1** guidance or recommendations offered with regard to future action. **2** a formal notice of a sale, delivery, or other transaction. **3** (**advices**) archaic news.

– ORIGIN Middle English: from Old French *avis*, from Latin *ad* 'to' + *visum*, past participle of *videre* 'to see'.

advice office ■ n. S. African a centre offering free paralegal assistance and advice on civil matters to the community, originally established to help those with problems caused by apartheid laws.

advisable ■ adj. to be recommended; sensible.
– DERIVATIVES **advisability** n. **advisably** adv.

advise ■ v. **1** recommend (a course of action). ▸ offer advice to. **2** inform about a fact or situation.
– DERIVATIVES **adviser** (also **advisor**) n.
– ORIGIN Middle English: from Latin *ad-* 'to' + *visere*, from *videre* 'to see'.

advised ■ adj. prudent. ▸ considered.
– DERIVATIVES **advisedly** adv.

advisement ■ n. archaic or N. Amer. careful consideration. ▸ advice or counsel.
– PHRASES **take something under advisement** N. Amer. reserve judgement while considering something.

advisory ■ adj. having the power to make recommendations but not to enforce them. ▸ recommended. ■ n. (pl. **-ies**) an official announcement, especially a warning of bad weather.

advocaat /ˈadvəkɑː/ ■ n. a liqueur made with eggs, sugar, and brandy.
– ORIGIN 1930s: from Dutch, 'advocate' (being orig. considered a lawyer's drink).

advocate ■ n. /ˈadvəkət/ **1** a person who publicly supports or recommends a particular cause or policy. **2** a person who pleads a case on someone else's behalf. ▸ S. African & Scottish Law a lawyer qualified to represent a client in the higher courts. Compare with ATTORNEY. ■ v. /ˈadvəkeɪt/ publicly recommend or support.
– DERIVATIVES **advocacy** n. **advocateship** n. **advocation** n.
– ORIGIN Middle English: from Old French *avocat*, from Latin *advocare* 'call (to one's aid)', from *ad-* 'to' + *vocare* 'to call'.

adze /adz/ (US **adz**) ■ n. a tool similar to an axe, with an arched blade at right angles to the handle.
– ORIGIN Old English *adesa*.

adzuki /ədˈzuːki/ (also **aduki**) ■ n. (pl. **adzukis**) **1** a small, round dark-red edible bean. **2** the bushy Asian plant which produces this bean. [*Vigna angularis*.]
– ORIGIN C18: from Japanese *azuki*.

A & E ■ abbrev. accident and emergency.

-ae /iː, ʌɪ/ ■ suffix forming plural nouns: **1** used in names of animal and plant families and other groups: *Felidae*. **2** used instead of *-as* in the plural of many non-naturalized nouns ending in *-a* derived from Latin or Greek: *larvae*.
– ORIGIN Latin pl. suffix, or representing Greek pl. ending *-ai*.

Aegean /iːˈdʒiːən, ɪ-/ ■ adj. relating to or denoting the region comprising the Aegean Sea and its coasts and islands. ■ n. (**the Aegean**) this region.

aegis /ˈiːdʒɪs/ ■ n. the protection, backing, or support of someone.
– ORIGIN C17: from Greek *aigis* 'shield of Zeus'.

aegrotat /ʌɪˈgrəʊtat, ˈiː-, iːˈgrəʊ-/ ■ n. a certificate stating that a student is too ill to attend an examination.
– ORIGIN C18: Latin, 'he is sick'.

-aemia (also **-haemia**, US **-emia** or **-hemia**) ■ comb. form in nouns denoting that a substance is present in the blood: *septicaemia*.
– ORIGIN from Greek, from *haima* 'blood'.

aeolian /iːˈəʊlɪən/ (US **eolian**) ■ adj. chiefly Geology relating to or arising from the action of the wind.
– ORIGIN C17: from *Aeolus*, the god of the winds in Greek mythology.

aeolian harp ■ n. a stringed instrument that produces musical sounds when a current of air passes through it.

Aeolian mode /iːˈəʊlɪən/ ■ n. Music the mode represented by the natural diatonic scale A–A (containing a minor 3rd, 6th, and 7th).
– ORIGIN C18: from Latin *Aeolius* 'from Aeolis', an ancient coastal district of Asia Minor.

aeon /ˈiːən/ ■ n. (US or technical also **eon**) **1** an indefinite and very long period of time. **2** Astronomy & Geology a unit of time equal to a thousand million years. **3** Geology a major

VOWELS a cat ɑː arm ɛ bed ɛː hair ə ago əː her ɪ sit i cosy iː see ɒ hot ɔː saw ʌ run

division of geological time, subdivided into eras.
–ORIGIN C17: from Greek *aiōn* 'age'.

aepyornis /ˌiːpɪˈɔːnɪs/ ■ n. an extinct giant flightless bird, found in Madagascar. [Genus *Aepyornis*.]
–ORIGIN C19: from Greek *aipus* 'high' + *ornis* 'bird'.

aerate /ˈɛːreɪt/ ■ v. introduce air into.
–DERIVATIVES **aeration** n. **aerator** n.
–ORIGIN C18: from Latin *aer* 'air'.

aerated ■ adj. (of a liquid) made effervescent by being charged with carbon dioxide or some other gas.

aerenchyma /ɛːˈrɛŋkɪmə/ ■ n. Botany a soft plant tissue containing air spaces, found especially in many aquatic plants.
–DERIVATIVES **aerenchymatous** adj.
–ORIGIN C19: from Greek *aēr* 'air' + *enkhuma* 'infusion'.

aerial /ˈɛːrɪəl/ ■ n. 1 a structure that transmits or receives radio or television signals. 2 (**aerials**) a type of freestyle skiing in which the skier jumps from a ramp and carries out manoeuvres in the air. ■ adj. 1 existing or taking place in the air or atmosphere. ▸ (of a bird) spending much of its time in flight. 2 involving the use of aircraft. 3 (of a part of a plant) growing above ground.
–DERIVATIVES **aerially** adv.
–ORIGIN C16: from Greek *aerios*, from *aēr* 'air'.

aerialist ■ n. a person who performs acrobatics high above the ground on a tightrope or trapezes.

aerie ■ n. US spelling of EYRIE.

aero- /ˈɛːrəʊ/ ■ comb. form 1 of or relating to air: *aerobic*. 2 of or relating to aircraft: *aerodrome*.
–ORIGIN from Greek *aēr* 'air'.

aerobatics ■ pl. n. [treated as sing. or pl.] feats of flying performed for an audience on the ground.
–DERIVATIVES **aerobatic** adj.
–ORIGIN FIRST WORLD WAR: from AERO- + a shortened form of ACROBATICS.

aerobe /ˈɛːrəʊb/ ■ n. Biology an aerobic micro-organism.
–ORIGIN C19: coined in French from Greek *aēr* + *bios* 'life'.

aerobic /ɛːˈrəʊbɪk/ ■ adj. 1 denoting physical exercise intended to improve the efficiency of the cardiovascular system in absorbing and transporting oxygen. 2 Biology relating to, involving, or requiring free oxygen.
–DERIVATIVES **aerobically** adv.
–ORIGIN C19: from AERO- + Greek *bios* 'life'.

aerobics ■ pl. n. [treated as sing. or pl.] aerobic exercises.

aerobiology ■ n. the study of the aerial transport of micro-organisms, spores, seeds, etc.

aerobraking ■ n. the process of slowing down a spacecraft by flying through a planet's atmosphere to produce aerodynamic drag.

aerodrome ■ n. Brit. a small airport or airfield.

aerodynamic ■ adj. 1 of or relating to aerodynamics. 2 having a shape which reduces the drag from air moving past.
–DERIVATIVES **aerodynamically** adv.

aerodynamics ■ pl. n. 1 [treated as sing.] the branch of science concerned with the properties of moving air and the interaction between the air and solid bodies moving through it. 2 [treated as pl.] aerodynamic properties.
–DERIVATIVES **aerodynamicist** n.

aerofoil (N. Amer. **airfoil**) ■ n. a structure with curved surfaces designed to give the most favourable ratio of lift to drag in flight.

aerogramme (US **aerogram**) ■ n. another term for AIR LETTER.

aerology ■ n. dated the study of the atmosphere.
–DERIVATIVES **aerological** adj.

aeronautics ■ pl. n. [usu. treated as sing.] the study or practice of travel through the air.
–DERIVATIVES **aeronautic** adj. **aeronautical** adj.
–ORIGIN C19: from Greek, from *aēr* 'air' + *nautēs* 'sailor'.

aeronomy /ɛːˈrɒnəmi/ ■ n. the branch of science concerned with the properties of the upper atmosphere.

aerophone ■ n. Music a wind instrument.

aeroplane (N. Amer. **airplane**) ■ n. a powered flying vehicle with fixed wings and a weight greater than that of the air it displaces.

–ORIGIN C19: from French *aéroplane*, from *aéro-* 'air' + Greek *-planos* 'wandering'.

aeroshell ■ n. a casing which protects a spacecraft during re-entry.

aerosol ■ n. 1 a substance enclosed under pressure and released as a fine spray by means of a propellant gas. 2 Chemistry a colloidal suspension of particles dispersed in air or gas.
–ORIGIN 1920s: from AERO- + SOL².

aerospace ■ n. the branch of technology and industry concerned with aviation and space flight.

aesthete /ˈiːsθiːt, ˈɛs-/ (US also **esthete**) ■ n. a person who is appreciative of or sensitive to art and beauty.
–ORIGIN C19: from Greek *aisthētēs* 'a person who perceives'.

aesthetic /iːsˈθɛtɪk, ɛs-/ (US also **esthetic**) ■ adj. concerned with beauty or the appreciation of beauty. ▸ of pleasing appearance. ▸ (**Aesthetic**) relating to or denoting a literary and artistic movement in England during the 1880s, devoted to 'art for art's sake' and rejecting the notion that art should have a social or moral purpose. ■ n. a set of principles underlying the work of a particular artist or artistic movement.
–DERIVATIVES **aesthetically** adv. **aestheticism** n. **aestheticize** (also **-ise**) v.
–ORIGIN C18: from Greek *aisthētikos*, from *aisthesthai* 'perceive'.

aesthetics (US also **esthetics**) ■ pl. n. [usu. treated as sing.] a set of principles concerned with the nature and appreciation of beauty, especially in art. ▸ the branch of philosophy which deals with questions of beauty and artistic taste.

aestivation /ˌiːstɪˈveɪʃ(ə)n, ˌɛst-/ (US **estivation**) ■ n. 1 Zoology prolonged torpor or dormancy of an insect, fish, or amphibian during a hot or dry period. 2 Botany the arrangement of petals and sepals in a flower bud before it opens. Compare with VERNATION.
–DERIVATIVES **aestivate** v.
–ORIGIN C17: from Latin *aestivare* 'spend the summer', from *aestus* 'heat'.

aether ■ n. variant spelling of ETHER (in senses 3 and 4).

aetiology /ˌiːtɪˈɒlədʒi/ (US **etiology**) ■ n. 1 Medicine the cause, set of causes, or manner of causation of a disease or condition. 2 the investigation or attribution of cause or a reason.
–DERIVATIVES **aetiologic** adj. **aetiological** adj. **aetiologically** adv.
–ORIGIN C16: from Greek, from *aitia* 'a cause' + *-logia* (see -LOGY).

AF ■ abbrev. 1 audio frequency. 2 autofocus.

af- ■ prefix variant spelling of AD- assimilated before *f* (as in *affiliate*, *affirm*).

Afar /ˈɑːfɑː/ ■ n. (pl. same or **Afars**) 1 a member of a people living in Djibouti and NE Ethiopia. 2 the Cushitic language of this people.
–ORIGIN from Afar *qafar*.

afar ■ adv. chiefly poetic/literary at or to a distance.
–ORIGIN Middle English *of feor* 'from far'.

afeared ■ adj. archaic afraid.
–ORIGIN Old English, from *āfǣran* 'frighten'.

affable ■ adj. good-natured and sociable.
–DERIVATIVES **affability** n. **affably** adv.
–ORIGIN Middle English: from Latin *affabilis*, from *ad-* 'to' + *fari* 'speak'.

affair ■ n. 1 an event or sequence of events of a specified kind or that has previously been referred to. 2 a matter that is a particular person's concern or responsibility.
▸ (**affairs**) matters of public interest and importance.
▸ (**affairs**) business and financial dealings. 3 a love affair.
–ORIGIN Middle English from Old French *afaire*, from *à faire* 'to do'.

affaire /aˈfɛː/ (also **affaire de** or **du cœur** /də ˈkəː, djuː/) ■ n. a love affair.
–ORIGIN C19: French, 'affair (of the heart)'.

affect

affect¹ /əˈfɛkt/ ■ v. have an effect on; make a difference to. ▸ touch the feelings of.
– DERIVATIVES **affecting** adj. **affectingly** adv.
– ORIGIN Middle English ('attack as a disease'): from Latin *afficere* 'affect'.

> **USAGE**
> **Affect** and **effect** are commonly confused. **Affect** is primarily a verb meaning 'make a difference to'. **Effect** is used both as a noun and a verb, meaning 'a result' or 'bring about (a result)'.

affect² /əˈfɛkt/ ■ v. pretend to have or feel. ▸ use, wear, or assume pretentiously or so as to impress.
– ORIGIN Middle English ('like, love'): from Latin *affectare* 'aim at', from *afficere* 'affect, influence'.

affect³ /ˈafɛkt/ ■ n. Psychology emotion or desire as influencing behaviour.
– ORIGIN C19: from German *Affekt*, from Latin *affectus* 'disposition', from *afficere* (see **AFFECT²**).

affectation ■ n. behaviour, speech, or writing that is artificial and designed to impress. ▸ a studied display of feeling.
– ORIGIN C16: from Latin, from *affectare* (see **AFFECT²**).

affected ■ adj. artificial, pretentious, and designed to impress.
– DERIVATIVES **affectedly** adv. **affectedness** n.

affection ■ n. 1 a feeling of fondness or liking. 2 archaic the action or process of affecting or being affected.
– ORIGIN Middle English: from Latin, from *afficere* (see **AFFECT²**).

affectionate ■ adj. readily showing affection.
– DERIVATIVES **affectionately** adv.

affective ■ adj. chiefly Psychology relating to moods, feelings, and attitudes.
– ORIGIN Middle English: from late Latin *affectivus*, from *afficere* (see **AFFECT²**).

afferent /ˈaf(ə)r(ə)nt/ Physiology ■ adj. relating to or denoting the conduction of nerve impulses or blood inwards or towards something. The opposite of **EFFERENT**. ■ n. an afferent nerve fibre or vessel.
– ORIGIN C19: from Latin *afferre* 'bring towards'.

affiance /əˈfʌɪəns/ ■ v. (**be affianced**) poetic/literary be engaged to marry.
– ORIGIN C15: from Old French *afiancer*, from *afier* 'promise, entrust', from medieval Latin *affidare* 'declare on oath'.

affidavit /ˌafɪˈdeɪvɪt/ ■ n. Law a written statement confirmed by oath or affirmation, for use as evidence in court.
– ORIGIN C16: from medieval Latin, 'he has stated on oath', from *affidare*.

affiliate ■ v. /əˈfɪlɪeɪt/ (usu. **be affiliated to/with**) officially attach or connect to an organization. ▸ (of an organization) admit as a member. ■ n. /əˈfɪlɪət/ an affiliated person or organization.
– DERIVATIVES **affiliation** n.
– ORIGIN C18: from medieval Latin *affiliare* 'adopt as a son'.

affinal /əˈfʌɪn(ə)l/ ■ adj. Anthropology concerning or having a family relationship by marriage.
– ORIGIN C19: from Latin *affinis* (see **AFFINITY**).

affine /əˈfʌɪn/ ■ adj. Mathematics allowing for or preserving parallel relationships. ■ n. Anthropology a relative by marriage.
– ORIGIN C16: from Latin *affinis* (see **AFFINITY**).

affinity ■ n. (pl. **-ies**) 1 a spontaneous or natural liking or sympathy. ▸ a close relationship based on a common origin or structure. ▸ relationship by marriage. 2 chiefly Biochemistry the degree to which a substance tends to combine with another.
– ORIGIN Middle English: from Latin *affinitas*, from *affinis* 'related' (literally 'bordering on').

affinity card ■ n. a cheque card or credit card for which the bank donates a portion of the money spent using the card to a specific charity.

affirm ■ v. state emphatically or publicly. ▸ Law ratify (a judgement or agreement). ▸ Law make a formal declaration rather than taking an oath.
– DERIVATIVES **affirmation** n. **affirmatory** adj. **affirmer** n.
– ORIGIN Middle English: from Latin *affirmare*, from *ad-* 'to' + *firmus* 'strong'.

affirmative ■ adj. 1 agreeing with or consenting to a statement or request. ▸ Grammar & Logic stating that a fact is so. Contrasted with **NEGATIVE** and **INTERROGATIVE**. 2 relating to affirmative action. ■ n. 1 an affirmative statement or word. ▸ Logic a statement asserting that something is true of the subject of a proposition. 2 derogatory a person who has benefited from affirmative action. ■ exclam. chiefly N. Amer. yes.
– PHRASES **in the affirmative** so as to accept or agree to a statement or request.
– DERIVATIVES **affirmatively** adv.
– ORIGIN Middle English ('assertive, positive'): from late Latin *affirmativus*, from *affirmare* (see **AFFIRM**).

affirmative action ■ n. chiefly S. African & N. Amer. action favouring those who suffer or have suffered from discrimination.

affix ■ v. /əˈfɪks/ attach or fasten to something else. ■ n. /ˈafɪks/ Grammar an addition to the base form or stem of a word in order to modify its meaning or create a new word.
– DERIVATIVES **affixation** n.
– ORIGIN Middle English: from medieval Latin *affixare*, from Latin, from *ad-* 'to' + *figere* 'to fix'.

afflict ■ v. cause pain or suffering to.
– ORIGIN Middle English: from Latin *afflictare* 'knock about, harass' or *affligere* 'knock down, weaken'.

affliction ■ n. a cause of pain or harm. ▸ the state of being in pain.

affluent ■ adj. wealthy.
– DERIVATIVES **affluence** n. **affluently** adv.
– ORIGIN Middle English: from Latin *affluere* 'flow towards, flow freely'.

afford ■ v. 1 (**can/could afford**) have sufficient money, time, or means for. ▸ be able to do something without risk of adverse consequences. 2 provide (an opportunity or facility).
– DERIVATIVES **affordability** n. **affordable** adj.
– ORIGIN Old English *geforthian* 'manage to do', from *ge-* (implying completeness) + *forthian* 'to further'.

afforest /əˈfɒrɪst/ ■ v. convert (land) into forest for commercial exploitation.
– DERIVATIVES **afforestation** n.

affray ■ n. Law, dated a breach of the peace by fighting in a public place.
– ORIGIN Middle English: from Anglo-Norman French *afrayer* 'disturb, startle'.

affricate /ˈafrɪkət/ ■ n. Phonetics a phoneme which combines a plosive with an immediately following fricative or spirant sharing the same place of articulation, e.g. *ch* as in *chair* and *j* as in *jar*.
– ORIGIN C19: from Latin, from *ad-* 'to' + *fricare* 'to rub'.

affront ■ n. an action or remark that causes outrage or offence. ■ v. offend the modesty or values of.
– ORIGIN Middle English: from Old French *afronter* 'to slap in the face, insult', from Latin *ad frontem* 'to the face'.

Afghan /ˈafɡan/ ■ n. 1 a native or national of Afghanistan, or a person of Afghan descent. 2 another term for **PASHTO**. 3 (**afghan**) a knitted or crocheted blanket or shawl. ■ adj. of or relating to Afghanistan or the Pashto language.
– ORIGIN from Pashto *afghānī*.

Afghan hound ■ n. a tall hunting dog of a breed with long silky hair.

aficionado /əˌfɪʃəˈnɑːdəʊ, -ˌfɪsjə-/ ■ n. (pl. **-os**) a person who is very knowledgeable and enthusiastic about an activity or subject.
– ORIGIN C19: from Spanish, 'amateur', from *aficionar* 'become fond of', from Latin *afficere* (see **AFFECT²**).

afield ■ adv. to or at a distance.

afire ■ adv. & adj. chiefly poetic/literary on fire.

aflame ■ adv. & adj. in flames.

aflatoxin /ˌaflaˈtɒksɪn/ ■ n. Chemistry a toxic compound produced by certain moulds found in food, which can cause liver damage and cancer.
– ORIGIN 1960s: from the taxonomic name of a mould (*Aspergillus flavus*) + **TOXIN**.

AFL-CIO ■ abbrev. American Federation of Labor and Congress of Industrial Organizations.

afloat ■ adj. & adv. **1** floating in water. ▸ on board a ship or boat. **2** out of debt or difficulty.

aflutter ■ adj. in a state of tremulous excitement.

afoot ■ adv. & adj. **1** in preparation or progress. **2** chiefly N. Amer. on foot.

afore- ■ prefix before; previously: *aforementioned*.

aforementioned ■ adj. denoting a thing or person previously mentioned.

a fortiori /ˌeɪ fɔːtɪˈɔːrʌɪ, ˌɑː, -riː/ ■ adv. & adj. with a yet stronger reason than a conclusion previously accepted.
– ORIGIN C17: Latin, from *a fortiori argumento* 'from stronger argument'.

AFP ■ abbrev. Agence France Presse.

afraid ■ adj. (often **afraid of/to do**) fearful or anxious. ▸ (**afraid for**) anxious about the well-being of.
– PHRASES **I'm afraid** expressing polite apology or regret.
– ORIGIN Middle English: from Anglo-Norman French *afrayer* 'disturb, startle'.

A-frame ■ n. a timber frame shaped like a capital letter A. ▸ a house built around such a frame.

afresh ■ adv. in a new or different way.

African ■ n. a person from Africa, especially a black person. ▸ a person of black African descent. ■ adj. of or relating to Africa or people of African descent.

Africana /ˌafrɪˈkɑːnə/ ■ pl. n. things connected with Africa.

African American chiefly US ■ n. an American of African origin. ■ adj. of or relating to African Americans.

Africander /ˌafrɪˈkandə/ ■ n. variant spelling of **AFRIKANDER**.

African harrier hawk ■ n. a large hawk with a bare yellow face and mostly grey plumage. [*Polyboroides typus*.]

African horse sickness ■ n. an often fatal insect-borne viral disease of equines that occurs in sub-Saharan Africa, characterized by fever and swelling of the head and tongue.

Africanis /afrɪˈkɑːnɪs/ ■ n. a slender, short-coated dog of a breed indigenous to Africa.

Africanism ■ n. **1** the belief that black Africans and their culture should predominate in Africa. **2** a feature of language or culture regarded as characteristically African.
– DERIVATIVES **Africanist** n. & adj.

Africanize (also **-ise**) ■ v. **1** make African in character. ▸ (in Africa) restructure (an organization) by replacing white employees with black Africans. **2** [usu. as adj. **Africanized**] hybridize (honeybees of European stock) with bees of African stock, producing an aggressive strain.
– DERIVATIVES **Africanization** (also **-isation**) n.

African olive ■ n. another term for **WILD OLIVE**.

African penguin ■ n. a penguin with a black and white face, a white belly, and a narrow black band across the chest, that breeds along the coast of Namibia and South Africa. [*Spheniscus demersus*.]

African potato ■ n. a perennial African plant with bright yellow flowers and strap-like leaves, the corms of which are used medicinally. [Genus *Hypoxis*: several species.]

African Renaissance ■ n. the concept of a revival of African cultural and political identity, especially as achieved through economic growth.

African salad ■ n. S. African another term for **UMPHOKOQO** or **UMVUBO**.

African time ■ n. S. African, often derogatory a disregard for strict punctuality.

African violet ■ n. a small East African plant with heart-shaped velvety leaves and violet, pink, or white flowers. [Genus *Saintpaulia*: several species.]

Afrikaans /ˌafrɪˈkɑːns/ ■ n. the modified form of Dutch spoken in South Africa. ■ adj. of or relating to Afrikaans-speaking people or their language.
– ORIGIN Afrikaans, from Dutch, 'African'.

Afrikander /ˌafrɪˈkandə/ (also **Africander**) ■ n. an animal of a South African breed of sheep or longhorn cattle.
– ORIGIN C19 (early form of **AFRIKANER**): from S. African Dutch.

Afrikaner /ˌafrɪˈkɑːnə/ ■ n. **1** an Afrikaans-speaking white person in South Africa, especially one of Dutch or Huguenot descent. **2** S. African a gladiolus or related plant.
– DERIVATIVES **Afrikanerdom** n.
– ORIGIN Afrikaans, from S. African Dutch *Afrikander*, from Dutch *Afrikaan* 'an African'.

Afrikanerbond /ˌafrɪˈkɑːnəbɒnt/ ■ n. S. African an organization promoting the political and economic advancement of the Afrikaner people.
– ORIGIN from **AFRIKANER** + Afrikaans *bond* 'league'.

Afrikaner Broederbond /afrɪˌkɑːnə ˈbruːdəbɒnt/ ■ n. former name for **AFRIKANERBOND**.
– ORIGIN *Broederbond* from Afrikaans *broeder* 'brother' + *bond* 'league'.

Afrino ■ n. (pl. **-os**) an animal of a hardy South African breed of sheep, a cross between Afrikander and merino stock.
– ORIGIN 1980: from S. African Dutch *Afrikander* + **MERINO**.

Afro ■ n. a hairstyle consisting of a mass of very tight curls all round the head, like the natural hair of some black people.

Afro- ■ comb. form African; African and ...: *Afro-Asiatic*. ▸ relating to Africa: *Afrocentric*.

Afro-American ■ adj. & n. chiefly N. Amer. another term for **AFRICAN AMERICAN**.

Afro-Asiatic ■ adj. relating to or denoting a family of languages spoken in the Middle East and North Africa.

Afro-Caribbean ■ n. a person of African descent living in or coming from the Caribbean. ■ adj. of or relating to Afro-Caribbeans.

Afrocentric ■ adj. regarding African or black culture as pre-eminent.
– DERIVATIVES **Afrocentrism** n. **Afrocentrist** n.

Afro-pessimism ■ n. a belief that everything is bad in Africa and there is little hope for successful economic development.

Afrotropical ■ adj. another term for **ETHIOPIAN** (in sense 2 of the adjective).

aft /ɑːft/ ■ adv. & adj. at, near, or towards the stern of a ship or tail of an aircraft.
– ORIGIN C17: prob. from obsolete *baft* 'in the rear'.

after ■ prep. **1** in the time following (an event or another period of time). ▸ N. Amer. past (used in specifying a time). **2** behind. ▸ in the direction of someone who is moving away. **3** in pursuit or quest of. **4** next to and following in order or importance. **5** in allusion or reference to: *he was named after his grandfather*. ▸ in the style or following the example of. ■ conj. & adv. in the time following (an event).
– PHRASES **after all** in spite of any indications or expectations to the contrary. **after hours** after normal working or opening hours. **after you** a polite formula offering precedence.
– ORIGIN Old English *æfter*, of Germanic origin.

afterbirth ■ n. the placenta and fetal membranes discharged from the womb after a birth.

afterburner ■ n. an auxiliary burner in which extra fuel is burned in the exhaust of a jet engine to increase thrust.

aftercare ■ n. **1** care of a person after a stay in hospital or on release from prison. **2** support or advice offered to a customer following a purchase.

afterdamp ■ n. choking gas left after an explosion of firedamp in a mine.

afterdeck ■ n. an open deck towards the stern of a ship.

after-effect ■ n. an effect that follows after the primary action of something.

afterglow ■ n. **1** light remaining in the sky after the sun has set. **2** good feelings remaining after a pleasurable experience.

after-image ■ n. an impression of a vivid image retained by the eye after the stimulus has ceased.

afterlife ■ n. **1** (in some religions) life after death. **2** later life.

aftermarket ■ n. **1** chiefly N. Amer. the market for spare

aftermath

parts and accessories for motor vehicles. **2** Stock Exchange the market for shares and bonds after their original issue.

aftermath ■ n. the consequences of an unpleasant or disastrous event.
– ORIGIN C15: from AFTER + *math* 'mowing', of Germanic origin.

aftermost ■ adj. nearest the stern of a ship or tail of an aircraft.

afternoon ■ n. the time from noon or lunchtime to evening. ■ adv. (**afternoons**) informal in the afternoon; every afternoon.

afterpains ■ pl. n. pains after childbirth caused by contraction of the womb.

aftershave ■ n. an astringent scented lotion for applying to the skin after shaving.

aftershock ■ n. a smaller earthquake following the main shock of a large earthquake.

aftersun ■ adj. denoting a product applied to the skin after exposure to the sun.

aftertaste ■ n. a strong or unpleasant taste lingering in the mouth after eating or drinking.

after tears party ■ n. S. African a party held by friends and relatives after a funeral.

afterthought ■ n. something thought of or added later.

afterwards (also **afterward** /ˈɑːftəwəd/) ■ adv. at a later or future time.
– ORIGIN Old English, from *æftan* 'aft' + -WARDS.

afterword ■ n. a concluding section in a book, typically by a person other than the author.

afterworld ■ n. a world entered after death.

AG ■ abbrev. **1** Adjutant General. **2** Attorney General. **3** S. African Auditor General.

Ag[1] ■ symb. the chemical element silver.
– ORIGIN from Latin *argentum*.

Ag[2] ■ abbrev. Biochemistry antigen.

ag /ax, ʌx/ (also **ach**) ■ exclam. S. African informal used to express impatience, sympathy, or resignation: *Ag man, just take it then!*

ag- ■ prefix variant spelling of AD- assimilated before *g* (as in *aggravate*, *aggression*).

Aga /ˈɑːɡə/ ■ n. trademark a type of heavy heat-retaining cooking stove or range intended for continuous heating.
– ORIGIN 1930s: from the original maker's name (*Svenskaa*) *A*(*ktiebolaget*) *Ga*(*sackumulator*) 'Swedish Gas Accumulator Company'.

again /əˈɡen, əˈɡeɪn/ ■ adv. **1** once more. **2** returning to a previous position or condition. **3** in addition to what has already been mentioned. ▸ on the other hand.
– PHRASES **again and again** repeatedly.
– ORIGIN Old English, of Germanic origin.

against /əˈɡenst, əˈɡeɪnst/ ■ prep. **1** in opposition to. ▸ to the disadvantage of. ▸ in resistance to. **2** in anticipation of and preparation for (a difficulty). ▸ (in betting) in anticipation of the failure of: *the odds were 5–1 against South Africa*. **3** in relation to (money owed, due, or lent) so as to reduce, cancel, or secure it. **4** in or into contact with. **5** in contrast to.
– PHRASES **have something against** dislike or bear a grudge against.
– ORIGIN Middle English: from AGAIN + -s (adverbial genitive) + -*t*, prob. by association with superlatives.

Aga Khan /ˌɑːɡə ˈkɑːn/ ■ n. the title of the spiritual leader of the Nizari sect of Ismaili Muslims.

agama /əˈɡɑːmə/ ■ n. a lizard of a large group with long tails and large heads. [Genus *Agama*, family Agamidae.]
– ORIGIN C18: perhaps from Carib.

agamic /əˈɡamɪk/ ■ adj. Biology asexual; reproducing asexually.
– ORIGIN C19: from Greek *agamos* 'unmarried'.

agamospermy /ˈaɡəmə(ʊ)ˌspɜːmi/ ■ n. Botany asexual reproduction in which seeds are produced from unfertilized ovules.
– DERIVATIVES **agamospermous** adj.
– ORIGIN 1930s: from Greek *agamos* 'unmarried' + *sperma* 'seed'.

agapanthus /ˌaɡəˈpanθəs/ ■ n. a South African plant of the lily family, with funnel-shaped bluish flowers which grow in rounded clusters. [Genus *Agapanthus*.]
– ORIGIN from Greek *agapē* 'love' + *anthos* 'flower'.

agape[1] /əˈɡeɪp/ ■ adj. (of a person's mouth) wide open.

agape[2] /ˈaɡəpi, -peɪ/ ■ n. **1** Christian love as distinct from erotic love or simple affection. **2** a communal meal in token of Christian fellowship.
– ORIGIN C17: from Greek *agapē* 'brotherly love'.

agar /ˈeɪɡɑː/ (also **agar-agar** /ˌeɪɡɑːrˈeɪɡɑː/) ■ n. a gelatinous substance obtained from various kinds of red seaweed and used in biological culture media and as a thickener in foods.
– ORIGIN C19: from Malay.

agaric /ˈaɡ(ə)rɪk, əˈɡarɪk/ ■ n. a fungus of an order (Agaricales) including all those with a cap with gills on the underside, e.g. mushrooms.
– ORIGIN Middle English: from Greek *agarikon* 'tree fungus'.

agarose /ˈaɡərəʊz, -s/ ■ n. Biochemistry a polysaccharide which is the main constituent of agar.

agate /ˈaɡət/ ■ n. an ornamental stone consisting of a hard variety of chalcedony, typically banded in appearance.
– ORIGIN C15: from Greek *akhatēs*.

agave /əˈɡeɪvi/ ■ n. a succulent plant with rosettes of narrow spiny leaves and tall flower spikes, native to the southern US and tropical America. [Genus *Agave*: numerous species.]
– ORIGIN from Greek *Agauē*, one of the daughters of Cadmus in Greek mythology.

AGC ■ abbrev. Electronics automatic gain control.

age ■ n. **1** the length of time that a person or thing has existed. ▸ a particular stage in someone's life. ▸ old age. **2** a distinct period of history. ▸ a division of geological time that is a subdivision of an epoch. ▸ (**ages/an age**) informal a very long time. ■ v. (**ageing** or **aging**) grow or cause to appear old or older. ▸ (with reference to an alcoholic drink, cheese, etc.) mature.
– PHRASES **act** (or **be**) **one's age** behave in a manner appropriate to someone of one's age. **come of age** reach adult status (in South African law at 18). **of an age 1** old enough to be able or expected to do something. **2** (of two or more people or things) of a similar age.
– DERIVATIVES **ageing** n. & adj.
– ORIGIN Middle English: from Latin, from *aevum* 'age, era'.

-age ■ suffix forming nouns: **1** denoting an action or its result: *leverage*. ▸ a function; a sphere of action: *homage*. ▸ a state or condition: *bondage*. **2** denoting an aggregate or number of: *mileage*. ▸ a set or group of: *baggage*. ▸ fees payable for: *postage*. **3** denoting a place or abode: *orphanage*.
– ORIGIN from Latin -*aticum*, neuter adjectival ending.

aged ■ adj. **1** /eɪdʒd/ of a specified age: *he died aged 60*. ▸ (of a horse or farm animal) over a certain defined age of maturity, typically 6 to 12 years for horses, 3 or 4 years for cattle. **2** /ˈeɪdʒɪd/ old. **3** /eɪdʒd/ having been subjected to ageing.

age group ■ n. a number of people or things classed together as being of similar age.

ageism (also **agism**) ■ n. prejudice or discrimination on the grounds of age.
– DERIVATIVES **ageist** adj. & n.

ageless ■ adj. not ageing or appearing to age.
– DERIVATIVES **agelessness** n.

agency ■ n. **1** a business or organization providing a particular service. ▸ a government office or department providing a specific service for a state. **2** action or intervention so as to produce a particular result. ▸ a thing or person that acts to produce a particular result.
– ORIGIN C17: from medieval Latin *agentia*, from *agere* 'to do'.

agenda /əˈdʒɛndə/ ■ n. a list of items of business to be discussed at a meeting. ▸ a list of matters to be addressed.
– ORIGIN C17: from Latin, from *agere* 'to do'.

agent ■ n. **1** a person who provides a particular service, typically one organizing transactions between two other parties. ▸ a person who manages financial or contractual matters for an actor, performer, or writer. **2** a person who

---

VOWELS   a cat   ɑː arm   ɛ bed   ɛː hair   ə ago   əː her   ɪ sit   i cosy   iː see   ɒ hot   ɔː saw   ʌ run

works in secret to obtain information for a government. **3** a person or thing that takes an active role or produces a specified effect. ▶ Grammar the doer of an action.
–ORIGIN Middle English: from Latin *agere* 'to do'.

agent noun ■ n. a noun denoting a person or thing that performs the action of a verb, usually ending in *-er* or *-or* (e.g. *worker, accelerator*).

Agent Orange ■ n. a defoliant chemical used by the US in the Vietnam War.

agent provocateur /ˌaʒɒ̃ prəˌvɒkəˈtəː/ ■ n. (pl. **agents provocateurs** pronunc. same) a person employed to induce suspected offenders to commit criminal acts and thus be convicted.
–ORIGIN C19: French, 'provocative agent'.

age of consent ■ n. the age at which a person's consent to sexual intercourse is valid in law.

age of discretion ■ n. the age at which someone is considered able to take responsibility for their actions or affairs.

age of reason ■ n. **1** the Enlightenment. **2** (especially in the Roman Catholic Church) the age at which a child is held capable of discerning right from wrong.

age-old ■ adj. having existed for a very long time.

agglomerate ■ v. /əˈglɒməreɪt/ collect or form into a mass or group. ■ n. /əˈglɒmərət/ **1** a mass or collection of things. **2** Geology a volcanic rock consisting of large fragments bonded together. ■ adj. /əˈglɒmərət/ collected or formed into a mass.
–DERIVATIVES **agglomeration** n. **agglomerative** adj.
–ORIGIN C17: from Latin *agglomerare* 'add to', from *ad-* 'to' + *glomerare*, from *glomus* 'ball'.

agglutinate /əˈgluːtɪneɪt/ ■ v. **1** firmly stick or be stuck together to form a mass. **2** Linguistics (of a language) combine (word elements) to express compound ideas.
–DERIVATIVES **agglutination** n.
–ORIGIN C16: from Latin *agglutinare* 'cause to adhere'.

agglutinin /əˈgluːtɪnɪn/ ■ n. Biology an antibody, lectin, or other substance that causes agglutination.

aggradation /ˌagrəˈdeɪʃ(ə)n/ ■ n. Geology the deposition of material by a river, stream, or current.
–ORIGIN C19: from AG- + (*de*)*gradation*.

aggrandize /əˈgrandʌɪz/ (also **-ise**) ■ v. increase the power, status, or wealth of. ▶ artificially enhance the reputation of.
–DERIVATIVES **aggrandizement** (also **-isement**) n.
–ORIGIN C17: from French *agrandir*, from Latin *grandis* 'large'.

aggravate ■ v. **1** make worse. **2** informal annoy or exasperate.
–DERIVATIVES **aggravating** adj. **aggravatingly** adv. **aggravation** n.
–ORIGIN C16: from Latin *aggravare* 'make heavy'.

aggravated ■ adj. Law (of an offence) made more serious by attendant circumstances. ▶ (of a penalty) made more severe in recognition of the seriousness of an offence.

aggregate ■ n. /ˈagrɪgət/ **1** a whole formed by combining several disparate elements. **2** the total score of a player or team in a fixture comprising more than one game or round. **3** a material or structure formed from a loosely compacted mass of fragments or particles. ▶ pieces of broken or crushed stone or gravel used to make concrete. ■ adj. /ˈagrɪgət/ **1** formed or calculated by the combination of many separate units or items. **2** Botany (of a group of species) comprising several very similar species formerly regarded as a single species. ■ v. /ˈagrɪgeɪt/ combine into a whole.
–DERIVATIVES **aggregation** n.
–ORIGIN Middle English: from Latin *aggregare* 'herd together', from *ad-* 'towards' + *grex, greg-* 'a flock'.

aggregate fruit ■ n. Botany a fruit formed from several carpels derived from the same flower, e.g. a raspberry.

aggression ■ n. hostile or violent behaviour or attitudes. ▶ the action of attacking without provocation, especially in beginning a war.
–DERIVATIVES **aggressor** n.
–ORIGIN C17: from Latin *aggredi* 'to attack', from *ad-* 'towards' + *gradi* 'proceed, walk'.

aggressive ■ adj. characterized by or resulting from aggression. ▶ unduly forceful.

agonistic

–DERIVATIVES **aggressively** adv. **aggressiveness** n.

aggrieved ■ adj. resentful because of unfair treatment.
–DERIVATIVES **aggrievedly** adv.
–ORIGIN Middle English: from Old French *agrever* 'make heavier', from Latin *aggravare* (see AGGRAVATE).

aggro ■ n. informal **1** aggressive behaviour. **2** difficulties.
–ORIGIN 1960s: abbrev. of *aggravation* or of *aggression*.

aghast /əˈɡɑːst/ ■ adj. filled with horror or shock.
–ORIGIN Middle English: from obsolete verb *agast, gast* 'frighten', from Old English *gǣsten*.

agile ■ adj. able to move quickly and easily.
–DERIVATIVES **agilely** adv. **agility** n.
–ORIGIN Middle English: from Latin *agilis*, from *agere* 'do'.

agin /əˈɡɪn/ ■ prep. dialect form of AGAINST.
–ORIGIN C19: var. of obsolete prep. *again*, with the same meaning.

aging ■ adj. & n. variant spelling of ageing (see AGE).

agism ■ n. variant spelling of AGEISM.

agitate ■ v. **1** [often as adj. **agitated**] make troubled or nervous. **2** campaign to arouse public concern about an issue. **3** stir or disturb (a liquid) briskly.
–DERIVATIVES **agitatedly** adv. **agitation** n. **agitator** n.
–ORIGIN Middle English: from Latin *agitare* 'agitate, drive', from *agere* 'do, drive'.

agitprop /ˈadʒɪtprɒp/ ■ n. political propaganda, especially in art or literature.
–ORIGIN 1930s: Russian, blend of *agitatsiya* 'agitation' and *propaganda* 'propaganda'.

AGM ■ abbrev. annual general meeting.

agnate /ˈaɡneɪt/ chiefly Law ■ n. a person descended from the same male ancestor as another, especially through the male line. ■ adj. descended in this way. Compare with COGNATE (in sense 2). ▶ of the same clan or nation.
–ORIGIN C15: from Latin *agnatus*, from *ad-* 'to' + *gnatus, natus* 'born'.

Agnatha /ˈaɡneɪθə/ ■ pl. n. Zoology a group of primitive jawless vertebrates which includes the lampreys, hagfishes, and many fossil fishlike forms.
–ORIGIN from Greek *a-* 'without' + *gnathos* 'jaw'.

agnosia /aɡˈnəʊsɪə/ ■ n. Medicine inability to interpret sensations and hence to recognize things, typically as a result of brain damage.
–ORIGIN C20: coined in German from Greek *agnōsia* 'ignorance'.

agnostic /aɡˈnɒstɪk/ ■ n. a person who believes that nothing is known or can be known of the existence or nature of God. ■ adj. of or relating to agnostics or agnosticism.
–DERIVATIVES **agnosticism** n.
–ORIGIN C19: from Greek *a-* 'without, not' + GNOSTIC.

Agnus Dei /ˌaɡnʊs ˈdeɪiː, ˌanjʊs ˈdiːʌɪ/ ■ n. Christian Church **1** a figure of a lamb bearing a cross or flag, as an emblem of Christ. **2** an invocation beginning with the words 'Lamb of God' forming a set part of the Mass.
–ORIGIN Middle English: from Latin, 'Lamb of God'.

ago ■ adv. before the present (used with a measurement of time).
–ORIGIN Middle English: from obsolete verb *ago* 'pass', used of time.

USAGE
When **ago** is followed by a clause, the clause should be introduced by *that* rather than *since*, e.g. *it was sixty years ago that I left this place* (not *it was sixty years ago since I left this place*).

agog ■ adj. very eager or curious to hear or see something.
–ORIGIN C16: from Old French *en gogues*, from *en* 'in' + *gogue* 'fun'.

agonist /ˈaɡənɪst/ ■ n. **1** Biochemistry a substance which initiates a physiological response when combined with a receptor. **2** Anatomy a muscle whose contraction moves a part of the body directly. **3** a protagonist.
–ORIGIN C20: from Greek *agōnistēs* 'contestant', from *agōn* 'contest'.

agonistic ■ adj. **1** polemical; combative. ▶ Zoology (of

animal behaviour) associated with conflict. **2** Biochemistry of, relating to, or acting as an agonist.
– ORIGIN C17: from Greek *agōnistikos*, from *agōn* 'contest'.

agonize (also **-ise**) ■ v. **1** undergo great mental anguish through worrying over something. **2** [usu. as adj. **agonizing** (also **-ising**)] cause agony to.
– DERIVATIVES **agonizingly** (also **-isingly**) adv.
– ORIGIN C16: from French *agoniser*, from Greek *agōnizesthai* 'contend', from *agōn* 'contest'.

agony ■ n. (pl. **-ies**) extreme suffering.
– ORIGIN Middle English: from Greek *agōnia*, from *agōn* 'contest'.

agony aunt (or **agony uncle**) ■ n. informal a person who answers letters in an agony column.

agony column ■ n. informal a column in a newspaper or magazine offering advice on readers' personal problems.

agora /'agɒrə/ ■ n. (pl. **agorae** /-riː/ or **agoras**) (in ancient Greece) a public open space used for assemblies and markets.
– ORIGIN from Greek.

agoraphobia /ˌag(ə)rə'fəʊbɪə/ ■ n. extreme or irrational fear of open or public places.
– DERIVATIVES **agoraphobe** n. **agoraphobic** adj. & n.
– ORIGIN C19: from Greek *agora* (see AGORA) + -PHOBIA.

AGR ■ abbrev. advanced gas-cooled (nuclear) reactor.

agranulocytosis /əˌgranjʊlə(ʊ)sʌɪ'təʊsɪs/ ■ n. Medicine a deficiency of granulocytes in the blood, causing increased vulnerability to infection.

agraphia /ə'grafɪə, eɪ-/ ■ n. Medicine inability to write, as a language disorder resulting from brain damage.
– ORIGIN C19: from Greek *a-* 'without, not' + *-graphia* 'writing'.

agrarian /ə'grɛːrɪən/ ■ adj. of or relating to cultivated land or agriculture. ▸ relating to landed property. ■ n. a person who advocates a redistribution of landed property.
– ORIGIN C17: from Latin *agrarius*, from *ager* 'field'.

agree ■ v. (**agrees**, **agreed**, **agreeing**) **1** have the same opinion about something. ▸ (**be agreed**) (of two or more parties) be in agreement. **2** (**agree to/to do something**) consent to do something. ▸ reach agreement about. **3** (**agree with**) be consistent with. ▸ [usu. with neg.] be good for. ▸ Grammar have the same number, gender, case, or person as.
– ORIGIN Middle English: from Old French *agreer*, from Latin *ad-* 'to' + *gratus* 'pleasing'.

agreeable ■ adj. **1** pleasant. **2** willing to agree to something. ▸ acceptable.
– DERIVATIVES **agreeableness** n. **agreeably** adv.

agreement ■ n. **1** accordance in opinion or feeling. ▸ consistency. ▸ Grammar the condition of agreeing with another word. **2** a negotiated and typically legally binding arrangement.

agribusiness ■ n. **1** agriculture conducted on strictly commercial principles. **2** the group of industries concerned with agricultural produce and services.

agriculture ■ n. the science or practice of farming, including the rearing of crops and animals.
– DERIVATIVES **agricultural** adj. **agriculturalist** n. **agriculturally** adv. **agriculturist** n.
– ORIGIN Middle English: from Latin *agricultura*, from *ager* 'field' + *cultura* 'growing, cultivation'.

agrimony /'agrɪməni/ ■ n. (pl. **-ies**) a plant of the rose family with slender flower spikes of yellow flowers. [Genus *Agrimonia*.]
– ORIGIN Middle English: from Latin *agrimonia*, from Greek *argemōnē* 'poppy'.

agriscience ■ n. the application of science to agriculture.
– DERIVATIVES **agriscientist** n.

agro- /'agrəʊ/ ■ comb. form agricultural: *agro-industry*. ▸ agriculture and ...: *agroforestry*.
– ORIGIN from Greek *agros* 'field'.

agrobiology ■ n. the branch of biology concerned with soil science and plant nutrition and its application to crop production.
– DERIVATIVES **agrobiological** adj. **agrobiologist** n.

agrochemical ■ n. a chemical used in agriculture.

agroforestry ■ n. agriculture incorporating the cultivation of trees.

agro-industry ■ n. industry connected with agriculture. ▸ agriculture developed along industrial lines.
– DERIVATIVES **agro-industrial** adj.

agronomy /ə'grɒnəmi/ ■ n. the science of soil management and crop production.
– DERIVATIVES **agronomic** adj. **agronomical** adj. **agro-nomically** adv. **agronomist** n.
– ORIGIN C19: from Greek *agros* 'field' + *-nomos* 'arranging', from *nemoein* 'arrange'.

aground ■ adj. & adv. (with reference to a ship) on or on to the bottom in shallow water.

agterryer /'ʌxtərɛɪə/ ■ n. S. African historical a mounted attendant of a military officer.
– ORIGIN C19: Afrikaans, from S. African Dutch *achter* 'rear' + *rijder* 'rider'.

ague /'eɪɡjuː/ ■ n. archaic malaria or some other illness involving fever and shivering. ▸ a fever or shivering fit.
– ORIGIN Middle English: from medieval Latin *acuta (febris)* 'acute (fever)'.

Agulhas current ■ n. a warm ocean current flowing along the eastern and southern coasts of southern Africa.
– ORIGIN from Cape *Agulhas*, the most southerly point of Africa, from Portuguese *agulha* 'needle'.

ah (also **aah**) ■ exclam. expressing surprise, sympathy, realization, etc.

AHA ■ abbrev. alpha-hydroxy acid.

aha ■ exclam. expressing triumph or surprise.

ahead ■ adv. further forward in space or time. ▸ in advance. ▸ in the lead.
– PHRASES **ahead of 1** before: *we have a long drive ahead of us*. **2** earlier than planned or expected. **ahead of** (or **behind**) **the curve** (especially of a business or politician) ahead of (or lagging behind) current thinking or trends.

ahem ■ exclam. used to attract attention or express disapproval or embarrassment.

AHI ■ abbrev. (in South Africa) Afrikaanse Handelsinstituut (the Afrikaner Chamber of Commerce).

ahistorical ■ adj. lacking historical perspective or context.

-aholic (also **-oholic**) ■ suffix denoting a person addicted to something: *shopaholic*.
– ORIGIN on the pattern of *(alc)oholic*.

ahoy ■ exclam. Nautical a call to attract attention.

AI ■ abbrev. **1** Amnesty International. **2** artificial insemination. **3** artificial intelligence.

AID ■ abbrev. artificial insemination by donor.

aid ■ n. **1** help or support. **2** material help given to a country in need. ■ v. help.
– PHRASES **in aid of** in support of. **what's (all) this in aid of?** informal what is the purpose of this?
– ORIGIN Middle English: from Old French *aide* (n.), from Latin *adjuvare*, from *ad-* 'towards' + *juvare* 'to help'.

aid climbing ■ n. rock climbing using objects such as pegs placed in the rock. Compare with FREE CLIMBING.

aide /eɪd/ ■ n. an assistant to a political leader. ▸ short for AIDE-DE-CAMP.

aide-de-camp /ˌeɪdə'kɒ̃/ ■ n. (pl. **aides-de-camp** pronunc. same) a military officer acting as a confidential assistant to a senior officer.
– ORIGIN C17: from French, 'camp adjutant'.

aide-memoire /ˌeɪd mɛm'wɑː/ ■ n. (pl. **aides-memoires** or **aides-memoire** pronunc. same) **1** a book or note used to aid the memory. **2** a diplomatic memorandum.
– ORIGIN C19: from French, from *aider* 'to help' and *mémoire* 'memory'.

Aids (also **AIDS**) ■ n. a disease, caused by a virus transmitted in body fluids, in which there is a severe loss of cellular immunity leaving the sufferer susceptible to infection and malignancy.
– ORIGIN 1980s: acronym from *acquired immune deficiency syndrome*.

Aids orphan ■ n. a child whose parent or parents have died of an Aids-related illness.

Aids-related complex ■ n. the symptoms of a person who is affected with the Aids virus but does not necessarily develop the disease.

AIH ■ abbrev. artificial insemination by husband.

aikido /aɪˈkiːdəʊ/ ■ n. a Japanese form of self-defence and martial art that uses locks, holds, throws, and the opponent's own movements.
– ORIGIN 1950S: from Japanese *aikidō* 'way of adapting the spirit', from *ai* 'together, unify' + *ki* 'spirit' + *dō* 'way'.

aikona /aɪˈkɔnə/ (also **haikona** /hʌɪ-/) ■ exclam. S. African informal expressing denial or surprised disbelief: *Aikona! You want me to go in there?*
– ORIGIN C19: Fanagalo, from isiXhosa *hayikhona* 'no', from *hayi* 'no, not' + *khona* 'here, there'.

ail ■ v. archaic trouble or afflict in mind or body.
– ORIGIN Old English, from *egle* 'troublesome', of Germanic origin.

ailanthus /eɪˈlanθəs/ ■ n. a tall large-leaved deciduous tree native to Asia and Australasia, especially the tree of heaven. [Genus *Ailanthus*: several species.]
– ORIGIN from Amboinese (an Indonesian language) *ailanto* 'tree of heaven', influenced by Greek *anthos* 'flower'.

aileron /ˈeɪlərɒn/ ■ n. a hinged surface in the trailing edge of an aircraft's wing, used to control the roll of the aircraft about its longitudinal axis.
– ORIGIN C20: from French, 'small wing'.

ailing ■ adj. in poor health.

ailment ■ n. a minor illness.

aim ■ v. 1 point (a weapon or camera) at a target. ▸ direct at someone or something. 2 try to achieve something. ■ n. 1 a purpose or intention. 2 the aiming of a weapon or missile.
– PHRASES **take aim** point a weapon or camera at a target.
– DERIVATIVES **aimless** adj. **aimlessly** adv. **aimlessness** n.
– ORIGIN Middle English: from Old French *amer*, from Latin *aestimare* 'assess, estimate'.

ain't ■ contr. informal 1 am not; are not; is not. 2 has not; have not.

aïoli /ʌɪˈəʊli/ (also **aioli**) ■ n. mayonnaise seasoned with garlic.
– ORIGIN from Provençal *ai* 'garlic' + *oli* 'oil'.

air ■ n. 1 the invisible gaseous substance surrounding the earth, a mixture mainly of oxygen and nitrogen. 2 the open space above the surface of the earth. ▸ [as modifier] indicating the use of aircraft. ▸ the earth's atmosphere as a medium for transmitting radio waves. 3 a breeze or light wind. 4 (**air of**) an impression given. ▸ (**airs**) an annoyingly affected and condescending manner. 5 Music a tune or short melodious composition. ■ v. 1 express (an opinion or grievance) publicly. ▸ broadcast (a programme) on radio or television. 2 expose (a room) to the open air. ▸ put (washed laundry) in the open air or a warm place to remove dampness.
– PHRASES **airs and graces** an affectation of superiority. **in the air** noticeable all around. **on** (or **off**) **the air** being (or not being) broadcast on radio or television. **take the air** go out of doors. **up in the air** unresolved. **walk** (or **tread**) **on air** feel elated.
– DERIVATIVES **airing** n. **airless** adj. **airlessness** n.
– ORIGIN Middle English: from Old French *air*, from Greek *aēr*; sense 4 from Old French *aire* 'disposition'; sense 5 from Italian *aria*.

air bag ■ n. a safety device that inflates rapidly on impact to protect the occupants of a vehicle in a collision.

air ball ■ n. Basketball a shot which misses the basket and backboard entirely.

airbase ■ n. a base for military aircraft.

air bed ■ n. an inflatable mattress.

airboat ■ n. a shallow-draught boat powered by an aircraft engine, for use in swamps.

airborne ■ adj. 1 transported by air. 2 (of an aircraft) flying.

air brake ■ n. 1 a brake worked by air pressure. 2 a movable flap or other device on an aircraft to reduce its speed.

airbrick ■ n. a brick perforated with small holes for ventilation.

air bridge ■ n. 1 a link provided by air transport, especially as part of a rescue operation. 2 a portable bridge or walkway put against an aircraft door.

airbrush ■ n. an artist's device for spraying paint by means of compressed air. ■ v. paint with an airbrush. ▸ alter or conceal (a photograph) using an airbrush.

airburst ■ n. an explosion in the air, especially of a nuclear bomb.

air chief marshal ■ n. a high rank of RAF officer, above air marshal and below Marshal of the RAF.

air commodore ■ n. a rank of RAF officer, above group captain and below air vice-marshal.

air conditioning ■ n. a system for controlling the humidity, ventilation, and temperature in a building or vehicle.
– DERIVATIVES **air-conditioned** adj. **air conditioner** n.

air corridor ■ n. a route over a foreign country to which aircraft are restricted.

air cover ■ n. protection by aircraft for land-based or naval operations in war situations.

aircraft ■ n. (pl. same) an aeroplane, helicopter, or other machine capable of flight.

aircraft carrier ■ n. a large warship equipped to serve as a base for aircraft.

aircraftman (or **aircraftwoman**) ■ n. (pl. **-men** or **-women**) the lowest RAF rank.

aircrew ■ n. (pl. **aircrews**) [treated as sing. or pl.] the crew manning an aircraft. ▸ (pl. same) a member of such a crew.

air cushion ■ n. 1 an inflatable cushion. 2 the layer of air supporting a hovercraft or similar vehicle.

airdrop ■ n. an act of dropping supplies, troops, or equipment by parachute. ■ v. (**-dropped**, **-dropping**) drop by parachute.

air-dry ■ v. make or become dry through contact with air.

Airedale /ˈɛːdeɪl/ ■ n. a large terrier of a rough-coated black-and-tan breed.
– ORIGIN C19: from *Airedale*, a district in Yorkshire, England.

airfare ■ n. the price to be paid by an aircraft passenger for a particular journey.

airfield ■ n. an area of land set aside for the take-off, landing, and maintenance of aircraft.

air filter ■ n. a device for filtering particles from the air passing into an internal-combustion engine.

airflow ■ n. the flow of air encountered by a moving aircraft or vehicle.

airfoil ■ n. North American term for **AEROFOIL**.

air force ■ n. a branch of the armed forces concerned with fighting or defence in the air.

airframe ■ n. the body of an aircraft as distinct from its engine.

airfreight ■ n. the carriage of goods by aircraft. ▸ goods carried by aircraft. ■ v. carry or send by aircraft.

air-freshener ■ n. a scented substance or device for masking unpleasant odours in a room.

airglow ■ n. a glow in the night sky caused by radiation from the upper atmosphere.

air gun ■ n. 1 a gun which uses compressed air to fire pellets. 2 a tool using very hot air to strip paint.

airhead ■ n. informal a stupid person.

air hostess ■ n. a stewardess in a passenger aircraft.

air layering ■ n. Horticulture layering of a plant in which the branch is potted or wrapped in a moist growing medium to promote root growth.

air letter ■ n. a sheet of light paper folded and sealed to form a letter for sending by airmail.

airlift ■ n. an act of transporting supplies by aircraft, typically in an emergency. ■ v. transport in this way.

airline ■ n. 1 an organization providing a regular passenger air service. 2 (usu. **air line**) a pipe supplying air.

airliner ■ n. a large passenger aircraft.

airlock ■ n. 1 a stoppage of the flow in a pump or pipe,

airmail

caused by an air bubble. **2** a compartment with controlled pressure and parallel sets of doors, to permit movement between areas at different pressures.

airmail ■ n. a system of transporting mail overseas by air. ■ v. send by airmail.

airman (or **airwoman**) ■ n. (pl. **-men** or **-women**) a pilot or member of the crew of an aircraft in an air force. ▶ the lowest rank in the South African and US air forces. ▶ a member of the RAF below commissioned rank.
– DERIVATIVES **airmanship** n.

air marshal ■ n. a high rank of RAF officer, above air vice-marshal and below air chief marshal.

air mass ■ n. Meteorology a body of air with horizontally uniform levels of temperature, humidity, and pressure.

air mattress ■ n. another term for AIR BED.

air mile ■ n. **1** a nautical mile used as a measure of distance flown by aircraft. **2** (**Air Miles**) trademark points (equivalent to miles of free air travel) accumulated by buyers of airline tickets and other products.

airmiss ■ n. Brit. an instance of two or more aircraft in flight on different routes being less than a prescribed safe distance apart.

airmobile /ɛːˈməʊbʌɪl/ ■ adj. (of troops) moved about by air.

air officer ■ n. any rank of RAF officer above that of group captain.

air pistol (or **air rifle**) ■ n. a gun which uses compressed air to fire pellets.

airplane ■ n. North American term for AEROPLANE.

air plant ■ n. an epiphytic tropical American plant with long narrow leaves that absorb water and nutrients from the atmosphere. [Genus *Tillandsia*: several species.]

airplay ■ n. broadcasting time devoted to a particular record, performer, or musical genre.

air pocket ■ n. **1** a cavity containing air. **2** a region of low pressure causing an aircraft to lose height suddenly.

airport ■ n. a complex for civil aircraft comprising runways, hangars, and passenger facilities.

air pump ■ n. a device for pumping air into or out of an enclosed space.

air quality ■ n. the degree to which the ambient air is pollution-free.

air raid ■ n. an attack in which bombs are dropped from aircraft on to a ground target.

air sac ■ n. an alveolus. ▶ an extension of a bird's lung cavity into a bone or other part of the body.

air-sea rescue ■ n. a rescue from the sea using aircraft.

airship ■ n. a power-driven aircraft kept buoyant by a body of gas (usually helium) which is lighter than air.

airsick ■ adj. affected with nausea due to air travel.
– DERIVATIVES **airsickness** n.

airside ■ n. the area beyond passport and customs control in an airport terminal.

airspace ■ n. the part of the air above and subject to the jurisdiction of a particular country.

airspeed ■ n. the speed of an aircraft relative to the air through which it is moving.

airstream ■ n. a current of air.

airstrip ■ n. a strip of ground for the take-off and landing of aircraft.

airtight ■ adj. not allowing air to escape or pass through.

airtime ■ n. **1** the time during which a broadcast is being transmitted. **2** the time during which a cellphone is able to be used.

air-to-air ■ adj. directed or operating from one aircraft to another in flight.

air-to-ground ■ adj. directed or operating from an aircraft in flight to the land surface.

air-to-surface ■ adj. directed or operating from an aircraft in flight to the surface of the sea.

air traffic control ■ n. the ground-based personnel and equipment concerned with controlling and monitoring air traffic within a particular area.
– DERIVATIVES **air traffic controller** n.

air vice-marshal ■ n. a high rank of RAF officer, above air commodore and below air marshal.

airwaves ■ pl. n. the radio frequencies used for broadcasting.

airway ■ n. **1** the passage by which air reaches the lungs. ▶ a tube for supplying air to the lungs in an emergency. **2** a recognized route followed by aircraft.

airworthy ■ adj. (of an aircraft) safe to fly.
– DERIVATIVES **airworthiness** n.

airy ■ adj. (**-ier, -iest**) **1** spacious and well ventilated. **2** light as air; delicate. **3** casual; dismissive.
– DERIVATIVES **airily** adv. **airiness** n.

airy-fairy ■ adj. informal foolishly idealistic and vague.

aish ■ n. variant spelling of EISH.

aisle /ʌɪl/ ■ n. **1** a passage between rows of seats, pews, or supermarket shelves. **2** Architecture a lateral division of a church parallel to, and divided by pillars from, a nave, choir, or transept.
– ORIGIN Middle English, from Old French *ele*, from Latin *ala* 'wing'.

aitch ■ n. the letter H.
– PHRASES **drop one's aitches** fail to pronounce the letter *h* at the beginning of words.
– ORIGIN C16: from Old French *ache*.

aitchbone ■ n. the buttock or rump bone of cattle. ▶ a cut of beef lying over this.
– ORIGIN C15: from dialect *nache* 'rump', from Latin *natis* 'buttock(s)', + BONE; the initial *n* was lost by wrong division of *a nache bone*.

ajar ■ adv. & adj. (of a door or window) slightly open.
– ORIGIN C17: from a-² + obsolete *char* (Old English *cerr*) 'a turn'.

ajuga /əˈdʒuːɡə/ ■ n. a plant of a genus that includes bugle. [Genus *Ajuga*.]
– ORIGIN from medieval Latin.

AK ■ n. short for AK 47.

AK 47 ■ n. a type of Kalashnikov assault rifle.

aka ■ abbrev. also known as.

Akan /ˈɑːk(ə)n/ ■ n. (pl. same) **1** a member of a people inhabiting southern Ghana and adjacent parts of Ivory Coast. **2** the language of this people, belonging to the Kwa group.
– ORIGIN the name in Akan.

Akela /ɑːˈkeɪlə/ ■ n. informal the adult leader of a group of Cub Scouts.
– ORIGIN 1920s: from the name of the leader of a wolf pack in Kipling's *Jungle Books*.

akimbo /əˈkɪmbəʊ/ ■ adv. with hands on the hips and elbows turned outwards.
– ORIGIN Middle English *in kenebowe*: from Old Norse.

akin ■ adj. **1** of similar character. **2** related by blood.
– ORIGIN C16: contracted form of *of kin*.

akinesia /ˌeɪkɪˈniːsɪə, a-/ ■ n. Medicine loss or impairment of the power of voluntary movement.
– ORIGIN C19: from Greek *akinēsia* 'quiescence'.

Akkadian /əˈkeɪdɪən, -ˈkad-/ ■ n. **1** an inhabitant of Akkad in ancient Babylonia. **2** the extinct Semitic language of Akkad.

akrasia /əˈkreɪzɪə, əˈkrasɪə/ (also **acrasia**) ■ n. chiefly Philosophy weakness of will, leading to someone acting against their better judgement.
– ORIGIN C19: from Greek, from *a-* 'without' + *kratos* 'power, strength'.

Al ■ symb. the chemical element aluminium.

-al ■ suffix **1** (forming adjectives from Latin, Greek, or English words) relating to; of the kind of: *tidal*. **2** forming nouns chiefly denoting verbal action: *arrival*.
– ORIGIN from Latin *-alis*.

al- ■ prefix variant spelling of AD- assimilated before *-l* (as in *alleviate*).

à la /ɑː lɑː, a la/ ■ prep. cooked or prepared in a specified style or manner: *fish cooked à la meunière*.
– ORIGIN French, from À LA MODE.

alabaster /ˈaləbɑːstə, -bastə, ˌaləˈbɑːstə, -ˈbastə/ ■ n. **1** a

aldehyde

translucent form of gypsum, typically white, often carved into ornaments. **2** [as modifier] poetic/literary smooth and white.
– ORIGIN Middle English: from Greek *alabastos, alabastros*.

à la carte /ɑː lɑː ˈkɑːt, a la/ ■ adj. (of a menu) listing food that can be ordered as separate items, rather than part of a set meal. ■ adv. as à la carte items from a menu.
– ORIGIN C19: French, 'according to the (menu) card'.

alack ■ exclam. archaic an expression of regret or dismay.
– ORIGIN Middle English: prob. from AH + LACK.

alacrity /əˈlakrɪti/ ■ n. brisk and cheerful readiness.
– ORIGIN Middle English: from Latin *alacritas*, from *alacer* 'brisk'.

Aladdin's cave ■ n. a place filled with a great number of interesting or precious items.
– ORIGIN from *Aladdin* in the *Arabian Nights' Entertainments*.

à la mode /ɑː lɑː ˈməʊd, a la/ ■ adv. & adj. **1** up to date. **2** (of beef) braised in wine with vegetables. **3** N. Amer. served with ice cream.
– ORIGIN C16: French, 'in the fashion'.

alanine /ˈalaniːn/ ■ n. Biochemistry an amino acid which is a constituent of most proteins.
– ORIGIN C19: from German as *Alanin*, from ALDEHYDE.

alar /ˈeɪlə/ ■ adj. chiefly Zoology of or relating to a wing or wings.
– ORIGIN C19: from Latin *alaris*, from *ala* 'wing'.

alarm ■ n. **1** anxious or frightened awareness of danger. ▸ a warning of danger. **2** a warning sound or device. ■ v. **1** frighten or disturb. **2** (**be alarmed**) be fitted or protected with an alarm.
– DERIVATIVES **alarming** adj. **alarmingly** adv.
– ORIGIN Middle English (as exclam. 'to arms!'): from Old French *alarme*, from Italian, from *all' arme!*

alarm clock ■ n. a clock with a device that can be made to sound at the time set in advance.

alarmist ■ n. a person who exaggerates a danger, so causing needless alarm. ■ adj. creating needless alarm.
– DERIVATIVES **alarmism** n.

alarum /əˈlɑːrəm/ ■ n. archaic term for ALARM.
– PHRASES **alarums and excursions** humorous confused activity and uproar.

alas ■ exclam. poetic/literary or humorous an expression of grief, pity, or concern.
– ORIGIN Middle English: from Old French, from *a* 'ah' + *las(se)*, from Latin *lassus* 'weary'.

Alaskan ■ n. a native or inhabitant of the US state of Alaska. ■ adj. of or relating to Alaska.

alate /ˈeɪleɪt/ ■ adj. Entomology (chiefly of insects) having wings or wing-like appendages.
– ORIGIN C17: from Latin *alatus*, from *ala* 'wing'.

alb /alb/ ■ n. a white vestment reaching to the feet, worn by clergy and servers in some Christian Churches.
– ORIGIN Old English, from eccles. Latin *tunica* (or *vestis*) *alba* 'white garment'.

alba /ˈalbə/ ■ n. a shrub rose of a variety with grey-green leaves and pinkish-white, sweet-scented flowers.
– ORIGIN C19: from Latin *albus* 'white'.

albacore /ˈalbəkɔː/ ■ n. a tuna of warm seas which travels in large schools and is an important food fish. [*Thunnus alalunga*.]
– ORIGIN C16: from Portuguese *albacora*, from Arabic *al-bakūra*.

Albanian ■ n. **1** a native or national of Albania, or a person of Albanian descent. **2** the Indo-European language of Albania. ■ adj. of or relating to Albania or its language.

albatross /ˈalbətrɒs/ ■ n. (pl. **albatrosses**) **1** a very large seabird with long narrow wings, found chiefly in the southern oceans. [Genera *Diomedea* and *Phoebetria*.] **2** a burden or encumbrance (in allusion to Coleridge's *The Rime of the Ancient Mariner*). **3** Golf a double eagle.
– ORIGIN C17: variant, influenced by Latin *albus* 'white', of C16 *alcatras*, from Spanish and Portuguese *alcatraz*, from Arabic *al-ġaṭṭās* 'the diver'.

albedo /alˈbiːdəʊ/ ■ n. (pl. **-os**) the proportion of the incident light or radiation that is reflected by a surface.
– ORIGIN C19: eccles. Latin, 'whiteness', from Latin *albus* 'white'.

albeit /ɔːlˈbiːɪt/ ■ conj. though.
– ORIGIN Middle English: from the phr. *all be it* 'although it be (that)'.

albino /alˈbiːnəʊ/ ■ n. (pl. **-os**) a person or animal having a congenital absence of pigment in the skin and hair (which are white) and the eyes (which are usually pink).
– DERIVATIVES **albinism** /ˈalbɪnɪz(ə)m/ n.
– ORIGIN C18: from Latin *albus* 'white'.

Albion /ˈalbɪən/ ■ n. poetic/literary Britain or England.
– ORIGIN Old English, prob. of Celtic origin, from Latin *albus* 'white' (in allusion to the white cliffs of Dover).

albite /ˈalbʌɪt/ ■ n. a sodium-rich, typically white mineral of the feldspar group.
– ORIGIN C19: from Latin *albus* 'white'.

albizzia /alˈbɪzɪə/ (also **albizia**) ■ n. a leguminous tree or shrub with feathery leaves and puff-like flowers, found in warm parts of Africa, Asia, and Australia. [*Albizia anthelmintica* and other species.]
– ORIGIN named after the Italian nobleman Filippo delgi Albizzi.

album ■ n. **1** a blank book for the insertion of photographs, stamps, or pictures. **2** a collection of recordings issued as a single item.
– ORIGIN C17: from Latin, neuter of *albus* 'white' used as noun meaning 'a blank tablet'.

albumen /ˈalbjʊmɪn/ ■ n. egg white, or the protein contained in it.
– ORIGIN C16: from Latin, from *albus* 'white'.

albumin /ˈalbjʊmɪn/ ■ n. Biochemistry a water-soluble form of protein, coagulable by heat, found especially in blood serum and egg white.
– DERIVATIVES **albuminous** /alˈbjuːmɪnəs/ adj.
– ORIGIN C19: from Latin *albumen, albumin-* (see ALBUMEN).

albuminuria /ˌalbjʊmɪˈnjʊərɪə/ ■ n. Medicine the presence of albumin in the urine, typically as a symptom of kidney disease.

alchemilla /ˌalkəˈmɪlə/ ■ n. lady's mantle or a related plant. [Genus *Alchemilla*.]
– ORIGIN from a medieval Latin diminutive of *alchimia* 'alchemy', from the belief that dew from the leaves of the plant could turn base metals into gold.

alchemy /ˈalkɪmi/ ■ n. **1** the medieval forerunner of chemistry, concerned particularly with attempts to convert base metals into gold or to find a universal elixir. **2** a process by which paradoxical results are achieved or incompatible elements combined.
– DERIVATIVES **alchemist** n. **alchemic** /alˈkɛmɪk/ adj. **alchemical** adj. **alchemize** (also **-ise**) v.
– ORIGIN Middle English: from Arabic *alkīmiyā*, from *al* 'the' + *kīmiyā*, from Greek *khēmia* 'art of transmuting metals'.

alcohol ■ n. **1** a colourless volatile flammable liquid which is the intoxicating constituent of wine, beer, spirits, etc. Also called ETHANOL, ETHYL ALCOHOL. [C_2H_5OH.] **2** drink containing this. **3** Chemistry any organic compound containing a hydroxyl group -OH: *propyl alcohol*.
– ORIGIN C16 ('a fine powder, especially kohl, produced by sublimation'): from Arabic *al-kuḥl* 'the kohl'.

alcoholic ■ adj. containing, relating to, or caused by the consumption of alcohol. ■ n. a person suffering from alcoholism.

alcoholism ■ n. addiction to alcoholic liquor.

alcopop ■ n. Brit. informal a ready-mixed soft drink containing alcohol.

alcove ■ n. a recess, typically in the wall of a room.
– ORIGIN C16: from French *alcôve*, from Arabic *al-kubba* 'the vault'.

aldehyde /ˈaldɪhʌɪd/ ■ n. Chemistry an organic compound containing the group -CHO, formed by the oxidation of alcohols.
– DERIVATIVES **aldehydic** /ˌaldɪˈhɪdɪk/ adj.
– ORIGIN C19: from Latin *alcohol dehydrogenatum* 'alcohol deprived of hydrogen'.

al dente

al dente /al 'dɛnteɪ, -ti/ ■ adj. & adv. (of food) cooked so as to be still firm when bitten.
– ORIGIN Italian, 'to the tooth'.

alder /'ɔːldə/ ■ n. a catkin-bearing tree of the birch family with toothed leaves, found especially on damp ground and riverbanks. [*Alnus glutinosa* and other species.]
– ORIGIN Old English, of Germanic origin.

alderfly ■ n. (pl. **-flies**) a brownish neuropterous insect that lives near water and has predatory aquatic larvae. [*Sialis* and other genera.]

alderman (or **alderwoman**) ■ n. (pl. **-men** or **-women**) **1** S. African a senior or long-serving elected member of a municipal council. **2** chiefly historical a co-opted member of an English county or borough council, next in status to the Mayor.
– DERIVATIVES **aldermanic** adj. **aldermanship** n.
– ORIGIN Old English, from *aldor* 'chief, patriarch', from *ald* 'old', + **MAN**.

Aldis lamp /'ɔːldɪs/ ■ n. trademark a hand-held lamp for signalling in Morse code.
– ORIGIN FIRST WORLD WAR: named after the British inventor Arthur C. W. *Aldis*.

aldosterone /al'dɒstərəʊn/ ■ n. Biochemistry a corticosteroid hormone which stimulates absorption of sodium by the kidneys and so regulates water and salt balance.
– ORIGIN 1950s: blend of **ALDEHYDE** and **STEROID**.

aldosteronism /ˌaldə(ʊ)'stɛrənɪz(ə)m/ ■ n. Medicine a condition in which there is excessive secretion of aldosterone, disturbing the salt balance of the blood and leading to high blood pressure.

ale ■ n. chiefly Brit. beer other than lager, stout, or porter. ▸ N. Amer. beer brewed by top fermentation.
– ORIGIN Old English, of Germanic origin.

alee /ə'liː/ ■ adj. & adv. Nautical on the leeward side of a ship. ▸ (of the helm) moved round to leeward.

alehouse ■ n. dated an inn or public house.

alembic /ə'lɛmbɪk/ ■ n. an apparatus formerly used for distilling, consisting of a gourd-shaped container and a cap with a long beak for conveying the products to a receiver.
– ORIGIN Middle English: from medieval Latin *alembicus*, from Arabic, from *al-* 'the' + *'anbīk* 'still', from Greek *ambix* 'cup'.

alert ■ adj. quick to notice and respond to potential danger or problems. ▸ intellectually active. ■ n. **1** (often in phr. **on the alert**) the state of being alert. **2** a warning of danger. ■ v. warn of a danger or problem.
– DERIVATIVES **alertly** adv. **alertness** n.
– ORIGIN C16: from French *alerte*, from Italian *all' erta* 'to the watchtower'.

-ales /'eɪliːz/ ■ suffix Botany forming the names of orders of plants: *Rosales*.
– ORIGIN pl. of the Latin adjectival suffix *-alis*.

alethic /ə'liːθɪk/ ■ adj. Philosophy denoting modalities of truth, such as necessity, contingency, or impossibility.
– ORIGIN 1950s: from Greek *alētheia* 'truth'.

aleurone /ə'ljʊərəʊn/ ■ n. Botany protein stored as granules in the cells of plant seeds.
– ORIGIN C19: from Greek *aleuron* 'flour'.

Aleut /ə'ljuːt, 'aluːt/ ■ n. **1** a member of a people chiefly inhabiting the Aleutian Islands and parts of western Alaska. **2** the language of this people, related to Eskimo.

A level ■ n. Brit. short for **ADVANCED LEVEL**.

Alexander technique ■ n. a system designed to promote well-being by retraining one's awareness and habits of posture to ensure minimum effort and strain.
– ORIGIN 1930s: named after the Australian-born actor and elocutionist Frederick Matthias *Alexander*.

Alexandrian ■ adj. of or relating to Alexandria in Egypt. ▸ belonging to or characteristic of the schools of literature and philosophy of ancient Alexandria, especially in being allusive or imitative.

alexandrine /ˌalɪg'zɑːndrɪn, -ʌɪn/ Prosody ■ adj. (of a line of verse) having six iambic feet. ■ n. an alexandrine line.

– ORIGIN C16: from French, from *Alexandre* referring to Alexander the Great, the subject of an Old French poem in this metre.

alexia /ə'lɛksɪə, eɪ-/ ■ n. Medicine inability to recognize or read written words or letters, typically as a result of brain damage. Compare with **DYSLEXIA**.
– ORIGIN C19: from Greek *a-* 'without' + *lexis* 'speech', from *legein* 'speak', which was confused with Latin *legere* 'read'.

alfalfa /al'falfə/ ■ n. a leguminous plant with clover-like leaves and bluish flowers, native to SW Asia and grown for fodder. [*Medicago sativa*.]
– ORIGIN C19: from Arabic *al-faṣfaṣa*.

alfisol /'alfɪsɒl/ ■ n. Soil Science a leached basic or slightly acid soil with a clay-enriched B horizon.
– ORIGIN 1960s: from the arbitrary element *Alfi-* + **-SOL**.

Alfredo /al'freɪdəʊ/ ■ n. a sauce for pasta incorporating butter, cream, garlic, and Parmesan cheese.
– ORIGIN named after the Italian chef and restaurateur *Alfredo di Lelio*.

alfresco /al'frɛskəʊ/ ■ adv. & adj. in the open air.
– ORIGIN C18: from Italian *al fresco* 'in the fresh (air)'.

alga /'algə/ ■ n. (pl. **algae** /'aldʒiː, 'algiː/) any of a large group of simple, non-flowering plants containing chlorophyll but lacking true stems, roots, leaves, and vascular tissue, e.g. the seaweeds and many single-celled forms.
– DERIVATIVES **algal** adj.
– ORIGIN C16: from Latin, 'seaweed'.

algebra /'aldʒɪbrə/ ■ n. the part of mathematics in which letters and other general symbols are used to represent numbers and quantities in formulae and equations. ▸ a system of this based on given axioms.
– DERIVATIVES **algebraic** /aldʒɪ'breɪɪk/ adj. **algebraical** adj. **algebraically** adv. **algebraist** n.

> **HISTORY**
> The word **algebra** comes from Arabic *al-jabr* 'the mending of broken parts', entering Middle English, via Italian, Spanish, and medieval Latin, in the sense 'the setting of broken bones'. The modern mathematical sense comes from the title of a book, *ilm al-jabr wa'l-muḳābala* 'the science of restoring what is missing and equating like with like', by the 9th-century Muslim mathematician Abū Ja'far Muhammad ibn Mūsa. His nickname, *al-Ḵwārizmī* (literally 'the man from Ḵwārizm', now Khiva in Uzbekistan) is the root of the word **algorithm**.

Algerian /al'dʒɪərɪən/ ■ n. a native or inhabitant of Algeria. ■ adj. of or relating to Algeria.

-algia ■ comb. form denoting pain in a specified part of the body: *neuralgia*.
– DERIVATIVES **-algic** comb. form in corresponding adjectives.
– ORIGIN from Greek *algos* 'pain'.

algicide /'aldʒɪsʌɪd, 'algɪ-/ ■ n. a substance which is poisonous to algae.

alginic acid /al'dʒɪnɪk/ ■ n. Chemistry an insoluble gelatinous carbohydrate found in many brown seaweeds, chiefly as salts which are used as thickening agents.
– DERIVATIVES **alginate** n.
– ORIGIN C19: *alginic* from **ALGA**.

Algol /'algɒl/ ■ n. an early, high-level computer programming language which was devised to carry out scientific calculations.
– ORIGIN 1950s: from *algo*(*rithmic*) + *the initial letter of* **LANGUAGE**.

algology /al'gɒlədʒi/ ■ n. the study of algae.
– DERIVATIVES **algological** adj. **algologist** n.

Algonquian /al'gɒŋkwɪən, -kɪ-/ (also **Algonkian** /-kɪən/) ■ n. **1** a large family of North American Indian languages, including Cree, Blackfoot, and Cheyenne. **2** a speaker of any of these languages. ■ adj. relating to or denoting this family of languages or its speakers.

algorithm /'algərɪð(ə)m/ ■ n. a process or set of rules to be followed in calculations or other problem-solving operations, especially by a computer.
– DERIVATIVES **algorithmic** adj. **algorithmically** adv.

– ORIGIN C17: var. of Middle English *algorism*, from Arabic *al-Ḵwārizmī* 'the man of Ḵwārizm', the cognomen of a C9 mathematician.

alias /'eɪlɪəs/ ■ adv. also known as. ■ n. **1** a false or assumed identity. **2** Computing an alternative name or label that refers to a file, command, or address, and can be used to locate or access it. **3** Physics & Telecommunications each of a set of signal frequencies which, when sampled at a given uniform rate, would give the same set of sampled values and thus be indistinguishable. ■ v. Physics & Telecommunications misidentify (a signal frequency), introducing distortion or error.
– DERIVATIVES **aliasing** n.
– ORIGIN Middle English: from Latin 'at another time, otherwise'.

alibi /'alɪbʌɪ/ ■ n. (pl. **alibis**) a claim or piece of evidence that one was elsewhere when an alleged act took place. ▸ informal an excuse. ■ v. (**alibis, alibied, alibiing**) informal provide an alibi for.
– ORIGIN C17: from Latin, 'elsewhere'.

Alice band ■ n. a flexible band worn to hold back the hair.
– ORIGIN from the name of the heroine of *Alice's Adventures in Wonderland* by Lewis Carroll.

alidade /'alɪdeɪd/ ■ n. a sighting device or pointer for determining directions or measuring angles, used in surveying.
– ORIGIN Middle English: from Arabic *al-'iḍāda* 'the revolving radius'.

alien ■ adj. **1** belonging to a foreign country. **2** unfamiliar and distasteful. **3** (of a plant or animal species) introduced from another country and later naturalized. **4** relating to or denoting beings from other worlds. ■ n. **1** a foreigner, especially one who is not a naturalized citizen of the country where they are living. **2** an alien plant or animal species. **3** a being from another world.
– DERIVATIVES **alienage** n. **alienness** n.
– ORIGIN Middle English: from Latin *alienus* 'belonging to another', from *alius* 'other'.

alienable ■ adj. Law able to be transferred to new ownership.
– DERIVATIVES **alienability** n.

alienate ■ v. **1** cause to feel isolated. ▸ lose or destroy the support or sympathy of. **2** Law transfer ownership of (property rights) to another.
– PHRASES **alienate someone's affections** US Law induce someone to transfer their affection from a person with legal rights or claims on them.
– DERIVATIVES **alienator** n.
– ORIGIN C16: from Latin *alienare* 'estrange', from *alienus* (see **ALIEN**).

alienation ■ n. **1** the state or experience of being alienated. ▸ Psychiatry a state of depersonalization or loss of identity in which the self seems unreal. **2** Law the transfer of the ownership of property rights.

alienist ■ n. former term for **PSYCHIATRIST**. ▸ chiefly US a psychiatrist who assesses the competence of a defendant in a law court.
– ORIGIN C19: from French *aliéniste*, from Latin *alienus* (see **ALIEN**).

aliform /'eɪlɪfɔːm/ ■ adj. wing-shaped.
– ORIGIN C18: from Latin *ala* 'wing' + *-formis* (see **-FORM**).

alight¹ ■ v. **1** formal, chiefly Brit. descend from public transport. **2** (**alight on**) chance to notice.
– ORIGIN Old English, from *ā-* (as an intensifier) + *līhtan* 'descend' (see **LIGHT³**).

alight² ■ adv. & adj. **1** on fire. **2** shining brightly.
– ORIGIN Middle English: prob. from phrase *on a light* (= lighted) *fire*.

align ■ v. **1** place or arrange in a straight line or into correct relative positions. **2** (**align oneself with**) ally oneself to. ▸ come together in alliance.
– DERIVATIVES **alignment** n.
– ORIGIN C17: from French *aligner*, from *à ligne* 'into line'.

alike ■ adj. similar. ■ adv. in a similar way.
– ORIGIN Old English *gelīc*, of Germanic origin; reinforced in Middle English by Old Norse *álíkr*.

alikreukel /ˌalɪ'krɪəkəl/ (also **ollycrock**) ■ n. (pl. same) S. African an edible periwinkle-like mollusc, also used by fishermen as bait. [*Turbo sarmaticus*.]

– ORIGIN 1910s: from Afrikaans *alikruik, arikreukel* from Dutch *alikruik* 'periwinkle'.

alimentary ■ adj. of or providing nourishment or sustenance.

alimentary canal ■ n. the whole passage along which food passes through the body from mouth to anus during digestion.

alimentation ■ n. formal the provision of nourishment or other necessities of life.

alimony /'alɪməni/ ■ n. chiefly N. Amer. maintenance for a spouse after separation or divorce.
– ORIGIN C17: from Latin *alimonia* 'nutriment', from *alere* 'nourish'.

A-line ■ adj. (of a garment) slightly flared from a narrow waist or shoulders.

aliphatic /ˌalɪ'fatɪk/ ■ adj. Chemistry relating to or denoting organic compounds in which carbon atoms form open chains (as in the alkanes), not aromatic rings.
– ORIGIN C19: from Greek *aleiphar* 'fat'.

aliquot /'alɪkwɒt/ ■ n. a portion of a larger whole, especially a sample taken for chemical analysis or other treatment. ■ v. divide (a whole) into aliquots; take aliquots from (a whole).
– ORIGIN C16: from Latin *aliquot* 'some, so many', from *alius* 'one of two' + *quot* 'how many'.

A-list (or **B-list**) ■ n. a real or imaginary list of the most (or second most) celebrated individuals, especially in show business: [as modifier] *an A-list celebrity*.

alive ■ adj. **1** living, not dead. ▸ continuing in existence or use. **2** alert and active. ▸ having interest and meaning. ▸ (**alive to**) aware of and interested in. **3** (**alive with**) swarming or teeming with.
– PHRASES **alive and kicking** informal prevalent and very active. **alive and well** still existing or active.
– DERIVATIVES **aliveness** n.
– ORIGIN Old English *on life* 'in life'.

aliyah /'alɪjə/ ■ n. (pl. **aliyoth** /'alɪjəʊt/) Judaism **1** immigration to Israel. **2** the honour of being called upon to read from the Torah.
– ORIGIN from Hebrew *'ăliyyāh* 'ascent'.

alizarin /ə'lɪz(ə)rɪn/ ■ n. Chemistry a red pigment present in madder root, used in making dyes.
– ORIGIN C19: from French, from *alizari* 'madder', from Arabic *al-'iṣāra* 'pressed juice'.

alkali /'alkəlʌɪ/ ■ n. (pl. **alkalis** or US also **alkalies**) a compound, e.g. lime or caustic soda, with particular chemical properties including turning litmus blue and neutralizing or effervescing with acids.
– DERIVATIVES **alkalization** (also **-isation**) n. **alkalize** (also **-ise**) v.
– ORIGIN Middle English (a saline substance derived from the ashes of plants): from Arabic *al-kalī*, from *kalā* 'fry, roast'.

alkali feldspar ■ n. Geology any of the group of feldspars rich in sodium and/or potassium.

alkali metal ■ n. Chemistry any of the reactive metals lithium, sodium, potassium, rubidium, caesium, and francium, occupying Group IA (1) of the periodic table and forming strongly alkaline hydroxides.

alkaline ■ adj. containing an alkali or having the properties of an alkali; having a pH greater than 7.
– DERIVATIVES **alkalinity** n.

alkaline earth ■ n. Chemistry any of the reactive metals beryllium, magnesium, calcium, strontium, barium, and radium, occupying Group IIA (2) of the periodic table and forming basic oxides and hydroxides.

alkaloid /'alkəlɔɪd/ ■ n. Chemistry any of a class of nitrogenous organic compounds of plant origin which have pronounced physiological actions on humans.

alkalosis /ˌalkə'ləʊsɪs/ ■ n. Medicine an excessively alkaline condition of the body fluids or tissues, which may cause weakness or cramp.

alkane /'alkeɪn/ ■ n. Chemistry any of the series of saturated hydrocarbons including methane, ethane, propane, and higher members.
– ORIGIN C19: from **ALKYL**.

alkene

alkene /'alkiːn/ ■ n. Chemistry any of the series of unsaturated hydrocarbons containing a double bond, including ethylene and propene.
– ORIGIN C19: from ALKYL.

alkyd /'alkɪd/ ■ n. Chemistry any of a group of synthetic polyester resins.
– ORIGIN 1920s: blend of ALKYL and ACID.

alkyl /'alkʌɪl, -kɪl/ ■ n. [as modifier] Chemistry of or denoting a hydrocarbon radical derived from an alkane by removal of a hydrogen atom.
– ORIGIN C19: German, from *Alkohol* 'alcohol'.

alkylate /'alkɪleɪt/ ■ v. Chemistry introduce an alkyl group into (a molecule).
– DERIVATIVES **alkylation** n.

alkyne /'alkʌɪn/ ■ n. Chemistry any of the series of unsaturated hydrocarbons containing a triple bond, including acetylene.
– ORIGIN C20: from ALKYL.

all ■ predet., det., & pron. the whole quantity or extent of. ▸ [det.] any whatever. ▸ [det.] the greatest possible. ▸ [pron.] everything. ■ adv. **1** completely. **2** (in games) used after a number to indicate an equal score.
– PHRASES **all along** from the beginning. **all and sundry** everyone. **all but 1** very nearly. **2** all except. **all for** informal strongly in favour of. **all in** informal exhausted. **all in all** on the whole. **all of** often ironic as much as. **all one to** making no difference to. **all out** using all one's strength or resources. **all over 1** informal everywhere. **2** informal typical of the person mentioned: *that's our management all over!* **all over the place** (or N. Amer. also **map**, Brit. also **shop**) informal **1** everywhere. **2** in a state of disorder. **all round 1** in all respects. **2** for or by each person. **all there** [with neg.] informal in full possession of one's mental faculties: *he's not quite all there*. **all together** all in one place or in a group. **all told** in total. **all very well** informal used to express criticism or scepticism. **all the way** informal without limit or reservation. **at all** [with neg. or in questions] in any way; to any extent. **for all ——** in spite of ——. **in all** in total. **on all fours** on hands and knees. **one's all** one's whole strength or resources.
– ORIGIN Old English, of Germanic origin.

Allah /'alə, əl'lɑː/ ■ n. the name of God among Muslims (and Arab Christians).
– ORIGIN from Arabic *'all'h*, contraction of *al-'il'h* 'the god'.

allamanda /ˌaləˈmandə/ ■ n. a tropical shrub or climber with showy flowers, typically of yellow or purple. [*Allamanda cathartica* and other species.]
– ORIGIN named after the Swiss naturalist Jean-Nicholas-Sébastien *Allamand*.

all-American ■ adj. US denoting a sports player honoured as one of the best amateur competitors in the US.

allantoin /əˈlantəʊɪn/ ■ n. Biochemistry a crystalline compound formed in the nitrogen metabolism of many mammals.
– ORIGIN C19: from ALLANTOIS (because it was discovered in the allantoic fluid of cows).

allantois /əˈlantəʊɪs/ ■ n. (pl. **allantoides** /-ɪdiːz/) the fetal membrane lying below the chorion in many vertebrates, formed as an outgrowth of the embryo's gut.
– DERIVATIVES **allantoic** adj. **allantoid** adj.
– ORIGIN C17: from Greek *allantoeidēs* 'sausage-shaped'.

allay /əˈleɪ/ ■ v. diminish or end (fear or concern). ▸ alleviate (pain or hunger).
– ORIGIN Old English, of Germanic origin.

all-clear ■ n. a signal that danger or difficulty is over.

allée /'aleɪ/ ■ n. an alley in a formal garden or park, bordered by trees or bushes.
– ORIGIN C18: from French.

allegation /alɪˈɡeɪʃ(ə)n/ ■ n. a claim that someone has done something wrong, typically an unfounded one.

allege /əˈlɛdʒ/ ■ v. claim that someone has done something wrong, typically without proof.
– DERIVATIVES **alleged** adj. **allegedly** adv.
– ORIGIN Middle English: from Old French *esligier*, from Latin *lis* 'lawsuit'; confused in sense with Latin *allegare* 'allege'.

allegiance ■ n. loyalty or commitment of a subordinate to a superior or of an individual to a group or cause.
– ORIGIN Middle English: from Old French *ligeance*, from *lige* (see LIEGE), perhaps by association with Anglo-Latin *alligantia* 'alliance'.

allegorical ■ adj. constituting or containing allegory.
– DERIVATIVES **allegoric** adj. **allegorically** adv.

allegory ■ n. (pl. **-ies**) a story, poem, or picture which can be interpreted to reveal a hidden meaning.
– DERIVATIVES **allegorist** n. **allegorization** (also **-isation**) n. **allegorize** (also **-ise**) v.
– ORIGIN Middle English: from Greek *allēgoria*, from *allos* 'other' + *-agoria* 'speaking'.

allegro /əˈlɛɡrəʊ, -ˈleɪɡ-/ Music ■ adv. & adj. at a brisk speed. ■ n. (pl. **-os**) an allegro movement, passage, or composition.
– ORIGIN Italian, 'lively'.

allele /əˈliːl/ ■ n. Genetics one of two or more alternative forms of a gene that arise by mutation and are found at the same place on a chromosome.
– DERIVATIVES **allelic** adj.
– ORIGIN 1930s: from German *Allel*, abbrev. of ALLELOMORPH.

allelochemical /əˌliːləʊˈkɛmɪk(ə)l/ ■ n. Biology a chemical produced by a living organism which exerts a detrimental physiological effect on another species.
– ORIGIN 1970s: from Greek *allēl-* 'one another' + CHEMICAL.

allelomorph /əˈliːləʊmɔːf/ ■ n. another term for ALLELE.
– DERIVATIVES **allelomorphic** adj.
– ORIGIN C20: from Greek *allēl-* 'one another' + *morphē* 'form'.

alleluia /ˌalɪˈluːjə/ ■ exclam. & n. variant spelling of HALLELUJAH.

allemande /ˈalmɑːnd/ ■ n. **1** a German court dance popular in the 16th century. **2** a figure in country dancing in which adjacent dancers make a turn.
– ORIGIN C17: from French, 'German (dance)'.

Allen key ■ n. trademark a spanner designed to fit into and turn an Allen screw.

Allen screw ■ n. trademark a screw with a hexagonal socket in the head.
– ORIGIN 1930s: from the name of the *Allen* Manufacturing Company, Connecticut.

allergen /ˈalədʒ(ə)n/ ■ n. a substance that causes an allergic reaction.
– DERIVATIVES **allergenic** adj. **allergenicity** n.

allergic /əˈləːdʒɪk/ ■ adj. of, caused by, or relating to an allergy. ▸ having an allergy: *allergic to bee stings*.

allergy /ˈalədʒi/ ■ n. (pl. **-ies**) a damaging immune response by the body to a substance to which it has become hypersensitive.
– DERIVATIVES **allergist** n.
– ORIGIN C20: from German *Allergie*, from Greek *allos* 'other'.

alleviate /əˈliːvɪeɪt/ ■ v. make (pain or difficulty) less severe.
– DERIVATIVES **alleviation** n. **alleviative** adj. **alleviator** n.
– ORIGIN Middle English: from late Latin *alleviare* 'lighten', from Latin, from *ad-* 'to' + *levare* 'raise'.

alley ■ n. (pl. **-eys**) **1** a narrow passageway between or behind buildings. ▸ a path in a park or garden. **2** a long, narrow area in which skittles and bowling are played. **3** N. Amer. Tennis either of the two side strips between the service court and the sidelines. ▸ Baseball the area between the outfielders in left-centre or right-centre field.
– ORIGIN Middle English: from Old French *alee* 'walking or passage', from *aler* 'go', from Latin *ambulare* 'to walk'.

alley cat ■ n. a stray urban cat.

alley-oop ■ exclam. used to encourage or draw attention to the performance of an acrobatic feat. ■ n. (also **alley-oop pass**) Basketball a high pass caught by a leaping teammate who tries to dunk the ball before landing.
– ORIGIN C20: from French *allez!* 'go on!' + a supposedly French pronunciation of UP.

alleyway ■ n. another term for ALLEY (in sense 1).

All Fools' Day ■ n. another term for APRIL FOOL'S DAY.

All Hallows ■ n. another term for ALL SAINTS' DAY.

VOWELS a cat ɑː arm ɛ bed ɛː hair ə ago əː her ɪ sit i cosy iː see ɒ hot ɔː saw ʌ run

alliance ■ n. a union or association formed for mutual benefit. ▶ a relationship based on an affinity. ▶ the state of being joined or associated.
– ORIGIN Middle English: from Old French *aliance*, from *alier* (see ALLY).

allied /'alʌɪd, ə'lʌɪd/ ■ adj. **1** joined by or relating to an alliance. ▶ (usu. **Allied**) of or relating to Britain and its allies in the First and Second World Wars and after. **2** (**allied to/with**) in combination or working together with. ▶ connected or related.

alligator ■ n. **1** a large semiaquatic reptile similar to a crocodile but with a broader and shorter head, native to the Americas and China. [Genus *Alligator*: two species.] **2** the skin of the alligator.
– ORIGIN C16: from Spanish *el lagarto* 'the lizard'.

alligator clip ■ n. chiefly N. Amer. another term for CROCODILE CLIP.

alligator pear ■ n. North American term for AVOCADO.

all-in ■ adj. Brit. (especially of a price) inclusive of everything.

all-inclusive ■ adj. including everything or everyone. ▶ denoting or relating to a holiday or resort in which all or most meals, drinks, and activities are included in the overall price. ■ n. an all-inclusive holiday resort.

all-in-one ■ adj. combining two or more items or functions in a single unit.

all-in wrestling ■ n. chiefly Brit. wrestling with few or no restrictions.

alliteration ■ n. the occurrence of the same letter or sound at the beginning of adjacent or closely connected words.
– DERIVATIVES **alliterate** v. **alliterative** adj. **alliteratively** adv.
– ORIGIN C17: from medieval Latin *alliteratio(n-)*, from Latin *ad-* (expressing addition) + *littera* 'letter'.

allium /'alɪəm/ ■ n. (pl. **alliums**) a bulbous plant of a genus that includes the onion and its relatives (e.g. garlic and chives). [Genus *Allium*.]
– ORIGIN Latin, 'garlic'.

allo- /'aləʊ/ ■ comb. form other; different: *allopatric*.
– ORIGIN from Greek *allos* 'other'.

allocate ■ v. assign or distribute (resources or duties) to.
– DERIVATIVES **allocable** adj. **allocation** n. **allocative** adj. **allocator** n.
– ORIGIN C17 (*allocation* Middle English): from medieval Latin *allocare* 'allot'.

allochthonous /ə'lɒkθənəs/ ■ adj. Geology denoting a deposit or formation that originated at a distance from its present position. Often contrasted with AUTOCHTHONOUS.
– ORIGIN C20: from Greek *allos* 'other' + *khthōn* 'earth'.

allocution /ˌaləˈkjuːʃ(ə)n/ ■ n. a formal speech giving advice or a warning.
– ORIGIN C17: from Latin, from *alloqui* 'speak to'.

allogamy /ə'lɒɡəmi/ ■ n. Botany the fertilization of a flower by pollen from another flower, especially one on a different plant. Compare with AUTOGAMY.
– DERIVATIVES **allogamous** adj.
– ORIGIN C19: from Greek *allos* 'other' + *gamos* 'marriage'.

allogeneic /ˌalə(ʊ)dʒɪˈniːɪk, -dʒɪˈneɪk/ ■ adj. Physiology relating to or denoting tissues which are genetically dissimilar and hence immunologically incompatible, although from individuals of the same species.
– ORIGIN 1960s: from Greek *allos* 'other' + *genea* 'race, stock'.

allogenic /ˌaləˈdʒɛnɪk/ ■ adj. **1** Geology (of a mineral or sediment) transported to its present position from elsewhere. Often contrasted with AUTHIGENIC. **2** Ecology (of a successional change) caused by non-living factors in the environment.

allograph /'aləɡrɑːf/ ■ n. **1** Linguistics each of two or more alternative forms of a letter of an alphabet or other unit of a writing system. **2** Phonetics each of two or more letters or letter combinations representing a single phoneme in different words (e.g. the (f) of 'fake' and the (ph) of 'phase').
– ORIGIN 1950s: from Greek *allos* 'other' + GRAPHEME.

allometry /ə'lɒmɪtri/ ■ n. Biology the growth of body parts at different rates, resulting in a change of proportions.
– DERIVATIVES **allometric** adj.

29 **all-rounder**

allomorph /'aləmɔːf/ ■ n. Linguistics any of two or more representations of a morpheme, such as the plural endings /s/ (as in *bats*) and /z/ (as in *bugs*).
– DERIVATIVES **allomorphic** adj.
– ORIGIN 1940s: from Greek *allos* 'other' + MORPHEME.

allopathy /ə'lɒpəθi/ ■ n. the treatment of disease by conventional means, i.e. with drugs having effects opposite to the symptoms. Often contrasted with HOMEOPATHY.
– DERIVATIVES **allopath** n. **allopathic** adj. **allopathist** n.

allopatric /ˌaləˈpatrɪk/ ■ adj. Biology (of animal or plant species or populations) occurring in separate non-overlapping geographical areas. Compare with SYMPATRIC.
– DERIVATIVES **allopatry** n.
– ORIGIN 1940s: from Greek *allos* 'other' + *patra* 'fatherland'.

allophone /'aləfəʊn/ ■ n. Phonetics any of the various phonetic realizations of a phoneme in a language, which do not contribute to distinctions of meaning.
– DERIVATIVES **allophonic** adj.
– ORIGIN 1930s: from Greek *allos* 'other' + PHONEME.

allosaurus /ˌaləˈsɔːrəs/ ■ n. a large bipedal carnivorous dinosaur of the late Jurassic period.
– ORIGIN from Greek *allos* 'other' + *sauros* 'lizard'.

allosteric /ˌaləˈstɛrɪk, -ˈstɪərɪk/ ■ adj. Biochemistry relating to or denoting the alteration of the activity of an enzyme by means of a conformational change induced by a different molecule.
– DERIVATIVES **allosterically** adv.

allot ■ v. (**allotted**, **allotting**) apportion or assign (something) to someone.
– ORIGIN C15: from Old French *aloter*, from *a-* 'to' + *loter* 'divide into lots'.

allotment ■ n. **1** Brit. a plot of land rented by an individual from a local authority, for growing vegetables or flowers. **2** the action of allotting. ▶ an amount of something allotted.

allotrope /'alətrəʊp/ ■ n. Chemistry each of two or more different physical forms in which an element can exist (e.g. graphite, charcoal, and diamond as forms of carbon).
– DERIVATIVES **allotropic** adj. **allotropy** /ə'lɒtrəpi/ n.
– ORIGIN C19: from Greek, from *allos* 'other' + *tropos* 'manner'.

allow ■ v. **1** admit as legal or acceptable. ▶ permit to do something. **2** (often **allow for**) take into consideration when making plans or calculations. ▶ provide or set aside for a particular purpose. **3** admit the truth of.
– DERIVATIVES **allowable** adj. **allowably** adv.
– ORIGIN Middle English: from Old French *alouer*, reinforced by medieval Latin *allocare* 'allot'.

allowance ■ n. the amount of something allowed. ▶ a sum of money paid regularly to a person, typically to meet specified expenses. ▶ an amount of money that can be earned or received free of tax. ▶ Horse Racing a deduction in the weight that a horse is required to carry in a race.
– PHRASES **make allowance(s) for 1** take into consideration. **2** treat leniently on account of mitigating circumstances.

allowedly ■ adv. as is generally admitted to be true.

alloy ■ n. /'alɔɪ/ a metal made by combining two or more metallic elements, especially to give greater strength or resistance to corrosion. ▶ an inferior metal mixed with a precious one. ■ v. /ə'lɔɪ/ **1** mix (metals) to make an alloy. **2** spoil by adding something inferior.
– ORIGIN C16: from Old French *aloi* (n.) and *aleier* 'combine', from Latin *alligare* 'bind'.

all-points bulletin ■ n. (in the US) a radio message sent to every officer in a police force giving details of a suspected criminal or stolen vehicle.

all right ■ adj. satisfactory; acceptable. ▶ permissible. ■ adv. fairly well. ■ exclam. expressing or asking for agreement or acceptance.

all-round ■ adj. having a great many abilities or uses. ▶ in many or all respects.

all-rounder ■ n. a person competent in a range of skills, especially a cricketer who can both bat and bowl well.

All Saints' Day

All Saints' Day ■ n. a Christian festival in honour of all the saints, held in the Western Church) on 1 November.

All Souls' Day ■ n. a Catholic festival with prayers for the souls of the dead in Purgatory, held on 2 November.

allspice ■ n. **1** the dried aromatic fruit of a Caribbean tree, used as a culinary spice. **2** a tree of the myrtle family from which this spice is obtained. [*Pimenta dioica*.] **3** an aromatic North American tree or shrub. [Genus *Calycanthus*.]

all-terrain vehicle ■ n. a small open motor vehicle fitted with large tyres, designed for use on rough ground.

all-ticket ■ adj. denoting or relating to a sports match for which tickets must be bought in advance.

all-time ■ adj. hitherto unsurpassed: *the all-time record.*

allude ■ v. (**allude to**) hint at. ▸ mention in passing.
– ORIGIN C15: from Latin *alludere*, from *ad-* 'towards' + *ludere* 'to play'.

allure ■ n. powerful attraction or fascination. ■ v. [often as adj. **alluring**] powerfully attract.
– DERIVATIVES **allurement** n. **alluringly** adv.
– ORIGIN Middle English: from Old French *aleurier* 'attract', from *a-* 'to' + *lure* 'a lure' (orig. a falconry term).

allusion ■ n. the practice or device of making indirect or implicit references. ▸ a reference of this type.
– DERIVATIVES **allusive** adj. **allusively** adv. **allusiveness** n.

alluvium /ə'l(j)uːvɪəm/ ■ n. a deposit of clay, silt, and sand left by flowing flood water in a river valley or delta, typically producing fertile soil.
– DERIVATIVES **alluvial** adj.
– ORIGIN C17: Latin, neuter of *alluvius* 'washed against', from *ad-* 'towards' + *luere* 'to wash'.

ally /'alʌɪ/ ■ n. (pl. **-ies**) a person or organization that cooperates with another. ▸ a state formally cooperating with another for a military or other purpose. ▸ (**the Allies**) the countries that fought with Britain in the First and Second World Wars. ■ v. /also ə'lʌɪ/ (**-ies, -ied**) (**ally something to/with**) combine a resource or commodity with (another) for mutual benefit. ▸ (**ally oneself with**) side with.
– ORIGIN Middle English: from Old French *alier*, from Latin *alligare* 'bind together'.

-ally ■ suffix forming adverbs from adjectives ending in *-al* (such as *radically* from *radical*).

allyl /'alʌɪl, -lɪl/ ■ n. [as modifier] Chemistry of or denoting the unsaturated hydrocarbon radical -C₃H₄.
– DERIVATIVES **allylic** adj.
– ORIGIN C19: from Latin *allium* 'garlic' (because identified in compounds from alliums).

alma mater /ˌalmə 'mɑːtə, 'meɪt-/ ■ n. the school, college, or university that one once attended.
– ORIGIN C17: Latin, 'bounteous mother'.

almanac /'ɔːlmənak, 'ɒl-/ (also **almanack**) ■ n. an annual calendar containing important dates and statistical information such as astronomical data. ▸ an annual handbook containing information of general or specialist interest.
– ORIGIN Middle English: from Greek *almenikhiaka*.

almighty ■ adj. **1** omnipotent. **2** informal enormous. ■ n. (**the Almighty**) a name or title for God.

almond ■ n. **1** the oval edible nut-like kernel of the almond tree, growing in a woody shell. **2** the tree that produces this, related to the peach and plum. [*Prunus dulcis*.]
– ORIGIN Middle English: from Old French *alemande*, from medieval Latin *amandula*, from Greek *amugdalē*.

almond eyes ■ pl. n. eyes that are narrow and oval with pointed ends.

almond oil ■ n. oil obtained from bitter almonds, used in cosmetic and medicinal preparations and as a flavouring.

almond paste ■ n. marzipan.

almoner /'ɑːmənə, 'alm-/ ■ n. historical an official distributor of alms.
– ORIGIN Middle English: from Old French *aumonier*, from medieval Latin *eleemosynarius*, from *eleemosyna* (see ALMS).

almost ■ adv. very nearly.
– ORIGIN Old English *æl mæst* 'for the most part', of Germanic origin.

alms /ɑːmz/ ■ pl. n. (in historical contexts) charitable donations of money or food to the poor.
– ORIGIN Old English *ælmysse*, from Greek *eleēmosunē* 'compassion', from *eleos* 'mercy'.

almshouse ■ n. a house founded by charity, offering accommodation for the poor.

aloe /'aləʊ/ ■ n. **1** a succulent plant native to Africa with a rosette of thick tapering leaves and tubular flowers on long stems. (Genus *Aloe*.) ▸ (**aloes** or **bitter aloes**) a strong laxative obtained from the bitter juice of various kinds of aloe. **2** (also **aloes wood**) the fragrant heartwood of a tropical Asian tree. ▸ the resin obtained from this wood, used in perfume, incense, and medicine.
– ORIGIN Old English *alewe*, from Greek *aloē*; reinforced by Old French *aloes* 'aloe', hence freq. used in the pl.

aloe vera /'vɪərə/ ■ n. **1** a gelatinous substance obtained from a kind of aloe, used in cosmetics as an emollient. **2** the plant that yields this substance, grown chiefly in the Caribbean and the southern US. [*Aloe vera*.]
– ORIGIN C20: modern Latin, 'true aloe', prob. in contrast to the American agave.

aloft ■ adj. & adv. up in or into the air. ▸ up the mast or into the rigging of a ship.
– ORIGIN Middle English: from Old Norse *á lopt*, from *á* 'in, on, to' + *lopt* 'air'.

aloha /ə'ləʊhə/ ■ exclam. & n. a Hawaiian word used when greeting or parting.
– ORIGIN C19: from Maori *aroha* 'love, pity'.

alone ■ adj. & adv. **1** on one's own; by oneself. ▸ isolated and lonely. **2** only; exclusively.
– PHRASES **go it alone** informal act without assistance. **leave** (or **let**) **alone 1** abandon or desert. **2** stop interfering with.
– DERIVATIVES **aloneness** n.
– ORIGIN Middle English: from ALL + ONE.

along ■ prep. & adv. **1** moving in a constant direction on (a more or less horizontal surface). **2** extending in a more or less horizontal line on. **3** in or into company with others.
– PHRASES **along with** in company with or at the same time as. **be** (or **come**) **along** arrive.
– ORIGIN Old English, of West Germanic origin; rel. to LONG¹.

alongshore ■ adv. along or by the shore.

alongside ■ prep. (N. Amer. also **alongside of**) close to the side of; next to. ▸ at the same time as or in coexistence with.

aloof ■ adj. cool and distant.
– DERIVATIVES **aloofly** adv. **aloofness** n.
– ORIGIN C16: from **a-²** + LUFF, orig. in nautical use meaning 'away and to windward!', i.e. with the ship's head kept close to the wind away from a lee shore or other hazard.

alopecia /ˌaləʊ'piːʃə/ ■ n. Medicine the absence of hair from areas of the body where it normally grows.
– ORIGIN Middle English: from Greek *alōpekia* 'fox mange', from *alōpēx* 'fox'.

aloud ■ adv. audibly. ▸ archaic loudly.

alp ■ n. a high mountain. ▸ (**the Alps**) the high range of mountains in Switzerland and adjoining countries.
– ORIGIN Middle English (orig. pl.): from Greek *Alpeis*.

alpaca /al'pakə/ ■ n. (pl. same or **alpacas**) a long-haired domesticated South American mammal related to the llama. [*Lama pacos*.] ▸ the wool of the alpaca, or fabric made from it.
– ORIGIN C18: from Aymara *allpaca*.

alpenhorn /'alpənhɔːn/ (also **alphorn**) ■ n. a very long valveless wooden wind instrument played like a horn and used for signalling in the Alps.
– ORIGIN C19: from German, 'Alp horn'.

alpenstock /'alpənstɒk/ ■ n. a long iron-tipped stick used by hillwalkers.
– ORIGIN C19: from German, 'Alp stick'.

alpha /'alfə/ ■ n. **1** the first letter of the Greek alphabet (A, α), transliterated as 'a'. ▸ [as modifier] denoting the first of a series of items or categories. ▸ [as modifier] denoting the dominant animal or person in a group: *an alpha male.* **2** a code word representing the letter A, used in radio

---

CONSONANTS   **b** but   **d** dog   **f** few   **g** get   **h** he   **j** yes   **k** cat   **l** leg   **m** man   **n** no   **p** pen   **r** red

communication.
- PHRASES **alpha and omega** the beginning and the end (used by Christians as a title for Jesus).
- ORIGIN from Greek.

alphabet ■ n. a set of letters or symbols in a fixed order used to represent the basic set of speech sounds of a language.
- DERIVATIVES **alphabetization** (also **-isation**) n. **alphabetize** (also **-ise**) v.
- ORIGIN C16: from Greek *alpha*, *bēta*, the first two letters of the Greek alphabet.

alphabetical ■ adj. of or relating to an alphabet. ▸ in the order of the letters of the alphabet.
- DERIVATIVES **alphabetic** adj. **alphabetically** adv.

alphabet soup ■ n. informal a confusing or confused mixture of things.
- ORIGIN C20: alluding to a clear soup containing pasta in the shapes of letters.

alpha blocker ■ n. Medicine any of a class of drugs which prevent the stimulation of the adrenergic receptors responsible for increased blood pressure.

alphafetoprotein /ˌalfəˌfiːtəʊˈprəʊtiːn/ ■ n. Medicine a protein produced by a fetus which is present in amniotic fluid and the bloodstream of the mother, levels of which can be measured to detect certain congenital defects such as spina bifida.

alpha-hydroxy acid ■ n. Chemistry an organic acid containing a hydroxyl group adjacent to the carboxylic acid group, especially any of a group used in skincare preparations for their exfoliating properties.

alphanumeric ■ adj. consisting of or using both letters and numerals. ■ n. a character that is either a letter or a number.
- DERIVATIVES **alphanumerical** adj.

alpha particle ■ n. Physics a helium nucleus, especially as emitted by some radioactive substances.

alpha radiation ■ n. ionizing radiation consisting of alpha particles, emitted by some substances undergoing radioactive decay.

alpha rhythm ■ n. Physiology the normal electrical activity of the brain when conscious and relaxed, consisting of oscillations (alpha waves) with a frequency of 8 to 13 hertz.

alpha test ■ n. a trial of machinery or software carried out before a product is made available for beta-testing. ■ v. (**alpha-test**) subject to an alpha test.

alpine ■ adj. 1 of or relating to high mountains. ▸ (in the names of plants and animals) growing or found on high mountains. ▸ (**Alpine**) of or relating to the Alps. 2 (also **Alpine**) relating to or denoting skiing downhill. ■ n. an alpine plant.

alpinist ■ n. a climber of high mountains, especially in the Alps.

alprazolam /alˈpreɪzə(ʊ)lam/ ■ n. Medicine a drug of the benzodiazepine group, used in the treatment of anxiety.
- ORIGIN 1970s: from *al-* of unknown origin + *p(henyl)* + *(t)r(i)azol(e)* + *(-azep)am*.

already ■ adv. 1 before the time in question. ▸ as surprisingly soon or early as this. 2 N. Amer. informal an expression of impatience: *enough already with these crazy kids!*
- ORIGIN Middle English: from ALL + READY; sense 2 influenced by Yiddish use.

alright ■ adj., adv., & exclam. variant spelling of ALL RIGHT.

USAGE
The spelling **alright** (rather than **all right**) is still considered by many to be unacceptable in formal writing, even though other single-word forms such as **altogether** have long been accepted.

Alsatian ■ n. 1 a German shepherd dog. 2 a native or inhabitant of Alsace. ■ adj. of or relating to Alsace.

also ■ adv. in addition.
- ORIGIN Old English *alswā* 'quite so, in that manner, similarly'.

also-ran ■ n. a loser in a race or contest. ▸ informal an undistinguished or unsuccessful person or thing.

alstroemeria /ˌalstrəˈmɪərɪə/ ■ n. a South American plant widely cultivated for its showy lily-like flowers. [Genus *Alstroemeria*.]
- ORIGIN C18: named after the Swedish naturalist Klas von Alstroemer.

altar /ˈɔːltə, ˈɒl-/ ■ n. the table in a Christian church at which the bread and wine are consecrated in communion services. ▸ a table or flat-topped block used as the focus for a religious ritual.
- ORIGIN Old English, from late Latin *altar*, from Latin *altus* 'high'.

altar boy ■ n. a boy who acts as a priest's assistant during a service.

altarpiece ■ n. a painting or other work of art designed to be set above and behind an altar.

altazimuth /alˈtazɪməθ/ ■ n. 1 Astronomy a telescope mounting that moves in azimuth (about a vertical axis) and in altitude (about a horizontal axis). 2 a surveying instrument for measuring vertical and horizontal angles.
- ORIGIN C19: blend of ALTITUDE and AZIMUTH.

alter /ˈɔːltə, ˈɒl-/ ■ v. change in character, appearance, direction, etc. ▸ N. Amer. & Austral. castrate or spay (a domestic animal).
- DERIVATIVES **alterable** adj. **alteration** n.
- ORIGIN Middle English: from Old French *alterer*, from Latin *alter* 'other'.

altercation ■ n. a noisy argument or disagreement.
- ORIGIN Middle English: from Latin *altercatio(n-)*, from *altercari* 'to wrangle'.

alter ego /ˌaltər ˈɛɡəʊ, ˌɒlt-, -ˈiːɡ-/ ■ n. 1 a person's secondary or alternative personality. 2 a close friend who is very like oneself.
- ORIGIN C16: Latin, 'other self'.

alternate ■ v. /ˈɔːltəneɪt, ˈɒl-/ occur or do in turn repeatedly. ▸ (of a thing) change repeatedly between two contrasting conditions. ■ adj. /ɔːlˈtəːnət, ɒl-/ 1 every other. ▸ (of two things) each following and succeeded by the other in a regular pattern. ▸ Botany (of leaves or shoots) placed alternately on the two sides of the stem. 2 chiefly N. Amer. another term for ALTERNATIVE. ■ n. /ɔːlˈtəːnət, ɒl-/ N. Amer. a deputy or substitute.
- DERIVATIVES **alternately** adv. **alternation** n.
- ORIGIN C16 (*alternation* Middle English): from Latin *alternare* 'do by turns', from *alternus* 'every other', from *alter* 'other'.

alternate angles ■ pl. n. Mathematics two equal angles formed when a line crosses two parallel lines, lying on opposite sides of the transversal line and on opposite relative sides of the other lines.

alternating current (abbrev.: **AC**) ■ n. an electric current that reverses its direction many times a second at regular intervals. Compare with DIRECT CURRENT.

alternation of generations ■ n. Biology a pattern of reproduction shown by some lower plants and invertebrates, involving a regular alternation between sexual and asexual forms (as in ferns) or dioecious and par-thenogenetic forms (as in some jellyfishes).

alternative ■ adj. 1 (of one or more things) available as another possibility. ▸ (of two things) mutually exclusive. 2 of or relating to activities that depart from or challenge traditional norms. ■ n. one of two or more available possibilities.
- DERIVATIVES **alternatively** adv.
- ORIGIN C16: from medieval Latin *alternativus*, from Latin *alternare* (see ALTERNATE).

USAGE
Some traditionalists maintain that, because of the word's origin, you can only have a maximum of two alternatives, and that uses where there are more than two are wrong. Such uses are, however, normal in modern standard English.

alternative dispute resolution ■ n. chiefly N. Amer. the use of methods such as mediation to resolve a dispute without resort to litigation.

alternative energy ■ n. energy fuelled in ways that do not use up the earth's natural resources or otherwise harm the environment, especially by avoiding the use of fossil fuels or nuclear power.

alternative fuel

alternative fuel ■ n. a fuel other than petrol or diesel for powering motor vehicles, such as natural gas or electricity.

alternative medicine ■ n. medical therapy regarded as unorthodox by the medical profession, e.g. herbalism and naturopathy. See also COMPLEMENTARY MEDICINE.

alternator ■ n. a dynamo that generates an alternating current.

although ■ conj. **1** in spite of the fact that. **2** but.

altimeter /'altɪmiːtə/ ■ n. an instrument for determining altitude attained, especially a barometric or radar device fitted in an aircraft.
– ORIGIN C20: from Latin *altus* 'high' + -METER.

altiplano /ˌaltɪˈplɑːnəʊ/ ■ n. (pl. **-os**) the high tableland of central South America.
– ORIGIN C20: from Spanish.

altitude ■ n. the height of an object or point in relation to sea level or ground level. ▸ Astronomy the apparent height of a celestial object above the horizon, measured in angular distance. ▸ Geometry the length of the perpendicular line from a vertex to the opposite side of a figure.
– DERIVATIVES **altitudinal** adj.
– ORIGIN Middle English: from Latin *altitudo*, from *altus* 'high'.

altitude sickness ■ n. illness caused by ascent to high altitude, characterized chiefly by hyperventilation, nausea, and exhaustion resulting from shortage of oxygen.

Alt key ■ n. Computing a key on a keyboard which, when pressed simultaneously with another key, gives the latter an alternative function.

alto /'altəʊ/ ■ n. (pl. **-os**) **1** (especially in church music) the highest adult male singing voice. ▸ the lowest female singing voice; contralto. **2** [as modifier] denoting the member of a family of instruments pitched second or third highest.
– ORIGIN C16: from Italian *alto (canto)* 'high (song)'.

alto clef ■ n. Music a clef placing middle C on the middle line of the stave, used chiefly for viola music.

altogether ■ adv. completely. ▸ in total. ▸ on the whole.
– PHRASES **in the altogether** informal naked.

USAGE
Altogether and all together do not mean the same thing. **Altogether** means 'in total', as in *there are six bedrooms altogether*, whereas **all together** means 'all in one place' or 'all at once', as in *they came in all together*.

alto-relievo /ˌaltəʊrɪˈliːvəʊ/ (also **-rilievo** /-rɪˈljeɪvəʊ/) ■ n. (pl. **-os**) Art high relief.
– ORIGIN C17: from Italian *alto-rilievo*.

altricial /əlˈtrɪʃ(ə)l/ ■ adj. Zoology relating to or denoting a bird or other animal whose young are hatched or born in an undeveloped state and require care and feeding by the parents. Often contrasted with PRECOCIAL.
– ORIGIN C19: from Latin *altrix*, feminine of *altor* 'nourisher', from *alere* 'nourish'.

altruism /'altrʊɪz(ə)m/ ■ n. selfless concern for the well-being of others. ▸ Zoology behaviour of an animal that benefits another at its own expense.
– DERIVATIVES **altruist** n. **altruistic** adj. **altruistically** adv.
– ORIGIN C19: from French *altruisme*, from Italian *altrui* 'somebody else', from Latin *alteri huic* 'to this other'.

ALU ■ abbrev. Computing arithmetic logic unit.

alum /'aləm/ ■ n. Chemistry **1** (also **potash alum**) a colourless astringent compound which is a hydrated double sulphate of aluminium and potassium, used in solution in dyeing and tanning. **2** any of a series of analogous compounds of other metals.
– ORIGIN Middle English: from Latin *alumen*, rel. to *aluta* 'tawed leather'.

alumina /əˈluːmɪnə/ ■ n. aluminium oxide, a white solid that is a major constituent of many clays and is found crystallized as corundum and sapphire. [Al_2O_3.]
– ORIGIN C18: from Latin *alumen* (see ALUM), on the pattern of *magnesia*.

aluminium /al(j)ʊˈmɪnɪəm/ (US **aluminum**) ■ n. a strong, light, corrosion-resistant silvery-grey metal, the chemical element of atomic number 13. (Symbol: **Al**)
– ORIGIN C19: from ALUMINA.

aluminium bronze ■ n. an alloy of copper and aluminium.

aluminosilicate /əˌluːmɪnə(ʊ)ˈsɪlɪkeɪt/ ■ n. Mineralogy a silicate in which aluminium replaces some of the silicon, especially as a constituent of minerals such as feldspar.

aluminum /əˈluːmɪnəm/ ■ n. US spelling of ALUMINIUM.

alumnus /əˈlʌmnəs/ ■ n. (fem. **alumna**; pl. **alumni** /-niː/ or fem. **alumnae** /-niː/) a former pupil or student of a particular school, college, or university.
– ORIGIN C17: from Latin, 'nursling, pupil', from *alere* 'nourish'.

a luta continua /aˌluːtə kɒntɪˈnuːə/ ■ exclam. a political rallying cry used by populist movements in some Portuguese-speaking countries and adopted by anti-apartheid campaigners in South Africa.
– ORIGIN Portuguese, 'the struggle continues'.

alveolar /alˈvɪələ, ˌalvɪˈəʊlə/ ■ adj. **1** Anatomy of or relating to an alveolus. **2** Phonetics (of a consonant) pronounced with the tip of the tongue on or near the bony ridge containing the alveoli of the upper teeth (e.g. *n*, *s*, *d*, *t*). ■ n. Phonetics an alveolar consonant.

alveolitis /ˌalvɪə(ʊ)ˈlʌɪtɪs/ ■ n. Medicine inflammation of the air sacs of the lungs.

alveolus /alˈvɪələs, ˌalvɪˈəʊləs/ ■ n. (pl. **alveoli** /-lʌɪ, -liː/) Anatomy **1** any of the many tiny air sacs of the lungs which allow for rapid gaseous exchange. **2** the bony socket for the root of a tooth. **3** a sac-like cavity in a gland.
– DERIVATIVES **alveolate** /alˈvɪələt/ adj.
– ORIGIN C17: from Latin, 'small cavity', diminutive of *alveus*.

always ■ adv. **1** on all occasions. ▸ throughout a long period of the past. ▸ forever. ▸ repeatedly. **2** failing all else.
– ORIGIN Middle English: from *all way*.

alyssum /'alɪs(ə)m, əˈlɪs(ə)m/ ■ n. (pl. **alyssums**) a herbaceous plant, often cultivated, which typically bears small white or yellow flowers. [Genera *Alyssum* and *Lobularia*: many species.]
– ORIGIN C16: from Greek *alusson*, from *a-* 'without' + *lussa* 'rabies' (referring to early herbalist use).

Alzheimer's disease /'altshʌɪməz/ ■ n. a form of progressive mental deterioration due to generalized degeneration of the brain, occurring in middle or old age.
– ORIGIN C20: named after the German neurologist Alois Alzheimer.

AM ■ abbrev. **1** amplitude modulation. **2** US Master of Arts. [Latin *artium magister*.]

Am ■ symb. the chemical element americium.

am first person singular present of BE.

a.m. ■ abbrev. before noon.
– ORIGIN from Latin *ante meridiem*.

ama- ■ prefix denoting the plural form of some nouns in isiXhosa, isiZulu, and isiNdebele. ▸ S. African informal, often humorous added to some English or Afrikaans nouns to Africanize them: *amagents* | *Amabokoboko*.

amadumbe /amaˈdʊmbi/ ■ n. variant spelling of MADUMBE.

amah /'ɑːmə/ ■ n. a nursemaid or maid in the Far East or India.
– ORIGIN from Portuguese *ama* 'nurse'.

amahubo /ˌamaˈhuːbɒ/ ■ pl. n. (pl. same) S. African Music ceremonial songs, hymns, or psalms.
– ORIGIN from isiZulu, pl. of *ihubo* 'hymn'.

amakhosi /ˌamaˈkɒsi/ (also **amakosi**) ■ pl. n. S. African traditional leaders regarded collectively. See TRADITIONAL LEADER.
– ORIGIN pl. of isiXhosa and isiZulu *ink(h)osi* 'ruler, chief'.

amakwerekwere /ˌamakwɛrɛˈkwɛrɛ/ ■ pl. n. variant spelling of MAKWEREKWERE.
– ORIGIN from isiXhosa, pl. of *ikwerekwere* 'foreigner'.

amalgam /əˈmalgəm/ ■ n. **1** a mixture or blend. **2** Chemistry an alloy of mercury with another metal, especially one used for dental fillings.
– ORIGIN C15: from medieval Latin *amalgama*, from Greek *malagma* 'an emollient'.

amalgamate /əˈmalgəmeɪt/ ■ v. **1** combine or unite to form one organization or structure. **2** Chemistry alloy (a

metal) with mercury.
— DERIVATIVES **amalgamation** n.
— ORIGIN C17: from medieval Latin *amalgamare* 'form into a soft mass', from *amalgama* (see **AMALGAM**).

amandla /a'mandxlə/ ■ exclam. S. African a political rallying cry used chiefly by anti-apartheid organizations in pre-democratic South Africa.
— ORIGIN isiXhosa and isiZulu, 'power, strength'.

amanuensis /əˌmanjʊ'ɛnsɪs/ ■ n. (pl. **amanuenses** /-siːz/) a literary assistant, in particular one who takes dictation.
— ORIGIN C17: Latin, from (*servus*) *a manu* '(slave) at hand (writing), secretary' + -*ensis* 'belonging to'.

amaranth /'aməranθ/ ■ n. a plant of a chiefly tropical family (Amaranthaceae), some species of which are grown for their edible leaves, and others, such as love-lies-bleeding, for their attractive flowers.
— DERIVATIVES **amaranthine** /ˌamə'ranθʌɪn/ adj.
— ORIGIN C16: var. (on the pattern of plant names ending in -*anthus*) of Latin *amarantus*, from Greek *amarantos* 'not fading'.

amaretti /ˌamə'rɛti/ ■ pl. n. Italian almond-flavoured biscuits.
— ORIGIN Italian, from *amaro* 'bitter'.

amaretto /ˌamə'rɛtəʊ/ ■ n. a brown almond-flavoured liqueur produced in Italy.
— ORIGIN Italian, diminutive of *amaro* 'bitter' (with ref. to bitter almonds).

amaryllis /ˌamə'rɪlɪs/ ■ n. a bulbous plant with showy trumpet-shaped flowers and strap-shaped leaves. [*Amaryllis belladonna* (South Africa) or genus *Hippeastrum* (S. America).]
— ORIGIN from Latin *Amaryllis*, from Greek *Amarullis*, a name for a country girl in pastoral poetry.

amasi /a'mɑːsi/ ■ n. another term for **MAAS**.
— ORIGIN isiXhosa and isiZulu, 'thickened curdled milk'.

amass ■ v. accumulate over time.
— ORIGIN C15: from French *amasser*, from Latin *massa* (see **MASS**).

amateur /'amətə, -tʃə, -tjʊə, ˌamə'təː/ ■ n. a person who engages in a pursuit, especially a sport, on an unpaid basis. ▸ a person considered inept at a particular activity. ■ adj. non-professional. ▸ inept.
— DERIVATIVES **amateurism** n.
— ORIGIN C18: from Latin *amator* 'lover', from *amare* 'to love'.

amateurish ■ adj. inept.
— DERIVATIVES **amateurishly** adv. **amateurishness** n.

amatol /'amətɒl/ ■ n. a high explosive consisting of a mixture of TNT and ammonium nitrate.
— ORIGIN C20: from *am*(*monium*) + *tol*(*uene*).

amatory /'amət(ə)ri/ ■ adj. relating to or induced by sexual love or desire.
— ORIGIN C16: from Latin *amatorius*, from *amator* (see **AMATEUR**).

amatungulu (also **amatungula**) ■ n. (pl. same) S. African another term for **NUM-NUM**.
— ORIGIN isiZulu, pl. of *itungulu*, var. of *ithungulu*.

amaze ■ v. surprise greatly.
— DERIVATIVES **amazement** n.
— ORIGIN Old English.

amazing ■ adj. **1** causing great surprise. **2** informal very impressive; excellent.
— DERIVATIVES **amazingly** adv.

Amazon /'aməz(ə)n/ ■ n. **1** a member of a legendary race of female warriors believed by the ancient Greeks to exist in Scythia or elsewhere. ▸ a very tall, strong woman. **2** (**amazon**) a green parrot with a broad rounded tail, found in Central and South America. [Genus *Amazona*.]
— ORIGIN Middle English: from Greek *Amazōn*, explained by the Greeks as 'breastless' (as if from *a*- 'without' + *mazos* 'breast'), referring to the fable that the Amazons cut off the right breast so as to draw a bow more easily.

Amazonian /aməˈzəʊnɪən/ ■ adj. **1** of or relating to the River Amazon. **2** (of a woman) very tall and strong.

ambassador ■ n. a diplomat sent by a state as its permanent representative in a foreign country. ▸ a representative or promoter of a specified activity.
— DERIVATIVES **ambassadorial** adj. **ambassadorship** n. **ambassadress** n.

— ORIGIN Middle English: from French *ambassadeur*, from Italian *ambasciator*, from Latin *ambactus* 'servant'.

ambatch /'ambatʃ/ ■ n. a tropical African tree with light spongy wood that is used chiefly for rafts and floats. [*Aeschynomene elaphroxylon*.]
— ORIGIN C19: of Ethiopic origin.

amber ■ n. **1** hard translucent fossilized resin originating from extinct coniferous trees, typically yellowish in colour and used in jewellery. **2** a honey-yellow colour. ▸ a yellow light used as a cautionary signal between green for 'go' and red for 'stop'.
— ORIGIN Middle English: from Arabic '*anbar* 'ambergris', later 'amber'.

ambergris /'ambəgrɪs, -iːs/ ■ n. a wax-like secretion of the intestines of the sperm whale, found floating in tropical seas and used in perfume manufacture.
— ORIGIN Middle English: from Old French *ambre gris* 'grey amber', as distinct from *amber jaune* 'yellow amber' (the resin).

amberjack ■ n. a large game fish with a yellowish tail, found in inshore tropical and subtropical waters of the Atlantic and South Pacific. [Genus *Seriola*: several species.]

ambidextrous /ˌambɪˈdɛkstrəs/ ■ adj. able to use the right and left hands equally well.
— DERIVATIVES **ambidexterity** n. **ambidextrously** adv. **ambidextrousness** n.
— ORIGIN C17: from Latin *ambi*- 'on both sides' + *dexter* 'right-handed'.

ambience /'ambɪəns/ (also **ambiance**) ■ n. **1** the character and atmosphere of a place. **2** quality or character given to a sound recording by the space in which the sound occurs.

ambient /'ambɪənt/ ■ adj. **1** of or relating to the immediate environs of something. **2** denoting a style of instrumental music with electronic textures and no persistent beat, used to create atmosphere.
— ORIGIN C16: from Latin *ambire* 'go round'.

ambiguous /am'bɪɡjʊəs/ ■ adj. (of language) having more than one meaning. ▸ unclear because not distinguishing between alternatives.
— DERIVATIVES **ambiguity** /ˌambɪˈɡjuːɪti/ n. **ambiguously** adv. **ambiguousness** n.
— ORIGIN C16: from Latin *ambiguus* 'doubtful', from *ambigere* 'waver, go around', from *ambi*- 'both ways' + *agere* 'to drive'.

ambit /'ambɪt/ ■ n. the scope, extent, or bounds of something.
— ORIGIN Middle English: from Latin *ambitus* 'circuit', from *ambire* 'go round'.

ambition ■ n. a strong desire to do or achieve something. ▸ desire for success, wealth, or fame.
— ORIGIN Middle English: from Latin *ambitio*(*n*-), from *ambire* 'go around (canvassing for votes)'.

ambitious ■ adj. having or showing ambition. ▸ (of a plan or piece of work) intended to satisfy high aspirations and therefore difficult to achieve.
— DERIVATIVES **ambitiously** adv. **ambitiousness** n.

ambivalent /amˈbɪv(ə)l(ə)nt/ ■ adj. having mixed feelings or contradictory ideas about something or someone.
— DERIVATIVES **ambivalence** n. **ambivalently** adv.
— ORIGIN C20: from German *Ambivalenz*, on the pattern of *equivalent*.

amble ■ v. walk or move at a leisurely pace. ■ n. a leisurely walk.
— DERIVATIVES **ambler** n.
— ORIGIN Middle English: from Old French *ambler*, from Latin *ambulare* 'to walk'.

amblyopia /ˌamblɪˈəʊpɪə/ ■ n. Medicine impaired or dim vision without obvious defect or change in the eye.
— DERIVATIVES **amblyopic** adj.
— ORIGIN C18: from Greek, from *amblus* 'dull' + *ōps, ōp*- 'eye'.

amboyna /am'bɔɪnə/ ■ n. the decorative wood of a fast-growing SE Asian tree (*Pterocarpus indicus*), used for cabinetmaking.
— ORIGIN C19: named after *Amboina* Island in Indonesia.

ambrosia ■ n. **1** Greek & Roman Mythology the food of the gods. ▸ something very pleasing to taste or smell. **2** a

ambulance

fungal product used as food by ambrosia beetles or their larvae. ▸ another term for BEE BREAD.
– DERIVATIVES **ambrosial** adj.
– ORIGIN C16: from Greek, 'elixir of life'.

ambulance ■ n. a vehicle equipped for taking sick or injured people to and from hospital. ■ v. convey in an ambulance.
– ORIGIN C19: French, from *hôpital ambulant* 'mobile field hospital', from Latin *ambulare* 'walk'.

ambulance-chaser ■ n. derogatory, chiefly N. Amer. a lawyer who specializes in bringing cases seeking damages for personal injury.

ambulant /'ambjʊl(ə)nt/ ■ adj. Medicine able to walk about; not confined to bed.
– ORIGIN C17: from Latin *ambulare* 'walk'.

ambulate /'ambjʊleɪt/ ■ v. formal or technical walk; move about.
– DERIVATIVES **ambulation** n.
– ORIGIN C17: from Latin *ambulare* 'walk'.

ambulatory /'ambjʊlət(ə)ri/ ■ adj. **1** relating to walking or able to walk. **2** movable; mobile. ■ n. (pl. -**ies**) an aisle or cloister in a church or monastery.

ambuscade /ˌambə'skeɪd/ ■ n. an ambush.
– ORIGIN C16: from French *embuscade*, from a late Latin word meaning 'to place in a wood'; rel. to BUSH[1].

ambush ■ n. a surprise attack by people lying in wait in a concealed position. ■ v. attack in such a way.
– ORIGIN Middle English: from Old French *embuschier* (v.), from late Latin 'to place in a wood'.

ameba ■ n. (pl. **amebae** or **amebas**) US spelling of AMOEBA.

amebiasis ■ n. US spelling of AMOEBIASIS.

ameliorate /ə'miːlɪəreɪt/ ■ v. make better; reduce the undesirable effect of.
– DERIVATIVES **amelioration** n. **ameliorative** adj.
– ORIGIN C18: from French *améliorer*, from *meilleur* 'better'.

amen /ɑːˈmɛn, eɪ-/ ■ exclam. said at the end of a prayer or hymn, meaning 'so be it'.
– ORIGIN Old English: from Hebrew *'āmēn* 'truth, certainty'.

amenable /ə'miːnəb(ə)l/ ■ adj. responsive to suggestion. ▸ (**amenable to**) capable of being acted on.
– DERIVATIVES **amenability** n. **amenably** adv.
– ORIGIN C16 (in the sense 'liable to answer to a tribunal'): from Old French *amener* 'bring to', from Latin *minari* 'threaten'.

amend ■ v. **1** make minor improvements (a document, proposal, piece of legislation, etc.). **2** archaic put right.
– DERIVATIVES **amendable** adj.
– ORIGIN Middle English: from Old French *amender*, from Latin *emendare* (see EMEND).

amendment ■ n. **1** a minor improvement. ▸ the action of amending something. **2** (**Amendment**) an article added to the US Constitution.

amends ■ pl. n. (in phr. **make amends**) compensate or make up for a wrongdoing.
– ORIGIN Middle English: from Old French *amendes* 'penalties, fine', from *amender* (see AMEND).

amenity /ə'miːnɪti, -'mɛn-/ ■ n. (pl. -**ies**) a useful or desirable feature of a place. ▸ the pleasantness or attractiveness of a place.
– ORIGIN Middle English: from Latin *amoenitas*, from *amoenus* 'pleasant'.

amenorrhoea /əˌmɛnə'riːə/ (US **amenorrhea**) ■ n. an abnormal absence of menstruation.

amensalism /eɪ'mɛnsəlɪzm, ə-/ ■ n. Botany competition between two species which adversely affects one of them.

Amerasian /ˌamə'reɪʃ(ə)n, -ʒ(ə)n/ ■ adj. having one American and one Asian parent. ■ n. an Amerasian person.

American ■ adj. relating to or characteristic of the United States. ▸ relating to the continents of America. ■ n. a native or citizen of the United States. ▸ a native or inhabitant of any of the countries of North, South, or Central America.
– PHRASES **the American dream** the ideal by which equality of opportunity is available to any American, allowing the highest aspirations and goals to be achieved.
– DERIVATIVES **Americanization** (also **-isation**) n. **Americanize** (also **-ise**) v. **Americanness** n.

Americana /əˌmɛrɪ'kɑːnə/ ■ pl. n. things associated with the United States.

American aloe ■ n. another term for CENTURY PLANT.

American football ■ n. a kind of football played with an oval ball by teams of eleven players, on a field marked out as a gridiron.

American Indian ■ n. a member of any of the groups of indigenous peoples of North, Central, and South America, especially those of North America.

> USAGE
> The term **American Indian** has been steadily replaced in the US by the term **Native American**, especially in official contexts; **American Indian** is still widespread in general use even in the US, however, and is not normally regarded as offensive by American Indians themselves.

Americanism ■ n. **1** a word or phrase peculiar to or originating in the United States. **2** the qualities typical of America and Americans.

americium /ˌamə'rɪsɪəm/ ■ n. the chemical element of atomic number 95, an artificially made radioactive metal of the actinide series. (Symbol: **Am**)
– ORIGIN 1940s: from *America* (where it was first made).

Amerindian /ˌamə'rɪndɪən/ (also **Amerind** /'amərɪnd/) ■ n. another term for AMERICAN INDIAN, used chiefly in anthropological and linguistic contexts.

amethyst /'aməθɪst/ ■ n. a precious stone consisting of a violet or purple variety of quartz.
– ORIGIN Middle English: from Greek *amethustos* 'not drunken' (because the stone was believed to prevent intoxication).

Amex ■ abbrev. **1** trademark American Express. **2** American Stock Exchange.

Amhara /am'hɑːrə/ ■ n. (pl. same or **Amharas**) a member of a Semitic people of central Ethiopia.
– ORIGIN from *Amhara*, a region of Ethiopia.

Amharic /am'harɪk/ ■ n. the official language of Ethiopia, a Semitic language descended from Ge'ez.

amiable ■ adj. friendly and pleasant in manner.
– DERIVATIVES **amiability** n. **amiableness** n. **amiably** adv.
– ORIGIN Middle English: from late Latin *amicabilis* (see AMICABLE).

amicable /'amɪkəb(ə)l/ ■ adj. characterized by friendliness and absence of discord.
– DERIVATIVES **amicability** n. **amicableness** n. **amicably** adv.
– ORIGIN Middle English: from late Latin *amicabilis*, from Latin *amicus* 'friend'.

amice /'amɪs/ ■ n. a cap, hood, or cape worn by members of certain religious orders.
– ORIGIN Middle English: from Old French *aumusse*, from medieval Latin *almucia*.

amicus /əˈmʌɪkəs/ (in full **amicus curiae** /'kjʊəriː/) ■ n. (pl. **amici** /-siː/) an impartial adviser to a court of law in a particular case.
– ORIGIN C17: Latin, 'friend (of the court)'.

amid ■ prep. surrounded by; in the middle of.

Amidah /ɑː'miːdə/ ■ n. Judaism a prayer consisting of a varying number of blessings recited while the worshippers stand.
– ORIGIN C19: Hebrew, 'standing'.

amide /'eɪmʌɪd, 'amʌɪd/ ■ n. Chemistry **1** an organic compound containing the group $-C(O)NH_2$. **2** a salt-like compound containing the anion NH_2^-.
– ORIGIN C19: from AMMONIA.

amidships (US also **amidship**) ■ adv. & adj. in the middle of a ship, either longitudinally or laterally.
– ORIGIN C17: from a-[2] + MIDSHIP.

amidst ■ prep. poetic/literary variant of AMID.

amine /'eɪmiːn/ ■ n. Chemistry an organic compound derived from ammonia by replacement of one or more

hydrogen atoms by organic radicals.
- ORIGIN C19: from AMMONIA.

amino ■ n. Chemistry the -NH₂ group, found in amino acids and amines.
- ORIGIN C19: from AMINE.

amino acid ■ n. Biochemistry any of a class of about twenty simple organic compounds which form the basic constituents of proteins and contain both a carboxyl (-COOH) and an amino (-NH₂) group.

amino group /əˈmiːnəʊ, əˈmʌɪnəʊ/ ■ n. Chemistry the group -NH₂, present in amino acids, amides, and many amines.

amir /əˈmiːə/ ■ n. variant spelling of EMIR.
- ORIGIN C16: from Arabic *amīr* 'commander'.

Amish /ˈɑːmɪʃ, ˈɑː-, ˈeɪ-/ ■ pl. n. (**the Amish**) a strict US Mennonite sect living mainly in Pennsylvania and Ohio. ■ adj. of or relating to this sect.
- ORIGIN C19: from German *amisch*, from the name of the Swiss preacher Jakob *Amman*.

amiss ■ adj. not quite right; inappropriate. ■ adv. wrongly or inappropriately.
- PHRASES **take something amiss** be offended through misinterpreting something said. **not go** (or **come**) **amiss** be welcome and useful.
- ORIGIN Middle English: from Old Norse *á mis* 'so as to miss'.

amitriptyline /ˌamɪˈtrɪptɪliːn/ ■ n. Medicine a mild tranquillizer of the tricyclic antidepressant group.
- ORIGIN 1960s: from *ami(ne)* + TRI- + *(he)ptyl*.

amity /ˈamɪti/ ■ n. friendly relations.
- ORIGIN Middle English: from Old French *amitie*, from Latin *amicus* 'friend'.

ammeter /ˈamɪtə/ ■ n. an instrument for measuring electric current in amperes.

ammo /ˈaməʊ/ ■ n. informal ammunition.

ammonia /əˈməʊnɪə/ ■ n. a colourless, intensely pungent gas which dissolves in water to give a strongly alkaline solution. [NH₃.] ▶ a solution of this, used as a cleaning fluid.
- DERIVATIVES **ammoniacal** adj.

HISTORY
The word **ammonia** was applied in the 18th century to the gas obtained from **sal ammoniac** (ammonium chloride), a term which derives from Latin *sal ammoniacus* 'salt of Ammon'. This name refers to the salt obtained in ancient times near the temple of Jupiter Ammon at Siwa in Egypt (Ammon is a romanized version of the name of the supreme god of the ancient Egyptians, Amun). Ammonite is also connected with Jupiter Ammon: the word comes from Latin *cornu Ammonis* 'horn of Ammon', because of the fossil's resemblance to the ram's horn associated with the god.

ammoniated ■ adj. combined or treated with ammonia.

ammonite /ˈamənʌɪt/ ■ n. Palaeontology an extinct marine cephalopod mollusc with a flat-coiled spiral shell, found as fossils chiefly in Jurassic and Cretaceous deposits.
- DERIVATIVES **ammonoid** n.
- ORIGIN C18: from medieval Latin *cornu Ammonis* 'horn of Ammon', from the fossil's resemblance to the ram's horn associated with the god Jupiter Ammon.

ammonium /əˈməʊnɪəm/ ■ n. [as modifier] Chemistry of or denoting the cation NH₄⁺, present in solutions of ammonia and in salts derived from ammonia.

ammunition ■ n. a supply or quantity of bullets and shells.
- ORIGIN C16: from obsolete French *amunition*, by wrong division of *la munition* (see MUNITION).

amnesia /amˈniːzɪə/ ■ n. a partial or total loss of memory.
- DERIVATIVES **amnesiac** n. & adj. **amnesic** adj. & n.
- ORIGIN C18: from Greek *amnēsia* 'forgetfulness'.

amnesty ■ n. (pl. **-ies**) an official pardon for people convicted of political offences. ▶ an undertaking by the authorities to take no action against specified offences during a fixed period. ■ v. (**-ies**, **-ied**) grant an amnesty to.
- ORIGIN C16: from Greek *amnēstia* 'forgetfulness'.

amniocentesis /ˌamnɪəʊsɛnˈtiːsɪs/ ■ n. (pl. **amniocenteses** /-siːz/) a process in which amniotic fluid is sampled using a hollow needle inserted into the uterus, to screen for abnormalities in the developing fetus.
- ORIGIN 1950s: from AMNION + Greek *kentēsis* 'pricking'.

amnion /ˈamnɪən/ ■ n. (pl. **amnions** or **amnia**) the innermost membrane that encloses the embryo of a mammal, bird, or reptile.
- DERIVATIVES **amniotic** adj.
- ORIGIN C17: from Greek, 'caul', diminutive of *amnos* 'lamb'.

amniote /ˈamnɪəʊt/ ■ n. Zoology an animal whose embryo develops in an amnion and chorion and has an allantois, i.e. a mammal, bird, or reptile.
- ORIGIN C19: back-formation from *amniotic* (see AMNION).

amniotic fluid ■ n. the fluid surrounding a fetus within the amnion.

amoeba /əˈmiːbə/ (US also **ameba**) ■ n. (pl. **amoebas** or **amoebae** /-biː/) a single-celled animal which catches food and moves about by extending finger-like projections of protoplasm. [Phylum Rhizopoda.]
- DERIVATIVES **amoebic** adj. **amoeboid** adj.
- ORIGIN C19: from Greek *amoibē* 'change, alternation'.

amoebiasis /ˌamiːˈbʌɪəsɪs/ (US also **amebiasis**) ■ n. Medicine infection with amoebas, especially as causing dysentery.

amok /əˈmɒk/ (also **amuck**) ■ adv. (in phr. **run amok**) behave uncontrollably and disruptively.
- ORIGIN C17: from Malay *amok* 'rushing in a frenzy'.

among (also **amongst**) ■ prep. **1** situated more or less centrally in relation to (several others). **2** being a member or members of (a larger set). **3** occurring in or practised by (some members of a community). **4** indicating a division, choice, or differentiation involving three or more participants.
- ORIGIN Old English, from *on* 'in' + *gemang* 'assemblage, mingling'.

amontillado /əˌmɒntɪˈlɑːdəʊ, -ˈljɑː-/ ■ n. (pl. **-os**) a medium dry sherry.
- ORIGIN Spanish, from *Montilla*, a town in southern Spain.

amoral /eɪˈmɒr(ə)l/ ■ adj. lacking a moral sense; unconcerned whether something is right or wrong.
- DERIVATIVES **amoralism** n. **amoralist** n. **amorality** n.

amorous ■ adj. showing or feeling sexual desire.
- DERIVATIVES **amorously** adv. **amorousness** n.
- ORIGIN Middle English: from Latin *amor* 'love'.

amorphous /əˈmɔːfəs/ ■ adj. **1** without a clearly defined shape or form. **2** Mineralogy & Chemistry not crystalline, or not apparently crystalline.
- DERIVATIVES **amorphously** adv. **amorphousness** n.
- ORIGIN C18: from Greek, from *a-* 'without' + *morphē* 'form'.

amortize /əˈmɔːtʌɪz/ (also **-ise**) ■ v. gradually write off the initial cost of (an asset) over a period. ▶ reduce or cancel (a debt) by money regularly put aside.
- DERIVATIVES **amortization** (also **-isation**) n.
- ORIGIN Middle English: from Old French *amortir*, from Latin *ad* 'to, at' + *mors* 'death'.

amount ■ n. the total of something in number, size, value, or extent. ▶ a quantity: *a small amount of water*. ■ v. (**amount to**) **1** come to be (a total) when added together. **2** be the equivalent of.
- PHRASES **any amount of** a great deal or number of.
- ORIGIN Middle English: from Old French *amont* 'upward, uphill', from Latin *ad montem*.

amour /əˈmʊə/ ■ n. a love affair or lover, especially a secret one.
- ORIGIN Middle English: from Latin *amor* 'love'.

amour propre /aˌmʊə ˈprɒpr(ə)/ ■ n. self-respect.
- ORIGIN from French.

amoxycillin /əˌmɒksɪˈsɪlɪn/ (also **amoxicillin**) ■ n. Medicine a semi-synthetic penicillin closely related to ampicillin and with similar properties.
- ORIGIN 1970s: from am(ino) + OXY-² + (PENI)CILLIN.

amp¹ ■ n. short for AMPERE.

amp² ■ n. informal short for AMPLIFIER.

ampelopsis /ˌampɪˈlɒpsɪs/ ■ n. (pl. same) a bushy climbing plant of the vine family. [Genus *Ampelopsis*: two species.]
- ORIGIN from Greek *ampelos* 'vine' + *opsis* 'appearance'.

amperage /ˈamp(ə)rɪdʒ/ ■ n. the strength of an electric current in amperes.

ampere /ˈampɛː/ (abbrev.: **A**) ■ n. the SI base unit of electric current, equal to a flow of one coulomb per second.
– ORIGIN C19: named after the French physicist André-Marie *Ampère*.

ampersand /ˈampəsand/ ■ n. the sign & (standing for *and*, as in *Smith & Co.*, or the Latin *et*, as in *&c.*).
– ORIGIN C19: alteration of *and per se and* '& by itself is *and*', chanted as an aid to learning the sign.

amphetamine /amˈfɛtəmiːn, -ɪn/ ■ n. a synthetic mood-altering drug, used illegally as a stimulant.
– ORIGIN 1930s: abbrev. of its chemical name, *a(lpha-)m(ethyl) phe(ne)t(hyl)amine*.

amphi- /ˈamfi/ ■ comb. form **1** both: *amphibian*. ▶ of both kinds: *amphipod*. ▶ on both sides. **2** around: *amphitheatre*.
– ORIGIN from Greek.

amphibian ■ n. Zoology a cold-blooded vertebrate animal of a class (Amphibia) that comprises the frogs, toads, newts, salamanders, and caecilians, distinguished by an aquatic gill-breathing larval stage followed by a terrestrial lung-breathing adult stage. **2** a seaplane, tank, or other vehicle that can operate on land and on water.
– ORIGIN C17: from Greek *amphibios* 'living both in water and on land', from *amphi* 'both' + *bios* 'life'.

amphibious /amˈfɪbɪəs/ ■ adj. **1** living in or suited for both land and water. **2** (of a military operation) involving forces landed from the sea.
– DERIVATIVES **amphibiously** adv.

amphibole /ˈamfɪbəʊl/ ■ n. any of a class of rock-forming silicate or aluminosilicate minerals typically occurring as fibrous or columnar crystals.
– ORIGIN C19: from Latin *amphibolus* 'ambiguous' (because of the varied structure of the minerals).

amphibolite /amˈfɪbəlʌɪt/ ■ n. Geology a granular metamorphic rock consisting mainly of hornblende and plagioclase.

amphimixis /ˌamfɪˈmɪksɪs/ ■ n. Botany sexual reproduction involving the fusion of two different gametes to form a zygote. Often contrasted with **APOMIXIS**.
– DERIVATIVES **amphimictic** adj.
– ORIGIN C19: from Greek *amphi* 'of both kinds' + *mixis* 'mingling'.

amphipathic /ˌamfɪˈpaθɪk/ ■ adj. Biochemistry (of a molecule, especially a protein) having both hydrophilic and hydrophobic parts.
– ORIGIN 1930s: from Greek *amphi* 'of both kinds' + *pathikos*, from *pathos* 'experience'.

amphiphilic /ˌamfɪˈfɪlɪk/ ■ adj. Biochemistry another term for **AMPHIPATHIC**.

Amphipoda /ˌamfɪˈpəʊdə/ ■ pl. n. Zoology an order of chiefly marine crustaceans with a laterally compressed body and a large number of leg-like appendages.
– DERIVATIVES **amphipod** /ˈamfɪpɒd/ n.
– ORIGIN from Greek *amphi* 'of both kinds' (because some legs are specialized for swimming and some for feeding) + *pous, pod-* 'foot'.

Amphisbaenia /ˌamfɪsˈbiːnɪə/ ■ pl. n. Zoology a suborder of reptiles which comprises the worm lizards.
– DERIVATIVES **amphisbaenian** n. & adj.
– ORIGIN from Greek, from *amphis* 'both ways' + *bainein* 'go'.

amphitheatre (US **amphitheater**) ■ n. (especially in Greek and Roman architecture) a round building consisting of tiers of seats surrounding a central space for dramatic or sporting events. ▶ a semicircular seating gallery in a theatre.
– ORIGIN Middle English: from Greek, from *amphi* 'on both sides' + *theatron* (see **THEATRE**).

amphora /ˈamfɔːrə/ ■ n. (pl. **amphorae** /-riː/ or **amphoras**) a tall ancient Greek or Roman jar or jug with two handles and a narrow neck.
– ORIGIN from Greek, from *amphi* 'on both sides' + *phoreus* 'bearer', from *pherein* 'to bear'.

amphoteric /ˌamfəˈtɛrɪk/ ■ adj. Chemistry able to react both as a base and as an acid.
– ORIGIN C19: from Greek *amphoteros*, comparative of *amphō* 'both'.

ampicillin /ˌampɪˈsɪlɪn/ ■ n. Medicine a semi-synthetic form of penicillin used chiefly to treat respiratory and urinary infections.
– ORIGIN 1960s: blend of *amino* (see **AMINO GROUP**) and **PENICILLIN**.

ample ■ adj. (**-er**, **-est**) enough or more than enough; plentiful. ▶ large and accommodating. ▶ euphemistic (of a person) stout.
– DERIVATIVES **ampleness** n. **amply** adv.
– ORIGIN Middle English: from Latin *amplus* 'large, abundant'.

amplexus /amˈplɛksəs/ ■ n. Zoology the mating position of frogs and toads, in which the male clasps the female about the back.
– ORIGIN 1930s: from Latin, 'an embrace'.

amplifier ■ n. **1** an electronic device for increasing the amplitude of electrical signals, used chiefly in sound reproduction. **2** a device of this kind combined with a loudspeaker, used to amplify electric guitars and other musical instruments.

amplify ■ v. (**-ies**, **-ied**) **1** increase the volume of (sound), especially using an amplifier. ▶ increase the amplitude of (an electrical signal or other oscillation). **2** add detail to (a story or statement). **3** Genetics make multiple copies of (a gene or DNA sequence).
– DERIVATIVES **amplification** n.
– ORIGIN Middle English: from Latin *amplificare*, from *amplus* 'large, abundant'.

amplitude ■ n. **1** Physics the maximum extent or magnitude of a vibration or other oscillating phenomenon, measured from the equilibrium position or average value. **2** breadth, range, or magnitude. **3** Astronomy the angular distance of a celestial object from the true east or west point of the horizon at rising or setting.
– ORIGIN C16: from Latin *amplitudo*, from *amplus* 'large, abundant'.

amplitude modulation ■ n. the modulation of a wave by varying its amplitude, used especially as a means of broadcasting an audio signal by combining it with a radio carrier wave.

ampoule /ˈampuːl/ (US also **ampul** or **ampule** /ˈampjuːl/) ■ n. Medicine a small sealed glass capsule containing a measured quantity of liquid ready for injecting.
– ORIGIN C20: from Latin *ampulla* (see **AMPULLA**).

ampulla /amˈpʊlə/ ■ n. (pl. **ampullae** /-liː/) **1** a roughly spherical ancient Roman flask with two handles. ▶ a flask for holding consecrated oil. **2** Anatomy & Zoology a cavity or enclosure shaped like a Roman ampulla.
– ORIGIN Middle English: from Latin, diminutive of *ampora*, var. of **AMPHORA**.

amputate /ˈampjʊteɪt/ ■ v. cut off (a limb) by surgical operation.
– DERIVATIVES **amputation** n. **amputator** n.
– ORIGIN C16: from Latin *amputare* 'lop off'.

amputee ■ n. a person who has had a limb amputated.

AMRAAM ■ abbrev. advanced medium range air-to-air missile.

amu ■ abbrev. atomic mass unit.

amuck /əˈmʌk/ ■ adv. variant spelling of **AMOK**.

amulet /ˈamjʊlɪt/ ■ n. an ornament or small piece of jewellery thought to give protection against evil or danger.
– ORIGIN C16: from Latin *amuletum*.

amuse ■ v. **1** cause to find something funny. **2** entertain.
– DERIVATIVES **amused** adj. **amusedly** adv. **amusing** adj. **amusingly** adv.
– ORIGIN C15: from Old French *amuser* 'entertain, deceive', from *a-* (expressing causal effect) + *muser* 'stare stupidly'.

amusement ■ n. **1** the state or experience of finding something funny. **2** the provision or enjoyment of entertainment. ▶ Brit. a game machine or other mechanical device for providing entertainment.

amusement arcade ■ n. an indoor area containing coin-operated game machines.

amusement park ■ n. a large outdoor area with fairground rides and other entertainments.

VOWELS a cat ɑː arm ɛ bed ɛː hair ə ago əː her ɪ sit i cosy iː see ɒ hot ɔː saw ʌ run

amyl /'eɪmʌɪl, 'amɪl/ ■ n. **1** [as modifier] Chemistry of or denoting the straight-chain pentyl radical -C$_5$H$_{11}$. **2** informal short for **AMYL NITRITE**.
– ORIGIN C19: from Latin *amylum* 'starch'.

amylase /'amɪleɪz/ ■ n. Biochemistry an enzyme, found chiefly in saliva and pancreatic fluid, that converts starch and glycogen into simple sugars.

amyl nitrate ■ n. Chemistry a colourless synthetic liquid used as an additive in diesel fuel to improve its ignition properties.

amyl nitrite ■ n. Chemistry a yellowish volatile synthetic liquid used medicinally as a vasodilator and sometimes inhaled for its stimulatory effects.

amyloid /'amɪlɔɪd/ ■ n. Medicine a starch-like protein which is deposited in the liver, kidneys, spleen, or other tissues in certain diseases.
– DERIVATIVES **amyloidosis** n.

amylopectin /,amɪləʊ'pɛktɪn/ ■ n. Biochemistry the non-crystallizable form of starch, consisting of branched polysaccharide chains.

amylose /'amɪləʊs/ ■ n. Biochemistry the crystallizable form of starch, consisting of long unbranched polysaccharide chains.

amyotrophic lateral sclerosis ■ n. a form of motor neuron disease.

Amytal /'amɪt(ə)l/ ■ n. trademark a barbiturate drug used as a sedative and a hypnotic.

an ■ det. the form of the indefinite article (see A[1]) used before words beginning with a vowel sound.

-an ■ suffix **1** forming adjectives and nouns, especially from: ▸ names of places: *Cuban*. ▸ names of systems: *Anglican*. ▸ names of zoological classes or orders: *crustacean*. ▸ names of founders: *Lutheran*. **2** /an/ Chemistry forming names of organic compounds, chiefly polysaccharides: *dextran*.
– ORIGIN from Latin adj. endings *-anus, -ana, -anum*.

an-[1] ■ prefix variant spelling of A-[1] before a vowel (as in *anaemia*).

an-[2] ■ prefix variant spelling of AD- assimilated before *n* (as in *annihilate, annotate*).

an-[3] ■ prefix variant spelling of ANA- shortened before a vowel (as in *aneurysm*).

-ana ■ suffix (forming plural nouns) denoting things associated with a person, place, or field of interest: *Victoriana*.
– ORIGIN from Latin, neuter pl. adj. ending of *-anus*.

ana- (usu. **an-** before a vowel) ■ prefix **1** up: *anabatic*. **2** back: *anamnesis*. **3** again: *anabiosis*.
– ORIGIN from Greek *ana* 'up'.

Anabaptism /,anə'baptɪz(ə)m/ ■ n. the doctrine that baptism should only be administered to believing adults, held by a Protestant sect of the 16th century.
– DERIVATIVES **Anabaptist** n. & adj.
– ORIGIN C16: from Greek *anabaptismos*, from *ana-* 'over again' + *baptismos* 'baptism'.

anabatic /,anə'batɪk/ ■ adj. Meteorology (of a wind) caused by local upward motion of warm air.
– ORIGIN C20: from Greek *anabatikos*, from *anabatēs* 'a person who ascends'.

anabiosis /,anəbʌɪ'əʊsɪs/ ■ n. Zoology a temporary state of suspended animation or greatly reduced metabolism.
– DERIVATIVES **anabiotic** /-'ɒtɪk/ adj.
– ORIGIN C19: from Greek *anabiōsis*, from *anabioein* 'return to life'.

anabolic steroid ■ n. any of a class of synthetic steroid hormones which are used medicinally to promote the growth of muscle and (illegally) to enhance performance in athletics and other sports.

anabolism /ə'nabəlɪz(ə)m/ ■ n. Biochemistry the synthesis of complex molecules in living organisms from simpler ones together with the storage of energy.
– DERIVATIVES **anabolic** adj.
– ORIGIN C19: from Greek *anabolē* 'ascent', from *ana-* 'up' + *ballein* 'to throw'.

anachronism /ə'nakrə,nɪz(ə)m/ ■ n. **1** a thing appropriate to a period other than that in which it exists. **2** the attribution of something to a period to which it does not belong.
– DERIVATIVES **anachronic** /,anə'krɒnɪk/ adj. **anachronistic** adj. **anachronistically** adv.
– ORIGIN C17: from Greek, from *ana-* 'backwards' + *khronos* 'time'.

anaconda /,anə'kɒndə/ ■ n. a very large semiaquatic snake of the boa family, native to tropical South America. [*Eunectes murinus* and other species.]
– ORIGIN C18: alteration of Latin *anacandaia* 'python', from Sinhalese *henakan̆dayā*.

anacrusis /,anə'kruːsɪs/ ■ n. (pl. **anacruses** /-siːz/) Prosody & Music one or more unstressed notes or syllables at the beginning of a verse or passage of music.
– ORIGIN C19: from Greek *anakrousis* 'prelude', from *ana-* 'up' + *krousis* 'striking'.

anadromous /ə'nadrəməs/ ■ adj. Zoology (of a fish) migrating up rivers from the sea to spawn. The opposite of **CATADROMOUS**.
– ORIGIN C18: from Greek, from *ana-* 'up' + *dromos* 'running'.

anaemia /ə'niːmɪə/ (US **anemia**) ■ n. a condition in which there is a deficiency of red cells or haemoglobin in the blood, resulting in pallor and weariness.
– ORIGIN C19: from Greek *anaimia*, from *an-* 'without' + *haima* 'blood'.

anaemic /ə'niːmɪk/ (US **anemic**) ■ adj. **1** suffering from anaemia. **2** lacking in colour or vitality.

anaerobic ■ adj. Biology relating to, involving, or requiring the absence of free oxygen.
– DERIVATIVES **anaerobically** adv.

anaesthesia /,anɪs'θiːzɪə/ (US **anesthesia**) ■ n. insensitivity to pain, especially as artificially induced by the administration of gases or drugs before a surgical operation.
– DERIVATIVES **anaesthesiologist** n. **anaesthesiology** n.
– ORIGIN C18: from Greek, from *an-* 'without' + *aisthēsis* 'sensation'.

anaesthetic /,anɪs'θɛtɪk/ (US **anesthetic**) ■ n. **1** a substance that induces insensitivity to pain. **2** (**anaesthetics**) [treated as sing.] the study or practice of anaesthesia. ■ adj. inducing or relating to anaesthesia.

anaesthetist /ə'niːsθətɪst/ (US **anesthetist**) ■ n. a medical specialist who administers anaesthetics.
– DERIVATIVES **anaesthetization** (also **-isation**) n. **anaesthetize** (also **-ise**) v.

anaglyph /'anəglɪf/ ■ n. **1** a stereoscopic photograph having two images superimposed and printed in different colours, producing a stereo effect when viewed with appropriate filters over each eye. **2** an object, such as a cameo, embossed or carved in low relief.
– ORIGIN C16: from Greek, from *ana-* 'up' + *gluphein* 'carve'.

anagram /'anəgram/ ■ n. a word, phrase, or name formed by rearranging the letters of another, such as *spar*, formed from *rasp*. ■ v. (**anagrammed, anagramming**) make an anagram of.
– DERIVATIVES **anagrammatic** adj. **anagrammatical** adj.
– ORIGIN C16: from Greek *ana-* 'back, anew' + *gramma* 'letter'.

anal /'eɪn(ə)l/ ■ adj. **1** of, relating to, or situated near the anus. **2** Psychoanalysis denoting a stage of infantile psychosexual development in which defecation is the major source of sensuous pleasure. ▸ anal-retentive.
– DERIVATIVES **anally** adv.

analects /'anəlɛkts/ (also **analecta** /,anə'lɛktə/) ■ pl. n. a collection of short literary or philosophical extracts.
– ORIGIN Middle English: from Greek *analekta* 'things gathered up', from *ana-* 'up' + *legein* 'gather'.

analeptic /,anə'lɛptɪk/ Medicine ■ adj. restorative, especially through stimulating the central nervous system. ■ n. an analeptic drug.
– ORIGIN C16: from Greek *analēptikos*.

anal fin ■ n. Zoology an unpaired fin located on the underside of a fish posterior to the anus.

analgesia /,an(ə)l'dʒiːzɪə/ ■ n. Medicine relief of pain through administration of drugs or other methods.
– ORIGIN C18: from Greek, from *an-* 'not' + *algein* 'feel pain'.

analgesic

analgesic /ˌan(ə)lˈdʒiːzɪk, -sɪk/ Medicine ■ adj. acting to relieve pain. ■ n. an analgesic drug.

analogize /əˈnalədʒʌɪz/ (also **-ise**) ■ v. compare by analogy.

analogous /əˈnaləgəs/ ■ adj. 1 comparable in certain respects. 2 Biology performing a similar function but having a different evolutionary origin, such as the wings of insects and birds. Often contrasted with HOMOLOGOUS.
– DERIVATIVES **analogously** adv.
– ORIGIN C17: from Greek *analogos* 'proportionate'.

analogue /ˈanəlɒg/ (US also **analog**) ■ n. a person or thing seen as analogous to another. ■ adj. (also **analog**) relating to or using information represented by a continuously variable physical quantity (such as spatial position, voltage, etc.) rather than digitally.
– ORIGIN C19: from Greek *analogos* 'proportionate'.

analogy /əˈnalədʒi/ ■ n. (pl. **-ies**) a comparison between one thing and another made for the purpose of explanation or clarification. ▸ the process of making such a comparison. ▸ a thing regarded as analogous to another; an analogue.
– DERIVATIVES **analogical** adj. **analogically** adv.
– ORIGIN Middle English: from Greek *analogos* 'proportionate'.

analphabetic ■ adj. 1 representing sounds by composite signs rather than by single letters or symbols. 2 completely illiterate.

anal-retentive ■ adj. often humorous excessively orderly and fussy (supposedly owing to conflict over toilet-training in infancy).
– DERIVATIVES **anal retention** n. **anal retentiveness** n.

analysand /əˈnalɪsand/ ■ n. a person undergoing psychoanalysis.

analyse (US **analyze**) ■ v. 1 examine methodically and in detail the constitution or structure of. ▸ identify and measure the chemical constituents of. 2 psychoanalyse.
– DERIVATIVES **analysable** adj. **analyser** n.
– ORIGIN C16: from medieval Latin *analysis*, from Greek (see ANALYSIS).

analysis /əˈnalɪsɪs/ ■ n. (pl. **analyses** /-siːz/) 1 a detailed examination of the elements or structure of something. 2 the process of separating something into its constituent elements. Often contrasted with SYNTHESIS. ▸ the process of analysing the chemical constituents of a substance. 3 short for PSYCHOANALYSIS. 4 Mathematics the part of mathematics concerned with the theory of functions and the use of limits, continuity, and the operations of calculus.
– ORIGIN C16: from Greek *analusis*, from *analuein* 'unloose'.

analyst ■ n. 1 a person who conducts analysis. 2 a psychoanalyst.

analytic ■ adj. 1 another term for ANALYTICAL. 2 Logic true by virtue of the meaning of the words or concepts used to express it, so that its denial would be a self-contradiction. Compare with SYNTHETIC. 3 Linguistics (of a language) tending to use word order to express grammatical structure. Contrasted with SYNTHETIC.
– ORIGIN C17: from Greek *analutikos*, from *analuein* 'unloose'.

analytical ■ adj. relating to or using analysis or logical reasoning.
– DERIVATIVES **analytically** adv.

analytical geometry ■ n. geometry using coordinates.

analytical philosophy ■ n. a method of approaching philosophical problems through analysis of the terms in which they are expressed.

analytical psychology ■ n. the psychoanalytical system of psychology developed and practised by the Swiss psychologist Carl Jung (1875–1961).

analyze ■ v. US spelling of ANALYSE.

anamnesis /ˌanəmˈniːsɪs/ ■ n. (pl. **anamneses** /-siːz/) 1 recollection, especially of a supposed previous existence. 2 Christian Church the part of the Eucharist in which the Passion, Resurrection, and Ascension of Christ are recalled.
– ORIGIN C16: from Greek *anamnēsis*.

anamorphosis /ˌanəˈmɔːfəsɪs/ ■ n. a distorted image which appears normal when viewed from a particular point or with a suitable mirror or lens. ▸ the process by which such images are produced.
– DERIVATIVES **anamorphic** adj.
– ORIGIN C18: from Greek *anamorphōsis* 'transformation'.

ananda /ɑːˈnʌndə/ ■ n. (in Hinduism, Buddhism, and Jainism) extreme happiness, as one of the highest states of being.
– ORIGIN from Sanskrit *ānanda*.

anapaest /ˈanəpiːst, -pɛst/ (US **anapest**) ■ n. Prosody a metrical foot consisting of two short or unstressed syllables followed by one long or stressed syllable.
– DERIVATIVES **anapaestic** /-ˈpiːstɪk, -ˈpɛstɪk/ adj.
– ORIGIN C16: from Greek *anapaistos* 'reversed', from *ana-* 'back' + *paiein* 'strike' (because it is the reverse of a dactyl).

anaphase /ˈanəfeɪz/ ■ n. Genetics the third stage of cell division, between metaphase and telophase, during which the chromosomes move away from one another to opposite poles of the spindle.

anaphora /əˈnaf(ə)rə/ ■ n. 1 Grammar the use of a word that refers back to a word used earlier in a text or conversation to avoid repetition, for example the pronouns *it* and *they* and the verb *do* in *I like it and so do they*. Compare with CATAPHORA. 2 Rhetoric the repetition of a word or phrase at the beginning of successive clauses. 3 Christian Church the part of the Eucharist which contains the consecration, anamnesis, and communion.
– DERIVATIVES **anaphoric** /ˌanəˈfɒrɪk/ adj. **anaphorically** adv.
– ORIGIN C16: from Greek, from *ana-* 'back' + *pherein* 'to bear'.

anaphrodisiac /əˌnafrəˈdɪzɪak/ Medicine ■ adj. tending to reduce sexual desire. ■ n. an anaphrodisiac drug.

anaphylaxis /ˌanəfɪˈlaksɪs/ ■ n. Medicine an extreme allergic reaction to an antigen to which the body has become hypersensitive following an earlier exposure.
– DERIVATIVES **anaphylactic** adj.
– ORIGIN C20: from Greek *ana-* 'again' + *phulaxis* 'guarding'.

anarchic ■ adj. with no controlling rules or principles to give order.
– DERIVATIVES **anarchical** adj. **anarchically** adv.

anarchism ■ n. belief in the abolition of all government and the organization of society on a voluntary, cooperative basis.
– DERIVATIVES **anarchist** n. & adj. **anarchistic** adj.
– ORIGIN C17: from Greek *anarkhos* (see ANARCHY).

anarchy ■ n. 1 a state of disorder due to lack of government or control. 2 a society or political system founded on the principles of anarchism.
– ORIGIN C16: from Greek *anarkhia*, from *an-* 'without' + *arkhos* 'chief, ruler'.

Anasazi /ˌanəˈsɑːzi/ ■ n. (pl. same or **Anasazis**) a member of an ancient American Indian people of the south-western US.
– ORIGIN from Navajo, 'ancient one' or 'enemy ancestor'.

anastigmatic /ˌanəstɪɡˈmatɪk/ ■ adj. (of a lens system) constructed so that the astigmatism of each element is cancelled out.

anastomosis /əˌnastəˈməʊsɪs/ ■ n. (pl. **anastomoses** /-siːz/) technical a cross-connection between adjacent channels, tubes, fibres, or other parts of a network. ▸ Medicine a connection made surgically between adjacent blood vessels, parts of the intestine, or other channels of the body.
– DERIVATIVES **anastomotic** adj. & n.
– ORIGIN C16: from Greek *anastomōsis*, from *anastomoun* 'provide with a mouth'.

anastrophe /əˈnastrəfi/ ■ n. Rhetoric the inversion of the usual order of words or clauses.
– ORIGIN C16: from Greek *anastrophē* 'turning back'.

anathema /əˈnaθəmə/ ■ n. 1 something that one vehemently dislikes: *racism was anathema to her*. 2 a formal curse of the Christian Church, excommunicating a person or denouncing a doctrine.
– ORIGIN C16: from Greek *anathema* 'thing dedicated', (later) 'thing devoted to evil'.

CONSONANTS **b** but **d** dog **f** few **g** get **h** he **j** yes **k** cat **l** leg **m** man **n** no **p** pen **r** red

anathematize /əˈnaθəmətʌɪz/ (also **-ise**) ■ v. curse; condemn.

Anatolian ■ n. **1** a native or inhabitant of Anatolia in western Asia Minor. **2** an extinct group of ancient languages constituting a branch of the Indo-European language family. ■ adj. of or relating to Anatolia.

anatomize (also **-ise**) ■ v. **1** dissect (a body). **2** examine and analyse in detail.
– ORIGIN Middle English: from medieval Latin *anatomizare*, from *anatomia* (see **ANATOMY**).

anatomy ■ n. (pl. **-ies**) **1** the branch of biology and medicine concerned with bodily structure, especially as revealed by dissection. ▸ the bodily structure of a person, animal, or plant. **2** a detailed examination: *the anatomy of change*. ▸ a complex structure.
– DERIVATIVES **anatomical** adj. **anatomically** adv. **anatomist** n.
– ORIGIN Middle English: from Greek, from *ana-* 'up' + *tomia* 'cutting'.

Ana tree ■ n. a large African leguminous tree which bears pale cream flowers in elongated spikes. [*Faidherbia albida*.]

anatto ■ n. variant spelling of **ANNATTO**.

ANC ■ abbrev. **1** African National Congress. **2** antenuptial contract.

-ance ■ suffix forming nouns: **1** denoting a quality or state: *perseverance*. **2** denoting an action: *utterance*.
– ORIGIN from French *-ance*, from Latin pres. participial stems *-ant-*, *-ent-*.

ancestor ■ n. **1** a person, typically one more remote than a grandparent, from whom one is descended. ▸ something from which a later species or version has evolved. **2** (in some traditional societies) the spirit of someone who is deceased, especially an elder or other respected person, who is venerated in the belief that they continue to have an influence on the welfare of the living.
– DERIVATIVES **ancestral** adj. **ancestrally** adv. **ancestress** n.
– ORIGIN Middle English: from Old French *ancestre*, from Latin *antecedere*, from *ante* 'before' + *cedere* 'go'.

ancestry ■ n. (pl. **-ies**) a person's ancestors or ethnic descent.

ancho /ˈantʃəʊ/ ■ n. a large aromatic variety of chilli, used in Mexican dishes.
– ORIGIN from Mexican Spanish (*chile*) *ancho* 'wide (chilli)'.

anchor ■ n. **1** a heavy object used to moor a ship to the sea bottom, typically having a metal shank with a pair of curved, barbed flukes. ▸ (**anchors**) informal the brakes of a car. **2** an anchorman or anchorwoman. ■ v. **1** moor with an anchor. ▸ secure firmly in position. **2** present and coordinate (a television or radio programme).
– PHRASES **at anchor** moored with an anchor.
– ORIGIN Old English: from Greek *ankura*.

anchorage ■ n. **1** an area suitable for a ship to anchor at. ▸ the action or state of anchoring or being anchored. **2** historical an anchorite's dwelling place.

anchorite /ˈaŋkərʌɪt/ ■ n. historical a religious recluse.
– DERIVATIVES **anchoress** n.
– ORIGIN Middle English: from eccles. Greek *anakhōrētēs*, from *anakhōrein* 'retire'.

anchorman (or **anchorwoman**) ■ n. (pl. **-men** or **-women**) **1** a person who presents and coordinates a live television or radio programme involving other contributors. **2** the member of a relay team who runs the last leg.

anchovy /ˈantʃəvi, anˈtʃəʊvi/ ■ n. (pl. **-ies**) a small shoaling fish of the herring family, an important food fish with a strong flavour. [Genus *Engraulis*: several species.]
– ORIGIN C16: from Spanish and Portuguese *anchova*.

ancien régime /ˌɒsiɛ̃ reɪˈʒiːm/ ■ n. (pl. **anciens régimes** pronunc. same) a political or social system that has been displaced by a more modern one. ▸ (**the Ancien Régime**) the political and social system in France before the Revolution of 1789.
– ORIGIN French, 'old rule'.

ancient ■ adj. belonging to or originating in the very distant past. ▸ chiefly humorous very old. ■ n. **1** archaic or humorous an old man. **2** (**the ancients**) the people of ancient times, especially the classical Greeks and Romans.
– PHRASES **the Ancient of Days** a biblical title for God.
– DERIVATIVES **anciently** adv. **ancientness** n.
– ORIGIN Middle English: from Old French *ancien*, from Latin *ante* 'before'.

ancillary /anˈsɪləri/ ■ adj. providing support to the primary activities of an organization. ▸ additional; subsidiary. ■ n. (pl. **-ies**) an ancillary person or thing.
– ORIGIN C17: from Latin, from *ancilla* 'maidservant'.

-ancy ■ suffix (forming nouns) denoting a quality or state: *expectancy*.
– ORIGIN from Latin *-antia* (see also **-ENCY**).

ancylostomiasis /ˌaŋkɪlə(ʊ)stə(ʊ)ˈmʌɪəsɪs, ˌansɪ-/ (also **ankylostomiasis**) ■ n. Medicine hookworm infection of the small intestine, often leading to anaemia.
– ORIGIN C19: from *Ancylostoma* a genus of hookworms.

and ■ conj. **1** used to connect words of the same part of speech, clauses, or sentences. ▸ connecting two identical comparatives, to emphasize a progressive change. ▸ connecting two identical words, implying great duration or great extent. **2** used to connect two numbers to indicate that they are being added together. ▸ archaic connecting two numbers, implying succession. **3** used to introduce an additional comment or interjection. **4** informal used after some verbs and before another verb to indicate intention, instead of 'to'. ■ n. (**AND**) **1** a logical operation which gives the value one if and only if all the operands are one, and otherwise gives a value of zero. **2** [as modifier] Electronics denoting a gate circuit which produces an output only when signals are received simultaneously through all input connections.
– ORIGIN Old English, of Germanic origin.

-and ■ suffix (forming nouns) denoting a person or thing to be treated in a specified way: *analysand*.
– ORIGIN from Latin gerundive ending *-andus*.

andalusite /ˌandəˈluːsʌɪt/ ■ n. a grey, green, brown, or pink aluminosilicate mineral occurring as elongated rhombic prisms.

Andean /anˈdiːən, ˈandɪən/ ■ adj. of or relating to the Andes.

andesite /ˈandɪzʌɪt, -sʌɪt/ ■ n. Geology a dark, fine-grained volcanic rock which is a common constituent of lava in some areas.
– DERIVATIVES **andesitic** adj.
– ORIGIN C19: named after the *Andes* mountains.

andiron /ˈandʌɪən/ ■ n. a metal support, typically one of a pair, for wood burning in a fireplace.
– ORIGIN Middle English: from Old French *andier*.

andouille /ɒˈduːj/ ■ n. (in France) a pork sausage made from chitterlings. ▸ (in Cajun cooking) a spicy smoked-pork sausage.
– ORIGIN from French.

andro- ■ comb. form of men; male: *androcentric*.
– ORIGIN from Greek *anēr*, *andr-* 'man'.

androcentric /ˌandrə(ʊ)ˈsɛntrɪk/ ■ adj. focused or centred on men.

androecium /anˈdriːsɪəm/ ■ n. (pl. **androecia** /-sɪə/) Botany the stamens of a flower collectively.
– ORIGIN C19: from **ANDRO-** + Greek *oikion* 'house'.

androgen /ˈandrədʒ(ə)n/ ■ n. Biochemistry a male sex hormone, such as testosterone.
– DERIVATIVES **androgenic** adj.
– ORIGIN 1930s: from Greek *anēr*, *andr-* 'man'.

androgenize /anˈdrɒdʒənʌɪz/ (also **-ise**) ■ v. treat with or expose to male sex hormones.
– DERIVATIVES **androgenization** (also **-isation**) n.

androgyne /ˈandrədʒʌɪn/ ■ n. an androgynous individual. ▸ a hermaphrodite.

androgynous /anˈdrɒdʒɪnəs/ ■ adj. partly male and partly female in appearance; of indeterminate sex. ▸ hermaphrodite.
– DERIVATIVES **androgyny** n.
– ORIGIN C17: from Greek, from *anēr*, *andr-* 'man' + *gunē* 'woman'.

android /ˈandrɔɪd/ ■ n. (in science fiction) a robot with a human appearance.

androsterone /ˌandrə(ʊ)ˈstɪərəʊn, anˈdrɒstərəʊn/ ■ n. Biochemistry a relatively inactive male sex hormone produced by metabolism of testosterone.

-androus

-androus ■ comb. form Botany having male organs or stamens of a specified number: *polyandrous*.
– ORIGIN from Greek *-andros* 'male'.

-ane¹ ■ suffix variant spelling of -AN, often with a distinction of sense (such as *humane* compared with *human*).

-ane² ■ suffix Chemistry forming names of saturated hydrocarbons: *propane*.

anecdotage /ˈanɪkdəʊtɪdʒ/ ■ n. **1** anecdotes collectively. **2** humorous old age in someone who is garrulous.

anecdote /ˈanɪkdəʊt/ ■ n. a short entertaining story about a real incident or person. ▶ an account regarded as unreliable or as being hearsay.
– DERIVATIVES **anecdotal** adj. **anecdotally** adv.
– ORIGIN C17: from Greek *anekdota* 'things unpublished'.

anele /əˈniːl/ ■ v. archaic anoint, especially as part of the Christian rite of extreme unction.
– ORIGIN Middle English: from *an-* 'on' + archaic *elien* 'to oil'.

anemia ■ n. US spelling of ANAEMIA.

anemic ■ adj. US spelling of anaemic (see ANAEMIA).

anemograph /əˈnɛməɡrɑːf/ ■ n. an anemometer which records the speed, duration, and sometimes also the direction of the wind.

anemometer /ˌanɪˈmɒmɪtə/ ■ n. an instrument for measuring the speed of the wind or other flowing gas.
– DERIVATIVES **anemometric** adj. **anemometry** n.
– ORIGIN C18: from Greek *anemos* 'wind' + -METER.

anemone /əˈnɛməni/ ■ n. **1** a plant of the buttercup family, which typically has brightly coloured flowers and deeply divided leaves. [Genus *Anemone*: numerous species.] **2** short for SEA ANEMONE.
– ORIGIN C16: prob. from Greek *anemōnē* 'windflower', because the flowers open only when the wind blows.

anemone fish ■ n. another term for CLOWNFISH.

anemophilous /ˌanɪˈmɒfɪləs/ ■ adj. Botany pollinated by the wind.
– DERIVATIVES **anemophily** n.
– ORIGIN C19: from Greek *anemos* 'wind' + *-philous* (see -PHILIA).

anencephalic /ˌanɛnsɪˈfalɪk, -kɛˈfalɪk/ Medicine ■ adj. having part or all of the cerebral hemispheres and the rear of the skull congenitally absent. ■ n. an anencephalic fetus or infant.
– DERIVATIVES **anencephaly** n.
– ORIGIN C19: from Greek *anenkephalos* 'without brain'.

-aneous ■ suffix forming adjectives from Latin words: *spontaneous*.
– ORIGIN from the Latin suffix *-aneus*.

anergy /ˈanədʒi/ ■ n. Medicine absence of the normal immune response to a particular antigen or allergen.
– ORIGIN C20: from German *Anergie*, from Greek *an-* 'not', on the pattern of *Allergie* 'allergy'.

aneroid /ˈanərɔɪd/ ■ adj. relating to or denoting a barometer that measures air pressure by the action of the air in deforming the elastic lid of an evacuated box.
– ORIGIN C19: from Greek *a-* 'without' + *nēros* 'water'.

anesthesia etc. ■ n. US spelling of ANAESTHESIA etc.

aneurysm /ˈanjʊrɪz(ə)m/ (also **aneurism**) ■ n. Medicine an excessive localized swelling of the wall of an artery.
– ORIGIN Middle English: from Greek *aneurusma* 'dilatation'.

anew ■ adv. chiefly poetic/literary in a new or different way. ▶ once more; again.

angel ■ n. **1** a spiritual being believed to act as an attendant or messenger of God, conventionally represented as being of human form with wings. **2** a person of great beauty, kindness, or virtue. **3** informal (especially in the theatre) a financial backer. **4** informal an unexplained radar signal.
– PHRASES **on the side of the angels** on the side of what is right.
– ORIGIN Old English: from Greek *angelos* 'messenger'.

angel cake (N. Amer. also **angel food cake**) ■ n. a very light, pale sponge cake typically baked in a ring shape and covered with soft icing.

angel dust ■ n. informal **1** the hallucinogenic drug phencyclidine hydrochloride. **2** another term for CLENBUTEROL.

angelfish ■ n. (pl. same or **-fishes**) **1** a freshwater fish with a deep, laterally compressed body and large dorsal and anal fins, often vividly coloured or patterned. [*Pterophyllum scalare* (Amazon basin) and other species.] **2** a similar marine or reef-dwelling fish. [Family Pomacanthidae: several genera.]

angel hair ■ n. a type of pasta consisting of very fine long strands.

angelic ■ adj. **1** of or relating to angels. **2** exceptionally beautiful, innocent, or kind.
– DERIVATIVES **angelical** adj. **angelically** adv.

angelica /anˈdʒɛlɪkə/ ■ n. a tall aromatic plant of the parsley family, the candied stalks of which are used in confectionery and cake decoration. [Genus *Angelica*: many species.]
– ORIGIN C16: from medieval Latin (*herba*) *angelica* 'angelic (herb)', so named because it was believed to be efficacious against poisoning and disease.

angelology ■ n. theological doctrine concerning angels.

angel shark ■ n. a large, active bottom-dwelling cartilaginous fish with broad wing-like pectoral fins. [*Squatina africana* and other species.]

angels on horseback ■ pl. n. an appetizer consisting of oysters individually wrapped in bacon and served on toast.

angel's trumpet ■ n. a South American shrub or small tree with large pendulous trumpet-shaped flowers. [Genus *Brugmansia*.]

angelus /ˈandʒ(ə)ləs/ ■ n. a Roman Catholic devotion commemorating the Incarnation of Jesus and including the Hail Mary. ▶ a ringing of bells announcing this.
– ORIGIN C17: from Latin *Angelus domini* 'the angel of the Lord', the opening words of the devotion.

anger ■ n. a strong feeling of annoyance, displeasure, or hostility. ■ v. provoke anger in.
– ORIGIN Middle English: from Old Norse *angr* 'grief', *angra* 'vex'.

angina /anˈdʒʌɪnə/ ■ n. Medicine **1** (also **angina pectoris** /ˈpɛkt(ə)rɪs/) a condition marked by severe pain in the chest, arising from an inadequate blood supply to the heart. **2** used in names of disorders involving pain in the throat: *Ludwig's angina*.
– ORIGIN C16: from Greek *ankhonē* 'strangling' (+ *pectoris* 'of the chest').

angio- ■ comb. form **1** relating to blood vessels: *angiography*. **2** relating to seed vessels: *angiosperm*.
– ORIGIN from Greek *angeion* 'vessel'.

angiogenesis ■ n. Physiology the development of new blood vessels.

angiogram /ˈandʒɪə(ʊ)ɡram/ ■ n. an X-ray photograph of blood or lymph vessels, made by angiography.

angiography /ˌandʒɪˈɒɡrəfi/ ■ n. radiography of blood or lymph vessels, carried out after introduction of a radiopaque substance.
– DERIVATIVES **angiographic** adj. **angiographically** adv.

angioma /ˌandʒɪˈəʊmə/ ■ n. (pl. **angiomas** or **angiomata** /-mətə/) Medicine an abnormal growth produced by the dilatation or new formation of blood vessels.

angioneurotic ■ adj. Medicine (of oedema) marked by swelling and itching of areas of skin.

angioplasty /ˈandʒɪə(ʊ)ˌplasti/ ■ n. (pl. **-ies**) Medicine surgical repair or unblocking of a blood vessel, especially a coronary artery.

angiosperm ■ n. Botany a plant of a large group (subdivision Angiospermae) that comprises those that have flowers and produce seeds enclosed within a carpel, including many herbaceous plants, grasses, shrubs, and trees. Compare with GYMNOSPERM.
– DERIVATIVES **angiospermous** /-ˈspəːməs/ adj.

angiotensin /ˌandʒɪə(ʊ)ˈtɛnsɪn/ ■ n. Biochemistry a protein whose presence in the blood promotes aldosterone secretion and tends to lead to hypertension.

Angle ■ n. a member of an ancient Germanic people that

founded English kingdoms in Mercia, Northumbria, and East Anglia.
– ORIGIN from Latin *Anglus* 'inhabitant of *Angul*' (in northern Germany).

angle¹ ■ n. **1** the space (usually measured in degrees) between two intersecting lines or surfaces at or close to the point where they meet. ▶ a corner, especially an external projection or internal recess. ▶ a measure of the inclination of one line or surface with respect to another. **2** a position from which something is viewed or along which it travels or acts. ▶ a particular way of approaching an issue or problem. **3** Astrology each of the four cardinal points of a chart. **4** angle iron or a similar constructional material. ■ v. **1** direct, move, or incline at an angle. **2** present (information) to reflect a particular view or have a particular focus.
– DERIVATIVES **angled** adj.
– ORIGIN Middle English: from Latin *angulus* 'corner'.

angle² ■ v. **1** [often as noun **angling**] fish with a rod and line. **2** seek something desired by indirectly prompting someone to offer it: *she was angling for sympathy*.
– DERIVATIVES **angler** n.
– ORIGIN Old English *angul* (n.).

angle bead ■ n. a strip of metal or wood fixed to an external corner before it is plastered to reinforce it.

angle bracket ■ n. **1** either of a pair of marks in the form < >, used to enclose words or figures so as to separate them from their context. **2** another term for BRACKET (in sense 3).

angle grinder ■ n. a device with a rotating abrasive disc, used to grind, polish, or cut metal and other materials.

angle iron ■ n. a constructional material consisting of pieces of iron or steel with an L-shaped cross section, able to be bolted together.

angle of attack ■ n. Aeronautics the angle between the line of the chord of an aerofoil and the relative airflow.

angle of incidence ■ n. Physics the angle which an incident line or ray makes with a perpendicular to the surface at the point of incidence.

angle of reflection ■ n. Physics the angle made by a reflected ray with a perpendicular to the reflecting surface.

angle of refraction ■ n. Physics the angle made by a refracted ray with a perpendicular to the refracting surface.

anglerfish ■ n. (pl. same or **-fishes**) a marine fish that lures prey within reach of its mouth with a fleshy lobe on a filament arising from its snout. [*Lophius piscatorius* and many other species.]

Anglian /ˈaŋglɪən/ ■ adj. of or relating to the ancient Angles.

Anglican ■ adj. relating to or denoting the Church of England or any Church in communion with it. ■ n. a member of any of these Churches.
– DERIVATIVES **Anglicanism** n.
– ORIGIN C17: from medieval Latin *Anglicanus*, from Latin *Anglus* 'Angle'.

Anglican communion ■ n. the group of Christian Churches derived from or related to the Church of England.

Anglicism ■ n. **1** a word or phrase that is peculiar to British English. **2** the quality of being typically English or of favouring English things.

anglicize (also **-ise**) ■ v. [often as adj. **anglicized** (also **-ised**)] make English in form or character.
– DERIVATIVES **anglicization** (also **-isation**) n.

Anglo ■ n. (pl. **Anglos**) a white English-speaking person, especially one of British or (US) non-Hispanic origin.

Anglo- ■ comb. form English: *anglophone*. ▶ of English origin: *Anglo-Saxon*. ▶ English and ...: *Anglo-Latin*. ▶ British and ...: *Anglo-Indian*.
– ORIGIN from Latin *Anglus* 'English'.

Anglo-Boer War ■ n. **1** a conflict between the British and the Boers, occurring from 1899–1902. **2** the 1880–81 conflict between the same parties.

Anglo-Catholicism ■ n. a tradition within the Anglican Church which is close to Catholicism in its doctrine and worship and is broadly identified with High Church Anglicanism.
– DERIVATIVES **Anglo-Catholic** adj. & n.

Anglo-Celt ■ n. a person of British or Irish descent.
– DERIVATIVES **Anglo-Celtic** adj.

Anglocentric ■ adj. centred on or considered in terms of England or Britain.

Anglo-Indian ■ adj. relating to or involving both Britain and India. ▶ of mixed British and Indian parentage. ▶ chiefly historical of British descent or birth but having lived long in India. ■ n. an Anglo-Indian person.

Anglo-Irish ■ adj. of or relating to both Britain and Ireland (or specifically the Republic of Ireland). ▶ of English descent but born or resident in Ireland. ▶ of mixed English and Irish parentage.

Anglo-Latin ■ n. Latin as used in medieval England.

Anglomania ■ n. excessive admiration of English customs.
– DERIVATIVES **Anglomaniac** n.

Anglo-Norman French ■ n. the variety of Norman French used in England after the Norman Conquest.

Anglophile ■ n. a person who is fond of or greatly admires England or Britain.
– DERIVATIVES **Anglophilia** n.

Anglophobe ■ n. a person who hates or fears England or Britain.
– DERIVATIVES **Anglophobia** n.

anglophone ■ adj. English-speaking. ■ n. an English-speaking person.

Anglo-Saxon ■ n. **1** a Germanic inhabitant of England between the 5th century and the Norman Conquest. ▶ a person of English descent. ▶ chiefly N. Amer. any white,English-speaking person. **2** the Old English language. ▶ informal plain English, in particular vulgar slang.

Angolan /aŋˈɡəʊlən/ ■ n. a native or inhabitant of Angola. ■ adj. of or relating to Angola.

angora /aŋˈɡɔːrə/ ■ n. **1** a cat, goat, or rabbit of a long-haired breed. **2** a fabric made from the hair of the angora goat or rabbit.
– ORIGIN C19: from *Angora* (Ankara) in Turkey.

angora wool ■ n. a mixture of sheep's wool and angora rabbit hair.

angostura /ˌaŋɡəˈstjʊərə/ ■ n. **1** an aromatic bitter bark from South America, used as a flavouring. **2** (also **Angostura bitters** trademark) a kind of tonic.
– ORIGIN C18: from *Angostura* (Ciudad Bolívar) in Venezuela.

angry ■ adj. (**-ier**, **-iest**) **1** feeling or showing anger. **2** (of a wound or sore) red and inflamed.
– DERIVATIVES **angrily** adv.

angst /aŋst/ ■ n. a profound feeling of generalized anxiety or dread.
– DERIVATIVES **angsty** adj.
– ORIGIN 1920s: from German, 'fear'.

angstrom /ˈaŋstrəm/ (also **ångström** /ˈɒŋstrɜːm/) (abbrev.: **Å**) ■ n. Physics a unit of length equal to one hundred-millionth of a centimetre, 10^{-10} metre.
– ORIGIN C19: named after the Swedish physicist A. J. Ångström.

anguilliform /aŋˈɡwɪlɪfɔːm/ ■ adj. Zoology relating to or denoting eels or related fish.
– ORIGIN C17: from Latin *anguilla* 'eel'.

anguish ■ n. severe mental or physical pain or suffering.
– ORIGIN Middle English: from Latin *angustia* 'straits, distress', from *angustus* 'narrow'.

anguished ■ adj. experiencing or expressing anguish.
– ORIGIN C17: from Old French *anguissier*, from Latin *angustia* (see ANGUISH).

angular /ˈaŋɡjʊlə/ ■ adj. having angles or sharp corners. ▶ (of a person) lean and having a prominent bone structure. ▶ placed or directed at an angle. ▶ Physics measured with reference to angles, especially those associated with rotation: *angular momentum*.
– DERIVATIVES **angularity** n. **angularly** adv.
– ORIGIN Middle English: from Latin *angularis*, from *angulus* (see ANGLE¹).

angulate /ˈaŋɡjʊleɪt/ ■ v. technical hold or bend (a part of the body) so as to form an angle or angles. ▶ Skiing incline

(the upper body) sideways and outwards during a turn.
– DERIVATIVES **angulation** n.
– ORIGIN C15: from Latin *angulare*, from *angulus* 'angle'.

Angus /'aŋgəs/ ■ n. short for ABERDEEN ANGUS.

anhedonia /ˌanhɪˈdəʊnɪə/ ■ n. Psychiatry inability to feel pleasure in normally pleasurable activities.
– DERIVATIVES **anhedonic** adj.
– ORIGIN C19: from French *anhédonie*, from Greek *an-* 'without' + *hēdonē* 'pleasure'.

anhedral /anˈhiːdr(ə)l, -ˈhɛd-/ ■ adj. chiefly Geology (of a crystal) having no plane faces. ■ n. Aeronautics downward inclination of an aircraft's wing.
– ORIGIN C19: from Greek *an-* 'without' + *-hedral* (see -HEDRON).

anhinga /anˈhɪŋgə/ ■ n. another term for DARTER (in sense 1).
– ORIGIN C18: from Tupi *áyinga*.

anhydride /anˈhʌɪdrʌɪd/ ■ n. Chemistry a compound obtained by removing the elements of water from a particular acid: *acetic anhydride*.
– ORIGIN C19: from Greek *anudros* (see ANHYDROUS).

anhydrous /anˈhʌɪdrəs/ ■ adj. Chemistry containing no water.
– ORIGIN C19: from Greek *anudros*, from *an-* 'without' + *hudōr* 'water'.

aniline /'anɪliːn, -lɪn/ ■ n. Chemistry a colourless oily liquid present in coal tar, used in the manufacture of dyes, drugs, and plastics.
– ORIGIN C19: from *anil*, another name for 'indigo', from Arabic *an-nīl*.

anima /'anɪmə/ ■ n. Psychoanalysis **1** (in Jungian psychology) the feminine part of a man's personality. Compare with ANIMUS. **2** the part of the psyche which is directed inwards, in touch with the subconscious. Compare with PERSONA.
– ORIGIN 1920s: from Latin, 'mind, soul'.

animadvert /ˌanɪmədˈvəːt/ ■ v. (**animadvert on/upon/against**) formal criticize or censure.
– DERIVATIVES **animadversion** n.
– ORIGIN Middle English: from Latin, from *animus* 'mind' + *advertere* 'to turn'.

animal ■ n. **1** a living organism which is typically distinguished from a plant by feeding on organic matter, having specialized sense organs and nervous system, and being able to move about and to respond rapidly to stimuli. ▶ a mammal, as opposed to a bird, reptile, fish, or insect. **2** a very cruel, violent, or uncivilized person. **3** [as modifier] pertaining to the flesh rather than the spirit or intellect: *animal lust*. **4** a particular type of person or thing: *a political animal*. ■ adj. Biology denoting the pole or extremity of an embryo containing the more active cytoplasm. The opposite of VEGETAL.
– ORIGIN Middle English: from Latin *animal*, from *anima* 'breath'.

animality ■ n. behaviour or nature characteristic of animals, especially in being physical and instinctive.

animal liberation ■ n. the freeing of animals from exploitation and cruel treatment by humans.
– DERIVATIVES **animal liberationist** n.

animal magnetism ■ n. a quality of powerful sexual attractiveness.

animal spirits ■ pl. n. natural exuberance.

animate ■ v. /'anɪmeɪt/ **1** bring to life or activity. **2** give (a film or character) the appearance of movement using animation techniques. ■ adj. /'anɪmət/ alive; having life.
– DERIVATIVES **animator** n.
– ORIGIN Middle English: from Latin *animare*, from *anima* 'life, soul'.

animated ■ adj. **1** lively. **2** (of a film) made using animation techniques.
– DERIVATIVES **animatedly** adv.

animateur /ˌanɪməˈtəː/ ■ n. a person who promotes or encourages something, especially artistic projects.
– ORIGIN 1950s: French, from medieval Latin *animator*.

animation ■ n. **1** the state of being full of life or vigour. ▶ chiefly archaic the state of being alive. **2** the technique of filming successive drawings, or positions of models, to create a film giving an illusion of movement. ▶ (also **computer animation**) the manipulation of electronic images by means of a computer to create moving images.

animatronics /ˌanɪməˈtrɒnɪks/ ■ pl. n. [treated as sing.] the technique of making and operating lifelike robots, especially for use in films.
– DERIVATIVES **animatronic** adj.

anime /'anɪmeɪ, 'anɪmə/ ■ n. Japanese film and television animation, typically having a science fiction theme.
– ORIGIN 1980s: Japanese.

animism /'anɪmɪz(ə)m/ ■ n. **1** the attribution of a living soul to plants, inanimate objects, and natural phenomena. **2** belief in a supernatural power that organizes and animates the material universe.
– DERIVATIVES **animist** n. **animistic** adj.
– ORIGIN C19: from Latin *anima* 'life, soul'.

animosity /ˌanɪˈmɒsɪti/ ■ n. (pl. **-ies**) strong hostility.
– ORIGIN Middle English: from Latin *animosus* 'spirited'.

animus /'anɪməs/ ■ n. **1** hostility or ill feeling. **2** motivation to do something. **3** Psychoanalysis (in Jungian psychology) the masculine part of a woman's personality. Compare with ANIMA.
– ORIGIN C19: from Latin, 'spirit, mind'.

anion /'anʌɪən/ ■ n. Chemistry a negatively charged ion. The opposite of CATION.
– DERIVATIVES **anionic** adj.
– ORIGIN C19: from Greek *ana-* 'up' + ION.

anise /'anɪs/ ■ n. **1** a Mediterranean plant of the parsley family, cultivated for its aromatic seeds (aniseed). [*Pimpinella anisum*.] **2** used in names of Asian or American trees or shrubs bearing fruit with an aniseed-like odour, e.g. star anise. [Genus *Illicium*.]
– ORIGIN Middle English: from Greek *anison* 'anise, dill'.

aniseed ■ n. the seed of the anise, used as a flavouring and in herbal medicine.

anisette /ˌanɪˈzɛt/ ■ n. a liqueur flavoured with aniseed.
– ORIGIN C19: from French, diminutive of *anis* 'anise'.

anisogamy /ˌanʌɪˈsɒgəmi/ ■ n. Biology sexual reproduction by the fusion of dissimilar gametes. Compare with ISOGAMY.
– DERIVATIVES **anisogamous** adj.
– ORIGIN C19: from Greek *anisos* 'unequal' + *gamos* 'marriage'.

Anisoptera /ˌanʌɪˈzɒptərə/ ■ pl. n. Entomology a suborder of insects which comprises the dragonflies.
– DERIVATIVES **anisopteran** n. & adj.
– ORIGIN from Greek *anisos* 'unequal' + *pteron* 'wing'.

anisotropic /ˌanʌɪsə(ʊ)ˈtrɒpɪk/ ■ adj. Physics having a different magnitude or properties when measured in different directions.
– DERIVATIVES **anisotropically** adv. **anisotropy** /-ˈsɒtrəpi/ n.
– ORIGIN C19: from Greek *anisos* 'unequal' + *tropos* 'turn'.

ankh /aŋk/ ■ n. an object or design resembling a cross with a loop instead of the top arm, used in ancient Egypt as a symbol of life.
– ORIGIN C19: from Egyptian, 'life, soul'.

ankle ■ n. the joint connecting the foot with the leg. ▶ the narrow part of the leg between this and the calf.
– ORIGIN Old English, of Germanic origin.

anklet ■ n. an ornament worn round an ankle.

ankylose /'aŋkɪləʊz/ ■ v. (**be/become ankylosed**) Medicine (of bones or a joint) be or become stiffened or united by ankylosis.
– ORIGIN C18: back-formation from ANKYLOSIS.

ankylosing spondylitis ■ n. Medicine a form of spinal arthritis, chiefly affecting young males, that eventually causes ankylosis of vertebral and sacro-iliac joints.

ankylosis /ˌaŋkɪˈləʊsɪs/ ■ n. Medicine abnormal stiffening and immobility of a joint due to fusion of the bones.
– DERIVATIVES **ankylotic** adj.
– ORIGIN C18: from Greek *ankulos* 'crooked'.

ankylostomiasis /ˌaŋkɪlə(ʊ)stə(ʊ)mʌɪəsɪs/ ■ n. variant spelling of ANCYLOSTOMIASIS.

anlage /'anlɑːgə/ ■ n. (pl. **anlagen** /-g(ə)n/) Biology the rudimentary basis of a particular organ or other part, especially in an embryo.
– ORIGIN C19: from German, 'foundation, basis'.

anna /'anə/ ■ n. a former monetary unit of India and

Pakistan, equal to one sixteenth of a rupee.
- ORIGIN from Hindi *ānā*.

annals ■ pl. n. a record of events year by year. ▶ historical records.
- DERIVATIVES **annalist** n.
- ORIGIN C16: from Latin *annales (libri)* 'yearly (books)', from *annus* 'year'.

annatto /əˈnatəʊ/ (also **anatto**) ■ n. an orange-red dye obtained from the seed coat of a tropical tree (*Bixa orellana*), used for colouring foods.
- ORIGIN C17: from Carib.

anneal /əˈniːl/ ■ v. **1** heat (metal or glass) and allow it to cool slowly, in order to remove internal stresses and toughen it. **2** Biochemistry recombine (DNA) in the double-stranded form.
- DERIVATIVES **annealer** n.
- ORIGIN Old English 'set on fire', from *āl* 'fire, burning'.

Annelida /əˈnɛlɪdə/ ■ pl. n. Zoology a large phylum that comprises the segmented worms, which include earthworms, lugworms, ragworms, and leeches.
- DERIVATIVES **annelid** /ˈan(ə)lɪd/ n. & adj. **annelidan** n. & adj.
- ORIGIN from Latin *anellus*, diminutive of *anulus* 'a ring'.

annex ■ v. /əˈnɛks/ add as an extra or subordinate part. ▶ add (territory) to one's own territory by appropriation. ■ n. & exclam. /ˈanɛks/. (chiefly Brit. also **annexe**) (pl. **annexes**) **1** a building joined to or associated with a main building. **2** (also **annexure**) an addition or attachment to a document.
- DERIVATIVES **annexation** n. **annexationist** n. & adj.
- ORIGIN Middle English: from Old French *annexer*, from Latin *annectere* 'connect'.

annihilate /əˈnʌɪɪleɪt/ ■ v. destroy utterly. ▶ informal defeat utterly.
- DERIVATIVES **annihilation** n. **annihilator** n.
- ORIGIN Middle English: from late Latin *annihilare* 'reduce to nothing'.

anniversary ■ n. (pl. **-ies**) the date on which an event took place in a previous year or in the past.
- ORIGIN Middle English: from Latin *annus* 'year' + *versus* 'turning'.

Anno Domini /ˌanəʊ ˈdɒmɪnʌɪ/ ■ adv. full form of **AD**.
- ORIGIN Latin, 'in the year of the Lord'.

annotate /ˈanəteɪt/ ■ v. add notes to (a text or diagram) giving explanation or comment.
- DERIVATIVES **annotation** n. **annotator** n.
- ORIGIN C16 (*annotation* Middle English): from Latin *annotare* 'mark'.

announce ■ v. make a formal public declaration about a fact, occurrence, or intention. ▶ make known the arrival of (a guest) at a formal social occasion.
- DERIVATIVES **announcement** n. **announcer** n.
- ORIGIN C15: from French *annoncer*, from Latin *annuntiare* 'declare, announce'.

annoy ■ v. **1** make a little angry. **2** archaic harm or attack repeatedly.
- DERIVATIVES **annoyance** n. **annoyer** n. **annoying** adj. **annoyingly** adv.
- ORIGIN Middle English: from Old French *anoi* (n.), based on Latin *(mihi) in odio (est)* '(it is) hateful to me)'.

annual ■ adj. **1** occurring once every year. **2** calculated over or covering a year. **3** (of a plant) living only for a year or less, perpetuating itself by seed. Compare with BIENNIAL, PERENNIAL. ■ n. **1** a book or magazine of a series published once a year. **2** an annual plant.
- DERIVATIVES **annually** adv.
- ORIGIN Middle English: from late Latin *annualis*, from Latin *annus* 'year'.

annual general meeting ■ n. a yearly meeting of the members or shareholders of an organization.

annualized (also **-ised**) ■ adj. (of a rate of return or inflation) recalculated as an annual rate.

annuity ■ n. (pl. **-ies**) a fixed sum of money paid to someone each year, typically for the rest of their life. ▶ a form of insurance or investment entitling the investor to a series of annual sums.
- ORIGIN Middle English: from French *annuité*, from Latin *annuus* 'yearly'.

annul /əˈnʌl/ ■ v. (**annulled**, **annulling**) declare (a law or contract, especially that of marriage) invalid.

- DERIVATIVES **annulment** n.
- ORIGIN Middle English: from late Latin, from *ad-* 'to' + *nullum* 'nothing'.

annular /ˈanjʊlə/ ■ adj. technical ring-shaped.
- DERIVATIVES **annularly** adv.
- ORIGIN C16: from Latin *annularis*, from *anulus* 'ring'.

annular eclipse ■ n. an eclipse of the sun in which the edge of the sun remains visible as a bright ring around the moon.

annulate /ˈanjʊlət/ ■ adj. chiefly Zoology marked with or formed of rings.
- DERIVATIVES **annulated** adj. **annulation** n.
- ORIGIN C19: from Latin *anulus* 'ring'.

annulet /ˈanjʊlɪt/ ■ n. **1** Architecture a small band encircling a column. **2** Heraldry a charge in the form of a small ring.
- ORIGIN Middle English: from Latin *anulus* 'ring'.

annulus /ˈanjʊləs/ ■ n. (pl. **annuli** /-lʌɪ, -liː/) technical a ring-shaped object, structure, or region.
- ORIGIN C16: from Latin *anulus* 'ring'.

annunciation ■ n. (**the Annunciation**) Christian Church the announcement of the Incarnation by the angel Gabriel to Mary (Luke 1:26–38). ▶ a Church festival commemorating this, held on 25 March.
- ORIGIN Middle English: from Latin *annuntiare* 'announce'.

annus horribilis /ˌanəs hɒˈriːbɪlɪs/ ■ n. a year of disaster or misfortune.
- ORIGIN modern Latin, suggested by ANNUS MIRABILIS.

annus mirabilis /mɪˈrɑːbɪlɪs/ ■ n. a remarkable or auspicious year.
- ORIGIN modern Latin, 'wonderful year'.

anode /ˈanəʊd/ ■ n. a positively charged electrode. The opposite of CATHODE.
- DERIVATIVES **anodal** adj. **anodic** adj.
- ORIGIN C19: from Greek *anodos* 'way up'.

anodize /ˈanədʌɪz/ (also **-ise**) ■ v. [usu. as adj. **anodized** (also **-ised**)] coat (a metal, especially aluminium) with a protective oxide layer by an electrolytic process in which the metal forms the anode.
- DERIVATIVES **anodizer** (also **-iser**) n.

anodyne /ˈanədʌɪn/ ■ adj. unlikely to cause offence or disagreement but somewhat dull. ■ n. a painkilling drug or medicine.
- ORIGIN C16: from Greek *anōdunos* 'painless'.

anogenital /ˌeɪnəʊˈdʒɛnɪt(ə)l/ ■ adj. Medicine & Anatomy of or relating to the anus and genitals.

anoint ■ v. smear or rub with oil, especially as part of a religious ceremony. ▶ ceremonially confer office on (a priest or monarch) by anointing. ▶ [often as adj. **anointed**] nominate as successor: *his officially anointed heir*.
- PHRASES **Anointing of the Sick** (in the Roman Catholic Church) the sacramental anointing of the ill or infirm with blessed oil; unction.
- DERIVATIVES **anointer** n.
- ORIGIN Middle English: from Old French *enoindre*, from Latin *inungere* 'anoint, smear with oil'.

anomaly /əˈnɒm(ə)li/ ■ n. (pl. **-ies**) **1** something that deviates from what is standard, normal, or expected. **2** Astronomy the angular distance of a planet or satellite from its last perihelion or perigee.
- DERIVATIVES **anomalous** n. **anomalously** adv. **anomalousness** n.
- ORIGIN C16: from Greek, from *an-* 'not' + *homalos* 'even'.

anomie /ˈanəmi/ (also **anomy**) ■ n. lack of the usual social or ethical standards.
- DERIVATIVES **anomic** /əˈnɒmɪk/ adj.
- ORIGIN 1930s: from Greek *anomia*, from *anomos* 'lawless'.

anon ■ adv. archaic or informal soon; shortly.
- ORIGIN Old English 'in or into (one state or course)'.

anon. ■ abbrev. anonymous.

anonymous ■ adj. **1** not identified by name; of unknown identity. **2** having no individual or unusual features.
- DERIVATIVES **anonymity** /anəˈnɪmɪti/ n. **anonymously** adv.
- ORIGIN C16: from Greek, from *an-* 'without' + *onoma* 'name'.

anopheles

anopheles /əˈnɒfɪliːz/ ■ n. a mosquito of a genus which includes the species that transmits the malarial parasite to humans.
– DERIVATIVES **anopheline** /əˈnɒfɪlʌɪn, -liːn/ adj. & n.
– ORIGIN C19: from Greek *anōphelēs* 'unprofitable'.

anorak ■ n. **1** a waterproof jacket, usually with a hood. **2** Brit. informal a socially inept person with unfashionable and largely solitary interests.
– ORIGIN 1920s: from Greenland Eskimo *anoraq*.

anorectal /ˌeɪnəʊˈrɛkt(ə)l/ ■ adj. Medicine & Anatomy of or relating to the anus and rectum.

anorexia /ˌanəˈrɛksɪə/ ■ n. lack of appetite for food, in particular (also **anorexia nervosa**) an emotional disorder characterized by an obsessive desire to lose weight by refusing to eat.
– ORIGIN C16: from Greek, from *an-* 'without' + *orexis* 'appetite'.

anorexic (also **anorectic**) ■ adj. relating to or suffering from anorexia. ■ n. **1** a person suffering from anorexia. **2** (**anorectic**) a medicine which produces a loss of appetite.

anorthite /əˈnɔːθʌɪt/ ■ n. a calcium-rich mineral of the feldspar group, typically white.
– ORIGIN C19: from AN-¹ + Greek *orthos* 'straight'.

anorthosite /əˈnɔːθəsʌɪt/ ■ n. Geology a granular igneous rock composed largely of labradorite or another plagioclase.
– ORIGIN C19: from French *anorthose* 'plagioclase'.

anosmia /aˈnɒzmɪə/ ■ n. Medicine the loss of the sense of smell, caused by head injury, infection, or blockage of the nose.
– DERIVATIVES **anosmic** adj.
– ORIGIN C19: from Greek *an-* 'without' + *osmē* 'smell'.

another ■ det. & pron. **1** one more; a further. **2** used to refer to a different person or thing from one already referred to.
– ORIGIN Middle English: orig. *an other*.

ANOVA /aˈnəʊvə/ ■ n. analysis of variance, a statistical method in which the variation in a set of observations is divided into distinct components.
– ORIGIN 1960s: acronym.

anovulant /aˈnɒvjʊl(ə)nt/ ■ adj. Medicine denoting a drug or other agent that prevents ovulation.

anovulatory /ˌanɒvjʊˈleɪt(ə)ri/ ■ adj. Medicine (of a menstrual cycle) in which ovulation does not occur.

anoxia /aˈnɒksɪə/ ■ n. chiefly Medicine an absence or deficiency of oxygen in a tissue, medium, etc.
– DERIVATIVES **anoxic** adj.

answer ■ n. **1** something said, written, or done as a reaction to a question, statement, or situation. **2** the solution to a problem or dilemma. ■ v. **1** respond with an answer. ▸ (**answer back**) respond impudently. ▸ (**answer to**) be responsible or report to. ▸ (**answer to the name of**) be called. **2** defend oneself against (a charge or accusation). ▸ (**answer for**) be responsible or to blame for. **3** be suitable for fulfilling (a need); satisfy.
– PHRASES **have** (or **know**) **all the answers** informal be very confident in one's knowledge. **in answer to** as a response to or as a result of.
– ORIGIN Old English, of Germanic origin.

answerable ■ adj. **1** (**answerable to/for**) responsible to or for. **2** (of a question) able to be answered.

answering machine ■ n. a device which supplies a recorded answer to a telephone call and can record a message from the caller.

answering service ■ n. a business that receives and answers telephone calls for its clients.

answerphone ■ n. Brit. a telephone answering machine.

ant ■ n. a small insect, usually wingless and with a sting, living in a complex social colony with one or more breeding queens. [Family Formicidae.]
– PHRASES **have ants in one's pants** informal be fidgety.
– ORIGIN Old English, of Germanic origin.

-ant ■ suffix **1** (forming adjectives) denoting attribution of an action or state: *arrogant*. **2** (forming nouns) denoting an agent: *deodorant*.

– ORIGIN from French or Latin pres. participial verb stems.

ant- ■ prefix variant spelling of ANTI- shortened before a vowel or *h* (as in *Antarctic*).

antacid /anˈtasɪd/ ■ adj. preventing or correcting acidity in the stomach. ■ n. an antacid medicine.

antagonism /anˈtag(ə)nɪz(ə)m/ ■ n. active hostility or opposition.

antagonist ■ n. **1** a person who actively opposes or is hostile. **2** Biochemistry a substance which interferes with the physiological action of another. **3** Anatomy a muscle whose action counteracts that of another muscle.
– DERIVATIVES **antagonistic** adj. **antagonistically** adv.
– ORIGIN C16: from Greek *antagōnistēs*, from *antagōnizesthai* (see ANTAGONIZE).

antagonize (also **-ise**) ■ v. **1** cause to become hostile. **2** Biochemistry act as an antagonist of.
– ORIGIN C18: from Greek, from *ant-* 'against' + *agōnizesthai* 'struggle'.

Antarctic ■ adj. of or relating to the south polar region or Antarctica.
– ORIGIN Middle English: from Greek, from *ant-* 'against, opposite' + *arktikos* (see ARCTIC).

antbear ■ n. another term for AARDVARK.

ante /ˈanti/ ■ n. a stake put up by a player in poker or brag before receiving cards. ■ v. (**antes**, **anted**, **anteing**) (**ante up**) put up (an amount) as an ante in poker or brag. ▸ N. Amer. informal pay an amount of money in advance.
– PHRASES **up** (or **raise**) **the ante** increase what is at stake or under discussion.
– ORIGIN C19: from Latin, 'before'.

ante- /ˈanti/ ■ prefix before; preceding: *antecedent*.
– ORIGIN from Latin *ante* 'before'.

anteater ■ n. a mammal that feeds on ants and termites, with a long snout and sticky tongue. [Many species, chiefly in the family Myrmecophagidae.] **2** S. African another term for AARDVARK.

antebellum /ˌantiˈbɛləm/ ■ adj. occurring or existing before a particular war, especially the US Civil War.
– ORIGIN C19: from Latin, from *ante* 'before' + *bellum* 'war'.

antecedent /ˌantɪˈsiːd(ə)nt/ ■ n. **1** a thing that existed before or logically precedes another. **2** (**antecedents**) a person's ancestors and social background. **3** Grammar an earlier word, phrase, or clause to which a following pronoun refers back. **4** Logic the statement contained in the 'if' clause of a conditional proposition. ■ adj. preceding in time or order.
– DERIVATIVES **antecedence** n. **antecedently** adv.
– ORIGIN Middle English: from Latin, from *ante* 'before' + *cedere* 'go'.

antechamber ■ n. a small room leading to a main one.
– ORIGIN C17: from French *antichambre*, from Italian, from *anti-* 'preceding' + *camera* (see CHAMBER).

antedate ■ v. come before in date. ▸ indicate that (a document or event) should be assigned to an earlier date.

antediluvian /ˌantɪdɪˈluːvɪən/ ■ adj. **1** of or belonging to the time before the biblical Flood. **2** chiefly humorous ridiculously old-fashioned.
– ORIGIN C17: from Latin, from *ante* 'before' + *diluvium* 'deluge'.

antelope ■ n. (pl. same or **antelopes**) a swift-running deer-like ruminant animal with upward-pointing horns, of a group including the gazelles, impala, gnu, and eland.
– ORIGIN Middle English (orig. the name of a fierce mythical creature): from late Greek *antholops*.

antenatal ■ adj. before birth; during or relating to pregnancy. ■ n. informal a medical examination during pregnancy.
– DERIVATIVES **antenatally** adv.

antenna ■ n. (pl. **antennae** /-niː/) **1** Zoology a long, thin sensory appendage found in pairs on the heads of insects and some other arthropods. **2** (pl. also **antennas**) chiefly N. Amer. or technical an aerial.
– DERIVATIVES **antennal** adj.
– ORIGIN C17: from Latin *antemna* 'yard' (of a ship).

antenuptial ■ adj. S. African & Brit. before marriage.
– ORIGIN C19: from late Latin *antenuptialis* (see ANTE-, NUPTIAL).

antenuptial contract ■ n. S. African Law a contract drawn up by a notary for a couple intending to marry, determining who retains control over the assets of the marriage. Compare with COMMUNITY OF PROPERTY.

antepartum /antɪˈpɑːtəm/ ■ adj. Medicine occurring not long before childbirth.
– ORIGIN C19: from Latin, 'before birth'.

antepenultimate ■ adj. last but two in a series.

anterior ■ adj. **1** chiefly Anatomy & Biology nearer the front, especially in the front of the body or nearer to the head. The opposite of POSTERIOR. ▸ Botany situated further away from the main stem. **2** (**anterior to**) formal prior to. **3** Phonetics pronounced with an obstruction located in front of the palato-alveolar region of the mouth, e.g. *b*, *p*, *d*, *t*.
– DERIVATIVES **anteriority** n. **anteriorly** adv.
– ORIGIN C16: from Latin *anterior*, comparative of *ante* 'before'.

antero- /ˈantərəʊ/ ■ comb. form chiefly Anatomy representing ANTERIOR: *anteroposterior*.

anterolateral ■ adj. chiefly Anatomy both anterior and lateral.

ante-room ■ n. an antechamber, especially one serving as a waiting room.

anteroposterior ■ adj. chiefly Anatomy relating to or directed towards both front and back.

anteverted /ˈantɪvɜːtɪd/ ■ adj. Anatomy & Medicine (of an organ of the body, especially the womb) inclined forward.
– ORIGIN C19: from Latin, from *ante* 'before' + *vertere* 'to turn'.

ant heap ■ n. **1** another term for ANTHILL. **2** S. African, chiefly historical material from crushed anthills, traditionally used for floors, tennis courts, and similar surfaces.

anthelmintic /ˌanθ(ə)lˈmɪntɪk/ ■ adj. Medicine denoting a preparation used to destroy parasitic worms.
– ORIGIN C17: from *anth-* (var. of *anti-* 'against') + Greek *helmins* 'worm'.

anthem ■ n. **1** a rousing or uplifting song identified with a particular group or cause. ▸ short for NATIONAL ANTHEM. **2** a musical setting of a religious text to be sung by a choir during a church service.
– DERIVATIVES **anthemic** n.
– ORIGIN Old English: from late Latin *antiphona* (see ANTIPHON).

anther ■ n. Botany the part of a stamen that contains the pollen.
– ORIGIN C18: from Greek *anthēra* 'flowery'.

antheridium /ˌanθəˈrɪdɪəm/ ■ n. (pl. **antheridia** /-dɪə/) Botany the male sex organ of algae, mosses, ferns, fungi, and other non-flowering plants.
– DERIVATIVES **antheridial** adj.
– ORIGIN C19: from Greek *anthera* 'flowery' + *-idion* (diminutive suffix).

anthesis /anˈθiːsɪs/ ■ n. Botany the flowering period of a plant, from the opening of the flower bud.
– ORIGIN C19: from Greek *anthēsis* 'flowering'.

anthill ■ n. a nest in the form of a mound built by ants or termites.

anthocyanin /ˌanθə(ʊ)ˈsʌɪənɪn/ ■ n. Chemistry a blue, violet, or red flavonoid pigment found in plants.
– ORIGIN C19: from Greek *anthos* 'flower' + *kuanos* 'blue'.

anthology ■ n. (pl. **-ies**) a collection of poems or other pieces of writing or music.
– DERIVATIVES **anthologist** n. **anthologize** (also **-ise**) v.
– ORIGIN C17: from Greek, from *anthos* 'flower' + *-logia* 'collection'.

Anthozoa /ˌanθəˈzəʊə/ ■ pl. n. Zoology a large class of marine coelenterates that includes the sea anemones and corals.
– DERIVATIVES **anthozoan** n. & adj.
– ORIGIN from Greek *anthos* 'flower' + *zōia* 'animals'.

anthracene /ˈanθrəsiːn/ ■ n. Chemistry a crystalline aromatic hydrocarbon obtained by the distillation of crude oils. [$C_{14}H_{10}$.]
– ORIGIN C19: from Greek *anthrax* 'coal'.

anthracite /ˈanθrəsʌɪt/ ■ n. coal of a hard variety that contains relatively pure carbon and burns with little flame and smoke.

---

45 **antibiosis**

– DERIVATIVES **anthracitic** adj.
– ORIGIN C16: from Greek, from *anthrax* 'coal'.

anthrax /ˈanθraks/ ■ n. a serious bacterial disease of sheep and cattle, typically affecting the skin and lungs and able to be transmitted to humans.
– ORIGIN Middle English, 'carbuncle': from Greek *anthrax* 'coal, carbuncle'.

anthropic principle /anˈθrɒpɪk/ ■ n. the cosmological principle that theories of the universe are constrained by the necessity to allow human existence.
– ORIGIN 1970s: from Greek, from *anthrōpos* 'human being'.

anthropo- /ˈanθrəpəʊ/ ■ comb. form human; relating to human beings: *anthropology*.
– ORIGIN from Greek *anthrōpos* 'human being'.

anthropocentric ■ adj. regarding humankind as the most important element of existence.
– DERIVATIVES **anthropocentrically** adv. **anthropocentrism** n.

anthropogenic /ˌanθrəpə(ʊ)ˈdʒɛnɪk/ ■ adj. (chiefly of pollution) originating in human activity.
– DERIVATIVES **anthropogenically** adv.

anthropoid ■ adj. resembling a human being in form.
– ORIGIN C19: from Greek, from *anthrōpos* 'human being'.

anthropology /ˌanθrəˈpɒlədʒi/ ■ n. the study of humankind, including the comparative study of societies and cultures and the science of human zoology and evolution.
– DERIVATIVES **anthropological** adj. **anthropologist** n.

anthropometry /ˌanθrəˈpɒmɪtri/ (also **anthropometrics**) ■ n. the scientific study of the measurements and proportions of the human body.
– DERIVATIVES **anthropometric** adj.

anthropomorphic /ˌanθrəpəˈmɔːfɪk/ ■ adj. relating to or characterized by anthropomorphism. ▸ having human characteristics.
– DERIVATIVES **anthropomorphically** adv.

anthropomorphism /ˌanθrəpəˈmɔːfɪz(ə)m/ ■ n. the attribution of human characteristics or behaviour to a god, animal, or object.
– DERIVATIVES **anthropomorphize** (also **-ise**) v.

anthropomorphous ■ adj. human in form or nature.
– ORIGIN C18: from Greek, from *anthrōpos* 'human being' + *morphē* 'form'.

anthropophagi /ˌanθrəˈpɒfəɡʌɪ/ ■ pl. n. (in legends or fables) cannibals.
– ORIGIN C16: from Greek *anthrōpophagos* 'man-eating'.

anthropophagy /ˌanθrəˈpɒfədʒi/ ■ n. cannibalism.
– DERIVATIVES **anthropophagous** /-ɡəs/ adj.

anthroposophy /ˌanθrəˈpɒsəfi/ ■ n. a system established by the Austrian philosopher Rudolf Steiner that seeks to optimize physical and mental health and well-being.
– DERIVATIVES **anthroposophical** adj.
– ORIGIN C20: from Greek, from *anthrōpos* 'human being' + *sophia* 'wisdom'.

anthurium /anˈθ(j)ʊərɪəm/ ■ n. (pl. **anthuriums**) a tropical American plant grown for its ornamental foliage or brightly coloured flowering spathes. [Genus *Anthurium*.]
– ORIGIN from Greek *anthos* 'flower' + *oura* 'tail'.

anti ■ prep. opposed to; against. ■ n. (pl. **antis**) informal an opponent of something.

anti- (also **ant-**) ■ prefix **1** opposed to; against: *anti-aircraft*. ▸ preventing or relieving: *antibacterial*. ▸ the opposite of: *anticlimax*. ▸ acting as a rival: *anti-pope*. **2** Physics the antiparticle of a specified particle.
– ORIGIN from Greek *anti* 'against'.

anti-Aids ■ adj. intended to prevent or hinder the development or spread of Aids.

anti-aircraft ■ adj. (of a gun or missile) used to attack enemy aircraft.

anti-apartheid ■ adj. relating to organizations or activities which opposed apartheid.

antibacterial ■ adj. active against bacteria.

antibiosis /ˌantɪbʌɪˈəʊsɪs/ ■ n. Biology an antagonistic association between two organisms (especially

antibiotic

micro-organisms), in which one is adversely affected. Compare with SYMBIOSIS.
– ORIGIN C19: from Greek *anti* 'against' + SYMBIOSIS.

antibiotic ■ n. a medicine that inhibits the growth of or destroys micro-organisms.
– ORIGIN C19: from Greek *anti* 'against' + *bios* 'life'.

antibody ■ n. (pl. -ies) a blood protein produced by the body in response to and counteracting an antigen.

antic ■ adj. archaic grotesque or bizarre.
– ORIGIN C16: from Italian *antico* 'antique, grotesque'.

Antichrist ■ n. (**the Antichrist**) a postulated opponent of Christ expected by the early Christian Church to appear before the end of the world.

anticipate ■ v. 1 be aware of (a future event) and take action. ▸ regard as probable. ▸ look forward to. 2 act or happen before.
– DERIVATIVES **anticipative** adj. **anticipator** n. **anticipatory** adj.
– ORIGIN C16 (*anticipation* Middle English): from Latin, from *ante-* 'before' + *capere* 'take'.

anticipation /antɪsɪˈpeɪʃ(ə)n/ ■ n. the action of anticipating; expectation or prediction. ▸ Music the introduction in a composition of part of a chord which is about to follow in full.
– ORIGIN Middle English: from Latin *anticipatio(n-)*, from the verb *anticipare* (see ANTICIPATE).

anticlerical ■ adj. chiefly historical opposed to the power or influence of the clergy.
– DERIVATIVES **anticlericalism** n.

anticlimax ■ n. a disappointing end to an exciting series of events.
– DERIVATIVES **anticlimactic** adj. **anticlimactically** adv.

anticline /ˈantɪklʌɪn/ ■ n. Geology a ridge or fold of stratified rock in which the strata slope downwards from the crest. Compare with SYNCLINE.
– DERIVATIVES **anticlinal** adj.
– ORIGIN C19: from Greek, from *anti-* 'against' + *klinein* 'lean'.

anticlockwise ■ adv. & adj. in the opposite direction to the way in which the hands of a clock move round.

anticoagulant ■ adj. having the effect of retarding the coagulation of the blood. ■ n. an anticoagulant substance.

anticonvulsant ■ adj. preventing or reducing the severity of epileptic fits or other convulsions. ■ n. an anticonvulsant drug.

antics ■ pl. n. foolish, outrageous, or amusing behaviour.
– ORIGIN C16: from ANTIC.

anticyclone ■ n. a weather system with high barometric pressure at its centre, around which air slowly circulates (typically associated with calm, fine weather).
– DERIVATIVES **anticyclonic** adj.

antidepressant ■ adj. used to alleviate depression. ■ n. an antidepressant drug.

antidiarrhoeal ■ adj. used to alleviate diarrhoea.

antidiuretic hormone ■ n. another term for VASOPRESSIN.

antidote ■ n. 1 a medicine taken to counteract a particular poison. 2 something that counteracts an unpleasant feeling or situation: *laughter is a good antidote to stress.*
– DERIVATIVES **antidotal** adj.
– ORIGIN Middle English: from Greek, from *anti-* 'against' + *didonai* 'give'.

anti-emetic ■ adj. preventing vomiting. ■ n. an anti-emetic drug.

antifouling ■ n. a substance applied to a boat's hull to prevent fouling.

antifreeze ■ n. a liquid added to water to lower the freezing point, especially in the radiator of a motor vehicle.

antigen ■ n. a substance which the body recognizes as alien and which induces an immune response. Compare with ANTIBODY.
– DERIVATIVES **antigenic** adj.
– ORIGIN C20: from Greek, from *anti-* 'against' + -GEN.

Antiguan /anˈtiːɡwən/ ■ n. a native or inhabitant of Antigua, or the country of Antigua and Barbuda, in the West Indies. ■ adj. of or relating to Antigua or Antigua and Barbuda.

anti-hero (or **anti-heroine**) ■ n. a central character in a story, film, or drama who lacks conventional heroic attributes.

antihistamine ■ n. a drug or other compound that inhibits the physiological effects of histamine, used especially in the treatment of allergies.

anti-infective ■ adj. used to prevent infection. ■ n. an anti-infective drug.

anti-inflammatory ■ adj. (of a drug) used to reduce inflammation. ■ n. (pl. -ies) an anti-inflammatory drug.

anti-knock ■ n. a substance added to petrol to inhibit pre-ignition.

anti-lock ■ adj. (of brakes) designed so as to prevent the wheels locking and the vehicle skidding if applied suddenly.

antilogarithm ■ n. the number of which a given number is the logarithm.

antimacassar /ˌantɪməˈkasə/ ■ n. a piece of cloth put over the back of an upholstered chair to protect it from grease and dirt.
– ORIGIN C19: from Greek *anti-* 'against' + MACASSAR.

antimalarial ■ adj. used to prevent malaria. ■ n. an antimalarial drug.

antimatter ■ n. Physics matter consisting of elementary particles which are the antiparticles of those making up normal matter.

antimicrobial ■ adj. active against microbes. ■ n. an antimicrobial substance.

antimony /ˈantɪməni/ ■ n. the chemical element of atomic number 51, a brittle silvery-white semimetal. (Symbol: **Sb**)
– DERIVATIVES **antimonial** adj. **antimonic** adj. **antimonious** adj.
– ORIGIN Middle English: from medieval Latin *antimonium*.

antinode ■ n. Physics the position of maximum displacement in a standing wave system.

antinomian /antɪˈnəʊmɪən/ ■ adj. holding or relating to the view that Christians are released by grace from the obligation of observing the moral law. ■ n. a person holding such a view.
– DERIVATIVES **antinomianism** n.
– ORIGIN C17: from medieval Latin *Antinomi*, a C16 German sect.

antinomy /anˈtɪnəmi/ ■ n. (pl. -ies) a paradox.
– ORIGIN C16: from Greek, from *anti* 'against' + *nomos* 'law'.

antioxidant ■ n. a substance that prevents or inhibits oxidation. ▸ a substance such as vitamin C or E that removes potentially damaging oxidizing agents in a living organism.

antiparallel ■ adj. Physics parallel but moving or oriented in opposite directions.

antiparticle ■ n. Physics a subatomic particle with the same mass as a given particle but opposite electric or magnetic properties (e.g. a positron in relation to an electron).

antipasto /ˌantɪˈpastəʊ/ ■ n. (pl. **antipasti** /-ti/) (in Italian cookery) an hors d'oeuvre.
– ORIGIN Italian, from *anti-* 'before' + *pasto*, from Latin *pastus* 'food'.

antipathy /anˈtɪpəθi/ ■ n. (pl. -ies) a deep-seated feeling of aversion.
– DERIVATIVES **antipathetic** adj.
– ORIGIN C16: from Greek *antipathēs* 'opposed in feeling'.

anti-personnel ■ adj. (of weapons) designed to kill or injure people rather than to damage buildings or equipment.

antiperspirant ■ n. a substance applied to prevent or reduce perspiration.

antiphon /ˈantɪf(ə)n/ ■ n. a short sentence sung or recited before or after a psalm or canticle. ▸ a musical setting of an antiphon.
– ORIGIN Middle English: from Greek *antiphōna* 'harmonies', from *anti* 'in return' + *phōnē* 'sound'.

CONSONANTS **b** but **d** dog **f** few **g** get **h** he **j** yes **k** cat **l** leg **m** man **n** no **p** pen **r** red

antiphonal ■ adj. (of church music) sung, recited, or played alternately by two groups.
– DERIVATIVES **antiphonally** adv.

Antipodes /anˈtɪpədiːz/ ■ pl. n. **1** (**the Antipodes**) Australia and New Zealand (used by inhabitants of the northern hemisphere). **2** (**antipodes** or **antipode**) the direct opposite of something.
– DERIVATIVES **antipodal** adj. **Antipodean** adj. & n.
– ORIGIN Middle English: from Greek *antipodes* 'having the feet opposite', from *anti* 'against, opposite' + *pous, pod-* 'foot'.

antipope ■ n. a person established as pope in opposition to one held by others to be canonically chosen.
– ORIGIN Middle English: from medieval Latin *antipapa*.

antipruritic /ˌantɪprʊˈrɪtɪk/ ■ adj. used to relieve itching. ■ n. an antipruritic drug.
– ORIGIN C19: from Greek *anti-* 'against' + *pruritic* (see PRURITUS).

antipsychotic ■ adj. used to treat psychotic disorders. ■ n. an antipsychotic drug.

antipyretic ■ adj. used to prevent or reduce fever. ■ n. an antipyretic drug.

antiquarian /ˌantɪˈkwɛːrɪən/ ■ adj. relating to or studying antiques, rare books, or antiquities. ■ n. (also **antiquary**) a person who studies or collects antiques or antiquities.
– DERIVATIVES **antiquarianism** n.
– ORIGIN C17: from Latin *antiquarius*, from *antiquus* (see ANTIQUE).

antiquated ■ adj. old-fashioned or outdated.
– ORIGIN C16: from eccles. Latin *antiquare* 'make old', from *antiquus* (see ANTIQUE).

antique ■ n. a decorative object or piece of furniture that is valuable because of its age. ■ adj. **1** valuable because of its age. **2** belonging to the distant past. ▸ old-fashioned or outdated. ■ v. (**antiques, antiqued, antiquing**) cause to resemble an antique by artificial means.
– ORIGIN C15: from Latin *antiquus, anticus* 'former, ancient', from *ante* 'before'.

antiquity ■ n. (pl. **-ies**) **1** the distant past, especially the classical and other civilizations before the Middle Ages. **2** (usu. **antiquities**) an object or building from the distant past. **3** great age.
– ORIGIN Middle English: from Latin *antiquitas*, from *antiquus* (see ANTIQUE).

antiretroviral /ˌantɪretrə(ʊ)ˈvʌɪrəl/ Medicine ■ adj. (of a drug or treatment) inhibiting the growth of retroviruses. ■ n. an antiretroviral drug, used to combat HIV.

anti-roll bar ■ n. a rubber-mounted bar fitted in the suspension of a vehicle to increase its stability, especially when cornering.

antirrhinum /ˌantɪˈrʌɪnəm/ ■ n. (pl. **antirrhinums**) a plant of a genus that includes the snapdragon. [Genus *Antirrhinum*.]
– ORIGIN from Greek, from *anti-* 'counterfeiting' + *rhis, rhin-* 'nose', from the resemblance of the flower to an animal's snout.

anti-self ■ n. an adopted persona that is the opposite of one's conscious normal self. ■ adj. Physiology (of antibodies) directed against the body's own tissues.

anti-Semitism ■ n. hostility to or prejudice against Jews.
– DERIVATIVES **anti-Semite** n. **anti-Semitic** adj.

antisepsis ■ n. the practice of using antiseptics to eliminate the micro-organisms that cause disease. Compare with ASEPSIS.

antiseptic ■ adj. **1** relating to or denoting substances that prevent the growth of disease-causing micro-organisms. **2** so clean or pure as to be bland or characterless. ■ n. an antiseptic compound or preparation.
– DERIVATIVES **antiseptically** adv.

antiserum ■ n. (pl. **antisera**) a blood serum containing antibodies against specific antigens, injected to treat or protect against specific diseases.

antisocial ■ adj. **1** contrary to the customs of society and causing annoyance to others. ▸ Psychiatry sociopathic. **2** not sociable.
– DERIVATIVES **antisocially** adv.

antispasmodic ■ adj. used to relieve spasm of involuntary muscle. ■ n. an antispasmodic drug.

anvil

anti-static ■ adj. preventing the build-up of static electricity or reducing its effects.

antisymmetric ■ adj. Mathematics & Physics unaltered in magnitude but changed in sign by an arithmetical or symmetry operation.

antithesis /anˈtɪθəsɪs/ ■ n. (pl. **antitheses** /-siːz/) **1** a person or thing that is the direct opposite of another. ▸ a contrast or opposition between two things. **2** a rhetorical or literary device in which an opposition or contrast of ideas is expressed.
– ORIGIN Middle English: from Greek *antitithenai* 'set against'.

antithetical /ˌantɪˈθɛtɪk(ə)l/ ■ adj. **1** mutually incompatible. **2** relating to or using the rhetorical device of antithesis.
– DERIVATIVES **antithetic** adj. **antithetically** adv.
– ORIGIN C16: from Greek, from *antithetos* 'placed in opposition'.

antitoxin ■ n. Physiology an antibody that counteracts a toxin.
– DERIVATIVES **antitoxic** adj.

antitrust ■ adj. chiefly US (of legislation) preventing or controlling monopolies.

antitype ■ n. a person or thing that represents the opposite of another.
– DERIVATIVES **antitypical** adj.
– ORIGIN C17: from Greek, from *anti* 'against, opposite' + *tupos* 'type, a stamp'.

antivenin /ˌantɪˈvɛnɪn/ ■ n. an antiserum containing antibodies against specific poisons, especially those in the venom of snakes.
– DERIVATIVES **antivenom** n.
– ORIGIN C19: from Greek *anti-* 'against' + *ven(om)*.

antiviral ■ adj. Medicine (of a drug or treatment) effective against viruses.

antivirus ■ adj. Computing (of software) designed to detect and destroy computer viruses.

antivivisection ■ adj. opposed to the use of live animals for scientific research.
– DERIVATIVES **antivivisectionism** n. **antivivisectionist** n. & adj.

antler ■ n. a branched horn on the head of an adult deer. ▸ one of the branches on an antler.
– DERIVATIVES **antlered** adj.
– ORIGIN Middle English: from Old French *antoillier*.

ant lion ■ n. an insect that resembles a dragonfly, with predatory larvae that construct conical pits into which insects fall. [Family Myrmeleontidae.]

antonym /ˈantənɪm/ ■ n. a word opposite in meaning to another.
– DERIVATIVES **antonymous** adj.
– ORIGIN C19: from French *antonyme*, from *anti-* 'against' + *onoma* 'a name'.

antrum /ˈantrəm/ ■ n. (pl. **antra** /-trə/) Anatomy **1** a natural chamber or cavity in a bone. **2** the pyloric end of the stomach.
– DERIVATIVES **antral** adj.
– ORIGIN C19: from Greek *antron* 'cave'.

antsy /ˈantsi/ ■ adj. (**-ier, -iest**) N. Amer. informal agitated, impatient, or restless.
– ORIGIN C19: prob. from the phr. *have ants in one's pants* (see ANT).

Anura /əˈnjʊərə/ ■ pl. n. Zoology an order of tailless amphibians that comprises the frogs and toads.
– DERIVATIVES **anuran** n. & adj.
– ORIGIN from Greek *an-* 'without' + *oura* 'tail'.

anuria /əˈnjʊərɪə/ ■ n. Medicine failure of the kidneys to produce urine.
– DERIVATIVES **anuric** adj.

anus /ˈeɪnəs/ ■ n. the opening at the end of the alimentary canal through which solid waste matter leaves the body.
– ORIGIN Middle English: from Latin, 'a ring'.

anvil ■ n. **1** a heavy iron block on which metal can be hammered and shaped. **2** the horizontally extended upper

anxiety

part of a cumulonimbus cloud. **3** Anatomy another term for **INCUS**.
– ORIGIN Old English, of Germanic origin.

anxiety ■ n. (pl. **-ies**) a feeling of being anxious. ▸ Psychiatry a nervous disorder marked by excessive uneasiness.
– ORIGIN C16: from Latin *anxietas*, from *anxius* (see **ANXIOUS**).

anxiolytic /ˌaŋzɪəˈlɪtɪk/ Medicine ■ adj. used to reduce anxiety. ■ n. an anxiolytic drug.

anxious ■ adj. **1** experiencing worry or unease. **2** very eager and concerned to do something.
– DERIVATIVES **anxiously** adv. **anxiousness** n.
– ORIGIN C17: from Latin *anxius*, from *angere* 'to choke'.

any ■ det. & pron. **1** used to refer to one or some of a thing or number of things, no matter how much or how many. **2** whichever of a specified class might be chosen. ■ adv. at all; in some degree (used for emphasis).
– PHRASES **any more** (also chiefly N. Amer. **anymore**) to any further extent; any longer. **any time** (also **anytime**) at whatever time. **any time** (or **day** or **minute**) now informal very soon. **be not having any** (**of it**) informal be unwilling to cooperate.
– ORIGIN Old English, of Germanic origin.

anybody ■ pron. anyone.

anyhow ■ adv. **1** another term for **ANYWAY**. **2** in a careless or haphazard way.

anyone ■ pron. any person or people.

anyplace ■ adv. chiefly N. Amer. informal term for **ANYWHERE**.

any road ■ adv. chiefly N. English informal term for **ANYWAY**.

anything ■ pron. used to refer to a thing, no matter what.
– PHRASES **anything but** not at all (used for emphasis). **anything like** —— [with neg.] at all like a specified thing (used for emphasis). (**as**) —— **as anything** informal extremely ——.

anyway ■ adv. **1** used to confirm or support a point. **2** used in conversations to change the subject or to resume after interruption. **3** used to indicate that something happened or will happen in spite of something else.

anyways ■ adv. N. Amer. informal or dialect form of **ANYWAY**.

anywhere ■ adv. in or to any place. ■ pron. any place.

anywheres ■ adv. & pron. chiefly N. Amer. informal or dialect form of **ANYWHERE**.

anywise ■ adv. archaic in any manner or way.

Anzac ■ n. a soldier in the Australian and New Zealand Army Corps (1914–18). ▸ informal a person from Australia or New Zealand.

AOB ■ abbrev. (at the end of an agenda for a meeting) any other business.

A-OK (also **A-okay**) ■ adj. & adv. N. Amer. informal in a good order or manner; all right.
– ORIGIN 1960s (orig. an astronauts' term): from *a*ll systems *OK*.

AOR ■ n. a style of popular music in which a hard rock background is combined with more melodic elements.
– ORIGIN 1970s (US): from *album-oriented/adult-oriented rock*.

aorta /eɪˈɔːtə/ ■ n. the main artery of the body, supplying oxygenated blood from the heart to the circulatory system.
– DERIVATIVES **aortic** adj.
– ORIGIN C16: from Greek *aortē*, from *aeirein* 'raise'.

à outrance /ɑː ˈuːtrɒs/ ■ adv. poetic/literary to the death or the very end.
– ORIGIN French, 'to the utmost'.

AP ■ abbrev. Associated Press.

ap-¹ ■ prefix variant spelling of **AD-** assimilated before *p* (as in *apposite*, *apprehend*).

ap-² ■ prefix variant spelling of **APO-** shortened before a vowel or *h* (as in *aphelion*).

apace ■ adv. poetic/literary swiftly; quickly.

– ORIGIN Middle English: from Old French *a pas* 'at (a considerable) pace'.

Apache /əˈpætʃi/ ■ n. (pl. same or **Apaches**) **1** a member of an American Indian people living chiefly in New Mexico and Arizona. **2** any of the Athabaskan languages of this people.
– ORIGIN from Mexican Spanish, from Zuñi *Apachu* 'enemy'.

apart ■ adv. **1** separated by a specified distance. ▸ no longer living together or close emotionally. **2** to or on one side. **3** into pieces.
– PHRASES **apart from 1** except for. **2** as well as.
– DERIVATIVES **apartness** n.
– ORIGIN Middle English: from Latin *a parte* 'at the side'.

apartheid /əˈpɑːtheɪt, əˈpɑːtʌɪd/ ■ n. the system of segregation or discrimination on grounds of race in force in South Africa 1948–91. ▸ any system, policy, or action which segregates people.
– ORIGIN 1940s: Afrikaans 'separateness', from Dutch *apart* 'separate' + *-heid* (equivalent of **-HOOD**).

aparthotel (also **apartotel**) ■ n. a type of hotel providing self-catering apartments as well as ordinary hotel facilities.

apartment ■ n. **1** chiefly N. Amer. a suite of rooms forming one residence; a flat. ▸ a block of apartments. **2** (**apartments**) a private suite of rooms in a very large house.
– ORIGIN C17: from Italian *appartamento*, from *appartare* 'to separate'.

apathetic ■ adj. not interested or enthusiastic.
– DERIVATIVES **apathetically** adv.

apathy /ˈapəθi/ ■ n. lack of interest or enthusiasm.
– ORIGIN C17: from Greek *apatheia*, from *apathēs* 'without feeling'.

apatite /ˈapətʌɪt/ ■ n. a pale green to purple mineral consisting chiefly of calcium phosphate.
– ORIGIN C19: from Greek *apatē* 'deceit' (from the mineral's diverse forms and colours).

apatosaurus /əˌpatəˈsɔːrəs/ ■ n. a huge herbivorous dinosaur of the late Jurassic period, with a long neck and tail.
– ORIGIN from Greek *apatē* 'deceit' (because of a deceptive similarity between its bones and those of other dinosaurs) + *sauros* 'lizard'.

APB ■ abbrev. US all-points bulletin.

ape ■ n. **1** a large tailless primate of a group including the gorilla, chimpanzees, orangutan, and gibbons. [Families Pongidae and Hylobatidae.] **2** informal an unintelligent or clumsy person. **3** archaic an inferior imitator. ■ v. imitate, especially in an absurd or unthinking way.
– PHRASES **go ape** (or N. Amer. vulgar slang **apeshit**) informal go wild.
– ORIGIN Old English, of Germanic origin.

APEC ■ abbrev. Asia Pacific Economic Cooperation.

apeman ■ n. (pl. **-men**) an extinct ape-like primate believed to be related to present-day humans.

aperçu /ˌapɛːˈsjuː/ ■ n. (pl. **aperçus**) a comment which makes an illuminating or entertaining point.
– ORIGIN C19: from French, past participle of *apercevoir* 'perceive'.

aperient /əˈpɪərɪənt/ Medicine ■ adj. used to relieve constipation. ■ n. an aperient drug.
– ORIGIN C17: from Latin *aperire* 'to open'.

aperiodic ■ adj. chiefly Physics **1** not periodic; irregular. **2** damped to prevent oscillation or vibration.
– DERIVATIVES **aperiodicity** n.

aperitif /əˈpɛrɪtiːf, əˌpɛrɪˈtiːf/ ■ n. an alcoholic drink taken before a meal to stimulate the appetite.
– ORIGIN C19: from French *apéritif*, from Latin *aperire* 'to open'.

aperture /ˈapətʃə, -tj(ʊ)ə/ ■ n. chiefly technical an opening, hole, or gap. ▸ the variable opening by which light enters a camera.
– ORIGIN Middle English: from Latin *apertura*, from *aperire* 'to open'.

apetalous /eɪˈpɛt(ə)ləs, ə-/ ■ adj. Botany having no petals.
– ORIGIN C18: from Greek *apetalos* 'leafless'.

Apex /ˈeɪpɛks/ ■ n. a system of reduced fares for scheduled airline flights and railway journeys which must be booked

and paid for in advance.
- ORIGIN 1970s: from *Advance* P*urchase* E*xcursion*.

apex /'eɪpeks/ ■ n. (pl. **apexes** or **apices** /'eɪpɪsiːz/) **1** the top or highest part of something, especially one forming a point. ▶ Botany the growing point of a shoot. **2** the highest level of a hierarchy. ■ v. reach a high point or climax.
- ORIGIN C17: from Latin, 'peak, tip'.

Apgar score /'apgə/ ■ n. Medicine a number expressing the physical condition of a newborn infant (a score of ten representing the best possible condition).
- ORIGIN 1960s: named after the American anaesthesiologist Virginia *Apgar*.

aphasia /ə'feɪzɪə/ ■ n. Medicine inability to understand or produce speech as a result of brain damage.
- DERIVATIVES **aphasic** adj. & n.
- ORIGIN C19: from Greek, from *aphatos* 'speechless'.

aphelion /ap'hiːlɪən/ ■ n. (pl. **aphelia** /-lɪə/) Astronomy the point in a body's orbit at which it is furthest from the sun. The opposite of **PERIHELION**.
- ORIGIN C17: from Greek *aph' hēlion* 'from the sun'.

aphicide /'eɪfɪsʌɪd/ ■ n. an insecticide used against aphids.

aphid /'eɪfɪd/ ■ n. a small bug which feeds by sucking sap from plants, especially a blackfly or greenfly. [*Aphis* and other genera: many species.]
- ORIGIN C19: back-formation from *aphides*, pl. of **APHIS**.

aphis /'eɪfɪs/ ■ n. (pl. **aphides** /-diːz/) another term for **APHID**.
- ORIGIN C18: from Greek.

aphorism /'afərɪz(ə)m/ ■ n. a pithy observation which contains a general truth.
- DERIVATIVES **aphorist** n. **aphoristic** adj. **aphoristically** adv. **aphorize** (also **-ise**) v.
- ORIGIN C16: from Greek *aphorismos* 'definition'.

aphrodisiac /ˌafrə'dɪzɪak/ ■ n. a food, drink, or drug that stimulates sexual desire.
- ORIGIN C18: from Greek *aphrodisiakos*, from *Aphroditē* 'Aphrodite', the goddess of love.

API ■ abbrev. Computing application programming interface.

apian /'eɪpɪən/ ■ adj. of or relating to bees.
- ORIGIN C17: from Latin *apianus*, from *apis* 'bee'.

apiary /'eɪpɪəri/ ■ n. (pl. **-ies**) a place where bees are kept.
- DERIVATIVES **apiarian** adj. **apiarist** n.
- ORIGIN C17: from Latin *apiarium*, from *apis* 'bee'.

apical /'eɪpɪk(ə)l, 'ap-/ ■ adj. **1** technical relating to or denoting an apex. **2** Phonetics (of a consonant) formed with the tip of the tongue at or near the front teeth or the alveolar ridge, for example *th* or trilled *r*.
- ORIGIN C19: from Latin **APEX**.

apices plural form of **APEX**.

apiculture /'eɪpɪˌkʌltʃə/ ■ n. technical term for **BEE-KEEPING**.
- DERIVATIVES **apicultural** adj. **apiculturist** n.
- ORIGIN C19: from Latin *apis* 'bee' + **CULTURE**.

apiece ■ adv. to, for, or by each one.

apish /'eɪpɪʃ/ ■ adj. resembling or likened to an ape. ▶ foolish or silly.
- DERIVATIVES **apishly** adv. **apishness** n.

Apla /'aplə/ (also **APLA**) ■ abbrev. historical (in South Africa) Azanian People's Liberation Army.

aplasia /ə'pleɪzɪə/ ■ n. Medicine the failure of an organ or tissue to develop or to function normally.
- DERIVATIVES **aplastic** adj.
- ORIGIN C19: from Greek *a-* 'without' + *plasis* 'formation'.

aplastic anaemia ■ n. Medicine deficiency of all types of blood cell caused by failure of bone marrow development.

aplenty ■ adj. [postpos.] in abundance: *he has work aplenty*.

aplomb /ə'plɒm/ ■ n. self-confidence or assurance.
- ORIGIN C18: from French, from *à plomb* 'according to a plummet'.

apnoea /ap'niːə/ (US **apnea**) ■ n. Medicine temporary cessation of breathing, especially during sleep.
- ORIGIN C18: from Greek *apnoia*, from *apnous* 'breathless'.

apo- /'apəʊ/ ■ prefix **1** away from or separate: *apocrine*. **2** Astronomy denoting the furthest point in the orbit of a body in relation to the primary: *apolune*. Compare with **PERI-**.
- ORIGIN from Greek *apo* 'from, away, quite, un-'.

apocalypse /ə'pɒkəlɪps/ ■ n. **1** an event involving destruction or damage on a catastrophic scale. **2** (**the Apocalypse**) the complete final destruction of the world, as described in the biblical book of Revelation.
▶ (especially in the Vulgate Bible) the book of Revelation.
- ORIGIN Old English: from Greek *apokalupsis*, from *apokaluptein* 'uncover, reveal'.

apocalyptic ■ adj. **1** momentous or catastrophic. **2** of or resembling the biblical Apocalypse.
- DERIVATIVES **apocalyptically** adv.

apocope /ə'pɒkəpi/ ■ n. Linguistics omission of the final sound of a word, as when *cup of tea* is pronounced as *cuppa tea*.
- ORIGIN C16: from Greek *apokoptein* 'cut off'.

apocrine /'apəkrʌɪn, -krɪn/ ■ adj. Physiology relating to or denoting glands which release some cytoplasm in their secretions, especially sweat glands in the armpits and pubic regions.
- ORIGIN C20: from Greek, from *apo* 'from, away' + *krinein* 'to separate'.

Apocrypha /ə'pɒkrɪfə/ ■ pl. n. [treated as sing. or pl.] **1** (**the Apocrypha**) biblical or related writings appended to the Old Testament in the Septuagint and Vulgate versions, not forming part of the accepted canon of Scripture. **2** (**apocrypha**) writings or reports not considered genuine.
- ORIGIN Middle English: from Greek *apokruphos*, from *apokruptein* 'hide away'.

apocryphal ■ adj. **1** (of a report) of doubtful authenticity, although widely circulated as being true. **2** of or belonging to the Apocrypha.

apodictic /ˌapə'dɪktɪk/ (also **apodeictic** /-'dʌɪktɪk/) ■ adj. formal clearly established or beyond dispute.
- ORIGIN C17: from Greek *apodeiktikos*, from *apodeiknunai* 'show off, demonstrate'.

apodous /'apədəs/ ■ adj. Zoology without feet or having only rudimentary feet.
- ORIGIN C19: from Greek *apous, apod-* 'footless'.

apogee /'apədʒiː/ ■ n. **1** Astronomy the point in the orbit of the moon or a satellite at which it is furthest from the earth. The opposite of **PERIGEE**. **2** the culmination or climax of something.
- ORIGIN C16: from French *apogée*, from Greek *apogaion* (*diastēma*) '(distance) away from earth'.

apolar ■ adj. chiefly Biochemistry having no electrical polarity.

apolitical ■ adj. not interested or involved in politics.

Apollonian /ˌapə'ləʊnɪən/ ■ adj. **1** Greek & Roman Mythology of or relating to the god Apollo. **2** of or relating to the rational, ordered, and self-disciplined aspects of human nature. Compare with **DIONYSIAC**.

apologetic ■ adj. **1** expressing an apology. **2** constituting a formal justification of a theory or doctrine.
- DERIVATIVES **apologetically** adv.

apologetics ■ pl. n. [treated as sing. or pl.] reasoned arguments in justification of a theory or doctrine.

apologia /ˌapə'ləʊdʒɪə/ ■ n. a formal written defence of one's opinions or conduct.
- ORIGIN C18: from Latin (see **APOLOGY**).

apologist ■ n. a person who offers an argument in defence of something controversial.

apologize (also **-ise**) ■ v. express regret for something that one has done wrong.

apology ■ n. (pl. **-ies**) **1** a regretful acknowledgement of an offence or failure. ▶ (**apologies**) a formal expression of regret at being unable to attend a meeting or social function. **2** (**an apology for**) a very poor example of. **3** a justification or defence.
- ORIGIN C16: from Greek *apologia* 'a speech in one's own defence', from *apo* 'away'+ *-logia* (see **-LOGY**).

apomixis /ˌapə'mɪksɪs/ ■ n. Botany asexual reproduction in plants, in particular agamospermy. Often contrasted with **AMPHIMIXIS**.
- DERIVATIVES **apomictic** adj.
- ORIGIN C20: from Greek *apo* 'un-' + *mixis* 'mingling'.

apomorphine

apomorphine /ˌapəˈmɔːfiːn/ ■ n. Medicine a compound derived from morphine, used as an emetic and in the treatment of Parkinsonism.

apophatic /ˌapəˈfatɪk/ ■ adj. Theology (of knowledge of God) obtained through negation. The opposite of CATAPHATIC.
– ORIGIN C19: from Greek *apophatikos* 'negative', from *apophasis* 'denial'.

apophthegm /ˈapəθɛm/ (US **apothegm**) ■ n. a concise saying or maxim.
– DERIVATIVES **apophthegmatic** /-θɛɡˈmatɪk/ adj.
– ORIGIN C16: from French *apophthegme*, from Greek, from *apophthengesthai* 'speak out'.

apoplectic /ˌapəˈplɛktɪk/ ■ adj. 1 informal overcome with anger. 2 dated relating to or denoting apoplexy (stroke).
– DERIVATIVES **apoplectically** adv.

apoplexy /ˈapəplɛksi/ ■ n. (pl. **-ies**) 1 dated unconsciousness or incapacity resulting from a cerebral haemorrhage or stroke. 2 informal inability to act or speak caused by extreme anger.
– ORIGIN Middle English: from Greek *apoplēxia*, from *apoplēssein* 'disable by a stroke'.

apoprotein /ˌapəˈprəʊtiːn/ ■ n. Biochemistry a protein which together with a prosthetic group forms a particular biochemical molecule such as a hormone or enzyme.

apoptosis /ˌapə(p)ˈtəʊsɪs/ ■ n. Physiology the death of cells which occurs as a normal part of an organism's development.
– DERIVATIVES **apoptotic** /-ˈtɒtɪk/ adj.
– ORIGIN 1970s: from Greek *apoptōsis* 'falling off'.

aporia /əˈpɔːrɪə, əˈpɒrɪə/ ■ n. 1 an irresolvable internal contradiction or logical disjunction in a text, argument, or theory. 2 Rhetoric the expression of doubt.
– ORIGIN C16: from Greek, from *aporos* 'impassable'.

aposematic /ˌapə(ʊ)sɪˈmatɪk/ ■ adj. Zoology denoting coloration or markings serving to warn or repel predators.
– DERIVATIVES **aposematism** n.
– ORIGIN C19: from Greek *apo* 'away, from' + *sēma* 'sign'.

aposiopesis /ˌapə(ʊ)ˌsʌɪəˈpiːsɪs/ ■ n. (pl. **aposiopeses** /-siːz/) Rhetoric the device of suddenly breaking off in speech.
– DERIVATIVES **aposiopetic** adj.
– ORIGIN C16: from Greek *aposiōpēsis*, from *aposiōpan* 'be silent'.

apostasy /əˈpɒstəsi/ ■ n. the abandonment or renunciation of a belief or principle.
– ORIGIN Middle English: from Greek *apostasis* 'defection'.

apostate /ˈapəsteɪt/ ■ n. a person who renounces a belief or principle. ■ adj. abandoning a belief or principle.
– ORIGIN Middle English: from Greek *apostatēs* 'apostate, runaway slave'.

apostatize /əˈpɒstətʌɪz/ (also **-ise**) ■ v. renounce a belief or principle.

a posteriori /eɪ, ɑː, pɒˌstɛriˈɔːrʌɪ, pɒˌstɪə-/ ■ adj. & adv. 1 (with reference to reasoning or knowledge) proceeding from observations or experiences to the deduction of probable causes. 2 as an afterthought or with hindsight.
– ORIGIN C17: Latin, 'from what comes after'.

apostle ■ n. 1 (**Apostle**) each of the twelve chief disciples of Jesus Christ. ▶ an important early Christian teacher or missionary. 2 a vigorous and pioneering supporter of an idea or cause.
– DERIVATIVES **apostleship** n.
– ORIGIN Old English, from Greek *apostolos* 'messenger', from *apostellein* 'send forth'.

Apostle spoon ■ n. a teaspoon with the figure of an Apostle or saint on the handle.

apostolate /əˈpɒstələɪt/ ■ n. 1 the position or authority of an apostle. ▶ a group of apostles. 2 evangelistic activity or works.

apostolic /ˌapəˈstɒlɪk/ ■ adj. 1 of or relating to the Apostles. 2 of or relating to the Pope, especially when he is regarded as the successor to St Peter.

Apostolic Fathers ■ pl. n. the Christian leaders immediately succeeding the Apostles.

apostolic succession ■ n. the uninterrupted transmission of spiritual authority from the Apostles through successive popes and bishops, taught by the Roman Catholic Church but denied by most Protestants.

apostrophe¹ /əˈpɒstrəfi/ ■ n. a punctuation mark (') used to indicate either possession (e.g. *Harry's book*) or the omission of letters or numbers (e.g. *can't*; *1 Jan. '99*).
– ORIGIN C16: from Greek *apostrophos*, from *apostrephein* 'turn away'.

> **USAGE**
> Do not use the apostrophe to form the plural of ordinary words, as in *apple's*, or in possessive pronouns such as **hers, yours, theirs,** or **its**. See **Apostrophe** in *Guide to Good English* p. SP 22.

apostrophe² /əˈpɒstrəfi/ ■ n. Rhetoric an exclamatory passage in a speech or poem addressed to a person or personified thing.
– ORIGIN C16: from Greek *apostrophē* 'turning away', from *apostrephein* 'turn away'.

apostrophize /əˈpɒstrəfʌɪz/ (also **-ise**) ■ v. 1 Rhetoric address with an exclamatory passage. 2 punctuate with an apostrophe.

apothecaries' measure (also **apothecaries' weight**) ■ n. historical a system of units formerly used in pharmacy for liquid volume (or weight), based on the fluid ounce and the ounce troy.

apothecary /əˈpɒθɪk(ə)ri/ ■ n. (pl. **-ies**) archaic a person who prepared and sold medicines.
– ORIGIN Middle English: from late Latin *apothecarius*, from Greek *apothēkē* 'storehouse'.

apothegm ■ n. US spelling of APOPHTHEGM.

apotheosis /əˌpɒθɪˈəʊsɪs/ ■ n. (pl. **apotheoses** /-siːz/) 1 the highest point in the development of something. 2 elevation to divine status.
– DERIVATIVES **apotheosize** (also **-ise**) v.
– ORIGIN C16: from Greek, from *apotheoun* 'make a god of', from *apo-* 'from' + *theos* 'god'.

apotropaic /ˌapətrəˈpeɪɪk/ ■ adj. supposedly having the power to avert evil or bad luck.
– ORIGIN C19: from Greek *apotropaios*, from *apotrepein* 'turn away or from'.

app. ■ abbrev. 1 appendix (in a book). 2 Computing informal application.

appal (US **appall**) ■ v. (**appalled, appalling**) 1 greatly dismay or horrify. 2 [as adj. **appalling**] informal very bad or displeasing.
– DERIVATIVES **appallingly** adv.
– ORIGIN Middle English: from Old French *apalir* 'grow pale'.

Appaloosa /ˌapəˈluːsə/ ■ n. a horse of a North American breed having dark spots on a light background.
– ORIGIN 1920s: from *Opelousas* in Louisiana, or *Palouse*, a river in Idaho.

appanage /ˈap(ə)nɪdʒ/ ■ n. historical a provision made for the maintenance of the younger children of kings and princes.
– ORIGIN C17: from medieval Latin *appanare* 'provide with the means of subsistence', from *ad-* 'to' + *panis* 'bread'.

apparat /ˌapəˈrɑːt/ ■ n. chiefly historical the administrative system of a communist party.
– ORIGIN Russian, from German, 'apparatus'.

apparatchik /ˌapəˈratʃɪk/ ■ n. (pl. **apparatchiks** or **apparatchiki** /-kiː/) 1 chiefly historical a member of a communist party apparat. 2 derogatory or humorous an official in a large political organization.
– ORIGIN 1940s: from Russian, from *apparat* (see APPARAT).

apparatus /ˌapəˈreɪtəs/ ■ n. (pl. **apparatuses**) 1 the equipment needed for a particular activity or purpose. 2 a complex structure within an organization: *the apparatus of government*. 3 (also **critical apparatus, apparatus criticus**) a collection of notes accompanying a printed text.
– ORIGIN C17: from Latin, from *apparare* 'make ready for'.

apparel /əˈparəl/ ■ n. formal clothing. ▶ (**apparels**) embroidered ornamentation on ecclesiastical vestments. ■ v. (**apparelled, apparelling**; US **appareled, appareling**) archaic clothe.
– ORIGIN Middle English: from Old French *apareillier*, from Latin *ad-* 'to' (expressing change) + *par* 'equal'.

apparent ■ adj. **1** readily perceived or understood; obvious. **2** seeming real or true.
– DERIVATIVES **apparently** adv.
– ORIGIN Middle English: from Old French *aparant*, from Latin *apparere* (see APPEAR).

apparent horizon ■ n. see HORIZON (sense 1).

apparent wind ■ n. the wind as it is experienced on board a moving sailing vessel.

apparition ■ n. a remarkable thing making a sudden appearance. ▶ a ghost.
– DERIVATIVES **apparitional** adj.
– ORIGIN Middle English: from Latin *apparitio(n-)*, from *apparere* (see APPEAR).

appeal ■ v. **1** make a serious or heartfelt request. ▶ Cricket (of the bowler or fielders) call on the umpire to declare a batsman out. **2** Law apply to a higher court for a reversal of the decision of a lower court. **3** (usu. **appeal to**) be attractive or interesting. ■ n. **1** an act of appealing. **2** Law an application to a higher court for a decision to be reversed. **3** the quality of being attractive or interesting.
– DERIVATIVES **appealable** adj. **appealer** n. **appealing** adj. **appealingly** adv.
– ORIGIN Middle English: from Old French *apel* (n.), *apeler* (v.), from Latin *appellare* 'to address'.

appear ■ v. **1** come into sight. ▶ come into existence or use. ▶ be published. ▶ informal arrive. **2** present oneself publicly or formally, especially on stage or as the accused or counsel in a law court. **3** seem; give a specified impression.
– ORIGIN Middle English: from Latin *apparere*, from *ad-* 'towards' + *parere* 'come into view'.

appearance ■ n. **1** the way that someone or something appears. ▶ an impression given: *she read it with every appearance of interest.* **2** an act of performing in a public event. **3** an act of arriving or becoming visible.
– PHRASES **keep up appearances** maintain an impression of wealth or well-being. **make** (or **put in**) **an appearance** attend an event briefly. **to** (or **by**) **all appearances** as far as can be seen.

appease ■ v. placate (someone) by acceding to their demands.
– DERIVATIVES **appeasement** n. **appeaser** n.
– ORIGIN Middle English: from Old French *apaisier*, from *a-* 'to, at' + *pais* 'peace'.

appellant /ə'pɛl(ə)nt/ ■ n. Law a person who appeals against a court ruling.
– ORIGIN Middle English: from French *apelant* 'appealing', from *apeler* (see APPEAL).

appellate /ə'pɛlət/ ■ adj. Law (of a court) dealing with appeals.
– ORIGIN Middle English: from Latin *appellare* (see APPEAL).

appellation /ˌapə'leɪʃ(ə)n/ ■ n. formal a name or title.
– ORIGIN Middle English: from Latin *appellatio(n-)*, from *appellare* (see APPEAL).

appellation contrôlée /apaˌlasjɔ̃ kɒn'trɒleɪ/ (also **appellation d'origine** /ˌdɒrɪ'ʒiːn/ **contrôlée**) ■ n. a guarantee of the description of a French wine, in conformity with statutory regulations as to its origin.
– ORIGIN French, 'controlled appellation'.

append ■ v. add to the end of a document or piece of writing.
– ORIGIN Middle English: from Latin *appendere* 'hang on'.

appendage ■ n. a thing attached to something larger or more important.

appendectomy /ˌap(ə)n'dɛktəmi/ (also **appendicectomy** /əˌpɛndɪ'sɛktəmi/) ■ n. (pl. **-ies**) a surgical operation to remove the appendix.

appendicitis ■ n. inflammation of the appendix.

appendix ■ n. (pl. **appendices** or **appendixes**) **1** (also **vermiform appendix**) Anatomy a tube-shaped sac attached to the lower end of the large intestine. **2** a section of subsidiary matter at the end of a book.
– ORIGIN C16: from Latin, from *appendere* (see APPEND).

appertain /ˌapə'teɪn/ ■ v. **1** (**appertain to**) relate to. **2** be appropriate.
– ORIGIN Middle English: from late Latin *appertinere*, from *ad-* 'to' + Latin *pertinere* 'to pertain'.

appetite ■ n. a natural desire to satisfy a bodily need, especially for food.
– ORIGIN Middle English: from Old French *apetit*, from Latin *appetitus* 'desire for', from *appetere* 'seek after'.

appetizer (also **-iser**) ■ n. a small dish of food or a drink taken before a meal to stimulate the appetite.

appetizing (also **-ising**) ■ adj. stimulating the appetite.
– DERIVATIVES **appetizingly** (also **-isingly**) adv.
– ORIGIN C17: from French *appétissant*, from Old French *apetit* (see APPETITE).

applaud ■ v. show approval by clapping. ▶ praise or approve of.
– ORIGIN C15: from Latin *applaudere*, from *ad-* 'to' + *plaudere* 'to clap'.

applause ■ n. approval expressed by clapping.
– ORIGIN Middle English: from medieval Latin *applausus*, from *applaudere* (see APPLAUD).

apple ■ n. **1** the rounded fruit of a tree of the rose family, with green or red skin and crisp flesh. **2** the tree bearing such fruit. [Genus *Malus*: numerous cultivated forms.] **3** used in names of similar unrelated fruits, e.g. custard apple.
– PHRASES **the apple of one's eye** a person of whom one is extremely fond and proud. [orig. denoting the pupil of the eye, extended as a symbol of something cherished.] **a rotten** (or **bad**) **apple** informal a corrupt person in a group, likely to have a detrimental influence on the others. **upset the apple cart** spoil a plan.
– DERIVATIVES **appley** adj.
– ORIGIN Old English, of Germanic origin.

apple butter ■ n. N. Amer. a paste of spiced stewed apple.

applejack ■ n. N. Amer. a spirit distilled from cider.

apple-pie bed ■ n. a bed which, as a practical joke, has been made with a sheet folded so that the legs cannot be stretched out.

apple-pie order ■ n. perfect order.

applesauce ■ n. **1** (**apple sauce**) a purée of stewed apples, typically served with pork or as a dessert. **2** N. Amer. informal nonsense.

applet /'aplɪt/ ■ n. Computing a small application running within a larger program.

appliance ■ n. **1** a device designed to perform a specific task. **2** a fire engine.
– DERIVATIVES **applianced** adj.

applicable ■ adj. relevant; appropriate.
– DERIVATIVES **applicability** n. **applicably** adv.
– ORIGIN C16 ('compliant'): from medieval Latin *applicabilis*, from *applicare* (see APPLY).

applicant ■ n. a person who applies for something.

application ■ n. **1** a formal request to an authority. **2** the action of putting something into operation. ▶ practical use or relevance. **3** the action of applying something to a surface. **4** sustained effort. **5** Computing a program or piece of software designed to fulfil a particular purpose.
– DERIVATIVES **applicational** adj.

application programming interface ■ n. Computing a system of tools and resources in an operating system, enabling creation of software applications.

applicator ■ n. a device for inserting something or applying a substance to a surface.

applied ■ adj. (of a subject) practical rather than theoretical. Compare with PURE.

appliqué /ə'pliːkeɪ/ ■ n. ornamental needlework in which pieces of fabric are attached to a fabric ground. ■ v. (**appliqués**, **appliquéd**, **appliquéing**) decorate with appliqué.
– ORIGIN C18: from French, from *appliquer* 'apply', from Latin *applicare* (see APPLY).

apply ■ v. (**-ies**, **-ied**) **1** make a formal request. ▶ put oneself forward as a candidate for a job. **2** bring into operation or use. ▶ be relevant. **3** put (a substance) on a surface. **4** (**apply oneself**) work hard.
– DERIVATIVES **applier** n.
– ORIGIN Middle English: from Old French *aplier*, from Latin *applicare* 'fold, fasten to'.

appoggiatura /əˌpɒdʒə'tjʊərə/ ■ n. (pl. **appoggiaturas** or **appoggiature**) Music a grace note which delays the next

appoint

note of the melody, taking half or more of its written time value.
– ORIGIN Italian, from *appoggiare* 'lean upon, rest'.

appoint ■ v. **1** assign a job or role to. **2** determine or decide on (a time or place). ▶ archaic decree. **3** Law determine the disposal of (property) under powers granted by the owner.
– DERIVATIVES **appointee** n. **appointer** n.
– ORIGIN Middle English: from Old French *apointer*, from *a point* 'to a point'.

appointed ■ adj. **1** (of a time or place) designated. **2** equipped or furnished in a specified way.

appointment ■ n. **1** an arrangement to meet at a particular time and place. **2** a job or position. ▶ the action or process of appointing someone. **3** (**appointments**) furniture or fittings.
– PHRASES **by appointment (to the Queen)** selling goods or services to the British Queen.

apport /əˈpɔːt/ ■ n. an object produced supposedly by occult means at a seance.
– ORIGIN C19: from French *apport* 'something brought', from *apporter* 'bring to'.

apportion ■ v. share out; assign.
– DERIVATIVES **apportionable** adj.
– ORIGIN C16: from medieval Latin *apportionare*, from *ad-* 'to' + *portionare* 'divide into portions'.

apportionment ■ n. the action or result of apportioning. ▶ the determination of the proportional number of members each US state sends to the House of Representatives.

appose /əˈpəʊz/ ■ v. technical place next to.
– ORIGIN C16: from Latin *apponere* 'put near'.

apposite /ˈapəzɪt/ ■ adj. (especially of language) very appropriate; apt.
– DERIVATIVES **appositely** adv. **appositeness** n.
– ORIGIN C16: from Latin *apponere* 'apply'.

apposition ■ n. **1** chiefly technical the positioning of things next to each other. **2** Grammar a relationship between two or more words in which the units are grammatically parallel and have the same referent (e.g. *my friend Sue*).
– DERIVATIVES **appositional** adj. & n.
– ORIGIN Middle English: from late Latin, from *apponere* (see APPOSITE).

appraisal ■ n. an assessment of someone or something, especially the performance of an employee.

appraise ■ v. assess the value, quality, or performance of. ▶ (of an official valuer) set a price on.
– DERIVATIVES **appraisable** adj. **appraisee** n. **appraisement** n. **appraiser** n. **appraising** adj. **appraisingly** adv.
– ORIGIN Middle English: alteration of archaic *apprize*, from Latin *ad* 'to, at' + *prisier* 'to price, prize', by association with PRAISE.

USAGE
Appraise is frequently confused with **apprise**. **Appraise** means 'assess', while **apprise** means 'inform' and is often used in the structure **apprise someone of something**.

appreciable ■ adj. large or important enough to be noticed.
– DERIVATIVES **appreciably** adv.

appreciate /əˈpriːʃɪeɪt, -sɪ-/ ■ v. **1** recognize the value or significance of. ▶ be grateful for. **2** rise in value or price.
– DERIVATIVES **appreciatory** /-ʃ(ɪ)ət(ə)ri/ adj.
– ORIGIN C16: from late Latin *appretiare* 'set at a price, appraise', from *ad-* 'to' + *pretium* 'price'.

appreciation ■ n. **1** recognition of the value or significance of something. ▶ gratitude. **2** a written assessment of an artist or work, especially a favourable one. **3** increase in monetary value.

appreciative ■ adj. feeling or showing gratitude or pleasure.
– DERIVATIVES **appreciatively** adv. **appreciativeness** n.

apprehend ■ v. **1** intercept (someone) in the course of harmful or illicit action. ▶ seize or arrest (someone). **2** understand; perceive.

– ORIGIN Middle English: from Latin *apprehendere*, from *ad-* 'towards' + *prehendere* 'lay hold of'.

apprehensible ■ adj. archaic or poetic/literary capable of being understood or perceived.

apprehension ■ n. **1** anxious or fearful anticipation. **2** understanding. **3** the action of arresting someone.

apprehensive ■ adj. anticipating with anxiety or fear.
– DERIVATIVES **apprehensively** adv. **apprehensiveness** n.
– ORIGIN Middle English: from medieval Latin *apprehensivus*, from Latin *apprehendere* (see APPREHEND).

apprentice ■ n. **1** a person learning a trade from a skilled employer. **2** S. African historical a servant, often a former slave, registered to a particular master for a fixed period. ■ v. **1** employ as an apprentice. **2** S. African historical register a former slave, or child of a slave, as one's servant.
– DERIVATIVES **apprenticeship** n.
– ORIGIN Middle English: from Old French *aprentis*, from *aprendre* 'learn', from Latin *apprehendere* (see APPREHEND).

appress /əˈprɛs/ ■ v. technical [usu. as adj. **appressed**] press (something) close to something else.
– ORIGIN C17: from Latin *appress-*, *apprimere* 'press close'.

apprise /əˈprʌɪz/ ■ v. (usu. **apprise someone of**) inform; tell.
– ORIGIN C17: from French *appris*, from *apprendre* 'learn, teach', from Latin *apprehendere* (see APPREHEND).

USAGE
On the confusion of **apprise** with **appraise**, see APPRAISE.

approach ■ v. **1** come near or nearer to in distance, time, or standard. **2** make an initial proposal to or request of. **3** start to deal with in a certain way. ■ n. **1** a way of dealing with something. **2** an initial proposal or request. **3** the action of approaching. ▶ a way leading to a place: *the northern approaches*.
– ORIGIN Middle English: from Old French *aprochier*, from eccles. Latin *appropiare* 'draw near'.

approachable ■ adj. **1** friendly and easy to talk to. **2** able to be reached from a particular direction or by a particular means.
– DERIVATIVES **approachability** n.

approach shot ■ n. Golf a stroke which sends the ball from the fairway on to or nearer the green.

approbation ■ n. approval; praise.
– DERIVATIVES **approbatory** adj.
– ORIGIN Middle English: from Latin *approbatio(n-)*, from *approbare* 'approve', from *ad-* 'to' + *probare* 'try, test'.

appropriate ■ adj. /əˈprəʊprɪət/ suitable; proper. ■ v. /əˈprəʊprɪeɪt/ **1** take for one's own use without permission. **2** devote (money) to a special purpose.
– DERIVATIVES **appropriately** adv. **appropriateness** n. **appropriation** n. **appropriator** n.
– ORIGIN Middle English: from late Latin *appropriare* 'make one's own', from *ad-* 'to' + *proprius* 'own, proper'.

appropriate technology ■ n. technological development employing simple methods, local resources, and affordable materials or equipment to improve the standard of living in a community, especially in underdeveloped areas.

approval ■ n. the action of approving of something. ▶ a favourable opinion.
– PHRASES **on approval** (of goods) able to be returned if unsatisfactory. **seal** (or **stamp**) **of approval** an official indication that something is approved of.

approve ■ v. officially accept as satisfactory. ▶ (often **approve of**) believe that someone or something is good or acceptable.
– DERIVATIVES **approving** adj. **approvingly** adv.
– ORIGIN Middle English: from Old French *aprover*, from Latin *approbare* (see APPROBATION).

approx. ■ abbrev. approximate(ly).

approximate ■ adj. /əˈprɒksɪmət/ fairly accurate but not totally precise. ■ v. /əˈprɒksɪmeɪt/ come close in quality or quantity. ▶ estimate fairly accurately.
– DERIVATIVES **approximately** adv. **approximation** n.
– ORIGIN Middle English: from late Latin *approximare*, from *ad-* 'to' + *proximus* 'very near'.

appurtenance /əˈpəːt(ɪ)nəns/ ■ n. an accessory associated with a particular activity.
– ORIGIN Middle English: from Old French *apertenance*, from late Latin *appertinere* (see APPERTAIN).

appy ■ n. (pl. **-ies**) S. African informal an apprentice.

APR ■ abbrev. annual(ized) percentage rate.

Apr. ■ abbrev. April.

apraxia /əˈpraksɪə/ ■ n. Medicine inability to perform particular activities as a result of brain damage.
– DERIVATIVES **apraxic** adj.
– ORIGIN C19: from Greek *apraxia* 'inaction'.

après-ski ■ n. social activities following a day's skiing.
– ORIGIN 1950s: from French, 'after skiing'.

apricot /ˈeɪprɪkɒt, ˈaprɪ-/ ■ n. **1** an orange-yellow soft fruit, resembling a small peach. **2** the tree bearing this fruit. [*Prunus armeniaca*.] **3** an orange-yellow colour.
– ORIGIN C16: from Portuguese *albricoque*, from Spanish Arabic *al* 'the' + *barkūk*, from Latin *praecoquum* 'early-ripe'.

April ■ n. the fourth month of the year.
– ORIGIN Old English, from Latin *Aprilis*.

April Fool ■ n. **1** a victim of a hoax on April Fool's Day. ▶ a trick played on April Fool's Day. **2** S. African a bulbous plant whose large flower consists of many small florets. [Several species in the family Amaryllidaceae, especially *Haemanthus rotundifolius*.]

April Fool's Day ■ n. 1 April, traditionally an occasion for playing tricks.

a priori /ˌeɪ prʌɪˈɔːrʌɪ, ˌɑː prɪˈɔːri/ ■ adj. & adv. based on theoretical deduction rather than empirical observation.
– DERIVATIVES **apriorism** /eɪˈprʌɪərɪz(ə)m/ n.
– ORIGIN C16: Latin, 'from what is before'.

apron ■ n. **1** a protective garment covering the front of one's clothes and tied at the back. **2** a small area adjacent to another larger area or structure. ▶ an area on an airfield used for manoeuvring or parking aircraft. ▶ (also **apron stage**) a strip of stage projecting in front of the curtain. **3** an endless conveyor made of overlapping plates.
– PHRASES **tied to someone's apron strings** under someone's influence and control to an excessive extent.
– DERIVATIVES **aproned** adj.
– ORIGIN Middle English *naperon*: from Old French, diminutive of *nape* 'tablecloth', from Latin *mappa* 'napkin'; the *n* was lost by wrong division of *a napron*.

apropos /ˌaprəˈpəʊ, ˈaprəpəʊ/ ■ prep. with reference to.
– PHRASES **apropos of nothing** having no relevance to any previous discussion or situation.
– ORIGIN C17: from French *à propos* '(with regard) to (this) purpose'.

apse /aps/ ■ n. a large semicircular or polygonal recess with a domed roof, typically at a church's eastern end.
– DERIVATIVES **apsidal** /ˈapsɪd(ə)l/ adj.
– ORIGIN C19: from Latin *apsis* 'arch, vault'.

apt ■ adj. **1** appropriate; suitable. **2** (**apt to do something**) having a specified tendency. **3** quick to learn.
– DERIVATIVES **aptly** adv. **aptness** n.
– ORIGIN Middle English: from Latin *aptus* 'fitted', from *apere* 'fasten'.

apterous /ˈapt(ə)rəs/ ■ adj. Entomology (of an insect) having no wings.
– ORIGIN C18: from Greek *apteros*, from *a-* 'without' + *pteron* 'wing'.

Apterygota /apˌtɛrɪˌɡəʊtə/ ■ pl. n. Entomology a group of primitive wingless insects including the bristletails and springtails.
– DERIVATIVES **apterygote** n.
– ORIGIN from Greek *a-* 'not' + *pterugōtos* 'winged'.

aptitude ■ n. a natural ability or propensity.
– ORIGIN Middle English: from late Latin *aptitudo*, from Latin *aptus* (see APT).

APU ■ abbrev. auxiliary power unit.

aqua /ˈakwə/ ■ n. the colour aquamarine.

aqua- /ˈakwə/ ■ comb. form relating to water: *aquaculture*.
– ORIGIN from Latin *aqua* 'water'.

aquaculture ■ n. the rearing or cultivation of aquatic animals or plants.

aqualung ■ n. a portable breathing apparatus for divers, which feeds compressed air from cylinders on the diver's back through a mask or mouthpiece.

aquamarine ■ n. **1** a light bluish-green variety of beryl. **2** a light bluish-green colour.
– ORIGIN C18: from Latin *aqua marina* 'seawater'.

aquanaut ■ n. a diver.
– ORIGIN C19: from Latin *aqua* 'water' + Greek *nautēs* 'sailor'.

aquaplane ■ n. a board for riding on water, pulled by a speedboat. ■ v. **1** ride on an aquaplane. **2** (of a vehicle) slide uncontrollably on a wet surface.

aqua regia /ˈriːdʒə/ ■ n. Chemistry a highly corrosive mixture of concentrated nitric and hydrochloric acids.
– ORIGIN C17: Latin, 'royal water'.

aquarelle /ˌakwəˈrɛl/ ■ n. the technique of painting with thin, transparent watercolours.
– ORIGIN C19: from Italian *acquarella* 'watercolour'.

aquarist /ˈakwərɪst/ ■ n. a person who keeps an aquarium.

aquarium ■ n. (pl. **aquaria** /-rɪə/ or **aquariums**) a transparent tank of water in which live fish and other water creatures and plants are kept.
– ORIGIN C19: from Latin, neuter of *aquarius* 'of water'.

Aquarius /əˈkwɛːrɪəs/ ■ n. **1** Astronomy a large constellation (the Water Carrier or Water Bearer), said to represent a man pouring water from a jar. **2** Astrology the eleventh sign of the zodiac, which the sun enters about 21 January.
– PHRASES **Age of Aquarius** an astrological age which is about to begin, marked by the precession of the vernal equinox into Aquarius, believed to herald worldwide peace and harmony.
– DERIVATIVES **Aquarian** n. & adj.
– ORIGIN Latin *aquarius* 'of water'.

aquarobics /ˌakwəˈrəʊbɪks/ ■ pl. n. [treated as sing. or pl.] aerobic exercises performed in water.

aquatic /əˈkwatɪk, -ˈkwɒt-/ ■ adj. of or relating to water. ▶ living in or near water. ■ n. an aquatic plant or animal.
– ORIGIN C15: from Latin *aquaticus*, from *aqua* 'water'.

aquatint ■ n. a print resembling a watercolour, made using a copper plate etched with nitric acid.
– ORIGIN C18: from French *aquatinte*, from Italian *acqua tinta* 'coloured water'.

aquavit /ˌakwəˈviːt/ ■ n. an alcoholic spirit made from potatoes.
– ORIGIN C19: from Norwegian, Swedish, and Danish *akvavit* 'water of life'.

aqua vitae /ˈvʌɪtiː, ˈviːtʌɪ/ ■ n. strong alcoholic spirit, especially brandy.
– ORIGIN Middle English: from Latin, 'water of life'.

aqueduct /ˈakwɪdʌkt/ ■ n. an artificial channel for conveying water, especially a bridge or viaduct carrying a waterway.
– ORIGIN C16: from Latin *aquae ductus* 'conduit', from *aqua* 'water' + *ducere* 'to lead'.

aqueous /ˈeɪkwɪəs/ ■ adj. of, resembling, or containing water.
– ORIGIN C17: from medieval Latin *aqueus*, from Latin *aqua* 'water'.

aqueous humour ■ n. the clear fluid in the eyeball in front of the lens.

aquifer /ˈakwɪfə/ ■ n. a body of permeable rock able to hold or transmit water.
– ORIGIN C20: from Latin, from *aqua* 'water' + *-fer* 'bearing'.

aquilegia /ˌakwɪˈliːdʒə/ ■ n. a plant bearing showy flowers with backward-pointing spurs. [Genus *Aquilegia*.]
– ORIGIN prob. from Latin *aquilegus* 'water-collecting'.

Aquilian liability ■ n. S. African Law liability arising from pecuniary loss caused by negligence.
– ORIGIN *Aquilian* from the Roman Lex *Aquilia* of 286 BC, later much extended.

aquiline /ˈakwɪlʌɪn/ ■ adj. **1** like an eagle. **2** (of a nose) curved like an eagle's beak.
– ORIGIN C17: from Latin *aquilinus*, from *aquila* 'eagle'.

Ar ■ symb. the chemical element argon.

-ar[1] ■ suffix **1** (forming adjectives) of the kind specified:

molecular. **2** forming nouns such as *scholar.* Compare with -ER⁵.
– ORIGIN from Latin *-aris*.

-ar² ▪ suffix forming nouns such as *pillar.*
– ORIGIN from Latin *-are* (neuter of *-aris*).

-ar³ ▪ suffix forming nouns such as *bursar.*
– ORIGIN from Latin *-arius, -arium.*

-ar⁴ ▪ suffix alteration of -ER¹, -OR¹ (as in *liar*).

ar- ▪ prefix variant spelling of AD- assimilated before *r* (as in *arrive*).

Arab /'arəb, 'eɪrab/ ▪ n. **1** a member of a Semitic people inhabiting much of the Middle East and North Africa. **2** a horse of a breed originating in Arabia.
– DERIVATIVES **Arabization** (also **-isation**) n. **Arabize** (also **-ise**) v.
– ORIGIN from Arabic *'arab.*

arabesque /ˌarəˈbɛsk/ ▪ n. **1** Ballet a posture in which one leg is extended horizontally backwards, the torso extended forwards, and the arms outstretched. **2** an ornamental design consisting of intertwined flowing lines. ▸ Music a passage with a highly ornamented melody.
– ORIGIN C17: from Italian *arabesco* 'in the Arabic style', from *arabo* 'Arab'.

Arabian ▪ n. **1** historical a native or inhabitant of Arabia. **2** an Arab horse. ▪ adj. of or relating to Arabia or its people.

Arabic ▪ n. the Semitic language of the Arabs, spoken in many dialects in much of North Africa and the Middle East and written from right to left in a cursive script also used for other languages such as Persian, Urdu, and Malay. ▪ adj. of or relating to the Arabs or Arabic.

arabica /əˈrabɪkə/ ▪ n. coffee beans from a widely grown coffee plant native to the Old World tropics (*Coffea arabica*).
– ORIGIN 1920S: from Latin, feminine of *arabicus* 'Arabic'.

Arabic numeral ▪ n. any of the numerals 0, 1, 2, 3, 4, 5, 6, 7, 8, and 9.

Arabism ▪ n. **1** Arab culture or identity. **2** an Arabic word or phrase.
– DERIVATIVES **Arabist** n. & adj.

arable ▪ adj. (of land) suitable for growing crops. ▸ (of crops) able to be grown on such land. ▪ n. arable land or crops.
– ORIGIN Middle English: from Latin *arabilis,* from *arare* 'to plough'.

arachidonic acid /əˌrakɪˈdɒnɪk/ ▪ n. Biochemistry a fatty acid present in animal fats which is an essential constituent of the human diet.
– ORIGIN C20: from modern Latin *arachis* 'peanut', from Greek *arak(h)os.*

Arachnida /əˈraknɪdə/ ▪ pl. n. Zoology a class of arthropods including spiders, scorpions, mites, and ticks.
– DERIVATIVES **arachnid** n. & adj.
– ORIGIN from Greek *arakhnē* 'spider'.

arachnoid /əˈraknɔɪd/ ▪ adj. like a spider or arachnid. ▪ n. (also **arachnoid membrane**) Anatomy the fine middle membrane of the three surrounding the brain and spinal cord, situated between the dura mater and the pia mater.
– ORIGIN C18: from Greek *arakhnoeidēs* 'like a cobweb', from *arakhnē* 'spider'.

arachnophobia /əˌraknəˈfəʊbɪə/ ▪ n. extreme or irrational fear of spiders.
– DERIVATIVES **arachnophobe** n. **arachnophobic** adj.
– ORIGIN 1920s: from Greek *arakhnē* 'spider' + -PHOBIA.

aragonite /ˈarəɡ(ə)nʌɪt/ ▪ n. a mineral consisting of calcium carbonate, occurring as colourless prisms in deposits from hot springs.
– ORIGIN C19: from the region of *Aragon* in Spain.

arak /əˈrak/ ▪ n. variant spelling of ARRACK.

aralia /əˈreɪlɪə/ ▪ n. a tree or shrub of a diverse group cultivated for their foliage, profuse tiny flowers, or herbal properties. [Genus *Aralia*.]

Aramaic /ˌarəˈmeɪɪk/ ▪ n. a branch of the Semitic family of languages, used as a lingua franca in the Near East from the 6th century BC and still spoken in some communities. ▪ adj. of or relating to this language.
– ORIGIN C19: from Greek *Aramaios* 'of Aram' (the biblical name of Syria).

Aran /ˈar(ə)n/ ▪ adj. denoting a type of knitwear with patterns of cable stitch and large diamond designs, traditionally associated with the Aran Islands off the west coast of Ireland.

araneid /əˈreɪnɪɪd/ ▪ n. Zoology an invertebrate of the order (Araneae) that comprises the spiders.
– ORIGIN C19: from Latin *aranea* 'spider'.

Arapaho /əˈrapəhəʊ/ ▪ n. (pl. same or **-os**) **1** a member of a North American Indian people living on the Great Plains. **2** the Algonquian language of this people.
– ORIGIN from Crow *alappahó* 'many tattoo marks'.

arational ▪ adj. unconcerned with or outside rationality.

Araucanian /ˌarɔːˈkeɪnɪən/ ▪ n. **1** a member of a group of American Indian peoples of Chile and parts of Argentina. **2** the language of these peoples. ▪ adj. relating to or denoting these peoples or their language.
– ORIGIN from Spanish *Araucania,* a region in Chile.

araucaria /ˌarɔːˈkɛːrɪə/ ▪ n. an evergreen conifer with stiff sharp leaves, e.g. the monkey puzzle. [Genus *Araucaria*.]
– ORIGIN from Spanish *Arauco,* a province of Araucania, Chile.

Arawak /ˈarəwak/ ▪ n. (pl. same or **Arawaks**) **1** a member of a group of native peoples of the Greater Antilles and northern and western South America. **2** any of the languages of these peoples.
– DERIVATIVES **Arawakan** adj. & n.
– ORIGIN from Carib *aruac.*

arb S. African informal ▪ adj. random. ▪ v. (also **arb around**) relax; spend time aimlessly.
– ORIGIN C20: prob. from ARBITRARY.

arbiter /ˈɑːbɪtə/ ▪ n. **1** a person who settles a dispute. **2** a person who has influence over something: *an arbiter of taste.*
– ORIGIN Middle English: from Latin, 'judge, supreme ruler'.

arbitrage /ˈɑːbɪtrɪdʒ, ˌɑːbɪˈtrɑːʒ/ ▪ n. Economics the simultaneous buying and selling of assets in different markets or in derivative forms, taking advantage of the differing prices.
– DERIVATIVES **arbitrageur** n.
– ORIGIN Middle English: from French, from *arbitrer* 'give judgement'.

arbitral /ˈɑːbɪtr(ə)l/ ▪ adj. of, relating to, or resulting from the use of an arbitrator.

arbitrary /ˈɑːbɪt(rə)ri/ ▪ adj. **1** based on random choice or personal whim. **2** (of power or a ruling body) autocratic.
– DERIVATIVES **arbitrarily** adv. **arbitrariness** n.
– ORIGIN Middle English: from Latin *arbitrarius,* from *arbiter* 'judge, supreme ruler'.

arbitration ▪ n. the use of an arbitrator to settle a dispute.
– DERIVATIVES **arbitrate** v.
– ORIGIN Middle English: from Latin *arbitratio(n-),* from *arbitrari,* from *arbiter* 'judge, supreme ruler'.

arbitrator ▪ n. an independent person or body officially appointed to settle a dispute.

arbor ▪ n. US spelling of ARBOUR.

arboreal /ɑːˈbɔːrɪəl/ ▪ adj. of, relating to, or living in trees.
– ORIGIN C17: from Latin *arboreus,* from *arbor* 'tree'.

arborescent /ˌɑːbəˈrɛs(ə)nt/ ▪ adj. Botany tree-like.
– DERIVATIVES **arborescence** n.
– ORIGIN C17: from Latin *arborescere* 'grow into a tree', from *arbor* 'tree'.

arboretum /ˌɑːbəˈriːtəm/ ▪ n. (pl. **arboretums** or **arboreta** /-tə/) a botanical garden devoted to trees.
– ORIGIN C19: from Latin, 'a place with trees', from *arbor* 'tree'.

arboriculture /ˈɑːb(ə)rɪˌkʌltʃə, ɑːˈbɔː-/ ▪ n. the cultivation of trees and shrubs.
– DERIVATIVES **arboricultural** adj. **arboriculturist** n.

Arborio /ɑːˈbɔːrɪəʊ/ ▪ n. a variety of round-grained Italian rice used in making risotto.
– ORIGIN named after *Arborio* in northern Italy.

arborist ▪ n. a tree surgeon.

arborization /ˌɑːb(ə)rʌɪˈzeɪʃ(ə)n/ (also **-isation**) ■ n. Anatomy a fine branching structure at the end of a nerve fibre.

arbour /ˈɑːbə/ (US **arbor**) ■ n. a garden alcove with the sides and roof formed by trees or climbing plants.
– DERIVATIVES **arboured** adj.
– ORIGIN Middle English: from Old French *erbier*, from *erbe* 'grass, herb', influenced by Latin *arbor* 'tree'.

arbovirus /ˈɑːbə(ʊ)ˌvʌɪrəs/ ■ n. Medicine any of a group of viruses (e.g. that causing yellow fever) transmitted by mosquitoes, ticks, or other arthropods.
– ORIGIN 1950s: from *ar(thropod)-bo(rne)* + VIRUS.

arbutus /ɑːˈbjuːtəs, ˈɑːbjʊtəs/ ■ n. an evergreen tree or shrub of a genus that includes the strawberry tree. [Genus *Arbutus*.]
– ORIGIN from Latin.

ARC ■ abbrev. Medicine Aids-related complex.

arc /ɑːk/ ■ n. **1** a curve forming part of the circumference of a circle or other figure. ▸ a curving trajectory. ▸ [as modifier] Mathematics indicating the inverse of a trigonometrical function: *arc cosine*. **2** a luminous electrical discharge between two points. ■ v. (**arced** /ɑːkt/, **arcing** /ˈɑːkɪŋ/) **1** move with a curving trajectory. **2** [as noun **arcing**] the forming of an electric arc.
– ORIGIN Middle English: from Latin *arcus* 'bow, curve'.

arcade ■ n. **1** a covered passage with arches along one or both sides. ▸ chiefly Brit. a covered walk with shops along one or both sides. ▸ Architecture a series of arches supporting a wall. **2** short for AMUSEMENT ARCADE.
– ORIGIN C17: from Provençal *arcada*, from Latin *arcus* 'bow'.

Arcadian ■ n. **1** a native of Arcadia, a mountainous region of southern Greece. **2** poetic/literary an idealized country dweller. ■ adj. of or relating to Arcadia, especially as regarded as an ideal rustic paradise.

Arcady /ˈɑːkədi/ ■ n. poetic/literary an ideal rustic paradise.
– ORIGIN C16: from Greek *Arkadia*, a region of Greece.

arcana /ɑːˈkeɪnə/ ■ pl. n. [treated as sing. or pl.] (sing. **arcanum**) **1** secrets; mysteries. **2** either of the two groups of cards in a tarot pack: the twenty-two trumps (the major arcana) and the fifty-six suit cards (the minor arcana).
– ORIGIN C16: from Latin, neuter pl. of *arcanus* (see ARCANE).

arcane /ɑːˈkeɪn/ ■ adj. understood by few; mysterious.
– DERIVATIVES **arcanely** adv.
– ORIGIN C16: from Latin *arcanus*, from *arcere* 'to shut up', from *arca* 'chest'.

arch[1] ■ n. **1** a curved symmetrical structure spanning an opening and supporting the weight of a bridge, roof, or wall. ▸ an arch-shaped curve. **2** the inner side of the foot. ■ v. form or cause to form an arch.
– DERIVATIVES **arched** adj.
– ORIGIN Middle English: from Old French *arche*, from Latin *arcus* 'bow'.

arch[2] ■ adj. self-consciously playful or teasing.
– DERIVATIVES **archly** adv. **archness** n.
– ORIGIN C17: from ARCH-, by association with the sense 'rogue' in words such as *arch-scoundrel*.

-arch /ɑːk/ ■ comb. form (forming nouns) denoting a ruler or leader: *monarch*.
– ORIGIN Greek *arkhos* 'ruling', from *arkhein* 'to rule'.

arch- ■ comb. form chief; principal: *archbishop*.
▸ pre-eminent of its kind: *arch-enemy*.
– ORIGIN from Greek *arkhi-*, from *arkhos* 'chief'.

archaea /ɑːˈkiːə/ ■ pl. n. Biology micro-organisms which are similar to bacteria in size and simplicity of structure but constitute an ancient group intermediate between the bacteria and eukaryotes.
– DERIVATIVES **archaean** adj. & n.
– ORIGIN from Greek *arkhaios* 'primitive'.

Archaean /ɑːˈkiːən/ (US **Archean**) ■ adj. Geology relating to or denoting the earlier part of the Precambrian aeon (before about 2 500 million years ago), in which there was no life on the earth.
– ORIGIN C19: from Greek *arkhaios* 'ancient'.

archaeo- /ˈɑːkɪəʊ/ ■ comb. form relating to archaeology or prehistoric times: *archaeopteryx*.
– ORIGIN from Greek *arkhaios* 'ancient'.

archaeology (US also **archeology**) ■ n. the study of human history and prehistory through the excavation of sites and the analysis of physical remains.
– DERIVATIVES **archaeologic** adj. **archaeological** adj. **archaeologically** adv. **archaeologist** n.

archaeopteryx /ˌɑːkɪˈɒptərɪks/ ■ n. the oldest known fossil bird, of the late Jurassic period, which had feathers and wings like a bird, but teeth and a bony tail like a dinosaur.
– ORIGIN from ARCHAEO- + Greek *pterux* 'wing'.

archaic /ɑːˈkeɪɪk/ ■ adj. very old or old-fashioned. ▸ (of language) used to give an old-fashioned flavour.
▸ belonging to an early period of art or culture.
– DERIVATIVES **archaically** adv.
– ORIGIN C19: from French *archaïque*, from Greek, from *arkhaios* 'ancient'.

archaism /ˈɑːkeɪɪz(ə)m/ ■ n. a thing that is archaic, especially a word or style of art. ▸ the use of archaic features in language or art.
– ORIGIN C17: from Greek *arkhaismos*, from *arkhaios* 'ancient'.

archaize (also **-ise**) ■ v. consciously imitate an archaic word or style of art.

archangel /ˈɑːkeɪndʒ(ə)l, ɑːkˈeɪn-/ ■ n. an angel of high rank.
– DERIVATIVES **archangelic** adj.

archbishop ■ n. the chief bishop responsible for a large district.

archbishopric ■ n. the office or district of an archbishop.

archdeacon ■ n. a senior Christian cleric to whom a bishop delegates certain responsibilities.

archdeaconry ■ n. (pl. **-ies**) the office or district of an archdeacon.

archdiocese ■ n. the district for which an archbishop is responsible.
– DERIVATIVES **archdiocesan** adj.

archduchess ■ n. historical **1** the wife or widow of an archduke. **2** a daughter of the Emperor of Austria.

archduke ■ n. a chief duke, in particular (historical) the son of the Emperor of Austria.
– DERIVATIVES **archducal** adj. **archduchy** n.

Archean ■ adj. US spelling of ARCHAEAN.

archegonium /ˌɑːkɪˈɡəʊnɪəm/ ■ n. (pl. **archegonia** /-ɪə/) Botany the female sex organ in mosses, liverworts, ferns, and most conifers.
– ORIGIN C19: from Greek *arkhegonos*, from *arkhe-* 'chief' + *gonos* 'race'.

arch-enemy ■ n. a chief enemy.

archeology ■ n. US spelling of ARCHAEOLOGY.

archer ■ n. a person who shoots with a bow and arrows.
– ORIGIN Middle English: from Old French *archier*, from Latin *arcus* 'bow'.

archerfish ■ n. (pl. same or **-fishes**) a freshwater fish, native to Asia, Australia, and the Philippines, that knocks insect prey off vegetation by shooting water from its mouth. [Genus *Toxotes*: several species.]

archery ■ n. shooting with a bow and arrows.

archetype /ˈɑːkɪtʌɪp/ ■ n. **1** a very typical example. **2** an original model. **3** Psychoanalysis (in Jungian theory) a primitive mental image inherited from the earliest human ancestors and supposed to be present in the collective unconscious. **4** a recurrent motif in literature or art.
– DERIVATIVES **archetypal** adj. **archetypally** adv. **archetypical** adj.
– ORIGIN C16: from Greek *arkhetupon* 'something moulded first as a model', from *arkhe-* 'primitive' + *tupos* 'a model'.

archiepiscopal /ˌɑːkɪɪˈpɪskəp(ə)l/ ■ adj. of or relating to an archbishop.
– DERIVATIVES **archiepiscopacy** n. (pl. **-ies**). **archiepiscopate** n.

archimandrite /ˌɑːkɪˈmandrʌɪt/ ■ n. the superior of a large monastery or group of monasteries in the Orthodox Church. ▸ an honorary title given to a monastic priest.
– ORIGIN C17: from eccles. Greek *arkhimandrítēs*, from *arkhi-* 'chief' + *mandra* 'monastery'.

Archimedean screw ■ n. a device invented by the

Archimedes' principle

Greek mathematician Archimedes (c.287–212 BC) for raising water by means of a helix rotating within a tube.

Archimedes' principle /ˌɑːkɪˈmiːdiːz/ ■ n. Physics a law stating that a body immersed in a fluid is subject to an upward force equal in magnitude to the weight of fluid it displaces.

archipelago /ˌɑːkɪˈpɛləgəʊ/ ■ n. (pl. -os or -oes) an extensive group of islands.
– ORIGIN C16: from Greek *arkhi-* 'chief' + *pelagos* 'sea' (orig. a name for the Aegean Sea, notable for its large number of islands).

architect ■ n. 1 a person who designs buildings and supervises their construction. 2 a person responsible for the invention or realization of something. ■ v. Computing design and make (a program or system).
– ORIGIN C16: from French *architecte*, from Greek *arkhitektōn* 'chief builder'.

architectonic /ˌɑːkɪtɛkˈtɒnɪk/ ■ adj. 1 of or relating to architecture or architects. 2 having a clearly defined and artistically pleasing structure. ■ n. (**architectonics**) [treated as sing.] the scientific study of architecture.
– DERIVATIVES **architectonically** adv.
– ORIGIN C17: from Greek *arkhitektonikos*, from *arkhitektōn* (see ARCHITECT).

architecture ■ n. 1 the art or practice of designing and constructing buildings. ▸ the style in which a building is designed and constructed. 2 the complex structure of something. ▸ the conceptual structure and logical organization of a computer or computer-based system.
– DERIVATIVES **architectural** adj. **architecturally** adv.

architrave /ˈɑːkɪtreɪv/ ■ n. 1 (in classical architecture) a main beam resting across the tops of columns. 2 the frame around a doorway or window. ▸ a moulding round the exterior of an arch.
– ORIGIN C16: from Italian, from *archi-* 'chief' + *-trave*, from Latin *trabs* 'a beam'.

archive /ˈɑːkʌɪv/ ■ n. a collection of historical documents or records. ▸ a complete record of the data in part or all of a computer system, stored on a less frequently used medium. ■ v. place in an archive.
– DERIVATIVES **archival** adj.
– ORIGIN C17: from French *archives* (pl.), from Latin *archia*, from Greek *arkheia* 'public records'.

archivist /ˈɑːkɪvɪst/ ■ n. a person who maintains and is in charge of archives.

archosaur /ˈɑːkəsɔː/ ■ n. Zoology & Palaeontology a reptile of a large group that includes the crocodilians together with the extinct dinosaurs and pterosaurs.
– ORIGIN 1930s: from Greek *arkhos* 'chief' or *arkhōn* 'ruler' + -SAUR.

archway ■ n. a curved structure forming a passage or entrance.

-archy /ˈɑːki/ ■ comb. form (forming nouns) denoting a type of rule or government, corresponding to nouns ending in *-arch*: *monarchy*.

arc lamp (also **arc light**) ■ n. a light source using an electric arc.

arcos ■ abbrev. the inverse of a cosine.

arcsin ■ abbrev. the inverse of a sine.

arctan ■ abbrev. the inverse of a tangent.

Arctic ■ adj. 1 of or relating to the regions around the North Pole. ▸ living or growing in such regions. 2 (**arctic**) informal (of weather) very cold. ■ n. 1 (**the Arctic**) the regions around the North Pole. 2 N. Amer. a thick waterproof overshoe.
– ORIGIN Middle English: from Latin *arcticus*, from Greek *arktos* 'bear, Ursa Major, pole star'.

arcuate /ˈɑːkjʊət/ ■ adj. technical curved.
– ORIGIN Middle English: from Latin *arcuare* 'to curve'.

arcus senilis /ˌɑːkəs sɪˈnʌɪlɪs/ ■ n. Medicine a narrow opaque band encircling the cornea, common in old age.
– ORIGIN Latin, 'senile bow'.

arc welding ■ n. welding using the heat generated by an electric arc.

-ard ■ suffix 1 forming nouns such as *bollard*. 2 forming nouns having a depreciatory sense: *drunkard*.
– ORIGIN from German *-hard* 'hard, hardy'.

ardent /ˈɑːd(ə)nt/ ■ adj. 1 very enthusiastic or passionate. 2 archaic or poetic/literary burning; glowing.
– DERIVATIVES **ardency** n. **ardently** adv.
– ORIGIN Middle English: from Old French *ardant* from Latin, from *ardere* 'to burn'.

ardour /ˈɑːdə/ (US **ardor**) ■ n. great enthusiasm or passion.
– ORIGIN Middle English: from Latin *ardor*, from *ardere* 'to burn'.

arduous /ˈɑːdjʊəs/ ■ adj. difficult and tiring.
– DERIVATIVES **arduously** adv. **arduousness** n.
– ORIGIN C16: from Latin *arduus* 'steep, difficult'.

are second person singular present and first, second, third person plural present of BE.

area ■ n. 1 a region of an expanse or surface. ▸ a space allocated for a specific use. 2 a subject or range of activity. 3 the extent or measurement of a surface. 4 a sunken enclosure giving access to a basement.
– DERIVATIVES **areal** adj.
– ORIGIN C16: from Latin, 'vacant piece of level ground'.

area code ■ n. another term for DIALLING CODE.

areaway ■ n. N. Amer. 1 a sunken enclosure giving access to a basement. 2 a passageway between buildings.

areca palm /ˈarɪkə, əˈriːkə/ ■ n. a tropical Asian palm yielding astringent nuts which are chewed with betel leaves. [Genus *Areca*.]
– ORIGIN from Malayalam *áḍekka*.

arena ■ n. 1 a level area surrounded by seating, in which public events and entertainments are held. 2 a sphere of activity.
– ORIGIN C17: from Latin *harena, arena* 'sand, sand-strewn place of combat'.

arenaceous /ˌarɪˈneɪʃəs/ ■ adj. Geology consisting of sand or sand-like particles. ▸ Biology living or growing in sand.
– ORIGIN C17: from Latin, from *arena* 'sand'.

arenavirus /əˈriːnəˌvʌɪrəs/ ■ n. Medicine any of a group of RNA viruses (e.g. that causing Lassa fever) appearing to contain sand-like granules.
– ORIGIN 1970s: from Latin *arenosus* 'sandy' + VIRUS.

aren't ■ contr. 1 are not. 2 am not (only used in questions).

areola /əˈrɪːələ/ ■ n. (pl. **areolae** /-liː/) 1 Anatomy a small circular area, in particular the pigmented skin surrounding a nipple. ▸ Medicine a reddened patch around a spot or papule. 2 Biology any of the small spaces between lines or cracks on a leaf or an insect's wing.
– DERIVATIVES **areolar** adj. **areolate** adj.
– ORIGIN C17: from Latin, 'small open space', diminutive of *area* (see AREA).

areole /ˈɛːrɪəʊl/ ■ n. Biology an areola, especially a small area bearing spines or hairs on a cactus.
– ORIGIN C19: from French *aréole*, from Latin (see AREOLA).

arête /əˈrɛt, əˈreɪt/ ■ n. a sharp mountain ridge.
– ORIGIN C19: from Latin *arista* 'ear of corn, spine'.

Argand diagram /ˈɑːɡənd/ ■ n. Mathematics a graph on which complex numbers can be represented, the horizontal coordinate representing the real part of the number and the vertical coordinate the imaginary part.
– ORIGIN C20: named after the French mathematician J. R. Argand.

argent /ˈɑːdʒ(ə)nt/ ■ adj. & n. poetic/literary & Heraldry silver.
– ORIGIN Middle English: from Latin *argentum* 'silver'.

argentiferous /ˌɑːdʒ(ə)nˈtɪf(ə)rəs/ ■ adj. (of rocks or minerals) containing silver.
– ORIGIN C18: from Latin *argentum* 'silver' + -FEROUS.

Argentine ■ n. & adj. another term for ARGENTINIAN.

Argentine ant ■ n. a predatory ant native to South America and introduced elsewhere. [*Iridomyrmex humilis*.]

Argentinian /ˌɑːdʒənˈtɪnɪən/ ■ n. a native or national of Argentina, or a person of Argentinian descent. ■ adj. of or relating to Argentina.

argillaceous /ˌɑːdʒɪˈleɪʃəs/ ■ adj. Geology (of rocks or sediment) consisting of or containing clay.
– ORIGIN C17: from Latin *argilla* 'clay'.

argillite /'ɑːdʒɪlʌɪt/ ■ n. Geology a sedimentary rock formed from consolidated clay.
– ORIGIN C18: from Latin *argilla* 'clay'.

arginine /'ɑːdʒmiːn/ ■ n. Biochemistry a basic amino acid which is an essential nutrient in the diet of vertebrates.
– ORIGIN C19: from German *Arginin*, perhaps from Greek *arginoeis* 'bright-shining, white'.

Argive /'ɑːɡʌɪv, -dʒʌɪv/ ■ adj. of or relating to the ancient city of Argos in Greece. ▸ (especially in Homer) Greek. ■ n. a citizen of Argos. ▸ (especially in Homer) a Greek person.

argol /'ɑːɡ(ə)l/ ■ n. tartar obtained from wine fermentation.
– ORIGIN Middle English: from Anglo-Norman French *argoile*.

argon /'ɑːɡɒn/ ■ n. the chemical element of atomic number 18, an inert gaseous element of the noble gas group. (Symbol: **Ar**)
– ORIGIN C19: from Greek, neuter of *argos* 'idle', from *a-* 'without' + *ergon* 'work'.

argot /'ɑːɡəʊ/ ■ n. the jargon or slang of a particular group.
– ORIGIN C19: from French.

arguable ■ adj. able to be argued or asserted. ▸ open to disagreement.
– DERIVATIVES **arguably** adv.

argue ■ v. (**argues**, **argued**, **arguing**) 1 exchange diverging or opposite views heatedly. 2 give reasons or cite evidence in support of something.
– PHRASES **argue the toss** informal, chiefly Brit. dispute a decision already made.
– DERIVATIVES **arguer** n.
– ORIGIN Middle English: from Old French *arguer*, from Latin *arguere* 'make clear, prove, accuse'.

argument ■ n. 1 a heated exchange of diverging or opposite views. 2 a set of reasons given in support of something. 3 Mathematics & Logic an independent variable associated with a function or proposition and determining its value, e.g. *x* in *y* = F(*x*). 4 Linguistics any of the noun phrases in a clause that are related directly to the verb. 5 archaic a summary of the subject matter of a book.
– ORIGIN Middle English: from Latin *argumentum*, from *arguere* 'make clear, prove, accuse'.

argumentation ■ n. the action of reasoning systematically in support of something.

argumentative ■ adj. 1 given to arguing. 2 using or characterized by systematic reasoning.
– DERIVATIVES **argumentatively** adv. **argumentativeness** n.

argy-bargy /ˌɑːdʒɪˈbɑːdʒi, ˌɑːɡrˈbɑːɡi/ ■ n. (pl. **-ies**) informal, chiefly Brit. noisy quarrelling.
– ORIGIN C19: rhyming jingle based on **ARGUE**.

argyle /ɑːˈɡʌɪl/ ■ n. a pattern on knitted garments composed of coloured diamonds on a plain background.
– ORIGIN 1940s: from the *Argyll* branch of the Scottish Campbell clan, on whose tartan the pattern is based.

arhythmic ■ adj. variant spelling of **ARRHYTHMIC**.

aria /'ɑːrɪə/ ■ n. Music a long accompanied song for a solo voice in an opera or oratorio.
– ORIGIN C18: from Latin *aer* 'air'.

Arian /'ɛːrɪən/ ■ n. 1 an adherent of Arianism. 2 (also **Arien**) a person born under the sign of Aries. ■ adj. 1 of or concerning Arianism. 2 (also **Arien**) of or relating to a person born under the sign of Aries.

-arian ■ suffix (forming adjectives and corresponding nouns) having a concern or belief in a specified thing: *vegetarian*.
– ORIGIN from the Latin suffix *-arius*.

Arianism ■ n. Christian Church the main heresy denying the divinity of Christ, originating with the Alexandrian priest Arius (*c*.250–*c*.336).

arid /'arɪd/ ■ adj. 1 (of land or a climate) very dry; having little or no rain. 2 uninteresting: *arid prose*.
– DERIVATIVES **aridity** n. **aridly** adv. **aridness** n.
– ORIGIN C17: from Latin *aridus*, from *arere* 'be dry or parched'.

aridisol /əˈrɪdɪsɒl/ ■ n. Soil Science a saline or alkaline soil with very little organic matter, characteristic of arid regions.

Arien ■ n. & adj. variant spelling of **ARIAN** (in sense 2).

Aries /'ɛːriːz/ ■ n. 1 Astronomy a small constellation (the Ram), said to represent the ram whose Golden Fleece was sought by Jason and the Argonauts. 2 Astrology the first sign of the zodiac, which the sun enters about 20 March.
– PHRASES **First Point of Aries** Astronomy the point on the celestial sphere (formerly in Aries but now in Pisces owing to precession) where the path of the sun crosses the celestial equator at the vernal equinox.
– ORIGIN from Latin.

aright ■ adv. dialect correctly; properly.
– ORIGIN Old English *on riht*, *ariht* (see **a-²** + **RIGHT**).

aril /'arɪl/ ■ n. Botany an extra seed covering, typically coloured and hairy or fleshy.
– ORIGIN C18: from modern Latin *arillus*.

-arious ■ suffix forming adjectives such as *gregarious*.
– ORIGIN from the Latin suffix *-arius*.

arise ■ v. (past **arose**; past part. **arisen**) 1 originate or become apparent. ▸ (**arise from/out of**) occur as a result of. 2 formal or poetic/literary get or stand up.
– ORIGIN Old English *ārīsan*, from *ā-* 'away' (as an intensifier) + **RISE**.

aristea ■ n. a southern African perennial of the iris family which bears blue star-shaped flowers on tall spikes, widely grown as an ornamental. [*Aristea major* and related species.]

aristocracy ■ n. (pl. **-ies**) [treated as sing. or pl.] the highest class in some societies, comprising people of noble birth with hereditary titles. ▸ a form of government in which power is held by the nobility.
– ORIGIN C15: from Greek *aristokratia*, from *aristos* 'best' + *-kratia* 'power'.

aristocrat /'arɪstəkrat, əˈrɪst-/ ■ n. a member of the aristocracy.
– DERIVATIVES **aristocratic** adj. **aristocratically** adv.

Aristotelian /ˌarɪstəˈtiːlɪən/ ■ adj. of or relating to the Greek philosopher Aristotle (384–322 BC) or his theories. ■ n. a student or follower of Aristotle or his philosophy.

Aristotelian logic ■ n. the traditional system of logic expounded by Aristotle and developed in the Middle Ages.

Aristotle's lantern /ˈarɪstɒt(ə)l/ ■ n. Zoology a conical structure of calcareous plates and muscles supporting the teeth of a sea urchin.

arithmetic ■ n. /əˈrɪθmətɪk/ the branch of mathematics concerned with the properties and manipulation of numbers. ▸ the use of numbers in counting and calculation. ■ adj. /ˌarɪθˈmɛtɪk/ of or relating to arithmetic.
– DERIVATIVES **arithmetical** adj. **arithmetically** adv. **arithmetician** n.
– ORIGIN Middle English: from Greek *arithmētikē* (*tekhnē*) '(art) of counting', from *arithmos* 'number'.

arithmetic mean ■ n. see **MEAN³** (sense 1).

arithmetic progression (also **arithmetic series**) ■ n. a sequence of numbers in which each differs from the preceding one by a constant quantity (e.g. 1, 2, 3, 4, etc.; 9, 7, 5, 3, etc.).

arithmetize /əˈrɪθmətʌɪz/ (also **-ise**) ■ v. express arithmetically.

-arium /'ɛːrɪəm/ ■ suffix forming nouns usually denoting a place: *planetarium*.
– ORIGIN from Latin, neuter of *-arius*, adjectival ending.

ark ■ n. 1 (in the Bible) the ship built by Noah to save his family and of every kind of animal from the Flood. 2 short for **ARK OF THE COVENANT**. ▸ (also **Holy Ark**) a chest or cupboard housing the Torah scrolls in a synagogue.
– PHRASES **out of the ark** informal very old or old-fashioned.
– ORIGIN Old English, from Latin *arca* 'chest'.

Ark of the Covenant (also **Ark of the Testimony**) ■ n. the wooden chest which contained the tablets of the laws of the ancient Israelites.

arkose /'ɑːkəʊs, -z/ ■ n. Geology a coarse-grained sandstone which is at least 25 per cent feldspar.
– DERIVATIVES **arkosic** adj.
– ORIGIN C19: prob. from Greek *arkhaios* 'ancient'.

arlie ■ n. S. African a child's word for a marble.
– ORIGIN C20: from obsolete *ally* 'choice marble', perhaps a diminutive of 'alabaster', or from Afrikaans *albaster* 'marble'.

arm¹ ■ v. **1** supply with weapons. ▸ provide with essential equipment for a task or situation. **2** activate the fuse of (a bomb) so that it is ready to explode.
– ORIGIN Middle English: from Latin *armare*, from *arma* 'armour, arms'.

arm² ■ n. **1** each of the two upper limbs of the human body from the shoulder to the hand. ▸ a limb of an octopus, starfish, or other animal. **2** a side part of a chair supporting a sitter's arm. **3** a narrow strip of water or land projecting from a larger body. **4** a branch or division of an organization. ▸ one of the types of troops of which an army is composed. **5** Mathematics each of the lines enclosing an angle. **6** S. African informal a thick roll of cannabis.
– PHRASES **arm in arm** with arms linked. **cost an arm and a leg** informal be extremely expensive. **would give one's right arm for** informal wish for desperately. **in arms** (of a baby) too young to walk. **keep at arm's length** avoid intimacy or close contact with. **the long** (or **strong**) **arm of the law** the far-reaching power of the law. **put the arm on** N. Amer. informal attempt to coerce (someone) to do something. **with open arms** with great affection or enthusiasm.
– DERIVATIVES **armful** n. (pl. **-fuls**). **armless** adj.
– ORIGIN Old English, of Germanic origin.

armada /ɑːˈmɑːdə/ ■ n. a fleet of warships.
– ORIGIN C16: from Latin *armata*, from *armare* 'to arm'.

armadillo /ˌɑːməˈdɪləʊ/ ■ n. (pl. **-os**) a nocturnal insectivorous mammal native to Central and South America, with large claws and a body covered in bony plates. [Family Dasypodidae: numerous species.]
– ORIGIN C16: from Spanish *armado* 'armed man', from Latin *armare* 'to arm'.

Armageddon /ˌɑːməˈɡɛd(ə)n/ ■ n. **1** (in the New Testament) the last battle between good and evil before the Day of Judgement. **2** a catastrophic conflict.
– ORIGIN from Hebrew *har měgiddōn* 'hill of Megiddo' (Revelation 16:16).

Armagnac /ˈɑːmənjak/ ■ n. a type of brandy made in Aquitaine in SW France.
– ORIGIN from the name of a district in Aquitaine.

armament /ˈɑːməm(ə)nt/ ■ n. **1** (also **armaments**) military weapons and equipment. **2** the process of equipping military forces for war.
– ORIGIN C17: from Latin *armamentum*, from *armare* 'to arm'.

armature /ˈɑːmətʃə, -tj(ʊ)ə/ ■ n. **1** the rotating coil or coils of a dynamo or electric motor. ▸ any moving part of an electrical machine in which a voltage is induced by a magnetic field. **2** a framework on which a clay sculpture is moulded.
– ORIGIN Middle English: from Latin *armatura* 'armour', from *armare* 'to arm'.

armband ■ n. **1** a band worn around the upper arm to hold up a shirtsleeve or as a form of identification. **2** an inflatable plastic band worn around the upper arm as a swimming aid.

armchair ■ n. **1** a large, comfortable chair with side supports for the sitter's arms. **2** [as modifier] lacking direct experience of or involvement in a particular subject or activity: *an armchair traveller*.

Armco /ˈɑːmkəʊ/ ■ n. trademark a very pure soft iron used for roadside crash barriers.
– ORIGIN C20: acronym from *American Rolling Mill Company*.

armed ■ adj. **1** equipped with or involving a firearm or firearms. **2** Heraldry having claws or a beak of a specified tincture.

armed forces (also **armed services**) ■ pl. n. a country's army, navy, and air force.

Armenian /ɑːˈmiːnɪən/ ■ n. **1** a native of Armenia or a person of Armenian descent. **2** the Indo-European language of Armenia. ■ adj. of or relating to Armenia, its language, or its Church.

armhole ■ n. an opening in a garment through which the wearer puts an arm.

armiger /ˈɑːmɪdʒə/ ■ n. a person entitled to heraldic arms.
– ORIGIN C16: Latin, 'bearing arms'.

armillary sphere ■ n. a revolving model of the celestial sphere constructed from metal rings representing the equator, the tropics, etc.
– ORIGIN C17: from *armillaris* 'relating to an *armilla*', a similar instrument used by ancient astronomers, from Latin *armilla* 'bracelet'.

Arminian /ɑːˈmɪnɪən/ ■ adj. of or relating to the doctrines of Jacobus Arminius (1560–1609), a Dutch Protestant theologian who rejected the Calvinist doctrine of predestination. ■ n. an adherent of these doctrines.
– DERIVATIVES **Arminianism** n.

armistice /ˈɑːmɪstɪs/ ■ n. a truce.
– ORIGIN C18: from Latin *arma* 'arms' + *-stitium* 'stoppage'.

Armistice Day ■ n. the anniversary of the armistice of 11 November 1918, now replaced by Remembrance Sunday.

armlet ■ n. a bracelet worn round the upper arm.

armlock ■ n. a method of restraining someone by holding their arm tightly behind their back.

armoire /ɑːˈmwɑː/ ■ n. a cupboard or wardrobe.
– ORIGIN C16: from Old French *armarie*, from Latin *armarium* 'closet'.

armor ■ n. US spelling of **ARMOUR**.

armorer ■ n. US spelling of **ARMOURER**.

armory¹ /ˈɑːməri/ ■ n. heraldry.
– DERIVATIVES **armorial** adj.
– ORIGIN Middle English: from Old French *armoierie* (see **ARMOURY**).

armory² ■ n. US spelling of **ARMOURY**.

armour (US **armor**) ■ n. **1** the metal coverings formerly worn by soldiers to protect the body in battle. **2** (also **armour plate**) the tough metal layer covering a military vehicle or ship. ▸ military vehicles collectively. **3** the protective layer or shell of some animals and plants.
– DERIVATIVES **armoured** adj. **armour-plated** adj.
– ORIGIN Middle English: from Old French *armure*, from Latin *armare* 'to arm'.

armourer (US **armorer**) ■ n. **1** a maker or supplier of weapons or armour. **2** an official in charge of the arms of a warship or regiment.

armoury (US **armory**) ■ n. (pl. **-ies**) **1** a store or supply of arms. **2** an array of resources available for a particular purpose.
– ORIGIN Middle English: from Old French *armoierie*, from *armoier* 'to blazon', from Latin *arma* 'arms'.

armpit ■ n. a hollow under the arm at the shoulder.
– PHRASES **up to one's armpits** deeply involved in something unpleasant.

armrest ■ n. an arm of a chair.

arms ■ pl. n. **1** weapons; armaments. **2** distinctive emblems originally borne on shields in battle and now forming heraldic insignia.
– PHRASES **a call to arms** a call to make ready for fighting. **under arms** equipped and ready for war or battle. **up in arms** (**about** or **over**) protesting vigorously (about).
– ORIGIN Middle English: from Latin *arma*.

arms control ■ n. international disarmament or arms limitation, especially by mutual consent.

arms race ■ n. a competition between nations for superiority in the development and accumulation of weapons.

arm-twisting ■ n. informal persuasion by the use of physical force or moral pressure.

arm-wrestling ■ n. a contest in which two people sit opposite each other with one elbow resting on a table and try to force each other's arm down on to the table.
– DERIVATIVES **arm-wrestle** v.

army ■ n. (pl. **-ies**) [treated as sing. or pl.] **1** an organized military force equipped for fighting on land. **2** a large number of similar people or things.
– ORIGIN Middle English: from Latin *armare* 'to arm'.

army ant ■ n. a blind nomadic tropical ant that forages in large columns, preying on insects. [Subfamily Dorylinae: many species.]

army worm ■ n. the larva of some moths of the Noctuidae family, which feed on crops and move en masse when the food is exhausted. [*Spodoptera exempta* and other species.]

arnica /ˈɑːnɪkə/ ■ n. a preparation made from arnica, a plant of the daisy family, used medicinally for the treatment of bruises.
– ORIGIN C18: of unknown origin.

aroma ■ n. a pleasant and distinctive smell.
– ORIGIN Middle English: from Greek *arōma* 'spice'.

aromatherapy ■ n. the use of aromatic plant extracts and essential oils for therapeutic purposes.
– DERIVATIVES **aromatherapeutic** adj. **aromatherapist** n.

aromatic ■ adj. 1 having an aroma. 2 Chemistry (of an organic compound) containing a planar unsaturated ring of atoms which is stabilized by an interaction of the bonds forming the ring. ■ n. an aromatic plant, substance, or compound.
– DERIVATIVES **aromatically** adv. **aromaticity** n. (Chemistry).

aromatize (also **-ise**) ■ v. Chemistry convert (a compound) into an aromatic structure.

arose past of ARISE.

around ■ adv. 1 located or situated on every side. 2 so as to face in the opposite direction. 3 in or to many places throughout a locality. 4 here and there. 5 available or present. 6 approximately. ■ prep. 1 on every side of. 2 in or to many places throughout (a locality). 3 so as to encircle or embrace. ▶ following an approximately circular route.
– ORIGIN Middle English: from A-² + ROUND.

arouse ■ v. 1 evoke (a feeling or response). ▶ provoke to anger or strong emotions. ▶ excite sexually. 2 awaken from sleep.
– DERIVATIVES **arousal** n.
– ORIGIN C16: from ROUSE, on the pattern of *rise*, *arise*.

arpeggio /ɑːˈpɛdʒɪəʊ/ ■ n. (pl. **-os**) Music the notes of a chord played in rapid succession.
– ORIGIN Italian, from *arpeggiare* 'play the harp', from *arpa* 'harp'.

arquebus /ˈɑːkwɪbəs/ ■ n. variant spelling of HARQUEBUS.

arr. ■ abbrev. 1 (of a piece of music) arranged by. 2 (in a transport timetable) arrives.

arrack /ˈarək, əˈrak/ (also **arak**) ■ n. an alcoholic spirit made from the sap of the coco palm or from rice.
– ORIGIN C17: from Arabic *'araḳ* 'sweat', from *'arak al-tamr*, an alcoholic spirit made from dates.

arraign /əˈreɪn/ ■ v. call before a court to answer a criminal charge.
– DERIVATIVES **arraignment** n.
– ORIGIN Middle English: from Old French *araisnier*, from Latin *ad-* 'to' + *ratio(n-)* 'reason, account'.

arrange ■ v. 1 put in a neat, attractive, or required order. 2 organize or plan. ▶ reach agreement about an action or event in advance. 3 Music adapt (a composition) for performance with instruments or voices other than those originally specified.
– DERIVATIVES **arrangeable** adj. **arranger** n.
– ORIGIN Middle English: from Latin *ad* 'to, at' + *rangier* (see RANGE).

arrangement ■ n. 1 the action, process, or result of arranging. 2 a plan for a future event. 3 Music an arranged composition.

arrant /ˈar(ə)nt/ ■ adj. utter; complete: *what arrant nonsense!*
– DERIVATIVES **arrantly** adv.
– ORIGIN Middle English: var. of ERRANT.

arras /ˈarəs/ ■ n. a tapestry wall hanging.
– ORIGIN Middle English: named after the French town *Arras*.

array /əˈreɪ/ ■ n. 1 an impressive display or range of a particular thing. 2 an ordered arrangement of troops. 3 Mathematics an arrangement of quantities or symbols in rows and columns; a matrix. 4 Computing an ordered set of related elements. 5 poetic/literary elaborate or beautiful clothing. ■ v. 1 display or arrange in a neat or impressive way. 2 (**be arrayed in**) be elaborately clothed in.

59

– ORIGIN Middle English: from Latin *ad-* 'towards' + a Germanic base meaning 'prepare'.

arrears ■ pl. n. payments or debts that are outstanding and due.
– PHRASES **in arrears** behind with paying money that is owed. ▶ (of wages or rent) paid at the end of each period of work or occupation.
– ORIGIN Middle English: from Old French *arere*, from medieval Latin *adretro*, from *ad-* 'towards' + *retro* 'backwards'.

arrest ■ v. 1 seize (someone) by legal authority and take them into custody. ▶ seize and detain (a ship) by legal authority. 2 stop or check (progress or a process). 3 [usu. as adj. **arresting**] attract the attention of. ■ n. 1 the action of arresting. 2 a sudden cessation of motion.
– DERIVATIVES **arrestee** n. (chiefly N. Amer.). **arrestingly** adv.
– ORIGIN Middle English: from Old French *arester*, from Latin *ad-* 'at, to' + *restare* 'remain, stop'.

arrhythmia /əˈrɪðmɪə/ ■ n. Medicine a condition in which the heart beats with an irregular or abnormal rhythm.
– ORIGIN C19: from Greek, from *a-* 'without' + *rhuthmos* (see RHYTHM).

arrhythmic (also **arhythmic**) ■ adj. not rhythmic.
▶ Medicine relating to or suffering from cardiac arrhythmia.
– DERIVATIVES **arrhythmical** adj. **arrhythmically** adv.

arris /ˈarɪs/ ■ n. Architecture a sharp edge formed by the meeting of two flat or curved surfaces.
– ORIGIN C17: from French *areste* 'sharp ridge', earlier form of ARÊTE.

arrive ■ v. 1 reach a destination. 2 be brought or delivered. 3 (of a particular moment) come about. 4 (**arrive at**) reach (a conclusion or decision). 5 informal become successful and well known.
– DERIVATIVES **arrival** n.
– ORIGIN Middle English: from Old French *ariver*, from Latin *ad-* 'to' + *ripa* 'shore'.

arriviste /ˌariːˈviːst/ ■ n. a person bent on improving their social or financial status; a parvenu.
– DERIVATIVES **arrivisme** /ˌariːˈviːzm(ə)/ n.
– ORIGIN C20: from French *arriver* (see ARRIVE).

arrogant ■ adj. having an exaggerated sense of one's own importance or abilities.
– DERIVATIVES **arrogance** n. **arrogantly** adv.
– ORIGIN Middle English: from Latin *arrogare* (see ARROGATE).

arrogate /ˈarəgeɪt/ ■ v. take or claim for oneself without justification.
– DERIVATIVES **arrogation** n.
– ORIGIN C16: from Latin *arrogare* 'claim for oneself', from *ad-* 'to' + *rogare* 'ask'.

arrondissement /əˈrɒndiːsmɑ̃, ˌarɒ̃ˈdiːsmɑ̃/ ■ n. (in France) a subdivision of a local government department.
▶ an administrative district of Paris.
– ORIGIN French, from *arrondir* 'make round'.

arrow ■ n. a stick with a sharp pointed head, designed to be shot from a bow. ▶ a symbol resembling this, used to show direction or position. ■ v. move swiftly and directly.
– DERIVATIVES **arrowed** adj.
– ORIGIN Old English, from Old Norse.

arrowhead ■ n. 1 the pointed end of an arrow. 2 Geometry a quadrilateral in which one internal angle is more than 180°.

arrowroot ■ n. a fine-grained starch made from a herbaceous Caribbean plant (*Maranta arundinacea*), used in cookery and medicine.
– ORIGIN C17: from Arawak *aru-aru* 'meal of meals' by association with ARROW and ROOT¹, the plant's tubers being used to absorb poison from arrow wounds.

arse vulgar slang ■ n. a person's buttocks or anus. ■ v. (**arse about/around**) behave in a stupid way.
– ORIGIN Old English, of Germanic origin.

arsenal ■ n. a store of weapons and ammunition. ▶ a military establishment where weapons and ammunition are made and stored.
– ORIGIN C16 (in the sense 'a dockyard'): from French, or

arsenic

from obsolete Italian *arzanale*, based on Arabic *dār-aṣ-ṣinā'a*, from *dār* 'house' + *al-* '(of) the' + *sinā'a* 'art, industry'.

arsenic /'ɑːs(ə)nɪk/ ■ n. the chemical element of atomic number 33, a brittle steel-grey semimetal with many highly poisonous compounds. (Symbol: **As**)
– DERIVATIVES **arsenical** adj. **arsenide** n.
– ORIGIN Middle English: from Greek *arsenikon*, from Arabic *al-zarnīk*.

arsine /'ɑːsiːn/ ■ n. Chemistry a poisonous gas made by the reaction of some arsenic compounds with acids. [AsH₃.]
– ORIGIN C19: from ARSENIC.

arson ■ n. the criminal act of deliberately setting fire to property.
– DERIVATIVES **arsonist** n.
– ORIGIN C17: from medieval Latin *arsio(n-)*, from Latin *ardere* 'to burn'.

art¹ ■ n. **1** the expression or application of creative skill and imagination, especially through a visual medium such as painting or sculpture. ▸ works produced in this way. **2** (**the arts**) the various branches of creative activity, such as painting, music, literature, and dance. **3** (**arts**) subjects of study primarily concerned with human creativity and social life (as contrasted with scientific or technical subjects). **4** a skill at doing a specified thing.
– ORIGIN Middle English: from Latin *ars, art-*.

art² archaic or dialect second person singular present of BE.

art deco /'dɛkəʊ/ ■ n. a style of decorative art characterized by precise and boldly delineated geometric shapes.
– ORIGIN 1960s: from French *art décoratif* 'decorative art'.

artefact /'ɑːtɪfakt/ (US **artifact**) ■ n. **1** an object made by a human being. **2** something observed in a scientific investigation that is not naturally present but occurs as a result of the investigative procedure.
– DERIVATIVES **artefactual** adj.
– ORIGIN C19: from Latin *arte* 'by or using art' + *factum* 'something made'.

artemisia /,ɑːtɪ'mɪzɪə/ ■ n. an aromatic or bitter-tasting plant of a genus that includes wormwood, some species of which are used in herbal medicine. [Genus *Artemisia*.]
– ORIGIN Middle English: from Greek, 'wormwood', named after the goddess Artemis.

arterial /ɑː'tɪərɪəl/ ■ adj. **1** relating to an artery or arteries. **2** denoting an important route in a system of roads, railways, or rivers.

arterialized (also **-ised**) ■ adj. Physiology (of blood) converted from venous to arterial by oxygenation.
– DERIVATIVES **arterialization** (also **-isation**) n.

arterio- ■ comb. form of or relating to the arteries: *arteriosclerosis*.

arteriography /ɑː,tɪərɪ'ɒɡrəfi/ ■ n. Medicine radiography of an artery, carried out after injection of a radiopaque substance.

arteriole /ɑː'tɪərɪəʊl/ ■ n. Anatomy a small branch of an artery leading into capillaries.
– DERIVATIVES **arteriolar** adj.
– ORIGIN C19: from French *artériole*, diminutive of *artère* (see ARTERY).

arteriosclerosis /ɑː,tɪərɪəʊskliə'rəʊsɪs, -sklə-/ ■ n. Medicine thickening and hardening of the walls of the arteries.
– DERIVATIVES **arteriosclerotic** adj.

artery ■ n. (pl. **-ies**) **1** any of the muscular-walled tubes forming part of the circulation system by which blood is conveyed from the heart to all parts of the body. **2** an important route in a traffic or transport system.
– DERIVATIVES **arteritis** n.
– ORIGIN Middle English: from Greek *artēria*, prob. from *airein* 'raise'.

artesian /ɑː'tiːzɪən, -ʒ(ə)n/ ■ adj. relating to or denoting a well that is bored perpendicularly into water-bearing strata lying at an angle, so that water is supplied by natural pressure.
– ORIGIN C19: from French *artésien* 'from Artois', a region in France.

Artex /'ɑːtɛks/ ■ n. trademark a kind of plaster applied to walls and ceilings to give a textured finish.
– ORIGIN 1950s: blend of ART¹ and TEXTURE.

art form ■ n. a conventionally established form of artistic composition, such as the novel.

artful ■ adj. cunningly clever or skilful.
– DERIVATIVES **artfully** adv. **artfulness** n.

art history ■ n. the academic study of the history and development of the visual arts.
– DERIVATIVES **art historian** n.

art house ■ n. a cinema which shows artistic or experimental films.

arthralgia /ɑː'θraldʒə/ ■ n. Medicine pain in a joint.
– ORIGIN C19: from Greek *arthron* 'joint' + -ALGIA.

arthritis /ɑː'θrʌɪtɪs/ ■ n. a disease causing painful inflammation and stiffness of the joints.
– DERIVATIVES **arthritic** adj. & n.
– ORIGIN C16: from Greek, from *arthron* 'joint'.

arthro- ■ comb. form of a joint; relating to joints: *arthroscope*.
– ORIGIN from Greek *arthron* 'joint'.

Arthropoda /,ɑː'θrəpəʊdə/ ■ pl. n. Zoology a large phylum of invertebrate animals having a segmented body, external skeleton, and jointed limbs, including insects, spiders, and crustaceans.
– DERIVATIVES **arthropod** /'ɑːθrəpɒd/ n.
– ORIGIN from Greek *arthron* 'joint' + *pous, pod-* 'foot'.

arthroscope /'ɑːθrəskəʊp/ ■ n. Medicine an instrument for inspecting or operating on the interior of a joint.
– DERIVATIVES **arthroscopic** adj. **arthroscopy** n.

Arthurian /ɑː'θjʊərɪən/ ■ adj. of or relating to the reign of the legendary King Arthur of Britain.

artichoke /'ɑːtɪtʃəʊk/ ■ n. **1** a plant with large, thistle-like flower heads. [*Cynara scolymus*.] **2** (also **globe artichoke**) the unopened flower head of this plant, of which the heart and the fleshy bases of the bracts are edible. **3** see JERUSALEM ARTICHOKE.
– ORIGIN C16: from northern Italian *articiocco*, from Arabic *al-karšūfa*.

article ■ n. **1** a particular object. **2** a piece of writing included with others in a newspaper or magazine. **3** a separate clause or paragraph of a legal document. **4** (**articles**) a period of training with a firm as an attorney or accountant. ▸ the terms on which crew members take service on a ship. **5** Grammar the definite or indefinite article. ■ v. bind by articles in order to become qualified.
– PHRASES **an article of faith** a firmly held belief.
– ORIGIN Middle English: from Latin *articulus* 'small connecting part', diminutive of *artus* 'joint'.

articled clerk ■ n. a trainee attorney or accountant.

articulate ■ adj. /ɑː'tɪkjʊlət/ **1** fluent and clear in speech. **2** technical having joints or jointed segments. ▸ Zoology denoting a brachiopod which has projections and sockets that form a hinge joining the two halves of the shell. ■ v. /ɑː'tɪkjʊleɪt/ **1** pronounce (words) distinctly. ▸ clearly express (an idea or feeling). **2** form a joint. ▸ (**be articulated**) be connected by joints.
– DERIVATIVES **articulable** adj. **articulacy** n. **articulated** adj. **articulately** adv. **articulateness** n. **articulatory** adj.
– ORIGIN C16: from Latin *articulare* 'divide into joints, utter distinctly', from *articulus* (see ARTICLE).

articulation ■ n. **1** the action of articulating. ▸ Music clarity in the production of successive notes. ▸ Phonetics the formation of a speech sound by constriction of the air flow in the vocal organs. **2** the state of being jointed. ▸ a specified joint.

artifact ■ n. US spelling of ARTEFACT.

artifice /'ɑːtɪfɪs/ ■ n. clever devices or expedients, especially to trick or deceive others.
– ORIGIN Middle English: from Latin *artificium*, from *ars* 'art' + *facere* 'make'.

artificer /ɑː'tɪfɪsə/ ■ n. a skilled mechanic in the armed forces.

artificial ■ adj. **1** made as a copy of something natural. **2** contrived or affected. **3** Bridge (of a bid) conventional as opposed to natural.
– DERIVATIVES **artificiality** n. **artificially** adv.
– ORIGIN Middle English: from Latin *artificialis*, from *artificium* (see ARTIFICE).

VOWELS a cat ɑː arm ɛ bed eː hair ə ago əː her ɪ sit i cosy iː see ɒ hot ɔː saw ʌ run

artificial horizon ▪ n. a gyroscopic instrument or a fluid surface providing the pilot of an aircraft with a horizontal reference plane for navigational measurement when the natural horizon is obscured.

artificial insemination ▪ n. the veterinary or medical procedure of injecting semen into the vagina or uterus.

artificial intelligence ▪ n. the performance by computer systems of tasks normally requiring human intelligence, such as visual perception or decision-making.

artificial respiration ▪ n. the restoration or maintenance of someone's breathing by manual, mechanical, or mouth-to-mouth methods.

artillery /ɑːˈtɪləri/ ▪ n. (pl. **-ies**) large-calibre guns used in warfare on land. ▸ a branch of the armed forces trained to use artillery.
– DERIVATIVES **artillerist** n.
– ORIGIN Middle English: from Old French *artillerie*, from *artiller* 'equip, arm', from *a-* + *tire* 'rank, order'.

Artiodactyla /ˌɑːtɪə(ʊ)ˈdaktɪlə/ ▪ pl. n. Zoology an order of mammals that comprises the ruminants, camels, pigs, and hippopotamuses (the even-toed ungulates).
– DERIVATIVES **artiodactyl** n. & adj.
– ORIGIN from Greek *artios* 'even' + *daktulos* 'finger, toe'.

artisan /ˌɑːtɪˈzan, ˈɑːtɪzan/ ▪ n. a skilled worker who makes things by hand.
– DERIVATIVES **artisanal** adj.
– ORIGIN C16: from Italian *artigiano*, from Latin *artire* 'instruct in the arts'.

artist ▪ n. 1 a person who paints or draws as a profession or hobby. ▸ a person who practises or performs any of the creative arts. 2 informal a habitual practitioner of a specified activity: *a con artist*.
– DERIVATIVES **artistry** n.
– ORIGIN C16: from Italian *artista*, from Latin *ars*, *art-* 'art'.

artiste /ɑːˈtiːst/ ▪ n. a professional entertainer, especially a singer or dancer.
– ORIGIN C19: from French (see **ARTIST**).

artistic ▪ adj. 1 having or revealing natural creative skill. 2 relating to or characteristic of art or artists.
– DERIVATIVES **artistically** adv.

artless ▪ adj. 1 without guile or pretension. 2 clumsy.
– DERIVATIVES **artlessly** adv.

art nouveau /ˌɑː(t) nuːˈvəʊ/ ▪ n. a style of decorative art and architecture characterized by intricate linear designs and flowing curves.
– ORIGIN C20: from French, 'new art'.

arts and crafts ▪ pl. n. decorative design and handicraft.

artwork ▪ n. illustrations or other non-textual material prepared for inclusion in a publication.

arty (chiefly N. Amer. also **artsy**) ▪ adj. (**-ier**, **-iest**) informal artistic or interested in the arts, especially in a pretentious or affected way.
– DERIVATIVES **artiness** n.

arty-farty (also **artsy-fartsy**) ▪ adj. informal pretentiously or affectedly artistic.

arugula /əˈruːɡjʊlə/ ▪ n. N. Amer. the salad vegetable rocket.
– ORIGIN 1970s: from Italian *arucula*, from *rucola*, diminutive of *ruca* **ROCKET**².

arum /ˈɛːrəm/ ▪ n. a plant of a large family with typically arrow-shaped leaves and a broad leafy spathe enclosing a club-shaped spadix. [*Arum maculatum* and other species, family Araceae.]
– ORIGIN Middle English: from Greek *aron*.

arum lily ▪ n. a tall lily-like African plant which bears a large showy spathe. [Genus *Zantedeschia*.]

ARV ▪ abbrev. antiretroviral.

-ary¹ ▪ suffix 1 forming adjectives such as *budgetary*. 2 forming nouns such as *dictionary*.
– ORIGIN from Latin *-arius* 'connected with'.

-ary² ▪ suffix forming adjectives such as *capillary*.
– ORIGIN from Latin *-aris* 'relating to'.

Aryan /ˈɛːrɪən/ ▪ n. 1 a member of a people speaking an Indo-European language who invaded northern India in the 2nd millennium BC. 2 the language of this people. 3 (in Nazi ideology) a person of Caucasian race not of Jewish descent. ▪ adj. relating to or denoting the Aryan people or their language.
– ORIGIN from Sanskrit *ārya* 'noble'.

aryl /ˈarʌɪl, -rɪl/ ▪ n. [as modifier] Chemistry of or denoting a radical derived from an aromatic hydrocarbon by removal of a hydrogen atom.
– ORIGIN C20: from **AROMATIC** + **-YL**.

As ▪ symb. the chemical element arsenic.

as /az, əz/ ▪ adv. used in comparisons to refer to the extent or degree of something. ▸ used to emphasize an amount. ▪ conj. 1 used to indicate simultaneous occurrence. 2 used to indicate by comparison the way that something happens. 3 because. 4 even though. ▪ prep. 1 used to refer to the function or character of someone or something. 2 during the time of being.
– PHRASES **as for** (or **to**) with regard to. **as from** (or **of**) chiefly Brit. from a particular time or date. **as if** (or **though**) as would be the case if. **as** (**it**) **is** in the existing circumstances. **as yet** until now or that time.
– ORIGIN Middle English: from Old English *alswā* 'similarly'.

as- ▪ prefix variant spelling of **AD-** assimilated before *s* (as in *assemble*).

asafoetida /ˌasəˈfiːtɪdə, -ˈfɛt-/ (US **asafetida**) ▪ n. 1 a fetid resinous gum obtained from the roots of a herbaceous plant, used in herbal medicine and Indian cooking. 2 a plant of the parsley family, from which this gum is obtained. [*Ferula assa-foetida*.]
– ORIGIN Middle English: from Persian *azā* 'mastic' + *foetida* (see **FETID**).

Asante ▪ n. variant spelling of **ASHANTI**.

asap ▪ abbrev. as soon as possible.

asbestos /azˈbɛstɒs, as-, -təs/ ▪ n. a highly heat-resistant fibrous silicate mineral able to be woven into fabrics, used in brake linings and in fire-resistant and insulating materials.
– ORIGIN C17: from Greek *asbestos* 'unquenchable'.

asbestosis /ˌazbɛˈstəʊsɪs, ˌas-/ ▪ n. a lung disease resulting from the inhalation of asbestos particles, marked by severe fibrosis and a high risk of cancer of the pleura.

ascarid /ˈaskərɪd/ (also **ascaris** /-rɪs/) ▪ n. Zoology a member of a family of parasitic nematode worms (Ascaridae) that live in the intestines of vertebrates.
– ORIGIN C17: from Greek *askaris* 'intestinal worm'.

ascend ▪ v. 1 go up; climb or rise. 2 rise in status. 3 (of a voice or sound) rise in pitch.
– PHRASES **ascend the throne** become king or queen.
– ORIGIN Middle English: from Latin, from *ad-* 'to' + *scandere* 'to climb'.

ascendant (also **ascendent**) ▪ adj. 1 holding a position of increasing status or influence. 2 Astrology (of a planet, zodiacal degree, or sign) on or close to the intersection of the ecliptic with the eastern horizon. ▪ n. Astrology the ascendant point.
– PHRASES **in the ascendant** rising in power or influence.
– DERIVATIVES **ascendancy** n.

ascender ▪ n. 1 a person or thing that ascends. 2 a lower-case letter (or part of it) that extends above the level of the top of an *x* (such as *b* and *f*). 3 Climbing a device which can be clipped to a rope to act as a foothold or handhold.

ascension ▪ n. 1 the action of ascending in status. 2 (**Ascension**) Christian Church the ascent of Christ into heaven on the fortieth day after the Resurrection.
– DERIVATIVES **ascensional** adj.
– ORIGIN Middle English: from Latin *ascensio(n-)*, from *ascendere* (see **ASCEND**).

Ascension Day ▪ n. the Thursday forty days after Easter, on which Christ's Ascension is celebrated in the Christian Church.

ascent ▪ n. an instance of ascending. ▸ a climb to the summit of a mountain. ▸ an upward slope.
– ORIGIN C16: from **ASCEND**, on the pattern of *descend*, *descent*.

ascertain /ˌasəˈteɪn/ ■ v. find out for certain.
– DERIVATIVES **ascertainable** adj. **ascertainment** n.
– ORIGIN Middle English: from Old French *acertener*, from Latin *certus* 'settled, sure'.

ascetic /əˈsɛtɪk/ ■ adj. characterized by the practice of severe self-discipline. ■ n. an ascetic person.
– DERIVATIVES **ascetically** adv. **asceticism** n.
– ORIGIN C17: from Greek, from *askētēs* 'monk', from *askein* 'to exercise'.

aschelminth /ˈaʃkɛlmɪnθ, ˈask-/ ■ n. (pl. **aschelminths** or **aschelminthes**) Zoology a typically worm-like invertebrate of a large group that lack a well-developed coelom and blood vessels and include the nematodes, rotifers, and water bears.
– ORIGIN from Greek *askos* 'sac' + *helminth* 'worm' (from a belief that such animals had a fluid-filled internal sac).

asci plural form of ASCUS.

ascidian /əˈsɪdɪən/ ■ n. Zoology a sea squirt.
– ORIGIN C19: from Greek *askidion*, diminutive of *askos* 'wineskin'.

ASCII /ˈaski/ ■ abbrev. Computing American Standard Code for Information Interchange.

ascites /əˈsaɪtiːz/ ■ n. Medicine the accumulation of fluid in the peritoneal cavity, causing abdominal swelling.
– DERIVATIVES **ascitic** adj.
– ORIGIN Middle English: from Greek, from *askos* 'wineskin'.

ascomycete /ˌaskəˈmaɪsiːt/ ■ n. (pl. **ascomycetes** /-ˈmaɪsiːts, -maɪˈsiːtiːz/) Botany a fungus of a large group whose spores develop within asci and which includes most moulds, mildews, and yeasts, the fungal component of most lichens, and the morels and truffles.
– ORIGIN C19: from Greek *askos* 'sac' + *mukētes* 'fungi'.

ascorbic acid /əˈskɔːbɪk/ ■ n. vitamin C, a compound found in citrus fruits and green vegetables which is essential in maintaining healthy connective tissue and of which a deficiency causes scurvy.
– DERIVATIVES **ascorbate** n.
– ORIGIN 1930s: from Greek *a-* 'without' + medieval Latin *scorbutus* 'scurvy'.

ascribe ■ v. (**ascribe something to**) attribute something to a particular cause, person or period. ▸ regard a quality as belonging to.
– DERIVATIVES **ascribable** adj. **ascription** n.
– ORIGIN Middle English: from Latin, from *ad-* 'to' + *scribere* 'write'.

ascus /ˈaskəs/ ■ n. (pl. **asci** /ˈaskaɪ, -iː/) Botany a sac in which the spores of ascomycete fungi develop.
– ORIGIN C19: from Greek *askos* 'bag'.

asdic /ˈazdɪk/ ■ n. chiefly Brit. a form of sonar developed in the Second World War to detect enemy submarines.
– ORIGIN acronym from *Allied Submarine Detection Investigation Committee*.

-ase ■ suffix Biochemistry forming names of enzymes: *amylase*.
– ORIGIN from (*diast*)*ase*.

ASEAN /ˈasɪən/ ■ abbrev. Association of South-East Asian Nations.

aseismic /eɪˈsaɪzmɪk/ ■ adj. Geology not characterized by earthquake activity.

asepsis /eɪˈsɛpsɪs/ ■ n. the absence or exclusion of bacteria, viruses, and other micro-organisms. Compare with ANTISEPSIS.

aseptic /eɪˈsɛptɪk/ ■ adj. free from contamination by bacteria, viruses, or other microorganisms; sterile.
– DERIVATIVES **aseptically** adv.

asexual ■ adj. **1** Biology without sex or sexual organs. ▸ (of reproduction) not involving the fusion of gametes. **2** without sexual feelings or associations.
– DERIVATIVES **asexuality** n. **asexually** adv.

AsgiSA (also **Asgisa**) ■ abbrev. Accelerated Shared Growth Initiative (for) South Africa.

ash¹ ■ n. **1** the powdery residue left after the burning of a substance. ▸ (**ashes**) the remains of a human body after cremation or burning. ▸ (in chemical analysis) the mineral component of an organic substance (indicated by the residue left after burning). **2** (**the Ashes**) a notional cricket trophy awarded for a test match series between England and Australia. [from a mock obituary notice referring to the symbolical remains of English cricket.] ■ v. **1** (in chemical analysis) burn to ash. **2** cover or sprinkle with ash.
– PHRASES **ashes in one's mouth** something that is bitterly disappointing or worthless. **rise from the ashes** be renewed after destruction.
– DERIVATIVES **ashy** adj.
– ORIGIN Old English, of German origin.

ash² ■ n. **1** a tree with compound leaves, winged fruits, and hard pale wood. [Genus *Fraxinus*: many species.] ▸ used in names of other trees, e.g. mountain ash. **2** an Old English runic letter, ᚫ. ▸ the symbol æ or Æ, used in the Roman alphabet in place of the runic letter and as a phonetic symbol. See also Æ.
– ORIGIN Old English, of Germanic origin.

ashamed ■ adj. embarrassed or guilty because of one's actions or characteristics.
– DERIVATIVES **ashamedly** adv.
– ORIGIN Old English, from *āscamian* 'feel shame'.

Ashanti /əˈʃanti/ (also **Asante**) ■ n. (pl. same) **1** a member of a people of south central Ghana. **2** the dialect of Akan spoken by the Ashanti.
– ORIGIN the name in Akan.

ash blonde (also **ash blond**) ■ adj. denoting hair that is a very pale blonde colour.

ashcan ■ n. US a rubbish bin.

ashen¹ ■ adj. **1** (of a person's face) very pale with shock, fear, or illness. **2** poetic/literary having the appearance or colour of ash.

ashen² ■ adj. archaic or poetic/literary made of wood from the ash tree.

Ashkenazi /ˌaʃkəˈnɑːzi/ ■ n. (pl. **Ashkenazim** /-zɪm/) a Jew of central or eastern European descent. Compare with SEPHARDI.
– ORIGIN from modern Hebrew, from *Ashkenaz*, son of Japheth, one of the sons of Noah (Genesis 10:3).

ash key ■ n. the winged fruit of an ash tree, growing in clusters resembling keys.

ashore ■ adv. to or on the shore or land from the direction of the sea. ▸ on land as opposed to at sea.

ashplant ■ n. a sapling from an ash tree used as a walking stick or whip.

ashram /ˈaʃrəm/ ■ n. a place of religious retreat or community life in or modelled on those in India.
– ORIGIN from Sanskrit *āśrama* 'hermitage'.

ashrama /ˈaʃrəmə/ ■ n. Hinduism any of the four stages of an ideal life, ascending from the status of pupil to the total renunciation of the world.
– ORIGIN from Sanskrit *āśrama*.

ashtanga /aʃˈtɑːŋə/ (also **astanga** /asˈtɑːŋə/) ■ n. a type of yoga based on eight principles and consisting of a series of poses executed in swift succession, combined with deep, controlled breathing.
– ORIGIN from Hindi *aṣṭan* or its source, Sanskrit *ashtáṅga* 'having eight parts', from *ashtán* 'eight'.

ashtray ■ n. a small receptacle for tobacco ash and cigarette ends.

Ash Wednesday ■ n. the first day of Lent in the Western Christian Church, marked by services of penitence.
– ORIGIN from the custom of marking the foreheads of penitents with ashes on that day.

Asian /ˈeɪʃ(ə)n, -ʒ(ə)n/ ■ n. a native of Asia or a person of Asian descent. ▸ S. African historical (under apartheid) a South African of Indian or Pakistani descent. ■ adj. of or relating to Asia or its people or languages. ▸ S. African historical (under apartheid) of or relating to people classified as Asians.

USAGE
In South Africa, during the period of apartheid, the classification **Asian** latterly replaced the wider term **Asiatic**, which had included Chinese and other nationals. In Britain **Asian** is used to refer to people who come from (or whose parents came from) the Indian subcontinent, while in North America it is used to refer to people from the Far East.

Asian American ■ n. an American who is of Asian (chiefly Far Eastern) descent. ■ adj. of or relating to Asian Americans.

Asiatic /ˌeɪʃɪˈatɪk, ˌeɪzɪ-/ ■ n. S. African historical (under apartheid) a South African of Asian descent, especially a person of Indian, Pakistani, or Chinese origin. Compare with ASIAN. ■ adj. relating to or deriving from Asia. ▸ S. African historical (under apartheid) of or relating to people classified as Asiatics.

ASIC ■ abbrev. Electronics application specific integrated circuit.

aside ■ adv. 1 to one side; out of the way. 2 in reserve or out of consideration. ■ n. 1 an actor's remark that is heard by the audience but is supposed not to be heard by the other characters. 2 an incidental remark.
– PHRASES **aside from** apart from. **set something aside** 1 remove land from agricultural production for fallow or other use. 2 annul a legal decision or process.
– ORIGIN Middle English: see A-², SIDE.

asinine /ˈasɪnʌɪn/ ■ adj. extremely stupid or foolish.
– DERIVATIVES **asininity** n.
– ORIGIN C15: from Latin *asininus*, from *asinus* 'ass'.

-asis (often **-iasis**) ■ suffix forming the names of diseases: *psoriasis*.
– ORIGIN from Greek.

ask ■ v. 1 say something in order to obtain an answer or some information. ▸ (**ask after**) enquire about the well-being of. 2 request to do or give something. ▸ request permission. ▸ (**ask for**) request to speak to. ▸ request (a specified amount) as a price for selling something. 3 expect or demand (something) of someone. 4 invite to a social occasion. ▸ (**ask someone out**) invite someone out on a date. ■ n. chiefly N. Amer. the asking price of a financial security.
– PHRASES **for the asking** for little or no effort or cost. **I ask you!** informal an exclamation of shock or disapproval.
– DERIVATIVES **asker** n.
– ORIGIN Old English, of West Germanic origin.

askance /əˈskans, əˈskɑːns/ (also **askant** /-ˈskant, -ˈskɑːnt/) ■ adv. with a look of suspicion or disapproval.
– ORIGIN C15.

askari /əˈskɑːri/ ■ n. (pl. same or **askaris**) 1 (in East Africa) a soldier or police officer. 2 (**Askari**) S. African historical an Umkhonto we Sizwe soldier who changed loyalties and joined the South African Police Force.
– ORIGIN C19: from Arabic *'askarī* 'soldier'.

askew /əˈskjuː/ ■ adv. & adj. not in a straight or level position.
– ORIGIN C16: from A-² + SKEW.

asking price ■ n. the price at which something is offered for sale.

aslant ■ adv. at a slant. ■ prep. across at a slant.

asleep ■ adj. & adv. 1 in or into a state of sleep. ▸ not attentive or alert. 2 (of a limb) numb.

ASM ■ abbrev. air-to-surface missile.

asocial ■ adj. avoiding or inconsiderate of others.

asp /asp/ ■ n. 1 (also **asp viper**) a small southern European viper with an upturned snout. [*Vipera aspis*.] 2 the Egyptian cobra. [*Naja haje*.]
– ORIGIN Middle English: from Latin *aspis*.

asparagine /əˈsparədʒiːn/ ■ n. Biochemistry a hydrophilic amino acid which is a constituent of most proteins.
– ORIGIN C19: from ASPARAGUS (which contains it).

asparagus /əˈsparəɡəs/ ■ n. 1 the tender young shoots of a plant, eaten as a vegetable. 2 the tall plant with feathery foliage from which these shoots are obtained. [*Asparagus officinalis*.]
– ORIGIN C16: from Greek *asparagos*.

asparagus fern ■ n. a decorative plant with feathery foliage, related to the edible asparagus. [Genus *Asparagus*: several species.]

aspartame /əˈspɑːteɪm/ ■ n. an artificial sweetener derived from aspartic acid and phenylalanine.

aspartic acid /əˈspɑːtɪk/ ■ n. Biochemistry an acidic amino acid present in many proteins and in sugar cane, important in the metabolism of nitrogen in animals and also acting as a neurotransmitter.
– DERIVATIVES **aspartate** n.

– ORIGIN C19: from French *aspartique*, from Greek *asparagos* 'asparagus'.

aspect ■ n. 1 a particular part or feature. ▸ a particular appearance or quality. 2 the positioning of a building in a particular direction. ▸ the side of a building facing a particular direction. 3 Astrology any of a number of particular angular relationships between one celestial body or point on the ecliptic and another. 4 Grammar a category or form of a verb which expresses a feature of the action related to time, such as completion or duration.
– DERIVATIVES **aspectual** adj.
– ORIGIN Middle English: from Latin *aspectus*, from *aspicere* 'look at'.

aspect ratio ■ n. 1 the ratio of the width to the height of an image on a television screen. 2 Aeronautics the ratio of the span to the mean chord of an aerofoil.

aspen ■ n. a poplar tree with small rounded long-stalked leaves noted for trembling in the breeze. [*Populus tremula* (Europe), *P. tremuloides* (N. America), and other species.]
– ORIGIN Middle English: from dialect *asp*.

asperges /əˈspɜːdʒiːz/ ■ n. Christian Church the rite of sprinkling holy water at the beginning of the Mass. ▸ another term for ASPERGILLUM.
– ORIGIN C16: from the Latin text of Psalms 50(51):9 ('thou shalt purge'), recited during the sprinkling of the holy water.

aspergillosis /ˌaspədʒɪˈləʊsɪs/ ■ n. Medicine a condition in which certain fungi infect the lungs or other tissues, especially through inhalation of spores from mouldy hay.
– ORIGIN C19: from *Aspergillus*, genus name of the fungi.

aspergillum /ˌaspəˈdʒɪləm/ ■ n. (pl. **aspergilla** or **aspergillums**) Christian Church an implement for sprinkling holy water.
– ORIGIN C17: from Latin, from *aspergere* 'sprinkle'.

asperity /əˈsperɪti/ ■ n. (pl. **-ies**) 1 harshness of tone or manner. ▸ (**asperities**) harsh qualities or conditions. 2 a rough edge on a surface.
– ORIGIN Middle English: from Latin *asperitas*, from *asper* 'rough'.

aspersion /əˈspɜːʃ(ə)n/ ■ n. an attack on someone's character or reputation.
– ORIGIN Middle English (denoting the sprinkling of water at baptism): from Latin *aspersio(n-)*, from *aspergere* 'sprinkle'.

asphalt /ˈasfalt, -əlt/ ■ n. a dark bituminous pitch occurring naturally or derived from crude oil, used in surfacing roads or as waterproofing in building. ■ v. surface with asphalt.
– DERIVATIVES **asphaltic** adj.
– ORIGIN Middle English: from French *asphalte*, from Greek *asphalton*.

aspherical ■ adj. not spherical.
– DERIVATIVES **aspheric** adj.

asphodel /ˈasfədɛl/ ■ n. 1 a Eurasian plant of the lily family with long, slender leaves and flowers borne on a spike. [*Asphodelus* and other genera.] 2 poetic/literary an everlasting flower said to grow in the Elysian fields.
– ORIGIN Middle English: from Greek *asphodelos*.

asphyxia /əsˈfɪksɪə/ ■ n. a condition arising when the body is deprived of oxygen, causing unconsciousness or death.
– DERIVATIVES **asphyxial** adj. **asphyxiant** adj. & n.
– ORIGIN C18: from Greek *asphuxia*, from *a-* 'without' + *sphuxis* 'pulse'.

asphyxiate ■ v. kill or be killed by asphyxia.
– DERIVATIVES **asphyxiation** n. **asphyxiator** n.

aspic ■ n. a clear savoury jelly made with meat stock.
– ORIGIN C18: from French, 'asp', from the colours of the jelly as compared with those of the snake.

aspidistra /ˌaspɪˈdɪstrə/ ■ n. a bulbous plant of the lily family with broad tapering leaves, native to East Asia. [Genus *Aspidistra*.]
– ORIGIN C19: from Greek *aspis* 'shield' (because of the shape of the stigma).

aspirant /əˈspʌɪr(ə)nt, ˈasp(ɪ)r-/ ■ adj. aspiring towards a particular achievement or status. ■ n. a person who has such aspirations.

aspirate ■ v. /ˈaspəreɪt/ **1** Phonetics pronounce (a sound) with an exhalation of breath. ▸ pronounce the sound of *h* at the beginning of a word. **2** chiefly Medicine draw (fluid) by suction from a bodily vessel or cavity. **3** inhale. **4** [as adj. **aspirated**] (of an internal-combustion engine) provided with air. ■ n. /ˈasp(ə)rət/ Phonetics an aspirated consonant. ▸ a sound of *h*.
– ORIGIN C16: from Latin *aspiratus* 'breathed', from *aspirare* (see ASPIRE).

aspiration ■ n. **1** a hope or ambition. **2** the action of aspirating.

aspirational ■ adj. /ˌaspɪˈreɪʃ(ə)n(ə)l/ having or characterized by aspirations to be successful.
– DERIVATIVES **aspirationally** adv.

aspirator ■ n. Medicine an instrument or apparatus for aspirating fluid from a vessel or cavity.

aspire ■ v. (usu. **aspire to/to do something**) direct one's hopes or ambitions towards achieving something.
– ORIGIN Middle English: from Latin *aspirare*, from *ad-* 'to' + *spirare* 'breathe'.

aspirin ■ n. (pl. same or **aspirins**) a synthetic compound (acetylsalicylic acid) used to relieve pain and reduce fever and inflammation.
– ORIGIN C19: from German, from *acetylierte Spirsäure* 'acetylated salicylic acid'.

ass[1] /as/ ■ n. **1** an animal of the horse family which is smaller than a horse and has longer ears and a braying call. [*Equus africanus* (Africa) and *E. hemionus* (Asia).] ▸ (in general use) a donkey. **2** informal a foolish or stupid person.
– ORIGIN Old English, from a Celtic word rel. to Welsh *asyn*, from Latin *asinus*.

ass[2] /ɑːs, as/ ■ n. N. Amer. vulgar slang a person's buttocks or anus.
– ORIGIN var. of ARSE.

assagai ■ n. & v. variant spelling of ASSEGAI.

assail /əˈseɪl/ ■ v. **1** make a concerted or violent attack on. **2** (of an unpleasant feeling) come upon (someone) strongly.
– DERIVATIVES **assailable** adj.
– ORIGIN Middle English: from Old French *asalir*, from Latin *assilire*, from *ad-* 'to' + *salire* 'to leap'.

assailant ■ n. a person who physically attacks another.

assassin /əˈsasɪn/ ■ n. **1** a person who assassinates. **2** (**Assassin**) a member of the fanatical Nizari branch of Ismaili Muslims dominant at the time of the Crusades.

HISTORY
In the literal sense an **assassin** was a person who used cannabis. The root of the word, which entered English in the 16th century from either French or medieval Latin, is the Arabic *ašīšī* 'hashish eater', and it was first used in reference to the Nizari branch of Ismaili Muslims who ruled part of northern Persia in the 12th and 13th centuries, during the time of the Crusades. Renowned as militant fanatics, they were reputed to use hashish before being sent to murder the Christian leaders. The word's current use still reflects the idea of someone who is either paid to kill a prominent person, or who does so because of a fanatical commitment to a cause.

---

assassinate ■ v. murder (a political or religious leader).
– DERIVATIVES **assassination** n.

assassin bug ■ n. a long-legged predatory or bloodsucking bug occurring chiefly in the tropics, some kinds of which can transmit diseases to humans. [Family Reduviidae: numerous species.]

assault ■ n. **1** a violent attack. ▸ Law the unlawful infliction of physical force on a person, or the immediate threat to do so. **2** a concerted attempt to do something demanding. ■ v. make an assault on.
– DERIVATIVES **assaulter** n.
– ORIGIN Middle English: from Old French *assauter* (v.), from Latin *ad-* 'to' + *saltare*, from *salire* 'to leap'.

assault course ■ n. a course providing a series of physical challenges, used for training soldiers.

assault rifle ■ n. a short lightweight rifle capable of automatic and semi-automatic fire, designed for close combat.

assay /əˈseɪ, ˈaseɪ/ ■ n. **1** the testing of a metal or ore to determine its ingredients and quality. **2** a procedure for measuring the biochemical or immunological activity of a sample. ■ v. **1** carry out an assay on. **2** archaic attempt.
– DERIVATIVES **assayer** n.
– ORIGIN Middle English: from Old French *assai* (n.), *assaier* (v.), var. of *essai* 'trial', *essayer* (see ESSAY).

assay office ■ n. **1** an establishment for the assaying of ores and metals. **2** Brit. an institution authorized to award hallmarks to articles made from precious metals.

assegai /ˈasəɡʌɪ/ (also **assagai**) ■ n. (pl. **assegais**) **1** a slender iron-tipped hardwood spear used chiefly by southern African peoples. **2** (also **assegai wood**) a southern African tree of the dogwood family, yielding a hard wood. [*Curtisia dentata*.] ■ v. wound or be wounded, or kill or be killed with an assegai.
– ORIGIN C17: from Arabic *az-zaġāyah*, from *az*, *al* 'the' + Berber *zaġāyah* 'spear'.

assemblage ■ n. a collection or gathering. ▸ a machine or object made of pieces fitted together. ▸ a work of art made by grouping together found or unrelated objects.

assemble ■ v. **1** come or bring together. **2** fit together the component parts of.
– ORIGIN Middle English: from Old French *asembler*, from Latin *ad-* 'to' + *simul* 'together'.

assemblé /ˌasɒ̃ˈbleɪ/ ■ n. (pl. pronounced same) Ballet a leap in which the feet are brought together before landing.
– ORIGIN French, past participle of *assembler* 'assemble, put together'.

assembler ■ n. **1** a person who assembles component parts. **2** Computing a program for converting instructions written in symbolic code into machine code. ▸ another term for ASSEMBLY LANGUAGE.

assembly ■ n. (pl. **-ies**) **1** a group of people gathered together. ▸ a group having legislative or decision-making powers. ▸ a regular gathering of teachers and pupils in a school. **2** the action of assembling component parts. ▸ a unit consisting of assembled components.

assembly language ■ n. Computing the symbolic code converted by an assembler.

assembly line ■ n. a series of workers and machines in a factory by which a succession of identical items is progressively assembled.

assembly rooms ■ pl. n. chiefly Brit. a public room or hall in which meetings or social functions are held.

assent /əˈsɛnt/ ■ n. the expression of approval or agreement. ■ v. (usu. **assent to**) express assent.
– ORIGIN Middle English: from Latin *assentire*, from *ad-* 'towards' + *sentire* 'feel, think'.

assert ■ v. **1** state a fact or belief confidently and forcefully. **2** cause others to recognize (one's authority or a right) by confident and forceful behaviour. ▸ (**assert oneself**) behave or speak in a confident and forceful manner.
– DERIVATIVES **asserter** (also **-or**) -.
– ORIGIN C17 (*assertion* Middle English): from Latin *asserere* 'claim, affirm', from *ad-* 'to' + *serere* 'to join'.

assertion /əˈsəːʃ(ə)n/ ■ n. a confident statement of fact or belief. ▸ the action of asserting.

assertive ■ adj. having or showing a confident and forceful personality.
– DERIVATIVES **assertively** adv. **assertiveness** n.

assess ■ v. evaluate or estimate the nature, value, or quality of. ▸ set the value of a tax, fine, etc., for (a person or property) at a specified level.
– DERIVATIVES **assessable** adj. **assessment** n.
– ORIGIN Middle English: from Old French *assesser*, from medieval Latin *assidere* 'levy tax', from *ad-* 'to, at' + *sedere* 'sit'.

assessment standard ■ n. S. African the level of proficiency expected of a pupil for a particular subject in a specific grade at school.

assessor ■ n. **1** a person who assesses. **2** a specialist who is called upon for advice by a judge or committee of inquiry.

asset ■ n. **1** a useful or valuable thing or person. **2** (**assets**)

property owned by a person or company, regarded as having value and being available to meet debts, commitments, or legacies.
– ORIGIN C16 ('sufficient estate to allow discharge of a will'): from Old French *asez* 'enough', from Latin *ad* 'to' + *satis* 'enough'.

asset-backed ■ adj. denoting securities having as collateral the return on a series of mortgages, credit agreements, or other forms of lending.

asset-stripping ■ n. the practice of taking over a company in financial difficulties and selling each of its assets at a profit.
– DERIVATIVES **asset-stripper** n.

asseveration /əˌsevəˈreɪʃ(ə)n/ ■ n. a solemn or emphatic declaration or statement.
– ORIGIN C16: from Latin *asseveratio(n-)*, from *asseverare*, from *ad-* 'to' + *severus* 'serious'.

assiduity /ˌasɪˈdjuːɪti/ ■ n. (pl. **-ies**) constant or close attention to what one is doing.
– ORIGIN Middle English: from Latin *assiduitas*, from *assiduus* (see **ASSIDUOUS**).

assiduous /əˈsɪdjuəs/ ■ adj. showing great care and perseverance.
– DERIVATIVES **assiduously** adv. **assiduousness** n.
– ORIGIN C16: from Latin *assiduus*, from *assidere* (see **ASSESS**).

assign ■ v. 1 allocate (a task or duty) to someone. ▶ appoint to a particular task. 2 designate or set aside for a specific purpose. ▶ attribute (something) to a group or person. 3 transfer (legal rights or liabilities). ■ n. Law another term for **ASSIGNEE**.
– DERIVATIVES **assignable** adj. **assigner** n. **assignor** n.
– ORIGIN Middle English: from Latin *assignare*, from *ad-* 'to' + *signare* 'to sign'.

assignation ■ n. 1 a secret arrangement to meet. 2 the action of assigning.

assignee ■ n. chiefly Law 1 a person to whom a right or liability is legally transferred. 2 a person appointed to act for another.

assignment ■ n. 1 a task or duty assigned as part of a job or course of study. 2 the action of assigning or fact of being assigned. 3 an act of assigning a right or liability. ▶ a document effecting such a transfer.

assimilate ■ v. 1 take in and fully understand (information or ideas). ▶ (of a society or culture) absorb and integrate (people, ideas, or culture). 2 absorb and digest (food or nutrients). 3 regard as similar. 4 Phonetics make (a sound) more like another in the same or next word.
– DERIVATIVES **assimilable** adj. **assimilation** n. **assimilative** adj. **assimilator** n. **assimilatory** adj.
– ORIGIN Middle English: from Latin *assimilare* 'absorb, incorporate', from *ad-* 'to' + *similis* 'like'.

assimilationist ■ n. a person who advocates or participates in racial or cultural integration.

assist ■ v. help by doing a share of work or by providing money or information. ■ n. chiefly N. Amer. 1 an act of helping, especially by providing money. 2 (chiefly in ice hockey, basketball, or baseball) an act of touching the ball in a play in which a teammate scores or an opposing batter is put out.
– DERIVATIVES **assister** n.
– ORIGIN Middle English: from Latin *assistere* 'take one's stand by'.

assistance ■ n. the provision of money, resources, or information to help someone. ▶ the action of helping.

assistant ■ n. 1 a person who ranks below a senior person. 2 a person who helps in particular work.

assistant professor ■ n. N. Amer. an academic ranking immediately below an associate professor.

assize /əˈsaɪz/ ■ n. historical a court which sat at intervals in each county of England and Wales to administer the civil and criminal law.
– ORIGIN Middle English: from Old French *assise*, from *asseeir* 'sit, settle, assess', from Latin *assidere* (see **ASSESS**).

Assoc. ■ abbrev. Association.

associate ■ v. /əˈsəʊʃɪeɪt, -sɪeɪt/ 1 make a conceptual connection between. 2 (usu. **associate with**) meet or have dealings with. ▶ (**associate oneself with**) allow oneself to be connected with or seen to be supportive of. ▶ (**be associated with**) be involved with. ■ n. /əˈsəʊʃɪət, -sɪət/ 1 a partner or companion in business or at work. 2 a person with limited or subordinate membership of an organization. ■ adj. /əˈsəʊʃɪət, -sɪət/ 1 connected with an organization or business. 2 having shared function or membership but with a lesser status.
– DERIVATIVES **associability** n. **associable** adj. **associateship** n. **associator** n.
– ORIGIN Middle English: from Latin *associare* 'join', from *ad-* 'to' + *socius* 'sharing, allied'.

associate professor ■ n. an academic ranking immediately below full professor.

association ■ n. 1 a group of people organized for a joint purpose. 2 a connection or cooperative link between people or organizations. ▶ Chemistry a weak interaction between molecules, such as hydrogen bonding. 3 a conceptual connection. 4 Ecology a stable plant community including a characteristic group of dominant plant species.
– DERIVATIVES **associational** adj.

Association Football ■ n. Brit. more formal term for SOCCER.

associative ■ adj. 1 of or involving association. 2 Mathematics involving the condition that a group of quantities connected by operators gives the same result in whichever order the operations are performed, as long as the order of the quantities remains the same, e.g. $(a \times b) \times c = a \times (b \times c)$.

assonance /ˈas(ə)nəns/ ■ n. the resemblance of sound between syllables in nearby words arising from the rhyming of stressed vowels (e.g. *sonnet, porridge*), and also from the use of identical consonants with different vowels (e.g. *killed, cold, culled*).
– DERIVATIVES **assonant** adj. **assonate** /-neɪt/ v.
– ORIGIN C18: from Latin *assonare* 'respond to'.

assort ■ v. Genetics (of genes or characteristics) become distributed among cells or progeny.
– ORIGIN C15: from Old French *assorter*, from *a-* + *sorte* 'sort, kind'.

assortative ■ adj. denoting or involving the preferential mating of animals or marriage between people with similar characteristics.

assorted ■ adj. of various sorts put together.

assortment ■ n. a miscellaneous collection.

Asst ■ abbrev. Assistant.

assuage /əˈsweɪdʒ/ ■ v. 1 make (an unpleasant feeling) less intense. 2 satisfy (an appetite or desire).
– DERIVATIVES **assuagement** n.
– ORIGIN Middle English: from Old French *assouagier*, from Latin *ad-* 'to' + *suavis* 'sweet'.

assume ■ v. 1 accept as true without proof. 2 take (responsibility or control). 3 begin to have (a specified quality, appearance, or extent). ▶ adopt falsely.
– DERIVATIVES **assumable** adj. **assumed** adj. **assumedly** adv.
– ORIGIN Middle English: from Latin, from *ad-* 'towards' + *sumere* 'take'.

assuming ■ conj. based on the assumption. ■ adj. archaic arrogant or presumptuous.

assumption ■ n. 1 a thing that is assumed as true. 2 the action of assuming responsibility or control. 3 (**Assumption**) the reception of the Virgin Mary bodily into heaven, according to Roman Catholic doctrine. ▶ the feast in honour of this, celebrated on 15 August.

assurance ■ n. 1 a positive declaration intended to give confidence. 2 confidence in one's own abilities. ▶ certainty. 3 life insurance (with reference to policies under whose terms a payment is guaranteed).

assure ■ v. 1 tell someone something positively in order to dispel potential doubts. 2 make (something) certain to happen. 3 chiefly Brit. cover by assurance. ▶ secure the future payment of (an amount) with insurance.
– DERIVATIVES **assurer** n.
– ORIGIN Middle English: from Old French *assurer*, from Latin *ad-* 'to' + *securus* (see **SECURE**).

assured ■ adj. **1** confident. **2** protected against discontinuance or change.
– DERIVATIVES **assuredly** adv.

Assyrian ■ n. **1** an inhabitant of ancient Assyria. **2** the language of ancient Assyria. **3** a dialect of Aramaic still spoken in parts of Syria and northern Iraq. ■ adj. **1** of or relating to ancient Assyria or its language. **2** relating to or denoting modern Assyrian or its speakers.

Assyriology /ə͵sɪrɪˈɒlədʒi/ ■ n. the study of the language, history, and antiquities of ancient Assyria.
– DERIVATIVES **Assyriological** adj. **Assyriologist** n.

AST ■ abbrev. Atlantic Standard Time.

astable /əˈsteɪb(ə)l, eɪ-/ ■ adj. chiefly Electronics of or relating to a system or electric circuit which oscillates spontaneously between unstable states.

astatine /ˈastəti:n/ ■ n. the chemical element of atomic number 85, a very unstable radioactive member of the halogen group. (Symbol: **At**)
– ORIGIN 1940s: from Greek *astatos* 'unstable'.

aster /ˈastə/ ■ n. a plant of a large genus that includes the Michaelmas daisy, with characteristic purple or pink rayed flowers. [Genus *Aster*: numerous species.]
– ORIGIN C17: from Greek *astēr* 'star'.

-aster ■ suffix forming nouns denoting poor quality: *poetaster*.
– ORIGIN from Latin.

asterisk ■ n. a symbol (*) used in text as a pointer to an annotation or footnote. ■ v. mark with an asterisk.
– ORIGIN Middle English: from Greek *asteriskos* 'small star', diminutive of *astēr*.

astern ■ adv. behind or towards the rear of a ship or aircraft. ▶ (of a ship's engine) backwards.

asteroid /ˈastərɔɪd/ ■ n. **1** a small rocky body orbiting the sun. **2** Zoology an echinoderm of a class (Asteroidea) comprising the starfishes.
– DERIVATIVES **asteroidal** adj.
– ORIGIN C19: from Greek *asteroeidēs* 'starlike', from *astēr* 'star'.

asthenia /əsˈθiːnɪə/ ■ n. Medicine abnormal physical weakness or lack of energy.
– DERIVATIVES **asthenic** adj.
– ORIGIN C18: from Greek, from *asthenēs* 'weak'.

asthenosphere /əsˈθɛnəsfɪə/ ■ n. Geology the upper layer of the earth's mantle, below the lithosphere, in which there is relatively low resistance to plastic flow and convection is thought to occur.
– DERIVATIVES **asthenospheric** adj.
– ORIGIN C20: from Greek *asthenēs* 'weak' + SPHERE.

asthma /ˈasmə/ ■ n. a respiratory condition marked by attacks of spasm in the bronchi of the lungs, causing difficulty in breathing and usually associated with allergic reaction.
– DERIVATIVES **asthmatic** adj. & n. **asthmatically** adv.
– ORIGIN Middle English: from Greek *asthma*, from *azein* 'breathe hard'.

astigmatism /əˈstɪɡmətɪz(ə)m/ ■ n. a deviation in the spherical curvature of the eye or a lens, resulting in distorted images.
– DERIVATIVES **astigmatic** /͵astɪɡˈmatɪk/ adj.
– ORIGIN C19: from Greek *a-* 'without' + *stigma* 'point'.

astir ■ adj. **1** in a state of excited movement. **2** awake and out of bed.

astonish ■ v. surprise or impress greatly.
– DERIVATIVES **astonishing** adj. **astonishingly** adv. **astonishment** n.
– ORIGIN C16: from obsolete *astone* 'stun, stupefy', from Old French *estoner*, from Latin *ex-* 'out' + *tonare* 'thunder'.

astound ■ v. shock or greatly surprise.
– DERIVATIVES **astounding** adj. **astoundingly** adv.
– ORIGIN Middle English: from *astoned*, past participle of *astone* (see ASTONISH).

astragal /ˈastrəɡ(ə)l/ ■ n. **1** Architecture a convex moulding or wooden strip, of semicircular section. **2** a bar separating panes of glass in cabinetmaking.
– ORIGIN C17: from ASTRAGALUS, via French *astragale*.

astragalus /əˈstraɡ(ə)ləs/ ■ n. (pl. **astragali** /-lʌɪ/) chiefly Zoology another term for TALUS¹.
– ORIGIN C16: from Greek *astragalos* 'ankle bone, moulding'.

astrakhan /͵astrəˈkan/ ■ n. the dark curly fleece of young karakul lambs from central Asia.
– ORIGIN C18: named after the city of *Astrakhan* in Russia.

astral /ˈastr(ə)l/ ■ adj. **1** of, relating to, or resembling the stars. **2** of or relating to a supposed non-physical realm of existence to which various psychic and paranormal phenomena are ascribed, and in which the physical human body is said to have a counterpart.
– ORIGIN C17: from late Latin *astralis*, from *astrum* 'star'.

astrantia /əˈstrantɪə/ ■ n. a plant of the parsley family with small compact starlike heads of tiny flowers surrounded by prominent bracts. [Genus *Astrantia*: several species.]
– ORIGIN perhaps from Greek *astēr* 'star'.

astray ■ adv. away from the correct path or direction.
– PHRASES **go astray** become lost or mislaid.
– ORIGIN Middle English: from an Anglo-Norman French var. of Old French *estraier*, from Latin *extra* 'out of bounds' + *vagari* 'wander'.

astride ■ prep. & adv. with a leg on each side of. ▶ [adv.] (of a person's legs) apart.

astringent /əˈstrɪn(d)ʒ(ə)nt/ ■ adj. **1** causing the contraction of skin cells and other body tissues. **2** sharp or severe in manner or style. ▶ (of taste or smell) sharp or bitter. ■ n. an astringent lotion applied to the skin for cosmetic purposes or to reduce bleeding from minor abrasions.
– DERIVATIVES **astringency** n. **astringently** adv.
– ORIGIN C16: from Latin *astringere* 'pull tight'.

astro- /ˈastrəʊ/ ■ comb. form relating to the stars or celestial objects: *astrodome*. ▶ relating to outer space: *astrochemistry*.
– ORIGIN from Greek *astron* 'star'.

astrobiology ■ n. the branch of biology concerned with the discovery or study of life on other planets or in space.
– DERIVATIVES **astrobiological** adj. **astrobiologist** n.

astrochemistry ■ n. the study of molecules and ions occurring in stars and interstellar space.
– DERIVATIVES **astrochemical** adj. **astrochemist** n.

astrocyte /ˈastrə(ʊ)sʌɪt/ ■ n. Anatomy a star-shaped glial cell of the central nervous system.
– DERIVATIVES **astrocytic** adj.

astrodome ■ n. **1** chiefly US an enclosed stadium with a domed roof. **2** a domed window in an aircraft for astronomical observations.

astrolabe /ˈastrəleɪb/ ■ n. an instrument formerly used in making astronomical measurements and in navigation for calculating latitude, consisting of a disc with the edge marked in degrees and a pivoted pointer.
– ORIGIN Middle English: from Old French *astrelabe*, from Greek *astrolabos* 'star-taking'.

astrology ■ n. the study of the movements and relative positions of celestial bodies interpreted as having an influence on human affairs and the natural world.
– DERIVATIVES **astrologer** n. **astrological** adj. **astrologically** adv. **astrologist** n.

astronaut ■ n. a person trained to travel in a spacecraft.
– DERIVATIVES **astronautical** adj.
– ORIGIN 1920s: from ASTRO-, on the pattern of *aeronaut*.

astronautics ■ pl. n. [treated as sing.] the science and technology of space travel and exploration.

astronomical ■ adj. **1** of or relating to astronomy. **2** informal (of an amount) extremely large.
– DERIVATIVES **astronomic** adj. **astronomically** adv.

astronomical unit ■ n. Astronomy a unit of measurement equal to 149.6 million kilometres, the mean distance from the centre of the earth to the centre of the sun.

astronomical year ■ n. another term for SOLAR YEAR.

astronomy ■ n. the branch of science which deals with celestial objects, space, and the physical universe as a whole.
– DERIVATIVES **astronomer** n.

astrophysics ■ pl. n. [treated as sing.] the branch of astronomy concerned with the physical nature of stars

and other celestial bodies, and the application of the laws and theories of physics to the interpretation of astronomical observations.
– DERIVATIVES **astrophysical** adj. **astrophysicist** n.

AstroTurf ■ n. trademark an artificial grass surface, used for sports fields.
– ORIGIN 1960s: from sense 1 of ASTRODOME + TURF.

astute ■ adj. having an ability to assess situations or people accurately.
– DERIVATIVES **astutely** adv. **astuteness** n.
– ORIGIN C17: from Latin *astutus*, from *astus* 'craft'.

asunder ■ adv. archaic or poetic/literary apart.
– ORIGIN Old English *on sundran* 'in or into a separate place'.

asura /ˈʌsʊrə/ ■ n. (in Vedic religion) a member of a class of divine beings which in Indian mythology tend to be evil and in Zoroastrianism are benevolent. Compare with DEVA.
– ORIGIN Sanskrit, prob. from *ásu* 'breath, life'.

ASV ■ abbrev. American Standard Version (of the Bible).

asylum ■ n. 1 the protection granted by a state to someone who has left their native country as a political refugee. ▶ shelter or protection from danger. 2 dated an institution for the care of the mentally ill.
– ORIGIN Middle English: from Greek *asulon* 'refuge', from *a-* 'without' + *sulon* 'right of seizure'.

asymmetrical warfare ■ n. warfare involving surprise attacks by small, simply armed groups on a nation armed with modern high-tech weaponry.

asymmetric bars ■ pl. n. a pair of bars of different heights used in women's gymnastics.

asymmetry /əˈsɪmɪtri, eɪ-/ ■ n. (pl. -ies) lack of symmetry.
– DERIVATIVES **asymmetric** adj. **asymmetrical** adj. **asymmetrically** adv.

asymptomatic ■ adj. Medicine producing or showing no symptoms.

asymptote /ˈasɪm(p)təʊt/ ■ n. a straight line that continually approaches a given curve but does not meet it at any finite distance.
– DERIVATIVES **asymptotic** /ˌasɪm(p)ˈtɒtɪk/ adj. **asymptotically** adv.
– ORIGIN C17: from Greek *asumptōtos* 'not falling together'.

asynchronous ■ adj. 1 not existing or occurring at the same time. 2 Computing & Telecommunications making use of pulses to control the timing of operations that are sent when the previous operation is completed, rather than at regular intervals. 3 (of a machine or motor) not working in time with the alternations of current. 4 Astronomy (of a satellite) revolving round the parent planet at a different rate from that at which the planet rotates.
– DERIVATIVES **asynchronously** adv.

@ ■ symb. 'at', used: 1 to indicate cost or rate per unit: *thirty items @ R29.99 each.* 2 in Internet addresses between the user's name and the domain name: *jsmith@oup.com.*

At ■ symb. the chemical element astatine.

at ■ prep. 1 expressing location or arrival in a particular place or position. 2 expressing the time when an event takes place. 3 expressing attendance of an educational institution or a workplace. 4 denoting a particular point or segment on a scale. ▶ referring to someone's age. 5 expressing a particular state or condition. ▶ expressing a relationship between an individual and a skill. 6 expressing the object or target of a look, shot, action, or plan. ▶ expressing an incomplete or attempted action. 7 expressing the means by which something is done.
– PHRASES **at that** in addition; furthermore. **where it's at** informal the focus of fashion or style.
– ORIGIN Old English, of Germanic origin.

at- ■ prefix variant spelling of AD- assimilated before *t* (as in *attend*).

atavistic /ˌatəˈvɪstɪk/ ■ adj. relating to or characterized by reversion to something ancient or ancestral.
– DERIVATIVES **atavism** n. **atavistically** adv.
– ORIGIN C19: from Latin *atavus* 'forefather'.

ataxia /əˈtaksɪə/ (also **ataxy** /-si/) ■ n. Medicine the loss of full control of bodily movements.
– DERIVATIVES **ataxic** adj.
– ORIGIN C19: from Greek, from *a-* 'without' + *taxis* 'order'.

atchar ■ n. variant spelling of ATJAR.

ate past of EAT.

-ate[1] ■ suffix forming nouns: 1 denoting status or office: *doctorate.* ▶ denoting a state or function: *mandate.* 2 denoting a group: *electorate.* 3 Chemistry denoting a salt or ester, especially of an acid with a corresponding name ending in *-ic*: *chlorate.* 4 denoting a product of a chemical process: *condensate.*
– ORIGIN from Latin *-atus, -ata, -atum.*

-ate[2] ■ suffix 1 forming adjectives and nouns such as *associate.* 2 forming adjectives from Latin: *caudate.*
– ORIGIN from Latin *-atus, -ata, -atum.*

-ate[3] ■ suffix forming verbs such as *fascinate.*
– ORIGIN from -ATE[2].

atelectasis /ˌatɪˈlɛktəsɪs/ ■ n. Medicine partial collapse or incomplete inflation of the lung.
– ORIGIN C19: from Greek *atelēs* 'imperfect' + *ektasis* 'extension'.

atelier /əˈtɛlɪeɪ/ ■ n. a workshop or studio.
– ORIGIN C17: from Old French *astelle* 'splinter of wood'.

Athabaskan /ˌaθəˈbask(ə)n/ (also **Athapaskan**) ■ n. a family of North American Indian languages, including Navajo and Apache. ■ adj. of or relating to these languages.
– ORIGIN from *Athabasca*, a lake in western Canada.

Atharva Veda /əˌtɑːvə ˈveɪdə, ˈviːdə/ ■ n. a collection of hymns and ritual utterances added at a later stage to the existing Veda material.
– ORIGIN from Sanskrit *Atharvan* (Brahma's eldest son, said to be the author of the collection) + VEDA.

atheism /ˈeɪθɪɪz(ə)m/ ■ n. the theory or belief that God does not exist.
– DERIVATIVES **atheist** n. **atheistic** adj. **atheistical** adj.
– ORIGIN C16: from French *athéisme*, from Greek *a-* 'without' + *theos* 'god'.

Athenian ■ n. a native or inhabitant of Athens. ■ adj. of or relating to Athens.

atheroma /ˌaθəˈrəʊmə/ ■ n. Medicine degeneration of the walls of the arteries, leading to restriction of the circulation and a risk of thrombosis.
– DERIVATIVES **atheromatous** adj.
– ORIGIN C16: from Greek *athērōma*, from *athērē* 'groats'.

atherosclerosis /ˌaθərəʊsklɪəˈrəʊsɪs, -sklə-/ ■ n. Medicine a disease of the arteries characterized by the deposition of plaques of fatty material on their inner walls.
– DERIVATIVES **atherosclerotic** adj.
– ORIGIN C20: from Greek *athērē* 'groats' + SCLEROSIS.

athetosis /ˌaθɪˈtəʊsɪs/ ■ n. Medicine a condition in which abnormal muscle contraction causes involuntary writhing movements.
– DERIVATIVES **athetoid** adj. **athetotic** adj.
– ORIGIN C19: from Greek *athetos* 'without position'.

athlete ■ n. a person who is proficient in sports, especially one who competes in track and field events.
– ORIGIN Middle English: from Greek, from *athlein* 'compete for a prize', from *athlon* 'prize'.

athlete's foot ■ n. a form of ringworm infection affecting mainly the skin between the toes.

athletic ■ adj. 1 physically strong and fit. 2 relating to athletes or athletics.
– DERIVATIVES **athletically** adv. **athleticism** n.

athletics ■ pl. n. [usu. treated as sing.] 1 the sport of competing in track and field events. 2 N. Amer. physical sports and games of any kind.

-athon ■ suffix forming nouns denoting an action or activity which is carried on for a very long time or on a very large scale, typically to raise funds for charity: *a talkathon.*
– ORIGIN on the pattern of *(mar)athon.*

athwart /əˈθwɔːt/ ■ prep. 1 from side to side of; across. 2 counter to. ■ adv. across from side to side; transversely.
– ORIGIN Middle English: from *a-*[2] + THWART.

-atic ■ suffix forming adjectives and nouns: *aquatic.*
– ORIGIN from Latin *-aticus.*

-ation ■ suffix (forming nouns) denoting an action or its result: *exploration*.
– ORIGIN from Latin *-ation-*.

-ative ■ suffix (forming adjectives) denoting a characteristic or propensity: *pejorative*.
– ORIGIN from French *-atif, -ative* or Latin *-ativus* (from past participial stems ending in *-at*).

atjar /'atʃa, 'atʃɑː/ (also *achar, atchar*) ■ n. a spicy pickle made from vegetables or fruit, often eaten with curry.
– ORIGIN from Persian *āchār* 'pickles'.

atlantes plural form of ATLAS (sense 3).

Atlantic ■ adj. 1 of or adjoining the Atlantic Ocean. 2 Geology relating to or denoting the third climatic stage of the postglacial period in northern Europe (about 7 500 to 5 000 years ago), with a moist oceanic climate.
– ORIGIN Middle English: from Greek *Atlantikos*, from *Atlas, Atlant-* (see ATLAS).

atlas ■ n. 1 a book of maps or charts. 2 Anatomy the topmost vertebra of the backbone, articulating with the occipital bone of the skull. 3 (pl. **atlantes** /at'lantiːz/) Architecture a stone carving of a male figure, used as a column to support the entablature of a Greek or Greek-style building.
– ORIGIN C16: from Greek *Atlas*, the Greek god who held up the pillars of the universe.

ATM ■ abbrev. automated teller machine.

atman /'ɑːtmən/ ■ n. Hinduism the spiritual life principle of the universe, especially when regarded as immanent in the real self of the individual. ▶ a person's soul.
– ORIGIN from Sanskrit *ātman* 'essence'.

atmosphere ■ n. 1 the envelope of gases surrounding the earth or another planet. ▶ the air in a particular place. 2 a pervading tone or mood. ▶ a pleasurable and interesting or exciting mood. 3 Physics a unit of pressure equal to mean atmospheric pressure at sea level, 101 325 pascals (roughly 14.7 pounds per square inch).
– DERIVATIVES **atmospheric** adj. **atmospherical** adj. (archaic). **atmospherically** adv.
– ORIGIN C17: from Greek, from *atmos* 'vapour' + *sphaira* 'globe'.

atmospherics ■ pl. n. electrical disturbances in the atmosphere, especially as they interfere with telecommunications.

atoll /'atɒl, ə'tɒl/ ■ n. a ring-shaped reef or chain of islands formed of coral.
– ORIGIN C17: from Maldivian *atoḷu*.

atom ■ n. 1 the smallest particle of a chemical element, consisting of a positively charged nucleus (containing protons and typically also neutrons) surrounded by negatively charged electrons. 2 [usu. with neg.] an extremely small amount.
– ORIGIN C15: from Greek *atomos* 'indivisible', from *a-* 'not' + *temnein* 'to cut'.

atom bomb (also **atomic bomb**) ■ n. a bomb which derives its destructive power from the rapid release of energy by fission of heavy atomic nuclei.

atomic ■ adj. 1 of or relating to an atom or atoms. 2 relating to or denoting nuclear energy.
– DERIVATIVES **atomically** adv.

atomic clock ■ n. an extremely accurate type of clock which is regulated by the vibrations of an atomic or molecular system such as caesium or ammonia.

atomicity ■ n. 1 Chemistry the number of atoms in the molecule of an element. 2 the state or fact of being composed of atoms.

atomic mass ■ n. the mass of an atom of a chemical element expressed in atomic mass units.

atomic mass unit ■ n. a unit of mass used to express atomic and molecular weights, equal to one twelfth of the mass of an atom of carbon-12.

atomic number ■ n. Chemistry the number of protons in the nucleus of an atom, which is characteristic of a chemical element and determines its place in the periodic table.

atomic theory ■ n. the theory that all matter is made up of tiny indivisible particles (atoms).

atomic volume ■ n. Chemistry the volume occupied by one gram-atom of an element under standard conditions.

atomic weight ■ n. Chemistry another term for RELATIVE ATOMIC MASS.

atomism ■ n. chiefly Philosophy a theoretical approach that regards something as interpretable through analysis into distinct, separable, and independent elementary components. The opposite of HOLISM.
– DERIVATIVES **atomist** n. **atomistic** adj.

atomize (also **-ise**) ■ v. 1 convert (a substance) into very fine particles or droplets. 2 fragment.
– DERIVATIVES **atomization** (also **-isation**) n. **atomizer** (also **-iser**) n.

atonal /eɪ'təʊn(ə)l, ə-/ ■ adj. Music not written in any key or mode.
– DERIVATIVES **atonalism** n. **atonalist** n. **atonality** n.

atone ■ v. (**atone for**) make amends or reparation for.
– ORIGIN Middle English: from *at one* and back-formation from ATONEMENT.

atonement ■ n. 1 reparation for a wrong or injury. 2 (**the Atonement**) Christian Church the reconciliation of God and mankind through the death of Jesus Christ.
– ORIGIN C16: from *at one* + -MENT.

atonic /ə'tɒnɪk/ ■ adj. Physiology lacking muscular tone.
– DERIVATIVES **atony** /'atəni/ n.

atop poetic/literary ■ prep. on the top of. ■ adv. on the top.

atopic /eɪ'tɒpɪk/ ■ adj. denoting a form of allergy in which a hypersensitivity reaction such as eczema or asthma may occur in a part of the body not in contact with the allergen.
– DERIVATIVES **atopy** /'atəpi/ n.
– ORIGIN C20: from Greek *atopia* 'unusualness'.

-ator ■ suffix forming agent nouns such as *agitator*.
– ORIGIN from Latin.

-atory ■ suffix (forming adjectives) relating to or involving an action: *explanatory*.
– ORIGIN from Latin *-atorius*.

atrazine /'atrəziːn/ ■ n. a synthetic compound derived from triazine, used as an agricultural herbicide.
– ORIGIN 1960s: blend of *amino* (see AMINO GROUP) and TRIAZINE.

atrioventricular /ˌeɪtrɪə(ʊ)ven'trɪkjʊlə/ ■ adj. Anatomy & Physiology of or relating to the atrial and ventricular chambers of the heart.

atrium /'eɪtrɪəm/ ■ n. (pl. **atria** /'eɪtrɪə/ or **atriums**) 1 Architecture an open-roofed central court in an ancient Roman house. ▶ a central hall or court in a modern building, typically rising through several stories and having a glazed roof. 2 Anatomy each of the two upper cavities of the heart from which blood is passed to the ventricles.
– DERIVATIVES **atrial** adj.
– ORIGIN C16: from Latin.

atrocious ■ adj. 1 horrifyingly wicked. 2 informal extremely bad or unpleasant.
– DERIVATIVES **atrociously** adv. **atrociousness** n.
– ORIGIN C17: from Latin *atrox, atroc-* 'cruel'.

atrocity ■ n. (pl. **-ies**) an extremely wicked or cruel act.
– ORIGIN C16: from Latin *atrocitas*, from *atrox, atroc-* 'cruel'.

atrophy /'atrəfi/ ■ v. (**-ies, -ied**) 1 (of body tissue or an organ) waste away, especially as a result of the degeneration of cells, or become vestigial during evolution. 2 gradually decline in effectiveness or vigour. ■ n. (pl. **-ies**) the condition or process of atrophying.
– DERIVATIVES **atrophic** /ə'trɒfɪk/ adj.
– ORIGIN C16: from Greek *atrophia* 'lack of food'.

atropine /'atrəpiːn, -ɪn/ ■ n. Chemistry a poisonous compound found in deadly nightshade, used in medicine as a muscle relaxant.
– ORIGIN C19: from *Atropa belladonna*, the plant 'deadly nightshade', from *Atropos* 'inflexible', the name of one of the Fates.

attaboy ■ exclam. an informal expression of encouragement or admiration.
– ORIGIN C20: from casual pronunciation of *that's the boy*.

attach ■ v. 1 fasten; join. ▶ include (a condition) as part of

an agreement. ▸ assign or attribute: *he doesn't attach much importance to fixed ideas.* **2** [as adj. **attached**] full of affection or fondness. **3** appoint for special or temporary duties.
– DERIVATIVES **attachable** adj.
– ORIGIN Middle English: from Old French *atachier* 'fasten, fix'.

attaché /əˈtaʃeɪ/ ■ n. a person on the staff of an ambassador, having a specialized area of responsibility.
– ORIGIN C19: from French, 'attached', from *attacher*.

attaché case ■ n. a small, flat briefcase for carrying documents.

attachment ■ n. **1** an extra part or extension attached to perform a function. **2** affection or fondness. ▸ an affectionate relationship. **3** the action of attaching. **4** Brit. temporary secondment to an organization.

attack ■ v. **1** take aggressive action against. ▸ (of a disease, chemical, etc.) act harmfully on. **2** criticize or oppose fiercely and publicly. **3** begin to deal with (a problem or task) in a determined way. **4** (in sport) make a forceful attempt to score goals or points. ■ n. **1** an instance of attacking. ▸ destructive action by a disease or chemical. **2** a sudden short bout of an illness or disorder. **3** the players in a team whose role is to attack.
– DERIVATIVES **attacker** n.
– ORIGIN C17: from Italian *attacco* 'an attack', *attaccare* 'join battle'.

attain ■ v. **1** succeed in accomplishing. **2** reach (a specified age, size, or amount).
– DERIVATIVES **attainability** n. **attainable** adj.
– ORIGIN Middle English: from Old French *ateindre*, from Latin, from *ad-* 'at, to' + *tangere* 'to touch'.

attainder /əˈteɪndə/ ■ n. historical the forfeiture of land and civil rights suffered as a consequence of a sentence of death for treason or felony.
– PHRASES **act** (or **bill**) **of attainder** an item of legislation inflicting attainder without judicial decision.
– ORIGIN Middle English: from Old French *ateindre* in the sense 'convict' (see ATTAIN).

attainment ■ n. the action or fact of attaining a goal. ▸ a skill or educational achievement.

attar /ˈatə/ (also **otto**) ■ n. a fragrant essential oil, typically made from rose petals.
– ORIGIN C17: from Arabic '*iṭr* 'perfume, essence'.

attempt ■ v. make an effort to achieve or complete. ▸ try to climb to the top of (a mountain). ■ n. an act of attempting. ▸ a bid to kill someone.
– DERIVATIVES **attemptable** adj.
– ORIGIN Middle English: from Latin *attemptare*, from *ad-* 'to' + *temptare* 'to tempt'.

attend ■ v. **1** be present at. ▸ go regularly to (a school, church, or service). **2** (**attend to**) deal with. ▸ pay attention to. **3** (usu. **be attended**) occur at the same time as or as a result of. **4** escort and wait on (a member of royalty or other important person).
– DERIVATIVES **attendee** n. **attender** n.
– ORIGIN Middle English: from Latin *attendere*, from *ad-* 'to' + *tendere* 'stretch'.

attendance ■ n. **1** the action or state of attending. **2** the number of people present at a particular occasion.

attendant ■ n. **1** a person employed to provide a service to the public. ▸ an assistant to an important person. **2** a person who attends a particular occasion. ■ adj. occurring at the same time or as a result of.

attention ■ n. **1** the mental faculty of considering or taking notice. ▸ notice taken. **2** special care or consideration. ▸ (**attentions**) a person's behaviour to another as an indication of affection or sexual interest. **3** Military a position assumed by a soldier, standing very straight with the feet together and the arms straight down the sides of the body.
– DERIVATIVES **attentional** adj.
– ORIGIN Middle English: from Latin *attentio(n-)*, from *attendere* (see ATTEND).

attention deficit disorder ■ n. any of a range of behavioural disorders occurring principally in children, including such symptoms as poor concentration, hyperactivity, and learning difficulties.

attentive ■ adj. **1** paying close attention. **2** assiduously attending to the comfort or wishes of others.
– DERIVATIVES **attentively** adv. **attentiveness** n.
– ORIGIN Middle English: from Old French *attentif, -ive*, from Latin *attendere* (see ATTEND).

attenuate /əˈtɛnjʊeɪt/ ■ v. **1** reduce the strength, effect, or value of. **2** make thin or thinner.
– DERIVATIVES **attenuation** n.
– ORIGIN C16: from Latin *attenuare* 'make slender'.

attest /əˈtɛst/ ■ v. **1** provide or serve as clear evidence of. **2** declare that something exists or is the case.
– DERIVATIVES **attestable** adj. **attestation** n. **attestor** n.
– ORIGIN C16: from Latin *attestari*, from *ad-* 'to' + *testari* 'to witness'.

Attic /ˈatɪk/ ■ adj. of or relating to Attica in Eastern Greece, or ancient Athens, or the dialect of Greek spoken there.
– ORIGIN C16: from Greek *Attikos*.

attic ■ n. a space or room inside or partly inside the roof of a building.
– ORIGIN C17 (designating a small structure above a much taller one, usu. in Attic style): from Greek *Attikos*.

attire ■ n. clothes, especially fine or formal ones. ■ v. (**be attired**) be dressed in clothes of a specified kind.
– ORIGIN Middle English: from Old French *atirier* 'equip', from *a tire* 'in order'.

attitude ■ n. **1** a settled way of thinking or feeling. ▸ a position of the body indicating a particular mental state. **2** informal, chiefly N. Amer. truculent behaviour. ▸ self-confident behaviour. **3** the orientation of an aircraft or spacecraft.
– DERIVATIVES **attitudinal** adj.
– ORIGIN C17: from Italian *attitudine* 'fitness, posture'.

attitudinize /ˌatɪˈtjuːdɪnaɪz/ (also **-ise**) ■ v. adopt or express a particular attitude or attitudes, typically just for effect.
– DERIVATIVES **attitudinizer** (also **-iser**) n.

atto- /ˈatəʊ/ ■ comb. form denoting a factor of 10^{-18}: *attowatt*.
– ORIGIN from Danish or Norwegian *atten* 'eighteen'.

attorney /əˈtəːni/ ■ n. (pl. **-eys**) a person, typically a lawyer, appointed to act for another in legal matters. ▸ a member of the legal profession qualified to act as a conveyancer and notary, as well as to instruct advocates, advise clients, and represent clients in lower and (under certain circumstances) higher courts.
– DERIVATIVES **attorneyship** n.
– ORIGIN Middle English: from Old French *atorner* 'assign', from *a* 'towards' + *torner* 'turn'.

Attorney-General ■ n. (pl. **Attorneys-General**) the principal legal officer of a national government, state, or province, who advises and represents it in legal proceedings.

attract ■ v. **1** draw or bring in by offering something of interest or advantage. **2** evoke (a specified reaction). ▸ (often **be attracted to**) cause to have a liking for or interest in. **3** exert a pull on.
– DERIVATIVES **attractable** adj. **attractor** n.
– ORIGIN Middle English: from Latin *attrahere* 'draw near'.

attractant ■ n. a substance which attracts. ■ adj. tending to attract.

attraction ■ n. **1** the action or power of attracting. ▸ a quality or feature that attracts. ▸ a building or place which draws visitors. **2** Physics a force under the influence of which objects tend to move towards each other.

attractive ■ adj. **1** pleasing or appealing to the senses. ▸ having qualities or features which arouse interest. **2** of or relating to attraction between physical objects.
– DERIVATIVES **attractively** adv. **attractiveness** n.

attribute ■ v. /əˈtrɪbjuːt/ (**attribute something to**) regard something as belonging to or being caused by. ■ n. /ˈatrɪbjuːt/ **1** a quality or feature regarded as characteristic or inherent. **2** a material object recognized as representative of a person, status, or office.
– DERIVATIVES **attributable** /əˈtrɪbjʊtəb(ə)l/ adj. **attribution** n.
– ORIGIN C15: from Latin *attribuere*, from *ad-* 'to' + *tribuere* 'assign'.

attributive /əˈtrɪbjʊtɪv/ ■ adj. Grammar (of an adjective or other modifier) preceding the word that it modifies and expressing an attribute, as *old* in *the old dog*. Contrasted

attrition

with **PREDICATIVE**.
– DERIVATIVES **attributively** adv.

attrition /ə'trɪʃ(ə)n/ ■ n. **1** the action or process of gradually wearing down through sustained attack or pressure. **2** wearing away by friction. **3** (in scholastic theology) sorrow for sin falling short of contrition.
– DERIVATIVES **attritional** adj.
– ORIGIN Middle English: from late Latin *attritio(n-)*, from *atterere* 'to rub'.

attune ■ v. adjust or accustom to a particular situation.
– ORIGIN C16: from AD- + TUNE.

atypical ■ adj. not typical.
– DERIVATIVES **atypically** adv.

AU ■ abbrev. African Union (formerly the OAU).

Au ■ symb. the chemical element gold.
– ORIGIN from Latin *aurum*.

aubergine /'əʊbəʒiːn/ ■ n. chiefly Brit. another term for BRINJAL.
– ORIGIN C18: from Arabic *al-bāḏinjān*.

aubretia /ɔː'briːʃə/ (also **aubrietia**) ■ n. a dwarf evergreen trailing plant with dense masses of foliage and purple, pink, or white flowers. [*Aubrieta deltoidea*.]
– ORIGIN C19: named after the French botanist Claude Aubriet.

auburn /'ɔːbən, 'ɔːbəːn/ ■ n. a reddish-brown colour.
– ORIGIN Middle English: from Old French *auborne*, from Latin *alburnus* 'whitish'. The word came to mean *brown* because in the 16th and 17th centuries it was often written *abrune* or *abroun*.

Auckland Park ■ n. S. African informal the SABC.
– ORIGIN the district of Johannesburg where the organization has its headquarters.

au courant /ˌəʊ kuˈrɒ̃/ ■ adj. up to date and well informed.
– ORIGIN C18: from French, literally 'in the (regular) course'.

auction /'ɔːkʃ(ə)n/ ■ n. **1** a public sale in which goods or property are sold to the highest bidder. **2** Bridge the part of the game in which players bid to decide the contract in which the hand shall be played. ■ v. sell or offer for sale at an auction.
– ORIGIN C16: from Latin *auctio(n-)* 'increase, auction'.

auctioneer ■ n. a person who conducts auctions by accepting bids and declaring goods sold.
– DERIVATIVES **auctioneering** n.

audacious /ɔːˈdeɪʃəs/ ■ adj. **1** recklessly daring. **2** impudent.
– DERIVATIVES **audaciously** adv. **audaciousness** n. **audacity** n.
– ORIGIN C16: from Latin *audax, audac-* 'bold'.

audible ■ adj. able to be heard. ■ n. American Football a change of playing tactics called by the quarterback at the line of scrimmage.
– DERIVATIVES **audibility** n. **audibly** adv.
– ORIGIN C15: from late Latin *audibilis*, from *audire* 'hear'.

audience ■ n. **1** the assembled spectators or listeners at an event. **2** the readership of a book, magazine, or newspaper. **3** a formal interview with a person in authority.
– ORIGIN Middle English: from Latin *audientia*, from *audire* 'hear'.

audio ■ n. [usu. as modifier] sound, especially when recorded, transmitted, or reproduced: *audio player*.

audio- ■ comb. form relating to hearing or sound, especially when recorded, transmitted, or reproduced: *audio-visual*.
– ORIGIN from Latin *audire* 'hear'.

audiobook ■ n. an audio cassette recording of a reading of a book.

audio frequency ■ n. a frequency of oscillation capable of being perceived by the human ear, generally between 20 and 20 000 Hz.

audiogram ■ n. a graphic record produced by audiometry.

audiology /ˌɔːdɪˈɒlədʒi/ ■ n. the branch of science and medicine concerned with the sense of hearing.

– DERIVATIVES **audiological** adj. **audiologist** n.

audiometry /ˌɔːdɪˈɒmɪtri/ ■ n. measurement of the range and sensitivity of a person's sense of hearing.
– DERIVATIVES **audiometer** n. **audiometric** adj.

audio player ■ an electronic device that stores, organizes, and plays audio files.

audio tape ■ n. magnetic tape on which sound can be recorded. ■ v. (**audiotape**) record (sound) on tape.

audio typist ■ n. a typist who transcribes from recorded dictation.

audio-visual ■ adj. using both sight and sound, typically in the form of slides or video and speech or music.

audit ■ n. an official inspection of an organization's accounts, typically by an independent body. ■ v. (**audited**, **auditing**) **1** conduct an audit of. **2** N. Amer. attend (a class) informally, without working for credit.
– ORIGIN Middle English: from medieval Latin *auditus* (*compoti*) 'audit (of an account)' from Latin *auditus* 'hearing', an audit orig. being presented orally.

audition /ɔːˈdɪʃ(ə)n/ ■ n. an interview for a musician, actor, etc., consisting of a practical demonstration of the candidate's suitability and skill. ■ v. assess or be assessed by an audition.
– ORIGIN C16: from Latin *auditio(n-)*, from *audire* 'hear'.

auditor ■ n. **1** a person who conducts an audit. **2** a listener.
– DERIVATIVES **auditorial** adj.

Auditor-General ■ n. (pl. **Auditors-General**) a senior official of a national government, state, or province, appointed to audit government finances and public expenditure.

auditorium ■ n. (pl. **auditoriums** or **auditoria**) **1** the part of a theatre or hall in which the audience sits. **2** chiefly N. Amer. a large hall used for public gatherings.
– ORIGIN C17: from Latin *auditorius* (see AUDITORY).

auditory ■ adj. of or relating to the sense of hearing.
– ORIGIN C16: from Latin *auditorius*, from *audire* 'hear'.

au fait /əʊ ˈfeɪ/ ■ adj. (**au fait with**) having a good or detailed knowledge of.
– ORIGIN C18: from French, 'to the point'.

au fond /əʊ ˈfɒ̃/ ■ adv. in essence.
– ORIGIN from French.

Aug. ■ abbrev. August.

auger /'ɔːɡə/ ■ n. a tool resembling a large corkscrew, for boring holes.
– ORIGIN Old English: from *nafu* (see NAVE[2]) + *gār* 'piercer'; the *n* was lost by wrong division of *a nauger*.

auger shell ■ n. a marine mollusc with a slender tapering spiral shell, often brightly coloured. [*Terebra* and other genera.]

aught /ɔːt/ (also **ought**) ■ pron. archaic anything at all.
– ORIGIN Old English (see AYE[2], WIGHT).

augite /'ɔːdʒʌɪt/ ■ n. a dark green or black aluminosilicate mineral found in many igneous rocks.
– ORIGIN C19: from Latin *augites*, denoting a precious stone, from Greek *augitēs*, from *augē* 'lustre'.

augment /ɔːɡˈmɛnt/ ■ v. **1** make greater by addition; increase. **2** [as adj. **augmented**] Music denoting an interval which is one semitone greater than the corresponding major or perfect interval.
– DERIVATIVES **augmenter** n.
– ORIGIN Middle English: from late Latin *augmentare*, from Latin *augere* 'to increase'.

augmentation ■ n. the action or process of augmenting.

au gratin /əʊ ˈɡratɑ̃/ ■ adj. [postpos.] sprinkled with breadcrumbs or grated cheese and browned.
– ORIGIN French, 'by grating', from *gratter* 'to grate'.

augur /'ɔːɡə/ ■ v. portend (a specified outcome): *the cessation of hostilities seemed to augur well*. ■ n. (in ancient Rome) a religious official who interpreted natural signs so as to determine divine approval or disapproval of a proposed action.
– DERIVATIVES **augural** /'ɔːɡjʊr(ə)l/ adj. (archaic).
– ORIGIN Middle English: from Latin, 'diviner'.

augury /'ɔːɡjʊri/ ■ n. (pl. **-ies**) **1** an omen. **2** the interpretation of omens.

August ■ n. the eighth month of the year.

– ORIGIN Old English, from Latin *augustus* 'consecrated, venerable'; named after *Augustus* Caesar, the first Roman emperor.

august /ɔːˈɡʌst/ ■ adj. inspiring respect and admiration.
– DERIVATIVES **augustly** adv. **augustness** n.
– ORIGIN C17: from Latin *augustus* 'consecrated, venerable'.

Augustan /ɔːˈɡʌst(ə)n/ ■ adj. **1** connected with or occurring during the reign of the Roman emperor Augustus, especially as a notable period of Latin literature. **2** relating to or denoting a refined and classical style of 17th- and 18th-century English literature. ■ n. a writer of the Augustan age.

Augustinian /ˌɔːɡəˈstɪnɪən/ ■ adj. of or relating to St Augustine (354–430) or his doctrines. ▶ relating to or denoting a religious order observing a rule derived from St Augustine's writings. ■ n. a member of an Augustinian order. ▶ an adherent of the doctrines of St Augustine.

auk /ɔːk/ ■ n. a short-winged diving seabird of a family including the guillemot and puffin, typically black and white. [Family Alcidae.]
– ORIGIN C17: from Old Norse *álka* 'razorbill'.

auld /ɔːld, ɑːld/ ■ adj. Scottish form of OLD.
– PHRASES **auld lang syne** times long past.
– ORIGIN Old English, Anglian form of OLD.

au naturel /ˌəʊ natjʊˈrɛl/ ■ adj. & adv. **1** in the most simple or natural way. **2** naked; in the nude.
– ORIGIN from French.

aunt ■ n. **1** the sister of one's father or mother or the wife of one's uncle. **2** informal an unrelated adult female friend of a child.
– ORIGIN Middle English: from Old French *ante*, from Latin *amita*.

auntie (also **aunty**) ■ n. (pl. **-ies**) informal **1** aunt. **2** S. African a friendly but respectful form of address for an older woman, used chiefly by young people. **3** S. African informal, often derogatory an old woman. **4** S. African the female owner of a shebeen.

Aunt Sally ■ n. (pl. **-ies**) **1** a game played in parts of Britain in which players throw sticks or balls at a wooden dummy (formerly a figure of a woman). **2** a person or thing set up as an easy target for criticism.

au pair /əʊ ˈpɛː/ ■ n. a young foreign person, typically a woman, who helps with housework and childcare in exchange for board and lodging.
– ORIGIN C19: from French, 'on equal terms'.

aura /ˈɔːrə/ ■ n. (pl. **aurae** /-riː/ or **auras**) **1** the distinctive atmosphere or quality that seems to be generated by someone or something. **2** (in spiritualism and some forms of alternative medicine) a supposed emanation surrounding the body of a living creature. **3** Medicine a warning sensation experienced before an attack of epilepsy or migraine.
– ORIGIN Middle English, 'a gentle breeze': from Greek, 'breeze, breath'.

aural /ˈɔːr(ə)l/ ■ adj. of or relating to the ear or the sense of hearing.
– DERIVATIVES **aurally** adv.
– ORIGIN C19: from Latin *auris* 'ear'.

aureate /ˈɔːrɪət/ ■ adj. made of or having the colour of gold.
– ORIGIN Middle English: from late Latin *aureatus*, from Latin *aurum* 'gold'.

aureole /ˈɔːrɪəʊl/ (also **aureola** /ɔːˈrɪələ/) ■ n. **1** (in paintings) a radiant circle surrounding a person's head or body as a way of representing holiness. **2** a corona around the sun or moon. **3** Geology the zone of metamorphosed rock surrounding an igneous intrusion.
– ORIGIN Middle English: from Latin *aureola* (*corona*) 'golden (crown)', from *aurum* 'gold'.

au revoir /ˌəʊ rəˈvwɑː/ ■ exclam. goodbye.
– ORIGIN C17: from French, 'to the seeing again'.

auric /ˈɔːrɪk/ ■ adj. Chemistry of gold with a valency of three; of gold(III).
– ORIGIN C19: from Latin *aurum* 'gold'.

auricle /ˈɔːrɪk(ə)l/ ■ n. Anatomy & Zoology **1** the external part or pinna of the ear. **2** an atrium of the heart.
– DERIVATIVES **auriculate** adj.
– ORIGIN Middle English: from Latin *auricula*, diminutive of *auris* 'ear'.

Australopithecus

auricula /ɔːˈrɪkjʊlə/ ■ n. an Alpine primula with leaves said to resemble bears' ears. [*Primula auricula*.]
– ORIGIN C17: from Latin, diminutive of *auris* 'ear'.

auricular /ɔːˈrɪkjʊlə/ ■ adj. **1** of or relating to the ear or hearing. **2** of, relating to, or shaped like an auricle.
– ORIGIN Middle English: from late Latin *auricularis*, from *auris* 'ear'.

auriferous /ɔːˈrɪf(ə)rəs/ ■ adj. (of rocks or minerals) containing gold.
– ORIGIN C17: from Latin *aurifer* 'gold-bearing'.

Aurignacian /ˌɔːrɪɡˈneɪʃ(ə)n, ˌɔːrɪɡˈneɪ-/ ■ adj. Archaeology relating to or denoting the early stages of the Upper Palaeolithic culture in Europe and the Near East, dated to about 34 000–29 000 years ago.
– ORIGIN C20: from French, from *Aurignac* in SW France, where objects from this culture were found.

aurochs /ˈɔːrɒks, ˈaʊ-/ ■ n. (pl. same) a large extinct wild ox that was the ancestor of domestic cattle. [*Bos primigenius.*]
– ORIGIN C18: from German *Auerochs*, from Old High German, from *ūr* + *ohso* 'ox'.

aurora /ɔːˈrɔːrə/ ■ n. (pl. **auroras** or **aurorae** /-riː/) **1** the northern lights (aurora borealis) or southern lights (aurora australis), a natural phenomenon characterized by the appearance of streamers of coloured light in the sky near the earth's magnetic poles and caused by the interaction of charged particles from the sun with atoms in the upper atmosphere. **2** poetic/literary the dawn.
– DERIVATIVES **auroral** adj.
– ORIGIN Middle English: from Latin, 'dawn, goddess of the dawn'.

Auslese /ˈaʊsleɪzə/ ■ n. a white wine of German origin or style made from selected bunches of grapes picked later than the general harvest.
– ORIGIN from German, from *aus* 'out' + *Lese* 'picking'.

auspice /ˈɔːspɪs/ ■ n. archaic an omen.
– PHRASES **under the auspices of** with the support or protection of.
– ORIGIN C16, 'the observation of bird-flight in divination': from Latin *auspicium*, from *auspex* 'observer of birds'.

auspicious /ɔːˈspɪʃəs/ ■ adj. indicating a good chance of success; favourable.
– DERIVATIVES **auspiciously** adv. **auspiciousness** n.

Aussie /ˈɒzi, ˈɒsi/ (also **Ozzie**) ■ n. (pl. **-ies**) & adj. informal Australia or Australian.

austenite /ˈɒstɪnʌɪt, ˈɔː-/ ■ n. Metallurgy a relatively soft component of steel consisting of a solid solution of carbon in iron.
– DERIVATIVES **austenitic** adj.
– ORIGIN C20: named after the English metallurgist Sir William Roberts-*Austen*.

austere /ɒˈstɪə, ɔː-/ ■ adj. (**-er**, **-est**) **1** severe or strict in appearance or manner. **2** lacking comforts, luxuries, or adornment.
– DERIVATIVES **austerely** adv. **austerity** n.
– ORIGIN Middle English: from Greek *austēros* 'severe'.

austral /ˈɒstr(ə)l, ˈɔː-/ ■ adj. of the southern hemisphere.
– ORIGIN C15: from Latin *australis*, from *Auster* 'the south, the south wind'.

Australasian /ˌɒstrəˈleɪʒ(ə)n, -ʃ(ə)n/ ■ adj. of or relating to Australasia, a region consisting of Australia, New Zealand, and islands of the SW Pacific. ■ n. a person from Australasia.

Australian ■ n. a native or national of Australia, or a person of Australian descent. ■ adj. of or relating to Australia.
– ORIGIN from Latin (*Terra*) *Australis* 'southern (land)', the name of the supposed southern continent.

Australian bug ■ n. S. African a scale insect, native to Australia, with a large fluted cottony egg sac, which infests citrus trees and other plants. [*Icerya purchasi*.]

Australian Rules ■ n. a form of football played on an oval field with an oval ball by teams of eighteen players.

Australopithecus /ˌɒstrələʊˈpɪθɪkəs, ˌɔː-/ ■ n. a genus of fossil bipedal primates with both ape-like and human characteristics, found in Pliocene and Lower Pleistocene

deposits in Africa.
– DERIVATIVES **australopithecine** /-ɪsiːn/ n. & adj.
– ORIGIN from Latin *australis* (see **AUSTRAL**) + Greek *pithēkos* 'ape'.

Austrian ▪ n. a native or inhabitant of Austria, or a person of Austrian descent. ▪ adj. of or relating to Austria or its people.

Austrian blind ▪ n. a ruched blind extending about a third of the way down a window.

Austro- /'ɒstrəʊ, 'ɔː-/ ▪ comb. form Austrian; Austrian and ...: *Austro-Hungarian*.

Austronesian /ˌɒstrə(ʊ)'niːziən, -ʒ(ə)n, ˌɔː-/ ▪ adj. relating to or denoting a family of languages spoken in an area extending from Madagascar in the west to the Pacific islands in the east. ▪ n. this family of languages.
– ORIGIN from Latin *australis* (see **AUSTRAL**) + Greek *nēsos* 'island'.

aut- ▪ prefix variant spelling of **AUTO-**[1].

autarchy /'ɔːtɑːki/ ▪ n. (pl. **-ies**) **1** another term for **AUTOCRACY**. **2** variant spelling of **AUTARKY**.
– DERIVATIVES **autarch** n. **autarchic** adj.

autarky (also **autarchy**) ▪ n. **1** economic independence or self-sufficiency. **2** a state or society which is economically independent.
– DERIVATIVES **autarkic** adj.
– ORIGIN C17: from Greek, from *autarkēs* 'self-sufficiency'.

autecology /ˌɔːtɪ'kɒlədʒi/ (also **autoecology**) ▪ n. Biology the ecological study of a particular species. Contrasted with **SYNECOLOGY**.
– DERIVATIVES **autecological** adj.

auteur /əʊ'təː, ɔː-/ ▪ n. a film director who influences their films so much that they rank as their author.
– ORIGIN 1960s: from French, 'author'.

authentic ▪ adj. of undisputed origin or veracity; genuine.
– DERIVATIVES **authentically** adv. **authenticity** /ɔː'θɛntɪsɪti/ n.
– ORIGIN Middle English: from Greek *authentikos* 'principal, genuine'.

authenticate ▪ v. prove or show to be authentic.
– DERIVATIVES **authentication** /-ˈkeɪʃ(ə)n/ n. **authenticator** n.

authigenic /ˌɔːθɪ'dʒɛnɪk/ ▪ adj. Geology (of minerals and other materials) formed in their present position. Often contrasted with **ALLOGENIC**.
– ORIGIN C19: from Greek *authigenēs* 'born on the spot'.

author ▪ n. **1** a writer of a book, article, or report. **2** an originator of a plan or idea. ▪ v. be the author or the originator of.
– DERIVATIVES **authoress** n. **authorial** /ɔː'θɔːrɪəl/ adj. **authorship** n.
– ORIGIN Middle English: from Old French *autor*, from Latin *auctor*, from *augere* 'increase, originate'.

authoring ▪ n. Computing the creation of programs and databases for computer applications such as multimedia products.

authoritarian /ɔːˌθɒrɪ'tɛːrɪən/ ▪ adj. favouring or enforcing strict obedience to authority at the expense of personal freedom. ▪ n. an authoritarian person.
– DERIVATIVES **authoritarianism** n.

authoritative /ɔː'θɒrɪtətɪv, -ˌteɪtɪv/ ▪ adj. **1** reliable because true or accurate: *an authoritative source*. **2** commanding and self-confident. **3** supported by authority.
– DERIVATIVES **authoritatively** adv. **authoritativeness** n.

authority ▪ n. (pl. **-ies**) **1** the power or right to give orders and enforce obedience. **2** a person or organization exerting control in a particular political or administrative sphere. **3** the power to influence others based on recognized knowledge or expertise. ▸ an authoritative person, book, or other source.
– ORIGIN Middle English: from Old French *autorite*, from Latin *auctoritas*, from *auctor* (see **AUTHOR**).

authorize (also **-ise**) ▪ v. give official permission for or approval to.
– DERIVATIVES **authorization** (also **-isation**) n.

– ORIGIN Middle English: from Old French *autoriser*, from Latin *auctor* (see **AUTHOR**).

Authorized Version ▪ n. an English translation of the Bible produced in Britain in 1611 at the order of King James I and still widely used.

autism /'ɔːtɪz(ə)m/ ▪ n. Psychiatry a mental condition characterized by great difficulty in communicating with others and in using language and abstract concepts.
– DERIVATIVES **autistic** adj. & n.
– ORIGIN C20: from Greek *autos* 'self'.

auto-[1] (usu. **aut-** before a vowel) ▪ comb. form **1** self: *autocrat*. **2** one's own: *autograph*. **3** automatic; spontaneous: *autoxidation*.
– ORIGIN from Greek *autos* 'self'.

auto-[2] ▪ comb. form relating to cars: *autocross*.
– ORIGIN C19: from **AUTOMOBILE**.

autoantibody ▪ n. (pl. **-ies**) Physiology an antibody produced by an organism in response to a constituent of its own tissues.

autobiography ▪ n. (pl. **-ies**) an account of a person's life written by that person.
– DERIVATIVES **autobiographer** n. **autobiographic** adj. **autobiographical** adj.

autocatalysis ▪ n. Chemistry catalysis of a reaction by one of its products.
– DERIVATIVES **autocatalytic** adj.

autochthonous /ɔː'tɒkθənəs/ ▪ adj. **1** indigenous. **2** Geology (of a deposit or formation) formed in its present position. Often contrasted with **ALLOCHTHONOUS**.

autoclave /'ɔːtə(ʊ)kleɪv/ ▪ n. a strong heated container used for chemical reactions and processes using high pressures and temperatures, e.g. steam sterilization. ▪ v. heat in an autoclave.
– ORIGIN C19: from Greek *autos* 'self' + Latin *clavus* 'nail' or *clavis* 'key' (so named because it is self-fastening).

autocorrelation ▪ n. Statistics correlation between the elements of a series and others from the same series separated from them by a given interval.

autocracy /ɔː'tɒkrəsi/ ▪ n. (pl. **-ies**) **1** a system of government by one person with absolute power. **2** a country, state, or society governed in this way.
– ORIGIN C17: from Greek *autokrateia*, from *autos* 'self' + *kratos* 'power'.

autocrat ▪ n. **1** a ruler who has absolute power. **2** a domineering person.
– DERIVATIVES **autocratic** adj. **autocratically** adv.

autocross ▪ n. Brit. a motor racing sport in which cars are driven over courses on rough terrain or unmade roads.

autocue ▪ n. trademark a device used as a television prompt in which a script is projected on to a screen visible only to the speaker or performer.

auto-da-fé /ˌɔːtəʊdɑː'feɪ/ ▪ n. (pl. **autos-da-fé** /ˌɔːtəʊz-/) the burning of a heretic by the Spanish Inquisition.
– ORIGIN C18: from Portuguese, 'act of the faith'.

autodidact /'ɔːtəʊdɪdakt/ ▪ n. a self-taught person.
– DERIVATIVES **autodidactic** adj.

autoecology /ˌɔːtəʊɪ'kɒlədʒi/ ▪ n. variant spelling of **AUTECOLOGY**.

auto-exposure ▪ n. a device which sets the exposure automatically on a camera or other device.

autofocus ▪ n. a device focusing a camera or other device automatically.
– DERIVATIVES **autofocusing** n.

autogamy /ɔː'tɒɡəmi/ ▪ n. Biology self-fertilization. Compare with **ALLOGAMY**.
– DERIVATIVES **autogamous** adj.
– ORIGIN C19: from Greek *autos* 'self' + *gamos* 'marriage'.

autogiro (also **autogyro**) ▪ n. (pl. **autogiros**) a form of aircraft with unpowered freely rotating horizontal blades and a propeller.
– ORIGIN 1920s: from Spanish, from *auto-* 'self' + *giro* 'gyration'.

autograft ▪ n. a graft of tissue from one point to another of the same individual's body.

autograph ▪ n. **1** a celebrity's signature written for an admirer. **2** a manuscript or musical score in an author's or composer's own handwriting. **3** a person's handwriting. ▪ v. write one's signature on. ▪ adj. written

in the author's own handwriting.
–DERIVATIVES **autographic** adj.
–ORIGIN C17: from Greek *autographos* 'written with one's own hand'.

autoimmune ■ adj. Medicine relating to or denoting disease caused by antibodies or lymphocytes produced against substances naturally present in the body.
–DERIVATIVES **autoimmunity** n.

autointoxication ■ n. Medicine poisoning by a toxin formed within the body itself.

autolysis /ɔːˈtɒlɪsɪs/ ■ n. Biology the destruction of cells or tissues by their own enzymes.
–DERIVATIVES **autolytic** adj.

automated teller machine (also **automatic teller machine**) ■ n. a machine that automatically provides cash and performs other banking services on insertion of a special card.

automatic ■ adj. 1 (of a device or process) working by itself with little or no direct human control. ▸ (of a firearm) self-loading and able to fire continuously. 2 done or occurring without conscious thought. ▸ (of a penalty or legal sanction) necessary and inevitable, as a result of a fixed rule or particular set of circumstances. ■ n. an automatic machine or device.
–DERIVATIVES **automatically** adv. **automaticity** n. **automatization** (also **-isation**) n. **automatize** (also **-ise**) v.
–ORIGIN C18: from Greek *automatos* (see AUTOMATON).

automatic pilot ■ n. 1 a device for keeping an aircraft on a set course. 2 in phr. **on automatic pilot**) a state of doing something out of routine or habit, without concentration or conscious thought.

automation ■ n. the use or introduction of automatic equipment in a manufacturing or other process or facility.
–DERIVATIVES **automate** v.

automatism /ɔːˈtɒmətɪz(ə)m/ ■ n. Psychiatry action which does not involve conscious thought or intention.
–ORIGIN C19: from French *automatisme*, from Greek *automatos* (see AUTOMATON).

automaton /ɔːˈtɒmət(ə)n/ ■ n. (pl. **automata** /-tə/ or **automatons**) 1 a moving mechanical device made in imitation of a human being. 2 a machine which performs a function according to a set of coded instructions.
–ORIGIN C17: from Greek, neuter of *automatos* 'acting of itself', from *autos* 'self'.

automobile ■ n. chiefly N. Amer. a motor car.

automotive /ˌɔːtəˈməʊtɪv/ ■ adj. relating to motor vehicles.

autonomic /ˌɔːtəˈnɒmɪk/ ■ adj. Physiology relating to or denoting the part of the nervous system responsible for control of breathing, circulation, digestion, and other bodily functions not consciously directed.

autonomy /ɔːˈtɒnəmi/ ■ n. (pl. **-ies**) 1 the possession or right of self-government. 2 freedom of action.
–DERIVATIVES **autonomist** n. & adj. **autonomous** adj. **autonomously** adv.
–ORIGIN C17: from Greek *autonomos* 'having its own laws', from *autos* 'self' + *nomos* 'law'.

autopilot ■ n. short for AUTOMATIC PILOT.

autopsy /ˈɔːtɒpsi, ɔːˈtɒpsi/ ■ n. (pl. **-ies**) a post-mortem examination to discover the cause of death or the extent of disease.
–ORIGIN C17 (in the sense 'personal observation'): from French *autopsie*, from Greek, from *autoptēs* 'eyewitness'.

autorotation ■ n. rotation of an object caused by the flow of moving air or water around it.
–DERIVATIVES **autorotate** v.

autosave ■ n. Computing a software facility which automatically saves a user's work at regular intervals.

autosome /ˈɔːtəsəʊm/ ■ n. Biology any chromosome that is not a sex chromosome.
–DERIVATIVES **autosomal** adj.

auto-suggestion ■ n. the hypnotic or subconscious adoption of an idea which one has originated oneself.

autotomy /ɔːˈtɒtəmi/ ■ n. Zoology the casting off of a part of the body (e.g. the tail of a lizard) by an animal under threat.

autotoxin ■ n. a substance produced by an organism which is toxic to itself.
–DERIVATIVES **autotoxic** adj.

autotransformer ■ n. an electrical transformer which has a single winding of which part is common to both primary and secondary circuits.

autotransplantation ■ n. transplantation of tissue from one site to another in the same individual.
–DERIVATIVES **autotransplant** n. **autotransplanted** adj.

autotroph /ˈɔːtə(ʊ)trəʊf, -trɒf/ ■ n. Biology an organism that synthesizes nutrients from simple inorganic substances. Compare with HETEROTROPH.
–DERIVATIVES **autotrophic** adj. **autotrophy** n.

autoxidation /ˌɔːtɒksɪˈdeɪʃ(ə)n/ ■ n. Chemistry spontaneous oxidation of a substance in the presence of oxygen.
–DERIVATIVES **autoxidize** (also **-ise**) v.

autumn ■ n. 1 the season after summer and before winter. 2 Astronomy the period from the autumn equinox to the winter solstice.
–DERIVATIVES **autumnal** adj.
–ORIGIN Middle English: from Latin *autumnus*.

autumn crocus ■ n. a plant of the lily family with autumn-blooming flowers. [Genus *Colchicum*.]

auxiliary /ɔːɡˈzɪliəri, ɒɡ-/ ■ adj. providing supplementary or additional help and support. ■ n. (pl. **-ies**) an auxiliary person or thing.
–ORIGIN Middle English: from Latin *auxiliarius*, from *auxilium* 'help'.

auxiliary verb ■ n. Grammar a verb used in forming the tenses, moods, and voices of other verbs (in English primarily *be*, *do*, and *have*).

auxotroph /ˈɔːksətrəʊf, -trɒf/ ■ n. Biology a mutant organism that requires a particular additional nutrient which the normal strain does not.
–DERIVATIVES **auxotrophic** adj.
–ORIGIN 1950s: from Latin *auxilium* 'help' + Greek *trophos* 'feeder'.

AV ■ abbrev. 1 audio-visual (teaching aids). 2 Authorized Version.

avail ■ v. 1 (**avail oneself of**) use or take advantage of. 2 help or benefit. ■ n. (usu. in phr. **of/to no avail**) use or benefit.
–ORIGIN Middle English: from Latin *valere* 'be strong, be of value'.

available ■ adj. 1 able to be used or obtained. 2 not otherwise occupied; free.
–DERIVATIVES **availability** n. **availableness** n.
–ORIGIN Middle English: from AVAIL.

avalanche /ˈavəlɑːnʃ/ ■ n. 1 a mass of snow, ice, and/or rocks falling rapidly down a mountainside. 2 an overwhelming deluge. 3 Physics a cumulative process in which an ion or electron generates further ions or electrons by collision. ■ v. 1 fall in an avalanche. 2 Physics undergo a rapid increase in conductivity due to an avalanche process.
–ORIGIN C18: from French dialect form *lavanche*, influenced by *avaler* 'descend'.

avant-garde /ˌavɒ̃ˈɡɑːd/ ■ adj. (in the arts) new and unusual or experimental. ■ n. (**the avant-garde**) avant-garde ideas or artists.
–DERIVATIVES **avant-gardism** n. **avant-gardist** n.
–ORIGIN Middle English: from French, 'vanguard'.

avarice ■ n. extreme greed for wealth or material gain.
–DERIVATIVES **avaricious** adj. **avariciously** adv. **avariciousness** n.
–ORIGIN Middle English: from Latin *avaritia*, from *avarus* 'greedy'.

avascular /əˈvaskjʊlə, eɪ-/ ■ adj. Medicine characterized by or associated with a lack of blood vessels.

avatar /ˈavətɑː/ ■ n. 1 chiefly Hinduism a manifestation of a deity or released soul in bodily form on earth. 2 Computing a movable icon representing a person in cyberspace or virtual reality graphics.
–ORIGIN from Sanskrit *avatāra* 'descent'.

avaunt /əˈvɔːnt/ ■ exclam. archaic go away.
–ORIGIN Middle English: from Old French *avant*, from Latin *ab* 'from' + *ante* 'before'.

Ave.

Ave. ▪ abbrev. Avenue.

ave /'ɑːveɪ/ ▪ exclam. poetic/literary used to express good wishes on meeting or parting.
– ORIGIN Middle English: from Latin, 'fare well!', from *avere*.

Ave Maria /ˌɑːveɪ məˈriːə/ ▪ n. Christian Church a prayer to the Virgin Mary used in Catholic worship; a Hail Mary.
– ORIGIN the opening words in Latin, 'hail, Mary!'

avenge ▪ v. inflict harm in return for (an injury or wrong). ▸ inflict retribution on behalf of (a wronged person).
– DERIVATIVES **avenger** n.
– ORIGIN Middle English: from Old French *avengier*, from Latin *vindicare* 'vindicate'.

aventurine /əˈvɛntʃərɪn/ ▪ n. 1 brownish glass containing sparkling particles of copper or gold. 2 translucent quartz or feldspar containing small reflective mineral particles.
– ORIGIN C18: from Italian *avventurino*, from *avventura* 'chance'.

avenue ▪ n. 1 a broad road or path, especially one lined with trees. 2 a means of approach.
– ORIGIN C17: from French, from *avenir* 'arrive, approach'.

aver /əˈvɜː/ ▪ v. (**averred**, **averring**) formal state or assert to be the case. ▸ Law allege as a fact in support of a plea.
– ORIGIN Middle English: from Old French *averer*, from Latin *ad* 'to' + *verus* 'true'.

average ▪ n. 1 the result obtained by adding several amounts together and then dividing the total by the number of amounts. 2 a usual or ordinary amount, level, or rate. 3 Law the apportionment of financial liability resulting from loss of or damage to a ship or its cargo. 4 Law downward adjustment of an insurance claim because of inadequate valuation of the goods which are insured. ▪ adj. 1 constituting an average. 2 of the usual or ordinary amount, level, or rate. ▸ mediocre: *a very average movie*. ▪ v. 1 amount to or achieve as an average. ▸ calculate or estimate the average of. 2 (**average out**) result in an even distribution.
– DERIVATIVES **averagely** adv. **averageness** n.
– ORIGIN C15: from French *avarie* 'damage to ship or cargo', from Arabic *'awār*; the modern sense arose from the equitable sharing of liability for losses at sea between the owners of the vessel and of the cargo.

averment /əˈvɜːm(ə)nt/ ▪ n. Law a formal statement including an offer of proof or substantiation.

averse ▪ adj. (usu. **averse to**) strongly disliking or opposed.
– ORIGIN C16: from Latin *avertere* (see AVERT).

USAGE
On the confusion of **averse** with **adverse**, see ADVERSE.

aversion ▪ n. a strong dislike or disinclination.
– DERIVATIVES **aversive** adj.

aversion therapy ▪ n. a type of behaviour therapy designed to make patients give up a habit by causing them to associate it with an unpleasant effect.

avert ▪ v. 1 turn away (one's eyes or thoughts). 2 prevent or ward off (an undesirable occurrence).
– DERIVATIVES **avertable** adj.
– ORIGIN Middle English: from Latin *avertere*, from *ab-* 'from' + *vertere* 'to turn'.

Aves /ˈeɪviːz, ˈɑːveɪz/ ▪ pl. n. Zoology the class of vertebrates which comprises the birds.
– ORIGIN Latin, pl. of *avis* 'bird'.

Avesta /əˈvɛstə/ ▪ n. the sacred texts of Zoroastrianism.
– ORIGIN from Persian.

avgas /ˈavɡas/ ▪ n. aircraft fuel.

avian /ˈeɪvɪən/ ▪ adj. relating to birds. ▪ n. a bird.
– ORIGIN C19: from Latin *avis* 'bird'.

aviary /ˈeɪvɪəri/ ▪ n. (pl. **-ies**) a large enclosure for keeping birds in.
– ORIGIN C16: from Latin *aviarium*, from *avis* 'bird'.

aviation ▪ n. the activity or business of operating and flying aircraft.
– DERIVATIVES **aviate** v.
– ORIGIN C19: from Latin *avis* 'bird'.

aviator ▪ n. (fem. **aviatrix** /ˌeɪvɪˈeɪtrɪks/, pl. **-trices** /-trɪsiːz/) dated a pilot.

aviculture /ˈeɪvɪˌkʌltʃə/ ▪ n. the breeding and rearing of birds.
– DERIVATIVES **avicultural** adj. **aviculturalist** n. **aviculturist** n.
– ORIGIN C19: from Latin *avis* 'bird' + CULTURE.

avid /ˈavɪd/ ▪ adj. keenly interested or enthusiastic.
– DERIVATIVES **avidly** adv.
– ORIGIN C19 (*avidity* Middle English): from Latin *avidus*, from *avere* 'crave'.

avidin /ˈavɪdɪn/ ▪ n. Biochemistry a protein found in raw egg white, which combines with biotin and hinders its absorption.
– ORIGIN 1940s: from AVID.

avidity ▪ n. 1 keen interest or enthusiasm. 2 Biochemistry the overall strength of binding between an antibody and an antigen.

avifauna /ˈeɪvɪfɔːnə/ ▪ n. Zoology the birds of a particular region, habitat, or geological period.
– DERIVATIVES **avifaunal** adj.
– ORIGIN C19: from Latin *avis* 'bird' + FAUNA.

avionics /ˌeɪvɪˈɒnɪks/ ▪ pl. n. [usu. treated as sing.] electronics or electronic equipment as applied to aviation.

avitaminosis /eɪˌvɪtəmɪˈnəʊsɪs, -ˌvaɪt-/ ▪ n. (pl. **avit-aminoses** /-siːz/) Medicine a condition resulting from a deficiency of a particular vitamin.

avo ▪ n. S. African & Austral. informal an avocado.

avocado /ˌavəˈkɑːdəʊ/ ▪ n. (pl. **-os**) 1 a pear-shaped fruit with a rough leathery skin, smooth oily edible flesh, and a large stone. 2 the tropical evergreen tree which bears this fruit. [*Persea americana*.] 3 a light green colour like that of an avocado's flesh.
– ORIGIN C17: from Spanish, from *aguacate*, from Nahuatl *ahuacatl*.

avocation /ˌavəˈkeɪʃ(ə)n/ ▪ n. a hobby or minor occupation.
– DERIVATIVES **avocational** adj.
– ORIGIN C17: from Latin, from *avocare* 'call away'.

avocet /ˈavəsɛt/ ▪ n. a long-legged wading bird, largely black and white, with a slender upturned bill. [Genus *Recurvirostra*: four species.]
– ORIGIN C17: from Italian *avosetta*.

Avogadro's constant (also **Avogadro's number**) ▪ n. Chemistry the number of atoms or molecules in one mole of a substance, equal to 6.023×10^{23}.
– ORIGIN named after the Italian physicist A. *Avogadro* (1776–1856).

Avogadro's law (also **Avogadro's hypothesis**) ▪ n. Chemistry a law stating that equal volumes of gases at the same temperature and pressure contain equal numbers of molecules.

avoid ▪ v. 1 keep away or refrain from. ▸ prevent from doing or happening. 2 Law repudiate, nullify, or render void (a decree or contract).
– DERIVATIVES **avoidable** adj. **avoidably** adv. **avoidance** n. **avoider** n.
– ORIGIN Middle English: from Old French *evuider* 'clear out, get rid of', from *vuide* (see VOID).

avoirdupois /ˌavwɑːdjuːˈpwɑː, ˌavədəˈpɔɪz/ ▪ n. a system of weights based on a pound of 16 ounces or 7000 grains. Compare with TROY.
– ORIGIN Middle English: from Old French *aveir de peis* 'goods of weight', from Latin *habere* + *peis* (see POISE[1]).

avouch ▪ v. archaic affirm or assert.
– DERIVATIVES **avouchment** n.
– ORIGIN C15: from Old French *avochier*, from Latin *advocare* 'summon in defence'.

avow ▪ v. assert or confess openly.
– DERIVATIVES **avowal** n. **avowed** adj. **avowedly** adv.
– ORIGIN Middle English: from Old French *avouer* 'acknowledge', from Latin *advocare* (see AVOUCH).

avuncular /əˈvʌŋkjʊlə/ ▪ adj. like an uncle in being kind and friendly towards a younger or less experienced person.
– ORIGIN C19: from Latin *avunculus* 'maternal uncle'.

avunculate /əˈvʌŋkjʊlət/ ▪ n. (**the avunculate**) Anthropology the special relationship in some societies

between a man and his sister's son.
−ORIGIN C20: from Latin *avunculus* 'maternal uncle'.

AWACS /'eɪwaks/ ■ abbrev. airborne warning and control system.

await ■ v. wait for.
−ORIGIN Middle English: from Anglo-Norman French *awaitier*, from *a-* 'to, at' + *waitier* 'to wait'.

awake ■ v. (past **awoke**; past part. **awoken**) 1 stop sleeping. 2 make or become active again. ■ adj. 1 not asleep. 2 (**awake to**) aware of.
−ORIGIN Old English: (see **a-²**, **WAKE¹**).

awaken ■ v. 1 stop or cause to stop sleeping. 2 rouse (a feeling).
−DERIVATIVES **awakening** n. & adj.
−ORIGIN Old English, from *on* 'on' + **WAKEN**.

award ■ v. give or grant officially as a prize or reward. ■ n. something awarded.
−DERIVATIVES **awarder** n.
−ORIGIN Middle English: from Anglo-Norman French *awarder*, var. of Old French *esguarder* 'consider, ordain', from *es-* 'thoroughly' + *guarder* 'watch (over)'.

aware ■ adj. having knowledge or perception of a situation or fact.
−DERIVATIVES **awareness** n.
−ORIGIN Old English, of Germanic origin.

awash ■ adj. covered or flooded with water.

away ■ adv. 1 to or at a distance. ▶ at a specified future distance in time. 2 towards a lower level. 3 into an appropriate place for storage or safe keeping. 4 towards or into non-existence. 5 constantly, persistently, or continuously. 6 (of a sports fixture) at the opponents' ground. ■ adj. (of a sports fixture) played at the opponents' ground. ■ n. an away game.
−ORIGIN Old English 'on one's way' (see **a-²**, **WAY**).

awe ■ n. a feeling of reverential respect mixed with fear or wonder. ■ v. inspire with awe.
−ORIGIN Old English *ege* 'terror, dread, awe'.

awesome ■ adj. 1 inspiring awe. 2 informal excellent.
−DERIVATIVES **awesomely** adv. **awesomeness** n.

awful ■ adj. 1 very bad or unpleasant. 2 used for emphasis: *an awful lot of letters.* 3 archaic inspiring awe.
−DERIVATIVES **awfulness** n.

awfully ■ adv. 1 informal very or very much: *I'm awfully sorry.* 2 very badly or unpleasantly.

awhile ■ adv. for a short time.

awkward ■ adj. 1 hard to do or deal with. 2 uneasy embarrassed. 3 not smooth or graceful.
−DERIVATIVES **awkwardly** adv. **awkwardness** n.
−ORIGIN Middle English: from dialect form *awk*, from Old Norse *afugr*.

awl /ɔːl/ ■ n. a small pointed tool used for piercing holes, especially in leather.
−ORIGIN Old English, of Germanic origin.

awn /ɔːn/ ■ n. Botany a stiff bristle growing from the ear or flower of barley, rye, and grasses.
−DERIVATIVES **awned** adj.
−ORIGIN Old English, from Old Norse *ǫgn*.

awning ■ n. a sheet of canvas or similar material stretched on a frame and used to shelter a shop window or doorway.
−ORIGIN C17: orig. in nautical use.

awoke past of **AWAKE**.

awoken past participle of **AWAKE**.

AWOL /'eɪwɒl/ ■ adj. Military absent but without intent to desert.
−ORIGIN 1920S: acronym from *absent without (official) leave*.

awry /ə'rʌɪ/ ■ adv. & adj. away from the appropriate or expected course or position.
−ORIGIN Middle English: from **a-²** + **WRY**.

axe (US also **ax**) ■ n. 1 a heavy-bladed tool used for chopping wood. 2 (**the axe**) cost-cutting action, especially redundancy: *thirty staff are facing the axe.* ■ v. 1 end, cancel, or dismiss suddenly and ruthlessly. 2 cut or strike with an axe.
−PHRASES **have an axe to grind** have a private reason for doing something.
−ORIGIN Old English, of Germanic origin.

axe kick ■ n. a type of kick used in martial arts, in which the opponent's head is struck with the heel of the foot.

axel /'aks(ə)l/ ■ n. a jump in skating with one (or more) and a half turns in the air.
−ORIGIN 1930S: named after the Norwegian skater *Axel R. Paulsen*.

axenic /eɪ'zɛnɪk/ ■ adj. Biology (of a culture) free from living organisms other than the species required.
−DERIVATIVES **axenically** adv.
−ORIGIN 1940S: from *a-* 'not' + *xenikos* 'alien, strange'.

axes plural form of **AXIS**.

axial /'aksɪəl/ ■ adj. forming, relating to, or around an axis.
−DERIVATIVES **axially** adv.

axil /'aksɪl/ ■ n. Botany the upper angle between a leaf stalk or branch and the stem or trunk from which it is growing.
−ORIGIN C18: from Latin *axilla* (see **AXILLA**).

axilla /ak'sɪlə/ ■ n. (pl. **axillae** /-liː/) Anatomy an armpit, or the corresponding part in a bird or other animal.
−DERIVATIVES **axillary** adj.
−ORIGIN C17: from Latin, diminutive of *ala* 'wing'.

axiom /'aksɪəm/ ■ n. 1 an accepted statement or proposition regarded as being self-evidently true. 2 chiefly Mathematics a statement or proposition on which an abstractly defined structure is based.
−DERIVATIVES **axiomatic** adj. **axiomatically** adv.
−ORIGIN C15: from Greek *axiōma*, from *axios* 'worthy'.

axion /'aksɪɒn/ ■ n. Physics a hypothetical subatomic particle postulated to account for the rarity of processes which break charge–parity symmetry.
−ORIGIN 1970S: from **AXIAL**.

axis /'aksɪs/ ■ n. (pl. **axes** /-siːz/) 1 an imaginary line about which a body rotates or with respect to which it possesses rotational symmetry. 2 an imaginary line which divides something in half, especially in the direction of its greatest length. 3 Mathematics a fixed reference line for the measurement of coordinates. 4 a straight central part in a structure to which other parts are connected. 5 Anatomy the second cervical vertebra, below the atlas at the top of the backbone. 6 (**the Axis**) the alliance between Germany and Italy in the Second World War.
−ORIGIN Middle English: from Latin, 'axle, pivot'.

axisymmetric /ˌaksɪsɪ'mɛtrɪk/ ■ adj. Geometry symmetrical about an axis.

axle /'aks(ə)l/ ■ n. a rod or spindle passing through the centre of a wheel or group of wheels.
−ORIGIN Middle English (orig. *axle-tree*): from Old Norse *ǫxultré*.

axolotl /'aksəlɒt(ə)l/ ■ n. a Mexican salamander which retains its aquatic newt-like larval form throughout life but is able to breed. [*Ambystoma mexicanum*.]
−ORIGIN C18: from Nahuatl, from *atl* 'water' + *xolotl* 'servant'.

axon /'aksɒn/ ■ n. the long thread-like part of a nerve cell along which impulses are conducted from the cell body to other cells. Compare with **DENDRITE**.
−DERIVATIVES **axonal** adj.
−ORIGIN C19: from Greek *axōn* 'axis'.

axoneme /'aksə(ʊ)niːm/ ■ n. Biology the central strand of a cilium or flagellum, consisting of an array of micro-tubules.
−DERIVATIVES **axonemal** adj.
−ORIGIN C20: from Greek *axōn* 'axis' + *nēma* 'thread'.

ay ■ exclam. & n. variant spelling of **AYE¹**.

ayah /'ʌɪə/ ■ n. a nanny employed by Europeans in India or another former British territory.
−ORIGIN Anglo-Indian, from Portuguese *aia* 'nurse'.

ayatollah /ˌʌɪə'tɒlə/ ■ n. a high-ranking Shiite religious leader in Iran.
−ORIGIN 1950S: from Arabic *'āyatu-llāh*, 'token of God'.

aye¹ /ʌɪ/ (also **ay**) ■ exclam. archaic or dialect yes. ▶ (**aye aye**) Nautical a response accepting an order. ▶ (in voting) I assent. ■ n. an affirmative answer, especially in voting.
−ORIGIN C16: prob. from *I*, personal pronoun, expressing assent.

aye

aye² /eɪ, ʌɪ/ ■ adv. archaic or Scottish always; still.
– PHRASES **for aye** forever.
– ORIGIN Middle English: from Old Norse *ei*, *ey*.

aye-aye /'ʌɪʌɪ/ ■ n. a rare nocturnal Madagascan primate related to the lemurs. [*Daubentonia madagascariensis*.]
– ORIGIN C18: from Malagasy *aiay*.

Aylesbury /'eɪlzb(ə)ri/ ■ n. (pl. **Aylesburys**) a domestic duck of a breed with white plumage.
– ORIGIN named after the town of *Aylesbury* in England, where the ducks were bred.

Aymara /'ʌɪmərɑː/ ■ n. (pl. same or **Aymaras**) 1 a member of an American Indian people inhabiting the high plateau region of Bolivia and Peru near Lake Titicaca. 2 the language of this people, perhaps related to Quechua.
– ORIGIN from Bolivian Spanish.

Ayrshire /'ɛːʃə/ ■ n. an animal of a mainly white breed of dairy cattle.
– ORIGIN named after the former Scottish county of *Ayrshire*, where the cattle were bred.

Ayurveda /ˌɑːjʊə'veɪdə, -'viːdə/ ■ n. the traditional Hindu system of medicine, which is based on the idea of balance in bodily systems and uses diet, herbal treatment, and yogic breathing.
– DERIVATIVES **Ayurvedic** adj.
– ORIGIN from Sanskrit *āyus* 'life' + *veda* '(sacred) knowledge'.

azalea /ə'zeɪlɪə/ ■ n. a deciduous flowering shrub with clusters of brightly coloured flowers, related to rhododendrons but generally smaller. [Genus *Rhododendron*: many species.]
– ORIGIN C18: from Greek, from *azaleos* 'dry' (because the shrubs flourish in dry soil).

azan /ə'zɑːn/ ■ n. the Muslim call to prayer made by a muezzin from the minaret of a mosque.
– ORIGIN C19: from Arabic *'aḏān* 'announcement'.

Azanian /ə'zeɪnɪən/ ■ n. an inhabitant of Azania, the name for South Africa proposed by supporters of black consciousness. ■ adj. denoting or relating to Azania.
– ORIGIN from Greek *Azania*, the name given by classical geographers to eastern and southern Africa, prob. from Arabic *Zanj* 'a black African'.

Azapo /ə'zɑːpəʊ/ (also **AZAPO**) ■ abbrev. (in South Africa) Azanian People's Organization.

azeotrope /'eɪzɪətrəʊp, ə'ziːə-/ ■ n. Chemistry a mixture of two liquids which has a constant boiling point and composition throughout distillation.
– DERIVATIVES **azeotropic** /-trəʊpɪk, -'trɒpɪk/ adj.
– ORIGIN C20: from Greek *a-* 'not' + *zein* 'to boil' + *tropos* 'turning'.

Azerbaijani ■ n. (pl. **Azerbaijanis**) 1 a native or national of Azerbaijan or a person of Azerbaijani descent. 2 the Turkic language of Azerbaijan and adjacent regions. ■ adj. of or relating to Azerbaijan or its people or their language.

Azeri /ə'zɛːri/ ■ n. (pl. **Azeris**) 1 a member of a Turkic people forming the majority population of Azerbaijan, and also living in Armenia and northern Iran. 2 the Azerbaijani language. ■ adj. relating to or denoting this people or their language.
– ORIGIN from Turkish *azerî*.

azide /'eɪzʌɪd/ ■ n. Chemistry a compound containing the anion N_3^- or the group $-N_3$.

azidothymidine /ˌeɪzɪdəʊ'θʌɪmɪdiːn, eɪˌzʌɪdəʊ-/ ■ n. trademark for **ZIDOVUDINE**.

azimuth /'azɪməθ/ ■ n. 1 Astronomy the horizontal component of the direction of a celestial object from the observer, expressed as an angular distance from the north or south point of the horizon. 2 the horizontal angle or direction of a compass bearing.
– ORIGIN Middle English: from Old French *azimut*, from Arabic *as-samt*, from *al* 'the' + *samt* 'way, direction'.

azine /'eɪziːn/ ■ n. Chemistry a cyclic organic compound having a ring including one or (usually) more nitrogen atoms.

azo- /'eɪzəʊ/ ■ prefix Chemistry containing two adjacent nitrogen atoms between carbon atoms: *azobenzene*.
– ORIGIN from obsolete *azote* 'nitrogen', from Greek *a-* 'without' + *zōē* 'life'.

azo dye ■ n. Chemistry any of a large class of synthetic dyes whose molecules contain two adjacent nitrogen atoms between carbon atoms.

azonal /eɪ'zəʊn(ə)l/ ■ adj. (especially of soils) having no zonal organization or structure.

azoospermia /ˌeɪzəʊə'spəːmɪə, ə'zəʊ-/ ■ n. Medicine absence of viable motile sperm in the semen.

AZT ■ abbrev. azidothymidine.

Aztec /'aztɛk/ ■ n. 1 a member of the American Indian people dominant in Mexico before the Spanish conquest of the 16th century. 2 the extinct language of this people, from which modern Nahuatl is descended.
– ORIGIN from Spanish *Azteca*, from Nahuatl *aztecatl* 'person of Aztlan', their legendary place of origin.

azulejo /ˌazjuː'leɪhəʊ/ ■ n. (pl. **azulejos**) a kind of glazed coloured tile traditionally used in Spanish and Portuguese buildings.
– ORIGIN from Spanish, from *azul* 'blue'.

azure /'aʒə, -ʒjʊə, 'eɪ-/ ■ adj. bright blue in colour like a cloudless sky. ▶ Heraldry blue. ■ n. a bright blue colour.
– ORIGIN Middle English: from Old French *asur*, from Arabic *al* 'the' + *lāzaward* (from Persian *lāžward* 'lapis lazuli').

azurite /'aʒʊrʌɪt, -ʒj(ʊ)ə-/ ■ n. a blue mineral consisting of basic copper carbonate.

azygous /'azɪɡəs/ ■ adj. Biology (of an organic structure) not existing in pairs; single.
– ORIGIN C19: from Greek *azugos*, from *a-* 'without' + *zugon* 'yoke'.

Bb

B[1] (also **b**) ▪ n. (pl. **Bs** or **B's**) **1** the second letter of the alphabet. **2** denoting the second, second-best, or secondary item in a set. **3** Music the seventh note of the diatonic scale of C major. **4** the human blood type (in the ABO system) containing the B antigen and lacking the A.

B[2] ▪ abbrev. **1** (in chess) bishop. **2** black (used in describing grades of pencil lead). **3** bomber (in designations of US aircraft types). ▪ symb. **1** the chemical element boron. **2** Physics magnetic flux density.

b ▪ abbrev. **1** (**b.**) born. **2** Cricket bowled by. **3** Cricket bye(s).

BA ▪ abbrev. **1** Bachelor of Arts. **2** British Airways.

Ba ▪ symb. the chemical element barium.

ba /bɑː/ ▪ n. (in ancient Egypt) the supposed soul of a person or god, which survived death but had to be sustained with offerings of food. See also **KA**.

baa ▪ v. (**baas**, **baaed**, **baaing**) (of a sheep or lamb) bleat. ▪ n. the cry of a sheep or lamb.
– ORIGIN C16: imitative.

baas /bɑːs/ ▪ n. S. African, often offensive a supervisor or employer, especially a white man in charge of coloured or black people.
– ORIGIN C18: Dutch, 'master'.

baasie /ˈbɑːsi/ ▪ n. S. African, often offensive a form of address to a young white man.
– ORIGIN C19: Afrikaans, from earlier Dutch *baasje* 'little master'.

baasskap /ˈbɑːskəp/ ▪ n. S. African historical domination of black people by white people under apartheid.
– ORIGIN 1930s: Afrikaans, from Dutch *baas* 'master' + *-skap* '-ship'.

Baathist /ˈbɑːθɪst/ (also **Ba'athist**) ▪ n. a member or supporter of the Baath Party, a pan-Arab socialist party founded in Syria in 1943. ▪ adj. of or relating to the Baath Party.
– ORIGIN from *Baath*, from Arabic *ba'ṯ* 'resurrection, renaissance'.

baba[1] /ˈbɑːbɑː/ (also **rum baba**) ▪ n. a small rich sponge cake, soaked in rum-flavoured syrup.
– ORIGIN from Polish, 'married peasant woman'.

baba[2] /ˈbɑːbɑː/ ▪ n. S. African a respectful title or form of address for an older man.
– ORIGIN C19: isiZulu, 'father'.

babalaas /ˈbʌbəlɑːs/ (also **babelaas**) S. African informal ▪ n. a hangover. ▪ adj. hung-over.
– ORIGIN 1940s: from isiZulu *ibhabhalazi* 'hangover'.

babble ▪ v. **1** talk rapidly and continuously in a foolish, excited, or incomprehensible way. ▸ reveal something secret. **2** [usu. as adj. **babbling**] (of a stream) make a continuous murmur as the water flows over stones. ▪ n. the sound of babbling. ▸ foolish, excited, or confused talk.
– ORIGIN Middle English: from Middle Low German *babbelen*, or an English formation based on the repeated syllable *ba*.

babbler ▪ n. **1** a person who babbles. **2** a thrush-like songbird with short rounded wings, and a loud voice. [Family Timaliidae: many species.]

babby ▪ n. (pl. **-ies**) dialect form of **BABY**.

babe ▪ n. **1** poetic/literary a baby. **2** informal an affectionate form of address for a lover. **3** informal a sexually attractive young woman.
– ORIGIN Middle English: prob. imitative of an infant's first attempts at speech.

babel /ˈbeɪb(ə)l/ ▪ n. a confused noise made by a number of voices.
– ORIGIN C16: from the Tower of *Babel*, where, according to the biblical story, God confused the languages of the builders.

babelaas ▪ n. variant spelling of **BABALAAS**.

babesiosis /bəˌbiːzɪˈəʊsɪs/ (also **babesiasis** /ˌbɑːbɪˈzaɪəsɪs/) ▪ n. a protozoal disease of livestock transmitted by tick bites, affecting the red blood cells and causing red or blackish urine.
– ORIGIN C20: from *Babesia*, a genus of protozoans, from the name of the Romanian bacteriologist Victor *Babès*.

Babism /ˈbɑːbɪz(ə)m/ ▪ n. a religion founded in 1844 by the Persian Mirza Ali Muhammad, who taught that a new prophet would follow Muhammad. See also **BAHA'I**.
– DERIVATIVES **Babi** n.
– ORIGIN C19: from Arabic *bāb* 'intermediary', literally 'gate' (taken as a name by the founder).

baboon ▪ n. a large ground-dwelling social monkey with a long doglike snout and large teeth. [Genera *Papio* and *Mandrillus*: several species.]
– ORIGIN Middle English: from Old French *babuin*, perhaps from *baboue* 'muzzle, grimace'.

baboon spider ▪ n. a large hairy burrowing spider of southern Africa. [Family Theraphosidae: several genera.]
– ORIGIN 1900s: prob. a translation of Afrikaans *baviaan spinnekop*.

babu /ˈbɑːbuː/ ▪ n. (pl. **babus**) Indian a respectful title or form of address for a man.
– ORIGIN from Hindi *bābū* 'father'.

babushka /bəˈbʊʃkə, ˈbabʊʃkə/ ▪ n. **1** (in Russia) an old woman or grandmother. **2** N. Amer. a headscarf tied under the chin.
– ORIGIN Russian, 'grandmother'.

baby ▪ n. (pl. **-ies**) **1** a child or animal that is newly or recently born. **2** a timid or childish person. **3** informal a person with whom one is having a romantic relationship (often as a form of address). ▪ adj. comparatively small or immature of its kind. ▪ v. (**-ies**, **-ied**) pamper or be overprotective towards.
– PHRASES **throw the baby out with the bathwater** discard something valuable along with other things that are undesirable.
– DERIVATIVES **babyhood** n.
– ORIGIN Middle English: prob. imitative of an infant's first attempts at speech.

baby blue ▪ n. **1** a pale shade of blue. **2** (**baby blues**) informal blue eyes. **3** (**baby blues**) informal post-natal depression.

baby boom ▪ n. informal a temporary marked increase in the birth rate.
– DERIVATIVES **baby boomer** n.

baby bouncer ▪ n. a harness suspended by elastic or a spring, into which a baby is put, with its feet within reach of the floor, to exercise its legs.

baby buggy ▪ n. trademark, chiefly Brit. a light collapsible pushchair.

baby carriage ▪ n. N. Amer. a pram.

baby doll ▪ adj. (especially of pyjamas) denoting a style of women's clothing resembling that traditionally worn by a doll or young child.

baby grand ▪ n. the smallest size of grand piano.

Babygro ▪ n. (pl. **-os**) trademark an all-in-one stretch garment for babies.

babyish ▪ adj. childish; immature.
– DERIVATIVES **babyishly** adv. **babyishness** n.

Babylon /ˈbabɪlɒn/ ▪ n. derogatory (chiefly among Rastafarians) aspects of white culture seen as degenerate or oppressive.
– ORIGIN 1940s: by association with the ancient city of *Babylon* (see **BABYLONIAN**).

Babylonian /ˌbabɪˈləʊnɪən/ ▪ n. **1** an inhabitant of

Babylon or Babylonia, an ancient city and kingdom in Mesopotamia. **2** the dialect of Akkadian spoken in ancient Babylon. ■ adj. of or relating to Babylon or Babylonia.

baby marrow ■ n. a variety of marrow harvested and eaten at an early stage of growth.

baby's breath ■ n. a herbaceous plant of delicate appearance which bears tiny scented pink or white flowers. [*Gypsophila paniculata*.]

baby shower ■ n. a party at which presents are given to a woman who is about to have a baby.

babysit ■ v. (**-sitting**; past and past part. **-sat**) look after a child or children while the parents are out.
– DERIVATIVES **babysitter** n.

baby walker ■ n. a device for helping a baby learn to walk, consisting of a harness set into a frame on wheels.

bacalhau /ˌbakəˈlaʊ/ ■ n. dried or salted codfish, as used in Portuguese cookery.
– ORIGIN from Portuguese.

baccalaureate /ˌbakəˈlɔːrɪət/ ■ n. an examination qualifying successful candidates for higher education. See also **INTERNATIONAL BACCALAUREATE**.
– ORIGIN C17: from medieval Latin, from *baccalaureus* 'bachelor'.

baccarat /ˈbakəraː/ ■ n. a gambling card game in which players hold two- or three-card hands, the winning hand being that giving the highest remainder when its face value is divided by ten.
– ORIGIN C19: from French *baccara*.

bacchanal /ˈbakən(ə)l, -nal/ chiefly poetic/literary ■ n. an occasion of wild and drunken revelry. ■ adj. bacchanalian.
– ORIGIN C16: from Latin *bacchanalis*, from the name of the god *Bacchus*.

Bacchanalia /ˌbakəˈneɪlɪə/ ■ pl. n. [also treated as sing.] **1** the Roman festival of Bacchus, the god of wine. **2** (**bacchanalia**) drunken revelry.
– DERIVATIVES **bacchanalian** adj.
– ORIGIN C16: from Latin *bacchanalia*, from *bacchanalis* (see **BACCHANAL**).

bacchant /ˈbakənt/ ■ n. (pl. **bacchants** or **bacchantes** /bəˈkantiːz/; fem. **bacchante** /bəˈkant, bəˈkanti/) a priest, priestess, or follower of Bacchus.
– ORIGIN C16: from French *bacchante*, from Latin *bacchari* 'celebrate the feast of Bacchus'.

baccy ■ n. Brit. informal term for **TOBACCO**.

bachelor ■ n. **1** a man who is not and has never been married. **2** a person who holds a first degree from a university or other academic institution (only in titles or set expressions). **3** historical a young knight serving under another's banner.
– DERIVATIVES **bachelorhood** n.
– ORIGIN Middle English: from Old French *bacheler* 'a young man aspiring to knighthood'.

bachelorette ■ n. N. Amer. a young unmarried woman.

bachelor girl ■ n. an independent, unmarried young woman.

bachelor party ■ n. N. Amer. a men-only party given for a man who is about to get married.

Bach flower remedies /batʃ/ ■ pl. n. preparations of the flowers of various plants used in a system of complementary medicine intended to relieve ill health by influencing underlying emotional states.
– ORIGIN 1970s: named after the British physician Edward *Bach*.

bacilliform /bəˈsɪlɪfɔːm/ ■ adj. chiefly Biology rod-shaped.

bacillus /bəˈsɪləs/ ■ n. (pl. **bacilli** /-lʌɪ, -liː/) a rod-shaped bacterium.
– DERIVATIVES **bacillary** adj.
– ORIGIN C19: from late Latin, diminutive of Latin *baculus* 'stick'.

back ■ n. **1** the rear surface of the human body from the shoulders to the hips. ▸ the corresponding upper surface of an animal's body. ▸ the part of a chair against which the sitter's back rests. **2** the side or part of something away from the spectator or from the direction in which it moves or faces. ▸ the side or part of an object opposed to the one that is normally seen or used. **3** a player in a team game who plays in a defensive position behind the forwards. **4** the main structure of a ship's hull or an aircraft's fuselage. ■ adv. **1** in the opposite direction from the one that one is facing or travelling towards. ▸ at a distance away. ▸ (also **back of**) N. Amer. behind. **2** so as to return to an earlier or normal position or condition. **3** in or into the past. **4** in return. ■ v. **1** give material or moral support to. ▸ bet money on (a person or animal) winning a race or contest. **2** cover the back of for support, protection, or decoration. **3** (especially in popular music) provide musical accompaniment to (a singer or musician). **4** walk or drive backwards. ▸ (of the wind) change direction anticlockwise around the points of the compass. The opposite of **VEER**. ▸ Nautical put (a sail) aback in order to slow down or assist in turning through the wind. **5** (**back on/on to**) (of a building or other structure) have its back facing or adjacent to. ▸ lie behind. ■ adj. **1** of or at the back. **2** in a remote or subsidiary position. **3** from or relating to the past. **4** directed towards the rear or in a reversed course. **5** Phonetics (of a sound) articulated at the back of the mouth.
– PHRASES **at someone's back** in pursuit or support of someone. **back and forth** to and fro. **the back of beyond** a very remote or inaccessible place. **back to front** with the back at the front and the front at the back. **back water** reverse the action of the oars to slow down or stop a boat. **behind someone's back** without a person's knowledge and in an unfair way. **get** (or **put**) **someone's back up** annoy or anger someone. **put one's back into** approach (a task) with vigour. **turn one's back on** ignore; reject. **with one's back to** (or **up against**) **the wall** in a desperate situation.
– PHRASAL VERBS **back down** concede defeat. **back off** draw back from action or confrontation. **back out** withdraw from a commitment. **back up 1** Computing make a spare copy of (data or a disk). **2** (of vehicles) form into a queue due to congestion.
– DERIVATIVES **backer** n. **backless** adj.
– ORIGIN Old English, of Germanic origin.

backache ■ n. prolonged pain in one's back.

backbeat ■ n. Music a strong accent on one of the normally unaccented beats of the bar, used especially in jazz and popular music.

back bench ■ n. any of the benches behind the front benches on either side of the British House of Commons, or a similar chamber of parliament elsewhere, occupied by members who do not hold office.
– DERIVATIVES **back-bencher** n.

backbiting ■ n. malicious talk about an absent person.
– DERIVATIVES **backbiter** n.

backboard ■ n. **1** a board used to support or straighten a person's back, especially after an accident. **2** Basketball an upright board behind the basket, off which the ball may rebound.

back boiler ■ n. Brit. a boiler supplying hot water, built in behind a fireplace or integral to a gas fire.

backbone ■ n. **1** the spine. **2** the chief support of a system or organization. ▸ strength of character.

back-breaking ■ adj. (especially of manual labour) physically demanding.

back-burner ■ v. US postpone action on.
– PHRASES **on the back burner** having low priority.

backchat ■ n. Brit. informal rude or impudent remarks.

backcloth ■ n. Brit. another term for **BACKDROP**.

backcomb ■ v. chiefly Brit. comb (the hair) from the ends of the strands towards the scalp to make it look thicker.

backcountry ■ n. chiefly N. Amer. sparsely inhabited rural areas.

backcourt ■ n. **1** (in tennis, basketball, and other games) the part of each side of the court nearest the back wall or back boundary line. **2** the defensive players in a basketball team.

backcross Genetics ■ v. cross (a hybrid) with one of its parents or an organism with the same genetic characteristics as one of the parents. ■ n. an instance of or the result of this.

backdate ■ v. make (something, especially a pay increase) retrospectively valid. ▸ put an earlier date to (a document or agreement) than the actual one.

back door ▪ adj. underhand; clandestine.
– PHRASES **by** (or **through**) **the back door** in a clandestine or underhand way.

backdraught (US **backdraft**) ▪ n. **1** a current of air or water that flows backwards down a chimney, pipe, etc. **2** a phenomenon in which a fire that has consumed all available oxygen suddenly explodes when more oxygen is made available.

backdrop ▪ n. **1** a painted cloth hung at the back of a theatre stage as part of the scenery. **2** the setting or background for a scene or event.

back-end ▪ adj. **1** relating to the end of a project, process, or investment. **2** Computing denoting a specialized subordinate processor or program, not directly accessed by the user.

back-fanged ▪ adj. denoting a snake (such as a boomslang) in which the rear pair or pairs of teeth have grooves to conduct the venom. Compare with FRONT-FANGED.

backfield ▪ n. American Football the area of play behind the line of scrimmage.

backfill ▪ v. refill (an excavated hole) with the material dug out of it. ▪ n. material used for backfilling.

backfire /bakˈfʌɪə/ ▪ v. **1** (of a vehicle or its engine) undergo a mistimed explosion in the cylinder or exhaust. **2** (of a plan or action) rebound adversely on the originator.

backflip ▪ n. a backward somersault done in the air with the arms and legs stretched out straight.

back focus ▪ n. Photography the distance between the back of a lens and the image of an object at infinity.

back-formation ▪ n. a word that is formed from its seeming derivative, typically by removal of a suffix (e.g. *edit* from *editor*).

backgammon ▪ n. **1** a board game in which two players move their pieces around twenty-four triangular points according to the throw of dice. **2** the most complete form of win in this game.
– ORIGIN C17: from BACK + GAMMON².

background ▪ n. **1** part of a scene, picture, or description that forms a setting for the main figures, events, etc. **2** a persistent low level of radioactivity, radiation, noise, etc. present in a particular environment. **3** explanatory or contributory information or circumstances. ▸ a person's education, experience, and social circumstances. **4** Computing tasks or processes running on a computer that do not need input from the user.

backgrounder ▪ n. an official briefing or handout giving background information.

backhand ▪ n. (in tennis and other racket sports) a stroke played with the back of the hand facing in the direction of the stroke, with the arm across the body. ▪ v. strike with a backhanded blow or stroke.

backhanded ▪ adj. **1** made with the back of the hand facing in the direction of movement. **2** indirect or ambiguous: *a backhanded compliment*. ▪ adv. with the back of the hand or with the hand turned backwards.

backhander ▪ n. **1** a backhand stroke or blow. **2** an indirect or ambiguous insult. **3** Brit. informal a bribe.

back-heel ▪ v. kick backwards with the heel.

backhoe (Brit. also **backhoe loader**) ▪ n. a mechanical excavator which draws towards itself a bucket attached to a hinged boom.

backing ▪ n. **1** support. ▸ a layer of material that forms, protects, or strengthens the back of something. **2** (especially in popular music) musical or vocal accompaniment to the main singer or soloist.

backing track ▪ n. a recorded musical accompaniment, especially one for a soloist to play or sing along with.

backlash ▪ n. **1** a strong and adverse reaction by a large number of people. **2** recoil or degree of play arising between parts of a mechanism.

backlight ▪ n. illumination from behind. ▪ v. (past **-lit**; past part. **-lit** or **-lighted**) illuminate from behind.
– DERIVATIVES **backlighting** n.

backline ▪ n. **1** a line marking the back of something, especially the area of play in a game. **2** Rugby the players lined out across the field behind a scrum or line-out.

backlist ▪ n. a publisher's list of books published before the current season and still in print.

backload ▪ n. a load transported on the return journey of a delivery truck. ▪ v. **1** transport such a load. **2** place more charges at the later stages of (a financial agreement) than at the earlier stages.

backlog ▪ n. an accumulation of work or matters needing to be dealt with.

backmarker ▪ n. a competitor who is among the last in a race.

backpack ▪ n. a rucksack. ▪ v. [usu. as noun **backpacking**] travel or hike carrying one's belongings in a rucksack.
– DERIVATIVES **backpacker** n.

back pass ▪ n. Soccer a deliberate pass to one's own goalkeeper.

back passage ▪ n. Brit. euphemistic a person's rectum.

back-pedal ▪ v. **1** move the pedals of a bicycle backwards in order to brake. **2** hastily reverse one's previous action or opinion.

back-projection ▪ n. the projection of a picture on to the back of a translucent screen.

backrest ▪ n. a support for a person's back when they are seated.

back room ▪ n. a place where secret, administrative, or supporting work is done.

back row ▪ n. [treated as sing. or pl.] Rugby the forwards who are in the second row in a scrum.
– DERIVATIVES **back-rower** n.

backscatter ▪ n. **1** Physics deflection of radiation or particles through an angle of 180°. **2** Photography light from a flashgun or other light source that is deflected directly into a lens. ▪ v. Physics deflect (radiation or particles) through an angle of 180°.

backscratching ▪ n. informal the reciprocal provision of help, typically in an underhand manner.

back-seat driver ▪ n. informal a passenger in a car who gives the driver unwanted advice.
– DERIVATIVES **back-seat driving** n.

backside ▪ n. **1** informal a person's buttocks or anus. **2** chiefly N. Amer. the reverse or rearward side.

backsight ▪ n. **1** the sight of a rifle or other weapon that is nearer the eye of the person aiming. **2** Surveying a sight or reading taken backwards or towards the point of starting.

back slang ▪ n. slang in which words are spoken as though they were spelled backwards (e.g. *redraw* for *warder*).

backslapping ▪ n. the action of offering hearty congratulations or praise. ▪ adj. vigorously hearty.
– DERIVATIVES **backslapper** n.

backslash ▪ n. a backward-sloping diagonal line (\).

backslide ▪ v. (past **-slid**; past part. **-slid** or **-slidden**) relapse into bad ways.
– DERIVATIVES **backslider** n. **backsliding** n.

backspace ▪ n. **1** a key on a typewriter or computer keyboard used to cause the carriage or cursor to move backwards. **2** a device on a video recorder or camcorder which produces a slight backward run between shots to eliminate disturbance caused by the interruption of the scanning process. ▪ v. move a typewriter carriage or computer cursor backwards.

backspin ▪ n. a backward spin given to a moving ball, causing it to stop more quickly or rebound at a steeper angle on hitting a surface.

back-stabbing ▪ n. the action of criticizing someone while feigning friendship. ▪ adj. behaving in such a way.
– DERIVATIVES **back-stabber** n.

backstage ▪ adv. in or to the area behind the stage in a theatre. ▪ adj. of or relating to this area in a theatre.

backstairs ▪ pl. n. **1** stairs at the back or side of a building. **2** [as modifier] underhand; clandestine.

backstay ▪ n. a stay on a sailing ship leading downwards and aft from the upper part of a mast.

backstitch

backstitch ■ n. a method of sewing with overlapping stitches. ■ v. sew using backstitch.

backstop ■ n. **1** a person or thing placed at the rear of something as a barrier or support. **2** Baseball a high fence or similar structure behind the home plate area. **3** Baseball a catcher. ■ v. Baseball act as backstop for.

back straight ■ n. the part of a racecourse, athletics track, etc. that is parallel to the home straight.

backstreet ■ n. **1** a minor street. **2** [as modifier] secret, especially because illegal.

backstretch ■ n. N. Amer. another term for BACK STRAIGHT.

backstroke ■ n. **1** a swimming stroke performed on the back with the arms lifted alternately out of the water in a backward circular motion and the legs extended and kicking. **2** Bell-ringing a pull of the tail end of the rope from its highest position so as to swing the bell through a full circle.
– DERIVATIVES **backstroker** n.

backswing ■ n. Golf a backward swing of the arm or the golf club when about to hit a ball.

back talk ■ n. informal North American term for BACKCHAT.

back-to-back ■ adj. **1** chiefly Brit. (of houses) built in a terrace backing on to another terrace, with a party wall or a narrow alley between. **2** consecutive. ■ adv. (**back to back**) **1** (of two people) facing in opposite directions with their backs touching. **2** consecutively.

back-to-nature ■ adj. advocating or relating to reversion to a simpler way of life.

backtrack ■ v. **1** retrace one's steps. ▸ reverse one's previous position or opinion. **2** US pursue; track.

back-up ■ n. **1** support. ▸ a reserve. **2** Computing the procedure for backing up data. ▸ a copy made in such a way. **3** N. Amer. a traffic jam.

backveld /ˈbakfɛlt/ ■ n. S. African remote country districts, especially when considered unsophisticated or conservative.
– DERIVATIVES **backvelder** n.
– ORIGIN partial translation of Afrikaans *agterveld* 'back countryside'.

backward ■ adj. **1** directed behind or to the rear. **2** having made less progress than is normal or expected. ▸ having learning difficulties. **3** [with neg.] (**backward in**) lacking the confidence to do: *he was not backward in displaying his talents*. **4** Cricket (of a fielding position) behind an imaginary line passing through the stumps at the batsman's end at right angles to the wicket. ■ adv. variant of BACKWARDS.
– DERIVATIVES **backwardly** adv. **backwardness** n.
– ORIGIN Middle English: from earlier *abackward*, from ABACK.

backwardation ■ n. Brit. Stock Exchange **1** a situation in which the spot or cash price of a commodity is higher than the forward price. **2** a situation in which the offer price for stock is lower than the bid.

backwards (also **backward**) ■ adv. **1** in the direction of one's back. **2** back towards the starting point. **3** in reverse of the usual direction or order. ▸ towards the past. ▸ towards a worse state.
– PHRASES **backwards and forwards** to and fro. **bend** (or **fall** or **lean**) **over backwards** informal make every effort, especially to be fair or helpful. **know something backwards** be entirely familiar with something.

backwash ■ n. **1** the motion of receding waves. **2** a backward current created by an object moving through water or air. ■ v. clean (a filter of a swimming pool) by sending fluid through it in a reverse direction.

backwater ■ n. **1** a part of a river not reached by the current, where the water is stagnant. **2** a place or state in which no development or progress is taking place.

backwind Nautical ■ v. (of a sail or vessel) deflect a flow of air into the back of (another sail or vessel). ■ n. a flow of air so deflected.

backwoods ■ pl. n. chiefly N. Amer. remote uncleared forest land. ▸ a remote or sparsely inhabited region, especially one considered backward or conservative.
– DERIVATIVES **backwoodsman** n.

backyard ■ n. **1** a yard at the back of a house or other building. ▸ S. African such an area used as the site for additional accommodation, especially for a domestic worker or low income tenant. **2** S. African & N. Amer. a back garden. **3** informal the area close to where one lives, regarded with proprietorial concern.

backyard dweller ■ n. S. African a tenant occupying an improvised building or shelter erected in a backyard.

backyarder ■ n. S. African another term for BACKYARD DWELLER.

bacon ■ n. cured meat from the back or sides of a pig.
– PHRASES **bring home the bacon** informal **1** supply material provision or support. **2** achieve success.
– ORIGIN Middle English: from Old French, from a Germanic word meaning 'ham, flitch'.

baconer ■ n. a pig suitable for being made into bacon and ham, typically heavier than both a porker and a cutter.

bacteraemia /ˌbaktəˈriːmɪə/ (US **bacteremia**) ■ n. Medicine the presence of bacteria in the blood.
– DERIVATIVES **bacteraemic** adj.

bacteria plural form of BACTERIUM.

bactericide /bakˈtɪərɪsʌɪd/ ■ n. a substance which kills bacteria.
– DERIVATIVES **bactericidal** adj.

bacteriological ■ adj. **1** of or relating to bacteriology or bacteria. **2** relating to or denoting germ warfare.
– DERIVATIVES **bacteriologic** adj. **bacteriologically** adv.

bacteriology ■ n. the study of bacteria.
– DERIVATIVES **bacteriologist** n.

bacteriolysis /bakˌtɪərɪˈɒlɪsɪs/ ■ n. Biology the rupture of bacterial cells, especially by an antibody.

bacteriophage /bakˈtɪərɪə(ʊ)feɪdʒ, -fɑːʒ/ ■ n. Biology a kind of virus which parasitizes a bacterium by infecting it and reproducing inside it.
– ORIGIN 1920s: from BACTERIUM + Greek *phagein* 'eat'.

bacterium /bakˈtɪərɪəm/ ■ n. (pl. **bacteria** /-rɪə/) a member of a large group of unicellular micro-organisms (prokaryotes) which have cell walls but lack an organized nucleus and other structures, and include numerous disease-causing forms.
– DERIVATIVES **bacterial** adj.
– ORIGIN C19: from Greek *baktērion*, diminutive of *baktēria* 'rod, cane' (because the first ones to be discovered were rod-shaped).

> **USAGE**
> **Bacteria**, the plural form of **bacterium**, is sometimes mistakenly treated as a singular form.

Bactrian camel ■ n. see CAMEL.

baculovirus /ˈbakjʊlə(ʊ)ˌvʌɪrəs/ ■ n. Biology a member of a family of DNA viruses infecting invertebrates.
– ORIGIN 1980s: from Latin *baculum* 'rod, stick' + VIRUS.

bad ■ adj. (**worse, worst**) **1** of poor quality or a low standard. **2** unwelcome; unpleasant. ▸ severe; serious. ▸ (**bad for**) harmful to. **3** offending moral standards or accepted conventions. **4** injured, ill, or diseased. **5** (of food) decayed. **6** guilty; ashamed. **7** inappropriate.
– PHRASES **in a bad way** ill or in trouble. **to the bad 1** to ruin. **2** in deficit. **too bad** informal indicating that something is regrettable but now beyond retrieval.
– DERIVATIVES **baddish** adj. **badness** n.
– ORIGIN Middle English: perhaps from Old English *bæddel* 'hermaphrodite, womanish man'.

bad blood ■ n. ill feeling.

bad break ■ n. informal a piece of bad luck.

bad debt ■ n. a debt that cannot be recovered.

baddy (also **baddie**) ■ n. (pl. **-ies**) informal a villain or criminal in a book, film, etc.

bade /beɪd, bad/ past of BID².

bad faith ■ n. intent to deceive: *the company had acted in bad faith*.

bad form ■ n. an offence against current social conventions.

badge ■ n. **1** a small piece of metal, plastic, or cloth bearing a design or words, typically worn to identify a

person or to indicate support for a cause. **2** a sign or feature revealing a quality or condition: *he converts the macho stereotype into a badge of honour.* ■ v. mark with a badge.
– ORIGIN Middle English.

badger ■ n. a heavily built omnivorous nocturnal mammal of the weasel family, typically having a grey and black coat and a white-striped head. [*Meles meles* (Eurasia) and *Taxidea taxus* (N. America).] ■ v. repeatedly and annoyingly ask (someone) to do something.
– ORIGIN C16: perhaps from **BADGE**, with ref. to its distinctive head markings.

bad hair day ■ n. informal a day on which everything goes wrong.

badinage /'badɪnɑːʒ/ ■ n. witty conversation.
– ORIGIN C17: from French, from *badiner* 'to joke'.

badlands ■ pl. n. extensive tracts of heavily eroded, uncultivable land with little vegetation.

badly ■ adv. (**worse**, **worst**) **1** in a bad manner. **2** severely; seriously. **3** very much.
– PHRASES **badly off** at a disadvantage, especially by being poor.

badminton ■ n. a game with rackets in which a shuttlecock is hit back and forth across a net.
– ORIGIN named after *Badminton* in SW England, where the game was first played.

bad-mouth ■ v. informal criticize maliciously.

bad-tempered ■ adj. easily annoyed or angered.
– DERIVATIVES **bad-temperedly** adv.

Baedeker /'beɪdɪkə/ ■ n. a travel guidebook published by the firm founded by the German publisher Karl Baedeker (1801–59).

baffle ■ v. **1** totally bewilder. **2** restrain or regulate (a fluid, a sound, etc.). ■ n. a device used to restrain the flow of a fluid, gas, or loose material or to prevent the spreading of sound or light in a particular direction.
– DERIVATIVES **bafflement** n. **baffler** n. **baffling** adj. **bafflingly** adv.
– ORIGIN C16: perhaps rel. to French *bafouer* 'ridicule' or obsolete French *beffer* 'mock, deceive'.

BAFTA /'baftə/ ■ abbrev. British Academy of Film and Television Arts.

bag ■ n. **1** a flexible container with an opening at the top. ▸ a piece of luggage. **2** (**bags**) loose folds of skin under a person's eyes. **3** (**bags**) Brit. dated loose-fitting trousers. **4** (**bags of**) informal plenty of. **5** the amount of game shot by a hunter. **6** (usu. **old bag**) informal an unpleasant or unattractive woman. **7** (**one's bag**) informal one's particular interest or taste. **8** Baseball a padded square marking each of the first, second, and third bases. ■ v. (**bagged**, **bagging**) **1** put in a bag. **2** succeed in killing or catching (an animal). ▸ succeed in securing. **3** (of clothes) form loose bulges due to wear.
– PHRASES **bag and baggage** with all one's belongings. **a bag of tricks** informal a set of ingenious plans, techniques, or resources. **bags** (or **bags I**) informal a child's expression used to make a claim to something. **in the bag** informal **1** (of something desirable) as good as secured. **2** US drunk.
– DERIVATIVES **bagful** n. (pl. -**fuls**)
– ORIGIN Middle English: perhaps from Old Norse *baggi*.

Baganda /bə'gandə/ ■ pl. n. (sing. **Muganda**) an African people of the kingdom of Buganda, now forming part of Uganda.
– ORIGIN a local name; cf. Kiswahili *Waganda*.

bagasse /bə'gas/ ■ n. the dry pulpy residue left after the extraction of juice from sugar cane.
– ORIGIN C19: from Spanish *bagazo* 'pulp'.

bagatelle /ˌbagə'tɛl/ ■ n. **1** a game in which small balls are hit into numbered holes on a board, with pins as obstructions. **2** something trifling or negligible. **3** a short, light piece of music.
– ORIGIN C17: from Italian *bagatella*, perhaps from *baga* 'baggage' or from Latin *baca* 'berry'.

bagel /'beɪɡ(ə)l/ ■ n. **1** a dense, ring-shaped bread roll that is simmered before baking. **2** S. African humorous or derogatory an affluent young Jewish man.
– ORIGIN C20: from Yiddish *beygel*.

baggage ■ n. **1** personal belongings packed in suitcases for travelling. **2** past experiences or long-held opinions perceived as encumbrances: *emotional baggage.*
– ORIGIN Middle English: from Old French *bagage*, from *baguer* 'tie up' or *bagues* 'bundles'.

baggy ■ adj. (-**ier**,-**iest**) (of clothing) loose and hanging in folds. ▸ (of eyes) having folds of puffy skin below them. ■ n. (**baggies**) loose, wide-legged trousers.
– DERIVATIVES **baggily** adv. **bagginess** n.

bag lady ■ n. informal a homeless woman who carries her possessions around in shopping bags.

bagman ■ n. (pl. -**men**) **1** Brit. informal, dated a travelling salesman. **2** Austral. a tramp. **3** Canadian a political fundraiser. **4** US & Austral. informal an agent who collects or distributes the proceeds of illicit activities.

bagpipe ■ n. a musical instrument with reed pipes that are sounded by the pressure of wind emitted from a bag squeezed by the player's arm.
– DERIVATIVES **bagpiper** n.

ba gua /bɑː 'ɡwɑː/ ■ n. variant spelling of **PA KUA**.

baguette /ba'ɡɛt/ ■ n. **1** a long, narrow French loaf. **2** a gem, especially a diamond, cut in a long rectangular shape.
– ORIGIN C18: from French, from Italian *bacchetto*, from Latin *baculum* 'staff'.

bagworm ■ n. a moth, the caterpillar and flightless female of which live in a portable protective case constructed out of plant debris. [Family Psychidae.]

bah ■ exclam. an expression of contempt or disagreement.
– ORIGIN C19: prob. from French.

Baha'i /bɑː'hɑːi/ (also **Bahai**) ■ n. (pl. **Baha'is**) **1** a monotheistic religion founded in the 19th century as a development of Babism, emphasizing the essential oneness of humankind and of all religions and seeking world peace. **2** an adherent of the Baha'i faith.
– DERIVATIVES **Baha'ism** /bɑː'hɑːɪz(ə)m/ n.
– ORIGIN Persian, from Arabic *bahā'* 'splendour'.

Bahamian /bə'heɪmɪən/ ■ n. a native or inhabitant of the Bahamas. ■ adj. of or relating to the Bahamas or its inhabitants.

Bahasa Indonesia /bə'hɑːsə/ ■ n. the official language of Indonesia. See **INDONESIAN**.
– ORIGIN from Malay *bahasa* 'language'.

Bahasa Malaysia ■ n. the official language of Malaysia. See **MALAY**.

Bahraini /bɑː'reɪni/ ■ n. a native or inhabitant of Bahrain. ■ adj. of or relating to Bahrain or its inhabitants.

baht /bɑːt/ ■ n. (pl. same) the basic monetary unit of Thailand.
– ORIGIN from Thai *bāt*.

bail[1] ■ n. **1** the temporary release of an accused person awaiting trial, sometimes on condition that a sum of money is lodged to guarantee their appearance in court. **2** money paid by or for such a person as security. ■ v. release or secure the release of (an accused person) on payment of bail.
– PHRASES **go** (or **stand**) **bail** act as surety for an accused person. **jump bail** informal fail to appear for trial after being released on bail.
– DERIVATIVES **bailable** adj.
– ORIGIN Middle English: from Old French, 'custody, jurisdiction', from *bailler* 'take charge of', from Latin *bajulare* 'bear a burden'.

bail[2] ■ n. **1** Cricket either of the two crosspieces bridging the stumps. **2** a bar on a typewriter or computer printer which holds the paper steady. **3** a bar separating horses in an open stable.
– ORIGIN Middle English: from Old French *baile* 'palisade, enclosure', from *baillier* 'enclose'.

bail[3] (also **bale**) ■ v. **1** scoop water out of (a ship or boat). **2** (**bail out**) make an emergency parachute descent from an aircraft. **3** (**bail someone/thing out**) rescue someone or something from a difficulty.
– DERIVATIVES **bailer** n.
– ORIGIN C17: from obsolete *bail* 'bucket', from French *baille*, from Latin *bajulus* 'carrier'.

bailey

bailey ■ n. (pl. **-eys**) the outer wall of a castle.
– ORIGIN Middle English: prob. from Old French *baile* (see **BAIL**²).

Bailey bridge ■ n. a temporary bridge of lattice steel designed for rapid assembly from prefabricated standard parts, used especially in military or emergency situations.
– ORIGIN SECOND WORLD WAR: named after its designer, the English engineer Sir D. *Bailey*.

bailie /'beɪli/ ■ n. (pl. **-ies**) chiefly historical a municipal officer and magistrate in Scotland.
– ORIGIN Middle English: from Old French *bailli*.

bailiff /'beɪlɪf/ ■ n. **1** chiefly Brit. a sheriff's officer who executes writs and processes and carries out seizure of property and arrests. **2** Brit. the agent of a landlord. **3** N. Amer. an official in a court of law who keeps order and looks after prisoners.
– ORIGIN Middle English: from Old French *baillif*, *bailli* (see **BAILIE**), from Latin *bajulus* 'carrier, manager'.

bailiwick /'beɪlɪwɪk/ ■ n. **1** Law the district or jurisdiction of a bailie or bailiff. **2** informal one's sphere of operations or particular area of interest.
– ORIGIN Middle English: from **BAILIE** + **WICK**².

Baily's beads ■ pl. n. Astronomy a string of bright points seen at the edge of the darkened moon at the beginning or end of totality in an eclipse of the sun, caused by the uneven lunar topography.
– ORIGIN C19: named after the English astronomer Francis *Baily*.

bain-marie /ˌbanmə'riː/ ■ n. (pl. **bains-marie** or **bain-maries** pronunc. same) a pan of hot water in which a cooking container is placed for slow cooking.
– ORIGIN C18: French, translation of medieval Latin *balneum Mariae* 'bath of Maria', translating Greek *kaminos Marias* 'furnace of Maria', said to be a Jewish alchemist.

Bairam /baɪ'rɑːm/ ■ n. either of two annual Muslim festivals, Greater Bairam at the end of the Islamic year and Lesser Bairam at the end of Ramadan.
– ORIGIN from Turkish *baïram*, from Persian *bazrām*.

bairn /bɛːn/ ■ n. chiefly Scottish & N. English a child.
– ORIGIN Old English, of Germanic origin.

bait ■ n. food used to entice fish or other animals as prey. ■ v. **1** deliberately annoy or taunt. **2** allow dogs to attack (a trapped or restrained animal). **3** put bait on (a hook) or in (a trap, net, or fishing area).
– PHRASES **rise to the bait** react to a provocation or temptation exactly as intended.
– ORIGIN Middle English: from Old Norse *beit* 'pasture, food', *beita* 'to hunt or chase'.

baitcasting ■ n. fishing by throwing a bait or lure into the water on the end of a line using a rod and reel.
– DERIVATIVES **baitcaster** n.

baize /beɪz/ ■ n. a coarse felt-like woollen material that is typically green, used chiefly for covering billiard and card tables.
– ORIGIN C16: from French *baies*, from *bai* (see **BAY**⁴).

Bajan /'beɪdʒ(ə)n/ ■ adj. & n. informal term for **BARBADIAN**.

bake ■ v. **1** cook (food) by dry heat without direct exposure to a flame, typically in an oven. **2** (of the sun or other agency) subject to dry heat. ▶ informal be or become extremely hot in prolonged hot weather. ■ n. a dish consisting of a number of ingredients mixed together and baked.
– ORIGIN Old English, of Germanic origin.

baked Alaska ■ n. a dessert consisting of sponge cake and ice cream in a meringue covering, cooked briefly in a hot oven.

baked beans ■ pl. n. baked haricot beans, typically cooked in tomato sauce and tinned.

bakehouse ■ n. dated a building or area in which bread is made.

Bakelite /'beɪk(ə)lʌɪt/ ■ n. trademark an early brittle form of plastic made from formaldehyde and phenol.
– ORIGIN C20: named after Leo H. *Baekeland*, the Belgian-born American chemist who invented it.

baker ■ n. a person whose trade is making and selling bread and cakes.
– PHRASES **baker's dozen** a group of thirteen. [from the former bakers' custom of adding an extra loaf to a dozen sold to a retailer, this constituting the latter's profit.]

bakery ■ n. (pl. **bakeries**) a place where bread and cakes are made or sold.

bakgat /'bakxat/ ■ adj. S. African informal excellent.
– ORIGIN C20: Afrikaans.

baking powder ■ n. a mixture of sodium bicarbonate and cream of tartar, used as a raising agent in baking.

baking soda ■ n. sodium bicarbonate.

bakkie /'bʌki/ ■ n. S. African **1** a pickup truck. **2** a bowl or other small container.
– ORIGIN diminutive of Afrikaans *bak* 'container'.

baklava /'bɑːkləvə, 'bak-/ ■ n. a Middle Eastern dessert made of filo pastry filled with chopped nuts and soaked in honey.
– ORIGIN from Turkish.

baksheesh /bak'ʃiːʃ/ ■ n. (in parts of the Middle and Far East and the Indian subcontinent) a small sum of money given as alms, a tip, or a bribe.
– ORIGIN from Persian *bakšiš*, from *bakšīdan* 'give'.

balaclava /ˌbalə'klɑːvə/ ■ n. a close-fitting woollen hat covering the whole head and encircling the neck.
– ORIGIN C19 (worn orig. by soldiers in the Crimean War): named after the village of *Balaclava* in the Crimea.

balafon /'balafɒn/ ■ n. a large xylophone with hollow gourds as resonators, used in West African music.
– ORIGIN C18: from Mande *bala* 'xylophone' + *fo* 'to play'.

balalaika /ˌbalə'lʌɪkə/ ■ n. a Russian musical instrument like a guitar with a triangular body and typically three strings.
– ORIGIN C18: from Russian, of Tartar origin.

balance ■ n. **1** an even distribution of weight ensuring stability. **2** mental or emotional stability. **3** a condition in which different elements are equal or in the correct proportions. **4** Nautical the ability of a boat to stay on course without adjustment of the rudder. **5** an apparatus for weighing, especially one with a central pivot, beam, and two scales. **6** a counteracting weight or force. ▶ (also **balance wheel**) the regulating device in a clock or watch. **7** a preponderance: *the balance of opinion was that work was important*. **8** a figure representing the difference between credits and debits in an account; the amount of money held in an account. ▶ the difference between an amount due and an amount paid. ■ v. **1** be or put in a steady position. **2** offset or compare the value of (one thing) with another. ▶ [often as adj. **balanced**] establish equal or appropriate proportions of elements in: *a balanced diet*. **3** compare debits and credits in (an account) to ensure that they are equal.
– PHRASES **balance of payments** the difference in total value between payments into and out of a country over a period. **balance of power 1** a situation in which states of the world have roughly equal power. **2** the power held by a small group when larger groups are of equal strength. **balance of trade** the difference in value between a country's imports and exports. **be** (or **hang**) **in the balance** be in an uncertain or critical state. **on balance** when all factors are taken into consideration. **throw** (or **catch**) **someone off balance** cause (or find) someone to be unsteady.
– DERIVATIVES **balancer** n.
– ORIGIN Middle English: from Old French *balance* (n.), from late Latin (*libra*) *bilanx* '(balance) having two scale-pans'.

balance sheet ■ n. a written statement of the assets, liabilities, and capital of a business.

balance wheel ■ n. another term for **BALANCE** (see sense 6).

balanitis /ˌbalə'nʌɪtɪs/ ■ n. Medicine inflammation of the glans penis.
– ORIGIN C19: from Greek *balanos* 'glans penis', literally 'acorn'.

balcony ■ n. (pl. **-ies**) **1** a platform enclosed by a wall or balustrade on the outside of a building. **2** the highest tier of seats in a theatre or cinema. ▶ N. Amer. the dress circle in a theatre.
– DERIVATIVES **balconied** adj.
– ORIGIN C17: from Italian *balcone*.

bald ■ adj. **1** having a scalp wholly or partly lacking hair. **2** (of an animal) not covered by the usual fur, hair, or feathers. **3** (of a tyre) having the tread worn away. **4** (of language) plain; blunt.
– DERIVATIVES **balding** adj. **baldish** adj. **baldly** adv. **baldness** n.
– ORIGIN Middle English: prob. from an Old English base meaning 'white patch'.

baldachin /ˈbaldəkɪn, ˈbɔːld-/ (also **baldaquin** /ˈbɔːldəkɪn/) ■ n. a ceremonial canopy over an altar, throne, or doorway.
– ORIGIN C16 (denoting a rich brocade): from Italian *baldacchino*, from *Baldacco* 'Baghdad', from where the brocade originated.

bald eagle ■ n. a white-headed North American eagle, the national bird of the US. [*Haliaeetus leucocephalus*.]

balderdash /ˈbɔːldədaʃ/ ■ n. senseless talk or writing.

baldy (also **baldie**) ■ n. (pl. **-ies**) informal, derogatory a bald-headed person. ■ adj. chiefly Scottish & Irish bald.

bale[1] ■ n. **1** a large wrapped or bound bundle of paper, hay, or cotton. **2** the quantity in a bale as a measure, specifically (in the US) 500 lb of cotton. ■ v. make up into bales.
– DERIVATIVES **baler** n.
– ORIGIN Middle English: prob. from Middle Dutch, of Germanic origin and rel. to **BALL**[1].

bale[2] ■ n. archaic **1** evil considered as a destructive force. **2** physical or mental torment.
– ORIGIN Old English, of Germanic origin.

bale[3] ■ v. variant spelling of **BAIL**[3].

baleen /bəˈliːn/ ■ n. whalebone.
– ORIGIN Middle English: from Latin *balaena* 'whale'.

baleen whale ■ n. any of the group of whales that have plates of whalebone in the mouth for straining plankton from the water. [Suborder Mysticeti.]

baleful ■ adj. menacing. ▶ having a harmful effect.
– DERIVATIVES **balefully** adv. **balefulness** n.
– ORIGIN Old English (see **BALE**[2]).

Balinese /ˌbɑːlɪˈniːz/ ■ n. (pl. same) **1** a native or inhabitant of Bali. **2** the Indonesian language of Bali. ■ adj. of or relating to Bali or its people or language.

balk ■ v. & n. variant spelling of **BAULK**.

Balkan /ˈbɔːlkən/ ■ adj. of or relating to the countries occupying the part of SE Europe forming a peninsula bounded by the Adriatic, Ionian, Aegean, and Black Seas. ■ n. (**the Balkans**) the Balkan countries.
– ORIGIN from Turkish.

Balkanize /ˈbɔːlkənaɪz, ˈbɒl-/ (also **-ise**) ■ v. divide (a region or body) into smaller mutually hostile states or groups.
– DERIVATIVES **Balkanization** (also **-isation**) /-ˈzeɪʃ(ə)n/ n.
– ORIGIN 1920s: from *Balkan* Peninsula (where this was done in the late 19th and early 20th century).

balky /ˈbɔːlki, ˈbɒːki/ (Brit. also **baulky**) ■ adj. (**-ier, -iest**) chiefly N. Amer. awkward; uncooperative.

ball[1] ■ n. **1** a solid or hollow sphere, especially one that is kicked, thrown, or hit in a game. ▶ N. Amer. a game played with a ball, especially baseball. **2** a single throw or kick of the ball in a game. ▶ Cricket a delivery of the ball by the bowler to the batsman. ▶ Baseball a pitch delivered outside the strike zone which the batter does not attempt to hit. ■ v. **1** squeeze or form into a ball. **2** N. Amer. vulgar slang (of a man) have sexual intercourse with. **3** Brit. (of a flower) fail to open properly, decaying in the half-open bud.
– PHRASES **the ball is in your court** it is up to you to make the next move. **the ball of the foot** the rounded protuberant part of the foot at the base of the big toe. **the ball of the thumb** the rounded protuberant part of the hand at the base of the thumb. **have a lot** (or **not much**) **on the ball** US have a lot of (or not much) ability. **keep the ball rolling** maintain the momentum of an activity. **keep one's eye on** (or **take one's eye off**) **the ball** keep (or fail to keep) one's attention focused on the matter in hand. **on the ball** alert to new ideas, methods, and trends. **play ball** informal cooperate. **start** (or **get** or **set**) **the ball rolling** make a start. **the whole ball of wax** N. Amer. informal everything.
– ORIGIN Middle English: from Old Norse *bǫllr*, of Germanic origin.

ball[2] ■ n. a formal social gathering for dancing.
– PHRASES **have a ball** informal enjoy oneself greatly.
– ORIGIN C17: from French *bal* 'a dance'.

ballad ■ n. **1** a poem or song narrating a popular story in short stanzas. **2** a slow sentimental or romantic song.
– DERIVATIVES **balladeer** n. **balladry** n.
– ORIGIN C15: from Old French *balade*, from Provençal *balada* 'dance, song to dance to'.

ballade /baˈlɑːd/ ■ n. **1** a poem consisting of one or more triplets of stanzas with a repeated refrain and an envoy. **2** a short, lyrical piece of music, especially one for piano.
– ORIGIN Middle English: earlier spelling of **BALLAD**.

ball and chain ■ n. a heavy metal ball secured by a chain to the leg of a prisoner to prevent escape.

ball-and-socket joint ■ n. a joint in which a partially spherical end lies in a socket, allowing movement and rotation in all directions.

ballast /ˈbaləst/ ■ n. **1** a heavy substance, such as gravel or lead, placed in the bilge of a ship to ensure its stability. ▶ a substance carried in an airship or on a hot-air balloon to stabilize it. **2** gravel or coarse stone used to form the bed of a railway track or the substratum of a road. ▶ a mixture of coarse and fine aggregate for making concrete. **3** a passive component used in an electric circuit to moderate changes in current. ■ v. provide with ballast.
– ORIGIN C16: prob. of Low German or Scandinavian origin.

ball bearing ■ n. a bearing in which the parts are separated by a ring of small metal balls which reduce friction. ▶ a ball used in such a bearing.

ballboy (or **ballgirl**) ■ n. a boy (or girl) who retrieves balls that go out of play during a tennis match or baseball game.

ball-breaker (also **ball-buster**) ■ n. informal a sexually demanding woman who destroys men's self-confidence.
– DERIVATIVES **ball-breaking** adj.

ball clay ■ n. a fine-textured clay used in the manufacture of ceramics.

ballcock ■ n. a valve which automatically tops up a cistern when liquid is drawn from it, especially in a flushing toilet.

ballerina ■ n. a female ballet dancer.
– ORIGIN C18: from Italian, feminine of *ballerino* 'dancing master'.

ballet ■ n. **1** an artistic dance form performed to music, using precise and formalized set steps and gestures. **2** a creative work of this form or the music written for it.
– DERIVATIVES **balletic** adj. **balletically** adv.
– ORIGIN C17: from Italian *balletto*, diminutive of *ballo* 'a dance'.

balletomane /ˈbalɪtəʊˌmeɪn/ ■ n. a ballet enthusiast.
– DERIVATIVES **balletomania** n.

ball float ■ n. the spherical float attached to a hinged arm in the ballcock of a water cistern.

ball game ■ n. **1** a game played with a ball. ▶ N. Amer. a baseball match. **2** informal a situation that is completely different from a previous one: *a whole new ball game*.

ballistic /bəˈlɪstɪk/ ■ adj. **1** of or relating to projectiles or their flight. **2** moving under the force of gravity only.
– PHRASES **go ballistic** informal fly into a rage.
– DERIVATIVES **ballistically** adv.

ballistic missile ■ n. a missile which is initially powered and guided but falls under gravity on to its target.

ballistics ■ pl. n. [treated as sing.] the science of projectiles and firearms.

ball lightning ■ n. a rare form of lightning in the shape of a moving luminous globe.

ballocks ■ pl. n. variant spelling of **BOLLOCKS**.

balloon ■ n. **1** a small rubber sac which is inflated and used as a child's toy or a decoration. ▶ a rounded outline in which the words or thoughts of characters in a comic strip or cartoon are written. **2** a large bag filled with hot air or gas to make it rise in the air, typically having a basket for passengers. **3** a large rounded drinking glass, used especially for brandy. ■ v. **1** swell out in a spherical shape. ▶ increase rapidly. **2** lob or be lobbed high in the air.
– PHRASES **when the balloon goes up** informal when the

balloon angioplasty

action or trouble starts.
- DERIVATIVES **ballooning** n. **balloonist** n.
- ORIGIN C16: from French *ballon* or Italian *ballone* 'large ball'.

balloon angioplasty ■ n. Medicine surgical widening of a blood vessel by means of a balloon catheter, an instrument incorporating a small balloon which is introduced into the blood vessel and then inflated in order to clear an obstruction or dilate a narrowed region.

balloonfish ■ n. (pl. same or **-fishes**) a tropical porcupine fish which lives in shallow water and can inflate itself when threatened. [*Diodon holocanthus*.]

balloon tyre ■ n. a large tyre containing air at low pressure.
- DERIVATIVES **balloon-tyred** adj.

balloon whisk ■ n. a hand whisk made of loops of metal wire.

ballot ■ n. 1 a procedure by which people vote secretly on an issue. ▸ (**the ballot**) the total number of votes cast in such a process. 2 a lottery held to decide the allocation of tickets or other things among a number of applicants. ■ v. (**balloted**, **balloting**) 1 elicit a secret vote from (members). ▸ cast one's vote. 2 allocate by drawing lots.
- ORIGIN C16 (orig. denoting a small coloured ball placed in a container to register a vote): from Italian *ballotta*, diminutive of *balla*.

ballot box ■ n. a sealed box into which voters put completed ballot papers.

ballpark ■ n. chiefly N. Amer. 1 a baseball ground. 2 informal a particular area or range. ■ adj. informal approximate: *the ballpark figure is $400–500.*

ballpoint pen ■ n. a pen with a tiny ball as its writing point.

ballroom ■ n. a large room for formal dancing.

ballroom dancing ■ n. formal social dancing in couples.

balls vulgar slang ■ pl. n. 1 testicles. 2 courage; nerve. 3 [treated as sing.] Brit. nonsense; rubbish. ■ v. (**balls something up**) bungle something.

balls-up ■ n. vulgar slang a bungled task or action.

ballsy ■ adj. (**-ier**, **-iest**) informal bold and confident.
- DERIVATIVES **ballsiness** n.

ball valve ■ n. a one-way valve opened and closed by pressure on a ball which fits into a cup-shaped opening.

bally /'bali/ ■ adj. & adv. Brit. old-fashioned euphemism for BLOODY[2].

ballyhoo informal ■ n. extravagant publicity or fuss. ■ v. (**ballyhoos**, **ballyhooed**) chiefly N. Amer. praise or publicize extravagantly.
- ORIGIN C19: American coinage.

balm /bɑːm/ ■ n. 1 a fragrant ointment used to heal or soothe the skin. ▸ something that has a soothing or restorative effect. 2 a tree which yields a fragrant resinous substance, especially one used in medicine. [Genus *Commiphora*: numerous species.] ▸ used in names of other fragrant plants, chiefly of the mint family, e.g. lemon balm.
- ORIGIN Middle English: from Old French *basme*, from Latin *balsamum* (see BALSAM).

balmoral /bal'mɒr(ə)l/ ■ n. 1 a round brimless hat with a cockade or ribbons attached, worn by certain Scottish regiments. 2 a heavy laced leather walking boot.
- ORIGIN C19: named after *Balmoral* Castle in Scotland.

balmy /'bɑːmi/ ■ adj. (**-ier**, **-iest**) 1 (of the weather) pleasantly warm. 2 old-fashioned spelling of BARMY.
- DERIVATIVES **balmily** adv. **balminess** n.

balneotherapy /ˌbalnɪə(ʊ)'θɛrəpi/ ■ n. the treatment of disease by bathing in mineral springs.

baloney /bə'ləʊni/ (also **boloney**) ■ n. informal nonsense.
- ORIGIN C20: perhaps a corruption of BOLOGNA.

balsa /'bɒlsə/ ■ n. 1 (also **balsa wood**) very lightweight timber used chiefly for making models and rafts. 2 the fast-growing tropical American tree from which this wood is obtained. [*Ochroma lagopus*.]
- ORIGIN C17: from Spanish, 'raft'.

balsam /'bɔːlsəm, 'bɒl-/ ■ n. 1 an aromatic resinous substance exuded by various trees and shrubs, used as a base for certain fragrances and medical preparations. ▸ a tree or shrub which yields balsam. 2 a herbaceous plant cultivated for its helmeted pink or purple flowers. [Genus *Impatiens*.]
- DERIVATIVES **balsamic** /-'samɪk/ adj.
- ORIGIN Old English, from Greek *balsamon*.

balsamic vinegar ■ n. dark, sweet Italian vinegar that has been matured in wooden barrels.

Balt /bɔːlt, bɒlt/ ■ n. 1 a speaker of a Baltic language. 2 a native or inhabitant of one of the Baltic States of Lithuania, Latvia, and Estonia.

Balti /'balti/ ■ n. 1 a native or inhabitant of Baltistan, a region in the Himalayas. 2 the Tibetan language of this people. ■ adj. of or relating to the Baltis or their language.
- ORIGIN the name in Ladakhi dialect.

balti /'bɔːlti, 'balti/ ■ n. (pl. **baltis**) a type of Pakistani cuisine in which the food is cooked in a small two-handled pan known as a karahi.
- ORIGIN from Urdu *bāltī* 'pail'.

Baltic /'bɔːltɪk, 'bɒlt-/ ■ n. 1 (**the Baltic**) an almost landlocked sea of northern Europe. ▸ (also **the Baltic States**) a small group of states on the eastern shores of this sea, consisting of Latvia, Lithuania, and Estonia. 2 an Indo-European branch of languages consisting of Lithuanian, Latvian, and Old Prussian. ■ adj. of or relating to this sea or group of languages.
- ORIGIN C16: from medieval Latin *Balticus*, from late Latin *Balthae* 'dwellers near the Baltic Sea'.

baluster /'baləstə/ ■ n. a short pillar forming part of a series supporting a rail or coping.
- ORIGIN C17: from French *balustre*, from Italian *balaust(r)a* 'wild pomegranate flower' (because of the resemblance to the curving calyx tube of the flower).

balustrade /ˌbalə'streɪd/ ■ n. a railing supported by balusters.
- DERIVATIVES **balustraded** adj.
- ORIGIN C17: from French, from *balustre* (see BALUSTER).

bam ■ exclam. used to imitate the sound of a hard blow or convey the idea of something happening abruptly.

Bambara /bam'bɑːrə/ ■ n. (pl. same or **Bambaras**) 1 a member of a West African people living chiefly in Mali. 2 the Mande language of this people.

bamboo ■ n. a giant woody grass with hollow jointed stems, growing chiefly in the tropics for use in furniture and implements. [*Bambusa* and other genera.]
- ORIGIN C16: from Dutch *bamboes*, from Malay *mambu*.

bamboo shoot ■ n. a young shoot of bamboo, eaten as a vegetable.

bamboozle /bam'buːz(ə)l/ ■ v. informal cheat or mystify.
- DERIVATIVES **bamboozler** n.
- ORIGIN C18.

ban ■ v. (**banned**, **banning**) officially or legally prohibit. ■ n. an official or legal prohibition.
- ORIGIN Old English *bannan* 'summon by a public proclamation', of Germanic origin; the noun is partly from Old French *ban* 'proclamation, banishment'.

banal /bə'nɑːl, -'nal/ ■ adj. tediously unoriginal or commonplace.
- DERIVATIVES **banality** n. (pl. **-ies**). **banally** adv.
- ORIGIN C18 (orig. relating to feudal service in the sense 'compulsory', hence 'common to all'): from French, from *ban* (see BAN).

banana ■ n. 1 a long curved fruit which grows in clusters and has soft pulpy flesh and yellow skin when ripe. 2 (also **banana plant** or **banana tree**) the tropical and subtropical palm-like plant which bears this fruit. [Genus *Musa*: several species.] 3 [as modifier] S. African informal denoting the province of KwaZulu-Natal.
- PHRASES **go** (or **be**) **bananas** informal become (or be) mad, angry, or excited. **top banana** informal, chiefly N. Amer. the most important person in an organization.
- ORIGIN C16: via Portuguese or Spanish from Mande.

banana plug ■ n. Electronics a single-pole connector with a curved strip of metal forming a spring along its tip.

banana republic ■ n. derogatory a small state that is politically unstable as a result of the domination of its economy by a single export controlled by foreign capital.

banana split ■ n. a sweet dish made with bananas cut down the middle and filled with ice cream, sauce, and nuts.

bancassurance /ˈbaŋkəˌʃɔːrəns/ (also **bankassurance**) ■ n. the selling of life assurance and other insurance products by banking institutions.
– DERIVATIVES **bancassurer** n.

band¹ ■ n. **1** a flat, thin strip or loop of material used as a fastener, for reinforcement, or as decoration. ▶ a belt or strap transmitting motion between two wheels or pulleys. ▶ N. Amer. Ornithology a ring of metal placed round a bird's leg to identify it. **2** a stripe, line, or elongated area of a different colour or composition from its surroundings: *a band of cloud*. **3** (especially in financial contexts) a range of values or a specified category within a series. ▶ a range of frequencies or wavelengths in a spectrum: *channels in the UHF band*. ▶ any of several groups into which school pupils of the same age are divided on the basis of similar ability. **4** (**bands**) a collar with two hanging strips, worn by certain lawyers, clerics, and academics as part of their formal dress. ■ v. **1** surround or fit with a band. **2** mark with a stripe or stripes of a different colour. **3** allocate to a range or category.
– DERIVATIVES **bander** n. **banding** n.
– ORIGIN Old English, from Old Norse, reinforced by Old French *bande*, of Germanic origin.

band² ■ n. **1** a small group of musicians and vocalists who play pop, jazz, or rock music. ▶ a group of musicians who play brass, wind, or percussion instruments. **2** a group of people having a common interest or purpose or characterized by a common feature. **3** N. Amer. a herd or flock. ■ v. form a group for a mutual purpose.
– ORIGIN Middle English: from Old French *bande*, of Germanic origin; rel. to BANNER.

bandage ■ n. a strip of woven material used to bind up a wound or to protect an injured part of the body. ■ v. bind with a bandage.
– DERIVATIVES **bandaging** n.
– ORIGIN C16: from French, from *bande* (see BAND¹).

bandanna /banˈdanə/ ■ n. a large coloured handkerchief or neckerchief.
– ORIGIN C18: prob. via Portuguese from Hindi.

bandbox ■ n. a circular cardboard box for carrying hats.
– ORIGIN C17: orig. denoting a box used for carrying neckbands.

bandeau /ˈbandəʊ/ ■ n. (pl. **bandeaux** /-dəʊz/) **1** a narrow band worn round the head to hold the hair in position. **2** a woman's strapless top formed from a band of fabric fitting around the bust.
– ORIGIN C18: from Old French *bandel*, diminutive of *bande* (see BAND¹).

bandicoot /ˈbandɪkuːt/ ■ n. a mainly insectivorous marsupial native to Australia and New Guinea. [Family Peramelidae: several species.]
– ORIGIN C18: from Telugu *pandikokku* 'pig-rat'.

bandiet /banˈdiːt/ ■ n. (pl. **bandiets** or **bandiete**) S. African informal a prisoner.
– ORIGIN 1920s: Afrikaans, from Dutch, 'robber, brigand'.

bandit ■ n. (pl. **bandits** or **banditti** /banˈdiːtiː/) **1** a violent robber or outlaw belonging to a gang. **2** military slang an enemy aircraft.
– DERIVATIVES **banditry** n.
– ORIGIN C16: from Italian *bandito*, *bandire* 'ban'.

bandleader ■ n. a player at the head of a musical band.

bandmaster ■ n. the conductor of a musical band, especially a brass or military one.

bandolier /ˌbandəˈlɪə/ (also **bandoleer**) ■ n. a shoulder belt with loops or pockets for cartridges.
– ORIGIN C16: from French *bandoulière*; perhaps from Spanish *bandolera*, from *banda* 'sash'.

bandpass ■ n. Electronics the range of frequencies which are transmitted through a filter.

bandsaw ■ n. a saw consisting of an endless moving steel belt with a serrated edge.

bandshell ■ n. chiefly N. Amer. a bandstand in the form of a large concave shell with special acoustic properties.

bandstand ■ n. a covered outdoor platform for a band to play on.

bandwagon ■ n. **1** historical a wagon used for carrying a band in a parade or procession. **2** a particular activity or cause that has suddenly become fashionable or popular: *the company is jumping on the environmental bandwagon*.

bandwidth ■ n. a range of frequencies, especially one used in telecommunications. ▶ the transmission capacity of a computer network or other telecommunication system.

bandy¹ ■ adj. (**-ier**, **-iest**) (of a person's legs) curved outwards so that the knees are wide apart.
– ORIGIN C17: perhaps from obsolete *bandy*, a curved stick used in hockey.

bandy² ■ v. (**-ies**, **-ied**) (usu. **be bandied about/around**) pass on or discuss (an idea or rumour) in a casual or uninformed way.
– PHRASES **bandy words** argue pointlessly or rudely.
– ORIGIN C16 ('pass (a ball) to and fro'): perhaps from French *bander* 'take sides at tennis', from *bande* (see BAND¹).

bane ■ n. **1** a cause of great distress or annoyance: *the telephone was the bane of my life*. **2** archaic poison.
– DERIVATIVES **baneful** adj. (archaic).
– ORIGIN Old English, of Germanic origin.

bang¹ ■ n. **1** a sudden loud, sharp noise. ▶ a sudden painful blow. **2** (**bangs**) chiefly N. Amer. a fringe of hair cut straight across the forehead. **3** Computing, chiefly N. Amer. the character '!'. ■ v. **1** strike or put down forcefully and noisily. ▶ make or cause to make a sudden loud noise. **2** vulgar slang (of a man) have sexual intercourse with. ■ adv. informal, chiefly Brit. exactly: *the train arrived bang on time*.
– PHRASES **bang for one's** (or **the**) **buck** US informal value for money. **bang goes** —— informal a plan or hope is suddenly or completely destroyed. **bang on** Brit. informal exactly right. **get a bang out of** informal, chiefly N. Amer. derive excitement or pleasure from. **with a bang 1** abruptly. **2** impressively or spectacularly.
– PHRASAL VERBS **bang away at** informal do persistently or doggedly. **bang on about** informal talk at tedious length about. **bang something out** informal **1** play music noisily and unskilfully. **2** produce something hurriedly or in great quantities. **bang someone up** Brit. informal imprison someone.
– ORIGIN C16: imitative, perhaps of Scandinavian origin.

bang² /baŋ/ ■ n. variant spelling of BHANG.

banger ■ n. **1** informal, chiefly Brit. a sausage. **2** informal an old car. **3** S. African & US informal a boxer who hits hard. **4** a loud explosive firework.

Bangla /ˈbaŋlə/ ■ n. the Bengali language.
– ORIGIN from Bengali *bāṅglā*.

Bangladeshi /ˌbaŋgləˈdɛʃi/ ■ n. (pl. same or **Bangladeshis**) a native or inhabitant of Bangladesh. ■ adj. of or relating to Bangladesh or its people.

bangle ■ n. a rigid ornamental band worn around the arm.
– ORIGIN C18: from Hindi *baṅglī* 'glass bracelet'.

banish ■ v. **1** send (someone) away, especially from a country, as an official punishment. **2** dismiss from one's mind.
– DERIVATIVES **banishment** n.
– ORIGIN Middle English: from Old French *banir*; rel. to BAN.

banister /ˈbanɪstə/ (also **bannister**) ■ n. the uprights and handrail at the side of a staircase. ▶ a single upright at the side of a staircase.
– ORIGIN C17: from earlier *barrister*, var. of BALUSTER.

banjax /ˈbandʒaks/ ■ v. ruin or incapacitate.
– ORIGIN 1930s: orig. Anglo-Irish.

banjo ■ n. (pl. **-os** or **-oes**) a stringed instrument of the guitar family, with an open-backed soundbox of vellum (or plastic) stretched over a round hoop.
– DERIVATIVES **banjoist** n.
– ORIGIN C18: orig. a black American var. of rare *bandore*, denoting a kind of lute, rel. to Dutch *bandoor* and Spanish *bandurria*, prob. from Greek *pandoura* 'three-stringed lute'.

bank¹ ■ n. **1** the land alongside or sloping down to a river or lake. **2** a long, high mound or elevation. **3** a transverse

bank

slope given to a road, railway, or sports track to enable vehicles or runners to maintain speed round a curve. **4** the sideways tilt of an aircraft when turning in flight. **5** a set of similar things grouped together in rows. **6** the cushion of a pool table. ■ v. **1** heap or form into a mass or mound. **2** (of an aircraft or vehicle) tilt sideways in making a turn. **3** build (a road, railway, or sports track) with a bank on a bend. **4** Brit. (of a locomotive) provide additional power for (a train) in ascending an incline. **5** (of an angler) land (a fish).
– ORIGIN Middle English: from Old Norse *bakki*, of Germanic origin; rel. to BENCH.

bank² ■ n. **1** a financial establishment that uses money deposited by customers for investment, pays it out when required, makes loans at interest, and exchanges currency. ▸ a site or receptacle where something may be deposited for recycling: *a paper bank*. ▸ (**the bank**) the store of money or tokens held by the banker in some gambling or board games. **2** a stock of something available for use when required: *a blood bank*. ■ v. **1** deposit (money or valuables) in a bank. ▸ have an account at a particular bank. **2** (**bank on**) base one's hopes or confidence on.
– PHRASES **break the bank** [usu. with neg.] informal cost more than one can afford.
– ORIGIN C15 (orig. denoting a money dealer's table): from French *banque*, from medieval Latin *banca*; rel. to BANK¹.

bankable ■ adj. certain to bring profit and success.
– DERIVATIVES **bankability** /-ə'bɪlɪti/ n.

bankassurance ■ n. variant spelling of BANCASSURANCE.

bank bill ■ n. **1** a bill of exchange drawn by one bank on another. **2** chiefly US a banknote.

bank card ■ n. another term for CASH CARD or CHEQUE CARD.

bank draft ■ n. a cheque drawn by a bank on its own funds.

banker ■ n. **1** a person who manages or owns a bank or group of banks. ▸ the person running the table, controlling play, or acting as dealer in some gambling or board games. **2** Brit. a supposedly certain bet.
– ORIGIN C16: from French *banquier*, from *banque* (see BANK²).

banker's order ■ n. an instruction to a bank to make payments of a stated sum at regular intervals.

bank guaranteed cheque ■ n. a cheque which is guaranteed by a bank.

bank holiday ■ n. Brit. a day on which banks are officially closed, kept as a public holiday.

banking¹ ■ n. the business conducted or services offered by a bank.

banking² ■ n. an embankment or artificial bank.

banknote ■ n. a piece of paper money, constituting a central bank's promissory note.

bank rate ■ n. another term for DISCOUNT RATE.

bankroll chiefly N. Amer. ■ n. a roll of banknotes. ■ v. informal support financially.

bankrupt ■ adj. **1** declared in law unable to pay one's debts. **2** completely lacking in a particular good quality or value: *the cause is morally bankrupt*. ■ n. a person judged by a court to be bankrupt. ■ v. reduce to a bankrupt state.
– DERIVATIVES **bankruptcy** n.
– ORIGIN C16: from Italian *banca rotta* 'broken bench'.

banksia /'baŋksɪə/ ■ n. an evergreen Australian shrub with flowers resembling bottlebrushes. [Genus *Banksia*.]
– ORIGIN named after the English botanist Sir Joseph *Banks*.

bank statement ■ n. a printed record of the transactions in and balance of a bank account.

banner ■ n. a long strip of cloth bearing a slogan or design. ▸ a flag on a pole used as the standard of a king, knight, or army. ■ adj. N. Amer. excellent; outstanding.
– DERIVATIVES **bannered** adj.
– ORIGIN Middle English: from Old French *baniere*, of Germanic origin and rel. to BAND².

banning order ■ n. S. African historical a document issued in terms of security legislation by which a person's freedom of movement, association, speech, and action were restricted.

bannister ■ n. variant spelling of BANISTER.

bannock /'banək/ ■ n. a round, flat loaf, typically unleavened, associated with Scotland and northern England.
– ORIGIN Old English, of Celtic origin.

banns ■ pl. n. a notice read out on three successive Sundays in a Christian parish church, announcing an intended marriage and giving the opportunity for objections.
– ORIGIN Middle English: pl. of BAN.

banoffi pie /bə'nɒfi/ (also **banoffee pie**) ■ n. a pie or tart made with bananas, toffee, and cream.
– ORIGIN 1970s: from BANANA + TOFFEE.

banquet /'baŋkwɪt/ ■ n. an elaborate and formal meal for many people. ■ v. (**banqueted, banqueting**) entertain with a banquet.
– ORIGIN C15: from French, diminutive of *banc* (see BANK¹).

banquette /baŋ'kɛt/ ■ n. an upholstered bench along a wall.
– ORIGIN C17: from French, from Italian *banchetta*, diminutive of *banca* (see BANK²).

banshee /ban'ʃiː, 'banʃiː/ ■ n. (in Irish legend) a female spirit whose wailing warns of a death in a house.
– ORIGIN C17: from Irish *bean sídhe*, from Old Irish *ben síde* 'woman of the fairies'.

bantam ■ n. a chicken of a small breed.
– ORIGIN C18: apparently named after the province of *Bantam* in Java, although the fowl is not native there.

bantamweight ■ n. a weight in boxing and other sports intermediate between the flyweight and featherweight categories.

banter ■ n. the playful and friendly exchange of teasing remarks. ■ v. engage in banter.
– ORIGIN C17.

Bantu /ban'tuː, 'bantuː/ ■ n. (pl. same or **Bantus**) **1** a member of an extensive group of indigenous peoples of central and southern Africa. **2** the group of Niger–Congo languages spoken by these peoples, including Kiswahili, isiXhosa, and isiZulu.
– ORIGIN pl. (in certain Bantu languages) of -*ntu* 'person'.

> **USAGE**
> **Bantu** is a strongly offensive word in South African English, especially when used of individual people, but is still used to refer to the group of languages and their speakers collectively.

Bantu education ■ n. S. African historical, offensive the system of education for black South Africans introduced in 1953, considered inferior to that provided for white children.

bantustan ■ n. S. African historical another term for HOMELAND.
– ORIGIN 1940s: from *Bantu* + Hindi -*stān* 'country', on the pattern of *Hindustan, Pakistan*.

banyan /'banɪən, -njən/ (also **banian**) ■ n. **1** (also **banyan tree**) an Indian fig tree, whose branches produce wide-ranging aerial roots which later become accessory trunks. [*Ficus benghalensis*.] **2** a loose flannel jacket, shirt, or gown worn in India.
– ORIGIN C16: from Gujarati *vāṇiyo* 'man of the trading caste', from Sanskrit (orig. applied by Europeans to a tree under which traders had built a pagoda).

baobab /'beɪə(ʊ)bab/ ■ n. a short African or Australian tree with a very thick trunk and large edible fruit, living to a great age. [Genus *Adansonia*: several species.]
– ORIGIN C17: prob. from an African language.

bap ■ n. Brit. a large, round, flattish bread roll, typically with a floury top.
– ORIGIN C16.

Bapedi /bə'pɛdi/ plural form of PEDI.

baptism ■ n. the Christian rite of sprinkling water on to a person's forehead or of immersing them in water, symbolizing purification or regeneration and admission to the Christian Church.
– PHRASES **baptism of fire** a difficult or painful new

undertaking or experience.
-DERIVATIVES **baptismal** adj.
-ORIGIN Middle English: from Old French *baptesme*, from Greek *baptizein* 'immerse, baptize'.

baptismal name ■ n. a personal name given at baptism.

baptist ■ n. 1 (**Baptist**) a member of a Protestant Christian denomination advocating baptism only of adult believers by total immersion. 2 a person who baptizes someone.

baptistery (also **baptistry**) ■ n. (pl. **-ies**) the part of a church used for baptism. ▸ (in a Baptist chapel) a sunken receptacle used for baptism by total immersion.

baptize (also **-ise**) ■ v. 1 administer baptism to. 2 give a specified name or nickname to.
-ORIGIN Middle English: from eccles. Latin *baptizare*, from Greek *baptizein* 'immerse, baptize'.

bar¹ ■ n. 1 a long rigid piece of wood, metal, or similar material, typically used as an obstruction, fastening, or weapon. ▸ a sandbank or shoal at the mouth of a harbour or an estuary. ▸ a metal strip below the clasp of a medal, awarded as an additional distinction. ▸ Heraldry a charge in the form of a narrow horizontal stripe across the shield. 2 a counter in a public house or café across which alcoholic drinks or refreshments are served. ▸ a room in a public house, restaurant, or hotel in which alcohol is served. ▸ an establishment where alcohol and other refreshments are served. ▸ a small shop or stall serving refreshments or providing a specified service: *a snack bar*. 3 a barrier or restriction to action or advance: *a bar to promotion*. ▸ a plea arresting an action or claim in a law case. 4 Music any of the short sections or measures into which a piece of music is divided, shown on a score by vertical lines across the stave. 5 (**the bar**) a partition in a court room, now usually notional, beyond which most people may not pass and at which an accused person stands. ▸ Brit. a rail marking the end of each chamber in the Houses of Parliament. 6 (**the Bar**) the profession of advocate or barrister. ▸ advocates, barristers, or lawyers collectively. ■ v. (**barred**, **barring**) 1 fasten with a bar or bars. 2 prohibit from doing something or going somewhere. ▸ exclude from consideration. ▸ Law prevent or delay (an action) by objection. 3 mark with bars or stripes. ■ prep. chiefly Brit. except for. ▸ Brit. Horse Racing except the horses indicated (used when stating the odds).
-PHRASES **bar none** with no exceptions. **be called** (or **go**) **to the Bar** Brit. be admitted as a barrister. **be called within the Bar** Brit. be appointed a Queen's Counsel. **behind bars** in prison.
-DERIVATIVES **barred** adj.
-ORIGIN Middle English: from Old French *barre* (n.), *barrer* (v.).

bar² ■ n. a unit of pressure equivalent to a hundred thousand newtons per square metre or approximately one atmosphere.
-ORIGIN C20: from Greek *baros* 'weight'.

barathea /ˌbærəˈθiːə/ ■ n. a fine woollen cloth, sometimes mixed with silk or cotton, used for coats and suits.
-ORIGIN C19.

barb¹ ■ n. 1 a sharp projection near the end of an arrow, fish hook, or similar object, which is angled away from the main point so as to make extraction difficult. ▸ a barbel at the mouth of some fish. ▸ one of the hair-like filaments growing from the shaft of a feather, forming the vane. 2 a deliberately hurtful remark. 3 a freshwater fish with barbels around the mouth. [Genus *Barbus*: many species.]
-DERIVATIVES **barbed** adj. **barbless** adj.
-ORIGIN Middle English (denoting a piece of linen worn around the chin by nuns): from Old French *barbe*, from Latin *barba* 'beard'.

barb² ■ n. a small horse of a hardy breed originally from North Africa.
-ORIGIN C17: from French *barbe*, from Italian *barbero* 'of Barbary'.

Barbadian /bɑːˈbeɪdiən/ ■ n. a native or inhabitant of Barbados. ■ adj. of or relating to Barbados or its people.

barbarian ■ n. 1 (in ancient times) a member of a people not belonging to one of the great civilizations (Greek, Roman, Christian). 2 an uncultured or brutish person. ■ adj. 1 of or relating to ancient barbarians. 2 uncultured; brutish.
-ORIGIN Middle English: from Old French *barbarien*, from *barbare*, or from Greek *barbaros* 'foreign'.

barbaric ■ adj. 1 savagely cruel. 2 primitive; unsophisticated.
-DERIVATIVES **barbarically** adv.

barbarism ■ n. 1 absence of culture and civilization. 2 extreme cruelty or brutality. 3 a word or expression which is badly formed according to traditional philological rules, e.g. a word formed from elements of different languages, such as *breathalyser* (English and Greek).
-DERIVATIVES **barbarity** n. **barbarization** (also **-isation**) n. **barbarize** (also **-ise**) v.

barbarous ■ adj. 1 exceedingly brutal. 2 primitive; uncivilized.
-DERIVATIVES **barbarously** adv. **barbarousness** n.

Barbary ape ■ n. a tailless macaque monkey that is native to NW Africa and also found on the Rock of Gibraltar. [*Macaca sylvana*.]
-ORIGIN from *Barbary*, a former name for the western part of N. Africa.

Barbary sheep ■ n. a short-coated sheep with a long neck ruff, found in the high deserts of northern Africa. [*Ammotragus lervia*.]

barbecue ■ n. 1 an outdoor meal or gathering at which meat, fish, or other food is grilled on a rack over an open fire. 2 a structure for grilling food at a barbecue. ■ v. (**barbecues**, **barbecued**, **barbecuing**) cook (food) on a barbecue.
-ORIGIN C17 ('wooden framework for storing meat or fish to be dried'): from Spanish *barbacoa*, perhaps from Arawak *barbacoa* 'wooden frame on posts'.

barbecue sauce ■ n. a highly seasoned sauce containing vinegar, spices, and usually chillies.

barbed wire ■ n. wire with clusters of short, sharp spikes set at short intervals along it, used as a defensive barrier.

barbel /ˈbɑːb(ə)l/ ■ n. 1 a fleshy filament growing from the mouth or snout of a fish. 2 a large European freshwater fish of the carp family, with barbels hanging from the mouth. [*Barbus barbus*.] ▸ another term for **CATFISH**.
-ORIGIN Middle English: from late Latin *barbellus*, diminutive of *barbus* 'barbel', from *barba* 'beard'.

barbell /ˈbɑːbɛl/ ■ n. a long metal bar to which discs of varying weights are attached at each end, used for weightlifting.
-ORIGIN C19: from **BAR¹** + **BELL¹**.

barber ■ n. a person who cuts men's hair and shaves or trims beards as an occupation. ■ v. cut or trim (a man's hair).
-ORIGIN Middle English: from Old French *barbe* (see **BARB¹**).

barberry ■ n. (pl. **-ies**) a spiny shrub with yellow flowers and red berries. [*Berberis vulgaris* and other species.]
-ORIGIN Middle English: from Old French *berberis* (see **BERBERIS**).

barbershop ■ n. a popular style of close harmony singing, typically for four male voices.
-ORIGIN from the former custom of passing time in a barber's shop by harmonizing to a lute or guitar.

barber's pole ■ n. a pole painted with spiralling red and white stripes and hung outside barbers' shops as a business sign.

Barberton daisy ■ n. a perennial South African plant, hybrids of which are widely cultivated for their red or orange daisy-like flowers. [*Gerbera jamesonii*.]
-ORIGIN named after the S. African town of *Barberton*.

barbet /ˈbɑːbɪt/ ■ n. a brightly coloured fruit-eating songbird, chiefly tropical, that has a stout bill with tufts of bristles at the base. [Family Capitonidae: numerous species.]
-ORIGIN C16 (orig. denoting a poodle): from French *barbe* (see **BARB¹**).

barbican /ˈbɑːbɪk(ə)n/ ■ n. the outer defence of a city or castle, especially a double tower above a gate or drawbridge.
-ORIGIN Middle English: from Old French *barbacane*; prob. from Arabic.

barbie

barbie ■ n. (pl. **-ies**) informal, chiefly Austral./NZ a barbecue.

Barbie doll ■ n. **1** trademark a doll representing a conventionally attractive young woman. **2** informal an attractive but characterless or unintelligent young woman.

bar billiards ■ pl. n. [treated as sing.] Brit. a form of billiards played on a small table, in which balls are struck into holes guarded by pegs.

barbiturate /bɑːˈbɪtjʊrət, -reɪt/ ■ n. **1** any of a class of sedative drugs derived from barbituric acid. **2** Chemistry a salt or ester of barbituric acid.

barbituric acid /ˌbɑːbɪˈtjʊərɪk, -ˈtʃʊərɪk/ ■ n. Chemistry a synthetic organic compound from which the barbiturates are derived.
– ORIGIN C19: from French *barbiturique*, from German *Barbitursäure*, from the given name *Barbara* + *Säure* 'acid'.

barbotine /ˈbɑːbətɪn/ ■ n. slip (liquid clay) used to decorate pottery.
– ORIGIN C19: from French.

Barbour /ˈbɑːbə/ ■ n. (also **Barbour jacket**) ■ n. trademark a type of green waxed outdoor jacket.
– ORIGIN named after John *Barbour*, a draper in NE England.

Barbudan /bɑːˈbuːdən/ ■ n. a native or inhabitant of Barbuda, an island in the West Indies. ■ adj. of or relating to Barbuda or its inhabitants.

barbule /ˈbɑːbjuːl/ ■ n. a minute filament projecting from the barb of a feather.
– ORIGIN C19: from Latin *barbula*, diminutive of *barba* 'beard'.

barbwire ■ n. N. Amer. barbed wire.

barcarole /ˈbɑːkərəʊl, ˌbɑːkəˈrəʊl/ (also **barcarolle** /-rɒl, -ˈrɒl/) ■ n. a song traditionally sung by Venetian gondoliers. ▸ a musical composition in the style of such a song.
– ORIGIN C18: from Venetian Italian *barcarola* 'boatman's song', from *barca* 'boat'.

barchan /ˈbɑːk(ə)n/ ■ n. a crescent-shaped shifting sand dune.
– ORIGIN C19: from Turkic *barkhan*.

bar chart (also **bar graph**) ■ n. a diagram in which the numerical values of variables are represented by the height or length of lines or rectangles.

bar code ■ n. a machine-readable code in the form of a pattern of parallel lines of varying widths, printed on and identifying a commodity for stock control.

bard[1] ■ n. **1** archaic or poetic/literary a poet, traditionally one reciting epics. ▸ (**the Bard**) Shakespeare. **2** the winner of a prize for Welsh verse at an Eisteddfod.
– DERIVATIVES **bardic** adj.
– ORIGIN Middle English: from Scottish Gaelic *bàrd*, Irish *bard*, Welsh *bardd*.

bard[2] ■ n. a rasher of fat bacon placed on meat or game before roasting. ■ v. cover with bards.
– ORIGIN C18: from French *barde* in sense 'armour for the breast of a warhorse'.

bardo /ˈbɑːdəʊ/ ■ n. (in Tibetan Buddhism) a state of existence between death and rebirth.
– ORIGIN Tibetan *bár-do*, from *bar* 'interval' + *do* 'two'.

Bardolino /ˌbɑːdəˈliːnəʊ/ ■ n. a red wine from the Veneto region of Italy.
– ORIGIN from Italian.

bare ■ adj. **1** (of a person or part of the body) not clothed or covered. ▸ without the appropriate or usual covering or contents. ▸ (**bare of**) without. **2** without elaboration; basic. ▸ only just sufficient: *a bare majority*. ■ v. uncover (a part of the body) and expose it to view.
– PHRASES **bare one's teeth** show one's teeth, typically when angry. **with one's bare hands** without using tools or weapons.
– DERIVATIVES **bareness** n.
– ORIGIN Old English, of Germanic origin.

bareback ■ adj. & adv. on an unsaddled horse.

bareboat ■ adj. (of a boat or ship) hired without a crew.

barefaced ■ adj. shameless and undisguised: *a barefaced lie.*
– DERIVATIVES **barefacedly** adv. **barefacedness** n.

barefoot (also **barefooted**) ■ adj. & adv. wearing nothing on one's feet.

barehanded ■ adj. & adv. with nothing in or covering one's hands.

bareheaded ■ adj. & adv. without a covering for one's head.

bare-knuckle (also **bare-knuckled**) ■ adj. (of a boxer or boxing match) without gloves.

barely ■ adv. **1** only just; almost not: *he was barely able to speak*. **2** only a very short time before. **3** in a simple and sparse way.

barf informal, chiefly N. Amer. ■ v. vomit. ■ n. vomited food.
– ORIGIN 1960s (orig. US).

barfly /ˈbɑːflaɪ/ ■ n. (pl. **-flies**) informal a person who spends much of their time drinking in bars.

bargain ■ n. **1** an agreement between two or more people as to what each will do for the other. **2** a thing bought or offered for sale for a lower price than normal. ■ v. **1** negotiate the terms and conditions of a transaction. **2** (**bargain for/on**) expect.
– PHRASES **drive a hard bargain** be uncompromising in making a deal. **into** (N. Amer. **in**) **the bargain** in addition.
– DERIVATIVES **bargainer** n.
– ORIGIN Middle English: from Old French *bargaine* (n.), *bargaignier* (v.); prob. of Germanic origin.

barge ■ n. **1** a long flat-bottomed boat for carrying freight on canals and rivers. ▸ a long ornamental boat used for pleasure or on ceremonial occasions. **2** a boat used by the chief officers of a warship. ■ v. **1** move forcefully or roughly. ▸ (**barge in**) intrude or interrupt rudely or awkwardly. **2** convey by barge.
– ORIGIN Middle English: from Old French, perhaps from Greek *baris* 'Egyptian boat'.

bargeboard ■ n. an ornamental board fixed to the gable end of a roof to hide the ends of the roof timbers.
– ORIGIN C19: perhaps from medieval Latin *bargus* 'gallows'.

bargee /bɑːˈdʒiː/ ■ n. chiefly Brit. a person in charge of or working on a barge.

bargepole ■ n. a long pole used to propel a barge and fend off obstacles.
– PHRASES **would not touch someone/thing with a bargepole** informal would refuse to have anything to do with someone or something.

bar graph ■ n. another term for BAR CHART.

barista /bəˈrɪstə/ ■ n. a person who serves in a coffee bar.
– ORIGIN 1980s: Italian, 'barman'.

barite /ˈbɑːraɪt, ˈbeː-/ ■ n. variant spelling of BARYTE.

baritone ■ n. **1** an adult male singing voice between tenor and bass. **2** [as modifier] denoting an instrument that is second lowest in pitch in its family.
– ORIGIN C17: from Italian *baritono*, from Greek, from *barus* 'heavy' + *tonos* (see TONE).

barium /ˈbɛːrɪəm/ ■ n. the chemical element of atomic number 56, a soft white reactive metal of the alkaline earth group. (Symbol: **Ba**) ▸ Medicine a mixture of barium sulphate and water, opaque to X-rays, which is swallowed to permit radiological examination of the stomach or intestines.
– ORIGIN C19: from *baryta* (barium hydroxide).

bark[1] ■ n. the sharp explosive cry of a dog, fox, or seal. ■ v. **1** (of a dog, fox, or seal) give a bark. **2** utter (a command or question) abruptly or aggressively.
– PHRASES **one's bark is worse than one's bite** one is not as ferocious as one seems. **be barking up the wrong tree** informal be pursuing a mistaken line of thought or course of action.
– ORIGIN Old English, of Germanic origin.

bark[2] ■ n. the tough protective outer sheath of the trunk, branches, and twigs of a tree or woody shrub. ■ v. **1** strip the bark from. **2** scrape the skin off (one's shin) by accidentally hitting it. **3** tan or dye (leather or other materials) using the tannins found in bark.
– DERIVATIVES **-barked** adj.
– ORIGIN Middle English: from Old Norse *bǫrkr*; perhaps rel. to BIRCH.

bark³ ■ n. archaic or poetic/literary a ship or boat.
– ORIGIN Middle English: var. of BARQUE.

bark beetle ■ n. a small wood-boring beetle that tunnels under the bark of trees. [Family Scolytidae: many species.]

barkcloth ■ n. cloth made from the inner bark of the paper mulberry or similar tree.

barking ■ adj. Brit. informal completely mad.

barley ■ n. a hardy cereal with coarse bristles extending from the ears, cultivated chiefly for use in brewing and stockfeed. [Genus *Hordeum*.]
– ORIGIN Old English, from *bære*, *bere* 'barley'.

barleymow ■ n. Brit. archaic a stack of barley.

barley sugar ■ n. an amber-coloured sweet made of boiled sugar, traditionally shaped as a twisted stick.

barley water ■ n. a drink made from water and a boiled barley mixture.

bar line ■ n. Music a vertical line used in a musical score to mark a division between bars.

barm ■ n. the froth on fermenting malt liquor.
– ORIGIN Old English, of West Germanic origin.

barmaid ■ n. 1 Brit. a woman serving behind the bar of a public house. 2 N. Amer. a waitress who serves drinks in a bar.

barman ■ n. (pl. **-men**) a man serving behind the bar of a public house.

bar mitzvah /baːˈmɪtsvə/ ■ n. the religious initiation ceremony of a Jewish boy who has reached the age of 13. ■ v. administer this ceremony to.
– ORIGIN from Hebrew *bar miṣwāh* 'son of the commandment'.

barmy ■ adj. (**-ier**, **-iest**) informal, chiefly Brit. extremely foolish.
– DERIVATIVES **barmily** adv. **barminess** n.
– ORIGIN C15 ('frothy'): from BARM.

barn¹ ■ n. 1 a large farm building used for storage or for housing livestock. 2 N. Amer. a large shed for storing road or railway vehicles.
– ORIGIN Old English, from *bere* 'barley' + *ern*, *ærn* 'house'.

barn² (abbrev.: **b**) ■ n. Physics a unit of area, 10⁻²⁸ square metres, used especially in particle physics.
– ORIGIN 1940s: apparently from the phr. *as big as a barn door*.

barnacle /ˈbɑːnək(ə)l/ ■ n. a marine crustacean with an external shell, which attaches itself permanently to underwater surfaces and feeds by using modified feathery legs as filters. [Class Cirripedia: many species.]
– DERIVATIVES **barnacled** adj.
– ORIGIN C16: from medieval Latin *bernaca*.

barnacle goose ■ n. a goose with a white face and black neck, breeding in arctic tundra. [*Branta leucopsis*.]
– ORIGIN C18: from the former belief that the bird hatched from barnacles.

barn dance ■ n. 1 an informal social gathering for country dancing. 2 a dance for a number of couples moving round a circle, typically involving changes of partner.

barn owl ■ n. a pale-coloured owl with a heart-shaped face, typically nesting in farm buildings. [*Tyto alba* and related species.]

barnstorm ■ v. chiefly N. Amer. 1 tour rural districts giving theatrical performances, formerly often in barns. ▶ travel around giving exhibitions of flying and performing aeronautical stunts. 2 make a rapid tour as part of a political campaign.
– DERIVATIVES **barnstormer** n.

barnstorming ■ adj. flamboyantly vigorous and effective.

barnyard ■ n. N. Amer. a farmyard.

baro- /ˈbarəʊ/ ■ comb. form relating to pressure: *barometer*.
– ORIGIN from Greek *baros* 'weight'.

barograph ■ n. a barometer that records its readings on a moving chart.

Barolo /bəˈrəʊləʊ/ ■ n. a full-bodied red Italian wine from Barolo, a region of Piedmont.

barometer ■ n. 1 an instrument measuring atmospheric pressure, used especially in forecasting the weather and determining altitude. 2 an indicator of change: *furniture is a barometer of changing tastes.*
– DERIVATIVES **barometric** adj. **barometrical** adj. **barometry** n.

baron ■ n. 1 a member of the lowest order of the British nobility. ▶ historical a person who held lands or property from the sovereign or a powerful overlord. 2 a powerful person in business or industry: *a press baron*.
– DERIVATIVES **baronial** /bəˈrəʊnɪəl/ adj.
– ORIGIN Middle English: from medieval Latin *baro* 'man, warrior', prob. of Germanic origin.

baronage ■ n. 1 [treated as sing. or pl.] barons or nobles collectively. 2 an annotated list of barons or peers.

baroness ■ n. the wife or widow of a baron. ▶ a woman holding the rank of baron either as a life peerage or as a hereditary rank.

baronet /ˈbar(ə)nɪt/ ■ n. a member of the lowest hereditary titled British order.
– DERIVATIVES **baronetcy** n.
– ORIGIN Middle English: from Anglo-Latin *baronettus*, from medieval Latin *baro* (see BARON).

baronetage ■ n. 1 [treated as sing. or pl.] baronets collectively. 2 an annotated list of baronets.

baron of beef ■ n. Brit. a joint of beef consisting of two sirloins joined at the backbone.

baroque /bəˈrɒk, -ˈrəʊk/ ■ adj. relating to or denoting a style of European architecture, music, and art of the 17th and 18th centuries characterized by ornate detail. ▶ highly ornate and extravagant in style. ■ n. the baroque style or period.
– ORIGIN C18, from French (orig. denoting a pearl of irregular shape).

baroreceptor ■ n. Zoology a receptor sensitive to changes in pressure.

barotitis /ˌbarə(ʊ)ˈtʌɪtɪs/ ■ n. Medicine discomfort and inflammation in the ear caused by the changes of pressure occurring during air travel.

barouche /bəˈruːʃ/ ■ n. historical a four-wheeled horse-drawn carriage with a collapsible hood over the rear half.
– ORIGIN C19: from German dialect *Barutsche*, from Italian *baroccio*, from Latin *birotus* 'two-wheeled'.

barque /bɑːk/ ■ n. 1 a sailing ship, typically with three masts, in which the foremast and mainmast are square-rigged and the mizzenmast is rigged fore and aft. 2 poetic/literary a boat.
– ORIGIN Middle English: from Old French, from late Latin *barca* 'ship's boat'.

barrack¹ ■ v. provide (soldiers) with accommodation.

barrack² ■ v. jeer loudly at (a performer or speaker).
– ORIGIN C19: prob. from Northern Irish dialect.

barrack-room lawyer ■ n. Brit. a person who makes authoritative-sounding pronouncements on subjects in which they are not qualified.

barracks ■ pl. n. [often treated as sing.] a large building or group of buildings used to house soldiers.
– ORIGIN C17: from French *baraque*, from Italian *baracca* or Spanish *barraca* 'soldier's tent'.

barracouta /ˌbarəˈkuːtə/ ■ n. (pl. same or **barracoutas**) another term for SNOEK.
– ORIGIN C19: var. of BARRACUDA.

barracuda /ˌbarəˈkuːdə/ ■ n. (pl. same or **barracudas**) a large predatory tropical marine fish with a slender body and large jaws and teeth. [Genus *Sphyraena*: several species.]
– ORIGIN C17.

barrage /ˈbarɑːʒ/ ■ n. 1 a concentrated artillery bombardment over a wide area. 2 an overwhelming number of questions or complaints delivered in rapid succession. 3 an artificial barrier across a river, to prevent flooding or to aid irrigation or navigation. ■ v. bombard with questions or complaints.
– ORIGIN C19: from French, from *barrer* 'to bar'.

barrage balloon ■ n. a large anchored balloon, typically with netting suspended from it, serving as an obstacle to low-flying enemy aircraft.

Barr body ■ n. Physiology a densely staining structure in the cell nuclei of females, consisting of a condensed, inactive X chromosome and regarded as diagnostic of genetic femaleness.
– ORIGIN 1960s: named after the Canadian anatomist M. L. Barr.

barre /bɑː/ ■ n. a horizontal bar at waist level used as a support by ballet dancers during certain exercises.
– ORIGIN from French.

barrel ■ n. 1 a cylindrical container bulging out in the middle, traditionally made of wooden staves enclosed by metal hoops, now more usually made of metal. ▸ Brit. & US a measure of capacity for oil and beer, equal to 36 imperial gallons for beer and 35 imperial gallons or 42 US gallons (roughly 192 litres) for oil. 2 a cylindrical tube forming part of an object such as a gun or a pen. 3 the belly and loins of a four-legged animal such as a horse. ■ v. (**barrelled**, **barrelling**; US **barreled**, **barreling**) 1 informal, chiefly N. Amer. drive or move very fast. 2 put into a barrel or barrels.
– PHRASES **over a barrel** informal in a severely disadvantageous position. **with both barrels** informal, chiefly US with unrestrained force.
– ORIGIN Middle English: from Old French *baril*, from medieval Latin *barriclus* 'small cask'.

barrel-chested ■ adj. having a large rounded chest.

barrel distortion ■ n. a type of defect in optical or electronic images in which vertical or horizontal straight lines appear as convex curves.

barrelhead ■ n. the flat top of a barrel.
– PHRASES **on the barrelhead** North American term for on the nail (see NAIL).

barrel organ ■ n. a small pipe organ played by turning a handle, which rotates a cylinder studded with pegs that open the valves to produce a preset tune.

barrel roll ■ n. an aerobatic manoeuvre in which an aircraft follows a single turn of a spiral while rolling once about its longitudinal axis.

barrel vault ■ n. Architecture a vault forming a half cylinder.
– DERIVATIVES **barrel-vaulted** adj.

barren ■ adj. 1 (of land) too poor to produce much or any vegetation. ▸ (of a tree or plant) not producing fruit or seed. 2 (of a female animal) unable to bear young. 3 bleak and lifeless. 4 (**barren of**) devoid of. ■ n. (**barrens**) chiefly N. Amer. barren tracts of land.
– DERIVATIVES **barrenly** adv. **barrenness** n.
– ORIGIN Middle English: from Old French *barhaine*.

barricade /ˌbarɪˈkeɪd/ ■ n. an improvised barrier erected to obstruct the movement of opposing forces. ■ v. block or defend with a barricade.
– ORIGIN C16: from French, from *barrique* 'cask', from Spanish *barrica*; rel. to BARREL.

barrier ■ n. a fence or other obstacle that prevents movement or access. ▸ an obstacle to communication, understanding, or progress: *a language barrier*.
– ORIGIN Middle English: from Old French *barriere*; rel. to BARRE.

barrier cream ■ n. a cream used to protect the skin from damage or infection.

barrier method ■ n. a method of contraception using a device or preparation which prevents sperm from reaching an ovum.

barrier reef ■ n. a coral reef close and running parallel to the shore but separated from it by a channel of deep water.

barring ■ prep. except for; if not for.

barrio /ˈbarɪəʊ/ ■ n. (pl. **-os**) a district of a town in Spanish-speaking countries. ▸ (in the US) the Spanish-speaking quarter of a town or city.
– ORIGIN from Spanish.

barrister (also **barrister-at-law**) ■ n. chiefly Brit. a person called to the bar and entitled to practise as an advocate, particularly in the higher courts. Compare with SOLICITOR.
– ORIGIN Middle English: from BAR¹, perhaps on the pattern of *minister*.

barroom ■ n. chiefly N. Amer. a room with a bar selling alcoholic drinks.

barrow¹ ■ n. Brit. a two-wheeled handcart used especially by street vendors.
– ORIGIN Old English *bearwe* 'stretcher, bier', of Germanic origin; rel. to BEAR¹.

barrow² ■ n. Archaeology an ancient burial mound.
– ORIGIN Old English, of Germanic origin.

Barsac /ˈbɑːsak/ ■ n. a sweet white wine from the district of Barsac in SW France.

bar sinister ■ n. popular term for BEND SINISTER.

Bart ■ abbrev. Baronet.

bar tack ■ n. a stitch made to strengthen a potential weak spot in a garment or other sewn item.
– DERIVATIVES **bar-tacked** adj. **bar tacking** n.

bartender ■ n. a person serving drinks at a bar.

barter ■ v. exchange (goods or services) for other goods or services. ■ n. the action or system of bartering.
– DERIVATIVES **barterer** n.
– ORIGIN Middle English: prob. from Old French *barater* 'deceive'.

Bartholin's gland /ˈbɑːtəlɪnz/ ■ n. Anatomy either of a pair of glands near the entrance of the vagina, which secrete a fluid that lubricates the vulva.
– DERIVATIVES **bartholinitis** n.
– ORIGIN C18: named by the Danish anatomist Caspar Bartholin.

bar tracery ■ n. Architecture tracery with strips of stone across an aperture.

barycentric /ˌbarɪˈsɛntrɪk/ ■ adj. of or relating to the centre of gravity.
– DERIVATIVES **barycentre** n.
– ORIGIN C19: from Greek *barus* 'heavy' + -CENTRIC.

baryon /ˈbarɪɒn/ ■ n. Physics a subatomic particle with a mass equal to or greater than that of a proton, such as a nucleon or hyperon.
– DERIVATIVES **baryonic** adj.
– ORIGIN 1950s: from Greek *barus* 'heavy'.

baryte /ˈbarʌɪt, ˈbɛː-/ (also **barytes** /bəˈrʌɪtiːz/, **barite**) ■ n. a colourless or white mineral consisting of barium sulphate.
– ORIGIN C19: from BARIUM.

basal /ˈbeɪs(ə)l/ ■ adj. forming or belonging to a base.

basal cell carcinoma ■ n. technical term for RODENT ULCER.

basal ganglia ■ pl. n. Anatomy a group of structures linked to the thalamus in the base of the brain and involved in coordination of movement.

basal metabolic rate ■ n. the rate at which the body uses energy while at rest to maintain vital functions such as breathing and keeping warm.
– DERIVATIVES **basal metabolism** n.

basalt /ˈbasɔːlt, -(ə)lt/ ■ n. a dark fine-grained volcanic rock composed largely of plagioclase with pyroxene and olivine.
– DERIVATIVES **basaltic** /bəˈsɔːltɪk/ adj.
– ORIGIN C17: from Latin *basaltes*, from Greek *basanitēs*, from *basanos* 'touchstone'.

Basarwa /bəˈsɑːwə/ ■ n. a member of the San people of Botswana.

bascule bridge /ˈbaskjuːl/ ■ n. a type of bridge with a section which can be raised and lowered using counterweights.
– ORIGIN C19: from French 'see-saw', from *battre* 'to bump' + *cul* 'buttocks'.

base¹ ■ n. 1 the lowest part or edge of something, especially the part on which it rests or is supported. ▸ Architecture the part of a column between the shaft and pedestal or pavement. ▸ Botany & Zoology the end at which a part or organ is attached to the trunk or main part. 2 a conceptual structure or entity on which something draws or depends: *the town's economic base collapsed*. ▸ a foundation or starting point. 3 the main place where a person works or stays. ▸ a centre of operations for military or other activity. 4 a main or important element or ingredient to which other things are added. ▸ a substance into which a pigment is mixed to form paint. 5 Chemistry a substance capable of reacting with an acid to form a salt and water, or of accepting or neutralizing hydrogen ions.

6 Electronics the middle part of a bipolar transistor, separating the emitter from the collector. **7** Linguistics the root or stem of a word or a derivative. ▸ the uninflected form of a verb. **8** Mathematics a number used as the basis of a numeration scale. ▸ a number in terms of which other numbers are expressed as logarithms. **9** Baseball one of the four stations that must be reached in turn to score a run. ■ v. **1** use something as the foundation for: *the film is based on a novel.* **2** situate at a place as the centre of operations.
– PHRASES **get to first base** informal, chiefly N. Amer. achieve the first step towards one's objective. **off base** informal, chiefly N. Amer. mistaken. **touch base** informal, chiefly N. Amer. briefly make or renew contact.
– DERIVATIVES **-based** adj.
– ORIGIN Middle English: from Latin *basis* 'base, pedestal'.

base² ■ adj. **1** without moral principles; ignoble. **2** archaic denoting or befitting a person of low social class. **3** (of coins or other articles) not made of precious metal.
– DERIVATIVES **basely** adv. **baseness** n.
– ORIGIN Middle English: from Old French *bas*, from medieval Latin *bassus* 'short'.

baseball ■ n. a ball game played chiefly in the US and Canada between two teams of nine on a diamond-shaped circuit of four bases.

baseball cap ■ n. a cotton cap with a large peak.

base dressing ■ n. the application of manure or fertilizer to the earth, which is then ploughed or dug in.

base hit ■ n. Baseball a hit that allows the batter to advance safely to a base without an error by the team in the field.

base hospital ■ n. **1** a military hospital situated away from the area of active operations during a war. **2** Austral./NZ a hospital serving a large rural area.

base jump ■ n. a parachute jump from a fixed point, e.g. a high building or promontory, rather than an aircraft. ■ v. [often as noun **base jumping**] perform such a jump.
– DERIVATIVES **base jumper** n.
– ORIGIN 1980s: *base* from *b*uilding, *a*ntenna-tower, *s*pan, *e*arth (denoting the types of structure used).

baseless ■ adj. without foundation in fact.
– DERIVATIVES **baselessly** adv. **baselessness** n.

baseline ■ n. **1** a minimum or starting point used for comparisons. **2** (in tennis, volleyball, etc.) the line marking each end of a court. **3** Baseball the line between bases which a runner must stay close to when running.

baseload ■ n. the permanent minimum load that a power supply system is required to deliver.

baseman ■ n. (pl. **-men**) Baseball a fielder designated to cover either first, second, or third base.

basement ■ n. **1** a room or floor which is partly or entirely below ground level. **2** Geology the oldest formation of rocks underlying a particular area.
– ORIGIN C18: prob. from archaic Dutch *basement* 'foundation', perhaps from Italian *basamento* 'column base'.

base metal ■ n. a common metal that is not considered precious, such as copper, tin, or zinc.

basenji /bəˈsɛndʒi/ ■ n. (pl. **basenjis**) a smallish hunting dog of a central African breed, which growls and yelps but does not bark.
– ORIGIN 1930s: a local word.

base pair ■ n. Biochemistry a pair of complementary bases in a double-stranded nucleic acid molecule, consisting of cytosine and guanine or adenine in one strand linked to (respectively) guanine or thymine in the other.

base rate ■ n. chiefly Brit. another term for REPO RATE.

bases plural form of BASE¹ and BASIS.

bash informal ■ v. **1** strike hard and violently. ▸ criticize severely. **2** (**bash something out**) produce something rapidly and carelessly. ■ n. **1** a heavy blow. **2** a party or social event. **3** an attempt: *she'll have a bash at anything.*
– ORIGIN C17: imitative, perhaps a blend of BANG¹ and SMASH.

bashful ■ adj. shy and easily embarrassed.
– DERIVATIVES **bashfully** adv. **bashfulness** n.
– ORIGIN C15: from obsolete *bash* 'make or become abashed' (from ABASH).

basho /ˈbaʃəʊ/ ■ n. (pl. same or **-os**) a sumo wrestling tournament.
– ORIGIN Japanese, from *ba* 'place' + *shō* 'victory, win'.

BASIC ■ n. a simple high-level computer programming language, formerly widely used on microcomputers.
– ORIGIN 1960s: acronym from *Beginners' All-purpose Symbolic Instruction Code.*

basic ■ adj. **1** forming an essential foundation; fundamental. **2** consisting of the minimum required or offered: *the food was good, if a bit basic.* **3** Chemistry containing or having the properties of a base; alkaline. ■ n. (**basics**) the essential facts or principles of a subject or skill.

basically ■ adv. fundamentally. ▸ in fact; actually.

Basic English ■ n. a simplified form of English limited to 850 selected words, intended for international communication.

basicity /beɪˈsɪsɪti/ ■ n. Chemistry the number of hydrogen atoms replaceable by a base in a particular acid.

basic oxygen process ■ n. a steel-making process in which carbon and other impurities are burned away from iron by a jet of oxygen in a retort lined with a basic refractory.

basic wage ■ n. **1** Brit. a minimum wage earned before additional payments such as overtime. **2** Austral./NZ the minimum living wage, as determined by industrial tribunal.

basidiomycete /bəˌsɪdɪəˈmaɪsiːt/ ■ n. (pl. **basidiomycetes** /-ˈmaɪsiːts, -ˌmaɪˈsiːtiːz/) Botany a fungus of a large group whose spores develop within basidia and which includes the majority of familiar mushrooms and toadstools.
– ORIGIN C19: from *basidium* (see BASIDIUM) + Greek *mukētes* 'fungi'.

basidium /bəˈsɪdɪəm/ ■ n. (pl. **basidia** /-dɪə/) a microscopic club-shaped spore-bearing structure produced by certain fungi.
– ORIGIN C19: from Greek *basidion*, diminutive of *basis* (see BASIS).

basil /ˈbaz(ə)l, -zɪl/ ■ n. an aromatic plant of the mint family, native to tropical Asia, used as a culinary herb. [*Ocimum basilicum* (sweet basil) and other species.]
– ORIGIN Middle English: from Old French *basile*, from Greek *basilikos* (see BASILICA).

basilar /ˈbasɪlə/ ■ adj. Anatomy & Zoology of or situated at the base of something, especially the skull.
– ORIGIN C16: from Latin *basis* (see BASIS).

basilect /ˈbasɪlɛkt, ˈbeɪsɪ-/ ■ n. Linguistics a less prestigious dialect or variety of a particular language. Contrasted with ACROLECT.
– DERIVATIVES **basilectal** /ˈlɛkt(ə)l/ adj.
– ORIGIN 1960s: from BASIS + *-lect* as in *dialect.*

Basilian /bəˈzɪlɪən/ ■ adj. of or relating to St Basil the Great (c.330–79), or the order of monks and nuns following his monastic rule. ■ n. a Basilian monk or nun.

basilica /bəˈsɪlɪkə, -ˈzɪl-/ ■ n. a large oblong hall or building with double colonnades and a semicircular apse, used in ancient Rome as a law court or for public assemblies. ▸ a similar building used as a Christian church.
– DERIVATIVES **basilican** adj.
– ORIGIN C16: from Latin, 'royal palace', from Greek *basilikos* 'royal', from *basileus* 'king'.

basilisk /ˈbazɪlɪsk/ ■ n. **1** a mythical reptile with a lethal gaze or breath, hatched by a serpent from a cock's egg. **2** a long, slender Central American lizard, the male of which has a crest running from the head to the tail. [*Basiliscus plumifrons*.]
– ORIGIN Middle English: from Greek *basiliskos* 'little king, serpent', from *basileus* 'king'.

basin ■ n. **1** a large bowl or open container for washing in, preparing food, or holding liquid. **2** a broadly circular valley or natural depression on the earth's surface. ▸ an area drained by a river and its tributaries. ▸ an enclosed area of water where boats can be moored.
– DERIVATIVES **basinful** n. (pl. **-fuls**).
– ORIGIN Middle English: from Old French *bacin*, from medieval Latin, from *bacca* 'water container'.

basipetal /beɪˈsɪpɪt(ə)l/ ■ adj. Botany (of growth or development) downwards towards the base or point of attachment. Often contrasted with ACROPETAL.
– DERIVATIVES **basipetally** adv.
– ORIGIN C19: from BASIS + Latin *petere* 'seek'.

basis ■ n. (pl. **bases** /-siːz/) the underlying support for an idea, argument, or process. ▶ the principles according to which an activity is carried on: *she needed coaching on a regular basis*.
– ORIGIN C16: from Greek, 'stepping'; cf. BASE¹.

basis point ■ n. Finance one hundredth of one per cent.

bask ■ v. **1** lie exposed to warmth and sunlight for pleasure. **2** (**bask in**) revel in (something pleasing).
– ORIGIN Middle English: perhaps rel. to Old Norse *batha* 'bathe'.

basket ■ n. **1** a container used to hold or carry things, made from interwoven strips of cane or wire. **2** Basketball a net fixed on a hoop used as the goal. ▶ a goal scored. **3** Finance a group or range of currencies or investments.
– DERIVATIVES **basketful** n. (pl. **-fuls**).
– ORIGIN Middle English: from Old French *basket*.

basketball ■ n. a game played between two teams of five players in which goals are scored by throwing a ball through a netted hoop fixed at each end of the court.

basket case ■ n. informal a person or thing regarded as useless or unable to cope.
– ORIGIN C20: orig. US slang denoting a soldier who had lost all four limbs.

basketry ■ n. **1** the craft of basket-making. **2** baskets collectively.

basking shark ■ n. a large shark which feeds exclusively on plankton and typically swims slowly close to the surface. [*Cetorhinus maximus*.]

basmati rice /basˈmɑːti, -zˈ-/ ■ n. a kind of long-grain Indian rice with a delicate fragrance.
– ORIGIN from Hindi *bāsmati* 'fragrant'.

basophil /ˈbeɪsə(ʊ)fɪl/ ■ n. Physiology a basophilic white blood cell.

basophilic /ˌbeɪsə(ʊ)ˈfɪlɪk/ ■ adj. Physiology (of a cell or its contents) readily stained with basic dyes.

Basotho /bəˈsuːtuː/ ■ pl. n. (sing. **Mosotho**) the Sotho people collectively.
– ORIGIN the name in Sesotho.

Basotho blanket ■ n. S. African a multi-coloured, traditionally patterned blanket, worn round the shoulders by Basotho men and women; sometimes presented and worn as a badge of honour.

Basotho hat ■ n. S. African a conical hat, woven of reeds, with a decorative topknot, traditionally worn by Basotho men.

Basotho pony ■ n. a hardy mountain pony bred in Lesotho from the Cape horse.

Basque /bask, bɑːsk/ ■ n. **1** a member of a people living in the western Pyrenees in both France and Spain. **2** the language of this people, which is thought to be unrelated to any other language.
– ORIGIN from Latin *Vasco*.

basque /bask, bɑːsk/ ■ n. a close-fitting bodice extending from the shoulders to the waist and typically having a short continuation below waist level.
– ORIGIN C19: from BASQUE, referring to traditional Basque dress.

bas-relief /ˈbasrɪˌliːf, ˈbɑː(s)-/ ■ n. Art low relief.
– ORIGIN C17: from Italian *basso-rilievo* 'low relief', later altered to the French form.

bass¹ /beɪs/ ■ n. **1** the lowest adult male singing voice. **2** [as modifier] denoting the member of a family of instruments that is the lowest in pitch. ▶ informal a bass guitar or double bass. **3** the low-frequency output of a radio or audio system, corresponding to the bass in music.
– DERIVATIVES **bassist** n.
– ORIGIN Middle English: form of BASE², influenced by BASSO.

bass² /bas/ ■ n. (pl. same or **basses**) **1** any of several predatory marine or freshwater fish. [Families Serranidae and Centrarchidae.] See also SEA BASS. **2** Brit. the common freshwater perch.
– ORIGIN Middle English: var. of dialect *barse*, of Germanic origin.

bass clef ■ n. Music a clef placing F below middle C on the second-highest line of the stave.

basset (also **basset hound**) ■ n. a sturdy hunting dog of a breed with a long body, short legs, and long, drooping ears.
– ORIGIN C17: from French, diminutive of *bas* 'low'.

basset horn ■ n. an alto clarinet in F, typically with a bent mouthpiece and upturned bell.
– ORIGIN C19: from German, from Italian *corno di bassetto*, from *corno* 'horn' + *di* 'of' + *bassetto* (diminutive of *basso* 'low').

bassinet /ˌbasɪˈnɛt/ ■ n. a child's wicker cradle.
– ORIGIN C19: from French, diminutive of *bassin* 'basin'.

basso /ˈbasəʊ/ ■ n. (pl. **bassos** or **bassi** /-siː/) a bass voice or vocal part.
– ORIGIN C18: Italian, 'low', from Latin *bassus* 'short, low'.

bassoon ■ n. a large bass woodwind instrument of the oboe family, played with a double reed.
– DERIVATIVES **bassoonist** n.
– ORIGIN C18: from French *basson*, from Italian *bassone*, from *basso* 'low'.

basso profundo /prəˈfʌndəʊ/ ■ n. (pl. **bassos profundos** or **bassi profundi** /-diː/) a bass singer with an exceptionally low range.
– ORIGIN C19: Italian, from *basso* 'low' + *profundo* 'deep'.

basso-relievo /ˌbasəʊrɪˈliːvəʊ/ ■ n. (pl. **-os**) Art low relief.
– ORIGIN C17: from Italian *basso-rilievo*.

bass viol ■ n. **1** a viola da gamba. **2** N. Amer. a double bass.

bast /bast/ ■ n. fibre obtained from plants and used for matting and cord, in particular the inner bark of a lime tree.
– ORIGIN Old English.

bastard /ˈbɑːstəd, ˈbast-/ ■ n. **1** archaic or derogatory an illegitimate person. **2** informal an unpleasant or despicable person. ■ adj. **1** archaic or derogatory illegitimate. **2** no longer in its pure or original form.
– DERIVATIVES **bastardy** n.

> **HISTORY**
> The word **bastard** came into English from Old French in the medieval period and derives from medieval Latin *bastardus*, which probably came from *bastum* 'packsaddle'. The reason for such a dramatic change of meaning is uncertain: however, there could be a parallel in the Old French term for an illegitimate child, *fils de bast*, literally 'packsaddle son', i.e. the son of a mule driver who had a brief sexual encounter with a woman, using a packsaddle for a pillow, and was gone by morning.

bastardize (also **-ise**) ■ v. **1** [often as adj. **bastardized** (also **-ised**)] debase by adding new elements. **2** archaic declare (someone) illegitimate.
– DERIVATIVES **bastardization** (also **-isation**) n.

bastard wing ■ n. a group of small quill feathers on the first digit of a bird's wing.

baste¹ ■ v. pour fat or juices over (meat) during cooking.
– DERIVATIVES **baster** n.
– ORIGIN C15.

baste² ■ v. tack with long, loose stitches in preparation for sewing.
– ORIGIN Middle English: from Old French *bastir* 'sew lightly', of Germanic origin.

baste³ ■ v. informal, dated beat soundly; thrash.
– DERIVATIVES **basting** n.
– ORIGIN C16: perhaps a figurative use of BASTE¹.

Baster (also **Rehoboth Baster**) ■ n. a member of an Afrikaans-speaking people descended from trekboers and the Khoisan, living in the Rehoboth area of central Namibia.
– ORIGIN from Afrikaans, 'bastard, half-caste'.

bastinado /ˌbastɪˈneɪdəʊ, -ˈnɑːdəʊ/ chiefly historical ■ n. a form of punishment or torture that involves caning the soles of someone's feet. ■ v. (**-oes**, **-oed**) punish or torture in such a way.

–ORIGIN C16: from Spanish, from *bastón* 'stick, cudgel', from late Latin *bastum* 'stick'.

bastion /ˈbastɪən/ ■ n. **1** a projecting part of a fortification allowing an increased angle of fire. **2** an institution or person strongly maintaining particular principles, attitudes, or activities.
–ORIGIN C16: from Italian *bastione*, from *bastire* 'build'.

bat[1] ■ n. **1** an implement with a handle and a solid surface, used in sports such as cricket or baseball for hitting the ball. **2** a slab on which pottery is formed, dried, or fired. ■ v. (**batted**, **batting**) **1** (in sport) take the role of hitting rather than throwing the ball. **2** hit with the flat of one's hand. **3** (**bat around/about**) informal, chiefly N. Amer. casually discuss (an idea or proposal). **4** (**bat around/about**) informal travel widely, frequently, or casually.
–PHRASES **off one's own bat** informal at one's own instigation. **right off the bat** informal at the very beginning.
–ORIGIN Old English *batt* 'club, stick, staff', perhaps partly from Old French, from *battre* 'to strike'.

bat[2] ■ n. **1** a mainly nocturnal mammal capable of sustained flight, with membranous wings that extend between the fingers and limbs. [Order Chiroptera: many species.] **2** (**old bat**) informal an unattractive and unpleasant woman.
–PHRASES **have bats in the belfry** informal, chiefly Brit. be eccentric or mad.
–ORIGIN C16: alteration, perhaps by association with medieval Latin *blacta*, of Middle English *bakke*, of Scandinavian origin; sense 2 is from *bat*, a slang term for 'prostitute', or from BATTLEAXE.

bat[3] ■ v. (**batted**, **batting**) flutter (one's eyelashes).
–PHRASES **not bat** (or **without batting**) **an eyelid** (or **eye**) informal show (or showing) no surprise or concern.
–ORIGIN C19: from dialect and US *bat* 'to wink, blink', var. of obsolete *bate* 'to flutter'.

Batavian historical or archaic ■ n. a member of an ancient Germanic people who inhabited the island of Betuwe, now part of the Netherlands. ■ adj. **1** of or relating to this people. **2** of or relating to the people of the Netherlands. **3** of or relating to Djakarta in Indonesia (formerly the Dutch East Indies).
–ORIGIN from Latin *Batavia*, from *Batavi* 'the people of Betuwe'.

batch ■ n. a quantity or consignment of goods produced at one time. ▸ Computing a group of records processed as a single unit. ■ v. arrange (things) in sets or groups.
–ORIGIN C15: from an Old English word rel. to *bacan* 'bake'.

batch file ■ n. a computer file containing a list of instructions to be carried out in turn.

bate ■ v. Falconry (of a hawk) beat the wings in agitation and flutter off the perch.
–ORIGIN Middle English: from Old French *batre* 'to beat'.

bat-eared fox ■ n. a small fox found in southern and East Africa, with very large ears that are used to locate insect prey. [*Otocyon megalotis*.]

bateau mouche /ˌbatəʊ ˈmuːʃ/ ■ n. (pl. **bateaux mouches** pronunc. same) a type of pleasure boat used on the Seine in Paris.
–ORIGIN French, 'fly boat', because of the boat's mobility.

bated ■ adj. (in phr. **with bated breath**) in great suspense.
–ORIGIN C16: from obsolete *bate* 'restrain', from ABATE.

> USAGE
> The correct phrase is **with bated breath** not **with baited breath**.

bateleur eagle /ˈbat(ə)lə/ ■ n. a short-tailed African eagle with mainly black plumage and a bare red face. [*Terathopius ecaudatus*.]
–ORIGIN C19: *bateleur* from French, 'acrobat, juggler'.

Batesian mimicry /ˈbeɪtsɪən/ ■ n. Zoology mimicry in which an animal is protected by its resemblance to one avoided by predators.
–ORIGIN C19: named after the English naturalist Henry W. Bates.

batfish ■ n. (pl. same or **-fishes**) **1** a sea fish with a flattened body that is round or almost triangular when viewed from above. [Family Ogcocephalidae: many species.]

2 a deep-bodied, laterally compressed sea fish of the Indo-Pacific region, resembling an angelfish. [Genus *Platax*.]

bath /bɑːθ/ ■ n. (pl. **baths**) **1** a large tub that is filled with water for immersing and washing the body. ▸ an act of immersing and washing one's body in a bath. **2** (also **baths**) Brit. a building containing a public swimming pool. **3** a container holding a liquid in which an object is immersed in chemical or industrial processing. ■ v. wash while immersed in a bath.
–PHRASES **take a bath** informal suffer a heavy financial loss.
–ORIGIN Old English, of Germanic origin.

Bath bun ■ n. Brit. a round yeast bun containing currants and topped with icing or sugar.
–ORIGIN named after the city of *Bath* in SW England, where it was orig. made.

bath chair ■ n. dated an invalid's wheelchair.
–ORIGIN C19: named after the city of *Bath* in SW England, frequented for its supposedly curative hot springs.

bathe /beɪð/ ■ v. **1** wash by immersing one's body in water. ▸ soak or wipe gently with liquid to clean or soothe. ▸ N. Amer. wash (someone) in a bath. **2** chiefly Brit. take a swim. ■ n. a spell of swimming.
–DERIVATIVES chiefly Brit. **bather** n.
–ORIGIN Old English, of Germanic origin.

bathhouse ■ n. a building containing baths for communal use.

bathing suit (also **bathing costume**) ■ n. a swimming costume.

batholith /ˈbaθəlɪθ/ ■ n. Geology a very large igneous intrusion extending to an unknown depth in the earth's crust.
–ORIGIN C20: coined in German from Greek *bathos* 'depth' + -LITH.

bathos /ˈbeɪθɒs/ ■ n. (in literature) an unintentional change in mood from the important and serious to the trivial or ridiculous.
–DERIVATIVES **bathetic** /bəˈθɛtɪk/ adj.
–ORIGIN C17: from Greek, 'depth'.

bathrobe ■ n. a dressing gown, especially one made of towelling.

bathroom ■ n. **1** a room containing a bath and usually also a washbasin and toilet. **2** chiefly N. Amer. a room containing a toilet.

bath salts ■ pl. n. a crystalline substance that is dissolved in bathwater to soften or perfume it.

bath sponge ■ n. a marine sponge of warm waters, the fibrous skeleton of which is used as a sponge for washing. [Genera *Spongia* and *Hippospongia*.]

bathtub ■ n. a bath.

bathy- /ˈbaθi/ ■ comb. form relating to depth: *bathysphere*.
–ORIGIN from Greek *bathus* 'deep'.

bathymeter /bəˈθɪmɪtə/ ■ n. an instrument used to measure the depth of water in seas or lakes.
–DERIVATIVES **bathymetric** adj. **bathymetry** n.

bathypelagic /ˌbaθɪpɪˈladʒɪk/ ■ adj. Biology (of fish and other organisms) inhabiting the sea at a depth of between about 1 000 and 3 000 metres (approximately 3 300 and 9 800 ft), where it is dark and cold.

bathysphere ■ n. a manned spherical chamber for deep-sea observation, lowered by cable from a ship.

batik /ˈbatɪk, bəˈtiːk/ ■ n. a method of producing coloured designs on textiles using wax to resist dye, originating in Java.
–ORIGIN C19: from Javanese, 'painted'.

batis /ˈbatɪs/ ■ n. a genus of small insect-eating birds native to sub-Saharan Africa. [Genus *Batis*: numerous species.]

batiste /bəˈtiːst/ ■ n. a fine, light linen or cotton fabric resembling cambric.
–ORIGIN C19: from French; prob. rel. to *battre* 'to beat'.

batman (also **batwoman**) ■ n. (pl. **-men** or **-women**) dated (in the British armed forces) an officer's personal valet or attendant.
–ORIGIN C18 (orig. denoting an orderly in charge of the *bat*

horse which carried the officer's baggage): from Old French *bat* (from medieval Latin *bastum* 'packsaddle') + MAN.

bat mitzvah /bɑːt ˈmɪtzvə/ ■ n. a religious initiation ceremony for a Jewish girl at the age of religious maturity (twelve years and one day).
– ORIGIN from Hebrew *baṯ miṣwāh* 'daughter of the commandment'.

baton ■ n. 1 a thin stick used by a conductor to direct an orchestra or choir. 2 a short stick passed from runner to runner in a relay race. 3 a stick carried and twirled by a drum major. 4 a police officer's truncheon. 5 a staff of office or authority. 6 (**batons**) one of the suits in some tarot packs, corresponding to wands in others. 7 a short bar replacing some figures on the dial of a clock or watch.
– PHRASES **pass** (or **take up**) **the baton** hand over (or take up) a duty or responsibility.
– ORIGIN C16: from French *bâton*, from late Latin *bastum* 'stick'.

baton round ■ n. a large rubber or plastic projectile shot from a special gun, used especially in riot control.

bats ■ adj. informal, chiefly Brit. mad.
– ORIGIN C20: from the phr. *have bats in the belfry* (see BAT²).

batsman ■ n. (pl. **-men**) a player who bats in cricket.
– DERIVATIVES **batsmanship** n.

Batswana plural form of TSWANA.

batt /bat/ ■ n. a piece of felted material or fibreglass used for insulation.
– ORIGIN Middle English (in the general sense 'lump, piece').

battalion /bəˈtalɪən/ ■ n. a large body of troops, forming part of a brigade.
– ORIGIN C16: from French *bataillon*, from Italian, from *battaglia* 'battle', from Latin (see BATTLE).

battement /ˈbat(ə)mɒ̃/ ■ n. Ballet a movement in which one leg is moved outward from the body and in again.
– ORIGIN French, 'beating'.

batten¹ ■ n. a long, flat wooden or metal strip for strengthening, stiffening, or securing something. ■ v. strengthen, stiffen, or fasten with battens.
– PHRASES **batten down the hatches** Nautical secure a ship's tarpaulins.
– DERIVATIVES **battening** n.
– ORIGIN C15: from Old French *batant*, from *batre* 'to beat', from Latin *battuere*.

batten² ■ v. (**batten on**) thrive or prosper at the expense of.
– ORIGIN C16: from Old Norse *batna* 'get better', rel. to BETTER.

batter¹ ■ v. strike repeatedly with hard blows. ▶ subject (one's spouse, partner, or child) to repeated violence and assault.
– DERIVATIVES **batterer** n. **battering** n.
– ORIGIN Middle English: from Old French *batre* 'to beat', from Latin *battuere*.

batter² ■ n. a mixture of flour, egg, and milk or water, used for making pancakes or coating food before frying. ▶ a mixture of ingredients for a cake.
– ORIGIN Middle English: from Old French *bateure* 'the action of beating', from *batre* 'to beat'.

batter³ ■ n. a player who bats in baseball.

battered¹ ■ adj. (of food) coated in batter and fried.

battered² ■ adj. injured by repeated blows. ▶ (of a thing) damaged by age and repeated use.

batterie /ˌbat(ə)ˈriː/ ■ n. Ballet the action of beating the feet or calves together during a leap.
– ORIGIN French, 'beating'.

battering ram ■ n. a heavy object swung or rammed against a door to break it down. ▶ historical a heavy beam, originally with an end in the form of a carved ram's head, used in breaching fortifications.

battery ■ n. (pl. **-ies**) 1 a container consisting of one or more cells, in which chemical energy is converted into electricity and used as a source of power. 2 an extensive series, sequence, or range of things. 3 chiefly Brit. a series of small cages for the intensive rearing and housing of poultry. 4 a fortified emplacement for heavy guns. ▶ an artillery subunit of guns, men, and vehicles.
– ORIGIN Middle English: from Old French *baterie*, from *battre* 'to strike', from Latin *battuere* ('metal articles wrought by hammering' later 'a collection of artillery', whence 'Leyden jars connected up so as to discharge simultaneously').

batting ■ n. cotton wadding in sheets for use in quilts.

battle ■ n. 1 a sustained fight between organized armed forces. 2 a lengthy and difficult conflict or struggle. ■ v. fight or struggle tenaciously with an enemy or to achieve something.
– PHRASES **battle royal** (pl. **battles royal**) a fiercely contested fight or dispute. **battle stations** the positions taken by military personnel in preparation for battle.
– DERIVATIVES **battler** n.
– ORIGIN Middle English: from Old French *bataille* (n.), from late Latin *battualia* 'military or gladiatorial exercises', from *battuere* 'to beat'.

battleaxe ■ n. 1 a large axe used in ancient warfare. 2 informal a formidably aggressive older woman.

battlecruiser ■ n. an early 20th-century warship that was faster and more lightly armoured than a battleship.

battledore /ˈbat(ə)ldɔː/ ■ n. 1 (also **battledore and shuttlecock**) a game played with a shuttlecock and rackets, a forerunner of badminton. ▶ the small racket used in this. 2 a wooden paddle-shaped implement formerly used to beat and stir washing.
– ORIGIN Middle English: perhaps from Provençal *batedor* 'beater', from *batre* 'to beat'.

battledress ■ n. combat dress worn by soldiers.

battlefield (also **battleground**) ■ n. the piece of ground on which a battle is fought.

battlement ■ n. a parapet with openings at regular intervals along the top of a wall, forming part of a fortification.
– DERIVATIVES **battlemented** adj.
– ORIGIN Middle English: from Old French *bataillier* 'fortify with movable defence turrets'.

battleship ■ n. a heavy warship with extensive armour protection and large-calibre guns.

batty ■ adj. (**-ier**, **-iest**) informal mad.
– DERIVATIVES **battily** adv. **battiness** n.
– ORIGIN C20: from BAT².

Batwa plural form of TWA.

batwing ■ adj. (of a sleeve) having a deep armhole and a tight cuff.

bauble /ˈbɔːb(ə)l/ ■ n. 1 a small, showy trinket or decoration. ▶ a decorative hollow ball hung on a Christmas tree. 2 a baton formerly used as an emblem by jesters.
– ORIGIN Middle English: from Old French *baubel* 'child's toy'.

baud /bɔːd/ ■ n. (pl. same or **bauds**) Computing a unit of transmission speed for electronic signals, corresponding to one information unit or event per second.
– ORIGIN 1930s: French, from the name of the French engineer Jean M. E. Baudot.

bauhinia /bəʊˈhɪnɪə/ ■ n. a leguminous tree or shrub which has deeply notched leaves and bears large showy flowers. [Genus *Bauhinia*: many species.]

baulk /bɔːlk, bɔːk/ (chiefly US also **balk**) ■ v. (**baulk at**) 1 hesitate to accept an idea or undertaking. ▶ thwart or hinder (a plan or person). 2 (of a horse) refuse to go on. ■ n. 1 a roughly squared timber beam. 2 the area on a billiard table between the baulk line and the bottom cushion. 3 Baseball an illegal action made by a pitcher that may deceive a base runner. 4 a ridge left unploughed between furrows.
– ORIGIN Old English ('unploughed ridge', later 'obstacle'), from Old Norse *bálkr* 'partition'.

baulky ■ adj. British spelling of BALKY.

bauxite /ˈbɔːksaɪt/ ■ n. an amorphous clayey rock that is the chief ore of aluminium, consisting of hydrated alumina with variable proportions of iron oxides.
– DERIVATIVES **bauxitic** adj.
– ORIGIN C19: from *Les Baux*, a village in SE France, near which it was first found.

bavarois /ˌbavəˈwɑː/ (also **bavaroise** /-ˈwɑːz/) ■ n. a dessert

containing gelatin and whipped cream.
– ORIGIN French, 'Bavarian'.

bawd /bɔːd/ ■ n. archaic a woman in charge of a brothel.
– ORIGIN Middle English: from Old French *baudestroyt* 'procuress', from *baude* 'shameless'.

bawdry ■ n. obscenity in speech or writing.

bawdy ■ adj. (**-ier**, **-iest**) humorously indecent. ■ n. humorously indecent talk or writing.
– DERIVATIVES **bawdily** adv. **bawdiness** n.

bawdy house ■ n. archaic a brothel.

bawl ■ v. 1 shout out noisily. ▸ (**bawl someone out**) reprimand someone angrily. 2 weep noisily. ■ n. a loud shout.
– ORIGIN Middle English ('howl, bark'): imitative.

bay[1] ■ n. a broad curved inlet of the sea.
– ORIGIN Middle English: from Old French *baie*, from Old Spanish *bahia*.

bay[2] (also **bay laurel** or **sweet bay**) ■ n. an evergreen, purple-berried Mediterranean shrub, with aromatic leaves that are used in cookery. [*Laurus nobilis*.]
– ORIGIN Middle English: from Old French *baie*, from Latin *baca* 'berry'.

bay[3] ■ n. 1 a window area that projects outwards from a wall. 2 a section of wall in the nave of a church between two buttresses or columns. 3 an area specially allocated or marked off.
– ORIGIN Middle English: from Old French, from *baer* 'to gape', from medieval Latin *batare*.

bay[4] ■ adj. (of a horse) brown with black points. ■ n. a bay horse.
– ORIGIN Middle English: from Old French *bai*, from Latin *badius*.

bay[5] ■ v. (of a dog) bark or howl loudly, especially in pursuit of quarry. ■ n. the sound of baying.
– PHRASES **at bay** trapped or cornered. **bay for blood** demand retribution. **hold** (or **keep**) **at bay** prevent from approaching or having an effect.
– ORIGIN Middle English: from Old French (*a*)*bai* (n.) 'bark'; imitative.

bayberry ■ n. (pl. **-ies**) a North American shrub with aromatic leathery leaves and waxy berries. [Genus *Myrica*: several species.]

Bayes' theorem ■ n. Statistics a theorem expressing the conditional probability of each of a set of possible causes for a given observed outcome in terms of the known probability of each cause and the conditional probability of the outcome of each cause.
– DERIVATIVES **Bayesian** adj.
– ORIGIN C19: named after the English mathematician Thomas *Bayes*.

bayonet ■ n. 1 a long blade fixed to the muzzle of a rifle for use in hand-to-hand fighting. 2 [as modifier] denoting a type of fitting for a light bulb or other appliance which is pushed into a socket and then twisted into place. ■ v. (**bayoneted**, **bayoneting**) stab with a bayonet.
– ORIGIN C17 (denoting a short dagger): from French *baïonnette*, from *Bayonne*, the name of a town in SW France, where they were first made.

bayou /'baɪuː/ ■ n. (pl. **bayous**) (in the southern US) a marshy outlet of a lake or river.
– ORIGIN C18: from Choctaw *bayuk*.

bay rum ■ n. a perfume for the hair, distilled originally from rum and bayberry leaves.

bay window ■ n. a window built to project outwards from a wall.

bazaar /bə'zɑː/ ■ n. 1 a market in a Middle-Eastern country. 2 a fund-raising sale of goods.
– ORIGIN C16: from Persian *bāzār* 'market'.

bazoo /bə'zuː/ ■ n. US informal a person's mouth.
– ORIGIN C19: perhaps from Dutch *bazuin* 'trombone, trumpet'.

bazooka ■ n. 1 a short-range tubular rocket launcher used against tanks. 2 a kazoo shaped like a trumpet.
– ORIGIN 1930s: from BAZOO.

bazoom ■ n. informal, chiefly N. Amer. a woman's breast.
– ORIGIN 1950s: prob. var. of BOSOM.

BB ■ symb. 1 double-black (used in describing grades of pencil lead). 2 N. Amer. a standard size of lead pellet used in air rifles.

B & B ■ abbrev. bed and breakfast.

BBBEE S. African ■ abbrev. broad-based black economic empowerment.

BBC ■ abbrev. British Broadcasting Corporation.

bbl. ■ abbrev. barrels (especially of oil).

BBQ ■ abbrev. informal a barbecue.

BBS ■ abbrev. Computing bulletin board system.

BC ■ abbrev. 1 before Christ (placed after a date, indicating that it is before the Christian era). 2 S. African Black Consciousness. 3 British Columbia.

bcc ■ abbrev. blind carbon copy.

BCE ■ abbrev. before the Common Era (indicating dates before the Christian era, used especially by non-Christians).

B-cell ■ n. Physiology another term for **B-LYMPHOCYTE**.

BCG ■ abbrev. Bacillus Calmette-Guérin, an anti-tuberculosis vaccine.

BCI ■ abbrev. business confidence index.

BD ■ abbrev. Bachelor of Divinity.

Bde ■ abbrev. Brigade.

bdellium /'dɛlɪəm/ ■ n. a fragrant resin produced by a number of trees related to myrrh, used in perfumes.
– ORIGIN Middle English: from Greek *bdellion*, of Semitic origin.

BDS ■ abbrev. Bachelor of Dental Surgery.

BE ■ abbrev. 1 Bachelor of Education. 2 Bachelor of Engineering.

Be ■ symb. the chemical element beryllium.

be ■ v. (sing. present **am**; **are**; **is**; pl. present **are**; 1st and 3rd sing. past **was**; 2nd sing. past and pl. past **were**; present subjunctive **be**; past subjunctive **were**; present part. **being**; past part. **been**) 1 (usu. **there is/are**) exist; be present. 2 take place. ▸ occupy a position in space. ▸ stay in the same place or condition. ▸ come; go; visit. 3 (when connecting a subject and complement) having the specified state, nature, or role. ▸ represent or signify. ■ aux. v. 1 used with a present participle to form continuous tenses. 2 used with a past participle to form the passive voice. 3 used to indicate something that is due to happen. ▸ used to express obligation or necessity. ▸ used to hypothesize about something that might happen.
– PHRASES **the be-all and end-all** informal a feature of an activity that is of greater importance than any other. **not be oneself** not feel in one's usual physical or mental state. **-to-be** of the future: *his bride-to-be*.
– ORIGIN Old English *bēon*, from several orig. distinct verbs; the forms *am* and *is* are rel. to Latin *sum* and *est*.

be- ■ prefix forming verbs: 1 all over; all round: *bespatter*. ▸ thoroughly; excessively: *bewilder*. 2 (added to intransitive verbs and to adjectives and nouns) expressing transitive action: *bemoan* | *befriend*. 3 (added to nouns) affect with: *befog*. ▸ (added to adjectives) cause to be: *befoul*. 4 (forming adjectives ending in *-ed*) having; covered with: *bejewelled*.
– ORIGIN Old English, weak form of *bī* 'by'.

beach ■ n. a pebbly or sandy shore at the edge of the sea or a lake. ■ v. bring on to a beach from the water. ▸ (with reference to a whale) become or cause to become stranded on a beach.
– ORIGIN C16: perhaps rel. to Old English *bæce* 'brook'.

beachcomber ■ n. 1 a person who searches beaches for articles of value. 2 a long wave rolling in from the sea.

beachfront ■ n. the part of a coastal town next to and directly facing the sea.

beachhead ■ n. a fortified position on a beach taken by landing forces.

beacon ■ n. 1 a fire lit on the top of a hill as a signal. 2 a light serving as a signal, warning, or guide for ships or aircraft. ▸ a radio transmitter signalling the position of a ship, aircraft, or spacecraft. 3 (also **trig beacon**) S. African a

bead

marker used for surveying boundaries; a trig point.
– ORIGIN Old English *bēacn* 'sign, portent', of West Germanic origin.

bead ■ n. **1** a small, rounded piece of glass, stone, plastic, etc., perforated and threaded in a string with others to make a necklace or rosary. **2** a drop of a liquid on a surface. **3** an ornamental plaster moulding resembling a string of beads. **4** a narrow moulding of circular cross section. **5** a small knob forming the foresight of a gun. **6** the reinforced inner edge of a pneumatic tyre. ■ v. **1** decorate or cover with beads. **2** form into a string like beads.
– DERIVATIVES **beaded** adj. **beading** n.
– ORIGIN Old English *gebed* 'prayer', of Germanic origin; current senses derive from the use of a rosary.

beadle ■ n. Brit. **1** a ceremonial officer of a church, college, or similar institution. **2** historical a minor parish officer dealing with petty offenders.
– ORIGIN Old English *bydel* 'a person who makes a proclamation', of Germanic origin.

beady ■ adj. (of a person's eyes) small, round, and observing things clearly.
– DERIVATIVES **beadily** adv. **beadiness** n.

beagle ■ n. a small, short-legged hound, kept as a pet or for hunting hares. ■ v. hunt with beagles.
– DERIVATIVES **beagler** n. **beagling** n.
– ORIGIN C15: perhaps from Old French *beegueule* 'open-mouthed'.

beak¹ ■ n. **1** a bird's horny projecting jaws; a bill. ▸ a projecting jaw in some other animals. **2** a projection at the prow of an ancient warship, used to pierce the hulls of enemy ships.
– DERIVATIVES **beaked** adj. **beaky** adj.
– ORIGIN Middle English: from Old French *bec*, from Latin *beccus*, of Celtic origin.

beak² ■ n. informal, chiefly Brit. a magistrate or schoolmaster.
– ORIGIN C18: prob. from criminals' slang.

beaked whale ■ n. a whale of a group with elongated jaws that form a beak, including the bottlenose whales. [Family Ziphiidae: several species.]

beaker ■ n. a tall plastic cup. ▸ a lipped cylindrical glass container for laboratory use. ▸ archaic or poetic/literary a large drinking container with a wide mouth.
– ORIGIN Middle English: from Old Norse *bikarr*, perhaps from Greek *bikos* 'drinking bowl'.

Beaker folk ■ pl. n. Archaeology a late Neolithic and early Bronze Age European people named after the distinctive waisted pots (Beaker ware) associated with their burials.

beam ■ n. **1** a long sturdy piece of squared timber or metal used horizontally in building to support a load above. ▸ a narrow horizontal length of squared timber used for balancing exercises in gymnastics. **2** a horizontal beam supporting the deck and joining the sides of a ship. ▸ the direction of an object visible from the side of a ship when it is perpendicular to the centre line of the vessel: *there was land in sight on the port beam*. ▸ a ship's breadth at its widest point. **3** a ray or shaft of light. ▸ a directional flow of particles or radiation. ▸ a series of radio or radar signals emitted as a navigational guide. **4** a radiant smile. **5** the crossbar of a balance. **6** an oscillating shaft in a beam engine. **7** the shank of an anchor. ■ v. **1** transmit (a radio signal or broadcast) in a specified direction. **2** shine brightly. **3** smile radiantly.
– PHRASES **a beam in one's eye** a fault that is greater in oneself than in the person one is finding fault with. [with biblical allusion to Matthew 7:3.] **off beam** informal on the wrong track. **on her** (or **its**) **beam ends** (of a ship) heeled over on its side.
– ORIGIN Old English 'tree, beam', of West Germanic origin.

beam compass ■ n. a compass for drawing large circles, consisting of a horizontal rod connected by sliding sockets to two vertical legs.

beam engine ■ n. a stationary steam engine with a large oscillating shaft that transmits the vertical movement of the pistons to a crank or pump.

Beamer ■ n. another term for BEEMER.

beamer ■ n. Cricket a ball bowled directly at a batsman's head or upper body without bouncing.

beam sea ■ n. Nautical a sea which is rolling against a ship's side approximately at right angles.

bean ■ n. **1** an edible kidney-shaped seed growing in long pods on certain leguminous plants. ▸ the hard seed of coffee, cocoa, and certain other plants. **2** a leguminous plant bearing beans. [*Phaseolus* and other genera: numerous species.] **3** (chiefly N. Amer. also **beans**) [with neg.] informal a very small amount or nothing at all. ■ v. informal, chiefly N. Amer. hit on the head.
– PHRASES **full of beans** informal lively; in high spirits. **old bean** Brit. informal, dated a friendly form of address.
– ORIGIN Old English, of Germanic origin.

beanbag ■ n. **1** a small bag filled with dried beans and used in children's games. **2** a large cushion filled with polystyrene beads.

bean counter ■ n. informal an accountant or bureaucrat who places excessive emphasis on controlling expenditure and budgets.

bean curd ■ n. another term for TOFU.

beanfeast ■ n. Brit. informal a celebratory party with plentiful food and drink.
– ORIGIN C19: orig. denoting an annual dinner given to employees, which always featured beans and bacon.

beanie ■ n. (pl. **-ies**) a small close-fitting hat worn on the back of the head.
– ORIGIN 1940s: perhaps from BEAN 'head'.

beanpole ■ n. informal a tall, thin person.

bean sprouts ■ pl. n. the edible sprouting seeds of certain beans.

beanstalk ■ n. the stem of a bean plant.

bear¹ ■ v. (past **bore**; past part. **borne**) **1** carry. ▸ have as an attribute or visible mark. ▸ (**bear oneself**) conduct oneself in a specified manner. **2** support (a weight). **3** [with neg.] manage to tolerate: *I can't bear it*. **4** give birth to (a child). ▸ (of a tree or plant) produce (fruit or flowers). **5** turn and proceed in a specified direction: *bear left*.
– PHRASES **bear fruit** yield positive results. **bear someone a grudge** nurture a feeling of resentment against someone. **bear in mind** remember and take into account. **bear someone malice** (or **ill will**) wish someone harm. **bear witness** (or **testimony**) to testify to. **be borne in upon** come to be realized by. **bring to bear 1** muster and use to effect. **2** aim (a weapon).
– PHRASAL VERBS **bear down** (of a woman in labour) exert downwards pressure in order to push the baby out. **bear down on** approach in a purposeful or intimidating manner. **bear off** (or **away**) Nautical change course away from the wind. **bear on** be relevant to. **bear something out** support or confirm something. **bear up** remain cheerful in the face of adversity. **bear with** be patient or tolerant with.
– DERIVATIVES **bearable** adj. **bearability** n. **bearably** adv.
– ORIGIN Old English, of Germanic origin.

bear² ■ n. **1** a large, heavy mammal which walks on the soles of its feet, having thick fur and a very short tail. [Family Ursidae: several species.] **2** Stock Exchange a person who sells shares hoping to buy them back later at a lower price. Often contrasted with BULL¹. [said to be from a proverb warning against 'selling the bear's skin before one has caught the bear'.] **3** a brutish, coarse, or ill-mannered person.
– PHRASES **like a bear with a sore head** very irritable.
– ORIGIN Old English, of West Germanic origin.

bear-baiting ■ n. historical a form of entertainment which involved setting dogs to attack a captive bear.

bearcat ■ n. a bear-like climbing mammal, especially the red panda.

beard ■ n. a growth of hair on the chin and lower cheeks of a man's face. ▸ an animal's growth or marking that is likened to a beard, such as the gills of an oyster. ▸ a tuft of hairs or bristles on certain plants. ■ v. boldly confront or challenge (someone formidable).
– DERIVATIVES **bearded** adj. **beardless** adj.
– ORIGIN Old English, of West Germanic origin.

bearded vulture ■ n. a long-winged, long-tailed vulture, noted for dropping bones to break them and get at the marrow. [*Gypaetus barbatus*.]

bearer ■ n. **1** a person or thing that carries something. **2** a person who presents a cheque or other order to pay money. ▶ [as modifier] payable to the possessor: *bearer bonds*.

bear garden (also **bear pit**) ■ n. a scene of uproar and confusion.
– ORIGIN C16, denoting a place set apart for bear-baiting.

bear hug ■ n. a rough, tight embrace.

bearing ■ n. **1** a person's way of standing, moving, or behaving. **2** relation; relevance: *the case has no bearing on the issues*. **3** (**bearings**) a device in a machine that allows two parts to rotate or move in contact with each other with reduced friction. **4** the direction or position of something relative to a fixed point, normally measured in degrees and with magnetic north as zero. ▶ (**one's bearings**) awareness of one's position relative to one's surroundings. **5** Heraldry a device or charge.

bearing rein ■ n. a fixed rein which causes a horse to raise its head and arch its neck.

bearish ■ adj. **1** resembling or likened to a bear. **2** Stock Exchange characterized by falling share prices. ▶ inclined to sell because of an anticipated fall in prices.
– DERIVATIVES **bearishly** adv. **bearishness** n.

bear market ■ n. Stock Exchange a market in which share prices are falling, encouraging selling.

Béarnaise sauce /ˌbeɪəˈneɪz/ ■ n. a rich sauce thickened with egg yolks and flavoured with tarragon.
– ORIGIN from French *béarnais* 'of *Béarn*', a region of SW France.

bearskin ■ n. a tall cap of black fur worn ceremonially by certain troops.

beast ■ n. **1** an animal, especially a large or dangerous mammal. ▶ a bovine farm animal. **2** an inhumanly cruel or depraved person.
– ORIGIN Middle English: from Old French *beste*, from Latin *bestia*.

beastie ■ n. (pl. **-ies**) Scottish or humorous a small animal or insect.

beastly Brit. informal ■ adj. (**-ier**, **-iest**) very unpleasant. ■ adv. dated to an extreme and unpleasant degree.
– DERIVATIVES **beastliness** n.

beast of burden ■ n. an animal that is used for carrying loads.

beast of prey ■ n. an animal, especially a mammal, that kills and eats other animals.

beat ■ v. (past **beat**; past part. **beaten**) **1** strike (a person or an animal) repeatedly and violently so as to hurt or punish them. ▶ strike repeatedly so as to make a noise. ▶ flatten or shape (metal) by striking it repeatedly with a hammer. **2** defeat in a game or other competitive situation. ▶ surpass (a record or score). ▶ overcome (a problem). ▶ informal baffle: *it beats me how you manage it*. **3** (of the heart) pulsate. **4** (of a bird) move (the wings) up and down. **5** stir (cooking ingredients) vigorously. **6** move across (an area of land) repeatedly striking at the ground cover in order to raise game birds for shooting. **7** Nautical sail into the wind, with repeated tacking. ■ n. **1** a main accent or rhythmic unit in music or poetry. ▶ a rhythm or rhythmic sound or movement. ▶ a pulsation of the heart. **2** the movement of a bird's wings. **3** an area allocated to a police officer and patrolled on foot. ▶ a spell of duty allocated to a police officer. ▶ a stretch of water fished by an angler. **4** a brief pause or moment of hesitation. ■ adj. informal completely exhausted.
– PHRASES **beat about the bush** discuss a matter without coming to the point. **beat the clock** perform a task within a fixed time limit. **beat a** (**hasty**) **retreat** withdraw. **beat time** indicate or follow a musical tempo with a baton or other means. **off the beaten track** in or into an isolated place. **to beat the band** informal, chiefly N. Amer. so as to surpass all competition.
– PHRASAL VERBS **beat someone down** force someone to reduce the price of something. **beat it** informal leave a place. **beat off** vulgar slang (of a man) masturbate. **beat someone/thing off** succeed in resisting an attacker or an attack. **beat someone up** (N. Amer. **beat up on someone**) assault and severely injure someone by hitting them repeatedly.
– DERIVATIVES **beatable** adj. **beater** n. **beating** n.
– ORIGIN Old English, of Germanic origin.

beatbox ■ n. informal **1** a drum machine. **2** a radio or radio cassette player used to play loud music.

beat generation ■ n. a movement of young people in the 1950s and early 1960s who rejected conventional society, valuing self-expression and favouring modern jazz.

beatific /biːəˈtɪfɪk/ ■ adj. feeling or expressing blissful happiness.
– DERIVATIVES **beatifically** adv.

beatification /bɪˌatɪfɪˈkeɪʃ(ə)n/ ■ n. (in the Roman Catholic Church) declaration by the Pope that a dead person is in a state of bliss, constituting a first step towards canonization and permitting public veneration.

beatify /bɪˈatɪfʌɪ/ ■ v. (**-ies**, **-ied**) (in the Roman Catholic Church) announce the beatification of.
– ORIGIN C16: from Old French *beatifier*, from Latin *beatus* 'blessed'.

beatitude /bɪˈatɪtjuːd/ ■ n. supreme blessedness. ▶ (**the Beatitudes**) Christian Church the blessings listed by Jesus in the Sermon on the Mount (Matthew 5:3–11).
– ORIGIN Middle English: from Latin *beatitudo*, from *beatus* 'blessed'.

beatnik ■ n. dated a young person belonging to a subculture associated with the beat generation.

beat-up ■ adj. informal worn out by overuse.

beau /bəʊ/ ■ n. (pl. **beaux** or **beaus** /bəʊz, bəʊ/) dated a boyfriend or male admirer.
– ORIGIN C17: from French, 'handsome'.

beau geste /bəʊ ˈʒɛst/ ■ n. (pl. **beaux gestes** pronunc. same) a noble and generous act.
– ORIGIN French, literally 'splendid gesture'.

beau idéal /ˌbəʊ iːdeɪˈal/ ■ n. a person or thing representing the highest possible standard of excellence in a particular respect.
– ORIGIN French, literally 'ideal beauty'.

Beaujolais /ˈbəʊʒəleɪ/ ■ n. a light red or burgundy wine produced in the Beaujolais district of SE France.

Beaujolais Nouveau /ˌbəʊʒəleɪ nuːˈvəʊ/ ■ n. a Beaujolais wine sold in the first year of a vintage.
– ORIGIN from BEAUJOLAIS + French *nouveau* 'new'.

beau monde /bəʊ ˈmɒnd/ ■ n. (**the beau monde**) fashionable society.
– ORIGIN French, 'fine world'.

Beaune /bəʊn/ ■ n. a red burgundy wine from the region around Beaune in eastern France.

beaut /bjuːt/ informal, chiefly Austral./NZ ■ n. an excellent or beautiful person or thing. ■ adj. excellent.

beauteous ■ adj. poetic/literary beautiful.

beautician ■ n. a person whose job is to give facials and other beauty treatments.

beautiful ■ adj. **1** pleasing the senses or mind aesthetically. **2** of a very high standard; excellent.
– DERIVATIVES **beautifully** adv.

beautify ■ v. (**-ies**, **-ied**) make beautiful.
– DERIVATIVES **beautification** n. **beautifier** n.

beauty ■ n. (pl. **-ies**) **1** a combination of qualities that delights the aesthetic senses. **2** [as modifier] denoting something intended to make someone more attractive: *beauty treatment*. **3** a beautiful woman. **4** an excellent example. ▶ an attractive feature or advantage.
– ORIGIN Middle English: from Old French *beaute*, from Latin *bellus* 'beautiful, fine'.

beauty contest ■ n. a contest in which the winner is the woman judged the most beautiful.

beauty queen ■ n. a woman judged most beautiful in a beauty contest.

beauty salon (also **beauty parlour**) ■ n. an establishment in which hairdressing, make-up, and similar cosmetic treatments are carried out professionally.

beauty sleep ■ n. humorous sleep considered to be essential in keeping one looking young and attractive.

beauty spot ■ n. **1** a place known for its beautiful

beaux

scenery. **2** a small natural or artificial mark such as a mole on a woman's face, considered to enhance her attractiveness.

beaux plural form of BEAU.

beaux arts /bəʊz 'ɑː/ ■ pl. n. **1** fine arts. **2** (usu. **Beaux Arts**) [as modifier] relating to the classical decorative style maintained by the École des Beaux-Arts in Paris in the 19th century.
– ORIGIN from French *beaux-arts*.

beaver¹ ■ n. (pl. same or **beavers**) **1** a large semiaquatic broad-tailed rodent, noted for its habit of gnawing through trees to fell them in order to make lodges and dams. [*Castor canadensis* (N. America) and *C. fiber* (Eurasia).] ▸ the soft light brown fur of the beaver. ▸ (also **beaver hat**) chiefly historical a hat made of felted beaver fur. ▸ (also **beaver cloth**) a heavy woollen cloth resembling felted beaver fur. **2** a very hard-working person. ■ v. (often **beaver away**) informal work hard.
– ORIGIN Old English, of Germanic origin.

beaver² ■ n. vulgar slang, chiefly N. Amer. a woman's genitals or pubic area.
– ORIGIN C20.

bebop /'biːbɒp/ ■ n. a type of jazz originating in the 1940s and characterized by complex harmony and rhythms.
– DERIVATIVES **bebopper** n.
– ORIGIN 1940s (orig. US): imitative of the typical rhythm of this music.

becalm ■ v. leave (a sailing ship) unable to move through lack of wind.

became past participle of BECOME.

because ■ conj. for the reason that; since.
– PHRASES **because of** by reason of.
– ORIGIN Middle English: from the phr. *by cause*, influenced by Old French *par cause de* 'by reason of'.

béchamel /'beɪʃəmɛl/ ■ n. a rich white sauce made with milk infused with herbs and other flavourings.
– ORIGIN named after the Marquis Louis de Béchamel, who is said to have invented a similar sauce.

beck¹ ■ n. N. English a stream.
– ORIGIN Middle English: from Old Norse *bekkr*, of Germanic origin.

beck² ■ n. archaic or poetic/literary a gesture requesting attention, such as a nod or wave.
– PHRASES **at someone's beck and call** always having to be ready to obey someone's orders.
– ORIGIN Middle English: abbr. of BECKON.

beckon ■ v. make a gesture to encourage or instruct someone to approach or follow. ▸ summon in this way.
– ORIGIN Old English, of West Germanic origin.

become ■ v. (past **became**; past part. **become**) **1** begin to be. ▸ develop into. ▸ (of a person) qualify or be accepted as. ▸ (**become of**) (in questions) happen to. **2** (of clothing) look well on. ▸ be appropriate to (someone).
– ORIGIN Old English *becuman* 'come to a place, come to be or do something', of Germanic origin.

becoming ■ adj. **1** (of clothing) looking well on someone. **2** decorous.
– DERIVATIVES **becomingly** adv. **becomingness** n.

becquerel /'bɛkərɛl/ (abbrev.: **Bq**) ■ n. Physics the SI unit of radioactivity, corresponding to one disintegration per second.
– ORIGIN C19: named after the French physicist A-H. Becquerel.

BEd ■ abbrev. Bachelor of Education.

bed ■ n. **1** a piece of furniture incorporating a mattress or other surface for sleeping or resting on. ▸ a place for a patient in a hospital. ▸ informal used with reference to a bed as a place for sexual activity. **2** an area of ground where flowers and plants are grown: *a flower bed*. **3** a flat base or foundation on which something rests or is supported. ▸ chiefly N. Amer. the open part of a truck or cart, where goods are carried. **4** a stratum or layer of rock. **5** the bottom of the sea or a lake or river. ▸ a place on the seabed where shellfish breed or are bred. ■ v. (**bedded**, **bedding**) **1** provide with sleeping accommodation. ▸ (**bed down**) settle down for the night in an improvised place. **2** informal have sexual intercourse with. **3** (**bed out**) transfer (a plant) from a pot or seed tray to the ground. **4** fix firmly; embed. ▸ lay or arrange in a layer.
– PHRASES **bed of nails** a board with nails pointing out of it, as lain on by fakirs and ascetics. **a bed of roses** [usu. with neg.] a situation or activity that is comfortable or easy. **be brought to bed** archaic (of a woman) give birth to a child. **get out of bed on the wrong side** start the day in a bad mood, which continues all day long. **put something to bed** informal make a newspaper ready for press.
– DERIVATIVES **bedded** adj.
– ORIGIN Old English, of Germanic origin.

bed and board ■ n. lodging and food.

bed and breakfast ■ n. guest house or hotel provision consisting of sleeping accommodation and breakfast. ▸ a guest house.

bedaub ■ v. poetic/literary smear or daub with a sticky substance.

bedazzle ■ v. greatly impress with brilliance or skill.
– DERIVATIVES **bedazzlement** n.

bedbug ■ n. a bloodsucking wingless bug which sucks the blood of sleeping humans. [*Cimex lectularius*.]

bedchamber ■ n. archaic a bedroom.

bedclothes ■ pl. n. coverings for a bed, such as sheets and blankets.

beddable /'bɛdəb(ə)l/ ■ adj. informal sexually attractive or available.

bedding ■ n. **1** bedclothes. ▸ straw or similar material for animals to sleep on. **2** a base or bottom layer. **3** Geology the stratification or layering of rocks.

bedding plant ■ n. an annual plant produced for planting in a bed in the spring.

bedeck ■ v. decorate lavishly.

bedevil ■ v. (**bedevilled**, **bedevilling**; US **bedeviled**, **bedeviling**) cause continual trouble to.
– DERIVATIVES **bedevilment** n.

bedew /bɪˈdjuː/ ■ v. poetic/literary cover or sprinkle with drops of water.

bedfellow ■ n. a person or thing that is closely connected with another.

bedhead ■ n. Brit. an upright board or panel fixed at the head of a bed.

bed-hop ■ v. informal engage in successive casual sexual affairs.
– DERIVATIVES **bed-hopper** n.

bedizen /bɪˈdaɪz(ə)n, -ˈdɪz-/ ■ v. poetic/literary dress up or decorate gaudily.
– ORIGIN C17: from BE- + obsolete *dizen* 'deck out'.

bedjacket ■ n. a soft loose jacket worn for extra warmth when sitting up in bed.

bedlam /'bɛdləm/ ■ n. **1** a scene of uproar and confusion. **2** archaic an asylum.
– ORIGIN Middle English: early form of *Bethlehem*, referring to the hospital of St Mary of Bethlehem in London, used as an asylum for the insane.

bedlinen ■ n. sheets, pillowcases, and duvet covers.

Bedlington terrier /'bɛdlɪŋt(ə)n/ ■ n. a terrier of a breed with a narrow head, long legs, and curly grey hair.
– ORIGIN C19: named after the village of *Bedlington* in northern England, where the breed originated.

Bedouin /'bɛdʊɪn/ (also **Beduin**) ■ n. (pl. same) a nomadic Arab of the desert.
– ORIGIN from Old French *beduin*, from Arabic *badawī*, (pl.) *badawīn* 'dwellers in the desert', from *badw* 'desert'.

bedpan ■ n. a receptacle used by a bedridden patient for urine and faeces.

bedplate ■ n. a metal plate forming the base of a machine.

bedpost ■ n. any of the four upright supports of a bedstead.

bedraggled ■ adj. dishevelled.

bedridden ■ adj. confined to bed by sickness or old age.
– ORIGIN Middle English: from archaic *bedrid* 'bedridden person', from RIDE.

bedrock ■ n. **1** solid rock underlying loose deposits such as soil or alluvium. **2** the fundamental principles on which something is based.

bedroll ■ n. chiefly N. Amer. a sleeping bag or other bedding rolled into a bundle.

bedroom ■ n. **1** a room for sleeping in. **2** [as modifier] N. Amer. denoting a dormitory town or suburb.

bedside ■ n. the space beside a bed.
– PHRASES **bedside manner** the manner in which a doctor attends a patient.

bedsit (also **bedsitter** or **bed-sitting room**) ■ n. informal a rented room consisting of a combined bedroom and living room, with cooking facilities.

bedsock ■ n. chiefly Brit. each of a pair of thick socks worn for extra warmth in bed.

bedsore ■ n. a sore that develops as a result of lying in bed in one position for a prolonged period.

bedspread ■ n. a decorative cloth used to cover a bed.

bedstead ■ n. the framework of a bed.

bedstraw ■ n. a herbaceous plant with small flowers and whorls of slender leaves, formerly used for stuffing mattresses. [Genus *Galium*: several species.]

bedtime ■ n. the usual time when someone goes to bed.

Bedu /ˈbɛduː/ ■ n. another term for BEDOUIN.
– ORIGIN from Arabic *badw*.

Beduin ■ n. variant spelling of BEDOUIN.

bed-wetting ■ n. involuntary urination during the night.
– DERIVATIVES **bed-wetter** n.

BEE S. African ■ abbrev. black economic empowerment.

bee ■ n. **1** (also **honeybee** or **hive bee**) a stinging social insect which collects nectar and pollen from flowers and produces wax and honey. [*Apis mellifera* and other species.] **2** an insect of a large group to which the honeybee belongs, including many solitary as well as social kinds. [Superfamily Apoidea.] **3** a meeting for communal work or amusement: *a sewing bee*.
– PHRASES **the bee's knees** informal an outstandingly good person or thing. **have a bee in one's bonnet** informal be preoccupied or obsessed with something.
– ORIGIN Old English, of Germanic origin.

bee bread ■ n. honey or pollen used as food by bees.

beech ■ n. a large tree with smooth grey bark, glossy leaves, and hard, pale, fine-grained wood. [*Fagus sylvaticus* (Europe) and other species.]
– ORIGIN Old English, of Germanic origin.

beechmast ■ n. the angular brown nuts of the beech tree, pairs of which are enclosed in a prickly case.

beedi ■ n. (pl. **beedis**) variant spelling of BIDI.

bee-eater ■ n. a brightly coloured insectivorous bird with a downcurved bill and long central tail feathers. [*Merops apiaster* and other species.]

beef ■ n. **1** the flesh of a cow, bull, or ox, used as food. ▸ (pl. **beeves** /biːvz/ or US also **beefs**) Farming a cow, bull, or ox fattened for its meat. **2** informal flesh with well-developed muscle. ▸ strength or power. ▸ the substance of a matter. **3** (pl. **beefs**) informal a complaint or grievance. ■ v. informal **1** (**beef something up**) give something more substance or strength. **2** complain.
– ORIGIN Middle English: from Old French *boef*, from Latin *bos, bov-* 'ox'.

beefburger ■ n. a flat round cake of minced beef, fried or grilled and typically eaten in a bun.

beefcake ■ n. informal men with well-developed muscles.

beefeater ■ n. a Yeoman Warder or Yeoman of the Guard in the Tower of London.
– ORIGIN C17 (orig. a derogatory term for a well-fed servant).

beefsteak fungus ■ n. a reddish-brown bracket fungus which resembles raw beef. [*Fistulina hepatica*.]

beef tea ■ n. Brit. a hot drink made with a beef extract.

beef tomato (chiefly N. Amer. also **beefsteak tomato**) ■ n. a tomato of a large, firm variety.

beef Wellington ■ n. a dish consisting of beef coated in pâté and wrapped in puff pastry.

beefwood ■ n. a tropical hardwood tree with close-grained red wood. [Species in several families, in particular *Casuarina equisetifolia*.]

beefy ■ adj. (**-ier, -iest**) **1** informal muscular or robust. ▸ large and impressively powerful. **2** tasting like beef.
– DERIVATIVES **beefily** adv. **beefiness** n.

beehive ■ n. **1** a structure in which bees are kept, typically in the form of a dome or box. **2** a woman's domed and lacquered hairstyle popular in the 1960s.
– DERIVATIVES **beehived** adj.

beehive hut ■ n. S. African a traditional dome-shaped dwelling of some African peoples, usually constructed of thatch or leaves on a timber frame.

bee-keeping ■ n. the occupation of owning and breeding bees for their honey.
– DERIVATIVES **bee-keeper** n.

beeline ■ n. (in phr. **make a beeline for**) hurry directly to.
– ORIGIN C19: with ref. to the straight line supposedly taken instinctively by a bee when returning to the hive.

Beelzebub /bɪˈɛlzɪbʌb/ ■ n. a name for the Devil.
– ORIGIN from late Latin *Beëlzebub*, translating Hebrew *baʿal zĕḇūḇ* 'lord of flies', the name of a Philistine god, and Greek *Beelzeboul* 'the Devil'.

Beemer (also **Beamer**) ■ n. informal a car or motorcycle manufactured by BMW.
– ORIGIN representing a pronunciation of the first two letters of *BMW*.

been past participle of BE.

bee orchid ■ n. an orchid with a flower that resembles a bee. [*Ophrys apifera* and related species.]

beep ■ n. a short, high-pitched sound emitted by electronic equipment or a vehicle horn. ■ v. produce a beep. ▸ chiefly N. Amer. summon with a device that beeps.
– DERIVATIVES **beeper** n.
– ORIGIN 1920s: imitative.

beer ■ n. an alcoholic drink made from yeast-fermented malt flavoured with hops. ▸ used in names of certain other fermented drinks, e.g. *ginger beer*.
– PHRASES **beer and skittles** Brit. amusement or enjoyment.
– DERIVATIVES **beerily** adv. **beeriness** n. **beery** adj.
– ORIGIN Old English, of West Germanic origin, from Latin *bibere* 'to drink'.

beer belly (or **beer gut**) ■ n. informal a man's protruding stomach, caused by excessive consumption of beer.
– DERIVATIVES **beer-bellied** adj.

beer boep /ˈbɪə bʊp/ ■ n. S. African another term for BEER BELLY.
– ORIGIN *boep* from Afrikaans *boepens* 'paunch'.

beer cellar ■ n. **1** an underground room for storing beer. **2** a basement bar where beer is served.

beer garden ■ n. a garden attached to a public house, where beer is served.

beerhall ■ n. S. African historical (under apartheid) government-controlled drinking premises in townships, selling only sorghum beer.

beer mat ■ n. a small cardboard mat for resting glasses on in a public house.

beer money ■ n. informal a small amount of money allowed or earned.

beestings ■ pl. n. [treated as sing.] the first milk produced by a cow or goat after giving birth.
– ORIGIN Old English, of West Germanic origin.

bee-stung ■ adj. informal (of a woman's lips) full and red.

beeswax ■ n. the wax secreted by bees to make honeycombs, used in making wood polishes and candles.

beet ■ n. a herbaceous plant cultivated as a source of food for humans and livestock, and for processing into sugar. [*Beta vulgaris*.]
– ORIGIN Old English, of West Germanic origin, from Latin *beta*.

beetle[1] ■ n. **1** an insect of a large order distinguished by having forewings modified into hard wing cases that cover and protect the hindwings and abdomen. [Order Coleoptera: many species.] **2** Brit. a dice game in which a picture of a beetle is drawn or assembled. ■ v. informal make one's way hurriedly or with short, quick steps.
– ORIGIN Old English *bitula* 'biter', from *bītan* 'to bite'.

beetle

beetle² ■ v. [usu. as adj. **beetling**] (especially of a person's eyebrows) project or overhang.
– DERIVATIVES **beetle-browed** adj.
– ORIGIN C16: back-formation from *beetle-browed* (Middle English).

beetroot ■ n. **1** the edible dark-red spherical root of a variety of beet. **2** the variety of beet which produces this root. [*Beta vulgaris*.]

beeves plural form of BEEF (in sense 1 of the noun).

BEF ■ abbrev. British Expeditionary Force.

befall ■ v. (past **befell**; past part. **befallen**) poetic/literary (especially of something bad) happen to.
– ORIGIN Old English *befeallan* 'to fall'.

befit ■ v. (**befitted**, **befitting**) be appropriate for.
– DERIVATIVES **befitting** adj. **befittingly** adv.

befog ■ v. (**befogged**, **befogging**) make confused.

before ■ prep., conj., & adv. **1** during the period of time preceding. **2** in front of. ▸ in front of and required to answer to (a court of law, tribunal, or other authority). **3** in preference to; with a higher priority than.
– ORIGIN Old English, of Germanic origin.

beforehand ■ adv. in advance.
– ORIGIN Middle English: prob. influenced by Old French *avant main*.

befoul ■ v. make dirty; pollute.

befriend ■ v. act as or become a friend to.

befuddle ■ v. [usu. as adj. **befuddled**] muddle or confuse.
– DERIVATIVES **befuddlement** n.

beg ■ v. (**begged**, **begging**) **1** ask (someone) earnestly or humbly for something. ▸ ask for (something) earnestly or humbly. ▸ (**beg off**) withdraw from a promise or undertaking. **2** ask for food or money as charity. **3** (of a dog) sit up with the front paws raised expectantly in the hope of a reward.
– PHRASES **beg the question 1** (of a fact or action) invite a question or point that has not been dealt with. **2** assume the truth of an argument or proposition to be proved, without arguing it. **beg yours** S. African & Austral./NZ I beg your pardon. **go begging** (of an article or opportunity) be available because unwanted by others.
– ORIGIN Middle English: prob. from Old English *bedecian*, of Germanic origin.

begat archaic past of BEGET.

beget ■ v. (**begetting**; past **begot**; past part. **begotten**) archaic or poetic/literary **1** produce (a child). **2** cause.
– DERIVATIVES **begetter** n.
– ORIGIN Old English *begietan* 'get, obtain by effort'.

beggar ■ n. **1** a person who lives by begging for food or money. **2** informal a person of a specified type: *lucky beggar!* ■ v. reduce to poverty.
– PHRASES **beggar belief** (or **description**) be too extraordinary to be believed or described.

beggarly ■ adj. **1** meagre and ungenerous. **2** poverty-stricken.
– DERIVATIVES **beggarliness** n.

beggar-my-neighbour ■ n. a card game for two players in which the object is to acquire one's opponent's cards. ■ adj. (of national policy) self-aggrandizing at the expense of competitors.

beggary ■ n. a state of extreme poverty.

begging letter ■ n. a letter asking for a gift or donation.

begin ■ v. (**beginning**; past **began**; past part. **begun**) **1** perform or undergo the first part of (an action or activity). ▸ come into being. ▸ start speaking. ▸ (**begin with**) have as a first element. ▸ (**begin on/upon**) set to work on. ▸ (**begin at**) (of a commodity) have as its lowest price. **2** [with neg.] informal have any chance or likelihood of doing: *circuitry that they could not begin to comprehend*.
– DERIVATIVES **beginner** n.
– ORIGIN Old English, of Germanic origin.

beginning ■ n. the time or place at which something begins. ▸ the first or earliest part. ▸ (**beginnings**) a person's background or origin.

begone ■ exclam. archaic go away at once!

begonia /bɪˈɡəʊnɪə/ ■ n. a herbaceous plant grown for its striking foliage and for its flowers, which have brightly coloured sepals but no petals. [Genus *Begonia*.]
– ORIGIN named after the French amateur botanist Michel Bégon, who discovered the plant.

begorra /bɪˈɡɒrə/ ■ exclam. an exclamation of surprise traditionally attributed to the Irish.
– ORIGIN C19: alteration of *by God*.

begot past of BEGET.

begotten past participle of BEGET.

begrime ■ v. blacken with ingrained dirt.

begrudge ■ v. **1** envy (someone) the possession or enjoyment of. **2** give reluctantly or resentfully.
– DERIVATIVES **begrudging** adj. **begrudgingly** adv.

beguile ■ v. **1** charm or enchant. ▸ trick into doing something. **2** archaic or poetic/literary help (time) pass pleasantly.
– DERIVATIVES **beguilement** n. **beguiler** n. **beguiling** adj. **beguilingly** adv.
– ORIGIN Middle English: from BE- + obsolete *guile* 'to deceive'.

begum /ˈbeɪɡəm/ ■ n. Indian a Muslim woman of high rank. ▸ (**Begum**) the title of a married Muslim woman, equivalent to Mrs.
– ORIGIN from Urdu *begam*, from Turkish *bigim* 'princess'.

begun past participle of BEGIN.

behalf ■ n. (in phr. **on** (US also **in**) **behalf of** or **on someone's behalf**) **1** in the interests of a person, group, or principle. **2** as a representative of.
– ORIGIN Middle English: from *on his halve* and *bihalve him*, both meaning 'on his side'.

behave ■ v. **1** act or conduct oneself in a specified way. **2** (also **behave oneself**) conduct oneself in accordance with accepted norms.
– ORIGIN Middle English: from BE- + HAVE in the sense 'bear (oneself) in a particular way'.

behaved ■ adj. conducting oneself in a specified way: *a well-behaved child*.

behaviour (US **behavior**) ■ n. the way in which someone behaves. ▸ the way in which an animal or person responds to a situation or stimulus: *the feeding behaviour of predators*.
– ORIGIN Middle English: from BEHAVE, on the pattern of *demeanour*, influenced by obsolete *haviour* from HAVE.

behavioural (US **behavioral**) ■ adj. involving, relating to, or emphasizing behaviour.

behaviouralism (US **behavioralism**) ■ n. **1** the methods and principles of the scientific study of animal (and human) behaviour. **2** advocacy of or adherence to a behavioural approach to social phenomena.
– DERIVATIVES **behaviouralist** n. & adj.

behavioural science ■ n. the scientific study of human and animal behaviour.

behaviourism (US **behaviorism**) ■ n. Psychology the theory that human and animal behaviour can be explained in terms of conditioning, and that psychological disorders are best treated by altering behaviour patterns.
– DERIVATIVES **behaviourist** n. & adj. **behaviouristic** adj.

behaviour therapy ■ n. the treatment of neurotic symptoms by training the patient's reactions to stimuli.

behead ■ v. cut off the head of (someone), especially as a form of execution.
– ORIGIN Old English, from BE- + *hēafod* 'head'.

beheld past and past participle of BEHOLD.

behemoth /bɪˈhiːmɒθ, ˈbiːhɪˌməʊθ/ ■ n. a huge or monstrous creature.
– ORIGIN Middle English: from Hebrew *bĕhēmōt*, intensive pl. of *bĕhēmāh* 'beast'.

behest /bɪˈhɛst/ ■ n. (usu. **at the behest of**) poetic/literary a person's orders or command.
– ORIGIN Old English *behǣs* 'a vow', from a Germanic base meaning 'bid'.

behind ■ prep. & adv. **1** at or to the far side of. ▸ hidden by. **2** further back than other members of a moving group. **3** in support of or giving guidance to. ▸ guiding, controlling, or responsible for (an event or plan). **4** after the departure or death of. **5** less advanced than in achievement or development. **6** having a lower score than (another competitor). **7** late in accomplishing a task. ▸ in

arrears. ■ n. 1 informal a person's bottom. 2 Australian Rules a kick that sends the ball over a behind line, or a touch that sends it between the inner posts, scoring one point.
– ORIGIN Old English, from BE- + *hindan* 'from behind'.

behindhand ■ adj. late or slow in doing something.
– ORIGIN C16: on the pattern of *beforehand*.

behind line ■ n. Australian Rules the line between an inner and outer goalpost.

behold ■ v. (past and past part. **beheld**) archaic or poetic/literary see or observe.
– DERIVATIVES **beholder** n.
– ORIGIN Old English, from *bi-* 'thoroughly' + *haldan* 'to hold'.

beholden ■ adj. (usu. **beholden to**) indebted.
– ORIGIN Middle English: from BEHOLD.

behove /bɪˈhəʊv/ (US **behoove** /-ˈhuːv/) ■ v. (**it behoves someone to do something**) formal it is a duty, responsibility, or appropriate response for someone to do something.
– ORIGIN Old English, from *behōf*, of West Germanic origin.

beige ■ n. a pale sandy fawn colour.
– ORIGIN C19: from French.

being ■ n. 1 existence. ▸ living; being alive. 2 the nature or essence of a person. 3 a real or imaginary living creature: *alien beings*.

beira /ˈbeɪrə/ ■ n. a rare antelope found in Somalia and Ethiopia. [*Dorcatragus megalotis*.]
– ORIGIN a local name.

beisa oryx /ˈbeɪzə/ ■ n. a gemsbok native to the Horn of Africa. [*Oryx gazella beisa*.]
– ORIGIN C19: from Amharic.

Beja /ˈbedʒə/ ■ n. (pl. same) 1 a member of a nomadic people living between the Nile and the Red Sea. 2 the Cushitic language of this people.

bejewelled (US **bejeweled**) ■ adj. adorned with jewels.

bel ■ n. a unit of measurement used in comparing two sound intensities or electrical power levels, corresponding to an intensity ratio of 10 to 1.
– ORIGIN 1920s: named after Alexander Graham *Bell*, inventor of the telephone.

belabour (US **belabor**) ■ v. 1 attack physically or verbally. 2 argue or discuss in excessive detail.

Belarusian /ˌbelə(ʊ)ˈrʌʃn, ˌbelə(ʊ)ruːsɪən/ (also **Belarussian**) ■ n. 1 a native or inhabitant of Belarus in eastern Europe. 2 the Eastern Slavic language of Belarus. ■ adj. relating to Belarus, its people, or their language.

belated ■ adj. coming late or too late.
– DERIVATIVES **belatedly** adv. **belatedness** n.
– ORIGIN C17 ('overtaken by darkness'): from obsolete *belate* 'delay'.

belay /ˈbiːleɪ, bɪˈleɪ/ ■ v. 1 fix (a rope) round a rock, pin, or other object to secure it. 2 secure (a rock climber) using a belay. 3 nautical slang stop! ■ n. 1 an act of belaying. 2 a spike of rock or other object used for belaying.
– DERIVATIVES **belayer** n.
– ORIGIN C16: from BE- + LAY[1].

belaying pin ■ n. a fixed pin used on board ship and in rock climbing to secure a rope fastened around it.

bel canto /bɛl ˈkantəʊ/ ■ n. a lyrical style of operatic singing using a full, rich, broad tone.
– ORIGIN C19: Italian, 'fine song'.

belch ■ v. 1 emit wind noisily from the stomach through the mouth. 2 expel (smoke or flames) forcefully out or up. ■ n. an act of belching.
– ORIGIN Old English *belcettan*, prob. imitative.

beleaguer ■ v. [usu. as adj. **beleaguered**] 1 lay siege to. 2 make difficulties for; harass.
– ORIGIN C16: from Dutch *belegeren* 'camp round'.

belfry ■ n. (pl. **-ies**) the place in a bell tower or steeple in which bells are housed.
– ORIGIN Middle English: from Old French *berfrei*, later *belfrei*, of West Germanic origin.

Belgian ■ n. a native or national of Belgium or a person of Belgian descent. ■ adj. of or relating to Belgium.

Belial /ˈbiːlɪəl/ ■ n. a name for the Devil.
– ORIGIN from Hebrew *bĕliyyaʻal* 'worthlessness'.

belle époque

belie ■ v. (**belying**) 1 fail to give a true notion of. 2 fail to justify (a claim or expectation).
– ORIGIN Old English 'deceive by lying', from BE- + *lēogan* 'to lie'.

belief ■ n. 1 an acceptance that something exists or is true, especially one without proof. ▸ a firmly held opinion or conviction. ▸ a religious conviction. 2 (**belief in**) trust or confidence in.
– PHRASES **beyond belief** astonishing; incredible.
– ORIGIN Middle English: from Old English *gelēafa*; cf. BELIEVE.

believe ■ v. 1 feel sure of the truth of. ▸ accept the statement of (someone) as true. ▸ have religious faith. 2 (**believe in**) have faith in the truth or existence of. 3 think or suppose.
– DERIVATIVES **believability** n. **believable** adj. **believably** adv. **believer** n.
– ORIGIN Old English *belȳfan*, alteration of *gelēfan*, of Germanic origin.

Belisha beacon /bəˈliːʃə/ ■ n. (in the UK) an orange ball containing a flashing light, mounted on a post at each end of a zebra crossing.
– ORIGIN 1930s: named after Leslie Hore-*Belisha*, Minister of Transport when the beacons were introduced.

belittle ■ v. dismiss as unimportant.
– DERIVATIVES **belittler** n. **belittlement** n. **belittling** adj. **belittlingly** adv.

Belizean /bɛˈliːzɪən/ (also **Belizian**) ■ n. a native or inhabitant of Belize, a country on the Caribbean coast of Central America. ■ adj. of or relating to Belize.

bell[1] ■ n. 1 a hollow object, typically made of metal and in the shape of a deep inverted cup, that sounds a clear musical note when struck. ▸ the sound or stroke of a bell, used as a signal. 2 (**bells**) a musical instrument consisting of a set of metal tubes, suspended in a frame and played by being struck. 3 Nautical (preceded by a numeral) the time as indicated every half-hour of a watch by the striking of the ship's bell one to eight times: *at five bells in the forenoon of June 11*. 4 something bell-shaped, in particular the end of a trumpet. ■ v. 1 summon or indicate with a bell. 2 spread or flare outwards in the shape of a bell.
– PHRASES **bells and whistles** attractive additional features or trimmings. (**as**) **clear** (or **sound**) **as a bell** perfectly clear (or sound). **give someone a bell** informal telephone someone. **ring a bell** informal revive a distant recollection.
– ORIGIN Old English *belle*, of Germanic origin; perhaps rel. to BELL[2].

bell[2] ■ n. the cry of a stag or buck at rutting time. ■ v. (of a stag or buck) make this cry.
– ORIGIN Old English *bellan* 'to bellow', of Germanic origin.

belladonna /ˌbeləˈdɒnə/ ■ n. deadly nightshade. ▸ a drug made from this plant, containing atropine.
– ORIGIN C18: from Italian *bella donna* 'fair lady'.

belladonna lily ■ n. a South African lily with scented trumpet-shaped pink and white flowers. [*Amaryllis belladonna*.]

bellbird ■ n. 1 a tropical American bird with a loud explosive call. [Genus *Procnias*.] 2 an Australasian songbird with ringing bell-like calls. [*Anthornis melanura* (New Zealand) and other species.]

bell-bottoms ■ pl. n. trousers with a marked flare below the knee.
– DERIVATIVES **bell-bottomed** adj.

bellboy ■ n. chiefly N. Amer. a porter in a hotel or club.

bell captain ■ n. N. Amer. the supervisor of a group of bellboys.

bell curve ■ n. Mathematics a graph of a normal (Gaussian) distribution, with a large rounded peak tapering away at each end.

belle /bɛl/ ■ n. a beautiful girl or woman: *the belle of the ball*.
– ORIGIN C17: from French, feminine of *beau* 'beautiful, handsome'.

belle époque /ˌbɛl eɪˈpɒk/ ■ n. the period of settled and comfortable life preceding the First World War.
– ORIGIN French, 'fine period'.

belles-lettres

belles-lettres /bɛl'lɛtr(ə)/ ▪ pl. n. literary works written and read primarily for their aesthetic effect.
– ORIGIN C17: from French, 'fine letters'.

bellflower ▪ n. a plant with blue, purple, or white bell-shaped flowers. [Genus *Campanula*: many species.]

bellhop ▪ n. N. Amer. another term for BELLBOY.

bellicose /'bɛlɪkəʊs/ ▪ adj. aggressive and ready to fight.
– DERIVATIVES **bellicosity** /-'kɒsɪti/ n.
– ORIGIN Middle English: from Latin *bellicus* 'warlike', from *bellum* 'war'.

belligerence /bə'lɪdʒ(ə)r(ə)ns/ (also **belligerency**) ▪ n. aggressive or warlike behaviour.

belligerent ▪ adj. hostile and aggressive. ▸ engaged in a war or conflict. ▪ n. a nation or person engaged in war or conflict.
– DERIVATIVES **belligerently** adv.
– ORIGIN C16: from Latin *belligerare* 'wage war', from *bellum* 'war'.

bell jar ▪ n. a bell-shaped glass cover for use in a laboratory.

bellow ▪ v. emit a loud, deep roar, typically in pain or anger. ▸ shout or sing very loudly. ▪ n. a loud, deep shout or sound.
– ORIGIN Middle English: perhaps from Old English *bylgan*.

bellows ▪ pl. n. 1 a device with an air bag that emits a stream of air when squeezed together with two handles, used for blowing air into a fire. ▸ a similar device used in a harmonium or small organ. 2 an object or device with concertinaed sides to allow it to expand and contract, such as a tube joining a lens to a camera body.
– ORIGIN Middle English: prob. from Old English *belig* (see BELLY).

bell-ringing ▪ n. the activity or pastime of ringing church bells or handbells.
– DERIVATIVES **bell-ringer** n.

Bell's palsy ▪ n. paralysis of the facial nerve causing muscular weakness in one side of the face.
– ORIGIN C19: named after the Scottish anatomist Sir Charles *Bell*, who first described it.

bell tent ▪ n. a cone-shaped tent supported by a central pole.

bellwether ▪ n. 1 the leading sheep of a flock, often with a bell on its neck. 2 a leader or indicator of something.

belly ▪ n. (pl. **-ies**) 1 the front part of the human trunk below the ribs, containing the stomach and bowels. ▸ the stomach, especially as representing the body's need for food. ▸ (also **belly pork**) a cut of pork from the underside between the legs. 2 the rounded underside of a ship or aircraft. 3 the top surface of an instrument of the violin family, over which the strings are placed. ▪ v. (**-ies, -ied**) swell or cause to swell or bulge.
– PHRASES **go belly up** informal go bankrupt.
– DERIVATIVES **-bellied** adj.
– ORIGIN Old English *belig* 'bag', of Germanic origin.

bellyache informal ▪ n. a stomach pain. ▪ v. complain noisily or persistently.
– DERIVATIVES **bellyacher** n.

belly button ▪ n. informal a person's navel.

belly dance ▪ n. a style of dance originating in the Middle East, performed by women and involving undulating movements of the belly and gyration of the hips.
– DERIVATIVES **belly dancer** n. **belly dancing** n.

bellyflop informal ▪ n. a dive into water, landing flat on one's front. ▪ v. (**-flopped, -flopping**) perform a belly-flop.

bellyful ▪ n. (pl. **-fuls**) a sufficient amount to eat.
– PHRASES **have a** (or **one's**) **bellyful** informal have more than enough of something.

belly laugh ▪ n. a loud unrestrained laugh.

belong ▪ v. 1 (of a thing) be rightly placed in or assigned to a specified position. 2 (of a person) fit or be acceptable in a specified place or environment. ▸ (**belong to**) be a member of. 3 (**belong to**) be the property of. ▸ be the rightful possession of; be due to.
– DERIVATIVES **belonging** n.

– ORIGIN Middle English: from BE- + *long* 'belong', from Old English *gelang* 'together with'.

belongings ▪ pl. n. a person's movable possessions.

Belorussian (also **Byelorussian**) ▪ n. & adj. another term for BELARUSIAN.

beloved ▪ adj. dearly loved. ▪ n. a much-loved person.
– ORIGIN Middle English: past participle of obsolete *belove* 'be pleasing', later 'love'.

below ▪ prep. & adv. 1 at a lower level than. ▸ [as adv.] Nautical below deck. 2 lower than (a specified amount, rate, or norm). 3 (in printed text) mentioned further down.
– PHRASES **below stairs** Brit. dated in the basement of a house as occupied by servants.
– ORIGIN Middle English: from BE- + LOW[1].

below decks (also **below deck**) ▪ adj. & adv. in or into the space below the main deck of a ship. ▪ n. (**belowdecks**) the space below the main deck of a ship.

Bel Paese /ˌbɛl pɑː'eɪzeɪ, -ziː/ ▪ n. trademark a rich, mild, creamy white cheese of a kind originally made in Italy.
– ORIGIN Italian, 'fair country'.

belt ▪ n. 1 a strip of leather or other material worn round the waist to support or hold in clothes or to carry weapons. ▸ a belt worn as a sign of rank or achievement, as in judo, karate, or similar sports. ▸ (**the belt**) the punishment of being struck with a belt. 2 a continuous band of material used in machinery for transferring motion from one wheel to another. 3 a strip or encircling area of a specified kind: *the asteroid belt*. 4 informal a heavy blow. ▪ v. 1 fasten or secure with a belt. 2 beat or hit very hard. ▸ (**belt something out**) informal sing or play something loudly and without finesse. 3 informal rush or dash in a specified direction. 4 (**belt up**) informal be quiet.
– PHRASES **below the belt** unfair; disregarding the rules. **belt and braces** Brit. providing double security, by using more than one means to the same end. **tighten one's belt** cut one's expenditure. **under one's belt** safely or satisfactorily achieved, experienced, or acquired.
– DERIVATIVES **belted** adj. **belting** n.
– ORIGIN Old English, of Germanic origin, from Latin *balteus* 'girdle'.

belter ▪ n. informal 1 an outstanding example of something. 2 a loud, forceful singer or song.

beltway ▪ n. US a ring road.

beluga /bə'luːɡə/ ▪ n. (pl. same or **belugas**) 1 a small white toothed whale of Arctic coastal waters, related to the narwhal. [*Delphinapterus leucas*.] 2 a very large sturgeon occurring in the inland seas and rivers of central Eurasia, from which caviar is obtained. [*Huso huso*.]
– ORIGIN C16: from Russian *belukha*, from *belyĭ* 'white'.

belvedere /'bɛlvɪdɪə/ ▪ n. a summer house or other building positioned to command a fine view.
– ORIGIN C16: from Italian, 'fair sight'.

belying present participle of BELIE.

BEM ▪ abbrev. British Empire Medal.

Bemba /'bɛmbə/ ▪ n. (pl. same) 1 a member of an African people of Zambia. 2 the Bantu language of this people.
– ORIGIN the name in Bemba.

bemoan ▪ v. lament or express sorrow for.

bemuse ▪ v. [usu. as adj. **bemused**] confuse or bewilder.
– DERIVATIVES **bemusedly** adv. **bemusement** n.
– ORIGIN C18: from BE- + MUSE[2].

ben ▪ n. Scottish a high mountain: *Ben Nevis*.
– ORIGIN C18: from Scottish Gaelic and Irish *beann*.

bench ▪ n. 1 a long seat for more than one person. 2 a long, sturdy work table in a workshop or laboratory. 3 (**the bench**) the office of judge or magistrate. ▸ judges or magistrates collectively. 4 a platform on which dogs are exhibited at shows. 5 (**the bench**) a seat at the side of a sports field for coaches and players not taking part in a game. ▪ v. 1 exhibit (a dog) at a show. 2 N. Amer. withdraw (a sports player) from play.
– ORIGIN Old English, of Germanic origin; rel. to BANK[1].

benchmark ▪ n. 1 a standard or point of reference against which things may be compared or assessed. 2 a surveyor's mark cut in a wall or building and used as a reference point in measuring altitudes. ▪ v. evaluate or check by comparison with a benchmark.

bench press ▪ n. a bodybuilding and weightlifting

exercise in which a lifter lies on a bench with feet on the floor and raises a weight with both arms. ■ v. (**bench-press**) raise (a weight) in a bench press.

bench test (also **bench run**) ■ n. a test carried out on a machine, a component, or software before it is released. ■ v. (**bench-test**) run a bench test on.

bend[1] ■ v. (past and past part. **bent**) 1 shape or force (something straight) into a curve or angle. ▸ (of a road, river, or path) deviate from a straight line. 2 (of a person) incline the body downwards; stoop. 3 interpret or modify (a rule) to suit oneself. 4 direct (one's attention or energies) to a task. 5 Nautical attach (a sail or cable) by means of a knot. ■ n. 1 a curved or angled part of something. ▸ a curve in a road, path, or river. 2 a kind of knot used to join two ropes together, or one rope to another object. 3 (**the bends**) [treated as sing.] decompression sickness.
– PHRASES **bend someone's ear** informal talk to someone, especially at length or when unwelcome to the listener. **bend one's elbow** informal drink alcohol. **round** (or US **around**) **the bend** informal mad.
– DERIVATIVES **bendable** adj. **bendiness** n. (informal). **bendy** adj. (informal).
– ORIGIN Old English *bendan* 'tension a bow by means of a string', of Germanic origin.

bend[2] ■ n. Heraldry a broad diagonal stripe from top left to bottom right of a shield.
– ORIGIN Middle English: from Old French *bende* 'flat strip'.

bender ■ n. informal 1 a drinking bout. 2 derogatory a male homosexual.

bendlet ■ n. Heraldry a bend of half the normal width, usually borne in groups of two or three.
– ORIGIN C16: prob. from Old French *bendel* 'little bend'.

bend sinister ■ n. Heraldry a broad diagonal stripe from top right to bottom left of a shield (a supposed sign of bastardy).

beneath ■ prep. & adv. 1 extending or directly underneath. 2 [as prep.] of lower status or worth than: *he is rather beneath her*.
– ORIGIN Old English, from *bi* (see BY) + *nithan* 'below', of Germanic origin.

benedicite /ˌbɛnɪˈdaɪsɪti/ ■ n. a blessing, especially a grace said at table in religious communities.
– ORIGIN Latin, 'bless you!', from *benedicere* 'wish well'; the first word of the Latin canticle *Benedicite, omnia opera*.

Benedictine ■ n. 1 /ˌbɛnɪˈdɪktɪn/ a monk or nun of a Christian religious order following the rule of St Benedict. 2 /ˌbɛnɪˈdɪktiːn/ trademark a liqueur based on brandy, originally made by Benedictine monks in France. ■ adj. /ˌbɛnɪˈdɪktɪn/ of St Benedict or the Benedictines.

benediction ■ n. the utterance or bestowing of a blessing. ▸ (**Benediction**) a Catholic service in which the congregation is blessed with the sacrament. ▸ the state of being blessed.
– DERIVATIVES **benedictory** adj.
– ORIGIN Middle English: from Latin *benedictio(n-)*, from *benedicere* 'bless', from *bene* 'well' + *dicere* 'say'.

Benedictus /ˌbɛnɪˈdɪktəs/ ■ n. Christian Church 1 an invocation beginning *Benedictus qui venit in nomine Domini* (Blessed is he who comes in the name of the Lord), forming a set part of the Mass. 2 a canticle beginning *Benedictus Dominus Deus* (Blessed be the Lord God), from Luke 1:68–79.
– ORIGIN Latin, 'blessed', from *benedicere* 'bless'.

benefaction /ˌbɛnɪˈfakʃ(ə)n/ ■ n. formal a donation or gift.
– ORIGIN C17: from late Latin *benefactio(n-)*, from *bene facere* 'do good (to)'.

benefactor ■ n. a person who gives money or other help to a person or cause.
– DERIVATIVES **benefactress** n.
– ORIGIN Middle English: from Latin, from *bene facere* 'do good (to)'.

benefice /ˈbɛnɪfɪs/ ■ n. a Church office, typically that of a rector or vicar, for which property and income are provided in respect of pastoral duties.
– DERIVATIVES **beneficed** adj.
– ORIGIN Middle English: from Latin *beneficium* 'favour, support', from *bene facere* 'do good (to)'.

beneficent /bɪˈnɛfɪs(ə)nt/ ■ adj. doing good or resulting in good.

Beninese

– DERIVATIVES **beneficence** n. **beneficently** adv.
– ORIGIN C17: from Latin, from *bene facere* 'do good (to)'.

beneficial ■ adj. 1 favourable or advantageous. 2 Law of or relating to rights to the use or benefit of property, other than legal title.
– DERIVATIVES **beneficially** adv.

beneficiary ■ n. (pl. **-ies**) a person who gains benefit from something, especially a trust or will.

beneficiate ■ v. 1 process raw materials to extract minerals or other substances in preparation for further processing. 2 S. African [often as n. **beneficiation**] add value to raw materials, especially minerals, by processing them in the region where they originate, rather than exporting them.
– DERIVATIVES **beneficiating** adj. **beneficiation** n.

HISTORY
The word **beneficiate** comes from the Spanish *beneficiar*, meaning 'to do good to something', or 'to make it productive', from Latin *bene facere*, through which it is linked to **benefit**. It was originally a technical mining term used to describe the treatment of mineral ores to extract impurities, and was rarely used outside this context. In the 1990s, however, it began to appear in South Africa in an extended form, particularly with reference to developing gold into jewellery and cutting and polishing locally mined diamonds. One of the earliest occurrences in this sense was in a speech by Nelson Mandela in 1993, when addressing a conference on oil and minerals in Cape Town. While originally the term was only applied to mineral resources, more recently it has also been used when describing the commercial development of plant and animal products.

benefit ■ n. 1 an advantage or profit gained from something. 2 a payment made by the state or an insurance scheme to someone entitled to receive it, e.g. an unemployed person. 3 a public performance designed to raise money for a charity. ■ v. (**benefited** or **benefitted**, **benefiting** or **benefitting**) receive an advantage; profit.
– PHRASES **the benefit of the doubt** a concession that a person or fact must be regarded as correct if the contrary has not been proven.
– ORIGIN Middle English: from Old French *bienfet*, from Latin, from *bene facere* 'do good (to)'.

benevolent ■ adj. 1 well meaning and kindly. 2 (of an organization) serving a charitable rather than a profit-making purpose.
– DERIVATIVES **benevolence** n. **benevolently** adv.
– ORIGIN Middle English: from Old French *benivolent*, from Latin, from *bene* 'well' + *velle* 'to wish'.

BEng ■ abbrev. Bachelor of Engineering.

Bengali /bɛŋˈɡɔːli/ ■ n. (pl. **Bengalis**) 1 a native of Bengal. 2 the Indic language of Bangladesh and West Bengal, written in a script similar to the Devanagari script. ■ adj. of or relating to Bengal, its people, or their language.
– ORIGIN from Hindi *baṅgālī*.

Benguela current /bɛŋˈɡwɛlə, -ˈɡɛlə/ ■ n. a cold current of the Atlantic Ocean flowing northwards along the west coast of southern Africa.
– ORIGIN named after the port of *Benguela* in Angola.

benighted ■ adj. 1 in a state of intellectual or moral ignorance. 2 archaic overtaken by darkness.
– DERIVATIVES **benightedness** n.
– ORIGIN C16: from archaic *benight*.

benign ■ adj. 1 genial and kindly. 2 favourable; not harmful. ▸ Medicine (of a tumour) not malignant.
– DERIVATIVES **benignity** n. **benignly** adv.
– ORIGIN Middle English: from Latin *benignus*, prob. from *bene* 'well' + *-genus* '-born'.

benignant /bɪˈnɪɡnənt/ ■ adj. less common term for BENIGN.
– DERIVATIVES **benignancy** n. **benignantly** adv.

benign neglect ■ n. non-interference which has the effect of being more beneficial than continual attention.

Beninese /ˌbɛnɪˈniːz/ ■ n. a native of Benin, a country in West Africa. ■ adj. of or relating to Benin or its people.

benison /ˈbɛnɪz(ə)n, -s-/ ■ n. poetic/literary a blessing.
– ORIGIN Middle English: from Old French *beneiçun*, from Latin *benedictio* (see BENEDICTION).

bent[1] past and past participle of BEND[1]. ■ adj. **1** sharply curved or having an angle. **2** informal, chiefly Brit. dishonest; corrupt. **3** informal, derogatory, chiefly Brit. homosexual. **4** (**bent on**) determined to do or have. ■ n. a natural talent or inclination.
– PHRASES **bent out of shape** N. Amer. informal angry or agitated.

bent[2] ■ n. a stiff grass which is used for lawns and in hay grasses. [*Agrostis capillaris* and other species.]
– ORIGIN Middle English: from Old English *beonet*, of West Germanic origin.

benthos /ˈbɛnθɒs/ ■ n. Ecology the flora and fauna found on the bottom of a sea or lake.
– DERIVATIVES **benthic** adj.
– ORIGIN C19: from Greek, 'depth of the sea'.

bentonite /ˈbɛntənʌɪt/ ■ n. a kind of absorbent clay formed by breakdown of volcanic ash, used especially as a filler.
– ORIGIN C19: from the name of Fort *Benton* in Montana, US, where it is found.

bentwood ■ n. wood that is artificially shaped for use in making furniture.

Benue-Congo /ˈbenweɪ/ ■ n. a major branch of the Niger–Congo family of languages, including Efik and Fula.
– ORIGIN from the names of rivers.

benumb ■ v. deprive of feeling.
– ORIGIN C15: from obsolete *benim* 'deprive', from BE- + Old English *niman* 'take'.

Benzedrine /ˈbɛnzɪdriːn/ ■ n. trademark for AMPHETAMINE.
– ORIGIN 1930S: from BENZOIC ACID and EPHEDRINE.

benzene /ˈbɛnziːn/ ■ n. Chemistry a volatile liquid hydrocarbon present in coal tar and petroleum, having a hexagonal ring-shaped molecule which is the basis of most aromatic organic compounds. [C_6H_6.]
– DERIVATIVES **benzenoid** adj.
– ORIGIN C19: from BENZOIC ACID.

benzine /ˈbɛnziːn/ (also **benzin** /-zɪn/) ■ n. a mixture of liquid hydrocarbons obtained from petroleum.
– ORIGIN C19 (denoting benzene): from BENZOIN.

benzodiazepine /ˌbɛnzəʊdʌɪˈeɪzɪpiːn, -ˈazəpiːn/ ■ n. Medicine any of a class of heterocyclic organic compounds used as tranquillizers, such as Librium and Valium.
– ORIGIN 1930S: from BENZENE.

benzoic acid ■ n. Chemistry a white crystalline compound present in benzoin and other plant resins, used as a food preservative.
– DERIVATIVES **benzoate** n.

benzoin /ˈbɛnzəʊɪn/ ■ n. (also **gum benzoin**) a fragrant gum resin obtained from certain East Asian storax trees.
– ORIGIN C16: from French *benjoin*, from Arabic *lubānjāwī* 'incense of Java'.

benzol /ˈbɛnzɒl/ (also **benzole** /-zəʊl/) ■ n. crude benzene, formerly used as a fuel.

benzoyl /ˈbɛnzəʊʌɪl, -zəʊɪl/ ■ n. [as modifier] Chemistry of or denoting the acyl radical -C(O)C_6H_5, derived from benzoic acid.

benzyl /ˈbɛnzʌɪl, -zɪl/ ■ n. [as modifier] Chemistry of or denoting the radical -$CH_2C_6H_5$, derived from toluene.

bequeath /bɪˈkwiːð/ ■ v. leave (property) to a person or other beneficiary by a will. ▸ hand down or pass on.
– ORIGIN Old English, from BE- + *cwethan* 'say'.

bequest ■ n. the action of bequeathing. ▸ something that is bequeathed.
– ORIGIN Middle English: from BE- + Old English *cwis* 'speech'.

berate ■ v. scold or criticize angrily.
– ORIGIN C16: from BE- + RATE[2].

Berber /ˈbəːbə/ ■ n. **1** a member of the indigenous peoples of North Africa. **2** the Afro-Asiatic language of these peoples.
– ORIGIN from Arabic *barbar*, from Greek *barbaros* 'foreigner'.

berberis /ˈbəːbərɪs/ ■ n. a plant of a genus that comprises the barberries. [Genus *Berberis*.]
– ORIGIN from medieval Latin *barbaris*.

bereave ■ v. (**be bereaved**) be deprived of a close relation or friend through their death.
– DERIVATIVES **bereavement** n.
– ORIGIN Old English *berēafian*.

bereft ■ adj. deprived of something: *her room was bereft of colour*. ▸ lonely and abandoned.
– ORIGIN C16: archaic past participle of BEREAVE.

beret /ˈbɛreɪ, -ri/ ■ n. a round flattish cap of felt or cloth.
– ORIGIN C19: from French *béret* 'Basque cap', from late Latin *birrus* 'hooded cape'.

berg[1] /bəːg/ ■ n. short for ICEBERG.

berg[2] /bəːx, bəːg/ ■ n. S. African a mountain or hill. ▸ (**the Berg**) the Drakensberg mountain range.
– ORIGIN from Dutch.

bergamot /ˈbəːgəmɒt/ ■ n. **1** an oily substance extracted from a variety of Seville orange, used in cosmetics and as flavouring in Earl Grey tea. **2** (also **bergamot orange**) the tree bearing this fruit. **3** an aromatic North American herb of the mint family. [*Monarda didyma* and other species.]
– ORIGIN C17: named after *Bergamo* in northern Italy.

bergie /ˈbəːxi, ˈbəːgi/ ■ n. S. African informal a (Cape Town) vagrant.
– ORIGIN from BERG.

bergschrund /ˈbəːgʃrʊnd/ ■ n. a crevasse at the head of a glacier.
– ORIGIN C19: from German, from *Berg* 'mountain' + *Schrund* 'crevice'.

berg wind ■ n. S. African a hot dry northerly wind blowing from the interior to coastal districts.

beriberi /ˌbɛrɪˈbɛri/ ■ n. a disease causing inflammation of the nerves and heart failure, ascribed to a deficiency of vitamin B_1.
– ORIGIN C18: from Sinhalese, from *beri* 'weakness'.

Beringian /bɛˈrɪndʒɪən/ ■ adj. of or relating to Beringia, the region surrounding the Bering Strait, especially in the geological past when a land bridge connected Siberia and Alaska in this area.

berk /bəːk/ ■ n. informal, chiefly Brit. a stupid person.
– ORIGIN 1930S: abbrev. of *Berkeley* or *Berkshire Hunt*, rhyming slang for 'cunt'.

berkelium /bəːˈkiːlɪəm, ˈbəːklɪəm/ ■ n. the chemical element of atomic number 97, an unstable radioactive metal of the actinide series. (Symbol: **Bk**)
– ORIGIN 1949: from the University of *Berkeley* in California, where it was first made.

berm /bəːm/ ■ n. a raised bank or flat strip of land bordering a river, canal, or road. ▸ an artificial ridge or embankment. ▸ a narrow ledge, especially one between a ditch and the base of a parapet.
– ORIGIN C18: from French *berme*.

Bermuda grass ■ n. a creeping grass common in warmer parts of the world. [*Cynodon dactylon*.]

Bermudan /bəˈmjuːd(ə)n/ ■ n. a native or inhabitant of Bermuda. ■ adj. of or relating to Bermuda or its people.
– DERIVATIVES **Bermudian** adj. & n.

Bermuda shorts (also **Bermudas**) ■ pl. n. casual knee-length shorts.

berry ■ n. (pl. **-ies**) **1** a small roundish juicy fruit without a stone. ▸ Botany any fruit that has its seeds enclosed in a fleshy pulp, for example a banana or tomato. **2** a fish egg or roe of a lobster or similar creature.
– DERIVATIVES **berried** adj. **berrying** n.
– ORIGIN Old English, of Germanic origin.

berserk /bəˈsəːk, -z-/ ■ adj. out of control; wild or frenzied.

berth ■ n. **1** a ship's allotted place at a wharf or dock. **2** a fixed bunk on a ship or train, or in a caravan. ■ v. **1** moor or be moored in a berth. **2** provide a berth for (a passenger).
– PHRASES **give someone/thing a wide berth** stay well away from someone or something.
– DERIVATIVES **berthing** n.

betatron

– ORIGIN C17: prob. from a nautical use of BEAR¹ + -TH².

beryl /'bɛrɪl/ ■ n. a transparent pale green, blue, or yellow mineral consisting of a silicate of beryllium and aluminium, sometimes used as a gemstone.
– ORIGIN Middle English: from Old French *beril*, from Greek *bērullos*.

beryllium /bə'rɪliəm/ ■ n. the chemical element of atomic number 4, a hard grey metal which is the lightest of the alkaline earth metals. (Symbol: **Be**)

beseech ■ v. (past and past part. **besought** or **beseeched**) chiefly poetic/literary ask (someone) urgently and fervently for something.
– DERIVATIVES **beseeching** adj. **beseechingly** adv.
– ORIGIN Middle English: from BE- + Old English *sēcan*.

beset ■ v. (**besetting**; past and past part. **beset**) **1** trouble or harass persistently. ▶ surround or attack from all sides. **2** (**be beset with**) archaic be covered or studded with.
– ORIGIN Old English, from BE- + *settan*.

beside ■ prep. **1** at the side of; next to. ▶ compared with. **2** in addition to; apart from.
– PHRASES **beside oneself** distraught.
– ORIGIN Old English *be sīdan* 'by the side'.

besides ■ prep. in addition to; apart from. ■ adv. in addition; as well. ▶ used to introduce an additional idea or explanation.

besiege ■ v. **1** surround (a place) with armed forces in order to capture it or force its surrender. ▶ crowd round oppressively. **2** (**be besieged**) be inundated by large numbers of requests or complaints.
– DERIVATIVES **besieger** n.
– ORIGIN Middle English: from Old French *asegier*.

beskuit /bəs'keɪt/ ■ n. S. African a rusk.
– ORIGIN Afrikaans.

besmear ■ v. poetic/literary smear or cover with.

besmirch /bɪ'smɜːtʃ/ ■ v. **1** damage (someone's reputation). **2** poetic/literary make dirty; soil.

besom /'biːz(ə)m, 'bɪz-/ ■ n. a broom made of twigs tied round a stick.
– ORIGIN Old English, of West Germanic origin.

besotted /bɪ'sɒtɪd/ ■ adj. strongly infatuated.
– ORIGIN C16: from obsolete *besot* 'make foolishly affectionate'.

besought past and past participle of BESEECH.

bespangle ■ v. poetic/literary adorn with something that glitters or sparkles.

bespatter ■ v. spatter with liquid.

bespeak ■ v. (past **bespoke**; past part. **bespoken**) **1** be evidence of. **2** order or reserve in advance. **3** archaic speak to.
– ORIGIN Old English *bisprecan* 'speak out', later 'discuss, decide on'.

bespectacled ■ adj. wearing glasses.

bespoke ■ adj. Brit. (of goods) made to order. ▶ (of a computer program) written or adapted for a specific user or purpose.

besprinkle ■ v. poetic/literary sprinkle with liquid, powder, etc.

best ■ adj. of the most excellent or desirable type or quality. ▶ most appropriate, advantageous, or well advised. ▶ S. African informal favourite. ■ adv. to the highest degree; most. ▶ to the highest standard. ▶ most suitably, appropriately, or usefully. ■ n. (**the best**) that which is the most excellent or desirable. ▶ (**one's best**) the highest standard or level attainable. ▶ (in sport) a record performance. ■ v. informal outwit.
– PHRASES **all the best** best wishes. **at best** taking the most optimistic view. **be for the best** be desirable in the end, although not at first seeming so. **best end** Brit. the rib end of a neck of lamb or other meat. **the best of three** (or **five** etc.) victory achieved by winning the majority of a specified odd number of games. **the best part of** most of. **best wishes** a conventional expression of hope for someone's future happiness. **get the best of** overcome (someone). **give someone/thing best** Brit. admit the superiority of someone or something. **had best** find it most sensible or well advised to. **make the best of** derive what limited advantage one can from (something unsatisfactory or unwelcome). **six of the best** a caning as a punishment,
traditionally with six strokes of the cane.
– ORIGIN Old English, of Germanic origin.

best ball ■ n. Golf the better score at a hole of two or more players competing as a team.

best boy ■ n. the assistant to the chief electrician of a film crew.

bestial /'bɛstɪəl/ ■ adj. of or like a beast. ▶ savagely cruel and depraved.
– DERIVATIVES **bestialize** (also -**ise**) v. **bestially** adv.
– ORIGIN Middle English: from late Latin *bestialis*, from Latin *bestia* 'beast'.

bestiality ■ n. **1** savagely cruel or depraved behaviour. **2** sexual intercourse between a person and an animal.

bestiary /'bɛstɪəri/ ■ n. (pl. -**ies**) a treatise on animals, especially a medieval work with a moralizing tone.
– ORIGIN C19: from medieval Latin *bestiarium*, from Latin *bestia* 'beast'.

bestir ■ v. (**bestirred, bestirring**) (**bestir oneself**) exert or rouse oneself.

best man ■ n. a male friend or relative chosen by a bridegroom to assist him at his wedding.

bestow ■ v. confer (an honour, right, or gift).
– DERIVATIVES **bestowal** n.
– ORIGIN Middle English: from BE- + Old English *stōw* 'place'.

bestrew ■ v. (past part. **bestrewed** or **bestrewn**) poetic/literary scatter or lie scattered over (a surface).
– ORIGIN Old English *bestrēowian* (see BE-, STREW).

bestride ■ v. (past **bestrode**; past part. **bestridden**) span or straddle.
– ORIGIN Old English *bestrīdan* (see BE-, STRIDE).

best-seller ■ n. a book or other product that sells in very large numbers.
– DERIVATIVES **best-selling** adj.

bet ■ v. (**betting**; past and past part. **bet** or **betted**) **1** risk a sum of money or other valued item against someone else's on the basis of the outcome of an unpredictable event such as a race or game. **2** informal used to express certainty: *he'll be surprised to see me, I'll bet*. ■ n. an act of betting. ▶ a sum of money staked. ▶ informal a candidate or option offering a specified likelihood of success: *Allen looked a good bet for victory*. ▶ (**one's bet**) informal one's opinion.
– PHRASES **you bet** informal you may be sure.
– DERIVATIVES **betting** n. **bettor** (also **better**) n.
– ORIGIN C16: perhaps from obsolete noun *abet* 'abetment'.

beta /'biːtə/ ■ n. **1** the second letter of the Greek alphabet (Β, β), transliterated as 'b'. ▶ [as modifier] denoting the second of a series of items or categories. **2** [as modifier] relating to beta decay or beta particles. **3** (also **beta coefficient**) a measure of the movement in price of a security relative to the stock market, used to indicate possible risk.
– ORIGIN from Greek.

beta blocker ■ n. any of a class of drugs which inhibit the stimulation of the adrenergic receptors responsible for increased cardiac action, used to control heart rhythm, treat angina, and reduce high blood pressure.

beta decay ■ n. radioactive decay in which an electron is emitted.

betake ■ v. (past **betook**; past part. **betaken**) (**betake oneself to**) poetic/literary go to.

beta particle (also **beta ray**) ■ n. Physics a fast-moving electron emitted by radioactive decay of substances (originally regarded as rays).

beta rhythm ■ n. Physiology the normal electrical activity of the brain when conscious and alert, consisting of oscillations (beta waves) with a frequency of 18 to 25 hertz.

beta test ■ n. an independent trial of machinery or software, carried out in the final stages of development (after alpha-testing). ■ v. (**beta-test**) subject to a beta test.

betatron /'biːtətrɒn/ ■ n. Physics an apparatus for accelerating electrons in a circular path by magnetic induction.
– ORIGIN 1940s: from BETA + -TRON.

betel

betel /ˈbiːt(ə)l/ ■ n. **1** the leaf of an Asian evergreen climbing plant, which in the East is chewed and used as a mild stimulant. **2** the plant, related to pepper, from which these leaves are taken. [*Piper betle.*]
– ORIGIN C16: from Malayalam *verrila*.

betel nut ■ n. the astringent seed of an areca palm, chewed with betel leaves.

bête noire /bɛt ˈnwɑː, bɛt/ ■ n. (pl. **bêtes noires** pronunc. same) (**one's bête noire**) a person or thing that one particularly dislikes.
– ORIGIN French, 'black beast'.

bethink ■ v. (past and past part. **bethought**) (**bethink oneself**) formal come to think.

betide ■ v. poetic/literary happen; befall.
– ORIGIN Middle English: from BE- + obsolete *tide* 'befall', from Old English *tīdan* 'happen'.

betimes ■ adv. poetic/literary in good time; early.
– ORIGIN Middle English: from obsolete *betime* (see BY, TIME).

betoken ■ v. poetic/literary be a warning or sign of.
– ORIGIN Old English, from BE- + *tācnian* 'signify', of Germanic origin.

betook past of BETAKE.

betray ■ v. **1** act treacherously towards (one's country) by aiding the enemy. ▸ be disloyal to or inform on. **2** unintentionally reveal; be evidence of: *she drew a deep breath that betrayed her indignation.*
– DERIVATIVES **betrayal** n. **betrayer** n.
– ORIGIN Middle English: from BE- + obsolete *tray* 'betray', from Old French *traïr*, from Latin *tradere* 'hand over'.

betroth /bɪˈtrəʊð, -θ/ ■ v. [as adj. **betrothed**] formally engaged to be married. ■ n. (**one's betrothed**) the person to whom one is engaged.
– DERIVATIVES **betrothal** n.
– ORIGIN Middle English *betreuthe*: from BE- + TRUTH.

better ■ adj. **1** more desirable, satisfactory, or effective. [comparative of the adj. GOOD.] ▸ more appropriate, advantageous, or well advised. **2** partly or fully recovered from illness or injury. [comparative of the adj. WELL¹.] ■ adv. more excellently or effectively. ▸ to a greater degree; more. ▸ more suitably or usefully. ■ n. **1** that which is better; the better one. **2** (**one's betters**) chiefly dated or humorous one's superiors in social class or ability. ■ v. improve on or surpass. ▸ (**better oneself**) achieve a higher social position or status. ▸ overcome or defeat (someone).
– PHRASES **better off** in a more advantageous position, especially in financial terms. **the better part of** almost all of; most of. **better than** N. Amer. more than. **the better to —** so as to do the specified thing better. **for better or (for) worse** whether the outcome is good or bad. **get the better of** defeat or overcome. **go one better** narrowly outdo or surpass. **had better** would find it wiser to.
– ORIGIN Old English, of Germanic origin.

better half ■ n. informal a person's spouse or partner.

betterment ■ n. **1** improvement. **2** Law the enhanced value of real property arising from local improvements.

between ■ prep. & adv. **1** at, into, or across the space separating (two objects, places, or points). **2** in the period separating (two points in time). **3** [as prep.] indicating a connection or relationship involving two or more parties. **4** [as prep.] by combining the resources or actions of (two or more parties).
– PHRASES **between ourselves** (or **you and me**) in confidence. (**in**) **between times** (or **whiles**) in the intervals between other actions.
– ORIGIN Old English, from *be* 'by' + a Germanic word rel. to TWO.

USAGE
Say **between you and me**, not **between you and I**. See **Personal pronouns** in *Guide to Good English* p. SP 20.

betwixt ■ prep. & adv. archaic term for BETWEEN.
– PHRASES **betwixt and between** informal neither one thing nor the other.
– ORIGIN Old English, from *be* 'by' + a Germanic word rel. to TWO.

bevel /ˈbɛv(ə)l/ ■ n. **1** (in carpentry) a surface or edge which slopes away from a horizontal or vertical surface. **2** (also **bevel square**) a tool for marking angles in carpentry and stonework. ■ v. (**bevelled**, **bevelling**; US **beveled**, **beveling**) [usu. as adj. **bevelled**] cut a bevel on.
– ORIGIN C16: from Old French *baif* 'open-mouthed', from *baer* (see BAY³).

beverage /ˈbɛv(ə)rɪdʒ/ ■ n. a drink other than water.
– ORIGIN Middle English: from Old French *bevrage*, from Latin *bibere* 'to drink'.

bevy /ˈbɛvi/ ■ n. (pl. **-ies**) a large group of people or things.
– ORIGIN Middle English.

bewail ■ v. greatly regret or lament.

beware ■ v. be cautious and alert to risks or dangers.
– ORIGIN Middle English: from the phr. *be ware* (see BE-, WARE³).

bewilder ■ v. [often as adj. **bewildered**] perplex or confuse.
– DERIVATIVES **bewilderedly** adv. **bewildering** adj. **bewilderingly** adv. **bewilderment** n.
– ORIGIN C17: from BE- + obsolete *wilder* 'lead or go astray'.

bewitch ■ v. **1** cast a spell over. **2** enchant and delight.
– DERIVATIVES **bewitching** adj. **bewitchingly** adv. **bewitchment** n.
– ORIGIN Middle English: from BE- + WITCH.

beyond ■ prep. & adv. **1** at or to the further side of. ▸ more extensive or extreme than. **2** happening or continuing after. **3** having reached or progressed further than (a specified level or amount). **4** to or in a degree where a specified action is impossible. ▸ too advanced for. **5** [with neg.] apart from; except. ■ n. (**the beyond**) the unknown, especially in references to life after death.
– ORIGIN Old English, from *be* 'by' + *geondan*, of Germanic origin.

bezant /ˈbɛz(ə)nt/ ■ n. Heraldry a roundel or (i.e. a solid gold circle).
– ORIGIN Middle English: from Old French *besant*, from Latin *Byzantius* 'Byzantine'.

bezel /ˈbɛz(ə)l/ ■ n. a grooved ring holding the cover of a watch face or other instrument in position. ▸ a groove holding the crystal of a watch or the stone of a gem in its setting.
– ORIGIN C16: from Old French.

bezique /bɪˈziːk/ ■ n. a trick-taking card game for two, played with a double pack of 64 cards, including the seven to ace only in each suit. ▸ the holding of the queen of spades and the jack of diamonds in this game.
– ORIGIN C19: from French *bésigue*, perhaps from Persian *bāzīgar* 'juggler' or *bāzī* 'game'.

b.f. ■ abbrev. (in bookkeeping) brought forward.

BGH ■ abbrev. bovine growth hormone.

Bh ■ symb. the chemical element bohrium.

Bhagavadgita /ˌbʌɡəvədˈɡiːtə/ ■ n. Hinduism a sacred text which is part of an epic Sanskrit poem, the Mahabharata, and which stresses the importance of doing one's duty and of faith in God.
– ORIGIN Sanskrit, 'Song of God'.

Bhagwan /bʌɡˈwɑːn/ ■ n. Indian God.
– ORIGIN from Hindi *bhagwān*.

bhajan /ˈbʌdʒ(ə)n/ ■ n. Hinduism a devotional song.
– ORIGIN from Sanskrit *bhajana*.

bhaji /ˈbɑːdʒi/ ■ n. **1** (in Indian cuisine) a spicy side dish of vegetables. **2** (chiefly in South Africa and India) any leafy green vegetable, especially when cooked. **3** another term for BHAJIA.
– ORIGIN from Hindi *bhājī* 'fried vegetables'.

bhajia /ˈbʌdʒ(j)ə/ (also **bhaji**) ■ n. (in Indian cuisine) a small flat cake or ball of vegetables, fried in batter.
– ORIGIN from Urdu *bhajya*.

bhakti /ˈbʌkti/ ■ n. Hinduism devotional worship directed to one supreme deity, usually Vishnu or Shiva.
– ORIGIN from Sanskrit.

bhang /baŋ/ ■ n. (also **bang**) ■ n. the leaves and flower-tops of cannabis, used as a narcotic in India.
– ORIGIN from Hindi *bhāṅg*.

bhangra /ˈbɑːŋɡrə/ ■ n. a type of popular music combining Punjabi folk traditions with Western pop music.
– ORIGIN 1960s: from Punjabi *bhāṅgrā*.

CONSONANTS   **b** but   **d** dog   **f** few   **g** get   **h** he   **j** yes   **k** cat   **l** leg   **m** man   **n** no   **p** pen   **r** red

Bharatanatyam /ˌbʌrʌtəˈnɑːtjʌm/ ■ n. a classical dance form originating in southern India.
– ORIGIN from Sanskrit *bharatanātya* 'the dance of Bharata', reputed to be the author of the *Nātyaśāstra*, a manual of dramatic art.

Bhutanese /ˌbuːtəˈniːz/ ■ n. a native or inhabitant of Bhutan, a small kingdom on the slopes of the Himalayas. ■ adj. of or relating to Bhutan or its people.

bhuti /ˈbuːti/ (also **buti**) ■ n. S. African a brother. ▸ a friendly form of address to a man or boy.
– ORIGIN from isiXhosa *ubuthi* 'brother'.

Bi ■ symb. the chemical element bismuth.

bi /baɪ/ ■ abbrev. informal bisexual.

bi- /baɪ/ (also **bin-** before a vowel) ■ comb. form two; having two: *biathlon*. ▸ occurring twice in every one or once in every two: *bicentennial*. ▸ lasting for two: *biennial*. ▸ Chemistry (in names of compounds) containing two atoms or groups of a specified kind: *bicarbonate*.
– ORIGIN from Latin, 'doubly, having two'; rel. to Greek *di-* 'two'.

> **USAGE**
> The meaning of **bimonthly** (and similar words such as **biyearly**) is ambiguous. Such words can either mean 'occurring or produced twice a month' or 'occurring or produced every two months'. The only way to avoid this ambiguity is to use alternative expressions like *every two months* and *twice a month*.

biannual ■ adj. occurring twice a year. Compare with BIENNIAL.
– DERIVATIVES **biannually** adv.

bias ■ n. **1** inclination or prejudice for or against one thing or person. ▸ a systematic distortion of a statistical result due to a factor not allowed for in its derivation. **2** a diagonal across the grain of a fabric. **3** Electronics a steady voltage, magnetic field, or other factor applied to a system to cause it to operate over a predetermined range. **4** Bowls the irregular shape given to one side of a bowl. ■ v. (**biased**, **biasing** or **biassed**, **biassing**) **1** influence unfairly; prejudice. **2** Electronics give a bias to.
– ORIGIN C16 ('oblique line'): from French *biais*, from Provençal.

bias binding ■ n. a narrow strip of fabric cut on the bias, used to bind edges or for decoration.

bias-ply ■ adj. North American term for CROSS-PLY.

biathlon ■ n. a sporting event in which the competitors combine cross-country skiing and rifle shooting.
– DERIVATIVES **biathlete** n.
– ORIGIN 1950s: from BI- + Greek *athlon* 'contest', on the pattern of *pentathlon*.

biaxial ■ adj. having or relating to two axes.
– DERIVATIVES **biaxially** adv.

bib ■ n. a piece of cloth or plastic fastened round a child's neck to keep its clothes clean while eating. ▸ a loose-fitting sleeveless garment worn for identification, e.g. by competitors and officials at sporting events. ▸ the part above the waist of the front of an apron or pair of dungarees.
– PHRASES **one's best bib and tucker** informal one's smartest clothes.
– ORIGIN C16: prob. from archaic *bib* 'drink', from Latin *bibere* 'to drink'.

Bible ■ n. **1** (**the Bible**) the Christian scriptures, consisting of the Old and New Testaments. ▸ the Jewish scriptures, consisting of the Torah or Law, the Prophets, and the Hagiographa or Writings. **2** (**bible**) informal a book regarded as authoritative.
– ORIGIN Middle English: from Greek (*ta*) *biblia* '(the) books', from *biblion* 'book'.

Bible-basher (also **Bible-thumper**) ■ n. informal a person who expounds the teachings of the Bible in an aggressively evangelical way.
– DERIVATIVES **Bible-bashing** n. & adj.

Bible Belt ■ n. those areas of the southern and middle western US and western Canada where Protestant fundamentalism is strong.

biblical ■ adj. of, relating to, or contained in the Bible. ▸ resembling the language or style of the Bible.
– DERIVATIVES **biblically** adv.

biblio- /ˈbɪblɪəʊ/ ■ comb. form relating to a book or books: *bibliophile*.
– ORIGIN from Greek *biblion* 'book'.

bibliography /ˌbɪblɪˈɒɡrəfi/ ■ n. (pl. **-ies**) **1** a list of sources referred to in a particular work. ▸ a list of the books of a specific author or on a specific subject. **2** the study of books in terms of their classification, printing, and publication.
– DERIVATIVES **bibliographer** n. **bibliographic** /-əˈɡrafɪk/ adj. **bibliographical** adj. **bibliographically** adv.

bibliomancy /ˈbɪblɪə(ʊ)mansi/ ■ n. the practice of foretelling the future by interpreting a randomly chosen passage from a book, especially the Bible.

bibliomania ■ n. passionate enthusiasm for collecting and possessing books.
– DERIVATIVES **bibliomaniac** n. & adj.

bibliometrics ■ pl. n. [treated as sing.] statistical analysis of books or other publications.
– DERIVATIVES **bibliometric** adj.

bibliophile ■ n. a person who collects or has a great love of books.
– DERIVATIVES **bibliophilic** adj. **bibliophily** /-ˈɒfɪli/ n.

bibulous /ˈbɪbjʊləs/ ■ adj. formal excessively fond of drinking alcohol.
– DERIVATIVES **bibulously** adv. **bibulousness** n.
– ORIGIN C17: from Latin *bibulus* 'freely drinking'.

bicameral /baɪˈkam(ə)r(ə)l/ ■ adj. (of a legislative body) having two chambers.
– DERIVATIVES **bicameralism** n.
– ORIGIN C19: from BI- + Latin *camera* 'chamber'.

bicarb ■ n. informal sodium bicarbonate.

bicarbonate /baɪˈkɑːbənɛɪt, -nət/ ■ n. **1** Chemistry a salt containing the anion HCO_3^-. **2** (also **bicarbonate of soda**) sodium bicarbonate.

bicentenary /ˌbaɪsɛnˈtiːnəri, -ˈtɛn-/ ■ n. (pl. **-ies**) the two-hundredth anniversary of a significant event.
– DERIVATIVES **bicentennial** n. & adj.

bicephalous /baɪˈsɛf(ə)ləs, -ˈkɛf-/ ■ adj. having two heads.
– ORIGIN C19: from BI- + Greek *kephalē* 'head'.

biceps /ˈbaɪsɛps/ ■ n. (pl. same) a large muscle in the upper arm which turns the hand to face palm uppermost and flexes the arm and forearm. ▸ (also **leg biceps**) a muscle in the back of the thigh which helps to flex the leg.
– ORIGIN C17: from Latin, 'two-headed' (because the muscle has two points of attachment).

bichir /ˈbɪʃɪr/ ■ n. an elongated African freshwater fish with hard shiny scales and a series of separate fins along its back. [Genus *Polypterus*: several species.]
– ORIGIN 1960s: from dialect Arabic *abu shīr*.

bicker ■ v. argue about petty and trivial matters.
– ORIGIN Middle English.

bicky (also **bikky**) ■ n. (pl. **-ies**) informal a biscuit.

bicolour (US **bicolor**) ■ adj. (also **bicoloured**) having two colours. ■ n. a bicolour flower or breed.

biconcave ■ adj. concave on both sides.

biconvex ■ adj. convex on both sides.

bicultural ■ adj. having or combining the cultures and customs of two nations or ethnic groups.
– DERIVATIVES **biculturalism** n.

bicuspid ■ adj. having two cusps or points. ■ n. a tooth with two cusps, especially a human premolar tooth.
– ORIGIN C19: from BI- + Latin *cuspis* 'sharp point'.

bicuspid valve ■ n. Anatomy the mitral valve.

bicycle ■ n. a vehicle consisting of two wheels held in a frame one behind the other, propelled by pedals and steered with handlebars attached to the front wheel. ■ v. ride a bicycle.
– DERIVATIVES **bicyclist** n.
– ORIGIN C19: from BI- + Greek *kuklos* 'wheel'.

bicyclic /baɪˈsaɪklɪk, -ˈsɪk-/ ■ adj. Chemistry having two rings of atoms in its molecule.

bid[1] ■ v. (**bidding**; past and past part. **bid**) **1** offer (a certain price) for something, especially at an auction. ▸ (**bid for**) (of a contractor) tender for (work). **2** (often **bid for**) make

bid

an effort to obtain or achieve. **3** Bridge make a statement during the auction undertaking to make (a certain number of tricks). ▪ n. **1** an offer to buy something. ▶ an offer to do work or supply goods at a stated price. **2** an effort to obtain or achieve. **3** Bridge an undertaking by a player in the auction to make a stated number of tricks with a stated suit as trumps.
– DERIVATIVES **bidder** n. **bidding** n.
– ORIGIN Old English *bēodan* 'to offer, command', of Germanic origin.

bid² ▪ v. (**bidding**; past **bid** or **bade**; past part. **bid**) **1** utter (a greeting or farewell) to. **2** archaic command (someone) to do something.
– ORIGIN Old English *biddan* 'ask', of Germanic origin.

biddable ▪ adj. meekly ready to accept and follow instructions.

bidden archaic or poetic/literary past participle of BID².

biddy ▪ n. (pl. **-ies**) informal a woman, especially an old one.
– ORIGIN C17 (orig. denoting a chicken).

bide ▪ v. archaic or dialect remain or stay in a certain place.
– PHRASES **bide one's time** wait quietly for a good opportunity to do something.
– ORIGIN Old English: of Germanic origin.

bidet ▪ n. a low oval basin used for washing one's genital and anal area.
– ORIGIN C17: from French, 'pony'.

bidi /ˈbiːdiː/ (also **beedi** or **biri**) ▪ n. (pl. **bidis**) (in the Indian subcontinent) a type of cheap cigarette made using unprocessed tobacco.
– ORIGIN from Hindi *bīḍī* 'betel plug, cigar'.

bidirectional ▪ adj. functioning in two directions.

Biedermeier /ˈbiːdəˌmaɪə/ ▪ adj. denoting a 19th-century German style of furniture and decoration characterized by restraint and utilitarianism.
– ORIGIN from the name of a fictitious German schoolmaster created by L. Eichrodt (1854).

biennial /baɪˈɛnɪəl/ ▪ adj. **1** taking place every other year. Compare with BIANNUAL. **2** (of a plant) taking two years to grow from seed to fruition and die. Compare with ANNUAL, PERENNIAL. ▪ n. **1** a biennial plant. **2** an event celebrated or taking place every two years.
– DERIVATIVES **biennially** adv.
– ORIGIN C17: from Latin *biennis*, from *bi-* 'twice' + *annus* 'year'.

biennium /baɪˈɛnɪəm/ ▪ n. (pl. **biennia** /-nɪə/ or **bienniums**) a period of two years.

bier /bɪə/ ▪ n. a movable platform on which a coffin or corpse is placed before burial.
– ORIGIN Old English, of Germanic origin.

bietou /ˈbiːtəʊ/ ▪ n. S. African an African shrub or small tree which bears yellow daisy-like flowers and edible purplish-black berries. [*Chrysanthemoides monilifera*.]
– ORIGIN Afrikaans, from Khoikhoi.

bifacial ▪ adj. having two faces, or two different faces.

biff informal ▪ v. strike (someone) roughly with the fist. ▪ n. a sharp blow with the fist.
– ORIGIN C19: prob. imitative.

bifid /ˈbaɪfɪd/ ▪ adj. Botany & Zoology (of a part of a plant or animal) divided by a deep cleft or notch into two parts.
– ORIGIN C17: from Latin *bifidus*, from *bi-* 'doubly' + *fidus*, from *findere* 'to split'.

bifilar /baɪˈfaɪlə/ ▪ adj. consisting of or involving two threads or wires.
– ORIGIN C19: from BI- + *filum* 'thread'.

bifocal ▪ adj. of or relating to lenses with two parts with different focal lengths, one for distant vision and one for near vision. ▪ n. (**bifocals**) a pair of glasses with bifocal lenses.

bifurcate ▪ v. /ˈbaɪfəkeɪt/ divide into two branches or forks. ▪ adj. /baɪˈfəːkət/ forked; branched.
– DERIVATIVES **bifurcation** n.
– ORIGIN C17: from medieval Latin *bifurcare* 'divide into two forks', from Latin *bifurcus* 'two-forked'.

big ▪ adj. (**bigger**, **biggest**) **1** of considerable size, power, or extent. ▶ larger than others of the same kind. ▶ informal exciting great interest or popularity. **2** of considerable importance or seriousness. **3** informal, often ironic generous: *'That's big of you!'* **4** (**big with**) archaic advanced in pregnancy with.
– PHRASES **big money** (also **big bucks**) informal large amounts of money. **the big screen** informal the cinema. **in a big way** informal to a great extent or high degree. **talk big** informal talk confidently or boastfully. **think big** informal be ambitious. **too big for one's boots** informal conceited.
– DERIVATIVES **biggish** adj. **bigness** n.
– ORIGIN Middle English.

bigamy ▪ n. the offence of marrying someone while already married to another person.
– DERIVATIVES **bigamist** n. **bigamous** adj.
– ORIGIN Middle English: from Old French *bigamie*, from Latin *bi-* 'twice' + Greek *-gamos* 'married'.

big band ▪ n. a large group of musicians playing jazz or swing music.

big bang ▪ n. Astronomy the rapid expansion of matter from a state of extremely high density and temperature which according to current cosmological theories marked the origin of the universe.

Big Brother ▪ n. informal a person or organization exercising total control over people's lives.
– ORIGIN 1950s: from the name of the head of state in George Orwell's *Nineteen Eighty-four* (1949).

big business ▪ n. large-scale financial or commercial activity.

big cheese ▪ n. informal an important person.
– ORIGIN 1920s: *cheese*, prob. from Persian *čīz* 'thing'.

big end ▪ n. (in a piston engine) the larger end of the connecting rod, encircling the crankpin.

bigeye ▪ n. **1** a large migratory tuna found in warm seas. [*Thunnus obesus*.] **2** a sea fish with large eyes which lives in tropical and temperate regions. [Family Priacanthidae: several species.]

big five ▪ n. (also **the Big Five**) (in tourism or hunting) the five largest and most dangerous African mammals: the elephant, lion, leopard, rhinoceros, and buffalo.

Bigfoot ▪ n. (pl. **Bigfeet**) a large, hairy ape-like creature, supposedly found in NW America.

big game ▪ n. large animals hunted for sport.

big gun ▪ n. informal a powerful person.

big-head ▪ n. informal a conceited person.
– DERIVATIVES **big-headed** adj. **big-headedness** n.

bight /baɪt/ ▪ n. a curve or recess in a coastline or other geographical feature.
– ORIGIN Old English *byht* 'a bend or angle', of Germanic origin.

big league ▪ n. a top league in a professional sport, especially baseball.
– DERIVATIVES **big leaguer** n.

big mouth ▪ n. informal an indiscreet or boastful person.
– DERIVATIVES **big-mouthed** adj.

bigot /ˈbɪɡət/ ▪ n. a person who is prejudiced in their views and intolerant of the opinions of others.
– DERIVATIVES **bigoted** adj. **bigotry** n.
– ORIGIN C16: from French.

big shot (also **big noise**) ▪ n. informal an important person.

big time ▪ n. (**the big time**) informal the highest or most successful level in a career.
– DERIVATIVES **big-timer** n.

big top ▪ n. the main tent in a circus.

big wheel ▪ n. a Ferris wheel.

bigwig ▪ n. informal an important person.
– ORIGIN C18: so named from the large wigs formerly worn by distinguished men.

bijou /ˈbiːʒuː/ ▪ adj. (especially of a house or flat) small and elegant. ▪ n. (pl. **bijoux** pronunc. same) archaic a jewel or trinket.
– ORIGIN French, from Breton *bizou* 'finger-ring', from *biz* 'finger'.

bike informal ▪ n. a bicycle or motorcycle. ▪ v. ride a bicycle or motorcycle.
– DERIVATIVES **biker** n.
– ORIGIN C19: abbrev.

bikini ▪ n. (pl. **bikinis**) a women's two-piece swimsuit.

– ORIGIN 1940s: named after *Bikini*, an atoll in the western Pacific, where an atom bomb was exploded in 1946 (because of the supposed 'explosive' effect of the garment).

bikini briefs ■ pl. n. scanty briefs worn by women as underwear.

bikini line ■ n. the area of skin around the edge of the bottom half of a bikini.

bikky ■ n. (pl. **-ies**) variant spelling of BICKY.

bilabial ■ adj. Phonetics denoting a speech sound formed by closure or near closure of the lips, e.g. *p*, *b*, *m*, *w*.

bilateral ■ adj. **1** having or relating to two sides. **2** involving two parties.
– DERIVATIVES **bilaterally** adv.

bilateral symmetry ■ n. the property of being divisible into symmetrical halves on either side of a unique plane.

bilayer ■ n. Biochemistry a film two molecules thick, especially one formed by lipid molecules with their hydrophilic ends directed outwards.

bilberry ■ n. (pl. **-ies**) **1** the small blue edible berry of a hardy dwarf shrub found on heathland and high ground in the northern hemisphere. **2** the shrub on which these berries grow. [*Vaccinium myrtilus* and other species.]
– ORIGIN C16: prob. of Scandinavian origin.

bilbo ■ n. (pl. **-os** or **-oes**) historical a sword noted for the temper and elasticity of its blade.
– ORIGIN C16: from *Bilboa*, an earlier English form of *Bilbao*, the Spanish seaport noted for the manufacture of fine blades.

bilboes ■ pl. n. an iron bar with sliding shackles, formerly used for confining a prisoner's ankles.
– ORIGIN C16.

Bildungsroman /ˈbɪldʊŋzrəʊˌmɑːn/ ■ n. a novel dealing with someone's formative years or spiritual education.
– ORIGIN German, from *Bildung* 'education' + *Roman* 'a novel'.

bile ■ n. **1** a bitter greenish-brown alkaline fluid secreted by the liver and stored in the gall bladder, which aids digestion. **2** anger; irritability.
– ORIGIN C16: from Latin *bilis*.

bile duct ■ n. the duct which conveys bile from the liver and the gall bladder to the duodenum.

bilge ■ n. **1** the area on the outer surface of a ship's hull where the bottom curves to meet the vertical sides. ▸ (**bilges**) the lowest internal portion of the hull. ▸ (also **bilge water**) dirty water that collects inside the bilges. **2** informal nonsense; rubbish.
– ORIGIN C15: prob. a var. of BULGE.

bilharzia /bɪlˈhɑːtsɪə/ ■ n. a chronic disease caused by infestation with blood flukes (schistosomes), endemic in parts of Africa and South America.
– ORIGIN C19: former name of the genus *Schistosoma*, named after the German physician T. *Bilharz*, who discovered the parasite.

bilharziasis /ˌbɪlhɑːˈtsaɪəsɪs/ ■ n. Medicine another term for BILHARZIA (the disease).

biliary /ˈbɪlɪəri/ ■ adj. Medicine of or relating to bile or the bile duct.

biliary fever (also **biliary**) ■ n. chiefly S. African babesiosis in horses or dogs.

bilinear ■ adj. Mathematics **1** rare relating to or contained by two straight lines. **2** denoting a function of two variables that is linear and homogeneous in both independently.

bilingual ■ adj. speaking two languages fluently. ▸ expressed in or using two languages.
– DERIVATIVES **bilingualism** n.

bilious ■ adj. **1** affected by or associated with nausea or vomiting. ▸ (of a colour) lurid or sickly. **2** spiteful; bad-tempered. **3** Physiology of or relating to bile.
– DERIVATIVES **biliously** adv. **biliousness** n.

bilirubin /ˌbɪlɪˈruːbɪn/ ■ n. Biochemistry an orange-yellow pigment formed in the liver by the breakdown of haemoglobin and excreted in bile.
– ORIGIN C19: from Latin *bilis* 'bile' + *ruber* 'red'.

biliverdin /ˌbɪlɪˈvɜːdɪn/ ■ n. Biochemistry a green pigment excreted in bile, an oxidized derivative of bilirubin.
– ORIGIN C19: from Latin *bilis* 'bile' + French *vert* 'green'.

bill of exchange

bilk ■ v. informal cheat or defraud. ▸ obtain (money) fraudulently.
– ORIGIN C17: perhaps a var. of BAULK.

Bill ■ n. (**the Bill** or **the Old Bill**) [treated as sing. or pl.] Brit. informal the police.
– ORIGIN 1960s: familiar form of the given name *William*.

bill¹ ■ n. **1** a printed or written statement of the money owed for goods or services. **2** a draft of a proposed law presented to parliament for discussion. **3** a programme of entertainment at a theatre or cinema. **4** N. Amer. a banknote. **5** a poster or handbill. ■ v. **1** list (a person or event) in a programme. ▸ (**bill someone/thing as**) proclaim someone or something as. **2** send a bill to. ▸ charge (a sum of money).
– PHRASES **fit** (or **fill**) **the bill** be suitable for a particular purpose.
– DERIVATIVES **billable** adj. **billing** n.
– ORIGIN Middle English: from Anglo-Norman French *bille*, prob. from medieval Latin *bulla* 'seal, sealed document'.

bill² ■ n. the beak of a bird, especially when it is slender, flattened, or weak, or belongs to a web-footed bird or a bird of the pigeon family. ■ v. (of birds, especially doves) stroke bill with bill during courtship.
– PHRASES **bill and coo** informal behave or talk in a loving and sentimental way.
– DERIVATIVES **-billed** adj.
– ORIGIN Old English *bile*.

billabong ■ n. Austral. a branch of a river forming a backwater or stagnant pool.
– ORIGIN C19: from Wiradhuri (an extinct Aboriginal language) *bilabang* (orig. as the name of the Bell River, NSW), from *billa* 'water' + *bang* 'channel that is dry except after rain'.

billboard ■ n. a hoarding.

billet¹ ■ n. a civilian house where soldiers are lodged temporarily. ■ v. (**billeted**, **billeting**) lodge (soldiers) in a civilian house.
– ORIGIN Middle English: from Anglo-Norman French *billette*, diminutive of *bille* (see BILL¹).

billet² ■ n. **1** a thick piece of wood. ▸ a small bar of metal for further processing. **2** Heraldry a rectangle placed vertically as a charge.
– ORIGIN Middle English: from Old French *billette*, diminutive of *bille*, from medieval Latin *billa* 'branch, trunk', prob. of Celtic origin.

billet-doux /ˌbɪlɪˈduː/ ■ n. (pl. **billets-doux** /-ˈduːz/) dated or humorous a love letter.
– ORIGIN C17: French, 'sweet note'.

billfish ■ n. (pl. same or **-fishes**) a marlin, sailfish, spearfish, or similar fish. [Family Istiophoridae.]

billfold ■ n. N. Amer. a wallet.

billhook ■ n. a tool having a sickle-shaped blade with a sharp inner edge, used for pruning or lopping branches.

billiards /ˈbɪljədz/ ■ pl. n. [treated as sing.] a game played on a billiard table, for two people using three balls.
– ORIGIN C16: from French *billard*, denoting both the game and the cue, diminutive of *bille* (see BILLET²).

billiard table ■ n. a smooth cloth-covered rectangular table used for billiards, snooker, and some forms of pool, with six pockets at the corners and sides into which balls are struck with cues.

billion ■ cardinal number (pl. **billions** or (with numeral or quantifying word) same) **1** the number equivalent to the product of a thousand and a million; 1 000 000 000 or 10^9. ▸ dated, chiefly Brit. a million million (1 000 000 000 000 or 10^{12}). **2** (**billions**) informal a very large number or amount.
– DERIVATIVES **billionth** ordinal number.
– ORIGIN C17: from French, from *million*, by substitution of the prefix *bi-* 'two' for the initial letters.

billionaire ■ n. a person possessing assets worth at least a billion pounds or dollars.
– ORIGIN C19: from BILLION, on the pattern of *millionaire*.

bill of exchange ■ n. a written order requiring a person to make a specified payment to the signatory or to a named payee.

bill of fare

bill of fare ■ n. dated a menu.

bill of health ■ n. a certificate relating to the incidence of infectious disease on a ship or in a port.
– PHRASES **a clean bill of health** a declaration or confirmation of good health or condition.

bill of lading ■ n. a detailed list of a ship's cargo given by the master of the ship to the person consigning the goods.

bill of quantities ■ n. a detailed statement of work, prices, dimensions, and other details, for the erection of a building by contract.

bill of rights ■ n. a statement of rights, in particular the English constitutional settlement of 1689 and the first ten amendments to the Constitution of the US, ratified 1791. ▸ a statement of rights which forms part of the South African Constitution of 1996.

bill of sale ■ n. a certificate of transfer of personal property, used especially where something is transferred as security for a debt.

billow ■ n. **1** a large undulating mass of cloud, smoke, or steam. **2** archaic a large sea wave. ■ v. (of fabric) fill with air and swell outwards. ▸ (of smoke, cloud, or steam) move or flow outward with an undulating motion.
– DERIVATIVES **billowy** adj.
– ORIGIN C16: from Old Norse *bylgja*.

billposter (also **billsticker**) ■ n. a person who pastes up advertisements on hoardings.
– DERIVATIVES **billposting** n.

billy (also **billycan**) ■ n. (pl. **-ies**) a tin or enamel cooking pot with a lid and folding handle, used in camping.
– ORIGIN C19: perhaps from Aboriginal *billa* 'water'.

billy goat ■ n. a male goat.

bilobed (also **bilobate**) ■ adj. having or consisting of two lobes.

biltong /'bɪltɒŋ, 'bəl-/ ■ n. chiefly S. African lean meat which is salted and dried in strips.
– ORIGIN Afrikaans, from Dutch *bil* 'buttock' + *tong* 'tongue'.

bimbo ■ n. (pl. **-os**) informal, derogatory an attractive but unintelligent or frivolous young woman.
– DERIVATIVES **bimbette** n.
– ORIGIN C20 (orig. 'fellow, chap'): from Italian, 'little child'.

bimetallic ■ adj. made or consisting of two metals.

bimodal ■ adj. having or involving two modes, in particular (of a statistical distribution) having two maxima.

bimonthly ■ adj. & adv. appearing or taking place twice a month or every two months.

bin Brit. ■ n. a receptacle in which to deposit rubbish. ▸ a capacious receptacle for storing a specified substance. ▸ a partitioned stand for storing bottles of wine. ■ v. (**binned**, **binning**) throw (something) away by putting it in a bin. ▸ store (wine) in a bin.
– ORIGIN Old English, of Celtic origin.

binary /'baɪnəri/ ■ adj. **1** composed of, or involving two things. **2** using or denoting a system of numerical notation with two as its base, employing the digits 0 and 1. ■ n. (pl. **-ies**) **1** the binary system of notation. **2** Astronomy a system of two stars revolving round their common centre.
– ORIGIN Middle English: from late Latin *binarius*, from *bini* 'two together'.

binary tree ■ n. Computing a data structure in which each record is linked to two successor records.

bind ■ v. (past and past part. **bound**) **1** tie or fasten (something) tightly together. ▸ restrain (someone) by tying their hands and feet. ▸ wrap or encircle (something) tightly. **2** hold in a united or cohesive group or mass. ▸ hold or combine with (a substance) by chemical bonding. **3** impose a legal or contractual obligation on. ▸ indenture (someone) as an apprentice. ▸ secure (a contract), typically with a sum of money. ▸ (**bind someone over**) (of a court of law) require someone to fulfil an obligation, typically by paying a sum of money as surety. **4** fix together and enclose (the pages of a book) in a cover. **5** trim (the edge of a piece of material) with a fabric strip. ▸ (**bind off**) N. Amer. cast off in knitting. **6** Logic (of a quantifier) be applied to (a given variable) so that the variable falls within its scope. **7** (of a food or medicine) make (someone) constipated. ■ n. **1** informal an annoyance. ▸ a problematical situation. **2** a statutory constraint. **3** Music another term for TIE.
– ORIGIN Old English, of Germanic origin.

binder ■ n. **1** a cover for holding magazines or loose sheets of paper together. **2** a reaping machine that binds grain into sheaves. **3** a bookbinder.

bindery ■ n. (pl. **-ies**) a workshop or factory in which books are bound.

bindi /'bɪndiː/ ■ n. (pl. **bindis**) a decorative mark worn in the middle of the forehead by Indian women, especially Hindus.
– ORIGIN from Hindi *bindī*.

binding ■ n. **1** a strong covering holding the pages of a book together. **2** fabric cut or woven in a strip, used for binding the edges of a piece of material. **3** (also **ski binding**) Skiing a device fixed to a ski to grip a ski boot. ■ adj. (of an agreement) involving a contractual obligation.

binding energy ■ n. Physics the energy that holds a nucleus together, equal to the mass defect of the nucleus.

bindweed /'baɪndwiːd/ ■ n. a twining plant with trumpet-shaped flowers, several kinds of which are invasive weeds. [*Convolvulus* and other genera: many species.]

bin-end ■ n. Brit. one of the last bottles from a bin of wine.

binge informal ■ n. a period of excessive indulgence. ■ v. (**bingeing** or US also **binging**) indulge in an activity, especially eating, to excess.
– DERIVATIVES **binger** n.
– ORIGIN C19.

bingo ■ n. a game in which players mark off randomly called numbers on printed cards, the winner being the first to mark off all their numbers. ■ exclam. **1** a call by someone who wins a game of bingo. **2** expressing satisfaction at a sudden positive event or outcome.
– ORIGIN 1920s (as an interjection).

binnacle /'bɪnək(ə)l/ ■ n. a built-in housing for a ship's compass.
– ORIGIN C15 (as *bittacle*): from Spanish *bitácula*, or Portuguese *bitacola*, from Latin *habitaculum* 'dwelling place'.

binocular /bɪ'nɒkjʊlə/ ■ adj. adapted for or using both eyes.
– ORIGIN C18: from Latin *bini* 'two together' | *oculus* 'eye'.

binoculars ■ pl. n. an optical instrument with a lens for each eye, used for viewing distant objects.

binocular vision ■ n. vision using two eyes with overlapping fields of view, allowing good perception of depth.

binomial /baɪ'nəʊmɪəl/ ■ n. **1** Mathematics an algebraic expression of the sum or the difference of two terms. **2** the two-part Latin name of a species of living organism (consisting of the genus followed by the specific epithet). ■ adj. consisting of or relating to a binomial.
– ORIGIN C16: from French *binôme*, from Latin *bi-* 'having two' + Greek *nomos* 'part, portion'.

binomial distribution ■ n. Statistics a frequency distribution of the possible number of successful outcomes in a given number of trials in each of which there is the same probability of success.

binomial theorem ■ n. a formula for finding any power of a binomial without multiplying at length.

binominal ■ adj. another term for BINOMIAL (in sense 2).

binucleate /baɪ'njuːklɪət/ ■ adj. Biology (of a cell) having two nuclei.

bio- /'baɪəʊ/ ■ comb. form of or relating to life: *biosynthesis*. ▸ biological; relating to biology: *biohazard*. ▸ of living beings: *biogenesis*.
– ORIGIN from Greek *bios* 'human life', the sense being extended to mean 'organic life'.

bioaccumulate ■ v. (of a substance) become concentrated inside the bodies of living things.
– DERIVATIVES **bioaccumulation** n.

bioactive ■ adj. (of a substance) having a biological effect.
– DERIVATIVES **bioactivity** n.

bioavailability ■ n. Physiology the proportion of a drug or

other substance which enters the circulation when introduced into the body and so is able to have an active effect.
– DERIVATIVES **bioavailable** adj.

biocenosis ■ n. US spelling of BIOCOENOSIS.

biochemistry ■ n. the branch of science concerned with the chemical and physico-chemical processes which occur within living organisms.
– DERIVATIVES **biochemical** adj. **biochemically** adv. **biochemist** n.

biocide ■ n. a substance that is poisonous to living organisms, such as a pesticide.

bioclimatic ■ adj. Ecology of or relating to the interrelation of climate and the activities and distribution of living organisms.

biocoenosis /ˌbaɪə(ʊ)sɪˈnəʊsɪs/ (US **biocenosis**) ■ n. (pl. -noses /-siːz/) Ecology an association of different organisms forming a closely integrated community.
– ORIGIN C19: from BIO- + Greek *koinōsis* 'sharing'.

biocomputer ■ n. a computer based on circuits and components formed from biological molecules or structures. ▸ the brain regarded as a computer.

biocontrol ■ n. short for BIOLOGICAL CONTROL.

biodata ■ pl. n. [treated as sing. or pl.] biographical details.

biodegradable ■ adj. capable of being decomposed by bacteria or other living organisms.
– DERIVATIVES **biodegradability** n. **biodegradation** n. **biodegrade** v.

biodiversity ■ n. the variety of plant and animal life in the world or in a particular habitat.

biodynamics ■ pl. n. [treated as sing.] **1** the study of physical motion or dynamics in living systems. **2** a method of organic farming that incorporates certain astrological and spiritual principles and practices.
– DERIVATIVES **biodynamic** adj.

bioelectric ■ adj. of or relating to electricity or electrical phenomena produced within living organisms.
– DERIVATIVES **bioelectrical** adj.

bioenergetics ■ pl. n. [treated as sing.] **1** the study of the transformation of energy in living organisms. **2** a system of alternative psychotherapy based on the belief that emotional healing can be aided through the resolution of bodily tension.
– DERIVATIVES **bioenergetic** adj.

bioengineering ■ n. **1** another term for GENETIC ENGINEERING. **2** the use of artificial tissues or organs in the body. **3** the use in engineering or industry of organisms or biological processes. **4** another term for BIOMECHANICS.
– DERIVATIVES **bioengineer** n. & v.

bioethics ■ pl. n. [treated as sing.] the ethics of medical and biological research.
– DERIVATIVES **bioethical** adj. **bioethicist** n.

biofeedback ■ n. the use of electronic monitoring of a normally automatic bodily function in order to train someone to acquire voluntary control of that function.

bioflavonoid ■ n. any of a group of compounds occurring mainly in citrus fruits and blackcurrants, sometimes regarded as vitamins.

biofuel ■ n. fuel derived directly from living matter.

biogas ■ n. gaseous fuel, especially methane, produced by the fermentation of organic matter.

biogenesis /ˌbaɪə(ʊ)ˈdʒɛnɪsɪs/ ■ n. **1** the synthesis of substances by living organisms. **2** historical the hypothesis that living matter arises only from other living matter.
– DERIVATIVES **biogenetic** adj.

biogeochemical ■ adj. relating to or denoting the cycle in which chemical elements and simple substances are transferred between living systems and the environment.
– DERIVATIVES **biogeochemist** n. **biogeochemistry** n.

biogeography ■ n. the branch of biology concerned with the geographical distribution of plants and animals.
– DERIVATIVES **biogeographer** n. **biogeographic** adj. **biogeographical** adj. **biogeographically** adv.

biography ■ n. (pl. -ies) an account of someone's life written by someone else.
– DERIVATIVES **biographer** n. **biographic** adj. **biographical** adj. **biographically** adv.

– ORIGIN C17: from French *biographie*, from medieval Greek, from *bios* 'life' + *-graphia* 'writing'.

biohazard ■ n. a risk to human health or the environment arising from biological research.

bioinformatics ■ pl. n. [treated as sing.] the science of collecting and analysing complex biological data such as genetic codes.

biokinetics /ˌbaɪə(ʊ)kɪˈnɛtɪks/ ■ pl. n. [treated as sing.] the study of the mechanics of human movement, typically in relation to sport and exercise. ▸ a paramedical discipline concerned with health and fitness assessment and rehabilitation exercise.
– DERIVATIVES **biokinetic** adj. **biokineticist** n.
– ORIGIN C20: from BIO- + Greek *kinētikos*, from *kinein* 'to move'.

biological ■ adj. **1** of or relating to biology or living organisms. ▸ (of a detergent) containing enzymes to assist the process of cleaning. **2** (of a parent or child) related by blood; natural. **3** relating to, involving, or denoting the use of micro-organisms or toxins of biological origin as weapons of war.
– DERIVATIVES **biologically** adv.

biological clock ■ n. an innate mechanism that controls the cyclical physiological activities of an organism.

biological control ■ n. the control of a pest by the introduction of a natural enemy or predator.

biology ■ n. the scientific study of living organisms. ▸ the plants and animals of a particular area. ▸ the features of a particular organism or class of organisms.
– DERIVATIVES **biologist** n.
– ORIGIN C19: coined in German from Greek *bios* 'life' + -LOGY.

bioluminescence ■ n. the biochemical emission of light by living organisms such as glow-worms and deep-sea fishes.
– DERIVATIVES **bioluminescent** adj.

biomass ■ n. **1** the total quantity or weight of organisms in a given area or volume. **2** organic matter used as a fuel, especially in the generation of electricity.

biome /ˈbaɪəʊm/ ■ n. Ecology a large naturally occurring community of flora and fauna occupying a major habitat, e.g. forest or grassland.
– ORIGIN C20: from BIO- + -OME.

biomechanics ■ pl. n. [treated as sing.] the study of the mechanical laws relating to the movement or structure of living organisms.

biometry /baɪˈɒmɪtri/ (also **biometrics** /ˌbaɪə(ʊ)ˈmɛtrɪks/) ■ n. the application of statistical analysis to biological data.
– DERIVATIVES **biometric** adj. **biometrical** adj. **biometrician** n.

biomimetic ■ adj. Biochemistry relating to or denoting synthetic methods which mimic biochemical processes.

bionic ■ adj. **1** relating to or denoting the use of electro-mechanical body parts instead of or as well as living ones. **2** informal having ordinary human powers increased by or as if by the aid of such devices.
– DERIVATIVES **bionically** adv. **bionics** pl. n.
– ORIGIN 1960s: from BIO-, on the pattern of *electronic*.

bionomics /ˌbaɪə(ʊ)ˈnɒmɪks/ ■ pl. n. [treated as sing.] the study of the behaviour and adaptation of organisms in their natural habitat; ecology.
– DERIVATIVES **bionomic** adj.
– ORIGIN C19: from BIO-, on the pattern of *economics*.

biophysics ■ pl. n. [treated as sing.] the science of the application of the laws of physics to biological phenomena.
– DERIVATIVES **biophysical** adj. **biophysicist** n.

biopic ■ n. informal a biographical film.

biopiracy ■ n. derogatory bioprospecting, regarded as a form of exploitation of developing countries.

bioprospecting ■ n. the search for plant and animal species from which medicinal drugs and other commercially valuable compounds can be obtained.
– DERIVATIVES **bioprospector** n.

biopsy /ˈbaɪɒpsi/ ■ n. (pl. -ies) an examination of tissue

taken from the body, to discover the presence, cause, or extent of a disease.
– ORIGIN C19: coined in French from Greek *bios* 'life' + *opsis* 'sight'.

bioreactor ■ n. an apparatus in which a biological reaction or process is carried out, especially on an industrial scale.

bioregion ■ n. a region defined by characteristics of the natural environment rather than by man-made divisions.
– DERIVATIVES **bioregional** adj.

bioremediation /ˌbaɪə(ʊ)rɪˌmiːdɪˈeɪʃ(ə)n/ ■ n. the use of either naturally occurring or deliberately introduced micro-organisms to consume and break down environmental pollutants.

biorhythm ■ n. a recurring cycle in the physiology or functioning of an organism, such as the daily cycle of sleeping and waking.
– DERIVATIVES **biorhythmic** adj.

BIOS /ˈbaɪɒs/ ■ n. Computing a set of computer instructions in firmware which control input and output operations.
– ORIGIN acronym from *Basic Input-Output System*.

bioscience ■ n. any of the life sciences.
– DERIVATIVES **bioscientist** n.

bioscope ■ n. dated, chiefly S. African a cinema or film.

biosensor ■ n. a device which uses a living organism or biological molecules, especially enzymes or antibodies, to detect the presence of chemicals.

biosolids ■ pl. n. organic matter recycled from sewage, especially for use in agriculture.

biosphere ■ n. the regions of the surface and atmosphere of the earth occupied by living organisms.
– DERIVATIVES **biospheric** adj.

biosynthesis ■ n. the production of complex molecules within living organisms or cells.
– DERIVATIVES **biosynthetic** adj.

biota /baɪˈəʊtə/ ■ n. Ecology the animal and plant life of a particular region, habitat, or geological period.
– ORIGIN C20: from Greek *biotē* 'life'.

biotech ■ n. short for BIOTECHNOLOGY.

biotechnology ■ n. the exploitation of biological processes for industrial and other purposes, especially the genetic manipulation of micro-organisms for the production of antibiotics, hormones, etc.
– DERIVATIVES **biotechnological** adj. **biotechnologist** n.

bioterrorism /ˌbaɪəʊˈtɛrərɪz(ə)m/ ■ n. the use of infectious agents or other harmful biological or biochemical substances as weapons of terrorism.
– DERIVATIVES **bioterrorist** n.

biotic /baɪˈɒtɪk/ ■ adj. of, relating to, or resulting from living things, especially in their ecological relations.
– ORIGIN C19: from Greek *biōtikos*, from *bios* 'life'.

biotin /ˈbaɪətɪn/ ■ n. Biochemistry a vitamin of the B complex, found in egg yolk, liver, and yeast, involved in the synthesis of fatty acids and glucose.
– ORIGIN 1930s: coined in German from Greek *bios* 'life'.

biotite /ˈbaɪətaɪt/ ■ n. a black, dark brown, or greenish black micaceous mineral, occurring as a constituent of many igneous and metamorphic rocks.
– ORIGIN C19: named after J.-B. *Biot* (1774–1862), French mineralogist.

biotope /ˈbaɪətəʊp/ ■ n. Ecology the region of a habitat associated with a particular ecological community.
– ORIGIN 1920s: from German *Biotop*, from Greek *topos* 'place'.

bioturbation /ˌbaɪətɜːˈbeɪʃ(ə)n/ ■ n. Geology the disturbance of sedimentary deposits by living organisms.
– DERIVATIVES **bioturbated** adj.

biotype ■ n. a group of organisms having an identical genetic constitution.

biowarfare ■ n. biological warfare.

bipartisan /ˌbaɪpɑːtɪˈzan/ ■ adj. of or involving the agreement or cooperation of two political parties.
– DERIVATIVES **bipartisanship** n.

bipartite /baɪˈpɑːtaɪt/ ■ adj. **1** involving or made by two separate parties. **2** technical consisting of two parts.

biped /ˈbaɪpɛd/ ■ n. an animal which walks on two feet.
– DERIVATIVES **bipedal** /baɪˈpiːd(ə)l/ adj. **bipedalism** n. **bipedality** /ˌbaɪpɪˈdalɪti/ n.
– ORIGIN C17: from Latin, from *bi-* 'having two' + *pes*, *ped-* 'foot'.

biphasic /baɪˈfeɪzɪk/ ■ adj. having two phases.

biphenyl /baɪˈfiːnʌɪl, baɪˈfɛnɪl/ ■ n. Chemistry an organic compound containing two phenyl groups bonded together, e.g. the PCBs.

bipinnate /baɪˈpɪneɪt/ ■ adj. Botany (of a pinnate leaf) having leaflets that are further subdivided in a pinnate arrangement.

biplane ■ n. an early type of aircraft with two pairs of wings, one above the other.

bipolar ■ adj. **1** having or relating to two poles or extremities. ▶ (of a plant or animal species) of or occurring in both polar regions. **2** (of psychiatric illness) characterized by both manic and depressive episodes, or manic ones only. **3** (of a nerve cell) having two axons, one either side of the cell body. **4** Electronics (of a transistor or other device) using both positive and negative charge carriers.
– DERIVATIVES **bipolarity** n.

biramous /baɪˈreɪməs/ ■ adj. Zoology (especially of crustacean limbs and antennae) dividing to form two branches.
– ORIGIN C19: from BI- + RAMUS.

birch ■ n. **1** a slender hardy tree of north temperate regions, which has thin, peeling, typically silver-grey or white bark and yields a hard, pale, fine-grained wood. [*Betula pendula* (silver birch) and related species.] **2** (**the birch**) chiefly historical a formal punishment in which a person is flogged with a bundle of birch twigs. ■ v. chiefly historical punish with the birch.
– DERIVATIVES **birchen** adj. (archaic).
– ORIGIN Old English, of Germanic origin.

bird ■ n. **1** a warm-blooded egg-laying vertebrate animal of a class distinguished by the possession of feathers, wings, and a beak, and typically by being able to fly. [Class Aves.] **2** informal a person of a specified kind or character: *she's a sharp old bird*. **3** Brit. informal a young woman or girlfriend.
– PHRASES **the bird has flown** the person one is looking for has escaped or left. **the birds and the bees** informal basic facts about sex and reproduction, as told to a child. **do (one's) bird** Brit. informal serve a prison sentence. [*bird* from rhyming slang *birdlime* 'time'.] **flip someone the bird** US stick one's middle finger up at someone as a sign of contempt or anger. (**strictly**) **for the birds** informal not worthy of consideration. **give someone the bird** Brit. informal boo or jeer at someone.
– ORIGIN Old English *brid* 'chick, fledgling'.

birdbrain ■ n. informal a stupid person.
– DERIVATIVES **birdbrained** adj.

bird cherry ■ n. a small wild cherry tree, with bitter black fruit that is eaten by birds. [*Prunus padus*.]

bird-eating spider (also **bird spider**) ■ n. another term for TARANTULA (in sense 1).

birder ■ n. informal a birdwatcher.

bird flu ■ n. a severe, often fatal, type of influenza that affects birds, especially poultry, and that can also be fatal to humans.

birdie ■ n. (pl. -ies) **1** informal a little bird. **2** Golf a score of one stroke under par at a hole. ■ v. (**birdying**) Golf play (a hole) with a score of one stroke under par.
– ORIGIN C18: diminutive of BIRD; the golf term from US slang *bird*, denoting any first-rate thing.

birding ■ n. informal birdwatching.

birdlime ■ n. a sticky substance spread on to twigs to trap small birds.

bird of paradise ■ n. **1** (pl. **birds of paradise**) a tropical Australasian bird, the male of which is noted for the beauty and brilliance of its plumage and its spectacular courtship display. [Family Paradisaeidae: many species.] **2** (also **bird of paradise flower**) a southern African plant which bears a showy flower with a long projecting tongue. [*Strelitzia regina* and related species.]

bird of passage ■ n. **1** dated a migratory bird. **2** a person who passes through a place without staying for long.

bird of prey ■ n. a bird that feeds on animal flesh and typically has a hooked bill and sharp talons (e.g. an eagle, hawk, falcon, or owl); a raptor.

bird pepper ■ n. a tropical American capsicum pepper which is thought to be the ancestor of both sweet and chilli peppers. [*Capsicum annuum* var. *glabriusculum*.]
▶ the small, red, very hot fruit of this plant.

bird's-eye chilli ■ n. a small very hot chilli pepper.

bird's-eye maple ■ n. the wood of an American maple with eye-like markings, used in decorative woodwork.

bird's-eye view ■ n. a general view from above.

bird's-foot trefoil ■ n. a small leguminous plant which has three-lobed leaves, yellow flowers streaked with red, and triple pods that resemble the feet of a bird. [*Lotus corniculatus*.]

birdshot ■ n. the smallest size of shot for sporting rifles or other guns.

bird snake ■ n. another term for TWIG SNAKE.

bird's-nesting ■ n. the practice of hunting for birds' nests in order to take the eggs.

bird's nest soup ■ n. (in Chinese cookery) a soup made from the dried gelatinous coating of the nests of swifts and other birds.

birdsong ■ n. the musical vocalizations of birds.

birdstrike ■ n. a collision of a bird and an aircraft.

bird table ■ n. a small platform or table in a garden on which food for birds is placed.

birdwatching ■ n. the practice of observing birds in their natural environment as a hobby.
–DERIVATIVES **birdwatcher** n.

birefringent /ˌbaɪrɪˈfrɪn(d)ʒ(ə)nt/ ■ adj. Physics having two different refractive indices.
–DERIVATIVES **birefringence** n.

biretta /bɪˈretə/ ■ n. a square cap with three flat projections on top, worn by Roman Catholic clergymen.
–ORIGIN C16: from Italian *berretta* or Spanish *birreta*, from late Latin *birrus* 'hooded cape'.

biriani /ˌbɪrɪˈɑːni/ (also **biriyani, biryani**, or S. African **breyani**) ■ n. an Indian dish made with highly seasoned rice and meat, fish, or vegetables.
–PHRASES (**want**) **breyani every day** S. African (expect) endless good fortune or success.
–ORIGIN Urdu, from Persian, from *biriyān* 'fried, grilled'.

Birman /ˈbɜːmən/ ■ n. a cat of a long-haired breed, typically with a cream body and dark head, tail, and legs.
–ORIGIN var. of BURMAN.

biro /ˈbaɪrəʊ/ ■ n. (pl. **-os**) Brit. trademark a kind of ballpoint pen.
–ORIGIN 1940s: named after László József *Biró*, Hungarian inventor of the ballpoint.

birth ■ n. **1** the emergence of a baby or other young from the body of its mother; the start of life as a physically separate being. **2** the beginning of something. ▶ origin, descent, or ancestry: *he is of noble birth*. ■ v. chiefly N. Amer. give birth to.
–PHRASES **give birth** bear a child or young.
–DERIVATIVES **birthing** n.
–ORIGIN Middle English: from Old Norse *byrth*; rel. to BEAR¹.

birth certificate ■ n. an official document recording a person's birth and identifying them by name, place and date of birth, and parentage.

birth control ■ n. the practice of preventing unwanted pregnancies, especially by use of contraception.

birthday ■ n. the annual anniversary of the day on which a person was born. ▶ the day of one's birth.
–PHRASES **in one's birthday suit** humorous naked.

Birthday Honours ■ pl. n. (in Britain) the titles and decorations awarded on a sovereign's official birthday.

birthing pool ■ n. a large circular bath in which a woman may give birth.

birthmark ■ n. a coloured mark on the body which is there from birth.

birth mother ■ n. a woman who has given birth to a child, as opposed to an adoptive mother.

birth parent ■ n. a biological as opposed to an adoptive parent.

birthplace ■ n. the place where a person was born.

birth rate ■ n. the number of live births per thousand of population per year.

birthright ■ n. a particular right of possession or privilege that a person has from birth, especially as an eldest son.
▶ a natural or moral right, possessed by everyone.

birth sign ■ n. Astrology the zodiacal sign through which the sun is passing when a person is born.

birthstone ■ n. a gemstone popularly associated with the month or astrological sign of a person's birth.

biryani ■ n. variant spelling of BIRIANI.

bis- /bɪs/ ■ comb. form Chemistry forming the names of compounds containing two groups identically substituted or coordinated: *bis(2-aminoethyl) ether*.

biscotti /bɪˈskɒti/ ■ pl. n. small rectangular Italian biscuits made with nuts.
–ORIGIN from Italian.

biscuit ■ n. **1** Brit. a small, flat, crisp unleavened cake. ▶ N. Amer. a small, soft round cake like a scone. **2** porcelain or other pottery which has been fired but not glazed. **3** a light brown colour. **4** a small flat piece of wood used in carpentry to join two larger pieces of wood together, fitting into slots in each.
–PHRASES **take the biscuit** (or chiefly N. Amer. **cake**) informal be the most remarkable or foolish of its kind.
–DERIVATIVES **biscuity** adj.
–ORIGIN Middle English: from Old French *bescuit*, from Latin *bis* 'twice' + *coctus*, from *coquere* 'to cook' (because biscuits were orig. first baked and then dried out in a slow oven).

bisect ■ v. divide into two parts.
–DERIVATIVES **bisection** n. **bisector** n.
–ORIGIN C17: from BI- + Latin *secare* 'to cut'.

bisexual ■ adj. **1** sexually attracted to both men and women. **2** Biology having characteristics of both sexes. ■ n. a person who is sexually attracted to both men and women.
–DERIVATIVES **bisexuality** n.

bishop ■ n. **1** a senior member of the Christian clergy, usually in charge of a diocese and empowered to confer holy orders. **2** (also **bishop bird**) an African weaver bird, the male of which has red, orange, yellow, or black plumage. [Genus *Euplectes*: several species.] **3** a chess piece, typically with its top shaped like a mitre, that can move in any direction along a diagonal.
–ORIGIN Old English *biscop*, from Greek *episkopos* 'overseer', from *epi* 'above' + *-skopos* '-looking'.

bishopric /ˈbɪʃəprɪk/ ■ n. the office or rank of a bishop.
▶ a diocese.
–ORIGIN Old English, from *bisceop* (see BISHOP) + *rīce* 'realm'.

bishop suffragan ■ n. see SUFFRAGAN.

bisley ■ n. S. African any full-bore target rifle-shooting competition.
–ORIGIN 1920s: named after *Bisley* in southern England, the site of the British national rifle range.

bismillah /bɪsˈmɪlə/ ■ exclam. in the name of God (an invocation used by Muslims at the beginning of an undertaking).
–ORIGIN from Arabic *bi-smi-llāh(i)*, the first word of the Koran.

bismuth /ˈbɪzməθ/ ■ n. the chemical element of atomic number 83, a brittle reddish-tinged grey metal. (Symbol: **Bi**)
–ORIGIN C17: from German *Wismut*.

bison /ˈbaɪs(ə)n/ ■ n. (pl. same) a humpbacked shaggy-haired wild ox. [*Bison bison* (the N. American buffalo) and *B. bonasus* (Europe, now only Poland).]
–ORIGIN Middle English: from Latin, of Germanic origin.

bisque¹ /bɪsk, biːsk/ ■ n. a rich soup made from lobster or other shellfish.
–ORIGIN French, 'crayfish soup'.

bisque² /bɪsk/ ■ n. another term for **BISCUIT** (in sense 2).

bistre /ˈbɪstə/ (US also **bister**) ■ n. a brownish-yellow pigment made from the soot of burnt wood.
– ORIGIN C18: from French.

bistro /ˈbiːstrəʊ, ˈbɪs-/ ■ n. (pl. **-os**) a small, inexpensive restaurant.
– ORIGIN 1920S: French; perhaps rel. to *bistouille* 'bad alcohol', perhaps from Russian *bystro* 'rapidly'.

bisulphate (US **bisulfate**) ■ n. Chemistry a salt of the anion HSO_4^-.

bit¹ ■ n. **1** a small piece, quantity, or extent of something. **2** informal a set of actions or ideas associated with a specific group or activity: *she did her theatrical bit*. **3** informal a girl or young woman.
– PHRASES **a bit** somewhat. **bit by bit** gradually. **a bit of a —— 1** used to suggest that something is not severe or extreme: *a bit of an accident*. **2** denoting a young person or one of slight build: *you're just a bit of a girl yourself*. **a bit of all right** Brit. informal an attractive or pleasing person or thing. **bit of fluff** (or **skirt** or **stuff**) Brit. informal a woman regarded in sexual terms. **bit on the side** informal **1** a person with whom one is unfaithful to one's partner. **2** money earned outside one's normal job. **do one's bit** informal make a useful contribution. **to bits 1** into pieces. **2** informal very much; to a great degree.
– ORIGIN Old English *bita* 'bite, mouthful', of Germanic origin.

bit² past of **BITE**.

bit³ ■ n. **1** a metal mouthpiece attached to a bridle, used to control a horse. **2** a tool or piece for boring or drilling. ▸ the cutting or gripping part of a plane, pincers, or other tool. ▸ the part of a key that engages with the lock lever. ▸ the copper head of a soldering iron. ■ v. put a bit into the mouth of (a horse).
– PHRASES **above** (or **behind**) **the bit** (of a horse) carrying its head too high (or with the chin tucked in) so that it evades correct contact with the bit. **get** (or **take** or **have**) **the bit between** (or N. Amer. **in**) **one's teeth** begin to tackle a problem or task in a determined way. **off the bit** (or **bridle**) (of a horse) ridden on a loose rein to allow it to gallop freely. **on the bit** (or **bridle**) (of a horse) ridden with (and calmly accepting) a light but firm contact on the mouth.
– DERIVATIVES **-bitted** adj.
– ORIGIN Old English *bite* 'biting, a bite', of Germanic origin.

bit⁴ ■ n. Computing a unit of information expressed as either a 0 or 1 in binary notation.
– ORIGIN 1940S: blend of **BINARY** and **DIGIT**.

bitch ■ n. **1** a female dog, wolf, fox, or otter. **2** informal a woman whom one dislikes or considers to be malicious or unpleasant. **3** (**a bitch**) informal a difficult or unpleasant thing or situation. ■ v. informal make malicious or spitefully critical comments.
– ORIGIN Old English, of Germanic origin.

bitching (also **bitchen**) informal, chiefly US ■ adj. excellent. ■ adv. extremely.

bitchy ■ adj. (**-ier**, **-iest**) informal malicious or spitefully critical.
– DERIVATIVES **bitchily** adv. **bitchiness** n.

bite ■ v. (past **bit**; past part. **bitten**) **1** (of a person or animal) use the teeth to cut into something. ▸ (of a snake, insect, or spider) wound with a sting, pincers, or fangs. **2** (**bite something back**) refrain with difficulty from saying something. **3** (of a tool, tyre, boot, etc.) grip or take hold on a surface. ▸ (of an object) press into a part of the body, causing pain. **4** (of an acid) corrode a surface. **5** (of a fish) take the bait or lure on the end of a fishing line into the mouth. **6** (of a policy or situation) take effect, with unpleasant consequences: *the cuts in art education were starting to bite*. ▸ informal annoy or worry: *what's biting you today?* ■ n. **1** an act or instance of biting. ▸ a piece cut off by biting. ▸ Dentistry the bringing together of the teeth in occlusion. **2** informal a quick snack. **3** a sensation of sharpness or pungency. ▸ a feeling of cold in the air or wind.
– PHRASES **be bitten by the —— bug** develop a passionate interest in a specified activity. **bite the bullet** decide to do something difficult or unpleasant that one has been hesitating over. [from the old custom of giving wounded soldiers a bullet to bite on when undergoing surgery without anaesthetic.] **bite the dust** informal die or be killed. **bite the hand that feeds one** deliberately hurt or offend a benefactor. **bite off more than one can chew** take on a commitment one cannot fulfil. **the biter bitten** (or **bit**) indicating that someone is being treated in the same way as they have treated others. **bite one's tongue** make a desperate effort to avoid saying something. **once bitten, twice shy** an unpleasant experience induces caution. **one could have bitten one's tongue off** one profoundly regrets having said something.
– DERIVATIVES **biter** n.
– ORIGIN Old English, of Germanic origin.

biting ■ adj. **1** (of wind or air) painfully cold. **2** (of wit or criticism) harsh or cruel.
– DERIVATIVES **bitingly** adv.

bitmap Computing ■ n. a representation in which each item corresponds to one or more bits of information, especially the information used to control the display of a computer screen. ■ v. (**-mapped**, **-mapping**) represent as a bitmap.

bit part ■ n. a small acting role in a play or a film.

bit rate ■ n. Electronics the number of bits per second that can be transmitted along a digital network.

bitstream /ˈbɪtstriːm/ ■ n. Electronics a stream of data in binary form.

bitten past participle of **BITE**.

bitter ■ adj. **1** having a sharp, pungent taste or smell; not sweet. **2** causing pain or unhappiness. ▸ feeling or showing angry hurt or resentment. ▸ (of a conflict) harsh and acrimonious. **3** (of wind or weather) intensely cold. ■ n. **1** Brit. beer that is strongly flavoured with hops and has a bitter taste. **2** (**bitters**) [treated as sing.] liquor that is flavoured with bitter plant extracts and used as an additive in cocktails.
– PHRASES **to the bitter end** to the very end, in spite of harsh difficulties.
– DERIVATIVES **bitterly** adv. **bitterness** n.
– ORIGIN Old English, of Germanic origin.

bitter aloes ■ n. another term for aloes (see **ALOE** (sense 1)).

bitter apple ■ n. another term for **COLOCYNTH**.

bitter-ender ■ n. **1** a diehard. **2** (also **bitter-einder**) S. African historical a Boer who refused to surrender at the end of the Anglo-Boer War of 1899–1902.
– ORIGIN C19 (orig. US).

bitter lemon ■ n. Brit. a carbonated semi-sweet soft drink flavoured with lemons.

bittern /ˈbɪtən/ ■ n. a marshbird of the heron family with brown streaked plumage, noted for the male's deep booming call. [*Botaurus stellaris* (southern Africa and Eurasia), *B. lentiginosus* (N. America), and other species.]
– ORIGIN Middle English *bitore*, from Latin *butio* 'bittern' + *taurus* 'bull' (because of its call).

bitter orange ■ n. another term for **SEVILLE ORANGE**.

bittersweet ■ adj. **1** sweet with a bitter aftertaste. **2** arousing pleasure tinged with sadness or pain.

bitty ■ adj. (**-ier**, **-iest**) informal **1** chiefly Brit. made up of small parts that seem unrelated. **2** [in combination] N. Amer. tiny: *a little-bitty girl*.
– DERIVATIVES **bittily** adv. **bittiness** n.

bitumen /ˈbɪtjʊmən/ ■ n. a black viscous mixture of hydrocarbons obtained naturally or as a residue from petroleum distillation, used for road surfacing and roofing.
– DERIVATIVES **bituminous** adj.
– ORIGIN Middle English: from Latin.

bituminize /bɪˈtjuːmɪnaɪz/ (also **-ise**) ■ v. convert into or treat with bitumen.
– DERIVATIVES **bituminization** (also **-isation**) n.

bituminous coal ■ n. black coal having a relatively high volatile content and burning with a characteristically bright smoky flame.

bitwise ■ adj. Computing denoting an operator in a programming language which manipulates the individual bits in a byte or word.

bivalence /baɪˈveɪl(ə)ns/ ■ n. Logic the existence of only two states or truth values (e.g. true and false).

bivalent ■ adj. **1** /'bɪv(ə)l(ə)nt/ Biology (of homologous chromosomes) associated in pairs. **2** /baɪ'veɪl(ə)nt/ Chemistry another term for DIVALENT. ■ n. /'bɪv(ə)l(ə)nt/ Biology a pair of homologous chromosomes.
– ORIGIN C19: from BI- + Latin *valent-*, *valere* 'be strong'.

bivalve ■ n. an aquatic mollusc which has a compressed body enclosed within two hinged shells, such as an oyster, mussel, or scallop. [Class Bivalvia.] ■ adj. **1** (also **bivalved**) (of a mollusc or other aquatic invertebrate) having a hinged double shell. **2** Botany having two valves.

bivariate /baɪ'vɛːrɪət/ ■ adj. Statistics involving or depending on two variates.

bivouac /'bɪvʊak, 'bɪvwak/ ■ n. a temporary camp without tents or cover. ■ v. (**bivouacked,**) **bivouacking** stay in such a camp.
– ORIGIN C18: from French, prob. from Swiss German *Bîwacht* 'additional guard at night'.

bivvy informal ■ n. (pl. **-ies**) a small tent or temporary shelter. ■ v. (**-ies, -ied**) use such a tent or shelter.
– ORIGIN C20: abbrev. of BIVOUAC.

biweekly ■ adj. & adv. appearing or taking place every two weeks or twice a week. ■ n. (pl. **-ies**) a periodical that appears biweekly.

biyearly ■ adj. & adv. appearing or taking place every two years or twice a year.

biz ■ n. informal short for BUSINESS.
– ORIGIN C19 (orig. US): abbrev.

bizarre /bɪ'zɑː/ ■ adj. strange; unusual.
– DERIVATIVES **bizarrely** adv. **bizarreness** n.
– ORIGIN C17: from Italian *bizzarro* 'angry'.

Bk ■ symb. the chemical element berkelium.

bk ■ abbrev. book.

blab informal ■ v. (**blabbed, blabbing**) reveal secrets by indiscreet talk. ■ n. a person who blabs.
– ORIGIN Middle English: prob. of Germanic origin; imitative.

blabber informal ■ v. talk indiscreetly or excessively. ■ n. a person who blabbers. ▶ indiscreet or excessive talk.

blabbermouth ■ n. informal a person who talks excessively or indiscreetly.

black ■ adj. **1** of the very darkest colour due to the absence of or complete absorption of light. ▶ deeply stained with dirt. ▶ (of coffee or tea) served without milk. **2** of or relating to a human group having dark-coloured skin, especially of African ancestry. **3** characterized by tragedy, disaster, or despair. ▶ (of humour) presenting tragic or harrowing situations in comic terms. ▶ full of anger or hatred. **4** (of a ski run) of the highest level of difficulty. **5** of or denoting the suits spades and clubs in a pack of cards. ■ n. **1** black colour or pigment. ▶ black clothes or material, worn as a sign of mourning. **2** a member of a dark-skinned people, especially one of African ancestry. ▶ S. African ((**the**) **blacks**) chiefly offensive black South Africans. **3** (**Black**) the player of the black pieces in chess or draughts. ■ v. **1** make black, especially by the application of black polish, make-up, etc. **2** (**black something out**) make a room or building dark by extinguishing lights, covering windows, etc. ▶ obscure something completely. ▶ (of a television screen) go blank. **3** (**black out**) (of a person) undergo a sudden and temporary loss of consciousness. **4** Brit. dated refuse to deal with (goods or people) or undertake (work), as a form of industrial action. **5** (of a television company) decide not to broadcast a controversial programme.
– PHRASES **black someone's eye** hit someone in the eye so as to cause bruising. **in the black** not owing any money. **in someone's black books** informal in disfavour with someone. **look on the black side** informal view a situation from a pessimistic angle.
– DERIVATIVES **blackish** adj. **blackly** adv. **blackness** n.
– ORIGIN Old English, of Germanic origin.

blackamoor /'blakəmɔː, -mʊə/ ■ n. archaic a black African or a very dark-skinned person.
– ORIGIN C16: from BLACK + MOOR.

black and tan ■ n. (**Black and Tans**) historical an armed force recruited by the British government to fight against republican groups in Ireland in 1921.
– ORIGIN 1920S: so named because of the khaki and black colours of their uniform.

black empowerment

black and white ■ adj. **1** consisting of or displaying images in black, white, and shades of grey rather than in colour. **2** (of a situation or debate) involving clearly defined opposing principles or issues. ■ n. US informal a police car.

black art ■ n. **1** (also **black arts**) another term for BLACK MAGIC. **2** a technique or practice considered mysterious and sinister.

blackball ■ v. reject or vote against (a candidate applying to become a member of a private club).
– ORIGIN C18: from the practice of registering an adverse vote by placing a black ball in a ballot box.

black bean ■ n. **1** a cultivated variety of soy bean, used fermented in oriental cooking. **2** a variety of the common bean used widely in Latin American and Creole cooking. [*Phaseolus vulgaris.*]

black bear ■ n. a medium-sized forest-dwelling bear with blackish fur and a paler face. [*Ursus americanus* (America) and *Selenarctos thibetanus* (E. Asia).]

black belt ■ n. a black belt worn by an expert in judo, karate, and other martial arts.

blackberry ■ n. (pl. **-ies**) **1** an edible soft fruit consisting of a cluster of soft purple-black drupels. **2** the prickly climbing shrub of the rose family which bears this fruit. [*Rubus fruticosus.*] ■ v. (**-ies, -ied**) [usu. as noun **blackberrying**] gather blackberries.

black bile ■ n. (in medieval science and medicine) one of the four bodily humours, believed to be associated with a melancholy temperament.
– ORIGIN C18: translation of Greek *melankholia* (see MELANCHOLY).

blackbird ■ n. **1** a Eurasian thrush of which the male has all-black plumage and a yellow bill, and the female is brown. [*Turdus merula.*] **2** an American songbird with largely black plumage. [*Agelaius phoeniceus* (red-winged blackbird) and other species, family Icteridae.]

blackboard ■ n. a large board with a smooth dark surface for writing on with chalk.

black body ■ n. Physics a hypothetical perfect absorber and radiator of energy, with no reflecting power.

black box ■ n. a flight recorder in an aircraft.

black bread ■ n. a coarse dark-coloured type of rye bread.

black bun ■ n. rich fruit cake in a pastry case, traditionally eaten in Scotland at New Year.

black-chip ■ adj. S. African denoting a company owned or managed by black people, or controlled by black shareholders.
– DERIVATIVES **black chip** n.

blackcock ■ n. (pl. same) the male of the black grouse.

black consciousness (also **Black Consciousness**) ■ n. a political movement and ideology seeking to unite black people in affirming their common identity. ▶ S. African a campaign based on this ideology initiated amongst black students in the 1960s with the aim of fighting apartheid.

blackcurrant ■ n. **1** a small round edible black berry which grows in loose hanging clusters. **2** the widely cultivated shrub which bears this fruit. [*Ribes nigrum.*]

black diamond ■ n. **1** S. African a middle-class black professional or business person. **2** informal a lump of coal. **3** a dark, opaque form of diamond.

black dog ■ n. informal melancholy or depression represented metaphorically: *I'm happier, but the black dog is still there.*
– ORIGIN C19: from a name used during the British Queen Anne's reign for a base silver coin.

black eagle ■ n. another term for VERREAUX'S EAGLE.

black economy ■ n. the part of a country's economic activity which is not recorded or taxed by its government.

black empowerment (also **black economic empowerment**) ■ n. S. African the encouragement of black ownership and control of South Africa's economic assets. ■ adj. denoting companies, organizations, or policies committed to encouraging control by black people of South Africa's economic assets.

blacken

blacken ■ v. **1** become or make black or dark. **2** damage or destroy (someone's reputation).

black eye ■ n. an area of bruised skin around the eye resulting from a blow.

black-eyed bean (also **black-eye bean**, US **black-eyed pea**) ■ n. **1** a creamy-white edible bean with a black mark at the point where it was attached to the pod. **2** the plant which produces these beans. [*Vigna sinensis*.]

black-eyed Susan ■ n. **1** a slender tropical climbing plant having flowers with yellowish petals and a dark centre. [*Thunbergia alata*.] **2** a type of cultivated rudbeckia. [*Rudbeckia hirta*.]

blackface ■ n. **1** a sheep of a breed with a black face. **2** the make-up used by a non-black performer playing a black role.

blackfish ■ n. (pl. same or **-fishes**) **1** a large, dark open-ocean fish related to the perches. [*Centrolophus niger*.] **2** a salmon just after spawning. **3** any of various other dark-coloured fish. **4** another term for **PILOT WHALE**.

black flag ■ n. **1** historical a pirate's ensign, featuring a white skull and crossbones on a black background. **2** historical a black flag hoisted outside a prison to announce an execution. **3** Motor Racing a black flag used to signal to a driver that he must stop at the pits as a punishment for a misdemeanour.

blackfly ■ n. (pl. same or **-flies**) **1** a black or dark green aphid which is a common pest of crops and gardens. [*Aphis fabae* and other species.] **2** a small black bloodsucking fly which can transmit a number of serious diseases. [*Simulium* and other genera.]

Blackfoot ■ n. (pl. same or **Blackfeet**) **1** a member of a confederacy of North American Indian peoples of the north-western plains consisting of three closely related peoples: the Blackfoot proper or Siksika, the Bloods, and the Peigan. **2** the Algonquian language of this people.

Black Forest gateau (N. Amer. **Black Forest cake**) ■ n. a chocolate sponge layered with cherries and cream and topped with chocolate icing.

Black Friar ■ n. a friar of the Dominican order (who wear black habits).

black frost ■ n. frost which does not have a white surface.

black grouse ■ n. (pl. same) a large European grouse of which the male has glossy blue-black plumage and a lyre-shaped tail. [*Tetrao tetrix*.]

blackguard /ˈblagɑːd, -gəd/ dated ■ n. a man who behaves in a dishonourable or contemptible way. ■ v. disparage or denounce.
– DERIVATIVES **blackguardly** adj.
– ORIGIN C16: from **BLACK** + **GUARD**.

blackhead ■ n. a plug of sebum in a hair follicle, darkened by oxidation.

blackhead Persian (also **blackheaded Persian**) ■ n. a fat-tailed sheep of an African breed, with a distinctive black head and neck.

black hole ■ n. Astronomy a region of space having a gravitational field so intense that no matter or radiation can escape.

black ice ■ n. a transparent coating of ice on a road surface.

blacking ■ n. black paste or polish, especially that used on shoes.

blackjack ■ n. **1** chiefly N. Amer. a gambling card game in which players try to acquire cards with a face value totalling 21 and no more. **2** a weed related to the bur-marigold, with barbed black seeds. [*Bidens pilosa*.] **3** N. Amer. a flexible lead-filled truncheon. **4** historical a pirate's black flag.

Black Jew ■ n. another term for **FALASHA**.

black kite ■ n. a bird of prey with dark plumage and a slightly forked tail, feeding mainly by scavenging. [*Milvus migrans*.]

blacklead ■ n. another term for **GRAPHITE**. ■ v. polish (metal, especially cast iron) with graphite.

blackleg Brit. derogatory ■ n. a person who continues working when fellow workers are on strike. ■ v. (**-legged**, **-legging**) continue working when one's fellow workers are on strike.

black letter ■ n. an ornate early bold style of type.

black light ■ n. ultraviolet or infrared radiation, invisible to the eye.

blacklist ■ n. a list of people or groups regarded as unacceptable or untrustworthy. ■ v. put on a blacklist.

black locust ■ n. a tree native to North America with compound leaves and dense hanging clusters of fragrant white flowers, widely grown as an ornamental. [*Robinia pseudoacacia*.]

black lung ■ n. chiefly N. Amer. pneumoconiosis caused by inhalation of coal dust.

black magic ■ n. magic involving the supposed invocation of evil spirits for evil purposes.

blackmail ■ n. the action of demanding money from someone in return for not revealing discreditable information. ▸ the use of threats or unfair manipulation in an attempt to influence someone's actions. ■ v. subject to blackmail.
– DERIVATIVES **blackmailer** n.
– ORIGIN C16 (denoting protection money levied by Scottish chiefs): from **BLACK** + obsolete *mail* 'tribute, rent', from Old Norse *mál* 'speech, agreement'.

Black Maria ■ n. **1** informal a police vehicle for transporting prisoners. **2** a card game in which players try to avoid winning tricks containing the queen of spades or any hearts. ▸ a name for the queen of spades in this game.
– ORIGIN C19 (orig. US): said to be named after a black woman, *Maria* Lee, who kept a boarding house in Boston and helped police in escorting drunk and disorderly customers to jail.

black mark ■ n. informal a note or record of a person's misdemeanour or discreditable action.

black market ■ n. an illegal trade in officially controlled or scarce commodities.
– DERIVATIVES **black marketeer** n.

black mass ■ n. a travesty of the Roman Catholic Mass in worship of the Devil.

black money ■ n. income illegally obtained or not declared for tax purposes.

black Muslim ■ n. a member of the Nation of Islam, a black Islamic sect advocating a separate black nation.

black nationalism ■ n. the advocacy of the national civil rights of black people, especially in the US.

blackout ■ n. **1** a period when all lights must be turned out or covered to prevent them being seen by the enemy during an air raid. ▸ (**blackouts**) dark curtains put up in windows during an air raid. ▸ a sudden failure or dimming of electric lights. **2** a temporary loss of consciousness. **3** an official suppression of information: *a total news blackout*.

Black Panther ■ n. a member of a US Black Power organization.

black powder ■ n. gunpowder.

Black Power ■ n. a movement in support of rights and political power for black people.

black pudding ■ n. Brit. a black sausage containing pork, dried pig's blood, and suet.

black rhinoceros ■ n. an African rhinoceros with a prehensile upper lip and two horns. [*Diceros bicornis*.]

black rot ■ n. a fungal or bacterial disease of plants producing blackening, shrivelling, and rotting.

black sheep ■ n. informal a member of a family or group who is regarded as a disgrace to it.

blackshirt ■ n. a member of a Fascist organization, in particular of an Italian paramilitary group before and during the Second World War.

blacksmith ■ n. a person who makes and repairs things in iron by hand. ▸ a farrier.

black spot ■ n. **1** a place marked by a particular problem: *an accident black spot*. **2** S. African historical land lived on by black people in an area predominantly owned by white people, which was destined for expropriation under apartheid legislation. **3** a fungal or bacterial disease of plants, producing black blotches on the leaves.

black swan ■ n. a mainly black swan with white flight feathers, native to Australia and introduced widely elsewhere. [*Cygnus atratus*.]

black tea ■ n. tea of the most usual type, that is fully fermented before drying. Compare with GREEN TEA.

blackthorn ■ n. **1** a southern African tree with short hooked thorns. [*Acacia mellifera*.] **2** a thorny European shrub which bears white flowers before the leaves appear, followed by astringent blue-black fruits (sloes). [*Prunus spinosa*.]

black tie ■ n. men's formal evening wear.

blacktop ■ n. chiefly N. Amer. asphalt, tarmacadam, or other black material used for surfacing roads.

black turf ■ n. another term for TURF (in sense 2).

black velvet ■ n. a drink consisting of a mixture of stout and champagne.

black water ■ n. technical waste water and sewage from toilets. Compare with GREY WATER.

blackwater fever ■ n. a severe form of malaria in which blood cells are rapidly destroyed, resulting in dark urine.

black widow ■ n. a highly venomous spider having a black body with red markings on the dorsal side of the abdomen. [Genus *Latrodectus*, especially *L. indistinctus*.]

blackwood ■ n. **1** a tropical hardwood tree which produces high-quality dark wood. [*Dalbergia melanoxylon* (Africa) and other species.] **2** a species of wattle, native to eastern Australia, commonly found in South Africa. [*Acacia melanoxylon*.]

bladder ■ n. **1** a muscular membranous sac in the abdomen which receives urine from the kidneys and stores it for excretion. **2** an inflated or hollow flexible bag or chamber.
– ORIGIN Old English, of Germanic origin, rel. to BLOW¹.

bladder nut ■ n. a shrub or small tree which bears white flowers and inflated seed capsules. [*Diospyros whyteana* (southern Africa) and other species.]

bladderwrack ■ n. a common brown shoreline seaweed with tough strap-like fronds containing air bladders that give buoyancy. [*Fucus vesiculosus*.]

bladdy ■ adj. & adv. S. African variant spelling of BLOODY².

blade ■ n. **1** the flat cutting edge of a knife or other tool or weapon. **2** the broad flat part of an oar, leaf, or other object. **3** a long narrow leaf of grass. **4** a shoulder bone in a joint of meat, or the joint itself. **5** informal, dated a dashing or energetic young man.
– DERIVATIVES **bladed** adj.
– ORIGIN Old English, of Germanic origin.

blag Brit. informal ■ n. **1** a violent robbery or raid. **2** an act of using clever talk or lying to obtain something. ■ v. (**blagged, blagging**) **1** steal in a violent robbery or raid. **2** obtain by clever talk or lying.
– ORIGIN C19: perhaps from French *blaguer* 'tell lies'.

blah informal ■ used to substitute for actual words where they are felt to be too tedious or lengthy to give in full.

blame ■ v. assign responsibility for a fault or wrong to. ■ n. responsibility for a fault or wrong.
– PHRASES **be to blame** be responsible for a fault or wrong.
– DERIVATIVES **blameable** (US also **blamable**) adj. **blameful** adj. **blameworthiness** n. **blameworthy** adj.
– ORIGIN Middle English: from Old French *blamer*, *blasmer*, from var. of eccles. Latin *blasphemare*, from Greek *blasphēmein* (see BLASPHEME).

blame game ■ n. informal a situation in which one party blames others rather than attempting to seek a solution.
– DERIVATIVES **blame-gaming** n.

blameless ■ adj. innocent of wrongdoing.
– DERIVATIVES **blamelessly** adv. **blamelessness** n.

blanch /blɑːn(t)ʃ/ ■ v. **1** make or become white or pale. **2** prepare (vegetables) for freezing or further cooking by immersing briefly in boiling water. ▸ [often as adj. **blanched**] peel (almonds) by scalding them.
– ORIGIN Middle English: from Old French *blanchir*, from *blanc* 'white', of Germanic origin.

blancmange /bləˈmɒnʒ, -ˈmɑːnʒ/ ■ n. a sweet opaque gelatinous dessert made with flavoured cornflour and milk.
– ORIGIN Middle English *blancmanger*: from Old French *blanc mangier*, from *blanc* 'white' + *mangier* 'eat'.

blanco /ˈblaŋkəʊ/ ■ n. Brit. a white substance used for whitening belts and other items of military equipment. ■ v. (**-oes, -oed**) whiten with blanco.
– ORIGIN C19: from French *blanc* 'white', of Germanic origin.

bland ■ adj. lacking strong features or characteristics and therefore uninteresting. ▸ (of food or drink) lacking flavour or seasoning; insipid.
– DERIVATIVES **blandly** adv. **blandness** n.
– ORIGIN Middle English: from Latin *blandus* 'soft, smooth'.

blandishments ■ pl. n. flattery intended to persuade or cajole.

blank ■ adj. **1** not marked or decorated; bare, empty, or plain. **2** not comprehending or reacting. **3** complete; absolute: *a blank refusal to discuss the issue.* **4** used euphemistically in place of an adjective regarded as obscene. ■ n. **1** a space left to be filled in a document. **2** (also **blank cartridge**) a cartridge containing gunpowder but no bullet. **3** an empty space or period of time: *my mind was a total blank.* **4** an object with no mark or design on it, in particular a roughly cut disc or block intended for stamping or finishing. **5** a dash written instead of a word or letter, especially to avoid spelling out an obscene word. ■ v. **1** cause to appear blank or empty. **2** N. Amer. defeat without allowing the opponent to score.
– PHRASES **draw a blank** elicit no successful response.
– DERIVATIVES **blankly** adv. **blankness** n.
– ORIGIN Middle English: from Old French *blanc* 'white', of Germanic origin.

blank cheque ■ n. **1** a cheque with the amount left for the payee to fill in. **2** an unlimited freedom of action.

blanket ■ n. **1** a large piece of thick material used as a covering for warmth, as on a bed. **2** a thick mass or layer of a specified material: *a blanket of cloud.* **3** Printing a rubber surface used for transferring the image in ink from the plate to the paper in offset printing. ■ adj. covering all cases or instances; total: *a blanket ban on tobacco advertising.* ■ v. (**blanketed, blanketing**) **1** cover completely with a thick layer. **2** Nautical take wind from the sails of (another craft) by passing to windward.
– DERIVATIVES **blanketing** n.
– ORIGIN Middle English: from Old French *blanc* 'white', of Germanic origin.

blanket bog ■ n. an extensive flat peat bog formed in cool regions of high rainfall or humidity.

blanket finish ■ n. a very close finish in a race.

blanket stitch ■ n. a buttonhole stitch used on the edges of a blanket or other material too thick to be hemmed.

blanket weed ■ n. a common green freshwater alga forming mats of long filaments. [Genus *Spirogyra*.]

blank verse ■ n. verse without rhyme, especially that which uses iambic pentameters.

blanquette /blɒ̃ˈkɛt/ ■ n. a dish consisting of white meat in a white sauce.
– ORIGIN French, from *blanc* 'white'.

blaps /blaps/ ■ n. S. African informal a blunder.
– ORIGIN Afrikaans.

blare ■ v. sound loudly and harshly. ■ n. a loud, harsh sound.
– ORIGIN Middle English (in the sense 'roar, bellow'): from Middle Dutch *blaren* or Low German *blaren*; imitative.

blarney ■ n. talk intended to be charming or flattering (often considered especially typical of Irish people).
– ORIGIN C18: named after *Blarney* Castle in Ireland, where there is a stone said to give the gift of persuasive speech to anyone who kisses it.

blasé /ˈblɑːzeɪ/ ■ adj. unimpressed with or indifferent to something because of over-familiarity.
– ORIGIN C19: French, from *blaser* 'cloy', prob. of Germanic origin.

blaspheme /blasˈfiːm/ ■ v. speak irreverently about God or sacred things.
– DERIVATIVES **blasphemer** n.
– ORIGIN Middle English: from eccles. Latin *blasphemare* 'reproach, blaspheme', from Greek *blasphēmein*, from *blasphēmos* 'evil-speaking'.

blasphemy ■ n. (pl. **-ies**) profane or sacrilegious talk about God or sacred things.
– DERIVATIVES **blasphemous** adj. **blasphemously** adv.

blast /blɑːst/ ■ n. **1** a destructive wave of highly compressed air spreading outwards from an explosion. **2** a strong gust of wind or air. ▶ a strong current of air used in smelting. **3** a single loud note of a horn or whistle. **4** informal a severe reprimand. **5** informal an enjoyable experience or lively party. ■ v. **1** blow up or break apart with explosives. **2** (**blast off**) (of a rocket or spacecraft) take off from a launching site. **3** produce loud continuous music or noise. **4** informal criticize fiercely. **5** kick or strike (a ball) hard. **6** strike with divine anger (used as a curse): *damn and blast this awful place!* **7** chiefly poetic/literary (of wind) wither or shrivel (a plant). ■ exclam. informal expressing annoyance.
– PHRASES (**at**) **full blast** at maximum power or intensity.
– DERIVATIVES **blaster** n.
– ORIGIN Old English, of Germanic origin.

-blast ■ comb. form Biology denoting an embryonic cell or tissue: *erythroblast*. Compare with -CYTE.
– ORIGIN from Greek *blastos* 'germ, sprout'.

blasted ■ adj. informal **1** used to express annoyance: *make your own blasted coffee!* **2** drunk.

blast furnace ■ n. a smelting furnace in the form of a tower into which a blast of hot compressed air can be introduced, especially for smelting iron.

blasto- /ˈblæstəʊ/ ■ comb. form relating to germination: *blastoderm*.
– ORIGIN from Greek *blastos* 'germ, sprout'.

blastocyst ■ n. Embryology a mammalian blastula in which some differentiation of cells has occurred.

blastoderm ■ n. Embryology a blastula having the form of a disc of cells on top of the yolk.

blastomycosis /ˌblæstə(ʊ)maɪˈkəʊsɪs/ ■ n. Medicine a disease of the skin or internal organs caused by infection with parasitic fungi.
– ORIGIN from genus name *Blastomyces*.

blastula /ˈblæstjʊlə/ ■ n. (pl. **blastulae** /-liː/ or US **blastulas**) Embryology an animal embryo at the early stage of development when it is a hollow ball of cells.
– ORIGIN C19: from Greek *blastos* 'sprout'.

blatant /ˈbleɪt(ə)nt/ ■ adj. open and unashamed; flagrant.
– DERIVATIVES **blatancy** n. **blatantly** adv.
– ORIGIN C16: perhaps from Scots *blatand* 'bleating'.

blather /ˈblæðə/ (also **blither**) ■ v. talk long-windedly without making much sense. ■ n. long-winded talk with no real substance.
– ORIGIN Middle English: from Old Norse *blathra* 'talk nonsense', from *blathr* 'nonsense'.

blatjang /ˈblætjæŋ/ ■ n. S. African a relish made of dried fruit, vinegar, and chillies; chutney.
– ORIGIN C19: Afrikaans, from Malay *belachan*, a fish condiment.

blaxploitation /ˌblæksplɔɪˈteɪʃ(ə)n/ ■ n. the exploitation of black people with regard to stereotyped roles in films.

blaze[1] ■ n. **1** a very large or fiercely burning fire. **2** a very bright light or display of colour. **3** (**blazes**) informal used as a euphemism for 'hell': *go to blazes!* ■ v. **1** burn or shine fiercely or brightly. **2** shoot repeatedly or indiscriminately.
– PHRASES **like blazes** informal very fast or forcefully.
– DERIVATIVES **blazing** adj. **blazingly** adv.
– ORIGIN Old English 'torch, bright fire', of Germanic origin.

blaze[2] ■ n. **1** a white stripe down the face of a horse or other animal. **2** a cut made on a tree to mark a route. ■ v. (**blaze a trail**) **1** mark out a path or route. **2** be the first to do something; pioneer.
– ORIGIN C17: of Germanic origin; rel. to BLAZE[1].

blaze[3] ■ v. present (news) in a prominent or sensational manner.
– ORIGIN Middle English ('blow out on a trumpet'): from Middle Low German or Middle Dutch *blāzen* 'to blow'.

blazer ■ n. **1** a coloured jacket worn by schoolchildren or sports players as part of a uniform. **2** a man's plain jacket not forming part of a suit but considered appropriate for formal wear.

blazon /ˈbleɪz(ə)n/ ■ v. **1** display or report prominently or vividly. **2** Heraldry describe or depict (armorial bearings) in a correct heraldic manner. ■ n. Heraldry a correct description of armorial bearings. ▶ archaic a coat of arms.
– ORIGIN Middle English: from Old French *blason* 'shield'; verb influenced by BLAZE[3].

blazonry ■ n. Heraldry the art of describing or painting heraldic devices or armorial bearings. ▶ devices or bearings of this type.

bleach ■ v. **1** cause to become white or much lighter by a chemical process or by exposure to sunlight. **2** clean or sterilize with bleach. ■ n. a chemical used to bleach things and also to sterilize drains, sinks, etc.
– ORIGIN Old English, from *blǣc* 'pale', of Germanic origin.

bleacher ■ n. **1** a person or thing that bleaches. **2** N. Amer. a cheap bench seat in an uncovered part of a sports ground.

bleaching powder ■ n. a powder containing calcium hypochlorite, used to bleach materials.

bleak ■ adj. **1** bare and exposed to the elements. ▶ charmless and inhospitable; dreary. **2** (of a situation) not hopeful or encouraging.
– DERIVATIVES **bleakly** adv. **bleakness** n.
– ORIGIN Old English *blāc* 'shining, white', or from Old Norse *bleikr*; of Germanic origin.

bleary ■ adj. (**-ier**, **-iest**) (of the eyes) dull and unfocused from sleep or tiredness.
– DERIVATIVES **blearily** adv. **bleariness** n.

bleat ■ v. **1** (of a sheep or goat) make a characteristic weak, wavering cry. **2** speak or complain in a weak or foolish way. ■ n. **1** the weak, wavering cry of a sheep or goat. **2** a person's weak or foolish cry or complaint.
– ORIGIN Old English, imitative.

bleb ■ n. **1** a small blister on the skin. **2** a small bubble in glass or in a fluid.
– ORIGIN C17: var. of BLOB.

bleed ■ v. (past and past part. **bled**) **1** lose blood from the body as a result of injury or illness. **2** draw blood from (someone) as a former method of medical treatment. **3** (often in phr. **bleed someone dry**) informal drain of money or resources. **4** (of dye or colour) seep into an adjacent colour or area. ▶ Printing (of a design) be printed so that it runs off the page after trimming. **5** allow (fluid or gas) to escape from a closed system through a valve. ■ n. the action or an instance of bleeding.
– ORIGIN Old English, of Germanic origin.

bleeder ■ n. **1** Brit. informal a person regarded with contempt, disrespect, or pity: *poor little bleeder!* **2** informal a haemophiliac.

bleeding ■ adj. Brit. informal used for emphasis, or to express annoyance.

bleeding heart ■ n. **1** informal, derogatory a person considered to be excessively soft-hearted or liberal. **2** a cultivated plant with red or partly red heart-shaped flowers. [*Dicentra spectabilis* and other species.]

bleep ■ n. a short high-pitched sound made by an electronic device as a signal or to attract attention. ■ v. **1** (of an electronic device) make a bleep. **2** (in broadcasting) censor (a word or phrase) by substituting a bleep.
– DERIVATIVES **bleeper** n.
– ORIGIN 1950s: imitative.

blemish ■ n. **1** a small mark or flaw which spoils the appearance of something. **2** a moral defect or fault. ■ v. [often as adj. **blemished**] spoil the appearance of.
– ORIGIN Middle English: from Old French *ble(s)mir* 'make pale, injure'.

blench /blen(t)ʃ/ ■ v. make a sudden flinching movement out of fear or pain.
– ORIGIN Old English *blencan* 'deceive', of Germanic origin.

blend ■ v. **1** mix and combine (something) with something else. **2** form a harmonious combination or part of a whole: *a bodyguard has to blend in*. ■ n. **1** a mixture of different things or people. **2** a word made up of the parts and combining the meanings of two others, for example *motel* from *motor* and *hotel*.

CONSONANTS   **b** but   **d** dog   **f** few   **g** get   **h** he   **j** yes   **k** cat   **l** leg   **m** man   **n** no   **p** pen   **r** red

–ORIGIN Middle English: prob. of Scandinavian origin and rel. to Old Norse *blanda* 'to mix'.

blender ■ n. an electric device used for liquidizing, chopping, or puréeing food.

blenny ■ n. (pl. **-ies**) a small spiny-finned fish with scaleless skin and a blunt head, typically found in shallow coastal waters. [*Blennius* and other genera, family Blenniidae.]
–ORIGIN C18: from Latin *blennius*, from Greek *blennos* 'mucus' (because of its mucous coating).

blent poetic/literary past and past participle of **BLEND**.

bleomycin /ˌbliːəʊˈmʌɪsɪn/ ■ n. Medicine a bacterial antibiotic used to treat Hodgkin's disease and other cancers.
–ORIGIN 1960s: alteration of *phleomycin*, a similar antibiotic.

blepharitis /ˌblɛfəˈrʌɪtɪs/ ■ n. Medicine inflammation of the eyelid.
–ORIGIN C19: from Greek *blepharon* 'eyelid'.

blepharoplasty /ˈblɛf(ə)rə(ʊ)ˌplasti/ ■ n. Medicine surgical repair or reconstruction of an eyelid.
–ORIGIN C19: from Greek *blepharon* 'eyelid' + -PLASTY.

blerry /ˈblɛri/ ■ adj. & adv. S. African informal used to express anger, or for emphasis.
–ORIGIN 1920s: alteration of *bloody*, reflecting the pronunciation of Afrikaans speakers.

blesbok /ˈblɛsbɒk/ ■ n. an antelope with a mainly reddish-brown coat and white face, found in south-western South Africa. [*Damaliscus dorcas phillipsi*.]
–ORIGIN C19: from Afrikaans, from Dutch *bles* 'blaze' + *bok* 'buck'.

bless ■ v. 1 consecrate or invoke divine favour upon (someone) by means of a religious rite. ▸ call (God) holy; praise (God). ▸ (**bless oneself**) dated make the sign of the cross. 2 (**bless someone with**) endow someone with (a particular valued attribute); grant (health, prosperity, etc.) to someone.
–PHRASES **bless you!** said to a person who has just sneezed. [from the phr. *(may) God bless you*.]
–ORIGIN Old English *blēdsian*, from *blōd* 'blood' (orig. perhaps 'mark or consecrate with blood').

blessed /ˈblɛsɪd, blɛst/ ■ adj. 1 made holy; consecrated. ▸ a title preceding the name of a dead person considered to have led a holy life, especially a person formally beatified by the Roman Catholic Church. 2 endowed with divine favour and protection. 3 informal used in mild expressions of annoyance or exasperation.
–DERIVATIVES **blessedly** adv. **blessedness** n.

blessing ■ n. 1 God's favour and protection. ▸ a prayer asking for such favour and protection. ▸ grace said before or after a meal. 2 a beneficial thing for which one is grateful: *it's a blessing we're alive*. 3 a person's sanction or support: *he gave the plan his blessing*.
–PHRASES **a blessing in disguise** an apparent misfortune that eventually has good results.

blest ■ adj. archaic or poetic/literary term for **BLESSED**.

blether /ˈblɛðə/ ■ n. chiefly Scottish another term for **BLATHER**.

blew past of **BLOW**[1].

blight ■ n. 1 a plant disease, especially one caused by fungi such as mildews, rusts, and smuts. 2 a thing that spoils or damages something. ▸ ugly or neglected urban landscape. ■ v. 1 infect (plants) with blight. 2 spoil, harm, or destroy. ▸ [usu. as adj. **blighted**] subject (an urban area) to neglect.
–ORIGIN C16 (denoting inflammation of the skin).

blighter ■ n. informal a person regarded with contempt, irritation, or pity.

Blighty ■ n. Brit. informal Britain or England, used especially by soldiers serving abroad in the First and Second World Wars.
–ORIGIN first used by soldiers in the Indian army; Anglo-Indian from Urdu *bilāyatī*, *wilāyatī* 'foreign, European'.

bliksem /ˈblɪksəm/ S. African informal ■ n. a scoundrel. ■ v. beat (someone) up.
–ORIGIN 1950s: Afrikaans, 'lightning'.

blimey ■ exclam. Brit. informal expressing surprise, excitement, or alarm.

blindworm

–ORIGIN C19: altered form of (*God*) *blind* (or *blame*) *me*!

blimp ■ n. informal 1 (also **Colonel Blimp**) Brit. a pompous, reactionary person. 2 a small airship or barrage balloon. 3 N. Amer. an obese person.
–DERIVATIVES **blimpish** adj.
–ORIGIN FIRST WORLD WAR; sense 1 derives from a character invented by the cartoonist David Low.

blind ■ adj. 1 unable to see because of injury, disease, or a congenital condition. 2 done without being able to see or without certain information. ▸ (of flying) using instruments only. 3 lacking perception, judgement, or reason. 4 concealed, closed, or blocked off. ▸ (of a corner or bend) impossible to see round. 5 (of a plant) without buds, eyes, or terminal flowers. 6 [with neg.] informal the slightest: *it didn't do a blind bit of good*. ■ v. 1 cause (someone) to be unable to see. 2 deprive of understanding or judgement. ▸ (**blind someone with**) confuse or overawe someone with (something they do not understand). ■ n. 1 a screen for a window, especially one on a roller or made of slats. ▸ Brit. an awning over a shop window. 2 something designed to conceal one's real intentions. 3 N. Amer. a hide, as used by hunters. ■ adv. without being able to see clearly.
–PHRASES **bake something blind** bake a pastry without a filling. (**as**) **blind as a bat** informal having very bad eyesight. **blind drunk** informal extremely drunk. **turn a blind eye** pretend not to notice. [said to be in allusion to Nelson, who lifted a telescope to his blind eye at the Battle of Copenhagen (1801), thus not seeing the signal to 'discontinue the action'.]
–DERIVATIVES **blindly** adv. **blindness** n.
–ORIGIN Old English, of Germanic origin.

blind alley ■ n. 1 a cul-de-sac. 2 a course of action leading nowhere.

blind date ■ n. a social engagement with a person one has not previously met, designed to have a romantic or sexual aim.

blinder ■ n. 1 informal an excellent performance in a game or race. 2 (**blinders**) N. Amer. blinkers on a horse's bridle.

blindfold ■ n. a piece of cloth tied around the head to cover someone's eyes. ■ v. deprive of sight with a blindfold. ■ adv. with a blindfold covering the eyes.
–ORIGIN C16: from obsolete *blindfell* 'strike blind, blindfold', from Old English *geblindfellan*.

blind gut ■ n. the caecum.

blinding ■ adj. 1 (of light) very bright. 2 suddenly and overwhelmingly obvious. 3 informal (of an action) remarkably skilful and exciting. ■ n. the process of covering a newly made road with grit to fill cracks.
–DERIVATIVES **blindingly** adv.

blind man's buff (US also **blind man's bluff**) ■ n. a game in which a blindfold player tries to catch others while being pushed about by them.
–ORIGIN C17: from *buff* 'a blow', from Old French *bufe*.

blind side ■ n. a direction in which a person has a poor view, especially of approaching danger. ▸ Rugby the side of the scrum nearest the touchline. ■ v. (**blindside**) N. Amer. 1 hit or attack on the blind side. 2 cause to be unable to perceive the truth of a situation.

blindsight ■ n. Medicine a condition in which the sufferer responds to visual stimuli without consciously perceiving them.

blind snake ■ n. a small burrowing insectivorous snake of a group which lacks a distinct head and has very small inefficient eyes. [Typhlopidae and other families: many species.]

blind spot ■ n. 1 Anatomy the point of entry of the optic nerve on the retina, insensitive to light. 2 an area where a person's view is obstructed. ▸ an area in which a person lacks understanding or impartiality. 3 Telecommunications a point within the normal range of a transmitter where there is unusually weak reception.

blind stitch ■ n. a sewing stitch producing stitches visible on one side only.

blind trust ■ n. chiefly N. Amer. a trust independently administering the private business interests of a person in public office to prevent conflict of interest.

blindworm ■ n. another term for **SLOW-WORM**.

bling-bling

bling-bling /blɪŋ 'blɪŋ/ (also **bling**) ■ n. & adj. informal used to refer to ostentatiously expensive clothing or jewellery, or the style or attitudes associated with them: *the bling-bling mentality dominated his early songs.*
– ORIGIN 1990s: perhaps imitative of light reflecting off jewellery, or of jewellery clashing together.

blini /'blɪni, 'bliːni/ (also **bliny** or **blinis**) ■ pl. n. pancakes made from buckwheat flour and served with sour cream.
– ORIGIN from Russian.

blink ■ v. 1 shut and open the eyes quickly. 2 [usu. with neg.] react with surprise or disapproval: *he doesn't blink at the unsavoury aspects of his subject.* 3 (of a light) shine unsteadily or intermittently. ■ n. 1 an act of blinking. 2 a momentary gleam of light.
– PHRASES **in the blink of an eye** (or **in a blink**) informal very quickly. **on the blink** informal (of a machine) not working properly; out of order.
– ORIGIN Middle English: from *blenk*, Scots var. of BLENCH.

blinker ■ n. 1 (**blinkers**) a pair of small screens attached to a horse's bridle to prevent the horse seeing sideways and behind and being startled during a race. 2 a thing that prevents someone from understanding a situation fully. 3 a vehicle indicator light that flashes on and off. ■ v. 1 put blinkers on (a horse). 2 [often as adj. **blinkered**] cause to have a narrow or limited outlook.

blinking ■ adj. Brit. informal used to express annoyance.

blintze /blɪn(t)s/ ■ n. a thin rolled pancake filled with cheese or fruit and then fried or baked.
– ORIGIN from Yiddish *blintse*, from Russian *blinets* 'little pancake'.

bliny ■ pl. n. variant spelling of BLINI.

blip ■ n. 1 a very short high-pitched sound made by an electronic device. ▸ a small flashing point of light on a radar screen representing an object. 2 an unexpected, minor, and usually temporary deviation from a general trend. ■ v. (**blipped**, **blipping**) 1 (of an electronic device) make a blip. 2 open (the throttle of a motor vehicle) momentarily.
– ORIGIN C19 (denoting a sudden rap or tap): imitative.

bliss ■ n. perfect happiness; great joy. ▸ a state of spiritual blessedness. ■ v. (**bliss out** or **be blissed out**) informal be in a state of perfect happiness, oblivious to everything else.
– ORIGIN Old English, of Germanic origin.

blissful ■ adj. extremely happy; full of joy.
– DERIVATIVES **blissfully** adv. **blissfulness** n.

blister ■ n. 1 a small bubble on the skin filled with serum and typically caused by friction or burning. 2 a similar swelling, filled with air or fluid, on a surface. 3 Medicine, chiefly historical a preparation applied to the skin to form a blister. ■ v. be or cause to be affected with blisters.
– ORIGIN Middle English: perhaps from Old French *blestre* 'swelling, pimple'.

blister beetle ■ n. a beetle that, when it is alarmed, secretes a substance that causes blisters. [*Lytta* and other genera: several species.]

blistering ■ adj. 1 (of heat) intense. 2 (of criticism) very vehement. 3 (in sport) extremely fast, forceful, or impressive.
– DERIVATIVES **blisteringly** adv.

blithe /blaɪð/ ■ adj. 1 cheerfully or thoughtlessly indifferent. 2 poetic/literary happy or joyous.
– DERIVATIVES **blithely** adv. **blitheness** n. **blithesome** /-s(ə)m/ adj. (poetic/literary).
– ORIGIN Old English, of Germanic origin.

blither /'blɪðə/ ■ v.& n. variant spelling of BLATHER.

blithering ■ adj. informal complete; utter: *a blithering idiot.*

BLitt ■ abbrev. Bachelor of Letters.
– ORIGIN from Latin *Baccalaureus Litterarum*.

blitz ■ n. 1 an intensive or sudden military attack. ▸ (**the Blitz**) the German air raids on Britain in 1940. 2 informal a sudden and concerted effort or course of action. 3 American Football a play in which one or more defensive backs charge the quarterback of the opposing team. ■ v. 1 attack or seriously damage in a blitz. 2 succeed in overwhelming or defeating utterly. 3 American Football charge in a blitz.
– ORIGIN abbrev. of BLITZKRIEG.

blitzkrieg /'blɪtskriːg/ ■ n. an intense military campaign intended to bring about a swift victory.
– ORIGIN SECOND WORLD WAR: from German, 'lightning war'.

blizzard ■ n. a severe snowstorm with high winds.
– ORIGIN C19 (orig. US, denoting a violent blow).

bloat ■ v. cause to swell with fluid or gas. ■ n. a disease of livestock characterized by an accumulation of gas in the stomach.
– ORIGIN C17: from obsolete *bloat* 'swollen, soft', perhaps from Old Norse *blautr* 'soft, flabby'.

bloated ■ adj. 1 swollen with fluid or gas. 2 excessively large or wealthy.

bloater ■ n. a herring cured by salting and light smoking.

blob ■ n. 1 a drop of a thick liquid or viscous substance. 2 an indeterminate roundish mass or shape. 3 informal a score of 0 in a game. ■ v. (**blobbed**, **blobbing**) splash or mark with blobs.
– DERIVATIVES **blobby** adj.
– ORIGIN Middle English: cf. BLOTCH.

bloc ■ n. a group of countries or political parties who have formed an alliance.
– ORIGIN C20: from French, 'block'.

block ■ n. 1 a large solid piece of hard material with flat surfaces on each side. ▸ a starting block. ▸ Printing a piece of wood or metal engraved for printing on paper or fabric. ▸ a head-shaped mould used for shaping hats or wigs. 2 a large single building subdivided into separate flats or offices. ▸ a group of buildings bounded by four streets. ▸ the length of one side of such a block: *he lives a few blocks away.* 3 a large quantity or allocation of things regarded as a unit. 4 an obstacle to the normal progress or functioning of something. ▸ a chock for stopping the motion of a wheel. 5 a flat area of something, especially a solid area of colour. 6 a pulley or system of pulleys mounted in a case. 7 (also **cylinder block** or **engine block**) a large metal moulding containing the cylinders of an internal-combustion engine. 8 (also **blockhole**) Cricket the spot on which a batsman rests the end of the bat while waiting to receive a ball. ■ v. 1 prevent movement or flow in. 2 impede or prevent (an action or movement). ▸ (in sport) impede with one's body. ▸ Cricket stop (a ball) with the bat defensively. 3 impress a design on (a book cover). 4 (**block something out/in**) mark out an outline or shade something in roughly. 5 shape (a hat) using a wooden mould.
– PHRASES **knock someone's block off** informal hit someone about the head; give someone a beating. **on the (auction) block** chiefly N. Amer. for sale at auction. **put one's head** (or **neck**) **on the block** informal put one's standing or reputation at risk by proceeding with an action.
– DERIVATIVES **blocker** n. **blocky** adj.
– ORIGIN Middle English (denoting a log or tree stump): from Old French *bloc*, from Middle Dutch *blok*.

blockade ■ n. 1 an act of sealing off a place to prevent goods or people from entering or leaving. 2 an obstruction of a biochemical or other physiological function. ■ v. set up a blockade of.
– PHRASES **run a blockade** (of a ship) manage to enter or leave a blockaded port.
– ORIGIN C17: from BLOCK.

blockage ■ n. an obstruction which makes movement or flow difficult or impossible.

block and tackle ■ n. a lifting mechanism consisting of ropes, a pulley block, and a hook.

blockboard ■ n. a building material consisting of a core of wooden strips between two layers of plywood.

blockbuster ■ n. informal a film or book that is a great commercial success.
– ORIGIN 1940s (denoting a huge aerial bomb): from BLOCK + BUSTER.

blockbusting ■ adj. informal very successful commercially.

block capitals ■ pl. n. plain capital letters.

block diagram ■ n. a diagram showing the general arrangement of parts of a complex system or process.

blockhead ■ n. informal a very stupid person.
– DERIVATIVES **blockheaded** adj.

blockhole ■ n. see BLOCK (sense 8).

blockhouse ■ n. 1 a reinforced concrete shelter used as an observation point. ▸ historical a one-storeyed timber building used as a fort. 2 US a house made of squared logs.

blocking ■ n. 1 Psychiatry the sudden halting of the flow of thought or speech, as a symptom of schizophrenia or other mental disorder. ▸ failure to recall or consider an unpleasant memory or train of thought. 2 the physical arrangement of actors on a stage or film set.

blockish ■ adj. 1 bulky or crude in form. 2 unintelligent; stupid.

block letters ■ pl. n. block capitals.

block plane ■ n. a carpenter's plane with a blade set at an acute angle, used especially for planing across the end grain of wood.

block release ■ n. Brit. a system of allowing employees the whole of a stated period off work for education.

block vote ■ n. Brit. a vote proportional in power to the number of people a delegate represents, used particularly at a trade-union conference.

blog ■ n. a weblog. ■ v. (**blogs**, **blogging**, **blogged**) [usu. as noun **blogging**] add new material to or regularly update a weblog.
– DERIVATIVES **blogger** n.

bloke ■ n. informal a man.
– ORIGIN C19: from Shelta (an ancient secret language used by Irish and Welsh gypsies, based on altered Irish or Gaelic words).

blokeish (also **blokish** or **blokey**) ■ adj. Brit. informal stereotypically male in behaviour and interests.

blonde ■ adj. (also **blond**) (of hair) fair or pale yellow. ▸ having fair hair and a light complexion. ■ n. 1 a woman with blonde hair. ▸ informal, humorous a person, usually a woman, stereotypically perceived to be attractive but not intelligent. 2 the colour of blonde hair.
– DERIVATIVES **blondish** adj. **blondness** n.
– ORIGIN C17: from French, feminine of *blond*.

blood ■ n. 1 the red liquid that circulates in the arteries and veins, carrying oxygen to and carbon dioxide from the tissues of the body. 2 violence involving bloodshed. 3 fiery or passionate temperament. 4 family background; descent or lineage: *she must have Irish blood.* 5 dated a fashionable and dashing young man. ■ v. 1 initiate in a particular activity. 2 Hunting smear the face of (a novice hunter) with the blood of the kill. ▸ give (a hound) a first taste of blood.
– PHRASES **blood and thunder** informal unrestrained and violent action or behaviour. **one's blood is up** one is in a fighting mood. **blood, sweat, and tears** extremely hard work. **first blood 1** the first shedding of blood in a fight or (formerly) a duel. **2** the first point or advantage gained in a contest. **give blood** allow blood to be removed medically from one's body in order to be stored for use in transfusions. **have blood on one's hands** be responsible for someone's death. **in one's blood** ingrained in or fundamental to one's character. **make someone's blood boil** make someone infuriate someone. **make someone's blood run cold** horrify someone. **new** (or **fresh**) **blood** new members admitted to a group. **of the blood** (*royal*) poetic/literary royal. **young blood** a younger member or members of a group.
– ORIGIN Old English, of Germanic origin.

blood bank ■ n. a place where supplies of blood or plasma for transfusion are stored.

bloodbath ■ n. an event in which many people are killed violently.

blood brother ■ n. a man who has sworn to treat another man as a brother, typically by a ceremonial mingling of blood.

blood count ■ n. a determination of the number of corpuscles in a specific volume of blood.

blood-curdling ■ adj. horrifying; very frightening.

blood diamond ■ n. another term for CONFLICT DIAMOND.

blood donor ■ n. a person who gives blood.

blood doping (also **blood boosting**) ■ n. the injection of oxygenated blood into an athlete before an event in an (illegal) attempt to enhance performance.

---

121 **bloody**

blooded ■ adj. 1 having blood or a temperament of a specified kind: *thin-blooded*. 2 chiefly N. Amer. (of horses or cattle) of good pedigree.

blood feud ■ n. a lengthy conflict between families involving a cycle of retaliatory killings.

blood fluke ■ n. another term for SCHISTOSOME.

blood group ■ n. any of the various types of human blood whose antigen characteristics determine compatibility in transfusion, especially those of the ABO system.

bloodhound ■ n. a large hound of a breed with a very keen sense of smell, used in tracking.

bloodless ■ adj. 1 (of a conflict) without violence or killing. 2 (of the skin) drained of colour. ▸ lacking in vitality; feeble. 3 (of a person) cold or ruthless.
– DERIVATIVES **bloodlessly** adv. **bloodlessness** n.

bloodletting ■ n. 1 historical the surgical removal of some of a patient's blood for therapeutic purposes. 2 violence during a war or conflict.

bloodline ■ n. a pedigree or set of ancestors.

bloodlust ■ n. uncontrollable desire to kill.

blood meal ■ n. dried blood used for feeding animals and as a fertilizer.

blood money ■ n. 1 money paid in compensation to the family of someone who has been killed. 2 money paid to a hired killer.

blood orange ■ n. an orange of a variety with red or red-streaked flesh.

blood poisoning ■ n. a diseased state due to the presence of micro-organisms or their toxins in the blood.

blood pressure ■ n. the pressure of the blood in the circulatory system, which is closely related to the force and rate of the heartbeat and the diameter and elasticity of the arterial walls.

blood pudding (also **blood sausage**) ■ n. black pudding.

blood relation (also **blood relative**) ■ n. a person who is related to another by birth rather than by marriage.

bloodshed ■ n. the killing or wounding of people.

bloodshot ■ adj. (of the eyes) inflamed or tinged with blood, typically as a result of tiredness.

blood sport ■ n. a sport involving the hunting, wounding, or killing of animals.

bloodstain ■ n. a mark or discoloration caused by blood.
– DERIVATIVES **bloodstained** adj.

bloodstock ■ n. [treated as sing. or pl.] thoroughbred horses considered collectively.

bloodstream ■ n. the blood circulating through the body of a person or animal.

bloodsucker ■ n. an animal or insect that sucks blood, especially a leech or a mosquito.
– DERIVATIVES **bloodsucking** adj.

blood sugar ■ n. the concentration of glucose in the blood.

bloodthirsty ■ adj. (**-ier**, **-iest**) eager to kill and maim.
– DERIVATIVES **bloodthirstily** adv. **bloodthirstiness** n.

blood vessel ■ n. a tubular structure carrying blood through the tissues and organs; a vein, artery, or capillary.

bloodwood ■ n. 1 an Australian hardwood tree with deep red wood. [*Eucalyptus gummifera.*] 2 another term for KIAAT.

bloodworm ■ n. 1 the bright red aquatic larva of a midge. 2 another term for TUBIFEX.

bloody[1] ■ adj. (**-ier**, **-iest**) 1 covered with or composed of blood. 2 involving much violence or cruelty. ■ v. (**-ies**, **-ied**) cover or stain with blood.
– DERIVATIVES **bloodily** adv. **bloodiness** n.

bloody

bloody² (S. African also **bladdy**) ■ adj. informal used to express anger or shock, or for emphasis.

> **HISTORY**
> Although widely believed to be a blasphemous reference to the blood of God or Christ, as in the archaic oath *'s-blood* or *God's blood*, the informal use of **bloody** was probably, in the first place, simply a reference to young bloods (that is 'young aristocrats', or children of 'good blood'), who behaved in a rowdy manner; in the 17th century the phrase *bloody drunk* meant 'drunk as a blood' or 'drunk as a lord'.

Bloody Mary ■ n. (pl. **Bloody Marys**) a drink consisting of vodka and tomato juice.

bloody-minded ■ adj. informal deliberately uncooperative.
– DERIVATIVES **bloody-mindedly** adv. **bloody-mindedness** n.

bloom ■ v. **1** produce flowers; be in flower. **2** be or become very healthy; flourish. **3** coat (a lens) with a special surface layer to reduce reflection. ■ n. **1** a flower, especially one cultivated for its beauty. ▸ the state or period of blooming: *the apple trees were in bloom*. **2** a youthful or healthy glow in a person's complexion. **3** a delicate powdery surface deposit on fruits, leaves, or stems. **4** a rapid growth of microscopic algae or cyanobacteria in water resulting in a coloured scum on the surface.
– ORIGIN Middle English: from Old Norse *blóm* 'flower, blossom', *blómi* 'prosperity'.

bloomer¹ ■ n. informal, chiefly Brit. a stupid mistake.
– ORIGIN C19: equivalent to *blooming error*.

bloomer² ■ n. Brit. a large loaf with diagonal slashes on a rounded top.
– ORIGIN 1930S.

bloomer³ ■ n. [in combination] a plant that blooms at a specified time.

bloomers ■ pl. n. **1** women's loose-fitting knee-length knickers. **2** historical women's loose-fitting trousers, gathered at the knee or ankle.
– ORIGIN C19: named after Mrs Amelia J. *Bloomer*, an American social reformer who advocated a similar garment.

blooming ■ adj. Brit. informal used to express annoyance or for emphasis.

blooper ■ n. informal, chiefly N. Amer. **1** an embarrassing error. **2** Baseball a poorly hit fly ball landing just beyond the reach of the infielders.

blossom ■ n. a flower or a mass of flowers on a tree or bush. ▸ the state or period of flowering. ■ v. **1** (of a tree or bush) produce blossom. **2** mature or develop in a promising or healthy way.
– DERIVATIVES **blossomy** adj.
– ORIGIN Old English, of Germanic origin; rel. to BLOOM.

blot ■ n. **1** a dark mark or stain, especially one made by ink. **2** a thing that mars something that is otherwise good. **3** Biochemistry a procedure in which proteins or nucleic acids separated on a gel are transferred directly to an immobilizing medium for identification. ■ v. (**blotted**, **blotting**) **1** dry with an absorbent material. **2** mark, stain, or mar. **3** (**blot something out**) obscure a view. ▸ obliterate or disregard a painful memory or thought. **4** Biochemistry transfer by means of a blot.
– PHRASES **blot** (or **a blot on**) **one's copybook** damage (to) one's good reputation.
– ORIGIN Middle English: prob. of Scandinavian origin and rel. to Old Norse *blettr*.

blotch ■ n. a large irregular patch or unsightly mark. ■ v. cover or mark with blotches.
– DERIVATIVES **blotchiness** n. **blotchy** adj.
– ORIGIN C17: partly an alteration of obsolete *plotch*, partly a blend of BLOT and BOTCH.

blotter ■ n. **1** a sheet or pad of blotting paper inserted into a frame and kept on a desk. **2** N. Amer. a temporary recording book, especially a police charge sheet.

blotting paper ■ n. absorbent paper used for soaking up excess ink when writing.

blotto ■ adj. informal extremely drunk.
– ORIGIN C20: from BLOT + -O.

blouse ■ n. **1** a woman's upper garment resembling a shirt. **2** a loose smock or tunic of a type worn by peasants and manual workers. **3** a type of jacket worn as part of military uniform. ■ v. make (a garment) hang in loose folds.
– ORIGIN C19: from French.

blouson /ˈbluːzɒn/ ■ n. a short loose-fitting jacket, typically bloused and finishing at the waist.
– ORIGIN C20: from French, diminutive of BLOUSE.

blow¹ ■ v. (past **blew**; past part. **blown**) **1** (of wind) move creating an air current. ▸ be carried or driven by the wind. **2** expel air through pursed lips. ▸ force air through the mouth into (an instrument) to make a sound. ▸ force air through a tube into (molten glass) to create an artefact. ▸ remove the contents of (an egg) by forcing air through it. **3** sound (the hooter of a vehicle). **4** (of a whale) eject air and vapour through the blowhole. **5** (of an explosion) displace violently or send flying. ▸ burst or burn out through pressure or overheating. ▸ (of a vehicle tyre) burst suddenly while the vehicle is in motion. **6** informal spend recklessly. **7** informal completely bungle (an opportunity). ▸ expose (a stratagem): *his cover was blown*. **8** (past part. **blowed**) Brit. informal damn: *'Well, blow me,' he said*. **9** (of flies) lay eggs in or on. **10** informal play jazz or rock music in an unrestrained style. **11** [as adj. **blown**] breathing hard; exhausted. ■ n. **1** a strong wind. **2** an act of blowing.
– PHRASES **blow a fuse** (or **gasket**) informal lose one's temper. **blow hot and cold** vacillate. **blow someone a kiss** kiss the tips of one's fingers then blow across them towards someone as a gesture of affection. **blow someone's mind** informal impress or otherwise affect someone very strongly. **blow one's nose** clear one's nose of mucus by blowing through it into a handkerchief. **blow one's top** (or chiefly N. Amer. **lid** or **stack**) informal lose one's temper. **blow up in one's face** (of an action) go drastically wrong with damaging effects to oneself. **blow with the wind** be incapable of maintaining a consistent course of action.
– PHRASAL VERBS **blow someone away** informal **1** kill someone using a firearm. **2** cause someone to be extremely impressed. **blow in** informal arrive casually and unannounced. **blow off** informal **1** lose one's temper and shout. **2** break wind noisily. **blow someone off** N. Amer. informal fail to keep an appointment with someone. **blow something off** N. Amer. informal ignore or fail to attend something. **blow over** (of trouble) fade away without serious consequences. **blow up 1** explode. **2** lose one's temper. **3** (of a wind or storm) begin to develop. **4** (of a scandal or dispute) emerge or become public. **5** inflate. **blow something up 1** cause something to explode. **2** inflate or enlarge something.
– ORIGIN Old English, of Germanic origin.

blow² ■ n. **1** a powerful stroke with a hand or weapon. **2** a sudden shock or disappointment.
– PHRASES **come to blows** start fighting after a disagreement.
– ORIGIN Middle English.

blowback ■ n. **1** a process in which gases expand or travel in a direction opposite to the usual one. **2** chiefly US the unintended adverse results of a political action or situation.

blow-by-blow ■ adj. (of a description of an event) giving all the details in the order in which they occurred.

blow-dry ■ v. arrange (the hair) into a particular style while drying it with a hand-held dryer.
– DERIVATIVES **blow-dryer** n.

blower ■ n. **1** a device for creating a current of air to dry or heat something. **2** informal, chiefly Brit. a telephone.

blowfish ■ n. (pl. same or **-fishes**) a fish that is able to inflate its body when alarmed, especially a globefish.

blowfly ■ n. (pl. **-flies**) a bluebottle or similar large fly which lays its eggs on meat and carcasses. [Family Calliphoridae.]

blowgun ■ n. another term for BLOWPIPE.

blowhole ■ n. **1** the nostril of a whale or dolphin on the top of its head. **2** a hole in ice for breathing or fishing through. **3** a vent for air or smoke in a tunnel or other

---

CONSONANTS **b** but **d** dog **f** few **g** get **h** he **j** yes **k** cat **l** leg **m** man **n** no **p** pen **r** red

structure. ▶ a natural chimney in the roof of a coastal cave through which rising tides force air and seawater.

blow job ■ n. vulgar slang an act of fellatio.

blowlamp ■ n. British term for BLOWTORCH.

blown past participle of BLOW¹. ■ adj. informal (of a vehicle) provided with a turbocharger.

blowout ■ n. 1 an occasion when a vehicle tyre bursts or an electric fuse melts. ▶ an uprush of oil or gas from a well. 2 informal, chiefly N. Amer. an argument or outburst of anger. 3 N. Amer. informal an easy victory. 4 informal a large, lavish meal.

blowpipe ■ n. 1 a primitive weapon consisting of a long tube through which an arrow or dart is blown. 2 a long tube by means of which molten glass is blown. ▶ a tube used to intensify the heat of a flame by blowing air or other gas through it at high pressure.

blowsy /ˈblaʊzi/ (also **blowzy**) ■ adj. (of a woman) coarse, untidy, and red-faced.
– DERIVATIVES **blowsiness** n.
– ORIGIN C17: from obsolete *blowze* 'beggar's female companion'.

blowtorch ■ n. a portable device producing a hot flame which can be directed on to a surface, typically to burn off paint.

blow-up ■ n. 1 an enlargement of a photograph. 2 informal an outburst of anger. ■ adj. inflatable.

blowy ■ adj. (-ier, -iest) windy or windswept.

BLT ■ n. informal a sandwich filled with bacon, lettuce, and tomato.

blub ■ v. (**blubbed, blubbing**) informal sob noisily and uncontrollably.
– ORIGIN C19: abbrev. of BLUBBER².

blubber¹ ■ n. the fat of sea mammals, especially whales and seals.
– DERIVATIVES **blubbery** adj.
– ORIGIN Middle English (denoting the foaming of the sea): perhaps symbolic.

blubber² ■ v. informal sob noisily and uncontrollably.
– DERIVATIVES **blubberer** n.
– ORIGIN Middle English: prob. symbolic.

bludgeon /ˈblʌdʒ(ə)n/ ■ n. a thick stick with a heavy end, used as a weapon. ■ v. 1 beat with a bludgeon. 2 bully into doing something.
– ORIGIN C18.

blue¹ ■ adj. (**bluer, bluest**) 1 of a colour intermediate between green and violet, as of the sky or sea on a sunny day. ▶ (of a cat, fox, or rabbit) having fur of a smoky grey colour. 2 informal melancholy, sad, or depressed. 3 informal (of a film, joke, or story) with sexual or pornographic content. 4 Brit. informal politically conservative. ■ n. 1 blue colour, pigment, or material. ▶ (**the blue**) poetic/literary the sky or sea, or the unknown. ▶ another term for BLUING. 2 Brit. a person who has represented Cambridge University or Oxford University in a particular sport. 3 used in names of small butterflies with predominantly blue wings. [Family Lycaenidae.] ■ v. (**blues, blued, bluing** or **blueing**) 1 make or become blue. 2 chiefly historical wash (white clothes) with bluing.
– PHRASES **once in a blue moon** informal very rarely. [because a 'blue moon' is a phenomenon that never occurs.] **out of the blue** (or **out of a clear blue sky**) informal without warning; unexpectedly.
– DERIVATIVES **blueness** n.
– ORIGIN Middle English: from Old French *bleu*, of Germanic origin.

blue² ■ v. (**blues, blued, bluing** or **blueing**) Brit. informal, dated squander or spend recklessly.
– ORIGIN C19: perhaps a var. of BLOW¹.

blue antelope ■ n. another term for BLUEBUCK.

blue baby ■ n. a baby with cyanosis, generally due to a congenital heart or circulatory defect.

Bluebeard ■ n. a man who murders his wives.
– ORIGIN from the name of a fairytale character who killed several wives in turn for disobeying his order to avoid a locked room, which contained the bodies of his previous wives.

bluebell ■ n. 1 a Eurasian woodland plant of the lily family, which produces clusters of blue bell-shaped flowers in spring. [*Hyacinthoides nonscripta*.] 2 Scottish term for HAREBELL. 3 any of various other plants with blue bell-shaped flowers. [Genera *Mertensia* (N. America), *Gladiolus* (South Africa), and *Wahlenbergia* (South Africa and Australia).]

blueberry ■ n. (pl. **-ies**) 1 the small blue-back berry of a North American dwarf shrub, related to the bilberry. 2 the shrub that produces this berry. [Genus *Vaccinium*: several species.]

bluebird ■ n. an American songbird, the male of which has a blue head, back, and wings. [Genus *Sialis*.]

blue blood ■ n. noble birth.
– DERIVATIVES **blue-blooded** adj.

blue book ■ n. 1 (in the UK) a report bound in a blue cover and issued by Parliament or the Privy Council. 2 (in the US) an official book listing government officials.

bluebottle ■ n. 1 S. African & Austral. the Portuguese man-of-war. 2 a common blowfly with a metallic-blue body. [*Calliphora vomitoria*.]

bluebuck ■ n. an extinct South African antelope related to the sable antelope. [*Hippotragus leucophaeus*.]

blue cheese ■ n. cheese containing veins of blue mould, such as Stilton and Danish Blue.

blue-chip ■ adj. 1 denoting companies or their shares considered to be a reliable investment, though less secure than gilt-edged stock. 2 of the highest quality.
– DERIVATIVES **blue chipper** n.
– ORIGIN C20 (orig. US): from the *blue chip* used in gambling games, which usu. has a high value.

blue coat ■ n. a person wearing a blue coat or uniform, especially a US soldier of the 19th century.

blue-collar ■ adj. of or relating to manual work or workers, particularly in industry.

blue crane ■ n. a large South African crane with blue-grey plumage, the national bird of South Africa. [*Anthropoides paradisea*.]

blue duiker ■ n. a small slate-grey African antelope with short horns and a long wagging tail, found in forests and dense bush. [*Philantomba monticola*.]

blue-eyed boy ■ n. informal, chiefly derogatory a person highly regarded and treated with special favour.

bluefin ■ n. the commonest large tuna, which occurs worldwide in warm seas. [*Thunnus thynnus*.]

bluefish ■ n. (pl. same or **-fishes**) a predatory blue-coloured marine fish, which inhabits tropical and temperate waters and is popular as a game fish. [*Pomatomus saltatrix*.]

blue flag ■ n. 1 a European award for beaches based on cleanliness and safety. 2 Motor Racing a blue flag used to indicate to a driver that there is another driver trying to lap him.

bluegrass ■ n. 1 (also **Kentucky bluegrass**) a European meadow grass introduced elsewhere, and used for fodder. [*Poa pratensis* and other species.] 2 a kind of country music characterized by virtuosic playing of banjos and guitars and high-pitched close-harmony vocals.

blue-green algae ■ pl. n. another term for CYANOBACTERIA.

blue ground ■ n. another term for KIMBERLITE.

bluegum ■ n. a eucalyptus tree with blue-green aromatic leaves and smooth bark. [Genus *Eucalyptus*: several species.]

blue helmet ■ n. a member of a United Nations peacekeeping force.

blueing ■ n. variant spelling of BLUING.

blueish ■ adj. variant spelling of BLUISH.

blue law ■ n. N. Amer. a law prohibiting certain activities, such as shopping, on a Sunday.
– ORIGIN C18: in ref. to strict puritanical laws in colonial New England, orig. printed on blue paper.

blue line ■ n. Ice Hockey either of the two lines running across the ice between the centre line and the goal line.

blue mould ■ n. a bluish fungus which grows on food, especially the mould producing blue cheeses. [*Penicillium* and other genera.]

blue note ■ n. Music a minor interval where a major would be expected, used especially in jazz.

blue pencil ■ n. a blue pencil as traditionally used to censor a text.

Blue Peter ■ n. a blue flag with a white square in the centre, raised by a ship about to leave port.

blue pointer ■ n. another term for MAKO.

blueprint ■ n. **1** a design plan or other technical drawing. **2** something which acts as a plan, model, or template. ■ v. N. Amer. draw up (a plan or model).
– ORIGIN C19: from the original process in which prints were composed of white lines on a blue ground or of blue lines on a white ground.

blue riband ■ n. **1** (also **blue ribbon**) a ribbon of blue silk given to the winner of a competition or as a mark of great distinction. **2** (**Blue Riband** or **Ribbon**) a trophy for the ship making the fastest eastward sea crossing of the Atlantic Ocean on a regular commercial voyage. ■ adj. (**blue-ribbon**) N. Amer. **1** of the highest quality; first-class. **2** (of a jury or committee) carefully or specially selected.

blue rinse ■ n. a preparation used as a rinse on grey or white hair to give it a temporary blue tint.

blue roan ■ n. an animal with a coat of black and white hairs evenly mixed, giving it a blue-grey hue.

blues ■ pl. n. **1** [treated as sing. or pl.] melancholic music of black American folk origin, typically in a twelve-bar sequence. **2** (**the blues**) informal feelings of melancholy, sadness, or depression.
– DERIVATIVES **bluesy** adj.
– ORIGIN C18: from *blue devils* 'depression or delirium tremens'.

blue shift ■ n. Astronomy the displacement of the spectrum to shorter wavelengths in the light coming from distant celestial objects moving towards the observer. Compare with RED SHIFT.

blue-sky ■ adj. informal not yet practicable or profitable: *blue-sky research*.

blue soap ■ n. S. African & W. Indian a coarse laundry or kitchen soap made with a mixture of washing blue, caustic soda, and starch.

bluestocking ■ n. often derogatory an intellectual or literary woman.
– ORIGIN C17: in ref. to literary assemblies held in London by society ladies, where some of the men favoured less formal dress.

blue tick ■ n. S. African any of several tick species which transmit a number of diseases, especially among cattle. [Genus *Boophilus*.]

blue tit ■ n. a common titmouse with a blue cap, greenish-blue back, and yellow underparts. [*Parus caeruleus*.]

bluetongue ■ n. an insect-borne viral disease of sheep, characterized by fever, lameness, and a blue, swollen mouth and tongue.

blue vitriol ■ n. archaic crystalline copper sulphate.

blue whale ■ n. a mottled bluish-grey rorqual which is the largest living animal and reaches lengths of up to 27 m (90 ft). [*Balaenoptera musculus*.]

bluff[1] ■ n. an attempt to deceive someone into believing that one can or will do something. ■ v. try to deceive someone as to one's abilities or intentions.
– PHRASES **call someone's bluff** challenge someone to carry out a stated intention, in the expectation of being able to expose it as a pretence. ▸ (in poker or brag) make an opponent show their hand in order to reveal that its value is weaker than their heavy betting suggests.
– DERIVATIVES **bluffer** n.
– ORIGIN C17: from Dutch *bluffen* 'brag'.

bluff[2] ■ adj. good-naturedly frank and direct.
– DERIVATIVES **bluffly** adv. **bluffness** n.
– ORIGIN C18 ('surly'): figurative use of BLUFF[3].

bluff[3] ■ n. a steep cliff, bank, or promontory. ■ adj. (of a cliff or a ship's bows) having a vertical or steep broad front.
– ORIGIN C17 (in nautical use).

bluing (also **blueing**) ■ n. **1** chiefly historical blue powder used to preserve the whiteness of laundry. **2** a greyish-blue finish on metal produced by heating.

bluish (also **blueish**) ■ adj. having a blue tinge.

blunder ■ n. a stupid or careless mistake. ■ v. **1** make a blunder. **2** move clumsily or as if unable to see.
– DERIVATIVES **blunderer** n. **blundering** adj. **blunderingly** adv.
– ORIGIN Middle English: prob. of Scandinavian origin and rel. to BLIND.

blunderbuss ■ n. **1** historical a short large-bored gun firing balls or slugs. **2** an unsubtle and imprecise action or method.
– ORIGIN C17: alteration of Dutch *donderbus* 'thunder gun'.

blunt ■ adj. **1** lacking a sharp edge or point. ▸ having a flat or rounded end. **2** uncompromisingly forthright in manner. ■ v. **1** make or become less sharp. **2** weaken or reduce the force of. ■ n. informal a hollowed-out cigar filled with cannabis.
– DERIVATIVES **bluntly** adv. **bluntness** n.
– ORIGIN Middle English ('dull, insensitive'): perhaps rel. to Old Norse *blunda* 'shut the eyes'.

blur ■ v. (**blurred**, **blurring**) make or become unclear or less distinct. ■ n. something that cannot be seen, heard, or recalled clearly.
– DERIVATIVES **blurry** adj. (**-ier**, **-iest**).
– ORIGIN C16 ('smear'): perhaps rel. to archaic *blear* 'dim, dull' and Middle High German *blerre* 'blurred vision'.

blurb ■ n. a short description of a book, film, or other product written for promotional purposes. ■ v. informal, chiefly N. Amer. write a blurb for.
– ORIGIN C20: coined by the American humorist Gelett Burgess.

blurt ■ v. (usu. **blurt out**) say suddenly and without careful consideration.
– ORIGIN C16: prob. imitative.

blush ■ v. **1** become red in the face through shyness, embarrassment, or shame. **2** poetic/literary be or become pink or pale red. ■ n. **1** an instance of blushing. **2** poetic/literary a pink or pale red tinge. **3** a wine with a slight pink tint made in the manner of white wine but from red grape varieties.
– DERIVATIVES **blushing** adj. **blushingly** adv.
– ORIGIN Old English: rel. to Dutch *blozen*.

blusher ■ n. **1** a cosmetic used to give a warm reddish tinge to the cheeks. **2** a toadstool with a buff cap bearing fluffy white spots and with white flesh that turns pink when bruised or cut. [*Amanita rubescens*.]

blushing bride ■ n. a South African shrub which bears drooping, pale pink flowers, widely cultivated as an ornamental. [*Serruria florida*, family Proteaceae.]

bluster ■ v. **1** talk in a loud, aggressive, or indignant way with little effect. **2** (of wind or rain) blow or beat fiercely and noisily. ■ n. blustering talk.
– DERIVATIVES **blusterer** n. **blustery** adj.
– ORIGIN Middle English: imitative.

B-lymphocyte ■ n. Physiology a lymphocyte of a type not processed by the thymus gland, responsible for producing antibodies. Compare with T-LYMPHOCYTE.
– ORIGIN *B* for BURSA, referring to the organ in birds where it was first identified.

BM ■ abbrev. Bachelor of Medicine.

BMI ■ abbrev. body mass index.

B-movie ■ n. a low-budget film of poor quality made for use as a supporting feature in a cinema programme.

BMR ■ abbrev. basal metabolic rate.

BMus ■ abbrev. Bachelor of Music.

BMX ■ n. [as modifier] denoting or relating to bicycles of a robust design suitable for cross-country racing.
– ORIGIN 1970s: from the initial letters of *bicycle motocross*, with *X* standing for *cross*.

Bn ■ abbrev. **1** Baron. **2** Battalion.

bn ■ abbrev. billion.

BO ■ abbrev. informal body odour.

bo ■ exclam. another term for BOO.
– ORIGIN Middle English: imitative.

boa /ˈbəʊə/ ■ n. **1** a large snake which kills its prey by constriction and bears live young. [*Boa constrictor*

(tropical America) and other species, family Boidae.] **2** a long, thin stole of feathers or fur worn around a woman's neck, usually as part of evening dress.
– ORIGIN Middle English: from Latin.

boab /ˈbəʊab/ ■ n. Austral. another term for BAOBAB.

boar ■ n. (pl. same or **boars**) **1** (also **wild boar**) a tusked wild pig from which domestic pigs are descended. [*Sus scrofa*.] ▸ the full-grown male of other wild pig species. **2** an uncastrated domestic male pig. **3** ▸ the full-grown male of certain other animals, especially a badger, guinea pig, or hedgehog.
– ORIGIN Old English, of West Germanic origin.

board ■ n. **1** a long, thin, flat piece of wood used for floors or other building purposes. ▸ (**the boards**) informal the stage of a theatre. **2** a thin, flat, rectangular piece of stiff material, e.g. a chopping board or noticeboard. ▸ the piece of equipment on which one stands in surfing, skateboarding, etc. **3** [treated as sing. or pl.] the decision-making body of an organization. **4** the provision of regular meals in return for payment or services. ▸ archaic a table set for a meal. **5** Nautical a distance covered by a vessel in a single tack. ■ v. **1** get on or into (a ship, aircraft, or other vehicle). ▸ (**be boarding**) (of an aircraft) be ready for passengers to get on. **2** live somewhere and receive meals in return for payment or services. ▸ (of a pupil) live in school during term time in return for payment. **3** (**board something up/over**) cover or seal a window or building with pieces of wood. **4** (also **board out**) certify someone as being medically unfit to continue in their current employment. **5** [as adj. **boarded**] made of wooden boards. **6** ride on a snowboard or skateboard.
– PHRASES **go by the board** (of a plan or principle) be abandoned, rejected, or ignored. [from nautical use meaning 'fall overboard', *board* meaning the side of the ship.] **on board** on or in a ship, aircraft, or other vehicle. **take something on board** informal fully consider or assimilate a new idea or situation. **tread** (or **walk**) **the boards** informal appear on stage as an actor.
– DERIVATIVES **boarding** n.
– ORIGIN Old English *bord*, of Germanic origin; reinforced in Middle English by Old French *bort* 'edge, ship's side' and Old Norse *borth* 'board, table'.

boarder ■ n. **1** a person who boards, in particular a pupil who lives in school during term time in return for payment. **2** a person who forces their way on to a ship in an attack.

board game ■ n. a game that involves the movement of counters or other objects around a board.

boarding house ■ n. a private house providing food and lodging for paying guests.

boarding kennel ■ n. a place in which dogs are kept and looked after while their owners are away.

boarding pass (also **boarding card**) ■ n. a passenger's pass for boarding an aircraft.

boarding school ■ n. a school in which the pupils live during term time.

boardroom ■ n. a room in which a board of directors meets regularly.

boardsailing ■ n. another term for WINDSURFING.
– DERIVATIVES **boardsailor** n.

board shorts ■ pl. n. long shorts of a kind originally worn by surfers.

boardwalk ■ n. a wooden walkway across sand or marshy ground. ▸ chiefly N. Amer. a promenade along a beach or waterfront.

boast¹ ■ v. **1** talk with excessive pride and self-satisfaction about oneself. **2** possess (a feature that is a source of pride). ■ n. an act of boasting.
– DERIVATIVES **boaster** n. **boastful** adj. **boastfully** adv. **boastfulness** n. **boasting** adj. **boastingly** adv.
– ORIGIN Middle English.

boast² ■ n. (in squash) a stroke in which the ball hits a side wall before hitting the front wall.
– ORIGIN C19: perhaps from French *bosse*, denoting a rounded projection in the wall of a court for real tennis.

boat ■ n. a small vessel propelled by oars, sails, or an engine. ▸ a vessel of any size. ■ v. travel in a boat. ▸ transport in a boat.
– PHRASES **be in the same boat** informal be in the same difficult circumstances as others. **miss the boat** see MISS. **push the boat out** Brit. informal be extravagant. **rock the boat** informal disturb an existing situation.
– DERIVATIVES **boatful** n. (pl. **-fuls**). **boating** n. **boatload** n.
– ORIGIN Old English *bāt*, of Germanic origin.

boat deck ■ n. the deck from which a ship's lifeboats are launched.

boater ■ n. **1** a flat-topped hardened straw hat with a brim. [orig. worn while boating.] **2** a person who travels in a boat.

boathook ■ n. a long pole with a hook and a spike at one end, used for moving boats.

boathouse ■ n. a shed at the edge of a river or lake used for housing boats.

boatman ■ n. (pl. **-men**) a person who provides transport by boat.

boat people ■ pl. n. refugees who have left a country by sea.

boat race ■ n. **1** a race between rowing crews. **2** Brit. rhyming slang a person's face.

boatswain /ˈbəʊs(ə)n/ (also **bo'sun** or **bosun**) ■ n. a ship's officer in charge of equipment and the crew.
– ORIGIN Old English *bātswegen* (see BOAT, SWAIN).

boatswain's chair ■ n. a seat suspended from ropes, used for work on the body or masts of a ship or the face of a building.

boat train ■ n. a train scheduled to connect with the arrival or departure of a boat.

boatyard ■ n. a place where boats are built or stored.

Bob ■ n. (in phr. **Bob's your uncle**) Brit. informal an expression signifying the simplicity of completing a task.

bob¹ ■ v. (**bobbed**, **bobbing**) **1** make or cause to make a quick, short movement up and down. ▸ make a sudden move so as to appear or disappear. **2** curtsy briefly. ■ n. **1** a quick, short movement up and down. **2** a brief curtsy.
– PHRASES **bob and weave** (of a boxer) move rapidly up and down and from side to side as an evasive tactic. **bob for apples** try to catch floating apples with one's mouth, as a game.
– ORIGIN Middle English.

bob² ■ n. **1** a short hairstyle hanging evenly all round. **2** a weight on a pendulum, plumb line, or kite-tail. **3** a bobsleigh. ■ v. (**bobbed**, **bobbing**) **1** cut (hair) in a bob. **2** ride on a bobsleigh.
– ORIGIN Middle English (denoting a bunch or cluster).

bob³ ■ n. (pl. same) Brit. informal, dated a shilling.
– ORIGIN C18.

bob⁴ ■ n. a change of order in bell-ringing.
– ORIGIN C17: perhaps connected with BOB¹.

bobbejaan spanner /ˌbɒbəˈjɑːn/ ■ n. S. African informal another term for MONKEY WRENCH.
– ORIGIN 1960s: *bobbejaan* from Afrikaans 'baboon, monkey'; partial translation of *bobbejaansleutel* 'monkey wrench'.

bobbin ■ n. **1** a cylinder, cone, or reel holding thread or yarn. **2** a small bar attached to a string used for raising a door latch.
– ORIGIN C16: from French *bobine*.

bobbinet /ˈbɒbɪnɛt/ ■ n. machine-made cotton net (imitating bobbin lace).

bobbin lace ■ n. lace made by hand with thread wound on bobbins.

bobble¹ ■ n. a small ball made of strands of wool, as used as a decoration on a hat or as forming on the surface of knitted fabric.
– DERIVATIVES **bobbly** adj.
– ORIGIN 1920s: diminutive of BOB².

bobble² /ˈbɒb(ə)l/ informal ■ v. move with an irregular bouncing motion. ■ n. an irregular bouncing motion.
– ORIGIN C19: from BOB¹.

bobby ■ n. (pl. **-ies**) Brit. informal, dated a police officer.
– ORIGIN C19: after Sir *Robert* Peel, the British Prime Minister who established the Metropolitan Police.

bobby pin ■ n. S. African & N. Amer. a sprung hairpin or small clip. ■ v. (**bobby-pin**) fix (hair) in place with a bobby pin.

–ORIGIN 1930s: from BOB² (because orig. used with bobbed hair).

bobby socks ▪ pl. n. N. Amer. socks reaching just above the ankle, worn by teenage girls in the 1940s and 1950s.
–ORIGIN cf. BOB² in the sense 'cut short'.

bobby-soxer ▪ n. N. Amer. informal, dated a teenage girl.

bobcat ▪ n. a small North American lynx with a barred and spotted coat and a short tail. [*Felis rufus*.]
–ORIGIN C19: from BOB² (with ref. to its short tail) + CAT¹.

bobotie /bəˈbuːti, -ˈbʊəti/ ▪ n. a South African dish of curried minced meat baked with a savoury custard topping.
–ORIGIN Afrikaans, prob. of Malay or Javanese origin.

bobsled /ˈbɒbslɛd/ ▪ n. North American term for BOBSLEIGH.
–DERIVATIVES **bobsledding** n.

bobsleigh ▪ n. chiefly Brit. a mechanically steered and braked sledge used for racing down an ice-covered run.
–DERIVATIVES **bobsleighing** n.
–ORIGIN C19: from BOB² in the sense 'short' + SLEIGH.

bobtail ▪ n. a docked tail of a horse or dog.
–ORIGIN C16: prob. from BOB² + TAIL¹.

bobweight ▪ n. a counterweight to a moving part in a machine.

bocconcini /ˌbɒkɒnˈtʃiːni/ ▪ pl. n. small balls of mozzarella cheese.
–ORIGIN from Italian.

Boche /bɒʃ/ ▪ n. (**the Boche**) informal, dated, chiefly Brit. Germans, especially German soldiers, collectively.
–ORIGIN from French soldiers' slang, orig. 'rascal'.

bod ▪ n. informal **1** a body. **2** chiefly Brit. a person.
–ORIGIN C18: orig. Scots.

bodacious /bəʊˈdeɪʃəs/ ▪ adj. N. Amer. informal excellent, admirable, or attractive.
–ORIGIN C19: perhaps a var. of SW dialect *boldacious*, blend of BOLD and AUDACIOUS.

bode ▪ v. (**bode well/ill**) be a portent of a good or bad outcome.
–ORIGIN Old English *bodian* 'proclaim, foretell', from *boda* 'messenger', of Germanic origin.

bodega /bəˈdeɪɡə/ ▪ n. a cellar or shop selling wine and food, especially in a Spanish-speaking country.
–ORIGIN C19: from Spanish, from Greek *apothēkē* 'storehouse'.

bodge ▪ v. Brit. informal make or repair badly or clumsily.
–DERIVATIVES **bodger** n.
–ORIGIN C16: alteration of BOTCH.

bodhrán /ˈbaʊrɑːn, baʊˈrɑːn/ ▪ n. a shallow one-sided Irish drum typically played using a short stick.
–ORIGIN from Irish.

bodh tree ▪ n. variant of BO TREE.

bodice ▪ n. the part of a woman's dress (excluding sleeves) above the waist. ▸ a woman's sleeveless undergarment, often laced at the front.
–ORIGIN C16 orig. *bodies*, pl. of BODY, retaining the original pronunciation.

bodice-ripper ▪ n. informal, humorous a sexually explicit historical novel or film.
–DERIVATIVES **bodice-ripping** adj.

bodiless ▪ adj. **1** lacking a body. **2** incorporeal; insubstantial.

bodily ▪ adj. **1** of or concerning the body. **2** material or physical. ▪ adv. by taking hold of a person's body with force.

bodkin ▪ n. a thick, blunt needle with a large eye, used for drawing tape through a hem. ▸ historical a long pin used to fasten women's hair.
–ORIGIN Middle English: perhaps of Celtic origin and rel. to Irish *bod* 'dagger'.

body ▪ n. (pl. **-ies**) **1** the physical structure, including the bones, flesh, and organs, of a person or an animal. ▸ informal, dated a person. ▸ the trunk apart from the head and the limbs. ▸ a corpse. **2** the main or central part of something. ▸ a mass or collection of something. **3** an organized group of people with a common function: *a regulatory body.* **4** a full flavour in wine. **5** fullness of a person's hair. **6** a bodysuit.
–PHRASES **in a body** as a group. **keep body and soul together** stay alive in difficult circumstances. **over my dead body** informal used to express strong opposition.
–DERIVATIVES **-bodied** adj.
–ORIGIN Old English *bodig*.

body armour ▪ n. clothing worn by the army and police to protect against gunfire.

body art ▪ n. **1** the practice of decorating the body by means of tattooing, piercing, etc. **2** an artistic genre in which the actual body of the artist or model is integral to the work.

body bag ▪ n. a bag used for carrying a corpse from the scene of an accident or crime.

body blow ▪ n. **1** a heavy punch to the body. **2** a severe setback.

bodyboard ▪ n. a short, light surfboard ridden in a prone position.
–DERIVATIVES **bodyboarder** n. **bodyboarding** n.

bodybuilder ▪ n. **1** a person who strengthens and enlarges their muscles through exercise such as weight-lifting. **2** a person or company that builds the bodies of vehicles.
–DERIVATIVES **bodybuilding** n.

body-check ▪ n. (especially in ice hockey) an attempt to obstruct a player by bumping into them. ▪ v. obstruct (a player) in such a way.

body clock ▪ n. a person's biological clock.

body corporate ▪ n. formal term for CORPORATION.

body double ▪ n. a stand-in for a film actor during stunt or nude scenes.

bodyguard ▪ n. a person employed to protect a rich or famous person.

body language ▪ n. the conscious and unconscious bodily movements by which feelings are communicated.

bodyline ▪ n. Cricket, historical fast short-pitched bowling on the leg side, threatening the batsman's body.

body louse ▪ n. a louse which infests the human body and is able to transmit several diseases through its bite, including typhus. [*Pediculus humanus humanus*.]

body mass index ▪ n. (pl. **body mass indices**) an approximate measure of whether someone is over- or underweight, calculated by dividing their weight in kilograms by the square of their height in metres.

body odour ▪ n. the unpleasant smell of a person's unwashed body.

body piercing ▪ n. the decorative piercing of parts of the body other than the ear lobes.

body politic ▪ n. the people of a nation or society considered as an organized group of citizens.

body scrub ▪ n. an exfoliating and cleansing cosmetic preparation applied to the skin.

body shop ▪ n. a garage where repairs to the bodywork of vehicles are carried out.

bodysnatcher ▪ n. historical a person who illicitly disinterred corpses for dissection.
–DERIVATIVES **bodysnatching** n.

body stocking ▪ n. a woman's one-piece undergarment covering the torso and legs.

bodysuit ▪ n. a woman's close-fitting stretch garment for the upper body, fastening at the crotch.

bodysurf ▪ v. surf without using a board.

body warmer ▪ n. a sleeveless padded jacket worn outdoors.

bodywork ▪ n. the metal outer shell of a vehicle.

body wrap ▪ n. a beauty treatment intended to result in a reduction body measurements, involving wrapping the body in hot bandages.

boeber /ˈbuːbə/ (also **boeboer**) ▪ n. S. African a sweet Cape Malay dessert usually made of milk, sago, vermicelli, sugar, and spices.

boekenhout /ˈbʊkənhaʊt/ ▪ n. S. African **1** a tree which resembles the European beech. [*Rapanea melanophloeos* (Cape beech), *Faurea saligna*, and other species.] **2** the wood of these trees.

– ORIGIN C18: S. African Dutch, from Dutch *beuke* 'beech' + *hout* 'wood'.

boep /bʊp/ ■ n. S. African informal a pot belly or paunch. ▶ short for BEER BOEP.
– ORIGIN 1970s: shortened form of Afrikaans *boepens* 'paunch', from Dutch, from *boeg* 'bow (of ship)' + *pens* 'stomach'.

Boer /buːr, bʊə/ (also **boer**) ■ n. (pl. **-s** or **-e**) **1** a member of the Dutch and Huguenot population which settled in southern Africa in the late 17th century. ▶ a burgher of the former Afrikaner republics, especially one who fought the British in the Anglo-Boer Wars. **2** S. African an Afrikaner farmer or country person. **3** S. African, often derogatory any person of Afrikaner origin. **4** S. African informal (under apartheid) a member of the police, prison service, or security forces. ■ adj. of or relating to the Boers.
– ORIGIN from Dutch *boer* 'farmer'.

boer- /ˈbuːr-, ˈbʊə-/ (also **Boer-**, **boere-**) ■ comb. form **1** of Afrikaner origin. ▶ associated with farmers; country-style. **2** (of animals and plants) indigenous to South Africa.

boerbean /ˈbuːrbiːn, ˈbʊə-/ (also **boerboon** /ˈbuːrbʊən/) ■ n. S. African an indigenous tree with nectar-rich red flowers and flat woody seed pods. [Genus *Schotia*: several species.]
– ORIGIN 1900s: from Afrikaans, partial translation of *boerboon*, from BOER- + *boon* 'bean'.

boerbok /ˈbuːrbɒk, ˈbʊə-/ ■ n. (pl. same or **boerbokke**) S. African another term for BOER GOAT.
– ORIGIN Afrikaans, from BOER- + *bok* 'goat'.

boerbull /ˈbuːrbʊl, ˈbʊə-/ (also **boerbul**) ■ n. S. African a large cross-breed dog bred from the mastiff and indigenous African dogs.
– ORIGIN 1960s: from Afrikaans *boerboel*, from BOER- + *boel*, from Dutch *bul* (as in *bulhond* 'mastiff').

boere- /ˈbuːrə-, ˈbʊərə-/ (also **Boere-**) ■ comb. form S. African variant spelling of BOER-.

boerekos /ˈbuːrəkɔs, ˈbʊər-/ ■ n. S. African traditional Afrikaner food.
– ORIGIN Afrikaans, from BOERE- + *kos* 'food'.

boeremeisie /ˈbuːrəˌmeɪsi, ˈbʊər-/ ■ n. S. African **1** an Afrikaner girl. ▶ an unsophisticated country girl. **2** (**boeremeisies**) brandied apricots.
– ORIGIN Afrikaans, from BOERE- + *meisie* 'girl'.

boeremusiek /ˈbuːrəmuːsɪk, ˈbʊər-/ ■ n. S. African popular traditional Afrikaans folk or light music, often for dancing.
– ORIGIN Afrikaans, from BOERE- + *musiek* 'music'.

boereqanga /ˈbuːrəkɑːŋɡa, ˈbʊərəˈɑːŋɡa/ ■ n. S. African a style of contemporary South African music which combines elements of boeremusiek and mbaqanga.
– ORIGIN blend of BOEREMUSIEK and MBAQANGA.

boereseun /ˈbuːrəsɪən, ˈbʊər-/ (also **boerseun** /ˈbuːrsɪʊn, ˈbʊər-/) ■ n. S. African an Afrikaner boy or man. ▶ a farm boy.
– ORIGIN Afrikaans, from BOERE- + *seun* 'boy, son'.

boeresport /ˈbuːrəˌspɔːt, ˈbʊə-/ ■ n. S. African any of several games played traditionally by Afrikaners, such as jukskei.
– ORIGIN Afrikaans, from BOERE- + *sport* 'sport, games'.

boerewors /ˈbuːrəˌvɔːs, ˈbʊər-/ ■ n. S. African a traditional sausage containing coarsely ground meat seasoned with spices.
– ORIGIN Afrikaans, from BOERE- + *wors* 'sausage'.

boerewors curtain ■ n. informal, often derogatory S. African an imaginary cultural barrier that separates predominantly white Afrikaans-speaking communities from others.

boer goat ■ n. a goat of a hardy indigenous breed, well adapted to arid terrain.

boerie /ˈbʊri/ ■ n. S. African informal short for BOEREWORS.

Boerperd /ˈbuːrpɜːt, ˈbʊər-/ ■ n. (pl. **Boerperde**) S. African a horse of a breed descended from indigenous horses cross-bred with those introduced to the Cape by early European settlers. See also NOOITGEDACHT PONY.
– ORIGIN Afrikaans, from BOERE- + *perd* 'horse'.

Boer War ■ n. short for ANGLO-BOER WAR.

boet /bʊt, buːt/ ■ n. S. African informal **1** used before a man's first name as an informal title. **2** (also **boetie** /ˈbuːti, ˈbʊti/, **ouboet** /ˈəʊbʊt/) a familiar or affectionate term of address for a male friend; pal or buddy. **3** used familiarly or affectionately of or to one's brother.
– ORIGIN Afrikaans, from Dutch *boet* 'youngster'.

boeuf bourguignon /ˌbəːf ˈbɔːɡɪnjɒ̃/ ■ n. a dish consisting of beef stewed in red wine.
– ORIGIN French, 'Burgundy beef'.

boffin ■ n. informal, chiefly Brit. a person engaged in scientific or technical research.
– DERIVATIVES **boffiny** adj.
– ORIGIN SECOND WORLD WAR.

bog ■ n. **1** an area of very soft wet muddy ground. **2** Brit. informal a toilet. ■ v. (**bogged**, **bogging**) **1** (usu. **be bogged down**) cause to become stuck; hinder the progress of. **2** (**bog off**) Brit. informal go away.
– DERIVATIVES **bogginess** n. **boggy** adj.
– ORIGIN Middle English: from Irish or Scottish Gaelic *bogach*, from *bog* 'soft'.

bogey[1] Golf ■ n. (pl. **-eys**) a score of one stroke over par at a hole. ■ v. (**-eys**, **-eyed**) play (a hole) in one stroke over par.
– ORIGIN C19: perhaps from *Bogey*, denoting the Devil (see BOGEY[2]).

bogey[2] (also **bogy**) ■ n. (pl. **-eys**) an evil or mischievous spirit.
– ORIGIN C19 (as a name applied to the Devil).

bogeyman (also **bogyman**) ■ n. (pl. **-men**) an evil spirit.

boggart /ˈbɒɡət/ ■ n. Scottish & N. English an evil or mischievous spirit.
– ORIGIN C16: rel. to obsolete *bog* 'bugbear'.

boggle ■ v. informal be startled or baffled: *the mind boggles at the spectacle.* ▶ (**boggle at**) hesitate or be anxious at.
– ORIGIN C16: prob. of dialect origin and rel. to BOGEY[2].

bog oak ■ n. an ancient oak tree preserved in peat, with hard black wood.

bog-standard ■ adj. informal, derogatory ordinary; basic.

bogtrotter ■ n. informal, offensive an Irish person.

bogus /ˈbəʊɡəs/ ■ adj. not genuine or true.
– DERIVATIVES **bogusly** adv. **bogusness** n.
– ORIGIN C18 (orig. US, denoting a machine for making counterfeit money).

bogy ■ n. (pl. **-ies**) variant spelling of BOGEY[2].

bogyman ■ n. variant spelling of BOGEYMAN.

Bohemian ■ n. **1** a native or inhabitant of Bohemia, a region of the Czech Republic. **2** a socially unconventional person, especially an artist or writer. [C19: from French *bohémien* 'gypsy' (because gypsies were thought to come from Bohemia).] ■ adj. **1** of or relating to Bohemia or its people. **2** socially unconventional.
– DERIVATIVES **Bohemianism** n.

bohrium /ˈbɔːrɪəm/ ■ n. the chemical element of atomic number 107, a very unstable element made by high-energy atomic collisions. (Symbol: **Bh**)
– ORIGIN C20: named after the Danish physicist Niels *Bohr*.

boil[1] ■ v. **1** (with reference to a liquid) reach or cause to reach the temperature at which it bubbles and turns to vapour. **2** (with reference to food) cook or be cooked by immersing in boiling water. **3** (of the sea or clouds) be turbulent and stormy. ▶ (of a person or emotion) be stirred up or inflamed. ▶ (**boil over**) become so excited or tense as to lose control. **4** (**boil down to**) amount to. ■ n. **1** the act or process of boiling; boiling point. **2** Fishing a sudden rise of a fish at a fly.
– PHRASES **keep the pot boiling** maintain the momentum or interest value of something.
– ORIGIN Middle English: from Old French *boillir*, from Latin, from *bulla* 'bubble'.

boil[2] ■ n. an inflamed pus-filled swelling on the skin.
– ORIGIN Old English, of West Germanic origin.

boiled sweet ■ n. Brit. a hard sweet made of boiled sugar.

boiler ■ n. a fuel-burning apparatus for heating water, especially a device providing a domestic hot-water supply or serving a central heating system. ▶ a tank for generating steam in a steam engine.

boilermaker ■ n. a person who makes boilers. ▶ a metalworker in heavy industry.

boilerplate ■ n. **1** rolled steel plates for making boilers.

boiler suit

2 (**boilerplates**) Climbing smooth, overlapping slabs of rock. **3** chiefly N. Amer. stereotyped or clichéd writing.
▸ standardized pieces of text for use as clauses in contracts or as part of a computer program.

boiler suit ■ n. Brit. a one-piece suit worn as overalls for heavy manual work.

boilie /ˈbɔɪli/ ■ n. (pl. **-ies**) a flavoured fishing bait, spherical in shape, used to catch carp.

boiling ■ adj. at or near boiling point. ▸ informal extremely hot. ■ n. boiling point.

boiling point ■ n. **1** the temperature at which a liquid boils. **2** the point at which anger or excitement breaks out into violence.

boiling-water reactor ■ n. a nuclear reactor in which the coolant and moderator is water, which is boiled to produce steam.

boisterous ■ adj. **1** noisy, energetic, and cheerful. **2** (of weather or water) wild or stormy.
– DERIVATIVES **boisterously** adv. **boisterousness** n.
– ORIGIN Middle English: var. of *boistuous* 'rustic, boisterous'.

bok ■ n. S. African **1** another term for BUCK[1] (sense 2). **2** a goat.
– ORIGIN Afrikaans, from S. African Dutch, 'antelope, goat'.

bok choy /bɒk ˈtʃɔɪ/ ■ n. US spelling of PAK CHOI.

bokkem /ˈbɒkəm/ ■ n. S. African a salted, dried, and sometimes smoked whole fish, usually a small mullet.
▸ the flesh of a fish prepared in this way.
– ORIGIN C19: from Dutch *bokking*, *bokkem* 'smoked herring'.

bokkie /ˈbɒki/ ■ n. S. African informal **1** an affectionate form of address, usually for a woman. **2** a girl. ▸ a girlfriend. **3** a small antelope or goat.
– ORIGIN Afrikaans: 'kid', diminutive of *bok* 'antelope, goat'.

bokmakierie /ˌbɒkməˈkɪəri/ ■ n. (pl. **-ies**) a shrike with yellow underparts and a black band across the breast, common in southern Africa. [*Telophorus zeylonus*.]
– ORIGIN C19: from Afrikaans, imitative of its call.

bold ■ adj. **1** confident and daring or courageous. ▸ dated audacious; impudent. **2** (of a colour or design) strong or vivid. ▸ (of type) having thick strokes. ■ n. a typeface with thick strokes.
– PHRASES **be** (or **make**) **so bold as to do something** dare to do something that might be considered audacious. (**as**) **bold as brass** confident to the point of impudence.
– DERIVATIVES **boldly** adv. **boldness** n.
– ORIGIN Old English, of Germanic origin.

boldface ■ n. a typeface with thick strokes.
– DERIVATIVES **boldfaced** adj.

bole ■ n. a tree trunk.
– ORIGIN Middle English: from Old Norse *bolr*.

bolection /bəˈlɛkʃ(ə)n/ ■ n. Architecture a decorative moulding above or around a panel.
– ORIGIN C17.

bolero /bəˈlɛːrəʊ/ ■ n. (pl. **-os**) **1** a Spanish dance in simple triple time. ▸ the music for such a dance. **2** /also ˈbɒlərəʊ/ a woman's short open jacket.
– ORIGIN C18: from Spanish.

boletus /bəˈliːtəs/ (also **bolete**) ■ n. (pl. **boletuses**) a toadstool with pores rather than gills on the underside of the cap, and a thick stem. [Genus *Boletus*.]
– ORIGIN from Greek *bōlitēs*, perhaps from *bōlos* 'lump'.

Bolivian /bəˈlɪvɪən/ ■ n. a native or inhabitant of Bolivia. ■ adj. of or relating to Bolivia or its inhabitants.

boll /bəʊl/ ■ n. the rounded seed capsule of plants such as cotton or flax.
– ORIGIN Middle English: from Middle Dutch *bolle* 'rounded object'.

bollard /ˈbɒlɑːd, -ləd/ ■ n. **1** Brit. a short post used to prevent traffic from entering an area. **2** a short post on a ship or quayside for securing a rope.
– ORIGIN Middle English: perhaps from Old Norse *bolr*.

bollocking (also **ballocking**) ■ n. Brit. vulgar slang a severe reprimand.
– DERIVATIVES **bollock** v.

bollocks (also **ballocks**) ■ pl. n. Brit. vulgar slang **1** the testicles. **2** [treated as sing.] nonsense; rubbish.
– ORIGIN C18: pl. of *bollock*, var. of *ballock*, of Germanic origin; rel. to BALL[1].

boll weevil ■ n. a small weevil which feeds on the fibres of the cotton boll. [*Anthonomus grandis*.]

bollworm ■ n. a moth caterpillar which is a pest of cotton and other crops in North America.

Bollywood ■ n. informal the Indian popular film industry, based in Bombay.

bolo ■ n. S. African coarse boneless meat cut from the forequarter of beef or big game, usually used for stewing.

bologna /bəˈləʊnjə, bəˈlɒnjə/ ■ n. a large smoked sausage made chiefly of bacon, veal, and pork suet.
– ORIGIN named after *Bologna*, a city in northern Italy.

boloney ■ n. variant spelling of BALONEY.

Bolshevik /ˈbɒlʃɪvɪk/ ■ n. historical **1** a member of the majority faction of the Russian Social Democratic Party, which seized power in the Revolution of 1917. **2** a person with politically subversive or radical views. ■ adj. of, relating to, or characteristic of Bolsheviks or Bolshevism.
– DERIVATIVES **Bolshevism** n. **Bolshevist** n.
– ORIGIN Russian: from *bolʹshe* 'greater' (with ref. to the greater faction).

bolshie (also **bolshy**) informal ■ adj. deliberately combative or uncooperative. ■ n. (pl. **-ies**) (**Bolshie**) dated a Bolshevik or socialist.
– DERIVATIVES **bolshiness** n.
– ORIGIN C20: abbrev. of BOLSHEVIK.

bolster /ˈbəʊlstə/ ■ n. **1** a long, thick pillow. **2** a part on a vehicle or tool providing structural support or reducing friction. ▸ Building a short timber cap over a post increasing the bearing of the beams it supports. ■ v. support or strengthen.
– ORIGIN Old English, of Germanic origin.

bolt[1] ■ n. **1** a long pin with a head that screws into a nut, used to fasten things together. ▸ a bar that slides into a socket to fasten a door or window. ▸ the sliding piece of the breech mechanism of a rifle. **2** a short, heavy arrow shot from a crossbow. **3** a flash of lightning across the sky. ■ v. fasten with a bolt.
– PHRASES **a bolt from** (or **out of**) **the blue** a sudden and unexpected event. **bolt upright** with the back very straight. **have shot one's bolt** informal have done everything possible but still not succeeded.
– ORIGIN Old English.

bolt[2] ■ v. **1** run away suddenly. ▸ (in hunting) cause (a rabbit or fox) to run out of its burrow or hole. **2** (of a plant) grow quickly upwards and stop flowering as seeds develop. **3** eat (food) quickly.
– PHRASES **make a bolt for** try to escape by running suddenly towards.
– ORIGIN Middle English: from BOLT[1].

bolt[3] ■ n. a roll of fabric, originally as a measure.
– ORIGIN Middle English: transferred use of BOLT[1].

bolt-action ■ adj. (of a gun) having a breech which is opened by turning a bolt and sliding it back.

bolter ■ n. **1** a person or animal that bolts or runs away. **2** a plant that bolts.

bolt hole ■ n. chiefly Brit. an escape route or hiding place.

Boltzmann's constant ■ n. Chemistry the ratio of the gas constant to Avogadro's constant, equal to 1.381×10^{-23} joule per kelvin.
– ORIGIN named after the Austrian physicist Ludwig *Boltzmann*.

bolus /ˈbəʊləs/ ■ n. (pl. **boluses**) **1** a small rounded mass of a substance, especially of food being swallowed. **2** a large pill used in veterinary medicine. ▸ Medicine a single dose of a drug given all at once.
– ORIGIN C16: from Greek *bōlos* 'clod'.

boma[1] /ˈbəʊmə/ ■ n. (in eastern and southern Africa) an enclosure.
– ORIGIN from Kiswahili.

boma[2] /ˈbəʊmə/ ■ n. S. African a hut where initiates stay in seclusion during circumcision rituals.
– ORIGIN from isiXhosa *ibhoma* 'circumcision lodge'.

bomb ■ n. **1** a container of explosive or incendiary material, designed to explode on impact or when

detonated by a timing or remote-control device. ▶ (**the bomb**) nuclear weapons collectively. **2** (**a bomb**) Brit. informal a large sum of money. **3** informal a thing that fails badly. **4** a pear-shaped weight used to anchor a fishing line to the bottom. ■ v. **1** attack with a bomb or bombs. **2** informal move very quickly. **3** informal fail badly.
– PHRASES **go down a bomb** Brit. informal be very well received. **go like a bomb** informal **1** be very successful. **2** move very fast.
– ORIGIN C17: from French *bombe*, prob. from Latin *bombus* 'booming, humming', from Greek *bombos*, of imitative origin.

bombard /bɒmˈbɑːd/ ■ v. **1** attack continuously with bombs or other missiles. **2** subject to a continuous flow of questions or information. **3** direct a stream of high-speed particles at (a substance).
– DERIVATIVES **bombardment** n.
– ORIGIN Middle English: from Old French *bombarde*, prob. from Latin *bombus* (see BOMB).

bombardier /ˌbɒmbəˈdɪə/ ■ n. **1** a rank of non-commissioned officer in artillery regiments, equivalent to corporal. **2** a member of a bomber crew in the US air force responsible for sighting and releasing bombs.
– ORIGIN C16: from Old French *bombarde* (see BOMBARD).

bombardier beetle ■ n. a beetle that discharges a puff of irritant vapour from its anus with an audible pop when alarmed. [*Brachinus crepitans* and other species.]

bombast /ˈbɒmbast/ ■ n. high-sounding language with little meaning.
– DERIVATIVES **bombastic** adj. **bombastically** adv.
– ORIGIN C16 (denoting cotton wool used as padding, later used figuratively): from Old French *bombace*, from Latin *bombyx* 'silkworm'.

Bombay duck ■ n. the bummalo (fish), dried and eaten as an accompaniment with curries.
– ORIGIN C19: alteration of BUMMALO by association with the city of *Bombay* in India, from which bummalo were exported; the reason for the use of *duck* is unknown.

Bombay mix ■ n. an Indian spiced snack consisting of lentils, peanuts, and deep-fried strands of gram flour.

bomb bay ■ n. a compartment in the fuselage of an aircraft used to hold bombs.

bomb disposal ■ n. the defusing or controlled detonation of unexploded bombs.

bombe /bɒmb/ ■ n. a frozen dome-shaped dessert.
– ORIGIN French, 'bomb'.

bombed ■ adj. **1** subjected to bombing. **2** informal intoxicated by drink or drugs.

bomber ■ n. **1** an aircraft that drops bombs. **2** a person who plants bombs, especially as a terrorist.

bomber jacket ■ n. a short jacket gathered at the waist and cuffs by elasticated bands and having a zip front.

bombshell ■ n. **1** an overwhelming surprise or disappointment. **2** informal a very attractive woman. **3** dated an artillery shell.

bombsight ■ n. a device used in an aircraft for aiming bombs.

bomb squad ■ n. a division of a police force investigating the planting of terrorist bombs.

bona fide /ˌbəʊnə ˈfʌɪdi/ ■ adj. genuine; real. ■ adv. chiefly Law without intention to deceive.
– ORIGIN Latin, 'with good faith', from BONA FIDES.

bona fides /ˌbəʊnə ˈfʌɪdiːz/ ■ n. **1** honesty and sincerity of intention. **2** [treated as pl.] informal a person's credentials.
– ORIGIN Latin, 'good faith'.

bonanza /bəˈnanzə/ ■ n. a source of wealth, good fortune, or profits.
– ORIGIN C19 (orig. US, with ref. to success when mining): from Spanish, 'fair weather, prosperity', from Latin *bonus* 'good'.

bon appétit /ˌbɒn apeˈtiː/ ■ exclam. used as a salutation to a person about to eat.
– ORIGIN French, 'good appetite'.

bonbon ■ n. a sweet.
– ORIGIN C18: from French, reduplication of *bon* 'good', from Latin *bonus*.

bond /bɒnd/ ■ n. **1** a thing used to tie or fasten things together. ▶ (**bonds**) physical restraints used to hold someone prisoner. **2** a force or feeling that unites people. **3** a binding agreement, especially one which commits someone to make a payment to another. ▶ S. African short for MORTGAGE BOND. ▶ a certificate issued by a government or a public company promising to repay borrowed money at a fixed rate of interest at a specified time. ▶ an insurance policy held by a company, which protects against losses resulting from circumstances such as bankruptcy. **4** (also **chemical bond**) a strong force of attraction holding atoms together in a molecule. **5** Building a pattern in which bricks are laid to ensure the strength of a structure. ■ v. **1** join or be joined securely to something else. **2** establish a relationship based on shared feelings or experiences. **3** join or be joined by a chemical bond. **4** [usu. as adj. **bonding**] lay (bricks) in a strong overlapping pattern. **5** [usu. as noun **bonding**] place (dutiable goods) in bond.
– PHRASES **in bond** (of dutiable goods) stored in a bonded warehouse.
– DERIVATIVES **bonding** n. & adj.
– ORIGIN Middle English: var. of BAND¹.

bondage ■ n. **1** the state of being a slave or serf. **2** sexual practice that involves the tying up or restraining of one partner.
– ORIGIN Middle English: from *bond* 'serf', from Old Norse *bóndi* 'tiller of the soil'; influenced by BOND.

bonded ■ adj. **1** joined securely together, especially by an adhesive, heat process, or pressure. **2** bound by a legal agreement. **3** (of dutiable goods) placed in bond.

bonded warehouse ■ n. a customs-controlled warehouse for the retention of imported goods until the duty owed is paid.

bond paper ■ n. high-quality writing paper.

bondsman ■ n. (pl. -men) **1** a person who stands surety for a bond. **2** archaic a slave or feudal serf.

bondstone ■ n. a stone or brick running through a wall to strengthen it.

bone ■ n. **1** any of the pieces of hard, whitish tissue making up the skeleton in vertebrates. ▶ (**one's bones**) one's body. **2** the calcified material of which bones consist. ▶ a thing made of a substance resembling bone, e.g. a strip of stiffening for an undergarment. **3** (in southern Africa) one of a set of carved dice or bones used by traditional healers in divination. ■ v. **1** remove the bones from (meat or fish) before cooking. **2** (**bone up on**) informal study (a subject) intensively.
– PHRASES **bone of contention** a source of continuing disagreement. **close to the bone** (of a remark) accurate to the point of causing discomfort. ▶ (of a joke or story) near the limit of decency. **cut** (or **pare**) **something to the bone** reduce something to the bare minimum. **have a bone to pick with someone** informal have reason to disagree or be annoyed with someone. **in one's bones** felt or believed deeply or instinctively. **make no bones about** have no hesitation in stating or dealing with (something unpleasant). **off** (or **on**) **the bone** (of meat or fish) having had the bones removed (or left in). **to the bone 1** (of a wound) so deep as to expose a bone. **2** (especially of cold) affecting a person in a penetrating way. **work one's fingers to the bone** work very hard.
– DERIVATIVES **boned** adj. **boneless** adj.
– ORIGIN Old English, of Germanic origin.

bone ash ■ n. the mineral residue of calcined bones, used in making bone china and in fertilizer.

bone china ■ n. white porcelain containing bone ash.

bone dry ■ adj. extremely dry.

bonefish ■ n. (pl. same or **-fishes**) a silvery game fish of warm coastal waters. [*Albula vulpes* and other species.]

bonehead ■ n. informal a stupid person.
– DERIVATIVES **boneheaded** adj.

bone idle ■ adj. extremely idle.
– ORIGIN C19: expressing *idle through to the bone*.

bonemeal ■ n. crushed or ground bones used as a fertilizer.

boner ■ n. informal **1** a stupid mistake. **2** an erection of the penis.

bone-setter ■ n. historical a person who set broken or dislocated bones without being a qualified surgeon.

boneshaker ■ n. Brit. informal an old vehicle with poor suspension. ▸ an early type of bicycle without rubber tyres.

bone-thrower ■ n. S. African a traditional healer who uses bones in divination.
– DERIVATIVES **bone-throwing** n.

boney (also **bony**) ■ n. S. African informal **1** a motorcycle. **2** a bicycle.

boneyard ■ n. informal, chiefly US a cemetery.

bonfire ■ n. a large open-air fire.
– ORIGIN Middle English (denoting a fire on which bones were burnt, or for burning heretics): from BONE + FIRE.

Bonfire Night ■ n. another term for GUY FAWKES NIGHT.

bong ■ n. a low-pitched resonant sound. ■ v. make this sound.
– ORIGIN 1920s: imitative.

bongo¹ /ˈbɒŋɡəʊ/ ■ n. (pl. **-os** or **-oes**) each of a pair of small drums, held between the knees and played with the fingers.
– ORIGIN 1920s: from Latin American Spanish *bongó*.

bongo² /ˈbɒŋɡəʊ/ ■ n. (pl. same or **-os**) an African forest antelope having a chestnut coat with white stripes. [*Tragelaphus eurycerus*.]
– ORIGIN C19: from Kikongo.

bonhomie /ˈbɒnəmiː, ˌbɒnəˈmiː/ ■ n. good-natured friendliness.
– ORIGIN C18: from French, from *bonhomme* 'good fellow'.

bonito /bəˈniːtəʊ/ ■ n. (pl. **-os**) a small tuna with dark stripes, important as a food and game fish. [*Sarda sarda* (Mediterranean), *Katsuwonus pelamis* (the skipjack, worldwide), and other species.]
– ORIGIN C16: from Spanish.

bonk informal ■ v. **1** hit so as to cause a reverberating sound. **2** have sexual intercourse. ■ n. **1** a reverberating sound. **2** an act of sexual intercourse.
– ORIGIN 1930s: imitative.

bonkers ■ adj. informal mad; crazy.
– ORIGIN 1940s.

bon mot /bɒn ˈməʊ/ ■ n. (pl. **bons mots** pronunc. same or /-ˈməʊz/) a clever or witty remark.
– ORIGIN C18: French, 'good word'.

bonne bouche /bɒn ˈbuːʃ/ ■ n. (pl. **bonne bouches** or **bonnes bouches** pronunc. same) an appetizing item of food eaten at the end of a meal.
– ORIGIN French, from *bon* 'good' + *bouche* 'mouth'.

bonne femme /bɒn ˈfam/ ■ adj. [postpos.] (of fish, stews, and soups) cooked in a simple way.
– ORIGIN French, from the phr. *à la bonne femme* 'in the manner of a good housewife'.

bonnet ■ n. **1** a woman's or child's hat tied under the chin and with a brim framing the face. **2** a soft brimless hat like a beret. **3** (also **war bonnet**) the ceremonial headdress of an American Indian. **4** the hinged metal canopy covering the engine of a motor vehicle. **5** a cowl on a chimney.
– DERIVATIVES **bonneted** adj.
– ORIGIN Middle English: from Old French *bonet*, from medieval Latin *abonnis* 'headgear'.

bonny (also **bonnie**) ■ adj. (**-ier**, **-iest**) chiefly Scottish physically attractive; healthy-looking.
– DERIVATIVES **bonnily** adv.
– ORIGIN C15: perhaps rel. to Old French *bon* 'good'.

bonobo /ˈbɒnəbəʊ/ ■ n. (pl. **-os**) a chimpanzee with a black face and black hair, found in the rainforests of the Democratic Republic of Congo. [*Pan paniscus*.]
– ORIGIN 1950s: a local word.

bonsai /ˈbɒnsʌɪ/ ■ n. the art of growing ornamental, artificially dwarfed varieties of trees or shrubs.
– ORIGIN 1950s: from Japanese, from *bon* 'tray' + *sai* 'planting'.

bonsella /bɒnˈsɛlə/ ■ n. S. African a gift or gratuity.
– ORIGIN 1900s: from isiZulu *bansela* 'offer a gift in gratitude'.

Bonsmara /bɒnsˈmɑːrə/ ■ n. an animal of a South African breed of beef cattle, cross-bred from Shorthorn, Hereford, and Afrikander cattle.
– ORIGIN from the name of Jan *Bonsma*, a developer of the breed, and *Mara* Research Station, at which the cattle were first bred.

bontebok /ˈbɒntəbɒk/ (also **bontebuck**) ■ n. (pl. same, or **bonteboks** or **-bucks**) an antelope with a reddish-brown coat and white face, native to parts of south-western South Africa. [*Damaliscus dorcas dorcas*.]
– ORIGIN C18: from Afrikaans, from Dutch *bont* 'pied' + *bok* 'buck'.

bont-legged tick ■ n. a tick with reddish-brown and white bands on the legs, which transmits Congo fever. [Genus *Hyalomma*: several species.]
– ORIGIN 1970s: *bont* from Afrikaans, from Dutch, 'variegated'.

bont tick ■ n. a large, brightly-patterned tick, which transmits heartwater amongst livestock and antelope, and causes tick-bite fever amongst humans. [*Amblyomma hebraeum* and other species.]
– ORIGIN C19: *bont* from Afrikaans, from Dutch, 'variegated'.

bonus ■ n. **1** a sum of money added seasonally to a person's wages for good performance. ▸ an extra dividend or issue paid to shareholders. **2** an extra and unexpected welcome event.
– ORIGIN C18: from Latin *bonus* 'good'.

bonus issue ■ n. an issue of additional shares to shareholders instead of a dividend.

bon vivant /ˌbɒ̃ viːˈvɒ̃/ ■ n. (pl. **bon vivants** or **bons vivants** pronunc. same) a person indulging in a sociable and luxurious lifestyle.
– ORIGIN C17: from French, 'person living well'.

bon viveur /ˌbɒ̃ viːˈvəː/ ■ n. (pl. **bon viveurs** or **bons viveurs** pronunc. same) another term for BON VIVANT.
– ORIGIN C19: pseudo-French, from French *bon* 'good' and *viveur* 'a living person'.

bon voyage /ˌbɒn vɔɪˈjɑːʒ/ ■ exclam. have a good journey.
– ORIGIN C17: French, 'good journey'.

bony ■ adj. (**-ier**, **-iest**) **1** of, like, or containing bones. **2** so thin that the bones can be seen. ■ n. variant spelling of BONEY.
– DERIVATIVES **boniness** n.

bony fish ■ n. a fish of a large class distinguished by a skeleton of bone, and comprising the majority of modern fishes. [Class Osteichthyes.]

bonze /bɒnz/ ■ n. a Japanese or Chinese Buddhist religious teacher.
– ORIGIN C16: prob. from Japanese *bonzō*, *bonsō* 'priest'.

boo ■ exclam. **1** said suddenly to surprise someone. **2** said to show disapproval or contempt. ■ v. (**boos**, **booed**) say 'boo' to show disapproval or contempt.
– PHRASES **wouldn't say boo to a goose** is very shy or reticent.
– ORIGIN C19: imitative of the lowing of oxen.

boob¹ informal ■ n. **1** Brit. an embarrassing mistake. **2** N. Amer. a stupid person. ■ v. Brit. make an embarrassing mistake.
– ORIGIN C20: abbrev. of BOOBY¹.

boob² ■ n. informal a woman's breast.
– ORIGIN 1950s: abbrev. of BOOBY²; from dialect *bubby*; perhaps rel. to German *Bübbi* 'teat'.

boo-boo ■ n. informal a mistake.
– ORIGIN 1950s: reduplication of BOOB¹.

boob tube ■ n. informal **1** Brit. a woman's tight-fitting strapless top. **2** chiefly N. Amer. television; a television set.

booby¹ ■ n. (pl. **-ies**) **1** informal a stupid person. **2** a large tropical seabird of the gannet family, with brown, black, or white plumage and brightly coloured feet. [Genus *Sula*: several species.]
– ORIGIN C17: prob. from Spanish *bobo*, from Latin *balbus* 'stammering'.

booby² ■ n. (pl. **-ies**) informal a woman's breast.
– ORIGIN 1930s: from dialect *bubby* (see BOOB²).

booby prize ■ n. a prize given to the person who comes last in a contest.

booby trap ■ n. an object containing a concealed

explosive device designed to detonate when someone touches it. ■ v. (**booby-trap**) place a booby trap in or on.

boodle ■ n. informal money, especially that gained or spent dishonestly.
– ORIGIN C17 (denoting a pack or crowd): from Dutch *boedel*, *boel* 'possessions, disorderly mass'.

boogie ■ n. (also **boogie-woogie**) (pl. **-ies**) **1** a style of blues played on the piano with a strong, fast beat. **2** informal a dance to pop or rock music. ■ v. (**boogieing**) informal dance to pop or rock music.
– ORIGIN C20 (orig. US in the sense 'party').

boogie board ■ n. a short, light surfboard ridden in a prone position.
– DERIVATIVES **boogie-boarder** n.

boohoo ■ exclam. representing the sound of someone crying noisily.
– ORIGIN C19: imitative.

boojum /'buːdʒəm/ ■ n. an imaginary dangerous animal.
– ORIGIN 1876: nonsense word coined by Lewis Carroll in *The Hunting of the Snark*.

book ■ n. **1** a written or printed work consisting of pages glued or sewn together along one side and bound in covers. ▸ a main division of a literary work or of the Bible. **2** (**books**) a set of records or accounts. ▸ a bookmaker's record of bets accepted and money paid out. **3** a set of tickets, stamps, matches, etc., bound together. **4** (**the book**) the first six tricks taken by the declarer in a hand of bridge. ■ v. **1** reserve (accommodation, a ticket, etc.). ▸ (**book in**) register one's arrival at a hotel. ▸ engage (a performer or guest) for an event. ▸ (**be booked up**) have all places reserved. **2** make an official note of the details of (someone who has broken a law or rule).
– PHRASES **bring someone to book** officially call someone to account for their behaviour. **by the book** strictly according to the rules. **in someone's bad** (or **good**) **books** in disfavour (or favour) with someone. **in my book** in my opinion. **make** (or **open**) **a book** take bets and pay out winnings on the outcome of a contest or other event. **on the books** contained in a list of members, employees, or clients. **People of the Book** Jews and Christians as regarded by Muslims. **take a leaf out of someone's book** imitate someone in a particular way. **throw the book at** informal charge or punish (someone) as severely as possible.
– DERIVATIVES **booker** n. **booking** n.
– ORIGIN Old English *bōc*, *bōcian* 'to grant by charter', of Germanic origin.

bookable ■ adj. **1** able to be reserved. **2** Soccer (of an offence) serious enough for the offending player to be cautioned by the referee.

bookbinder ■ n. a person who binds books.
– DERIVATIVES **bookbinding** n.

bookcase ■ n. an open cabinet containing shelves on which to keep books.

book club ■ n. a society which sells its members selected books at reduced prices.

bookend ■ n. a support placed at the end of a row of books to keep them upright.

book hand ■ n. a formal style of handwriting used by professional copiers of books before the invention of printing.

bookie ■ n. (pl. **-ies**) informal a bookmaker.

bookish ■ adj. **1** devoted to reading and studying. **2** (of language) literary in style.
– DERIVATIVES **bookishly** adv. **bookishness** n.

bookkeeping ■ n. the activity of keeping records of financial affairs.
– DERIVATIVES **bookkeeper** n.

book learning ■ n. knowledge gained from study rather than personal experience.

booklet ■ n. a small, thin book with paper covers.

booklouse ■ n. (pl. **booklice**) a minute insect with no or rudimentary wings, capable of causing damage to books and paper. [*Liposcelis bostrychophilus* and other species.]

book lung ■ n. Zoology (in an arachnid) each of a pair of respiratory organs in the abdomen, composed of many fine leaves.

bookmaker ■ n. a person whose job is to take bets, calculate odds, and pay out winnings.
– DERIVATIVES **bookmaking** n.

booster

bookmark ■ n. a strip of leather or card used to mark a place in a book. ▸ Computing a record of the address of a file, Internet page, etc. enabling quick access by a user. ■ v. Computing make a record of (the address of a file, Internet page, etc.) to enable quick access.

bookmobile /'bʊkmə‚biːl/ ■ n. N. Amer. a mobile library.

book of hours ■ n. a book of prayers appointed for particular canonical hours or times of day, used by Roman Catholics for private devotions.

Book of Life ■ n. S. African informal, dated a personal identity document.

bookplate ■ n. a decorative label in the front of a book, bearing the name of its owner.

bookrest ■ n. Brit. a support for an open book on a table.

book token ■ n. a voucher which can be exchanged for books costing up to a specified amount.

book value ■ n. the value of a security or asset as entered in a firm's books. Often contrasted with MARKET VALUE.

bookworm ■ n. **1** informal a person who enjoys reading. **2** the larva of a wood-boring beetle which feeds on the paper and glue in books.

Boolean /'buːlɪən/ ■ adj. denoting a system of algebraic notation used to represent logical propositions by means of the binary digits 0 (false) and 1 (true), especially in computing and electronics. ■ n. Computing a binary variable with these possible values.
– ORIGIN C19: from the name of the English mathematician G. *Boole*.

boom[1] ■ n. a loud, deep, resonant sound. ■ v. make this sound.
– DERIVATIVES **booming** adj. **boomy** adj.
– ORIGIN Middle English: imitative; perhaps from Dutch *bommen* 'to hum, buzz'.

boom[2] ■ n. a period of great prosperity. ■ v. experience a boom: *business is booming*.
– DERIVATIVES **boomy** adj.
– ORIGIN C19: prob. from BOOM[1].

boom[3] ■ n. **1** a pivoted spar to which the foot of a vessel's sail is attached. **2** a movable arm carrying a microphone or film camera. **3** a floating beam used to contain oil spills or to form a barrier across the mouth of a harbour.
– ORIGIN C16: from Dutch, 'beam, tree, pole'.

boomerang ■ n. a curved flat piece of wood that can be thrown so as to return to the thrower, used by Australian Aboriginals as a hunting weapon.
– ORIGIN C19: from Dharuk (an extinct Aboriginal language).

boomslang ■ n. a large, highly venomous southern African tree snake. [*Dispholidus typus*.]
– ORIGIN C18: from Afrikaans, from Dutch *boom* 'tree' + *slang* 'snake'.

boon ■ n. **1** a thing that is helpful or beneficial. **2** archaic a favour or request.
– ORIGIN Middle English: from Old Norse *bón*.

boon companion ■ n. dated or poetic/literary a close friend.
– ORIGIN C16: *boon* from Old French *bon*, from Latin *bonus* 'good'.

boondocks /'buːndɒks/ ■ pl. n. (**the boondocks**) informal, chiefly N. Amer. rough or isolated country.
– ORIGIN 1940s: *boondock* from Tagalog *bundok* 'mountain'.

boonies /'buːnɪz/ ■ pl. n. short for BOONDOCKS.

boor /bʊə/ ■ n. a rough and bad-mannered person.
– DERIVATIVES **boorish** adj. **boorishly** adv. **boorishness** n.
– ORIGIN C16: from Low German *būr* or Dutch *boer* 'farmer'.

boost ■ v. help or encourage to increase or improve. ■ n. a source of help or encouragement towards improvement.
– ORIGIN C19 (orig. US, in the sense 'push from below').

booster ■ n. **1** Medicine a dose of a vaccine increasing or renewing the effect of an earlier one. **2** the first stage of a rocket or spacecraft, used to give initial acceleration. **3** a source of help or encouragement. **4** a device for increasing electrical voltage or signal strength.

booster seat

booster seat ■ n. an extra seat placed on an existing seat for a small child.

boot[1] ■ n. **1** a sturdy item of footwear covering the foot and ankle, and sometimes the lower leg. **2** informal a hard kick. **3** a space at the back of a car for carrying luggage. ■ v. **1** kick hard. **2** (**boot someone out**) informal force someone to leave unceremoniously. **3** start (a computer) and put it into a state of readiness for operation. [from BOOTSTRAP.]
– PHRASES **the boot** (or N. Amer. **shoe**) **is on the other foot** the situation has reversed. **die with one's boots on** die in battle or while actively occupied. **give** (or **get**) **the boot** informal dismiss (or be dismissed) from a job. **old boot** informal an ugly or disliked old woman. **put the boot in** informal kick or attack someone when they are already on the ground. **with one's heart in one's boots** very depressed or anxious.
– DERIVATIVES **bootable** adj. **booted** adj.
– ORIGIN Middle English: from Old Norse *bóti* or Old French *bote*.

boot[2] ■ n. (in phr. **to boot**) as well.
– ORIGIN Old English *bōt* 'advantage, remedy', of Germanic origin.

bootblack ■ n. historical a person who polished boots and shoes.

bootboy ■ n. **1** informal a rowdy youth with close-cropped hair and heavy boots. **2** Brit. historical a boy who cleaned boots and shoes.

boot camp ■ n. chiefly N. Amer. a military training camp with very harsh discipline. ▸ a prison for young offenders, run on military lines.

bootee /buːˈtiː/ (also **bootie**) ■ n. **1** a baby's soft woollen shoe. **2** a woman's short boot.

booth /buːð, buːθ/ ■ n. **1** a small temporary structure used for selling goods or staging shows at a market or fair. **2** an enclosed compartment allowing privacy when telephoning, voting, etc.
– ORIGIN Middle English: from Old Norse *buth*, from *búa* 'dwell'.

bootjack ■ n. a device for holding a boot by the heel to ease withdrawal of one's foot.

bootlace ■ n. a cord or leather strip for lacing boots.

bootleg ■ adj. **1** (of alcoholic drink or a recording) made or distributed illegally. **2** (of trousers) shaped below the knee so as to fit over boots. ■ n. an illegal musical recording.
– DERIVATIVES **bootlegged** adj. **bootlegger** n. **bootlegging** n.
– ORIGIN C19: from the smugglers' practice of hiding bottles in their boots.

bootlicker ■ n. informal an obsequious person.
– DERIVATIVES **bootlicking** n.

bootstrap ■ n. **1** a loop at the back of a boot, used to pull it on. **2** Computing the action of loading a program into a computer by means of a few initial instructions which enable the introduction of the rest of the program from an input device.
– PHRASES **pull oneself up by one's bootstraps** improve one's position by one's own efforts.

booty ■ n. valuable stolen goods.
– ORIGIN Middle English: from Middle Low German *būte*, *buite* 'exchange, distribution'.

booze informal ■ n. alcoholic drink. ■ v. drink large quantities of alcohol.
– ORIGIN Middle English *bouse*, from Middle Dutch *būsen* 'drink to excess'.

boozer ■ n. informal **1** a person who drinks large quantities of alcohol. **2** Brit. a pub.

booze-up ■ n. informal a heavy drinking session.

boozy ■ adj. (**-ier**, **-iest**) informal drinking or involving large quantities of alcohol.
– DERIVATIVES **boozily** adv. **booziness** n.

bop[1] informal ■ n. **1** chiefly Brit. a dance to pop music. ▸ an organized social occasion with such dancing. **2** short for BEBOP. ■ v. (**bopped**, **bopping**) dance to pop music.
– DERIVATIVES **bopper** n.
– ORIGIN 1940s: shortening of BEBOP.

bop[2] informal ■ v. (**bopped**, **bopping**) hit or punch quickly. ■ n. a quick blow or punch.
– ORIGIN 1930s (orig. US): imitative.

boracic /bəˈrasɪk/ ■ adj. consisting of, containing, or denoting boric acid.
– ORIGIN C18: from medieval Latin *borax* (see BORAX).

borage /ˈbɒrɪdʒ/ ■ n. a European herbaceous plant with bright blue flowers and hairy leaves. [*Borago officinalis*.]
– ORIGIN Middle English: from medieval Latin *borrago*, perhaps from Arabic *'abū ḥurāš* 'father of roughness'.

borane /ˈbɔːreɪn/ ■ n. Chemistry any of a series of unstable compounds of boron and hydrogen.

borate /ˈbɔːreɪt/ ■ n. Chemistry a salt in which the anion contains both boron and oxygen, as in borax.

borax /ˈbɔːraks/ ■ n. a white mineral consisting of hydrated sodium borate, found in some alkaline salt deposits and used in making glass and as a metallurgical flux.
– ORIGIN Middle English: from Arabic *būrak*.

borborygmus /ˌbɔːbəˈrɪɡməs/ ■ n. (pl. **borborygmi** /-mʌɪ/) technical a rumbling noise made by fluid and gas in the intestines.
– DERIVATIVES **borborygmic** adj.
– ORIGIN C18: from Greek *borborugmos*.

Bordeaux /bɔːˈdəʊ/ ■ n. (pl. same /-ˈdəʊz/) a wine from Bordeaux, a district of SW France.

bordello /bɔːˈdɛləʊ/ ■ n. (pl. **-os**) chiefly N. Amer. a brothel.
– ORIGIN C16: prob. from Old French *bordel*, diminutive of *borde* 'small farm, cottage', of Germanic origin.

border ■ n. **1** a line separating two countries or other areas. ▸ (also **the Border**) S. African, chiefly historical the region of the Eastern Cape lying south of the Great Kei River and east of the Kat River. ▸ (also **the Border**) S. African historical areas in which the South African Defence Force fought members of Umkhonto we Sizwe (or the South West African People's Organization), especially the border between Namibia and Angola. **2** a decorative band around the edge of something. ▸ a strip of ground along the edge of a lawn for planting flowers or shrubs. ■ v. **1** form a border around or along. **2** (of a country or area) be adjacent to (another). **3** (**border on**) come close to (an extreme condition).
– ORIGIN Middle English: from Old French *bordeure*; of Germanic origin.

borderer ■ n. a person living near the border between two countries.

borderline ■ n. a boundary separating two countries or areas. ■ adj. only just acceptable in quality or as belonging to a category.

borderline personality disorder ■ n. Psychiatry a condition in which a person's behaviour fluctuates between normal patterns and psychological instability, manifested in emotional difficulties, mood swings, and problems with interpersonal relations.

bordure /ˈbɔːdjʊə/ ■ n. Heraldry a broad border used as a charge in a coat of arms, often as a mark of difference.
– ORIGIN Middle English: var. of BORDER.

bore[1] ■ v. **1** make (a hole) in something with a drill or other tool. ▸ hollow out (a gun barrel or other tube). **2** (of an athlete or racehorse) push another competitor out of the way. ■ n. the hollow part inside a gun barrel or other tube. ▸ the diameter of this: *a small-bore rifle*.
– ORIGIN Old English, of Germanic origin.

bore[2] ■ n. a dull and uninteresting person or activity. ■ conj. & adv. cause to feel weary and uninterested by being dull and tedious.
– ORIGIN C18.

bore[3] ■ n. a steep-fronted wave caused by the meeting of two tides or by a tide rushing up a narrow estuary.
– ORIGIN C17: perhaps from Old Norse *bára* 'wave'.

bore[4] past of BEAR[1].

boreal /ˈbɔːrɪəl/ ■ adj. chiefly Ecology of the North or northern regions, adjacent to or including the Arctic.
– ORIGIN Middle English: from late Latin *borealis*, from Latin *Boreas*, the god of the north wind, from Greek.

bored ■ adj. weary and impatient because one is unoccupied or lacks interest in something.

-bored ■ adj. (of a gun) having a specified bore.

boredom ■ n. the state of feeling bored.

borehole ▪ n. a deep, narrow hole in the ground made to locate water or oil.

borer ▪ n. 1 a worm, mollusc, or insect which bores into plant material or rock. ▸ (also **borer beetle**) S. African the furniture beetle. [*Anobium punctatum*.] 2 a tool for boring.

boric /ˈbɔːrɪk/ ▪ adj. Chemistry of boron.

boric acid ▪ n. Chemistry a weakly acid crystalline compound derived from borax, used as a mild antiseptic. [B(OH)$_3$.]

boring ▪ adj. not interesting; tedious.
– DERIVATIVES **boringly** adv. **boringness** n.

borlotti bean /bɔːˈlɒti/ ▪ n. a type of kidney bean with a pink speckled skin that turns brown when cooked.
– ORIGIN Italian *borlotti*, pl. of *borlotto* 'kidney bean'.

born ▪ adj. 1 existing as a result of birth. 2 (**born of**) existing as a result of (a situation or feeling). 3 having a natural ability to do a particular job or task: *a born engineer.* 4 (**-born**) having a specific nationality: *a German-born philosopher.*
– PHRASES **born and bred** by birth and upbringing. **in all one's born days** throughout one's life (used for emphasis). **not know one is born** not realize how easy one's life is. **I** (or **she**, etc.) **wasn't born yesterday** I am (or she, etc. is) not foolish or gullible.
– ORIGIN Old English, from *beran* (see BEAR^1).

born-again ▪ adj. 1 relating to or denoting a person who has converted to a personal faith in Christ. 2 newly converted to and very enthusiastic about (an idea, cause, etc.).

borne past participle of BEAR^1.

-borne ▪ adj. carried by the thing specified.

Bornean /ˈbɔːnɪən/ ▪ n. a native or inhabitant of Borneo. ▪ adj. of or relating to Borneo or its people.

born free ▪ n. (in Africa) a member of a generation born in a country after its transition to democracy (e.g. post-apartheid South Africa or post-independence Zimbabwe).

bornite /ˈbɔːnʌɪt/ ▪ n. a brittle reddish-brown mineral with an iridescent purple tarnish, consisting of a sulphide of copper and iron.
– ORIGIN from the name of the Austrian mineralogist Ignatius von *Born*.

boro- /ˈbɔːrəʊ/ ▪ comb. form Chemistry representing BORON: *borosilicate.*

boron /ˈbɔːrɒn/ ▪ n. the chemical element of atomic number 5, a non-metal which can be isolated as a brown, amorphous powder or (if pure) a black crystalline semiconductor. (Symbol: **B**)
– DERIVATIVES **boride** n.
– ORIGIN C19: from BORAX, on the pattern of *carbon* (which it resembles).

borough /ˈbʌrə/ ▪ n. 1 Brit. a town (as distinct from a city) with a corporation and privileges granted by a royal charter. ▸ historical a town sending representatives to Parliament. 2 a municipal corporation in certain US states.
– ORIGIN Old English *burg*, *burh* 'fortress', later 'fortified town', of Germanic origin.

borrie ▪ n. S. African turmeric.
– ORIGIN Afrikaans, from Malay *boreh* 'turmeric'.

borrow ▪ v. 1 take and use (something belonging to someone else) with the intention of returning it. ▸ take and use (money) from a person or bank under agreement to pay it back later. 2 Golf allow (a certain distance) when playing a shot to compensate for a slope or other irregularity. ▪ n. Golf a slope or other irregularity on a golf course.
– PHRASES **be (living) on borrowed time** be surviving against expectations. **borrow trouble** N. Amer. take needless action that may have detrimental effects.
– DERIVATIVES **borrower** n. **borrowing** n.
– ORIGIN Old English, of Germanic origin.

USAGE
Reciprocal pairs of words such as **borrow** and **lend** are often confused. A person asking for the temporary use of something says: *may I borrow your pen?* The person whom he asks may then *lend* it to him.

borrow pit ▪ n. a pit resulting from the excavation of material for use in embankments.

borscht /bɔːʃt/ (also **borsch** /bɔːʃ/) ▪ n. a Russian or Polish soup made with beetroot.
– ORIGIN from Russian *borshch*.

borstal /ˈbɔːst(ə)l/ ▪ n. Brit. historical a custodial institution for young offenders.
– ORIGIN C20: named after the village of *Borstal* in southern England, where the first of these was established.

borzoi /ˈbɔːzɔɪ/ ▪ n. (pl. **borzois**) a large Russian wolfhound of a breed with a narrow head and silky coat.
– ORIGIN C19: from Russian, from *borzy* 'swift'.

bosberaad /ˈbɒsbərɑːt/ ▪ n. (pl. **-ade**) S. African a long-term planning or strategy meeting, held away from the workplace.
– ORIGIN Afrikaans, from *bos* 'bush' + *beraad* 'deliberation'.

boscage /ˈbɒskɪdʒ/ (also **boskage**) ▪ n. a mass of trees or shrubs.
– ORIGIN Middle English: from Old French, of Germanic origin.

bosch ▪ n. S. African (in place names) bush; forest.
– ORIGIN from Dutch.

bosh ▪ n. informal nonsense.
– ORIGIN C19: from Turkish *boş* 'empty, worthless'.

Bosnian /ˈbɒznɪən/ ▪ n. a native or inhabitant of Bosnia. ▪ adj. of or relating to Bosnia or its people.

bosom ▪ n. 1 a woman's breast or chest. 2 the breast as the seat of emotions: *quivering dread was settling in her bosom.* ▸ a person's loving care or protection: *Bruno went home each night to the bosom of his family.* ▪ adj. (of a friend) very close.
– DERIVATIVES **-bosomed** adj. **bosomy** adj.
– ORIGIN Old English, of West Germanic origin.

boson /ˈbəʊzɒn/ ▪ n. Physics a subatomic particle, such as a photon, which has zero or integral spin.
– ORIGIN 1940s: named after the Indian physicist S. N. *Bose*.

boss^1 informal ▪ n. a person who is in charge of an employee or organization. ▪ v. give orders in a domineering manner.
– ORIGIN C19 (orig. US): from Dutch *baas* 'master'.

boss^2 ▪ n. 1 a stud on the centre of a shield. 2 Architecture an ornamental carving at the point where the ribs in a ceiling cross. 3 the central part of a propeller.
– ORIGIN Middle English: from Old French *boce*.

bossa nova /ˌbɒsə ˈnəʊvə/ ▪ n. a dance like the samba, originating in Brazil. ▸ a piece of music for this dance.
– ORIGIN 1960s: from Portuguese, from *bossa* 'tendency' and *nova* 'new'.

bossies /ˈbɒsiz/ ▪ adj. S. African informal traumatized or crazed, especially as a result of the stress of military action.
– ORIGIN 1970s: from Afrikaans army slang *bosbefok* 'deranged', from *bos* 'bush' + *befok* 'fucked'.

bossy ▪ adj. (**-ier**, **-iest**) informal fond of giving orders; domineering.
– DERIVATIVES **bossily** adv. **bossiness** n.

bossyboots ▪ n. Brit. informal a bossy person.

Boston ivy ▪ n. a Virginia creeper with three-lobed leaves, cultivated for its foliage. [*Parthenocissus tricuspidata.*]

Boston terrier ▪ n. a small terrier of a breed originating in Massachusetts from a crossing of the bulldog and terrier.

bosun /ˈbəʊs(ə)n/ (also **bo'sun**) ▪ n. variant spelling of BOATSWAIN.

bot^1 ▪ n. the larva of a botfly.
– ORIGIN C16: prob. of Low German origin.

bot^2 ▪ n. Computing an autonomous program on a network which can interact with systems or users, especially in the manner of a player in some computer games.
– ORIGIN 1980s: shortening of ROBOT.

bot. ▪ abbrev. 1 botanic; botanical; botany. 2 bottle. 3 bought.

botanical ▪ adj. of or relating to botany. ▪ n. a substance obtained from a plant and used as an additive.
– DERIVATIVES **botanically** adv.

botanic garden (also **botanical garden**) ■ n. a place where plants are grown for scientific study and display to the public.

botanizing (also -**ising**) ■ n. the studying of plants in their natural habitat.
– DERIVATIVES **botanize** (also -**ise**) v.

Botany /'bɒt(ə)ni/ (also **Botany wool**) ■ n. merino wool.
– ORIGIN C19: named after *Botany* Bay in Australia, from where the wool orig. came.

botany /'bɒt(ə)ni/ ■ n. the scientific study of the structure, ecology, distribution, classification, and economic importance of plants. ▸ the plant life of a particular region or geological period.
– DERIVATIVES **botanic** adj. **botanist** n.
– ORIGIN C17: from earlier *botanic*, from Greek *botanikos*, from *botanē* 'plant'.

botch informal ■ v. carry out (a task) badly or carelessly. ■ n. (also **botch-up**) a badly carried out task.
– DERIVATIVES **botcher** n.
– ORIGIN Middle English (in the sense 'repair' but orig. not implying clumsiness).

botfly /'bɒtflʌɪ/ ■ n. (pl. -**flies**) a stout hairy-bodied fly whose larvae are internal parasites of horses and other mammals. [*Gasterophilus* and other genera.]

both ■ predet., det., & pron. two people or things, regarded and identified together. ■ adv. applying equally to each of two alternatives.
– ORIGIN Middle English: from Old Norse *báthir*.

bother ■ v. 1 [with neg.] take the trouble to do something. 2 worry, disturb, or upset (someone). ▸ [usu. with neg.] feel concern about or interest in. ■ n. trouble; fuss. ▸ a cause of trouble or fuss. ■ exclam. chiefly Brit. used to express mild irritation.
– ORIGIN C17: of Anglo-Irish origin; prob. rel. to Irish *bodhaire* 'noise', *bodhraim* 'deafen, annoy'.

bothersome ■ adj. annoying; troublesome.

both ways ■ adv. & adj. another term for EACH-WAY.
– PHRASES **have it both ways** benefit from two incompatible ways of thinking or behaving.

bo tree /bəʊ/ (also **bodh tree**) ■ n. a fig tree native to India and SE Asia, regarded as sacred by Buddhists. [*Ficus religiosa*.]
– ORIGIN C19: representing Sinhalese *bōgaha* 'tree of knowledge' (Buddha's enlightenment having occurred beneath such a tree), from *bō* (from Sanskrit *budh* 'understand thoroughly') + *gaha* 'tree'.

botryoidal /ˌbɒtrɪ'ɔɪd(ə)l/ ■ adj. (chiefly of minerals) shaped like a cluster of grapes.
– ORIGIN C18: from Greek *botruoeidēs*, from *botrus* 'bunch of grapes'.

botrytis /bə'trʌɪtɪs/ ■ n. a greyish powdery mould of plants, deliberately cultivated on the grapes for certain wines.
– ORIGIN the name of a genus of moulds, from Greek *botrus* 'cluster of grapes'.

Botswanan /bɒ'tswɑːnən/ ■ n. a native or inhabitant of Botswana. ■ adj. of or relating to Botswana.

botte /bɒt/ ■ n. Fencing an attack or thrust.
– ORIGIN from French.

bottle ■ n. 1 a container with a narrow neck, used for storing liquids. ▸ a large metal cylinder holding liquefied gas. ▸ a baby's feeding bottle. 2 Brit. informal one's courage or confidence. ■ v. 1 place in bottles for storage. 2 (**bottle something up**) repress or conceal feelings.
– PHRASES **hit the bottle** informal start to drink alcohol heavily.
– ORIGIN Middle English: from Old French *boteille*, from medieval Latin *butticula*, from *buttis* (see BUTT⁴).

bottle blonde ■ adj. (of a woman's hair) of a shade of blonde that looks artificial. ■ n. a woman with such hair.

bottlebrush ■ n. 1 a cylindrical brush for cleaning inside bottles. 2 an Australian shrub or small tree with spikes of scarlet or yellow flowers resembling bottlebrushes. [Genus *Callistemon*.] ▸ S. African any of several shrubs or trees bearing brush-like flowers. [Families Greyiaceae and Proteaceae.]

bottle-feed ■ v. feed (a baby) with milk from a bottle.

bottle green ■ n. dark green.

bottle jack ■ n. a jack for lifting heavy objects.

bottleneck ■ n. 1 the neck or mouth of a bottle.
▸ S. African informal a bottleneck used as a pipe, especially for smoking dagga. 2 a narrow section of road where traffic flow is restricted. 3 a device shaped like a bottleneck, worn on a guitarist's finger and used to produce sliding effects on the strings.

bottlenose dolphin (also **bottle-nosed dolphin**) ■ n. a stout-bodied dolphin with a distinct short beak, found in tropical and temperate coastal waters. [*Tursiops truncatus*.]

bottlenose whale (also **bottle-nosed whale**) ■ n. a beaked whale with a bulbous forehead. [Genus *Hyperoodon*: two species.]

bottler ■ n. a person who bottles drinks.

bottle store (also **bottle shop**) ■ n. S. African & Austral./NZ a shop selling liquor for consumption off the premises.

bottle tree ■ n. an Australian tree with a swollen bottle-shaped trunk containing water. [*Adansonia gregorii* (a baobab) and *Brachychiton rupestre*.]

bottom ■ n. 1 the lowest point, position, or part of something. ▸ the furthest part or point of something.
▸ (also **bottoms**) the lower half of a two-piece garment. 2 a person's buttocks. ■ adj. in the lowest position. ▸ in the furthest position away in a downhill direction. ■ v. 1 (of a ship) touch the bottom of the sea. 2 (**bottom out**) (of a situation) reach the lowest point before stabilizing or improving.
– PHRASES **at bottom** fundamentally. **be at the bottom of** be the fundamental cause or origin of. **the bottom falls** (or **drops**) **out** something suddenly fails or collapses. **bottoms up!** informal said as a toast before drinking. **get to the bottom of** find an explanation for (a mystery). **you (can) bet your bottom dollar** informal, chiefly N. Amer. a particular thing is bound to happen.
– DERIVATIVES -**bottomed** adj. **bottomless** adj. **bottom-most** adj.
– ORIGIN Old English, of Germanic origin.

bottom drawer ■ n. Brit. dated household linen and other items stored by a woman in preparation for her marriage.

bottom fermentation ■ n. the process by which lagers are fermented, proceeding at low temperature with the yeast falling to the bottom.

bottom line ■ n. informal 1 the final total of an account or balance sheet. 2 the underlying and most important factor.

bottom-up ■ adj. proceeding from the bottom or beginning of a hierarchy or process upwards.

botty ■ n. (pl. -**ies**) informal, chiefly Brit. a person's bottom.

botulin /'bɒtjʊlɪn/ ■ n. the bacterial toxin involved in botulism.

botulism /'bɒtjʊlɪz(ə)m/ ■ n. a dangerous form of food poisoning caused by a bacterium (*Clostridium botulinum*) growing on improperly sterilized foods.
– ORIGIN C19: from German *Botulismus* 'sausage poisoning', from Latin *botulus* 'sausage'.

bouclé /'buːkleɪ/ ■ n. yarn with a looped or curled ply.
– ORIGIN C19: French, 'buckled, curled'.

boudin /'buːdã/ ■ n. 1 (pl. same) a French type of black pudding. 2 /also 'buːdɪn/ (**boudins**) Geology a series of elongated parallel sections formed by the fracturing of a sedimentary rock stratum during folding.
– ORIGIN from French.

boudoir /'buːdwɑː/ ■ n. a woman's bedroom or small private room.
– ORIGIN C18: French, 'sulking-place', from *bouder* 'pout, sulk'.

bouffant /'buːfɒ̃/ ■ adj. (of hair) styled so as to stand out from the head in a rounded shape. ■ n. a bouffant hairstyle.
– ORIGIN C19: from French, 'swelling', from *bouffer*.

bougainvillea /ˌbuːg(ə)n'vɪlɪə/ (also **bougainvillaea**) ■ n. an ornamental shrubby climbing plant widely cultivated in the tropics, with brightly coloured papery bracts surrounding the flowers. [Genus *Bougainvillea*.]

–ORIGIN named after the French explorer L. A. de *Bougainville*.

bough /baʊ/ ■ n. a main branch of a tree.
–ORIGIN Old English *bōg*, *bōh* 'bough or shoulder', of Germanic origin.

bought past and past participle of BUY.

bouillabaisse /ˈbuːjəˌbeɪs/ ■ n. a rich, spicy stew or soup made with fish, originally from Provence.
–ORIGIN French, from Provençal *bouiabaisso*.

bouillon /ˈbuːjɒ̃/ ■ n. thin soup or stock made by stewing meat, fish, or vegetables.
–ORIGIN French, from *bouillir* 'to boil'.

boulder ■ n. a large rock.
–DERIVATIVES **bouldery** adj.
–ORIGIN Middle English: shortened from *boulderstone*, of Scandinavian origin.

bouldering ■ n. Climbing climbing on large boulders, either for practice or as a sport in its own right.

boule /buːl/ (also **boules** pronunc. same) ■ n. a French form of bowls, played with metal balls.
–ORIGIN C20 (orig. a form of roulette): French, 'bowl'.

boulevard /ˈbuːləvɑːd/ ■ n. a wide street, typically one lined with trees.
–ORIGIN C18: French, 'a rampart', later 'a promenade on the site of one'; from German *Bollwerk* (see BULWARK).

boulle /buːl/ (also **buhl**) ■ n. brass, tortoiseshell, or other material used for inlaying furniture.
–ORIGIN C19: from French *boule*, from the name of the French cabinetmaker André *Boulle*.

bounce ■ v. 1 (of an object, especially a ball) spring quickly up or away from a surface after hitting it. ▸ move or jump up and down repeatedly. ▸ (also **bounce back**) (of an email) be returned to its sender after failing to reach its destination. 2 (of light, sound, or an electronic signal) reflect back from a surface. 3 (**bounce back**) recover well after a setback or problem. 4 move in an energetic or enthusiastic manner. 5 informal (of a cheque) be returned by a bank when there are insufficient funds in an account to meet it. 6 informal, chiefly N. Amer. dismiss from a job. 7 Brit. informal pressurize (someone) into doing something. ■ n. 1 a rebound of a ball or other object. ▸ an act of jumping or moving up and down. 2 exuberant self-confidence. 3 health and body in a person's hair.
–PHRASES **bounce an idea off someone** informal discuss an idea with another person in order to test or improve it.
–ORIGIN Middle English *bunsen* 'beat, thump', perhaps imitative, or from Low German *bunsen* 'beat'.

bouncer ■ n. 1 a person employed by a nightclub or pub to prevent troublemakers entering or to eject them from the premises. 2 Cricket a ball bowled fast and short so as to rise high after pitching.

bouncing ■ adj. (of a baby) vigorous and healthy.

bouncy ■ adj. (-ier, -iest) 1 able to bounce or making something bounce well. 2 confident and lively.
–DERIVATIVES **bouncily** adv. **bounciness** n.

bouncy castle ■ n. another term for JUMPING CASTLE.

bound¹ ■ v. walk or run with leaping strides. ■ n. a leaping movement towards or over something.
–ORIGIN C16: from French *bondir* (v.) 'resound', later 'rebound', from late Latin *bombitare*, from Latin *bombus* 'humming'.

bound² ■ n. 1 a boundary. 2 a limitation or restriction. ▸ technical a limiting value. ■ v. 1 form the boundary of. 2 restrict.
–PHRASES **out of bounds** 1 beyond the acceptable or permitted limits. 2 (in sport) beyond the field of play.
–ORIGIN Middle English: from Old French *bodne*, from medieval Latin *butina*.

bound³ ■ adj. going towards somewhere: *a train bound for Durban*.
–ORIGIN Middle English *boun*, from Old Norse *búinn*, from *búa* 'get ready'.

bound⁴ past and past participle of BIND. ■ adj. 1 (-**bound**) restricted, confined to or by a place or situation: *his job kept him city-bound*. 2 destined or certain to be, do, or have something. ▸ obliged to do something. 3 (-**bound**) (of a book) having a specified binding. 4 (of a grammatical element) occurring only in combination with another form.

–PHRASES **I'll be bound** I am sure.

boundary ■ n. (pl. -ies) 1 a line marking the limits of an area. 2 Cricket a hit crossing the limits of the field, scoring four or six runs.
–ORIGIN C17: var. of dialect *bounder*, from BOUND².

boundless ■ adj. unlimited.
–DERIVATIVES **boundlessly** adv. **boundlessness** n.

bounteous ■ adj. archaic bountiful.
–DERIVATIVES **bounteously** adv. **bounteousness** n.
–ORIGIN Middle English: from Old French *bontif* 'benevolent', from *bonte* 'bounty', on the pattern of *plenteous*.

bountiful ■ adj. 1 abundant. 2 giving generously.
–PHRASES **Lady Bountiful** a woman who engages in ostentatious acts of charity.
–DERIVATIVES **bountifully** adv.

bounty ■ n. (pl. -ies) 1 a reward paid for killing or capturing someone. 2 historical a sum paid by the state to encourage trade. ▸ chiefly historical a sum paid by the state to enlisting army or navy recruits. 3 poetic/literary something given or occurring in generous amounts.
–ORIGIN Middle English: from Old French *bonte* 'goodness', from Latin, from *bonus* 'good'.

bounty hunter ■ n. a person who pursues a criminal for a reward.

bouquet /bʊˈkeɪ, bəʊˈkeɪ, ˈbʊkeɪ/ ■ n. 1 a bunch of flowers. 2 the characteristic scent of a wine or perfume.
–ORIGIN C18: from French, from dialect of Old French *bos* 'wood'.

bouquet garni /ˌbʊˌkeɪ ˈɡɑːni, bəʊˈkeɪ, ˈbʊkeɪ/ ■ n. (pl. **bouquets garnis**) a bunch of herbs used for flavouring a stew or soup.
–ORIGIN French, 'garnished bouquet'.

bourbon /ˈbəːb(ə)n, ˈbʊə-/ ■ n. a kind of American whisky distilled from maize and rye.
–ORIGIN C19: named after *Bourbon* County, Kentucky, where it was first made.

bourgeois /ˈbʊəʒwɑː/ (also **bourgeoise** /ˈbʊəʒwɑːz/) ■ adj. of or characteristic of the middle class, especially in having materialistic values or conventional attitudes. ▸ (in Marxist contexts) capitalist. ■ n. (pl. same) a bourgeois person.
–ORIGIN C16: from French, from late Latin *burgus* 'castle', of Germanic origin.

bourgeoisie /ˌbʊəʒwɑːˈziː/ ■ n. [treated as sing. or pl.] the middle class. ▸ (in Marxist contexts) the capitalist class.
–ORIGIN C18: French, from BOURGEOIS.

bourrée /ˈbʊəreɪ/ ■ n. 1 a lively French dance like a gavotte. 2 Ballet a series of very fast little steps performed on the tips of the toes with the feet close together. ■ v. perform a bourrée.
–ORIGIN C17: French, 'faggot of twigs' (the dance being performed around a twig fire).

bourse /bʊəs/ ■ n. a stock market, especially in a francophone country.
–ORIGIN C16: from French, 'purse', from Greek *bursa* 'leather'.

bout /baʊt/ ■ n. 1 a short period of intense activity. ▸ an attack of illness or strong emotion. 2 a wrestling or boxing match. 3 a curve in the side of a violin or other musical instrument.
–ORIGIN C16: from dialect *bought* 'bend, loop'; prob. of Low German origin.

boutique /buːˈtiːk/ ■ n. a small shop selling fashionable clothes.
–ORIGIN C18: from French, 'small shop', from Greek *apothēkē* 'storehouse'.

boutonnière /ˌbuːtɒnˈjɛː/ ■ n. a spray of flowers worn in a buttonhole.
–ORIGIN C19: French, 'buttonhole', from *bouton* 'button'.

bouzouki /bʊˈzuːki/ ■ n. (pl. **bouzoukis**) a long-necked Greek form of mandolin.
–ORIGIN 1950s: from modern Greek *mpouzouki*, perhaps rel. to Turkish *bozuk* 'spoilt' (with ref. to roughly made instruments).

bovid /ˈbəʊvɪd/ ▪ n. Zoology a mammal of the cattle family (Bovidae).
– ORIGIN C19: from Latin *bos, bov-* 'ox'.

bovine /ˈbəʊvaɪn/ ▪ adj. of, relating to, or resembling cattle. ▪ n. an animal of the cattle family.
– ORIGIN C19: from late Latin *bovinus*, from Latin *bos, bov-* 'ox'.

bovine spongiform encephalopathy ▪ n. see BSE.

Bovril ▪ n. trademark a dark savoury spread made chiefly from beef extract.

bow¹ /bəʊ/ ▪ n. 1 a knot tied with two loops and two loose ends. 2 a weapon for shooting arrows, made of a curved piece of wood joined at both ends by a taut string. ▸ (musical bow) a simple musical instrument made this way. 3 a partially curved rod with horsehair stretched along its length, used for playing some stringed instruments. 4 a curved stroke forming part of a letter (e.g. *b, p*). 5 a metal ring forming the handle of a key or pair of scissors. ▪ v. play (a stringed instrument) using a bow.
– PHRASES **have** (or **add**) **another string to one's bow** chiefly Brit. have a further resource available.
– ORIGIN Old English *boga* 'bend, bow, arch', of Germanic origin.

bow² /baʊ/ ▪ v. 1 bend the head or upper body as a sign of respect, greeting, or shame. 2 cause to bend with age or under a heavy weight. 3 submit to pressure or demands. 4 (**bow out**) withdraw or retire from something. ▪ n. an act of bowing.
– PHRASES **bow and scrape** behave in an obsequious way. **make one's bow** make one's first formal appearance in a particular role. **take a bow** acknowledge applause by bowing.
– ORIGIN Old English *būgan* 'bend, stoop', of Germanic origin.

bow³ /baʊ/ (also **bows**) ▪ n. the front end of a ship.
– PHRASES **on the bow** Nautical within 45° of the point directly ahead. **a shot across the bows** a warning statement or gesture.
– ORIGIN Middle English: from Low German *boog*, Dutch *boeg* 'shoulder or ship's bow'.

bow compass ▪ n. a compass with jointed legs.

bowdlerize /ˈbaʊdləraɪz/ (also **-ise**) ▪ v. remove from (a text) material regarded as improper or offensive.
– DERIVATIVES **bowdlerism** n. **bowdlerization** n.
– ORIGIN C19: from the name of Dr Thomas *Bowdler*, an American who published an expurgated edition of Shakespeare.

bowel /ˈbaʊəl/ ▪ n. 1 the intestine. 2 (**bowels**) the deepest inner parts of something.
– ORIGIN Middle English: from Old French *bouel*, from Latin *botellus*, diminutive of *botulus* 'sausage'.

bowel movement ▪ n. an act of defecation.

bower¹ /ˈbaʊə/ ▪ n. 1 a pleasant shady place under trees. 2 poetic/literary a summer house or country cottage. 3 poetic/literary a lady's private room. ▪ v. poetic/literary shade; enclose.
– ORIGIN Old English, of Germanic origin.

bower² /ˈbaʊə/ ▪ n. an anchor carried at a ship's bow.
– ORIGIN C15: from BOW³.

bowerbird ▪ n. an Australasian bird noted for the male's habit of constructing an elaborate bower adorned with feathers, shells, etc. to attract the female. [Family Ptilonorhynchidae: several species.]

bow-fronted ▪ adj. having a convexly curved front.
– DERIVATIVES **bow front** n.

bowhead whale /ˈbəʊhɛd/ ▪ n. a black Arctic right whale, feeding by skimming the surface for plankton. [*Balaena mysticetus*.]

bowie knife /ˈbəʊi/ ▪ n. (pl. **-ies**) a long knife with a blade double-edged at the point.
– ORIGIN C19: named after the American frontiersman Jim *Bowie*.

bowl¹ ▪ n. 1 a round, deep dish or basin. ▸ a rounded, concave part of an object. ▸ Geography a natural basin. 2 [in names] chiefly N. Amer. a stadium for sporting or musical events. ▸ an American football game played after the season between leading teams.
– DERIVATIVES **bowlful** n. (pl. **-fuls**).
– ORIGIN Old English *bolle, bolla*, of Germanic origin.

bowl² ▪ n. 1 a wooden or hard rubber ball used in the game of bowls. ▸ a large ball used in tenpin bowling or skittles. 2 a spell of bowling in cricket. ▪ v. 1 roll (a round object) along the ground. 2 Cricket (of a bowler) propel (the ball) towards the wicket for the batsman to attempt to hit. ▸ dismiss (a batsman) by knocking down the wicket with a bowled ball. 3 move rapidly and smoothly. 4 (**bowl someone over**) knock someone down. 5 (usu. **be bowled over**) informal completely overwhelm or astonish.
– DERIVATIVES **bowling** n.
– ORIGIN Middle English: from Old French *boule*, from Latin *bulla* 'bubble'.

bow-legged ▪ adj. having legs that curve outwards at the knee.
– DERIVATIVES **bow legs** pl. n.

bowler¹ ▪ n. 1 Cricket a member of the fielding side who bowls. 2 a player at bowls, tenpin bowling, or skittles.

bowler² (also **bowler hat**) ▪ n. a man's hard felt hat with a round dome-shaped crown.
– ORIGIN C19: named after the English hatter William *Bowler*.

bowline /ˈbəʊlɪn/ ▪ n. 1 a rope attaching the weather side of a square sail to a ship's bow. 2 a simple knot for forming a non-slipping loop at the end of a rope.
– ORIGIN Middle English: from Middle Dutch *boechlijne*, from *boeg* 'ship's bow' + *lijne* 'line'.

bowling alley ▪ n. a long narrow track along which balls are rolled in skittles or tenpin bowling.

bowling crease ▪ n. Cricket the line from behind which a bowler delivers the ball.

bowling green ▪ n. an area of closely mown grass on which the game of bowls is played.

bowls /bəʊlz/ ▪ pl. n. [treated as sing.] a game played with heavy wooden bowls, the object of which is to propel one's bowl as close as possible to a small white ball (the jack).

bowman¹ /ˈbəʊmən/ ▪ n. (pl. **-men**) an archer.

bowman² /ˈbaʊmən/ ▪ n. (pl. **-men**) the rower who sits nearest the bow of a boat.

bowsaw /ˈbəʊsɔː/ ▪ n. a saw with a narrow blade stretched on a light curved frame.

bowser /ˈbaʊzə/ ▪ n. trademark a tanker used for fuelling aircraft or supplying water.
– ORIGIN 1920s: from the name of a company of oil storage engineers.

bowshot /ˈbəʊʃɒt/ ▪ n. the distance to which a bow can send an arrow.

bowsprit /ˈbaʊsprɪt/ ▪ n. a spar running out from a ship's bow, to which the forestays are fastened.
– ORIGIN Middle English: from Middle Dutch *boechspriet*, from *boech* 'bow' + *spriet* 'sprit'.

Bow Street Runner /ˈbəʊ/ ▪ n. historical, informal a London policeman.
– ORIGIN named after *Bow Street* in London, site of the chief metropolitan magistrates' court.

bow tie ▪ n. a necktie in the form of a bow.

bow window ▪ n. a curved bay window.

bow-wow ▪ exclam. /baʊˈwaʊ/ an imitation of a dog's bark. ▪ n. /ˈbaʊwaʊ/ informal a dog.

bowyer /ˈbəʊjə/ ▪ n. a person who makes or sells archers' bows.

box¹ ▪ n. 1 a container with a flat base and sides and a lid. 2 (**the box**) informal television. 3 an area enclosed within straight lines on a page or computer screen, to be filled in with or containing information. 4 (**the box**) Soccer the penalty area. ▸ (**the box**) Baseball the area occupied by the batter. 5 an enclosed area reserved for people in a theatre or sports ground, or for witnesses or the jury in a law court. 6 a protective casing for part of a mechanism. ▸ a shield for protecting a man's genitals in sport, especially cricket. 7 a facility at a newspaper office for receiving replies to an advertisement. ▸ a facility at a post office whereby letters are kept until collected by the addressee. 8 historical a coachman's seat. ▪ v. 1 [often as adj. **boxed**] put in or provide with a box. 2 (**box someone in**) restrict someone's ability to move freely.

–PHRASES **think outside the box** informal have ideas that are original or creative.
–DERIVATIVES **boxful** n. (pl. **-fuls**). **box-like** adj.
–ORIGIN Old English, prob. from late Latin *buxis*, from Latin *pyxis* 'boxwood box', from Greek *puxos*.

box² ■ v. fight an opponent with the fists in padded gloves as a sport. ■ n. a slap on the side of a person's head.
–PHRASES **box clever** Brit. informal outwit someone. **box someone's ears** slap someone on the side of the head.
–DERIVATIVES **boxing** n.
–ORIGIN Middle English.

box³ (also **box tree**) ■ n. a slow-growing evergreen shrub with small glossy leaves, yielding hard wood. [*Buxus sempervirens*.] ▸ any of various other trees with similar foliage or wood.
–ORIGIN Old English, from Greek *puxos*.

boxboard ■ n. stiff cardboard used to make boxes.

box camera ■ n. a simple box-shaped hand camera.

box canyon ■ n. a narrow canyon with a flat bottom and vertical walls.

boxcar ■ n. N. Amer. an enclosed railway freight wagon.

Boxer ■ n. a member of a fiercely nationalistic Chinese secret society which flourished in the 19th century.
–ORIGIN from BOXER, translating Chinese *yì hé quán* 'righteous harmony fists'.

boxer ■ n. 1 a person who boxes as a sport. 2 a medium-sized dog of a breed with a smooth brown coat and pug-like face.

boxer shorts ■ pl. n. men's underpants resembling shorts.

boxfish ■ n. (pl. same or **-fishes**) a tropical marine fish with a shell of bony plates covered in spines enclosing the body. [*Tetrosomus gibbosus* and other species.]

box girder ■ n. a hollow girder square in cross section.

Boxing Day ■ n. a public holiday on the first day (or first weekday) after Christmas Day.
–ORIGIN C19: from the former custom of giving tradespeople a Christmas box on this day.

boxing glove ■ n. a heavily padded mitten worn in boxing.

box kite ■ n. a tailless kite in the form of a long box open at each end.

box number ■ n. a number identifying an advertisement in a newspaper, used as an address for replies.

box office ■ n. a place at a theatre, cinema, etc. where tickets are sold.

box pew ■ n. a church pew enclosed by wooden partitions.

box pleat ■ n. a pleat consisting of two parallel creases facing opposite directions and forming a raised band.

boxroom ■ n. Brit. a very small room.

box spanner ■ n. a cylindrical spanner with a hexagonal end fitting over the head of a nut.

box spring ■ n. each of a set of vertical springs housed in a frame in a mattress.

box turtle ■ n. a land-living turtle having a lower shell with hinged lobes that can be drawn up tightly. [Genus *Terrapene*: several species.]

box wine ■ n. S. African wine contained in a carton rather than a bottle.

boxy ■ adj. (**-ier**, **-iest**) 1 squarish in shape. 2 (of a room or space) cramped.

boy ■ n. 1 a male child or youth. 2 (**boys**) informal men who mix socially or belong to a particular group. 3 dated, offensive a black male servant or worker. ■ exclam. informal used to express strong feelings: *Oh boy, that's wonderful!*
–DERIVATIVES **boyhood** n. **boyish** adj. **boyishly** adv. **boyishness** n.
–ORIGIN Middle English.

boycott ■ v. withdraw from commercial or social relations with, as a punishment or protest. ▸ refuse to buy or handle (goods) for this reason. ■ n. an act of boycotting.
–ORIGIN from the name of Captain Charles C. *Boycott*, an Irish land agent so treated in 1880 in an attempt to get rents reduced.

brachial

boyfriend ■ n. a person's regular male companion in a romantic or sexual relationship.

boykie ■ n. S. African informal a friendly form of address for a boy or man.
–ORIGIN 1970s: from *boy* + Afrikaans diminutive suffix -*ie*.

Boyle's law ■ n. Chemistry a law stating that the pressure of a given mass of an ideal gas is inversely proportional to its volume at a constant temperature.
–ORIGIN from the name of the English scientist Robert *Boyle* (1627–91).

boyo ■ n. (pl. **-os**) informal a boy or man.

boy racer ■ n. informal a young man fond of driving very fast in high-powered cars.

Boy Scout ■ n. old-fashioned term for SCOUT (in sense 2).

boysenberry /'bɔɪz(ə)n,b(ə)ri, -,bɛri/ ■ n. (pl. **-ies**) 1 a large red edible blackberry-like fruit. 2 the shrubby hybrid bramble plant that bears this fruit. [*Rubus loganobaccus*.]
–ORIGIN 1930s: named after the American horticulturalist Robert *Boysen*.

boy wonder ■ n. an exceptionally talented young man.

bozo /'bəʊzəʊ/ ■ n. (pl. **-os**) informal, chiefly N. Amer. a stupid or insignificant person.
–ORIGIN 1920s.

BP ■ abbrev. 1 before the present (era). 2 blood pressure.

Bp ■ abbrev. Bishop.

bp ■ abbrev. 1 Finance basis point(s). 2 boiling point.

BPhil ■ abbrev. Bachelor of Philosophy.

bps ■ abbrev. Computing bits per second.

Bq ■ abbrev. Physics becquerel.

Br ■ symb. the chemical element bromine.

Br. ■ abbrev. 1 British. 2 (in religious orders) Brother.

bra¹ ■ n. a woman's undergarment worn to support the breasts.
–DERIVATIVES **braless** adj.
–ORIGIN 1930s: abbrev. of BRASSIERE.

bra² ■ n. S. African informal a title or friendly form of address for a man: *Bra Pat | my bra.*
–ORIGIN 1950s: shortening of *brother*.

braai /'brʌɪ/ S. African ■ n. (pl. **braais**) a picnic or barbecue where meat is grilled over an open fire. ▸ a structure on which a fire can be made, used for grilling meat outdoors. ■ v. (**braaied**, **braaiing** or **braaing**) grill (meat) over an open fire.
–ORIGIN from Afrikaans.

braaivleis /'brʌɪˌfleɪs/ ■ n. (pl. same) S. African full form of BRAAI. ▸ meat cooked in this way.
–ORIGIN Afrikaans, 'grilled meat', from *braai* 'to grill' + *vleis* 'meat'.

brace ■ n. 1 (**braces**) a pair of straps passing over the shoulders and fastening to the top of trousers at the front and back to hold them up. 2 a device supporting a weak or injured part of the body. ▸ a wire device fitted in the mouth to straighten the teeth. ▸ a strengthening piece of iron or timber in building or carpentry. 3 (also **brace and bit**) a drilling tool with a crank handle and a socket to hold a bit. 4 a rope attached to the yard of a ship for trimming the sail. 5 (pl. same) a pair of things, especially birds or mammals killed in hunting. 6 either of two connecting marks { and }, used in printing. ■ v. 1 make stronger or firmer with wood, iron, etc. 2 press (one's body) firmly against something in order to stay balanced. 3 (**brace oneself**) prepare for something difficult or unpleasant.
–ORIGIN Middle English: from Old French *brace* 'two arms', from Latin *bracchium* 'arm', from Greek *brakhiōn*.

bracelet ■ n. an ornamental band or chain worn on the wrist or arm.
–ORIGIN Middle English: from Old French, from *bras* 'arm', from Latin *bracchium*.

brachial /'breɪkɪəl/ ■ adj. 1 Anatomy of or relating to the arm or an arm-like structure. 2 Zoology denoting the upper valve of a brachiopod's shell.
–ORIGIN Middle English: from Latin *brachialis*, from *brac(c)hium* 'arm'.

Brachiopoda

Brachiopoda /ˌbrakɪəˈpəʊdə/ ■ pl. n. Zoology a phylum of marine invertebrates that comprises the lamp shells.
– DERIVATIVES **brachiopod** /ˈbrakɪə(ʊ)ppd/ n.
– ORIGIN from Greek *brakhiōn* 'arm' + *pous, pod-* 'foot'.

brachiosaurus /ˌbrakɪə(ʊ)ˈsɔːrəs/ ■ n. a huge herbivorous dinosaur of the late Jurassic to mid-Cretaceous periods, with forelegs much longer than the hind legs. [Genus *Brachiosaurus*.]
– ORIGIN from Greek *brakhiōn* 'arm' + *sauros* 'lizard'.

brachycephalic /ˌbrakɪsɪˈfalɪk, -kɛˈfalɪk/ ■ adj. having a relatively broad, short skull.
– DERIVATIVES **brachycephaly** n.

bracing ■ adj. **1** fresh and invigorating. **2** (of a support) serving as a brace.
– DERIVATIVES **bracingly** adv.

bracken ■ n. a tall fern with coarse lobed fronds. [*Pteridium aquilinum*.]
– ORIGIN Middle English: of Scandinavian origin.

bracket ■ n. **1** each of a pair of marks ( ) [ ] { } < > used to enclose words or figures and separate them from the surrounding context. **2** a category of similar people or things. **3** a right-angled support projecting from a wall, holding a shelf, lamp, etc. **4** Military the distance between two artillery shots fired either side of the target to establish range. ■ v. (**bracketed, bracketing**) **1** enclose (words or figures) in brackets. ▸ Mathematics enclose (a complex expression) in brackets to denote that the whole of the expression has a particular relation to another expression. **2** place in the same category or group. **3** hold or attach by means of a bracket. **4** Military establish the range of (a target) by firing preliminary shots short of and beyond it.
– ORIGIN C16: from French *braguette* or Spanish *bragueta* 'codpiece, bracket', from Latin *braca*, (pl.) *bracae* 'breeches'.

bracket fungus ■ n. a fungus which forms shelf-like projections on the trunks of trees. [Order Aphyllophorales: many species.]

brackish ■ adj. (of water) slightly salty, as in river estuaries. ▸ living in or requiring such water.
– DERIVATIVES **brackishness** n.
– ORIGIN C16: from obsolete *brack* 'salty', from Middle Dutch *brac*.

bract ■ n. Botany a modified leaf or scale with a flower or flower cluster in its axil.
– ORIGIN C18: from Latin *bractea* 'thin plate of metal'.

bracteate /ˈbraktɪət, -tɪeɪt/ ■ adj. having or bearing bracts. ■ n. Archaeology a coin or ornament of thinly beaten precious metal.

brad ■ n. a nail of rectangular cross section with a flat tip and a small asymmetrical head.
– ORIGIN Middle English: from Old Norse *broddr* 'spike'.

bradawl /ˈbradɔːl/ ■ n. a tool for boring holes, resembling a screwdriver.

bradycardia /ˌbradɪˈkɑːdɪə/ ■ n. Medicine abnormally slow heart action.
– ORIGIN C19: from Greek *bradus* 'slow' + *kardia* 'heart'.

bradykinin /ˌbradɪˈkaɪnɪn/ ■ n. Biochemistry a compound released in the blood which causes contraction of smooth muscle and dilation of blood vessels.
– ORIGIN 1940s: from Greek *bradus* 'slow' + *kinēsis* 'motion'.

brae /breɪ/ ■ n. Scottish a steep bank or hillside.
– ORIGIN Middle English: from Old Norse *brá* 'eyelash', of Germanic origin.

brag ■ v. (**bragged, bragging**) boast. ■ n. **1** a simplified form of poker. **2** an act of bragging.
– DERIVATIVES **bragger** n. **bragging** adj. **braggingly** adv.
– ORIGIN Middle English.

braggadocio /ˌbragəˈdəʊtʃɪəʊ/ ■ n. boastful or arrogant behaviour.
– ORIGIN C16: from *Braggadocchio*, the name of a braggart in Spenser's *Faerie Queene*, from **BRAG** or **BRAGGART** + the Italian suffix *-occio*, denoting something large.

braggart /ˈbragət, -ɑːt/ ■ n. a person who brags.
– ORIGIN C16: from French *bragard*, from *braguer* 'to brag'.

Brahman /ˈbrɑːmən/ ■ n. (pl. -mans) **1** (also **Brahmin**) a member of the highest Hindu caste, that of the priesthood. **2** the ultimate reality underlying all phenomena in the Hindu scriptures. **3** US spelling of **BRAHMIN** (in sense 3).
– DERIVATIVES **Brahmanic** /-ˈmanɪk/ adj.
– ORIGIN sense 1 from Sanskrit *brāhmaṇa*; sense 2 from Sanskrit *brahman*.

Brahmana /ˈbrɑːmənə/ ■ n. (in Hinduism) any of the lengthy commentaries on the Vedas.

Brahmanism /ˈbrɑːməˌnɪz(ə)m/ (also **Brahminism**) ■ n. the early form of Hinduism that emerged in India (c.900 BC) under the influence of the Brahmans.

Brahmin /ˈbrɑːmɪn/ ■ n. **1** variant spelling of **BRAHMAN** (in sense 1). **2** US a socially or culturally superior person. **3** (also **Brahminy bull** or US **Brahman**) another term for ZEBU.
– DERIVATIVES **Brahminical** adj.

braid ■ n. **1** threads of silk, cotton, etc. woven into a decorative band. **2** a length of hair made up of three or more interlaced strands. ■ v. **1** form a braid with three or more strands of (hair). **2** [usu. as adj. **braided**] edge or trim with braid. **3** [usu. as adj. **braided**] (of a river or stream) flow into shallow interconnected channels divided by deposited earth.
– DERIVATIVES **braiding** n.
– ORIGIN Old English *bregdan* 'make a sudden movement, interweave', of Germanic origin.

Braille /breɪl/ ■ n. a written language for the blind, in which characters are represented by patterns of raised dots. ■ v. print or transcribe in Braille.
– ORIGIN C19: named after the blind French educationist Louis *Braille*, who developed it.

brain ■ n. **1** an organ of soft nervous tissue contained in the skull, functioning as the coordinating centre of sensation and intellectual and nervous activity. ▸ (**brains**) the substance of an animal's brain used as food. **2** intellectual capacity. **3** (**the brains**) informal the main organizer or planner within a group; the person who supplies the ideas. ■ v. informal hit hard on the head with an object.
– PHRASES **have something on the brain** informal be obsessed with something.
– DERIVATIVES **-brained** adj.
– ORIGIN Old English, of West Germanic origin.

brainbox ■ n. informal a very clever person.

brainchild ■ n. (pl. -children) informal an idea or invention considered to be the creation of a particular person.

brain coral ■ n. a compact coral with a convoluted surface resembling that of the brain. [*Diploria* and other genera.]

brain death ■ n. irreversible brain damage causing the end of independent respiration.
– DERIVATIVES **brain-dead** adj.

brain drain ■ n. informal the emigration of highly skilled or qualified people from a country.

brainless ■ adj. stupid; foolish.
– DERIVATIVES **brainlessly** adv. **brainlessness** n.

brainpower ■ n. intellectual power or ability.

brainstem ■ n. Anatomy the central trunk of the mammalian brain, consisting of the medulla oblongata, pons, and midbrain.

brainstorm ■ n. **1** informal a moment or period in which one is suddenly unable to think clearly. **2** a spontaneous group discussion to produce ideas and ways of solving problems. ▸ informal, chiefly N. Amer. a sudden clever idea. ■ v. [often as noun **brainstorming**] produce an idea or solution by having a spontaneous discussion.

brain-teaser (also **brain-twister**) ■ n. informal a problem or puzzle.
– DERIVATIVES **brain-teasing** adj.

brain trust ■ n. N. Amer. a group of experts advising a government or politician.

brainwash ■ v. indoctrinate systemically and so completely as to effect a radical transformation of attitudes and beliefs.

brainwave ■ n. **1** an electrical impulse in the brain. **2** informal a sudden clever idea.

brainy ■ adj. (-ier, -iest) informal intelligent.
- DERIVATIVES **brainily** adv. **braininess** n.

braise ■ v. fry (food) lightly and then stew slowly in a closed container.
- ORIGIN C18: from French *braiser*, from *braise* 'live coals'.

brak[1] ■ adj. S. African (of water or soil) brackish or alkaline.
- ORIGIN Afrikaans, 'alkaline'.

brak[2] ■ n. S. African a mongrel dog.
- ORIGIN 1950s: Afrikaans, from Dutch *brak* 'setter'.

brake[1] ■ n. a device for slowing or stopping a moving vehicle, typically by applying pressure to the wheels. ■ v. slow or stop a moving vehicle using a brake.
- ORIGIN C18.

brake[2] ■ n. archaic or poetic/literary a thicket.
- ORIGIN Old English (orig. *fearnbraca* 'thickets of fern'), rel. to Middle Low German *brake* 'branch, stump'.

brake[3] ■ n. a coarse fern of warm countries, typically with fronds divided into long segments. [Genus *Pteris*.]
- ORIGIN Middle English: perhaps an abbrev. of BRACKEN.

brake block ■ n. a block of hard material pressed against the rim of a wheel to slow it down by friction.

brake disc ■ n. the disc attached to the wheel in a disc brake.

brake drum ■ n. a broad, short cylinder attached to a wheel, against which the brake shoes press to cause braking.

brake horsepower ■ n. (pl. same) an imperial unit equal to one horsepower, used in expressing the power available at the shaft of an engine.

brake lining ■ n. a layer of hard material attached to a brake shoe or pad to increase friction against the drum or disc.

brakeman ■ n. (pl. -men) 1 (Brit. also **brakesman**) chiefly N. Amer. a railway worker responsible for a train's brakes. 2 a person in charge of the brakes in a bobsleigh.

brake pad ■ n. a thin block which presses on to the disc in a disc brake.

brake shoe ■ n. a long curved block which presses on to a brake drum.

bramble ■ n. a prickly scrambling shrub of the rose family, especially a blackberry. ▶ chiefly Brit. the fruit of the blackberry. ■ v. [usu. as noun **brambling**] Brit. gather blackberries.
- DERIVATIVES **brambly** adj.
- ORIGIN Old English, of Germanic origin.

Bramley ■ n. (pl. -eys) an English cooking apple.
- ORIGIN C20: named after the English butcher Matthew Bramley, in whose garden it first grew.

bran ■ n. pieces of grain husk separated from flour after milling.
- ORIGIN Middle English: from Old French.

branch ■ n. 1 a woody extending part of a tree which grows out from the trunk or a bough. 2 a subdivision extending from a river, road, or railway. ▶ a division of a large organization. ▶ a conceptual subdivision of a group of languages, subject, etc. ■ v. 1 (of a road or path) divide into one or more subdivisions. ▶ (of a tree or plant) bear or send out branches. 2 (**branch out**) extend one's activities or interests in a new direction.
- DERIVATIVES **branchlet** n. **branch-like** adj. **branchy** adj.
- ORIGIN Middle English: from Old French *branche*, from late Latin *branca* 'paw'.

branchia /'braŋkɪə/ ■ n. (pl. **branchiae** /-kɪiː/) the gills of fish and some invertebrates.
- DERIVATIVES **branchial** adj.
- ORIGIN C17: from Latin *branchia*, from Greek *brankhia* (pl.).

Branchiopoda /ˌbraŋkɪəˈpəʊdə/ ■ pl. n. Zoology a class of small aquatic crustaceans having gills on the feet, including water fleas and fairy shrimps.
- DERIVATIVES **branchiopod** /'braŋkɪə(ʊ)pɒd/ n.
- ORIGIN from Greek *brankhia* 'gills' + *pous, pod-* 'foot'.

branch line ■ n. a secondary railway line running from a main line to a terminus.

brand ■ n. 1 a type of product manufactured by a company under a particular name. ▶ a particular type of something: *the Finnish brand of socialism*. 2 an identifying mark or characteristic common to the products of a particular company. 3 an identifying mark burned on livestock with a branding iron. 4 a piece of burning or smouldering wood. 5 poetic/literary a sword. ■ v. 1 mark with a branding iron. 2 mark out as having a particular shameful quality: *she was branded a liar*. 3 [usu. as adj. **branded**] assign a brand name to.
- DERIVATIVES **brander** n.
- ORIGIN Old English *brand* 'burning', of Germanic origin.

brandewyn /'brandəveɪn/ ■ n. S. African brandy.
- ORIGIN Afrikaans, from Dutch *brandewijn*, from *branden* 'distil' + *wijn* 'wine'.

branding iron ■ n. a metal implement which is heated and used to brand livestock.

brandish ■ v. wave or flourish as a threat or in anger or excitement.
- DERIVATIVES **brandisher** n.
- ORIGIN Middle English: from Old French *brandir*, of Germanic origin.

brand leader ■ n. the best-selling or most highly regarded product of its type.

brand name ■ n. a name given by the maker to a product or range of products.

brand new ■ adj. completely new.
- ORIGIN C16: from BRAND + NEW, with the idea 'straight from the fire'.

brandy ■ n. (pl. -ies) a strong alcoholic spirit distilled from wine or fermented fruit juice.
- DERIVATIVES **brandied** adj.
- ORIGIN C17: from earlier *brandwine*, from Dutch *brandewijn*, from *branden* 'burn, distil' + *wijn* 'wine'.

brandy butter ■ n. a stiff sauce of brandy, butter, and sugar.

brandy snap ■ n. a crisp rolled gingerbread wafer.

brash[1] ■ adj. self-assertive in a rude, noisy, or overbearing way.
- DERIVATIVES **brashly** adv. **brashness** n.
- ORIGIN C19: perhaps a form of RASH[1].

brash[2] ■ n. 1 loose broken rock or ice. 2 clippings from hedges or other plants.
- ORIGIN C18.

brass ■ n. 1 a yellow alloy of copper and zinc. 2 (also **horse brass**) a flat brass ornament for the harness of a draught horse. ▶ Brit. a memorial consisting of a flat piece of inscribed brass set into the wall or floor of a church. ▶ a brass block used for stamping a design on a book binding. 3 brass wind instruments forming a band or section of an orchestra. 4 (also **top brass**) informal people in authority. 5 Brit. informal money.
- PHRASES **brassed off** Brit. informal disgruntled. **brass monkey** informal used to indicate extremely cold weather: [from a type of brass rack or 'monkey' in which cannonballs were stored and which contracted in very cold weather, ejecting the balls.] *cold enough to freeze the balls off a brass monkey*. **get down to brass tacks** informal start to consider the basic facts or practical details.
- ORIGIN Old English *bræs*.

brassard /'brɑːsɑːd/ ■ n. a band or badge worn on the upper sleeve.
- ORIGIN C16: from French, from *bras* 'arm'.

brass band ■ n. a group of musicians playing brass instruments.

brasserie /'brasəri/ ■ n. (pl. -ies) a restaurant in France or in a French style, serving inexpensive food.
- ORIGIN C19: French, 'brewery'.

brass hat ■ n. Brit. informal a high-ranking officer in the armed forces.

brassica /'brasɪkə/ ■ n. a plant of a genus that includes cabbage, swede, rape, and mustard. [Genus *Brassica*.]
- ORIGIN from Latin, 'cabbage'.

brassie /'brasi, 'brɑːsiː/ (also **brassy**) ■ n. (pl. -ies) Golf, informal a number two wood.
- ORIGIN C19: so named because the wood was orig. shod with brass.

brassiere /'brazɪə, -s-, 'brazɪɛː/ ■ n. full form of BRA.
- ORIGIN C20: from French, 'bodice, child's vest'.

brass rubbing

brass rubbing ■ n. the action of rubbing heelball or chalk over paper laid on an engraved brass to reproduce its design.

brassy[1] ■ adj. (-ier, -iest) 1 resembling brass in colour. 2 sounding harsh or loud like a brass instrument. 3 tastelessly showy or loud.
– DERIVATIVES **brassily** adv. **brassiness** n.

brassy[2] ■ n. variant spelling of BRASSIE.

brat ■ n. informal a badly behaved child.
– DERIVATIVES **brattish** adj. **brattishness** n. **bratty** adj.
– ORIGIN C16: perhaps an abbrev. of synonymous Scots *bratchet*, from Old French *brachet* 'hound, bitch'.

brat pack ■ n. informal a rowdy and ostentatious group of young celebrities.
– DERIVATIVES **brat packer** n.

brattice /ˈbratɪs/ ■ n. a partition or shaft lining in a coal mine.
– DERIVATIVES **bratticed** adj.
– ORIGIN Middle English: from Old French *bretesche*, from Old English *brittisc* 'British'.

bratwurst /ˈbratvəːst/ ■ n. a type of fine German pork sausage.
– ORIGIN German, from *Brat* 'a spit' + *Wurst* 'sausage'.

bravado ■ n. boldness intended to impress or intimidate.
– ORIGIN C16: from Spanish *bravada*, from *bravo* (see BRAVE).

brave ■ adj. showing courage. ■ n. dated an American Indian warrior. ■ v. endure or face (unpleasant conditions) with courage.
– DERIVATIVES **bravely** adv. **braveness** n. **bravery** n.
– ORIGIN C15: from Italian *bravo* 'bold' or Spanish *bravo* 'courageous, untamed, savage'.

bravo /brɑːˈvəʊ, ˈbrɑːvəʊ/ ■ exclam. used to express approval for a performer. ■ n. (pl. -os) a code word representing the letter B, used in radio communication.
– ORIGIN C18: from Italian, 'bold' (see BRAVE).

bravura /brəˈv(j)ʊərə/ ■ n. 1 great skill and brilliance. 2 the display of great daring.
– ORIGIN C18: from Italian, from *bravo* 'bold'.

brawl ■ n. a rough or noisy fight or quarrel. ■ v. take part in a brawl.
– DERIVATIVES **brawler** n.
– ORIGIN Middle English: perhaps imitative and rel. to BRAY[1].

brawn ■ n. 1 physical strength as opposed to intelligence. 2 chiefly Brit. cooked meat from a pig's or calf's head, pressed with jelly.
– DERIVATIVES **brawniness** n. **brawny** adj.
– ORIGIN Middle English: from Old French *braon* 'fleshy part of the leg', of Germanic origin.

Braxton Hicks contractions /ˌbrakstən ˈhɪks/ ■ pl. n. Medicine intermittent weak contractions of the uterus occurring during pregnancy.
– ORIGIN C20: named after the English gynaecologist John Braxton Hicks.

bray[1] ■ n. the loud, harsh cry of a donkey. ■ v. make such a sound.
– ORIGIN Middle English: from Old French *braire* 'to cry', perhaps of Celtic origin.

bray[2] ■ n. & v. variant spelling of BREI[1].

bray[3] (also **brei**, **brey**) ■ v. S. African soften leather by twisting, pounding, and working it until pliable.
– ORIGIN from S. African Dutch *breien* 'prepare skins', from Dutch *bereiden* 'prepare'.

braze ■ v. form, fix, or join by soldering with an alloy of copper and zinc. ■ n. a brazed joint.
– ORIGIN C17: from French *braser* 'solder'.

brazen ■ adj. 1 bold and shameless. 2 chiefly poetic/literary made of brass. ■ v. (**brazen it out**) endure a difficult situation with apparent confidence and lack of shame.
– DERIVATIVES **brazenly** adv. **brazenness** /ˈbreɪz(ə)nnɪs/ n.
– ORIGIN Old English, from *bræs* 'brass'.

brazier /ˈbreɪzɪə, -ʒə/ ■ n. a portable heater consisting of a pan or stand holding lighted coals.
– ORIGIN C17: from French *brasier*, from *braise* 'hot coals'.

brazil ■ n. 1 (also **Brazil nut**) the large three-sided nut of a South American forest tree (*Bertholletia excelsa*). 2 (also **Brazil wood**) the hard red wood of a tropical tree (genus *Caesalpinia*) from which dye is obtained.

Brazilian ■ n. 1 a native or inhabitant of Brazil. 2 a style of waxing a woman's pubic hair so that only a narrow central strip remains. ■ adj. of or relating to Brazil.

breach ■ n. 1 an act of breaking a law, agreement, or code of conduct. ▸ a break in relations. 2 a gap in a wall or barrier, especially one made by an attacking army. ■ v. 1 make a breach in. 2 break (a law, agreement, or code of conduct).
– PHRASES **breach of the peace** an act of violent or noisy behaviour causing a public disturbance, considered a criminal offence. **breach of promise** the action of breaking a sworn assurance. **step into the breach** replace someone who is suddenly unable to do a job.
– ORIGIN Middle English: from Old French *breche*, of Germanic origin.

bread ■ n. 1 food made of flour, water, and yeast mixed together and baked. 2 informal money.
– PHRASES **bread and butter** a person's livelihood or main source of income. **break bread** Christian Church celebrate the Eucharist. **cast one's bread upon the waters** do good without expecting gratitude or reward. [with biblical allusion to Ecclesiastes 11:1.] **know which side one's bread is buttered** informal know where one's advantage lies.
– ORIGIN Old English, of Germanic origin.

bread-and-butter letter ■ n. a letter expressing thanks for hospitality.

breadbasket ■ n. a region that supplies cereals to another.

breadboard ■ n. Electronics a board for making an experimental model of an electric circuit.

breadcrumb ■ n. a small fragment of bread.
– DERIVATIVES **breadcrumbed** adj.

breaded ■ adj. (of food) coated with breadcrumbs and fried.

breadfruit ■ n. 1 the large round starchy fruit of a tree (*Artocarpus altilis*) native to Pacific islands, used as a vegetable and to make a substitute for flour. 2 S. African (also **breadfruit tree**) another term for BREAD TREE.

breadline ■ n. 1 the poorest condition in which it is acceptable to live. 2 N. Amer. a queue of people waiting to receive free food.

bread sauce ■ n. sauce made with milk and breadcrumbs, typically eaten with roast turkey.

breadstick ■ n. a crisp stick of baked dough.

breadth ■ n. the distance or measurement from side to side of something. ▸ wide range: *breadth of experience*.
– DERIVATIVES **breadthways** (also **breadthwise**) adv.
– ORIGIN C16: from obsolete *brede*, on the pattern of *length*.

bread tree (also **bread palm**) ■ n. a cycad native to southern Africa, which yields an edible sago-like starch. [Genus *Encephalartos*.]

breadwinner ■ n. a person who earns money to support their family.
– DERIVATIVES **breadwinning** n.

break ■ v. (past **broke**; past part. **broken**) 1 separate or cause to separate into pieces as a result of a blow, shock, or strain. 2 make or become inoperative. 3 interrupt (a continuity, sequence, or course). ▸ lessen the impact of (a fall). ▸ disconnect or interrupt (an electric circuit). 4 fail to observe (a law, regulation, or agreement). 5 crush the strength, spirit, or resistance of. 6 surpass (a record). 7 (of an attacking player or a military force) make a rush or dash. 8 (of the weather) change suddenly, especially after a fine spell. ▸ (of a storm) begin violently. ▸ (of dawn or a day) begin as the sun rises. ▸ (of waves) curl over and dissolve into foam. 9 (of a person's voice) falter and change tone. ▸ (of a boy's voice) change in tone and register at puberty. 10 (of news or a scandal) suddenly become public. ▸ (**break something to**) make bad news known to. 11 Phonetics (of a vowel) develop into a diphthong, under the influence of an adjacent sound. 12 (of two boxers or wrestlers) come out of a clinch. 13 make the first stroke at the beginning of a game of billiards, pool, or snooker. 14 unfurl (a flag or sail). 15 succeed in deciphering (a code). ■ n. 1 an interruption

or pause. ▸ a short holiday. **2** a rush or dash, especially by an attacking player or team. **3** informal an opportunity or chance. **4** a gap or opening: *a break in the hedge*. **5** an instance of breaking, or the point where something is broken. **6** (also **break of serve** or **service break**) Tennis the winning of a game against an opponent's serve. **7** Snooker & Billiards a consecutive series of successful shots, scoring a specified number of points. ▸ a player's turn to make the opening shot of a game. **8** a short solo or instrumental passage in jazz or popular music.
–PHRASES **break ship** Nautical fail to rejoin one's ship after absence on leave. **break wind** release gas from the anus. **break one's back** (or **neck**) put great effort into achieving something. **break the back of** accomplish the main or hardest part of (a task). **break cover** (of game being hunted) emerge into the open. **break a leg!** theatrical slang good luck! **break of day** dawn. **break someone's serve** win a game in a tennis match against an opponent's service. **give someone a break** informal stop putting pressure on someone. **make a clean break** remove oneself completely from a situation.
–PHRASAL VERBS **break away** escape from the control or influence of a person, group, or practice. **break down** **1** suddenly cease to function. **2** cease to continue; collapse. **3** lose control of one's emotions when in distress. **break in 1** force entry to a building. **2** interject. **break something in 1** accustom a horse to being ridden. **2** wear shoes until they become supple and comfortable. **break into 1** enter forcibly. **2** suddenly or unexpectedly burst forth into (laughter, song, or faster movement). **break something off** abruptly end or discontinue something. **break out 1** (of fighting or another undesirable thing) start suddenly. **2** escape. **break something out** informal open and start using something. **break out in** be suddenly affected by an unpleasant sensation or condition. **break up 1** (of a gathering or relationship) end or part. ▸ Brit. end the school term. **2** informal start laughing uncontrollably. **break with 1** quarrel or cease relations with. **2** act in a way that is not in accordance with (a custom or tradition).
–DERIVATIVES **breakable** adj. **breakage** n.
–ORIGIN Old English, of Germanic origin.

breakaway ▪ n. **1** a divergence or secession from something established or long-standing. **2** a sudden attack or forward movement, especially in sport.

break-dancing ▪ n. an energetic and acrobatic style of street dancing, developed in the US.
–DERIVATIVES **break-dance** v. & n. **break dancer** n.

breakdown ▪ n. **1** a failure or collapse. **2** chemical or physical decomposition. **3** an explanatory analysis, especially of statistics.

breaker ▪ n. **1** a heavy sea wave that breaks on the shore. **2** a Citizens' Band radio user.

breakfast ▪ n. a meal eaten in the morning, the first of the day. ▪ v. eat this meal.
–PHRASES **have** (or **eat**) **someone for breakfast** informal deal with or defeat someone with contemptuous ease.
–DERIVATIVES **breakfaster** n.
–ORIGIN Middle English: from BREAK + FAST².

breakfast run ▪ n. S. African informal an early morning motorcycle rally, usually held on a Sunday.

breakfront ▪ n. [usu. as modifier] a piece of furniture having the line of its front broken by a curve or angle.

break-in ▪ n. an illegal forced entry in order to steal something.

breaking and entering ▪ n. the crime of entering a building by force to commit burglary.

breakneck ▪ adj. dangerously or extremely fast.

break point ▪ n. Tennis the state of a game when the player receiving service needs only one more point to win the game.

breakthrough ▪ n. a sudden important development or success.

breakthrough bleeding ▪ n. bleeding from the uterus occurring abnormally between menstrual periods.

breakwater ▪ n. a barrier built out into the sea to protect a coast or harbour from the force of waves.

bream ▪ n. (pl. same) a European freshwater fish of the carp family. [Family Cyprinidae.] ▸ used in names of other fishes, e.g. sea bream.

breccia

–ORIGIN Middle English: from Old French *bresme*, of Germanic origin.

breast ▪ n. **1** either of the two soft, protruding organs on the upper front of a woman's body which secrete milk after pregnancy. **2** a person's or animal's chest region. ▸ a joint of meat or poultry cut from such a part. ▪ v. face and move forwards against or through. ▸ reach the top of (a hill).
–DERIVATIVES **-breasted** adj.
–ORIGIN Old English, of Germanic origin.

breastbone ▪ n. a thin flat bone running down the centre of the chest and connecting the ribs; the sternum.

breastfeed ▪ v. (past and past part. **-fed**) feed (a baby) with milk from the breast. ▸ (of a baby) feed from the breast.

breast implant ▪ n. Medicine a prosthesis implanted behind or in place of a female breast in reconstructive or cosmetic surgery.

breastplate ▪ n. a piece of armour covering the chest.

breast pump ▪ n. a device for drawing milk from a woman's breasts by suction.

breaststroke ▪ n. a style of swimming on one's front, in which the arms are pushed forwards and then swept back in a circular movement, while the legs are alternately tucked in and kicked out.

breath ▪ n. **1** air taken into or expelled from the lungs. ▸ an inhalation or exhalation of air from the lungs. **2** a slight movement of air.
–PHRASES **breath of fresh air** a refreshing change. **catch one's breath 1** cease breathing momentarily in surprise or fear. **2** rest after exercise to restore normal breathing. **draw breath** breathe in. **hold one's breath** cease breathing temporarily. **out of breath** gasping for air, typically after exercise. **take breath** pause to recover normal breathing. **take someone's breath away** astonish or inspire someone with awed respect or delight. **under** (or **below**) **one's breath** in a very quiet voice. **waste one's breath** talk or give advice without effect.
–ORIGIN Old English *brǣth* 'smell, scent', of Germanic origin.

breathable ▪ adj. **1** (of air) fit to breathe. **2** (of clothing) admitting air to the skin and allowing sweat to evaporate.

breathalyser (US trademark **Breathalyzer**) ▪ n. a device used by police for measuring the amount of alcohol in a driver's breath.
–DERIVATIVES **breathalyse** (US **breathalyze**) v.
–ORIGIN 1960s: blend of BREATH and ANALYSE.

breathe ▪ v. **1** take air into the lungs and then expel it as a regular physiological process. ▸ (of a plant or invertebrate animal) respire or exchange gases. **2** (of wine) be exposed to fresh air. **3** (of material or soil) admit or emit air or moisture.
–PHRASES **breathe** (**freely**) **again** relax after being frightened or tense. **breathe down someone's neck** follow closely behind. ▸ constantly check up on someone. **breathe one's last** die. **breathe** (**new**) **life into** reinvigorate. **not breathe a word** remain silent about something secret.
–ORIGIN Middle English: from BREATH.

breather ▪ n. **1** informal a brief pause for rest. **2** a vent or valve to release pressure or to allow air to move freely.

breathing space ▪ n. an opportunity to pause, relax, or decide what to do next.

breathless ▪ adj. **1** gasping for breath, typically due to exertion. ▸ feeling or causing great excitement, fear, etc. **2** (of air) stiflingly still.
–DERIVATIVES **breathlessly** adv. **breathlessness** n.

breathtaking ▪ adj. astonishing or awe-inspiring.
–DERIVATIVES **breathtakingly** adv.

breath test ▪ n. a test in which a driver is made to blow into a breathalyser. ▪ v. (**breath-test**) test with a breathalyser.

breathy ▪ adj. (**-ier**, **-iest**) (of a voice) having an audible sound of breathing.
–DERIVATIVES **breathily** adv. **breathiness** n.

breccia /ˈbretʃə, -tʃɪə/ ▪ n. Geology rock consisting of

bred

angular fragments of stones cemented by finer calcareous material.
– DERIVATIVES **brecciate** v. **brecciation** n.
– ORIGIN C18: from Italian, 'gravel', rel. to BREAK.

bred past and past participle of BREED.

bredie /'briːdi/ ■ n. S. African a traditional Cape dish of meat, usually mutton or lamb, stewed with vegetables.
– ORIGIN Afrikaans, perhaps from Portuguese *bredo* denoting any of several species of *Amaranthus* cooked as a vegetable.

breech ■ n. **1** the part of a cannon behind the bore. **2** the back part of a rifle or gun barrel.
– ORIGIN Old English *brēc* 'garment covering the loins and thighs', of Germanic origin.

breech birth (also **breech delivery**) ■ n. a delivery of a baby which is so positioned in the womb that the buttocks or feet are delivered first.

breeches ■ pl. n. short trousers fastened just below the knee, now chiefly worn for riding or as part of ceremonial dress. ▶ informal trousers.

breeches buoy ■ n. a lifebuoy on a rope with a canvas support resembling a pair of breeches, by means of which a person may be held and transported.

breech-loader ■ n. a gun designed to have ammunition inserted at the breech rather than through the muzzle.
– DERIVATIVES **breech-loading** adj.

breed ■ v. (past and past part. **bred**) **1** (of animals) mate and then produce offspring. ▶ cause (an animal) to produce offspring. **2** bring up to behave in a particular way. **3** produce or lead to: *success had bred a certain arrogance.* **4** Physics create (fissile material) by nuclear reaction. ■ n. **1** a distinctive stock of animals or plants within a species, typically one deliberately developed. **2** a sort or kind.
– ORIGIN Old English, of Germanic origin.

breeder ■ n. **1** a person who breeds specific types of animals or plants. **2** an animal that breeds at a particular time or in a particular way: *emperor penguins are winter breeders.*

breeder reactor ■ n. a nuclear reactor which creates fissile material (typically plutonium-239 by irradiation of uranium-238) at a faster rate than it uses another fissile material (typically uranium-235) as fuel.

breeding ■ n. good manners regarded as characteristic of the aristocracy and conferred by heredity.

breeding ground ■ n. a thing that favours the development or occurrence of something.

breeze ■ n. **1** a gentle wind. **2** informal something easy to do. ■ v. informal come, go, or proceed in a casual or light-hearted manner.
– ORIGIN C16: prob. from Old Spanish and Portuguese *briza*.

breeze block ■ n. a lightweight building brick made from small cinders mixed with sand and cement.
– ORIGIN from French *braise, brese* 'live coals' + BLOCK.

breezeway ■ n. N. Amer. a roofed outdoor passage, as between a house and a garage.

breezy ■ adj. (**-ier, -iest**) **1** pleasantly windy. **2** relaxed, informal, and cheerily brisk.
– DERIVATIVES **breezily** adv. **breeziness** n.

brei¹ /breɪ/ (also **bray**) S. African ■ n. a guttural pronunciation of the 'r' sound, as in some Cape regional accents. ■ v. pronounce the letter 'r' in the back of the throat.
– ORIGIN 1950s: from Afrikaans *bry*, from Dutch *brouwen* 'speak thickly'.

brei² /breɪ/ variant spelling of BRAY³.

breker /'brɪəkə/ ■ n. S. African informal a tough, rough, and aggressive man.
– ORIGIN 1970s: Afrikaans, 'destroyer', from *breek* 'to break'.

bremsstrahlung /'brɛmzˌʃtrɑːlʊŋ/ ■ n. Physics electromagnetic radiation emitted by a charged particle on passing through the electric and magnetic fields of a nucleus.

– ORIGIN 1940s: from German, from *bremsen* 'to brake' + *Strahlung* 'radiation'.

Bren gun ■ n. a lightweight quick-firing machine gun used by the Allied forces in the Second World War.
– ORIGIN blend of *Brno* in the Czech Republic (where it was orig. made) and *Enfield*, England (where it was later made).

brethren archaic plural of BROTHER. ■ pl. n. fellow Christians or members of a male religious order.

Breton /'brɛt(ə)n/ ■ n. a native of Brittany.
– ORIGIN from Old French, 'Briton'.

breve ■ n. Music a note having the time value of two semibreves, represented as a semibreve with two short bars either side, or as a square.
– ORIGIN Middle English: var. of BRIEF: orig. in a series where a *long* was of greater time value than a *breve*.

brevet /'brɛvɪt/ ■ n. a former type of military commission conferred especially for outstanding service, by which an officer was promoted to a higher rank without the corresponding pay. ■ v. (**breveted** or **brevetted**, **breveting** or **brevetting**) confer a brevet rank on.
– ORIGIN Middle English: from Old French *brievet* 'little letter', diminutive of *bref*.

breviary /'briːvɪəri/ ■ n. (pl. **-ies**) a book containing the service for each day, to be recited by those in orders in the Roman Catholic Church.
– ORIGIN Middle English: from Latin *breviarium* 'summary, abridgement', from *breviare* 'abridge'.

brevity /'brɛvɪti/ ■ n. **1** concise and exact use of words. **2** shortness of time.
– ORIGIN C15: from Latin *brevitas*, from *brevis* 'brief'.

brew ■ v. **1** make (beer) by soaking, boiling, and fermentation. **2** make (tea or coffee) by mixing it with hot water. **3** (of an unwelcome situation) begin to develop. ■ n. **1** a kind of beer. **2** informal a drink of tea.
– DERIVATIVES **brewer** n.
– ORIGIN Old English, of Germanic origin.

brewery ■ n. (pl. **-ies**) a place where beer is made commercially.

brey ■ v. variant spelling of BRAY³.

breyani ■ n. S. African variant spelling of BIRIANI.

briar¹ (also **brier**) ■ n. a prickly scrambling shrub, especially a wild rose. [*Rosa eglanteria* (sweetbriar) and other species.]
– DERIVATIVES **briary** adj.
– ORIGIN Old English.

briar² (also **brier**) ■ n. **1** (also **briar pipe**) a tobacco pipe made from woody nodules borne by the tree heath. **2** another term for TREE HEATH.
– ORIGIN C19: from French *bruyère* 'heath, heather'.

bribe ■ v. dishonestly persuade (someone) to act in one's favour by a payment or other inducement. ■ n. an inducement offered in an attempt to bribe.
– DERIVATIVES **bribable** adj. **briber** n. **bribery** n.
– ORIGIN Middle English: from Old French *briber, brimber* 'beg'.

bric-a-brac ■ n. miscellaneous objects and ornaments of little value.
– ORIGIN C19: from French, from obsolete *à bric et à brac* 'at random'.

brick ■ n. **1** a small rectangular block of fired or sun-dried clay, used in building. ▶ bricks collectively as a building material. **2** Brit. informal, dated a generous, helpful, and reliable person. ■ v. block or enclose with a wall of bricks.
– PHRASES **bricks and mortar** buildings, especially housing. **like a ton of bricks** informal with crushing weight, force, or authority.
– ORIGIN Middle English: from Middle Dutch *bricke, brike*; prob. reinforced by Old French *brique*.

brickbat ■ n. **1** a piece of brick used as a missile. **2** a highly critical remark or reaction.

bricklayer ■ n. a person whose job is to build structures with bricks.
– DERIVATIVES **bricklaying** n.

brick red ■ n. a deep brownish red.

bridal ■ adj. of or concerning a bride or a newly married couple.
– ORIGIN Middle English: from Old English *brȳd-ealu* 'wedding feast', from *brȳd* 'bride' + *ealu* 'ale-drinking'.

bride ■ n. a woman on her wedding day or just before and after the event.
– ORIGIN Old English, of Germanic origin.

bridegroom ■ n. a man on his wedding day or just before and after the event.
– ORIGIN Old English *brýdguma*, from *brýd* 'bride' + *guma* 'man'; influenced by GROOM.

bride price ■ n. (in some traditional societies) a payment made to a bride's family by that of the groom.

bridesmaid ■ n. a girl or woman who accompanies a bride on her wedding day.

bridge[1] ■ n. 1 a structure carrying a road, path, or railway across a river, road, etc. 2 the elevated, enclosed platform on a ship from which the captain and officers direct operations. 3 the upper bony part of a person's nose. 4 an electric circuit used chiefly to measure an unknown resistance or impedance by equalizing the potentials in two parts of the circuit. 5 a partial denture supported by natural teeth on either side. 6 Music the part on a stringed instrument over which the strings are stretched. 7 Music a bridge passage or middle eight. ■ v. be or make a bridge over or between.
– DERIVATIVES **bridgeable** adj.
– ORIGIN Old English, of Germanic origin.

bridge[2] ■ n. a card game related to whist, played by two partnerships of two players who at the beginning of each hand bid for the right to name the trump suit, the highest bid also representing a contract to make a specified number of tricks.
– ORIGIN C19.

bridgehead ■ n. a strong position secured by an army inside enemy territory from which to advance or attack.

bridge roll ■ n. Brit. a small, soft bread roll with a long, thin shape.

bridging loan ■ n. a sum of money lent by a bank to cover an interval between two transactions.

bridie ■ n. (pl. -ies) Scottish a meat pasty.
– ORIGIN perhaps from obsolete *bride's pie*.

bridle ■ n. 1 the headgear used to control a horse, consisting of buckled straps to which a bit and reins are attached. 2 Nautical a mooring cable. ■ v. 1 put a bridle on. 2 bring under control. 3 show resentment or anger.
– PHRASES **off** (or **on**) **the bridle** see BIT[3].
– ORIGIN Old English, of Germanic origin.

bridleway (also **bridle path**) ■ n. Brit. a path or track along which horse riders have right of way.

Brie /briː/ ■ n. a kind of soft, mild, creamy cheese with a firm, white skin.
– ORIGIN named after *Brie* in northern France.

brief ■ adj. 1 of short duration. 2 concise; using few words. 3 (of clothing) not covering much of the body. ■ n. 1 chiefly Brit. a summary of the facts and legal points in a case given to an advocate to argue in court. ▶ a piece of work for an advocate. ▶ US a written summary of a case, for presentation to a court. 2 Brit. informal an attorney or advocate. 3 a set of instructions given to a person about a task. ■ v. instruct or inform thoroughly in preparation for a task. ▶ instruct (an advocate) by brief.
– PHRASES **hold a brief for** Brit. be retained as counsel for. **hold no brief for** not support. **in brief** in short.
– DERIVATIVES **briefless** adj. (Brit. Law). **briefly** adv. **briefness** n.
– ORIGIN Middle English: from Old French *brief*, from Latin *brevis* 'short'.

briefcase ■ n. a flat rectangular case for carrying books and documents.

briefing ■ n. a meeting for giving information or instructions.

briefs ■ pl. n. short, close-fitting underpants or knickers.

brier[1] ■ n. variant spelling of BRIAR[1].

brier[2] ■ n. variant spelling of BRIAR[2].

Brig. ■ abbrev. Brigadier.

brig ■ n. 1 a two-masted square-rigged ship, typically having an additional lower fore-and-aft sail on the gaff and a boom to the mainmast. 2 informal a prison, especially on a warship.
– ORIGIN C18: abbrev. of BRIGANTINE.

brigade ■ n. 1 a subdivision of an army, typically consisting of a small number of battalions and forming part of a division. 2 an organization with a quasi-military structure. 3 informal, often derogatory a group of people with a characteristic in common: *the anti-smoking brigade*.
– ORIGIN C17: from French, from Italian *brigata* 'company'.

brigadier ■ n. a rank of officer in the British army, above colonel and below major general.
– ORIGIN C17: from French (see BRIGADE).

brigadier general ■ n. a rank of officer in the army and air force, above colonel and below major general.

brigand /ˈbrɪɡ(ə)nd/ ■ n. a member of a gang that ambushes and robs people in forests and mountains.
– DERIVATIVES **brigandage** n. **brigandry** n.
– ORIGIN Middle English: from Italian *brigante* '(person) contending', from *brigare*.

brigantine /ˈbrɪɡ(ə)ntiːn/ ■ n. a two-masted sailing ship with a square-rigged foremast and a mainmast rigged fore and aft.
– ORIGIN C16: from Italian *brigantino*, from *brigante* (see BRIGAND).

bright ■ adj. 1 giving out much light, or filled with light. 2 (of colour) vivid and bold. 3 intelligent and quick-witted. 4 (of sound) clear and typically high-pitched. 5 cheerfully lively. 6 (of prospects) good. ■ n. (**brights**) N. Amer. headlights switched to full beam.
– PHRASES **bright and early** very early in the morning. (**as**) **bright as a button** informal intelligently alert and lively. **bright-eyed and bushy-tailed** informal alert and lively. **look on the bright side** be optimistic or cheerful in spite of difficulties.
– DERIVATIVES **brighten** v. **brightish** adj. **brightly** adv. **brightness** n.
– ORIGIN Old English, of Germanic origin.

bright spark ■ n. informal, often ironic a clever or witty person.

brightwork ■ n. polished metalwork on ships or other vehicles.

brilliant ■ adj. 1 (of light or colour) very bright or vivid. 2 exceptionally clever or talented. 3 Brit. informal excellent; marvellous. ■ n. a diamond of brilliant cut.
– DERIVATIVES **brilliance** (also **brilliancy**) n. **brilliantly** adv.
– ORIGIN C17: from French *brillant*, from *briller* 'shine', prob. from Latin *beryllus* (see BERYL).

brilliant cut ■ n. a circular cut for gemstones in the form of two many-faceted pyramids joined at their bases, the upper one truncated near its apex.

brilliantine ■ n. 1 dated scented oil used on men's hair to make it look glossy. 2 US shiny dress fabric made from cotton and mohair or cotton and worsted.
– DERIVATIVES **brilliantined** adj.
– ORIGIN C19: from French *brillantine*, from *brillant* (see BRILLIANT).

brim ■ n. 1 the projecting edge around the bottom of a hat. 2 the lip of a cup, bowl, etc. ■ v. (**brimmed**, **brimming**) [often as adj. **brimming**] fill or be full to the point of overflowing.
– DERIVATIVES **brimful** adj. **brimless** adj. **-brimmed** adj.
– ORIGIN Middle English: perhaps rel. to German *Bräme* 'trimming'.

brimstone /ˈbrɪmst(ə)n, -stəʊn/ ■ n. 1 archaic sulphur. 2 a large butterfly, the male of which is bright yellow and the female greenish-white. [*Gonepteryx rhamni*.]
– ORIGIN Old English, prob. from *bryne* 'burning' + *stān* 'stone'.

brimstone moth ■ n. a small bright yellow moth. [*Opisthograptis luteolata*.]

brindle (also **brindled**) ■ adj. (especially of a domestic animal) brownish or tawny with streaks of other colour.
– ORIGIN C17: from Middle English *brinded*, prob. of Scandinavian origin.

brine ■ n. water saturated or strongly impregnated with salt; seawater. ▶ technical a strong solution of a salt or salts. ■ v. [often as adj. **brined**] soak in or saturate with brine.
– ORIGIN Old English.

brine shrimp

brine shrimp ■ n. a small fairy shrimp which lives in brine pools and salt lakes and is used as food for aquarium fish. [*Artemia salina*.]

bring ■ v. (past and past part. **brought**) 1 carry or accompany to a place. 2 cause to be in a particular state or condition. 3 cause someone to receive (money) as income or profit: *the two novels brought him R600 000.* 4 [usu. with neg.] (**bring oneself to do something**) force oneself to do something unpleasant. 5 initiate (legal action).
– PHRASES **bring the house down** make an audience laugh or applaud very enthusiastically. **bring something to bear** exert influence or pressure.
– PHRASAL VERBS **bring something about** 1 cause something to happen. 2 cause a ship to head in a different direction. **bring someone/thing down** cause someone or something to fall over or down. ▶ cause someone to lose power. **bring something forth** archaic or poetic/literary give birth to something. **bring something forward** 1 [often as adj. **brought forward**] (in bookkeeping) transfer a total sum from the bottom of one page to the top of the next. 2 propose an idea for consideration. **bring someone off** vulgar slang give someone an orgasm. **bring something off** achieve something successfully. **bring someone on** encourage or help someone who is learning to develop or improve. **bring something on** 1 cause something unpleasant to occur. ▶ (**bring something on/upon**) be responsible for something unpleasant that happens to (someone). 2 (of the weather) promote the growth of crops. **bring someone out** encourage someone to feel more confident. **bring something out** 1 produce and launch a new product or publication. 2 emphasize a feature. **bring someone round** (or US **around**) 1 restore someone to consciousness. 2 persuade someone to adopt one's own point of view. **bring someone to** restore someone to consciousness. **bring something to** cause a boat to stop, especially by turning into the wind. **bring up** (chiefly of a ship) come to a stop. **bring someone up** look after a child until it is an adult. **bring something up** 1 vomit something. 2 raise a matter for discussion or consideration.
– DERIVATIVES **bringer** n.
– ORIGIN Old English, of Germanic origin.

bring and buy sale ■ n. Brit. a charity sale at which people donate things to sell and buy those brought by others.

brinjal /'brɪndʒəl/ ■ n. S. African & Indian 1 the purple egg-shaped fruit of a tropical plant, eaten as a vegetable; an aubergine. 2 the plant of the nightshade family which bears this fruit. [*Solanum melongena*.]
– ORIGIN from Portuguese *berinjela*, from Arabic *al-bāḏinjān*.

brink ■ n. 1 the extreme edge of land before a steep slope or a body of water. 2 the verge of a state or situation, typically a bad one.
– ORIGIN Middle English: of Scandinavian origin.

brinkmanship /'brɪŋkmənʃɪp/ (US also **brinksmanship**) ■ n. the pursuit of a dangerous policy to the limits of safety before stopping.

briny /'braɪni/ ■ adj. (-**ier**, -**iest**) of salty water or the sea; salty. ■ n. (**the briny**) Brit. informal the sea.

brio /'briːəʊ/ ■ n. vigour or vivacity.
– ORIGIN C18: from Italian.

brioche /briː'ɒʃ, 'briːɒʃ/ ■ n. a small round French roll made from a light sweet yeast bread.
– ORIGIN French, from Norman French *brier* 'split up into small pieces'.

briquette /brɪ'kɛt/ (also **briquet**) ■ n. a block of compressed organic fuel, often used for braai fires.
– ORIGIN C19: from French, diminutive of *brique* 'brick'.

brisé /'briːzeɪ/ ■ n. Ballet a jump in which the dancer sweeps one leg into the air to the side while jumping off the other and brings both legs together in the air before landing.
– ORIGIN French, 'broken'.

brisk ■ adj. 1 active and energetic. 2 slightly brusque.
– DERIVATIVES **brisken** v. **briskly** adv. **briskness** n.
– ORIGIN C16: prob. from French *brusque* (see BRUSQUE).

brisket ■ n. meat from the breast of a cow.

– ORIGIN Middle English: perhaps from Old Norse *brjósk* 'cartilage, gristle'.

bristle /'brɪs(ə)l/ ■ n. a short, stiff hair on an animal's skin or a man's face. ▶ a bristle, or a man-made substitute, used to make a brush. ■ v. 1 (of hair or fur) stand upright away from the skin, typically as a sign of anger or fear. 2 react angrily or defensively. 3 (**bristle with**) be covered with or abundant in.
– DERIVATIVES **bristly** adj.
– ORIGIN Middle English: from Old English *byrst*, of Germanic origin.

bristletail ■ n. a small primitive wingless insect which has two or three bristles at the end of the abdomen. [Orders Thysanura (with three bristles, including the silverfish) and Diplura (with two bristles).]

Brit informal ■ n. a British person. ■ adj. British.

Britannia /brɪ'tanjə/ ■ n. the personification of Britain, usually depicted as a helmeted woman with shield and trident.
– ORIGIN the Latin name for Britain.

Britannic /brɪ'tanɪk/ ■ adj. dated (chiefly in names or titles) of Britain or the British Empire.

Briticism /'brɪtɪsɪz(ə)m/ (also **Britishism** /-ʃɪz(ə)m/) ■ n. an idiom used in Britain but not in other English-speaking countries.

British ■ adj. of or relating to Great Britain or the United Kingdom.
– DERIVATIVES **Britishness** n.
– ORIGIN Old English *Brettisc*, from *Bret* 'Briton', from Latin *Britto* or its Celtic equivalent.

British thermal unit ■ n. dated a unit of heat equal to the amount of heat needed to raise 1 lb of water at maximum density through one degree Fahrenheit. [1.055×10^3 joules.]

Briton ■ n. 1 a native or inhabitant of Great Britain, or a person of British descent. 2 one of the people of southern Britain before and during Roman times.
– ORIGIN from Old French *Breton*, from Latin *Britto* or its Celtic equivalent.

Britpop ■ n. pop music by British groups of the mid 1990s, typically influenced by the Beatles and other British groups of the 1960s.

brittle ■ adj. 1 hard but liable to break or shatter easily. 2 (of a voice) unpleasantly hard and sharp and showing signs of nervousness or instability. 3 superficial or unfeeling. ■ n. a brittle sweet made from nuts and set melted sugar.
– DERIVATIVES **brittlely** (or **brittly**) adv. **brittleness** n.
– ORIGIN Middle English: of Germanic origin and rel. to Old English *brēotan* 'break up'.

brittle bone disease ■ n. another term for the diseases OSTEOGENESIS IMPERFECTA or OSTEOPOROSIS.

brittlestar ■ n. a marine animal related to a starfish, with long thin flexible arms radiating from a small central disk. [*Ophiura* and other genera, class Ophiuroidea.]

bro /brəʊ/ ■ n. informal short for BROTHER. ▶ S. African & N. Amer. a friendly greeting or form of address for a man.

broach[1] ■ v. 1 raise (a sensitive subject) for discussion. 2 pierce or open (a cask or container) to draw liquor.
– ORIGIN Middle English: from Old French *brochier*, from Latin *brocchus*, *broccus* 'projecting'.

broach[2] ■ v. Nautical (of a ship) veer and pitch forward, presenting a side to the wind and waves and losing steerage control.
– ORIGIN C18.

broad ■ adj. 1 having a distance larger than usual from side to side; wide. ▶ of a specified distance wide. 2 large in area or scope. 3 without detail. 4 (of a hint) clear and unambiguous. 5 (of a regional accent) very noticeable and strong. 6 somewhat coarse and indecent. ■ n. N. Amer. informal a woman.
– PHRASES **broad daylight** full daylight; day.
– DERIVATIVES **broaden** v. **broadly** adv. **broadness** n.
– ORIGIN Old English, of Germanic origin.

broadband ■ adj. of or using signals over a wide range of frequencies in high-capacity telecommunications.

broad-based ■ adj. involving the participation of a wide range of people or political groups; having great scope.

broad bean ■ n. **1** a large flat edible green bean which is usually eaten without the pod. **2** the plant which yields these beans. [*Vicia faba*.]

broadbill ■ n. a small, colourful songbird of the Old World tropics, with a large head and a wide, flattened bill. [Family Eurylaimidae: numerous species.]

broad-brush ■ adj. lacking in detail and finesse.

broadcast ■ v. (past **broadcast**; past part. **broadcast** or **broadcasted**) **1** transmit by radio or television. **2** tell to many people. **3** scatter (seeds) rather than placing in drills or rows. ■ n. a radio or television programme or transmission. ■ adv. by scattering.
– DERIVATIVES **broadcaster** n. **broadcasting** n.

broadcloth ■ n. clothing fabric of fine twilled wool or worsted, or plain-woven cotton.

broad gauge ■ n. a railway gauge which is wider than the standard gauge of 4 ft 8½ in (1.435 m).

broadleaved (also **broadleaf**) ■ adj. denoting trees or herbaceous plants with relatively wide flat leaves, as opposed to conifers or grasses respectively.

broadloom ■ n. carpet woven in wide widths.

broad-minded ■ adj. tolerant or liberal.
– DERIVATIVES **broad-mindedly** adv. **broad-mindedness** n.

broad money ■ n. Economics money in any form, including bank or other deposits as well as notes and coins.

broadsheet ■ n. **1** a large piece of paper printed with information on one side only. **2** a newspaper with a large format, regarded as more serious than tabloids.

broadside ■ n. **1** historical a firing of all the guns from one side of a warship. **2** the side of a ship above the water between the bow and quarter. **3** a strongly worded critical attack. **4** another term for **BROADSHEET** (sense 1). ■ adv. with the side turned in a particular direction. ▶ on the side. ■ v. N. Amer. collide with the side of (a vehicle).
– PHRASES **broadside on** sideways on.

broadsword ■ n. a sword with a wide blade, used for cutting rather than thrusting.

Brobdingnagian /ˌbrɒbdɪŋˈnaɡɪən/ ■ adj. gigantic. ■ n. a giant.
– ORIGIN C18: from *Brobdingnag*, a land in *Gulliver's Travels* where everything is of huge size.

brocade ■ n. a rich fabric woven with a raised pattern, usually with gold or silver thread. ■ v. (usu. as adj. **brocaded**) weave with this design.
– ORIGIN C16: from Italian *broccato*, from *brocco* 'twisted thread'.

Broca's area /ˈbrəʊkəz/ ■ n. Anatomy a region of the brain concerned with the production of speech, located in the cortex of the dominant frontal lobe.
– ORIGIN C19: named after the French surgeon Paul *Broca*.

broccoli /ˈbrɒkəli/ ■ n. a cultivated variety of cabbage with heads of small green or purplish flower buds, eaten as a vegetable.
– ORIGIN C17: from Italian, pl. of *broccolo* 'cabbage sprout, head'.

brochure /ˈbrəʊʃə, brɒˈʃʊə/ ■ n. a small book or magazine containing pictures and information about a product or service.
– ORIGIN C18: from French, 'something stitched', from *brocher*.

brock ■ n. Brit. a name for the badger.
– ORIGIN Old English, of Celtic origin.

broderie anglaise /ˌbrəʊd(ə)ri ˈɒ̃ɡleɪz/ ■ n. open embroidery, typically in floral patterns, on fine white cotton or linen.
– ORIGIN C19: French, 'English embroidery'.

Broeder /ˈbruːdə/ ■ n. S. African a member of the Afrikaner Broederbond.
– ORIGIN Afrikaans, 'brother'.

Broederbond /ˈbruːdəbɒnd/ short for **AFRIKANER BROEDERBOND**.
– DERIVATIVES **Broederbonder** n.

broedertwis /ˈbruːdətvəs/ ■ n. S. African friction between individuals or groups, especially within a political party.
– ORIGIN Afrikaans, from *broeder* 'brother' + *twis* 'quarrel'.

broekielace /ˈbrʊkɪleɪs/ ■ n. S. African a border of decorative wrought iron or woodwork used especially around the roof of a Victorian house or its veranda.
– ORIGIN C20: from Afrikaans *broekie* 'panties' + **LACE**.

brogue[1] ■ n. a strong outdoor shoe with ornamental perforated patterns in the leather. ▶ a rough shoe of untanned leather, formerly worn in Ireland and the Scottish Highlands.
– ORIGIN C16: from Scottish Gaelic and Irish *bróg*, from Old Norse *brók*.

brogue[2] ■ n. a marked accent, especially Irish or Scottish, when speaking English.
– ORIGIN C18: perhaps allusively from **BROGUE**[1].

broil[1] ■ v. **1** cook (meat or fish) by exposure to direct heat. **2** become very hot, especially from the sun.
– ORIGIN Middle English: from Old French *bruler* 'to burn'.

broil[2] ■ n. archaic a quarrel or a commotion.
– ORIGIN C16: from obsolete *broil* 'to muddle'; cf. **EMBROIL**.

broiler ■ n. **1** a young chicken suitable for roasting, grilling, or barbecuing. **2** N. Amer. a gridiron, grill, or special part of a stove for broiling meat or fish.

broiler house ■ n. a building for rearing broiler chickens in close confinement.

broke past (and archaic past participle) of **BREAK**. ■ adj. informal having completely run out of money.
– PHRASES **go for broke** informal risk everything in an all-out effort.

broken past participle of **BREAK**. ■ adj. (of a language) spoken falteringly and with many mistakes, as by a foreigner.
– DERIVATIVES **brokenly** adv. **brokenness** /ˈbrəʊk(ə)nnɪs/ n.

broken chord ■ n. Music a chord in which the notes are played successively.

broken-down ■ adj. **1** worn out and dilapidated. **2** not working.

broken-hearted ■ adj. overwhelmed by grief or disappointment.
– DERIVATIVES **broken-heartedness** n.

broken home ■ n. a family in which the parents are divorced or separated.

broken reed ■ n. see **REED**.

broken wind ■ n. another term for **COPD** in horses.
– DERIVATIVES **broken-winded** adj.

broker ■ n. a person who buys and sells goods or assets for others. Compare with **BROKER-DEALER**. ■ v. arrange or negotiate (a deal or plan).
– DERIVATIVES **brokerage** n.
– ORIGIN Middle English: from Anglo-Norman French *brocour*.

broker-dealer ■ n. (in the UK) a person combining the former functions of a broker and jobber on the Stock Exchange.

broking ■ n. the business or service of buying and selling goods or assets for others.

brolly ■ n. (pl. **-ies**) informal, chiefly Brit. an umbrella.

brome /brəʊm/ ■ n. an oat-like grass which is sometimes grown for fodder or ornamental purposes. [Genus *Bromus*.]
– ORIGIN C18: from Greek *bromos* 'oat'.

bromeliad /brəˈmiːlɪad/ ■ n. a plant of a tropical and subtropical American family (Bromeliaceae), typically with short stems with rosettes of stiff, spiny leaves.
– ORIGIN C19: from *Bromelia*, a genus, named after the Swedish botanist Olaf *Bromel*.

bromide /ˈbrəʊmʌɪd/ ■ n. **1** Chemistry a compound of bromine with another element or group: *methyl bromide*. **2** a reproduction or piece of typesetting on bromide paper. **3** dated a sedative preparation containing potassium bromide. **4** a trite statement intended to soothe or placate.
– DERIVATIVES **bromidic** adj.

bromide paper ■ n. photographic printing paper coated with silver bromide emulsion.

bromine /ˈbrəʊmiːn/ ■ n. the chemical element of atomic number 35, a dark red toxic liquid halogen with a choking irritating smell. (Symbol: **Br**)
– ORIGIN C19: from Greek *brōmos* 'a stink'.

bronchi

bronchi plural form of **BRONCHUS**.
bronchial /'brɒŋkɪəl/ ■ adj. of or relating to the bronchi or bronchioles.
bronchiole /'brɒŋkɪəʊl/ ■ n. Anatomy any of the minute branches into which a bronchus divides.
– DERIVATIVES **bronchiolar** adj.
– ORIGIN C19: from *bronchiolus*, diminutive of late Latin *bronchia*, denoting the branches of the main bronchi.
bronchiolitis /ˌbrɒŋkɪə'laɪtɪs/ ■ n. Medicine inflammation of the bronchioles.
bronchitis ■ n. inflammation of the mucous membrane in the bronchial tubes, typically with spasm of bronchial muscle and coughing.
– DERIVATIVES **bronchitic** adj. & n.
broncho- /'brɒŋkəʊ/ ■ comb. form of or relating to the bronchi: *bronchopneumonia*.
– ORIGIN from Greek, from *bronkhos* 'windpipe'.
bronchodilator /ˌbrɒŋkə(ʊ)daɪ'leɪtə/ ■ n. Medicine a drug that causes widening of the bronchi, for example any of those taken by inhalation for the alleviation of asthma.
bronchopneumonia /ˌbrɒŋkə(ʊ)njuː'məʊnɪə/ ■ n. inflammation of the lungs, arising in the bronchi or bronchioles.
bronchus /'brɒŋkəs/ ■ n. (pl. **bronchi** /-kaɪ/) any of the major air passages of the lungs which diverge from the windpipe.
– ORIGIN C17: from Greek *bronkhos* 'windpipe'.
bronco ■ n. (pl. **-os**) a wild or half-tamed horse of the western US.
– ORIGIN C19: from Spanish, 'rough, rude'.
brontosaurus /ˌbrɒntə'sɔːrəs/ (also **brontosaur** /'brɒntəsɔː/) ■ n. another term for **APATOSAURUS**.
– ORIGIN from Greek *brontē* 'thunder' + *sauros* 'lizard'.
Bronx cheer ■ n. N. Amer. a sound of derision made by blowing through closed lips with the tongue between them.
bronze ■ n. **1** a yellowish-brown alloy of copper with up to one-third tin. **2** a yellowish-brown colour. **3** a work of sculpture or other object made of bronze. ■ v. **1** give a bronze surface to. **2** make suntanned.
– DERIVATIVES **bronzy** adj.
– ORIGIN C17: from French *bronze*, from Italian *bronzo*, prob. from Persian *birinj* 'brass'.
Bronze Age ■ n. a prehistoric period that followed the Stone Age and preceded the Iron Age, when weapons and tools were made of bronze rather than stone.
bronze medal ■ n. a medal made of or coloured bronze, customarily awarded for third place in a race or competition.
brooch /brəʊtʃ/ ■ n. an ornament fastened to clothing with a hinged pin and catch.
– ORIGIN Middle English: var. of *broach* 'skewer, bodkin', from Old French *broche* 'spit for roasting', from Latin *brocchus, broccus* 'projecting'.
brood ■ n. **1** a family of young animals, especially birds, produced at one hatching or birth. **2** bee or wasp larvae. ■ v. **1** think deeply about something that makes one unhappy. **2** [as adj. **brooding**] appearing darkly menacing. **3** (of a bird) sit on (eggs) to hatch them. ▸ (of a fish, frog, or invertebrate) hold (developing eggs) within the body. ■ adj. (of an animal) kept to be used for breeding.
– DERIVATIVES **broodingly** adv.
– ORIGIN Old English, of Germanic origin.
brooder ■ n. a heated house for chicks or piglets.
broody ■ adj. (**-ier**, **-iest**) **1** (of a hen) inclined to incubate eggs. **2** informal (of a woman) having a strong desire to have a baby. **3** thoughtful and unhappy.
– DERIVATIVES **broodily** adv. **broodiness** n.
brook[1] ■ n. a small stream.
– DERIVATIVES **brooklet** n.
– ORIGIN Old English *brōc*.
brook[2] ■ v. [with neg.] formal tolerate or allow (opposition).
– ORIGIN Old English *brūcan* 'use, possess' or 'digest, stomach', of Germanic origin.

broom ■ n. **1** a long-handled brush of bristles or twigs, used for sweeping. **2** a shrub typically having many yellow flowers, long, thin green stems, and small or few leaves. [*Cytisus, Genista*, and other genera.]
– ORIGIN Old English, of Germanic origin.
broomrape ■ n. a leafless parasitic plant of the northern hemisphere with tubular flowers, which attaches itself to the roots of its host plant. [Genus *Orobanche*.]
– ORIGIN C16: from **BROOM** + Latin *rapum* 'tuber'.
broomstick ■ n. the handle of a broom, on which witches are said to fly.
Bros /brɒs/ ■ pl. n. brothers (in names of companies).
broth ■ n. a thin soup of meat or vegetable stock, sometimes thickened with barley or other cereals. ▸ meat or fish stock.
– ORIGIN Old English, of Germanic origin; rel. to **BREW**.
brothel ■ n. a house where men visit prostitutes.
– ORIGIN C16: from Middle English *brothel* 'worthless man, prostitute'.
brothel creepers ■ pl. n. informal soft-soled suede shoes.
brother ■ n. **1** a man or boy in relation to other sons and daughters of his parents. **2** a male associate or fellow member of an organization. **3** informal a black man. **4** something which resembles or is equivalent to another. **5** (pl. also **brethren**) Christian Church a (male) fellow Christian. ▸ a member of a religious order of men. ■ exclam. used to express annoyance or surprise.
– DERIVATIVES **brotherliness** n. **brotherly** adj.
– ORIGIN Old English, of Germanic origin.
brotherhood ■ n. **1** the relationship between brothers. ▸ a feeling of kinship and closeness. **2** an association or community of people with a common interest, religion, or trade. ▸ N. Amer. a trade union.
– ORIGIN Middle English: prob. from obsolete *brotherred*, from Old English *-rǣden* 'condition, state'.
brother-in-law ■ n. (pl. **brothers-in-law**) **1** the brother of one's wife or husband. **2** the husband of one's sister or sister-in-law.
brougham /'bruː(ə)m/ ■ n. historical a horse-drawn carriage with a roof, four wheels, and an open driver's seat in front.
– ORIGIN C19: named after Lord *Brougham*, who designed the carriage.
brought past and past participle of **BRING**.
brouhaha /'bruːhɑːhɑː/ ■ n. a noisy and overexcited reaction.
– ORIGIN C19: from French, prob. imitative.
brow ■ n. **1** a person's forehead. **2** an eyebrow. **3** the summit of a hill or pass.
– DERIVATIVES **-browed** adj.
– ORIGIN Old English *brū* 'eyelash, eyebrow', of Germanic origin.
browbeat ■ v. (past **-beat**; past part. **-beaten**) intimidate or cajole with words or looks.
– DERIVATIVES **browbeater** n.
brown ■ adj. **1** of a colour produced by mixing red, yellow, and blue, as of dark wood or rich soil. **2** dark-skinned or suntanned. **3** S. African another term for **COLOURED** (in sense 2). ■ n. **1** brown colour, pigment, or material. **2** used in names of various butterflies with mainly brown wings and small eyespots. **3** (**browns**) the brown uniform worn by members of the former South African Defence Force. ■ v. **1** make or become brown by cooking. **2** (**be browned off**) informal be irritated or depressed.
– DERIVATIVES **brownish** adj. **brownness** n. **browny** adj.
– ORIGIN Old English, of Germanic origin.
brown ale ■ n. Brit. dark, mild beer sold in bottles.
brown algae ■ pl. n. a large group of algae that are typically olive brown or greenish in colour, including many seaweeds. [Class Phaeophyceae.]
brown bear ■ n. a large bear with a coat colour ranging from cream to black. [*Ursus arctos*.]
brown belt ■ n. a belt of a brown colour marking a level of proficiency below that of a black belt in judo, karate, or other martial arts.
brown coal ■ n. another term for **LIGNITE**.
brown dwarf ■ n. Astronomy a celestial object

intermediate in size between a giant planet and a small star, believed to emit mainly infrared radiation.

brown fat ■ n. dark-coloured adipose tissue with many blood vessels, able to provide bodily heat quite rapidly.

brownfield ■ adj. (of an urban site) having had previous development on it. Compare with GREENFIELD.

brown goods ■ pl. n. television sets, audio equipment, and similar household appliances. Compare with WHITE GOODS.

brown haze ■ n. a brownish layer of smog caused by pollutant chemicals combined with airborne particles.

brown hyena ■ n. a southern African hyena with a dark brown shaggy coat. [*Hyaena brunnea*.]

Brownian motion /ˈbraʊnɪən/ ■ n. Physics the erratic random movement of microscopic particles in a fluid, as a result of continuous bombardment from molecules of the surrounding medium.
– ORIGIN C19: named after the Scottish botanist Robert *Brown*.

Brownie ■ n. (pl. -ies) 1 (Brit. also **Brownie Guide**) a member of the junior branch of the Girl Guides Association, for girls aged between about 7 and 10. 2 (**brownie**) a small square of rich chocolate cake, with nuts. 3 (**brownie**) a benevolent elf supposedly haunting houses and doing housework secretly.
– PHRASES **brownie point** informal, humorous a notional award given for a good deed or an attempt to please.

Browning ■ n. 1 a type of water-cooled automatic machine gun. 2 a type of automatic pistol.
– ORIGIN C20: named after the American designer John M. *Browning*.

browning ■ n. Brit. darkened flour for colouring gravy.

brown-nose informal ■ n. (also **brown-noser**) a person who acts in a grossly obsequious way. ■ v. curry favour with (someone) by acting in such a way.

brownout ■ n. a partial blackout.

Brown Owl ■ n. informal, chiefly Brit. the adult leader of a group of Brownies (officially termed the Brownie Guider).

brown rice ■ n. unpolished rice with only the husk of the grain removed.

brown rot ■ n. 1 a fungal disease producing discoloration and shrivelling of apples, pears, and other fruit. 2 a fungal disease resulting in the softening and cracking of timber.

brown sauce ■ n. a commercially prepared relish containing vinegar and spices.

Brownshirt ■ n. a member of a Nazi militia founded by Hitler in 1921 and suppressed in 1934, who wore brown uniforms.

brownstone ■ n. N. Amer. 1 a kind of reddish-brown sandstone used for building. 2 a building faced with such sandstone.

brown sugar ■ n. 1 unrefined or partially refined sugar. 2 informal heroin.

brown trout ■ n. (pl. same) the common trout of European lakes and rivers, typically with dark spotted skin. [*Salmo trutta*.]

browse /braʊz/ ■ v. 1 survey goods or text in a leisurely and superficial fashion. ▶ Computing read or survey (data files) via a network. 2 (of an animal) feed on leaves, twigs, etc. ■ n. 1 an act of browsing. 2 vegetation eaten by animals.
– DERIVATIVES **browsable** adj.
– ORIGIN Middle English: from Old French *broster*, from *brost* 'young shoot', prob. of Germanic origin.

browser ■ n. 1 a person or animal that browses. 2 Computing a program with a graphical user interface for displaying HTML files, used to navigate the World Wide Web.

brrr ■ exclam. used to express a reaction to feeling cold.

bru /ˌbruː/ ■ n. S. African informal another term for BRO.

brucellosis /ˌbruːsəˈləʊsɪs/ ■ n. a bacterial disease chiefly affecting cattle and causing undulant fever in humans.
– ORIGIN 1930s: from *Brucella*, genus name of the bacterium responsible, named after the Scottish physician Sir David *Bruce*.

bruise ■ n. an injury appearing as an area of discoloured skin on the body, caused by a blow or impact rupturing underlying blood vessels. ▶ a similar area of damage on a fruit, vegetable, or plant. ■ v. 1 inflict a bruise on. ▶ be susceptible to bruising. 2 crush or pound (food).
– ORIGIN Old English *brȳsan* 'crush, injure', reinforced in Middle English by Old French *bruisier* 'break'.

bruiser ■ n. informal, derogatory a tough, aggressive person.

bruising ■ adj. (of a contest) aggressively conducted and likely to be damaging. ■ n. bruises on the skin.

bruit /bruːt/ ■ v. spread (a report or rumour) widely. ■ n. Medicine a sound, especially an abnormal one, heard through a stethoscope.
– ORIGIN Middle English: from Old French *bruit* 'noise', from *bruire* 'to roar'.

Brummie (also **Brummy**) Brit. informal ■ n. (pl. -ies) a person from Birmingham. ■ adj. of, from, or relating to Birmingham.

brunch ■ n. a late morning meal eaten instead of breakfast and lunch.

Bruneian /bruːˈnʌɪən/ ■ n. a native or inhabitant of the sultanate of Brunei on the NW coast of Borneo. ■ adj. of or relating to Brunei.

brunette /bruːˈnet, bru-/ (US also **brunet**) ■ n. a woman or girl with dark brown hair.
– ORIGIN C16: from French, feminine of *brunet*, diminutive of *brun* 'brown'.

brunt /brʌnt/ ■ n. (usu. in phr. **bear the brunt**) the chief impact of something bad.
– ORIGIN Middle English.

bruschetta /bruˈskɛtə/ ■ n. toasted Italian bread drenched in olive oil, usually served with garlic or tomatoes.
– ORIGIN from Italian.

brush¹ ■ n. 1 an implement with a handle and a block of bristles, hair, or wire, used especially for cleaning, smoothing, or painting. 2 an act of brushing. 3 a slight and fleeting touch. 4 a brief encounter with something bad or unwelcome: *a brush with death*. 5 a piece of carbon or metal serving as an electrical contact with a moving part in a motor or alternator. 6 a drumstick with long wire bristles, used to make a soft hissing sound. 7 the bushy tail of a fox. ■ v. 1 clean, smooth, or apply with a brush. 2 touch or push lightly and gently. 3 (**brush someone/thing off**) dismiss someone or something in an abrupt, contemptuous way. 4 (**brush up on**) or **brush something up** work to regain a previously learned skill.
– DERIVATIVES **brushless** adj. (chiefly technical). **brushy** adj.
– ORIGIN Middle English: from Old French *broisse* (n.) and *brosser* (v.) 'to sweep'.

brush² ■ n. undergrowth, small trees, and shrubs. ▶ N. Amer. cut brushwood. ▶ Austral./NZ dense forest.
– ORIGIN Middle English: from Old French *broce*, perhaps from Latin *bruscum*, denoting an excrescence on a maple.

brushed ■ adj. 1 (of fabric) having a soft raised nap. 2 (of metal) finished with a non-reflective surface.

brushwood ■ n. undergrowth, twigs, and small branches.

brusque /brʊsk, bruːsk/ ■ adj. abrupt or offhand.
– DERIVATIVES **brusquely** adv. **brusqueness** n.
– ORIGIN C17: from French, 'lively, fierce', from Italian *brusco* 'sour'.

Brussels lace ■ n. an elaborate kind of lace, typically with a raised design, made using a needle or lace pillow.

Brussels sprout (also **Brussel sprout**) ■ n. a vegetable consisting of the small compact bud of a variety of cabbage which bears many such buds along a tall single stem.

brut /bruːt/ ■ adj. (of sparkling wine) very dry.
– ORIGIN French, 'raw, rough'.

brutal ■ adj. 1 savagely violent. 2 without any attempt to disguise unpleasantness: *brutal honesty*.
– DERIVATIVES **brutality** /-ˈtalɪti/ n. **brutally** adv.
– ORIGIN C15: from medieval Latin *brutalis*, from *brutus* (see BRUTE).

brutalism ■ n. 1 cruelty and savageness. 2 a stark style of functionalist architecture that makes use of steel and concrete in massive blocks.
– DERIVATIVES **brutalist** n. & adj.

brutalize

brutalize (also **-ise**) ▪ v. **1** make brutal by repeated exposure to violence. **2** treat brutally.
– DERIVATIVES **brutalization** (also **-isation**) n.

brute ▪ n. **1** a violent or savage person or animal. ▸ informal a cruel or insensitive person. **2** an animal as opposed to a human being. ▪ adj. **1** unreasoning and animal-like. **2** merely physical: *brute force*. **3** harsh or inescapable: *brute necessity*.
– DERIVATIVES **brutish** adj. **brutishly** adv. **brutishness** n.
– ORIGIN Middle English: from Old French *brut(e)*, from Latin *brutus* 'dull, stupid'.

bruxism /ˈbrʌksɪz(ə)m/ ▪ n. Medicine involuntary habitual grinding of the teeth, typically during sleep.
– ORIGIN 1930s: from Greek *brukhein* 'gnash the teeth'.

Brylcreem /ˈbrɪlkriːm/ ▪ n. trademark a cream used on men's hair to give it a smooth, shiny appearance.
– DERIVATIVES **Brylcreemed** adj.

bryology /brʌɪˈɒlədʒi/ ▪ n. the study of mosses and liverworts.
– DERIVATIVES **bryological** adj. **bryologist** n.
– ORIGIN C19: from Greek *bruon* 'moss' + -LOGY.

bryony /ˈbrʌɪəni/ ▪ n. (pl. **-ies**) a climbing Eurasian hedgerow plant with red berries. [*Bryonia dioica* (white bryony) and *Tamus communis* (black bryony).]
– ORIGIN Old English, from Greek *bruōnia*.

Bryophyta /ˌbrʌɪə(ʊ)ˈfʌɪtə/ ▪ pl. n. Botany a division of small flowerless green plants which comprises the mosses and liverworts.
– DERIVATIVES **bryophyte** n.
– ORIGIN from Greek *bruon* 'moss' + *phuta* 'plants'.

Bryozoa /ˌbrʌɪəˈzəʊə/ ▪ pl. n. Zoology a phylum of sedentary aquatic invertebrates that comprises the moss animals.
– DERIVATIVES **bryozoan** n. & adj.
– ORIGIN from Greek *bruon* 'moss' + *zōia* 'animals'.

BS ▪ abbrev. **1** US Bachelor of Science. **2** Bachelor of Surgery. **3** Blessed Sacrament. **4** British Standard(s). **5** N. Amer. vulgar slang bullshit.

BSc ▪ abbrev. Bachelor of Science.

BSE ▪ abbrev. bovine spongiform encephalopathy, a fatal disease of cattle which affects the central nervous system, causing agitation and staggering, and is believed to be related to Creutzfeldt–Jakob disease in humans.

BST ▪ abbrev. **1** bovine somatotrophin, especially as an additive in cattle feed. **2** British Summer Time.

Bt ▪ abbrev. Baronet.

Btu (also **BTU**) ▪ abbrev. British thermal unit(s).

btw ▪ abbrev. by the way.

bubba /ˈbʌbə/ ▪ n. N. Amer. informal, derogatory an uneducated conservative white male of the southern US.
– ORIGIN C20: alteration of **BROTHER**.

bubble ▪ n. **1** a thin sphere of liquid enclosing air or another gas. ▸ an air- or gas-filled spherical cavity in a liquid or a solidified liquid such as glass. **2** a transparent domed cover or enclosure. ▪ v. **1** (of a liquid) be agitated by rising bubbles of air or gas. **2** (**bubble with**) be filled with (an irrepressible positive feeling). **3** (**bubble up**) (of a feeling) intensify to the point of being expressed.
– ORIGIN Middle English: partly imitative, partly an alteration of **BURBLE**.

bubble and squeak ▪ n. Brit. a dish of cooked cabbage fried with cooked potatoes.

bubble bath ▪ n. fragrant liquid added to bathwater to make it foam.

bubble car ▪ n. a small car with a transparent domed canopy and typically three wheels.

bubble chamber ▪ n. Physics an apparatus in which the tracks of ionizing particles are visible as a row of bubbles in a liquid.

bubblegum ▪ n. **1** chewing gum that can be blown into bubbles. **2** [as modifier] chiefly N. Amer. simplistic or adolescent in style: *bubblegum pop music*.

bubblehead ▪ n. informal a foolish person.

bubblejet printer ▪ n. a form of ink-jet printer.

bubble memory ▪ n. Computing a type of memory in which data is stored as a pattern of magnetized regions in a thin layer of magnetic material.

bubble shell ▪ n. a marine mollusc with a thin scroll-like shell. [Bullidae and related families: many species.]

bubble wrap ▪ n. (trademark in the US) protective plastic packaging in sheets containing numerous small air cushions.

bubbly ▪ adj. (**-ier**, **-iest**) **1** containing bubbles. **2** cheerful and high-spirited. ▪ n. informal champagne.

bubo /ˈbjuːbəʊ/ ▪ n. (pl. **-oes**) a swollen inflamed lymph node in the armpit or groin.
– DERIVATIVES **bubonic** /bjuːˈbɒnɪk/ adj.
– ORIGIN Middle English: from Greek *boubōn* 'groin or swelling in the groin'.

bubonic plague ▪ n. a form of plague transmitted by rat fleas and characterized by fever, delirium, and the formation of buboes.

buccal /ˈbʌk(ə)l/ ▪ adj. technical of or relating to the cheek or mouth.
– ORIGIN C19: from Latin *bucca* 'cheek'.

buccaneer /ˌbʌkəˈnɪə/ ▪ n. historical **1** a pirate, originally one preying on ships in the Caribbean. **2** a recklessly adventurous and unscrupulous person.
– DERIVATIVES **buccaneering** adj.
– ORIGIN C17: from French *boucanier*, from *boucan* 'a frame on which to cook or cure meat', from Tupi *mukem*.

buchu /ˈbuxuː/ ▪ n. **1** a heather-like South African shrub, cultivated for its essential oil and medicinal properties. [*Agathosma betulina* and other species.] **2** a herbal remedy made from buchu leaves.
– ORIGIN C18: from Khoikhoi.

buck[1] ▪ n. **1** the male of some animals, especially deer and antelopes. ▸ S. African & US a (male) goat. **2** S. African an antelope (of either sex). **3** a vertical jump performed by a horse, with the head lowered, back arched, and back legs thrown out behind. **4** archaic a fashionable and daring young man. ▪ v. **1** (of a horse) perform a buck. **2** oppose or resist: *buck the trend*. **3** (**buck up**) informal make or become more cheerful. ▪ adj. US military slang lowest of a particular rank.
– PHRASES **buck up one's ideas** become more serious, energetic, and hard-working.
– ORIGIN Old English: partly from *buc* 'male deer', of Germanic origin; reinforced by *bucca* 'male goat'.

buck[2] ▪ n. informal **1** N. Amer. & Austral./NZ a dollar. **2** S. African a rand. **3** Indian a rupee.
– PHRASES **a fast buck** easily and quickly earned money.
– ORIGIN C19.

buck[3] ▪ n. an object placed as a reminder in front of a poker player whose turn it is to deal.
– PHRASES **the buck stops here** informal the responsibility for something cannot be passed to someone else. **pass the buck** informal shift responsibility to someone else.
– ORIGIN C19.

buckboard ▪ n. N. Amer. an open horse-drawn carriage with four wheels and seating that is attached to a plank between the front and rear axles.
– ORIGIN C19: from *buck* 'body of a cart', perhaps a var. of obsolete *bouk* 'belly, body', + **BOARD**.

bucket ▪ n. **1** a cylindrical open container with a handle, used to carry liquids. ▸ a compartment on the outer edge of a waterwheel. ▸ the scoop of a dredger or grain elevator, or one attached to the front of a digger or tractor. **2** (**buckets**) informal large quantities of liquid. ▪ v. (**bucketed**, **bucketing**) informal **1** (**bucket down**) rain heavily. **2** (of a vehicle) move quickly and jerkily.
– DERIVATIVES **bucketful** n. (pl. **-fuls**).
– ORIGIN Middle English: from Anglo-Norman French *buquet* 'tub, pail', perhaps from Old English *būc* 'belly, pitcher'.

bucket list ▪ n. informal a list of things to do before dying.
– ORIGIN C21: from the phr. *kick the bucket* (see **KICK**).

bucket seat ▪ n. a vehicle seat with a rounded back to fit one person.

bucket shop ▪ n. informal **1** derogatory an unauthorized office speculating in stocks or currency using the funds of unwitting investors. **2** Brit. a travel agency providing cheap air tickets.

VOWELS a cat ɑː arm ɛ bed ɛː hair ə ago əː her ɪ sit i cosy iː see ɒ hot ɔː saw ʌ run

bucket system (also **bucket toilet system**) ■ n. S. African a sanitation system using bucket toilets that are emptied by municipal waste removal services, common in areas without sewerage.

bucket toilet ■ n. a simple, unplumbed toilet made with a bucket and a seat.

buckle ■ n. a flat rectangular or oval frame with a hinged pin, used for joining the ends of a belt or strap. ■ v. **1** fasten or decorate with a buckle. ▶ (**buckle up**) fasten one's seat belt. **2** bend and give way under pressure. **3** (**buckle down**) tackle a task with determination.
– ORIGIN Middle English: from Old French *bocle*, from Latin *buccula* 'cheek strap of a helmet', from *bucca* 'cheek'; sense 2 is from French *boucler* 'to bulge'.

buckler ■ n. historical a small round shield held by a handle or worn on the forearm.
– ORIGIN Middle English: from Old French (*escu*) *bocler* '(shield) with a boss', from *bocle* (see **BUCKLE**).

buckminsterfullerene /ˌbʌkmɪnstəˈfʊləriːn/ ■ n. Chemistry a form of carbon having molecules of 60 atoms arranged in a polyhedron resembling a geodesic sphere. See also **FULLERENE**.
– ORIGIN 1980s: named after the American designer and architect Richard *Buckminster Fuller*.

buck naked ■ adj. informal, chiefly N. Amer. completely naked.

buckram /ˈbʌkrəm/ ■ n. coarse linen or other cloth stiffened with paste, used as interfacing and in bookbinding.
– ORIGIN Middle English: from Old French *boquerant*, perhaps from *Bukhoro*, a city in Uzbekistan.

Buck's Fizz ■ n. Brit. champagne or sparkling white wine mixed with orange juice as a cocktail.
– ORIGIN 1930s: from the name *Buck's Club*, in London, + **FIZZ**.

buckshot ■ n. coarse lead shot used in shotgun shells.

buckskin ■ n. **1** the skin of an antelope or a male deer. ▶ (**buckskins**) clothes or shoes made from buckskin. **2** thick smooth cotton or woollen fabric. **3** N. Amer. a horse of a greyish-yellow colour.
– DERIVATIVES **buckskinned** adj.

buckthorn ■ n. a thorny Eurasian shrub or small tree which bears black berries, some of which have been used medicinally as purgatives. [*Rhamnus cathartica* and other species.]

buck-tooth ■ n. an upper tooth that projects over the lower lip.
– DERIVATIVES **buck-toothed** adj.

buckwheat ■ n. an Asian plant of the dock family, producing starchy seeds used for fodder or milled into flour. [*Fagopyrum esculentum*.]
– ORIGIN C16: from Middle Dutch *boecweite* 'beech wheat', its grains being shaped like beechmast.

buckyballs ■ pl. n. Chemistry, informal spherical molecules of a fullerene, especially buckminsterfullerene.

buckytubes ■ pl. n. Chemistry, informal cylindrical molecules of a fullerene.

bucolic /bjuːˈkɒlɪk/ ■ adj. of or relating to rural or pastoral life. ■ n. a pastoral poem.
– DERIVATIVES **bucolically** adv.
– ORIGIN C16: from Greek, from *boukolos* 'herdsman', from *bous* 'ox'.

bud[1] ■ n. **1** a compact knob-like growth on a plant which develops into a leaf, flower, or shoot. **2** Biology an outgrowth from an organism that separates to form a new individual asexually. **3** Zoology a rudimentary leg or other appendage. ■ v. (**budded**, **budding**) Biology form a bud. ▶ graft a bud of (a plant) on to another plant.
– ORIGIN Middle English.

bud[2] ■ n. N. Amer. informal another term for **BUDDY**.

Buddhism /ˈbʊdɪz(ə)m/ ■ n. a widespread Asian religion or philosophy, founded by Siddartha Gautama (Buddha; c.563–c.460 BC) in NE India in the 5th century BC, which teaches that elimination of the self and earthly desires is the route to enlightenment.
– DERIVATIVES **Buddhist** n. & adj. **Buddhistic** adj.

budding ■ adj. beginning and showing signs of promise.

buddleja /ˈbʌdlɪjə/ (also **buddleia**) ■ n. a shrub of a genus with clusters of fragrant flowers. [Genus *Buddleja*: many species.]
– ORIGIN named in honour of the English botanist Adam *Buddle* (died 1715).

buddy informal ■ n. (pl. **-ies**) a close friend. ▶ a working companion with whom close cooperation is required. ▶ a person who befriends and helps another with an incapacitating disease, typically Aids. ■ v. (**-ies**, **-ied**) become friendly.
– ORIGIN C19: perhaps an alteration of **BROTHER**.

budge ■ v. **1** [usu. with neg.] make or cause to make the slightest movement. **2** change or cause to change an opinion.
– ORIGIN C16: from French *bouger* 'to stir', from Latin *bullire* 'to boil'.

budgerigar ■ n. a small gregarious Australian parakeet which is green with a yellow head in the wild, but has been bred in a variety of colours as a pet. [*Melopsittacus undulatus*.]
– ORIGIN C19: perhaps an alteration of Kamilaroi (an extinct Aboriginal language) *gijirrigaa*.

budget ■ n. **1** an estimate of income and expenditure for a set period of time. ▶ (**Budget**) a regular estimate of national revenue and expenditure put forward by a finance minister. **2** the amount of money needed or available for a purpose. ■ v. (**budgeted**, **budgeting**) allow or provide for in a budget. ■ adj. inexpensive.
– DERIVATIVES **budgetary** adj.

> **HISTORY**
> The word **budget** entered Middle English from Old French in the sense 'a leather pouch or bag'. In the 18th century the British Chancellor of the Exchequer, in presenting his annual statement, was said to 'open the budget', thus giving rise to the modern financial sense. The word itself comes from Old French *bougette*, meaning 'small leather bag', from Latin *bulga* 'leather bag'. **Bulge**, which also derives from *bulga*, was similarly first used in the sense 'leather sack or bag'.

budget account ■ n. Brit. an account with a bank, store, or public utility into which one makes regular payments to cover bills.

budgie ■ n. (pl. **-ies**) informal term for **BUDGERIGAR**.

budwood ■ n. lengths of young branches with buds prepared for grafting on to the rootstock of another plant.

buff[1] ■ n. **1** a yellowish-beige colour. **2** a dull yellow leather with a velvety surface. **3** a cloth or pad used for polishing. ■ v. polish. ▶ give (leather) a velvety finish by removing the surface of the grain. ■ adj. (also **buffed**) N. Amer. informal in good physical shape; muscular.
– PHRASES **in the buff** informal naked.
– ORIGIN C16: prob. from French *buffle*, from late Latin *bufalus* (see **BUFFALO**).

buff[2] ■ n. informal a person who is interested in and very knowledgeable about a particular subject.
– ORIGIN C20: from **BUFF**[1], orig. applied to fire-watchers, because of the buff uniforms worn by New York firemen.

buffalo ■ n. (pl. same or **-oes**) **1** a heavily built wild ox with backswept horns. [*Synceros caffer* (sub-Saharan Africa) and genus *Bubalus* (India and SE Asia, four species).] **2** the North American bison.
– ORIGIN C16: prob. from Portuguese *bufalo*, from late Latin *bufalus*, from Greek *boubalos* 'antelope, wild ox'.

buffalo grass ■ n. **1** any of various tropical and subtropical grasses used for pasture and lawns. [*Steno-taphrum secundatum*, *Panicum maximum*, and other species.] **2** a creeping grass of the North American plains. [*Buchloe dactyloides*.]

buffalo thorn ■ n. a small thorny African tree, the leaves, bark, roots, and berries of which are used medicinally and as food. [Genus *Ziziphus*, especially *Z. mucronata*.]

Buffalo wings ■ pl. n. N. Amer. deep-fried chicken wings in a spicy sauce, served with blue cheese dressing.
▶ S. African spiced chicken wings on a skewer, cooked over an open fire.

buffer

buffer¹ ■ n. **1** (**buffers**) a pair of shock-absorbing pistons projecting from a cross-beam at the end of a railway track or on a railway vehicle. **2** a person or thing that reduces a shock or forms a barrier between adversaries. **3** (also **buffer solution**) Chemistry a solution which resists changes in pH when acid or alkali is added to it. **4** Computing a temporary memory area or queue used when creating or editing text, or when transferring data. ■ v. **1** lessen or moderate the impact of. **2** treat with a chemical buffer.
– ORIGIN C19: prob. from obsolete *buff* (v.), imitative of the sound of a blow to a soft body.

buffer² ■ n. informal an unworldly or incompetent elderly man.
– ORIGIN C18: prob. from obsolete *buff* (see BUFFER¹), or from dial. *buff* 'stutter, splutter'.

buffer stock ■ n. a reserve of a commodity that can be used to offset price fluctuations.

buffet¹ /'bʊfeɪ, 'bʌfeɪ/ ■ n. **1** a meal consisting of several dishes from which guests serve themselves. **2** a room or counter in a station, hotel, etc. selling light meals or snacks. ► (also **buffet car**) Brit. a railway carriage selling light meals or snacks. **3** /also 'bʌfɪt/ a piece of dining-room furniture with cupboards and open shelves for crockery.
– ORIGIN C18: from Old French *bufet* 'stool'.

buffet² /'bʌfɪt/ ■ v. (**buffeted**, **buffeting**) (especially of wind or waves) strike repeatedly and violently. ■ n. **1** dated a blow. **2** Aeronautics another term for BUFFETING.
– ORIGIN Middle English: from Old French *buffeter* (v.), *buffet* (n.), diminutive of *bufe* 'a blow'.

buffeting ■ n. Aeronautics irregular oscillation of part of an aircraft, caused by turbulence.

buffo /'bʊfəʊ/ ■ n. (pl. -**os**) a comic part or actor in Italian opera. ■ adj. of or typical of Italian comic opera.
– ORIGIN C18: Italian, 'puff of wind, buffoon'.

buffoon /bə'fuːn/ ■ n. a ridiculous but amusing person.
– DERIVATIVES **buffoonery** n. **buffoonish** adj.
– ORIGIN C16: from French *bouffon*, from medieval Latin *buffo* 'clown'.

bug ■ n. **1** Entomology an insect of a large order having piercing and sucking mouthparts, including aphids, leafhoppers, cicadas, and many other insects. [Order Hemiptera.] ► informal any small insect. **2** informal a harmful micro-organism. ► an illness caused by a micro-organism. **3** informal an enthusiasm for something: *they caught the sailing bug*. **4** a concealed miniature microphone used for secret recording. **5** an error in a computer program or system. ■ v. (**bugged**, **bugging**) **1** conceal a miniature microphone in. **2** informal annoy; bother. **3** (**bug off**) N. Amer. informal go away. **4** (**bug out**) N. Amer. informal bulge outwards.
– ORIGIN C17.

bugbear ■ n. a cause of obsessive fear or anxiety. ► archaic an imaginary being invoked to frighten children.
– ORIGIN C16: prob. from obsolete *bug* 'bogey' + BEAR².

bug-eyed ■ adj. & adv. with bulging eyes.

bugger ■ n. **1** vulgar slang, chiefly Brit. a person who commits buggery. **2** informal, often humorous a man or boy. ► a person of a specified type: *cheeky bugger!* **3** informal an annoyingly awkward thing. ■ v. **1** vulgar slang, chiefly Brit. practise buggery with. **2** informal cause serious harm or trouble to. ► (**bugger about/around**) act stupidly or carelessly. **3** (**bugger off**) informal go away. ■ exclam. informal used to express annoyance.
– PHRASES **bugger all** nothing.

HISTORY
The word **bugger** entered Middle English in the sense 'heretic', from Old French *bougre*. It was used of members of a heretical Christian sect based in Albi in southern France in the 12th and 13th centuries (the Albigensians). The word ultimately comes from Latin *Bulgarus*, meaning 'Bulgarian': Bulgarians belonging to the Orthodox Church were regarded as heretical by Roman Catholics. The sexual meaning of the term arose in the 16th century from an association of heresy with forbidden sexual practices.

buggery ■ n. anal intercourse.

buggy¹ ■ n. (pl. -**ies**) **1** a small motor vehicle with an open top. **2** a baby buggy. **3** historical a light horse-drawn vehicle for one or two people.
– ORIGIN C18.

buggy² ■ adj. (-**ier**, -**iest**) infested with bugs.

bughouse ■ n. S. African a second-rate cinema.

bugle¹ ■ n. (also **bugle-horn**) a brass instrument like a small trumpet, traditionally used for military signals. ■ v. sound a bugle.
– DERIVATIVES **bugler** n.
– ORIGIN Middle English ('wild ox'): from Latin *buculus*, diminutive of *bos* 'ox'; hence *bugle-horn*, denoting the horn of an ox used to give signals.

bugle² ■ n. a creeping Eurasian plant with blue flowers on upright stems. [*Ajuga reptans* and other species.]
– ORIGIN Middle English: from late Latin *bugula*.

bugle³ ■ n. an ornamental tube-shaped bead on clothing.
– ORIGIN C16.

bugweed (also **bugtree**) ■ n. an Asian plant with red berries and large hairy leaves, a declared weed in South Africa. [*Solanum mauritianum*.]

buhl /buːl/ ■ n. variant spelling of BOULLE.

build ■ v. (past and past part. **built**) **1** construct by putting parts or materials together. ► (**build something in/into**) incorporate something as a permanent part of. **2** increase in size or intensity over time. ► (**build on**) use as a basis for further development. ■ n. the proportions of a person's or animal's body. ► the style or form of construction of something.
– DERIVATIVES **builder** n.
– ORIGIN Old English, from *bold*, *botl* 'dwelling', of Germanic origin.

building ■ n. **1** a structure with a roof and walls. **2** the process or trade of building houses and other structures.

building society ■ n. a financial organization which pays interest on members' investments and lends capital for mortgages.

build-up ■ n. **1** a gradual accumulation or increase. **2** a period of excitement and preparation before a significant event.

built past and past participle of BUILD. ■ adj. of a specified physical build: *a slightly built woman*.

built-in ■ adj. forming an integral part of a structure. ► inherent; innate.

built-up ■ adj. **1** (of an area) densely covered by buildings. **2** increased in height by the addition of parts.

bulb ■ n. **1** a rounded underground storage organ present in lilies and some other plants, consisting of a short stem surrounded by fleshy leaf bases and lying dormant over winter. **2** short for LIGHT BULB. **3** an expanded or rounded part at the end of something. **4** a hollow container from which air can be expelled by squeezing, used to fill a syringe, pipette, etc.
– ORIGIN Middle English: from Greek *bolbos* 'onion, bulbous root'.

bulbil /'bʌlbɪl/ ■ n. Botany a small bulb-like structure, especially in the axil of a leaf, which may fall to form a new plant.
– ORIGIN C19: from modern Latin *bulbillus*, diminutive of *bulbus*, from Greek.

bulbous ■ adj. **1** round or bulging in shape. **2** (of a plant) growing from a bulb.

bulbul /'bʊlbʊl/ ■ n. a tropical African and Asian songbird, typically with drab plumage. [Family Pycnonotidae: numerous species.]
– ORIGIN C17: from Persian; imitative.

Bulgarian ■ n. **1** a native or national of Bulgaria. **2** the Southern Slavic language spoken in Bulgaria. ■ adj. of or relating to Bulgaria, its people, or their language.

bulgar wheat /'bʌlgə/ (also **bulgur wheat**) ■ n. a cereal food made from whole wheat partially boiled then dried.
– ORIGIN 1930s: from Turkish *bulgur* 'bruised grain'.

bulge ■ n. **1** a rounded swelling distorting a flat surface. **2** informal a temporary increase. ■ v. swell or protrude to an unnatural extent. ► be full of and distended with.
– DERIVATIVES **bulging** adj. **bulgy** adj.

– ORIGIN Middle English: from Old French *boulge*, from Latin *bulga* (see BUDGET).

bulimia /bjʊˈlɪmɪə, bʊ-/ (also **bulimia nervosa**) ■ n. an emotional disorder characterized by bouts of overeating, typically alternating with fasting or self-induced vomiting or purging.
– DERIVATIVES **bulimic** adj. & n.
– ORIGIN Middle English: from medieval Latin *bolismos*, from Greek *boulimia* 'ravenous hunger', from *bous* 'ox' + *limos* 'hunger'.

bulk ■ n. 1 the mass or magnitude of something large. ▸ a large mass or shape. ▸ [as modifier] large in quantity: *bulk supplier.* 2 the greater part. 3 roughage in food. 4 cargo not divided into individual units. ■ v. 1 be of great size or importance. 2 treat (a product) so that its quantity appears greater than it is. 3 combine (shares or commodities for sale).
– PHRASES **in bulk 1** (of goods) in large quantities. 2 (of a cargo or commodity) not packaged.
– ORIGIN Middle English: prob. from Old Norse *búlki* 'cargo'.

bulk carrier ■ n. a ship that carries non-liquid cargoes in bulk.

bulker ■ n. a bulk carrier.

bulkhead ■ n. a barrier between separate compartments inside a ship, aircraft, etc.
– ORIGIN C15: from Old Norse *bálkr* 'partition' + HEAD.

bulk modulus ■ n. Physics the relative change in the volume of a body produced by a unit compressive or tensile stress acting uniformly over its surface.

bulky ■ adj. (**-ier**, **-iest**) large and unwieldy.
– DERIVATIVES **bulkily** adv. **bulkiness** n.

bull[1] ■ n. 1 an uncastrated male bovine animal. 2 the male of other animals, e.g. whales, elephants, and seals. 3 Brit. a bullseye. 4 Stock Exchange a person who buys shares hoping to sell them at a higher price later. Often contrasted with BEAR[2]. ■ v. 1 informal move powerfully or violently. 2 (**be bulling**) (of a cow) be on heat.
– PHRASES **like a bull at a gate** acting hastily and without thought. **like a bull in a china shop** behaving clumsily in a delicate situation. **take the bull by the horns** deal decisively with a difficult or unpleasant situation.
– ORIGIN Old English *bula*, from Old Norse *boli*.

bull[2] ■ n. a papal edict.
– ORIGIN Middle English: from Latin *bulla* 'bubble, rounded object', in medieval Latin 'seal or sealed document'.

bull[3] ■ n. informal nonsense.
– ORIGIN C17.

bulla /ˈbʊlə/ ■ n. (pl. **bullae** /ˈbʊliː/) 1 Medicine a large blister or other cavity containing fluid or air. 2 Anatomy a rounded prominence. 3 a round seal attached to a papal bull.
– DERIVATIVES **bullate** adj. (Botany). **bullous** adj. (Medicine).
– ORIGIN Latin, 'bubble'.

bull bar ■ n. a strong metal grille fitted to the front of a motor vehicle to protect it against impact damage.

bulldog ■ n. a dog of a sturdy breed with a powerful protruding lower jaw, a flat wrinkled face, and a broad chest. ■ v. (**-dogged**, **-dogging**) N. Amer. wrestle (a steer) to the ground by holding its horns and twisting its neck.

bulldog ant ■ n. a large Australian ant with large jaws and a powerful sting. [Genus *Myrmecia*.]

bulldog clip ■ n. trademark a sprung metal device with two flat plates that close to hold papers together.

bulldoze ■ v. 1 clear or destroy with a bulldozer. 2 informal intimidate or coerce.
– ORIGIN C19: from BULL[1] + *-doze*, alteration of the noun DOSE.

bulldozer ■ n. a powerful tractor with caterpillar tracks and a broad curved blade at the front for clearing ground.

bullet ■ n. 1 a projectile fired from a small firearm, typically metal, cylindrical, and pointed. 2 (**the bullet**) informal dismissal from employment. 3 Printing a small solid circle printed before each in a list of items.
– ORIGIN C16: from French *boulet*, *boulette* 'small ball', diminutive of *boule*, from Latin *bulla* 'bubble'.

bulletin ■ n. a short official statement or summary of news. ▸ a regular newsletter or report.

bulrush

– ORIGIN C17: from Italian *bullettino*, diminutive of *bulletta* 'passport', diminutive of *bulla* 'seal, bull'.

bulletin board ■ n. 1 a noticeboard. 2 a computer-based system, typically dedicated to a particular topic, by which users can read or download files supplied by others and add their own files.

bullet train ■ n. informal a Japanese high-speed passenger train.

bullfighting ■ n. the sport of baiting and often killing a bull as a public spectacle in an outdoor arena, associated particularly with Spanish- and Portuguese-speaking countries.
– DERIVATIVES **bullfight** n. **bullfighter** n.

bullfinch ■ n. a stocky Eurasian finch with mainly grey and black plumage and a white rump, of which the male has a pink breast. [*Pyrrhula pyrrhula* and other species.]

bullfrog ■ n. a very large frog with a deep booming croak. [*Rana adspersa* (Africa), *R. catesbiana* (N. America), and other species elsewhere.]

bullheaded ■ adj. determined and obstinate.
– DERIVATIVES **bullheadedly** adv. **bullheadedness** n.

bullhorn ■ n. chiefly N. Amer. a megaphone.

bullion ■ n. 1 gold or silver in bulk before coining, or valued by weight. 2 ornamental braid or fringing of gold or silver thread.
– ORIGIN Middle English: from Anglo-Norman French, in the sense 'a mint', from Latin *bullire* 'to boil'.

bullish ■ adj. 1 aggressively confident and self-assertive. 2 Stock Exchange characterized or influenced by rising share prices.
– DERIVATIVES **bullishly** adv. **bullishness** n.

bull market ■ n. Stock Exchange a market in which share prices are rising.

bull-nose ■ n. technical a surface or object having a rounded end.
– DERIVATIVES **bull-nosed** adj.

bullock ■ n. a castrated male bovine animal raised for beef. ■ v. informal rush aggressively; charge: *he bullocked his way over the goal line.*
– ORIGIN Old English *bulluc*, diminutive of *bula* (see BULL[1]).

bullpen ■ n. chiefly N. Amer. 1 an exercise area for baseball pitchers. 2 a large cell in which prisoners are held before a court hearing.

bullring ■ n. an arena where bullfights are held.

bullrush ■ n. variant spelling of BULRUSH.

bullseye ■ n. 1 the centre of the target in sports such as archery and darts. 2 a large, hard peppermint-flavoured sweet. 3 dated a thick disc of glass forming a small window in a ship or the glass of a lamp.

bullshit vulgar slang ■ n. nonsense. ■ v. (**-shitted**, **-shitting**) talk nonsense in an attempt to deceive.
– DERIVATIVES **bullshitter** n.

bull terrier ■ n. a dog that is a cross-breed of bulldog and terrier.

bully[1] ■ n. (pl. **-ies**) a person who deliberately intimidates or persecutes those who are weaker. ■ v. (**-ies**, **-ied**) intimidate.
– ORIGIN C16 (orig. a term of endearment, then a form of address to a male friend): prob. from Middle Dutch *boele* 'lover'.

bully[2] ■ adj. informal, chiefly N. Amer. excellent.
– PHRASES **bully for you!** (or **him** etc.) often ironic an expression of admiration or approval.
– ORIGIN C16 (orig. 'admirable, jolly'): from BULLY[1].

bully[3] ■ n. (pl. **-ies**) (also **bully off**) the start of play in field hockey. ■ v. (**-ies**, **-ied**) start play in this way.
– ORIGIN C19.

bully[4] (also **bully beef**) ■ n. informal corned beef.
– ORIGIN C18: alteration of obsolete *bouilli* 'boiled meat', from French, 'boiled'.

bulrush (also **bullrush**) ■ n. a reed mace, clubrush, or similar waterside plant.
– ORIGIN Middle English: prob. from BULL[1] meaning 'large, coarse'.

bult /bʌlt/ ■ n. S. African a low ridge; a hillock.
– ORIGIN Afrikaans, 'hump, hill'.

bulwark /ˈbʊlwək/ ■ n. 1 a defensive wall. 2 an extension of a ship's sides above deck level.
– ORIGIN Middle English: from Middle Low German and Middle Dutch *bolwerk*, rel. to BOLE.

bum¹ ■ n. informal a person's buttocks or anus.
– ORIGIN Middle English.

bum² informal ■ n. chiefly N. Amer. 1 a vagrant. 2 a lazy or worthless person. 3 a devotee of a particular activity: *a ski bum*. ■ v. (**bummed**, **bumming**) 1 get by asking or begging. 2 (**bum around**) chiefly N. Amer. pass one's time idly. ■ adj. bad; wrong.
– PHRASES **give someone the bum's rush** chiefly N. Amer. forcibly eject someone. **on the bum** N. Amer. vagrant.
– ORIGIN C19: prob. from BUMMER.

bumbag ■ n. British term for MOONBAG.

bumble ■ v. 1 act or speak in an awkward or confused manner. 2 (of an insect) buzz or hum.
– DERIVATIVES **bumbler** n.
– ORIGIN Middle English: from BOOM¹.

bumblebee ■ n. a large hairy bee with a loud hum, living in small colonies underground. [Genus *Bombus*: many species.]

bumf (also **bumph**) ■ n. informal 1 useless or tedious printed information. 2 dated toilet paper.
– ORIGIN C19: abbrev. of slang *bum-fodder*, in the same sense.

bumfluff ■ n. informal the first beard growth of an adolescent.

bummalo /ˈbʌməloʊ/ ■ n. (pl. same) a small elongated South Asian fish, dried as food. [*Harpodon nehereus*.]
– ORIGIN C17: perhaps from Marathi *bombīl*.

bummer ■ n. informal 1 an annoying or disappointing thing. 2 N. Amer. a vagrant or loafer.
– ORIGIN C19: perhaps from German *Bummler*, from *bummeln* 'stroll, loaf about'.

bump ■ n. 1 a light blow or a jolting collision. ▸ Rowing (in races where boats make a spaced start one behind another) the point at which a boat begins to overtake or touch the boat ahead, thereby defeating it. 2 a protuberance on a level surface. ▸ a lump on a person's skull, formerly thought to indicate a particular mental faculty. 3 Aeronautics a rising air current causing an irregularity in an aircraft's motion. ■ v. 1 knock or run into with a jolt. ▸ (**bump into**) meet by chance. ▸ Rowing gain a bump against. 2 move or cause to move with much jolting. 3 (**bump someone off**) informal murder someone. 4 (**bump something up**) informal make something larger or appear to be larger. 5 refuse (a passenger) a reserved place on a flight because of deliberate overbooking by the airline. 6 N. Amer. displace from a job or position.
– DERIVATIVES **bumpily** adv. **bumpiness** n. **bumpy** adj. (**-ier**, **-iest**).
– ORIGIN C16: imitative, perhaps of Scandinavian origin.

bumper ■ n. a horizontal bar across the front or back of a motor vehicle to reduce damage in a collision. ■ adj. exceptionally large or successful.
– PHRASES **bumper-to-bumper** very close together.

bumper car ■ n. a dodgem.

bumph ■ n. variant spelling of BUMF.

bumpkin ■ n. an unsophisticated rustic.
– ORIGIN C16: perhaps from Dutch *boomken* 'little tree' or Middle Dutch *bommekijn* 'little barrel', denoting a dumpy person.

bump-start ■ n. & v. another term for PUSH-START.

bumptious ■ adj. irritatingly self-assertive or proud.
– DERIVATIVES **bumptiously** adv. **bumptiousness** n.
– ORIGIN C19: from BUMP, on the pattern of *fractious*.

bum rap ■ n. informal, chiefly N. Amer. a false charge leading to imprisonment.

bum steer ■ n. N. Amer. informal a piece of false information.

bun ■ n. 1 a small cake or bread roll. 2 a hairstyle in which the hair is drawn into a tight coil at the back of the head. 3 (**buns**) informal, chiefly N. Amer. a person's buttocks.
– PHRASES **have a bun in the oven** informal be pregnant.
– ORIGIN Middle English.

bunch ■ n. 1 a number of things growing or fastened together. ▸ informal a group of people. ▸ informal, chiefly N. Amer. a lot. 2 (**bunches**) Brit. a hairstyle in which the hair is tied back into two clumps. ■ v. collect, form, or fasten into a bunch.
– DERIVATIVES **bunchy** adj.
– ORIGIN Middle English.

bund ■ n. (in India and Pakistan) an embankment or causeway.
– ORIGIN C19: from Persian.

bundle ■ n. 1 a collection of things or quantity of material tied or wrapped up together. ▸ a set of nerve, muscle, or other fibres running in parallel close together. 2 informal a large amount of money. ■ v. 1 tie or roll up in or as if in a bundle. ▸ Computing sell (items of hardware and software) as a package. 2 (usu. **be bundled up**) dress in many warm clothes. 3 informal push or carry forcibly. ▸ (of a group) move in a disorganized way.
– PHRASES **a bundle of fun** (or **laughs**) informal, often ironic something extremely amusing or pleasant. **go a bundle on** [usu. with neg.] Brit. informal be very keen on.
– DERIVATIVES **bundler** n.
– ORIGIN Middle English: perhaps orig. from Old English *byndelle* 'a binding', reinforced by Low German and Dutch *bundel*.

bundu /ˈbʊndu:/ ■ n. (in eastern and southern Africa) an area remote from large cities; a wilderness region.
– ORIGIN prob. from Shona *bundo* 'grasslands'.

bundu-bash ■ v. (in Africa) travel into the wild; force one's way through rough terrain.
– DERIVATIVES **bundu-basher** n. **bundu-bashing** n.

bunfight ■ n. informal, humorous a grand or official tea party or other function.

bung¹ ■ n. a stopper for a hole in a container. ■ v. close with a bung. ▸ (**bung something up**) block something up.
– ORIGIN Middle English: from Middle Dutch *bonghe* (n.).

bung² Brit. informal ■ v. put or throw somewhere carelessly or casually. ■ n. a bribe.
– ORIGIN C19: symbolic; the noun sense dates from the 1950s.

bungalow /ˈbʌŋɡəloʊ/ ■ n. 1 a house with only one main storey. 2 S. African an army barracks.
– ORIGIN C17: from Hindi *banglā* 'belonging to Bengal'.

bungee /ˈbʌndʒi/ (also **bungy**) ■ n. (also **bungee cord** or **rope**) a long nylon-cased rubber cord.
– ORIGIN 1930s.

bungee jumping (also **bungy jumping**) ■ n. the sport of leaping from a high place, secured by a bungee around the ankles.
– DERIVATIVES **bungee jump** (also **bungy jump**) n. **bungee jumper** (also **bungy jumper**) n.

bungle ■ v. carry out (a task) clumsily or incompetently. ▸ [as adj. **bungling**] prone to making mistakes. ■ n. a mistake or failure.
– DERIVATIVES **bungler** n.
– ORIGIN C16: cf. with BUMBLE.

bunion /ˈbʌnjən/ ■ n. a painful swelling on the first joint of the big toe.
– ORIGIN C18: from Old French *buignon*, from *buigne* 'bump on the head'.

bunk¹ ■ n. a narrow shelf-like bed. ■ v. sleep in a bunk or improvised bed in shared quarters.
– ORIGIN C18: perhaps rel. to BUNKER.

bunk² ■ v. informal abscond from school or work.
– PHRASES **do a bunk** make a hurried departure.
– ORIGIN C19.

bunk³ ■ n. informal, dated nonsense.
– ORIGIN C20: abbrev. of BUNKUM.

bunk bed ■ n. a piece of furniture consisting of two beds, one above the other.

bunker ■ n. 1 a large container or compartment for storing fuel. 2 a reinforced underground shelter for use in wartime. 3 a hollow filled with sand, used as an obstacle on a golf course. ■ v. 1 refuel (a ship). 2 Golf hit (the ball) into a bunker.

– ORIGIN C16 (orig. Scots, denoting a seat or bench): perhaps rel. to BUNK¹.

bunkhouse ■ n. a building with basic sleeping accommodation.

bunkum ■ n. informal, dated nonsense.
– ORIGIN C19: named after *Buncombe* County in North Carolina, mentioned in a speech made by its congressman solely to please his constituents.

bunk-up ■ n. informal a helping push or pull up.

bunny ■ n. (pl. -ies) informal **1** a child's word for a rabbit. **2** (also **bunny girl**) a club hostess or waitress wearing a skimpy costume with ears and a tail.
– ORIGIN C17: from dialect *bun* 'squirrel, rabbit'.

bunny chow ■ n. S. African a takeaway food consisting of a hollowed-out half loaf of bread filled with vegetable or meat curry.
– ORIGIN 1970s: prob. from Hindi *banya*, from Gujarati *vaniya* denoting a Hindi merchant, + CHOW.

bunny-hop ■ v. jump forward in a crouched position. ■ n. an act of bunny-hopping.

Bunsen burner ■ n. a small adjustable gas burner used in laboratories.
– ORIGIN named after the German chemist R. *Bunsen*.

bunt /bʌnt/ Baseball ■ v. (of a batter) gently tap (a pitched ball) so that it does not roll beyond the infield. ■ n. an act of bunting a ball.
– ORIGIN C18: prob. rel. to BUTT¹.

bunting¹ ■ n. any of a large group of seed-eating songbirds related to the finches, typically with brown streaked plumage and a boldly marked head. [*Emberiza* and other genera, family Emberizidae: numerous species.]
– ORIGIN Middle English.

bunting² ■ n. flags and other colourful festive decorations.
– ORIGIN C18.

buoy /bɔɪ/ ■ n. an anchored float serving as a navigation mark, to show hazards, or for mooring. ■ v. **1** (usu. **be buoyed up**) keep afloat. **2** cause (a price) to rise or to remain high. **3** mark with a buoy.
– ORIGIN Middle English: prob. from Middle Dutch *boye*, *boeie*, from a Germanic base meaning 'signal'.

buoyancy aid ■ n. a sleeveless jacket lined with buoyant material, worn for water sports.

buoyant ■ adj. **1** able or tending to keep afloat. **2** cheerful and optimistic. **3** (of an economy or market) engaged in much activity.
– DERIVATIVES **buoyancy** n. **buoyantly** adv.
– ORIGIN C16: from Spanish *boyante*, *boyar* 'to float'.

buppie ■ n. (pl. -ies) informal a young urban black professional; a black yuppie.

bur ■ n. see BURR.

Burberry /ˈbɜːb(ə)ri/ ■ n. (pl. -ies) trademark a lightweight belted raincoat.
– ORIGIN C20: from *Burberrys Ltd*, the manufacturer.

burble ■ v. **1** make a continuous murmuring noise. **2** speak unintelligibly and at unnecessary length. ■ n. continuous murmuring noise. ▶ rambling speech.
– DERIVATIVES **burbler** n.
– ORIGIN Middle English: imitative.

burden ■ n. **1** a heavy load. **2** a cause of hardship, worry, or grief. ▶ the main responsibility for a task. **3** a ship's carrying capacity. **4** the main theme. ■ v. **1** (usu. **be burdened**) load heavily. **2** cause worry, hardship, or grief.
– PHRASES **burden of proof** the obligation to prove an assertion.
– DERIVATIVES **burdensome** adj.
– ORIGIN Old English, of West Germanic origin.

burdock /ˈbɜːdɒk/ ■ n. a herbaceous Eurasian plant of the daisy family, with large leaves and prickly flowers which cling to fur or clothing. [*Arctium pubens* and other species.]

bureau /ˈbjʊərəʊ/ ■ n. (pl. **bureaux** or **bureaus**) **1** Brit. a writing desk with drawers and an angled top opening downwards to form a writing surface. **2** N. Amer. a chest of drawers. **3** an office for transacting particular business. **4** a government department.
– ORIGIN C17: from French, orig. 'baize' (covering writing desks).

bureaucracy /ˌbjʊə(ə)ˈrɒkrəsi/ ■ n. (pl. -ies) **1** a system of government in which most decisions are taken by state officials rather than by elected representatives. ▶ a state or organization governed according to such a system. **2** excessively complicated administrative procedure.
– DERIVATIVES **bureaucratization** (also **-isation**) n. **bureaucratize** (also **-ise**) v.
– ORIGIN C19: from French *bureaucratie*, from *bureau* (see BUREAU).

bureaucrat ■ n. a government official perceived as being overly concerned with procedural correctness.
– DERIVATIVES **bureaucratic** adj. **bureaucratically** adv.

bureau de change /ˌbjʊərəʊ də ˈʃɒ̃ʒ/ ■ n. (pl. **bureaux de change** pronunc. same) a place where one can exchange foreign money.
– ORIGIN 1950s: French, 'office of exchange'.

burette /bjʊˈrɛt/ (US also **buret**) ■ n. a graduated glass tube with a tap at one end, for delivering known volumes of a liquid.
– ORIGIN C19: from French, from *buire* 'jug'.

burg /bɜːɡ/ ■ n. an ancient or medieval fortress or walled town.
– ORIGIN C18: from late Latin *burgus* (see BURGESS).

burgee /bɜːˈdʒiː/ ■ n. a triangular flag flown from the mast of a yacht to indicate the owner's membership of a particular sailing club.
– ORIGIN C18: perhaps from French *bourgeois* in the sense 'owner, master'.

burgeon /ˈbɜːdʒ(ə)n/ ■ v. [often as adj. **burgeoning**] grow or increase rapidly.
– ORIGIN Middle English: from Old French *bourgeonner* 'put out buds', from *borjon* 'bud', from late Latin *burra* 'wool'.

burger ■ n. a hamburger.

burgess ■ n. **1** Brit. historical a Member of Parliament for a borough, corporate town, or university. **2** (in the US and historically in the UK) a magistrate or member of the governing body of a town.
– ORIGIN Middle English: from Anglo-Norman French *burgeis*, from late Latin *burgus* 'castle, fort' (in medieval Latin 'fortified town').

burgh /ˈbʌrə/ ■ n. archaic or Scottish a borough or chartered town.
– ORIGIN Middle English: Scots form of BOROUGH.

burgher /ˈbɜːɡə/ ■ n. **1** archaic a citizen of a town or city. **2** S. African historical a citizen of a Boer Republic. **3** S. African historical a civilian member of a local militia unit.
– ORIGIN Middle English: from BURGH, reinforced by Dutch *burger*, from *burg* (see BOROUGH).

burghul /bɜːˈɡuːl/ ■ n. another term for BULGAR WHEAT.
– ORIGIN from Persian.

burglar ■ n. a person who commits burglary.
– ORIGIN C16: from legal French *burgler* or Anglo-Latin *burgulator*; rel. to Old French *burgier* 'pillage'.

burglar bars ■ pl. n. metal bars fixed over a window to prevent illegal entry into a building.

burglarize (also **-ise**) ■ v. North American term for BURGLE.

burglary ■ n. (pl. -ies) illegal entry into a building with intent to commit a crime such as theft.

burgle ■ v. commit burglary in (a building).
– ORIGIN C19: orig. a back-formation from BURGLAR.

burgomaster /ˈbɜːɡə(ʊ)mɑːstə/ ■ n. the mayor of a Dutch, Flemish, German, Austrian, or Swiss town.
– ORIGIN C16: from Dutch, from *burg* (see BOROUGH) + *meester* 'master'.

Burgundian /bɜːˈɡʌndɪən/ ■ n. **1** a native or inhabitant of Burgundy, a region of east central France. **2** a member of a Germanic people that invaded Gaul and established the kingdom of Burgundy in the 5th century AD. ■ adj. of or relating to Burgundy or the Burgundians.

burgundy ■ n. (pl. -ies) **1** a red wine from Burgundy, a region of east central France. **2** a deep red colour.

burial ■ n. **1** the burying of a dead body. ▶ a funeral. **2** Archaeology a grave or the remains found in it.
– ORIGIN Old English *byrgels* 'place of burial, grave', of Germanic origin.

burin

burin /ˈbjʊərɪn/ ■ n. **1** a hand-held steel tool used for engraving. **2** Archaeology a flint tool with a chisel point.
– ORIGIN C17: from French.

burka /ˈbʊəkə/ (also **burkha**) ■ n. a long, loose garment covering the whole body, worn in public by some Muslim women.
– ORIGIN from Urdu and Persian *burḳa'*, from Arabic *burḳu'*.

Burkinan /bɜːˈkiːnən/ ■ n. a native or national of Burkina Faso. ■ adj. of or relating to Burkina Faso or its people.

Burkitt's lymphoma /ˈbɜːkɪts/ ■ n. Medicine cancer of the lymphatic system, caused by the Epstein–Barr virus.
– ORIGIN 1960s: named after the British surgeon Denis P. Burkitt.

burl /bɜːl/ ■ n. **1** a lump in wool or cloth. **2** a rounded knotty growth on a tree.
– ORIGIN Middle English: from Old French *bourle* 'tuft of wool', diminutive of *bourre*, from late Latin *burra* 'wool'.

burlap /ˈbɜːlap/ ■ n. coarse canvas woven from jute or hemp, used for sacking. ▸ a similar, lighter material used in dressmaking and furnishing.
– ORIGIN C17.

burlesque /bɜːˈlɛsk/ ■ n. **1** a comically exaggerated imitation, especially in a literary or dramatic work. ▸ absurdity. **2** N. Amer. a variety show, typically including striptease.
– ORIGIN C17: from French, from Italian *burlesco*, from *burla* 'mockery'.

burly ■ adj. (**-ier**, **-iest**) (of a person) large and strong.
– DERIVATIVES **burliness** n.
– ORIGIN Middle English: prob. from Old English word meaning 'stately, fit for the bower'.

Burman ■ n. (pl. **Burmans**) & adj. another term for BURMESE.

Burmese ■ n. (pl. same) **1** a member of the largest ethnic group of Burma (now Myanmar) in SE Asia. **2** a native or national of Burma. **3** the Sino-Tibetan official language of Burma. **4** (also **Burmese cat**) a cat of a short-coated breed originating in Asia. ■ adj. of or relating to Burma, its people, or their language.

burn¹ ■ v. (past and past part. **burned** or **burnt**) **1** (of a fire) flame or glow while consuming a fuel. ▸ use (a fuel) as a source of heat or energy. **2** be or cause to be harmed or destroyed by fire. ▸ destroy (vegetation) by fire in a controlled manner, so as to allow new shoots to grow. **3** (of the skin) become red and painful through exposure to the sun. ▸ feel hot as a result of illness, injury, or emotion. ▸ (**be burning with**) be entirely possessed by (a desire or emotion). **5** (**burn out**) become exhausted through overwork. **6** informal drive very fast. **7** (**burn someone up**) N. Amer. informal make someone very angry. **8** informal copy or create a compact disc. ■ n. **1** an injury or area of damage caused by burning. **2** an act of clearing vegetation by burning. **3** a firing of a rocket engine in flight.
– PHRASES **burn one's boats** (or **bridges**) do something which makes turning back impossible. **burn the candle at both ends** go to bed late and get up early. **burn a hole in one's pocket** (of money) tempt one to spend it quickly or extravagantly. **burn the midnight oil** work late into the night. **burn rubber** informal drive very quickly.
– ORIGIN Old English *birnan* 'be on fire' and *bærnan* 'consume by fire', of Germanic origin.

burn² ■ n. Scottish & N. English a small stream.
– ORIGIN Old English, of Germanic origin.

burned ■ adj. variant spelling of BURNT.

burner ■ n. **1** a part of a cooker, lamp, etc. that emits a flame. **2** an apparatus for burning something.
– PHRASES **on the back burner** having low priority.

burnet /ˈbɜːnɪt/ ■ n. **1** a day-flying moth, typically having greenish-black wings with crimson markings. [*Zygaena* and other genera.] **2** a Eurasian plant of the rose family with globular pink flower heads and leaves composed of many small leaflets. [Genus *Sanguisorba*: several species.]
– ORIGIN Middle English: from Old French *brunete*, *burnete*, diminutive of *brun* 'brown'.

burnet rose ■ n. a small wild Eurasian rose with white flowers and leaves like those of burnet. [*Rosa pimpinellifolia*.]

burning ■ adj. **1** very deeply felt. **2** of urgent interest and importance.
– DERIVATIVES **burningly** adv.

burning bush ■ n. **1** a shrub with bright red fruit or autumn foliage. **2** an aromatic Eurasian plant of the rue family with showy white flowers and fragrant leaves that emit a flammable vapour. [*Dictamnus albus*.]
– ORIGIN C19: with biblical allusion to Exodus 3:2.

burning glass ■ n. a lens for concentrating the sun's rays on an object so as to set fire to it.

burnish ■ v. [usu. as adj. **burnished**] polish by rubbing. ■ n. the shine on a polished surface.
– ORIGIN Middle English: from Old French *burnir*, var. of *brunir* 'make brown', from *brun* 'brown'.

burnous /bɜːˈnuːs/ (US also **burnoose**) ■ n. a long loose hooded cloak worn by Arabs.
– ORIGIN C16: from Arabic *burnus*, from Greek *birros* 'cloak'.

burnout ■ n. **1** the reduction of a fuel or substance to nothing. **2** overheating of an electrical device or component. **3** physical or mental collapse.

burnt (also **burned**) past and past participle of BURN¹.

burnt ochre ■ n. a deep yellow-brown pigment made by calcining ochre.

burnt offering ■ n. **1** a religious sacrifice burnt on an altar. **2** humorous burnt food.

burp informal ■ v. belch. ▸ make (a baby) belch after feeding. ■ n. a belch.
– ORIGIN 1930s: imitative.

burpee /ˈbɜːpiː/ ■ n. a squat thrust made from and ending in a standing position.
– ORIGIN 1930s (orig. in *Burpee test*, a test of agility in which a series of burpees were executed rapidly): named after the American psychologist Royal H. Burpee.

burr ■ n. **1** a whirring sound. ▸ a rough pronunciation of the letter *r*, as in some regional accents. **2** (also **bur**) a rough edge left on a metal object by the action of a tool. **3** (also **bur**) a small drill used in woodworking, dentistry, or surgery. **4** a siliceous rock used for millstones. ▸ a whetstone. **5** (also **bur**) a prickly seed case or flower head that clings to clothing and animal fur. **6** (also **bur**) [as modifier] denoting wood containing a pattern of dense swirls in the grain. **7** the coronet of a deer's antler. ■ v. **1** make a whirring sound. ▸ speak with a burr. **2** form a rough edge on (metal).
– ORIGIN Middle English: prob. of Scandinavian origin; sense 1 is prob. imitative.

burrito /bʊˈriːtəʊ/ ■ n. (pl. **-os**) a Mexican dish consisting of a tortilla rolled round a filling of minced beef or beans.
– ORIGIN Latin American Spanish, diminutive of Spanish *burro* 'donkey'.

burro /ˈbʊrəʊ/ ■ n. (pl. **-os**) chiefly US a small donkey used as a pack animal.
– ORIGIN C19: from Spanish.

burrow ■ n. a hole or tunnel dug by a small animal as a dwelling. ■ v. **1** make a burrow. ▸ dig into or through something solid. **2** hide underneath or delve into something.
– DERIVATIVES **burrower** n.
– ORIGIN Middle English: var. of BOROUGH.

bursa /ˈbɜːsə/ ■ n. (pl. **bursae** /-siː/ or **bursas**) Anatomy a fluid-filled sac or cavity, especially one countering friction at a joint.
– DERIVATIVES **bursal** adj.
– ORIGIN C19: from medieval Latin, 'bag, purse'.

bursar ■ n. chiefly Brit. a person who manages the financial affairs of a college or school.
– ORIGIN Middle English: from French *boursier* or medieval Latin *bursarius*, from *bursa* (see BURSA).

bursary /ˈbɜːsəri/ ■ n. (pl. **-ies**) a grant, especially one awarded to a student.
– DERIVATIVES **bursarial** /-ˈsɛːrɪəl/ adj.

bursitis /bɜːˈsʌɪtɪs/ ■ n. Medicine inflammation of a bursa, typically in a shoulder joint.

burst ■ v. (past and past part. **burst**) **1** break or cause to break

suddenly and violently apart. **2** be very full: *the wardrobe was bursting with clothes*. ▶ (**be bursting with**) feel (an irrepressible emotion or impulse). **3** move or be opened suddenly and forcibly. ▶ issue suddenly and uncontrollably. **4** separate (continuous stationery) into single sheets. ■ *n*. **1** an instance or the result of bursting. **2** a sudden brief outbreak of something violent or noisy. **3** a period of continuous effort.
– PHRASES **burst someone's bubble** shatter someone's illusions.
– ORIGIN Old English, of Germanic origin.

burthen ■ *n*. archaic form of BURDEN.

Burundian /bʊˈrʊndiən/ ■ *n*. a native or national of Burundi, a country in central Africa. ■ *adj*. of or relating to Burundi or its people.

bury ■ *v*. (**-ies, -ied**) **1** put or hide underground. ▶ place (a dead body) in the earth or a tomb. **2** cause to disappear or become unnoticeable. **3** (**bury oneself**) involve oneself deeply in something.
– PHRASES **bury one's head in the sand** ignore unpleasant realities.
– ORIGIN Old English, of West Germanic origin.

burying beetle ■ *n*. a black beetle which buries small animal carcasses to provide food for its larvae. [*Nicrophorus* and other genera.]

bus ■ *n*. (pl. **buses**; US also **busses**) **1** a large motor vehicle carrying paying passengers on a fixed route. **2** Computing a distinct set of conductors within a computer system, to which pieces of equipment may be connected in parallel. ■ *v*. (**buses** or **busses**, **bused** or **bussed**, **busing** or **bussing**) **1** transport or travel in a bus. ▶ N. Amer. transport (a child of one race) to a school where another race is predominant. **2** chiefly N. Amer. clear (dirty crockery) in a restaurant or cafeteria.
– ORIGIN C19: shortening of OMNIBUS.

busbar /ˈbʌsbɑː/ ■ *n*. a system of electrical conductors in a generating or receiving station into which power is fed for distribution.

busboy /ˈbʌsbɔɪ/ ■ *n*. chiefly N. Amer. a man who clears tables in a restaurant or café.

busby /ˈbʌzbi/ ■ *n*. (pl. **-ies**) a tall fur hat with a cloth flap hanging down on the right-hand side, worn by certain regiments of hussars and artillerymen. ▶ popular term for BEARSKIN (the cap).
– ORIGIN C18 (denoting a bushy wig).

bush[1] ■ *n*. **1** a shrub or clump of shrubs with stems of moderate length. **2** (**the bush**) (in Africa and Australia) wild or uncultivated country. ▶ the vegetation of such a district. ▶ [as modifier] chiefly S. African of inferior quality or skill: *bush justice | a bush mechanic*. **3** vulgar slang a woman's pubic hair.
– PHRASES **go bush** informal run wild; live without the trappings of civilization. **go to the bush** S. African (of young Xhosa men) withdraw from the community to take part in a traditional period of initiation and be circumcised.
– ORIGIN Middle English: from Old French *bos*, *bosc* 'wood', reinforced by Old Norse *buski*, of Germanic origin.

bush[2] ■ *n*. **1** a metal lining for a round hole, especially one in which an axle revolves. **2** a sleeve that protects an electric cable where it passes through a panel.
– ORIGIN C15: from Middle Dutch *busse*.

bushbaby ■ *n*. (pl. **-ies**) a small nocturnal tree-dwelling African primate with very large eyes. [Genus *Galago*: several species.]

bushbuck ■ *n*. a small African antelope with a reddish-brown coat with scattered white markings. [*Tragelaphus scriptus*.]
– ORIGIN C19: from BUSH[1] + BUCK[1], influenced by Dutch *bosbok*.

bush cricket ■ *n*. a mainly carnivorous insect related to the grasshoppers, with very long antennae. [Family Tettigoniidae: many species.]

bushed ■ *adj*. informal exhausted.

bushel /ˈbʊʃ(ə)l/ ■ *n*. **1** Brit. a measure of capacity equal to 8 gallons (equivalent to 36.4 litres). **2** US a measure of capacity equal to 64 US pints (equivalent to 35.2 litres).
– DERIVATIVES **bushelful** *n*. (pl. **-fuls**).
– ORIGIN Middle English: from Old French *boissel*, perhaps of Gaulish origin.

bush fire ■ *n*. a fire in scrub or a forest.

businesslike

bushido /ˈbuːʃɪdəʊ, buˈʃiːdəʊ/ ■ *n*. the code of honour and morals of the Japanese samurai.
– ORIGIN Japanese, from *bushi* 'samurai' + *dō* 'way'.

bush jacket ■ *n*. another term for SAFARI JACKET.

Bushman ■ *n*. (pl. **-men**) **1** a member of any of several aboriginal peoples of southern Africa, especially of the Kalahari Desert. **2** old-fashioned term for SAN (the languages of these people). **3** (**bushman**) a person who lives or travels in the Australian bush.

Bushman painting ■ *n*. (in southern Africa) a cave painting done with red or black pigment, considered to be the work of early Bushmen.

Bushman's candle ■ *n*. a southern African succulent plant yielding a flammable resinous secretion. [Genus *Sarcocaulon*: several species.]

Bushman's poison ■ *n*. a southern African shrub with small white or pale pink flowers and large purple fruits, traditionally used by Bushmen for making poison for arrows. [Genus *Acokanthera*: three species.]

bushmaster ■ *n*. a very large American pit viper. [*Lachesis muta*.]
– ORIGIN C19: perhaps from Dutch *bosmeester*, from *bos* 'bush' + *meester* 'master'.

bush meat ■ *n*. (in Africa) meat from wild animals, especially monkeys and gorillas, which are often illegally hunted.

bush pig ■ *n*. a wild forest-dwelling pig native to Africa and Madagascar. [*Potamochoerus porcus*.]

bush sickness ■ *n*. a deficiency disease of animals caused by a lack of cobalt in the soil.

bush tea ■ *n*. chiefly S. African a tea made from the dried leaves and twigs of various aromatic shrubs, especially *Aspalathus linearis* and *Cyclopia* species.

bush telegraph ■ *n*. a rapid informal network by which information or gossip is spread.

bush-tick berry ■ *n*. another term for BIETOU.

bushveld /ˈbʊʃfelt/ ■ *n*. **1** S. African wild or uncultivated country. ▶ Ecology a southern African vegetation type characterized by grassland interspersed with shrubs and trees. **2** (**the Bushveld**) the hot, dry areas of northern South Africa. **3** (**the Bushveld**, also **the Bushveld Complex**) a layered mafic intrusion and associated granite suite in northern South Africa containing extensive deposits of chromium, platinum-group elements, titanium, and vanadium.
– ORIGIN C19: partial translation of Afrikaans *bosveld* 'bush land'.

bushwhack ■ *v*. [often as noun **bushwhacking**] travel or live in the bush.
– DERIVATIVES **bushwhacker** *n*.

bushwhacked ■ *adj*. exhausted.

bushwillow ■ *n*. a combretum which bears flowers in small spikes, native to southern Africa. [Genus *Combretum*: many species.]

bushy ■ *adj*. (**-ier, -iest**) **1** growing thickly. **2** covered with bush or bushes.
– DERIVATIVES **bushily** *adv*. **bushiness** *n*.

business ■ *n*. **1** a person's regular occupation or trade. ▶ work to be done or matters to be attended to. **2** a person's concern. **3** commercial activity. ▶ a commercial organization. **4** informal a matter: *the business of trying to find her mother*. **5** (**the business**) informal an excellent person or thing.
– PHRASES **in business** informal able to begin something. **in the business of** engaged in or prepared to engage in. **like nobody's business** informal extraordinarily. **mind one's own business** refrain from meddling in other people's affairs. **send someone about their business** dated tell someone to go away.
– ORIGIN Old English *bisignis* 'anxiety' (see BUSY).

business card ■ *n*. a small card printed with one's name, occupation, and business address.

business end ■ *n*. informal the functional part of a tool or device.

businesslike ■ *adj*. efficient and practical.

businessman

businessman (or **businesswoman**) ■ n. (pl. **-men** or **-women**) a person who works in commerce, especially at executive level.

business park ■ n. an area composed of company offices and light industrial premises.

business process re-engineering ■ n. the process of restructuring a company's organization and methods, especially so as to exploit the capabilities of computers.

business studies ■ pl. n. [treated as sing.] the study of economics and management.

busk ■ v. **1** play music in the street for voluntary donations. **2** (**busk it**) informal improvise.
– DERIVATIVES **busker** n.
– ORIGIN C17: from obsolete French *busquer* 'seek'.

busman ■ n. (pl. **-men**) a bus driver.
– PHRASES **a busman's holiday** leisure time spent doing the same thing that one does at work.

buss archaic or N. Amer. informal ■ n. a kiss. ■ v. kiss.
– ORIGIN C16: alteration of Middle English *bass*, prob. from French *baiser*, from Latin *basiare*.

bus stop ■ n. a regular stopping place on a bus route.

bust¹ ■ n. **1** a woman's breasts. **2** a sculpture of a person's head, shoulders, and chest.
– ORIGIN C17: from French *buste*, from Latin *bustum* 'tomb, sepulchral monument'.

bust² informal ■ v. (past and past part. **busted** or **bust**) **1** break, split, or burst. ▶ (**bust up**) (of a group or couple) separate. **2** chiefly N. Amer. strike violently. **3** raid or search (premises). ▶ arrest. **4** chiefly US demote (a soldier). ■ n. **1** a period of economic difficulty or depression. **2** a police raid. **3** chiefly N. Amer. a violent blow. ■ adj. **1** damaged; broken. **2** bankrupt.
– ORIGIN C18 (orig. US): var. of BURST.

bustard /ˈbʌstəd/ ■ n. a large, heavily built, swift-running bird of open country. [Family Otididae: several species.]
– ORIGIN C15: perhaps an Anglo-Norman French blend of Old French *bistarde* and *oustarde*, both from Latin *avis tarda* 'slow bird'.

buster ■ n. informal **1** a person or thing that breaks, destroys, or overpowers something: *drug busters | stress busters*. **2** chiefly N. Amer. a form of address to a man or boy. **3** a violent gale.

bustier /ˈbʌstɪeɪ, ˈbuːst-/ ■ n. a close-fitting strapless top for women.
– ORIGIN 1970s: from French, from *buste* (see BUST¹).

bustle¹ ■ v. move energetically or noisily. ▶ [often as adj. **bustling**] (of a place) be full of activity. ■ n. excited activity and movement.
– ORIGIN Middle English: perhaps a var. of obsolete *buskle*, from *busk* 'prepare', from Old Norse.

bustle² ■ n. historical a pad or frame worn under a skirt to puff it out behind.
– ORIGIN C18.

bust-up ■ n. informal a serious quarrel or fight.

busty ■ adj. (**-ier, -iest**) informal having large breasts.
– DERIVATIVES **bustiness** n.

busy ■ adj. (**-ier, -iest**) **1** having a great deal to do. ▶ (of a place) full of activity or people. **2** (of a person) presently occupied; engaged. ▶ (of a telephone line) engaged. **3** S. African in the process of: *busy having convulsions*. ▶ (**busy with**) engaged in. **4** excessively detailed or decorated. ■ v. (**-ies, -ied**) (**busy oneself**) keep occupied.
– DERIVATIVES **busily** adv. **busyness** n.
– ORIGIN Old English *bisgian* (v.), *bisig* (n.).

busybody ■ n. (pl. **-ies**) a meddling or prying person.

busy Lizzie ■ n. (pl. **-ies**) an East African plant with abundant red, pink, or white flowers, often grown as a house plant. [*Impatiens walleriana*.]

but ■ conj. **1** nevertheless. ▶ on the contrary. **2** [with neg. or in questions] other than; otherwise than. ■ prep. except; apart from. ■ adv. only. ■ n. an objection.
– PHRASES **but for** except for. ▶ if it were not for. **but then** on the other hand.
– ORIGIN Old English *be-ūtan, būtan, būta* 'outside, without, except'.

butadiene /ˌbjuːtəˈdʌiiːn/ ■ n. Chemistry a gaseous unsaturated hydrocarbon, used in the manufacture of synthetic rubber. [C_4H_6.]

butane /ˈbjuːteɪn/ ■ n. Chemistry a flammable hydrocarbon gas of the alkane series, present in petroleum and natural gas and used as a fuel. [C_4H_{10}.]
– ORIGIN C19: from BUTYL + -ANE².

butch informal ■ adj. masculine in appearance or behaviour, often aggressively or ostentatiously so. ■ n. a mannish lesbian.
– ORIGIN 1940s: perhaps an abbrev. of BUTCHER.

butcher ■ n. **1** a person whose trade is cutting up and selling meat in a shop. ▶ a person who slaughters and cuts up animals for food. **2** N. Amer. informal a person selling refreshments, newspapers, etc. on a train or in a theatre. ■ v. **1** slaughter or cut up (an animal) for food. ▶ kill (someone) brutally. **2** ruin deliberately or through incompetence.
– PHRASES **have** (or **take**) **a butcher's** Brit. informal have a look. [*butcher's* from **butcher's hook**, rhyming slang for a 'look'.]
– DERIVATIVES **butchery** n.
– ORIGIN Middle English: from an Anglo-Norman French var. of Old French *bochier*, from *boc* 'he-goat', prob. rel. to BUCK¹.

butcher-bird ■ n. a shrike, so called from its habit of impaling prey on thorns.

butcher's broom ■ n. a low evergreen Eurasian shrub, with flat shoots that give the appearance of stiff spine-tipped leaves. [*Ruscus aculeatus*.]

buti ■ n. variant spelling of BHUTI.

butler ■ n. the chief manservant of a house.
– ORIGIN Middle English: from Old French *bouteillier* 'cup-bearer', from *bouteille* 'bottle'.

butt¹ ■ v. **1** hit with the head or horns. **2** (**butt in**) interrupt or intrude on a conversation or activity. ▶ (**butt out**) N. Amer. informal stop interfering. ■ n. a rough push with the head.
– ORIGIN Middle English: from Old French *boter*, of Germanic origin.

butt² ■ n. **1** an object of criticism or ridicule. **2** an archery or shooting target or range. ▶ a mound on or in front of which a target is set up for archery or shooting.
– ORIGIN Middle English: from Old French *but*.

butt³ ■ n. **1** (also **butt-end**) the thicker end of something, especially a tool or a weapon. ▶ the square end of a plank or plate meeting the end or side of another. **2** (also **butt-end**) the stub of a cigar or a cigarette. **3** informal a person's bottom. **4** the trunk of a tree, especially the part just above the ground. ■ v. meet end to end: *the shop butted up against the row of houses*. ▶ join (pieces of stone, timber, and other building materials) with the ends or sides flat against each other.
– ORIGIN Middle English: rel. to Dutch *bot* 'stumpy', also to BUTTOCK; the verb is partly from BUTT², reinforced by ABUT.

butt⁴ ■ n. **1** a cask used for wine, ale, or water. **2** US a liquid measure equal to 126 US gallons (equivalent to 477.5 litres).
– ORIGIN Middle English: from late Latin *buttis*.

butte /bjuːt/ ■ n. N. Amer. & technical an isolated hill with steep sides and a flat top.
– ORIGIN C19: from French, 'mound', from Old French *but* (cf. BUTT²).

butter ■ n. a pale yellow edible fatty substance made by churning cream and used as a spread or in cooking. ■ v. **1** spread with butter. **2** (**butter someone up**) informal flatter someone.
– PHRASES **look as if butter wouldn't melt in one's mouth** informal appear innocent while being the opposite.
– ORIGIN Old English *butere*, of West Germanic origin, from Greek *bouturon*.

butterball ■ n. N. Amer. **1** a plump bird, especially a turkey. **2** informal, derogatory a fat person.

butter bean ■ n. a lima bean, especially one of a variety with large flat white seeds.

buttercream ■ n. a mixture of butter and icing sugar used as a filling or topping for a cake.

buttercup ■ n. a herbaceous plant with bright yellow cup-shaped flowers, common in grassland. [Genus *Ranunculus*: many species.]

butterfat ■ n. the natural fat contained in milk and dairy products.

butterfingers ■ n. (pl. same) informal a clumsy person, especially one who fails to hold a catch.
– DERIVATIVES **butterfingered** adj.

butterfish ■ n. (pl. same or **-fishes**) any of various fishes with oily flesh or slippery skin. [Genera *Stromateus* and *Chirodactylus* (southern Africa).]

butterfly ■ n. (pl. **-flies**) **1** any of a large group of nectar-feeding lepidopterous insects with two pairs of large, typically colourful wings, distinguished from moths by having clubbed or dilated antennae, holding their wings erect when at rest, and being active by day. **2** [as modifier] having a two-lobed shape resembling the spread wings of a butterfly: *a butterfly clip*. **3** a showy or frivolous person: *a social butterfly*. **4** (**butterflies**) informal a fluttering and nauseous sensation felt in the stomach when one is nervous. **5** a stroke in swimming in which both arms are raised out of the water and lifted forwards together. ■ v. (**-flies**, **-flied**) split (a piece of meat) almost in two and spread it out flat.
– ORIGIN Old English: perhaps from the cream or yellow colour of common species, or from a former belief that the insects stole butter.

butterfly bush ■ n. **1** a buddleja cultivated for its large spikes of fragrant purplish-lilac or white flowers. [*Buddleja davidii* and other species.] **2** another term for CAMEL'S FOOT.

butterfly effect ■ n. (with reference to chaos theory) the phenomenon whereby a minute localized change in a complex system can have large effects elsewhere.
– ORIGIN 1980s: from the notion that a butterfly fluttering in Rio de Janeiro could change the weather in Chicago.

butterfly fish ■ n. **1** a brightly coloured reef-dwelling fish popular in marine aquaria. [*Chaetodon* and related genera.] **2** another term for FIREFISH.

butterfly net ■ n. a fine-meshed bag supported on a frame at the end of a handle, used for catching butterflies.

butterfly nut ■ n. another term for WING NUT.

butterhead lettuce ■ n. a class of lettuce varieties having soft leaves that grow in a loose head and are said to have the flavour of butter.

butter icing ■ n. another term for BUTTERCREAM.

buttermilk ■ n. **1** the slightly sour liquid left after butter has been churned, used in baking or consumed as a drink. **2** a pale yellow colour.

butter muslin ■ n. loosely woven cotton cloth, formerly used for wrapping butter.

butternut (also **butternut squash**) ■ n. a winter squash of a pear-shaped variety with light yellowish-brown rind and orange flesh.

butterscotch ■ n. a brittle yellow-brown sweet made with butter and brown sugar.

buttery[1] ■ adj. containing, tasting like, or covered with butter.
– DERIVATIVES **butteriness** n.

buttery[2] ■ n. (pl. **-ies**) Brit. a room in a college where food is kept and sold to students.
– ORIGIN Middle English: from Anglo-Norman French *boterie* 'butt-store', from late Latin *buttis* (see BUTT[4]).

buttock ■ n. either of the two round fleshy parts of the human body that form the bottom.
– ORIGIN Old English, prob. from the base of BUTT[3].

button ■ n. **1** a small disc or knob sewn on to a garment, either to fasten it by being pushed through a buttonhole or for decoration. **2** a decorative badge pinned to clothing. **3** a knob on a piece of electrical or electronic equipment which is pressed to operate it. **4** Fencing a knob fitted to the point of a foil to make it harmless. **5** S. African informal a Mandrax tablet. ■ v. **1** fasten or be fastened with buttons. **2** (**button something up**) informal complete something satisfactorily.
– PHRASES **button one's lip** informal stop or refrain from talking. **on the button** informal, chiefly N. Amer. precisely. **push** (or **press**) **someone's buttons** informal provoke a reaction in someone.
– DERIVATIVES **-buttoned** adj. **buttonless** adj. **buttony** adj.
– ORIGIN Middle English: from Old French *bouton*, of Germanic origin.

button-back ■ n. [as modifier] denoting a chair or sofa with a quilted back, the stitching being hidden by buttons.

button chrysanthemum ■ n. a variety of chrysanthemum with small spherical flowers.

button-down ■ adj. (of a collar) having points which are buttoned to the garment. ▸ (of a shirt) having such a collar.

buttonhole ■ n. **1** a slit made in a garment to receive a button for fastening. **2** a flower or spray worn in a lapel buttonhole. ■ v. **1** informal accost and detain (a reluctant person) in conversation. **2** make buttonholes in.
– DERIVATIVES **buttonholer** n.

buttonhole stitch ■ n. a looped stitch used for edging buttonholes or pieces of material.

buttonhook ■ n. **1** a small hook with a long handle for fastening tight buttons (often formerly on buttoned boots). **2** American Football a play in which a pass receiver runs straight downfield and then doubles back sharply towards the line of scrimmage.

button mushroom ■ n. a young unopened mushroom.

button-quail ■ n. a small quail-like bird related to the rails, with only three toes. [Genus *Turnix*: several species.]

Buttons ■ n. Brit. informal a nickname for a liveried pageboy, especially in a pantomime.
– ORIGIN C19: from the rows of buttons on his jacket.

button spider ■ n. a highly venomous African spider with a round black or brown body and a red spot or hourglass mark on the abdomen. [Genus *Latrodectus*: several species.]

button-through ■ adj. (of clothing) fastened with buttons from top to bottom.

buttress /ˈbʌtrɪs/ ■ n. **1** a projecting support of stone or brick built against a wall. **2** a projecting portion of a hill or mountain. ■ v. support with buttresses. ▸ support or strengthen: *authority was buttressed by religious belief*.
– ORIGIN Middle English: from Old French (*ars*) *bouterez* 'thrusting (arch)', from *boter* (see BUTT[1]).

butty ■ n. (pl. **-ies**) informal, chiefly N. English a sandwich.
– ORIGIN C19: from BUTTER.

butyl /ˈbjuːtʌɪl, -tɪl/ ■ n. [as modifier] Chemistry of or denoting an alkyl radical -C_4H_9, derived from butane: *butyl acetate*.

butyl rubber ■ n. a synthetic rubber made by polymerizing isobutylene and isoprene.

buxom /ˈbʌks(ə)m/ ■ adj. (of a woman) full-figured with large breasts.
– DERIVATIVES **buxomness** n.
– ORIGIN Middle English ('compliant', later 'lively and good-tempered'): from Old English *būgan* 'to bend'.

buy ■ v. (**buys**, **buying**; past and past part. **bought**) **1** obtain in exchange for payment. ▸ (**buy someone out**) pay someone to give up an ownership, interest, or share. ▸ (**buy oneself out**) obtain one's release from the armed services by payment. ▸ (**buy something in**) withdraw something at auction because it fails to reach the reserve price. **2** get by sacrifice or great effort. **3** informal accept the truth of. ■ n. informal a purchase.
– PHRASES **buy time** delay an event temporarily so as to have longer to improve one's own position. **have bought it** informal be killed.
– ORIGIN Old English, of Germanic origin.

buy-back ■ n. the buying back of goods by the original seller, especially a form of borrowing in which shares or bonds are sold with an agreement to repurchase them later.

buyer ■ n. a person who buys. ▸ a person employed to select and purchase stock for a retail or manufacturing business.
– PHRASES **a buyer's market** an economic situation in which goods or shares are plentiful and buyers can keep prices down.

buy-in ■ n. **1** a purchase of shares by a broker after a seller has failed to deliver similar shares, the original seller being charged any difference in cost. **2** a purchase of

buyout

shares in a company by managers who are not employed by it. **3** the buying back by a company of its own shares. **4** agreement with, or acceptance of, a policy, suggestion, etc.

buyout ■ n. the purchase of a controlling share in a company, especially by its own managers.

buzz ■ n. **1** a low, continuous humming or murmuring sound, made by or similar to that made by an insect. ► the sound of a buzzer or telephone. ► informal a telephone call. **2** an atmosphere of excitement and activity. ► informal a feeling of excitement or euphoria. **3** informal a rumour. ■ v. **1** make a humming sound. ► signal with a buzzer. **2** move quickly. ► (**buzz off**) informal go away. ► Aeronautics, informal fly very close to (another aircraft, the ground, etc.) at high speed. **3** have an air of excitement or purposeful activity.
– ORIGIN Middle English: imitative.

buzzard /ˈbʌzəd/ ■ n. **1** a large hawklike bird of prey with broad wings and a rounded tail, typically seen soaring in wide circles. [*Buteo buteo* and other species.] **2** N. Amer. a vulture.
– ORIGIN Middle English: from Old French *busard*, from Latin *buteo* 'falcon'.

buzzer ■ n. an electrical device that makes a buzzing noise to attract attention.
– PHRASES **at the buzzer** at the end of a game or period of play, especially in basketball.

buzz saw ■ n. North American term for CIRCULAR SAW.

buzzword ■ n. informal a technical word or phrase that has become fashionable.

b/w ■ abbrev. black and white (used to describe printing, film, photographs, or television pictures).

bwana /ˈbwɑːnə/ ■ n. (in East Africa) a boss or master (often used as a title or form of address).
– ORIGIN from Kiswahili.

by ■ prep. **1** through the agency or means of. ► indicating how something happens. **2** indicating a quantity or amount, or the size of a margin. ► identifying a parameter. ► expressing multiplication, especially in dimensions. **3** indicating the end of a time period. **4** near to; beside. ► past and beyond. **5** during. **6** according to. **7** used in mild oaths. ■ adv. so as to go past. ■ n. (pl. **byes**) variant spelling of BYE[1].
– PHRASES **by and by** before long. **by the by** (or **bye**) incidentally. **by and large** on the whole. **by oneself 1** alone. **2** unaided. **by way of** see WAY.
– ORIGIN Old English *bī*, *bi*, *be*, of Germanic origin.

by- (also **bye-**) ■ prefix subordinate; incidental; secondary: *by-election*.

by-blow ■ n. Brit. dated a man's illegitimate child.

by-catch ■ n. the unwanted fish and other marine creatures trapped by commercial fishing nets during fishing for a different species.

bye[1] ■ n. **1** the transfer of a competitor directly to the next round of a competition in the absence of an assigned opponent. **2** Cricket a run scored from a ball that passes the batsman without being hit (recorded as an extra). **3** Golf one or more holes remaining unplayed after a match has been decided.
– PHRASES **by the bye** variant spelling of by the by (see BY).
– ORIGIN C16: from BY.

bye[2] ■ exclam. informal goodbye.

bye- ■ prefix variant spelling of BY-.

bye-bye ■ exclam. informal goodbye.
– ORIGIN C18: child's reduplication.

bye-byes ■ n. a child's word for sleep.
– ORIGIN C19: from the sound *bye-bye*, long used as a refrain in lullabies.

by-election ■ n. an election for a single member of Parliament or councillor to fill a vacancy arising during the term of office of a government or council.

byeline ■ n. variant spelling of BYLINE (in sense 2).

Byelorussian /ˌbjɛlə(ʊ)ˈrʌʃ(ə)n/ ■ adj. & n. variant spelling of BELORUSSIAN.

by-form ■ n. a secondary form of a word.

bygone ■ adj. belonging to an earlier time.
– PHRASES **let bygones be bygones** forget past differences or offences and be reconciled.

by-law (also **bye-law**) ■ n. **1** a regulation made by a local or municipal authority or corporation. **2** a rule made by a company or society to control the actions of its members.
– ORIGIN Middle English: prob. from obsolete *byrlaw* 'local law', from Old Norse *býr* 'town', but associated with BY.

byline ■ n. **1** a line in a newspaper naming the writer of an article. **2** (also **byeline**) (chiefly in soccer) the part of the goal line to either side of the goal.

byname ■ n. a sobriquet or nickname.

bypass ■ n. **1** a road passing round a town to provide an alternative route for through traffic. **2** a secondary channel, pipe, or connection to allow a flow when the main one is closed or blocked. **3** a surgical operation to make an alternative passage to aid the circulation of blood. ■ v. go past or round. ► provide (a town) with a bypass.

byplay ■ n. subsidiary action in a play or film.

by-product ■ n. **1** an incidental or secondary product made in the manufacture of something else. **2** an unintended but inevitable secondary result.

byre ■ n. chiefly Brit. a cowshed.
– ORIGIN Old English.

byroad ■ n. a minor road.

Byronic /baɪˈrɒnɪk/ ■ adj. characteristic of Lord Byron (1788–1824) or his poetry. ► (of a man) alluringly dark, mysterious, and moody.

byssus /ˈbɪsəs/ ■ n. (pl. **byssuses** or **byssi** /-sʌɪ/) Zoology a tuft of tough silky filaments by which mussels and some other bivalves adhere to rocks and other objects.
– DERIVATIVES **byssal** adj.
– ORIGIN Middle English: from Greek *bussos*, of Semitic origin.

bystander ■ n. a person who is present at an event or incident but does not take part.

byte /bʌɪt/ ■ n. Computing a group of binary digits or bits (usually eight) operated on as a unit. ► such a group as a unit of memory size.
– ORIGIN 1960s: an arbitrary formation based on BIT[4] and BITE.

byway ■ n. **1** a minor road or path. **2** a little-known area of knowledge.

bywoner /ˈbeɪvʊənə, ˈbʌɪ-/ ■ n. S. African historical a white tenant farmer who laboured in return for the right to cultivate an area of land.
– ORIGIN C19: Afrikaans, from *by-* 'with, at' + *woon* 'dwell'.

byword ■ n. **1** a person or thing cited as a notable example or embodiment of something. **2** a word or expression summarizing a thing's characteristics or a person's principles.

Byzantine /bɪˈzantʌɪn, bʌɪ-/ ■ adj. **1** of or relating to Byzantium, the Byzantine Empire, or the Eastern Orthodox Church. ► of a rich and highly decorated artistic and architectural style which developed in the Byzantine Empire and spread to Italy, Russia, and elsewhere. **2** excessively complicated and detailed. ► characterized by deviousness or underhand methods. ■ n. a citizen of Byzantium or the Byzantine Empire.
– ORIGIN C16: from Latin, from *Byzantium*, the city later called Constantinople and now Istanbul.

Cc

C¹ (also **c**) ■ n. (pl. **Cs** or **C's**) **1** the third letter of the alphabet. **2** denoting the third in a set of items, categories, sizes, etc. **3** Music the first note of the diatonic scale of C major, the major scale having no sharps or flats. **4** the Roman numeral for 100. [abbrev. of Latin *centum* 'hundred'.] **5** (**C**) a computer programming language originally developed for implementing the UNIX operating system. [formerly known as *B*, abbrev. of *BCPL*.]

C² ■ abbrev. **1** (**C.**) Cape (chiefly on maps). **2** Celsius or centigrade. **3** (in Britain) Conservative. **4** (©) copyright. **5** Physics coulomb(s). ■ symb. **1** Physics capacitance. **2** the chemical element carbon.
– PHRASES **the Big C** informal cancer.

c ■ abbrev. **1** Cricket caught by. **2** cent(s). **3** centi-. **4** (**c.**) century or centuries. **5** (preceding a date or amount) circa. **6** colt. ■ symb. Physics the speed of light in a vacuum: $E = mc^2$.

c/- ■ abbrev. Austral./NZ care of (used chiefly in addresses on envelopes).

CA ■ abbrev. chartered accountant.

Ca ■ symb. the chemical element calcium.

ca ■ abbrev. (preceding a date or amount) circa.

cab ■ n. **1** (also **taxi cab**) a private taxi. **2** the driver's compartment in a truck, bus, or train. **3** historical a horse-drawn vehicle for public hire.
– ORIGIN C19: abbrev. of **CABRIOLET**.

cabal /kəˈbal/ ■ n. a secret political clique or faction.
– ORIGIN C16: from French *cabale*, from medieval Latin *cabala* (see **KABBALAH**).

Cabala ■ n. variant spelling of **KABBALAH**.

cabana /kəˈbɑːnə/ ■ n. chiefly N. Amer. a hut, cabin, or shelter at a beach or swimming pool.
– ORIGIN C19: from Spanish *cabaña*.

cabaret /ˈkabəreɪ, ˌkabəˈreɪ/ ■ n. entertainment held in a nightclub or restaurant while the audience eat or drink at tables. ▶ a nightclub or restaurant where such entertainment is performed.
– ORIGIN C17 (denoting a French inn): from Old French, 'wooden structure'.

cabbage ■ n. **1** a cultivated plant eaten as a vegetable, having thick green or purple leaves surrounding a spherical heart or head of young leaves. [*Brassica oleracea*.] **2** informal, derogatory a person whose physical or mental activity is impaired or destroyed as a result of injury or illness. **3** S. African informal a ten-rand note.
– DERIVATIVES **cabbagy** adj.
– ORIGIN Middle English: from Old French *caboche* 'head', var. of *caboce*.

cabbage lettuce ■ n. lettuce of a variety which has broad, rounded leaves forming a globular head close to the ground.

cabbage moth ■ n. a brown moth whose caterpillars are pests of cabbages and related plants. [*Mamestra brassicae*.]

cabbage palm ■ n. **1** another term for **CABBAGE TREE**. **2** any of several palms or palm-like plants that resemble a cabbage in some way.

cabbage rose ■ n. a kind of rose with a large, round, compact double flower.

cabbage tree ■ n. **1** an African tree with succulent roots and stems, and large leaves which grow at the ends of the branches. [Genus *Cussonia*: several species.] **2** a cabbage palm, especially a New Zealand tree grown for its sugary sap or for ornament. [*Cordyline australis*.]

Cabbala ■ n. variant spelling of **KABBALAH**.

cabbalistic /ˌkabəˈlɪstɪk/ ■ adj. relating to or associated with mystical interpretation or esoteric doctrine. See also **KABBALAH**.
– DERIVATIVES **cabbalism** n. **cabbalist** n.
– ORIGIN var. of *Kabbalistic*: see **KABBALAH**.

cabby (also **cabbie**) ■ n. (pl. **-ies**) informal a taxi driver.

caber /ˈkeɪbə/ ■ n. a roughly trimmed tree trunk used in the Scottish Highland sport of tossing the caber.
– ORIGIN C16: from Scottish Gaelic *cabar* 'pole'.

Cabernet Franc /ˈkabəneɪ frɒ̃/ ■ n. a variety of black wine grape. ▶ a red wine made from this grape.
– ORIGIN from French.

Cabernet Sauvignon /ˈsəʊvɪnjɒ̃/ ■ n. a variety of black wine grape originally from the Bordeaux area of France. ▶ a red wine made from this grape.
– ORIGIN from French.

cabin ■ n. **1** a private room or compartment on a ship. **2** the passenger compartment in an aircraft. **3** a small wooden shelter or house.
– ORIGIN Middle English: from Old French *cabane*, from late Latin *capanna, cavanna*.

cabin boy ■ n. chiefly historical a boy employed to wait on a ship's officers or passengers.

cabin class ■ n. the intermediate class of accommodation on a passenger ship.

cabin crew ■ n. [treated as sing. or pl.] the members of an aircraft crew who attend to passengers or cargo.

cabin cruiser ■ n. a motor boat with living accommodation.

cabinet ■ n. **1** a cupboard with drawers or shelves for storing or displaying articles. ▶ a wooden box, container, or piece of furniture housing a radio, television set, or speaker. **2** (also **Cabinet**) (in South Africa and other countries) the committee of senior ministers responsible for controlling government policy. ▶ (in the US) a body of advisers to the President, composed of the heads of the executive departments of the government.
– ORIGIN C16: from **CABIN**, influenced by French *cabinet*; sense 2 derives from the obsolete sense 'a small private room'.

cabinetmaker ■ n. a skilled joiner who makes furniture or similar high-quality woodwork.
– DERIVATIVES **cabinetmaking** n.

cabinet pudding ■ n. a steamed suet pudding containing dried fruit.

cabin fever ■ n. informal, chiefly N. Amer. lassitude and irritability resulting from long confinement indoors during the winter.

cable ■ n. **1** a thick rope of wire or hemp, typically used for construction, mooring ships, and towing vehicles. ▶ the chain of a ship's anchor. ▶ (also **cable moulding**) Architecture a moulding resembling twisted rope. **2** an insulated wire or wires having a protective casing and used for transmitting electricity or telecommunication signals. **3** a cablegram. **4** Nautical a length of 200 yards (182.9 m) or (in the US) 240 yards (219.4 m). ■ v. **1** dated send a cablegram to. **2** provide (an area) with power lines or other equipment necessary for cable television.
– ORIGIN Middle English: from var. of Old French *chable*, from late Latin *capulum* 'halter'.

cable car ■ n. **1** a transport system, typically one on a mountainside, in which cabins are suspended on a continuous moving cable driven by a motor at one end of the route. **2** a carriage on a cable railway.

cablegram ■ n. historical a telegraph message sent by cable.

cable-laid ■ adj. (of rope) made of three triple strands.

cable railway ■ n. **1** a tramway on which the unpowered

cable release

cars are attached to a continuously moving cable running in a slot in the street. **2** a funicular.

cable release ■ n. Photography a cable attached to the shutter release of a camera, allowing the photographer to open the shutter without touching the camera.

cable stitch ■ n. a combination of knitted stitches resembling twisted rope.

cable television ■ n. a system in which television programmes are transmitted to the sets of subscribers by cable.

cableway ■ n. a transport system in which goods are carried suspended from a continuous moving cable.

cabochon /ˈkabəʃɒn/ ■ n. a gem polished but not faceted.
– ORIGIN C16: from French, diminutive of *caboche* 'head'.

caboodle ■ n. (in phr. **the whole caboodle** or **the whole kit and caboodle**) informal the whole number or quantity of people or things in question.
– ORIGIN C19 (orig. US): perhaps from the phr. *kit and boodle*, in the same sense.

caboose ■ n. N. Amer. a railway wagon with accommodation for the train crew, typically attached to the end of the train.
– ORIGIN C18: from Dutch *kabuis*, *kombuis*.

caboshed /kəˈbɒʃt/ ■ adj. [usu. postpos.] Heraldry (of the head of a stag, bull, etc.) shown full face with no neck visible.
– ORIGIN C16: from French *caboché*, in the same sense.

cabotage /ˈkabətɑːʒ, -ɪdʒ/ ■ n. **1** the right to operate sea, air, or other transport services within a particular territory. **2** restriction of the operation of transport services within or into a particular country to that country's own transport services.
– ORIGIN C19: from French, from *caboter* 'sail along a coast'.

cabriole /ˈkabrɪəʊl/ ■ n. Ballet a jump in which one leg is extended into the air forwards or backwards, the other is brought up to meet it, and the dancer lands on the second foot.
– ORIGIN French, 'light leap', from *cabrioler*, from Italian *capriolare* (see CAPRIOLE).

cabriole leg ■ n. a kind of curved leg characteristic of Chippendale and Queen Anne furniture.
– ORIGIN C18: so named from the resemblance to the front leg of a leaping animal (see CABRIOLE).

cabriolet /ˈkabrɪə(ʊ)leɪ/ ■ n. **1** a car with a roof that folds down. **2** a light two-wheeled carriage with a hood, drawn by one horse.
– ORIGIN C18: from French, from *cabriole* (see CABRIOLE); so named because of the carriage's motion.

cacao /kəˈkɑːəʊ, -ˈkeɪəʊ/ ■ n. (pl. **-os**) **1** bean-like seeds from which cocoa, cocoa butter, and chocolate are made. **2** the small tropical American evergreen tree which bears these seeds, which are contained in large oval pods growing on the trunk. [*Theobroma cacao*.]
– ORIGIN C16: from Nahuatl *cacaua*.

cacciatore /ˌkatʃəˈtɔːreɪ, -riː/ (also **cacciatora** /-rə/) ■ adj. [postpos.] prepared in a spicy tomato sauce with mushrooms and herbs.
– ORIGIN Italian, 'hunter'.

cache /kaʃ/ ■ n. **1** a hidden store of things. **2** Computing an auxiliary memory from which high-speed retrieval is possible. ■ v. store in a cache.
– ORIGIN C18: from French, from *cacher* 'to hide'.

cachectic /kəˈkɛktɪk/ ■ adj. Medicine relating to or having the symptoms of cachexia.

cachepot /ˈkaʃpəʊ, ˈkaʃpɒt/ ■ n. (pl. pronounced same) an ornamental holder for a flowerpot.
– ORIGIN C19: from French *cache-pot*, from *cacher* 'to hide' + *pot* 'pot'.

cachet /ˈkaʃeɪ/ ■ n. **1** prestige. **2** a distinguishing mark or seal. **3** a flat capsule enclosing a dose of unpleasant-tasting medicine.
– ORIGIN C17: from French, from *cacher* in the sense 'to press'.

cachexia /kəˈkɛksɪə/ ■ n. Medicine weakness and wasting of the body due to severe chronic illness.
– ORIGIN C16: from Greek, from *kakos* 'bad' + *hexis* 'habit'.

cachinnate /ˈkakɪneɪt/ ■ v. poetic/literary laugh loudly.
– DERIVATIVES **cachinnation** n.
– ORIGIN C19 (*cachinnation* C17): from Latin *cachinnare* 'laugh loudly'; imitative.

cack-handed ■ adj. Brit. informal **1** inept; clumsy. **2** derogatory left-handed.
– DERIVATIVES **cack-handedly** adv. **cack-handedness** n.

cackle ■ v. **1** (of a hen or goose) give a raucous clucking cry. ▸ make a similar sound when laughing. **2** talk inconsequentially and at length. ■ n. a cackling sound.
– PHRASES **cut the cackle** informal stop talking aimlessly and come to the point.
– ORIGIN Middle English: prob. from Middle Low German *kākelen*, partly imitative.

cacophony /kəˈkɒf(ə)ni/ ■ n. (pl. **-ies**) a harsh discordant mixture of sounds.
– DERIVATIVES **cacophonous** adj.
– ORIGIN C17: from French *cacophonie*, from Greek, from *kakophōnos* 'ill-sounding'.

cactus ■ n. (pl. **cacti** /-taɪ/ or **cactuses**) a succulent plant of a large family native to arid regions of the New World, with a thick fleshy stem which typically bears spines, lacks leaves, and has brilliantly coloured flowers. [Family Cactaceae.]
– DERIVATIVES **cactaceous** adj.
– ORIGIN C17: from Latin, from Greek *kaktos* 'cardoon'.

CAD ■ abbrev. computer-aided design.

cad ■ n. dated or humorous a man who behaves dishonourably, especially towards a woman.
– DERIVATIVES **caddish** adj. **caddishly** adv. **caddishness** n.
– ORIGIN C18: abbrev. of CADDIE or CADET.

cadastral /kəˈdastr(ə)l/ ■ adj. (of a map or survey) showing the extent, value, and ownership of land, especially for taxation.
– ORIGIN C19: from French, from *cadastre* 'register of property'.

cadaver /kəˈdɑːvə, -ˈdeɪ-/ ■ n. Medicine or poetic/literary a corpse.
– DERIVATIVES **cadaveric** adj.
– ORIGIN Middle English: from Latin, from *cadere* 'to fall'.

cadaverous ■ adj. resembling a corpse in being very pale, thin, or bony.

CADCAM ■ abbrev. computer-aided design, computer-aided manufacture.

caddie (also **caddy**) ■ n. (pl. **-ies**) a person who carries a golfer's clubs and provides other assistance during a match. ■ v. (**caddying**) work as a caddie.
– ORIGIN C17: from French CADET.

caddis /ˈkadɪs/ (also **caddis fly**) ■ n. a small moth-like insect of an order having aquatic larvae that build protective cases of sticks, stones, etc. [Order Trichoptera.]
– ORIGIN C17.

caddis worm ■ n. the soft-bodied aquatic larva of a caddis fly, used as fishing bait.

caddy[1] ■ n. (pl. **-ies**) a small storage container.
– ORIGIN C18: from earlier *catty*, a unit of weight of 1⅓ lb (0.61 kg), from Malay *kati*.

caddy[2] ■ n. & v. variant spelling of CADDIE.

cadence /ˈkeɪd(ə)ns/ ■ n. **1** a modulation or inflection of the voice. **2** Music a sequence of notes or chords comprising the close of a musical phrase. **3** rhythm.
– DERIVATIVES **cadenced** adj.
– ORIGIN Middle English: from Italian *cadenza*, from Latin *cadere* 'to fall'.

cadency ■ n. chiefly Heraldry the status of a younger branch of a family.
– ORIGIN C17: from Latin *cadere* 'to fall'; the current sense by association with CADET.

cadential ■ adj. of or relating to a cadenza or cadence.

cadenza /kəˈdɛnzə/ ■ n. Music a virtuoso solo passage inserted into a movement in a concerto or other work, typically near the end.
– PHRASES **have a cadenza** S. African informal be in a state of agitation.
– ORIGIN C18: from Italian (see CADENCE).

cadet ■ n. **1** a young trainee in the armed services or police. ▸ a secondary school pupil or student who

VOWELS a cat ɑː arm ɛ bed ɛː hair ə ago əː her ɪ sit i cosy iː see ɒ hot ɔː saw ʌ run

undergoes voluntary training in the armed services. **2** formal or archaic a junior branch of a family.
– DERIVATIVES **cadetship** n.
– ORIGIN C17: from French, from Gascon dialect *capdet*, from Latin *caput* 'head'.

cadge ■ v. informal ask for or obtain (something to which one is not strictly entitled). ■ n. Falconry a padded wooden frame on which hooded hawks are carried to the field.
– PHRASES **on the cadge** informal seeking to obtain something without paying for it.
– DERIVATIVES **cadger** n.
– ORIGIN C17: back-formation from the noun *cadger*, denoting an itinerant dealer; the noun may be an alteration of CAGE.

cadmium /ˈkadmɪəm/ ■ n. the chemical element of atomic number 48, a silvery-white metal resembling zinc. (Symbol: **Cd**)
– ORIGIN C19: from Latin *cadmia* 'calamine', so named because it is found with calamine in zinc ore.

cadmium yellow ■ n. a bright yellow pigment containing cadmium sulphide.

cadre /ˈkɑːdə, ˈkɑːdr(ə), ˈkadrɪ/ ■ n. **1** a small group of people trained for a particular purpose or profession. **2** /also ˈkeɪdə/ a group of activists in a communist or other revolutionary organization. **3** a member of a cadre.
– ORIGIN C19: from Italian *quadro*, from Latin *quadrus* 'square'.

caduceus /kəˈdjuːsɪəs/ ■ n. (pl. **caducei** /-sɪaɪ/) an ancient Greek or Roman herald's wand, typically one with two serpents twined round it, carried by the messenger god Hermes or Mercury.
– ORIGIN from Doric Greek *karukeion*, from Greek *kērux* 'herald'.

caducous /kəˈdjuːkəs/ ■ adj. chiefly Botany (of an organ or part) easily detached and shed at an early stage.
– ORIGIN C17: from Latin *caducus* 'liable to fall', from *cadere* 'to fall'.

CAE ■ abbrev. computer-aided engineering.

caecilian /sɪˈsɪlɪən/ (also **coecilian**) ■ n. Zoology a burrowing worm-like amphibian of a tropical order distinguished by poorly developed eyes and the lack of limbs. [Order Gymnophiona: many species.]
– ORIGIN from Latin *caecilia* 'slow-worm'.

caecum /ˈsiːkəm/ (US **cecum**) ■ n. (pl. **caeca**) Anatomy a pouch connected to the junction of the small and large intestines.
– DERIVATIVES **caecal** adj.
– ORIGIN Middle English: from Latin (*intestinum*) *caecum* 'blind (gut)', translation of Greek *tuphlon enteron*.

Caerphilly /keːˈfɪli, kɑː-, kə-/ ■ n. a kind of mild white cheese, originally made in Caerphilly in Wales.

Caesar /ˈsiːzə/ ■ n. **1** a title of Roman emperors, especially those from Augustus to Hadrian. **2** informal a Caesarean section.
– PHRASES **Caesar's wife** a person required to be above suspicion.
– ORIGIN Middle English: from Latin *Caesar*, family name of the Roman statesman, Gaius Julius *Caesar*.

Caesarean /sɪˈzɛːrɪən/ (also **Caesarian**) ■ adj. (US also **Cesarean**) of or effected by Caesarean section. ■ n. a Caesarean section.

Caesarean section ■ n. a surgical operation for delivering a child by cutting through the wall of the mother's abdomen.
– ORIGIN C17: from the story that Julius Caesar was delivered by this method.

Caesar salad ■ n. a salad consisting of cos lettuce and croutons served with a dressing of olive oil, lemon juice, raw egg, and Worcester sauce.
– ORIGIN named after *Caesar* Cardini, the Mexican restaurateur who invented it.

caesium /ˈsiːzɪəm/ (US **cesium**) ■ n. the chemical element of atomic number 55, a soft, silvery, rare, extremely reactive metal of the alkali metal group. (Symbol: **Cs**)
– ORIGIN C19: from Latin *caesius* 'greyish-blue' (because it has characteristic lines in the blue part of the spectrum).

caesium clock ■ n. an atomic clock that uses the vibrations of caesium atoms as a time standard.

caesura /sɪˈzjʊərə/ ■ n. (in modern verse) a pause near the middle of a line.
– ORIGIN C16: from Latin, from *caedere* 'cut, hew'.

CAF ■ abbrev. Confederation of African Football.

café /ˈkafeɪ, ˈkafi, or informal kaf/ ■ n. **1** a small restaurant selling light meals and drinks. **2** S. African a small shop selling sweets, cigarettes, newspapers, and perishable goods, usually staying open late. **3** N. Amer. a bar or nightclub.
– ORIGIN C19: from French *café* 'coffee or coffee house'.

café au lait /ˌkafeɪ əʊ ˈleɪ, ˌkafi/ ■ n. **1** coffee with milk. **2** the light brown colour of this.
– ORIGIN from French *café au lait*.

café curtain ■ n. a curtain covering the lower half of a window.

café noir /ˌkafeɪ ˈnwɑː, ˌkafi/ ■ n. black coffee.
– ORIGIN from French *café noir*.

café society ■ n. the regular patrons of fashionable restaurants and nightclubs.

cafeteria ■ n. a self-service restaurant.
– ORIGIN C19 (orig. US): from Latin American Spanish *cafetería* 'coffee shop'.

cafetière /ˌkaf(ə)ˈtjɛː/ ■ n. a coffee pot containing a plunger with which the grounds are pushed to the bottom before the coffee is poured.
– ORIGIN C19: from French, from *café* 'coffee'.

caffeine /ˈkafiːn/ ■ n. a crystalline compound of the alkaloid type which is found in tea and coffee plants and is a stimulant of the central nervous system.
– DERIVATIVES **caffeinated** adj.
– ORIGIN C19: from French *caféine*, from *café* 'coffee'.

caffè latte /ˌkafeɪ ˈlɑːteɪ, ˈlateɪ/ ■ n. a drink of frothy steamed milk to which a shot of espresso coffee is added.
– ORIGIN Italian, 'milk coffee'.

caftan ■ n. variant spelling of KAFTAN.

cage ■ n. **1** a structure of bars or wires in which birds or other animals are confined. **2** an open framework forming the compartment in a lift. **3** a structure of crossing bars or wires designed to hold or support something. ▶ Baseball a portable mesh backstop used for batting practice. ■ v. confine in or as in a cage.
– ORIGIN Middle English: from Latin *cavea*.

cage bird ■ n. a bird of a kind customarily kept in a cage.

cagey (also **cagy**) ■ adj. informal uncommunicative owing to caution or suspicion.
– DERIVATIVES **cagily** adv. **caginess** (also **cageyness**) n.
– ORIGIN C20 (orig. US).

cagoule /kəˈɡuːl/ (also **kagoul**) ■ n. a lightweight, hooded, thigh-length waterproof jacket.
– ORIGIN 1950s: from French, 'cowl'.

cahoots /kəˈhuːts/ ■ pl. n. (in phr. **in cahoots**) informal colluding or conspiring together secretly.
– ORIGIN C19 (orig. US).

CAI ■ abbrev. computer-assisted (or -aided) instruction.

caiman /ˈkeɪmən/ (also **cayman**) ■ n. a semiaquatic tropical American reptile similar to an alligator, with a heavily armoured belly. [*Caiman sclerops* (spectacled caiman) and other species.]
– ORIGIN C16: from Spanish *caimán*, from Carib *acayuman*.

Cain ■ n. (in phr. **raise Cain**) informal create trouble or a commotion.
– ORIGIN *Cain*, eldest son of Adam and Eve and murderer of his brother Abel (Genesis 4).

Cainozoic /ˌkʌɪnəˈzəʊɪk/ ■ adj. variant spelling of CENOZOIC.

caique /kʌɪˈiːk, kɑː-/ ■ n. **1** a light rowing boat used on the Bosporus. **2** a small eastern Mediterranean sailing ship.
– ORIGIN C17: from French *caïque*, from Turkish *kayik*.

cairn ■ n. a mound of rough stones built as a memorial or landmark. ▶ a prehistoric burial mound made of stones.
– ORIGIN Middle English: from Scottish Gaelic *carn*.

caitiff /ˈkeɪtɪf/ ■ n. archaic a contemptible or cowardly person.
– ORIGIN Middle English: from Old French *caitif* 'captive', from Latin *captivus* (see CAPTIVE).

cajole

cajole /kəˈdʒəʊl/ ■ v. persuade (someone) to do something by sustained coaxing or flattery.
– DERIVATIVES **cajolement** n. **cajolery** n.
– ORIGIN C17: from French *cajoler*.

Cajun /ˈkeɪdʒ(ə)n/ ■ n. a member of any of the communities in the bayou areas of southern Louisiana formed by descendants of French Canadians, speaking an archaic form of French. ■ adj. of or relating to the Cajuns, especially with reference to their folk music or cuisine.
– ORIGIN alteration of obsolete *Acadian*, denoting a person from the former French colony of Acadia (now Nova Scotia) in Canada.

cake ■ n. **1** an item of soft sweet food made from baking a mixture of flour, fat, eggs, sugar, etc. **2** an item of savoury food formed into a flat round shape, and baked or fried. **3** the amount of money or assets regarded as available for sharing: *a fair slice of the education cake*. ■ v. (of a thick or sticky substance) cover and become encrusted on.
– PHRASES **a piece of cake** informal something easily achieved. **sell like hot cakes** informal be sold quickly and in large quantities. **take the cake** see *take the biscuit* at BISCUIT.
– ORIGIN Middle English: of Scandinavian origin.

cake flour ■ n. S. African & N. Amer. flour that does not contain a raising agent.

cakehole ■ n. informal a person's mouth.

cakewalk ■ n. **1** informal a very easy task. **2** a strutting dance popular at the end of the 19th century, developed from an American black contest in graceful walking which had a cake as a prize. ■ v. **1** informal achieve something easily. **2** do a cakewalk.

CAL ■ abbrev. computer-assisted (or -aided) learning.

Cal ■ abbrev. large calorie(s).

cal ■ abbrev. small calorie(s).

calabash /ˈkaləbaʃ/ ■ n. **1** (also **calabash tree**) an evergreen tropical American tree which bears fruit in the form of large woody gourds. [*Crescentia cujete*.] **2** a water container, tobacco pipe, or other object made from the dried shell of a gourd.
– ORIGIN C17: from French *calebasse*, perhaps from Persian *karbuz* 'melon'.

calabrese /ˈkaləbriːs, ˌkaləˈbriːs, -ˈbreɪsɪ/ ■ n. a bright green dense-headed variety of broccoli.
– ORIGIN 1930s: from Italian, 'of or from Calabria', a region of SW Italy.

calamari /ˌkaləˈmɑːri/ (also **calamares** /ˌkaləˈmɑːreɪz/) ■ pl. n. squid served as food.
– ORIGIN Italian, pl. of *calamaro*, from Greek *kalamos* 'pen' (with ref. to the squid's long tapering internal shell and its ink).

calamine /ˈkaləmʌɪn/ ■ n. a pink powder consisting of zinc carbonate and ferric oxide, used to make a soothing lotion or ointment.
– ORIGIN Middle English: from medieval Latin *calamina*, alteration of Latin *cadmia*, from Greek *kadmeia* (*gē*) 'Cadmean (earth)', named after Cadmus, the legendary founder of Thebes.

calamint /ˈkaləmɪnt/ ■ n. an aromatic herbaceous plant or shrub with blue or lilac flowers. [Genus *Calamintha*.]
– ORIGIN Middle English: from Old French *calament*, from Greek *kalaminthē*.

calamity ■ n. (pl. **-ies**) an event causing great and often sudden damage or distress.
– DERIVATIVES **calamitous** adj. **calamitously** adv.
– ORIGIN Middle English: from Latin *calamitas*.

calamus /ˈkaləməs/ ■ n. (pl. **calami** /-mʌɪ/) Zoology the hollow lower part of the shaft of a feather.
– ORIGIN Middle English: from Greek *kalamos*.

calathea /ˌkaləˈθɪə/ ■ n. a tropical American plant which typically has variegated and ornamental leaves, often grown as a greenhouse or pot plant. [Genus *Calathea*: many species.]
– ORIGIN from Greek *kalathos* 'basket'.

calc- ■ comb. form (used chiefly in geological terms) of lime or calcium: *calcareous*.
– ORIGIN from German *Kalk* 'lime'.

calcaneus /kalˈkeɪnɪəs/ (also **calcaneum** /-nɪəm/) ■ n. (pl. **calcanei** /-nɪʌɪ/ or **calcanea** /-nɪə/) Anatomy the large bone forming the heel.
– ORIGIN C18: from Latin.

calcareous /kalˈkɛːrɪəs/ ■ adj. **1** containing calcium carbonate; chalky. **2** Ecology (of vegetation) occurring on chalk or limestone.
– ORIGIN C17: from Latin *calcarius*, from *calx* 'lime'.

calceolaria /ˌkalsɪəˈlɛːrɪə/ ■ n. a South American plant which is cultivated for its brightly coloured slipper- or pouch-shaped flowers. [Genus *Calceolaria*.]
– ORIGIN C18: from Latin *calceolus*, diminutive of *calceus* 'shoe'.

calces plural form of CALX.

calci- ■ comb. form relating to calcium or its compounds: *calcifuge*.
– ORIGIN from Latin *calx* 'lime'.

calcic /ˈkalsɪk/ ■ adj. (chiefly of minerals) containing or relatively rich in calcium.

calcicole /ˈkalsɪkəʊl/ ■ n. Botany a plant that grows best in calcareous soil.
– DERIVATIVES **calcicolous** adj.
– ORIGIN C19: from CALCI- + Latin *colere* 'inhabit'.

calciferol /kalˈsɪfərɒl/ ■ n. Biochemistry vitamin D_2, essential for the deposition of calcium in bones.

calciferous /kalˈsɪf(ə)rəs/ ■ adj. containing or producing calcium salts, especially calcium carbonate.

calcifuge /ˈkalsɪfjuːdʒ/ ■ n. Botany a plant that is intolerant of calcareous soil.

calcify /ˈkalsɪfʌɪ/ ■ v. (**-ies, -ied**) [usu. as adj. **calcified**] harden by deposition of or conversion into calcium carbonate or some other insoluble calcium compounds.
– DERIVATIVES **calcific** adj. **calcification** n.

calcine /ˈkalsʌɪn, -sɪn/ ■ v. [usu. as adj. **calcined**] reduce, oxidize, or desiccate by roasting or strong heat.
– DERIVATIVES **calcination** n.
– ORIGIN Middle English: from medieval Latin *calcinare*, from Latin *calx* 'lime'.

calcite /ˈkalsʌɪt/ ■ n. a white or colourless mineral consisting of calcium carbonate.
– DERIVATIVES **calcitic** adj.
– ORIGIN C19: from German *Calcit* from Latin *calx* 'lime'.

calcitonin /ˌkalsɪˈtəʊnɪn/ ■ n. Biochemistry a thyroid hormone that has the effect of lowering blood calcium.

calcium ■ n. the chemical element of atomic number 20, a soft grey reactive metal of the alkaline earth metal group. (Symbol: **Ca**)
– ORIGIN C19: from Latin *calx* 'lime'.

calcium carbonate ■ n. a white insoluble compound occurring naturally as chalk, limestone, marble, and calcite, and forming mollusc shells. [$CaCO_3$.]

calcium hydroxide ■ n. a soluble white crystalline compound commonly produced in the form of slaked lime. [$Ca(OH)_2$.]

calcium oxide ■ n. a white caustic alkaline solid commonly produced in the form of quicklime. [CaO.]

calcrete /ˈkalkriːt/ ■ n. Geology a breccia or conglomerate cemented together by calcareous material, formed in soils in semi-arid conditions.
– ORIGIN C20: from CALC- + a shortened form of CONCRETE.

calculable ■ adj. able to be measured or assessed.
– DERIVATIVES **calculability** n. **calculably** adv.

calculate ■ v. **1** determine mathematically. **2** (**calculate on**) include as an essential element in one's plans. **3** intend (an action) to have a particular effect.
– ORIGIN Middle English: from late Latin *calculare* 'count', from *calculus* 'a small pebble (as used on an abacus)'.

calculated ■ adj. done with awareness of the likely consequences.
– DERIVATIVES **calculatedly** adv.

calculating ■ adj. selfishly scheming.
– DERIVATIVES **calculatingly** adv.

calculation ■ n. **1** a mathematical determination of quantity or extent. **2** an assessment of the risks or effects of a course of action.

calculator ■ n. something used for making mathematical

calculations, in particular a small electronic device with a keyboard and a visual display.

calculus /ˈkalkjʊləs/ ■ n. **1** (pl. **calculuses**) (also **infinitesimal calculus**) the branch of mathematics concerned with the determination and properties of derivatives and integrals of functions, by methods based on the summation of infinitesimal differences. ▶ a particular method or system of calculation or reasoning. **2** (pl. **calculi** /-lʌɪ, -liː/) Medicine a concretion of minerals formed in the kidney, gall bladder, or other organ. ▶ another term for TARTAR.
– ORIGIN C17: from Latin, 'small pebble (as used on an abacus)'.

caldera /kɒlˈdɛːrə, -ˈdɪərə/ ■ n. a large volcanic crater, especially one formed by a major eruption leading to the collapse of the mouth of the volcano.
– ORIGIN C17: from late Latin *caldaria* 'boiling pot'.

caldron ■ n. chiefly US variant spelling of CAULDRON.

Caledonian /ˌkalɪˈdəʊnɪən/ ■ adj. (chiefly in names or geographical terms) of or relating to Scotland or the Scottish Highlands. ■ n. humorous or poetic/literary a person from Scotland.
– ORIGIN from *Caledonia*, the Latin name for northern Britain.

calendar /ˈkalɪndə/ ■ n. **1** a chart or series of pages showing the days, weeks, and months of a particular year. **2** a system by which the beginning, length, and subdivisions of the year are fixed. See also JULIAN CALENDAR and GREGORIAN CALENDAR. **3** a list or schedule of special days, events, or activities. ■ v. enter in a calendar.
– DERIVATIVES **calendric** /-ˈlɛndrɪk/ adj. **calendrical** adj.
– ORIGIN Middle English: from Latin *kalendarium* 'account book', from *kalendae* (see CALENDS).

calendar month ■ n. see MONTH.

calendar year ■ n. see YEAR (sense 2).

calender /ˈkalɪndə/ ■ n. a machine in which cloth or paper is pressed by rollers to glaze or smooth it. ■ v. press in such a machine.
– ORIGIN C15: from French *calendre* (n.).

calends /ˈkalɪndz/ (also **kalends**) ■ pl. n. the first day of the month in the ancient Roman calendar.
– ORIGIN Old English: from Old French *calendes*, from Latin *kalendae* 'first day of the month' (when the order of days was proclaimed).

calendula /kəˈlɛndjʊlə/ ■ n. a plant of a genus that includes the common or pot marigold. [Genus *Calendula*.]
– ORIGIN diminutive of *kalendae* (see CALENDS), perhaps because it flowers for most of the year.

calf¹ ■ n. (pl. **calves**) **1** a young bovine animal, especially a domestic cow or bull in its first year. **2** the young of some other large mammals, such as elephants. **3** a floating piece of ice detached from an iceberg.
– DERIVATIVES **calf-like** adj.
– ORIGIN Old English: of Germanic origin.

calf² ■ n. (pl. **calves**) the fleshy part at the back of a person's leg below the knee.
– ORIGIN Middle English: from Old Norse *kálfi*.

calf love ■ n. another term for PUPPY LOVE.

calibrate /ˈkalɪbreɪt/ ■ v. **1** mark (a gauge or instrument) with a standard scale of readings. **2** correlate the readings of (an instrument) with those of a standard. **3** adjust (experimental results) to take external factors into account or to allow comparison with other data.
– DERIVATIVES **calibration** n. **calibrator** n.
– ORIGIN C19: from CALIBRE.

calibre /ˈkalɪbə/ (US **caliber**) ■ n. **1** quality of character or level of ability. ▶ the standard reached by something. **2** the internal diameter of a gun barrel. ▶ the diameter of a bullet, shell, or rocket.
– DERIVATIVES **calibred** adj.
– ORIGIN C16: from Italian *calibro*, perhaps from Arabic *ḵālib* 'mould'.

calico /ˈkalɪkəʊ/ ■ n. (pl. **-oes** or US also **-os**) a type of plain white or unbleached cotton cloth. ▶ chiefly N. Amer. printed cotton fabric. ■ adj. chiefly N. Amer. (of an animal, typically a cat) multicoloured or piebald.
– ORIGIN C16: alteration of *Calicut*, a seaport in SW India where the fabric originated.

California poppy ■ n. an annual poppy native to western North America, cultivated for its brilliant yellow or orange flowers. [*Eschscholtzia californica*.]

californium /ˌkalɪˈfɔːnɪəm/ ■ n. the chemical element of atomic number 98, an unstable radioactive metal of the actinide series. (Symbol: **Cf**)
– ORIGIN 1950s: named after *California University* (where it was first made).

caliper /ˈkalɪpə/ (also **calliper**) ■ n. **1** an instrument for measuring external or internal dimensions, typically with two hinged legs and in-turned or out-turned points. **2** a motor-vehicle or bicycle brake consisting of two or more hinged components. **3** a metal support for a person's leg.
– ORIGIN C16: prob. an alteration of CALIBRE.

caliph /ˈkeɪlɪf, ˈka-/ ■ n. historical the chief Muslim civil and religious ruler, regarded as the successor of Muhammad.
– DERIVATIVES **caliphate** n.
– ORIGIN Middle English: from Old French *caliphe*, from Arabic *ḵalīfa* 'deputy (of God)'.

calisthenics ■ pl. n. US spelling of CALLISTHENICS.

calix ■ n. variant spelling of CALYX.

calk ■ n. & v. US spelling of CAULK.

call ■ v. **1** cry out to (someone) in order to summon them or attract their attention. ▶ telephone. **2** pay a brief visit. ▶ (**call for**) stop to collect. ▶ (**call at**) (of a train or coach) stop at (a specified station) on a particular route. **3** give a specified name; address by a specified name, title, etc. ▶ consider or describe (someone or something) as being: *he's the only person I would call a friend*. **4** fix a date or time for (a meeting, strike, or election). ▶ predict the result of (an election or a vote). **5** Computing cause the execution of (a subroutine). **6** bring (a witness) into court to give evidence. **7** dated inspire or urge to do something. **8** Bridge make (a particular bid) during the auction: *her partner called 6♠*. **9** Cricket (of an umpire) no-ball (a bowler) for throwing. ■ n. **1** a cry made as a summons or to attract attention. ▶ a telephone communication. **2** (**a call for**) an appeal or demand for. ▶ [usu. with neg.] a demand or need for: *there is little call for antique furniture*. **3** a vocation: *his call to be a disciple*. **4** a brief visit. **5** a shout by an official in a game indicating that the ball has gone out of play or that a rule has been breached. **6** Bridge a bid, response, or double.
– PHRASES **at call** see *on call* (sense 2). **call attention to** cause people to notice. **call collect** N. Amer. make a telephone call reversing the charges. **call something into** (or **in**) **question** cast doubt on something. **call of nature** euphemistic a need to urinate or defecate. **call the shots** (or **tune**) take the initiative in deciding how something should be done. **call someone/thing to order** ask those present at a meeting to be silent so that business may proceed. **on call 1** available to provide a professional service if necessary, but not formally on duty. **2** (of money lent) repayable on demand.
– PHRASAL VERBS **call for** require; demand. **call someone/thing down** cause someone or something to appear or occur. **call something in** require payment of a loan or promise of money. **call something off** cancel an event or agreement. **call on/upon** have recourse to. **call someone up** summon someone to serve in the army or to play in a team. **call something up** summon for use something that is stored or kept available.
– DERIVATIVES **caller** n.
– ORIGIN Old English, from Old Norse *kalla* 'summon loudly'.

calla lily ■ n. chiefly N. Amer. another term for ARUM LILY.
– ORIGIN C19.

Callanetics /ˌkaləˈnɛtɪks/ ■ pl. n. [treated as sing. or pl.] trademark a system of physical exercises based on small repeated movements.
– ORIGIN C20: named after *Callan* Pinckney, the American deviser of the system.

callback ■ n. **1** chiefly N. Amer. an invitation to return for a second audition or interview. **2** a telephone call made to return one that someone has received.

call centre ■ n. an office in which large numbers of telephone calls are handled, especially one providing the customer services functions of a large organization.

call changes ▪ pl. n. Bell-ringing changes rung in response to spoken commands.

call girl ▪ n. a female prostitute who accepts appointments by telephone.

calligraph /ˈkalɪɡrɑːf/ ▪ v. write decoratively.

calligraphy ▪ n. decorative handwriting or handwritten lettering. ▸ the art of producing this.
– DERIVATIVES **calligrapher** n. **calligraphic** adj. **calligraphist** n.
– ORIGIN C17: from Greek, from *kalligraphos* 'person who writes beautifully'.

calling ▪ n. a strong urge towards a particular way of life or career; a vocation. ▸ a profession or occupation.

calling card ▪ n. 1 chiefly N. Amer. a visiting card or business card. 2 N. Amer. a phonecard or telephone charge card.

calliper /ˈkalɪpə/ ▪ n. variant spelling of CALIPER.

callistemon /ˌkalɪˈstiːmən/ ▪ n. a plant of a genus that comprises the bottlebrushes. [Genus *Callistemon*.]
– ORIGIN from Greek *kallos* 'beauty' + *stēmōn* 'thread or stamen'.

callisthenics /ˌkalɪsˈθɛnɪks/ (US **calisthenics**) ▪ pl. n. gymnastic exercises to achieve bodily fitness and grace of movement.
– DERIVATIVES **callisthenic** adj.
– ORIGIN C19: from Greek *kallos* 'beauty' + *sthenos* 'strength'.

call money ▪ n. money loaned by a bank or other institution which is repayable on demand.

call option ▪ n. Stock Exchange an option to buy assets at an agreed price on or before a particular date.

callous ▪ adj. insensitive and cruel. ▪ n. variant spelling of CALLUS.
– DERIVATIVES **callously** adv. **callousness** n.
– ORIGIN Middle English: from Latin *callosus* 'hard-skinned'.

callow ▪ adj. (of a young person) inexperienced and immature.
– DERIVATIVES **callowly** adv. **callowness** n.
– ORIGIN Old English *calu* 'bald', of West Germanic origin, prob. from Latin *calvus* 'bald, unfledged'.

call sign (also **call signal**) ▪ n. a message, code, or tune that is broadcast by radio to identify the broadcaster or transmitter.

callus /ˈkaləs/ (also **callous**) ▪ n. 1 a thickened and hardened part of the skin or soft tissue, especially one caused by friction. ▸ Medicine the bony healing tissue which forms around the ends of broken bone. 2 Botany a hard formation of tissue, especially new tissue formed over a wound.
– DERIVATIVES **callused** adj.
– ORIGIN C16: from Latin *callum* 'hardened skin'.

calm ▪ adj. 1 not showing or feeling nervousness, anger, or other emotions. 2 peaceful and undisturbed. ▪ n. 1 the state or fact of being peaceful or tranquil. 2 (**calms**) an area of the sea without wind. ▪ v. (often **calm down**) make or become tranquil and quiet.
– DERIVATIVES **calmly** adv. **calmness** n.
– ORIGIN Middle English: from Greek *kauma* 'heat (of the day)'.

calmative /ˈkɑːmətɪv, ˈkal-/ ▪ adj. (of a drug) having a sedative effect. ▪ n. a calmative drug.

calmodulin /kalˈmɒdjʊlɪn/ ▪ n. Biochemistry a protein which binds calcium and is involved in regulating a variety of activities in cells.
– ORIGIN 1970s: from *cal(cium)* + *modul(ate)*.

calomel /ˈkaləmɛl/ ▪ n. mercurous chloride, a white powder formerly used as a purgative. [Hg_2Cl_2.]
– ORIGIN C17: perhaps from Greek *kalos* 'beautiful' + *melas* 'black' (perhaps because orig. obtained from a black mixture of mercury and mercuric chloride).

Calor gas /ˈkalə/ ▪ n. Brit. trademark liquefied butane stored under pressure in portable containers, used as a substitute for mains gas and in camping.
– ORIGIN 1930s: *Calor* from Latin *calor* 'heat'.

caloric /kəˈlɒrɪk, ˈkalərɪk/ ▪ adj. chiefly N. Amer. or technical of or relating to heat; calorific. ▪ n. Physics a hypothetical fluid substance formerly thought to be responsible for the phenomenon of heat.
– ORIGIN C18: from French *calorique*, from Latin *calor* 'heat'.

calorie ▪ n. (pl. **-ies**) 1 (also **small calorie**) the energy needed to raise the temperature of 1 gram of water through 1 °C (now usually defined as 4.1868 joules). 2 (also **large calorie**) the energy needed to raise the temperature of 1 kilogram of water through 1 °C, equal to one thousand small calories and often used to measure the energy value of foods.
– ORIGIN C19: from Latin *calor* 'heat'.

calorific ▪ adj. chiefly Brit. relating to the amount of energy contained in food or fuel. ▸ high in calories.
– DERIVATIVES **calorifically** adv.

calorific value ▪ n. the energy contained in a fuel or food (now usually expressed in joules per kilogram), determined by burning a specified amount.

calorimeter /ˌkaləˈrɪmɪtə/ ▪ n. an apparatus for measuring the amount of heat involved in a chemical reaction or other process.
– DERIVATIVES **calorimetric** adj. **calorimetry** n.

calque /kalk/ Linguistics ▪ n. another term for LOAN TRANSLATION. ▪ v. (**be calqued on**) be a calque of.
– ORIGIN 1930s: from French, 'copy, tracing'.

caltrop /ˈkaltrəp/ (also **caltrap**) ▪ n. 1 a spiked metal ball thrown on the ground to impede wheeled vehicles or (formerly) cavalry horses. 2 a creeping plant with woody carpels that typically have hard spines. ▸ another term for DEVIL'S THORN. 3 (also **water caltrop**) another term for WATER CHESTNUT (in sense 2).
– ORIGIN Old English *calcatrippe*, from medieval Latin *calcatrippa*, from *calx* 'heel' or *calcare* 'to tread' + a word rel. to TRAP.

calumet /ˈkaljʊmɛt/ ▪ n. a North American Indian peace pipe.
– ORIGIN C17: from late Latin *calamellus* 'little reed'.

calumniate /kəˈlʌmnɪeɪt/ ▪ v. formal make false and defamatory statements about.
– DERIVATIVES **calumniation** n. **calumniator** n.

calumny /ˈkaləmni/ ▪ n. (pl. **-ies**) the making of false and defamatory statements about someone. ▪ v. (**-ies, -ied**) formal calumniate.
– DERIVATIVES **calumnious** /kəˈlʌmnɪəs/ adj.
– ORIGIN Middle English: from Latin *calumnia*.

calutron /ˈkaljuːtrɒn/ ▪ n. a device that uses large electromagnets to separate uranium isotopes from uranium ore.
– ORIGIN 1940s: from *Cal(ifornia) U(niversity) (cyclo)tron*.

Calvados /ˈkalvədɒs/ ▪ n. apple brandy, traditionally made in the Calvados region of Normandy, France.

calve ▪ v. 1 give birth to a calf. 2 (of a mass of ice) split off from an iceberg or glacier.
– ORIGIN Old English, from *cælf* 'calf'.

calves plural form of CALF[1], CALF[2].

Calvinism ▪ n. (in Christianity) the Protestant theological system of John Calvin (1509–64) and his successors, a development of Lutheranism and centring on the doctrine of predestination.
– DERIVATIVES **Calvinist** n. **Calvinistic** adj. **Calvinistical** adj.

calx /kalks/ ▪ n. (pl. **calces** /ˈkalsiːz/) Chemistry, archaic a powdery metallic oxide formed when an ore or mineral has been heated.
– ORIGIN Middle English: from Latin, 'lime', prob. from Greek *khalix* 'pebble, limestone'.

calypso /kəˈlɪpsəʊ/ ▪ n. (pl. **-os**) a kind of West Indian music or song in syncopated African rhythm, typically with words improvised on a topical theme.
– DERIVATIVES **calypsonian** adj. & n.
– ORIGIN 1930s.

calyx /ˈkalɪks, ˈkeɪ-/ (also **calix**) ▪ n. (pl. **calyces** /-lɪsiːz/ or **calyxes**) 1 Botany the sepals of a flower, typically forming a whorl that encloses the petals and forms a protective layer around a flower in bud. 2 Zoology a cup-like cavity or structure, in particular part of the pelvis of a mammalian kidney.

– ORIGIN C17: from Greek *kalux* 'case of a bud, husk', rel. to *kaluptein* 'to hide'.

calzone /kalˈtsəʊneɪ, -niː/ ■ n. (pl. **calzoni** or **calzones**) a type of pizza that is folded in half before cooking to contain a filling.
– ORIGIN Italian dialect, prob. a special use of *calzone* 'trouser leg'.

CAM ■ abbrev. computer-aided manufacturing.

cam ■ n. 1 a projection on a rotating part in machinery, designed to make sliding contact with another part while rotating and impart reciprocal or variable motion to it. 2 short for **CAMSHAFT**.
– ORIGIN C18: from Dutch *kam* 'comb'.

camaraderie /ˌkaməˈrɑːd(ə)ri, -riː/ ■ n. mutual trust and friendship.
– ORIGIN C19: from French, from *camarade* 'comrade'.

camber /ˈkambə/ ■ n. 1 a slightly convex or arched shape of a road or other horizontal surface. ▸ a tilt built into a road at a bend or curve. 2 the slight sideways inclination of the front wheels of a motor vehicle. 3 Aeronautics the extent of curvature of a section of an aerofoil.
– DERIVATIVES **cambered** adj.
– ORIGIN Middle English: from Old French *cambre*, from Latin *camurus* 'curved inwards'.

cambium /ˈkambɪəm/ ■ n. (pl. **cambia** or **cambiums**) Botany a cellular plant tissue from which phloem, xylem, or cork grows by division.
– DERIVATIVES **cambial** adj.
– ORIGIN C16: from medieval Latin, 'change, exchange'.

Cambodian ■ n. 1 a native or national of Cambodia, or a person of Cambodian descent. 2 another term for **KHMER** (the language). ■ adj. of or relating to Cambodia.

cambozola /ˌkambəˈzəʊlə/ (also **cabazola**) ■ n. trademark a type of German blue soft cheese with a rind like Camembert.
– ORIGIN blend of **CAMEMBERT** and **GORGONZOLA**.

Cambrian /ˈkambrɪən/ ■ adj. 1 (chiefly in names or geographical terms) Welsh. 2 Geology relating to or denoting the first period in the Palaeozoic era (between the Precambrian aeon and the Ordovician period, about 570 to 510 million years ago), a time when there was extensive invertebrate life.
– ORIGIN C17: from Latin *Cambria* 'Wales', from Welsh *Cymru* 'Wales'.

cambric /ˈkambrɪk, ˈkeɪm-/ ■ n. a lightweight, closely woven white linen or cotton fabric.
– ORIGIN Middle English: from *Kamerijk*, Flemish form of *Cambrai*, a town in northern France, where it was orig. made.

camcorder ■ n. a portable combined video camera and video recorder.

came¹ past tense of **COME**.

came² ■ n. each of a number of strips forming a framework for enclosing a pane of glass, especially in a leaded window.
– ORIGIN C16.

camel ■ n. 1 a large, long-necked, mainly domesticated ungulate mammal of arid country, with long slender legs, broad cushioned feet, and either one or two humps on the back. [*Camelus dromedarius* (Arabian camel, N. Africa and SW Asia, with one hump) and *C. ferus* (Bactrian camel, central Asia, two humps).] 2 a fabric made from camel hair. 3 an apparatus for raising a sunken ship, consisting of one or more watertight chests to provide buoyancy.
– ORIGIN Old English, from Latin *camelus*, from Greek *kamēlos*, of Semitic origin.

camel cricket ■ n. a wingless humpbacked insect related to the grasshoppers, typically living in caves or holes. [Family Rhaphidophoridae: many species.]

cameleer /ˌkaməˈlɪə/ ■ n. a person who controls or rides a camel.

camel hair (also **camel's hair**) ■ n. 1 a fabric made from the hair of a camel. 2 fine, soft hair from a squirrel's tail, used in artists' brushes.

camelid /kəˈmiːlɪd, ˈkamɪlɪd/ ■ n. Zoology a mammal of a family (Camelidae) comprising the camels together with the llama and its relatives.

camellia /kəˈmiːlɪə, -ˈmɛlɪə/ ■ n. an evergreen East Asian shrub related to the tea plant, grown for its showy flowers and shiny leaves. [*Camellia japonica* and related species.]
– ORIGIN named by Linnaeus after the C17 Moravian botanist Joseph Kamel (Latinized as *Camellus*).

camelopard /ˈkamɪlə(ʊ)pɑːd, kəˈmɛləpɑːd/ ■ n. archaic a giraffe.
– ORIGIN Middle English: from Greek *kamēlopardalis*, from *kamēlos* 'camel' + *pardalis*, from *pardos* 'leopard'.

Camelot /ˈkamɪlɒt/ ■ n. a place associated with glittering romance and optimism.
– ORIGIN the place where King Arthur held his legendary court.

camel's foot ■ n. a spreading deciduous tree with kidney-shaped leaves and purple flowers. [*Bauhinia purpurea*.]

camel thorn ■ n. a spiny leguminous shrub occurring in arid country. [*Acacia giraffae* (southern Africa) and *Alhagi camelorum* (Middle East).]

Camembert /ˈkaməmbɛː/ ■ n. a kind of rich, soft, creamy cheese with a whitish rind, originally made near Camembert in Normandy, France.

cameo /ˈkamɪəʊ/ ■ n. (pl. **-os**) 1 a piece of jewellery consisting of a portrait in profile carved in relief on a background of a different colour. 2 a short piece of writing which neatly encapsulates something. 3 a small distinctive part in a play or film, played by a distinguished actor.
– ORIGIN Middle English: from Old French *camahieu*, from medieval Latin *cammaeus*.

camera¹ ■ n. a device for recording visual images in the form of photographs, cinema film, or video signals.
– PHRASES **on** (or **off**) **camera** while being (or not being) filmed or televised.
– DERIVATIVES **cameraman** n. **camerawork** n.

HISTORY
The two meanings of the word **camera**, though apparently quite different, are closely linked historically, both deriving from Latin *camera*, 'vaulted roof or chamber', also the root of English **chamber**. **Camera** entered English in the 17th century in the sense 'legislative chamber', and is still used in the phrase **in camera**, now meaning 'in private chambers'. The application of the word to the device for taking photographs dates from the earliest years of photography; the precursor of the cameras of today was the **camera obscura** or 'dark chamber'.

camera² ■ n. [in names] a chamber or round building.
– PHRASES **in camera** chiefly Law in private, in particular taking place in the private chambers of a judge, with the press and public excluded.
– ORIGIN C17: from Latin, 'vault, arched chamber'.

camera obscura /ɒbsˈkjʊərə/ ■ n. 1 a darkened box with a convex lens or aperture for projecting the image of an external object on to a screen inside. 2 a small round building with a rotating angled mirror at the apex of the roof, projecting an image of the landscape on to a horizontal surface inside.
– ORIGIN C18: from Latin, 'dark chamber'.

camera phone ■ n. a cellphone with a built-in camera.

camera-ready ■ adj. Printing in the right form to be reproduced photographically on to a printing plate.

Cameroonian /ˌkaməˈruːnɪən/ ■ n. a native or inhabitant of Cameroon, a country on the west coast of Africa. ■ adj. of or relating to Cameroon.

camisole /ˈkamɪsəʊl/ ■ n. a woman's loose-fitting undergarment for the upper body.
– ORIGIN C19: from Italian *camiciola* or from Spanish *camisola*, both from late Latin *camisia* 'shirt or nightgown'.

camomile ■ n. variant spelling of **CHAMOMILE**.

camouflage /ˈkaməflɑːʒ/ ■ n. 1 the disguising of military personnel and equipment by painting or covering them to make them blend in with their surroundings. ▸ the clothing or materials used for such a purpose. 2 the natural colouring or form of an animal which enables it to

camp

blend in with its surroundings. ■ v. hide or disguise by means of camouflage.
– ORIGIN First World War: from French, from *camoufler* 'to disguise'.

camp[1] ■ n. **1** a place with temporary accommodation used by soldiers, refugees, or travelling people. ▸ a complex of buildings for holiday accommodation. **2** (also **summer camp**) N. Amer. a summer holiday programme for children, offering a range of activities. **3** the supporters of a particular party or doctrine regarded collectively. **4** Brit. Archaeology a prehistoric enclosed or fortified site, especially an Iron Age hill fort. **5** S. African a fenced field or enclosed area for grazing. ■ v. **1** lodge temporarily, especially in a tent or caravan while on holiday. **2** S. African divide (land) and enclose with fences.
– PHRASES **break camp** take down a tent or the tents of an encampment ready to leave.
– ORIGIN C16: from French *camp*, *champ*, from Latin *campus* 'level ground'.

camp[2] informal ■ adj. (of a man) ostentatiously and extravagantly effeminate. ▸ deliberately exaggerated and theatrical in style. ■ n. camp behaviour or style. ■ v. (usu. **camp it up**) (of a man) behave in a camp way.
– DERIVATIVES **campily** adv. **campiness** n. **campy** adj.
– ORIGIN C20.

campaign ■ n. **1** a series of military operations intended to achieve an objective in a particular area. **2** an organized course of action to achieve a goal. ■ v. work in an organized and active way towards a goal.
– DERIVATIVES **campaigner** n.
– ORIGIN C17 (denoting a tract of open country): from French *campagne*, from late Latin *campania*, from *campus* (see **CAMP**[1]).

campanile /ˌkampəˈniːleɪ/ ■ n. a bell tower, especially a free-standing one.
– ORIGIN C17: from Italian, from *campana* 'bell'.

campanology /ˌkampəˈnɒlədʒi/ ■ n. the art or practice of bell-ringing.
– DERIVATIVES **campanological** adj. **campanologist** n.
– ORIGIN C19: from modern Latin *campanologia*, from Latin *campana* 'bell'.

campanula /kamˈpanjʊlə/ ■ n. another term for BELLFLOWER.
– ORIGIN diminutive of late Latin *campana* 'bell'.

campanulate /kamˈpanjʊlət/ ■ adj. Botany (of a flower) bell-shaped, as in a campanula.

Campari /kamˈpɑːri/ ■ n. trademark a pinkish aperitif flavoured with bitters.

camp bed ■ n. a folding portable bed.

camper ■ n. **1** a person who spends a holiday in a tent or holiday camp. **2** (also **camper van**) a large motor vehicle with living accommodation.

campesino /ˌkampəˈsiːnəʊ/ ■ n. (pl. **-os** /-əʊz/) (in Spanish-speaking countries) a peasant farmer.
– ORIGIN from Spanish.

campfire ■ n. an open-air fire in a camp.

camp follower ■ n. **1** a civilian working in or attached to a military camp. **2** a person who associates with a group without being a full member of it.

campground ■ n. North American term for CAMPSITE.

camphor /ˈkamfə/ ■ n. a white volatile crystalline substance with an aromatic smell and bitter taste, occurring in certain essential oils.
– ORIGIN Middle English: from Old French *camphore* or medieval Latin *camphora*, from Sanskrit *karpūra*.

camphorate ■ v. impregnate or treat with camphor.

camphor tree ■ n. an East Asian tree, the chief natural source of camphor. [*Cinnamomum camphora*.]

campion /ˈkampɪən/ ■ n. a plant of the pink family, typically having pink or white flowers with notched petals. [Genera *Silene* and *Lychnis*.]
– ORIGIN C16: perhaps rel. to CHAMPION, applied to a plant of this kind said to have been used for victors' garlands in ancient times.

campsite ■ n. a place used for camping, especially one equipped for holidaymakers.

campus ■ n. (pl. **campuses**) the grounds and buildings of a university or college. ▸ N. Amer. the grounds of a college, school, hospital, or other institution.
– ORIGIN C18 (orig. US): from Latin *campus* (see **CAMP**[1]).

campylobacter /ˈkampɪləʊˌbaktə, ˌkampɪləʊˈbaktə/ ■ n. a bacterium of a genus including species responsible for abortion in animals and food poisoning in humans. [Genus *Campylobacter*.]
– ORIGIN modern Latin, from Greek *kampulos* 'bent' + BACTERIUM.

camshaft /ˈkamʃɑːft/ ■ n. a shaft with one or more cams attached to it, especially one operating the valves in an internal-combustion engine.

camwood ■ n. the hard red wood of the African padauk tree.
– ORIGIN C17: prob. from Temne *k'am* + WOOD.

can[1] ■ modal v. (3rd sing. present **can**; past **could**) **1** be able to. ▸ [with neg. or in questions] used to express doubt or surprise: *he can't have finished*. ▸ used to indicate that something is typically the case: *he could be very moody*. **2** be permitted to.
– ORIGIN Old English *cunnan* 'know'.

can[2] ■ n. **1** a cylindrical metal container, in particular one in which food or drink is hermetically sealed for storage over long periods. ▸ S. African a bottle for wine, usually containing two litres. **2** (**the can**) N. Amer. informal prison. **3** (**the can**) N. Amer. informal the toilet. ■ v. (**canned**, **canning**) **1** preserve in a can. **2** N. Amer. informal dismiss from a job or reject as inadequate. **3** [as adj. **canned**] referring to the commercial hunting of tame or drugged animals, especially lions, within an enclosed area. ▸ denoting animals hunted in this way.
– PHRASES **a can of worms** a complicated matter likely to prove awkward or embarrassing. **in the can** informal on tape or film and ready to be broadcast or released.
– DERIVATIVES **canner** n.
– ORIGIN Old English, of Germanic origin or from late Latin *canna*.

Canaanite /ˈkeɪnənʌɪt/ ■ n. a native or inhabitant of Canaan, the biblical name for the area of ancient Palestine west of the River Jordan, the Promised Land of the Israelites.

Canada balsam ■ n. a yellowish resin obtained from the balsam fir (*Abies balsamea*), used for mounting specimens on microscope slides.

Canada goose ■ n. a common brownish-grey North American goose, introduced in Britain and elsewhere. [*Branta canadensis*.]

Canadian ■ n. a native or inhabitant of Canada. ■ adj. of or relating to Canada.
– DERIVATIVES **Canadianism** n.

canal ■ n. **1** an artificial waterway allowing the passage of boats inland or conveying water for irrigation. **2** a tubular duct in a plant or animal conveying food, liquid, or air.
– ORIGIN Middle English: from Old French, alteration of *chanel* 'channel', from Latin *canalis* 'pipe, channel', from *canna* 'cane'.

canalize /ˈkan(ə)lʌɪz/ (also **-ise**) ■ v. **1** convert (a river) into a navigable canal. **2** convey through a duct or channel. **3** give a direction or purpose to.
– DERIVATIVES **canalization** (also **-isation**) n.
– ORIGIN C19: from French *canaliser*, from *canal* (see CANAL).

canapé /ˈkanəpeɪ/ ■ n. a small piece of bread or pastry with a savoury topping, often served with drinks.
– ORIGIN from French.

canard /kəˈnɑːd, ˈkanɑːd/ ■ n. **1** an unfounded rumour or story. **2** a small wing-like projection on an aircraft forward of the main wing, for extra stability or control.
– ORIGIN C19: from French, 'duck', also 'hoax', from Old French *caner* 'to quack'.

canary ■ n. (pl. **-ies**) **1** a bright yellow finch with a melodious song, popular as a cage bird. [*Serinus canaria* (Canary Islands, Azores, and Madeira) and related species in Africa.] **2** (also **canary yellow**) a bright yellow colour.
– ORIGIN C16: from Spanish *canario* 'canary' or 'person from the Canary Islands'.

canary creeper ■ n. a climbing plant bearing bright yellow flowers. [*Tropaeolum peregrinum* (South America) and *Senecio tamoides* (southern Africa).]

canary grass ■ n. a tall grass of NW Africa and the Canary Islands, grown for its seeds which are fed to cage birds. [Genus *Phalaris*: several species.]

canasta /kəˈnastə/ ■ n. a card game resembling rummy, using two packs and usually played by two pairs of partners. ▸ a meld of seven cards in this game.
– ORIGIN 1940s: from Spanish (of Uruguayan origin), 'basket', from Latin *canistrum* (see CANISTER).

cancan ■ n. a lively, high-kicking stage dance originating in 19th-century Parisian music halls and performed by women in long skirts and petticoats.
– ORIGIN C19: from French, child's word for *canard* 'duck', from Old French *caner* 'to quack'.

cancel ■ v. (**cancelled, cancelling**; US also **canceled, canceling**) **1** decide that (a planned event) will not take place. ▸ annul or revoke: *his visa had been cancelled*. **2** mark or tear (a ticket or stamp) to show that it has been used or invalidated. **3** (often **cancel something out**) (of a factor or circumstance) neutralize or negate the effect of (another). **4** Mathematics delete (an equal factor) from both sides of an equation or from the numerator and denominator of a fraction. ■ n. **1** a mark made on a postage stamp to show that it has been used. **2** US (in music) a natural sign (c).
– DERIVATIVES **cancellation** n. **canceller** n.
– ORIGIN Middle English: from Old French *canceller*, from Latin, from *cancelli* 'crossbars'.

Cancer ■ n. **1** Astronomy a constellation (the Crab), said to represent a crab crushed under the foot of Hercules. **2** Astrology the fourth sign of the zodiac, which the sun enters at the northern summer solstice (about 21 June).
– DERIVATIVES **Cancerian** /-ˈsɪərɪən, -ˈsɛːrɪən/ n. & adj.
– ORIGIN from Latin.

cancer ■ n. **1** a disease caused by an uncontrolled division of abnormal cells in a part of the body. ▸ a malignant growth or tumour resulting from such a division of cells. **2** something evil or destructive that is hard to contain or eradicate.
– DERIVATIVES **cancerous** adj.
– ORIGIN Old English, from Latin, 'crab or creeping ulcer', translating Greek *karkinos*, said to have been applied to tumours because the swollen veins around them resembled the limbs of a crab.

cancer bush ■ n. a southern African shrub which bears bright red pea-shaped flowers and inflated pods, used medicinally. [*Sutherlandia frutescens* and related species.]

candela /kanˈdelə, -ˈdiːlə, ˈkandɪlə/ (abbrev.: **cd**) ■ n. Physics the SI unit of luminous intensity.
– ORIGIN 1950s: from Latin, 'candle'.

candelabra tree ■ n. a tree with upward-curving boughs, resembling a candelabrum. [Genus *Euphorbia* (Africa) and *Araucaria angustifolia* (S. America).]

candelabrum /ˌkandɪˈlɑːbrəm, -ˈleɪ-/ ■ n. (pl. **candelabra** /-brə/) a large branched candlestick or holder for several candles or lamps.
– ORIGIN C19: from Latin, from *candela* (see CANDLE).

USAGE
Based on the Latin forms, the correct singular is **candelabrum** and the correct plural is **candelabra**, but these forms are often not observed in practice: the singular form is assumed to be **candelabra** and hence its plural is interpreted as **candelabras**.

candid ■ adj. **1** truthful and straightforward; frank. **2** (of a photograph or film) taken informally, especially without the subject's knowledge.
– DERIVATIVES **candidly** adv. **candidness** n.
– ORIGIN C17: from Latin *candidus* cf. CANDOUR.

candida /ˈkandɪdə/ ■ n. a yeast-like parasitic fungus that sometimes causes thrush. [Genus *Candida*.]
– ORIGIN from Latin *candidus* 'white'.

candidate /ˈkandɪdeɪt, -dət/ ■ n. **1** a person who applies for a job or is nominated for election. **2** a person taking an examination. **3** a person or thing suitable for or likely to receive a particular fate, treatment, or position.
– DERIVATIVES **candidacy** n. **candidature** n. (chiefly Brit.)
– ORIGIN C17: from Latin *candidatus* 'white-robed', also denoting a candidate for office (who traditionally wore a white toga), from *candidus* 'white'.

candidate attorney ■ n. S. African a trainee articled to a firm of attorneys or performing supervised community service at a law clinic.

candidate officer ■ n. chiefly S. African a trainee officer in the South African army, air force, or police.

candidiasis /ˌkandɪˈdʌɪəsɪs/ ■ n. infection with candida, especially as causing oral or vaginal thrush.

candle ■ n. **1** a cylinder of wax or tallow with a central wick which is lit to produce light as it burns. **2** (also **international candle**) Physics a unit of luminous intensity, superseded by the candela.
– PHRASES **be unable to hold a candle to** informal be not nearly as good as. **(the game's) not worth the candle** the potential advantages to be gained from doing something do not justify the cost or trouble involved.
– ORIGIN Old English, from Latin *candela*, from *candere* 'be white or glisten'.

candleberry ■ n. (pl. **-ies**) a bayberry, or other tree or shrub whose berries yield wax.

candlelight ■ n. dim light provided by a candle or candles.
– DERIVATIVES **candlelit** adj.

Candlemas /ˈkand(ə)lməs, -məs/ ■ n. a Christian festival held on 2 February to commemorate the purification of the Virgin Mary (after childbirth, according to Jewish law) and the presentation of Christ in the Temple.
– ORIGIN Old English (see CANDLE, MASS).

candlepower ■ n. illuminating power expressed in candelas or candles.

candlestick ■ n. a support or holder for one or more candles.

candlewick ■ n. a thick, soft cotton fabric with a raised, tufted pattern. ▸ the yarn used to make such a fabric.

can-do ■ adj. informal willing or determined to take action and achieve results: *a can-do attitude*.

candour (US **candor**) ■ n. the quality of being open and honest.
– ORIGIN Middle English (in the sense 'whiteness', hence 'purity, honesty'): from Latin *candor*.

candy ■ n. (pl. **-ies**) (also **sugar candy**) **1** N. Amer. sweets; confectionery. **2** sugar crystallized by repeated boiling and slow evaporation. ■ v. (**-ies, -ied**) [often as adj. **candied**] preserve (fruit) by coating and impregnating it with a sugar syrup.
– ORIGIN C17: as n. from Middle English *sugar-candy*, from French *sucre candi* 'crystallized sugar', from Arabic *sukkar* 'sugar' + *kandī* 'candied'.

candy cane ■ n. N. Amer. a stick of striped sweet rock with a curved end, resembling a walking stick.

candyfloss ■ n. **1** a mass of pink or white fluffy spun sugar wrapped round a stick. **2** something worthless or insubstantial.

candyman ■ n. (pl. **-men**) N. Amer. informal a person who sells illegal drugs.

candy-striped ■ adj. patterned with alternating stripes of white and another colour, typically pink.
– DERIVATIVES **candy-stripe** adj. & n.

candytuft ■ n. a plant with small heads of white, pink, or purple flowers, grown as a garden or rockery plant. [Genus *Iberis*.]
– ORIGIN C17: from *Candy* (obsolete form of *Candia*, former name of Crete) + TUFT.

cane ■ n. **1** the hollow jointed stem of tall reeds, grasses, etc., especially bamboo or the slender, pliant stem of plants such as rattan. ▸ a woody stem of a raspberry or related plant. **2** a length of cane or a slender stick used as a support for plants, a walking stick, or an instrument of punishment. **3** (also **cane spirit**) chiefly S. African a spirit distilled from sugar cane. ■ v. **1** beat with a cane as a punishment. **2** [usu. as adj. **caned**] make or repair (furniture) with cane.
– DERIVATIVES **caner** n.
– ORIGIN Middle English: from Latin *canna*, from Greek *kannē*, of Semitic origin.

cane rat ■ n. a large rat-like African rodent found in wetlands south of the Sahara. [Genus *Thryonomys*.]

cane toad ■ n. a large brown toad of tropical America, introduced elsewhere for pest control. [*Bufo marinus*.]

canid /'kanɪd/ ■ n. Zoology a mammal of the dog family (Canidae).

canine /'keɪnʌɪn, 'ka-/ ■ adj. of, relating to, or resembling a dog. ■ n. 1 a dog or other animal of the dog family. 2 (also **canine tooth**) a pointed tooth between the incisors and premolars, often greatly enlarged in carnivores.
– ORIGIN Middle English: from Latin *caninus*, from *canis* 'dog'.

caning ■ n. 1 a beating with a cane as a punishment. 2 informal a resounding defeat.

canister ■ n. a round or cylindrical container used for storing food, chemicals, rolls of film, etc.
– ORIGIN C15: from Latin *canistrum*, from Greek *kanastron* 'wicker basket', from *kanna* (see CANE).

canker ■ n. 1 a destructive fungal disease of trees that results in damage to the bark. ▶ an open lesion in plant tissue caused by infection or injury. ▶ fungal rot in parsnips, tomatoes, or other vegetables. 2 an ulcerous condition of an animal, especially an inflammation of the ear caused by a mite infestation. ▶ chiefly N. Amer. a small ulcer of the mouth or lips. ■ v. 1 become infected with canker. 2 [usu. as adj. **cankered**] infect with a pervasive and corrupting bitterness.
– DERIVATIVES **cankerous** adj.
– ORIGIN Middle English: from Old French *chancre*, from Latin *cancer* (see CANCER).

canna /'kanə/ ■ n. a lily-like tropical American plant with bright flowers and ornamental strap-like leaves. [Genus *Canna*: several species.]
– ORIGIN from Latin *canna* (see CANE).

cannabinol /'kanəbɪˌnɒl, kə'nab-/ ■ n. Chemistry a crystalline compound whose derivatives, especially THC, are the active constituents of cannabis.
– DERIVATIVES **cannabinoid** n.

cannabis ■ n. 1 a dried preparation or resinous extract made from a plant, used (generally illegally) as a psychotropic drug (chiefly in cigarettes). 2 the plant from which this substance comes, also used to produce hemp fibre. [*Cannabis sativa*.]
– ORIGIN from Greek *kannabis*.

canned ■ adj. 1 preserved in a sealed can. 2 informal, chiefly derogatory (of music, applause, etc.) pre-recorded.

cannellini bean /ˌkanə'liːni/ ■ n. a kidney-shaped bean of a medium-sized creamy-white variety.
– ORIGIN Italian *cannellini* 'small tubes'.

cannelloni /ˌkanə'ləʊni/ ■ pl. n. rolls of pasta stuffed with a meat or vegetable mixture, usually cooked in a cheese sauce.
– ORIGIN Italian, 'large tubes', from *cannello* 'tube'.

cannelure /'kan(ə)ljʊə/ ■ n. a groove round the cylindrical part of a bullet.
– ORIGIN C18: from French, from *canneler* 'provide with a channel', from *canne* 'reed, cane'.

cannery ■ n. (pl. **-ies**) a factory where food is canned.

cannibal ■ n. a person who eats the flesh of other human beings. ▶ an animal that eats the flesh of its own species.
– DERIVATIVES **cannibalism** n. **cannibalistic** adj. **cannibalistically** adv.
– ORIGIN C16: from Spanish *Canibales*, var. of *Caribes*, a West Indian people reputed to eat humans (see CARIB).

cannibalize (also **-ise**) ■ v. 1 use (a machine) as a source of spare parts for another, similar machine. 2 (of a company) reduce (the sales of one of its products) by introducing a similar, competing product. 3 (of an animal) eat (an animal of its own kind).
– DERIVATIVES **cannibalization** (also **-isation**) n.

cannon ■ n. 1 (pl. usu. same) a large, heavy piece of artillery formerly used in warfare. ▶ an automatic heavy gun that fires shells from an aircraft or tank. 2 Billiards & Snooker, chiefly Brit. a stroke in which the cue ball strikes two balls successively. 3 Engineering a heavy cylinder or hollow drum rotating independently on a shaft. ■ v. chiefly Brit. collide with something forcefully or at an angle. ▶ Billiards & Snooker make a cannon shot.
– ORIGIN Middle English: from Italian *cannone* 'large tube', from *canna* (see CANE).

cannonade /ˌkanə'neɪd/ ■ n. a period of continuous heavy gunfire. ■ v. discharge heavy guns continuously.
– ORIGIN C16: from Italian *cannonata*, from *cannone* (see CANNON).

cannonball ■ n. a round metal or stone projectile fired from a cannon.

cannon bone ■ n. a long tube-shaped bone in the lower leg of a horse, between the fetlock and the knee or hock.

cannoneer ■ n. historical an artilleryman who positioned and fired a cannon.

cannon fodder ■ n. soldiers regarded merely as material to be expended in war.

cannot ■ contr. can not.

cannula /'kanjʊlə/ ■ n. (pl. **cannulae** /-liː/ or **cannulas**) Surgery a thin tube inserted into the body to administer medication, drain off fluid, or introduce a surgical instrument.
– ORIGIN C17: from Latin, diminutive of *canna* (see CANE).

cannulate ■ v. Surgery introduce a cannula into.
– DERIVATIVES **cannulation** n.

canny ■ adj. (**-ier**, **-iest**) shrewd, especially in financial or business matters.
– DERIVATIVES **cannily** adv. **canniness** n.
– ORIGIN C16 (orig. Scots): from CAN¹ (in obsolete sense 'know').

canoe ■ n. a narrow keelless boat with pointed ends, propelled with a paddle. ■ v. (**-oes**, **-oed**, **canoeing**) travel in or paddle a canoe.
– DERIVATIVES **canoeing** n. **canoeist** n.
– ORIGIN C16: from Spanish *canoa*, from Carib *canaoua*.

canola /kə'nəʊlə/ ■ n. oilseed rape of a variety grown in North America.
– ORIGIN 1970s: from *Canada* + *-ola* (from Latin *oleum* 'oil').

canon¹ ■ n. 1 a general rule or principle by which something is judged. ▶ a Church decree or law. 2 a collection or list of sacred books accepted as genuine. ▶ the works of a particular author or artist that are recognized as genuine. ▶ a list of literary works considered to be permanently established as being of the highest quality. 3 Music a piece in which the same melody is begun in different parts successively, so that the imitations overlap.
– ORIGIN Old English: from Greek *kanōn* 'rule'.

canon² ■ n. a member of the clergy on the staff of a cathedral, especially one who is a member of the chapter.
– ORIGIN Middle English: from Old French *canonie*, from Latin *canonicus* (see CANONIC).

canonic /kə'nɒnɪk/ ■ adj. another term for CANONICAL.
– ORIGIN Old English: from Latin *canonicus* 'canonical', from Greek *kanōn* 'rule'.

canonical /kə'nɒnɪk(ə)l/ ■ adj. 1 according to or ordered by canon law. 2 accepted as being accurate and authoritative. 3 of or relating to a cathedral chapter or a member of it. ■ n. (**canonicals**) the prescribed official dress of the clergy.
– DERIVATIVES **canonically** adv. **canonicity** n.

canonical hours ■ pl. n. 1 the times of daily Christian prayer appointed in the breviary, or the offices set for them. 2 (in the Church of England) the time during which a marriage may lawfully be celebrated (usually between 8 a.m. and 6 p.m.).

canonize (also **-ise**) ■ v. 1 (in the Roman Catholic Church) officially declare (a dead person) to be a saint. 2 sanction by Church authority.
– DERIVATIVES **canonization** (also **-isation**) n.
– ORIGIN Middle English: from late Latin *canonizare* 'admit as authoritative', from *canon*, from Greek *kanōn* 'rule'.

canon law ■ n. ecclesiastical law, especially that laid down by papal pronouncements.

canonry ■ n. (pl. **-ies**) the office or benefice of a canon.

canoodle ■ v. informal kiss and cuddle amorously.
– ORIGIN C19 (orig. US).

Canopic jar /kə'nəʊpɪk/ ■ n. a covered urn used in ancient Egyptian burials to hold the visceral organs from an embalmed body.

–ORIGIN C19: *Canopic* from Latin, from *Canopus*, a town in ancient Egypt.

canopy ■ n. (pl. **-ies**) **1** a cloth covering over a throne, bed, etc. ▸ a roof-like projection or shelter. ▸ the expanding, umbrella-like part of a parachute. **2** the transparent plastic or glass cover of an aircraft's cockpit. **3** a fibreglass or metal cover for the back of a bakkie or truck. **4** the uppermost branches of the trees in a forest, forming a more or less continuous layer of foliage. ■ v. (**-ies**, **-ied**) [usu. as adj. **canopied**] cover or provide with a canopy.
–ORIGIN Middle English: from medieval Latin *canopeum*, from Greek *kōnōpeion* 'couch with mosquito curtains', from *kōnōps* 'mosquito'.

canst archaic second person singular present of **CAN**[1].

cant[1] /kant/ ■ n. **1** hypocritical and sanctimonious talk. **2** derogatory language peculiar to a specified group: *thieves' cant.* ▸ [as modifier] denoting a phrase or catchword temporarily current.
–ORIGIN C16 (in sense 'singing', later 'whining speech'): prob. from Latin *cantare* (see **CHANT**).

cant[2] /kant/ ■ v. be or cause to be in a slanting or oblique position; tilt. ▸ (of a ship) swing round. ■ n. **1** a slope or tilt. **2** a wedge-shaped block of wood remaining after the better-quality pieces have been cut off.
–ORIGIN Middle English: from Middle Low German *kant*, *cant* 'point, edge', rel. to medieval Latin *cantus* 'corner, side'.

can't ■ contr. cannot.

Cantab. /'kantab/ ■ abbrev. of Cambridge University.
–ORIGIN from Latin *Cantabrigiensis*, from *Cantabrigia* 'Cambridge'.

Cantabrigian /ˌkantəˈbrɪdʒɪən/ ■ adj. of or relating to Cambridge or Cambridge University. ■ n. a member of Cambridge University.
–ORIGIN C16: from Latin *Cantabrigia* 'Cambridge'.

cantaloupe /'kantəluːp/ ■ n. a small round melon of a variety with orange flesh and ribbed skin.
–ORIGIN C18: from French *cantaloup*, from *Cantaluppi* near Rome.

cantankerous ■ adj. bad-tempered, argumentative, and uncooperative.
–DERIVATIVES **cantankerously** adv. **cantankerousness** n.
–ORIGIN C18: perhaps a blend of Anglo-Irish *cant* 'auction' and *rancorous* (see **RANCOUR**).

cantata /kanˈtɑːtə/ ■ n. a medium-length narrative or descriptive piece of music with vocal solos and normally a chorus and orchestra.
–ORIGIN C18: from Italian *cantata* (*aria*) 'sung (air)', from *cantare* 'sing'.

canteen ■ n. **1** a restaurant in a workplace or educational establishment. **2** chiefly Brit. a specially designed case or box containing a set of cutlery. **3** a small water bottle, as used by soldiers or campers.
–ORIGIN C18: from Italian *cantina* 'cellar'.

canter ■ n. a pace of a horse between a trot and a gallop, with not less than one foot on the ground at any time. ▸ a ride on a horse at such a speed. ■ v. move at this pace.
–PHRASES **in** (or **at**) **a canter** Brit. without much effort; easily.
–ORIGIN C18: short for *Canterbury pace*, from the supposed easy pace of medieval pilgrims to Canterbury in southern England.

canterbury ■ n. (pl. **-ies**) a low open-topped cabinet with partitions for holding music or books.

Canterbury bell ■ n. a tall cultivated bellflower with large pale blue flowers. [*Campanula medium*.]
–ORIGIN C16: named after the bells on Canterbury pilgrims' horses.

canthus /'kanθəs/ ■ n. (pl. **canthi** /-θʌɪ/) the outer or inner corner of the eye, where the upper and lower lids meet.
–ORIGIN C17: from Greek *kanthos*.

canticle /'kantɪk(ə)l/ ■ n. a hymn or chant forming a regular part of a church service.
–ORIGIN Middle English: from Latin *canticulum* 'little song', from *canere* 'sing'.

cantilever /'kantɪliːvə/ ■ n. a long projecting beam or girder fixed at only one end, used chiefly in bridge construction. ▸ a bracket or beam projecting from a wall to support a balcony, cornice, etc. ■ v. [usu. as adj.

cap

cantilevered] support by a cantilever or cantilevers.
–ORIGIN C17.

canting arms ■ pl. n. Heraldry arms containing an allusion to the name of the bearer.

cantle /'kant(ə)l/ ■ n. the raised curved part at the back of a horse's saddle.
–ORIGIN Middle English: from Anglo-Norman French *cantel*, from medieval Latin *cantellus*, from *cantus* 'corner, side'.

canto /'kantəʊ/ ■ n. (pl. **-os**) one of the sections into which some long poems are divided.
–ORIGIN C16: from Italian, 'song', from Latin *cantus*.

canton ■ n. **1** /'kantɒn, kanˈtɒn/ a political or administrative subdivision of a country. **2** /'kant(ə)n/ Heraldry a square charge smaller than a quarter and positioned in the upper (usually dexter) corner of a shield.
–ORIGIN C16: from Old French, 'corner', rel. to medieval Latin *cantus* (see **CANT**[2]).

Cantonese ■ n. (pl. same) **1** a native or inhabitant of Canton (Guangzhou), a city in China. **2** a form of Chinese spoken mainly in SE China and Hong Kong. ■ adj. of or relating to Canton or Cantonese.

cantonment /kanˈtɒnm(ə)nt, -ˈtuːn-/ ■ n. a military camp, especially a permanent military station in British India.
–ORIGIN C18: from French *cantonnement*, from *cantonner* 'to quarter'.

cantor /'kantɔː, -ə/ ■ n. **1** (in Jewish worship) an official who sings liturgical music and leads prayer in a synagogue. **2** (in formal Christian worship) a person who sings solo verses to which the choir or congregation respond.
–ORIGIN C16: from Latin, 'singer', from *canere* 'sing'.

cantorial ■ adj. **1** of or relating to a cantor. **2** relating to or denoting the north side of the choir in a church, on which the cantor sits. The opposite of **DECANAL**.

cantus /'kantəs/ ■ n. the highest voice in polyphonic choral music.
–ORIGIN C16: from Latin.

canvas ■ n. (pl. **canvases** or **canvasses**) **1** a strong, coarse unbleached cloth used to make sails, tents, etc. and as a surface for oil painting. ▸ a piece of canvas prepared for use as the surface for an oil painting. ▸ (**the canvas**) the floor of a boxing or wrestling ring, having a canvas covering. **2** either of a racing boat's tapering ends, originally covered with canvas. ■ v. (**canvassed**, **canvassing**; US **canvased**, **canvasing**) cover with canvas.
–PHRASES **under canvas 1** in a tent or tents. **2** with sails spread.

HISTORY
The word **canvas** came into Middle English, via Old Northern French *canevas*, from the Latin name for hemp, *cannabis*: hemp is the raw material traditionally used in making canvas, and is also the source of **cannabis** itself. The noun **canvas** (earlier spelled with a double -s) is also linked with the verb **canvass**, which originally meant 'toss in a canvas sheet' (a practice carried out both in fun and as a punishment); **canvass** then came to mean 'assault, attack' or 'criticize', and later 'scrutinize in order to reject invalid votes', from which developed the modern sense, 'solicit votes'.

canvass ■ v. solicit votes from (electors). ▸ question (someone) in order to ascertain their opinion on something.
–DERIVATIVES **canvasser** n.
–ORIGIN C16 (in the sense 'toss in a canvas sheet' (as a sport or punishment)): from **CANVAS**.

canyon ■ n. a deep gorge, especially one with a river flowing through it.
–ORIGIN C19: from Spanish *cañón* 'tube', from Latin *canna* 'reed, cane'.

canyoning ■ n. another term for **KLOOFING**.

cap ■ n. **1** a soft, flat hat without a brim and usually with a peak. ▸ a soft, close-fitting head covering worn for a particular purpose: *a shower cap.* ▸ an academic mortar board. **2** a protective lid or cover for a bottle, pen, etc.

cap.

▶ Dentistry an artificial protective covering for a tooth. **3** an upper limit imposed on spending or borrowing. **4** a cap awarded to members of a sports team, especially a national team. **5** (also **Dutch cap**) Brit. informal a contraceptive diaphragm. **6** the broad upper part of the fruiting body of a mushroom or toadstool. **7** short for **PERCUSSION CAP**. ■ v. (**capped**, **capping**) **1** put or form a lid or cover on. ▶ put a cap on (a tooth). **2** provide a fitting climax or conclusion to. ▶ follow or reply to (a story or remark) with a still better one. **3** place a limit on (prices, expenditure, etc.). **4** (**be capped**) be chosen as a member of a sports team, especially a national one.
– PHRASES **cap in hand** humbly asking for a favour. **set one's cap at** (or US **for**) dated (of a woman) try to attract (a particular man) as a suitor. **to cap it all** as the final unfortunate incident in a long series.
– DERIVATIVES **capful** n. (pl. **-fuls**). **capper** n.
– ORIGIN Old English *cæppe* 'hood', from late Latin *cappa*, perhaps from Latin *caput* 'head'.

cap. ■ abbrev. **1** capacity. **2** capital (city). **3** capital letter.

capability ■ n. (pl. **-ies**) power or ability to do something. ▶ an undeveloped or unused faculty.

capable ■ adj. **1** (**capable of doing something**) having the ability or quality necessary to do something. ▶ open to or admitting of something. **2** (of a person) competent.
– DERIVATIVES **capably** adv.
– ORIGIN C16: from late Latin *capabilis*, from Latin *capere* 'take or hold'.

capacious ■ adj. having a lot of space inside; roomy.
– DERIVATIVES **capaciously** adv. **capaciousness** n.
– ORIGIN C17: from Latin *capax* 'capable'.

capacitance /kəˈpasɪt(ə)ns/ ■ n. Physics ability to store electric charge, equivalent to the ratio of the change in electric charge in a system or component to the corresponding change in electric potential.
– ORIGIN C19: from CAPACITY.

capacitate ■ v. make someone capable or legally competent. ▶ train and empower (a group of people previously disadvantaged).
– DERIVATIVES **capacitation** n.

capacitor /kəˈpasɪtə/ ■ n. a device used to store electric charge, consisting of one or more pairs of conductors separated by an insulator.

capacity ■ n. (pl. **-ies**) **1** the maximum amount that something can contain or produce. ▶ [as modifier] fully occupying the available space: *a capacity crowd*. ▶ the total cylinder volume that is swept by the pistons in an internal-combustion engine. **2** the ability or power to do something. ▶ a person's legal competence. **3** a specified role or position. **4** dated capacitance.
– DERIVATIVES **capacitive** (also **capacitative**) adj. (chiefly Physics).
– ORIGIN Middle English: from Latin *capacitas*, from *capax* 'that can contain', from *capere* 'take or hold'.

capacity building ■ n. skills training and empowerment, usually of disadvantaged people.

caparison /kəˈparɪs(ə)n/ ■ v. (**be caparisoned**) be decked out in rich decorative coverings.
– ORIGIN C16: from obsolete French *caparasson*, from Spanish *caparazón* 'saddlecloth', from *capa* 'hood'.

Cap Classique /ˌkap klaˈsiːk/ ■ n. short for **MÉTHODE CAP CLASSIQUE**.

cape¹ ■ n. a sleeveless cloak, especially a short one. ▶ a part of a longer coat or cloak that falls loosely over the shoulders from the neckband.
– DERIVATIVES **caped** adj.
– ORIGIN C16: from Provençal *capa*, from late Latin *cappa* 'covering for the head'.

cape² ■ n. **1** a headland or promontory. **2** S. African (**the Cape**) the Cape of Good Hope. ▶ the Cape Peninsula. ▶ the Western Cape province. ▶ Cape Town. **3** historical the Cape Colony. ■ adj. (**Cape**) S. African originating in or relating to the Cape.
– ORIGIN Middle English: from Old French *cap*, from Latin *caput* 'head'.

Cape aloe ■ n. **1** a winter-flowering South African aloe. [*Aloe ferox*.] **2** (also **Cape aloes**) a medicinal product made from the dried leaf sap of this plant, used primarily as a purgative.

Cape ash ■ n. a southern African tree which bears small white flowers and bright red fruits, popularly cultivated as a shade tree. [*Ekebergia capensis*.]

Cape beech ■ n. S. African a large evergreen tree with smooth grey bark and leathery leaves. [*Rapanea melanophloeos*.] ▶ the wood of this tree, used for furniture.

Cape cart ■ n. S. African historical a two-wheeled hooded carriage, drawn by between one and eight horses or mules.

Cape chestnut ■ n. an African tree with large pink flower clusters, commonly planted as an ornamental. [*Calodendrum capense*.] ▶ the pale yellow wood of this tree.

Cape Colony (also **the Cape Colony**, **the Colony**) ■ n. historical the official designation of the areas around the Cape Peninsula colonised by early European settlers, which became the Cape Province when South Africa was unified in 1910.

Cape Coloured ■ n. S. African historical (under apartheid) an official racial sub-group for people of mixed ethnic descent living in the former Cape Province, who were Afrikaans or English first-language speakers and usually Christian. Compare with **CAPE MALAY**.

Cape cottage ■ n. S. African a single-storey whitewashed house, often with a gabled roof. ▶ [as modifier] denoting a style of furniture made of indigenous woods.

Cape Doctor ■ n. S. African informal the strong prevailing SE wind in the Western Cape.

Cape Dutch ■ adj. S. African **1** denoting the gabled, whitewashed style of early Cape architecture. **2** relating to the furniture made by early Cape colonists, usually of indigenous woods, in a style blending Dutch and English tradition. ■ n. historical the form of Dutch spoken by the early settlers at the Cape of Good Hope, which developed into Afrikaans.

Cape Floral Kingdom ■ n. Ecology the smallest of the world's six floristic regions, which extends across South Africa's Western and Eastern Cape provinces and is dominated by flora known as fynbos.

Cape Frontier War ■ n. another term for **FRONTIER WAR** (in sense 2).

Cape gooseberry ■ n. **1** a soft edible yellow berry enclosed in a lantern-shaped husk. **2** the tropical South American plant which bears this fruit. [*Physalis peruviana*.]

Cape griffon (also **Cape griffon vulture**) ■ n. another term for **CAPE VULTURE**.

Cape hen ■ n. the white-chinned petrel. [*Procellaria aequinoctialis*.]

Cape honeysuckle ■ n. S. African an evergreen shrub bearing clusters of orange tubular flowers with protruding stamens, commonly grown in gardens. [*Tecomaria capensis*.]

Cape horse ■ n. S. African a hardy horse bred predominantly from oriental and English stock, from which the Boerperd and the Basotho pony breeds were developed.

Cape jasmine ■ n. a fragrant Chinese gardenia with flowers that are used to perfume tea. [*Gardenia jasminioides*.]

Cape jazz ■ n. a style of music fusing Cape Malay folk elements with African rhythms and jazz.

Cape Malay S. African ■ n. (also **Cape Muslim**) a member of a predominantly Afrikaans-speaking and Muslim group resident mainly in the Western Cape. ■ adj. of or relating to the Cape Malays.

Cape minstrel ■ n. S. African a performer in a traditional Cape band, characterized by the use of blackface make-up and colourful costumes.

Cape minstrel carnival ■ n. a parade of Cape minstrel troupes, held in Cape Town on 1 and 2 January each year.

Cape primrose ■ n. another term for **STREPTOCARPUS**.

caper¹ ■ v. skip or dance about in a lively or playful way. ■ n. **1** a playful skipping movement. **2** informal an illicit or ridiculous activity or escapade.

– PHRASES **cut a caper** make a playful, skipping movement.
– DERIVATIVES **caperer** n.
– ORIGIN C16: abbrev. of CAPRIOLE.

caper[2] ■ n. **1** a cooked and pickled flower bud of a bramble-like southern European shrub, used in pickles and sauces. **2** the shrub from which these buds are taken. [*Capparis spinosa*.]
– ORIGIN Middle English: from French *câpres*, from Greek *kapparis*.

capercaillie /ˌkapəˈkeɪli/ (Scottish also **capercailzie** /-ˈkeɪlzi/) ■ n. (pl. **-ies**) a large turkey-like grouse of mature pine forests in northern Europe. [*Tetrao urogallus*.]
– ORIGIN C16: from Scottish Gaelic *capull coille* 'horse of the wood'.

Cape reed ■ n. S. African **1** another term for RESTIO. **2** (also **Cape thatching reed**) any of several species of restio used for thatching. [Genera *Elegia* and *Thamnochortus*.]

Cape salmon ■ n. S. African another term for GEELBEK.

Cape Triangular ■ n. Philately any of several rare triangular postage stamps issued in the Cape Colony between 1853 and 1900.

Cape Velvet ■ n. S. African trademark an alcoholic drink made from brandy and cream.

Cape Verdean /ˈvəːdɪən/ ■ n. a native or inhabitant of the Cape Verde Islands, a small country off the coast of Senegal. ■ adj. of or relating to the Cape Verde Islands.

Cape vulture (also **Cape griffon** or **Cape griffon vulture**) ■ n. a large southern African vulture with a pale body and dark wing and tail feathers. [*Gyps coprotheres*.]

Capey ■ n. S. African informal **1** a person from Cape Town. **2** dated, offensive a Cape Coloured person.

capillarity ■ n. the tendency of a liquid in a narrow tube or pore to rise or fall as a result of surface tension.

capillary /kəˈpɪləri/ ■ n. **1** Anatomy any of the fine branching blood vessels that form a network between the arterioles and venules. **2** (also **capillary tube**) a tube with an internal diameter of hair-like thinness. ■ adj. of or relating to capillaries or capillarity.
– ORIGIN C17: from Latin, from *capillus* 'hair', influenced by Old French *capillaire*.

capillary action ■ n. another term for CAPILLARITY.

capillary joint ■ n. a joint made between two pipes by putting their ends into a slightly larger joining piece and filling the gaps with molten solder.

capital[1] ■ n. **1** the most important city or town of a country or region, usually its seat of government and administrative centre. ▸ a place particularly associated with a specified activity: *the fashion capital of the world*. **2** wealth owned by a person or organization or invested, lent, or borrowed. ▸ the excess of a company's assets over its liabilities. **3** a capital letter. ■ adj. **1** (of an offence or charge) liable to the death penalty. **2** (of a letter of the alphabet) large in size and of the form used to begin sentences and names. **3** informal, dated excellent.
– PHRASES **make capital out of** use to one's own advantage. **with a capital ——** used for emphasis: *this is life with a capital L*.
– DERIVATIVES **capitally** adv.
– ORIGIN Middle English: from Latin *capitalis*, from *caput* 'head'.

capital[2] ■ n. Architecture the distinct, typically broader section at the head of a pillar or column.
– ORIGIN Middle English: from late Latin *capitellum* 'little head', diminutive of Latin *caput*.

capital gains tax ■ n. a tax levied on profit from the sale of property or an investment.

capital goods ■ pl. n. goods that are used in producing other goods, rather than being bought by consumers.

capital-intensive ■ adj. requiring the investment of large sums of money.

capitalism ■ n. an economic and political system in which a country's trade and industry are controlled by private owners for profit, rather than by the state.
– DERIVATIVES **capitalist** n. & adj. **capitalistic** adj. **capitalistically** adv.

capitalize (also **-ise**) ■ v. **1** (**capitalize on**) take the chance to gain advantage from. **2** provide with capital. **3** convert into capital. ▸ reckon (the value of an asset) by setting future benefits against the cost of maintenance. **4** write or print (a word or letter) in capital letters. ▸ begin (a word) with a capital letter.
– DERIVATIVES **capitalization** (also **-isation**) n.

capital levy ■ n. a tax by means of which the state appropriates a fixed proportion of private wealth.

capital punishment ■ n. the legally authorized killing of someone as punishment for a crime.

capital sum ■ n. a lump sum of money payable to an insured person or paid as an initial fee or investment.

capital territory ■ n. a territory containing the capital city of a country, as in Australia, Nigeria, and Pakistan.

capitate /ˈkapɪteɪt/ ■ adj. Botany ending in a distinct compact head.
– ORIGIN C17: from Latin *capitatus*, from *caput* 'head'.

capitation ■ n. the payment of a fee or grant to a doctor, school, etc., the amount being determined by the number of patients, pupils, etc.
– ORIGIN C17: from late Latin *capitatio* 'poll tax', from *caput* 'head'.

capitol /ˈkapɪt(ə)l/ ■ n. **1** (in the US) a building housing a legislative assembly. ▸ (**the Capitol**) the seat of the US Congress in Washington DC. **2** (**the Capitol**) the temple of Jupiter on the Capitoline Hill in ancient Rome.
– ORIGIN from Old French *capitolie*, *capitoile*, from *caput* 'head'.

capitulate /kəˈpɪtjʊleɪt/ ■ v. cease to resist an opponent or an unwelcome demand; surrender.
– DERIVATIVES **capitulator** n.
– ORIGIN C16: from medieval Latin *capitulare* 'draw up under headings', from Latin *capitulum*, diminutive of *caput* 'head'.

capitulation ■ n. the action of capitulating.

capitulum /kəˈpɪtjʊləm/ ■ n. (pl. **capitula** /-lə/) Biology a compact head of a structure, in particular a dense flat cluster of small flowers or florets.
– ORIGIN C18: from Latin, diminutive of *caput* 'head'.

cap'n /ˈkapn/ ■ n. informal contraction of CAPTAIN.

capo /ˈkapəʊ/ (also **capo tasto**) ■ n. (pl. **-os**) a clamp fastened across all the strings of a fretted musical instrument to raise their tuning.
– ORIGIN C19: from Italian *capo tasto* 'head stop'.

Capo di Monte /ˌkapəʊ dɪ ˈmɒnteɪ, ˈmɒnti/ ■ n. a type of porcelain that is generally white with richly coloured rococo decoration.
– ORIGIN from the *Capo di Monte* palace near Naples, Italy.

capon /ˈkeɪp(ə)n/ ■ n. a castrated domestic cock fattened for eating.
– DERIVATIVES **caponize** (also **-ise**) v.
– ORIGIN Old English: from Latin *capo*.

capo tasto /ˌkapəʊ ˈtastəʊ/ ■ n. see CAPO.

cappuccino /ˌkapʊˈtʃiːnəʊ/ ■ n. (pl. **-os**) coffee made with milk that has been frothed up with pressurized steam.
– ORIGIN 1940s: from Italian, 'Capuchin', because its colour resembles that of a Capuchin's habit.

caprice /kəˈpriːs/ ■ n. a sudden and unaccountable change of mood or behaviour.
– ORIGIN C17: from Italian *capriccio* 'head with the hair standing on end', from *capo* 'head' + *riccio* 'hedgehog'.

capricious /kəˈprɪʃəs/ ■ adj. given to sudden and unaccountable changes of mood or behaviour.
– DERIVATIVES **capriciously** adv. **capriciousness** n.
– ORIGIN C17: from French *capricieux*, from Italian *capriccio* (see CAPRICE).

Capricorn /ˈkaprɪkɔːn/ ■ n. Astrology the tenth sign of the zodiac (the Goat), which the sun enters at the northern winter solstice (about 21 December).
– DERIVATIVES **Capricornian** n. & adj.
– ORIGIN Old English: from Latin *capricornus*, from *caper* 'goat' + *cornu* 'horn'.

caprine /ˈkapraɪn/ ■ adj. relating to or resembling a goat or goats.
– ORIGIN Middle English, from Latin *caprinus*, from *caper* 'goat'.

capriole /ˈkaprɪəʊl/ ■ n. a leap or caper in dancing, especially a cabriole.
– ORIGIN C16: from Italian *capriola* 'leap', from *capriolo* 'roebuck', from Latin, from *caper* 'goat'.

capri pants /kəˈpriː/ (also **capris**) ■ pl. n. close-fitting tapered trousers for women.
– ORIGIN 1950s: named after the island of *Capri*, Italy.

caps ■ abbrev. capital letters.

capsaicin /kapˈseɪɪsɪn/ ■ n. a cyclic compound responsible for the pungency of capsicums.
– ORIGIN C19: alteration of *capsicine*, another substance formerly thought to have the same property.

Capsian /ˈkapsɪən/ ■ adj. Archaeology relating to or denoting a Palaeolithic culture of North Africa and southern Europe, dated to c.8000–4500 BC.
– ORIGIN C20: from Latin *Capsa* (now *Gafsa* in Tunisia), where objects from this culture were found.

capsicum /ˈkapsɪkəm/ ■ n. (pl. **capsicums**) 1 the fruit of a tropical American plant, of which sweet peppers and chilli peppers are varieties. 2 the plant of the nightshade family from which such fruits come. [Genus *Capsicum*.]
– ORIGIN C16: perhaps from Latin *capsa* (see CASE²).

capsid¹ ■ n. another term for MIRID.
– ORIGIN C19: from *Capsus* (genus name).

capsid² ■ n. Microbiology the protein coat or shell of a virus particle.
– ORIGIN 1960s: coined in French from Latin *capsa* (see CASE²).

capsize ■ v. (of a boat) be overturned in the water.
– ORIGIN C18: perhaps from Spanish *capuzar* 'sink (a ship) by the head', from *cabo* 'head' + *chapuzar* 'to dive or duck'.

cap sleeve ■ n. a short sleeve which tapers to nothing under the arm.

capstan /ˈkapst(ə)n/ ■ n. a broad revolving cylinder with a vertical axis used for winding a rope or cable.
– ORIGIN Middle English: from Provençal *cabestan*, from *cabestre* 'halter', from Latin, from *capere* 'seize'.

capstone ■ n. a stone placed on top of a wall, tomb, or other structure.

capsule /ˈkapsjuːl, -sjʊl/ ■ n. 1 a small soluble case of gelatin containing a dose of medicine, swallowed whole. ▸ a small case or container. 2 Anatomy a sheath or membrane that encloses an organ or other structure, such as a kidney. ▸ Botany a dry fruit that releases its seeds by bursting open when ripe. ▸ Botany the spore-producing structure of mosses and liverworts. 3 the foil or plastic covering the cork of a wine bottle.
– DERIVATIVES **capsular** adj. **capsulate** adj.
– ORIGIN Middle English: from Latin *capsula*, diminutive of *capsa* (see CASE²).

Capt. ■ abbrev. Captain.

captain ■ n. 1 the person in command of a ship. ▸ the pilot in command of a civil aircraft. ▸ a rank of naval officer above commander and below rear admiral (junior grade). 2 a rank of officer in the army and in the air force, above lieutenant and below major. 3 (in the US) a police officer in charge of a precinct. 4 the leader of a team, especially in sports. ■ v. serve as the captain of.
– DERIVATIVES **captaincy** n.
– ORIGIN Middle English: from Old French *capitain*, from late Latin *capitaneus* 'chief', from Latin *caput* 'head'.

caption ■ n. 1 a title or brief explanation appended to an illustration or cartoon. ▸ a piece of text appearing on screen as part of a film or broadcast. 2 Law the heading of a legal document. ■ v. provide with a caption.
– ORIGIN Middle English: from Latin *captio*(n-), from *capere* 'take, seize'.

captious /ˈkapʃəs/ ■ adj. formal tending to find fault or raise petty objections.
– DERIVATIVES **captiously** adv. **captiousness** n.
– ORIGIN Middle English: from Latin *captiosus*, from *captio*(n-) (see CAPTION).

captivate ■ v. attract and hold the interest and attention of; charm.
– DERIVATIVES **captivating** adj. **captivatingly** adv.

captivation n.
– ORIGIN C16: from late Latin *captivare* 'take captive', from *captivus* (see CAPTIVE).

captive ■ n. a person who has been taken prisoner or confined. ■ adj. 1 imprisoned or confined. 2 having no freedom to choose an alternative: *a captive audience*. 3 (of a facility or service) controlled by and reserved for a particular organization.
– DERIVATIVES **captivity** n.
– ORIGIN Middle English: from Latin *captivus*, from *capere* 'seize, take'.

captor ■ n. a person who imprisons or confines another.

capture ■ v. 1 take into one's possession or control by force. ▸ (in chess and other board games) make a move that secures the removal of (an opposing piece). 2 Physics absorb (a particle). 3 record or express accurately in words or pictures. 4 cause (data) to be stored in a computer. ■ n. the action of capturing or of being captured. ▸ a person or thing that has been captured.
– DERIVATIVES **capturer** n.
– ORIGIN C16 (as n.): from Latin *captura*, from *capere* 'seize, take'.

Capuchin /ˈkapʊtʃɪn/ ■ n. 1 Christian Church a friar belonging to a strict branch of the Franciscan order. 2 (**capuchin**) a South American monkey with a cowl-like cap of hair on the head. [Genus *Cebus*: four species.] 3 (**capuchin**) a pigeon of a breed with head and neck feathers resembling a cowl.
– ORIGIN C16: from French *capucin*, from Italian, from *cappuccio* 'hood, cowl', from *cappa* (see CAPE¹).

capybara /ˌkapɪˈbɑːrə/ ■ n. (pl. same or **capybaras**) a large South American rodent resembling a long-legged guinea pig. [*Hydrochaerus hydrochaeris*.]
– ORIGIN C17: from Spanish *capibara*, from Tupi *capiuára*, from *capĩ* 'grass' + *uára* 'eater'.

car ■ n. 1 a powered road vehicle designed to carry a small number of people. 2 a railway carriage or (N. Amer.) wagon. ▸ the passenger compartment of a lift, cableway, or balloon.
– DERIVATIVES **carful** n. (pl. **-fuls**). **carload** n.
– ORIGIN Middle English: from Old Northern French *carre*, from Latin *carrum*, of Celtic origin.

carabid /ˈkarəbɪd/ ■ n. Entomology a beetle of a family (Carabidae) comprising the predatory ground beetles.
– ORIGIN C19: from Latin *carabus*, denoting a kind of crab.

carabineer /ˌkarəbɪˈnɪə/ (also **carabinier**) ■ n. historical a cavalry soldier whose principal weapon was a carbine.
– ORIGIN C17: from French *carabinier*, from *carabine* (see CARBINE).

carabiner ■ n. variant spelling of KARABINER.

carabiniere /ˌkarəbɪˈnjɛːri/ ■ n. (pl. **carabinieri** pronunc. same) a member of the Italian paramilitary police.
– ORIGIN Italian, 'carabineer'.

caracal /ˈkarəkal/ ■ n. a long-legged lynx-like cat with black tufted ears, native to Africa and western Asia. [*Caracal caracal*.]
– ORIGIN C19: from Turkish *karakulak*, from *kara* 'black' + *kulak* 'ear'.

caracul ■ n. variant spelling of KARAKUL.

carafe /kəˈraf, -ˈrɑːf/ ■ n. an open-topped glass flask typically used for serving wine in a restaurant.
– ORIGIN C18: from Italian *caraffa*, prob. from Arabic *ġarafa* 'draw water'.

carambola /ˌkar(ə)mˈbəʊlə/ ■ n. 1 a golden-yellow fruit with a star-shaped cross section; starfruit. 2 the tropical tree which bears this fruit. [*Averrhoa carambola*.]
– ORIGIN C16: from Portuguese, prob. from Marathi *karambal*.

caramel /ˈkarəm(ə)l, -mɛl/ ■ n. 1 sugar or syrup heated until it turns brown, used as a flavouring or colouring for food or drink. 2 a soft toffee made with sugar and butter that have been melted and further heated.
– DERIVATIVES **caramelization** (also **-isation**) n. **caramelize** (also **-ise**) v.
– ORIGIN C18: from Spanish *caramelo*.

carapace /ˈkarəpeɪs/ ■ n. the hard upper shell of a tortoise or crustacean.
– ORIGIN C19: from Spanish *carapacho*.

carat /ˈkarət/ ■ n. 1 a unit of weight for precious stones

and pearls, equivalent to 200 milligrams. **2** (US also **karat**) a measure of the purity of gold, pure gold being 24 carats.
– ORIGIN Middle English: from Italian *carato*, from Arabic *ḳīrāṭ*, from Greek *keration* 'fruit of the carob'.

caravan ■ n. **1** a vehicle equipped for living in, usually designed to be towed. **2** N. Amer. a covered truck. **3** chiefly historical a group of people travelling together across a desert in Asia or North Africa.
– DERIVATIVES **caravanner** n. **caravanning** n.
– ORIGIN C15: from French *caravane*, from Persian *kārwān*.

caravanserai /ˌkarəˈvansərʌɪ, -ri/ (US also **caravansary**) ■ n. (pl. **caravanserais** or **caravansaries**) **1** historical an inn with a central courtyard for travellers in the desert regions of Asia or North Africa. **2** a group of people travelling together; a caravan.
– ORIGIN C16: from Persian *kārwānsarāy*, from *kārwān* 'caravan' + *sarāy* 'palace'.

caravel /ˈkarəvel/ (also **carvel**) ■ n. historical a small, fast Spanish or Portuguese ship of the 15th–17th centuries.
– ORIGIN C16: from Portuguese *caravela*, diminutive of *caravo*, from Greek *karabos* 'horned beetle' or 'light ship'.

caraway /ˈkarəweɪ/ ■ n. **1** the seeds of a plant of the parsley family, used for flavouring and as a source of oil. **2** the white-flowered Mediterranean plant which bears these seeds. [*Carum carvi*.]
– ORIGIN Middle English: from medieval Latin *carui*, from Arabic *alkarāwiyā*, prob. from Greek *karon* 'cumin'.

carb[1] ■ n. informal short for CARBURETTOR.

carb[2] ■ n. informal short for CARBOHYDRATE.

carbamate /ˈkɑːbəmeɪt/ ■ n. Chemistry a salt or ester containing the anion NH_2COO^- or the group $-OOCNH_2$.
– ORIGIN C19: from CARBO- + AMIDE.

carbanion /kɑːˈbanʌɪən/ ■ n. Chemistry an organic ion with a negative charge located on a carbon atom.

carbaryl /ˈkɑːbərɪl/ ■ n. a synthetic insecticide used to protect crops and in the treatment of fleas and lice.
– ORIGIN C20: from CARBAMATE.

carbide /ˈkɑːbʌɪd/ ■ n. Chemistry a compound of carbon with a metal or other element: *silicon carbide*.

carbine /ˈkɑːbʌɪn/ ■ n. a light automatic rifle. ▸ historical a short rifle or musket used by cavalry.
– ORIGIN C17: from French *carabine*, from *carabin* 'mounted musketeer'.

carbo- ■ comb. form representing CARBON.

carbocation /ˌkɑːbə(ʊ)ˈkatʌɪən/ ■ n. Chemistry another term for CARBONIUM ION.

carbohydrate ■ n. any of a large group of compounds (including sugars, starch, and cellulose) which contain carbon, hydrogen, and oxygen, occur in foods and living tissues, and can be broken down to release energy in the body.

carbolic acid (also **carbolic**) ■ n. phenol, especially when used as a disinfectant.

carbo-load ■ v. informal consume a large quantity of carbohydrate-rich food to give energy, especially before a long-distance running or cycling race.

car bomb ■ n. a terrorist bomb concealed in a parked car. ■ v. (**car-bomb**) attack with such a bomb.
– DERIVATIVES **car bomber** n.

carbon ■ n. **1** the chemical element of atomic number 6, a non-metal which has two main forms (diamond and graphite), occurs in impure form in charcoal, soot, and coal, and is present in all organic compounds. (Symbol: **C**) **2** a piece of carbon paper; a carbon copy.
– DERIVATIVES **carbonaceous** adj.
– ORIGIN C18: from French *carbone*, from Latin *carbo* 'coal, charcoal'.

carbonara /ˌkɑːbəˈnɑːrə/ ■ adj. denoting a pasta sauce made with bacon or ham, egg, and cream.
– ORIGIN Italian, 'charcoal kiln', perhaps influenced by *carbonata*, a dish of charcoal-grilled pork.

carbonate /ˈkɑːbəneɪt/ ■ n. a salt of the anion CO_3^{2-}, typically formed by reaction of carbon dioxide with bases. ■ v. [usu. as adj. **carbonated**] dissolve carbon dioxide in.
– DERIVATIVES **carbonation** n.

carbonatite /kɑːˈbɒnətʌɪt/ ■ n. Geology a lava or other igneous rock composed chiefly of carbonates.

carbon copy ■ n. a copy made with carbon paper. ▸ a person or thing identical to another.

carbon dating ■ n. the determination of the age of an organic object from the relative proportions of the isotopes carbon-12 and carbon-14 that it contains.

carbon dioxide ■ n. a colourless, odourless gas produced by burning carbon and organic compounds and by respiration, and absorbed by plants in photosynthesis. [CO_2.]

carbon fibre ■ n. a material consisting of thin, strong crystalline filaments of carbon.

carbonic /kɑːˈbɒnɪk/ ■ adj. of or relating to carbon or carbon dioxide.

carbonic acid ■ n. a very weak acid formed when carbon dioxide dissolves in water. [H_2CO_3.]

Carboniferous /ˌkɑːbəˈnɪf(ə)rəs/ ■ adj. Geology relating to or denoting the fifth period of the Palaeozoic era (between the Devonian and Permian periods, about 363 to 290 million years ago), a time when extensive coal-bearing strata were formed.

carbonium ion /kɑːˈbəʊnɪəm/ ■ n. Chemistry an organic ion with a positive charge located on a carbon atom.
– ORIGIN C20: from CARBO-, on the pattern of *ammonium*.

carbonize (also **-ise**) ■ v. convert into carbon, by heating or burning.
– DERIVATIVES **carbonization** (also **-isation**) n.

carbon monoxide ■ n. a colourless, odourless toxic flammable gas formed by incomplete combustion of carbon. [CO.]

carbon paper ■ n. thin paper coated with carbon, used for making copies of written or typed documents.

carbon steel ■ n. steel in which the main alloying element is carbon, and whose properties depend on the percentage of carbon present.

carbon tetrachloride ■ n. a colourless toxic volatile liquid used as a solvent. [CCl_4.]

carbonyl /ˈkɑːbənʌɪl, -nɪl/ ■ n. [as modifier] Chemistry of or denoting the divalent radical :C=O, present in aldehydes, ketones, and many other organic compounds.

car boot sale ■ n. an outdoor sale at which people sell things, typically from the boots of their cars.

carborundum /ˌkɑːbəˈrʌndəm/ ■ n. a very hard black solid consisting of silicon carbide, used as an abrasive.
– ORIGIN C19: blend of CARBON and CORUNDUM.

carboxyl /kɑːˈbɒksʌɪl, -sɪl/ ■ n. [as modifier] Chemistry of or denoting the radical -COOH, present in organic acids.
– ORIGIN C19: from CARBO- + OX-.

carboxylate /kɑːˈbɒksɪleɪt/ Chemistry ■ n. a salt or ester of a carboxylic acid. ■ v. add a carboxyl group to (a compound).
– DERIVATIVES **carboxylation** n.

carboxylic acid /ˌkɑːbɒkˈsɪlɪk/ ■ n. Chemistry an acid containing a carboxyl group, such as formic and acetic acids.

carboy ■ n. a large globular glass bottle with a narrow neck, used for holding acids or other corrosive liquids.
– ORIGIN C18: from Persian *ḳarāba* 'large glass flagon'.

carbuncle /ˈkɑːbʌŋk(ə)l/ ■ n. a severe abscess or multiple boil in the skin.
– DERIVATIVES **carbuncular** adj.
– ORIGIN Middle English: from Latin *carbunculus* 'small coal', from *carbo* 'coal, charcoal'.

carburettor /ˌkɑːbjʊˈrɛtə, -bə-/ (also **carburetter**, US **carburetor**) ■ n. a device in an internal-combustion engine for mixing air with a fine spray of liquid fuel.
– ORIGIN C19: from archaic *carburet* 'combine or charge with carbon'.

carcajou /ˈkɑːkədʒuː, -ʒuː/ ■ n. North American term for WOLVERINE.
– ORIGIN C18: from Canadian French, perhaps of Algonquian origin.

carcass (Brit. also **carcase**) ■ n. **1** the dead body of an animal, especially one prepared for cutting up as meat. ▸ the remains of a cooked bird after all the edible parts have been removed. ▸ derogatory or humorous a person's

body, living or dead. **2** the structural framework of a building, ship, or piece of furniture.
– ORIGIN Middle English: from Anglo-Norman French *carcois*, var. of Old French *charcois*.

carcinogen /kɑːˈsɪnədʒ(ə)n/ ■ n. a substance capable of causing cancer.

carcinogenic /ˌkɑːsɪ(ɪ)nəˈdʒɛnɪk/ ■ adj. having the potential to cause cancer.
– DERIVATIVES **carcinogenesis** n. **carcinogenicity** n.

carcinoma /ˌkɑːsɪˈnəʊmə/ ■ n. (pl. **carcinomas** or **carcinomata** /-mətə/) a cancer arising in the epithelial tissue of the skin or of the lining of the internal organs.
– DERIVATIVES **carcinomatous** adj.
– ORIGIN C18: from Greek *karkinōma*, from *karkinos* 'crab' (cf. CANCER).

car coat ■ n. a short, square-cut style of coat designed to be worn when driving a car.

card[1] ■ n. **1** thick, stiff paper or thin cardboard. **2** a piece of card for writing on, especially a postcard or greetings card. ▸ a business card or visiting card. **3** a small rectangular piece of plastic containing machine-readable personal data, e.g. a credit card or cash card. **4** a playing card. ▸ (**cards**) a game played with playing cards. **5** a scorecard, in particular a list of holes on a golf course. ▸ a programme of events at a race meeting. **6** Computing a circuit board that can be inserted in a computer to give extra facilities. **7** informal, dated or N. Amer. a person regarded as odd or amusing.
– PHRASES **a card up one's sleeve** a plan or asset that is kept secret until it is needed. **give someone their cards** (or **get one's cards**) Brit. informal dismiss someone (or be dismissed) from employment. **hold all the cards** be in a very strong position. **on** (or N. Amer. **in**) **the cards** informal possible or likely. **play the —— card** exploit the specified issue or idea mentioned, especially for political advantage: *he saw an opportunity to play the peace card*. **play one's cards right** make the best use of one's assets and opportunities. **put** (or **lay**) **one's cards on the table** be completely open and honest in declaring one's intentions.
– ORIGIN Middle English: from Latin *carta*, from Greek *khartēs* 'papyrus leaf'.

card[2] ■ v. comb and clean (raw wool or similar material) with a sharp-toothed instrument to disentangle the fibres before spinning. ■ n. a toothed implement or machine for this purpose.
– DERIVATIVES **carder** n.
– ORIGIN Middle English: from Provençal *carda*, from *cardar* 'tease, comb', from Latin *carere* 'to card'.

cardamom /ˈkɑːdəməm/ (also **cardamum**) ■ n. **1** the aromatic seeds of a plant of the ginger family, used as a spice. **2** the SE Asian plant which bears these seeds. [*Elettaria cardamomum*.]
– ORIGIN Middle English: from Old French *cardamome*, from Greek, from *kardamon* 'cress' + *amōmon*, the name of a kind of spice plant.

cardboard ■ n. **1** pasteboard or stiff paper. **2** [as modifier] (of a fictional character) lacking depth and realism.

card-carrying ■ adj. registered as a member of a political party or trade union.

cardia /ˈkɑːdɪə/ ■ n. Anatomy the upper opening of the stomach, where the oesophagus enters.
– ORIGIN C18: from Greek *kardia*.

cardiac /ˈkɑːdɪak/ ■ adj. **1** of or relating to the heart. **2** of or relating to the cardia of the stomach.
– ORIGIN Middle English: from Latin *cardiacus*, from Greek, from *kardia* 'heart, cardia'.

cardigan ■ n. a knitted jumper fastening with buttons down the front.
– ORIGIN C19 (Crimean War): named after the 7th Earl of *Cardigan*, whose troops first wore such garments.

cardinal ■ n. **1** a leading dignitary of the Roman Catholic Church, nominated by and having the power to elect the Pope. **2** a deep scarlet colour like that of a cardinal's cassock. **3** an American songbird of which the male is partly or mostly red and which typically has a crest. [*Cardinalis cardinalis* and other species, subfamily Cardinalinae.] ■ adj. of the greatest importance; fundamental.

– DERIVATIVES **cardinalate** n. **cardinally** adv. **cardinalship** n.
– ORIGIN Old English, from Latin *cardinalis*, from *cardo* 'hinge'.

cardinal flower ■ n. a tall scarlet-flowered lobelia found in North America. [*Lobelia cardinalis*.]

cardinality ■ n. (pl. **-ies**) Mathematics the number of elements in a particular set or other grouping.

cardinal number ■ n. a number denoting quantity (one, two, three, etc.), as opposed to an ordinal number (first, second, third, etc.).

cardinal point ■ n. each of the four main points of the compass (north, south, east, and west).

cardinal sin ■ n. any of the seven deadly sins. ▸ chiefly humorous a serious error of judgement: *he committed the cardinal sin of criticizing his teammates*.

cardinal virtue ■ n. each of the chief moral attributes of scholastic philosophy: justice, prudence, temperance, and fortitude.

cardinal vowel ■ n. Phonetics each of a series of vowel sounds used as a standard reference point to assist in the description and classification of vowel sounds.

card index ■ n. a catalogue in which each item is entered on a separate card. ■ v. (**card-index**) catalogue (information) in the form of a card index.

carding wool ■ n. short-stapled pieces of wool which result from the carding process, spun and woven to make standard-quality fabrics. Compare with COMBING WOOL.

cardio ■ n. informal cardiovascular exercise.

cardio- /ˈkɑːdɪəʊ/ ■ comb. form of or relating to the heart: *cardiograph*.
– ORIGIN from Greek *kardia* 'heart'.

cardiogram /ˈkɑːdɪə(ʊ)gram/ ■ n. a record of muscle activity within the heart made by a cardiograph.

cardiograph /ˈkɑːdɪə(ʊ)grɑːf/ ■ n. an instrument for recording heart muscle activity.
– DERIVATIVES **cardiographer** n. **cardiography** n.

cardiology ■ n. the branch of medicine concerned with diseases and abnormalities of the heart.
– DERIVATIVES **cardiological** adj. **cardiologist** n.

cardiomegaly /ˌkɑːdɪəʊˈmɛɡəli/ ■ n. Medicine abnormal enlargement of the heart.
– ORIGIN 1960s: from CARDIO- + Greek *megas* 'great'.

cardiomyopathy /ˌkɑːdɪəʊmaɪˈɒpəθi/ ■ n. Medicine chronic disease of the heart muscle.

cardiopulmonary ■ adj. Medicine of or relating to the heart and the lungs.

cardiorespiratory ■ adj. Medicine relating to the action of both heart and lungs.

cardiovascular ■ adj. Medicine of or relating to the heart and blood vessels.

carditis /kɑːˈdaɪtɪs/ ■ n. Medicine inflammation of the heart.

card key ■ n. another term for KEY CARD.

cardoon /kɑːˈduːn/ ■ n. a tall thistle-like plant related to the globe artichoke, with edible leaves and roots. [*Cynara cardunculus*.]
– ORIGIN C17: from French *cardon*, from *carde* 'edible part of an artichoke', from Latin *carduus* 'thistle, artichoke'.

card sharp (also **card sharper**) ■ n. a person who cheats at cards.

card table ■ n. a table for playing cards on, typically having legs that fold flat for storage and a baize surface.

cardy (also **cardie**) ■ n. (pl. **-ies**) Brit. informal a cardigan.

care ■ n. **1** the provision of what is necessary for the health, welfare, maintenance, and protection of someone or something. ▸ Brit. protective custody or guardianship provided for children by a local authority. **2** serious attention or consideration applied to an action or plan. ▸ a feeling of or occasion for anxiety. ■ v. **1** feel concern or interest. ▸ feel affection or liking. ▸ (**care for/to do something**) like to have or be willing to do something. **2** (**care for**) look after and provide for the needs of.
– PHRASES **care of** at the address of. **take care 1** be cautious; keep oneself safe. **2** make sure of doing something. **take care of 1** keep safe and provided for. **2** deal with.

–DERIVATIVES **caring** n. & adj.
–ORIGIN Old English, of Germanic origin.

careen /kəˈriːn/ ■ v. **1** turn (a ship) on its side for cleaning or repair. ▸ (of a ship) tilt; lean over. **2** another term for CAREER v.
–ORIGIN C16: from French *carène*, from Latin *carina* 'a keel'.

career ■ n. an occupation undertaken for a significant period of a person's life, usually with opportunities for progress. ▸ the progress through history of an institution or organization. ▸ [as modifier] working with commitment in a particular profession: *a career diplomat.* ▸ [as modifier] (of a woman) pursuing a profession. ■ v. move swiftly and in an uncontrolled way in a specified direction.
–ORIGIN C16 (denoting a road or racecourse): from French *carrière*, from Latin *carrus* 'wheeled vehicle'.

careerist ■ n. a person whose main concern is for advancement in their profession.
–DERIVATIVES **careerism** n.

carefree ■ adj. free from anxiety or responsibility.
–DERIVATIVES **carefreeness** n.

careful ■ adj. **1** taking care to avoid mishap or harm; cautious. ▸ (**careful of/about**) protective of. ▸ (**careful with**) prudent in the use of. **2** done with or showing thought and attention.
–DERIVATIVES **carefully** adv. **carefulness** n.
–ORIGIN Old English *carful* (see CARE).

caregiver ■ n. chiefly N. Amer. another term for CARER.
–DERIVATIVES **caregiving** n. & adj.

care label ■ n. a label giving instructions for the washing and care of a fabric or garment.

careless ■ adj. **1** not giving sufficient attention or thought to avoiding harm or mistakes. **2** (**careless of/about**) not concerned or worried about. ▸ showing no interest or effort; casual.
–DERIVATIVES **carelessly** adv. **carelessness** n.
–ORIGIN Old English *carlēas* 'free from care' (see CARE).

careline ■ n. Brit. a telephone complaints and advice service.

carer ■ n. Brit. a family member or paid helper who regularly looks after a sick, elderly, or disabled person.

caress ■ v. touch or stroke gently or lovingly. ■ n. a gentle or loving touch.
–DERIVATIVES **caressing** adj. **caressingly** adv.
–ORIGIN C17: from French *caresser* (v.), *caresse* (n.), from Latin *carus* 'dear'.

caret /ˈkarət/ ■ n. a mark (‸, ⋀) placed below a line of text to indicate a proposed insertion.
–ORIGIN C17: from Latin, 'is lacking'.

caretaker ■ n. **1** a person employed to look after a public building. **2** [as modifier] holding power temporarily: *he was to act as caretaker Prime Minister.* **3** chiefly N. Amer. a person employed to look after people or animals.

careworn ■ adj. tired and unhappy because of prolonged worry.

cargo ■ n. (pl. **-oes** or **-os**) goods carried commercially on a ship, aircraft, or truck.
–ORIGIN C17: from Spanish *cargo*, from late Latin *carricare* 'to load', from Latin *carrus* 'wheeled vehicle'.

cargo cult ■ n. (in the Melanesian Islands) a system of beliefs based around the expected arrival of benevolent spirits in aircraft or ships bringing cargoes of food and other goods.

car guard ■ n. S. African a person paid to watch over parked cars to prevent theft or break-ins.

Carib /ˈkarɪb/ ■ n. **1** a member of an indigenous South American people living mainly in coastal regions of French Guiana, Suriname, Guyana, and Venezuela. **2** the language of the Carib.
–ORIGIN from Spanish *caribe*, from Haitian Creole.

Caribbean /ˌkarɪˈbiːən, kəˈrɪbɪən/ ■ adj. of or relating to the region consisting of the Caribbean Sea, its islands (including the West Indies), and the surrounding coasts.

caribou /ˈkarɪbuː/ ■ n. (pl. same) N. Amer. a reindeer.
–ORIGIN C17: from Canadian French, from Micmac (an Algonquian language) *ɣalipu* 'snow-shoveller'.

caricature /ˈkarɪkəˌtjʊə/ ■ n. a depiction of a person in which distinguishing characteristics are exaggerated for comic or grotesque effect. ■ v. make a caricature of.
–DERIVATIVES **caricatural** adj. **caricaturist** n.
–ORIGIN C18: from Italian *caricatura*, from *caricare* 'load, exaggerate', from Latin *carricare* (see CHARGE).

caries /ˈkɛːriːz/ ■ n. decay and crumbling of a tooth or bone.
–ORIGIN C16: from Latin.

carillon /ˈkarɪljən, -lɒn, kəˈrɪljən/ ■ n. **1** a set of bells sounded from a keyboard or by an automatic mechanism. **2** a tune played on such bells.
–DERIVATIVES **carillonneur** /ˌkarɪljəˈnəː, -ˈrɪlə-, kə-/ n.
–ORIGIN C18: from Old French *quarregnon* 'peal of four bells', from Latin *quattuor* 'four'.

carina /kəˈrʌɪnə, -ˈriː-/ ■ n. (pl. **carinae** /-niː/ or **carinas**) Anatomy a cartilage situated at the point where the trachea (windpipe) divides into the two bronchi.
–DERIVATIVES **carinal** adj.
–ORIGIN C18: from Latin, 'keel'.

carious /ˈkɛːrɪəs/ ■ adj. (of bones or teeth) decayed.
–ORIGIN C16: from Latin *cariosus* (see CARIES).

caritas /ˈkarɪtɑːs/ ■ n. Christian love of humankind; charity.
–ORIGIN C19: from Latin.

carjacking ■ n. chiefly N. Amer. the action of stealing a car after violently ejecting its driver.
–DERIVATIVES **carjack** v. **carjacker** n.
–ORIGIN 1990s: blend of CAR and *hijacking* (see HIJACK).

Carmelite /ˈkɑːmɛlʌɪt/ ■ n. Christian Church a friar or nun of an order founded at Mount Carmel during the Crusades. ■ adj. of or relating to the Carmelites.

carminative /ˈkɑːmɪnətɪv, kɑːˈmɪnətɪv/ Medicine ■ adj. relieving flatulence. ■ n. a carminative drug.
–ORIGIN Middle English: from medieval Latin *carminare* 'heal (by incantation)' from Latin *carmen* (see CHARM).

carmine /ˈkɑːmʌɪn, -mɪn/ ■ n. a vivid crimson pigment made from cochineal.
–ORIGIN C18: from French *carmin*, from Arabic *ḳirmiz* (see KERMES).

carnage /ˈkɑːnɪdʒ/ ■ n. the killing of a large number of people.
–ORIGIN C17: from Italian *carnaggio*, from medieval Latin *carnaticum*, from Latin *caro* 'flesh'.

carnal /ˈkɑːn(ə)l/ ■ adj. relating to physical, especially sexual, needs and activities.
–DERIVATIVES **carnality** n. **carnally** adv.
–ORIGIN Middle English: from eccles. Latin *carnalis*, from *caro, can-* 'flesh'.

carnal knowledge ■ n. dated, chiefly Law sexual intercourse.

carnassial /kɑːˈnasɪəl/ ■ adj. Zoology denoting the large upper premolar and lower molar teeth of a carnivore, adapted for shearing flesh.
–ORIGIN C19: from French *carnassier* 'carnivorous', from Latin *caro* 'flesh'.

Carnatic /kɑːˈnatɪk/ ■ adj. of or denoting the main style of classical music in southern India, as distinct from the Hindustani music of the north.
–ORIGIN Anglicization of *Karnataka*, a state in SW India.

carnation ■ n. a double-flowered cultivated variety of clove pink, with grey-green leaves and showy pink, white, or red flowers.
–ORIGIN C16: perhaps from Arabic *ḳaranful* 'clove or clove pink', influenced by French *carnation* 'flesh colour, rosy pink', from Latin *caro* 'flesh'.

carnauba /kɑːˈnɔːbə, -ˈnaʊbə/ ■ n. **1** a NE Brazilian fan palm, the leaves of which exude a yellowish wax. [*Copernicia cerifera.*] **2** wax from this palm.
–ORIGIN C19: from Tupi.

carnelian /kɑːˈniːlɪən/ (also **cornelian**) ■ n. a dull red or reddish-white semi-precious variety of chalcedony.
–ORIGIN Middle English: from Old French *corneline*; influenced by Latin *caro* 'flesh'.

carnet /ˈkɑːneɪ/ ■ n. **1** a permit for a particular purpose, especially one allowing a motor vehicle to be taken across a frontier for a limited period. **2** a book of tickets for use on public transport in some countries.
–ORIGIN 1920s: from French, 'notebook'.

carnival

carnival ▪ n. **1** an annual period of public revelry involving processions, music, dancing, etc. **2** N. Amer. a travelling funfair or circus.
– DERIVATIVES **carnivalesque** adj.
– ORIGIN C16: from Italian *carnevale*, from medieval Latin *carnelevamen* 'Shrovetide', from Latin *caro* 'flesh' + *levare* 'put away'.

Carnivora /kɑːˈnɪvərə/ ▪ pl. n. Zoology an order of mammals comprising the cats, dogs, bears, hyenas, weasels, civets, raccoons, and mongooses, having powerful jaws and teeth adapted for tearing and eating flesh.

carnivore /ˈkɑːnɪvɔː/ ▪ n. an animal that feeds on flesh.
– ORIGIN C19: from Latin *carnivorus* (see **CARNIVOROUS**).

carnivorous /kɑːˈnɪv(ə)rəs/ ▪ adj. (of an animal) feeding on flesh.
– DERIVATIVES **carnivorously** adv. **carnivorousness** n.
– ORIGIN C16: from Latin *carnivorus*, from *caro* 'flesh' + *-vorus* (see **-VOROUS**).

carnosaur /ˈkɑːnəsɔː/ ▪ n. a large bipedal carnivorous dinosaur of a group including tyrannosaurus, allosaurus, and megalosaurus.
– ORIGIN 1930s: from Latin *caro, carn-* 'flesh' + Greek *sauros* 'lizard'.

carob /ˈkarɒb/ ▪ n. **1** the edible brownish-purple pod of an Arabian tree, from which a powder is extracted for use as a substitute for chocolate. **2** the tree which yields this pod. [*Ceratonia siliqua*.]
– ORIGIN Middle English: from Old French *carobe*, from Arabic *ḵarrūba*.

carol ▪ n. a religious song or popular hymn associated with Christmas. ▪ v. (**carolled, carolling**; US **caroled, caroling**) **1** (go carolling) sing carols in the streets. **2** sing or say (something) happily.
– DERIVATIVES **caroller** (US **caroler**) n. **carolling** (US **caroling**) n.
– ORIGIN Middle English: from Old French *carole* (n.), *caroler* (v.).

Caroline /ˈkarəlʌɪn/ ▪ adj. (also **Carolean** /-ˈliːən/) of or relating to the reigns of Charles I and II of England (1625–49; 1660–85).
– ORIGIN C17: from medieval Latin *Carolus* 'Charles'.

carol-singing ▪ n. the singing of carols, especially by groups going from door to door at Christmas with the object of raising money.
– DERIVATIVES **carol-singer** n.

carotene /ˈkarətiːn/ ▪ n. Chemistry an orange or red plant pigment found notably in carrots and of which one form (beta-carotene) is important in the diet as a precursor of vitamin A.
– DERIVATIVES **carotenoid** /kəˈrɒtɪnɔɪd/ n.
– ORIGIN C19: coined in German from Latin *carota* 'carrot'.

carotid /kəˈrɒtɪd/ ▪ adj. Anatomy relating to or denoting the two main arteries carrying blood to the head and neck.
– ORIGIN C17: from French *carotide*, from Greek *karōtides*, from *karoun* 'stupefy' (because compression of these arteries was thought to cause stupor).

carouse /kəˈraʊz/ ▪ v. drink alcohol and enjoy oneself with others in a noisy, lively way. ▪ n. a noisy, lively drinking party.
– DERIVATIVES **carousal** n. **carouser** n. **carousing** n.
– ORIGIN C16: orig. as adv. meaning 'right out, completely' in the phr. *drink carouse*, from German *gar aus trinken*.

carousel /ˌkarəˈsɛl, -ˈzɛl/ ▪ n. **1** a merry-go-round at a fair. **2** a rotating machine or device, in particular a conveyor system for baggage collection at an airport.
– ORIGIN C17: from French *carrousel*, from Italian *carosello*.

carp[1] ▪ n. (pl. same) a deep-bodied freshwater fish, often kept in ponds and sometimes farmed for food. [*Cyprinus carpio* and other species, family Cyprinidae.]
– ORIGIN Middle English: from Old French *carpe*, from late Latin *carpa*.

carp[2] ▪ v. complain or find fault continually.
– DERIVATIVES **carper** n.
– ORIGIN Middle English: from Old Norse *karpa* 'brag'; later influenced by Latin *carpere* 'pluck at, slander'.

carpaccio /kɑːˈpatʃɪəʊ/ ▪ n. an Italian hors d'oeuvre consisting of thin slices of raw beef or fish served with a sauce.
– ORIGIN Italian, named after the painter Vittore *Carpaccio* (from his use of red pigments, resembling raw meat).

carpal /ˈkɑːp(ə)l/ Anatomy & Zoology ▪ adj. of or relating to the carpus. ▪ n. a bone of the carpus.

carpal tunnel syndrome ▪ n. a painful condition of the hand and fingers caused by compression of a major nerve where it passes over the carpal bones.

carpe diem /ˌkɑːpeɪ ˈdiːɛm, ˈdʌɪɛm/ ▪ exclam. make the most of the present time.
– ORIGIN Latin, 'seize the day!', a quotation from Horace (*Odes* I.xi).

carpel /ˈkɑːp(ə)l/ ▪ n. Botany the female reproductive organ of a flower, consisting of an ovary, a stigma, and usually a style.
– DERIVATIVES **carpellary** adj.
– ORIGIN C19: from French *carpelle*, from Greek *karpos* 'fruit'.

carpenter[1] ▪ n. a person who makes wooden objects and structures. ▪ v. make by shaping wood.
– DERIVATIVES **carpentry** n.
– ORIGIN Middle English: from Old French *charpentier*, from late Latin *carpentarius* (*artifex*) 'carriage(-maker)', from *carpentum* 'wagon', of Gaulish origin.

carpenter[2] (also **karpenter**) ▪ n. S. African a small edible sea bream fished commercially off the Cape to KwaZulu-Natal coast. [*Argyrozona argyrozona*.]
– ORIGIN 1910s: prob. from S. African Dutch *kaapenaar* 'one from the Cape'.

carpenter bee ▪ n. a large solitary black bee with purplish wings, which nests in tunnels bored in dead wood or plant stems. [Genus *Xylocopa*.]

carpet ▪ n. **1** a floor covering made from thick woven fabric. ▸ a large rug. **2** a thick or soft expanse or layer of something: *a carpet of bluebells*. ▪ v. (**carpeted, carpeting**) **1** cover with a carpet. **2** Brit. informal reprimand severely.
– PHRASES **on the carpet** informal being severely reprimanded by someone in authority. [from *carpet* referring to the covering of the council table, before which one would be summoned for reprimand.] **sweep (a problem or difficulty) under the carpet** conceal or ignore a problem or difficulty in the hope that it will be forgotten.
– DERIVATIVES **carpeting** n.
– ORIGIN Middle English: from Old French *carpite*, from obsolete Italian *carpita* 'woollen counterpane', from Latin *carpere* 'pluck'.

carpet bag ▪ n. a travelling bag of a kind originally made of carpet-like material. ▪ v. (**carpet-bag**) N. Amer. act as a carpetbagger.

carpetbagger ▪ n. derogatory, chiefly N. Amer. a politician who seeks election in an area where they have no local connections, originally a northerner who went to the South after the Civil War. ▸ an unscrupulous opportunist.

carpet beetle ▪ n. a small beetle whose larva (a woolly bear) is destructive to carpets, fabrics, etc. [Genus *Anthrenus*.]

carpet-bomb ▪ v. bomb (an area) intensively.
– DERIVATIVES **carpet-bombing** n.

carpet shark ▪ n. a small shallow-water shark of the Indo-Pacific region, typically with a conspicuous colour pattern. [Family Orectolobidae: several species.]

carpet slipper ▪ n. a soft slipper whose upper part is made of wool or thick cloth.

carpet sweeper ▪ n. a manual household implement with revolving brushes for sweeping carpets.

carpology /kɑːˈpɒlədʒi/ ▪ n. the study of fruits and seeds.
– DERIVATIVES **carpological** adj.
– ORIGIN C19: from Greek *karpos* 'fruit'.

carpool chiefly N. Amer. ▪ n. a group of people who arrange to make a journey or journeys in a single car. ▪ v. take part in a carpool.

carport ▪ n. a shelter for a car consisting of a roof supported on posts, built beside a house.

carpus /ˈkɑːpəs/ ▪ n. (pl. **carpi** /-pʌɪ/) the group of small bones between the main part of the forelimb and the

metacarpus, forming the wrist in humans.
– ORIGIN Middle English: from Greek *karpos* 'wrist'.

carrageenan /ˌkarəˈgiːnən/ ■ n. a carbohydrate extracted from carrageen, an edible seaweed, and used as a thickening or emulsifying agent in food products.

carrel /ˈkar(ə)l/ ■ n. **1** a small cubicle with a desk for the use of a reader in a library. **2** historical a small enclosure or study in a cloister.
– ORIGIN C16: rel. to CAROL in the old sense 'ring'.

carriage ■ n. **1** a four-wheeled passenger vehicle pulled by two or more horses. ▸ a wheeled support for moving a heavy object such as a gun. **2** any of the separate vehicles of a passenger train. **3** the conveying of items or merchandise from one place to another. **4** a moving part of a machine that carries other parts into the required position. **5** a person's bearing or deportment.
– ORIGIN Middle English: from Old Northern French *cariage*, from *carier* (see CARRY).

carriage and pair ■ n. a carriage pulled by two horses.

carriage clock ■ n. Brit. a portable clock in a rectangular case with a handle on top.

carriage return ■ n. see RETURN (sense 8).

carriageway ■ n. Brit. **1** each of the two sides of a dual carriageway or motorway, consisting of two or more lanes. **2** the part of a road intended for vehicles.

carrier ■ n. **1** a person or thing that carries, holds, or conveys something. **2** a person or company that undertakes the professional conveyance of goods or people. **3** a person or animal that transmits a disease-causing organism to others, especially without suffering from it themselves.

carrier bag ■ n. a plastic or paper bag with handles, for carrying purchased goods.

carrier pigeon ■ n. a pigeon trained to carry messages tied to its neck or leg.

carrier wave ■ n. a high-frequency electromagnetic wave modulated in amplitude or frequency to convey a signal.

carrion ■ n. the decaying flesh of dead animals.
– ORIGIN Middle English: from Anglo-Norman French *caroine*, from Latin *caro* 'flesh'.

carrion beetle ■ n. a beetle that feeds on decaying animal and plant matter. [Family Silphidae: many species.]

carrion crow ■ n. a common Eurasian black crow. [*Corvus corone*.]

carrion flower ■ n. a plant with a flower that emits an odour like that of rotting flesh to attract insects as pollinators. [Numerous genera and species, including the stapelias.]

carrot ■ n. **1** a tapering orange-coloured root eaten as a vegetable. **2** a cultivated plant of the parsley family with feathery leaves, which yields this vegetable. [*Daucus carota*.] **3** an offer of something enticing as a means of persuasion (as contrasted with the 'stick' or punishment). **4** (**carrots**) informal, chiefly derogatory a nickname for a red-haired person.
– DERIVATIVES **carroty** adj.
– ORIGIN C15: from French *carotte*, from Greek *karōton*.

carry ■ v. (**-ies, -ied**) **1** move or transport from one place to another. ▸ have on one's person wherever one goes. ▸ conduct; transmit. ▸ be infected with (a disease) and liable to transmit it to others. **2** support the weight of. ▸ be pregnant with. ▸ (**carry oneself**) stand and move in a specified way. ▸ assume or accept (responsibility or blame). **3** have as a feature or consequence. **4** take or develop (an idea or activity) to a specified point. ▸ propel (a missile) to a specified distance. ▸ Golf & Cricket hit the ball over and beyond (a particular point). **5** (often **be carried**) approve (a proposed measure) by a majority of votes. ▸ persuade to support one's policy. ▸ N. Amer. gain (a state or district) in an election. **6** (of a newspaper, television station, etc.) publish or broadcast. ▸ (of a retailing outlet) keep a regular stock of. **7** (of a sound or voice) be audible at a distance. ■ n. (pl. **-ies**) **1** an act of carrying. ▸ American Football an act of running or rushing with the ball. **2** Golf the distance a ball travels before reaching the ground. **3** the range of a gun or similar weapon.
– PHRASES **carry all before one** overcome all opposition. **carry one's bat** Cricket (especially of an opening batsman) be not out at the end of one's side's completed innings. **carry the can** Brit. informal take responsibility for a mistake or misdeed. **carry the day** be victorious or successful. **carry weight** be influential or important.
– PHRASAL VERBS **be/get carried away** lose self-control. **carry away** Nautical lose (a mast or other part of a ship) through breakage. **carry forward** transfer (figures) to a new page or account. ▸ keep to use or deal with at a later time. **carry off 1** take away by force. ▸ (of a disease) kill (someone). **2** succeed in doing (something difficult). **carry on 1** continue an activity or task. ▸ continue to move in the same direction. **2** informal behave in a specified way. **3** informal, derogatory, chiefly Brit. be engaged in a love affair. **carry out** perform (a task or planned operation). **carry over 1** extend beyond the normal or original area of application. **2** keep to use or deal with in a new context. ▸ postpone. **carry through** bring to completion.
– ORIGIN Middle English: from Anglo-Norman French *carier*, from Latin *carrus* 'wheeled vehicle'.

carryall ■ n. chiefly N. Amer. a large bag or case.

carrycot ■ n. Brit. a small portable cot for a baby.

carry-on ■ n. Brit. informal **1** a display of excitement or fuss. ▸ (also **carryings-on**) questionable or improper behaviour. **2** a bag or suitcase suitable for taking on to an aircraft as hand luggage.

carry-over ■ n. something transferred or resulting from a previous situation or context.

carsick ■ adj. affected with nausea caused by the motion of a car in which one is travelling.
– DERIVATIVES **carsickness** n.

cart ■ n. **1** a horse-drawn open vehicle with two or four wheels, used for carrying loads. ▸ a light two-wheeled open vehicle for driving in, pulled by a single horse. **2** a shallow open container on wheels, pulled or pushed by hand. ▸ N. Amer. a supermarket trolley. ■ v. **1** convey or put in a cart or similar vehicle. **2** informal carry (a heavy or cumbersome object) somewhere with difficulty. ▸ convey or propel unceremoniously.
– PHRASES **put the cart before the horse** reverse the proper order or procedure.
– DERIVATIVES **carter** n. **cartful** n. (pl. **-fuls**). **cartload** n.
– ORIGIN Middle English: from Old Norse *kartr*, prob. influenced by Anglo-Norman French *carete*, diminutive of *carre* (see CAR).

cartage ■ n. the conveyance of something in a cart or other vehicle.

carte ■ n. variant spelling of QUART (in sense 2).

carte blanche /ˌkɑːt ˈblɑːnʃ/ ■ n. complete freedom to act as one wishes or thinks best.
– ORIGIN C17: French, 'blank paper'.

cartel /kɑːˈtɛl/ ■ n. **1** an association of manufacturers or suppliers formed to maintain high prices and restrict competition. **2** chiefly historical a political coalition intended to promote a mutual interest.
– DERIVATIVES **cartelize** (also **-ise**) v.
– ORIGIN C19: from German *Kartell*, from Latin *carta* (see CARD[1]).

Cartesian /kɑːˈtiːziən, -3(ə)n/ ■ adj. of or relating to the French philosopher René Descartes (1596–1650) and his ideas. ■ n. a follower of Descartes.
– DERIVATIVES **Cartesianism** n.
– ORIGIN C17: from *Cartesius*, Latinized form of the name *Descartes*.

Cartesian coordinates ■ pl. n. coordinates which locate a point in terms of its perpendicular distance from two (or three) mutually perpendicular axes.

Carthaginian /ˌkɑːθəˈdʒɪniən/ ■ n. a native or inhabitant of the ancient city of Carthage on the coast of North Africa. ■ adj. of or relating to Carthage or its people.

carthorse ■ n. Brit. a large, strong horse suitable for heavy work.

Carthusian /kɑːˈθjuːziən/ ■ n. Christian Church a monk or nun of an austere contemplative order founded by St Bruno in 1084. ■ adj. of or relating to this order.
– ORIGIN from medieval Latin, from *Cart(h)usia*, Latin name of *Chartreuse*, near Grenoble, where the order was founded.

cartilage /ˈkɑːt(ɪ)lɪdʒ/ ■ n. a firm, whitish, flexible

cartilaginous fish

connective tissue which is the main component of the articulating surfaces of joints and of structures such as the larynx and respiratory tract and the external ear.
- DERIVATIVES **cartilaginoid** /-'ladʒɪnɔɪd/ adj. **cartilaginous** /-'ladʒɪnəs/ adj.
- ORIGIN Middle English: from Latin *cartilago*.

cartilaginous fish ▪ n. a fish of a large class distinguished by having a skeleton of cartilage rather than bone and including the sharks, rays, and chimaeras. [Class Chondrichthyes.]

cartogram /'kɑːtəgram/ ▪ n. a map on which statistical information is shown in diagrammatic form.
- ORIGIN C19: from French, from *carte* 'map or card' + *-gramme*, from Greek *gramma* 'thing written'.

cartography /kɑːˈtɒgrəfi/ ▪ n. the science or practice of drawing maps.
- DERIVATIVES **cartographer** n. **cartographic** adj. **cartographical** adj. **cartographically** adv.
- ORIGIN C19: from French, from *carte* (see CARD¹) + *-graphie* (see -GRAPHY).

cartomancy /'kɑːtə(ʊ)mansi/ ▪ n. fortune telling involving the interpretation of playing cards.
- DERIVATIVES **cartomancer** n.
- ORIGIN C19: from French *cartomancie*, from *carte* 'card' + *-mancie* (see -MANCY).

carton ▪ n. a light cardboard container.
- ORIGIN C19: from Italian *cartone* (see CARTOON).

cartoon ▪ n. 1 a drawing executed in an exaggerated style for humorous or satirical effect. 2 a film made from a sequence of such images, using animation techniques to produce the appearance of movement. 3 a full-size drawing made as a preliminary design for a painting or other work of art. ▪ v. represent in a cartoon.
- DERIVATIVES **cartooning** n. **cartoonish** adj. **cartoonist** n. **cartoony** adj.
- ORIGIN C16: from Italian *cartone*, from Latin *carta* (see CARD¹).

cartophily /kɑːˈtɒfɪli/ ▪ n. the collecting of picture cards, such as postcards or cigarette cards, as a hobby.
- DERIVATIVES **cartophilist** n.
- ORIGIN 1930s: from French *carte* 'card' + -PHILY.

cartouche /kɑːˈtuːʃ/ ▪ n. a carved tablet or drawing representing a scroll with rolled-up ends, used ornamentally or bearing an inscription. ▸ a decorative architectural feature resembling a scroll. ▸ an ornate frame around a design or inscription.
- ORIGIN C17: from French *cartouche*, from Italian *cartoccio*, from Latin *carta* (see CARD¹).

cartridge ▪ n. 1 a container holding a spool of photographic film, a quantity of ink, or other item or substance, designed for insertion into a mechanism. 2 a casing containing a charge and a bullet or shot for small arms or an explosive charge for blasting.
- ORIGIN C16: from French *cartouche*, from Italian *cartoccio* (see CARTOUCHE).

cartridge belt ▪ n. a belt holding cartridges of ammunition.

cartridge paper ▪ n. thick, rough-textured paper used for drawing and for strong envelopes.
- ORIGIN C17: orig. used to make cartridge casing.

cartwheel ▪ n. 1 the wheel of a cart. 2 a circular sideways handspring with the arms and legs extended. ▪ v. perform cartwheels.

cartwright ▪ n. chiefly historical a person whose job is making carts.

carve ▪ v. 1 cut into or shape (a hard material) in order to produce an object or design. ▸ produce in such a way. 2 cut (cooked meat) into slices for eating. 3 (**carve something out**) develop a career, reputation, etc. through painstaking effort. 4 (**carve something up**) cut into or divide up something ruthlessly. ▸ (**carve someone up**) aggressively overtake another driver.
- DERIVATIVES **carving** n.
- ORIGIN Old English *ceorfan* 'cut, carve', of West Germanic origin.

carvel /'kɑːv(ə)l/ ▪ n. variant spelling of CARAVEL.

carvel-built ▪ adj. (of a boat) having external planks which do not overlap. Compare with CLINKER-BUILT.

carver ▪ n. 1 a person or tool that carves. 2 Brit. the principal chair, with arms, in a set of dining chairs, intended for the person carving meat.

carvery ▪ n. (pl. -ies) a buffet or restaurant where cooked joints are carved as required.

car wash ▪ n. a structure through which a vehicle is driven while being washed automatically.

caryatid /ˌkarɪˈatɪd/ ▪ n. (pl. **caryatides** /-diːz/ or **caryatids**) Architecture a pillar in the form of a draped female figure, supporting an entablature.
- ORIGIN C16: from Latin *caryatides*, from Greek, from *karuatis* 'priestess of Artemis at Caryae' from *Karuai* in Laconia.

caryopsis /ˌkarɪˈɒpsɪs/ ▪ n. (pl. **caryopses** /-siːz/) Botany a dry one-seeded fruit in which the ovary wall is united with the seed coat, typical of grasses and cereals.
- ORIGIN C19: from Greek *karuon* 'nut' + *opsis* 'appearance'.

Casanova /ˌkasəˈnəʊvə, -z-/ ▪ n. a man notorious for seducing women.
- ORIGIN C20: from the name of the Italian adventurer Giovanni Jacopo *Casanova* (1725–98).

casbah ▪ n. variant spelling of KASBAH.

cascade ▪ n. 1 a small waterfall, especially one in a series. 2 a mass of something that falls, hangs, or occurs in copious quantities. 3 a process by which information or knowledge is passed on successively. 4 a succession of devices or stages in a process, each of which triggers or initiates the next. ▪ v. 1 pour downwards rapidly and in large quantities. 2 pass (information or knowledge) on to a succession of others. 3 arrange in a series or sequence.
- ORIGIN C17: from Italian *cascata*, from *cascare* 'to fall', from Latin *casus* (see CASE¹).

case¹ ▪ n. 1 an instance of a particular situation; an example of something occurring. ▸ the situation affecting or relating to a particular person or thing. ▸ an incident under official investigation by the police. 2 an instance of a disease, injury, or problem. ▸ a person or their particular problem as a subject of medical or welfare attention. 3 a legal action, especially one that is to be decided in a court of law. ▸ a set of facts or arguments supporting one side in such a legal action. ▸ a legal action that has been decided and may be cited as a precedent. 4 a set of facts or arguments supporting one side of a debate or controversy. 5 Grammar any of the inflected forms of a noun, adjective, or pronoun that express the semantic relation of the word to other words in the sentence. ▸ such a relation whether indicated by inflection or not.
- PHRASES **be the case** be so. **on** (or **off**) **someone's case** informal continually (or no longer) criticizing or harassing someone.
- ORIGIN Middle English: from Old French *cas*, from Latin *casus* 'fall', rel. to *cadere* 'to fall'.

case² ▪ n. 1 a container designed to hold or protect something. ▸ the outer protective covering of a natural or manufactured object. 2 a suitcase. 3 a box containing twelve bottles of wine or other drink, sold as a unit. 4 Printing each of the two forms, capital or minuscule, in which a letter of the alphabet may be written or printed. ▪ v. 1 enclose within a case. 2 informal reconnoitre (a place) before carrying out a robbery.
- ORIGIN Middle English: from Old French *casse*, *chasse* (modern *caisse* 'trunk, chest'), from Latin *capsa*, rel. to *capere* 'to hold'.

caseation /ˌkeɪsɪˈeɪʃ(ə)n/ ▪ n. Medicine a form of necrosis characteristic of tuberculosis, in which diseased tissue forms a firm, dry mass like cheese.
- ORIGIN C19: from medieval Latin *caseatio(n-)*, from Latin *caseus* 'cheese'.

casebook ▪ n. 1 Brit. a written record of cases, kept by a doctor, investigator, lawyer, etc. ▸ a book containing extracts of important legal cases. 2 US a book containing a selection of source materials on a particular subject.

case-bound ▪ adj. (of a book) hardback.

case-harden ▪ v. 1 harden the surface of (a material). 2 [as adj. **case-hardened**] made callous or tough by experience.

case history ■ n. a record of a person's background or medical history kept by a doctor or social worker.

casein /'keɪsiːn, -sɪɪn/ ■ n. the main protein present in milk and (in coagulated form) in cheese.
–ORIGIN C19: from Latin *caseus* 'cheese'.

case law ■ n. the law as established by the outcome of former cases.

caseload ■ n. the number of cases with which a doctor, lawyer, or social worker is concerned at one time.

casemate /'keɪsmeɪt/ ■ n. historical **1** a small room in the thickness of the wall of a fortress, with embrasures from which guns or missiles can be fired. **2** an armoured enclosure for guns on a warship.
–ORIGIN C16: from Italian *casamatta*, perhaps from Greek *khasma* (see CHASM).

casement ■ n. a window set on a vertical hinge so that it opens like a door.
–ORIGIN Middle English: from Anglo-Latin *cassimentum*, from *casa*, from Latin *capsa* (see CASE²).

case-sensitive ■ adj. Computing differentiating between capital and lower-case letters.

case study ■ n. **1** a detailed study of the development of a particular person, group, or situation over a period of time. **2** a particular instance of something illustrating a thesis or principle.

casework ■ n. social work directly concerned with individuals and their personal circumstances.
–DERIVATIVES **caseworker** n.

cash ■ n. money in coins or notes. ▸ money in any form as an available resource. ■ v. **1** give or obtain notes or coins for (a cheque or money order). **2** (**cash something in**) convert an insurance policy, savings account, etc. into money. ▸ (**cash in on**) informal take advantage of or exploit (a situation). **3** (**cash up**) count and check takings at the end of a day's trading.
–PHRASES **cash down** with immediate and full payment at the time of purchase. **cash in one's chips** informal die. **cash in hand** payment in cash rather than by cheque or other means.
–DERIVATIVES **cashable** adj. **cashless** adj.
–ORIGIN C16: from Old French *casse* or Italian *cassa* 'box', from Latin *capsa* (see CASE²).

cash and carry ■ n. a system of wholesale trading whereby goods are paid for in full at the time of purchase and taken away by the purchaser.

cashback ■ n. **1** a cash refund offered as an incentive to buyers. **2** a facility whereby a customer may withdraw cash when making a debit card purchase.

cash book ■ n. a book in which receipts and payments of money are recorded.

cash box ■ n. a lockable metal box for keeping cash in.

cash card ■ n. a plastic card issued by a bank or building society which enables the holder to withdraw money and perform other banking activities at an automated teller machine.

cash cow ■ n. informal a business or investment that provides a steady income or profit.

cash crop ■ n. a crop produced for its commercial value rather than for use by the grower.
–DERIVATIVES **cash cropping** n.

cash desk ■ n. Brit. a counter or compartment in a shop or restaurant where payments are made.

cash dispenser ■ n. Brit. another term for AUTOMATED TELLER MACHINE.

cashew /'kaʃuː, kəˈʃuː/ ■ n. **1** (also **cashew nut**) an edible kidney-shaped nut, rich in oil and protein. **2** the bushy tropical American tree that bears these nuts. [*Anacardium occidentale.*]
–ORIGIN C16: from Tupi *acajú, cajú*.

cashew apple ■ n. the swollen edible fruit of the cashew tree, from which the cashew nut hangs.

cash flow ■ n. the total amount of money passing into and out of a business, especially as affecting liquidity.

cashier¹ ■ n. a person handling payments and receipts in a shop, bank, or business.
–ORIGIN C16: from Dutch *cassier* or French *caissier*, from *caisse* 'cash'.

cashier² ■ v. dismiss from the armed forces because of a serious misdemeanour.
–ORIGIN C16: from Flemish *kasseren* 'disband (troops)' or 'revoke (a will)', from Latin *quassare* (see QUASH).

cash-in-transit ■ n. [often as modifier] money or valuables being transported securely from one commercial premises to another, typically a bank: *a cash-in-transit heist.*

cash loan company ■ n. chiefly S. African a business that lends small amounts of money to people.

cashmere ■ n. fine soft wool, originally that from the Kashmir goat.
–ORIGIN C17: an early spelling of *Kashmir*.

cash on delivery ■ n. the system of paying for goods when they are delivered.

cashpoint ■ n. Brit. another term for AUTOMATED TELLER MACHINE.

cash register ■ n. a machine used in shops for totalling and recording the amount of each sale and storing the money received.

cash-strapped ■ adj. informal extremely short of money.

casing ■ n. **1** a cover or shell that protects or encloses something. **2** the frame round a door or window.

casino ■ n. (pl. **-os**) an establishment where gambling games are played.
–ORIGIN C18: from Italian, diminutive of *casa* 'house', from Latin.

cask ■ n. a large barrel-like container for the storage of liquid, especially alcoholic drinks.
–ORIGIN C16: from French *casque* or Spanish *casco* 'helmet'.

casket ■ n. a small ornamental box or chest for holding valuable objects. ▸ Brit. a small wooden box for cremated ashes. ▸ a coffin.
–ORIGIN Middle English: perhaps an Anglo-Norman French form of Old French *cassette*, diminutive of *casse* (see CASE²).

Cassandra /kəˈsandrə/ ■ n. a prophet of disaster.
–ORIGIN from the name in Greek mythology of *Cassandra*, who was given the gift of prophecy by Apollo.

cassata /kəˈsɑːtə/ ■ n. Neapolitan ice cream containing candied or dried fruit and nuts.
–ORIGIN 1920s: Italian.

cassava /kəˈsɑːvə/ ■ n. **1** a starchy tuberous root used as food in tropical countries but requiring careful preparation to remove traces of cyanide. **2** the shrubby tree from which this root is obtained, native to tropical America. [Genus *Manihot*: several species.]
–ORIGIN C16: from Taino *casávi, cazábbi*, influenced by French *cassave*.

casserole ■ n. **1** a large dish with a lid, used for cooking food slowly in an oven. **2** a kind of stew cooked slowly in an oven. ■ v. cook slowly in a casserole.
–ORIGIN C18: from French, diminutive of *casse* 'spoon-like container', from late Latin *cattia* 'ladle, pan', from Greek, from *kuathos* 'cup'.

cassette ■ n. a sealed plastic unit containing a length of audio tape, videotape, film, etc. wound on a pair of spools, for insertion into a recorder, playback device, etc.
–ORIGIN C18: from French, diminutive of *casse* (see CASE²).

cassette deck ■ n. a hi-fi unit for playing or recording audio cassettes.

cassette player (also **cassette recorder**) ■ n. a machine for playing back or recording audio cassettes.

cassette tape ■ n. a cassette of audio tape.

cassia /'kasɪə/ ■ n. **1** a leguminous tree or plant of warm climates, producing senna and other valuable products. [Genus *Cassia*: numerous species.] **2** the aromatic bark of an East Asian tree (*Cinnamomum aromaticum*), yielding an inferior kind of cinnamon.
–ORIGIN from Latin, prob. orig. denoting wild cinnamon, from Hebrew *qĕṣīʿāh*.

cassis /kaˈsiːs, ˈkasɪs/ (also **crème de cassis**) ■ n. a syrupy blackcurrant liqueur produced mainly in Burgundy.
–ORIGIN French, 'blackcurrant', prob. from Latin *cassia* (see CASSIA).

cassiterite /kəˈsɪtərʌɪt/ ■ n. a reddish, brownish, or

cassock

yellowish mineral consisting of tin dioxide.
– ORIGIN C19: from Greek *kassiteros* 'tin'.

cassock ■ n. a long garment worn by some Christian clergy and members of church choirs.
– DERIVATIVES **cassocked** adj.
– ORIGIN C16: from French *casaque* 'long coat', prob. from Turkic *kazak* 'vagabond'.

cassoulet /'kasʊleɪ/ ■ n. a stew made with meat and beans.
– ORIGIN French, diminutive of dialect *cassolo* 'stew pan', from Old Provençal *cassa* 'pan'.

cassowary /'kasəwəri, -weːri/ ■ n. (pl. **-ies**) a very large flightless bird related to the emu, native mainly to New Guinea. [Genus *Casuarius*: five species.]
– ORIGIN C17: from Malay *kesuari*.

cast[1] ■ v. (past and past part. **cast**) 1 throw forcefully in a specified direction. ▸ throw so as to spread over an area. 2 cause (light or shadow) to appear on a surface. ▸ direct (one's eyes or thoughts) towards something. ▸ cause to be associated with something: *journalists cast doubt on this version of events.* 3 discard. 4 shape (metal or other material) by pouring it into a mould while molten. ▸ arrange and present in a specified form or style. 5 register (a vote). 6 throw the hooked and baited end of (a fishing line) out into the water. 7 cause (a magic spell) to take effect. 8 Hunting let loose (hounds) on a scent. ▸ search around for a scent. ■ n. 1 an object made by casting metal or other material. ▸ (also **plaster cast**) a mould used to make such an object. ▸ (also **plaster cast**) a bandage stiffened with plaster of Paris, moulded to support and protect a broken limb. 2 an act of casting something. ▸ the leader of a fishing line. 3 the form, appearance, or character of something. 4 a slight squint. 5 short for **WORM CAST**. 6 a pellet regurgitated by a hawk or owl.
– PHRASAL VERBS **cast about** (or **around** or **round**) search far and wide. **be cast away** be stranded after a shipwreck. **be cast down** feel depressed. **cast off** (or **cast something off**) 1 Knitting take the stitches off the needle by looping each over the next to finish the edge. 2 set a boat or ship free from her moorings. 3 let loose a hunting hound or hawk. 4 Printing estimate the space that will be taken in print by manuscript copy. **cast on** (or **cast something on**) Knitting make the first row of a specified number of loops on the needle.
– DERIVATIVES **casting** n.
– ORIGIN Middle English: from Old Norse *kasta* 'to cast or throw'.

cast[2] ■ n. the actors taking part in a play or film. ■ v. (past and past part. **cast**) assign a part to (an actor). ▸ allocate parts in (a play or film).
– ORIGIN C17: a special use of **CAST**[1].

castanets ■ pl. n. small concave pieces of wood, ivory, or plastic, joined in pairs by a cord and clicked together by the fingers as a rhythmic accompaniment to Spanish dancing.
– ORIGIN C17: from Spanish *castañeta*, diminutive of *castaña*, from Latin *castanea* 'chestnut'.

castaway ■ n. a person who has been shipwrecked and stranded in an isolated place.

caste ■ n. 1 each of the hereditary classes of Hindu society, distinguished by relative degrees of ritual purity or pollution and of social status. 2 Entomology (in some social insects) a physically distinct kind of individual with a particular function.
– PHRASES **lose caste** descend in status.
– DERIVATIVES **casteism** n.
– ORIGIN C16: from Spanish and Portuguese *casta* 'lineage, breed', from Latin *castus* 'pure, chaste'.

castellated /'kastəleɪtɪd/ ■ adj. 1 having battlements. 2 (of a nut or other mechanical part) having grooves or slots on its upper face.
– DERIVATIVES **castellation** n.
– ORIGIN C17: from medieval Latin *castellatus*, from Latin *castellum* (see **CASTLE**).

caste mark ■ n. a symbol on the forehead denoting membership of a particular Hindu caste.

caster ■ n. 1 a person or machine that casts. 2 Fishing a fly pupa used as bait. 3 variant spelling of **CASTOR**.

caster sugar (also **castor sugar**) ■ n. finely granulated white sugar.
– ORIGIN C19: so named because it was suitable for sprinkling using a castor.

castigate /'kastɪɡeɪt/ ■ v. reprimand severely.
– DERIVATIVES **castigation** n. **castigator** n. **castigatory** adj.
– ORIGIN C17 (*castigation* Middle English): from Latin *castigare* 'reprove', from *castus* 'pure, chaste'.

Castilian /ka'stɪlɪən/ ■ n. 1 a native of the central Spanish region of Castile. 2 the language of Castile, being the standard spoken and literary Spanish. ■ adj. of or relating to Castile or Castilian.

casting couch ■ n. informal used in reference to the supposed practice whereby parts in films are awarded by the director in return for sexual favours.

casting vote ■ n. an extra vote used by a chairperson to decide an issue when votes on each side are equal.
– ORIGIN C17: from an obsolete sense of *cast* 'turn the scale'.

cast iron ■ n. 1 a hard, relatively brittle alloy of iron and carbon which can be readily cast in a mould. 2 [as modifier] firm and unchangeable: *there are no cast-iron guarantees.*

castle ■ n. 1 a large building, typically of the medieval period, which is (or was formerly) fortified as a stronghold. 2 Chess, informal old-fashioned term for **ROOK**[2]. ■ v. Chess move one's king from its original square two squares along the back rank towards a rook on its corner square which is simultaneously moved to the square passed over by the king.
– PHRASES **castles in the air** (or **in Spain**) visionary unattainable schemes; daydreams.
– DERIVATIVES **castled** adj.
– ORIGIN Old English: from Anglo-Norman French *castel*, from Latin *castellum*, diminutive of *castrum* 'fort'.

cast net ■ n. Fishing a round net with weights along the edge that is thrown out and drawn in again, as opposed to one that is set up and left.

cast-off ■ adj. no longer wanted; abandoned or discarded. ■ n. a cast-off garment.

castor /'kɑːstə/ (also **caster**) ■ n. 1 each of a set of small swivelling wheels fixed to the legs or base of a heavy piece of furniture. 2 a small container with holes in the top, used for sprinkling the contents.
– ORIGIN C17: orig. a var. of **CASTER**.

castor bean ■ n. the seed of the castor oil plant, containing the poisonous compound ricin.

castor oil ■ n. a pale yellow purgative oil obtained from the seeds of an African shrub (*Ricinus communis*).
– ORIGIN C18: perhaps so named because it succeeded *castor*, an oily substance secreted by beavers, in medicinal use.

castor sugar ■ n. variant spelling of **CASTER SUGAR**.

castrate ■ v. remove the testicles of (a male animal or man). ■ n. a castrated man or male animal.
– DERIVATIVES **castration** n. **castrator** n.
– ORIGIN C16 (*castration* Middle English): from Latin *castrare*.

castrato /ka'strɑːtəʊ/ ■ n. (pl. **castrati** /-tiː/) historical a male singer castrated in boyhood so as to retain a soprano or alto voice.
– ORIGIN C18: from Italian, from *castrare* (see **CASTRATE**).

casual /'kaʒjʊəl, -zj-/ ■ adj. 1 relaxed and unconcerned. ▸ made, done, or acting without much care or thought. 2 not regular or firmly established. ▸ (of a worker) employed on a temporary or irregular basis. 3 happening by chance; accidental. 4 without formality of style, manner, or procedure. ■ n. 1 a casual worker. 2 (**casuals**) clothes or shoes suitable for everyday wear rather than formal occasions.
– DERIVATIVES **casually** adv. **casualness** n.
– ORIGIN Middle English: from Old French *casuel* and Latin *casualis*, from *casus* 'fall'.

casualization (also **-isation**) ■ n. the replacement of a permanently employed workforce by casual workers.

casualty ■ n. (pl. **-ies**) 1 a person killed or injured in a war or accident. ▸ the casualty department of a hospital. 2 (chiefly in insurance) an accident, mishap, or disaster.
– ORIGIN Middle English: from medieval Latin *casualitas*, from *casualis* (see **CASUAL**), on the pattern of *penalty*.

casualty department (also **casualty ward**) ■ n. the department of a hospital providing immediate treatment for emergency cases.

casual water ■ n. Golf a temporary expanse of water which is not a recognized hazard of the course and from which a player may remove a ball without penalty.

casuarina /ˌkasjʊəˈriːnə/ ■ n. a tree with slender, jointed, drooping twigs bearing tiny scale-like leaves, native to Australia and SE Asia. [Genus *Casuarina*.]
– ORIGIN from modern Latin *casuarius* 'cassowary', from the resemblance of the branches to the bird's feathers.

casuist /ˈkazjuɪst, -ʒj-/ ■ n. a person who uses clever but false reasoning.
– DERIVATIVES **casuistic** adj. **casuistical** adj. **casuistically** adv. **casuistry** n.
– ORIGIN C17: from French *casuiste*, from Latin *casus* (see CASE¹).

casus belli /ˌkeɪsəs ˈbɛlʌɪ, ˌkɑːsʊs ˈbɛli/ ■ n. (pl. same) an act or situation provoking or justifying war.
– ORIGIN Latin, from *casus* (see CASE¹) and *belli*, from *bellum* 'war'.

CAT ■ abbrev. **1** Central African Time. **2** clear air turbulence. **3** computer-assisted testing. **4** Medicine computerized axial tomography.

cat¹ ■ n. **1** a small domesticated carnivorous mammal with soft fur, a short snout, and retractile claws. [*Felis catus*.] ▶ a wild animal resembling this, in particular any member of the cat family (Felidae), which includes the lion, tiger, leopard, etc. **2** informal a malicious or spiteful woman. **3** historical short for CAT-O'-NINE-TAILS. ■ v. (**catted, catting**) Nautical raise (an anchor) from the surface of the water to the cathead.
– PHRASES **let the cat out of the bag** informal reveal a secret carelessly or by mistake. **like a cat on a hot tin roof** (Brit. also **on hot bricks**) informal very agitated or anxious. **not have a cat in hell's chance** informal have no chance at all. **put** (or **set**) **the cat among the pigeons** say or do something likely to cause trouble or controversy. **see which way the cat jumps** informal see what direction events are taking before committing oneself.
– DERIVATIVES **catlike** adj.
– ORIGIN Old English, of Germanic origin.

cat² ■ n. a catalytic converter.

cat³ ■ n. a catamaran.

cata- (also **cat-**) ■ prefix **1** down; downwards: *catadromous*. **2** wrongly; badly: *catachresis*. **3** completely: *cataclysm*. **4** against; alongside: *catapult*.
– ORIGIN from Greek *kata* 'down'.

catabolism /kəˈtabəlɪz(ə)m/ (also **katabolism**) ■ n. Biology the breakdown of complex molecules in living organisms to form simpler ones, together with the release of energy; destructive metabolism.
– DERIVATIVES **catabolic** /katəˈbɒlɪk/ adj.
– ORIGIN C19: from Greek *katabolē* 'throwing down'.

catachresis /ˌkatəˈkriːsɪs/ ■ n. (pl. **catachreses** /-siːz/) the incorrect use of a word.
– DERIVATIVES **catachrestic** /-ˈkriːstɪk, -ˈkrɛstɪk/ adj.
– ORIGIN C16: from Greek, from *katakhrēsthai* 'misuse'.

cataclasis /ˌkatəˈkleɪsɪs/ ■ n. Geology the fracture and breaking up of rock by natural processes.
– DERIVATIVES **cataclastic** /-ˈklastɪk/ adj.
– ORIGIN 1950s: from CATA- + Greek *klasis* 'breaking'.

cataclysm /ˈkatəˌklɪz(ə)m/ ■ n. a violent upheaval or disaster.
– DERIVATIVES **cataclysmic** adj. **cataclysmically** adv.
– ORIGIN C17 (orig. denoting the biblical Flood): from French *cataclysme*, from Greek *kataklusmos* 'deluge'.

catacomb /ˈkatəkuːm, -kəʊm/ ■ n. an underground cemetery consisting of a gallery with recesses for tombs.
– ORIGIN Old English, from late Latin *catacumbas*, the subterranean cemetery of St Sebastian near Rome.

catadromous /kəˈtadrəməs/ ■ adj. Zoology (of a fish) migrating down rivers to the sea to spawn. The opposite of ANADROMOUS.
– ORIGIN C19: from CATA- + Greek *dromos* 'running', on the pattern of *anadromous*.

catafalque /ˈkatəfalk/ ■ n. a decorated wooden framework to support a coffin.
– ORIGIN C17: from Italian *catafalco*.

Catalan /ˈkatəlan/ ■ n. **1** a native of Catalonia in NE Spain. **2** the Romance language of Catalonia closely related to Castilian Spanish and Provençal. ■ adj. of or relating to Catalonia, its people, or their language.
– ORIGIN from Spanish *catalán*, rel. to Catalan *català* 'Catalan'.

catalase /ˈkatəleɪz/ ■ n. Biochemistry an enzyme that promotes the reduction of hydrogen peroxide.
– ORIGIN C20: from CATALYSIS.

catalectic /ˌkatəˈlɛktɪk/ ■ adj. Prosody denoting a metrical line of verse lacking one syllable in the last foot.
– ORIGIN C16: from Greek *katalēktikos*, from *katalēgein* 'leave off'.

catalepsy /ˈkat(ə)lɛpsi/ ■ n. a medical condition characterized by a trance or seizure with a loss of sensation and consciousness accompanied by rigidity of the body.
– DERIVATIVES **cataleptic** adj. & n.
– ORIGIN Middle English: from French *catalepsie*, from Greek *katalēpsis*, from *katalambanein* 'seize upon'.

catalogue (US also **catalog**) ■ n. a complete list of items arranged in alphabetical or other systematic order. ▶ a publication containing details of items for sale. ▶ a series of unfortunate or bad things: *a catalogue of dismal failures*. ■ v. (**catalogues, catalogued, cataloguing**; US also **catalogs, cataloged, cataloging**) list in a catalogue.
– DERIVATIVES **cataloguer** (US also **cataloger**) n.
– ORIGIN Middle English: from Greek *katalogos*, from *katalegein* 'pick out or enrol'.

Catalonian /ˌkatəˈləʊnɪən/ ■ adj. & n. another term for CATALAN.

catalyse /ˈkat(ə)lʌɪz/ (US **catalyze**) ■ v. cause or accelerate (a reaction) by acting as a catalyst.
– DERIVATIVES **catalyser** n.
– ORIGIN C19: from CATALYSIS, on the pattern of *analyse*.

catalysis /kəˈtalɪsɪs/ ■ n. Chemistry & Biochemistry the acceleration of a chemical reaction by a catalyst.
– DERIVATIVES **catalytic** /ˌkatəˈlɪtɪk/ adj. **catalytically** adv.
– ORIGIN C19: from Greek *katalusis*, from *kataluein* 'dissolve'.

catalyst ■ n. a substance that increases the rate of a chemical reaction without itself undergoing any permanent chemical change. ▶ a person or thing that precipitates an event.
– ORIGIN C20: from CATALYSIS, on the pattern of *analyst*.

catalytic converter ■ n. a device in the exhaust system of a motor vehicle, containing a catalyst for converting pollutant gases into less harmful ones.

catamaran ■ n. a yacht or other boat with twin hulls in parallel.
– ORIGIN C17: from Tamil *kaṭṭumaram* 'tied wood'.

catamite /ˈkatəmʌɪt/ ■ n. archaic a boy kept for homosexual practices.
– ORIGIN C16: from Latin *catamitus*, from Greek *Ganumēdēs* 'Ganymede', the name of Zeus's cup-bearer in Greek mythology.

cataphatic /ˌkatəˈfatɪk/ ■ adj. Theology (of knowledge of God) obtained through affirmation. The opposite of APOPHATIC.
– ORIGIN C19: from Greek *kataphatikos* 'affirmative', from *kataphasis* 'affirmation'.

cataphora /kəˈtaf(ə)rə/ ■ n. Grammar the use of a word referring to a word used later (e.g. the pronoun *he* in *he may be approaching 60, but Jeff has no plans to retire yet*). Compare with ANAPHORA.
– DERIVATIVES **cataphoric** /katəˈfɒrɪk/ adj. **cataphorically** adv.
– ORIGIN 1970s: from CATA- on the pattern of *anaphora*.

cataplexy /ˈkatəˌplɛksi/ ■ n. a medical condition in which strong emotion or laughter causes a person to suffer sudden physical collapse though remaining conscious.
– DERIVATIVES **cataplectic** adj.
– ORIGIN C19: from Greek *kataplēxis* 'stupefaction', from *kataplessein*, from *kata-* 'down' + *plēssein* 'strike'.

catapult ■ n. **1** a forked stick with an elastic band fastened to the two prongs, used for shooting small stones. **2** historical a machine worked by a lever and ropes for

hurling large stones or other missiles. **3** a mechanical device for launching a glider or aircraft. ▪ v. hurl or launch with or as if with a catapult. ▸ move suddenly or at great speed.
– ORIGIN C16: from Latin *catapulta*, from Greek *katapeltēs*, from *kata-* 'down' + *pallein* 'hurl'.

cataract /ˈkatərakt/ ▪ n. **1** a large waterfall. **2** a medical condition in which the lens of the eye becomes progressively opaque, resulting in blurred vision.
– ORIGIN Middle English: from Latin *cataracta* 'waterfall, floodgate', from Greek *kataraktēs* 'down-rushing'.

catarrh /kəˈtɑː/ ▪ n. excessive discharge of mucus in the nose or throat.
– DERIVATIVES **catarrhal** adj.
– ORIGIN C16: from late Latin *catarrhus*, from Greek *katarrhous*, from *katarrhein* 'flow down'.

catarrhine /ˈkatərʌɪn/ ▪ adj. Zoology relating to or denoting primates of a group distinguished by having close, downwardly directed nostrils and lacking a prehensile tail, comprising the Old World monkeys, gibbons, great apes, and humans. Compare with **PLATYRRHINE**.
– ORIGIN C19: from **CATA-** + Greek *rhis* 'nose'.

catastrophe /kəˈtastrəfi/ ▪ n. **1** an event causing great damage or suffering. **2** the denouement of a drama, especially a classical tragedy.
– ORIGIN C16: from Greek *katastrophē* 'overturning, sudden turn'.

catastrophe theory ▪ n. a branch of mathematics concerned with systems displaying abrupt discontinuous change.

catastrophic ▪ adj. /katəˈstrɒfɪk/ involving or causing sudden great damage or suffering. ▸ extremely unfortunate or unsuccessful.
– DERIVATIVES **catastrophically** adv.

catastrophism ▪ n. Geology the theory that changes in the earth's crust during geological history have resulted chiefly from sudden violent and unusual events. Often contrasted with **UNIFORMITARIANISM**.
– DERIVATIVES **catastrophist** n. & adj.

catatonia /ˌkatəˈtəʊnɪə/ ▪ n. Psychiatry abnormality of movement and behaviour arising from a disturbed mental state. ▸ informal a state of immobility and stupor.
– DERIVATIVES **catatonic** adj.
– ORIGIN C19: from **CATA-** + Greek *tonos* 'tone or tension'.

catawba /kəˈtɔːbə/ ▪ n. a North American variety of grape. ▸ a white wine made from this grape.
– ORIGIN named after the river *Catawba* in North and South Carolina.

catboat ▪ n. a sailing boat with a single mast placed well forward and carrying only one sail.
– ORIGIN C19: perhaps from *cat* (denoting a type of merchant ship) + **BOAT**.

cat burglar ▪ n. a thief who enters a building by climbing to an upper storey.

catcall ▪ n. a shrill whistle or shout of mockery or disapproval. ▪ v. make a catcall.
– ORIGIN C17: from **CAT**[1] + **CALL**.

catch ▪ v. (past and past part. **caught**) **1** intercept and hold (something which has been thrown, propelled, or dropped). ▸ seize or take hold of. ▸ Cricket dismiss (a batsman) by catching the ball before it touches the ground. **2** capture (a person or animal that tries or would try to escape). **3** accidentally become entangled or trapped in something. ▸ have (a part of one's body or clothing) become entangled or trapped in something. **4** reach in time and board (a train, bus, or aircraft). ▸ reach or be in a place in time to see (a person, performance, etc.). **5 (be caught in)** unexpectedly find oneself in (an unwelcome situation). ▸ surprise (someone) in an awkward or incriminating situation. **6** engage (a person's interest or imagination). ▸ perceive fleetingly. ▸ hear or understand (something said), especially with effort. ▸ succeed in evoking or representing. **7** strike (someone) on a part of the body. ▸ accidentally strike (a part of one's body) against something. **8** contract (an illness) through infection or contagion. **9** become ignited and start burning. ▪ n. **1** an act or instance of catching. ▸ an amount of fish caught. ▸ informal a person considered desirable as a partner or spouse. **2** a device for securing something such as a door, window, or box. **3** a hidden problem or disadvantage. **4** an unevenness in a person's voice caused by emotion.
– PHRASES **catch one's breath 1** draw one's breath in sharply as a reaction to an emotion. **2** recover one's breath after exertion. **catch someone's eye 1** be noticed by someone. **2** attract someone's attention by making eye contact. **catch the light** shine or glint in the light. **catch sight of** suddenly notice; glimpse. **catch the sun 1** be in a sunny position. **2** become tanned or sunburnt. **catch a tan** S. African informal become brown or browner after exposure to the sun.
– PHRASAL VERBS **catch on** informal **1** (of a practice or fashion) become popular. **2** understand what is meant or how to do something. **catch someone out 1** detect that someone has done something wrong. **2** (often **be caught out**) put someone in a difficult situation for which they are unprepared. **catch up** (or **catch someone up**) **1** succeed in reaching a person who is ahead of one. **2** do work or other tasks which one should have done earlier. ▸ (**be/get caught up in**) become involved in. **catch up with 1** exchange news with (someone whom one has not seen for some time). **2** begin to have a damaging effect on.
– ORIGIN Middle English: from Anglo-Norman French *cachier*, var. of Old French *chacier*, from Latin *captare* 'try to catch'.

catch-22 ▪ n. a difficult situation from which there is no escape because it involves mutually conflicting or dependent conditions.
– ORIGIN 1970s: title of a novel by Joseph Heller (1961).

catch-all ▪ n. a term or category that includes a variety of different possibilities.

catch-as-catch-can ▪ n. **1** wrestling in which all holds are permitted. **2** [usu. as modifier] a situation of using whatever is available.

catcher ▪ n. a person or thing that catches. ▸ Baseball a fielder positioned to catch pitches not hit by the batter.

catching ▪ adj. informal (of a disease) infectious.

catchline ▪ n. Brit. **1** a short, eye-catching headline or title. **2** an advertising slogan.

catchment (also **catchment area**) ▪ n. **1** the area from which a hospital's patients or a school's pupils are drawn. **2** the area from which rainfall flows into a river, lake, or reservoir.

catchpenny ▪ adj. having a cheap superficial attractiveness designed to encourage quick sales.

catchphrase ▪ n. a well-known sentence or phrase.

catchup /ˈkatʃʌp/ ▪ n. variant spelling of **KETCHUP**.

catchweight ▪ n. unrestricted weight, as a weight category in sport.

catchword ▪ n. **1** a popular word or phrase encapsulating a particular concept. **2** a word printed or placed so as to attract attention. ▸ Printing the first word of a page given at the foot of the previous one.

catchy ▪ adj. (**-ier**, **-iest**) (of a tune or phrase) instantly appealing and memorable.
– DERIVATIVES **catchily** adv. **catchiness** n.

catechism /ˈkatɪkɪz(ə)m/ ▪ n. a summary of the principles of Christian religion in the form of questions and answers, used for teaching.
– DERIVATIVES **catechismal** adj.
– ORIGIN C16: from eccles. Latin *catechismus*, from eccles. Greek, from *katēkhizein* (see **CATECHIZE**).

catechist ▪ n. a Christian teacher, especially one using a catechism.
– ORIGIN C16: from eccles. Greek *katēkhistēs*, from *katēkhein* (see **CATECHIZE**).

catechize (also **-ise**) ▪ v. instruct by means of question and answer, especially by using a catechism.
– DERIVATIVES **catechizer** (also **-iser**) n.
– ORIGIN Middle English: from eccles. Greek *katēkhizein*, from *katēkhein* 'instruct orally, make hear'.

catechumen /ˌkatɪˈkjuːmɛn/ ▪ n. a Christian preparing for baptism or confirmation.
– ORIGIN Middle English: from Greek *katēkhoumenos* 'being instructed', from *katēkhein* (see **CATECHIZE**).

categorical ▪ adj. unambiguously explicit and direct.

–DERIVATIVES **categoric** adj. **categorically** adv.
–ORIGIN C16: from Greek *katēgorikos*, from *katēgoria* (see CATEGORY).

categorical imperative ■ n. Philosophy (in Kantian ethics) an unconditional and binding moral obligation which is not dependent on a person's inclination or purpose.

categorize (also **-ise**) ■ v. place in a particular category; classify.
–DERIVATIVES **categorization** (also **-isation**) n.

category ■ n. (pl. **-ies**) **1** a class or division of people or things having particular shared characteristics. **2** Philosophy each of a possibly exhaustive set of classes among which all things might be distributed. ▶ an a priori conception applied by the mind to sense impressions.
–DERIVATIVES **categorial** adj.
–ORIGIN Middle English: from Greek *katēgoria* 'statement, accusation', from *katēgoros* 'accuser'.

catenary /kəˈtiːnəri/ ■ n. (pl. **-ies**) a curve formed by a chain hanging freely from two points on the same horizontal level. ▶ a chain forming such a curve. ■ adj. of, involving, or denoting a catenary.
–ORIGIN C18: from Latin *catenarius* 'relating to a chain', from *catena* 'chain'.

catenated /ˈkatɪneɪtɪd/ ■ adj. connected in a chain or series.
–DERIVATIVES **catenation** n.
–ORIGIN C19: from Latin *catenare* 'to chain, fetter'.

cater ■ v. **1** provide food and drink at a social event. **2** (**cater for/to**) provide with what is needed or required. ▶ (**cater for**) take into account or make allowances for. ▶ (**cater to**) satisfy (a need or demand).
–DERIVATIVES **caterer** n. **catering** n.
–ORIGIN C16: from obsolete *cater* 'caterer', from Old French *acateor* 'buyer', from *acater* 'buy'.

cater-cornered /ˈkeɪtəˌkɔːnəd/ (also **cater-corner**, **catty-cornered**, **kitty-corner**) ■ adj. & adv. chiefly N. Amer. situated diagonally opposite.
–ORIGIN C19: from dialect *cater* 'diagonally', from *cater* denoting the four on dice, from Latin *quattuor*.

caterpillar ■ n. **1** the larva of a butterfly or moth. **2** (also **caterpillar track** or **tread**) trademark an articulated steel band passing round the wheels of a vehicle for travel on rough ground.
–ORIGIN Middle English: perhaps from a var. of Old French *chatepelose* 'hairy cat', influenced by obsolete *piller* 'ravager'.

caterwaul /ˈkatəwɔːl/ ■ v. make a shrill howling or wailing noise. ■ n. such a noise.
–DERIVATIVES **caterwauling** n. & adj.
–ORIGIN Middle English: from CAT[1] + rare *waul* 'give a cry like that of a cat', of imitative origin.

catfish ■ n. (pl. same or **-fishes**) a freshwater or marine fish with whisker-like barbels round the mouth, typically bottom-dwelling. [Order Siluriformes: many species.]

cat flap ■ n. a small hinged flap through which a cat may enter or leave a building.

catgut ■ n. a material used for the strings of musical instruments and for surgical sutures, made of the dried twisted intestines of sheep or horses (but not cats).
–ORIGIN C16: the association with CAT[1] remains unexplained.

Cath. ■ abbrev. **1** Cathedral. **2** Catholic.

catharsis /kəˈθɑːsɪs/ ■ n. the process of releasing pent-up emotions, for example through drama.
–DERIVATIVES **cathartic** adj. & n. **cathartically** adv.
–ORIGIN C19: from Greek *katharsis*, from *kathairein* 'cleanse', from *katharos* 'pure'.

cathead ■ n. a horizontal beam at each side of a ship's bow, used for raising and carrying an anchor.

cathedral ■ n. the principal church of a diocese.
–ORIGIN Middle English (*cathedral church* 'the church which contains the bishop's throne'): from Latin *cathedra* 'seat', from Greek *kathedra*.

Catherine wheel ■ n. **1** a firework in the form of a spinning coil. **2** Heraldry a wheel with curved spikes projecting around the circumference.
–ORIGIN C16: named after St *Catherine*, with ref. to her martyrdom on a spiked wheel.

catheter /ˈkaθɪtə/ ■ n. Medicine a flexible tube inserted through a narrow opening into a body cavity, particularly the bladder, for removing fluid.
–DERIVATIVES **catheterization** (also **-isation**) n. **catheterize** (also **-ise**) v.
–ORIGIN C17: from Greek *kathetēr*, from *kathienai* 'send or let down'.

cathode /ˈkaθəʊd/ ■ n. a negatively charged electrode. The opposite of ANODE.
–DERIVATIVES **cathodal** adj. **cathodic** /kəˈθɒdɪk/ adj.
–ORIGIN C19: from Greek *kathodos* 'way down', from *kata-* 'down' + *hodos* 'way'.

cathode ray ■ n. a beam of electrons emitted from the cathode of a high-vacuum tube.

cathode ray tube ■ n. a high-vacuum tube in which cathode rays produce a luminous image on a fluorescent screen.

cathodic protection ■ n. protection of a metal structure from corrosion under water by making it act as an electrical cathode.

catholic ■ adj. **1** including a wide variety of things. **2** (**Catholic**) of the Roman Catholic faith. ▶ of or including all Christians. ▶ of or relating to the historic doctrine and practice of the Western Church. ■ n. (**Catholic**) a member of the Roman Catholic Church.
–DERIVATIVES **Catholicism** n. **catholicity** n. **Catholicize** (also **-ise**) v.
–ORIGIN Middle English: from Old French *catholique*, from Greek *katholikos* 'universal', from *kata* 'in respect of' + *holos* 'whole'.

cathouse ■ n. informal, chiefly N. Amer. a brothel.

cation /ˈkatʌɪən/ ■ n. Chemistry a positively charged ion. The opposite of ANION.
–DERIVATIVES **cationic** /katʌɪˈɒnɪk/ adj.
–ORIGIN C19: from CATA- or CATHODE.

catkin ■ n. a downy, hanging, wind-pollinated flowering spike of trees such as willow and hazel.
–ORIGIN C16: from obsolete Dutch *katteken* 'kitten'.

cat ladder ■ n. a ladder used for working on a sloping roof, with a hook at one end.

catlick ■ n. a perfunctory wash.

catmint ■ n. a plant with downy leaves, purple-spotted white flowers, and a pungent smell attractive to cats. [*Nepeta cataria* and related species.]

catnap ■ n. a short sleep during the day. ■ v. (**-napped**, **-napping**) have a catnap.

catnip ■ n. another term for CATMINT.
–ORIGIN C18 (orig. US): from CAT[1] + *nip*, var. of dialect *nep*, from Latin *nepeta* 'catmint'.

cat-o'-nine-tails ■ n. historical a rope whip with nine knotted cords, used for flogging.

cat's cradle ■ n. a child's game in which patterns are constructed in a loop of string held between the fingers of each hand.

cat's eye ■ n. **1** a semi-precious stone, especially chalcedony, with a chatoyant lustre. **2** (**catseye**) trademark a light-reflecting stud set in a series into a road to mark traffic lanes or the edge of the carriageway.

cat shark ■ n. a small bottom-dwelling shark that has catlike eyes and small dorsal fins set well back. [Family Scyliorhinidae: several genera.]

cat's paw ■ n. a person who is used by another to carry out an unpleasant or dangerous task.

cat's tail (also **cattail**) ■ n. a plant, such as a reed mace or grass, with long thin parts suggestive of a cat's tail.

catsuit ■ n. chiefly Brit. a woman's close-fitting one-piece garment with trouser legs.

catsup /ˈkatsəp/ ■ n. US another term for KETCHUP.

cat's whisker ■ n. a fine adjustable wire in a crystal radio receiver.
–PHRASES **the cat's whiskers** informal an excellent person or thing.

cattery ■ n. (pl. **-ies**) a boarding or breeding establishment for cats.

cattle ▪ pl. n. large ruminant animals with horns and cloven hoofs, chiefly domesticated for meat or milk or as beasts of burden; cows and oxen. [Family Bovidae: several species, including *Bos taurus* and *B. indicus*.]
– ORIGIN Middle English: from Anglo-Norman French *catel*, var. of Old French *chatel* (see **CHATTEL**).

cattle call ▪ n. N. Amer. informal an open audition for parts in a play or film.

cattle egret ▪ n. a small egret which normally feeds around grazing cattle and game herds. [*Bubulcus ibis*.]

cattle grid (N. Amer. **cattle guard**) ▪ n. a metal grid covering a ditch, allowing vehicles and pedestrians to cross but not animals.

cattleya /ˈkatlɪə/ ▪ n. a tropical American orchid with brightly coloured showy flowers and thick leaves. [Genus *Cattleya*.]
– ORIGIN C19: named after William *Cattley*, English patron of botany.

catty¹ ▪ adj. (**-ier, -iest**) **1** spiteful. **2** of or relating to cats; catlike.
– DERIVATIVES **cattily** adv. **cattiness** n.

catty² ▪ n. S. African informal a catapult.

catty-cornered ▪ adj. see **CATER-CORNERED**.

catwalk ▪ n. **1** a narrow walkway or open bridge, especially in an industrial installation. **2** a platform extending into an auditorium, along which models walk to display clothes.

Caucasian /kɔːˈkeɪzɪən, -ʒ(ə)n/ ▪ adj. **1** relating to or denoting a broad division of humankind covering peoples from Europe, western Asia, and parts of India and North Africa. ▸ white-skinned; of European origin. **2** of or relating to the region of the Caucasus in SE Europe. ▪ n. a Caucasian person.

USAGE
Caucasian (or **Caucasoid**) belonged to a set of terms introduced by 19th-century anthropologists attempting to categorize human races. Although such classification is now outdated and potentially offensive, the term **Caucasian** has acquired a more restricted meaning, especially in the US, as a synonym for 'white or of European origin', as in *the police are looking for a Caucasian male in his forties*.

Caucasoid /ˈkɔːkəsɔɪd/ ▪ adj. of or relating to the Caucasian division of humankind. ▪ n. a Caucasian.

caucus /ˈkɔːkəs/ ▪ n. (pl. **caucuses**) **1** a meeting of the members of a legislative body who belong to a particular political party, to select candidates or decide policy. **2** a group of people with shared concerns within a larger organization. ▪ v. (**caucused, caucusing**) hold or form a caucus.
– ORIGIN C18: perhaps from Algonquian *cau'-cau'-as'u* 'adviser'.

caudal /ˈkɔːd(ə)l/ ▪ adj. of or like a tail. ▸ at or near the tail or the posterior part of the body.
– DERIVATIVES **caudally** adv.
– ORIGIN C17: from Latin *cauda* 'tail'.

caudal fin ▪ n. Zoology another term for **TAIL FIN**.

Caudata /kɔːˈdeɪtə/ ▪ pl. n. Zoology another term for **URODELA**.
– ORIGIN from Latin *cauda* 'tail'.

caudate /ˈkɔːdeɪt/ ▪ adj. Anatomy relating to or denoting the upper of the two grey nuclei of the corpus striatum in the cerebrum of the brain.
– ORIGIN C17: from medieval Latin *caudatus*, from *cauda* 'tail'.

caught past and past participle of **CATCH**.

caul /kɔːl/ ▪ n. **1** the amniotic membrane enclosing a fetus. ▸ part of this membrane occasionally found on a child's head at birth, thought to bring good luck. **2** historical a woman's close-fitting indoor headdress or hairnet. **3** Anatomy the omentum.
– ORIGIN Middle English: perhaps from Old French *cale* 'head covering'.

cauldron (also **caldron**) ▪ n. **1** a large metal pot, used for cooking over an open fire. **2** a situation characterized by instability and strong emotions.
– ORIGIN Middle English: from Anglo-Norman French *caudron*, from Latin *caldarium* 'cooking-pot', from *calidus* 'hot'.

caul fat ▪ n. a lacy membrane of fat taken from the abdominal lining of an animal, used in cookery.

cauliflower ▪ n. a cabbage of a variety which bears a large immature flower head of small creamy-white flower buds, eaten as a vegetable.
– ORIGIN C16: from obsolete French *chou fleuri* 'flowered cabbage', prob. from Italian *cavolfiore*.

cauliflower cheese ▪ n. a savoury dish of cauliflower in a cheese sauce.

cauliflower ear ▪ n. a person's ear that has become thickened or deformed as a result of repeated blows.

caulk /kɔːk/ (US also **calk**) ▪ n. a waterproof filler and sealant, used in building work and repairs. ▪ v. **1** seal with caulk. **2** make (a boat or its seams) watertight.
– ORIGIN Middle English: from Old Northern French *cauquer* 'tread, press with force', from Latin *calcare* 'tread', from *calx* 'heel'.

causal ▪ adj. of, relating to, or acting as a cause.
– DERIVATIVES **causally** adv.
– ORIGIN Middle English: from late Latin *causalis*, from Latin *causa* 'cause'.

causality ▪ n. **1** the relationship between cause and effect. **2** the principle that everything has a cause.

causation ▪ n. **1** the action of causing something. **2** the relationship between cause and effect.

causative ▪ adj. **1** acting as a cause. **2** Grammar expressing causation.
– ORIGIN Middle English: from late Latin *causativus*, from *causare* 'to cause'.

cause ▪ n. **1** a person or thing that gives rise to an action, phenomenon, or condition. ▸ reasonable grounds for a belief or action. **2** a principle or movement which one is prepared to defend or advocate. ▸ something deserving of support. **3** a matter to be resolved in a court of law. ▸ an individual's case offered at law. ▪ v. be the cause of; make happen.
– PHRASES **cause and effect** the principle of causation. **cause of action** Law a fact or facts that enable a person to bring an action against another. **make common cause** unite in order to achieve a shared aim.
– DERIVATIVES **causeless** adj. **causer** n.
– ORIGIN Middle English: from Latin *causa* (n.), *causare* (v.).

'cause ▪ conj. informal because.

cause célèbre /ˌkɔːz sɛˈlɛbr(ə)/ ▪ n. (pl. **causes célèbres** pronunc. same) a controversial issue that attracts a great deal of public attention.
– ORIGIN C18: French, 'famous case'.

causeway ▪ n. a raised road or track across low or wet ground.
– DERIVATIVES **causewayed** adj.
– ORIGIN Middle English: from dialect *causey*, from Anglo-Norman French *causee*, from Latin *calx* 'lime, limestone' + **WAY**.

caustic /ˈkɔːstɪk, ˈkɒst-/ ▪ adj. **1** able to burn or corrode organic tissue by chemical action. **2** scathingly sarcastic. **3** Physics formed by the intersection of reflected or refracted parallel rays from a curved surface. ▪ n. **1** a caustic substance. **2** Physics a caustic surface or curve.
– DERIVATIVES **caustically** adv. **causticity** n.
– ORIGIN Middle English: from Greek *kaustos* 'combustible', from *kaiein* 'to burn'.

caustic potash ▪ n. potassium hydroxide.

caustic soda ▪ n. sodium hydroxide.

cauterize /ˈkɔːtəraɪz/ (also **-ise**) ▪ v. burn the skin or flesh of (a wound) to stop bleeding or prevent infection.
– DERIVATIVES **cauterization** (also **-isation**) n.
– ORIGIN Middle English: from Old French *cauteriser*, from Greek *kautēriazein*, from *kautērion* 'branding iron', from *kaiein* 'to burn'.

cautery /ˈkɔːt(ə)ri/ ▪ n. (pl. **-ies**) Medicine **1** an instrument or caustic substance used for cauterizing. **2** the action of cauterizing.
– ORIGIN Middle English: from Greek *kautērion* (see **CAUTERIZE**).

caution ■ n. **1** care taken to avoid danger or mistakes. **2** an official or legal warning given to someone who has committed a minor offence that has not been charged. ■ v. **1** say something as a warning. ▸ (**caution against**) warn or advise against. **2** issue an official or legal warning to. ▸ (of a police officer) advise (someone) of their legal rights when arresting them.
– PHRASES **throw caution to the wind** act in a reckless manner.
– ORIGIN Middle English: from Latin *cautio(n-)*, from *cavere* 'take heed'.

cautionary ■ adj. serving as a warning.

cautious ■ adj. careful to avoid potential problems or dangers.
– DERIVATIVES **cautiously** adv. **cautiousness** n.

cava /'kɑːvə/ ■ n. a Spanish sparkling wine made in the same way as champagne.
– ORIGIN from Spanish.

cavalcade /ˌkav(ə)l'keɪd, 'kav(ə)lkeɪd/ ■ n. a procession of people walking, on horseback, or riding in vehicles.
– ORIGIN C16: from Italian *cavalcata*, from *cavalcare* 'to ride', from Latin *caballus* 'horse'.

cavalier ■ n. **1** (**Cavalier**) historical a supporter of King Charles I in the English Civil War. **2** archaic or poetic/literary a gallant. **3** archaic a cavalryman. ■ adj. showing a lack of proper concern.
– DERIVATIVES **cavalierly** adv.
– ORIGIN C16: from Italian *cavaliere*, from Latin *caballus* 'horse'.

cavalry ■ n. (pl. **-ies**) [usu. treated as pl.] historical soldiers who fought on horseback. ▸ modern soldiers who fight in armoured vehicles.
– DERIVATIVES **cavalryman** n. (pl. **-men**).
– ORIGIN C16: from French *cavallerie*, from Italian, from *cavallo* 'horse', from Latin *caballus*.

cavalry twill ■ n. strong woollen twill of a khaki or light brown colour.

cave[1] /keɪv/ ■ n. a large natural underground chamber. ■ v. **1** explore caves as a sport. **2** (**cave in**) (US **cave**) (of a roof or walls) subside or collapse.
– DERIVATIVES **caver** n. **caving** n.
– ORIGIN Middle English: from Latin *cava*, from *cavus* 'hollow'.

cave[2] /'keɪvi/ ■ exclam. Brit. school slang, dated look out!
– PHRASES **keep cave** act as lookout.
– ORIGIN Latin, from *cavere* 'beware'.

caveat /'kavɪat, 'keɪ-/ ■ n. a warning or proviso of specific stipulations, conditions, or limitations.
– ORIGIN C16: from Latin, 'let a person beware'.

caveat emptor /'ɛmptɔː/ ■ n. the principle that the buyer is responsible for checking the quality and suitability of goods before purchase.
– ORIGIN Latin, 'let the buyer beware'.

caveman (or **cavewoman**) ■ n. (pl. **-men** or **-women**) a prehistoric person who lived in caves.

cavern /'kav(ə)n/ ■ n. **1** a large cave, or chamber in a cave. **2** a vast, dark space.
– DERIVATIVES **cavernous** adj. **cavernously** adv.
– ORIGIN Middle English: from Latin *caverna*, from *cavus* 'hollow'.

caviar /'kavɪɑː, ˌkavɪ'ɑː/ (also **caviare**) ■ n. the pickled roe of sturgeon or other large fish, eaten as a delicacy.
– ORIGIN C16: from Italian *caviale*, *caviaro* or French *caviar*, prob. from medieval Greek *khaviari*.

cavil /'kav(ə)l/ ■ v. (**cavilled**, **cavilling**; US **caviled**, **caviling**) make petty or unnecessary objections. ■ n. an objection of this kind.
– DERIVATIVES **caviller** n.
– ORIGIN C16: from French *caviller*, from Latin, from *cavilla* 'mockery'.

cavitation /ˌkavɪ'teɪʃ(ə)n/ ■ n. Physics **1** the formation of an empty space within a solid object or body. **2** the formation of bubbles in a liquid.

cavity ■ n. (pl. **-ies**) an empty space within a solid object. ▸ a decayed part of a tooth.
– ORIGIN C16: from French *cavité* or late Latin *cavitas*, from Latin *cavus* 'hollow'.

cavity wall ■ n. a wall formed from two thicknesses of bricks with a space between them.

cavort ■ v. prance around excitedly or self-indulgently.
– ORIGIN C18 (orig. US): perhaps from Italian, from *corvetta* 'little curve', from Latin *curvus* 'bent'.

caw ■ n. the harsh cry of a rook, crow, or similar bird. ■ v. utter a caw.
– ORIGIN C16: imitative.

cay /keɪ, kiː/ ■ n. (in Spanish America) a low bank or reef of coral, rock, or sand.
– ORIGIN C17: from Spanish *cayo* 'shoal, reef', from French *quai* 'quay'.

cayenne /keɪ'ɛn/ (also **cayenne pepper**) ■ n. a pungent, hot-tasting red powder prepared from dried chillies.
– ORIGIN C18: from Tupi *kyynha*, *quiynha*, later associated with *Cayenne* in French Guiana.

cayman ■ n. variant spelling of CAIMAN.

CB ■ abbrev. Citizens' Band.

CBC ■ abbrev. Canadian Broadcasting Corporation.

CBD ■ abbrev. chiefly S. African the central business district of a town or city.

CBE ■ abbrev. (in the UK) Commander of the Order of the British Empire.

CBS ■ abbrev. (in the US) Columbia Broadcasting System.

CC ■ abbrev. **1** (also **cc**) (after a name) close corporation. **2** Cricket Club.

cc (also **c.c.**) ■ abbrev. **1** carbon copy (an indication that a duplicate has been or should be sent to another person). **2** cubic centimetre(s).

CCB ■ abbrev. S. African historical Civil Cooperation Bureau.

CCD ■ abbrev. Electronics charge-coupled device.

CCMA ■ abbrev. (in South Africa) Commission for Conciliation, Mediation, and Arbitration.

CCTV ■ abbrev. closed-circuit television.

CD ■ abbrev. **1** civil defence. **2** compact disc. **3** corps diplomatique.

Cd ■ symb. the chemical element cadmium.

cd ■ abbrev. candela.

CDC ■ abbrev. Commonwealth Development Corporation.

CD4 cell ■ n. Physiology a type of T-lymphocyte containing CD4 receptor-molecules, which orchestrates the body's response to micro-organisms such as viruses.
– ORIGIN *CD4*: 'cluster of *d*ifferentiation' (a set of antibodies that reacts with and thereby identifies the particular antigen present on a cell) + *4* (a number identifying the cluster).

Cde ■ abbrev. Comrade.

cDNA ■ abbrev. complementary DNA.

Cdr ■ abbrev. (in a navy or air force) Commander.

CD-ROM ■ n. a compact disc used in a computer as a read-only device for displaying data.
– ORIGIN 1980s: acronym from *compact disc read-only memory*.

CDV ■ abbrev. compact disc video.

CE ■ abbrev. **1** Church of England. **2** civil engineer. **3** Common Era.

Ce ■ symb. the chemical element cerium.

ceanothus /ˌsiːə'nəʊθəs/ ■ n. a shrub with dense clusters of small blue flowers, native to North America. [Genus *Ceanothus*.]
– ORIGIN from Greek *keanōthos*, a kind of thistle.

cease ■ v. come or bring to an end; stop.
– PHRASES **without cease** without stopping.
– ORIGIN Middle English: from Old French *cesser*, from Latin *cessare*, from *cedere* 'to yield'.

ceasefire ■ n. a temporary suspension of fighting.

ceaseless ■ adj. constant and unending.
– DERIVATIVES **ceaselessly** adv.

cecum ■ n. (pl. **ceca**) US spelling of CAECUM.

cedar ■ n. a tall, elegant coniferous tree yielding typically fragrant, durable wood. [*Cedrus libani* (cedar of Lebanon) and other species in the genera *Cedrus* and *Thuja*.] ▸ used in names of similar trees.
– DERIVATIVES **cedarn** adj. (poetic/literary).
– ORIGIN Old English: from Old French *cedre* or Latin

cedrus, from Greek *kedros*.

cede /siːd/ ■ v. give up (power or territory).
– ORIGIN C16: from French *céder* or Latin *cedere* 'to yield'.

cedilla /sɪˈdɪlə/ ■ n. a mark (,) written under the letter *c*, especially in French, to show that it is pronounced like an *s* rather than a *k* (e.g. *façade*). ▸ a similar mark under *s* in Turkish and other languages.
– ORIGIN C16: from obsolete Spanish, earlier form of *zedilla*, diminutive of *zeda* (the letter Z), from Greek *zēta*.

ceiba /ˈsʌɪbə/ ■ n. a very tall tropical American tree from which kapok is obtained. [*Ceiba pentandra*.]
– ORIGIN from Taino, 'giant tree'.

ceilidh /ˈkeɪli/ ■ n. a social event with Scottish or Irish folk music and singing, traditional dancing, and storytelling.
– ORIGIN C19: from Scottish Gaelic *ceilidh* and Irish *céilidhe*, from Old Irish *céilide* 'visit, visiting', from *céile* 'companion'.

ceiling ■ n. 1 the upper interior surface of a room. 2 an upper limit set on prices, wages, etc. 3 the maximum altitude that an aircraft can reach. ▸ the altitude of the base of a cloud layer. 4 the inside planking of a ship's bottom and sides.
– ORIGIN Middle English: perhaps rel. to Latin *celare* 'conceal'.

celadon /ˈsɛlədɒn/ ■ n. a willow-green colour. ▸ a grey-green glaze used in pottery.
– ORIGIN C18: from French *céladon*, a colour named after the hero in d'Urfé's pastoral romance *L'Astrée* (1607–27).

-cele (also **-coele**) ■ comb. form Medicine denoting a swelling or hernia in a specified part: *hydrocele*.
– ORIGIN from Greek *kēlē* 'tumour'.

celeb /sɪˈlɛb/ ■ n. informal a celebrity.
– ORIGIN C20 (orig. US): abbrev.

celebrant /ˈsɛlɪbr(ə)nt/ ■ n. 1 a person who performs a rite, especially a priest at the Eucharist. 2 a person who celebrates something.
– ORIGIN C19: from French *célébrant* or from Latin *celebrare* (see CELEBRATE).

celebrate ■ v. 1 mark (a significant time or event) with an enjoyable activity. ▸ engage in festivities. 2 perform (a religious ceremony), in particular officiate at (the Eucharist). 3 honour or praise publicly.
– DERIVATIVES **celebration** n. **celebrator** n. **celebratory** adj.
– ORIGIN Middle English: from Latin *celebrare* 'celebrate', from *celeber, celebr-* 'frequented or honoured'.

celebrity ■ n. (pl. **-ies**) 1 a famous person. 2 the state of being famous.
– ORIGIN Middle English: from Latin *celebritas*, from *celeber* 'frequented or honoured'.

celeriac /sɪˈlɛrɪak/ ■ n. celery of a variety which forms a large swollen turnip-like root.
– ORIGIN C18: from CELERY.

celerity /sɪˈlɛrɪti/ ■ n. formal or poetic/literary swiftness of movement.
– ORIGIN C15: from Latin *celeritas*, from *celer* 'swift'.

celery ■ n. a cultivated plant of the parsley family, with closely packed succulent leaf stalks that are eaten raw or cooked. [*Apium graveolens* var. *dulce*.]
– ORIGIN C17: from French *céleri*, from Italian dialect *selleri*, from Greek *selinon* 'parsley'.

celery salt ■ n. a mixture of salt and ground celery seed used for seasoning.

celesta /sɪˈlɛstə/ (also **celeste** /sɪˈlɛst/) ■ n. a small keyboard instrument in which felted hammers strike a row of steel plates suspended over wooden resonators, giving an ethereal bell-like sound.
– ORIGIN C19: from French *céleste* 'heavenly'.

celestial ■ adj. 1 positioned in or relating to the sky or outer space. 2 belonging or relating to heaven.
– DERIVATIVES **celestially** adv.
– ORIGIN Middle English: from medieval Latin *caelestialis*, from Latin, from *caelum* 'heaven'.

celestial equator ■ n. Astronomy the projection into space of the earth's equator.

celestial latitude ■ n. Astronomy the angular distance of a point north or south of the ecliptic.

celestial longitude ■ n. Astronomy the angular distance of a point east of the First Point of Aries, measured along the ecliptic.

celestial mechanics ■ pl. n. [treated as sing.] the branch of astronomy concerned with the calculation of the motions of celestial objects such as planets.

celestial navigation ■ n. navigation using the sun, moon, and stars.

celestial pole ■ n. Astronomy the point on the celestial sphere directly above either of the earth's geographic poles, around which the stars appear to rotate.

celestial sphere ■ n. an imaginary sphere of which the observer is the centre and on which all celestial objects are considered to lie.

celiac ■ n. US spelling of COELIAC.

celibate /ˈsɛlɪbət/ ■ adj. 1 abstaining from marriage and sexual relations for religious reasons. 2 having or involving no sexual relations. ■ n. a person who is celibate.
– DERIVATIVES **celibacy** n.
– ORIGIN C19: from *celibacy* (C17), from French *célibat* or Latin *caelibatus* 'unmarried state'.

cell ■ n. 1 a small room in which a prisoner is locked up or in which a monk or nun sleeps. ▸ a small compartment in a larger structure such as a honeycomb. 2 Biology the smallest structural and functional unit of an organism, typically microscopic, consisting of cytoplasm and a nucleus enclosed in a membrane. 3 a small group forming a nucleus of political activity. 4 a device containing electrodes immersed in an electrolyte, used for current generation or electrolysis. ▸ a unit in a device for converting chemical energy or light into electricity. 5 short for CELLPHONE.
– DERIVATIVES **-celled** adj.
– ORIGIN Old English, from Old French *celle* or Latin *cella* 'storeroom, chamber'.

cellar ■ n. a storage space or room below ground level in a house. ▸ a stock of wine. ■ v. store in a cellar.
– ORIGIN Middle English: from Old French *celier*, from late Latin *cellarium* 'storehouse', from *cella* 'storeroom, chamber'.

cellarer /ˈsɛlərə/ ■ n. 1 the person in a monastery who is responsible for provisions and catering. 2 a person in charge of a wine cellar.

cell-mediated ■ adj. Physiology (of immunity) involving the action of white blood cells. Often contrasted with HUMORAL.

cello /ˈtʃɛləʊ/ ■ n. (pl. **-os**) a bass instrument of the violin family, held upright on the floor between the legs of the seated player.
– DERIVATIVES **cellist** n.
– ORIGIN C19: shortening of VIOLONCELLO.

cellophane /ˈsɛləfeɪn/ ■ n. trademark a thin transparent wrapping material made from viscose.
– ORIGIN C20: from CELLULOSE + *-phane*, from *diaphane*, a kind of semi-transparent woven silk (from medieval Latin *diaphanus* 'diaphanous').

cellphone (also **cellular phone**) ■ n. a portable telephone using a cellular radio system.

cellular /ˈsɛljʊlə/ ■ adj. 1 of, relating to, or consisting of living cells. 2 denoting or relating to a mobile telephone system that uses a number of short-range radio stations. 3 (of fabric) knitted so as to form holes or hollows that trap air and provide extra insulation. 4 consisting of small compartments or rooms.
– DERIVATIVES **cellularity** n.
– ORIGIN C18: from French *cellulaire*, from late Latin, from *cellula* 'little chamber', diminutive of *cella*.

cellulase /ˈsɛljʊleɪz/ ■ n. Biochemistry an enzyme that converts cellulose into glucose or a disaccharide.

cellulite /ˈsɛljʊlʌɪt/ ■ n. persistent subcutaneous fat causing dimpling of the skin.
– ORIGIN 1960s: from French, from *cellule* 'small cell'.

cellulitis ■ n. Medicine inflammation of subcutaneous connective tissue.

celluloid ■ n. a transparent flammable plastic made in sheets from camphor and nitrocellulose, formerly used for cinematographic film. ► the cinema as a genre.
– ORIGIN C19: from CELLULOSE.

cellulose /'sɛljʊləʊz, -s/ ■ n. **1** an insoluble substance which is a polysaccharide derived from glucose and is the main constituent of plant cell walls and of vegetable fibres such as cotton. **2** paint or lacquer consisting principally of cellulose acetate or nitrate in solution.
– DERIVATIVES **cellulosic** adj.
– ORIGIN C19: from French, from *cellule* 'small cell'.

cellulose acetate ■ n. Chemistry a non-flammable polymer made by acetylating cellulose, used as the basis of artificial fibres and plastic.

cellulose nitrate ■ n. Chemistry nitrocellulose.

Celsius /'sɛlsɪəs/ ■ adj. [postpos. when used with a numeral] of or denoting a scale of temperature on which water freezes at 0° and boils at 100°.
– ORIGIN from the name of the Swedish astronomer Anders Celsius (1701–44).

Celt /kɛlt, s-/ ■ n. **1** a member of a group of peoples inhabiting much of Europe and Asia Minor in pre-Roman times. **2** a native of a modern nation or region in which a Celtic language is (or was until recently) spoken.
– ORIGIN from Latin *Celtae* (pl.), from Greek *Keltoi*.

celt /sɛlt/ ■ n. Archaeology a prehistoric stone or metal implement with a bevelled cutting edge.
– ORIGIN C18: from medieval Latin *celtis* 'chisel'.

Celtic /'kɛltɪk, 's-/ ■ n. a group of languages including Irish, Scottish Gaelic, Welsh, Breton, Manx, and Cornish. ■ adj. of or relating to this language group or to the Celts.
– DERIVATIVES **Celticism** /-sɪz(ə)m/ n.
– ORIGIN C16: from Latin *Celticus* (from *Celtae* 'Celts'), or from French *Celtique* (from *Celte* 'Breton').

> **USAGE**
> In standard English the normal pronunciation of **Celt** and **Celtic** is with an initial **k** rather than an **s**, except in the names of some sporting clubs, as in *Bloemfontein Celtic*.

Celtic cross ■ n. a Latin cross with a circle round the centre.

Celtic fringe ■ n. the Highland Scots, Irish, Welsh, and Cornish or their land, in relation to the rest of Britain.

cembalo /'tʃɛmbələʊ/ ■ n. (pl. **-os**) another term for HARPSICHORD.
– DERIVATIVES **cembalist** n.
– ORIGIN C19: from Italian, shortening of *clavicembalo*, from *clavis* 'key' + *cymbalum* 'cymbal'.

cement ■ n. **1** a powdery substance made by calcining lime and clay, used in making mortar and concrete. **2** a soft glue that hardens on setting. **3** (also **cementum**) Anatomy a thin layer of bony material that fixes teeth to the jaw. **4** Geology the material which binds particles together in sedimentary rock. ■ v. fix with cement; bind together.
– DERIVATIVES **cementer** n.
– ORIGIN Middle English: from Old French *ciment* (n.), from Latin *caementum* 'quarry stone', from *caedere* 'hew'.

cementation /ˌsiːmɛnˈteɪʃ(ə)n/ ■ n. **1** the binding together of particles or other things by cement. **2** Metallurgy a process of heating iron in contact with charcoal to make steel.

cementite /sɪˈmɛntaɪt/ ■ n. Metallurgy a hard, brittle iron carbide present in cast iron and most steels.
– ORIGIN C19: from CEMENT.

cement mixer ■ n. a machine with a revolving drum used for mixing cement with sand, gravel, and water to make concrete.

cemetery ■ n. (pl. **-ies**) a large burial ground.
– ORIGIN Middle English: from Greek *koimētērion* 'dormitory', from *koiman* 'put to sleep'.

CEng ■ abbrev. chartered engineer.

cenotaph /'sɛnətɑːf, -taf/ ■ n. a monument to someone buried elsewhere, especially a war memorial.
– ORIGIN C17: from French *cénotaphe*, from Greek, from *kenos* 'empty' + *taphos* 'tomb'.

Cenozoic /ˌsiːnəˈzəʊɪk/ (also **Cainozoic**) ■ adj. Geology relating to or denoting the era following the Mesozoic era (from about 65 million years ago to the present).
– ORIGIN C19: from Greek *kainos* 'new' + *zōion* 'animal'.

censer ■ n. a container in which incense is burnt.
– ORIGIN Middle English: from Old French *censier*, from *encensier*, from *encens* (see INCENSE[1]).

censor ■ n. an official who examines material that is to be published and suppresses parts considered offensive or a threat to security. ■ v. examine (a book, film, etc.) officially and suppress unacceptable parts of it.
– DERIVATIVES **censorial** adj. **censorship** n.
– ORIGIN C16: from Latin, from *censere* 'assess'.

censorious /sɛnˈsɔːrɪəs/ ■ adj. severely critical.
– DERIVATIVES **censoriously** adv. **censoriousness** n.
– ORIGIN C16: from Latin *censorius*, from *censor* 'magistrate'.

censure /'sɛnʃə/ ■ v. express severe disapproval of; formally reprove. ■ n. formal disapproval.
– DERIVATIVES **censurable** adj.
– ORIGIN Middle English: from Latin *censura* 'judgement, assessment', from *censere* 'assess'.

census ■ n. (pl. **censuses**) an official count or survey of a population.
– ORIGIN C17 (denoting a poll tax): from Latin, from *censere* 'assess'.

cent ■ n. **1** a monetary unit equal to one hundredth of a rand, dollar, or other decimal currency unit. **2** Music one hundredth of a semitone.
– ORIGIN Middle English: from French *cent* or Latin *centum* 'hundred'.

cent. ■ abbrev. century.

centaur /'sɛntɔː/ ■ n. Greek & Roman Mythology a creature with the head, arms, and torso of a man and the body and legs of a horse.
– ORIGIN from Greek *kentauros*, the Greek name for a Thessalonian tribe of expert horsemen.

centaury /'sɛntɔːri/ ■ n. (pl. **-ies**) a plant of the gentian family, typically having pink flowers. [*Centaurium minus* and other species.]
– ORIGIN Middle English: from late Latin *centaurea*, from Greek *kentauros* 'centaur'.

centenarian /ˌsɛntɪˈnɛːrɪən/ ■ n. a person a hundred or more years old. ■ adj. a hundred or more years old.

centenary /sɛnˈtiːnəri, -ˈtɛn-/ ■ n. (pl. **-ies**) the hundredth anniversary of a significant event.
– ORIGIN C17: from Latin *centenarius* 'containing a hundred', from *centum* 'a hundred'.

centennial /sɛnˈtɛnɪəl/ ■ adj. of or relating to a hundredth anniversary. ■ n. a hundredth anniversary.
– ORIGIN C18: from Latin *centum* 'a hundred', on the pattern of *biennial*.

center etc. ■ n. US spelling of CENTRE etc.

centering ■ n. US spelling of CENTRING.

centesimal /sɛnˈtɛsɪm(ə)l/ ■ adj. of or relating to division into hundredths.
– ORIGIN C17: from Latin *centesimus* 'hundredth', from *centum* 'a hundred'.

centi- ■ comb. form **1** one hundredth: *centilitre*. **2** hundred: *centipede*.
– ORIGIN from Latin *centum* 'a hundred'.

centigrade ■ adj. [postpos. when used with a numeral] of or denoting a scale of a hundred degrees, in particular the Celsius scale of temperature.
– ORIGIN C19: from Latin *centum* 'a hundred' + *gradus* 'step'.

centigram (also **centigramme**) (abbrev.: **cg**) ■ n. one hundredth of a gram.

centile /'sɛntaɪl/ ■ n. another term for PERCENTILE.

centilitre (US **centiliter**) (abbrev.: **cl**) ■ n. one hundredth of a litre.

centime /'sɒtiːm/ ■ n. a monetary unit of Switzerland, and formerly also of France and Belgium, equal to one hundredth of a franc or other decimal currency unit.
– ORIGIN from Latin *centesimus* 'hundredth', from *centum* 'a hundred'.

centimetre

centimetre (US **centimeter**) (abbrev.: **cm**) ■ n. one hundredth of a metre.

centipede /ˈsɛntɪpiːd/ ■ n. a predatory arthropod with a flattened, elongated body composed of many segments, most of which bear a pair of legs. [Class Chilopoda: many species.]
– ORIGIN C17: from Latin, from *centum* 'a hundred' + *pes*, *ped-* 'foot'.

central ■ adj. **1** in or near the centre of something. **2** most important; principal.
– DERIVATIVES **centrality** n. **centrally** adv.
– ORIGIN C17: from Latin *centralis*, from *centrum* (see **CENTRE**).

Central American ■ adj. of or relating to the countries of Guatemala, Belize, Honduras, El Salvador, Nicaragua, Costa Rica, and Panama, in the southernmost part of North America. ■ n. a native or inhabitant of a Central American country.

central bank ■ n. a national bank that provides financial and banking services for its country's government and commercial banking system, and issues currency.

central heating ■ n. a system for warming a building by heating water or air in one place and circulating it through pipes and radiators or vents.

centralize (also **-ise**) ■ v. [often as adj. **centralized** (also **-ised**)] concentrate (control or power) under a single authority.
– DERIVATIVES **centralism** n. **centralist** n. & adj. **centralization** (also **-isation**) n.

central nervous system ■ n. Anatomy the complex of nerve tissues that controls the activities of the body, in vertebrates comprising the brain and spinal cord.

central processing unit (also **central processor**) ■ n. Computing the part of a computer in which operations are controlled and executed.

central reservation ■ n. British term for **MEDIAN** n. (sense 2).

centre (US **center**) ■ n. **1** a point in the middle of something that is equally distant from all of its sides, ends, or surfaces. ▸ the middle player in some team games. ▸ (in some team games) a kick, hit, or throw of the ball from the side to the middle of field. **2** a place or group of buildings where a specified activity is concentrated. ▸ a point to or from which an activity or process is directed. ■ v. **1** place in the centre. ▸ (in some team games) kick, hit, or throw (the ball) from the side to the middle of field. ▸ chiefly N. Amer. play as the middle player in some team games. **2** (**centre on/around**) have as a major concern or theme. ▸ (**be centred in**) occur mainly in or around.
– DERIVATIVES **centremost** adj.
– ORIGIN Middle English: from Latin *centrum*, from Greek *kentron* 'sharp point, stationary point of a pair of compasses', rel. to *kentein* 'to prick'.

centre back ■ n. Soccer a defender who plays in the middle of the field.

centre bit ■ n. a drill bit with a central point and side cutters.

centreboard (US **centerboard**) ■ n. a pivoted board that can be lowered through the keel of a sailing boat to reduce sideways movement.

centred (US **centered**) ■ adj. **1** (**-centred**) taking a specified subject as the most important element: *a child-centred school*. **2** chiefly US (of a person) well balanced and confident.
– DERIVATIVES **centredness** n.

centrefield (US **centerfield**) ■ n. Baseball the central part of the outfield.
– DERIVATIVES **centrefielder** n.

centrefold (US **centerfold**) ■ n. the two middle pages of a magazine. ▸ an illustration on a centrefold, typically a picture of a naked or scantily clad model.

centre forward ■ n. Soccer & Hockey an attacker who plays in the middle of the field.

centre half ■ n. Soccer another term for **CENTRE BACK**.

centre of curvature ■ n. Mathematics the centre of a circle which passes through a curve at a given point and has the same tangent and curvature at that point.

centre of gravity ■ n. the point from which the weight of a body may be considered to act (in uniform gravity the same as the centre of mass).

centre of mass ■ n. a point representing the mean position of all the matter in a body.

centrepiece ■ n. an item serving as a central or principal ornament or display.

centre spread ■ n. the two facing middle pages of a newspaper or magazine.

centre stage ■ n. the centre of a stage. ▸ the most prominent position. ■ adv. in or towards this position.

centric ■ adj. in or at the centre; central.
– DERIVATIVES **centrical** adj. **centricity** /-ˈtrɪsɪti/ n.

-centric ■ comb. form **1** having a specified centre: *geocentric*. **2** originating from a specified viewpoint: *Eurocentric*.
– DERIVATIVES **-centricity** comb. form in corresponding nouns.
– ORIGIN from Greek *kentrikos*.

centrifugal /ˌsɛntrɪˈfjuːɡ(ə)l, sɛnˈtrɪfjʊɡ(ə)l/ ■ adj. Physics moving away from a centre.
– DERIVATIVES **centrifugally** adv.
– ORIGIN C18: from Latin *centrum* (see **CENTRE**) + *-fugus* 'fleeing', from *fugere* 'flee'.

centrifugal force ■ n. Physics a force, arising from the body's inertia, which appears to act on a body moving in a circular path and is directed away from the centre around which the body is moving.

centrifugal pump ■ n. a pump that uses an impeller to move water or other fluids.

centrifuge /ˈsɛntrɪfjuːdʒ/ ■ n. a machine with a rapidly rotating container that applies centrifugal force to its contents, used chiefly to separate liquids from solids. ■ v. subject to the action of a centrifuge.
– DERIVATIVES **centrifugation** /-fjuːˈɡeɪʃ(ə)n/ n.

centring (US **centering**) ■ n. **1** the action or process of placing in the centre. **2** Architecture framing used to support an arch or dome under construction.

centriole /ˈsɛntrɪəʊl/ ■ n. Biology each of a pair of minute cylindrical structures near the nucleus in animal cells, involved in the development of spindle fibres in cell division.
– ORIGIN C19: from modern Latin *centriolum*, diminutive of *centrum* (see **CENTRE**).

centripetal /ˌsɛntrɪˈpiːt(ə)l, sɛnˈtrɪpɪt(ə)l/ ■ adj. Physics moving towards a centre.
– DERIVATIVES **centripetally** adv.
– ORIGIN C18: from Latin *centrum* (see **CENTRE**) + *-petus* 'seeking', from *petere* 'seek'.

centripetal force ■ n. Physics a force which acts on a body moving in a circular path and is directed towards the centre around which the body is moving.

centrist ■ n. a person having moderate political views or policies.
– DERIVATIVES **centrism** n.

centroid ■ n. Mathematics the centre of mass of a geometric object of uniform density.

centromere /ˈsɛntrə(ʊ)mɪə/ ■ n. Biology the point on a chromosome by which it is attached to a spindle fibre during cell division.
– ORIGIN 1920s: from Latin *centrum* (see **CENTRE**) + Greek *meros* 'part'.

centrosome /ˈsɛntrəsəʊm/ ■ n. Biology a structure near the nucleus of a cell which contains the centrioles and from which the spindle fibres develop in cell division.
– ORIGIN C19: from Latin *centrum* (see **CENTRE**) + Greek *sōma* 'body'.

centuple /ˈsɛntjʊp(ə)l/ ■ v. multiply by a hundred.
– ORIGIN C17: from eccles. Latin *centuplus*, from Latin *centum* 'hundred'.

centurion /sɛnˈtjʊərɪən/ ■ n. the commander of a century in the ancient Roman army.
– ORIGIN Middle English: from Latin *centurio(n-)*, from *centuria* (see **CENTURY**).

century ■ n. (pl. **-ies**) **1** a period of one hundred years, in particular each of a number of such periods from the date

of the birth of Christ. **2** a batsman's score of a hundred runs in cricket. **3** a company of a hundred men in the ancient Roman army.
– ORIGIN Middle English: from Latin *centuria*, from *centum* 'a hundred'.

century plant ■ n. a large agave which produces a very tall flowering stem after many years of growth and then dies. [*Agave americana*.]

CEO ■ abbrev. chief executive officer.

cep /sɛp/ ■ n. an edible mushroom with a smooth brown cap and pores rather than gills. [*Boletus edulis*.]
– ORIGIN C19: from French *cèpe*, from Gascon dialect *cep* 'tree trunk, mushroom', from Latin *cippus* 'stake'.

cephalic /sɪˈfalɪk, kɛ-/ ■ adj. of, in, or relating to the head.
– ORIGIN Middle English: from Latin *cephalicus*, from Greek, from *kephalē* 'head'.

cephalic index ■ n. Anthropology the ratio of the maximum breadth of a skull to its maximum length.

cephalo- /ˈsɛfələʊ, ˈkɛf-/ ■ comb. form relating to the head or skull:
– ORIGIN from Greek *kephalē* 'head'.

Cephalopoda /ˌsɛfələˈpəʊdə, ˌkɛ-/ ■ pl. n. Zoology a large class of active predatory molluscs comprising octopuses, squids, and cuttlefish.
– DERIVATIVES **cephalopod** /ˈsɛf(ə)ləpɒd, ˈkɛ-/ n.
– ORIGIN from Greek *kephalē* 'head' + *pous, pod-* 'foot'.

cephalosporin /ˌsɛfələ(ʊ)ˈspɔːrɪn, ˌkɛ-/ ■ n. any of a group of semi-synthetic antibiotics resembling penicillin.
– ORIGIN 1950S: from *Cephalosporium*, the name of the genus providing moulds for this.

cephalothorax /ˌsɛf(ə)ləʊˈθɔːraks, ˌkɛf-/ ■ n. (pl. **-thoraces** /-ˈθɔːrəsiːz/ or **-thoraxes**) Zoology the fused head and thorax of spiders and other chelicerate arthropods.

cepheid /ˈsiːfiɪd, ˈsɛ-/ ■ n. Astronomy a star whose brightness varies on a regular cycle whose frequency is related to its luminosity, so allowing estimation of its distance from the earth.
– ORIGIN C20: from the name of the variable star *Delta Cephei*, which typifies this class.

ceramic /sɪˈramɪk/ ■ adj. **1** made of clay that is permanently hardened by heat. **2** of or relating to ceramics. ■ n. (**ceramics**) **1** ceramic articles. ▸ [usu. treated as sing.] the art of making ceramics. **2** clay used in this way. ▸ any non-metallic solid which remains hard when heated.
– DERIVATIVES **ceramicist** n.
– ORIGIN C19: from Greek *keramikos*, from *keramos* 'pottery'.

ceramic hob ■ n. an electric cooker hob made of ceramic, with heating elements fixed to its underside.

ceratopsian /ˌsɛrəˈtɒpsɪən, ˌkɛr-/ ■ n. Palaeontology a gregarious quadrupedal herbivorous dinosaur of a group including triceratops, with a bony frill protecting the neck.
– ORIGIN C20: from Greek *keras, kerat-* 'horn' + *ops* 'face'.

cercaria /səˈkɛːrɪə/ ■ n. (pl. **cercariae** /-iiː/) Zoology a free-swimming larval stage in which a parasitic fluke passes from an intermediate host (typically a snail) to another host.
– ORIGIN C19: from Greek *kerkos* 'tail'.

cercopithecine /ˌsəːkə(ʊ)ˈpɪθɪsiːn/ ■ adj. Zoology relating to or denoting monkeys of a subfamily (Cercopithecinae) that includes the macaques, mangabeys, baboons, and guenons.
– ORIGIN based on Greek *kerkopithēkos* 'long-tailed monkey', from *kerkos* 'tail' + *pithēkos* 'ape'.

cercus /ˈsəːkəs/ ■ n. (pl. **cerci** /-kʌɪ/) Zoology either of a pair of small appendages at the end of the abdomen of some insects and other arthropods.
– ORIGIN C19: from Greek *kerkos* 'tail'.

cere /sɪə/ ■ n. Ornithology a waxy fleshy covering at the base of the upper beak in some birds.
– ORIGIN C15: from Latin *cera* 'wax'.

cereal ■ n. **1** a grain used for food, for example wheat, maize, or rye. ▸ a grass producing such grain, grown as an agricultural crop. **2** a breakfast food made from a cereal grain or grains.
– ORIGIN C19: from Latin, from *Ceres*, the name of the Roman goddess of agriculture.

cerebellum /ˌsɛrɪˈbɛləm/ ■ n. (pl. **cerebellums** or **cerebella**) Anatomy the part of the brain at the back of the skull, which coordinates and regulates muscular activity.
– DERIVATIVES **cerebellar** adj.
– ORIGIN C16: from Latin, diminutive of **CEREBRUM**.

cerebral /ˈsɛrɪbr(ə)l/ ■ adj. of the cerebrum of the brain. ▸ intellectual rather than emotional or physical.
– DERIVATIVES **cerebrally** adv.
– ORIGIN C19: from Latin *cerebrum* 'brain'.

cerebral palsy ■ n. a condition marked by impaired muscle coordination and spastic paralysis, caused by damage to the brain before or at birth.

cerebration /ˌsɛrɪˈbreɪʃ(ə)n/ ■ n. the working of the brain; thinking.

cerebro- ■ comb. form of or relating to the brain: *cerebrospinal*.
– ORIGIN from Latin *cerebrum* 'brain'.

cerebrospinal /ˌsɛrɪbrə(ʊ)ˈspʌɪn(ə)l/ ■ adj. Anatomy of or relating to the brain and spine.

cerebrospinal fluid ■ n. Anatomy clear watery fluid which fills the space between the arachnoid membrane and the pia mater.

cerebrovascular /ˌsɛrɪbrə(ʊ)ˈvaskjʊlə/ ■ adj. Anatomy of or relating to the brain and its blood vessels.

cerebrum /ˈsɛrɪbrəm/ ■ n. (pl. **cerebra** /-brə/) Anatomy the principal part of the brain, located in the front area of the skull and consisting of left and right hemispheres.
– ORIGIN C17: from Latin, 'brain'.

cerement /ˈsɪəm(ə)nt/ ■ n. (**cerements**) historical waxed cloth for wrapping a corpse.
– ORIGIN C17: from obsolete *cere* 'to wax', from Latin, from *cera* 'wax'.

ceremonial ■ adj. **1** relating to or used for ceremonies. **2** (of a post or role) involving only nominal authority or power. ■ n. another term for **CEREMONY**.
– DERIVATIVES **ceremonialism** n. **ceremonially** adv.

ceremonious ■ adj. relating or appropriate to grand and formal occasions.
– DERIVATIVES **ceremoniously** adv. **ceremoniousness** n.
– ORIGIN C16: from French *cérémonieux* or late Latin *caerimoniosus*, from Latin *caerimonia* (see **CEREMONY**).

ceremony ■ n. (pl. **-ies**) **1** a formal religious or public occasion, typically celebrating a particular event, achievement, or anniversary. ▸ an act or series of acts performed according to a traditional or prescribed form. **2** the ritual procedures observed at such occasions: *graduate with due ceremony*.
– PHRASES **stand on ceremony** observe formalities. **without ceremony** without formality or politeness.
– ORIGIN Middle English: from Old French *ceremonie* or Latin *caerimonia* 'religious worship, ritual observances'.

cereology /ˌsɪərɪˈɒlədʒɪ/ ■ n. the study or investigation of crop circles.
– DERIVATIVES **cereologist** n.
– ORIGIN C20: from *Ceres* (see **CEREAL**).

ceresin /ˈsɛrɪsɪn/ ■ n. a hard whitish paraffin wax used with or instead of beeswax.
– ORIGIN C19: from Latin *cera* 'wax'.

cerise /səˈriːs, -z/ ■ n. a light, clear red colour.
– ORIGIN C19: from French, 'cherry'.

cerium /ˈsɪərɪəm/ ■ n. the chemical element of atomic number 58, a silvery-white metal of the lanthanide series. (Symbol: **Ce**)
– ORIGIN C19: named after the asteroid *Ceres*, discovered shortly before.

cermet /ˈsəːmɛt/ ■ n. any of a class of heat-resistant materials made of ceramic and sintered metal.
– ORIGIN 1950S: blend of **CERAMIC** and **METAL**.

cero- /ˈsɪərəʊ/ ■ comb. form of or relating to wax: *ceroplastic*.
– ORIGIN from Latin *cera* or Greek *kēros* 'wax'.

ceroplastic ■ adj. of or relating to modelling in wax.

cert ■ n. informal, chiefly Brit. **1** an event regarded as inevitable. **2** a competitor, candidate, etc. regarded as certain to win.
– ORIGIN C19: abbrev. of **CERTAINTY**.

cert. ■ abbrev. **1** certificate. **2** certified.

certain

certain /'sə:t(ə)n, -tɪn/ ■ adj. **1** able to be firmly relied on to happen or be the case. **2** completely convinced of something. **3** specific but not explicitly named or stated: *certain problems*. ▶ not known to the reader or hearer: *a certain Mr Percy*. ■ pron. (**certain of**) some but not all.
– PHRASES **for certain** without any doubt. **make certain** take action to ensure that something happens. ▶ establish whether something is definitely correct.
– ORIGIN Middle English: via Old French from Latin *certus* 'settled, sure'.

certainly ■ adv. definitely; undoubtedly. ▶ yes; by all means.

certainty ■ n. (pl. **-ies**) **1** the quality or state of being certain. **2** a true fact or an event that is definitely going to take place.
– PHRASES **for a certainty** beyond the possibility of doubt.
– ORIGIN Middle English: from Old French *certainete*, from *certain* (see CERTAIN).

certifiable ■ adj. able or needing to be certified.

certificate ■ n. /sə'tɪfɪkət/ **1** an official document attesting or recording a particular fact or event, a level of achievement, the fulfilment of a legal requirement, etc. **2** an official classification awarded to a cinema film by a board of censors, indicating its suitability for a particular age group. ■ v. /sə'tɪfɪkeɪt/ provide with or attest in an official document.
– DERIVATIVES **certification** n.
– ORIGIN Middle English: from late Latin *certificare* (see CERTIFY).

certified cheque ■ n. another term for BANK GUARANTEED CHEQUE.

certified mail ■ n. another term for RECORDED DELIVERY.

certify ■ v. (**-ies, -ied**) **1** formally attest or confirm. **2** officially recognize as possessing certain qualifications or meeting certain standards. **3** officially declare insane.
– ORIGIN Middle English: from late Latin *certificare*, from Latin *certus* 'certain'.

certitude /'sə:tɪtjuːd/ ■ n. a feeling of absolute certainty. ▶ something considered with certainty to be true.
– ORIGIN Middle English: from late Latin *certitudo*, from *certus* 'certain'.

cerulean /sɪ'ruːlɪən/ ■ adj. deep blue in colour like a clear sky.
– ORIGIN C17: from Latin *caeruleus*, from *caelum* 'sky'.

cervelat /'sə:vəlɑː, -lat/ ■ n. a kind of smoked pork sausage.
– ORIGIN C17: from Italian *cervellata*.

cervical /'sə:vɪk(ə)l, sə:'vʌɪk(ə)l/ ■ adj. Anatomy **1** of or relating to the cervix. **2** of or relating to the neck.
– ORIGIN C17: from Latin *cervix, cervic-* 'neck'.

cervical smear ■ n. another term for PAP SMEAR.

cervicitis /ˌsə:vɪ'sʌɪtɪs/ ■ n. Medicine inflammation of the cervix.

cervid /'sə:vɪd/ ■ n. Zoology a mammal of the deer family (Cervidae).
– ORIGIN C19: from Latin *cervus* 'deer'.

cervix /'sə:vɪks/ ■ n. (pl. **cervices** /-siːz/) **1** the narrow neck-like passage forming the lower end of the womb. **2** technical the neck.
– ORIGIN C18: from Latin.

Cesarean (also **Cesarian**) ■ adj. & n. US spelling of CAESAREAN.

cesium ■ n. US spelling of CAESIUM.

cessation /sɛ'seɪʃ(ə)n/ ■ n. the fact or process of ceasing.
– ORIGIN Middle English: from Latin *cessatio(n-)*, from *cessare* 'cease'.

cession /'sɛʃ(ə)n/ ■ n. the formal giving up of rights, property, or territory by a state. ▶ S. African Law the transferral of a right, claim, etc. from one party to another.
– ORIGIN Middle English: from Latin *cessio(n-)*, from *cedere* 'cede'.

cesspit ■ n. a pit for the disposal of liquid waste and sewage.

– ORIGIN C19: from *cess* (the supposed base of CESSPOOL) + PIT[1].

cesspool ■ n. an underground container for the temporary storage of liquid waste and sewage.
– ORIGIN C17: prob. an alteration, influenced by POOL[1], of archaic *suspiral* 'vent, settling tank', from Old French *souspirail* 'air hole', from Latin *sub-* 'from below' + *spirare* 'breathe'.

c'est la guerre /ˌseɪ lɑː 'gɛːr/ ■ exclam. that's war; such is war.
– ORIGIN from French.

c'est la vie /ˌseɪ lɑː 'viː/ ■ exclam. that's life; such is life.
– ORIGIN from French.

Cestoda /sɛs'təʊdə/ (also **Cestoidea**) ■ pl. n. Zoology a class of parasitic flatworms comprising the tapeworms.
– DERIVATIVES **cestode** /'sɛstəʊd/ n.
– ORIGIN from Greek *kestos* 'stitched', used as a noun in the sense 'girdle'.

CET ■ abbrev. Central European Time.

Cetacea /sɪ'teɪʃə/ ■ pl. n. Zoology an order of marine mammals comprising the whales, dolphins, and porpoises.
– DERIVATIVES **cetacean** n. & adj.
– ORIGIN from Latin *cetus*, from Greek *kētos* 'whale'.

ceviche /sɛ'viːtʃeɪ/ (also **seviche**) ■ n. a South American dish of marinated raw fish or seafood.
– ORIGIN from Latin American Spanish.

CF ■ abbrev. cystic fibrosis.

Cf ■ symb. the chemical element californium.

c.f. ■ abbrev. carried forward (referring to figures transferred to a new page or account).

cf. ■ abbrev. compare with.
– ORIGIN from Latin *confer* 'compare'.

CFA (also **CFA franc**) ■ n. the basic monetary unit of Cameroon, Congo, Gabon, and the Central African Republic, equal to 100 centimes.
– ORIGIN *CFA* from French *Communauté Financière Africaine* 'African Financial Community'.

CFC ■ abbrev. Chemistry chlorofluorocarbon, any of a class of synthetic compounds of carbon, hydrogen, chlorine, and fluorine formerly used as refrigerants and aerosol propellants and known to be harmful to the ozone layer.

CFS ■ abbrev. chronic fatigue syndrome.

cg ■ abbrev. centigram(s).

cgs ■ abbrev. centimetre-gram-second (denoting a system of measurement using these as basic units).

CGT ■ abbrev. capital gains tax.

ch. ■ abbrev. **1** chapter. **2** church.

Chablis /'ʃabliː/ ■ n. a dry white burgundy wine from Chablis in eastern France.

cha-cha /'tʃɑːtʃɑː/ ■ n. a ballroom dance with small steps and swaying hip movements, performed to a Latin American rhythm. ■ v. (**cha-chas, cha-chaed** /-tʃɑːd/ or **cha-cha'd, cha-chaing** /-tʃɑː(r)ɪŋ/) dance the cha-cha.
– ORIGIN 1950s: Latin American Spanish.

chacma baboon /'tʃakmə/ ■ n. a dark grey baboon inhabiting savannah in southern Africa. [*Papio ursinus*.]
– ORIGIN from Khoikhoi.

chacun à son goût /ˌʃakœ̃ a sɒn 'guː/ ■ exclam. each to their own taste.
– ORIGIN from French.

Chadian /'tʃadɪən/ ■ n. a native or inhabitant of Chad in central Africa. ■ adj. of or relating to Chad or Chadians.

Chadic /'tʃadɪk/ ■ n. a group of Afro-Asiatic languages spoken in the region of Lake Chad in north central Africa, of which the most important is Hausa. ■ adj. of or relating to this group of languages.

chador /'tʃɑːdɔː, 'tʃʌdə, 'tʃʌdə/ (also **chadar** or **chuddar**) ■ n. a large piece of dark-coloured cloth that is wrapped around the head and upper body leaving only the face exposed, worn by Muslim women.
– ORIGIN C17: from Urdu *chādar, chaddar*, from Persian *čādar* 'sheet or veil'.

Chaetognatha /ˌkiːtəg'nɑːθə, -'neɪθə/ ■ pl. n. Zoology a small phylum of marine invertebrates that comprises the arrow worms.
– DERIVATIVES **chaetognath** n.
– ORIGIN from Greek *khaitē* 'long hair' + *gnathos* 'jaw'.

chafe /tʃeɪf/ ■ v. **1** make or become sore by rubbing. ▸ (of an object) rub abrasively against another. **2** rub (a part of the body) to restore warmth or sensation. **3** become annoyed or impatient because of a restriction or inconvenience. ■ n. wear or damage caused by rubbing.
– ORIGIN Middle English: from Old French *chaufer* 'make hot', from Latin *calefacere*, from *calere* 'be hot' + *facere* 'make'.

chafer /'tʃeɪfə/ ■ n. a large flying beetle, many of which are destructive to plants. [Family Scarabaeidae.]
– ORIGIN Old English, of Germanic origin.

chaff¹ /tʃɑːf, tʃaf/ ■ n. **1** the husks of grain or other seed separated by winnowing or threshing. ▸ chopped hay and straw used as fodder. **2** strips of metal foil released in the air to obstruct radar detection.
– PHRASES **separate** (or **sort**) **the wheat from the chaff** distinguish valuable people or things from worthless ones.
– DERIVATIVES **chaffy** adj.
– ORIGIN Old English, prob. from a Germanic base meaning 'gnaw'.

chaff² /tʃɑːf, tʃaf/ ■ n. light-hearted joking. ■ v. tease. ▸ S. African informal flirt with (someone).
– ORIGIN C19: perhaps from CHAFE.

chaffinch ■ n. a common finch, native to Eurasia and North Africa, the male of which has a bluish head, pink underparts, and dark wings with a white flash. [*Fringilla coelebs*.]
– ORIGIN Old English *ceaffinc* 'chaff finch'.

Chagas' disease /'tʃɑːɡəsɪz/ ■ n. a disease caused by trypanosomes transmitted by bloodsucking bugs, endemic in South America and causing damage to the heart and central nervous system.
– ORIGIN C20: named after Carlos *Chagas*, the Brazilian physician who first described it.

chagrin /'ʃaɡrɪn, ʃə'ɡrɪn/ ■ n. annoyance or shame at having failed. ■ v. (**be chagrined**) feel annoyed or ashamed.
– ORIGIN C17 (in the sense 'melancholy'): from French *chagrin* 'rough skin, shagreen'.

chai /tʃʌɪ/ ■ n. Indian tea made by boiling tea leaves with milk, sugar, and cardamoms.
– ORIGIN a term in various Indian languages.

chain ■ n. **1** a connected flexible series of metal links used for fastening, pulling, etc., or in jewellery. ▸ (**chains**) such a series of links used to confine a prisoner. ▸ a restricting force or factor. **2** a sequence of items of the same type forming a line. ▸ a series of connected elements. ▸ a group of hotels or shops owned by the same company. ▸ a part of a molecule consisting of a number of atoms bonded together in a linear sequence. **3** a jointed measuring line consisting of linked metal rods. ▸ the length of this (66 ft). **4** (**chains**) a structure projecting horizontally from a sailing ship's sides abreast of the masts, used to widen the basis for the shrouds. ■ v. fasten, secure, or confine with a chain.
– ORIGIN Middle English: from Old French *chaine*, from Latin *catena* 'a chain'.

chain drive ■ n. a mechanism in which power is transmitted from an engine to the wheels of a vehicle or a boat's propeller by means of an endless chain.
– DERIVATIVES **chain-driven** adj.

chain gang ■ n. a group of convicts chained together while working outside the prison.

chain gear ■ n. a gear transmitting motion by means of a moving endless chain, as typically used in bicycles.

chain letter ■ n. one of a sequence of letters, each recipient in the sequence being requested to send copies to a specific number of other people.

chain-link ■ adj. made of wire in a diamond-shaped mesh.

chain mail ■ n. historical armour made of small metal rings linked together.

chainplate ■ n. a strong link or plate on a sailing ship's side, to which the shrouds are secured.

chain reaction ■ n. **1** a chemical or other reaction in which the products themselves promote or spread the reaction, especially a self-sustaining nuclear fission process spread by neutrons. **2** a series of events, each caused by the previous one.

chainsaw ■ n. a mechanical power-driven saw with teeth set on a chain moving around the edge of a blade.

chain shot ■ n. historical pairs of cannonballs or half balls joined by a chain, fired from cannons in sea battles.

chain-smoke ■ v. smoke continually, typically by lighting a cigarette from the stub of the last one smoked.
– DERIVATIVES **chain-smoker** n.

chain stitch ■ n. an ornamental embroidery or crochet stitch resembling a chain.

chain store ■ n. one of a series of shops owned by one firm and selling the same goods.

chain wheel ■ n. a wheel transmitting power by means of a chain fitted to its edges.

chair ■ n. **1** a separate seat for one person, typically with a back and four legs. **2** the person in charge of a meeting or an organization (used as a neutral alternative to chairman or chairwoman). ▸ an official position of authority, especially on a board of directors. **3** a professorship. **4** (**the chair**) short for ELECTRIC CHAIR. ■ v. **1** act as chairperson of. **2** chiefly Brit. carry (someone) aloft in a chair or in a sitting position to celebrate a victory.
– ORIGIN Middle English: from Old French *chaiere*, (modern French *chaire* 'bishop's throne'), from Latin *cathedra* 'seat', from Greek *kathedra*.

chairlift ■ n. **1** a series of chairs hung from a moving cable, used for carrying passengers up and down a mountain. **2** a device for carrying people in wheelchairs from one floor of a building to another.

chairman (or **chairwoman**) ■ n. (pl. **-men** or **-women**) a person in charge of a meeting, committee, company, or other organization.
– DERIVATIVES **chairmanship** n.

chairperson ■ n. a chairman or chairwoman (used as a neutral alternative).

chaise /ʃeɪz/ ■ n. **1** chiefly historical a horse-drawn carriage for one or two people, especially one with an open top and two wheels. ▸ another term for POST-CHAISE. **2** US term for CHAISE LONGUE.
– ORIGIN C17: from French, var. of *chaire* 'bishop's throne'.

chaise longue /'lɒŋɡ/ (US also **chaise lounge**) ■ n. (pl. **chaises longues** pronunc. same) **1** a sofa with a backrest at only one end. **2** N. Amer. a sunbed or other chair with a lengthened seat for reclining on.
– ORIGIN C19: French, 'long chair'.

chakalaka ■ n. S. African a spicy sauce of chopped tomatoes, chillies, and onions.

chakra /'tʃʌkrə/ ■ n. (in Indian thought) each of the centres of spiritual power in the human body, usually considered to be seven in number.
– ORIGIN from Sanskrit *cakra* 'wheel, circle'.

chalcedony /kal'sɛdəni/ ■ n. (pl. **-ies**) quartz occurring in a microcrystalline form such as onyx and agate.
– DERIVATIVES **chalcedonic** /ˌkalsɪ'dɒnɪk/ adj.
– ORIGIN Middle English: from Latin *calcedonius*, from Greek *khalkēdōn*.

chalcid /'kalsɪd/ ■ n. Entomology a minute parasitic wasp of a large group (superfamily Chalcidoidea) typically having a metallic colouration.
– ORIGIN C19: from *Chalcis* (genus name), from Greek *khalkos* 'copper, brass'.

Chalcolithic /ˌkalkə(ʊ)'lɪθɪk/ ■ adj. Archaeology relating to or denoting a period in the 4th and 3rd millennia BC, during which some weapons and tools were made of copper.
– ORIGIN C20: from Greek *khalkos* 'copper' + *lithos* 'stone'.

chalcopyrite /ˌkalkə(ʊ)'pʌɪrʌɪt/ ■ n. a yellow mineral consisting of a sulphide of copper and iron, the principal ore of copper.
– ORIGIN C19: from Greek, from *khalkos* 'copper' + *puritēs* (see PYRITES).

Chaldean ■ n. **1** a member of a people who lived in Chaldea, an ancient country in what is now southern Iraq. **2** the Semitic language of the ancient Chaldeans. ▸ a language related to Aramaic and spoken in parts of Iraq. ■ adj. of or relating to ancient Chaldea or its people or language.

chalet /ˈʃaleɪ/ ■ n. **1** a wooden house with overhanging eaves, typically found in the Swiss Alps. **2** a small wooden cabin used by holidaymakers, typically one in a holiday camp.
– ORIGIN C18: from Swiss French, diminutive of Old French *chasel* 'farmstead'.

chalice ■ n. **1** historical a goblet. **2** the wine cup used in the Christian Eucharist.
– ORIGIN Middle English: from Latin *calix, calic-* 'cup'.

chalk ■ n. a white soft earthy limestone formed from the skeletal remains of sea creatures. ▸ a similar substance (calcium sulphate), made into white or coloured sticks and used for drawing or writing. ■ v. **1** draw or write with chalk. ▸ rub the tip of (a snooker cue) with chalk. **2** Brit. charge (drinks bought in a pub or bar) to a person's account. **3 (chalk something up)** achieve something noteworthy.
– PHRASES **as different as chalk and cheese** fundamentally different or incompatible. **by a long chalk** by far. **chalk and talk** teaching by traditional methods focusing on the blackboard. **not by a long chalk** not at all.
– DERIVATIVES **chalkiness** n. **chalky** adj. (**-ier, -iest**).
– ORIGIN Old English, from Latin *calx* 'lime', prob. from Greek *khalix* 'pebble, limestone'.

chalkboard ■ n. North American term for **BLACKBOARD**.

chalkdown ■ n. S. African a teachers' strike.

chalk-stripe ■ adj. (of a garment or material) having a pattern of thin white stripes on a dark background.
– DERIVATIVES **chalk-striped** adj.

challah /ˈhɑːlə, xɑːˈlɑː/ ■ n. (pl. **challahs** or **chalot**(**h**) /xɑːˈlɒt/) another term for **KITKE**.
– ORIGIN 1920s: from Hebrew *ḥallah*.

challenge ■ n. **1** a call to someone to participate in a contest or fight to decide who is superior. ▸ a demanding task or situation. ▸ an attempt to win a sporting contest. **2** a call to prove or justify something. **3** Medicine exposure of the immune system to pathogenic organisms or antigens. ■ v. **1** dispute the truth or validity of. ▸ Law object to (a jury member). ▸ (of a sentry) call on (someone) to prove their identity. **2** invite (someone) to engage in a contest. ▸ compete with. ▸ [usu. as adj. **challenging**] test the abilities of. **3** Medicine expose (the immune system) to pathogenic organisms or antigens.
– DERIVATIVES **challengeable** adj. **challenger** n. **challengingly** adv.
– ORIGIN Middle English: from Old French *chalenge* (n.), *chalenger* (v.), from Latin *calumnia* 'calumny', *calumniari* 'calumniate'.

challenged ■ adj. **1** euphemistic suffering from impairment or disability in a specified respect: *physically challenged*. **2** humorous lacking or deficient in a specified respect: *vertically challenged*.

challis /ˈʃalɪs, ˈʃali/ ■ n. a lightweight soft clothing fabric made from silk and worsted.
– ORIGIN C19.

chalybeate /kəˈlɪbɪət/ ■ adj. of or denoting natural mineral springs containing iron salts.
– ORIGIN C17: from Latin *chalybs*, from Greek *khalups, khalub-* 'steel'.

chamaeleon ■ n. variant spelling of **CHAMELEON**.

chamber ■ n. **1** a large room used for formal or public events. **2** one of the houses of a parliament. **3** (**chambers**) Law a judge's room used for official proceedings not required to be held in open court. **4** (**chambers**) Brit. Law rooms used by a barrister, especially in the Inns of Court. **5** poetic/literary or archaic a private room, especially a bedroom. **6** an enclosed space or cavity. ▸ the part of a gun bore that contains the charge. **7** [as modifier] Music of or for a small group of instruments: *a chamber orchestra*.
– DERIVATIVES **chambered** adj.
– ORIGIN Middle English: from Old French *chambre*, from Latin *camera* 'vault, arched chamber', from Greek *kamara* 'object with an arched cover'.

chamberlain /ˈtʃeɪmbəlɪn/ ■ n. historical **1** an officer who managed the household of a monarch or noble. **2** Brit. an officer who received revenue on behalf of a corporation or public body.
– DERIVATIVES **chamberlainship** n.
– ORIGIN Middle English (denoting a servant in a bedchamber): from Old Saxon *kamera*, from Latin *camera* (see **CHAMBER**).

chambermaid ■ n. a woman who cleans bedrooms and bathrooms in a hotel.

chamber music ■ n. instrumental music played by a small ensemble, such as a string quartet, with one player to a part.

Chamber of Commerce ■ n. a local association to promote and protect the interests of the business community.

Chamber of Deputies ■ n. the lower legislative assembly in some parliaments.

chamber of horrors ■ n. a place of entertainment containing instruments or scenes of torture or execution.
– ORIGIN C19: from the name given to a room in Madame Tussaud's waxwork exhibition.

chamber organ ■ n. a movable pipe organ for playing in a small concert hall, chapel, or private house.

chamber pot ■ n. a bowl kept in a bedroom and used as a toilet.

Chambertin /ˈʃɒbətã/ ■ n. a dry red burgundy wine of high quality from Gevrey Chambertin in eastern France.

chambray /ˈʃambreɪ/ ■ n. a linen-finished gingham cloth with a white weft and a coloured warp, producing a mottled appearance.
– ORIGIN C19 (orig. US): from *Cambrai* (see **CAMBRIC**).

chambré /ˈʃɒmbreɪ, ˈsɔ̃-/ ■ adj. (of red wine) at room temperature.
– ORIGIN 1950s: French, from *chambrer* 'bring to room temperature', from *chambre* (see **CHAMBER**).

chameleon /kəˈmiːlɪən/ (also **chamaeleon**) ■ n. a small slow-moving lizard with a prehensile tail, long extensible tongue, protruding eyes, and the ability to change colour. [*Chamaeleo* and other genera, family Chamaeleonidae: numerous species.]
– DERIVATIVES **chameleonic** adj.
– ORIGIN Middle English: from Greek *khamaileōn*, from *khamai* 'on the ground' + *leōn* 'lion'.

chametz /hɑːˈmɛts, ˈxɑːmɛts/ (also **chometz**) ■ n. Judaism leaven or food mixed with leaven, prohibited during Passover.
– ORIGIN C19: from Hebrew *ḥāmēṣ*.

chamfer /ˈtʃamfə/ ■ v. (in carpentry) cut away (a right-angled edge or corner) to make a symmetrical sloping edge. ■ n. a chamfered edge or corner.
– ORIGIN C16: from French *chamfrain*, from *chant* (see **CANT**²) + *fraint* 'broken'.

chamois ■ n. **1** /ˈʃamwɑː/ (pl. same /-wɑːz/) an agile goat-antelope with short hooked horns, found in mountainous areas of southern Europe. [Genus *Rupicapra*: two species.] **2** /ˈʃami, ˈʃamwɑː/ (pl. same /-mɪz, -wɑːz/) (also **chamois leather**) soft pliable leather made from the skin of sheep, goats, or deer.
– ORIGIN C16: from French.

chamomile /ˈkaməmʌɪl/ (also **camomile**) ■ n. an aromatic plant of the daisy family, with white and yellow flowers. [*Chamaemelum nobile* (sweet chamomile) and other species.]
– ORIGIN Middle English: from Old French *camomille*, from Greek *khamaimēlon* 'earth-apple' (because of the apple-like smell of its flowers).

champ¹ ■ v. **1** munch enthusiastically or noisily. ▸ (of a horse) make a noisy biting or chewing action. **2** fret impatiently.
– PHRASES **champ (or chafe) at the bit** be restlessly impatient to start doing something.
– ORIGIN Middle English: prob. imitative.

champ² ■ n. informal a champion.

champagne /ʃamˈpeɪn/ ■ n. a white sparkling wine from Champagne, a region in NE France.

champagne socialist ■ n. Brit. derogatory a person who espouses socialist ideals while enjoying a wealthy and luxurious lifestyle.
– DERIVATIVES **champagne socialism** n.

champers ■ n. informal, chiefly Brit. champagne.

champerty /ˈtʃampəti/ ■ n. Law an illegal agreement in

which a person with no previous interest in a lawsuit finances it with a view to sharing the disputed property if the suit succeeds.
– ORIGIN Middle English: from Anglo-Norman French *champartie*, from Old French *champart* 'feudal lord's share of produce', from Latin *campus* 'field' + *pars* 'part'.

champion ■ n. 1 a person who has surpassed all rivals in a sporting contest or other competition. 2 a defender of a cause or person. ▶ historical a knight who fought in single combat on behalf of the monarch. ■ v. support the cause of.
– ORIGIN Middle English: from medieval Latin *campio(n-)* 'fighter', from Latin *campus* (see **CAMP¹**).

championship ■ n. 1 a sporting contest for the position of champion. 2 the vigorous defence of a person or cause.

chana /ˈtʃʌnə/ (also **channa**) ■ n. Indian chickpeas.
– ORIGIN from Hindi *canā*.

chance ■ n. 1 a possibility of something happening. 2 (**chances**) the probability of something happening. 3 an opportunity. 4 the occurrence of events in the absence of any obvious design or cause: *he met his brother by chance.* ■ v. 1 do something by accident. ▶ (**chance upon/on/across**) find or see by accident. 2 informal risk.
– PHRASES **by any chance** possibly. **chance one's arm** (or **luck**) chiefly Brit. informal risk doing something. **on the (off) chance** just in case. **stand a chance** [usu. with neg.] have a prospect of success or survival. **take a chance** (or **chances**) expose oneself to the risk of danger or failure. ▶ (**take a chance on**) risk trusting. **take one's chance** do something risky with the hope of success.
– ORIGIN Middle English: from Old French *cheance*, from *cheoir* 'fall, befall', from Latin *cadere*.

chancel /ˈtʃɑːns(ə)l/ ■ n. the part of a church near the altar, reserved for the clergy and choir, and typically separated from the nave by steps or a screen.
– ORIGIN Middle English: from Latin *cancelli* 'crossbars'.

chancellery /ˈtʃɑːns(ə)l(ə)ri, -ˈsləri/ ■ n. (pl. **-ies**) 1 the position, office, or department of a chancellor. 2 chiefly US an office attached to an embassy or consulate.

chancellor ■ n. a senior state or legal official of various kinds. ▶ (**Chancellor**) the head of the government in some European countries, e.g. Germany. ▶ the non-resident honorary head of a university. ▶ US the presiding judge of a chancery court.
– DERIVATIVES **chancellorship** n.
– ORIGIN Old English, from late Latin *cancellarius* 'porter, secretary' (orig. a court official stationed at the grating separating public from judges), from *cancelli* 'crossbars'.

Chancellor of the Exchequer ■ n. the finance minister of the United Kingdom.

chancer ■ n. informal a person who exploits any opportunity to the utmost.

chancery ■ n. (pl. **-ies**) 1 (**Chancery** or **Chancery Division**) Law (in the UK) the Lord Chancellor's court, a division of the High Court of Justice. 2 US a court of equity. ▶ equity. 3 chiefly Brit. an office attached to an embassy or consulate. 4 a public record office.
– ORIGIN Middle English: contraction of **CHANCELLERY**.

chancre /ˈʃaŋkə/ ■ n. Medicine a painless ulcer, particularly one developing on the genitals in venereal disease.
– ORIGIN C16: from Latin *cancer* 'creeping ulcer'.

chancroid /ˈʃaŋkrɔɪd/ ■ n. a venereal infection causing ulceration of the lymph nodes in the groin.

chancy ■ adj. (**-ier**, **-iest**) informal uncertain; risky.
– DERIVATIVES **chancily** adv. **chanciness** n.

chandelier /ˌʃandəˈlɪə/ ■ n. a large decorative hanging light with branches for several light bulbs or candles.
– ORIGIN C18: from French, from *chandelle* 'candle'.

chandler /ˈtʃɑːndlə/ ■ n. 1 (also **ship chandler**) a dealer in supplies and equipment for ships and boats. 2 historical a dealer in household items such as oil and groceries.
– DERIVATIVES **chandlery** n.
– ORIGIN Middle English: from Old French *chandelier*, from *chandelle* 'candle'.

change ■ v. 1 make or become different. ▶ (of the moon) arrive at a fresh phase; become new. 2 take or use another instead of. ▶ move from one to (another): *she had to change trains.* ▶ (**change over**) move from one system or situation to another. ▶ remove (something dirty or faulty) and replace it with another of the same kind. ▶ engage a different gear in a motor vehicle. 3 exchange (a sum of money) for the same sum in a different currency or denomination. ■ n. 1 the action of changing. ▶ an instance of becoming different. ▶ (**the change** or **the change of life**) informal the menopause. 2 a clean garment or garments as a replacement for something one is wearing. 3 coins as opposed to banknotes. ▶ money given in exchange for the same sum in larger units. ▶ money returned to someone as the balance of the sum paid. 4 an order in which a peal of bells can be rung.
– PHRASES **change colour** blanch or flush. **change hands** (of a business or building) pass to a different owner. ▶ (of money or a marketable commodity) pass to another person in the course of a business transaction. **a change of air** a different climate, typically as means of improving one's health. **change step** alter one's step so that the opposite leg is the one that marks time when marching. **change one's tune** express a very different opinion or behave in a very different way. **for a change** contrary to how things usually happen or in order to introduce variety. **get no change out of** Brit. informal fail to get information or a desired reaction from. **ring the changes** vary the ways of doing something. [with allusion to the different orders in which a peal of bells may be rung.]
– DERIVATIVES **changeless** adj. **changelessly** adv. **changelessness** n. **changer** n.
– ORIGIN Middle English: from Old French *change* (n.), *changer* (v.), from Latin *cambire* 'barter'.

changeable ■ adj. 1 liable to unpredictable variation. 2 able to be changed or exchanged.
– DERIVATIVES **changeability** n. **changeableness** n. **changeably** adv.

changeling ■ n. a child believed to have been secretly substituted by fairies for the parents' real child in infancy.

changeover ■ n. a change from one system or situation to another.

change-ringing ■ n. the ringing of sets of church bells or handbells in a constantly varying order.
– DERIVATIVES **change-ringer** n.

change-up ■ n. Baseball an unexpectedly slow pitch designed to throw off the batter's timing.

channa /ˈtʃʌnə/ ■ n. variant spelling of **CHANA**.

channel ■ n. 1 a length of water wider than a strait, joining two larger areas of water, especially two seas. ▶ (**the Channel**) the English Channel. ▶ a navigable passage in a stretch of water otherwise unsafe for vessels. 2 an electric circuit which acts as a path for a signal. 3 a band of frequencies used in radio and television transmission, especially as used by a particular station. 4 a medium for communication or the passage of information. ■ v. (**channelled**, **channelling**; US **channeled**, **channeling**) 1 direct towards a particular end. ▶ cause to pass along or through a specified route or medium. 2 [usu. as adj. **channelled**] form channels or grooves in.
– ORIGIN Middle English: from Old French *chanel*, from Latin *canalis* 'pipe, groove, channel', from *canna* (see **CANE**).

channel-hop ■ v. informal change frequently from one television channel to another, using a remote control device.
– DERIVATIVES **channel-hopper** n.

channel-surf ■ v. informal, chiefly N. Amer. another term for **CHANNEL-HOP**.

chanson /ˈʃɒ̃sɒ̃/ ■ n. a French song.
– ORIGIN French, from Latin *cantio(n-)* 'singing', from *canere* 'sing'.

chant ■ n. 1 a repeated rhythmic phrase, typically one shouted or sung in unison by a crowd. 2 a monotonous or repetitive song, typically an incantation or part of a ritual. 3 Music a short musical passage in two or more phrases used for singing unmetrical words; a psalm or canticle sung to such music. ■ v. say or shout repeatedly in a sing-song tone. ▶ sing or intone (a psalm, canticle, or sacred text).
– ORIGIN Middle English: from Old French *chanter* 'sing', from Latin *cantare*, *canere* 'sing'.

chanterelle /ˈtʃɑːntərɛl, ˌtʃɑːntəˈrɛl/ ■ n. an edible

woodland mushroom of Eurasia and North America which has a yellow funnel-shaped cap and a faint smell of apricots. [*Cantharellus cibarius*.]
– ORIGIN C18: from French, from Greek *kantharos*, denoting a kind of drinking container.

Chantilly cream /ʃanˈtɪli/ ■ n. sweetened or flavoured whipped cream.
– ORIGIN C19: named after *Chantilly*, a town near Paris, France, where it originated.

Chantilly lace ■ n. a delicate kind of bobbin lace.

chantry /ˈtʃɑːntri/ ■ n. (pl. **-ies**) a chapel, altar, or other part of a Christian church endowed for the celebration of masses for the donor's soul.
– ORIGIN Middle English: from Old French *chanterie*, from *chanter* 'to sing'.

Chanukkah ■ n. variant spelling of **HANUKKAH**.

chaos /ˈkeɪɒs/ ■ n. **1** complete disorder and confusion. ▸ Physics behaviour so unpredictable as to appear random, owing to great sensitivity to small changes in conditions. **2** the formless matter supposed to have existed before the creation of the universe.
– DERIVATIVES **chaotic** adj. **chaotically** adv.
– ORIGIN C15 (denoting a gaping void): from Greek *khaos* 'vast chasm, void'.

chap[1] ■ v. (**chapped**, **chapping**) (of the skin) crack and become sore, typically through exposure to cold weather. ▸ [usu. as adj. **chapped**] (of the wind or cold) cause (skin) to crack in this way. ■ n. a chapped area.
– ORIGIN Middle English.

chap[2] ■ n. informal a man or a boy.
– ORIGIN C16: abbrev. of archaic *chapman* 'pedlar', from Old English *cēap* 'bargaining, trade'.

chap[3] ■ n. the lower jaw or half of the cheek, especially that of a pig used as food.
– ORIGIN C16.

chap. ■ abbrev. chapter.

chaparajos /ˌʃapəˈreɪhəʊs, ˌtʃ-/ (also **chaparejos**) ■ pl. n. N. Amer. leather trousers without a seat, worn by a cowboy over ordinary trousers to protect the legs.
– ORIGIN C19: from Mexican Spanish *chaparreras*, from *chaparra* (with ref. to protection from thorny vegetation: see **CHAPARRAL**).

chaparral /ˌʃapəˈral, ˌtʃ-/ ■ n. N. Amer. vegetation consisting chiefly of tangled shrubs and thorny bushes.
– ORIGIN C19: from Spanish, from *chaparra* 'dwarf evergreen oak'.

chapatti /tʃəˈpɑːti, -ˈpati/ ■ n. (pl. **chapattis**) (in Indian cookery) a thin pancake of unleavened wholemeal bread cooked on a griddle.
– ORIGIN from Hindi *capātī*, from *capānā* 'roll out'.

chapbook ■ n. historical a small pamphlet containing tales, ballads, or tracts, sold by pedlars.
– ORIGIN C19: from archaic *chapman* 'pedlar' + **BOOK**.

chapeau /ˈʃapəʊ/ ■ n. (pl. **chapeaux**) Heraldry a hat or cap, typically a red one with an ermine lining, on which the crests of some peers are borne.
– ORIGIN C15: from French, from Latin *cappellum*, diminutive of *cappa* 'cap'.

chapel ■ n. **1** a small building for Christian worship, typically one attached to an institution or private house. ▸ a part of a large church or cathedral with its own altar and dedication. ▸ chiefly Brit. a place of worship for Nonconformist congregations. **2** Brit. the members or branch of a print or newspaper trade union at a particular place of work.
– ORIGIN Middle English: from Old French *chapele*, from medieval Latin *cappella*, diminutive of *cappa* 'cap, cape' (the first chapel being a sanctuary in which St Martin's cloak was preserved).

chapel of rest ■ n. Brit. an undertaker's mortuary.

chaperone /ˈʃapərəʊn/ (also **chaperon** /ˈʃapərɒn/) ■ n. dated an older woman responsible for the decorous behaviour of a young unmarried girl at social occasions. ■ v. accompany and look after.
– DERIVATIVES **chaperonage** /ˈʃap(ə)r(ə)ˌnɪdʒ/ n.

– ORIGIN Middle English: from French, from *chaperon* 'hood', diminutive of Old French *chape* 'cape'.

chaplain ■ n. a member of the clergy attached to a private chapel, institution, regiment, etc.
– DERIVATIVES **chaplaincy** n.
– ORIGIN Middle English: from Old French *chapelain*, from medieval Latin *cappellanus*, orig. denoting a custodian of the cloak of St Martin, from *cappella* (see **CHAPEL**).

chaplet /ˈtʃaplɪt/ ■ n. **1** a circlet for a person's head. **2** Christian Church a string of 55 beads (one third of the rosary number) for counting prayers.
– ORIGIN Middle English: from Old French *chapelet*, diminutive of *chapel* 'hat', from late Latin *cappa* 'cap'.

chaps ■ pl. n. short for **CHAPARAJOS**.

chaptalization /ˌtʃaptəlʌɪˈzeɪʃ(ə)n/ (also **-isation**) ■ n. (in winemaking) the correction or improvement of must by the addition of calcium carbonate or sugar.
– DERIVATIVES **chaptalize** (also **-ise**) v.
– ORIGIN C19: from the name of Jean A. *Chaptal*, the French chemist who invented the process.

Chapter 11 ■ n. (in the US) protection from creditors given to a company in financial difficulties for a limited period to allow it to reorganize.
– ORIGIN with allusion to chapter 11 of the US bankruptcy code.

chapter ■ n. **1** a main division of a book. **2** a particular period in history or in a person's life. **3** the governing body of a cathedral or other religious community. **4** a local branch of a society.
– PHRASES **chapter and verse** an exact reference or authority. **a chapter of accidents** a series of unfortunate events.
– ORIGIN Middle English: from Old French *chapitre*, from Latin *capitulum*, diminutive of *caput* 'head'.

chapter house ■ n. a building used for the meetings of a chapter. ▸ US a place where a college fraternity or sorority meets.

char[1] /tʃɑː/ ■ v. (**charred**, **charring**) partially burn so as to blacken the surface. ■ n. charred material.
– ORIGIN C17: prob. a back-formation from **CHARCOAL**.

char[2] /tʃɑː/ informal ■ n. a charwoman. ■ v. (**charred**, **charring**) work as a charwoman.

char[3] /tʃɑː/ (also **cha** /tʃɑː/ or **chai** /tʃʌɪ/) ■ n. Brit. informal tea.
– ORIGIN C16: from Chinese (Mandarin) *chá*.

char[4] ■ n. variant spelling of **CHARR**.

charabanc /ˈʃarəbaŋ/ ■ n. Brit. an early form of bus.
– ORIGIN C19: from French *char-à-bancs* 'carriage with benches'.

characin /ˈkarəsɪn/ ■ n. a small freshwater fish of a family native to Africa and tropical America, including the piranhas and tetras. [Family Characidae.]
– ORIGIN C19: from Greek *kharax* 'pointed stake'.

character ■ n. **1** the mental and moral qualities distinctive to an individual. ▸ strength and originality in a person's nature. ▸ a person's good reputation. **2** the distinctive nature of something. **3** a person in a novel, play, or film. ▸ a part played by an actor. **4** informal an interesting, eccentric, or amusing person. **5** a printed or written letter or symbol. ▸ Computing a symbol representing a letter or number. **6** chiefly Biology a characteristic, especially one that assists in the identification of a species.
– DERIVATIVES **characterful** adj. **characterless** adj.
– ORIGIN Middle English ('distinctive mark', later 'feature, trait'): from Old French *caractere*, from Greek *kharaktēr* 'a stamping tool'.

character actor ■ n. an actor who specializes in playing eccentric or unusual people rather than leading roles.

characteristic ■ adj. typical of a particular person, place, or thing. ■ n. **1** a feature or quality typical of a person, place, or thing. **2** Mathematics the whole number or integral part of a logarithm.
– DERIVATIVES **characteristically** adv.

characteristic curve ■ n. a graph showing the relationship between two variable but interdependent quantities.

characterize (also **-ise**) ■ v. **1** describe the distinctive character of. **2** (of a feature or quality) be characteristic of.
– DERIVATIVES **characterization** (also **-isation**) n.

character recognition ■ n. the identification by electronic means of printed or written characters.

charade /ʃəˈrɑːd/ ■ n. **1** an absurd pretence intended to create a pleasant impression. **2** (**charades**) [treated as sing.] a game of guessing a word or phrase from a written or acted clue given for each syllable and for the whole item.
–ORIGIN C18: from modern Provençal *charrado* 'conversation'.

charas /ˈtʃɑːrəs/ ■ n. cannabis resin.
–ORIGIN from Hindi *caras*.

charbroil ■ v. [usu. as adj. **charbroiled**] N. Amer. grill (food, especially meat) on a rack over charcoal.

charcoal ■ n. **1** a porous black form of carbon obtained as a residue when wood or other organic matter is heated in the absence of air. ▸ a stick of this used for drawing. **2** a dark grey colour.
–ORIGIN Middle English: prob. rel. to COAL.

charcuterie /ʃɑːˈkuːt(ə)ri/ ■ n. (pl. **-ies**) **1** cold cooked meats collectively. **2** a shop selling such meats.
–ORIGIN French, from obsolete *char* 'flesh' + *cuite* 'cooked'.

chard /tʃɑːd/ (also **Swiss chard**) ■ n. a beet of a variety with edible broad white leaf stalks and green blades.
–ORIGIN C17: from French *carde*, perhaps influenced by *chardon* 'thistle'.

Chardonnay /ˈʃɑːdəneɪ/ ■ n. a variety of white wine grape used for making champagne and other wines. ▸ a wine made from this grape.
–ORIGIN from French.

charge ■ v. **1** demand (an amount) as a price for a service rendered or goods supplied. **2** accuse (someone) of something, especially an offence under law. **3** entrust with a task. **4** store electrical energy in (a battery or battery-operated device). **5** technical or formal load or fill (a container, gun, etc.) to the full or proper extent. ▸ fill with a quality or emotion: *the air was charged with menace*. **6** rush forward in attack. ▸ move quickly and with impetus. **7** Heraldry place a charge on. ■ n. **1** a price asked. ▸ a financial liability or commitment. **2** a formal accusation made against a prisoner brought to trial. **3** responsibility for care or control. ▸ a person or thing entrusted to someone's care. **4** the property of matter that is responsible for electrical phenomena, existing in a positive or negative form. ▸ the quantity of this carried by a body. ▸ energy stored chemically in a battery for conversion into electricity. **5** a quantity of explosive to be detonated in order to fire a gun or similar weapon. **6** a headlong rush forward, typically in attack. **7** an official instruction given by a judge to a jury regarding points of law. **8** Heraldry a device or bearing placed on a shield or crest.
–PHRASES **press** (or **prefer**) **charges** accuse someone formally of a crime so that they can be brought to trial. **put someone on a charge** Brit. charge someone with a specified offence.
–DERIVATIVES **chargeable** adj. **charged** adj.
–ORIGIN Middle English, from Old French *charger* (v.), *charge* (n.), from late Latin *carricare* 'to load', from Latin *carrus* 'wheeled vehicle'.

charge account ■ n. an account to which goods and services may be charged on credit.

charge card ■ n. a credit card for use with an account which must be paid in full when a statement is issued.

charge carrier ■ n. an electron, ion, etc. which carries electric charge in a conductor or semiconductor.

charge-coupled device ■ n. a high-speed semiconductor device used chiefly in image detection.

chargé d'affaires /ˌʃɑːʒeɪ daˈfɛː/ (also **chargé**) ■ n. (pl. **chargés** pronunc. same) an ambassador's deputy. ▸ a state's diplomatic representative in a minor country.
–ORIGIN C18: French, '(a person) in charge of affairs'.

chargehand ■ n. Brit. a worker with supervisory duties ranking below a foreman.

charge nurse ■ n. Brit. a nurse in charge of a ward in a hospital.

charger[1] ■ n. **1** a device for charging a battery or battery-powered equipment. **2** a horse ridden by a knight or cavalryman.

charger[2] ■ n. archaic a large flat dish.

195

charm

–ORIGIN Middle English: from Anglo-Norman French *chargeour*, from *chargier* 'to load', from late Latin *carricare* (see CHARGE).

chargrill ■ v. [usu. as adj. **chargrilled**] grill (food, typically meat or fish) quickly at a very high heat.
–ORIGIN C20: on the pattern of *charbroil*.

chariot ■ n. **1** a two-wheeled vehicle drawn by horses, used in ancient warfare and racing. **2** poetic/literary a stately or triumphal carriage.
–DERIVATIVES **charioteer** n.
–ORIGIN Middle English: from Old French *char* 'cart', from Latin *carrus* 'wheeled vehicle'.

charisma /kəˈrɪzmə/ ■ n. **1** compelling attractiveness or charm that can inspire devotion. **2** (pl. **charismata** /kəˈrɪzmətə/) a divinely conferred power or talent.
–ORIGIN C17: from Greek *kharisma*, from *kharis* 'favour, grace'.

charismatic ■ adj. **1** having charisma. **2** of or relating to the charismatic movement. ▸ (of a power or talent) divinely conferred. ■ n. an adherent of the charismatic movement. ▸ a person who claims divine inspiration.
–DERIVATIVES **charismatically** adv.

charismatic movement ■ n. a fundamentalist movement within the Roman Catholic, Anglican, and other Christian Churches that emphasizes talents held to be conferred by the Holy Spirit.

charitable ■ adj. **1** of or relating to the assistance of those in need. ▸ officially recognized as a charity. ▸ generous in giving to those in need. **2** tolerant in judging others.
–DERIVATIVES **charitableness** n. **charitably** adv.

charity ■ n. (pl. **-ies**) **1** an organization set up to provide help and raise money for those in need. **2** the voluntary giving of money to those in need. ▸ help or money given in this way. **3** tolerance in judging others. **4** archaic love of humankind, typically in a Christian context.
–ORIGIN Old English: from Old French *charite*, from Latin *caritas*, from *carus* 'dear'.

charlady ■ n. (pl. **-ies**) Brit. a charwoman.

charlatan /ˈʃɑːlət(ə)n/ ■ n. a person falsely claiming to have a special knowledge or skill.
–DERIVATIVES **charlatanism** n. **charlatanry** n.
–ORIGIN C17 (denoting an itinerant seller of supposed remedies): from Italian *ciarlatano*, from *ciarlare* 'to babble'.

Charles's law ■ n. Chemistry a law stating that the volume of an ideal gas at constant pressure is directly proportional to the absolute temperature.
–ORIGIN C19: named after the French physicist Jacques A. C. *Charles*.

charleston ■ n. a lively dance of the 1920s which involved turning the knees inwards and kicking out the lower legs.
–ORIGIN 1920s: named after the city of *Charleston* in South Carolina, US.

charley horse ■ n. N. Amer. informal a cramp or feeling of stiffness in a limb.
–ORIGIN C19.

charlie ■ n. (pl. **-ies**) **1** Brit. informal a fool. **2** a code word representing the letter C, used in radio communication.
–ORIGIN C19: diminutive of the male given name *Charles*.

charlotte ■ n. a pudding made of stewed fruit with a casing or covering of bread, sponge cake, biscuits, or breadcrumbs.
–ORIGIN French: from the female given name *Charlotte*.

charlotte russe /ˈruːs/ ■ n. a pudding consisting of custard enclosed in sponge cake or a casing of sponge fingers.
–ORIGIN French, 'Russian charlotte'.

charm ■ n. **1** the power or quality of delighting, attracting, or fascinating others. ▸ an attractive characteristic or feature. **2** a small ornament worn on a necklace or bracelet. **3** an object, act, or saying believed to have magic power. **4** Physics one of six flavours of quark. ■ v. **1** delight greatly. ▸ use one's charm in order to influence someone. **2** control or achieve by or as if by magic.
–DERIVATIVES **charmer** n. **charmless** adj. **charmlessly** adv.

charmed

charmlessness n.
– ORIGIN Middle English: from Old French *charme* (n.), *charmer* (v.), from Latin *carmen* 'song, incantation'.

charmed ■ adj. (of a person's life) unusually lucky as though protected by magic. ■ exclam. dated expressing polite pleasure at an introduction: *charmed, I'm sure*.

charmeuse /ʃɑːˈməːz/ ■ n. a soft smooth silky dress fabric.
– ORIGIN C20: from French, feminine of *charmeur* 'charmer'.

charming ■ adj. **1** delightful; attractive. **2** very polite, friendly, and likeable. ■ exclam. used as an ironic expression of displeasure or disapproval.
– DERIVATIVES **charmingly** adv.

charm offensive ■ n. a campaign of flattery, friendliness, and cajolement designed to achieve the support of others.

charm school ■ n. a school where young women are taught social graces such as deportment and etiquette.

charnel house ■ n. historical a building or vault in which corpses or bones are piled.
– ORIGIN C16: from Middle English *charnel* 'burying place', from late Latin *carnalis* 'relating to flesh', from *caro*, *carn-* 'flesh'.

Charolais /ˈʃarə(ʊ)leɪ/ ■ n. (pl. same) an animal of a breed of large white beef cattle.
– ORIGIN C19: named after the *Monts du Charollais*, hills in eastern France where the breed originated.

charophyte /ˈkɑːrə(ʊ)fʌɪt, ˈkarə(ʊ)-, ˈtʃarə(ʊ)-/ ■ n. Botany a plant of a division (Charophyta) that includes the stoneworts.
– ORIGIN from *Chara* (genus name) + Greek *phuta* 'plants'.

charpoy /ˈtʃɑːpɔɪ/ ■ n. Indian a light bedstead.
– ORIGIN C17: from Urdu *cārpāī* 'four-legged', from Persian.

charr /tʃɑː/ (also **char**) ■ n. (pl. same) a trout-like northern freshwater or marine fish. [Genus *Salvelinus*: several species.]
– ORIGIN C17: perhaps of Celtic origin.

chart ■ n. **1** a sheet of information in the form of a table, graph, or diagram. ▶ (**the charts**) a weekly listing of the current best-selling pop records. **2** a geographical map, especially one used for navigation by sea or air. ■ v. **1** make a map of. ▶ plot (a course) on a chart. **2** (of a record) sell enough copies to enter the charts at a particular position.
– ORIGIN C16: from French *charte*, from Latin *charta* (see **CARD**[1]).

charter ■ n. **1** a written grant by a sovereign or legislature, by which a body such as a university is created or its rights and privileges defined. **2** a written constitution or description of an organization's functions. **3** (in the UK) a written statement of the rights of a specified group of people: *the patient's charter*. **4** (**Charter**) S. African short for **FREEDOM CHARTER**. **5** the hiring of an aircraft, ship, or motor vehicle. ■ v. **1** [usu. as adj. **chartered**] grant a charter to (a city, university, etc.). **2** hire (an aircraft, ship, or motor vehicle).
– DERIVATIVES **charterer** n.
– ORIGIN Middle English: from Old French *chartre*, from Latin *chartula*, diminutive of *charta* (see **CARD**[1]).

chartered ■ adj. (of an accountant, quantity surveyor, company secretary, etc.) qualified as a member of a professional body that has a royal charter.

charter flight ■ n. a flight by an aircraft chartered for a specific journey, not part of an airline's regular schedule.

charter party ■ n. a deed between a shipowner and a merchant for the hire of a ship and the delivery of cargo.
– ORIGIN Middle English: from French *charte partie*, from medieval Latin *charta partita* 'divided charter'.

Chartism ■ n. a UK parliamentary reform movement of 1837–48, the principles of which were set out in a manifesto called *The People's Charter*.
– DERIVATIVES **Chartist** n. & adj.

chartreuse /ʃɑːˈtrəːz/ ■ n. **1** a pale green or yellow liqueur made from brandy and aromatic herbs. **2** a pale green or yellow colour.

– ORIGIN named after *La Grande Chartreuse*, the Carthusian monastery near Grenoble, France, where the liqueur was first made.

charwoman ■ n. (pl. **-women**) Brit. dated a woman employed as a cleaner in a house or office.
– ORIGIN C16: from obsolete *char* or *chare* 'a chore' + **WOMAN**.

chary /ˈtʃɛːri/ ■ adj. (**-ier**, **-iest**) cautiously or suspiciously reluctant: *leaders are chary of major reform*.
– DERIVATIVES **charily** adv.
– ORIGIN Old English *cearig* 'sorrowful, anxious', of West Germanic origin.

Chas ■ abbrev. Charles.

chase[1] ■ v. **1** pursue in order to catch or catch up with. **2** rush or cause to go in a specified direction. **3** try to obtain (something owed or required). ▶ make further investigation of (an unresolved matter). ■ n. **1** an act of chasing. **2** (**the chase**) hunting as a sport.
– PHRASES **give chase** go in pursuit.
– ORIGIN Middle English: from Old French *chacier* (v.), from Latin *captare* 'continue to take', from *capere* 'take'.

chase[2] ■ v. [usu. as adj. **chased**] decorate (metal) by engraving or inlaying.
– ORIGIN Middle English: from Old French *enchasser* 'encase, set gems'.

chaser ■ n. **1** a person or thing that chases. **2** a horse for steeplechasing. **3** informal a strong alcoholic drink taken after a weaker one.

Chasidism /ˈxasɪdɪz(ə)m/ ■ n. variant spelling of **HASIDISM**.

chasm /ˈkaz(ə)m/ ■ n. **1** a deep fissure. **2** a profound difference between people, viewpoints, feelings, etc.
– ORIGIN C16: from Greek *khasma* 'gaping hollow'.

chassé /ˈʃaseɪ/ ■ n. a gliding step in dancing in which one foot displaces the other. ■ v. (**chasséd**, **chasséing**) make such a step.
– ORIGIN French, 'chased'.

chasseur sauce ■ n. a rich, dark sauce with wine and mushrooms, typically served with poultry or game.

Chassidism /ˈxasɪˌdɪz(ə)m/ ■ n. variant spelling of **HASIDISM**.

chassis /ˈʃasi, -iː/ ■ n. (pl. same /-sɪz/) **1** the base frame of a motor vehicle, carriage, or other wheeled conveyance. **2** the outer structural framework of a piece of audio, radio, or computer equipment.
– ORIGIN C20: from French *châssis* 'frame', from Latin *capsa* (see **CASE**[2]).

chaste ■ adj. **1** abstaining from extramarital, or from all, sexual intercourse. **2** without unnecessary ornamentation.
– DERIVATIVES **chastely** adv. **chasteness** n.
– ORIGIN Middle English: from Latin *castus*.

chasten /ˈtʃeɪs(ə)n/ ■ v. **1** (of a reproof or misfortune) have a restraining or demoralizing effect on. **2** archaic (especially of God) discipline; punish.
– DERIVATIVES **chastener** n.
– ORIGIN C16: from the obsolete verb *chaste*, from Old French *chastier*, from Latin *castigare* 'castigate', from *castus* 'chaste'.

chastise ■ v. reprimand severely. ▶ dated punish, especially by beating.
– DERIVATIVES **chastisement** n. **chastiser** n.
– ORIGIN Middle English: from the obsolete verb *chaste* (see **CHASTEN**).

chastity ■ n. the state or practice of abstaining from extramarital, or from all, sexual intercourse.

chastity belt ■ n. historical a garment or device designed to prevent the woman wearing it from having sexual intercourse.

chasuble /ˈtʃazjʊb(ə)l/ ■ n. Christian Church an ornate sleeveless outer vestment worn by a Catholic priest when celebrating Mass.
– ORIGIN Middle English: from Old French *chesible*, from late Latin *casubla*, from Latin *casula* 'hooded cloak or little cottage', diminutive of *casa* 'house'.

chat[1] ■ v. (**chatted**, **chatting**) talk in a friendly and informal way. ▶ (**chat someone up**) informal engage someone in flirtatious conversation. ■ n. an informal conversation.
– ORIGIN Middle English: shortening of **CHATTER**.

chat² ■ n. used in names of various songbirds with harsh, chattering calls, e.g. stonechat.
– ORIGIN C17: prob. imitative of their calls.

chateau /ˈʃatəʊ/ ■ n. (pl. **chateaux** pronunc. same or /-təʊz/) a large French country house or castle.
– ORIGIN C18: French: from Old French *chastel* (see **CASTLE**).

chateaubriand /ˌʃatəʊˈbriːɒ̃/ ■ n. a thick fillet of beef steak.
– ORIGIN C19: named after the French writer and statesman François-René, Vicomte de *Chateaubriand*, whose chef is said to have created the dish.

Chateau Cardboard ■ n. S. African & Austral./NZ informal, humorous another term for **BOX WINE**.

chatelaine /ˈʃatəleɪn/ ■ n. 1 dated a woman in charge of a large house. 2 historical a set of short chains attached to a woman's belt, used for carrying keys or other items.
– ORIGIN C19: from French *châtelaine*, feminine of *châtelain* 'castellan'.

chatline ■ n. a telephone service which allows conversation among a number of separate callers.

chatoyant /ʃəˈtɔɪənt/ ■ adj. (of a gem, especially when cut en cabochon) showing a band of bright lustre caused by reflection from inclusions in the stone.
– DERIVATIVES **chatoyance** n. **chatoyancy** n.
– ORIGIN C18: French, from *chatoyer* 'to shimmer'.

chat room ■ n. an area on the Internet or other computer network where users can communicate, typically one dedicated to a particular topic.

chat show ■ n. a television or radio programme in which celebrities are invited to talk informally about various topics.

chattel /ˈtʃat(ə)l/ ■ n. (in general use) a personal possession. ▸ Law an item of property other than freehold land, including tangible goods (chattels personal) and leasehold interests (chattels real). See also **GOODS AND CHATTELS**.
– ORIGIN Middle English: from Old French *chatel*, from Latin *capitalis*, from *caput* 'head'.

chattel mortgage ■ n. a mortgage on a movable item of property.

chatter ■ v. 1 talk rapidly or incessantly about trivial matters. 2 (of a person's teeth) click repeatedly together from cold or fear. ■ n. 1 incessant trivial talk. 2 a series of short quick high-pitched sounds.
– PHRASES **the chattering classes** derogatory educated or intellectual people considered as a social group given to the expression of liberal opinions.
– DERIVATIVES **chatterer** n. **chattery** adj.
– ORIGIN Middle English: imitative.

chatterbox ■ n. informal a person who chatters.

chatty ■ adj. (-ier, -iest) 1 fond of chatting. 2 (of a conversation, letter, etc.) informal and lively.
– DERIVATIVES **chattily** adv. **chattiness** n.

Chaucerian /tʃɔːˈsɪərɪən/ ■ adj. of or relating to Geoffrey Chaucer (c.1342–1400) or his writing. ■ n. a student or admirer of Chaucer.

chauffeur ■ n. a person employed to drive a car. ■ v. drive (a car or a passenger in a car) as a chauffeur.
– DERIVATIVES **chauffeuse** n. (rare).
– ORIGIN C19: from French, 'stoker' (by association with steam engines).

chauvinism /ˈʃəʊv(ɪ)nɪz(ə)m/ ■ n. 1 exaggerated or aggressive patriotism. 2 excessive or prejudiced support or loyalty for one's own cause, group, or sex.
– DERIVATIVES **chauvinist** n. & adj. **chauvinistic** adj. **chauvinistically** adv.
– ORIGIN C19: named after Nicolas *Chauvin*, a Napoleonic veteran noted for his extreme patriotism.

chayote /tʃeɪˈəʊti/ ■ n. 1 a succulent green pear-shaped tropical fruit resembling a cucumber in flavour. 2 the tropical American vine which yields chayotes, also producing an edible tuberous root. [*Sechium edule*.]
– ORIGIN C19: from Spanish, from Nahuatl *chayotli*.

ChB ■ abbrev. Bachelor of Surgery.
– ORIGIN from Latin *Chirurgiae Baccalaureus*.

cheap ■ adj. 1 low in price. ▸ charging low prices. ▸ inexpensive because of inferior quality. 2 of little worth because achieved in a discreditable way requiring little effort: *her moment of cheap triumph*. ▸ contemptible. 3 N. Amer. informal miserly. ■ adv. at or for a low price.

197

– PHRASES **on the cheap** informal at a low cost.
– DERIVATIVES **cheapish** adj. **cheaply** adv. **cheapness** n.
– ORIGIN C15: from an obsolete phr. *good cheap* 'a good bargain', from Old English *cēap* 'bargaining, trade', from Latin *caupo* 'small trader, innkeeper'.

cheapen ■ v. 1 reduce the price of. 2 degrade.

cheapjack ■ adj. chiefly N. Amer. of inferior quality. ■ n. a seller of cheap inferior goods, typically one at a fair or market.

cheapskate ■ n. informal a miserly person.
– ORIGIN C19 (orig. US): from **CHEAP** + **SKATE³**.

cheat ■ v. 1 act dishonestly or unfairly in order to gain an advantage. ▸ deprive of something by unfair or unfair means. 2 avoid (something undesirable) by luck or skill: *she cheated death in a spectacular crash*. ■ n. 1 a person who cheats. 2 an act of cheating.
– ORIGIN Middle English: shortening of *escheat*, from Old French *eschete*, from Latin *excidere* 'fall away'.

cheater ■ n. a person who cheats.

Chechen /ˈtʃetʃen/ ■ n. (pl. same or **Chechens**) 1 a member of the largely Muslim people inhabiting Chechnya, an autonomous republic in SW Russia. 2 the North Caucasian language of this people.
– ORIGIN from obsolete Russian *chechen*.

check¹ ■ v. 1 examine the accuracy, quality, or condition of. ▸ verify or establish to one's satisfaction. 2 stop or slow the progress of. ▸ Ice Hockey hamper or neutralize (an opponent) with one's body or stick. 3 Chess move a piece or pawn to a square where it attacks (the opposing king). ■ n. 1 an examination to check accuracy, quality, or condition. 2 an act of checking progress. ▸ a means of control or restraint. 3 Chess an act of checking the opposing king. 4 N. Amer. the bill in a restaurant. 5 (also **baggage/luggage check**) a token of identification for left luggage. 6 (also **check mark**) North American term for **TICK¹** (in sense 1). ■ exclam. Chess used by a player to announce that the opponent's king has been placed in check.
– PHRASES **in check 1** under control. 2 Chess (of a king) directly attacked by an opponent's piece or pawn. **keep a check on** monitor.
– PHRASAL VERBS **check in** (or **check someone in**) arrive and register at a hotel or airport. **check something in** have one's baggage weighed and consigned to the hold of an aircraft. **check into** register one's arrival at (a hotel). **check something off** mark an item on a list to show that it has been dealt with. **check on** verify, ascertain, or monitor the state or condition of. **check out** settle one's hotel bill before leaving. **check someone/thing out** establish the truth or inform oneself about someone or something. **check up on** investigate to establish the truth about or accuracy of.
– DERIVATIVES **checkable** adj.
– ORIGIN Middle English: noun and exclamation from Old French *eschec*, from medieval Latin *scaccus*, from Persian *šāh* 'king'; verb from Old French *eschequier* 'play chess, put in check'.

check² ■ n. a pattern of small squares. ■ adj. (also **checked**) having such a pattern.
– ORIGIN Middle English: prob. from **CHEQUER**.

check³ ■ n. US spelling of **CHEQUE**.

checkbox ■ n. Computing a small area on a computer screen which, when selected by the user, shows that a particular feature has been enabled.

checker¹ ■ n. a person or thing that checks.

checker² ■ n. & v. US spelling of **CHEQUER**.

checkerboard ■ n. US spelling of **CHEQUERBOARD**.

checking account (Canadian **chequing account**) ■ n. N. Amer. a current account at a bank.
– ORIGIN 1920s: from **CHECK³**.

checklist ■ n. a list of items required, things to be done, or points to be considered.

check mark ■ n. another term for **CHECK¹** (in sense 8).

checkmate ■ n. 1 Chess a position of check from which a king cannot escape. 2 a final defeat or deadlock. ■ v. 1 Chess put into checkmate. 2 defeat or frustrate totally.
– ORIGIN Middle English: from Old French *eschec mat*,

checkout

from Persian *šāh māt* 'the king is dead'.

checkout ▪ n. a point at which goods are paid for in a supermarket or similar store.

checkpoint ▪ n. a barrier or manned entrance, typically at a border, where security checks are carried out on travellers.

checksum ▪ n. a digit representing the sum of the correct digits in a piece of data, against which comparisons can be made to detect errors.

check-up ▪ n. a thorough medical or dental examination to detect any problems.

check valve ▪ n. a valve that closes to prevent backward flow of liquid.

Cheddar ▪ n. a kind of firm smooth yellow, white, or orange cheese, originally made in Cheddar in SW England.

cheek ▪ n. 1 either side of the face below the eye. 2 either of the buttocks. 3 either of two side pieces or parts arranged in lateral pairs in a structure. 4 impertinence; audacity. ▪ v. speak impertinently to.
– PHRASES **cheek by jowl** close together. **cheek to cheek** (of two people dancing) with their heads close together in an intimate and romantic way. **turn the other cheek** refrain from retaliating after an attack or insult. [with biblical allusion to Matthew 5:39.]
– DERIVATIVES **-cheeked** adj.
– ORIGIN Old English *cē(a)ce* 'cheek, jaw', of West Germanic origin.

cheekbone ▪ n. the bone below the eye.

cheeky ▪ adj. (-ier, -iest) impudent or irreverent.
– DERIVATIVES **cheekily** adv. **cheekiness** n.

cheep ▪ n. 1 a shrill squeaky cry made by a young bird. 2 [with neg.] informal the slightest sound: *there hasn't been a cheep from anybody.* ▪ v. make a cheep.
– ORIGIN C16 (orig. Scots): imitative.

cheer ▪ v. 1 shout in praise or encouragement. ▸ praise or encourage with shouts. 2 give comfort or support to. ▸ (**cheer someone up** or **cheer up**) make someone or become less miserable. ▪ n. 1 a shout of encouragement, praise, or joy. 2 (also **good cheer**) cheerfulness; optimism.
– PHRASES **three cheers** three successive hurrahs expressing appreciation or congratulation.
– ORIGIN Middle English (in the sense 'face', hence 'expression, mood', later 'a good mood'): from Old French *chiere* 'face', from Greek *kara* 'head'.

cheerful ▪ adj. 1 noticeably happy and optimistic. 2 causing happiness because pleasant.
– DERIVATIVES **cheerfully** adv. **cheerfulness** n.

cheerio ▪ exclam. Brit. informal goodbye.

cheerleader ▪ n. a member of a team of girls who perform organized cheering, chanting, and dancing in support of a sports team at matches in the US and elsewhere.

cheerless ▪ adj. gloomy; depressing.
– DERIVATIVES **cheerlessly** adv. **cheerlessness** n.

cheers ▪ exclam. informal expressing good wishes before drinking or (Brit.) on parting. ▸ chiefly Brit. expressing gratitude or acknowledgement.

cheery ▪ adj. (-ier, -iest) happy and optimistic.
– DERIVATIVES **cheerily** adv. **cheeriness** n.

cheese[1] ▪ n. 1 a food made from the pressed curds of milk, having a texture either firm and elastic or soft and semi-liquid. 2 Brit. a conserve having the consistency of soft cheese: *lemon cheese.*
– PHRASES **hard cheese** Brit. informal, dated used to express sympathy over a petty matter.
– ORIGIN Old English, of West Germanic origin; from Latin *caseus.*

cheese[2] ▪ v. (usu. **be cheesed off**) Brit. informal exasperate, frustrate, or bore.
– ORIGIN C19.

cheeseboard ▪ n. 1 a board on which cheese is served and cut. 2 a selection of cheeses served as a course of a meal.

cheeseburger ▪ n. a beefburger with a slice of cheese on it, served in a bread roll.

cheesecake ▪ n. 1 a kind of rich sweet tart made with cream and soft cheese on a biscuit base, typically topped with fruit. 2 informal images portraying women according to a stereotypical ideal of sexual attractiveness.

cheesecloth ▪ n. thin, loosely woven, unsized cotton cloth, used typically for light clothing and in preparing or protecting food.

cheese-paring ▪ adj. very careful or mean with money. ▪ n. meanness.

cheese straw ▪ n. a thin strip of cheese-flavoured pastry, eaten as a snack.

cheesy ▪ adj. (-ier, -iest) 1 like cheese in taste, smell, or consistency. 2 informal cheap, unpleasant, or blatantly inauthentic. ▸ hackneyed and trite. ▸ (of a smile) exaggerated and insincere.
– DERIVATIVES **cheesiness** n.

cheetah /ˈtʃiːtə/ ▪ n. a large swift-running spotted cat found in Africa and parts of Asia. [*Acinonyx jubatus.*]
– ORIGIN C18: from Hindi *cītā*, perhaps from Sanskrit *citraka* 'leopard'.

chef ▪ n. a professional cook, typically the chief cook in a restaurant or hotel. ▪ v. (**chefs, cheffing, cheffed**) work as a chef.
– ORIGIN C19: French, 'head'.

chef-d'œuvre /ʃeɪ ˈdəːvr(ə)/ ▪ n. (pl. **chefs-d'œuvre** pronunc. same) a masterpiece.
– ORIGIN French, 'chief work'.

Chekhovian /tʃɛˈkəʊvɪən/ ▪ adj. of, relating to, or characteristic of the work of the Russian dramatist Anton Chekhov (1860–1904).

chela[1] /ˈkiːlə/ ▪ n. (pl. **chelae** /-liː/) Zoology a pincer-like claw, especially of a crab or other crustacean.
– ORIGIN C17: from Latin *chele* or Greek *khēlē* 'claw'.

chela[2] /ˈtʃeɪlə/ ▪ n. a follower and pupil of a guru.
– ORIGIN from Hindi *celā.*

chelate /ˈkiːleɪt/ ▪ n. Chemistry a compound containing an organic ligand bonded to a central metal atom at two or more points. ▪ v. Chemistry form a chelate with.
– DERIVATIVES **chelation** n. **chelator** n.

chelicera /kəˈlɪs(ə)rə/ ▪ n. (pl. **chelicerae** /-riː/) Zoology either of a pair of appendages in front of the mouth in arachnids and some other arthropods, usually modified as pincer-like claws.
DERIVATIVES **cheliceral** adj.
– ORIGIN C19: from Greek *khēlē* 'claw' + *keras* 'horn'.

Chelicerata /kəˌlɪsəˈreɪtə/ ▪ n. Zoology a large subphylum of arthropods which possess chelicerae, comprising the arachnids, sea spiders, and horseshoe crabs.
– DERIVATIVES **chelicerate** /kəˈlɪsəreɪt, -(ə)rət/ n. & adj.

Chelsea boot ▪ n. an elastic-sided boot with a pointed toe.
– ORIGIN named after *Chelsea*, a district of London.

Chelsea bun ▪ n. Brit. a flat, spiral-shaped currant bun sprinkled with sugar.

Chelsea pensioner ▪ n. (in the UK) an inmate of the Chelsea Royal Hospital for old or disabled soldiers.

chemi- ▪ comb. form representing CHEMICAL. See also CHEMO-.

chemical ▪ adj. of or relating to chemistry or chemicals. ▸ relating to or denoting the use of poison gas or other chemicals as weapons of war. ▪ n. a distinct compound or substance, especially one which has been artificially prepared or purified.
– DERIVATIVES **chemically** adv.
– ORIGIN C16: from French *chimique*, from medieval Latin *alchymicus*, from *alchimia* (see ALCHEMY).

chemical bond ▪ n. see BOND (sense 4).

chemical compound ▪ n. see COMPOUND[1].

chemical engineering ▪ n. the branch of engineering concerned with the design and operation of industrial chemical plants.
– DERIVATIVES **chemical engineer** n.

chemical formula ▪ n. see FORMULA (sense 1).

chemico- ▪ comb. form representing CHEMICAL.

CONSONANTS　**b** but　**d** dog　**f** few　**g** get　**h** he　**j** yes　**k** cat　**l** leg　**m** man　**n** no　**p** pen　**r** red

chemin de fer /ˌʃæˌmã də 'fɛː/ ■ n. a card game which is a variety of baccarat.
– ORIGIN C19: French, 'railway'.

chemise /ʃə'miːz/ ■ n. 1 a dress hanging straight from the shoulders, popular in the 1920s. 2 a woman's loose-fitting undergarment or nightdress.
– ORIGIN Middle English: from Old French, from late Latin *camisia* 'shirt or nightgown'.

chemisorption /ˌkɛmɪ'sɔːpʃ(ə)n, -'zɔːp-/ ■ n. Chemistry adsorption in which the adsorbed substance is held by chemical bonds.
– DERIVATIVES **chemisorbed** adj.

chemist ■ n. 1 Brit. another term for PHARMACY. ▸ another term for PHARMACIST. 2 a person engaged in chemical research or experiments.
– ORIGIN Middle English: from French *chimiste*, from medieval Latin *alchimista* 'alchemist', from *alchimia* (see ALCHEMY).

chemistry ■ n. (pl. -ies) 1 the branch of science concerned with the properties and interactions of the substances of which matter is composed. 2 the chemical properties of a substance or body. 3 the emotional or psychological interaction between two people, especially when experienced as a powerful mutual attraction.

chemo- ■ comb. form representing CHEMICAL. See also CHEMI-.

chemoautotroph /ˌkiːməʊ'ɔːtətrəʊf, -trɒf, ˌkɛm-/ ■ n. Biology an organism which derives energy from the oxidation of inorganic compounds.
– DERIVATIVES **chemoautotrophic** /-'trəʊfɪk, -'trɒfɪk/ adj. **chemoautotrophy** /-'trəʊfi, -'trɒfi/ n.

chemoreceptor /ˈkiːməʊrɪˌsɛptə, ˌkɛm-/ ■ n. Physiology a sensory cell or organ responsive to chemical stimuli.
– DERIVATIVES **chemoreception** n.

chemosynthesis /ˌkiːmə(ʊ)'sɪnθɪsɪs, ˌkɛm-/ ■ n. Biology the metabolic synthesis of organic compounds by living organisms using energy derived from reactions involving inorganic chemicals.
– DERIVATIVES **chemosynthetic** adj.

chemotaxis /ˌkiːmə(ʊ)'taksɪs, ˌkɛm-/ ■ n. Biology movement of an organism in response to the changing concentration of a particular substance.
– DERIVATIVES **chemotactic** adj.

chemotherapy /ˌkiːmə(ʊ)'θɛrəpi, ˌkɛm-/ ■ n. the treatment of disease, especially cancer, by the use of chemical substances.
– DERIVATIVES **chemotherapist** n.

chenille /ʃə'niːl/ ■ n. a tufty velvety cord or yarn, used for trimming furniture and made into carpets or clothing.
– ORIGIN C18: from French, 'hairy caterpillar'.

Chenin Blanc /ˌʃɛnɪn ˌblɒŋk/ ■ n. a variety of wine grape grown mainly in France, South Africa, and the Americas. ▸ a white wine made from this grape.

cheongsam /tʃɪɒŋ'sam, tʃɒŋ-/ ■ n. a straight, close-fitting silk dress with a high neck and slit skirt, worn by Chinese and Indonesian women.
– ORIGIN Chinese (Cantonese).

cheque (US **check**) ■ n. an order to a bank to pay a stated sum from the drawer's account, written on a specially printed form.
– ORIGIN C18: var. of CHECK[1], in the sense 'device for checking an amount'.

cheque account ■ n. another term for CURRENT ACCOUNT.

chequebook journalism ■ n. the payment of a large amount of money to acquire the exclusive right to publish a person's story in a newspaper.

cheque card ■ n. Brit. a card issued by a bank to guarantee the honouring of cheques up to a stated amount.

chequer (US **checker**) ■ n. 1 (**chequers**) a pattern of alternately coloured squares. 2 (**checkers**) [treated as sing.] N. Amer. the game of draughts. ■ v. 1 (usu. **be chequered**) divide into or mark with chequers. 2 [as adj. **chequered**] marked by periods of fluctuating fortune: *a chequered career*.
– ORIGIN Middle English (in the sense 'chessboard', giving rise to *chequered* meaning 'marked like a chessboard'): from EXCHEQUER.

chequerboard (US **checkerboard**) ■ n. a board for playing checkers and similar games, having a regular chequered pattern, typically in black and white.

chequered flag ■ n. Motor Racing a flag with a black-and-white chequered pattern, displayed to drivers at the end of a race.

cherchez la femme /ˌʃɛrʃeɪ lɑ: 'fam/ ■ exclam. used to indicate that a woman is certain to be at the source of a problem or mystery.
– ORIGIN French, literally 'look for the woman'.

cherish ■ v. 1 protect and care for lovingly. 2 nurture (a hope or ambition).
– ORIGIN Middle English: from Old French *cherir*, from *cher* 'dear', from Latin *carus*.

chernozem /'tʃɜːnəzɛm/ ■ n. Soil Science a fertile black soil rich in humus, typical of temperate grassland.
– ORIGIN C19: from Russian, from *chërnyi* 'black' + *zemlya* 'earth'.

Cherokee /ˌtʃɛrə'kiː/ ■ n. (pl. same or **Cherokees**) 1 a member of an American Indian people formerly inhabiting much of the southern US. 2 the Iroquoian language of this people.
– ORIGIN from obsolete Cherokee *tsaraki*.

cheroot /ʃə'ruːt/ ■ n. a cigar with both ends open.
– ORIGIN C17: from French *cheroute*, from Tamil *curuṭṭu* 'roll of tobacco'.

cherry ■ n. (pl. -ies) 1 a small, soft round stone fruit that is typically bright or dark red. 2 the tree that bears such fruit. [*Prunus avium* (sweet cherry), *P. cerasus* (sour cherry), and other species and varieties.] 3 a bright deep red colour. 4 (**one's cherry**) informal one's virginity. 5 S. African informal a young woman; a (man's) girlfriend.
– PHRASES **a bite at the cherry** an attempt or opportunity. **a bowl of cherries** [with neg.] a very pleasant situation. **the cherry on the cake** a desirable thing providing the finishing touch to something already good.
– ORIGIN Middle English: from Old Northern French *cherise*, from Greek *kerasos* 'cherry tree, cherry'.

cherry brandy ■ n. a sweet, dark red cherry-flavoured liqueur made with brandy in which cherries have been steeped, or with crushed cherry stones.

cherry-pick ■ v. selectively choose (the best things or people) from those available.

cherry picker ■ n. informal 1 a hydraulic crane with a railed platform for raising and lowering people. 2 a person who cherry-picks.

cherry pie ■ n. a garden heliotrope with fragrant blue flowers. [*Heliotropium arborescens*.]

cherry plum ■ n. 1 a SW Asian shrub or small tree with white flowers and small red and yellow edible fruit. [*Prunus cerasifera*.] 2 the fruit of this tree.

cherry tomato ■ n. a miniature tomato with a strong flavour.

chert /tʃɜːt/ ■ n. a hard, dark, opaque rock composed of silica (chalcedony) with an amorphous or microscopically fine-grained texture.
– DERIVATIVES **cherty** adj.
– ORIGIN C17 (orig. dialect).

cherub ■ n. 1 (pl. **cherubim** or **cherubs**) a winged angelic being described in biblical tradition as attending on God, conventionally represented as a chubby child with wings. 2 (pl. **cherubs**) a beautiful or innocent-looking child.
– DERIVATIVES **cherubic** adj. **cherubically** adv.
– ORIGIN Old English *cherubin*, from Hebrew *kĕrūb*, pl. *kĕrūbīm*.

chervil /'tʃɜːvɪl/ ■ n. a plant of the parsley family, with delicate fern-like leaves which are used as a culinary herb. [*Anthriscus cerefolium*.]
– ORIGIN Old English, from Latin *chaerephylla*, from Greek *khairephullon*.

Cheshire /'tʃɛʃə/ ■ n. a kind of firm crumbly cheese, originally made in the English county of Cheshire.

Cheshire cat ■ n. a cat depicted with a broad fixed grin, as popularized through Lewis Carroll's *Alice's Adventures*

chess

in Wonderland (∞815).
- ORIGIN C18: it is said that *Cheshire* cheeses used to be marked with the face of a smiling cat.

chess ■ n. a board game of strategic skill for two players, the object of which is to put the opponent's king under a direct attack, leading to checkmate.
- ORIGIN Middle English: from Old French *esches*, pl. of *eschec* (see CHECK[1]).

chessboard ■ n. a square board divided into sixty-four alternating dark and light squares, used for playing chess or draughts.

chessman ■ n. (pl. **-men**) a solid figure used as a chess piece.

chest ■ n. **1** the front surface of a person's or animal's body between the neck and the stomach. ▸ the whole of a person's upper trunk. **2** a large strong box for storage or transport.
- PHRASES **get something off one's chest** informal say something that one has wanted to say for a long time. **keep** (or **play**) **one's cards close to one's chest** (or N. Amer. **vest**) informal be extremely secretive about one's intentions.
- DERIVATIVES **-chested** adj.
- ORIGIN Old English *cest*, *cyst*, from Greek *kistē* 'box'.

chesterfield ■ n. **1** a sofa with padded arms and back of the same height and curved outwards at the top. **2** a man's plain straight overcoat, typically with a velvet collar.
- ORIGIN C19: named after an Earl of *Chesterfield*.

chestnut ■ n. **1** a glossy hard brown nut which develops within a bristly case and can be roasted and eaten. **2** (also **chestnut tree**, **sweet chestnut**, or **Spanish chestnut**) the large tree that produces these nuts. [*Castanea sativa*.] ▸ used in names of similar nuts, and trees and plants that produce them, e.g. horse chestnut, water chestnut. **3** a deep reddish-brown colour. **4** a horse of a reddish-brown or yellowish-brown colour. **5** a small horny patch on the inside of a horse's leg.
- PHRASES **an old chestnut** a joke, story, or subject that has become uninteresting through constant repetition.
- ORIGIN C16: from Old English, from Old French *chastaine*, from Greek *kastanea* + NUT.

chest of drawers ■ n. a piece of furniture used for storage, consisting of an upright frame into which drawers are fitted.

chesty ■ adj. informal having a lot of catarrh in the lungs.
- DERIVATIVES **chestily** adv. **chestiness** n.

Chetnik /ˈtʃɛtnɪk/ ■ n. a member of a Slavic nationalist guerrilla force in the Balkans, especially during the Second World War.
- ORIGIN C20: from Serbo-Croat *četnik*, from *četa* 'band, troop'.

cheval glass /ʃəˈval/ (also **cheval mirror**) ■ n. a tall mirror fitted at its middle to an upright frame so that it can be tilted.
- ORIGIN C19: *cheval* from French, in the sense 'frame'.

chevalier /ˌʃɛvəˈlɪə/ ■ n. historical a knight. ▸ a member of certain orders of knighthood or of modern French orders such as the Legion of Honour.
- ORIGIN Middle English: from Old French, from medieval Latin *caballarius*, from Latin *caballus* 'horse'.

Cheviot /ˈtʃɛvɪət, ˈtʃiːv-/ ■ n. a large sheep of a breed with short thick wool.
- ORIGIN from the *Cheviot* Hills in northern England and Scotland.

chèvre /ʃɛvr(ə)/ ■ n. French cheese made with goat's milk.
- ORIGIN 1960s: French, 'goat, she-goat'.

chevron ■ n. a V-shaped line or stripe, especially one on the sleeve of a uniform indicating rank or length of service. ▸ Heraldry an ordinary in the form of a broad inverted V-shape.
- ORIGIN Middle English: from Old French, based on Latin *caper* 'goat'; cf. Latin *capreoli* (diminutive of *caper*) used to mean 'pair of rafters'.

chevrotain /ˈʃɛvrətein/ ■ n. a small deer-like mammal with small tusks, found in tropical rainforests. [Genera *Tragulus* (Asia) and *Hyemoschus* (Africa): four species.]
- ORIGIN C18: from Old French *chevrot*, diminutive of *chèvre* 'goat'.

chew ■ v. **1** bite and work (food) in the mouth to make it easier to swallow. **2** (**chew something over**) discuss or consider something at length. **3** (**chew someone out**) N. Amer. informal reprimand someone severely. ■ n. an instance of chewing. ▸ a thing for chewing.
- PHRASES **chew the fat** informal chat in a leisurely way.
- DERIVATIVES **chewable** adj. **chewer** n. **chewiness** n. **chewy** adj.
- ORIGIN Old English, of West Germanic origin.

chewing gum ■ n. flavoured gum for chewing.

Cheyenne /ʃaɪˈan/ ■ n. (pl. same or **Cheyennes**) a member of an American Indian people formerly living between the Missouri and Arkansas Rivers.
- ORIGIN Canadian French, from Dakota *šahíyena*, from *šaia* 'speak incoherently'.

Cheyne-Stokes breathing /tʃeɪn/ ■ n. Medicine an abnormal cyclical pattern of breathing in which the rate gradually decreases to a complete stop and then increases again.
- ORIGIN C19: named after the physicians John *Cheyne* and William *Stokes*.

chez /ʃeɪ/ ■ prep. chiefly humorous at the home of.
- ORIGIN C18: French, from Old French *chiese*, from Latin *casa* 'cottage'.

chi[1] /kʌɪ/ ■ n. the twenty-second letter of the Greek alphabet (Χ, χ), transliterated as 'kh' or 'ch'.
- PHRASES **chi-square test** a statistical method assessing the goodness of fit between a set of observed values and those expected theoretically.
- ORIGIN from Greek.

chi[2] /kiː/ (also **qi** or **ki**) ■ n. the circulating life force whose existence and properties are the basis of much Chinese philosophy and medicine.
- ORIGIN from Chinese *qì* 'air, breath'.

Chianti /kɪˈanti/ ■ n. (pl. **Chiantis**) a dry red Italian wine produced in Tuscany.
- ORIGIN named after the *Chianti* Mountains, Italy.

chiaroscuro /kɪˌɑːrəˈskʊərəʊ/ ■ n. the treatment of light and shade in drawing and painting.
- ORIGIN C17: from Italian, from *chiaro* 'clear, bright' + *oscuro* 'dark, obscure'.

chiasma /kʌɪˈazmə, kɪ-/ ■ n. (pl. **chiasmata** /-tə/) Biology a point at which paired chromosomes remain in contact during the first metaphase of meiosis.
- ORIGIN C19: from Greek *chiasma* 'crosspiece, cross-shaped mark', from *khiazein* 'mark with the letter chi'.

chiasmus /kʌɪˈazməs, kɪ-/ ■ n. the inversion in a second phrase or clause of the order of words in the first.
- DERIVATIVES **chiastic** adj.
- ORIGIN C17: from Greek *khiasmos*, from *khiazein* (see CHIASMA).

chic /ʃiːk/ ■ adj. (**-er**, **-est**) elegantly and stylishly fashionable. ■ n. stylishness and elegance.
- DERIVATIVES **chicly** adv.
- ORIGIN C19: from French, prob. from German *Schick* 'skill'.

chicane /ʃɪˈkeɪn/ ■ n. a sharp double bend created to form an obstacle on a motor-racing track.

chicanery ■ n. the use of trickery to achieve one's purpose.

Chichewa /tʃɪˈtʃeɪwə/ ■ n. another term for NYANJA (the language).

chichi /ˈʃiːʃiː/ ■ adj. attempting stylish elegance but achieving only an over-elaborate affectedness.
- ORIGIN C20: from French, of imitative origin.

chick ■ n. **1** a young bird, especially one newly hatched. ▸ a newly hatched young domestic fowl. **2** informal a young woman.
- ORIGIN Middle English: abbrev. of CHICKEN.

chickadee ■ n. North American term for TIT[1].
- ORIGIN C19: imitative of its call.

chicken ■ n. **1** a domestic fowl kept for its eggs or meat, especially a young one. **2** a coward. **3** informal a game in which the first person to lose their nerve and withdraw from a dangerous situation is the loser. ■ adj. informal cowardly. ■ v. (**chicken out**) informal be too scared to do something.
- PHRASES **chicken-and-egg** denoting a situation in which

each of two things appears to be necessary to the other. [from the question 'What came first, the chicken or the egg?'] **like a headless chicken** informal frenziedly.
–ORIGIN Old English, of Germanic origin.

chicken à la king ■ n. cooked breast of chicken in a cream sauce with mushrooms and peppers.
–ORIGIN said to be named after E. Clark *King*, proprietor of a New York hotel.

chicken feed ■ n. informal a paltry sum of money.

chickenpox ■ n. an infectious disease causing a mild fever and a rash of itchy inflamed pimples, caused by the herpes zoster virus; varicella.
–ORIGIN C18: prob. so named because of its mildness, as compared to smallpox.

chicken run ■ n. S. African informal, chiefly derogatory the emigration of people and businesses from South Africa since the early 1990s, because of fear for their future in the country.

chickenshit informal, chiefly N. Amer. ■ adj. worthless or contemptible. ■ n. a worthless or contemptible person.

chicken wire ■ n. light wire netting with a hexagonal mesh.

chick flick ■ n. informal, chiefly derogatory a film which appeals to young women.

chick lit ■ n. informal, chiefly derogatory literature which appeals to young women.

chickpea ■ n. 1 a round yellowish seed which is a pulse of major importance as food. 2 the leguminous plant which bears these seeds. [*Cicer arietinum*.]
–ORIGIN C18: from Middle English *chiche*, from Old French *cice*, from Latin *cicer* 'chickpea' + **PEASE**.

chickweed ■ n. a small white-flowered plant, often growing as a garden weed. [*Stellaria media* and numerous related species.]

chicle /ˈtʃɪk(ə)l/ ■ n. the milky latex of the sapodilla tree, used to make chewing gum.
–ORIGIN via Latin American Spanish, from Nahuatl *tzictli*.

chicory /ˈtʃɪk(ə)ri/ ■ n. (pl. **-ies**) 1 a blue-flowered Mediterranean plant of the daisy family, cultivated for its edible salad leaves and its carrot-shaped root, which is used as an additive to or substitute for coffee. [*Cichorium intybus*.] 2 North American term for **ENDIVE**.
–ORIGIN Middle English: from obsolete French *cicorée* 'endive', from Greek *kikhorion*.

chide /tʃaɪd/ ■ v. (past **chided** or **chid** /tʃɪd/; past part. **chided**) scold or rebuke.
–DERIVATIVES **chider** n. **chiding** adj. **chidingly** adv.
–ORIGIN Old English.

chief ■ n. 1 a leader or ruler of a people. ▶ the head of an organization. 2 Heraldry an ordinary consisting of a broad horizontal band across the top of the shield. ▶ the upper third of the field. ■ adj. 1 having the highest rank or authority. 2 most important: *the chief reason*.
–DERIVATIVES **chiefdom** n.
–ORIGIN Middle English: from Old French *chief, chef*, from Latin *caput* 'head'.

chief constable ■ n. Brit. the head of the police force of a county or other region.

chief inspector ■ n. Brit. a police officer ranking above inspector and below superintendent.

chiefly ■ adv. mainly; especially. ▶ for the most part; mostly.

chief of staff ■ n. the senior staff officer of a service, command, or formation.

chief petty officer ■ n. a rank of non-commissioned officer in the navy, above petty officer and below warrant officer.

chieftain ■ n. the leader of a people or clan.
–DERIVATIVES **chieftaincy** /-si/ n. (pl. **-ies**). **chieftainship** n.
–ORIGIN Middle English and Old French *chevetaine*, from late Latin *capitaneus*; the spelling was assimilated to **CHIEF**.

chiffchaff ■ n. a common Eurasian warbler with drab plumage and a repetitive call. [*Phylloscopus collybita*.]
–ORIGIN C18: imitative of its call.

chiffon ■ n. a light, transparent fabric typically made of silk or nylon.
–ORIGIN C18: from French *chiffe* 'rag'.

chiffonade /ˌʃɪfəˈnɑːd/ (also **chiffonnade**) ■ n. (pl. same) a preparation of shredded or finely cut leaf vegetables, used as a garnish for soup.
–ORIGIN French, from *chiffonner* 'to crumple'.

chiffonier /ˌʃɪfəˈnɪə/ ■ n. 1 Brit. a low cupboard either used as a sideboard or with a raised bookshelf on top. 2 N. Amer. a tall chest of drawers.
–ORIGIN C18: from French *chiffonnier, chiffonnière* 'ragpicker', also denoting a chest of drawers for oddments.

chifforobe /ˈʃɪfərəʊb/ ■ n. US a piece of furniture with drawers on one side and hanging space on the other.
–ORIGIN C20: blend of **CHIFFONIER** and **WARDROBE**.

chigger /ˈtʃɪɡə, ˈdʒ-/ (also **jigger**) ■ n. a tropical flea, the female of which burrows and lays eggs beneath the host's skin, causing painful sores. [*Tunga penetrans*.]
–ORIGIN C18: var. of **CHIGOE**.

chignon /ˈʃiːnjɒ̃/ ■ n. a knot or coil of hair arranged on the back of a woman's head.
–ORIGIN C18: from French, orig. 'nape of the neck'.

chigoe /ˈtʃɪɡəʊ/ ■ n. another term for **CHIGGER**.
–ORIGIN C17: from French *chique*, from a West African language.

chihuahua /tʃɪˈwɑːwə/ ■ n. a very small dog of a smooth-haired large-eyed breed originating in Mexico.
–ORIGIN C19: named after *Chihuahua* in northern Mexico.

chikungunya /ˌtʃɪk(ə)nˈɡʌnjə/ ■ n. a viral disease resembling dengue, transmitted by mosquitoes and endemic in East Africa and parts of Asia.
–ORIGIN 1950s: a local African word.

chilblain ■ n. a painful, itching swelling on a hand or foot caused by poor circulation in the skin when exposed to cold.
–DERIVATIVES **chilblained** adj.

child ■ n. (pl. **children**) 1 a young human being below the age of full physical development. ▶ a son or daughter of any age. 2 derogatory an immature or irresponsible person. 3 (**children**) archaic the descendants of a family or people. –PHRASES **child's play** a task which is easily accomplished. **with child** archaic pregnant.
–DERIVATIVES **childhood** n. **childless** adj. **childlessness** n.
–ORIGIN Old English, of Germanic origin.

childbearing ■ n. the process of giving birth to children.

childbed ■ n. archaic term for **CHILDBIRTH**.

child benefit ■ n. (in the UK) regular payment by the state to the parents of a child up to a certain age.

childbirth ■ n. the action of giving birth to a child.

child-centred ■ adj. giving priority to the interests and needs of children.

Childe /tʃaɪld/ ■ n. archaic or poetic/literary a youth of noble birth.
–ORIGIN Old English, var. of **CHILD**.

childish ■ adj. of, like, or appropriate to a child. ▶ silly and immature.
–DERIVATIVES **childishly** adv. **childishness** n.

childlike ■ adj. (of an adult) having the good qualities, such as innocence, associated with a child.

childminder ■ n. a person who looks after children in their own house for payment.

childproof ■ adj. designed to prevent children from injuring themselves or doing damage.

children plural form of **CHILD**.

chile ■ n. variant spelling of **CHILLI**.

Chilean /ˈtʃɪlɪən/ ■ n. a native or inhabitant of Chile. ■ adj. of or relating to Chile.

Chile pine ■ n. another term for **MONKEY PUZZLE**.

chile relleno /ˌtʃɪlɪ rɛˈljeɪnəʊ/ ■ n. (pl. **chiles rellenos**) (in Mexican cuisine) a stuffed chilli pepper, typically battered and deep-fried.
–ORIGIN Spanish, 'stuffed chilli'.

chili ■ n. (pl. **chilies**) US spelling of **CHILLI**.

chill ■ n. 1 an unpleasant feeling of coldness. 2 a feverish cold. ■ v. 1 make cold. ▶ cool (food or drink) in a refrigerator. 2 horrify or frighten. 3 (usu. **chill out**) informal

chiller

calm down and relax. ■ adj. chilly.
– DERIVATIVES **chilling** adj. **chillingly** adv. **chillness** n. **chillsome** adj. (poetic/literary).
– ORIGIN Old English *cele, ciele* 'cold, coldness', of Germanic origin.

chiller ■ n. **1** a cold cabinet or refrigerator for keeping stored food a few degrees above freezing point. **2** short for SPINE-CHILLER.

chill factor ■ n. a quantity expressing the perceived lowering of the air temperature caused by the wind.

chilli /'tʃɪli/ (also **chilli pepper**, **chile**, US **chili**) ■ n. (pl. **chillies**, **chiles**, or US **chilies**) **1** a small hot-tasting pod of a variety of capsicum, used in sauces, relishes, and spice powders. **2** short for CHILLI POWDER or CHILLI CON CARNE.
– ORIGIN C17: from Spanish *chile*, from Nahuatl *chilli*.

chilli-bite (also **chili-bite**, **chillie-bite**) ■ n. S. African another term for BHAJIA.

chilli con carne /kɒn 'kɑːneɪ, -ni/ ■ n. a stew of minced beef and beans flavoured with chilli powder.
– ORIGIN from Spanish *chile con carne*, 'chilli pepper with meat'.

chilli powder ■ n. a hot-tasting mixture of ground dried red chillies and other spices.

chillum /'tʃɪləm/ ■ n. (pl. **chillums**) **1** a hookah. **2** a pipe used for smoking cannabis.
– ORIGIN from Hindi *cilam*.

chilly ■ adj. (**-ier, -iest**) **1** unpleasantly cold. **2** unfriendly.
– DERIVATIVES **chilliness** n.

Chilopoda /ˌkaɪlə'pəʊdə/ ■ pl. n. Zoology a class of myriapod arthropods which comprises the centipedes.
– DERIVATIVES **chilopod** /'kaɪləpɒd/ n.
– ORIGIN from Greek *kheilos* 'lip' + *pous, pod-* 'foot'.

chimaera ■ n. variant spelling of CHIMERA.

chime ■ n. **1** a bell or a metal bar or tube tuned and used in a set to produce melodious ringing sounds when struck. ▸ a sound made by such an instrument. **2** Bell-ringing a stroke of the clapper against one or both sides of a scarcely moving bell. ■ v. **1** (of a bell or clock) make chimes. **2** (**chime with**) be in agreement with. **3** (**chime in**) interject a remark.
– DERIVATIVES **chimer** n.
– ORIGIN Middle English: prob. from Old English *cimbal* (see CYMBAL), later interpreted as *chime bell*.

chimera /kaɪ'mɪərə, kɪ-/ (also **chimaera**) ■ n. **1** Greek & Roman Mythology a fire-breathing female monster with a lion's head, a goat's body, and a serpent's tail. **2** something hoped for but illusory or impossible to achieve. **3** (**chimaera**) a long-tailed cartilaginous marine fish with an erect spine before the first dorsal fin. [*Chimaera* and other genera, family Chimaeridae.]
– DERIVATIVES **chimeric** /-'mɛrɪk/ adj. **chimerical** adj. **chimerically** adv.
– ORIGIN Middle English: from Greek *khimaira* 'she-goat or chimera'.

chimney ■ n. (pl. **-eys**) **1** a vertical pipe which conducts smoke and gases up from a fire or furnace. ▸ a chimney stack. **2** a glass tube protecting the flame of a lamp. **3** a very steep narrow cleft by which a rock face may be climbed.
– ORIGIN Middle English: from Old French *cheminee*, from late Latin, perhaps from (*camera*) *caminata* '(room) with a fireplace', from Latin *caminus* 'forge, furnace', from Greek *kaminos* 'oven'.

chimney breast ■ n. a part of an interior wall that projects to surround a chimney.

chimney corner ■ n. a warm seat within an old-fashioned fireplace.

chimney pot ■ n. an earthenware or metal pipe at the top of a chimney.

chimney stack ■ n. the part of a chimney that projects above a roof.

chimney sweep ■ n. a person whose job is cleaning out the soot from chimneys.

chimp ■ n. informal term for CHIMPANZEE.

chimpanzee ■ n. an anthropoid ape with large ears, mainly black coloration, and lighter skin on the face, native to west and central Africa. [*Pan troglodytes* and *P. paniscus* (the bonobo or pygmy chimpanzee).]
– ORIGIN C18: from French *chimpanzé*, from Kikongo.

Chimu /tʃɪ'muː/ ■ n. (pl. same or **Chimus**) a member of a native people of Peru that developed the most important civilization before the Incas.
– ORIGIN from Spanish.

chin ■ n. the protruding part of the face below the mouth, formed by the apex of the lower jaw. ■ v. draw one's body up so that one's chin is level with (a horizontal bar), as an exercise.
– PHRASES **keep one's chin up** informal remain cheerful in difficult circumstances. **take it on the chin** informal accept misfortune stoically.
– DERIVATIVES **-chinned** adj.
– ORIGIN Old English, of Germanic origin.

china ■ n. **1** a fine white or translucent vitrified ceramic material. ▸ household tableware or other objects made from china. **2** S. African & Brit. informal a friend. ▸ a term of address: *my china*. [from rhyming slang *china plate* 'mate'.]
– ORIGIN C16: from Persian *chīnī* 'relating to China'.

China aster ■ n. a Chinese plant of the daisy family, cultivated for its bright showy flowers. [*Callistephus chinensis*.]

chinaberry ■ n. (pl. **-ies**) another term for SYRINGA.

china blue ■ n. a pale greyish blue.

china clay ■ n. another term for KAOLIN.

chinagraph pencil ■ n. Brit. a waxy pencil used to write on china, glass, or other hard surfaces.

China rose ■ n. **1** a Chinese rose from which various garden rose varieties have been derived. [*Rosa chinensis*.] **2** a shrubby tropical hibiscus cultivated for its large showy flowers. [*Hibiscus rosa-sinensis*.]

China syndrome ■ n. a hypothetical sequence of events following the meltdown of a nuclear reactor, in which the core melts through its containment structure and deep into the earth.
– ORIGIN 1970s: so named because China is on the opposite side of the earth from a reactor in the US.

China tea ■ n. tea made from a small-leaved type of tea plant grown in China, typically flavoured by smoke curing or the addition of flower petals.

Chinatown ■ n. a district of a non-Chinese town in which the population is predominantly of Chinese origin.

chincherinchee /ˌtʃɪntʃərɪn'tʃiː/ ■ n. a white-flowered South African lily. [*Ornithogalum thyrsoides*.]
– ORIGIN C20: imitative of the squeaky sound made by rubbing its stalks together.

chinchilla /tʃɪn'tʃɪlə/ ■ n. **1** a small South American rodent with soft grey fur and a long bushy tail. [Genus *Chinchilla*: two species.] **2** a cat or rabbit of a breed with silver-grey or grey fur. **3** the highly valued fur of the chinchilla, or of the chinchilla rabbit.
– ORIGIN C17: from Spanish, from Aymara or Quechua.

chin-chin ■ exclam. Brit. informal, dated a toast made before drinking.
– ORIGIN C18: representing a pronunciation of Chinese *qing qing*.

Chindit /'tʃɪndɪt/ ■ n. a member of the Allied forces behind the Japanese lines in Burma (now Myanmar) in 1943–5.
– ORIGIN SECOND WORLD WAR: from Burmese *chinthé*, a mythical creature.

chine /tʃaɪn/ ■ n. **1** the backbone of an animal as it appears in a joint of meat. ▸ a joint of meat containing all or part of this. **2** a mountain ridge. ■ v. cut (meat) across or along the backbone.
– ORIGIN Middle English: from Old French *eschine*, from a blend of Latin *spina* 'spine' and a Germanic word meaning 'narrow piece'.

Chinese ■ n. (pl. same) **1** the language of China. **2** a native or national of China, or a person of Chinese descent. ■ adj. of or relating to China, its people or their language. ▸ belonging to the dominant ethnic group of China (the Han).

Chinese box ■ n. each of a nest of boxes.

Chinese burn ■ n. informal a burning sensation inflicted on a person by placing both hands on their arm and then twisting it.

Chinese cabbage ■ n. another term for **CHINESE LEAVES**.

Chinese chequers (US **Chinese checkers**) ■ pl. n. [usu. treated as sing.] a board game for two to six players who attempt to move marbles or counters from one corner to the opposite one on a star-shaped board.

Chinese gooseberry ■ n. former term for **KIWI FRUIT**.

Chinese lantern ■ n. 1 a collapsible paper lantern. 2 a plant with white flowers and globular orange fruits enclosed in an orange-red papery calyx. [*Physalis alkekengi*.] 3 (also **Chinese lantern flower**) a shrub with bell-shaped white, pink, red, yellow, or orange flowers. [*Abutilon megapotamicum*.]

Chinese leaves (also **Chinese cabbage**) ■ pl. n. an oriental variety of cabbage which does not form a firm heart. [*Brassica chinensis* (pak choi) and *B. pekinensis* (pe tsai).]

Chinese puzzle ■ n. an intricate puzzle consisting of many interlocking pieces.

Chinese red ■ n. a vivid orange-red.

Chinese wall ■ n. an insurmountable barrier, especially to the passage of information.

Chinese whispers ■ pl. n. [treated as sing.] a game in which a message is distorted by being passed around in a whisper.

Chinese white ■ n. white pigment consisting of zinc oxide.

Chink ■ n. informal, offensive a Chinese person.

chink[1] ■ n. 1 a narrow opening or crack. 2 a beam of light admitted by a chink.
– ORIGIN C16: perhaps rel. to Old English *cinu* 'chink, cleft', of Germanic origin.

chink[2] ■ v. make a light, high-pitched ringing sound, as of glasses or coins striking together. ■ n. a high-pitched ringing sound.
– ORIGIN C16: imitative.

Chinky ■ n. (pl. **-ies**) informal 1 offensive a Chinese person. 2 a Chinese restaurant.

chinless ■ adj. 1 lacking a well-defined chin. 2 informal lacking strength of character.

Chino- /'tʃaɪnəʊ/ ■ comb. form equivalent to **SINO-**.

chino /'tʃiːnəʊ/ ■ n. (pl. **-os**) 1 a cotton twill fabric, typically khaki-coloured. 2 (**chinos**) casual trousers made from such fabric.
– ORIGIN 1940s: from Latin American Spanish, 'toasted' (referring to the typical colour).

chinoiserie /ʃɪn'wɑːzəri/ ■ n. (pl. **-ies**) the use of Chinese motifs and techniques in Western art, furniture, and architecture. ▸ objects or decorations in this style.
– ORIGIN C19: from French, from *chinois* 'Chinese'.

Chinook /tʃɪ'nuːk, -nʊk, ʃɪ-/ ■ n. (pl. same or **Chinooks**) a member of an American Indian people originally inhabiting the region around the Columbus River in Oregon.
– ORIGIN from Salish *tsinúk*.

chinook /tʃɪ'nuːk, -nʊk, ʃɪ-/ ■ n. 1 (also **chinook wind**) a warm, dry wind which blows down the east side of the Rocky Mountains at the end of winter. 2 (also **chinook salmon**) a large North Pacific salmon which is an important commercial food fish. [*Oncorhynchus tshawytscha*.]

chintz ■ n. printed multicoloured cotton fabric with a glazed finish, used especially for curtains and upholstery.
– ORIGIN C17 (as *chints*, denoting a stained or painted calico cloth imported from India): from Hindi *chīṇṭ* 'spattering, stain'.

chintzy ■ adj. (**-ier**, **-iest**) 1 decorated with or resembling chintz. 2 gaudy and tasteless. 3 N. Amer. informal miserly.
– DERIVATIVES **chintzily** adv. **chintziness** n.

chin-up ■ n. chiefly N. Amer. another term for **PULL-UP**.

chinwag Brit. informal ■ n. a chat. ■ v. (**-wagged**, **-wagging**) have a chat.

chip ■ n. 1 a small, thin piece removed in the course of chopping, cutting, or breaking a hard material. ▸ a blemish left by the removal of such a piece. ▸ Brit. wood or woody fibre split into thin strips and used for weaving hats or baskets. 2 a long rectangular piece of deep-fried potato. ▸ (also **potato chip**) a potato crisp. 3 short for **MICROCHIP**. 4 a counter used in certain gambling games to represent money. 5 (in football or golf) a short lofted kick or shot. ■ v. (**chipped**, **chipping**) 1 cut or break (a chip) from a hard material. ▸ (of a hard material or object) break at the edge or on the surface. 2 (**chip away**) gradually and relentlessly make something smaller or weaker: *rivals may chip away at one's profits*. 3 (**chip in**) contribute one's share of a joint activity. ▸ informal make an interjection. 4 [usu. as adj. **chipped**] chiefly Brit. cut (a potato) into chips. 5 (in football or golf) strike (the ball) to produce a short lofted shot or pass.
– PHRASES **a chip off the old block** informal someone who resembles their parent in character. **a chip on one's shoulder** informal a deeply ingrained grievance. **when the chips are down** informal when a very serious situation arises.
– ORIGIN Middle English: rel. to Old English *forcippian* 'cut off'.

chipboard ■ n. material made in rigid sheets from compressed wood chips and resin and used for furniture and in buildings.

chipmunk ■ n. a burrowing ground squirrel with cheek pouches and light and dark stripes running down the body, found in North America and northern Eurasia. [Genus *Tamias*: many species.]
– ORIGIN C19: from Ojibwa.

chipolata ■ n. Brit. a small thin sausage.
– ORIGIN C19: from Italian *cipollata* 'a dish of onions', from *cipolla* 'onion'.

Chippendale /'tʃɪp(ə)ndeɪl/ ■ adj. (of furniture) designed by or in the style of Thomas Chippendale (1718–79), neoclassical with elements of French rococo and chinoiserie.

chipper[1] ■ adj. informal cheerful and lively.
– ORIGIN C19: perhaps from northern English dialect *kipper* 'lively'.

chipper[2] ■ n. a thing that turns something into chips.

chipping ■ n. a small fragment of stone, wood, or similar material.

chippy informal ■ n. (also **chippie**) (pl. **-ies**) 1 Brit. a fish-and-chip shop. 2 Brit. a carpenter. ■ adj. touchy and irritable.

chiral /'kaɪr(ə)l/ ■ adj. Chemistry (of a molecule) not able to be superimposed on its mirror image.
– ORIGIN C19: from Greek *kheir* 'hand'.

chiro- /'kaɪrəʊ/ (also **cheiro-**) ■ comb. form of the hand or hands: *chiromancy*.
– ORIGIN from Greek *kheir* 'hand'.

chirography /kaɪ'rɒgrəfi/ ■ n. handwriting, especially as distinct from typography.

chiromancy /'kaɪrə(ʊ)mansi/ ■ n. the prediction of a person's future from the lines on the palms of their hands; palmistry.

chironomid /kaɪ'rɒnəmɪd/ ■ n. Entomology an insect of a family (Chironomidae) which comprises the non-biting midges.
– ORIGIN C19: from *Chironomus* (genus name), from Greek *kheironomos* 'pantomime dancer'.

chiropody ■ n. the treatment of the feet and their ailments.
– DERIVATIVES **chiropodist** n.
– ORIGIN C19: from **CHIRO-** + Greek *pous*, *pod-* 'foot'.

chiropractic /ˌkaɪrə(ʊ)'praktɪk/ ■ n. a system of complementary medicine based on the diagnosis and manipulative treatment of misalignments of the joints, especially those of the spinal column.
– DERIVATIVES **chiropractor** n.
– ORIGIN C19: from **CHIRO-** + Greek *praktikos* 'practical'.

Chiroptera /kaɪ'rɒpt(ə)rə/ ■ pl. n. Zoology an order of mammals that comprises the bats.
– ORIGIN from **CHIRO-** + Greek *pteron* 'wing'.

chirp ■ v. 1 (of a small bird or a grasshopper) utter a short, sharp, high-pitched sound. 2 say something in a lively and cheerful way. ▸ informal taunt; complain. ■ n. 1 a chirping

chirpy

sound. **2** informal a taunt or complaint.
— DERIVATIVES **chirper** n.
— ORIGIN Middle English: imitative.

chirpy ■ adj. (**-ier**, **-iest**) informal cheerful and lively.
— DERIVATIVES **chirpily** adv. **chirpiness** n.

chirr /tʃəː/ (also **churr**) ■ v. (especially of an insect) make a prolonged low trilling sound. ■ n. a low trilling sound.
— ORIGIN C17: imitative.

chirrup ■ v. (**chirruped**, **chirruping**) (of a small bird) make repeated short high-pitched sounds. ■ n. a chirruping sound.
— DERIVATIVES **chirrupy** adj.
— ORIGIN C16: alteration of **CHIRP**.

chisel /ˈtʃɪz(ə)l/ ■ n. a long-bladed hand tool with a bevelled cutting edge, struck with a hammer or mallet to cut or shape wood, stone, or metal. ■ v. (**chiselled**, **chiselling**; US **chiseled**, **chiseling**) **1** cut or shape with a chisel. **2** [as adj. **chiselled**] (of a man's facial features) strongly and clearly defined.
— DERIVATIVES **chiseller** n.
— ORIGIN Middle English: from Old Northern French, from Latin *cis-*, var. of *caes-*, *caedere* 'to cut'.

chit[1] ■ n. derogatory an impudent or arrogant young woman: *a chit of a girl*.
— ORIGIN Middle English: perhaps rel. to dialect *chit* 'sprout'.

chit[2] ■ n. a short official note, memorandum, or voucher, typically recording a sum owed.
— ORIGIN C18: Anglo-Indian, from Hindi *ciṭṭhī* 'note, pass'.

chit-chat informal ■ n. inconsequential conversation. ■ v. talk about trivial matters.
— ORIGIN C17: reduplication of **CHAT**[1].

chitin /ˈkaɪtɪn/ ■ n. Biochemistry a fibrous carbohydrate which forms the exoskeleton of arthropods and the cell walls of fungi.
— DERIVATIVES **chitinous** adj.
— ORIGIN C19: from French *chitine*, from Greek *khitōn* (see **CHITON**).

chiton /ˈkaɪtɒn, -t(ə)n/ ■ n. **1** a long woollen tunic worn in ancient Greece. **2** a marine mollusc that has an oval flattened body with a shell of overlapping plates. [*Chiton* and other genera, class Polyplacophora.]
— ORIGIN from Greek *khitōn* 'tunic'.

chitter ■ v. make a twittering or chattering sound.
— ORIGIN Middle English: imitative.

chitterlings /ˈtʃɪtəlɪŋz/ ■ pl. n. the smaller intestines of a pig, cooked for food.
— ORIGIN Middle English: perhaps rel. to German *Kutteln*.

chivalry ■ n. **1** (in Europe) the medieval knightly system with its religious, moral, and social code. **2** the combination of qualities expected of an ideal knight, especially courage, honour, courtesy, justice, and a readiness to help the weak. ▸ courteous behaviour, especially that of a man towards women.
— DERIVATIVES **chivalric** adj. **chivalrous** adj. **chivalrously** adv.
— ORIGIN Middle English: from Old French *chevalerie*, from medieval Latin *caballerius*, from Latin *caballus* 'horse'.

chives ■ pl. n. a small plant related to the onion, with long tubular leaves used as a culinary herb. [*Allium schoenoprasum*.]
— ORIGIN Middle English: from Old French, var. of *cive*, from Latin *cepa* 'onion'.

chivvy (also **chivy**) ■ v. (**-ies**, **-ied**) tell repeatedly to do something.
— ORIGIN C18: orig. denoting a hunting cry, prob. from the ballad *Chevy Chase*, celebrating a skirmish on the Scottish border.

chlamydia /kləˈmɪdɪə/ ■ n. (pl. same or **chlamydiae** /-diː/) a very small parasitic bacterium which, like a virus, requires the biochemical mechanisms of another cell in order to reproduce. [Genus *Chlamydia*, order Chlamydiales.]
— DERIVATIVES **chlamydial** adj.
— ORIGIN 1960s: from Greek *khlamus, khlamud-* 'cloak'.

chlamydomonas /ˌklamɪdəˈməʊnəs/ ■ n. Biology a common single-celled green alga living in water and moist soil. [Genus *Chlamydomonas*.]

— ORIGIN C19: from Greek *khlamus, khlamud-* 'cloak' + *monas* (see **MONAD**).

chloasma /kləʊˈazmə/ ■ n. Medicine a temporary condition, typically caused by hormones, in which large brown patches form on the skin.
— ORIGIN C19: from Greek *khloazein* 'become green'.

chlor- ■ comb. form variant spelling of **CHLORO-** before a vowel.

chloramphenicol /ˌklɔːramˈfɛnɪkɒl/ ■ n. Medicine a bacterial antibiotic used against serious infections such as typhoid fever.
— ORIGIN 1940s: from **CHLOR-** + *am(ide)* + **PHENO-** + *ni(tro)-* + *(gly)col*.

chlordane /ˈklɔːdeɪn/ ■ n. a toxic, viscous, synthetic compound used as an insecticide.
— ORIGIN 1940s: from **CHLOR-** + *(in)dene* + **-ANE**[2].

chlordiazepoxide /ˌklɔːdʌɪazɪˈpɒksʌɪd/ ■ n. Medicine a tranquillizer used chiefly to treat anxiety and alcoholism.
— ORIGIN 1960s: from **CHLOR-** + *diazo-* + **EPOXIDE**.

chlorella /kləˈrɛlə/ ■ n. Biology a common single-celled green alga, responsible for turning stagnant water an opaque green. [Genus *Chlorella*.]
— ORIGIN diminutive of Greek *khlōros* 'green'.

chlorhexidine /klɔːˈhɛksɪdiːn/ ■ n. a synthetic compound used as a mild antiseptic.
— ORIGIN C20: from **CHLOR-** + *hex(ane)* + *-id(e)* + *(am)ine*.

chloride /ˈklɔːrʌɪd/ ■ n. Chemistry a compound of chlorine with another element or group: *sodium chloride*.

chlorinate /ˈklɔːrɪneɪt, ˈklɒ-/ ■ v. impregnate or treat with chlorine.
— DERIVATIVES **chlorination** n. **chlorinator** n.

chlorine /ˈklɔːriːn/ ■ n. the chemical element of atomic number 17, a toxic, irritant, pale green gas of the halogen group. (Symbol: **Cl**)
— ORIGIN C19: from Greek *khlōros* 'green'.

chlorite[1] /ˈklɔːrʌɪt/ ■ n. a dark green mineral found in many rocks, consisting of an aluminosilicate of magnesium and iron.
— ORIGIN C18: from Greek *khlōritis*, a green precious stone.

chlorite[2] /ˈklɔːrʌɪt/ ■ n. Chemistry a salt of chlorous acid ($HClO_2$), containing the anion ClO_2^-.

chloro- ■ comb. form **1** Biology green: *chlorophyll*. **2** Chemistry representing **CHLORINE**: *chloroquine*.

chlorofluorocarbon /ˌklɔːrə(ʊ)ˌflʊərə(ʊ)ˈkɑːb(ə)n, -ˌflɒː-/ ■ n. see **CFC**.

chloroform ■ n. a volatile sweet-smelling liquid used as a solvent and formerly as a general anaesthetic. [$CHCl_3$.] ■ v. make unconscious with this substance.
— ORIGIN C19: from **CHLORO-** + *form-* from **FORMIC ACID**.

chlorophyll /ˈklɔːrəfɪl, ˈklɒ-/ ■ n. a green pigment which is responsible for the absorption of light by plants to provide energy for photosynthesis.
— DERIVATIVES **chlorophyllous** adj.
— ORIGIN C19: coined in French from Greek *khlōros* 'green' + *phullon* 'leaf'.

Chlorophyta /ˈklɔːrə(ʊ)ˌfʌɪtə, ˈklɒ-/ ■ pl. n. Botany a division of lower plants that comprises the green algae.
— DERIVATIVES **chlorophyte** n.
— ORIGIN from Greek *khlōros* 'green' + *phuton* 'plant'.

chloroplast /ˈklɔːrə(ʊ)plast, -plɑːst, ˈklɒ-/ ■ n. Botany a structure in green plant cells which contains chlorophyll and in which photosynthesis takes place.
— ORIGIN C19: from Greek *khlōros* 'green' + *plastos* 'formed'.

chloroquine /ˈklɔːrə(ʊ)kwiːn, ˈklɒ-/ ■ n. Medicine a synthetic drug related to quinoline, chiefly used against malaria.

chlorosis /klɒˈrəʊsɪs/ ■ n. Botany loss of the normal green coloration of leaves, caused by mineral deficiency, disease, or lack of light.
— DERIVATIVES **chlorotic** adj.

chlorpromazine /klɔːˈprəʊməzɪn, -ziːn/ ■ n. Medicine a synthetic drug used as a tranquillizer, sedative, and anti-emetic.
— ORIGIN 1950s: from **CHLORO-** + *prom(eth)azine*.

ChM ■ abbrev. Master of Surgery.
— ORIGIN from Latin *Chirurgiae Magister*.

| VOWELS | a cat | ɑː arm | ɛ bed | ɛː hair | ə ago | əː her | ɪ sit | i cosy | iː see | ɒ hot | ɔː saw | ʌ run |

chocaholic ■ n. variant spelling of **CHOCOHOLIC**.

choc ice ■ n. Brit. a small block of ice cream with a thin coating of chocolate.

chock ■ n. **1** a wedge or block placed against a wheel or rounded object to prevent it from moving or to support it. **2** a ring with a gap at the top, through which a rope or line is run. ■ v. support or make fast with a chock.
– ORIGIN Middle English: prob. from Old French *çouche*, *çoche* 'block, log'.

chocka ■ adj. Brit. short for **CHOCK-A-BLOCK**.

chock-a-block ■ adj. informal crammed full.
– ORIGIN C19: from *chock* (in **CHOCK-FULL**) and **BLOCK**.

chock-full ■ adj. informal filled to overflowing.
– ORIGIN Middle English: later associated with **CHOCK**.

chockstone ■ n. Climbing a stone that has become wedged in a vertical cleft.

chocoholic (also **chocaholic**) ■ n. informal a person who is very fond of chocolate.

chocolate ■ n. **1** a food made from roasted and ground cacao seeds, typically sweetened and eaten as confectionery. ▸ a sweet covered with chocolate. **2** a drink made by mixing milk or water with chocolate. **3** a deep brown colour.
– DERIVATIVES **chocolatey** (also **chocolaty**) adj.
– ORIGIN C17: from Spanish *chocolate*, from Nahuatl *chocolatl*, influenced by unrelated *cacaua-atl* 'drink made from cacao'.

chocolate-box ■ adj. (of a view or picture) pretty in a trite, conventional way.

chocolate spot ■ n. a fungal disease of field and broad beans, characterized by dark brown spots.

chocolatier /ˌtʃɒkəˈlatɪə/ ■ n. (pl. pronounced same) a maker or seller of chocolate.
– ORIGIN C19: from French.

Choctaw /ˈtʃɒktɔː/ ■ n. (pl. same or **Choctaws**) **1** a member of an American Indian people now living mainly in Mississippi. **2** the Muskogean language of this people.
– ORIGIN from Choctaw *čahta*.

CHOGM ■ abbrev. Commonwealth Heads of Government Meeting.

choice ■ n. **1** an act of choosing. ▸ the right or ability to choose. **2** a range from which to choose. ▸ something chosen. ■ adj. **1** (especially of food) of very good quality. **2** (of language) rude and abusive.
– ORIGIN Middle English: from Old French *chois*, from *choisir* 'choose', of Germanic origin.

choir ■ n. **1** an organized group of singers, especially one that takes part in church services. **2** a group of instruments of one family playing together. **3** the part of a cathedral or large church between the altar and the nave, used by the choir and clergy.
– ORIGIN Middle English: from Old French *quer*, from Latin *chorus* (see **CHORUS**).

choirboy (or **choirgirl**) ■ n. a boy (or girl) who sings in a church or cathedral choir.

choke¹ ■ v. **1** prevent from breathing by constricting or blocking the throat or depriving of air. ▸ have trouble breathing in such a way. **2** fill (a space) so as to make movement difficult or impossible. **3** make speechless with strong emotion. **4** enrich the fuel mixture in (a petrol engine) by reducing the intake of air. ■ n. **1** a valve in the carburettor of a petrol engine used to reduce the amount of air in the fuel mixture. **2** a narrowed part of a shotgun bore serving to restrict the spread of the shot. **3** an inductance coil used to smooth the variations of an alternating current or to alter its phase.
– ORIGIN Middle English: from Old English *ācēocian* (v.), from *cēoce* 'cheek, jaw'.

choke² ■ n. the inedible mass of silky fibres at the centre of a globe artichoke.
– ORIGIN C17: prob. a confusion of the ending of *artichoke* with **CHOKE¹**.

choke chain ■ n. a chain formed into a loop by passing one end through a ring on the other, placed round a dog's neck to exert control.

choke-damp ■ n. choking or suffocating gas, typically carbon dioxide, that is found in mines and other underground spaces.

205

Chomskyan

chokehold ■ n. a tight grip round a person's neck, used to restrain them by restricting their breathing.

choker ■ n. **1** a close-fitting necklace or ornamental neckband. ▸ a clerical or other high collar. **2** N. Amer. a cable looped round a log to drag it.

chokey (also **choky**) ■ n. (pl. **-eys** or **-ies**) Brit. informal, dated prison.
– ORIGIN C17: Anglo-Indian, from Hindi *caukī* 'customs or toll house, police station'; influenced by **CHOKE¹**.

chokka ■ n. S. African squid, especially when used as bait.
– ORIGIN 1900s: from Afrikaans *tjokka*, perhaps from Portuguese *choco*, a species of cuttlefish.

choky¹ ■ adj. (**-ier**, **-iest**) **1** having or causing difficulty in breathing. **2** breathless with emotion.

choky² ■ n. variant spelling of **CHOKEY**.

chole- /ˈkɒli/ (also **chol-** before a vowel) ■ comb. form Medicine & Chemistry relating to bile or the bile ducts: *cholesterol*.
– ORIGIN from Greek *kholē* 'gall, bile'.

cholecalciferol /ˌkɒlɪkalˈsɪf(ə)rɒl/ ■ n. Biochemistry vitamin D₃, a compound essential for the deposition of calcium in bones and formed in the skin by the action of sunlight on dehydrocholesterol.

cholecystectomy ■ n. (pl. **-ies**) surgical removal of the gall bladder.
– ORIGIN from modern Latin *cholecystis* 'gall bladder', from Greek *kholē* 'gall, bile' + **-ECTOMY**.

cholelithiasis /ˌkɒlɪlɪˈθʌɪəsɪs/ ■ n. Medicine the formation of gallstones.

cholent /ˈtʃɒl(ə)nt, ˈʃɒ-/ ■ n. a Jewish Sabbath dish of slowly baked meat and vegetables.
– ORIGIN from Yiddish *tsholnt*.

choler /ˈkɒlə/ ■ n. **1** (in medieval science and medicine) one of the four bodily humours, identified with bile, believed to be associated with a peevish or irascible temperament. **2** archaic or poetic/literary anger or irascibility.
– ORIGIN Middle English: from Old French *colere*, from Latin *cholera* 'diarrhoea', which in late Latin acquired the senses 'bile or anger', from Greek *kholē* 'bile'.

cholera /ˈkɒlərə/ ■ n. **1** an infectious and often fatal bacterial disease of the small intestine, typically contracted from infected water supplies and causing severe vomiting and diarrhoea. **2** (usu. **chicken cholera**) an infectious form of pasteurellosis affecting fowls.
– ORIGIN Middle English: from Latin (see **CHOLER**).

choleric /ˈkɒlərɪk/ ■ adj. **1** bad-tempered or irritable. **2** (in medieval belief) influenced by or predominating in choler.

cholesterol /kəˈlɛstərɒl/ ■ n. a compound which is present in most body tissues and is important in metabolism, and of which high concentrations in the blood are thought to promote atherosclerosis.
– ORIGIN C19: from Greek *kholē* 'bile' + *stereos* 'stiff'.

choli /ˈtʃəʊli/ ■ n. (pl. **cholis**) a short-sleeved bodice worn under a sari by Indian women.
– ORIGIN from Hindi *colī*.

choline /ˈkəʊliːn, -lɪn/ ■ n. Biochemistry a strongly basic compound important in the synthesis and transport of lipids in the body.
– ORIGIN C19: coined in German from Greek *kholē* 'bile'.

cholinesterase /ˌkəʊlɪˈnɛstəreɪz/ ■ n. Biochemistry an enzyme which breaks down esters of choline.

cholla /ˈtʃɔɪə/ ■ n. a cactus with a cylindrical stem, native to Mexico and the south-western US. [Genus *Opuntia*.]
– ORIGIN C19: Mexican Spanish use of Spanish *cholla* 'skull, head'.

chometz /hɔːˈmɛts, ˈxɔːmɛts/ ■ n. variant spelling of **CHAMETZ**.

chommie ■ n. S. African informal a friend.
– ORIGIN 1950s: from Afrikaans *tjommie* 'pal, chum', from English *chummy* 'friend'.

chomp ■ v. munch or chew noisily or vigorously.
– ORIGIN C17: imitative.

Chomskyan /ˈtʃɒmskiən/ (also **Chomskian**) ■ adj. of or relating to the American theoretical linguist Noam Chomsky (b. 1928). ■ n. a follower of Chomsky.

chondrite

chondrite /ˈkɒndrʌɪt/ ■ n. a stony meteorite containing small mineral granules (chondrules).
– DERIVATIVES **chondritic** adj.
– ORIGIN C19: from Greek *khondros* 'granule'.

chondro- /ˈkɒndrə(ʊ)/ ■ comb. form of or relating to cartilage: *chondrocyte*.
– ORIGIN from Greek *khondros* 'grain or cartilage'.

chondrocyte /ˈkɒndrə(ʊ)sʌɪt/ ■ n. Biology a cell which has secreted the matrix of cartilage and become embedded in it.

chondroitin /kɒnˈdrəʊɪtɪn/ ■ n. Biochemistry a substance which is the major constituent of cartilage and other connective tissue.

choose ■ v. (past **chose**; past part. **chosen**) **1** pick out as being the best of two or more alternatives. **2** decide on a course of action.
– DERIVATIVES **chooser** n.
– ORIGIN Old English, of Germanic origin.

choosy ■ adj. (**-ier**, **-iest**) informal overly fastidious in making a choice.
– DERIVATIVES **choosily** adv. **choosiness** n.

chop[1] ■ v. (**chopped**, **chopping**) **1** cut with repeated sharp, heavy blows of an axe or knife. ▸ strike with a short, heavy blow. **2** ruthlessly abolish or reduce in size. ■ n. **1** a downward cutting blow or movement. **2** (**the chop**) informal dismissal, cancellation, or killing. **3** a thick slice of meat, especially pork or lamb, adjacent to and usually including a rib. **4** a broken motion of waves.
– PHRASES **chop logic** argue in a tiresomely pedantic way. [C16: from a dialect use of *chop* meaning 'bandy words'.]
– ORIGIN Middle English: var. of **CHAP**[1].

chop[2] ■ v. (**chopped**, **chopping**) (in phr. **chop and change**) informal change one's opinions or behaviour repeatedly and abruptly.
– ORIGIN Middle English: perhaps rel. to Old English *cēap* 'bargaining, trade'.

chop-chop ■ adv. & exclam. quickly.
– ORIGIN C19: pidgin English, based on Chinese dialect *kuai-kuai*.

chophouse ■ n. a restaurant specializing in meat chops.

chopper ■ n. **1** a short axe with a large blade. ▸ a machine for chopping. **2** a device for regularly interrupting a current or beam. **3** (**choppers**) informal teeth. **4** informal a helicopter. **5** informal a type of motorcycle with high handlebars. **6** vulgar slang a man's penis.

choppy ■ adj. (**-ier**, **-iest**) (of the sea) having many small waves.
– DERIVATIVES **choppily** adv. **choppiness** n.

chops ■ pl. n. informal **1** a person's or animal's mouth, jaws, or cheeks. **2** the technical skill of a jazz or rock musician.
– PHRASES **bust someone's chops** N. Amer. informal nag or criticize someone.
– ORIGIN Middle English: var. of **CHAP**[3].

chopsocky /ˈtʃɒpsɒki/ ■ n. N. Amer. informal kung fu or a similar martial art, especially as depicted in violent action films.
– ORIGIN 1970s: humorous, perhaps suggested by **CHOP SUEY**.

chopstick ■ n. each of a pair of small, thin, tapered sticks held in one hand and used as eating utensils by the Chinese and Japanese.
– ORIGIN C17: pidgin English, from *chop* 'quick' + **STICK**[1], translating Chinese dialect *kuaizi* 'nimble ones'.

chop suey /tʃɒpˈsuːi/ ■ n. a Chinese-style dish of meat stewed and fried with bean sprouts, bamboo shoots, and onions, and served with rice.
– ORIGIN C19: from Chinese *tsaap sui* 'mixed bits'.

choral ■ adj. of, for, or sung by a choir or chorus.
– DERIVATIVES **chorally** adv.
– ORIGIN C16: from medieval Latin *choralis*, from Latin *chorus* (see **CHORUS**).

chorale ■ n. **1** a simple, stately hymn tune, or a composition consisting of a harmonized version of one. **2** chiefly US a choir or choral society.
– ORIGIN C19: from German *Choral(gesang)*, translating medieval Latin *cantus choralis*.

chord[1] ■ n. a group of notes (usually three or more) sounded together in harmony. ■ v. [usu. as noun **chording**] play, sing, or arrange notes in chords.
– DERIVATIVES **chordal** adj.
– ORIGIN Middle English *cord*, from **ACCORD**; the spelling changed due to confusion with **CHORD**[2].

chord[2] ■ n. **1** a straight line joining the ends of an arc. **2** Aeronautics the width of an aerofoil from leading to trailing edge. **3** Engineering each of the two principal members of a truss. **4** Anatomy variant spelling of **CORD**. **5** poetic/literary a string on a harp or other instrument.
– PHRASES **strike** (or **touch**) **a chord** affect or stir someone's emotions.
– ORIGIN C16: a later spelling (influenced by Latin *chorda* 'rope') of **CORD**.

Chordata /kɔːˈdeɪtə/ ■ pl. n. Zoology a large phylum of animals including the vertebrates together with the sea squirts and lancelets, distinguished by possessing a notochord.
– DERIVATIVES **chordate** /ˈkɔːdeɪt/ n. & adj.
– ORIGIN from Latin *chorda* (see **CHORD**[2]).

chordophone ■ n. any musical instrument using strings to produce sound.

chore ■ n. a routine or tedious task, especially a household one.
– ORIGIN C18 (orig. dialect and US): var. of obsolete *char* or *chare* (see **CHARWOMAN**).

chorea /kɒˈrɪə/ ■ n. Medicine a neurological disorder characterized by jerky involuntary movements affecting especially the shoulders, hips, and face.
– ORIGIN C17: from Greek *khoreia* 'dancing in unison', from *khoros* 'chorus'.

choreograph /ˈkɒrɪəgrɑːf/ ■ v. compose the sequence of steps and moves for (a dance performance).
– DERIVATIVES **choreographer** n.

choreography /ˌkɒrɪˈɒɡrəfi/ ■ n. the sequence of steps and movements in dance, especially ballet. ▸ the practice of designing such sequences.
– DERIVATIVES **choreographic** adj. **choreographically** adv.
– ORIGIN C18: from Greek *khoreia* 'dancing in unison', from *khoros* 'chorus' + **-GRAPHY**.

choreology /ˌkɒrɪˈɒlədʒi/ ■ n. the notation of dance movement.
– DERIVATIVES **choreologist** n.

choric /ˈkɒrɪk, ˈkɔːrɪk/ ■ adj. of or resembling a chorus in drama or recitation.

chorine /ˈkɔːriːn/ ■ n. a chorus girl.

chorio- /ˈkɔːrɪəʊ/ ■ comb. form representing **CHORION** or **CHOROID**.

choriocarcinoma /ˌkɔːrɪə(ʊ)ˌkɑːsɪˈnəʊmə, ˌkɒrɪəʊ-/ ■ n. (pl. **choriocarcinomas** or **choriocarcinomata** /-mətə/) Medicine a malignant tumour of the uterus originating in the fetal chorion.

chorion /ˈkɔːrɪən/ ■ n. Embryology the outermost membrane surrounding the embryo of a reptile, bird, or mammal.
– DERIVATIVES **chorionic** adj.
– ORIGIN C16: from Greek *khorion*.

chorister ■ n. **1** a member of a choir, especially a choirboy or choirgirl. **2** US a person who leads the singing of a church choir or congregation.
– ORIGIN Middle English *queristre*, from var. of Old French *cueriste*, from *quer* (see **CHOIR**), associated with obsolete *chorist* 'member of a choir or chorus'.

chorizo /tʃəˈriːzəʊ/ ■ n. (pl. **-os**) a spicy Spanish pork sausage.
– ORIGIN from Spanish.

choroid /ˈkɔːrɔɪd, ˈkɒr-/ ■ adj. resembling the chorion, particularly in containing many blood vessels. ■ n. (also **choroid coat**) the pigmented vascular layer of the eyeball between the retina and the sclera.
– DERIVATIVES **choroidal** adj.
– ORIGIN C17: from Greek *khoroeidēs*, from *khorion* (see **CHORION**).

choroid plexus /ˈkɔːrɔɪd, ˈkɒr-/ ■ n. (pl. same or **plexuses**) a network of blood vessels in each ventricle of the brain, producing the cerebrospinal fluid.

choropleth map /ˈkɒrə(ʊ)plɛθ/ ■ n. a map which uses shading, colouring, or symbols to show the average values of a particular quantity in different areas.
– ORIGIN 1930s: from Greek *khōra* 'region' + *plēthos* 'multitude'.

chorrie ■ n. variant spelling of TJORRIE.

chortle ■ v. laugh in a breathy, gleeful way. ■ n. a breathy, gleeful laugh.
– ORIGIN 1871: coined by Lewis Carroll in *Through the Looking Glass*; prob. a blend of CHUCKLE and SNORT.

chorus ■ n. (pl. **choruses**) **1** a large group of singers, especially one performing with an orchestra. **2** a piece of choral music, especially one forming part of an opera or oratorio. **3** a part of a song which is repeated after each verse. **4** (in ancient Greek tragedy) a group of performers who comment on the main action, typically speaking and moving together. **5** a simultaneous utterance by many people. **6** a device used with an amplified musical instrument to give the impression that more than one instrument is being played. ■ v. (**chorused**, **chorusing**) (of a group of people) say the same thing at the same time.
– ORIGIN C16: from Latin *chorus*, from Greek *khoros*.

chorus girl ■ n. a young woman who sings or dances in the chorus of a musical.

chose past of CHOOSE.

chosen past participle of CHOOSE.

chou chou ■ n. another term for CHAYOTE.

choucroute /ˈʃuːkruːt/ ■ n. sauerkraut.
– ORIGIN French, from German dialect *Surkrut* 'sauerkraut', influenced by French *chou* 'cabbage'.

chough /tʃʌf/ ■ n. **1** a black bird of the crow family with a red or yellow downcurved bill, typically frequenting mountains and sea cliffs. [*Pyrrhocorax pyrrhocorax* and other species.] **2** (**white-winged chough**) a black and white Australian songbird. [*Corcorax melanorhamphos*.]
– ORIGIN Middle English: prob. imitative.

choux pastry /ʃuː/ ■ n. very light pastry made with egg, typically used for eclairs and profiteroles.
– ORIGIN C19: from *choux* or *chou*, denoting a round cream-filled pastry, from French *chou* (pl. *choux*) 'cabbage, rosette'.

chow /tʃaʊ/ ■ n. **1** informal, chiefly N. Amer. food. **2** (also **chow chow**) a dog of a sturdy Chinese breed with a tail curled over its back, a bluish-black tongue, and typically a dense thick coat. ■ v. (**chow down**) informal, chiefly N. Amer. eat.
– ORIGIN C19: shortening of pidgin English *chow chow*.

chowder ■ n. a rich soup typically containing fish, clams, or corn with potatoes and onions.
– ORIGIN C18: perhaps from French *chaudière* 'stew pot', rel. to Old Northern French *caudron* (see CAULDRON).

chowk /tʃaʊk/ ■ n. (in the Indian subcontinent) an open market area at the junction of two roads.
– ORIGIN from Hindi *cauk*.

chowkidar /ˈtʃaʊkɪdɑː/ ■ n. (in the Indian subcontinent) a watchman or gatekeeper.
– ORIGIN from Urdu *caukīdār*, from *caukī* 'toll house' + *-dār* 'keeper'.

chow mein /tʃaʊ ˈmeɪn/ ■ n. a Chinese-style dish of fried noodles with shredded meat or seafood and vegetables.
– ORIGIN C19: from Chinese *chǎo miàn* 'stir-fried noodles'.

chrism /ˈkrɪz(ə)m/ ■ n. a consecrated oil used for anointing in the Catholic, Orthodox, and Anglican Churches.
– ORIGIN Old English, from medieval Latin *crisma*, from Greek *khrisma* 'anointing', from *khriein* 'anoint'.

chrisom /ˈkrɪz(ə)m/ (also **chrisom-cloth**) ■ n. historical a white robe put on a child at baptism, and used as its shroud if it died within the month.
– ORIGIN Middle English: alteration of CHRISM.

Christ ■ n. the title, also treated as a name, given to Jesus. ■ exclam. an oath used to express irritation, dismay, or surprise.
– DERIVATIVES **Christhood** n. **Christlike** adj. **Christly** adj.
– ORIGIN Old English, from Greek *Khristos*, noun use of an adjective meaning 'anointed', from *khriein* 'anoint', translating Hebrew *māšīaḥ* 'Messiah'.

christen ■ v. **1** give (a baby) a Christian name at baptism as a sign of admission to a Christian Church. **2** informal use for the first time.
– DERIVATIVES **christener** n. **christening** n.
– ORIGIN Old English *crīstnian* 'make Christian', from *crīsten* 'Christian', from Latin *Christianus*, from *Christus* 'Christ'.

Christendom ■ n. dated the worldwide body or society of Christians.

Christian /ˈkrɪstɪən, -tʃ(ə)n/ ■ adj. **1** of, relating to, or professing Christianity or its teachings. **2** informal having qualities associated with Christians, e.g. kindness or fairness. ■ n. a person who has received Christian baptism or is a believer in Christianity.
– DERIVATIVES **Christianization** (also **-isation**) n. **Christianize** (also **-ise**) v.
– ORIGIN Middle English: from Latin *Christianus*, from *Christus* 'Christ'.

Christian era ■ n. the era beginning with the traditional date of Christ's birth.

Christianity ■ n. the religion based on the person and teachings of Jesus Christ; its beliefs and practices.

Christian name ■ n. a first name, especially one given at baptism.

> **USAGE**
> In recognition of the fact that English-speaking societies have many religions and cultures, not just Christian ones, the term **Christian name** has largely given way to alternative terms such as **given name**, **first name**, or **forename**.

Christian Nationalism ■ n. S. African historical an ideology grounded in and promoting Afrikaner religion, culture, and language.
– DERIVATIVES **Christian Nationalist** n. & adj.

Christian Science ■ n. the beliefs and practices of the Church of Christ Scientist, a Christian sect holding that only God and the mind have ultimate reality.
– DERIVATIVES **Christian Scientist** n.

Christmas ■ n. (pl. **Christmases**) **1** (also **Christmas Day**) the annual Christian festival celebrating Christ's birth, held on 25 December. **2** the period immediately before and after this.
– DERIVATIVES **Christmassy** adj.
– ORIGIN Old English *Crīstes mæsse* (see CHRIST, MASS).

Christmas beetle ■ n. S. African & Austral./NZ any of several species of cicada, the males of which produce a shrill mating song in summer. [Family Cicadidae.]

Christmas box ■ n. S. African & Brit. a present given at Christmas, usually to tradespeople and employees.

Christmas cake ■ n. a rich fruit cake covered with marzipan and icing, eaten at Christmas.

Christmas flower ■ n. S. African any of several species of hydrangea with pink, white, or blue flowers, which typically flower at Christmas time. [Genus *Hydrangea*: several species.]

Christmas pudding ■ n. a rich boiled pudding eaten at Christmas, made with flour, suet, and dried fruit.

Christmas rose ■ n. **1** a small white-flowered hellebore. [*Helleborus niger*.] **2** S. African another term for CHRISTMAS FLOWER.

Christmas tree ■ n. an evergreen or artificial tree decorated with lights and ornaments at Christmas.

Christology ■ n. the branch of Christian theology relating to Christ.

Christ's thorn ■ n. **1** a thorny shrub, popularly held to have formed Christ's crown of thorns. [*Ziziphus spina-christi* (Mediterranean region) and other species.] **2** another term for CROWN OF THORNS (in sense 2).

chroma /ˈkrəʊmə/ ■ n. purity or intensity of colour.
– ORIGIN C19: from Greek *khrōma* 'colour'.

chromakey /ˈkrəʊməkiː/ ■ n. a digital technique by which a block of a particular colour in a video image can be replaced by another colour or image. ■ v. (**-eys**, **-eyed**) manipulate using chromakey.

chromate

chromate /ˈkrəʊmeɪt/ ■ n. Chemistry a salt in which the anion contains both chromium and oxygen: *potassium chromate.*

chromatic ■ adj. **1** Music relating to or using notes not belonging to the diatonic scale of the key of a passage. ▶ (of a scale) ascending or descending by semitones. **2** of, relating to, or produced by colour.
– DERIVATIVES **chromatically** adv.
– ORIGIN C17: from Latin *chromaticus*, from Greek *khrōmatikos*, from *khrōma* 'colour, chromatic scale'.

chromatic aberration ■ n. Optics the effect produced by the refraction of different wavelengths of light through slightly different angles, resulting in a failure to focus.

chromaticity /ˌkrəʊməˈtɪsɪti/ ■ n. the quality of colour, independent of brightness.

chromatid /ˈkrəʊmətɪd/ ■ n. Biology each of the two thread-like strands into which a chromosome divides during cell division.
– ORIGIN C20: from Greek *khrōma, khrōmat-* 'colour'.

chromatin /ˈkrəʊmətɪn/ ■ n. Biology the material of which non-bacterial chromosomes are composed, consisting of protein, RNA, and DNA.
– ORIGIN C19: coined in German from Greek *khrōma, khrōmat-* 'colour'.

chromato- /ˈkrəʊmətəʊ/ (also **chromo-**) ■ comb. form colour; of or in colours: *chromatography.*
– ORIGIN from Greek *khrōma, khrōmat-* 'colour'.

chromatography /ˌkrəʊməˈtɒɡrəfi/ ■ n. Chemistry a technique for the separation of a mixture by passing it in solution or suspension through a medium in which the components move at different rates.
– DERIVATIVES **chromatogram** n. **chromatograph** n. **chromatographic** adj.
– ORIGIN 1930s: from CHROMATO- + -GRAPHY (early separations being displayed as a number of coloured bands or spots).

chrome ■ n. **1** chromium plate as a decorative or protective finish. **2** [as modifier] denoting compounds or alloys of chromium: *chrome steel.*
– DERIVATIVES **chromed** adj.
– ORIGIN C19: from Greek *khrōma* 'colour' (some chromium compounds having brilliant colours).

chrome yellow ■ n. a bright yellow pigment made from lead chromate.

chromite /ˈkrəʊmʌɪt/ ■ n. the main ore of chromium, a brownish-black oxide of chromium and iron.

chromium ■ n. the chemical element of atomic number 24, a hard white metal used in stainless steel and other alloys. (Symbol: **Cr**)
– DERIVATIVES **chromic** adj. **chromous** adj.
– ORIGIN C19: from CHROME.

chromium plate ■ n. metallic chromium electroplated on to an object as a decorative or protective coating.

chromo-¹ /ˈkrəʊməʊ/ ■ comb. form Chemistry representing CHROMIUM.

chromo-² /ˈkrəʊməʊ/ ■ comb. form variant spelling of CHROMATO-.

chromodynamics ■ pl. n. see QUANTUM CHROMODYNAMICS.

chromogenic ■ adj. **1** involving the production of colour or pigments. **2** Photography denoting a modern process of developing film which uses couplers to produce black-and-white images of very high definition.

chromolithograph historical ■ n. a coloured picture printed by lithography. ■ v. produce (a coloured picture) by lithography.

chromoly /ˈkrəʊmpli/ ■ n. steel containing chromium and molybdenum, used to make strong, lightweight components such as bicycle frames.
– ORIGIN 1980s: blend of CHROMIUM and MOLYBDENUM.

chromoplast /ˈkrəʊməplast, -plɑːst/ ■ n. Botany a coloured plastid other than a chloroplast, typically containing a yellow or orange pigment.
– ORIGIN C19: from CHROMO-² + Greek *plastos* 'formed'.

chromosome ■ n. Biology a thread-like structure of nucleic acids and protein found in the nuclei of most living cells, carrying genetic information in the form of genes.
– DERIVATIVES **chromosomal** adj.
– ORIGIN C19: coined in German from Greek *khrōma* 'colour' + *sōma* 'body'.

chromosphere ■ n. Astronomy a reddish gaseous layer immediately above the photosphere of the sun or another star.
– DERIVATIVES **chromospheric** adj.
– ORIGIN C19: from CHROMO-² + SPHERE.

chronic ■ adj. **1** (of an illness or problem) persisting for a long time. **2** having a persistent illness or bad habit. **3** informal, chiefly Brit. very bad.
– DERIVATIVES **chronically** adv. **chronicity** n.
– ORIGIN Middle English: from French *chronique*, from Greek *khronikos* 'of time', from *khronos* 'time'.

chronic fatigue syndrome ■ n. a medical condition of unknown cause, with fever, aching, and prolonged tiredness and depression.

chronicle ■ n. a written account of important or historical events in the order of their occurrence. ■ v. record (a series of events) in a factual and detailed way.
– DERIVATIVES **chronicler** n.
– ORIGIN Middle English: from Anglo-Norman French *cronicle*, var. of Old French *cronique*, from Greek *khronika* 'annals', from *khronikos* (see CHRONIC).

chrono- /ˈkrɒnəʊ/ ■ comb. form relating to time: *chronometry.*
– ORIGIN from Greek *khronos* 'time'.

chronobiology ■ n. the branch of biology concerned with natural physiological rhythms and other cyclical phenomena.
– DERIVATIVES **chronobiologist** n.

chronograph ■ n. an instrument for recording time with great accuracy.
– DERIVATIVES **chronographic** adj.

chronology /krəˈnɒlədʒi/ ■ n. (pl. **-ies**) **1** the study of records to establish the dates of past events. **2** the arrangement of events or dates in the order of their occurrence.
– DERIVATIVES **chronological** adj. **chronologically** adv. **chronologist** n.
– ORIGIN C16: from Greek *khronos* 'time' + *-logia* (see -LOGY).

chronometer /krəˈnɒmɪtə/ ■ n. an instrument for measuring time accurately in spite of motion or variations in temperature, humidity, and air pressure.

chronometry ■ n. the science of accurate time measurement.
– DERIVATIVES **chronometric** adj. **chronometrical** adj. **chronometrically** adv.

chrysalid /ˈkrɪs(ə)lɪd/ ■ n. another term for CHRYSALIS.
– ORIGIN C18: from Latin *chrysal(l)is, chrysal(l)id-* (see CHRYSALIS).

chrysalis /ˈkrɪs(ə)lɪs/ ■ n. (pl. **chrysalises**) a quiescent insect pupa, especially of a butterfly or moth. ▶ the hard outer case enclosing this.
– ORIGIN C17: from Latin *chrysal(l)is, chrysal(l)id-*, from Greek *khrusallis*, from *khrusos* 'gold' (because of the metallic sheen of some pupae).

chrysanthemum /krɪˈsanθɪməm, -z-/ ■ n. (pl. **chrysanthemums**) a plant of the daisy family with brightly coloured ornamental flowers. [Genera *Chrysanthemum* or (most cultivated species) *Dendranthema*.]
– ORIGIN from Greek, from *khrusos* 'gold' + *anthemon* 'flower'.

chrysocolla /ˌkrɪsə(ʊ)ˈkɒlə/ ■ n. a greenish-blue mineral consisting of hydrated copper silicate.
– ORIGIN C16: from Greek *khrusokolla*, denoting a mineral used in ancient times for soldering gold.

chrysolite /ˈkrɪsəlʌɪt/ ■ n. a yellowish-green or brownish variety of olivine, used as a gemstone.
– ORIGIN Middle English: from Old French *crisolite*, from Latin *chrysolithus*, from Greek *khrusos* 'gold' + *lithos* 'stone'.

chrysoprase /ˈkrɪsə(ʊ)preɪz/ ■ n. an apple-green variety of chalcedony containing nickel.
– ORIGIN Middle English: from Old French *crisopace*, from Greek *khrusoprasos*, from *khrusos* 'gold' + *prason* 'leek'.

chrysotile /ˈkrɪsə(ʊ)tʌɪl/ ■ n. a fibrous form of the mineral serpentine.
– ORIGIN C19: from Greek *khrusos* 'gold' + *tilos* 'fibre'.

chthonic /ˈ(k)θɒnɪk/ (also **chthonian** /ˈ(k)θəʊnɪən/) ■ adj. of, belonging to, or inhabiting the underworld.
– ORIGIN C19: from Greek *khthōn* 'earth'.

chub ■ n. a thick-bodied European river fish with a grey-green back and white underparts, popular with anglers. [*Leuciscus cephalus*.]
– ORIGIN Middle English.

Chubb ■ n. trademark a lock with a device for fixing the bolt immovably to prevent it from being picked.
– ORIGIN C19: named after the London locksmith Charles *Chubb*.

chubby ■ adj. (-ier, -iest) plump and rounded.
– DERIVATIVES **chubbily** adv. **chubbiness** n.
– ORIGIN C17: from CHUB.

chuck[1] informal ■ v. 1 throw (something) carelessly or casually. ▸ (**chuck something out**) throw something away. 2 (usu. **chuck something in**) give up suddenly. 3 S. African informal depart. 4 (**chuck up**) vomit. ■ n. (**the chuck**) Brit. a dismissal or rejection.
– PHRASES **chuck it down** rain heavily.
– DERIVATIVES **chucker** n.
– ORIGIN C17: from CHUCK[2].

chuck[2] ■ v. touch playfully under the chin. ■ n. a playful touch under the chin.
– ORIGIN C17: prob. from Old French *chuquer*, later *choquer* 'to knock, bump'.

chuck[3] ■ n. 1 a device for holding a workpiece in a lathe or a tool in a drill. 2 a cut of beef extending from the neck to the ribs.
– ORIGIN C17, as a var. of CHOCK; see also CHUNK[1].

chuckle ■ v. laugh quietly or inwardly. ■ n. a quiet or suppressed laugh.
– ORIGIN C16: from Middle English *chuck* 'to cluck'.

chuddar ■ n. variant spelling of CHADOR.

chuff ■ v. (of a steam engine) move with a regular sharp puffing sound.
– ORIGIN C20: imitative.

chuffed ■ adj. informal very pleased.
– ORIGIN 1950s: from dialect *chuff* 'plump or pleased'.

chug ■ v. (**chugged**, **chugging**) emit a series of regular muffled explosive sounds, as of an engine running slowly. ■ n. a sound of this type.
– ORIGIN C19: imitative.

chukar /ˈtʃuːkɑː/ (also **chukor**) ■ n. a partridge with conspicuous black barring on the flanks and a black band around the head and breast, with a call like a domestic hen. [Genus *Alectoris*.]
– ORIGIN from Sanskrit *cakora*.

chukka /ˈtʃʌkə/ (US also **chukker**) ■ n. each of a number of periods (typically six, of 7½ minutes each) into which play in a game of polo is divided.
– ORIGIN C19: from Hindi *cakkar*, from Sanskrit *cakra* 'circle or wheel'.

chum[1] informal ■ n. dated a close friend. ■ v. (**chummed**, **chumming**) (**chum up**) form a friendship with someone.
– DERIVATIVES **chummily** adv. **chumminess** n. **chummy** adj.
– ORIGIN C17: prob. short for *chamber-fellow*; cf. COMRADE.

chum[2] chiefly N. Amer. ■ n. chopped fish and other material used as bait. ▸ the remains of fish, especially after oil has been expressed. ■ v. fish using chum as bait.
– ORIGIN C19.

chum[3] ■ n. (pl. same or **chums**) a large North Pacific salmon that is commercially important as a food fish. [*Oncorhynchus keta*.]
– ORIGIN C20: from Chinook Jargon (an extinct pidgin) *tzum* (*samun*) 'spotted (salmon)'.

chump ■ n. 1 informal, dated a foolish person. 2 Brit. the thick end of something, especially a loin of lamb or mutton.
– PHRASES **off one's chump** Brit. informal, dated mad.
– ORIGIN C18: prob. a blend of CHUNK[1] and LUMP[1] or STUMP.

chump change ■ n. N. Amer. informal a very small amount of money.
– ORIGIN 1960s: orig. US black English.

chunder informal, chiefly Austral./NZ ■ v. vomit. ■ n. vomit.
– ORIGIN 1950s: prob. from rhyming slang *Chunder Loo* 'spew', from the name of a cartoon character *Chunder Loo of Akim Foo* in advertisements in the Sydney *Bulletin*.

chunk[1] ■ n. a thick, solid piece. ▸ a large amount. ■ v. divide into chunks.
– ORIGIN C17: prob. an alteration of CHUCK[3].

chunk[2] ■ v. make a muffled, metallic sound.
– ORIGIN C19: imitative.

chunky ■ adj. (-ier, -iest) 1 (of a person) short and sturdy. ▸ bulky; thick. 2 containing chunks.
– DERIVATIVES **chunkily** adv. **chunkiness** n.

chunter ■ v. Brit. informal 1 chatter or grumble monotonously. 2 move slowly and noisily.
– ORIGIN C17: prob. imitative.

chuppah /ˈxʊpə/ (also **chuppa**) ■ n. (pl. **chuppot** /ˈxʊpəʊt/) a canopy beneath which Jewish marriage ceremonies are performed.
– ORIGIN C19: from Hebrew *ḥuppāh* 'cover, canopy'.

church ■ n. 1 a building used for public Christian worship. 2 (**Church**) a particular Christian organization with its own distinctive doctrines. 3 institutionalized religion as a political or social force.
– ORIGIN Old English *cir(i)ce*, from Greek *kuriakon (dōma)* 'Lord's (house)', from *kurios* 'master or lord'.

churchman (or **churchwoman**) ■ n. (pl. **-men** or **-women**) a member of the Christian clergy or of a Church.

Church of England ■ n. the English branch of the Western Christian Church, which combines Catholic and Protestant traditions, rejects the Pope's authority, and has the British monarch as its titular head.

churchwarden ■ n. either of two elected lay representatives in an Anglican parish. ▸ US a church administrator.

churchy ■ adj. 1 excessively pious. 2 resembling a church.
– DERIVATIVES **churchiness** n.

churchyard ■ n. an enclosed area surrounding a church, especially as used for burials.

churidars /ˈtʃʊrɪdɑːz/ ■ pl. n. tight trousers worn by people from the Indian subcontinent.
– ORIGIN from Hindi *cūṛīdār* 'having a series of gathered rows'.

churinga /tʃəˈrɪŋɡə/ ■ n. (pl. same or **churingas**) (among Australian Aboriginals) a sacred amulet or other object.
– ORIGIN C19: from Aranda (an Aboriginal language), 'object from the dreaming'.

churl ■ n. 1 an impolite and mean-spirited person. 2 archaic a peasant.
– ORIGIN Old English, of West Germanic origin.

churlish ■ adj. rude, mean-spirited, and surly.
– DERIVATIVES **churlishly** adv. **churlishness** n.

churn ■ n. 1 a machine for making butter by agitating milk or cream. 2 chiefly Brit. a large metal milk can. 3 [often as modifier] Finance a rapid turnover, especially of investors, subscribers, or customers. ■ v. 1 agitate (milk or cream) in a churn to produce butter. 2 move (liquid) about vigorously. 3 (**churn something out**) produce something mechanically in large quantities. 4 [as adj. **churned up**] upset or nervous.
– ORIGIN Old English, of Germanic origin.

churr ■ v. & n. variant spelling of CHIRR.

chute[1] (also **shoot**) ■ n. a sloping channel or slide for conveying things to a lower level. ▸ a water slide into a swimming pool.
– ORIGIN C19: from French, 'fall' (of water or rocks).

chute[2] ■ n. informal 1 a parachute. 2 Nautical a spinnaker.

chutney ■ n. (pl. **-eys**) 1 a spicy condiment made of fruits or vegetables with vinegar, spices, and sugar. 2 Music traditional Indian folk songs accompanied by rhythmic music and dancing.
– ORIGIN C19: from Hindi *caṭnī*.

chutzpah /ˈxʊtspə, ˈhʊ-/ ■ n. informal shameless audacity.
– ORIGIN C19: Yiddish, from Aramaic *ḥu ṣpā*.

chyle /kʌɪl/ ■ n. Physiology a milky fluid which drains from

chyme

the small intestine into the lymphatic system during digestion.
– DERIVATIVES **chylous** adj.
– ORIGIN Middle English: from Greek *khūlos* 'juice'.

chyme /kaɪm/ ■ n. Physiology the fluid which passes from the stomach to the small intestine, consisting of gastric juices and partly digested food.
– DERIVATIVES **chymous** adj.
– ORIGIN Middle English: from Greek *khūmos* 'juice'.

chymotrypsin /ˌkaɪmə(ʊ)ˈtrɪpsɪn/ ■ n. Biochemistry a pancreatic enzyme which breaks down proteins in the small intestine.

chypre /ˈʃiːpr(ə)/ ■ n. a heavy perfume made from sandalwood.
– ORIGIN C19: from French, 'Cyprus', perhaps where it was first made.

Ci ■ abbrev. curie.

CIA ■ abbrev. Central Intelligence Agency.

ciabatta /tʃəˈbɑːtə/ ■ n. a flattish, open-textured Italian bread, made with olive oil.
– ORIGIN Italian, 'slipper' (from its shape).

ciao /tʃaʊ/ ■ exclam. informal used as a greeting at meeting or parting.
– ORIGIN 1920s: Italian, dialect form of *schiavo* '(I am your) slave'.

cicada /sɪˈkɑːdə/ ■ n. a large bug with long transparent wings, the males of which make a loud shrill droning noise after dark. [Family Cicadidae: many species.]
– ORIGIN Middle English: from Latin *cicada*, *cicala*.

cicatrix /ˈsɪkətrɪks/ (also **cicatrice** /ˈsɪkətrɪs/) ■ n. (pl. **cicatrices** /-ˈtraɪsiːz/) **1** a scar. **2** Botany a mark on a stem left after a leaf or other part has become detached.
– ORIGIN Middle English: from Latin *cicatrix* or Old French *cicatrice*.

cicatrize /ˈsɪkətrʌɪz/ (also **-ise**) ■ v. heal by scar formation.
– DERIVATIVES **cicatrization** (also **-isation**) n.

cicely /ˈsɪsɪli/ (also **sweet cicely**) ■ n. (pl. **-ies**) an aromatic white-flowered plant of the parsley family, with fern-like leaves. [*Myrrhis odorata* (Europe), *Osmorhiza claytoni* (N. America), and other species.]
– ORIGIN C16: from Latin *seselis*, from Greek; influenced by the given name *Cicely*.

cichlid /ˈsɪklɪd/ ■ n. Zoology a perch-like freshwater fish of a large tropical family (Cichlidae).
– ORIGIN C19: from Greek *kikhlē*, denoting a kind of fish.

CID ■ abbrev. (in the UK) Criminal Investigation Department.

-cide ■ comb. form **1** denoting a person or substance that kills: *insecticide*. **2** denoting an act of killing: *suicide*.
– DERIVATIVES **-cidal** comb. form in corresponding adjectives. **-cidally** comb. form in corresponding adverbs.
– ORIGIN sense 1 from Latin *-cida*; sense 2 from Latin *-cidium*, both from *caedere* 'kill'.

cider ■ n. an alcoholic drink made from fermented apple juice. ▶ (also **apple cider**) chiefly N. Amer. a cloudy unfermented drink made from crushed apples.
– ORIGIN Middle English: from Old French *sidre*, from eccles. Greek *sikera*, from Hebrew *šēḵār* 'strong drink'.

c.i.f. ■ abbrev. cost, insurance, freight (as included in a price).

cigar ■ n. a cylinder of tobacco rolled in tobacco leaves for smoking.
– PHRASES **close but no cigar** N. Amer. informal almost but not quite successful.
– ORIGIN C18: from French *cigare*, or from Spanish *cigarro*, prob. from Mayan *sik'ar* 'smoking'.

cigarette (US also **cigaret**) ■ n. a thin cylinder of finely cut tobacco rolled in paper for smoking.
– ORIGIN C19: from French, diminutive of *cigare* (see **CIGAR**).

cigarette card ■ n. a small collectable card with a picture on it, formerly included in packets of cigarettes.

cigarette paper ■ n. a piece of thin paper with a gummed edge for rolling around tobacco to make a cigarette.

cigarillo /ˌsɪɡəˈrɪləʊ/ ■ n. (pl. **-os**) a small cigar.
– ORIGIN C19: from Spanish, diminutive of *cigarro* (see **CIGAR**).

ciggy ■ n. (pl. **-ies**) informal a cigarette.

cilia plural form of **CILIUM**.

ciliary /ˈsɪlɪəri/ ■ adj. **1** Biology of, relating to, or involving cilia. **2** Anatomy of or relating to the eyelashes or eyelids.

ciliary body ■ n. Anatomy the part of the eye that connects the iris to the choroid.

ciliate /ˈsɪlɪeɪt/ ■ n. Zoology a single-celled animal of a phylum (Ciliophora) distinguished by the possession of cilia. ■ adj. **1** Zoology bearing cilia. **2** Botany having a fringe of hairs.
– DERIVATIVES **ciliated** adj.

cilium /ˈsɪlɪəm/ ■ n. (pl. **cilia** /-lɪə/) **1** Biology a short microscopic hair-like vibrating structure, occurring in large numbers on the surface of certain cells. **2** Anatomy an eyelash.
– ORIGIN C18: from Latin.

cill ■ n. chiefly Building variant spelling of **SILL**.

cimetidine /saɪˈmɛtɪdiːn/ ■ n. Medicine an antihistamine drug used to treat stomach acidity and peptic ulcers.
– ORIGIN 1970s: from *ci*- (alteration of *cy*- in *cyano*-) + *met(hyl)* + -IDE + -INE[4].

C.-in-C. ■ abbrev. Commander-in-Chief.

cinch ■ n. **1** informal an extremely easy task. ▶ a certainty. **2** chiefly N. Amer. a girth for a Western saddle or pack, used in Mexico and the western US. ■ v. chiefly N. Amer. **1** secure with a belt or girth. **2** informal make certain of.
– ORIGIN C19: from Spanish *cincha* 'girth'.

cinchona /sɪŋˈkəʊnə/ ■ n. a medicinal drug containing quinine and related compounds, made from the dried bark of various South American trees.
– ORIGIN C18: genus name, named after the Countess of Chinchón, who brought the drug to Spain.

cinder ■ n. a piece of burnt coal or wood that has stopped giving off flames but still has combustible matter in it.
– DERIVATIVES **cindery** adj.
– ORIGIN Old English *sinder* 'slag', of Germanic origin; influenced by French *cendre* (from Latin *cinis* 'ashes').

cinder block ■ n. North American term for **BREEZE BLOCK**.

cinder cone ■ n. a cone formed round a volcanic vent by fragments of lava from eruptions.

cine ■ adj. cinematographic.

cine- ■ comb. form representing cinematographic (see **CINEMATOGRAPHY**).

cineaste /ˈsɪnɪast/ (also **cineast**) ■ n. an enthusiast of the cinema.
– ORIGIN 1920s: from French *cinéaste*, from *ciné* (from *cinéma*).

cinema ■ n. **1** a theatre where films are shown. **2** the production of films as an art or industry.
– ORIGIN C20: from French *cinéma*, abbrev. of *cinématographe* (see **CINEMATOGRAPH**).

cinematheque /ˌsɪnɪməˈtɛk/ ■ n. **1** a film library or archive. **2** a small cinema.
– ORIGIN 1960s: from French *cinémathèque*, from *cinéma* 'cinema'.

cinematic ■ adj. of, relating to, or characteristic of the cinema.
– DERIVATIVES **cinematically** adv.

cinematograph /ˌsɪnɪˈmatəɡrɑːf/ (also **kinematograph**) ■ n. historical, chiefly Brit. an apparatus for showing films.
– ORIGIN C19: from French *cinématographe*, from Greek *kinēma, kinēmat-* 'movement', from *kinein* 'to move'.

cinematography /ˌsɪnɪməˈtɒɡrəfi/ ■ n. the art of photography and camerawork in film-making.
– DERIVATIVES **cinematographer** n. **cinematographic** adj.

cinéma-vérité /ˌsɪnɪmɑːˈvɛrɪteɪ/ ■ n. a style of film-making characterized by realistic films avoiding artistic effect.
– ORIGIN French, 'cinema truth'.

cinephile ■ n. an enthusiast of the cinema.

cineplex ■ n. trademark, chiefly N. Amer. a multiplex cinema.

cineraria /ˌsɪnəˈrɛːrɪə/ ■ n. a plant of the daisy family, sometimes cultivated as a pot plant. [Genus *Pericallis* (formerly *Cineraria*).]
– ORIGIN feminine of Latin *cinerarius* 'of ashes' (because of the ash-coloured down on the leaves).

cinerary urn /ˈsɪnərəri/ ■ n. an urn for holding a person's ashes after cremation.
– ORIGIN C18: *cinerary* from Latin *cinerarius* 'of ashes'.

cinereous /sɪˈnɪərɪəs/ ■ adj. ash-grey.
– ORIGIN Middle English: from Latin *cinereus* 'similar to ashes', from *cinis, ciner-* 'ashes'.

cinnabar /ˈsɪnəbɑː/ ■ n. 1 a bright red mineral consisting of mercury sulphide. 2 (also **cinnabar moth**) a European day-flying moth with black and red wings. [*Tyria jacobaeae*.]
– ORIGIN Middle English: from Latin *cinnabaris*, from Greek *kinnabari*, of oriental origin.

cinnamon ■ n. 1 an aromatic spice made from the dried and rolled bark of a SE Asian tree. 2 the tree which yields this spice. [*Cinnamomum zeylanicum* and related species.] 3 a yellowish-brown colour resembling cinnamon.
– ORIGIN Middle English: from Old French *cinnamome* and Latin *cinnamon*, both from a Semitic language and perhaps based on Malay.

cinque /sɪŋk/ (also **cinq**) ■ n. the five on dice.
– ORIGIN Middle English: from Old French *cinc, cink*, from Latin *quinque* 'five'.

cinquecento /ˌtʃɪŋkwɪˈtʃɛntəʊ/ ■ n. the 16th century as a period of Italian art and literature with a reversion to classical forms.
– ORIGIN Italian, '500' (shortened from *milcinquecento* '1500') used with ref. to the years 1500–99.

cinquefoil /ˈsɪŋkfɔɪl/ ■ n. 1 a herbaceous plant of the rose family, with compound leaves of five leaflets and five-petalled yellow flowers. [Genus *Potentilla*.] 2 Art an ornamental design of five lobes arranged in a circle.
– ORIGIN Middle English: from Latin *quinquefolium*, from *quinque* 'five' + *folium* 'leaf'.

Cinzano /tʃɪnˈzɑːnəʊ/ ■ n. trademark an Italian vermouth.

cipher[1] /ˈsaɪfə/ (also **cypher**) ■ n. 1 a code. ▶ a key to a code. 2 dated a zero. 3 an unimportant person or thing. 4 a monogram. ■ v. encode (a message).
– ORIGIN Middle English: from Old French *cifre*, from Arabic *ṣifr* 'zero'.

cipher[2] ■ n. a continuous sounding of an organ pipe, caused by a defect. ■ v. (of an organ pipe) sound continuously.
– ORIGIN C18: perhaps from CIPHER[1].

circa /ˈsəːkə/ ■ prep. approximately.
– ORIGIN C19: Latin.

circadian /səːˈkeɪdɪən/ ■ adj. (of biological processes) recurring naturally on a twenty-four-hour cycle.
– ORIGIN 1950s: from Latin *circa* 'about' + *dies* 'day'.

circinate /ˈsəːsɪnət, -eɪt/ ■ adj. 1 Botany rolled up with the tip in the centre. 2 Medicine circular.
– ORIGIN C19: from Latin *circinare* 'make round'.

circle ■ n. 1 a round plane figure whose boundary consists of points equidistant from the centre. ▶ a group of people or things forming a circle. 2 a curved upper tier of seats in a theatre. 3 a group of people with a shared profession, interests, or acquaintances. ■ v. move or be situated all the way around. ▶ draw a line around.
– PHRASES **circle the wagons** N. Amer. informal unite in defence of something. [with ref. to the defensive position of a wagon train under attack.] **come** (or **turn**) **full circle** return to a past position or situation. **go** (or **run**) **round in circles** informal do something for a long time without achieving anything.
– ORIGIN Old English, from Old French *cercle*, from Latin *circulus*, diminutive of *circus* 'ring'.

circlet ■ n. 1 an ornamental circular band worn on the head. 2 a small circular arrangement or object.

circlip /ˈsəːklɪp/ ■ n. a metal ring sprung into a slot in a bar to hold something in place.
– ORIGIN C20: blend of CIRCLE or CIRCULAR and CLIP[1].

circuit ■ n. 1 a roughly circular line, route, or movement. 2 a track used for motor racing, horse racing, or athletics. 3 a system of electrical conductors and components forming a complete path around which an electric current can flow. 4 an established series of sporting events or entertainments. 5 a series of athletic exercises performed in one training session. 6 (in the UK) a regular journey by a judge around a district to hear court cases. 7 a group of Methodist Churches forming an administrative unit. 8 a chain of theatres or cinemas under a single management. ■ v. move all the way around.
– ORIGIN Middle English: from Latin *circuitus*, from *circuire*, var. of *circumire* 'go round'.

circuit board ■ n. a thin rigid board containing an electric circuit.

circuit-breaker ■ n. an automatic safety device for stopping the flow of current in an electric circuit.

circuit court ■ n. 1 a court that holds sessions in different parts of a judicial district, typically able to hear cases beyond the jurisdiction of the lower courts. 2 (**Circuit Court**) (in the US) the court of general jurisdiction in some states.

circuitous /səˈkjuːɪtəs/ ■ adj. (of a route) longer than the most direct way.
– DERIVATIVES **circuitously** adv. **circuitousness** n.

circuitry ■ n. (pl. **-ies**) electric circuits collectively.

circular ■ adj. 1 having the form of a circle. 2 Logic (of an argument) already containing an assumption of what is to be proved. 3 (of a letter or advertisement) for distribution to a large number of people. ■ n. a circular letter or advertisement.
– DERIVATIVES **circularity** n. **circularly** adv.

circularize (also **-ise**) ■ v. 1 distribute a large number of letters, leaflets, etc. to. 2 make circular.
– DERIVATIVES **circularization** (also **-isation**) n.

circular saw ■ n. a power saw with a rapidly rotating toothed disc.

circulate ■ v. 1 move or cause to move continuously or freely through a closed area. ▶ move around a social function and talk to many people. 2 pass or cause to pass from place to place or person to person.
– DERIVATIVES **circulator** n.
– ORIGIN C15: from Latin *circulare* 'move in a circular path', from *circulus* (see CIRCLE).

circulating medium ■ n. a commodity used in commercial exchange, especially coins or gold.

circulation ■ n. 1 movement to and fro or around something. ▶ the continuous motion by which blood travels through the body. 2 the public availability or knowledge of something. 3 the number of copies sold of a newspaper or magazine.
– PHRASES **in** (or **out of**) **circulation** 1 available (or unavailable) for general use. 2 (of a person) seen (or not seen) in public.
– DERIVATIVES **circulatory** adj.

circum- /ˈsəːkəm/ ■ prefix about; around (functioning within the word as an adverb as in *circumambulate*, or as a preposition as in *circumpolar*).
– ORIGIN from Latin *circum* 'round'.

circumambient /ˌsəːkəmˈambɪənt/ ■ adj. chiefly poetic/literary surrounding.

circumambulate /ˌsəːkəmˈambjʊleɪt/ ■ v. formal walk all the way round.
– DERIVATIVES **circumambulation** n. **circumambulatory** adj.

circumcircle ■ n. Geometry a circle touching all the vertices of a triangle or polygon.

circumcise /ˈsəːkəmsʌɪz/ ■ v. 1 cut off the foreskin of (a young boy or man) for medical reasons, or as a traditional or religious rite. 2 cut off the clitoris, and sometimes the labia, of (a girl or young woman) as a traditional practice.
– DERIVATIVES **circumcision** n.
– ORIGIN Middle English: from Old French *circonciser* or from Latin *circumcidere* 'cut about'.

circumcision school ■ n. another term for INITIATION SCHOOL.

circumference /səˈkʌmf(ə)r(ə)ns/ ■ n. 1 the enclosing boundary of a circle. 2 the distance around something.
– DERIVATIVES **circumferential** adj. **circumferentially** adv.
– ORIGIN Middle English: from Latin *circumferentia*, from

circumflex

circum 'around' + *ferre* 'carry'.

circumflex /ˈsəːkəmflɛks/ ■ n. a mark (^) placed over a vowel in some languages to indicate contraction, length, or another quality. ■ adj. Anatomy curved.
– ORIGIN C16: from Latin *circumflexus* (from *circum* 'around' + *flectere* 'to bend'), translating Greek *perispōmenos* 'drawn around'.

circumlocution /ˌsəːkəmləˈkjuːʃ(ə)n/ ■ n. the use of many words where fewer would do.
– DERIVATIVES **circumlocutory** /-ˈlɒkjʊt(ə)ri/ adj.
– ORIGIN Middle English: from Latin *circumlocutio(n-)*, from *circum* 'around' + *locutio(n-)* from *loqui* 'speak'.

circumnavigate ■ v. sail all the way around.
– DERIVATIVES **circumnavigation** n. **circumnavigator** n.

circumpolar /səːkəmˈpəʊlə/ ■ adj. 1 situated or occurring around one of the earth's poles. 2 Astronomy (of a star) above the horizon at all times in a given latitude.

circumscribe ■ v. 1 restrict; limit. 2 Geometry draw (a figure) round another, touching it at points but not cutting it. Compare with INSCRIBE.
– DERIVATIVES **circumscription** n.
– ORIGIN Middle English: from Latin *circumscribere*, from *circum* 'around' + *scribere* 'write'.

circumspect ■ adj. cautious or prudent.
– DERIVATIVES **circumspection** n. **circumspectly** adv.
– ORIGIN Middle English: from Latin *circumspectus*, from *circumspicere* 'look around'.

circumstance ■ n. 1 a fact or condition connected with or relevant to an event or action. 2 (**circumstances**) one's state of financial or material welfare.
– PHRASES **under** (or **in**) **the circumstances** given the difficult nature of the situation. **under** (or **in**) **no circumstances** never.
– DERIVATIVES **circumstanced** adj.
– ORIGIN Middle English: from Latin *circumstantia*, from *circumstare* 'encircle, encompass'.

circumstantial ■ adj. 1 (of evidence or a legal case) pointing indirectly towards someone's guilt. 2 (of a description) containing full details.
– DERIVATIVES **circumstantiality** n. **circumstantially** adv.

circumvent /səːkəmˈvɛnt/ ■ v. 1 find a way around (an obstacle). 2 archaic outwit.
– DERIVATIVES **circumvention** n.
– ORIGIN Middle English: from Latin *circumvenire* 'skirt around'.

circus ■ n. (pl. **circuses**) 1 a travelling company of acrobats, trained animals, and clowns, giving performances typically in a large tent. 2 (in ancient Rome) a rounded sporting arena lined with tiers of seats. 3 informal a scene of lively activity. 4 Brit. a rounded open space in a town where several streets converge: *Piccadilly Circus*.
– ORIGIN Middle English: from Latin, 'ring, circus'.

cire perdue /ˌsɪə pəːˈdjuː/ ■ n. formal term for LOST WAX.
– ORIGIN French, 'lost wax'.

cirque /səːk/ ■ n. 1 a steep-sided hollow at the head of a valley or on a mountainside. 2 poetic/literary a ring, circlet, or circle.
– ORIGIN C17: from French, from Latin *circus*.

cirrhosis /sɪˈrəʊsɪs/ ■ n. a chronic liver disease marked by degeneration of cells, inflammation, and thickening of tissue.
– DERIVATIVES **cirrhotic** /sɪˈrɒtɪk/ adj.
– ORIGIN C19: from Greek *kirrhos* 'tawny' (the colour of the liver in many cases).

cirriped /ˈsɪrɪpɛd/ (also **cirripede** /ˌsɪrɪˈpiːd/) ■ n. Zoology a crustacean of a class (Cirripedia) that comprises the barnacles.
– ORIGIN from Latin *cirrus* 'a curl' (because of the form of the legs) + *pes, ped-* 'foot'.

cirrocumulus /ˌsɪrəʊˈkjuːmjʊləs/ ■ n. cloud forming a broken layer of small fleecy clouds at high altitude.

cirrostratus /ˌsɪrəʊˈstrɑːtəs, -ˈstreɪtəs/ ■ n. cloud forming a thin, uniform semi-translucent layer at high altitude.

cirrus /ˈsɪrəs/ ■ n. (pl. **cirri** /-rʌɪ/) cloud forming wispy filamentous tufted streaks at high altitude.

– ORIGIN C18: from Latin, 'a curl'.

CIS ■ abbrev. Commonwealth of Independent States.

cis- ■ prefix 1 on this side of: *cislunar*. 2 closer to the present. 3 Chemistry (usu. *cis-*) denoting molecules in which two particular atoms or groups lie on the same side of a given plane, in particular denoting an isomer in which substituents at opposite ends of a carbon–carbon double bond are on the same side of the bond: *cis-1,2-dichloroethene*.
– ORIGIN from Latin *cis*.

cisalpine /sɪsˈalpʌɪn/ ■ adj. on the southern side of the Alps.
– ORIGIN C16: from Latin *cisalpinus*.

Ciskeian /sɪsˈkʌɪən/ ■ n. a native or inhabitant of the Ciskei region in the Eastern Cape. ▸ an inhabitant of the former Ciskei homeland. ■ adj. of or relating to the Ciskei.
– ORIGIN C19: from CIS- + *Kei* (the name of a river).

cislunar /sɪsˈluːnə/ ■ adj. between the earth and the moon.

cissy ■ n. & adj. variant spelling of SISSY.

cist /sɪst/ (also **kist**) ■ n. Archaeology a coffin or burial chamber made from stone or a hollowed tree.
– ORIGIN Welsh, 'chest'.

Cistercian /sɪˈstəːʃ(ə)n/ ■ n. a monk or nun of an order that is a stricter branch of the Benedictines. ■ adj. of or relating to this order.
– ORIGIN from French *cistercien*, from *Cistercium*, the Latin name of *Cîteaux* near Dijon in France, where the order was founded.

cistern ■ n. 1 a water storage tank, especially as part of a flushing toilet. 2 an underground reservoir for rainwater.
– ORIGIN Middle English: from Latin *cisterna*, from *cista*, from Greek *kistē* 'box'.

cisticola /sɪˈstɪkələ/ ■ n. any of a number of very similar small brown birds of the warbler family, found mainly in Africa. [Genus *Cisticola*: many species.]

cistron /ˈsɪstrɒn/ ■ n. Biochemistry a section of a DNA or RNA molecule that codes for a specific polypeptide in protein synthesis.
– ORIGIN 1950s: from CIS- + TRANS- (because of the possibility of two genes being on the same or different chromosomes).

cistus /ˈsɪstəs/ ■ n. a Mediterranean shrub with large white or red flowers, the twigs of which yield ladanum. [Genus *Cistus*.]
– ORIGIN from Greek *kistos*.

citadel /ˈsɪtəd(ə)l, -dɛl/ ■ n. 1 a fortress protecting or dominating a city. 2 a meeting hall of the Salvation Army.
– ORIGIN C16: from French *citadelle* or Italian *cittadella*, from Latin *civitas* (see CITY).

citation /sʌɪˈteɪʃ(ə)n/ ■ n. 1 a quotation from or reference to a book or author. 2 a mention of a praiseworthy act in an official report. ▸ a note accompanying an award, giving reasons for it. 3 Law a reference to a former case, used as guidance or in support of an argument. 4 Law, chiefly N. Amer. a summons.

cite /sʌɪt/ ■ v. 1 quote (a book or author) as evidence for an argument. 2 praise for a courageous act in an official dispatch. 3 Law summon to appear in a law court.
– DERIVATIVES **citable** adj.
– ORIGIN Middle English: from Old French *citer*, from Latin *citare*, from *ciere* 'to call'.

CITES /ˈsʌɪtiːz/ ■ abbrev. Convention on International Trade in Endangered Species.

citified (also **cityfied**) ■ adj. chiefly derogatory characteristic of or adjusted to a city.

citizen ■ n. 1 a legally recognized subject or national of a state or commonwealth. 2 an inhabitant of a town or city.
– DERIVATIVES **citizenry** n. **citizenship** n.
– ORIGIN Middle English: from Anglo-Norman French *citezein*, alteration of Old French *citeain*, from Latin *civitas* (see CITY).

Citizens' Advice Bureau ■ n. an office at which the public can receive free advice on civil matters.

citizen's arrest ■ n. an arrest by an ordinary person without a warrant, allowable in certain cases.

Citizens' Band ■ n. a range of radio frequencies which are allocated for local communication by private individuals.

citrate /ˈsɪtreɪt/ ■ n. Chemistry a salt or ester of citric acid.

citric ■ adj. derived from or related to citrus fruit.
– ORIGIN C18: from Latin *citrus* 'citron tree'.

citric acid ■ n. Chemistry a sharp-tasting crystalline acid present in the juice of lemons and other sour fruits, used commercially as a flavouring and setting agent.

citrine /ˈsɪtrɪn/ ■ n. a glassy yellow variety of quartz.
– ORIGIN Middle English: from Old French *citrin* 'lemon-coloured', from Latin *citrus* 'citron tree'.

citron /ˈsɪtr(ə)n/ ■ n. **1** a shrubby Asian tree bearing large lemon-like fruits with thick fragrant peel. [*Citrus medica*.] **2** the fruit of this tree.
– ORIGIN C16: from Latin *citrus* 'citron tree'.

citronella ■ n. **1** a fragrant natural oil used as an insect repellent and in perfume. **2** the South Asian grass from which this oil is obtained. [*Cymbopogon nardus*.]
– ORIGIN C19: from CITRON + the diminutive suffix *-ella*.

citrus ■ n. (pl. **citruses**) **1** a tree of a genus that includes citron, lemon, lime, orange, and grapefruit. [Genus *Citrus*.] **2** (also **citrus fruit**) a fruit from such a tree.
– DERIVATIVES **citrous** adj. **citrusy** adj.
– ORIGIN Latin, 'citron tree, thuja'.

cittern /ˈsɪt(ə)n/ ■ n. a lute-like stringed instrument with a flattened back and wire strings, used in 16th- and 17th-century Europe.
– ORIGIN C16: from Latin *cithara*, from Greek *kithara*, denoting a kind of harp.

city ■ n. (pl. **-ies**) **1** S. African a town that has been given the status and title of a city by the state. ▶ Brit. a town created a city by charter and containing a cathedral. ▶ N. Amer. a municipal centre incorporated by the state or province. **2** (**the City**) the part of London governed by the Lord Mayor and the Corporation. ▶ the financial and commercial institutions in this part of London.
– DERIVATIVES **cityward** adj. & adv. **citywards** adv.
– ORIGIN Middle English: from Old French *cite*, from Latin *civitas*, from *civis* 'citizen'.

city desk ■ n. Brit. the department of a newspaper dealing with business news. ▶ N. Amer. the department of a newspaper dealing with local news.

city father ■ n. a person concerned with the administration of a city.

cityfied ■ adj. variant spelling of CITIFIED.

city hall ■ n. [treated as sing.] municipal offices or officers collectively.

cityscape ■ n. a city landscape.

city slicker ■ n. a person with the sophisticated tastes or values associated with city dwellers.

city state ■ n. a city and surrounding territory that forms an independent state.

civet /ˈsɪvɪt/ ■ n. **1** a slender nocturnal carnivorous mammal with a barred or spotted coat, native to Africa and Asia. [*Civetticis civetta* (Africa), and other species.] **2** a strong musky perfume obtained from the scent glands of the civet.
– ORIGIN C16: from French *civette*, from Arabic *zabād*.

civic ■ adj. of or relating to a city or town. ■ n. S. African informal term for CIVIC ASSOCIATION (in sense 2).
– DERIVATIVES **civically** adv.
– ORIGIN C16: from Latin *civicus*, from *civis* 'citizen'.

civic association ■ n. **1** a volunteer organization which coordinates activities regarded as beneficial to a community. **2** (in South Africa) an organization formed to represent community interests to local government.

civic centre ■ n. **1** the area of a town where municipal offices are situated. **2** a building containing municipal offices.

civics ■ pl. n. [treated as sing.] the study of the rights and duties of citizenship.

civil ■ adj. of or relating to ordinary citizens, as distinct from military or ecclesiastical matters. **2** Law non-criminal: *a civil court*. **3** courteous and polite. **4** (of time measurement) fixed by custom or law, not natural or astronomical.
– DERIVATIVES **civilly** adv.

cladistics

– ORIGIN Middle English: from Latin *civilis*, from *civis* 'citizen'.

civil defence ■ n. the organization and training of civilians for their protection during and after attacks in wartime.

civil disobedience ■ n. the refusal to comply with certain laws or to pay taxes, as a political protest.

civil engineer ■ n. an engineer who designs roads, bridges, dams, etc.
– DERIVATIVES **civil engineering** n.

civilian ■ n. a person not in the armed services or the police force. ■ adj. of, denoting, or relating to a civilian.
– DERIVATIVES **civilianization** (also **-isation**) n. **civilianize** (also **-ise**) v.
– ORIGIN Middle English: from Old French *civilien*, in the phr. *droit civilien* 'civil law'.

civility ■ n. (pl. **-ies**) politeness and courtesy. ▶ (**civilities**) polite remarks used in formal conversation.

civilization (also **-isation**) ■ n. **1** an advanced stage or system of human social development. ▶ the process of achieving this. **2** a civilized nation or region.

civilize (also **-ise**) ■ v. **1** [usu. as adj. **civilized** (also **-ised**)] bring to an advanced stage of social development. **2** [as adj. **civilized** (also **-ised**)] polite and good-mannered.
– DERIVATIVES **civilizer** (also **-iser**) n.

civil law ■ n. **1** law concerned with ordinary citizens, rather than criminal, military, or religious affairs. **2** the system of law predominant on the European continent, influenced by that of ancient Rome.

civil liberty ■ n. freedom of action and speech subject to laws established for the good of the community. ▶ (**civil liberties**) one's rights to this.
– DERIVATIVES **civil libertarian** n.

Civil List ■ n. (in the UK) an annual allowance voted by Parliament for the royal family's household expenses.

civil marriage ■ n. a marriage without religious ceremony.

civil partnership (also **civil union**) ■ n. a legally recognized union of a same-sex couple, with rights similar to those of marriage.

civil rights ■ pl. n. the rights of citizens to political and social freedom and equality.

civils ■ pl. n. [usu. treated as sing.] short for civil engineering.

civil servant ■ n. a member of the civil service.

civil service ■ n. the permanent professional branches of state administration, excluding military and judicial branches and elected politicians.

civil union ■ n. another term for CIVIL PARTNERSHIP.

civil war ■ n. a war between citizens of the same country.

civil wrong ■ n. Law an infringement of a person's rights.

civil year ■ n. see YEAR (sense 2).

civvy ■ n. (pl. **-ies**) informal **1** a civilian. **2** (**civvies**) civilian clothes, as opposed to uniform.
– PHRASES **Civvy Street** informal civilian life.

CJD ■ abbrev. Creutzfeldt–Jakob disease.

Cl ■ symb. the chemical element chlorine.

cl ■ abbrev. centilitre.

clack ■ v. make or cause to make a sharp sound as of a hard object striking another. ■ n. a clacking sound.
– DERIVATIVES **clacker** n.
– ORIGIN Middle English: imitative.

clad[1] archaic or poetic past participle of CLOTHE. ■ adj. **1** clothed. **2** provided with cladding.

clad[2] ■ v. (**cladding**; past and past part. **cladded** or **clad**) cover with cladding.
– ORIGIN C16: prob. from CLAD[1].

cladding ■ n. a covering or coating on a structure or material.

clade /kleɪd/ ■ n. Biology a group of organisms comprising all the evolutionary descendants of a common ancestor.
– ORIGIN 1950s: from Greek *klados* 'branch'.

cladistics /kləˈdɪstɪks/ ■ pl. n. [treated as sing.] Biology a

method of classification of animals and plants into groups based on characteristics which originated in a common evolutionary ancestor.
– DERIVATIVES **cladism** /'kladɪz(ə)m/ n. **cladistic** adj.

clado- /'kleɪdəʊ, 'kladəʊ/ ■ comb. form relating to a branch or branching: *cladogram*.
– ORIGIN from Greek *klados* 'branch or shoot'.

Cladocera /klə'dɒsərə/ ■ pl. n. Zoology an order of minute branchiopod crustaceans which includes the water fleas.
– DERIVATIVES **cladoceran** n. & adj.
– ORIGIN from Greek *klados* 'branch or root' + *keras* 'horn' (because of the branched antennae).

cladode /'kleɪdəʊd/ ■ n. Botany a flattened leaf-like stem.
– ORIGIN C19: from Greek *kladōdēs* 'with many shoots'.

cladogenesis /ˌkleɪdə(ʊ)'dʒɛnɪsɪs, ˌkladə(ʊ)-/ ■ n. Biology the formation of a new group of organisms by evolutionary divergence from an ancestral form.
– DERIVATIVES **cladogenetic** adj.

cladogram /'kleɪdə(ʊ)gram, 'kladə(ʊ)-/ ■ n. Biology a branching diagram showing the cladistic relationship between species.

cladophyll /'kleɪdəfɪl, 'kladə-/ ■ n. another term for CLADODE.

claim ■ v. **1** assert that something is the case. **2** demand as one's property or earnings. ▸ request (money) under the terms of an insurance policy. **3** call for (someone's) attention. **4** cause the loss of (someone's life). ■ n. **1** an assertion of the truth of something. **2** a demand for something considered one's due. ▸ a request for compensation under the terms of an insurance policy. **3** (also **mining claim**) a piece of land allotted to or taken by someone in order to be mined.
– DERIVATIVES **claimable** adj. **claimant** n.
– ORIGIN Middle English: from Old French *claime* (n.), *clamer* (v.), from Latin *clamare* 'call out'.

clairvoyance ■ n. the supposed faculty of perceiving events in the future or beyond normal sensory contact.
– ORIGIN C19: from French, from *clair* 'clear' + *voir* 'to see'.

clairvoyant ■ n. a person claiming to have clairvoyance. ■ adj. having clairvoyance.
– DERIVATIVES **clairvoyantly** adv.
– ORIGIN C17: from French, from *clair* 'clear' + *voyant* 'seeing'.

clam ■ n. a large marine bivalve mollusc with shells of equal size, several kinds of which are edible. [*Mya arenaria* (softshell clam), *Venus mercenaria* (hardshell clam) (both N. America), *Tridacna gigas* (giant clam, Indo-Pacific), and many other species.] ■ v. (**clammed, clamming**) **1** chiefly N. Amer. dig for or collect clams. **2** (**clam up**) informal abruptly stop talking.
– ORIGIN C16: from earlier *clam* 'a clamp', from Old English *clam* 'a bond or bondage', of Germanic origin.

clamant /'kleɪm(ə)nt, 'klam-/ ■ adj. forcing itself urgently on the attention.
– DERIVATIVES **clamantly** adv.
– ORIGIN C17: from Latin *clamare* 'cry out'.

clambake ■ n. N. Amer. a social gathering outdoors, especially for eating seafood.

clamber ■ v. climb or move in an awkward and laborious way. ■ n. an act of clambering.
– ORIGIN Middle English: prob. from *clamb*, obsolete past tense of CLIMB.

clammy ■ adj. (**-ier, -iest**) unpleasantly damp and sticky or slimy. ▸ (of air) cold and damp.
– DERIVATIVES **clammily** adv. **clamminess** n.
– ORIGIN Middle English: from dialect *clam* 'to be sticky or adhere', of Germanic origin.

clamour (US **clamor**) ■ n. a loud and confused noise, especially of vehement shouting. ▸ a vehement protest or demand. ■ v. (of a group) make a clamour.
– DERIVATIVES **clamorous** adj. **clamorously** adv. **clamorousness** n.
– ORIGIN Middle English: from Latin *clamor*, from *clamare* 'cry out'.

clamp ■ n. **1** a brace, band, or clasp for strengthening or holding things together. **2** an electric circuit maintaining the voltage limits of a signal at prescribed levels. ■ v. **1** fasten in place or together with a clamp. ▸ hold tightly against another thing. ▸ fit a wheel clamp to (an illegally parked car). **2** (**clamp down**) suppress or prevent something. **3** maintain the voltage limits of (an electrical signal) at prescribed values.
– DERIVATIVES **clamper** n.
– ORIGIN Middle English: prob. of Dutch or Low German origin and rel. to CLAM.

clampdown ■ n. informal a concerted attempt to suppress something.

clan ■ n. **1** a group of close-knit and interrelated families. **2** a group with a strong common interest.
– ORIGIN Middle English: from Scottish Gaelic *clann* 'offspring, family', from Old Irish *cland*, from Latin *planta* 'sprout'.

clandestine /klan'dɛstɪn, 'klandɛstɪn/ ■ adj. surreptitious.
– DERIVATIVES **clandestinely** adv. **clandestinity** n.
– ORIGIN C16: from Latin *clandestinus*, from *clam* 'secretly'.

clang ■ n. a loud, resonant metallic sound. ■ v. make or cause to make a clang.
– ORIGIN C16: imitative, influenced by Latin *clangere* 'resound'.

clanger ■ n. informal a mistake.

clangour /'klaŋgə/ (US **clangor**) ■ n. a continuous clanging sound.
– DERIVATIVES **clangorous** adj. **clangorously** adv.
– ORIGIN C16: from Latin *clangor*, from *clangere* 'resound'.

clank ■ n. a loud, sharp sound as of pieces of metal being struck together. ■ v. make or cause to make a clank.
– DERIVATIVES **clanking** adj. **clankingly** adv.
– ORIGIN Middle English: imitative.

clan name ■ n. a surname shared by members of clan. ▸ a name shared by members of a kinship group, often that of an ancestor or totemic animal or plant.

clannish ■ adj. tending to exclude others outside the group.
– DERIVATIVES **clannishly** adv. **clannishness** n.

clanship ■ n. the system of clan membership or loyalty.

clansman ■ n. (pl. **-men**) a male member of a clan.

clap¹ ■ v. (**clapped, clapping**) **1** strike the palms of (one's hands) together repeatedly, especially to applaud. **2** slap encouragingly on the back. **3** place (a hand) briefly over one's face as a gesture of dismay or regret. **4** (of a bird) flap (its wings) audibly. **5** (**clap something on**) abruptly impose a restrictive or punitive measure on. **6** S. African variant spelling of KLAP. ■ n. **1** an act of clapping. **2** an explosive sound, especially of thunder.
– PHRASES **clap someone in jail** (or **irons**) put someone in prison (or in chains).
– ORIGIN Old English *clappan* 'throb, beat'; imitative.

clap² ■ n. informal a venereal disease, especially gonorrhoea.
– ORIGIN C16: from Old French *clapoir* 'venereal bubo'.

clapboard /'klapbɔːd, 'klabəd/ ■ n. chiefly N. Amer. one of a series of long planks of wood with edges horizontally overlapping, covering the outer walls of buildings.
– DERIVATIVES **clapboarded** adj.
– ORIGIN C16: partial translation of Low German *klappholt* 'barrel stave', from *klappen* 'to crack' + *holt* 'wood'.

clapped-out ■ adj. informal worn out from age or heavy use.

clapper ■ n. the tongue or striker of a bell.
– PHRASES **like the clappers** Brit. informal very fast or hard.

clapperboard ■ n. a device of hinged boards that are struck together before filming to synchronize the starting of picture and sound machinery.

claptrap ■ n. nonsense.
– ORIGIN C18: from CLAP¹ + TRAP¹.

claque /klak, klɑːk/ ■ n. a group of people hired to applaud or heckle a performer.
– ORIGIN C19: French, from *claquer* 'to clap'.

claret /'klarət/ ■ n. **1** a red wine, especially from Bordeaux. **2** a deep purplish red colour.
– ORIGIN Middle English: from Old French (*vin*) *claret* and medieval Latin *claratum* (*vinum*) 'clarified (wine)', from Latin *clarus* 'clear'.

clarify /ˈklarɪfʌɪ/ ■ v. (-ies, -ied) 1 make more comprehensible. 2 [usu. as adj. **clarified**] melt (butter) to separate out the impurities.
– DERIVATIVES **clarification** n. **clarificatory** adj. **clarifier** n.
– ORIGIN Middle English: from Old French *clarifier*, from Latin *clarus* 'clear'.

clarinet ■ n. a woodwind instrument with a single-reed mouthpiece, a cylindrical tube of dark wood with a flared end, and holes stopped by keys.
– DERIVATIVES **clarinettist** (US **clarinetist**) n.
– ORIGIN C18: from French *clarinette*, diminutive of *clarine*, denoting a kind of bell.

clarion /ˈklarɪən/ ■ n. chiefly historical a shrill narrow-tubed war trumpet. ■ adj. loud and clear.
– PHRASES **clarion call** a strongly expressed demand for action.
– ORIGIN Middle English: from medieval Latin *clario(n-)*, from Latin *clarus* 'clear'.

clarity ■ n. 1 the state or quality of being clear, distinct, and easily perceived or understood. 2 the quality of transparency or purity.
– ORIGIN Middle English: from Latin *claritas*, from *clarus* 'clear'.

clarsach /ˈklaːrsəx, ˈklaːsək/ ■ n. a small harp with wire strings, used in the folk and early music of Scotland and Ireland.
– ORIGIN C15: from Scottish Gaelic, perhaps from *clar* 'table, board'.

clary /ˈklɛːri/ ■ n. an aromatic plant of the mint family, used as a culinary and medicinal herb. [*Salvia sclarea* (S. Europe) and related species.]
– ORIGIN Middle English: from obsolete French *clarie*.

clash ■ v. 1 (of two opposing groups) come abruptly into violent conflict. ▶ have a forceful disagreement. 2 be incompatible. 3 (of colours) appear discordant when placed together. 4 (of dates or events) occur inconveniently at the same time. 5 strike (cymbals) together, producing a loud discordant sound. ■ n. an instance of clashing.
– DERIVATIVES **clasher** n.
– ORIGIN C16: imitative.

clasp ■ v. 1 grasp tightly with one's hand. ▶ place (one's arms) around something so as to hold it tightly. ▶ hold tightly. ▶ press (one's hands) together with the fingers interlaced. 2 fasten with a clasp. ■ n. 1 a small device with interlocking parts used for fastening things together. 2 an inscribed silver bar on a medal ribbon. 3 an act of clasping.
– PHRASES **clasp hands** shake hands with fervour or affection.
– ORIGIN Middle English.

clasp knife ■ n. a knife with a blade that folds into the handle.

class ■ n. 1 a set or category of things having some property in common and differentiated from others by kind or quality. ▶ Biology a principal taxonomic grouping that ranks above order and below phylum or division, such as Mammalia or Insecta. ▶ a division of candidates according to merit in a university examination. 2 a system that divides members of a society into sets based on perceived social or economic status. ▶ such a set. 3 a group of students or pupils who are taught together. ▶ a lesson. ▶ all of the college or school students of a particular year. 4 informal impressive stylishness in appearance or behaviour. ■ v. assign or regard as belonging to a particular category. ■ adj. informal showing stylish excellence: *he's a class player*.
– PHRASES **class act** a person or thing displaying impressive and stylish excellence.
– ORIGIN C16: from Latin *classis* 'a division of the Roman people, a grade, or a class of pupils'.

class action ■ n. Law a law suit filed or defended by an individual acting on behalf of a group.

class consciousness ■ n. awareness of one's place in a system of social class, especially (in Marxist terms) as it relates to the class struggle.
– DERIVATIVES **class-conscious** adj.

classic ■ adj. 1 judged over a period of time to be of the highest quality. ▶ (of a garment) of a simple, elegant style not greatly subject to changes in fashion. 2 remarkably typical: *the classic symptoms of flu*. ■ n. 1 a work of art of recognized and established value: *his books have become classics*. 2 (**Classics**) the study of ancient Greek and Latin literature, philosophy, and history. ▶ (**the classics**) the works of ancient Greek and Latin writers and philosophers. 3 (**Classic**) a major sports tournament or competition, especially in golf or tennis.
– ORIGIN C17: from Latin *classicus* 'belonging to a class or division', later 'of the highest class'.

classical ■ adj. 1 of or relating to ancient Greek or Latin literature, art, or culture. ▶ (of art or architecture) influenced by ancient Greek or Roman forms or principles. 2 (of a form of art or a language) representing an exemplary standard within a traditional and long-established form or style. ▶ (of music) of traditional and long-established form or style or (more specifically) written in the European tradition during a period lasting approximately from 1750 to 1830, when forms such as the symphony were standardized. 3 of or relating to the first significant period of an area of study: *classical Marxism*. 4 Physics relating to or based upon concepts and theories which preceded the theories of relativity and quantum mechanics; Newtonian.
– DERIVATIVES **classicality** n. **classically** adv.

classicism ■ n. the following of ancient Greek or Roman principles and style in art and literature, generally associated with harmony, restraint, and adherence to recognized standards of form and craftsmanship.

classicist ■ n. 1 a person who studies Classics. 2 a follower of classicism.

classicize (also **-ise**) ■ v. [usu. as adj. **classicizing** (also **-ising**)] imitate a classical style: *the classicizing strains in Guercino's art*.

classification ■ n. 1 the action or process of classifying. 2 a category into which something is put. ▶ S. African historical (under apartheid) the registration of a person as a member of a particular racial group.
– DERIVATIVES **classificatory** adj.

classified ■ adj. 1 (of newspaper or magazine advertisements) organized in categories according to what is being advertised. 2 (of information or documents) designated as officially secret. ■ n. (**classifieds**) classified advertisements.

classify ■ v. (-ies, -ied) 1 arrange (a group) in classes or categories according to shared qualities or characteristics. ▶ assign (someone or something) to a particular class or category. 2 designate (documents or information) as officially secret or to which only authorized people may have access.
– DERIVATIVES **classifiable** adj. **classifier** n. **classifying** adj.
– ORIGIN C18: back-formation from CLASSIFICATION, from French, from *classe* 'class', from Latin *classis* 'division'.

classism ■ n. prejudice against or in favour of people belonging to a particular social class.
– DERIVATIVES **classist** adj. & n.

classless ■ adj. 1 (of a society) not divided into social classes. 2 not showing characteristics of a particular social class: *a classless accent*.
– DERIVATIVES **classlessness** n.

classroom ■ n. a room in which a class of pupils or students is taught.

class struggle ■ n. (in Marxist ideology) the conflict of interests between the workers and the ruling class in a capitalist society.

classy ■ adj. (-ier, -iest) informal stylish and sophisticated.
– DERIVATIVES **classily** adv. **classiness** n.

clast /klast/ ■ n. Geology a constituent fragment of a clastic rock.
– ORIGIN C20: back-formation from CLASTIC.

clastic ■ adj. Geology denoting rocks composed of broken pieces of older rocks.
– ORIGIN C19: from French *clastique*, from Greek *klastos* 'broken in pieces'.

clathrate /ˈklaθreɪt/ ■ n. Chemistry a compound in which molecules of one component are physically trapped within the crystal structure of another.
– ORIGIN 1940s: from Latin *clathratus*, from *clathri* 'lattice-bars'.

clatter

clatter ■ n. a loud rattling sound as of hard objects falling or striking each other. ■ v. make or cause to make a clatter. ▸ fall or move with a clatter.
– ORIGIN Old English (as v.); imitative.

clause ■ n. **1** a unit of grammatical organization next below the sentence in rank, and in traditional grammar said to consist of a subject and predicate. **2** a particular and separate article, stipulation, or proviso in a treaty, bill, or contract.
– DERIVATIVES **clausal** adj.
– ORIGIN Middle English: from Latin *claus-*, *claudere* 'shut, close'.

claustrophobia /klɔːstrəˈfəʊbɪə/ ■ n. extreme or irrational fear of confined places.
– DERIVATIVES **claustrophobe** n.
– ORIGIN C19: from Latin *claustrum* 'lock, bolt' + -PHOBIA.

claustrophobic ■ adj. suffering from claustrophobia. ▸ (of a place or situation) inducing claustrophobia. ■ n. a claustrophobic person.
– DERIVATIVES **claustrophobically** adv.

clave[1] /kleɪv, klɑːv/ ■ n. one of a pair of hardwood sticks used in music to make a hollow sound when struck together.
– ORIGIN 1920s: from Spanish *clave* 'keystone', from Latin *clavis* 'key'.

clave[2] archaic past of CLEAVE[2].

clavichord /ˈklavɪkɔːd/ ■ n. a small, rectangular keyboard instrument with a soft tone.
– ORIGIN Middle English: from medieval Latin *clavichordium*, from Latin *clavis* 'key' + *chorda* 'string'.

clavicle /ˈklavɪk(ə)l/ ■ n. Anatomy technical term for COLLARBONE.
– DERIVATIVES **clavicular** /kləˈvɪkjʊlə/ adj.
– ORIGIN C17: from Latin *clavicula* 'small key', diminutive of *clavis* (because of its shape).

claw ■ n. **1** a curved, pointed horny nail on each digit of the foot in birds, lizards, and some mammals. ▸ either of a pair of small hooked appendages on an insect's foot. **2** the pincer of a crab, scorpion, or other arthropod. **3** a mechanical device resembling a claw, used for gripping or lifting. ■ v. **1** (usu. **claw at**) scratch or tear at with the claws or fingernails. ▸ clutch at with the hands. ▸ (**claw something away**) try desperately to move something with the hands. **2** (**claw one's way**) haul oneself forward with one's hands. **3** (**claw something back**) regain or recover money, power, etc. laboriously or harshly. **4** (of a sailing ship) beat to windward.
– PHRASES **get one's claws into** informal have a controlling influence over.
– DERIVATIVES **-clawed** adj. **clawless** adj.
– ORIGIN Old English, of West Germanic origin.

clawback ■ n. an act of retrieving money already paid out, typically by a government using taxation.

claw hammer ■ n. a hammer with one side of the head split and curved, used for extracting nails.

clay ■ n. **1** a stiff, sticky fine-grained impermeable earth that can be moulded when wet and baked to make bricks and pottery. **2** poetic/literary the substance of the human body: *this lifeless clay.*
– DERIVATIVES **clayey** adj. **clayish** adj.
– ORIGIN Old English, of West Germanic origin.

claymore ■ n. **1** historical a type of two-edged or single-edged broadsword used in Scotland. **2** a type of anti-personnel mine.
– ORIGIN C18: from Scottish Gaelic *claidheamh* 'sword' + *mór* 'great'.

clay pigeon ■ n. a saucer-shaped piece of baked clay or other material thrown up in the air from a trap as a target for shooting.

clay pipe ■ n. a tobacco pipe made of hardened clay.

clean ■ adj. **1** free from dirt, pollutants, or harmful substances. ▸ attentive to personal hygiene. **2** morally pure. ▸ not obscene: *good clean fun.* ▸ showing or having no record of offences or crimes. ▸ played or done according to the rules. **3** free from irregularities; smooth; well defined. ▸ (of timber) free from knots. **4** (of an action) smoothly and skilfully done. **5** (of a taste, sound, or smell) distinctive and fresh. ■ adv. **1** so as to be free from dirt. **2** informal completely: *I clean forgot her birthday.* ■ v. **1** make clean; make free of mess. **2** (**clean someone out**) informal use up or take all someone's money or resources. ▸ (**clean something out**) strip a place of and steal all its contents. **3** (**clean up**) informal make a substantial gain or profit. ■ n. an act of cleaning.
– PHRASES **a clean sheet** (or **slate**) an absence of existing restraints or commitments. ▸ (**keep a clean sheet**) (in a soccer match) prevent the opposing side from scoring. **come clean** informal fully confess something. **keep one's hands clean** remain uninvolved in an immoral or illegal act. **make a clean breast of it** fully confess one's mistakes or wrongdoings. **make a clean sweep 1** remove all unwanted people or things ready to start afresh. **2** win all of a group of related sporting contests.
– DERIVATIVES **cleanable** adj. **cleaning** n. **cleanish** adj. **cleanness** n.
– ORIGIN Old English, of West Germanic origin.

clean-cut ■ adj. **1** sharply outlined. **2** (of a person) clean and neat.

cleaner ■ n. a person or thing that cleans. ▸ (**the cleaners**) a shop where clothes and fabrics are dry-cleaned.
– PHRASES **take someone to the cleaners** informal **1** unscrupulously take a large portion of someone's money or resources. **2** inflict a crushing defeat on someone.

cleaner fish ■ n. a small fish that removes parasites from the skin, gills, and mouth of larger fishes. [*Labroides dimidiatus* and other species.]

cleanly /ˈkliːnli/ ■ adv. in a clean manner.
– DERIVATIVES **cleanliness** n.

clean room ■ n. an environment free from dust and other contaminants, used chiefly for the manufacture of electronic components.

cleanse ■ v. **1** make thoroughly clean. **2** archaic (in biblical translations) cure (a leper). ■ n. an act of cleansing.
– DERIVATIVES **cleanser** n. **cleansing** adj.
– ORIGIN Old English.

clean-shaven ■ adj. (of a man) without a beard or moustache.

clean-up ■ n. **1** an act of making a place clean or restoring order. **2** (also **cleanup**) Baseball the fourth position in a team's batting order, usually reserved for a strong batter whose hits are likely to enable any runner who is on base to score.

clear ■ adj. **1** easy to perceive or understand. ▸ leaving or feeling no doubt. **2** transparent; unclouded. ▸ free of mist; having good visibility. ▸ (of a person's skin) free from blemishes. ▸ (of a colour) pure and intense. **3** free of any obstructions or unwanted objects. ▸ (of a period of time) free of any commitments. **4** free from disease, contamination, or guilt. **5** (**clear of**) not touching; away from: *the lorry had one wheel clear of the ground.* **6** complete: *seven clear days' notice.* ▸ (of a sum of money) net. ■ adv. **1** so as to be out of the way of, away from, or uncluttered by. **2** with clarity: *I heard the message loud and clear.* ■ v. **1** make or become clear. ▸ cause people to leave (a building or place). ▸ chiefly Soccer send (the ball) away from the area near one's goal. ▸ discharge (a debt). **2** get past or over (something) safely or without touching it. **3** show or declare officially to be innocent. **4** give official approval or authorization to or for. ▸ (of a person or goods) satisfy the necessary requirements to pass through (customs). ▸ (with reference to a cheque) pass or cause to pass through a clearing house so that the money goes into the payee's account. **5** earn or gain (an amount of money) as a net profit. **6** (of a person's face or expression) assume a happier or less confused aspect.
– PHRASES **clear the air 1** make the air less sultry. **2** defuse or clarify a tense situation by frank discussion. **clear the decks** prepare for something by dealing beforehand with anything that might hinder progress. **in the clear** no longer in danger or suspected of something. **out of a clear sky** as a complete surprise.
– PHRASAL VERBS **clear away** remove the remains of a meal from the table. **clear off** informal go away. **clear out** informal leave quickly. **clear something out** empty something. **clear up 1** (of an illness or other medical condition) become cured. **2** (of the weather) become brighter; stop raining. **clear something up 1** (also **clear up**) tidy something up by removing unwanted items.

VOWELS a cat ɑː arm ɛ bed ɛː hair ə ago əː her ɪ sit i cosy iː see ɒ hot ɔː saw ʌ run

2 solve or explain something. **3** cure an illness or other medical condition.
– DERIVATIVES **clearable** adj. **clearness** n.
– ORIGIN Middle English: from Old French *cler*, from Latin *clarus*.

clearance ■ n. **1** the action or process of clearing or of being dispersed. **2** (in soccer and other games) a kick or hit that sends the ball out of a defensive zone. **3** Snooker the potting of all the balls remaining on the table in a single break. **4** official authorization for something to proceed or take place. **5** clear space allowed for a thing to move past or under another.

clear-cut ■ adj. **1** sharply defined; easy to perceive or understand. **2** (of an area) from which every tree has been cut down and removed. ■ v. cut down and remove every tree from (an area).

clearer ■ n. **1** a person or thing that clears away obstructions. **2** a clearing bank.

clear-fell ■ v. another term for CLEAR-CUT.

clearing ■ n. an open space in a forest.

clearing bank ■ n. a bank which is a member of a clearing house.

clearing house ■ n. **1** a bankers' establishment where cheques and bills from member banks are exchanged, so that only the balances need be paid in cash. **2** an agency which collects and distributes something, especially information.

clearly ■ adv. **1** with clarity. **2** obviously; without doubt.

clear-sighted ■ adj. thinking clearly; perspicacious.

clearstory ■ n. (pl. **-ies**) US spelling of CLERESTORY.

clearwing ■ n. a day-flying moth with mainly transparent wings, resembling a wasp or bee. [Family Sesiidae: many species.]

cleat /kliːt/ ■ n. **1** a T-shaped or similar projection to which a rope may be attached. **2** a projecting wedge on a spar, tool, etc., to prevent slippage. ▶ one of a number of projections on the sole of a boot, to increase its grip.
– DERIVATIVES **cleated** adj.
– ORIGIN Middle English, of West Germanic origin.

cleavage ■ n. **1** a sharp division; a split. **2** the cleft between a woman's breasts. **3** Biology cell division, especially of a fertilized egg cell. **4** the splitting of rocks or crystals along definite parallel, closely-spaced planes.

cleave[1] ■ v. (past **clove** or **cleft** or **cleaved**; past part. **cloven** or **cleft** or **cleaved**) **1** split or sever along a natural grain or line. ▶ split (a molecule) by breaking a particular chemical bond. ▶ Biology (of a cell) divide. **2** make a way through: *they watched a coot cleave the smooth water.*
– DERIVATIVES **cleavable** adj.
– ORIGIN Old English, of Germanic origin.

cleave[2] ■ v. (**cleave to**) poetic/literary **1** stick fast to. **2** become strongly involved with or emotionally attached to.
– ORIGIN Old English: of West Germanic origin.

cleaver ■ n. a tool with a heavy broad blade, used for chopping meat.

cleavers ■ pl. n. [treated as sing. or pl.] another term for GOOSEGRASS.
– ORIGIN Old English.

clef ■ n. Music any of several symbols placed at the left-hand end of a stave, indicating the pitch of the notes written on the stave.
– ORIGIN C16: from French, from Latin *clavis* 'key'.

cleft[1] past participle of CLEAVE[1]. ■ adj. split, divided, or partially divided into two.
– PHRASES **be** (or **be caught**) **in a cleft stick** chiefly Brit. be in a situation in which any action one takes will have adverse consequences.

cleft[2] ■ n. **1** a fissure or split in rock or the ground. **2** an indentation or deep hollow in a person's forehead or chin, or between two parts of the body.
– ORIGIN Middle English, of Germanic origin.

cleft lip ■ n. a congenital split in the upper lip on one or both sides of the centre, often associated with a cleft palate.

cleft palate ■ n. a congenital split in the roof of the mouth.

cleft sentence ■ n. Grammar a sentence in which an element is emphasized by being put in a separate clause,

---

217

---

with the use of an empty introductory word such as *it* or *that*, e.g. *it was today that I saw him.*

cleg /klɛg/ ■ n. another term for HORSEFLY.
– ORIGIN Middle English: from Old Norse *kleggi*.

cleistogamy /klʌɪˈstɒɡəmi/ ■ n. Botany self-fertilization that occurs within a permanently closed flower.
– DERIVATIVES **cleistogamous** adj.
– ORIGIN C19: from Greek *kleistos* 'closed' + *gamos* 'marriage'.

clematis /ˈklɛmətɪs, kləˈmeɪtɪs/ ■ n. an ornamental climbing plant of the buttercup family which bears white, pink, or purple flowers and feathery seeds. [Genus *Clematis*.]
– ORIGIN from Greek *klēmatis*, from *klēma* 'vine branch'.

clemency ■ n. the quality of being clement or merciful.

clement ■ adj. **1** (of weather) mild. **2** merciful.
– ORIGIN Middle English: from Latin.

clementine /ˈklɛm(ə)ntʌɪn, -tiːn/ ■ n. a tangerine of a deep orange-red North African variety which is grown around the Mediterranean and in South Africa.
– ORIGIN 1920s: from French *clémentine*, from the male given name *Clément*.

clenbuterol /klɛnˈbjuːtərɒl/ ■ n. Medicine a synthetic drug used to treat respiratory diseases, also used illegally by athletes to enhance performance.
– ORIGIN 1970s: from *c(h)l(oro-)* + *(ph)en(yl)* + *but(yl)* + *er* + *-ol*.

clench ■ v. **1** (with reference to one's fist or teeth) close or press together tightly, in response to stress or anger. ▶ (with reference to a set of muscles) contract or cause to contract sharply. **2** grasp tightly with the hands or between the teeth. ■ n. the action or state of clenching or being clenched.
– DERIVATIVES **clenched** adj.
– ORIGIN Old English, of Germanic origin.

clerestory /ˈklɪəˌstɔːri/ (US also **clearstory**) ■ n. (pl. **-ies**) the upper part of the nave, choir, and transepts of a large church, containing a series of windows and admitting light to the central parts of the building.
– ORIGIN Middle English: from CLEAR + STOREY.

clergy /ˈkləːdʒi/ ■ n. (pl. **-ies**) [usu. treated as pl.] the body of people ordained for religious duties in the Christian Church.
– ORIGIN Middle English: from eccles. Latin *clericus* (see CLERIC).

clergyman (or **clergywoman**) ■ n. (pl. **-men** or **-women**) a priest or minister of a Christian church.

cleric ■ n. a priest or religious leader.
– ORIGIN C17: from eccles. Latin *clericus* 'clergyman', from Greek *klērikos* 'belonging to the Christian clergy', from *klēros* 'lot, heritage' (Acts 1:26).

clerical ■ adj. **1** concerned with or relating to the routine work of an office clerk. **2** of or relating to the clergy.
– DERIVATIVES **clericalism** n. **clericalist** n. **clerically** adv.

clerical collar ■ n. a stiff upright white collar which fastens at the back, worn by the clergy in some churches.

clerical error ■ n. a mistake made in copying or writing out a document.

clerihew /ˈklɛrɪhjuː/ ■ n. a short comic or nonsensical verse, typically in two rhyming couplets with lines of unequal length and referring to a famous person.
– ORIGIN 1920s: named after Edmund *Clerihew* Bentley, the English writer who invented it.

clerk ■ n. **1** a person employed in an office or bank to keep records or accounts and to undertake other routine administrative duties. **2** an official in charge of the records of a local council or court. ▶ a senior official in Parliament. ▶ a lay officer of a cathedral, church, or chapel. **3** (also **desk clerk**) N. Amer. a receptionist in a hotel. ▶ an assistant in a shop; a sales clerk. **4** (also **clerk in holy orders**) formal a member of the clergy. ■ v. N. Amer. work as a clerk.
– PHRASES **clerk of the course** an official who assists the judges in horse racing or motor racing.
– DERIVATIVES **clerkship** n.
– ORIGIN Old English, from eccles. Latin *clericus* (see CLERIC).

ʊ put　uː too　ʌɪ my　aʊ how　eɪ day　əʊ no　ɪə near　ɔɪ boy　ʊə poor　ʌɪə fire　aʊə sour

clever ■ adj. (-er, -est) 1 quick to understand, learn, and devise or apply ideas. ▸ skilful; adroit. 2 [with neg.] Brit. informal healthy; well: *I didn't feel too clever.* ■ n. S. African informal a young streetwise black man.
– PHRASES **too clever by half** informal annoyingly proud of one's cleverness, and bound to overreach oneself.
– DERIVATIVES **cleverly** adv. **cleverness** n.
– ORIGIN Middle English ('quick to catch hold', later 'manually skilful', then 'possessing mental agility'): perhaps of Dutch or Low German origin.

clever-clever ■ adj. derogatory seeking to appear clever.

clever clogs ■ n. another term for CLEVER DICK.

clever Dick ■ n. informal, chiefly Brit. a person who is irritatingly and ostentatiously knowledgeable or intelligent.

clew /kluː/ ■ n. 1 the lower or after corner of a sail. 2 (**clews**) Nautical the cords by which a hammock is suspended. ■ v. (**clew a sail up/down**) draw a sail up or let it down by the clews when preparing for furling or when unfurling.
– ORIGIN Old English, of Germanic origin.

cliché /ˈkliːʃeɪ/ (also **cliche**) ■ n. a hackneyed or overused phrase or opinion. ▸ a very predictable or unoriginal thing or person.
– ORIGIN C19: French, from *clicher* 'to stereotype'.

clichéd (also **cliché'd** or **cliched**) ■ adj. showing a lack of originality; hackneyed or overused.

click ■ n. a short, sharp sound as of two metallic or plastic objects coming smartly into contact. ▸ a speech sound produced by sudden withdrawal of the tongue from the soft palate, front teeth, or back teeth and hard palate, occurring in some southern African and other languages. ▸ Computing an act of pressing one of the buttons on a mouse. ■ v. 1 make or cause to make a click. ▸ move or become secured with such a sound: *it clicked into place.* ▸ Computing press (one of the buttons on a mouse). 2 informal become suddenly clear and understandable. ▸ become friendly and compatible.
– DERIVATIVES **clickable** adj. **clicker** n. **clicky** adj.
– ORIGIN C16 (as v.): imitative.

click beetle ■ n. a long, narrow beetle which can spring up with a click as a means of startling predators and escaping. [Family Elateridae.]

click-clack ■ n. a repeated clicking sound as of shoe heels on a hard surface. ■ v. move with a click-clack.

client ■ n. 1 a person using the services of a professional person or organization. 2 Computing (in a network) a computer or workstation that obtains information and applications from a server. ▸ (also **client application** or **program**) a program that obtains a service provided by another program.
– ORIGIN Middle English: from Latin *cliens*, from *cluere* 'hear or obey'.

clientele /ˌkliːɒnˈtɛl/ ■ n. [treated as sing. or pl.] clients collectively. ▸ the customers of a shop, restaurant, etc.
– ORIGIN C16: from Latin *clientela* 'clientship', from *cliens* (see CLIENT).

clientelism /ˌkliːɒnˈtɛlɪz(ə)m/ (also **clientism** /ˈklʌɪəntɪz(ə)m/) ■ n. a social order which depends on relations of patronage, especially one that is exploitative of these relations.
– DERIVATIVES **clientelistic** adj.

cliff ■ n. a steep rock face, especially at the edge of the sea.
– DERIVATIVES **cliffy** adj.
– ORIGIN Old English, of Germanic origin.

cliffhanger ■ n. a dramatic story or climactic ending that leaves an audience in suspense.
– DERIVATIVES **cliffhanging** adj.

climacteric /klʌɪˈmaktərɪk, ˌklʌɪmakˈtɛrɪk/ ■ n. 1 a critical period or event. 2 Medicine the period of life when fertility is in decline; (in women) the menopause. 3 Botany the ripening period while still on the tree of certain fruits such as apples, involving increased metabolism. ■ adj. 1 having extreme and far-reaching implications or results; critical. 2 Medicine & Botany occurring at, characteristic of, or undergoing a climacteric.
– ORIGIN C16: from Greek *klimaktērikos*, from *klimaktēr* 'critical period', from *klimax* 'ladder, climax'.

climactic /klʌɪˈmaktɪk/ ■ adj. forming an exciting climax.
– DERIVATIVES **climactically** adv.

climate ■ n. 1 the general weather conditions prevailing in an area over a long period. 2 a prevailing trend or public attitude.
– DERIVATIVES **climatic** adj. **climatical** adj. **climatically** adv.
– ORIGIN Middle English: from late Latin *clima, climat-*, from Greek *klima* 'slope, zone'.

climate control ■ n. another term for AIR CONDITIONING.

climatology ■ n. the scientific study of climate.
– DERIVATIVES **climatological** adj. **climatologically** adv. **climatologist** n.

climax ■ n. 1 the most intense, exciting, or important point of something. 2 an orgasm. 3 Rhetoric a sequence of propositions or ideas in order of increasing importance, force, or effectiveness of expression. 4 Ecology the final stage in a succession in a given environment, at which a plant community reaches a state of equilibrium. ■ v. reach or bring to a climax.
– ORIGIN C16: from Greek *klimax* 'ladder, climax'.

climb ■ v. 1 go or come up to a higher position. ▸ go up mountains as a sport. ▸ slope or lead up. ▸ (of a plant) grow up (a supporting structure) by clinging to or twining round it. 2 move with effort into or out of a confined space. 3 increase in scale, value, or power. 4 (**climb down**) withdraw from a position taken up in argument or negotiation. ■ n. 1 an instance of climbing; an ascent. 2 a recognized route up a mountain or cliff.
– PHRASES **be climbing the walls** informal feel frustrated, helpless, and trapped.
– DERIVATIVES **climbable** adj. **climber** n. **climbing** n.
– ORIGIN Old English, of West Germanic origin.

climbdown ■ n. a withdrawal from a position taken up in argument or negotiation.

climbing frame ■ n. a structure of joined bars for children to climb on.

climbing irons ■ pl. n. a set of spikes attached to boots for climbing trees or ice slopes.

climbing wall ■ n. a wall simulating a rock face, used for climbing practice.

clime /klʌɪm/ ■ n. poetic/literary or humorous a region considered with reference to its climate: *jetting off to sunnier climes.*
– ORIGIN Middle English: from late Latin *clima* (see CLIMATE).

climograph (also **climagraph**) ■ n. a graph depicting climatic factors for a particular period, especially average temperatures and precipitation.
– DERIVATIVES **climography** n. **climographic** adj.

clinch ■ v. 1 conclusively settle (a contract or contest). 2 secure (a nail or rivet) by driving the point sideways when it has penetrated. 3 (of two people) grapple at close quarters. ▸ come together in an embrace. ■ n. 1 a struggle or scuffle at close quarters. ▸ an embrace. 2 (also **clinch knot**) a knot used to fasten ropes or angling lines, using a half hitch with the end seized back on its own part.
– ORIGIN C16: var. of CLENCH.

clincher ■ n. informal a fact, argument, or event that settles a matter conclusively.

cline /klʌɪn/ ■ n. a continuum with an infinite number of gradations from one extreme to the other. ▸ Biology a gradation in one or more characteristics within a species or other taxon, especially between different populations.
– ORIGIN 1930s: from Greek *klinein* 'to slope'.

cling ■ v. (past and past part. **clung**) (**cling to/on to**) 1 hold on tightly to. ▸ adhere or stick to. 2 remain persistently faithful to: *she clung to her convictions.* 3 be emotionally dependent on. ■ n. (also **cling peach**) a clingstone peach.
– DERIVATIVES **clinger** n. **clinging** adj.
– ORIGIN Old English *clingan* 'stick together', of Germanic origin.

cling film (also **cling wrap**) ■ n. a thin transparent plastic film that adheres to surfaces and to itself, used as a wrapping or covering for food.

clingfish ■ n. (pl. same or **-fishes**) a small fish with a sucker for attachment to rocks and other surfaces. [Family Gobiesocidae.]

clingstone ■ n. a peach or nectarine of a variety in which the flesh adheres to the stone. Contrasted with **FREESTONE**.

clingy ■ adj. (**-ier**, **-iest**) **1** (of a garment) liable to cling to the body. **2** too emotionally dependent.
– DERIVATIVES **clinginess** n.

clinic ■ n. **1** a place where specialized medical treatment or advice is given. **2** a gathering at a hospital bedside for the teaching of medicine or surgery. **3** chiefly N. Amer. a conference or short course on a particular subject: *a drum clinic.*
– ORIGIN C19: from French *clinique*, from Greek *klinikē (tekhnē)* 'bedside (art)', from *klinē* 'bed'.

clinical ■ adj. **1** relating to the observation and treatment of patients (rather than theoretical or laboratory studies). ▸ (of a disease or condition) causing observable and recognizable symptoms. **2** efficient and coldly detached. ▸ (of a place) bare, functional, and clean.
– DERIVATIVES **clinically** adv.

clinical death ■ n. death as judged by the medical observation of the cessation of respiration and the beating of the heart.

clinical psychology ■ n. the branch of psychology concerned with the assessment and treatment of mental illness.
– DERIVATIVES **clinical psychologist** n.

clinician ■ n. a doctor having direct contact with and responsibility for treating patients, rather than one involved with theoretical or laboratory studies.

clink[1] ■ n. a sharp ringing sound, such as that made when metal or glass are struck. ■ v. make or cause to make a clink.
– ORIGIN Middle English (as v.): prob. from Middle Dutch *klinken*.

clink[2] ■ n. informal prison.
– ORIGIN C16 (orig. denoting a prison in Southwark, London).

clinker (S. African also **klinker**) ■ n. **1** the stony residue from burnt coal or from a furnace. **2** a brick with a vitrified surface.
– ORIGIN C17: from obsolete Dutch *klinckaerd*, from *klinken* 'to clink'.

clinker-built ■ adj. (of a boat) having external planks which overlap downwards and are secured with clinched nails. Compare with **CARVEL-BUILT**.
– ORIGIN C18: *clinker* from *clink*, northern English var. of **CLINCH**.

clinometer /klaɪˈnɒmɪtə, klɪ-/ ■ n. Surveying an instrument used for measuring the angle or elevation of slopes.
– ORIGIN C19: from Greek *klinein* 'to slope' + **-METER**.

clip[1] ■ n. **1** a flexible or spring-loaded device for holding an object or objects together or in place. **2** a piece of jewellery fastened by a clip. **3** a metal holder containing cartridges for an automatic firearm. ■ v. (**clipped**, **clipping**) fasten or be fastened with a clip or clips.
– ORIGIN Old English: of West Germanic origin.

clip[2] ■ v. (**clipped**, **clipping**) **1** cut, trim, or excise with shears or scissors. ▸ trim the hair or wool of (an animal). **2** strike smartly or with a glancing blow. **3** informal, chiefly US move quickly in a specified direction. **4** Electronics truncate the amplitude of (a signal) above or below predetermined levels. ■ n. **1** an act of clipping. ▸ a short sequence taken from a film or broadcast. ▸ the quantity of wool clipped from a sheep or flock. **2** informal a smart or glancing blow. **3** informal a rapid or specified speed.
– PHRASES **clip the wings of** trim the feathers of (a bird) to disable it from flight. ▸ hamper the aspirations of.
– DERIVATIVES **clipping** n.
– ORIGIN Middle English, from Old Norse *klippa*, prob. imitative.

clip art ■ n. pre-drawn pictures and symbols provided with word-processing software and drawing packages.

clipboard ■ n. **1** a small board with a spring clip at the top, used for holding papers and providing support for writing. **2** Computing a temporary storage area where text or other data cut or copied from a file is kept until it is pasted into another file.

clip-clop ■ n. the sound of a horse's hoofs beating on a hard surface. ■ v. move with a clip-clop.

clip-on ■ adj. attached by a clip so as to be easy to fasten or remove.

clipped ■ adj. (of speech) having short, sharp vowel sounds and clear pronunciation.

clipper ■ n. **1** (**clippers**) an instrument for clipping. **2** a fast sailing ship, especially one of 19th-century design with concave bows and raked masts.

clique /kliːk/ ■ n. a small group of people who spend time together and do not readily allow others to join them.
– DERIVATIVES **cliquey** adj. (**-ier**, **-iest**). **cliquish** adj. **cliquishness** n.
– ORIGIN C18: from Old French *cliquer* 'make a noise'.

clitoridectomy /ˌklɪt(ə)rɪˈdɛktəmi/ ■ n. (pl. **-ies**) excision of the clitoris; female circumcision.

clitoris /ˈklɪt(ə)rɪs/ ■ n. a small sensitive and erectile part of the female genitals at the anterior end of the vulva.
– DERIVATIVES **clitoral** adj.
– ORIGIN C17: from Greek *kleitoris*.

clivia /ˈklɪvɪə/ ■ n. a southern African plant of the lily family, with dark green strap-like leaves and trumpet-shaped orange, red, or yellow flowers. [Genus *Clivia.*]
– ORIGIN from *Clive*, maiden name of Charlotte, Duchess of Northumberland (1787–1866).

Cllr ■ abbrev. Councillor.

cloaca /kləʊˈeɪkə/ ■ n. (pl. **cloacae** /-siː, -kiː/) Zoology a common cavity at the end of the digestive tract for the release of both excretory and genital products in vertebrates (except most mammals) and certain invertebrates.
– DERIVATIVES **cloacal** adj.
– ORIGIN C16: from Latin, rel. to *cluere* 'cleanse'.

cloak ■ n. **1** an overgarment that hangs loosely from the shoulders over the arms to the knees or ankles. **2** something that hides or covers: *a cloak of secrecy.* ■ v. dress or hide in a cloak.
– ORIGIN Middle English: from Old French *cloke*, from medieval Latin *clocca* 'bell'.

cloak-and-dagger ■ adj. involving intrigue and secrecy.

cloakroom ■ n. **1** a room in a public building where outdoor clothes and bags may be left. **2** a room that contains a toilet or toilets.

clobber[1] ■ n. informal clothing and personal belongings.
– ORIGIN C19.

clobber[2] ■ v. informal **1** hit hard. **2** defeat heavily.
– ORIGIN SECOND WORLD WAR.

cloche /klɒʃ, kləʊʃ/ ■ n. **1** a small translucent cover for protecting or forcing outdoor plants. **2** (also **cloche hat**) a woman's close-fitting, bell-shaped hat.
– ORIGIN C19: from French, 'bell'.

clock[1] ■ n. **1** an instrument that measures and indicates the time by means of a dial or a digital display. ▸ informal a measuring device resembling a clock, such as a speedometer. **2** the downy spherical seed head of a dandelion. ■ v. informal **1** attain or register (a specified time, distance, or speed). ▸ achieve (a victory). **2** (**clock in/out**) or Brit. **on/off** register by means of an automatic recording clock one's arrival at or departure from work. **3** informal hit on the head.
– PHRASES **round** (or **around**) **the clock** all day and all night. **turn** (or **put**) **back the clock** return to the past or to a previous way of doing things.
– DERIVATIVES **clocker** n.
– ORIGIN Middle English: from Middle Low German and Middle Dutch *klocke*, from medieval Latin *clocca* 'bell'.

clock[2] ■ n. an ornamental pattern woven or embroidered on the side of a stocking or sock near the ankle.
– ORIGIN C16.

clock golf ■ n. a lawn game in which the players putt to a hole in the centre of a circle from successive points on its circumference.

clock radio ■ n. a combined bedside radio and alarm clock.

clock speed ■ n. the operating speed of a computer or its microprocessor, expressed in cycles per second (megahertz).

clock tower ■ n. a tower, especially that of a church or civic building, displaying a large clock.

clock-watch ■ v. take care not to work more than the hours prescribed.
– DERIVATIVES **clock-watcher** n. **clock-watching** n.

clockwise ■ adv. & adj. in a curve corresponding in direction to the movement of the hands of a clock.

clockwork ■ n. a mechanism with a spring and toothed gearwheels, used to drive a mechanical clock, toy, or other device.
– PHRASES **like clockwork** very smoothly and easily.

clod ■ n. **1** a lump of earth or clay. **2** informal a stupid person.
– ORIGIN Middle English: var. of CLOT.

cloddish ■ adj. foolish, awkward, or clumsy.
– DERIVATIVES **cloddishly** adv. **cloddishness** n.

clodhopper ■ n. informal **1** a large, heavy shoe. **2** a foolish, awkward, or clumsy person.
– DERIVATIVES **clodhopping** adj.

clog ■ n. **1** a shoe with a thick wooden sole. **2** an encumbrance. ■ v. (**clogged**, **clogging**) (often **clog up**) block or become blocked with something thick or sticky.
– ORIGIN Middle English (in the sense 'block of wood to impede an animal's movement').

clog dance ■ n. a traditional dance for which clogs are worn.
– DERIVATIVES **clog dancer** n. **clog dancing** n.

cloggy ■ adj. (**-ier**, **-iest**) thick, lumpy, or sticky.

cloisonné /ˈklwɑːzɒneɪ, -ˈzɒneɪ/ ■ n. enamel work in which different colours are separated by strips of flattened wire placed edgeways on a metal backing.
– ORIGIN C19: French, 'partitioned', from *cloisonner*, from *cloison* 'division'.

cloister /ˈklɔɪstə/ ■ n. **1** a covered, and typically colonnaded, passage round an open court in a convent, monastery, college, or cathedral. **2** a convent or monastery. ▸ (**the cloister**) monastic life. ■ v. seclude or shut up in a convent or monastery.
– ORIGIN Middle English: from Old French *cloistre*, from Latin *claustrum* 'lock, enclosed place', from *claudere* 'to close'.

cloistered ■ adj. **1** having or enclosed by a cloister. **2** sheltered from the outside world: *a cloistered upbringing*.

clomiphene /ˈklɒmɪfiːn/ ■ n. Medicine a synthetic non-steroidal drug used to treat infertility in women by stimulating ovulation.
– ORIGIN C20: from *chlo(ro-)* + *(a)mi(ne)* + *phen(yl)*.

clomp ■ v. walk with a heavy tread. ■ n. the sound of a heavy tread.
– ORIGIN C19: imitative; cf. CLUMP.

clone ■ n. **1** Biology an organism or cell, or a group of organisms or cells, produced asexually from one ancestor to which they are genetically identical. **2** a person or thing regarded as identical with another; a copy or double. ■ v. **1** propagate (an organism or cell) as a clone. ▸ Biochemistry replicate (a fragment of DNA placed in an organism). **2** make an identical copy of. **3** illegally copy the security codes from (a cellphone) to others as a way of obtaining free calls.
– DERIVATIVES **clonal** adj.
– ORIGIN C20: from Greek *klōn* 'twig'.

clonus /ˈkləʊnəs/ ■ n. Medicine muscular spasm involving repeated, often rhythmic, contractions.
– DERIVATIVES **clonic** adj.
– ORIGIN C19: from Greek *klonos* 'turmoil'.

clop ■ n. a sound made by a horse's hooves on a hard surface. ■ v. (**clopped**, **clopping**) move with such a sound.

cloqué /ˈklɒkeɪ/ ■ n. a fabric with an irregularly raised or embossed surface.
– ORIGIN French, 'blistered'.

close¹ /kləʊs/ ■ adj. **1** only a short distance away or apart in space or time. ▸ dense: *close print*. ▸ (**close to**) very near to (being or doing something). **2** denoting someone who is part of a person's immediate family, typically a parent or sibling. ▸ (of a connection or resemblance) strong. **3** (of a relationship or the people conducting it) very affectionate or intimate. **4** (of observation or examination) done in a careful and thorough way. **5** (of information) carefully guarded: *a close secret*. ▸ (of a person) not willing to give away money or information. **6** uncomfortably humid or airless. **7** Phonetics another term for HIGH (sense 7). ■ adv. so as to be very near; with very little space between. ■ n. **1** a residential street without through access. **2** Brit. the precinct surrounding a cathedral. **3** Scottish an entry from the street to a common stairway or to a court at the back of a building.
– PHRASES **close-fisted** unwilling to spend money; mean. **close-knit** (of a group of people) united or bound together by strong relationships and common interests. **close-mouthed** reticent; discreet. **at** (or **from**) **close quarters** (or **range**) close to or from a position close to someone or something. **close-run** (of a contest or objective) won or lost by a very small margin. **close shave** (also **close call**) informal a narrow escape from danger or disaster.
– DERIVATIVES **closely** adv. **closeness** n. **closish** adj.
– ORIGIN Middle English: from Old French *clos*, from Latin *clausum* 'enclosure' and *clausus* 'closed', from *claudere*.

close² /kləʊz/ ■ v. **1** move so as to cover an opening. **2** (also **close something up**) bring two parts of (something) together. ▸ grow or cause to grow smaller; make or become blocked: *she felt her throat close up*. **3** (**close on/in on/up on**) gradually get nearer to or surround. ▸ (**close with**) come near, especially so as to engage with (an enemy force). ▸ (**close in**) (of days) get successively shorter with the approach of the winter solstice. **4** (**close around/over**) encircle and hold. **5** make (an electric circuit) continuous. **6** bring or come to an end. ▸ finish speaking or writing. ▸ (often **close down/up**) (of a business or other organization) cease to be open to the public or in operation. ▸ bring (a transaction or arrangement) to a conclusion. ▸ (**close something out**) N. Amer. bring something to an end. ■ n. **1** the end of an event or of a period of time or activity. **2** the shutting of a door, window, etc.
– DERIVATIVES **closable** adj. **closer** n. **closing** adj.
– ORIGIN Middle English: from Old French *clore*, from Latin *claudere* 'to shut'.

close corporation ■ n. S. African a business registered in terms of the Close Corporations Act of 1984, consisting of not more than ten members who share its ownership and management.

closed ■ adj. **1** not open or allowing access. **2** not communicating with or influenced by others. **3** Mathematics (of a set) having the property that the result of a specified operation on any element of the set is itself a member of the set. **4** Geometry (of a curve or figure) formed from a single unbroken line. **5** Phonetics (of a syllable) ending in a consonant.
– PHRASES **behind closed doors** taking place secretly. **a closed book** a subject or person about which one knows nothing.

closed caption chiefly N. Amer. ■ n. one of a series of subtitles to a television programme, accessible through a decoder. ■ v. (**closed-caption**) [usu. as noun **closed-captioning**] provide (a programme) with such captions.
– DERIVATIVES **closed-captioned** adj.

closed-circuit television ■ n. a television system in which the video signals are transmitted from one or more cameras by cable to a restricted set of monitors.

closed-end ■ adj. S. African & N. Amer. denoting an investment trust or company that issues a fixed number of shares.

closed season (also Brit. **close season**) ■ n. **1** a period between specified dates when fishing or the killing of particular game is officially forbidden. **2** a part of the year when a particular sport is not played.

closed shop ■ n. a place of work where all employees must belong to an agreed trade union.

close harmony ■ n. Music harmony in which the notes of the chord are close together, typically in vocal music.

VOWELS　a cat　ɑː arm　ɛ bed　ɛː hair　ə ago　əː her　ɪ sit　i cosy　iː see　ɒ hot　ɔː saw　ʌ run

close-hauled ■ adj. & adv. Nautical with the sails hauled aft to sail close to the wind.

close season ■ n. Brit. another term for **CLOSED SEASON**.

closet ■ n. **1** chiefly N. Amer. a tall cupboard or wardrobe. **2** a small room. **3** archaic a toilet. **4** (**the closet**) (especially with reference to homosexuality) a state of secrecy or concealment. **5** [as modifier] secret; covert: *a closet socialist*. ■ v. (**closeted**, **closeting**) shut away in private conference or study. ▶ [as adj. **closeted**] keeping something secret.
– ORIGIN Middle English: from Old French, diminutive of *clos* (see **CLOSE**[1]).

close-up ■ n. a photograph or film sequence taken at close range and showing the subject on a large scale.

clostridium /klɒˈstrɪdɪəm/ ■ n. (pl. **clostridia** /-dɪə/) Biology an anaerobic bacterium of a large genus that includes many pathogenic species, e.g. those causing tetanus and botulism.
– DERIVATIVES **clostridial** adj.
– ORIGIN from Greek *klōstēr* 'spindle'.

closure ■ n. **1** an act or process of closing something. **2** a device that closes or seals something. **3** (in a legislative assembly) a procedure for ending a debate and taking a vote. **4** a feeling that an emotional or traumatic experience has been resolved. ■ v. apply the closure to (a debate or speaker) in a legislative assembly.
– ORIGIN Middle English: from late Latin *clausura*, from *claudere* 'to close'.

clot ■ n. **1** a thick mass of coagulated liquid, especially blood, or of material stuck together. **2** Brit. informal a foolish or clumsy person. ■ v. (**clotted**, **clotting**) form or cause to form into clots. ▶ cover with sticky matter.
– ORIGIN Old English, of Germanic origin.

cloth ■ n. (pl. **cloths**) **1** woven, knitted, or felted fabric made from a soft fibre such as wool or cotton. **2** a piece of cloth for a particular purpose. **3** (**the cloth**) the clergy; the clerical profession.
– ORIGIN Old English *clāth*.

cloth cap ■ n. Brit. a man's flat woollen cap with a peak.
▶ [as modifier] relating to or associated with the working class: *Labour's traditional cloth-cap image*.

clothe ■ v. (past and past part. **clothed** or archaic or poetic/literary **clad**) (often **be clothed in**) put clothes on; dress.
▶ provide (someone) with clothes.
– ORIGIN Old English (only in the past participle *geclāded*).

clothes ■ pl. n. items worn to cover the body.
– ORIGIN Old English *clāthas*, pl. of *clāth*.

clothes horse ■ n. **1** a frame on which washed clothes are hung to dry. **2** informal a person who wears or models fashionable clothes.

clothes line ■ n. a rope or wire on which washed clothes are hung to dry.

clothes moth ■ n. a small drab moth whose larvae can be destructive to textile fibres. [*Tineola bisselliella* and related species.]

clothes peg (also N. Amer. **clothespin**) ■ n. a clip or forked device for securing clothes to a clothes line.

clothier /ˈkləʊðɪə/ ■ n. a person who makes or sells clothes or cloth.
– ORIGIN Middle English *clother*, from **CLOTH**.

clothing ■ n. clothes collectively.

cloth of gold ■ n. fabric made of wool or silk interwoven with gold threads.

clotted cream ■ n. chiefly Brit. thick cream obtained by heating milk slowly and then allowing it to cool while the cream content rises to the top in coagulated lumps.

clotting factor ■ n. Physiology any of a number of substances in blood plasma which are involved in the clotting process, such as factor VIII.

cloud ■ n. **1** a visible mass of condensed watery vapour floating in the atmosphere, typically high above the general level of the ground. ▶ an indistinct or billowing mass of smoke, dust, or something consisting of numerous particles. ▶ an opaque patch within a transparent substance. **2** an oppressive burden of gloom or anxiety. ■ v. **1** (usu. **cloud over**) (of the sky) become full of clouds. **2** make or become less clear or transparent. **3** (of someone's face or eyes) become expressive of sadness, anxiety, or anger. **4** make unclear or uncertain.
– PHRASES **in** (or **with one's head in**) **the clouds** full of idealistic dreams; out of touch with reality. **on cloud nine** (or **seven**) extremely happy. [with ref. to a ten-part classification of clouds in which 'nine' was next to the highest.] **under a cloud** under suspicion or discredited.
– DERIVATIVES **cloudless** adj. **cloudlessly** adv. **cloudlet** n.
– ORIGIN Old English *clūd* 'mass of rock or earth'.

cloud base ■ n. the level or altitude of the lowest part of a general mass of clouds.

cloudberry ■ n. (pl. -**ies**) a dwarf bramble with white flowers and edible orange fruit, growing on high, open land. [*Rubus chamaemorus*.]
– ORIGIN C16: prob. from the noun **CLOUD** in the obsolete sense 'hill' + **BERRY**.

cloudburst ■ n. a sudden violent rainstorm.

cloud cover ■ n. a mass of cloud covering all or most of the sky.

cloud cuckoo land ■ n. a state of unrealistic or absurdly over-optimistic fantasy.
– ORIGIN C19: translation of Greek *Nephelokokkugia*, the name of a city built by the birds in Aristophanes' comedy *Birds*, from *nephelē* 'cloud' + *kokkux* 'cuckoo'.

clouded leopard ■ n. a large spotted cat found in forests in SE Asia. [*Neofelis nebulosa*.]

clouded yellow ■ n. a migratory butterfly which has yellowish wings with black margins. [*Colias electo* and related species.]

cloudy ■ adj. (-**ier**, -**iest**) **1** (of the sky or weather) covered with or characterized by clouds. **2** (of a liquid) not transparent or clear. **3** uncertain or unclear.
– DERIVATIVES **cloudily** adv. **cloudiness** n.

clout ■ n. **1** informal a heavy blow. **2** informal influence or power. **3** archaic a piece of cloth or clothing. **4** Archery a large target placed flat on the ground with a flag marking its centre and used in long-distance shooting. **5** (also **clout nail**) a nail with a large, flat head, used especially in securing roofing felt. ■ v. informal hit hard.
– ORIGIN Old English *clūt* 'a patch or metal plate'.

clove[1] ■ n. **1** the dried flower bud of a tropical tree, used as a pungent aromatic spice. ▶ (**oil of cloves**) aromatic analgesic oil extracted from these buds and used medicinally, especially for the relief of dental pain. **2** the Indonesian tree from which these buds are obtained. [*Syzygium aromaticum* (also called *Eugenia caryophyllus*).] **3** (also **clove pink** or **clove gillyflower**) a clove-scented pink which is the original type from which the carnation and other double pinks have been bred. [*Dianthus caryophyllus*.]
– ORIGIN Middle English: from Old French *clou de girofle* 'nail of gillyflower' (from its shape), **GILLYFLOWER** being orig. the name of the spice and later applied to the pink.

clove[2] ■ n. any of the small bulbs making up a compound bulb of garlic, shallot, etc.
– ORIGIN Old English, of Germanic origin.

clove[3] past of **CLEAVE**[1].

clove hitch ■ n. a knot by which a rope is secured by passing it twice round a spar or another rope that it crosses at right angles in such a way that both ends pass under the loop of rope at the front.
– ORIGIN C18: *clove*, past tense of **CLEAVE**[1] (because the rope appears as separate parallel lines at the back of the knot).

cloven past participle of **CLEAVE**[1].

cloven hoof (also **cloven foot**) ■ n. the divided hoof or foot of ruminants such as cattle, sheep, goats, antelopes, and deer.
– DERIVATIVES **cloven-hoofed** adj.

clover ■ n. a herbaceous leguminous plant with dense white or red globular flower heads and leaves which are typically three-lobed. [Genus *Trifolium*: many species.]
– PHRASES **in clover** in ease and luxury.
– ORIGIN Old English, of Germanic origin.

cloverleaf ■ n. chiefly N. Amer. a junction of roads intersecting at different levels and forming the pattern of a four-leaved clover.

Clovis /ˈkləʊvɪs/ ■ n. [as modifier] Archaeology denoting a

clown

Palaeo-Indian culture of Central and North America, dated to about 11 500–11 000 years ago and earlier.
– ORIGIN named after *Clovis* in New Mexico.

clown ■ n. **1** a comic entertainer, especially one in a circus, wearing a traditional costume and exaggerated make-up. **2** a playful, extrovert person. **3** archaic an unsophisticated country person. ■ v. act comically or playfully.
– DERIVATIVES **clownish** adj. **clownishly** adv. **clownishness** n.
– ORIGIN C16: perhaps of Low German origin.

clownfish ■ n. (pl. same or **-fishes**) a small, brightly coloured tropical fish that lives in close association with sea anemones. [*Amphiprion percula* and other species.]

cloy ■ v. [usu. as adj. **cloying**] disgust or sicken with an excess of sweetness, richness, or sentiment.
– DERIVATIVES **cloyingly** adv.
– ORIGIN Middle English: shortening of obsolete *accloy* 'stop up, choke', from Old French *encloyer* 'drive a nail into'.

cloze test /kləʊz/ ■ n. a procedure in which a subject is asked to supply words that have been removed from a passage as a test of their ability to comprehend text.
– ORIGIN 1950s: *cloze* representing a spoken abbrev. of CLOSURE.

club¹ ■ n. **1** an association dedicated to a particular interest or activity. ▸ an organization constituted to play matches in a particular sport. **2** an organization offering members social amenities, meals, and temporary residence. **3** a nightclub with dance music. ■ v. (**clubbed**, **clubbing**) **1** (**club together**) combine with others to do something, especially to collect a sum of money. **2** informal go out to nightclubs.
– DERIVATIVES **clubber** n. **clubbing** n.
– ORIGIN C17: prob. from CLUB².

club² ■ n. **1** a heavy stick with a thick end, used as a weapon. **2** (also **golf club**) a club used to hit the ball in golf, with a heavy wooden or metal head on a slender shaft. **3** (**clubs**) one of the four suits in a conventional pack of playing cards, denoted by a black trefoil. ▸ a card of such a suit. ■ v. (**clubbed**, **clubbing**) beat with a club or similar implement.
– ORIGIN Middle English: from Old Norse *clubba*, var. of *klumba*; rel. to CLUMP.

club car ■ n. chiefly N. Amer. a railway carriage equipped with a lounge and other amenities.

club class ■ n. Brit. the intermediate class of seating on an aircraft, designed especially for business travellers.

club foot ■ n. a deformed foot which is twisted so that the sole cannot be placed flat on the ground.
– DERIVATIVES **club-footed** adj.

clubhouse ■ n. a building having a bar and other facilities for the members of a club.

clubmoss ■ n. a low-growing flowerless plant belonging to a group of pteridophytes resembling large mosses. [Class Lycopsida: many species.]

clubroot ■ n. a fungal disease of cabbages, turnips, etc. in which the root becomes swollen and distorted.

club sandwich ■ n. a sandwich consisting typically of chicken and bacon, tomato, and lettuce, layered between three slices of bread.

club soda ■ n. trademark North American term for SODA (in sense 1).

cluck ■ n. **1** the characteristic short, guttural sound made by a hen. **2** N. Amer. informal a silly or foolish person. ■ v. **1** (of a hen) make a cluck. **2** (**cluck over/around**) express fussy concern about.
– DERIVATIVES **clucky** adj.
– ORIGIN C15: imitative.

clue ■ n. a fact or piece of evidence serving to reveal a hidden truth or solve a problem. ■ v. (**clues**, **clued**, **clueing**) (**clue someone in**) informal inform someone about a particular matter.
– PHRASES **not have a clue** informal know nothing about something or about how to do something.
– ORIGIN Middle English (orig. 'a ball of thread', hence one used to guide a person out of a labyrinth): var. of CLEW.

clued-up (also chiefly N. Amer. **clued-in**) ■ adj. informal well informed about a particular subject.

clueless ■ adj. informal having no knowledge, understanding, or ability.
– DERIVATIVES **cluelessly** adv. **cluelessness** n.

clump ■ n. **1** a small group of trees or plants growing closely together. ▸ a compacted mass or lump of something. ▸ Physiology an agglutinated mass of blood cells or bacteria, especially as an indicator of the presence of an antibody to them. **2** another term for CLOMP. ■ v. **1** form into a clump or mass. **2** another term for CLOMP.
– ORIGIN Middle English (denoting a heap or lump): partly imitative.

clumpy ■ adj. (**-ier**, **-iest**) **1** (of shoes or boots) heavy and inelegant. **2** forming or showing a tendency to form clumps.

clumsy ■ adj. (**-ier**, **-iest**) awkward in movement or performance. ▸ tactless. ▸ unwieldy.
– DERIVATIVES **clumsily** adv. **clumsiness** n.
– ORIGIN C16: from obsolete *clumse* 'make or be numb', prob. of Scandinavian origin.

clung past and past participle of CLING.

clunk ■ n. a dull, heavy sound such as that made by thick pieces of metal striking together. ■ v. move with or make a clunk.
– ORIGIN C18 (orig. Scots): imitative; cf. CLANK.

clunky ■ adj. (**-ier**, **-iest**) informal **1** chiefly N. Amer. solid, heavy, and old-fashioned. ▸ (of shoes) clumpy. **2** making a clunking sound.

clupeoid /ˈkluːpɔɪd/ ■ adj. Zoology relating to or denoting fish of an order (Clupeiformes) including the herrings and anchovies.
– ORIGIN C19: from Latin *clupea*, the name of a river fish.

cluster ■ n. **1** a group of similar things positioned or occurring closely together. **2** a natural subgroup of a population, used for statistical sampling or analysis. **3** Chemistry a group of atoms of the same element, typically a metal, bonded closely together in a molecule. ■ v. **1** form a cluster. **2** Statistics (of data points) have similar numerical values.
– DERIVATIVES **clustered** adj.
– ORIGIN Old English *clyster*; prob. rel. to CLOT.

cluster bean ■ n. another term for GUAR.

cluster bomb ■ n. a bomb which releases a number of projectiles on impact.

cluster pine ■ n. another term for MARITIME PINE.

clutch¹ ■ v. grasp tightly. ■ n. **1** a tight grasp. **2** (**clutches**) power; control: *she was about to fall into his clutches*. **3** a mechanism for connecting and disconnecting the engine and the transmission system in a vehicle, or the working parts of any machine.
– ORIGIN Middle English: var. of obsolete *clitch* 'close the hand', from Old English *clyccan* 'crook, clench', of Germanic origin.

clutch² ■ n. **1** a group of eggs fertilized at the same time, laid in a single session and (in birds) incubated together. ▸ a brood of chicks. **2** a small group of people or things.
– ORIGIN C18: prob. a var. of northern English dialect *cletch*, rel. to Middle English *cleck* 'to hatch', from Old Norse *klekja*.

clutch bag ■ n. a slim, flat handbag without handles or a strap.

clutter ■ n. things lying about untidily. ▸ an untidy state. ■ v. cover or fill with clutter.
– ORIGIN Middle English: var. of dialect *clotter* 'to clot', influenced by CLUSTER.

Clydesdale ■ n. **1** a horse of a heavy, powerful British breed, used for pulling heavy loads. **2** a dog of a small breed of terrier.
– ORIGIN from the name of the river *Clyde* in Scotland, in the area of which they were orig. bred.

clypeus /ˈklɪpɪəs/ ■ n. (pl. **clypei** /-pɪaɪ/) Entomology a broad plate at the front of an insect's head.
– DERIVATIVES **clypeal** adj.
– ORIGIN C19: from Latin, 'round shield'.

Cm ■ symb. the chemical element curium.

cm ■ abbrev. centimetre(s).

Cmdr ■ abbrev. Commander.

Cmdre ■ abbrev. Commodore.

CMG ■ abbrev. (in the UK) Companion (of the Order) of St Michael and St George.

CMOS ■ n. Electronics a technology for making low-power integrated circuits. ▸ a chip based on such technology.
– ORIGIN 1980s: from *Complementary Metal Oxide Semiconductor*.

Cn ■ symb. the chemical element copernicium.

Cnidaria /(k)nʌɪˈdɛːrɪə/ ■ pl. n. Zoology a phylum of aquatic invertebrate animals that comprises the coelenterates.
– DERIVATIVES **cnidarian** n. & adj.
– ORIGIN from Greek *knidē* 'nettle'.

CNN ■ abbrev. Cable News Network.

CO ■ abbrev. Commanding Officer.

Co ■ symb. the chemical element cobalt.

Co. ■ abbrev. **1** company. **2** county.

c/o ■ abbrev. care of.

co- /kəʊ/ ■ prefix **1** (forming nouns) joint; mutual; common: *co-driver*. **2** (forming adjectives) jointly; mutually: *coequal*. **3** (forming verbs) together with another or others: *co-produce*. **4** Mathematics of the complement of an angle: *cosine*. ▸ the complement of: *co-latitude*.
– ORIGIN from Latin, orig. a form of **COM-**.

coacervate /kəʊˈasəveɪt/ ■ n. Chemistry a colloid-rich viscous liquid phase which may separate from a colloidal solution on addition of a third component.
– ORIGIN C20: back-formation from *coacervation*, from Latin *cum* '(together) with' + *acervus* 'heap'.

coach[1] ■ n. **1** a comfortably equipped single-decker bus used for longer journeys. **2** a railway carriage. **3** [as modifier] N. Amer. denoting economy-class seating in an aircraft or train. **4** chiefly historical a closed horse-drawn carriage.
– ORIGIN C16: from French *coche*, from Hungarian *kocsi (szekér)* '(wagon) from *Kocs*', a town in Hungary.

coach[2] ■ n. **1** an instructor or trainer in sport. **2** a tutor who gives private or specialized teaching. ■ v. train or teach as a coach.
– ORIGIN C18: figuratively from **COACH**[1].

coach-built ■ adj. (of a vehicle) having specially or individually built bodywork.
– DERIVATIVES **coachbuilder** n.

coach house ■ n. a building formerly used for the storage of coaches.

coaching inn ■ n. Brit. historical an inn along a route followed by horse-drawn coaches, at which horses could be changed.

coachman ■ n. (pl. **-men**) historical a driver of a horse-drawn carriage.

coachwork ■ n. the bodywork of a road or railway vehicle.

coadjutor /kəʊˈadʒʊtə/ ■ n. Christian Church a bishop appointed to assist and often to succeed a diocesan bishop.
– ORIGIN Middle English: from late Latin, from **CO-** + *adjutor* 'assistant'.

coagulant /kəʊˈagjʊlənt/ ■ n. a substance that causes coagulation.

coagulase /kəʊˈagjʊleɪz, -s/ ■ n. Biochemistry a bacterial enzyme which brings about the coagulation of blood or plasma and is produced by disease-causing forms of staphylococcus.

coagulate /kəʊˈagjʊleɪt/ ■ v. (of a fluid, especially blood) change to a solid or semi-solid state.
– DERIVATIVES **coagulable** adj. **coagulation** n. **coagulative** adj. **coagulator** n.
– ORIGIN Middle English: from Latin *coagulare* 'curdle'.

coal ■ n. **1** a combustible black rock consisting mainly of carbonized plant matter and used as fuel. **2** (usu. **coals**) the glowing embers of a wood or charcoal fire.
– PHRASES **coals to Newcastle** something supplied to a place where it is already plentiful. **haul someone over the coals** reprimand someone severely.
– ORIGIN Old English, of Germanic origin.

coalesce /ˌkəʊəˈlɛs/ ■ v. come or bring together to form one mass or whole.

223 **coati**

– DERIVATIVES **coalescence** n. **coalescent** adj.
– ORIGIN C16: from Latin *coalescere*, from **CO-** + *alescere* 'grow up'.

coalface ■ n. an exposed surface of coal in a mine.
– PHRASES **at the coalface** engaged in work at an active rather than theoretical level in a particular field.

coalfield ■ n. an extensive area containing a number of underground coal strata.

coal gas ■ n. a mixture of gases (chiefly hydrogen, methane, and carbon monoxide) obtained by distilling coal and formerly used for lighting and heating.

coalition /ˌkəʊəˈlɪʃ(ə)n/ ■ n. a temporary alliance, especially of political parties forming a government.
– DERIVATIVES **coalitionist** n.
– ORIGIN C17: from medieval Latin *coalitio(n-)*, from Latin *coalescere* (see **COALESCE**).

coal measures ■ pl. n. Geology a series of strata of the Carboniferous period, including coal seams.

Coalport ■ n. a kind of porcelain produced at Coalport in Shropshire, England, from the late 18th century.

coal tar ■ n. a thick black liquid produced by distilling bituminous coal, containing organic chemicals including benzene, naphthalene, phenols, and aniline.

coaming /ˈkəʊmɪŋ/ (also **coamings**) ■ n. a raised border round the cockpit or hatch of a yacht or other boat to keep out water.
– ORIGIN C17.

coarctate /kəʊˈɑːkteɪt/ ■ adj. chiefly Anatomy & Biology compressed; contracted.
– ORIGIN Middle English: from Latin *coarctare* 'press or draw together'.

coarctation ■ n. Medicine congenital narrowing of a short section of the aorta.

coarse ■ adj. **1** rough or harsh in texture; unrefined. ▸ consisting of large grains or particles. **2** (of a person's features) not elegantly formed or proportioned. **3** (of a person or their speech) rude or vulgar.
– DERIVATIVES **coarsely** adv. **coarseness** n. **coarsish** adj.
– ORIGIN Middle English ('ordinary or inferior'): perhaps rel. to **COURSE**.

coarse fish ■ n. (pl. same) any freshwater fish other than salmon and trout. Compare with **GAME FISH**.

coarsen ■ v. make or become coarse.

coast ■ n. **1** the part of the land adjoining or near the sea. **2** the easy movement of a vehicle without the use of power. ■ v. **1** move easily without using power. ▸ act or make progress with little effort: *they coasted to victory*. **2** sail along the coast.
– PHRASES **the coast is clear** there is no danger of being observed or caught.
– DERIVATIVES **coastal** adj. **coastwise** adj. & adv.
– ORIGIN Middle English: from Old French *coste* (n.), *costeier* (v.), from Latin *costa* 'rib, flank, side'.

coaster ■ n. **1** a ship carrying cargo along the coast from port to port. **2** a small mat for a glass.

coastguard ■ n. a person or organization that keeps watch over coastal waters to assist people or ships in danger and to prevent smuggling.

coastline ■ n. a length of coast, with reference to its shape or character: *a rugged coastline*.

coat ■ n. **1** a full-length outer garment with sleeves. **2** an animal's covering of fur or hair. **3** an enclosing or covering layer or structure. **4** a single application of paint or similar material. ■ v. provide with or form a layer or covering.
– DERIVATIVES **-coated** adj.
– ORIGIN Middle English: from Old French *cote*.

coat dress ■ n. a woman's tailored dress that resembles a coat.

coati /kəʊˈɑːti/ ■ n. (pl. **coatis**) a raccoon-like animal found in Central and South America, with a long flexible snout and a ringed tail. [Genera *Nasua* and *Nasuella*.]
– ORIGIN C17: from Tupi *kua'ti*, from *cua* 'belt' + *tim* 'nose'.

coatimundi /ˌkəʊəˌtiːˈmʌndi/ ■ n. (pl. **coatimundis**) another term for COATI.
– ORIGIN C17: from Tupi *kuatimu'ne*, from *kua'ti* (see COATI) + *mu'ne* 'snare or trick'.

coating ■ n. a thin layer or covering of something.

coat of arms ■ n. the distinctive heraldic bearings or shield of a person, family, corporation, or country.

coat of mail ■ n. historical a jacket composed of metal rings or plates, serving as armour.

coat-tail ■ n. each of the flaps formed by the back of a tailcoat.

co-author ■ n. a joint author. ■ v. be a joint author of.

coax /kəʊks/ ■ v. persuade (someone) gradually or by flattery to do something. ▸ use such persuasion to obtain (something). ▸ manipulate (something) carefully into a particular situation or position.
– DERIVATIVES **coaxer** n. **coaxing** adj. **coaxingly** adv.
– ORIGIN C16 ('pet, fondle'): from obsolete *cokes* 'simpleton'.

coaxial /kəʊˈaksɪəl/ ■ adj. **1** having a common axis. **2** (of a cable or line) transmitting by means of two concentric conductors separated by an insulator.
– DERIVATIVES **coaxially** adv.

cob[1] ■ n. **1** short for CORNCOB. ▸ S. African informal a quantity of dagga wrapped in maize leaves. **2** a powerfully built, short-legged horse. **3** a male swan.
– ORIGIN Middle English (denoting a strong man).

cob[2] ■ n. variant spelling of KOB[1].

cobalamin /kə(ʊ)ˈbaləmɪn/ ■ n. Biochemistry any of a group of cobalt-containing substances including cyanocobalamin (vitamin B_{12}).
– ORIGIN 1950s: blend of COBALT and VITAMIN.

cobalt /ˈkəʊbɔːlt, -ɒlt/ ■ n. the chemical element of atomic number 27, a hard silvery-white magnetic metal. (Symbol: **Co**)
– DERIVATIVES **cobaltic** /kə(ʊ)ˈbɔːltɪk, -ˈbɒlt-/ adj. **cobaltous** /kə(ʊ)ˈbɔːltəs, -ˈbɒlt-/ adj.
– ORIGIN C17: from German *Kobalt* 'imp, demon' (from the belief that cobalt was harmful to the ores with which it occurred).

cobalt blue ■ n. a deep blue pigment containing cobalt and aluminium oxides.

cobber ■ n. Austral./NZ informal a companion or friend.
– ORIGIN C19: perhaps rel. to English dialect *cob* 'take a liking to'.

cobble[1] ■ n. (also **cobblestone**) a small round stone used to cover road surfaces.
– DERIVATIVES **cobbled** adj.
– ORIGIN Middle English: from COB[1].

cobble[2] ■ v. (**cobble something together**) roughly assemble something from available parts or elements.
– ORIGIN C15: back-formation from COBBLER.

cobbler ■ n. **1** a person whose job is mending shoes. **2** an iced drink made with wine or sherry, sugar, and lemon. **3** chiefly N. Amer. a fruit pie with a rich, cake-like crust. **4** (**cobblers**) Brit. informal a man's testicles. [from rhyming slang *cobbler's awls* 'balls'.] ▸ nonsense.
– ORIGIN Middle English.

cobby ■ adj. (of a horse or other animal) stocky.
– ORIGIN C17: from COB[1].

co-belligerent ■ n. any of two or more nations engaged in war as allies.
– DERIVATIVES **co-belligerence** n.

cobia /ˈkəʊbɪə/ ■ n. (pl. same) a large edible game fish living in the open ocean. [*Rachycentron canadum*.]
– ORIGIN C19.

COBOL /ˈkəʊbɒl/ ■ n. a computer programming language designed for use in commerce.
– ORIGIN 1960s: from *co(mmon) b(usiness) o(riented) l(anguage)*.

cobra /ˈkəʊbrə, ˈkɒbrə/ ■ n. a highly venomous African or Asian snake that spreads the skin of its neck into a hood when disturbed. [*Naja nivea* (Cape cobra), *N. haje* (Egyptian cobra), and other species.]
– ORIGIN C17: from Portuguese *cobra de capello* 'snake with hood'.

cobweb ■ n. a spider's web, especially an old or dusty one.
– DERIVATIVES **cobwebbed** adj. **cobwebby** adj.
– ORIGIN Middle English: from obsolete *coppe* 'spider' + WEB.

coca /ˈkəʊkə/ ■ n. **1** a tropical American shrub grown for its leaves, which are the source of cocaine. [*Erythroxylum coca*.] **2** the dried leaves of this shrub mixed with lime and chewed as a stimulant by the native people of western South America.
– ORIGIN C16: from Aymara *kuka* or Quechua *koka*.

cocaine /kə(ʊ)ˈkeɪn/ ■ n. an addictive drug derived from coca or prepared synthetically, used as an illegal stimulant and sometimes medicinally as a local anaesthetic.
– ORIGIN C19: from COCA.

coccidia /kɒkˈsɪdɪə/ ■ pl. n. Biology parasitic protozoans of a group responsible for toxoplasmosis and other diseases. [Suborder Eimeriorina.]
– DERIVATIVES **coccidian** adj. & n. **coccidiosis** n.
– ORIGIN C19: from Greek *kokkis*, diminutive of *kokkos* 'berry'.

coccolith /ˈkɒkəlɪθ/ ■ n. Biology a minute rounded calcareous platelet, numbers of which form the spherical shells of some planktonic flagellates (coccolithophores).
– ORIGIN C19: from Greek *kokkos* 'grain or berry' + *lithos* 'stone'.

coccyx /ˈkɒksɪks/ ■ n. (pl. **coccyges** /-ɪdʒiːz/ or **coccyxes**) a small triangular bone at the base of the spinal column in humans and some apes, formed of fused vestigial vertebrae.
– DERIVATIVES **coccygeal** /kɒkˈsɪdʒɪəl/ adj.
– ORIGIN C16: from Greek *kokkux* 'cuckoo' (because the shape of the human bone resembles the cuckoo's bill).

cochineal /ˌkɒtʃɪˈniːl, ˈkɒtʃɪniːl/ ■ n. **1** a scarlet dye used for colouring food, made from the crushed dried bodies of a female scale insect. **2** (**cochineal insect**) the scale insect that is used for cochineal, native to Mexico and formerly widely cultivated on cacti. [*Dactylopius coccus*.]
– ORIGIN C16: from French *cochenille* or Spanish *cochinilla*, from Latin *coccinus* 'scarlet'.

cochlea /ˈkɒklɪə/ ■ n. (pl. **cochleae** /-kliː/) the spiral cavity of the inner ear containing the organ of Corti, which produces nerve impulses in response to sound vibrations.
– DERIVATIVES **cochlear** adj.
– ORIGIN C16: from Latin, 'snail shell or screw'.

cock ■ n. **1** a male bird, especially of a domestic fowl. ▸ Brit. a male lobster, crab, or salmon. ▸ Brit. informal a friendly form of address among men. **2** vulgar slang a man's penis. **3** Brit. informal nonsense. **4** a firing lever in a gun which can be raised to be released by the trigger. **5** a stopcock. ■ v. **1** tilt (something) in a particular direction. ▸ bend (a limb or joint) at an angle. **2** raise the cock of (a gun) in order to make it ready for firing. **3** (**cock something up**) informal spoil or ruin something.
– PHRASES **at full cock** (of a gun) with the cock lifted to the position at which the trigger will act. **cock one's ear** (of a dog) raise its ears to an erect position. **cock one's eye** glance in a quizzical or knowing manner with a raised eyebrow. **cock of the walk** someone who dominates others within a group.
– ORIGIN Old English, from medieval Latin *coccus*; reinforced in Middle English by Old French *coq*.

cockade /kɒˈkeɪd/ ■ n. a rosette or knot of ribbons worn in a hat as a badge of office or as part of a livery.
– DERIVATIVES **cockaded** adj.
– ORIGIN C17: from French *cocarde*, orig. in *bonnet à la coquarde*, from the obsolete *coquard* 'saucy'.

cock-a-doodle-doo ■ exclam. used to represent the sound made by a cock when it crows.

cock-a-hoop ■ adj. extremely pleased.
– ORIGIN C17: from the phr. *set cock a hoop*, apparently denoting the action of turning on a tap and allowing liquor to flow.

cock-a-leekie ■ n. a soup traditionally made in Scotland with chicken and leeks.

cockamamie /ˈkɒkəˌmeɪmi/ (also **cockamamy**) ■ adj. informal, chiefly N. Amer. ridiculous; nonsensical.
– ORIGIN 1940s (denoting a design left by a transfer).

cock and bull story ■ n. informal a ridiculous and implausible story.

cockatiel /ˌkɒkəˈtiːl/ ■ n. a slender long-crested

Australian parrot related to the cockatoos, with a mainly grey body and a yellow and orange face. [*Nymphicus hollandicus*.]
– ORIGIN C19: from Dutch *kaketielje*, prob. a diminutive of *kaketoe* 'cockatoo'.

cockatoo /ˌkɒkəˈtuː/ ■ n. a parrot with an erectile crest, found in Australia, eastern Indonesia, and neighbouring islands. [Family Cacatuidae: numerous species.]
– ORIGIN C17: from Dutch *kaketoe*, from Malay *kakatua*.

cockatrice /ˈkɒkətrʌɪs, -trɪs/ ■ n. another term for BASILISK (in sense 1).
– ORIGIN Middle English: from Old French *cocatris*, from Latin *calcatrix* 'tracker', translating Greek *ikhneumōn* (see ICHNEUMON).

cockchafer /ˈkɒkˌtʃeɪfə/ ■ n. a large brown dusk-flying beetle which is a destructive plant pest. [*Melolontha melolontha*.]
– ORIGIN C18: from COCK (expressing size) + CHAFER.

cockcrow ■ n. poetic/literary dawn.

cocked hat ■ n. a brimless triangular hat pointed at the front, back, and top. ▸ historical a hat with a wide brim permanently turned up towards the crown.
– PHRASES **knock something into a cocked hat** utterly defeat or outdo something.

cockerel ■ n. a young domestic cock.
– ORIGIN Middle English: diminutive of COCK.

cocker spaniel ■ n. a small spaniel of a breed with a silky coat.
– ORIGIN C19: from COCK (because the dog was bred to flush game birds such as woodcock).

cock-eyed ■ adj. informal **1** crooked or askew; not level. ▸ absurd; impractical. **2** having a squint.

cockfighting ■ n. the sport (illegal in some countries) of setting two cocks to fight each other.
– DERIVATIVES **cockfight** n.

cockle[1] ■ n. **1** an edible burrowing bivalve mollusc with a strong ribbed shell. [Genus *Cardium*.] **2** (also **cockleshell**) poetic/literary a small shallow boat.
– PHRASES **warm the cockles of one's heart** give one a comforting feeling of contentment.
– ORIGIN Middle English: from Old French *coquille* 'shell', from Greek *konkhulion*, from *konkhē* 'conch'.

cockle[2] ■ v. wrinkle or pucker.
– ORIGIN C16: from French *coquiller* 'blister (bread in cooking)', from *coquille* (see COCKLE[1]).

cocklebur ■ n. a plant of the daisy family with broad leaves and burred fruits, native to tropical America. [*Xanthium strumarium*.]
– ORIGIN C19: from COCKLE[2] + BUR.

cockney /ˈkɒkni/ ■ n. (pl. **-eys**) a native of the East End of London, traditionally one born within hearing of Bow Bells. ▸ the dialect or accent typical of such people.
– DERIVATIVES **cockneyism** n.
– ORIGIN Middle English (denoting a pampered child, later a town-dweller regarded as affected or puny).

cockpit ■ n. **1** a compartment for the pilot and crew in an aircraft or spacecraft. ▸ the driver's compartment in a racing car. **2** a place where a battle or other conflict takes place.
– ORIGIN C16: from COCK + PIT[1]; from a C18 nautical use denoting an area in the aft lower deck where the wounded were taken, later coming to mean 'the 'pit' or well from which a yacht was steered'.

cockroach /ˈkɒkrəʊtʃ/ ■ n. a beetle-like scavenging insect with long antennae and legs, some kinds of which are household pests. [*Blatta orientalis* and other species, suborder Blattodea.]
– ORIGIN C17: from Spanish *cucaracha*.

cockscomb ■ n. **1** the crest or comb of a domestic cock. **2** (also **coxcomb**) a tropical plant with a crest of tiny yellow, orange, or red flowers. [*Celosia cristata*.]

cocksfoot ■ n. a pasture grass with broad leaves and green or purplish flowering spikes. [*Dactylis glomerata*.]

cockshy /ˈkɒkʃʌɪ/ ■ n. (pl. **-ies**) Brit. dated a target for throwing sticks or stones at as a game.
– ORIGIN from the original use of a replica of a cockerel as a target.

cocksure ■ adj. presumptuously or arrogantly confident.
– DERIVATIVES **cocksurely** adv. **cocksureness** n.

225

cod

– ORIGIN C16: from archaic *cock* (a euphemism for *God*) + SURE.

cocktail ■ n. **1** an alcoholic drink consisting of a spirit mixed with other ingredients, such as fruit juice. ▸ [as modifier] relating to or associated with cocktail drinking or formal social occasions: *a cocktail dress*. ▸ a dish consisting of small pieces of food, typically served as an hors d'oeuvre: *a prawn cocktail*. **2** a mixture of diverse substances or factors, especially when dangerous or unpleasant: *a potent cocktail of tranquillizers*.
– ORIGIN C17: from COCK + TAIL; denoting a horse with a docked tail, later a racehorse which was not a thoroughbred.

cock-up ■ n. informal something done badly or inefficiently.

cocky ■ adj. (**-ier**, **-iest**) conceited in a bold or cheeky way.
– DERIVATIVES **cockily** adv. **cockiness** n.
– ORIGIN C16 ('lecherous'): from COCK.

cocoa ■ n. a powder made from roasted and ground cacao seeds. ▸ a hot drink made from such a powder mixed with milk or water.
– ORIGIN C18: alteration of CACAO.

cocoa bean ■ n. a cacao seed.

cocoa butter ■ n. a fatty substance obtained from cocoa beans, used in making confectionery and cosmetics.

cocoanut ■ n. old-fashioned spelling of COCONUT.

coco de mer /ˌkəʊkəʊdəˈmeː/ ■ n. a tall palm tree native to the Seychelles, having an immense nut in a hard woody shell. [*Lodoicea maldivica*.]
– ORIGIN C19: from French *coco-de-mer* 'coco from the sea' (because the tree was first known from nuts found floating in the sea).

coconut ■ n. **1** the large oval brown seed of a tropical palm, consisting of a hard woody husk surrounded by fibre, lined with edible white flesh and containing a clear liquid (coconut milk). ▸ the flesh of a coconut, often shredded and used as food. **2** (also **coconut palm** or **tree**) the tall palm tree that yields this nut, and also other products such as copra and coir. [*Cocos nucifera*.] **3** S. African informal, derogatory a black or coloured person who is seen, especially by other black people, as wishing to be part of the white establishment.
– DERIVATIVES **coconutness** n.

coconut butter ■ n. a solid fat obtained from the flesh of the coconut, and used in the manufacture of soap, candles, ointment, etc.

coconut shy ■ n. Brit. a fairground sideshow where balls are thrown at coconuts in an attempt to knock them off stands.

cocoon /kəˈkuːn/ ■ n. **1** a silky case spun by the larvae of many insects for protection as pupae. ▸ something that envelops, especially in a protective or comforting way. **2** a covering that prevents the corrosion of metal equipment. ■ v. **1** wrap in a cocoon. **2** N. Amer. retreat from the stressful conditions of public life.
– DERIVATIVES **cocooner** n.
– ORIGIN C17: from French *cocon*, from medieval Provençal *coucoun* 'eggshell, cocoon', diminutive of *coca* 'shell'.

cocooning ■ n. the tendency to spend more of one's leisure time enjoying one's home.
– ORIGIN 1980s (orig. US).

cocopan /ˈkʊkʊpan/ ■ n. S. African Mining a small V-shaped tipper truck, usually on rails, used for transporting ore.
– ORIGIN 1910s: from isiZulu *ingqukumbana* 'stumpy wagon'.

cocotte /kɒˈkɒt/ ■ n. **1** (usu. in phr. **en cocotte**) a small casserole in which individual portions of food can be cooked and served. [C20: from French *cocasse*, from Latin *cucuma* 'cooking container'.] **2** dated a fashionable prostitute. [C19: French, from a child's name for a hen.]

COD ■ abbrev. cash on delivery.

cod ■ n. (pl. same) a large marine fish with a small barbel on the chin, important as a food fish. [*Gadus morhua* (N. Atlantic) and other species, family Gadidae.]
– ORIGIN Middle English: perhaps from Old English *cod*(*d*) 'bag', because of the fish's appearance.

ʊ put　uː too　ʌɪ my　aʊ how　eɪ day　əʊ no　ɪə near　ɔɪ boy　ʊə poor　ʌɪə fire　aʊə sour

coda /ˈkəʊdə/ ■ n. Music the concluding passage of a piece or movement, typically forming an addition to the basic structure.
– ORIGIN C18: Italian, from Latin *cauda* 'tail'.

coddle ■ v. **1** treat in an indulgent or overprotective way. **2** cook (an egg) in water below boiling point.
– DERIVATIVES **coddler** n.
– ORIGIN C16: sense 1 is prob. a dialect var. of obsolete *caudle* 'administer invalids' gruel'.

code ■ n. **1** a system of words, figures, or symbols used to represent others, especially for the purposes of secrecy. ▸ a series of letters or numbers assigned to something to classify or identify it. ▸ short for DIALLING CODE. **2** Computing program instructions. **3** a systematic collection of laws or statutes: *the penal code*. ▸ a set of conventions governing behaviour or activity in a particular sphere. **4** short for SPORTING CODE. ■ v. **1** convert into a code. ▸ assign a code to for purposes of classification or identification. **2** (**code for**) Biochemistry be the genetic code for (an amino acid or protein). ▸ be the genetic determiner of (a characteristic). **3** write code for (a computer program).
– DERIVATIVES **coder** n. **coding** n. & adj.
– ORIGIN Middle English: from Latin *codex*, *codic*- (see CODEX).

codec /ˈkəʊdɛk/ ■ n. Electronics a microchip that compresses data to enable faster transmission or decompresses received data.
– ORIGIN 1960s: blend of *coder* and *decoder*.

codeine /ˈkəʊdiːn, -diːɪn/ ■ n. Medicine a sleep-inducing and analgesic drug derived from morphine.
– ORIGIN C19: from Greek *kōdeia* 'poppy head'.

codependency ■ n. excessive emotional or psychological reliance on a partner, typically one with an illness or addiction who requires support.
– DERIVATIVES **codependence** n. **codependent** adj. & n.

Codesa /kəˈdɛsə/ (also **CODESA**) ■ n. (in South Africa) either of two all-party conventions held between 1991 and 1993 to draw up a new constitution and establish guidelines for the transition to democratic government.
– ORIGIN acronym from *Convention for a Democratic South Africa*.

codex /ˈkəʊdɛks/ ■ n. (pl. **codices** /ˈkəʊdɪsiːz, ˈkɒd-/ or **codexes**) **1** an ancient manuscript text in book form. **2** an official list of medicines, chemicals, etc.
– ORIGIN C16: from Latin, 'block of wood', later denoting a block split into tablets for writing on, hence a book.

codger ■ n. informal, derogatory an elderly man.
– ORIGIN C18: perhaps a var. of *cadger* (see CADGE).

codicil /ˈkɒdɪsɪl, ˈkəʊ-/ ■ n. an addition or supplement that explains, modifies, or revokes a will or part of one.
– DERIVATIVES **codicillary** /ˌkɒdɪˈsɪləri/ adj.
– ORIGIN Middle English: from Latin *codicillus*, diminutive of *codex* (see CODEX).

codify /ˈkəʊdɪfʌɪ/ ■ v. (**-ies**, **-ied**) organize (procedures or rules) into a system or code.
– DERIVATIVES **codification** n. **codifier** n.

codling moth ■ n. a small greyish moth whose larvae feed on apples. [*Cydia pomonella*.]

cod liver oil ■ n. oil pressed from the fresh liver of cod, which is rich in vitamins D and A.

codon /ˈkəʊdɒn/ ■ n. Biochemistry a sequence of three nucleotides which together form a unit of genetic code in a DNA or RNA molecule.
– ORIGIN 1960s: from CODE.

codpiece ■ n. a pouch to cover the genitals on a pair of man's breeches, worn in the 15th and 16th centuries.
– ORIGIN from earlier *cod* 'scrotum' (from Old English *codd* 'bag, pod') + PIECE.

codswallop ■ n. Brit. informal nonsense.
– ORIGIN 1960s: perhaps named after Hiram *Codd*, who invented a bottle for fizzy drinks (1875).

coecilian ■ n. variant spelling of CAECILIAN.

co-ed /ˈkəʊɛd, ˌkəʊˈɛd/ ■ adj. informal co-educational.

co-education ■ n. the education of pupils of both sexes together.
– DERIVATIVES **co-educational** adj.

coefficient /ˌkəʊɪˈfɪʃ(ə)nt/ ■ n. **1** Mathematics a numerical or constant quantity placed before and multiplying the variable in an algebraic expression (e.g. 4 in 4x^y). **2** Physics a multiplier or factor that measures some property.
– ORIGIN C17: from COM- + Latin *efficient*- (see EFFICIENT).

coelacanth /ˈsiːləkanθ/ ■ n. a large bony marine fish with a three-lobed tail fin and fleshy pectoral fins, known only from fossils until one was found alive in 1938. [*Latimeria chalumnae*.]
– ORIGIN C19: from *Coelacanthus* (genus name), from Greek *koilos* 'hollow' + *akantha* 'spine' (because its fins have hollow spines).

-coele ■ comb. form variant spelling of -CELE.

coelenterate /siːˈlɛnt(ə)rət, -reɪt/ ■ n. Zoology an aquatic invertebrate animal, typically having a tube- or cup-shaped body with a single opening ringed with tentacles, belonging to a phylum (Cnidaria, formerly Coelenterata) that includes jellyfishes, corals, and sea anemones.
– ORIGIN C19: from Greek *koilos* 'hollow' + *enteron* 'intestine'.

coeliac /ˈsiːlɪak/ (US **celiac**) ■ adj. Anatomy & Medicine of or relating to the abdomen.
– ORIGIN C17: from Greek *koiliakos*, from *koilia* 'belly'.

coeliac disease ■ n. a disease in which chronic failure to digest food is triggered by hypersensitivity of the small intestine to gluten.

coelom /ˈsiːləm/ ■ n. (pl. **-oms** or **-omata** /-ˈləʊmətə/) Zoology the principal body cavity in most animals, located between the intestinal canal and the body wall.
– DERIVATIVES **coelomate** adj. & n. **coelomic** /səˈlɒmɪk/ adj.
– ORIGIN C19: from Greek *koilōma* 'cavity'.

coelurosaur /sɪˈljʊərəsɔː/ ■ n. a small slender bipedal carnivorous dinosaur with long forelimbs, believed to be an evolutionary ancestor of birds.
– ORIGIN 1950s: from Greek *koilos* 'hollow' + *oura* 'tail' + *sauros* 'lizard'.

coenocyte /ˈsiːnəʊsʌɪt/ ■ n. Botany a body of algal or fungal cytoplasm containing several nuclei, enclosed in a single membrane.
– DERIVATIVES **coenocytic** /-ˈsɪtɪk/ adj.
– ORIGIN C20: from Greek *koinos* 'common' + -CYTE.

coenzyme /ˌkəʊˈɛnzʌɪm/ ■ n. Biochemistry a non-protein compound that is necessary for the functioning of an enzyme.

coequal ■ adj. having the same rank or importance. ■ n. a person or thing equal with another.
– DERIVATIVES **coequality** /ˌkəʊɪˈkwɒlɪti/ n.

coerce /kəʊˈəːs/ ■ v. persuade (an unwilling person) to do something by using force or threats.
– DERIVATIVES **coercible** adj. **coercion** n. **coercive** adj.
– ORIGIN Middle English: from Latin *coercere* 'restrain', from *co-* 'jointly, together' + *arcere* 'restrain'.

coercivity /ˌkəʊəˈsɪvɪti/ ■ n. Physics the resistance of a magnetic material to changes in magnetization, equivalent to the field intensity necessary to demagnetize the fully magnetized material.

coeval /kəʊˈiːv(ə)l/ ■ adj. having the same age or date of origin; contemporary. ■ n. a person of roughly the same age as oneself; a contemporary.
– DERIVATIVES **coevality** n. **coevally** adv.
– ORIGIN C17: from late Latin *coaevus*, from *co-* 'jointly, in common' + Latin *aevum* 'age'.

coexist ■ v. exist at the same time or in the same place. ▸ exist in harmony.
– DERIVATIVES **coexistence** n. **coexistent** adj.

coextensive ■ adj. extending over the same area, extent, or time.

cofactor ■ n. Biochemistry a substance whose presence is essential for the activity of an enzyme.

C. of E. ■ abbrev. Church of England.

coffee ■ n. **1** a hot drink made from the roasted and ground bean-like seeds of a tropical shrub. ▸ the processed, roasted, and ground seeds used to make this drink. **2** the shrub which yields these seeds. [Genus *Coffea*: several species.]
– ORIGIN C16: from Turkish *kahveh*, from Arabic *ḳahwa*.

coffee morning ■ n. Brit. a morning social gathering at which coffee is served.

coffee table ■ n. a small, low table.

coffee-table book ■ n. a large, lavishly illustrated book, especially one intended only for casual reading.

coffer ■ n. **1** a small chest for holding valuables. ▶ (**coffers**) the funds or financial reserves of an institution. **2** a decorative sunken panel in a ceiling. ■ v. [usu. as adj. **coffered**] decorate with a coffer or coffers.
– ORIGIN Middle English: from Old French *coffre* 'chest', from Greek *kophinos* 'basket'.

cofferdam ■ n. a watertight enclosure pumped dry to permit construction work below the waterline, as when building bridges or repairing a ship.

coffin ■ n. a long, narrow box in which a dead body is buried or cremated. ■ v. (**coffined**, **coffining**) place in a coffin.
– ORIGIN Middle English: from Old French *cofin* 'little basket', from Latin *cophinus* (see COFFER).

coffret /ˈkɒfrɪt/ ■ n. a small container.
– ORIGIN C15: from Old French, 'small chest', diminutive of *coffre* (see COFFER).

cog ■ n. a wheel or bar with a series of projections on its edge, which transfers motion by engaging with projections on another wheel or bar. ▶ each of such a series of projections.
– DERIVATIVES **cogged** adj.
– ORIGIN Middle English: prob. of Scandinavian origin.

cogeneration ■ n. the generation of electricity and useful heat jointly, especially the utilization of the steam left over from electricity generation for heating.

cogent /ˈkəʊdʒ(ə)nt/ ■ adj. (of an argument or case) clear, logical, and convincing.
– DERIVATIVES **cogency** n. **cogently** adv.
– ORIGIN C17: from Latin *cogere* 'compel'.

cogitate /ˈkɒdʒɪteɪt/ ■ v. formal meditate or reflect.
– DERIVATIVES **cogitation** n. **cogitative** adj. **cogitator** n.
– ORIGIN C16 (Middle English *cogitation*): from Latin *cogitare* 'to consider'.

cogito /ˈkɒɡɪtəʊ, -dʒɪ-/ ■ n. Philosophy the principle establishing the existence of a being from the fact of its thinking or awareness.
– ORIGIN Latin, as in Descartes' formula (1641) *cogito, (ergo sum)* 'I think, (therefore I am)'.

cognac /ˈkɒnjak/ ■ n. a high-quality brandy, strictly speaking that distilled in Cognac in western France.

cognate /ˈkɒɡneɪt/ ■ adj. **1** Linguistics (of a word) having the same linguistic derivation as another (e.g. English *father*, German *Vater*, Latin *pater*). **2** formal related; connected. ▶ related to or descended from a common ancestor. Compare with AGNATE. ■ n. **1** Linguistics a cognate word. **2** Law a blood relative.
– DERIVATIVES **cognately** adv. **cognateness** n.
– ORIGIN C17: from Latin *cognatus*, from *co-* 'together with' + *natus* 'born'.

cognition /kɒɡˈnɪʃ(ə)n/ ■ n. the mental action or process of acquiring knowledge through thought, experience, and the senses. ▶ a perception, sensation, or intuition resulting from this.
– DERIVATIVES **cognitional** adj.
– ORIGIN Middle English: from Latin *cognitio(-)*, from *cognoscere* 'get to know'.

cognitive /ˈkɒɡnɪtɪv/ ■ adj. of or relating to cognition.
– DERIVATIVES **cognitively** adv.

cognitive dissonance ■ n. Psychology the state of having inconsistent thoughts, beliefs, or attitudes.

cognitive science ■ n. the study of thought, learning, and mental organization.
– DERIVATIVES **cognitive scientist** n.

cognitive therapy ■ n. a type of psychotherapy in which negative patterns of thought about the self and the world are challenged.

cognizable /ˈkɒ(ɡ)nɪzəb(ə)l/ (also **-isable**) ■ adj. **1** formal perceptible; clearly identifiable. **2** Law within the jurisdiction of a court.

cognizance /ˈkɒ(ɡ)nɪz(ə)ns/ (also **cognisance**) ■ n. formal knowledge or awareness. ▶ Law the action of taking judicial notice.

– PHRASES **take cognizance of** formal attend to; take account of.
– DERIVATIVES **cognizant** (also **-isant**) adj. **cognize** (also **-ise**) v.
– ORIGIN Middle English *conisance*, from Old French *conoisance*, from Latin *cognoscere* 'get to know'.

cognoscenti /ˌkɒnjəˈʃɛnti/ ■ pl. n. people who are considered to be especially well informed about a particular subject.
– ORIGIN C18: Italian, 'people who know', from Latin *cognoscere* 'get to know'.

cohabit ■ v. (**cohabited**, **cohabiting**) **1** live together and have a sexual relationship without being married. **2** coexist.
– DERIVATIVES **cohabitant** n. **cohabitation** /-ˈteɪʃ(ə)n/ n. **cohabitee** /-ˈtiː/ n. **cohabiter** n.
– ORIGIN C16 (Middle English *cohabitation*): from Latin, from *co-* 'together' + *habitare* 'dwell'.

cohen ■ n. variant spelling of KOHEN.

cohere /kə(ʊ)ˈhɪə/ ■ v. **1** hold firmly together; form a whole. **2** (of an argument or theory) be logically consistent.
– ORIGIN C16: from Latin, from *co-* 'together' + *haerere* 'to stick'.

coherent ■ adj. **1** (of an argument or theory) logical and consistent. ▶ able to speak clearly and logically. **2** holding together to form a whole. **3** Physics (of waves) having a constant phase relationship.
– DERIVATIVES **coherence** n. **coherency** n. (rare). **coherently** adv.

cohesion /kə(ʊ)ˈhiːʒ(ə)n/ ■ n. the action or fact of forming a united whole. ▶ Physics the sticking together of particles of the same substance.
– ORIGIN C17: from Latin *cohaerere* (see COHERE).

cohesive ■ adj. characterized by or causing cohesion.
– DERIVATIVES **cohesively** adv. **cohesiveness** n.

cohort /ˈkəʊhɔːt/ ■ n. **1** [treated as sing. or pl.] an ancient Roman military unit. **2** [treated as sing. or pl.] a group of people banded together or treated as a group. **3** a supporter or companion.
– ORIGIN Middle English: from Latin *cohors*, *cohort-* 'yard, retinue'.

coif ■ n. /kɔɪf/ a woman's close-fitting cap, worn under a veil by nuns. ■ v. /kwɑːf, kwɒf/ (**coiffed**, **coiffing**; US also **coifed**, **coifing**) style or arrange (someone's hair).
– ORIGIN Middle English: from Old French *coife* 'headdress', from late Latin *cofia* 'helmet'.

coiffeur /kwɑːˈfəː, kwɒ-/ ■ n. (fem. **coiffeuse** /kwɑːˈfəːz, kwɒ-/) a hairdresser.
– ORIGIN C19: French, from *coiffer* 'arrange the hair'.

coiffure /kwɑːˈfjʊə, kwɒ-/ ■ n. a person's hairstyle.
– DERIVATIVES **coiffured** adj.

coign /kɔɪn/ ■ n. a projecting corner or angle of a wall.
– ORIGIN Middle English: var. of COIN.

coil ■ n. **1** a length of something wound in a joined sequence of concentric rings. **2** an intrauterine contraceptive device in the form of a coil. **3** an electrical device consisting of a coiled wire, for converting the level of a voltage, producing a magnetic field, or adding inductance to a circuit. ■ v. arrange or form into a coil.
– ORIGIN C16: from Old French *coillir*, from Latin *colligere* (see COLLECT[1]).

coin ■ n. **1** a flat disc or piece of metal with an official stamp, used as money. ▶ money in the form of coins. **2** (**coins**) one of the suits in some tarot packs, corresponding to pentacles in others. ■ v. **1** make (coins) by stamping metal. ▶ Brit. informal earn (large amounts of money) quickly and easily: *the company was coining it in*. **2** invent or devise (a new word or phrase).
– PHRASES **pay someone back in their own coin** retaliate by similar behaviour. **to coin a phrase** said when introducing a new expression or a variation on a familiar one.
– DERIVATIVES **coiner** n.
– ORIGIN Middle English: from Old French *coin* 'wedge, corner, die', *coigner* 'to mint', from Latin *cuneus* 'wedge'.

coinage ■ n. **1** coins collectively. ▶ the action or process of producing coins. ▶ a system or type of coins in use. **2** the invention of a new word or phrase. ▶ a newly invented word or phrase.

coincide /ˌkəʊɪnˈsaɪd/ ■ v. **1** occur at the same time or place. **2** correspond in nature; tally. ▶ be in agreement.
– ORIGIN C18: from medieval Latin, from *co-* 'together with' + *incidere* 'fall upon or into'.

coincidence ■ n. **1** a remarkable concurrence of events or circumstances without apparent causal connection. **2** correspondence in nature or in time of occurrence. **3** Physics the presence of ionizing particles or other objects in two or more detectors simultaneously, or of two or more signals simultaneously in a circuit.
– DERIVATIVES **coincidental** adj. **coincidentally** adv.

coincident ■ adj. **1** occurring together in space or time. **2** in agreement or harmony.
– DERIVATIVES **coincidently** adv.

coin-op ■ n. a machine operated by the insertion of coins.

Cointreau /ˈkwʌntrəʊ/ ■ n. trademark a colourless orange-flavoured liqueur.
– ORIGIN named after the *Cointreau* family, liqueur producers based in Angers, France.

coir /ˈkɔɪə/ ■ n. fibre from the outer husk of the coconut, used in potting compost and for making ropes and matting.
– ORIGIN C16: from Malayalam *kayaṟu* 'cord, coir'.

coition /kəʊˈɪʃ(ə)n/ ■ n. another term for COITUS.
– ORIGIN C16: from Latin *coitio(n-)*, from *coire* 'go together'.

coitus /ˈkəʊɪtəs/ ■ n. technical sexual intercourse.
– DERIVATIVES **coital** adj.
– ORIGIN C19: from Latin, from *coire* 'go together'.

coitus interruptus /ˌɪntəˈrʌptəs/ ■ n. sexual intercourse in which the penis is withdrawn before ejaculation.

cojones /kəˈhəʊneɪz/ ■ pl. n. informal, chiefly N. Amer. **1** a man's testicles. **2** courage; guts.
– ORIGIN from Spanish.

coke[1] ■ n. a solid fuel made by heating coal in the absence of air so that the volatile components are driven off. ▶ carbon residue left after the incomplete combustion or distillation of petrol or other fuels. ■ v. [usu. as noun **coking**] convert (coal) into coke.
– ORIGIN Middle English.

coke[2] ■ n. informal term for COCAINE.

Col. ■ abbrev. Colonel.

col ■ n. the lowest point of a ridge or saddle between two peaks.
– ORIGIN C19: from French, 'neck', from Latin *collum*.

col- ■ prefix variant spelling of COM- assimilated before *l* (as in *collocate, collude*).

cola ■ n. **1** a brown carbonated drink that is flavoured with an extract of cola nuts, or with a similar flavouring. **2** (also **kola**) a small evergreen African tree cultivated in the tropics, whose seed (the cola nut) contains caffeine. [*Cola acuminata* and related species.]
– ORIGIN from Temne *k'ola* 'cola nut'.

colander /ˈkʌləndə, ˈkɒl-/ ■ n. a perforated bowl used to strain off liquid from food.
– ORIGIN Middle English: from Latin *colare* 'to strain'.

co-latitude ■ n. Astronomy the difference between a given latitude and 90°.

cold ■ adj. **1** of or at a low or relatively low temperature. **2** lacking affection or warmth of feeling; unemotional. ▶ not affected by emotion; objective. ▶ (of a colour) containing pale blue or grey and giving no impression of warmth. **3** (of a scent or trail) no longer fresh and easy to follow: *the trail went cold.* ▶ (in children's games) far from finding or guessing what is sought. **4** without preparation or rehearsal; unawares. **5** informal unconscious: *she was out cold.* ■ n. **1** a low temperature; cold weather; a cold environment. **2** a common infection in which the mucous membrane of the nose and throat becomes inflamed, causing running at the nose and sneezing.
– PHRASES **catch a cold** informal encounter trouble or difficulties. **cold comfort** poor or inadequate consolation. **cold feet** loss of nerve or confidence. **the cold light of day** the objective realities of a situation. **the cold shoulder** a show of intentional unfriendliness; rejection. **in cold blood** without feeling or mercy. **leave someone cold** fail to interest or excite someone. **out in the cold** ignored; neglected.
– DERIVATIVES **coldish** adj. **coldly** adv. **coldness** n.
– ORIGIN Old English, of Germanic origin.

cold-blooded ■ adj. **1** denoting animals whose body temperature varies with that of the environment (e.g. reptiles and fish). **2** without emotion; deliberately cruel.
– DERIVATIVES **cold-bloodedly** adv. **cold-bloodedness** n.

cold-call ■ v. [usu. as noun **cold-calling**] make an unsolicited visit or telephone call to (someone), in an attempt to sell goods or services.

cold chisel ■ n. a toughened chisel used for cutting metal.

cold cream ■ n. a cosmetic preparation used for cleansing and softening the skin.

cold cuts ■ pl. n. slices of cold cooked meats.

cold frame ■ n. a frame with a glass top in which small plants are grown and protected without artificial heat.

cold-hearted ■ adj. lacking affection or warmth; unfeeling.
– DERIVATIVES **cold-heartedly** adv. **cold-heartedness** n.

cold-rolled ■ adj. (of metal) having been rolled into sheets while cold, resulting in a smooth, hard finish.
– DERIVATIVES **cold-rolling** n.

cold sore ■ n. an inflamed blister in or near the mouth, caused by infection with the herpes simplex virus.

cold storage ■ n. the keeping of something in a refrigerator or other cold place for preservation.

cold store ■ n. a large refrigerated room for preserving food stocks at very low temperatures.

cold sweat ■ n. a state of sweating induced by nervousness or illness.

cold turkey informal ■ n. the abrupt and complete cessation of taking a drug to which one is addicted. ▶ withdrawal symptoms, typically sweating and nausea, caused by this.

cold war ■ n. (**the cold war**) a state of political hostility existing between the Soviet bloc countries and the Western powers after the Second World War.

colectomy /kə(ʊ)ˈlɛktəmi/ ■ n. (pl. **-ies**) surgical removal of all or part of the colon.

Coleoptera /ˌkɒlɪˈɒpt(ə)rə/ ■ pl. n. Entomology an order of insects that comprises the beetles (including weevils), forming the largest order of animals on the earth.
– DERIVATIVES **coleopteran** n. & adj. **coleopterous** adj.
– ORIGIN from Greek, from *koleos* 'sheath' + *pteron* 'wing'.

coleoptile /ˌkɒlɪˈɒptaɪl/ ■ n. Botany a sheath protecting a young shoot tip in a grass or cereal.
– ORIGIN C19: from Greek *koleon* 'sheath' + *ptilon* 'feather'.

coleslaw ■ n. a salad dish of shredded raw cabbage, carrots, and other vegetables mixed with mayonnaise.
– ORIGIN C18: from Dutch *koolsla*, from *kool* 'cabbage' + *sla* (see SLAW).

coleus /ˈkəʊlɪəs/ ■ n. a tropical SE Asian plant of the mint family, with brightly coloured variegated leaves. [Genus *Solenostemon* (formerly *Coleus*).]
– ORIGIN from Greek *koleos* 'sheath' (because the stamens are joined together, resembling a sheath).

colic ■ n. severe pain in the abdomen caused by wind or obstruction in the intestines.
– DERIVATIVES **colicky** adj.
– ORIGIN Middle English: from Old French *colique*, from late Latin *colicus*, from *colon* (see COLON[2]).

coliform /ˈkɒlɪfɔːm/ ■ adj. Biology belonging to a group of rod-shaped bacteria typified by *E. coli*.
– ORIGIN C20: from Latin *coli* 'of the colon'.

colitis /kəˈlaɪtɪs/ ■ n. Medicine inflammation of the lining of the colon.

collaborate /kəˈlabəreɪt/ ■ v. **1** work jointly on an activity or project. **2** cooperate traitorously with an enemy.
– DERIVATIVES **collaboration** n. **collaborationist** n. & adj. **collaborative** adj. **collaboratively** adv. **collaborator** n.
– ORIGIN C19: from Latin *collaborare* 'work together'.

collage /'kɒlɑːʒ, kə'lɑːʒ/ ■ n. **1** a form of art in which various materials such as photographs and pieces of paper or fabric are arranged and stuck to a backing. **2** a combination or collection of various things.
– DERIVATIVES **collagist** n.
– ORIGIN C20: from French, 'gluing'.

collagen /'kɒlədʒ(ə)n/ ■ n. Biochemistry the main structural protein found in animal connective tissue, yielding gelatin when boiled.
– ORIGIN C19: from French *collagène*, from Greek *kolla* 'glue'.

collapse ■ v. **1** (of a structure) suddenly fall down or give way. ▸ [usu. as adj. **collapsed**] (of a lung or blood vessel) fall inwards and become flat and empty. **2** (of a person) fall down as a result of physical breakdown. **3** fail suddenly and completely. ■ n. **1** an instance of a structure collapsing. **2** a sudden failure or breakdown.
– ORIGIN C17: from medical Latin *collaps-, collabi*, from *col-* 'together' + *labi* 'to slip'.

collapsible ■ adj. able to be folded down.
– DERIVATIVES **collapsibility** n.

collar ■ n. **1** a band of material around the neck of a shirt or other garment, either upright or turned over. **2** a band put around the neck of a domestic animal, used to restrain or control. **3** a connecting band or pipe in a piece of machinery. ■ v. informal seize or apprehend (someone).
– DERIVATIVES **collared** adj. **collarless** adj.
– ORIGIN Middle English: from Latin *collare* 'band for the neck', from *collum* 'neck'.

collarbone ■ n. either of the pair of bones joining the breastbone to the shoulder blades; the clavicle.

collate /kɒ'leɪt/ ■ v. collect and combine (texts or information). ▸ compare and analyse (two or more sources of information). ▸ Printing verify the number and order of (the sheets of a book).
– DERIVATIVES **collator** n.

collateral /kɒ'lat(ə)r(ə)l/ ■ n. **1** something pledged as security for repayment of a loan. **2** a person descended from the same ancestor as another but through a different line. ■ adj. **1** descended from the same stock but by a different line. **2** additional but subordinate; secondary. **3** situated side by side; parallel: *collateral veins*.
– DERIVATIVES **collaterality** n. **collaterally** adv.
– ORIGIN Middle English: from medieval Latin, from *col-* 'together with' + *lateralis* (from *latus* 'side').

collateral damage ■ n. inadvertent casualties and destruction in civilian areas caused by military operations.

collateralize (also **-ise**) ■ v. provide something as collateral for (a loan).

collation /kə'leɪʃ(ə)n/ ■ n. **1** the action of collating. **2** a light informal meal.
– ORIGIN Middle English: via Old French from Latin *collatio(n-)*, from *conferre* (see **CONFER**).

colleague ■ n. a person with whom one works in a profession or business.
– ORIGIN C16: from French *collègue*, from Latin *collega* 'partner in office'.

collect[1] /kə'lɛkt/ ■ v. **1** bring or gather together. ▸ systematically seek and acquire (items of a particular kind) as a hobby. **2** call for and take away; fetch. ▸ call for and receive (something) as a right or due. **3** (**collect oneself**) regain control of oneself, typically after a shock. **4** archaic conclude; infer. ■ adv. & adj. chiefly N. Amer. (with reference to a telephone call) to be paid for by the person receiving it.
– ORIGIN Middle English: from Latin *collect-, colligere* 'gather together'.

collect[2] /'kɒlɛkt, -lɪkt/ ■ n. Christian Church a short prayer, especially one assigned to a particular day or season.
– ORIGIN Middle English: from Latin *collecta* 'gathering', from *colligere* 'gather together'.

collectable /kə'lɛktəb(ə)l/ (also **collectible**) ■ adj. **1** worth collecting; of interest to a collector. **2** able to be collected. ■ n. an item valued and sought by collectors.
– DERIVATIVES **collectability** /-'bɪlɪti/ n.

collected ■ adj. **1** not perturbed or distracted. **2** (of works) brought together in one volume or edition.

collection ■ n. **1** the action or process of collecting. ▸ a regular removal of mail for dispatch or of refuse for disposal. ▸ an instance of collecting money, as in a church service. **2** a group of things collected or accumulated.

collective ■ adj. done by or belonging to all the members of a group. ▸ taken as a whole; aggregate. ■ n. a co-operative enterprise. ▸ a collective farm.
– DERIVATIVES **collectively** adv. **collectiveness** n. **collectivity** n.

collective bargaining ■ n. negotiation of wages and other conditions of employment by an organized body of employees.

collective farm ■ n. a jointly operated amalgamation of several smallholdings, especially one owned by the state.

collective noun ■ n. Grammar a count noun that denotes a group of individuals (e.g. *assembly, family, crew*).

USAGE
A collective noun can be used with either a singular verb (*my family was always hard-working*) or a plural verb (*his family were disappointed in him*), depending on whether the emphasis is on the group as a whole or on the individuals within the group. See **Singular and plural nouns** in *Guide to Good English* p. SP 19.

collective unconscious ■ n. (in Jungian psychology) the part of the unconscious mind which is derived from ancestral memory and experience and is common to all humankind, as distinct from the individual's unconscious.

collectivism ■ n. **1** the practice or principle of giving the group priority over each individual in it. **2** the ownership of land and the means of production by the people or the state.
– DERIVATIVES **collectivist** adj. & n. **collectivization** (also **-isation**) n. **collectivize** (also **-ise**) v.

collector /kə'lɛktə/ ■ n. **1** a person who collects things of a specified type, professionally or as a hobby. **2** an official who is responsible for collecting money owed.

colleen /kɒ'liːn, 'kɒliːn/ ■ n. Irish a girl or young woman.
– ORIGIN C19: from Irish *cailin*, diminutive of *caile* 'countrywoman'.

college ■ n. **1** an educational establishment providing higher education or specialized professional or vocational training. ▸ (in Britain) any of the independent institutions into which some universities are separated. **2** an organized group of professional people with particular aims, duties, and privileges.
– ORIGIN Middle English: from Latin *collegium* 'partnership', from *collega* (see **COLLEAGUE**).

College of Arms ■ n. (in the UK) a corporation which officially records and grants armorial bearings.

college of education ■ n. an institution where schoolteachers are trained.

collegial /kə'liːdʒɪəl, -dʒ(ə)l/ ■ adj. **1** another term for **COLLEGIATE** (in sense 1). **2** relating to or involving shared responsibility.
– DERIVATIVES **collegiality** n.

collegiate /kə'liːdʒ(ɪ)ət/ ■ adj. **1** belonging to, relating to, or appropriate for a college or for college students. **2** (of a university) composed of different colleges.

collenchyma /kə'lɛŋkɪmə/ ■ n. Botany tissue strengthened by the thickening of cell walls, as in young shoots.
– ORIGIN C19: from Greek *kolla* 'glue' + *enkhuma* 'infusion'.

Colles' fracture /'kɒlɪs/ ■ n. Medicine a fracture of the radius in the wrist with a characteristic backward displacement of the hand.
– ORIGIN C19: named after the Irish surgeon Abraham Colles.

collide ■ v. **1** hit by accident when moving. **2** come into conflict or opposition.
– ORIGIN C17: from Latin *collidere*, from *col-* 'together' + *laedere* 'to strike'.

collider ■ n. Physics an accelerator in which two beams of particles are made to collide.

collie ■ n. (pl. **-ies**) a sheepdog of a breed having a long,

collier

pointed nose and thick long hair.
- ORIGIN C17: perhaps from COAL (the breed orig. being black).

collier /ˈkɒlɪə/ ■ n. chiefly Brit. **1** a coal miner. **2** a ship carrying coal.
- ORIGIN Middle English: from COAL.

colliery ■ n. (pl. **-ies**) a coal mine and the buildings and equipment associated with it.

colligative /kəˈlɪɡətɪv/ ■ adj. Chemistry of or relating to the binding together of molecules.
- ORIGIN C20: from Latin *colligare* 'bind together'.

collinear /kɒˈlɪnɪə/ ■ adj. Geometry (of points) lying in the same straight line.
- DERIVATIVES **collinearity** n.

collision ■ n. an instance of colliding.
- DERIVATIVES **collisional** adj.
- ORIGIN Middle English: from late Latin *collisio(n-)*, from Latin *collidere* (see COLLIDE).

collocation ■ n. **1** Linguistics the habitual juxtaposition of a particular word with another word or words with a frequency greater than chance. **2** the action of placing things together according to some system or order.
- DERIVATIVES **collocate** v.
- ORIGIN Middle English: from Latin *collocatio(n-)*, from *collocare* 'place together'.

colloid /ˈkɒlɔɪd/ ■ n. a homogeneous non-crystalline substance consisting of large molecules or ultramicroscopic particles of one substance dispersed in a second substance, as in gels, sols, and emulsions. ▸ Anatomy & Medicine a substance of gelatinous consistency.
- DERIVATIVES **colloidal** adj.
- ORIGIN C19: from Greek *kolla* 'glue'.

colloquial /kəˈləʊkwɪəl/ ■ adj. (of language) used in ordinary or familiar conversation; not formal or literary.
- DERIVATIVES **colloquially** adv.
- ORIGIN C18: from Latin *colloquium* 'conversation'.

colloquialism ■ n. a colloquial word or phrase.

colloquium /kəˈləʊkwɪəm/ ■ n. (pl. **colloquiums** or **colloquia** /-kwɪə/) an academic conference or seminar.
- ORIGIN C16: from Latin, from *colloqui* 'to converse'.

colloquy /ˈkɒləkwi/ ■ n. (pl. **-ies**) **1** a formal conference or conversation. **2** a gathering for discussion of theological questions.
- ORIGIN Middle English: from Latin *colloquium* 'conversation'.

collude /kəˈl(j)uːd/ ■ v. come to a secret understanding; conspire.
- DERIVATIVES **colluder** n.
- ORIGIN C16: from Latin *colludere* 'have a secret agreement', from *col-* 'together' + *ludere* 'to play'.

collusion ■ n. secret or illegal cooperation in order to cheat or deceive others.
- DERIVATIVES **collusive** adj. **collusively** adv.
- ORIGIN Middle English: from Latin *collusio(n-)*, from *colludere* (see COLLUDE).

collywobbles ■ pl. n. informal, chiefly humorous stomach pain or queasiness. ▸ intense anxiety.
- ORIGIN C19: fanciful form from COLIC and WOBBLE.

colobus /ˈkɒləbəs/ ■ n. (pl. same) a slender leaf-eating African monkey with silky fur. [Genera *Colobus* and *Procolobus*: several species.]
- DERIVATIVES **colobine** n.
- ORIGIN from Greek *kolobos* 'curtailed' (with ref. to its shortened thumbs).

colocynth /ˈkɒləsɪnθ/ ■ n. a tropical climbing plant with pulpy fruits which yield a bitter purgative drug. [*Citrullus colocynthis*.]
- ORIGIN C16: from Greek *kolokunthis*.

cologne /kəˈləʊn/ ■ n. eau de cologne or similarly scented toilet water.

Colombian /kəˈlɒmbɪən/ ■ n. a native or inhabitant of Colombia. ■ adj. of or relating to Colombia or its people.

colon[1] /ˈkəʊlən/ ■ n. **1** a punctuation mark (:) used to precede a list of items, a quotation, or an expansion or explanation. **2** this mark used in various technical and formulaic contexts, for example a statement of proportion between two numbers.
- ORIGIN C16: from Greek *kōlon* 'limb, clause'.

colon[2] /ˈkəʊlən, -lɒn/ ■ n. Anatomy the main part of the large intestine, which passes from the caecum to the rectum.
- ORIGIN Middle English: from Greek *kolon*.

colonel /ˈkəːn(ə)l/ ■ n. a rank of officer in the army and air force, above a lieutenant colonel and below a brigadier general.
- DERIVATIVES **colonelcy** n. (pl. **-ies**).
- ORIGIN C16: from obsolete French *coronel*, from Italian *colonnello* 'column of soldiers'.

colonial ■ adj. **1** of, relating to, or characteristic of a colony or colonies. **2** (of architecture or furniture) in the style of the period of the British colonies in America before independence. **3** (of animals or plants) living in colonies. ■ n. a person who lives in a colony.
- DERIVATIVES **colonially** adv.

colonialism ■ n. the policy or practice of acquiring political control over another country, occupying it with settlers, and exploiting it economically.
- DERIVATIVES **colonialist** n. & adj.

colonic /kəˈlɒnɪk/ ■ adj. Anatomy of, relating to, or affecting the colon.

colonic irrigation ■ n. the practice of inserting water via the anus to flush out the colon, used as a therapeutic treatment.

colonist ■ n. a settler in or inhabitant of a colony.

colonize (also **-ise**) ■ v. **1** establish a colony in (a place). ▸ establish control over the indigenous people of a colony). **2** appropriate (a place or domain) for one's own use. **3** Ecology (of a plant or animal) establish itself in (an area).
- DERIVATIVES **colonization** (also **-isation**) n. **colonizer** (also **-iser**) n.

colonnade /ˌkɒləˈneɪd/ ■ n. a row of evenly spaced columns supporting a roof or other structure.
- DERIVATIVES **colonnaded** adj.
- ORIGIN C18: from French, from *colonne* 'column', from Latin *columna*.

colonoscopy /ˌkəʊləˈnɒskəpi/ ■ n. (pl. **-ies**) Medicine examination of the colon with a fibre-optic instrument inserted through the anus.

colony ■ n. (pl. **-ies**) **1** a country or area under the political control of another country and occupied by settlers from that country. ▸ (**the colonies**) all the foreign places formerly under British political control. ▸ (**the colonies**) the thirteen areas on the east coast of North America that gained independence and founded the United States of America. ▸ (**the Colony**) S. African historical another term for CAPE COLONY. **2** a group of people of one nationality or race living in a foreign place. ▸ a group of people separated by occupation or interest: *a nudist colony*. **3** a community of animals or plants of one kind living close together or forming a physically connected structure.
- ORIGIN Middle English: from Latin *colonia* 'settlement, farm', from *colere* 'cultivate'.

color ■ n. & v. US spelling of COLOUR.

Colorado beetle ■ n. a yellow- and black-striped beetle, native to America, whose larvae are highly destructive to potato plants. [*Leptinotarsa decemlineata*.]

coloration (also **colouration**) ■ n. **1** arrangement or scheme of colour; colouring. **2** the character or tone of something, especially musical expression.
- ORIGIN C17: from late Latin *coloratio(n-)*, from *colorare* 'to colour'.

coloratura /ˌkɒlərəˈtjʊərə/ ■ n. elaborate ornamentation of a vocal melody. ▸ a soprano skilled in such singing.
- ORIGIN Italian, 'colouring'.

color bar ■ n. US spelling of COLOUR BAR.

colossal ■ adj. **1** extremely large. **2** Architecture (of an order) having more than one storey of columns.
- DERIVATIVES **colossally** adv.
- ORIGIN C18: from Latin *colossus* (see COLOSSUS).

colossus /kəˈlɒsəs/ ■ n. (pl. **colossi** /-saɪ/ or **colossuses**) a person or thing of enormous size, in particular a statue that is much bigger than life size.
- ORIGIN Middle English: via Latin from Greek *kolossos* (used by Herodotus of the statues of Egyptian temples).

colostomy /kəˈlɒstəmi/ ■ n. (pl. **-ies**) a surgical operation in which the colon is shortened to remove a damaged part and the cut end diverted to an opening in the abdominal wall.
– ORIGIN C19: from **COLON**[2] + Greek *stoma* 'mouth'.

colostrum /kəˈlɒstrəm/ ■ n. the first secretion from the mammary glands after giving birth, rich in antibodies.
– ORIGIN C16: from Latin.

colour (US **color**) ■ n. **1** the property possessed by an object of producing different sensations on the eye as a result of the way it reflects or emits light. ▸ one, or any mixture, of the constituents into which light can be separated in a spectrum or rainbow. ▸ the use of all colours, not only black and white, in photography or television. ▸ Heraldry any of the major conventional colours used in coats of arms (gules, vert, sable, azure, purpure). ▸ Snooker any of the balls other than the white cue ball and the reds. **2** pigmentation of the skin, especially as an indication of someone's race. **3** redness of the complexion, as indicating health or an emotion such as anger. **4** interest, excitement, and vitality: *a town full of colour and character*. **5** (**colours**) an item of a particular colour worn to identify or distinguish, in particular the clothes worn by a jockey or the members of sports team. ▸ a badge or cap awarded to a pupil representing a school in sport. ▸ the flag of a regiment or ship. **6** Physics a property of quarks which can take three values designated blue, green, and red. ■ v. **1** give a colour to. **2** show embarrassment by becoming red; blush. **3** influence, especially in a negative way; distort: *the experiences had coloured her whole existence*.
– PHRASES **sail under false colours** disguise one's true nature or intentions. **show one's true colours** reveal one's real character or intentions, especially when these are disreputable. **under colour of** under the pretext of.
– ORIGIN Middle English: from Old French *colour* (n.), *colourer* (v.), from Latin *color* (n.), *colorare* (v.).

colourant (US **colorant**) ■ n. a dye or pigment used to colour something.

colouration ■ n. variant spelling of **COLORATION**.

colour bar (US **color bar**) ■ n. a social system which denies black people the same rights as white people. ▸ S. African historical (under apartheid) a policy which excluded non-white people from skilled jobs.

colour-blind ■ adj. unable to distinguish certain colours.
– DERIVATIVES **colour blindness** n.

colour code ■ n. a system of marking things with different colours as a means of identification. ■ v. (**colour-code**) mark using a colour code.

coloured (US **colored**) ■ adj. **1** having a colour or colours. **2** (also **Coloured**) chiefly offensive wholly or partly of non-white descent. ▸ S. African of mixed descent. ■ n. **1** (also **Coloured**) S. African historical, offensive (under apartheid) an official racial grouping for people of mixed ethnic descent. ▸ an English- or Afrikaans-speaking person of mixed descent. **2** (**coloureds**) clothes, sheets, etc. that are any colour but white.

colour-fast ■ adj. dyed in colours that will not fade or be washed out.
– DERIVATIVES **colour fastness** n.

colourful (US **colorful**) ■ adj. **1** having many or varied colours. **2** lively and exciting. ▸ (of language) vulgar or rude.
– DERIVATIVES **colourfully** adv. **colourfulness** n.

colouring (US **coloring**) ■ n. **1** the process or art of applying colour. **2** visual appearance with regard to colour. ▸ the natural hues of a person's skin, hair, and eyes. **3** a substance used to colour something, especially food.

colourist (US **colorist**) ■ n. an artist or designer who uses colour in a special or skilful way.

colouristic (US **coloristic**) ■ adj. **1** showing or relating to a special use of colour. **2** having or showing a variety of musical expression.
– DERIVATIVES **colouristically** adv.

colourless (US **colorless**) ■ adj. **1** without colour. **2** lacking character or interest; dull.
– DERIVATIVES **colourlessly** adv.

colour scheme ■ n. an arrangement or combination of colours.

231

colourway (US **colorway**) ■ n. any of a range of combinations of colours in which something is available.

colposcope /ˈkɒlpəskəʊp/ ■ n. a surgical instrument used to examine the vagina and the cervix of the womb.
– DERIVATIVES **colposcopy** /kɒlˈpɒskəpi/ n.
– ORIGIN C20: from Greek *kolpos* 'womb' + **-SCOPE**.

colt /kəʊlt/ ■ n. **1** a young uncastrated male horse, in particular one less than four years old. **2** a member of a junior sports team.
– ORIGIN Old English; perhaps rel. to Swedish *kult*, applied to boys or half-grown animals.

coltan ■ n. informal deposits of columbite-tantalite, minerals which contain niobium and tantalum, elements used in the manufacture of electronic components.
– ORIGIN blend of **COLUMBITE** and **TANTALITE**.

coltish ■ adj. energetic but awkward in one's movements or behaviour.
– DERIVATIVES **coltishly** adv. **coltishness** n.

colubrid /ˈkɒljʊbrɪd/ ■ n. Zoology a snake of a very large family (Colubridae) which includes the majority of harmless species, such as grass snakes.

colubrine /ˈkɒljʊbrʌɪn/ ■ adj. of or resembling a snake.
– ORIGIN C16: from Latin *colubrinus*, from *coluber* 'snake'.

columbarium /ˌkɒl(ə)mˈbɛːrɪəm/ ■ n. (pl. **columbaria**) a room or building with niches for funeral urns to be stored.
– ORIGIN C18: from Latin, 'pigeon house'.

columbine /ˈkɒl(ə)mbʌɪn/ ■ n. a plant with long-spurred, typically purplish-blue flowers. [*Aquilegia vulgaris* and related species.]
– ORIGIN Middle English: from Old French *colombine*, from Latin *columba* 'dove' (from the supposed resemblance of the flower to a cluster of five doves).

columbite /kəˈlʌmbʌɪt/ ■ n. a black mineral consisting of an oxide of iron, manganese, niobium, and tantalum.
– ORIGIN C19: from *columbium*, an older name for **NIOBIUM**.

columella /ˌkɒljʊˈmɛlə/ ■ n. (pl. **columellae** /-liː/) **1** Zoology the central pillar or axis of a spiral structure such as a shell. **2** Botany the axis of the spore-producing body of some lower plants.
– DERIVATIVES **columellar** adj.
– ORIGIN C16: from Latin, 'small column'.

column ■ n. **1** an upright pillar supporting an arch or other structure or standing alone as a monument. ▸ an upright shaft used for controlling a machine. **2** a vertical division of a page or text. ▸ a regular section of a newspaper or magazine on a particular subject or by a particular person. **3** a line of people or vehicles moving in the same direction. ▸ Military a narrow-fronted deep formation of troops in successive lines.
– DERIVATIVES **columnar** adj. **columned** adj.
– ORIGIN Middle English: partly from Old French *columpne*, reinforced by Latin *columna* 'pillar'.

columnist /ˈkɒl(ə)m(n)ɪst/ ■ n. a journalist who writes a column in a newspaper or magazine.

coly /ˈkəʊli/ ■ n. (pl. **-ies**) another term for **MOUSEBIRD**.
– ORIGIN C19: from Greek *kolios*, denoting a type of woodpecker.

com- (also **co-**, **col-**, **con-**, or **cor-**) ■ prefix with; together; jointly; altogether: *combine*.
– ORIGIN from Latin *cum* 'with'.

coma[1] /ˈkəʊmə/ ■ n. a state of prolonged deep unconsciousness, caused especially by severe injury or illness.
– ORIGIN C17: from Greek *kōma* 'deep sleep'.

coma[2] /ˈkəʊmə/ ■ n. (pl. **comae** /-miː/) **1** Astronomy a diffuse cloud of gas and dust surrounding the nucleus of a comet. **2** Optics aberration which causes an off-axis image to be flared like a comet.
– ORIGIN C17: from Greek *komē* 'hair of the head'.

Comanche /kəˈmantʃi/ ■ n. (pl. same or **Comanches**) a member of an American Indian people of the south-western US.
– ORIGIN Spanish: from Comanche.

comatose /ˈkəʊmətəʊs, -z/ ■ adj. of or in a state of coma. ▸ humorous extremely tired or lethargic.

comb ■ n. **1** an article with a row of narrow teeth, used for untangling or arranging the hair. ▶ a short curved comb worn by women to hold the hair in place. **2** a device for separating and dressing textile fibres. **3** the red fleshy crest on the head of a domestic fowl, especially a cock. **4** a honeycomb. ■ v. **1** untangle or arrange (the hair) by drawing a comb through it. **2** prepare (wool, flax, or cotton) for manufacture with a comb. **3** search carefully and systematically.
– ORIGIN Old English: of Germanic origin.

combat ■ n. fighting, especially between armed forces. ■ v. (**combated** or **combatted, combating** or **combatting**) take action to reduce or prevent (something bad or undesirable).
– ORIGIN C16: from French *combattre*, from late Latin, from *com-* 'together with' + *battere*, var. of Latin *batuere* 'to fight'.

combatant /ˈkɒmbət(ə)nt, ˈkʌm-/ ■ n. a person or nation engaged in fighting during a war. ■ adj. engaged in fighting during a war.

combat fatigue ■ n. **1** more recent term for SHELL SHOCK. **2** (**combat fatigues**) uniform worn by soldiers in combat.

combative /ˈkɒmbətɪv, ˈkʌm-/ ■ adj. ready or eager to fight or argue.
– DERIVATIVES **combatively** adv. **combativeness** n.

combe /kuːm/ (also **coomb** or **coombe**) ■ n. Brit. a short valley or hollow on a hillside or coastline, especially in southern England.
– ORIGIN Old English *cumb*, of Celtic origin.

comber[1] /ˈkəʊmə/ ■ n. **1** a long curling sea wave. **2** a person or machine that combs cotton or wool.

comber[2] /ˈkɒmbə/ ■ n. a small coastal sea bass. [*Serranus cabrilla*.]
– ORIGIN C18.

combi ■ n. variant spelling of KOMBI.

combination ■ n. **1** the action of combining two or more different things. **2** a union in which the component elements are individually distinct. **3** Mathematics a group of things chosen from a larger number without regard to their arrangement. **4** a sequence of numbers or letters used to open a combination lock. **5** (**combinations**) dated a single undergarment covering the body and legs.
– DERIVATIVES **combinational** adj. **combinative** adj. **combinatory** adj.

combination lock ■ n. a lock that is opened by rotating a set of dials, marked with letters or numbers, to show a specific sequence.

combination therapy ■ n. treatment in which a patient is given two or more drugs for one disease.

combinatorial /ˌkɒmbɪnəˈtɔːrɪəl/ ■ adj. Mathematics of or relating to combinations of items.
– DERIVATIVES **combinatorially** adv. **combinatorics** pl. n.

combine ■ v. /kəmˈbaɪn/ unite; merge. ▶ Chemistry unite to form a compound. ■ n. /ˈkɒmbaɪn/ a group of people or companies acting together for a commercial purpose.
– DERIVATIVES **combinable** adj. **combiner** n.
– ORIGIN Middle English: from Old French *combiner* or late Latin *combinare* 'join two by two', from *com-* 'together' + Latin *bini* 'two together'.

combine harvester ■ n. an agricultural machine that reaps, threshes, and cleans a cereal crop in one operation.

combing wool ■ n. long-stapled wool with straight, parallel fibres, suitable for combing and making into high-quality fabrics. Compare with CARDING WOOL.

combining form ■ n. Grammar a form of a word normally used in compounds in combination with another element to form a word (e.g. *bio-* 'life' in *biology*).

comb jelly ■ n. a marine animal with a jellyfish-like body bearing rows of fused cilia for propulsion. [Phylum Ctenophora.]

combo ■ n. (pl. **-os**) informal **1** a small jazz, rock, or pop band. **2** a combination. ▶ a guitar amplifier with an integral speaker rather than a separate one.

combretum /kɒmˈbriːtəm/ ■ n. a shrub or tree with characteristic winged fruits, common in African savannah. [Family Combretaceae: numerous species.]

combust /kəmˈbʌst/ ■ v. consume or be consumed by fire.
– DERIVATIVES **combustible** adj. & n.
– ORIGIN C15 (earlier Middle English as *combustion*): from obsolete *combust* 'burnt, calcined', from Latin *combust-*, *comburere* 'burn up'.

combustion ■ n. the process of burning. ▶ Chemistry rapid chemical combination with oxygen, involving the production of heat and light.
– DERIVATIVES **combustive** adj.

combustion chamber ■ n. an enclosed space in which combustion takes place, especially in an engine or furnace.

come ■ v. (past **came**; past part. **come**) **1** move or travel towards or into a place thought of as near or familiar to the speaker. ▶ arrive. ▶ (of a thing) reach or extend to a specified point. ▶ join in a specified activity: *do you want to come fishing?* ▶ (**come along/on**) make progress; develop. ▶ said to correct, reassure, or urge on someone. **2** occur; happen; take place. ▶ (**come across** or chiefly Brit. **over** or US **off**) give a specified impression. **3** occupy or achieve a specified position in space, order, or priority: *she came second*. **4** pass into a specified state, especially one of separation: *his shirt had come undone*. ▶ (**come to/into**) reach or be brought to a specified situation. **5** be sold or available in a specified form. **6** informal have an orgasm. ■ prep. informal when a specified time is reached or event happens. ■ n. informal semen ejaculated at an orgasm.
– PHRASES **come again?** informal used to ask someone to repeat or explain something they have said. **come off it** informal said when vigorously expressing disbelief. **come right** informal have a good outcome; end well. **come right with someone** S. African informal respond appropriately or receive satisfactory treatment: *Tell me if he doesn't come right with you*. **come the ——** informal play the part of; behave like: *don't come the innocent with me*. **come to nothing** have no significant or successful result. **come to pass** chiefly poetic/literary happen; occur. **come to that** (or **if it comes to that**) informal in fact; if that is the case. **come to think of it** on reflection. **come what may** no matter what happens. **have it coming (to** one) informal be due for retribution. **how come?** informal said when asking how or why something happened. **not know if one is coming or going** informal be confused, especially through being very busy. **to come** in the future.
– PHRASAL VERBS **come about 1** happen; take place. **2** (of a ship) change direction. **come across 1** meet or find by chance. **2** informal hand over what is wanted. **come around** see *come round*. **come at** launch oneself at; attack. **come away** be left with a specified feeling or result. **come back** chiefly N. Amer. reply or respond, especially vigorously. **come before** be dealt with by (a judge or court). **come by** manage to acquire or obtain. **come down on 1** criticize or punish harshly. **2** reach a decision or recommendation in favour of one side or another. **come down to** be dependent on (a factor). **come for** launch oneself at in order to attack. **come forward** volunteer for a task or to give evidence. **come from** originate in; have as a source or place of birth. **come in 1** have a useful role or function. **2** (of money) be earned or received regularly. **3** join others in speaking or playing music. **4** (of the tide) rise; advance to high tide. **come in for** receive (a reaction), typically a negative one. **come into** inherit (money or property). **come of 1** result from. **2** be descended from. **come off 1** succeed; be accomplished. ▶ fare in a specified way. **2** become detached. **3** Brit. informal have an orgasm. **come on 1** (of a state or condition) start to arrive or happen. **2** (also **come upon**) meet or find by chance. **3** said to encourage or correct someone or hurry them up. **come on to** informal make sexual advances towards. **come out 1** (of a fact) emerge; become known. ▶ happen as a result. ▶ (of a photograph) be produced satisfactorily or in a specified way. ▶ (of the result of a calculation or measurement) emerge at a specified figure. ▶ (of patience or a similar card game) be played to a finish with all cards dealt with. **2** (of a book or other work) be released or published. **3** declare oneself as being for or against something. **4** achieve a specified placing in an examination or contest. ▶ acquit oneself in a specified way. **5** (of a stain) be removed or able to be removed. **6** Brit. go on strike. **7** informal openly declare that one is homosexual. **8** Brit. dated (of a young upper-class

woman) make one's debut in society. **come out in** Brit. (of a person's skin) break out in (spots or a similar condition). **come out with** say in a sudden, rude, or incautious way. **come over 1** (of a feeling) begin to affect. ▸ Brit. informal suddenly start to feel a specified way. **2** change to another side or point of view. **come round** chiefly Brit. (chiefly US also **come around**) **1** recover consciousness. **2** be converted to another person's opinion. **3** (of a date or regular occurrence) recur; be imminent again. **come through 1** succeed in surviving or dealing with. **2** (of a message) be sent and received. ▸ (of an official decree) be processed and notified. **come to 1** recover consciousness. **2** (of an expense) reach in total; amount to. **3** (of a ship) come to a stop. **come under 1** be classified as or among. **2** be subject to. **come up** (of a situation or problem) occur or present itself, especially unexpectedly. ▸ (of a time or event) approach or draw near. **come up against** be faced with or opposed by. **come up with** produce (something), especially when pressured or challenged. **come upon 1** attack by surprise. **2** see *come on* (sense 2).
– ORIGIN Old English: of Germanic origin.

comeback ▪ n. **1** a return to prominence or fashion. **2** informal a quick reply to a critical remark. ▸ opportunity to seek redress.

comedian ▪ n. (fem. **comedienne**) an entertainer whose act is designed to arouse laughter. ▸ a comic playwright.

comedogenic /ˌkɒmɪdə(ʊ)ˈdʒɛnɪk/ ▪ adj. tending to block the pores of the skin and thereby cause black-heads.
– ORIGIN C19: from Latin *comedo* 'glutton' (a former name for parasitic worms, the term now refers to the matter squeezed from a blackhead).

comedown ▪ n. informal **1** a loss of status or importance. **2** a feeling of disappointment or depression. ▸ a lessening of the sensations generated by a narcotic drug as its effects wear off.

comedy ▪ n. (pl. **-ies**) **1** entertainment consisting of jokes and sketches intended to make an audience laugh. ▸ a film, play, or programme intended to arouse laughter. **2** a play with a humorous or satirical tone, in which the characters ultimately triumph over adversity.
– DERIVATIVES **comedic** /kəˈmiːdɪk, -ˈmɛ-/ adj.
– ORIGIN Middle English: from Old French *comedie*, from Greek *kōmōidia*, from *kōmos* 'revel' + *aoidos* 'singer'.

comedy of manners ▪ n. a play, novel, or film that gives a satirical portrayal of behaviour in a particular social group.

come-hither ▪ adj. informal flirtatious or coquettish: *a come-hither look.*

comely /ˈkʌmli/ ▪ adj. (**-ier**, **-iest**) **1** archaic or humorous (typically of a woman) pleasant to look at; attractive. **2** archaic agreeable; suitable.
– DERIVATIVES **comeliness** n.
– ORIGIN Middle English: prob. shortened from *becomely* 'fitting, becoming', from BECOME.

come-on ▪ n. informal **1** a gesture or remark intended to attract someone sexually. **2** a marketing ploy, such as a free or cheap offer.

COMESA /kəˈmɛsə/ (also **Comesa**) ▪ abbrev. Common Market for Eastern and Southern Africa.

comestible /kəˈmɛstɪb(ə)l/ formal or humorous ▪ n. an item of food. ▪ adj. edible.
– ORIGIN C15: from medieval Latin *comestibilis*, from Latin *comedere* 'eat up'.

comet /ˈkɒmɪt/ ▪ n. a celestial object which consists of a nucleus of ice and dust and, when near the sun, a diffuse tail, and typically follows a highly eccentric orbit around the sun.
– DERIVATIVES **cometary** adj.
– ORIGIN Old English, from Latin *cometa*, from Greek *komētēs* 'long-haired (star)', from *komē* 'hair'.

comeuppance ▪ n. informal a punishment or fate that someone deserves.

comfit /ˈkʌmfɪt/ ▪ n. archaic a sweet consisting of a nut, seed, or other centre coated in sugar.
– ORIGIN Middle English: from Old French *confit*, from Latin *conficere* (see CONFECT).

comfort ▪ n. **1** a state of physical ease and freedom from pain or constraint. ▸ (**comforts**) things that contribute to comfort. ▸ prosperity and a pleasant lifestyle. **2** consolation for grief or anxiety. ▸ a person or thing that gives such consolation. ▪ v. cause to feel less unhappy; console.
– DERIVATIVES **comforting** adj. **comfortingly** adv. **comfortless** adj.
– ORIGIN Middle English: from Old French *confort* (n.), *conforter* (v.), from late Latin *confortare* 'strengthen'.

comfortable ▪ adj. **1** providing or enjoying physical comfort. ▸ relaxed and free from constraint. **2** free from financial worry. **3** (of a victory) with a wide margin.
– DERIVATIVES **comfortableness** n. **comfortably** adv.

comforter ▪ n. **1** a person or thing that provides consolation. **2** dated a woollen scarf. **3** S. African & N. Amer. a warm quilt.

comfrey /ˈkʌmfri/ ▪ n. (pl. **-eys**) a plant with large hairy leaves and clusters of purplish or white bell-shaped flowers. [*Symphytum officinale* and related species.]
– ORIGIN Middle English: from Anglo-Norman French *cumfirie*, from Latin *conferva*, from *confervere* 'heal' (referring to the plant's medicinal use).

comfy ▪ adj. (**-ier**, **-iest**) informal comfortable.

comic ▪ adj. causing or meant to cause laughter. ▸ relating to or in the style of comedy. ▪ n. **1** a comedian. **2** a children's periodical containing comic strips. ▸ (**comics**) N. Amer. comic strips.
– ORIGIN C16: from Greek *kōmikos*, from *kōmos* 'revel'.

comical ▪ adj. amusing.
– DERIVATIVES **comically** adv.

comic opera ▪ n. an opera that portrays humorous situations and characters, with much spoken dialogue.

comic relief ▪ n. humorous content in a dramatic or literary work which offsets more serious portions.

comic strip ▪ n. a sequence of drawings in boxes that tell an amusing story.

COMINT /ˈkɒmɪnt/ ▪ abbrev. communications intelligence.

comity /ˈkɒmɪti/ ▪ n. (pl. **-ies**) **1** an association of nations for their mutual benefit. ▸ (also **comity of nations**) the mutual recognition by nations of the laws and customs of others. **2** formal courtesy and considerate behaviour towards others.
– ORIGIN C16: from Latin *comitas*, from *comis* 'courteous'.

comma ▪ n. **1** a punctuation mark (,) indicating a pause between parts of a sentence or separating items in a list. ▸ S. African a mark (,) representing a decimal comma: *two comma five* (2,5) *metres*. **2** a widespread butterfly that has orange and brown wings and a white comma-shaped mark on the underside of the hindwing. [*Polygonia c-album*.]
– ORIGIN C16: from Greek *komma* 'piece cut off, short clause', from *koptein* 'cut'.

command ▪ v. **1** give an authoritative or peremptory order. ▸ Military be in charge of (a unit). ▸ archaic control or restrain (oneself or one's feelings). **2** dominate (a strategic position) from a superior height. **3** be in a position to receive (something such as respect). ▪ n. **1** an authoritative order. ▸ authority, especially over armed forces: *the officer in command.* ▸ [treated as sing. or pl.] a group of officers exercising control over a particular group or operation. ▸ a body of troops or a district under the control of a particular officer. **2** the ability to use or control something: *his command of English*. **3** Computing an instruction causing a computer to perform one of its basic functions.
– ORIGIN Middle English: from late Latin *commandare*, from *com-* (expressing intensive force) + *mandare* 'commit, command'.

commandant /ˌkɒmənˈdant, ˈkɒmənˌdant, -dɑːnt/ ▪ n. an officer in charge of a particular force or institution. ▸ S. African historical (especially in the Anglo-Boer Wars) the chief military officer of a district; a leader of a commando.

command economy ▪ n. another term for PLANNED ECONOMY.

commandeer /ˌkɒmənˈdɪə/ ▪ v. officially take possession or control of for military purposes. ▸ seize for one's own purposes.
– ORIGIN C19: from Afrikaans *kommandeer*, from Dutch *commanderen*, from French *commander* 'command'.

commander ▪ n. a person in authority, especially in a

commander-in-chief

military context. ▸ a rank of naval officer, above lieutenant commander and below captain.
– DERIVATIVES **commandership** n.

commander-in-chief ■ n. (pl. **commanders-in-chief**) an officer in charge of all of the armed forces of a country, or a major subdivision of them.

commanding ■ adj. **1** having a position of authority. ▸ indicating or expressing authority. **2** possessing or giving superior strength: *a commanding lead.*
– DERIVATIVES **commandingly** adv.

commandment ■ n. a divine rule, especially one of the Ten Commandments.

command module ■ n. the detachable control compartment of a manned spacecraft.

commando ■ n. (pl. **-os**) a soldier specially trained for carrying out raids. ▸ a unit of such troops. ▸ S. African a community-based reserve unit of the South African defence forces, with the primary task of regional protection. ▸ S. African historical a unit of the Boer forces during the Anglo-Boer Wars.
– PHRASES **on commando** S. African historical engaged in military service or on a military expedition.
– ORIGIN C18: from S. African Dutch, from Portuguese, from *commandar* 'to command'.

commando knife ■ n. a long, slender knife suitable for hand-to-hand combat.

commedia dell'arte /kɒˈmeɪdɪə delˈɑːteɪ/ ■ n. an improvised kind of popular comedy in Italian theatres in the 16th–18th centuries, based on stock characters.
– ORIGIN Italian, 'comedy of art'.

comme il faut /ˌkɒm iːl ˈfəʊ/ ■ adj. correct in behaviour or etiquette.
– ORIGIN French, 'as is necessary'.

commemorate ■ v. honour the memory of as a mark of respect, especially with a ceremony or memorial.
– DERIVATIVES **commemoration** n. **commemorative** adj.
– ORIGIN C16 (*commemoration* Middle English): from Latin *commemorare* 'bring to remembrance'.

commence ■ v. begin.
– ORIGIN Middle English: from Old French *commencier*, from Latin *com-* (expressing intensive force) + *initiare* 'begin'.

commencement ■ n. **1** the beginning of something. **2** N. Amer. a ceremony in which degrees or diplomas are conferred.

commend ■ v. **1** praise formally or officially. **2** present as suitable or good; recommend. **3** (**commend someone/thing to**) archaic or formal entrust someone or something to. ▸ pass on someone's good wishes to.
– DERIVATIVES **commendation** n. **commendatory** adj.
– ORIGIN Middle English: from Latin *commendare*, from *com-* (expressing intensive force) + *mandare* 'commit, entrust'.

commendable ■ adj. deserving praise.
– DERIVATIVES **commendably** adv.

commensal /kəˈmɛns(ə)l/ Biology ■ adj. relating to or denoting an association between two organisms in which one benefits and the other derives neither benefit nor harm. ■ n. a commensal organism, such as many bacteria.
– DERIVATIVES **commensalism** n.
– ORIGIN C19: from medieval Latin *commensalis*, from *com-* 'sharing' + *mensa* 'a table'.

commensurable /kəˈmɛnʃ(ə)rəb(ə)l, -sjə-/ ■ adj. **1** measurable by the same standard. **2** (**commensurable to**) proportionate to. **3** Mathematics (of numbers) in a ratio equal to a ratio of integers.
– DERIVATIVES **commensurably** adv.
– ORIGIN C16: from late Latin, from *com-* 'together' + *mensurare*, from *mensurare* 'to measure'.

commensurate /kəˈmɛnʃ(ə)rət, -sjə-/ ■ adj. corresponding in size or degree; in proportion.
– DERIVATIVES **commensurately** adv.
– ORIGIN C17: from late Latin *commensuratus*, from *com-* 'together' + *mensurare* 'to measure'.

comment ■ n. a remark expressing an opinion or reaction. ▸ discussion, especially of a critical nature, of an issue or event. ▸ an explanatory note in a book or other written text. ■ v. express an opinion or reaction.
– DERIVATIVES **commenter** n.
– ORIGIN Middle English: from Latin *commentum* 'contrivance', from *comminisci* 'devise'.

commentary ■ n. (pl. **-ies**) **1** the expression of opinions or offering of explanations about an event or situation. ▸ a set of explanatory or critical notes on a text. **2** a descriptive spoken account (especially on radio or television) of a sports match or other event as it happens.

commentate ■ v. provide a commentary on a sports match or other event.

commentator ■ n. **1** a person who comments on events or texts, especially in the media. **2** a person who provides a commentary on a sports match or other event.

commerce ■ n. **1** the activity of buying and selling, especially on a large scale. **2** dated social dealings between people.
– ORIGIN C16: from Latin *commercium* 'trade, trading', from *com-* 'together' + *merx*, *merc-* 'merchandise'.

commercial ■ adj. **1** concerned with or engaged in commerce. **2** making or intended to make a profit. **3** (of television or radio) funded by the revenue from broadcast advertisements. **4** (of chemicals) supplied in bulk and not of the highest purity. ■ n. a television or radio advertisement.
– DERIVATIVES **commerciality** n. **commercially** adv.

commercial art ■ n. art used in advertising and selling.

commercial bank ■ n. a bank that offers services to the general public and to companies.

commercial bill ■ n. a bill of exchange issued by a commercial organization to raise money for short-term needs.

commercial break ■ n. an interruption in a radio or television broadcast for advertisements.

commercialism ■ n. emphasis on the maximizing of profit.

commercialize (also **-ise**) ■ v. manage or exploit in a way designed to make a profit.
– DERIVATIVES **commercialization** (also **-isation**) n.

commercial paper ■ n. short-term unsecured promissory notes issued by companies.

commercial traveller ■ n. dated, chiefly Brit. a travelling sales representative.

commercial vehicle ■ n. a vehicle used for carrying goods or fare-paying passengers.

Commie ■ n. (pl. **-ies**) informal, derogatory a communist.

commingle /kɒˈmɪŋg(ə)l/ ■ v. poetic/literary mix; blend.

comminuted /ˈkɒmɪnjuːtɪd/ ■ adj. Medicine (of a fracture) producing multiple bone splinters.
– ORIGIN C17: from Latin *comminuere* 'break into pieces'.

commis chef /ˈkɒmɪ/ ■ n. (pl. same /ˈkɒmɪ, ˈkɒmɪz/) a junior chef.
– ORIGIN 1930s: from French, 'deputy, clerk'.

commiserate /kəˈmɪzəreɪt/ ■ v. express sympathy or pity; sympathize.
– DERIVATIVES **commiseration** n. **commiserative** adj.
– ORIGIN C16: from Latin, from *com-* 'with' + *miserari* 'to lament'.

commissar /ˌkɒmɪˈsɑː/ ■ n. a Communist official, especially in Soviet Russia or China, responsible for political education. ▸ a head of a government department in the Soviet Union before 1946.
– ORIGIN C20: from Russian *komissar*, from French *commissaire*.

commissariat /ˌkɒmɪˈsɛːrɪət/ ■ n. **1** chiefly Military a department for the supply of food and equipment. **2** a government department of the Soviet Union before 1946.
– ORIGIN C16: from French *commissariat*, from medieval Latin *commissarius* (see **COMMISSARY**).

commissary /ˈkɒmɪs(ə)ri/ ■ n. (pl. **-ies**) **1** a deputy or delegate. ▸ a representative or deputy of a bishop. **2** N. Amer. a restaurant or food store in a military base or other institution.
– DERIVATIVES **commissarial** /-ˈsɛːrɪəl/ adj.
– ORIGIN Middle English: from medieval Latin *commissarius* 'person in charge', from Latin *committere* (see **COMMIT**).

commission ■ n. **1** an instruction or command. ▶ an order for something, especially a work of art, to be produced specially. **2** a group of people given official authority to do something. **3** a sum paid to an agent in a commercial transaction. **4** a warrant conferring the rank of military officer. **5** the action of committing a crime or offence. ■ v. **1** order or authorize the production of. ▶ order or authorize (someone) to do or produce something. **2** bring into working order. **3** appoint to the rank of military officer.
– PHRASES **in** (or **out of**) **commission** in (or not in) use or working order.
– ORIGIN Middle English: from Latin *commissio(n-)*, from *committere* (see COMMIT).

commissionaire /kəˌmɪʃəˈnɛː/ ■ n. chiefly Brit. a uniformed door attendant at a hotel, theatre, or other building.
– ORIGIN C17: from medieval Latin *commissarius* (see COMMISSARY).

commissioner ■ n. a person appointed to a role on or by a commission. ▶ a representative of the supreme authority in an area. ▶ N. Amer. a person appointed to regulate a particular sport.

commissioner for oaths (also **commissioner of oaths**) ■ n. a person authorized to administer an oath to a person making an affidavit.

commit ■ v. (**committed, committing**) **1** perpetrate or carry out (a mistake, crime, or immoral act). **2** pledge or bind to a course, policy, or use. ▶ [often as adj. **committed**] dedicate to a cause: *a committed Christian*. ▶ (**be committed**) be in a long-term emotional relationship. **3** transfer for safe keeping or permanent preservation. ▶ send to prison or psychiatric hospital, or for trial in a higher court. ▶ refer (a parliamentary or legislative bill) to a committee.
– DERIVATIVES **committer** n.
– ORIGIN Middle English: from Latin *committere* 'join, entrust', from *com-* 'with' + *mittere* 'put or send'.

commitment ■ n. **1** the state or quality of being dedicated to a cause or policy. ▶ a pledge or undertaking. **2** an engagement or obligation that restricts freedom of action.

committal ■ n. **1** the sending of someone to prison or psychiatric hospital, or for trial. **2** the burial of a corpse.

committee ■ n. **1** /kəˈmɪti/ [treated as sing. or pl.] a group of people appointed for a specific function by a larger group. **2** /ˌkɒmɪˈtiː/ chiefly US a person who has been judicially committed to the charge of another because of insanity or mental retardation.

committee stage ■ n. the third of five stages of a bill's progress through Parliament, when it may be debated and amended.

commode ■ n. **1** a piece of furniture containing a concealed chamber pot. ▶ N. Amer. a toilet. **2** a chest of drawers or chiffonier of a decorative type popular in the 18th century. **3** N. Amer. historical a movable washstand.
– ORIGIN C18: from French, 'convenient, suitable'.

commodify /kəˈmɒdɪfʌɪ/ ■ v. (**-ies, -ied**) turn into or treat as a mere commodity.

commodious /kəˈməʊdɪəs/ ■ adj. **1** formal roomy and comfortable. **2** archaic convenient.
– DERIVATIVES **commodiously** adv. **commodiousness** n.
– ORIGIN Middle English: from medieval Latin *commodiosus*, from Latin *commodus* 'convenient'.

commodity /kəˈmɒdɪti/ ■ n. (pl. **-ies**) **1** a raw material or primary agricultural product that can be bought and sold. **2** something useful or valuable.
– ORIGIN Middle English: from Old French *commodite* or Latin *commoditas*, from *commodus* 'convenient'.

commodore /ˈkɒmədɔː/ ■ n. a naval rank above captain and below rear admiral, generally given temporarily to an officer commanding a squadron or division of a fleet. ▶ the president of a yacht club.
– ORIGIN C17: prob. from Dutch *komandeur*, from French *commandeur* 'commander'.

common ■ adj. (**-er, -est**) **1** occurring, found, or done often; not rare. ▶ without special rank or position; ordinary. ▶ (of a quality) of a sort to be generally expected: *common decency*. ▶ of the most familiar type. **2** showing a lack of taste and refinement supposedly typical of the lower classes; vulgar. **3** shared by two or more people or things. ▶ belonging to or affecting the whole of a community: *common land*. ▶ Mathematics belonging to two or more quantities. **4** Grammar of or denoting a noun that refers to individuals of either sex (e.g. *teacher*) or belongs to a gender conventionally regarded as masculine or feminine. **5** Prosody (of a syllable) able to be either short or long. **6** Law (of a crime) of lesser importance. ■ n. **1** a piece of open land for public use. **2** (also **right of common**) English Law a person's right over another's land, e.g. for pasturage or mineral extraction.
– PHRASES **common ground** views shared by each of two or more differing parties. **common or garden** informal of the usual or ordinary type. **in common** in joint use or possession; shared. **in common with** in the same way as. **out of the common** rarely occurring; unusual.
– DERIVATIVES **commonness** n.
– ORIGIN Middle English: from Old French *comun*, from Latin *communis*.

commonage ■ n. **1** chiefly Brit. the right of pasturing animals on common land. ▶ land held in common. **2** the common people; the commonalty.

commonality ■ n. (pl. **-ies**) **1** the state of sharing features or attributes. ▶ a shared feature or attribute. **2** (**the commonality**) another term for COMMONALTY.

commonalty /ˈkɒmən(ə)lti/ ■ n. [treated as pl.] (**the commonalty**) Brit., chiefly historical people without special rank or position, usually viewed as an estate of the realm.
– ORIGIN Middle English: from medieval Latin *communalitas*, from Latin *communis* (see COMMON).

common carrier ■ n. **1** a person or company undertaking to transport any goods or passengers on regular routes at agreed rates. **2** a company providing public telecommunications facilities.

common denominator ■ n. **1** Mathematics a common multiple of the denominators of several fractions. **2** a feature shared by all members of a group.

commoner ■ n. **1** one of the ordinary or common people, as opposed to the aristocracy or to royalty. **2** a person who has the right of common.

Common Era ■ n. another term for CHRISTIAN ERA.

common fiscal ■ n. an African shrike with black-and-white plumage. [*Lanius collaris*.]

common fraction ■ n. a fraction expressed by numerator and denominator, not decimally.

common law ■ n. **1** the part of South African and English law that is derived from custom and judicial precedent rather than statutes. **2** [as modifier] denoting a partner in a marriage recognized in some jurisdictions as valid by common law, though not brought about by a civil or ecclesiastical ceremony. ▶ denoting a partner in a relationship in which a man and woman cohabit for a period long enough to suggest stability.

common logarithm ■ n. a logarithm to the base 10.

commonly ■ adv. very often; frequently.

common market ■ n. a group of countries imposing few or no duties on trade with one another and a common tariff on trade with other countries.

common noun ■ n. Grammar a noun denoting a class of objects or a concept as opposed to a particular individual. Often contrasted with PROPER NOUN.

commonplace ■ adj. not unusual; ordinary. ▶ not interesting or original; trite. ■ n. **1** a usual or ordinary thing. ▶ a trite saying or topic; a platitude.
– ORIGIN C16: translation of Latin *locus communis*, rendering Greek *koinos topos* 'general theme'.

common room ■ n. a room in an educational institution for use of students or staff outside teaching hours.

commons ■ pl. n. **1** (**the Commons**) short for HOUSE OF COMMONS. **2** [treated as sing.] land or resources belonging to or affecting the whole of a community. **3** archaic provisions shared in common; rations.
– PHRASES **short commons** insufficient allocation of food.

common seal ■ n. an official seal of a corporate body.

common sense ■ n. good sense and sound judgement in practical matters.
– DERIVATIVES **commonsensical** adj.

common stock (also **common stocks**) ■ pl. n. chiefly N. Amer. ordinary shares.

commonweal /ˈkɒmənwiːl/ ■ n. (**the commonweal**) archaic the welfare of the public.

commonwealth ■ n. **1** an independent state or community, especially a democratic republic. ▸ a formal title of certain US states. ▸ the title of the federated Australian states. **2** (**the Commonwealth**) (in full **the Commonwealth of Nations**) an international association consisting of the UK together with states that were previously part of the British Empire, and dependencies.

commotion ■ n. **1** a state of confused and noisy disturbance. **2** civil insurrection.
– ORIGIN Middle English: from Latin *commotio(n-)*, from *com-* 'altogether' + *motio* (see MOTION).

communal /ˈkɒmjun(ə)l, kəˈmjuː-/ ■ adj. **1** shared or done by all members of a community. ▸ involving the sharing of work and property: *communal living*. **2** (of conflict) between different communities, especially those having different religions or ethnic origins.
– DERIVATIVES **communality** n. **communalization** (also **-isation**) n. **communally** adv.
– ORIGIN C19: from late Latin *communalis*, from *communis* (see COMMON).

communalism ■ n. **1** a principle of political organization based on federated communes. ▸ the principle or practice of living together communally. **2** allegiance to one's own ethnic group rather than to the wider society.
– DERIVATIVES **communalist** adj. & n.

commune[1] /ˈkɒmjuːn/ ■ n. a group of people living together and sharing possessions and responsibilities. ▸ a communal settlement in a communist country. ▸ a dwelling shared by a group of people.
– ORIGIN C17: from medieval Latin *communia*, from Latin *communis* (see COMMON).

commune[2] /kəˈmjuːn/ ■ v. (**commune with**) share one's intimate thoughts or feelings with. ▸ feel in close spiritual contact with.
– ORIGIN Middle English: from Old French *comuner* 'to share', from *comun* (see COMMON).

communicable ■ adj. (especially of a disease) able to be communicated to others.
– DERIVATIVES **communicability** n.

communicant ■ n. a person who receives Holy Communion.

communicate ■ v. **1** share or exchange information or ideas. ▸ convey (an emotion or feeling) in a non-verbal way. ▸ pass on (an infectious disease). ▸ transmit (heat or motion). **2** [often as adj. **communicating**] (of two rooms) have a common connecting door.
– DERIVATIVES **communicator** n.
– ORIGIN C16 (*communication* Middle English): from Latin *communicare* 'share', from *communis* (see COMMON).

communication ■ n. **1** the action of communicating. ▸ a letter or message containing information or news. ▸ social contact. **2** (**communications**) the means of sending or receiving information, such as telephone lines or computers. ▸ the means of travelling or of transporting goods, such as roads or railways.
– PHRASES **line of communications** the connections between an army in the field and its bases.
– DERIVATIVES **communicational** adj.

communication cord ■ n. a cord or chain which a train passenger may pull in an emergency, causing the train to brake.

communications satellite ■ n. a satellite placed in orbit round the earth in order to relay television, radio, and telephone signals.

communicative ■ adj. **1** willing, eager, or able to talk or impart information. **2** relating to the conveyance or exchange of information.
– DERIVATIVES **communicatively** adv.

communion ■ n. **1** the sharing or exchanging of intimate thoughts and feelings. **2** (also **Holy Communion**) the service of Christian worship at which bread and wine are consecrated and shared; the Eucharist. **3** a relationship of recognition and acceptance between Christian Churches or denominations.
– ORIGIN Middle English: from Latin *communio(n-)*, from *communis* (see COMMON).

communiqué /kəˈmjuːnɪkeɪ/ ■ n. an official announcement or statement, especially one made to the media.
– ORIGIN C19: from French *communiquer* 'communicate'.

communism ■ n. a theory or system of social organization in which all property is vested in the community and each person contributes and receives according to their ability and needs. ▸ a theory or system of this kind derived from Marxism and established in the Soviet Union, China, and elsewhere.
– DERIVATIVES **communist** n. & adj. **communistic** adj.
– ORIGIN C19: from French *communisme*, from *commun* (see COMMON).

communitarianism /kəˌmjuːnɪˈtɛːrɪənɪz(ə)m/ ■ n. **1** a system of social organization based on small self-governing communities. **2** an ideology which emphasizes the responsibility of the individual to the community and the social importance of the family unit.
– DERIVATIVES **communitarian** adj. & n.

community ■ n. (pl. **-ies**) **1** a group of people living together in one place, especially one practising common ownership. ▸ a place considered together with its inhabitants: *a rural community*. ▸ (**the community**) the people of an area or country considered collectively; society. **2** a group of people having a religion, race, or profession in common: *the scientific community*. **3** the condition of having certain attitudes and interests in common. ▸ joint ownership or liability. **4** Ecology a group of interdependent plants or animals growing or living together.
– ORIGIN Middle English: from Old French *comunete* and Latin *communitas*, from *communis* (see COMMON).

community care ■ n. long-term care for the mentally ill, the elderly, and people with disabilities provided within the community rather than in hospitals or institutions.

community centre ■ n. a place providing educational or recreational activities for a neighbourhood.

community chest ■ n. a fund for charitable activities among the people in a particular area.

community home ■ n. Brit. a centre for housing young offenders and other young people in need of custodial care.

community of property ■ n. S. African Law a marriage contract in which the possessions of the partners are merged in a joint estate, and disposed of by means of a joint will. Compare with ANTENUPTIAL CONTRACT.

community service ■ n. unpaid work, intended to be of social use, that an offender is required to do instead of going to prison.

commutate /ˈkɒmjʊteɪt/ ■ v. regulate or reverse the direction of (an alternating electric current), especially to make it a direct current.
– ORIGIN C19: from Latin *commutare* (see COMMUTE).

commutation ■ n. **1** the action or process of commuting a judicial sentence or a legal obligation or entitlement. **2** the process of commutating an electric current. **3** Mathematics the property of having a commutative relation.

commutative /kəˈmjuːtətɪv, ˈkɒmjʊˌtətɪv/ ■ adj. Mathematics involving the condition that a group of quantities connected by operators gives the same result whatever the order of the quantities involved, e.g. $a \times b = b \times a$.

commutator /ˈkɒmjʊˌteɪtə/ ■ n. **1** an attachment, connected with the armature of a motor or dynamo, through which electrical connection is made and which ensures the current flows as direct current. **2** a device for reversing the direction of flow of electric current.

commute ■ v. **1** travel some distance between one's home and place of work on a regular basis. **2** reduce (a judicial sentence, especially a sentence of death) to a less severe one. ▸ change one kind of payment or obligation for (another). ▸ replace (an annuity or other series of payments) with a single payment. **3** Mathematics (of two

operations or quantities) have a commutative relation.
– DERIVATIVES **commutable** adj. **commuter** n.
– ORIGIN Middle English: from Latin *commutare*, from *com-* 'altogether' + *mutare* 'to change'; sense 1 derives from *commutation ticket*, the US term for a season ticket (because the daily fare is commuted to a single payment).

Comoran /'kɒmərən/ ■ n. a native or inhabitant of the Comoros, a country consisting of a group of islands to the north of Madagascar. ■ adj. of or relating to the Comoros.

co-morbid ■ adj. Medicine relating to or denoting a medical condition that co-occurs with another.
– DERIVATIVES **co-morbidity** n.

comp ■ abbrev. informal **1** a competition. **2** S. African & N. Amer. a complimentary ticket or voucher. ■ v. **1** [as noun **comping**] Brit. informal the practice of entering competitions. **2** N. Amer. give away as part of a promotion. ■ adj. N. Amer. complimentary; free.

compact[1] ■ adj. /kəm'pakt/ closely and neatly packed together; dense. ▶ having all the necessary components or features neatly fitted into a small space. ■ v. /kəm'pakt/ exert force on to make more dense; compress. ■ n. /'kɒmpakt/ a small flat case containing face powder, a mirror, and a powder puff.
– DERIVATIVES **compaction** n. **compactly** adv. **compactness** n. **compactor** n.
– ORIGIN Middle English: from Latin *compact-*, *compingere*, from *com-* 'together' + *pangere* 'fasten'.

compact[2] /'kɒmpakt/ ■ n. a formal agreement or contract between two or more parties. ■ v. make or enter into (a formal agreement).
– ORIGIN C16: from Latin *compact-*, *compacisci*, from *com-* 'with' + *pacisci* 'make a covenant'.

compact disc ■ n. a small plastic disc on which music or other digital information is stored in the form of a pattern of metal-coated pits from which it can be read using laser light reflected off the disc.

compand /kɒm'pand/ ■ v. reduce the signal-to-noise ratio of (a signal) using a compander.

compander (also **compandor**) ■ n. a device that improves the signal-to-noise ratio of an electrical signal by compressing the range of amplitudes of the signal before transmission, and then expanding it on reproduction or reception.
– ORIGIN 1930s: blend of **COMPRESSOR** and *expander*.

companion[1] ■ n. **1** a person with whom one spends time or travels. ▶ a person employed to live with and assist someone old or unwell. **2** each of a pair of things intended to complement or match each other.
– DERIVATIVES **companionship** n.
– ORIGIN Middle English: from Old French *compaignon* 'one who breaks bread with another', from Latin *com-* 'together with' + *panis* 'bread'.

companion[2] ■ n. Nautical **1** a covering over the hatchway leading to a companionway. **2** short for **COMPANIONWAY**.
– ORIGIN C18: from obsolete Dutch *kompanje* 'quarterdeck'.

companionable ■ adj. friendly and sociable.
– DERIVATIVES **companionableness** n. **companionably** adv.
– ORIGIN C17: from obsolete *companiable*, influenced by **COMPANION**[1].

companionate /kəm'panjənət/ ■ adj. formal (of a marriage or relationship) between partners or spouses as equal companions.

companion-in-arms ■ n. a fellow soldier.

companion set ■ n. a collection of fireside implements on a stand.

companionway ■ n. a set of steps leading from a ship's deck down to a cabin or lower deck.

company ■ n. (pl. **-ies**) **1** a commercial business. **2** the fact or condition of being with another or others. ▶ a person as a source of friendship and entertainment: *she is excellent company.* ▶ a visitor or visitors: *I'm expecting company.* **3** a number of individuals gathered together. ▶ a body of soldiers, especially the smallest subdivision of an infantry battalion. ▶ a group of actors, singers, or dancers who perform together. **4** (**the Company**) short for **DUTCH EAST INDIA COMPANY**.
– PHRASES **in company with** together with. **keep someone company** spend time with someone to prevent them feeling lonely or bored. **keep company with** associate

with habitually.
– ORIGIN Middle English: from Old French *compainie*; rel. to *compaignon* (see **COMPANION**[1]).

company car ■ n. a car provided by a firm for the business and private use of an employee.

comparable /'kɒmp(ə)rəb(ə)l/ ■ adj. able to be likened to another; similar. ▶ of equivalent quality.
– DERIVATIVES **comparability** n. **comparably** adv.

comparative /kəm'parətɪv/ ■ adj. **1** measured or judged by comparison; relative. **2** involving comparison between two or more subjects or branches of science: *comparative religion*. **3** Grammar (of an adjective or adverb) expressing a higher degree of a quality, but not the highest possible (e.g. *braver, more fiercely*). Contrasted with **POSITIVE**, **SUPERLATIVE**.

comparative advantage ■ n. Economics the ability of an individual or group to carry out a particular economic activity more efficiently than another activity.

comparative linguistics ■ pl. n. [treated as sing.] the study of similarities and differences between languages, in particular the comparison of related languages with a view to reconstructing forms in their lost parent languages.

comparatively ■ adv. to a moderate degree as compared to something else; relatively.

comparator /kəm'parətə/ ■ n. a device for comparing something measurable with a reference or standard. ▶ something used as a standard for comparison.

compare ■ v. **1** (often **compare something to/with**) estimate, measure, or note the similarity or dissimilarity between. ▶ (**compare something to**) point out or describe the resemblances of something with; liken to. ▶ (usu. **compare with**) be similar to or have a specified relationship with another thing or person: *salaries compare favourably with those of other professions*.
2 Grammar form the comparative and superlative degrees of (an adjective or an adverb).
– PHRASES **beyond** (or **without**) **compare** surpassing all others of the same kind. **compare notes** exchange ideas or information about a particular subject.
– ORIGIN Middle English: from Old French *comparer*, from Latin *comparare*, from *compar* 'like, equal'.

comparison ■ n. **1** the action of comparing. ▶ the quality of being similar or equivalent. **2** Grammar the formation of the comparative and superlative forms of adjectives and adverbs.
– PHRASES **beyond comparison** another way of saying beyond compare (see **COMPARE**).
– ORIGIN Middle English: from Old French *comparesoun*, from Latin, from *comparare* (see **COMPARE**).

compartment ■ n. **1** a separate section of a structure or container. ▶ a division of a railway carriage marked by partitions. **2** Heraldry a grassy mound or other support depicted below a shield. ■ v. divide into compartments.
– DERIVATIVES **compartmental** adj. **compartmentally** adv. **compartmentation** n.
– ORIGIN C16: from French *compartiment*, from late Latin *compartiri* 'divide'.

compartmentalize (also **-ise**) ■ v. divide into categories or sections.
– DERIVATIVES **compartmentalism** n. **compartmentalization** (also **-isation**) n.

compass ■ n. **1** an instrument containing a magnetized pointer which shows the direction of magnetic north and bearings from it. **2** (also **compasses**) an instrument for drawing circles and arcs and measuring distances between points, consisting of two arms linked by a movable joint. **3** range or scope. ■ v. archaic circle or surround.
– ORIGIN Middle English: from Old French *compas* (n.), *compasser* (v.), from Latin *com-* 'together' + *passus* 'a step or pace'.

compass card ■ n. a circular rotating card showing the thirty-two principal bearings, forming the indicator of a magnetic compass.

compassion ■ n. sympathetic pity and concern for the sufferings or misfortunes of others.
– ORIGIN Middle English: from eccles. Latin *compassio(n-)*, from *compati* 'suffer with'.

compassionate ■ adj. feeling or showing compassion.
– DERIVATIVES **compassionately** adv.

compassionate leave ■ n. a period of absence from work granted as the result of particular personal circumstances, especially the death of a close relative.

compassion fatigue ■ n. indifference to charitable appeals on behalf of those who are suffering, experienced as a result of the frequency of such appeals.

compass rose ■ n. a graduated circle printed on a map or chart from which bearings can be taken.

compass saw ■ n. a handsaw with a narrow blade for cutting curves.

compatible ■ adj. 1 able to exist or be used together without problems or conflict. ▸ (of two people) able to have a harmonious relationship; well suited. 2 (usu. **compatible with**) consistent or in keeping.
– DERIVATIVES **compatibility** n. **compatibly** adv.
– ORIGIN Middle English: from medieval Latin *compatibilis*, from *compati* 'suffer with'.

compatriot /kəm'patrɪət, -'peɪt-/ ■ n. a fellow citizen or national of a country.
– ORIGIN C16: from French *compatriote*, from late Latin *com-* 'together with' + *patriota* (see **PATRIOT**).

compel ■ v. (**compelled**, **compelling**) 1 force or oblige to do something. ▸ bring about by force or pressure. ▸ poetic/literary force to move in a particular direction. 2 [as adj. **compelling**] powerfully evoking attention or admiration.
– DERIVATIVES **compellingly** adv.
– ORIGIN Middle English: from Latin *compellere*, from *com-* 'together' + *pellere* 'drive'.

compellable ■ adj. Law (of a witness) able to be made to attend court or give evidence.

compendious ■ adj. formal presenting the essential facts in a comprehensive but concise way.
– DERIVATIVES **compendiously** adv. **compendiousness** n.
– ORIGIN Middle English: from Latin *compendiosus* 'advantageous, brief', from *compendium* 'profit, saving, abbreviation'.

compendium ■ n. (pl. **compendiums** or **compendia** /-dɪə/) 1 a collection of concise but detailed information about a particular subject. 2 a collection of similar items. 3 a package of stationery for writing letters.
– ORIGIN C16: from Latin, 'profit, saving' (literally 'what is weighed together'), from *compendere* 'weigh together'.

compensable /kəm'pɛnsəb(ə)l/ ■ adj. (of a loss or hardship) for which compensation can be obtained.

compensate ■ v. 1 give something to reduce or balance the bad effect of loss, suffering, or injury. 2 (**compensate for**) make up for (something undesirable) by exerting an opposite force or effect.
– DERIVATIVES **compensatory** adj.
– ORIGIN C17 (*compensation* Middle English): from Latin *compensare* 'weigh against'.

compensation ■ n. 1 something awarded to compensate for loss, suffering, or injury. ▸ something that compensates for an undesirable state of affairs. ▸ the action or process of compensating. 2 chiefly N. Amer. money received as salary or wages.

compère /'kɒmpɛː/ ■ n. a person who introduces the acts in a variety show. ■ v. act as a compère for.
– ORIGIN C20: French, 'godfather'.

compete ■ v. strive to gain or win something by defeating or establishing superiority over others.
– ORIGIN C17 (*competitor* C16): from Latin, from *com-* 'together' + *petere* 'aim at, seek'.

competence (also **competency**) ■ n. 1 the quality or extent of being competent. 2 Linguistics a person's subconscious knowledge of the rules governing the formation of speech in their first language. Often contrasted with **PERFORMANCE**. 3 dated an income large enough to live on.

competent ■ adj. having the necessary ability or knowledge to do something successfully. ▸ (of a person) efficient and capable. ▸ (of a court or other body) having legal authority to deal with a particular matter.
– DERIVATIVES **competently** adv.
– ORIGIN Middle English ('suitable, adequate'): from Latin *competere* in the sense 'be fit or proper' (see **COMPETE**).

competition ■ n. 1 the activity or condition of competing against others. ▸ Ecology interaction between species or organisms which share a limited environmental resource. 2 an event or contest in which people compete. ▸ the person or people with whom one is competing.

competitive ■ adj. 1 relating to or characterized by competition. ▸ strongly desiring to be more successful than others. 2 as good as or better than others of a comparable nature.
– DERIVATIVES **competitively** adv. **competitiveness** n.

competitor ■ n. 1 a person who takes part in a sporting contest. 2 an organization engaged in commercial or economic competition with others.

compilation ■ n. 1 the action or process of compiling something. 2 a thing, especially a book or record, compiled from different sources.

compile ■ v. 1 produce (a collection) by assembling material from other sources. ▸ accumulate (a specified score). 2 Computing convert (a program) into a lower-level form in which the program can be executed.
– DERIVATIVES **compiler** n.
– ORIGIN Middle English: from Old French *compiler* or Latin *compilare* 'plunder or plagiarize'.

complacent /kəm'pleɪs(ə)nt/ ■ adj. smug and uncritically satisfied with oneself or one's achievements.
– DERIVATIVES **complacency** (also **complacence**) n. **complacently** adv.
– ORIGIN C17 (*complacence* Middle English): from Latin *complacere* 'to please'.

USAGE
The words **complacent** and **complaisant** are sometimes confused: **complacent** means 'smug and self-satisfied', whereas **complaisant** means 'willing to please'.

complain ■ v. 1 express dissatisfaction or annoyance. 2 (**complain of**) state that one is suffering from (a symptom of illness).
– DERIVATIVES **complainer** n. **complaining** adj. **complainingly** adv.
– ORIGIN Middle English: from Old French *complaindre*, from medieval Latin *complangere* 'bewail', from Latin *com-* (expressing intensive force) + *plangere* 'to lament'.

complainant ■ n. Law a plaintiff in certain lawsuits.

complaint ■ n. 1 an act or the action of complaining. ▸ a reason for dissatisfaction. ▸ Law the plaintiff's reasons for proceeding in a civil action. 2 an illness or medical condition, especially a relatively minor one.

complaisant /kəm'pleɪz(ə)nt/ ■ adj. willing to please others or to accept their behaviour without protest.
– DERIVATIVES **complaisance** n.
– ORIGIN C17: French, from *complaire* 'acquiesce in order to please', from Latin *complacere* 'to please'.

USAGE
On the confusion of **complaisant** with **complacent**, see **COMPLACENT**.

compleat ■ adj. & v. archaic spelling of **COMPLETE**.

complement ■ n. /'kɒmplɪm(ə)nt/ 1 a thing that contributes extra features to something else so as to enhance or improve it. 2 the number or quantity that makes something complete. 3 Grammar a word, phrase, or clause governed by a verb that completes the meaning of the predicate. ▸ an adjective or noun that has the same reference as either the subject or object (as *mad* in *he is mad* or *he drove her mad*). 4 Physiology protein present in blood plasma which combines with an antigen–antibody complex to bring about the destruction of foreign cells. 5 Geometry the amount by which an angle is less than 90°. ■ v. /'kɒmplɪmɛnt/ serve as a complement to.
– ORIGIN Middle English: from Latin *complementum*, from

complere (see **COMPLETE**).

USAGE
Complement and **compliment** (together with related words such as **complementary** and **complimentary**) are frequently confused. **Complement** means 'add to in a way that enhances or improves', while **compliment** means 'politely congratulate or praise'.

complementarity ■ n. (pl. **-ies**) a situation in which two or more different things enhance each other or form a balanced whole.

complementary ■ adj. **1** combining in such a way as to form a complete whole or enhance each other. **2** of or relating to complementary medicine.
–DERIVATIVES **complementariness** n.

complementary angle ■ n. either of two angles whose sum is 90°.

complementary colour ■ n. a colour that combined with a given colour makes white or black.

complementary DNA ■ n. synthetic DNA in which the sequence of bases is complementary to that of a given example of DNA.

complementary medicine ■ n. medical therapy that falls outside the scope of scientific medicine but may be used alongside it in the treatment of disease and ill health, e.g. acupuncture and osteopathy.

complementation ■ n. **1** the action of complementing. **2** Grammar all the clause constituents that are governed by a verb. **3** Genetics the phenomenon by which the effects of two different non-allelic mutations in a gene are partly or entirely cancelled out when they occur together.

complete ■ adj. **1** having all the necessary or appropriate parts; entire. ▸ (**complete with**) having as an additional part or feature. **2** having run its full course; finished. **3** to the greatest extent or degree; total: *a complete surprise.* **4** (also **compleat**) chiefly humorous skilled at every aspect of an activity; consummate. ■ v. **1** finish making or doing. ▸ conclude the sale of a property. **2** provide with the items necessary to make (something) complete. ▸ write the required information on (a form).
–DERIVATIVES **completeness** n.
–ORIGIN Middle English: from Latin *complet-, complere* 'fill up, finish, fulfil', from *com-* (expressing intensive force) + *plere* 'fill'.

completely ■ adv. totally; utterly.

completion ■ n. the action or state of completing or being completed. ▸ the final stage in the sale of a property, at which point it legally changes ownership.

complex ■ adj. **1** consisting of many different and connected parts. **2** not easy to analyse or understand; complicated or intricate. **3** Mathematics (of a number) containing both a real and an imaginary part. ■ n. **1** a group of similar buildings or facilities on the same site. ▸ an interlinked system; a network. **2** Psychoanalysis a related group of repressed or partly repressed emotionally significant ideas which lead to abnormal mental states or behaviour. ▸ informal a feeling of disproportionate anxiety about something. **3** Chemistry an ion or molecule in which one or more groups are linked to a metal atom by coordinate bonds. ■ v. Chemistry form or cause to form a complex with another.
–DERIVATIVES **complexation** n. (Chemistry). **complexity** n. **complexly** adv.
–ORIGIN C17: from Latin *complexus*, from *complectere* 'embrace, comprise', later associated with *complexus* 'plaited'; the adjective is partly via French *complexe*.

complexion ■ n. **1** the natural tone and texture of the skin of a person's face. **2** the general aspect or character of something.
–DERIVATIVES **-complexioned** adj.
–ORIGIN Middle English (denoting temperament or constitution): from Latin *complexio(n-)* 'combination', from *complectere* 'embrace, comprise'.

complex sentence ■ n. a sentence containing a subordinate clause or clauses.

compliance /kəmˈplʌɪəns/ ■ n. the action or fact of being compliant.

compliant ■ adj. **1** disposed to agree with others or obey rules, especially to an excessive degree; acquiescent.

2 meeting or in accordance with rules or standards.
–DERIVATIVES **compliantly** adv.

complicate /ˈkɒmplɪkeɪt/ ■ v. **1** make more complicated. **2** Medicine introduce complications in (an existing condition).
–ORIGIN C17 (in the sense 'combine, intertwine'): from Latin *complicare* 'fold together'.

complicated ■ adj. **1** consisting of many interconnecting parts or elements; intricate. ▸ involving many different and confusing aspects. **2** Medicine involving complications.
–DERIVATIVES **complicatedly** adv.

complication ■ n. **1** a circumstance that complicates something; a difficulty. ▸ an involved or confused condition or state. **2** Medicine a secondary disease or condition aggravating an already existing one.

complicit /kəmˈplɪsɪt/ ■ adj. involved with others in an unlawful activity; having complicity.

complicity ■ n. the fact or condition of being involved with others in an unlawful activity.
–ORIGIN C17: from Middle English *complice* 'an associate', from late Latin *complex, complic-* 'allied', from Latin *complicare* 'fold together'.

compliment ■ n. /ˈkɒmplɪm(ə)nt/ a polite expression of praise or admiration. ▸ (**compliments**) congratulations or praise expressed to someone. ▸ (**compliments**) formal greetings, especially when sent as a message. ■ v. /ˈkɒmplɪment/ politely congratulate or praise (someone).
–PHRASES **return the compliment** give a compliment in return for another. ▸ retaliate or respond in kind. **with the compliments of someone** given without charge; free.
–ORIGIN C17: from French *compliment* (n.), *complimenter* (v.), from Italian *complimento* 'fulfilment of the requirements of courtesy', from Latin *complementum* 'completion, fulfilment'.

USAGE
On the confusion of **compliment** with **complement**, see **COMPLEMENT**.

complimentary ■ adj. **1** expressing a compliment; praising or approving. **2** given or supplied free of charge.

compliments slip ■ n. a small piece of paper printed with a company's name and address, sent out with goods or information in place of a covering letter.

compline /ˈkɒmplɪn, -lʌɪn/ ■ n. a service of evening prayers forming part of the Divine Office of the Western Christian Church, traditionally said before retiring for the night.
–ORIGIN Middle English: from Old French *complie*, from Latin *complere* (see **COMPLETE**).

comply /kəmˈplʌɪ/ ■ v. (**-ies, -ied**) **1** act in accordance with a wish or command. **2** meet specified standards.
–ORIGIN C16: from Italian *complire*, from Latin *complere* (see **COMPLETE**).

compo ■ n. (pl. **-os**) **1** a composite material. **2** (also **compo rations**) a supply of food designed to last a specified number of man-days and made up of various tinned items carried in a large pack.

component /kəmˈpəʊnənt/ ■ n. **1** a part or element of a larger whole, especially a part of a machine or vehicle. **2** Physics each of two or more forces, velocities, or other vectors acting in different directions which are together equivalent to a given vector. ■ adj. constituting part of a larger whole; constituent.
–ORIGIN C17: from Latin *componere* 'put together'.

componential analysis /ˌkɒmpəˈnɛnʃ(ə)l/ ■ n. Linguistics the analysis of the meaning of a word or other linguistic unit into discrete semantic components.

compony /kɒmˈpəʊni/ ■ adj. Heraldry divided into a single row of squares in alternating tinctures.
–ORIGIN C16: from French *componé*, from Latin *componere* 'put together'.

comport /kəmˈpɔːt/ ■ v. (**comport oneself**) formal conduct oneself; behave.
–ORIGIN Middle English: from Latin *comportare*, from *com-* 'together' + *portare* 'carry, bear'.

comportment ■ n. formal behaviour or bearing.

compose

compose ■ v. **1** write or create (a work of art, especially music or poetry). ▸ order or arrange in order to form an artistic whole. **2** (of elements) constitute or make up (a whole). **3** [often as adj. **composed**] calm or settle (one's features or thoughts). **4** prepare (a text) for printing by setting up the characters to be printed.
– DERIVATIVES **composedly** adv.
– ORIGIN Middle English: from Old French *composer*, from Latin *componere* (see COMPONENT).

composer ■ n. a person who writes music.

composite /'kɒmpəzɪt/ ■ adj. **1** made up of various parts or elements. ▸ (of a constructional material) made up of recognizable constituents. **2** /usu. 'kɒmpəzʌɪt/ Botany relating to or denoting plants of the family Compositae, which have composite flower heads consisting of numerous florets and include daisies, dandelions, thistles, and chrysanthemums. **3** Mathematics (of an integer) being the product of two or more factors greater than unity;not prime. ■ n. **1** a thing made up of several parts or elements. ▸ a composite constructional material. ▸ /'kɒmpəzʌɪt/ a motion for debate composed of two or more related resolutions. **2** /'kɒmpəzʌɪt/ Botany a plant of the daisy family (Compositae). ■ v. [usu. as noun **compositing**] combine (two or more images) to make a single picture, especially electronically.
– ORIGIN Middle English: from Latin *composit-*, *componere* 'put together'.

composition ■ n. **1** the way in which a whole or mixture is made up; ingredients or constituents. ▸ a thing composed of various elements. ▸ a compound artificial substance. **2** a work of music, literature, or art. **3** the action of composing. **4** a legal agreement to pay a sum in lieu of a larger debt or other obligation. **5** Mathematics the successive application of functions to a variable. **6** Physics the process of finding the resultant of a number of forces.
– DERIVATIVES **compositional** adj. **compositionally** adv.

compositor /kəm'pɒzɪtə/ ■ n. a person who arranges type for printing or keys text into a composing machine.
– ORIGIN Middle English: from Anglo-Norman French *compositour*, from Latin, from *componere* (see COMPOSE).

compos mentis /ˌkɒmpɒs 'mɛntɪs/ ■ adj. having full control of one's mind.
– ORIGIN C17: Latin.

compost ■ n. decayed organic material used as a fertilizer for growing plants. ▸ a mixture of compost with loam soil used as a growing medium. ■ v. make into or treat with compost.
– ORIGIN Middle English: from Old French *composte*, from Latin *compositum* 'something put together', from *componere*.

compost heap (N. Amer. also **compost pile**) ■ n. a pile of garden and kitchen refuse which decomposes to produce compost.

composure ■ n. the state or feeling of being calm and composed.

compote /'kɒmpəʊt, -ɒt/ ■ n. **1** fruit preserved or cooked in syrup. **2** a bowl-shaped dessert dish with a stem.
– ORIGIN C17: from Old French *composte* (see COMPOST).

compound¹ ■ n. /'kɒmpaʊnd/ a thing composed of two or more separate elements. ▸ Chemistry a substance formed from two or more elements chemically united in fixed proportions. ▸ a word made up of two or more existing words. ■ adj. /'kɒmpaʊnd/ made up of or consisting of several parts or elements. ▸ (of interest) payable on both capital and the accumulated interest. ▸ Biology (of a leaf, flower, or eye) consisting of two or more simple parts or entities in combination. Compare with SIMPLE. ■ v. /kəm'paʊnd/ **1** make up (a composite whole); constitute. ▸ mix or combine (ingredients or constituents). ▸ reckon (interest) on previously accumulated interest. **2** make (something bad) worse. **3** Law forbear from prosecuting (a felony) in exchange for money or other consideration. ▸ settle (a debt or other matter) in this way.
– ORIGIN Middle English *compoune* (v.), from Old French *compondre*, from Latin *componere* 'put together'.

compound² /'kɒmpaʊnd/ ■ n. a large open area enclosed by a fence, e.g. around a factory or within a prison. ▸ a group of houses enclosed by a security fence. ▸ another term for POUND³.
– ORIGIN C17: from Portuguese *campon* or Dutch *kampoeng*, from Malay *kampong* 'enclosure, hamlet'.

compound eye ■ n. an eye consisting of an array of numerous small visual units, as found in insects and crustaceans. Contrasted with SIMPLE EYE.

compound fracture ■ n. an injury in which a broken bone pierces the skin.

compound interval ■ n. Music an interval greater than an octave.

compound sentence ■ n. a sentence with more than one subject or predicate.

compound time ■ n. Music musical rhythm or metre in which each beat in a bar is subdivided into three smaller units, so having the value of a dotted note. Compare with SIMPLE TIME.

comprehend /ˌkɒmprɪ'hɛnd/ ■ v. **1** grasp mentally; understand. **2** formal include, comprise, or encompass.
– ORIGIN Middle English: from Latin *comprehendere*, from *com-* 'together' + *prehendere* 'grasp'.

comprehensible ■ adj. able to be understood; intelligible.
– DERIVATIVES **comprehensibility** n. **comprehensibly** adv.

comprehension ■ n. the action or capability of understanding. ▸ the school exercise of answering questions on a set text to test understanding.

comprehensive ■ adj. **1** including or dealing with all or nearly all aspects of something. ▸ of large content or scope; wide-ranging. ▸ (of a victory or defeat) by a large margin. ▸ (of motor-vehicle insurance) providing cover for most risks, including damage to the policyholder's own vehicle. **2** denoting a system of secondary education in which children of all abilities from a particular area are educated in one school. ■ n. Brit. a comprehensive school.
– DERIVATIVES **comprehensively** adv. **comprehensiveness** n.

compress ■ v. /kəm'prɛs/ flatten by pressure; squeeze into less space. ▸ [as adj. **compressed**] chiefly Biology having a narrow shape as if flattened, especially sideways. ▸ squeeze or press (two things) together. ■ n. /'kɒmprɛs/ a pad of absorbent material pressed on to part of the body to relieve inflammation or stop bleeding.
– DERIVATIVES **compressibility** /-'bɪlɪti/ n. **compressible** /kəm'prɛsɪb(ə)l/ adj.
– ORIGIN Middle English: from Old French *compresser* or late Latin *compressare*, from Latin *comprimere*.

compressed air ■ n. air that is at more than atmospheric pressure.

compression ■ n. **1** the action of compressing or being compressed. **2** the reduction in volume (causing an increase in pressure) of the fuel mixture in an internal-combustion engine before ignition.

compressive strength ■ n. the resistance of a material to breaking under compression. Compare with TENSILE STRENGTH.

compressor ■ n. **1** an instrument or device for compressing something. ▸ a machine used to supply air or other gas at increased pressure. **2** an electrical device which reduces the dynamic range of a sound signal.

comprise ■ v. consist of; be made up of. ▸ (also **be comprised of**) make up; constitute.
– ORIGIN Middle English: from French, 'comprised', from *comprendre* (see COMPREHEND).

compromise ■ n. **1** an agreement reached by each side making concessions. ▸ an intermediate state between conflicting opinions. **2** the expedient acceptance of standards that are lower than is desirable. ■ v. **1** settle a dispute by mutual concession. **2** expediently accept standards that are lower than is desirable. **3** bring into disrepute or danger by indiscreet or reckless behaviour. ▸ [as adj. **compromising**] revealing an embarrassing or incriminating secret: *a compromising situation*.
– ORIGIN Middle English: from Old French *compromis*, from late Latin *compromittere*, from *com-* 'together' + *promittere* (see PROMISE).

comptroller /kən'trəʊlə, kɒmp-/ ■ n. a controller (used in the title of some financial officers).
– ORIGIN C15: var. of *controller* (see CONTROL), associated with French *compte* 'calculation'.

compulsion ▪ n. **1** the action or state of compelling or being compelled; constraint. **2** an irresistible urge to behave in a certain way, especially against one's conscious wishes.

compulsive ▪ adj. **1** resulting from or acting on an irresistible urge or compulsion. **2** irresistibly interesting or exciting; compelling.
– DERIVATIVES **compulsively** adv. **compulsiveness** n.

compulsory ▪ adj. required by law or a rule; obligatory. ▸ involving or exercising compulsion; coercive.
– DERIVATIVES **compulsorily** adv. **compulsoriness** n.

compulsory purchase ▪ n. the officially enforced purchase of privately owned land or property for public use.

compunction ▪ n. a feeling of guilt or moral scruple that prevents or follows the doing of something bad.
– ORIGIN Middle English: from Old French *componction*, from Latin *compungere* 'prick sharply'.

computation ▪ n. **1** the action of mathematical calculation. **2** the use of computers, especially as a subject of research or study.
– DERIVATIVES **computational** adj. **computationally** adv.

computational linguistics ▪ pl. n. [treated as sing.] the branch of linguistics in which the techniques of computer science are applied to the analysis and synthesis of language and speech.

compute ▪ v. reckon or calculate (a figure or amount).
– DERIVATIVES **computable** adj.
– ORIGIN C17: from French *computer* or Latin *computare*, from *com-* 'together' + *putare* 'to settle (an account)'.

computer ▪ n. an electronic device which is capable of receiving information (data) and performing a sequence of logical operations in accordance with a predetermined but variable set of procedural instructions (program) to produce a result in the form of information or signals.

computerate /kəmˈpjuːtərət/ ▪ adj. informal another term for COMPUTER-LITERATE.

computer dating ▪ n. the use of computer databases to identify potentially compatible partners for people.

computer game ▪ n. a game played using a computer, especially a video game.

computerize (also **-ise**) ▪ v. [often as adj. **computerized** (also **-ised**)] convert to a system or form which is controlled, stored, or processed by computer.
– DERIVATIVES **computerization** (also **-isation**) n.

computer-literate ▪ adj. having sufficient knowledge and skill to be able to use computers.
– DERIVATIVES **computer literacy** n.

computer science ▪ n. the study of the principles and use of computers.

computing ▪ n. the use or operation of computers.

comrade ▪ n. (among men) a companion who shares one's activities or is a fellow member of an organization. ▸ (also **comrade-in-arms**) a fellow soldier or serviceman. ▸ a fellow socialist or communist. ▸ S. African historical a member of a group of young left-wing militants active in the townships.
– DERIVATIVES **comradely** adj. **comradeship** n.
– ORIGIN C16: from French *camerade*, from Spanish *camarada* 'room-mate'.

Comrades Marathon (also **the Comrades**) ▪ n. (in South Africa) an annual long-distance race for runners, from Pietermaritzburg to Durban, or vice versa.
– ORIGIN named in commemoration of soldiers who died in the First World War.

con¹ informal ▪ v. (**conned**, **conning**) deceive (someone) into doing or believing something by lying to them. ▪ n. a deception of this kind.
– ORIGIN C19 (orig. US): abbrev. of CONFIDENCE, as in *confidence trick*.

con² ▪ n. (usu. in phr. **pros and cons**) a disadvantage or argument against something.
– ORIGIN C16: from Latin *contra* 'against'.

con³ (US also **conn**) Nautical ▪ v. (**conned**, **conning**) direct the steering of (a ship). ▪ n. (**the con**) the action or post of conning a ship.
– ORIGIN C17: from obsolete *cond* 'conduct, guide', from Old French *conduire*.

con- ▪ prefix variant spelling of COM- assimilated before *c, d, f, g, j, n, q, s, t, v*, and sometimes before vowels (as in *concord, condescend, confide*, etc.).

concatenate /kənˈkatɪneɪt/ ▪ v. formal or technical link together in a chain or series.
– DERIVATIVES **concatenation** n.
– ORIGIN C15 (as adj.): from late Latin *concatenare* 'link together'.

concave /ˈkɒnkeɪv/ ▪ adj. having an outline or surface that curves inwards like the interior of a circle or sphere. Compare with CONVEX.
– DERIVATIVES **concavely** adv. **concavity** n.
– ORIGIN Middle English: from Latin, from *con-* 'together' + *cavus* 'hollow'.

conceal ▪ v. not allow to be seen; hide. ▸ keep secret; prevent from being known.
– DERIVATIVES **concealment** n.
– ORIGIN Middle English: from Old French *conceler*, from Latin, from *con-* 'completely' + *celare* 'hide'.

concealer ▪ n. a flesh-toned cosmetic used to cover spots and blemishes.

concede ▪ v. **1** finally admit or agree that something is true. ▸ admit (defeat) in a match or contest. **2** surrender or yield (a possession, advantage, or right). ▸ fail to prevent an opponent scoring (a goal or point).
– ORIGIN C15: from Latin *concedere*, from *con-* 'completely' + *cedere* 'yield'.

conceit ▪ n. **1** excessive pride in oneself. **2** an elaborate metaphor or artistic effect. ▸ a fanciful notion.
– ORIGIN Middle English: from CONCEIVE, on the pattern of *deceive, deceit*.

conceited ▪ adj. excessively proud of oneself.
– DERIVATIVES **conceitedly** adv. **conceitedness** n.

conceivable ▪ adj. capable of being imagined or understood.
– DERIVATIVES **conceivably** adv.

conceive ▪ v. **1** become pregnant with (a child). **2** devise in the mind; imagine.
– ORIGIN Middle English: from Old French *concevoir*, from Latin *concipere*, from *com-* 'together' + *capere* 'take'.

concentrate ▪ v. **1** focus all one's attention or mental effort on. ▸ (**concentrate on**) do (one particular thing) above all others. **2** gather together in numbers or a mass at one point. **3** increase the strength of (a solution). ▪ n. a concentrated form of something, especially food.
– DERIVATIVES **concentrated** adj. **concentrator** n.
– ORIGIN C17: from French *concentrer* 'to concentrate'.

concentration ▪ n. **1** the action or power of concentrating. **2** a close gathering of people or things. **3** the relative amount of a particular substance contained within a solution or mixture.

concentration camp ▪ n. a camp for detaining political prisoners.

concentric ▪ adj. of or denoting circles, arcs, or other shapes which share the same centre.
– DERIVATIVES **concentrically** adv.
– ORIGIN Middle English: from Old French *concentrique*, from Latin *com-* 'together' + *centrum* 'centre'.

concept ▪ n. **1** an abstract idea. ▸ an idea to help sell or publicize a commodity. **2** Philosophy an idea or mental picture of a group or class of objects, formed by combining all their aspects.
– ORIGIN C16: from Latin *conceptum* 'something conceived', from *concipere* (see CONCEIVE).

conception ▪ n. **1** the action of conceiving a child or of one being conceived. ▸ the devising of a plan or idea. **2** the way in which something is perceived. ▸ a concept. ▸ ability to imagine or understand.
– ORIGIN Middle English: from Latin *conceptio(n-)*, from *concipere* (see CONCEIVE).

conceptual ▪ adj. of, relating to, or based on mental concepts.
– DERIVATIVES **conceptually** adv.

conceptualize (also **-ise**) ▪ v. form a concept or idea of.
– DERIVATIVES **conceptualization** (also **-isation**) n.

concern ▪ v. **1** relate to; be about. ▸ affect or involve.

concerned

2 worry (someone). ■ n. **1** worry; anxiety. **2** a matter of interest or importance. **3** a business.
-PHRASES **as** (or **so**) **far as —— is concerned** as regards the interests or case of ——. **have no concern with** have nothing to do with. **to whom it may concern** used to address a reader whose identity is unknown.
-ORIGIN Middle English: from French *concerner* or late Latin *concernere*, from *con-* (expressing intensive force) + *cernere* 'sift, discern'.

concerned ■ adj. worried; anxious.
-DERIVATIVES **concernedly** adv.

concerning ■ prep. about.

concert /ˈkɒnsət/ ■ n. **1** a musical performance given in public, typically of several compositions. **2** formal agreement; harmony.
-PHRASES **in concert 1** acting jointly. **2** giving a live public performance.
-ORIGIN C16: from French *concerter*, from Italian *concertare* 'harmonize'; noun from French *concert*.

concerted ■ adj. **1** jointly arranged or carried out. ▶ done with great effort. **2** (of music) arranged in several parts of equal importance.

concert grand ■ n. the largest size of grand piano, used for concerts.

concertina /ˌkɒnsəˈtiːnə/ ■ n. **1** a small musical instrument played by stretching and squeezing a central bellows between the hands to blow air over reeds, each note being sounded by a button. **2** [as modifier] opening or closing in multiple folds. ■ v. (**concertinas, concertinaed** or **concertina'd, concertining**) extend or compress in folds like those of a concertina.

concertino /ˌkɒntʃəˈtiːnəʊ/ ■ n. (pl. **-os**) a simple or short concerto.
-ORIGIN C18: Italian, diminutive of *concerto* (see CONCERTO).

concertmaster ■ n. chiefly N. Amer. the leading first-violin player in some orchestras.

concerto /kənˈtʃɛːtəʊ, -ˈtʃɛːtəʊ/ ■ n. (pl. **concertos** or **concerti**) a musical composition for a solo instrument accompanied by an orchestra.
-ORIGIN C18: Italian, from *concertare* 'harmonize'.

concerto grosso /ˈɡrɒsəʊ/ ■ n. (pl. **concerti grossi** /-siː/) a musical composition for a group of solo instruments accompanied by an orchestra.
-ORIGIN C18: Italian, 'big concerto'.

concert party ■ n. a group of performers giving variety concerts.

concert performance ■ n. a performance of a piece of music written for an opera or ballet without the accompanying dramatic action.

concert pitch ■ n. Music a standard for the tuning of musical instruments, in which the note A above middle C has a frequency of 440 Hz.

concession ■ n. **1** a thing that is conceded. ▶ a gesture made in recognition of a demand or prevailing standard. **2** a reduction in price for a certain category of person. **3** the right to use land or other property for a specified purpose. ▶ a commercial operation set up within the premises of a larger concern.
-DERIVATIVES **concessional** adj. **concessionary** adj.
-ORIGIN Middle English: from Latin *concessio(n-)*, from *concedere* (see CONCEDE).

concessionaire /kənˌsɛʃəˈnɛː/ (also **concessionnaire**) ■ n. the holder of a concession or grant, especially for the use of land or trading rights.
-ORIGIN C19: from French *concessionnaire*, from Latin *concessio* (see CONCESSION).

concessive ■ adj. of, characterized by, or tending to concession.

conch /kɒŋk, kɒn(t)ʃ/ ■ n. (pl. **conchs** /kɒŋks/ or **conches** /ˈkɒntʃɪz/) **1** a tropical marine mollusc with a robust spiral shell which may bear long projections and have a flared lip. [*Strombus* and other genera: many species.] **2** Architecture the roof of a semicircular apse.

-ORIGIN Middle English: from Latin *concha* 'shellfish, shell', from Greek *konkhē* 'mussel, cockle, shell-like cavity'.

conchology /kɒŋˈkɒlədʒi/ ■ n. the scientific study or collection of mollusc shells.
-DERIVATIVES **conchological** adj. **conchologist** n.

concierge /ˈkɒnsɪɛːʒ/ ■ n. **1** (especially in France) a resident caretaker of a block of flats or small hotel. **2** a hotel employee who assists guests by booking tours, making theatre and restaurant reservations, etc.
-ORIGIN C16: French, prob. from Latin *conservus* 'fellow slave'.

conciliate /kənˈsɪlɪeɪt/ ■ v. placate; pacify. ▶ act as a mediator. ▶ formal reconcile.
-DERIVATIVES **conciliation** n. **conciliatory** adj.
-ORIGIN C16: from Latin *conciliare* 'combine, gain', from *concilium* (see COUNCIL).

concise ■ adj. giving a lot of information clearly and in few words.
-DERIVATIVES **concisely** adv. **conciseness** n.
-ORIGIN C16: from French *concis* or Latin *concisus*, from *concidere* 'cut up, cut down'.

conclave /ˈkɒŋkleɪv/ ■ n. a private meeting.
-ORIGIN Middle English: from Latin *conclave* 'lockable room', from *con-* 'with' + *clavis* 'key'.

conclude ■ v. **1** bring or come to an end. ▶ formally settle or arrange (a treaty or agreement). **2** arrive at a judgement or opinion by reasoning.
-ORIGIN Middle English: from Latin *conclus-, concludere*, from *con-* 'completely' + *claudere* 'to shut'.

conclusion ■ n. **1** the end or finish of something. ▶ the summing-up of an argument or text. ▶ the settling of a treaty or agreement. **2** a judgement or decision reached by reasoning. ▶ Logic a proposition that is reached from given premises.
-PHRASES **jump to conclusions** make a hasty judgement before considering all the facts.

conclusive ■ adj. (of evidence or argument) decisive or convincing.
-DERIVATIVES **conclusively** adv. **conclusiveness** n.

concoct /kənˈkɒkt/ ■ v. make (a dish or meal) by combining ingredients. ▶ create or devise (a story or plan).
-DERIVATIVES **concoction** n.
-ORIGIN C16: from Latin *concoct-, concoquere* 'cook together'.

concomitance /kənˈkɒmɪt(ə)ns/ (also **concomitancy**) ■ n. the fact of existing or occurring with something else.
-ORIGIN C16: from medieval Latin *concomitantia*, from *concomitari* 'accompany'.

concomitant /kənˈkɒmɪt(ə)nt/ formal ■ adj. naturally accompanying or associated. ■ n. a concomitant phenomenon.
-DERIVATIVES **concomitantly** adv.

concord ■ n. **1** formal agreement; harmony. ▶ a treaty. **2** Grammar agreement between words in gender, number, case, or person. **3** Music a chord that is pleasing or satisfactory in itself.
-ORIGIN Middle English: from Old French *concorde*, from Latin *concordia*, from *concors* 'of one mind'.

concordance /kənˈkɔːd(ə)ns/ ■ n. **1** an alphabetical list of the important words in a text, usually with citations of the passages concerned. **2** Medicine the inheritance by two related individuals of the same genetic characteristic.
-ORIGIN Middle English: from medieval Latin *concordantia*, from Latin *concordare* 'agree on'.

concordant ■ adj. **1** in agreement; consistent. **2** Medicine (of twins) inheriting the same genetic characteristic.
-DERIVATIVES **concordantly** adv.

concordat /kənˈkɔːdat/ ■ n. an agreement or treaty, especially one between the Vatican and a secular government.
-ORIGIN C17: from French, or from Latin *concordatum* 'something agreed upon'.

concourse ■ n. **1** a large open central area inside or in front of a public building. **2** formal a crowd or assembly. ▶ the action of coming together.
-ORIGIN Middle English: from Old French *concours*, from Latin *concursus*, from *concurrere* (see CONCUR).

ConCourt (also **Concourt**) ■ n. short for CONSTITUTIONAL COURT.

concrete /ˈkɒŋkriːt/ ■ adj. existing in a material or physical form. ▸ specific; definite. ▸ (of a noun) denoting a material object as opposed to an abstract quality, state, or action. ■ n. a building material made from a mixture of gravel, sand, cement, and water, forming a stone-like mass on hardening. ■ v. cover or fix solidly with concrete.
– DERIVATIVES **concretely** adv. **concreteness** n.
– ORIGIN Middle English: from French *concret* or Latin *concretus*, from *concrescere* 'grow together'.

concrete jungle ■ n. an area with a high density of large, unattractive, modern buildings.

concrete mixer ■ n. a cement mixer.

concretion ■ n. a hard solid mass formed by accumulation of matter.
– ORIGIN C16: from Latin *concretio(n-)*, from *concrescere* 'grow together'.

concretize /ˈkɒŋkrɪtʌɪz/ (also **-ise**) ■ v. make concrete instead of abstract.
– DERIVATIVES **concretization** (also **-isation**) n.

concubinage /kɒnˈkjuːbɪnɪdʒ/ ■ n. chiefly historical the practice of keeping or the state of being a concubine.

concubine /ˈkɒŋkjʊbʌɪn/ ■ n. **1** chiefly historical (in polygamous societies) a woman who lives with a man but has lower status than his wife or wives. **2** archaic a mistress.
– ORIGIN Middle English: from Latin *concubina*, from *con-* 'with' + *cubare* 'to lie'.

concupiscence /kənˈkjuːpɪs(ə)ns/ ■ n. formal lust.
– DERIVATIVES **concupiscent** adj.
– ORIGIN Middle English: from late Latin *concupiscentia*, from Latin *concupiscere* 'begin to desire'.

concur ■ v. (**concurred**, **concurring**) **1** (often **concur with**) agree. **2** happen at the same time.
– ORIGIN Middle English: from Latin *concurrere* 'run together, assemble in crowds'.

concurrent ■ adj. **1** existing or happening at the same time. **2** Mathematics (of three or more lines) meeting at or tending towards one point.
– DERIVATIVES **concurrence** n. **concurrently** adv.

concussion ■ n. temporary unconsciousness or confusion caused by a blow on the head.
– DERIVATIVES **concuss** v.
– ORIGIN Middle English: from Latin *concussio(n-)*, from *concutere* 'dash together, shake'.

condemn ■ v. **1** express complete disapproval of. **2** (usu. **condemn someone to**) sentence to a punishment, especially death. ▸ force (someone) to endure something unpleasant. ▸ prove the guilt of. **3** officially declare to be unfit for use.
– DERIVATIVES **condemnation** n. **condemnatory** adj.
– ORIGIN Middle English: from Old French *condemner*, from Latin *condemnare*, from *con-* (expressing intensive force) + *damnare* (see DAMN).

condensation ■ n. **1** water from humid air collecting as droplets on a cold surface. **2** the conversion of a vapour or gas to a liquid. **3** Chemistry a reaction in which two molecules combine to form a larger molecule, producing a small molecule such as H$_2$O as a by-product. **4** a concise version of something.

condense ■ v. **1** make denser or more concentrated. ▸ [usu. as adj. **condensed**] thicken (a liquid) by heating it to reduce the water content. ▸ express (a piece of writing or speech) in fewer words; make concise. **2** change from a gas or vapour to a liquid.
– ORIGIN Middle English: from Old French *condenser* or Latin *condensare*, from *condensus* 'very thick'.

condensed milk ■ n. milk that has been thickened by evaporation and sweetened.

condenser ■ n. **1** an apparatus for condensing vapour. **2** a lens or system of lenses for collecting and directing light. **3** another term for CAPACITOR.

condescend ■ v. show that one feels superior. ▸ do something despite regarding it as below one's dignity: *he condescended to meet me.*
– DERIVATIVES **condescending** adj. **condescendingly** adv. **condescension** n.
– ORIGIN Middle English: from Old French *condescendre*, from eccles. Latin *condescendere*, from *con-* 'together' + *descendere* 'descend'.

condiment ■ n. a substance such as salt or pepper, used to flavour food.
– ORIGIN Middle English: from Latin *condimentum*, from *condire* 'to pickle'.

condition ■ n. **1** the state of something or someone, with regard to appearance, fitness, or working order. ▸ an illness or medical problem. ▸ archaic social position. **2** (**conditions**) circumstances affecting the functioning or existence of something. **3** a state of affairs that must exist before something else is possible. ■ v. **1** have a significant influence on. ▸ train or accustom to behave in a certain way. ▸ [as adj. **conditioned**] relating to or denoting automatic responses established by training to an ordinarily neutral stimulus. **2** bring into the desired state for use. ▸ [often as adj. **conditioned**] make fit and healthy. **3** apply conditioner to (the hair).
– PHRASES **in** (or **out of**) **condition** in a fit (or unfit) physical state. **on condition that** with the stipulation that.
– ORIGIN Middle English: from Old French *condicion*, from Latin *condicio(n-)* 'agreement', from *condicere* 'agree upon', from *con-* 'with' + *dicere* 'say'.

conditional ■ adj. **1** subject to one or more conditions being met. **2** Grammar expressing a condition. ■ n. **1** Grammar & Philosophy a conditional clause or conjunction. **2** Grammar the conditional mood of a verb, for example *should* in *if I should die*.
– DERIVATIVES **conditionality** n. **conditionally** adv.

conditional discharge ■ n. an order made by a criminal court whereby an offender will not be sentenced for an offence unless a further offence is committed within a stated period.

conditioner ■ n. a thing used to improve the condition of something, especially a liquid applied to the hair after shampooing.

condo /ˈkɒndəʊ/ ■ n. (pl. **-os**) N. Amer. informal short for CONDOMINIUM (in sense 2).

condole /kənˈdəʊl/ ■ v. (**condole with**) express sympathy for.
– ORIGIN C16: from Christian Latin *condolere*, from *con-* 'with' + *dolere* 'grieve, suffer'.

condolence ■ n. an expression of sympathy, especially on the occasion of a death.

condom ■ n. a thin rubber sheath worn on the penis during sexual intercourse as a contraceptive or to protect against infection.
– ORIGIN C18.

condominium /ˌkɒndəˈmɪnɪəm/ ■ n. (pl. **condominiums**) **1** the joint control of a state's affairs by other states. **2** chiefly N. Amer. a building or complex containing a number of individually owned flats or houses. ▸ each of the flats or houses in such a building.
– ORIGIN C18: from *con-* 'together with' + *dominium* (see DOMINION).

condomize (also **-ise**) ■ v. use a condom, especially in order to prevent sexually transmitted diseases.
– DERIVATIVES **condomization** (also **-isation**) n.

condone /kənˈdəʊn/ ■ v. **1** [usu. with neg.] accept or forgive (behaviour considered wrong or offensive). **2** approve or sanction, especially reluctantly. ▸ [often as adj. **condoned**] S. African grant the status of a pass in an examination, despite the candidate having failed it.
– DERIVATIVES **condonation** /ˌkɒndəˈneɪʃ(ə)n/ n. **condoner** n.
– ORIGIN C19 (*condonation* C17): from Latin *condonare* 'refrain from punishing'.

condor ■ n. a very large American vulture with a bare head and mainly black plumage. [*Vultur gryphus* (Andean condor) and *Gymnogyps californianus* (California condor).]
– ORIGIN C17: from Spanish *cóndor*, from Quechua *kuntur*.

conduce ■ v. (**conduce to**) formal help to bring about.
– ORIGIN Middle English: from Latin *conducere* (see CONDUCT).

conducive ■ adj. (**conducive to**) contributing or helping towards.

conduct ■ n. /ˈkɒndʌkt/ **1** the manner in which a person behaves. **2** the directing or managing of something. ■ v. /kənˈdʌkt/ **1** organize and carry out. ▸ direct the performance of (a piece of music or an orchestra or choir). ▸ guide to or around a place. **2** Physics transmit by conduction. **3** (**conduct oneself**) behave in a specified way.
– DERIVATIVES **conductible** /kənˈdʌktɪb(ə)l/ adj.
– ORIGIN Middle English (as *conduit*): from Old French *conduit* (n.), *conduire* (v.), from Latin *conduct-*, *conducere* 'bring together'.

conductance ■ n. the degree to which a material conducts electricity.

conduction ■ n. **1** the transmission of heat through a medium from a region of higher temperature to a region of lower temperature. **2** the transmission of electricity or sound through a medium. **3** the conveying of fluid through a channel.
– DERIVATIVES **conductive** adj. **conductively** adv.

conductivity ■ n. (pl. **-ies**) the degree to which a specified material conducts electricity or heat.

conductor ■ n. **1** a person who conducts an orchestra or choir. **2** a person who collects fares on a bus or train. ▸ N. Amer. a guard on a train. **3** Physics a material or device that conducts heat or electricity.
– DERIVATIVES **conductorship** n. **conductress** n.

conductor rail ■ n. a rail transmitting current to an electric train or other vehicle.

conduct sheet ■ n. a military form recording someone's offences and punishments.

conduit /ˈkɒndɪt, -jʊɪt/ ■ n. **1** a channel for conveying water or other fluid. **2** a tube or trough protecting electric wiring.
– ORIGIN Middle English: from medieval Latin *conductus*, from Latin *conducere* (see CONDUCT).

condyle /ˈkɒndɪl, -dʌɪl/ ■ n. Anatomy a rounded protuberance at the end of some bones, forming an articulation with another bone.
– DERIVATIVES **condylar** adj. **condyloid** adj.
– ORIGIN C17: from Latin *condylus*, from Greek *kondulos* 'knuckle'.

cone ■ n. **1** an object which tapers from a circular or roughly circular base to a point. ▸ (also **traffic cone**) a plastic cone-shaped object used to separate off sections of a road. ▸ a cone-shaped wafer container in which ice cream is served. ▸ the peak of a volcano. **2** the dry fruit of a conifer, formed of a tight array of overlapping scales on a central axis. **3** Anatomy one of two types of light-sensitive cell present in the retina of the eye, responding to bright light and responsible for sharpness of vision and colour perception. Compare with ROD (in sense 4). ■ v. (**cone something off**) Brit. separate off part of a road with traffic cones.
– DERIVATIVES **coned** adj. **conic** adj.
– ORIGIN Middle English: from French *cône*, from Greek *kōnos*.

conebush ■ n. a shrub or small tree of the protea family with cone-shaped flower heads. [Genera *Leucadendron* (South Africa) and *Isopogon* (Australia).]

cone shell ■ n. a predatory marine mollusc with a conical shell. [Genus *Conus*: numerous species.]

coney /ˈkəʊni/ (also **cony**) ■ n. (pl. **-eys**) chiefly Brit. a rabbit.
– ORIGIN Middle English: from Old French *conin*, from Latin *cuniculus*.

confab informal ■ n. an informal private conversation or discussion. ■ v. (**confabbed**, **confabbing**) engage in such conversation.

confabulate /kənˈfabjʊleɪt/ ■ v. formal converse.
– DERIVATIVES **confabulation** n.
– ORIGIN C17 (*confabulation* Middle English): from Latin *confabulari* 'chat together'.

confect /kənˈfɛkt/ ■ v. make (something elaborate or dainty).
– ORIGIN Middle English: from Latin *confect-*, *conficere* 'put together'.

confection ■ n. **1** an elaborate sweet dish or delicacy. **2** an elaborate article of women's dress. **3** the action of mixing or compounding something.

confectioner ■ n. a person who makes or sells confectionery.

confectioner's custard ■ n. thick sweet custard used as a filling for cakes and pastries.

confectioner's sugar ■ n. US term for ICING SUGAR.

confectionery ■ n. (pl. **-ies**) sweets and chocolates collectively.

confederacy ■ n. (pl. **-ies**) **1** a league or alliance, especially of confederate states. ▸ (**the Confederacy**) the Confederate states of the US. **2** a league formed for an unlawful purpose.

confederal ■ adj. relating to or denoting a confederation.

confederate ■ adj. /kənˈfɛd(ə)rət/ joined by an agreement or treaty. ▸ (**Confederate**) denoting the southern states which separated from the US in 1860–1. ■ n. /kənˈfɛd(ə)rət/ an accomplice or fellow worker. ■ v. /kənˈfɛdəreɪt/ [usu. as adj. **confederated**] bring into an alliance.
– ORIGIN Middle English: from late Latin *confoederatus*, from *con-* 'together' + *foederatus* (see FEDERATE).

confederation ■ n. **1** an alliance of a number of parties or groups. ▸ a more or less permanent union of states with some political power vested in a central authority. **2** the action of confederating or state of being confederated.

confer /kənˈfəː/ ■ v. (**conferred**, **conferring**) **1** grant (a title, degree, benefit, or right). **2** have discussions.
– DERIVATIVES **conferment** n. **conferrable** adj. **conferral** n.
– ORIGIN Middle English: from Latin *conferre*, from *con-* 'together' + *ferre* 'bring'.

Conference ■ n. a dessert pear of a firm-fleshed variety.
– ORIGIN C19: apparently named after the National Pear Conference of 1885.

conference ■ n. **1** a formal meeting of people with a shared interest, typically taking place over several days. ▸ a linking of several telephones or computers, so that each user may communicate with the others simultaneously. **2** an association in commerce for regulation or exchange of information. ▸ a league of sports teams or clubs. **3** the governing body of Methodist and other Christian Churches. ■ v. [usu. as noun **conferencing**] take part in a conference.
– PHRASES **in conference** in a meeting.
– ORIGIN C16: from French *conférence* or medieval Latin *conferentia*, from Latin *conferre* (see CONFER).

confess ■ v. **1** admit to a crime or wrongdoing. ▸ acknowledge reluctantly: *I must confess that I was surprised.* **2** declare one's sins formally to a priest. ▸ (of a priest) hear the confession of.
– ORIGIN Middle English: from Old French *confesser*, from Latin *confess-*, *confiteri* 'acknowledge'.

confessedly ■ adv. by one's own admission.

confession ■ n. **1** a formal statement admitting to a crime. ▸ a reluctant acknowledgement. **2** a formal admission of one's sins privately to a priest. **3** (also **confession of faith**) a statement setting out essential religious doctrine. ▸ the religious body or Church sharing a confession of faith.
– DERIVATIVES **confessionary** adj.

confessional ■ n. **1** an enclosed stall in a church, divided by a screen, in which a priest sits to hear confessions. **2** a confession. ■ adj. **1** (of speech or writing) in which a person reveals or admits to private thoughts or incidents in their past. **2** of or relating to religious confession. **3** of or relating to confessions of faith.

confessor ■ n. **1** a priest who hears confessions. **2** a person who makes a confession. **3** a person who avows religious faith in the face of opposition.

confetti ■ n. small pieces of coloured paper traditionally thrown over a bride and groom after a marriage ceremony.
– ORIGIN C19 (orig. denoting real or imitation sweets thrown during Italian carnivals): from Italian.

confetti bush ■ n. an evergreen South African shrub with fine, aromatic leaves and small pink or white flowers. [Genus *Coleonema*.]

confidant /ˈkɒnfɪdant, ˌkɒnfɪˈdant, -dɑːnt/ ■ n. (fem. **confidante** pronunc. same) a person in whom one confides.

– ORIGIN C17: alteration of **CONFIDENT** (as a noun), prob. to represent the pronunciation of French *confidente* 'having full trust'.

confide /kənˈfʌɪd/ ■ v. **1** (often **confide in**) tell someone about a secret or private matter in confidence. **2** (**confide something to**) dated entrust something to the care of.
– DERIVATIVES **confiding** adj. **confidingly** adv.
– ORIGIN Middle English: from Latin *confidere* 'have full trust'.

confidence ■ n. **1** the belief that one can have faith in or rely on someone or something. ▸ a feeling of self-assurance arising from an appreciation of one's own abilities. **2** the telling of private matters or secrets with mutual trust. ▸ a secret or private matter told to someone under a condition of trust.
– PHRASES **in someone's confidence** in a position of trust with someone. **take someone into one's confidence** tell someone one's secrets.
– ORIGIN Middle English: from Latin *confidentia*, from *confidere* (see **CONFIDENT**).

confidence interval ■ n. Statistics a range of values so defined that there is a specified probability that the value of a parameter lies within it.

confidence trick (N. Amer. also **confidence game**) ■ n. an act of cheating or tricking someone by persuading them to believe something that is not true.
– DERIVATIVES **confidence trickster** n.

confident ■ adj. **1** feeling confidence in oneself. **2** feeling certainty about something.
– DERIVATIVES **confidently** adv.

confidential ■ adj. **1** intended to be kept secret. **2** entrusted with private information: *a confidential secretary*.
– DERIVATIVES **confidentiality** n. **confidentially** adv.

configuration /kənˌfɪɡəˈreɪʃ(ə)n, -ɡjuː-/ ■ n. an arrangement of parts or elements in a particular form or figure. ▸ Chemistry the fixed three-dimensional relationship of the atoms in a molecule.
– DERIVATIVES **configurational** adj.

configure ■ v. (often **be configured**) arrange in a particular configuration. ▸ Computing arrange or order (a computer system) so as to fit it for a designated task.
– DERIVATIVES **configurable** adj.
– ORIGIN Middle English: from Latin *configurare* 'shape after a pattern', from *con-* 'together' + *figurare* 'to shape', from *figura* 'shape, figure'.

confine ■ v. /kənˈfʌɪn/ (**confine someone/thing to**) keep or restrict someone or something within certain limits of (space, scope, or time). ▸ (**be confined to**) be unable to leave (one's bed, home, etc.) due to illness or disability. ▸ (**be confined**) dated (of a woman) remain in bed for a period before, during, and after giving birth. ■ n. /ˈkɒnfʌɪn/ (**confines**) limits or boundaries.
– ORIGIN Middle English: from French *confins*, from Latin *confinis* 'bordering', from *con-* 'together' + *finis* 'end, limit'; verb from French *confiner*, from Latin *confinis*.

confined ■ adj. (of a space) enclosed; cramped.

confinement ■ n. **1** the action of confining or state of being confined. **2** dated the condition of being in childbirth.

confirm ■ v. **1** establish the truth or correctness of. ▸ state with assurance that something is true. ▸ (**confirm someone in**) reinforce someone in (an opinion or feeling). **2** make (a provisional arrangement) definite. ▸ declare formally to be appointed to a post. **3** (usu. **be confirmed**) administer the religious rite of confirmation to.
– DERIVATIVES **confirmative** adj. **confirmatory** adj.
– ORIGIN Middle English: from Old French *confermer*, from Latin *confirmare*, from *con-* 'together' + *firmare* 'strengthen', from *firmus* 'firm'.

confirmand /ˈkɒnfəmand/ ■ n. a person about to undergo the religious rite of confirmation.

confirmation ■ n. **1** the action of confirming or state of being confirmed. **2** (in the Christian Church) the rite at which a baptized person affirms Christian belief and is admitted as a full member of the Church. **3** the Jewish ceremony of bar mitzvah.

confirmed ■ adj. firmly established in a habit, belief, or way of life: *a confirmed bachelor*.

confiscate /ˈkɒnfɪskeɪt/ ■ v. take or seize (property) with authority. ▸ appropriate to the public treasury as a penalty.
– DERIVATIVES **confiscation** n. **confiscator** n. **confiscatory** adj.
– ORIGIN C16: from Latin *confiscare* 'put away, consign to the public treasury', from *con-* 'together' + *fiscus* 'chest, treasury'.

conflagration /ˌkɒnfləˈɡreɪʃ(ə)n/ ■ n. an extensive and destructive fire.
– ORIGIN C15: from Latin *conflagratio(n-)*, from *conflagrare*, from *con-* (expressing intensive force) + *flagrare* 'to blaze'.

conflate ■ v. combine into one.
– DERIVATIVES **conflation** n.
– ORIGIN Middle English: from Latin *conflare* 'kindle, fuse', from *con-* 'together' + *flare* 'to blow'.

conflict ■ n. /ˈkɒnflɪkt/ a serious disagreement or argument. ▸ a prolonged armed struggle. ▸ an incompatibility between opinions, principles, etc. ■ v. /kənˈflɪkt/ (often as adj. **conflicting**) be incompatible or at variance with.
– DERIVATIVES **conflictual** adj.
– ORIGIN Middle English: from Latin *conflict-*, *confligere* 'strike together, fight', from *con-* 'together' + *fligere* 'to strike'; the noun is via Latin *conflictus* 'a contest'.

conflict diamond ■ n. a rough diamond traded illicitly to finance armed insurgency, especially in Africa. ▸ [as modifier] relating to such diamonds.

confluence /ˈkɒnfluəns/ ■ n. **1** the junction of two rivers. **2** an act or process of merging.
– DERIVATIVES **confluent** adj.
– ORIGIN Middle English: from late Latin *confluentia*, from Latin *confluere*, from *con-* 'together' + *fluere* 'to flow'.

conform ■ v. **1** comply with rules, standards, or laws. ▸ behave according to social convention. **2** be similar in form or type.
– ORIGIN Middle English: from Old French *conformer*, from Latin *conformare*, from *con-* 'together' + *formare* 'to form'.

conformable ■ adj. (usu. **conformable to**) **1** disposed or accustomed to conform. **2** similar in nature; consistent. **3** Geology (of strata) deposited in a continuous sequence, and having the same direction of stratification.
– DERIVATIVES **conformability** n. **conformably** adv.

conformation ■ n. the shape or structure of something. ▸ Chemistry any of the spatial arrangements which the atoms in a molecule may adopt, especially by rotation about individual single bonds.
– DERIVATIVES **conformational** adj.
– ORIGIN C16: from Latin *conformatio(n-)*, from *conformare* (see **CONFORM**).

conformist ■ n. a person who conforms to social convention. ■ adj. conforming to accepted behaviour or established practices.
– DERIVATIVES **conformism** n.

conformity ■ n. **1** compliance with conventions, rules, or laws. ▸ Brit., chiefly historical compliance with the practices of the Church of England. **2** similarity in form or type.

confound ■ v. **1** surprise or confuse. ▸ prove wrong. ▸ defeat (a plan, aim, or hope). **2** (often **be confounded with**) mix up with something else. ■ exclam. (**confound it!**) dated used to express annoyance.
– ORIGIN Middle English: from Old French *confondre*, from Latin *confundere* 'pour together, mix up'.

confounded ■ adj. informal, dated used for emphasis to express annoyance: *a confounded nuisance*.
– DERIVATIVES **confoundedly** adv.

confraternity ■ n. (pl. **-ies**) a brotherhood, especially with a religious or charitable purpose.
– ORIGIN Middle English: from Old French *confraternite*, from medieval Latin *confraternitas*, from Latin *con-* 'together with' + *frater* 'brother'.

confront ■ v. **1** stand or meet face to face with hostile intent. **2** (of a problem) present itself to (someone). ▸ face up to and deal with (a problem). ▸ compel to face or consider something.
– DERIVATIVES **confrontation** n. **confrontational** adj.
– ORIGIN C16: from French *confronter*, from medieval Latin

Confucian

confrontare, from Latin *con-* 'with' + *frons* 'face'.

Confucian /kənˈfjuːʃ(ə)n/ ■ adj. of or relating to Confucius or Confucianism. ■ n. an adherent of Confucianism.

Confucianism /kənˈfjuːʃənɪz(ə)m/ ■ n. a system of philosophical and ethical teachings founded by the Chinese philosopher Confucius (551–479 BC).
— DERIVATIVES **Confucianist** n. & adj.

confuse ■ v. 1 cause to become bewildered or perplexed. 2 make less easy to understand. ▸ identify wrongly.
— DERIVATIVES **confusability** n. **confusable** adj. **confusing** adj. **confusingly** adv.
— ORIGIN Middle English: from Old French *confus*, from Latin *confusus*, from *confundere* (see **CONFOUND**).

confused ■ adj. 1 bewildered. 2 lacking order and so difficult to understand or distinguish.
— DERIVATIVES **confusedly** adv.

confusion ■ n. 1 uncertainty. ▸ a situation of panic. ▸ a disorderly jumble. 2 the state of being bewildered. ▸ the mistaking of one person or thing for another.

confute ■ v. formal prove to be wrong.
— DERIVATIVES **confutation** n.
— ORIGIN C16 (*confutation* Middle English): from Latin *confutare* 'restrain, answer conclusively', from *con-* 'altogether' + the base of *refutare* 'refute'.

conga /ˈkɒŋɡə/ ■ n. 1 a Latin American dance of African origin, typically with several people in a line, one behind the other. 2 (also **conga drum**) a tall, narrow drum beaten with the hands. ■ v. (**congas, congaed** or **conga'd, congaing**) perform the conga.
— ORIGIN 1930s: from Latin American Spanish, from Spanish, from *congo* 'Congolese'.

congeal /kənˈdʒiːl/ ■ v. become semi-solid, especially on cooling.
— DERIVATIVES **congealable** adj. **congelation** /ˌkɒndʒəˈleɪʃ(ə)n/ n.
— ORIGIN Middle English: from Old French *congeler*, from Latin *congelare*, from *con-* 'together' + *gelare* 'freeze', from *gelu* 'frost'.

congener /ˈkɒndʒɪnə, kənˈdʒiːnə/ ■ n. a person or thing of the same kind as another. ▸ an animal or plant of the same genus as another.
— DERIVATIVES **congeneric** /ˌkɒndʒɪˈnɛrɪk/ adj.
— ORIGIN C18: from Latin, from *con-* 'together with' + *genus, gener-* 'race, stock'.

congenial /kənˈdʒiːnɪəl/ ■ adj. pleasant because of qualities or interests similar to one's own. ▸ suited to one's taste or inclination.
— DERIVATIVES **congeniality** n. **congenially** adv.

congenital /kənˈdʒɛnɪt(ə)l/ ■ adj. (especially of a disease or abnormality) present from birth. ▸ having a particular trait from birth or by established habit.
— DERIVATIVES **congenitally** adv.
— ORIGIN C18: from Latin *congenitus*, from *con-* 'together' + *genitus*, from *gignere* 'beget'.

conger /ˈkɒŋɡə/ (also **conger eel**) ■ n. a large edible predatory eel of shallow coastal waters. [Family Congridae: several species.]
— ORIGIN Middle English: from Old French *congre*, from Greek *gongros*.

congeries /kɒnˈdʒɪəriːz, -ɪz/ ■ n. (pl. same) a disorderly collection.
— ORIGIN C16: from Latin *congeries* 'heap, pile', from *congerere* 'heap up'.

congested ■ adj. so crowded as to hinder freedom of movement. ▸ (of a part of the body) abnormally full of blood. ▸ (of the respiratory tract) blocked with mucus.
— DERIVATIVES **congestion** n.
— ORIGIN Middle English: from Latin *congest-, congerere* 'heap up', from *con-* 'together' + *gerere* 'bring'.

congestion charge ■ n. chiefly Brit. a charge made to drive into an area, typically a city centre, that suffers heavy traffic.
— DERIVATIVES **congestion-charging** n.

congestive ■ adj. Medicine involving or produced by congestion.

conglomerate ■ n. /kənˈɡlɒm(ə)rət/ 1 a number of different things grouped together to form a whole while remaining distinct entities. ▸ a large corporation formed by the merging of separate firms. 2 Geology a coarse-grained sedimentary rock composed of rounded rock fragments cemented together. ■ adj. /kənˈɡlɒm(ə)rət/ of or relating to a conglomerate. ■ v. /kənˈɡlɒməreɪt/ gather into or form a conglomerate.
— DERIVATIVES **conglomeration** n.
— ORIGIN Middle English: from Latin *conglomerare*, from *con-* 'together' + *glomus* 'ball'.

Congo fever (in full **Crimean-Congo haemorrhagic fever**) ■ n. a tick-borne viral fever which is mild in livestock, but acute and sometimes fatal in humans.

Congolese /ˌkɒŋɡəˈliːz/ ■ n. (pl. same) 1 a native or inhabitant of the Congo or the Democratic Republic of Congo. 2 any of the Bantu languages spoken in the Congo region. ■ adj. of or relating to the Congo or the Democratic Republic of Congo.

congrats ■ pl. n. informal congratulations.

congratulate ■ v. express pleasure at the happiness or good fortune of. ▸ praise for an achievement.
▸ (**congratulate oneself**) feel pride or satisfaction.
— DERIVATIVES **congratulator** n. **congratulatory** adj.
— ORIGIN C16: from Latin *congratulari* 'congratulate', from *con-* 'with' + *gratulari* 'show joy', from *gratus* 'pleasing'.

congratulation ■ n. 1 (**congratulations**) praise or good wishes on a special occasion. 2 the action of congratulating.

congregant /ˈkɒŋɡrɪɡ(ə)nt/ ■ n. a member of a congregation.

congregate ■ v. gather into a crowd or mass.
— ORIGIN Middle English: from Latin *congregare* 'collect (into a flock), unite', from *con-* 'together' + *gregare*, from *grex* 'a flock'.

congregation ■ n. 1 a group of people assembled for religious worship. ▸ a group of people obeying a common religious rule. 2 a gathering or collection of people or things. ▸ the action of congregating. 3 (in the Roman Catholic Church) a permanent committee of the College of Cardinals.

congregational ■ adj. 1 of or relating to a congregation. 2 (**Congregational**) of or adhering to Congregationalism.

Congregationalism ■ n. a system of organization among Christian churches whereby individual churches are largely self-governing.
— DERIVATIVES **Congregationalist** n. & adj.

congress ■ n. 1 a formal meeting or series of meetings between delegates. 2 (**Congress**) a national legislative body, especially that of the US. 3 a society or organization. 4 the action of coming together.
— DERIVATIVES **congressional** adj.
— ORIGIN Middle English: from Latin *congressus*, from *congredi* 'meet', from *con-* 'together' + *gradi* 'walk'.

congressman (or **congresswoman**) ■ n. (pl. **-men** or **-women**) a male (or female) member of the US Congress.

congruent /ˈkɒŋɡruənt/ ■ adj. 1 in agreement or harmony. 2 Geometry (of figures) identical in form.
— DERIVATIVES **congruence** n. **congruency** n. **congruently** adv.
— ORIGIN Middle English: from Latin *congruere* 'agree, meet together', from *con-* 'together' + *ruere* 'fall, rush'.

congruous /ˈkɒŋɡruəs/ ■ adj. in agreement or harmony.
— DERIVATIVES **congruity** /-ˈɡruːɪti/ n. **congruously** adv.

conical ■ adj. shaped like a cone.
— DERIVATIVES **conically** adv.

conical projection ■ n. a map projection in which an area of the earth is projected on to a cone.

conic section ■ n. the figure of a circle, ellipse, parabola, or hyperbola formed by the intersection of a plane and a circular cone.

conidium /kəʊˈnɪdɪəm/ ■ n. (pl. **conidia** /-dɪə/) Botany a spore produced asexually by various fungi at the tip of a specialized hypha.
— ORIGIN C19: from Greek *konis* 'dust' + the diminutive suffix *-idium*.

conifer /ˈkɒnɪfə, ˈkəʊn-/ ■ n. a tree bearing cones and evergreen needle-like or scale-like leaves, e.g. a pine, fir, or cypress. [Order Coniferales.]

connotation

– DERIVATIVES **coniferous** adj.
– ORIGIN C19: from Latin, 'cone-bearing', from *conus* (see **CONE**).

conjecture /kən'dʒɛktʃə/ ■ n. an opinion or conclusion based on incomplete information. ▶ an unproven mathematical or scientific theorem. ■ v. form a conjecture.
– DERIVATIVES **conjecturable** adj. **conjectural** adj. **conjecturally** adv.
– ORIGIN Middle English: from Latin *conjectura*, from *conicere* 'put together in thought', from *con-* 'together' + *jacere* 'throw'.

conjoin ■ v. formal join; combine.
– ORIGIN Middle English: from Old French *conjoindre*, from Latin *conjungere*, from *con-* 'together' + *jungere* 'to join'.

conjoint ■ adj. combining all people or things involved.
– DERIVATIVES **conjointly** adv.

conjugal /'kɒndʒʊg(ə)l/ ■ adj. of or relating to marriage or the relationship between husband and wife.
– DERIVATIVES **conjugality** n. **conjugally** adv.
– ORIGIN C16: from Latin *conjugalis*, from *conjux* 'spouse', from *con-* 'together' + *jugum* 'a yoke'.

conjugal rights ■ pl. n. the rights, especially to sexual relations, regarded as exercisable in law by each partner in a marriage.

conjugate ■ v. /'kɒndʒʊgeɪt/ **1** Grammar give the different forms of (a verb). **2** Biology (of bacteria or unicellular organisms) become temporarily united in order to exchange genetic material. **3** Chemistry be combined with or joined to reversibly. ■ adj. /'kɒndʒʊgət/ **1** Chemistry (of an acid or base) related by loss or gain of a proton. **2** Mathematics joined in a reciprocal relation, especially having the same real parts and equal magnitudes but opposite signs of imaginary parts. **3** Geometry (of angles) adding up to 360°. **4** Biology (of gametes) fused. ■ n. /'kɒndʒʊgət/ **1** chiefly Biochemistry a conjugated substance. **2** a conjugate mathematical value or entity.
– DERIVATIVES **conjugacy** n.
– ORIGIN C15: from Latin *conjugare* 'yoke together', from *con-* 'together' + *jugum* 'yoke'.

conjugation ■ n. /kɒndʒʊ'geɪʃ(ə)n/ **1** Grammar the variation of the form of a verb, by which the voice, mood, tense, number, and person are identified. ▶ the class in which a verb is put according to the manner of this variation. **2** the temporary union of two bacteria or unicellular organisms for the exchange of genetic material. ▶ the fusion of two gametes. **3** the sharing of electron density between nearby multiple bonds in a molecule.
– DERIVATIVES **conjugational** adj.

conjunct ■ adj. /kən'dʒʌŋ(k)t/ joined together, combined, or associated. ■ n. /'kɒndʒʌŋ(k)t/ **1** each of two or more joined or associated things. **2** Logic each of the terms of a conjunctive proposition. **3** Grammar an adverbial joining two sentences or clauses (e.g. *however*).
– ORIGIN Middle English: from Latin *conjunctus*, from *conjungere* (see **CONJOIN**).

conjunction ■ n. Grammar **1** a word used to connect clauses or sentences or to coordinate words in the same clause (e.g. *and*, *if*). **2** an instance of two or more events occurring at the same point in time or space. ▶ Astronomy & Astrology an alignment of two planets so that they appear to be in the same place in the sky.
– PHRASES **in conjunction** together.
– DERIVATIVES **conjunctional** adj.

conjunctiva /,kɒndʒʌŋ(k)'tʌɪvə, kən'dʒʌŋ(k)tɪvə/ ■ n. Anatomy the mucous membrane that covers the front of the eye and lines the inside of the eyelids.
– DERIVATIVES **conjunctival** adj.
– ORIGIN Middle English: from medieval Latin (*membrana*) *conjunctiva* 'conjunctive (membrane)', from Latin, from *conjungere* (see **CONJOIN**).

conjunctive ■ adj. of, relating to, or forming a conjunction. ▶ involving the combination or co-occurrence of two or more things. ■ n. Grammar a conjunction.
– DERIVATIVES **conjunctively** adv.

conjunctivitis /kən,dʒʌŋ(k)tɪ'vʌɪtɪs/ ■ n. Medicine inflammation of the conjunctiva.

conjuncture ■ n. **1** a combination of events. **2** a state of affairs.

conjure /'kʌndʒə/ ■ v. **1** (usu. **conjure up**) cause to appear as if by magic. ▶ call to the mind. ▶ call upon (a spirit) to appear by means of a magic ritual. **2** /kən'dʒʊə/ archaic implore to do something.
– PHRASES **a name to conjure with** a name of great importance within a particular field.
– DERIVATIVES **conjuration** /,kʌndʒə'reɪʃ(ə)n, ,kɒndʒʊ(ə)-/ n. **conjuring** n.
– ORIGIN Middle English: from Old French *conjurer*, from Latin *conjurare* 'band together by an oath, conspire', from *con-* 'together' + *jurare* 'swear'.

conjuror (also **conjurer**) ■ n. a performer of conjuring tricks.

conk[1] ■ v. (**conk out**) informal **1** (S. African also **conk in**) (of a machine) break down. **2** faint or go to sleep. ▶ die.
– ORIGIN FIRST WORLD WAR.

conk[2] informal ■ n. a person's nose. ▶ dated a person's head.
– ORIGIN C19: perhaps an alteration of **CONCH**.

conker ■ n. Brit. the hard shiny dark brown nut of a horse chestnut tree. ▶ (**conkers**) [treated as sing.] a children's game in which each has a conker on a string and tries to break another's with it.
– ORIGIN C19 (a dialect word denoting a snail shell, with which the game was orig. played): perhaps from **CONCH**.

con man ■ n. informal a man who cheats others using confidence tricks.

conn ■ v. US spelling of **CON**[3].

connect ■ v. **1** bring together so as to establish a link. ▶ be related in some respect. ▶ join together so as to provide access and communication. ▶ put into contact by telephone. **2** (of a train, bus, etc.) arrive at its destination just before another departs so that passengers can transfer. **3** informal (of a blow) hit the intended target.
– DERIVATIVES **connectable** adj. **connectedly** adv. **connectedness** n. **connector** n.
– ORIGIN Middle English: from Latin *connectere*, from *con-* 'together' + *nectere* 'bind'.

connecting rod ■ n. the rod connecting the piston and the crankpin in an engine or pump.

connection (Brit. also **connexion**) ■ n. **1** a link or relationship between people or things. **2** an opportunity for catching a connecting train, bus, etc. **3** (**connections**) people with whom one has contact. **4** S. African informal a friend.
– PHRASES **in connection with** concerning. **in this** (or **that**) **connection** with reference to this (or that).
– DERIVATIVES **connectional** adj.

connective ■ adj. connecting. ■ n. **1** Grammar a word or phrase linking other linguistic units. **2** Anatomy a bundle of nerve fibres connecting two nerve centres or ganglia, especially in invertebrates.

connective tissue ■ n. Anatomy tissue that connects, supports, binds, or separates other tissues or organs, including cartilaginous, fatty, and elastic tissues.

connectivity ■ n. the state or extent of being connected. ▶ Computing capacity for the interconnection of platforms, systems, and applications.

connexion ■ n. variant spelling of **CONNECTION**.

conning tower /'kɒnɪŋ/ ■ n. the superstructure of a submarine, containing the periscope.

connive /kə'nʌɪv/ ■ v. (**connive at/in**) secretly allow (a wrongdoing). ▶ conspire.
– DERIVATIVES **connivance** n. **conniver** n. **conniving** adj.
– ORIGIN C17: from Latin *connivere* 'shut the eyes (to)', from *con-* 'together' + a word rel. to *nictare* 'to wink'.

connoisseur /,kɒnə'sə:/ ■ n. an expert judge in matters of taste.
– DERIVATIVES **connoisseurship** n.
– ORIGIN C18: from obsolete French, from *conoistre* 'know'.

connotation /kɒnə'teɪʃ(ə)n/ ■ n. an idea or feeling which a word invokes in addition to its primary meaning. ▶ Philosophy the abstract meaning of a term, determining which objects or concepts it applies to.
– ORIGIN C16: from medieval Latin *connotatio(n-)*, from *connotare* (see **CONNOTE**).

---

s sit   t top   v voice   w we   z zoo   ʃ she   ʒ decision   θ thin   ð this   ŋ ring   x loch   tʃ chip   dʒ jar

connote /kə'nəʊt/ ■ v. (of a word) imply or suggest. ▸ imply as a consequence or condition.
– DERIVATIVES **connotative** /'kɒnəteɪtɪv, kə'nəʊtətɪv/ adj.
– ORIGIN C17: from medieval Latin *connotare* 'mark in addition', from *con-* 'together with' + *notare* 'to note'.

connubial /kə'nju:bɪəl/ ■ adj. poetic/literary conjugal.
– ORIGIN C17: from Latin *connubialis*, from *connubium* 'marriage', from *con-* 'with' + *nubere* 'marry'.

conodont /'kəʊnədɒnt/ ■ n. Palaeontology an extinct marine invertebrate with a long worm-like body and numerous small teeth.
– ORIGIN C19: from *Conodonta* (name of a class), from Greek *kōnos* 'cone' + *odous* 'tooth'.

conquer ■ v. **1** overcome and take control of by military force. **2** successfully overcome (a problem). **3** climb (a mountain) successfully.
– DERIVATIVES **conquerable** adj. **conqueror** n.
– ORIGIN Middle English: from Old French *conquerre*, from Latin *conquirere* 'gain, win', from *con-* (expressing completion) + *quaerere* 'seek'.

conquest ■ n. **1** the action of conquering. ▸ a territory gained in such a way. **2** a person whose affection or favour has been won.
– PHRASES **make a conquest of** win the affections of.
– ORIGIN Middle English: from Old French *conquest(e)*, from Latin *conquirere* (see CONQUER).

conquistador /kɒn'kwɪstədɔ:, -kɪst-/ ■ n. (pl. **conquistadores** /-'dɔ:reɪz/ or **conquistadors**) a conqueror, especially a Spanish conqueror of Mexico or Peru in the 16th century.
– ORIGIN C19: from Spanish.

con rod ■ n. informal term for CONNECTING ROD.

consanguineous /,kɒnsaŋ'gwɪnɪəs/ ■ adj. relating to or denoting people descended from the same ancestor.
– DERIVATIVES **consanguine** adj. **consanguinity** n.
– ORIGIN C17: from Latin *consanguineus* 'of the same blood', from *con-* 'together with' + *sanguis* 'blood'.

conscience ■ n. a person's moral sense of right and wrong.
– PHRASES **in (all) conscience** in fairness. **on one's conscience** causing feelings of guilt.
– DERIVATIVES **conscienceless** adj.
– ORIGIN Middle English: from Latin *conscientia*, from *conscire* 'be privy to', from *con-* 'with' + *scire* 'know'.

conscience money ■ n. money paid due to feelings of guilt.

conscientious /,kɒnʃɪ'ɛnʃəs/ ■ adj. **1** wishing to do what is right. **2** relating to a person's conscience.
– DERIVATIVES **conscientiously** adv. **conscientiousness** n.
– ORIGIN C17: from French *consciencieux*, from medieval Latin *conscientiosus*, from Latin *conscientia* (see CONSCIENCE).

conscientious objector ■ n. a person who for reasons of conscience objects to serving in the armed forces.
– DERIVATIVES **conscientious objection** n.

conscientize (also **-ise**) ■ v. develop a person's consciousness of their rights, especially in order to free themselves from oppression.
– DERIVATIVES **conscientization** (also **-isation**) n.

conscious ■ adj. **1** aware of and responding to one's surroundings. **2** (usu. **conscious of**) having knowledge of something. ▸ [in combination] concerned about a matter: *security-conscious*. **3** deliberate.
– DERIVATIVES **consciously** adv.
– ORIGIN C16: from Latin *conscius* 'knowing with others or in oneself', from *conscire* 'be privy to'.

consciousness ■ n. **1** the state of being conscious. ▸ the fact of awareness by the mind of itself and the world. **2** one's awareness or perception of something.

conscript ■ v. /kən'skrɪpt/ enlist compulsorily, typically into the armed services. ■ n. /'kɒnskrɪpt/ a conscripted person.
– DERIVATIVES **conscription** n.
– ORIGIN C18 (*conscription* Middle English): from French *conscrit*, from Latin *conscriptus*, from *conscribere* 'enrol'.

consecrate /'kɒnsɪkreɪt/ ■ v. (usu. **be consecrated**) **1** make or declare sacred. ▸ (in Christian belief) make (bread or wine) into the body and blood of Christ. **2** ordain to a sacred office, typically that of bishop.
– DERIVATIVES **consecration** n. **consecrator** n. **consecratory** adj.
– ORIGIN Middle English: from Latin *consecrare* 'dedicate', from *con-* (expressing intensive force) + *sacrare* 'dedicate', from *sacer* 'sacred'.

consecutive /kən'sɛkjʊtɪv/ ■ adj. **1** following continuously. ▸ in sequence. **2** Grammar expressing consequence or result.
– DERIVATIVES **consecutively** adv. **consecutiveness** n.
– ORIGIN C17: from French *consécutif*, from medieval Latin *consecutivus*, from Latin *consequi* 'follow closely'.

consensual /kən'sɛnsjʊəl, -ʃʊəl/ ■ adj. relating to or involving consent or consensus.
– DERIVATIVES **consensually** adv.

consensus /kən'sɛnsəs/ ■ n. general agreement.
– ORIGIN C17: from Latin, 'agreement', from *consentire* 'agree'.

consent ■ n. permission. ■ v. give permission. ▸ agree to do something.
– PHRASES **informed consent** permission granted in the knowledge of the possible consequences.
– ORIGIN Middle English: from Old French *consente* (n.), *consentir* (v.), from Latin *consentire*, from *con-* 'together' + *sentire* 'feel'.

consenting adult ■ n. an adult who willingly agrees to engage in a sexual act.

consequence ■ n. **1** a result or effect. **2** [usu. with neg.] importance or relevance. ▸ dated social distinction. **3** (**consequences**) [treated as sing.] a game in which a narrative is made up by the players in turn, each ignorant of what has already been contributed.
– PHRASES **in consequence** as a result. **take** (or **bear**) **the consequences** accept responsibility for negative results or effects.
– ORIGIN Middle English: from Latin *consequentia*, from *consequi* 'follow closely'.

consequent ■ adj. following as a consequence. ■ n. Logic the second part of a conditional proposition, whose truth is stated to be implied by that of the antecedent.
– DERIVATIVES **consequential** adj. **consequentiality** n. **consequentially** adv.

consequentialism ■ n. Philosophy the doctrine that the morality of an action is to be judged solely by its consequences.
– DERIVATIVES **consequentialist** adj. & n.

consequently /'kɒnsɪkw(ə)ntli/ ■ adv. as a result; therefore.

conservancy /kən'sə:v(ə)nsi/ ■ n. (pl. **-ies**) **1** a body concerned with the preservation of natural resources. **2** (in the UK) a commission controlling a port, river, or catchment area. **3** conservation.
– ORIGIN C18: from Anglo-Norman French *conservacie*, from Latin *conservatio* (see CONSERVATION).

conservation ■ n. **1** preservation or restoration of the natural environment and wildlife. ▸ preservation and repair of archaeological, historical, and cultural sites and artefacts. **2** careful use of a resource. **3** Physics the principle by which the total value of a quantity remains constant in a system which is not subject to external influence.
– DERIVATIVES **conservational** adj. **conservationist** n.
– ORIGIN Middle English: from Latin *conservatio(n-)*, from *conservare* (see CONSERVE).

conservative ■ adj. **1** averse to change or innovation and holding traditional values. ▸ (of dress or taste) sober and conventional. **2** (in a political context) favouring free enterprise, private ownership, and socially conservative ideas. ▸ (**Conservative**) of or relating to a Conservative Party. **3** (of an estimate) purposely low for the sake of caution. **4** (of surgery or medical treatment) intended to control rather than eliminate a condition, and preserve existing tissue. ■ n. **1** a conservative person. **2** (**Conservative**) a supporter or member of a Conservative Party.
– DERIVATIVES **conservatism** n. **conservatively** adv. **conservativeness** n.

Conservative Judaism ■ n. a form of Judaism seeking to preserve Jewish tradition and ritual but with a more flexible approach than Orthodox Judaism.

conservatoire /kənˈsəːvətwɑː/ ■ n. a college for the study of classical music or other arts.
– ORIGIN C18: French, from Italian *conservatorio*.

conservator /ˈkɒnsəˌveɪtə, kənˈsəːvətə/ ■ n. a person involved in conservation.

conservatory ■ n. (pl. **-ies**) **1** chiefly Brit. a room with a glass roof and walls, attached to a house and used as a sun lounge or for growing delicate plants. **2** another term for **CONSERVATOIRE**.
– ORIGIN C16: from late Latin *conservatorium*, from *conservare* (see **CONSERVE**).

conserve /kənˈsəːv/ ■ v. **1** protect from harm or destruction. ▸ prevent the wasteful overuse of. ▸ preserve (food, typically fruit) with sugar. **2** Physics maintain (a quantity) at a constant overall total. ■ n. /also ˈkɒnsəːv/ jam.
– ORIGIN Middle English: from Old French *conserver* (v.), from Latin *conservare* 'to preserve', from *con-* 'together' + *servare* 'to keep'.

consider ■ v. **1** think carefully about. ▸ believe to be. ▸ take into account when making a judgement. **2** look attentively at.
– PHRASES **all things considered** taking everything into account.
– ORIGIN Middle English: from Old French *considerer*, from Latin *considerare* 'examine', perhaps from *sidus, sider-* 'star'.

considerable ■ adj. **1** notably large. **2** having merit or distinction.
– DERIVATIVES **considerably** adv.

considerate ■ adj. careful not to harm or inconvenience others.
– DERIVATIVES **considerately** adv. **considerateness** n.

consideration ■ n. **1** careful thought. ▸ a fact taken into account when making a decision. **2** thoughtfulness towards others. **3** a payment or reward. ▸ Law anything given or promised by one party in exchange for the promise or undertaking of another. **4** archaic importance.
– PHRASES **in consideration of** in return for. **take into consideration** take into account. **under consideration** being considered.

considering ■ prep. & conj. taking into consideration. ■ adv. informal taking everything into account.

consign /kənˈsʌɪn/ ■ v. deliver to someone's custody. ▸ send (goods) by a public carrier. ▸ (**consign someone/thing to**) put someone or something in (a place) in order to be rid of them.
– DERIVATIVES **consignee** n. **consignor** n.
– ORIGIN Middle English: from French *consigner* or Latin *consignare* 'mark with a seal'.

consignment ■ n. a batch of goods consigned.

consist ■ v. /kənˈsɪst/ (**consist of**) be composed of. ▸ (**consist in**) have as an essential feature. ■ n. /ˈkɒnsɪst/ the set of vehicles forming a complete train.
– ORIGIN Middle English: from Latin *consistere* 'stand firm, exist', from *con-* 'together' + *sistere* 'stand (still)'.

consistency (also **consistence**) ■ n. (pl. **-ies**) **1** the state of being consistent. **2** the thickness or viscosity of a substance.

consistent ■ adj. **1** unchanging over time. **2** (usu. **consistent with**) congruous or in agreement. **3** not containing any logical contradictions.
– DERIVATIVES **consistently** adv.
– ORIGIN C16: from Latin *consistere* (see **CONSIST**).

consistory /kənˈsɪst(ə)ri/ ■ n. (pl. **-ies**) **1** (in the Roman Catholic Church) the council of cardinals, with or without the Pope. **2** (also **consistory court**) (in the Church of England) a court presided over by a bishop, for the administration of ecclesiastical law in a diocese. **3** (in other Churches) a local administrative body.
– DERIVATIVES **consistorial** /ˌkɒnsɪˈstɔːrɪəl/ adj.
– ORIGIN Middle English: from Anglo-Norman French *consistorie*, from late Latin *consistorium*, from *consistere* (see **CONSIST**).

consociation ■ n. **1** a political system formed by the cooperation of different social groups on the basis of shared power. **2** Ecology a small climax community of plants having a characteristic dominant species.
– DERIVATIVES **consociational** adj.

– ORIGIN C16: from Latin *consociatio(n-)*, from *consociare*, from *con-* 'together' + *sociare* 'to associate', from *socius* 'fellow'.

consolation /ˌkɒnsəˈleɪʃ(ə)n/ ■ n. comfort received by someone after a loss or disappointment. ▸ a source of such comfort.
– DERIVATIVES **consolatory** /kənˈsɒlət(ə)ri, -ˈsəʊl-/ adj.
– ORIGIN Middle English: from Latin *consolatio(n-)*, from *consolari* (see **CONSOLE**[1]).

consolation prize ■ n. a prize given to a competitor who just fails to win.

console[1] /kənˈsəʊl/ ■ v. give consolation to.
– DERIVATIVES **consolable** adj. **consoler** n. **consoling** adj. **consolingly** adv.
– ORIGIN C17: from French *consoler*, from Latin *consolari*, from *con-* 'with' + *solari* 'soothe'.

console[2] /ˈkɒnsəʊl/ ■ n. **1** a panel or unit accommodating a set of controls. ▸ a cabinet for television or radio equipment. ▸ (also **games console**) a small machine for playing computerized video games. ▸ the cabinet or enclosure containing the keyboards, stops, etc. of an organ. **2** an ornamented bracket.
– ORIGIN C17: from French, perhaps from *consolider*, from Latin *consolidare* (see **CONSOLIDATE**).

console table ■ n. a table top supported by ornamented brackets against a wall.

consolidate /kənˈsɒlɪdeɪt/ ■ v. **1** make stronger or more solid. **2** combine into a single unit.
– DERIVATIVES **consolidation** n. **consolidator** n.
– ORIGIN C16: from Latin *consolidare*, from *con-* 'together' + *solidare* 'make firm', from *solidus* 'solid'.

consommé /kənˈsɒmeɪ/ ■ n. a clear soup made with concentrated stock.
– ORIGIN French: from *consommer* 'consume, consummate', from Latin *consummare* (see **CONSUMMATE**).

consonance /ˈkɒns(ə)nəns/ ■ n. **1** agreement or compatibility. **2** the recurrence of similar-sounding consonants, especially in prosody. **3** Music a harmonious combination of notes.
– ORIGIN Middle English: from Latin *consonantia*, from *consonare* (see **CONSONANT**).

consonant /ˈkɒns(ə)nənt/ ■ n. a speech sound in which the breath is at least partly obstructed and which can be combined with a vowel to form a syllable. ▸ a letter representing such a sound. ■ adj. **1** denoting or relating to a consonant. **2** (**consonant with**) in agreement or harmony with.
– DERIVATIVES **consonantal** adj. **consonantly** adv.
– ORIGIN Middle English: from Latin *consonare* 'sound together', from *con-* 'with' + *sonare* 'to sound', from *sonus* 'sound'.

consort[1] ■ n. /ˈkɒnsɔːt/ **1** a wife, husband, or companion, in particular the spouse of a monarch. **2** a ship sailing in company with another. ■ v. /kənˈsɔːt/ (**consort with**) habitually associate with.
– ORIGIN Middle English: from Latin *consors* 'sharing, partner', from *con-* 'together with' + *sors, sort-* 'lot, destiny'.

consort[2] /ˈkɒnsɔːt/ ■ n. a small group of musicians performing together, typically playing Renaissance music.
– ORIGIN C16: earlier form of **CONSORT**[1].

consortium /kənˈsɔːtɪəm/ ■ n. (pl. **consortia** /-tɪə/ or **consortiums**) **1** an association, typically of several companies. **2** Law the right of association and companionship with one's spouse.
– ORIGIN C19: from Latin, from *consors* (see **CONSORT**[1]).

conspecific /ˌkɒnspəˈsɪfɪk/ Biology ■ adj. belonging to the same species. ■ n. a member of the same species.
– DERIVATIVES **conspecificity** n.

conspectus /kənˈspɛktəs/ ■ n. a summary or overview of a subject.
– ORIGIN C19: from Latin, from *conspicere* (see **CONSPICUOUS**).

conspicuous /kənˈspɪkjʊəs/ ■ adj. clearly visible. ▸ attracting notice or attention.
– PHRASES **conspicuous by one's absence** obviously not

conspiracist

present where one should be.
– DERIVATIVES **conspicuity** n. **conspicuously** adv. **conspicuousness** n.
– ORIGIN C16: from Latin *conspicuus*, from *conspicere*, from *con-* (expressing intensive force) + *spicere* 'look at'.

conspiracist ■ n. a supporter of a conspiracy theory.

conspiracy ■ n. (pl. **-ies**) a secret plan by a group to do something unlawful or harmful. ▸ the action of conspiring.
– PHRASES **a conspiracy of silence** an agreement to say nothing.
– ORIGIN Middle English: from Anglo-Norman French *conspiracie*, alteration of Old French *conspiration*, from Latin *conspirare* (see CONSPIRE).

conspiracy theory ■ n. a belief that some covert but influential organization is responsible for an unexplained event.

conspire ■ v. make secret plans jointly to commit an unlawful or harmful act. ▸ (of circumstances) seem to be acting together, especially with unfortunate results.
– DERIVATIVES **conspirator** n. **conspiratorial** adj. **conspiratorially** adv.
– ORIGIN Middle English: from Old French *conspirer*, from Latin *conspirare* 'agree, plot', from *con-* 'together with' + *spirare* 'breathe'.

constable /ˈkʌnstəb(ə)l, ˈkɒn-/ ■ n. **1** (also **police constable**) a police officer of the lowest rank. **2** the governor of a royal castle. ▸ historical the highest-ranking official in a royal household.
– ORIGIN Middle English: from Old French *conestable*, from late Latin *comes stabuli* 'count (head officer) of the stable'.

constabulary /kənˈstabjʊləri/ ■ n. (pl. **-ies**) chiefly Brit. a police force.
– ORIGIN C15: from medieval Latin *constabularia (dignitas)* '(rank) of constable', from *constabulus*, from Latin *comes stabuli* (see CONSTABLE).

constant ■ adj. **1** occurring continuously. **2** remaining the same. ▸ faithful and dependable. ■ n. an unchanging situation. ▸ Mathematics a component of a relationship between variables that does not change its value. ▸ Physics a number expressing a relation or property which remains the same in all circumstances, or for the same substance under the same conditions.
– DERIVATIVES **constancy** n. **constantly** adv.
– ORIGIN Middle English: from Latin *constare* 'stand firm', from *con-* 'with' + *stare* 'stand'.

constellation ■ n. **1** a group of stars forming a recognized pattern and typically named after a mythological or other figure. **2** a group of associated people or things.
– DERIVATIVES **constellate** v. (poetic/literary).
– ORIGIN Middle English: from late Latin *constellatio(n-)*, from Latin *stella* 'star'.

consternation ■ n. anxiety or dismay.

constipate /ˈkɒnstɪpeɪt/ ■ v. (usu. **be constipated**) affect with constipation.
– ORIGIN C16: from Latin *constipare*, from *con-* 'together' + *stipare* 'press, cram'.

constipation ■ n. a difficulty in emptying the bowels, associated with hardened faeces.

constituency /kənˈstɪtjʊənsi/ ■ n. (pl. **-ies**) **1** a body of voters in a specified area who elect a representative to a legislative body. ▸ the area represented in this way. **2** a body of customers or supporters.

constituent ■ adj. **1** being a part of a whole. **2** having the power to appoint or elect. ▸ able to make or change a political constitution. ■ n. **1** a member of a constituency. **2** a component part.
– ORIGIN C15: from Latin *constituere* (see CONSTITUTE).

constitute /ˈkɒnstɪtjuːt/ ■ v. **1** be (a part) of a whole. ▸ be or be equivalent to. **2** (usu. **be constituted**) establish by law.
– ORIGIN Middle English: from Latin *constituere* 'establish, appoint', from *con-* 'together' + *statuere* 'set up'.

constitution ■ n. **1** a body of fundamental principles or established precedents according to which a state or organization is governed. ▸ historical a decree, ordinance, or law. **2** the composition or forming of something. **3** a person's physical or mental state.

constitutional ■ adj. **1** of, relating to, or in accordance with a constitution. **2** of or relating to a person's physical or mental state. ■ n. dated a walk taken regularly to maintain good health.
– DERIVATIVES **constitutionality** n. **constitutionally** adv.

Constitutional Court ■ n. (in South Africa) a court dealing with matters that include the interpretation and enforcement of the constitution.

constitutionalism ■ n. constitutional government. ▸ adherence to such a system.
– DERIVATIVES **constitutionalist** n.

constitutive ■ adj. **1** having the power to establish something. **2** forming a constituent of something.
– DERIVATIVES **constitutively** adv.

constrain ■ v. compel or force towards a course of action. ▸ [as adj. **constrained**] appearing forced. ▸ severely restrict the scope, extent, or activity of. ▸ poetic/literary imprison.
– DERIVATIVES **constrainedly** adv.
– ORIGIN Middle English: from Old French *constraindre*, from Latin *constringere* 'bind tightly together'.

constraint ■ n. **1** a limitation or restriction. **2** stiffness of manner and inhibition.

constrict ■ v. make or become narrower, especially by encircling pressure. ▸ (of a snake) coil round (prey) in order to asphyxiate it.
– DERIVATIVES **constriction** n. **constrictive** adj.
– ORIGIN C18 (*constriction* Middle English): from Latin *constringere* (see CONSTRAIN).

constrictor ■ n. **1** a snake that kills by constricting its prey, such as a boa or python. **2** Anatomy a muscle whose contraction narrows a vessel or passage.

construct ■ v. /kənˈstrʌkt/ **1** build or erect. **2** form (a theory) from various conceptual elements. **3** Grammar form (a sentence) according to grammatical rules. **4** Geometry draw or delineate (a geometrical figure). ■ n. /ˈkɒnstrʌkt/ **1** an idea or theory. **2** Linguistics a group of words forming a phrase. **3** a thing constructed.
– DERIVATIVES **constructor** n.
– ORIGIN Middle English: from Latin *construere*, from *con-* 'together' + *struere* 'pile, build'.

construction ■ n. **1** the action or process of constructing. ▸ the industry of erecting buildings. **2** an interpretation or explanation.
– DERIVATIVES **constructional** adj. **constructionally** adv.

constructionism ■ n. another term for CONSTRUCTIVISM.

constructionist ■ n. another term for constructivist (see CONSTRUCTIVISM).

constructive ■ adj. **1** serving a useful purpose. **2** Law not stated explicitly. **3** of or relating to construction.
– DERIVATIVES **constructively** adv. **constructiveness** n.

constructive dismissal ■ n. the changing of an employee's job with the aim of forcing resignation.

constructivism ■ n. Art a style in which mechanical objects are combined into abstract mobile forms.
– DERIVATIVES **constructivist** n.

construe ■ v. (**construes, construed, construing**) (often **be construed**) interpret in a particular way. ▸ dated analyse the construction of (a text, sentence, or word). ▸ dated translate word for word.
– DERIVATIVES **construable** adj. **construal** n.
– ORIGIN Middle English: from Latin *construere* (see CONSTRUCT).

consubstantial ■ adj. (especially of the three persons of the Trinity in Christian theology) of the same substance.
– ORIGIN Middle English: from eccles. Latin *consubstantialis* (translating Greek *homoousios* 'of one substance'), from *con-* 'with' + *substantialis*, from *substantia* 'being, essence'.

consubstantiation /ˌkɒnsəbstanʃɪˈeɪʃ(ə)n, -sɪ-/ ■ n. Christian Church the doctrine that the substance of the bread and wine coexists with the body and blood of Christ in the Eucharist. Compare with TRANSUBSTANTIATION.

consul /ˈkɒns(ə)l/ ■ n. **1** a state official living in a foreign city and protecting the state's citizens and interests there. **2** (in ancient Rome) one of the two annually elected chief magistrates who ruled the republic.
– DERIVATIVES **consular** /ˈkɒnsjʊlə/ adj. **consulship** n.
– ORIGIN Middle English: from Latin, rel. to *consulere* 'take counsel'.

CONSONANTS **b** but **d** dog **f** few **g** get **h** he **j** yes **k** cat **l** leg **m** man **n** no **p** pen **r** red

consulate ■ n. the place where a consul works.

consult ■ v. seek information or advice from (someone, especially an expert or professional). ▸ seek permission or approval from. ▸ [as adj. **consulting**] engaged in the business of giving advice to others in the same field: *a consulting engineer*.
–DERIVATIVES **consultation** n. **consultative** adj.
–ORIGIN C16 (*consultation* Middle English): from French *consulter*, from Latin *consultare*, from *consulere* 'take counsel'.

consultancy ■ n. (pl. **-ies**) a professional practice giving expert advice in a particular field.

consultant ■ n. **1** a person who provides expert advice professionally. **2** Brit. a hospital doctor of senior rank.

consumable ■ adj. intended to be used up and then replaced. ■ n. a consumable commodity.

consume ■ v. **1** eat, drink, or ingest. **2** buy (goods or services) for personal use. ▸ use up. **3** (especially of a fire) completely destroy. **4** (usu. **be consumed**) (of a feeling) absorb all of the attention and energy of.
–DERIVATIVES **consuming** adj.
–ORIGIN Middle English: from Latin *consumere*, from *con-* 'altogether' + *sumere* 'take up'.

consumer ■ n. **1** a person or thing that eats or uses something. **2** a person who buys goods and services for personal use: [as modifier] *consumer demand*.

consumer durable ■ n. a product expected to have a long useful life.

consumerism ■ n. **1** the protection or promotion of the interests of consumers. **2** the preoccupation of society with the acquisition of goods.
–DERIVATIVES **consumerist** adj. & n. **consumeristic** adj.

consumer price index ■ n. an index of the average change in prices of a fixed list of goods and services over a specified period.

consummate ■ v. /ˈkɒnsəmeɪt, -sjʊ-/ **1** make (a marriage or relationship) complete by having sexual intercourse. **2** complete (a transaction). ■ adj. /kənˈsʌmət, ˈkɒnsʌmət/ showing great skill and flair.
–DERIVATIVES **consummately** adv. **consummation** n. **consummator** n.
–ORIGIN Middle English: from Latin *consummare* 'bring to completion', from *con-* 'altogether' + *summa* 'sum total', from *summus* 'highest, supreme'.

consumption ■ n. **1** the action or process of consuming. ▸ an amount consumed. **2** dated a wasting disease, especially tuberculosis.
–DERIVATIVES **consumptive** adj. & n. (dated). **consumptively** adv. (dated).
–ORIGIN Middle English: from Latin *consumptio(n-)*, from *consumere* (see **CONSUME**).

cont. ■ abbrev. **1** contents. **2** continued.

contact ■ n. /ˈkɒntakt/ **1** the state or condition of physical touching. ▸ [as modifier] caused by or operating through physical touch: *contact dermatitis*. **2** the action of communicating or meeting. ▸ a communication or relationship. ▸ a person whom one may ask for information or assistance. ▸ a person who has associated with a person with a contagious disease. **3** a connection for the passage of an electric current from one thing to another. **4** (**contacts**) contact lenses. ■ v. /ˈkɒntakt, kənˈtakt/ **1** get in touch or communication with. **2** touch.
–DERIVATIVES **contactable** adj.
–ORIGIN C17: from Latin *contactus*, from *contingere* 'touch, grasp, border on', from *con-* 'together with' + *tangere* 'to touch'.

contact lens ■ n. a thin plastic lens placed directly on the surface of the eye to correct visual defects.

contact print ■ n. a photographic print made by placing a negative directly on to sensitized paper, glass, or film and illuminating it. ■ v. (**contact-print**) make a photograph from (a negative) in this way.

contact sheet ■ n. a sheet of contact prints.

contact sport ■ n. a sport in which the participants necessarily come into bodily contact with one another.

contagion /kənˈteɪdʒ(ə)n/ ■ n. the communication of disease from one person to another by close contact. ▸ dated a disease spread in such a way.

251

contemptible

–ORIGIN Middle English: from Latin *contagio(n-)*, from *con-* 'together with' + the base of *tangere* 'to touch'.

contagious ■ adj. **1** (of a disease) spread by direct or indirect contact of people or organisms. ▸ having a contagious disease. **2** (of an emotion, attitude, etc.) likely to spread to and affect others.
–DERIVATIVES **contagiously** adv. **contagiousness** n.

contagious abortion ■ n. a type of brucellosis which causes spontaneous abortion in cattle.

contain ■ v. **1** have or hold within. **2** control or restrain. ▸ prevent (a problem) from becoming worse. **3** (of a number) be divisible by (a factor) without a remainder.
–DERIVATIVES **containable** adj.
–ORIGIN Middle English: from Old French *contenir*, from Latin *continere*, from *con-* 'altogether' + *tenere* 'to hold'.

container ■ n. an object for holding or transporting something. ▸ a large standard-sized metal box for the transport of goods by road, rail, sea, or air.

containerize (also **-ise**) ■ v. [usu. as adj. **containerized** (also **-ised**)] pack into or transport by container.
–DERIVATIVES **containerization** (also **-isation**) n.

containment ■ n. the action of keeping something harmful under control. ▸ the action of preventing the expansion of a hostile country or influence.

contaminate ■ v. make impure by exposure to or addition of a poisonous or polluting substance.
–DERIVATIVES **contaminant** n. **contamination** n. **contaminator** n.
–ORIGIN Middle English: from Latin *contaminare* 'make impure', from *contamen* 'contact, pollution', from *con-* 'together with' + the base of *tangere* 'to touch'.

Conté /ˈkɒnteɪ/ ■ n. a kind of hard grease-free crayon used for artwork.
–ORIGIN C19: named after the French inventor Nicolas J. Conté.

contemplate /ˈkɒntəmpleɪt, -təm-/ ■ v. look at thoughtfully. ▸ think about. ▸ think profoundly and at length. ▸ have as a probable intention.
–DERIVATIVES **contemplator** n.
–ORIGIN C16: from Latin *contemplari* 'survey, contemplate', from *templum* 'place for observation'.

contemplation ■ n. **1** the action of contemplating. **2** religious meditation. ▸ (in Christian spirituality) a form of prayer in which a person seeks a direct experience of the divine.

contemplative /kənˈtɛmplətɪv/ ■ adj. expressing or involving contemplation. ■ n. a person whose life is devoted to prayer, especially in a monastery or convent.
–DERIVATIVES **contemplatively** adv.

contemporaneous /kənˌtɛmpəˈreɪnɪəs, kɒn-/ ■ adj. existing at or occurring in the same period of time.
–DERIVATIVES **contemporaneity** n. **contemporaneously** adv. **contemporaneousness** n.
–ORIGIN C17: from Latin, from *con-* 'together with' + *temporaneus*, from *tempus* 'time'.

contemporary /kənˈtɛmp(ə)r(ər)i/ ■ adj. **1** living, occurring, or originating at the same time. **2** belonging to or occurring in the present. ▸ modern in style or design. ■ n. (pl. **-ies**) a person or thing existing at the same time as another. ▸ a person of roughly the same age as another.
–DERIVATIVES **contemporarily** adv. **contemporariness** n.
–ORIGIN C17: from medieval Latin *contemporarius*, from *con-* 'together with' + *tempus* 'time'.

contempt ■ n. **1** the feeling that a person or a thing is worthless or beneath consideration. **2** (also **contempt of court**) the offence of being disobedient to or disrespectful of a court of law.
–PHRASES **beneath contempt** utterly worthless or despicable. **hold someone in contempt** judge someone to be in contempt of court. **hold someone/thing in contempt** despise someone or something.
–ORIGIN Middle English: from Latin *contemptus*, from *contemnere*, from *con-* (expressing intensive force) + *temnere* 'despise'.

contemptible ■ adj. deserving contempt.
–DERIVATIVES **contemptibly** adv.

---

s sit   t top   v voice   w we   z zoo   ʃ she   ʒ decision   θ thin   ð this   ŋ ring   x loch   tʃ chip   dʒ jar

contemptuous ▪ adj. showing contempt.
– DERIVATIVES **contemptuously** adv. **contemptuousness** n.

contend ▪ v. **1** (**contend with/against**) struggle to surmount (a difficulty). ▶ (**contend for**) engage in a struggle or campaign to achieve. **2** assert.
– DERIVATIVES **contender** n.
– ORIGIN Middle English: from Latin *contendere*, from *con-* 'with' + *tendere* 'stretch, strive'.

content[1] /kənˈtɛnt/ ▪ adj. in a state of peaceful happiness or satisfaction. ▪ v. satisfy. ▶ (**content oneself with**) accept as adequate despite wanting more or better. ▪ n. a state of satisfaction.
– PHRASES **to one's heart's content** to the full extent of one's desires.
– DERIVATIVES **contented** adj. **contentedly** adv. **contentedness** n. **contentment** n.
– ORIGIN Middle English: from Latin *contentus* 'satisfied', from *continere* (see CONTAIN).

content[2] /ˈkɒntɛnt/ ▪ n. **1** (**contents**) the things that are contained in something. ▶ (**contents** or **table of contents**) a list of chapters or sections at the front of a book or periodical. **2** the material dealt with in a speech, literary work, etc. as distinct from its form or style.
– DERIVATIVES **contentless** adj.
– ORIGIN Middle English: from medieval Latin *contentum* (pl. *contenta* 'things contained'), from *continere* (see CONTAIN).

contention ▪ n. **1** heated disagreement. **2** an assertion.
– PHRASES **in contention** having a good chance of success in a contest.
– ORIGIN Middle English: from Latin *contentio(n-)*, from *contendere* (see CONTEND).

contentious ▪ adj. causing or likely to cause disagreement or controversy. ▶ Law of, relating to, or involving differences between contending parties. ▶ given to provoking argument.
– DERIVATIVES **contentiously** adv. **contentiousness** n.
– ORIGIN Middle English: from Old French *contentieux*, from Latin *contentiosus*, from *contendere* 'strive'.

conterminous /kɒnˈtəːmɪnəs/ ▪ adj. **1** sharing a common boundary. **2** having the same area, context, or meaning.
– DERIVATIVES **conterminously** adv.
– ORIGIN C17: from Latin *conterminus*, from *con-* 'with' + *terminus* 'boundary'.

contest ▪ n. /ˈkɒntɛst/ an event in which people compete for supremacy. ▶ a dispute or conflict. ▪ v. /kənˈtɛst/ **1** compete to attain (a position of power). ▶ take part in (a competition or election). **2** challenge or dispute.
– PHRASES **no contest** a decision to declare a boxing match invalid on the grounds that one or both of the boxers are not making serious efforts. ▶ a competition or comparison of which the outcome is a foregone conclusion.
– DERIVATIVES **contestable** adj. **contester** n.
– ORIGIN C16: from Latin *contestari* 'call upon to witness', from *con-* 'together' + *testare* 'to witness'.

contestant ▪ n. a person who takes part in a contest.

contestation ▪ n. formal the action or process of disputing or arguing.
– ORIGIN C16: from Latin *contestatio(n-)*, from *contestari* (see CONTEST).

context /ˈkɒntɛkst/ ▪ n. the circumstances that form the setting for an event, statement, or idea, and in terms of which it can be fully understood. ▶ the parts that immediately precede and follow a word or passage and clarify its meaning.
– DERIVATIVES **contextual** adj. **contextualization** (also **-isation**) n. **contextualize** (also **-ise**) v. **contextually** adv.
– ORIGIN Middle English: from Latin *contextus*, from *con-* 'together' + *texere* 'to weave'.

contiguity /ˌkɒntɪˈɡjuːɪti/ ▪ n. the state of being contiguous with something.

contiguous /kənˈtɪɡjʊəs/ ▪ adj. sharing a common border. ▶ next or together in sequence.
– DERIVATIVES **contiguously** adv.
– ORIGIN C16: from Latin *contiguus* 'touching', from *contingere* (see CONTINGENT).

continent[1] ▪ n. **1** any of the world's main continuous expanses of land (Europe, Asia, Africa, North and South America, Australia, Antarctica). **2** (also **the Continent**) Brit. the mainland of Europe as distinct from the British Isles.
– ORIGIN C16: from Latin *terra continens* 'continuous land'.

continent[2] ▪ adj. **1** able to control movements of the bowels and bladder. **2** exercising self-restraint, especially sexually.
– DERIVATIVES **continence** n. **continently** adv.
– ORIGIN Middle English: from Latin *continere* (see CONTAIN).

continental ▪ adj. **1** forming or belonging to a continent. **2** (also **Continental**) Brit. coming from or characteristic of mainland Europe. ▪ n. an inhabitant of mainland Europe.
– DERIVATIVES **continentally** adv.

continental breakfast ▪ n. a light breakfast of coffee and bread rolls with butter and jam.

continental climate ▪ n. a relatively dry climate with very hot summers and very cold winters, characteristic of the central parts of Asia and North America.

continental drift ▪ n. the gradual movement of the continents across the earth's surface through geological time.

continental shelf ▪ n. an area of seabed around a large land mass where the sea is relatively shallow.

contingency /kənˈtɪndʒ(ə)nsi/ ▪ n. (pl. **-ies**) **1** a future event or circumstance which is possible but cannot be predicted with certainty. ▶ a provision for such an event or circumstance. **2** the absence of certainty in events. **3** Philosophy the absence of necessity.

contingency table ▪ n. Statistics a table showing the distribution of one variable in rows and another in columns, used to study the correlation between the two.

contingent /kənˈtɪndʒ(ə)nt/ ▪ adj. **1** subject to chance. ▶ (**contingent on/upon**) dependent on. ▶ (of losses, liabilities, etc.) that can be anticipated to arise if a particular event occurs. **2** Philosophy true by virtue of the way things in fact are and not by logical necessity. ▪ n. a group of people within a larger group. ▶ a body of troops or police sent to join a larger force.
– DERIVATIVES **contingently** adv.
– ORIGIN Middle English: from Latin *contingere* 'befall', from *con-* 'together with' + *tangere* 'to touch'.

continual ▪ adj. constantly or frequently occurring.
– DERIVATIVES **continually** adv.
– ORIGIN Middle English: from Old French *continuel*, from *continuer* 'continue', from Latin, from *continuus* (see CONTINUOUS).

> USAGE
> For an explanation of the difference between **continual** and **continuous**, see usage at CONTINUOUS.

continuance ▪ n. **1** formal the state of continuing. ▶ the time for which a situation or action lasts. **2** US Law a postponement or adjournment.

continuant ▪ n. Phonetics a consonant which is sounded with the vocal tract only partly closed, allowing the breath to pass through and the sound to be prolonged (as with *f*, *l*, *m*, *n*, *r*, *s*, *v*). ▪ adj. relating to or denoting a continuant.
– ORIGIN C17: from French, from *continuer* 'continue', reinforced by Latin *continuare* 'continue', from *continuus* (see CONTINUOUS).

continuation ▪ n. **1** the action of continuing or state of being continued. **2** a part that is attached to and is an extension of something else.

continuative /kənˈtɪnjʊətɪv/ Linguistics ▪ adj. (of a word or phrase) having the function of moving a discourse or conversation forward. ▪ n. a word or phrase of this type (e.g. *yes*, *well*, *as I was saying*).
– ORIGIN C16: from late Latin *continuativus*, from *continuare* (see CONTINUE).

continue ▪ v. (**continues**, **continued**, **continuing**) **1** persist in an activity or process. ▶ remain in existence, operation, or a specified state. **2** carry on with. ▶ carry on travelling in the same direction. **3** recommence or resume.
– ORIGIN Middle English: from Old French *continuer*, from Latin *continuare*, from *continuus* (see CONTINUOUS).

continuing education ▪ n. education provided for adults after they have left the formal education system.

continuity /ˌkɒntɪˈnjuːɪti/ ▪ n. (pl. **-ies**) **1** the unbroken and consistent existence or operation of something. ▸ a connection or line of development with no sharp breaks. **2** the maintenance of continuous action and self-consistent detail in the scenes of a film or broadcast. **3** the linking of broadcast items by a spoken commentary.

continuo /kənˈtɪnjuəʊ/ (also **basso continuo**) ■ n. (pl. **-os**) (in baroque music) an accompanying part which includes a bass line and harmonies, typically played on a keyboard instrument.
– ORIGIN C18: Italian *basso continuo* 'continuous bass'.

continuous ■ adj. **1** without interruption. ▸ forming a series with no exceptions or reversals. ▸ Mathematics (of a function) of which the graph is a smooth unbroken curve. **2** Grammar another term for **PROGRESSIVE** (in sense 4).
– DERIVATIVES **continuously** adv. **continuousness** n.
– ORIGIN C17: from Latin *continuus* 'uninterrupted', from *continere* 'hang together', from *con-* 'together with' + *tenere* 'hold'.

> **USAGE**
> **Continuous** and **continual** can both mean roughly 'without interruption' (*five years of continuous/continual warfare*), but **continuous** is much more prominent in this sense and can be used to refer to space as well as time, as in *the development forms a continuous line along the coast*. **Continual**, on the other hand, typically means 'happening frequently, with intervals between', as in *the bus service has been disrupted by continual breakdowns*.

continuous assessment ■ n. the evaluation of a pupil's progress throughout a course of study, as distinct from by examination.

continuous creation ■ n. the creation of matter as a continuing process throughout time, especially as postulated in steady-state theories of the universe.

continuous stationery (also **continuous paper**) ■ n. a long continuous strip of paper that is usually perforated to form sheets.

continuum ■ n. (pl. **continua**) a continuous sequence in which adjacent elements are not perceptibly different from each other, but the extremes are quite distinct.
– ORIGIN C17: from Latin, from *continuus* (see **CONTINUOUS**).

contort /kənˈtɔːt/ ■ v. twist or bend out of its normal shape.
– DERIVATIVES **contortion** n.
– ORIGIN Middle English: from Latin *contorquere* 'twist round, brandish', from *con-* 'together' + *torquere* 'twist'.

contortionist ■ n. an entertainer who twists and bends their body into strange and unnatural positions.

contour ■ n. **1** an outline, especially one representing or bounding the shape or form of something. ▸ (also **contour line**) a line on a map joining points of equal height above or below sea level. ▸ a line joining points on a diagram at which some property has the same value. **2** a way in which something varies, especially the pitch of music or the pattern of tones in an utterance. ■ v. **1** mould into a specific shape. **2** (usu. as adj. **contoured**) mark (a map or diagram) with contours. **3** (of a road or railway) follow the outline of (a topographical feature).
– ORIGIN C17: from Italian *contorno*, from *contornare* 'draw in outline', from *con-* 'together' + *tornare* 'to turn'.

contra- /ˈkɒntrə/ ■ prefix against; opposite: *contraception*.
– ORIGIN from Latin *contra* 'against'.

contraband /ˈkɒntrəband/ ■ n. goods that have been imported or exported illegally. ▸ trade in smuggled goods. ▸ (also **contraband of war**) goods forbidden to be supplied by neutrals to those engaged in war. ■ adj. imported or exported illegally. ▸ relating to traffic in illegal goods.
– DERIVATIVES **contrabandist** n.
– ORIGIN C16: from Italian *contrabando*, from *contra-* 'against' + *bando* 'proclamation, ban'.

contrabass ■ n. another term for **DOUBLE BASS**. ■ adj. denoting a musical instrument with a range an octave lower than the normal bass range.
– ORIGIN C18: from Italian *contrabasso*, from *contra-* 'pitched an octave below' + *basso* (see **BASS**[1]).

contrabassoon ■ n. another term for **DOUBLE BASSOON**.

contralateral

contraception ■ n. the use of artificial methods or other techniques to prevent pregnancy.

contraceptive ■ adj. serving to prevent pregnancy. ▸ of or relating to contraception. ■ n. a contraceptive device or drug.

contract ■ n. /ˈkɒntrakt/ **1** a written or spoken agreement intended to be enforceable by law. **2** informal an arrangement for someone to be killed by a hired assassin. **3** Bridge the declarer's undertaking to win the number of tricks bid with a stated suit as trumps. ■ v. /kənˈtrakt/ **1** decrease in size, number, or range. **2** (of a muscle) become shorter and tighter in order to effect movement of part of the body. **3** shorten (a word or phrase) by combination or elision. **4** enter into a formal and legally binding agreement. ▸ (**contract in/into**) choose to be involved in. ▸ (**contract out**) choose to withdraw from or not become involved in. ▸ (**contract something out**) arrange for work to be done by another organization. **5** catch or develop (a disease). **6** become liable to pay (a debt).
– DERIVATIVES **contractive** adj.
– ORIGIN Middle English: from Latin *contractus*, from *contrahere* 'draw together, tighten'.

contractable ■ adj. (of a disease) able to be caught.

contract bridge ■ n. the standard form of the card game bridge, in which only tricks bid and won count towards the game.

contractible ■ adj. able to be shrunk or capable of contracting.

contraction ■ n. **1** the process of contracting. **2** a shortening of the uterine muscles occurring at intervals before and during childbirth. **3** a word or group of words resulting from contracting an original form.

contract note ■ n. a certificate confirming the terms of a sale of specified assets or securities.

contractor ■ n. a person who undertakes a contract to provide materials or labour for a job.

contractual /kənˈtraktʃʊəl/ ■ adj. relating to or agreed by a contract.
– DERIVATIVES **contractually** adv.

contractural ■ adj. **1** Medicine relating to or involving contracture. **2** another term for contractual (see **CONTRACT**). [formed by erroneous insertion of *-r-*.]

contracture /kənˈtraktʃə/ ■ n. Medicine a condition of shortening and hardening of muscles, tendons, or other tissue, often leading to deformity and rigidity of joints.
– ORIGIN C17: from Latin *contractura*, from *contrahere* 'draw together'.

contradict ■ v. deny the truth of (a statement) by asserting the opposite. ▸ assert the opposite of a statement made by (someone).
– DERIVATIVES **contradictor** n.
– ORIGIN C16: from Latin *contradicere* 'speak against'.

contradiction ■ n. a combination of statements, ideas, or features which are opposed to one another. ▸ the statement of a position opposite to one already made.
– PHRASES **contradiction in terms** a statement or group of words associating incompatible objects or ideas.

contradictory ■ adj. mutually opposed or inconsistent. ▸ containing inconsistent elements. ▸ Logic (of two propositions) so related that one and only one must be true. Compare with **CONTRARY**.
– DERIVATIVES **contradictorily** adv. **contradictoriness** n.

contradistinction ■ n. distinction made by contrasting the different qualities of two things.

contrafactual /ˌkɒntrəˈfaktʃʊəl, -tjʊəl/ ■ adj. another term for **COUNTERFACTUAL**.

contrail /ˈkɒntreɪl/ ■ n. another term for **VAPOUR TRAIL**.
– ORIGIN 1940s: abbrev. of *condensation trail*.

contraindicate ■ v. (usu. **be contraindicated**) Medicine (of a condition or circumstance) suggest or indicate that (a particular technique or drug) should not be used.
– DERIVATIVES **contraindication** n.

contralateral /ˌkɒntrəˈlat(ə)r(ə)l/ ■ adj. Medicine relating to or denoting the side of the body opposite to that on which a particular structure or condition occurs.

Contralesa

Contralesa /ˌkɒntrəˈlɛsə/ (also **CONTRALESA**) ■ abbrev. Congress of Traditional Leaders of South Africa.

contralto /kənˈtrɑltəʊ/ ■ n. (pl. **-os**) the lowest female singing voice.
– ORIGIN C18: Italian.

contrapposto /ˌkɒntrəˈpɒstəʊ/ ■ n. (pl. **contrapposti** /-ti/) (in sculpture) an asymmetrical arrangement of the human figure in which the line of the arms and shoulders contrasts with, while balancing, that of the hips and legs.
– ORIGIN Italian, from *contrapporre*, from Latin *contraponere* 'place against'.

contraption ■ n. a machine or device that appears strange or unnecessarily complicated.
– ORIGIN C19: perhaps from CONTRIVE (on the pattern of *conceive*, *conception*), by association with TRAP.

contrapuntal /ˌkɒntrəˈpʌnt(ə)l/ ■ adj. Music of or in counterpoint.
– DERIVATIVES **contrapuntally** adv. **contrapuntist** n.
– ORIGIN C19: from Italian *contrapunto* (see COUNTERPOINT).

contrarian /kənˈtrɛːrɪən/ ■ n. a person who opposes or rejects popular opinion, especially in stock exchange dealing.
– DERIVATIVES **contrarianism** n.

contrariety /ˌkɒntrəˈraɪəti/ ■ n. opposition or inconsistency between two things.
– ORIGIN Middle English: from Old French *contrariete*, from late Latin *contrarietas*, from *contrarius* (see CONTRARY).

contrariwise /kənˈtrɛːrɪwaɪz, ˈkɒntrərɪˌwaɪz/ ■ adv. in the opposite way. ▶ on the other hand.

contrary /ˈkɒntrəri/ ■ adj. **1** (often **contrary to**) opposite in nature, direction, or meaning. **2** of two or more statements, beliefs, etc.) opposed to one another. ▶ Logic (of two propositions) so related that one or neither but not both must be true. Compare with CONTRADICTORY. **3** /kənˈtrɛːri/ perversely inclined to do the opposite of what is expected or desired. ■ n. (pl. **-ies**) (**the contrary**) the opposite.
– PHRASES **on** (or **quite**) **the contrary** used to intensify a denial of what has just been implied or stated. **to the contrary** with the opposite meaning or implication.
– DERIVATIVES **contrarily** /ˈkɒntrərɪli, kənˈtrɛːrɪli/ adv. **contrariness** /ˈkɒntrərɪnɪs, kənˈtrɛːrɪnɪs/ n.
– ORIGIN Middle English: from Anglo-Norman French *contrarie*, from Latin *contrarius*, from *contra* 'against'.

contrast ■ n. /ˈkɒntrɑːst/ **1** the state of being strikingly different from something else in juxtaposition or close association. **2** the degree of difference between tones in a television picture, photograph, etc. **3** enhancement of the apparent brightness or clarity of a design provided by the juxtaposition of different colours or textures. **4** a thing or person noticeably different from another. ■ v. /kənˈtrɑːst/ differ strikingly. ▶ compare so as to emphasize differences.
– DERIVATIVES **contrasting** adj. **contrastingly** adv. **contrastive** adj.
– ORIGIN C17: from French *contraste* (n.), *contraster* (v.), from medieval Latin *contrastare*, from Latin *contra-* 'against' + *stare* 'stand'.

contrast medium ■ n. Medicine a substance introduced into a part of the body in order to improve the visibility of internal structure during radiography.

contravene /ˌkɒntrəˈviːn/ ■ v. offend against the prohibition or order of (a law, treaty, etc.). ▶ conflict with (a right, principle, etc.), especially to its detriment.
– DERIVATIVES **contravener** n. **contravention** n.
– ORIGIN C16: from late Latin *contravenire*, from Latin *contra-* 'against' + *venire* 'come'.

contretemps /ˈkɒntrətɒ̃/ ■ n. (pl. same /-tɒ̃z/) a minor dispute or disagreement.
– ORIGIN C17 (orig. denoting a thrust in fencing made at an inopportune moment): French, from *contre-* 'against' + *temps* 'time'.

contribute /kənˈtrɪbjuːt, ˈkɒntrɪbjuːt/ ■ v. give in order to help achieve or provide something. ▶ (**contribute to**) help to cause or bring about.
– DERIVATIVES **contribution** n. **contributive** /kənˈtrɪb-/ adj. **contributor** n.
– ORIGIN C16 (*contribution* Middle English): from Latin *contribuere* 'bring together, add', from *con-* 'with' + *tribuere* 'bestow'.

USAGE
The first pronunciation, which puts the stress on **-tri-**, is held to be the only correct one, despite the fact that the alternative, with the stress on **con-**, is older.

contributory ■ adj. **1** playing a part in bringing something about. **2** (of a pension or insurance scheme) operated by means of a fund into which people pay. ■ n. (pl. **-ies**) Law a person liable to contribute towards the payment of a wound-up company's debts.

contributory negligence ■ n. Law failure of an injured party to act prudently, considered to be a contributory factor in the injury suffered.

con trick ■ n. informal term for CONFIDENCE TRICK.

contrite /kənˈtrʌɪt, ˈkɒntrʌɪt/ ■ adj. feeling or expressing remorse.
– DERIVATIVES **contritely** adv. **contriteness** n.
– ORIGIN Middle English: from Old French *contrit*, from Latin *contritus*, from *conterere* 'grind down, wear away'.

contrition ■ n. the state of feeling contrite. ▶ (in the Roman Catholic Church) the repentance of past sins during or after confession.

contrivance ■ n. **1** the action of contriving something. **2** an ingenious device or scheme.

contrive /kənˈtrʌɪv/ ■ v. **1** devise or plan using skill and artifice. **2** manage to do something foolish.
– DERIVATIVES **contrivable** adj. **contriver** n.
– ORIGIN Middle English: from Old French *controuve-*, *controver* 'imagine, invent', from medieval Latin *contropare* 'compare'.

contrived ■ adj. deliberately created rather than arising spontaneously.

control ■ n. **1** the power to influence people's behaviour or the course of events. ▶ the restriction of an activity, tendency, or phenomenon. **2** a device by which a machine is regulated. **3** the place where something is verified or from which an activity is directed. **4** Bridge a high card that will prevent the opponents from establishing a particular suit. **5** a person or thing used as a standard of comparison for checking the results of a survey or experiment. **6** a member of an intelligence organization who personally directs the activities of a spy. ■ v. (**controlled**, **controlling**) **1** have control or command of. ▶ regulate. **2** [as adj. **controlled**] (of a drug) restricted by law in respect of use and possession. **3** (**control for**) take into account (an extraneous factor that might affect the results of an experiment).
– PHRASES **in control** able to direct a situation, person, or activity. **out of control** no longer possible to manage. **under control** (of a danger or emergency) being dealt with or contained successfully.
– DERIVATIVES **controllability** n. **controllable** adj. **controllably** adv. **controller** n. **controllership** n.
– ORIGIN Middle English: from Anglo-Norman French *contreroller* 'keep a copy of a roll of accounts', from medieval Latin, from *contrarotulus* 'copy of a roll', from *contra-* 'against' + *rotulus* 'a roll'.

control character ■ n. Computing a character that does not represent a printable character but serves to initiate a particular action.

control key ■ n. Computing a key which alters the function of another key if they are pressed at the same time.

controlling interest ■ n. the holding by one person or group of a majority of the stock of a business.

control tower ■ n. a tall building at an airport from which the movements of air traffic are controlled.

controversial ■ adj. causing or likely to cause controversy.
– DERIVATIVES **controversialist** n. **controversially** adv.

controversy /ˈkɒntrəvəːsi, kənˈtrɒvəsi/ ■ n. (pl. **-ies**) disagreement, typically when prolonged and public.
– ORIGIN Middle English: from Latin *controversia*, from

controversus 'turned against, disputed'.

USAGE
The second pronunciation, putting the stress on **-trov-**, is widely held to be incorrect in standard English.

controvert ■ v. deny the truth of.
– DERIVATIVES **controvertible** adj.
– ORIGIN C16: from Latin *controversus* (see **CONTROVERSY**).

contumacious /ˌkɒntjʊˈmeɪʃəs/ ■ adj. archaic or Law stubbornly or wilfully disobedient to authority.
– DERIVATIVES **contumaciously** adv. **contumacy** n.
– ORIGIN C16: from Latin *contumax, contumac-*, perhaps from *con-* 'with' + *tumere* 'to swell'.

contumely /ˈkɒntjuːmɪli, -tjuːmli/ ■ n. (pl. **-ies**) archaic insolent or insulting language or treatment.
– ORIGIN Middle English: from Latin *contumelia*, perhaps from *con-* 'with' + *tumere* 'to swell'.

contusion /kənˈtjuːʒ(ə)n/ ■ n. Medicine a bruise.
– DERIVATIVES **contuse** v.
– ORIGIN Middle English: from Latin *contusio(n-)*, from *contundere*, from *con-* 'together' + *tundere* 'to beat, thump'.

conundrum /kəˈnʌndrəm/ ■ n. (pl. **conundrums**) a confusing and difficult problem or question. ▸ a riddle.
– ORIGIN C16 (in the sense 'a crank or pedant').

conurbation /ˌkɒnəˈbeɪʃ(ə)n/ ■ n. an extended urban area, typically consisting of several towns merging with the suburbs of a central city.
– ORIGIN C20: from **CON-** + Latin *urbs* 'city'.

convalesce /ˌkɒnvəˈlɛs/ ■ v. gradually recover one's health after an illness or medical treatment.
– ORIGIN C15: from Latin *convalescere*, from *con-* 'altogether' + *valescere* 'grow strong'.

convalescent ■ adj. recovering from an illness or medical treatment. ■ n. a convalescent person.
– DERIVATIVES **convalescence** n.

convection ■ n. transference of mass or heat within a fluid caused by the tendency of warmer and less dense material to rise.
– DERIVATIVES **convect** v. **convectional** adj. **convective** adj.
– ORIGIN C19: from late Latin *convectio(n-)*, from Latin *convehere*, from *con-* 'together' + *vehere* 'carry'.

convector ■ n. a heating appliance that circulates warm air by convection.

convene /kənˈviːn/ ■ v. call people together for (a meeting). ▸ assemble for a common purpose.
– DERIVATIVES **convenable** adj.
– ORIGIN Middle English: from Latin *convenire* 'assemble, agree, fit', from *con-* 'together' + *venire* 'come'.

convener (also **convenor**) ■ n. a person who convenes meetings of a committee.

convenience ■ n. 1 freedom from effort or difficulty. ▸ a useful or helpful device or situation. 2 Brit. a public toilet.
– PHRASES **at one's convenience** when or where it suits one. **at one's earliest convenience** as soon as one can without difficulty.
– DERIVATIVES **conveniency** n. (rare).
– ORIGIN Middle English: from Latin *convenientia*, from *convenire* (see **CONVENE**).

convenience food ■ n. a food that has been pre-prepared commercially and so requires little preparation by the consumer.

convenience store ■ n. chiefly N. Amer. a small local shop with extended opening hours.

convenient ■ adj. fitting in well with a person's needs, activities, and plans.
– DERIVATIVES **conveniently** adv.
– ORIGIN Middle English: from Latin *convenire* (see **CONVENE**).

convenor ■ n. variant spelling of **CONVENER**.

convent ■ n. a Christian community under monastic vows, especially one of nuns. ▸ (also **convent school**) a school attached to and run by a convent.
– ORIGIN Middle English: from Latin *conventus* 'assembly, company', from *convenire* (see **CONVENE**).

convention ■ n. 1 a way in which something is usually done. ▸ socially acceptable behaviour. 2 an agreement between states, especially one less formal than a treaty. 3 a large meeting, especially of members of a political party or a particular profession. ▸ N. Amer. an assembly of the delegates of a political party to select candidates for office. ▸ a body set up by agreement to deal with a particular issue. 4 Bridge a bid or system of bidding by which the bidder tries to convey specific information about the hand to their partner.
– ORIGIN Middle English: from Latin *conventio(n-)* 'meeting, covenant', from *convenire* (see **CONVENE**).

conventional ■ adj. 1 based on or in accordance with convention. ▸ overly concerned with convention. 2 (of weapons or power) non-nuclear.
– DERIVATIVES **conventionalism** n. **conventionalist** n. **conventionality** n. **conventionalize** (also **-ise**) v. **conventionally** adv.

converge /kənˈvəːdʒ/ ■ v. 1 come together from different directions so as eventually to meet. ▸ (**converge on/upon**) come from different directions and meet at. 2 Mathematics (of a series) approximate in the sum of its terms towards a definite limit.
– ORIGIN C17: from late Latin *convergere*, from *con-* 'together' + Latin *vergere* 'incline'.

convergent ■ adj. 1 converging. 2 Biology (of unrelated animals and plants) showing a tendency to evolve superficially similar characteristics under similar environmental conditions. 3 (of thought) tending to follow well-established patterns.
– DERIVATIVES **convergence** n. **convergency** n.

conversant ■ adj. familiar with or knowledgeable about something.
– DERIVATIVES **conversance** n. **conversancy** n.
– ORIGIN Middle English: from Old French, from *converser* (see **CONVERSE**[1]).

conversation ■ n. an informal spoken exchange of news and ideas between two or more people.
– DERIVATIVES **conversational** adj. **conversationally** adv.

conversationalist ■ n. a person who is good at or fond of engaging in conversation.

conversation piece ■ n. 1 a type of genre painting in which a group of figures are posed in a landscape or domestic setting. 2 an object whose unusual quality makes it a topic of conversation.

converse[1] ■ v. /kənˈvəːs/ engage in conversation. ■ n. /ˈkɒnvəːs/ archaic conversation.
– DERIVATIVES **converser** n.
– ORIGIN Middle English: from Old French *converser*, from Latin *conversari* 'keep company (with)', from *con-* 'with' + *versare*, from *vertere* 'to turn'.

converse[2] /ˈkɒnvəːs/ ■ n. a situation, object, or statement that is the opposite of another. ▸ Mathematics a theorem whose hypothesis and conclusion are the conclusion and hypothesis of another. ■ adj. opposite.
– DERIVATIVES **conversely** adv.
– ORIGIN Middle English: from Latin *conversus* 'turned about', from *convertere* (see **CONVERT**).

conversion ■ n. 1 the process or action of converting or of being converted. 2 Rugby & American Football the action of converting a try, touchdown, or down.
– ORIGIN Middle English: from Latin *conversio(n-)*, from *convertere* (see **CONVERT**).

conversion factor ■ n. an arithmetical multiplier for converting a quantity expressed in one set of units into an equivalent expressed in another.

convert ■ v. /kənˈvəːt/ 1 change or cause to change in form, character, or function. ▸ change (money, stocks, or units in which a quantity is expressed) into others of a different kind. ▸ adapt (a building) to make it suitable for a new purpose. 2 change one's religious faith or other beliefs. 3 Logic transpose the subject and predicate of (a proposition) according to certain rules to form a new proposition by inference. 4 Rugby score extra points after (a try) by a successful kick at goal. ■ n. /ˈkɒnvəːt/ a person who has changed their religious faith or other beliefs.
– ORIGIN Middle English: from Old French *convertir*, from Latin *convertere* 'turn about'.

converter (also **convertor**) ■ n. 1 a person or thing that converts something. 2 a retort used in steel-making.

converter reactor ■ n. a nuclear reactor that converts fertile material into fissile material.

convertible ■ adj. **1** able to be converted. ▶ (of currency) able to be converted into other forms, especially into gold or US dollars. ▶ (of a bond or stock) able to be converted into ordinary or preference shares. **2** (of a car) having a folding or detachable roof. **3** Logic (of terms) synonymous. ■ n. **1** a convertible car. **2** a convertible bond or stock.
– DERIVATIVES **convertibility** n.

convex /'kɒnvɛks/ ■ adj. having an outline or surface curved like the exterior of a circle or sphere. Compare with CONCAVE.
– DERIVATIVES **convexity** n. **convexly** adv.
– ORIGIN C16: from Latin *convexus* 'vaulted, arched'.

convey /kən'veɪ/ ■ v. **1** transport or carry to a place. **2** communicate (an idea, impression, or feeling). **3** Law transfer the title to (property).
– DERIVATIVES **conveyable** adj. **conveyor** (also **conveyer**) n.
– ORIGIN Middle English: from Old French *conveier*, from medieval Latin *conviare*, from *con-* 'together' + Latin *via* 'way'.

conveyance ■ n. **1** the action or process of conveying. **2** formal or humorous a vehicle. **3** the legal process of transferring property from one owner to another.
– DERIVATIVES **conveyancer** n. **conveyancing** n.

conveyor belt ■ n. a continuous moving band of fabric, rubber, or metal used for transporting objects from one place to another.

convict ■ v. /kən'vɪkt/ declare to be guilty of a criminal offence by the verdict of a jury or the decision of a judge in a court of law. ■ n. /'kɒnvɪkt/ a person convicted of a criminal offence and serving a sentence of imprisonment.
– ORIGIN Middle English: from Latin *convict-*, *convincere* (see CONVINCE).

conviction ■ n. **1** an instance of being convicted. ▶ the action or process of convicting someone. **2** a firmly held belief or opinion. ▶ the quality of showing that one is firmly convinced of something.

convince ■ v. cause to believe firmly in the truth of something. ▶ persuade to do something. ▶ [as adj. **convinced**] firm in one's belief with regard to a particular cause: *a convinced pacifist.*
– DERIVATIVES **convincer** n. **convincible** adj.
– ORIGIN C16: from Latin *convincere*, from *con-* 'with' + *vincere* 'conquer'.

convincing ■ adj. **1** able to convince. **2** (of a victory or a winner) leaving no margin of doubt.
– DERIVATIVES **convincingly** adv.

convivial /kən'vɪvɪəl/ ■ adj. (of an atmosphere or event) friendly, lively, and enjoyable. ▶ cheerful and sociable.
– DERIVATIVES **conviviality** n. **convivially** adv.
– ORIGIN C17: from Latin *convivialis*, from *convivium* 'a feast'.

convocation /ˌkɒnvə'keɪʃ(ə)n/ ■ n. **1** Brit. a legislative or deliberative assembly of a university. ▶ N. Amer. a formal ceremony for the conferment of university awards. **2** the action of convoking a large formal assembly.
– DERIVATIVES **convocational** adj.
– ORIGIN Middle English: from Latin *convocare* 'call together'.

convoke /kən'vəʊk/ ■ v. formal call together (an assembly or meeting).
– ORIGIN C16: from Latin *convocare*.

convoluted /ˌkɒnvə'l(j)uːtɪd/ ■ adj. **1** (especially of an argument, story, or sentence) extremely complex. **2** chiefly technical intricately folded, twisted, or coiled.
– DERIVATIVES **convolutedly** adv.

convolution ■ n. **1** a coil or twist. ▶ a sinuous fold in the surface of the brain. ▶ the state of being or process of becoming coiled or twisted. **2** a complex argument, story, etc.
– DERIVATIVES **convolutional** adj.
– ORIGIN C16: from medieval Latin *convolutio(n-)*, from *convolvere* 'roll together'.

convolvulus /kən'vɒlvjʊləs/ ■ n. (pl. **convolvuluses**) a twining plant with trumpet-shaped flowers, some kinds of which are invasive weeds; bindweed. [Genus *Convolvulus*.]
– ORIGIN Latin, 'bindweed', from *convolvere* 'roll together'.

convoy /'kɒnvɔɪ/ ■ n. a group of ships or vehicles travelling together and accompanied by armed troops or warships for protection. ■ v. (of a warship or armed troops) accompany (a group of ships or vehicles) for protection.
– PHRASES **in convoy** (of travelling vehicles) as a group.
– ORIGIN Middle English: from French *convoyer*, from medieval Latin *conviare* (see CONVEY).

convulse /kən'vʌls/ ■ v. suffer convulsions. ▶ (usu. **be convulsed**) (of an emotion, laughter, or physical stimulus) cause to make sudden, violent, uncontrollable movements.
– DERIVATIVES **convulsive** adj. **convulsively** adv.
– ORIGIN C17: from Latin *convuls-*, *convellere* 'pull violently, wrench'.

convulsion ■ n. **1** a sudden, violent, irregular movement of the body caused by involuntary contraction of muscles, associated especially with epilepsy or toxins. **2** (**convulsions**) uncontrollable laughter. **3** a violent social or natural upheaval.

coo ■ v. (**coos**, **cooed**) **1** (of a pigeon or dove) make a soft murmuring sound. **2** (of a person) speak in a soft gentle voice. ▶ make a cooing sound.
– ORIGIN C17: imitative.

cooee informal ■ exclam. used to attract attention. ■ v. (**cooees**, **cooeed**, **cooeeing**) make such a call.
– ORIGIN C18: imitative of a signal used by Australian Aboriginals.

cook ■ v. **1** prepare (food) by mixing, combining, and heating the ingredients. ▶ (of food) be heated so as to reach an edible state. **2** informal alter dishonestly. ▶ (**cook something up**) concoct a story, excuse, or plan, especially an ingenious or devious one. **3** (**be cooking**) informal be happening or planned. **4** N. Amer. informal perform or proceed vigorously or very well. ■ n. a person who cooks, especially as a job.
– PHRASES **cook someone's goose** informal spoil someone's plans.
– DERIVATIVES **cookable** adj. **cooking** n.
– ORIGIN Old English: from popular Latin *cocus*, from Latin *coquus*.

cooker ■ n. Brit. an appliance for cooking food, typically consisting of an oven, hob, and grill.

cookery ■ n. the practice or skill of preparing and cooking food.

cookhouse ■ n. a building used for cooking, especially on a ranch, military camp, etc.

cookie ■ n. (pl. **-ies**) **1** N. Amer. a sweet biscuit. **2** informal a person of a specified kind: *she's a tough cookie.* **3** Computing a packet of data sent by an Internet server to a browser and used to identify the user or track their access to the server.
– PHRASES **the way the cookie crumbles** informal, chiefly N. Amer. the way things turn out, especially when undesirable.
– ORIGIN C18: from Dutch *koekje* 'little cake', diminutive of *koek*.

cookie cutter ■ n. N. Amer. **1** a device with sharp edges for cutting biscuit dough into a particular shape. **2** [as modifier] denoting something mass-produced or lacking any distinguishing characteristics.

cookout ■ n. N. Amer. a party or gathering where a meal is cooked and eaten outdoors.

Cook's tour ■ n. informal a rapid tour of many places.
– ORIGIN C20: from the name of the English travel agent Thomas *Cook*.

cookware ■ n. pots, pans, or dishes in which food can be cooked.

cool ■ adj. **1** of or at a fairly low temperature. ▶ (especially of clothing) keeping one from becoming too hot. **2** unfriendly or unenthusiastic. ▶ free from anxiety or excitement. **3** (of jazz, especially modern jazz) restrained and relaxed. **4** informal fashionably attractive or impressive. ▶ excellent. **5** (**a cool ——**) informal used to emphasize a specified large amount of money. ■ n. (**the cool**) a fairly low temperature, or a place or time characterized by this. ■ v. become or cause to become cool.
– PHRASES **keep** (or **lose**) **one's cool** informal maintain (or fail to maintain) a calm and controlled attitude.

–DERIVATIVES **-cooled** adj. **coolish** adj. **coolly** adv. **coolness** n.
–ORIGIN Old English, of Germanic origin.

coolant ■ n. a fluid used to cool an engine, nuclear reactor, or other device.
–ORIGIN 1930s: from **COOL**, on the pattern of *lubricant*.

cool bag (also **cool box**) ■ n. an insulated container for keeping food and drink cool.

cooldrink ■ n. S. African a soft drink.

cooler ■ n. **1** a device or container for keeping things cool. ▸ N. Amer. a refrigerator. **2** a long drink, especially a mixture of wine, fruit juice, and soda water. **3** (**the cooler**) informal prison or a prison cell.

coolibah /'kuːlɪbɑː/ ■ n. a North Australian gum tree which typically grows near watercourses and yields very strong, hard wood. [*Eucalyptus microtheca*.]
–ORIGIN C19: from Kamilaroi (an extinct Aboriginal language) *gulubaa*.

coolie /'kuːli/ ■ n. (pl. **-ies**) **1** dated an unskilled native labourer in India, China, and some other Asian countries. **2** offensive a person from the Indian subcontinent or of Indian descent.
–ORIGIN C17: from Hindi and Telugu *kūlī* 'day-labourer', prob. associated with Urdu *kulī* 'slave'.

coolie hat ■ n. a broad conical hat as worn by labourers in some Asian countries.

cooling-off period ■ n. **1** an interval during which the parties in a dispute can try to settle their differences before taking further action. **2** an interval after a sale contract is agreed during which the purchaser can decide to cancel without loss.

cooling tower ■ n. a tall, open-topped, cylindrical concrete tower, used for cooling water or condensing steam from an industrial process.

coolth /kuːlθ/ ■ n. **1** pleasantly low temperature. **2** informal articles, activities, or people perceived as fashionable.

coombe (also **coomb**) ■ n. variant spelling of **COMBE**.

coon ■ n. **1** another term for **CAPE MINSTREL**. **2** N. Amer. short for **RACCOON**. **3** informal, offensive a black person.

Coon Carnival ■ n. S. African another term for **CAPE MINSTREL CARNIVAL**.

coonhound ■ n. a dog of a black-and-tan American breed, used to hunt raccoons.

coop ■ n. a cage or pen for confining poultry. ■ v. (usu. **be cooped up**) confine in a small space.
–ORIGIN Middle English *cowpe*, from Latin *cupa*; cf. **COOPER**.

co-op /'kəʊɒp/ ■ n. informal a cooperative organization.

cooper ■ n. a maker or repairer of casks and barrels. ■ v. make or repair (a cask or barrel).
–DERIVATIVES **cooperage** n. **coopery** n.
–ORIGIN Middle English *cowper*, from Middle Dutch, Middle Low German *kūper*, from *kūpe* 'tub, vat', from Latin *cupa*.

cooperate /kəʊˈɒpəreɪt/ (also **co-operate**) ■ v. work jointly towards the same end. ▸ assist someone or comply with their requests.
–DERIVATIVES **cooperant** n. **cooperator** n.
–ORIGIN C16: from eccles. Latin *cooperari* 'work together'.

cooperation (also **co-operation**) ■ n. **1** the action or process of cooperating. **2** Economics the formation and operation of cooperatives.

cooperative (also **co-operative**) ■ adj. **1** involving cooperation. **2** willing to be of assistance. **3** (of a farm, business, etc.) owned and run jointly by its members, with profits or benefits shared among them. ■ n. a cooperative organization.
–DERIVATIVES **cooperatively** adv. **cooperativeness** n.

co-opt ■ v. **1** appoint to membership of a committee or other body by invitation of the existing members. **2** divert to a role different from the usual or original one. **3** adopt (an idea or policy) for one's own use.
–DERIVATIVES **co-optation** n. **co-option** n. **co-optive** adj.
–ORIGIN C17: from Latin *cooptare*, from *co-* 'together' + *optare* 'choose'.

coordinate (also **co-ordinate**) ■ v. /kəʊˈɔːdɪneɪt/ **1** bring the different elements of (a complex activity or organization) into a harmonious or efficient relationship.

copernicium

2 negotiate with others in order to work together effectively. **3** match or harmonize attractively. **4** Chemistry form a coordinate bond to. ■ adj. /kəʊˈɔːdɪnət/ **1** equal in rank or importance. ▸ Grammar (of parts of a compound sentence) equal in rank and fulfilling identical functions. **2** Chemistry denoting a covalent bond in which one atom provides both the shared electrons. ■ n. /kəʊˈɔːdɪnət/ **1** Mathematics each of a group of numbers used to indicate the position of a point, line, or plane. **2** (**coordinates**) matching items of clothing.
–DERIVATIVES **coordinative** adj. **coordinator** n.
–ORIGIN C17: from **CO-** + Latin *ordinare*, from *ordo* 'order'.

coordinating conjunction ■ n. a conjunction placed between words, phrases, clauses, or sentences of equal rank, e.g. *and*, *but*, *or*. Contrasted with **SUBORDINATING CONJUNCTION**.

coordination (also **co-ordination**) ■ n. **1** the action or process of coordinating. ▸ the ability to move different parts of the body smoothly and at the same time. **2** Chemistry the linking of atoms by coordinate bonds.

coot ■ n. **1** (pl. same) an aquatic bird of the rail family with black plumage and a white bill that extends back on to the forehead as a horny shield. [*Fulica cristata* and related species.] **2** (usu. **old coot**) informal a stupid or eccentric person, typically an old man.
–ORIGIN Middle English: prob. of Dutch or Low German origin.

cootie /'kuːti/ ■ n. N. Amer. informal a body louse.
–ORIGIN FIRST WORLD WAR: perhaps from Malay *kutu*, denoting a parasitic biting insect.

co-own ■ v. own jointly.
–DERIVATIVES **co-owner** n. **co-ownership** n.

cop informal ■ n. a police officer. ■ v. (**copped**, **copping**) **1** catch or arrest (an offender). **2** incur (something unwelcome). **3** (**cop out**) avoid doing something that one ought to do.
–PHRASES **cop hold of** Brit. take hold of. **cop it** Brit. **1** get into trouble. **2** be killed. **cop a plea** N. Amer. engage in plea bargaining. **not much cop** Brit. not very good.
–ORIGIN C18 (as v.): perhaps from obsolete *cap* 'arrest', from Old French *caper* 'seize', from Latin *capere*.

copal /'kəʊp(ə)l/ ■ n. resin from any of a number of tropical trees, used to make varnish.
–ORIGIN C16: from Nahuatl *copalli* 'incense'.

co-parent ■ v. (especially of a separated or unmarried couple) share the duties of bringing up (a child). ■ n. a person who co-parents a child.

co-partner ■ n. a partner or associate, especially an equal partner in a business.
–DERIVATIVES **co-partnership** n.

COPD ■ abbrev. Medicine chronic obstructive pulmonary disease, involving constriction of the airways and difficulty or discomfort in breathing.

cope[1] ■ v. deal effectively with something difficult.
–DERIVATIVES **coper** n.
–ORIGIN Middle English (in the sense 'come to blows'): from Old French *coper*, from *cop*, *colp* 'a blow', from Greek *kolaphos* 'a blow with the fist'.

cope[2] ■ n. a long, loose cloak worn by a priest or bishop on ceremonial occasions.
–ORIGIN Middle English: from medieval Latin *capa*, var. of late Latin *cappa* (see **CAP**).

copeck ■ n. variant spelling of **KOPEK**.

Copepoda /ˌkəʊpɪˈpəʊdə/ ■ pl. n. Zoology a large class of small aquatic crustaceans, many of which occur in plankton.
–DERIVATIVES **copepod** /ˈkəʊpɪpɒd/ n.
–ORIGIN from Greek *kōpē* 'handle, oar' + *pous*, *pod-* 'foot' (because of their paddle-like feet).

Copernican system /kəˈpəːnɪk(ə)n/ (also **Copernican theory**) ■ n. Astronomy the theory proposed by the Polish astronomer Nicolaus Copernicus (1473–1543) that the sun is the centre of the solar system, with the planets (including the earth) orbiting round it. Compare with **PTOLEMAIC SYSTEM**.

copernicium /kəˌpəːˈnɪkɪəm/ ■ n. the chemical element of

copiable

atomic number 112, a very unstable element made by high-energy atomic collisions. (Symbol: **Cn**)
– ORIGIN C21: named after the Polish astronomer, Nicolaus Copernicus.

copiable ■ adj. able to be copied, especially legitimately.

copier ■ n. a machine that makes exact copies of something.

co-pilot ■ n. a second pilot in an aircraft.

coping ■ n. the top, typically sloping, course of a brick or stone wall.
– ORIGIN C16: from COPE², orig. meaning 'dress in a cope', hence 'to cover'.

coping saw ■ n. a saw with a very narrow blade stretched across a D-shaped frame, used for cutting curves in wood.
– ORIGIN 1920s: *coping* from COPE², describing likeness to a vault, arch, etc.

coping stone ■ n. a flat stone forming part of a coping.

copious ■ adj. abundant; plentiful.
– DERIVATIVES **copiously** adv. **copiousness** n.
– ORIGIN Middle English: from Old French *copieux* or Latin *copiosus*, from *copia* 'plenty'.

coplanar /kəʊˈpleɪnə/ ■ adj. Geometry in the same plane.
– DERIVATIVES **coplanarity** n.

copolymer /kəʊˈpɒlɪmə/ ■ n. Chemistry a polymer made by reaction of two different monomers, with units of more than one kind.
– DERIVATIVES **copolymerization** (also **-isation**) n. **copolymerize** (also **-ise**) v.

cop-out ■ n. informal an instance of avoiding a commitment or responsibility.

copper¹ ■ n. **1** a red-brown metal, the chemical element of atomic number 29, which is a good conductor of electricity and heat and is used for electrical wiring and as a component of brass and bronze. (Symbol: **Cu**) **2** (**coppers**) Brit. coins of low value made of copper or bronze. **3** Brit. dated a large copper or iron container for boiling laundry. **4** a reddish-brown colour. **5** a small butterfly with bright orange-brown wings. [Genus *Aloeides*: many species.] ■ v. cover or coat with copper.
– DERIVATIVES **coppery** adj.
– ORIGIN Old English, from late Latin *cuprum*, from Latin *cyprium aes* 'Cyprus metal' (because Cyprus was the chief source).

copper² ■ n. Brit. informal a police officer.
– ORIGIN C19: from COP.

copper beech ■ n. a beech tree of a variety with purplish-brown leaves.

copper-bottomed ■ adj. Brit. thoroughly reliable.
– ORIGIN from earlier usage referring to the copper sheathing of the bottom of a ship.

copperhead ■ n. a venomous snake with reddish-brown coloration. [*Agkistrodon contortrix* (N. America) and *Austrelaps superbus* (Australia).]

copperplate ■ n. **1** a polished copper plate with a design engraved or etched into it. **2** a style of neat, round handwriting, usually slanted and looped. [**the copybooks for this were orig. printed from copperplates.**] ■ adj. of or in copperplate writing.

copper pyrites ■ n. another term for CHALCOPYRITE.

coppersmith ■ n. a person who makes things out of copper.

copper sulphate ■ n. a blue crystalline solid used in electroplating and as a fungicide.

coppice ■ n. an area of woodland in which the trees or shrubs are periodically cut back to ground level to stimulate growth and provide wood. ■ v. cut back (a tree or shrub) in this way.
– ORIGIN Middle English: from Old French *copeiz*, from medieval Latin *colpus* (see COPE¹).

copra /ˈkɒprə/ ■ n. dried coconut kernels, from which oil is obtained.
– ORIGIN C16: from Malayalam *koppara* 'coconut'.

co-precipitation ■ n. Chemistry the simultaneous precipitation of more than one compound from a solution.

– DERIVATIVES **co-precipitate** v.

coprocessor ■ n. Computing a microprocessor designed to supplement the capabilities of the primary processor.

co-produce ■ v. produce (a theatrical work or a radio or television programme) jointly.
– DERIVATIVES **co-producer** n. **co-production** n.

coprolite /ˈkɒprə(ʊ)laɪt/ ■ n. Palaeontology a piece of fossilized dung.

coprophagy /kɒˈprɒfədʒi/ (also **coprophagia** /ˌkɒprə(ʊ)ˈfeɪdʒɪə/) ■ n. Zoology the eating of faeces.
– DERIVATIVES **coprophagic** adj. **coprophagous** adj.

copse ■ n. a small group of trees.
– ORIGIN C16: shortened form of COPPICE.

cop shop ■ n. informal a police station.

Copt /kɒpt/ ■ n. a member of the Coptic Church, the native Christian Church in Egypt.
– ORIGIN from French *Copte*, from Arabic *al-ḳibṭ, al-ḳubṭ* 'Copts', from Coptic *Gyptios*, from Greek *Aiguptios* 'Egyptian'.

Coptic ■ n. the language of the Copts, which survives only in the Coptic Church. ■ adj. of or relating to the Copts or their language.

copula /ˈkɒpjʊlə/ ■ n. Logic & Grammar a connecting word, in particular a form of the verb *be* connecting a subject and complement.
– DERIVATIVES **copular** adj.
– ORIGIN C17: from Latin, 'connection, linking of words', from *co-* 'together' + *apere* 'fasten'.

copulate /ˈkɒpjʊleɪt/ ■ v. have sexual intercourse.
– DERIVATIVES **copulation** n. **copulatory** adj.
– ORIGIN Middle English: from Latin *copulare* 'fasten together', from *copula* (see COPULA).

copulative ■ adj. **1** Grammar (of a word) connecting words or clauses linked in sense. ▸ connecting a subject and predicate. **2** of or relating to sexual intercourse.
– DERIVATIVES **copulatively** adv.

copy ■ n. (pl. **-ies**) **1** a thing made to be similar or identical to another. **2** a single specimen of a particular book, record, etc. **3** matter to be printed. ▸ material for a newspaper or magazine article. ■ v. (**-ies**, **-ied**) make a copy of. ▸ imitate the behaviour or style of.
– ORIGIN Middle English: from Old French *copie* (n.), *copier* (v.), from Latin *copia* 'abundance', later 'transcript'.

copybook ■ n. a book containing models of handwriting for learners to imitate. ■ adj. exactly in accordance with established standards.

copycat ■ n. informal **1** a person who copies another, especially slavishly. **2** [as modifier] denoting an action, typically a crime, carried out in imitation of another.

copy-edit ■ v. edit (text) by checking its consistency and accuracy.
– DERIVATIVES **copy editor** n.

copyist ■ n. **1** a person who makes copies. **2** a person who imitates the styles of others, especially in art.

copyleft ■ n. Computing an agreement allowing software to be used, modified, and distributed freely on condition that a notice to this effect is included with it.
– DERIVATIVES **copylefted** adj.
– ORIGIN 1980s: after COPYRIGHT.

copyread ■ v. read and edit (text) for a newspaper, magazine, or book.
– DERIVATIVES **copyreader** n.

copyright ■ n. the exclusive legal right, given to the originator or their assignee for a fixed number of years, to publish, perform, film, or record literary, artistic, or musical material, and to authorize others to do the same. ■ v. secure copyright for (such material).

copyright library ■ n. a library entitled to a free copy of each book published in the UK.

copy typist ■ n. a person whose job is to type transcripts of written drafts.

copywriter ■ n. a person who writes the text of advertisements or publicity material.
– DERIVATIVES **copywriting** n.

coq au vin /ˌkɒk əʊ ˈvã/ ■ n. a casserole of chicken pieces cooked in red wine.
– ORIGIN French, 'cock in wine'.

coquette /kɒˈket/ ■ n. a woman who flirts.
– DERIVATIVES **coquetry** n. **coquettish** adj. **coquettishly** adv. **coquettishness** n.
– ORIGIN C17: from French *coquet* 'wanton', diminutive of *coq* 'cock'.

cor- ■ prefix variant spelling of COM- assimilated before *r* (as in *corrode*, *corrugate*).

coracle /ˈkɒrək(ə)l/ ■ n. (especially in Wales and Ireland) a small, round boat made of wickerwork covered with a watertight material, propelled with a paddle.
– ORIGIN C16: from Welsh *corwgl*, rel. to Scottish Gaelic and Irish *curach* 'small boat'.

coral ■ n. 1 a hard stony substance secreted by certain colonial marine animals as an external skeleton, typically forming large reefs. ▸ precious red coral, used in jewellery. 2 the pinkish-red colour of red coral. 3 an anthozoan of a large group including those that form coral reefs, secreting a calcareous, horny, or soft skeleton. [Orders Scleractinia or Madreporaria (the reef-forming stony corals), Alcyonacea (soft corals), and Gorgonacea (horny corals).] 4 the edible unfertilized roe of a lobster or scallop, reddening when cooked.
– DERIVATIVES **coralloid** adj. (chiefly Biology & Zoology).
– ORIGIN Middle English: from Latin *corallum*, from Greek *kouralion*.

Corallian /kɒˈralɪən/ ■ adj. Geology relating to or denoting an age in the Upper Jurassic period when extensive coral-derived limestone deposits were laid down.
– ORIGIN from Latin *corallium* 'coral'.

coralline /ˈkɒrəlʌɪn/ ■ adj. 1 derived or formed from coral. 2 of the pinkish-red colour of red coral. 3 resembling coral. ■ n. a branching reddish seaweed with a calcareous jointed stem. [*Corallina officinalis* and other species.]
– ORIGIN C16: the adjective from late Latin *corallinus*, the noun from Italian, diminutive of *corallo* 'coral', both from Latin *corallum* 'coral'.

corallite /ˈkɒrəlʌɪt/ ■ n. Palaeontology the cup-like calcareous skeleton of a single coral polyp. ▸ a fossil coral.

coral snake ■ n. a brightly banded venomous snake of the cobra family. [*Aspidelaps* and other genera.]

coral tree ■ n. a tropical or subtropical thorny shrub or tree with showy red or orange flowers that are pollinated by birds. [Genus *Erythrina*.]

coral vine ■ n. a pink-flowered climbing vine native to Mexico and the Caribbean, grown as an ornamental. [*Antigonon leptopus*.]

cor anglais /ˌkɔːr ˈɑːŋɡleɪ, ˈɒŋɡleɪ/ ■ n. (pl. **cors anglais** pronunc. same) an alto woodwind instrument of the oboe family, having a bulbous bell and sounding a fifth lower than the oboe.
– ORIGIN C19: French, 'English horn'.

corbel /ˈkɔːb(ə)l/ ■ n. a projection jutting out from a wall to support a structure above it. ■ v. (**corbelled**, **corbelling**; US **corbeled**, **corbeling**) [often as adj. **corbelled**] support on corbels.
– ORIGIN Middle English: from Old French, diminutive of *corp* 'crow', from Latin *corvus* 'raven'.

corbel table ■ n. a projecting course of bricks or stones resting on corbels.

cord ■ n. 1 long thin string or rope made from several twisted strands. ▸ a length of such material. 2 (also **chord**) an anatomical structure resembling a cord (e.g. the spinal cord). 3 an electric flex. 4 corduroy. ▸ (**cords**) corduroy trousers. 5 a measure of cut wood (usually 3.62 cubic metres). ■ v. [usu. as adj. **corded**] attach a cord to.
– DERIVATIVES **cording** n. **cord-like** adj.
– ORIGIN Middle English: from Old French *corde*, from Latin *chorda*, from Greek *khordē* 'gut, string of a musical instrument'.

cordate /ˈkɔːdeɪt/ ■ adj. Botany heart-shaped.
– ORIGIN C17: from Latin *cordatus* 'wise' (in modern Latin 'heart-shaped'), from *cor* 'heart'.

corded ■ adj. 1 (of cloth) ribbed. 2 (of a muscle) tensed and standing out. 3 equipped with a cord or flex.

cordgrass ■ n. a coarse wiry coastal grass which is sometimes used to stabilize mudflats. [Genus *Spartina*.]

cordial ■ adj. 1 warm and friendly. 2 strongly felt: *cordial loathing*. ■ n. 1 Brit. a sweet fruit-flavoured drink, sold as a concentrate. 2 chiefly N. Amer. another term for LIQUEUR. 3 a pleasant-tasting medicine.
– DERIVATIVES **cordiality** n. **cordially** adv.
– ORIGIN Middle English: from medieval Latin *cordialis*, from Latin *cor* 'heart'.

cordierite /ˈkɔːdɪərʌɪt/ ■ n. a dark blue mineral consisting of an aluminosilicate of magnesium and iron.
– ORIGIN C19: named after the French geologist Pierre L. A. Cordier.

cordillera /ˌkɔːdɪˈljeːrə/ ■ n. a system or group of parallel mountain ranges together with the intervening plateaux and other features, especially in the Andes or the Rocky Mountains.
– ORIGIN C18: from Spanish, from *cordilla*, diminutive of *cuerda* 'cord', from Latin *chorda* (see CORD).

cordite ■ n. a smokeless explosive made from nitrocellulose, nitroglycerine, and petroleum jelly.
– ORIGIN C19: from CORD (because of its appearance).

cordless ■ adj. (of an electrical appliance or telephone) working without connection to a mains supply or central unit.

cordon /ˈkɔːd(ə)n/ ■ n. 1 a line or circle of police, soldiers, or guards preventing access to or from an area or building. 2 a fruit tree trained to grow as a single stem. 3 Architecture a raised horizontal band or course of bricks on a building. ■ v. (**cordon something off**) prevent access to or from an area by means of a cordon.
– ORIGIN Middle English: from Italian *cordone*, from *corda*, and French *cordon*, diminutive of *corde*, both from Latin *chorda* (see CORD).

cordon bleu /ˌkɔːdɔ̃ ˈblɜː/ ■ adj. Cookery of the highest class. ■ n. 1 (pl. **cordons bleus** pronounced same) a cook of the highest class. 2 (**cordon-bleu**) (pl. **cordon-bleus**) an African waxbill popular as a cage bird, the male of which has a blue face, breast, and tail. [Genus *Uraeginthus*.]
– ORIGIN C18: French, 'blue ribbon' (once signifying the highest order of chivalry).

cordon sanitaire /ˌkɔːdɔ̃ sanɪˈtɛː/ ■ n. (pl. **cordons sanitaires** pronunc. same) 1 a guarded line preventing anyone from leaving an area infected by a disease. 2 a measure designed to prevent communication or the spread of undesirable influences.
– ORIGIN C19: French, 'sanitary line'.

cordovan /ˈkɔːdəv(ə)n/ ■ n. a kind of soft leather made originally from goatskin and now from horsehide.
– ORIGIN C16: from Spanish *cordován*, former spelling of *cordobán* 'of Cordoba' (a city in Spain).

corduroy /ˈkɔːdərɔɪ, -djuː-/ ■ n. a thick cotton fabric with velvety ribs.
– ORIGIN C18: prob. from CORD + *duroy*, denoting a former kind of lightweight worsted.

cordwood ■ n. wood cut into cords or uniform lengths.

core ■ n. 1 the tough central part of various fruits, containing the seeds. 2 the central or most important part. ▸ the dense metallic or rocky central region of a planet. ▸ the central part of a nuclear reactor, which contains the fissile material. ▸ a piece of soft iron forming the centre of an electromagnet or an induction coil. 3 an internal mould filling a space to be left hollow in a casting. 4 Archaeology a piece of flint from which flakes or blades have been removed. 5 a cylindrical sample of rock, ice, or other material obtained by boring with a hollow drill. ■ v. remove the core from (a fruit).
– PHRASES **to the core** to the depths of one's being.
– DERIVATIVES **corer** n.
– ORIGIN Middle English.

coreferential /ˌkəʊrɛfəˈrɛnʃ(ə)l/ ■ adj. Linguistics (of two elements or units) having the same reference.
– DERIVATIVES **coreference** n.

co-religionist (also **coreligionist**) ■ n. an adherent of the same religion as another person.

coreopsis /ˌkɒrɪˈɒpsɪs/ ■ n. a plant of the daisy family, cultivated for its rayed, typically yellow, flowers. [Genus *Coreopsis*.]
– ORIGIN from Greek *koris* 'bug' + *opsis* 'appearance' (because of the shape of the seed).

co-respondent (also **corespondent**) ▪ n. a person cited in a divorce case as having committed adultery with the respondent.

core time ▪ n. chiefly Brit. the central part of the working day in a flexitime system, when an employee must be present.

corgi (also **Welsh corgi**) ▪ n. (pl. **corgis**) a dog of a short-legged breed with a foxlike head.
– ORIGIN 1920s: from Welsh, from *cor* 'dwarf' + *ci* 'dog'.

coriaceous /ˌkɒrɪˈeɪʃəs/ ▪ adj. technical resembling or having the texture of leather.
– ORIGIN C17: from late Latin *coriaceus*, from Latin *corium* 'leather'.

coriander /ˌkɒrɪˈandə/ ▪ n. an aromatic Mediterranean plant of the parsley family, the leaves and seeds of which are used as culinary herbs. [*Coriandrum sativum*.]
– ORIGIN Middle English: from Latin *coriandrum*, from Greek *koriannon*.

Corinthian /kəˈrɪnθɪən/ ▪ adj. 1 belonging or relating to Corinth, a city in southern Greece and a city state in ancient Greece. 2 relating to or denoting the most ornate of the classical orders of architecture, characterized by flared capitals with rows of acanthus leaves. 3 involving the highest standards of amateur sportsmanship. ▪ n. 1 a native or inhabitant of Corinth. 2 the Corinthian order of architecture. 3 historical a wealthy amateur of sport.

Coriolis effect /ˌkɒrɪˈəʊlɪs/ ▪ n. an effect whereby a mass moving in a rotating system experiences a force perpendicular to the direction of motion and to the axis of rotation (influencing, for example, the formation of cyclonic weather systems).
– ORIGIN C20: named after the French engineer Gaspard Coriolis.

cork ▪ n. 1 the buoyant, light brown substance obtained from the outer layer of the bark of the cork oak. 2 a bottle stopper made of cork. 3 a piece of cork used as a float for a fishing line or net. 4 Botany a protective layer of dead cells immediately below the bark of woody plants. ▪ v. (often **be corked**) close or seal (a bottle) with a cork. ▸ [as adj. **corked**] (of wine) spoilt by tannin from the cork.
– DERIVATIVES **cork-like** adj.
– ORIGIN Middle English: from Dutch *kork*, from Spanish *alcorque* 'cork-soled sandal', from Arabic *al-* 'the' + Spanish Arabic *ḳorḳ*, from Latin *quercus* 'oak, cork oak'.

corkage ▪ n. a charge made by a restaurant or hotel for serving wine that has been brought in by a customer.

corker ▪ n. informal an excellent person or thing.
– DERIVATIVES **corking** adj.

cork oak ▪ n. an evergreen Mediterranean oak, the outer layer of the bark of which is the source of cork. [*Quercus suber*.]

corkscrew ▪ n. a device for pulling corks from bottles, consisting of a spiral metal rod that is inserted into the cork, and a handle. ▪ v. move or twist in a spiral.

corky ▪ adj. (**-ier**, **-iest**) 1 cork-like. 2 (of wine) corked.

corm ▪ n. a rounded underground storage organ present in plants such as crocuses and cyclamens, consisting of a swollen stem base covered with scale leaves.
– DERIVATIVES **cormlet** n.
– ORIGIN C19: from Greek *kormos* 'trunk stripped of its boughs'.

cormorant /ˈkɔːm(ə)r(ə)nt/ ▪ n. a large diving seabird with a long neck, long hooked bill, short legs, and mainly black plumage. [*Phalacrocorax carbo* and other species.]
– ORIGIN Middle English: from Old French *cormaran*, from medieval Latin *corvus marinus* 'sea-raven'; the final *-t* is on the pattern of *peasant*.

corn[1] ▪ n. 1 chiefly Brit. the chief cereal crop of a district, especially (in England) wheat or (in Scotland) oats. ▸ informal the grain of any cereal, especially as fed to livestock. ▸ N. Amer. & Austral./NZ maize. 2 informal something banal or sentimental. ▪ v. [as adj. **corned**] preserved with salt or brine.
– ORIGIN Old English, of Germanic origin.

corn[2] ▪ n. a small, painful area of thickened skin on the foot, especially on the toes, caused by pressure.
– ORIGIN Middle English: from Latin *cornu* 'horn'.

cornball ▪ adj. N. Amer. informal trite and sentimental.

cornbread ▪ n. a type of bread made from maize meal.

corncob ▪ n. the central cylindrical woody part of the maize ear to which the grains are attached.

corncrake ▪ n. a secretive crake inhabiting coarse grasslands, with mainly brown streaked plumage and a distinctive double rasping call. [*Crex crex*.]

corn dog ▪ n. N. Amer. a hot dog covered in maize-flour batter, fried, and served on a stick.

corn dolly ▪ n. Brit. a symbolic or decorative model of a human figure, made of plaited straw.

cornea /ˈkɔːnɪə/ ▪ n. the transparent layer forming the front of the eye.
– DERIVATIVES **corneal** adj.
– ORIGIN Middle English: from medieval Latin *cornea tela* 'horny tissue', from Latin *cornu* 'horn'.

corned beef ▪ n. 1 S. African & N. Amer. beef brisket cured in brine and boiled, typically served cold. 2 Brit. beef preserved in brine, chopped and pressed and sold in tins.

cornelian /kɔːˈniːlɪən/ ▪ n. variant spelling of **CARNELIAN**.

corner ▪ n. 1 a place or angle where two or more sides or edges meet. ▸ a place where two streets meet. 2 a secluded or remote region or area. 3 a difficult or awkward position. 4 (also **corner kick**) Soccer a free kick taken by the attacking side from a corner of the field after the ball has been sent over the byline by a defender. ▸ a similar free hit in field hockey. 5 Boxing & Wrestling each of the diagonally opposite ends of the ring, where a contestant rests between rounds. ▸ a contestant's supporters or seconds. ▪ v. 1 force into a place or situation from which it is hard to escape. 2 control (a market) by dominating the supply of a particular commodity. 3 go round a bend in a road.
– PHRASES (**just**) **around the corner** very near. **fight one's corner** defend one's position or interests. **in someone's corner** supporting and encouraging someone.
– DERIVATIVES **-cornered** adj.
– ORIGIN Middle English: from Anglo-Norman French, from Latin *cornu* 'horn, tip, corner'.

cornerback ▪ n. American Football a defensive back positioned to the outside of the linebackers.

corner shop ▪ n. Brit. a small shop selling groceries and general goods in a mainly residential area.

cornerstone ▪ n. 1 a stone that forms the base of a corner of a building, joining two walls. 2 an important quality or feature on which something is based.

cornerwise ▪ adv. at an angle of 45°; diagonally.

cornet[1] /ˈkɔːnɪt/ ▪ n. 1 a brass instrument resembling a trumpet but shorter and wider. 2 Brit. a cone-shaped wafer for holding ice cream.
– DERIVATIVES **cornetist** /kɔːˈnɛtɪst/ (also **cornettist**) n.
– ORIGIN Middle English (orig. denoting a wind instrument made of a horn): from Old French, from Latin *cornu* 'horn'.

cornet[2] /ˈkɔːnɪt/ ▪ n. (formerly) the fifth grade of commissioned officer in a cavalry troop, who carried the colours.
– ORIGIN C16 (earlier denoting the pennant of a cavalry troop): from French *cornette*, diminutive of *corne*, from Latin *cornua* 'horns'.

corn exchange ▪ n. (in the UK) a building where corn is or was traded.

corn-fed ▪ adj. fed on grain, especially maize.

cornflakes ▪ pl. n. a breakfast cereal consisting of toasted flakes made from maize flour.

cornflour ▪ n. finely ground maize flour, used for thickening sauces.

cornflower ▪ n. a slender plant related to the knapweeds, with flowers that are typically a deep, vivid blue. [*Centaurea cyaneus* and related species.]

cornice /ˈkɔːnɪs/ ▪ n. 1 an ornamental moulding round the wall of a room just below the ceiling. ▸ a horizontal moulded projection crowning a building or structure, especially the uppermost member of the entablature of an order, surmounting the frieze. 2 an overhanging mass of hardened snow at the edge of a mountain precipice.
– DERIVATIVES **corniced** adj. **cornicing** n.

–ORIGIN C16: from French *corniche*, from Italian *cornice*, perhaps from Latin *cornix* 'crow' but influenced by Greek *korōnis* 'coping stone'.

corniche /'kɔːnɪʃ, kɔː'niːʃ/ ■ n. a road cut into the edge of a cliff, especially one running along a coast.
–ORIGIN C19: from French (see CORNICE).

Cornish ■ adj. of or relating to Cornwall, or its people or language.
–DERIVATIVES **Cornishman** n. (pl. **-men**). **Cornishwoman** n. (pl. **-women**).

Cornish pasty ■ n. Brit. a pasty containing seasoned meat and vegetables, especially potato.

corn marigold ■ n. a daisy-like yellow-flowered plant, formerly a common weed of cornfields. [*Chrysanthemum segetum*.]

cornmeal ■ n. meal made from maize flour.

corn oil ■ n. an oil obtained from the germ of maize, used in cookery and salad dressings.

corn pone N. Amer. ■ n. unleavened maize bread. ■ adj. rustic; unsophisticated.

cornrows ■ pl. n. (especially among black people) a style of braiding and plaiting the hair in narrow strips to form geometric patterns on the scalp.

corn snake ■ n. a long North American rat snake with a spear-shaped mark between the eyes. [*Elaphe guttata*.]
–ORIGIN C17: so named because often found in cornfields.

cornstarch ■ n. North American term for CORNFLOUR.

cornu /'kɔːnjuː/ ■ n. (pl. **cornua** /'-njʊə/) Anatomy 1 a horn-shaped projection of the thyroid cartilage or of certain bones. 2 either of the two lateral cavities of the womb, into which the Fallopian tubes pass. 3 each of three elongated parts of the lateral ventricles of the brain.
–DERIVATIVES **cornual** adj.
–ORIGIN C17: from Latin, 'horn'.

cornucopia /ˌkɔːnjʊ'kəʊpɪə/ ■ n. 1 a symbol of plenty consisting of a goat's horn overflowing with flowers, fruit, and corn. 2 an abundant supply of good things.
–DERIVATIVES **cornucopian** adj.
–ORIGIN C16: from Latin *cornu copiae* 'horn of plenty' (a mythical horn providing whatever is desired).

corny ■ adj. (**-ier, -iest**) informal trite or mawkishly sentimental.
–DERIVATIVES **cornily** adv. **corniness** n.
–ORIGIN 1930s: from an earlier sense 'rustic'.

corolla /kə'rɒlə/ ■ n. Botany the petals of a flower, typically forming a whorl within the sepals and enclosing the reproductive organs.
–ORIGIN C17: from Latin, diminutive of *corona* 'wreath, crown'.

corollary /kə'rɒləri/ ■ n. (pl. **-ies**) 1 Logic a proposition that follows from (and is often appended to) one already proved. 2 a direct consequence or result. ■ adj. 1 Logic forming a corollary. 2 associated; supplementary.
–ORIGIN Middle English: from Latin *corollarium* 'money paid for a garland or chaplet; gratuity', later 'deduction', from *corolla* (see COROLLA).

coromandel /ˌkɒrə'mand(ə)l/ ■ n. (also **coromandel wood** or **coromandel ebony**) a fine-grained, greyish-brown ebony streaked with black, used in furniture. 2 the Sri Lankan tree yielding this wood. [*Diospyros quaesita*.] ■ adj. denoting a form of oriental lacquerware with intaglio designs.
–ORIGIN from the *Coromandel* Coast, the southern part of India's east coast, from which oriental lacquerware was exported.

corona[1] /kə'rəʊnə/ ■ n. (pl. **coronae** /-niː/) 1 Astronomy the rarefied gaseous envelope of the sun or a star. ▸ (also **corona discharge**) Physics the glow around a conductor at high potential. ▸ a small circle of light seen round the sun or moon. 2 Anatomy a crown or crown-like structure. 3 Botany a whorl of floral parts between the corolla and the stamens, as in flowers of Asclepiadaceae. 4 a circular chandelier in a church. 5 Architecture a part of a cornice having a broad vertical face.
–ORIGIN C16: from Latin, 'wreath, crown'.

corona[2] /kə'rəʊnə/ ■ n. a long, straight-sided cigar.
–ORIGIN C19: from Spanish *La Corona* 'the crown', orig. a proprietary name.

coronagraph ■ n. an instrument that blocks out light emitted by the sun's actual surface so that the corona can be observed.

coronal /kə'rəʊn(ə)l, 'kɒr(ə)n(ə)l/ ■ adj. 1 of or relating to the crown or corona of something. 2 Anatomy of or in the coronal plane. 3 Phonetics (of a consonant) formed by raising the tip or blade of the tongue towards the hard palate. ■ n. Phonetics a coronal consonant.

coronal plane ■ n. Anatomy an imaginary plane dividing the body into dorsal and ventral parts.

coronal suture ■ n. Anatomy the transverse suture in the skull separating the frontal bone from the parietal bones.

coronary ■ adj. Anatomy 1 relating to or denoting the arteries which surround and supply the heart. 2 relating to or denoting a structure encircling a part of the body. ■ n. (pl. **-ies**) short for CORONARY THROMBOSIS.
–ORIGIN C17: from Latin *coronarius*, from *corona* 'wreath, crown'.

coronary thrombosis ■ n. a blockage of the flow of blood to the heart, caused by a blood clot in a coronary artery.

coronation ■ n. the ceremony of crowning a sovereign or a sovereign's consort.
–ORIGIN Middle English: from medieval Latin *coronatio(n-)*, from *coronare* 'to crown', from *corona* (see CROWN).

coronation chicken ■ n. a cold dish of cooked chicken served in a sauce flavoured with apricots and curry powder.
–ORIGIN so named because the dish was created for the coronation of Queen Elizabeth II of Britain.

coroner /'kɒr(ə)nə/ ■ n. an official who holds inquests into violent, sudden, or suspicious deaths.
–DERIVATIVES **coronership** n. **coronial** adj.
–ORIGIN Middle English: from Anglo-Norman French *coruner*, from *corune* (see CROWN).

coronet /'kɒr(ə)nɪt/ ■ n. 1 a small or simple crown, especially as worn by lesser royalty and nobles. ▸ a circular decoration for the head. 2 a ring of bone at the base of a deer's antler. 3 the band of tissue containing the horn-producing cells from which a horse's hoof grows.
–DERIVATIVES **coroneted** adj.
–ORIGIN Middle English: from Old French *coronete*, diminutive of *corone* (see CROWN).

Corp. ■ abbrev. 1 (**Corp**) informal Corporal. 2 N. Amer. Corporation.

corpora /'kɔːpərə/ ■ plural form of CORPUS.

corporal[1] ■ n. a rank of non-commissioned officer in the army and air force, above lance corporal and below sergeant.
–ORIGIN C16: from French, obsolete var. of *caporal*, from Italian *caporale*, prob. from Latin *corpus* 'body (of troops)'.

corporal[2] ■ adj. of or relating to the human body.
–DERIVATIVES **corporally** adv.
–ORIGIN Middle English: from Latin *corporalis*, from *corpus* 'body'.

corporal punishment ■ n. physical punishment, such as caning or flogging.

corporate ■ adj. 1 of or relating to a large company or group. 2 Law (of a large company or group) authorized to act as a single entity and recognized as such in law. 3 of or shared by all the members of a group. ■ n. a corporate company or group.
–DERIVATIVES **corporately** adv.
–ORIGIN C15: from Latin *corporare* 'form into a body', from *corpus* 'body'.

corporate raider ■ n. a financier who makes a practice of making hostile takeover bids for companies.

corporate social responsibility ■ n. the involvement of business in ethical practices, and activities of wider benefit to society. ▸ (also **corporate social investment**, **corporate responsibility**) [often as modifier] denoting funds which a business allocates specifically to socially beneficial programmes.

corporation ■ n. 1 a large company or group of companies authorized to act as a single entity and

corporation tax

recognized as such in law. **2** Brit. a group of people elected to govern a city, town, or borough.
– ORIGIN Middle English: from late Latin *corporatio(n-)*, from Latin *corporare* (see **CORPORATE**).

corporation tax ■ n. tax levied on companies' profits.

corporatism ■ n. the control of a state or organization by large interest groups.
– DERIVATIVES **corporatist** adj. & n.

corporative ■ adj. relating to or denoting a state, typically a fascist one, organized into corporations representing employers and workers in various spheres.
– DERIVATIVES **corporativism** n. **corporativist** adj. & n.

corporatize (also **-ise**) ■ v. convert (a state organization) into an independent commercial company.

corporeal /kɔːˈpɔːrɪəl/ ■ adj. **1** of or relating to a person's body, especially as opposed to their spirit. ▸ having a body. **2** Law consisting of material objects.
– DERIVATIVES **corporeality** /-ˈalɪti/ n. **corporeally** adv.
– ORIGIN Middle English: from late Latin *corporealis*, from Latin *corporeus* 'bodily, physical', from *corpus* 'body'.

corps /kɔː/ ■ n. (pl. **corps** /kɔːz/) a main subdivision of an army in the field, consisting of two or more divisions. ▸ a branch of an army assigned to a particular kind of work. ▸ a body of people engaged in a particular activity.
– ORIGIN C16: from French, from Latin *corpus* 'body'.

corps de ballet /ˌkɔː də ˈbaleɪ/ ■ n. [treated as sing. or pl.] the members of a ballet company who dance together as a group. ▸ the lowest rank of dancers in a ballet company.
– ORIGIN C19: French.

corpse ■ n. a dead body, especially of a human. ■ v. theatrical slang spoil a piece of acting by forgetting one's lines or laughing uncontrollably.
– ORIGIN Middle English: alteration of archaic *corse* by association with Latin *corpus*.

corpse-candle ■ n. a lambent flame seen just above the ground in a churchyard or over a grave, superstitiously regarded as an omen of death.

corpulent /ˈkɔːpjul(ə)nt/ ■ adj. (of a person) fat.
– DERIVATIVES **corpulence** n. **corpulency** n.
– ORIGIN Middle English: from Latin *corpulentus*, from *corpus* 'body'.

cor pulmonale /ˌkɔː pʌlməˈnɑːli, -eɪli/ ■ n. Medicine abnormal enlargement of the right side of the heart as a result of disease of the lungs or the pulmonary blood vessels.
– ORIGIN C19: from Latin *cor* 'heart' + modern Latin *pulmonalis*, from Latin *pulmo(n-)* 'lung'.

corpus /ˈkɔːpəs/ ■ n. (pl. **corpora** or **corpuses**) **1** a body or collection of written texts. ▸ a collection of written or spoken material in machine-readable form. **2** Anatomy the main body or mass of a structure. ▸ the central part of the stomach, between the fundus and the antrum.
– ORIGIN Middle English: from Latin, 'body'.

corpus callosum /kəˈləʊsəm/ ■ n. (pl. **corpora callosa** /-sə/) Anatomy a broad band of nerve fibres joining the two hemispheres of the brain.
– ORIGIN C18: from **CORPUS** + Latin *callosum*, from *callosus* 'tough'.

corpus cavernosum /ˌkavəˈnəʊsəm/ ■ n. (pl. **corpora cavernosa** /-sə/) Anatomy either of two masses of erectile tissue forming the bulk of the penis and the clitoris.
– ORIGIN from **CORPUS** + Latin *cavernosum*, from *cavernosus* 'containing hollows'.

Corpus Christi /ˌkɔːpəs ˈkrɪsti/ ■ n. Christian Church a feast commemorating the institution of the Eucharist, observed on the Thursday after Trinity Sunday.
– ORIGIN Latin, 'body of Christ'.

corpuscle /ˈkɔːpʌs(ə)l/ ■ n. **1** Biology a minute body or cell in an organism, especially a red or white blood cell. **2** historical a minute particle regarded as the basic constituent of matter or light.
– DERIVATIVES **corpuscular** /kɔːˈpʌskjʊlə/ adj.
– ORIGIN C17: from Latin *corpusculum* 'small body', diminutive of *corpus*.

corpus delicti /dɪˈlɪktʌɪ/ ■ n. Law the facts and circumstances constituting a breach of a law.

– ORIGIN Latin, 'body of offence'.

corpus luteum /ˈluːtɪəm/ ■ n. (pl. **corpora lutea** /ˈluːtɪə/) Anatomy a hormone-secreting structure that develops in an ovary after an ovum has been discharged but degenerates after a few days unless pregnancy has begun.
– ORIGIN C18: from **CORPUS** + Latin *luteum*, from *luteus* 'yellow'.

corpus spongiosum /ˌspʌndʒɪˈəʊsəm/ ■ n. (pl. **corpora spongiosa** /-sə/) Anatomy a mass of erectile tissue alongside the corpora cavernosa of the penis and terminating in the glans.
– ORIGIN from **CORPUS** + Latin *spongiosum*, from *spongiosus* 'porous'.

corpus striatum /strʌɪˈeɪtəm/ ■ n. (pl. **corpora striata** /-sə/) Anatomy part of the basal ganglia of the brain, comprising the caudate and lentiform nuclei.
– ORIGIN from **CORPUS** + Latin *striatum*, from *striatus* 'grooved'.

corral /kəˈrɑːl/ ■ n. N. Amer. **1** a pen for livestock on a farm or ranch. **2** historical a defensive enclosure of wagons in an encampment. ■ v. (**corralled**, **corralling**) **1** chiefly N. Amer. put or keep (livestock) in a corral. ▸ gather (a group) together. **2** N. Amer. historical form (wagons) into a corral.
– ORIGIN C16: from Spanish and Old Portuguese, perhaps from Latin *currere* 'to run'.

correct ■ adj. **1** free from error; true; right. ▸ conforming to a particular political or ideological orthodoxy: *environmentally correct.* **2** conforming to accepted social standards. ■ v. put right. ▸ mark the errors in (a text). ▸ adjust (an instrument) to function accurately or accord with a standard. ▸ adjust (a numerical result or reading) to allow for departure from standard conditions.
– DERIVATIVES **correctable** adj. **correctly** adv. **correctness** n. **corrector** n.
– ORIGIN Middle English: from Latin *correct-*, *corrigere* 'make straight, amend', from *cor-* 'together' + *regere* 'guide'.

correction ■ n. **1** the action or process of correcting something. ▸ a change that rectifies an error or inaccuracy. ▸ a quantity adjusting a numerical result to allow for a departure from standard conditions. **2** N. Amer or dated punishment, especially that of criminals in prison.
– DERIVATIVES **correctional** adj.

correction fluid ■ n. an opaque liquid painted over a typed or written error to allow for the insertion of the correct character.

correctitude /kəˈrektɪtjuːd/ ■ n. correctness, especially conscious correctness in one's behaviour.

corrective ■ adj. designed to correct or counteract something undesirable. ■ n. a corrective measure.
– DERIVATIVES **correctively** adv.

correlate /ˈkɒrəleɪt, -rɪ-/ ■ v. have a relationship or connection in which one thing affects or depends on another. ▸ establish a correlation between. ■ n. each of two or more related or complementary things.
– ORIGIN C17: back-formation from **CORRELATION**.

correlation ■ n. **1** a mutual relationship or connection. ▸ the process of correlating two or more things. **2** Statistics interdependence of variable quantities.
– DERIVATIVES **correlational** adj.
– ORIGIN C16: from medieval Latin *correlatio(n-)*, from *cor-* 'together' + *relatio*, from *referre* 'bring back'.

correlation coefficient ■ n. Statistics a number between +1 and −1 calculated so as to represent the linear interdependence of two variables or sets of data. (Symbol: **r**.)

correlative /kəˈrelətɪv/ ■ adj. having a correlation.
– DERIVATIVES **correlatively** adv. **correlativity** n.
– ORIGIN C16: from medieval Latin *correlativus*, from *cor-* 'together' + late Latin *relativus* 'having reference or relation' (see **RELATE**).

correspond ■ v. **1** have a close similarity; match or agree almost exactly. ▸ be analogous or equivalent. **2** communicate by exchanging letters.
– DERIVATIVES **corresponding** adj. **correspondingly** adv.
– ORIGIN Middle English: from medieval Latin *correspondere*, from *cor-* 'together' + Latin *respondere* (see **RESPOND**).

correspondence ■ n. **1** the action or fact of corresponding. **2** letters sent or received.

correspondence course ■ n. a course of study in which student and tutors communicate by post.

correspondence theory ■ n. Philosophy the theory that states that the definition or criterion of truth is that true propositions correspond to the facts.

correspondent ■ n. 1 a person who writes letters, especially on a regular basis. 2 a journalist reporting on a particular subject or from a particular country. ■ adj. corresponding.

corresponding member ■ n. an honorary member of a learned society who has no voice in the society's affairs.

corridor ■ n. 1 a long passage from which doors lead into rooms. ▶ Brit. a passage along the side of a railway carriage giving access to compartments. 2 a belt of land linking two other areas or following a road or river.
– PHRASES **the corridors of power** the senior levels of government or administration.
– ORIGIN C16: from French, from Italian *corridore*, from *correre* 'to run', from Latin *currere*.

corrie /'kɒri/ ■ n. (pl. -ies) a cirque, especially one in the mountains of Scotland.
– ORIGIN C16: from Scottish Gaelic and Irish *coire* 'cauldron, hollow'.

corrigendum /ˌkɒrɪ'dʒɛndəm/ ■ n. (pl. corrigenda /-də/) a thing to be corrected, especially an error in a book.
– ORIGIN C19: Latin, from *corrigere* (see CORRECT).

corrigible /'kɒrɪdʒɪb(ə)l/ ■ adj. capable of being corrected or reformed.
– DERIVATIVES **corrigibility** n.
– ORIGIN Middle English: from medieval Latin *corrigibilis*, from Latin *corrigere* 'to correct'.

corroborate /kə'rɒbəreɪt/ ■ v. confirm or give support to (a statement or theory).
– DERIVATIVES **corroboration** n. **corroborative** adj. **corroborator** n. **corroboratory** adj.
– ORIGIN C16 (*corroboration* Middle English): from Latin *corroborare*, from *cor-* 'together' + *roborare*, from *robur* 'strength'.

corroboree /kə'rɒbəri/ ■ n. an Australian Aboriginal dance ceremony in the form of a sacred ritual or informal gathering.
– ORIGIN from Dharuk (an extinct Aboriginal language) *garaabara*, denoting a style of dancing.

corrode /kə'rəʊd/ ■ v. destroy or damage (metal or other hard material) slowly by chemical action. ▶ be destroyed or damaged in this way. ▶ gradually weaken or erode.
– DERIVATIVES **corrodible** adj.
– ORIGIN Middle English: from Latin *corrodere*, from *cor-* (expressing intensive force) + *rodere* 'gnaw'.

corrosion ■ n. the process of corroding or being corroded. ▶ damage caused by corrosion.

corrosive ■ adj. tending to cause corrosion. ■ n. a corrosive substance.
– DERIVATIVES **corrosively** adv. **corrosiveness** n.

corrugate /'kɒrʊgeɪt/ ■ v. contract into wrinkles or folds.
– ORIGIN Middle English: from Latin *corrugare* 'to wrinkle', from *cor-* (expressing intensive force) + *rugare*, from *ruga* 'a wrinkle'.

corrugated ■ adj. shaped into alternate ridges and grooves.
– DERIVATIVES **corrugation** n.

corrugated iron ■ n. iron which has been corrugated for added rigidity, typically produced in galvanized sheets.

corrugated paper ■ n. packaging material made from layers of thick paper, the top layer of which is corrugated for added strength and rigidity.

corrupt ■ adj. 1 willing to act dishonestly in return for money or personal gain. ▶ evil or morally depraved. 2 (of a text or a computer database or program) made unreliable by errors or alterations. 3 archaic rotten or putrid. ■ v. 1 cause to become corrupt. 2 debase by making errors. 3 archaic infect; contaminate.
– DERIVATIVES **corrupter** n. **corruptibility** n. **corruptible** adj. **corruptive** adj. **corruptly** adv.
– ORIGIN Middle English: from Latin *corrupt-, corrumpere* 'mar, bribe, destroy', from *cor-* 'altogether' + *rumpere* 'to break'.

corruption ■ n. 1 the action of corrupting or the state of being corrupt. 2 archaic the process of decay.

corsage /kɔː'sɑːʒ, 'kɔːsɑːʒ/ ■ n. 1 a spray of flowers worn pinned to a woman's clothes. 2 the upper part of a woman's dress.
– ORIGIN C19: French, from Old French *cors* 'body', from Latin *corpus*.

corsair /kɔː'sɛː, 'kɔːsɛː/ ■ n. archaic a pirate. ▶ historical a privateer, especially one operating along the southern shore of the Mediterranean.
– ORIGIN C16: from French *corsaire*, from medieval Latin *cursarius*, from *cursus* 'a raid', earlier 'course', from *currere* 'to run'.

corset ■ n. a woman's tightly fitting undergarment extending from below the chest to the hips, formerly worn to shape the figure. ▶ a similar garment worn to support a weak or injured back. ▶ historical a tightly fitting laced or stiffened outer bodice or dress.
– DERIVATIVES **corseted** adj. **corsetry** n.
– ORIGIN Middle English: from Old French, diminutive of *cors* 'body', from Latin *corpus*.

Corsican ■ n. 1 a native of Corsica. 2 the language of Corsica, which originated as a dialect of Italian. ■ adj. of or relating to Corsica or its language.

cortège /kɔː'teɪʒ, -'tɛʒ/ ■ n. 1 a solemn procession, especially for a funeral. 2 a person's entourage or retinue.
– ORIGIN C17: from Italian *corteggio*, from *corteggiare* 'attend court', from *corte* 'court', from Latin *cohors* 'retinue'.

cortex /'kɔːtɛks/ ■ n. (pl. cortices /-tɪˌsiːz/) 1 Anatomy the outer layer of an organ or structure, such as a kidney or adrenal gland. ▶ (also **cerebral cortex**) the outer, folded layer of the cerebrum, which plays an important role in consciousness. 2 Botany an outer layer of tissue immediately below the epidermis of a stem or root.
– DERIVATIVES **cortical** adj.
– ORIGIN Middle English: from Latin, 'bark'.

cortico- ■ comb. form representing CORTEX, used especially with reference to the adrenal and cerebral cortices.

corticosteroid /ˌkɔːtɪkəʊ'stɪərɔɪd, -'stɛrɔɪd/ ■ n. Biochemistry any of a group of steroid hormones produced in the adrenal cortex.

corticosterone /ˌkɔːtɪkəʊ'stɛrəʊn/ ■ n. Biochemistry a hormone secreted by the adrenal cortex, one of the glucocorticoids.

cortisol /'kɔːtɪsɒl/ ■ n. Biochemistry another term for HYDROCORTISONE.

cortisone /'kɔːtɪzəʊn/ ■ n. Biochemistry a hormone produced by the adrenal cortex or made synthetically, used as an anti-inflammatory and anti-allergy agent.
– ORIGIN 1940s: from elements of its chemical name *17-hydroxy-11-dehydrocorticosterone*.

corundum /kə'rʌndəm/ ■ n. extremely hard crystallized alumina, used as an abrasive.
– ORIGIN C18: from Tamil *kuruntam* and Telugu *kuruvindam*.

coruscate /'kɒrəskeɪt/ ■ v. poetic/literary (of light) flash or sparkle.
– DERIVATIVES **coruscation** n.
– ORIGIN C18: from Latin *coruscare* 'glitter'.

corvette /kɔː'vɛt/ ■ n. a small warship designed for convoy escort duty. ▶ historical a flush-decked sailing warship with one tier of guns.
– ORIGIN C17: from Dutch *korf*, denoting a kind of ship, + -ETTE.

corvid /'kɔːvɪd/ ■ n. Ornithology a bird of the crow family (Corvidae); a crow.
– ORIGIN C20: from Latin *corvus* 'raven'.

corvine /'kɔːvaɪn/ ■ adj. of or like a raven or crow, especially in colour.
– ORIGIN C17: from Latin *corvinus*, from *corvus* 'raven'.

corybantic /ˌkɒrɪ'bantɪk/ ■ adj. wild; frenzied.
– ORIGIN C17: from *Corybantes*, Latin name of the priests of Cybele, a Phrygian goddess of nature who performed wild dances, from Greek *Korubantes*.

corymb /'kɒrɪmb/ ■ n. Botany a flower cluster whose lower stalks are proportionally longer so that the flowers form a

coryphée

flat or slightly convex head.
- DERIVATIVES **corymbose** adj.
- ORIGIN C18: from Latin *corymbus*, from Greek *korumbos* 'cluster'.

coryphée /'kɒrɪfeɪ/ ■ n. a leading dancer in a corps de ballet.
- ORIGIN French, from Greek *koruphaios* 'leader of a chorus', from *koruphē* 'head'.

cos[1] /kɒs/ ■ n. lettuce of a variety with crisp narrow leaves that form a tall head.
- ORIGIN C17: named after the Aegean island of *Cos*, where it originated.

cos[2] /kɒz, kɒs/ ■ abbrev. cosine.

cos[3] /kɒz, kəz/ (also **'cos** or **coz**) ■ conj. informal short for BECAUSE.

Cosa Nostra /ˌkəʊzə ˈnɒstrə/ ■ n. a US criminal organization resembling and related to the Mafia.
- ORIGIN Italian, 'our affair'.

COSATU /kɒˈsɑːtuː/ (also **Cosatu**) ■ abbrev. Congress of South African Trade Unions.

cosec /ˈkəʊsɛk/ ■ abbrev. cosecant.

cosecant /kəʊˈsiːk(ə)nt, -ˈsɛk-/ ■ n. Mathematics the ratio of the hypotenuse (in a right-angled triangle) to the side opposite an acute angle; the reciprocal of sine.
- ORIGIN C18: from **co-** + Latin *secant-*, *secare* 'to cut'.

cosh[1] ■ n. a thick heavy stick or bar used as a weapon. ■ v. hit on the head with a cosh.
- PHRASES **under the cosh** under threat, at the mercy of someone or something.
- ORIGIN C19.

cosh[2] /kɒʃ, kɒsˈeɪtʃ/ ■ abbrev. Mathematics hyperbolic cosine.
- ORIGIN from **cos**[2] + **-h** for *hyperbolic*.

co-signatory ■ n. a person or state signing a treaty or other document jointly with others.

cosine /ˈkəʊsaɪn/ ■ n. Mathematics the trigonometric function that is equal to the ratio of the side adjacent to an acute angle (in a right-angled triangle) to the hypotenuse.

co-sleeping ■ n. the practice of parents allowing a young child to sleep in the same bed as them.
- DERIVATIVES **co-sleep** v.

cosmetic ■ adj. 1 relating to treatment intended to improve a person's appearance. 2 affecting only the appearance of something. ■ n. (**cosmetics**) cosmetic preparations, especially for the face.
- DERIVATIVES **cosmetically** adv.
- ORIGIN C17: from French *cosmétique*, from Greek, from *kosmein* 'arrange, adorn', from *kosmos* 'order, adornment'.

cosmetician /ˌkɒzməˈtɪʃ(ə)n/ ■ n. N. Amer. a person who sells or applies cosmetics as an occupation.

cosmetology /ˌkɒzmɪˈtɒlədʒi/ ■ n. the professional application of cosmetic preparations and techniques.
- DERIVATIVES **cosmetological** adj. **cosmetologist** n.

cosmic ■ adj. of or relating to the universe or cosmos, especially as distinct from the earth.
- DERIVATIVES **cosmical** adj. **cosmically** adv.

cosmic dust ■ n. small particles of matter distributed throughout space.

cosmic radiation ■ n. radiation consisting of cosmic rays.

cosmic ray ■ n. a highly energetic atomic nucleus or other particle travelling through space at a speed approaching that of light.

cosmic string ■ n. see STRING (in sense 7).

cosmo- /ˈkɒzməʊ/ ■ comb. form of or relating to the world or the universe: *cosmography*.
- ORIGIN from Greek *kosmos* 'order, world'.

cosmogenesis /ˌkɒzməˈ(ʊ)dʒɛnɪsɪs/ ■ n. the origin or evolution of the universe.
- DERIVATIVES **cosmogenetic** adj. **cosmogenic** adj.

cosmogony /kɒzˈmɒɡəni/ ■ n. (pl. **-ies**) the branch of science concerned with the origin of the universe, especially the solar system.
- DERIVATIVES **cosmogonic** /-məˈɡɒnɪk/ adj. **cosmogonical** /-məˈɡɒnɪk(ə)l/ adj. **cosmogonist** n.
- ORIGIN C17: from Greek *kosmogonia*, from *kosmos* 'order, world' + *-gonia* '-begetting'.

cosmography ■ n. (pl. **-ies**) 1 the branch of science which deals with the general features of the universe, including the earth. 2 a description or representation of the universe or the earth.
- DERIVATIVES **cosmographer** n. **cosmographic** adj. **cosmographical** adj.

cosmology ■ n. (pl. **-ies**) the science of the origin and development of the universe. ▸ an account or theory of the origin of the universe.
- DERIVATIVES **cosmological** adj. **cosmologist** n.

cosmonaut ■ n. a Russian astronaut.
- ORIGIN 1950s: from **COSMOS**[1], on the pattern of *astronaut* and Russian *kosmonavt*.

cosmopolis /kɒzˈmɒp(ə)lɪs/ ■ n. a city inhabited by people from many different countries.
- ORIGIN C19: from Greek *kosmos* 'world' + *polis* 'city'.

cosmopolitan /ˌkɒzməˈpɒlɪt(ə)n/ ■ adj. 1 familiar with or representative of many different countries and cultures. ▸ having an exciting and glamorous character associated with travel and a mixture of cultures. 2 (of a plant or animal) found all over the world. ■ n. a cosmopolitan person, plant, or animal.
- DERIVATIVES **cosmopolitanism** n. **cosmopolitanize** (also **-ise**) v.
- ORIGIN C17: from Greek *kosmopolitēs*, from *kosmos* 'world' + *politēs* 'citizen'.

cosmos[1] ■ n. the universe seen as a well-ordered whole.
- ORIGIN Middle English: from Greek *kosmos* 'order, world'.

cosmos[2] ■ n. a plant of the daisy family with white, pink, or red flowers, which is native to Central America but a common weed in southern Africa. [Genus *Cosmos*.]
- ORIGIN from Greek *kosmos* in the sense 'ornament'.

Cossack /ˈkɒsak/ ■ n. a member of a people of southern Russia, Ukraine, and Siberia, noted for their horsemanship and military skill. ▸ a member of a Cossack military unit.
- ORIGIN from Russian *kazak*, from Turkic, 'vagabond, nomad'; later influenced by French *Cosaque*.

cosset ■ v. (**cosseted**, **cosseting**) care for and protect in an overindulgent way.
- ORIGIN C16: prob. from Anglo-Norman French *coscet* 'cottager', from Old English *cotsǣta*.

cossie (also **cozzie**) ■ n. (pl. **-ies**) informal a swimming costume or a pair of swimming trunks.

cost ■ v. (past and past part. **cost**) 1 require the payment of (a specified sum) in order to be bought or obtained. ▸ cause or require the expenditure or loss of. ▸ informal be expensive for: *it'll cost you*. 2 (past and past part. **costed**) estimate the price or cost of. ■ n. the amount that something costs. ▸ the effort or loss necessary to achieve something. ▸ (**costs**) legal expenses, especially those allowed in favour of the winning party or against the losing party in a suit.
- PHRASES **at all costs** (or **at any cost**) regardless of the price or the effort needed. **at cost** at cost price. **cost someone dear** (or **dearly**) involve someone in a serious loss or a heavy penalty. **to someone's cost** with loss or disadvantage to someone.
- ORIGIN Middle English: from Old French *coust* (n.), *couster* (v.), from Latin *constare* 'stand firm, stand at a price'.

costa ■ n. (pl. **costae** /ˈkɒstiː/) 1 Botany & Zoology a rib, midrib, or rib-like structure. 2 Entomology the main vein running along the leading edge of an insect's wing.
- DERIVATIVES **costal** adj.
- ORIGIN C19: from Latin.

cost accounting ■ n. the recording of all the costs incurred in a business in a way that can be used to improve its management.
- DERIVATIVES **cost accountant** n.

co-star ■ n. a performer appearing with another or others of equal importance. ■ v. appear in a production as a co-star. ▸ (of a production) include as a co-star.

Costa Rican /ˈriːkən/ ■ n. a native of inhabitant of Costa Rica, a republic in Central America. ■ adj. of or relating to Costa Rica.

cost centre ■ n. a department or other unit within an organization to which costs may be charged for accounting purposes.

cost-effective ■ adj. effective or productive in relation to its cost.
– DERIVATIVES **cost-effectively** adv. **cost-effectiveness** n.

cost-efficient ■ adj. another term for COST-EFFECTIVE.
– DERIVATIVES **cost-efficiency** n.

costermonger /ˈkɒstəmʌŋɡə/ ■ n. Brit. dated a person who sells goods, especially fruit and vegetables, from a handcart in the street.
– ORIGIN C16: from *Costard*, denoting a kind of apple + -MONGER.

costing ■ n. the estimated cost of producing or undertaking something.

costive /ˈkɒstɪv/ ■ adj. constipated.
– DERIVATIVES **costively** adv. **costiveness** n.
– ORIGIN Middle English: from Latin *constipare* (see CONSTIPATE).

costly ■ adj. (-ier, -iest) 1 expensive. 2 causing suffering, loss, or disadvantage.
– DERIVATIVES **costliness** n.

costmary /ˈkɒstmɛːri/ ■ n. (pl. -ies) an aromatic plant of the daisy family, formerly used in medicine and for flavouring ale prior to the use of hops. [*Balsamita major*.]
– ORIGIN Middle English: from obsolete *cost*, from Greek *kostos*, from Sanskrit *kuṣṭha*, denoting an aromatic plant, + *Mary*, the mother of Christ.

cost-benefit ■ adj. relating to a process that assesses the relation between the cost of an undertaking and the value of the resulting benefits: *a cost–benefit analysis*.

cost of living ■ n. the level of prices relating to a range of everyday items.

cost-plus ■ adj. denoting a method of pricing something in which a fixed profit factor is added to the costs.

cost price ■ n. the price at which goods are bought by a retailer.

cost-push ■ adj. relating to or denoting inflation caused by increased labour or raw material costs.

costume ■ n. a set of clothes in a style typical of a particular country or historical period. ▶ a set of clothes worn by an actor or performer for a role. ▶ Brit. dated a woman's matching jacket and skirt. ■ v. dress in a particular set of clothes.
– ORIGIN C18: from French, from Italian *custume* 'custom, fashion', from Latin *consuetudo* (see CUSTOM).

costume drama ■ n. a television or cinema production set in a historical period.

costume jewellery ■ n. jewellery made with inexpensive materials or imitation gems.

costumier /kɒˈstjuːmɪə/ (US also **costumer** /-mə/) ■ n. a maker or supplier of theatrical or fancy-dress costumes.
– ORIGIN C19: French, from *costumer* (see COSTUME).

cosy (US **cozy**) ■ adj. (-ier, -iest) 1 comfortable, warm, and secure. 2 not seeking or offering challenge or difficulty. ▶ informal, derogatory (of a transaction or arrangement) beneficial to all those involved and possibly somewhat unscrupulous. ■ n. (pl. -ies) a cover to keep a teapot or a boiled egg hot. ■ v. (-ies, -ied) informal make (someone) feel cosy. ▶ (**cosy up to**) snuggle up to or ingratiate oneself with.
– DERIVATIVES **cosily** adv. **cosiness** n.
– ORIGIN C18 (orig. Scots).

cot[1] ■ n. a small bed with high barred sides for a baby or very young child. ▶ a plain narrow bed. ▶ N. Amer. a camp bed. ▶ Nautical a bed resembling a hammock hung from deck beams, formerly used by officers.
– ORIGIN C17: from Hindi *khāṭ* 'bedstead, hammock'.

cot[2] ■ abbrev. Mathematics cotangent.

cotangent /kəʊˈtandʒ(ə)nt/ ■ n. Mathematics (in a right-angled triangle) the ratio of the side (other than the hypotenuse) adjacent to a particular acute angle to the side opposite the angle.

cot death ■ n. the unexplained death of a baby in its sleep.

coterie /ˈkəʊt(ə)ri/ ■ n. (pl. -ies) a small exclusive group of people with shared interests or tastes.
– ORIGIN C18: from French, from Middle Low German *kote* 'cote'.

coterminous /kəʊˈtəːmɪnəs/ ■ adj. having the same boundaries or extent.
– ORIGIN C18: from Latin *conterminus*, from *con-* 'with' + *terminus* 'boundary'.

coth /kɒθ, kɒtˈeɪtʃ/ ■ abbrev. hyperbolic cotangent.
– ORIGIN from COT[2] + *-h* for *hyperbolic*.

cotillion /kəˈtɪljən/ ■ n. 1 an 18th-century French dance based on the contredanse. ▶ US a quadrille. 2 US a formal ball, especially one at which debutantes are presented.
– ORIGIN C18: from French *cotillon* 'petticoat dance', diminutive of *cotte*, from Old French *cote*.

cotoneaster /kəˌtəʊnɪˈastə/ ■ n. a small-leaved shrub of the rose family, cultivated as a hedging plant or for its bright red berries. [Genus *Cotoneaster*.]
– ORIGIN C18: from Latin *cotoneum* (see QUINCE) + -ASTER.

cotta /ˈkɒtə/ ■ n. a short garment resembling a surplice, worn typically by Catholic priests and servers.
– ORIGIN C19: from Italian; rel. to COAT.

cottage ■ n. 1 a small simple house, typically one in the country. 2 informal (in the context of casual homosexual encounters) a public toilet. ■ v. [usu. as noun **cottaging**] informal perform homosexual acts in a public toilet.
– DERIVATIVES **cottagey** adj.
– ORIGIN Middle English: from Anglo-Norman French *cotage* and Anglo-Latin *cotagium*.

cottage cheese ■ n. soft, lumpy white cheese made from the curds of skimmed milk.

cottage garden ■ n. chiefly Brit. an informal garden stocked typically with colourful flowering plants.

cottage industry ■ n. Brit. a business or manufacturing activity carried on in people's homes.

cottage loaf ■ n. Brit. a loaf made from two round pieces of dough, the smaller on top of the larger.

cottage pie ■ n. a dish of minced meat topped with browned mashed potato.

cottager ■ n. a person living in a cottage.

cotter pin ■ n. a metal pin used to fasten two parts of a mechanism together. ▶ a split pin that is opened out after being passed through a hole.
– ORIGIN C17.

cotton ■ n. 1 a soft white fibrous substance which surrounds the seeds of the cotton plant and is used as textile fibre and thread for sewing. 2 (also **cotton batting**) N. Amer. cotton wool. 3 (also **cotton plant**) the tropical and subtropical plant commercially grown for this product. [Genus *Gossypium*.] ■ v. informal 1 (**cotton on**) begin to understand. 2 (**cotton to**) N. Amer. have a liking for.
– DERIVATIVES **cottony** adj.
– ORIGIN Middle English: from Old French *coton*, from Arabic *kuṭn*.

cotton bud ■ n. a small wad of cotton wool on a short thin stick, used for cosmetic purposes or cleaning the ears.

cotton candy ■ n. N. Amer. candyfloss.

cotton lavender ■ n. a shrubby aromatic plant of the daisy family, with lavender-like foliage and yellow button flowers. [Genus *Santolina*: several species.]

cottonmouth (also **cottonmouth moccasin**) ■ n. a large, dangerous semiaquatic pit viper of the south-eastern US, which opens its mouth wide to display the white interior when threatening. [*Agkistrodon piscivorus*.]

cottonseed cake (also Brit. **cotton cake**) ■ n. compressed cotton seed, used as food for cattle.

cotton swab ■ n. N. Amer. a cotton bud.

cottontail ■ n. an American rabbit which has a speckled brownish coat and a white underside to the tail. [Genus *Sylvilagus*.]

cottonwood ■ n. a North American poplar with seeds covered in white cottony hairs. [*Populus deltoides* and other species.]

cotton wool ■ n. 1 fluffy wadding of a kind originally made from raw cotton, used especially for cleaning the skin or bathing wounds. 2 US raw cotton.
– PHRASES **wrap someone in cotton wool** be overprotective towards someone.

cottony-cushion scale ▪ n. another term for AUSTRALIAN BUG.

cotyledon /ˌkɒtɪˈliːd(ə)n/ ▪ n. **1** Botany an embryonic leaf in seed-bearing plants, one or more of which are the first leaves to appear from a germinating seed. **2** a succulent plant of the stonecrop family. [Genus *Cotyledon*.]
–DERIVATIVES **cotyledonary** adj.
–ORIGIN C16: from Latin, 'navelwort', from Greek *kotulēdōn* 'cup-shaped cavity'.

coucal /ˈkuːk(ə)l, ˈkʊkɑːl/ ▪ n. a large, ungainly ground-dwelling bird of the cuckoo family. [Genera *Centropus* and *Coua*: numerous species.]
–ORIGIN C19: from French, perhaps a blend of *coucou* 'cuckoo' and *alouette* 'lark'.

couch[1] /kaʊtʃ/ ▪ n. a long upholstered piece of furniture for several people to sit on. ▸ a reclining seat with a headrest at one end on which a psychoanalyst's subject or doctor's patient lies while undergoing treatment. ▪ v. **1** (usu. **be couched in**) express in language of a specified style. **2** poetic/literary lie down. **3** (in embroidery) fix (a thread) to a fabric by stitching it down flat with another thread.
–ORIGIN Middle English: from Old French *couche* (n.), *coucher* (v.), from Latin *collocare* (see COLLOCATION).

couch[2] /kaʊtʃ, kuːtʃ/ (also **couch grass**) ▪ n. a coarse grass with long creeping roots. [*Elymus repens* and other species.]
–ORIGIN C16.

couchant /ˈkaʊtʃ(ə)nt/ ▪ adj. [usu. postpos.] Heraldry (of an animal) lying with the body resting on the legs and the head raised.
–ORIGIN Middle English: French, 'lying', from *coucher* (see COUCH[1]).

couchette /kuːˈʃɛt/ ▪ n. a railway carriage with seats convertible into sleeping berths. ▸ a berth in such a carriage.
–ORIGIN 1920s: French, diminutive of *couche* 'a couch'.

couch potato ▪ n. informal a person who spends a great deal of time watching television.

cougar /ˈkuːɡə/ ▪ n. North American term for PUMA.
–ORIGIN C18: from French *couguar*, abbrev. of modern Latin *cuguarcuarana*, from Guarani *guaçuarana*.

cough /kɒf/ ▪ v. **1** expel air from the lungs with a sudden sharp sound. **2** (of an engine) make a sudden harsh noise, especially as a sign of malfunction. **3** (**cough up**) informal give something, especially money, reluctantly. ▸ informal reveal information; confess. ▪ n. an act or sound of coughing. ▸ a condition of the respiratory organs causing coughing.
–DERIVATIVES **cougher** n.
–ORIGIN Middle English: imitative.

cough drop (also **cough sweet**) ▪ n. a medicated lozenge sucked to relieve a cough.

cough mixture ▪ n. liquid medicine taken to relieve a cough.

could ▪ modal v. past of CAN[1]. ▸ used in making suggestions or polite requests: *could I use the phone?*

couldn't ▪ contr. could not.

coulis /ˈkuːli/ ▪ n. (pl. same) a thin fruit or vegetable purée, used as a sauce.
–ORIGIN French, from *couler* 'to flow'.

coulisse /kuːˈliːs/ ▪ n. a flat piece of scenery at the side of the stage in a theatre. ▸ (**the coulisses**) the wings.
–ORIGIN C19: from French *coulis* 'sliding'.

couloir /ˈkuːlwɑː/ ▪ n. a steep, narrow gully on a mountainside.
–ORIGIN C19: French, 'gully, corridor'.

coulomb /ˈkuːlɒm/ (abbrev.: **C**) ▪ n. Physics the SI unit of electric charge, equal to the quantity of electricity conveyed in one second by a current of one ampere.
–ORIGIN C19: named after the French military engineer Charles-Augustin de *Coulomb*.

Coulomb's law /ˈkuːlɒmz/ ▪ n. Physics a law stating that like electric charges repel and opposite charges attract, with a force proportional to the product of the charges and inversely proportional to the square of the distance between them.

coulter /ˈkəʊltə/ (US **colter**) ▪ n. a vertical cutting blade fixed in front of a ploughshare. ▸ the part of a seed drill that makes the furrow for the seed.
–ORIGIN Old English, from Latin *culter* 'knife, ploughshare'.

council ▪ n. **1** a formally constituted advisory, deliberative, or administrative body. ▸ a body elected to manage the affairs of a city, county, or district. **2** [as modifier] Brit. denoting housing provided by a local council.
–ORIGIN Old English: from Anglo-Norman French *cuncile*, from Latin *concilium* 'convocation, assembly'.

councillor (US also **councilor**) ▪ n. a member of a council.
–DERIVATIVES **councillorship** n.

USAGE
On the difference between **councillor** and **counsellor**, see usage at COUNSELLOR.

councilman (or **councilwoman**) ▪ n. (pl. **-men** or **-women**) chiefly US a councillor.

council of war ▪ n. a gathering of military officers in wartime. ▸ a meeting held to plan a response to an emergency.

counsel ▪ n. **1** advice, especially that given formally. **2** (pl. same) an advocate or other legal adviser conducting a case. ▪ v. (**counselled**, **counselling**; US **counseled**, **counseling**) **1** give advice to. ▸ recommend (a course of action). **2** [often as noun **counselling**] give professional help and advice to (someone) to resolve personal, social, or psychological problems.
–PHRASES **a counsel of despair** an action to be taken when all else fails. **a counsel of perfection** advice that is ideal but not feasible. **keep one's own counsel** not confide in others. **take counsel** discuss a problem.
–ORIGIN Middle English: via Old French *counseil* (n.), *conseiller* (v.), from Latin *consilium* 'consultation, advice'.

counsellor (US **counselor**) ▪ n. **1** a person trained to give guidance on personal, social, or psychological problems. **2** a senior officer in the diplomatic service. **3** (also **counselor-at-law**) US & Irish an advocate.

USAGE
The words **counsellor** and **councillor** are often confused. A **counsellor** is a person who gives advice or counsel, especially on personal problems (*a marriage counsellor*), whereas a **councillor** is a member of a city, county, or other council (*she stood as an ANC candidate for city councillor*).

count[1] ▪ v. **1** determine the total number of. **2** recite numbers in ascending order. ▸ (**count down**) recite or display numbers backwards to zero to indicate remaining time, especially before the launch of a rocket. **3** (**count someone out**) complete a count of ten seconds over a fallen boxer to indicate defeat. **4** (**count something out**) take out items one by one, keeping a note of how many one takes. **5** take into account; include. ▸ (**count someone in**) or **out** include (or not include) someone in a planned activity. **6** regard or be regarded as possessing a quality or fulfilling a role: *people she had counted as her friends*. **7** matter: *it was the critics that counted*. **8** (**count on/upon**) rely on. ▪ n. **1** an act of counting. ▸ the total determined by counting. ▸ a referee's count of up to ten seconds when a boxer is knocked down. **2** a point for discussion or consideration. ▸ Law a separate charge in an indictment.
–PHRASES **count one's blessings** be grateful for what one has. **count the cost** calculate the consequences of a careless or foolish action. **count the days** (or **hours**) be impatient for time to pass. **keep** (or **lose**) **count** take note of (or forget) the number or amount when counting. **out** (or N. Amer. also **down**) **for the count** Boxing defeated by being knocked to the ground and unable to rise within ten seconds.
–DERIVATIVES **countable** adj.
–ORIGIN Middle English: from Old French *counte* (n.), *counter* (v.), from Latin *computare* (see COMPUTE).

count[2] ▪ n. a foreign nobleman whose rank corresponds to that of an earl.

– ORIGIN Middle English: from Old French *conte*, from Latin *comes*, *comit-* 'companion, overseer, attendant'.

countback ■ n. a method of deciding the winner of a tied game or competition by awarding it to the contestant with the better score in the later part.

countdown ■ n. **1** an act of counting down to zero, especially before the launching of a rocket. **2** the final moments before a significant event. **3** a digital display that counts down.

countenance /ˈkaʊnt(ə)nəns, -tɪn-/ ■ n. a person's face or facial expression. ■ v. admit as acceptable or possible.
– PHRASES **keep one's countenance** maintain one's composure. **out of countenance** disconcerted or unpleasantly surprised.
– ORIGIN Middle English: from Old French *contenance* 'bearing, behaviour', from *contenir* (see **CONTAIN**).

counter[1] ■ n. **1** a long flat-topped fitment across which business is conducted in a shop or food and drinks are served. ▸ chiefly N. Amer. a worktop. **2** a small disc used in board games for keeping the score or as a place marker. ▸ a token representing a coin. **3** a factor used to give one party an advantage in negotiations. **4** a person or thing that counts something. ▸ Physics an apparatus used for counting individual ionizing particles or events.
– PHRASES **over the counter** by ordinary retail purchase, with no need for a prescription or licence. ▸ (of share transactions) taking place outside the stock exchange system. **under the counter** (or **table**) (with reference to goods bought or sold) surreptitiously and illegally.
– ORIGIN Middle English: from Old French *conteor*, from medieval Latin *computatorium*, from Latin *computare* (see **COMPUTE**).

counter[2] ■ v. **1** speak or act in opposition or response to. **2** Boxing give a return blow while parrying. ■ adv. (**counter to**) in the opposite direction to or in conflict with. ■ adj. responding to something of the same kind, especially in opposition: *argument and counter argument*. ■ n. **1** an act or speech which counters something else. **2** Boxing a counterpunch. **3** the curved part of the stern of a ship projecting aft above the waterline. **4** Printing the white space enclosed by a letter such as *O* or *c*.
– ORIGIN Middle English: from Old French *contre*, from Latin *contra* 'against'.

counter- ■ prefix denoting opposition, retaliation, or rivalry: *counter-attack*. ▸ denoting movement or effect in the opposite direction: *counterpoise*. ▸ denoting correspondence, duplication, or substitution: *counterpart*.
– ORIGIN from Anglo-Norman French *countre-*, Old French *contre*, from Latin *contra* 'against'.

counteract ■ v. act against (something) in order to reduce its force or neutralize it.
– DERIVATIVES **counteraction** n. **counteractive** adj.

counter-attack ■ n. an attack made in response to one by an enemy or opponent. ■ v. attack in response.
– DERIVATIVES **counter-attacker** n.

counter-attraction ■ n. a rival attraction.

counterbalance ■ n. /ˈkaʊntəˌbal(ə)ns/ **1** a weight that balances another. **2** a factor having the opposite effect to that of another, preventing it from exercising a disproportionate influence. ■ v. /ˌkaʊntəˈbal(ə)ns/ be a counterbalance to.

counterblast ■ n. a strongly worded reply to someone else's views.

counterbore ■ n. **1** a drilled hole which has a wider section at the top. **2** a drill whose bit has a uniform smaller diameter near the tip, for drilling counterbores. ■ v. drill a counterbore in.

counterchange ■ v. Heraldry interchange the tinctures of (a charge) with that of a divided field. ■ n. **1** change that is opposite in effect to a previous change. **2** patterning in which a dark motif on a light ground alternates with the same motif light on a dark ground.

counterclaim ■ n. a claim made to rebut a previous claim. ▸ Law a claim made by a defendant against the plaintiff. ■ v. chiefly Law make a counterclaim.

counterclockwise ■ adv. & adj. North American term for **ANTICLOCKWISE**.

counterculture ■ n. a way of life and set of attitudes at variance with the prevailing social norm.

countersink

counter-espionage ■ n. activities designed to prevent or thwart spying by an enemy.

counterfactual Philosophy ■ adj. relating to or expressing what has not happened or is not the case. ■ n. a counterfactual conditional statement (e.g. *If kangaroos had no tails, they would topple over*).

counterfeit ■ adj. made in exact imitation of something valuable with the intention to deceive or defraud. ▸ archaic pretended; sham. ■ n. a forgery. ■ v. imitate fraudulently. ▸ poetic/literary resemble closely.
– DERIVATIVES **counterfeiter** n.
– ORIGIN Middle English: from Anglo-Norman French *countrefeter*, from Old French *contrefaire*, from Latin *contra-* 'in opposition' + *facere* 'make'.

counterfoil ■ n. the part of a cheque, ticket, etc. that is kept as a record by the person issuing it.

counter-insurgency ■ n. military or political action taken against guerrillas or revolutionaries.

counter-intelligence ■ n. counter-espionage.

counter-intuitive ■ adj. contrary to intuition or to common-sense expectation.
– DERIVATIVES **counter-intuitively** adv.

countermand /ˌkaʊntəˈmɑːnd/ ■ v. revoke (an order).
– ORIGIN Middle English: from Old French *contremander* (v.), from medieval Latin *contramandare*, from Latin *contra-* 'against' + *mandare* 'to order'.

countermeasure ■ n. an action taken to counteract a danger or threat.

counterpane ■ n. dated a bedspread.
– ORIGIN C17: alteration of **COUNTERPOINT**, from medieval Latin *culcitra puncta* 'quilted mattress'.

counterpart ■ n. a person or thing that corresponds to or has the same function as another.

counterpoint ■ n. **1** Music the technique of setting, writing, or playing a melody or melodies in conjunction with another, according to fixed rules. ▸ a melody played in conjunction with another. **2** an idea or theme contrasting with the main element. ■ v. **1** Music add counterpoint to (a melody). **2** emphasize by contrast. **3** compensate for.
– ORIGIN Middle English: from Old French *contrepoint*, from medieval Latin *contrapunctum*.

counterpoise ■ n. a factor or force that balances or neutralizes another. ▸ a counterbalancing weight. ■ v. have an opposing and balancing effect on. ▸ bring into contrast.
– ORIGIN Middle English: from Old French *contrepois*, from *contre* 'against' + *pois*, from Latin *pensum* 'weight'.

counterpose ■ v. set against or in opposition to.
– DERIVATIVES **counterposition** n.

counterproductive ■ adj. having the opposite of the desired effect.

counterpunch Boxing ■ n. a punch thrown in return for one received. ■ v. throw a counterpunch.
– DERIVATIVES **counterpuncher** n.

Counter-Reformation ■ n. the reform of the Church of Rome in the 16th and 17th centuries which was stimulated by the Protestant Reformation.

counter-revolution ■ n. a revolution opposing a former one or reversing its results.
– DERIVATIVES **counter-revolutionary** adj. & n.

counterrotate ■ v. rotate in opposite directions, especially about the same axis.
– DERIVATIVES **counterrotation** n.

countershading ■ n. Zoology protective coloration used by some animals in which parts normally in shadow are light and those exposed to the sky are dark.
– DERIVATIVES **countershaded** adj.

countershaft ■ n. a machine driveshaft that transmits motion from the main shaft to where it is required.

countersign ■ v. add a signature to (a document already signed by another person).
– DERIVATIVES **countersignature** n.

countersink ■ v. (past and past part. **-sunk**) enlarge and bevel the rim of (a drilled hole) so that a screw or bolt can be inserted flush with the surface. ▶ drive (a screw or bolt) into such a hole.

countertenor ■ n. Music the highest male adult singing voice.

counterterrorism ■ n. political or military activities designed to prevent or thwart terrorism.
–DERIVATIVES **counterterrorist** n.

countertop ■ n. chiefly N. Amer. a worktop.

countertrade ■ n. international trade by exchange of goods rather than by currency purchase.

counter-transference ■ n. Psychoanalysis the emotional reaction of the analyst to the subject's contribution.

countervail /ˌkaʊntəˈveɪl/ ■ v. [usu. as adj. **countervailing**] offset the effect of (something) by countering it with something of equal force.
–ORIGIN Middle English: from Anglo-Norman French *contrevaloir*, from Latin *contra valere* 'be of worth against'.

counterweight ■ n. a counterbalancing weight.

countess ■ n. the wife or widow of a count or earl. ▶ a woman holding the rank of count or earl.

counting ■ prep. taking account of; including: *there were three of us, or four counting the baby.*

counting house ■ n. historical a place where the accounts and money of a person or company were kept.

countless ■ adj. too many to be counted; very many.

count noun ■ n. Grammar a noun that can form a plural and, in the singular, can be used with the indefinite article (e.g. *books, a book*). Contrasted with MASS NOUN.

countrified ■ adj. chiefly Brit. characteristic of the country, especially in being unsophisticated.

country ■ n. (pl. **-ies**) **1** a nation with its own government, occupying a particular territory. **2** districts outside large urban areas. **3** an area or region with regard to its physical features: *a tract of wild country.*
–PHRASES **across country** not keeping to roads. **go to the country** Brit. dissolve Parliament and hold a general election. **line of country** Brit. a subject in which a person is skilled or knowledgeable.
ORIGIN Middle English: from Old French *cuntree*, from medieval Latin *contrata* (*terra*) '(land) lying opposite', from Latin *contra* 'against, opposite'.

country and western ■ n. country music.

country club ■ n. a club with sporting and social facilities, set in a rural area.

country cousin ■ n. an unsophisticated and provincial person.

country dance ■ n. a traditional type of social English dance, in particular one performed by couples facing each other in long lines.

country house ■ n. a large house in the country, typically the seat of a wealthy or aristocratic family.

countryman (or **countrywoman**) ■ n. (pl. **-men** or **-women**) **1** a person living or born in the country. **2** a person from the same country as someone else: *my fellow countryman.*

country mile ■ n. informal a very long way.

country music ■ n. a form of popular music originating in the rural southern US, characteristically featuring guitar and pedal steel guitar.

country rock[1] ■ n. Geology the rock which encloses a mineral deposit, igneous intrusion, or other feature.

country rock[2] ■ n. a type of popular music that is a blend of rock and country music.

countryside ■ n. the land and scenery of a rural area.

countrywide ■ adj. & adv. extending throughout a nation.

county ■ n. (pl. **-ies**) **1** a territorial division of some countries, forming the chief unit of local administration. ▶ US a political and administrative division of a state. **2** [as modifier] Brit. of or denoting aristocratic people with an ancestral home in a particular county.
–ORIGIN Middle English: from Old French *conte*, from Latin *comitatus*, from *comes* (see COUNT[2]).

county council ■ n. (in the UK) the elected governing body of an administrative county.
–DERIVATIVES **county councillor** n.

county court ■ n. (in England and Wales) a judicial court for civil cases. ▶ US a court for civil and criminal cases.

county town (N. Amer. **county seat**) ■ n. the town that is the administrative capital of a county.

coup /kuː/ ■ n. (pl. **coups** /kuːz/) **1** (also **coup d'état**) a sudden violent seizure of power from a government. **2** an unexpected and notably successful act. **3** Billiards a direct pocketing of the cue ball, which is a foul stroke.
–ORIGIN C18: from French, from medieval Latin *colpus* (see COPE[1]).

coup de foudre /ˌkuː də ˈfuːdr(ə)/ ■ n. (pl. **coups de foudre** pronunc. same) a sudden unforeseen event, especially love at first sight.
–ORIGIN French, 'stroke of lightning'.

coup de grâce /ˌkuː də ˈɡrɑːs/ ■ n. (pl. **coups de grâce** pronunc. same) a final blow or shot given to kill a wounded person or animal.
–ORIGIN French, 'stroke of grace'.

coup de main /ˌkuː də ˈmã/ ■ n. (pl. **coups de main** pronunc. same) a sudden surprise attack.
–ORIGIN French, 'stroke of hand'.

coup d'état /ˌkuː deɪˈtɑː/ ■ n. (pl. **coups d'état** pronunc. same) see COUP (sense 1).
–ORIGIN French, 'blow of state'.

coup de théâtre /ˌkuː də teɪˈɑːtr(ə)/ ■ n. (pl. **coups de théâtre** pronunc. same) **1** a dramatically sudden action or turn of events, especially in a play. **2** a successful theatrical production.
–ORIGIN French, 'blow of theatre'.

coupe /kuːp/ ■ n. **1** a shallow glass or glass dish, typically with a stem, in which desserts or champagne are served. **2** a dessert served in such a dish.
–ORIGIN French, 'goblet'.

coupé /ˈkuːpeɪ/ (also **coupe** /kuːp/) ■ n. **1** S. African an end compartment in a railway carriage, with seats (or beds) on one side only. **2** a car with a fixed roof, two doors, and a sloping rear. **3** historical a four-wheeled enclosed carriage for two passengers and a driver.
–ORIGIN C19: from French *carrosse coupé* 'cut carriage'.

couped /kuːpt/ ■ adj. Heraldry cut off or truncated in a straight line.
–ORIGIN C16: from French *couper* 'to cut'.

couple ■ n. **1** two individuals of the same sort considered together. **2** informal an indefinite small number. **3** [treated as sing. or pl.] two people who are married or otherwise closely associated romantically or sexually. **4** Mechanics a pair of equal and parallel forces acting in opposite directions, and tending to cause rotation about an axis perpendicular to the plane containing them. ■ v. **1** join to form a pair.
▶ (often **be coupled to/with**) combine. ▶ connect (a railway vehicle or a piece of equipment) to another. **2** have sexual intercourse.
–DERIVATIVES **coupledom** n.
–ORIGIN Middle English: from Old French *cople* (n.), *copler* (v.), from Latin *copula* (n.), *copulare* (v.), from *co-* 'together' + *apere* 'fasten'.

coupler ■ n. **1** something that connects or couples two things. **2** Photography a compound in a developer or an emulsion which combines with the products of development to form an insoluble dye, part of the image. **3** (also **acoustic coupler**) a modem which interconverts digital signals from a computer and audible sound signals for transmission over telephone lines.

couplet ■ n. a pair of successive lines of verse, typically rhyming and of the same length.
–ORIGIN C16: from French, diminutive of *couple*, from Old French *cople* (see COUPLE).

coupling ■ n. a device for coupling railway vehicles or parts of machinery together.

coupling rod ■ n. a rod which couples the driving wheels of a locomotive, enabling them to act as a unit.

coupon ■ n. **1** a voucher entitling the holder to a discount on a product or a quantity of something rationed. **2** a detachable portion of a bond which is given up in return

for a payment of interest. ▶ the nominal rate of interest on a fixed-interest security. **3** a detachable form used to send for a purchase or information or to enter a competition.
– ORIGIN C19: from French, 'piece cut off', from *couper* 'cut'.

courage ■ n. the ability to do something that frightens one. ▶ strength in the face of pain or grief.
– PHRASES **have the courage of one's convictions** act on one's beliefs despite danger or disapproval. **take courage** make an effort to do something that frightens one. **take one's courage in both hands** nerve oneself to do something that frightens one.
– ORIGIN Middle English: from Old French *corage*, from Latin *cor* 'heart'.

courageous ■ adj. having courage; brave.
– DERIVATIVES **courageously** adv. **courageousness** n.

courant /kʊ'rant/ ■ adj. Heraldry represented as running.
– ORIGIN C17: French, 'running'.

courbette /kʊə'bɛt/ ■ n. (in classical riding) a movement in which the horse performs a series of jumps on the hind legs without the forelegs touching the ground.
– ORIGIN C17: French, from Italian *corvetta* 'little curve', from Latin *curvus* 'curved'.

courgette /kʊə'ʒɛt/ ■ n. Brit. a baby marrow.
– ORIGIN 1930s: from French, diminutive of *courge* 'gourd', from Latin *cucurbita*.

courier /'kʊrɪə/ ■ n. **1** a messenger who transports goods or documents. **2** a person employed to guide and assist a group of tourists. ■ v. send or transport by courier.
– ORIGIN Middle English: from Old French *coreor*, or from Italian *corriere*, from Latin *currere* 'to run'.

course ■ n. **1** the route or direction followed by a ship, aircraft, road, or river. **2** the way in which something progresses or develops. ▶ a procedure adopted to deal with a situation. **3** a dish forming one of the successive parts of a meal. **4** a series of lectures or lessons in a particular subject. ▶ Medicine a series of repeated treatments or doses of medication. **5** an area of land prepared for racing, golf, or another sport. **6** Architecture a continuous horizontal layer of brick or stone. **7** Bell-ringing a series of changes which brings the bells back to their original order, or the changes of a particular bell. ■ v. **1** (of liquid) flow. **2** [often as noun **coursing**] pursue (game, especially hares) with greyhounds using sight rather than scent.
– PHRASES **the course of nature** normal and expected events or processes. **in (the) course of 1** undergoing (the specified process). **2** during (the specified period). **of course** as expected. ▶ used to give or emphasize agreement or permission. ▶ admittedly. **on (or off) course** following (or not following) the intended route. **run (or take) its course** complete its natural development without interference.
– ORIGIN Middle English: from Old French *cours*, from Latin *cursus*, from *currere* 'run'.

coursebook ■ n. a textbook designed for use on a particular course of study.

courser[1] ■ n. poetic/literary a swift horse.
– ORIGIN Middle English: from Old French *corsier*, from Latin *cursus* (see **COURSE**).

courser[2] ■ n. a fast-running plover-like bird found in open country in Africa and Asia. [*Cursorius rufus* (Burchell's courser) and other species.]
– ORIGIN C18: from *Cursorius* 'adapted for running', from Latin *cursor* 'runner'.

courseware ■ n. computer programs or other material designed for use in an educational or training course.

coursework ■ n. work done during a course of study, typically counting towards a final mark.

court ■ n. **1** (also **court of law**) a body of people before whom judicial cases are heard. ▶ the place where they meet. **2** a quadrangular area marked out for ball games such as tennis. ▶ a quadrangle surrounded by a building or group of buildings. **3** the establishment, retinue, and courtiers of a sovereign. **4** the qualified members of a company or a corporation. ■ v. **1** dated be involved with romantically, typically with the intention of marrying. ▶ (of a male bird or other animal) try to attract (a mate). **2** attempt to win the support or favour of. ▶ go to great lengths to win (favourable attention). **3** risk incurring (misfortune) because of the way one behaves.
– PHRASES **out of court** before a legal hearing can take place. **pay court to** pay flattering attention to.
– ORIGIN Middle English: from Old French *cort*, from Latin *cohors, cohort-* 'yard, retinue'; the verb is influenced by Old Italian *corteare*, Old French *courtoyer*.

court bouillon /kɔːt 'buːjɒn/ ■ n. a stock made from wine and vegetables, typically used in fish dishes.
– ORIGIN French, from *court* 'short' + **BOUILLON**.

court card ■ n. Brit. a playing card that is a king, queen, or jack of a suit.
– ORIGIN C17: alteration of C16 *coat card*, from the decorative dress of the figures depicted.

court circular ■ n. Brit. a daily report of the activities and public engagements of royal family members.

courteous /'kəːtjəs/ ■ adj. polite, respectful, and considerate.
– DERIVATIVES **courteously** adv. **courteousness** n.
– ORIGIN Middle English (meaning 'having manners fit for a royal court'): from Old French *corteis*, from Latin *cohors* (see **COURT**).

courtesan /ˌkɔːtɪ'zan, 'kɔːtɪ-/ ■ n. a prostitute, especially one with wealthy or upper-class clients.
– ORIGIN C16: from French *courtisane*, from obsolete Italian *cortigiana*, *cortigiano* 'courtier'.

courtesy /'kəːtɪsi/ ■ n. (pl. **-ies**) **1** courteous behaviour. ▶ a polite speech or action, especially one required by convention. **2** archaic a curtsy.
– PHRASES **(by) courtesy of** given or allowed by.

courtesy light ■ n. a small light in a car that is automatically switched on when one of the doors is opened.

courtesy title ■ n. Brit. a title given to someone, especially the son or daughter of a peer, that has no legal validity.

courthouse ■ n. **1** a building in which a judicial court is held. **2** US a building containing the administrative offices of a county.

courtier /'kɔːtɪə/ ■ n. a companion or adviser to a king or queen.
– ORIGIN Middle English: from Old French *cortoyer* 'be present at court', from *cort* (see **COURT**).

courtly ■ adj. (**-ier**, **-iest**) very polite and refined.
– DERIVATIVES **courtliness** n.

courtly love ■ n. a highly conventionalized medieval tradition of love between a knight and a married noblewoman.

court martial ■ n. (pl. **courts martial** or **court martials**) a judicial court for trying members of the armed services accused of offences against military law. ■ v. (**court-martial**) (**-martialled**, **-martialling**; US **-martialed**, **-martialing**) try by court martial.

Court of Appeal ■ n. (in England and Wales) a court of law that hears appeals against judgements from the Crown Courts, High Court, and County Courts. ▶ (also **Supreme Court of Appeal**) (in South Africa) the highest court of law besides the Constitutional Court, where appeals are heard against judgements from the High Courts and Magistrates' Courts. ▶ (**court of appeals**) US a court of law in a federal circuit or state to which appeals are taken.

court of first instance ■ n. a court in which legal proceedings are begun or first heard.

court of record ■ n. a court whose proceedings are recorded and available as evidence of fact.

Court of St James's ■ n. the British sovereign's court.

court order ■ n. a direction issued by a court or a judge requiring a person to do or not do something.

courtroom ■ n. the room or building in which a court of law meets.

courtship ■ n. **1** a period of courting, especially with a view to marriage. ▶ the courting behaviour of male birds and other animals. **2** the process of courting favour or support.

court shoe ■ n. a woman's plain, lightweight shoe that has a low-cut upper and no fastening.

courtyard ■ n. an open area enclosed by walls or buildings, especially in a castle or large house.

COUSCOUS 270

couscous /'kʊskʊs, 'kuːskuːs/ ■ n. a North African dish of steamed or soaked semolina, usually served with spicy meat or vegetables.
– ORIGIN C17: from French, from Arabic *kuskus*, from *kaskasa* 'to pound', prob. of Berber origin.

cousin ■ n. 1 (also **first cousin**) a child of one's uncle or aunt. 2 a person of a kindred people or nation. 3 historical a title formerly used by a sovereign in addressing another sovereign or a noble of their own country.
– PHRASES **first cousin once removed 1** a child of one's first cousin. **2** one's parent's first cousin. **first cousin twice removed 1** a grandchild of one's first cousin. **2** one's grandparent's first cousin. **second cousin** a child of one's parent's first cousin. **second cousin once removed 1** a child of one's second cousin. **2** one's parent's second cousin. **third cousin** a child of one's parent's second cousin.
– DERIVATIVES **cousinhood** n. **cousinly** adj. **cousinship** n.
– ORIGIN Middle English: from Old French *cosin*, from Latin *consobrinus* 'mother's sister's child', from *con-* 'with' + *sobrinus* 'second cousin', from *soror* 'sister'.

couta (also **cuda**) S. African ■ n. a large mackerel of the Indo-Pacific region, popular as a food and game fish, also known as king mackerel. [*Scomberomorus commerson*.]

couth /kuːθ/ ■ adj. humorous refined and well mannered.
– ORIGIN C19: back-formation from **UNCOUTH**.

couture /kuːˈtjʊə/ ■ n. the design and manufacture of fashionable clothes to a client's specific requirements. ▸ clothes of this type.
– ORIGIN 1920s: French, 'sewing, dressmaking'.

couturier /kuːˈtjʊərɪeɪ/ ■ n. (fem. **couturière** /kuːˈtjʊərɪɛː/) a person who makes and sells couture clothes.

couverture /ˈkuːvətjʊə/ ■ n. chocolate with extra cocoa butter to give a high gloss, used to cover sweets and cakes.
– ORIGIN 1930s: French, 'covering', from *couvrir* 'to cover'.

covalent /kəʊˈveɪl(ə)nt/ ■ adj. Chemistry relating to or denoting chemical bonds formed by the sharing of electrons between atoms. Often contrasted with **IONIC**.
– DERIVATIVES **covalence** n. **covalency** n. **covalently** adv.

covariance /kəʊˈvɛːrɪəns/ ■ n. 1 Mathematics the property of a function of retaining its form when the variables are linearly transformed. 2 Statistics the mean value of the product of the deviations of two variates from their respective means.

covariant ■ adj. Mathematics changing in such a way that mathematical interrelations with another simultaneously changing quantity remains unchanged.

cove ■ n. 1 a small sheltered bay. 2 Architecture a concave arch or arched moulding, especially one formed at the junction of a wall with a ceiling. ■ v. [usu. as adj. **coved**] Architecture fit with a cove.
– DERIVATIVES **coving** n.
– ORIGIN Old English *cofa* 'chamber, cave', of Germanic origin.

covellite /kəʊˈvɛlʌɪt/ ■ n. a blue mineral consisting of copper sulphide.
– ORIGIN C19: named after the Italian chemist Nicolò Covelli.

coven /ˈkʌv(ə)n/ ■ n. a group of witches who meet regularly.
– ORIGIN C17: var. of archaic *covin* 'deception', from Latin *convenire* (see **CONVENE**).

covenant /ˈkʌv(ə)nənt/ ■ n. a solemn agreement. ▸ Theology an agreement held to be the basis of a relationship of commitment with God.
– DERIVATIVES **covenantor** n.
– ORIGIN Middle English: from Old French *covenir* 'agree', from Latin *convenire* (see **CONVENE**).

cover ■ v. 1 put something on top of or in front of (something) in order to protect or conceal it. ▸ envelop in a layer of something. 2 extend over (an area): *the grounds covered eight acres.* 3 deal with (a subject). ▸ (of a rule or law) apply to. 4 travel a specified distance. 5 (of money) be enough to pay (a cost). ▸ (of insurance) protect against a liability, loss, or accident. ▸ (**cover oneself**) take precautions against future blame or liability. 6 (**cover up**) try to hide or deny the fact of (a wrongful action). ▸ (**cover for**) temporarily take over the job or role of. 7 aim a gun at. ▸ protect (an exposed person) by shooting at the enemy. ▸ (in team games) take up a position ready to defend against (an opponent). 8 Bridge play a higher card on (a high card). 9 record or perform a cover version of (a song). 10 (of a male animal, especially a stallion) copulate with (a female animal). ■ n. 1 something that covers or protects. ▸ a lid. ▸ a thick protective outer part or page of a book or magazine. ▸ (**the covers**) bedclothes. 2 physical shelter: *they ran for cover.* ▸ vegetation used as a shelter by hunted animals. See also **COVERT** (sense 1). 3 military support for someone in danger or under attack. 4 a means of concealing an illegal or secret activity. ▸ an identity adopted by a spy to conceal their true activities. 5 Ecology the amount of ground covered by a vertical projection of the vegetation. 6 protection by insurance. 7 a place setting at a table in a restaurant. 8 Cricket short for **COVER POINT**. ▸ (**the covers**) an area of the field consisting of cover point and extra cover. 9 (also **cover version**) a recording or performance of a song previously recorded by a different artist.
– PHRASES **break cover** suddenly leave a place of shelter when being hunted or pursued. **cover all the bases** informal deal with something thoroughly. **cover one's back** informal take steps to avoid attack or criticism. **cover one's tracks** conceal evidence of one's actions. **from cover to cover** from beginning to end of a book or magazine. **take cover** take shelter from an attack. **under cover** under a roof or other shelter. **under cover of** concealed by. ▸ while pretending to do something. **under separate cover** in a separate envelope.
– DERIVATIVES **coverable** adj. **covering** n.
– ORIGIN Middle English: from Old French *covrir*, from Latin *cooperire*, from **CO-** + *operire* 'to cover'.

coverage ■ n. the extent to which something is covered.

cover charge ■ n. a fee paid for admission to a restaurant, bar, or club.

cover crop ■ n. a crop grown to protect and enrich the soil.

covering letter (N. Amer. **cover letter**) ■ n. a letter explaining the contents of an accompanying enclosure.

coverlet ■ n. a bedspread.
– ORIGIN Middle English: from Anglo-Norman French *covrelet*, from Old French *covrir* 'to cover' + *lit* 'bed'.

cover note ■ n. a temporary certificate showing that a person has a current insurance policy.

cover point ■ n. Cricket a fielding position a little in front of the batsman on the off side and halfway to the boundary.

coverslip ■ n. a thin piece of glass used to cover and protect a specimen on a microscope slide.

covert ■ adj. /ˈkʌvət, ˈkəʊvəːt/ not openly acknowledged or displayed. ■ n. /ˈkʌvət, ˈkʌvə/ 1 a thicket in which game can hide. 2 Ornithology a feather covering the base of a main flight or tail feather of a bird.
– DERIVATIVES **covertly** adv. **covertness** n.
– ORIGIN Middle English: from Old French, 'covered', from *covrir* (see **COVER**).

coverture /ˈkʌvətjʊə/ ■ n. poetic/literary protective or concealing covering.
– ORIGIN Middle English: from Old French, from *covrir* 'to cover'.

cover-up ■ n. an attempt to conceal the truth about a mistake or crime.

covet /ˈkʌvɪt/ ■ v. (**coveted**, **coveting**) yearn to possess (something belonging to someone else).
– DERIVATIVES **covetable** adj. **covetous** adj. **covetously** adv. **covetousness** n.
– ORIGIN Middle English: from Old French *cuveitier*, from Latin *cupiditas* (see **CUPIDITY**).

covey /ˈkʌvi/ ■ n. (pl. **-eys**) a small flock of birds, especially partridge.
– ORIGIN Middle English: from Old French *covee*, from *cover*, from Latin *cubare* 'lie down'.

cow[1] ■ n. 1 a fully grown female animal of a domesticated breed of ox. ▸ (in farming) an animal of this type which has borne more than one calf. Compare with **HEIFER**. ▸ the female of certain other large animals, e.g. elephant, rhinoceros, or whale. 2 informal, derogatory a woman.
– PHRASES **have a cow** N. Amer. informal become angry or

CONSONANTS b but d dog f few g get h he j yes k cat l leg m man n no p pen r red

excited. **till the cows come home** informal for an indefinitely long time.

cow² ■ v. (usu. **be cowed**) cause (someone) to submit to one's wishes by intimidation.
– ORIGIN C16: prob. from Old Norse *kúga* 'oppress'.

coward ■ n. a person contemptibly lacking in courage.
– DERIVATIVES **cowardice** n. **cowardliness** n. **cowardly** adj.
– ORIGIN Middle English: from Old French *couard*, from Latin *cauda* 'tail', perhaps with ref. to an animal with its tail between its legs.

cowbell ■ n. a bell hung round a cow's neck.

cowboy ■ n. **1** a man on horseback who herds cattle, especially in the western US. **2** informal an unscrupulous or unqualified tradesman.

cowcatcher ■ n. a metal frame at the front of a locomotive for pushing aside obstacles on the line.

cower ■ v. crouch down in fear.
– ORIGIN Middle English: from Middle Low German *kūren* 'lie in wait'.

cowfish ■ n. (pl. same or **-fishes**) a boxfish with horn-like spines on its head. [*Lactoria diaphana* and other species.]

cowherd ■ n. a person who tends grazing cattle.
– ORIGIN Old English, from COW¹ + obsolete *herd* 'herdsman'.

cowl ■ n. **1** a large loose hood forming part of a monk's habit. **2** a hood-shaped covering for a chimney or ventilation shaft. ▶ another term for COWLING.
– DERIVATIVES **cowled** adj.
– ORIGIN Old English *cugele*, *cūle*, from Latin *cucullus*.

cowlick ■ n. a lock of hair hanging over the forehead.

cowling ■ n. a removable cover for a vehicle or aircraft engine.

cowl neck ■ n. a neckline on a woman's garment that hangs in draped folds.

cow parsley ■ n. a European hedgerow plant of the parsley family with fern-like leaves and large, lacy heads of tiny white flowers. [*Anthriscus sylvestris*.]

cowpat ■ n. a flat, round piece of cow dung.

cowpea ■ n. a tropical leguminous plant cultivated for its edible pods and seeds. [*Vigna unguiculata*.] ▶ the seed of this plant as food.

cowpox ■ n. a viral disease of cows' udders which can be contracted by humans and resembles mild smallpox.

cowrie /ˈkaʊ(ə)ri/ (also **cowry**) ■ n. (pl. **-ies**) a marine gastropod mollusc with a smooth, glossy, domed shell with a long, narrow opening. [Genus *Cypraea*: numerous species.]
– ORIGIN C17: from Hindi *kaurī*.

co-write ■ v. write together with another person.
– DERIVATIVES **co-writer** n.

cowslip ■ n. a European wild primula with clusters of drooping fragrant yellow flowers in spring. [*Primula veris*.]
– ORIGIN Old English *cūslyppe*, from *cū* 'cow' + *slyppe* 'slime'.

Cox (in full **Cox's orange pippin**) ■ n. an English eating apple of a variety with a red-tinged green skin.
– ORIGIN C19: named after the English fruit grower R. *Cox*.

cox ■ n. a coxswain. ■ v. act as a coxswain for.
– DERIVATIVES **coxless** adj.

coxa /ˈkɒksə/ ■ n. (pl. **coxae** /-siː/) Anatomy the hip bone or hip joint. ▶ Entomology the first or basal segment of the leg of an insect.
– DERIVATIVES **coxal** adj.
– ORIGIN C17: from Latin, 'hip'.

coxcomb /ˈkɒkskəʊm/ ■ n. **1** archaic a vain and conceited man; a dandy. **2** variant spelling of COCKSCOMB (in sense 2).
– ORIGIN C16.

Coxsackie virus /kɒkˈsaki, kʊk-/ ■ n. Medicine an enterovirus of a group causing various respiratory, neurological, and muscular diseases.
– ORIGIN 1940s: named after *Coxsackie*, New York State, where the first cases were diagnosed.

coxswain /ˈkɒks(ə)n/ ■ n. the steersman of a boat.
– ORIGIN Middle English: from obsolete *cock* 'small boat' + SWAIN.

coy ■ adj. (**coyer**, **coyest**) pretending shyness or modesty. ▶ reluctant to give details about something sensitive.
– DERIVATIVES **coyly** adv. **coyness** n.
– ORIGIN Middle English: from Old French *coi*, *quei*, from Latin *quietus* (see QUIET).

coyote /ˈkɔɪəʊt, kɔɪˈəʊti/ ■ n. (pl. same or **coyotes**) a wolf-like wild dog native to North America. [*Canis latrans*.]
– ORIGIN C18: from Mexican Spanish, from Nahuatl *coyotl*.

coypu /ˈkɔɪpuː/ ■ n. (pl. **coypus**) a large semiaquatic beaver-like South American rodent, farmed for its fur (nutria). [*Myocastor coypus*.]
– ORIGIN C18: from Araucanian.

coz /kʌz/ ■ n. informal, archaic or N. Amer. cousin.

cozen /ˈkʌz(ə)n/ ■ v. poetic/literary trick or deceive.
– DERIVATIVES **cozenage** n. **cozener** n.
– ORIGIN C16: perhaps from obsolete Italian *cozzonare* 'to cheat'.

cozy ■ adj. US spelling of COSY.

cozzie ■ n. (pl. **-ies**) variant spelling of COSSIE.

CP ■ abbrev. **1** cerebral palsy. **2** Finance commercial paper. **3** Communist Party.

cp. ■ abbrev. compare.

CPA ■ abbrev. N. Amer. certified public accountant.

CPI ■ abbrev. consumer price index.

CPIX ■ abbrev. chiefly S. African consumer price index, excluding mortgage interest rates.

Cpl ■ abbrev. Corporal.

CPR ■ abbrev. cardiopulmonary resuscitation.

CPU ■ abbrev. Computing central processing unit.

Cr¹ ■ symb. the chemical element chromium.

Cr² ■ abbrev. **1** Councillor. **2** credit.

crab ■ n. **1** a crustacean, found chiefly on seashores, with a broad carapace, stalked eyes, and five pairs of legs, the first of which are modified as pincers. [Order Decapoda: many species.] **2** (**crabs**) informal an infestation of crab lice. **3** a machine with pincer-like arms for picking up heavy weights. ■ v. **1** move sideways or obliquely. **2** fish for crabs.
– PHRASES **catch a crab** Rowing make a faulty stroke.
– DERIVATIVES **crablike** adj. & adv.
– ORIGIN Old English, of Germanic origin.

crab apple ■ n. **1** a small, sour kind of apple. **2** (also **crab tree**) a small tree bearing such apples. [*Malus sylvestris* and other species.]
– ORIGIN Middle English: perhaps an alteration of Scots and northern English *scrab*.

crabbed ■ adj. **1** (of writing) hard to read or understand. **2** crabby.
– ORIGIN Middle English: from CRAB, because of the crab's sideways gait and habit of snapping.

crabby ■ adj. (**-ier**, **-iest**) bad-tempered; morose.
– DERIVATIVES **crabbily** adv. **crabbiness** n.

crabgrass ■ n. a creeping grass that can become a serious weed. [*Digitaria sanguinalis* and other species.]

crab louse ■ n. a louse that infests human body hair. [*Phthirus pubis*.]

crab spider ■ n. a spider with long front legs that moves with a crablike sideways motion. [Family Thomisidae: many species.]

crab stick ■ n. a stick of mixed compressed fish pieces flavoured with crab.

crabwise ■ adv. & adj. (of movement) sideways, especially in an awkward way.

crack ■ n. **1** a narrow opening between two parts of something which has split or been broken. **2** a sudden sharp or explosive noise. ▶ a sharp blow. **3** informal a joke or jibe. **4** informal an attempt to do something. **5** (also **crack cocaine**) a potent hard crystalline form of cocaine broken into small pieces. ■ v. **1** break or cause to break with little or no separation of the parts. **2** give way under pressure or

crackdown

strain. ▸ (**crack up**) informal suffer an emotional breakdown under pressure. ▸ (**crack up**) informal burst into laughter. **3** make or cause to make a sudden sharp or explosive sound. ▸ hit hard. **4** (of a person's voice) suddenly change in pitch, especially through strain. **5** (**crack down on**) informal take severe measures against. **6** (**crack on**) informal proceed or progress quickly. **7** informal solve, interpret, or decipher. ▸ break into (a safe or a computer system). **8** decompose (hydrocarbons) by heat and pressure to produce lighter hydrocarbons. ■ adj. very good or skilful: *he is a crack shot.*
– PHRASES **crack of dawn** daybreak. **crack of doom** a thunder peal announcing the Day of Judgement. **a fair crack of the whip** Brit. informal a chance to try or participate in something. **cracked up to be** [with neg.] informal asserted to be: *acting is not as glamorous as it's cracked up to be.* **get cracking** informal act quickly and energetically.
– ORIGIN Old English *cracian* 'make an explosive noise', of Germanic origin.

crackdown ■ n. a series of severe measures against undesirable or illegal behaviour.

cracked ■ adj. **1** having cracks. **2** informal crazy.

cracked wheat ■ n. grains of wheat that have been crushed into small pieces.

cracker ■ n. **1** a decorated paper cylinder which, when pulled apart, makes a sharp noise and releases a small toy or other novelty. **2** a firework exploding with a crack. **3** a thin dry biscuit, typically eaten with cheese. **4** Brit. informal a fine example of something. **5** an installation for cracking hydrocarbons. **6** a person who breaks into a computer system with malicious intent.

crackers ■ adj. informal insane; crazy.

cracking ■ adj. Brit. informal excellent. ▸ fast and exciting: *a cracking pace.*

crackle ■ v. make a rapid succession of slight cracking noises. ■ n. **1** a cracking sound of this type. **2** a pattern of minute surface cracks.
– DERIVATIVES **crackly** adj.
– ORIGIN Middle English: from CRACK.

crackling ■ n. the crisp fatty skin of roast pork.

crackpot informal ■ n. an eccentric or foolish person. ■ adj. eccentric; impractical.

-cracy ■ comb. form denoting a particular form of government or rule: *democracy.*
– ORIGIN from French *-cratie*, from Greek *-kratia* 'power, rule'.

cradle ■ n. **1** a baby's bed or cot, especially one mounted on rockers. **2** a supporting framework resembling this, in particular for a boat under repair or for workers on the side of high building. ■ v. **1** hold gently and protectively. **2** place in a cradle.
– DERIVATIVES **cradling** n.
– ORIGIN Old English.

cradle cap ■ n. a skin condition in babies in which there are areas of yellowish or brownish scales on the top of the head.

cradle-snatcher ■ n. derogatory a person who marries or has a sexual relationship with a much younger person.

craft ■ n. **1** an activity involving skill in making things by hand. ▸ (**crafts**) things made by hand. ▸ skill in carrying out one's work. ▸ the members of a skilled profession. **2** cunning. **3** (pl. same) a boat or ship. ▸ an aircraft or spacecraft. ■ v. exercise skill in making (something).
– DERIVATIVES **crafter** n. **craftwork** n. **craftworker** n.
– ORIGIN Old English *cræft* 'strength, skill', of Germanic origin.

craftsman (or **craftswoman**) ■ n. (pl. **-men** or **-women**) a worker skilled in a particular craft.
– DERIVATIVES **craftsmanship** n.

crafty ■ adj. (**-ier, -iest**) **1** cunning or deceitful. **2** informal of or relating to the making of objects by hand.
– DERIVATIVES **craftily** adv. **craftiness** n.
– ORIGIN Old English *cræftig* 'strong, powerful' (see CRAFT).

crag ■ n. a steep or rugged cliff or rock face.
– ORIGIN Middle English: of Celtic origin.

craggy ■ adj. (**-ier, -iest**) **1** having many crags. ▸ (of a rock face) rough and uneven. **2** (of a man's face) attractively rugged and rough-textured.
– DERIVATIVES **craggily** adv. **cragginess** n.

crake ■ n. a bird of the rail family with a short bill, such as the corncrake.
– ORIGIN Middle English: from Old Norse *kráka*, of imitative origin.

cram ■ v. (**crammed, cramming**) **1** force too many (people or things) into a room or container. ▸ fill to the point of overflowing. **2** study intensively just before an examination.
– ORIGIN Old English, of Germanic origin.

crammer ■ n. Brit. a college or school that prepares pupils intensively for a particular examination.

cramp ■ n. **1** painful involuntary contraction of a muscle or muscles, typically caused by fatigue or strain. ▸ (**cramps**) abdominal pain caused by menstruation. **2** a tool, typically shaped like a capital G, for clamping two objects together. ▸ (also **cramp-iron**) a metal bar with bent ends for holding masonry together. ■ v. **1** restrict or inhibit the development of. **2** fasten with a cramp or cramps. **3** suffer from cramp.
– PHRASES **cramp someone's style** informal prevent a person from acting freely or naturally.
– ORIGIN Middle English: from Middle Low German and Middle Dutch *krampe*.

cramped ■ adj. **1** uncomfortably small or crowded. **2** (of handwriting) small and difficult to read.

crampon /'krampɒn, -pən/ ■ n. a metal plate with spikes fixed to a boot for climbing on ice or rock.
– ORIGIN Middle English: from Old French, of Germanic origin.

cranberry ■ n. (pl. **-ies**) **1** a small red acid berry used in cooking. **2** an evergreen dwarf shrub which yields this fruit. [*Vaccinium oxycoccos* (Europe), *V. macrocarpon* (N. America), and other species.]
– ORIGIN C17: from German *Kranbeere* or Low German *kraneberre* 'crane-berry'.

crane[1] ■ n. a large, tall machine used for moving heavy objects by suspending them from a projecting arm. ▸ a moving platform supporting a camera. ■ v. **1** stretch out (one's neck) in order to see better. **2** move (an object) by means of a crane.
– DERIVATIVES **cranage** n.
– ORIGIN Middle English: figuratively from CRANE[2].

crane[2] ■ n. a tall, long-legged, long-necked bird, typically with white or grey plumage and tail plumes. [*Anthropoides paradisea* (blue crane) and related species, family Gruidae.]
– ORIGIN Old English, of Germanic origin.

crane flower ■ n. another term for BIRD OF PARADISE (in sense 2).

crane fly ■ n. a slender two-winged fly with very long legs. [*Tipula maxima* and related species, family Tipulidae.]

cranesbill ■ n. a herbaceous plant with lobed leaves and typically purple or violet five-petalled flowers. [*Geranium pratense* (meadow cranesbill) and related species.]
– ORIGIN C16: so named because of the shape of the fruit.

cranial /'kreɪnɪəl/ ■ adj. Anatomy of or relating to the skull or cranium.

cranial index ■ n. another term for CEPHALIC INDEX.

cranial nerves ■ pl. n. Anatomy the twelve pairs of nerves which arise directly from the brain and pass through separate apertures in the skull.

craniate /'kreɪnɪət/ ■ adj. Zoology relating to or denoting animals that possess a skull.
– ORIGIN C19: from modern Latin *craniatus*, from medieval Latin *cranium*.

cranio- /'kreɪnɪəʊ/ ■ comb. form relating to the cranium: *craniotomy.*

craniometry /ˌkreɪnɪ'ɒmɪtri/ ■ n. the measurement of the dimensions of skulls.
– DERIVATIVES **craniometric** adj.

craniosacral therapy /ˌkreɪnɪəʊ'seɪkr(ə)l, -'sak-/ ■ n. a system of alternative medicine intended to relieve pain and tension by gentle manipulations of the skull.

craniotomy /ˌkreɪnɪˈɒtəmi/ ■ n. surgical removal of a portion of the skull.

cranium /ˈkreɪnɪəm/ ■ n. (pl. **craniums** or **crania** /-nɪə/) Anatomy the skull, especially the part enclosing the brain.
–ORIGIN Middle English: from Greek *kranion*.

crank[1] ■ v. **1** turn a crankshaft or handle, especially in order to start an engine. **2** (**crank up**) informal increase the intensity of. **3** (**crank out**) informal, derogatory produce regularly and routinely. **4** give a bend to (a shaft or bar). ■ n. a part of an axle or shaft bent out at right angles, for converting reciprocal to circular motion and vice versa.
–ORIGIN Old English *cranc*, rel. to *crincan* (see **CRINGE**).

crank[2] ■ n. a person with eccentric or obsessive views. ▸ N. Amer. a bad-tempered person.
–ORIGIN back-formation from **CRANKY**.

crankcase ■ n. a case or covering enclosing a crankshaft.

crankpin ■ n. a pin by which a connecting rod is attached to a crank.

crankshaft ■ n. a shaft driven by a crank.

cranky ■ adj. (**-ier**, **-iest**) informal **1** eccentric, odd. ▸ chiefly N. Amer. ill-tempered; irritable. **2** (of a machine) working erratically.
–DERIVATIVES **crankily** adv. **crankiness** n.
–ORIGIN C18: perhaps from Dutch or German *krank* 'sick'.

cranny ■ n. (pl. **-ies**) a small, narrow space or opening.
–ORIGIN Middle English: from Old French *crane* 'notched', from popular Latin *crena* 'notch'.

crap[1] vulgar slang ■ n. **1** nonsense; rubbish. **2** excrement. ▸ an act of defecation. ■ v. (**crapped**, **crapping**) defecate. ■ adj. extremely poor in quality.
–DERIVATIVES **crappy** adj.
–ORIGIN Middle English: rel. to Dutch *krappe*, from *krappen* 'pluck, cut off', and perhaps also to Old French *crappe* 'siftings', Anglo-Latin *crappa* 'chaff'.

crap[2] N. Amer. ■ v. (**crap out**) informal make a losing throw at craps. ▸ give up; fail.

crape ■ n. **1** variant spelling of **CRÊPE**. **2** black silk, formerly used for mourning clothes.
–ORIGIN C16: from French *crêpe* (see **CRÊPE**).

crape myrtle (also **crepe myrtle**) ■ n. an ornamental Chinese shrub or small tree with pink, white, or purplish crinkled petals. [*Lagerstroemia indica*.]

craps ■ pl. n. [treated as sing.] a North American gambling game played with two dice, in which 7 or 11 is a winning throw, 2, 3, or 12 is a losing throw.
–ORIGIN C19: perhaps from **CRAB** or *crab's eyes*, denoting a throw of two ones.

crapshoot ■ n. N. Amer. a game of craps.

crash ■ v. **1** collide violently with an obstacle or another vehicle. ▸ (of an aircraft) fall from the sky and violently hit the land or sea. **2** informal (of a company's shares) fall suddenly and disastrously in value. ▸ Computing fail suddenly. **3** (also **crash out**) informal fall deeply asleep. **4** move with force, speed, and sudden loud noise. ▸ make a sudden loud, deep noise. **5** informal gatecrash (a party). ■ n. **1** an instance of crashing. **2** a sudden loud discordant noise. ■ adj. done rapidly and involving a concentrated effort: *a crash course in Italian*.
–ORIGIN Middle English: imitative.

crash-dive ■ v. **1** (of a submarine) dive rapidly to a deeper level in an emergency. **2** (of an aircraft) plunge steeply downwards into a crash. ■ n. (**crash dive**) a steep dive of this kind.

crash helmet ■ n. a helmet worn by a motorcyclist to protect the head in case of a crash.

crashing ■ adj. informal complete; total: *a crashing bore*.

crash-land ■ v. land roughly in an emergency.

crash pad ■ n. informal a place to sleep, especially for emergency use.

crash-test ■ v. deliberately crash (a new vehicle) under controlled conditions in order to evaluate and improve its ability to withstand impact. ■ n. (**crash test**) a test of this kind.

crashworthiness ■ n. the degree to which a vehicle will protect its occupants from the effects of an accident.

crass ■ adj. showing a grossly insensitive lack of intelligence.
–DERIVATIVES **crassly** adv. **crassness** n.
–ORIGIN C15: from Latin *crassus* 'solid, thick'.

crassula ■ n. a succulent with thick, fleshy leaves, native to southern Africa. [Genus *Crassula*: many species.]

-crat ■ comb. form denoting a member or supporter of a particular form of government or rule: *plutocrat*.
–ORIGIN from French *-crate*, from adjectives ending in *-cratique* (see **-CRATIC**).

crate ■ n. a slatted wooden case used for transporting goods. ▸ a square container divided into small individual units for holding bottles. ■ v. pack in a crate for transportation.
–DERIVATIVES **crateful** n. (pl. **-fuls**).
–ORIGIN Middle English: perhaps rel. to Dutch *krat* 'tailboard of a wagon'.

crater ■ n. a large bowl-shaped cavity, especially one caused by an explosion or impact or forming the mouth of a volcano. ■ v. form a crater or craters in.
–ORIGIN C17: from Greek *kratēr* 'mixing-bowl'.

-cratic ■ comb. form relating to a particular kind of government or rule: *democratic*.
–DERIVATIVES **-cratically** comb. form in corresponding adverbs.
–ORIGIN from French *-cratique*, from *-cratie* (see **-CRACY**).

craton /ˈkratɒn/ ■ n. Geology a large stable block of the earth's crust forming the nucleus of a continent.
–ORIGIN 1930s: alteration of *kratogen* in the same sense, from Greek *kratos* 'strength'.

cravat ■ n. a short, wide strip of fabric worn by men round the neck and tucked inside an open-necked shirt.
–DERIVATIVES **cravatted** adj.
–ORIGIN C17: from French *cravate*, from *Cravate* 'Croat', because of the scarf worn by Croatian mercenaries.

crave ■ v. **1** feel a powerful desire for. **2** dated ask for: *I must crave your indulgence*.
–DERIVATIVES **craving** n.
–ORIGIN Old English, of Germanic origin.

craven ■ adj. contemptibly lacking in courage; cowardly. ■ n. archaic a cowardly person.
–DERIVATIVES **cravenly** adv. **cravenness** n.
–ORIGIN Middle English *cravant* 'defeated', perhaps from Old French *cravanter* 'crush, overwhelm', from Latin *crepare* 'burst'.

craw ■ n. dated the crop of a bird or insect.
–PHRASES **stick in one's craw** see **STICK**[2].
–ORIGIN Middle English: rel. to Middle Dutch *crāghe* or Middle Low German *krage* 'neck, throat'.

crawfish ■ n. (pl. same or **-fishes**) **1** another term for **SPINY LOBSTER**. **2** chiefly N. Amer. a freshwater crayfish.
–ORIGIN C17: var. of **CRAYFISH**.

crawl ■ v. **1** move forward on the hands and knees or by dragging the body close to the ground. ▸ (of an insect or small animal) move slowly along a surface. ▸ move at an unusually slow pace. **2** informal behave obsequiously or ingratiatingly. **3** (**be crawling with**) be unpleasantly covered or crowded with: *the place was crawling with soldiers*. ▸ feel an unpleasant sensation resembling something moving over the skin. ■ n. **1** an act of crawling. ▸ a slow rate of movement. **2** a swimming stroke involving alternate overarm movements and rapid kicks of the legs.
–DERIVATIVES **crawling** adj. **crawly** adj.
–ORIGIN Middle English: possibly rel. to Swedish *kravla* and Danish *kravle*.

crawler ■ n. **1** a person or thing that crawls. ▸ a vehicle moving on an endless caterpillar track. **2** Computing a program that searches the World Wide Web in order to create an index of data.

crayfish ■ n. (pl. same or **-fishes**) **1** a nocturnal freshwater crustacean resembling a lobster. [*Astacus* (Europe), *Cambarus* (N. America), and other genera.] **2** another term for **SPINY LOBSTER**.
–ORIGIN Middle English: from Old French *crevice*, rel. to German *Krebs* 'crab'.

crayon ■ n. a pencil or stick of coloured chalk or wax, used for drawing. ■ v. draw with a crayon or crayons.
–ORIGIN C17: from French, from *craie* 'chalk'.

craze ■ n. a widespread but short-lived enthusiasm for

crazy

something. ▪v. **1** [usu. as adj. **crazed**] make or become wildly insane: *a crazed killer*. **2** (usu. **be crazed**) produce a network of fine cracks on (a surface).
– DERIVATIVES **crazing** n.
– ORIGIN Middle English (in the sense 'break, shatter, crack'): perhaps of Scandinavian origin.

crazy informal ▪adj. (**-ier, -iest**) **1** insane or unbalanced, especially as manifested in wild or aggressive behaviour. **2** extremely enthusiastic about something. **3** appearing absurdly out of place or unlikely: *the monument leaned at a crazy angle*. ▪n. (pl. **-ies**) chiefly N. Amer. an insane person.
– PHRASES **like crazy** to a great degree.
– DERIVATIVES **crazily** adv. **craziness** n.

crazy paving ▪n. paving made of irregular pieces of flat stone.

creak ▪v. **1** make a harsh high-pitched sound when being moved or when pressure is applied. **2** show weakness or frailty under strain. ▪n. a creaking sound.
– DERIVATIVES **creaking** adj. **creakingly** adv. **creaky** adj.
– ORIGIN Middle English (in the sense 'croak'): imitative.

cream ▪n. **1** the thick white or pale yellow fatty liquid which rises to the top when milk is left to stand. ▸ a sauce, soup, dessert, or other food containing cream or having the consistency of cream. **2** a thick liquid or semi-solid cosmetic or medical preparation. **3** the very best of a group of people or things: *the cream of American society*. **4** a very pale yellow or off-white colour. ▪v. **1** work (butter) to form a smooth soft paste. ▸ mash (a cooked vegetable) and mix with milk or cream. ▸ add cream to (coffee). **2** (**cream off**) take away (the best part of a group of people or things). **3** rub a cosmetic cream into (the skin). **4** informal, chiefly N. Amer. defeat heavily. ▸ hit or beat.
– ORIGIN Middle English: from Old French *cresme*, from a blend of late Latin *cramum* and eccles. Latin *chrisma* (see CHRISM).

cream cheese ▪n. soft, rich cheese made from unskimmed milk and cream.

cream cracker ▪n. a dry unsweetened biscuit eaten chiefly with cheese.

creamer ▪n. **1** a cream or milk substitute for adding to coffee or tea. **2** N. Amer. a jug for cream. **3** historical a flat dish for skimming the cream off milk. ▸ a machine for separating cream from milk.

creamery ▪n. (pl. **-ies**) a factory that produces butter and cheese.

cream of tartar ▪n. potassium hydrogen tartrate, an acidic crystalline compound used in baking powder.

cream puff ▪n. **1** a cake made of puff pastry filled with cream. **2** informal a weak or ineffectual person.

cream sherry ▪n. a full-bodied mellow sweet sherry.

cream soda ▪n. a carbonated soft drink.

cream tea ▪n. Brit. an afternoon meal consisting of tea to drink with scones, jam, and cream.

creamy ▪adj. (**-ier, -iest**) resembling cream in consistency or colour. ▸ containing a lot of cream.
– DERIVATIVES **creamily** adv. **creaminess** n.

creance /'kriːəns/ ▪n. Falconry a long fine cord attached to a hawk's leash to prevent escape during training.
– ORIGIN C15: from French *créance* 'faith'.

crease ▪n. **1** a line or ridge produced on paper or cloth by folding, pressing, or crushing. ▸ a wrinkle or furrow in the skin, especially of the face. **2** Cricket any of a number of lines marked on the pitch at specified places. ▪v. **1** make a crease in. **2** (of a bullet) graze.
– ORIGIN C16: prob. a var. of CREST.

create ▪v. **1** bring into existence. **2** invest with a title of nobility. **3** Brit. informal make a fuss; complain.
– ORIGIN Middle English: from Latin *creare* 'produce'.

creatine /'kriːətiːn/ ▪n. Biochemistry a compound formed in protein metabolism and involved in the supply of energy for muscular contraction.
– ORIGIN C19: from Greek *kreas* 'meat'.

creation ▪n. **1** the action or process of creating. ▸ a thing which has been made or invented, especially something showing artistic talent. **2** (**the Creation**) the creating of the universe, especially when regarded as an act of God. ▸ the universe.

creationism ▪n. the belief that the universe and living organisms originated from specific acts of divine creation.
– DERIVATIVES **creationist** n. & adj.

creation science ▪n. the reinterpretation of scientific knowledge in accord with belief in the literal truth of the Bible.

creative ▪adj. relating to or involving the use of imagination or original ideas in order to create something. ▪n. a person engaged in creative work.
– DERIVATIVES **creatively** adv. **creativeness** n. **creativity** n.

creative accountancy (also **creative accounting**) ▪n. informal the exploitation of loopholes in financial regulation to gain advantage or to present figures in a misleadingly favourable light.

creator ▪n. a person or thing that creates. ▸ (**the Creator**) God.

creature ▪n. **1** an animal, as distinct from a human being. ▸ an animal or person. **2** a person or organization considered to be under the complete control of another.
– DERIVATIVES **creaturely** adv.
– ORIGIN Middle English (in the sense 'something created'): from late Latin *creatura*, from *creare* (see CREATE).

creature comforts ▪pl. n. material comforts that contribute to physical ease and well-being, such as good food and accommodation.

crèche /krɛʃ, kreɪʃ/ ▪n. **1** a nursery where babies and young children are cared for during the working day. **2** chiefly N. Amer. a representation of the nativity scene.
– ORIGIN C18: French, of Germanic origin and rel. to CRIB.

cred ▪n. informal short for STREET CREDIBILITY.

credence /'kriːd(ə)ns/ ▪n. belief in or acceptance of something as true. ▸ the likelihood of something being true; plausibility.
– ORIGIN Middle English: from medieval Latin *credentia*, from Latin *credere* 'believe'.

credential /krɪ'dɛnʃ(ə)l/ ▪n. **1** a qualification, achievement, etc., especially when used to indicate suitability. **2** a letter of introduction given by a government to an ambassador before a new posting.
– ORIGIN Middle English: from medieval Latin *credentialis*, from *credentia* (see CREDENCE).

credenza /krɪ'dɛnzə/ ▪n. a sideboard or cupboard.
– ORIGIN C19: Italian, from medieval Latin *credentia* (see CREDENCE).

credibility ▪n. the quality of being credible.

credibility gap ▪n. an apparent difference between what is said or promised and what happens or is true.

credible ▪adj. able to be believed; convincing.
– DERIVATIVES **credibly** adv.
– ORIGIN Middle English: from Latin *credibilis*, from *credere* 'believe'.

credit ▪n. **1** the ability of a customer to obtain goods or services before payment, based on the trust that payment will be made in the future. ▸ money lent or made available under such an arrangement. **2** an entry in an account recording a sum received. **3** public acknowledgement or praise given for an achievement or quality. ▸ a source of pride. **4** (also **credit title**) an item in a list displayed at the beginning or end of a film or programme, acknowledging a contributor's role. **5** the acknowledgement of a student's completion of a course or activity that counts towards a degree or diploma. ▸ chiefly Brit. a grade above a pass in an examination. ▪v. (**credited, crediting**) **1** publicly acknowledge someone as a participant in the production of (something published or broadcast). ▸ (**credit someone with**) ascribe (an achievement or good quality) to someone. **2** add (an amount of money) to an account. **3** believe (something surprising or unlikely).
– PHRASES **be in credit** (of an account) have money in it. **do someone credit** make someone worthy of praise or respect. **have something to one's credit** have achieved something notable. **on credit** with an arrangement to pay later.
– ORIGIN C16: from French *crédit*, from Latin *creditum*, from *credere* 'believe, trust'.

creditable ▪ adj. deserving public acknowledgement and praise but not necessarily outstanding or successful.
– DERIVATIVES **creditability** n. **creditably** adv.

credit card ▪ n. a small plastic card issued by a bank or building society, allowing the holder to make purchases on credit.

creditor ▪ n. a person or company to whom money is owing.

credit title ▪ n. see **CREDIT** (sense 4).

credit transfer ▪ n. a direct payment of money from one bank account to another.

credit union ▪ n. a non-profit-making money co-operative whose members can borrow from pooled deposits at low interest rates.

creditworthy ▪ adj. considered suitable to receive commercial credit.
– DERIVATIVES **creditworthiness** n.

credo /'kriːdəʊ, 'kreɪ-/ ▪ n. (pl. **-os**) **1** a statement of a person's beliefs or aims. **2** (**Credo**) a creed of the Christian Church in Latin.
– ORIGIN Middle English: Latin, 'I believe'.

credulous /'krɛdjʊləs/ ▪ adj. having or showing too great a readiness to believe things.
– DERIVATIVES **credulity** /krɪ'djuːlɪti/ n. **credulously** adv. **credulousness** n.
– ORIGIN C16: from Latin *credulus*, from *credere* 'believe'.

Cree /kriː/ ▪ n. (pl. same or **Crees**) **1** a member of an American Indian people living in central Canada. **2** the Algonquian language of this people.
– ORIGIN from Canadian French *Cris*, abbrev. of *Cristinaux*, from Algonquian.

creed ▪ n. **1** a system of religious belief; a faith. ▸ a formal statement of Christian beliefs. **2** a credo.
– ORIGIN Old English, from Latin **CREDO**.

Creek /kriːk/ ▪ n. (pl. same) **1** a member of a confederacy of American Indian peoples of the south-eastern US in the 16th to 19th centuries. **2** the language spoken by these peoples.
– ORIGIN from **CREEK**, because they lived beside the waterways of the flatlands of Georgia and Alabama.

creek ▪ n. a narrow, sheltered waterway such as an inlet in a shoreline or channel in a marsh. ▸ N. Amer. & Austral./NZ a stream or minor tributary of a river.
– PHRASES **up the creek** informal **1** in severe difficulty or trouble. **2** Brit. stupid or misguided.
– ORIGIN Middle English: from Old French *crique* or from Old Norse *kriki* 'nook'.

creel ▪ n. **1** a large basket for carrying fish. **2** a rack holding bobbins or spools when spinning.
– ORIGIN Middle English; orig. Scots and northern English.

creep ▪ v. (past and past part. **crept** /krɛpt/) **1** move slowly and carefully, especially in order to avoid being heard or noticed. ▸ move or progress very slowly and steadily. ▸ (of a plant) grow along the ground or other surface by extending stems or branches. **2** (of a plastic solid) undergo gradual deformation under stress. **3** (**creep to**) informal behave obsequiously towards. ▪ n. **1** informal a contemptible person, especially one who behaves obsequiously in the hope of advancement. **2** very slow, steady movement or progress. ▸ gradual deformation of a plastic solid under stress.
– PHRASES **give someone the creeps** informal induce a feeling of revulsion or fear in someone. **make one's flesh creep** cause one to feel revulsion and have a sensation like that of something crawling over the skin.
– DERIVATIVES **creeping** adj.
– ORIGIN Old English, of Germanic origin.

creeper ▪ n. **1** any plant that grows along the ground, around another plant, or up a wall by means of extending stems or branches. **2** any of a number of small birds that creep around in trees or vegetation.

creepy ▪ adj. (**-ier**, **-iest**) informal causing an unpleasant feeling of fear or unease.
– DERIVATIVES **creepily** adv. **creepiness** n.

creepy-crawly informal ▪ n. (pl. **-ies**) a spider, worm, or other small flightless creature, especially when considered unpleasant or frightening. ▪ adj. creepy.

cremaster /krɪ'mɑːstə/ ▪ n. Entomology the hook-like tip of a butterfly pupa.

– ORIGIN C17: from Greek *kremastēr*, from *krema-* 'hang'.

cremate ▪ v. dispose of (a dead person's body) by burning it to ashes.
– DERIVATIVES **cremation** n. **cremator** n.
– ORIGIN C19 (*cremation* C17): from Latin *cremare* 'burn'.

crematorium /ˌkrɛmə'tɔːrɪəm/ ▪ n. (pl. **crematoria** or **crematoriums**) a building where the dead are cremated.
– ORIGIN C19: from Latin *cremare* 'burn'.

crematory /'krɛmət(ə)ri/ ▪ adj. of or relating to cremation. ▪ n. (pl. **-ies**) North American term for **CREMATORIUM**.

crème anglaise /ˌkrɛm ɒ'ɡlɛɪz/ ▪ n. a rich egg custard.
– ORIGIN French, 'English cream'.

crème brûlée /ˌkrɛm bruː'leɪ/ ▪ n. (pl. **crèmes brûlées** pronunc. same or **crème brûlées** /-'leɪz/) a dessert of custard topped with caramelized sugar.
– ORIGIN French, 'burnt cream'.

crème caramel /krɛm ˌkarə'mɛl, 'karəməl/ ▪ n. (pl. **crèmes caramel** pronunc. same or **crème caramels**) a custard dessert made with whipped cream and eggs and topped with caramel.
– ORIGIN from French.

crème de cassis /ˌkrɛm də ka'siːs/ ▪ n. see **CASSIS**.

crème de la crème /ˌkrɛm də la 'krɛm/ ▪ n. the best person or thing of a particular kind.
– ORIGIN French, 'cream of the cream'.

crème de menthe /ˌkrɛm də 'mɒnθ, 'mɒt/ ▪ n. a green peppermint-flavoured liqueur.
– ORIGIN French, 'cream of mint'.

crème fraiche /krɛm 'frɛʃ/ ▪ n. a type of thick cream made from double cream with the addition of buttermilk, sour cream, or yogurt.
– ORIGIN from French *crème fraîche* 'fresh cream'.

crenate /'kriːneɪt/ ▪ adj. Botany & Zoology having a round-toothed or scalloped edge.
– ORIGIN C18: from modern Latin *crenatus*, from popular Latin *crena* 'notch'.

crenellate /'krɛn(ə)leɪt/ (also **crenelate**) ▪ v. [usu. as adj. **crenellated**] chiefly historical provide with battlements.

crenellations ▪ pl. n. battlements.

creodont /'kriːədɒnt/ ▪ n. a fossil carnivorous mammal of the early Tertiary period, ancestral to modern carnivores.
– ORIGIN C19: from *Creodonta* (name of an order), from Greek *kreas* 'flesh' + *odous, odont-* 'tooth'.

Creole /'kriːəʊl/ (also **creole**) ▪ n. **1** a person of mixed European and black descent. **2** a descendant of European settlers in the Caribbean or Central or South America. **3** a white descendant of French settlers in Louisiana. **4** a mother tongue formed from the contact of a European language with a local language (especially African languages spoken by slaves in the West Indies). ▪ adj. of or relating to a Creole or Creoles.
– ORIGIN from French *créole, criole*, from Spanish *criollo*, prob. from Portuguese *crioulo* 'black person born in Brazil'.

creosol /'kriːəsɒl/ ▪ n. Chemistry a colourless liquid which is the chief constituent of wood-tar creosote.
– ORIGIN C19: from **CREOSOTE**.

creosote ▪ n. **1** a dark brown oil containing various phenols and other compounds distilled from coal tar, used as a wood preservative. **2** a colourless, pungent, oily liquid distilled from wood tar and used as an antiseptic. ▪ v. treat with creosote.
– ORIGIN C19: coined in German from Greek *kreas* 'flesh' + *sōtēr* 'preserver'.

creosote bush ▪ n. a common shrub of arid parts of Mexico and the western US, whose leaves yield a pungent antiseptic. [*Larrea tridentata*.]

crêpe /kreɪp/ (also **crape**) ▪ n. **1** a light, thin fabric with a wrinkled surface. **2** (also **crêpe rubber**) hard-wearing wrinkled rubber, used especially for the soles of shoes. **3** /also krɛp/ a thin pancake.
– DERIVATIVES **crêpey** (also **crêpy**) adj.
– ORIGIN C18: French, from Old French *crespe* 'curled, frizzed'.

crêpe de Chine /də ˈʃiːn/ ■ n. a fine crêpe of silk or similar fabric.
– ORIGIN C19: French, 'crêpe of China'.

crepe myrtle ■ n. variant spelling of **CRAPE MYRTLE**.

crêpe paper ■ n. thin, crinkled paper used chiefly for making decorations.

crêpe Suzette ■ n. (pl. **crêpes Suzette**) a thin dessert pancake flamed and served in alcohol.

crepitus /ˈkrɛpɪtəs/ ■ n. Medicine a grating sound or sensation produced by friction between bone and cartilage or the fractured parts of a bone. ▸ the production of rattling sounds in the lungs.
– ORIGIN C19: from Latin, from *crepare* 'rattle'.

crept past and past participle of **CREEP**.

crepuscular /krɪˈpʌskjʊlə, krɛ-/ ■ adj. of, resembling, or relating to twilight.
– ORIGIN C17: from Latin *crepusculum* 'twilight'.

Cres. ■ abbrev. crescent.

crescendo /krɪˈʃɛndəʊ/ ■ n. **1** (pl. **crescendos** or **crescendi** /-di/) a gradual increase in loudness in a piece of music. **2** the loudest or climactic point. ■ v. (**-oes**, **-oed**) increase in loudness or intensity.
– ORIGIN C18: Italian, from *crescere* 'to increase'.

crescent /ˈkrɛz(ə)nt, -s-/ ■ n. **1** the curved sickle shape of the waxing or waning moon. **2** a thing which has the shape of a single curve, especially when broad in the centre and tapering to a point at each end. ▸ a street or terrace of houses forming an arc. ■ adj. **1** having the shape of a crescent: *a crescent moon.* **2** poetic/literary growing, increasing, or developing.
– DERIVATIVES **crescentic** /-ˈsɛntɪk/ adj.
– ORIGIN Middle English, from Old French *creissant*, from Latin *crescere* 'grow'.

cresol /ˈkriːsɒl/ ■ n. Chemistry each of three isomeric crystalline compounds present in coal-tar creosote.
– ORIGIN C19: from **CREOSOTE**.

cress ■ n. a plant of the cabbage family with small white flowers and pungent leaves. [*Barbarea* and other genera.] ▸ young sprouts of garden cress eaten in salads.
– ORIGIN Old English, of West Germanic origin.

cresset /ˈkrɛsɪt/ ■ n. historical a metal container of oil, grease, wood, or coal set alight for illumination and typically mounted on a pole.
– ORIGIN Middle English: from Old French, from *craisse*, var. of *graisse* 'oil, grease'.

crest ■ n. **1** a comb or tuft of feathers, fur, or skin on the head of a bird or other animal. ▸ a plume of feathers on a helmet. **2** the top of a ridge, wave, etc. ▸ Anatomy a ridge along the surface of a bone. **3** a distinctive heraldic device representing a family or corporate body, displayed above the shield of a coat of arms or separately. ■ v. reach the top of. ▸ (of a wave) form a curling foamy top. ▸ (**be crested with**) have attached at the top.
– PHRASES **on the crest of a wave** at a very successful point.
– DERIVATIVES **crested** adj.
– ORIGIN Middle English: from Old French *creste*, from Latin *crista* 'tuft, plume'.

crestfallen ■ adj. sad and disappointed.
– ORIGIN C16: orig. with ref. to an animal with a fallen or drooping crest.

Cretaceous /krɪˈteɪʃəs/ ■ adj. Geology relating to or denoting the last period of the Mesozoic era (between the Jurassic and Tertiary periods, about 146 to 65 million years ago), a time when the first flowering plants appeared and at the end of which dinosaurs, ammonites, and many other organisms died out.
– ORIGIN C17: from Latin *cretaceus*, from *creta* 'chalk'.

Cretan /ˈkriːtən/ ■ n. an inhabitant or native of the Greek island of Crete. ■ adj. of or relating to Crete or its inhabitants.

cretin /ˈkrɛtɪn/ ■ n. a stupid person.
– DERIVATIVES **cretinous** adj.
– ORIGIN C18: from French *crétin*, from Swiss French *crestin* 'Christian', apparently used to convey a reminder that handicapped people are human.

cretonne /krɛˈtɒn, ˈkrɛtɒn/ ■ n. a heavy cotton fabric, typically with a floral pattern, used for upholstery.
– ORIGIN C19: from French.

Creutzfeldt–Jakob disease /ˌkrɔɪtsfɛltˈjakɒb/ ■ n. a fatal degenerative disease affecting nerve cells in the brain, believed to be caused by a prion.
– ORIGIN 1930s: named after the German neurologists H. G. *Creutzfeldt* and A. *Jakob*.

crevasse /krɪˈvas/ ■ n. a deep open crack in a glacier or ice field.
– ORIGIN C19: from French, from Old French *crevace* (see **CREVICE**).

crevice /ˈkrɛvɪs/ ■ n. a narrow opening or fissure, especially in a rock or wall.
– ORIGIN Middle English: from Old French *crevace*, from *crever* 'to burst', from Latin *crepare* 'to rattle, crack'.

crew[1] ■ n. [treated as sing. or pl.] **1** a group of people who work on and operate a ship, boat, aircraft, or train. ▸ such a group other than the officers. **2** informal, often derogatory a group of people. ■ v. provide with a crew. ▸ act as a member of a crew.
– DERIVATIVES **crewman** n. (pl. **-men**).
– ORIGIN Middle English: from Old French *creue* 'augmentation, increase', from *croistre* 'grow', from Latin *crescere*.

crew[2] past of **CROW**[2].

crew cut ■ n. a very short haircut for men and boys.
– ORIGIN 1940s: apparently first adopted by boat crews of Harvard and Yale universities.

crewel /ˈkruːəl/ ■ n. a thin, loosely twisted, worsted yarn used for tapestry and embroidery.
– ORIGIN C15.

crew neck ■ n. a close-fitting round neckline.
– DERIVATIVES **crew-necked** adj.

crib ■ n. **1** a child's bed with barred or latticed sides; a cot. ▸ a manger. ▸ a model of the Nativity of Christ. **2** informal a translation of a text for use by students, especially in a surreptitious way. ▸ a thing that has been plagiarized. **3** short for **CRIBBAGE**. **4** (also **cribwork**) a heavy timber framework used in foundations. ■ v. (**cribbed**, **cribbing**) informal copy illicitly or without acknowledgement.
– ORIGIN Old English, of Germanic origin.

cribbage ■ n. a card game for two players, in which the objective is to play so that the pip value of one's cards played reaches exactly 15 or 31.
– ORIGIN C17: rel. to **CRIB**.

crib death ■ n. North American term for **COT DEATH**.

cribellum /krɪˈbɛləm/ ■ n. (pl. **cribella** /-lə/) Zoology (in some spiders) an additional spinning organ with numerous fine pores, situated in front of the spinnerets.
– ORIGIN C19: from late Latin, diminutive of *cribrum* 'sieve'.

crick ■ n. a painful stiff feeling in the neck or back. ■ v. twist or strain (one's neck or back), causing painful stiffness.
– ORIGIN Middle English.

cricket[1] ■ n. an open-air game played on a large grass field with bat and ball between teams of eleven players, the batsmen attempting to score runs by hitting the ball and running between the wickets.
– PHRASES **not cricket** Brit. informal contrary to traditional standards of fairness or rectitude.
– DERIVATIVES **cricketer** n. **cricketing** adj.
– ORIGIN C16.

cricket[2] ■ n. an insect related to the grasshoppers but with shorter legs, of which the male produces a characteristic musical chirping sound. [Family Gryllidae: many species.] ▸ used in names of similar insects of related families, e.g. bush cricket.
– ORIGIN Middle English: from Old French *criquet*, from *criquer* 'to crackle', of imitative origin.

cricoid /ˈkraɪkɔɪd/ ■ n. (also **cricoid cartilage**) Anatomy the ring-shaped cartilage of the larynx.
– ORIGIN C18: from modern Latin *cricoides* 'ring-shaped'.

cri de cœur /ˌkriː də ˈkəː/ ■ n. (pl. **cris de cœur** pronunc. same) a passionate appeal or complaint.
– ORIGIN French, 'cry from the heart'.

cried past and past participle of **CRY**.

crikey ■ exclam. informal an expression of surprise.
– ORIGIN C19: euphemism for **CHRIST**.

crime ■ n. **1** an action which constitutes a serious offence against an individual or the state and is punishable by law. ▸ such actions collectively: *the victims of crime.* **2** informal a shameful or deplorable action or state of affairs.
– ORIGIN Middle English: from Latin *crimen* 'judgement, offence', from *cernere* 'to judge'.

Crimean /krʌɪˈmiːən/ ■ adj. of or relating to the Crimea, a peninsula of Ukraine between the Sea of Azov and the Black Sea.

crimen injuria ■ n. S. African Law wilful injury to the dignity of another, especially through the use of obscene language or gestures, or insults based on race or gender.
– ORIGIN from Latin *crimen* 'accusation, charge' + *iniuria* 'indignity, affront'.

criminal ■ n. a person who has committed a crime. ■ adj. **1** of, relating to, or constituting a crime. **2** informal deplorable and shocking.
– DERIVATIVES **criminality** /-ˈnalɪti/ n. **criminally** adv.
– ORIGIN Middle English: from late Latin *criminalis*, from Latin *crimen* (see CRIME).

criminalize /ˈkrɪmɪn(ə)lʌɪz/ (also **-ise**) ■ v. make (an activity) illegal. ▸ turn (someone) into a criminal by making their activities illegal.
– DERIVATIVES **criminalization** (also **-isation**) (/-ˈzeɪʃ(ə)n/) n.

criminal law ■ n. a system of law concerned with the punishment of offenders.

criminal libel ■ n. Law a malicious defamatory statement in a permanent form, rendering the maker liable to criminal prosecution.

criminology /ˌkrɪmɪˈnɒlədʒi/ ■ n. the scientific study of crime and criminals.
– DERIVATIVES **criminological** adj. **criminologist** n.

crimp ■ v. **1** compress into small folds or ridges. ▸ connect by squeezing together. ▸ [often as adj. **crimped**] make waves in (hair) with a hot iron. **2** N. Amer. informal have a limiting or adverse effect on. ■ n. **1** a curl, wave, or folded or compressed edge. **2** a small connecting piece for crimping wires or lines together.
– DERIVATIVES **crimper** n.
– ORIGIN Old English, of Germanic origin.

crimplene /ˈkrɪmpliːn/ ■ n. trademark a synthetic crease-resistant fibre and fabric.
– ORIGIN 1950s: prob. from CRIMP + a shortened form of TERYLENE.

crimson /ˈkrɪmz(ə)n/ ■ n. a rich deep red colour inclining to purple. ■ v. become flushed, especially through embarrassment.
– ORIGIN Middle English: from obsolete French *cramoisin* or Old Spanish *cremesin*, from Arabic *ḳirmiz* (see KERMES).

cringe /krɪn(d)ʒ/ ■ v. (**cringing**) **1** bend one's head and body in fear or apprehension or in a servile manner. **2** experience an inward shiver of embarrassment or disgust. ■ n. an act of cringing.
– ORIGIN Middle English *crenge* rel. to Old English *cringan*, *crincan* 'bend, yield, fall in battle', of Germanic origin and rel. to CRANK[1].

cringle ■ n. Nautical a ring of rope containing a thimble, for another rope to pass through.
– ORIGIN C17: from Low German *kringel*, diminutive of *kring* 'ring'.

crinkle ■ v. form or cause to form small creases or wrinkles. ■ n. a small crease or wrinkle.
– DERIVATIVES **crinkly** adj.
– ORIGIN Middle English: rel. to Old English *crincan* (see CRINGE).

crinoid /ˈkrɪnɔɪd, ˈkrʌɪnɔɪd/ ■ n. Zoology an echinoderm of a class (Crinoidea) that comprises the sea lilies and feather stars.
– ORIGIN from Greek *krinoeidēs* 'lily-like', from *krinon* 'lily'.

crinoline /ˈkrɪn(ə)lɪn/ ■ n. **1** historical a stiffened or hooped petticoat worn to make a long skirt stand out. **2** a stiff fabric made of horsehair and cotton or linen thread, used for stiffening petticoats or as a lining.
– ORIGIN C19: from French, from Latin *crinis* 'hair' + *linum* 'thread'.

cripes /krʌɪps/ ■ exclam. dated, informal used as a euphemism for Christ.

cripple ■ n. archaic or offensive a person who is unable to walk or move properly through disability or injury. ■ v. (usu. **be crippled**) make unable to move or walk properly. ▸ cause severe and disabling damage to.
– ORIGIN Old English, of Germanic origin.

crisis ■ n. (pl. **crises**) **1** a time of intense difficulty or danger. **2** the turning point of a disease when an important change takes place, indicating either recovery or death.
– ORIGIN Middle English: medical Latin, from Greek *krisis* 'decision', from *krinein* 'decide'.

crisp ■ adj. **1** firm, dry, and brittle, especially in a way considered pleasing. ▸ (of hair) having tight curls, giving an impression of rigidity. **2** (of the weather) cool, fresh, and invigorating. **3** (of a way of speaking) briskly decisive and matter-of-fact. ■ n. (also **potato crisp**) Brit. a wafer-thin slice of potato fried until crisp and eaten as a snack. ■ v. give (food) a crisp surface by placing it in an oven or grill.
– PHRASES **burn to a crisp** burn so as to leave only a charred remnant.
– DERIVATIVES **crispiness** n. **crisply** adv. **crispness** n. **crispy** adj. (**-ier**, **-iest**)
– ORIGIN Old English: from Latin *crispus* 'curled'.

crispbread ■ n. a thin crisp biscuit made from crushed rye or wheat.

crisper ■ n. a compartment at the bottom of a refrigerator for storing fruit and vegetables.

criss-cross ■ n. a pattern of intersecting straight lines or paths. ■ adj. (of a pattern) containing a number of intersecting straight lines or paths. ■ v. **1** form a criss-cross pattern on (a place). **2** move or travel around (a place) by going back and forth repeatedly.
– ORIGIN C17: from *Christ-cross*, later treated as a reduplication of CROSS.

crista /ˈkrɪstə/ ■ n. (pl. **cristae** /-tiː/) **1** Zoology a ridge or crest. **2** Biology an infolding of the inner membrane of a mitochondrion.
– DERIVATIVES **cristate** adj.
– ORIGIN C19: from Latin, 'tuft, plume, crest'.

criterion /krʌɪˈtɪəriən/ ■ n. (pl. **criteria** /-rɪə/) a principle or standard by which something may be judged or decided.
– DERIVATIVES **criterial** adj.
– ORIGIN C17: from Greek *kritērion* 'means of judging', from *kritēs* (see CRITIC).

> **USAGE**
> The singular form is **criterion** and the plural form is **criteria**. It is a common mistake to use **criteria** as if it were a singular, as in *a further criteria needs to be considered*.

critic ■ n. **1** a person who expresses an unfavourable opinion of something. **2** a person who judges the merits of literary, artistic, or musical works, especially one who does so professionally.
– ORIGIN C16: from Latin *criticus*, from Greek *kritikos*, from *kritēs* 'a judge'.

critical ■ adj. **1** expressing adverse or disapproving comments or judgements. **2** expressing or involving an analysis of the merits and faults of a work of literature, music, or art. **3** (of a situation or problem) at a point of crisis. ▸ extremely ill and at risk of death. ▸ having a decisive importance in the success or failure of something. **4** Mathematics & Physics relating to or denoting a point of transition from one state to another. **5** (of a nuclear reactor or fuel) maintaining a self-sustaining chain reaction.
– DERIVATIVES **criticality** n. **critically** adv.

critical angle ■ n. Optics the angle of incidence beyond which rays of light passing through a denser medium to the surface of a less dense medium are no longer refracted but totally reflected.

critical apparatus ■ n. see APPARATUS (sense 3).

critical damping ■ n. Physics damping just sufficient to prevent oscillations.

critical mass ■ n. **1** Physics the minimum amount of fissile material needed to maintain a nuclear chain reaction. **2** the minimum size or amount of resources required to start or maintain a venture.

critical outcome ■ n. any of a defined set of results expected to be achieved within a specific time frame, especially as used for performance evaluation. ▶ (in education) any of a set of clearly defined skills expected to be acquired by a student in the course of their studies.

critical path ■ n. the sequence of stages determining the minimum time needed for a complex operation.

critical point ■ n. **1** Chemistry a set of conditions at which both the liquid and gas phases of a substance have the same density, and are therefore indistinguishable. **2** Mathematics US term for **STATIONARY POINT**.

critical pressure ■ n. Chemistry the pressure of a gas or vapour in its critical state.

critical state ■ n. Chemistry the state of a substance when it is at the critical point.

critical temperature ■ n. Chemistry the temperature of a gas in its critical state, above which it cannot be liquefied by pressure alone.

criticism ■ n. **1** the expression of disapproval of someone or something based on perceived faults or mistakes. **2** the critical assessment of a literary or artistic work.

criticize (also **-ise**) ■ v. **1** indicate the faults of in a disapproving way. **2** form and express a critical assessment of (a literary or artistic work).
–DERIVATIVES **criticizer** (also **-iser**) n.

critique /krɪˈtiːk/ ■ n. a detailed analysis and assessment. ■ v. (**critiques, critiqued, critiquing**) evaluate in a detailed and analytical way.
–ORIGIN C17: from French, from Greek *kritikē tekhnē* 'critical art'.

critter ■ n. informal or dialect, chiefly N. Amer. a living creature.
–ORIGIN C19: var. of **CREATURE**.

croak ■ n. a characteristic deep hoarse sound made by a frog or a crow. ■ v. **1** (of a frog or crow) utter a croak. **2** informal die.
–DERIVATIVES **croakily** adv. **croaky** adj. (**-ier, -iest**).
–ORIGIN Middle English: imitative.

Croatian /krəʊˈeɪʃ(ə)n/ ■ n. (also **Croat** /ˈkrəʊat/) **1** a native or national of Croatia, or a person of Croatian descent. **2** the Southern Slavic language of the Croats, almost identical to Serbian but written in the Roman alphabet. ■ adj. of or relating to Croatia, its people, or their language.

crochet /ˈkrəʊʃeɪ, -ʃi/ ■ n. a handicraft in which yarn is made up into a patterned fabric by means of a hooked needle. ▶ fabric or items made in this way. ■ v. (**crocheted** /-ʃeɪd/ , **crocheting** /-ʃeɪɪŋ/) make (a garment or piece of fabric) in this way.
–ORIGIN C19: from French, diminutive of *croc* 'hook'.

croci plural form of **CROCUS**.

crocidolite /krə(ʊ)ˈsɪdəlʌɪt/ ■ n. a fibrous blue or green mineral consisting of a silicate of iron and sodium.
–ORIGIN C19: from Greek *krokis, krokid-* 'nap of cloth'.

crock[1] informal ■ n. an old person considered to be feeble and useless. ▶ Brit. an old and worn-out vehicle.
–ORIGIN Middle English: perhaps from Flemish, and prob. rel. to **CRACK**.

crock[2] ■ n. an earthenware pot or jar. ▶ a broken piece of earthenware. ▶ a plate, cup, or other item of crockery.
–ORIGIN Old English, of Germanic origin.

crockery ■ n. plates, dishes, cups, and similar items made of earthenware or china.
–ORIGIN C18: from obsolete *crocker* 'potter', from **CROCK**[2].

crocodile ■ n. **1** a large predatory semiaquatic reptile with long jaws, long tail, short legs, and a horny textured skin. [*Crocodylus* and other genera.] **2** leather made from crocodile skin, used especially to make bags and shoes. **3** Brit. informal a line of schoolchildren walking in pairs.
–ORIGIN Middle English: from Old French *cocodrille*, from Latin *crocodilus*, from Greek *krokodilos* 'worm of the stones'.

crocodile clip ■ n. a sprung metal clip with long, serrated jaws, used to connect an electric cable temporarily to a battery or other component.

crocodile tears ■ pl. n. tears or expressions of sorrow that are insincere.
–ORIGIN C16: said to be so named from a belief that crocodiles wept while devouring or luring their prey.

crocodilian /ˌkrɒkəˈdɪliən/ ■ n. Zoology a reptile of the order Crocodylia, comprising the crocodiles, alligators, caimans, and gharial.

crocus /ˈkrəʊkəs/ ■ n. (pl. **crocuses** or **croci** /-kʌɪ, -kiː/) a small spring-flowering Eurasian plant of the iris family, which grows from a corm and bears bright yellow, purple, or white flowers. [Genus *Crocus*.]
–ORIGIN Middle English: from Greek *krokos*, of Semitic origin.

Croesus /ˈkriːsəs/ ■ n. a person of great wealth.
–ORIGIN C17: from the name of a famously wealthy king of Lydia c.560–546 BC.

croft Brit. ■ n. **1** a small rented farm, especially in Scotland, having a right of pasturage held in common with other such farms. **2** a small enclosed field, typically attached to a house. ■ v. farm (land) as a croft or crofts.
–DERIVATIVES **crofter** n. **crofting** n.
–ORIGIN Old English.

Crohn's disease /ˈkrəʊnz/ ■ n. a chronic inflammatory disease of the intestines, especially the colon and ileum, associated with ulcers and fistulae.
–ORIGIN 1930s: named after the American pathologist Burrill B. *Crohn*.

croissant /ˈkrwasɒ̃/ ■ n. a French crescent-shaped roll made of sweet flaky pastry, eaten for breakfast.
–ORIGIN C19: French (see **CRESCENT**).

Cro-Magnon /krəʊˈmanjɒ̃, -ˈmagnən/ ■ n. [as modifier] denoting the earliest form of modern human in Europe, appearing c.35 000 years ago and associated with the Aurignacian flint industry.
–ORIGIN the name of a hill in the Dordogne, France.

crombec /ˈkrɒmbɛk/ ■ n. a small African warbler with a very short tail. [Genus *Sylvietta*: several species.]
–ORIGIN C20: from French, from Dutch *krom* 'crooked' + *bek* 'beak'.

crone ■ n. an ugly old woman.
–ORIGIN Middle English: via Middle Dutch *croonje, caroonje* 'carcass, old ewe' from Old Northern French *caroigne* (see **CARRION**).

crony /ˈkrəʊni/ ■ n. (pl. **-ies**) informal, often derogatory a close friend or companion.
–ORIGIN C17: from Greek *khronios* 'long-lasting', here used to mean 'contemporary'.

cronyism (also **croneyism**) ■ n. derogatory the improper appointment of friends and associates to positions of authority.

crook ■ n. **1** a shepherd's hooked staff. ▶ a bishop's crozier. **2** a bend, especially at the elbow in a person's arm. **3** informal a person who is dishonest or a criminal. ■ v. bend (something, especially a finger as a signal). ■ adj. Austral./NZ informal bad, unsound, or unwell.
–ORIGIN Middle English: from Old Norse *krókr* 'hook'.

crooked /ˈkrʊkɪd/ ■ adj. **1** bent or twisted out of shape or position. **2** informal dishonest or illegal.
–DERIVATIVES **crookedly** adv. **crookedness** n.

croon ■ v. hum, sing, or speak in a soft, low voice. ■ n. a soft, low voice or tone.
–DERIVATIVES **crooner** n.
–ORIGIN C15: from Middle Low German and Middle Dutch *krōnen* 'groan, lament'.

crop ■ n. **1** a plant cultivated on a large scale for food or other use, especially a cereal, fruit, or vegetable. ▶ an amount of a crop harvested at one time. **2** an amount of related people or things appearing at one time: *the current crop of students*. **3** a hairstyle in which the hair is cut very short. **4** a riding crop or hunting crop. **5** a pouch in a bird's gullet where food is stored or prepared for digestion. ■ v. (**cropped, cropping**) **1** cut (something, especially a person's hair) very short. ▶ (of an animal) bite off and eat the tops of (plants). ▶ trim off the edges of (a photograph). **2** harvest (a crop) from an area. ▶ sow or plant (land) with plants that will produce a crop. ▶ (of land or a plant) yield a harvest. **3** (**crop up**) appear or occur unexpectedly. **4** (**crop out**) (of rock) appear or be exposed at the surface of the earth.

–ORIGIN Old English, of Germanic origin.

crop circle ■ n. an area of standing crops which has been flattened in the form of a circle or more complex pattern by an unexplained agency.

crop dusting ■ n. the spraying of powdered insecticide or fertilizer on crops, especially from the air.

cropper ■ n. 1 a plant which yields a specified crop. 2 a machine or person that cuts or trims something. 3 chiefly US a person who raises a crop, especially as a share-cropper.
–PHRASES **come a cropper** informal fall heavily. ▸ suffer a defeat or disaster.

crop top (also **cropped top**) ■ n. a woman's casual garment for the upper body, cut short so that it reveals the stomach.

croquet /'krəʊkeɪ, -ki/ ■ n. a game played on a lawn, in which wooden balls are driven through a series of square-topped hoops by means of mallets. ▸ an act of croqueting a ball. ■ v. (**croqueted** /-keɪd/, **croqueting** /-keɪɪŋ/) drive away (an opponent's ball) by holding one's own ball against it and striking one's own.
–ORIGIN C19: perhaps a dialect form of French *crochet* 'hook'.

croquette /krə(ʊ)'kɛt/ ■ n. a small ball or roll of vegetables, minced meat, or fish, fried in breadcrumbs.
–ORIGIN French, from *croquer* 'to crunch'.

crosier /'krəʊzɪə, -ʒə/ ■ n. variant spelling of CROZIER.

cross ■ n. 1 a mark, object, or figure formed by two short intersecting lines or pieces (+ or ×). 2 an upright post with a transverse bar, as used in antiquity for crucifixion. ▸ (**the Cross**) the cross on which Christ was crucified. ▸ a cross-shaped decoration awarded for personal valour or indicating rank in some orders of knighthood. 3 a thing that is unavoidable and has to be endured: *she's just a cross we have to bear*. 4 an animal or plant resulting from cross-breeding; a hybrid. ▸ (**a cross between**) a mixture or compromise of two things. 5 (in soccer) a pass of the ball across the field towards the centre close to one's opponents' goal. 6 (in boxing) a blow given with a crosswise movement of the fist. ■ v. 1 go or extend across or to the other side of (a path, obstacle, or area). ▸ (**cross over**) (of an artist) begin to appeal to a wider audience. 2 pass in an opposite or different direction; intersect. ▸ place crosswise: *Michele crossed her arms*. 3 draw a line or lines across; mark with a cross. ▸ mark or annotate (a cheque), typically with a pair of parallel lines, to indicate that it must be paid into a named bank account. ▸ (**cross something off**) delete an item on a list. ▸ (**cross something out/through**) delete a word or phrase by drawing a line through it. 4 (**cross oneself**) make the sign of the cross in front of one's chest as a sign of Christian reverence or to invoke divine protection. 5 Soccer pass (the ball) across the field towards the centre when attacking. 6 cause (an animal of one species, breed, or variety) to interbreed with one of another. ▸ cross-fertilize (a plant). 7 oppose or stand in the way of. ■ adj. annoyed.
–PHRASES **at cross purposes** misunderstanding or having different aims from one another. **cross one's fingers** put one finger across another as a sign of hoping for good luck. **cross the floor** join the opposing side in Parliament. **cross my heart (and hope to die)** used to emphasize the truthfulness and sincerity of what one is saying. **cross someone's palm with silver** often humorous pay someone for a favour or service, especially having one's fortune told. **cross swords** have an argument or dispute. **crossed line** a telephone connection that has been wrongly made with the result that another call can be heard. **get one's wires (or lines) crossed** have a misunderstanding.
–DERIVATIVES **crosser** n. **crossly** adv. **crossness** n.
–ORIGIN Old English: from Old Norse *kross*, from Old Irish *cros*, from Latin *crux*.

cross- ■ comb. form 1 denoting movement or position across: *cross-channel*. ▸ denoting interaction: *cross-pollinate*. ▸ passing from side to side; transverse: *crosspiece*. 2 describing the form of a cross: *crossbones*.

crossbar ■ n. a horizontal bar, in particular one between the two upright posts of a football goal or between the handlebars and saddle on a bicycle.

cross-bedding ■ n. Geology layering within a stratum and at an angle to the main bedding plane.

cross bench ■ n. a seat in the British House of Lords occupied by a member who is independent of any political party.
–DERIVATIVES **cross-bencher** n.

cross-berry ■ n. a southern African shrub or small tree bearing mauve-pink flowers and four-lobed berries. [*Grewia occidentalis*.]

crossbow ■ n. a medieval bow of a kind fixed across a wooden support, having a groove for the bolt and a mechanism for drawing and releasing the string.
–DERIVATIVES **crossbowman** n. (pl. **-men**).

cross-breed ■ n. an animal or plant produced by mating or hybridizing two different species, breeds, or varieties. ■ v. breed or cause to breed in this way.

cross-check ■ v. verify (figures or information) by using an alternative source or method. ■ n. an instance of cross-checking figures or information.

cross-contamination ■ n. the process by which bacteria or other microorganisms are unintentionally transferred from one substance or object to another.
–DERIVATIVES **cross-contaminate** v.

cross-country ■ adj. 1 across fields or countryside, as opposed to on roads or tracks: *cross-country running*. 2 across a region or country, in particular not keeping to main or direct routes. ■ n. the sport of cross-country running, riding, skiing, or motoring.

cross-current ■ n. 1 a current in a river or sea which flows across another. 2 a process or tendency which is in conflict with another.

cross-cut ■ v. 1 cut (wood or stone) across its main grain or axis. 2 alternate (one sequence) with another when editing a film. ■ n. an instance of cross-cutting. ■ adj. (of a file) having two sets of grooves crossing each other diagonally.

cross-cut saw ■ n. a saw used for cutting across the grain of timber.

cross-dating ■ n. Archaeology the dating of objects by correlation with the chronology of another culture or site.

cross-dress ■ v. wear clothing typical of the opposite sex.
–DERIVATIVES **cross-dresser** n.

crosse /krɒs/ ■ n. the stick used in women's field lacrosse.
–ORIGIN C19: from French, from Old French *croce* 'bishop's crook'.

cross-examine ■ v. question (a witness called by the other party) in a court of law to check or extend testimony already given.
–DERIVATIVES **cross-examination** n. **cross-examiner** n.

cross-eyed ■ adj. having one or both eyes turned inwards towards the nose, either temporarily or as a permanent condition (convergent strabismus).

cross-fade ■ v. (in sound or film editing) make a picture or sound appear or be heard gradually as another disappears or becomes silent. ■ n. an act or instance of cross-fading.

cross-fertilize (also **-ise**) ■ v. 1 fertilize (a plant) using pollen from another plant of the same species. 2 stimulate the development of with an exchange of ideas or information.
–DERIVATIVES **cross-fertilization** (also **-isation**) n.

crossfire ■ n. gunfire from two or more directions passing through the same area.

cross-grain ■ adj. running across the regular grain in timber.

cross-grained ■ adj. 1 (of timber) having a cross-grain. 2 stubbornly contrary or bad-tempered.

cross hairs ■ pl. n. a pair of fine wires crossing at right angles at the focus of an optical instrument or gunsight.

cross-hatch ■ v. shade (an area) with intersecting sets of parallel lines.
–DERIVATIVES **cross-hatching** n.

cross head ■ n. 1 a bar or block between the piston rod and connecting rod in a steam engine. 2 a screw with an indented cross shape in its head. 3 a paragraph heading printed across a column in the body of a newspaper article.

cross infection ■ n. the transfer of infection, especially

crossing

to a hospital patient with a different infection or between different species of animal or plant.

crossing ■ n. **1** a place where things, especially roads or railway lines, cross. ▶ Architecture the intersection of a church nave and the transepts. **2** a place at which one may safely cross something, especially a street.

crossing over ■ n. Genetics the exchange of genes between homologous chromosomes, resulting in a mixture of parental characteristics in offspring.

cross-legged ■ adj. & adv. (of a seated person) with the legs crossed at the ankles and the knees bent outwards.

cross link ■ n. a transverse link, especially between chains of atoms in a polymeric molecule. ■ v. (**cross-link**) connect by a series of transverse links.
– DERIVATIVES **cross-linkage** n.

crossmatch ■ v. Medicine test the compatibility of (a donor's and a recipient's blood or tissue).

cross member ■ n. a transverse structural piece which adds support to a motor-vehicle chassis or other construction.

crossover ■ n. **1** a point or place of crossing from one side to the other. **2** the process of producing work or achieving success in a new field or style, especially in popular music.

crosspatch ■ n. informal a bad-tempered person.
– ORIGIN C18: from **CROSS** + obsolete *patch* 'fool, clown', perhaps from Italian *pazzo* 'madman'.

crosspiece ■ n. a beam or bar fixed or placed across something else.

cross-platform ■ adj. Computing able to be used on different types of computers or with different software packages.

cross-ply ■ adj. (of a tyre) having fabric layers with their threads running diagonally, crosswise to each other.

cross-pollinate ■ v. pollinate (a flower or plant) with pollen from another flower or plant.
– DERIVATIVES **cross-pollination** n.

cross-question ■ v. question in great detail.

cross-rate ■ n. an exchange rate between two currencies computed by reference to a third currency, usually the US dollar.

cross reference ■ n. a reference to another text or part of a text, typically given in order to elaborate on a point. ■ v. (**cross-reference**) provide with cross references.
– DERIVATIVES **cross-refer** v.

cross-rhythm ■ n. Music a rhythm used simultaneously with another rhythm or rhythms.

crossroads ■ n. **1** an intersection of two or more roads. **2** (**crossroad**) N. Amer. a road that crosses a main road or joins two main roads.

cross section ■ n. **1** a surface or shape exposed by making a straight cut through something, especially at right angles to an axis. **2** a typical or representative sample of a larger group. **3** Physics a quantity having the dimensions of an area which expresses the probability of a given interaction between particles. ■ v. (**cross-section**) make a cross section of.
– DERIVATIVES **cross-sectional** adj.

cross-sell ■ v. sell (a different product or service) to an existing customer.

cross stitch ■ n. a needlework stitch formed of two stitches crossing each other. ■ v. (**cross-stitch**) sew or embroider using such stitches.

cross-subsidize (also **-ise**) ■ v. subsidize (a business or activity) out of the profits of another business or activity.
– DERIVATIVES **cross-subsidization** (also **-isation**) n. **cross-subsidy** n.

crosstalk ■ n. **1** unwanted transfer of signals between communication channels. **2** witty conversation.

cross-train ■ v. **1** learn another skill, especially one related to one's current job. **2** [as noun **cross-training**] training in two or more sports in order to improve fitness and performance.

crosstrees ■ pl. n. a pair of horizontal struts attached to a sailing ship's mast to spread the rigging, especially at the head of a topmast.

cross-voting ■ n. voting for a party one does not belong to, or for more than one party.

crosswalk ■ n. N. Amer. & Austral. a pedestrian crossing.

crossways ■ adv. another term for **CROSSWISE**.

crosswind ■ n. a wind blowing across one's direction of travel.

crosswise ■ adv. **1** in the form of a cross. **2** diagonally; transversely.

crossword ■ n. a puzzle consisting of a grid of squares and blanks into which words crossing vertically and horizontally are written according to clues.

crostini /krɒˈstiːni/ ■ pl. n. small pieces of toasted or fried bread served with a topping as a starter or canapé.
– ORIGIN Italian, pl. of *crostino* 'little crust'.

crotch ■ n. **1** the part of the human body between the legs where they join the torso. **2** a fork in a tree, road, or river.
– DERIVATIVES **crotched** adj. **crotchless** adj.
– ORIGIN C16: perhaps rel. to Old French *croche* 'shepherd's crook', from Old Norse *krókr* 'hook'; partly also a var. of **CRUTCH**.

crotchet /ˈkrɒtʃɪt/ ■ n. Music a musical note having the time value of a quarter of a semibreve or half a minim, represented by a large solid dot with a plain stem.
– ORIGIN Middle English: from Old French *crochet*, diminutive of *croc*, from Old Norse *krókr* 'hook'.

crotchety ■ adj. irritable.
– DERIVATIVES **crotchetiness** n.
– ORIGIN C19: from rare *crotchet* 'perverse belief or notion'.

croton /ˈkrəʊt(ə)n/ ■ n. **1** a strong-scented tree, shrub, or herbaceous plant, native to tropical and warm regions. [Genus *Croton*.] **2** a small evergreen tree or shrub of the Indo-Pacific region, with colourful foliage. [Genus *Codiaeum*.]
– ORIGIN from Greek *krotōn* 'sheep tick' (from the shape of the seeds of the croton in sense 1).

crouch ■ v. adopt a position where the knees are bent and the upper body is brought forward and down. ▶ (**crouch over**) bend over so as to be close to. ■ n. a crouching stance or posture.
– ORIGIN Middle English: perhaps from Old French *crochir* 'be bent', from *croche* (see **CROTCH**).

croup[1] /kruːp/ ■ n. inflammation of the larynx and trachea in children, associated with infection and causing breathing difficulties.
– DERIVATIVES **croupy** adj.
– ORIGIN C18: from dialect *croup* 'to croak', of imitative origin.

croup[2] /kruːp/ ■ n. the rump or hindquarters of a horse.
– ORIGIN Middle English: from Old French *croupe*, of Germanic origin and rel. to **CROP**.

croupier /ˈkruːpɪə, -pɪeɪ/ ■ n. the person in charge of a gaming table, gathering in and paying out money or tokens.
– ORIGIN C18 (denoting a person standing behind a gambler to give advice): French, from Old French *cropier* 'pillion rider', rel. to Old French *croupe* (see **CROUP**[2]).

croustade /kruːˈstɑːd/ ■ n. a crisp piece of bread or pastry hollowed to receive a savoury filling.
– ORIGIN French: from Old French *crouste* or Italian *crostata* 'tart'.

crouton /ˈkruːtɒn/ ■ n. a small piece of fried or toasted bread served with soup or used as a garnish.
– ORIGIN from French *croûton*, from *croûte* (see **CRUST**).

Crow ■ n. (pl. same or **Crows**) **1** a member of an American Indian people inhabiting eastern Montana. **2** the Siouan language of this people.
– ORIGIN suggested by French *gens de corbeaux*, translating Siouan *apsáaloke* 'crow people'.

crow[1] ■ n. **1** a large perching bird with mostly glossy black plumage, a heavy bill, and a raucous voice. [Genus *Corvus*: several species; family Corvidae.] **2** informal an old or ugly woman.
– PHRASES **as the crow flies** in a straight line across country. **eat crow** N. Amer. informal be humiliated by having to admit one's defeats or mistakes.

–ORIGIN Old English *crāwe*, of West Germanic origin; rel. to CROW².

crow² ■ v. (past **crowed** or **crew**) **1** (of a cock) utter its characteristic loud cry. **2** express great pride or triumph, especially in a tone of gloating satisfaction. ■ n. **1** the cry of a cock. **2** a sound expressing great pride or triumph.
–ORIGIN Old English *crāwan*, of West Germanic origin, rel. to CROW¹; ultimately imitative.

crowbar ■ n. an iron bar with a flattened end, used as a lever. ■ v. (**-barred**, **-barring**) strike or open with a crowbar.

crowberry ■ n. (pl. **-ies**) **1** a creeping heather-like dwarf shrub of the northern hemisphere with small leaves and black berries. [*Empetrum nigrum*.] **2** the edible but flavourless black berry of this plant.

crowd ■ n. a large number of people gathered together. ▸ a large audience, especially at a sporting event. ▸ informal, often derogatory a group of people with a common interest. ■ v. **1** [often as adj. **crowded**] (of a number of people) fill (a space) almost completely, leaving little or no room for movement. ▸ move or come together as a crowd. **2** move too close to: *don't crowd her, she needs air.* **3** (**crowd someone/thing out**) exclude by taking the place of someone or something.
–DERIVATIVES **crowdedness** n.
–ORIGIN Old English *crūdan* 'press, hasten', of Germanic origin.

crowd-puller ■ n. informal an event or person that attracts a large audience.
–DERIVATIVES **crowd-pulling** adj.

crowfoot ■ n. a plant related to the buttercups, typically aquatic and having lobed or divided leaves and white or yellow flowers. [*Ranunculus aquatilis* (water crowfoot) and related species.]

crown ■ n. **1** a circular ornamental headdress worn by a monarch as a symbol of authority. ▸ (**the Crown**) the monarchy or reigning monarch. ▸ a wreath of leaves or flowers, especially that worn as an emblem of victory in ancient Greece or Rome. **2** an award or distinction gained by a victory or achievement, especially in sport. **3** the top or highest part. ▸ the top part of a person's head or a hat. ▸ the upper branching part of a tree or other plant. ▸ the upper part of a cut gem, above the girdle. **4** the part of a tooth projecting from the gum. ▸ an artificial replacement or covering for the upper part of a tooth. **5** a British coin with a face value of five shillings or 25 pence, now minted only for commemorative purposes. ■ v. **1** ceremonially place a crown on the head of (someone) to invest them as a monarch. ▸ declare to be the best, especially at a sport: *he was crowned world champion.* ▸ (in draughts) promote (a piece) to king by placing another on the top of it. **2** rest on or form the top of. **3** be the triumphant culmination of (an effort or endeavour). **4** fit a crown to (a tooth). **5** (of a baby's head during labour) fully appear in the vaginal opening prior to emerging.
–ORIGIN Middle English: from Anglo-Norman French *corune* (n.), *coruner* (v.), Old French *corone*, *coroner*, from Latin *corona* 'wreath, chaplet'.

crown cap ■ n. another term for CROWN CORK.

Crown Colony ■ n. a British colony whose legislature and administration is controlled by the Crown, represented by a governor.

crown cork ■ n. a metal bottle cap with a crimped edge.

Crown Court ■ n. (in England and Wales) a court of criminal jurisdiction, which deals with serious offences and appeals referred from the magistrates' courts.

Crown Derby ■ n. a kind of soft-paste porcelain made at Derby, England and often marked with a crown above the letter 'D'.

crowned head ■ n. a king or queen.

crown gall ■ n. a large tumour-like gall on the roots or lower trunk of a tree, caused by a bacterium.

crown glass ■ n. glass made without lead or iron, originally in a circular sheet, and used as optical glass.

crown green ■ n. Brit. a kind of bowling green which rises slightly towards the middle.

crown imperial ■ n. an Asian plant of the lily family with a cluster of bell-like flowers at the top of a tall, largely bare stem. [*Fritillaria imperialis*.]

Crown jewels ■ pl. n. the crown and other ornaments and jewellery worn or carried by the sovereign on certain state occasions.

crown moulding ■ n. US term for CORNICE (in sense 1).

crown of thorns ■ n. **1** a large spiky starfish of the tropical Indo-Pacific, feeding on coral. [*Acanthaster planci*.] **2** a thorny shrub, native to Madagascar. [*Euphorbia milii* (a popular house plant), and other species.]

Crown prince ■ n. (in some countries) a male heir to a throne.

Crown princess ■ n. the wife of a Crown prince. ▸ (in some countries) a female heir to a throne.

Crown prosecutor ■ n. (in England, Wales, and Canada) a lawyer who acts for the Crown, especially a prosecutor in a criminal court.

crown wheel ■ n. a gearwheel or cogwheel with teeth that project from the face of the wheel at right angles, used especially in the gears of motor vehicles.

crow's foot ■ n. (pl. **feet**) **1** a branching wrinkle at the outer corner of a person's eye. **2** a mark, symbol, or design formed of lines diverging from a point.

crow's-nest ■ n. a platform at the masthead of a vessel for a lookout to watch from.

crozier /ˈkrəʊzɪə/ (also **crosier**) ■ n. **1** a hooked staff carried by a bishop as a symbol of pastoral office. **2** the curled top of a young fern.
–ORIGIN Middle English: from Old French *croisier* 'cross-bearer', reinforced by Old French *crocier* 'bearer of a bishop's crook'.

CRT ■ abbrev. cathode ray tube.

cru /kruː/ ■ n. (pl. **crus** pronunc. same) (in France) a vineyard or group of vineyards, especially one of recognized superior quality. See also GRAND CRU (in sense 1), PREMIER CRU (in sense 1).
–ORIGIN French, from *crû* 'growth', from *croître*.

cruces plural form of CRUX.

crucial /ˈkruːʃ(ə)l/ ■ adj. **1** decisive or critical, especially in the success or failure of something. **2** informal excellent.
–DERIVATIVES **cruciality** /-ʃɪˈalɪti/ n. **crucially** adv.

HISTORY
The word **crucial** entered English in the 18th century in the sense 'cross-shaped', coming via French from Latin *crux* (stem *cruc-*) 'cross'. The sense 'decisive' developed from the Latin phrase *instantia crucis* 'crucial instance', coined by the philosopher Francis Bacon (1561–1626): Bacon was using the *crux*, or fingerpost marking a fork at a crossroads, as a metaphor for the moment at which one has to take a decision. The scientists Sir Isaac Newton and Robert Boyle took up the metaphor in *experimentum crucis* 'crucial experiment'. Latin *crux* is the root of a number of words, including cross, crucible, crucify, cruise, crusade, and excruciate.

cruciate ligament ■ n. Anatomy either of a pair of ligaments in the knee which cross each other and connect the femur to the tibia.

crucible /ˈkruːsɪb(ə)l/ ■ n. **1** a container in which metals or other substances may be melted or subjected to very high temperatures. **2** a situation of severe trial, or in which different elements interact to produce something new.
–ORIGIN Middle English: from medieval Latin *crucibulum* 'night lamp, crucible', from Latin *crux, cruc-* 'cross'.

cruciferous /kruːˈsɪf(ə)rəs/ ■ adj. Botany relating to or denoting plants of the cabbage family (Cruciferae), with four equal petals arranged in a cross.
–ORIGIN C19: from Latin *crux, cruc-* 'cross' + *-fer* 'bearing'.

crucifix /ˈkruːsɪfɪks/ ■ n. a representation of a cross with a figure of Christ on it.
–ORIGIN Middle English: from Latin *cruci fixus* 'fixed to a cross'.

cruciform /ˈkruːsɪfɔːm/ ■ adj. having the shape of a cross.
–ORIGIN C17: from Latin *crux, cruc-* 'cross' + -IFORM.

crucify /ˈkruːsɪfʌɪ/ ■ v. (**-ies**, **-ied**) **1** put (someone) to death

crud | 282

by nailing or binding them to a cross. **2** criticize severely and unrelentingly. ▶ cause anguish to.
– DERIVATIVES **crucifier** n. **crucifixion** n.
– ORIGIN Middle English: from Old French *crucifier*, from late Latin *crucifigere*, from Latin *crux, cruc-* 'cross' + *figere* 'fix'.

crud ■ n. informal **1** an unpleasantly dirty or messy substance. **2** nonsense.
– DERIVATIVES **cruddy** adj.
– ORIGIN Middle English: var. of CURD (the original sense).

crude ■ adj. **1** in a natural or raw state; not yet processed or refined. **2** (of an estimate or guess) likely to be only approximately accurate. **3** constructed or carried out in a rudimentary or makeshift way. **4** offensively coarse or rude, especially in relation to sexual matters. ■ n. natural mineral oil.
– DERIVATIVES **crudely** adv. **crudeness** n. **crudity** n.
– ORIGIN Middle English: from Latin *crudus* 'raw, rough'.

crudités /'kru:dɪteɪ/ ■ pl. n. mixed raw vegetables served as an hors d'oeuvre, typically with a sauce into which they may be dipped.
– ORIGIN pl. of French *crudité* 'rawness, crudity'.

cruel ■ adj. (**crueller, cruellest** or **crueler, cruelest**) disregarding or taking pleasure in the pain or suffering of others. ▶ causing pain or suffering.
– DERIVATIVES **cruelly** adv.
– ORIGIN Middle English: from Latin *crudelis*, rel. to *crudus* (see CRUDE).

cruelty ■ n. (pl. **-ies**) cruel behaviour or attitudes.

cruelty-free ■ adj. (of cosmetics) manufactured or developed by methods which do not involve cruelty to animals.

cruet /'kru:ɪt/ ■ n. **1** a small container for salt, pepper, oil, or vinegar for use at a dining table. ▶ (also **cruet stand**) Brit. a stand holding such containers. **2** (in church use) a small container for the wine or water to be used in the celebration of the Eucharist.
– ORIGIN Middle English: from Anglo-Norman French, diminutive of Old French *crue* 'pot', from Old Saxon *krūka*; rel. to CROCK².

cruise ■ v. **1** sail, travel, or move slowly around without a precise destination, especially for pleasure. ▶ travel smoothly at a moderate or economical speed. **2** achieve an objective with ease: *Sundowns cruised to a 2-0 win.* **3** informal wander about in search of a sexual partner. ■ n. an instance of cruising. ▶ a voyage on a ship taken as a holiday and usually calling in at several places.
– ORIGIN C17: prob. from Dutch *kruisen* 'to cross'.

cruise control ■ n. a device in a motor vehicle which can be switched on to maintain a selected constant speed without the use of the accelerator pedal.

cruise missile ■ n. a low-flying missile which is guided to its target by an on-board computer.

cruiser ■ n. **1** a relatively fast warship larger than a destroyer and less heavily armed than a battleship. **2** a yacht or motor boat with passenger accommodation, designed for leisure use.

cruiserweight ■ n. another term for LIGHT HEAVYWEIGHT.

crumb ■ n. a small fragment of bread, cake, or biscuit. ▶ the soft inner part of a loaf of bread. ■ v. [often as adj. **crumbed**] cover (food) with breadcrumbs.
– DERIVATIVES **crumby** adj.
– ORIGIN Old English, of Germanic origin.

crumble ■ v. break or fall apart into small fragments, especially as part of a gradual process of deterioration. ▶ cause (something, especially food) to crumble. ■ n. a pudding made with fruit and a topping of flour and fat rubbed to the texture of breadcrumbs.
– ORIGIN Middle English: prob. from Old English, rel. to CRUMB.

crumbly ■ adj. (**-ier, -iest**) easily crumbling. ■ n. (pl. **-ies**) informal, humorous an old person.
– DERIVATIVES **crumbliness** n.

crumbs ■ exclam. informal used to express dismay or surprise.
– ORIGIN C19: euphemism for *Christ*.

crumhorn ■ n. variant spelling of KRUMMHORN.

crummy ■ adj. (**-ier, -iest**) informal bad, unpleasant, or of poor quality.
– DERIVATIVES **crummily** adv. **crumminess** n.
– ORIGIN var. of *crumby* (see CRUMB).

crump ■ n. a loud thudding sound, especially one made by an exploding bomb or shell.
– ORIGIN C17: imitative.

crumpet ■ n. **1** a thick, flat, savoury cake with a soft, porous texture, made from a yeast mixture cooked on a griddle and eaten toasted and buttered. **2** Brit. informal women regarded as objects of sexual desire.
– ORIGIN C17.

crumple ■ v. **1** crush or become crushed so as to become creased and wrinkled. **2** suddenly lose force, effectiveness, or composure. ■ n. a crushed fold, crease, or wrinkle.
– DERIVATIVES **crumply** adj.
– ORIGIN Middle English: from obsolete *crump* 'make curved', from Old English *crump* 'bent, crooked', of West Germanic origin.

crumple zone ■ n. a part of a motor vehicle, especially the extreme front and rear, designed to crumple easily in a crash and absorb the main force of an impact.

crunch ■ v. **1** crush (a hard or brittle foodstuff) with the teeth, making a marked grinding sound. **2** make or move with such a sound. **3** (especially of a computer) process (large quantities of data). ■ n. **1** a crunching sound. **2** (**the crunch**) informal the crucial point of a situation. **3** a sit-up.
– ORIGIN C19: var. of C17 *cranch* (prob. imitative), associated with CRUSH and MUNCH.

cruncher ■ n. informal **1** a crucial or difficult point or question. **2** a computer, system, or person able to perform operations of great complexity or size. See also NUMBER CRUNCHER.

crunchy ■ adj. (**-ier, -iest**) **1** making a crunching noise when bitten or crushed. **2** N. Amer. informal politically liberal and environmentally aware.
– DERIVATIVES **crunchily** adv. **crunchiness** n.

crura cerebri plural form of CRUS CEREBRI.

crural /'krʊər(ə)l/ ■ adj. Anatomy & Zoology of or relating to the leg or the thigh. ▶ of or relating to the crura cerebri.
– ORIGIN C16: from Latin *cruralis*, from *crus, crur-* 'leg'.

crusade /kru:'seɪd/ ■ n. **1** any of a series of medieval military expeditions made by Europeans to recover the Holy Land from the Muslims. ▶ a war instigated for alleged religious ends. **2** an energetic organized campaign with a political, social, or religious aim: *a crusade against crime.* ■ v. [often as adj. **crusading**] lead or take part in a crusade.
– DERIVATIVES **crusader** n.
– ORIGIN C16: from French *croisade*, alteration of earlier *croisée* 'the state of being marked with the cross', from Latin *crux* 'cross'.

crus cerebri /krʌs 'serɪbraɪ/ ■ n. (pl. **crura cerebri**) Anatomy either of two symmetrical tracts of nerve fibres at the base of the midbrain, linking the pons and the cerebral hemispheres.
– ORIGIN C18: from Latin, 'leg of the brain'.

crush ■ v. **1** deform, pulverize, or force inwards by compressing forcefully. ▶ crease or crumple (cloth or paper). **2** violently subdue (opposition or a rebellion). **3** cause to feel overwhelming disappointment or embarrassment. ■ n. **1** a crowd of people pressed closely together. **2** informal an intense infatuation. **3** a drink made from the juice of pressed fruit. **4** (also **crush pen**) a fenced passage with one narrow end used for handling cattle or sheep.
– DERIVATIVES **crushable** adj. **crusher** n. **crushing** adj. **crushingly** adv.
– ORIGIN Middle English: from Old French *cruissir* 'gnash (teeth) or crack'.

crush barrier ■ n. Brit. a barrier, especially a temporary one, for restraining a crowd.

crushed velvet ■ n. velvet which has its nap pointing in different directions in irregular patches.

crush zone ■ n. another term for CRUMPLE ZONE.

crust ■ n. **1** the tough outer part of a loaf of bread. ▶ a hard, dry scrap of bread. **2** a hardened layer, coating, or deposit on something soft. ▶ a layer of pastry covering a

pie. **3** the outermost layer of rock of which a planet consists, especially the part of the earth above the mantle. **4** a deposit of tartrates and other substances formed in wine aged in the bottle, especially port. **5** informal a living or livelihood: *earning a crust.* ■ v. [often as adj. **crusted**] form into or cover with a crust: *crusted port.*
– DERIVATIVES **crustal** adj. (Geology).
– ORIGIN Middle English: from Old French *crouste*, from Latin *crusta* 'rind, shell, crust'.

Crustacea /krʌˈsteɪʃ(ə)/ ■ pl. n. Zoology a large group of mainly aquatic arthropods including crabs, lobsters, shrimps, woodlice, and barnacles.
– DERIVATIVES **crustacean** n. & adj. **crustaceous** adj.
– ORIGIN from Latin *crusta* (see CRUST).

crustose /ˈkrʌstəʊs/ ■ adj. Botany (of a lichen or alga) forming or resembling a crust.
– ORIGIN C19: from Latin *crustosus*, from *crusta* (see CRUST).

crusty ■ adj. (-ier, -iest) **1** having or consisting of a crust. **2** (of an old person) conservative and easily irritated. ■ n. (also **crustie**) (pl. **-ies**) informal a young person of a subculture characterized by a shabby appearance, a nomadic lifestyle, and a rejection of conventional values.
– DERIVATIVES **crustily** adv. **crustiness** n.

crutch ■ n. **1** a long stick with a crosspiece at the top, used as a support by a lame person. **2** something used for support or reassurance. **3** the crotch of the body or a garment.
– ORIGIN Old English, of Germanic origin.

crux /krʌks/ ■ n. (pl. **cruxes** or **cruces** /ˈkruːsiːz/) (**the crux**) the decisive or most important point at issue. ▶ a particular point of difficulty.
– ORIGIN C17: from Latin, 'cross'.

cry ■ v. (**-ies**, **-ied**) **1** shed tears. **2** shout or scream loudly. ▶ (of a hawker) proclaim (wares) for sale in the street. **3** (of a bird or other animal) make a loud characteristic call. **4** (**cry out for**) demand as a self-evident requirement or solution. **5** (**cry off**) informal go back on a promise or fail to keep to an arrangement. ■ n. (pl. **-ies**) **1** a spell of weeping. **2** a loud shout or scream. ▶ an urgent appeal, entreaty, or demand. **3** a distinctive call of a bird or other animal.
– PHRASES **cry for the moon** ask for what is unattainable or impossible. **for crying out loud** informal used to express irritation or impatience.
– ORIGIN Middle English: from Old French *crier* (v.), *cri* (n.), from Latin *quiritare* 'raise a public outcry', literally 'call on the *Quirites* (Roman citizens) for help'.

crybaby ■ n. (pl. **-ies**) a person, especially a child, who sheds tears frequently or readily.

crying ■ adj. very great: *it would be a crying shame.*

cryo- /ˈkraɪəʊ/ ■ comb. form involving or producing cold, especially extreme cold: *cryosurgery.*
– ORIGIN from Greek *kruos* 'frost'.

cryobiology ■ n. the branch of biology which deals with the properties of organisms and tissues at low temperatures.
– DERIVATIVES **cryobiological** adj. **cryobiologist** n.

cryogen /ˈkraɪə(ʊ)dʒ(ə)n/ ■ n. a substance used to produce very low temperatures.

cryogenics /ˌkraɪə(ʊ)ˈdʒɛnɪks/ ■ pl. n. [treated as sing.] the branch of physics concerned with the production and effects of very low temperatures. ▶ another term for CRYONICS.
– DERIVATIVES **cryogenic** adj.

cryonics /kraɪˈɒnɪks/ ■ pl. n. [treated as sing.] the practice or technique of deep-freezing the bodies of those who have died of an incurable disease, in the hope of a future cure.
– DERIVATIVES **cryonic** adj.
– ORIGIN 1960s: contraction of CRYOGENICS.

cryoprecipitate /ˌkraɪəʊprɪˈsɪpɪtət/ ■ n. chiefly Biochemistry a substance precipitated from a solution, especially from the blood, at low temperatures.

cryoprotectant ■ n. Physiology a substance that prevents the freezing of tissues, or prevents damage to cells during freezing.

cryosurgery ■ n. surgery using the local application of intense cold to destroy unwanted tissue.

crypt ■ n. **1** an underground room or vault beneath a church, used as a chapel or burial place. **2** Anatomy a small tubular gland, pit, or recess.
– ORIGIN Middle English: from Latin *crypta*, from Greek *kruptē* 'a vault', from *kruptos* 'hidden'.

cryptic ■ adj. **1** mysterious or obscure in meaning. ▶ (of a crossword) having difficult clues which indicate the solutions indirectly. **2** Zoology (of coloration or markings) serving to camouflage an animal in its natural environment.
– DERIVATIVES **cryptically** adv.
– ORIGIN C17: from late Latin *crypticus*, from Greek *kruptikos*, from *kruptos* 'hidden'.

crypto- /ˈkrɪptəʊ/ ■ comb. form concealed; secret: *cryptogram.*
– ORIGIN from Greek *kruptos* 'hidden'.

cryptobiont /ˌkrɪptəʊˈbaɪɒnt/ ■ n. Biology an organism capable of cryptobiosis.

cryptobiosis /ˌkrɪptə(ʊ)baɪˈəʊsɪs/ ■ n. Biology a physiological state in which metabolic activity is reduced to an undetectable level without disappearing altogether.
– DERIVATIVES **cryptobiotic** adj.

cryptocrystalline ■ adj. having a crystalline structure visible only when magnified.

cryptogam /ˈkrɪptə(ʊ)gam/ ■ n. Botany a plant with no true flowers or seeds, such as a fern, moss, liverwort, lichen, alga, or fungus.
– DERIVATIVES **cryptogamous** adj.
– ORIGIN C19: from French *cryptogame*, from modern Latin *cryptogamae* (*plantae*) from Greek *kruptos* 'hidden' + *gamos* 'marriage'.

cryptogamic ■ adj. **1** Botany relating to or denoting cryptogams. **2** Ecology relating to or denoting a fragile black surface layer of cyanobacteria, mosses, and lichens.

cryptogenic /ˌkrɪptəʊˈdʒɛnɪk/ ■ adj. (of a disease) of obscure or uncertain origin.

cryptogram /ˈkrɪptə(ʊ)gram/ ■ n. a text written in code.

cryptography ■ n. the art of writing or solving codes.
– DERIVATIVES **cryptographer** n. **cryptographic** adj. **cryptographically** adv.

cryptology ■ n. the study of codes, or the art of writing and solving them.
– DERIVATIVES **cryptological** adj. **cryptologist** n.

cryptomeria /ˌkrɪptə(ʊ)ˈmɪərɪə/ ■ n. a tall conical coniferous tree with long, curved leaves and short cones, native to China and Japan. [*Cryptomeria japonica*.]
– ORIGIN from CRYPTO- + Greek *meros* 'part' (because the seeds are concealed).

cryptonym /ˈkrɪptənɪm/ ■ n. a code name.
– DERIVATIVES **cryptonymous** adj.
– ORIGIN C19: from CRYPTO- + Greek *onoma* 'name'.

cryptorchidism ■ n. Medicine a condition in which one or both of the testes fail to descend from the abdomen into the scrotum.
– ORIGIN C19: from CRYPTO- + Greek *orkhis*, *orkhid-* 'testicle'.

cryptosporidium /ˌkrɪptə(ʊ)spɒˈrɪdɪəm/ ■ n. a parasitic coccidian protozoan found in the intestinal tract of many vertebrates, where it sometimes causes disease.
– ORIGIN C20: from CRYPTO- + modern Latin *sporidium* 'small spore'.

cryptozoology ■ n. the search for animals whose existence is disputed or unsubstantiated, such as the Loch Ness monster.
– DERIVATIVES **cryptozoological** adj. **cryptozoologist** n.

crystal ■ n. **1** a piece of a homogeneous solid substance having a natural geometrically regular form with symmetrically arranged plane faces. ▶ Chemistry any solid consisting of a symmetrical, ordered, three-dimensional aggregation of atoms or molecules. ▶ a clear transparent mineral, especially quartz. **2** (also **crystal glass**) highly transparent glass with a high refractive index. ▶ the glass over a watch face. **3** [as modifier] clear and transparent: *the crystal waters of the lake.*
– ORIGIN Old English: from Old French *cristal*, from Latin *crystallum*, from Greek *krustallos* 'ice, crystal'.

crystal ball ■ n. a solid globe of glass or rock crystal, used by fortune tellers and clairvoyants for crystal-gazing.

crystal class ■ n. each of thirty-two categories of crystals classified according to the possible combinations of symmetry elements possessed by the crystal lattice.

crystal-gazing ■ n. looking intently into a crystal ball with the aim of seeing images relating to future or distant events.

crystal lattice ■ n. the symmetrical three-dimensional arrangement of atoms inside a crystal.

crystalline /ˈkrɪst(ə)lʌɪn/ ■ adj. 1 having the structure and form of a crystal. 2 poetic/literary very clear.
– DERIVATIVES **crystallinity** n.

crystalline lens ■ n. the lens of the eye.

crystallite /ˈkrɪstəlʌɪt/ ■ n. an individual perfect crystal or region of regular crystalline structure in the substance of a material. ▸ a very small crystal.

crystallize (also **-ise**) ■ v. 1 form or cause to form crystals. ▸ [as adj. **crystallized** (also **-ised**)] (of fruit or petals) coated and impregnated with sugar. 2 make or become definite and clear.
– DERIVATIVES **crystallizable** (also **-isable**) adj. **crystallization** (also **-isation**) n.

crystallography /ˌkrɪstəˈlɒɡrəfi/ ■ n. the branch of science concerned with the structure and properties of crystals.
– DERIVATIVES **crystallographer** n. **crystallographic** adj. **crystallographically** adv.

crystalloid ■ adj. resembling a crystal in shape or structure. ■ n. Chemistry a substance that, when dissolved, forms a true solution rather than a colloid and is able to pass through a semipermeable membrane.

crystal meth ■ n. see METH.

crystal set ■ n. a simple early form of radio receiver with a crystal touching a metal wire as the rectifier and lacking an amplifier or loudspeaker, necessitating headphones or an earphone.

crystal system ■ n. each of seven categories of crystals (cubic, tetragonal, orthorhombic, trigonal, hexagonal, monoclinic, and triclinic) classified according to the possible relations of the crystal axes.

Cs ■ symb. the chemical element caesium.

c/s ■ abbrev. cycles per second.

CSE ■ abbrev. Brit. Certificate of Secondary Education.

C-section ■ n. a Caesarean section.

CS gas ■ n. a powerful form of tear gas used particularly in the control of riots.
– ORIGIN 1960s: from the initials of the American chemists Ben B. *Corson* and Roger W. *Stoughton*.

CSIR ■ abbrev. (in South Africa) Council for Scientific and Industrial Research.

CST ■ abbrev. Central Standard Time.

CT ■ abbrev. computerized (or computed) tomography.

ct ■ abbrev. 1 carat. 2 cent.

ctenidium /tɪˈnɪdɪəm/ ■ n. (pl. **ctenidia** /-dɪə/) Zoology a comb-like respiratory organ in a mollusc.
– ORIGIN C19: from Greek *ktenidion*, diminutive of *kteis, kten-* 'comb'.

ctenoid /ˈtiːnɔɪd/ ■ adj. Zoology (of fish scales) having many tiny projections on the edge like the teeth of a comb, as in many bony fishes. Compare with GANOID and PLACOID.
– ORIGIN C19: from Greek *kteis, kten-* 'comb'.

Ctenophora /tiːˈnɒfərə, tɛ-/ ■ pl. n. Zoology a small phylum of aquatic invertebrates that comprises the comb jellies.
– DERIVATIVES **ctenophore** /ˈtiːnəfɔː, ˈtɛ-/ n.
– ORIGIN from Greek *kteis, kten-* 'comb' + *pherein* 'to bear'.

CTS ■ abbrev. carpal tunnel syndrome.

Cu ■ symb. the chemical element copper.
– ORIGIN from late Latin *cuprum*.

cu. ■ abbrev. cubic.

cub ■ n. 1 the young of a fox, bear, lion, or other carnivorous mammal. 2 (**Cubs**) a junior branch of the Scout Association, for boys and girls aged about 8 to 10. ▸ (also **Cub Scout**) a member of this organization. ■ v.

(**cubbed**, **cubbing**) 1 give birth to cubs. 2 hunt fox cubs.
– ORIGIN C16.

cubage ■ n. cubic content or capacity.

Cuban /ˈkjuːbən/ ■ n. a native or inhabitant of Cuba. ■ adj. of or relating to Cuba.

cubby ■ n. (pl. **-ies**) a cubbyhole.

cubbyhole ■ n. a small enclosed space or room. ▸ S. African the glove compartment of a motor vehicle.
– ORIGIN C17: rel. to dialect *cub* 'stall, pen, hutch', of Low German origin.

cube ■ n. 1 a symmetrical three-dimensional shape contained by six equal squares. 2 Mathematics the product of a number multiplied by its square, represented by a superscript figure 3. ■ v. 1 Mathematics raise (a number or value) to its cube. 2 cut (food) into small cubes.
– ORIGIN C16: from Old French or from Greek *kubos*.

cube root ■ n. the number which produces a given number when cubed.

cubic /ˈkjuːbɪk/ ■ adj. 1 having the shape of a cube. ▸ denoting a crystal system with three equal axes at right angles. 2 denoting a unit of measurement equal to the volume of a cube whose side is one of the linear unit specified: *a cubic metre*. 3 involving the cube (and no higher power) of a quantity or variable.
– DERIVATIVES **cubical** adj. **cubically** adv.

cubicle ■ n. a small partitioned-off area of a room.
– ORIGIN Middle English (in the sense 'bedroom'): from Latin *cubiculum*, from *cubare* 'lie down'.

cubism ■ n. an early 20th-century style of painting in which perspective with a single viewpoint was abandoned and use was made of simple geometric shapes and interlocking planes.
– DERIVATIVES **cubist** n. & adj.

cubit /ˈkjuːbɪt/ ■ n. an ancient measure of length, approximately equal to the length of a forearm.
– ORIGIN Middle English: from Latin *cubitum* 'elbow, forearm, cubit'.

cubital /ˈkjuːbɪt(ə)l/ ■ adj. Anatomy of the forearm or the elbow.
– ORIGIN Middle English: from Latin *cubitalis*, from *cubitus* 'cubit'.

cuboid /ˈkjuːbɔɪd/ ■ adj. more or less cubic in shape. ■ n. 1 Geometry a solid which has six rectangular faces at right angles to each other. 2 (also **cuboid bone**) Anatomy a squat tarsal bone on the outer side of the foot, articulating with the heel bone and the fourth and fifth metatarsals.
– DERIVATIVES **cuboidal** adj.

cub reporter ■ n. informal a young or inexperienced newspaper reporter.

cuckold /ˈkʌk(ə)ld/ ■ n. the husband of an adulteress regarded as an object of derision. ■ v. make (a married man) a cuckold.
– DERIVATIVES **cuckoldry** n.
– ORIGIN Old English, from Old French *cucuault*, from *cucu* 'cuckoo' (from the cuckoo's habit of laying its egg in another bird's nest).

cuckoo ■ n. a grey or brown bird known for the far-carrying two-note call of the male and for the habit of laying its eggs in the nests of small songbirds. [*Cuculus canorus*.] ▸ used in names of other birds of the same family (Culicidae). ■ adj. informal crazy.
– ORIGIN Middle English: from Old French *cucu*, imitative of its call.

cuckoo bee ■ n. a parasitic bee which lays its eggs in the nest of another kind of bee. [*Nomada*, *Psithyrus*, and other genera.]

cuckoo clock ■ n. a clock with a mechanical cuckoo that pops out on the hour making a sound like a cuckoo's call.

cuckooflower ■ n. a spring-flowering European plant with pale lilac flowers, growing in damp habitats. [*Cardamine pratensis*.]
– ORIGIN C16: so named because it flowers at the time of year when the cuckoo is first heard calling.

cuckoo pint ■ n. the common European wild arum with a pale spathe and a purple or green spadix followed by bright red berries. [*Arum maculatum*.]
– ORIGIN Middle English: from earlier *cuckoo-pintle*, from PINTLE in the obsolete sense 'penis' (because of the shape of the spadix).

cuckoo spit Brit. ■ n. whitish froth found in compact masses on leaves and plant stems, exuded by the larvae of froghoppers.

cuckoo wasp ■ n. a ruby-tail or other wasp which lays its eggs in the nest of a bee or other wasp.

cucumber ■ n. **1** a long, green-skinned fruit with watery flesh, eaten raw in salads. **2** the widely cultivated climbing plant of the gourd family which yields this fruit, originally native to the Chinese Himalayan region. [*Cucumis sativus*.]
– PHRASES **(as) cool as a cucumber** very cool or calm.
– ORIGIN Middle English: from Old French *coucombre*, from Latin *cucumis, cucumer-*.

cucurbit /kjuːˈkəːbɪt/ ■ n. chiefly N. Amer. a plant of the gourd family (Cucurbitaceae), which includes melon, pumpkin, squash, and cucumber.
– DERIVATIVES **cucurbitaceous** adj.
– ORIGIN Middle English: from Latin *cucurbita*.

cud ■ n. partly digested food returned from the first stomach of ruminants to the mouth for further chewing.
– PHRASES **chew the cud** think or talk reflectively.
– ORIGIN Old English, of Germanic origin.

cuda ■ n. another term for COUTA.

cuddle ■ v. hold close in one's arms as a way of showing love or affection. ▸ (often **cuddle up to**) lie or sit close and snug. ■ n. a prolonged and affectionate hug.
– DERIVATIVES **cuddlesome** adj.
– ORIGIN C16.

cuddly ■ adj. (**-ier, -iest**) pleasantly soft or plump.

cudgel /ˈkʌdʒ(ə)l/ ■ n. a short thick stick used as a weapon. ■ v. (**cudgelled, cudgelling**; US **cudgeled, cudgeling**) beat with a cudgel.
– PHRASES **cudgel one's brain** think hard about a problem. **take up cudgels** start to defend or support someone or something strongly.
– ORIGIN Old English.

cudweed ■ n. a plant of the daisy family, with hairy or downy leaves and inconspicuous flowers. [Genus *Gnaphalium*.]

cue¹ ■ n. **1** a signal to an actor or other performer to enter or to begin their speech or performance. ▸ a signal or prompt for action. **2** Psychology a feature of something perceived that is used in the brain's interpretation of the perception. **3** a facility for playing through an audio or video recording very rapidly until a desired starting point is reached. ■ v. (**cues, cued, cueing** or **cuing**) **1** give a cue to or for. ▸ act as a prompt or reminder. **2** set a piece of audio or video equipment in readiness to play (a particular part of a recording).
– PHRASES **on cue** at the correct moment.
– ORIGIN C16.

cue² ■ n. a long tapering wooden rod for striking the ball in snooker, billiards, etc. ■ v. (**cues, cued, cueing** or **cuing**) use a cue to strike the ball.
– ORIGIN C18 (denoting a long plait or pigtail): var. of QUEUE.

cue ball ■ n. the ball, usually a white one, that is to be struck with the cue in snooker, billiards, etc.

cue bid ■ n. Bridge a bid intended to give specific information about the content of the hand to the bidder's partner rather than to advance the auction.

cue card ■ n. a card held beside a camera for a television broadcaster to read from while appearing to look into the camera.

cuesta /ˈkwɛstə/ ■ n. Geology a ridge formed by inclined strata, with a gentle slope on one side and a steep slope on the other.
– ORIGIN C19: from Spanish, 'slope'.

cuff¹ ■ n. **1** the end part of a sleeve, where the material of the sleeve is turned back or a separate band is sewn on. ▸ chiefly N. Amer. a trouser turn-up. **2** (**cuffs**) informal handcuffs. **3** an inflatable bag wrapped round the arm when blood pressure is measured. ■ v. informal secure with handcuffs.
– PHRASES **off the cuff** informal without preparation. [as if from impromptu notes made on one's shirt cuffs.]
– DERIVATIVES **cuffed** adj.
– ORIGIN Middle English (denoting a glove or mitten).

cuff² ■ v. strike with an open hand, especially on the head. ■ n. a blow given with an open hand.
– ORIGIN C16.

cufflink ■ n. a device for fastening together the sides of a shirt cuff, passed through a hole in each side of the cuff.

Cufic ■ n. & adj. variant spelling of KUFIC.

cui bono? /kwiː ˈbɒnəʊ, ˈbəʊ-/ ■ exclam. who stands to gain (i.e. from a crime, and so might have been responsible for it)?
– ORIGIN Latin, 'to whom (is it) a benefit?'

cuirass /kwɪˈras/ ■ n. historical a piece of armour consisting of breastplate and backplate fastened together.
– ORIGIN Middle English: from Old French *cuirace*, from late Latin *coriaceus*, from *corium* 'leather'.

cuisine /kwɪˈziːn/ ■ n. a style or method of cooking, especially as characteristic of a particular country or region. ▸ food cooked in a certain way.
– ORIGIN C18: French, 'kitchen'.

cul-de-sac /ˈkʌldəˌsak, ˈkʊl-/ ■ n. (pl. **culs-de-sac** pronunc. same) a street or passage closed at one end.
– ORIGIN C18: French, 'bottom of a sack'.

culex /ˈkjuːlɛks/ ■ n. (pl. **culices** /-lɪsiːz/) a mosquito of a genus which includes species that transmit filariasis and other diseases but not malaria.
– DERIVATIVES **culicine** /ˈkjuːlɪsʌɪn, -siːn/ adj. & n.
– ORIGIN Latin, 'gnat'.

culinary ■ adj. of or for cooking.
– DERIVATIVES **culinarily** adv.
– ORIGIN C17: from Latin *culinarius*, from *culina* 'kitchen'.

cull ■ v. **1** reduce the population of (a wild animal) by selective slaughter. ▸ send (an unwanted farm animal) to be slaughtered. **2** select from a large quantity; obtain from a variety of sources. ■ n. a selective slaughter of wild animals. ▸ a livestock animal selected for killing.
– ORIGIN Middle English: from Old French *coillier*, from Latin *colligere* (see COLLECT¹).

culm /kʌlm/ ■ n. the hollow stem of a grass or cereal plant, especially that bearing the flower.
– ORIGIN C17: from Latin *culmus* 'stalk'.

culminant ■ adj. at or forming the top or highest point.

culminate /ˈkʌlmɪneɪt/ ■ v. (usu. **culminate in**) reach or be a climax or point of highest development. **2** archaic or Astrology (of a celestial body) reach or be at the meridian.
– DERIVATIVES **culmination** n.
– ORIGIN C17: from late Latin *culminare*, from Latin *culmen* 'summit'.

culottes /kjuːˈlɒt(s)/ ■ pl. n. women's knee-length trousers, cut with very full legs to resemble a skirt.
– ORIGIN C19: French, 'knee breeches', diminutive of *cul* 'rump'.

culpable ■ adj. deserving blame.
– DERIVATIVES **culpability** n. **culpably** adv.
– ORIGIN Middle English: from Latin *culpabilis*, from *culpare* 'to blame', from *culpa* 'fault, blame'.

culpable homicide ■ n. Law (in some jurisdictions) an unlawful act which has resulted in a person's death but is held not to amount to murder.

culprit ■ n. a person who is responsible for a crime or other misdeed.
– ORIGIN C17: perhaps from a misinterpretation of the abbrev. *cul. prist* for the Anglo-Norman French judicial formula *Culpable: prest d'averrer notre bille* '(You are) guilty: (We are) ready to prove our indictment'.

cult ■ n. **1** a system of religious devotion directed towards a particular figure or object. ▸ a relatively small religious group regarded by others as strange or as imposing excessive control over members. **2** something popular or fashionable among a particular section of society.
– DERIVATIVES **cultic** adj. **cultish** adj. **cultishness** n. **cultism** n. **cultist** n.
– ORIGIN C17: from French *culte* or Latin *cultus* 'worship'.

cultivar /ˈkʌltɪvɑː/ ■ n. a plant variety that has been produced in cultivation by selective breeding.
– ORIGIN 1920s: blend of CULTIVATE and VARIETY.

cultivate ■ v. **1** prepare and use (land) for crops or gardening. ▸ raise or grow (plants), especially on a large scale for commercial purposes. **2** try to acquire or develop

cultivation

(a quality or skill). ▶ try to win the friendship or favour of. **3** [as adj. **cultivated**] refined and well educated.
– DERIVATIVES **cultivable** adj. **cultivatable** adj.
– ORIGIN C17: from medieval Latin *cultivare*, from *cultiva (terra)* 'arable (land)', from *colere* 'cultivate, inhabit'.

cultivation ■ n. **1** the action of cultivating land, or the state of being cultivated. **2** the process of acquiring or developing a quality or skill. **3** refinement and good education: *a person of cultivation and taste*.

cultivator ■ n. a person or thing that cultivates something. ▶ a mechanical implement for breaking up the ground.

cultural ■ adj. **1** of or relating to the culture of a society. **2** of or relating to the arts and to intellectual achievements.
– DERIVATIVES **culturally** adv.

cultural anthropology ■ n. another term for SOCIAL ANTHROPOLOGY.

culture ■ n. **1** the arts and other manifestations of human intellectual achievement regarded collectively. ▶ a refined understanding or appreciation of this. **2** the customs, institutions, and achievements of a particular nation, people, or group. **3** Biology the cultivation of bacteria, tissue cells, etc. in an artificial medium containing nutrients. ▶ a preparation of cells obtained in such a way. ▶ the cultivation of plants. **4** [in combination] denoting cultivation or husbandry: *aviculture*. ■ v. Biology maintain (tissue cells, bacteria, etc.) in conditions suitable for growth.
– ORIGIN C17: the noun from French *culture* or directly from Latin *cultura* 'growing, cultivation'; the verb from obsolete French *culturer* or medieval Latin *culturare*, both from Latin *colere* (see CULTIVATE).

cultured ■ adj. **1** refined and well educated. **2** (of a pearl) formed round a foreign body inserted into an oyster.

culture shock ■ n. the feeling of disorientation experienced when suddenly subjected to an unfamiliar culture or way of life.

culture vulture ■ n. informal a person who is very interested in the arts.

culverin /ˈkʌlv(ə)rɪn/ ■ n. **1** a 16th- or 17th-century cannon with a relatively long barrel for its bore. **2** a kind of handgun of the 15th and 16th centuries.
– ORIGIN C15: from Old French *coulevrine*, from *couleuvre* 'snake'.

culvert /ˈkʌlvət/ ■ n. a tunnel carrying a stream or open drain under a road or railway.
– ORIGIN C18.

cum¹ /kʌm/ ■ prep. combined with; also used as: *a study-cum-bedroom*.
– ORIGIN C19: Latin.

cum² /kʌm/ ■ n. informal variant spelling of COME.

cumber /ˈkʌmbə/ ■ v. dated hamper, hinder, or obstruct.
– ORIGIN Middle English: prob. from ENCUMBER.

Cumberland sauce ■ n. a piquant sauce made from redcurrant jelly, served with game and cold meats.

cumbersome ■ adj. **1** difficult to carry or use through size; unwieldy. **2** slow or complicated and therefore inefficient.
– DERIVATIVES **cumbersomely** adv. **cumbersomeness** n.

cumbrous /ˈkʌmbrəs/ ■ adj. poetic/literary cumbersome.
– DERIVATIVES **cumbrously** adv. **cumbrousness** n.

cum dividend ■ adv. (of share purchases) with a dividend about to be paid.

cumin /ˈkʌmɪn, ˈkjuːmɪn/ (also **cummin**) ■ n. **1** the aromatic seeds of a plant of the parsley family, used as a spice, especially in curry powder. **2** the plant which bears this fruit, occurring from the Mediterranean to central Asia. [*Cuminum cyminum*.]
– ORIGIN Old English *cymen*, Old French *cumon*, from Latin *cuminum*, from Greek *kuminon*, prob. of Semitic origin.

cum laude /kʌm ˈlɔːdi, kʊm ˈlaʊdeɪ/ ■ adv. & adj. with distinction (with reference to university degrees and diplomas).
– ORIGIN Latin, literally 'with praise'.

cummerbund /ˈkʌməbʌnd/ ■ n. a sash worn around the waist, especially as part of a man's formal evening suit.
– ORIGIN from Urdu and Persian *kamar-band*.

cumquat ■ n. variant spelling of KUMQUAT.

cumulate ■ v. /ˈkjuːmjʊleɪt/ accumulate or be accumulated. ■ n. /ˈkjuːmjʊlət/ Geology an igneous rock formed by gravitational settling of particles in a magma.
– DERIVATIVES **cumulation** n.
– ORIGIN C16 (in the sense 'gather in a heap'): from Latin *cumulare*, from *cumulus* 'a heap'.

cumulative ■ adj. increasing or increased in quantity or degree by successive additions.
– DERIVATIVES **cumulatively** adv. **cumulativeness** n.

cumulative preference share ■ n. a preference share whose annual fixed-rate dividend, if it cannot be paid in any year, accrues until it can.

cumulative voting ■ n. a system of voting in an election in which each voter is allowed as many votes as there are candidates.

cumulonimbus /ˌkjuːmjʊləʊˈnɪmbəs/ ■ n. (pl. **cumulonimbi** /-bʌɪ/) Meteorology cloud forming a towering mass with a flat base at fairly low altitude and often a flat top, as in thunderstorms.

cumulus /ˈkjuːmjʊləs/ ■ n. (pl. **cumuli** /-lʌɪ, -liː/) Meteorology cloud forming rounded masses heaped on each other above a flat base at fairly low altitude.
– ORIGIN C17: from Latin, 'heap'.

cuneiform /ˈkjuːnɪfɔːm, kjuːˈneɪfɔːm/ ■ adj. **1** denoting or relating to the wedge-shaped characters used in the ancient writing systems of Mesopotamia, Persia, and Ugarit. **2** chiefly Biology wedge-shaped. ▶ Anatomy denoting three bones of the tarsus between the navicular bone and the metatarsals. ■ n. cuneiform writing.
– ORIGIN C17: from French *cunéiforme* or modern Latin *cuneiformis*, from Latin *cuneus* 'wedge'.

cunnilingus /ˌkʌnɪˈlɪŋɡəs/ ■ n. stimulation of the female genitals using the tongue or lips.
– ORIGIN C19: from Latin, from *cunnus* 'vulva' + *lingere* 'lick'.

cunning ■ adj. **1** skilled in achieving one's ends by deceit or evasion. **2** ingenious. ■ n. **1** craftiness. **2** ingenuity.
– DERIVATIVES **cunningly** adv. **cunningness** n.
– ORIGIN Middle English: perhaps from Old Norse *kunnandi* 'knowledge', from *kunna* 'know', or perhaps from Middle English *cunne*, an obsolete var. of CAN¹.

cunt ■ n. vulgar slang **1** a woman's genitals. **2** an unpleasant or stupid person.
– ORIGIN Middle English: of Germanic origin.

cup ■ n. **1** a small bowl-shaped container for drinking from, typically having a handle and used with a matching saucer. ▶ (in church use) a chalice used at the Eucharist. ▶ a cup-shaped trophy, usually made of gold or silver and having a stem and two handles, awarded as a prize in a sports contest. ▶ (**cups**) one of the suits in a tarot pack. **2** a measure of capacity used in cookery, now usually equal to 250 millilitres. **3** either of the two parts of a bra shaped to contain or support one breast. **4** Golf the hole on a putting green or the metal container in it. **5** a long mixed drink made from wine or cider and fruit juice. ■ v. (**cupped, cupping**) form (one's hand or hands) into the curved shape of a cup. ▶ place the curved hand or hands around.
– PHRASES **in one's cups** informal drunk. **not one's cup of tea** informal not what one likes or is interested in.
– DERIVATIVES **cupful** n. (pl. **-fuls**).
– ORIGIN Old English: from popular Latin *cuppa*, prob. from Latin *cupa* 'tub'.

cup-bearer ■ n. historical or poetic/literary a person who serves wine, especially in a royal or noble household.

cupboard ■ n. a piece of furniture or small recess with a door and usually shelves, used for storage.
– PHRASES **cupboard love** affection that is feigned so as to obtain something.
– ORIGIN Middle English (denoting a table or sideboard on which cups, plates, etc. were displayed).

cupcake ■ n. **1** a small iced cake baked in a cup-shaped foil or paper container. **2** US informal a weak or effeminate man.

cupel /ˈkjuːp(ə)l/ ■ n. a shallow, porous container in which gold or silver can be refined or assayed by melting with a blast of hot air which oxidizes lead or other base

metals. ■ v. (**cupelled, cupelling**; US **cupeled, cupeling**) assay or refine (a metal) in a cupel.
–DERIVATIVES **cupellation** n.
–ORIGIN C17: from French *coupelle*, diminutive of *coupe* 'goblet'.

Cup Final ■ n. the final match in a sports competition in which the winners are awarded a cup.

cupidity /kjuːˈpɪdɪti/ ■ n. greed for money or possessions.
–ORIGIN Middle English: from Old French *cupidite* or Latin *cupiditas*, from *cupidus* 'desirous', from *cupere* 'to desire'.

Cupid's bow ■ n. a pronounced double curve at the top edge of a person's upper lip, resembling the shape of the bow carried by the Roman god of love Cupid.

cupola /ˈkjuːpələ/ ■ n. a rounded dome forming or adorning a roof or ceiling.
–DERIVATIVES **cupolaed** /-ləd/ adj.
–ORIGIN C16: Italian, from late Latin *cupula* 'small cask or burying vault', diminutive of *cupa* 'cask'.

cuppa ■ n. Brit. informal a cup of tea.

cuprammonium /ˌkjuːprəˈməʊnɪəm/ ■ n. [as modifier] Chemistry of or denoting a complex ion containing copper bonded to ammonia, solutions of which are deep blue in colour and able to dissolve cellulose.

cupreous /ˈkjuːprɪəs/ ■ adj. dated or poetic/literary of or like copper.
–ORIGIN C17: from late Latin *cupreus*, from *cuprum* 'copper'.

cupric /ˈkjuːprɪk/ ■ adj. Chemistry of copper with a valency of two; of copper(II).

cupro- /ˈkjuːprəʊ/ ■ comb. form of or relating to copper: *cupro-nickel*.
–ORIGIN from late Latin *cuprum*.

cupro-nickel ■ n. an alloy of copper and nickel, especially in the proportions 3:1 as used in 'silver' coins.

cuprous /ˈkjuːprəs/ ■ adj. Chemistry of copper with a valency of one; of copper(I).

cup-tied ■ adj. (of a soccer player) ineligible to play for one's club in a cup competition as a result of having played for another club in an earlier round.

cur /kɜː/ ■ n. 1 an aggressive dog, especially a mongrel. 2 informal a despicable man.
–ORIGIN Middle English: prob. orig. in *cur-dog*, perhaps from Old Norse *kurr* 'grumbling'.

curaçao /ˌkjʊərəˈsəʊ/ ■ n. (pl. **-os**) a liqueur flavoured with the peel of bitter oranges.
–ORIGIN C19: named after *Curaçao*, the Caribbean island where the oranges are grown.

curare /kjuˈrɑːri/ ■ n. a paralysing poison obtained from the bark and stems of some South American plants and traditionally used by Indian peoples as an arrow poison.
–ORIGIN C18: from a Carib word, partly via Spanish and Portuguese.

curate[1] /ˈkjʊərət/ ■ n. (also **assistant curate**) a member of the clergy engaged as assistant to a vicar, rector, or parish priest. ► archaic a minister with pastoral responsibility.
–PHRASES **curate's egg** something that is partly good and partly bad. [from a cartoon in *Punch* (1895) depicting a meek curate who, given a stale egg when dining with the bishop, assures his host that 'parts of it are excellent'.]
–DERIVATIVES **curacy** n. (pl. **-ies**)
–ORIGIN Middle English: from medieval Latin *curatus*, from Latin *cura* 'care'.

curate[2] /kjʊ(ə)ˈreɪt/ ■ v. select, organize, and look after the items in (a collection or exhibition).
–DERIVATIVES **curation** n.
–ORIGIN C19: back-formation from **CURATOR**.

curate-in-charge ■ n. another term for **PRIEST-IN-CHARGE**.

curative ■ adj. able to cure disease. ■ n. a curative medicine or agent.
–DERIVATIVES **curatively** adv.

curator ■ n. 1 a keeper or custodian of a museum or other collection. 2 S. African a person appointed to administer the affairs of a bank or other financial institution in the course of liquidation. ► a person legally appointed to administer the financial affairs of someone no longer able to do so for themselves.
–DERIVATIVES **curatorial** adj. **curatorship** n.

–ORIGIN Middle English: from Old French *curateur* or, in later use, directly from Latin *curator*, from *curare* (see **CURE**).

curb ■ n. 1 a check or restraint. ► (also **curb bit**) a type of bit with a strap or chain attached which passes under a horse's lower jaw, used as a check. 2 US variant spelling of **KERB**. ■ v. keep in check.
–ORIGIN C15: from Old French *courber* 'bend, bow', from Latin *curvare* (see **CURVE**).

curbstone ■ n. US spelling of **KERBSTONE**.

curd ■ n. 1 (also **curds**) a soft, white substance formed when milk coagulates, used as the basis for cheese. ► a fatty substance found between the flakes of poached salmon. 2 the edible head of a cauliflower or similar plant.
–DERIVATIVES **curdy** adj.
–ORIGIN Middle English.

curd cheese ■ n. chiefly Brit. a mild, soft, smooth cheese made from skimmed milk curd.

curdle ■ v. separate or cause to separate into curds or lumps.
–PHRASES **make one's blood curdle** fill one with horror.
–DERIVATIVES **curdler** n.
–ORIGIN C16: from of obsolete *curd* 'congeal'.

cure ■ v. 1 relieve of the symptoms of a disease or condition. ► end (a disease, condition, or problem) by treatment or remedial action. 2 preserve (meat, fish, tobacco, or an animal skin) by salting, drying, or smoking. ► harden (rubber, plastic, concrete, etc.) after manufacture by a chemical process such as vulcanization. ■ n. 1 a substance, treatment, or remedy that cures a disease, condition, or problem. ► restoration to health. 2 the process of curing meat, fish, rubber, etc.
–DERIVATIVES **curability** n. **curable** adj. **curer** n.
–ORIGIN Middle English: from Old French *curer* (v.), *cure* (n.), both from Latin *curare* 'take care of', from *cura* 'care'.

curé /ˈkjʊəreɪ/ ■ n. a parish priest in a French-speaking country.
–ORIGIN French: from medieval Latin *curatus* (see **CURATE**[1]).

cure-all ■ n. a remedy that will supposedly cure any ailment or problem.

curettage /kjʊəˈretɪdʒ, ˌkjʊərɪˈtɑːʒ/ ■ n. Surgery the use of a curette, especially on the lining of the uterus. See **DILATATION AND CURETTAGE**.
–ORIGIN C19: from French, from **CURETTE**.

curette /kjʊəˈret/ ■ n. a small surgical instrument used to remove material by a scraping action, especially from the uterus. ■ v. clean or scrape with a curette.
–ORIGIN C18: from French, from *curer* 'cleanse'.

curfew /ˈkɜːfjuː/ ■ n. a regulation requiring people to remain indoors between specified hours, typically at night. ► the time designated as the beginning of such a restriction.
–ORIGIN Middle English (denoting a regulation requiring fires to be extinguished at a fixed hour in the evening): from Old French *cuevrefeu*, from *cuvrir* 'to cover' + *feu* 'fire'.

Curia /ˈkjʊərɪə/ ■ n. the papal court at the Vatican, by which the Roman Catholic Church is governed.
–DERIVATIVES **Curial** adj.
–ORIGIN C17: from Latin *curia*, denoting a division of an ancient Roman tribe, (by extension) the senate of cities other than Rome, and later a feudal or Roman Catholic court of justice.

curie /ˈkjʊəri/ (abbrev.: **Ci**) ■ n. (pl. **-ies**) a unit of radioactivity, corresponding to 3.7×10^{10} disintegrations per second. ► the quantity of radioactive substance that has this amount of activity.
–ORIGIN C20: named after the French physicists Pierre and Marie *Curie*.

curio /ˈkjʊərɪəʊ/ ■ n. (pl. **-os**) a rare, unusual, or intriguing object.
–ORIGIN C19: abbrev. of **CURIOSITY**.

curiosa /ˌkjʊərɪˈəʊsə/ ■ pl. n. curiosities, especially erotica or pornography.
–ORIGIN C19: from Latin, from *curiosus* (see **CURIOUS**).

curiosity

curiosity ■ n. (pl. **-ies**) **1** a strong desire to know or learn something. **2** a unusual or interesting object or fact.

curious ■ adj. **1** eager to know or learn something. **2** strange; unusual.
– DERIVATIVES **curiously** adv. **curiousness** n.
– ORIGIN Middle English: from Old French *curios*, from Latin *curiosus* 'careful', from *cura* 'care'.

curium /ˈkjʊərɪəm/ ■ n. the chemical element of atomic number 96, an artificially made radioactive metal of the actinide series. (Symbol: **Cm**)
– ORIGIN 1940s: from the name of Marie and Pierre *Curie* (see CURIE).

curl ■ v. **1** form or cause to form a curved or spiral shape. **2** move or cause to move in a spiral or curved course. **3** (in weight training) lift (a weight) using only the hands, wrists, and forearms. **4** play at the game of curling. ■ n. **1** something in the shape of a spiral or coil, especially a lock of hair. **2** a curling movement. **3** a weightlifting exercise involving movement of only the hands, wrists, and forearms.
– PHRASES **make someone's hair curl** informal shock or horrify someone.
– DERIVATIVES **curly** adj. (**-ier**, **-iest**).
– ORIGIN Middle English: from obsolete *crulle* 'curly', from Middle Dutch *krul*.

curler ■ n. **1** a roller or clasp around which a lock of hair is wrapped to curl it. **2** a player in the game of curling.

curlew /ˈkɜːl(j)uː/ ■ n. (pl. same or **curlews**) a large wading bird of the sandpiper family, with a long downcurved bill and brown streaked plumage. [*Numenius arquata* and other species.]
– ORIGIN Middle English: from Old French *courlieu*, alteration (by associated with *courliu* 'courier') of imitative *courlis*.

curlicue /ˈkɜːlɪkjuː/ ■ n. a decorative curl or twist in calligraphy or in the design of an object.
– ORIGIN C19: from *curly* (see CURL) + CUE² (in the sense 'pigtail'), or *-cue* representing the letter *q*.

curling ■ n. a game played on ice, especially in Scotland and Canada, in which large circular flat stones are slid across the surface towards a mark.

curling tongs (also **curling iron**) ■ pl. n. a device incorporating a heated rod around which hair can be wound so as to curl it.

curmudgeon /kəˈmʌdʒ(ə)n/ ■ n. a bad-tempered or surly person.
– DERIVATIVES **curmudgeonliness** n. **curmudgeonly** adj.
– ORIGIN C16.

currant ■ n. **1** a small dried fruit made from a small seedless variety of grape, used in cookery. **2** used in names of various small edible berries and the shrubs which produce them, e.g. redcurrant.
– ORIGIN Middle English *raisons of Corauntz*, translating Anglo-Norman French *raisins de Corauntz* 'grapes of Corinth' (the original source).

currency ■ n. (pl. **-ies**) **1** a system of money in general use in a particular country. **2** the fact or quality of being current. ► the time during which something is current.

current ■ adj. happening or being used or done now. ► in common or general use. ■ n. **1** a body of water or air moving in a definite direction through a surrounding body of water or air in which there is less movement. **2** a flow of electricity which results from the ordered directional movement of electrically charged particles. ► a quantity representing the rate of flow of electric charge, usually measured in amperes.
– ORIGIN Middle English: from Old French *corant* 'running', from *courre* 'run', from Latin *currere* 'run'.

current account ■ n. an account with a bank or building society from which money may be withdrawn without notice.

current assets ■ pl. n. cash and other assets that are expected to be converted to cash within a year. Compare with FIXED ASSETS.

current liabilities ■ pl. n. amounts due to be paid to creditors within twelve months.

currently ■ adv. at the present time.

curricle /ˈkʌrɪk(ə)l/ ■ n. historical a light, open, two-wheeled carriage pulled by two horses side by side.
– ORIGIN C18: from Latin *curriculum* 'course, racing chariot'.

curriculum /kəˈrɪkjʊləm/ ■ n. (pl. **curricula** or **curriculums**) the subjects comprising a course of study in a school or college.
– DERIVATIVES **curricular** adj.
– ORIGIN C19: from Latin (see CURRICLE).

curriculum vitae /ˈviːtʌɪ, ˈvʌɪtiː/ ■ n. (pl. **curricula vitae**) a brief account of a person's education, qualifications, and previous occupations, typically sent with a job application.
– ORIGIN C20: Latin, 'course of life'.

currier /ˈkʌrɪə/ ■ n. a person who curries leather.
– ORIGIN Middle English: from Old French *corier*, from Latin *coriarius*, from *corium* 'leather'.

currish /ˈkəːrɪʃ/ ■ adj. like a cur, especially in being bad-tempered.
– DERIVATIVES **currishly** adv. **currishness** n.

curry¹ ■ n. (pl. **-ies**) a dish of meat, vegetables, etc., cooked in an Indian-style sauce of strong spices. ■ v. (**-ies**, **-ied**) [usu. as adj. **curried**] prepare or flavour with such a sauce.
– ORIGIN C16: from Tamil *karti*.

curry² ■ v. (**-ies**, **-ied**) chiefly N. Amer. groom (a horse) with a curry-comb.
– PHRASES **curry favour** ingratiate oneself through obsequious behaviour. [alteration of Middle English *curry favel*, from the name (*Favel*) of a horse in a C14 French romance who became a symbol of cunning and duplicity; hence 'to rub down Favel' meant to use cunning.]
– ORIGIN Middle English: from Old French *correier*, of Germanic origin.

curry-comb ■ n. a hand-held device with serrated ridges, used for grooming horses.

curry leaf ■ n. a shrub or small tree native to India and Sri Lanka, the leaves of which are widely used in Indian cooking. [*Murraya koenigii*.]

curry powder ■ n. a mixture of finely ground spices, such as turmeric and coriander, used for making curry.

curse ■ n. **1** a solemn appeal to a supernatural power to inflict harm on someone or something. ► a cause of harm or misery. **2** an offensive word or phrase used to express anger or annoyance. ■ v. **1** use a curse against. ► (**be cursed with**) be afflicted with. **2** utter or address with expletives.
– DERIVATIVES **curser** n.
– ORIGIN Old English.

cursed /ˈkəːsɪd, kəːst/ ■ adj. informal, dated used to express annoyance or irritation.
– DERIVATIVES **cursedly** adv. **cursedness** n.

cursive /ˈkəːsɪv/ ■ adj. written with the characters joined. ■ n. writing with such a style.
– DERIVATIVES **cursively** adv.
– ORIGIN C18: from medieval Latin *cursivus*, from Latin *curs-*, *currere* 'run'.

cursor ■ n. a movable indicator on a computer screen identifying the point that will be affected by input from the user.
– ORIGIN Middle English: from Latin, 'runner', from *curs-* (see CURSIVE).

cursorial /kəːˈsɔːrɪəl/ ■ adj. Zoology having limbs adapted for running.

cursory /ˈkəːs(ə)ri/ ■ adj. hasty and therefore not thorough.
– DERIVATIVES **cursorily** adv. **cursoriness** n.
– ORIGIN C17: from Latin *cursorius* 'of a runner', from *cursor* (see CURSOR).

curst ■ adj. archaic spelling of CURSED.

curt ■ adj. rudely brief.
– DERIVATIVES **curtly** adv. **curtness** n.
– ORIGIN Middle English: from Latin *curtus* 'cut short, abridged'.

curtail /kəːˈteɪl/ ■ v. reduce in extent or quantity.
– DERIVATIVES **curtailment** n.
– ORIGIN C15: from obsolete *curtal* 'horse with a docked tail', from French *courtault*, from *court* 'short', from Latin *curtus*.

curtain ■ n. **1** a piece of material suspended at the top to form a screen, typically movable sideways and found as

one of a pair at a window. ▸ **(the curtain)** a screen of heavy cloth or other material that can be raised or lowered at the front of a stage. ▸ a raising or lowering of such a screen at the beginning or end of an act or scene. **2 (curtains)** informal a disastrous outcome. ■ v. [often as adj. **curtained**] provide with a curtain or curtains. ▸ conceal with or as with a curtain.
– ORIGIN Middle English: from Old French *cortine*, from late Latin *cortina*, translation of Greek *aulaia*, from *aulē* 'court'.

curtain call ■ n. the appearance of one or more performers on stage after a performance to acknowledge the audience's applause.

curtain-raiser ■ n. an entertainment or other event happening just before a longer or more important one.
– ORIGIN C19: orig. used in the theatre to denote a short opening piece performed before a play.

curtain wall ■ n. **1** a fortified wall around a medieval castle, typically one linking towers together. **2** a wall which encloses the space within a building but does not support the roof.

curtsy (also **curtsey**) ■ n. (pl. **-ies** or **-eys**) a woman's or girl's formal greeting made by bending the knees with one foot in front of the other. ■ v. (**-ies, -ied** or **-eys, -eyed**) perform a curtsy.
– ORIGIN C16: var. of COURTESY.

curvaceous /kəːˈveɪʃəs/ ■ adj. (especially of a woman or a woman's figure) having an attractively curved shape.
– DERIVATIVES **curvaceousness** n.

curvature /ˈkəːvətʃə/ ■ n. the fact of being curved or the degree to which something is curved. ▸ Geometry the degree to which a curve deviates from a straight line, or a curved surface deviates from a plane.

curve ■ n. a line or outline which gradually deviates from being straight for some or all of its length. ▸ a line on a graph (whether straight or curved) showing how one quantity varies with respect to another. ▸ (also **curve ball**) Baseball a delivery in which the pitcher causes the ball to deviate from a straight path by imparting spin. ■ v. form or cause to form a curve.
– ORIGIN Middle English: from Latin *curvare* 'to bend', from *curvus* 'bent'.

curvilinear /ˌkəːvɪˈlɪnɪə/ ■ adj. contained by or consisting of a curved line or lines.
– DERIVATIVES **curvilinearly** adv.
– ORIGIN C18: from Latin *curvus* 'bent, curved', on the pattern of *rectilinear*.

curvy ■ adj. (**-ier, -iest**) having many curves. ▸ informal (especially of a woman's figure) shapely and voluptuous.
– DERIVATIVES **curviness** n.

Cushing's syndrome ■ n. Medicine a metabolic disorder caused by overproduction of corticosteroid hormones by the adrenal cortex and often involving obesity and high blood pressure.
– ORIGIN 1930s: named after the American surgeon Harvey W. *Cushing*.

cushion ■ n. **1** a bag of cloth stuffed with a mass of soft material, used as a comfortable support for sitting or leaning on. **2** something providing support or protection against impact. ▸ the elastic lining of the sides of a billiard table, from which the ball rebounds. ■ v. **1** soften the effect of an impact on. **2** mitigate the adverse effects of.
– DERIVATIVES **cushioned** adj. **cushiony** adj.
– ORIGIN Middle English: from Old French *cuissin*, from a Latin word meaning 'cushion for the hip', from *coxa* 'hip, thigh'.

cushion star ■ n. a small starfish with a broad body and very short blunt arms. [*Patiriella exigua*.]

Cushitic /kʊˈʃɪtɪk/ ■ n. a group of East African languages of the Afro-Asiatic family spoken mainly in Ethiopia and Somalia. ■ adj. of or relating to this group of languages.
– ORIGIN C20: from *Cush*, the name of part of ancient Nubia.

cushy ■ adj. (**-ier, -iest**) informal **1** (of a task or situation) undemanding, easy, or secure. **2** N. Amer. (of furniture) comfortable.
– DERIVATIVES **cushiness** n.
– ORIGIN FIRST WORLD WAR: from Urdu *ḳushī* 'pleasure'.

cusk-eel ■ n. a small eel-like marine fish with a tapering body and a pointed tail. [Family Ophidiidae: many species.]

cusp /kʌsp/ ■ n. **1** each of the pointed ends of a crescent, especially of the moon. ▸ Architecture a projecting point between small arcs in Gothic tracery. **2** a cone-shaped prominence on the surface of a tooth, especially of a molar or premolar. **3** Mathematics a point at which the direction of a curve is abruptly reversed. **4** Astrology the initial point of an astrological sign or house. ▸ a point of transition between two different states: *those on the cusp of adulthood*. **5** Anatomy a pocket or fold in the wall of the heart or a major blood vessel, forming part of a valve.
– DERIVATIVES **cuspate** adj. **cusped** adj. **cusping** n.
– ORIGIN C16: from Latin *cuspis* 'point, apex'.

cuspid ■ n. a tooth with a single cusp or point; a canine tooth.
– DERIVATIVES **cuspidate** adj.
– ORIGIN C18: from Latin *cuspis, cuspid-* 'point, apex'.

cuss informal ■ n. **1** an annoying or stubborn person or animal. **2** another term for CURSE (in sense 2). ■ v. another term for CURSE (in sense 2).

cussed /ˈkʌsɪd/ ■ adj. informal awkward; annoying.
– DERIVATIVES **cussedly** adv. **cussedness** n.
– ORIGIN C19: var. of CURSED.

custard ■ n. a dessert or sweet sauce made with milk and eggs and thickened with cornflour, or milk and a proprietary powder.
– ORIGIN Middle English *crustarde, custarde* (denoting an open pie containing meat or fruit in a sauce), from Old French *crouste* (see CRUST).

custard apple ■ n. **1** a large fleshy tropical fruit with a sweet yellow pulp. **2** the tree which bears this fruit, native to Central and South America. [Genus *Annona*: several species.]

custard marrow ■ n. a summer squash which has flattened round fruits with scalloped edges.

custard pie ■ n. an open pie containing cold set custard. ▸ a pie of this type, or a flat container of foam, used for throwing in someone's face in slapstick comedy.

custodian ■ n. a person who is responsible for protecting or guarding something.
– DERIVATIVES **custodianship** n.

custody /ˈkʌstədi/ ■ n. **1** the protective care or guardianship of someone or something. ▸ Law parental responsibility, especially as allocated to one of two divorcing parents. **2** imprisonment.
– DERIVATIVES **custodial** /kʌˈstəʊdɪəl/ adj.
– ORIGIN Middle English: from Latin *custodia*, from *custos* 'guardian'.

custom ■ n. **1** a traditional and widely accepted way of behaving or doing something that is specific to a particular society, place, or time. ▸ Law established usage having the force of law or right. **2** regular dealings with a shop or business by customers.
– ORIGIN Middle English: from Old French *coustume*, from Latin, from *consuetus*, from *consuescere* 'accustom'.

customary ■ adj. in accordance with custom; usual. ▸ Law established by or based on custom or cultural tradition rather than common law or statute.
– DERIVATIVES **customarily** adv. **customariness** n.

custom-built ■ adj. made to a particular customer's order.

customer ■ n. **1** a person who buys goods or services from a shop or business. **2** a person or thing of a specified kind that one has to deal with: *he's a tough customer*.

custom house (also **customs house**) ■ n. chiefly historical the office at a port or frontier where customs duty is collected.

customize (also **-ise**) ■ v. modify to suit a particular individual or task.

custom-made ■ adj. another term for CUSTOM-BUILT.

customs ■ pl. n. the official department that administers and collects the duties levied by a government on imported goods. ▸ (also **customs duties**) the duties levied by a government on imported goods.
– ORIGIN Middle English: orig. in the sing., denoting a customary due paid to a ruler, later duty levied on goods on their way to market.

customs union ■ n. a group of states that have agreed to charge the same import duties as each other and usually to allow free trade between themselves.

cut ■ v. (**cutting**; past and past part. **cut**) **1** make an opening, incision, or wound in (something) with a sharp tool or object. **2** remove (something) from something larger by using a sharp implement. **3** divide into pieces with a knife or other sharp implement. ▸ (**cut something down**) cause something to fall by cutting through at the base. **4** make or form by using a sharp tool to remove material. ▸ [often as adj. **cut**] make or design (a garment) in a particular way: *an impeccably cut suit*. **5** reduce the length of by using a sharp implement. **6** reduce the amount or quantity of. ▸ Computing delete (part of a text). ▸ end or interrupt the provision of (a supply). ▸ (**cut something off**) block the usual means of access to a place. ▸ chiefly N. Amer. absent oneself deliberately from: *Rod was cutting class*. **7** (of a line) cross or intersect (another line). **8** stop filming or recording. ▸ move to another shot in a film. ▸ make (a film) into a coherent whole by removing or reordering parts. **9** make (a sound recording). **10** divide a pack of playing cards by lifting a portion from the top. **11** strike or kick (a ball) quickly and abruptly. ▸ Golf slice (the ball). ▸ Cricket hit (the ball) to the off side with the bat held almost horizontally; play such a stroke against (the bowler). ▸ Cricket (of the ball) turn sharply on pitching. **12** chiefly N. Amer. adulterate (a drug) or dilute (alcohol) by mixing it with another substance: *speed cut with rat poison*. **13** (**cut it**) informal, chiefly N. Amer. come up to expectations. [shortened form of the idiom *cut the mustard*.] ■ n. **1** an act of cutting. ▸ a reduction in amount or size. **2** a result of cutting: *a cut on his jaw*. ▸ a piece of meat cut from a carcass. ▸ informal a share of profits. ▸ a version of a film after editing: *the director's cut*. **3** the way or style in which a garment or the hair is cut: *the elegant cut of his jacket*.
– PHRASES **be cut out for** (or **to be**) [usu. with neg.] informal have exactly the right qualities for a particular role. **a cut above** informal noticeably superior to. **cut and dried** (of a situation) completely settled. [C18: orig. used to distinguish the herbs of herbalists' shops from growing herbs.] **cut and run** informal make a speedy departure from a difficult situation rather than deal with it. [orig. a nautical phr., meaning 'cut the anchor cable because of an emergency and make sail immediately'.] **cut and thrust** a difficult or competitive atmosphere or environment: [orig. a fencing phr.] *the cut and thrust of political debate*. **cut both ways** (of a point or statement) serve both sides of an argument. ▸ (of an action or process) have both good and bad effects. **cut corners** undertake something perfunctorily so as to save time or money. **cut a dash** be stylish or impressive in one's dress or behaviour. **cut someone dead** completely ignore someone. **cut from the same cloth** of the same nature. **cut in line** US jump the queue. **cut it out** informal stop it. **cut the mustard** informal reach the required standard. **cut no ice** informal have no influence or effect. **cut one's teeth** acquire initial practice or experience of a particular sphere of activity. **cut a tooth** (of a baby) have a tooth appear through the gum. **cut to the chase** N. Amer. informal come to the point. **cut up rough** Brit. informal behave in an aggressive or awkward way. **make** (or **miss**) **the cut** Golf reach (or fail to reach) a required score, thus avoiding (or ensuring) elimination from the last two rounds of a four-round tournament.
– PHRASAL VERBS **cut in 1** interrupt. **2** pull in too closely in front of another vehicle. **3** (of a motor or other device) begin operating, especially when triggered automatically. **cut someone in** informal include someone in a deal and give them a share of the profits. **cut someone off 1** break the connection during a telephone call. **2** deprive someone of a supply of power, water, etc. **3** disinherit someone. **cut out** (of an engine) suddenly stop operating. **cut someone out** exclude someone. **cut someone up 1** informal (of a driver) overtake someone and pull in too closely. **2** informal, chiefly N. Amer. criticize someone severely.
– ORIGIN Middle English: prob. of Germanic origin.

cut and paste ■ n. a process used in assembling text on a word processor or computer, in which items are removed from one part and inserted elsewhere. ■ v. move (an item of text) using such a technique.

cutaneous /kjuːˈteɪnɪəs/ ■ adj. of, relating to, or affecting the skin.
– ORIGIN C16: from modern Latin *cutaneus*, from Latin *cutis* 'skin'.

cutaway ■ adj. **1** denoting a coat or jacket with the front cut away below the waist. **2** denoting a diagram or drawing with some external parts left out to reveal the interior. ■ n. a shot in a film which is of a different subject from those to which it is joined in editing.

cutback ■ n. a reduction, especially in expenditure.

cute ■ adj. **1** endearingly pretty. ▸ informal sexually attractive. **2** informal, chiefly N. Amer. clever; shrewd.
– DERIVATIVES **cutely** adv. **cuteness** n.
– ORIGIN C18: shortening of ACUTE.

cutesy ■ adj. informal cute to a sentimental or mawkish extent.

cut glass ■ n. glass that has been ornamented by having patterns cut into it by grinding and polishing.

cuticle /ˈkjuːtɪk(ə)l/ ■ n. **1** Botany & Zoology a protective layer covering the epidermis of a plant or of an insect or other invertebrate. **2** Anatomy the epidermis of the body. ▸ dead skin at the base of a fingernail or toenail. ▸ the outer cellular layer of a hair.
– DERIVATIVES **cuticular** /-ˈtɪkjʊlə/ adj.
– ORIGIN C15: from Latin *cuticula*, diminutive of *cutis* 'skin'.

cutie ■ n. (pl. **-ies**) informal an attractive or endearing person.

cutin /ˈkjuːtɪn/ ■ n. Biochemistry a waxy water-repellent substance in the cuticle of plants.
– ORIGIN C19: from CUTIS.

cutis /ˈkjuːtɪs/ ■ n. Anatomy the true skin or dermis.
– ORIGIN C17: from Latin, 'skin'.

cutlass /ˈkʌtləs/ ■ n. a short sword with a slightly curved blade, formerly used by sailors.
– ORIGIN C16: from French *coutelas*, from Latin *cultellus* (see CUTLER).

cutler ■ n. a person who makes or sells cutlery.
– ORIGIN Middle English: from Old French *coutelier*, from *coutel* 'knife', from Latin *cultellus*, diminutive of *culter* 'knife, ploughshare'.

cutlery ■ n. knives, forks, and spoons used for eating or serving food.

cutlet ■ n. a portion of meat, especially a lamb or veal chop from just behind the neck served grilled or fried. ▸ a flat croquette of minced meat, nuts, or pulses.
– ORIGIN C18: from French *côtelette*, earlier *costelette*, diminutive of *coste* 'rib'.

cutline ■ n. (in squash) the line above which a served ball must strike the front wall.

cut-off ■ n. **1** a point or level marking a designated limit. **2** a device for producing an interruption in flow of a power or fuel supply. ▸ a sudden drop in amplification or responsiveness of an electric device at a certain frequency. **3** (**cut-offs**) shorts made by cutting off the legs of a pair of jeans.

cut-out ■ n. **1** a shape cut out of board or another material. **2** a hole cut in something for decoration or to allow the insertion of something else. **3** a device that automatically breaks an electric circuit for safety.

cutover ■ n. a rapid transition from one phase of a project to another.

cut-price (chiefly N. Amer. also **cut-rate**) ■ adj. for sale at a reduced price; cheap.

cutpurse ■ n. archaic term for PICKPOCKET.
– ORIGIN Middle English: with ref. to stealing by cutting purses suspended from a waistband.

cutter ■ n. **1** a person or thing that cuts. **2** a light, fast coastal patrol boat. ▸ a ship's boat used for carrying light stores or passengers. ▸ historical a small fore-and-aft rigged sailing boat with one mast, more than one headsail, and a running bowsprit, used as a fast auxiliary. ▸ a yacht with one mainsail and two foresails. **3** Cricket & Baseball a ball that deviates sharply on pitching.

cut-throat ■ n. dated a murderer or other violent criminal. ■ adj. **1** ruthless and intense. **2** (of some card games) played by three rather than four players.

cut-throat razor ■ n. Brit. a razor with a long blade which folds like a penknife.

cutting ■ n. 1 a piece cut off from something. ▸ Brit. an article or other piece cut from a newspaper. ▸ a piece cut from a plant for propagation. 2 an open passage excavated through higher ground for a railway, road, or canal. ■ adj. 1 capable of cutting. 2 (of a remark) hurtful.
–DERIVATIVES **cuttingly** adv.

cutting edge ■ n. the latest or most advanced stage; the forefront. ▸ adj. (**cutting-edge**) innovative; pioneering.

cuttle ■ n. a cuttlefish.
–ORIGIN Old English *cudele* 'cuttlefish', of Germanic origin.

cuttlebone ■ n. the flattened internal skeleton of the cuttlefish, used as a dietary supplement for cage birds and for making casts for precious metal items.

cuttlefish ■ n. (pl. same or **-fishes**) a swimming marine mollusc that resembles a broad-bodied squid, having eight arms and two long tentacles that are used for grabbing prey. [*Sepia* and other genera, order Sepioidea.]

cut up ■ adj. informal very distressed. ■ n. (**cut-up**) a film or sound recording made by cutting and editing material from pre-existing recordings.

cutwater ■ n. 1 the forward edge of a ship's prow. 2 a wedge-shaped projection on the pier of a bridge.

cutwork ■ n. embroidery or lace with parts cut out and the edges oversewn or filled with needlework designs.

cutworm ■ n. a moth caterpillar that lives in the soil and eats through the stems of young plants at ground level.

cuvée /ˈkjuːveɪ/ ■ n. a type, blend, or batch of wine, especially champagne.
–ORIGIN C19: French, 'vatful'.

cuvette /kjuːˈvet/ ■ n. Biochemistry a straight-sided container for holding liquid samples in a spectrophotometer or other instrument.
–ORIGIN C18: from French, diminutive of *cuve* 'cask'.

CV ■ abbrev. curriculum vitae.

CVS ■ abbrev. chorionic villus sampling, a test made in early pregnancy to detect fetal abnormalities.

C & W ■ abbrev. country and western (music).

cwt. ■ abbrev. hundredweight.
–ORIGIN from Latin *centum* 'a hundred'.

-cy ■ suffix 1 denoting state or condition: *bankruptcy*. 2 denoting rank or status: *baronetcy*.
–ORIGIN from Latin *-cia*, *-tia* and Greek *-k(e)ia*, *-t(e)ia*.

cyan /ˈsaɪən/ ■ n. a greenish-blue colour which is one of the primary subtractive colours, complementary to red.
–ORIGIN C19: from Greek *kuaneos* 'dark blue'.

cyanamide /saɪˈanəmaɪd/ ■ n. Chemistry a weakly acidic crystalline compound made as an intermediate in ammonia manufacture.
–ORIGIN C19: blend of **CYANOGEN** and **AMIDE**.

cyanic acid ■ n. Chemistry a colourless, poisonous, volatile, strongly acidic liquid. [HOCN.]
–DERIVATIVES **cyanate** n.
–ORIGIN C19: from **CYANOGEN**.

cyanide /ˈsaɪənaɪd/ ■ n. Chemistry a salt or ester of hydrocyanic acid, examples of which are extremely toxic: *potassium cyanide*.
–ORIGIN C19: from **CYANOGEN**.

cyano- ■ comb. form 1 relating to the colour blue: *cyanosis*. 2 representing **CYANIDE**: *cyanogenic*.
–ORIGIN from Greek *kuan(e)os* 'dark blue'.

cyanoacrylate /ˌsaɪənəʊˈakrɪleɪt/ ■ n. Chemistry any of a class of compounds which are cyanide derivatives of acrylates, used to make quick-setting adhesives.

cyanobacteria /ˌsaɪənəʊbakˈtɪərɪə/ ■ pl. n. (sing. **cyanobacterium**) Biology micro-organisms of a division (Cyanobacteria) comprising the blue-green algae, related to bacteria but capable of photosynthesis.
–ORIGIN from Greek *kuaneos* 'dark blue' + **BACTERIUM**.

cyanocobalamin /ˌsaɪənəʊkəˈbaləmɪn/ ■ n. vitamin B_{12}, a cobalt-containing vitamin derived from liver, fish, and eggs, a deficiency of which can cause pernicious anaemia.
–ORIGIN 1950s: from **CYANO-** + *cobalamin* (blend of **COBALT** and **VITAMIN**).

cyanogen /saɪˈanədʒ(ə)n/ ■ n. Chemistry a colourless flammable highly poisonous gas made by oxidizing hydrogen cyanide. [C_2N_2.]
–ORIGIN C19: from French *cyanogène*, from Greek *kuanos* 'dark blue mineral' + *-gène* (see **-GEN**), so named because it is rel. to Prussian blue.

cyanosis /ˌsaɪəˈnəʊsɪs/ ■ n. Medicine a bluish discoloration of the skin due to poor circulation or inadequate oxygenation of the blood.
–DERIVATIVES **cyanotic** adj.
–ORIGIN C19: modern Latin, from Greek *kuanōsis* 'blueness'.

cyber- /ˈsaɪbə/ ■ comb. form relating to information technology, the Internet, and virtual reality: *cyberspace*.
–ORIGIN back-formation from **CYBERNETICS**.

cybernetics ■ pl. n. [treated as sing.] the science of communications and automatic control systems in both machines and living things.
–DERIVATIVES **cybernetic** adj. **cybernetician** n. **cyberneticist** n.
–ORIGIN 1940s: from Greek *kubernētēs* 'steersman'.

cyberphobia ■ n. extreme or irrational fear of computers or technology.
–DERIVATIVES **cyberphobe** n. **cyberphobic** adj. & n.

cyberpunk ■ n. 1 a genre of science fiction set in a lawless subculture of an oppressive society dominated by computer technology. 2 a person who accesses computer networks illegally.

cyberspace ■ n. the notional environment in which communication over computer networks occurs.

cyborg /ˈsaɪbɔːg/ ■ n. a fictional or hypothetical person whose physical abilities are extended beyond human limitations by mechanical elements built into the body.
–ORIGIN 1960s: blend of **CYBER-** and **ORGANISM**.

cycad /ˈsaɪkad/ ■ n. a tall, cone-bearing, palm-like plant of tropical and subtropical regions. [Genus *Cycas*, class Cycadopsida: several species.]
–ORIGIN C19: from supposed Greek *kukas*, scribal error for *koikas*, pl. of *koix* 'Egyptian palm'.

Cycladic /sɪˈkladɪk, saɪ-/ ■ adj. 1 of or relating to the Cyclades, a group of Greek islands in the southern Aegean. 2 Archaeology relating to or denoting a Bronze Age civilization that flourished in the Cyclades, dated to c.3000–1050 BC.

cyclamate /ˈsɪkləmeɪt, ˈsaɪk-/ ■ n. Chemistry a salt of a synthetic organic acid, formerly used as an artificial sweetener.
–ORIGIN 1950s: contraction of *cyclohexylsulphamate*.

cyclamen /ˈsɪkləmən/ ■ n. (pl. same or **cyclamens**) a plant of the primrose family, having pink, red, or white flowers with backward-curving petals. [Genus *Cyclamen*: several species.]
–ORIGIN from Latin *cyclaminos*, from Greek *kuklaminos*, perhaps from *kuklos* 'circle', with ref. to its bulbous roots.

cycle ■ n. 1 a series of events that are regularly repeated in the same order. ▸ the period of time taken to complete a single such series. 2 one complete sequence of changes associated with a recurring phenomenon such as an alternating current, wave, etc. 3 Ecology the movement of a simple substance through the soil, rocks, water, atmosphere, and living organisms of the earth: *the carbon cycle*. 4 a series of musical or literary works composed around a particular theme. 5 a bicycle. ■ v. 1 ride a bicycle. 2 move in or follow a cycle of events.
–DERIVATIVES **cycling** n. **cyclist** n.
–ORIGIN Middle English: from Old French, from late Latin *cyclus*, from Greek *kuklos* 'circle'.

cyclic /ˈsaɪklɪk, ˈsɪk-/ ■ adj. 1 occurring in cycles. 2 having the form of a circle or closed ring. ▸ Chemistry having a molecular structure containing one or more closed rings of atoms.
–DERIVATIVES **cyclical** adj. **cyclically** adv.

cyclic redundancy check (also **cyclic redundancy code**) ■ n. Computing a code added to data in order to detect errors occurring during transmission, storage, or retrieval.

cyclin /ˈsaɪklɪn/ ■ n. Biochemistry a protein which is thought to initiate certain processes of mitosis.

cyclize /ˈsaɪklaɪz/ (also **-ise**) ■ v. Chemistry undergo or cause to undergo a reaction in which one part of a molecule

cyclo-

becomes linked to another to form a closed ring.
– DERIVATIVES **cyclization** (also **-isation**) n.

cyclo- /'sʌɪkləʊ/ ■ comb. form **1** circular: *cyclorama*. **2** relating to a cycle or cycling: *cyclo-cross*. **3** cyclic: *cycloalkane*.
– ORIGIN from Greek *kuklos* 'circle', or directly from **CYCLE** or **CYCLIC**.

cycloalkane ■ n. Chemistry a hydrocarbon with a molecule containing a ring of carbon atoms joined by single bonds.

cyclo-cross ■ n. cross-country racing on bicycles.

cyclohexane ■ n. Chemistry a volatile cyclic hydrocarbon obtained from petroleum, used as a solvent. [C_6H_{12}.]

cyclometer /sʌɪ'klɒmɪtə/ ■ n. **1** an instrument for measuring circular arcs. **2** an instrument attached to a bicycle for measuring distance.

cyclone /'sʌɪkləʊn/ ■ n. Meteorology a system of winds rotating inwards to an area of low barometric pressure; a depression. ▸ another term for **TROPICAL STORM**.
– DERIVATIVES **cyclonic** adj. **cyclonically** adv.
– ORIGIN C19: prob. from Greek *kuklōma* 'wheel, coil of a snake'.

Cyclops /'sʌɪklɒps/ ■ n. **1** (pl. **Cyclops**, **Cyclopses**, or **Cyclopes** /sʌɪ'kləʊpiːz/) Greek & Roman Mythology a member of a race of savage one-eyed giants. **2** (**cyclops**) a minute predatory freshwater crustacean which has a cylindrical body with a single central eye. [*Cyclops* and other genera, order Cyclopoida.]
– ORIGIN from Greek *Kuklōps* 'round-eyed'.

cyclorama /ˌsʌɪklə'rɑːmə/ ■ n. **1** a panoramic scene set on the inside of a cylindrical surface, to be viewed by a central spectator. **2** a cloth stretched tight in an arc around the back of a stage set, often used to represent the sky.
– DERIVATIVES **cycloramic** /-'ramɪk/ adj.

cyclostome /'sʌɪkləʊ(u)stəʊm/ ■ n. Zoology an eel-like jawless vertebrate with a round sucking mouth, such as a lamprey or hagfish.
– ORIGIN C19: from **CYCLO-** + Greek *stoma* 'mouth'.

cyclotron /'sʌɪklətrɒn/ ■ n. Physics an apparatus in which charged atomic and subatomic particles are accelerated by an alternating electric field while following an outward spiral or circular path in a magnetic field.

cyder ■ n. archaic spelling of **CIDER**.

cygnet /'sɪɡnɪt/ ■ n. a young swan.
– ORIGIN Middle English: from Anglo-Norman French *cignet*, diminutive of Old French *cigne* 'swan', from Latin *cycnus*, from Greek *kuknos*.

cylinder /'sɪlɪndə/ ■ n. **1** a three-dimensional shape with straight parallel sides and a circular or oval cross section. **2** a piston chamber in a steam or internal-combustion engine. **3** a cylindrical container for liquefied gas under pressure. **4** a rotating metal roller in a printing press.
– DERIVATIVES **cylindric** /sə'lɪndrɪk/ adj. **cylindrical** adj. **cylindrically** adv.
– ORIGIN C16: from Latin *cylindrus*, from Greek *kulindros* 'roller'.

cylinder block ■ n. see **BLOCK** (sense 7).

cylinder head ■ n. the end cover of a cylinder in an internal-combustion engine, against which the piston compresses the cylinder's contents.

cylinder seal ■ n. Archaeology a small barrel-shaped stone object bearing an incised design or cuneiform inscription, used chiefly as a seal in ancient Mesopotamia.

cymbal /'sɪmb(ə)l/ ■ n. a musical instrument consisting of a slightly concave round brass plate which is either struck against another one or struck with a stick.
– DERIVATIVES **cymbalist** n.
– ORIGIN Old English, from Latin *cymbalum*, from Greek *kumbalon*, from *kumbē* 'cup'.

cymbidium /sɪm'bɪdɪəm/ ■ n. (pl. **cymbidiums**) a tropical orchid with long narrow leaves and arching stems bearing several flowers, growing chiefly as an epiphyte from Asia to Australasia. [Genus *Cymbidium*.]
– ORIGIN from Greek *kumbē* 'cup'.

cyme /sʌɪm/ ■ n. Botany a flower cluster with a central stem bearing a single terminal flower that develops first, the other flowers in the cluster developing as terminal buds of lateral stems. Compare with **RACEME**.
– DERIVATIVES **cymose** adj.
– ORIGIN C18: from French, 'summit', from a popular var. of Latin *cyma*.

cynic /'sɪnɪk/ ■ n. **1** a person who believes that people are motivated purely by self-interest. ▸ a sceptic. **2** (**Cynic**) a member of a school of ancient Greek philosophers characterized by an ostentatious contempt for wealth and pleasure.
– DERIVATIVES **cynicism** n.
– ORIGIN C16: from Latin *cynicus*, from Greek *kunikos*; prob. orig. from *Kunosarges*, the name of a gymnasium where the Cynic Antisthenes taught, but popularly taken to mean 'doglike, churlish', from *kuōn* 'dog'.

cynical ■ adj. **1** believing that people are motivated purely by self-interest. ▸ sceptical. ▸ contemptuous; mocking. **2** concerned only with one's own interests and disregarding accepted standards to achieve them: *a cynical foul*.
– DERIVATIVES **cynically** adv.

cynodont /'sʌɪnə(ʊ)dɒnt/ ■ n. a fossil carnivorous mammal-like reptile of the late Permian and Triassic periods, with well-developed specialized teeth.
– ORIGIN C19: from Greek *kuōn*, *kun-* 'dog' + *odous*, *odont-* 'tooth'.

cynosure /'sɪnəzjʊə, 'sʌɪn-, -sjʊə/ ■ n. a person or thing that is the centre of attention or admiration.
– ORIGIN C16 (orig. denoting the constellation Ursa Minor, or the pole star which it contains): from French, or from Latin *cynosura*, from Greek *kunosoura* 'dog's tail', also 'Ursa Minor'.

cypher ■ n. variant spelling of **CIPHER**[1].

cy-pres /siː'preɪ/ ■ adv. & adj. Law as near as possible to the testator's or donor's intentions when these cannot be precisely followed.
– ORIGIN C19: from a late Anglo-Norman French var. of French *si près* 'so near'.

cypress ■ n. an evergreen coniferous tree with flattened shoots bearing small scale-like leaves, whose dark foliage is sometimes associated with mourning. [*Cupressus sempervirens* (southern Europe) and other species, family Cupressaceae.]
– ORIGIN Middle English: from late Latin *cypressus*, from Greek *kuparissos*.

cyprinid /'sɪprɪnɪd/ ■ n. Zoology a fish of the carp family (Cyprinidae).
– ORIGIN C19: from Greek *kuprinos* 'carp'.

Cypriot ■ n. a native or national of Cyprus. ■ adj. of or relating to Cyprus or its people or the Greek dialect used there.
– ORIGIN from Greek *Kupriōtēs*, from *Kupros* 'Cyprus'.

Cyrillic /sɪ'rɪlɪk/ ■ adj. denoting the alphabet used by many Slavic peoples, chiefly those with a historical allegiance to the Orthodox Church; now used especially for Russian and Bulgarian. ■ n. the Cyrillic alphabet.
– ORIGIN C19: named after the C9 Greek missionary St Cyril, its reputed inventor.

cyst /sɪst/ ■ n. **1** Biology a thin-walled hollow organ or cavity in an animal or plant, containing a liquid secretion. **2** Medicine a membranous sac or cavity of abnormal character in the body, containing fluid. **3** a tough protective capsule enclosing the larva of a parasitic worm or the resting stage of an organism.
– ORIGIN C18: from late Latin *cystis*, from Greek *kustis* 'bladder'.

cysteine /'sɪstiːn, -tɪn, -teɪn, -tiːn/ ■ n. Biochemistry a sulphur-containing amino acid which occurs in keratins and other proteins.
– ORIGIN C19: from **CYSTINE** + *-eine*, var. of **-INE**[4].

cystic fibrosis ■ n. a hereditary disorder which affects the exocrine glands, and results in the production of abnormally thick mucus, leading to the blockage of the pancreatic ducts, intestines, and bronchi.

cystine /'sɪstiːn, -tɪn/ ■ n. Biochemistry an oxidized dimeric form of cysteine.
– ORIGIN C19: from Greek *kustis* 'bladder'.

cystitis /sɪ'stʌɪtɪs/ ■ n. Medicine inflammation of the urinary bladder, typically caused by infection and accompanied by frequent painful urination.

cysto- /ˈsɪstəʊ/ ■ comb. form of or relating to the urinary bladder: *cystotomy*.
– ORIGIN from Greek *kustis* 'bladder'.

cystoscope /ˈsɪstəskəʊp/ ■ n. Medicine an instrument inserted into the urethra for examining the urinary bladder.
– DERIVATIVES **cystoscopic** adj. **cystoscopy** n.

-cyte ■ comb. form Biology denoting a mature cell: *lymphocyte*. Compare with **-BLAST**.
– ORIGIN from Greek *kutos* 'vessel'.

cytidine /ˈsaɪtɪdiːn/ ■ n. Biochemistry a nucleoside consisting of cytosine combined with ribose.

cytisus /saɪˈtɪsəs, ˈsɪtɪsəs/ ■ n. a shrub of a large genus which includes many brooms. [Genus *Cytisus*.]
– ORIGIN from Greek *kutisos*.

cyto- /ˈsaɪtəʊ/ ■ comb. form Biology of a cell or cells: *cytology*.
– ORIGIN from Greek *kutos* 'vessel'.

cytochrome ■ n. Biochemistry any of a number of compounds consisting of haem bonded to a protein, involved in cellular respiration.

cytogenetics /ˌsaɪtəʊdʒəˈnɛtɪks/ ■ pl. n. [treated as sing.] Biology the study of inheritance in relation to the structure and function of chromosomes.
– DERIVATIVES **cytogenetic** adj. **cytogenetical** adj. **cytogenetically** adv. **cytogeneticist** n.

cytokine /ˈsaɪtə(ʊ)kaɪn/ ■ n. Physiology a substance, such as interferon and interleukin, which is secreted by the immune system and has an effect on other cells.

cytokinesis /ˌsaɪtə(ʊ)kʌɪˈniːsɪs/ ■ n. Biology the cytoplasmic division of a cell into two daughter cells at the end of mitosis or meiosis.

cytology /saɪˈtɒlədʒi/ ■ n. the branch of biology concerned with the structure and function of plant and animal cells.
– DERIVATIVES **cytological** adj. **cytologically** adv. **cytologist** n.

cytolysis /saɪˈtɒlɪsɪs/ ■ n. Biology the dissolution or disruption of cells, especially by an external agent.
– DERIVATIVES **cytolytic** adj.

cytomegalic /ˌsaɪtə(ʊ)mɪˈɡalɪk/ ■ adj. Medicine (of disease) characterized by enlarged cells.

cytomegalovirus /ˌsaɪtə(ʊ)ˈmɛɡ(ə)lə(ʊ)ˌvʌɪrəs/ ■ n. Medicine a kind of herpesvirus which usually produces very mild symptoms in an infected person but may cause severe neurological damage in people with weakened immune systems and in the newborn.

cytoplasm /ˈsaɪtə(ʊ)plaz(ə)m/ ■ n. Biology the material or protoplasm within a living cell, excluding the nucleus.
– DERIVATIVES **cytoplasmic** adj.

cytosine /ˈsaɪtəsiːn/ ■ n. Biochemistry a compound found in living tissue as a constituent base of DNA.

cytoskeleton ■ n. Biology a microscopic network of protein filaments and tubules in the cytoplasm of many living cells, giving them shape and coherence.
– DERIVATIVES **cytoskeletal** adj.

cytosol /ˈsaɪtə(ʊ)sɒl/ ■ n. Biology the aqueous component of the cytoplasm of a cell.
– DERIVATIVES **cytosolic** adj.

cytotoxic ■ adj. toxic to living cells.
– DERIVATIVES **cytotoxicity** n.

czar etc. ■ n. variant spelling of **TSAR** etc.

Czech /tʃɛk/ ■ n. 1 a native or national of the Czech Republic or (formerly) Czechoslovakia, or a person of Czech descent. 2 the Western Slavic language spoken in the Czech Republic, closely related to Slovak. ■ adj. of or relating to the Czechs or their language.
– ORIGIN Polish spelling of Czech *čech*.

Czechoslovak /-ˈsləʊvak/ (also **Czechoslovakian**) ■ n. a native or national of the former country of Czechoslovakia, now divided between the Czech Republic and Slovakia. ■ adj. of or relating to Czechoslovaks or the former country of Czechoslovakia.

Dd

D¹ (also **d**) ■ n. (pl. **Ds** or **D's**) **1** the fourth letter of the alphabet. **2** denoting the fourth in a set of items, categories, sizes, etc. **3** Music the second note of the diatonic scale of C major. **4** the Roman numeral for 500. [understood as half of CIƆ, an earlier form of M (= 1 000).]

D² ■ abbrev. **1** (in the US) Democrat or Democratic. **2** depth (in the sense of the dimension of an object from front to back). **3** Chemistry dextrorotatory. **4** (with a numeral) dimension(s) or dimensional. **5** (in tables of sports results) drawn. ■ symb. **1** Physics electric flux density. **2** Chemistry the hydrogen isotope deuterium.

d ■ abbrev. **1** (in genealogies) daughter. **2** day(s). **3** deci-. **4** (in travel timetables) departs. **5** (**d.**) died (used to indicate a date of death). **6** Brit. penny or pence (of pre-decimal currency). [from Latin *denarius* 'penny'.] **7** Chemistry denoting electrons and orbitals possessing two units of angular momentum. [*d* from *diffuse*, orig. applied to lines in atomic spectra.] ■ symb. **1** Mathematics diameter. **2** Mathematics denoting a small increment in a given variable.

'd ■ contr. **1** had. **2** would.

DA ■ abbrev. **1** (in South Africa) Democratic Alliance. **2** US district attorney.

D/A ■ abbrev. Electronics digital to analogue.

da ■ abbrev. deca-.

dab¹ ■ v. (**dabbed**, **dabbing**) press against (something) lightly several times with a piece of absorbent material. ▸ apply (a substance) with light quick strokes. ■ n. **1** a small amount: *she put a dab of perfume behind her ears*. ▸ a brief application of a piece of absorbent material to a surface. **2** (**dabs**) Brit. informal fingerprints.
– ORIGIN Middle English: symbolic of a light striking movement.

dab² ■ n. a small, commercially important flatfish found chiefly in the North Atlantic. [*Limanda limanda* and other species.]
– ORIGIN Middle English.

daba grass /'dɑːbɑː/ ■ n. S. African a coarse grass, often used for thatching. [*Miscanthus capensis*.]
– ORIGIN *daba*: from isiXhosa *idobo*, denoting any coarse long grass.

dabble ■ v. **1** move (one's hands or feet) around gently in water. ▸ (of a duck or other water bird) move the bill around in shallow water while feeding. **2** (often **dabble in**) take part in an activity in a casual or superficial way.
– DERIVATIVES **dabbler** n.
– ORIGIN C16: from obsolete Dutch *dabbelen*, or from **DAB¹**.

dabbling duck ■ n. a duck which typically feeds by dabbling and upending in fresh water, such as the mallard or teal.

dabchick ■ n. the little grebe. [*Tachybaptus ruficollis*.]
– ORIGIN C16 (as *dopchick*): the first element is perhaps rel. to **DIP**.

dab hand ■ n. Brit. informal a person who is an expert at a particular activity.
– ORIGIN C19.

DAC ■ abbrev. Electronics digital to analogue converter.

da capo /dɑːˈkɑːpəʊ/ ■ adv. & adj. Music repeat or repeated from the beginning. Compare with **DAL SEGNO**.
– ORIGIN Italian, 'from the head'.

dacha /'datʃə/ (also **datcha**) ■ n. a country house or cottage in Russia, typically used as a second or holiday home.
– ORIGIN Russian, orig. 'grant (of land)'.

dachshund /'dakshʊnd, -s(ə)nd/ ■ n. a dog of a very short-legged, long-bodied breed.
– ORIGIN C19: from German, 'badger dog' (the breed being orig. used to dig badgers out of their setts).

dacoit /dəˈkɔɪt/ ■ n. a member of a band of armed robbers in India or Burma (Myanmar).
– DERIVATIVES **dacoity** n. (pl. **-ies**)
– ORIGIN from Hindi *ḍakait*, from *ḍakaitī* 'robbery by a gang'.

Dacron ■ n. trademark a tough, elastic polyester fibre used as a fabric to make sails, etc.

dactyl /'daktɪl/ ■ n. Prosody a metrical foot consisting of one stressed syllable followed by two unstressed syllables or (in Greek and Latin) one long syllable followed by two short syllables.
– ORIGIN Middle English: from Greek *daktulos* 'finger' (the three bones of the finger corresponding to the three syllables).

dactylic Prosody ■ adj. of or using dactyls. ■ n. (**dactylics**) dactylic verse.

dad ■ n. informal one's father.
– ORIGIN C16: perhaps imitative of a young child's first syllables *da*, *da*.

Dada /'dɑːdɑː/ ■ n. an early 20th-century international movement in art, literature, music, and film, repudiating and mocking artistic and social conventions and emphasizing the illogical and absurd.
– DERIVATIVES **Dadaism** n. **Dadaist** n. & adj. **Dadaistic** adj.
– ORIGIN French, 'hobby horse', the title of a review which appeared in Zurich in 1916.

dada /'dɑːdɑː/ ■ n. Indian an older brother or male cousin. ▸ a respectful form of address for any familiar older male.
– ORIGIN from Hindi *dādā*.

daddy ■ n. (pl. **-ies**) informal one's father.

daddy-long-legs ■ n. **1** another term for **HARVESTMAN**. **2** Brit. informal a crane fly.

dado /'deɪdəʊ/ ■ n. (pl. **-os**) **1** the lower part of the wall of a room, when decorated differently from the upper part. **2** N. Amer. a groove cut in the face of a board, into which the edge of another board is fixed. **3** Architecture the cube of a pedestal between the base and the cornice.
– ORIGIN C17: from Italian, 'dice or cube'.

dado rail ■ n. a waist-high moulding round the wall of a room.

daemon¹ /'diːmən/ (also **daimon**) ■ n. **1** (in ancient Greek belief) a divinity or supernatural being of a nature between gods and humans. ▸ an inner or attendant spirit or inspiring force. **2** archaic spelling of **DEMON¹**.
– DERIVATIVES **daemonic** adj.
– ORIGIN C16: common spelling of **DEMON¹** until the 19th century.

daemon² /'diːmən/ (also **demon**) ■ n. Computing a background process that handles requests for services such as print spooling, and is dormant when not required.
– ORIGIN 1980s: perhaps from *d*(*isk*) *a*(*nd*) *e*(*xecution*) *mon*-(*itor*) or from *de*(*vice*) *mon*(*itor*), or merely a transferred use of **DEMON¹**.

daffodil ■ n. a bulbous plant bearing bright yellow flowers with a long trumpet-shaped centre. [*Narcissus pseudonarcissus* and related species.]
– ORIGIN C16: from Middle English *affodil*, from medieval Latin *affodilus*, var. of Latin *asphodilus* (see **ASPHODEL**).

daffy ■ adj. (**-ier**, **-iest**) informal silly; mildly eccentric.
– DERIVATIVES **daffiness** n.
– ORIGIN C19: from northern English dialect *daff* 'simpleton'.

daft ■ adj. informal, chiefly Brit. **1** silly; foolish. **2** (**daft about**) infatuated with.
– ORIGIN Old English *gedæfte* 'mild, meek', of Germanic origin.

dag Austral./NZ ■ n. a lock of wool matted with dung

hanging from the hindquarters of a sheep. ■ v. (**dagged**, **dagging**) cut dags from (a sheep).

daga /'dɑːɡə/ ■ n. **1** S. African (also **daga salmon**) an important food fish of tropical and temperate waters. [*Argyrosomus japonicus*.] **2** variant spelling of **DAGHA**.

dageraad /'dɑːxərɑːt/ ■ n. (pl. same) S. African a sea bream characterized by its colour changes when caught, fished commercially and for sport in Cape waters. [*Chrysoblephus cristiceps*.]
– ORIGIN S. African Dutch, prob. from French *daurade* 'sea bream' influenced by Dutch *dageraad* 'dawn'.

dagga[1] /'daxə/ ■ n. chiefly S. African cannabis.
– ORIGIN C17: from Afrikaans, from Khoikhoi *dachab*.

dagga[2] /'dɑːɡə/ ■ n. variant spelling of **DAGA** or **DAGHA**.

dagger ■ n. **1** a short knife with a pointed and edged blade, used as a weapon. **2** Printing another term for **OBELUS**.
– PHRASES **at daggers drawn** in bitter enmity. **look daggers at** glare angrily or venomously at.
– ORIGIN Middle English: perhaps from obsolete *dag* 'pierce', influenced by Old French *dague* 'long dagger'.

daggerboard ■ n. a kind of centreboard which slides vertically through the keel of a sailing boat.

daggerhead ■ n. another term for **DAGERAAD**.

dagha /'dɑːɡə, 'daɡə/ (also **daga**, **dagga**) ■ n. S. African building mortar or plaster traditionally made of mud or ant-hill soil and sometimes mixed with cow-dung or blood; now usually a mixture of soil, sand, and lime.
– ORIGIN Afrikaans: from isiXhosa or isiZulu *udaka* 'clay, mud'.

dago /'deɪɡəʊ/ ■ n. (pl. **-os** or **-oes**) informal, offensive a Spanish, Portuguese, or Italian-speaking person.
– ORIGIN C19: from the Spanish given name *Diego*.

daguerreotype /dəˈɡɛrətʌɪp/ (also **daguerrotype**) ■ n. a photograph taken by an early photographic process employing an iodine-sensitized silvered plate and mercury vapour.
– ORIGIN C19: from French *daguerréotype*, named after L.-J.-M. *Daguerre*, its French inventor.

dahlia /'deɪlɪə/ ■ n. a tuberous-rooted Mexican plant of the daisy family, cultivated for its brightly coloured single or double flowers. [Genus *Dahlia*.]
– ORIGIN modern Latin: named in honour of the Swedish botanist Andreas *Dahl*.

daikon /'dʌɪk(ə)n, -kɒn/ ■ n. another term for **MOOLI**.
– ORIGIN Japanese: from *dai* 'large' + *kon* 'root'.

daily ■ adj. done, produced, or occurring every day or every weekday. ■ adv. every day. ■ n. (pl. **-ies**) informal **1** a newspaper published every day except Sunday. **2** (also **daily help**) Brit. dated a daily charwoman.

daimon /'dʌɪməʊn/ ■ n. variant spelling of **DAEMON**[1].
– DERIVATIVES **daimonic** /-'məʊnɪk, -'mɒnɪk/ adj.

dainty ■ adj. (**-ier**, **-iest**) **1** delicately small and pretty. ▸ delicate and graceful in build or movement. **2** fastidious, typically concerning food. ■ n. (pl. **-ies**) a delicacy.
– DERIVATIVES **daintily** adv. **daintiness** n.
– ORIGIN Middle English: from Old French *daintie* 'choice morsel, pleasure', from Latin *dignitas* 'worthiness, beauty', from *dignus* 'worthy'.

daiquiri /'dʌɪkɪri, 'dak-/ ■ n. (pl. **daiquiris**) a cocktail containing rum and lime juice.
– ORIGIN named after *Daiquiri*, a rum-producing district in Cuba.

dairy ■ n. (pl. **-ies**) a building or room for the storage, processing, and distribution of milk and milk products. ■ adj. containing or made from milk.
▸ concerned with or involved in the production of milk.
– DERIVATIVES **dairying** n.
– ORIGIN Middle English *deierie*, from *deie* 'dairymaid' (in Old English *dǣge* 'female servant'), of Germanic origin.

dairymaid ■ n. archaic a woman employed in a dairy.

dairyman ■ n. (pl. **-men**) a man who is employed in a dairy or who sells dairy products.

dais /'deɪs, deɪs/ ■ n. a low platform for a lectern or throne.
– ORIGIN Middle English: from Old French *deis*, from Latin *discus* 'disc, dish', later 'table'.

daisy ■ n. (pl. **-ies**) a small grassland plant, native to Europe, with composite flowers having a yellow disc and white rays. [*Bellis perennis*.] ▸ used in names of other plants of the same family, e.g. Michaelmas daisy.
– PHRASES **pushing up (the) daisies** informal dead and buried.
– ORIGIN Old English *dæges ēage* 'day's eye' (because the flower opens in the morning and closes at night).

daisy chain ■ n. **1** a string of daisies threaded together by their stems. **2** a string of associated people or things. ■ v. (**daisy-chain**) Computing connect (several devices) together in a linear series.
– DERIVATIVES **daisy-chainable** adj.

daisy wheel ■ n. a device used as a printer in word processors and typewriters, consisting of a disc of spokes extending radially from a central hub, each terminating in a printing character.

dakkamer /'dʌkkɑːmə/ ■ n. S. African Architecture a small room built on the flat roof of a Cape Dutch house and set behind a gable, often used as a lookout.
– ORIGIN Afrikaans: from *dak* 'roof' + *kamer* 'room'.

Dakota /dəˈkəʊtə/ ■ n. (pl. same or **Dakotas**) **1** a member of a North American Indian people of the northern Mississippi valley and the surrounding plains. **2** the Siouan language of this people.
– ORIGIN the name in Dakota, 'allies'.

dakriet ■ n. S. African variant spelling of **DEKRIET**.
– ORIGIN C19: from Afrikaans (see **DEKRIET**).

dal ■ n. variant spelling of **DHAL**.

Dalai Lama /ˌdalʌɪ 'lɑːmə/ ■ n. the spiritual head of Tibetan Buddhism and, until the establishment of Chinese communist rule, the spiritual and temporal ruler of Tibet.
– ORIGIN from Tibetan, 'ocean monk', so named because he is regarded as 'the ocean of compassion'.

dale ■ n. a valley, especially in northern England.
– ORIGIN Old English, of Germanic origin.

Daliesque /dɑːlɪ'ɛsk/ ■ adj. resembling or characteristic of the work of the Spanish painter Salvador Dali (1904–89), especially in being surrealistic.

Dalit /'dɑːlɪt/ ■ n. (in the traditional Indian caste system) a member of the lowest caste. See also **UNTOUCHABLE**, **SCHEDULED CASTE**.
– ORIGIN from Sanskrit *dalita* 'oppressed'.

dalliance /'dalɪəns/ ■ n. a casual romantic or sexual relationship. ▸ a period of casual interest in something.

dally ■ v. (**-ies**, **-ied**) **1** act or move slowly. **2** (**dally with**) have a casual romantic or sexual liaison with. ▸ show a casual interest in.
– ORIGIN Middle English: from Old French *dalier* 'to chat'.

Dalmatian ■ n. a dog of a large, white short-haired breed with dark spots.
– ORIGIN C16: the dog is believed to have originated in Dalmatia in the 18th century.

dal segno /dal ˈsɛnjəʊ/ ■ adv. & adj. Music repeat or repeated from the point marked by a sign. Compare with **DA CAPO**.
– ORIGIN Italian, 'from the sign'.

dalton /'dɔːlt(ə)n/ ■ n. Chemistry a unit used in expressing the molecular weight of proteins, equivalent to atomic mass unit.
– ORIGIN 1930s: named after the English chemist John *Dalton*.

dam[1] ■ n. **1** a barrier constructed to hold back water and raise its level, forming a reservoir or preventing flooding. ▸ a barrier of branches in a stream, constructed by a beaver to provide a deep pool and a lodge. **2** ▸ S. African a man-made pond or reservoir where rain or spring water is collected for storage. **3** chiefly N. Amer. a rubber sheet used to keep saliva from the teeth during dental operations. ■ v. (**dammed**, **damming**) build a dam across.
▸ hold back or obstruct.
– ORIGIN Middle English: from Middle Low German or Middle Dutch, rel. to Old English *fordemman* 'close up'.

dam[2] ■ n. the female parent of an animal, especially a mammal.
– ORIGIN Middle English: alteration of **DAME**.

damage ■ n. **1** physical harm impairing the value,

damaged goods

usefulness, or normal function of something. ▸ unwelcome and detrimental effects. **2** (**damages**) a sum of money claimed or awarded in compensation for a loss or injury. ■ v. inflict damage on.
– PHRASES **what's the damage?** informal, humorous what does it cost?
– DERIVATIVES **damaging** adj. **damagingly** adv.
– ORIGIN Middle English: from Old French, from *dam*, *damne* 'loss, damage', from Latin *damnum* 'loss, hurt'.

damaged goods ■ pl. n. a person regarded as inadequate or impaired in some way.

damar /'damə/ ■ n. variant spelling of DAMMAR.

Damara /'damərə, də'mɑːrə/ ■ n. (pl. same or **Damaras**) **1** a member of a people inhabiting mountainous parts of Namibia and speaking the Nama language. **2** (also **Damara sheep**) a sheep of a short-haired southern African breed with long legs and a fat tail.
– ORIGIN the name in Nama.

Damascene /'daməsiːn, ˌdamə'siːn/ ■ adj. of or relating to the city of Damascus, the capital of Syria. ▸ of, relating to, or resembling the conversion of St Paul on the road to Damascus.

damascened /'daməsiːnd, ˌdamə'siːnd/ ■ adj. **1** (of iron or steel) given a wavy pattern by hammer-welding and repeated heating and forging. **2** (of a metal object) inlaid with gold or silver.

Damascus steel /də'mɑːskəs, -'maskəs/ ■ n. historical damascened steel, used chiefly for knife and sword blades.

damask /'daməsk/ ■ n. **1** a figured, lustrous fabric, with a pattern visible on both sides. ▸ a tablecloth made of damask. **2** (also **damask steel**) historical another term for DAMASCUS STEEL. ■ adj. poetic/literary of the colour of a damask rose. ■ v. poetic/literary decorate with or as if with a variegated pattern.
– ORIGIN Middle English: from *Damaske*, early form of the name of *Damascus*, the city in Syria where the fabric was first produced.

damask rose ■ n. a sweet-scented rose of an old variety, having pink or light red velvety petals which are used to make attar. [*Rosa damascena*.]

dame ■ n. **1** (**Dame**) (in the UK) the title given to a woman of high rank in the Orders of Chivalry. **2** archaic or humorous an elderly or mature woman. ▸ N. Amer. informal a woman. ▸ (also **pantomime dame**) Brit. a comic middle-aged female character in pantomime, typically played by a man.
– ORIGIN Middle English: from Latin *domina* 'mistress'.

dame school ■ n. historical a small primary school run by elderly women.

damfool informal, dated ■ adj. thoroughly foolish. ■ n. a foolish person.

dammar /'damə/ (also **damar**) ■ n. resin obtained from various mainly Indo-Malaysian trees, used to make varnish.
– ORIGIN C17: from Malay *damar* 'resin'.

damn /dam/ ■ v. **1** (**be damned**) (in Christian belief) be condemned by God to suffer eternal punishment in hell. ▸ be doomed to misfortune or failure. **2** condemn, especially publicly. **3** curse. ■ exclam. informal expressing anger or frustration. ■ adj. informal used to emphasize one's anger or frustration: *turn that damn thing off!*
– PHRASES **as near as damn it** as close to being accurate as makes no difference. **damn all** Brit. informal nothing. **damn with faint praise** praise so unenthusiastically as to imply condemnation. **I'm** (or **I'll be**) **damned if** informal used to express a strong negative: *I'm damned if I know.* **not be worth a damn** informal have no value. **well I'll be** (or **I'm**) **damned** informal used to express surprise.
– ORIGIN Middle English: from Old French *dam(p)ner*, from Latin *dam(p)nare* 'inflict loss on', from *damnum* 'loss, damage'.

damna /'damnə/ plural form of DAMNUM.

damnable /'damnəb(ə)l/ ■ adj. **1** very bad or unpleasant. **2** worthy of divine condemnation.
– DERIVATIVES **damnably** adv.

damnation /dam'neɪʃ(ə)n/ ■ n. condemnation to eternal punishment in hell. ■ exclam. expressing anger or frustration.

damnatory /'damnə,t(ə)ri/ ■ adj. conveying or causing censure or damnation.

damned /damd/ ■ adj. informal used to emphasize one's anger or frustration. ▸ (**damnedest**) used to emphasize the surprising nature of something.
– PHRASES **do** (or **try**) **one's damnedest** do (or try) one's utmost.

damning ■ adj. strongly suggestive of guilt or error.
– DERIVATIVES **damningly** adv.

damnum /'damnəm/ ■ n. (pl. **damna**) Law a loss.
– ORIGIN Latin, 'harm, damage'.

damp ■ adj. slightly wet. ■ n. moisture in the air, on a surface, or in a solid, typically with detrimental or unpleasant effects. ■ v. **1** make damp. **2** control or restrain (a feeling or a situation). **3** make (a fire) burn less strongly by reducing its air supply. **4** reduce or stop the vibration of (the strings of a musical instrument).
– DERIVATIVES **dampish** adj. **damply** adv. **dampness** n.
– ORIGIN Middle English (in the sense 'noxious inhalation'): of West Germanic origin.

damp course (also **damp-proof course**) ■ n. a layer of waterproof material in the wall of a building near the ground, to prevent rising damp.

dampen ■ v. **1** make damp. **2** make less strong or intense. ▸ reduce the amplitude of (a sound source).
– DERIVATIVES **dampener** n.

damper ■ n. Music a pad silencing a piano string except when removed by means of a pedal or by the note being struck. **2** a device for reducing vibration or oscillation. **3** a movable metal plate in a flue or chimney, used to regulate the draught and so control the rate of combustion. **4** chiefly Austral./NZ an unleavened loaf or cake of flour and water baked in wood ashes. [in the sense 'something that takes the edge off the appetite'.]
– PHRASES **put a** (or **the**) **damper on** have a subduing or inhibiting effect on.

damping ■ n. **1** a reduction in the amplitude of a vibration or oscillation. **2** (**damping off**) the death of young seedlings as a result of a fungal infection in damp conditions.

damp-proof ■ adj. impervious to damp. ■ v. make impervious to damp by using a damp course.

damp squib ■ n. Brit. something much less impressive than expected.

damsel /'damz(ə)l/ ■ n. archaic or poetic/literary a young unmarried woman.
– ORIGIN Middle English: from Old French *dameisele*, from Latin *domina* 'mistress'.

damselfish ■ n. (pl. same or **-fishes**) a small brightly coloured tropical fish living near coral reefs. [*Chromis chromis* and other species.]

damselfly ■ n. (pl. **-flies**) a slender insect related to the dragonflies, typically resting with the wings folded back along the body. [Suborder Zygoptera: many species.]

damson /'damz(ə)n/ ■ n. **1** a small purple-black plum-like fruit. **2** (also **damson tree**) the small tree which bears this fruit. [*Prunus domestica* subsp. *insititia*.]
– ORIGIN Middle English *damascene*, from Latin *damascenum* (*prunum*) '(plum) of Damascus'.

damson cheese ■ n. a solid preserve of damsons and sugar.

dan ■ n. any of ten degrees of advanced proficiency in judo or karate. ▸ a person who has achieved a dan.
– ORIGIN 1940s: from Japanese.

Danakil /'danəkɪl, də'nɑːk(ə)l/ ■ n. another term for AFAR.
– ORIGIN from Arabic *danākil*, pl. of *dankalī*.

dance ■ v. **1** move rhythmically to music, typically following a set sequence of steps. ▸ perform (a particular dance or a role in a ballet). **2** move in a quick and light or lively way. ▸ (of someone's eyes) sparkle with pleasure or excitement. ■ n. **1** a series of steps and movements that match the speed and rhythm of a piece of music. **2** a social gathering at which people dance. **3** (also **dance music**) music for dancing to, especially in a nightclub.
– PHRASES **dance attendance on** do one's utmost to please someone. **dance to someone's tune** comply with someone's demands and wishes. **lead someone a merry dance** Brit. cause someone a great deal of trouble or worry.

VOWELS   a cat   ɑː arm   ɛ bed   ɛː hair   ə ago   əː her   ɪ sit   i cosy   iː see   ɒ hot   ɔː saw   ʌ run

– DERIVATIVES **danceable** adj. **dancer** n. **dancing** n.
– ORIGIN Middle English: from Old French *dancer*, *dance*.

dance band ■ n. a band that plays music suitable for dancing to, especially swing.

dance floor ■ n. an area of floor in a nightclub, disco, or restaurant reserved for dancing.

dance hall ■ n. a large public hall or building where people pay to enter and dance.

dancercise (also **-ize**) ■ n. a system of aerobic exercise using dance movements.

dancing girl ■ n. a female professional dancer, especially a member of a chorus in a musical.

D and C ■ abbrev. dilatation and curettage.

dandelion ■ n. a widely distributed weed of the daisy family, with large bright yellow flowers followed by globular heads of seeds with downy tufts. [*Taraxacum officinale* and related species.]
– ORIGIN Middle English: from French *dent-de-lion* 'lion's tooth' (because of the jagged shape of the leaves).

dandelion clock ■ n. see CLOCK[1] (sense 2).

dander[1] ■ n. (in phr. **get/have one's dander up**) informal lose one's temper.
– ORIGIN C19.

dander[2] ■ n. skin flakes in an animal's fur.
– ORIGIN C18: rel. to DANDRUFF.

Dandie Dinmont /ˌdandɪ ˈdɪnmənt/ ■ n. a terrier of a breed from the Scottish Borders, with short legs, a long body, and a rough coat.
– ORIGIN C19: named after a character in Sir Walter Scott's *Guy Mannering* who owned a special breed of terriers.

dandified ■ adj. **1** (of a man) showing excessive concern about his appearance. **2** self-consciously elaborate: *dandified prose*.

dandle ■ v. move (a baby or young child) up and down in a playful or affectionate way.
– ORIGIN C16.

dandruff ■ n. small pieces of dead skin among a person's hair.
– DERIVATIVES **dandruffy** adj.
– ORIGIN C16: the first element is unknown; the second (*-ruff*) is perhaps rel. to Middle English *rove* 'scurfy skin'.

dandy ■ n. (pl. **-ies**) a man unduly concerned with a stylish and fashionable appearance. ■ adj. (**-ier**, **-iest**) informal, chiefly N. Amer. excellent.
– DERIVATIVES **dandyish** adj. **dandyism** n.
– ORIGIN C18: perhaps a shortened form of C17 *Jack-a-dandy* 'conceited fellow'.

dandy brush ■ n. a coarse brush used for grooming a horse.

Dane ■ n. a native or national of Denmark, or a person of Danish descent.
– ORIGIN Old English.

dang ■ adj., exclam., & v. informal, chiefly N. Amer. euphemism for DAMN.

danger ■ n. **1** the possibility of suffering harm or injury. ▶ a cause of harm or injury. **2** the possibility of something unwelcome or unpleasant: *there was no danger of the champagne running out.*
– ORIGIN Middle English (in the sense 'jurisdiction, power to harm'): from Old French *dangier*, from Latin *dominus* 'lord'.

danger list ■ n. Brit. a list of those who are dangerously ill in a hospital.

danger money (also **danger pay**) ■ n. extra payment for working under dangerous conditions.

dangerous ■ adj. able or likely to cause harm or injury. ▶ likely to cause problems or difficulties.
– DERIVATIVES **dangerously** adv. **dangerousness** n.

dangle ■ v. hang or cause to hang so as to swing freely.
– PHRASES **keep someone dangling** keep someone in an uncertain position.
– DERIVATIVES **dangler** n. **dangly** adj.
– ORIGIN C16.

dangling participle ■ n. Grammar a participle intended to modify a noun which is not actually present in the text (e.g. *arriving* in *arriving at the station, the sun came out*), regarded as a mistake in standard English.

dark

Danish /ˈdeɪnɪʃ/ ■ adj. of or relating to Denmark or its people or language. ■ n. the Scandinavian language spoken in Denmark.
– ORIGIN Old English, of Germanic origin.

Danish blue ■ n. a soft, salty, strong-flavoured white cheese with blue veins.

Danish pastry ■ n. a cake of sweetened yeast pastry with toppings or fillings of icing, fruit, or nuts.

dank ■ adj. damp, cold, and musty.
– DERIVATIVES **dankly** adv. **dankness** n.
– ORIGIN Middle English: prob. of Scandinavian origin and rel. to Swedish *dank* 'marshy spot'.

Dantean /ˈdantɪən, danˈtiːən/ ■ adj. of or reminiscent of the work of the Italian poet Dante (1265–1321), especially his vision of hell in *The Divine Comedy*. ■ n. an admirer of Dante or his work.
– DERIVATIVES **Dantesque** /ˌdantɪˈɛsk/ adj.

daphne /ˈdafni/ ■ n. a small, typically evergreen shrub with sweet-scented flowers. [Genus *Daphne*.]
– ORIGIN Middle English (denoting the laurel or bay tree): from Greek *daphnē*, from the name of *Daphne*, a nymph in Greek mythology who was turned into a laurel bush.

daphnia /ˈdafnɪə/ ■ n. (pl. same) a minute semi-transparent freshwater crustacean with long antennae and prominent eyes. [Genus *Daphnia*.]
– ORIGIN from the name of the nymph *Daphne* (see DAPHNE).

dapper ■ adj. (of a man) neat and trim in dress and appearance.
– DERIVATIVES **dapperly** adv. **dapperness** n.
– ORIGIN Middle English: prob. from a Middle Low German or Middle Dutch word meaning 'strong, stout'.

dapple ■ v. (usu. **be dappled**) mark with spots or rounded patches. ■ n. **1** a patch of colour or light. **2** an animal whose coat is dappled.
– ORIGIN C16: perhaps rel. to Old Norse *depill* 'spot'.

dapple grey ■ adj. (of a horse) grey or white with darker ring-like markings. ■ n. a horse of this type.

dapsone /ˈdapsəʊn/ ■ n. Medicine a sulphur-containing drug used to treat leprosy.
– ORIGIN 1950s: from elements of the systematic name *dipara-aminophenyl sulphone*.

dare ■ v. (3rd sing. present usu. **dare** before an expressed or implied infinitive without 'to') **1** have the courage to do something. ▶ (**how dare you**) used to express indignation. ▶ (**don't you dare**) used to order someone threateningly not to do something. **2** defy or challenge to do something. **3** poetic/literary take the risk of. ■ n. a challenge, especially to prove courage.
– PHRASES **I dare say** (or **daresay**) it is probable.
– DERIVATIVES **darer** n.
– ORIGIN Old English, of Germanic origin.

daredevil ■ n. a person who enjoys doing dangerous things.
– DERIVATIVES **daredevilry** n.

dargah /ˈdɑːɡə/ ■ n. the tomb or shrine of a Muslim holy man.
– ORIGIN from Urdu, from Persian.

daring ■ adj. adventurous or audaciously bold. ■ n. adventurous courage.
– DERIVATIVES **daringly** adv.

Darjeeling /dɑːˈdʒiːlɪŋ/ ■ n. a high-quality tea grown in the mountains of northern India.
– ORIGIN from *Darjeeling*, a hill station in West Bengal.

dark ■ adj. **1** with little or no light. **2** of a deep or sombre colour. ▶ (of skin, hair, or eyes) brown or black. ▶ (of a person) having such skin, hair, or eyes. **3** mysterious: *a dark secret*. ▶ (**darkest**) humorous (of a region) most remote, inaccessible, or uncivilized. ▶ archaic ignorant. **4** characterized by unhappiness or unpleasantness: *the dark days of the war*. ▶ (of an expression) angry. ▶ evil; sinister: *dark deeds*. ■ n. **1** (**the dark**) the absence of light. ▶ a dark colour or shade. **2** nightfall.
– PHRASES **in the dark** in a state of ignorance. **keep something dark** keep something secret. **a shot** (or **stab**) **in**

the dark a mere guess.
– DERIVATIVES **darkish** adj. **darkly** adv. **darkness** n. **darksome** adj. (poetic/literary).
– ORIGIN Old English, of Germanic origin.

Dark Ages ■ pl. n. the period in Europe between the fall of the Roman Empire and the Middle Ages, c.500–1100 AD, judged to have been a time of relative unenlightenment.

dark chocolate ■ n. plain chocolate.

dark current ■ n. the residual electric current flowing in a photoelectric device when there is no illumination.

darken ■ v. 1 make or become dark or darker. ▶ (of something unpleasant) cast a shadow over; spoil. 2 make or become unhappy or angry. ▶ (of someone's eyes or expression) show anger.
– PHRASES **never darken someone's door** keep away from someone's home.

dark horse ■ n. a person about whom little is known, especially one with unexpected abilities.
– ORIGIN C19: orig. racing slang.

darkie (also **darky**) ■ n. (pl. **-ies**) informal, offensive a black person.

darkling ■ adj. poetic/literary of or relating to growing darkness.

dark matter ■ n. Astronomy (in some cosmological theories) non-luminous material postulated to exist in space.

dark night of the soul ■ n. a period of spiritual desolation suffered by a mystic in which all sense of consolation is removed.
– ORIGIN C19: translating Spanish *noche oscura*.

darkroom ■ n. a room for developing photographs, from which normal light is excluded.

darky ■ n. variant spelling of DARKIE.

darling ■ n. used as an affectionate form of address. ▶ a lovable or endearing person. ▶ a favourite of a certain group: *the darling of the team*. ■ adj. beloved. ▶ pretty; charming.
– ORIGIN Old English *dēorling* (see DEAR, -LING).

darmstadtium /dɑːmˈstatiəm/ ■ n. the chemical element of atomic number 110, a radioactive element produced artificially. (Symbol: **Ds**)
– ORIGIN C21: named after the German city of *Darmstadt* (where it was discovered) + -IUM.

darn¹ ■ v. mend (knitted material or a hole in this) by interweaving yarn across it with a needle. ▶ embroider with a large running stitch. ■ n. a place in a garment that has been darned.
– DERIVATIVES **darning** n.
– ORIGIN C17: perhaps from dialect *dern* 'to hide', from Old English, of West Germanic origin.

darn² (US also **durn**) ■ v., adj., & exclam. informal euphemism for DAMN.

darned (US also **durned**) ■ adj. informal euphemism for DAMNED.

darnel /ˈdɑːn(ə)l/ ■ n. a ryegrass, formerly a common weed of cereals. [*Lolium temulentum* and other species.]
– ORIGIN Middle English.

darning needle ■ n. a long sewing needle with a large eye, used in darning.

darshan /ˈdɑːʃ(ə)n/ ■ n. Hinduism an opportunity of seeing a holy person or the image of a deity.
– ORIGIN from Sanskrit *darśana* 'sight, seeing'.

dart ■ n. 1 a small pointed missile thrown or fired as a weapon. ▶ a small pointed missile with a flight, used in the game of darts. 2 an act of moving suddenly and rapidly. 3 a tapered tuck in a garment. ■ v. 1 move suddenly or rapidly. 2 shoot (an animal) with a dart, in order to administer a drug.
– ORIGIN Middle English: from Old French, from *darz*, from a West Germanic word meaning 'spear, lance'.

dartboard ■ n. a circular board marked with numbered segments, used as a target in the game of darts.

darter ■ n. 1 a long-necked bird which spears fish with its long pointed bill. [Genus *Anhinga*.] 2 a broad-bodied dragonfly which darts out to grab prey. [Libellulidae and other families.]

Dartmoor pony ■ n. a pony of a small hardy breed with a long shaggy coat in winter.

darts ■ pl. n. [usu. treated as sing.] an indoor game in which darts are thrown at a dartboard to score points.

Darwinism ■ n. the theory of the evolution of species by natural selection, advanced by the English natural historian Charles Darwin (1809–82).
– DERIVATIVES **Darwinian** n. & adj. **Darwinist** n. & adj.

dash ■ v. 1 run or travel in a great hurry. 2 strike or fling with great force. 3 destroy or frustrate (hopes or expectations). 4 (**dash something off**) write something hurriedly and without much thought. ■ exclam. informal used to express mild annoyance. ■ n. 1 an act of dashing. ▶ chiefly N. Amer. a sprint. 2 a small quantity of a substance, added to something else. ▶ a small amount of a particular quality adding distinctiveness to something. 3 a horizontal stroke in writing, marking a pause or to represent omitted letters or words. ▶ the longer signal of the two used in Morse code. 4 panache. 5 short for DASHBOARD.
– ORIGIN Middle English: prob. symbolic of forceful movement.

dashboard ■ n. the panel of instruments and controls facing the driver of a vehicle.

dashed ■ adj. Brit. informal, dated used for emphasis: *it's a dashed shame*.

dasher ■ n. 1 informal a flamboyant or stylish person. 2 a plunger for agitating cream in a churn.

dashiki /ˈdɑːʃɪki/ ■ n. (pl. **dashikis**) a loose, brightly coloured shirt, originally from West Africa.
– ORIGIN from Yoruba or Hausa.

dashing ■ adj. (of a man) attractive in a romantic, adventurous way. ▶ stylish.
– DERIVATIVES **dashingly** adv.

dassie /ˈdasi/ ■ n. (pl. **-ies**) 1 South African term for ROCK HYRAX. 2 a silvery fish with dark fins and a black spot on the tail. [*Diplodus sargus*.]
– ORIGIN C18: from Afrikaans, from S. African Dutch *dasje*, diminutive of Dutch *das* 'badger'.

dastardly ■ adj. dated or humorous wicked and cruel.
– DERIVATIVES **dastardliness** n.

DAT ■ abbrev. digital audiotape.

data /ˈdeɪtə/ ■ n. 1 facts and statistics used for reference or analysis. ▶ Philosophy things known or assumed as facts, making the basis of reasoning. 2 the quantities, characters, or symbols on which operations are performed by a computer.
– ORIGIN C17: from Latin, pl. of DATUM.

> USAGE
> In Latin, **data** is the plural of **datum** and, historically and in specialized scientific fields, it is also treated as a plural in English. In modern non-scientific use, however, it is often treated as a mass noun, similar to a word like **information**, which cannot normally have a plural and which takes a singular verb. Sentences such as *data was collected over a number of years* are now widely accepted in standard English.

databank ■ n. Computing a large repository of data, sometimes formed from more than one database.

database ■ n. a structured set of data held in a computer.

datable (also **dateable**) ■ adj. able to be dated to a particular time.

data capture ■ n. Computing the action of gathering data from an automatic device, control system, or sensor.

data link ■ n. a telecommunications link over which data is transmitted.

data mining ■ n. the extraction of information from databases through computer analysis of data patterns and relationships.

data processing ■ n. a series of operations on data, especially by a computer, to retrieve, transform, or classify information.
– DERIVATIVES **data processor** n.

data protection ■ n. legal control over access to and use of data stored in computers.

date¹ ■ n. **1** the day of the month or year as specified by a number. **2** a day or year when a given event occurred or will occur. ▶ (**dates**) the years of a person's birth and death or of the beginning and end of a period or event. ▶ the period of time to which something belongs. **3** informal a social or romantic appointment. **4** a musical or theatrical performance, especially as part of a tour. ■ v. **1** establish or ascertain the date of. ▶ mark with a date. ▶ have existed since. **2** [often as adj. **dated**] appear or cause to appear old-fashioned. **3** informal, chiefly N. Amer. go on a date with.
–PHRASES **to date** until now.
–DERIVATIVES **dating** n.
–ORIGIN Middle English: from medieval Latin *data*, from *dare* 'give', from the Latin formula used in dating letters, *data* (*epistola*) '(letter) given or delivered'.

date² ■ n. **1** a sweet, dark brown, oval fruit with a hard stone, usually eaten dried. **2** (also **date palm**) a tall palm tree which bears clusters of this fruit, native to western Asia and North Africa. [*Phoenix dactylifera*.]
–ORIGIN Middle English: from Old French, from Greek *daktulos* 'finger' (because of the finger-like shape of its leaves).

dateable ■ adj. variant spelling of DATABLE.

datebook ■ n. N. Amer. an engagement diary.

Date Line (also **International Date Line**) ■ n. an imaginary North–South line through the Pacific Ocean, chiefly along the meridian furthest from Greenwich, to the east of which the date is a day earlier than it is to the west.

date line ■ n. a line at the head of a dispatch or special article in a newspaper showing the date and place of writing.

date rape ■ n. rape by a person with whom the victim has gone on a date. ■ v. (**date-rape**) rape in this way.

date stamp ■ n. a stamped mark indicating a date. ▶ an adjustable stamp used to make such a mark. ■ v. (**date-stamp**) mark with a date stamp.

dating agency ■ n. a service which arranges introductions for people seeking romantic partners or friends.

dative /ˈdeɪtɪv/ Grammar ■ adj. (in Latin, Greek, German, etc.) denoting a case of nouns and pronouns indicating an indirect object or recipient. ■ n. a dative noun, pronoun, etc.
–ORIGIN Middle English: from Latin (*casus*) *dativus* '(case) of giving', from *dat-*, *dare* 'give'.

datum /ˈdeɪtəm/ ■ n. (pl. **data**) See also DATA. **1** a piece of information. **2** an assumption or premise from which inferences may be drawn. See SENSE DATUM. **3** a fixed starting point of a scale or operation.
–ORIGIN C18: from Latin, 'something given'.

datum line (also **datum level**) ■ n. a standard of comparison or point of reference. ▶ Surveying an assumed surface used as a reference for the measurement of heights and depths.

datura /dəˈtjʊərə/ ■ n. a shrubby North American plant of a genus including the thorn apple. [Genus *Datura*.]
–ORIGIN from Hindi *dhatūrā*.

daub /dɔːb/ ■ v. coat or smear with a thick substance carelessly or liberally. ▶ spread (a thick substance) on a surface in such a way. ■ n. **1** plaster, clay, etc., especially when mixed with straw and applied to laths or wattles to form a wall. **2** a patch or smear of a thick substance. **3** a painting executed without much skill.
–DERIVATIVES **dauber** n.
–ORIGIN Middle English: from Old French *dauber*, from Latin *dealbare* 'whiten, whitewash', from *albus* 'white'.

daube /dəʊb/ ■ n. a stew of meat, typically beef, braised in wine.
–ORIGIN French.

daughter ■ n. **1** a girl or woman in relation to her parents. ▶ a female descendant. **2** a woman considered as the product of a particular influence or environment. **3** Physics a nuclide formed by the radioactive decay of another.
–DERIVATIVES **daughterly** adj.
–ORIGIN Old English, of Germanic origin.

Dayak

daughter cell ■ n. Biology a cell formed by the division or budding of another.

daughter-in-law ■ n. (pl. **daughters-in-law**) the wife of one's son.

daunt /dɔːnt/ ■ v. (usu. **be daunted**) cause to feel intimidated or apprehensive.
–DERIVATIVES **daunting** adj. **dauntingly** adv.
–ORIGIN Middle English: from Old French *danter*, from Latin *domitare*, from *domare* 'to tame'.

dauntless ■ adj. fearless and determined.
–DERIVATIVES **dauntlessly** adv. **dauntlessness** n.

dauphin /ˈdɔːfɪn, ˈdəʊfã/ ■ n. historical the eldest son of the King of France.
–ORIGIN French: from the family name of the lords of the Dauphiné, ultimately a nickname meaning 'dolphin'.

dauphinois /ˌdəʊfɪˈnwʌ/ (also **dauphinoise** /-ˈnwʌz/) ■ adj. (of potatoes) sliced and baked in milk, typically with a topping of cheese.
–ORIGIN French, 'from the province of Dauphiné'.

davenport /ˈdav(ə)npɔːt/ ■ n. **1** an ornamental writing desk with drawers and a sloping surface for writing. **2** N. Amer. a large heavily upholstered sofa or sofa bed.
–ORIGIN sense 1 is named after Captain *Davenport*, for whom a desk of this type was made in the late C18; sense 2 is prob. from a manufacturer's name.

davit /ˈdavɪt, ˈdeɪv-/ ■ n. a small crane on a ship, especially one of a pair for lowering a lifeboat.
–ORIGIN C15: from Old French *daviot*, diminutive of *david*, denoting a kind of carpenter's tool.

Davy Jones's locker ■ n. informal the bottom of the sea, especially regarded as the grave of those who drowned.
–ORIGIN from C18 nautical slang *Davy Jones*, denoting the evil spirit of the sea.

Davy lamp ■ n. historical a miner's portable safety lamp with the flame enclosed by wire gauze to reduce the risk of a gas explosion.
–ORIGIN named after the English chemist Sir Humphry *Davy* (1778–1829), who invented it.

dawdle ■ v. waste time. ▶ move slowly and idly.
–DERIVATIVES **dawdler** n.
–ORIGIN C17: rel. to dialect *daddle*, *doddle* 'dally'.

dawn ■ n. **1** the first appearance of light in the sky before sunrise. **2** the beginning of something. ▶ **1** (of a day) begin. **2** come into existence. ▶ (often **dawn on**) become evident or understood.
–ORIGIN C15: back-formation from DAWNING.

dawn chorus ■ n. the singing of a large number of birds before dawn each day.

dawning ■ n. **1** poetic/literary dawn. **2** the beginning or first appearance of something.
–ORIGIN Middle English: alteration of earlier *dawing*, from Old English *dagian* 'to dawn', of Germanic origin.

day ■ n. **1** a twenty-four-hour period as a unit of time, reckoned from one midnight to the next and corresponding to a rotation of the earth on its axis. ▶ the time between sunrise and sunset. ▶ Astronomy a single rotation of a planet in relation to its primary. **2** a particular period of the past. ▶ (**the day**) the present time. ▶ (**days**) a particular period in a person's life: *my student days*. ▶ (**one's day**) the successful or influential period of a person's life. ■ adj. working or done during the day.
–PHRASES **all in a day's work** part of someone's normal routine. **any day** informal at any time. ▶ under any circumstances. **call it a day** decide to stop doing something. **day and night** all the time. **day by day** gradually and steadily. **day in, day out** continuously or repeatedly over a long period. **day of reckoning** a testing time when the degree of one's success or failure will be revealed. [with allusion to Judgement Day.] **one day** (or **some day** or **one of these days**) at some time in the future. **one of those days** a day when things go badly. **that will be the day** informal that is very unlikely. **these days** at present.
–ORIGIN Old English, of Germanic origin.

Dayak /ˈdʌɪak/ (also **Dyak**) ■ n. (pl. same or **Dayaks**) **1** a member of a group of indigenous peoples inhabiting parts

| s sit | t top | v voice | w we | z zoo | ʃ she | ʒ decision | θ thin | ð this | ŋ ring | x loch | tʃ chip | dʒ jar |

of Borneo. **2** the group of Austronesian languages spoken by these peoples.
– ORIGIN Malay, 'up-country'.

dayan /daˈjɑːn/ (also **Dayan**) ■ n. (pl. **dayanim** /daˈjɑːnɪm/) Judaism a senior rabbi, especially one who acts as a religious judge.
– ORIGIN from Hebrew *dayyān*, from *dān* 'to judge'.

daybed ■ n. a bed for daytime rest. ▶ N. Amer. a couch that can be made into a bed.

daybook ■ n. an account book in which a day's transactions are entered for later transfer to a ledger.

day boy (or **day girl**) ■ n. a boy (or girl) who lives at home but attends a boarding school.

daybreak ■ n. dawn.

day care ■ n. daytime care for people who cannot be fully independent. ▶ (**daycare**) N. Amer. a day centre.

day centre (also **day-care centre**) ■ n. a place providing care and recreation facilities for those who cannot be fully independent.

daydream ■ n. a series of pleasant thoughts that distract one's attention from the present. ■ v. indulge in a daydream.
– DERIVATIVES **daydreamer** n.

Day-Glo ■ n. trademark a fluorescent paint or other colouring.

day labourer ■ n. an unskilled labourer paid by the day.

daylight ■ n. **1** the natural light of the day. ▶ dawn. **2** visible distance between one person or thing and another. **3** (**daylights**) used to emphasize the severity of an action: *he beat the living daylights out of them*.
– PHRASES **see daylight** begin to understand something.

daylight robbery ■ n. informal blatant and unfair overcharging.

daylight saving time (also **daylight time**) ■ n. time as advanced one hour ahead of standard time to achieve longer evening daylight in summer.

day lily ■ n. a lily which bears large yellow, red, or orange flowers, each lasting only one day. [Genus *Hemerocallis*.]

Day of Atonement ■ n. another term for **YOM KIPPUR**.

day off ■ n. (pl. **days off**) a day's holiday from work or school.

Day of Goodwill ■ n. S. African 26 December, a public holiday.

Day of Judgement ■ n. another term for **JUDGEMENT DAY**.

Day of Reconciliation ■ n. S. African 16 December, a public holiday instituted in 1995.

day of rest ■ n. a day set aside from normal activity, typically on religious grounds.

day out ■ n. (pl. **days out**) a trip or excursion for a day.

daypack ■ n. a small rucksack.

day return ■ n. Brit. a ticket at a reduced rate for a return journey on public transport in one day.

day room ■ n. a communal room in an institution, used during the day.

day school ■ n. **1** a non-residential school. **2** a short educational course.

dayside ■ n. Astronomy the side of a planet that is facing its primary star.

day surgery ■ n. minor surgery that does not require an overnight stay in hospital.

daytime ■ n. the time between sunrise and sunset.

day-to-day ■ adj. **1** happening regularly every day. ▶ ordinary. **2** short-term. ■ n. an ordinary, everyday routine. ■ adv. on a daily basis.

day trip ■ n. a journey or excursion completed in one day.
– DERIVATIVES **day tripper** n.

daywear ■ n. casual clothing suitable for informal or everyday occasions.

daze ■ v. (usu. **be dazed**) make unable to think or react properly. ■ n. a state of stunned confusion or bewilderment.
– DERIVATIVES **dazedly** /-zɪdli/ adv.
– ORIGIN Middle English: back-formation from *dazed* (adj.), from Old Norse *dasathr* 'weary'.

dazzle ■ v. **1** (of a bright light) blind temporarily. **2** overwhelm with an impressive quality. ■ n. blinding brightness.
– DERIVATIVES **dazzlement** n. **dazzler** n.
– ORIGIN C15: from **DAZE**.

dazzling ■ adj. **1** extremely bright. **2** extremely impressive.
– DERIVATIVES **dazzlingly** adv.

Db ■ symb. the chemical element dubnium.

dB ■ abbrev. decibel(s).

DBS ■ abbrev. **1** direct broadcasting by satellite. **2** direct-broadcast satellite.

dbx ■ n. trademark electronic circuitry designed to increase the dynamic range of reproduced sound.
– ORIGIN 1970s: from **DB** + *x* (representing *expander*).

DC ■ abbrev. **1** Music da capo. **2** direct current. **3** District Commissioner.

DCC ■ abbrev. digital compact cassette.

DD ■ abbrev. Doctor of Divinity.

D-Day ■ n. **1** the day (6 June 1944) in the Second World War on which Allied forces invaded northern France. **2** the day on which something important is to begin.
– ORIGIN from *D* for *day* + **DAY**.

DDE ■ n. Computing a standard allowing data to be shared between different programs.
– ORIGIN 1980s: abbrev. of *Dynamic Data Exchange*.

DDI ■ abbrev. didanosine.

DDR ■ abbrev. historical German Democratic Republic.
– ORIGIN abbrev. of German *Deutsche Demokratische Republik*.

DDT ■ abbrev. dichlorodiphenyltrichloroethane, a synthetic organic compound used as an insecticide but now banned in many countries.

de- ■ prefix **1** (forming verbs and their derivatives) down; away: *descend* | *deduct*. ▶ completely: *denude*. **2** (added to verbs and their derivatives) denoting removal or reversal: *de-ice*. **3** denoting formation from: *deverbal*.
– ORIGIN from Latin *de* 'off, from'; sense 2 via Old French *des-* from Latin *dis-*.

deaccession /ˌdiːəkˈsɛʃ(ə)n/ ■ v. officially remove (an item) from a library, museum, or art gallery in order to sell it. ■ n. the disposal of items in this way.

deacon /ˈdiːk(ə)n/ ■ n. (in Catholic, Anglican, and Orthodox Churches) an ordained minister of an order ranking below that of priest. ▶ (in some Protestant Churches) a lay officer assisting a minister. ■ v. appoint or ordain as a deacon.
– ORIGIN Old English, from Greek *diakonos* 'servant', in eccles. Greek, 'Christian minister'.

deaconess /ˌdiːkəˈnɛs, ˈdiːk(ə)nɪs/ ■ n. (in the early Church and some modern Churches) a woman with duties similar to those of a deacon.

deactivate ■ v. make (technical equipment or a virus) inactive by disconnecting or destroying it.
– DERIVATIVES **deactivation** n. **deactivator** n.

dead ■ adj. **1** no longer alive. ▶ devoid of living things. **2** (of a part of the body) numb. ▶ lacking emotion, sympathy, or sensitivity. **3** no longer relevant or important. **4** lacking activity or excitement. ▶ (of sound or a colour) dull. **5** (of equipment) not functioning. ▶ (of a glass or bottle) empty or no longer in use. ▶ (of the ball in a game) out of play. **6** complete; absolute: *dead silence*. ■ adv. absolutely. ▶ exactly. ▶ straight; directly: *dead ahead*. ▶ informal very: *dead easy*.
– PHRASES **dead and buried** over; finished. **dead in the water** (of a ship) unable to move. ▶ unable to function effectively. **dead meat** informal in serious trouble. **the dead of night** the quietest, darkest part of the night. **the dead of winter** the coldest part of winter. **dead on one's feet** informal extremely tired. **dead to the world** informal fast asleep. **from the dead** from a state of death. **wouldn't be seen** (or **caught**) **dead in** (or **with**, **at**, etc.) informal have a strong dislike for.
– DERIVATIVES **deadness** n.
– ORIGIN Old English, of Germanic origin.

dead-ball line ■ n. **1** Rugby a line behind the goal line, beyond which the ball is out of play. **2** Soccer the byline.

deadbeat ■ adj. **1** (**dead beat**) informal completely exhausted. **2** (of a mechanism) without recoil. ■ n. informal an idle or feckless person.

deadbolt ■ n. a bolt engaged by turning a knob or key, rather than by spring action.

dead duck ■ n. informal an unsuccessful or useless person or thing.
– ORIGIN from the old saying 'never waste powder on a dead duck'.

deaden ■ v. **1** make (a noise or sensation) less strong or intense. ▸ cause to be insensitive. **2** deprive of force or vitality.
– DERIVATIVES **deadening** adj.

dead end ■ n. an end of a road or passage from which no exit is possible.

dead hand ■ n. an undesirable persisting influence.

deadhead ■ n. a faded flower head. ■ v. remove dead flower heads from (a plant).

dead heat ■ n. a race in which two or more competitors are exactly level.

dead letter ■ n. a law or treaty which has not been repealed but is defunct in practice.

dead letter box ■ n. a place where messages can be left and collected without the sender and recipient meeting.

dead lift ■ n. Weightlifting a lift made from a standing position, without the use of a bench.

deadline ■ n. the latest time or date by which something should be completed.

deadlock ■ n. **1** a situation in which no progress can be made. **2** a lock operated by a key, as distinct from a spring lock. ■ v. cause to come to a deadlock.

dead loss ■ n. an unproductive or useless venture, person, or thing.

deadly ■ adj. (**-ier**, **-iest**) **1** causing or able to cause death. ▸ (of a voice, glance, etc.) filled with hate. **2** extremely accurate or effective. **3** informal extremely boring. **4** complete: *she was in deadly earnest*. ■ adv. **1** in a way that resembles or suggests death. **2** extremely: *deadly serious*.
– DERIVATIVES **deadliness** n.

deadly nightshade ■ n. a poisonous bushy plant with drooping purple flowers and black cherry-like fruit. [*Atropa belladonna*.]

deadly sin ■ n. (in Christian tradition) a sin regarded as leading to damnation. See the seven deadly sins at SEVEN.

dead man ■ n. **1** informal a bottle after the contents have been drunk. **2** (usu. **deadman**) an object secured to the ground to provide anchorage or leverage.

dead march ■ n. a slow, solemn piece of music suitable for a funeral procession.

dead-nettle ■ n. a Eurasian plant of the mint family, with leaves that resemble those of a nettle without stinging hairs. [*Lamium album* and other species.]

deadpan ■ adj. impassive or expressionless. ■ adv. in a deadpan manner. ■ v. (**-panned**, **-panning**) say something amusing while affecting a serious manner.

dead reckoning ■ n. the process of calculating one's position, especially at sea, by estimating the direction and distance travelled.

dead ringer ■ n. a person or thing closely resembling another.

dead set ■ n. see SET² (sense 2).

dead shot ■ n. an extremely accurate marksman or markswoman.

dead time ■ n. Physics the period after the recording of a particle or pulse when a detector is unable to record another.

deadweight ■ n. **1** the weight of an inert person or thing. ▸ the total weight of cargo, stores, etc. which a ship can carry. ▸ Farming animals sold by the estimated weight of saleable meat that they will yield. **2** Economics losses incurred because of the inefficient allocation of resources. ▸ a debt not covered by assets.

dead wood ■ n. useless or unproductive people or things.

deaf ■ adj. without hearing or having impaired hearing. ▸ (**deaf to**) unwilling to listen or respond to.
– PHRASES **fall on deaf ears** be ignored. **turn a deaf ear** refuse to listen or respond.
– DERIVATIVES **deafness** n.
– ORIGIN Old English, of Germanic origin.

deaf aid ■ n. Brit. a hearing aid.

deaf-blind ■ adj. having severely impaired hearing and vision.

deafen ■ v. cause to become deaf. ▸ [as adj. **deafening**] extremely loud. ▸ (**deafen someone to**) (of a sound) cause someone to be unaware of (other sounds).
– DERIVATIVES **deafeningly** adv.

deaf mute ■ n. a person who is deaf and unable to speak.

> USAGE
> In modern use **deaf mute** has acquired offensive connotations. It is advisable to avoid it in favour of other terms such as **profoundly deaf**.

deal¹ ■ v. (past and past part. **dealt**) **1** distribute (cards) to players for a game or round. ▸ (**deal someone in**) include a new player in a card game. **2** (**deal something out**) distribute or apportion something. **3** take part in commercial trading of a commodity. ▸ informal buy and sell illegal drugs. ▸ (**deal with**) have relations with in a commercial context. **4** (**deal with**) take measures concerning. ▸ cope with. ▸ have as a subject. **5** inflict (a blow) on. ■ n. **1** an agreement entered into by two or more parties for their mutual benefit. ▸ a particular form of treatment: *working mothers get a bad deal*. **2** the process of dealing cards in a card game.
– PHRASES **a big deal** informal [usu. with neg.] an important thing. ▸ (**big deal**) used ironically to express contempt for something regarded as unimpressive. **a raw deal** informal unfair or harsh treatment. **a deal of** a large amount of. **a good** (or **great**) **deal** a large amount. ▸ to a considerable extent: *a good deal better*. **a square deal** a fair bargain or treatment. **it's a deal** informal used to express assent to an agreement.
– DERIVATIVES **dealing** n.
– ORIGIN Old English *dǣlan* 'divide, participate', of Germanic origin.

deal² ■ n. fir or pine wood (as a building material).
– ORIGIN Middle English: from Middle Low German and Middle Dutch *dele* 'plank'.

deal-breaker ■ n. (in business and politics) a factor or issue which, if unresolved during negotiations, would cause one party to withdraw from a deal.

dealer ■ n. **1** a person who buys and sells goods. ▸ a person who buys and sells shares or other financial assets as a principal (rather than as a broker or agent). **2** a player who deals cards in a card game.
– DERIVATIVES **dealership** n.

dealt past participle of DEAL¹.

deamination /dɪˈamɪneɪʃ(ə)n/ ■ n. Biochemistry the removal of an amino group from an amino acid or other compound.

dean ■ n. **1** the head of the chapter of a cathedral or collegiate church. ▸ (also **rural dean**) chiefly Brit. a member of the clergy exercising supervision over a group of parochial clergy within a division of an archdeaconry. **2** the head of a university faculty or department or of a medical school. ▸ a college officer with a disciplinary role.
– DERIVATIVES **deanery** n.
– ORIGIN Middle English: from Old French *deien*, from late Latin *decanus* 'chief of a group of ten', from *decem* 'ten'.

dear ■ adj. **1** regarded with deep affection. ▸ endearing; sweet. ▸ used in the polite introduction to a letter. **2** expensive. ■ n. used as an affectionate form of address. ▸ an endearing person. ■ adv. at a high cost. ■ exclam. used in expressions of surprise, dismay, or sympathy.
– ORIGIN Old English, of Germanic origin.

dearest ■ adj. **1** most loved or cherished. **2** most expensive. ■ n. used as an affectionate form of address.

dearie ▪ n. (pl. **-ies**) informal, chiefly Brit. used as a friendly or condescending form of address.
– PHRASES **dearie me!** used to express surprise or dismay.

Dear John letter (also **Dear John**) ▪ n. informal a letter from a woman to a man, ending a personal relationship.

dearly ▪ adv. **1** very much. **2** at great cost.

dearth /dəːθ/ ▪ n. a scarcity or lack of something.
– ORIGIN Middle English *derthe* (see DEAR).

death ▪ n. **1** the action or fact of dying or being killed. ▸ an instance of a person or an animal dying. **2** the state of being dead. ▸ (**Death**) the personification of the power that destroys life, often represented as a skeleton or an old man holding a scythe. **3** the destruction or end of something.
– PHRASES **at death's door** so ill that one may die. **be the death of someone** cause someone's death. ▸ be present when something fails or ends. **catch one's death (of cold)** informal catch a severe cold. **die a (or the) death** fail utterly or come to an end. **do someone to death** kill someone. **do something to death** repeat something so frequently that it becomes tedious. **like death warmed up** (or N. Amer. **over**) informal extremely tired or ill. **put someone to death** execute someone. **to death** until dead. ▸ used to emphasize the extreme nature of a feeling or action: *I'm sick to death of you*.
– DERIVATIVES **deathless** adj. **deathlike** adj.
– ORIGIN Old English, of Germanic origin.

deathbed ▪ n. the bed where someone is dying or has died.

death camp ▪ n. a prison camp, especially for political prisoners or prisoners of war, in which many die.

death cap ▪ n. a deadly poisonous toadstool with a pale olive-green cap and white gills, growing in broadleaved woodland. [*Amanita phalloides*.]

death certificate ▪ n. an official statement, signed by a doctor, of the cause, date, and place of a person's death.

death duty ▪ n. a tax levied on property after the owner's death.

death knell ▪ n. **1** the tolling of a bell to mark someone's death. **2** an event that heralds the end of something.

deathly ▪ adj. (**-ier**, **-iest**) resembling or suggestive of death.

death mask ▪ n. a plaster cast of a dead person's face, used to make a mask or model.

death penalty ▪ n. punishment by death.

death rate ▪ n. the number of deaths per one thousand people per year.

death rattle ▪ n. a gurgling sound in a dying person's throat.

death row ▪ n. a prison block or section for those sentenced to death.

death's head ▪ n. a human skull as a symbol of mortality.

death toll ▪ n. the number of deaths resulting from a particular cause.

death trap ▪ n. a thing that is potentially very dangerous.

death warrant ▪ n. an order for the execution of a condemned person.

death-watch beetle ▪ n. a small beetle whose larvae bore into and damage dead wood and structural timbers, making a sound like a watch ticking which was formerly believed to portend death. [*Xestobium rufovillosum*.]

death wish ▪ n. an unconscious desire for one's own or another's death.

deb ▪ n. informal short for DEBUTANTE.

debacle /deɪˈbɑːk(ə)l/ ▪ n. an utter failure or disaster.
– ORIGIN C19: from French, from *débâcler* 'unleash', from *dé-* 'un-' + *bâcler* 'to bar', from Latin *baculum* 'staff'.

debar ▪ v. (**debarred**, **debarring**) exclude or prohibit from doing something.
– ORIGIN Middle English: from French *débarrer*, from Old French *desbarrer* 'remove the bars from', from *des-* (expressing reversal) + *barrer* 'to bar'.

debark¹ ▪ v. leave a ship or aircraft.
– DERIVATIVES **debarkation** n.
– ORIGIN C17: from French *débarquer*.

debark² ▪ v. remove (the bark) from a tree.

debase /dɪˈbeɪs/ ▪ v. lower the quality, value, or character of.
– DERIVATIVES **debasement** n.
– ORIGIN C16: from DE- + obsolete verb *base* expressing the notion 'bring down completely'.

debatable ▪ adj. open to discussion or argument.
– DERIVATIVES **debatably** adv.

debate ▪ n. a formal discussion in a public meeting or legislative assembly. ▸ an argument, especially one involving many people. ▪ v. discuss or argue about. ▸ consider; ponder.
– PHRASES **under debate** being discussed or disputed.
– DERIVATIVES **debater** n.
– ORIGIN Middle English: from Latin *dis-* (expressing reversal) + *battere* 'to fight'.

debauch /dɪˈbɔːtʃ/ ▪ v. destroy the moral purity of. ▪ n. a bout of excessive indulgence in sensual pleasures.
– DERIVATIVES **debauched** adj. **debaucher** n.
– ORIGIN C16: from French *débaucher* (v.) 'turn away from one's duty', from Old French *desbaucher*.

debauchery ▪ n. excessive indulgence in sensual pleasures.

debeak ▪ v. remove the upper part of the beak of (a bird) to prevent it injuring other birds.

debenture /dɪˈbɛntʃə/ ▪ n. a long-term security yielding a fixed rate of interest, issued by a company and secured against assets. ▸ (also **debenture bond**) N. Amer. an unsecured loan certificate issued by a company.
– ORIGIN Middle English: from Latin *debentur* 'are owing', from *debere* 'owe'.

debilitate /dɪˈbɪlɪteɪt/ ▪ v. [often as adj. **debilitating**] make very weak and infirm.
– DERIVATIVES **debilitatingly** adv. **debilitative** adj. **debilitation** n.
– ORIGIN C16: from Latin *debilitare* 'weaken', from *debilis* 'weak'.

debility ▪ n. (pl. **-ies**) weakness, especially as a result of illness.

debit ▪ n. an entry in an account recording a sum owed. ▸ a payment made or owed. ▪ v. (**debited**, **debiting**) (of a bank) remove (money) from a customer's account.
– ORIGIN Middle English: from French *débit*, from Latin *debitum* (see DEBT).

debit card ▪ n. a card allowing the holder to transfer money electronically from one bank account to another when making a purchase.

debit order ▪ n. S. African an arrangement made with a bank that allows a third party to transfer money from a customer's account on agreed dates.

debonair ▪ adj. (of a man) confident, stylish, and charming.
– DERIVATIVES **debonairly** adv.
– ORIGIN Middle English: from Old French, from *de bon aire* 'of good disposition'.

debouch /dɪˈbaʊtʃ, -ˈbuːʃ/ ▪ v. emerge from a confined space into a wide, open area.
– DERIVATIVES **debouchment** n.
– ORIGIN C18: from French *déboucher*, from *dé-* (expressing removal) + *bouche* 'mouth', from Latin *bucca* 'cheek'.

debrief ▪ v. question (someone, typically a soldier or spy) about a completed mission or undertaking.
– DERIVATIVES **debriefing** n.

debris /ˈdɛbriː, ˈdeɪbriː/ ▪ n. scattered rubbish or remains. ▸ loose natural material, e.g. broken rocks.
– ORIGIN C18: from French, from obsolete *débriser* 'break down'.

debt ▪ n. **1** money or services owed or due. **2** the state of owing money: *they are in debt*. ▸ a feeling of obligation or gratitude for a favour.
– PHRASES **be in someone's debt** owe gratitude to someone for a favour.
– ORIGIN Middle English *dette*: from Old French, from Latin *debitum* 'something owed', from *debere* 'owe'.

debt collector ▪ n. a person who collects debts for creditors.

debtor ▪ n. a person who owes money.

debug ■ v. (**debugged, debugging**) **1** remove errors from (computer hardware or software). **2** detect and remove concealed microphones from. **3** N. Amer. remove insects from.

debugger ■ n. a computer program for debugging other programs.

debunk ■ v. **1** expose the falseness of (an idea or belief). **2** reduce the inflated reputation of (someone).
– DERIVATIVES **debunker** n.

debut /'deɪbjuː, -buː/ ■ n. a person's first appearance in a capacity or role. ▶ [as modifier] denoting the first recording or publication of a singer or writer. ■ v. make a debut.
– ORIGIN C18: from French *début*, from *débuter* 'lead off'.

debutant /'dɛbjutɒ̃, deɪ-/ ■ n. a person making a debut.

debutante /'dɛbjutɑːnt, deɪ-/ ■ n. a young upper-class woman making her debut. ▶ a female debutante.

debye /dəˈbaɪ/ ■ n. Chemistry a unit of measurement used to express electric dipole moments of molecules, equal to 3.336×10^{-30} coulomb metre.
– ORIGIN C20: named after the Dutch-born US physicist Peter *Debye*.

Dec. ■ abbrev. December.

dec. ■ abbrev. **1** deceased. **2** Cricket declared.

deca- /'dɛkə/ (also **dec-** before a vowel) ■ comb. form ten; having ten: *decahedron*.
– ORIGIN from Greek *deka* 'ten'.

decade /'dɛkeɪd, dɪ'keɪd/ ■ n. **1** a period of ten years. **2** a set or group of ten. ▶ a range of electrical resistances or other quantities spanning from one to ten times a base value.
– DERIVATIVES **decadal** adj.
– ORIGIN Middle English: from Greek *deka* 'ten'.

decadence /'dɛkəd(ə)ns/ ■ n. **1** the process, period, or manifestation of moral or cultural decline. **2** luxurious self-indulgence.
– ORIGIN C16: from French *décadence*, from medieval Latin *decadentia*; rel. to DECAY.

decadent ■ adj. **1** characterized by or reflecting moral or cultural decline. **2** luxuriously self-indulgent. ■ n. a decadent person.
– DERIVATIVES **decadently** adv.

decaf /'diːkaf/ ■ n. informal (trademark in the UK) decaffeinated coffee.

decaffeinate /diːˈkafɪneɪt/ ■ v. [usu. as adj. **decaffeinated**] remove most or all of the caffeine from (coffee or tea).
– DERIVATIVES **decaffeination** n.

decagon /'dɛkəg(ə)n/ ■ n. a plane figure with ten straight sides and angles.
– DERIVATIVES **decagonal** adj.
– ORIGIN C17: from Greek *dekagōnon*, from *dekagōnos* 'ten-angled'.

decahedron /ˌdɛkəˈhiːdr(ə)n, -ˈhɛd-/ ■ n. (pl. **decahedra** or **decahedrons**) a solid figure with ten plane faces.
– DERIVATIVES **decahedral** adj.
– ORIGIN C19: from DECA- + -HEDRON.

decal /'diːkal/ ■ n. a design on prepared paper for transferring on to glass, porcelain, etc.
– ORIGIN 1950s: abbrev. of rare *decalcomania*, from French *décalcomanie*, from *décalquer* 'transfer a tracing' + *-manie* '-mania' (with ref. to the enthusiasm for the process in the 1860s).

decalcified ■ adj. (of rock or bone) containing a reduced quantity of calcium salts.
– DERIVATIVES **decalcification** n.

decalitre (US **decaliter**, **dekaliter**) (abbrev.: **dal**; US also **dkl**) ■ n. a metric unit of capacity, equal to 10 litres.

decametre (US **decameter**, **dekameter**) (abbrev.: **dam**; US also **dkm**) ■ n. a metric unit of length, equal to 10 metres.

decamp ■ v. **1** depart suddenly or secretly. **2** archaic break up or leave a military camp.
– ORIGIN C17: from French *décamper*, from *dé-* (expressing removal) + *camp* 'camp'.

decanal /dɪˈkeɪn(ə)l, ˈdɛk(ə)n(ə)l/ ■ adj. **1** of or relating to a dean or deanery. **2** relating to or denoting the south side of the choir of a church, on which the dean sits. The opposite of CANTORIAL.
– ORIGIN C18: from medieval Latin *decanalis*, from late Latin *decanus* (see DEAN).

303

decane /'dɛkeɪn/ ■ n. Chemistry a liquid hydrocarbon of the alkane series, present in petroleum spirit. [$C_{10}H_{22}$.]
– ORIGIN C19: from DECA- 'ten' (denoting ten carbon atoms) + -ANE².

decant /dɪˈkant/ ■ v. gradually pour from one container into another, typically in order to separate the liquid from the sediment.
– ORIGIN C17: from medieval Latin *decanthare*, from Latin *de-* 'away from' + *canthus* 'edge, rim'.

decanter ■ n. a stoppered glass container into which wine or spirit is decanted.

decapitate /dɪˈkapɪteɪt/ ■ v. cut off the head of.
– DERIVATIVES **decapitation** n.
– ORIGIN C17: from late Latin *decapitare* 'to decapitate', from *de-* + *caput*, *capit-* 'head'.

Decapoda /ˌdɛkəˈpəʊdə/ ■ pl. n. Zoology an order of crustaceans with five pairs of walking legs, including shrimps, crabs, and lobsters.
– DERIVATIVES **decapod** /'dɛkəpɒd/ n. & adj.
– ORIGIN from DECA- + Greek *pous, pod-* 'foot'.

decarbonize (also **-ise**) ■ v. remove carbon or carbonaceous deposits from.
– DERIVATIVES **decarbonization** (also **-isation**) n.

decarboxylase /ˌdiːkɑːˈbɒksɪleɪz/ ■ n. Biochemistry an enzyme that catalyses the decarboxylation of a particular organic molecule.

decarboxylate /ˌdiːkɑːˈbɒksɪleɪt/ ■ v. Chemistry eliminate a carboxylic acid group from (an organic compound).
– DERIVATIVES **decarboxylation** n.

decarburize /diːˈkɑːbjʊrʌɪz/ (also **-ise**) ■ v. Metallurgy remove carbon from (iron or steel).
– DERIVATIVES **decarburization** (also **-isation**) n.

decastyle /'dɛkəstʌɪl/ ■ adj. Architecture (of a temple or portico) having ten columns.
– ORIGIN C18: from Greek *dekastulos*, from *deka* 'ten' + *stulos* 'column'.

decasyllabic /ˌdɛkəsɪˈlabɪk/ ■ adj. Prosody (of a metrical line) consisting of ten syllables.

decathlon /dɪˈkaθlɒn, -lən/ ■ n. an athletic event in which each competitor takes part in the same ten events.
– DERIVATIVES **decathlete** n.
– ORIGIN C20: from DECA- + Greek *athlon* 'contest'.

decay ■ v. **1** rot or cause to rot through the action of bacteria and fungi; decompose. ▶ deteriorate; decline in quality or vigour. **2** Physics (of a radioactive substance, particle, etc.) undergo change to a different form by emitting radiation. ■ n. **1** the state or process of decaying. **2** rotten matter or tissue.
– ORIGIN Middle English: from Old French *decair*, from Latin *decidere* 'fall down', from *de-* 'from' + *cadere* 'fall'.

decease ■ n. formal or Law death.
– ORIGIN Middle English: from Old French *deces*, from Latin *decessus* 'death', from *decedere* 'to die'.

deceased formal or Law ■ n. (**the deceased**) the recently dead person in question. ■ adj. recently dead.

deceit ■ n. the action or practice of deceiving. ▶ a deceitful act or statement.
– ORIGIN Middle English: from Old French, from *deceveir* 'deceive'.

deceitful ■ adj. acting to deceive others.
– DERIVATIVES **deceitfully** adv. **deceitfulness** n.

deceive ■ v. deliberately mislead or misrepresent the truth to. ▶ (of a thing) give a mistaken impression: *the area may seem to offer nothing of interest, but don't be deceived*.
– DERIVATIVES **deceiver** n.
– ORIGIN Middle English: from Old French *deceivre*, from Latin *decipere* 'ensnare, cheat'.

decelerate /diːˈsɛləreɪt/ ■ v. begin to move more slowly.
– DERIVATIVES **deceleration** n.
– ORIGIN C19: from DE- + ACCELERATE.

December ■ n. the twelfth month of the year.
– ORIGIN Middle English: from Latin, from *decem* 'ten' (being orig. the tenth month of the Roman year).

decency ■ n. (pl. **-ies**) **1** decent behaviour. **2** (**decencies**) things required for a reasonable standard of living.

decennial /dɪˈsɛnɪəl/ ■ adj. lasting for or recurring every ten years.
– ORIGIN C17: from Latin *decennis*, from *decem* 'ten' + *annus* 'year'.

decent ■ adj. **1** conforming with generally accepted standards of morality or respectability. **2** of an acceptable or appropriate standard; satisfactory. ▸ informal obliging or generous: *that's very decent of you.*
– DERIVATIVES **decently** adv.
– ORIGIN C16: from Latin *decere* 'to be fit'.

decentralize (also **-ise**) ■ v. [often as adj. **decentralized** (also **-ised**)] transfer (authority) from central to local government. ▸ disperse or divide (a large organization) into smaller separate units.
– DERIVATIVES **decentralist** n. & adj. **decentralization** (also **-isation**) n.

decentre (US **decenter**) ■ v. displace from the centre or from a central position.

deception ■ n. the action of deceiving. ▸ a thing that deceives.
– ORIGIN Middle English: from late Latin *deceptio(n-)*, from *decipere* 'deceive'.

deceptive ■ adj. giving an appearance or impression different from the true one; misleading.
– DERIVATIVES **deceptiveness** n.

deceptively ■ adv. **1** to a lesser extent than appears the case: *the idea was deceptively simple*. **2** to a greater extent than appears the case: *the airy and deceptively spacious lounge*.

deci- ■ comb. form one tenth: *decilitre*.
– ORIGIN from Latin *decimus* 'tenth'.

decibel /ˈdɛsɪbɛl/ (abbrev.: **dB**) ■ n. a unit of measurement expressing the intensity of a sound or the power of an electrical signal, equal to one tenth of a bel.

decide ■ v. come to or cause to come to a resolution in the mind as a result of consideration. ▸ resolve or settle (an issue or contest).
– DERIVATIVES **deciding** adj.
– ORIGIN Middle English: from Latin *decidere* 'determine', from *de-* 'off' + *caedere* 'cut'.

decided ■ adj. definite; unquestionable: *a decided improvement*. ▸ (of a person) having clear opinions; resolute.
– DERIVATIVES **decidedly** adv.

decider ■ n. a contest that settles the outcome of a series of contests.

deciduous /dɪˈsɪdjʊəs/ ■ adj. **1** (of a tree or shrub) shedding its leaves annually. Often contrasted with **EVERGREEN**. **2** denoting the milk teeth of a mammal, which are shed after a time.
– ORIGIN C17: from Latin *deciduus*, from *decidere* 'fall off'.

decigram (abbrev.: **dg**) ■ n. one tenth of a gram.

decile /ˈdɛsʌɪl/ ■ n. Statistics each of ten equal groups into which a population can be divided according to the distribution of values of a particular variable.
– ORIGIN C17: from French *décile*, from Latin *decem* 'ten'.

decilitre (US **-liter**) (abbrev.: **dl**) ■ n. one tenth of a litre.

decimal ■ adj. relating to or denoting a system of numbers and arithmetic based on the number ten, tenth parts, and powers of ten. ■ n. a fraction whose denominator is a power of ten and whose numerator is expressed by figures placed to the right of a decimal point or comma. ▸ a system of decimal numerical notation.
– DERIVATIVES **decimalize** (also **-ise**) v. **decimalization** (also **-isation**) n. **decimally** adv.
– ORIGIN C17: from modern Latin *decimalis* (adj.), from Latin *decimus* 'tenth'.

decimal comma ■ n. a comma placed after the figure representing units in a decimal fraction.

decimal place ■ n. the position of a digit to the right of a decimal point or comma.

decimal point ■ n. a full point or dot placed after the figure representing units in a decimal fraction.

decimate /ˈdɛsɪmeɪt/ ■ v. kill or destroy a large proportion of. ▸ drastically reduce the strength of.
– DERIVATIVES **decimation** n.
– ORIGIN Middle English: from Latin *decimare* 'take as a tenth', from *decimus* 'tenth'.

decimetre (US **-meter**) (abbrev.: **dm**) ■ n. one tenth of a metre.

decipher /dɪˈsʌɪfə/ ■ v. convert from code into normal language. ▸ succeed in understanding or interpreting (something obscure or unclear).
– DERIVATIVES **decipherable** adj. **decipherment** n.

decision ■ n. **1** a conclusion or resolution reached after consideration. ▸ the action or process of deciding. **2** the quality of being decisive; resoluteness.
– ORIGIN Middle English: from Latin *decisio(n-)*, from *decidere* (see **DECIDE**).

decision theory ■ n. the mathematical study of strategies for optimal decision-making between options involving different risks or expectations of gain or loss depending on the outcome. Compare with **GAME THEORY**.

decisive ■ adj. acting to settle an issue quickly and effectively. ▸ tending or able to make decisions quickly.
– DERIVATIVES **decisively** adv. **decisiveness** n.

decitex ■ n. one tenth of a tex, an international unit by which the fineness of yarn is measured, equal to a mass of 1 decigram per 1 000 metres or 1 gram per 10 000 metres of thread.
– ORIGIN from **DECI-** + *tex*, a shortening of *textile*.

deck ■ n. **1** a floor of a ship, especially the upper, open level. ▸ a similar floor or platform, as in a bus or car park. ▸ (**the deck**) informal the ground or floor: *there was a big thud when I hit the deck*. **2** a component or unit in sound-reproduction equipment that incorporates a playing or recording mechanism for discs or tapes. **3** chiefly N. Amer. a pack of cards. ▸ N. Amer. informal a packet of narcotics. ■ v. **1** (usu. **be decked out**) decorate or dress brightly or festively. **2** informal knock to the ground with a punch.
– DERIVATIVES **-decked** adj.
– ORIGIN Middle English (orig. denoting a canvas covering, especially on a ship): from Middle Dutch *dec* 'covering, roof', from *dekken* 'to cover'.

deckchair ■ n. a folding chair with a frame of wood and a suspended seat of canvas.

-decker ■ comb. form having a specified number of decks or layers: *double-decker*.

deckhand ■ n. a member of a ship's crew whose duties include cleaning, mooring, and cargo handling.

deckhead ■ n. the underside of the deck of a ship.

decking ■ n. material used in making a deck.

deckle edge ■ n. the rough uncut edge of a sheet of paper.
– DERIVATIVES **deckle-edged** adj.

declaim ■ v. utter or deliver words or a speech in a rhetorical or impassioned way.
– DERIVATIVES **declaimer** n. **declamatory** adj.
– ORIGIN Middle English: from French *déclamer* or Latin *declamare*, from *de-* (expressing thoroughness) + *clamare* 'to shout'.

declamation ■ n. the action or art of declaiming. ▸ a rhetorical exercise or set speech.

declarant /dɪˈklɛːr(ə)nt/ ■ n. chiefly Law a person or party who makes a formal declaration.

declaration ■ n. **1** a formal or explicit statement or announcement. ▸ (also **declaration of the poll**) Brit. a public official announcement of the votes cast for candidates in an election. ▸ Law a plaintiff's statement of claims in proceedings. **2** Law an affirmation made instead of taking an oath. **3** an act or instance of declaring.

declarative /dɪˈklarətɪv/ ■ adj. of the nature of or making a declaration. ▸ Grammar (of a sentence or phrase) taking the form of a simple statement.
– DERIVATIVES **declaratively** adv.

declare ■ v. **1** announce solemnly or officially; make clearly known. ▸ (**declare for/against**) openly align oneself for or against (a party or position). **2** (**declare oneself**) reveal one's intentions or identity. ▸ express feelings of love to someone. **3** announce oneself as a candidate for an election. **4** acknowledge possession of (taxable income or

dutiable goods). **5** Cricket close an innings voluntarily before all the wickets have fallen. **6** announce that one holds (certain combinations of cards) in a card game.
– DERIVATIVES **declarable** adj. **declaratory** adj. **declared** adj. **declaredly** adv.
– ORIGIN Middle English: from Latin *declarare*, from *de-* 'thoroughly' + *clarare* 'make clear', from *clarus* 'clear'.

declarer ■ n. Bridge the player whose bid establishes the suit of the contract.

declassify ■ v. (**-ies, -ied**) (often **be declassified**) officially declare (information or documents) to be no longer secret.
– DERIVATIVES **declassification** n.

declension /dɪˈklɛnʃ(ə)n/ ■ n. **1** the variation of the form of a noun, pronoun, or adjective, by which its grammatical case, number, and gender are identified. ▶ the class to which a noun or adjective is assigned according to this variation. **2** poetic/literary a condition of decline or moral deterioration.
– ORIGIN Middle English *declinson*, from Old French *declinaison*, from *decliner* 'to decline'.

declination /ˌdɛklɪˈneɪʃ(ə)n/ ■ n. **1** Astronomy the angular distance of a point north or south of the celestial equator. ▶ the angular deviation of a compass needle from true north. **2** US formal refusal.

decline ■ v. **1** become smaller, fewer, or less; decrease. ▶ diminish in strength or quality; deteriorate. **2** politely refuse: *the company declined to comment*. **3** (especially of the sun) move downwards. **4** Grammar state the forms of (a noun, pronoun, or adjective) corresponding to cases, number, and gender. ■ n. a gradual and continuous loss of strength, numbers, or value.
– DERIVATIVES **declining** adj.
– ORIGIN Middle English: from Latin *declinare* 'bend down, turn aside', from *de-* 'down' + *clinare* 'to bend'.

declivity /dɪˈklɪvɪti/ ■ n. (pl. **-ies**) a downward slope.
– ORIGIN C17: from Latin *declivitas*, from *declivis* 'sloping down', from *de-* 'down' + *clivus* 'a slope'.

declutch ■ v. disengage the clutch of a motor vehicle.

decoction ■ n. a liquor containing the concentrated essence of a substance, produced as a result of heating or boiling, especially as used in medicinal and herbal preparations.

decode ■ v. convert (a coded message) into intelligible language. ▶ convert (audio or video signals), in particular from digital to analogue.
– DERIVATIVES **decodable** adj. **decoder** n.

decoke /diːˈkəʊk/ ■ v. informal remove carbon or carbonaceous material from.

decollement /deɪˈkɒlmɒ̃/ ■ n. Geology a process in which some strata become partly detached from those underneath and slide over them, causing folding and deformation.
– ORIGIN C19: from French *décoller* 'unstick'.

décolletage /ˌdeɪkɒlˈtɑːʒ/ ■ n. a low neckline on a woman's dress or top.
– ORIGIN C19: French, from *décolleter* 'expose the neck'.

décolleté /deɪˈkɒlteɪ/ ■ adj. (also **décolletée**) having a low neckline. ■ n. a décolletage.
– ORIGIN C19: French, from *décolleter* 'expose the neck'.

decolonize (also **-ise**) ■ v. withdraw from (a colony), leaving it independent.
– DERIVATIVES **decolonization** (also **-isation**) n.

decolorize (also **decolourize** or **-ise**) ■ v. remove the colour from.
– DERIVATIVES **decolorization** (also **decolourization** or **-isation**) n.

decommission ■ v. **1** take (a ship) out of service. **2** dismantle and make safe (a nuclear reactor or weapon).

decompensation ■ n. Medicine the failure of an organ (especially the liver or heart) to compensate for the functional overload resulting from disease.
– DERIVATIVES **decompensated** adj.

decompose ■ v. **1** (of organic matter) decay; become rotten. **2** break down or cause to break down into component elements. **3** Mathematics express (a number or function) as a combination of simpler components.
– DERIVATIVES **decomposable** adj. **decomposition** n.

decompress /ˌdiːkəmˈprɛs/ ■ v. **1** expand (compressed computer data) to its normal size. **2** subject (a diver) to decompression. **3** N. Amer. informal calm down and relax.
– DERIVATIVES **decompressor** n.

decompression ■ n. **1** reduction in air pressure. ▶ a gradual reduction of air pressure on a person who has been experiencing high pressure while diving. **2** the process of expanding computer data to its normal size.

decompression chamber ■ n. a small room in which the air pressure can be varied, used to allow deep-sea divers to adjust to normal air pressure.

decompression sickness ■ n. a condition that results when too rapid decompression causes nitrogen bubbles to form in the tissues of the body, characterized by pain in the muscles and joints, cramp, numbness, nausea, and paralysis.

decongest ■ v. relieve the congestion of.
– DERIVATIVES **decongestion** n.

decongestant ■ adj. (chiefly of a medicine) used to relieve nasal congestion. ■ n. a decongestant medicine.

deconsecrate ■ v. transfer (a building) from sacred to secular use.
– DERIVATIVES **deconsecration** n.

deconstruct /ˌdiːk(ə)nˈstrʌkt/ ■ v. **1** analyse (a text, conceptual system, etc.) by deconstruction. **2** dismantle and expose the workings of: *social forms will have to be deconstructed before socialism can develop*.
– DERIVATIVES **deconstructive** adj.

deconstruction ■ n. a method of critical analysis of philosophical and literary language which emphasizes the internal workings of language and conceptual systems, the relational quality of meaning, and the assumptions implicit in forms of expression.
– DERIVATIVES **deconstructionism** n. **deconstructionist** adj. & n.

decontaminate ■ v. remove dangerous substances from.
– DERIVATIVES **decontamination** n.

decontextualize (also **-ise**) ■ v. consider in isolation from its context.
– DERIVATIVES **decontextualization** (also **-isation**) n.

decontrol ■ v. (**decontrolled, decontrolling**) release (a commodity, market, etc.) from controls or restrictions. ■ n. the action of decontrolling.

decor /ˈdeɪkɔː, ˈdɛ-/ ■ n. **1** the furnishing and decoration of a room. **2** stage scenery.
– ORIGIN C19: from French *décor*, from Latin *decorare* (see DECORATE).

decorate ■ v. **1** add ornament to. ▶ apply paint or wallpaper to. **2** confer an award or medal on.
– ORIGIN C16: from Latin *decoratus* 'embellished', from *decus, decor-* 'honour, embellishment'.

decoration ■ n. **1** the process or art of decorating. **2** ornamentation. ▶ a thing that serves as an ornament. **3** a medal or award conferred as an honour.

decorative /ˈdɛk(ə)rətɪv/ ■ adj. serving to make something look more attractive; ornamental. ▶ relating to decoration.
– DERIVATIVES **decoratively** adv. **decorativeness** n.

decorator ■ n. a person who decorates. ▶ chiefly Brit. a person whose job is to decorate the interior of buildings by painting the walls or hanging wallpaper.

decorous /ˈdɛk(ə)rəs/ ■ adj. in keeping with good taste and propriety; polite and restrained.
– DERIVATIVES **decorously** adv. **decorousness** n.
– ORIGIN C17: from Latin *decorus* 'seemly'.

decorum /dɪˈkɔːrəm/ ■ n. behaviour in keeping with good taste and propriety. ▶ prescribed behaviour; etiquette.
– ORIGIN C16: from Latin, from *decorus* 'seemly'.

découpage /ˌdeɪkuːˈpɑːʒ, dɪˈkuːpɑːʒ, ˈdɛkuːpɑːʒ/ ■ n. the decoration of the surface of an object with paper cut-outs.
– ORIGIN 1960s: French, from *découper* 'cut out'.

decoy ■ n. /ˈdiːkɔɪ, dɪˈkɔɪ/ **1** a bird or mammal, or an imitation of one, used to lure game. **2** a person or thing used to mislead or lure someone into a trap. **3** a pond from which narrow netted channels lead, into which wild duck may be enticed for capture. ■ v. /dɪˈkɔɪ, ˈdiːkɔɪ/ lure

by means of a decoy.
–ORIGIN C16 (earlier as *coy*): from Dutch *de kooi* 'the decoy', from Middle Dutch *de kouw* 'the cage', from Latin *cavea* 'cage'.

decrease ■ v. /dɪˈkriːs/ make or become smaller or fewer in size, amount, intensity, or degree. ■ n. /ˈdiːkriːs/ an instance or example of decreasing. ▸ the action or process of decreasing.
–DERIVATIVES **decreasing** adj. **decreasingly** adv.
–ORIGIN Middle English: from Old French *decreis* (n.), *decreistre* (v.), from Latin *decrescere*, from *de-* 'down' + *crescere* 'grow'.

decree ■ n. an official order issued by a ruler or authority that has the force of law. ▸ a judgement or decision of certain law courts. ■ v. (**decrees**, **decreed**, **decreeing**) order by decree: *the government decreed a ban on contact with the guerrillas.*
–ORIGIN Middle English: from Old French *decret*, from Latin *decretum* 'something decided', from *decernere* 'decide'.

decree absolute ■ n. (pl. **decrees absolute**) English Law a final order by a court which officially ends a marriage.

decree nisi ■ n. (pl. **decrees nisi**) English Law **1** another term for RULE NISI. **2** an order by a court of law that states the date on which a marriage will end, unless a good reason to prevent a divorce is produced.
–ORIGIN C19: Latin *nisi* 'unless'.

decrement /ˈdɛkrɪm(ə)nt/ ■ n. **1** a reduction or diminution. **2** Physics the ratio of the amplitudes in successive cycles of a damped oscillation. ■ v. chiefly Computing cause a discrete reduction in (a numerical quantity).
–ORIGIN C17: from Latin *decrementum* 'diminution', from *decrescere* 'to decrease'.

decrepit /dɪˈkrɛpɪt/ ■ adj. elderly and infirm. ▸ worn out or ruined because of age or neglect.
–DERIVATIVES **decrepitude** n.
–ORIGIN Middle English: from Latin *decrepitus*, from *de-* 'down' + *crepitus*, from *crepare* 'rattle, creak'.

decriminalize (also **-ise**) ■ v. cease to treat as illegal.
–DERIVATIVES **decriminalization** (also **-isation**) n.

decry /dɪˈkrʌɪ/ ■ v. (**-ies**, **-ied**) publicly denounce.
–DERIVATIVES **decrier** n.
–ORIGIN C17 (in the sense 'decrease the value of coins by royal proclamation'): from DE- + CRY, on the pattern of French *décrier* 'cry down'.

decrypt /diːˈkrɪpt/ ■ v. make (a coded or unclear message) intelligible.
–DERIVATIVES **decryption** n.
–ORIGIN 1930s: from DE- + *crypt* as in *encrypt*.

decumbent /dɪˈkʌmb(ə)nt/ ■ adj. Botany (of a plant stem) lying along the ground, with the extremity upturned.
–ORIGIN C18: from Latin *decumbere* 'lie down'.

decurrent /dɪˈkʌr(ə)nt/ ■ adj. Botany extending down the stem below the point of attachment.
–ORIGIN C18: from Latin *decurrere* 'to run down'.

decurved ■ adj. Biology (especially of a bird's bill) curved downwards.

dedicate ■ v. **1** devote to a particular subject, task, or purpose: *Joan has dedicated her life to animals.* **2** address (a book) to a particular person, as a sign of respect or affection. ▸ ceremonially assign (a church or other building) to a deity or saint.
–DERIVATIVES **dedicatee** n. **dedicator** n. **dedicatory** adj.
–ORIGIN Middle English: from Latin *dedicare* 'to devote or consecrate'.

dedicated ■ adj. **1** devoted to a task or purpose. **2** exclusively assigned or allocated for a particular purpose: *a dedicated high-speed rail link.*
–DERIVATIVES **dedicatedly** adv.

dedication ■ n. **1** the quality of being dedicated. **2** the action of dedicating. ▸ an inscription dedicating a building. ▸ the words with which a book is dedicated.

deduce ■ v. arrive at (a fact or a conclusion) by reasoning.
–DERIVATIVES **deducible** adj.
–ORIGIN Middle English: from Latin *deducere*, from *de-* 'down' + *ducere* 'lead'.

deduct ■ v. subtract or take away from a total.
–ORIGIN Middle English: from Latin *deducere* 'to take or lead away'.

deductible ■ adj. able to be deducted, especially from taxable income. ■ n. chiefly N. Amer. the part of an insurance claim to be paid by the insured; an excess.
–DERIVATIVES **deductibility** n.

deduction ■ n. **1** the action of deducting: *paid without deduction of tax.* ▸ an amount that is or may be deducted. **2** the inference of particular instances by reference to a general law or principle. Often contrasted with INDUCTION. ▸ a conclusion that has been deduced.
–DERIVATIVES **deductive** adj. **deductively** adv.

deed ■ n. **1** an action that is performed intentionally or consciously. **2** (usu. **deeds**) a legal document, especially one relating to property ownership or legal rights. ■ v. N. Amer. convey or transfer by legal deed.
–ORIGIN Old English, of Germanic origin.

deed poll ■ n. English Law a legal deed made and executed by one party only, especially to formalize a change of a person's name.
–ORIGIN C16: so named because the parchment was 'polled' or cut even, not indented as in the case of a deed made by two parties.

deejay informal ■ n. a disc jockey. ■ v. perform as a disc jockey.
–ORIGIN 1950s: representing the pronunciation of the initials *DJ*.

deem ■ v. formal regard or consider in a specified way: *the event was deemed a great success.*
–ORIGIN Old English, of Germanic origin.

deep ■ adj. **1** extending far down or in from the top or surface. ▸ extending a specified distance from the top, surface, or outer edge. ▸ Cricket (of a fielding position) relatively distant from the batsman. ▸ (in ball games) to or from a position far down or across the field: *a deep cross from Neill.* **2** very intense, profound, or extreme. ▸ difficult to understand: *this is all getting too deep for me.* **3** (of sound) low in pitch and full in tone; not shrill. **4** (of colour) dark and intense. ■ n. **1** (**the deep**) poetic/literary the sea. **2** (usu. **deeps**) a deep part of something, especially the sea. ▸ (**the deep**) Cricket the part of the field distant from the batsman. ■ adv. far down or in; deeply. ▸ (in sport) distant from the batsman or forward line of one's team.
–PHRASES **go off** (or **go in off**) **the deep end** informal give way immediately to an emotional or irrational outburst. **in deep water** informal in trouble or difficulty. **jump** (or **be thrown**) **in at the deep end** informal face a difficult problem or undertaking with little experience.
–DERIVATIVES **deeply** adv. **deepness** n.
–ORIGIN Old English, of Germanic origin.

Deepavali /ˌdiːˈpɑːvəli, ˌdiːpəˈvɑːli/ ■ n. S. African another term for DIWALI.

deep-bodied ■ adj. (of an animal, especially a fish) having a body which is deeper (from back to belly) than it is wide.

deep-dyed ■ adj. informal thoroughgoing; complete.

deepen ■ v. make or become deep or deeper.

deep freeze ■ n. (also **deep freezer**) a freezer. ■ v. (**deep-freeze**) store in or free using a deep freeze.

deep-fry ■ v. [usu. as adj. **deep-fried**] fry (food) in an amount of fat or oil sufficient to cover it completely.

deep-rooted ■ adj. firmly established.
–DERIVATIVES **deep-rootedness** n.

deep-seated ■ adj. firmly established.

deep-set ■ adj. embedded or positioned firmly or deeply: *deep-set eyes.*

deep-six ■ v. N. Amer. informal get rid of; destroy utterly.
–ORIGIN 1920s (as *the deep six* 'the grave'): perhaps from the custom of burial at sea at a depth of six fathoms.

deep space ■ n. another term for OUTER SPACE.

deep structure ■ n. (in transformational grammar) the underlying logical relationships of the elements of a phrase or sentence. Contrasted with SURFACE STRUCTURE.

deep-vein thrombosis ■ n. thrombosis in a vein lying deep below the skin, especially in the legs.

deer ■ n. (pl. same) a hoofed grazing or browsing animal, with branched bony antlers that are shed annually (and

typically borne only by the male). [Family Cervidae: many species.]
– ORIGIN Old English *dēor*, also orig. denoting any quadruped; of Germanic origin.

deer fly ■ n. **1** a bloodsucking louse fly which is a parasite of deer. [*Lipoptena cervi*.] **2** a bloodsucking horsefly which attacks large mammals and can transmit various diseases. [Genus *Chrysops*.]

deerhound ■ n. a large dog of a rough-haired breed, resembling the greyhound.

deerstalker ■ n. **1** a soft cloth cap, originally worn for hunting, with peaks in front and behind and ear flaps which can be tied together over the top. **2** a person who stalks deer.

de-escalate ■ v. reduce the intensity of (a conflict or crisis).
– DERIVATIVES **de-escalation** n.

deface ■ v. spoil the surface or appearance of.
– DERIVATIVES **defacement** n. **defacer** n.
– ORIGIN Middle English: from Old French *desfacier*.

de facto /deɪ ˈfaktəʊ, diː/ ■ adv. in fact, whether by right or not. Often contrasted with DE JURE. ■ adj. existing in fact: *a de facto one-party system*.
– ORIGIN Latin, 'of fact'.

defalcate /ˈdiːfalˌkeɪt/ ■ v. formal embezzle (funds).
– DERIVATIVES **defalcation** n. **defalcator** n.
– ORIGIN C16 (in the sense 'deduct, subtract'): from medieval Latin *defalcare* 'to lop'.

defamation ■ n. Law the act of making a false statement, orally or through written publication, that is damaging to a person's reputation.
– DERIVATIVES **defamatory** adj.

defame ■ v. damage the good reputation of.
– DERIVATIVES **defamer** n.
– ORIGIN Middle English: from Old French *diffamer*, from Latin *diffamare* 'spread evil report', from *dis-* (expressing removal) + *fama* 'report'.

defang ■ v. [often as adj. **defanged**] render harmless or ineffectual.

default ■ n. **1** failure to fulfil an obligation, especially to repay a loan or appear in a law court. **2** a pre-selected option adopted by a computer program or other mechanism when no alternative is specified. ■ v. **1** fail to fulfil an obligation, especially to repay a loan or to appear in a law court: *some had defaulted on student loans*. ▶ declare (a party) in default and give judgement against that party. **2** (**default to**) revert automatically to (a pre-selected option).
– PHRASES **by default** because of a lack of opposition or positive action: *he became an actor by default*. **go by default** be decided in favour of one party because of lack of opposition by the other party. **in default** guilty of default. **in default of** in the absence of.
– ORIGIN Middle English: from Old French *defaut*, from *defaillir* 'to fail', from Latin *fallere* 'disappoint, deceive'.

defaulter ■ n. a person who defaults. ▶ chiefly Brit. a member of the armed forces guilty of a military offence.

defeasible /dɪˈfiːzɪb(ə)l/ ■ adj. Philosophy open in principle to revision or valid objection.
– DERIVATIVES **defeasibility** n. **defeasibly** adv.

defeat ■ v. **1** win a victory over. **2** prevent (an aim) from being achieved: *this defeats the object of the exercise*. ▶ thwart or frustrate. ▶ Law render null and void. ■ n. an instance of defeating or being defeated.
– DERIVATIVES **defeated** adj. **defeatedly** adv.
– ORIGIN Middle English: from Old French *desfait* 'undone', from *desfaire*, from medieval Latin *disfacere* 'undo'.

defeatist ■ n. a person who gives in to failure too readily. ■ adj. showing ready acceptance of failure.
– DERIVATIVES **defeatism** n.

defecate /ˈdɛfɪkeɪt, ˈdiːf-/ ■ v. discharge faeces from the body.
– DERIVATIVES **defecation** n. **defecator** n. **defecatory** adj.
– ORIGIN Middle English (orig. in the sense 'clear of dregs, purify'): from Latin *defaecare*, from *de-* + *faex, faec-* 'dregs'.

defect[1] ■ n. /ˈdiːfɛkt, dɪˈfɛkt/ a shortcoming, imperfection, or lack.

– ORIGIN Middle English: from Latin *defectus*, from *deficere* 'desert, fail', from *de-* (expressing reversal) + *facere* 'do'.

defect[2] /dɪˈfɛkt/ ■ v. abandon one's country or cause in favour of an opposing one.
– DERIVATIVES **defection** n. **defector** n.
– ORIGIN C16: from Latin *defect-* 'failed', from *deficere* (see DEFECT[1]).

defective ■ adj. **1** imperfect or faulty. **2** lacking or deficient.
– DERIVATIVES **defectively** adv. **defectiveness** n.

defence (US **defense**) ■ n. **1** the action of defending from or resisting attack. ▶ military measures or resources for protecting a country. ▶ (**defences**) fortifications against attack. **2** the case presented by or on behalf of the party being accused or sued in a lawsuit. ▶ (usu. **the defence**) [treated as sing. or pl.] the counsel for the defendant in a lawsuit. **3** attempted justification or vindication: *he spoke in defence of a disciplined approach*. **4** (in sport) the action or role of defending one's goal or wicket against the opposition. ▶ (**the defence**) the players in a team who perform this role.

defence force ■ n. **1** another term for ARMED FORCES. **2** (**Defence Force**) S. African the South African National Defence Force. ▶ historical (under apartheid) the South African Defence Force.

defenceless (US **defenseless**) ■ adj. without defence or protection; totally vulnerable.
– DERIVATIVES **defencelessness** n.

defence mechanism ■ n. an automatic reaction of the body against disease-causing organisms. ▶ a mental process initiated, typically unconsciously, to avoid conscious conflict or anxiety.

defend ■ v. **1** resist an attack on; protect from harm or danger. **2** conduct the case for (the party being accused or sued) in a lawsuit. **3** attempt to justify. **4** compete to retain (a title or seat). **5** (in sport) protect one's goal or wicket rather than attempt to score against one's opponents.
– DERIVATIVES **defendable** adj. **defender** n.
– ORIGIN Middle English: from Old French *defendre*, from Latin *defendere*, from *de-* 'off' + *-fendere* 'to strike'.

defendant ■ n. an individual, company, or institution sued or accused in a court of law. Compare with PLAINTIFF.

defenestration ■ n. formal or humorous the action of throwing someone out of a window.
– DERIVATIVES **defenestrate** v.
– ORIGIN C17: from modern Latin *defenestratio(n-)*, from *de-* 'from' + Latin *fenestra* 'window'.

defense ■ n. US spelling of DEFENCE.

defensible ■ adj. **1** justifiable by argument. **2** able to be defended or protected.
– DERIVATIVES **defensibility** n. **defensibly** adv.

defensive ■ adj. **1** used or intended to defend or protect. ▶ (in sport) relating to or intended as defence. **2** very anxious to challenge or avoid criticism.
– PHRASES **on the defensive** expecting or resisting criticism or attack.
– DERIVATIVES **defensively** adv. **defensiveness** n.

defer[1] /dɪˈfəː/ ■ v. (**deferred**, **deferring**) put off to a later time; postpone. ▶ Law (of a judge) postpone (a sentence) for a period of up to six months from conviction.
– DERIVATIVES **deferment** n. **deferrable** adj. **deferral** n.
– ORIGIN Middle English: from Old French *differer* 'defer, differ', from Latin *differre*, from *dis-* 'apart' + *ferre* 'bring, carry'.

defer[2] /dɪˈfəː/ ■ v. (**deferred**, **deferring**) (**defer to**) submit humbly to: *he deferred to Tim's superior knowledge*.
– DERIVATIVES **deferrer** n.
– ORIGIN Middle English: from Old French *deferer*, from Latin *deferre* 'carry away, refer', from *de-* 'away from' + *ferre* 'bring, carry'.

deference ■ n. humble submission and respect.

deferential ■ adj. showing deference; respectful.
– DERIVATIVES **deferentially** adv.

defiance ▪ n. open resistance; bold disobedience.
– DERIVATIVES **defiant** adj. **defiantly** adv.
– ORIGIN Middle English: from Old French, from *defier* 'defy'.

defiance campaign (also **Defiance Campaign**) ▪ n. S. African a national civil disobedience campaign, in particular that of 1952 or 1989.

defibrillation /ˌdiːfɪbrɪˈleɪʃ(ə)n/ ▪ n. Medicine the stopping of fibrillation of the heart by administering a controlled electric shock, to allow restoration of the normal rhythm.
– DERIVATIVES **defibrillate** v. **defibrillator** n.

deficiency ▪ n. (pl. **-ies**) a lack or shortage. ▸ a failing or shortcoming.

deficient /dɪˈfɪʃ(ə)nt/ ▪ adj. not having enough of a specified quality or ingredient: *this diet is deficient in vitamin B*. ▸ insufficient or inadequate.
– ORIGIN C16: from Latin *deficient-*, *deficere* (see DEFECT¹).

deficit /ˈdɛfɪsɪt, ˈdiː-/ ▪ n. 1 the amount by which something, especially a sum of money, falls short. ▸ an excess of expenditure or liabilities over income or assets in a given period. 2 technical a deficiency or failing, especially in a neurological or psychological function.
– ORIGIN C18: from Latin *deficit* 'it is lacking', from *deficere* (see DEFECT¹).

deficit spending ▪ n. government spending, in excess of revenue, of funds raised by borrowing rather than from taxation.

defilade /ˌdɛfɪˈleɪd/ ▪ n. Military the protection of a position, vehicle, or troops against enemy observation or gunfire.
– ORIGIN C19: from French *défiler* 'protect from the enemy'.

defile¹ /dɪˈfʌɪl/ ▪ v. sully, mar, or spoil. ▸ desecrate or profane (something sacred). ▸ archaic violate the chastity of (a woman).
– DERIVATIVES **defilement** n. **defiler** n.
– ORIGIN Middle English: alteration of obsolete *defoul*, from Old French *defouler* 'trample down', influenced by obsolete *befile* 'befoul, defile'.

defile² /dɪˈfʌɪl, ˈdiːfʌɪl/ ▪ n. a steep-sided narrow gorge or passage (originally one requiring troops to march in single file).
– ORIGIN C17: from French *défilé* (n.), from *dé* 'away from' + *file* 'column, file'.

define ▪ v. 1 state or describe exactly the nature, scope, or meaning of. ▸ give the meaning of (a word or phrase). 2 mark out the limits of.
– DERIVATIVES **definable** adj. **definer** n.
– ORIGIN Middle English: from Old French *definer*, from a var. of Latin *definire*, from *de-* (expressing completion) + *finire* 'finish'.

definite ▪ adj. 1 clearly stated or decided; not vague or doubtful. ▸ (of a person) certain or sure about something. 2 clearly true or real. 3 having exact and discernible physical limits.
– DERIVATIVES **definiteness** n.
– ORIGIN C16: from Latin *definitus* 'defined, set within limits', from *definire* (see DEFINE).

definite article ▪ n. Grammar a determiner (*the* in English) that introduces a noun phrase and implies that the thing mentioned has already been mentioned, or is common knowledge, or is about to be defined.

definite integral ▪ n. Mathematics an integral expressed as the difference between values at specified upper and lower limits of the independent variable.

definitely ▪ adv. without doubt (used for emphasis).

definition ▪ n. 1 a formal statement of the exact meaning of a word. ▸ an exact description of the nature, scope, or meaning of something. ▸ the action or process of defining. 2 the degree of distinctness in outline of an object or image.
– PHRASES **by definition** by its very nature; intrinsically.
– DERIVATIVES **definitional** adj.

definitive ▪ adj. 1 (of a conclusion or agreement) done or reached decisively and with authority. ▸ (of a book or other text) the most authoritative of its kind. 2 (of a postage stamp) for general use, not special or commemorative. ▪ n. a definitive postage stamp.
– DERIVATIVES **definitively** adv.
– ORIGIN Middle English: from Old French *definitif*, from Latin *definitivus*, from *definire* (see DEFINE).

deflagration ▪ n. Chemistry the action of heating a substance until it burns away rapidly.
– DERIVATIVES **deflagrate** v. **deflagrator** n.
– ORIGIN C17: from Latin *deflagratio(n-)*, from *deflagrare* 'burn up', from *de-* 'away, thoroughly' + *flagrare* 'to burn'.

deflate ▪ v. 1 let air or gas out of (a tyre, balloon, or similar object). ▸ be emptied of air or gas. 2 [usu. as adj. **deflated**] cause to feel suddenly dispirited.
– DERIVATIVES **deflator** n.
– ORIGIN C19: from DE- + *-flate*, from Latin *flare* 'to blow'.

deflation ▪ n. 1 the action or process of deflating or being deflated. 2 Economics reduction of the general level of prices in an economy. 3 Geology the removal of particles of rock, sand, etc. by the wind.
– DERIVATIVES **deflationary** adj. **deflationist** n. & adj.

deflect ▪ v. deviate or cause to deviate from a straight course.
– DERIVATIVES **deflective** adj. **deflector** n.
– ORIGIN C16: from Latin *deflectere*, from *de-* + *flectere* 'to bend'.

deflection (also **deflexion**) ▪ n. the action or process of deflecting or being deflected. ▸ the amount by which something is deflected.

deflocculate /diːˈflɒkjʊleɪt/ ▪ v. Chemistry break up (a suspended substance) into finer particles, producing a dispersion.
– DERIVATIVES **deflocculation** n.

deflower ▪ v. 1 dated or poetic/literary deprive (a woman) of her virginity. 2 strip of flowers.
– ORIGIN Middle English: from Old French *desflourer*, from a var. of late Latin *deflorare*, from *de-* + Latin *flos*, *flor-* 'a flower'.

defoliant ▪ n. a chemical that removes the leaves from trees and plants, often used in warfare.

defoliate /diːˈfəʊlɪeɪt/ ▪ v. remove leaves or foliage from (a plant or area).
– DERIVATIVES **defoliation** n. **defoliator** n.
– ORIGIN C18: from late Latin *defoliare* 'to strip of leaves', from *de-* + *folium* 'leaf'.

deforest ▪ v. clear of forest or trees.
– DERIVATIVES **deforestation** n.

deform ▪ v. [often as adj. **deformed**] distort the shape or form of; make or become misshapen.
– DERIVATIVES **deformable** adj. **deformation** n.
– ORIGIN Middle English: from Old French *desformer*, from Latin *deformare*, from *de-* + *forma* 'a shape'.

deformity ▪ n. (pl. **-ies**) a deformed part, especially of the body. ▸ the state of being deformed: *spinal deformity*.

defrag ▪ v. Computing (**defrags**, **defragging**, **defragged**) short for DEFRAGMENT.

defragment /ˌdiːfragˈmɛnt/ ▪ v. Computing reduce the fragmentation of (a file) by concatenating parts stored in separate locations.
– DERIVATIVES **defragmentation** n. **defragmenter** n.

defraud ▪ v. illegally obtain money from (someone) by deception.
– DERIVATIVES **defrauder** n.
– ORIGIN Middle English: from Latin *defraudare*, from *de-* + *fraudare* 'to cheat'.

defray /dɪˈfreɪ/ ▪ v. provide money to pay (a cost).
– DERIVATIVES **defrayable** adj. **defrayal** n. **defrayment** n.
– ORIGIN Middle English: from French *défrayer*, from *dé-* + obsolete *frai* 'cost, expenses'.

defrock ▪ v. deprive (a person in holy orders) of ecclesiastical status.

defrost ▪ v. 1 make or become free of accumulated ice. 2 thaw (frozen food).
– DERIVATIVES **defroster** n.

deft ▪ adj. quick and neatly skilful.
– DERIVATIVES **deftly** adv. **deftness** n.
– ORIGIN Middle English: var. of DAFT, in the obsolete sense 'meek'.

defunct /dɪˈfʌŋ(k)t/ ▪ adj. no longer existing or functioning.
– ORIGIN C16: from Latin *defunctus* 'dead', from *defungi* 'carry out, finish'.

defuse ■ v. **1** remove the fuse from (an explosive device) in order to prevent it from exploding. **2** reduce the danger or tension in (a difficult situation).

defy ■ v. (-ies, -ied) **1** openly resist or refuse to obey. **2** challenge to do or prove something: *he glowered at her, defying her to mock him.*
– DERIVATIVES **defier** n.
– ORIGIN Middle English: from Old French *desfier*, based on Latin *dis-* (expressing reversal) + *fidus* 'faithful'.

deg. ■ abbrev. degree(s).

degauss /diːˈgaʊs/ ■ v. Physics remove unwanted magnetism from.
– DERIVATIVES **degausser** n.
– ORIGIN C20: from **DE-** + the name of the C19 German physicist Karl Friedrich *Gauss*.

degenerate ■ adj. /dɪˈdʒɛn(ə)rət/ **1** having lost the physical or moral qualities considered normal and desirable; showing evidence of decline. **2** Physics relating to or denoting a quantized energy level corresponding to more than one state. ▸ denoting matter at such high density (e.g. in neutron stars) that quantum effects are dominant. ■ n. /dɪˈdʒɛn(ə)rət/ a morally degenerate person. ■ v. /dɪˈdʒɛnəreɪt/ decline or deteriorate physically or morally.
– DERIVATIVES **degeneracy** n. **degenerately** adv.
– ORIGIN C15: from Latin *degeneratus* 'no longer of its kind', from *degenerare*, from *degener* 'debased', from *de-* + *genus*, *gener-* 'race, kind'.

degeneration ■ n. the state or process of being or becoming degenerate; decline or deterioration.

degenerative ■ adj. (of a disease or symptom) characterized by progressive deterioration and loss of function.

deglaze ■ v. dilute meat sediments in (a pan) in order to make a gravy or sauce: *deglaze the pan with the wine.*
– ORIGIN C19: from French *déglacer*.

degradation /ˌdɛɡrəˈdeɪʃ(ə)n/ ■ n. **1** the condition or process of degrading or being degraded. **2** Geology the wearing down of rock by disintegration.

degrade ■ v. **1** cause to suffer a severe loss of dignity or respect; demean. ▸ lower the character or quality of. **2** cause to break down or deteriorate chemically. ▸ Physics reduce (energy) to a less readily convertible form.
– DERIVATIVES **degradability** n. **degradable** adj. **degradative** adj. **degrader** n.
– ORIGIN Middle English: from Old French *degrader*, from eccles. Latin *degradare*, from *de-* 'down' + Latin *gradus* 'grade'.

degrading ■ adj. causing a loss of self-respect; humiliating.

degree ■ n. **1** the amount, level, or extent to which something happens or is present. **2** a unit of measurement of angles, equivalent to one ninetieth of a right angle. (Symbol: °) **3** a unit in any of various scales of temperature, intensity, or hardness. (Symbol: °) **4** a stage in a scale or series, in particular: ▸ each of a set of grades (usually three) used to classify burns according to their severity. ▸ chiefly N. Amer. a legal grade of crime, especially murder. ▸ a step in direct genealogical descent: *second-degree relatives.* **5** an academic rank conferred by a college or university after examination or after completion of a course, or conferred as an honour. **6** archaic social or official rank.
– PHRASES **by degrees** a little at a time; gradually. **to a degree** to some extent. ▸ dated to a considerable extent.
– ORIGIN Middle English: from Latin *de-* 'down' + *gradus* 'grade'.

dehumanize (also **-ise**) ■ v. deprive of positive human qualities.
– DERIVATIVES **dehumanization** (also **-isation**) n.

dehumidify ■ v. (-ies, -ied) remove moisture from (the air or a gas).
– DERIVATIVES **dehumidification** n. **dehumidifier** n.

dehydrate /diːˈhaɪdreɪt, -haɪˈdreɪt/ ■ v. [often as adj. **dehydrated**] lose or cause to lose a large amount of water. ▸ remove water from (food) in order to preserve it.
– DERIVATIVES **dehydration** n. **dehydrator** n.
– ORIGIN C19: from **DE-** + Greek *hudros* 'water'.

dehydrogenase /ˌdiːhaɪˈdrɒdʒəneɪz/ ■ n. Biochemistry an enzyme that brings about the removal of hydrogen atoms from a molecule.

delectation

dehydrogenate ■ v. Chemistry remove a hydrogen atom or atoms from.
– DERIVATIVES **dehydrogenation** n.

de-ice ■ v. remove ice from.
– DERIVATIVES **de-icer** n.

deictic /ˈdeɪktɪk, ˈdʌɪktɪk/ ■ adj. Linguistics of or denoting a word or expression whose meaning is dependent on the context in which it is used (such as *here*, or *next week*).
– DERIVATIVES **deictically** adv.
– ORIGIN C19: from Greek *deiktos* 'capable of proof', from *deiknunai* 'to show'.

deify /ˈdeɪɪfʌɪ, ˈdiːɪ-/ ■ v. (-ies, -ied) make into or worship as a god.
– DERIVATIVES **deification** n.
– ORIGIN Middle English: from Old French *deifier*, from eccles. Latin *deificare*, from *deus* 'god'.

deign /deɪn/ ■ v. do something that one considers to be beneath one's dignity: *she did not deign to answer.*
– ORIGIN Middle English: from Old French *degnier*, from Latin *dignare* 'deem worthy', from *dignus* 'worthy'.

de-index ■ v. end the indexation to inflation of (pensions or other benefits).

deindustrialization (also **-isation**) ■ n. decline in industrial activity in a region or economy.
– DERIVATIVES **deindustrialize** (also **-ise**) v.

deinstall ■ v. remove (an application or file) from a computer.
– DERIVATIVES **deinstallation** n. **deinstaller** n.

deionize /diːˈʌɪənʌɪz/ (also **-ise**) ■ v. [usu. as adj. **deionized** (also **-ised**)] remove the ions or ionic constituents from.
– DERIVATIVES **deionization** (also **-isation**) n. **deionizer** (also **-iser**) n.

deity /ˈdeɪɪti, ˈdiːɪ-/ ■ n. (pl. **-ies**) **1** a god or goddess (especially in a polytheistic religion). ▸ **(the Deity)** the creator or supreme being. **2** divine status, quality, or nature.
– ORIGIN Middle English: from eccles. Latin *deitas*, from *deus* 'god'.

deixis /ˈdeɪksɪs, ˈdʌɪksɪs/ ■ n. Linguistics the function or use of deictic words or forms.
– ORIGIN 1940s: from Greek, 'reference', from *deiknunai* 'to show'.

déjà vu /ˌdeɪʒɑː ˈvuː/ ■ n. a feeling of having already experienced the present situation.
– ORIGIN C20: French, 'already seen'.

deject ■ v. [usu. as adj. **dejected**] make sad or dispirited.
– DERIVATIVES **dejectedly** adv. **dejection** n.
– ORIGIN Middle English: from Latin *deject-* 'thrown down', from *deicere*, from *de-* 'down' + *jacere* 'to throw'.

de jure /deɪ ˈjʊəreɪ, diː ˈdʒʊəri/ ■ adv. rightfully; by right. Often contrasted with **DE FACTO**. ■ adj. rightful.
– ORIGIN Latin, 'of law'.

dekaliter ■ n. US variant spelling of **DECALITRE**.

dekameter ■ n. US variant spelling of **DECAMETRE**.

dekriet ■ n. S. African another term for **CAPE REED** (in sense 2).
– ORIGIN C19: Afrikaans, from S. African Dutch *dek* 'to roof or cover' (or *dak* 'roof') + *riet* 'reed'.

delaminate /diːˈlamɪneɪt/ ■ v. divide or become divided into layers.
– ORIGIN C19: from **DE-** + Latin *lamina* 'thin plate'.

Delaware /ˈdɛləwɛː/ ■ n. (pl. same or **Delawares**) a member of an American Indian people formerly inhabiting the Delaware River valley of New Jersey and eastern Pennsylvania.

delay ■ v. **1** become or cause to become late or slow. **2** postpone or defer. ■ n. a period of time by which something is late or postponed.
– DERIVATIVES **delayer** n.
– ORIGIN Middle English: from Old French *delayer* (v.).

delectable ■ adj. (of food or drink) delicious. ▸ chiefly humorous lovely; delightful.
– DERIVATIVES **delectability** n. **delectably** adv.

delectation /ˌdiːlɛkˈteɪʃ(ə)n/ ■ n. formal, chiefly humorous pleasure and delight.
– ORIGIN Middle English: from Latin *delectatio(n-)*, from *delectare* (see **DELIGHT**).

delegacy /ˈdɛlɪɡəsi/ ■ n. (pl. **-ies**) [treated as sing. or pl.] a body of delegates; a committee or delegation.

delegate ■ n. /ˈdɛlɪɡət/ a person sent or authorized to represent others, in particular a representative sent to a conference. ▸ a member of a committee. ■ v. /ˈdɛlɪɡeɪt/ entrust (a task or responsibility) to another person. ▸ authorize (someone) to act as a representative or on one's behalf: *Edward was delegated to meet new arrivals.*
– DERIVATIVES **delegable** /ˈdɛlɪɡəb(ə)l/ adj. **delegator** n.
– ORIGIN Middle English: from Latin *delegatus* 'sent on a commission', from *delegare*, from *de-* 'down' + *legare* 'depute'.

delegation ■ n. [treated as sing. or pl.] **1** a body of delegates; a deputation. **2** the action or process of delegating or being delegated.

delete ■ v. remove or erase (text).
– DERIVATIVES **deletion** n.
– ORIGIN Middle English: from Latin *delere* 'to blot out'.

deleterious /ˌdɛlɪˈtɪərɪəs/ ■ adj. causing harm or damage.
– DERIVATIVES **deleteriously** adv.
– ORIGIN C17: from Greek *dēlētērios* 'noxious'.

delft /dɛlft/ ■ n. English or Dutch tin-glazed earthenware, typically decorated by hand in blue on a white background.
– DERIVATIVES **delftware** n.
– ORIGIN C17: from the name of the town of *Delft* in the Netherlands, where the pottery originated.

deli ■ n. (pl. **delis**) informal short for DELICATESSEN.

deliberate ■ adj. /dɪˈlɪb(ə)rət/ **1** done consciously and intentionally. ▸ fully considered; not impulsive. **2** done or acting in a careful, unhurried way. ■ v. /dɪˈlɪbəreɪt/ engage in long and careful consideration.
– DERIVATIVES **deliberately** adv. **deliberateness** n. **deliberator** n.
– ORIGIN Middle English: from Latin *deliberare* 'consider carefully'.

deliberation ■ n. **1** long and careful consideration. **2** slow and careful movement or thought.

deliberative ■ adj. relating to or involving consideration or discussion: *a deliberative assembly.*

delicacy ■ n. (pl. **-ies**) **1** fineness or intricacy of texture or structure. **2** susceptibility to illness or adverse conditions; fragility. **3** discretion and tact. *treat this matter with the utmost delicacy.* **4** a choice or expensive food.

delicate ■ adj. **1** very fine in texture or structure; of intricate workmanship or quality. ▸ (of food or drink) subtly and pleasantly flavoured. **2** easily broken or damaged; fragile. ▸ susceptible to illness or adverse conditions. **3** requiring sensitive or careful handling. ▸ skilful; deft. ■ n. (**delicates**) garments made from delicate fabric.
– PHRASES **in a delicate condition** archaic, euphemistic pregnant.
– DERIVATIVES **delicately** adv. **delicateness** n.
– ORIGIN Middle English (in the sense 'delightful, charming'): from French *délicat* or Latin *delicatus*, of unknown origin.

delicatessen /ˌdɛlɪkəˈtɛs(ə)n/ ■ n. a shop selling cooked meats, cheeses, and unusual or foreign prepared foods.
– ORIGIN C19: from German or Dutch, from French *délicatesse* 'delicateness'.

delicious ■ adj. **1** highly pleasant to the taste. **2** delightful: *a delicious irony.*
– DERIVATIVES **deliciously** adv. **deliciousness** n.
– ORIGIN Middle English: from late Latin *deliciosus*, from Latin *deliciae* (pl.) 'delight, pleasure'.

delicious monster ■ n. another term for SWISS CHEESE PLANT.

delict /dɪˈlɪkt, ˈdiːlɪkt/ ■ n. Law a civil violation of the law; a tort.
– ORIGIN Middle English: from Latin *delictum* 'something showing fault', from *delinquere* (see DELINQUENT).

delight ■ v. please greatly. ▸ (**delight in**) take great pleasure in. ■ n. great pleasure. ▸ a cause or source of great pleasure.
– DERIVATIVES **delighted** adj. **delightedly** adv.
– ORIGIN Middle English: from Old French *delitier* (v.), *delit* (n.), from Latin *delectare* 'to charm', from *delicere*.

delightful ■ adj. causing delight; charming.
– DERIVATIVES **delightfully** adv. **delightfulness** n.

delimit /dɪˈlɪmɪt/ ■ v. (**delimited, delimiting**) determine the limits or boundaries of.
– DERIVATIVES **delimitation** n. **delimiter** n.

delineate /dɪˈlɪnɪeɪt/ ■ v. describe or indicate precisely. ▸ trace the outline of (a border or boundary).
– DERIVATIVES **delineation** /-ˈeɪʃ(ə)n/ n. **delineator** n.
– ORIGIN C16: from Latin *delineare* 'to outline'.

delinquency ■ n. (pl. **-ies**) **1** minor crime, especially that committed by young people. **2** formal neglect of one's duty. **3** a failure to pay an outstanding debt.

delinquent /dɪˈlɪŋkw(ə)nt/ ■ adj. **1** (typically with reference to young people) showing or characterized by a tendency to commit crime. **2** formal failing in one's duty. **3** in arrears: *delinquent accounts.* ■ n. a delinquent person.
– DERIVATIVES **delinquently** adv.
– ORIGIN C15: from Latin *delinquere* 'to offend'.

deliquesce /ˌdɛlɪˈkwɛs/ ■ v. Chemistry (of a solid) become liquid by absorbing moisture from the air.
– DERIVATIVES **deliquescence** n. **deliquescent** adj.
– ORIGIN C18: from Latin *deliquescere* 'dissolve'.

delirious ■ adj. **1** suffering from delirium. **2** in a state of wild excitement or ecstasy.
– DERIVATIVES **deliriously** adv.

delirium /dɪˈlɪrɪəm/ ■ n. an acutely disturbed state of mind characterized by restlessness, illusions, and incoherence of thought and speech, occurring in fever, intoxication, and other disorders.
– ORIGIN C16: from Latin, from *delirare* 'deviate, be deranged' (literally 'deviate from the furrow'), from *de-* 'away' + *lira* 'ridge between furrows'.

delirium tremens /ˈtriːmɛnz, ˈtrɛ-/ ■ n. a psychotic condition typical of withdrawal in chronic alcoholics, involving tremors, hallucinations, anxiety, and disorientation.
– ORIGIN C19: from Latin, 'trembling delirium'.

delist ■ v. remove from a list, in particular remove (a security) from the official register of a stock exchange.

deliver ■ v. **1** bring and hand over (a letter or goods) to the appropriate recipient. ▸ formally hand over (someone). ▸ Law acknowledge that one intends to be bound by (a deed), either explicitly by declaration or implicitly by formal handover. **2** provide (something promised or expected). **3** save or set free: *deliver us from the nightmare of junk mail.* **4** state or present in a formal manner: *he will deliver a lecture on endangered species.* **5** assist in the birth of. ▸ (also **be delivered of**) give birth to. **6** launch or aim (a blow or attack).
– DERIVATIVES **deliverable** adj. & n. **deliverer** n.
– ORIGIN Middle English: from Old French *delivrer*, based on Latin *de-* 'away' + *liberare* 'set free'.

deliverance ■ n. **1** the process of being rescued or set free. **2** a formal or authoritative utterance.

delivery ■ n. (pl. **-ies**) **1** the action of delivering something, especially letters, goods, or services. ▸ a regular or scheduled occasion for this. ▸ Law the acknowledgement by the maker of a deed that they intend to be bound by it. **2** the process of giving birth. **3** an act of throwing or bowling a ball, especially a cricket ball. ▸ the style or manner of such an action. **4** the manner or style of giving a speech.
– PHRASES **take delivery of** receive at one's address (something purchased).

dell ■ n. poetic/literary a small valley.
– ORIGIN Old English, of Germanic origin.

Delphic /ˈdɛlfɪk/ ■ adj. **1** of or relating to the ancient Greek oracle at Delphi. **2** deliberately obscure or ambiguous.

delphinium /dɛlˈfɪnɪəm/ ■ n. (pl. **delphiniums**) a popular garden plant bearing tall spikes of blue flowers. [Genus *Delphinium*.]
– ORIGIN from Greek *delphinion* 'larkspur', from *delphin* 'dolphin' (because of the shape of the spur, thought to resemble a dolphin's back).

delta¹ ■ n. **1** the fourth letter of the Greek alphabet (Δ, δ), transliterated as 'd'. **2** a code word representing the letter D, used in radio communication. ■ **symb.** Mathematics variation of a variable or quantity.
– ORIGIN Greek: from Phoenician *daleth*.

delta² ■ n. a triangular tract of sediment deposited at the mouth of a river, typically where it diverges into several outlets.
– DERIVATIVES **deltaic** adj.
– ORIGIN C16: orig. *the Delta* (of the River Nile), from the shape of the Greek letter (see **DELTA¹**).

delta rays ■ pl. n. Physics rays of low penetrative power consisting of slow electrons or other particles ejected from atoms by the impact of ionizing radiation.

delta wing ■ n. the single triangular swept-back wing on some aircraft.

deltoid /ˈdɛltɔɪd/ ■ adj. technical **1** triangular. **2** denoting a thick triangular muscle covering the shoulder joint and used for raising the arm away from the body. ■ n. a deltoid muscle, or one of the three parts of a deltoid muscle.
– ORIGIN C18: from French *deltoïde*, or from Greek *deltoeidēs*.

delude /dɪˈl(j)uːd/ ■ v. impose a misleading belief upon.
– DERIVATIVES **deluded** adj. **deludedly** adv. **deluder** n.
– ORIGIN Middle English: from Latin *deludere* 'to mock', from *de-* + *ludere* 'to play'.

deluge /ˈdɛljuːdʒ/ ■ n. **1** a severe flood. ▶ a very heavy fall of rain. **2** a great quantity of something arriving at the same time: *a deluge of complaints*. ■ v. **1** inundate; overwhelm. **2** flood.
– ORIGIN Middle English: from Old French, var. of *diluve*, from Latin *diluvium*, from *diluere* 'wash away'.

delusion ■ n. **1** an idiosyncratic belief or impression that is not in accordance with a generally accepted reality. **2** the action of deluding or being deluded.
– DERIVATIVES **delusional** adj. **delusive** adj. **delusory** adj.

de luxe /dɪ ˈlʌks, ˈlʊks/ ■ adj. luxurious or sumptuous; of a superior kind.
– ORIGIN C19: French, 'of luxury'.

delve ■ v. **1** reach inside a receptacle and search for something. **2** research intensively into something.
– DERIVATIVES **delver** n.
– ORIGIN Old English *delfan* 'dig', of West Germanic origin.

Dem. ■ abbrev. US Democrat.

demagnetize (also **-ise**) ■ v. remove magnetic properties from.
– DERIVATIVES **demagnetization** (also **-isation**) n. **demagnetizer** (also **-iser**) n.

demagogue /ˈdɛməɡɒɡ/ ■ n. **1** a political leader who seeks support by appealing to popular desires and prejudices rather than by using rational argument. **2** (in ancient Greece and Rome) an orator who espoused the cause of the common people.
– DERIVATIVES **demagogic** /-ˈɡɒɡɪk/ adj. **demagoguery** /-ˈɡɒɡ(ə)ri/ n. **demagogy** n.
– ORIGIN C17: from Greek *dēmagōgos*, from *dēmos* 'the people' + *agōgos* 'leading'.

demand ■ n. **1** an insistent and peremptory request, made as of right. ▶ (**demands**) pressing requirements. **2** Economics the desire of purchasers, consumers, etc. for a particular commodity or service: *a recent slump in demand*. ■ v. ask authoritatively or brusquely. ▶ insist on having. ▶ require; need.
– PHRASES **in demand** sought after. **on demand** as soon as or whenever required.
– DERIVATIVES **demander** n.
– ORIGIN Middle English: from Old French *demande* (n.), *demander* (v.), from Latin *demandare* 'hand over, entrust'.

demand feeding ■ n. the practice of feeding a baby when it cries for a feed rather than at set times.

demanding ■ adj. requiring much skill or effort: *a demanding job*.
– DERIVATIVES **demandingly** adv.

demarcation (also **demarkation**) ■ n. the action of fixing boundaries or limits. ▶ a dividing line.
– DERIVATIVES **demarcate** v. **demarcator** n.
– ORIGIN C18: from Spanish *demarcación* (from *demarcar* 'mark the bounds of'), orig. used with ref. to the line dividing the New World between the Spanish and Portuguese, laid down by the Pope in 1493.

dematerialize (also **-ise**) ■ v. make or become no longer physically present, or spiritual rather than physical.
– DERIVATIVES **dematerialization** (also **-isation**) n.

deme /diːm/ ■ n. Biology a subdivision of a population consisting of closely related plants or animals.
– ORIGIN from Greek *dēmos* 'people'.

demean /dɪˈmiːn/ ■ v. cause to suffer a severe loss of dignity or respect. ▶ (**demean oneself**) do something that is beneath one's dignity.
– DERIVATIVES **demeaning** adj.
– ORIGIN C17: from **DE-** + adj. **MEAN²**, on the pattern of *debase*.

demeanour (US **demeanor**) ■ n. outward behaviour or bearing.
– ORIGIN C15: from **DEMEAN**, prob. influenced by obsolete *havour* 'behaviour'.

demented ■ adj. **1** suffering from dementia. **2** informal wild and irrational.
– DERIVATIVES **dementedly** adv. **dementedness** n.
– ORIGIN C17: from French *dément* or Latin *demens*, *dement-* 'insane'.

dementia /dɪˈmɛnʃə/ ■ n. Medicine a chronic or persistent mental disorder marked by memory failures, personality changes, and impaired reasoning.
– ORIGIN C18: from Latin, from *demens*, *dement-* 'out of one's mind'.

demerara sugar /ˌdɛməˈrɛːrə, -ˈrɑːrə/ ■ n. light brown cane sugar, originally from Demerara in Guyana.

demerge ■ v. separate (a company) from another with which it was merged.
– DERIVATIVES **demerger** n.

demerit ■ n. **1** a feature or fact deserving censure. **2** N. Amer. a mark awarded against someone for a fault or offence.
– DERIVATIVES **demeritorious** /-ˈtɔːrɪəs/ adj.

demersal /dɪˈmɜːs(ə)l/ ■ adj. (of fish) living close to the seabed.
– ORIGIN C19: from Latin *demersus*, from *demergere* 'submerge, sink'.

demesne /dɪˈmeɪn, dɪˈmiːn/ ■ n. historical land attached to a manor and retained by the owner for their own use. ▶ archaic a domain.
– ORIGIN Middle English: from Old French *demeine* 'belonging to a lord', from Latin *dominicus*, from *dominus* 'lord, master'.

demi- ■ prefix **1** half. **2** partially; in an inferior degree: *demigod*.
– ORIGIN from medieval Latin *dimedius* 'half', from earlier *dimidius*.

demigod (or **demigoddess**) ■ n. a being with partial or lesser divine status.

demijohn ■ n. a bulbous narrow-necked bottle holding from 3 to 10 gallons of liquid.
– ORIGIN C18: prob. an alteration of French *dame-jeanne* 'Lady Jane', associated with **DEMI-** and the given name *John*.

demilitarize (also **-ise**) ■ v. [usu. as adj. **demilitarized** (also **-ised**)] remove military forces from: *a demilitarized zone*.
– DERIVATIVES **demilitarization** (also **-isation**) n.

demi-mondaine /ˈdɛmɪmɒnˌdeɪn/ ■ n. a woman considered to belong to the demi-monde.
– ORIGIN from French.

demi-monde /ˌdɛmɪˈmɒnd/ ■ n. a group considered to be on the fringes of respectable society.
– ORIGIN C19: French (orig. with ref. to C19 France and the class of women considered morally dubious), 'half-world'.

demine ■ v. remove explosive mines from.
– DERIVATIVES **deminer** n.

demineralize (also **-ise**) ■ v. remove salts or minerals from.
– DERIVATIVES **demineralization** (also **-isation**) n.

demi-pension /ˌdɛmɪˈpɒ̃sjɔ̃/ ■ n. hotel accommodation

demise

with bed, breakfast, and one main meal per day.
– ORIGIN French, 'half board'.

demise /dɪˈmaɪz/ ■ n. **1** the end or failure of something. **2** a person's death. **3** Law the transfer of property or a title by demising. ■ v. Law convey or grant by will or lease.
– ORIGIN Middle English: from Anglo-Norman French, from Old French *desmettre* 'dismiss'.

demi-sec /ˈdɛmɪˌsɛk/ ■ adj. (of wine) medium dry.
– ORIGIN French, 'half-dry'.

demitasse /ˈdɛmɪtas/ ■ n. a small coffee cup.
– ORIGIN C19: from French, 'half-cup'.

demo informal ■ n. (pl. **-os**) **1** short for DEMONSTRATION. **2** a demonstration recording or piece of software. ■ v. (**-os**, **-oed**) give a demonstration of.

demob /diːˈmɒb/ Brit. informal ■ v. (**demobbed**, **demobbing**) demobilize. ■ n. demobilization.

demobilize /diːˈməʊbɪlʌɪz/ (also **-ise**) ■ v. (usu. **be demobilized**) take (troops) out of active service.
– DERIVATIVES **demobilization** (also **-isation**) n.

democracy /dɪˈmɒkrəsi/ ■ n. (pl. **-ies**) a form of government in which the people have a voice in the exercise of power, typically through elected representatives. ▸ a state governed in such a way. ▸ control of a group by the majority of its members.
– ORIGIN C16: from French *démocratie*, from Greek *dēmo-kratia*, from *dēmos* 'the people' + *-kratia* 'power, rule'.

democrat ■ n. **1** a supporter of democracy. **2** (**Democrat**) (in the US) a member of the Democratic Party.
– ORIGIN C18: from French *démocrate*, on the pattern of *aristocrate* 'aristocrat'.

democratic ■ adj. **1** of, relating to, or supporting democracy. ▸ egalitarian. **2** (**Democratic**) (in the US) of or relating to the Democratic Party.
– DERIVATIVES **democratically** adv.

democratize (also **-ise**) ■ v. introduce a democratic system or democratic principles to.
– DERIVATIVES **democratization** (also **-isation**) n.

démodé /ˌdeɪməʊˈdeɪ/ ■ adj. out of fashion.
– ORIGIN French: from *démoder* 'go out of fashion'.

demodulate ■ v. Electronics extract (a modulating signal) from its carrier.
– DERIVATIVES **demodulation** n. **demodulator** n.

demographic /ˌdɛməˈɡrafɪk/ ■ adj. relating to the structure of populations. ■ n. (**demographics**) statistical data relating to the population and particular groups within it. **2** a particular sector of a population: *the drink is popular with a young demographic.*
– DERIVATIVES **demographical** adj. **demographically** adv.

demography /dɪˈmɒɡrəfi/ ■ n. the study of the structure of human populations using statistics relating to births, deaths, wealth, disease, etc.
– DERIVATIVES **demographer** n.
– ORIGIN C19: from Greek *dēmos* 'the people' + -GRAPHY.

demoiselle /ˌdɛmwɑːˈzɛl/ ■ n. archaic or poetic/literary a young woman.
– ORIGIN C16: from French, from Old French *dameisele* 'damsel'.

demoiselle crane ■ n. a small crane, breeding in SE Europe and central Asia. [*Anthropoides virgo*].

demolish /dɪˈmɒlɪʃ/ ■ v. **1** pull or knock down (a building). **2** comprehensively refute or defeat. **3** humorous eat up (food) quickly.
– DERIVATIVES **demolisher** n.
– ORIGIN C16: from French *démoliss-*, *démolir*, from Latin *demoliri*, from *de-* (expressing reversal) + *moliri* 'construct'.

demolition /ˌdɛməˈlɪʃ(ə)n/ ■ n. the action or process of demolishing or being demolished.
– ORIGIN C16: from Latin *demolitio(n-)*, from *demoliri* (see DEMOLISH).

demon[1] ■ n. **1** an evil spirit or devil. ▸ often humorous an evil or destructive person or thing: *I was a little demon, I can tell you.* **2** [as modifier] denoting a person forceful or skilful in a specified role: *a demon cook.* **3** another term for DAEMON[1].

– PHRASES **like a demon** in a very forceful, fierce, or skilful way.
– ORIGIN Middle English: from medieval Latin, from Latin *daemon* (or its diminutive *daemonium*), from Greek *daimōn* 'deity, genius'.

demon[2] ■ n. variant spelling of DAEMON[2].

demoniac /dɪˈməʊnɪak/ ■ adj. demonic. ■ n. a person supposedly possessed by an evil spirit.
– DERIVATIVES **demoniacal** adj. **demoniacally** adv.
– ORIGIN Middle English: from eccles. Latin *daemoniacus*, from *daemonium* (see DEMON[1]).

demonic /dɪˈmɒnɪk/ ■ adj. of, resembling, or characteristic of demons or evil spirits.
– DERIVATIVES **demonically** adv.

demonism /ˈdiːməniz(ə)m/ ■ n. **1** belief in the power of demons. **2** demonic action or behaviour.

demonize (also **-ise**) ■ v. portray as wicked and threatening.
– DERIVATIVES **demonization** (also **-isation**) n.

demonolatry /ˌdiːməˈnɒlətri/ ■ n. the worship of demons.

demonology ■ n. the study of demons or demonism.
– DERIVATIVES **demonological** adj. **demonologist** n.

demonstrable /dɪˈmɒnstrəb(ə)l, ˈdɛmən-/ ■ adj. clearly apparent or capable of being logically proved.
– DERIVATIVES **demonstrability** n. **demonstrably** adv.
– ORIGIN Middle English: from Latin *demonstrabilis*.

demonstrate ■ v. **1** clearly show the existence or truth of. ▸ give a practical exhibition and explanation of. **2** take part in a public demonstration.
– DERIVATIVES **demonstrator** n.
– ORIGIN C16: from Latin *demonstrare* 'point out'.

demonstration ■ n. **1** the action of demonstrating something. **2** a public meeting or march expressing protest or other opinion on an issue.

demonstrative /dɪˈmɒnstrətɪv/ ■ adj. **1** tending to show affectionate or other feelings openly. **2** serving to demonstrate something. **3** Grammar (of a determiner or pronoun) indicating the person or thing referred to (e.g. *this, that, those*). ■ n. Grammar a demonstrative determiner or pronoun.
– DERIVATIVES **demonstratively** adv. **demonstrativeness** n.

demoralize (also **-ise**) ■ v. cause to lose confidence or hope.
– DERIVATIVES **demoralization** (also **-isation**) n. **demoralized** (also **-ised**) adj. **demoralizing** (also **-ising**) adj. **demoralizingly** (also **-isingly**) adv.
– ORIGIN C18: from French *démoraliser*.

demote ■ v. give a lower rank or less senior position to, often as a punishment.
– DERIVATIVES **demotion** n.
– ORIGIN C19: from DE- + a shortened form of PROMOTE.

demotic /dɪˈmɒtɪk/ ■ adj. **1** denoting or relating to the kind of language used by ordinary people; colloquial. **2** denoting or relating to the form of modern Greek used in everyday speech and writing. Compare with KATHAR-EVOUSA. **3** denoting a simplified, cursive form of ancient Egyptian script. Compare with HIERATIC. ■ n. demotic speech, language, or writing.
– ORIGIN C19: from Greek *dēmotikos*, from *dēmotēs* 'one of the people', from *dēmos* 'the people'.

demotivate ■ v. make less eager to work or study.
– DERIVATIVES **demotivation** n.

demountable ■ adj. able to be dismantled or removed and readily reassembled or repositioned.
– DERIVATIVES **demount** v.

demur /dɪˈməː/ ■ v. (**demurred**, **demurring**) raise doubts or objections; show reluctance. ■ n. the action of demurring: *they accepted this ruling without demur.*
– DERIVATIVES **demurral** n.
– ORIGIN Middle English: from Old French *demourer* (v.), *demeure* (n.), from Latin *de-* 'away, completely' + *morari* 'delay'.

demure /dɪˈmjʊə/ ■ adj. (**-er**, **-est**) (of a woman) reserved, modest, and shy.
– DERIVATIVES **demurely** adv. **demureness** n.
– ORIGIN Middle English: perhaps from Old French *demoure*, from *demourer* (see DEMUR); influenced by Old French *mur* 'grave'.

demurrage /dɪˈmʌrɪdʒ/ ■ n. Law a charge payable to the owner of a chartered ship in respect of delay in loading or discharging.

demutualize /diːˈmjuːtʃʊəlaɪz, -tjʊə-/ (also **-ise**) ■ v. change (a mutual organization such as a building society) to one of a different kind.
– DERIVATIVES **demutualization** (also **-isation**) n.

demystify ■ v. (**-ies**, **-ied**) make (a subject) easier to understand.
– DERIVATIVES **demystification** n.

demythologize (also **-ise**) ■ v. reinterpret (a subject) so that it is free of mythical elements.

den ■ n. **1** a wild animal's lair or habitation. **2** informal a person's private room. **3** a place where people meet secretly or illicitly: *an opium den*. ■ v. (**denned**, **denning**) (of an animal) live in or retreat to a den.
– ORIGIN Old English, of Germanic origin.

denarius /dɪˈnɛːrɪəs, dɪˈnɑːrɪəs/ ■ n. (pl. **denarii** /-rɪʌɪ, -riː/) an ancient Roman silver or gold coin.
– ORIGIN Latin, 'containing ten', from *deni* 'in tens'.

denationalize (also **-ise**) ■ v. **1** transfer from public to private ownership. **2** deprive of nationality or national characteristics.
– DERIVATIVES **denationalization** (also **-isation**) n.

denature /diːˈneɪtʃə/ ■ v. **1** take away or alter the natural qualities of. **2** make (alcohol) unfit for drinking by adding toxic or foul-tasting substances.
– DERIVATIVES **denaturant** n. **denaturation** n.

dendrite /ˈdɛndrʌɪt/ ■ n. **1** Physiology a short branched extension of a nerve cell conducting impulses to the cell body. **2** a crystalline mass with a branching, tree-like structure. ▸ a natural tree-like marking on a rock or mineral.
– DERIVATIVES **dendritic** /dɛnˈdrɪtɪk/ adj. **dendritically** adv.
– ORIGIN C18: from French, from Greek *dendritēs* 'tree-like'.

dendro- /ˈdɛndrəʊ/ ■ comb. form of or relating to a tree or trees: *dendrology*.
– ORIGIN from Greek *dendron* 'tree'.

dendrochronology ■ n. a technique of dating based on the investigation of annual growth rings in tree trunks.
– DERIVATIVES **dendrochronological** adj. **dendrochronologist** n.

dendrogram /ˈdɛndrə(ʊ)gram/ ■ n. a tree diagram.

dendroid /ˈdɛndrɔɪd/ ■ adj. Biology tree-shaped; branching. ■ n. Palaeontology a graptolite of a type that formed much-branched colonies.

dendrology /dɛnˈdrɒlədʒi/ ■ n. the scientific study of trees.
– DERIVATIVES **dendrological** adj. **dendrologist** n.

dendron /ˈdɛndrɒn/ ■ n. another term for **DENDRITE** (in sense 1).
– ORIGIN C19: from **DENDRITE**, on the pattern of *axon*.

denervate /diːˈnɜːveɪt/ ■ v. Medicine cut off the nerve supply from.
– DERIVATIVES **denervation** n.

dengue /ˈdɛŋgi/ (also **dengue fever**) ■ n. a debilitating tropical viral disease transmitted by mosquitoes, causing sudden fever and acute pains in the joints.
– ORIGIN C19: from West Indian Spanish, from Kiswahili *dinga*, influenced by Spanish *dengue* 'fastidiousness' (with ref. to the dislike of movement by affected patients).

deniable ■ adj. able to be denied.
– DERIVATIVES **deniability** n. **deniably** adv.

denial ■ n. **1** the action of denying something. **2** Psychology refusal to acknowledge an unacceptable truth or emotion, used as a defence mechanism.

denier[1] /ˈdɛnɪə/ ■ n. a unit by which the fineness of yarn is measured, equal to the weight in grams of 9 000 metres of the yarn.
– ORIGIN Middle English: from Latin *denarius* (see **DENARIUS**).

denier[2] /dɪˈnʌɪə/ ■ n. a person who denies something.

denigrate /ˈdɛnɪgreɪt/ ■ v. criticize unfairly; disparage.
– DERIVATIVES **denigration** n. **denigrator** n. **denigratory** /-ˈgreɪt(ə)ri/ adj.

– ORIGIN Middle English (in the sense 'blacken'): from Latin *denigrare*, from *de-* 'away, completely' + *nigare*, from *niger* 'black'.

denim ■ n. a hard-wearing cotton twill fabric, typically blue. ▸ (**denims**) jeans or other clothes made of such fabric.
– ORIGIN C17 (as *serge denim*): from French *serge de Nîmes*, denoting serge from the manufacturing town of Nîmes.

denitrify /diːˈnʌɪtrɪfʌɪ/ ■ v. (**-ies**, **-ied**) remove the nitrates or nitrites from (soil, water, etc.) by chemical reduction.
– DERIVATIVES **denitrification** n.

denizen /ˈdɛnɪz(ə)n/ ■ n. formal or humorous an inhabitant or occupant: *denizens of field and forest*.
– ORIGIN Middle English *deynseyn*, from Old French *deinz* 'within' + *-ein* (from Latin *-aneus* '-aneous'); influenced by **CITIZEN**.

denominate /dɪˈnɒmɪneɪt/ ■ v. **1** formal call; name. **2** (**be denominated**) (of sums of money) be expressed in a specified monetary unit.
– ORIGIN Middle English: from Latin *denominare*, from *de-* 'away, formally' + *nominare* 'to name'.

denomination ■ n. **1** a recognized autonomous branch of a church or religion. **2** the face value of a banknote, coin, or postage stamp. ▸ the rank of a playing card. **3** formal a name or designation.

denominational ■ adj. of or relating to a particular religious denomination.
– DERIVATIVES **denominationalism** n.

denominator ■ n. Mathematics the number below the line in a vulgar fraction; a divisor.
– ORIGIN C16: from French *dénominateur* or medieval Latin *denominator*.

de nos jours /ˌdə nəʊ ˈʒʊə/ ■ adj. [postpos.] contemporary.
– ORIGIN French, 'of our days'.

denote /dɪˈnəʊt/ ■ v. be a sign of; indicate. ▸ stand as a name or symbol for.
– DERIVATIVES **denotation** n. **denotational** adj. **denotative** /-tətɪv/ adj.
– ORIGIN C16: from French *dénoter* or Latin *denotare*, from *de-* 'away, thoroughly' + *notare* 'observe, note'.

denouement /deɪˈnuːmɒ̃/ ■ n. the final part of a play, film, or narrative in which matters are explained or resolved.
– ORIGIN C18: French *dénouement*, from *dénouer* 'unknot'.

denounce ■ v. publicly declare to be wrong or evil.
– DERIVATIVES **denouncement** n. **denouncer** n.
– ORIGIN Middle English: from Old French *denoncier*, from Latin *denuntiare*, from *nuntius* 'messenger'.

dense ■ adj. **1** closely compacted in substance. ▸ crowded closely together. **2** informal (of a person) stupid.
– DERIVATIVES **densely** adv. **denseness** n. **densification** n. **densify** v.
– ORIGIN Middle English: from Latin *densus*.

density ■ n. (pl. **-ies**) the degree of compactness of a substance. ▸ the opacity of a photographic image. ▸ the quantity of people or things in a given area or space.
– ORIGIN C17: from French *densité* or Latin *densitas*, from *densus* 'dense'.

dent ■ n. a slight hollow in a hard even surface made by a blow or pressure. ■ v. **1** mark with a dent. **2** have an adverse effect on.
– ORIGIN Middle English: var. of **DINT**.

dental ■ adj. **1** of or relating to the teeth or dentistry. **2** Phonetics (of a consonant) pronounced with the tip of the tongue against the upper front teeth (as *th*) or the alveolar ridge (as *n, d, t*).
– DERIVATIVES **dentalize** (also **-ise**) v. **dentally** adv.
– ORIGIN C16: from late Latin *dentalis*, from Latin *dens*, *dent-* 'tooth'.

dental surgeon ■ n. a dentist.

dental technician ■ n. a person who makes and repairs artificial teeth.

dentary /ˈdɛnt(ə)ri/ ■ n. (pl. **-ies**) Zoology the bone of the lower jaw which bears the teeth.
– ORIGIN C19: from late Latin *dentarius*.

ʊ put   uː too   ʌɪ my   aʊ how   eɪ day   əʊ no   ɪə near   ɔɪ boy   ʊə poor   ʌɪə fire   aʊə sour

dentate

dentate /ˈdɛnteɪt/ ■ adj. Botany & Zoology having a tooth-like or serrated edge.
– ORIGIN Middle English: from Latin *dentatus*.

dentelle /dɛnˈtɛl/ ■ n. (pl. pronounced same) ornamental tooling used in bookbinding, resembling lace edging.
– ORIGIN C19: from French, 'lace'.

denticle /ˈdɛntɪk(ə)l/ ■ n. Zoology a small tooth or tooth-like projection.
– ORIGIN Middle English: from Latin *denticulus*, diminutive of *dens, dent-* 'tooth'.

denticulate /dɛnˈtɪkjʊlət/ ■ adj. having small teeth or tooth-like projections.
– DERIVATIVES **denticulated** adj.

dentifrice /ˈdɛntɪfrɪs/ ■ n. a paste or powder for cleaning the teeth.
– ORIGIN Middle English: from French, from Latin *dentifricium*, from *dens, dent-* 'tooth' + *fricare* 'to rub'.

dentil /ˈdɛntɪl/ ■ n. Architecture one of a series of small tooth-like rectangular blocks used as a decoration under the moulding of a cornice.
– ORIGIN C16: from Italian *dentello* or obsolete French *dentille*, diminutive of *dent* 'tooth'.

dentine /ˈdɛntiːn/ (US **dentin** /-tɪn/) ■ n. hard dense bony tissue forming the bulk of a tooth.
– DERIVATIVES **dentinal** /ˈdɛntɪn(ə)l/ adj.
– ORIGIN C19: from Latin *dens, dent-* 'tooth'.

dentist ■ n. a person who is qualified to treat the diseases and conditions that affect the teeth and gums.
– DERIVATIVES **dentistry** n.
– ORIGIN C18: from French *dentiste*, from *dent* 'tooth'.

dentition /dɛnˈtɪʃ(ə)n/ ■ n. the arrangement or condition of the teeth in a particular species or individual.
– ORIGIN C16: from Latin *dentitio(n-)*, from *dentire* 'teethe'.

denture /ˈdɛntʃə/ ■ n. a removable plate or frame holding one or more artificial teeth.
– DERIVATIVES **denturist** n.
– ORIGIN C19: from French.

denuclearize (also -**ise**) ■ v. remove nuclear weapons from.
– DERIVATIVES **denuclearization** (also -**isation**) n.

denude ■ v. (often **be denuded of**) strip of covering or possessions; make bare.
– DERIVATIVES **denudation** n.
– ORIGIN Middle English: from Latin *denudare*, from *de-* 'completely' + *nudare* 'to bare'.

denumerable /dɪˈnjuːm(ə)rəb(ə)l/ ■ adj. Mathematics able to be counted by correspondence with the set of integers.
– DERIVATIVES **denumerability** n. **denumerably** adv.
– ORIGIN C20: from late Latin *denumerare* 'count out'.

denunciation /dɪˌnʌnsɪˈeɪʃ(ə)n/ ■ n. the action of denouncing someone or something.
– DERIVATIVES **denunciator** n. **denunciatory** adj.
– ORIGIN Middle English: from Latin *denuntiatio(n-)*, from *denuntiare* (see DENOUNCE).

deny /dɪˈnaɪ/ ■ v. (-**ies**, -**ied**) 1 refuse to admit the truth or existence of. 2 refuse to give (something requested or desired) to (someone). ▶ archaic refuse access to. ▶ (**deny oneself**) go without.
– ORIGIN Middle English: from Old French *deneier*, from Latin *denegare*, from *de-* 'formally' + *negare* 'say no'.

deodar /ˈdiːəʊdɑː/ ■ n. a tall cedar with drooping branches, native to the Himalayas. [*Cedrus deodara*.]
– ORIGIN C19: from Hindi, from Sanskrit *devadāru* 'divine tree'.

deodorant /dɪˈəʊd(ə)r(ə)nt/ ■ n. a substance which removes or conceals unpleasant bodily odours.
– ORIGIN C19: from DE- + Latin *odor* 'smell'.

deodorize (also -**ise**) ■ v. remove or conceal an unpleasant smell in.
– DERIVATIVES **deodorization** (also -**isation**) n. **deodorizer** (also -**iser**) n.

deontic /dɪˈɒntɪk/ ■ adj. Philosophy of or relating to duty and obligation as ethical concepts.
– ORIGIN C20: from Greek *deont-* 'being right', from *dei* 'it is right'.

deontology /ˌdiːɒnˈtɒlədʒi/ ■ n. Philosophy the study of the nature of duty and obligation.
– DERIVATIVES **deontological** adj. **deontologist** n.

Deo volente /ˌdeɪəʊ vɒˈlɛnteɪ/ ■ adv. God willing; if nothing prevents it.
– ORIGIN from Latin.

deoxygenate /diːˈɒksɪdʒəneɪt/ ■ v. remove oxygen from.
– DERIVATIVES **deoxygenation** n.

deoxyribonucleic acid /dɪˌɒksɪrʌɪbəʊnjuːˈkleɪɪk/ ■ n. see DNA.
– ORIGIN 1930s: from a blend of DEOXYRIBOSE and NUCLEIC ACID.

deoxyribose /dɪˌɒksɪˈrʌɪbəʊz, -s/ ■ n. Biochemistry a sugar derived from ribose by replacement of a hydroxyl group by hydrogen.
– ORIGIN 1930s: from DE- (expressing reduction) + OXY-^{2} + RIBOSE.

dep. ■ abbrev. 1 departs. 2 deputy.

depart ■ v. 1 leave, especially in order to start a journey. 2 (**depart from**) deviate from (a course of action).
– PHRASES **depart this life** archaic die.
– ORIGIN Middle English: from Old French *departir*, from Latin *dispertire* 'to divide'.

departed ■ adj. deceased.

department ■ n. 1 a division of a large organization or building, dealing with a specific area of activity. 2 an administrative district in France and other countries. 3 (**one's department**) informal an area of special expertise or responsibility. ▶ informal a specified aspect or quality: *he was a bit lacking in the height department*.
– DERIVATIVES **departmental** adj. **departmentalism** n. **departmentalization** (also -**isation**) n. **departmentalize** (also -**ise**) v. **departmentally** adv.
– ORIGIN Middle English: from Old French *departement*, from *departir* (see DEPART).

department store ■ n. a large shop stocking many varieties of goods in different departments.

departure ■ n. 1 the action of departing. 2 Nautical the amount of a ship's change of longitude.
– ORIGIN Middle English: from Old French *departeure*.

depend ■ v. 1 (**depend on**) be controlled or determined by. 2 (**depend on**) rely on.
– PHRASES **depending on** according to.
– ORIGIN Middle English: from Old French *dependre*, from Latin *dependere*, from *de-* 'down' + *pendere* 'hang'.

dependable ■ adj. trustworthy and reliable.
– DERIVATIVES **dependability** n. **dependably** adv.

dependant (also **dependent**) ■ n. a person who relies on another, especially a family member, for financial support.

dependency ■ n. (pl. -**ies**) 1 a country or province controlled by another. 2 the state of being dependent.

dependent ■ adj. 1 (**dependent on**) contingent on or determined by. 2 relying on someone or something for financial or other support. ▶ (**dependent on**) unable to do without: *dependent on drugs*. 3 Grammar subordinate to another clause, phrase, or word. ■ n. variant spelling of DEPENDANT.
– DERIVATIVES **dependence** n. **dependently** adv.
– ORIGIN Middle English *dependant* 'hanging down', from Old French, from *dependre* (see DEPEND).

dependent variable ■ n. Mathematics a variable (often denoted by *y*) whose value depends on that of another.

depersonalize (also -**ise**) ■ v. divest of human characteristics or individuality.
– DERIVATIVES **depersonalization** (also -**isation**) n.

depict /dɪˈpɪkt/ ■ v. represent by a drawing, painting, or other art form. ▶ portray in words.
– DERIVATIVES **depicter** n. **depiction** n.
– ORIGIN Middle English: from Latin *depict-, depingere*, from *de-* 'completely' + *pingere* 'to paint'.

depilate /ˈdɛpɪleɪt/ ■ v. remove the hair from.
– DERIVATIVES **depilation** n. **depilator** n.
– ORIGIN C16: from Latin *depilare*, from *de-* (expressing removal) + *pilare*, from *pilus* 'hair'.

depilatory /dɪˈpɪlət(ə)ri/ ■ adj. used to remove unwanted hair. ■ n. (pl. -**ies**) a depilatory cream or lotion.

deplete /dɪˈpliːt/ ■ v. reduce the number or quantity of: *fish stocks are severely depleted*. ▶ exhaust.
– DERIVATIVES **depletion** n.

–ORIGIN C19: from Latin *deplere* 'empty out', from *de-* (expressing reversal) + *plere* 'fill'.

depleted uranium ■ n. uranium from which most of the fissile isotope uranium-235 has been removed.

deplorable /dɪˈplɔːrəb(ə)l/ ■ adj. deserving strong condemnation; shockingly bad.
–DERIVATIVES **deplorably** adv.

deplore /dɪˈplɔː/ ■ v. feel or express strong disapproval of.
–DERIVATIVES **deploring** adj. **deploringly** adv.
–ORIGIN C16 (in the sense 'weep for'): from French or Italian, from Latin *deplorare*, from *de-* 'away, thoroughly' + *plorare* 'bewail'.

deploy /dɪˈplɔɪ/ ■ v. bring or move into position for military action. ▸ bring into effective action.
–DERIVATIVES **deployment** n.
–ORIGIN C18: from French *déployer*, from Latin *displicare* and late Latin *deplicare* 'unfold, explain'.

depolarize /diːˈpəʊləraɪz/ (also **-ise**) ■ v. Physics reduce or remove the polarization of.
–DERIVATIVES **depolarization** (also **-isation**) n.

depoliticize (also **-ise**) ■ v. remove from political activity or influence.
–DERIVATIVES **depoliticization** (also **-isation**) n.

depolymerize /diːˈpɒlɪməraɪz/ (also **-ise**) ■ v. Chemistry break (a polymer) down into smaller units.
–DERIVATIVES **depolymerization** (also **-isation**) n.

deponent /dɪˈpəʊnənt/ ■ n. Law a person who makes a deposition or affidavit under oath.
–ORIGIN Middle English: from Latin *deponere* 'lay aside, put down'.

depopulate ■ v. substantially reduce the population of (an area).
–DERIVATIVES **depopulation** n.

deport ■ v. **1** expel (a foreigner or immigrant) from a country. **2** (**deport oneself**) archaic conduct oneself in a specified manner.
–DERIVATIVES **deportable** adj. **deportation** n. **deportee** n.
–ORIGIN C16: from French *déporter*, from Latin *deportare*, from *de-* 'away' + *portare* 'carry'.

deportment ■ n. **1** chiefly Brit. the way a person stands and walks, particularly as an element of etiquette. **2** chiefly N. Amer. a person's behaviour or manners.

depose ■ v. **1** remove from office suddenly and forcefully. **2** Law testify to or give (evidence) on oath, especially in writing.
–ORIGIN Middle English: from Old French *deposer*, from Latin *deponere* (see **DEPONENT**), but influenced by Latin *depositus* and Old French *poser* 'to place'.

deposit ■ n. **1** a sum of money placed in a bank or other account. **2** a sum payable as a first instalment or as a pledge. ▸ a returnable sum paid to cover possible loss or damage. **3** a layer or body of accumulated matter. **4** the action of depositing something. ■ v. (**deposited**, **depositing**) **1** put or set down in a specific place. ▸ lay down naturally as a layer or covering. **2** store or entrust with someone for safe keeping. ▸ pay as a deposit.
–DERIVATIVES **depositor** n.
–ORIGIN C16: from Latin *depositum* (n.), medieval Latin *depositare* (v.), both from Latin *deponere* 'lay aside'.

deposit account ■ n. chiefly Brit. a bank account that pays interest and may not be drawn on without notice.

depositary (also **depository**) ■ n. (pl. **-ies**) a person to whom something is lodged in trust.

deposition /ˌdɛpəˈzɪʃ(ə)n, diː-/ ■ n. **1** the action of deposing a monarch. **2** Law the process of giving sworn evidence. ▸ a statement to be used as evidence. **3** the action of depositing something.
–ORIGIN Middle English: from Latin *depositio(n-)*, from *deponere* (see **DEPOSIT**).

depository ■ n. (pl. **-ies**) **1** a place where things are stored. **2** variant spelling of **DEPOSITARY**.

depot /ˈdɛpəʊ/ ■ n. **1** a place for the storage of large quantities of a commodity. **2** a place where buses, trains, or other vehicles are housed and maintained. ▸ N. Amer. a railway or bus station. **3** the headquarters of a regiment.
–ORIGIN C18: from French *dépôt*, from Latin *depositum* (see **DEPOSIT**).

depower ■ v. Nautical adjust a sail so that the wind no longer fills it.

depth

deprave /dɪˈpreɪv/ ■ v. lead away from what is natural or right; corrupt.
–DERIVATIVES **depravation** n. **depravity** /dɪˈpravɪti/ n.
–ORIGIN Middle English: from Old French *depraver* or Latin *depravare*, from *de-* 'down, thoroughly' + *pravus* 'crooked, perverse'.

depraved ■ adj. morally corrupt.

deprecate /ˈdɛprɪkeɪt/ ■ v. **1** express disapproval of. **2** another term for **DEPRECIATE** (in sense 2).
–DERIVATIVES **deprecating** adj. **deprecatingly** adv. **deprecation** n. **deprecative** /ˈdɛprɪkətɪv/ adj. **deprecator** n.
–ORIGIN C17 (*deprecation* Middle English, in the sense 'a prayer to ward off evil'): from Latin *deprecari*, from *de-* (expressing reversal) + *precari* 'pray'.

deprecatory /ˈdɛprɪkət(ə)ri, ˌdɛprɪˈkeɪt-/ ■ adj. expressing disapproval. ▸ apologetic or appeasing.

depreciate /dɪˈpriːʃɪeɪt, -sɪ-/ ■ v. **1** diminish in value over a period of time. ▸ reduce the recorded value of (an asset) over a predetermined period. **2** disparage or belittle.
–DERIVATIVES **depreciation** n. **depreciatory** / dɪˈpriːʃ(ɪ)ət(ə)ri/ adj.
–ORIGIN Middle English: from late Latin *depreciare*, from Latin *de-* 'down' + *pretium* 'price'.

depredation /ˌdɛprɪˈdeɪʃ(ə)n/ ■ n. (usu. **depredations**) an act of attacking or plundering.
–ORIGIN C15: from French *déprédation*, from late Latin *depraedatio(n-)*, from *depraedari* 'to plunder'.

depress ■ v. **1** cause to feel utterly dispirited or dejected. **2** reduce the level of activity in (a system). **3** push or pull down into a lower position.
–DERIVATIVES **depressible** adj.
–ORIGIN Middle English: from Old French *depresser*, from late Latin *depressare*, from Latin *deprimere* 'press down'.

depressant ■ adj. reducing functional or nervous activity. ■ n. a depressant drug or other agent.

depressed ■ adj. **1** in a state of unhappiness or despondency. ▸ suffering from clinical depression. **2** suffering from economic depression. **3** having been pushed down.

depressing ■ adj. causing a feeling of miserable dejection.
–DERIVATIVES **depressingly** adv.

depression ■ n. **1** severe despondency and dejection, especially when long-lasting. ▸ a long and severe recession in an economy or market. ▸ (**the Depression** or **the Great Depression**) the financial and industrial slump of 1929 and subsequent years. **3** the action of depressing something. ▸ a sunken place or hollow. **4** Meteorology a cyclonic weather system.
–ORIGIN Middle English: from Latin *depressio(n-)*, from *deprimere* (see **DEPRESS**).

depressive ■ adj. tending to causing depression. ■ n. a person who tends to suffer from depression.

depressor ■ n. **1** Anatomy a muscle whose contraction pulls down a part of the body. **2** Physiology a nerve whose stimulation results in a lowering of blood pressure. **3** an instrument for pressing something down.

depressurize (also **-ise**) ■ v. release the pressure inside (a compartment or container).
–DERIVATIVES **depressurization** (also **-isation**) n.

deprivation /ˌdɛprɪˈveɪʃ(ə)n/ ■ n. the damaging lack of basic material benefits. ▸ the lack or denial of something considered essential.

deprive /dɪˈpraɪv/ ■ v. deny (a person or place) the possession or use of something.
–DERIVATIVES **deprival** n. **deprived** adj.
–ORIGIN Middle English: from Old French *depriver*, from medieval Latin *deprivare*, from *de-* 'away, completely' + *privare* (see **PRIVATE**).

de profundis /ˌdeɪ prəˈfʊndɪs/ ■ adv. expressing one's deepest feelings. ■ n. a heartfelt appeal.
–ORIGIN Latin, 'from the depths', the opening words of Psalm 130.

Dept ■ abbrev. Department.

depth ■ n. **1** the distance from the top or surface to the bottom of something or to a specified point within it.
▸ distance from the front to the back of something. ▸ the

depth charge

apparent existence of three dimensions in a two-dimensional representation. **2** complexity and profundity of thought. ▶ comprehensiveness of study or detail: *third-year courses go into more depth.* ▶ creditable intensity of emotion. **3** (**the depths**) the deepest or lowest part of something.
– PHRASES **hidden depths** previously unnoticed qualities. **in depth** in great detail; comprehensively and thoroughly. **out of one's depth 1** in water too deep to stand in. **2** in a situation beyond one's capabilities.
– ORIGIN Middle English: from DEEP + -TH², on the pattern of *long, length*.

depth charge ■ n. an explosive charge designed to explode under water at a preset depth, used for attacking submarines.

deputation ■ n. a group of people who undertake a mission on behalf of a larger group.

depute /dɪˈpjuːt/ ■ v. appoint (someone) to perform a task for which one is responsible. ▶ delegate (authority or a task).
– ORIGIN Middle English: from Latin *deputare* 'consider to be, assign', from *de-* 'away' + *putare* 'think over'.

deputize /ˈdɛpjʊtʌɪz/ (also **-ise**) ■ v. temporarily act or speak on behalf of someone else. ▶ N. Amer. make (someone) a deputy.

deputy ■ n. (pl. **-ies**) **1** a person appointed to undertake the duties of a superior in the superior's absence. **2** a parliamentary representative in certain countries.
– ORIGIN Middle English: from Old French *depute*, from late Latin *deputatus*, from *deputare* (see DEPUTE).

deracinate /dɪˈrasɪneɪt/ ■ v. **1** tear up by the roots. **2** [as adj. **deracinated**] displaced from one's environment.
– DERIVATIVES **deracination** n.
– ORIGIN C16: from French *déraciner*, from *dé-* (expressing removal) + *racine* 'root'.

derail ■ v. cause (a train) to leave the tracks.
– DERIVATIVES **derailment** n.
– ORIGIN C19: from French *dérailler*.

derange ■ v. **1** [usu. as adj. **deranged**] cause to become insane. **2** throw into disorder.
– DERIVATIVES **derangement** n.
– ORIGIN C18: from French *déranger*, from Old French *desrengier* 'move from orderly rows'.

Derby /ˈdɑːbɪ/ ■ n. (pl. **-ies**) **1** Brit. an annual flat race at Epsom in Surrey for three-year-old horses, founded in 1780 by the 12th Earl of Derby. ▶ [in names] a similar race or other important sporting contest. **2** (**derby**; also **local derby**) a sports match between two rival teams from the same area. **3** (**derby**) N. Amer. a bowler hat.

derecognize (also **-ise**) ■ v. withdraw recognition of.
– DERIVATIVES **derecognition** n.

dereference /diːˈrɛfərəns/ ■ v. Computing obtain the address of a data item held in another location from (a pointer).

deregister ■ v. remove from a register.
– DERIVATIVES **deregistration** n.

deregulate ■ v. remove regulations or restrictions from.
– DERIVATIVES **deregulation** n. **deregulatory** adj.

derelict ■ adj. **1** in a very poor condition as a result of disuse and neglect. **2** chiefly N. Amer. shamefully negligent. ■ n. **1** a destitute person. **2** a ship or other piece of property abandoned by its owner.
– ORIGIN C17: from Latin *derelict-*, *derelinquere* 'abandon', from *de-* 'completely' + *relinquere* 'forsake'.

dereliction ■ n. **1** the state of having been abandoned and become dilapidated. **2** (usu. **dereliction of duty**) shameful failure to fulfil one's obligations.

derestrict ■ v. remove restrictions from.
– DERIVATIVES **derestriction** n.

deride /dɪˈrʌɪd/ ■ v. express contempt for; ridicule.
– DERIVATIVES **derider** n.
– ORIGIN C16: from Latin *deridere* 'scoff at'.

de-rig ■ v. dismantle the rigging of.

de rigueur /də rɪˈɡəː/ ■ adj. required by etiquette or current fashion.
– ORIGIN C19: French, 'in strictness'.

derision /dɪˈrɪʒ(ə)n/ ■ n. contemptuous ridicule or mockery.
– DERIVATIVES **derisible** /dɪˈrɪzɪb(ə)l/ adj.
– ORIGIN Middle English: from late Latin *derisio(n-)*, from Latin *deridere* 'scoff at'.

derisive /dɪˈrʌɪsɪv, -z-/ ■ adj. expressing contempt or ridicule.
– DERIVATIVES **derisively** adv. **derisiveness** n.

derisory /dɪˈrʌɪs(ə)ri, -z-/ ■ adj. **1** ridiculously small or inadequate. **2** another term for DERISIVE.

derivation ■ n. **1** the deriving of something from a source or origin. **2** the formation of a word from another word or from a root in the same or another language.
– DERIVATIVES **derivational** adj.

derivative /dɪˈrɪvətɪv/ ■ adj. **1** chiefly derogatory imitative of the work of another artist, writer, etc. **2** (of a financial product) having a value deriving from an underlying variable asset. ■ n. **1** something which is derived from another source. **2** (often **derivatives**) Finance a derivative future, option, or other financial product. **3** Mathematics an expression representing the rate of change of a function with respect to an independent variable.
– DERIVATIVES **derivatively** adv.
– ORIGIN Middle English: from French *dérivatif*, from Latin *derivativus*, from *derivare* (see DERIVE).

derive /dɪˈrʌɪv/ ■ v. **1** (**derive something from**) obtain something from (a specified source). ▶ base something on a modification of: *Marx derived his philosophy of history from Hegel*. ▶ Mathematics obtain a function or equation from another, especially by differentiation. **2** (**derive from**) have as a root or origin; originate from.
– DERIVATIVES **derivable** adj.
– ORIGIN Middle English (in the sense 'draw a fluid through or into a channel'): from Old French *deriver* or Latin *derivare*, from *de-* 'down, away' + *rivus* 'brook, stream'.

dermabrasion /ˌdəːməˈbreɪʒ(ə)n/ ■ n. (in cosmetic surgery) the removal of superficial layers of skin with an abrasive tool.
– ORIGIN 1950s: from Greek *derma* 'skin' + ABRASION.

dermatitis /ˌdəːməˈtʌɪtɪs/ ■ n. inflammation of the skin as a result of irritation by or allergic reaction to an external agent.
– ORIGIN C19: from Greek *derma*, *dermat-* 'skin' + -ITIS.

dermato- /ˈdəːmətəʊ/ ■ comb. form of or relating to the skin: *dermatomyositis*.
– ORIGIN from Greek *derma*, *dermat-* 'skin'.

dermatology /ˌdəːməˈtɒlədʒi/ ■ n. the branch of medicine concerned with skin disorders.
– DERIVATIVES **dermatological** adj. **dermatologically** adv. **dermatologist** n.

dermatomyositis /ˌdəːmətə(ʊ)mʌɪə(ʊ)ˈsʌɪtɪs/ ■ n. Medicine inflammation of the skin and underlying muscle tissue.

dermatosis /ˌdəːməˈtəʊsɪs/ ■ n. (pl. **dermatoses** /-siːz/) a disease of the skin, especially one that does not cause inflammation.

dermestid /dəːˈmɛstɪd/ ■ n. Entomology a small beetle of a family (Dermestidae) including many kinds destructive to materials such as hides and wool.
– ORIGIN C19: from the genus name *Dermestes*, from Greek *derma* 'skin' + *esthiein* 'eat'.

dermis /ˈdəːmɪs/ ■ n. technical the skin. ▶ Anatomy the thick layer of living tissue below the epidermis, containing blood capillaries, nerve endings, sweat glands, hair follicles, and other structures.
– DERIVATIVES **dermal** adj.
– ORIGIN C19: modern Latin, suggested by *epidermis*.

dermoid cyst ■ n. Medicine an abnormal growth containing epidermis, hair follicles, and sebaceous glands, derived from residual embryonic cells.

dernier cri /ˌdəːnjeɪ ˈkriː/ ■ n. the very latest fashion.
– ORIGIN C19: French, 'last cry'.

derogate /ˈdɛrəɡeɪt/ ■ v. formal **1** (**derogate from**) detract from. **2** (**derogate from**) deviate from: *one country derogated from the Rome Convention*. **3** disparage.
– DERIVATIVES **derogation** n. **derogative** adj.
– ORIGIN Middle English: from Latin *derogare* 'abrogate', from *de-* 'aside, away' + *rogare* 'ask'.

derogatory /dɪˈrɒɡət(ə)ri/ ■ adj. showing a critical or disrespectful attitude.

– DERIVATIVES **derogatorily** adv.

derrick /ˈdɛrɪk/ ■ n. **1** a kind of crane with a movable pivoted arm. **2** the framework over an oil well, holding the drilling machinery.
– ORIGIN C17 (denoting a hangman, also the gallows): from *Derrick*, the surname of a London hangman.

derrière /ˌdɛrɪˈɛː/ ■ n. euphemistic or humorous a person's buttocks.
– ORIGIN C18: French, 'behind'.

derring-do /ˌdɛrɪŋˈduː/ ■ n. dated or humorous action displaying heroic courage.
– ORIGIN C16: from Middle English *dorryng do* 'daring to do', misprinted as *derrynge do* and misinterpreted by the Elizabethan poet Edmund Spenser.

derringer /ˈdɛrɪn(d)ʒə/ ■ n. a small pistol with a large bore, effective at close range.
– ORIGIN C19: named after the American gunsmith Henry *Deringer*.

dervish /ˈdəːvɪʃ/ ■ n. a member of a Muslim fraternity vowed to poverty and known for their wild rituals.
– ORIGIN from Turkish *derviş*, from Persian *darvīš* 'poor'.

desacralize /diːˈsakrəlʌɪz/ (also **-ise**) ■ v. remove the religious or sacred status or significance from.
– DERIVATIVES **desacralization** (also **-isation**) n.

desalinate /diːˈsalɪneɪt/ ■ v. remove salt from (sea-water).
– DERIVATIVES **desalination** n. **desalinator** n.

desalinize (also **-ise**) ■ v. US term for DESALINATE.
– DERIVATIVES **desalinization** (also **-isation**) n.

desalt ■ v. another term for DESALINATE.

desaparecido /ˌdɛzəparəˈsiːdəʊ/ ■ n. (pl. **-os**) a person who has disappeared, presumed killed by soldiers or police.
– ORIGIN 1970s: Spanish (first used in Argentina), 'disappeared'.

desaturate ■ v. make less saturated or unsaturated.
– DERIVATIVES **desaturation** n.

descale ■ v. remove deposits of scale from.
– DERIVATIVES **descaler** n.

descant /ˈdɛskant/ ■ n. Music an independent treble melody sung or played above a basic melody. ▶ archaic or poetic/literary a melodious song.
– ORIGIN Middle English: from Old French *deschant*, from medieval Latin *discantus* 'part song, refrain'.

descant recorder ■ n. the most common size of recorder, with a range of two octaves above the C above middle C.

descend ■ v. **1** move downwards. ▶ (of a road or flight of steps) slope or lead down. **2** (**descend on**) make a sudden attack on or unwelcome visit to. **3** (**be descended from**) be a blood relative of (an ancestor). ▶ pass by inheritance.
– DERIVATIVES **descendent** adj.
– ORIGIN Middle English: from Old French *descendre*, from Latin *descendere*, from *de-* 'down' + *scandere* 'to climb'.

descendant ■ n. a person, animal, etc. that is descended from a particular ancestor.

descender ■ n. a part of a letter that extends below the line (as in g and p).

descent ■ n. **1** the action of descending. ▶ a downward slope. **2** a person's origin or nationality: *the settlers were of Cornish descent*. ▶ transmission by inheritance. **3** (**descent on**) a sudden violent attack.
– ORIGIN Middle English: from Old French *descente*, from *descendre* (see DESCEND).

descramble ■ v. restore (a signal) to intelligible form.
– DERIVATIVES **descrambler** n.

describe ■ v. **1** give a detailed account in words of. **2** mark out or draw (a geometrical figure).
– DERIVATIVES **describable** adj. **describer** n.
– ORIGIN Middle English: from Latin *describere*, from *de-* 'down' + *scribere* 'write'.

description ■ n. **1** a spoken or written account of a person, object, or event. ▶ the process of describing. **2** a sort, kind, or class: *people of any description*.
– PHRASES **beyond description** to a great and astonishing extent. **defy description** be so remarkable as to be impossible to describe.

descriptive ■ adj. **1** serving or seeking to describe. **2** describing or classifying without expressing judgement.
– DERIVATIVES **descriptively** adv. **descriptiveness** n.

descriptor ■ n. an element or term that serves to describe, identify, or index something.

descry /dɪˈskrʌɪ/ ■ v. (**-ies**, **-ied**) poetic/literary catch sight of.
– ORIGIN Middle English: perhaps confused with obsolete *descry* 'describe', var. of obsolete *descrive* 'perceive'.

desecrate /ˈdɛsɪkreɪt/ ■ v. treat (a sacred place or thing) with violent disrespect.
– DERIVATIVES **desecration** n. **desecrator** n.
– ORIGIN C17: from DE- (expressing reversal) + a shortened form of CONSECRATE.

deseed ■ v. remove the seeds from.
– DERIVATIVES **deseeder** n.

desegregate ■ v. end a policy of racial segregation in.
– DERIVATIVES **desegregation** n.

deselect ■ v. **1** Brit. reject the candidature of (an existing MP). **2** Computing turn off (a feature) on a list of options.
– DERIVATIVES **deselection** n.

desensitize (also **-ise**) ■ v. **1** make less sensitive. **2** make indifferent to cruelty or suffering.
– DERIVATIVES **desensitization** (also **-isation**) n. **desensitizer** (also **-iser**) n.

desert[1] /dɪˈzəːt/ ■ v. **1** callously or treacherously abandon. **2** [usu. as adj. **deserted**] leave (a place), causing it to appear empty. **3** illegally run away from military service.
– DERIVATIVES **desertion** n.
– ORIGIN Middle English: from Old French *deserter*, from late Latin *desertare*, from Latin *desertus* (see DESERT[2]).

desert[2] /ˈdɛzət/ ■ n. **1** a waterless, desolate area of land with little or no vegetation, typically covered with sand. **2** a situation or area considered dull and uninteresting: *a cultural desert*. ■ adj. like a desert; uninhabited and desolate.
– ORIGIN Middle English: from late Latin *desertum* 'something left waste', from Latin *deserere* 'leave, forsake'.

desert[3] /dɪˈzəːt/ ■ n. (usu. **deserts**) a person's worthiness or entitlement to reward or punishment.
– PHRASES **get** (or **receive**) **one's just deserts** receive the appropriate reward or (more usually) punishment.
– ORIGIN Middle English: from Old French *deservir* (see DESERVE).

deserter ■ n. a member of the armed forces who deserts.

desertification /dɪˌzəːtɪfɪˈkeɪʃ(ə)n/ ■ n. the process by which fertile land becomes desert.

desert pavement ■ n. Geology a hard surface layer of cemented rock fragments from which fine material has been removed by the wind in arid regions.

desert rose ■ n. **1** a flower-like aggregate of mineral crystals, occurring in arid areas. **2** another term for IMPALA LILY.

desert truffle ■ n. any of a number of truffles native to arid regions of Africa and the Middle East. [Family Terfeziaceae.]

desert varnish ■ n. Geology a dark hard film of oxides formed on exposed rock surfaces in arid regions.

deserve ■ v. do something or show qualities worthy of (a reward or punishment as appropriate).
– DERIVATIVES **deserved** adj. **deservedly** adv.
– ORIGIN Middle English: from Old French *deservir*, from Latin *deservire* 'serve well or zealously'.

deserving ■ adj. worthy of favourable treatment or assistance.
– DERIVATIVES **deservingly** adv. **deservingness** n.

déshabillé /ˌdeza'biːjeɪ/ ■ n. the state of being only partly or scantily clothed.
– ORIGIN French, 'undressed'.

desiccate /ˈdɛsɪkeɪt/ ■ v. remove the moisture from.
– DERIVATIVES **desiccation** n. **desiccative** adj.
– ORIGIN C16: from Latin *desiccare* 'make thoroughly dry'.

desideratum /dɪˌzɪdəˈrɑːtəm, -ˈreɪtəm, -ˌsɪd-/ ■ n. (pl. **desiderata** /-tə/) something that is needed or wanted.
– ORIGIN C17: from Latin, 'something desired', from *desiderare* 'to desire', perhaps from *de-* 'down' + *sidus* 'star'.

design ■ n. **1** a plan or drawing produced to show the look and function or workings of something before it is

designate

built or made. ▸ the art or action of conceiving of and producing such a plan or drawing. ▸ purpose or planning that exists behind an action or object. **2** a decorative pattern. ■ v. decide upon the look and functioning of (something), especially by making a detailed drawing of it. ▸ do or plan (something) with a specific purpose in mind.
– PHRASES **by design** as a result of a plan; intentionally. **have designs on** aim to obtain, especially in an underhand way.
– ORIGIN Middle English (as a verb in the sense 'to designate'): from Latin *designare*, reinforced by French *désigner*.

designate ■ v. /ˈdɛzɪɡneɪt/ give a specified position or status to: *he was designated as prime minister*. ■ adj. /ˈdɛzɪɡnət/ [postpos.] appointed to an office or position but not yet installed: *the Director designate*.
– DERIVATIVES **designator** n.
– ORIGIN C17: from Latin *designare* (see DESIGN).

designated driver ■ n. N. Amer. a person who abstains from alcohol at a social gathering so as to be fit to drive others home.

designated hitter ■ n. Baseball a non-fielding player named to bat instead of the pitcher.

designation ■ n. the choosing and naming of someone or something to have a specified position or status. ▸ an official title or description.

designedly ■ adv. deliberately in order to produce a specific effect.

designer ■ n. a person who designs things. ▸ [as modifier] made by a famous and prestigious fashion designer: *designer clothing*.

designing ■ adj. acting in a calculating, deceitful way.

desirable ■ adj. wished for as being attractive, useful, or necessary. ▸ (of a person) arousing sexual desire. ■ n. a desirable person or thing.
– DERIVATIVES **desirability** n. **desirableness** n. **desirably** adv.
– ORIGIN Middle English: from Old French, suggested by Latin *desiderabilis*, from *desiderare* (see DESIRE).

desire ■ n. a strong feeling of wanting to have something or wishing for something to happen. ▸ strong sexual feeling or appetite. ■ v. strongly wish for or want. ▸ want sexually. ▸ archaic request or entreat.
– DERIVATIVES **desirous** adj.
– ORIGIN Middle English: from Old French *desir* (n.), *desirer* (v.), from Latin *desiderare* 'to desire', perhaps from *de-* 'down' + *sidus* 'star'.

desist /dɪˈzɪst, dɪˈsɪst/ ■ v. cease; abstain.
– ORIGIN Middle English: from Old French *desister*, from Latin *desistere*, from *de-* 'down from' + *sistere* 'to stop'.

desk ■ n. **1** a piece of furniture with a flat or sloped surface and typically with drawers, at which one can read, write, or do other work. **2** Music a position in an orchestra at which two players share a music stand. **3** a counter in a hotel, bank, airport, etc. **4** a specified section of a news organization.
– ORIGIN Middle English: from medieval Latin *desca*, prob. from Provençal *desca* 'basket' or Italian *desco* 'table, butcher's block', both from Latin *discus*, from Greek *diskos* (see DISCUS).

desk job ■ n. a clerical or administrative job.

desktop ■ n. **1** the working surface of a desk. **2** a microcomputer suitable for use at an ordinary desk. **3** the working area of a computer screen regarded as representing a notional desktop.

desktop publishing ■ n. the production of high-quality printed matter by means of a printer linked to a desktop computer.

desmid /ˈdɛzmɪd/ ■ n. Biology a single-celled freshwater alga which appears to be composed of two rigid cells with a shared nucleus. [Family Desmidiaceae.]
– ORIGIN C19: from Greek *desmos* 'band, chain' (because the algae are often found united in chains or masses).

desolate ■ adj. /ˈdɛs(ə)lət/ giving an impression of bleak and dismal emptiness. ▸ utterly wretched and unhappy. ■ v. /ˈdɛsəleɪt/ make desolate.
– DERIVATIVES **desolately** adv. **desolateness** n. **desolation** n. **desolator** n.
– ORIGIN Middle English: from Latin *desolare* 'abandon', from *de-* 'thoroughly' + *solus* 'alone'.

desorb /diːˈsɔːb/ ■ v. Chemistry cause the release of (an adsorbed substance) from a surface.
– DERIVATIVES **desorbent** adj. & n. **desorber** n. **desorption** n.
– ORIGIN 1920s: orig. as *desorption*, from *de-* 'away' + *adsorption*.

despair ■ n. the complete loss or absence of hope. ■ v. lose or be without hope.
– PHRASES **be the despair of** be the cause of despair in (someone else).
– DERIVATIVES **despairing** adj. **despairingly** adv.
– ORIGIN Middle English: from Old French *desespeir* (n.), *desperer* (v.), from Latin *desperare*, from *de-* 'down from' + *sperare* 'to hope'.

despatch ■ v.& n. variant spelling of DISPATCH.

desperado /ˌdɛspəˈrɑːdəʊ/ ■ n. (pl. **-oes** or **-os**) dated a desperate or reckless criminal.
– DERIVATIVES **desperadoism** n.
– ORIGIN C17: pseudo-Spanish alteration of the obsolete noun *desperate*.

desperate ■ adj. **1** feeling, showing, or involving despair. ▸ tried in despair or when everything else has failed. **2** extremely bad or serious: *a desperate shortage*. **3** having a great need or desire for something. **4** violent or dangerous: *a desperate criminal*.
– DERIVATIVES **desperately** adv. **desperateness** n.
– ORIGIN Middle English: from Latin *desperatus* 'deprived of hope', from *desperare* (see DESPAIR).

desperation ■ n. a state of despair, especially as resulting in rash or extreme behaviour.

despicable /dɪˈspɪkəb(ə)l, ˈdɛspɪk-/ ■ adj. deserving hatred and contempt.
– DERIVATIVES **despicably** adv.
– ORIGIN C16: from late Latin *despicabilis*, from Latin *despicari* 'look down on'.

despise /dɪˈspaɪz/ ■ v. feel contempt or repugnance for.
– DERIVATIVES **despiser** n.
– ORIGIN Middle English: from Old French *despire*, from Latin *despicere*, from *de-* 'down' + *specere* 'look at'.

despite /dɪˈspaɪt/ ■ prep. without being affected by; in spite of. ■ n. archaic or poetic/literary **1** outrage; injury. **2** contempt; disdain.
– PHRASES **despite oneself** without intending to or expecting to.
– ORIGIN Middle English: from Old French *despit* (n.), from Latin *despectus* 'looking down on', from *despicere* (see DESPISE).

despoil /dɪˈspɔɪl/ ■ v. steal valuable or attractive possessions from (a place).
– DERIVATIVES **despoiler** n. **despoilment** n. **despoliation** /dɪˌspəʊlɪˈeɪʃ(ə)n/ n.
– ORIGIN Middle English: from Old French *despoillier*, from Latin *despoliare* 'rob, plunder', from *spolia* 'spoil'.

despondent ■ adj. in low spirits from loss of hope or courage.
– DERIVATIVES **despondence** n. **despondency** n. **despondently** adv.

despot /ˈdɛspɒt/ ■ n. a ruler who exercises absolute power, especially in a cruel or oppressive way.
– DERIVATIVES **despotic** adj. **despotically** adv. **despotism** n.
– ORIGIN C16: from French *despote*, from Greek *despotēs* 'master, absolute ruler'.

dessert /dɪˈzɜːt/ ■ n. the sweet course eaten at the end of a meal.
– ORIGIN C16: from French, from *desservir* 'clear the table'.

dessertspoon ■ n. a spoon used for dessert, smaller than a tablespoon and larger than a teaspoon.
– DERIVATIVES **dessertspoonful** n. (pl. **-fuls**).

dessert wine ■ n. a sweet wine drunk with or following dessert.

destabilize (also **-ise**) ■ v. upset the stability of.
– DERIVATIVES **destabilization** (also **-isation**) n.

destination ■ n. the place to which someone or something is going or being sent.

destine /ˈdɛstɪn/ ▪ v. (**be destined**) be intended or chosen for a particular purpose or end.
– ORIGIN Middle English: from Old French *destiner*, from Latin *destinare* 'make firm, establish'.

destiny ▪ n. (pl. **-ies**) the events that will necessarily happen to a particular person in the future. ▸ the hidden power believed to control this; fate.
– ORIGIN Middle English: from Old French *destinee*, from Latin *destinata*, from *destinare* 'make firm, establish'.

destitute /ˈdɛstɪtjuːt/ ▪ adj. **1** extremely poor and lacking the means to provide for oneself. **2** (**destitute of**) not having.
– DERIVATIVES **destitution** n.
– ORIGIN Middle English (in the sense 'deserted, abandoned'): from Latin *destituere* 'forsake'.

de-stress ▪ v. relax after a period of work or tension.

destrier /ˈdɛstrɪə, dɛˈstriːə/ ▪ n. a medieval knight's warhorse.
– ORIGIN Middle English: from Latin *dextera*, from *dexter* 'on the right' (because the squire led the knight's horse with his right hand).

destroy ▪ v. **1** put an end to the existence of (something) by damaging or attacking it. ▸ ruin emotionally or spiritually. **2** kill (an animal) by humane means.
– ORIGIN Middle English: from Old French *destruire*, from Latin *destruere*, from *de-* (expressing reversal) + *struere* 'build'.

destroyer ▪ n. **1** someone or something that destroys. **2** a small fast warship equipped for a defensive role against submarines and aircraft.

destructible ▪ adj. able to be destroyed.
– DERIVATIVES **destructibility** n.
– ORIGIN C18: from French, from late Latin *destructibilis*.

destruction ▪ n. the action or process of causing so much damage to something that it no longer exists or cannot be repaired. ▸ a cause of someone's ruin.
– ORIGIN Middle English: from Latin *destructio(n-)*, from *destruere* (see DESTROY).

destructive ▪ adj. **1** causing destruction. **2** tending to refute or disparage; negative and unhelpful.
– DERIVATIVES **destructively** adv. **destructiveness** n.

desuetude /dɪˈsjuːɪtjuːd, ˈdɛswɪ-/ ▪ n. formal a state of disuse.
– ORIGIN C17 (in the sense 'cessation'): from French, from Latin *desuetudo*, from *desuescere*, from *de-* (expressing reversal) + *suescere* 'be accustomed'.

desultory /ˈdɛs(ə)lt(ə)ri, -z-/ ▪ adj. lacking purpose or enthusiasm.
– DERIVATIVES **desultorily** adv. **desultoriness** n.
– ORIGIN C16 ('skipping about'): from Latin *desultorius* 'superficial', literally 'relating to a vaulter', from *desultor* 'vaulter'.

detach ▪ v. **1** disengage (something) and remove it. ▸ (**detach oneself from**) leave or separate oneself from (a group or place). **2** (**be detached**) Military be sent on a separate mission.
– DERIVATIVES **detachability** n. **detachable** adj.
– ORIGIN C16: from French *détacher*, from *des-* (expressing reversal) + *attacher* 'attach'.

detached ▪ adj. **1** separate or disconnected. ▸ (of a house) not joined to another on either side. **2** aloof and objective.
– DERIVATIVES **detachedly** adv.

detachment ▪ n. **1** the state of being objective or aloof. **2** Military a group of troops, ships, etc. sent away on a separate mission. **3** the action or process of detaching.

detail ▪ n. **1** a small individual feature, fact, or item. ▸ a small part of a picture reproduced separately for close study. **2** a small detachment of troops or police officers given a special duty. ▸ a special duty assigned to such a detachment. ▪ v. **1** describe item by item; give the full particulars of. **2** assign to undertake a particular task.
– PHRASES **go into detail** give a full account of something. **in detail** as regards every feature or aspect; fully.
– ORIGIN C17: from French *détail* (n.), *détailler* (v.), from *dé-* (expressing separation) + *tailler* 'to cut'.

detailed ▪ adj. including many details. ▸ showing attention to detail.

detailing ▪ n. small decorative features on a building, garment, or work of art.

detain ▪ v. **1** keep (someone) from proceeding by holding them back or making claims on their attention. **2** keep (someone) in official custody.
– DERIVATIVES **detainment** n.
– ORIGIN Middle English: from Old French *detenir*, from a var. of Latin *detinere*, from *de-* 'away, aside' + *tenere* 'to hold'.

detainee /ˌdiːteɪˈniː, ˌdiː-/ ▪ n. a person held in custody, especially for political reasons.

detect ▪ v. **1** discover or identify the presence or existence of. **2** discover or investigate (a crime or its perpetrators). **3** discern (something intangible or barely perceptible).
– DERIVATIVES **detectable** adj. **detectably** adv. **detection** n.
– ORIGIN Middle English: from Latin *detect-, detegere* 'uncover' from *de-* (expressing reversal) + *tegere* 'to cover'.

detective ▪ n. a person, especially a police officer, whose occupation is to investigate crimes.

detector ▪ n. a device designed to detect the presence of a particular object or substance and to emit a signal in response.

detent /dɪˈtɛnt/ ▪ n. a catch in a machine which prevents motion until released. ▸ (in a clock) a catch that regulates striking.
– ORIGIN C17: from French, from Old French *destente*, from *destendre* 'slacken'.

détente /deɪˈtɑːnt/ ▪ n. the easing of hostility or strained relations between countries.
– ORIGIN C20: French, 'loosening, relaxation'.

detention ▪ n. **1** the action or state of detaining or being detained. **2** the punishment of being kept in school after hours.
– ORIGIN Middle English: from late Latin *detentio(n-)*, from Latin *detinere* (see DETAIN).

detention centre ▪ n. an institution where people, in particular refugees and people awaiting trial, are detained for short periods.

deter /dɪˈtəː/ ▪ v. (**deterred**, **deterring**) discourage (someone) from doing something by instilling fear of the consequences. ▸ prevent the occurrence of.
– ORIGIN C16: from Latin *deterrere*, from *de-* 'away from' + *terrere* 'frighten'.

detergent ▪ n. a soluble cleansing agent which combines with impurities and dirt to make them more soluble. ▪ adj. of or relating to detergents or their action.
– DERIVATIVES **detergency** n.
– ORIGIN C17: from Latin *detergere* 'wipe away'.

deteriorate /dɪˈtɪərɪəreɪt/ ▪ v. become progressively worse.
– DERIVATIVES **deterioration** n.
– ORIGIN C16: from late Latin *deteriorare*, from Latin *deterior* 'worse'.

determinable ▪ adj. able to be determined.

determinant /dɪˈtəːmɪnənt/ ▪ n. a factor which determines the nature or outcome of something. ▪ adj. serving to determine or decide something.

determinate /dɪˈtəːmɪnət/ ▪ adj. **1** having exact and discernible limits or form. **2** Botany (of a flowering shoot) having the main axis ending in a flower, as in a cyme.
– DERIVATIVES **determinately** adv. **determinateness** n.

determination ▪ n. **1** the quality of being determined; firmness of purpose. **2** the process of determining something. ▸ Law the settlement of a dispute by the authoritative decision of a judge or arbitrator. ▸ Law a judicial decision or sentence.

determinative /dɪˈtəːmɪnətɪv/ ▪ adj. chiefly Law serving to define, qualify, or direct.

determine /dɪˈtəːmɪn/ ▪ v. **1** cause to occur in a particular way; be the decisive factor in. **2** firmly decide: *she determined to tackle Stephen the next day*. **3** ascertain or establish by research or calculation. **4** Mathematics specify the value, position, or form of (a mathematical or geometrical object) uniquely.
– ORIGIN Middle English: from Latin *determinare* 'limit, fix', from *de-* 'completely' + *terminare* 'terminate'.

determined

determined ■ adj. having firmness of purpose; resolute.
– DERIVATIVES **determinedly** adv. **determinedness** n.

determiner ■ n. **1** a person or thing that determines something. **2** Grammar a modifying word that determines the kind of reference a noun or noun group has, for example *a*, *the*, *every*.

determinism ■ n. Philosophy the doctrine that all events and actions are ultimately determined by causes regarded as external to the will.
– DERIVATIVES **determinist** n. & adj. **deterministic** adj. **deterministically** adv.

deterrent /dɪˈtɛr(ə)nt/ ■ n. a thing that deters or is intended to deter someone from doing something. ■ adj. able or intended to deter.
– DERIVATIVES **deterrence** n.

detest ■ v. dislike intensely.
– ORIGIN C16: from Latin *detestari*, from *de-* 'down' + *testari* '(call upon to) witness', from *testis* 'a witness'.

detestable ■ adj. deserving intense dislike.
– DERIVATIVES **detestably** adv.

detestation /ˌdiːtɛˈsteɪʃ(ə)n/ ■ n. intense dislike.

dethrone ■ v. remove (a monarch) from power. ▸ remove from a position of authority or dominance.
– DERIVATIVES **dethronement** n.

detonate /ˈdɛtəneɪt/ ■ v. explode or cause to explode.
– DERIVATIVES **detonation** n. **detonative** adj.
– ORIGIN C18: from Latin *detonare*, from *de-* 'down' + *tonare* 'to thunder'.

detonator ■ n. a device or small sensitive charge used to detonate an explosive.

detour ■ n. a roundabout route taken to avoid something or to visit somewhere along the way. ■ v. take a detour.
– ORIGIN C18: from French *détour* 'change of direction', from *détourner* 'turn away'.

detox informal ■ n. /ˈdiːtɒks/ detoxification. ■ v. /diːˈtɒks/ detoxify.

detoxify /diːˈtɒksɪfʌɪ/ ■ v. (**-ies**, **-ied**) **1** remove toxic substances or qualities from. **2** abstain or help to abstain from drink and drugs until the bloodstream is free of toxins.
– DERIVATIVES **detoxification** n. **detoxifier** n.
ORIGIN C20: from DE- | Latin *toxicum* 'poison'.

detract ■ v. (**detract from**) reduce or take away the worth or value of (a quality or achievement) so as to make it seem less impressive.
– DERIVATIVES **detraction** n.
– ORIGIN Middle English: from Latin *detract-*, *detrahere* 'draw away'.

detractor ■ n. a person who disparages someone or something.

detribalize (also **-ise**) ■ v. [usu. as adj. **detribalized** (also **-ised**)] remove from a traditional tribal social structure.
– DERIVATIVES **detribalization** (also **-isation**) n.

detriment /ˈdɛtrɪm(ə)nt/ ■ n. (often in phr. **to the detriment of**) the state of being harmed or damaged.
– ORIGIN Middle English: from Latin *detrimentum*, from *detri-*, *deterere* 'wear away'.

detrimental ■ adj. tending to cause harm.
– DERIVATIVES **detrimentally** adv.

detritivore /dɪˈtrɪtɪvɔː/ ■ n. Zoology an animal which feeds on dead organic material, especially plant detritus.
– DERIVATIVES **detritivorous** /ˌdɛtrɪˈtɪv(ə)rəs/ adj.
– ORIGIN 1960s: from DETRITUS + *-vore* 'eating' (see -VOROUS).

detritus /dɪˈtrʌɪtəs/ ■ n. waste or debris, in particular organic matter produced by decomposition or loose matter produced by erosion.
– DERIVATIVES **detrital** adj.
– ORIGIN C18: from French *détritus*, from Latin *detritus*, from *deterere* 'wear away'.

de trop /də ˈtrəʊ/ ■ adj. not wanted; unwelcome.
– ORIGIN C18: French, 'excessive'.

detrusor /dɪˈtruːsə/ ■ n. Anatomy a muscle which forms a layer of the wall of the bladder.

– ORIGIN C18: modern Latin, from Latin *detrus-*, *detrudere* 'thrust down'.

detumescence /ˌdiːtjʊˈmɛs(ə)ns/ ■ n. the process of subsiding from a state of tension, swelling, or sexual arousal.
– DERIVATIVES **detumescent** adj.
– ORIGIN C17: from Latin *detumescent-*, *detumescere*, from *de-* 'down, away' + *tumescere* 'to swell'.

detune ■ v. **1** cause (a musical instrument) to become out of tune. **2** change the frequency of (an oscillatory system such as a laser) away from a state of resonance. **3** [usu. as adj. **detuned**] reduce the performance of (a motor vehicle or engine) by adjustment.

deuce[1] /djuːs/ ■ n. **1** chiefly N. Amer. a thing representing, or represented by, the number two, in particular the two on dice or playing cards. **2** Tennis the score of 40 all in a game, at which each player needs two consecutive points to win the game.
– ORIGIN C15: from Old French *deus* 'two', from Latin *duos*.

deuce[2] /djuːs/ ■ n. (**the deuce**) informal used as a euphemism for 'devil' in exclamations or for emphasis.
– ORIGIN C17: from Low German *duus*, prob. of the same origin as DEUCE[1] (two aces at dice being the worst throw).

deurmekaar /ˌdɪəməˈkɑː/ ■ adj. S. African informal confused; disorganized.
– ORIGIN Afrikaans: from Dutch, from *door* 'through' + *malkaar* 'one another'.

deus ex machina /ˌdeɪʊs ɛks ˈmakɪnə, ˌdiːəs ɛks məˈʃiːnə/ ■ n. an unexpected power or event saving a seemingly hopeless situation, especially as a narrative device in a play or novel.
– ORIGIN C17: modern Latin, translation of Greek *theos ek mēkhanēs* 'god from the machinery' (with ref. to the actors representing gods suspended above the stage in ancient Greek theatre, who brought about the denouement of the play by their intervention).

deuteranopia /ˌdjuːt(ə)rəˈnəʊpɪə/ ■ n. colour blindness resulting from insensitivity to green light, causing confusion of greens, reds, and yellows. Compare with PROTANOPIA, TRITANOPIA.
– ORIGIN C20: from Greek *deuteros* 'second' (green being regarded as the second component of colour vision) + AN-[1] + -OPIA.

deuterated /ˈdjuːtəreɪtɪd/ (also **deuteriated** /djuːˈtɪərɪeɪtɪd/) ■ adj. Chemistry (of a compound) in which the ordinary isotope of hydrogen has been replaced with deuterium.
– DERIVATIVES **deuteration** n.

deuteric /djuːˈtɛrɪk/ ■ adj. Geology relating to or denoting alteration of the minerals of an igneous rock during the later stages of consolidation.
– ORIGIN C20: from Greek *deuteros* 'second'.

deuterium /djuːˈtɪərɪəm/ ■ n. Chemistry a stable isotope of hydrogen with a mass approximately twice that of the usual isotope. (Symbol: **D**)
– ORIGIN 1930s: modern Latin, from Greek *deuteros* 'second'.

Deutschmark /ˈdɔɪtʃmɑːk/ (also **Deutsche Mark** /ˈdɔɪtʃə mɑːk/) ■ n. the former basic monetary unit of Germany, equal to 100 pfennig.
– ORIGIN from German *deutsche Mark* 'German mark'.

deutzia /ˈdjuːtsɪə, ˈdɔɪt-/ ■ n. an ornamental shrub with white or pinkish flowers, native to Asia and Central America. [Genus *Deutzia*.]
– ORIGIN modern Latin, named after the C18 Dutch patron of botany Johann van der *Deutz*.

deva /ˈdeɪvə/ ■ n. a member of a class of divine beings in the Vedic period, which in Indian religion are benevolent and in Zoroastrianism are evil. Compare with ASURA.
– ORIGIN from Sanskrit, 'shining one'.

devalue ■ v. (**devalues**, **devalued**, **devaluing**) reduce or underestimate the worth or importance of. ▸ Economics reduce the official value of (a currency) in relation to other currencies.
– DERIVATIVES **devaluation** n.

Devanagari /ˌdeɪvəˈnɑːg(ə)ri, dɛv-/ ■ n. the alphabet used for Sanskrit, Hindi, and other Indian languages.
– ORIGIN from Sanskrit, 'divine town script', from *deva* 'god' + *nāgarī*, an earlier name of the script.

devastate /ˈdɛvəsteɪt/ ■ v. **1** destroy or ruin. **2** cause (someone) severe and overwhelming shock or grief.

VOWELS   **a** cat   **ɑː** arm   **ɛ** bed   **ɛː** hair   **ə** ago   **əː** her   **ɪ** sit   **i** cosy   **iː** see   **ɒ** hot   **ɔː** saw   **ʌ** run

–DERIVATIVES **devastation** n. **devastator** n.
–ORIGIN C17 (*devastation* Middle English): from Latin *devastare*, from *de-* 'thoroughly' + *vastare* 'lay waste'.

devastating ■ adj. 1 highly destructive or damaging. ▶ causing severe shock or grief. 2 informal extremely impressive, effective, or attractive.
–DERIVATIVES **devastatingly** adv.

develop ■ v. (**developed**, **developing**) 1 grow or cause to grow and become larger or more advanced. 2 convert (land) to a new purpose, especially by constructing buildings. 3 start to exist, experience, or possess: *I developed an interest in law.* 4 treat (a photographic film) with chemicals to make a visible image. 5 Chess bring (a piece) into play from its initial position on a player's back rank.
–DERIVATIVES **developable** adj. **developer** n.
–ORIGIN C17 (in the sense 'unfold, unfurl'): from French *développer*, based on Latin *dis-* 'un-' + a second element of unknown origin found also in ENVELOP.

developing country (also **less-developed country**) ■ n. a non-industrialized nation seeking to move towards a more advanced economy.

development ■ n. 1 the process of developing or being developed. ▶ a specified state of growth or advancement. 2 a new product or idea. 3 an event constituting a new stage in a changing situation. 4 an area of land with new buildings on it: *a major housing development.*
–DERIVATIVES **developmental** adj. **developmentally** adv.

développé /ˌdeɪvəlɒˈpeɪ/ ■ n. (pl. **développés** pronunc. same) Ballet a movement in which one leg is raised and then kept in a fully extended position.

devi /ˈdeɪvi/ ■ n. Indian a goddess.
–ORIGIN from Sanskrit.

deviant ■ adj. diverging from usual or accepted standards, especially in social or sexual behaviour. ■ n. a deviant person or thing.
–DERIVATIVES **deviance** n. **deviancy** n.
–ORIGIN Middle English: from late Latin *deviare* (see DEVIATE).

deviate ■ v. /ˈdiːvɪeɪt/ diverge from an established course or from usual or accepted standards. ■ n. & adj. /ˈdiːvɪət/ old-fashioned term for DEVIANT.
–DERIVATIVES **deviator** n.
–ORIGIN C16: from late Latin *deviare* 'turn out of the way', from Latin *de-* 'away from' + *via* 'way'.

deviation ■ n. 1 the action of deviating. 2 Statistics the amount by which a single measurement differs from a fixed value such as the mean. 3 the deflection of a ship's compass needle caused by iron in the ship.
–DERIVATIVES **deviationism** n. **deviationist** n.

device ■ n. 1 a thing made or adapted for a particular purpose, especially a mechanical or electronic contrivance. 2 a plan, scheme, or trick. ▶ a turn of phrase intended to produce a particular effect. 3 a drawing or design. ▶ an emblematic or heraldic design. 4 archaic design or look: *works of strange device.*
–PHRASES **leave someone to their own devices** leave someone to do as they wish without supervision.
–ORIGIN Middle English (in sense 'desire, intention'): from Old French *devis*, from Latin *divis-*, *dividere* 'to divide'.

devil ■ n. 1 (usu. **the Devil**) (in Christian and Jewish belief) the supreme spirit of evil; Satan. ▶ an evil spirit; a demon. 2 a very wicked or cruel person. ▶ a mischievously clever or self-willed person. 3 (**the devil**) fighting spirit; wildness: *he was born with the devil in him.* 4 (**the devil**) a thing that is very difficult or awkward to do or deal with. 5 informal a person characterized by particular circumstances: *the poor devil.* 6 (**the devil**) expressing surprise or annoyance in various questions or exclamations. 7 an instrument or machine used for tearing or other destructive work. ■ v. (**devilled**, **devilling**; US **deviled**, **deviling**) 1 informal, dated act as a junior assistant for a lawyer or other professional. 2 N. Amer. harass or worry.
–PHRASES **be a devil!** informal said when encouraging someone to do something that they are hesitating to do. **between the devil and the deep blue sea** caught in a dilemma. **devil-may-care** cheerful and reckless. **the devil's in the detail** the details of a matter are its most problematic aspect. **the devil to pay** serious trouble to be dealt with. **like the devil** with great speed or energy. **play the devil with** have a damaging or disruptive effect on. **speak** (or **talk**) **of the devil** said when a person appears just after being mentioned. [from the superstition that the devil will appear if his name is spoken.]
–ORIGIN Old English, from Greek *diabolos* 'accuser, slanderer' (used in the Septuagint to translate Hebrew *śāṭān* 'Satan'), from *diaballein* 'to slander'.

devilfish ■ n. (pl. same or **-fishes**) any of a number of marine creatures perceived as having a sinister appearance, in particular a devil ray, a stonefish, or an octopus or squid.

devilish ■ adj. of, like, or appropriate to a devil in evil and cruelty. ▶ mischievous and rakish. ▶ very difficult to deal with or use. ■ adv. informal, dated very; extremely.
–DERIVATIVES **devilishly** adv. **devilishness** n.

devilled ■ adj. (of food) cooked with hot seasoning.

devilment ■ n. reckless mischief; wild spirits.

devil ray ■ n. a manta or other large long-tailed ray with a fleshy horn-like projection on each side of the mouth. [Family Mobulidae: several species.]

devilry ■ n. wicked activity. ▶ reckless mischief. ▶ black magic; dealings with the devil.

devil's advocate ■ n. 1 a person who expresses a contentious opinion in order to provoke debate or test the strength of the opposing arguments. 2 historical a person appointed by the Roman Catholic Church to challenge a proposed beatification or canonization, or the verification of a miracle.

devil's claw ■ n. a plant whose seed pods bear claw-like hooks which can harm livestock. [Genus *Proboscidea* (warmer parts of America) and *Harpagophytum procumbens* (southern Africa).]

devil's food cake ■ n. chiefly N. Amer. a rich chocolate cake.

devils on horseback ■ pl. n. a savoury snack of prunes individually wrapped in slices of bacon.

devil's thorn ■ n. the hard sharp-pointed fruit of a herbaceous plant that can cause injury to livestock and people. [*Tribulus terrestris*, *T. zeyheri* and *Emex australis*.] ▶ the plant that bears this fruit.

deviltry ■ n. archaic variant of DEVILRY.

devious /ˈdiːvɪəs/ ■ adj. 1 skilfully using underhand tactics to achieve goals. 2 (of a route or journey) longer and less direct than the most straightforward way.
–DERIVATIVES **deviously** adv. **deviousness** n.
–ORIGIN C16: from Latin *devius*, from *de-* 'away from' + *via* 'way'.

devise /dɪˈvaɪz/ ■ v. 1 plan or invent (a complex procedure or mechanism). 2 Law leave (real property) to someone by the terms of a will.
–DERIVATIVES **devisable** adj. **deviser** n. **devisor** n.
–ORIGIN Middle English: from Old French *deviser*, from Latin *divis-*, *dividere* 'force apart, remove'.

devitalize (also **-ise**) ■ v. [usu. as adj. **devitalized** (also **-ised**)] deprive of strength and vigour.
–DERIVATIVES **devitalization** (also **-isation**) n.

devoice ■ v. Phonetics make (a vowel or voiced consonant) voiceless.

devoid /dɪˈvɔɪd/ ■ adj. (**devoid of**) entirely lacking or free from.
–ORIGIN Middle English: from obsolete *devoid* 'cast out', from Old French *devoidier*.

devolution /ˌdiːvəˈluːʃ(ə)n, dev-/ ■ n. 1 the devolving of power by central government to local or regional administration. 2 formal descent or degeneration to a lower or worse state. 3 Law the legal transfer of property from one owner to another. 4 Biology evolutionary degeneration.
–DERIVATIVES **devolutionary** adj. **devolutionist** n.

devolve /dɪˈvɒlv/ ■ v. 1 transfer or delegate (power) to a lower level, especially from central government to local or regional administration. 2 (**devolve on/upon/to**) (of duties or responsibility) pass to (a person or people at a lower level). 3 (**devolve on/upon**) Law (of property) be transferred from one owner to (another), especially by

Devonian

inheritance. **4** (**devolve into**) formal degenerate or be split into.
– DERIVATIVES **devolvement** n.
– ORIGIN Middle English (in the sense 'roll down'): from Latin *devolvere*, from *de-* 'down' + *volvere* 'to roll'.

Devonian /dɛˈvəʊnɪən, dɪ-/ ■ adj. Geology relating to or denoting the fourth period of the Palaeozoic era (between the Silurian and Carboniferous periods, about 409 to 363 million years ago), a time when the first amphibians appeared.

devoré /dəˈvɔːreɪ/ ■ n. a velvet fabric with a pattern formed by burning the pile away with acid.
– ORIGIN from French *dévoré* 'devoured', from *dévorer*.

devote ■ v. (**devote something to**) give time or resources to (a person or activity).
– ORIGIN C16 (in the sense 'dedicate formally'): from Latin *devot-*, *devovere*, from *de-* 'formally' + *vovere* 'to vow'.

devoted ■ adj. very loving or loyal.
– DERIVATIVES **devotedly** adv. **devotedness** n.

devotee /ˌdɛvə(ʊ)ˈtiː/ ■ n. **1** a person who is very interested in and enthusiastic about someone or something. **2** a follower of a particular religion or god.

devotion ■ n. **1** love, loyalty, or enthusiasm for a person or activity. **2** religious worship or observance.
▸ (**devotions**) prayers or religious observances.
– DERIVATIVES **devotional** adj.

devour /dɪˈvaʊə/ ■ v. **1** eat (food or prey) hungrily or quickly. ▸ (of fire or a similar force) consume destructively. **2** read quickly and eagerly. **3** (**be devoured**) be totally absorbed by a powerful feeling.
– DERIVATIVES **devourer** n. **devouring** adj. **devouringly** adv.
– ORIGIN Middle English: from Old French *devorer*, from Latin *devorare*, from *de-* 'down' + *vorare* 'to swallow'.

devout /dɪˈvaʊt/ ■ adj. **1** having or showing deep religious feeling or commitment. **2** earnest; sincere: *my devout hope*.
– DERIVATIVES **devoutly** adv. **devoutness** n.
– ORIGIN Middle English: from Old French *devot*, from Latin *devotus* 'devoted' from *devovere* (see **DEVOTE**).

dew ■ n. tiny drops of water that form on cool surfaces at night, when atmospheric vapour condenses. ▸ beaded or glistening liquid resembling dew. ■ v. wet with a beaded or glistening liquid.
– ORIGIN Old English, of Germanic origin.

dewan /dɪˈwɑːn/ ■ n. variant spelling of **DIWAN**.

dewar /ˈdjuːə/ ■ n. a double-walled flask of metal or silvered glass with a vacuum between the walls, used to hold liquids at well below ambient temperature.
– ORIGIN C19: named after the Scottish physicist Sir James Dewar.

dewberry ■ n. (pl. **-ies**) **1** a trailing bramble with soft prickles and edible blue-black fruit with a dewy white bloom. [*Rubus caesius* (Europe) and other species.] **2** the fruit of this plant. **3** another term for **CROSS-BERRY**.

dewclaw ■ n. a rudimentary inner toe present in some dogs. ▸ a false hoof on an animal such as a deer, which is formed by its rudimentary side toes.

dewdrop ■ n. a drop of dew.

Dewey decimal classification ■ n. an internationally applied decimal system of library classification which uses a three-figure code from 000 to 999 to represent the major branches of knowledge, with finer classifications made by adding figures after a decimal point.
– ORIGIN C19: named after the American librarian Melvil Dewey.

dewfall ■ n. poetic/literary the time of evening when dew begins to form.

dewlap ■ n. a fold of loose skin hanging from the neck or throat of an animal or bird, especially that present in many cattle.
– ORIGIN Middle English: from **DEW** and **LAP**[1].

deworm ■ v. treat (an animal) to free it of worms.
– DERIVATIVES **dewormer** n.

dew point ■ n. the atmospheric temperature below which water droplets begin to condense and dew can form.

dewy ■ adj. (**-ier, -iest**) **1** wet with dew. **2** (of a person's skin) appearing soft and lustrous.
– DERIVATIVES **dewily** adv. **dewiness** n.

dewy-eyed ■ adj. having eyes that are moist with tears (taken as indicating nostalgia, naivety, or sentimentality).

Dexedrine /ˈdɛksədriːn, -drɪn/ ■ n. trademark a form of amphetamine.
– ORIGIN 1940s: prob. from Latin *dexter* 'right', on the pattern of *Benzedrine*.

dexter[1] /ˈdɛkstə/ ■ adj. archaic & Heraldry on or towards the right-hand side (in a coat of arms, from the bearer's point of view, i.e. the left as it is depicted). The opposite of **SINISTER**.
– ORIGIN C16: from Latin, 'on the right'.

dexter[2] /ˈdɛkstə/ ■ n. an animal of a small, hardy breed of Irish cattle.
– ORIGIN C19: said to have been named after the breeder.

dexterity /dɛkˈstɛrɪti/ ■ n. skill in performing tasks, especially with the hands.
– ORIGIN C16: from French *dextérité*, from Latin *dexteritas*, from *dexter* 'on the right'.

dexterous /ˈdɛkst(ə)rəs/ (also **dextrous**) ■ adj. showing or having dexterity; adroit.
– DERIVATIVES **dexterously** adv. **dexterousness** n.

dextral /ˈdɛkstr(ə)l/ ■ adj. **1** of or on the right side or the right hand. The opposite of **SINISTRAL**. ▸ right-handed. **2** Geology relating to or denoting a strike-slip fault in which the motion of the block on the further side of the fault is towards the right. ■ n. a right-handed person.
– DERIVATIVES **dextrality** /-ˈstralɪti/ n. **dextrally** adv.
– ORIGIN C17: from medieval Latin *dextralis*, from Latin *dextra* 'the right hand', from *dexter* 'on the right'.

dextran /ˈdɛkstran/ ■ n. Chemistry a carbohydrate gum formed by the fermentation of sugars, used to make a substitute for blood plasma.
– ORIGIN C19: from Latin *dexter* 'right'.

dextrin /ˈdɛkstrɪn/ ■ n. a soluble gummy substance obtained by hydrolysis of starch, used as a thickening agent and in adhesives and dietary supplements.
– ORIGIN C19: from Latin *dexter* 'right'.

dextrorotatory /ˌdɛkstrəʊˈrəʊtət(ə)ri/ ■ adj. Chemistry (of a compound) having the property of rotating the plane of a polarized light ray to the right, i.e. clockwise facing the oncoming radiation. The opposite of **LAEVOROTATORY**.
– DERIVATIVES **dextrorotation** n.

dextrose /ˈdɛkstrəʊz, -s/ ■ n. Chemistry the dextrorotatory form of glucose (and the predominant naturally occurring form).

dextrous ■ adj. variant spelling of **DEXTEROUS**.

DF ■ abbrev. **1** Defender of the Faith. [from Latin *Defensor Fidei*.] **2** direction-finder.

DFC ■ abbrev. (in the UK) Distinguished Flying Cross.

Dfl ■ abbrev. Dutch florins.

DFM ■ abbrev. (in the UK) Distinguished Flying Medal.

DG ■ abbrev. **1** by the grace of God. [Latin *Dei gratia*.] **2** thanks be to God. [Latin *Deo gratias*.] **3** director general.

dg ■ abbrev. decigram(s).

dhal /dɑːl/ (also **dal**) ■ n. split pulses. ▸ (in Indian cookery) a purée or soup made with these.
– ORIGIN from Hindi *dāl*.

dhania /ˈdanjə/ (S. African also **dhunia**) ■ n. an Indian term for **CORIANDER**.
– ORIGIN from Hindi and Urdu.

dhansak /ˈdʌnsɑːk/ ■ n. an Indian dish of meat or vegetables cooked with lentils and coriander.
– ORIGIN from Gujarati.

dharma /ˈdɑːmə, ˈdəːmə/ (also **dhamma**) ■ n. (in Indian religion) the eternal law of the cosmos, inherent in the very nature of things.
– ORIGIN Sanskrit, 'decree, custom'.

dhikr /ˈdɪkʌr/ ■ n. (in Islam) a form of devotion, associated chiefly with Sufism, in which the worshipper is absorbed in the rhythmic repetition of the name of God or his attributes.

dholak /'dəʊlək/ ▪ n. a small, typically two-headed drum used primarily in the Indian subcontinent.
– ORIGIN from Hindi *ḍholak*.

dhoti /'dəʊti/ ▪ n. (pl. **dhotis**) a loincloth worn by male Hindus.
– ORIGIN from Hindi *dhotī*.

dhow /daʊ/ ▪ n. a lateen-rigged ship with one or two masts, used chiefly in the Arabian region.
– ORIGIN C18: from Arabic *dāwa*, prob. rel. to Marathi *dāw*.

dhunia /'dʌnjə/ ▪ n. variant spelling of **DHANIA**.

dhurrie /'dʌri/ ▪ n. (pl. **-ies**) a heavy cotton rug of Indian origin.
– ORIGIN from Hindi *darī*.

dhyana /dɪ'ɑːnə/ ▪ n. (in Hindu and Buddhist practice) profound meditation which is the penultimate stage of yoga.
– ORIGIN from Sanskrit *dhyāna*.

DI ▪ abbrev. **1** Defence Intelligence. **2** Detective Inspector. **3** direct injection.

di-¹ /dʌɪ, di/ ▪ comb. form twice; two-; double: *dichromatic*. ▸ Chemistry containing two atoms, molecules, or groups of a specified kind: *dioxide*.
– ORIGIN from Greek *dis* 'twice'.

di-² /di, dʌɪ/ ▪ prefix variant spelling of **DIS-** shortened before *l, m, n, r, s* (followed by a consonant), and *v*; also often shortened before *g*, and sometimes before *j*.
– ORIGIN from Latin.

di-³ /dʌɪ/ ▪ prefix variant spelling of **DIA-** shortened before a vowel (as in *dielectric*).

dia- (also **di-** before a vowel) ▪ prefix **1** through; across: *diaphanous*. **2** apart: *diakinesis*.
– ORIGIN from Greek *dia* 'through'.

dia. ▪ abbrev. diameter.

diabase /'dʌɪəbeɪs/ ▪ n. Geology another term for **DOLERITE**.
– ORIGIN C19: from French, formed as if from *di-* 'two' + *base* 'base', but perhaps associated later with Greek *diabasis* 'transition'.

diabetes /ˌdʌɪə'biːtiːz/ ▪ n. a disorder of the metabolism causing excessive thirst and the production of large amounts of urine.
– ORIGIN C16: from Greek, 'siphon', from *diabainein* 'go through'.

diabetes mellitus /mɪ'lʌɪtəs/ ▪ n. the commonest form of diabetes, caused by a deficiency of the pancreatic hormone insulin, which results in a failure to metabolize sugars and starch.
– ORIGIN C19: from **DIABETES** + Latin *mellitus* 'sweet'.

diabetic ▪ adj. having or relating to diabetes. ▪ n. a person suffering from diabetes.

diablerie /dɪ'ɑːbləri/ ▪ n. reckless mischief; charismatic wildness.
– ORIGIN C18: from French, from *diable*, from eccles. Latin *diabolus* 'devil'.

diabolical ▪ adj. **1** (also **diabolic**) characteristic of or associated with the Devil: *diabolical cunning*. **2** informal disgracefully bad or unpleasant.
– DERIVATIVES **diabolically** adv.
– ORIGIN Middle English: from Old French *diabolique* or eccles. Latin *diabolicus*, from *diabolus* 'devil'.

diabolism /dʌɪ'abəlɪz(ə)m/ ▪ n. worship of the Devil.
– DERIVATIVES **diabolist** n.
– ORIGIN C17: from eccles. Latin *diabolus* or Greek *diabolos* 'devil'.

diabolo /dɪ'abələʊ, dʌɪ-/ ▪ n. (pl. **-os**) a game in which a two-headed top is thrown up and caught with a string stretched between two sticks. ▸ the top used in this game.
– ORIGIN C20: from Italian, from eccles. Latin *diabolus* 'devil'.

diacetylmorphine /dʌɪˌasɪtʌɪl'mɔːfiːn/ ▪ n. technical term for **HEROIN**.

diachronic /ˌdʌɪə'krɒnɪk/ ▪ adj. concerned with the way in which something, especially language, has developed through time. Often contrasted with **SYNCHRONIC**.
– DERIVATIVES **diachronically** adv. **diachronistic** /dʌɪˌakrə'nɪstɪk/ adj.
– ORIGIN C19: from **DIA-** + Greek *khronos* 'time'.

diachronism /dʌɪ'akrənɪz(ə)m/ ▪ n. Geology the occurrence of a feature or phenomenon in different geological periods.

– DERIVATIVES **diachronous** adj. **diachronously** adv.

diaconal /dʌɪ'ak(ə)n(ə)l/ ▪ adj. relating to a deacon or deacons.
– ORIGIN C17: from eccles. Latin *diaconalis*, from Greek *diakonos* (see **DEACON**).

diaconate /dʌɪ'akəneɪt, -ət/ ▪ n. the office of deacon. ▸ a body of deacons collectively.
– ORIGIN C18: from eccles. Latin *diaconatus*, from Greek *diakonos* (see **DEACON**).

diacritic /ˌdʌɪ'krɪtɪk/ ▪ n. a sign such as an accent written above or below a letter to indicate a difference in pronunciation from the same letter when unmarked. ▪ adj. (of a mark or sign) indicating a difference in pronunciation.
– DERIVATIVES **diacritical** adj. **diacritically** adv.
– ORIGIN C17: from Greek *diakritikos*, from *diakrinein* 'distinguish'.

diadem /'dʌɪədɛm/ ▪ n. a jewelled crown or headband worn as a symbol of sovereignty.
– DERIVATIVES **diademed** adj.
– ORIGIN Middle English: from Greek *diadēma*, from *diadein* 'bind round'.

diaeresis /dʌɪ'ɪərɪsɪs, -'ɛr-/ (US **dieresis**) ▪ n. (pl. **diaereses** /-siːz/) **1** a mark (¨) placed over a vowel to indicate that it is sounded separately, as in *naïve*, *Brontë*. ▸ the division of a sound into two syllables, especially by sounding a diphthong as two vowels. **2** Prosody a natural rhythmic break in a line of verse where the end of a metrical foot coincides with the end of a phrase.
– ORIGIN C16: from Greek *diairesis* 'separation', from *diairein* 'take apart'.

diagenesis /ˌdʌɪə'dʒɛnɪsɪs/ ▪ n. Geology the physical and chemical changes occurring during the conversion of sediment to sedimentary rock.
– DERIVATIVES **diagenetic** adj. **diagenetically** adv.

diagnose /'dʌɪəgnəʊz, -'nəʊz/ ▪ v. make a diagnosis of (an illness or other problem). ▸ identify the medical condition of (someone): *she was diagnosed as having epilepsy*.
– DERIVATIVES **diagnosable** adj.

diagnosis /ˌdʌɪəg'nəʊsɪs/ ▪ n. (pl. **diagnoses** /-siːz/) **1** the identification of the nature of an illness or other problem by examination of the symptoms. **2** the distinctive characterization in precise terms of a genus, species, or phenomenon.
– ORIGIN C17: modern Latin, from Greek, from *diagignōskein* 'distinguish, discern'.

diagnostic /dʌɪəg'nɒstɪk/ ▪ adj. **1** concerned with the diagnosis of illness or other problems. ▸ (of a symptom) distinctive, and so indicating the nature of an illness. **2** characteristic of a particular species, genus, or phenomenon. ▪ n. **1** a distinctive symptom or characteristic. **2** (**diagnostics**) [treated as sing. or pl.] the practice or techniques of diagnosis. **3** Computing a program or routine that helps a user to identify errors.
– DERIVATIVES **diagnostically** adv. **diagnostician** /-nɒ'stɪʃ(ə)n/ n.

diagonal /dʌɪ'ag(ə)n(ə)l/ ▪ adj. denoting a straight line joining opposite corners of a rectangle, square, or other figure. ▸ (of a line) straight and at an angle; slanting. ▸ Mathematics denoting a matrix with non-zero elements only on the diagonal running from the upper left to the lower right. ▪ n. a diagonal line.
– DERIVATIVES **diagonally** adv.
– ORIGIN C16: from Latin *diagonalis*, from Greek *diagōnios* 'from angle to angle', from *dia* 'through' + *gōnia* 'angle'.

diagram /'dʌɪəgram/ ▪ n. a simplified drawing showing the appearance or structure of something. ▪ v. (**diagrammed**, **diagramming**; US **diagramed**, **diagraming**) represent in graphic form.
– DERIVATIVES **diagrammatic** /-grə'matɪk/ adj. **diagrammatically** adv.
– ORIGIN C17: from Latin *diagramma*, from Greek, from *diagraphein* 'mark out by lines'.

diakinesis /ˌdʌɪəkʌɪ'niːsɪs/ ▪ n. (pl. **diakineses** /-siːz/) Biology the final stage of the prophase of meiosis, following diplotene, when the separation of homologous chromosomes is complete and crossing over has occurred.
– ORIGIN C20: from **DIA-** + Greek *kinēsis* 'motion'.

dial

dial ■ n. a disc marked to show the time on a clock or indicate a reading or measurement by means of a pointer. ▶ a disc with numbered holes on a telephone, turned to make a call. ▶ a disc turned to select a setting on a radio, cooker, etc. ■ v. (**dialled**, **dialling**; US **dialed**, **dialing**) call (a telephone number) by turning a dial or using a keypad. ▶ indicate or regulate by means of a dial.
– ORIGIN Middle English: from medieval Latin *diale* 'clock dial', from Latin *dies* 'day'.

dialect /'dʌɪəlɛkt/ ■ n. a form of a language which is peculiar to a specific region or social group.
– DERIVATIVES **dialectal** /-'lɛkt(ə)l/ adj.
– ORIGIN C16: from Greek *dialektos* 'discourse, way of speaking', from *dialegesthai* (see **DIALOGUE**).

dialectic /ˌdʌɪə'lɛktɪk/ Philosophy ■ n. (also **dialectics**) [usu. treated as sing.] **1** the art of investigating or discussing the truth of opinions. **2** enquiry into metaphysical contradictions and their solutions. **3** the existence or action of opposing social forces, concepts, etc. ■ adj. of or relating to dialectic or dialectics; dialectical.
– ORIGIN Middle English: from Old French *dialectique* or Latin *dialectica*, from Greek *dialektikē (tekhnē)* '(art) of debate', from *dialegesthai* (see **DIALOGUE**).

dialectical ■ adj. **1** relating to the logical discussion of ideas and opinions. **2** concerned with or acting through opposing forces.
– DERIVATIVES **dialectically** adv.

dialectical materialism ■ n. the Marxist theory that political and historical events result from the conflict of social forces (as caused by material needs) and are interpretable as a series of contradictions and their solutions.

dialectician /ˌdʌɪəlɛk'tɪʃ(ə)n/ ■ n. a person skilled in philosophical debate.

dialectology /ˌdʌɪəlɛk'tɒlədʒi/ ■ n. the branch of linguistics concerned with the study of dialects.
– DERIVATIVES **dialectological** /-tə'lɒdʒɪk(ə)l/ adj. **dialectologist** n.

dialler (also **dialer**) ■ n. a device or piece of software for calling telephone numbers automatically.

dialling code ■ n. S. African & Brit. a sequence of numbers dialled to connect a telephone to an exchange in another area or country.

dialling tone (N. Amer. & Austral./NZ **dial tone**) ■ n. a sound produced by a telephone that indicates that a caller may start to dial.

dialog box (Brit. also **dialogue box**) ■ n. Computing a small area on screen in which the user is prompted to provide information or select commands.

dialogue (US also **dialog**) ■ n. conversation between two or more people as a feature of a book, play, or film. ▶ discussion directed towards exploration of a subject or resolution of a problem. ■ v. chiefly N. Amer. take part in dialogue. ▶ provide (a film or play) with dialogue.
– ORIGIN Middle English: from Old French *dialoge*, from Greek *dialogos*, from *dialegesthai* 'converse with', from *dia* 'through' + *legein* 'speak'.

dial tone ■ n. another term for **DIALLING TONE**.

dial-up ■ adj. (of a computer system or service) used remotely via a telephone line.

dialyse /'dʌɪəlʌɪz/ (US **dialyze**) ■ v. purify (a mixture) or treat (a patient) by means of dialysis.

dialysis /dʌɪ'alɪsɪs/ ■ n. (pl. **dialyses** /-siːz/) **1** Chemistry the separation of particles in a liquid on the basis of differences in their ability to pass through a membrane. **2** Medicine the clinical purification of blood by this technique, as a substitute for the normal function of the kidney.
– DERIVATIVES **dialytic** adj.
– ORIGIN C19: from Greek *dialusis*, from *dialuein* 'split, separate'.

diamagnetic ■ adj. Physics tending to become magnetized in a direction at 180° to the applied magnetic field.
– DERIVATIVES **diamagnet** n. **diamagnetically** adv. **diamagnetism** n.

diamanté /dɪə'mɒnteɪ/ ■ adj. decorated with artificial jewels. ■ n. fabric or costume jewellery decorated with artificial jewels.
– ORIGIN C20: French, 'set with diamonds'.

diamantine /ˌdʌɪə'mantɪn, -iːn/ ■ adj. made from or resembling diamonds.
– ORIGIN C16: from French *diamantin*, from *diamant* 'diamond'.

diameter /dʌɪ'amɪtə/ ■ n. **1** a straight line passing from side to side through the centre of a body or figure, especially a circle or sphere. ▶ a transverse measurement of something; width or thickness. **2** a unit of linear measurement of magnifying power.
– DERIVATIVES **diametral** adj.
– ORIGIN Middle English: from Old French *diametre*, from Greek *diametros (grammē)* '(line) measuring across'.

diametrical /ˌdʌɪə'mɛtrɪk(ə)l/ ■ adj. **1** (of opposites) complete; absolute: *he's the diametrical opposite of Gabriel*. **2** of or along a diameter.
– DERIVATIVES **diametric** adj. **diametrically** adv.

diamine /dʌɪ'eɪmiːn, dʌɪ'am-, 'dʌɪəmiːn/ ■ n. Chemistry a compound whose molecule contains two amino groups, especially when not part of amide groups.

diamond ■ n. **1** a precious stone consisting of a clear and often colourless crystalline form of pure carbon, the hardest naturally occurring substance. **2** a figure with four straight sides of equal length forming two opposite acute angles and two opposite obtuse angles; a rhombus. **3** (**diamonds**) one of the four suits in a conventional pack of playing cards, denoted by a red figure of such a shape. ▶ a card of this suit. **4** a baseball field. **5** a railway crossing in which two tracks cross over each other at an acute angle.
– PHRASES **diamond in the rough** North American term for **ROUGH DIAMOND**.
– DERIVATIVES **diamondiferous** /-'dɪf(ə)rəs/ adj.
– ORIGIN Middle English: from Old French *diamant*, from medieval Latin *diamas*, var. of Latin *adamans* (see **ADAMANT**).

diamondback ■ n. a large, common North American rattlesnake with diamond-shaped markings.

diamond-cut ■ adj. **1** cut with facets like a diamond. **2** cut into the shape of a diamond.

diamond jubilee ■ n. the sixtieth anniversary of a notable event.

diamond wedding ■ n. the sixtieth anniversary of a wedding.

diamorphine /dʌɪ'mɔːfiːn/ ■ n. technical term for **HEROIN**.

Dianetics /ˌdʌɪə'nɛtɪks/ ■ pl. n. [treated as sing.] a system developed by the founder of the Church of Scientology, L. Ron Hubbard, which aims to relieve psychosomatic disorder by cleansing the mind of harmful mental images.
– ORIGIN 1950s: from Greek *dianoētikos* 'relating to thought'.

dianthus /dʌɪ'anθəs/ ■ n. (pl. **dianthuses**) a flowering plant of a genus that includes the pinks and carnations. [Genus *Dianthus*.]
– ORIGIN from Greek *Dios* 'of Zeus' + *anthos* 'flower'.

diapause /'dʌɪəpɔːz/ ■ n. Zoology a period of suspended development in an organism.

diaper /'dʌɪəpə/ N. Amer. ■ n. a baby's nappy. ■ v. put a nappy on (a baby).
– ORIGIN Middle English: from Old French *diapre*, from medieval Greek *diaspros* (adj.), from *dia* 'across' + *aspros* 'white'.

diaphanous /dʌɪ'af(ə)nəs/ ■ adj. (of fabric) light, delicate, and translucent.
– ORIGIN C17: from Greek *diaphanēs*, from *dia* 'through' + *phainein* 'to show'.

diaphragm /'dʌɪəfram/ ■ n. **1** a dome-shaped muscular partition separating the thorax from the abdomen in mammals. **2** a thin sheet of material forming a partition. ▶ a taut flexible membrane in mechanical or acoustic systems. **3** a thin contraceptive cap fitting over the cervix. **4** a device for varying the effective aperture of the lens in a camera or other optical system.
– DERIVATIVES **diaphragmatic** adj.
– ORIGIN Middle English: from Greek, from *dia* 'through, apart' + *phragma* 'a fence'.

VOWELS a cat ɑː arm ɛ bed ɛː hair ə ago əː her ɪ sit i cosy iː see ɒ hot ɔː saw ʌ run

diaphragm pump ■ n. a pump using a flexible diaphragm in place of a piston.

diaphysis /dʌɪˈafɪsɪs/ ■ n. (pl. **diaphyses** /-siːz/) Anatomy the shaft or central part of a long bone.
– ORIGIN C19: from Greek *diaphusis* 'growing through'.

diapir /ˈdʌɪəpɪə/ ■ n. Geology a domed rock formation in which a core of rock has moved upward to pierce the overlying strata.
– DERIVATIVES **diapiric** adj. **diapirism** n.
– ORIGIN C20: from Greek *diapeirainein* 'pierce through'.

diapositive /ˌdʌɪəˈpɒzɪtɪv/ ■ n. a positive photographic slide or transparency.

diapsid /dʌɪˈapsɪd/ ■ n. Zoology a reptile of a large group having two temporal openings in the skull, including the lizards, snakes, crocodiles, dinosaurs, and pterosaurs.
– ORIGIN C20: from *Diapsida* (name of a subclass), from **DI-**[1] + Greek *apsis, apsid-* 'arch'.

diarist ■ n. a person who writes a diary.
– DERIVATIVES **diaristic** adj.

diarize (also **-ise**) ■ v. **1** note (an appointment or event) in a diary. **2** archaic keep a record of events in a diary.

diarrhoea /ˌdʌɪəˈrɪə/ (US **diarrhea**) ■ n. a condition in which faeces are discharged from the bowels frequently and in a liquid form.
– DERIVATIVES **diarrhoeal** adj. **diarrhoeic** adj.
– ORIGIN Middle English: from Greek *diarrhoia*, from *diarrhein* 'flow through'.

diary ■ n. (pl. **-ies**) a book in which one keeps a daily record of events and experiences. ▸ a book with spaces for each day of the year in which to note appointments.

HISTORY

As well as being synonyms, **diary** and **journal** come from the same Latin word, *dies* 'day'. The older word **journal** came into English in the 14th century from Old French *jurnal*, from Latin *diurnalis* 'daily'; the later word **diary**, which entered English in the 16th century, came directly from Latin *diarium* 'daily allowance', later 'diary'. **Dial** and **dismal** also derive from *dies*, the latter being a contraction of *dies mali* 'evil days'.

---

diaspora /dʌɪˈasp(ə)rə/ ■ n. (**the diaspora**) the dispersion of the Jews beyond Israel. ▸ Jews living outside Israel. ▸ a dispersion of people from their homeland.
– ORIGIN from Greek *diaspeirein* 'disperse'.

diaspore /ˈdʌɪəspɔː/ ■ n. Botany a spore, seed, or other structure that functions in plant dispersal; a propagule.

diastase /ˈdʌɪəsteɪz/ ■ n. Biochemistry another term for **AMYLASE**.
– ORIGIN C19: from Greek *diastasis* 'separation'.

diastema /ˌdʌɪəˈstiːmə, dʌɪˈastɪmə/ ■ n. (pl. **diastemata**) **1** Zoology a space separating teeth of different functions, especially that between the biting teeth and grinding teeth in rodents and ungulates. **2** a gap between a person's two upper front teeth.
– ORIGIN C19: from Greek *diastēma* 'space between'.

diastereoisomer /ˌdʌɪəstɛrɪəʊˈʌɪsəmə/ ■ n. Chemistry each of a pair of stereoisomeric compounds that are not mirror images of one another.
– DERIVATIVES **diastereoisomeric** adj.

diastole /dʌɪˈastəli/ ■ n. Physiology the phase of the heartbeat when the heart muscle relaxes and allows the chambers to fill with blood. Often contrasted with **SYSTOLE**.
– DERIVATIVES **diastolic** adj.
– ORIGIN C16: from Greek, 'separation, expansion'.

diathermy /ˈdʌɪəˌθəːmi/ ■ n. a medical and surgical technique involving the production of heat in a part of the body by high-frequency electric currents.
– ORIGIN C20: from **DIA-** + Greek *thermon* 'heat'.

diatom /ˈdʌɪətəm/ ■ n. Biology a single-celled alga which has a cell wall of silica. [Class Bacillariophyceae.]
– DERIVATIVES **diatomaceous** adj.
– ORIGIN C19: from *Diatoma* (genus name), from Greek *diatomos* 'cut in two'.

diatomaceous earth /ˌdʌɪətəˈmeɪʃəs/ ■ n. a soft, crumbly, porous sedimentary deposit formed from the fossil remains of diatoms.

diatomic /ˌdʌɪəˈtɒmɪk/ ■ adj. Chemistry consisting of two atoms.

diatomite /dʌɪˈatəmʌɪt/ ■ n. Geology a fine-grained sedimentary rock formed from consolidated diatomaceous earth.

diatonic /ˌdʌɪəˈtɒnɪk/ ■ adj. Music involving only notes proper to the prevailing key without chromatic alteration.
– ORIGIN C17: from Greek *diatonikos* 'at intervals of a tone'.

diatreme /ˈdʌɪətriːm/ ■ n. Geology a long vertical pipe or plug formed when gas-filled magma forced its way up through overlying strata.
– ORIGIN C20: from **DIA-** + Greek *trēma* 'perforation'.

diatribe /ˈdʌɪətrʌɪb/ ■ n. a forceful and bitter verbal attack.
– ORIGIN C16: from Greek *diatribē* 'spending of time, discourse'.

diazepam /dʌɪˈazɪpam, -ˈeɪz-/ ■ n. a tranquillizing muscle-relaxant drug used chiefly to relieve anxiety. Also called **VALIUM** (trademark).
– ORIGIN 1960s: blend of **BENZODIAZEPINE** and **AMIDE**.

diazo /dʌɪˈazəʊ, -ˈeɪzəʊ/ (also **diazotype**) ■ n. a copying or colouring process using a diazo compound decomposed by ultraviolet light.

diazo compound ■ n. Chemistry an organic compound containing two nitrogen atoms bonded together, especially a diazonium compound.
– ORIGIN C19: *diazo* from **DIAZONIUM**.

diazonium /ˌdʌɪəˈzəʊnɪəm/ ■ n. [as modifier] Chemistry of or denoting an organic cation containing two nitrogen atoms bonded together, present in many synthetic dyes.
– ORIGIN C19: coined in German from *diazo-* (indicating the presence of two nitrogen atoms) + *-onium* (from **AMMONIUM**).

dibasic /dʌɪˈbeɪsɪk/ ■ adj. Chemistry (of an acid) having two replaceable hydrogen atoms.

dibber ■ n. Brit. another term for **DIBBLE**.

dibble ■ n. a pointed hand tool for making holes in the ground for seeds or young plants. ■ v. dig or plant with a dibble.
– ORIGIN Middle English.

dibs ■ pl. n. informal **1** (often in phr. **have first dibs**) N. Amer. the right to share or choose something. **2** money.
– ORIGIN C18 (denoting pebbles used in a children's game): from earlier *dib-stones*.

dice ■ n. (pl. same; sing. also **die**) **1** a small cube with faces bearing from one to six spots, used in games of chance. See also **DIE**[2]. ▸ a game played with dice. **2** small cubes of food. ■ v. **1** [often as noun **dicing**] play or gamble with dice. **2** [often as adj. **diced**] cut (food) into small cubes. **3** S. African informal race against another vehicle.
– PHRASES **dice with death** take serious risks. **no dice** informal, chiefly N. Amer. used to refuse a request or indicate no chance of success.
– DERIVATIVES **dicer** n.
– ORIGIN Middle English: from Old French *des*, pl. of *de* (see **DIE**[2]).

USAGE

Historically, **dice** is the plural of **die**, but in modern standard English **dice** is used as both the singular and the plural.

---

dicentric /dʌɪˈsɛntrɪk/ ■ adj. Genetics (of a chromosome) having two centromeres.

dicey ■ adj. (**-ier**, **-iest**) informal unpredictable and potentially dangerous.

dichotomize /dʌɪˈkɒtəmʌɪz, dɪ-/ (also **-ise**) ■ v. regard or represent as divided or opposed.

dichotomy /dʌɪˈkɒtəmi, dɪ-/ ■ n. (pl. **-ies**) **1** a division or contrast between two things that are opposed or entirely different. **2** Botany repeated branching into two equal parts.
– DERIVATIVES **dichotomous** adj. **dichotomously** adv.
– ORIGIN C16: from Greek *dikhotomia*, from *dikho-* 'in two, apart' + *-tomia* 'cutting'.

dichroic /dʌɪˈkrəʊɪk/ ■ adj. (of a crystal) showing different

dichromate

colours when viewed from different directions or in light of differing polarization.
– DERIVATIVES **dichroism** n.
– ORIGIN C19: from Greek *dikhroos*, from *di-* 'twice' + *khrōs* 'colour'.

dichromate /ˈdaɪkrəʊmeɪt/ ■ n. Chemistry a salt, typically red or orange, containing the anion $Cr_2O_7^{2-}$.

dichromatism /daɪˈkrəʊmətɪz(ə)m/ ■ n. **1** the occurrence of two different kinds of colouring, especially in an animal species. **2** colour blindness in which only two of the three primary colours can be discerned.
– DERIVATIVES **dichromatic** adj.

dick¹ ■ n. **1** vulgar slang a man's penis. **2** Brit. vulgar slang a stupid or contemptible person. **3** [with neg.] N. Amer. informal anything at all: *you don't know dick about it!*
– ORIGIN C16 (in the sense 'fellow'): familiar form of the given name *Richard*.

dick² ■ n. informal, dated, chiefly N. Amer. a detective.
– ORIGIN C20: perhaps an arbitrary shortening of DETECTIVE, or from obsolete slang *dick* 'look', from Romany.

dickens /ˈdɪkɪnz/ ■ n. informal used for emphasis, or to express annoyance or surprise when asking questions: *what the dickens is going on?*
– ORIGIN C16: a euphemism for 'devil', prob. a use of the surname *Dickens*.

Dickensian /dɪˈkɛnzɪən/ ■ adj. reminiscent of the novels of Charles Dickens, especially in terms of the poverty and squalor that they portray.

dicker ■ v. **1** engage in petty argument or bargaining. **2** toy or fiddle with something.
– ORIGIN C19: perhaps from obsolete *dicker* 'set of ten (hides)', used as a unit of trade, from Latin *decem* 'ten'.

dickhead ■ n. vulgar slang a stupid, irritating, or ridiculous man.

dicky¹ (also **dickey**) ■ n. (pl. **-ies** or **-eys**) informal a false shirt front.
– ORIGIN C18 (denoting a petticoat): perhaps partly from *Dicky*, familiar form of *Richard*.

dicky² ■ adj. (**-ier**, **-iest**) informal not strong, healthy, or functioning reliably.
– ORIGIN C18: perhaps from the given name *Dick*, in the old saying *as queer as Dick's hatband*.

dicky bird ■ n. informal a child's word for a bird.
– PHRASES **not a dicky bird** not a word; nothing at all.

dicky bow ■ n. informal a bow tie.

dicotyledon /ˌdaɪkɒtɪˈliːd(ə)n/ ■ n. Botany a plant with an embryo bearing two cotyledons, such plants constituting the larger (Dicotyledoneae) of the two classes of flowering species. Compare with MONOCOTYLEDON.
– DERIVATIVES **dicotyledonous** adj.

dicta plural form of DICTUM.

Dictaphone /ˈdɪktəfəʊn/ ■ n. trademark a small cassette recorder used to record speech for transcription at a later time.

dictate ■ v. /dɪkˈteɪt/ **1** state or order authoritatively. ▸ control or decisively affect; determine. **2** say or read aloud (words to be typed or written down). ■ n. /ˈdɪkteɪt/ an order or principle that must be obeyed.
– DERIVATIVES **dictation** n.
– ORIGIN C16: from Latin *dictare*.

dictator ■ n. a ruler with total power over a country. ▸ an autocratic person.
– DERIVATIVES **dictatorial** adj. **dictatorially** adv.

dictatorship ■ n. **1** government by a dictator. **2** a country governed by a dictator.

diction ■ n. **1** the choice and use of words in speech or writing. **2** the style of enunciation in speaking or singing.
– ORIGIN C16: from Latin *dictio(n-)*, from *dicere* 'to say'.

dictionary ■ n. (pl. **-ies**) a book that lists the words of a language in alphabetical order and gives their meaning, or their equivalent in a different language.
– ORIGIN C16: from medieval Latin *dictionarium (manuale)* or *dictionarius (liber)* 'manual, book of words', from Latin *dictio* (see DICTION).

dictum /ˈdɪktəm/ ■ n. (pl. **dicta** /-tə/ or **dictums**) a formal pronouncement from an authoritative source. ▸ a short statement that expresses a general truth or principle. ▸ Law short for OBITER DICTUM.
– ORIGIN C16: from Latin, 'something said', from *dicere*.

Dictyoptera /ˌdɪktɪˈɒptərə/ ■ pl. n. Entomology an order of insects that comprises the cockroaches and mantises.
– DERIVATIVES **dictyopteran** n. & adj.
– ORIGIN from Greek *diktuon* 'net' + *pteron* 'wing'.

dicynodont /daɪˈsɪnədɒnt/ ■ n. a fossil herbivorous mammal-like reptile of the late Permian and Triassic periods, with beaked jaws and no teeth apart from two tusks in the upper jaw of the male.
– ORIGIN C19: from *Dicynodontia*, from Greek *di-* 'two' + *kuōn* 'dog' + *odous, odont-* 'tooth'.

did past of DO¹.

didactic /dɪˈdaktɪk, dʌɪ-/ ■ adj. intended to teach, in particular having moral instruction as an ulterior motive. ▸ in the manner of a teacher; patronizing or hectoring.
– DERIVATIVES **didactically** adv. **didacticism** n.
– ORIGIN C17: from Greek *didaktikos*, from *didaskein* 'teach'.

didanosine /dɪˈdanəʊsiːn/ ■ n. Medicine a drug used in the treatment of Aids, especially in combination with zidovudine.

diddle ■ v. informal **1** cheat or swindle. **2** chiefly N. Amer. pass time aimlessly or unproductively.
– ORIGIN C19: prob. from the name of Jeremy *Diddler*, a character in the farce *Raising the Wind* (1803) who constantly borrowed small sums of money.

diddly-squat /ˈdɪdlɪˌskwɒt/ ■ pron. [usu. with neg.] informal, chiefly N. Amer. anything at all.
– ORIGIN C20: prob. from US slang *doodle* 'excrement' + SQUAT in the sense 'defecate'.

diddy ■ n. (pl. **-ies**) Brit. informal a fool.
– ORIGIN C18: alteration of TITTY.

didgeridoo /ˌdɪdʒ(ə)rɪˈduː/ ■ n. an Australian Aboriginal wind instrument in the form of a long wooden tube, which is blown to produce a deep resonant sound.
– ORIGIN from an Aboriginal language of Arnhem Land, Australia.

didn't ■ contr. did not.

didst archaic second person singular past of DO¹.

didymium /dɪˈdɪmɪəm/ ■ n. Chemistry a mixture containing the rare-earth elements praseodymium and neodymium, used to colour glass for optical filters.
– ORIGIN C19: from Greek *didumos* 'twin'.

die¹ ■ v. (**dying**) **1** stop living. ▸ (**die out**) become extinct. ▸ be forgotten: *her name will never die.* ▸ (often **die away/down**) become less loud or strong. **2** informal used to emphasize strong feelings of desire, embarrassment, shock, etc.: *I nearly died when I saw them.* ▸ (**be dying for/to do something**) be very eager for something.
– PHRASES **die hard** disappear or change very slowly. **never say die** said to encourage someone not to give up hope. **to die for** informal extremely good or desirable.
– ORIGIN Middle English: from Old Norse *deyja*, of Germanic origin.

die² ■ n. **1** singular form of DICE. **2** (pl. **dies**) a device for cutting or moulding metal or for stamping a design on coins or medals. **3** (pl. **dies**) Architecture the cubic part of a pedestal between the base and the cornice; a dado or plinth.
– PHRASES **the die is cast** an event has happened or a decision has been taken that cannot be changed. (**as**) **straight as a die 1** completely straight. **2** entirely open and honest.
– ORIGIN Middle English: from Old French *de*, from Latin *datum* 'something given or played', from *dare*.

dieback ■ n. a condition in which a tree or shrub begins to die from the tip of its leaves or roots backwards.

die-cast ■ adj. (of a metal object) formed by pouring molten metal into a reusable mould. ■ v. [usu. as noun **die-casting**] make (a metal object) in this way.

Diederik cuckoo ■ n. a metallic green and white African cuckoo. [*Chrysococcyx caprius*.]
– ORIGIN *Diederik*: S. African Dutch adaptation of *didric*, the onomatopoeic name coined in 1790 by the explorer and ornithologist François Le Vaillant.

dieffenbachia /ˌdiːf(ə)nˈbakɪə/ ■ n. a plant of a genus that includes dumb cane and its relatives. [Genus *Dieffenbachia*.]
– ORIGIN named after the German horticulturalist Ernst Dieffenbach.

diehard ■ n. a person who strongly opposes change or who continues to support something in spite of opposition.

diel /ˈdiːl/ ■ adj. Biology denoting or involving a period of twenty-four hours.
– ORIGIN 1930s: from Latin *dies* 'day' + *-(a)l* (see -AL).

dieldrin /ˈdiːldrɪn/ ■ n. an insecticide made by the oxidation of aldrin, a chlorinated hydrocarbon, now largely banned.
– ORIGIN 1940s: from the name of the German chemist Otto *Diels* + *aldrin*, named after the German chemist Kurt *Alder*.

dielectric /ˌdaɪɪˈlɛktrɪk/ Physics ■ adj. having the property of transmitting electric force without conduction; insulating. ■ n. an insulator.
– DERIVATIVES **dielectrically** adv.
– ORIGIN C19: from DI-³ + ELECTRIC.

diene /ˈdaɪiːn/ ■ n. Chemistry an unsaturated hydrocarbon containing two double bonds between carbon atoms.
– ORIGIN C20: from DI-¹ + -ENE.

dieresis ■ n. US spelling of DIAERESIS.

diesel /ˈdiːz(ə)l/ ■ n. 1 an internal-combustion engine in which heat produced by the compression of air in the cylinder is used to ignite the fuel. 2 a heavy petroleum fraction used as fuel in diesel engines.
– ORIGIN C19: named after the German engineer Rudolf *Diesel*.

diesel-electric ■ adj. denoting or relating to a locomotive driven by the electric current produced by a diesel-engined generator. ■ n. a locomotive of this type.

diesel-hydraulic ■ adj. denoting or relating to a locomotive driven by a hydraulic transmission system powered by a diesel engine. ■ n. a locomotive of this type.

die-sinker ■ n. a person who engraves dies used to stamp designs on coins or medals.
– DERIVATIVES **die-sinking** n.

die-stamping ■ n. a method of embossing paper or another surface using a die.

Die Stem /diː stɛm/ (in full **Die Stem van Suid-Afrika**) ■ n. the former South African national anthem, a part of which has been retained in the current national anthem.

diestrus ■ n. US spelling of DIOESTRUS.

diet¹ ■ n. 1 the kinds of food that a person, animal, or community habitually eats. 2 a special course of food to which a person restricts themselves to lose weight or for medical reasons. ▶ [as modifier] (of food or drink) with reduced fat or sugar content. ■ v. (**dieted**, **dieting**) restrict oneself to a special diet to lose weight.
– DERIVATIVES **dietary** adj. **dieter** n.
– ORIGIN Middle English: from Old French *diete* (n.), *dieter* (v.), from Greek *diaita* 'a way of life'.

diet² ■ n. a legislative assembly in certain countries.
▶ historical a regular meeting of the states of a confederation.
– ORIGIN Middle English: from medieval Latin *dieta* 'day's work, wages'.

dietetic /ˌdaɪəˈtɛtɪk/ ■ adj. concerned with diet and nutrition.
– DERIVATIVES **dietetically** adv.

dietetics ■ pl. n. [treated as sing.] the branch of knowledge concerned with the diet and its effects on health.

dietitian /ˌdaɪəˈtɪʃ(ə)n/ (also **dietician**) ■ n. an expert on diet and nutrition.

Difaqane /ˌdɪfəˈkɑːni, ˌdɪfəˈlɑːni/ ■ n. another term for MFECANE.
– ORIGIN Sesotho, 'mass movement of warriors and people, time of calamity'.

differ ■ v. 1 be unlike or dissimilar. 2 disagree.
– PHRASES **agree to differ** amicably stop arguing about something because agreement will clearly not be reached. **beg to differ** politely disagree.

diffract

– ORIGIN Middle English: from Old French *differer* 'differ, defer', from Latin *different-*, *differre*, from *dis-* 'from, away' + *ferre* 'bring, carry'.

difference ■ n. 1 a way in which people or things are different. ▶ the state or condition of being different. 2 the remainder left after subtraction of one value from another. 3 a disagreement, quarrel, or dispute. 4 Heraldry an alteration in a coat of arms to distinguish members or branches of a family. ■ v. Heraldry alter (a coat of arms) to distinguish members or branches of a family.
– PHRASES **with a difference** having a new or unusual feature or treatment.
– ORIGIN Middle English: from Latin *differentia*, from *different-* (see DIFFER).

different ■ adj. 1 not the same as another or each other; unlike in nature, form, or quality. 2 informal novel and unusual. 3 distinct; separate.
– DERIVATIVES **differently** adv. **differentness** n.

> USAGE
> There is little difference in sense between **different from**, **different to**, and **different than**, and all have been used by respected writers. **Different from** is traditionally held to be the correct collocation, and is by far the commonest in written evidence; **different to** is commonly heard in speech; **different than** is largely restricted to North America.

differentia /ˌdɪfəˈrɛnʃɪə/ ■ n. (pl. **differentiae** /-ʃiː/) a distinguishing mark or characteristic. ▶ chiefly Philosophy an attribute that distinguishes a species of thing from other species of the same genus.
– ORIGIN C17: from Latin (see DIFFERENCE).

differentiable /ˌdɪfəˈrɛnʃɪəb(ə)l/ ■ adj. able to be differentiated.
– DERIVATIVES **differentiability** n.

differential /ˌdɪfəˈrɛnʃ(ə)l/ chiefly technical ■ adj. 1 of, constituting, or depending on a difference; differing or varying according to circumstances or relevant factors. 2 Mathematics relating to infinitesimal differences or to the derivatives of functions. ■ n. 1 a difference. ▶ Mathematics an infinitesimal difference between successive values of a variable. 2 a gear allowing a vehicle's driven wheels to revolve at different speeds in cornering.
– DERIVATIVES **differentially** adv.

differential coefficient ■ n. Mathematics another term for DERIVATIVE.

differential equation ■ n. an equation involving derivatives of a function or functions.

differentiate /ˌdɪfəˈrɛnʃɪeɪt/ ■ v. 1 recognize or identify as different; distinguish. ▶ cause to appear different or distinct. 2 technical make or become different in the process of growth or development. 3 Mathematics transform (a function) into its derivative.
– DERIVATIVES **differentiation** n. **differentiator** n.

differently abled ■ adj. euphemistic disabled.

difficult ■ adj. 1 needing much effort or skill to accomplish, deal with, or understand. 2 (of a person) not easy to please or satisfy; awkward.
– DERIVATIVES **difficultness** n.
– ORIGIN Middle English: back-formation from DIFFICULTY.

difficulty ■ n. (pl. **-ies**) 1 the state or condition of being difficult. 2 a difficult or dangerous situation or circumstance; a problem.
– ORIGIN Middle English: from Latin *difficultas*, from *dis-* (expressing reversal) + *facultas* 'ability, opportunity'.

diffident ■ adj. modest or shy because of a lack of self-confidence.
– DERIVATIVES **diffidence** n. **diffidently** adv.
– ORIGIN Middle English: from Latin *diffidere* 'fail to trust'.

diff lock (also formal **differential lock**) ■ n. a device which disables the differential of a motor vehicle in slippery conditions to improve grip.

diffract /dɪˈfrakt/ ■ v. Physics cause to undergo diffraction.
– DERIVATIVES **diffractive** adj. **diffractively** adv.
– ORIGIN C19: from Latin *diffract-*, *diffringere* 'break in pieces'.

diffraction

diffraction ■ n. Physics the process by which a beam of light or other system of waves is spread out as a result of passing through a narrow aperture or across an edge.

diffuse ■ v. /dɪˈfjuːz/ spread out or cause to spread over a wide area. ▶ Physics intermingle with another substance by movement of particles. ■ adj. /dɪˈfjuːs/ **1** spread out over a large area; not concentrated. ▶ (of disease) not localized in the body. **2** lacking clarity or conciseness.
– DERIVATIVES **diffusely** /dɪˈfjuːsli/ adv. **diffuseness** /dɪˈfjuːsnɪs/ n. **diffuser** (also **diffusor**) n. **diffusible** adj.
– ORIGIN Middle English: from Latin *diffus-*, *diffundere* 'pour out'; the adj. is via French *diffus* or Latin *diffusus* 'extensive'.

USAGE
The verbs **diffuse** and **defuse** sound similar but have different meanings. **Diffuse** means 'spread over a wide area', while **defuse** means 'reduce the danger or tension in'. Thus sentences such as *Cooper successfully diffused the situation* are wrong, while *Cooper successfully defused the situation* would be correct.

diffusion ■ n. the action or process of diffusing. ▶ Anthropology the dissemination of elements of culture to another region or people.
– DERIVATIVES **diffusionism** n. **diffusionist** adj. & n. **diffusive** adj.

dig ■ v. (**digging**; past and past part. **dug**) **1** break up and move earth with a tool or with hands, paws, etc. ▶ make (a hole) by digging. ▶ extract from the ground by digging. ▶ (**dig in**) begin eating heartily. ▶ (**dig in**) (of a soldier) protect oneself by making a trench or similar ground defence. **2** poke or jab sharply. **3** search, rummage, or investigate. ▶ (**dig something out/up**) bring out or uncover something hidden. **4** excavate (an archaeological site). **5** informal, dated like, appreciate, or understand.' ■ n. **1** an act or spell of digging. **2** an archaeological excavation. **3** a sharp push or poke. **4** informal a remark intended to mock or criticize. **5** (**digs**) informal lodgings.
– PHRASES **dig up dirt** informal discover and reveal damaging information about someone. **dig oneself into a hole** get oneself into an awkward or restrictive situation. **dig in one's heels** resist stubbornly; refuse to give in.
– ORIGIN Middle English: perhaps from Old English *dīc* 'ditch'.

digastric muscle /dʌɪˈgastrɪk/ ■ n. Anatomy each of a pair of muscles which run under the jaw and act to open it.
– ORIGIN C17: from modern Latin *digastricus*, from *di-* 'twice' + Greek *gastēr* 'belly' (because the muscle has two fleshy parts or 'bellies' connected by a tendon).

digenean /ˌdʌɪdʒɪˈniːən, dʌɪˈdʒɛnɪən/ ■ adj. Zoology relating to or denoting parasitic flukes which need from two to four hosts to complete their life cycle. Compare with MONOGENEAN.
– ORIGIN 1960s: from the name of the subclass *Digenea*, from Greek *di-* 'twice' + *genea* 'generation, race'.

digerati /ˌdɪdʒəˈrɑːti/ ■ pl. n. informal people with expertise or professional involvement in information technology.
– ORIGIN 1990s: blend of DIGITAL and LITERATI.

digest ■ v. /dʌɪˈdʒɛst, dɪ-/ **1** break down (food) in the stomach and intestines into substances that can be used by the body. **2** Chemistry treat (a substance) with heat, enzymes, or a solvent in order to break it down. **3** understand or assimilate (information) by reflection. **4** arrange in a systematic or convenient order, especially by reduction. ■ n. /ˈdʌɪdʒɛst/ **1** a compilation or summary of material or information. ▶ a methodical summary of a body of laws. ▶ (**the Digest**) the compendium of Roman law compiled in the reign of Justinian. **2** Chemistry a substance or mixture obtained by digestion.
– DERIVATIVES **digestibility** n. **digestible** adj.
– ORIGIN Middle English: from Latin *digest-*, *digerere* 'distribute, dissolve, digest'; the n. is from Latin *digesta* 'matters methodically arranged'.

digester ■ n. Chemistry a container in which substances are treated with heat, enzymes, or a solvent in order to promote decomposition or extract essential components.

digestif /dʌɪˈdʒɛstɪf, ˌdiːʒɛˈstiːf/ ■ n. a drink, especially an alcoholic one, taken before or after a meal in order to aid the digestion.
– ORIGIN French, 'digestive'.

digestion ■ n. the process of digesting. ▶ a person's capacity to digest food.

digestive ■ adj. of or relating to the process of digesting food. ▶ (of food or medicine) aiding or promoting the process of digestion. ■ n. **1** a food or medicine that aids or promotes the digestion of food. **2** Brit. a round semi-sweet biscuit made of wholemeal flour.
– DERIVATIVES **digestively** adv.
– ORIGIN Middle English: from Latin *digestivus*, from *digest-*, *digerere* (see DIGEST).

digger ■ n. a person, animal, or large machine that digs earth.

digger wasp ■ n. a solitary wasp which excavates a burrow, filling it with paralysed insects or spiders for its larvae to feed on. [Families Sphecidae and Pompilidae: many species.]

diggings ■ pl. n. a site such as a mine or goldfield that has been excavated. ▶ material that has been dug from the ground.

digit /ˈdɪdʒɪt/ ■ n. **1** any of the numerals from 0 to 9, especially when forming part of a number. **2** a finger or thumb. ▶ Zoology a finger, thumb, or toe.
– ORIGIN Middle English: from Latin *digitus* 'finger, toe'.

digital ■ adj. **1** relating to or using signals or information represented as digits using discrete values of a physical quantity such as voltage or magnetic polarization. Compare with ANALOGUE. ▶ involving or relating to the use of computer technology: *the digital revolution*. **2** (of a clock or watch) showing the time by means of displayed digits rather than hands or a pointer. **3** of or relating to a finger or fingers.
– DERIVATIVES **digitally** adv.

digital audiotape ■ n. magnetic tape used to make digital recordings.

digital camera ■ n. a camera which produces digital images that can be stored in a computer and displayed on screen.

digital divide ■ n. the gulf between those who have ready access to computers and the Internet and those who do not.

digitalin /ˌdɪdʒɪˈteɪlɪn/ ■ n. a drug containing the active constituents of digitalis.

digitalis /ˌdɪdʒɪˈteɪlɪs/ ■ n. a drug prepared from foxglove leaves, containing substances that stimulate the heart muscle.
– ORIGIN C18: from the genus name of the foxglove, from *digitalis* (*herba*) '(plant) relating to the finger', suggested by German *Fingerhut* 'thimble, foxglove'.

digitalize[1] (also **-ise**) ■ v. another term for DIGITIZE.
– DERIVATIVES **digitalization** (also **-isation**) n.

digitalize[2] (also **-ise**) ■ v. Medicine administer digitalis to (a patient with a heart complaint).
– DERIVATIVES **digitalization** (also **-isation**) n.

digital mapping ■ n. the process of converting geographic information from e.g. satellite images and aerial photography into digital form.

digitigrade /ˈdɪdʒɪtɪˌgreɪd/ ■ adj. Zoology (of a mammal) walking on its toes and not touching the ground with its heels, as a dog, cat, or rodent. Compare with PLANTIGRADE.
– ORIGIN C19: from Latin *digitus* 'finger, toe' + *-gradus* '-walking'.

digitize (also **-ise**) ■ v. [usu. as adj. **digitized** (also **-ised**)] convert (pictures or sound) into a digital form that can be processed by a computer.
– DERIVATIVES **digitization** (also **-isation**) n. **digitizer** (also **-iser**) n.

diglossia /dʌɪˈglɒsɪə/ ■ n. Linguistics a situation in which two languages (or two varieties of the same language) are used under different conditions within a community, often by the same speakers.
– DERIVATIVES **diglossic** adj.
– ORIGIN 1950s: from Greek *diglōssos* 'bilingual', on the pattern of French *diglossie*.

dignified ■ adj. having or showing dignity.
– DERIVATIVES **dignifiedly** adv.

dignify ■ v. (**-ies, -ied**) make (something) seem worthy and impressive. ▶ give an impressive name to (someone or something unworthy of it).
– ORIGIN Middle English: from late Latin *dignificare*, from Latin *dignus* 'worthy'.

dignitary /'dɪgnɪt(ə)ri/ ■ n. (pl. **-ies**) a person holding high rank or office.

dignity ■ n. (pl. **-ies**) 1 the state or quality of being worthy of honour or respect. 2 a composed or serious manner or style. ▶ a sense of pride in oneself: *it was beneath his dignity to shout*.
– PHRASES **stand on one's dignity** insist on being treated with due respect.
– ORIGIN Middle English: from Latin *dignitas*, from *dignus* 'worthy'.

digraph /'dʌɪgrɑːf/ ■ n. 1 a combination of two letters representing one sound, as in *ph* and *ey*. 2 Printing a ligature.
– DERIVATIVES **digraphic** adj.

digress /dʌɪ'grɛs/ ■ v. leave the main subject temporarily in speech or writing.
– DERIVATIVES **digresser** n. **digression** n. **digressive** adj. **digressively** adv. **digressiveness** n.
– ORIGIN C16: from Latin *digress-*, *digredi* 'step away', from *di-* 'aside' + *gradi* 'to walk'.

dihedral /dʌɪ'hiːdr(ə)l/ ■ adj. having or contained by two plane faces. ■ n. 1 an angle formed by two plane faces. 2 Aeronautics upward inclination of an aircraft's wing.
– ORIGIN C18: from **DI-**[1] + *-hedral* (see **-HEDRON**).

dihybrid /dʌɪ'hʌɪbrɪd/ ■ n. Genetics a hybrid that is heterozygous for alleles of two different genes.

dik-dik /'dɪkdɪk/ ■ n. a dwarf antelope found on the dry savannah of Africa. [Genus *Madoqua*: several species.]
– ORIGIN C19: a local word in East Africa, imitative of its call.

dike[1] ■ n. variant spelling of **DYKE**[1].

dike[2] ■ n. variant spelling of **DYKE**[2].

dikkop /'dɪkɒp, 'dɪkɔp/ ■ n. (pl. same or **dikkops**) S. African 1 another term for **THICK-KNEE**. 2 a form of African horse sickness, characterized by swelling of the animal's head and neck.
– ORIGIN S. African Dutch, from Dutch *dik* 'thick' + *kop* 'head'.

diktat /'dɪktat/ ■ n. an order or decree imposed by someone in power without popular consent.
– ORIGIN 1930s: from German.

dilapidated ■ adj. (of a building or object) in a state of disrepair or ruin as a result of age or neglect.

dilapidation ■ n. 1 the state or process of falling into decay or being in disrepair. 2 (**dilapidations**) repairs required during or at the end of a tenancy or lease.

dilatation /ˌdʌɪleɪ'teɪʃ(ə)n, dɪ-, -lə-/ ■ n. chiefly Medicine & Physiology the action of dilating a vessel or opening or the process of becoming dilated. ▶ a dilated part of a hollow organ or vessel.

dilatation and curettage ■ n. Medicine a surgical procedure involving dilatation of the cervix and curettage of the uterus, performed after a miscarriage or for the removal of cysts or tumours.

dilate /dʌɪ'leɪt, dɪ-/ ■ v. 1 become or make wider, larger, or more open. 2 (**dilate on**) speak or write at length on.
– DERIVATIVES **dilatable** adj. **dilation** n.
– ORIGIN Middle English: from Latin *dilatare* 'spread out'.

dilator ■ n. 1 (also **dilator muscle**) Anatomy a muscle whose contraction dilates an organ or aperture, such as the pupil of the eye. 2 a surgical instrument for dilating a tube or cavity in the body. ▶ a vasodilatory drug.

dilatory /'dɪlət(ə)ri/ ■ adj. given to or intended to cause delay.
– DERIVATIVES **dilatorily** adv. **dilatoriness** n.
– ORIGIN Middle English: from late Latin *dilatorius*, from Latin *dilator* 'delayer', from *dilat-*, *differre* 'defer'.

dildo ■ n. (pl. **-os** or **-oes**) an object shaped like an erect penis used for sexual stimulation.
– ORIGIN C16.

dilemma /dɪ'lɛmə, dʌɪ-/ ■ n. 1 a situation in which a difficult choice has to be made between two or more alternatives. ▶ informal a difficult situation or problem.

329

dimer

2 Logic an argument forcing an opponent to choose either of two unfavourable alternatives.
– ORIGIN C16: from Greek *dilēmma*, from *di-* 'twice' + *lēmma* 'premise'.

dilettante /ˌdɪlɪ'tanteɪ, -ti/ ■ n. (pl. **dilettanti** /-ti/ or **dilettantes**) 1 a person who cultivates an area of interest, such as the arts, without real commitment or knowledge. 2 archaic a person with an amateur interest in the arts.
– DERIVATIVES **dilettantish** adj. **dilettantism** n.
– ORIGIN C18: from Italian, 'person loving the arts'.

diligence[1] /'dɪlɪdʒ(ə)ns/ ■ n. careful and persistent work or effort.

diligence[2] /'dɪlɪdʒ(ə)ns/ ■ n. historical a public stagecoach.
– ORIGIN C17: from French, shortened from *carrosse de diligence* 'coach of speed'.

diligent ■ adj. careful and conscientious in one's work or duties.
– DERIVATIVES **diligently** adv.
– ORIGIN Middle English: from Latin *diligens* 'assiduous', from *diligere* 'take delight in'.

dill (also **dill weed**) ■ n. an aromatic culinary and medicinal herb of the parsley family, with yellow flowers. [*Anethum graveolens*.]
– ORIGIN Old English.

dill pickle ■ n. pickled cucumber flavoured with dill.

dilly-dally ■ v. (**-ies, -ied**) informal dawdle or vacillate.
– ORIGIN C17: reduplication of **DALLY**.

diluent /'dɪljʊənt/ technical ■ n. a substance used to dilute something. ■ adj. acting to cause dilution.
– ORIGIN C18: from Latin *diluere* 'dissolve'.

dilute /dʌɪ'l(j)uːt, dɪ-/ ■ v. 1 make (a liquid) thinner or weaker by adding water or another solvent. 2 make weaker or less forceful by modifying or adding other elements. ■ adj. /also 'dʌɪ-/ (of a liquid) diluted. ▶ Chemistry (of a solution) having a relatively low concentration of solute.
– DERIVATIVES **diluter** n. **dilution** n. **dilutive** adj.
– ORIGIN C16: from Latin *diluere* 'wash away, dissolve'.

diluvial /dʌɪ'l(j)uːvɪəl, dɪ-/ (also **diluvian**) ■ adj. of or relating to a flood or floods, especially the biblical Flood.
– ORIGIN C17: from late Latin *diluvialis*, from *diluvium* 'deluge'.

dim ■ adj. (**dimmer, dimmest**) 1 (of a light or illuminated object) not shining brightly or clearly. ▶ made difficult to see by darkness, shade, or distance. ▶ (of the eyes) not able to see clearly. 2 not clearly recalled or formulated in the mind. 3 informal stupid or slow to understand. ■ v. (**dimmed, dimming**) make or become dim. ▶ N. Amer. dip (a vehicle's headlights).
– PHRASES **take a dim view of** regard with disapproval.
– DERIVATIVES **dimly** adv. **dimmish** adj. **dimness** n.
– ORIGIN Old English, of Germanic origin.

dime /dʌɪm/ ■ n. N. Amer. a ten-cent coin. ▶ informal a small amount of money.
– PHRASES **a dime a dozen** informal very common and of little value. **drop a (or the) dime on** informal inform on. **on a dime** informal within a small area or short distance.
– ORIGIN Middle English: from Old French *disme*, from Latin *decima pars* 'tenth part'.

dimension /dɪ'mɛnʃ(ə)n, dʌɪ-/ ■ n. 1 a measurable extent, such as length, breadth, or height. ▶ Physics an expression for a derived physical quantity in terms of fundamental quantities such as mass, length, or time, raised to the appropriate power (acceleration, for example, having the dimension of $length \times time^{-2}$). 2 an aspect or feature: *water can add a new dimension to your garden*. ■ v. cut or shape to particular dimensions. ▶ [usu. as adj. **dimensioned**] mark (a diagram) with dimensions.
– DERIVATIVES **-dimensional** adj. **dimensionless** adj.
– ORIGIN Middle English: from Latin *dimensio(n)-*, from *dimetiri* 'measure out'.

dimer /'dʌɪmə/ ■ n. Chemistry a molecule or molecular complex consisting of two identical molecules linked together.
– DERIVATIVES **dimeric** adj.
– ORIGIN 1930s: from **DI-**[1], on the pattern of *polymer*.

dimerize /ˈdʌɪmərʌɪz/ (also **-ise**) ■ v. Chemistry combine with a similar molecule to form a dimer.
– DERIVATIVES **dimerization** (also **-isation**) n.

dime store ■ n. N. Amer. a shop selling cheap merchandise (originally one where the maximum price was a dime).
▶ [as modifier] cheap and inferior.

dimeter /ˈdɪmɪtə/ ■ n. Prosody a line of verse consisting of two metrical feet.
– ORIGIN C16: from Greek *dimetros* 'of two measures'.

dimethyl sulphoxide /dʌɪˌmiːθʌɪl sʌlˈfɒksʌɪd, -ˌmɛθ-, -θɪl/ (US **dimethyl sulfoxide**) ■ n. Chemistry a colourless liquid used as a solvent, especially for medicines applied to the skin (which it readily penetrates).

dimetrodon /dʌɪˈmiːtrədɒn/ ■ n. a large fossil carnivorous mammal-like reptile of the Permian period, with long spines on its back supporting a sail-like crest.
– ORIGIN modern Latin, from *di-* 'twice' + Greek *metron* 'measure' + *odous, odont-* 'tooth' (taken in the sense 'two long teeth').

diminish ■ v. **1** make or become less. **2** [as adj. **diminished**] Music denoting an interval which is one semitone less than the corresponding minor or perfect interval.
– PHRASES **(the law of) diminishing returns** the principle that as expenditure or investment increases each further increase produces a proportionately smaller return.
– DERIVATIVES **diminishable** adj.
– ORIGIN Middle English: blend of archaic *minish* 'diminish' (from Latin *minutia* 'smallness') and obsolete *diminue* 'speak disparagingly' (from Latin *deminuere* 'lessen').

diminished responsibility ■ n. English Law an unbalanced mental state which is recognized as grounds to reduce a charge of murder to that of manslaughter.

diminution /ˌdɪmɪˈnjuːʃ(ə)n/ ■ n. a reduction.

diminutive /dɪˈmɪnjʊtɪv/ ■ adj. **1** extremely or unusually small. **2** (of a word, name, or suffix) implying smallness, either actual or as an expression of affection or scorn (e.g. *teeny, -let*). ■ n. a shortened form of a name, typically used informally.
– DERIVATIVES **diminutively** adv. **diminutiveness** n.
– ORIGIN Middle English: from Old French *diminutif*, from late Latin *diminutivus*, from Latin *deminuere* 'lessen'.

dimity /ˈdɪmɪti/ ■ n. a hard-wearing cotton fabric woven with stripes or checks.
– ORIGIN Middle English: from Italian *dimito* or medieval Latin *dimitum*, from Greek *dimitos*, from *di-* 'twice' + *mitos* 'warp thread'.

dimmer ■ n. **1** (also **dimmer switch**) a device for varying the brightness of an electric light. **2** US a dipped headlight.

dimorphic /dʌɪˈmɔːfɪk/ ■ adj. chiefly Biology occurring in or representing two distinct forms.
– DERIVATIVES **dimorphism** n.
– ORIGIN C19: from Greek *dimorphos*, from *di-* 'twice' + *morphē* 'form'.

dimple ■ n. a small depression in the flesh, either permanent or forming in the cheeks when one smiles. ■ v. produce a dimple or dimples in the surface of. ▶ [usu. as adj. **dimpled**] form or show a dimple or dimples.
– DERIVATIVES **dimply** adj.
– ORIGIN Middle English: of Germanic origin.

dim sum /dɪm ˈsʌm/ (also **dim sim** /ˈsɪm/) ■ n. a Chinese dish of small steamed or fried savoury dumplings containing various fillings.
– ORIGIN from Chinese (Cantonese dialect) *tim sam*, from *tim* 'dot' + *sam* 'heart'.

dimwit ■ n. informal a stupid or silly person.
– DERIVATIVES **dim-witted** adj. **dim-wittedly** adv. **dim-wittedness** n.

DIN ■ n. any of a series of technical standards originating in Germany and used internationally, especially to designate electrical connections and film speeds.
– ORIGIN C20: acronym from *Deutsche Industrie-Norm* 'German Industrial Standard'.

din ■ n. a loud, unpleasant, and prolonged noise. ■ v. (**dinned, dinning**) **1** (**din something into**) instil information into (someone) by constant repetition. **2** make a din.
– ORIGIN Old English, of Germanic origin.

dinar /ˈdiːnɑː/ ■ n. the basic monetary unit of Algeria, Bahrain, Iran, Iraq, Jordan, Libya, Sudan, and the states of Yugoslavia.
– ORIGIN from Arabic and Persian *dīnār*, Turkish and Serbo-Croat *dinar*, from Latin *denarius* (see **DENARIUS**).

dine ■ v. **1** eat dinner. **2** (**dine out on**) regularly entertain friends with (a humorous or interesting anecdote).
– ORIGIN Middle English: from Old French *disner*, prob. from *desjëuner* 'to break fast'.

diner ■ n. **1** a person who dines. **2** a dining car on a train. **3** N. Amer. a small roadside restaurant, originally one designed to resemble a dining car.

dinette /dʌɪˈnɛt/ ■ n. **1** a small room or part of a room used for eating meals. **2** N. Amer. a set of table and chairs for such an area.
– ORIGIN 1930s: from **DINE** + **-ETTE**.

ding[1] ■ v. make the metallic ringing sound of a bell.

ding[2] informal, chiefly N. Amer. ■ n. a mark or dent on the bodywork of a car or other vehicle. ■ v. dent or hit.
– ORIGIN Middle English: prob. of Scandinavian origin.

ding-a-ling ■ n. **1** the ringing sound of a bell. **2** N. Amer. informal an eccentric or stupid person.

dingbat /ˈdɪŋbat/ ■ n. informal **1** N. Amer. & Austral./NZ a stupid or eccentric person. **2** (**dingbats**) Austral./NZ delusions or feelings of unease, particularly those induced by delirium tremens. **3** a typographical device other than a letter or numeral, used to signal divisions in text or to replace letters in a euphemistically presented vulgar word.
– ORIGIN C19: perhaps based on **DING**[2].

ding-dong ■ n. informal **1** Brit. a fierce argument or fight. **2** N. Amer. a silly or foolish person. ■ adv. & adj. **1** with the simple alternate chimes of a bell. **2** [as adj.] Brit. informal (of a contest) evenly matched and intensely waged.

dinger /ˈdɪŋə/ ■ n. Baseball a home run.
– ORIGIN C19: shortening of **HUMDINGER**.

dinghy /ˈdɪŋgi, ˈdɪŋi/ ■ n. (pl. **-ies**) **1** a small boat for recreation or racing, especially an open boat with a mast and sails. **2** a small inflatable rubber boat.
– ORIGIN C19 (denoting a rowing boat in India): from Hindi *ḍiṅgī*.

dingle ■ n. poetic/literary or dialect a deep wooded valley.
– ORIGIN Middle English.

dingo /ˈdɪŋgəʊ/ ■ n. (pl. **-oes** or **-os**) **1** a wild or semi-domesticated Australian dog with a sandy-coloured coat. [*Canis dingo*.] **2** Austral. Informal a cowardly or treacherous person.
– ORIGIN C18: from Dharuk (an extinct Aboriginal language) *din-gu* 'domesticated dingo'.

dingus /ˈdɪŋəs/ ■ n. (pl. **dinguses**) S. African & N. Amer. informal a thing one cannot or does not wish to name specifically.
– ORIGIN C19: from Dutch *ding* 'thing'.

dingy /ˈdɪn(d)ʒi/ ■ adj. (**-ier, -iest**) gloomy and drab.
– DERIVATIVES **dingily** adv. **dinginess** n.
– ORIGIN C18: perhaps from Old English *dynge* 'dung'.

dining car ■ n. a railway carriage equipped as a restaurant.

dining room ■ n. a room in a house or hotel in which meals are eaten.

dink chiefly Tennis ■ n. a drop shot. ■ v. hit (the ball) with a drop shot.
– ORIGIN 1930s: symbolic of the light action.

Dinka /ˈdɪŋkə/ ■ n. (pl. same or **Dinkas**) **1** a member of a Sudanese people of the Nile basin. **2** the Nilotic language of this people.
– ORIGIN from the local word *Jieng* 'people'.

dinkum /ˈdɪŋkəm/ (also **fair dinkum**) Austral./NZ informal ■ adj. genuine. ■ adv. [often in questions] really.
– ORIGIN C19.

dinky[1] ■ adj. (**-ier, -iest**) informal **1** Brit. small and neat in an attractive way. **2** N. Amer. disappointingly small; insignificant. ■ n. S. African a small bottle of wine, holding approximately 200 millilitres.
– ORIGIN C18: from Scots and northern English dialect *dink* 'neat, trim'.

dinky[2] ■ n. (pl. **-ies**) informal a partner in a well-off working couple with no children.
– ORIGIN 1980s: acronym from *double income, no kids*.

dinner ■ n. the main meal of the day, taken either around midday or in the evening. ▸ a formal evening meal, typically one in honour of a person or event.
– ORIGIN Middle English: from Old French *disner* (see DINE).

dinner jacket ■ n. a man's short jacket without tails, typically a black one, worn with a bow tie for formal evening occasions.

dinner lady ■ n. Brit. a woman who serves meals and supervises children at mealtimes in a school.

dinner theatre ■ n. N. Amer. a theatre in which a meal is included in the price of a ticket.

dinoflagellate /ˌdaɪnə(ʊ)ˈflædʒəleɪt/ ■ n. Biology a single-celled aquatic organism with two flagella, occurring in large numbers in marine plankton. [Division Dinophyta.]
– ORIGIN C19: from Greek *dinos* 'whirling' + Latin *flagellum* (see FLAGELLUM).

dinosaur /ˈdaɪnəsɔː/ ■ n. **1** a Mesozoic fossil reptile of a diverse group including large bipedal and quadrupedal forms such as tyrannosaurus, brachiosaurus, triceratops, etc. **2** a person or thing that is outdated or has become obsolete because of failure to adapt.
– DERIVATIVES **dinosaurian** adj. & n.
– ORIGIN C19: from Greek *deinos* 'terrible' + *sauros* 'lizard'.

dint ■ n. an impression or hollow in a surface.
– PHRASES **by dint of** by means of.
– ORIGIN Old English *dynt*, reinforced in Middle English by the rel. Old Norse word *dyntr*.

diocesan /daɪˈɒsɪs(ə)n/ ■ adj. of or concerning a diocese. ■ n. the bishop of a diocese.

diocese /ˈdaɪəsɪs/ ■ n. (pl. **dioceses** /ˈdaɪəsiːz, -sɪzɪz/) a district under the pastoral care of a bishop in the Christian Church.
– ORIGIN Middle English: from Old French *diocise*, from Latin *dioecesis* 'governor's jurisdiction, diocese'.

diode /ˈdaɪəʊd/ ■ n. Electronics **1** a semiconductor device with two terminals, typically allowing the flow of current in one direction only. **2** a thermionic valve with two electrodes.
– ORIGIN C20: from DI-[1] + a shortened form of ELECTRODE.

dioecious /daɪˈiːʃəs/ ■ adj. Biology (of a plant or invertebrate animal) having the male and female reproductive organs in separate individuals. Compare with MONOECIOUS.
– DERIVATIVES **dioecy** n.
– ORIGIN C18: from *Dioecia* (a class in Linnaeus's sexual system), from DI-[1] + Greek *-oikos* 'house'.

dioestrus /daɪˈiːstrəs/ (US **diestrus**) ■ n. Zoology (in most female mammals) a period of sexual inactivity between recurrent periods of oestrus.

diol /ˈdaɪɒl/ ■ n. Chemistry an alcohol containing two hydroxyl groups in its molecule.

Dionysiac /ˌdaɪəˈnɪzɪak/ (also **Dionysian** /-zɪən/) ■ adj. **1** Greek & Roman Mythology of or relating to the god Dionysus. **2** of or relating to the sensual, spontaneous, and emotional aspects of human nature. Compare with APOLLONIAN.

diopside /daɪˈɒpsaɪd/ ■ n. a pale green to white silicate mineral occurring in many metamorphic and igneous rocks.
– ORIGIN C19: from French, from DI-[3] + Greek *opsis* 'aspect', later interpreted as from Greek *diopsis* 'a view through'.

dioptre /daɪˈɒptə/ (US **diopter**) ■ n. Optics a unit of refractive power, which is equal to the reciprocal of the focal length (in metres) of a given lens.
– ORIGIN C16: from Latin *dioptra*, from Greek, from *di-* 'through' + *optos* 'visible'.

dioptric /daɪˈɒptrɪk/ ■ adj. of or relating to the refraction of light, especially in the organs of sight or in devices which aid or improve the vision.
– ORIGIN C17: from Greek *dioptrikos*, from *dioptra*, a kind of theodolite.

dioptrics ■ pl. n. [treated as sing.] the branch of optics concerned with refraction.

diorama /ˌdaɪəˈrɑːmə/ ■ n. **1** a model representing a scene with three-dimensional figures. ▸ a miniature film set used for special effects or animation. **2** chiefly historical a scenic painting, viewed through a peephole, in which changes in colour and direction of illumination simulate changes in the weather and time of day.
– ORIGIN C19: French, from DIA-, on the pattern of *panorama*.

diorite /ˈdaɪərʌɪt/ ■ n. Geology a speckled, coarse-grained igneous rock consisting typically of plagioclase, feldspar, and hornblende.
– DERIVATIVES **dioritic** adj.
– ORIGIN C19: from Greek *diorizein* 'distinguish'.

diosma /daɪˈɒzmə/ ■ n. a small evergreen heath-like shrub with tiny white or pink flowers and a strong aromatic scent, indigenous to South Africa. [Genus *Diosma*: several species.]
– ORIGIN C19: from Greek *dios* 'heavenly' + *osmē* 'fragrance'.

dioxane /daɪˈɒkseɪn/ (also **dioxan** /-an/) ■ n. Chemistry a colourless toxic heterocyclic compound used as an organic solvent.

dioxide /daɪˈɒksaɪd/ ■ n. Chemistry an oxide containing two atoms of oxygen in its molecule or empirical formula.

dioxin /daɪˈɒksɪn/ ■ n. a highly toxic organic compound produced as a by-product in some manufacturing processes.

DIP ■ abbrev. **1** Computing document image processing. **2** Electronics dual in-line package.

Dip. ■ abbrev. diploma.

dip ■ v. (**dipped**, **dipping**) **1** (**dip something in/into**) put or let something down quickly or briefly in or into (liquid). ▸ make (a candle) by immersing a wick repeatedly in hot wax. **2** sink, drop, or slope downwards. ▸ (of a level or amount) temporarily become lower or smaller. ▸ lower or move downwards. ▸ lower the beam of (a vehicle's headlights). **3** (**dip into**) put a hand or implement into (a bag or container) in order to take something out. **4** (**dip into**) spend from or make use of (one's financial resources). ■ n. **1** an act of dipping, especially a brief swim. **2** a thick sauce in which pieces of food are dipped before eating. **3** a brief downward slope followed by an upward one. ▸ an instance of dropping briefly before rising again. **4** the angle made with the horizontal at any point by the earth's magnetic field. ▸ Geology the angle a stratum makes with the horizontal. ▸ Astronomy & Surveying the apparent depression of the horizon from the line of observation, due to the curvature of the earth.
– ORIGIN Old English, of Germanic origin.

diphenhydramine /ˌdaɪfɛnˈhaɪdrəmiːn/ ■ n. Medicine an antihistamine compound used for the symptomatic relief of allergies.

diphtheria /dɪpˈθɪərɪə, dɪf-/ ■ n. a serious bacterial disease causing inflammation of the mucous membranes and formation of a false membrane in the throat which hinders breathing and swallowing.
– DERIVATIVES **diphtherial** adj. **diphtheritic** /-θəˈrɪtɪk/ adj. **diphtheroid** adj.
– ORIGIN C19: modern Latin, from French *diphthérie*, from Greek *diphthera* 'skin, hide'.

diphthong /ˈdɪfθɒŋ/ ■ n. a sound formed by the combination of two vowels in a single syllable, in which the sound begins as one vowel and moves towards another (as in *coin*). ▸ a digraph representing the sound of a diphthong or single vowel (as in *feat*). ▸ a ligature (such as æ).
– DERIVATIVES **diphthongal** /-ˈθɒŋɡ(ə)l/ adj. **diphthongization** (also **-isation**) n. **diphthongize** (also **-ise**) v.
– ORIGIN Middle English: from Greek *diphthongos*, from *di-* 'twice' + *phthongos* 'sound'.

diplegia /daɪˈpliːdʒə/ ■ n. Medicine paralysis of corresponding parts on both sides of the body, typically affecting the legs more severely than the arms.

diplo- ■ comb. form **1** double: *diplococcus*. **2** diploid: *diplotene*.
– ORIGIN from Greek *diplous* 'double'.

diplococcus /ˌdɪplə(ʊ)ˈkɒkəs/ ■ n. (pl. **diplococci** /-k(s)ʌɪ, -k(s)iː/) a bacterium that occurs as pairs of cocci, e.g. pneumococcus.

diplodocus

diplodocus /dɪˈplɒdəkəs, ˌdɪplə(ʊ)ˈdəʊkəs/ ■ n. a huge herbivorous dinosaur of the late Jurassic period, with a long slender neck and tail.
– ORIGIN modern Latin, from DIPLO- + Greek *dokos* 'wooden beam'.

diploid /ˈdɪplɔɪd/ ■ adj. Genetics (of a cell or nucleus) containing two complete sets of chromosomes, one from each parent. Compare with HAPLOID.
– DERIVATIVES **diploidy** n.
– ORIGIN C19: from Greek *diplous* 'double'.

diploma ■ n. 1 a certificate awarded by an educational establishment for passing an examination or completing a course of study. 2 historical an official document or charter.
– ORIGIN C17: from Greek *diplōma* 'folded paper'.

diplomacy ■ n. 1 the profession, activity, or skill of managing international relations. 2 skill and tact in dealing with people.
– ORIGIN C18: from French *diplomatie*, from *diplomatique* 'diplomatic', on the pattern of *aristocratie* 'aristocracy'.

diplomat ■ n. an official representing a country abroad.

diplomate /ˈdɪpləmeɪt/ ■ n. a holder of a diploma.

diplomatic ■ adj. 1 of or concerning diplomacy. 2 tactful. 3 (of an edition or copy) exactly reproducing the original.
– DERIVATIVES **diplomatically** adv.

diplomatic bag ■ n. a container in which official mail is sent to or from an embassy, which is not subject to customs inspection.

diplomatic corps ■ n. the body of diplomats representing other countries in a particular state.

diplomatic immunity ■ n. the privilege of exemption from certain laws and taxes granted to diplomats by the state in which they are working.

diplomatic pouch ■ n. US term for DIPLOMATIC BAG.

diplomatist ■ n. old-fashioned term for DIPLOMAT.

diplotene /ˈdɪplətiːn/ ■ n. Biology the fourth stage of the prophase of meiosis, following pachytene, during which the paired chromosomes begin to separate.
– ORIGIN 1920s: from DIPLO- + Greek *tainia* 'band'.

dipole /ˈdaɪpəʊl/ ■ n. 1 Physics a pair of equal and oppositely charged or magnetized poles separated by a distance. 2 an aerial consisting of a horizontal metal rod with a connecting wire at its centre.
– DERIVATIVES **dipolar** adj.

dipole moment ■ n. Physics & Chemistry the mathematical product of the separation of the ends of a dipole and the magnitude of the charges.

dip pen ■ n. a pen that has to be dipped in ink.

dipper ■ n. 1 a stocky, short-tailed songbird frequenting fast-flowing streams and able to dive or walk under water to feed. [*Cinclus cinclus* and related species.] 2 a ladle or scoop.

dippy ■ adj. (-ier, -iest) informal foolish or eccentric.
– ORIGIN C20.

dipshit ■ n. vulgar slang, chiefly N. Amer. a contemptible or inept person.
– ORIGIN 1970s: perhaps a blend of DIPPY + SHIT.

dip slope ■ n. Geology the gentler slope of a cuesta, following the underlying strata. Often contrasted with SCARP SLOPE.

dipsomania /ˌdɪpsə(ʊ)ˈmeɪnɪə/ ■ n. alcoholism, specifically in a form characterized by intermittent bouts of craving for alcohol.
– DERIVATIVES **dipsomaniac** n.
– ORIGIN C19: from Greek *dipso-* (from *dipsa* 'thirst') + -MANIA.

dipstick ■ n. 1 a graduated rod for measuring the depth of a liquid, especially oil in a vehicle's engine. 2 informal a stupid or inept person.

DIP switch ■ n. Computing an arrangement of switches in a dual in-line package used to select the operating mode of a device such as a printer.

Diptera /ˈdɪpt(ə)rə/ ■ pl. n. Entomology a large order of insects that comprises the two-winged or true flies, which have the hind wings reduced to form balancing organs (halteres).
– DERIVATIVES **dipteran** n. & adj.
– ORIGIN from Greek *dipteros* 'two-winged'.

dipterous /ˈdɪpt(ə)rəs/ ■ adj. Entomology of or relating to flies of the order Diptera.

diptych /ˈdɪptɪk/ ■ n. 1 a painting, especially an altarpiece, on two hinged wooden panels which may be closed like a book. 2 an ancient writing tablet consisting of two hinged leaves with waxed inner sides.
– ORIGIN C17: from late Greek *diptukha* 'pair of writing tablets', from Greek *diptukhos* 'folded in two'.

dire ■ adj. 1 extremely serious or urgent. 2 informal of a very poor quality.
– DERIVATIVES **direly** adv. **direness** n.
– ORIGIN C16: from Latin *dirus* 'fearful, threatening'.

direct /dɪˈrɛkt, dʌɪ-/ ■ adj. 1 going from one place to another without changing direction or stopping. ▸ Astronomy & Astrology (of apparent planetary motion) proceeding from west to east in accord with actual motion. 2 straightforward; frank. ▸ clear; unambiguous. 3 without intervening factors or intermediaries: *the complications are a direct result of bacteria spreading.* ▸ (of descent) proceeding in continuous succession from parent to child. ▸ Soccer denoting a free kick from which a goal may be scored without another player touching the ball. 4 perpendicular to a surface. ■ adv. in a direct way or by a direct route. ■ v. 1 control the operations of. ▸ supervise and control (a film, play, or other production). 2 aim (something) in a particular direction. ▸ tell or show (someone) the way. 3 give an order or authoritative instruction to.
– DERIVATIVES **directness** n.
– ORIGIN Middle English: from Latin *directus*, from *dirigere*, from *di-* 'distinctly' or *de-* 'down' + *regere* 'put straight'.

direct action ■ n. the use of strikes, demonstrations, or other public forms of protest rather than negotiation to achieve one's demands.

direct current (abbrev.: **DC**) ■ n. an electric current flowing in one direction only. Compare with ALTERNATING CURRENT.

direct debit ■ n. Brit. another term for DEBIT ORDER.

direct dialling ■ n. the facility of making a telephone call without connection by the operator.

direct-drive ■ adj. denoting or relating to mechanical parts driven directly by a motor, without a belt or other device to transmit power.

direct injection ■ n. (in diesel engines) the use of a pump to spray fuel into the cylinder at high pressure, without the use of compressed air.

direction /dɪˈrɛkʃ(ə)n, dʌɪ-/ ■ n. 1 a course along which someone or something moves, or which must be taken to reach a destination. ▸ a point to or from which a person or thing moves or faces. ▸ a trend or tendency. 2 the action of directing or managing people. ▸ (**directions**) instructions on how to reach a destination or about how to do something.
– DERIVATIVES **directionless** adj.

directional ■ adj. 1 relating to or indicating the direction in which someone or something is facing or moving. 2 having a particular direction of motion, progression, or orientation.
– DERIVATIVES **directionality** /-ˈnalɪti/ n. **directionally** adv.

direction-finder ■ n. a system of aerials for locating the source of radio signals, used as an aid to navigation.

directive ■ n. an official or authoritative instruction. ■ adj. involving the direction of operations.
– ORIGIN Middle English: from medieval Latin *directivus*, from *dirigere* (see DIRECT).

directly ■ adv. 1 in a direct manner. ▸ immediately. ▸ dated soon. 2 exactly in a specified position. ■ conj. Brit. as soon as.

direct mail ■ n. unsolicited commercial literature mailed to prospective customers.
– DERIVATIVES **direct mailing** n.

direct marketing ■ n. the business of selling products or services directly to the customer, e.g. by telephone selling.

direct object ■ n. a noun phrase denoting a person or

VOWELS a cat ɑː arm ɛ bed ɛː hair ə ago əː her ɪ sit i cosy iː see ɒ hot ɔː saw ʌ run

thing that is the recipient of the action of a transitive verb, for example *the dog* in *Jeremy fed the dog*.

director ■ n. **1** a person who is in charge of an activity, department, or organization. **2** a member of the managing board of a business. **3** a person who directs a film, play, etc.
– DERIVATIVES **directorial** adj. **directorship** n.

directorate ■ n. [treated as sing. or pl.] **1** the board of directors of a company. **2** a section of a government department in charge of a particular activity.

director-general ■ n. (pl. **directors-general**) **1** (**Director-General**) S. African a senior civil servant, especially the head of a government department. **2** chiefly Brit. the chief executive of a large organization.

directory ■ n. (pl. **-ies**) a book listing individuals or organizations alphabetically or thematically with details such as addresses and telephone numbers. ▸ Computing a file consisting solely of a set of other files.

directory enquiries (N. Amer. **directory assistance**) ■ pl. n. a telephone service used to find out someone's telephone number.

direct proportion (also **direct ratio**) ■ n. the relation between quantities whose ratio is constant.

directrix /dɪˈrektrɪks, daɪ-/ ■ n. (pl. **directrices** /-trɪsiːz/) Geometry a fixed line used in describing a curve or surface.
– ORIGIN C18: from medieval Latin, 'directress'.

direct speech ■ n. the reporting of speech by repeating the actual words of a speaker, for example *'I'm going,' she said*. Contrasted with REPORTED SPEECH.

direct tax ■ n. a tax, such as income tax, which is levied on the income or profits of the person who pays it.

dirge /dəːdʒ/ ■ n. **1** a lament for the dead, especially one forming part of a funeral rite. **2** a mournful song, piece of music, or sound.
– DERIVATIVES **dirgeful** adj.
– ORIGIN Middle English: from Latin *dirige!* 'direct!', the first word of an antiphon (Psalms 5:8) used in the Latin Office for the Dead.

dirham /ˈdɪər(h)əm/ ■ n. **1** the basic monetary unit of Morocco and the United Arab Emirates. **2** a monetary unit of Libya and Qatar.
– ORIGIN from Arabic: from Greek *drakhmē* (see DRACHMA).

dirigible /ˈdɪrɪdʒɪb(ə)l/ ■ n. an airship.
– ORIGIN C16: from Latin *dirigere* 'to direct'.

dirigisme /ˈdɪrɪʒɪz(ə)m/ ■ n. state control of economic and social matters.
– DERIVATIVES **dirigiste** adj.
– ORIGIN 1950s: from French, from *diriger* 'to direct'.

dirk /dəːk/ ■ n. a short dagger of a kind formerly carried by Scottish Highlanders.
– ORIGIN C16.

dirndl /ˈdəːnd(ə)l/ (also **dirndl skirt**) ■ n. a full, wide skirt with a tight waistband.
– ORIGIN 1930s: from German dialect, diminutive of *Dirne* 'girl'.

dirt ■ n. **1** a substance, such as mud, that causes uncleanliness. ▸ informal excrement: *dog dirt*. **2** loose soil or earth. **3** informal scandalous or sordid information or material.
– PHRASES **eat dirt** informal suffer insults or humiliation.
– ORIGIN Middle English: from Old Norse *drit* 'excrement'.

dirt bike ■ n. a motorcycle designed for use on rough terrain, especially in scrambling.

dirt cheap ■ adv. & adj. informal extremely cheap.

dirt poor ■ adv. & adj. extremely poor.

dirt track ■ n. a course made of rolled cinders for motorcycle racing or of earth for flat racing.
– DERIVATIVES **dirt tracker** n.

dirty ■ adj. (**-ier**, **-iest**) **1** covered or marked with an unclean substance. **2** lewd; obscene. **3** dishonest; dishonourable. **4** (of weather) rough, stormy, and unpleasant. ■ adv. Brit. informal very: *a dirty great stone*. ■ v. (**-ies**, **-ied**) make dirty.
– PHRASES **do the dirty on** Brit. informal cheat or betray. **get one's hands dirty** (or **dirty one's hands**) do manual, menial, or other hard work. **play dirty** informal act in a dishonest or unfair way.
– DERIVATIVES **dirtily** adv. **dirtiness** n.

dirty look ■ n. informal a look expressing disapproval, disgust, or anger.

dirty old man ■ n. informal an older man who is sexually interested in younger women or girls.

dirty weekend ■ n. Brit. informal a weekend spent away, especially in secret, with a lover.

dirty word ■ n. **1** an offensive or indecent word. **2** something regarded with dislike or disapproval.

dirty work ■ n. unpleasant or dishonest activities that are delegated to someone else.

dis /dɪs/ informal, chiefly US ■ v. (also **diss**) (**dissed**, **dissing**) speak disrespectfully to. ■ n. disrespectful talk.

dis- /dɪs/ ■ prefix **1** expressing negation: *disadvantage*. **2** denoting reversal or absence of an action or state: *diseconomy*. **3** denoting removal, separation, or expulsion: *disbar*. **4** expressing completeness or intensification of an action: *disgruntled*.
– ORIGIN from Latin: sometimes via Old French *des-*.

disa /ˈdaɪsə/ ■ n. a southern African orchid often found near streams in mountainous areas. [*Disa uniflora* and other species.]
– ORIGIN C19.

disability ■ n. (pl. **-ies**) **1** a physical or mental condition that limits a person's movements, senses, or activities. **2** a disadvantage or handicap, especially one imposed or recognized by the law.

disable ■ v. **1** (of a disease, injury, or accident) limit (someone) in their movements, senses, or activities. **2** put out of action.
– DERIVATIVES **disablement** n.

disabled ■ adj. (of a person) having a physical or mental disability. ▸ designed for or relating to disabled people: *disabled access*.

USAGE
The word **disabled** is the most generally accepted term in English today. It has superseded outmoded, now often offensive, terms such as **crippled** and **handicapped**.

disabuse /ˌdɪsəˈbjuːz/ ■ v. (usu. **disabuse someone of**) persuade (someone) that an idea or belief is mistaken.

disaccharide /daɪˈsakəraɪd/ ■ n. Chemistry any of a class of sugars whose molecules contain two monosaccharide residues.

disadvantage ■ n. an unfavourable circumstance or condition. ■ v. put in an unfavourable position. ▸ [as adj. **disadvantaged**] in socially or economically deprived circumstances. See also PREVIOUSLY DISADVANTAGED.

disadvantageous ■ adj. involving or creating unfavourable circumstances.
– DERIVATIVES **disadvantageously** adv.

disaffected ■ adj. dissatisfied with those in authority and no longer willing to support them.
– DERIVATIVES **disaffectedly** adv. **disaffection** n.
– ORIGIN C17: from *disaffect*, orig. in the sense 'dislike, disorder'.

disaffiliate /ˌdɪsəˈfɪlɪeɪt/ ■ v. (of a group or organization) end its affiliation with (a subsidiary group). ▸ (of a subsidiary group) end its affiliation.
– DERIVATIVES **disaffiliation** n.

disafforest /ˌdɪsəˈfɒrɪst/ ■ v. another term for DEFOREST.
– DERIVATIVES **disafforestation** n.

disaggregate /dɪsˈagrɪgeɪt/ ■ v. separate into component parts.
– DERIVATIVES **disaggregation** n.

disagree ■ v. (**disagrees**, **disagreed**, **disagreeing**) **1** have a different opinion. **2** (**disagree with**) be inconsistent with. ▸ affect adversely: *the sea crossing disagreed with her*.
– DERIVATIVES **disagreement** n.

disagreeable ■ adj. unpleasant. ▸ unfriendly and bad-tempered.
– DERIVATIVES **disagreeableness** n. **disagreeably** adv.

disallow ■ v. refuse to declare valid.
– DERIVATIVES **disallowance** n.

disambiguate

disambiguate ■ v. remove uncertainty of meaning from.
– DERIVATIVES **disambiguation** n.

disappear ■ v. cease to be visible. ▶ cease to exist or be in use. ▶ (of a person) go missing or (in coded political language) be killed.
– DERIVATIVES **disappearance** n.
– ORIGIN Middle English: from DIS- + APPEAR, on the pattern of French *disparaître*.

disappoint ■ v. fail to fulfil the hopes or expectations of. ▶ prevent (hopes or expectations) from being realized.
– DERIVATIVES **disappointing** adj. **disappointingly** adv. **disappointment** n.
– ORIGIN Middle English ('deprive of a position'): from Old French *desappointer*.

disappointed ■ adj. sad or displeased because one's hopes or expectations have not been fulfilled.
– DERIVATIVES **disappointedly** adv.

disapprobation /ˌdɪsˌæprəˈbeɪʃ(ə)n/ ■ n. strong disapproval, especially on moral grounds.

disapprove ■ v. (often **disapprove of**) have or express an unfavourable opinion. ▶ officially refuse to agree to.
– DERIVATIVES **disapproval** n. **disapprover** n. **disapproving** adj. **disapprovingly** adv.

disarm ■ v. **1** take a weapon or weapons away from. ▶ (of a country or force) give up or reduce its armed forces or weapons. ▶ remove the fuse from (a bomb). **2** deprive of the power to hurt. ▶ [often as adj. **disarming**] allay the hostility or suspicions of.
– DERIVATIVES **disarmer** n. **disarmingly** adv.

disarmament /dɪsˈɑːməm(ə)nt/ ■ n. the reduction or withdrawal of military forces and weapons.

disarrange ■ v. make untidy or disordered.
– DERIVATIVES **disarrangement** n.

disarray ■ n. a state of disorganization or untidiness. ■ v. make disorganized or untidy.

disarticulate ■ v. **1** separate (bones) at the joints. **2** break up and disrupt the logic of (an argument or opinion).
– DERIVATIVES **disarticulation** n.

disassemble ■ v. **1** take to pieces. **2** Computing translate (a program) from machine code into a symbolic language.
– DERIVATIVES **disassembler** n. **disassembly** n.

disassociate ■ v. another term for DISSOCIATE.
– DERIVATIVES **disassociation** n.

disaster ■ n. **1** a sudden accident or a natural catastrophe that causes great damage or loss of life. **2** an event or fact leading to ruin or failure.
– ORIGIN C16: from Italian *disastro* 'ill-starred event', from Latin *astrum* 'star'.

disastrous ■ adj. **1** causing great damage. **2** informal highly unsuccessful.
– DERIVATIVES **disastrously** adv.

disavow ■ v. deny any responsibility or support for.
– DERIVATIVES **disavowal** n.

disband ■ v. (with reference to an organized group) break up or cause to break up.
– DERIVATIVES **disbandment** n.
– ORIGIN C16: from obsolete French *desbander*.

disbar ■ v. (**disbarred**, **disbarring**) **1** expel (an advocate) from the Bar. **2** exclude from something.
– DERIVATIVES **disbarment** n.

disbelief ■ n. inability or refusal to accept that something is true or real. ▶ lack of faith.

disbelieve ■ v. be unable to believe. ▶ have no religious faith.
– DERIVATIVES **disbeliever** n. **disbelieving** adj. **disbelievingly** adv.

disburse /dɪsˈbɜːs/ ■ v. pay out (money from a fund).
– DERIVATIVES **disbursal** n. **disbursement** n. **disburser** n.
– ORIGIN C16: from Old French *desbourser*, from *des-* (expressing removal) + *bourse* 'purse'.

disc (US also **disk**) ■ n. **1** a flat, thin, round object. **2** (**disk**) an information storage device for a computer comprising a rotatable disc on which data is stored either magnetically or optically (as on a CD-ROM). **3** dated a gramophone record. **4** (**discs**) one of the suits in some tarot packs, corresponding to coins in others. **5** (also **intervertebral disc**) a layer of cartilage separating adjacent vertebrae in the spine. **6** Botany the central part of the flower of a daisy or other composite plant, consisting of a close-packed cluster of tubular florets.
– ORIGIN C17: from French *disque* or Latin *discus* (see DISCUS).

discard ■ v. /dɪˈskɑːd/ **1** get rid of as no longer useful or desirable. **2** (in bridge, whist, and similar card games) play (a card that is neither of the suit led nor a trump), when one is unable to follow suit. ■ n. /ˈdɪskɑːd/ a discarded item, especially a card in bridge or whist.
– DERIVATIVES **discardable** /dɪsˈkɑːdəb(ə)l/ adj.
– ORIGIN C16: from DIS- + CARD¹.

discarnate /dɪsˈkɑːnət/ ■ adj. not having a physical body.
– ORIGIN C19: from DIS- + Latin *caro, carn-* 'flesh' or late Latin *carnatus* 'fleshy'.

disc brake ■ n. a type of vehicle brake employing the friction of pads attached to a disc attached to the wheel.

discern /dɪˈsɜːn/ ■ v. recognize or find out. ▶ distinguish with difficulty by sight or with the other senses.
– DERIVATIVES **discerner** n. **discernible** adj. **discernibly** adv.
– ORIGIN Middle English: from Latin *discernere*, from *dis-* 'apart' + *cernere* 'to separate'.

discerning ■ adj. having or showing good judgement.
– DERIVATIVES **discerningly** adv. **discernment** n.

discharge ■ v. /dɪsˈtʃɑːdʒ/ **1** allow to go, especially from hospital. ▶ dismiss from a job. ▶ release from the custody or restraint of the law. **2** emit or send out (a liquid, gas, or other substance). ▶ Physics release or neutralize the electric charge of (an electric field, battery, or other object). ▶ fire (a gun or missile). ▶ unload (goods or passengers) from a ship. **3** do all that is required to fulfil (a responsibility) or perform (a duty). ▶ release from a contract or obligation. ▶ Law relieve (an insolvent) of residual liability. **4** Law (of a judge or court) cancel (an order of a court). ▶ S. African Law acquit (an accused). ■ n. /ˈdɪstʃɑːdʒ, dɪsˈtʃɑːdʒ/ **1** the action of discharging. **2** a substance that has been discharged. ▶ a flow of electricity through air or other gas, especially when accompanied by emission of light.
– DERIVATIVES **dischargeable** adj. **discharger** n.
– ORIGIN Middle English: from Old French *descharger*, from late Latin *discarricare* 'unload', from *dis-* (expressing reversal) + *carricare* (see CHARGE).

disciple /dɪˈsʌɪp(ə)l/ ■ n. **1** Christian Church a personal follower of Christ during his life, especially one of the twelve Apostles. **2** a follower or pupil of a teacher, leader, or philosophy.
– DERIVATIVES **discipleship** n. **discipular** /dɪˈsɪpjʊlə/ adj.
– ORIGIN Old English, from Latin *discipulus* 'learner', from *discere* 'learn'; reinforced by Old French *deciple*.

disciplinarian ■ n. a person who believes in or practises firm discipline.

discipline /ˈdɪsɪplɪn/ ■ n. **1** the practice of training people to obey rules or a code of behaviour. ▶ controlled behaviour resulting from such training. **2** a branch of knowledge, especially one studied in higher education. ■ v. **1** train in obedience or self-control by punishment or imposing rules. ▶ [as adj. **disciplined**] showing a controlled form of behaviour. **2** punish or rebuke formally for an offence.
– DERIVATIVES **disciplinable** adj. **disciplinal** /ˌdɪsɪˈplʌɪn(ə)l, ˈdɪsɪˌplɪn(ə)l/ adj. **disciplinary** adj.
– ORIGIN Middle English: from Latin *disciplina* 'instruction, knowledge', from *discipulus* (see DISCIPLE).

disc jockey ■ n. a person who introduces and plays recorded popular music, especially on radio or at a disco.

disclaim ■ v. **1** refuse to acknowledge. **2** Law renounce a legal claim to (a property or title).
– ORIGIN Middle English: from Anglo-Norman French *desclamer*, from *des-* (expressing reversal) + *clamer* (see CLAIM).

disclaimer ■ n. **1** a statement disclaiming something, especially responsibility. **2** Law an act of repudiating another's claim or renouncing one's own.

disclose ■ v. make (secret or new information) known. ▶ expose to view.
– DERIVATIVES **discloser** n. **disclosure** n.
– ORIGIN Middle English: from Old French *desclos-, desclore*, from Latin *claudere* 'to close'.

CONSONANTS b but d dog f few g get h he j yes k cat l leg m man n no p pen r red

disco ■ n. (pl. **-os**) informal **1** a club or party at which people dance to pop music. **2** (also **disco music**) soul-influenced, melodic pop music with a regular bass beat, intended for dancing to.

discography /dɪˈskɒɡrəfi/ ■ n. (pl. **-ies**) **1** a descriptive catalogue of musical recordings, particularly those of a particular performer or composer. **2** the study of musical recordings and compilation of descriptive catalogues.
– DERIVATIVES **discographer** n.

discolour (US **discolor**) ■ v. become or cause to become a different, less attractive colour.
– DERIVATIVES **discoloration** (also **discolouration**) n.

discombobulate /ˌdɪskəmˈbɒbjʊleɪt/ ■ v. humorous, chiefly N. Amer. disconcert or confuse.
– ORIGIN C19: prob. based on DISCOMPOSE or DISCOMFIT.

discomfit /dɪsˈkʌmfɪt/ ■ v. (**discomfited**, **discomfiting**) make uneasy or embarrassed.
– DERIVATIVES **discomfiture** n.
– ORIGIN Middle English: from Old French *desconfit*, from *desconfire*, from Latin *dis-* (expressing reversal) + *conficere* 'put together'.

discomfort ■ n. **1** slight pain. **2** slight anxiety or embarrassment. ■ v. cause discomfort to.
– ORIGIN Middle English: from Old French *desconforter* (v.), *desconfort* (n.), from *des-* (expressing reversal) + *conforter* (see COMFORT).

discompose ■ v. [often as adj. **discomposed**] disturb or agitate.
– DERIVATIVES **discomposure** n.

disconcert /ˌdɪskənˈsɜːt/ ■ v. disturb the composure of.
– DERIVATIVES **disconcerted** adj. **disconcertedly** adv. **disconcerting** adj. **disconcertingly** adv. **disconcertion** n.
– ORIGIN C17: from obsolete French *desconcerter*, from *des-* (expressing reversal) + *concerter* 'bring together'.

disconformity ■ n. (pl. **-ies**) **1** lack of conformity. **2** Geology a break in a sequence of strata which does not involve a difference of inclination on each side of the break.

disconnect ■ v. break the connection of or between. ▸ put (an electrical device) out of action by detaching it from a power supply.
– DERIVATIVES **disconnection** (also **disconnexion**) n.

disconnected ■ adj. (of speech, writing, or thought) lacking a logical sequence.
– DERIVATIVES **disconnectedly** adv. **disconnectedness** n.

disconsolate /dɪsˈkɒns(ə)lət/ ■ adj. very unhappy and unable to be comforted.
– DERIVATIVES **disconsolately** adv. **disconsolateness** n. **disconsolation** n.
– ORIGIN Middle English: from medieval Latin *disconsolatus*, from *dis-* (expressing reversal) + Latin *consolari* 'to console'.

discontent ■ n. lack of contentment or satisfaction. ▸ a person who is dissatisfied.
– DERIVATIVES **discontented** adj. **discontentedly** adv. **discontentedness** n. **discontentment** n.

discontinue ■ v. (**discontinues**, **discontinued**, **discontinuing**) stop doing, providing, or making.
– DERIVATIVES **discontinuance** n. **discontinuation** n.

discontinuous ■ adj. having intervals or gaps; not continuous.
– DERIVATIVES **discontinuity** n. **discontinuously** adv.

discord /ˈdɪskɔːd/ ■ n. **1** lack of agreement or harmony. **2** Music lack of harmony between notes sounding together. ▸ a chord which is regarded as displeasing or requiring resolution by another. ▸ any interval except unison, an octave, a perfect fifth or fourth, a major or minor third and sixth, or their octaves.
– DERIVATIVES **discordance** n. **discordancy** n. **discordant** adj. **discordantly** adv.
– ORIGIN Middle English: from Old French *descord* (n.), from Latin *discordare*, from *discors* 'discordant', from *dis-* (expressing negation) + *cor, cord-* 'heart'.

discotheque /ˈdɪskətɛk/ ■ n. another term for DISCO (in sense 1).
– ORIGIN 1950s: from French *discothèque*, orig. 'record library', on the pattern of *bibliothèque* 'library'.

discount ■ n. /ˈdɪskaʊnt/ a deduction from the usual cost of something. ▸ Finance a percentage deducted from the face value of a bill of exchange or promissory note when it changes hands before the due date. ■ v. /dɪsˈkaʊnt/ **1** deduct a discount from (the usual price of something). ▸ reduce (a product or service) in price. ▸ Finance buy or sell (a bill of exchange) before its due date at less than its maturity value. **2** disregard as lacking credibility or significance.
– DERIVATIVES **discountable** /dɪsˈkaʊntəb(ə)l/ adj. **discounter** /dɪsˈkaʊntə/ n.
– ORIGIN C17: from obsolete French *descompte* (n.), *descompter* (v.), or (in commercial contexts) from Italian *(di)scontare*, from Latin *dis-* (expressing reversal) + *computare* (see COMPUTE).

discounted cash flow ■ n. Finance a method of assessing investments taking into account the expected accumulation of interest.

discountenance ■ v. **1** refuse to approve of. **2** disturb the composure of.

discount rate ■ n. Finance **1** the minimum interest rate set by the US Federal Reserve (and some other national banks) for lending to other banks. **2** a rate used for discounting bills of exchange.

discount store ■ n. a shop that sells goods at less than the normal retail price.

discourage ■ v. **1** cause a loss of confidence or enthusiasm in. **2** prevent or seek to prevent by showing disapproval or creating difficulties. ▸ (**discourage someone from**) persuade someone against (an action).
– DERIVATIVES **discouragement** n. **discouraging** adj. **discouragingly** adv.
– ORIGIN Middle English: from Old French *descouragier*, from *des-* (expressing reversal) + *corage* 'courage'.

discourse ■ n. /ˈdɪskɔːs, -ˈkɔːs/ written or spoken communication or debate. ▸ a formal discussion of a topic in speech or writing. ▸ Linguistics a text or conversation. ■ v. /dɪsˈkɔːs/ speak or write authoritatively about a topic. ▸ engage in conversation.
– ORIGIN Middle English: from Old French *discours*, from Latin *discursus* 'running to and fro' (in medieval Latin 'argument'), from *discurrere* 'run away'.

discourse marker ■ n. Grammar a word or phrase whose function is to organize discourse into segments, for example *I mean*.

discourteous ■ adj. rude and lacking consideration for others.
– DERIVATIVES **discourteously** adv. **discourteousness** n. **discourtesy** n. (pl. **-ies**)

discover ■ v. find unexpectedly or in the course of a search. ▸ become aware of (a fact or situation). ▸ be the first to find or observe (a place, substance, or scientific phenomenon).
– DERIVATIVES **discoverable** adj. **discoverer** n.
– ORIGIN Middle English: from Old French *descovrir*, from late Latin *discooperire*, from Latin *dis-* (expressing reversal) + *cooperire* (see COVER).

discovered check ■ n. Chess a check which results when a player moves a piece or pawn so as to put the opponent's king in check from another piece.

discovery ■ n. (pl. **-ies**) **1** the action or process of discovering or being discovered. ▸ a person or thing discovered. **2** Law the compulsory disclosure, by a party to an action, of relevant documents referred to by the other party.

discredit ■ v. (**discredited**, **discrediting**) harm the good reputation of. ▸ cause (an idea or piece of evidence) to seem false or unreliable. ■ n. loss or lack of reputation.
– DERIVATIVES **discreditable** adj. **discreditably** adv.

discreet /dɪˈskriːt/ ■ adj. (**-er**, **-est**) **1** careful and prudent in one's speech or actions, especially so as to avoid giving offence or attracting attention. **2** unobtrusive.
– DERIVATIVES **discreetly** adv. **discreetness** n.
– ORIGIN Middle English: from Latin *discretus* 'separate',

discrepancy

from *discernere* 'discern', the sense arising from late Latin *discretio* (see DISCRETION).

USAGE
The words **discrete** and **discreet** are often confused. **Discrete** means 'separate' (*a discrete unit*), while **discreet** means 'careful and prudent'.

discrepancy /dɪsˈkrɛp(ə)nsi/ ■ n. (pl. **-ies**) an illogical or surprising lack of compatibility or similarity between two or more facts.
– DERIVATIVES **discrepant** adj.
– ORIGIN C17: from Latin *discrepantia*, from *discrepare* 'be discordant'.

discrete /dɪˈskriːt/ ■ adj. individually separate and distinct.
– DERIVATIVES **discretely** adv. **discreteness** n.
– ORIGIN Middle English: from Latin *discretus* 'separate'; cf. DISCREET.

discretion ■ n. **1** the quality of being discreet. **2** the freedom to decide what should be done in a particular situation.
– DERIVATIVES **discretionary** adj.
– ORIGIN Middle English: from Latin *discretio(n-)* 'separation' (in late Latin 'discernment'), from *discernere* (see DISCERN).

discretionary income ■ n. income remaining after deduction of taxes, social security charges, and basic living costs. Compare with DISPOSABLE INCOME.

discriminable /dɪˈskrɪmɪnəb(ə)l/ ■ adj. able to be discriminated; distinguishable.
– DERIVATIVES **discriminability** n. **discriminably** adv.

discriminate /dɪˈskrɪmɪneɪt/ ■ v. **1** recognize a distinction. ▸ perceive or constitute the difference in or between. **2** (usu. **discriminate against**) make an unjust distinction in the treatment of different categories of people, especially on the grounds of race, sex, or age.
– DERIVATIVES **discriminately** adv. **discriminative** adj.
– ORIGIN C17: from Latin *discriminare* 'distinguish between'.

discriminating ■ adj. having or showing good taste or judgement.
– DERIVATIVES **discriminatingly** adv.

discrimination ■ n. **1** the action of discriminating against people. **2** recognition and understanding of the difference between one thing and another. ▸ good judgement or taste.

discriminatory /dɪˈskrɪmɪnɪˌt(ə)ri, dɪˌskrɪmɪˈneɪt(ə)ri/ ■ adj. showing discrimination or prejudice.

discursive /dɪsˈkəːsɪv/ ■ adj. **1** digressing from subject to subject. **2** of or relating to discourse or modes of discourse.
– DERIVATIVES **discursively** adv. **discursiveness** n.
– ORIGIN C16: from medieval Latin *discursivus*, from Latin *discurrere* 'run away'.

discus /ˈdɪskəs/ ■ n. (pl. **discuses**) a heavy thick-centred disc thrown by an athlete, in ancient Greek games or in modern field events.
– ORIGIN from Greek *diskos*.

discuss ■ v. talk about so as to reach a decision. ▸ talk or write about (a topic) in detail.
– DERIVATIVES **discussable** adj. **discussant** n. **discusser** n.
– ORIGIN Middle English: from Latin *discutere* 'dash to pieces', later 'investigate', from *dis-* 'apart' + *quatere* 'shake'.

discussion ■ n. the action or process of discussing. ▸ a debate about or detailed written treatment of a topic.

disdain ■ n. the feeling that someone or something is unworthy of one's consideration or respect. ■ v. consider or reject with disdain.
– DERIVATIVES **disdainful** adj. **disdainfully** adv. **disdainfulness** n.
– ORIGIN Middle English: from Old French *desdeign* (n.), *desdeignier* (v.), from Latin *dedignari*, from *de-* (expressing reversal) + *dignari* 'consider worthy'.

disease ■ n. **1** a disorder of structure or function in a human, animal, or plant, especially one that produces specific symptoms or that affects a specific part. **2** a quality, habit, or disposition that adversely affects a person or group: *the British disease of self-deprecation.*
– DERIVATIVES **diseased** adj.
– ORIGIN Middle English: from Old French *desaise* 'lack of ease'.

diseconomy ■ n. (pl. **-ies**) Economics an economic disadvantage such as an increase in cost arising from an increase in the size of an organization.

disembark ■ v. leave a ship, aircraft, or train.
– DERIVATIVES **disembarkation** n.

disembarrass ■ v. (**disembarrass oneself of/from**) free oneself of (a burden or nuisance).
– DERIVATIVES **disembarrassment** n.

disembodied ■ adj. separated from or existing without the body. ▸ (of a sound) lacking any obvious physical source.
– DERIVATIVES **disembodiment** n. **disembody** v.

disembowel /ˌdɪsɪmˈbaʊəl, ˌdɪsɛm-/ ■ v. (**disembowelled**, **disembowelling**; US **disemboweled**, **disemboweling**) cut open and remove the internal organs of.
– DERIVATIVES **disembowelment** n.

disempower ■ v. make less powerful or confident.
– DERIVATIVES **disempowerment** n.

disenchant ■ v. make disillusioned.
– DERIVATIVES **disenchanting** adj. **disenchantingly** adv. **disenchantment** n.
– ORIGIN C16: from French *désenchanter*, from *dés-* (expressing reversal) + *enchanter* (see ENCHANT).

disencumber ■ v. free from an encumbrance.

disenfranchise /ˌdɪsɪnˈfran(t)ʃaɪz, ˌdɪsɛn-/ (also **disfranchise**) ■ v. deprive of the right to vote. ▸ deprive of a right or privilege.
– DERIVATIVES **disenfranchisement** n.

disengage /ˌdɪsɪnˈɡeɪdʒ, ˌdɪsɛn-/ ■ v. **1** separate, release, or detach. ▸ [as adj. **disengaged**] emotionally detached; uninvolved. **2** remove (troops) from an area of conflict.
– DERIVATIVES **disengagement** n.

disentangle ■ v. free from entanglement; untwist.
▸ remove knots or tangles from (wool, rope, or hair).
– DERIVATIVES **disentanglement** n.

disentitle ■ v. deprive of an entitlement.
– DERIVATIVES **disentitlement** n.

disequilibrium /ˌdɪsiːkwɪˈlɪbrɪəm, ˌdɪsɛk-/ ■ n. a loss or lack of equilibrium, especially in relation to supply, demand, and prices.

disestablish ■ v. deprive (an organization, especially a national Church) of its official status.
– DERIVATIVES **disestablishment** n.

disfavour (US **disfavor**) ■ n. disapproval or dislike. ■ v. regard or treat with disfavour.

disfigure ■ v. spoil the appearance of.
– DERIVATIVES **disfiguration** n. **disfigurement** n.
– ORIGIN Middle English: from Old French *desfigurer*, from Latin *figura* 'figure'.

disfranchise ■ v. another term for DISENFRANCHISE.

disgorge ■ v. **1** discharge; cause to pour out. ▸ bring up or vomit (food). ▸ yield or give up. **2** remove the sediment from (a sparkling wine) after fermentation.
– DERIVATIVES **disgorgement** n.
– ORIGIN C15: from Old French *desgorger*, from *des-* (expressing removal) + *gorge* 'throat'.

disgorger ■ n. Fishing a device for extracting a hook from a fish's throat.

disgrace ■ n. loss of reputation as the result of a dishonourable action. ▸ a person or thing regarded as shameful and unacceptable. ■ v. bring disgrace on.
▸ cause to fall from favour or a position of power or honour.
– ORIGIN C16: from Italian *disgrazia* (n.), *disgraziare* (v.).

disgraceful ■ adj. shockingly unacceptable.
– DERIVATIVES **disgracefully** adv.

disgruntled ■ adj. angry or dissatisfied.
– DERIVATIVES **disgruntlement** n.
– ORIGIN C17: from DIS- + dialect *gruntle* 'utter little grunts'.

disguise ■ v. alter the appearance, sound, taste, or smell of so as to conceal the identity. ▸ conceal the nature or existence of (a feeling or situation). ■ n. a means of

disguising one's identity. ▶ the state of being disguised.
– ORIGIN Middle English ('change one's usual style of dress'): from Old French *desguisier*.

disgust ■ n. strong revulsion or profound indignation. ■ v. cause disgust in.
– DERIVATIVES **disgusted** adj. **disgustedly** adv. **disgusting** adj. **disgustingly** adv. **disgustingness** n.
– ORIGIN C16: from early modern French *desgoust* or Italian *disgusto*, from Latin *dis-* (expressing reversal) + *gustus* 'taste'.

dish ■ n. 1 a shallow, typically flat-bottomed container for cooking or serving food. ▶ (**the dishes**) all the items that have been used in the preparation, serving, and eating of a meal. ▶ a shallow, concave receptacle: *a soap dish*. ▶ short for SATELLITE DISH. 2 a particular variety or preparation of food served as part of a meal. 3 informal a sexually attractive person. ■ v. 1 (**dish something out/up**) put food on to a plate or plates before a meal. ▶ (**dish something out**) dispense something in a casual or indiscriminate way. 2 N. Amer. informal gossip.
– PHRASES **dish the dirt** informal reveal or spread scandal or gossip.
– DERIVATIVES **dishful** n. (pl. **-fuls**).
– ORIGIN Old English *disc* 'plate, bowl', from Latin *discus* (see DISCUS).

disharmony ■ n. lack of harmony.
– DERIVATIVES **disharmonious** adj. **disharmoniously** adv.

dishearten ■ v. cause to lose determination or confidence.
– DERIVATIVES **disheartening** adj. **dishearteningly** adv. **disheartenment** n.

dishevelled /dɪˈʃɛv(ə)ld/ (US **disheveled**) ■ adj. (of a person's hair, clothes, or appearance) untidy; disordered.
– DERIVATIVES **dishevel** (**dishevelled**, **dishevelling**; US **disheveled**, **disheveling**) v. **dishevelment** n.
– ORIGIN Middle English (orig. 'having the hair uncovered'): from Old French *deschevele*, from *descheveler*, from *chevel* 'hair', from Latin *capillus*.

dishonest ■ adj. not honest, trustworthy, or sincere.
– DERIVATIVES **dishonestly** adv. **dishonesty** n.

dishonour (US **dishonor**) ■ n. a state of shame or disgrace. ■ v. 1 bring dishonour to. ▶ archaic rape (a woman). 2 fail to honour (an agreement, cheque, etc.).

dishonourable (US **dishonorable**) ■ adj. bringing shame or disgrace.
– DERIVATIVES **dishonourableness** n. **dishonourably** adv.

dishonourable discharge ■ n. dismissal from the armed forces as a result of criminal or morally unacceptable actions.

dishwasher ■ n. 1 a machine for washing dishes automatically. 2 a person employed to wash dishes.

dishwater ■ n. water in which dishes have been washed.

dishy ■ adj. (**-ier**, **-iest**) informal, chiefly Brit. sexually attractive.

disillusion /ˌdɪsɪˈl(j)uːʒ(ə)n/ ■ n. the disappointing loss of a belief or an ideal. ■ v. cause to experience disillusion.
– DERIVATIVES **disillusioned** adj. **disillusionment** n.

disincentive ■ n. a factor that discourages a particular action.

disinclination ■ n. a reluctance or unwillingness to do something.

disinclined ■ adj. reluctant; unwilling.

disinfect ■ v. make clean and free from infection, especially by the use of a chemical disinfectant.
– DERIVATIVES **disinfection** n.

disinfectant ■ n. a chemical liquid that destroys bacteria. ■ adj. causing disinfection.

disinformation ■ n. information which is intended to mislead.
– ORIGIN 1950s: formed on the pattern of Russian *dezinformatsiya*.

disingenuous /ˌdɪsɪnˈdʒɛnjʊəs/ ■ adj. not candid or sincere, especially in pretending that one knows less about something than one really does.
– DERIVATIVES **disingenuously** adv. **disingenuousness** n.

disinherit ■ v. (**disinherited**, **disinheriting**) dispossess of or bar from an inheritance.
– DERIVATIVES **disinheritance** n.

– ORIGIN Middle English: from DIS- + *inherit* in the obsolete sense 'make someone an heir'.

disinhibit ■ v. (**disinhibited**, **disinhibiting**) make less inhibited.
– DERIVATIVES **disinhibition** n.

disintegrate /dɪsˈɪntɪɡreɪt/ ■ v. 1 break up into small parts as a result of impact or decay. 2 lose strength or cohesion. 3 Physics undergo or cause to undergo disintegration at a subatomic level.
– DERIVATIVES **disintegrative** adj. **disintegrator** n.

disintegration ■ n. 1 the process of disintegrating. 2 Physics a process in which a nucleus or other subatomic particle emits a smaller particle or divides into smaller particles.

disinter /ˌdɪsɪnˈtəː/ ■ v. (**disinterred**, **disinterring**) dig up (something that has been buried).
– DERIVATIVES **disinterment** n.

disinterest ■ n. 1 impartiality. 2 lack of interest.

disinterested ■ adj. 1 not influenced by considerations of personal advantage; impartial. 2 having or feeling no interest or concern.
– DERIVATIVES **disinterestedly** adv. **disinterestedness** n.
– ORIGIN C17: from the rare verb *disinterest* 'rid of interest'.

USAGE
According to traditional guidelines, it is a mistake to use **disinterested** to mean 'not interested'. In fact, the earliest recorded use is for this sense, and today this use is widespread.

disintermediation ■ n. Economics reduction in the use of intermediaries between producers and consumers, e.g. by involvement in the securities market directly rather than through a bank.

disinvent ■ v. undo the invention of.

disinvest ■ v. withdraw or reduce an investment.
– DERIVATIVES **disinvestment** n.

disjoint ■ v. disturb the cohesion or organization of. ■ adj. Mathematics (of sets) having no elements in common.

disjointed ■ adj. lacking a coherent sequence or connection.
– DERIVATIVES **disjointedly** adv. **disjointedness** n.

disjunct /ˈdɪsdʒʌŋ(k)t/ ■ n. Logic each of the terms of a disjunctive proposition. ■ adj. disjoined and distinct from one another.
– ORIGIN Middle English: from Latin *disjunct-*, *disjungere* 'disjoin, separate'.

disjunction ■ n. 1 a lack of correspondence or consistency. 2 Logic the relation of two distinct alternatives, or a statement expressing this.

disjunctive ■ adj. 1 lacking connection. 2 Grammar (of a conjunction) expressing a choice between two mutually exclusive possibilities, for example *or* in *she asked if he was going or staying*. 3 Logic (of a proposition) expressing alternatives. ■ n. 1 Grammar a disjunctive conjunction. 2 Logic a disjunctive proposition.
– DERIVATIVES **disjunctively** adv.

disjuncture ■ n. a separation or disconnection.

disk ■ n. variant spelling in the US and in computing contexts of DISC.
– DERIVATIVES **diskless** adj.

disk drive ■ n. a device which allows a computer to read from and write on to computer disks.

diskette ■ n. another term for FLOPPY.

diski S. African informal ■ n. soccer.
– ORIGIN from township slang *diski* 'round', used of a soccer ball.

dislike ■ v. feel distaste for or hostility towards. ■ n. a feeling of dislike. ▶ a thing that is disliked.
– DERIVATIVES **dislikable** (also **dislikeable**) adj.

dislocate /ˈdɪslə(ʊ)keɪt/ ■ v. 1 disturb the normal arrangement or position of (a joint in the body). 2 disturb the organization of; disrupt.

dislocation /ˌdɪslə(ʊ)ˈkeɪʃ(ə)n/ ■ n. the process or state of dislocating or being dislocated.

dislodge ■ v. remove from an established or fixed position.
– DERIVATIVES **dislodgeable** adj. **dislodgement** n.

disloyal ■ adj. not loyal or faithful.
– DERIVATIVES **disloyally** adv. **disloyalty** n.

dismal /ˈdɪzm(ə)l/ ■ adj. **1** causing or demonstrating a mood of gloom or depression; dreary. **2** informal pitifully or disgracefully bad: *a dismal performance*.
– DERIVATIVES **dismally** adv. **dismalness** n.
– ORIGIN Middle English: from earlier *dismals*, the two days in each month which in medieval times were believed to be unlucky, from Anglo-Norman French *dis mal*, from medieval Latin *dies mali* 'evil days'.

dismantle ■ v. take to pieces.
– DERIVATIVES **dismantlement** n. **dismantler** n.
– ORIGIN C16 ('destroy the defensive capability of (a fortification)'): from Old French *desmanteler*, from *des-* (expressing reversal) + *manteler* 'fortify'.

dismast ■ v. break or force down the mast or masts of (a ship).

dismay ■ n. consternation and distress. ■ v. cause to feel dismay.
– ORIGIN Middle English: from Latin *dis-* (expressing negation) + the Germanic base of MAY[1].

dismember /dɪsˈmɛmbə/ ■ v. **1** tear or cut the limbs from. **2** partition or divide up (a territory or organization).
– DERIVATIVES **dismembered** adj. **dismemberment** n.
– ORIGIN Middle English: from Latin *dis-* 'apart' + *membrum* 'limb'.

dismiss ■ v. **1** order or allow to leave; send away. **2** discharge from employment. **3** Law refuse further hearing to (a case). **4** Cricket end the innings of (a batsman or side). **5** treat as being unworthy of serious consideration.
– DERIVATIVES **dismissal** n. **dismissible** adj.
– ORIGIN Middle English: from medieval Latin *dismiss-*, var. of Latin *dimiss-*, *dimittere* 'send away'.

dismissive ■ adj. feeling or showing that something is unworthy of serious consideration.
– DERIVATIVES **dismissively** adv. **dismissiveness** n.

dismount ■ v. **1** alight from a horse or bicycle. **2** remove (something) from its support. **3** Computing make (a disk or disk drive) unavailable for use.
– ORIGIN C16: from DIS- + MOUNT[1], prob. on the pattern of Old French *desmonter*, medieval Latin *dismontare*.

disobedient ■ adj. failing or refusing to be obedient.
– DERIVATIVES **disobedience** n. **disobediently** adv.

disobey ■ v. fail or refuse to obey.
– DERIVATIVES **disobeyer** n.

disoblige ■ v. offend (someone) by not acting in accordance with their wishes.
– DERIVATIVES **disobliging** adj.

disorder ■ n. **1** a lack of order; a confused or untidy state. **2** the disruption of peaceful and law-abiding behaviour. **3** Medicine a disruption of normal physical or mental functions: *a skin disorder*. ■ v. [usu. as adj. **disordered**] bring disorder to.
– ORIGIN C15: alteration, influenced by ORDER, of earlier *disordain*, from Old French *desordener*, ultimately from Latin *ordinare* 'ordain'.

disorderly ■ adj. **1** lacking organization; untidy. **2** involving or contributing to a breakdown of peaceful and law-abiding behaviour.
– DERIVATIVES **disorderliness** n.

disorderly conduct ■ n. Law unruly behaviour constituting a minor offence.

disorganized (also **-ised**) ■ adj. **1** not properly planned and controlled. **2** (of a person) inefficient.
– DERIVATIVES **disorganization** (also **-isation**) n.

disorient /dɪsˈɔːrɪənt/ ■ v. chiefly N. Amer. another term for DISORIENTATE.

disorientate ■ v. cause (someone) to lose their sense of direction or feel confused.
– DERIVATIVES **disorientated** adj. **disorientation** n.

disown ■ v. refuse to acknowledge or maintain any connection with.
– DERIVATIVES **disowner** n. **disownment** n.

disparage /dɪˈsparɪdʒ/ ■ v. represent as being of little worth; scorn.
– DERIVATIVES **disparagement** n. **disparaging** adj. **disparagingly** adv.
– ORIGIN Middle English: from Old French *desparagier* 'marry someone of unequal rank', from Latin *par* 'equal'.

disparate /ˈdɪsp(ə)rət/ ■ adj. essentially different in kind; not able to be compared. ■ n. (**disparates**) things so different that there is no basis for comparison between them.
– DERIVATIVES **disparately** adv. **disparateness** n.
– ORIGIN Middle English: from Latin *disparare* 'separate', influenced by *dispar* 'unequal'.

disparity ■ n. (pl. **-ies**) a great difference.
– ORIGIN C16: from late Latin *disparitas*, from Latin *paritas* 'parity'.

dispassionate ■ adj. not influenced by strong emotion; rational and impartial.
– DERIVATIVES **dispassion** n. **dispassionately** adv. **dispassionateness** n.

dispatch (also **despatch**) ■ v. **1** send off promptly to a destination or for a purpose. **2** deal with (a task or problem) quickly and efficiently. **3** kill. ■ n. **1** an instance of dispatching. **2** an official report on the latest situation in state or military affairs. ▸ a report sent in from abroad by a journalist. **3** promptness and efficiency: *he should proceed with dispatch*.
– DERIVATIVES **dispatcher** n.
– ORIGIN C16: from Italian *dispacciare* or Spanish *despachar* 'expedite'.

dispatch box (also **dispatch case**) ■ n. a container for state or military dispatches.

dispatch rider ■ n. a messenger who delivers urgent business documents or military dispatches by motor cycle or (formerly) on horseback.

dispel /dɪˈspɛl/ ■ v. (**dispelled**, **dispelling**) make (a doubt, feeling, or belief) disappear.
– DERIVATIVES **dispeller** n.
– ORIGIN Middle English: from Latin *dispellere* 'drive apart'.

dispensable ■ adj. **1** able to be replaced or done without. **2** (of a law or other rule) able to be relaxed in special cases.
– DERIVATIVES **dispensability** n.

dispensary /dɪˈspɛns(ə)ri/ ■ n. (pl. **-ies**) **1** a room where medicines are prepared and provided. **2** a clinic provided by public or charitable funds.

dispensation ■ n. **1** the action of dispensing. **2** exemption from a rule, usual requirement, or religious obligation. **3** a religious or political system prevailing at a particular time: *the Mosaic dispensation*.
– DERIVATIVES **dispensational** adj.

dispense /dɪˈspɛns/ ■ v. **1** distribute to a number of people. ▸ (of a machine or container) supply or release (a product). **2** (of a pharmacist) supply (medicine) according to a doctor's prescription. **3** (**dispense with**) get rid of or manage without.
– DERIVATIVES **dispenser** n.
– ORIGIN Middle English: from Latin *dispensare* 'continue to weigh out or disburse', from *dispendere*, from *pendere* 'weigh'.

dispersant ■ n. a liquid or gas used to disperse small particles in a medium.

disperse /dɪˈspəːs/ ■ v. **1** go or distribute in different directions or over a wide area. **2** thin out and eventually disappear. **3** Physics divide (light) into constituents of different wavelengths. ■ adj. Chemistry denoting a phase dispersed in another phase, as in a colloid.
– DERIVATIVES **dispersal** n. **disperser** n. **dispersible** adj. **dispersive** adj.
– ORIGIN Middle English: from Latin *dispers-*, *dispergere* 'scatter widely'.

dispersion ■ n. **1** the action, process, or state of dispersing or being dispersed. **2** (**the dispersion**) another term for DIASPORA. **3** a mixture of one substance dispersed in another medium. **4** Physics the separation of white light into colours or of any radiation according to wavelength. **5** Statistics the extent to which values of a variable differ from a fixed value such as the mean.

dispirit /dɪˈspɪrɪt/ ■ v. cause to lose enthusiasm or hope.
– DERIVATIVES **dispiritedly** adv. **dispiritedness** n. **dispiriting** adj. **dispiritingly** adv.

displace ■ v. **1** shift (something) from its proper or usual position. **2** take the place, position, or role of; oust. **3** [often as adj. **displaced**] (especially of war, persecution, or natural disaster) force (someone) to leave their home: *displaced persons*.

displacement ■ n. **1** the action or process of displacing. **2** the amount by which a thing is moved from a position. **3** the volume or weight of water that would fill the volume displaced by a floating ship, used as a measure of the ship's size. **4** the volume swept by a reciprocating system, as in a pump or engine. **5** Physics the component of an electric field due to free separated charges, regardless of any polarizing effects. **6** Psychoanalysis the unconscious transfer of an intense emotion from one object to another.

display ■ v. **1** place (something) prominently so that it may readily be seen. **2** show (data or an image) on a computer, television or cinema screen. **3** give a conspicuous demonstration of (a quality, emotion, or skill). **4** (of a male animal) engage in a specialized pattern of behaviour intended to attract a mate. ■ n. **1** an instance of displaying or being displayed. **2** a collection of objects being displayed. **3** an electronic device for the visual presentation of data.
– DERIVATIVES **displayer** n.
– ORIGIN Middle English: from Old French *despleier*, from Latin *displicare* 'scatter, disperse' (in medieval Latin 'unfold').

display case (also **display cabinet**) ■ n. a case, made all or partly of glass, for displaying items in a shop or museum for observation or inspection.

displayed ■ adj. Heraldry (of a bird of prey) depicted with the wings extended.

displease ■ v. annoy or upset.
– DERIVATIVES **displeased** adj. **displeasing** adj. **displeasingly** adv.

displeasure ■ n. a feeling of annoyance or dissatisfaction.

disport ■ v. (**disport oneself**) enjoy oneself unrestrainedly; frolic.
– ORIGIN Middle English: from Old French *desporter* 'carry away', from Latin *portare*.

disposable ■ adj. **1** (of an article) intended to be used once and then thrown away. ▸ (of a person or idea) able to be dispensed with. **2** (chiefly of financial assets) readily available for the owner's use as required. ■ n. a disposable article.
– DERIVATIVES **disposability** n.

disposable income ■ n. income remaining after deduction of taxes and social security charges, available to be spent or saved as one wishes. Compare with **DISCRETIONARY INCOME**.

disposal ■ n. **1** the action or process of disposing. **2** the sale of assets.
– PHRASES **at one's disposal** available for one to use whenever or however one wishes. **at someone's disposal** ready to assist the person concerned in any way they wish.

dispose ■ v. **1** (**dispose of**) get rid of. **2** arrange in a particular position. **3** incline (someone) towards a particular activity or frame of mind. **4** archaic or poetic/literary determine the course of events: *man proposes, but God disposes*.
– DERIVATIVES **disposer** n.
– ORIGIN Middle English: from Latin *disponere* 'arrange', influenced by *dispositus* 'arranged' and Old French *poser* 'to place'.

disposed ■ adj. **1** inclined or willing to do or feel something: *he was not disposed to take the hint*. **2** having a specified attitude to or towards: *he is favourably disposed towards the proposals*.

disposition ■ n. **1** a person's inherent qualities of mind and character. ▸ an inclination or tendency. **2** the action or result of arranging people or things in a particular way. ▸ (**dispositions**) the stationing of troops ready for military action. **3** Law the action of distributing or transferring property or money to someone, in particular by bequest. **4** the power to deal with something as one pleases. ▸ archaic the determination of events, especially by divine power.

339

dissect

dispossess ■ v. deprive of land or property. ▸ [as pl. n. **the dispossessed**] people who have been dispossessed.
– DERIVATIVES **dispossession** n.

disproof ■ n. action or evidence that proves something to be untrue.

disproportion ■ n. a lack of proportion.
– DERIVATIVES **disproportional** adj. **disproportionality** n. **disproportionally** adv.

disproportionate[1] /ˌdɪsprəˈpɔːʃ(ə)nət/ ■ adj. too large or too small in comparison with something else.
– DERIVATIVES **disproportionately** adv. **disproportionateness** n.

disproportionate[2] /ˌdɪsprəˈpɔːʃ(ə)neɪt/ ■ v. Chemistry undergo disproportionation.

disproportionation ■ n. Chemistry a reaction in which a substance is simultaneously oxidized and reduced, giving two different products.

disprove ■ v. prove to be false.
– DERIVATIVES **disprovable** adj.

disputable ■ adj. open to question or debate.
– DERIVATIVES **disputably** adv.

disputation ■ n. debate or argument.
– DERIVATIVES **disputative** adj.
– ORIGIN Middle English: from Latin *disputatio(n-)*, from *disputare* (see **DISPUTE**).

disputatious ■ adj. **1** fond of argument. **2** (of an argument or situation) motivated by or causing strong opinions.
– DERIVATIVES **disputatiously** adv. **disputatiousness** n.

dispute ■ v. /dɪˈspjuːt/ **1** argue about (something). ▸ question whether (a statement or alleged fact) is true or valid. **2** contend for. **3** resist (a military landing or advance). ■ n. /dɪˈspjuːt, ˈdɪspjuːt/ a disagreement or argument. ▸ a disagreement between management and employees that leads to industrial action.
– DERIVATIVES **disputant** n. **disputer** n.
– ORIGIN Middle English: from Latin *disputare* 'to estimate', in late Latin 'to dispute'.

disqualify ■ v. (**-ies**, **-ied**) pronounce (someone) ineligible for an office or activity because of an offence or infringement. ▸ (of a feature or characteristic) make (someone) unsuitable for an office or activity.
– DERIVATIVES **disqualification** n.

disquiet ■ n. a feeling of anxiety. ■ v. [usu. as adj. **disquieted**] make (someone) anxious.
– DERIVATIVES **disquieting** adj. **disquietingly** adv. **disquietude** n.

disregard ■ v. pay no attention to; ignore. ■ n. the action or state of disregarding or being disregarded.

disrepair ■ n. a poor condition due to neglect.

disreputable ■ adj. not respectable in appearance or character; sleazy or shabby.
– DERIVATIVES **disreputableness** n. **disreputably** adv.

disrepute /ˌdɪsrɪˈpjuːt/ ■ n. the state of being discredited.

disrespect ■ n. lack of respect or courtesy.
– DERIVATIVES **disrespectful** adj. **disrespectfully** adv.

disrobe ■ v. **1** take off one's clothes; undress. **2** take off official regalia or vestments.

disrupt ■ v. **1** disturb or interrupt. **2** drastically alter or destroy the structure of.
– DERIVATIVES **disrupter** (also **disruptor**) n. **disruption** n. **disruptive** adj. **disruptively** adv. **disruptiveness** n.
– ORIGIN Middle English: from Latin *disrupt-*, *disrumpere* 'break apart'.

diss ■ v. variant spelling of **DIS**.

dissatisfaction ■ n. lack of satisfaction.

dissatisfied ■ adj. not content or happy.
– DERIVATIVES **dissatisfiedly** adv.

dissatisfy ■ v. (**-ies**, **-ied**) fail to satisfy or give pleasure to.

dissaving ■ n. the action of spending more than one has earned in a given period. ▸ (**dissavings**) the excess amount spent.
– DERIVATIVES **dissaver** n.

dissect /dʌɪˈsɛkt, dɪ-/ ■ v. **1** methodically cut up (a body,

part, or plant) in order to study its internal parts. **2** analyse in minute detail.
– DERIVATIVES **dissection** n. **dissector** n.
– ORIGIN C16: from Latin *dissecare* 'cut up'.

dissected ■ adj. **1** Botany (of a leaf) divided into many deep lobes. **2** Geology (of a plateau or upland) divided by a number of deep valleys.

dissemble /dɪˈsɛmb(ə)l/ ■ v. hide or disguise one's true motives or feelings.
– DERIVATIVES **dissemblance** n. **dissembler** n.
– ORIGIN Middle English: alteration (suggested by SEMBLANCE) of obsolete *dissimule*, from Latin *dissimulare* 'disguise, conceal'.

disseminate /dɪˈsɛmɪneɪt/ ■ v. spread widely.
– DERIVATIVES **dissemination** n. **disseminator** n.
– ORIGIN Middle English: from Latin *disseminare* 'scatter', from *dis-* 'abroad' + *semen* 'seed'.

dissension /dɪˈsɛnʃ(ə)n/ ■ n. disagreement that leads to discord.
– ORIGIN Middle English: from Latin *dissensio(n-)*, from *dissentire* (see DISSENT).

dissent /dɪˈsɛnt/ ■ v. express disagreement with a prevailing view or official decision. ▸ disagree with the doctrine of an established or orthodox Church. ■ n. the holding or expression of a dissenting view.
– ORIGIN Middle English: from Latin *dissentire* 'differ in sentiment'.

dissenter ■ n. a person who dissents.

dissentient /dɪˈsɛnʃɪənt, -ʃ(ə)nt/ ■ adj. in opposition to a majority or official opinion. ■ n. a dissentient person.
– ORIGIN C17: from Latin *dissentire* 'differ in opinion'.

dissertation /ˌdɪsəˈteɪʃ(ə)n/ ■ n. a long essay, especially one written for a university degree or diploma.
– DERIVATIVES **dissertational** adj.
– ORIGIN C17: from Latin *dissertatio(n-)*, from *dissertare* 'continue to discuss'.

disservice ■ n. a harmful action.

dissident /ˈdɪsɪd(ə)nt/ ■ n. a person who opposes official policy. ■ adj. in opposition to official policy.
– DERIVATIVES **dissidence** n.
– ORIGIN C16: from Latin *dissidere* 'sit apart, disagree'.

dissimilar ■ adj. not similar; different.
– DERIVATIVES **dissimilarity** n. **dissimilarly** adv.

dissimilate /dɪˈsɪmɪleɪt/ ■ v. Linguistics change (a sound in a word) to another when the word originally had identical sounds near each other (e.g. in *taper*, which derives from *papyrus*, the *p* is dissimilated to *t*).
– DERIVATIVES **dissimilation** n. **dissimilatory** /dɪˈsɪmɪlət(ə)ri/ adj.
– ORIGIN C19: from DIS- + Latin *similis* 'like, similar', on the pattern of *assimilate*.

dissimulate /dɪˈsɪmjʊleɪt/ ■ v. hide or disguise one's thoughts or feelings.
– DERIVATIVES **dissimulation** n. **dissimulator** n.
– ORIGIN Middle English: from Latin *dissimulare* 'to conceal'.

dissipate /ˈdɪsɪpeɪt/ ■ v. **1** be dispelled or dispersed, or cause to be so. **2** waste (money, energy, or resources). **3** Physics cause (energy) to be lost through its conversion into heat.
– DERIVATIVES **dissipative** adj. **dissipator** (also **dissipater**) n.
– ORIGIN Middle English: from Latin *dissipare* 'scatter'.

dissipated ■ adj. overindulgent in sensual pleasures.

dissipation ■ n. **1** dissipated living. **2** the action of dissipating something.

dissociate /dɪˈsəʊʃɪeɪt, -sɪ-/ ■ v. **1** disconnect or separate. **2** Chemistry undergo or cause to undergo dissociation.
– DERIVATIVES **dissociative** adj.
– ORIGIN C16: from Latin *dissociare* 'separate'.

dissociation /dɪˌsəʊʃɪˈeɪʃ(ə)n, -sɪ-/ ■ n. **1** the action or process of disconnecting or separating. **2** Psychiatry separation of normally related mental processes, resulting in one group functioning independently from the rest and leading to disorders such as multiple personality. **3** Chemistry the splitting of a molecule into smaller molecules, atoms, or ions, especially by a reversible process.

dissolute /ˈdɪsəluːt/ ■ adj. overindulgent in sensual pleasures.
– DERIVATIVES **dissolutely** adv. **dissoluteness** n.
– ORIGIN Middle English: from Latin *dissolutus* 'disconnected, loose', from *dissolvere* (see DISSOLVE).

dissolution ■ n. **1** the closing down of an assembly, partnership, or official body. **2** the action or process of dissolving or being dissolved. **3** disintegration; decomposition. **4** debauched living; dissipation.
– ORIGIN Middle English: from Latin *dissolutio(n-)*, from *dissolvere* (see DISSOLVE).

dissolve ■ v. **1** (with reference to a solid) become or cause to become incorporated into a liquid so as to form a solution. **2** (with reference to an assembly or body) close down, dismiss, or annul. ▸ (of something abstract) disappear. **3** (**dissolve into/to**) (of an image or scene in a film) gradually blend into another. **4** (**dissolve into/in**) subside uncontrollably into (an expression of strong feelings).
– DERIVATIVES **dissolvable** adj.
– ORIGIN Middle English: from Latin *dissolvere*, from *dis-* 'apart' + *solvere* 'loosen, solve'.

dissonant ■ adj. **1** Music lacking harmony. **2** unsuitable in combination; clashing.
– DERIVATIVES **dissonance** n. **dissonantly** adv.
– ORIGIN Middle English: from Latin *dissonare* 'be discordant', from *dis-* 'apart' + *sonare* 'to sound'.

dissuade /dɪˈsweɪd/ ■ v. (**dissuade someone from**) advise someone against; persuade someone not to do something.
– DERIVATIVES **dissuader** n. **dissuasion** n. **dissuasive** adj.
– ORIGIN C15: from Latin *dissuadere*, from *dis-* (expressing reversal) + *suadere* 'advise, persuade'.

dissyllable /dɪˈsɪləb(ə)l/ ■ n. variant spelling of DISYLLABLE.
– DERIVATIVES **dissyllabic** adj.

distaff /ˈdɪstɑːf/ ■ n. **1** a stick or spindle on to which wool or flax is wound for spinning. **2** [as modifier] denoting or concerning women: *a family tree on the distaff side*. Compare with SPEAR (in sense 3).
– ORIGIN Old English *distæf*: the first element is apparently rel. to Middle Low German *dise*, *disene* 'distaff, bunch of flax'; the second is STAFF.

distal /ˈdɪst(ə)l/ ■ adj. chiefly Anatomy situated away from the centre of the body or an area or from the point of attachment. The opposite of PROXIMAL.
– ORIGIN C19: from DISTANT, on the pattern of *dorsal*.

distance ■ n. **1** the length of the space between two points. **2** the condition of being far off; remoteness. ▸ a far-off point or place. **3** the full length or time of a race or other contest. ▸ Brit. Horse Racing a space of more than twenty lengths between two finishers in a race. **4** an interval of time or relation. **5** aloofness or reserve. ■ v. make distant. ▸ (often **distance oneself from**) dissociate or separate.
– PHRASES **go the distance** last or continue to participate until the scheduled end of a contest. **keep one's distance** stay far away. ▸ maintain one's reserve.
– ORIGIN Middle English ('discord, debate'): from Latin *distantia*, from *distare* (see DISTANT).

distance learning ■ n. a method of studying in which lectures are broadcast and lessons are conducted by correspondence.

distant ■ adj. **1** far away in space or time. ▸ at a specified distance: *the town lay half a mile distant*. ▸ (of a sound) faint or vague because far away. **2** remote or far apart in resemblance or relationship. ▸ (of a person) not closely related: *a distant cousin*. **3** (of a person) cool or reserved. **4** remote; abstracted: *a distant look*.
– DERIVATIVES **distantly** adv.
– ORIGIN Middle English: from Latin *distare* 'stand apart'.

distaste ■ n. dislike or aversion.
– DERIVATIVES **distasteful** adj. **distastefully** adv. **distastefulness** n.
– ORIGIN C16: from DIS- + TASTE, on the pattern of early modern French *desgout*, Italian *disgusto*; cf. DISGUST.

distemper[1] /dɪˈstɛmpə/ ■ n. a kind of paint having a base of glue or size instead of oil, used on walls. ▸ a method of mural and poster painting using this. ■ v. [often as adj.]

distempered] paint with distemper.
– ORIGIN Middle English: from late Latin *distemperare* 'soak'.

distemper² /dɪˈstɛmpə/ ■ n. a viral disease of some animals, especially dogs, causing fever, coughing, and catarrh.
– ORIGIN C16: from Middle English *distemper* 'upset, derange', from late Latin *distemperare* 'soak, mix in the wrong proportions'.

distend /dɪˈstɛnd/ ■ v. swell or cause to swell because of pressure from inside.
– DERIVATIVES **distended** adj. **distensibility** n. **distensible** adj. **distension** n.
– ORIGIN Middle English: from Latin *distendere*, from *dis-* 'apart' + *tendere* 'to stretch'.

distil /dɪˈstɪl/ (US **distill**) ■ v. (**distilled**, **distilling**) 1 purify (a liquid) by heating it so that it vaporizes, then cooling and condensing the vapour and collecting the resulting liquid. ▸ make (spirits) in this way. ▸ extract a volatile component of (a substance) by heating, often with a solvent. 2 extract the essential meaning of.
– DERIVATIVES **distillate** n. **distillation** n. **distillatory** adj.
– ORIGIN Middle English: from Latin *distillare*, var. of *destillare*, from *de-* 'down, away' + *stillare*, from *stilla* 'a drop'.

distiller ■ n. a person or company that manufactures spirits.

distillery ■ n. (pl. **-ies**) a place where spirits are manufactured.

distinct ■ adj. 1 recognizably different in nature; individual or separate. 2 readily distinguishable by the senses.
– DERIVATIVES **distinctly** adv. **distinctness** n.
– ORIGIN Middle English: from Latin *distinctus* 'separated, distinguished', from *distinguere* (see **DISTINGUISH**).

distinction ■ n. 1 a marked difference or contrast. ▸ the action of distinguishing. 2 excellence that serves to mark someone or something out from others. ▸ special honour or recognition. ▸ an examination grade denoting excellence.

distinctive ■ adj. individually characteristic; distinct from others of its kind.
– DERIVATIVES **distinctively** adv. **distinctiveness** n.

distinguish /dɪˈstɪŋɡwɪʃ/ ■ v. 1 recognize, show, or treat as different. ▸ (**distinguish between**) perceive or point out a difference between. ▸ [often as adj. **distinguishing**] be an identifying characteristic of. 2 manage to discern (something barely perceptible). 3 (**distinguish oneself**) make oneself worthy of respect.
– DERIVATIVES **distinguishable** adj.
– ORIGIN C16: from Latin *distinguere*, from *dis-* 'apart' + *stinguere* 'put out'.

distinguished ■ adj. 1 noble and dignified in appearance. 2 successful and commanding great respect.

distort /dɪˈstɔːt/ ■ v. 1 pull or twist out of shape. 2 give a misrepresentative account or impression of. 3 change the form of (an electrical signal or sound wave) during transmission or amplification.
– DERIVATIVES **distorted** adj. **distortedly** adv. **distortedness** n.
– ORIGIN C15: from Latin *distort-*, *distorquere* 'twist apart'.

distortion ■ n. the action of distorting or the state of being distorted. ▸ a distorted form or part.
– DERIVATIVES **distortional** adj. **distortionless** adj.

distract /dɪˈstrakt/ ■ v. prevent (someone) from giving their full attention to something. ▸ divert (attention) from something.
– DERIVATIVES **distracted** adj. **distractedly** adv. **distracting** adj. **distractingly** adv.
– ORIGIN Middle English: from Latin *distract-*, *distrahere* 'draw apart'.

distraction ■ n. 1 a thing that diverts someone's attention. 2 a thing offering recreation or entertainment. 3 an agitated mental state: *her air of distraction.*
– PHRASES **to distraction** almost to a state of madness: *she loved him to distraction.*

distractor ■ n. 1 a person or thing that distracts. 2 an incorrect option in a multiple-choice question.

distrait /dɪˈstreɪ, ˈdɪstreɪ/ ■ adj. (fem. **distraite** /-ˈstreɪt/) distracted; absent-minded.
– ORIGIN C18: from Old French *destrait*, from *destraire* 'distract'.

distraught /dɪˈstrɔːt/ ■ adj. very worried and upset.
– ORIGIN Middle English: alteration of the obsolete adj. *distract*, from Latin *distractus* 'pulled apart'.

distress ■ n. 1 extreme anxiety or suffering. 2 the state of a ship or aircraft when in danger or difficulty. 3 Medicine a state of physical strain, especially difficulty in breathing. ■ v. 1 cause distress to. 2 give (furniture, leather, etc.) simulated marks of age and wear.
– DERIVATIVES **distressed** adj. **distressful** adj. **distressing** adj. **distressingly** adv.
– ORIGIN Middle English: from Old French *destresce* (n.), *destrecier* (v.), from Latin *distringere* 'stretch apart'.

distributary /dɪˈstrɪbjʊt(ə)ri/ ■ n. (pl. **-ies**) a branch of a river that does not return to the main stream after leaving it (as in a delta).

distribute /dɪˈstrɪbjuːt, ˈdɪstrɪbjuːt/ ■ v. 1 hand or share out to a number of recipients. 2 (**be distributed**) be spread over an area. 3 supply (goods) to retailers. 4 Logic use (a term) to include every individual of the class to which it refers.
– DERIVATIVES **distributable** adj.
– ORIGIN Middle English: from Latin *distribuere* 'divide up'.

distributed system ■ n. Computing a number of independent computers linked by a network.

distribution ■ n. 1 the action of distributing. 2 the way in which something is distributed: *changes in the area have affected the distribution of its wildlife.*
– DERIVATIVES **distributional** adj.

distributive /dɪˈstrɪbjʊtɪv/ ■ adj. 1 of or relating to the processes of distribution or things that are distributed. 2 Mathematics involving the condition that an operation performed on two or more quantities already combined by another operation gives the same result as when it is performed on each quantity individually and the products then combined, e.g. $a \times (b + c) = ab + ac$.
– DERIVATIVES **distributively** adv.

distributor /dɪˈstrɪbjʊtə/ ■ n. 1 an agent who supplies goods to retailers. 2 a device in a petrol engine for passing electric current to each spark plug in turn.

district ■ n. an area or part of a town or region.
– ORIGIN C17: from medieval Latin *districtus* '(territory of) jurisdiction', from Latin *distringere* 'draw apart'.

district attorney ■ n. (in the US) a public official who acts as prosecutor for the state or the federal government in court in a particular district.

district nurse ■ n. (in the UK) a nurse who visits and treats patients in their homes, operating within a particular district.

district surgeon ■ n. S. African a government-appointed doctor who conducts post-mortems and supervises the health care of people for whose welfare the state is responsible in a particular district.

distrust ■ n. lack of trust. ■ v. have little trust in; regard with suspicion.
– DERIVATIVES **distruster** n. **distrustful** adj. **distrustfully** adv.

disturb ■ v. 1 interfere with the normal arrangement or functioning of. 2 interrupt the sleep, relaxation, or privacy of. 3 cause to feel anxious.
– DERIVATIVES **disturber** n. **disturbing** adj. **disturbingly** adv.
– ORIGIN Middle English: from Latin *disturbare*, from *dis-* 'utterly' + *turbare* 'disturb'.

disturbance ■ n. 1 the action of disturbing or the process of being disturbed. 2 a breakdown of peaceful behaviour; a riot. 3 Law interference with rights or property; molestation.

disturbed ■ adj. suffering from emotional or psychological problems.

disubstituted /ˌdʌɪˈsʌbstɪtjuːtɪd/ ■ adj. Chemistry (of a molecule) having two substituent groups.

disulfiram /dʌɪˈsʌlfɪram/ ■ n. Medicine a synthetic compound used in the treatment of alcoholism, causing unpleasant after-effects after the drinking of alcohol.
– ORIGIN 1940s: blend of **DI-¹**, *sulfide* (see **SULPHIDE**), and *thiuram*, a radical (from **THIO-** + **UREA** + **AMIDE**).

disunited

disunited ■ adj. lacking unity.
–DERIVATIVES **disunity** n.

disuse /dɪsˈjuːs/ ■ n. the state of not being used; neglect.
–DERIVATIVES **disused** adj.

disutility /ˌdɪsjuːˈtɪlɪti/ ■ n. Economics the adverse qualities associated with a particular activity or process.

disyllable /dʌɪˈsɪləb(ə)l, ˈdʌɪsɪl-/ (also **dissyllable** /dɪˈsɪləb(ə)l/) ■ n. Prosody a word or metrical foot consisting of two syllables.
–DERIVATIVES **disyllabic** /ˌdʌɪsɪˈlabɪk/ adj.
–ORIGIN C16: alteration (influenced by SYLLABLE) of French *disyllabe*, from Greek *disullabos* 'of two syllables'.

ditch ■ n. a narrow channel dug to hold or carry water. ■ v. **1** provide with a ditch. **2** (with reference to an aircraft) bring or come down in a forced landing on the sea. **3** informal get rid of; give up. ▸ N. Amer. informal play truant from (school).
–DERIVATIVES **ditching** n.
–ORIGIN Old English, of Germanic origin.

diterpene /dʌɪˈtəːpiːn/ ■ n. Chemistry any of a group of terpenes with unsaturated molecules based on a unit with the formula $C_{20}H_{32}$.
–DERIVATIVES **diterpenoid** adj. & n.

dither ■ v. **1** be indecisive. **2** Computing display or print (a colour image) without sharp edges so that it appears to contain extra colours. ■ n. informal **1** a state of dithering. **2** a state of agitation.
–DERIVATIVES **ditherer** n. **dithery** adj.
–ORIGIN C17 (in the dialect sense 'tremble, quiver'): var. of dialect *didder*.

dithyramb /ˈdɪθɪram(b)/ ■ n. a wildly ecstatic choral hymn of ancient Greece, especially one dedicated to the god Dionysus. ▸ a passionate or inflated speech, poem, or text.
–DERIVATIVES **dithyrambic** adj.
–ORIGIN C17: from Greek *dithurambos*.

ditransitive /dʌɪˈtransɪtɪv, -ˈtrɑː-, -nz-/ ■ adj. Grammar denoting a verb that takes two objects, for example *give* as in *I gave her the book*.

ditsy ■ adj. variant spelling of DITZY.

ditto ■ n. **1** the same thing again (used in lists and often indicated by a ditto mark under the word or figure to be repeated). **2** (also **ditto mark**) a symbol consisting of two apostrophes (") representing a repetition.
–ORIGIN C17: from Tuscan dialect, var. of Italian *detto* 'said', from Latin *dictus* 'said'.

ditty ■ n. (pl. -**ies**) a short simple song.
–ORIGIN Middle English: from Old French *dite* 'composition', from Latin *dictatum*, from *dictare* 'to dictate'.

ditz ■ n. informal, chiefly N. Amer. a scatterbrained person.
–ORIGIN 1970s: back-formation from DITZY.

ditzy (also **ditsy**) ■ adj. informal, chiefly N. Amer. silly or scatterbrained.
–DERIVATIVES **ditziness** n.
–ORIGIN 1970s.

diuresis /ˌdʌɪjʊ(ə)ˈriːsɪs/ ■ n. Medicine increased or excessive production of urine.
–ORIGIN C17: modern Latin, from DI-³ + Greek *ourēsis* 'urination'.

diuretic /ˌdʌɪjʊ(ə)ˈrɛtɪk/ Medicine ■ adj. causing increased passing of urine. ■ n. a diuretic drug.
–ORIGIN Middle English: from Old French *diuretique*, or from Greek *diourētikos*, from *diourein* 'urinate'.

diurnal /dʌɪˈəːn(ə)l/ ■ adj. **1** of or during the daytime. **2** daily; of each day: *diurnal rhythms*.
–DERIVATIVES **diurnally** adv.
–ORIGIN Middle English: from Latin *diurnus* 'daily', from *dies* 'day'.

Div. ■ abbrev. Division.

div ■ abbrev. divergence (in mathematical equations).

diva /ˈdiːvə/ ■ n. a celebrated female opera singer.
–ORIGIN C19: from Latin, 'goddess'.

divalent /dʌɪˈveɪl(ə)nt/ ■ adj. Chemistry having a valency of two.

Divali ■ n. variant spelling of DIWALI.

divan /dɪˈvan, dʌɪˈvan, ˈdʌɪvan/ ■ n. **1** a bed consisting of a base and mattress but no footboard or headboard. **2** a long, low sofa without a back or arms.
–ORIGIN C16: from Turkish *dīvān*, from Persian *dīwān* 'register, court, or bench'.

dive ■ v. (past and past part. **dived**; US also **dove** /dəʊv/) **1** plunge head first and with arms outstretched into water. **2** go to a deeper level in water. ▸ swim under water using breathing equipment. **3** plunge steeply downwards through the air. ▸ move quickly or suddenly in a downward direction or under cover. ▸ Soccer deliberately fall when challenged in order to deceive the referee into awarding a foul. **4** (of prices or profits) drop suddenly. ■ n. **1** an act or instance of diving. **2** informal a disreputable nightclub or bar.
–DERIVATIVES **diving** n.
–ORIGIN Old English *dūfan* 'dive, sink' and *dȳfan* 'immerse', of Germanic origin.

dive-bomb ■ v. bomb (a target) while diving steeply downwards in an aircraft.
–DERIVATIVES **dive-bomber** n.

diver ■ n. **1** a person who dives under water as a sport or as part of their work. **2** a large diving waterbird with a sleek black or grey head, a straight pointed bill, and a wailing call. [Family Gaviidae.]

diverge /dʌɪˈvəːdʒ, dɪ-/ ■ v. **1** (of a road, route, or line) separate and go in a different direction. **2** (of an opinion or approach) differ. **3** (**diverge from**) depart from (a set course or standard). **4** Mathematics (of a series) increase without limit as more of its terms are added.
–DERIVATIVES **divergence** n.
–ORIGIN C17: from medieval Latin *divergere*, from Latin *dis-* 'in two ways' + *vergere* 'to turn or incline'.

divergent ■ adj. **1** diverging. **2** (of thought) using a variety of premises and avoiding common assumptions in making deductions.
–DERIVATIVES **divergently** adv. **diverging** adj.

divers /ˈdʌɪvəz/ ■ adj. archaic or poetic/literary of varying types; several.
–ORIGIN Middle English: from Latin *diversus* 'diverse', from *divertere* (see DIVERT).

diverse /dʌɪˈvəːs, ˈdʌɪvəːs/ ■ adj. widely varied.
–DERIVATIVES **diversely** adv.
–ORIGIN Middle English: var. of DIVERS.

diversify /dʌɪˈvəːsɪfʌɪ, dɪ-/ ■ v. (-**ies**, -**ied**) make or become more diverse. ▸ (of a company) enlarge or vary its range of products or field of operation.
–DERIVATIVES **diversification** n.

diversion /dʌɪˈvəːʃ(ə)n, dɪ-/ ■ n. **1** an instance of diverting. **2** an alternative route for use by traffic when the usual road is temporarily closed. **3** something intended to distract someone's attention: *a raid was carried out to create a diversion*. **4** a recreation or pastime.
–DERIVATIVES **diversionary** adj.

diversity /dʌɪˈvəːsɪti, dɪ-/ ■ n. (pl. -**ies**) the state of being diverse. ▸ a diverse range; a variety: *a diversity of views*.

divert /dʌɪˈvəːt, dɪ-/ ■ v. **1** cause to change course or take a different route. ▸ redirect (a telephone call) to a message service. **2** reallocate (a resource) to a different purpose. **3** draw the attention of; distract or entertain. ■ n. a facility on a cellphone enabling calls to be redirected to a message service.
–DERIVATIVES **diverting** adj.
–ORIGIN Middle English: from Latin *divertere*, from *di-* 'aside' + *vertere* 'to turn'.

diverticula plural form of DIVERTICULUM.

diverticular /ˌdʌɪvəˈtɪkjʊlə/ ■ adj. Medicine of or relating to diverticula.

diverticular disease ■ n. a condition in which muscle spasm in the colon (lower intestine) in the presence of diverticula causes abdominal pain and disturbance of bowel function without inflammation.

diverticulitis /ˌdʌɪvətɪkjʊˈlʌɪtɪs/ ■ n. Medicine inflammation of a diverticulum, especially in the colon, causing pain and disturbance of bowel function. Compare with DIVERTICULOSIS.

diverticulosis /ˌdʌɪvətɪkjʊˈləʊsɪs/ ■ n. Medicine a condition in which diverticula are present in the intestine without signs of inflammation. Compare with DIVERTICULITIS.

diverticulum /ˌdʌɪvəˈtɪkjʊləm/ ■ n. (pl. **diverticula** /-lə/) Anatomy **1** a blind tube leading from a cavity or passage. **2** Medicine an abnormal sac or pouch formed at a weak point in the wall of the alimentary tract.
– ORIGIN C19: from Latin *deverticulum* 'byway', from *devertere* 'turn down or aside'.

divertimento /dɪˌvəːtɪˈmɛntəʊ, -ˌvɛːt-/ ■ n. (pl. **divertimenti** /-ti/ or **divertimentos**) Music a light and entertaining composition, typically in the form of a suite for chamber orchestra.
– ORIGIN C18: Italian, 'diversion'.

divertissement /dɪˈvəːtɪsmənt, ˌdiːvɛːˈtiːsmɒ̃/ ■ n. **1** a minor entertainment or diversion. **2** Ballet a short discrete dance within a ballet, intended to display a dancer's technical skill.
– ORIGIN C18: French, from *divertiss-*, *divertir*, from Latin *divertere* 'turn in separate ways'.

divest /dʌɪˈvɛst, dɪ-/ ■ v. (**divest someone/thing of**) **1** deprive or dispossess someone or something of. **2** free or rid of.
– ORIGIN C17: alteration of *devest*, from Old French *desvestir*, from *des-* (expressing removal) + Latin *vestire*, from *vestis* 'garment'.

divestiture (also **divesture**) ■ n. another term for DIVESTMENT.

divestment ■ n. the action or process of selling off subsidiary business interests or investments.

divide ■ v. **1** separate or be separated into parts. ▶ (usu. **divide something between**) distribute or share out. ▶ form a boundary between. **2** disagree or cause to disagree. **3** Mathematics find how many times (a number) contains another: *36 divided by 2 equals 18.* ▶ (of a number) be susceptible of division without a remainder. ■ n. **1** an instance of dividing or being divided. **2** chiefly US a ridge or line of high ground forming the division between two valleys or river systems.
– PHRASES **divide and rule** (or **conquer**) maintain control over subordinates or opponents by encouraging dissent between them so that they do not unite in opposition.
– DERIVATIVES **divided** adj.
– ORIGIN Middle English: from Latin *dividere* 'force apart, remove'.

dividend /ˈdɪvɪdɛnd/ ■ n. **1** a sum of money that is divided among a number of people, such as the part of a company's profits paid to its shareholders or the winnings from a football pool. ▶ an individual's share of this money. **2** (**dividends**) a benefit from an action or policy: *the policy would pay dividends in the future*. **3** Mathematics a number to be divided by another number.
– ORIGIN C15: from Latin *dividendum* 'something to be divided', from *dividere* (see DIVIDE).

dividend cover ■ n. the ratio of a company's net profits to the total sum allotted in dividends to ordinary shareholders.

divider ■ n. **1** (also **room divider**) a screen or piece of furniture that divides a room into two parts. **2** (**dividers**) a measuring compass, especially one with a screw for making fine adjustments.

divination /ˌdɪvɪˈneɪʃ(ə)n/ ■ n. the practice of divining or seeking knowledge by supernatural means.

divine[1] ■ adj. (**-er**, **-est**) **1** of, from, or like God or a god. ▶ devoted to God; sacred. **2** informal excellent; delightful. ■ n. **1** dated a cleric or theologian. **2** (**the Divine**) providence or God.
– DERIVATIVES **divinely** adv.
– ORIGIN Middle English: from Latin *divinus*, from *divus* 'godlike', rel. to *deus* 'god'.

divine[2] ■ v. **1** discover by guesswork or intuition. **2** have supernatural or magical insight into (the future). **3** discover (water) by dowsing.
– DERIVATIVES **diviner** n.
– ORIGIN Middle English: from Old French *deviner* 'predict', from Latin *divinare*, from *divinus* (see DIVINE[1]).

divine service ■ n. public Christian worship.

diving beetle ■ n. a predatory water beetle which stores air under its wing cases for swimming underwater. [Family Dytiscidae: numerous species.]

diving bell ■ n. an open-bottomed chamber supplied with air, in which a person can be let down under water.

diving board ■ n. an elevated board projecting over a swimming pool or other body of water, from which people dive or jump in.

diving duck ■ n. a duck which typically feeds by diving underwater, such as a pochard or goldeneye.

diving suit ■ n. a watertight suit, typically with a helmet and an air supply, worn for working or exploring deep under water.

divining rod ■ n. a stick or rod used for dowsing.

divinity /dɪˈvɪnɪti/ ■ n. (pl. **-ies**) **1** the state or quality of being divine. **2** a divine being; a god or goddess. **3** (**the Divinity**) God. **4** the study of religion; theology.

divisible /dɪˈvɪzɪb(ə)l/ ■ adj. capable of being divided. ▶ Mathematics (of a number) containing another number a number of times without a remainder.
– DERIVATIVES **divisibility** n.

division ■ n. **1** the action or process of dividing or being divided. **2** the separation of members of a legislative body into groups to vote for or against a bill. **3** the action of splitting the roots of a perennial plant into parts to be replanted separately, as a means of propagation. **4** the process of dividing one number by another. ▶ Mathematics the process of dividing a matrix, vector, or other quantity by another under specific rules to obtain a quotient. **5** each of the parts into which something is divided. ▶ a major unit or section of an organization. ▶ a number of teams or competitors grouped together in a sport for competitive purposes. ▶ Botany a principal taxonomic category that ranks above class and below kingdom, equivalent to the phylum in zoology. ▶ Zoology any subsidiary category between major levels of classification. **6** a partition that divides two groups or things.
– PHRASES **division of labour** the assignment of different parts of a manufacturing process or task to different people in order to improve efficiency.

divisional ■ adj. **1** relating to an organizational or administrative division. **2** forming a partition.
– DERIVATIVES **divisionalize** (also **-ise**) v. **divisionally** adv.

division sign ■ n. the sign ÷, placed between two numbers showing that the first is to be divided by the second, as in $6 ÷ 3 = 2$.

divisive /dɪˈvʌɪsɪv/ ■ adj. causing disagreement or hostility.
– DERIVATIVES **divisively** adv. **divisiveness** n.
– ORIGIN C16: from late Latin *divisivus*, from Latin *dividere* (see DIVIDE).

divisor /dɪˈvʌɪzə/ ■ n. Mathematics a number by which another number is to be divided. ▶ a number that divides into another without a remainder.

divorce ■ n. the legal dissolution of a marriage. ▶ a legal decree dissolving a marriage. ■ v. **1** legally dissolve one's marriage with. **2** detach or dissociate: *religion cannot be divorced from morality*.
– ORIGIN Middle English: from Old French *divorce*, from Latin *divortium*, from *divertere* (see DIVERT).

divorcee /ˌdɪvɔːˈsiː/ ■ n. (US masc. **divorcé**, fem. **divorcée** /-ˈseɪ/) a divorced person.
– ORIGIN C19: from French *divorcé(e)* 'divorced man (or woman)'.

divot /ˈdɪvət/ ■ n. a piece of turf cut out of the ground by a golf club in making a stroke. ▶ a small hole made in this way.
– ORIGIN C16.

divulge /dʌɪˈvʌldʒ, dɪ-/ ■ v. make known.
– ORIGIN Middle English: from Latin *divulgare*, from *di-* 'widely' + *vulgare* 'publish', from *vulgus* 'common people'.

divvy informal ■ n. (pl. **-ies**) Brit. a dividend or share, especially of profits earned by a cooperative. ■ v. (**-ies**, **-ied**) share out.

Diwali /dɪˈwɑːli/ (also **Divali**) ■ n. a Hindu festival with lights, held in October and/or November.
– ORIGIN from Hindi *dīvālī*, from Sanskrit *dīpāvali* 'row of lights'.

diwan /dɪˈwɑːn/ (also **dewan**) ■ n. **1** (in Islamic societies) a

Dixie

central finance department, chief administrative office, or regional governing body. **2** a chief treasury official, finance minister, or Prime Minister in some Indian states.
– ORIGIN Urdu: from Persian *dīwān* 'fiscal register'.

Dixie ■ n. an informal name for the Southern states of the US.
– PHRASES **whistle Dixie** US informal engage in unrealistic fantasies; waste one's time.
– ORIGIN C19.

dixie ■ n. (pl. **-ies**) a large iron cooking pot used especially by campers or soldiers.
– ORIGIN C20: from Hindi *degcī* 'cooking pot', from Persian *degča*, diminutive of *deg* 'pot'.

Dixieland ■ n. a kind of jazz with a strong two-beat rhythm and collective improvisation, which originated in New Orleans in the early 20th century.

DIY ■ n. the activity of decorating and making fixtures and repairs in the home oneself rather than employing a professional.
– DERIVATIVES **DIY'er** n.
– ORIGIN 1950s: abbrev. of **DO-IT-YOURSELF**.

dizygotic /ˌdaɪzɪˈɡɒtɪk/ ■ adj. (of twins) derived from two separate ova, and so not identical.

dizzy ■ adj. (**-ier, -iest**) **1** having a sensation of spinning around and losing one's balance. **2** informal (of a woman) silly but attractive. ■ v. (**-ies, -ied**) [usu. as adj. **dizzying**] make (someone) feel unsteady, confused, or amazed: *the dizzying rate of change.*
– PHRASES **the dizzy heights** informal a position of great importance in a particular field.
– DERIVATIVES **dizzily** adv. **dizziness** n.
– ORIGIN Old English *dysig* 'foolish', of West Germanic origin.

DJ ■ n. a disc jockey. ▶ a person who uses samples of recorded music to make dance music. ■ v. (**DJ's, DJ'ing, DJ'd**) perform as a disc jockey.

djellaba /ˈdʒɛləbə/ (also **djellabah** or **jellaba**) ■ n. a loose hooded woollen cloak of a kind traditionally worn by Arabs.
– ORIGIN C19: from Moroccan Arabic *jellāba, jellābiyya.*

djembe /ˈʒɛmbə, ˈʒɛmbeɪ/ (also **jembe**) ■ n. a goblet-shaped hand drum originating in West Africa.
– ORIGIN French *djembé*, from Mande *jembe.*

djinn ■ n. variant spelling of **JINN**.

dl ■ abbrev. decilitre(s).

D-layer ■ n. the lowest layer of the ionosphere, able to reflect low-frequency radio waves.
– ORIGIN 1930s: from an arbitrary use of the letter *D*.

DLitt ■ abbrev. Doctor of Letters.
– ORIGIN from Latin *Doctor Litterarum.*

DLL ■ abbrev. Computing dynamic linked library.

DM (also **D-mark**) ■ abbrev. Deutschmark.

dm ■ abbrev. decimetre(s).

DMA ■ abbrev. Computing direct memory access.

DMSO ■ abbrev. Chemistry dimethyl sulphoxide.

DMus ■ abbrev. Doctor of Music.

DMZ ■ abbrev. N. Amer. demilitarized zone.

DNA ■ n. Biochemistry deoxyribonucleic acid, a substance present in nearly all living organisms as the carrier of genetic information, and typically consisting of a very long double-stranded chain of sugar and phosphate groups cross-linked by pairs of organic bases.

DNA fingerprinting (also **DNA profiling**) ■ n. another term for **GENETIC FINGERPRINTING**.

DNase /ˌdiːɛnˈeɪz/ ■ n. Biochemistry an enzyme which breaks down DNA into smaller molecules.
– ORIGIN 1940s: from **DNA** + **-ASE**.

DNA virus ■ n. a virus in which the genetic information is stored in the form of DNA (as opposed to RNA).

DNS ■ abbrev. Computing **1** domain name server, the system that automatically translates Internet addresses to the numeric machine addresses that computers use. **2** domain name system, the hierarchical method by which Internet addresses are constructed.

do[1] ■ v. (**does**; past **did**; past part. **done**) **1** perform or carry out (an action). ▶ work on (something) to bring it to completion or to a required state. ▶ make, produce, or provide. ▶ work at for a living or take as one's subject of study. ▶ informal regularly take (a narcotic drug). **2** achieve or complete (a specified target). ▶ informal visit as a tourist. ▶ informal spend (a specified period of time) in a particular occupation or in prison. ▶ (**be/have done with**) give up concern for; have finished with. **3** act or progress in a specified way. ▶ have a specified result or effect on. **4** be suitable or acceptable. **5** informal beat up or kill. ▶ swindle. **6** (usu. **be/get done for**) Brit. informal prosecute; convict. ■ aux. v. **1** used before a verb in questions and negative statements. **2** used to refer back to a verb already mentioned. **3** used in negative or positive commands, or to give emphasis to a positive verb. **4** used with inversion of a subject and verb when an adverbial phrase begins a clause for emphasis. ■ n. (pl. **dos** or **do's**) informal a party or other social event.
– PHRASES **be** (or **have**) **to do with** be concerned or connected with. **do one's head in** Brit. informal make one extremely angry or agitated. **do or die** persist, even if death is the result. **dos and don'ts** rules of behaviour. **that does it!** informal indicating that one will not tolerate something any longer.
– PHRASAL VERBS **do away with** informal put an end to; remove or kill. **do by** treat or deal with in a specified way: *she did well by them.* **do someone down** Brit. informal criticize someone. **do for 1** informal defeat, ruin, or kill. **2** suffice for. **do something** (or **nothing**) **for** informal enhance (or detract from) the appearance or quality of. **do someone in** informal **1** kill someone. **2** (usu. **be done in**) tire someone out. **do someone out of** informal deprive someone of (something) in an underhand or unfair way. **do someone/thing over** Brit. informal beat up or ransack. **be done up** be dressed elaborately or impressively. **do something up 1** fasten, wrap, or arrange something. **2** informal renovate or redecorate a room or building. **do with 1** (**can/could do with**) would find useful or would like to have or do: *I could do with a cup of coffee.* **2** (**can't/won't be doing with**) Brit. be unwilling to tolerate.
– DERIVATIVES **doable** adj. (informal).
– ORIGIN Old English, of Germanic origin.

do[2] ■ n. variant spelling of **DOH**[1].

do. ■ abbrev. ditto.

DOA ■ abbrev. dead on arrival.

dobby ■ n. (pl. **-ies**) a mechanism attached to a loom for weaving small patterns.
– ORIGIN C19: perhaps an application of the given name *Dobbie*, from *Dob* (alteration of *Rob*); the usage is prob. an extension of the earlier sense 'benevolent elf' (who performed household tasks secretly).

Dobermann /ˈdəʊbəmən/ (also **Dobermann pinscher** /ˈpɪnʃə/, **Doberman**) ■ n. a large dog of a German breed with powerful jaws and a smooth coat, typically black with tan markings.
– ORIGIN C20: from the name of the German dog-breeder Ludwig *Dobermann* (+ German *Pinscher* 'terrier').

doc ■ abbrev. informal **1** doctor. **2** Computing document.

docent /ˈdəʊs(ə)nt/ ■ n. **1** (in certain US and European universities and colleges) a member of the teaching staff immediately below professorial rank. **2** N. Amer. a person who acts as a guide in a museum, art gallery, or zoo.
– ORIGIN C19: from Latin *docent-, docere* 'teach'.

docile /ˈdəʊsaɪl/ ■ adj. ready to accept control or instruction; submissive.
– DERIVATIVES **docilely** adv. **docility** n.
– ORIGIN C15 ('apt or willing to learn'): from Latin *docilis*, from *docere* 'teach'.

dock[1] ■ n. **1** an enclosed area of water in a port for the loading, unloading, and repair of ships. ▶ N. Amer. a group of piers where a ship or boat may moor for loading and unloading. **2** (also **loading dock**) a platform for loading trucks or goods trains. ■ v. **1** (with reference to a ship) come or bring into a dock. **2** (of a spacecraft) join with a space station or another spacecraft in space. **3** attach (a piece of equipment) to another.
– ORIGIN Middle English: from Middle Dutch, Middle Low German *docke.*

dock[2] ■ n. the enclosure in a criminal court where a defendant stands or sits.

– ORIGIN C16: prob. orig. slang and rel. to Flemish *dok* 'chicken coop, rabbit hutch'.

dock³ ■ n. a coarse weed of temperate regions, with inconspicuous greenish or reddish flowers, and leaves that are popularly used to relieve nettle stings. [Genus *Rumex*.]
– ORIGIN Old English, of Germanic origin.

dock⁴ ■ v. 1 deduct (money or a point in a score). 2 cut short (an animal's tail). ■ n. the solid bony or fleshy part of an animal's tail. ▸ the stump left after a tail has been docked.
– ORIGIN Middle English (orig. 'the solid part of an animal's tail'): perhaps rel. to Frisian *dok* 'bunch, ball (of string)' and German *Docke* 'doll'.

docker ■ n. a person employed in a port to load and unload ships.

docket ■ n. 1 N. Amer. a list of cases for trial or people having cases pending. ▸ (also **police docket**) S. African a dossier relating to a particular case under investigation by the police. 2 Brit. a document accompanying a consignment of goods that lists its contents, certifies payment of duty, or entitles the holder to delivery. ■ v. (**docketed**, **docketing**) 1 N. Amer. enter (a case or suit) on to a list of those due to be heard. 2 mark (a consignment or package) with a document listing the contents.
– ORIGIN C15 (orig. denoting a short summary): perhaps from **DOCK⁴**.

docking station ■ n. a device to which a portable computer is connected so that it can be used like a desktop computer.

dockland (also **docklands**) ■ n. the area containing a city's docks.

dockyard ■ n. an area with docks and equipment for repairing and maintaining ships.

doctor ■ n. 1 a person who is qualified to practise medicine. ▸ N. Amer. a qualified dentist or veterinary surgeon. 2 (**Doctor**) a person who holds the highest university degree. 3 an artificial fishing fly. 4 a cool onshore breeze that blows regularly in a particular warm location. ■ v. 1 adulterate, tamper with, or falsify. 2 informal practise medicine. 3 remove the sexual organs of (an animal) so that it cannot reproduce. 4 repair (a machine).
– PHRASES **what the doctor ordered** informal something beneficial or desirable.
– DERIVATIVES **doctoring** n.
– ORIGIN Middle English (in the senses 'learned person' and 'Doctor of the Church'): from Latin *doctor* 'teacher'.

doctoral /ˈdɒkt(ə)r(ə)l/ ■ adj. relating to a doctorate.

doctorate /ˈdɒkt(ə)rət/ ■ n. the highest degree awarded by a university faculty or other approved educational organization.

Doctor of Philosophy ■ n. a person holding a doctorate in any faculty except law, medicine, or sometimes theology.

doctrinaire /ˌdɒktrɪˈnɛː/ ■ adj. seeking to impose a doctrine without questions or considerations. ■ n. a doctrinaire person.
– ORIGIN C19: from French, from *doctrine* (see **DOCTRINE**).

doctrine /ˈdɒktrɪn/ ■ n. a set of beliefs or principles held and taught by a Church, political party, or other group.
– DERIVATIVES **doctrinal** adj. **doctrinally** adv.
– ORIGIN Middle English: from Old French, from Latin *doctrina* 'teaching, learning', from *doctor*, from *docere* 'teach'.

docudrama /ˈdɒkjʊˌdrɑːmə/ ■ n. a dramatized film based on real events and incorporating documentary features.

document ■ n. /ˈdɒkjʊm(ə)nt/ a piece of written, printed, or electronic matter that provides information or evidence or that serves as an official record. ■ v. /ˈdɒkjʊmɛnt/ record in written, photographic, or other form.
– DERIVATIVES **documentable** adj.
– ORIGIN Middle English: from Latin *documentum* 'lesson, proof' (in medieval Latin 'written instruction, official paper'), from *docere* 'teach'.

documentary ■ adj. 1 consisting of documents, photographs, and other material providing a factual account. 2 using film, photographs, and sound recordings of real events. ■ n. (pl. **-ies**) a documentary film or television or radio programme.

documentation ■ n. 1 the documents required in the provision of information or evidence. 2 written specifications or instructions. 3 the process of classifying and annotating texts, photographs, etc.

DOD ■ abbrev. Department of Defence.

dodder¹ ■ v. be slow and unsteady.
– DERIVATIVES **dodderer** n. **doddering** adj. **doddery** adj.
– ORIGIN C17: var. of obsolete dialect *dadder*.

dodder² ■ n. a parasitic climbing plant of the convolvulus family, with leafless stems that are attached to the host plant by means of suckers. [Genus *Cuscuta*.]
– ORIGIN Middle English: rel. to Middle Low German *doder*, Middle High German *toter*.

doddle ■ n. Brit. informal a very easy task.
– ORIGIN 1930s: perhaps from dialect *doddle* 'toddle'.

dodeca- /ˈdəʊdɛkə/ ■ comb. form twelve; having twelve: *dodecahedron*.
– ORIGIN from Greek.

dodecagon /dəʊˈdɛkəɡ(ə)n/ ■ n. a plane figure with twelve straight sides and angles.
– ORIGIN C17: from Greek *dōdekagōnon*, neuter (used as a noun) of *dōdekagōnos* 'twelve-angled'.

dodecahedron /ˌdəʊdɛkəˈhiːdr(ə)n, -ˈhɛd-/ ■ n. (pl. **dodecahedra** /-drə/ or **dedecahedrons**) a three-dimensional shape having twelve plane faces, in particular a regular solid figure with twelve equal pentagonal faces.
– DERIVATIVES **dodecahedral** adj.
– ORIGIN C16: from Greek *dōdekaedron*, neuter (used as a noun) of *dōdekaedros* 'twelve-faced'.

dodge ■ v. 1 avoid by a sudden quick movement. ▸ move quickly to one side or out of the way. ▸ cunningly avoid doing or paying. 2 [often as noun **dodging**] Photography expose (one area of a print) less than the rest during processing or enlarging. ■ n. 1 an act or instance of dodging. 2 informal a cunning trick, especially one used to avoid something.
– ORIGIN C16.

dodgeball ■ n. N. Amer. a game in which a team of players forms a circle and tries to hit its opponents with a large ball.

dodgem (also **dodgem car**) ■ n. a small electrically powered car driven within an enclosure at a funfair, with the aim of bumping other such cars and avoiding being bumped by them.
– ORIGIN 1920s: US proprietary name (as *Dodg'em*), from the phr. *dodge them*.

dodger ■ n. 1 informal a person who evades something that is required of them: *a tax dodger*. 2 Nautical a canvas screen on a ship giving protection from spray. 3 US & Austral. a small handbill or leaflet.

dodgy ■ adj. (**-ier**, **-iest**) informal 1 dishonest. 2 risky; dangerous. 3 not good or reliable.

dodo /ˈdəʊdəʊ/ ■ n. (pl. **-os** or **-oes**) a large extinct flightless bird found on Mauritius until the end of the 17th century. [*Raphus cucullatus*.]
– PHRASES **as dead as a dodo** utterly dead or finished.
– ORIGIN C17: from Portuguese *doudo* 'simpleton' (because the birds were tame and easy to catch).

DoE ■ abbrev. Department of Education.

doe ■ n. 1 a female roe or fallow deer or reindeer. 2 a female hare, rabbit, rat, ferret, or kangaroo.
– ORIGIN Old English.

doedoe /ˈdʊdʊ/ ■ v. (often in phr. **go doedoes**) S. African informal a child's word for sleep.
– ORIGIN Afrikaans: perhaps from Dutch *dodijnen* or isiZulu *duduza* 'lull to sleep', or from Malay *dodoi* 'lullaby'.

doe-eyed ■ adj. having large gentle dark eyes.

doek /dʊk/ (also **doekie**) ■ n. S. African a headscarf.
– ORIGIN S. African Dutch: from Dutch *doek* 'cloth'.

doer¹ ■ n. a person who does something.

doer² /duːr/ ■ adv. (usu. in phr. **doer and gone**) S. African informal very far away.
– ORIGIN Afrikaans, 'yonder, far away'.

does third person singular present of **DO**[1].

doesn't ■ contr. does not.

doest archaic second person singular present of **DO**[1].

doeth archaic third person singular present of **DO**[1].

dof ■ adj. S. African informal dull, stupid, or uninformed.
– ORIGIN Afrikaans.

doff ■ v. remove (an item of clothing, especially a hat).
– ORIGIN Middle English: contraction of *do off*.

dog ■ n. 1 a domesticated carnivorous mammal probably descended from the wolf, with a barking or howling voice, an acute sense of smell, and non-retractile claws. [*Canis familiaris*.] ▶ a wild animal resembling this, in particular any member of the dog family (Canidae), which includes the wolf, fox, coyote, jackal, and other species. ▶ the male of such an animal. ▶ (**the dogs**) Brit. informal greyhound racing. 2 informal a contemptible man. ▶ dated a person of a specified kind: *you lucky dog!* 3 informal, derogatory an unattractive woman. 4 used in names of dogfishes, e.g. spurdog. 5 a mechanical device for gripping. ■ v. (**dogged**, **dogging**) 1 follow closely and persistently. 2 (of a problem) cause continual trouble for.
– PHRASES **a dog in the manger** a person who prevents others from having things that they do not need themselves. **a dog's dinner** (or **breakfast**) informal a mess. **a dog's life** an unhappy and oppressed existence. **go to the dogs** informal deteriorate badly. **not a dog's chance** no chance at all.
– ORIGIN Old English.

dogbox ■ n. (in phr. **in the dogbox**) S. African & NZ informal in disfavour.

dog cart ■ n. a two-wheeled cart for driving in, with cross seats back to back, originally incorporating a box under the seat for sportsmen's dogs.

dog collar ■ n. 1 a collar for a dog. 2 informal a clerical collar.

dog days ■ pl. n. chiefly poetic/literary the hottest period of the year (reckoned in antiquity from the heliacal rising of Sirius, the Dog Star.)

dog-eared ■ adj. having worn or battered corners.

dog-end ■ n. informal 1 a cigarette end. 2 the last and least pleasing part of something.

dogfight ■ n. 1 a close combat between military aircraft. 2 a ferocious struggle or fight.

dogfish ■ n. (pl. same or **-fishes**) a small bottom-dwelling shark with a long tail. [*Scyliorhinus canicula* and other species.]

dogged /'dɒgɪd/ ■ adj. tenacious; grimly persistent.
– DERIVATIVES **doggedly** adv. **doggedness** n.

doggerel /'dɒg(ə)r(ə)l/ ■ n. comic verse composed in irregular rhythm. ▶ badly written verse or words.
– ORIGIN Middle English: apparently from **DOG** (used contemptuously).

doggie ■ n. variant spelling of **DOGGY**.

doggone /'dɒgɒn/ N. Amer. informal ■ adj. damned. ■ v. damn (used to express surprise or irritation).
– ORIGIN C19: prob. from *dog on it*, euphemism for *God damn it*.

doggy ■ adj. 1 of or like a dog. 2 fond of dogs. ■ n. (also **doggie**) (pl. **-ies**) a child's word for a dog.

doggy bag ■ n. a bag used to take home leftover food from a restaurant, supposedly for one's dog.

doggy-paddle ■ n. an elementary swimming stroke resembling that of a dog. ■ v. swim using this stroke.

doghouse ■ n. 1 N. Amer. a dog's kennel. 2 Nautical a raised standing area at the after end of a yacht's coachroof.
– PHRASES **in the doghouse** informal in disgrace or disfavour.

dogie /'dəʊgi/ ■ n. (pl. **-ies**) N. Amer. a motherless or neglected calf.
– ORIGIN C19.

dog-leg ■ n. 1 a sharp bend. 2 Golf a hole where the fairway has a bend.

dogma /'dɒgmə/ ■ n. a principle or set of principles laid down by an authority as incontrovertible.

– ORIGIN C16: from Greek *dogma* 'opinion', from *dokein* 'seem good, think'.

dogmatic /dɒg'matɪk/ ■ adj. inclined to impose dogma; firmly asserting personal opinions as true.
– DERIVATIVES **dogmatically** adv. **dogmatism** n. **dogmatist** n.
– ORIGIN C17: from Greek *dogmatikos*, from *dogma*, *dogmat-* (see **DOGMA**).

dogmatics ■ pl. n. [treated as sing.] a system of dogma, especially one laid down by the Roman Catholic Church.

dogmatize /'dɒgmətʌɪz/ (also **-ise**) ■ v. represent as an incontrovertible truth.

do-gooder ■ n. a well-meaning but unrealistic or interfering person.

dog-paddle ■ n. & v. chiefly N. Amer. another term for **DOGGY-PADDLE**.

dog rose ■ n. a delicately scented wild rose with pink or white flowers, commonly growing in European hedgerows. [*Rosa canina* and other species.]

dogsbody ■ n. (pl. **-ies**) informal a person who is given boring, menial tasks.

dog sled ■ n. a sled pulled by dogs.

dogstail ■ n. a fodder grass with spiky flower heads. [Genus *Cynosurus*: several species.]

Dog Star ■ n. Sirius, the brightest star in the sky.
– ORIGIN translating Greek *kuon* or Latin *canicula* 'small dog'; so named as it appears to follow at the heels of Orion (the hunter).

dog tag ■ n. 1 a metal tag attached to a dog's collar, giving its name and owner's address. 2 informal, chiefly N. Amer. a soldier's metal identity tag.

dog-tired ■ adj. extremely tired.

dog-tooth ■ n. 1 Architecture a small pointed moulding forming one of a series radiating like petals from a raised centre. 2 (also **dogstooth**) a small check pattern with notched corners suggestive of a canine tooth.

dogtrot ■ n. a gentle easy trot.

dog violet ■ n. a scentless wild violet with purple or lilac flowers. [*Viola riviniana* and other species.]

dogwatch ■ n. either of two short watches on a ship (4–6 or 6–8 p.m.).

dogwood ■ n. 1 a flowering shrub or small tree with red stems, colourful berries, and hard wood. [*Cornus sanguinea* and related species.] 2 (in southern Africa) a shrub or small tree with glossy leaves and red berries. [*Rhamnus prinoides*.]
– ORIGIN so named because the wood was formerly used to make 'dogs' (i.e. skewers).

doh[1] /dəʊ/ (also **do**) ■ n. Music (in tonic sol-fa) the first and eighth note of a major scale. ▶ the note C in the fixed-doh system.
– ORIGIN C18: from Italian *do*, an arbitrarily chosen syllable.

doh[2] /dəː/ ■ exclam. informal used to comment on a foolish action.

DOI ■ abbrev. Computing digital object identifier, a unique alphanumeric string assigned to a text published online.

doily /'dɔɪli/ ■ n. (pl. **-ies**) a small ornamental mat made of lace or paper, put on a plate under sweet food.
– ORIGIN C17: from *Doiley* or *Doyley*, the name of a C17 London draper.

doing ■ n. 1 (also **doings**) the activities in which someone engages. ▶ [treated as sing. or pl.] informal, chiefly Brit. things whose name one has forgotten. 2 activity or effort: *it would take some doing to calm him down*.

do-it-yourself ■ n. full form of **DIY**.

dojo /'dəʊdʒəʊ/ ■ n. (pl. **-os**) a place in which judo and other martial arts are practised.
– ORIGIN Japanese: from *dō* 'way, pursuit' + *jō* 'a place'.

Dolby /'dɒlbi, 'dəʊl-/ ■ n. trademark 1 an electronic noise-reduction system used in tape recording. 2 an electronic system providing stereophonic sound for cinemas and televisions.
– ORIGIN 1960s: named after the American engineer Ray M. Dolby.

dolce far niente /,dɒltʃeɪ fɑː nɪ'ɛntɛɪ/ ■ n. pleasant idleness.
– ORIGIN Italian, 'sweet doing nothing'.

Dolcelatte /ˌdɒltʃəˈlɑːteɪ, -ˈlati/ ■ n. trademark a kind of soft creamy blue-veined cheese from Italy.
– ORIGIN Italian, 'sweet milk'.

dolce vita /ˌdɒltʃeɪ ˈviːtə/ ■ n. a life of pleasure and luxury.
– ORIGIN Italian, 'sweet life'.

doldrums /ˈdɒldrəmz/ ■ pl. n. (**the doldrums**) **1** a state of stagnation or depression. **2** an equatorial region of the Atlantic Ocean with calms, sudden storms, and light unpredictable winds.
– ORIGIN C18 (as *doldrum* 'dull, sluggish person'): perhaps from DULL.

dole ■ n. (often in phr. **on the dole**) Brit. informal benefit paid by the state to the unemployed. ■ v. (**dole something out**) distribute something.
– ORIGIN Old English *dāl* 'portion, share', of Germanic origin.

doleful ■ adj. **1** sorrowful. **2** causing grief or misfortune.
– DERIVATIVES **dolefully** adv. **dolefulness** n.

dolerite /ˈdɒlərʌɪt/ ■ n. Geology a dark, medium-grained igneous rock typically occurring in dykes and sills.
– ORIGIN C19: from French *dolérite*, from Greek *doleros* 'deceptive' (because it resembles diorite).

doli capax /ˌdɒlɪ ˈkapaks/ ■ adj. Law capable of intending to commit a crime, especially through having reached the age of criminal capacity.
– ORIGIN Latin, 'capable of evil'.

doli incapax /ɪnˈkapaks/ ■ adj. Law incapable of intending to commit a crime, especially through being under the age of criminal capacity.
– ORIGIN Latin, 'incapable of evil'.

doll ■ n. **1** a small model of a human figure, used as a child's toy. **2** informal an attractive young woman or man. ▶ S. African informal darling. ■ v. (**doll someone up**) informal dress someone smartly and attractively.
– ORIGIN C16 (denoting a mistress): familiar form of the given name *Dorothy*.

dollar ■ n. the basic monetary unit of the US, Canada, Australia, and certain countries in the Pacific, Caribbean, SE Asia, Africa, and South America.

dollar diplomacy ■ n. the use of a country's financial power to extend its international influence.

dollarization (also **-isation**) ■ n. **1** the process of aligning a country's currency with the US dollar. **2** the dominating effect of the US on a country's economy.

dollar sign (also **dollar mark**) ■ n. the sign $, representing a dollar.

dollop ■ n. informal a shapeless mass or lump, especially of soft food. ■ v. (**dolloped, dolloping**) add or serve out in large shapeless quantities.
– ORIGIN C16 (denoting a clump of grass or weeds in a field): perhaps of Scandinavian origin.

doll's house (N. Amer. also **dollhouse**) ■ n. a miniature toy house for dolls.

dolly ■ n. (pl. **-ies**) **1** a child's word for a doll. **2** informal, dated an attractive and stylish young woman. **3** a small platform on wheels for holding heavy objects, typically film cameras. ■ v. (**-ies, -ied**) (of a film camera) be moved on a dolly.

dolly bird ■ n. Brit. informal, dated an attractive but unintelligent young woman.

dolly mixtures ■ pl. n. Brit. a mixture of small variously shaped and coloured sweets.

dolly tub ■ n. historical a washtub.

dolma /ˈdɒlmə/ ■ n. (pl. **dolmas** or **dolmades** /-ˈmɑːðɛz/) a Greek and Turkish delicacy of spiced rice and meat wrapped in vine or cabbage leaves.
– ORIGIN from Turkish *dolma*, from *dolmak* 'fill, be filled'.

dolman /ˈdɒlmən/ ■ n. a long Turkish robe open in front. ▶ a woman's loose cloak with cape-like sleeves.
– ORIGIN C16: from Turkish *dolama, dolaman*.

dolman sleeve ■ n. a loose sleeve cut in one piece with the body of a garment.

dolmen /ˈdɒlmɛn/ ■ n. a megalithic tomb with a large flat stone laid on upright ones.
– ORIGIN C19: from French, from Cornish *tolmen* 'hole of a stone'.

347

Domesday Book

dolomite /ˈdɒləmʌɪt/ ■ n. a mineral or sedimentary rock consisting chiefly of a carbonate of calcium and magnesium.
– DERIVATIVES **dolomitic** adj.
– ORIGIN C18: from French, from the name of the French geologist *Dolomieu*.

dolorous /ˈdɒl(ə)rəs/ ■ adj. poetic/literary feeling great sorrow or distress.
– DERIVATIVES **dolorously** adv.
– ORIGIN Middle English: from late Latin *dolorosus*, from Latin *dolor* 'pain, grief'.

dolos /ˈdɒlɒs/ ■ n. (pl. same or **dolosse**) **1** a large concrete anchor block which interlocks with others to prevent erosion of coastlines and harbour walls. **2** S. African one of a set of animal knuckle bones, dice, or other objects used by traditional healers in divination.
– ORIGIN C19: perhaps from Dutch *dobbelos*, from *dobbel* 'to gamble' + *os* 'ox'.

dolostone /ˈdɒləstəʊn/ ■ n. Geology rock consisting of dolomite.

dolour /ˈdɒlə/ (US **dolor**) ■ n. poetic/literary a state of great sorrow or distress.
– ORIGIN Middle English: from Latin *dolor* 'pain, grief'.

dolphin ■ n. **1** a small gregarious and intelligent toothed whale with a beak-like snout and a curved fin on the back. [Families Delphinidae (marine) and Platanistidae (river dolphins): many species.] **2** (also **dolphinfish**) another term for DORADO. **3** a bollard, pile, or buoy for mooring. **4** a structure protecting the pier of a bridge.
– ORIGIN Middle English: from Old French *dauphin*, from Provençal *dalfin*, from Greek *delphin*.

dolphinarium /ˌdɒlfɪˈnɛːrɪəm/ ■ n. (pl. **dolphinariums** or **dolphinaria**) an aquarium in which dolphins are kept and trained for public entertainment.

dolt /dəʊlt/ ■ n. a stupid person.
– DERIVATIVES **doltish** adj. **doltishly** adv. **doltishness** n.
– ORIGIN C16: perhaps a var. of *dulled*, from DULL.

Dom /dɒm/ ■ n. a title prefixed to the names of some Roman Catholic dignitaries and Benedictine and Carthusian monks.
– ORIGIN from Latin *dominus* 'master'.

-dom ■ suffix forming nouns: **1** denoting a state or condition: *freedom*. **2** denoting rank or status: *earldom*. **3** denoting a domain: *fiefdom*. **4** denoting a class of people or attitudes associated with them: *officialdom*.
– ORIGIN Old English *-dōm*, orig. meaning 'decree, judgement'.

domain /də(ʊ)ˈmeɪn/ ■ n. **1** an area owned or controlled by a ruler or government. ▶ a sphere of activity or knowledge. **2** Physics a discrete region of magnetism in ferromagnetic material. **3** Computing a distinct subset of the Internet with addresses sharing a common suffix. **4** Mathematics the possible values of the independent variable or variables of a function.
– ORIGIN Middle English: from French *domaine*, alteration (by association with Latin *dominus* 'lord') of Old French *demeine* (see DEMESNE).

domaine /dəˈmeɪn/ ■ n. a vineyard.
– ORIGIN 1960s: from French, 'estate' (see DOMAIN).

domain name ■ n. Computing the part of a network address which identifies it as belonging to a particular domain.

domba ■ n. **1** a pre-marital initiation rite of the Venda people. **2** (also **domba dance**) a dance that mimics the movements of a snake, performed by unmarried girls as part of this rite.

dome ■ n. **1** a rounded vault forming the roof of a building or structure. ▶ the revolving openable hemispherical roof of an observatory. **2** the rounded summit of a hill or mountain. ▶ Geology a rounded uplifted landform or underground structure. **3** informal the top of the head. **4** poetic/literary a stately building. ■ v. [often as noun **doming**] form a rounded shape; swell out.
– DERIVATIVES **domed** adj.
– ORIGIN C16: from French *dôme*, from Italian *duomo* 'cathedral, dome', from Latin *domus* 'house'.

Domesday Book /ˈduːmzdeɪ/ ■ n. a comprehensive

domestic

record of the extent, value, ownership, and liabilities of land in England, made in 1086 by order of King William I.
– ORIGIN Middle English: var. of **DOOMSDAY**, because the book was regarded as a final authority.

domestic ■ adj. **1** of or relating to a home or family affairs or relations. ▸ of or for use in the home. **2** (of a person) fond of family life and running a home. **3** (of an animal) tame and kept by humans. **4** existing or occurring within a country. ■ n. **1** (also **domestic worker** or **domestic help**) a person who is employed to do domestic tasks. **2** informal a violent quarrel between family members. **3** N. Amer. a product not made abroad.
– DERIVATIVES **domestically** adv.
– ORIGIN Middle English: from Latin *domesticus*, from *domus* 'house'.

domesticate ■ v. **1** tame (an animal) and keep it as a pet or for farm produce. ▸ humorous accustom (someone) to home life and domestic tasks. **2** cultivate (a plant) for food.
– DERIVATIVES **domestication** n.

domesticity ■ n. home or family life.

domestic science ■ n. dated home economics.

domicile /ˈdɒmɪsʌɪl, -sɪl/ (also **domicil** /-sɪl/) ■ n. formal or Law **1** the country in which a person has permanent residence. ▸ chiefly S. African & N. Amer. a person's home. **2** the place at which a company or other body is registered. ■ v. (**be domiciled**) formal or Law treat a specified country as a permanent home. ▸ chiefly S. African & N. Amer. reside; be based.
– ORIGIN Middle English: from Latin *domicilium* 'dwelling', from *domus* 'home'.

domiciliary /ˌdɒmɪˈsɪlɪəri/ ■ adj. concerned with or occurring in someone's home.

domicilium citandi et executandi /ˌdɒmɪˈsɪliəm sɪˈtandi ɛt ɛksɛkjuˈtandi/ ■ n. S. African Law the address where a summons or other official notice can be served.
– ORIGIN Latin, 'the address at which legal proceedings may be instituted'.

dominance ■ n. **1** power and influence over others. **2** Genetics the phenomenon whereby one allelic form of a gene is expressed to the exclusion of the other. **3** Ecology the predominance of one or more species in a plant or animal community.
– DERIVATIVES **dominancy** n.

dominant ■ adj. **1** most important, powerful, or influential. **2** (of a high place or object) overlooking others. **3** Genetics relating to or denoting heritable characteristics which are controlled by genes that are expressed in offspring even when inherited from only one parent. Often contrasted with **RECESSIVE**. **4** Ecology denoting the predominant species in a plant or animal community.
■ n. Music the fifth note of the diatonic scale of any key, considered in relation to the key of the tonic.
– DERIVATIVES **dominantly** adv.

dominate /ˈdɒmɪneɪt/ ■ v. **1** have a commanding or controlling influence over. **2** (of something tall or high) overlook.
– DERIVATIVES **domination** n. **dominator** n.
– ORIGIN C17 (*domination* Middle English): from Latin *dominari* 'rule, govern', from *dominus* 'lord, master'.

dominatrix /ˌdɒmɪˈneɪtrɪks/ ■ n. (pl. **dominatrices** /-ˈtrɪsiːz/ or **dominatrixes**) a dominating woman, especially in sadomasochistic practices.
– ORIGIN C16: from Latin, feminine of *dominator*, from *dominari* (see **DOMINATE**).

dominee /ˈdʊəmini/ ■ n. S. African a minister, especially of the Dutch Reformed Church.
– ORIGIN Dutch, 'clergyman'.

domineer /ˌdɒmɪˈnɪə/ ■ v. [usu. as adj. **domineering**] behave in an arrogant and overbearing way.
– DERIVATIVES **domineeringly** adv.
– ORIGIN C16: from French *dominer*, from Latin *dominari* (see **DOMINATE**).

dominical /dəˈmɪnɪk(ə)l/ ■ adj. **1** (in Christianity) of Sunday as the Lord's day. **2** of Jesus Christ as the lord.
– ORIGIN Middle English: from late Latin *dominicalis*, from Latin *dominicus*, from *dominus* 'lord, master'.

Dominican /dəˈmɪnɪk(ə)n/ ■ n. a member of the Roman Catholic order of preaching friars founded by St Dominic, or of a similar religious order for women. ■ adj. of or relating to St Dominic or the Dominicans.

dominie /ˈdɒmɪni/ ■ n. (pl. **-ies**) **1** chiefly US a pastor or clergyman. **2** Scottish a schoolmaster.
– ORIGIN C17: alteration of Latin *domine!* (vocative) 'master!, sir!', from *dominus* 'lord'.

dominion ■ n. **1** sovereignty; control. **2** the territory of a sovereign or government.
– ORIGIN Middle English: from medieval Latin *dominio(n-)*, from Latin *dominium*, from *dominus* 'lord, master'.

dominium ■ n. Law ownership and rights over property, especially land.
– ORIGIN from Latin *dominium*, from *dominus* 'lord, master'.

domino /ˈdɒmɪnəʊ/ ■ n. (pl. **-oes**) any of 28 small oblong pieces marked with 0–6 pips in each half. ▸ (**dominoes**) [treated as sing.] the game played with such pieces, each player in turn trying to lay down a domino with a value matching that of a piece at either end of the line already formed.
– ORIGIN C17: from French, denoting a hood worn by priests in winter, prob. from Latin *dominus* 'lord, master'.

domino effect ■ n. the effect of the domino theory.

domino theory ■ n. the theory that a political event in one country will cause similar events in neighbouring countries, like a row of falling dominoes.

dompas /ˈdɒmpas/ (also **dompass**) ■ n. (pl. **dompasse**) S. African derogatory term for **PASSBOOK** (in sense 2).
– ORIGIN Afrikaans: from *dom* 'stupid' + *pas* 'pass'.

Dom Pedro (also **Don Pedro**) ■ n. S. African a drink made by mixing cream or ice cream with whisky or a whisky liqueur.
– ORIGIN Portuguese: perhaps named after the Brazilian emperor *Dom Pedro* II.

don¹ ■ n. **1** a university teacher, especially a senior member of a college at Oxford or Cambridge. **2** (**Don**) a Spanish title prefixed to a male forename. ▸ N. Amer. informal a high-ranking member of the Mafia.
– ORIGIN C16: from Spanish, from Latin *dominus* 'lord, master'.

don² ■ v. (**donned, donning**) put on (an item of clothing).
– ORIGIN Middle English: contraction of *do on*.

donate ■ v. **1** give (money or goods) for a good cause. **2** allow the removal of (blood or an organ) from one's body for transfusion or transplantation. **3** Chemistry & Physics provide or contribute (electrons or protons).

donation ■ n. something that is given to a charity, especially a sum of money.
– ORIGIN Middle English: from Latin *donatio(n-)*, from *donare* 'give', from *donum* 'gift'.

donder /ˈdɒnə/ (also **donner**) S. African ■ n. derogatory an unpleasant or despicable person; a blighter. ■ v. variant spelling of **DONNER**.
– ORIGIN Afrikaans, 'wretch'.

done past participle of **DO¹**. ■ adj. **1** (of food) cooked thoroughly. **2** no longer happening or existing. **3** informal socially acceptable: *the done thing*. ■ exclam. (in response to an offer) accepted.
– PHRASES **done for** informal in serious trouble. **done in** informal extremely tired.

donee /dəʊˈniː/ ■ n. a person who receives a gift. ▸ Law a person who is given a power of appointment.

doner kebab /ˈdɒnə, ˈdəʊnə/ ■ n. a Turkish dish consisting of spiced lamb cooked on a spit and served in slices, typically in pitta bread.
– ORIGIN from Turkish *döner kebap*, from *döner* 'rotating' and *kebap* 'roast meat'.

dong ■ v. (of a bell) make a deep resonant sound. ■ n. **1** a deep resonant sound. **2** vulgar slang a man's penis.

donga /ˈdɒŋɡə/ ■ n. S. African & Austral./NZ a ravine or dry watercourse.
– ORIGIN from isiXhosa and isiZulu *udonga*.

dongle /ˈdɒŋɡ(ə)l/ ■ n. Computing an electronic device which must be attached to a computer in order for protected software to be used.
– ORIGIN 1980s: an arbitrary formation.

donjon /ˈdɒndʒ(ə)n, ˈdʌn-/ ■ n. the great tower or

innermost keep of a castle.
- ORIGIN Middle English: var. of DUNGEON.

Don Juan /dɒn ˈdʒuːən, ˈhwɑːn/ ■ n. a seducer of women.
- ORIGIN C19: from the name of a legendary Spanish nobleman of dissolute life.

donkey ■ n. (pl. -eys) **1** a domesticated hoofed mammal of the horse family with long ears and a braying call, used as a beast of burden. [*Equus asinus*.] **2** informal a foolish person. **3** (also **donkey stool**) a low stool astride which an artist sits. **4** a children's card game. **5** (also **donkey boiler**) a device for heating domestic water consisting of a metal drum under which a fire is lit, typically used in areas with no mains electricity.
- PHRASES **donkey's years** informal a very long time. **talk the hind leg off a donkey** informal talk incessantly.
- ORIGIN C18: perhaps from DUN, or from the given name *Duncan*.

donkey jacket ■ n. Brit. a heavy jacket with a patch of waterproof leather or plastic across the shoulders.

donkeyman ■ n. (pl. -men) a man working in a ship's engine room.

donkey work ■ n. informal the laborious part of a job.

donnée /ˈdɒneɪ/ (also **donné**) ■ n. **1** a subject or theme of a narrative. **2** a basic fact or assumption.
- ORIGIN French, 'given'.

donner /ˈdɒnə/ (also **donder**) S. African ■ v. informal hit; beat up. ■ n. variant spelling of DONDER.
- ORIGIN Afrikaans, 'thrash'.

donnish ■ adj. resembling or likened to a college don, particularly in having a pedantic manner.
- DERIVATIVES **donnishly** adv. **donnishness** n.

donor /ˈdəʊnə, -nɔː/ ■ n. **1** a person who donates something. **2** Chemistry an atom or molecule that provides a pair of electrons in forming a coordinate bond. **3** Physics an impurity atom in a semiconductor which contributes conducting electrons to the material.
- ORIGIN Middle English: from Old French *doneur*, from Latin *donator*, from *donare* 'give'.

donor card ■ n. a card carried to indicate consent to the use of one's organs for transplant surgery in the event of one's death.

don't ■ contr. do not.

donut ■ n. US spelling of DOUGHNUT.

doodah /ˈduːdɑː/ (N. Amer. **doodad** /ˈduːdad/) ■ n. informal an object that the speaker cannot name precisely.
- ORIGIN C20: perhaps from the refrain of the song *Camptown Races*.

doodle ■ v. scribble absent-mindedly. ■ n. a drawing made absent-mindedly.
- DERIVATIVES **doodler** n.
- ORIGIN C17: from Low German *dudeltopf, dudeldopp* 'simpleton'.

doodlebug ■ n. informal **1** N. Amer. the larva of an ant lion. **2** US a divining rod. **3** a small car or other vehicle.
- ORIGIN C19: from C17 *doodle* 'ninny' + BUG.

doo-doo ■ n. a child's word for excrement.

doofus /ˈduːfəs/ (also **dufus**) ■ n. (pl. **doofuses**) chiefly N. Amer. informal a stupid person.
- ORIGIN 1960s: perhaps an alteration of US slang *goofus* 'foolish person' (from GOOF), or from Scots *doof* 'dolt'.

doolally /duːˈlali/ ■ adj. informal temporarily insane.
- ORIGIN C20: orig. *doolally tap*, Indian army slang, from *Deolali* (a town near Bombay) + Urdu *tap* 'fever'.

doom ■ n. death, destruction, or another terrible fate. ▶ archaic (in Christian belief) the Last Judgement. ■ v. (usu. **be doomed to**) condemn to certain destruction, death, or failure.
- ORIGIN Old English *dōm* 'statute, judgement', of Germanic origin, from a base meaning 'to put in place'.

doomsayer ■ n. a person who predicts disaster.
- DERIVATIVES **doomsaying** n.

doomsday ■ n. the last day of the world's existence. ▶ (in Christian belief) the day of the Last Judgement.

doomster ■ n. a doomsayer.

door ■ n. a hinged, sliding, or revolving barrier at the entrance to a building, room, or vehicle, or in the framework of a cupboard. ▶ used to refer to a house: *he lived two doors away*.
- PHRASES **lay something at someone's door** blame someone for something. **out of doors** in or into the open air.
- DERIVATIVES **-doored** adj. **doorless** adj.
- ORIGIN Old English, of Germanic origin.

doorbell ■ n. a bell in a building which can be rung by visitors arriving outside.

do-or-die ■ adj. showing or requiring a determination not to compromise or be deterred.

door frame (also **doorcase**) ■ n. the frame into which a door is fitted.

door furniture ■ n. the handles, lock, and other fixtures on a door.

doorkeeper ■ n. a person on duty at the entrance to a building.

doorknob ■ n. a door handle that is turned to release the latch.

doorman ■ n. (pl. -men) a man who is on duty at the entrance to a large building.

doormat ■ n. **1** a mat placed in a doorway for wiping the shoes. **2** informal a submissive person.

doornail ■ n. a stud in a door for strength or as decoration.
- PHRASES (**as**) **dead as a doornail** quite dead.

doorpost ■ n. an upright part of a door frame.

doorstep ■ n. **1** a step leading up to the outer door of a house. **2** Brit. informal a thick sandwich or slice. ■ v. (-stepped, -stepping) Brit. informal **1** (of a journalist) wait uninvited outside the home of (someone) for an interview or photograph. **2** go from door to door selling or canvassing.
- PHRASES **on one's** (or **the**) **doorstep** very close by.

doorstop (also **doorstopper**) ■ n. a fixed or heavy object that keeps a door open or in place.

doorway ■ n. an entrance with a door.

doos /ˈduːəs/ S. African vulgar slang ■ n. **1** a woman's genitals. **2** an unpleasant or stupid person.
- ORIGIN from Afrikaans, 'box'.

doo-wop /ˈduːwɒp/ ■ n. a style of pop music involving close harmony vocals and nonsense phrases, originating in the 1950s.
- ORIGIN imitative.

dop /dɒp/ S. African informal ■ n. a drink, especially of brandy or other spirits. ▶ a tot of spirits. ▶ [as modifier] chiefly historical denoting a system in which wine farmers pay their labourers with low quality wine. ■ v. (**dopped, dopping**) drink (alcohol).
- ORIGIN S. African Dutch, 'shell, husk'.

dopa /ˈdəʊpə/ ■ n. Biochemistry a compound which is present in nerve tissue as a precursor of dopamine and is used to treat Parkinsonism.
- ORIGIN C20: from German, acronym from the systematic name *dihydroxyphenylalanine*.

dopamine /ˈdəʊpəmiːn/ ■ n. Biochemistry a compound present in the body as a neurotransmitter and as a precursor of other substances including adrenalin.
- ORIGIN 1950s: blend of DOPA and AMINE.

dope ■ n. **1** informal an illegal drug, especially cannabis or (US) heroin. ▶ a drug used to enhance the performance of an athlete, racehorse, or greyhound. **2** informal, chiefly N. Amer. a stupid person. **3** informal, chiefly N. Amer. information. **4** a varnish used to strengthen the fabric surface of model aircraft. ▶ a lubricant. ▶ a substance added to petrol to increase its effectiveness. ■ v. **1** administer dope to (a racehorse, greyhound, or athlete). ▶ (**be doped up**) informal be heavily under the influence of drugs. **2** cover with varnish or other thick liquid. **3** Electronics add an impurity to (a semiconductor) to produce a desired electrical characteristic. ■ adj. N. Amer. informal very good.
- DERIVATIVES **doper** n.
- ORIGIN C19 (in the sense 'thick liquid'): from Dutch *doop* 'sauce', from *doopen* 'to dip, mix'.

dopey (also **dopy**) ■ adj. (-**ier**, -**iest**) informal **1** stupefied by sleep or a drug. **2** idiotic.
- DERIVATIVES **dopily** adv. **dopiness** n.

dopiaza /dəʊpɪˈɑːʒə/ ■ n. an Indian dish consisting of meat in an onion sauce.
– ORIGIN from Hindi *do* 'two' + *pyāz* 'onion'.

doppelgänger /ˈdɒp(ə)lˌɡɛŋə, -ˌɡaŋə/ ■ n. an apparition or double of a living person.
– ORIGIN C19: from German, 'double-goer'.

Dopper /ˈdɒpə/ ■ n. (in South Africa) a member of the Gereformeerde Kerk, a strictly orthodox Calvinistic denomination.
– ORIGIN Afrikaans.

doppie ■ n. S. African informal **1** a shell, lid, container, or other hollow object. ▸ a cartridge case. **2** a tot of spirits.
– ORIGIN Afrikaans, diminutive of **DOP**.

dopy ■ adj. variant spelling of **DOPEY**.

dorado /dəˈrɑːdəʊ/ (also **dorade**) ■ n. (pl. **-os**) a large edible fish of warm seas, with silver and bright blue or green coloration. [*Coryphaena hippurus*.]
– ORIGIN C17: from Spanish, 'gilded'.

dor beetle /dɔː/ ■ n. a large black dung beetle that makes a droning sound in flight. [*Geotrupes stercorarius* and other species.]
– ORIGIN Old English (denoting a bee or buzzing fly): prob. imitative.

dorcas gazelle /ˈdɔːkəs/ ■ n. a small gazelle found on semi-desert plains in North Africa and western Asia. [*Gazella dorcas*.]
– ORIGIN C19: from Greek *dorkas* 'gazelle'.

Dorian /ˈdɔːrɪən/ ■ n. a member of a people speaking the Doric dialect of Greek, thought to have entered Greece from the north *c*.1100 BC.
– ORIGIN from Greek *Dōrios* 'of Doris' (a district in Greece).

Dorian mode ■ n. Music the mode represented by the natural diatonic scale D–D (containing a minor 3rd and minor 7th).

Doric /ˈdɒrɪk/ ■ adj. **1** relating to or denoting a classical order of architecture characterized by a plain, sturdy column and a thick square abacus resting on a rounded moulding. **2** relating to or denoting the ancient Greek dialect of the Dorians. ■ n. **1** the Doric order of architecture. **2** the ancient Greek dialect of the Dorians. **3** a broad dialect, especially that spoken in the north-east of Scotland.

dork ■ n. **1** informal a socially inept person. **2** N. Amer. vulgar slang a man's penis.
– ORIGIN 1960S: perhaps a var. of **DIRK**, influenced by **DICK**[1].

dorm ■ n. informal a dormitory.

dormant ■ adj. **1** (of an animal) in or as if in a deep sleep. ▸ Heraldry (of an animal) lying with its head on its paws. **2** (of a plant or bud) alive but not growing. **3** (of a volcano) temporarily inactive. **4** (of a disease) causing no symptoms but liable to recur.
– DERIVATIVES **dormancy** n.
– ORIGIN Middle English: from Old French, 'sleeping', from *dormir*, from Latin *dormire* 'to sleep'.

dormer (also **dormer window**) ■ n. a window that projects vertically from a sloping roof.
– ORIGIN C16 (denoting a dormitory or bedroom window): from Old French *dormeor* 'dormitory', from *dormir* 'to sleep'.

dormitory /ˈdɔːmɪt(ə)ri/ ■ n. (pl. **-ies**) **1** a bedroom for a number of people in a school or institution. ▸ N. Amer. a college hall of residence. **2** [as modifier] denoting a small town or suburb from which people travel to work in a nearby city.
– ORIGIN Middle English: from Latin *dormitorium*, from *dormire* 'to sleep'.

dormouse ■ n. (pl. **dormice**) an agile mouse-like rodent with a bushy tail, noted for spending long periods in hibernation. [*Muscardinus avellanarius* and other species, family Gliridae.]
– ORIGIN Middle English: of unknown origin, but associated with Latin *dormire* 'to sleep'.

dorp /dɔːp/ (also **dorpie**) ■ n. S. African a small rural town or village.
– ORIGIN Dutch, 'village'.

Dorper ■ n. a sheep of a South African cross-breed, which is tolerant of arid conditions and commercially important for its meat.
– ORIGIN 1950S: blend of *Dorset* Horn and *Persian* from which the Dorper was bred.

dorsal /ˈdɔːs(ə)l/ ■ adj. Anatomy,, Zoology, & Botany of, on, or relating to the upper side or back. Compare with **VENTRAL**.
– DERIVATIVES **dorsally** adv.
– ORIGIN Middle English: from late Latin *dorsalis*, from Latin *dorsum* 'back'.

dorsal fin ■ n. Zoology an unpaired fin on the back of a fish or whale.

Dorset Horn ■ n. a sheep of a breed with a white face and horns.

dorsiflex /ˈdɔːsɪflɛks/ ■ v. Physiology bend (something) towards its upper surface.
– DERIVATIVES **dorsiflexion** n.

dorsiventral /ˌdɔːsɪˈvɛntr(ə)l/ ■ adj. chiefly Botany **1** having dissimilar dorsal and ventral surfaces. **2** another term for **DORSOVENTRAL**.
– DERIVATIVES **dorsiventrality** n. **dorsiventrally** adv.

dorsolateral /ˌdɔːsə(ʊ)ˈlat(ə)r(ə)l/ ■ adj. Anatomy & Biology of or relating to the dorsal and lateral surfaces.
– DERIVATIVES **dorsolaterally** adv.

dorsoventral /ˌdɔːsə(ʊ)ˈvɛntr(ə)l/ ■ adj. Anatomy & Biology extending along or denoting an axis joining the dorsal and ventral surfaces. ▸ of or relating to these surfaces.
– DERIVATIVES **dorsoventrally** adv.

dorsum /ˈdɔːsəm/ ■ n. (pl. **dorsa**) Anatomy & Zoology the dorsal part of an organism or structure.
– ORIGIN C18: from Latin, 'back'.

dory[1] /ˈdɔːri/ ■ n. (pl. **-ies**) a narrow deep-bodied marine fish with a large mouth. [Families Zeidae and Oreosomatidae: several species, including the John Dory.]
– ORIGIN Middle English: from French *dorée*, from *dorer* 'gild', based on Latin *aurum* 'gold'.

dory[2] /ˈdɔːri/ ■ n. (pl. **-ies**) a small flat-bottomed rowing boat with a high bow and stern.
– ORIGIN C18: perhaps from Miskito *dóri* 'dugout'.

DOS ■ abbrev. Computing disk operating system.

dosa /ˈdəʊsə/ ■ n. (pl. **dosas** or **dosai** /ˈdəʊsaɪ/) (in Indian cooking) a pancake made from rice flour.
– ORIGIN from Tamil *tôcai*.

dosage ■ n. the size of a dose of medicine or radiation.

dose ■ n. **1** a quantity of a medicine or drug taken at one time. ▸ an amount of ionizing radiation received or absorbed at one time. **2** informal a venereal infection. **3** informal a quantity of something necessary but unpleasant. ■ v. **1** administer a dose to. **2** adulterate or blend (a substance) with another.
– PHRASES **like a dose of salts** Brit. informal very fast and efficiently. [from the use of Epsom salts as an aperient.]
– ORIGIN Middle English: from Greek *dosis* 'gift', from *didonai* 'give'.

dosh ■ n. Brit. informal money.
– ORIGIN 1950S.

do-si-do /ˌdəʊzɪˈdəʊ, -sɪ-/ (also **do-se-do**) ■ n. (pl. **-os**) (in country dancing) a figure in which two dancers pass round each other back to back and return to their original positions.
– ORIGIN 1920S: from French *dos-à-dos* 'back to back'.

dosimeter /dəʊˈsɪmɪtə/ (also **dosemeter** /ˈdəʊsmiːtə/) ■ n. a device used to measure an absorbed dose of ionizing radiation.
– DERIVATIVES **dosimetric** adj. **dosimetry** n.

doss ■ v. informal **1** sleep in rough accommodation or on an improvised bed. **2** spend time idly.
– DERIVATIVES **dosser** n.
– ORIGIN C18: perhaps from Latin *dorsum* 'back'.

dosshouse ■ n. Brit. informal a cheap lodging house for homeless people.

dossier /ˈdɒsɪə, -ɪeɪ, -jeɪ/ ■ n. a collection of documents about a person or subject.
– ORIGIN C19: from French, denoting a bundle of papers with a label on the back, from *dos* 'back', from Latin *dorsum*.

dost /dʌst/ archaic second person singular present of **DO**[1].

dot ■ n. a small round mark or spot. ▸ a dot written as part

of an *i* or *j*, as one of a series of marks to signify omission, or as a full stop. ▶ the shorter signal of the two used in Morse code. ■ v. (**dotted**, **dotting**) **1** mark with a dot or dots. **2** scatter or be scattered over (an area). **3** Brit. informal hit (someone).
– PHRASES **dot the i's and cross the t's** informal ensure that all details are correct. **on the dot** informal exactly on time. **the year dot** Brit. informal a very long time ago.
– ORIGIN Old English *dott* 'head of a boil'; perhaps influenced by Dutch *dot* 'a knot'.

dotage /ˈdəʊtɪdʒ/ ■ n. the period of life in which a person is old and weak.
– ORIGIN Middle English: from DOTE.

dotard /ˈdəʊtəd/ ■ n. an old person, especially one who is weak or senile.

dotcom (also **dot.com**) ■ n. [often as modifier] informal a company which provides products or services on the Internet.
– ORIGIN 1990s: from the suffix *.com* used by companies as the final part of their Internet address.

dote ■ v. **1** (**dote on/upon**) be extremely and uncritically fond of. **2** archaic be silly or feeble-minded, especially as a result of old age.
– DERIVATIVES **doter** n. **doting** adj. **dotingly** adv.
– ORIGIN Middle English: rel. to Middle Dutch *doten* 'be silly'.

doth /dʌθ/ archaic third person singular present of DO¹.

dot matrix ■ n. a grid of dots which are filled selectively to produce an image on a screen or paper.

dot product ■ n. another term for SCALAR PRODUCT.

dotted line ■ n. a line of dots or dashes, especially as a space for a signature on a contract.

dotterel /ˈdɒt(ə)r(ə)l/ ■ n. a small migratory plover which breeds in northern mountains and tundra. [*Eudromias morinellus*.] ▶ chiefly Austral./NZ used in names of other small plovers.
– ORIGIN Middle English: from DOTE (with ref. to the birds' tameness).

dottle /ˈdɒt(ə)l/ ■ n. a remnant of tobacco left in a pipe after smoking.
– ORIGIN Middle English (denoting a plug for a barrel): from DOT.

dotty ■ adj. (**-ier**, **-iest**) informal, chiefly Brit. **1** slightly mad or eccentric. **2** (**dotty about**) infatuated with.
– DERIVATIVES **dottily** adv. **dottiness** n.
– ORIGIN C19: perhaps from obsolete *dote* 'simpleton, fool'.

double ■ adj. **1** consisting of two equal, identical, or similar parts or things. ▶ designed to be used by two people. ▶ having two different roles or interpretations. ▶ (of a domino) having the same number of pips on each half. **2** having twice the usual size, quantity, or strength. ▶ (of a flower) having more than one circle of petals. ■ predet. twice as much or as many. ■ adv. at or to twice the amount or extent. ■ n. **1** a thing which is twice as large as usual or is made up of two parts. **2** Brit. two sporting victories or championships in the same season, event, etc. **3** a system of betting in which the winnings from the first bet are transferred to a second. **4** Bridge a call that increases the penalty points for the defenders if the declarer fails to make the contract. **5** a hit on the ring enclosed by the two outer circles of a dartboard, scoring double. **6** a person who looks exactly like another. **7** (**doubles**) a game involving sides made up of two players. **8** (**Double**) Bell-ringing a system of change-ringing using five bells, with two pairs changing places each time. ■ pron. an amount twice as large as usual. ■ v. **1** make or become double. ▶ (**double up**) use the winnings from a bet as stake for another bet. ▶ (**double up**) share a room. **2** fold or bend over on itself. ▶ (**double up**) bend over or curl up, typically with pain or mirth. ▶ (usu. **double back**) go back in the direction one has come. **3** (**double** (**up**) **as**) be used in or play another, different role. **4** Bridge call a double.
– PHRASES **at** (or **on**) **the double** very fast. **double or nothing** (or Brit. **quits**) a gamble to decide whether a debt should be doubled or cancelled.
– DERIVATIVES **doubleness** n. **doubler** n. **doubly** adv.
– ORIGIN Middle English: from Latin *duplus*, from *duo* 'two'.

double act ■ n. a performance involving two people.

double agent ■ n. an agent who pretends to act as a spy for one country while in fact acting for its enemy.

double axe ■ n. an axe with two blades.

double bar ■ n. a pair of closely spaced lines marking the end of a piece of music.

double-barrelled ■ adj. **1** (of a gun) having two barrels. **2** Brit. (of a surname) having two parts joined by a hyphen.

double bass ■ n. the largest and lowest-pitched instrument of the violin family.

double bassoon ■ n. a bassoon that is larger and longer than usual and an octave lower in pitch.

double bill ■ n. a programme of entertainment with two main items.

double bind ■ n. a dilemma.

double-blind ■ adj. denoting a test or trial in which information which may influence the behaviour of the tester or subject is withheld.

double bluff ■ n. an action or statement intended to appear as a bluff, but which is in fact genuine.

double boiler ■ n. a saucepan with a detachable upper compartment heated by boiling water in the lower one.

double bond ■ n. a chemical bond in which two pairs of electrons are shared between two atoms.

double-book ■ v. inadvertently reserve (something) for two different customers at the same time.

double-breasted ■ adj. (of a jacket or coat) having a large overlap at the front and two rows of buttons.

double-check ■ v. check again.

double chin ■ n. a roll of flesh below a person's chin.
– DERIVATIVES **double-chinned** adj.

double cream ■ n. Brit. thick cream containing a high proportion of milk fat.

double-cross ■ v. deceive or betray (a person one is supposedly helping). ■ n. an act of double-crossing.
– DERIVATIVES **double-crosser** n.

double dagger (also **double obelus**, **double obelisk**) ■ n. a symbol (‡) used to introduce an annotation.

double-dealing ■ n. deceitful behaviour. ■ adj. acting deceitfully.
– DERIVATIVES **double-dealer** n.

double-decker ■ n. something, especially a bus, with two levels.

double decomposition ■ n. Chemistry a reaction in which two compounds exchange ions.

double-density ■ adj. Computing (of a disk) having twice the basic capacity.

double Dutch ■ n. Brit. informal incomprehensible language.

double-dyed ■ adj. thoroughly imbued with a particular quality: *a double-dyed Liberal*.

double-edged ■ adj. **1** (of a knife or sword) having two cutting edges. **2** having two contradictory aspects or possible outcomes.

double entendre /ˌduːbˈ(ə)l ɒ̃ˈtɒ̃dr(ə)/ ■ n. (pl. **double entendres** pronunc. same) a word or phrase open to two interpretations, one of which is usually indecent.
– ORIGIN C17: from obsolete French (now *double entente*), 'double understanding'.

double-entry ■ adj. denoting a system of bookkeeping in which each transaction is entered as a debit in one account and a credit in another.

double exposure ■ n. the repeated exposure of a photographic plate or film.

double fault ■ n. Tennis an instance of two consecutive faults in serving, counting as a point against the server. ■ v. (**double-fault**) serve a double fault.

double feature ■ n. a cinema programme with two films.

double figures ■ pl. n. a number between 10 and 99.

double first ■ n. Brit. a university degree with first-class honours in two subjects or examinations.

double flat

double flat ■ n. a sign (♭♭) placed before a musical note to indicate that it is to be lowered two semitones. ▸ a note so marked or lowered.

double-fronted ■ adj. (of a house) with principal windows either side of the front door.

double glazing ■ n. windows having two layers of glass with a space between them, designed to reduce heat loss and exclude noise.
– DERIVATIVES **double-glaze** v.

double-header ■ n. 1 a train pulled by two locomotives. 2 chiefly N. Amer. a sporting event in which two games are played in succession at the same venue.
– DERIVATIVES **double-headed** adj.

double helix ■ n. a pair of parallel helices intertwined about a common axis, especially that in the structure of DNA.

double jeopardy ■ n. Law the prosecution of a person twice for the same offence.

double-jointed ■ adj. (of a person) having unusually flexible joints.
– DERIVATIVES **double-jointedness** n.

double knitting ■ n. a grade of yarn of medium thickness, used in hand knitting.

double negative ■ n. Grammar 1 a negative statement containing two negative elements (e.g. *didn't say nothing*), regarded as incorrect in standard English. 2 a positive statement in which two negative elements are used to produce the positive force, e.g. *there is not nothing to worry about!*

double obelus (also **double obelisk**) ■ n. another term for DOUBLE DAGGER.

double-park ■ v. park (a vehicle) alongside one that is already parked.

double play ■ n. Baseball a defensive play in which two runners are put out.

double pneumonia ■ n. pneumonia affecting both lungs.

double quick ■ adj. & adv. informal very quick or quickly.

double reed ■ n. Music a reed with two slightly separated blades, used for playing a wind instrument such as an oboe or bassoon.

double salt ■ n. Chemistry a salt composed of two simple salts but with a different crystal structure from either.

double sharp ■ n. a sign (𝄪) placed before a musical note to indicate that it is to be raised two semitones. ▸ a note so marked or raised.

doublespeak ■ n. deliberately ambiguous or obscure language.
– ORIGIN 1949: coined by George Orwell (see DOUBLETHINK).

double standard ■ n. a rule or principle applied unfairly in different ways to different people.

double-stopping ■ n. the sounding of two strings at once on a violin or similar instrument.
– DERIVATIVES **double stop** n.

doublet ■ n. 1 a man's short close-fitting padded jacket, commonly worn from the 14th to the 17th century. 2 either of a pair of similar things, in particular either of two words having the same derivation but different meanings, for example *fashion* and *faction*. 3 technical a pair of similar things, e.g. lines in a spectrum. 4 (**doublets**) the same number on two dice thrown at once.
– ORIGIN Middle English: from Old French, 'something folded', from *double* 'double'.

double take ■ n. a delayed reaction to something unexpected, immediately after one's first reaction.

doubletalk ■ n. chiefly N. Amer. doublespeak.

doublethink ■ n. the acceptance of contrary opinions or beliefs at the same time.
– ORIGIN 1949: coined by George Orwell in his novel *Nineteen Eighty-Four*.

double time ■ n. 1 a rate of pay equal to double the standard rate. 2 Military a regulation running pace. 3 Music a rhythm twice as fast as an earlier one.

double vision ■ n. the perception of two overlapping images of a single scene.

double whammy ■ n. informal a twofold blow or setback.

doubloon /dʌˈbluːn/ ■ n. historical a Spanish gold coin.
– ORIGIN from Spanish *doblón*, from *doble* 'double' (because the coin was worth double the value of a pistole, a gold coin used in Europe in the 17th and 18th centuries).

doublure /duːˈbljʊə/ ■ n. an ornamental lining, especially of leather, in a book cover.
– ORIGIN French, 'lining', from *doubler* 'to line'.

doubt ■ n. a feeling of uncertainty or lack of conviction. ■ v. feel uncertain about. ▸ question the truth or fact of. ▸ disbelieve (someone).
– PHRASES **beyond doubt** allowing no uncertainty. **in doubt** 1 open to question. 2 feeling uncertain. **no doubt** certainly; probably.
– DERIVATIVES **doubtable** adj. **doubter** n. **doubting** adj. **doubtingly** adv.
– ORIGIN Middle English: from Old French *doute* (n.), *douter* (v.), from Latin *dubitare* 'hesitate', from *dubius* 'doubtful'.

doubtful ■ adj. 1 uncertain. 2 not known with certainty. ▸ improbable. ▸ not established as genuine or acceptable: *of doubtful legality*.
– DERIVATIVES **doubtfully** adv. **doubtfulness** n.

doubting Thomas ■ n. a person who refuses to believe something without proof.
– ORIGIN C17: with biblical allusion to the apostle Thomas (John 20: 24–29).

doubtless ■ adv. very probably.
– DERIVATIVES **doubtlessly** adv.

douce /duːs/ ■ adj. chiefly Scottish sober, gentle, and sedate.
– ORIGIN Middle English: from Old French *dous, douce*, from Latin *dulcis* 'sweet'.

douche /duːʃ/ ■ n. a shower of water. ▸ a jet of liquid applied to part of the body for cleansing or medicinal purposes. ▸ a device for washing out the vagina as a contraceptive measure. ■ v. spray or shower with water. ▸ use a contraceptive douche.
– ORIGIN C18: from Italian *doccia* 'conduit pipe'.

dough ■ n. 1 a thick, malleable mixture of flour and liquid, for baking into bread or pastry. 2 informal money.
– DERIVATIVES **doughiness** n. **doughy** adj. (**-ier, -iest**).
– ORIGIN Old English, of Germanic origin.

doughboy ■ n. 1 a boiled or deep-fried dumpling. 2 US informal (especially in the First World War) a United States infantryman.

doughnut (also US **donut**) ■ n. 1 a small fried cake or ring of sweetened dough. 2 a ring-shaped object.

doughty /ˈdaʊti/ ■ adj. (**-ier, -iest**) archaic or humorous brave and resolute.
– DERIVATIVES **doughtily** adv. **doughtiness** n.
– ORIGIN Old English, of Germanic origin.

Douglas fir ■ n. a tall, slender conifer native to western North America, valued for its wood. [*Pseudotsuga menziesii*.]
– ORIGIN C19: named after the Scottish botanist and explorer David *Douglas*.

doum palm /duːm/ (also **dom palm**) ■ n. an Egyptian palm tree producing edible fruit and a vegetable ivory substitute. [*Hyphaene thebaica*.]
– ORIGIN C18: from Arabic *dawm, dūm*.

dour /dʊə, ˈdaʊə/ ■ adj. very severe, stern, or gloomy.
– DERIVATIVES **dourly** adv. **dourness** n.
– ORIGIN Middle English: prob. from Scottish Gaelic *dúr* 'dull, obstinate', perhaps from Latin *durus* 'hard'.

douse /daʊs/ (also **dowse**) ■ v. 1 drench with liquid. 2 extinguish (a fire or light). 3 Nautical lower (a sail) quickly.
– ORIGIN C17: perhaps imitative, influenced by SOUSE, or perhaps from dialect *douse* 'strike, beat', from Middle Dutch and Low German *dossen*.

dove[1] /dʌv/ ■ n. 1 a stocky seed- or fruit-eating bird with a small head, short legs, and a cooing voice, similar to but generally smaller and more delicate than a pigeon. [Family Columbidae: many species.] 2 a person who advocates peaceful or conciliatory policies.
– DERIVATIVES **dovelike** adj. **dovish** adj.

VOWELS a cat ɑː arm ɛ bed ɛː hair ə ago əː her ɪ sit i cosy iː see ɒ hot ɔː saw ʌ run

– ORIGIN Middle English: from Old Norse *dúfa*.

dove² /dəʊv/ chiefly N. Amer. past of **DIVE**.

dovecote /'dʌvkɒt/ (also **dovecot**) ■ n. a shelter with nest holes for domesticated pigeons.

dove grey ■ n. light grey.

Dover sole ■ n. a marine flatfish which is highly valued as food. [*Solea solea* (Europe) and *Microstomus pacificus* (eastern Pacific).]

dove shell ■ n. a small mollusc with a robust shell, occurring in tropical and subtropical seas. [*Pyrene* and other genera.]

dovetail ■ n. a joint formed by one or more tapered tenons which interlock with corresponding mortises. ■ v. **1** join together by means of a dovetail. **2** fit together easily or conveniently.

dove tree ■ n. a slender deciduous Chinese tree with flowers that bear large white bracts resembling doves' wings. [*Davidia involucrata*.]

dowager /'daʊədʒə/ ■ n. **1** a widow with a title or property derived from her late husband. **2** informal a dignified elderly woman.
– ORIGIN C16: from Old French *douagiere*, from *douage* 'dower', from *douer*, from Latin *dotare* (see **DOWER**).

dowager's hump ■ n. forward curvature of the spine resulting in a stoop, especially in women with osteoporosis.

dowd /daʊd/ ■ n. a dowdy person.
– ORIGIN Middle English.

dowdy ■ adj. (**-ier**, **-iest**) (especially of a woman) unfashionable and dull in appearance.
– DERIVATIVES **dowdily** adv. **dowdiness** n.

dowel /'daʊəl/ ■ n. a headless peg used for holding together components. ■ v. (**dowelled**, **dowelling**; US **doweled**, **doweling**) fasten with a dowel.
– ORIGIN Middle English: perhaps from Middle Low German *dovel*.

dowelling (US **doweling**) ■ n. cylindrical rods for cutting into dowels.

dower /'daʊə/ ■ n. **1** a widow's share for life of her husband's estate. **2** archaic a dowry. ■ v. archaic give a dowry to.
– ORIGIN Middle English: from Old French *douaire*, from medieval Latin *dotarium*, from Latin *dotare* 'endow', from *dos*, *dot-* 'dowry'.

dower house ■ n. Brit. a house intended for a widow, typically one on her late husband's estate.

Dow Jones index /daʊ 'dʒəʊnz/ (also **Dow Jones average**) ■ n. an index of figures indicating the relative price of shares on the New York Stock Exchange.
– ORIGIN from the name of the American financial news agency *Dow Jones & Co, Inc.*

down¹ ■ adv. **1** towards or in a lower place or position. ▶ to or at a place perceived as lower. ▶ away from the north. ▶ Brit. away from a university, especially Oxford or Cambridge. ▶ so as to lie flush or flat. **2** to or at a lower level or value. ▶ to a smaller amount or size, or a simpler or more basic state. ▶ from an earlier to a later point in time or order. **3** in or into a weaker or worse position, mood, or condition. ▶ (of a computer system) out of action. **4** (**down with** ——) expressing strong dislike. **5** in or into writing. ▶ on or on to a list, schedule, or record. **6** (with reference to partial payment of a sum of money) made initially or on the spot. **7** (of sailing) with the current or the wind. ▶ (of a ship's helm) moved round to leeward. **8** American Football (of the ball or a player in possession) not in play. ■ prep. **1** from a higher to a lower point of. **2** at a point further along the course of. ▶ along the course or extent of. **3** throughout (a period of time). **4** informal at or to (a place). ■ adj. **1** directed or moving towards a lower place or position. **2** unhappy. **3** (of a computer system) out of action. **4** Physics denoting a flavour of quark having a charge of -⅓. ■ v. informal **1** knock or bring to the ground. **2** consume (a drink). **3** (of a golfer) sink (a putt). ■ n. **1** American Football a chance for a team to advance the ball, ending when the ball-carrier is tackled or the ball becomes out of play. **2** (**downs**) informal unwelcome events. **3** informal a period of unhappiness.
– PHRASES **be** (or **have a**) **down on** informal feel hostile towards. **be down to 1** be attributable to (a factor). ▶ be

downright

the responsibility of. **2** be left with only (the specified amount). **down in the mouth** informal unhappy. **down on one's luck** informal having a period of bad luck. **down tools** Brit. informal stop work. **have** (or **put**) **someone/thing down as** judge someone or something to be (a particular type).
– ORIGIN Old English *dūn*, *dūne*, shortened from *adūne* 'downward', from the phr. *of dūne* 'off the hill' (see **DOWN³**).

down² ■ n. **1** soft fine feathers forming the covering of a young bird or an insulating layer below the contour feathers of an adult bird, used for stuffing cushions and quilts. **2** fine soft hair on a person's skin. ▶ short soft hairs on leaves, fruit, or seeds.
– ORIGIN Middle English: from Old Norse *dúnn*.

down³ ■ n. a gently rolling hill. ▶ (**the Downs**) ridges of undulating chalk and limestone hills in southern England.
– ORIGIN Old English *dūn* 'hill', perhaps ultimately of Celtic origin and rel. to Old Irish *dún* and obsolete Welsh *din* 'fort'.

down-and-dirty ■ adj. informal, chiefly N. Amer. **1** highly competitive or unprincipled. **2** explicit.

down and out ■ adj. **1** destitute. **2** (of a boxer) knocked down and unable to continue fighting. ■ n. (**down-and-out**) a destitute person.

down at heel ■ adj. chiefly Brit. **1** (of a shoe) with the heel worn down. **2** shabby or impoverished.

downbeat ■ adj. **1** pessimistic; gloomy. **2** understated. ■ n. Music an accented beat, usually the first of the bar.

downcast ■ adj. **1** (of eyes) looking downwards. **2** (of a person) feeling despondent. ■ n. a shaft dug in a mine for ventilation.

downcomer ■ n. a pipe for the downward transport of water or gas from the top of a furnace or boiler.

downconverter ■ n. Electronics a device that converts a signal to a lower frequency.
– DERIVATIVES **downconversion** n.

downcurved ■ adj. curved downwards.

downdraught ■ n. a downward current or draught of air.

downer ■ n. informal **1** a depressant or tranquillizing drug. **2** something dispiriting or depressing.

downfall ■ n. a loss of power, prosperity, or status.

downforce ■ n. a force pressing a moving vehicle down towards the ground, giving increased stability.

downgrade ■ v. reduce to a lower grade, rank, or level of importance. ■ n. **1** an instance of downgrading. **2** chiefly N. Amer. a downward gradient.

downhearted ■ adj. discouraged; dejected.
– DERIVATIVES **downheartedly** adv. **downheartedness** n.

downhill ■ adv. & adj. /daʊn'hɪl/ **1** towards the bottom of a slope. **2** into a steadily worsening situation. ■ n. /'daʊnhɪl/ **1** a downward slope. **2** Skiing a downhill race.
– DERIVATIVES **downhiller** n. (Skiing).

down-home ■ adj. chiefly N. Amer. unpretentious; homely.

downland ■ n. gently rolling hill country.

downlink ■ n. a telecommunications link for signals coming to the earth from a satellite, spacecraft, or aircraft.

download Computing ■ v. copy (data) from one computer system to another or to a disk. ■ n. the act or process of downloading. ▶ a downloaded data file.
– DERIVATIVES **downloadable** adj.

downmarket ■ adj. & adv. towards or relating to the cheaper or less prestigious sector of the market.

down payment ■ n. an initial payment made when buying on credit.

downpipe ■ n. a pipe to carry rainwater from a roof to a drain or to ground level.

downplay ■ v. make (something) appear less important than it really is.

downpour ■ n. a heavy fall of rain.

downright ■ adj. **1** utter; complete: *it's a downright disgrace*. **2** so direct in manner as to be blunt. ■ adv. to an

downriver

extreme degree; thoroughly: *he was downright rude.*
– DERIVATIVES **downrightness** n.

downriver ■ adv. & adj. towards or situated at a point nearer the mouth of a river.

downscale N. Amer. ■ v. reduce in size, scale, or extent.

downshift ■ v. change to a lower gear. ■ n. an instance of downshifting.

downside ■ n. the negative aspect of something.

downsize ■ v. make (something) smaller. ▶ (of a company) shed staff.

downslope ■ n. a downward slope. ■ adv. & adj. at or towards a lower point on a slope.

downspout ■ n. North American term for **DOWNPIPE**.

Down's syndrome (also **Down syndrome**) ■ n. Medicine a congenital disorder causing intellectual impairment and physical abnormalities including short stature and a broad facial profile.
– ORIGIN 1960s: named after the C19 English physician John L. H. *Down*.

downstage ■ adj. & adv. at or towards the front of a stage.

downstairs ■ adv. & adj. down a flight of stairs; on or to a lower floor. ■ n. the ground floor or lower floors of a building.

downstream ■ adv. & adj. situated or moving in the direction in which a stream or river flows.

downstroke ■ n. a stroke made downwards.

downswing ■ n. **1** another term for **DOWNTURN**. **2** Golf the downward movement of a club when the player is about to hit the ball.

down time ■ n. time during which a computer or other machine is out of action.

down-to-earth ■ adj. practical and realistic.
– DERIVATIVES **down-to-earthness** n.

downtown chiefly N. Amer. ■ adj. & adv. of, in, or towards the central area or main business area of a city. ■ n. such an area of a city.
– DERIVATIVES **downtowner** n.

downtrodden ■ adj. oppressed or treated badly by people in power.

downturn ■ n. a decline in economic or other activity. ■ v. (usu. as adj. **downturned**) turn downwards.

down under informal ■ adv. in or to Australia or New Zealand. ■ n. Australia and New Zealand.

downward ■ adv. (also **downwards**) towards a lower point or level. ■ adj. moving or leading towards a lower point or level.
– DERIVATIVES **downwardly** adv.

downwash ■ n. the downward deflection of an airstream by a wing or rotor blade.

downwelling ■ n. the downward movement of fluid.

downwind ■ adv. & adj. in the direction in which the wind is blowing.

downy ■ adj. (**-ier**, **-iest**) covered with fine soft hair or feathers. ▶ soft and fluffy.
– DERIVATIVES **downily** adv. **downiness** n.

dowry /'daʊ(ə)ri/ ■ n. (pl. **-ies**) property or money brought by a bride to her husband on their marriage.
– ORIGIN Middle English: from Anglo-Norman French *dowarie*, from medieval Latin *dotarium* (see **DOWER**).

dowse¹ /daʊz/ ■ v. (usu. as noun **dowsing**) search for underground water or minerals by observing the motion of a pointer, supposedly in response to unseen influences.
– DERIVATIVES **dowser** n.
– ORIGIN C17.

dowse² ■ v. variant spelling of **DOUSE**.

doxastic /dɒk'sastɪk/ ■ adj. Philosophy of or relating to an individual's beliefs.
– ORIGIN C18: from Greek *doxastikos* 'conjectural'.

doxy /'dɒksi/ ■ n. (pl. **-ies**) archaic a mistress. ▶ a prostitute.
– ORIGIN C16.

doxycycline /ˌdɒksɪ'sʌɪkliːn/ ■ n. an orally administered broad-spectrum antibiotic of the tetracycline group, used also as an antimalarial drug.
– ORIGIN 1960s: from **DE-** + **OXY-²** + *-cycline*, from **TETRACYCLINE**.

doyen /'dɔɪən, 'dwɑːjã/ ■ n. (fem. **doyenne** /dɔɪ'ɛn, dwʌ'jɛn/) the most respected or prominent person in a particular field.
– ORIGIN C17: from Old French *deien* (see **DEAN**).

doz. ■ abbrev. dozen.

doze ■ v. sleep lightly. ■ n. a short light sleep.
– ORIGIN C17: perhaps rel. to Danish *døse* 'make drowsy'.

dozen ■ n. (pl. same) a group or set of twelve.
– PHRASES **talk nineteen to the dozen** Brit. talk incessantly.
– DERIVATIVES **dozenth** adj.
– ORIGIN Middle English: from Old French *dozeine*, from Latin *duodecim* 'twelve'.

dozy ■ adj. (**-ier**, **-iest**) feeling drowsy and lazy. ▶ Brit. informal not alert; stupid.
– DERIVATIVES **dozily** adv. **doziness** n.

DP ■ abbrev. **1** data processing. **2** (in South Africa) Democratic Party.

DPhil ■ abbrev. Doctor of Philosophy.

dpi ■ abbrev. Computing dots per inch.

DPT ■ abbrev. Medicine diphtheria, pertussis (whooping cough), and tetanus.

Dr ■ abbrev. **1** (as a title) Doctor. **2** (in street names) Drive.

drab¹ ■ adj. (**drabber**, **drabbest**) drearily dull. ■ n. a dull light brown colour.
– DERIVATIVES **drably** adv. **drabness** n.
– ORIGIN C16 (denoting undyed cloth): prob. from Old French *drap* 'cloth'.

drab² ■ n. archaic **1** a slovenly woman. **2** a prostitute.
– ORIGIN C16: perhaps rel. to Low German *drabbe* 'mire' and Dutch *drab* 'dregs'.

drachma /'drakmə/ ■ n. (pl. **drachmas** or **drachmae** /-miː/) the former basic monetary unit of Greece.
– ORIGIN from Greek *drakhmē*, an Attic weight and coin.

draconian /drə'kəʊnɪən, dreɪ-/ ■ adj. (of laws) excessively harsh and severe.
– DERIVATIVES **draconic** /-'kɒnɪk/ adj.
– ORIGIN C19: from *Draco*, name of an ancient Athenian legislator.

draft ■ n. **1** a preliminary version of a piece of writing. ▶ a plan or sketch. **2** a written order to pay a specified sum. **3** (**the draft**) chiefly US compulsory recruitment for military service. ▶ N. Amer. a procedure whereby sports players are made available for selection or reselection by the teams in a league. **4** US spelling of **DRAUGHT**. ■ v. **1** prepare a preliminary version of (a text). **2** select (a person or group) and bring them somewhere for a certain purpose. ▶ US conscript for military service.
– DERIVATIVES **drafter** n.
– ORIGIN C16: phonetic spelling of **DRAUGHT**.

draftsman ■ n. (pl. **-men**) **1** a person who drafts legal documents. **2** chiefly N. Amer. variant spelling of **DRAUGHTSMAN**.

drafty ■ adj. US spelling of **DRAUGHTY**.

drag ■ v. (**dragged**, **dragging**) **1** pull along forcefully, roughly, or with difficulty. ▶ take (someone) somewhere, despite their reluctance. ▶ move (an image) across a computer screen using a mouse. ▶ trail along the ground. ▶ (**drag at**) catch hold of and pull. ▶ search the bottom of (a body of water) with grapnels or nets. **2** (**drag something up**) informal deliberately mention something unwelcome. **3** (of time) pass slowly and tediously. ▶ (**drag something out**) protract something unnecessarily. **4** (**drag on**) informal inhale the smoke from (a cigarette). **5** (**drag someone up**) Brit. dated bring up a child badly. ■ n. **1** the action of dragging. **2** the longitudinal retarding force exerted by air or other fluid surrounding a moving object. **3** informal a boring or tiresome person or thing. **4** informal an act of inhaling smoke from a cigarette. **5** women's clothing worn by a man: *men in drag*. **6** short for **DRAG RACE**. **7** informal, chiefly N. Amer. a street or road: *the main drag*. **8** an apparatus for dredging or for recovering objects from the bottom of water.
– PHRASES **drag one's feet** **1** walk slowly and wearily or with difficulty. **2** be deliberately slow or reluctant to act.
– ORIGIN Middle English: from Old English *dragan* or Old Norse *draga* 'to draw'.

dragée /'drɑːʒeɪ/ ■ n. **1** a sweet consisting of a centre covered with a coating, such as a sugared almond. **2** a small silver ball for decorating a cake.
– ORIGIN C17: French, from Old French *dragie* (see DREDGE²).

draggy ■ adj. (-ier, -iest) informal dreary; tedious.

dragline ■ n. **1** a large excavator with a bucket pulled in by a wire cable. **2** a line of silk produced by a spider and acting as a safety line.

dragnet ■ n. **1** a net drawn through water or across ground to trap fish or game. **2** a systematic search for criminals or criminal activity.

dragoman /'drægə(ʊ)mən/ ■ n. (pl. **dragomans** or **dragomen**) an interpreter or guide in a country speaking Arabic, Turkish, or Persian.
– ORIGIN Middle English: from Italian *dragomanno*, from medieval Greek *dragoumanos*, from Arabic *tarjumān* 'interpreter'.

dragon ■ n. **1** a mythical monster like a giant reptile, typically with wings and claws and able to breathe out fire. ▸ used in names of various lizards, e.g. Komodo dragon. **2** derogatory a fierce and intimidating woman.
– PHRASES **chase the dragon** informal smoke heroin.
– ORIGIN Middle English: from Greek *drakōn* 'serpent'.

dragon boat ■ n. a boat of a traditional Chinese design resembling a dragon, propelled with paddles by a large crew.

dragonet /'dragənɪt/ ■ n. a small marine fish of which the male is brightly coloured. [*Callionymus lyra* and other species.]
– ORIGIN Middle English: from Old French, diminutive of *dragon* 'dragon'.

dragonfish ■ n. (pl. same or **-fishes**) a long, slender deep-sea fish with fang-like teeth, a barbel on the chin, and luminous organs. [Families Stomiatidae and Idiacanthidae: numerous species.]

dragonfly ■ n. (pl. **-flies**) a fast-flying long-bodied predatory insect with two pairs of large transparent wings (spread out sideways at rest) and voracious aquatic larvae. [Suborder Anisoptera: many species.]

dragon ship ■ n. a Viking longship ornamented with a beaked prow.

dragon tree ■ n. a slow-growing palm-like tree, grown for its ornamental foliage. [Genus *Dracaena*: several species.]

dragoon /drə'guːn/ ■ n. **1** a member of any of several British cavalry regiments. ▸ historical a mounted infantryman armed with a carbine. **2** a variety of pigeon. ■ v. coerce into doing something.
– ORIGIN C17 (denoting a kind of carbine, thought of as breathing fire): from French *dragon* 'dragon'.

drag queen ■ n. a man who ostentatiously dresses up in women's clothes.

drag race ■ n. a race between two cars over a short distance as a test of acceleration.
– DERIVATIVES **drag racer** n. **drag racing** n.

dragster ■ n. a car built or modified to take part in drag races.

drail /dreɪl/ ■ n. Fishing a weighted fish hook and line for dragging below the surface of the water.
– ORIGIN C16: from the obsolete v. *drail*, an alteration of TRAIL.

drain ■ v. **1** cause the water or other liquid in (something) to run out, leaving it empty or dry. ▸ (of liquid) run off or out. ▸ (of a river) carry off the superfluous water from (an area). ▸ become dry as liquid runs off. ▸ drink the entire contents of. **2** deprive of strength or vitality. ▸ cause to be lost or used up. ■ n. **1** a channel or pipe carrying off surplus liquid, especially rainwater or liquid waste. **2** a thing that uses up a particular resource. ▸ the continuous loss of a resource: *the drain of talented staff*.
– PHRASES **go down the drain** informal be totally wasted. **laugh like a drain** Brit. informal laugh raucously.
– ORIGIN Old English *drēhnian* 'strain (liquid)', of Germanic origin.

drainage ■ n. **1** the action or process of draining something. **2** a system of drains.

drainer ■ n. **1** a rack used to hold crockery while it drains. **2** a draining board.

draining board ■ n. a sloping grooved board or surface on which crockery is left to drain into an adjacent sink.

drainpipe ■ n. **1** a pipe for carrying off rainwater or liquid refuse from a building. **2** (**drainpipes**) or **drainpipe trousers** trousers with very narrow legs.

Draize test ■ n. a pharmacological test in which a potentially harmful substance is introduced into the eye or on to the skin of a laboratory animal.
– ORIGIN 1970s: named after the American pharmacologist John H. *Draize*.

drake ■ n. a male duck.
– ORIGIN Middle English: of West Germanic origin.

Drake equation ■ n. Astronomy a formula giving an estimate of the likelihood of discovering intelligent extraterrestrial life in the galaxy.
– ORIGIN 1960s: named after the American astronomer Frank *Drake*, who formulated it.

Drakensberg /'drɑːkənzbəːg/ ■ n. the highest mountain range in South Africa, located on the eastern side of the country.

Drakensberger /'drɑːkənsbəːgə/ ■ n. an animal of a South African indigenous breed of black cattle.
– ORIGIN 1940s: named after the region of South Africa where the breed was developed.

Dralon /'dreɪlɒn/ ■ n. trademark, chiefly Brit. a synthetic textile made from acrylic fibre.
– ORIGIN 1950s: on the pattern of *nylon*.

DRAM ■ abbrev. Electronics dynamic random-access memory.

dram /dram/ ■ n. chiefly Scottish a small drink of spirits.
– ORIGIN Middle English: from Old French *drame*, *dragme* or medieval Latin *drama*, *dragma*.

drama ■ n. **1** a play. ▸ plays as a genre or literary style. **2** an exciting or emotional series of events.
– ORIGIN C16: from Greek *drama*, from *dran* 'do, act'.

drama queen ■ n. informal a person who responds to situations in a melodramatic way.

dramatic ■ adj. **1** of or relating to drama. **2** sudden and striking: *a dramatic increase*. ▸ exciting or impressive. ▸ intended to create an effect; theatrical.
– DERIVATIVES **dramatically** adv.

dramatics ■ pl. n. **1** [treated as sing. or pl.] the study or practice of acting in and producing plays. **2** theatrically exaggerated or overemotional behaviour.

dramatis personae /ˌdramətɪs pəːˈsəʊnʌɪ, -niː/ ■ pl. n. the characters of a play, novel, or narrative.
– ORIGIN C18: from Latin, 'persons of the drama'.

dramatist ■ n. a person who writes plays.

dramatize (also **-ise**) ■ v. **1** present (a novel, event, etc.) as a play. **2** exaggerate the excitement or seriousness of.
– DERIVATIVES **dramatization** (also **-isation**) /-ˈzeɪʃ(ə)n/ n.

dramaturge /'dramətəːdʒ/ (also **dramaturg**) ■ n. **1** a dramatist. **2** a literary editor on the staff of a theatre who liaises with authors and edits texts.
– ORIGIN C19: from Greek *dramatourgos*, from *drama*, *dramat-* 'drama' + *-ergos* 'worker'.

dramaturgy /'draməˌtəːdʒi/ ■ n. the theory and practice of dramatic composition.
– DERIVATIVES **dramaturgic** adj. **dramaturgical** adj. **dramaturgically** adv.

Drambuie /dramˈbuːi, -ˈbjuːi/ ■ n. trademark a sweet Scotch whisky liqueur.
– ORIGIN from Scottish Gaelic *dram buidheach* 'satisfying drink'.

drank past of DRINK.

drape ■ v. arrange (cloth or clothing) loosely on or round something. ▸ adorn or wrap loosely with folds of cloth. ■ n. **1** (**drapes**) long curtains. **2** the way in which a garment or fabric hangs. **3** a cloth for covering a patient's body when a surgical operation is being performed.
– ORIGIN C17: back-formation from DRAPERY, influenced by French *draper* 'to drape'.

draper ■ n. Brit. dated a person who sells textile fabrics.
– ORIGIN Middle English: from Old French *drapier*, from *drap* 'cloth'.

drapery ▪ n. (pl. **-ies**) cloth, curtains, or clothing hanging in loose folds.
– ORIGIN Middle English: from Old French *draperie*, from *drap* 'cloth'.

drastic /'drastɪk, 'drɑː-/ ▪ adj. having a strong or far-reaching effect.
– DERIVATIVES **drastically** adv.
– ORIGIN C17: from Greek *drastikos*, from *dran* 'do'.

drat ▪ exclam. used to express mild annoyance.
– DERIVATIVES **dratted** adj.
– ORIGIN C19: shortening of *od rat*, euphemism for *God rot*.

draught /drɑːft/ (US **draft**) ▪ n. **1** a current of cool air in a room or confined space. **2** a single act of drinking or inhaling. ▸ poetic/literary or archaic a quantity of a liquid with medicinal properties: *a sleeping draught*. **3** the depth of water needed to float a particular ship: *her shallow draught*. **4** the drawing in of a fishing net. ▸ a catch of fish. ▪ v. variant spelling of DRAFT. ▪ adj. **1** denoting beer served from a cask rather than from a bottle or can. **2** denoting an animal used for pulling heavy loads.
– PHRASES **on draught** (of beer) ready to be drawn from a cask.
– ORIGIN Middle English ('drawing, pulling'): from Old Norse *dráttr*, of Germanic origin.

draughtboard ▪ n. a square chequered board of sixty-four small squares, used for playing draughts.

draughtproof ▪ adj. sealed so as to keep out draughts. ▪ v. make (a building, window, etc.) draughtproof.

draughts ▪ n. a game played on a chequered board by two players, who each start with twelve disc-shaped pieces and move them diagonally with the aim of capturing all the opponent's pieces.
– ORIGIN Middle English: from DRAUGHT; rel. to obsolete *draught* in the sense 'move' (in chess).

draughtsman (or **draughtswoman**) ▪ n. (pl. **-men** or **-women**) **1** a person who makes detailed technical plans or drawings. ▸ an artist skilled in drawing. **2** variant spelling of DRAFTSMAN.
– DERIVATIVES **draughtsmanship** n.

draughty (US **drafty**) ▪ adj. (**-ier**, **-iest**) cold and uncomfortable because of draughts of air.
– DERIVATIVES **draughtily** adv. **draughtiness** n.

Dravidian /drə'vɪdɪən/ ▪ n. **1** a family of languages spoken in southern India and Sri Lanka, including Tamil and Kannada. **2** a member of any of the peoples speaking these languages. ▪ adj. relating to or denoting this family of languages or its speakers.
– ORIGIN from Sanskrit *drāviḍa* 'relating to the Tamils', from *Dravida* 'Tamil'.

draw ▪ v. (past **drew**; past part. **drawn**) **1** produce (a picture or diagram) by making lines and marks on paper. ▸ trace or produce (a line) on a surface. **2** pull or drag (a vehicle) so as to make it follow behind. ▸ pull or move (something) in a specified direction. ▸ pull (curtains) shut or open. **3** arrive at a specified stage or point in time: *the campaign drew to a close*. **4** extract from a container or receptacle: *he drew his gun*. ▸ (**draw from**) obtain from (a particular source). ▸ (**draw on**) use as a resource: *Sue has a lot of experience to draw on*. ▸ Bridge cause to be played. **5** take in (a breath). ▸ (**draw on**) suck smoke from (a cigarette or pipe). ▸ (of a chimney or fire) allow air to flow in and upwards freely, so that a fire can burn. **6** be the cause of (a specified response). ▸ attract to come to a place or an event. ▸ induce to reveal or do something: *he refused to be drawn on what he would do next*. ▸ direct or attract (someone's attention). ▸ reach (a conclusion) by deduction or inference. ▸ formulate or perceive (a comparison or distinction). **7** finish (a contest or game) with an even score. **8** Bowls cause (a bowl) to travel in a curve to the desired point. ▸ Golf hit (the ball) so that it travels slightly to the left (for a left-handed player, the right). **9** make (wire) by pulling metal through successively smaller holes. **10** (of a ship) require (a specified depth of water) to float in. **11** (of a sail) be filled with wind. **12** historical disembowel. ▪ n. **1** an act of selecting names randomly, to decide winners in a lottery, opponents in a sporting contest, etc. **2** a game or match that ends with the scores even. ▸ Cricket a game which is left incomplete for lack of time. Compare with TIE. **3** a person or thing that is very attractive or interesting: *the big city was a powerful draw to youngsters*. **4** an act of inhaling smoke from a cigarette. ▸ informal cannabis. **5** Golf a shot which draws the ball.
– PHRASES **draw blood** cause someone to bleed, especially in the course of a fight. **draw someone's fire** attract hostile criticism away from a more important target. **draw the line at** set a limit of what one is willing to do or accept.
– PHRASAL VERBS **draw back** choose not to do something that one was expected to do. **draw in** (of successive days) become shorter or (of nights) start earlier, because of the changing seasons. **draw on** (of a period of time) pass by and approach its end. **draw out** (of successive days) become longer because of the changing seasons. **draw someone out** gently or subtly persuade someone to be more talkative. **draw something out** make something last longer. **draw up** come to a halt. **draw something up** prepare a plan or document in detail.
– ORIGIN Old English, of Germanic origin.

drawback ▪ n. **1** a disadvantage or problem. **2** (also **duty drawback**) excise or import duty remitted on goods exported.

drawbar ▪ n. **1** a bar on a vehicle to which something can be attached to pull it or be pulled. **2** a bar in a structure that can be pulled out to free something.

drawbridge ▪ n. a bridge, typically over a castle moat, which is hinged at one end so that it can be raised.

drawcard ▪ n. informal an attractive quality or feature.

drawcord ▪ n. another term for DRAWSTRING.

drawdown ▪ n. **1** a reduction in the quantity of something. **2** an act of drawing on available loan facilities.

drawee /drɔː'iː/ ▪ n. the person or organization who has to pay a draft or bill.

drawer ▪ n. **1** /drɔː/ a lidless box-like storage compartment made to slide horizontally in and out of a desk or chest. **2** (**drawers**) /drɔːz/ dated or humorous knickers or underpants. **3** /'drɔː(r)ə/ a person who draws something. ▸ the person who writes a cheque.

USAGE
The word **drawer**, which mainly means 'a sliding storage compartment', is often spelled incorrectly as **draw**.

drawing ▪ n. a picture or diagram made with a pencil, pen, or crayon rather than paint, especially one drawn in monochrome. ▸ the art or skill of making such pictures.

drawing board ▪ n. a large flat board on which paper can be spread for artists or designers to work on.
– PHRASES **back to the drawing board** a plan has failed and a new one is needed.

drawing pin ▪ n. Brit. a short flat-headed pin for fastening paper to a surface.

drawing room ▪ n. a room in a large private house in which guests can be received and entertained.
– ORIGIN C17: abbrev. of *withdrawing-room* 'a room to withdraw to'.

drawl ▪ v. speak in a slow, lazy way with prolonged vowel sounds. ▪ n. a drawling accent.
– DERIVATIVES **drawler** n. **drawly** adj.
– ORIGIN C16: prob. orig. slang, from Low German or Dutch *dralen* 'delay, linger'.

drawn past participle of DRAW. ▪ adj. looking strained from illness or exhaustion: *Cathy was pale and drawn*.

drawn-out ▪ adj. lasting longer than is necessary.

drawn work (also **drawn-thread-work**) ▪ n. ornamental work on fabric done by drawing out threads, usually with additional needlework.

draw sheet ▪ n. a sheet that can be taken from under a patient or invalid without disturbing the bedclothes.

drawstring ▪ n. a string in the seam of a garment or bag, which can be pulled to tighten or close it.

dray ▪ n. a low truck or cart without sides, for delivering barrels or other heavy loads.
– ORIGIN Middle English: perhaps from Old English *dræge* 'dragnet', rel. to *dragan* 'to pull'.

VOWELS a cat ɑː arm ɛ bed ɛː hair ə ago əː her ɪ sit i cosy iː see ɒ hot ɔː saw ʌ run

DRC ■ abbrev. **1** (in South Africa) Dutch Reformed Church. **2** Democratic Republic of Congo.

dread ■ v. **1** anticipate with great apprehension or fear. **2** archaic regard with great awe. ■ n. **1** great fear or apprehension. **2** (**dreads**) informal dreadlocks. ■ adj. **1** greatly feared; dreadful. **2** archaic regarded with awe.
– DERIVATIVES **dreaded** adj.
– ORIGIN Old English, of West Germanic origin.

dreadful ■ adj. **1** extremely bad or serious. **2** used for emphasis: *you're a dreadful flirt.*
– DERIVATIVES **dreadfully** adv. **dreadfulness** n.

dreadlocks ■ pl. n. a Rastafarian hairstyle in which the hair is twisted into tight braids or ringlets.
– DERIVATIVES **dreadlocked** adj.

dreadnought /ˈdrɛdnɔːt/ ■ n. **1** historical a type of battleship of the early 20th century, equipped entirely with large-calibre guns. [named after Britain's HMS *Dreadnought*, completed 1906.] **2** archaic a fearless person.

dream ■ n. **1** a series of thoughts, images, and sensations occurring in a person's mind during sleep. ▸ a state of mind in which someone is not fully aware of their surroundings: *he walked around in a dream.* **2** a cherished ambition or ideal; a fantasy. ▸ informal someone or something perceived as wonderful or perfect. ■ v. (past and past part. **dreamed** /drɛmd, driːmd/ or **dreamt** /drɛmt/) **1** experience dreams during sleep. **2** indulge in daydreams or fantasies. ▸ (**dream up**) imagine or invent. **3** [with neg.] contemplate the possibility of: *I never dreamed anyone would take offence.*
– PHRASES **like a dream** informal very easily or successfully.
– DERIVATIVES **dreamer** n. **dreamful** adj. (poetic/literary). **dreamless** adj. **dreamlike** adj.
– ORIGIN Middle English: of Germanic origin.

dreamboat ■ n. informal a very attractive person, especially a man.

dreamcatcher ■ n. a small hoop containing a decorated horsehair mesh, believed by American Indians to give its owner good dreams.

dreamland ■ n. sleep regarded as a world of dreams. ▸ an unrealistically ideal world.

dreamscape ■ n. a scene with the strangeness or mystery characteristic of dreams.

dreamtime ■ n. (in the mythology of some Australian Aboriginals) the 'golden age' when the first ancestors were created.

dreamy ■ adj. (**-ier, -iest**) **1** dreamlike; pleasantly distracting or unreal. **2** given to daydreaming.
– DERIVATIVES **dreamily** adv. **dreaminess** n.

drear /drɪə/ ■ adj. poetic/literary dreary.

dreary ■ adj. (**-ier, -iest**) dull, bleak, and depressing.
– DERIVATIVES **drearily** adv. **dreariness** n.
– ORIGIN Old English *drēorig* 'gory, cruel, melancholy', from *drēor* 'gore', of Germanic origin.

dreck /drɛk/ (also **drek**) ■ n. informal rubbish.
– ORIGIN C20: from Yiddish *drek* 'filth, dregs'.

dredge[1] ■ v. **1** clean out the bed of (a harbour, river, etc.) with a dredge. ▸ bring up or remove with a dredge. **2** (**dredge something up**) bring something unwelcome and forgotten or obscure to people's attention. ■ n. an apparatus for bringing up objects or mud from a river or seabed by scooping or dragging.
– DERIVATIVES **dredger** n.
– ORIGIN C15 (orig. in *dredge-boat*): perhaps rel. to Middle Dutch *dregghe* 'grappling hook'.

dredge[2] ■ v. sprinkle (food) with sugar or other powdered substance.
– ORIGIN C16: from obsolete *dredge* 'sweetmeat, mixture of spices', from Old French *dragie*, perhaps from Greek *tragēmata* 'spices'.

dregs ■ n. **1** the remnants of a liquid left in a container, together with any sediment. **2** the most worthless parts: *the dregs of society.*
– DERIVATIVES **dreggy** adj.
– ORIGIN Middle English: prob. of Scandinavian origin.

drek ■ n. variant spelling of DRECK.

drench ■ v. **1** wet thoroughly; soak. ▸ [often as adj. **drenched**] cover liberally with something: *a sun-drenched clearing.* **2** forcibly administer a liquid medicine to (an animal). ■ n. a dose of medicine administered to an animal.
– ORIGIN Old English *drencan* 'force to drink', *drenc* 'a drink or draught', of Germanic origin.

Dresden china /ˈdrɛzd(ə)n/ ■ n. porcelain ware with elaborate decoration and delicate colourings, made originally at Dresden in Germany.

dress ■ v. **1** put on one's clothes. ▸ put clothes on (someone). ▸ wear clothes in a particular way or of a particular type: *she dresses well.* ▸ (**dress up**) dress in smart or formal clothes, or in a special costume. **2** decorate in an artistic or attractive way. ▸ arrange or style (the hair). **3** clean, treat, or apply a dressing to (a wound). **4** clean and prepare (food) for cooking or eating. ▸ add a dressing to (a salad). **5** apply fertilizer to. **6** treat the surface of (leather or fabric) during manufacture. **7** smooth the surface of (stone). **8** Military draw up (troops) in the proper alignment. **9** make (an artificial fly) for use in fishing. **10** (**dress someone down**) informal reprimand someone. ■ n. **1** a one-piece garment for a woman or girl that covers the body and extends down over the legs. **2** clothing of a specified kind for men or women. ▸ [as modifier] denoting ceremonial clothing or uniform: *a dress suit.*
– PHRASES **dressed to kill** informal wearing glamorous clothes intended to create a striking impression.
– ORIGIN Middle English: from Old French *dresser* 'arrange, prepare', from Latin *directus* 'direct, straight'.

dressage /ˈdrɛsɑː(d)ʒ/ ■ n. the art of riding and training horses so as to develop obedience, flexibility, and balance.
– ORIGIN 1930s: from French, 'training', from *dresser* 'to train'.

dress circle ■ n. the first level of seats above the ground floor in a theatre.

dresser[1] ■ n. a sideboard with shelves above for storing and displaying crockery. ▸ N. Amer. a dressing table or chest of drawers.
– ORIGIN Middle English (denoting a sideboard or table on which food was prepared).

dresser[2] ■ n. **1** a person who dresses in a specified way: *a snappy dresser.* **2** a person who looks after theatrical costumes. **3** a person who dresses something.

dressing ■ n. **1** (also **salad dressing**) a sauce for salads, usually consisting of oil and vinegar with herbs or other flavourings. **2** N. Amer. stuffing. **3** a piece of material placed on a wound to protect it. **4** size or stiffening used in the finishing of fabrics. **5** a fertilizer spread over or ploughed into land.

dressing gown ■ n. a long loose robe worn after getting out of bed or bathing.

dressing room ■ n. a room in which actors or sports players change clothes. ▸ a small room attached to a bedroom, containing clothes.

dressing station ■ n. a place for giving emergency treatment to troops injured in battle.

dressing table ■ n. a table with a mirror and drawers, used while dressing or applying make-up.

dressmaker ■ n. a person who makes women's clothes.
– DERIVATIVES **dressmaking** n.

dress parade ■ n. a military parade in full dress uniform.

dress rehearsal ■ n. a final rehearsal in which everything is done as it would be in a real performance.

dress sense ■ n. a good instinct for selecting garments.

dress shirt ■ n. a man's white shirt worn with a bow tie and a dinner jacket on formal occasions. ▸ N. Amer. a shirt suitable for wearing with a tie.

dressy ■ adj. (**-ier, -iest**) (of clothes) suitable for a smart or formal occasion.
– DERIVATIVES **dressily** adv. **dressiness** n.

drew past of DRAW.

drey /dreɪ/ ■ n. (pl. **-eys**) a squirrel's nest of twigs in a tree.
– ORIGIN C17.

dribble ■ v. **1** (of a liquid) fall slowly in drops or a thin stream. ▸ allow saliva to run from the mouth. **2** (in soccer and hockey) take (the ball) forward past opponents with slight touches of the feet or the stick, or (in basketball) by

driblet

continuous bouncing. ■ n. **1** a thin stream of liquid. ▸ saliva running from the mouth. **2** (in soccer, hockey, and basketball) an act of dribbling.
– DERIVATIVES **dribbler** n. **dribbly** adj.
– ORIGIN C16: from obsolete *drib*, var. of DRIP.

driblet ■ n. **1** a thin stream or small drop of liquid. **2** a small or insignificant amount.
– ORIGIN C16: from obsolete *drib* (see DRIBBLE).

dribs and drabs ■ pl. n. (in phr. **in dribs and drabs**) informal in small scattered or sporadic amounts.
– ORIGIN C19: from obsolete *drib* (see DRIBBLE) and *drab* (by reduplication).

dried past and past participle of DRY.

drier[1] ■ adj. comparative of DRY.

drier[2] ■ n. variant spelling of DRYER.

drift ■ v. **1** be carried slowly by a current of air or water. **2** walk slowly or casually. ▸ move aimlessly or involuntarily into a certain situation or condition: *Lewis and his father drifted apart.* **3** (chiefly of snow) be blown into heaps by the wind. ■ n. **1** a continuous slow movement from one place to another. ▸ deviation from an intended or expected course because of currents or winds. **2** the general intention or meaning of someone's remarks: *he didn't understand much English, but he got her drift.* **3** a large mass of snow or other material piled up by the wind. **4** a state of inaction or indecision. **5** Mining a passage following a mineral vein or coal seam. **6** S. African a ford.
– DERIVATIVES **drifty** adj.
– ORIGIN Middle English: orig. from Old Norse *drift* 'snowdrift, something driven'; in later use from Middle Dutch *drift* 'course, current'.

drifter ■ n. **1** a person who is continually moving from place to place, without any fixed home or job. **2** a fishing boat equipped with a drift net.

driftfish ■ n. (pl. same or **-fishes**) a slender-bodied fish found in the deeper parts of warm seas. [Family Nomeidae.]

drift net ■ n. a large fishing net, kept upright by weights at the bottom and floats at the top and allowed to drift in the sea.
– DERIVATIVES **drift netter** n. **drift netting** n.

drift sand ■ n. sand picked up by the wind and deposited inland. ▸ (usu. **drift sands**) land covered by mounds of wind-blown sand.

driftwood ■ n. pieces of wood floating on the sea or washed ashore.

drill[1] ■ n. **1** a tool or machine with a rotating or reciprocating cutting tip, used for boring holes. **2** training in military exercises. ▸ instruction by means of repeated exercises. ▸ (**the drill**) informal the correct or recognized procedure. **3** a predatory mollusc that borers into the shells of other molluscs. [*Urosalpinx cinerea* (oyster drill, America) and other species.] ■ v. **1** bore (a hole) in something with a drill. ▸ sink a borehole. **2** subject to military training or other intensive instruction. **3** informal hit (something) so that it travels fast in a straight line.
– DERIVATIVES **driller** n.
– ORIGIN C17: from Middle Dutch *drillen* 'bore, turn in a circle'.

drill[2] ■ n. a machine which makes small furrows, sows seed in them, and then covers the sown seed. ▸ a small furrow made by such a machine. ■ v. sow with a drill.
– ORIGIN C18: perhaps from DRILL[1].

drill[3] ■ n. a West African baboon with a naked blue or purple rump. [*Mandrillus leucophaeus.*]
– ORIGIN C17: prob. a local word.

drill[4] ■ n. a coarse twilled cotton or linen fabric.
– ORIGIN C18: abbrev. of earlier *drilling*, from German *Drillich*, from Latin *trilix*, from *tri-* 'three' + *licium* 'thread'.

drilling rig ■ n. a large structure with equipment for drilling an oil well.

drill sergeant ■ n. a non-commissioned officer who trains soldiers in military parade exercises.

drily /ˈdrʌɪli/ (also **dryly**) ■ adv. **1** in a matter-of-fact or ironically humorous way. **2** in a dry way or condition.

drink ■ v. (past **drank**; past part. **drunk**) **1** take (a liquid) into the mouth and swallow. ▸ consume alcohol, especially to excess. ▸ (**drink up**) consume the rest of a drink. **2** (**drink something in**) watch or listen eagerly to something. **3** absorb (moisture). ■ n. **1** a liquid consumed as refreshment or nourishment. ▸ a quantity of liquid swallowed at one go. **2** the habitual or excessive consumption of alcohol. **3** (**the drink**) informal the sea.
– PHRASES **drink deep** take a large draught or draughts of something. **drink someone's health** (or **drink to someone**) express good wishes for someone by raising one's glass and drinking a small amount. **drink someone under the table** informal consume as much alcohol as one's drinking companion without becoming as drunk. **I'll drink to that** expressing agreement or approval. **in drink** when intoxicated.
– DERIVATIVES **drinkable** adj.
– ORIGIN Old English, of Germanic origin.

drink-driving ■ n. Brit. the crime of driving a vehicle with an excess of alcohol in the blood.
– DERIVATIVES **drink-driver** n.

drinker ■ n. **1** a person who drinks. **2** a container from which an animal can drink.

drinking chocolate ■ n. a mixture of cocoa powder, milk solids, and sugar, added to hot water to make a chocolate drink.

drinking fountain ■ n. a device producing a small jet of water for drinking.

drinking song ■ n. a hearty or bawdy song sung by a group while drinking alcohol.

drip ■ v. (**dripped**, **dripping**) let fall small drops of liquid. ▸ fall in small drops. ■ n. **1** a small drop of a liquid. **2** Medicine an apparatus which slowly passes fluid, nutrients, or drugs into a patient's body intravenously. **3** informal a weak and ineffectual person. **4** Architecture a projection on a moulding or cornice, channelled to prevent rain from running down the wall below.
– ORIGIN Old English, of Germanic origin.

drip-dry ■ v. (of fabric or a garment) become dry without forming creases when hung up after washing. ■ adj. capable of drip-drying.

drip feed ■ n. a device for introducing fluid drop by drop into a system. ■ v. (**drip-feed**) introduce (fluid) drop by drop. ▸ supply (a patient) with fluid through a drip.

dripping ■ n. **1** Brit. fat that has melted and dripped from roasting meat. **2** (**drippings**) chiefly N. Amer. wax, fat, or other liquid produced from something by the effect of heat. ■ adj. extremely wet.

drippy ■ adj. (**-ier**, **-iest**) **1** informal weak, ineffectual, or sloppily sentimental. **2** tending to drip.
– DERIVATIVES **drippily** adv. **drippiness** n.

dripstone ■ n. **1** Architecture a moulding over a door or window which deflects rain. **2** Geology rock deposited by precipitation from dripping water, e.g. as stalactites and stalagmites.

drive ■ v. (past **drove**; past part. **driven**) **1** operate and control the direction and speed of a motor vehicle. ▸ convey in a car. **2** propel or carry along by force in a specified direction. ▸ provide the energy to keep (an engine or machine) in motion. ▸ (in ball games) hit or kick (the ball) hard. **3** bore (a tunnel). **4** urge or force to move in a specified direction. **5** (usu. **be driven**) compel to act in a particular way: *he was driven by ambition.* ■ n. **1** a trip or journey in a car. **2** (also **driveway**) a short private road leading to a house. **3** an innate, biologically determined urge. ▸ determination and ambition. **4** an organized effort to achieve a particular purpose: *a recruitment drive.* ▸ Brit. a large organized gathering to play whist or another game. **5** the transmission of power to machinery or to the wheels of a vehicle. ▸ Computing short for DISK DRIVE. **6** an act of driving a ball. **7** an act of driving animals.
– PHRASES **what someone is driving at** the point that someone is attempting to make.
– DERIVATIVES **drivability** (also **driveability**) n. **drivable** (also **driveable**) adj.
– ORIGIN Old English, of Germanic origin.

drive-by ■ adj. denoting a shooting carried out from a passing vehicle.

drive-in ■ adj. denoting a cinema, restaurant, etc. that one can visit without leaving one's car.

drivel /ˈdrɪv(ə)l/ ■ n. nonsense. ■ v. (**drivelled, drivelling**; US **driveled, driveling**) **1** talk nonsense. **2** archaic let saliva or mucus flow from the mouth or nose.
– DERIVATIVES **driveller** (US **driveler**) n.
– ORIGIN Old English.

driveline /ˈdrʌɪvlʌɪn/ ■ n. another term for DRIVETRAIN.

driven past participle of DRIVE.

driver ■ n. **1** a person or thing that drives something. **2** a flat-faced golf club used for driving.
– PHRASES **in the driver's seat** in control.
– DERIVATIVES **driverless** adj.

driver ant ■ n. another term for ARMY ANT.

driveshaft ■ n. a rotating shaft which transmits torque in an engine.

drive-through ■ adj. chiefly N. Amer. another term for DRIVE-IN.

drivetrain ■ n. the system in a motor vehicle which connects the transmission to the drive axles.

driveway ■ n. see DRIVE (sense 2).

driving ■ adj. **1** having a strong and controlling influence: *she was the driving force behind the plan.* **2** being blown by the wind with great force: *driving rain.*
– PHRASES **in the driving seat** in control.

driving range ■ n. an area where golfers can practise drives.

drizzle ■ n. **1** light rain falling in very fine drops. **2** Cookery a thin stream of a liquid ingredient trickled over something. ■ v. **1** (**it drizzles**), **it is drizzling, etc.** rain lightly. **2** Cookery apply (an ingredient) as a drizzle.
– DERIVATIVES **drizzly** adj.
– ORIGIN C16: prob. from Old English *drēosan* 'to fall', of Germanic origin.

droëwors /ˈdruəvɒs/ ■ n. S. African a salted and spiced air-dried sausage.
– ORIGIN Afrikaans: from *droë* 'dry' + *wors* 'sausage'.

drogue /drəʊɡ/ ■ n. a device, typically conical or funnel-shaped, towed behind a boat, aircraft, etc., especially to reduce speed or improve stability.
– ORIGIN C18 (orig. denoting a board attached to a harpoon line, used to slow down or mark the position of a whale): perhaps rel. to DRAG.

drogue parachute ■ n. a small parachute used as a brake or to pull out a larger parachute.

droit de seigneur /ˌdrwʌ də sɛnˈjəː/ ■ n. the alleged right of a medieval feudal lord to have sexual intercourse with a vassal's bride on her wedding night.
– ORIGIN French, 'lord's right'.

droll /drəʊl/ ■ adj. amusing in a strange or quaint way. ■ n. archaic a jester; a buffoon.
– DERIVATIVES **drollery** n. **drollness** n. **drolly** /ˈdrəʊlli/ adv.
– ORIGIN C17: from French *drôle*, perhaps from Middle Dutch *drolle* 'imp, goblin'.

dromaeosaur /ˈdrəʊmɪə(ʊ)sɔː/ ■ n. a carnivorous bipedal dinosaur of a group including the velociraptors.
– DERIVATIVES **dromaeosaurid** n.
– ORIGIN 1970s: from *Dromaeosauridae* (name of a family), from Greek *dromaios* 'swift-running' + *sauros* 'lizard'.

-drome ■ comb. form **1** denoting a place for running or racing: *velodrome.* **2** denoting something that proceeds in a certain way: *palindrome.*
– ORIGIN from Greek *dromos* 'racecourse', rel. to *dramein* 'to run'.

dromedary /ˈdrɒmɪd(ə)ri, ˈdrʌm-/ ■ n. (pl. **-ies**) an Arabian camel (with one hump), especially one of a breed trained for riding or racing.
– ORIGIN Middle English: from late Latin *dromedarius* (*camelus*) 'swift camel', from Greek *dromas* 'runner'.

drone ■ v. make a continuous low humming sound. ▸ speak tediously and at length: *Jim droned on for an hour.* ■ n. **1** a low continuous humming sound. ▸ a pipe (especially in a set of bagpipes) or string used to sound a continuous note of low pitch. **2** a male bee which does no work in a colony but can fertilize a queen. ▸ an idler. **3** a remote-controlled pilotless aircraft.
– ORIGIN Old English *drān, drǣn* 'male bee', from a West Germanic verb meaning 'resound, boom'.

drone fly ■ n. a hoverfly resembling a honeybee. [*Eristalis tenax.*]

drop kick

drongo /ˈdrɒŋɡəʊ/ ■ n. (pl. **-os** or **-oes**) **1** a long-tailed, crested songbird with glossy black plumage, found in Africa, southern Asia, and Australia. [Family Dicruridae: several species.] **2** informal, chiefly Austral./NZ a stupid or incompetent person.
– ORIGIN C19: from Malagasy; sense 2 is said to be from the name of a very unsuccessful Australian racehorse of the 1920s.

drool ■ v. **1** drop saliva uncontrollably from the mouth. **2** informal make an excessive show of pleasure or desire: *enthusiasts drooled over old cars.* ■ n. saliva falling from the mouth.
– ORIGIN C19: contraction of DRIVEL.

droop ■ v. bend or hang downwards limply. ▸ sag down from weariness or dejection. ■ n. an act or instance of drooping.
– DERIVATIVES **droopily** adv. **droopiness** n. **droopy** adj. (**-ier, -iest**).
– ORIGIN Middle English: from Old Norse *drúpa* 'hang the head'.

drop ■ v. (**dropped, dropping**) **1** fall or cause to fall vertically. ▸ deliver by parachute. **2** (of an animal) give birth to. **3** sink to or towards the ground. ▸ informal collapse from exhaustion. **4** make or become lower, weaker, or less. **5** abandon or discontinue: *the charges against him were dropped.* ▸ discard or exclude. **6** set down or unload (a passenger or goods). ▸ place without ceremony: *drop it in the post.* ▸ mention in passing, particularly in order to impress. **7** lose (a point, a match, etc.). **8** Bridge be forced to play (a relatively high card) as a loser. **9** [usu. as adj. **dropped**] Rugby score by a drop kick. **10** informal take (a drug) orally. ■ n. **1** a small round or pear-shaped portion of liquid. ▸ (**drops**) liquid medication applied in very small amounts. **2** [usu. with neg.] a drink of alcohol. **3** an instance of falling or dropping. ▸ an abrupt fall or slope. **4** informal a delivery. ▸ US a letter box. **5** a sweet or lozenge: *a chocolate drop.* **6** a pendant earring. **7** a drop cloth. **8** the trapdoor on a gallows, through which the victim fell.
– PHRASES **at the drop of a hat** informal without delay or good reason. **drop one's aitches** omit the 'h' sound from the beginning of words. **drop asleep** fall gently asleep. **drop the ball** N. Amer. informal make a mistake. **drop a brick** Brit. informal make an indiscreet or embarrassing remark. **drop a clanger** Brit. informal make an embarrassing or foolish mistake. **drop a curtsy** Brit. make a curtsy. **drop dead** die suddenly and unexpectedly. **drop one's guard** abandon one's habitual defensive or watchful stance. **drop a hint** let fall a hint, as if casually or unconsciously. **a drop in the ocean** (or **in a bucket**) a very small amount compared with what is needed or expected. **drop someone a line** send someone an informal note or letter. **drop a stitch** let a stitch fall off the end of a knitting needle. **have the drop on** informal have the advantage over.
– PHRASAL VERBS **drop back/behind** fall back or get left behind. **drop by/in** visit informally and briefly. **drop off** fall asleep, especially without intending to. **drop out 1** cease to participate. **2** abandon a course of study. **3** pursue an alternative lifestyle. **4** Rugby restart play with a drop kick.
– DERIVATIVES **droppable** adj.
– ORIGIN Old English, of Germanic origin.

drop capital ■ n. a large opening capital letter occupying more than the depth of one line.

drop cloth ■ n. **1** (also **drop curtain**) a curtain or painted cloth lowered vertically on to a theatre stage. **2** N. Amer. a dust sheet.

drop-dead ■ adj. informal used to emphasize attractiveness: *drop-dead gorgeous.*

drop goal ■ n. Rugby a goal scored by drop-kicking the ball over the crossbar.

drop handlebars ■ pl. n. handlebars with the handles bent below the rest of the bar, used especially on racing cycles.

drop kick ■ n. **1** a kick made by dropping the ball and kicking it as it bounces. **2** (chiefly in martial arts) a flying kick made while dropping to the ground. ■ v. (**drop-kick**) kick using a drop kick.

droplet

droplet ■ n. a very small drop of a liquid.

drop-off ■ n. **1** a decline or decrease. **2** chiefly N. Amer. a sheer downward slope.

dropout ■ n. **1** a person who has dropped out of society or a course of study. **2** Rugby the restarting of play with a drop kick. **3** a momentary loss of recorded audio signal or an error in reading data.

dropper ■ n. **1** a short glass tube with a rubber bulb at one end, for measuring out drops of liquid. **2** S. African & Austral./NZ a light vertical stave in a fence. **3** Fishing a subsidiary line or loop of filament attached to a main line.

droppings ■ pl. n. the excrement of animals.

drop scone ■ n. a small thick pancake made by dropping batter on to a heated surface.

drop-ship ■ v. (**drop-ships**, **drop-shipping**, **drop-shipped**) provide (goods) by direct delivery from the manufacturer to the retailer or customer.
– DERIVATIVES **drop shipment** n.

drop shot ■ n. (in tennis or squash) a softly hit shot, usually with backspin, which drops abruptly to the ground.

drop shoulder ■ n. a style of shoulder on a garment cut with the seam positioned on the upper arm rather than the shoulder.

dropsy /'drɒpsi/ ■ n. (pl. **-ies**) old-fashioned or less technical term for OEDEMA.
– DERIVATIVES **dropsical** adj.
– ORIGIN Middle English: shortening of obsolete *hydropsy*, from Greek *hudrōps*, from *hudōr* 'water'.

drop tank ■ n. an external fuel tank on an aircraft which can be jettisoned when empty.

drop test ■ n. a test of the strength of an object, in which it is dropped under standard conditions or a set weight is dropped on it from a given height.
– DERIVATIVES **drop-testing** n.

drop waist ■ n. a style of waistline with the seam positioned at the hips rather than the waist.

drop zone ■ n. a designated area into which troops or supplies are dropped by parachute.

drosophila /drɒ'sɒfɪlə/ ■ n. a genus of fruit flies used extensively in genetic research.
– ORIGIN modern Latin: from Greek *drosos* 'dew, moisture' + *philos* 'loving'.

dross ■ n. **1** rubbish. **2** scum on the surface of molten metal.
– DERIVATIVES **drossy** adj.
– ORIGIN Old English, rel. to Dutch *droesem* and German *Drusen* 'dregs, lees'.

drostdy /'drɒstɪ, 'drɒsdeɪ/ ■ n. (pl. **drostdies** or **drostdys**) S. African historical a magisterial and administrative district in the Cape Colony. ▸ the residence or offices of the chief administrator (landdrost) of such a district.
– ORIGIN C18: S. African Dutch, from Dutch *drost* 'bailiff' + noun-forming suffix -(*d*)*ij*.

drought /draʊt/ ■ n. a prolonged period of abnormally low rainfall; a shortage of water. ▸ archaic thirst.
– DERIVATIVES **droughty** adj.
– ORIGIN Old English *drūgath* 'dryness', of Germanic origin.

drove¹ past of DRIVE.

drove² ■ n. a flock of animals being driven. ▸ a large number of people doing the same thing: *tourists arrived in droves*. ■ v. [usu. as noun **droving**] historical drive (livestock) to market.
– DERIVATIVES **drover** n.
– ORIGIN Old English *drāf*, rel. to *drīfan* 'to drive'.

drove road ■ n. (in the UK) an ancient roadway along which cattle were driven to market.

drown ■ v. **1** die or kill through submersion in water. **2** submerge or flood (an area). **3** (usu. **drown something out**) make inaudible by being much louder.
– PHRASES **drown one's sorrows** forget one's problems by getting drunk.
– ORIGIN Middle English: rel. to Old Norse *drukkna* 'to be drowned', also to DRINK.

drowse /draʊz/ ■ v. be half asleep; doze. ■ n. an instance of drowsing. ▸ a state of drowsiness.
– ORIGIN C16: back-formation from DROWSY.

drowsy ■ adj. (**-ier**, **-iest**) sleepy and lethargic.
– DERIVATIVES **drowsily** adv. **drowsiness** n.
– ORIGIN C15: prob. from the stem of Old English *drūsian* 'be languid or slow', of Germanic origin.

drub ■ v. (**drubbed**, **drubbing**) **1** hit or beat repeatedly. **2** informal defeat thoroughly.
– DERIVATIVES **drubbing** n.
– ORIGIN C17: prob. from Arabic *ḍaraba* 'to beat, bastinado'.

drudge ■ n. a person made to do hard, menial, or dull work. ■ v. archaic do such work.
– DERIVATIVES **drudgery** n.
– ORIGIN Middle English.

drug ■ n. a medicine or other substance which has a marked physiological effect when taken into the body. ▸ a substance with narcotic or stimulant effects. ■ v. (**drugged**, **drugging**) administer a drug to, in order to induce stupor or insensibility. ▸ informal take drugs.
– ORIGIN Middle English: from Old French *drogue*, perhaps from Middle Dutch *droge vate* 'dry vats', referring to the contents.

drugget /'drʌgɪt/ ■ n. a floor covering made of a coarse woven fabric.
– ORIGIN C16: from French *droguet*, from *drogue* in the sense 'poor-quality article'.

druggy (also **druggie**) ■ n. (pl. **-ies**) informal a drug addict.

drug lord ■ n. a person who controls an organization dealing in illegal drugs.

drugstore ■ n. N. Amer. a pharmacy which also sells toiletries and other articles.

Druid /'druːɪd/ ■ n. a priest, magician, or soothsayer in the ancient Celtic religion. ▸ a member of a present-day group claiming to be derived from this religion.
– DERIVATIVES **Druidic** adj. **Druidical** adj. **Druidism** n.
– ORIGIN from Latin *druidae*, *druides* (pl.), from Gaulish; rel. to Irish *draoidh* 'magician, sorcerer'.

drum¹ ■ n. **1** a percussion instrument sounded by being struck with sticks or the hands, typically cylindrical, barrel-shaped, or bowl-shaped with a taut membrane over one or both ends. ▸ a sound made by or resembling that of a drum. **2** historical a military drummer. **3** a cylindrical object or part, especially a container: *an oil drum*. ▸ Architecture the circular vertical wall supporting a dome. ■ v. (**drummed**, **drumming**) **1** play on a drum. ▸ make or cause to make a continuous rhythmic noise. **2** (**drum something into**) drive a lesson into (someone) by constant repetition. **3** (**drum someone out**) expel or dismiss someone with ignominy. **4** (**drum something up**) attempt to obtain something by canvassing or soliciting: *they drummed up support*.
– PHRASES **beat** (or **bang**) **the drum of** (or **for**) be ostentatiously in support of.
– ORIGIN Middle English: from Middle Dutch or Low German *tromme*, of imitative origin.

drum² (also **drumfish**) ■ n. (pl. same or **drums**) a coastal or estuarine fish that makes a drumming sound by vibrating its swim bladder. [Family Sciaenidae: many species.]

drumbeat ■ n. a stroke or pattern of strokes on a drum.

drumhead ■ n. **1** the membrane or skin of a drum. **2** a winter cabbage of a flat-topped variety. **3** chiefly historical the circular top of a ship's capstan. ■ adj. denoting a summary trial, as carried out by an army in the field.

drum kit ■ n. a set of drums, cymbals, and other percussion instruments.

drumlin /'drʌmlɪn/ ■ n. Geology an oval mound or small hill consisting of compacted boulder clay moulded by glacial action.
– ORIGIN C19: prob. from *drum* 'long narrow hill' (from Scottish Gaelic and Irish *druim* 'ridge') + *-lin* (from -LING).

drum major ■ n. **1** a non-commissioned officer commanding regimental drummers. **2** the male leader of a marching band, who twirls a baton.

drum majorette ■ n. the female leader of a marching band, who twirls a baton. ▸ a female member of such a band.

drummer ■ n. a person who plays a drum or drums.

drummie ■ n. S. African informal a drum majorette.

drum roll ■ n. a rapid succession of drumbeats, typically used to introduce an announcement or event.

drumstick ■ n. 1 a stick used for beating a drum. 2 the lower joint of the leg of a cooked fowl.

drunk past part. of DRINK. ■ adj. affected by alcohol to the extent of losing control of one's faculties or behaviour. ■ n. 1 a person who is drunk or who habitually drinks to excess. 2 informal a drinking bout.
– PHRASES **drunk and disorderly** creating a public disturbance under the influence of alcohol.

drunkard ■ n. a person who is habitually drunk.
– ORIGIN Middle English: from Middle Low German *drunkert*.

drunken ■ adj. drunk, especially habitually or frequently. ▸ caused by or showing the effects of drink.
– DERIVATIVES **drunkenly** adv. **drunkenness** n.
– ORIGIN Old English, from DRINK.

drupe /druːp/ ■ n. 1 Botany a fleshy fruit with thin skin and a central stone, e.g. a plum or olive. 2 a small marine mollusc with a thick knobbly shell. [Genus *Drupa*.]
– DERIVATIVES **drupaceous** adj. (Botany).
– ORIGIN C18: from Latin *drupa* 'overripe olive'.

druse /druːz/ ■ n. Geology a rock cavity lined with a crust of projecting crystals.
– DERIVATIVES **drusy** adj. (Geology).
– ORIGIN C19: from German *Druse* 'weathered ore'.

druther /ˈdrʌðə/ N. Amer. informal ■ n. (usu. **one's druthers**) a person's preference in a matter. ■ adv. rather.
– ORIGIN C19: from a US regional pronunciation of *I'd rather*.

Druze /druːz/ (also **Druse**) ■ n. (pl. same, **Druzes**, or **Druses**) a member of a political and religious sect of Islamic origin, living chiefly in Lebanon and Syria.
– ORIGIN from Arabic *durūz* (pl.), from the name of one of their founders, Muhammad ibn Ismail *al-Darazī* (died 1019).

dry ■ adj. (**drier**, **driest**) 1 free from moisture or liquid. ▸ not yielding water, oil, or milk: *a dry well*. ▸ without grease or other moisturizer or lubricator: *dry hair*. 2 (of information, writing, etc.) dully factual. ▸ unemotional or undemonstrative. ▸ (of humour) subtle and expressed in a matter-of-fact way. 3 prohibiting the sale or consumption of alcoholic drink. ▸ no longer drinking alcohol. 4 (of wine) not sweet. ■ v. (**-ies**, **-ied**) 1 become or cause to become dry. ▸ [usu. as adj. **dried**] preserve by evaporating the moisture from: *dried milk*. 2 (**dry up**) (of a supply or flow) decrease and stop. 3 theatrical slang forget one's lines. ▸ (**dry up**) informal cease talking. 4 (**dry out**) informal overcome alcoholism.
– PHRASES **come up dry** N. Amer. informal be unsuccessful.
– DERIVATIVES **dryish** adj. **dryness** n.
– ORIGIN Old English, of Germanic origin.

dryad /ˈdrʌɪəd, -ad/ ■ n. (in folklore and Greek mythology) a nymph inhabiting a tree or wood.
– ORIGIN from Greek *druas*, *druad-*, from *drus* 'tree'.

dry cell (also **dry battery**) ■ n. an electric cell (or battery) in which the electrolyte is absorbed in a solid to form a paste.

dry-clean ■ v. clean (a garment) with an organic solvent.
– DERIVATIVES **dry-cleaner** n.

dry cough ■ n. a cough not producing phlegm.

dry-cure ■ v. cure (meat or fish) with salt rather than in liquid.

dry dock ■ n. a dock which can be drained of water to allow repair of a ship's hull. ■ v. (**dry-dock**) place in a dry dock.

dryer (also **drier**) ■ n. 1 a machine or device for drying something, especially the hair or laundry. 2 a substance mixed with oil paint or ink to promote drying.

dry fly ■ n. an artificial fishing fly which floats lightly on the water.

dry-fry ■ v. fry in a pan without fat or oil.

dry goods ■ pl. n. 1 solid commodities traded in bulk, e.g. tea or sugar. 2 chiefly N. Amer. drapery and haberdashery.

dry ice ■ n. solid carbon dioxide. ▸ white mist produced with this as a theatrical effect.

dryly ■ adv. variant spelling of DRILY.

dry measure ■ n. a measure of volume for dry goods.

dry mounting ■ n. Photography a process in which a print is bonded to a mount using a layer of shellac in a hot press.

Dryopithecus /ˌdrʌɪəˈpɪθɪkəs/ ■ n. a genus of anthropoid apes of the middle Miocene to early Pliocene periods, including the supposed common ancestor of gorillas, chimpanzees, and humans.
– DERIVATIVES **dryopithecine** /-ɪsiːn/ n. & adj.
– ORIGIN from Greek *drus* 'tree' + *pithēkos* 'ape'.

dry rot ■ n. a fungus causing decay of wood in poorly ventilated conditions. [*Serpula lacrymans*.]

dry run ■ n. informal a rehearsal of a performance or procedure.

dry-shod ■ adj. & adv. without wetting one's shoes.

dry slope (also **dry-ski slope**) ■ n. an artificial ski slope.

drystone ■ adj. Brit. (of a stone wall) built without using mortar.

drysuit ■ n. a waterproof rubber suit for water sports, under which warm clothes can be worn.

drywall ■ n. N. Amer. plasterboard.

Ds¹ ■ abbrev. Dominee.

Ds² ■ symb. the chemical element darmstadtium.

DSC ■ abbrev. (in the UK) Distinguished Service Cross.

DSc ■ abbrev. Doctor of Science.

DSM ■ abbrev. (in the UK) Distinguished Service Medal.

DSO ■ abbrev. (in the UK) Distinguished Service Order.

DTI ■ abbrev. Department of Trade and Industry.

DTP ■ abbrev. desktop publishing.

DTs ■ pl. n. informal delirium tremens.

dual ■ adj. 1 consisting of two parts, elements, or aspects. 2 (often **dual to**) Mathematics related to another theorem or expression by the interchange of terms, such as 'point' and 'line'. ■ n. Mathematics a theorem or expression that is dual to another.
– DERIVATIVES **duality** n. **dually** adv.
– ORIGIN Middle English: from Latin *dualis*, from *duo* 'two'.

dual carriageway ■ n. S. African & Brit. a road consisting of two or more lanes in each direction and with a dividing strip separating the two directions.

dualism ■ n. 1 the division of something conceptually into two opposed or contrasted aspects, such as good and evil or mind and matter. 2 duality.
– DERIVATIVES **dualist** n. & adj. **dualistic** adj. **dualistically** adv.

dual-medium ■ adj. of or relating to an educational system or institution in which some subjects are taught in one language and others in another language. Compare with PARALLEL-MEDIUM.

dual-use ■ adj. chiefly US (of technology or equipment) suitable for both civilian and military purposes.

dub¹ ■ v. (**dubbed**, **dubbing**) 1 give an unofficial name or nickname to. 2 knight (someone) by the ritual touching of the shoulder with a sword.
– ORIGIN Old English: from Old French *adober* 'equip with armour'.

dub² ■ v. (**dubbed**, **dubbing**) 1 provide (a film) with a soundtrack in a different language from the original. ▸ add (sound effects or music) to a film or a recording. 2 make a copy of (a recording). ▸ transfer (a recording) from one medium to another. ▸ combine (two or more sound recordings) into one soundtrack. ■ n. 1 an instance of dubbing sound effects or music. 2 a style of popular music originating from the remixing of recorded music (especially reggae).
– DERIVATIVES **dubby** adj.
– ORIGIN 1920s: abbrev. of DOUBLE.

dubbeltjie /'dɪb(ə)lki/ ■ n. S. African another term for DEVIL'S THORN.

HISTORY
Dubbeltjie comes from Dutch *dubbeltje* 'little double (one)', perhaps referring to its two-pronged thorns. It seems to have taken its other English name **devil's thorn** from the alternative Afrikaans spelling, *duwweltjie*, which was corrupted to *duiveltje* 'little devil': an understandable interpretation in the light of the painful effects of the thorns. In Australia, where the plant was introduced in the late 19th century, it is known as *doublegee*, reflecting its South African origins.

dubbin /'dʌbɪn/ ■ n. prepared grease used for softening and waterproofing leather. ■ v. (**dubbined**, **dubbining**) apply dubbin to (leather).
– ORIGIN C19: alteration of *dubbing*, from *dub* in the rare sense 'smear (leather) with grease'.

dubbing ■ n. material used for the bodies of artificial fishing flies, especially fur or wool on waxed silk.
– ORIGIN C17: from rare *dub* 'dress an artificial fishing fly'.

dubiety /dju:'baɪɪti/ ■ n. formal uncertainty.
– ORIGIN C18: from late Latin *dubietas*, from Latin *dubium* 'a doubt'.

dubious /'dju:bɪəs/ ■ adj. **1** hesitating or doubting. **2** not to be relied upon. ▸ of questionable value.
– DERIVATIVES **dubiously** adv. **dubiousness** n.
– ORIGIN C16: from Latin *dubiosus*, from *dubium*, neuter of *dubius* 'doubtful'.

dubnium /'dʌbnɪəm/ ■ n. the chemical element of atomic number 105, a very unstable element made by high-energy atomic collisions. (Symbol: **Db**)
– ORIGIN 1990s: modern Latin, from *Dubna* in Russia, site of the Joint Nuclear Institute.

ducal /'dju:k(ə)l/ ■ adj. of, like, or relating to a duke or dukedom.
– ORIGIN C15: from Old French, from *duc* 'duke'.

ducat /'dʌkət/ ■ n. a gold coin formerly current in most European countries. ▸ (**ducats**) informal money.
– ORIGIN from Italian *ducato*, orig. referring to a silver coin minted by the Duke of Apulia in 1190: from medieval Latin *ducatus* (see DUCHY).

duchess ■ n. the wife or widow of a duke. ▸ a woman holding a rank equivalent to duke in her own right.
– ORIGIN Middle English: from medieval Latin *ducissa*, from Latin *dux* (see DUKE).

duchesse /du:'ʃes, 'dʌtʃɪs, -es/ (also **duchesse satin**) ■ n. a soft, heavy, glossy kind of satin.
– ORIGIN C18: from French, 'duchess'.

duchesse lace ■ n. a kind of Brussels pillow lace with bold floral patterns worked in a fine thread.

duchesse potatoes ■ pl. n. mashed potatoes mixed with egg yolk, piped into small shapes and baked.

duchy /'dʌtʃi/ ■ n. (pl. **-ies**) the territory of a duke or duchess.
– ORIGIN Middle English: from Old French *duche*, from medieval Latin *ducatus*, from Latin *dux*, *duc-* (see DUKE).

duck[1] ■ n. (pl. same or **ducks**) a waterbird with a broad blunt bill, short legs, webbed feet, and a waddling gait, some kinds of which are domesticated. [Family Anatidae: many species.] ▸ the female of such a bird. Contrasted with DRAKE.
– PHRASES **get** (or **have**) **one's ducks in a row** N. Amer. informal get (or have) everything organized. **like water off a duck's back** referring to a hurtful remark which has no effect. **take to something like a duck to water** take to something very readily.
– ORIGIN Old English *duce*, from the Germanic base of DUCK[2] (expressing the notion of 'diving bird').

duck[2] ■ v. **1** lower the head or body quickly to avoid a blow or missile or so as not to be seen. ▸ avoid (a blow or missile) by ducking. ▸ informal evade (an unwelcome duty). **2** push (someone) under water. **3** Bridge refrain from playing a winning card on a particular trick for tactical reasons. ■ n. a quick lowering of the head.
– PHRASES **duck and dive** use one's ingenuity to deal with or evade a situation.
– DERIVATIVES **ducker** n.
– ORIGIN Middle English: of Germanic origin; rel. to DUCK[1].

duck[3] ■ n. Cricket a batsman's score of nought.
– PHRASES **break one's duck** Cricket score the first run of one's innings.
– ORIGIN C19: short for *duck's egg*, used for the figure 0.

duck[4] (also **ducks**) ■ n. Brit. informal dear (used as an affectionate form of address).
– ORIGIN C16: from DUCK[1].

duck[5] ■ n. a strong untwilled linen or cotton fabric, used chiefly for work clothes and sails. ▸ (**ducks**) trousers made from such a fabric.
– ORIGIN C17: from Middle Dutch *doek* 'linen'.

duck-billed dinosaur ■ n. another term for HADROSAUR.

duck-billed platypus ■ n. see PLATYPUS.

duckboards ■ pl. n. wooden slats joined together to form a path over muddy ground.

ducking stool ■ n. historical a chair fastened to the end of a pole, used to plunge offenders into a pond or river as a punishment.

duckling ■ n. a young duck.

ducks and drakes ■ n. a game of throwing flat stones so that they skim along the surface of water.
– ORIGIN C16: from the movement of the stone over the water.

duck's arse (US **duck's ass**) ■ n. informal a man's hairstyle in which the hair is slicked back on both sides and tapered at the nape.

duck soup ■ n. N. Amer. informal an easy task.

ducktail ■ n. S. African dated a young white man having a duck's arse hairstyle and usually dressed in a leather jacket, narrow trousers, and pointed shoes; a Teddy boy.
– ORIGIN 1950s (orig. US).

duckweed ■ n. a tiny aquatic flowering plant that floats in large quantities on still water. [Family Lemnaceae.]

ducky[1] informal ■ n. (pl. **-ies**) Brit. dear (used as a form of address). ■ adj. chiefly N. Amer. delightful.
– ORIGIN C19: from DUCK[4].

ducky[2] (also **duckie**) ■ n. (pl. **-ies**) S. African short for RUBBER DUCK.

duct ■ n. a tube or passageway in a building or machine for air, cables, etc. ▸ a vessel in the body for conveying lymph or glandular secretions. ▸ a vessel in a plant for conveying water, sap, or air. ■ v. (usu. **be ducted**) convey through a duct.
– DERIVATIVES **ducting** n.
– ORIGIN C17: from Latin *ductus* 'leading, aqueduct' from *ducere* 'lead'.

ductile /'dʌktaɪl/ ■ adj. **1** (of a metal) able to be drawn out into a thin wire. **2** able to be deformed without losing toughness.
– DERIVATIVES **ductility** n.
– ORIGIN Middle English: from Latin *ductilis*, from *ducere* 'to lead'.

ductless ■ adj. Anatomy denoting a gland that secretes directly into the bloodstream, such as an endocrine gland.

duct tape ■ n. strong cloth-backed waterproof adhesive tape.
– ORIGIN 1970s: orig. used for repairing leaks in ducted ventilation and heating systems.

ductule /'dʌktju:l/ ■ n. Anatomy a minute duct.
– DERIVATIVES **ductular** adj.

dud informal ■ n. **1** a thing that fails to work properly. ▸ an ineffectual person. **2** (**duds**) clothes. ■ adj. failing to work or meet a standard.
– ORIGIN Middle English.

dude /d(j)u:d/ ■ n. informal **1** a man. ▸ a stylish and confident man. **2** a dandy.
– DERIVATIVES **dudish** adj.
– ORIGIN C19: prob. from German dialect *Dude* 'fool'.

dude ranch ■ n. (in the western US) a cattle ranch converted to a holiday centre for tourists.

dudgeon /'dʌdʒ(ə)n/ ■ n. deep resentment.
– ORIGIN C16.

due ■ adj. **1** expected at, planned for, or required by a

certain time. ▸ (of a person) at a point where something is owed or merited. ▸ required as a legal or moral obligation. **2** proper; appropriate. ■ n. **1 (one's due/dues)** a person's right. **2 (dues)** fees. ■ adv. (with reference to a point of the compass) directly.
– PHRASES **due to 1** caused by. **2** because of. **give someone their due** be fair to someone. **in due course** at the appropriate time. **pay one's dues** fulfil one's obligations.
– ORIGIN Middle English: from Old French *deu* 'owed', from Latin *debitus*, from *debere* 'owe'.

USAGE
Due to in the sense 'because of' has been condemned as incorrect on the grounds that **due** is an adjective and should not be used in a prepositional phrase. However, the prepositional use is now common in all types of literature and is regarded as part of standard English.

due diligence ■ n. Law reasonable steps taken by a person in order to avoid committing an offence, especially in buying or selling something.

duel ■ n. chiefly historical a pre-arranged contest with deadly weapons between two people to settle a point of honour. ▸ (in modern use) a contest between two parties. ■ v. (**duelled, duelling**; US **dueled, dueling**) fight a duel.
– DERIVATIVES **dueller** (US **dueler**) n. **duellist** (US **duelist**) n.
– ORIGIN C15: from Latin *duellum*, from *bellum* 'war', used in medieval Latin with the meaning 'combat between two persons', influenced by *dualis* 'of two'.

duenna /djuːˈɛnə/ ■ n. (in some Latin countries) an older woman acting as a governess and chaperone to the girls in a family.
– ORIGIN C17: earlier form of Spanish *dueña*, from Latin *domina* 'lady, mistress'.

due process (also **due process of law**) ■ n. fair treatment through the normal judicial system.

duet ■ n. a performance by two singers, instrumentalists, or dancers. ▸ a musical composition for two performers. ■ v. (**duetted, duetting**) perform a duet.
– DERIVATIVES **duettist** n.
– ORIGIN C18: from Italian *duetto*, diminutive of *duo* 'duet'.

duff[1] ■ n. a flour pudding boiled or steamed in a cloth bag.
– ORIGIN C19: northern English form of DOUGH.

duff[2] ■ adj. Brit. informal worthless or false.
– ORIGIN C18.

duff[3] ■ v. informal **1 (duff someone up)** chiefly Brit. beat someone up. **2** Golf mishit (a shot).
– ORIGIN sense 1 (1960s) of uncertain origin; sense 2 (C19) prob. a back-formation from DUFFER.

duff[4] ■ n. N. Amer. informal a person's buttocks.
– ORIGIN C19.

duffel (also **duffle**) ■ n. **1** a coarse woollen cloth with a thick nap. **2** N. Amer. sporting or camping equipment.
– ORIGIN C17: from *Duffel*, the name of a town in Belgium where the cloth was orig. made.

duffel bag ■ n. a cylindrical canvas bag closed by a drawstring.
– ORIGIN C20 (orig. US): from sense 2 of DUFFEL.

duffel coat ■ n. a hooded coat made of duffel, typically fastened with toggles.

duffer ■ n. informal an incompetent or stupid person.
– ORIGIN C19: from Scots *dowfart* 'stupid person'.

dufus ■ n. variant spelling of DOOFUS.

dug[1] past and past participle of DIG.

dug[2] ■ n. the udder, teat, or nipple of a female animal.
– ORIGIN C16: perhaps of Old Norse origin.

dugong /ˈduːɡɒŋ, ˈdjuː-/ ■ n. (pl. same or **dugongs**) a sea cow found in the Indian Ocean, distinguished from the manatees by its forked tail. [*Dugong dugon*.]
– ORIGIN C19: from Malay *duyong*.

dugout ■ n. **1** a trench that is roofed over as a shelter for troops. ▸ an underground air-raid or nuclear shelter. ▸ a low shelter at the side of a sports field for a team's coaches and substitutes. **2** (also **dugout canoe**) a canoe made from a hollowed tree trunk.

duh ■ exclam. another way of saying DOH[2].

duiker /ˈdʌɪkə, ˈdeɪkə/ ■ n. (pl. same or **duikers**) **1** a small African antelope, typically with a tuft of hair between the horns. [*Sylvicapra grimmia* and other species.] **2** S. African dated a cormorant.
– ORIGIN C18: from Dutch, 'diver', from the antelope's habit of plunging through bushes when pursued.

duke ■ n. **1** a male holding the highest hereditary title in the British and certain other peerages. **2** chiefly historical (in parts of Europe) a male ruler of a small independent state.
– PHRASES **duke it out** N. Amer. informal fight it out.
– DERIVATIVES **dukedom** n.
– ORIGIN Old English, from Old French *duc*, from Latin *dux* 'leader'.

dulcamara /ˌdʌlkəˈmɛːrə/ ■ n. an extract of woody nightshade, used in homeopathy especially for treating skin diseases and chest complaints.
– ORIGIN C16: from medieval Latin, from Latin *dulcis* 'sweet' + *amara* 'bitter'.

dulcet /ˈdʌlsɪt/ ■ adj. (of a sound) sweet and soothing.
– ORIGIN Middle English *doucet*: from Old French *doucet*, diminutive of *doux*, from Latin *dulcis* 'sweet'.

dulcimer /ˈdʌlsɪmə/ ■ n. a musical instrument with a sounding board or box over which strings of graduated length are stretched, played by striking the strings with hand-held hammers.
– ORIGIN C15: from Old French *doulcemer*, prob. from Latin *dulce melos* 'sweet melody'.

dull ■ adj. **1** lacking interest or excitement. **2** lacking brightness or sheen. ▸ (of the weather) overcast. **3** slow to understand. ▸ slow-moving. **4** indistinctly felt or heard. ■ v. make or become dull.
– DERIVATIVES **dullish** adj. **dullness** (also **dulness**) n. **dully** /ˈdʌl.li/ adv.
– ORIGIN Old English *dol* 'stupid', of Germanic origin.

dullard /ˈdʌləd/ ■ n. a slow or stupid person.
– ORIGIN Middle English: from Middle Dutch *dullaert*, from *dul* 'dull'.

duly ■ adv. in accordance with what is required or appropriate. ▸ as might be expected.

Duma /ˈduːmə/ ■ n. a legislative body in the ruling assembly of Russia and of some other republics of the former USSR.
– ORIGIN from Russian.

dumb ■ adj. **1** unable to speak, normally because of congenital deafness. ▸ (of animals) unable to speak as a natural state. ▸ temporarily unable or unwilling to speak. **2** informal, chiefly N. Amer. stupid. **3** (of a computer terminal) having no independent processing capability. ■ v. **1 (dumb something down)** informal reduce the intellectual content of something. ▸ (**dumb down**) become less intellectually challenging. **2** poetic/literary silence.
– DERIVATIVES **dumbly** adv. **dumbness** n.
– ORIGIN Old English, of Germanic origin.

USAGE
In the sense meaning 'not able to speak', **dumb** has been overwhelmed by the sense 'stupid' to such an extent that the use of the first sense is now almost certain to cause offence. Alternatives such as **speech-impaired** should be used instead.

dumb-bell ■ n. **1** a short bar with a weight at each end, used typically in pairs for exercise or muscle-building. **2** informal a stupid person.
– ORIGIN C18: orig. denoting an object similar to that used to ring a church bell (but without the bell, so 'dumb').

dumb cane ■ n. a thick-stemmed Caribbean plant with a poisonous sap that swells the tongue and destroys the power of speech. [*Dieffenbachia seguine*.]

dumbfound ■ v. (usu. **be dumbfounded**) astonish greatly.
– ORIGIN C17: blend of DUMB and CONFOUND.

dumbo ■ n. (pl. **-os**) informal a stupid person.
– ORIGIN 1950s (orig. US): from DUMB, popularized by the cartoon film *Dumbo*.

dumbshow ■ n. gestures used to convey something without speech. ▸ (especially in English drama of the 16th and 17th centuries) a part of a play acted in mime.

dumbstruck ■ adj. so shocked or surprised as to be unable to speak.

dumb waiter ■ n. **1** a small lift for carrying food and

dumdum

crockery between floors. **2** Brit. a movable table, typically with revolving shelves, used in a dining room.

dumdum (also **dumdum bullet**) ■ n. a kind of soft-nosed bullet that expands on impact and inflicts laceration.
— ORIGIN C19: from *Dum Dum*, name of a town and arsenal near Calcutta, India, where they were first produced.

dum-dum ■ n. informal a stupid person.
— ORIGIN 1970s (orig. US): reduplication of DUMB.

dummy ■ n. (pl. **-ies**) **1** a model or replica of a human being. **2** an object or item designed to resemble and serve as a substitute for the real item. ▸ a rubber or plastic teat for a baby to suck on. **3** (chiefly in rugby and soccer) a feigned pass or kick. **4** Bridge the declarer's partner, whose cards are exposed on the table after the opening lead and played by the declarer. ▸ (in whist) an imaginary fourth player. **5** informal a stupid person. ■ v. (**-ies, -ied**) **1** (chiefly in rugby and soccer) feign a pass or kick. **2** (**dummy up**) N. Amer. informal keep quiet.
— PHRASES **sell someone a dummy** (chiefly in rugby and soccer) deceive an opponent by feigning a pass or kick.
— ORIGIN C16 (orig. 'a person who cannot speak'): from DUMB.

dummy run ■ n. a practice or trial.

dump ■ n. a site for depositing rubbish or waste. ▸ a heap of rubbish left at a dump. ▸ informal an unpleasant or dreary place. ■ v. **1** deposit or dispose of (rubbish or something unwanted). ▸ put down firmly and carelessly. ▸ informal desert (someone). ▸ send (goods unsaleable in the home market) to a foreign market for sale at a low price. **2** Computing copy (stored data) to a different location, especially so as to protect against loss. ▸ print out the contents of (a store). **3** (**dump on**) N. Amer. informal treat badly or criticize harshly.
— ORIGIN Middle English (orig. 'fall suddenly'): in later use partly imitative.

dumper ■ n. **1** a person or thing that dumps something. **2** (also **dumper truck**) Brit. a dump truck. **3** S. African & Austral./NZ a large wave that hurls a swimmer or surfer onto the beach.

dumpling ■ n. **1** a small savoury ball of dough (usually made with suet) which may be boiled in water or a stew. **2** a pudding consisting of apple or other fruit enclosed in a sweet dough and baked.
— ORIGIN C17: apparently from the rare adjective *dump* 'of the consistency of dough', although *dumpling* is recorded much earlier.

dumps ■ pl. n. (in phr. (**down**) **in the dumps**) informal depressed or unhappy.
— ORIGIN C16 (orig. sing. 'a dazed or puzzled state'): prob. a figurative use of Middle Dutch *domp* 'haze, mist'.

dumpster ■ n. N. Amer. a rubbish skip.
— ORIGIN 1930s: orig. *Dempster Dumpster*, proprietary name (from DUMP) given by the American manufacturers, Dempster Brothers of Tennessee.

dump truck ■ n. S. African & N. Amer. a truck with a body that tilts or opens at the back for unloading.

dumpy ■ adj. (**-ier, -iest**) short and stout. ■ n. (pl. **-ies**) (also **dumpie**) S. African a small squat bottle of beer, holding 340 millilitres.
— DERIVATIVES **dumpily** adv. **dumpiness** n.
— ORIGIN C18: from DUMPLING.

dun ■ adj. of a dull greyish-brown colour. ■ n. **1** a dull greyish-brown colour. **2** a horse with a sandy coat, black mane, tail, and lower legs, and a dark dorsal stripe. **3** a sub-adult mayfly with drab, opaque wings, or a fishing fly imitating them.
— ORIGIN Old English, of Germanic origin.

dunce ■ n. a person who is slow at learning.

dunce's cap (N. Amer. also **dunce cap**) ■ n. a paper cone formerly put on the head of a dunce at school as a mark of disgrace.

Dundee cake ■ n. chiefly Brit. a rich fruit cake, decorated with almonds.

dunderhead ■ n. informal a stupid person.
— DERIVATIVES **dunderheaded** adj.
— ORIGIN C17: cf. obsolete Scots *dunder* 'resounding noise'.

dune ■ n. a mound or ridge of sand or other loose sediment formed by the wind, especially on the sea coast or in a desert.
— ORIGIN C18: from French, from Middle Dutch *dūne*; rel. to Old English *dūn* 'hill'.

dung ■ n. manure. ■ v. (of an animal) defecate.
— ORIGIN Old English, of Germanic origin.

dungaree /ˌdʌŋɡəˈriː/ ■ n. **1** (**dungarees**) trousers with a bib held up by straps over the shoulders, made of denim or a similar material and worn for work or leisure. **2** a kind of coarse Indian calico.
— ORIGIN C17: from Hindi *duṅgrī*.

dung beetle ■ n. a beetle whose larvae feed on dung, especially a scarab.

dungeon ■ n. **1** a strong underground prison cell, especially in a castle. **2** archaic term for DONJON. ■ v. poetic/literary imprison in a dungeon.
— ORIGIN Middle English: from Old French (perhaps orig. with the sense 'lord's tower'), from Latin *dominus* 'lord'.

dung fly ■ n. a hairy fly that lays its eggs in fresh dung. [*Scathophaga stercoraria* and other species.]

dunghill ■ n. a heap of dung or refuse, especially in a farmyard.

dunite /ˈdʌnʌɪt/ ■ n. Geology a green to brownish coarse-grained igneous rock consisting largely of olivine.
— ORIGIN C19: from the name of *Dun* Mountain, New Zealand.

dunk ■ v. **1** dip (bread or other food) into a drink or soup before eating it. ▸ immerse in water. **2** Basketball score a field goal by shooting the ball down through the basket with the hands above the rim. ■ n. Basketball a goal scored by dunking.
— DERIVATIVES **dunker** n.
— ORIGIN C20: from Pennsylvania German *dunke* 'dip', from German *tunken* 'dip, plunge'.

dunlin /ˈdʌnlɪn/ ■ n. (pl. same or **dunlins**) a common migratory sandpiper with a downcurved bill and greyish-brown upper parts. [*Calidris alpina*.]
— ORIGIN C16: prob. from DUN + -LING.

dunnage /ˈdʌnɪdʒ/ ■ n. **1** loose wood, matting, or similar material used to keep a cargo in position in a ship's hold. **2** informal baggage.
— ORIGIN Middle English.

dunnock /ˈdʌnək/ ■ n. a small European songbird of the accentor family, with a dark grey head and a reddish-brown back. [*Prunella modularis*.]
— ORIGIN Middle English: apparently from DUN + -OCK.

dunny /ˈdʌni/ ■ n. (pl. **-ies**) Austral./NZ informal a toilet.
— ORIGIN C19: from dialect *dunnekin* 'privy', prob. from DUNG + archaic slang *ken* 'house'.

duo ■ n. (pl. **-os**) **1** a pair of people or things, especially in music or entertainment. **2** Music a duet.
— ORIGIN C16: from Latin *duo* 'two'.

duo- ■ comb. form two; having two: *duopoly*.
— ORIGIN from Latin.

duodecimal /ˌdjuːə(ʊ)ˈdɛsɪm(ə)l/ ■ adj. relating to or denoting a system of counting or numerical notation that has twelve as a base.
— DERIVATIVES **duodecimally** adv.
— ORIGIN C17: from Latin *duodecimus* 'twelfth'.

duodecimo /ˌdjuːə(ʊ)ˈdɛsɪməʊ/ ■ n. (pl. **-os**) a size of book in which each leaf is one twelfth of the size of the printing sheet.
— ORIGIN C17: from Latin (*in*) *duodecimo* 'in a twelfth'.

duodenum /ˌdjuːəˈdiːnəm/ ■ n. (pl. **duodenums** or **duodena** /-ˈdiːnə/) Anatomy the first part of the small intestine immediately beyond the stomach.
— DERIVATIVES **duodenal** /ˌdjuːəˈdiːn(ə)l/, /-ˈnʌɪtɪs/ n.
— ORIGIN Middle English: from medieval Latin, from *duodeni* 'in twelves', its length being equivalent to the breadth of approximately twelve fingers.

duopoly /djuːˈɒpəli/ ■ n. (pl. **-ies**) a situation in which two suppliers dominate a market.
— DERIVATIVES **duopolistic** adj.
— ORIGIN 1920s: from DUO-, on the pattern of *monopoly*.

duotone /ˈdjuːətəʊn/ ■ n. a half-tone illustration made from a single original with two colours at different screen angles.

dupatta /dʊˈpʌtə/ ■ n. a length of material worn as a head covering by women from the Indian subcontinent.
– ORIGIN from Hindi *dupaṭṭā*.

dupe ■ v. deceive; trick. ■ n. a victim of deception.
– DERIVATIVES **dupable** adj. **duper** n.
– ORIGIN C17: from French dialect *dupe* 'hoopoe', from the bird's supposedly stupid appearance.

dupion /ˈdjuːpɪən/ ■ n. a rough slubbed silk fabric woven from the threads of double cocoons.
– ORIGIN C19 ('double cocoon'): from French *doupion*, from Italian *doppione*, from *doppio* 'double'.

duple /ˈdjuːp(ə)l/ ■ adj. Music (of rhythm) based on two main beats to the bar.
– ORIGIN C16: from Latin *duplus*, from *duo* 'two'.

duplet /ˈdjuːplɪt/ ■ n. a set of two things, especially a pair of equal musical notes to be performed in the time of three.
– ORIGIN C17: from Latin *duplus* 'duple', on the pattern of *doublet*.

duplex /ˈdjuːplɛks/ ■ n. 1 N. Amer. a residential building divided into two apartments. 2 a semi-detached house. 3 Biochemistry a double-stranded polynucleotide molecule. ■ adj. 1 having two parts. 2 (of a communications system, computer circuit, etc.) allowing the transmission of two signals simultaneously in opposite directions.
– ORIGIN C16: from Latin *duplex,, duplic-*, from *duo* 'two' + *plicare* 'to fold'.

duplicate ■ adj. /ˈdjuːplɪkət/ 1 exactly like something else. 2 having two corresponding parts. 3 twice the number or quantity. ■ n. /ˈdjuːplɪkət/ one of two or more identical things. ■ v. /ˈdjuːplɪkeɪt/ make or be an exact copy of. ▶ multiply by two. ▶ do again unnecessarily.
– DERIVATIVES **duplicable** adj. **duplication** n.
– ORIGIN Middle English: from Latin *duplicare* 'double', from *duplic-* (see DUPLEX).

duplicate bridge ■ n. a competitive form of bridge in which the same hands are played successively by different partnerships.

duplicator ■ n. a machine for copying something.

duplicitous ■ adj. deceitful.

duplicity /djuːˈplɪsɪti, djʊ-/ ■ n. deceitfulness.
– ORIGIN Middle English: from late Latin *duplicitas*, from Latin *duplic-* (see DUPLEX).

durable ■ adj. 1 hard-wearing. 2 (of goods) not for immediate consumption and so able to be kept.
– DERIVATIVES **durability** n. **durableness** n. **durably** adv.
– ORIGIN Middle English: from Latin *durabilis*, from *durare* (see DURATION).

dura mater /ˌdjʊərə ˈmeɪtə/ ■ n. Anatomy the tough outermost membrane enveloping the brain and spinal cord.
– DERIVATIVES **dural** adj.
– ORIGIN C19: from medieval Latin, 'hard mother', translation of Arabic *al-'umm al-jāfiya* 'coarse mother'.

duration ■ n. the time during which something continues.
– PHRASES **for the duration** informal for a very long time.
– DERIVATIVES **durational** adj.
– ORIGIN Middle English: from medieval Latin *duratio(n-)*, from *durare* 'to last', from *durus* 'hard'.

Durban July ■ n. see JULY sense 2.

Durban poison ■ n. S. African informal cannabis of a particularly potent variety, originating in KwaZulu-Natal.

durbar /ˈdəːbɑː/ ■ n. historical 1 the court of an Indian ruler. 2 a public reception held by an Indian prince or a British governor or viceroy in India.
– ORIGIN Urdu: from Persian *darbār* 'court'.

duress /djʊ(ə)rɛs, ˈdjʊərɛs/ ■ n. threats, violence, etc. used to coerce a person into doing something. ▶ Law constraint illegally exercised to force someone to perform an act.
– ORIGIN Middle English ('harshness, cruel treatment'): from Latin *duritia*, from *durus* 'hard'.

Durex ■ n. (pl. same) S. African & Brit. trademark a contraceptive sheath.
– ORIGIN 1930s: name invented by the manufacturers, prob. based on Latin *durare* 'to last'.

durian /ˈdʊərɪən/ ■ n. 1 an oval spiny tropical fruit containing a creamy pulp with a fetid smell but agreeable taste. 2 (also **durian tree**) the large Malaysian tree that bears this fruit. [*Durio zibethinus*.]
– ORIGIN C16: from Malay *durian*, from *duri* 'thorn'.

duricrust /ˈdjʊərɪkrʌst/ ■ n. Geology a hard mineral crust formed at or near the surface of soil in semi-arid regions by the evaporation of groundwater.
– ORIGIN 1920s: from Latin *durus* 'hard' + CRUST.

during ■ prep. throughout the course or duration of. ▶ at a particular point in the course of.
– ORIGIN Middle English: from the obsolete verb *dure* 'last, endure, extend', from Latin *durare* (see DURATION).

durned ■ adj. & adv. US dialect form of DARNED.

durra /ˈdʊrə, ˈdʊərə/ ■ n. sorghum of the principal variety grown from NE Africa to India.
– ORIGIN C18: from Arabic *ḍura*, *ḍurra*.

durst archaic or regional past of DARE.

durum wheat /ˈdjʊərəm/ ■ n. a kind of hard wheat grown in arid regions, yielding flour that is used to make pasta. [*Triticum durum*.]
– ORIGIN C20: from Latin, neuter of *durus* 'hard'.

dusk ■ n. the darker stage of twilight. ■ v. poetic/literary grow dark.
– ORIGIN Old English *dox* 'dark, swarthy' and *doxian* 'darken', of Germanic origin.

dusky ■ adj. (-ier, -iest) darkish in colour. ▶ euphemistic, dated or poetic/literary (of a person) black; dark-skinned.
– DERIVATIVES **duskily** adv. **duskiness** n.

dusky kob (also **dusky cob**) ■ n. S. African another term for DAGA (in sense 1).

dust ■ n. 1 fine, dry powder consisting of tiny particles of earth or waste matter. ▶ any material in the form of tiny particles: *coal dust*. ▶ poetic/literary a dead person's remains. 2 an act of dusting. ■ v. 1 remove dust from the surface of. ▶ (**dust something down/off**) bring something out for use again after a long period of neglect. 2 (usu. **be dusted**) cover lightly with a powdered substance.
– PHRASES **the dust settles** things quieten down. **eat someone's dust** N. Amer. informal fall far behind someone in a competitive situation. **leave someone/thing in the dust** surpass someone or something easily. **not see someone for dust** find that a person has made a hasty departure. **kick up a dust** (or US **kick up dust**) informal create a disturbance.
– DERIVATIVES **dustless** adj.
– ORIGIN Old English, of Germanic origin.

dust bath ■ n. a bird's rolling in dust to clean its feathers.

dustbin ■ n. S. African & Brit. a large container for refuse.

dust bowl ■ n. an area where vegetation has been lost and soil reduced to dust and eroded, especially as a consequence of drought or unsuitable farming practice.

dust bunny ■ n. informal, chiefly N. Amer. a ball of dust and fluff.

dustcart ■ n. Brit. a vehicle used for collecting household refuse.

dust cover ■ n. a dust jacket or dust sheet.

dust devil ■ n. a small whirlwind or air vortex over land, visible as a column of dust and debris. ▶ S. African a dust storm.

duster ■ n. a cloth for dusting furniture.

dusting powder ■ n. powder for dusting over something, especially talcum powder.

dust jacket ■ n. a removable paper cover on a book.

dustman ■ n. (pl. -men) a man employed to collect household refuse.

dustpan ■ n. a flat hand-held receptacle into which dust and waste can be swept.

dust sheet ■ n. Brit. a large sheet for covering furniture to protect it from dust or while decorating.

dust storm ■ n. a strong, turbulent wind which carries clouds of fine dust and sand over a large area.

dust-up ■ n. informal a fight or quarrel.

dusty ■ adj. (-ier, -iest) 1 covered with or resembling dust. 2 staid and uninteresting.
– DERIVATIVES **dustily** adv. **dustiness** n.

dusty miller ■ n. a plant of the daisy family with whitish or greyish foliage. [*Artemisia stellerana* (N. America), *Senecio cineraria* (Mediterranean), and other species.]
– ORIGIN C19: named from the fine powder on the flowers and leaves.

Dutch ■ adj. of or relating to the Netherlands, its people, or their language. ■ n. the West Germanic language of the Netherlands.
– PHRASES **go Dutch** share the cost of a meal equally.
– ORIGIN from Middle Dutch *dutsch* 'Dutch, Netherlandish, German'.

Dutch auction ■ n. a method of selling in which the price is reduced until a buyer is found.

Dutch barn ■ n. Brit. a farm building comprising a curved roof set on an open frame, used to cover hay.

Dutch courage ■ n. confidence gained from drinking alcohol.

Dutch door ■ n. N. Amer. a stable door.

Dutch East India Company ■ n. a Dutch trading company engaged in commerce with the East, which established a refreshment post for its ships at the Cape in 1652.

Dutch elm disease ■ n. a fungal disease of elm trees, spread by bark beetles.

Dutch hoe ■ n. a hoe used with a pushing action just under the surface of the soil.

Dutchman (or **Dutchwoman**) ■ n. (pl. **-men** or **-women**) 1 a native or national of the Netherlands, or a person of Dutch descent. 2 S. African derogatory an Afrikaner.

Dutchman's pipe ■ n. a vigorous climbing vine with hooked tubular flowers, native to Brazil. [*Aristolochia elegans*.]

Dutch metal ■ n. an alloy of copper and zinc used in imitation of gold leaf.

Dutch oven ■ n. 1 a covered earthenware or cast-iron container for cooking casseroles. 2 chiefly historical a large metal box serving as a simple oven, heated by being placed next to or under hot coals. 3 S. African, chiefly historical a large clay or brick oven with a domed roof, built outside the kitchen.

Dutch Reformed Church ■ n. any of the three mainstream Calvinist Churches in South Africa.

duteous /'dju:tɪəs/ ■ adj. archaic dutiful.
– DERIVATIVES **duteously** adv. **duteousness** n.
– ORIGIN C16: from DUTY, on the pattern of words such as *bounteous*.

dutiful ■ adj. conscientiously or obediently fulfilling one's duty. ▶ motivated by duty rather than enthusiasm: *dutiful applause*.
– DERIVATIVES **dutifully** adv. **dutifulness** n.

duty ■ n. (pl. **-ies**) 1 a moral or legal obligation. 2 a task required as part of one's job. ▶ (**duties**) performance of prescribed church services by a priest or minister. 3 a payment levied on the import, export, manufacture, or sale of goods. ▶ a payment levied on the transfer of property, for licences, and for the legal recognition of documents.
– PHRASES **do duty as** (or **for**) serve or act as a substitute for. **on** (or **off**) **duty** engaged (or not engaged) in one's regular work.
– DERIVATIVES **dutiable** adj.
– ORIGIN Middle English: from Anglo-Norman French *duete*, from Old French *deu* (see DUE).

duty drawback ■ n. see DRAWBACK (sense 2).

duty-free ■ adj. & adv. exempt from payment of duty.

duty-paid ■ adj. on which the duty has been met.

duvet /'d(j)uːveɪ/ ■ n. a soft thick quilt used instead of an upper sheet and blankets.
– ORIGIN C18: from French, 'down'.

dux /dʌks/ ■ n. (pl. **duces**) S. African, Scottish, & Austral./NZ the top pupil in a school or class.
– ORIGIN C18: from Latin, 'leader'.

duxelles /'dʌks(ə)lz, dʊk'sɛl/ ■ n. a stuffing made from chopped mushrooms, onions, shallots, and parsley.

– ORIGIN named after the Marquis *d'Uxelles*, a C17 French nobleman.

DVD ■ abbrev. digital videodisc.

DVD-R ■ abbrev. DVD recordable, a DVD which can be recorded on once only.

DVD-ROM ■ abbrev. DVD read-only memory, a DVD used in a computer for displaying data.

DVD-RW (also **DVD-RAM**) ■ abbrev. DVD rewritable (or random-access memory), a DVD on which recordings can be made and erased a number of times.

DVT ■ abbrev. deep-vein thrombosis.

dwaal /dwɑːl/ ■ n. S. African informal a dreamy, dazed, or absent-minded state.
– ORIGIN from Afrikaans.

dwang ■ n. (usu. in phr. **in/out of the dwang**) S. African informal trouble.
– ORIGIN Afrikaans, 'compulsion, constraint'.

dwarf ■ n. (pl. **dwarfs** or **dwarves**) 1 a member of a mythical race of short, stocky human-like creatures, skilled in mining and metalworking. 2 an abnormally small person. ▶ [as modifier] denoting an animal or plant that is much smaller than is usual for its type or species. 3 (also **dwarf star**) Astronomy a star of relatively small size and low luminosity. ■ v. cause to seem small in comparison. ▶ stunt the growth of.
– DERIVATIVES **dwarfish** adj.
– ORIGIN Old English, of Germanic origin.

dwarfism ■ n. (in medical or technical contexts) unusually low stature or small size.

dweeb ■ n. informal, chiefly N. Amer. a boring, studious, or socially inept person.
– ORIGIN 1980s: perhaps a blend of DWARF and *feeb* 'a feeble-minded person'.

dwell ■ v. (past and past part. **dwelt** or **dwelled**) 1 formal live in or at a place. 2 (**dwell on/upon**) think, speak, or write at length about. ■ n. technical a slight regular pause in the motion of a machine.
– DERIVATIVES **dweller** n.
– ORIGIN Old English *dwellan* 'lead astray, delay' (in Middle English 'remain in a place'), of Germanic origin.

dwelling (also **dwelling place**) ■ n. formal a house or other place of residence.

dwindle ■ v. diminish gradually.
– ORIGIN C16: from Scots and dialect *dwine* 'fade away', from Old English *dwīnan*, of Germanic origin.

dwt ■ abbrev. deadweight tonnage.

Dy ■ symb. the chemical element dysprosium.

dyad /'dʌɪad/ ■ n. technical something that consists of two elements or parts. ▶ Mathematics an operator which is a combination of two vectors.
– DERIVATIVES **dyadic** adj.
– ORIGIN C17: from late Latin *dyas, dyad-*, from Greek *duas*, from *duo* 'two'.

Dyak /'dʌɪak/ ■ n. & adj. variant spelling of DAYAK.

dye ■ n. a natural or synthetic substance used to colour something. ■ v. (**dyeing**) make a specified colour with dye.
– PHRASES **dyed in the wool** unchanging in a particular belief. [with allusion to the fact that yarn was dyed when raw, producing a more even and permanent colour.]
– DERIVATIVES **dyeable** adj. **dyer** n.
– ORIGIN Old English.

dyeline ■ n. a print made by the diazo process.

dyestuff ■ n. a substance used as or yielding a dye.

dying present participle of DIE¹. ■ adj. relating to or at the time of death.
– PHRASES **to one's dying day** for the rest of one's life.

dyke¹ (also **dike**) ■ n. 1 an embankment built to prevent flooding from the sea. ▶ an earthwork serving as a boundary or defence. 2 a ditch or watercourse. 3 Geology an intrusion of igneous rock cutting across existing strata. Compare with SILL. ■ v. (often as adj. **dyked**) provide (land) with a dyke to prevent flooding.
– ORIGIN Middle English: from Old Norse *dík*.

dyke² (also **dike**) ■ n. informal a lesbian.
– DERIVATIVES **dykey** adj.
– ORIGIN 1940s (earlier as *bulldyke*).

dyn ■ abbrev. dyne.

dynamic /daɪˈnæmɪk/ ■ adj. **1** (of a process or system) characterized by constant change or activity. ▶ full of energy and new ideas. **2** Physics of or relating to forces producing motion. Often contrasted with **STATIC**. **3** Linguistics (of a verb) expressing an action, activity, event, or process. ■ n. **1** an energizing or motive force. **2** Music another term for **DYNAMICS** (in sense 3).
– DERIVATIVES **dynamical** adj. **dynamically** adv.
– ORIGIN C19: from Greek *dunamikos*, from *dunamis* 'power'.

dynamic equilibrium ■ n. a state of balance between continuing processes.

dynamic range ■ n. the range of sound intensity that occurs in a piece of music or that can be satisfactorily handled by a piece of equipment.

dynamics ■ pl. n. **1** [treated as sing.] the branch of mechanics concerned with the motion of bodies under the action of forces. Compare with **KINEMATICS**, **STATICS**. **2** the forces which stimulate development or change within a system or process. **3** Music the varying levels of volume of sound in a musical performance.
– DERIVATIVES **dynamicist** n.

dynamic viscosity ■ n. a quantity measuring the force needed to overcome internal friction in a fluid.

dynamism ■ n. **1** the quality of being dynamic. **2** Philosophy, chiefly historical the theory that phenomena can be explained by an immanent force.
– DERIVATIVES **dynamist** n. **dynamization** (also **-isation**) n. **dynamize** (also **-ise**) v.

dynamite ■ n. **1** a high explosive consisting of nitroglycerine mixed with an absorbent material. **2** informal an extremely impressive or potentially dangerous person or thing. ■ v. blow up with dynamite.
– DERIVATIVES **dynamiter** n.
– ORIGIN C19: from Greek *dunamis* 'power'.

dynamo ■ n. (pl. **-os**) a machine for converting mechanical energy into electrical energy by rotating conducting coils in a magnetic field.
– ORIGIN C19: abbrev. of *dynamo-electric machine*, from Greek *dunamis* 'power'.

dynamometer /ˌdaɪnəˈmɒmɪtə/ ■ n. an instrument which measures the power output of an engine.

dynast /ˈdɪnəst, ˈdaɪnəst, -nast/ ■ n. a member of a dynasty, especially a hereditary ruler.
– ORIGIN C17: from Greek *dunastēs*, from *dunasthai* 'be able'.

dynasty /ˈdɪnəsti/ ■ n. (pl. **-ies**) a line of hereditary rulers. ▶ a succession of powerful or prominent people from the same family.
– DERIVATIVES **dynastic** adj. **dynastically** adv.
– ORIGIN Middle English: from French *dynastie*, from Greek *dunasteia* 'lordship', from *dunastēs* (see **DYNAST**).

dyne /daɪn/ ■ n. Physics a unit of force that, acting on a mass of one gram, increases its velocity by one centimetre per second every second along the direction in which it acts.
– ORIGIN C19: from French, from Greek *dunamis* 'force, power'.

dyno ■ n. (pl. **-os**) **1** short for **DYNAMOMETER**. **2** Climbing a rapid move across a rock face in order to reach a hold.

dys- /dɪs/ ■ comb. form bad; difficult (used especially in medical terms): *dyspepsia*.
– ORIGIN from Greek *dus-*.

dysarthria /dɪsˈɑːθrɪə/ ■ n. Medicine unclear articulation of speech that is otherwise linguistically normal.
– ORIGIN C19: from DYS- + Greek *arthron* 'joint, articulation'.

dysentery /ˈdɪs(ə)nt(ə)ri/ ■ n. infection of the intestines with bacteria or protozoans, resulting in severe diarrhoea with blood and mucus in the faeces.
– DERIVATIVES **dysenteric** /-ˈtɛrɪk/ adj.
– ORIGIN Middle English: from Old French *dissenterie*, from Greek *dusenteros* 'afflicted in the bowels'.

dysfunctional ■ adj. **1** not operating normally or properly. **2** unable to deal adequately with normal social relations.
– DERIVATIVES **dysfunction** n. **dysfunctionally** adv.

dysgenic /dɪsˈdʒɛnɪk/ ■ adj. exerting a detrimental effect on later generations.

dysuria

dyskinesia /ˌdɪskɪˈniːzɪə, -kaɪ-/ ■ n. Medicine abnormality or impairment of voluntary movement.
– ORIGIN C18: from DYS- + Greek *kinēsis* 'motion'.

dyslexia /dɪsˈlɛksɪə/ ■ n. a disorder involving difficulty in learning to read or interpret words, letters, and other symbols. Compare with **ALEXIA**.
– DERIVATIVES **dyslectic** adj. & n. **dyslexic** adj. & n.
– ORIGIN C19: German *Dyslexie* from DYS- + Greek *lexis* 'speech' (apparently by confusion of Greek *legein* 'to speak' and Latin *legere* 'to read').

dysmenorrhoea /ˌdɪsmɛnəˈriːə/ (US **dysmenorrhea**) ■ n. Medicine painful menstruation.

dysmorphia /dɪsˈmɔːfɪə/ ■ n. Medicine deformity or abnormality in the shape or size of a specified part of the body: *muscle dysmorphia*.
– DERIVATIVES **dysmorphic** adj.
– ORIGIN C19: from Greek *dusmorphia* 'misshapenness, ugliness', from *dus-* DYS- + *morphē* 'form'.

dyspepsia /dɪsˈpɛpsɪə/ ■ n. indigestion.
– ORIGIN C18: from Greek *duspepsia*, from *duspeptos* 'difficult to digest'.

dyspeptic ■ adj. of or relating to dyspepsia or the resulting irritableness. ■ n. a dyspeptic person.

dysphagia /dɪsˈfeɪdʒɪə/ ■ n. Medicine difficulty in swallowing, as a symptom of disease.
– ORIGIN C18: from DYS- + Greek *phagia* 'eating'.

dysphoria /dɪsˈfɔːrɪə/ ■ n. Psychiatry a state of unease or general dissatisfaction.
– DERIVATIVES **dysphoric** adj. & n.
– ORIGIN C19: from Greek *dusphoros* 'hard to bear'.

dysplasia /dɪsˈpleɪzɪə/ ■ n. Medicine the enlargement of an organ or tissue by the proliferation of abnormal cells.
– DERIVATIVES **dysplastic** adj.
– ORIGIN 1930s: from DYS- + Greek *plasis* 'formation'.

dyspnoea /dɪspˈniːə/ (US **dyspnea**) ■ n. Medicine laboured breathing.
– DERIVATIVES **dyspnoeic** adj.
– ORIGIN C17: from Greek *dus-* 'difficult' + *pnoē* 'breathing'.

dyspraxia /dɪsˈpraksɪə/ ■ n. a developmental disorder of the brain in childhood causing difficulty in activities requiring coordination and movement.
– ORIGIN C20: from Greek *dus-* 'bad, difficult' + *praxis* 'action'.

dysprosium /dɪsˈprəʊzɪəm/ ■ n. the chemical element of atomic number 66, a soft silvery-white metal of the lanthanide series. (Symbol: **Dy**)
– ORIGIN C19: from Greek *dusprositos* 'hard to get at'.

dysrhythmia /dɪsˈrɪðmɪə/ ■ n. Medicine abnormality in a physiological rhythm, especially of the brain or heart.
– DERIVATIVES **dysrhythmic** adj. **dysrhythmical** adj.

dysthymia /dɪsˈθaɪmɪə/ ■ n. Psychiatry persistent mild depression.
– DERIVATIVES **dysthymic** adj. & n.
– ORIGIN C19: from Greek *dusthumia*.

dystonia /dɪsˈtəʊnɪə/ ■ n. Medicine a state of abnormal muscle tone resulting in muscular spasm and abnormal posture.
– DERIVATIVES **dystonic** adj.

dystopia /dɪsˈtəʊpɪə/ ■ n. an imaginary place or society in which everything is bad.
– DERIVATIVES **dystopian** adj. & n.
– ORIGIN C18: from DYS- + UTOPIA.

dystrophin /dɪsˈtrəʊfɪn/ ■ n. Biochemistry a protein found in skeletal muscle, which is absent in sufferers from muscular dystrophy.

dystrophy /ˈdɪstrəfi/ ■ n. Medicine a disorder in which an organ or tissue of the body wastes away. See also **MUSCULAR DYSTROPHY**.
– ORIGIN C19: from modern Latin *dystrophia*, from Greek *dus-* 'bad' + *-trophia* 'nourishment'.

dysuria /dɪsˈjʊərɪə/ ■ n. Medicine painful or difficult urination.
– ORIGIN Middle English: from Greek *dusouria*, from *dus-* 'difficult' + *ouron* 'urine'.

Ee

E¹ (also **e**) ■ n. (pl. **Es** or **E's**) **1** the fifth letter of the alphabet. **2** denoting the fifth in a set. **3** Music the third note of the diatonic scale of C major.

E² ■ abbrev. **1** East or Eastern. **2** informal the drug Ecstasy or a tablet of Ecstasy. **3** denoting products, in particular food additives, which comply with European Union regulations. See also **E-NUMBER**. **4** exa- (10^{18}). ■ symb. Physics **1** electric field strength. **2** energy.

e ■ symb. **1** Chemistry (also **e⁻**) an electron. **2** (*e*) Mathematics the transcendental number that is the base of Napierian or natural logarithms, approximately equal to 2.71828.

e-¹ ■ prefix variant spelling of **EX-¹** (as in *elect, emit*).

e-² ■ prefix denoting the use of electronic data transfer, especially through the Internet: *e-cash*.
– ORIGIN from **ELECTRONIC**, on the pattern of *email*.

ea. ■ abbrev. each.

each ■ det. & pron. every one of two or more people or things, regarded and identified separately. ■ adv. to, for, or by every one of a group.
– PHRASES **each and every** every single.
– ORIGIN Old English, based on a West Germanic phr. meaning 'ever alike'.

each other ■ pron. the other one or ones.

each-way ■ adj. & adv. (of a bet) backing a horse or other competitor either to win or to finish in the first three.

eager ■ adj. strongly wanting to do or have. ▸ keenly expectant or interested.
– DERIVATIVES **eagerly** adv. **eagerness** n.
– ORIGIN Middle English: from Old French *aigre* 'keen', from Latin *acer* 'sharp, pungent'.

eagle ■ n. **1** a large bird of prey with a massive hooked bill and long broad wings, renowned for its keen sight and powerful soaring flight. [*Aquila* and other genera.] **2** Golf a score of two strokes under par at a hole. **3** US a former gold coin worth ten dollars. ■ v. Golf play (a hole) in two strokes under par.
– DERIVATIVES **eaglet** n.
– ORIGIN Middle English: from Old French *aigle*, from Latin *aquila*. The golf term was suggested by **BIRDIE**.

eagle eye ■ n. a close watch.
– DERIVATIVES **eagle-eyed** adj.

eagle owl ■ n. a very large owl with ear tufts and a deep hoot. [*Bubo bubo* (Eurasia) and other species.]

eagle ray ■ n. a large ray with long pointed pectoral fins, a long tail, and a distinct head. [Genera *Myliobatis* and *Aetobatus*; several species.]

EAK ■ abbrev. Kenya (international vehicle registration).
– ORIGIN from *East Africa Kenya*.

ear¹ ■ n. **1** the organ of hearing and balance in humans and other vertebrates, especially the external part of this. ▸ (in other animals) an organ sensitive to sound. **2** an ability to recognize and appreciate sounds. **3** willingness to listen and pay attention: *a sympathetic ear*.
– PHRASES **be all ears** informal be listening attentively. **one's ears are burning** one is subconsciously aware of being talked about. **have someone's ear** have access to and influence with someone. **have** (or **keep**) **an ear to the ground** be well informed about events and trends. **be out on one's ear** informal be dismissed ignominiously. **up to one's ears in** informal very busy with.
– DERIVATIVES **-eared** adj. **earless** adj.
– ORIGIN Old English, of Germanic origin.

ear² ■ n. the seed-bearing head or spike of a cereal plant.
– ORIGIN Old English, of Germanic origin.

earache ■ n. pain inside the ear.

earbud ■ n. **1** another term for **COTTON BUD**. **2** (usu. **earbuds**) a very small earphone.

eardrum ■ n. the membrane of the middle ear, which vibrates in response to sound waves.

eared seal ■ n. see **SEAL²**.

earful ■ n. informal a prolonged reprimand.

earhole ■ n. the external opening of the ear.

earl ■ n. a British nobleman ranking above a viscount and below a marquess.
– DERIVATIVES **earldom** n.
– ORIGIN Old English, of Germanic origin.

Earl Grey ■ n. a kind of China tea flavoured with bergamot.
– ORIGIN prob. named after the 2nd *Earl Grey* (1764–1845), said to have been given the recipe by a Chinese mandarin.

Earl Marshal ■ n. (in the UK) the officer presiding over the College of Arms, with ceremonial duties on various royal occasions.

ear lobe ■ n. a soft, rounded fleshy part hanging from the lower margin of the ear.

early ■ adj. (**-ier, -iest**) & adv. **1** before the usual or expected time. **2** of, at, or near the beginning of a particular time, period, or sequence.
– PHRASES **at the earliest** not before the time or date specified. **early bird** humorous a person who rises or arrives early. **early** (or **earlier**) **on** at an early (or earlier) stage. **it's** (or **these are**) **early days** informal it is too soon to be sure how a situation will develop.
– DERIVATIVES **earliness** n.
– ORIGIN Old English (as adv.) *ǣrlīce*, influenced by Old Norse *árliga*.

early closing ■ n. chiefly Brit. the practice of shutting business premises on a particular afternoon every week.

Early English ■ adj. denoting a style of English Gothic architecture typical of the late 12th and 13th centuries, characterized by pointed arches and simple lancet windows.

early music ■ n. medieval, Renaissance, and early baroque music, especially as revived and played on period instruments.

earmark ■ n. a mark on the ear of a domesticated animal indicating ownership or identity. ▸ an identifying feature. ■ v. **1** (usu. **be earmarked**) designate for a particular purpose. **2** mark (an animal) with an earmark.

earmuffs ■ pl. n. a pair of soft fabric coverings, connected by a band, worn over the ears to protect them from cold or noise.

earn ■ v. obtain (money) in return for labour or services. ▸ (of capital invested) gain (money) as interest or profit. ▸ gain as the reward for hard work or merit.
– ORIGIN Old English, of West Germanic origin.

earned income ■ n. money derived from paid work as opposed to profit from investments.

earned run ■ n. Baseball a run that is not the result of an error or passed ball.

earner ■ n. a person or thing earning money or income of a specified kind or level: *high earners*.

earnest¹ /ˈɜːnɪst/ ■ adj. intensely serious.
– PHRASES **in earnest** to a greater extent or more intensely than before. ▸ sincere and serious in intention.
– DERIVATIVES **earnestly** adv. **earnestness** n.
– ORIGIN Old English, of Germanic origin.

earnest² /ˈɜːnɪst/ ■ n. a sign or promise of what is to come.
– ORIGIN Middle English *ernes*, 'instalment paid to confirm a contract', from Old French *erres*, from Latin *arra*, from *arrabo* 'a pledge'.

earnest money ■ n. money paid by a buyer to a seller to confirm a contract.

VOWELS a cat ɑː arm ɛ bed ɛː hair ə ago əː her ɪ sit i cosy iː see ɒ hot ɔː saw ʌ run

earnings ▪ pl. n. money or income earned.

earphone ▪ n. an electrical device worn on the ear to receive radio or telephone communications. ▸ a similar device worn in the the ear to listen to a radio or portable audio player.

earpiece ▪ n. the part of a telephone, radio receiver, or other aural device that is applied to the ear during use.

ear-piercing ▪ adj. loud and shrill. ▪ n. the piercing of the lobes or edges of the ears to allow the wearing of earrings.

earplug ▪ n. a piece of wax, cotton wool, etc., placed in the ear as protection against noise, water, or cold air.

earring ▪ n. a piece of jewellery worn on the lobe or edge of the ear.

earshot ▪ n. the range or distance over which one can hear or be heard.

ear-splitting ▪ adj. extremely loud.

earth ▪ n. 1 (also **Earth**) the planet on which we live, the third planet of the solar system in order of distance from the sun. 2 the substance of the land surface; soil. ▸ used in names of stable, dense, non-volatile inorganic substances, e.g. fuller's earth. ▸ poetic/literary the substance of the human body: *earth to earth, ashes to ashes.* 3 electrical connection to the ground, regarded as having zero electrical potential. 4 the underground lair of a badger or fox. ▪ v. connect (an electrical device) to earth.
−PHRASES **bring** (or **come**) **back** (**down**) **to earth** cause to return (or return) to reality. **the earth** a very large amount: *her ha⎯⎯⎯t the earth.* **go to earth** go into hiding. **on earth** used for emphasis: *what on earth are you doing?*
−DERIVATIVES **earthward** adj. & adv. **earthwards** adv.
−ORIGIN Old English, of Germanic origin.

earthbound ▪ adj. 1 confined to the earth or earthly things. 2 moving towards the earth.

earthen ▪ adj. 1 made of compressed earth. 2 (of a pot) made of baked or fired clay.

earthenware ▪ n. pottery made of fired clay.

earthling ▪ n. (in science fiction) an inhabitant of the earth.

earthly ▪ adj. 1 of or relating to the earth or human life on the earth. ▸ material; worldly. 2 [with neg.] informal used for emphasis: *there was no earthly reason to rush.*
−PHRASES **not stand** (or **have**) **an earthly** Brit. informal have no chance at all.
−DERIVATIVES **earthliness** n.

earth mother ▪ n. (in mythology and primitive religion) a goddess symbolizing fertility and the source of life.

earthquake ▪ n. a sudden violent shaking of the ground as a result of movements within the earth's crust.

earth science ▪ n. the branch of science concerned with the physical constitution of the earth and its atmosphere. ▸ (**earth sciences**) the various branches of this subject, e.g. geology.

earth-shattering ▪ adj. informal very important or shocking.
−DERIVATIVES **earth-shatteringly** adv.

earthshine ▪ n. Astronomy the glow caused by sunlight reflected by the earth, especially on the darker portion of a crescent moon.

earthstar ▪ n. a brownish woodland fungus with a spherical fruiting body surrounded by a fleshy star-shaped structure. [*Geastrum* and other genera.]

earthwork ▪ n. a large artificial bank of soil, especially one built as a defence in ancient times.

earthworm ▪ n. a burrowing annelid worm that lives in the soil. [Family Lumbricidae.]

earthy ▪ adj. (**-ier**, **-iest**) 1 resembling or suggestive of soil. 2 direct and uninhibited, especially about sexual subjects or bodily functions.
−DERIVATIVES **earthily** adv. **earthiness** n.

ear trumpet ▪ n. a trumpet-shaped device formerly used as a hearing aid.

ear tuft ▪ n. each of a pair of tufts of longer feathers on the top of the head of some owls.

earwax ▪ n. the protective yellow waxy substance secreted in the passage of the outer ear.

East Indian

earwig ▪ n. a small elongated insect with a pair of terminal appendages that resemble pincers. [Order Dermaptera: many species.] ▪ v. (**earwigged**, **earwigging**) informal eavesdrop.
−ORIGIN Old English *ēarwicga*, from *ēare* 'ear' + *wicga* 'earwig'; the insect was once thought to crawl into the human ear.

ease ▪ n. 1 absence of difficulty or effort. ▸ freedom from worries or problems. ▪ v. 1 make or become less serious or severe. ▸ facilitate. 2 move carefully or gradually. ▸ (**ease something away/down/off**) Nautical slacken a rope or sail slowly or gently. 3 (of share prices, interest rates, etc.) decrease in value or amount.
−PHRASES **at** (**one's**) **ease** relaxed. ▸ (**at ease**) Military in a relaxed attitude with the feet apart and the hands behind the back.
−DERIVATIVES **easeful** adj. (poetic/literary). **easer** n.
−ORIGIN Middle English: from Old French *aise*, from Latin *adjacens, adjacere* 'lie close by'.

easel /ˈiːz(ə)l/ ▪ n. a wooden frame for holding an artist's work in progress.
−ORIGIN C16: from Dutch *ezel* 'ass'.

easement /ˈiːzm(ə)nt/ ▪ n. 1 Law another term for SERVITUDE. 2 poetic/literary comfort or peace.

easily ▪ adv. 1 without difficulty or effort. ▸ more quickly or frequently than is usual. 2 without doubt. ▸ very probably.

east ▪ n. (usu. **the east**) 1 the direction towards the point of the horizon where the sun rises at the equinoxes, on the right-hand side of a person facing north. 2 the eastern part of a country, region, or town. ▸ (**the East**) the regions or countries lying to the east of Europe, especially China, Japan, and India. ▸ (**the East**) historical the former communist states of eastern Europe. ▪ adj. 1 lying towards, near, or facing the east. 2 (of a wind) blowing from the east. ▪ adv. to or towards the east.
−DERIVATIVES **eastbound** adj. & adv.
−ORIGIN Old English, of Germanic origin.

East Coast Fever ▪ n. a feverish tick-borne disease of cattle, prevalent mostly in Africa and usually fatal.

Easter ▪ n. the festival of the Christian Church celebrating the resurrection of Christ, held (in the Western Church) on the first Sunday after the first full moon following the northern spring equinox.
−ORIGIN Old English, of Germanic origin and rel. to EAST; perhaps from *Ēastre*, the name of a goddess associated with spring.

Easter bunny ▪ n. an imaginary rabbit said to bring gifts to children at Easter.

Easter Day (also **Easter Sunday**) ▪ n. the day on which the festival of Easter is celebrated.

Easter egg ▪ n. an artificial chocolate egg or decorated hard-boiled egg given at Easter, especially to children.

easterly ▪ adj. & adv. 1 in an eastward position or direction. 2 (of a wind) blowing from the east. ▪ n. a wind blowing from the east.

eastern ▪ adj. 1 situated in, directed towards, or facing the east. 2 (usu. **Eastern**) living in, coming from, or characteristic of the east, in particular the regions to the east of Europe.
−DERIVATIVES **easternmost** adj.

Eastern Church (also **Eastern Orthodox Church**) ▪ n. another name for ORTHODOX CHURCH. ▸ any of the Christian Churches originating in eastern Europe and the Middle East.

easterner ▪ n. a native or inhabitant of the east of a particular region or country.

Eastertide ▪ n. the Easter period.

East Germanic ▪ n. the extinct eastern group of Germanic languages, including Gothic. ▪ adj. of or relating to this group of languages.

East Indiaman ▪ n. historical a trading ship belonging to the East India Company.

East Indian ▪ adj. of or relating to the islands of SE Asia or (archaic) the whole of SE Asia to the east of and including India.

easting ■ n. **1** distance travelled or measured eastward, especially at sea. **2** a figure or line representing eastward distance on a map.

east-north-east ■ n. the direction or compass point midway between east and north-east.

east-south-east ■ n. the direction or compass point midway between east and south-east.

eastward ■ adj. in an easterly direction. ■ adv. (also **eastwards**) towards the east. ■ n. (**the eastward**) the direction or region to the east.
– DERIVATIVES **eastwardly** adj. & adv.

easy ■ adj. (**-ier, -iest**) **1** achieved without great effort; presenting few difficulties. ▸ free from worry or problems. **2** informal, derogatory (of a woman) very receptive to sexual advances. **3** lacking anxiety or awkwardness. ■ exclam. be careful!
– PHRASES **easy on the eye** (or **ear**) informal pleasant to look at (or listen to). **go** (or **be**) **easy on** informal refrain from being harsh with or critical of. **of easy virtue** dated or humorous (of a woman) sexually promiscuous. **stand easy!** Military used to instruct soldiers standing at ease that they may relax their attitude further. **take it easy** make little effort; rest.
– DERIVATIVES **easiness** n.
– ORIGIN Middle English: from Old French *aisie*, from *aisier* 'put at ease, facilitate'.

easy chair ■ n. a large, comfortable chair, typically an armchair.

easy-going ■ adj. relaxed and tolerant.

easy listening ■ n. popular music that is tuneful and undemanding.

easy money ■ n. **1** money obtained by dubious means or for little work. **2** money available at relatively low interest.

easy-peasy ■ adj. Brit. informal very easy (used by children).
– ORIGIN 1970s: reduplication of EASY.

easy street ■ n. informal a state of financial comfort or security.

EAT ■ abbrev. Tanzania (international vehicle registration).
– ORIGIN from *East Africa Tanzania*.

eat ■ v. (past **ate** /ɛt, eɪt/; past part. **eaten**) **1** put (food) into the mouth and chew and swallow it. ▸ (**eat out**) or **in** have a meal in a restaurant (or at home). ▸ (**eat something away**) or **eat away at/into** erode or destroy something gradually. ▸ (**eat something up**) use resources in very large quantities. ▸ (**eat someone up**) dominate someone's thoughts completely. ■ n. (**eats**) informal light food or snacks.
– PHRASES **eat one's heart out** suffer from excessive longing, especially for something unattainable. **eat like a bird** (or **a horse**) informal eat very little (or a lot). **eat one's words** retract what one has said, especially in a humiliated way. **I'll eat my hat** informal said to indicate that one thinks something is extremely unlikely to happen. **what's eating you?** (or **him** etc.) informal what is worrying or annoying you?
– DERIVATIVES **eater** n.
– ORIGIN Old English, of Germanic origin.

eatable ■ adj. fit to be consumed as food. ■ n. (**eatables**) items of food.

eatery ■ n. (pl. **-ies**) informal a restaurant or café.

eating apple ■ n. an apple suitable for eating raw.

eau de cologne /ˌəʊ də kəˈləʊn/ ■ n. (pl. **eaux de cologne** pronunc. same) a toilet water with a strong, characteristic scent.
– ORIGIN C19: French, 'water of Cologne'.

eau de Nil /ˌəʊ də ˈniːl/ ■ n. a pale greenish colour.
– ORIGIN C19: from French *eau-de-Nil* 'water of the Nile'.

eau de toilette /ˌəʊ də twɑːˈlɛt/ ■ n. (pl. **eaux de toilette** pronunc. same) a dilute form of perfume.
– ORIGIN C20: French, 'toilet water'.

eau de vie /ˌəʊ də ˈviː/ ■ n. (pl. **eaux de vie** pronunc. same) brandy.
– ORIGIN from French *eau-de-vie* 'water of life'.

eaves ■ pl. n. the part of a roof that meets or overhangs the walls of a building.

– ORIGIN Old English, of Germanic origin.

eavesdrop ■ v. (**eavesdropped, eavesdropping**) secretly listen to a conversation.
– DERIVATIVES **eavesdropper** n.
– ORIGIN C17: from *eavesdropper* (Middle English), from the obsolete noun *eavesdrop* 'the ground on to which water drips from the eaves', prob. from Old Norse *upsardropi*.

ebb ■ n. the movement of the tide out to sea. ■ v. **1** (of tidewater) move away from the land; recede. Compare with FLOW. **2** (often **ebb away**) (of an emotion or quality) gradually lessen or reduce.
– PHRASES **at a low ebb** in a poor state.
– ORIGIN Old English, of West Germanic origin.

E-boat ■ n. a German torpedo boat used in the Second World War.
– ORIGIN from *E-* for enemy + BOAT.

Ebola fever /iːˈbəʊlə, əˈbəʊlə/ ■ n. an infectious and generally fatal viral disease marked by fever and severe internal bleeding.
– ORIGIN 1976: named after a river in the Democratic Republic of Congo.

Ebonics /ɛˈbɒnɪks/ ■ pl. n. [treated as sing.] American black English regarded as a language in its own right rather than as a dialect of standard English.
– ORIGIN blend of EBONY and PHONICS.

ebonize (also **-ise**) ■ v. [usu. as adj. **ebonized** (also **-ised**)] make (furniture) look like ebony.

ebony /ˈɛb(ə)ni/ ■ n. **1** heavy blackish or very dark brown wood from a tree of tropical and warm regions. **2** the tree which produces this wood. [*Diospyros ebenum* (India and Sri Lanka) and other species.] **3** a very dark brown or black colour.
– ORIGIN Middle English: from earlier *ebon*, from Greek *ebenos* 'ebony tree', perhaps on the pattern of *ivory*.

ebullient /ɪˈbʌljənt, -ˈbʊl-/ ■ adj. **1** cheerful and full of energy. **2** archaic or poetic/literary boiling or agitated as if boiling.
– DERIVATIVES **ebullience** n. **ebulliently** adv.
– ORIGIN C16: from Latin *ebullire* 'boil up'.

EC ■ abbrev. **1** European Commission. **2** European Community.

écarté /ˌeɪkɑːˈteɪ/ ■ n. Ballet a position in which the dancer extends one leg in the air to the side with the arm of the same side raised above the head and the other arm extended to the side.
– ORIGIN C19: French, from *écarter* 'discard, throw out'.

e-cash ■ n. electronic financial transactions conducted in cyberspace via computer networks.

Ecce Homo /ˌɛkeɪ ˈhɒməʊ, ˈhəʊməʊ/ ■ n. Art a painting of Christ wearing the crown of thorns.
– ORIGIN Latin, 'behold the man', the words of Pontius Pilate to the Jews after Jesus was crowned with thorns (John 19:5).

eccentric /ɪkˈsɛntrɪk, ɛk-/ ■ adj. **1** unconventional and slightly strange. **2** technical not placed centrally or not having its axis placed centrally. ▸ (of an orbit) not circular, especially to a marked degree. ■ n. **1** an eccentric person. **2** a cam or other part mounted eccentrically on a revolving shaft in order to transform rotation into backward-and-forward motion.
– DERIVATIVES **eccentrically** adv. **eccentricity** n.
– ORIGIN Middle English: from Greek *ekkentros*, from *ek* 'out of' + *kentron* 'centre'.

ecchymosis /ˌɛkɪˈməʊsɪs/ ■ n. (pl. **ecchymoses** /-siːz/) Medicine a discoloration of the skin resulting from bleeding underneath, typically caused by bruising.
– ORIGIN C16: modern Latin, from Greek *ekkhumōsis* 'escape of blood'.

Eccles cake ■ n. Brit. a round flat cake of sweetened pastry filled with currants.
– ORIGIN named after the town of *Eccles* near Manchester, England.

ecclesial /ɪˈkliːzɪ(ə)l/ ■ adj. formal relating to or constituting a Church or denomination.
– ORIGIN C17: from Greek *ekklēsia* (see ECCLESIASTICAL).

ecclesiastic formal ■ n. a priest or clergyman. ■ adj. another term for ECCLESIASTICAL.

ecclesiastical ■ adj. of or relating to the Christian Church or its clergy.

– DERIVATIVES **ecclesiastically** adv.
– ORIGIN Middle English: from Greek *ekklēsiastikos*, from *ekklēsiastēs* 'member of an assembly', from *ekklēsia* 'assembly, church'.

ecclesiology /ɪˌkliːzɪˈɒlədʒi/ ■ n. **1** the study of churches. **2** theology as applied to the nature and structure of the Christian Church.
– DERIVATIVES **ecclesiological** adj. **ecclesiologist** n.

eccrine /ˈɛkrʌɪn, -krɪn/ ■ adj. Physiology relating to or denoting multicellular glands which do not lose cytoplasm in their secretions, especially the sweat glands.
– ORIGIN 1930s: from Greek *ekkrinein* 'secrete'.

ECD ■ abbrev. early childhood development.

ecdysis /ˈɛkdɪsɪs, ɛkˈdʌɪsɪs/ ■ n. Zoology the process of shedding the old skin (in reptiles) or casting off the outer cuticle (in insects and other arthropods).
– DERIVATIVES **ecdysial** /ɛkˈdɪzɪəl/ adj.
– ORIGIN C19: from Greek *ekdusis* 'shedding'.

ecdysone /ˈɛkdɪsəʊn, ɛkˈdʌɪsəʊn/ ■ n. Biochemistry a steroid hormone that controls moulting in insects and other arthropods.
– ORIGIN 1950s: from Greek *ekdusis* 'shedding'.

ECG ■ abbrev. electrocardiogram or electrocardiograph.

echelon /ˈɛʃəlɒn, ˈeɪʃ-/ ■ n. **1** a level or rank in an organization, profession, or society. **2** Military a formation of troops, ships, aircraft, or vehicles in parallel rows with the end of each row projecting further than the one in front. ■ v. Military arrange in an echelon formation.
– ORIGIN C18: from French *échelon*, from *échelle* 'ladder'.

echidna /ɪˈkɪdnə/ ■ n. a spiny insectivorous egg-laying mammal with a long snout and claws, native to Australia and New Guinea. [*Tachyglossus aculeatus* and *Zaglossus bruijni*.]
– ORIGIN C19: modern Latin, from Greek *ekhidna* 'viper'; cf. *ekhinos* 'hedgehog'.

echinacea /ˌɛkɪˈneɪsɪə/ ■ n. a North American plant of the daisy family, whose flowers have a raised cone-like centre which appears to consist of soft spines. [Genus *Echinacea*: several species.]
– ORIGIN from Greek *ekhinos* 'hedgehog'.

Echinodermata /ɪˌkʌɪnə(ʊ)dəˈmɑːtə, ˌɛkɪn-, -ˈdəːmətə/ ■ pl. n. Zoology a phylum of marine invertebrates which includes starfishes, sea urchins, brittlestars, crinoids, and sea cucumbers.
– DERIVATIVES **echinoderm** /ɪˈkʌɪnə(ʊ)dəːm, ˈɛkɪn-/ n.
– ORIGIN from Greek *ekhinos* 'hedgehog, sea urchin' + *derma* 'skin'.

Echinoidea /ˌɛkɪˈnɔɪdɪə/ ■ pl. n. Zoology a class of echinoderms that comprises the sea urchins.
– DERIVATIVES **echinoid** /ˈɛkɪnɔɪd/ n. & adj.
– ORIGIN from *Echinus* (genus name), from Greek *ekhinos* (see ECHINUS).

echinus /ɪˈkʌɪnəs/ ■ n. Architecture a rounded moulding below an abacus on a Doric or Ionic capital.
– ORIGIN Middle English: from Greek *ekhinos* 'hedgehog, sea urchin'.

echo ■ n. (pl. **-oes**) **1** a sound caused by the reflection of sound waves from a surface back to the listener. **2** a reflected radio or radar beam. **3** something suggestive of or parallel to something else. **4** a code word representing the letter E, used in radio communication. ■ v. (**-oes, -oed**) **1** (of a sound) reverberate or be repeated after the original sound has stopped. **2** have a continued significance or influence. **3** repeat (someone's words or opinions).
– DERIVATIVES **echoer** n. **echoey** adj. **echoless** adj.
– ORIGIN Middle English: from Greek *ēkhō*, rel. to *ēkhē* 'a sound'.

echocardiography /ˌɛkəʊkɑːdɪˈɒɡrəfi/ ■ n. Medicine the use of ultrasound waves to investigate the action of the heart.
– DERIVATIVES **echocardiogram** n. **echocardiograph** n. **echocardiographic** adj.

echo chamber ■ n. an enclosed space for producing reverberation of sound.

echoic /ɛˈkəʊɪk/ ■ adj. **1** of or like an echo. **2** Linguistics representing a sound by imitation; onomatopoeic.
– DERIVATIVES **echoically** adv.

echolocation /ˈɛkə(ʊ)lə(ʊ)ˌkeɪʃ(ə)n/ ■ n. the location of objects by reflected sound, in particular as used by animals such as dolphins and bats.

echo sounder ■ n. a device for determining the depth of the seabed or detecting objects in water by measuring the time taken for echoes to return to the listener.
– DERIVATIVES **echo-sounding** n.

echovirus (also **ECHO virus**) ■ n. Medicine any of a group of enteroviruses which can cause respiratory infections and a mild form of meningitis.
– ORIGIN 1950s: *echo* is acronym from *enteric cytopathogenic human orphan*, because the virus was not orig. assignable to any known disease.

eclair /eɪˈklɛː, ɪ-/ ■ n. a small, soft cake of choux pastry filled with cream and typically topped with chocolate icing.
– ORIGIN C19: from French *éclair* 'lightning'.

eclampsia /ɪˈklam(p)sɪə/ ■ n. Medicine a condition in which one or more convulsions occur in a pregnant woman suffering from high blood pressure, often followed by coma and posing a threat to the health of mother and baby.
– DERIVATIVES **eclamptic** adj.
– ORIGIN C19: modern Latin, from Greek *eklampsis* 'sudden development'.

éclat /eɪˈklɑː/ ■ n. brilliant display or effect. ▸ social distinction or conspicuous success.
– ORIGIN C17: from French, from *éclater* 'burst out'.

eclectic /ɪˈklɛktɪk/ ■ adj. deriving ideas or style from a broad and diverse range of sources. ■ n. an eclectic person.
– DERIVATIVES **eclectically** adv. **eclecticism** n.
– ORIGIN C17: from Greek *eklektikos*, from *eklegein* 'pick out'.

eclipse /ɪˈklɪps/ ■ n. **1** an obscuring of the light from one celestial body by the passage of another between it and the observer or between it and its source of illumination. ▸ an instance of being eclipsed by another person or thing. **2** Ornithology a phase during which the distinctive markings of a bird (especially a male duck) are obscured by moulting of the breeding plumage. ■ v. **1** (of a celestial body) obscure the light from or to (another body). **2** deprive of significance, power, or prominence.
– ORIGIN Middle English: from Old French *e(s)clipse* (n.), *eclipser* (v.), from Greek *ekleipsis*, from *ekleipein* 'fail to appear, be eclipsed'.

ecliptic /ɪˈklɪptɪk/ ■ n. Astronomy a great circle on the celestial sphere representing the sun's apparent path during the year, so called because lunar and solar eclipses can only occur when the moon crosses it. ■ adj. of eclipses or the ecliptic.
– ORIGIN Middle English: from Greek *ekleiptikos*, from *ekleipein* (see ECLIPSE).

eclogite /ˈɛklɒdʒʌɪt/ ■ n. Geology a metamorphic rock composed essentially of garnet and pyroxene formed in the Earth's mantle.
– ORIGIN C19: from Greek *eklogē* 'selection'.

eclose /ɪˈkləʊz/ ■ v. Entomology (of an insect) emerge as an adult from the pupa or as a larva from the egg.
– DERIVATIVES **eclosion** n.
– ORIGIN C19 (as *eclosion*): from French *éclore* 'to hatch'.

eco- /ˈiːkəʊ, ˈɛkəʊ/ ■ comb. form representing ECOLOGY.

ecocide ■ n. destruction of the natural environment, especially when wilfully done.

eco-friendly ■ adj. not harmful to the environment.

eco-labelling ■ n. the use of labels to identify products conforming to recognized environmental standards.
– DERIVATIVES **eco-label** n.

E. coli /ˈkəʊlʌɪ/ ■ n. the bacterium *Escherichia coli*, commonly found in the intestines of humans and other animals, some strains of which can cause severe food poisoning.

ecology /ɪˈkɒlədʒi, ɛ-/ ■ n. the branch of biology concerned with the relations of organisms to one another and to their physical surroundings.
– DERIVATIVES **ecological** adj. **ecologically** adv. **ecologist** n.
– ORIGIN C19 (orig. as *oecology*): from Greek *oikos* 'house' + -LOGY.

econometrics

econometrics /ɪˌkɒnəˈmɛtrɪks/ ■ pl. n. [treated as sing.] the branch of economics concerned with the use of mathematical methods (especially statistics) in describing economic systems.
– DERIVATIVES **econometric** adj. **econometrical** adj. **econometrician** n. **econometrist** n.
– ORIGIN 1930s: from ECONOMY, on the pattern of words such as *biometrics*.

economic /ˌiːkəˈnɒmɪk, ɛk-/ ■ adj. 1 of or relating to economics or the economy. 2 justified in terms of profitability.
– ORIGIN Middle English: from Greek *oikonomikos*, from *oikonomia* (see ECONOMY).

economical ■ adj. giving good value or return in relation to the resources or money expended. ▸ sparing in the use of resources or money.
– PHRASES **economical with the truth** euphemistic lying or deliberately withholding information.

economically ■ adv. 1 in a way that relates to economics or finance. 2 in an economical way.

economic exclusion zone ■ n. another term for EXCLUSIVE ECONOMIC ZONE.

economic good ■ n. Economics a product or service which can command a price when sold.

economic rent ■ n. Economics the extra amount earned by a resource (e.g. land, capital, or labour) by virtue of its present use.

economics ■ pl. n. [often treated as sing.] the branch of knowledge concerned with the production, consumption, and transfer of wealth.

economism /ɪˈkɒnəmɪz(ə)m/ ■ n. belief in the primacy of economic causes or factors.

economist ■ n. an expert in economics.

economize (also **-ise**) ■ v. spend less; be economical.
– DERIVATIVES **economization** (also **-isation**) n. **economizer** (also **-iser**) n.

economy ■ n. (pl. **-ies**) 1 the state of a country or region in terms of the production and consumption of goods and services and the supply of money. ▸ a country or region having a particular economy: *a free-market economy*. 2 careful management of available resources. ▸ [as modifier] offering good value for money: *an economy pack of soap flakes*. ▸ a financial saving. 3 (also **economy class**) the cheapest class of air or rail travel.
– PHRASES **economy of scale** a proportionate saving in costs gained by an increased level of production. **economy of scope** a proportionate saving gained by producing two or more distinct goods, when the cost of doing so is less than that of producing each separately.
– ORIGIN C15: from Greek *oikonomia* 'household management', from *oikos* 'house' + *nemein* 'manage'.

ecosphere ■ n. a region in which life exists or could exist; the biosphere.

ecosystem ■ n. Ecology a biological community of interacting organisms and their physical environment.

ecotone /ˈiːkə(ʊ)təʊn, ˈɛk-/ ■ n. Ecology a region of transition between two biological communities.
– DERIVATIVES **ecotonal** adj.
– ORIGIN from ECO- + Greek *tonos* 'tension'.

ecotourism ■ n. tourism directed towards unspoiled natural environments and intended to support conservation efforts.
– DERIVATIVES **ecotour** n. & v. **ecotourist** n.

ecotype ■ n. Botany & Zoology a distinct form or race of a plant or animal species occupying a particular habitat.

ecru /ˈeɪkruː, ˈɛkruː/ ■ n. the light fawn colour of unbleached linen.
– ORIGIN C19: from French *écru* 'unbleached'.

ecstasy /ˈɛkstəsi/ ■ n. (pl. **-ies**) 1 an overwhelming feeling of great happiness or joyful excitement. 2 an emotional or religious frenzy or trancelike state. 3 (**Ecstasy**) an illegal amphetamine-based synthetic drug with euphoric effects.
– ORIGIN Middle English: from Greek *ekstasis* 'standing outside oneself'.

ecstatic /ɪkˈstatɪk, ɛk-/ ■ adj. feeling or characterized by ecstasy. ■ n. a person subject to mystical experiences.
– DERIVATIVES **ecstatically** adv.

ECT ■ abbrev. electroconvulsive therapy.

ecto- ■ comb. form outer; external: *ectoparasite*.
– ORIGIN from Greek *ektos* 'outside'.

ectoderm /ˈɛktə(ʊ)dəːm/ ■ n. Zoology & Embryology the outermost layer of cells or tissue of an embryo, or the parts derived from this (e.g. the epidermis, nerve tissue, and nephridia).
– DERIVATIVES **ectodermal** adj.
– ORIGIN C19: from ECTO- + Greek *derma* 'skin'.

ectomorph /ˈɛktə(ʊ)mɔːf/ ■ n. Physiology a person with a lean and delicate build of body. Compare with ENDOMORPH and MESOMORPH.
– DERIVATIVES **ectomorphic** adj. **ectomorphy** n.
– ORIGIN 1940s: *ecto-* from *ectodermal* (being the layer of the embryo giving rise to physical characteristics which predominate) + -MORPH.

-ectomy ■ comb. form denoting surgical removal of a specified part of the body: *appendectomy*.
– ORIGIN from Greek *ektomē* 'excision'.

ectoparasite /ˌɛktəʊˈparəsʌɪt/ ■ n. Biology a parasite, such as a flea, that lives on the outside of its host. Compare with ENDOPARASITE.
– DERIVATIVES **ectoparasitic** adj.

ectopic /ɛkˈtɒpɪk/ ■ adj. Medicine in an abnormal place or position.
– ORIGIN C19: from modern Latin *ectopia* 'presence of tissue, cells, etc. in an abnormal place', from Greek *ektopos* 'out of place'.

ectopic pregnancy ■ n. a pregnancy in which the fetus develops outside the womb, typically in a Fallopian tube.

ectoplasm /ˈɛktə(ʊ)plaz(ə)m/ ■ n. 1 Biology, dated the more viscous, clear outer layer of the cytoplasm in amoeboid cells. Compare with ENDOPLASM. 2 a viscous substance that supposedly exudes from the body of a medium during a spiritualistic trance and forms the material for the manifestation of spirits.
– DERIVATIVES **ectoplasmic** adj.

Ectoprocta /ˌɛktə(ʊ)ˈprɒktə/ ■ pl. n. Zoology another term for BRYOZOA.
– DERIVATIVES **ectoproct** n.
– ORIGIN modern Latin, from *ektos* 'outside, external' + *prōktos* 'anus'.

ectotherm /ˈɛktəʊθəːm/ ■ n. Zoology an animal that is dependent on external sources of body heat.
– DERIVATIVES **ectothermic** adj. **ectothermy** n.

ectropion /ɛkˈtrəʊpɪən/ ■ n. Medicine a condition, typically a consequence of advanced age, in which the eyelid is turned outwards away from the eyeball.
– ORIGIN C17: from Greek, from *ek-* 'out' + *trepein* 'to turn'.

ecu /ˈɛkjuː, ˈiː-, ˈeɪ-, -kuː/ (also **ECU**) ■ n. (pl. same or **ecus**) former term for EURO.
– ORIGIN acronym from *European currency unit*.

Ecuadorean /ˌɛkwəˈdɔːrɪən/ (also **Ecuadorian**) ■ n. a native or inhabitant of Ecuador. ■ adj. of or relating to Ecuador.

ecumenical /ˌiːkjʊˈmɛnɪk(ə)l, ˌɛk-/ ■ adj. representing a number of different Christian Churches. ▸ promoting or relating to unity among the world's Christian Churches.
– DERIVATIVES **ecumenically** adv.
– ORIGIN C16: from Greek *oikoumenikos* from *oikoumenē* 'the (inhabited) earth'.

ecumenism /ɪˈkjuːmənɪz(ə)m/ ■ n. the principle or aim of promoting unity among the world's Christian Churches.

eczema /ˈɛksɪmə, ˈɛkzɪmə/ ■ n. a medical condition in which patches of skin become rough and inflamed with blisters which cause itching and bleeding.
– DERIVATIVES **eczematous** /ɛkˈziːmətəs, ɛkˈzɛm-/ adj.
– ORIGIN C18: modern Latin, from Greek *ekzema*, from *ekzein* 'boil over, break out'.

-ed[1] ■ suffix forming adjectives: 1 (added to nouns) having; possessing; affected by: *talented*. 2 from phrases consisting of adjective and noun: *bad-tempered*.
– ORIGIN Old English.

-ed[2] ■ suffix forming: 1 the past tense and past participle of weak verbs: *landed*. 2 participial adjectives: *wounded*.
– ORIGIN Old English.

ed. ■ abbrev. 1 edited by. 2 edition. 3 editor.

Edam /ˈiːdam/ ▪ n. a round Dutch cheese, typically pale yellow with a red wax coating, traditionally made at Edam in the Netherlands.

edaphic /ɪˈdafɪk/ ▪ adj. Ecology of, produced by, or influenced by the soil.
– ORIGIN C19: from Greek *edaphos* 'floor'.

eddy ▪ n. (pl. **-ies**) a circular movement of water causing a small whirlpool. ▪ v. (**-ies, -ied**) (of water, air, or smoke) move in a circular way.
– ORIGIN Middle English: prob. from the Germanic base of the Old English prefix *ed-* 'again, back'.

edelweiss /ˈeɪd(ə)lvʌɪs/ ▪ n. a European mountain plant which has woolly white bracts around its small flowers and downy grey-green leaves. [*Leontopodium alpinum*.]
– ORIGIN C19: from German, from *edel* 'noble' + *weiss* 'white'.

edema ▪ n. US spelling of OEDEMA.

Eden /ˈiːd(ə)n/ ▪ n. **1** (also **Garden of Eden**) the place where Adam and Eve lived in the biblical account of the Creation. **2** a place or state of unspoilt happiness or beauty.
– ORIGIN from late Latin (Vulgate), Greek *Ēdēn* (Septuagint), and Hebrew *'Ēḏen*; perhaps ultimately from Sumerian *eden* 'plain, desert', but prob. rel. to Hebrew *'ēḏen* 'delight'.

edentate /iːˈdɛnteɪt/ ▪ n. Zoology a mammal of an order distinguished by the lack of incisor and canine teeth, including the anteaters, sloths, and armadillos. [Order Xenarthra (or Edentata).]
– ORIGIN C19: from Latin *edentare* 'make toothless'.

edentulous /ɪˈdɛntjʊləs/ ▪ adj. Medicine & Zoology lacking teeth.
– ORIGIN C18: from Latin *edentulus*.

edge ▪ n. **1** the outside limit of an object, area, or surface. ▶ an area next to a steep drop. **2** the sharpened side of a blade. **3** an intense or striking quality. ▶ a quality or factor which gives superiority over close rivals. ▶ the line along which two surfaces of a solid meet. ▪ v. **1** provide with a border or edge. **2** move carefully or furtively. **3** (usu. **edge out**) informal defeat by a small margin. **4** give an intense or sharp quality to. **5** Cricket strike (the ball) with the edge of the bat. **6** ski with one's weight on the edges of one's skis.
– PHRASES **on edge** tense, nervous, or irritable. **set someone's teeth on edge** (of a sound or taste) cause intense discomfort or irritation to someone.
– DERIVATIVES **-edged** adj. **edgeless** adj. **edger** n.
– ORIGIN Old English *ecg* 'sharpened side of a blade', of Germanic origin.

edgeways (also **edgewise**) ▪ adv. with the edge uppermost or towards the viewer.
– PHRASES **get a word in edgeways** [usu. with neg.] manage to contribute to a conversation with a voluble person.

edging ▪ n. something forming an edge or border.

edgy ▪ adj. (**-ier, -iest**) **1** tense, nervous, or irritable. **2** informal avant-garde and unconventional.
– DERIVATIVES **edgily** adv. **edginess** n.

edible /ˈɛdɪb(ə)l/ ▪ adj. fit to be eaten. ▪ n. (**edibles**) items of food.
– DERIVATIVES **edibility** n.
– ORIGIN C16: from late Latin *edibilis*, from Latin *edere* 'eat'.

edible snail ▪ n. a large snail which is widely collected or cultured for food, occurring chiefly in southern Europe. [*Helix pomatia*.]

edict /ˈiːdɪkt/ ▪ n. an official order or proclamation.
– DERIVATIVES **edictal** /ɪˈdɪkt(ə)l/ adj.
– ORIGIN Middle English: from Latin *edictum* 'something proclaimed', from *edicere*, from *e-* (var. of *ex-*) 'out' + *dicere* 'say, tell'.

edifice /ˈɛdɪfɪs/ ▪ n. **1** a building, especially a large, imposing one. **2** a complex system of beliefs.
– ORIGIN Middle English: from Latin *aedificium*, from *aedes* 'dwelling' + *facere* 'make'.

edify /ˈɛdɪfʌɪ/ ▪ v. (**-ies, -ied**) formal instruct or improve morally or intellectually.
– DERIVATIVES **edification** n. **edifying** adj. **edifyingly** adv.
– ORIGIN Middle English: from Old French *edifier*, from Latin *aedificare* 'build', from *aedis* 'dwelling' + *facere* 'make'.

edit ▪ v. (**edited, editing**) prepare (written material) for publication by correcting, condensing, or otherwise modifying it. ▶ prepare and arrange material for (a recording or broadcast). ▶ be editor of (a newspaper or magazine). ▶ (**edit something out**) remove material in preparing a recording or broadcast. ▪ n. a change or correction made as a result of editing.
– DERIVATIVES **editable** adj.
– ORIGIN C18: partly a back-formation from EDITOR, reinforced by French *éditer* 'to edit'.

edition ▪ n. a particular form or version of a published text. ▶ the total number of copies of a book, newspaper, etc. issued at one time. ▶ a particular version or instance of a regular programme or broadcast.
– ORIGIN Middle English: from Latin *editio(n-)*, from *edere* 'put out'.

editor ▪ n. **1** a person who is in charge of a newspaper, magazine, or multi-author book. **2** a person who commissions or prepares written or recorded material. **3** a computer program enabling the user to alter or rearrange online text.
– DERIVATIVES **editorship** n.
– ORIGIN C17: from Latin, 'producer (of games), publisher', from *edit-*, *edere* 'put out'.

editorial ▪ adj. of or relating to the commissioning or preparing of material for publication. ▪ n. a newspaper article giving an opinion on a topical issue.
– DERIVATIVES **editorialist** n. **editorially** adv.

editorialize (also **-ise**) ▪ v. (of a newspaper or editor) express opinions rather than just report news.

edit suite ▪ n. a room containing equipment for electronically editing video-recorded material.

-edly ▪ suffix (forming adverbs) in a manner characterized by the action expressed by the formative verb: *repeatedly*.

Edo /ˈɛdəʊ/ ▪ n. (pl. same or **-os**) **1** a member of a people inhabiting the district of Benin in Nigeria. **2** the Benue-Congo language of this people.
– ORIGIN the name of Benin City in Edo.

EDP ▪ abbrev. electronic data processing.

EDT ▪ abbrev. Eastern Daylight Time.

EDTA ▪ abbrev. Chemistry ethylenediamine tetra-acetic acid, an organic acid which is a strong chelating agent.

educate /ˈɛdjʊkeɪt/ ▪ v. give intellectual, moral, and social instruction to. ▶ train or give information on a particular subject.
– DERIVATIVES **educability** n. **educable** adj. **educative** adj.
– ORIGIN Middle English: from Latin *educare* 'lead out'.

educated guess ▪ n. a guess based on knowledge and experience.

education ▪ n. **1** the process of educating or being educated. ▶ the theory and practice of teaching. ▶ information about or training in a particular subject: *health education*. **2** (**an education**) informal an enlightening experience.
– DERIVATIVES **educational** adj. **educationalist** n. **educationally** adv. **educationist** n.

educator ▪ n. a person who teaches another, especially a school teacher.

edutainment /ˌɛdjʊˈteɪnm(ə)nt/ ▪ n. entertainment, especially computer games, with an educational aspect.

Edwardian /ɛdˈwɔːdɪən/ ▪ adj. relating to or characteristic of the reign of the British king Edward VII. ▪ n. a person who lived during this period.

-ee ▪ suffix forming nouns: **1** denoting the person affected directly or indirectly by the action of the formative verb: *employee*. **2** denoting a person described as or concerned with: *absentee*. **3** denoting an object of relatively smaller size: *bootee*.
– ORIGIN from Anglo-Norman French *-é*, from Latin *-atus* (past participial ending); some forms are anglicized modern French nouns (e.g. *refugee* from *réfugié*).

EEC ▪ abbrev. European Economic Community.

EEG ▪ abbrev. electroencephalogram or electroencephalograph.

eejit /ˈiːdʒɪt/ ▪ n. informal Irish and Scottish form of IDIOT.

eek ▪ exclam. informal used to express alarm or surprise.

eel

eel ■ n. a snake-like fish with a slender elongated body and poorly developed fins, proverbial for its slipperiness. [*Anguilla anguilla* (Europe) and related species, order Anguilliformes.] ▸ used in names of unrelated fishes that resemble the true eels, e.g. electric eel.
– DERIVATIVES **eel-like** adj. **eely** adj.
– ORIGIN Old English, of Germanic origin.

eelgrass ■ n. **1** a European marine plant with long ribbon-like leaves. [*Zostera marina*.] **2** a submerged aquatic plant with narrow, grass-like leaves. [Genus *Valisneria*.]

eelworm ■ n. a nematode, especially a small soil nematode that can become a serious pest of crops and ornamental plants.

e'en /iːn/ ■ adv. poetic/literary form of EVEN¹.

eensy /ˈiːnsi/ (also **eensy-weensy**) ■ adj. informal tiny.

EEPROM ■ n. Computing a read-only memory whose contents can be erased and reprogrammed using a pulsed voltage.
– ORIGIN acronym from *electrically erasable programmable ROM*.

-eer ■ suffix **1** (forming nouns) denoting a person concerned with or engaged in an activity: *auctioneer*. **2** (forming verbs) denoting concern or involvement with an activity: *electioneer*.
– ORIGIN from French *-ier*, from Latin *-arius*; verbs are often back-formations (e.g. *electioneer* from *electioneering*).

e'er /ɛː/ ■ adv. poetic/literary form of EVER.

eerie /ˈɪəri/ ■ adj. (**-ier, -iest**) strange and frightening.
– DERIVATIVES **eerily** adv. **eeriness** n.
– ORIGIN Middle English (orig. northern English and Scots in the sense 'fearful'): prob. from Old English *earg* 'cowardly', of Germanic origin.

ef- ■ prefix variant spelling of EX-¹ assimilated before *f* (as in *efface, effloresce*).

EFA ■ abbrev. essential fatty acid.

eff ■ n. & v. Brit. used as a euphemism for 'fuck'.
– PHRASES **eff and blind** informal swear. [*blind* from its use in expletives such as *blind me* (see BLIMEY).]
– DERIVATIVES **effing** adj. & adv.

efface /ɪˈfeɪs/ ■ v. erase (a mark) from a surface. **2** (**efface oneself**) make oneself appear insignificant or inconspicuous.
– DERIVATIVES **effacement** n.
– ORIGIN C15: from French *effacer*, from *e-* (from Latin *ex-* 'away from') + *face* 'face'.

effect ■ n. **1** a change which is a result or consequence of an action or other cause. ▸ the extent to which something succeeds or is operative. **2** (often in phr. **to that effect**) general sense or meaning. **3** the state of being or becoming operative: *the law came into effect*. **4** (**effects**) the lighting, sound, or scenery used in a play or film. **5** (**effects**) personal belongings. **6** Physics a physical phenomenon, typically named after its discoverer: *the Renner effect*. ■ v. cause to happen; bring about.
– PHRASES **for effect** in order to impress people. **in effect** in practice, even if not formally acknowledged.
– ORIGIN Middle English: from Latin *effectus*, from *efficere* 'accomplish'.

USAGE
On the confusion of **effect** with **affect**, see AFFECT¹.

effective ■ adj. **1** producing a desired or intended result. **2** (of a law or policy) operative. **3** existing in fact, though not formally acknowledged as such.
– DERIVATIVES **effectively** adv. **effectiveness** n. **effectivity** n.

effective demand ■ n. Economics the level of demand that represents a real intention to purchase by people with the means to pay.

effector ■ n. Biology an organ or cell that acts in response to a stimulus.

effectual /ɪˈfɛktʃʊəl, -tjʊəl/ ■ adj. effective.
– DERIVATIVES **effectually** n. **effectually** adv. **effectualness** n.

effectuate /ɪˈfɛktʃʊeɪt, -tjʊ-/ ■ v. formal put into force or operation.
– DERIVATIVES **effectuation** n.

effeminate /ɪˈfɛmɪnət/ ■ adj. derogatory (of a man) having characteristics regarded as typical of a woman.
– DERIVATIVES **effeminacy** n. **effeminately** adv.
– ORIGIN Middle English: from Latin *effeminare* 'make feminine'.

effendi /ɛˈfɛndi/ ■ n. (pl. **effendis**) a man of high education or social standing in an eastern Mediterranean or Arab country.
– ORIGIN C17: from Turkish *efendi*, from modern Greek *aphentēs*, from Greek *authentēs* 'lord, master'.

efferent /ˈɛf(ə)r(ə)nt/ Physiology ■ adj. relating to or denoting the conduction of nerve impulses or blood outwards or away from something. The opposite of AFFERENT. ■ n. an efferent nerve fibre or blood vessel.
– ORIGIN C19: from Latin *efferre* 'carry out'.

effervescent ■ adj. **1** (of a liquid) giving off bubbles; fizzy. **2** vivacious and enthusiastic.
– DERIVATIVES **effervesce** v. **effervescence** n.
– ORIGIN C17: from Latin *effervescere* 'boil up'.

effete /ɪˈfiːt/ ■ adj. **1** affected, over-refined, and ineffectual. **2** no longer capable of effective action.
– DERIVATIVES **effetely** adv. **effeteness** n.
– ORIGIN C17: from Latin *effetus* 'worn out by bearing young'; rel. to FETUS.

efficacious /ˌɛfɪˈkeɪʃəs/ ■ adj. formal effective.
– DERIVATIVES **efficaciously** adv. **efficaciousness** n. **efficacy** /ˈɛfɪkəsi/ n.
– ORIGIN C16: from Latin *efficax, efficac-*, from *efficere* 'accomplish'.

efficiency ■ n. (pl. **-ies**) **1** the state or quality of being efficient. **2** technical the ratio of the useful work performed by a machine or in a process to the total energy expended or heat taken in.

efficient ■ adj. working productively with minimum wasted effort or expense.
– DERIVATIVES **efficiently** adv.
– ORIGIN Middle English: from Latin *efficere* 'accomplish'.

efficient cause ■ n. Philosophy an agent that brings a thing into being or initiates a change.

effigy /ˈɛfɪdʒi/ ■ n. (pl. **-ies**) a sculpture or model of a person.
– ORIGIN C16: from Latin *effigies*, from *effingere* 'to fashion (artistically)'.

effloresce /ˌɛfləˈrɛs/ ■ v. **1** (of a substance) lose moisture and turn to a fine powder on exposure to air. **2** (of salts) come to the surface of brickwork or other material and crystallize. ▸ (of a surface) become covered with salt particles. **3** reach an optimum stage of development.
– DERIVATIVES **efflorescence** n. **efflorescent** adj.
– ORIGIN C18: from Latin *efflorescere*, from *e-* (var. of *ex-*) 'out' + *florescere* 'begin to bloom'.

effluence /ˈɛflʊəns/ ■ n. **1** a substance that flows out. **2** the action of flowing out.
– ORIGIN Middle English: from medieval Latin *effluentia*, from Latin *effluent-, effluere* 'flow out'.

effluent ■ n. liquid waste or sewage discharged into a river or the sea.

effluvium /ɪˈfluːvɪəm/ ■ n. (pl. **effluvia** /-vɪə/) an unpleasant or harmful odour or discharge.
– ORIGIN C17: from Latin, from *effluere* 'flow out'.

effluxion /ɪˈflʌkʃ(ə)n/ ■ n. Law the passing of time.

effort ■ n. **1** a vigorous or determined attempt. ▸ strenuous physical or mental exertion. **2** technical a force exerted by a machine or in a process.
– DERIVATIVES **effortful** adj. **effortfully** adv.
– ORIGIN C15: from Old French *esforcier*, from Latin *ex-* 'out' + *fortis* 'strong'.

effortless ■ adj. requiring no effort. ▸ achieved with admirable ease.
– DERIVATIVES **effortlessly** adv. **effortlessness** n.

effrontery /ɪˈfrʌnt(ə)ri/ ■ n. insolence or impertinence.
– ORIGIN C17: from French *effronterie*, from late Latin *effrons, effront-* 'shameless, barefaced', from *ex-* 'out' + *frons* 'forehead'.

effulgent /ɪˈfʌldʒ(ə)nt/ ■ adj. poetic/literary shining brightly.
– DERIVATIVES **effulgence** n. **effulgently** adv.
– ORIGIN C18: from Latin *effulgere* 'shine brightly'.

effusion ■ n. **1** an instance of giving off a liquid, light, or smell. **2** Medicine an escape of fluid into a body cavity. **3** an instance of unrestrained speech or writing.
– DERIVATIVES **effuse** v.
– ORIGIN Middle English: from Latin *effusio(n-)*, from *effus-*, *effundere* 'pour out'.

effusive ■ adj. expressing gratitude, pleasure, or approval in an unrestrained manner.
– DERIVATIVES **effusively** adv. **effusiveness** n.

EFL ■ abbrev. English as a foreign language.

e.g. ■ abbrev. for example.
– ORIGIN from Latin *exempli gratia* 'for the sake of example'.

egad /ɪˈgad/ ■ exclam. archaic expressing surprise, anger, or affirmation.
– ORIGIN C17: representing earlier *A God*.

egalitarian /ɪˌgalɪˈtɛːrɪən/ ■ adj. believing in or based on the principle that all people are equal and deserve equal rights and opportunities. ■ n. an egalitarian person.
– DERIVATIVES **egalitarianism** n.
– ORIGIN C19: from French *égalitaire*, from *égal* 'equal', from Latin *aequalis* (see EQUAL).

egg[1] ■ n. **1** an oval or round object laid by a female bird, reptile, fish, or invertebrate and containing an ovum which if fertilized can develop into a new organism. ▸ an infertile egg, typically of the domestic hen, used for food. **2** informal, dated a person of a specified kind: *a thoroughly bad egg*. **3** Architecture a decorative oval moulding, used alternately with triangular figures.
– PHRASES **kill the goose that lays the golden eggs** destroy a reliable and valuable source of income. [with allusion to one of Aesop's fables.] **with egg on one's face** informal appearing foolish or ridiculous.
– DERIVATIVES **eggless** adj. **eggy** adj.
– ORIGIN Middle English: from Old Norse.

egg[2] ■ v. (**egg someone on**) urge or encourage someone to do something foolish or risky.
– ORIGIN Middle English: from Old Norse *eggja* 'incite'.

eggar /ˈɛgə/ ■ n. a large brownish moth which is often active during the day. [*Lasiocampa quercus* (oak eggar) and other species.]
– ORIGIN C18: prob. from EGG[1] (from the shape of the moth's cocoons).

egg-bound ■ adj. (of a hen) unable through weakness or disease to expel its eggs.

egg custard ■ n. a custard made with milk and eggs, typically sweetened and baked.

egg-eater ■ n. a non-venomous African snake which feeds exclusively on birds' eggs. [*Dasypeltis scabra* and other species.]

egghead ■ n. informal a very academic or studious person.

egg-nog (Brit. also **egg-flip**) ■ n. a drink consisting of wine or other alcohol mixed with beaten egg and milk.

eggplant ■ n. another term for BRINJAL.

egg roll ■ n. N. Amer. a Chinese-style snack similar to a spring roll, encased in a dough made with egg and deep-fried.

eggs Benedict ■ pl. n. a dish consisting of poached eggs and sliced ham on toast, covered with hollandaise sauce.

eggshell ■ n. **1** the thin, hard, fragile outer layer of an egg. **2** [as modifier] (of china) extremely thin and delicate. **3** [as modifier] denoting an oil-based paint that dries with a slight sheen.

egg timer ■ n. a device, traditionally a small hourglass, for timing the cooking of a boiled egg.

egg tooth ■ n. a hard white protuberance on the beak or jaw of an embryo bird or reptile, used for breaking out of the shell.

egg white ■ n. the clear, viscous substance round the yolk of an egg that turns white when cooked or beaten.

eglantine /ˈɛglənˌtʌɪn/ ■ n. another term for SWEETBRIAR.
– ORIGIN Middle English: from Old French *eglantine*, from Provençal *aiglentina*, from Latin *acus* 'needle' or *aculeus* 'prickle'.

ego /ˈiːgəʊ, ˈɛ-/ ■ n. (pl. **-os**) **1** a person's sense of self-esteem or self-importance. **2** Psychoanalysis the part of the mind that mediates between the conscious and the unconscious and is responsible for reality testing and a sense of personal identity. Compare with ID and SUPEREGO. **3** Philosophy (in metaphysics) a conscious thinking subject.
– DERIVATIVES **egoless** adj.
– ORIGIN C19: from Latin, 'I'.

egocentric /ˌɛgəʊˈsɛntrɪk, ˌiː-/ ■ adj. **1** self-centred. **2** centred in or arising from a person's own individual existence or perspective. ■ n. an egocentric person.
– DERIVATIVES **egocentrically** adv. **egocentricity** n. **egocentrism** n.

ego-ideal ■ n. Psychoanalysis (in Freudian theory) the part of the mind which imposes on itself concepts of ideal behaviour developed from parental and social standards.

egoism /ˈɛgəʊɪz(ə)m, ˈiː-/ ■ n. **1** an ethical theory that treats self-interest as the foundation of morality. **2** another term for EGOTISM.
– DERIVATIVES **egoist** n. **egoistic** adj. **egoistical** adj. **egoistically** adv.

egomania /ˌɛgə(ʊ)ˈmeɪnɪə, ˌiː-/ ■ n. obsessive egotism.
– DERIVATIVES **egomaniac** n. **egomaniacal** adj.

egotism /ˈɛgətɪz(ə)m, ˈiː-/ ■ n. the quality of being excessively conceited or absorbed in oneself.
– DERIVATIVES **egotist** n. **egotistic** adj. **egotistical** adj. **egotistically** adv. **egotize** (also **-ise**) v.

ego trip ■ n. informal something done to increase one's sense of self-importance.

egregious /ɪˈgriːdʒəs/ ■ adj. **1** outstandingly bad; shocking. **2** archaic remarkably good.
– DERIVATIVES **egregiously** adv. **egregiousness** n.
– ORIGIN C16: from Latin *egregius* 'illustrious', literally 'standing out from the flock', from *ex-* 'out' + *grex* 'flock'.

egress /ˈiːgrɛs/ ■ n. formal the action of going out of or leaving a place. ▸ a way out. ■ v. chiefly US go out of or leave (a place).
– DERIVATIVES **egression** n.
– ORIGIN C16: from Latin *egress-*, *egredi* 'go out'.

egret /ˈiːgrɪt, ˈɛ-/ ■ n. a heron with mainly white plumage, having long plumes in the breeding season. [Genus *Egretta* (and *Bubulcus*): several species.]
– ORIGIN Middle English: from Provençal *aigreta*, from the Germanic base of HERON.

Egyptian ■ n. **1** a native of ancient or modern Egypt, or a person of Egyptian descent. **2** the Afro-Asiatic language used in ancient Egypt, represented in its oldest stages by hieroglyphic inscriptions. ■ adj. of or relating to Egypt or its people or language.

Egyptian cobra ■ n. a large African cobra with a thick body and large head. [*Naja haje*.]

Egyptian goose ■ n. a common pale brown and grey African goose with dark brown eye patches. [*Alopochen aegyptiaca*.]

Egyptology /ˌiːdʒɪpˈtɒlədʒi/ ■ n. the study of the language, history, and culture of ancient Egypt.
– DERIVATIVES **Egyptological** adj. **Egyptologist** n.

Eid /iːd/ (also **Id**) ■ n. **1** (in full **Eid ul-Fitr** /ˌiːdʊlˈfɪtrə/) the Muslim festival marking the end of the fast of Ramadan. **2** (in full **Eid ul-Adha** /ˌiːdʊlˈɑːdə/) the festival marking the culmination of the annual pilgrimage to Mecca.
– ORIGIN from Arabic '*īd* 'feast', from Aramaic.

eider /ˈʌɪdə/ ■ n. (pl. same or **eiders**) **1** (also **eider duck**) a northern sea duck of which the male is mainly black-and-white and the female brown. [*Somateria mollissima* and related species.] **2** (also **eider down**) small, soft feathers from the breast of the female eider duck.
– ORIGIN C17: from Icelandic *æthur*, from Old Norse *æthr*.

eiderdown ■ n. chiefly Brit. a quilt filled with down (originally from the eider) or some other soft material.

eight ■ cardinal number **1** equivalent to the product of two and four; one more than seven, or two less than ten; 8. (Roman numeral: **viii** or **VIII**.) **2** an eight-oared rowing boat or its crew.
– PHRASES **have one over the eight** Brit. informal have one drink too many.
– DERIVATIVES **eightfold** adj. & adv.
– ORIGIN Old English; of Germanic origin.

eight ball ■ n. chiefly N. Amer. a variety of the game of pool.
– PHRASES **behind the eight ball** informal at a disadvantage.

eighteen ■ cardinal number equivalent to the product of two and nine; one more than seventeen, or eight more than ten; 18. (Roman numeral: **xviii** or **XVIII**.)
– DERIVATIVES **eighteenth** ordinal number.
– ORIGIN Old English.

eighth ■ ordinal number constituting number eight in a sequence; 8th.
– DERIVATIVES **eighthly** adv.

eighthman ■ n. S. African Rugby a number eight forward.

eights ■ pl. n. a race for eight-oared rowing boats.

eightsome reel ■ n. a lively Scottish dance for eight people.

eighty ■ cardinal number (pl. **-ies**) equivalent to the product of eight and ten; ten less than ninety; 80. (Roman numeral: **lxxx** or **LXXX**.)
– DERIVATIVES **eightieth** ordinal number. **eightyfold** adj. & adv.
– ORIGIN Old English *hunde(a)htatig, from hund* (of uncertain origin) + *e(a)hta* 'eight' + *-tig* '-ty'.

eina /'eɪnɑː/ S. African ■ exclam. used as an expression of pain or distress. ■ n. pain or trouble.
– ORIGIN Afrikaans, perhaps from Khoikhoi /*é* + //*náu* or Nama *llei*.

einsteinium /ʌɪnˈstʌɪnɪəm/ ■ n. the chemical element of atomic number 99, an artificially made radioactive metal of the actinide series. (Symbol: **Es**)

eirenic /ʌɪˈrɛnɪk, -ˈriː-/ (also **irenic**) ■ adj. formal aiming or aimed at peace.
– DERIVATIVES **eirenical** adj.
– ORIGIN C19: from Greek *eirēnikos*, from *eirēnē* 'peace'.

eish /eɪʃ/ or **eiʃ**/ (also **aish** or **heish** /heɪʃ/) S. African ■ exclam. used to express a range of emotions including surprise, annoyance, or pain.
– ORIGIN 1990s: from Tsotsitaal.

eisteddfod /ʌɪˈstɛdvəd, Welsh ʌɪˈstɛWʊdd/ ■ n. (pl. **eisteddfods** or **eisteddfodau** /-ˈvɒdʌɪ/) a competitive festival of music and poetry, originating from Wales.
– ORIGIN Welsh, 'session', from *eistedd* 'sit'.

Eiswein /ˈʌɪsvʌɪn/ ■ n. (pl. **Eisweine** /-nə/ or **Eisweins**) wine made from ripe grapes picked while covered with frost.
– ORIGIN from German, from *Eis* 'ice' + *Wein* 'wine'.

either /ˈʌɪðə, ˈiː-/ ■ conj. & adv. 1 used before the first of two (or occasionally more) alternatives specified (the other being introduced by 'or'). 2 [adv. , with neg.] used to indicate a similarity or link with a statement just made.
▸ moreover. ■ det. & pron. one or the other of two people or things. ▸ each of two.
– ORIGIN Old English, of Germanic origin.

eiusdem generis /ˌeɪˌ(j)ʊsdəm ˈdʒɛnɛrɪs/ ■ adj. variant spelling of **EJUSDEM GENERIS**.

ejaculate ■ v. /ɪˈdʒakjʊleɪt/ 1 (of a man or male animal) eject semen from the body at the moment of sexual climax. 2 dated say something quickly and suddenly. ■ n. /ɪˈdʒakjʊlət/ semen that has been ejaculated.
– DERIVATIVES **ejaculation** n. **ejaculator** n. **ejaculatory** /ɪˈdʒakjʊlət(ə)ri/ adj.
– ORIGIN C16: from Latin *ejaculari* 'dart out', ultimately from *iacere* 'to throw'.

eject ■ v. force or throw out violently or suddenly. ▸ (of a pilot) escape from an aircraft by means of an ejection seat. ▸ compel (someone) to leave a place.
– DERIVATIVES **ejection** n. **ejector** n.
– ORIGIN Middle English: from Latin *eicere* 'throw out', from *e-* (var. of *ex-*) 'out' + *jacere* 'to throw'.

ejecta /ɪˈdʒɛktə/ ■ pl. n. [often treated as sing.] chiefly Geology & Astronomy material that is forced or thrown out, especially as a result of volcanic eruption or meteoritic impact.
– ORIGIN C19: from Latin, 'things thrown out', from *ejectus*, from *eicere* (see **EJECT**).

ejection seat (also **ejector seat**) ■ n. an aircraft seat that can propel its occupant from the craft in an emergency.

ejective /ɪˈdʒɛktɪv/ Phonetics ■ adj. denoting a type of consonant in some languages (e.g. Hausa) produced by sudden release of pressure from the glottis. ■ n. an ejective consonant.

ejusdem generis /eɪˌ(j)ʊsdəm ˈdʒɛnɛrɪs/ (also **eiusdem generis**) ■ adj. & adv. Law of or as the same kind.
– ORIGIN from Latin.

ekasi /ɛˈkɑːsi/ (also **ekasie**) S. African informal ■ adv. in, to, or from the township.
– ORIGIN from Nguni locative prefix *e-* + Tsotsitaal *kasi* 'township'.

eke¹ /iːk/ ■ v. (**eke something out**) make something last longer by using or consuming it frugally. ▸ manage to make a living with difficulty: *eke out a living*.
– ORIGIN Old English *ēacian, ēcan* (in the sense 'increase'), of Germanic origin.

eke² /iːk/ ■ adv. archaic term for **ALSO**.
– ORIGIN Old English, of Germanic origin.

EL ■ abbrev. (in South Africa) East London.

-el ■ suffix variant spelling of **-LE²**.

elaborate ■ adj. /ɪˈlab(ə)rət/ involving many carefully arranged parts; detailed and complicated. ■ v. /ɪˈlabəreɪt/ develop or present in further detail. ▸ (often **elaborate on**) add more detail to something already said.
– DERIVATIVES **elaborately** adv. **elaborateness** n. **elaboration** n. **elaborative** adj. **elaborator** n.
– ORIGIN C16 (*elaboration* Middle English): from Latin *elaborare* 'work out'.

elan /eɪˈlɒ̃, eɪˈlan/ ■ n. energy, style, and enthusiasm.
– ORIGIN C19: from French *élan*, from *élancer* 'to dart'.

eland /ˈiːlənd/ ■ n. a spiral-horned African antelope, the largest of the antelopes. [*Tragelaphus oryx* and *T. derbianus*.]
– ORIGIN C18: from Dutch, 'elk'.

elapse ■ v. (of time) pass.
– ORIGIN C16: from Latin *elaps-, elabi* 'slip away'.

elasmobranch /ɪˈlazmə(ʊ)braŋk/ ■ n. Zoology a cartilaginous fish of a group (subclass Elasmobranchii) that comprises the sharks, rays, and skates.
– ORIGIN C19: from Greek *elasmos* 'beaten metal' + *brankhia* 'gills'.

elastane /ɪˈlasteɪn/ ■ n. an elastic polyurethane material, used for close-fitting clothing.

elastase /ɪˈlasteɪz/ ■ n. Biochemistry a pancreatic enzyme which digests elastin.

elastic /ɪˈlastɪk/ ■ adj. 1 able to resume normal shape spontaneously after being stretched or squeezed. 2 flexible and adaptable: *the definition is elastic*. ▸ Economics (of demand or supply) sensitive to changes in price or income. 3 Physics (of a collision) involving no decrease of kinetic energy. ■ n. cord, tape, or fabric which returns to its original length or shape after being stretched.
– DERIVATIVES **elastically** adv. **elasticity** /ɛlaˈstɪsɪti, iː-, ɪ-/ n. **elasticize** (also **-ise**) v.
– ORIGIN C17: from modern Latin *elasticus*, from Greek *elastikos* 'propulsive'.

elasticated ■ adj. chiefly Brit. (of a garment or material) made elastic by the insertion of rubber thread or tape.

elastic band ■ n. a rubber band.

elastic limit ■ n. Physics the maximum extent to which a solid can be stretched without permanent alteration of size or shape.

elastic modulus ■ n. Physics the ratio of the force exerted upon a substance or body to the resultant deformation.

elastin /ɪˈlastɪn/ ■ n. Biochemistry an elastic, fibrous glycoprotein found in connective tissue.

elastomer /ɪˈlastəmə/ ■ n. a natural or synthetic polymer having elastic properties, e.g. rubber.
– DERIVATIVES **elastomeric** adj.

Elastoplast /ɪˈlastəplast, -plɑːst/ ■ n. trademark adhesive sticking plaster for covering cuts and wounds.

elate /ɪˈleɪt/ ■ v. [usu. as adj. **elated**] make ecstatically happy.
– DERIVATIVES **elatedly** adv. **elatedness** n.
– ORIGIN Middle English: from Latin *elat-, efferre* 'to raise'.

elation ■ n. great happiness and exhilaration.

E-layer ■ n. a layer of the ionosphere able to reflect medium-frequency radio waves.
– ORIGIN 1930s: arbitrary use of the letter *E*.

elbow ■ n. **1** the joint between the forearm and the upper arm. **2** a piece of piping or something similar bent through an angle. ■ v. **1** strike with one's elbow. ▸ (often **elbow one's way**) move by pushing past people with one's elbows. **2** informal summarily reject or dismiss.
– PHRASES **give someone the elbow** informal summarily reject or dismiss someone. **up to one's elbows in** informal deeply involved in.
– ORIGIN Old English, of Germanic origin.

elbow grease ■ n. informal hard physical work, especially vigorous polishing or cleaning.

elbow room ■ n. informal adequate space to move or work in.

elder[1] ■ adj. (of one or more out of a group of people) of a greater age. ■ n. **1** (**one's elder**) a person of greater age than one. **2** a leader or senior figure in a tribe. **3** an official in the early Christian Church, or of various Protestant Churches and sects.
– ORIGIN Old English, of Germanic origin.

elder[2] ■ n. a small tree or shrub with white flowers and bluish-black or red berries. [*Sambucus nigra* and related species.] ▸ used in names of other plants resembling this, e.g. ground elder.
– ORIGIN Old English.

elderberry ■ n. the berry of the elder, used for making jelly or wine. ▸ an elder tree or shrub.

elderflower ■ n. the flower of the elder, used to make wines and cordials.

elderly ■ adj. old or ageing.
– DERIVATIVES **elderliness** n.

elder statesman ■ n. an experienced and respected politician or other public figure.

eldest ■ adj. (of one out of a group of people) oldest.
– ORIGIN Old English, of Germanic origin.

El Dorado /ˌɛl dəˈrɑːdəʊ/ (also **eldorado**) ■ n. (pl. **-os**) a place of great abundance and wealth.
– ORIGIN Spanish, 'the gilded one', the name of a country or city formerly believed to exist in South America.

eldritch /ˈɛl(d)rɪtʃ/ ■ adj. weird and sinister or ghostly.
– ORIGIN C16 (orig. Scots).

elecampane /ˌɛlɪkamˈpeɪn/ ■ n. an Asian plant with yellow daisy-like flowers and bitter aromatic roots that are used in herbal medicine. [*Inula helenium*.]
– ORIGIN Middle English: from medieval Latin *enula* 'elecampane' + *campana* (prob. meaning 'of the fields').

elect /ɪˈlɛkt/ ■ v. **1** choose (someone) to hold a position, especially public office, by voting. **2** opt for or choose to do something. **3** Christian Church (of God) choose (someone) in preference to others for salvation. ■ adj. **1** chosen or singled out. ▸ Christian Church chosen by God for salvation. **2** [postpos.] elected to a position but not yet in office: *the President Elect.*
– DERIVATIVES **electable** adj.
– ORIGIN Middle English: from Latin *elect-*, *eligere* 'pick out'.

election ■ n. **1** a formal procedure whereby a person is elected, especially to a political office. **2** the action or fact of electing or being elected.

electioneer ■ v. [usu. as noun **electioneering**] campaign to be elected to public office. ■ n. a campaigning politician during an election.

elective ■ adj. **1** relating to or appointed by election. **2** (of a course of study) chosen by the student rather than compulsory. ▸ (of surgical or medical treatment) chosen by the patient rather than urgently necessary. ■ n. chiefly N. Amer. an optional course of study.
– DERIVATIVES **electively** adv.

elector ■ n. **1** a person who has the right to vote in an election. ▸ (in the US) a member of the electoral college. **2** historical a German prince entitled to take part in the election of the Holy Roman Emperor.
– DERIVATIVES **electorship** n.

electoral ■ adj. of or relating to elections or electors.
– DERIVATIVES **electorally** adv.

electoral college ■ n. a body of electors chosen or appointed by a larger group. ▸ (in the US) a body of people representing the states of the US, who formally cast votes for the election of the President and Vice-President.

electrochemistry

electoral roll (also **electoral register**) ■ n. another term for VOTERS' ROLL.

electorate /ɪˈlɛkt(ə)rət/ ■ n. **1** [treated as sing. or pl.] all the people in a country or area who are entitled to vote in an election. **2** Austral./NZ the area represented by one Member of Parliament. **3** historical the office or territories of a German elector.

Electra complex ■ n. Psychoanalysis old-fashioned term for the Oedipus complex as manifested in young girls.
– ORIGIN C20: named after *Electra* in Greek mythology, who persuaded her brother to kill their mother in revenge for the murder of their father.

electric /ɪˈlɛktrɪk/ ■ adj. **1** of, worked by, or producing electricity. **2** thrillingly exciting: *the atmosphere was electric.* ■ n. (**electrics**) Brit. the system of electric wiring and parts in a house or vehicle.
– DERIVATIVES **electrically** adv.
– ORIGIN C17: from modern Latin *electricus*, from Latin *electrum* 'amber', from Greek *ēlektron* (because rubbing amber causes electrostatic phenomena).

electrical ■ adj. concerned with, operating by, or producing electricity. ■ n. (**electricals**) electrical equipment or circuitry.

electric-arc furnace ■ n. a furnace using an electric arc as a heat source, especially for steel-making.

electric blanket ■ n. an electrically wired blanket used for heating a bed.

electric blue ■ n. a steely or brilliant light blue.

electric chair ■ n. a chair in which convicted criminals are executed by electrocution.

electric eel ■ n. a large eel-like freshwater fish of South America, using pulses of electricity to kill prey, assist in navigation, and for defence. [*Electrophorus electricus.*]

electric eye ■ n. informal a photoelectric cell operating a relay when the beam of light illuminating it is obscured.

electric fence ■ n. a fence through which an electric current can be passed, giving an electric shock to any person or animal touching it.

electric guitar ■ n. a guitar with a built-in pickup or pickups which convert sound vibrations into electrical signals for amplification.

electrician ■ n. a person who installs and maintains electrical equipment.

electricity /ˌɪlɛkˈtrɪsɪti, ˌɛl-, ˌiːl-/ ■ n. **1** a form of energy resulting from the existence of charged particles (such as electrons or protons), either statically as an accumulation of charge or dynamically as a current. **2** the supply of electric current to a building for heating, lighting, etc. **3** thrilling excitement.

electric ray ■ n. a sluggish bottom-dwelling marine ray that can produce an electric shock for the capture of prey and for defence. [*Torpedo* and other genera: many species.]

electric shock ■ n. a sudden discharge of electricity through a part of the body.

electric storm ■ n. a thunderstorm or other violent disturbance of the electrical condition of the atmosphere.

electrify /ɪˈlɛktrɪfʌɪ/ ■ v. (**-ies**, **-ied**) **1** charge with electricity. **2** convert to the use of electrical power. **3** (often as adj. **electrifying**) cause a sense of thrilling excitement in.
– DERIVATIVES **electrification** n. **electrifier** n.

electro /ɪˈlɛktrəʊ/ ■ n. (pl. **-os**) **1** short for ELECTROPLATE. **2** a style of dance music with a fast beat and synthesized backing track.

electro- ■ comb. form of, involving, or caused by electricity: *electroconvulsive.*

electro-acoustic ■ adj. **1** involving the interconversion of electrical and acoustic energy. **2** denoting a guitar with both a pickup and a reverberating hollow body.

electrocardiography /ɪˌlɛktrəʊˌkɑːdɪˈɒɡrəfi/ ■ n. the measurement and recording of electrical activity in the heart using electrodes placed on the skin.
– DERIVATIVES **electrocardiogram** n. **electrocardiograph** n. **electrocardiographic** adj.

electrochemistry ■ n. the branch of chemistry

electroconvulsive

concerned with the relations between electrical and chemical phenomena.
- DERIVATIVES **electrochemical** adj. **electrochemically** adv. **electrochemist** n.

electroconvulsive ■ adj. relating to or denoting the treatment of mental illness by applying electric shocks to the brain.

electrocorticogram /ɪˌlɛktrə(ʊ)ˈkɔːtɪkə(ʊ)gram/ ■ n. Physiology a record of the electrical activity of the brain made directly using electrodes.

electrocute ■ v. (often **be electrocuted**) injure or kill by electric shock.
- DERIVATIVES **electrocution** n.
- ORIGIN C19: from ELECTRO-, on the pattern of *execute*.

electrode /ɪˈlɛktrəʊd/ ■ n. a conductor through which electricity enters or leaves something.
- ORIGIN C19: from ELECTRIC + Greek *hodos* 'way', on the pattern of *anode* and *cathode*.

electrodynamics ■ pl. n. [usu. treated as sing.] the branch of mechanics concerned with the interaction of electric currents with magnetic or electric fields.
- DERIVATIVES **electrodynamic** adj.

electroencephalography /ɪˌlɛktrəʊɪnˌsɛfəˈlɒgrəfi, -ˌkɛf-/ ■ n. the measurement and recording of electrical activity in different parts of the brain.
- DERIVATIVES **electroencephalogram** n. **electroencephalograph** n.

electrojet ■ n. an intense electric current occurring in the lower ionosphere in the region of strong auroral displays.

electroluminescence /ɪˌlɛktrəʊluːmɪˈnɛs(ə)ns/ ■ n. luminescence produced by the application of a voltage.
- DERIVATIVES **electroluminescent** adj.

electrolyse /ɪˈlɛktrəlʌɪz/ (US **electrolyze**) ■ v. subject to electrolysis.
- DERIVATIVES **electrolyser** n.

electrolysis /ˌɪlɛkˈtrɒlɪsɪs, ˌɛl-/ ■ n. 1 Chemistry chemical decomposition produced by passing an electric current through a conducting liquid. 2 the removal of hair roots or small blemishes on the skin by the application of heat using an electric current.
- DERIVATIVES **electrolytic** /ɪˌlɛktrə(ʊ)ˈlɪtɪk/ adj. **electrolytical** adj. **electrolytically** adv.

electrolyte /ɪˈlɛktrəlʌɪt/ ■ n. 1 a liquid or gel which contains ions and can be decomposed by electrolysis, e.g. that present in a battery. 2 Physiology the ionic constituents of cells, blood, etc.
- ORIGIN C19: from ELECTRO- + Greek *lutos* 'released', from *luein* 'loosen'.

electromagnet ■ n. Physics a soft metal core made into a magnet by the passage of electric current through a surrounding coil.

electromagnetic ■ adj. of or relating to the interrelation of electric currents or fields and magnetic fields.
- DERIVATIVES **electromagnetically** adv. **electromagnetism** n.

electromagnetic radiation ■ n. Physics a kind of radiation including visible light, radio waves, gamma rays, and X-rays, in which electric and magnetic fields vary simultaneously.

electromechanical /ɪˌlɛktrəʊmɪˈkanɪk(ə)l/ ■ adj. relating to or denoting a mechanical device which is electrically operated.

electrometer /ˌɪlɛkˈtrɒmɪtə/ ■ n. Physics an instrument for measuring electrical potential without drawing any current from the circuit.
- DERIVATIVES **electrometric** adj. **electrometry** n.

electromotive /ɪˌlɛktrəˈməʊtɪv/ ■ adj. Physics tending to produce an electric current.

electromotive force ■ n. Physics a difference in potential that tends to give rise to an electric current.

electromyography /ɪˌlɛktrə(ʊ)mʌɪˈɒgrəfi/ ■ n. Medicine the recording of the electrical activity of muscle tissue by means of electrodes.
- DERIVATIVES **electromyogram** n. **electromyograph** n. **electromyographic** adj. **electromyographically** adv.

electron /ɪˈlɛktrɒn/ ■ n. Physics a stable negatively charged subatomic particle with a mass 1 836 times less than that of the proton, found in all atoms and acting as the primary carrier of electricity in solids.
- ORIGIN C19: from ELECTRIC.

electronegative ■ adj. 1 Physics electrically negative. 2 Chemistry (of an element) tending to acquire electrons and form negative ions in chemical reactions.
- DERIVATIVES **electronegativity** n.

electronic ■ adj. 1 having components such as microchips and transistors that control and direct electric currents. 2 (of music) produced by electronic instruments. 3 of or relating to electrons or electronics. 4 carried out using a computer, especially over a network: *electronic shopping*.
- DERIVATIVES **electronically** adv.
- ORIGIN C20: from ELECTRON.

electronic mail ■ n. another term for EMAIL.

electronic publishing ■ n. the issuing of texts in machine-readable form rather than on paper.

electronics ■ pl. n. 1 [usu. treated as sing.] the branch of physics and technology concerned with the behaviour and movement of electrons, especially in semiconductors and gases. 2 [treated as pl.] circuits or devices using transistors, microchips, etc.

electron microscope ■ n. Physics a microscope with high magnification and resolution, employing electron beams in place of light.

electronvolt ■ n. Physics a unit of energy equal to the work done on an electron in accelerating it through a potential difference of one volt.

electro-optics ■ pl. n. [treated as sing.] the branch of science concerned with the effect of electric fields on light and optics.
- DERIVATIVES **electro-optic** adj. **electro-optical** adj.

electrophilic /ɪˌlɛktrə(ʊ)ˈfɪlɪk/ ■ adj. Chemistry having a tendency to attract or acquire electrons. Often contrasted with NUCLEOPHILIC.
- DERIVATIVES **electrophile** n.

electrophoresis /ɪˌlɛktrə(ʊ)fəˈriːsɪs/ ■ n. Physics & Chemistry the movement of charged particles in a fluid or gel under the influence of an electric field.
- DERIVATIVES **electrophoretic** adj. **electrophoretically** adv.
- ORIGIN C20: from ELECTRO- + Greek *phorēsis* 'being carried'.

electrophorus /ˌɪlɛkˈtrɒf(ə)rəs, ɛl-/ ■ n. Physics a device for repeatedly generating static electricity by induction.
- ORIGIN C18: from ELECTRO- + Greek *-phoros* 'bearing'.

electrophysiology /ɪˌlɛktrəʊfɪzɪˈɒlədʒi/ ■ n. the branch of physiology concerned with electrical phenomena such as nerve impulses.
- DERIVATIVES **electrophysiological** adj. **electrophysiologically** adv. **electrophysiologist** n.

electroplate /ɪˈlɛktrə(ʊ)pleɪt, ɪˌlɛktrə(ʊ)ˈpleɪt/ ■ v. [usu. as noun **electroplating**] coat (a metal object) by electrolytic deposition with another metal. ■ n. electroplated articles.
- DERIVATIVES **electroplater** n.

electropositive ■ adj. 1 Physics electrically positive. 2 Chemistry (of an element) tending to lose electrons and form positive ions in chemical reactions.

electroscope ■ n. Physics an instrument for detecting and measuring electric charge, especially as an indication of the ionization of air by radioactivity.
- DERIVATIVES **electroscopic** adj.

electroshock ■ adj. another term for ELECTROCONVULSIVE.

electrostatic ■ adj. Physics of or relating to stationary electric charges or fields as opposed to electric currents.
- DERIVATIVES **electrostatics** pl. n.
- ORIGIN C19: from ELECTRO- + STATIC, on the pattern of *hydrostatic*.

electrotherapy ■ n. the use of electric currents passed through the body to treat paralysis and other disorders.
- DERIVATIVES **electrotherapeutic** adj. **electrotherapeutical** adj. **electrotherapist** n.

electrovalent /ɪˌlɛktrə(ʊ)ˈveɪl(ə)nt/ ■ adj. Chemistry (of bonding) ionic.
- DERIVATIVES **electrovalence** n. **electrovalency** n.

–ORIGIN 1920s: from **ELECTRO-** + -*valent*, on the pattern of *trivalent*.

electroweak ■ adj. Physics relating to or denoting electromagnetic and weak interactions regarded as manifestations of the same interaction.

electrum /ɪˈlɛktrəm/ ■ n. an alloy of gold with at least 20 per cent of silver, used for jewellery.
–ORIGIN Middle English: from Greek *ēlektron* 'amber, electrum'.

eleemosynary /ˌɛliːˈmɒsɪnəri, -ˈmɒz-/ ■ adj. formal charitable.
–ORIGIN C16: from late Latin *eleemosyna* 'alms', from Greek *eleēmosunē* (see **ALMS**).

elegant ■ adj. **1** graceful and stylish. **2** pleasingly ingenious and simple.
–DERIVATIVES **elegance** n. **elegantly** adv.
–ORIGIN C15: from Latin *elegans*, rel. to *eligere* (see **ELECT**).

elegiac /ˌɛlɪˈdʒʌɪək/ ■ adj. of, relating to, or characteristic of an elegy. ▸ wistfully mournful. ■ n. (**elegiacs**) verses in an elegiac metre.
–DERIVATIVES **elegiacally** adv.

elegize /ˈɛlɪdʒʌɪz/ (also **-ise**) ■ v. write elegiacally.
–DERIVATIVES **elegist** n.

elegy /ˈɛlɪdʒi/ ■ n. (pl. **-ies**) a mournful poem, typically a lament for the dead.
–ORIGIN C16: from Greek *elegeia*, from *elegos* 'mournful poem'.

element ■ n. **1** a basic constituent part. ▸ an aspect: *an element of danger*. ▸ a group of a particular kind within a larger group: *right-wing elements*. **2** (also **chemical element**) each of more than one hundred substances that cannot be chemically interconverted or broken down, each consisting of atoms with the same atomic number. **3** any of the four substances (earth, water, air, and fire) regarded as the fundamental constituents of the world in ancient and medieval philosophy. **4** (**the elements**) the weather, especially bad weather. **5** one's natural or preferred environment: *she was in her element*. **6** a part in an electric device consisting of a wire through which an electric current is passed to provide heat.
–ORIGIN Middle English: from Latin *elementum* 'principle, rudiment'.

elemental /ˌɛlɪˈmɛnt(ə)l/ ■ adj. **1** fundamental. **2** concerned with chemical elements. ▸ denoting uncombined chemical elements: *elemental sulphur*. **3** (of action or emotion) basic and primitive. ■ n. a supernatural entity or force thought to be physically manifested by occult means.
–DERIVATIVES **elementalism** n.

elementary ■ adj. **1** of or relating to the most rudimentary aspects of a subject; introductory. ▸ simple. **2** not decomposable into elements or other primary constituents.
–DERIVATIVES **elementarily** adv. **elementariness** n.

elementary school ■ n. a primary school, especially (N. Amer.) for the first six or eight grades.

elephant ■ n. (pl. same or **elephants**) a very large plant-eating mammal with a prehensile trunk, long curved ivory tusks, and large ears. [*Loxodonta africana* (African elephant, Africa) and *Elephas maximus* (Indian elephant, southern Asia).]
–ORIGIN Middle English: from Greek *elephas*, *elephant-* 'ivory, elephant'.

elephant bird ■ n. an aepyornis or related extinct giant bird.

elephant fish ■ n. (pl. same or **-fishes**) a cartilaginous marine fish with a trunk-like snout. [*Callorhinchus capensis* and other species.]

elephant grass ■ n. a very tall robust tropical African grass. [*Pennisetum purpureum*.]

elephantiasis /ˌɛlɪf(ə)nˈtʌɪəsɪs/ ■ n. Medicine a condition in which the limbs become grossly enlarged due to obstruction of the lymphatic vessels, especially by nematode parasites.
–ORIGIN C16: from Greek, from *elephas*, *elephant-* 'elephant'.

elephantine /ˌɛlɪˈfantʌɪn/ ■ adj. of, resembling, or characteristic of an elephant, especially in being large or clumsy.

elephant seal ■ n. a large seal that breeds on the west coast of North America and around Antarctica, the male of which has a very thick neck and an inflatable snout. [Genus *Mirounga*: two species.]

elephant shrew ■ n. a small insectivorous African mammal with a long mobile snout, long hindlimbs, and a rat-like tail. [Family Macroscelididae: many species.]

elevate /ˈɛlɪveɪt/ ■ v. lift to a higher position. ▸ raise to a higher level or status. ▸ Military raise the axis of (a piece of artillery) to increase its range.
–DERIVATIVES **elevated** adj. **elevatory** adj.
–ORIGIN Middle English: from Latin *elevare* 'to raise'.

elevation ■ n. **1** the action or fact of elevating or being elevated. **2** height above a given level, especially sea level. ▸ the angle of something with the horizontal. **3** Ballet the ability of a dancer to attain height in jumps. **4** a particular side of a building. ▸ a scale drawing showing the vertical projection of one side of a building.
–DERIVATIVES **elevational** adj.

elevator ■ n. **1** North American term for **LIFT** (in sense 1). **2** a hinged flap on the tailplane of an aircraft, used to control pitch. **3** a muscle whose contraction raises a part of the body. **4** a machine consisting of an endless belt with scoops attached, used for raising grain. ▸ N. Amer. a tall building used for storing grain.

eleven ■ cardinal number **1** equivalent to the sum of six and five; one more than ten; 11. (Roman numeral: **xi** or **XI**.) **2** a sports team of eleven players: *the first eleven*.
–DERIVATIVES **elevenfold** adj. & adv.
–ORIGIN Old English, of Germanic origin.

elevenses ■ pl. n. Brit. informal a break for light refreshments taken at about eleven o'clock in the morning.

eleventh ■ ordinal number constituting number eleven in a sequence; 11th.
–PHRASES **the eleventh hour** the latest possible moment.

elf[1] ■ n. (pl. **elves**) a supernatural creature of folk tales, represented as a small, delicate human figure with pointed ears and a capricious nature.
–DERIVATIVES **elfish** adj. **elven** adj. (poetic/literary) **elvish** adj.
–ORIGIN Old English, of Germanic origin.

elf[2] ■ n. (pl. same) S. African another term for **BLUEFISH**.

elfin ■ adj. of or resembling an elf.

elicit /ɪˈlɪsɪt/ ■ v. (**elicited**, **eliciting**) evoke or draw out (a response or answer).
–DERIVATIVES **elicitation** n. **elicitor** n.
–ORIGIN C17: from Latin *elicere* 'to draw out by trickery'.

elide /ɪˈlʌɪd/ ■ v. **1** [often as adj. **elided**] omit (a sound or syllable) when speaking. **2** join together; merge.
–ORIGIN C16: from Latin *elidere* 'crush out'.

eligible /ˈɛlɪdʒɪb(ə)l/ ■ adj. **1** (often **eligible for/to do something**) satisfying the appropriate conditions. **2** desirable as a spouse: *an eligible bachelor*.
–DERIVATIVES **eligibility** n. **eligibly** adv.
–ORIGIN Middle English: from late Latin *eligibilis*, from Latin *eligere* (see **ELECT**).

eliminate /ɪˈlɪmɪneɪt/ ■ v. **1** completely remove or get rid of. ▸ reject or exclude from consideration or further participation. **2** Chemistry generate (a simple substance) as a product in the course of a reaction involving larger molecules.
–DERIVATIVES **eliminable** adj. **elimination** n. **eliminator** n. **eliminatory** adj.
–ORIGIN C16: from Latin *eliminare* 'to turn out of doors'.

ELISA /ɪˈlʌɪzə/ ■ n. Biochemistry enzyme-linked immunosorbent assay, an immunological assay technique making use of an enzyme bonded to a particular antibody or antigen.

elision /ɪˈlɪʒ(ə)n/ ■ n. **1** the omission of a sound or syllable in speech. **2** the process of joining or merging things.
–ORIGIN C16: from late Latin *elisio(n-)*, from Latin *elidere* 'crush out'.

elite /eɪˈliːt, ɪ-/ ■ n. a group of people considered to be superior in a particular society or organization.
–ORIGIN C18: from French *élite* 'selection, choice'.

elitism ■ n. **1** the belief that a society or system should be

elixir

run by an elite. **2** the superior attitude or behaviour associated with an elite.
– DERIVATIVES **elitist** adj. & n.

elixir /ɪˈlɪksə, -sɪə/ ■ n. a magical or medicinal potion, especially (in former times) either one supposedly able to change metals into gold or (also called **elixir of life**) supposedly able to prolong life indefinitely.
– ORIGIN Middle English: from Arabic *al-'iksīr*, from *al* 'the' + *'iksīr*, from Greek *xērion* 'powder for drying wounds'.

Elizabethan /ɪˌlɪzəˈbiːθ(ə)n/ ■ adj. of, relating to, or characteristic of the reign of Queen Elizabeth I of England. ■ n. a person, especially a writer, of the Elizabethan age.

elk /ɛlk/ ■ n. (pl. same or **elks**) a large northern deer with palmate antlers and a growth of skin hanging from the neck. Called **MOOSE** in North America. [*Alces alces*.]
– ORIGIN C15: prob. from Old English *elh, eolh*, with substitution of *k* for *h*.

ellipse /ɪˈlɪps/ ■ n. a regular oval shape, traced by a point moving in a plane so that the sum of its distances from two other points (the foci) is constant, or resulting when a cone is cut by an oblique plane which does not intersect the base.
– ORIGIN C17: from Latin *ellipsis* (see **ELLIPSIS**).

ellipsis /ɪˈlɪpsɪs/ ■ n. (pl. **ellipses** /-siːz/) the omission of words from speech or writing. ▸ a set of dots indicating such an omission.
– ORIGIN C16: from Greek *elleipsis*, from *elleipein* 'leave out'.

elliptic ■ adj. of, relating to, or having the form of an ellipse.
– DERIVATIVES **ellipticity** n.

elliptical ■ adj. **1** another term for **ELLIPTIC**. **2** (of speech or text) using or involving ellipsis, especially so as to be difficult to understand.
– DERIVATIVES **elliptically** adv.

elm ■ n. a tall deciduous tree with rough serrated leaves. [*Ulmus procera* (English elm) and related species.]
– DERIVATIVES **elmy** adj.
– ORIGIN Old English, of Germanic origin.

El Niño /ɛl ˈniːnjəʊ/ ■ n. (pl. **-os**) an irregularly occurring and complex series of climatic changes affecting the equatorial Pacific region and beyond every few years, characterized by the appearance of unusually warm, nutrient-poor water off northern Peru and Ecuador.
– ORIGIN Spanish, 'the (Christ) child', because of its occurrence around Christmas time.

elocution /ˌɛləˈkjuːʃ(ə)n/ ■ n. the skill of clear and expressive speech, especially of distinct pronunciation and articulation. ▸ a particular style of speaking.
– DERIVATIVES **elocutionary** adj. **elocutionist** n.
– ORIGIN Middle English: from Latin *elocutio(n)-*, from *eloqui* (see **ELOQUENCE**).

elongate /ˈiːlɒŋɡeɪt/ ■ v. [usu. as adj. **elongated**] make or become longer. ■ adj. chiefly Biology long; elongated.
– ORIGIN Middle English: from late Latin *elongare* 'to place at a distance'.

elongation ■ n. the lengthening of something.
– ORIGIN Middle English: from late Latin *elongatio(n)-*, from *elongare* (see **ELONGATE**).

elope ■ v. run away secretly in order to get married.
– DERIVATIVES **elopement** n. **eloper** n.
– ORIGIN C16 ('abscond, run away'): from Anglo-Norman French *aloper*.

eloquence /ˈɛləkwəns/ ■ n. fluent or persuasive speaking or writing.
– ORIGIN Middle English: from Latin *eloquentia*, from *eloqui* 'speak out'.

eloquent ■ adj. **1** showing eloquence. **2** clearly expressive.
– DERIVATIVES **eloquently** adv.

else ■ adv. **1** in addition; besides. **2** different; instead.
– PHRASES **or else** used to introduce the second of two alternatives. ▸ in circumstances different from those mentioned. ▸ used as a threat or warning.
– ORIGIN Old English, of Germanic origin.

elsewhere ■ adv. in, at, or to some other place or other places. ■ pron. some other place.
– ORIGIN Old English (see **ELSE**, **WHERE**).

ELT ■ abbrev. English language teaching.

eluate /ˈɛljuːət, -eɪt/ ■ n. Chemistry a solution obtained by elution.
– ORIGIN 1930s: from Latin *eluere* 'wash out'.

elucidate /ɪˈl(j)uːsɪdeɪt/ ■ v. make clear; explain.
– DERIVATIVES **elucidation** n. **elucidative** adj. **elucidator** n. **elucidatory** adj.
– ORIGIN C16: from late Latin *elucidare* 'to make clear'.

elude /ɪˈl(j)uːd/ ■ v. **1** evade or escape from, typically in a skilful or cunning way. **2** fail to be attained or understood by; baffle.
– DERIVATIVES **elusion** n.
– ORIGIN C16: from Latin *eludere*, from *e-* 'out, away from' + *ludere* 'to play'.

elusive ■ adj. difficult to find, catch, or achieve.
– DERIVATIVES **elusively** adv. **elusiveness** n.
– ORIGIN C18: from Latin *elus-, eludere* 'elude'.

elutriate /ɪˈl(j)uːtrɪeɪt/ ■ v. Chemistry separate (particles in a mixture) by suspension in an upward flow of liquid or gas.
– DERIVATIVES **elutriation** n.
– ORIGIN C18: from Latin *elutriare* 'to wash out'.

elver /ˈɛlvə/ ■ n. a young eel, especially when undergoing mass migration upriver from the sea.
– ORIGIN C17: var. of dialect *eel-fare* 'the passage of young eels up a river', from **EEL** + **FARE** in its original sense 'a journey'.

elves plural form of **ELF**[1].

Elysian /ɪˈlɪzɪən/ ■ adj. of or relating to Elysium or the Elysian Fields, the place in Greek mythology where heroes were conveyed after death. ▸ of or like paradise.

elytron /ˈɛlɪtrɒn/ ■ n. (pl. **elytra** /-trə/) Entomology each of the two wing cases of a beetle.
– ORIGIN C18: from Greek *elutron* 'sheath'.

em ■ n. Printing a unit for measuring the width of printed matter, equal to the height of the type size being used. ▸ a unit of measurement equal to twelve points.
– ORIGIN C18: the letter *M*, since it is approx. this width.

em- /ɪm, ɛm/ ■ prefix variant spelling of **EN-**[1], **EN-**[2] assimilated before *b, p* (as in *emblazon, emplacement*).

emaciated /ɪˈmeɪsɪeɪtɪd, ɪˈmeɪʃ-/ ■ adj. abnormally thin and weak.
– DERIVATIVES **emaciation** n.
– ORIGIN C17: from Latin *emaciare* 'to make thin'.

email ■ n. the system of sending messages by electronic means from one computer user to one or more recipients via a network. ■ v. mail or send using email.
– DERIVATIVES **emailer** n.
– ORIGIN C20: abbrev. of *electronic mail*.

emalangeni plural form of **LILANGENI**.

emanate /ˈɛməneɪt/ ■ v. issue or spread out from a source. ▸ give out or emit.
– ORIGIN C18 (*emanation* C16): from Latin *emanare* 'to flow out'.

emanation ■ n. **1** something which emanates or is produced from a source. **2** (in various mystical traditions) a being or force which is a manifestation of God. **3** the action or process of emanating.

emancipate /ɪˈmansɪpeɪt/ ■ v. set free, especially from legal, social, or political restrictions. ▸ free from slavery. ▸ Law set (a child) free from the authority of its father or parents.
– DERIVATIVES **emancipation** n. **emancipator** n. **emancipatory** adj.
– ORIGIN C17: from Latin *emancipare* 'to transfer as property', from *e-* 'out' + *mancipium* 'slave'.

emasculate /ɪˈmaskjʊleɪt/ ■ v. **1** make weaker or less effective. **2** [usu. as adj. **emasculated**] deprive (a man) of his male role or identity.
– DERIVATIVES **emasculation** n. **emasculator** n. **emasculatory** /-lət(ə)ri/ adj.
– ORIGIN C17: from Latin *emasculare* 'to castrate'.

embalm /ɪmˈbɑːm, ɛm-/ ■ v. **1** [often as noun **embalming**] preserve (a corpse) from decay, originally with spices and now usually by injection of a preservative. **2** archaic give a pleasant fragrance to.

– DERIVATIVES **embalmer** n. **embalmment** n.
– ORIGIN Middle English: from Old French *embaumer*, from *em-* 'in' + *baume* 'balm', var. of *basme* (see **BALM**).

embankment ■ n. 1 a wall or bank built to prevent flooding by a river. 2 a bank of earth or stone built to carry a road or railway over an area of low ground.

embargo /ɛmˈbɑːɡəʊ, ɪm-/ ■ n. (pl. -**oes**) 1 an official ban, especially on trade or other commercial activity with a particular country. ▸ archaic a stoppage or impediment. 2 historical an order of a state forbidding foreign ships to enter, or any ships to leave, its ports. ▸ v. (-**oes**, -**oed**) 1 impose an embargo on. 2 archaic seize (a ship or goods) for state service.
– ORIGIN C17: from Spanish, from *embargar* 'arrest'.

embark ■ v. 1 go on board a ship or aircraft. 2 (**embark on/upon**) begin (a new project or course of action).
– DERIVATIVES **embarkation** n.
– ORIGIN C16: from French *embarquer*, from *em-* 'in' + *barque* 'bark, ship'.

embarras de richesses /ɒmbaˌrɑː də riːˈʃɛs/ (also **embarras de choix** /ˈʃwɑː/) ■ n. more options or resources than one knows what to do with.
– ORIGIN French, 'embarrassment of riches (or choice)'.

embarrass /ɪmˈbarəs, ɛm-/ ■ v. 1 cause to feel awkward, self-conscious, or ashamed. ▸ (**be embarrassed**) be caused financial difficulties. 2 archaic hamper or impede.
– DERIVATIVES **embarrassed** adj. **embarrassedly** adv. **embarrassing** adj. **embarrassingly** adv. **embarrassment** n.
– ORIGIN C17: from French *embarrasser*, from Spanish *embarazar*, prob. from Portuguese *embaraçar*, from *baraço* 'halter'.

embassy ■ n. (pl. -**ies**) 1 the official residence or offices of an ambassador. 2 chiefly historical a deputation or mission sent by one state to another.
– ORIGIN C16: from Old French *ambasse*, from Latin *ambactus* 'servant'.

embattled ■ adj. 1 prepared for battle. 2 fortified; having battlements. 3 [postpos.] Heraldry divided or edged by a line of square notches like battlements in outline. 4 beset by problems or difficulties.

embed (also **imbed**) ■ v. (**embedded, embedding**) 1 fix or become fixed firmly and deeply in the surrounding mass. 2 implant (an idea or feeling). 3 Computing incorporate within the body of a file or document.

embellish ■ v. 1 adorn; decorate. 2 add extra details to (a story or account) for interest.
– DERIVATIVES **embellisher** n. **embellishment** n.
– ORIGIN Middle English: from Old French *embelliss-*, *embellir*, from *bel* 'handsome', from Latin *bellus*.

ember /ˈɛmbə/ ■ n. a small piece of burning or glowing material in a dying fire.
– ORIGIN Old English, of Germanic origin.

embezzle ■ v. steal or misappropriate (money placed in one's trust or under one's control).
– DERIVATIVES **embezzlement** n. **embezzler** n.
– ORIGIN Middle English ('steal'): from Anglo-Norman French *embesiler*.

embitter ■ v. [usu. as adj. **embittered**] make bitter or resentful.
– DERIVATIVES **embitterment** n.

emblazon /ɪmˈbleɪz(ə)n, ɛm-/ ■ v. 1 (usu. **be emblazoned**) conspicuously display (a design) on something. ▸ depict (a heraldic device) on something. 2 archaic celebrate or extol publicly.
– DERIVATIVES **emblazonment** n.

emblem /ˈɛmbləm/ ■ n. a heraldic device or symbolic object as a distinctive badge of a nation, organization, or family. ▸ a symbol or symbolic representation.
– DERIVATIVES **emblematic** adj. **emblematical** adj. **emblematically** adv.
– ORIGIN C16: from Latin *emblema* 'inlaid work, raised ornament', from Greek *emblēma* 'insertion'.

embody /ɪmˈbɒdi, ɛm-/ ■ v. (-**ies**, -**ied**) 1 give a tangible or visible form to (an idea or quality). 2 include or contain as a constituent part.
– DERIVATIVES **embodiment** n.

embolden ■ v. 1 cause to have courage or confidence. 2 (of typeface) make bold.

embolism /ˈɛmbəlɪz(ə)m/ ■ n. Medicine obstruction of an artery, typically by a clot of blood or an air bubble.
– ORIGIN C19: from Greek *embolismos*, from *emballein* 'insert'.

embolus /ˈɛmbələs/ ■ n. (pl. **emboli** /-lʌɪ, iː/) a blood clot, air bubble, piece of fatty deposit, or other object obstructing a blood vessel.
– DERIVATIVES **embolic** adj.
– ORIGIN C17 (denoting the plunger of a syringe): from Latin, 'piston', from Greek *embolos* 'peg, stopper'.

embonpoint /ˌɒmbɔ̃ˈpwã/ ■ n. plumpness or fleshiness, especially with reference to a woman's bosom.
– ORIGIN C17: from French *en bon point* 'in good condition'.

emboss ■ v. [usu. as adj. **embossed**] carve a design in relief on (a surface).
– DERIVATIVES **embosser** n.
– ORIGIN Middle English: from the Old French base of obsolete French *embosser*, from *em-* 'into' + *boce* 'protuberance'.

embouchure /ˌɒmbʊˈʃʊə/ ■ n. Music the way in which a player applies the mouth and tongue in playing a brass or wind instrument.
– ORIGIN C18: French, from *s'emboucher*, from *emboucher* 'put in or to the mouth'.

embower /ɪmˈbaʊə, ɛm-/ ■ v. poetic/literary surround or enclose.

embrace ■ v. 1 hold closely in one's arms, especially as a sign of affection. 2 include or contain. 3 accept or support (a belief or change) willingly. ■ n. an act of embracing.
– DERIVATIVES **embraceable** adj. **embracement** n. **embracer** n.
– ORIGIN Middle English: from Old French *embracer*, from Latin *in-* 'in' + *bracchium* 'arm'.

embrasure /ɪmˈbreɪʒə, ɛm-/ ■ n. 1 an opening in a wall or parapet, used for shooting through. 2 an opening or recess around a window or door forming an enlargement of the area from the inside.
– DERIVATIVES **embrasured** adj.
– ORIGIN C18: from French, from obsolete *embraser* 'widen an opening'.

embrocation /ˌɛmbrəˈkeɪʃ(ə)n/ ■ n. a liquid medication rubbed on the body to relieve pain from sprains and strains.
– ORIGIN Middle English: from medieval Latin *embrocatio(n-)*, from *embrocare*, from Greek *embrokhē* 'lotion'.

embroider ■ v. 1 sew decorative needlework patterns on. 2 add fictitious or exaggerated details to.
– DERIVATIVES **embroiderer** n.
– ORIGIN Middle English: from Anglo-Norman French *enbrouder*.

embroidery ■ n. (pl. -**ies**) 1 the art or pastime of embroidering. 2 embroidered cloth.

embroil ■ v. [often as adj. **embroiled**] involve deeply in a conflict or difficult situation.
– DERIVATIVES **embroilment** n.
– ORIGIN C17: from French *embrouiller* 'to muddle'.

embryo /ˈɛmbrɪəʊ/ ■ n. (pl. -**os**) 1 an unborn or unhatched offspring in the process of development, especially an unborn human in the first eight weeks from conception. Compare with **FETUS**. 2 Botany the part of a seed which develops into a new plant.
– PHRASES **in embryo** at a rudimentary stage.
– DERIVATIVES **embryonal** /ˈɛmbrɪən(ə)l/ adj.
– ORIGIN Middle English: from Greek *embruon* 'fetus', from *em-* 'into' + *bruein* 'grow'.

embryogenesis /ˌɛmbrɪə(ʊ)ˈdʒɛnɪsɪs/ ■ n. Biology the formation and development of an embryo.
– DERIVATIVES **embryogenic** adj. **embryogeny** n.

embryology /ˌɛmbrɪˈɒlədʒi/ ■ n. the branch of biology and medicine concerned with the study of embryos.
– DERIVATIVES **embryologic** adj. **embryological** adj. **embryologist** n.

embryonic /ˌɛmbrɪˈɒnɪk/ ■ adj. 1 of or relating to an embryo. 2 in or at a rudimentary stage.
– DERIVATIVES **embryonically** adv.

emcee /ɛmˈsiː/ informal, chiefly N. Amer. ■ n. 1 a master of

emend

ceremonies. **2** an MC at a club or party. ■ v. (**emcees, emceed, emceeing**) act as a master of ceremonies for or at (an event, club, etc.).
– ORIGIN 1930s: representing the pronunciation of **MC**.

emend /ɪˈmɛnd/ ■ v. correct and revise (a text).
– DERIVATIVES **emendation** n.
– ORIGIN Middle English: from Latin *emendare*, from *e-* 'out of' + *menda* 'a fault'.

emerald ■ n. **1** a bright green precious stone consisting of a chromium-rich variety of beryl. **2** a bright green colour.
– ORIGIN Middle English: from Old French *e(s)meraud*, from Greek *(s)maragdos*, from Semitic.

emerge /ɪˈməːdʒ/ ■ v. **1** become gradually visible or apparent. ▸ (of facts) become known. **2** recover from or survive a difficult period. **3** (of an insect) break out from an egg, cocoon, or pupal case.
– DERIVATIVES **emergence** n. **emerging** adj.
– ORIGIN C16: from Latin *emergere*, from *e-* 'out, forth' + *mergere* 'to dip'.

emergency ■ n. (pl. **-ies**) **1** a serious, unexpected, and potentially dangerous situation requiring immediate action. ▸ [as modifier] arising from or used in an emergency: *an emergency exit*. **2** (also **Emergency**) S. African historical short for state of emergency at **STATE**. **3** N. Amer. the casualty department in a hospital.
– ORIGIN C17: from medieval Latin *emergentia*, from Latin *emergere* (see **EMERGE**).

emergent ■ adj. **1** in the process of coming into being; emerging. **2** Philosophy (of a property) arising as an effect of complex causes and not analysable simply as the sum of their effects. **3** denoting water plants with leaves and flowers that appear above the water surface. ■ n. Philosophy an emergent property.

emeritus /ɪˈmɛrɪtəs, iː-/ ■ adj. having retired but allowed to retain a title as an honour: *emeritus professor of microbiology*.
– ORIGIN C18: from Latin *emereri* 'earn one's discharge by service'.

emery /ˈɛm(ə)ri/ ■ n. a greyish-black form of corundum containing iron oxide, used in powdered form as an abrasive.
– ORIGIN C15: from Old French *esmeri*, from Italian *smeriglio*, from Greek *smuris* 'polishing powder'.

emery board ■ n. a strip of thin wood or card coated with emery or another abrasive and used as a nail file.

emetic /ɪˈmɛtɪk/ ■ adj. (of a substance) causing vomiting. ■ n. an emetic medicine or other substance.
– ORIGIN C17: from Greek *emetikos*, from *emein* 'to vomit'.

-emia ■ comb. form US spelling of **-AEMIA**.

emigrant ■ n. a person who leaves their own country in order to settle permanently in another.

emigrate /ˈɛmɪɡreɪt/ ■ v. leave one's own country in order to settle permanently in another.
– DERIVATIVES **emigration** n.
– ORIGIN C18: from Latin *emigrare* 'to emigrate'.

émigré /ˈɛmɪɡreɪ/ ■ n. a person who has emigrated, especially for political reasons.
– ORIGIN C18 (orig. denoting a person escaping the French Revolution): French, from *émigrer* 'emigrate'.

eminence /ˈɛmɪnəns/ ■ n. **1** acknowledged superiority within a particular sphere. **2** an important or distinguished person. ▸ (**His/Your Eminence**) a title given to a Roman Catholic cardinal. **3** formal or poetic/literary a piece of rising ground. **4** Anatomy a slight projection from the surface of the body.
– ORIGIN Middle English: from Latin *eminentia*, from *eminere* 'jut, project'.

éminence grise /ˌeminɒ̃s ˈɡriːz/ ■ n. (pl. **éminences grises** pronunc. same) a person who exercises power or influence without holding an official position.
– ORIGIN 1930s: French, 'grey eminence'; the term was orig. applied to Cardinal Richelieu's grey-cloaked private secretary, Père Joseph (1577–1638).

eminent ■ adj. **1** respected; distinguished. **2** notable; outstanding: *his eminent suitability for studio work*.
– DERIVATIVES **eminently** adv.

emir /ɛˈmɪə/ (also **amir**) ■ n. a title of various Muslim (mainly Arab) rulers. ▸ historical a Muslim (usually Arab) military commander or local chief.
– ORIGIN C16 (denoting a male descendant of Muhammad): from French *émir*, from Arabic *'amīr* 'commander'.

emirate /ˈɛmɪrət/ ■ n. the rank, lands, or reign of an emir.

emissary /ˈɛmɪs(ə)ri/ ■ n. (pl. **-ies**) a person sent as a diplomatic representative on a special mission.
– ORIGIN C17: from Latin *emissarius* 'scout, spy', from *emittere* (see **EMIT**).

emission /ɪˈmɪʃ(ə)n/ ■ n. the action of emitting something, especially heat, light, gas, or radiation. ▸ a substance which is emitted.
– ORIGIN Middle English: from Latin *emissio(n-)*, from *emittere* (see **EMIT**).

emit ■ v. (**emitted, emitting**) **1** discharge; send forth or give out. **2** make (a sound).
– ORIGIN C17: from Latin *emittere*, from *e-* 'out of' + *mittere* 'send'.

emitter ■ n. **1** a thing which emits. **2** Electronics the region in a bipolar transistor that produces carriers of current.

Emmental /ˈɛmənta:l/ (also **Emmenthal**) ■ n. a kind of hard Swiss cheese with holes in it, similar to Gruyère.
– ORIGIN from German *Emmentaler*, from *Emmental*, the name of a valley in Switzerland where the cheese was orig. made.

emmer /ˈɛmə/ ■ n. an old kind of wheat with bearded ears and spikelets that each contain two grains, now grown mainly for fodder and breakfast cereals. [*Triticum dicoccum*.]
– ORIGIN C20: from German, from Old High German *amer*.

Emmy ■ n. (pl. **Emmys**) (in the US) a statuette awarded annually to an outstanding television programme or performer.
– ORIGIN 1940s: said to be from *Immy*, short for *image orthicon tube* (a kind of television camera tube).

emollient /ɪˈmɒlɪənt/ ■ adj. **1** having the quality of softening or soothing the skin. **2** attempting to avoid confrontation or anger; soothing or calming. ■ n. an emollient preparation.
– DERIVATIVES **emollience** n.
– ORIGIN C17: from Latin *emollire* 'to make soft'.

emolument /ɪˈmɒljʊm(ə)nt, ɛ-/ ■ n. formal a salary, fee, or benefit from employment or office.
– ORIGIN Middle English: from Latin *emolumentum*, orig. prob. 'payment for grinding corn', from *emolere* 'grind up'.

emote /ɪˈməʊt/ ■ v. portray emotion theatrically.
– ORIGIN C20: back-formation from **EMOTION**.

emoticon /ɪˈməʊtɪkɒn, -ˈmɒtɪ-/ ■ n. a representation of a facial expression such as a smile or frown, formed with keyboard characters and used in electronic communications to convey the writer's feelings.
– ORIGIN 1990s: blend of **EMOTION** and **ICON**.

emotion ■ n. a strong feeling, such as joy, anger, or sadness. ▸ instinctive or intuitive feeling as distinguished from reasoning or knowledge.
– DERIVATIVES **emotionless** adj.
– ORIGIN C16: from French *émotion*, from *émouvoir* 'excite', from Latin *emovere*, from *e-* 'out' + *movere* 'move'.

emotional ■ adj. of or relating to emotions. ▸ arousing or showing intense feeling: *an emotional speech*.
– DERIVATIVES **emotionalism** n. **emotionality** n. **emotionally** adv.

emotive ■ adj. arousing intense feeling.
– DERIVATIVES **emotively** adv. **emotiveness** n.

empanada /ˌɛmpəˈnɑːdə/ ■ n. a pastry turnover filled with savoury ingredients and baked or fried, typical of South American cooking.
– ORIGIN Spanish: from *empanar* 'roll in pastry', from Latin *panis* 'bread'.

empathize (also **-ise**) ■ v. understand and share the feelings of another.

empathy /ˈɛmpəθi/ ■ n. the ability to empathize.
– DERIVATIVES **empathetic** adj. **empathetically** adv. **empathic** /ɛmˈpaθɪk/ adj. **empathically** adv.
– ORIGIN C20: from Greek *empatheia* (from *em-* 'in' + *pathos* 'feeling') translating German *Einfühlung*.

empennage /ɛmˈpɛnɪdʒ/ ■ n. Aeronautics an arrangement of stabilizing surfaces at the tail of an aircraft.
– ORIGIN C20: from French, from *empenner* 'to feather an arrow', from *em-* 'in' + *penne* 'a feather'.

emperor ■ n. **1** the ruler of an empire. **2** in names of certain large, strikingly marked butterflies, e.g. purple emperor.
– DERIVATIVES **emperorship** n.
– ORIGIN Middle English: from Old French *emperere*, from Latin *imperator* 'military commander', from *imperare* 'to command'.

emperor moth ■ n. a large moth of the silk moth family, with eyespots on all four wings. [*Saturnia pavonia* and related species.]

emperor penguin ■ n. the largest kind of penguin, which breeds in the Antarctic and has a yellow patch on each side of the head. [*Aptenodytes forsteri*.]

emphasis /ˈɛmfəsɪs/ ■ n. (pl. **emphases** /-siːz/) **1** special importance, value, or prominence given to something. **2** stress laid on a word or words in speaking.
– ORIGIN C16: from Greek, orig. 'appearance, show', later denoting a figure of speech in which more is implied than is said, from *emphainein* 'exhibit'.

emphasize (also **-ise**) ■ v. **1** give emphasis to. **2** make more clearly defined: *a jacket which emphasized her hips*.

emphatic ■ adj. showing or giving emphasis. ▸ definite and clear: *the answer was an emphatic 'yes'*.
– DERIVATIVES **emphatically** adv.

emphysema /ˌɛmfɪˈsiːmə/ ■ n. Medicine **1** (also **pulmonary emphysema**) a condition in which the air sacs of the lungs are damaged and enlarged, causing breathlessness. **2** a condition in which air is abnormally present within the body tissues.
– ORIGIN C17: from Greek *emphusēma*, from *emphusan* 'puff up'.

empire ■ n. **1** an extensive group of states ruled over by a single monarch, an oligarchy, or a sovereign state. **2** supreme political power: *his dream of empire in Asia Minor*. **3** a large commercial organization under the control of one person or group.
– ORIGIN Middle English: from Latin *imperium*, rel. to *imperare* (see **EMPEROR**).

empire line ■ n. a style of women's clothing characterized by a waistline cut just under the bust and typically a low neckline.

empiric /ɛmˈpɪrɪk, ɪm-/ ■ adj. another term for **EMPIRICAL**.
– ORIGIN Middle English: from Greek *empeirikos*, from *empeiria* 'experience'.

empirical ■ adj. based on, concerned with, or verifiable by observation or experience rather than theory or pure logic.
– DERIVATIVES **empirically** adv.

empirical formula ■ n. Chemistry a formula giving the proportions of the elements present in a compound but not the actual numbers or arrangement of atoms.

empiricism /ɛmˈpɪrɪsɪz(ə)m/ ■ n. Philosophy the theory that all knowledge is derived from sense-experience.
– DERIVATIVES **empiricist** n. & adj.

emplacement ■ n. **1** a structure or platform where a gun is placed for firing. **2** chiefly Geology the process or state of setting something in place.

employ ■ v. **1** give work to (someone) and pay them for it. ▸ keep occupied. **2** make use of. ■ n. the state of being employed; employment: *in the employ of a wine merchant*.
– DERIVATIVES **employability** n. **employable** adj.
– ORIGIN Middle English: from Old French *employer*, from Latin *implicari*, from *implicare* (see **IMPLY**).

employee ■ n. a person employed for wages or salary.

employer ■ n. a person that employs people.

employment ■ n. **1** the action or condition of employing. ▸ a person's work or profession. **2** the utilization of something.

emporium /ɛmˈpɔːrɪəm, ɪm-/ ■ n. (pl. **emporia** /-rɪə/ or **emporiums**) a large store selling a wide variety of goods.
– ORIGIN C16: from Latin, from Greek *emporion*, from *emporos* 'merchant'.

empower ■ v. give authority or power to; authorize. ▸ give strength and confidence to.

empowerment ■ n. **1** the action of empowering. **2** (in South Africa) a policy of creating opportunities in employment, training, etc., for people who were disadvantaged under apartheid. ▸ [as modifier] denoting or relating to such a policy: *a R230 million empowerment deal*.

empress /ˈɛmprɪs/ ■ n. a female emperor. ▸ the wife or widow of an emperor.
– ORIGIN Middle English: from Old French *emperesse*, feminine of *emperere* (see **EMPEROR**).

empty ■ adj. (**-ier**, **-iest**) **1** containing nothing; not filled or occupied. ▸ Mathematics (of a set) containing no members or elements. **2** (of words or a gesture) lacking sincerity. **3** having no value or purpose. ■ v. (**-ies**, **-ied**) **1** make or become empty. ▸ discharge (the contents) from a container. **2** (of a river) discharge itself into the sea or a lake. ■ n. (pl. **-ies**) informal a bottle or glass left empty of its contents.
– PHRASES **be running on empty** have exhausted all of one's resources.
– DERIVATIVES **emptily** adv. **emptiness** n.
– ORIGIN Old English *ǣmtig*, *ǣmetig* 'at leisure, empty', from *ǣmetta* 'leisure'.

empty-handed ■ adj. having failed to obtain or achieve what one wanted.

empty-headed ■ adj. unintelligent and foolish.

empty nester ■ n. informal a parent whose children have grown up and left home.

empyema /ˌɛmpʌɪˈiːmə/ ■ n. Medicine the collection of pus in a body cavity, especially in the pleural cavity.
– ORIGIN Middle English: from Greek *empuēma*, from *empuein* 'suppurate'.

empyrean /ˌɛmpʌɪˈriːən, -pɪ-, ɛmˈpɪrɪən/ ■ adj. of or relating to heaven. ■ n. (**the empyrean**) the highest part of heaven, thought by the ancients to be the realm of pure fire. ▸ poetic/literary the visible heavens; the sky.
– ORIGIN Middle English: from Greek *empurios*, from *en-* 'in' + *pur* 'fire'.

EMS ■ abbrev. European Monetary System.

EMU ■ abbrev. European Monetary Union.

emu[1] ■ n. a large flightless fast-running Australian bird resembling the ostrich, with shaggy grey or brown plumage, bare blue skin on the head and neck, and three-toed feet. [*Dromaius novaehollandiae*.]
– ORIGIN C17: from Portuguese *ema*.

emu[2] ■ abbrev. Brit. **1** electric multiple unit. **2** electromagnetic unit(s).

emulate /ˈɛmjʊleɪt/ ■ v. attempt to match or surpass, typically by imitation.
– DERIVATIVES **emulation** n. **emulative** adj. **emulator** n.
– ORIGIN C16: from Latin *aemulari* 'to rival or equal'.

emulsifier ■ n. a substance that stabilizes an emulsion, in particular an additive used to stabilize processed foods.

emulsify /ɪˈmʌlsɪfʌɪ/ ■ v. (**-ies**, **-ied**) make into or become an emulsion.

emulsion /ɪˈmʌlʃ(ə)n/ ■ n. **1** a fine dispersion of minute droplets of one liquid in another in which it is not soluble or miscible. **2** a type of paint consisting of pigment bound in a synthetic resin which forms an emulsion with water. **3** a light-sensitive coating for photographic films and plates, containing crystals of a silver compound dispersed in a medium such as gelatin.
– ORIGIN C17 (denoting a milky liquid made by crushing almonds in water): from modern Latin *emulsio(n-)*, from *emulgere* 'milk out'.

en ■ n. Printing a unit of measurement equal to half an em and approximately the average width of typeset characters.
– ORIGIN C18: the letter *N*, since it is approx. this width.

-en[1] ■ suffix forming verbs: **1** (from adjectives) denoting the development or intensification of a state: *widen*. **2** from nouns (such as *strengthen* from *strength*).
– ORIGIN Old English *-nian*, of Germanic origin.

-en[2] (also **-n**) ■ suffix forming adjectives from nouns:

-en¹ ■ suffix 1 made or consisting of: *earthen*. 2 resembling: *golden*.
– ORIGIN Old English, of Germanic origin.

-en³ (also **-n**) ■ suffix forming past participles of strong verbs: 1 as a regular inflection: *spoken*. 2 as an adjective: *mistaken*.
– ORIGIN Old English, of Germanic origin.

-en⁴ ■ suffix forming the plural of a few nouns such as *children*, *oxen*.
– ORIGIN Middle English reduction of the earlier suffix *-an*.

-en⁵ ■ suffix forming diminutives of nouns (such as *chicken*).
– ORIGIN Old English, of Germanic origin.

-en⁶ ■ suffix 1 forming feminine nouns such as *vixen*. 2 forming abstract nouns such as *burden*.
– ORIGIN Old English, of Germanic origin.

en-¹ (also **em-**) ■ prefix 1 (added to nouns) forming verbs meaning 'put into or on': *engulf*. 2 (added to nouns and adjectives) forming verbs (often with the suffix *-en*) meaning 'bring into the condition of': *enliven*. 3 (added to verbs) in; into; on: *ensnare*. ▶ as an intensifier: *entangle*.
– ORIGIN from French: from Latin *in-*.

en-² (also **em-**) ■ prefix within; inside: *enthusiasm*.
– ORIGIN from Greek.

enable ■ v. 1 give (someone) the ability or means to do something. ▶ make possible. 2 chiefly Computing make (a device or system) operational; activate. ▶ [as adj. **-enabled**] adapted for use with the specified application or system: *WAP-enabled cellphones*.
– DERIVATIVES **enablement** n. **enabler** n.
– ORIGIN Middle English: from EN-¹, IN-², + ABLE.

enabling act ■ n. Law a statute empowering a person or body to take certain action, especially to make regulations.

enact ■ v. 1 make (a bill or other proposal) law. 2 put into practice. 3 act out (a role or play).
– DERIVATIVES **enaction** n. **enactor** n.
– ORIGIN Middle English: from EN-¹, IN-², + ACT.

enactment ■ n. 1 the process of enacting. 2 a law that has been passed.

enamel ■ n. 1 an opaque or semi-transparent glassy substance applied to metallic or other hard surfaces for ornament or as a protective coating. 2 the hard glossy substance that covers the crown of a tooth. 3 a paint that dries to give a smooth, hard coat. ■ v. (**enamelled**, **enamelling**; US **enameled**, **enameling**) [usu. as adj. **enamelled**] coat or decorate with enamel.
– DERIVATIVES **enameller** n. **enamelware** n. **enamelwork** n.
– ORIGIN Middle English: from Anglo-Norman French *enamailler*, from *en-* 'in, on' + *amail* 'enamel'.

enamour /ɪˈnaməː, ɛ-/ (US **enamor**) ■ v. (**be enamoured of/with/by**) be filled with love or admiration for.
– ORIGIN Middle English: from Old French *enamourer*, from *en-* 'in' + *amour* 'love'.

enanthema /ˌɛnənˈθiːmə/ ■ n. Medicine an ulcer or eruption occurring on a mucus-secreting surface such as the inside of the mouth.
– ORIGIN C19: from EN-² + a shortened form of EXANTHEMA.

enantiomer /ɪˈnantɪə(ʊ)mə, ɛ-/ ■ n. Chemistry each of a pair of molecules that are mirror images of each other.
– ORIGIN 1930s: from Greek *enantios* 'opposite' + -MER.

en bloc /ɒ̃ ˈblɒk/ ■ adv. all together or all at the same time.
– ORIGIN C19: French.

enc. ■ abbrev. 1 enclosed. 2 enclosure.

encamp ■ v. settle in or establish a camp.

encampment ■ n. 1 a place where a camp is set up. 2 a prehistoric enclosed or fortified site, especially an Iron Age hill fort. 3 the process of setting up a camp.

encapsulate /ɪnˈkapsjʊleɪt, ɛn-/ ■ v. 1 enclose in or as if in a capsule. 2 express concisely and succinctly. 3 Computing enclose in a set of codes which allow transfer across networks.
– DERIVATIVES **encapsulation** n.
– ORIGIN C19: from EN-¹, IN-² + Latin *capsula* (see CAPSULE).

encase (also **incase**) ■ v. enclose or cover in a case or close-fitting surround.
– DERIVATIVES **encasement** n.

encash ■ v. Brit. convert (a cheque, bond, etc.) into money.
– DERIVATIVES **encashment** n.

encaustic /ɛnˈkɔːstɪk/ ■ adj. (in painting and ceramics) decorated by burning in colours as an inlay, especially using coloured clays or pigments mixed with hot wax. ■ n. the art or process of encaustic painting.
– ORIGIN C16: from Greek *enkaustikos*, from *enkaiein* 'burn in'.

-ence ■ suffix forming nouns: 1 denoting a quality: *impertinence*. 2 denoting an action or its result: *reference*.
– ORIGIN from French *-ence*, from Latin *-entia*, *-antia*.

encephalic /ˌɛnsɪˈfalɪk, ɛnˈkɛf(ə)lɪk/ ■ adj. Anatomy relating to or situated in the brain.
– ORIGIN C19: from Greek *enkephalos* 'brain', from *en-* 'in' + *kephalē* 'head'.

encephalitis /ɛnˌsɛfəˈlʌɪtɪs, -ˌkɛfə-/ ■ n. inflammation of the brain.

encephalization (also **-isation**) ■ n. Zoology an evolutionary increase in the complexity or relative size of the brain.

encephalo- /ɛnˈsɛf(ə)ləʊ, -ˈkɛf-/ ■ comb. form of or relating to the brain: *encephalopathy*.
– ORIGIN from Greek *enkephalos*.

encephalography /ɛnˌsɛfəˈlɒɡrəfi, -ˌkɛfə-/ ■ n. Medicine any of various techniques for recording the structure or electrical activity of the brain.
– DERIVATIVES **encephalogram** /ɛnˈsɛf(ə)lə(ʊ)ɡram, -ˈkɛf-/ n. **encephalograph** n. **encephalographic** adj.

encephalomyelitis /ɛnˌsɛf(ə)ləʊmʌɪəˈlʌɪtɪs, -ˌkɛf-/ ■ n. Medicine inflammation of the brain and spinal cord, typically due to acute viral infection.

encephalopathy /ɛnˌsɛfəˈlɒpəθi, -ˌkɛfə-/ ■ n. (pl. **-ies**) Medicine a disease in which the functioning of the brain is affected, especially by viral infection or toxins in the blood.

enchaînement /ɒ̃ˈʃɛnmɒ̃/ ■ n. (pl. pronounced same) Ballet a linked sequence of steps or movements constituting a phrase.
– ORIGIN C19: French, 'chaining together'.

enchant ■ v. 1 delight; charm. 2 [often as adj. **enchanted**] put under a spell: *an enchanted garden*.
– DERIVATIVES **enchanter** n. **enchanting** adj. **enchantingly** adv. **enchantment** n. **enchantress** n.
– ORIGIN Middle English: from French *enchanter*, from Latin *incantare*, from *in-* 'in' + *cantare* 'sing'.

enchilada /ˌɛntʃɪˈlɑːdə/ ■ n. a tortilla filled with meat or cheese and served with chilli sauce.
– ORIGIN Latin American Spanish: from *enchilar* 'season with chilli'.

encircle ■ v. form a circle around; surround.
– DERIVATIVES **encirclement** n.

encl. ■ abbrev. enclosed or enclosure.

enclave /ˈɛnkleɪv/ ■ n. 1 a portion of territory surrounded by a larger territory whose inhabitants are culturally or ethnically distinct. Compare with EXCLAVE. 2 a group that is different in character from those surrounding it: *a male enclave*.
– ORIGIN C19: from Old French *enclaver* 'enclose, dovetail', from Latin *clavis* 'key'.

enclose (also **inclose**) ■ v. 1 surround or close off on all sides. 2 place in an envelope together with a letter.
– ORIGIN Middle English: from Old French *enclos*, from *enclore*, from Latin *includere* 'shut in'.

enclosure /ɪnˈkləʊʒə, ɛn-/ (also **inclosure**) ■ n. 1 an area that is sealed off by a barrier. ▶ Brit. a section of a racecourse or stadium allocated to a particular group: *the members' enclosure*. 2 a document or object placed in an envelope together with a letter.

encode ■ v. convert into a coded form.
– DERIVATIVES **encoder** n.

encomiast /ɛnˈkəʊmɪast/ ■ n. formal a person who publicly praises or flatters someone else.
– DERIVATIVES **encomiastic** adj.
– ORIGIN C17: from Greek *enkōmiastēs*, from *enkōmiazein* 'to praise'.

encomium /ɛnˈkəʊmɪəm/ ■ n. (pl. **encomiums** or

encomia) formal a speech or piece of writing expressing praise.
– ORIGIN C16: Latin, from Greek *enkōmion* 'eulogy'.

encompass /ɪnˈkʌmpəs, ɛn-/ ■ v. **1** surround and have or hold within. **2** include comprehensively.

encopresis /ˌɛnkəʊˈpriːsɪs/ ■ n. Medicine involuntary defecation, especially associated with emotional or psychiatric disorder.

encore /ˈɒŋkɔː/ ■ n. a repeated or additional performance of an item at the end of a concert, as called for by an audience. ■ exclam. again! (as called by an audience at the end of a concert) ■ v. call for (an encore).
– ORIGIN C18: French, 'still, again'.

encounter ■ v. unexpectedly meet or be faced with. ■ n. **1** an unexpected or casual meeting. **2** a confrontation or unpleasant struggle.
– ORIGIN Middle English: from Old French *encontrer* (v.), *encontre* (n.), from Latin *in-* 'in' + *contra* 'against'.

encourage ■ v. give support, confidence, or hope to. ▸ help or stimulate the development of.
– DERIVATIVES **encourager** n. **encouragement** n. **encouraging** adj. **encouragingly** adv.
– ORIGIN Middle English: from French *encourager*, from *en-* 'in' + *corage* 'courage'.

encroach ■ v. (**encroach on/upon**) gradually and steadily intrude on (a person's territory, rights, etc.). ▸ advance gradually beyond expected or acceptable limits.
– DERIVATIVES **encroacher** n. **encroachment** n.
– ORIGIN Middle English: from Old French *encrochier* 'seize, fasten upon', from *en-* 'in, on' + *crochier*, from *croc* 'hook'.

en croute /ɒ̃ ˈkruːt/ ■ adj. & adv. in a pastry crust.
– ORIGIN French *en croûte*.

encrust /ɪnˈkrʌst, ɛn-/ ■ v. [usu. as adj. **encrusted**] cover with a hard crust.
– DERIVATIVES **encrustation** n.
– ORIGIN C17: from Latin *incrustare*, from *in-* 'into' + *crusta* 'a crust'.

encrypt /ɛnˈkrɪpt/ ■ v. convert into code.
– DERIVATIVES **encryption** n.
– ORIGIN 1950s: from **EN-**[1] + Greek *kruptos* 'hidden'.

enculturation (also **inculturation**) ■ n. the gradual acquisition of the norms of a culture or group.

encumber /ɪnˈkʌmbə, ɛn-/ ■ v. impede or burden.
– ORIGIN Middle English: from Old French *encombrer* 'block up', from *en-* 'in' + *combre* 'river barrage'.

encumbrance ■ n. **1** a burden or impediment. **2** Law a mortgage or other charge on property or assets.

-ency ■ suffix forming nouns: **1** denoting a quality: *efficiency*. **2** denoting a state: *presidency*.
– ORIGIN from Latin *-entia*.

encyclical /ɛnˈsɪklɪk(ə)l, ɪn-, -ˈsaɪk-/ ■ n. a letter sent by the pope to all bishops of the Roman Catholic Church.
– ORIGIN C17: from Greek *enkuklios* 'circular, general'.

encyclopedia /ɛnˌsaɪkləˈpiːdɪə, ɪn-/ (also **encyclopaedia**) ■ n. a book or set of books giving information on many subjects or on many aspects of one subject, typically arranged alphabetically.
– ORIGIN C16: modern Latin, from pseudo-Greek *enkuklopaideia* for *enkuklios paideia* 'all-round education'.

encyclopedic /ɛnˌsaɪkləˈ(ʊ)piːdɪk, ɪn-/ (also **encyclopaedic**) ■ adj. **1** comprehensive: *an encyclopedic knowledge of food*. **2** of or relating to encyclopedias or information suitable for an encyclopedia.

encyclopedist (also **encyclopaedist**) ■ n. a person who writes, edits, or contributes to an encyclopedia.

encyst /ɪnˈsɪst, ɛn-/ ■ v. Zoology enclose or become enclosed in a cyst.

end ■ n. **1** a final part of something. ▸ a termination of a state or situation. **2** the furthest or most extreme part of something. ▸ a small piece that is left after use. **3** a part or share of an activity. **4** a place linked to another by a telephone call, letter, or journey. **5** the part of a sports field or court defended by one team or player. **6** a goal or desired result. **7** Bowls a session of play in one particular direction across the playing area. **8** American Football a lineman positioned nearest the sideline. ■ v. come or bring to an end; finish.
– PHRASES **at the end of the day** informal when everything is taken into consideration. **be the end** informal be the limit of what one can tolerate: *you really are the end!* **end it all** commit suicide. **the end of the road** (or **line**) the point beyond which progress or survival cannot continue. **the end of one's tether** (or N. Amer. **rope**) having no patience or energy left. **end on** situated on or viewed from the end. **end to end** in a row with the ends touching or close together. **in the end** eventually. **keep** (or **hold**) **one's end up** informal perform well in a difficult or competitive situation. **make** (**both**) **ends meet** earn just enough money to live on. **never** (or **not**) **hear the end of** be continually reminded of (something unpleasant). **no end** informal to a great extent; very much. **no end of** informal a vast number or amount of. **on end 1** continuing without stopping. **2** in an upright position. **put an end to** cause to die or stop. **the sharp end** informal the most challenging and least safe part of an activity or system. **a —— to end all ——s** informal the most impressive or successful of its kind: *a party to end all parties*.
– ORIGIN Old English, of Germanic origin.

-end ■ suffix denoting a person or thing to be treated in a specified way: *dividend | reverend*.
– ORIGIN from Latin *-endus*, gerundive ending.

endanger ■ v. put at risk or in danger.
– DERIVATIVES **endangerment** n.

endangered ■ adj. at risk, especially of extinction.

endear /ɪnˈdɪə, ɛn-/ ■ v. cause to be loved or liked.

endearing ■ adj. inspiring love or affection.
– DERIVATIVES **endearingly** adv.

endearment ■ n. love or affection. ▸ a word or phrase expressing this.

endeavour /ɪnˈdɛvə, ɛn-/ (US **endeavor**) ■ v. try hard to do or achieve something. ■ n. **1** an act of endeavouring; an enterprise. **2** earnest and industrious effort.
– ORIGIN Middle English: from the obsolete phr. *put oneself in devoir* 'do one's utmost'; *devoir* from French 'duty', from Old French *deveir* 'to owe'.

endemic /ɛnˈdɛmɪk/ ■ adj. **1** (of a disease or condition) regularly found among particular people or in a certain area. **2** (of a plant or animal) native or restricted to a certain area. ■ n. an endemic plant or animal.
– DERIVATIVES **endemically** adv. **endemicity** /ˌɛndɪˈmɪsɪti/ n. **endemism** /ˈɛndɪmɪz(ə)m/ n.
– ORIGIN C17: modern Latin *endemicus*, from Greek *endēmios* 'native'.

endgame ■ n. the final stage of a game such as chess or bridge, when few pieces or cards remain.

end grain ■ n. the grain of wood seen when it is cut across the growth rings.

ending ■ n. an end or final part. ▸ the final part of a word, constituting a grammatical inflection or formative element.

endive /ˈɛndaɪv, -dɪv/ ■ n. an edible Mediterranean plant, the bitter leaves of which may be blanched and used in salads. [*Cichorium endivia*.]
– ORIGIN Middle English: from medieval Latin *endivia*, from Greek *entubon*.

endless ■ adj. **1** having or seeming to have no end or limit. **2** innumerable. **3** (of a belt, chain, or tape) having the ends joined to allow for continuous action.
– DERIVATIVES **endlessly** adv. **endlessness** n.

endmost ■ adj. nearest to the end.

endo- ■ comb. form internal; within: *endoderm*.
– ORIGIN from Greek *endon* 'within'.

endocardial /ˌɛndə(ʊ)ˈkɑːdɪəl/ ■ adj. Anatomy & Medicine **1** of or relating to the endocardium. **2** inside the heart.

endocardium /ˌɛndəʊˈkɑːdɪəm/ ■ n. the thin, smooth membrane which lines the chambers of the heart and forms the surface of the valves.
– ORIGIN C19: modern Latin, from **ENDO-** + Greek *kardia* 'heart'.

endocarp /ˈɛndə(ʊ)kɑːp/ ■ n. Botany the innermost layer of the pericarp which surrounds a seed in a fruit.

endocentric /ˌɛndəʊˈsɛntrɪk/ ■ adj. Linguistics denoting or

endocrine

being a construction in which the whole has the same syntactic function as the head, for example *big black dogs*. Contrasted with EXOCENTRIC.

endocrine /'endə(ʊ)krʌɪn, -krɪn/ ■ adj. Physiology of or denoting glands which secrete hormones or other products directly into the blood.
- ORIGIN C20: from ENDO- + Greek *krinein* 'sift'.

endocrinology /,endəʊkrɪ'nɒlədʒi/ ■ n. the branch of physiology and medicine concerned with endocrine glands and hormones.
- DERIVATIVES **endocrinologist** n.

endocytosis /,endəʊsʌɪ'təʊsɪs/ ■ n. Biology the taking in of matter by a living cell by enclosing it in a vacuole.

endoderm /'endə(ʊ)də:m/ ■ n. Zoology & Embryology the innermost layer of cells or tissue of an embryo, or the parts derived from this (e.g. the lining of the gut).
- DERIVATIVES **endodermal** adj.
- ORIGIN C19: from ENDO- + Greek *derma* 'skin'.

endogamy /ɛn'dɒɡəmi/ ■ n. 1 Anthropology the custom of marrying only within the limits of a community, clan, or tribe. Compare with EXOGAMY. 2 Biology inbreeding or self-pollination.
- DERIVATIVES **endogamous** adj.
- ORIGIN C19: from ENDO- + Greek *gamos* 'marriage'.

endogenic /,endəʊ'dʒɛnɪk/ ■ adj. Geology formed or occurring beneath the surface of the earth. Often contrasted with EXOGENIC.

endogenous /ɛn'dɒdʒɪnəs, ɪn-/ ■ adj. technical of or relating to an internal cause or origin. Often contrasted with EXOGENOUS.
- DERIVATIVES **endogenously** adv.

endolymph /'endə(ʊ)lɪmf/ ■ n. Anatomy the fluid in the membranous labyrinth of the ear.

endometriosis /,endə(ʊ)mi:trɪ'əʊsɪs/ ■ n. Medicine a condition resulting from the appearance of endometrial tissue outside the womb, causing pelvic pain.

endometrium /,endə(ʊ)'mi:trɪəm/ ■ n. Anatomy the mucous membrane lining the womb.
- DERIVATIVES **endometrial** adj.
- ORIGIN C19: modern Latin, from ENDO- + Greek *mētra* 'womb'.

endomorph /'endə(ʊ)mɔ:f/ ■ n. Physiology a person with a soft round build of body and a high proportion of fat tissue. Compare with ECTOMORPH and MESOMORPH.
- DERIVATIVES **endomorphic** adj. **endomorphy** n.
- ORIGIN 1940s: *endo-* from *endodermal* (being the layer of the embryo giving rise to these physical characteristics) + -MORPH.

endoparasite ■ n. Biology a parasite, such as a tapeworm, that lives inside its host. Compare with ECTOPARASITE.
- DERIVATIVES **endoparasitic** adj.

endoplasm /'endə(ʊ)plaz(ə)m/ ■ n. Biology, dated the more fluid, granular inner layer of the cytoplasm in amoeboid cells. Compare with ECTOPLASM (in sense 1).

endoplasmic reticulum /,endəʊ'plazmɪk/ ■ n. Biology a network of membranous tubules within the cytoplasm of a eukaryotic cell, continuous with the nuclear membrane.

endorphin /ɛn'dɔ:fɪn/ ■ n. Biochemistry any of a group of hormones secreted within the brain and nervous system and activating the body's opiate receptors, causing an analgesic effect.
- ORIGIN 1970s: blend of ENDOGENOUS and MORPHINE.

endorse /ɪn'dɔ:s, ɛn-/ (US & Law also **indorse**) ■ v. 1 declare one's public approval of. 2 sign (a cheque or bill of exchange) on the back to specify another as the payee or to accept responsibility for paying it. ▸ (usu. **be endorsed on**) write (a comment) on a document. 3 (**endorse out**) S. African historical order a black person to leave an urban area for failing to meet the requirements of the Native Laws Amendment Act. 4 Brit. enter an endorsement on (a driving licence).
- DERIVATIVES **endorsee** n. **endorser** n.
- ORIGIN C15: from medieval Latin *indorsare*, from Latin *in-* 'in, on' + *dorsum* 'back'.

endorsement ■ n. 1 an act of endorsing someone or something. 2 (in the UK) a note on a driving licence recording the penalty points incurred for a driving offence. 3 a clause in an insurance policy detailing an exemption from or change in cover. 4 the action of endorsing a cheque or bill of exchange.

endoscope /'endəskəʊp/ ■ n. Medicine an instrument which can be introduced into the body to view its internal parts.
- DERIVATIVES **endoscopic** adj. **endoscopically** adv. **endoscopy** n.

endoskeleton ■ n. Zoology an internal skeleton, such as that of vertebrates. Compare with EXOSKELETON.

endosperm ■ n. Botany the part of a seed which acts as a food store for the developing plant embryo.

endothelium /,endə(ʊ)'θi:lɪəm/ ■ n. the layer of cells lining the blood vessels, heart, and other organs and cavities of the body, and formed from the embryonic mesoderm. Compare with EPITHELIUM.
- DERIVATIVES **endothelial** adj.
- ORIGIN C19: modern Latin, from ENDO- + Greek *thēlē* 'nipple'.

endotherm /'endə(ʊ)θə:m/ ■ n. Zoology an animal that is dependent on the internal generation of heat.
- DERIVATIVES **endothermy** n.

endothermic ■ adj. Chemistry (of a reaction) accompanied by the absorption of heat. The opposite of EXOTHERMIC.

endotoxin /'endəʊ,tɒksɪn/ ■ n. Microbiology a toxin present inside a bacterial cell and released when the cell disintegrates. Compare with EXOTOXIN.

endow /ɪn'daʊ, ɛn-/ ■ v. 1 give or bequeath an income or property to. ▸ establish (a university post, annual prize, etc.) by donating funds. 2 (usu. **be endowed with**) provide with a quality, ability, or asset.
- ORIGIN Middle English: from Anglo-Norman French *endouer*, from *en-* 'in, towards' + Old French *douer* 'give as a gift', from Latin *dotare* (see DOWER).

endowment ■ n. 1 the action of endowing. ▸ an income or form of property endowed. 2 a quality or ability with which a person is endowed. 3 [as modifier] denoting a form of life insurance involving payment of a fixed sum to the insured person on a specified date, or to their estate should they die before this date.

endpaper ■ n. a leaf of paper at the beginning or end of a book, usually fixed to the inside of the cover.

endplay ■ n. Bridge a way of playing in the last few tricks which forces an opponent to make a disadvantageous lead.

end point ■ n. Chemistry the point in a titration at which a reaction is complete, often marked by a colour change.

end run ■ n. 1 American Football an attempt by the ball-carrier to run around the end of the defensive line. 2 N. Amer. an evasive tactic.

end-stopped ■ adj. (of verse) having a pause at the end of each line.

endure /ɪn'djʊə, ɛn-/ ■ v. 1 suffer (something painful and prolonged) patiently. ▸ tolerate. 2 remain in existence.
- DERIVATIVES **endurable** adj. **endurance** n. **enduring** adj. **enduringly** adv.
- ORIGIN Middle English: from Old French *endurer*, from Latin *indurare* 'harden'.

enduro /ɪn'djʊərəʊ, ɛn-/ ■ n. (pl. **-os**) a long-distance race for motor vehicles or bicycles over rough terrain, designed to test endurance.

end-user ■ n. the person who uses a particular product.

endways (also **endwise**) ■ adv. 1 with its end facing upwards, forwards, or towards the viewer. 2 end to end.

end zone ■ n. American Football the rectangular area at the end of the field into which the ball must be carried or passed to score a touchdown.

ENE ■ abbrev. east-north-east.

-ene suffix 1 denoting an inhabitant: *Nazarene*. 2 Chemistry forming names of unsaturated hydrocarbons containing a double bond: *benzene*.
- ORIGIN from Greek *-ēnos*.

enema /'ɛnɪmə/ ■ n. (pl. **enemas** or **enemata** /ɪ'nɛmətə/) a procedure in which fluid is injected into the rectum, typically to expel its contents.
- ORIGIN Middle English: from Greek, from *enienai* 'send or put in'.

enemy ■ n. (pl. **-ies**) a person who is actively opposed or

hostile to someone or something. ▸ **(the enemy)** [treated as sing. or pl.] a hostile nation or its armed forces in time of war.
– ORIGIN Middle English: from Old French *enemi*, from Latin *inimicus*, from *in-* 'not' + *amicus* 'friend'.

energetic /ˌɛnəˈdʒɛtɪk/ ■ adj. **1** showing or involving great energy or activity. **2** Physics of or relating to energy.
– DERIVATIVES **energetically** adv.
– ORIGIN C17: from Greek *energētikos*, from *energein* 'operate, work in or upon'.

energetics ■ pl. n. the properties or behaviour of something in terms of energy.

energy ■ n. (pl. **-ies**) **1** the strength and vitality required for sustained activity. ▸ **(energies)** a person's physical and mental powers as applied to a particular activity. **2** power derived from physical or chemical resources to provide light and heat or to work machines. **3** Physics the property of matter and radiation which is manifest as a capacity to perform work.
– DERIVATIVES **energize** (also **-ise**) v.
– ORIGIN C16: from Greek *energeia*, from *en-* 'in, within' + *ergon* 'work'.

energy audit ■ n. an assessment of the energy needs and efficiency of a building or buildings.

enervate /ˈɛnəveɪt/ ■ v. cause to feel drained of energy.
– DERIVATIVES **enervation** n.
– ORIGIN C17 (*enervation* Middle English): from Latin *enervare* 'weaken (by extraction of the sinews)'.

en famille /ˌɒ̃ faˈmiː/ ■ adv. with one's family. ▸ as or like a family; informally.
– ORIGIN French, 'in family'.

enfant terrible /ˌɒ̃fɒ̃ tɛˈriːbl(ə)/ ■ n. (pl. **enfants terribles** pronunc. same) a person who behaves in an unconventional or controversial way.
– ORIGIN French, 'terrible child'.

enfeeble ■ v. weaken.
– DERIVATIVES **enfeeblement** n.
– ORIGIN Middle English: from Old French *enfeblir*.

enfilade /ˌɛnfɪˈleɪd/ ■ n. **1** a volley of gunfire directed along a line from end to end. **2** a suite of rooms with doorways in line with each other. ■ v. direct an enfilade at.
– ORIGIN C18 (denoting a military post commanding the length of a line): from French, from *enfiler* 'thread on a string'.

enfold /ɪnˈfəʊld, ɛn-/ ■ v. surround; envelop.

enforce ■ v. compel compliance with (a law, rule, or obligation). ▸ cause to happen by necessity or force.
– DERIVATIVES **enforceability** n. **enforceable** adj. **enforced** adj. **enforcedly** adv. **enforcement** n. **enforcer** n.
– ORIGIN Middle English: from Old French *enforcir*, from Latin *in-* 'in' + *fortis* 'strong'.

enfranchise /ɪnˈfran(t)ʃʌɪz, ɛn-/ ■ v. **1** give the right to vote to. **2** historical free (a slave).
– DERIVATIVES **enfranchisement** n.
– ORIGIN Middle English: from Old French *enfranchiss-*, *enfranchir*, from *en-* (expressing a change of state) + *franc*, *franche* 'free'.

ENG ■ abbrev. electronic news-gathering.

engage ■ v. **1** attract or involve (someone's interest or attention). **2** chiefly Brit. employ or hire. ▸ enter into a contract to do. **3** (**engage in/with**) participate or become involved in. ▸ enter into combat with. ▸ (of fencers or swordsmen) bring (weapons) together preparatory to fighting. **4** (with reference to a part of a machine or engine) move or cause to move into position so as to come into operation.
– ORIGIN Middle English: from French *engager*, ultimately from the base of **GAGE**[1].

engaged ■ adj. **1** busy; occupied. ▸ (of a telephone line) unavailable because already in use. **2** having formally agreed to marry.

engagement ■ n. **1** a formal agreement to get married. **2** an appointment. **3** the action of engaging or being engaged. **4** a fight or battle between armed forces.

engaging ■ adj. charming and attractive.
– DERIVATIVES **engagingly** adv.

engender /ɪnˈdʒɛndə, ɛn-/ ■ v. **1** give rise to. **2** archaic beget (offspring).

387

– ORIGIN Middle English: from Old French *engendrer*, from Latin *ingenerare*, from *in-* 'in' + *generare* 'beget'.

engine ■ n. **1** a machine with moving parts that converts power into motion. ▸ historical a mechanical device or instrument, especially one used in warfare. **2** (also **railway engine**) a locomotive.
– DERIVATIVES **-engined** adj.

engine block ■ n. see **BLOCK** (sense 7).

engineer ■ n. **1** a person qualified in engineering. **2** a person who maintains or controls an engine or machine. **3** a skilful contriver. ■ v. **1** design and build. **2** contrive to bring about. **3** modify (an organism) by manipulating its genetic material.
– ORIGIN Middle English: from Old French *engigneor*, from medieval Latin *ingeniator*, from *ingeniare* 'contrive', from Latin *ingenium* (see **ENGINE**).

engineering ■ n. **1** the branch of science and technology concerned with the design, building, and use of engines, machines, and structures. ▸ the practical application of scientific ideas and principles. **2** a field of study or activity concerned with modification or development in a particular area: *software engineering*.

engineering brick ■ n. a strong, dense brick made of semi-vitreous material.

engineering science (also **engineering sciences**) ■ n. the parts of science concerned with the physical and mathematical basis of engineering and machine technology.

engine room ■ n. a room containing engines, especially in a ship.

engirdle (also **engird**) ■ v. poetic/literary encircle.

English ■ n. **1** the language of England, now used in many varieties throughout the world. **2** N. Amer. (in pool or billiards) spin or side given to a ball. ■ adj. of or relating to England or its people or language. ▸ (in South Africa) of or relating to white English-speaking people.
– DERIVATIVES **Englishness** n.
– ORIGIN Old English *Englisc* (see **ANGLE**, **-ISH**[1]).

English breakfast ■ n. a substantial breakfast including hot cooked food such as bacon and eggs.

English horn ■ n. chiefly N. Amer. another term for **COR ANGLAIS**.

Englishman (or **Englishwoman**) ■ n. (pl. **-men** or **-women**) a native or national of England, or a person of English descent. ▸ (in South Africa) a white English-speaking person.

English mustard ■ n. a kind of mustard with a very hot taste.

English oak ■ n. the common oak. [*Quercus robur*.]

English rose ■ n. an attractive English girl with a delicate, fair-skinned complexion.

engorge /ɪnˈɡɔːdʒ, ɛn-/ ■ v. swell or cause to swell with blood, water, etc.
– ORIGIN C15: from Old French *engorgier* 'feed to excess', from *en-* 'into' + *gorge* 'throat'.

engraft (also **ingraft**) ■ v. another term for **GRAFT**[1].

engrailed ■ adj. chiefly Heraldry having semicircular indentations along the edge. Compare with **INVECTED**.

engrain ■ v. variant spelling of **INGRAIN**.

engram /ˈɛnɡram/ ■ n. a hypothetical permanent change in the brain accounting for the existence of memory.
– ORIGIN C20: from German *Engramm*, from Greek *en-* 'within' + *gramma* 'letter of the alphabet'.

engrave ■ v. **1** cut or carve (a text or design) on a hard surface. ▸ cut or carve a text or design on. ▸ cut (a design) as lines on a metal plate for printing. **2** (**be engraved on** or **in**) be permanently fixed in (one's memory or mind).
– DERIVATIVES **engraver** n. **engraving** n.
– ORIGIN C15: from **EN-**[1], **IN-**[2] + **GRAVE**[3], influenced by obsolete French *engraver*.

engross /ɪnˈɡrəʊs, ɛn-/ ■ v. [often as adj. **engrossed**] absorb all the attention of.
– ORIGIN Middle English: from Old French *en gros*, from medieval Latin *in grosso* 'wholesale'.

engulf

engulf ■ v. (of a natural force) sweep over so as to completely surround or cover.
– DERIVATIVES **engulfment** n.

enhance /ɪnˈhɑːns, -hans, ɛn-/ ■ v. improve the quality, value, or extent of.
– DERIVATIVES **enhancement** n. **enhancer** n.
– ORIGIN Middle English: from Anglo-Norman French *enhauncer*, based on Latin *in-* (expressing intensive force) + *altus* 'high'.

enigma /ɪˈnɪɡmə/ ■ n. a mysterious or puzzling person or thing.
– DERIVATIVES **enigmatic** adj. **enigmatically** adv.
– ORIGIN C16: from Greek *ainigma* 'riddle'.

enjambement /ɪnˈdʒam(b)m(ə)nt, ɛn-, ɒ̃ˈʒɔ̃bmɒ̃/ (also **enjambment**) ■ n. (in verse) the continuation of a sentence without a pause beyond the end of a line, couplet, or stanza.
– ORIGIN C19: French, from *enjamber* 'stride over, go beyond'.

enjoin ■ v. instruct or urge to do something. ▸ (**enjoin someone from**) Law prohibit someone from performing (an action) by issuing an injunction.
– ORIGIN Middle English: from Old French *enjoindre*, from Latin *injungere* 'join, attach, impose'.

enjoy ■ v. 1 take pleasure in. 2 possess and benefit from.
– DERIVATIVES **enjoyer** n.
– ORIGIN Middle English: from Old French *enjoier* 'give joy to' or *enjoïr* 'enjoy', both based on Latin *gaudere* 'rejoice'.

enjoyable /ɪnˈdʒɔɪəb(ə)l, ɛn-/ ■ adj. (of an activity or occasion) giving enjoyment or pleasure.
– DERIVATIVES **enjoyability** n. **enjoyableness** n. **enjoyably** adv.

enjoyment ■ n. 1 the state or process of taking pleasure in something. ▸ a thing that gives pleasure. 2 the action of possessing and benefiting from something.

enlarge ■ v. 1 make or become bigger. 2 (**enlarge on/upon**) speak or write about in greater detail.
– ORIGIN Middle English: from Old French *enlarger*.

enlargement ■ n. the action or state of enlarging or being enlarged. ▸ a photograph that is larger than the original negative or than an earlier print.

enlarger ■ n. Photography an apparatus for enlarging or reducing negatives or positives.

enlighten ■ v. give greater knowledge and understanding to. ▸ give spiritual insight to. ▸ [as adj. **enlightened**] rational, tolerant, and well-informed.
– ORIGIN Middle English: in early use from Old English *inlīhtan* 'to shine'; later from EN-1, IN-2 + LIGHTEN2 or the noun LIGHT1.

enlightenment ■ n. 1 the action of enlightening or the state of being enlightened. ▸ the attainment of spiritual insight, in particular (in Buddhism) that awareness which frees a person from the cycle of rebirth. 2 (**the Enlightenment**) a European intellectual movement of the late 17th and 18th centuries emphasizing reason and individualism rather than tradition.

enlist ■ v. enrol or be enrolled in the armed services. ▸ engage (a person or their help).
– DERIVATIVES **enlistment** n.

enlisted man ■ n. US a member of the armed forces below the rank of officer.

enliven ■ v. make more entertaining or interesting. ▸ make more cheerful or animated.
– ORIGIN C17 ('give life to'): from C16 *enlive*, *inlive* (in the same sense).

en masse /ɒ̃ ˈmas/ ■ adv. all together.
– ORIGIN C18: French, 'in a mass'.

enmesh ■ v. (usu. **be enmeshed in**) entangle.

enmity ■ n. (pl. -ies) the state of being an enemy; hostility.
– ORIGIN Middle English: from Old French *enemi(s)tie*, from Latin *inimicus* (see ENEMY).

ennoble ■ v. give a noble rank or title to. ▸ give greater dignity to; elevate.
– DERIVATIVES **ennoblement** n.
– ORIGIN C15: from French *ennoblir*.

ennui /ɒnˈwiː/ ■ n. listlessness and dissatisfaction arising from boredom.
– ORIGIN C18: from Latin, from (*mihi*) *in odio* (*est*) '(it is) hateful (to me)'.

enormity ■ n. (pl. -ies) 1 (**the enormity of**) the large scale or extreme seriousness of (something bad). ▸ (in neutral use) great size or scale. 2 a grave crime or sin.
– ORIGIN Middle English: from Latin *enormitas*, from *enormis*, from *e-* 'out of' + *norma* 'pattern, standard'.

enormous ■ adj. very large.
– DERIVATIVES **enormously** adv.

enough ■ det. & pron. as much or as many as is necessary or desirable. ■ adv. 1 to the required degree or extent. 2 to a moderate degree.
– PHRASES **enough is enough** no more will be tolerated. **enough said** all is understood and there is no need to say more.
– ORIGIN Old English, of Germanic origin.

en passant /ɒ̃ paˈsɑ̃nt, ˈpasɒ̃/ ■ adv. by the way.
– PHRASES **en passant rule** (or **law**) Chess the rule that a pawn making a first move of two squares instead of one may nevertheless be immediately captured by an opposing pawn on the fifth rank.
– ORIGIN C17: French, 'in passing'.

en pointe ■ adj. & adv. Ballet on the tips of the toes. See POINTE.
– ORIGIN from French.

en primeur /ˌɒ̃ priːˈmɜː/ ■ adj. & adv. (of wine) newly produced and made available.
– ORIGIN French, 'as being new'.

en prise /ɒ̃ ˈpriːz/ ■ adj. Chess (of a piece or pawn) in a position to be taken.
– ORIGIN C19: French.

enquire ■ v. ask for information. ▸ (**enquire after**) ask about the health and well-being of. ▸ (**enquire into**) investigate. ▸ [as adj. **enquiring**] (of a look) suggesting that information is sought.
– DERIVATIVES **enquirer** n. **enquiringly** adv.
– ORIGIN Middle English *enquere*, from Latin *inquirere*, from *quaerere* 'seek'.

enquiry ■ n. (pl. -ies) an act of asking for information. ▸ an official investigation.

enrage ■ v. (usu. **be enraged**) make very angry.
– ORIGIN C15: from French *enrager*.

enrapture ■ v. give intense pleasure to.

enrich ■ v. 1 improve the quality or value of. 2 [usu. as adj. **enriched**] increase the proportion of a particular isotope in (an element), especially that of the fissile isotope U-235 in uranium. 3 make wealthy or wealthier.
– DERIVATIVES **enrichment** n.
– ORIGIN Middle English: from Old French *enrichir*.

enrol /ɪnˈrəʊl, ɛn-/ (chiefly US also **enroll**) ■ v. (**enrolled, enrolling**) officially register as a member or student. ▸ recruit. ▸ Law, chiefly historical enter (a deed or other document) among the rolls of a court of justice.
– ORIGIN Middle English: from Old French *enroller*, from *en-* 'in' + *rolle* 'a roll' (names being orig. written on a roll of parchment).

enrolment (chiefly US also **enrollment**) ■ n. the action of enrolling or being enrolled. ▸ the number of people enrolled, typically at a school or college.

en route /ɒn ˈruːt/ ■ adv. on the way.
– ORIGIN C18: French (see ROUTE).

ensconce /ɪnˈskɒns, ɛn-/ ■ v. (often **ensconce oneself**) establish in a comfortable, safe, or secret place.
– ORIGIN C16: from EN-1, IN-2 + SCONCE2.

ensemble /ɒnˈsɒmb(ə)l/ ■ n. 1 a group of musicians, actors, or dancers who perform together. ▸ a scene or passage written for performance by a whole cast, choir, or group of instruments. 2 a group of items viewed as a whole. ▸ a set of clothes worn together.
– ORIGIN Middle English: from French, from Latin *insimul*, from *in-* 'in' + *simul* 'at the same time'.

enshrine ■ v. (usu. **be enshrined**) 1 place (a revered or precious object) in an appropriate receptacle. 2 preserve (a right, tradition, or idea) in a form that ensures it will be respected.
– DERIVATIVES **enshrinement** n.

enshroud /ɪnˈʃraʊd, ɛn-/ ■ v. poetic/literary envelop completely and hide from view.

ensiform /ˈɛnsɪfɔːm/ ■ adj. chiefly Botany long and narrow with sharp edges and a pointed tip.
– ORIGIN C16: from Latin *ensis* 'sword' + -FORM.

ensign /ˈɛnsʌɪn/ ■ n. **1** a flag, especially a military or naval one indicating nationality. **2** the lowest rank of commissioned officer in the navy, below sub lieutenant. ▸ historical the lowest rank of commissioned infantry officer in the British army. **3** historical a standard-bearer.
– ORIGIN Middle English: from Old French *enseigne*, from Latin *insignia* (see INSIGNIA).

ensile /ɛnˈsʌɪl/ ■ v. put (grass or another crop) into a silo.
– ORIGIN C19: from French *ensiler*, from Spanish *ensilar*.

enslave ■ v. make a slave. ▸ cause to lose freedom of choice or action.
– DERIVATIVES **enslavement** n.
– ORIGIN C17: from EN-1, IN-2 + SLAVE.

ensnare ■ v. catch in or as in a trap.
– DERIVATIVES **ensnarement** n.

enstatite /ˈɛnstətʌɪt/ ■ n. a translucent mineral consisting of magnesium silicate, found in igneous rocks and some meteorites.
– ORIGIN C19: from Greek *enstatēs* 'adversary' (because of its refractory nature) + -ITE1.

ensue ■ v. (**ensues**, **ensued**, **ensuing**) happen or occur afterwards or as a result.
– ORIGIN Middle English: from Old French *ensivre*, from Latin *insequi*, from *sequi* 'follow'.

en suite /ɒn ˈswiːt/ ■ adj. & adv. (of a bathroom) immediately adjoining a bedroom and forming a single unit. ▸ (of a bedroom) having such a bathroom.
– ORIGIN C18: from French, 'in sequence'.

ensure /ɪnˈʃʊə, ɛn-/ ■ v. make certain that (something) will occur or be so. ▸ (**ensure against**) make sure that (a problem) does not occur.
– ORIGIN Middle English: from Anglo-Norman French *enseurer*, alteration of Old French *aseurer*, earlier form of *assurer* (see ASSURE).

ENT ■ abbrev. ear, nose, and throat (as a department in a hospital).

-ent ■ suffix **1** (forming adjectives) denoting an occurrence of action: *effervescent*. ▸ denoting a state: *convenient*. **2** (forming nouns) denoting an agent: *coefficient*.
– ORIGIN from French, or from the Latin present participial verb stem *-ent-*.

entablature /ɛnˈtablətʃə, ɪn-/ ■ n. Architecture the upper part of a classical building supported by columns or a colonnade, comprising the architrave, frieze, and cornice.
– ORIGIN C17: from Italian *intavolatura* 'boarding'.

entablement /ɛnˈteɪb(ə)lm(ə)nt, ɪn-/ ■ n. Architecture a platform supporting a statue, above the dado and base.
– ORIGIN C17: from French, from *table* 'table'.

entail ■ v. **1** involve as an inevitable part or consequence. **2** Law settle the inheritance of (property) over a number of generations so that ownership remains within a particular family. ■ n. Law an instance of entailing property. ▸ an entailed estate.
– DERIVATIVES **entailment** n.
– ORIGIN Middle English: from EN-1, IN-2 + Old French *taille* 'notch, tax', from *tailler* 'to cut'.

entangle ■ v. (usu. **be entangled in/with**) **1** cause to become tangled. **2** involve in complicated circumstances.
– DERIVATIVES **entanglement** n.

entasis /ˈɛntəsɪs/ ■ n. (pl. **entases**) Architecture a slight convex curve in the shaft of a column, introduced to correct the visual illusion of concavity produced by a straight shaft.
– ORIGIN C17: modern Latin, from Greek, from *enteinein* 'to stretch or strain'.

entelechy /ɛnˈtɛləki, ɪn-/ ■ n. (pl. **-ies**) Philosophy **1** the realization of potential. **2** the supposed vital principle that guides the development and functioning of an organism or other system.
– ORIGIN Middle English: from Greek *entelekheia*, from *en-* 'within' + *telos* 'end, perfection' + *ekhein* 'be in a certain state'.

entente /ɒnˈtɒnt, ɔ̃ˈtɒ̃t/ (also **entente cordiale** /ˌkɔːdɪˈɑːl/) ■ n. a friendly understanding or informal alliance between states or factions.
– ORIGIN C19: French *entente* (*cordiale*) '(friendly) understanding'.

enter ■ v. **1** come or go into. ▸ penetrate. ▸ (**enter on/upon**) Law (as a legal entitlement) go freely into (property) as or as if the owner. **2** (often **enter into**) begin to be involved in. ▸ (**enter on/upon**) begin (an activity or job). ▸ join (an institution or profession). ▸ register as a competitor or participant in. ▸ register to participate in a competition or examination. ▸ (**enter into**) undertake to bind oneself by (an agreement). **3** record (information) in a book, computer, etc. ▸ Law submit (a statement) in an official capacity, usually in a court of law.
– ORIGIN Middle English: from Old French *entrer*, from Latin *intrare*, from *intra* 'within'.

enteral /ˈɛntər(ə)l/ ■ adj. Medicine (chiefly of nutrition) involving or passing through the intestine. Often contrasted with PARENTERAL.
– DERIVATIVES **enterally** adv.
– ORIGIN C20: from Greek *enteron* 'intestine', partly as a back-formation from PARENTERAL.

enteric /ɛnˈtɛrɪk/ ■ adj. of, relating to, or occurring in the intestines.
– ORIGIN C19: from Greek *enterikos*, from *enteron* 'intestine'.

enteric fever ■ n. another term for TYPHOID or PARATYPHOID.

enteritis /ˌɛntəˈrʌɪtɪs/ ■ n. Medicine inflammation of the intestine, especially the small intestine, usually accompanied by diarrhoea.

entero- ■ comb. form of or relating to the intestine: *enterovirus*.
– ORIGIN from Greek *enteron*.

enterostomy /ˌɛntəˈrɒstəmi/ ■ n. (pl. **-ies**) a surgical operation in which the small intestine is diverted to an artificial opening, usually in the abdominal wall.

enterotoxin /ˌɛntərəʊˈtɒksɪn/ ■ n. Medicine a toxin produced in or affecting the intestines.

enterovirus /ˈɛntərəʊˌvʌɪrəs/ ■ n. Medicine any of a group of RNA viruses (e.g. those causing polio and hepatitis A) which occur chiefly in the gastrointestinal tract.

enterprise ■ n. **1** a project or undertaking, especially a bold one. ▸ bold resourcefulness. **2** a business or company.
– ORIGIN Middle English: from Old French, 'something undertaken', from *entreprendre*, from Latin *prendere*, *prehendere* 'to take'.

enterprise zone ■ n. an area in which tax concessions or other state incentives are offered to encourage business investment.

enterprising ■ adj. showing initiative and resourcefulness.
– DERIVATIVES **enterprisingly** adv.

entertain ■ v. **1** provide with amusement or enjoyment. ▸ show hospitality to. **2** give attention or consideration to.
– DERIVATIVES **entertaining** adj. **entertainingly** adv.
– ORIGIN Middle English: from French *entretenir*, from Latin *inter* 'among' + *tenere* 'to hold'.

entertainer ■ n. a person, such as a singer or comedian, whose job is to entertain others.

entertainment ■ n. the action of providing or being provided with amusement or enjoyment. ▸ an event or performance designed to entertain. ▸ the provision of hospitality.

enthalpy /ˈɛnθ(ə)lpi, ɛnˈθalpi/ ■ n. Physics a thermodynamic quantity equivalent to the total heat content of a system.
– ORIGIN 1920s: from Greek *enthalpein* (v.), from *en-* 'within' + *thalpein* 'to heat'.

enthral /ɪnˈθrɔːl, ɛn-/ (US **enthrall**) ■ v. (**enthralled**, **enthralling**) **1** (usu. **be enthralled**) capture the fascinated attention of. **2** (also **inthrall**) archaic enslave.
– DERIVATIVES **enthralment** (US **enthrallment**) n.
– ORIGIN Middle English: from EN-1, IN-2 + THRALL.

enthrone ■ v. install (a monarch or bishop) on a throne with due ceremony. ▸ treat with honour and respect.
– DERIVATIVES **enthronement** n.

enthuse

enthuse /ɪnˈθjuːz, ɛn-/ ■ v. be or make enthusiastic.

enthusiasm ■ n. intense enjoyment, interest, or approval. ▸ an object of such feelings.
– ORIGIN C17: from Greek *enthousiasmos*, from *enthous* 'possessed by a god', from *theos* 'god'.

enthusiast ■ n. a person who is full of enthusiasm for something.

enthusiastic ■ adj. having or showing intense enjoyment, interest, or approval.
– DERIVATIVES **enthusiastically** adv.

enthymeme /ˈɛnθɪmiːm/ ■ n. Logic an argument in which one premise is not explicitly stated.
– ORIGIN C16: from Greek *enthumēma*, from *enthumeisthai* 'consider'.

entice /ɪnˈtʌɪs, ɛn-/ ■ v. attract by offering pleasure or advantage.
– DERIVATIVES **enticement** n. **enticing** adj. **enticingly** adv.
– ORIGIN Middle English: from Old French *enticier*, prob. from a base meaning 'set on fire', based on an alteration of Latin *titio* 'firebrand'.

entire /ɪnˈtʌɪə, ɛn-/ ■ adj. 1 with no part left out; whole. 2 (of a male horse) not castrated. 3 Botany (of a leaf) without indentations or division into leaflets. 4 without qualification; absolute.
– ORIGIN Middle English: from Old French *entier*, from Latin *integer* 'untouched, whole', from *in-* 'not' + *tangere* 'to touch'.

entirely ■ adv. completely. ▸ solely.

entirety ■ n. (**the entirety**) the whole.
– PHRASES **in its entirety** as a whole.

entisol /ˈɛntɪsɒl/ ■ n. Soil Science a mineral soil that has not yet differentiated into distinct horizons.
– ORIGIN C20: from ENTIRE + -SOL.

entitle ■ v. 1 give a right to. 2 give a title to (a book, play, etc.).
– DERIVATIVES **entitlement** n.
– ORIGIN Middle English: from late Latin *intitulare*, from *in-* 'in' + Latin *titulus* 'title'.

entity /ˈɛntɪti/ ■ n. (pl. **-ies**) a thing with distinct and independent existence.
– ORIGIN C15: from medieval Latin *entitas*, from late Latin *ens, ent-* 'being'.

entomb ■ v. 1 place in a tomb. 2 bury in or under.
– DERIVATIVES **entombment** n.
– ORIGIN Middle English: from Old French *entomber*.

entomo- /ˈɛntəməʊ/ ■ comb. form of an insect; of or relating to insects: *entomophagous*.
– ORIGIN from Greek *entomon*, neuter (denoting an insect) of *entomos* 'cut up, segmented'.

entomology /ˌɛntəˈmɒlədʒi/ ■ n. the branch of zoology concerned with the study of insects.
– DERIVATIVES **entomological** adj. **entomologist** n.
– ORIGIN C18: from modern Latin *entomologia*, from Greek *entomon* (denoting an insect) + *-logia* (see -LOGY).

entomophilous /ˌɛntəˈmɒfɪləs/ ■ adj. Botany pollinated by insects.
– DERIVATIVES **entomophily** n.

Entoprocta /ˌɛntə(ʊ)ˈprɒktə/ ■ pl. n. Zoology a small phylum of sedentary aquatic invertebrates with a rounded body on a long stalk, bearing a ring of tentacles for filtering food from the water.
– ORIGIN modern Latin: from Greek *entos* 'within' + *prōktos* 'anus', the anus being within the ring of tentacles.

entoptic /ɪnˈtɒptɪk, ɛn-/ ■ adj. (of visual images) occurring or originating inside the eye.
– ORIGIN C19: from Greek *entos* 'within' + OPTIC.

entourage /ˈɒntʊrɑːʒ, ˌɒntʊ(ə)ˈrɑːʒ/ ■ n. a group of people attending or surrounding an important person.
– ORIGIN C19: French, from *entourer* 'to surround'.

entr'acte /ˈɒntrakt, 'ɔ̃-/ ■ n. an interval between two acts of a play or opera. ▸ a piece of music or a dance performed during such an interval.
– ORIGIN C19: French, from *entre* 'between' + *acte* 'act'.

entrails ■ pl. n. a person's or animal's intestines or internal organs.
– ORIGIN Middle English: from Old French *entrailles*, from medieval Latin *intralia*, alteration of Latin *interanea* 'internal things', from *inter* 'among'.

entrain¹ /ɪnˈtreɪn, ɛn-/ ■ v. board or put on board a train.

entrain² /ɪnˈtreɪn, ɛn-/ ■ v. 1 (of a current or fluid) incorporate and sweep along in its flow. 2 bring about as a consequence. 3 Biology cause to fall into synchronism with a rhythmic phenomenon.
– DERIVATIVES **entrainment** n.
– ORIGIN C16: from French *entraîner*, from *en-* 'in' + *traîner* 'to drag'.

entrance¹ /ˈɛntr(ə)ns/ ■ n. 1 an opening allowing access. 2 an act of entering. 3 the right, means, or opportunity to enter.
– ORIGIN C15: from Old French, from *entrer* 'enter'.

entrance² /ɪnˈtrɑːns, ɛn-/ ■ v. (usu. **be entranced**) fill with wonder and delight. ▸ cast a spell on.
– DERIVATIVES **entrancement** n. **entrancing** adj. **entrancingly** adv.

entrant ■ n. a person who enters something.
– ORIGIN C17: from French, 'entering', from *entrer* (see ENTER).

entrap ■ v. (**entrapped**, **entrapping**) catch in or as in a trap. ▸ (of a police officer) deceive (someone) into committing a crime in order to secure their prosecution.
– DERIVATIVES **entrapment** n.
– ORIGIN C16: from Old French *entraper*.

entreat ■ v. ask (someone) earnestly or anxiously. ▸ ask earnestly or anxiously for.
– DERIVATIVES **entreating** adj. **entreatingly** adv. **entreaty** n. (pl. **-ies**).
– ORIGIN Middle English: from Old French *entraitier*, from *traitier* 'to treat', from Latin *tractare* 'to handle'.

entrechat /ˈɒtrəʃɑː/ ■ n. Ballet a vertical jump during which the dancer repeatedly crosses the feet and beats them together.
– ORIGIN French: from Italian (*capriola*) *intrecciata* 'complicated (caper)'.

entrecôte /ˈɒntrəkəʊt/ ■ n. a boned steak cut off the sirloin.
– ORIGIN French: from *entre* 'between' + *côte* 'rib'.

entrée /ˈɒntreɪ/ ■ n. 1 the main course of a meal. ▸ Brit. a dish served between the fish and meat courses at a formal dinner. 2 right of entry.
– ORIGIN C18: French, from *entrer* (see ENTRY).

entrench (also **intrench**) ■ v. 1 (usu. **be entrenched**) establish so firmly that change is difficult. ▸ apply extra legal safeguards to (a constitutional right guaranteed by legislation). 2 establish (a military force, camp, etc.) in trenches or other fortified positions.
– DERIVATIVES **entrenchment** n.

entre nous /ˌɒtrə ˈnuː/ ■ adv. between ourselves.
– ORIGIN from French.

entrepôt /ˈɒntrəpəʊ/ ■ n. a port or other place which acts as a centre for import and export.
– ORIGIN C18: French, from *entreposer* 'to store'.

entrepreneur /ˌɒntrəprəˈnəː/ ■ n. a person who sets up a business or businesses, taking on greater than normal financial risks in order to do so.
– DERIVATIVES **entrepreneurial** /-ˈn(j)əːrɪəl -ˈnjʊərɪəl/ adj. **entrepreneurialism** n. **entrepreneurially** adv. **entrepreneurism** n. **entrepreneurship** n.
– ORIGIN C19: from French, from *entreprendre* (see ENTERPRISE).

entropy /ˈɛntrəpi/ ■ n. 1 Physics a thermodynamic quantity representing the unavailability of a system's thermal energy for conversion into mechanical work, often interpreted as the degree of disorder or randomness in the system. 2 (in information theory) a logarithmic measure of the rate of transfer of information in a particular message or language.
– DERIVATIVES **entropic** /-ˈtrɒpɪk/ adj. **entropically** adv.
– ORIGIN C19: from EN-² + Greek *tropē* 'transformation'.

entrust ■ v. assign a responsibility to. ▸ put into someone's care.

entry ■ n. (pl. **-ies**) 1 an act or the action of entering. 2 a place of entrance. 3 the right, means, or opportunity to enter. ▸ (also **entry into possession**) Law the action of taking up the legal right to property. ▸ Bridge a card providing an

opportunity to transfer the lead to a particular hand. **4** an item entered in a list, account book, reference book, etc. **5** an entrant to a competition. ▸ the number of entrants in a race or competition. **6** the forward part of a ship's hull below the waterline, considered in terms of breadth or narrowness.
– ORIGIN Middle English: from Old French *entree*, from Latin *intrata*, from *intrare* (see ENTER).

entry-level ■ adj. suitable for a beginner or first-time user.

entry permit ■ n. an official document that authorizes a foreign citizen to enter a country.

entryphone ■ n. Brit. trademark a type of intercom at the entrance to a building by which visitors may identify themselves before the door is unlocked.

entryway ■ n. N. Amer. an entrance.

entwine ■ v. wind or twist together.
– DERIVATIVES **entwinement** n.

enucleate /ɪˈnjuːklɪeɪt/ ■ v. **1** Biology remove the nucleus from (a cell). **2** surgically remove (an eyeball or other structure) from its surrounding capsule. ■ adj. Biology lacking a nucleus.
– DERIVATIVES **enucleation** n.
– ORIGIN C16: from Latin *enucleare* 'extract'.

E-number ■ n. Brit. a code number preceded by the letter E, denoting food additives numbered in accordance with EU directives.

enumerable /ɪˈnjuːm(ə)rəb(ə)l/ ■ adj. Mathematics able to be counted by one-to-one correspondence with the set of positive integers.

enumerate /ɪˈnjuːməreɪt/ ■ v. **1** mention one by one. **2** formal establish the number of.
– DERIVATIVES **enumeration** n.
– ORIGIN C17: from Latin *enumerare* 'count out'.

enumerator ■ n. a person employed in taking a census of the population.

enunciate /ɪˈnʌnsɪeɪt/ ■ v. **1** say or pronounce clearly. **2** set out precisely or definitely.
– DERIVATIVES **enunciation** n. **enunciator** n.
– ORIGIN C17 (*enunciation* C16): from Latin *enuntiare* 'announce clearly'.

enure /ɪˈnjʊə/ (also **inure**) ■ v. (**enure for/to**) Law (of a right or other advantage) belong or be available to.

enuresis /ˌɛnjʊəˈriːsɪs/ ■ n. Medicine involuntary urination, especially by children at night.
– DERIVATIVES **enuretic** adj. & n.
– ORIGIN C19: modern Latin, from Greek *enourein* 'urinate in'.

envelop /ɪnˈvɛləp, ɛn-/ ■ v. (**enveloped**, **enveloping**) wrap up, cover, or surround completely.
– DERIVATIVES **envelopment** n.
– ORIGIN Middle English: from Old French *envoluper*, from *en-* 'in' + a second element of unknown origin (also found in DEVELOP).

envelope /ˈɛnvələʊp, ˈɒn-/ ■ n. **1** a flat paper container with a sealable flap, used to enclose a letter or document. **2** a covering or containing structure or layer. **3** Electronics a curve joining the successive peaks of a modulated wave. **4** Mathematics a curve or surface tangent to each of a family of curves or surfaces.
– PHRASES **push the (edge of the) envelope** informal approach or extend the limits of what is possible. [orig. aviation slang, relating to graphs of aerodynamic performance.]
– ORIGIN C16: from French *enveloppe*, from *envelopper* 'envelop'.

envenomate ■ v. poison by biting or stinging.
– DERIVATIVES **envenomation** n.

enviable /ˈɛnvɪəb(ə)l/ ■ adj. arousing or likely to arouse envy.
– DERIVATIVES **enviably** adv.

envious ■ adj. feeling or showing envy.
– DERIVATIVES **enviously** adv.

environ /ɪnˈvʌɪrən, ɛn-/ ■ v. formal surround; enclose.
– ORIGIN Middle English: from Old French, from *environ* 'surroundings', from *en* 'in' + *viron* 'circuit'.

environment ■ n. **1** the surroundings or conditions in which a person, animal, or plant lives or operates. ▸ Computing the overall structure within which a user, computer, or program operates. **2** (**the environment**) the natural world, especially as affected by human activity.
– DERIVATIVES **environmental** adj. **environmentally** adv.

environmental audit ■ n. an assessment of the extent to which an organization is observing practices which seek to minimize harm to the environment.

environmentalist ■ n. **1** a person who is concerned with or advocates the protection of the environment. **2** a person who considers that environment has the primary influence on the development of a person or group.
– DERIVATIVES **environmentalism** n.

environs ■ pl. n. the surrounding area or district.
– ORIGIN C17: from French, pl. of *environ* (see ENVIRON).

envisage /ɪnˈvɪzɪdʒ, ɛn-/ ■ v. regard or conceive of as a possibility. ▸ form a mental picture of.
– ORIGIN C19: from French *envisager*, from *en-* 'in' + *visage* 'face'.

envision ■ v. visualize.

envoy /ˈɛnvɔɪ/ ■ n. a messenger or representative, especially one on a diplomatic mission.
– ORIGIN C17: from French *envoyé*, from *envoyer* 'send'.

envy ■ n. (pl. **-ies**) discontented or resentful longing aroused by another's possessions, qualities, or luck. ▸ (**the envy of**) a person or thing that inspires such a feeling. ■ v. (**-ies**, **-ied**) feel envy of.
– DERIVATIVES **envier** n.
– ORIGIN Middle English: from Old French *envie* (n.), *envier* (v.), from Latin *invidia*, from *invidere* 'regard maliciously', from *in-* 'into' + *videre* 'to see'.

enwrap (also **inwrap**) ■ v. (**enwrapped**, **enwrapping**) wrap; envelop.

enzootic /ˌɛnzəʊˈɒtɪk/ ■ adj. (of a disease) regularly affecting animals in a particular district or at a particular season.
– ORIGIN C19: from EN-[2] + Greek *zōion* 'animal'.

enzyme /ˈɛnzʌɪm/ ■ n. Biochemistry a substance produced by a living organism and acting as a catalyst to promote a specific biochemical reaction.
– DERIVATIVES **enzymatic** adj. **enzymic** adj. **enzymological** adj. **enzymologist** n. **enzymology** n.
– ORIGIN C19: German *Enzym*, from modern Greek *enzumos* 'leavened'.

Eocene /ˈiːə(ʊ)siːn/ ■ adj. Geology relating to or denoting the second epoch of the Tertiary period (between the Palaeocene and Oligocene epochs, 56.5 to 35.4 million years ago), a time when the first horses, bats, and whales appeared.
– ORIGIN C19: from Greek *ēōs* 'dawn' + *kainos* 'new'.

eolian ■ adj. US spelling of AEOLIAN.

eon ■ n. US and technical spelling of AEON.

eosin /ˈiːə(ʊ)sɪn/ ■ n. a red fluorescent dye that is a bromine derivative of fluorescein.
– ORIGIN C19: from Greek *ēōs* 'dawn'.

-eous ■ suffix (forming adjectives) resembling; displaying the nature of: *aqueous*.
– ORIGIN from the Latin suffix *-eus* + -OUS.

EP ■ abbrev. **1** electroplate. **2** European Parliament. **3** extended-play (of a record or compact disc). **4** extreme pressure (used in grading lubricants).

Ep. ■ abbrev. Epistle.

e.p. ■ abbrev. Chess en passant.

ep- /ɛp, ɪp, iːp/ ■ prefix variant spelling of EPI- shortened before a vowel or *h* (as in *eparch*, *ephod*).

EPA ■ abbrev. (in the US) Environmental Protection Agency.

epaulette /ˈɛpəlɛt, -ˌpɔːl-, ˌɛpəˈlɛt/ (US also **epaulet**) ■ n. an ornamental shoulder piece on a military uniform.
– ORIGIN C18: from French *épaulette*, diminutive of *épaule* 'shoulder'.

epaxial /ɛˈpaksɪəl/ ■ adj. Anatomy & Zoology situated on the dorsal side of an axis.

épée /ˈɛpeɪ, ˈɛp-/ ■ n. a sharp-pointed duelling sword, used, with the end blunted, in fencing.
– DERIVATIVES **épéeist** n.
– ORIGIN C19: French, 'sword'.

epergne

epergne /ɪˈpəːn/ ■ n. an ornamental centrepiece for a dining table, holding fruit or flowers.
– ORIGIN C18: perhaps an alteration of French *épargne* 'economy'.

ephedra /ɛˈfɛdrə/ ■ n. an evergreen trailing or climbing shrub of warm arid regions, some kinds of which are a source of the drug ephedrine. [Genus *Ephedra*.]
– ORIGIN from Latin, 'equisetum' (which it resembles).

ephedrine /ˈɛfədriːn/ ■ n. Medicine an alkaloid drug which causes constriction of the blood vessels and widening of the bronchial passages and is used to relieve asthma and hay fever.
– ORIGIN C19: from EPHEDRA.

ephemera /ɪˈfɛm(ə)rə, -ˈfiːm-/ ■ pl. n. items of short-lived interest or usefulness.
– DERIVATIVES **ephemerist** n.
– ORIGIN C16: pl. of *ephemeron*, from Greek, neuter of *ephēmeros* 'lasting only a day'.

ephemeral ■ adj. lasting or living for a very short time. ▶ (chiefly of plants) having a very short life cycle.
– DERIVATIVES **ephemerality** n. **ephemerally** adv. **ephemeralness** n.

ephemeris /ɪˈfɛm(ə)rɪs, -ˈfiːm-/ ■ n. (pl. **ephemerides** /ˌɛfɪˈmɛrɪdiːz/) Astronomy & Astrology a table of the calculated positions of a celestial object at regular intervals throughout a period.
– ORIGIN C16: from Latin, from Greek *ephēmeros* 'lasting only a day'.

Ephemeroptera /ɪˌfɛməˈrɒptərə, -ˌfiːm-/ ■ pl. n. Entomology an order of insects that comprises the mayflies.
– DERIVATIVES **ephemeropteran** n. & adj.
– ORIGIN from *Ephemera* (genus name) + *pteron* 'wing'.

epi- (also **ep-**) ■ prefix **1** upon: *epigraph*. **2** above: *epicotyl*. **3** in addition: *epiphenomenon*.
– ORIGIN from Greek *epi* 'upon, near to, in addition'.

epic ■ n. a long poem narrating the deeds of heroic or legendary figures or the past history of a nation. ▶ a long film, book, or other work portraying heroic deeds or covering an extended period of time. ■ adj. of, relating to, or characteristic of an epic or epics.
– DERIVATIVES **epical** adj. **epically** adv.
– ORIGIN C16: from Greek *epikos*, from *epos* 'word, song'.

epicanthic fold ■ n. a fold of skin from the upper eyelid covering the inner angle of the eye, typical in many peoples of eastern Asia.

epicardium /ˌɛpɪˈkɑːdɪəm/ ■ n. Anatomy a serous membrane that forms the innermost layer of the pericardium.
– DERIVATIVES **epicardial** adj.
– ORIGIN C19: from EPI- + Greek *kardia* 'heart', on the pattern of *pericardium*.

epicene /ˈɛpɪsiːn/ ■ adj. **1** having characteristics of both sexes or no characteristics of either sex. **2** effete. ■ n. an epicene person.
– ORIGIN Middle English: from Greek *epikoinos*, from *koinos* 'common'.

epicentre (US **epicenter**) ■ n. the point on the earth's surface vertically above the focus of an earthquake.
– DERIVATIVES **epicentral** adj.
– ORIGIN C19: from Greek *epikentros* 'situated on a centre'.

epicondyle /ˌɛpɪˈkɒndɪl/ ■ n. Anatomy a protuberance on the condyle of a long bone, especially the humerus.
– DERIVATIVES **epicondylar** adj.
– ORIGIN C19: from modern Latin *epicondylus*.

epicondylitis /ˌɛpɪkɒndɪˈlaɪtɪs/ ■ n. Medicine inflammation of tendons surrounding an epicondyle.

epicotyl /ˌɛpɪˈkɒtɪl/ ■ n. Botany the region of an embryo or seedling stem above the cotyledon.

epicure /ˈɛpɪkjʊə/ ■ n. a person who takes particular pleasure in fine food and drink.
– DERIVATIVES **epicurism** n.
– ORIGIN Middle English: from Greek *Epikouros* 'Epicurus' (see EPICUREAN).

Epicurean /ˌɛpɪkjʊˈriːən/ ■ n. **1** a disciple or student of the Greek philosopher Epicurus (341–270 BC), who taught that pleasure, particularly mental pleasure, was the highest good. **2** (**epicurean**) an epicure. ■ adj. **1** of or concerning Epicurus or his ideas. **2** (**epicurean**) relating to or suitable for an epicure.
– DERIVATIVES **Epicureanism** n.

epicycle /ˈɛpɪˌsaɪk(ə)l/ ■ n. Geometry a small circle whose centre moves round the circumference of a larger one.
– DERIVATIVES **epicyclic** adj.
– ORIGIN Middle English: from Greek *epikuklos*.

epidemic ■ n. a widespread occurrence of an infectious disease in a community at a particular time. ▶ a sudden, widespread occurrence of an undesirable phenomenon. ■ adj. relating to or of the nature of an epidemic.
– ORIGIN C17: from French *épidémique*, from Greek *epidēmia* 'prevalence of disease'.

epidemiology /ˌɛpɪdiːmɪˈɒlədʒi/ ■ n. the branch of medicine concerned with the incidence and distribution of diseases and other factors relating to health.
– DERIVATIVES **epidemiological** adj. **epidemiologist** n.
– ORIGIN C19: from Greek *epidēmia* 'prevalence of disease' + -LOGY.

epidermis /ˌɛpɪˈdəːmɪs/ ■ n. **1** Zoology & Anatomy the surface epithelium of the skin of an animal, overlying the dermis. **2** Botany the outer layer of tissue in a plant.
– DERIVATIVES **epidermal** adj. **epidermic** adj. **epidermoid** adj.
– ORIGIN C17: from Greek, from *epi* 'upon' + *derma* 'skin'.

epididymis /ˌɛpɪˈdɪdɪmɪs/ ■ n. (pl. **epididymides** /ˌɛpɪdɪˈdɪmɪdiːz/) Anatomy a highly convoluted duct behind the testis, along which sperm passes to the vas deferens.
– DERIVATIVES **epididymal** adj.
– ORIGIN C17: from Greek *epididumis*, from *epi* 'upon' + *didumos* 'testicle'.

epidote /ˈɛpɪdəʊt/ ■ n. a lustrous yellow-green mineral consisting of a silicate of calcium, aluminium, and iron.
– ORIGIN C19: from French *épidote*, from Greek *epididonai* 'give additionally' (because of the length of the crystals).

epidural /ˌɛpɪˈdjʊər(ə)l/ Anatomy & Medicine ■ adj. on or around the dura mater of the spinal cord. ■ n. an anaesthetic introduced into the space around the dura mater, used especially in childbirth.

epifauna ■ n. Ecology animals living on the bed of a body of water or on other submerged surfaces. Compare with INFAUNA.
– DERIVATIVES **epifaunal** adj.

epigastrium /ˌɛpɪˈɡastrɪəm/ ■ n. (pl. **epigastria** /-rɪə/) Anatomy the part of the upper abdomen immediately over the stomach.
– DERIVATIVES **epigastric** adj.
– ORIGIN C17: from Greek *epigastrios* 'over the belly'.

epigeal /ˌɛpɪˈdʒiːəl/ ■ adj. Botany growing or occurring above the ground surface. Compare with HYPOGEAL.
– ORIGIN C19: from Greek *epigeios*.

epigenesis /ˌɛpɪˈdʒɛnɪsɪs/ ■ n. Biology the progressive development of an embryo from an undifferentiated egg cell.

epigenetic /ˌɛpɪdʒɪˈnɛtɪk/ ■ adj. **1** Biology resulting from external rather than genetic influences. **2** Geology formed later than the surrounding or underlying rocks.
– DERIVATIVES **epigenetically** adv. **epigeneticist** n.

epiglottis /ˌɛpɪˈɡlɒtɪs/ ■ n. a flap of cartilage at the root of the tongue, which is depressed during swallowing to cover the opening of the windpipe.
– DERIVATIVES **epiglottal** adj. **epiglottic** adj.
– ORIGIN Middle English: from Greek *epiglōttis*, from *epi* 'upon, near to' + *glōtta* 'tongue'.

epigram /ˈɛpɪɡram/ ■ n. a concise and witty saying or remark. ▶ a short witty poem.
– DERIVATIVES **epigrammatic** adj. **epigrammatically** adv. **epigrammatist** n. **epigrammatize** (also **-ise**) v.
– ORIGIN Middle English: from Greek, from *epi* 'upon, in addition' + *gramma* (see -GRAM¹).

epigraph /ˈɛpɪɡrɑːf/ ■ n. **1** an inscription on a building, statue, or coin. **2** a short quotation or saying at the beginning of a book or chapter, intended to suggest its theme.
– ORIGIN C16: from Greek *epigraphē*, from *epigraphein* 'write on'.

epigraphy /ɪˈpɪɡrəfi, ɛ-/ ■ n. the study and interpretation of ancient inscriptions.

VOWELS a cat ɑː arm ɛ bed ɛː hair ə ago əː her ɪ sit i cosy iː see ɒ hot ɔː saw ʌ run

-DERIVATIVES **epigrapher** n. **epigraphic** adj. **epigraphical** adj. **epigraphically** adv. **epigraphist** n.

epigynous /ɪˈpɪdʒɪnəs, ɛ-/ ■ adj. Botany (of a plant or flower) having the ovary enclosed in the receptacle, with the stamens and other floral parts situated above. Compare with HYPOGYNOUS and PERIGYNOUS.
-DERIVATIVES **epigyny** n.

epilation /ˌɛpɪˈleɪʃ(ə)n/ ■ n. the removal of hair by the roots.
-DERIVATIVES **epilate** v. **epilator** n.
-ORIGIN C19: from French *épiler*, from *é-* (expressing removal) + Latin *pilus* 'strand of hair'.

epilepsy /ˈɛpɪlɛpsi/ ■ n. a neurological disorder marked by sudden recurrent episodes of sensory disturbance, loss of consciousness, or convulsions.
-DERIVATIVES **epileptic** adj. & n.
-ORIGIN C16: from Greek *epilēpsia*, from *epilambanein* 'seize, attack'.

epilogue /ˈɛpɪlɒɡ/ (US also **epilog**) ■ n. a section or speech at the end of a book or play serving as a comment on or a conclusion to what has happened.
-ORIGIN Middle English: from Greek *epilogos*, from *epi* 'in addition' + *logos* 'speech'.

epimer /ˈɛpɪmə/ ■ n. Chemistry each of two isomers with different configurations of atoms about one of several asymmetric carbon atoms present.
-DERIVATIVES **epimeric** /-ˈmɛrɪk/ adj. **epimerism** /ɪˈpɪm-, ɛ-/ n.

epimerize /ɪˈpɪməraɪz, ɛ-/ (also **-ise**) ■ v. Chemistry convert from one epimeric form into the other.

epinephrine /ˌɛpɪˈnɛfrɪn, -riːn/ ■ n. Biochemistry the hormone adrenalin.
-ORIGIN C19: from EPI- + Greek *nephros* 'kidney'.

epiphany /ɪˈpɪf(ə)ni, ɛ-/ ■ n. (pl. **-ies**) **1** (**Epiphany**) Christian Church the manifestation of Christ to the Gentiles as represented by the Magi (Matthew 2: 1-12). ▶ the festival commemorating this on 6 January. **2** a moment of sudden and great revelation.
-DERIVATIVES **epiphanic** /ɛpɪˈfanɪk/ adj.
-ORIGIN Middle English: from Greek *epiphainein* 'reveal'.

epiphenomenon /ˌɛpɪfəˈnɒmɪnən/ ■ n. (pl. **epiphenomena** /-nə/) **1** Medicine a secondary symptom, occurring simultaneously with a disease or condition but not directly related to it. **2** a mental state regarded as a by-product of brain activity.
-DERIVATIVES **epiphenomenal** adj.

epiphyte /ˈɛpɪfʌɪt/ ■ n. Botany a plant that grows non-parasitically on a tree or other plant.
-DERIVATIVES **epiphytal** /-ˈfʌɪt(ə)l/ adj. **epiphytic** /-ˈfɪtɪk/ adj.
-ORIGIN C19: from EPI- + Greek *phuton* 'plant'.

episcopacy /ɪˈpɪskəpəsi, ɛ-/ ■ n. (pl. **-ies**) government of a Church by bishops. ▶ (**the episcopacy**) the bishops of a region or church collectively.
-ORIGIN C17: from eccles. Latin *episcopatus* 'episcopate'.

episcopal /ɪˈpɪskəp(ə)l, ɛ-/ ■ adj. of a bishop or bishops. ▶ (of a Church) governed by or having bishops.
-DERIVATIVES **episcopalism** n. **episcopally** adv.
-ORIGIN Middle English: from eccles. Latin *episcopalis*, from *episcopus* 'bishop', from Greek *episkopos* (see BISHOP).

Episcopal Church ■ n. the Anglican Church in Scotland and the US.

episcopalian /ɪˌpɪskəˈpeɪlɪən, ɛ-/ ■ adj. of or advocating episcopacy. ▶ of or belonging to an episcopal or (**Episcopalian**) the Episcopal Church. ■ n. an adherent of episcopacy. ▶ (**Episcopalian**) a member of the Episcopal Church.
-DERIVATIVES **episcopalianism** n.

episcopate /ɪˈpɪskəpət, ɛ-/ ■ n. the office or term of office of a bishop. ▶ (**the episcopate**) the bishops of a church or region collectively.

episematic /ˌɛpɪsɪˈmatɪk/ ■ adj. Zoology (of coloration or markings) serving to help recognition by animals of the same species.
-ORIGIN C19: from EPI- + Greek *sēma* 'sign'.

episiotomy /ɪˌpɪsɪˈɒtəmi, ɛ-/ ■ n. (pl. **-ies**) a surgical cut made at the opening of the vagina during childbirth, to aid a difficult delivery.

393

epitope

-ORIGIN C19: from Greek *epision* 'pubic region' + -TOMY.

episode ■ n. an event or a group of events occurring as part of a sequence. ▶ each of the separate instalments into which a serialized story or radio or television programme is divided.
-ORIGIN C17: from Greek *epeisodion*, neuter of *epeisodios* 'coming in besides'.

episodic /ˌɛpɪˈsɒdɪk/ ■ adj. **1** occurring as or presented in episodes. **2** occurring at irregular intervals.
-DERIVATIVES **episodically** adv.

episome /ˈɛpɪsəʊm/ ■ n. Microbiology a genetic element inside some bacterial cells that can replicate independently of the host.

epistasis /ɪˈpɪstəsɪs/ ■ n. Genetics the suppression by a gene of the effect of another gene.
-DERIVATIVES **epistatic** /ˌɛpɪˈstatɪk/ adj.
-ORIGIN C19: from Greek, 'stoppage'.

epistaxis /ˌɛpɪˈstaksɪs/ ■ n. Medicine bleeding from the nose.
-ORIGIN C18: modern Latin, from Greek, from *epistazein* 'bleed from the nose'.

epistemology /ɪˌpɪstɪˈmɒlədʒi, ɛ-/ ■ n. Philosophy the theory of knowledge, especially with regard to its methods, validity, and scope.
-DERIVATIVES **epistemic** adj. **epistemically** adv. **epistemological** adj. **epistemologically** adv. **epistemologist** n.
-ORIGIN C19: from Greek *epistēmē* 'knowledge'.

epistle /ɪˈpɪs(ə)l/ ■ n. formal or humorous a letter. ▶ (**Epistle**) a book of the New Testament in the form of a letter from an Apostle.
-ORIGIN Old English, from Greek *epistolē*, from *epistellein* 'send news'.

epistolary /ɪˈpɪst(ə)ˌləri/ ■ adj. relating to or denoting the writing of letters or literary works in the form of letters.

epistyle /ˈɛpɪstʌɪl/ ■ n. Architecture an architrave.
-ORIGIN C16: from Greek *epistulion*, from *epi* 'upon' + *stulos* 'pillar'.

epitaph /ˈɛpɪtɑːf, -taf/ ■ n. words written in memory of a person who has died, especially as an inscription on a tombstone.
-ORIGIN Middle English: from Old French *epitaphe*, from Greek *epitaphion* 'funeral oration', neuter of *ephitaphios* 'over or at a tomb'.

epithalamium /ˌɛpɪθəˈleɪmɪəm/ ■ n. (pl. **epithalamiums** or **epithalamia**) a song or poem celebrating a marriage.
-DERIVATIVES **epithalamic** /-ˈlamɪk/ adj.
-ORIGIN C16: from Greek *epithalamion*, from *epi* 'upon' + *thalamos* 'bridal chamber'.

epithelium /ˌɛpɪˈθiːlɪəm/ ■ n. (pl. **epithelia** /-lɪə/) Anatomy the thin tissue forming the outer layer of the body's surface and lining the alimentary canal and other hollow structures, especially that part derived from the embryonic ectoderm and endoderm. Compare with ENDOTHELIUM.
-DERIVATIVES **epithelial** adj.
-ORIGIN C18: modern Latin, from EPI- + Greek *thēlē* 'teat'.

epithet /ˈɛpɪθɛt/ ■ n. an adjective or descriptive phrase expressing a quality or attribute of the person or thing mentioned.
-DERIVATIVES **epithetic** adj. **epithetical** adj. **epithetically** adv.
-ORIGIN C16: from Greek *epitheton*, neuter of *epithetos* 'attributed', from *epitithenai* 'add'.

epitome /ɪˈpɪtəmi, ɛ-/ ■ n. **1** (**the epitome of**) a person or thing that is a perfect example of a quality or type. **2** a summary of a written work.
-DERIVATIVES **epitomist** n.
-ORIGIN C16: from Greek *epitomē*, from *epitemnein* 'abridge'.

epitomize (also **-ise**) ■ v. **1** be a perfect example of. **2** archaic summarize (a written work).
-DERIVATIVES **epitomization** (also **-isation**) n.

epitope /ˈɛpɪtəʊp/ ■ n. Biochemistry the part of an antigen molecule to which an antibody attaches itself.
-ORIGIN 1960s: from EPI- + Greek *topos* 'place'.

epizoic

epizoic /ˌɛpɪˈzəʊɪk/ ■ adj. Biology living non-parasitically on the exterior of a living animal.
– DERIVATIVES **epizoite** /ɛpɪˈzəʊʌɪt/ n.
– ORIGIN C19: from EPI- + Greek *zōion* 'animal'.

epizootic /ˌɛpɪzəʊˈɒtɪk/ ■ adj. (of a disease) temporarily prevalent and widespread in an animal population. ■ n. an outbreak of such a disease.
– ORIGIN C18: from French, from *épizootie*, from Greek *epi* 'upon' + *zōion* 'animal'.

e pluribus unum /eɪ ˌplʊərɪbʊs ˈjuːnʊm/ ■ n. one out of many (the motto of the US).

EPNS ■ abbrev. electroplated nickel silver.

EPO ■ abbrev. erythropoietin (used especially when isolated as a drug).

epoch /ˈiːpɒk, ˈɛpɒk/ ■ n. a period of time marked by particular events or characteristics. ▸ Geology a division of time that is a subdivision of a period and is itself subdivided into ages, corresponding to a series. ▸ Astronomy an arbitrarily fixed date relative to which planetary or stellar measurements are expressed.
– DERIVATIVES **epochal** adj.
– ORIGIN C17: from modern Latin *epocha*, from Greek *epokhē* 'stoppage, fixed point of time', from *epekhein* 'stop, take up a position'.

epoch-making ■ adj. significant; historic.

eponym /ˈɛpənɪm/ ■ n. a word or name derived from the name of a person. ▸ a person after whom a discovery, invention, place, etc. is named.
– DERIVATIVES **eponymous** adj.
– ORIGIN C19: from Greek *epōnumos* 'given as a name, giving one's name to someone or something', from *epi* 'upon' + *onoma* 'name'.

EPOS /ˈiːpɒz, ˈiːpɒs/ ■ abbrev. electronic point of sale.

epoxide /ɪˈpɒksʌɪd/ ■ n. Chemistry an organic compound whose molecule contains a three-membered ring involving an oxygen atom and two carbon atoms.
– ORIGIN 1930s: from EPI- + OXIDE.

epoxy /ɪˈpɒksi, ɛ-/ ■ n. (pl. **-ies**) (also **epoxy resin**) an adhesive, plastic, paint, etc. made from a class of synthetic polymers containing epoxide groups. ■ v. (**-ies, -ied**) glue using an epoxy.
– ORIGIN C20: from EPI- + OXY-[2].

EPROM /ˈiːprɒm/ ■ n. Electronics a read-only memory whose contents can be erased by ultraviolet light or other means and reprogrammed using a pulsed voltage.
– ORIGIN 1970s: acronym from *erasable programmable ROM*.

eps ■ abbrev. earnings per share.

epsilon /ˈɛpsɪlɒn, ɛpˈsʌɪlɒn/ ■ n. the fifth letter of the Greek alphabet (Ε, ε), transliterated as 'e'. ▸ [as modifier] denoting the fifth in a series of items or categories.
– ORIGIN Greek, 'bare or simple E', from *psilos* 'bare'.

Epsom salts ■ pl. n. crystals of hydrated magnesium sulphate used as a purgative.
– ORIGIN C18: named after the town of Epsom in Surrey, England where the salts were first found.

Epstein.-Barr virus (abbrev.: **EBV**) ■ n. Medicine a herpesvirus causing glandular fever and associated with certain cancers.
– ORIGIN 1960s: named after British and Irish virologists Michael A. *Epstein* and Y. M. *Barr*.

equable /ˈɛkwəb(ə)l/ ■ adj. **1** calm and even-tempered. **2** not varying or fluctuating greatly.
– DERIVATIVES **equability** n. **equably** adv.
– ORIGIN C17: from Latin *aequabilis*, from *aequare* (see EQUATE).

equal ■ adj. **1** being the same in quantity, size, degree, value, or status. ▸ evenly or fairly balanced: *an equal contest*. **2** (**equal to something**) having the ability or resources to meet a challenge. ■ n. a person or thing that is equal to another. ■ v. (**equalled**, **equalling**; US **equaled**, **equaling**) be equal or equivalent to. ▸ match or rival.
– ORIGIN Middle English: from Latin *aequalis*, from *aequus* 'even, level, equal'.

equality ■ n. **1** the state of being equal. **2** Mathematics a symbolic expression of the fact that two quantities are equal; an equation.
– ORIGIN Middle English: from Latin *aequalitas*, from *aequalis* (see EQUAL).

equalize (also **-ise**) ■ v. make or become equal. ▸ level the score in a match by scoring a goal.
– DERIVATIVES **equalization** (also **-isation**) n.
– ORIGIN C16: from EQUAL, partly suggested by French *égaliser*.

equalizer (also **-iser**) ■ n. **1** a thing that has an equalizing effect. ▸ a goal that levels the score in a match. **2** N. Amer. informal a weapon, especially a gun. **3** Electronics a passive network designed to modify a frequency response, especially to compensate for distortion.

equally ■ adv. **1** in an equal manner. **2** in amounts or parts that are equal. **3** to an equal degree.

equals sign (also **equal sign**) ■ n. the symbol =.

equanimity /ˌɛkwəˈnɪmɪti, iː-/ ■ n. calmness; composure.
– DERIVATIVES **equanimous** /ɪˈkwanɪməs, iː-/ adj.
– ORIGIN C17: from Latin *aequanimitas*, from *aequus* 'equal' + *animus* 'mind'.

equate /ɪˈkweɪt/ ■ v. consider (one thing) as equal or equivalent to another. ▸ (**equate to/with**) be the same as or equivalent to. ▸ cause to be equal.
– DERIVATIVES **equatable** adj.
– ORIGIN Middle English: from Latin *aequare* 'make level or equal', from *aequus* (see EQUAL).

equation /ɪˈkweɪʒ(ə)n/ ■ n. **1** the process of equating one thing with another. **2** Mathematics a statement that the values of two mathematical expressions are equal (indicated by the sign =). **3** Chemistry a symbolic representation of the changes which occur in a chemical reaction, expressed in terms of the formulae of the molecules or other species involved.
– PHRASES **equation of the first** (or **second** etc.) **order** Mathematics an equation involving only the first derivative, second derivative, etc.
– ORIGIN Middle English: from Latin *aequatio(n-)*, from *aequare* (see EQUATE).

equation of state ■ n. Chemistry an equation showing the relationship between the values of the pressure, volume, and temperature of a quantity of a particular substance.

equator /ɪˈkweɪtə/ ■ n. a line notionally drawn on the earth equidistant from the poles, dividing the earth into northern and southern hemispheres and constituting the parallel of latitude 0°. ▸ Astronomy short for **CELESTIAL EQUATOR**.
– ORIGIN Middle English: from medieval Latin (*circulus*) *aequator* (*diei et noctis*) '(circle) equalizing (day and night)', from Latin *aequare* (see EQUATE).

equatorial /ˌɛkwəˈtɔːrɪəl/ ■ adj. of, at, or near the equator.
– DERIVATIVES **equatorially** adv.

Equatorial Guinean /ˈɡɪnɪən/ ■ n. a native or inhabitant of the West African country of Equatorial Guinea. ■ adj. of or relating to Equatorial Guinea or its people.

equerry /ɪˈkwɛri, ˈɛkwəri/ ■ n. (pl. **-ies**) an officer of the British royal household who attends members of the royal family.
– ORIGIN C16: from Old French *esquierie* 'company of squires, prince's stables', from Old French *esquier* 'esquire', perhaps associated with Latin *equus* 'horse'.

equestrian /ɪˈkwɛstrɪən, ɛ-/ ■ adj. **1** of or relating to horse riding. **2** depicting or representing a person on horseback. ■ n. (fem. **equestrienne** /ɪˌkwɛstrɪˈɛn/) a person on horseback.
– ORIGIN C17: from Latin *equester* 'belonging to a horseman', from *eques* 'horseman, knight', from *equus* 'horse'.

equestrianism ■ n. the skill or sport of horse riding.

equi- /ˈiːkwi, ˈɛkwi-/ ■ comb. form equal; equally: *equidistant*.
– ORIGIN from Latin *aequi-*, from *aequus* 'equal'.

equiangular ■ adj. having equal angles.

equid /ˈɛkwɪd/ ■ n. Zoology a mammal of the horse family (Equidae).
– ORIGIN C19: from Latin *equus* 'horse'.

equidistant ■ adj. at equal distances.
– DERIVATIVES **equidistance** n. **equidistantly** adv.

equilateral /ˌiːkwɪˈlat(ə)r(ə)l, ˌɛkwɪ-/ ■ adj. having all its sides of the same length.

– ORIGIN C16: from late Latin *aequilateralis*, from *aequilaterus* 'equal-sided', from Latin *latus, later-* 'side'.

equilibrate /ˌiːkwɪˈlʌɪbreɪt, ɪˈkwɪlɪ-, iːˈkwɪlɪ-/ ■ v. bring into, attain, or maintain a state of equilibrium.
– DERIVATIVES **equilibration** n.
– ORIGIN C17: from late Latin *aequilibrare*, from Latin *aequi-* 'equally' + *libra* 'balance'.

equilibrium /ˌiːkwɪˈlɪbrɪəm, ˌɛkwɪ-/ ■ n. (pl. **equilibria** /-rɪə/) **1** a state in which opposing forces or influences are balanced. ▶ the state of being physically balanced. **2** a calm state of mind. **3** Chemistry a state in which a process and its reverse are occurring at equal rates so that no overall change is taking place. **4** Economics a situation in which supply and demand are matched and prices stable.
– DERIVATIVES **equilibrial** adj.
– ORIGIN from Latin *aequilibrium*, from *aequi-* 'equal'+ *libra* 'balance'.

equine /ˈiːkwʌɪn, ˈɛ-/ ■ adj. of, relating to, or affecting horses or other members of the horse family. ▶ resembling a horse. ■ n. a horse or other member of the horse family.
– ORIGIN C18: from Latin *equinus*, from *equus* 'horse'.

equinoctial /ˌiːkwɪˈnɒkʃ(ə)l, ˌɛkwɪ-/ ■ adj. **1** of, relating to, or at the time of the equinox. **2** at or near the equator. ■ n. (also **equinoctial line**) another term for CELESTIAL EQUATOR.

equinoctial year ■ n. another term for SOLAR YEAR.

equinox /ˈiːkwɪnɒks, ˌɛkwɪ-/ ■ n. the time or date (twice each year, about 22 September and 20 March) at which the sun crosses the celestial equator, when day and night are of equal length.
– ORIGIN Middle English: from Old French *equinoxe* or Latin *aequinoctium*, from *aequi-* 'equal' + *nox* 'night'.

equip ■ v. (**equipped, equipping**) **1** supply with the items needed for a particular purpose. **2** prepare (someone) mentally for a particular situation or task.
– DERIVATIVES **equipper** n.
– ORIGIN C16: from French *équiper*, prob. from Old Norse *skipa* 'to man (a ship)', from *skip* 'ship'.

equipage /ˈɛkwɪpɪdʒ/ ■ n. **1** archaic equipment. **2** historical a carriage and horses with attendants.
– ORIGIN C16 (denoting the crew of a ship): from French *équipage*, from *équiper* 'equip'.

equipment ■ n. **1** the items needed for a particular purpose. **2** the process of supplying these items.
– ORIGIN C18: from French *équipement*, from *équiper* 'equip'.

equipoise /ˈɛkwɪpɔɪz, ˈiːkwɪ-/ ■ n. balance of forces or interests. ▶ a counterbalance or balancing force. ■ v. balance or counterbalance (something).
– ORIGIN C17: from EQUI- + the noun POISE[1], replacing the phr. *equal poise*.

equipotent /ˌiːkwɪˈpəʊt(ə)nt, ˌɛkwɪ-/ ■ adj. (chiefly of chemicals and medicines) having equal potencies.

equipotential ■ adj. Physics (of a surface or line) composed of points all at the same potential. ■ n. an equipotential line or surface.

equiprobable ■ adj. Mathematics & Logic (of two or more things) equally probable.
– DERIVATIVES **equiprobability** n.

equisetum /ˌɛkwɪˈsiːtəm/ ■ n. (pl. **equiseta** /-tə/ or **equisetums**) Botany a plant of a genus that comprises the horsetails. [Genus *Equisetum*.]
– ORIGIN from Latin *equus* 'horse' + *saeta* 'bristle'.

equitable /ˈɛkwɪtəb(ə)l/ ■ adj. **1** fair and impartial. **2** Law valid in equity as distinct from law.
– DERIVATIVES **equitability** n. **equitableness** n. **equitably** adv.
– ORIGIN C16: from French *équitable*, from *équité* (see EQUITY).

equitation /ˌɛkwɪˈteɪʃ(ə)n/ ■ n. formal the art and practice of horse riding.
– ORIGIN C16: from Latin *equitatio(n-)*, from *equitare* 'ride a horse', from *eques, equit-* 'horseman', from *equus* 'horse'.

equity /ˈɛkwɪti/ ■ n. (pl. **-ies**) **1** the quality of being fair and impartial. **2** Law a branch of law that developed alongside common law in order to remedy some of its defects in fairness and justice. **3** (**Equity**) a trade union for professional actors. **4** the value of the shares issued by a company. ▶ (**equities**) stocks and shares that carry no fixed interest. **5** the value of a mortgaged property after deduction of charges against it.
– ORIGIN Middle English: from Old French *equité*, from Latin *aequitas*, from *aequus* 'equal'.

equivalent /ɪˈkwɪv(ə)l(ə)nt/ ■ adj. equal in value, amount, function, meaning, etc. ▶ (**equivalent to**) having the same or a similar effect as. ■ n. **1** a person or thing that is equivalent to another. **2** (also **equivalent weight**) Chemistry the mass of a particular substance that can combine with or displace one gram of hydrogen or eight grams of oxygen, used in expressing combining powers of elements.
– DERIVATIVES **equivalence** n. **equivalency** n. **equivalently** adv.
– ORIGIN Middle English: from late Latin *aequivalere* 'be of equal worth'.

equivocal /ɪˈkwɪvək(ə)l/ ■ adj. unclear in meaning or intention; ambiguous.
– DERIVATIVES **equivocality** n. **equivocally** adv. **equivocalness** n.
– ORIGIN C16: from late Latin *aequivocus*, from Latin *aequus* 'equally' + *vocare* 'to call'.

equivocate /ɪˈkwɪvəkeɪt/ ■ v. use ambiguous or evasive language.
– DERIVATIVES **equivocation** n. **equivocator** n. **equivocatory** adj.
– ORIGIN Middle English: from late Latin *aequivocare* 'call by the same name', from *aequivocus* (see EQUIVOCAL).

Er ■ symb. the chemical element erbium.

-er[1] ■ suffix **1** denoting a person, animal, or thing that performs a specified action or activity: *farmer*. **2** denoting a person or thing that has a specified attribute or form: *two-wheeler*. **3** denoting a person concerned with a specified thing or subject: *milliner*. **4** denoting a person belonging to a specified place or group: *city-dweller*.
– ORIGIN Old English *-ere*, of Germanic origin.

-er[2] ■ suffix forming the comparative of adjectives (as in *bigger*) and adverbs (as in *faster*).
– ORIGIN Old English suffix *-ra* (adjectival), *-or* (adverbial), of Germanic origin.

-er[3] ■ suffix forming nouns used informally, usually by distortion of the root word: *footer*.
– ORIGIN prob. an extended use of -ER[1].

-er[4] ■ suffix forming frequentative verbs such as *patter*.
– ORIGIN Old English *-erian, -rian*, of Germanic origin.

-er[5] ■ suffix forming nouns: **1** such as *sampler*. Compare with -AR[1]. [ending corresponding to Latin *aris*.] ▶ such as *butler, danger*. [ending corresponding to Latin *arius, arium*.] ▶ such as *border*. [ending corresponding (via Old French *eure*) to Latin *atura*.] ▶ such as *laver*. See LAVER[2]. [ending corresponding (via Old French *eor*) to Latin *atorium*.] **2** equivalent to -OR[1].
– ORIGIN via Old French or Anglo-Norman French (see above).

-er[6] ■ suffix chiefly Law (forming nouns) denoting verbal action or a document effecting such action: *disclaimer*.
– ORIGIN from Anglo-Norman French (infinitive ending).

era /ˈɪərə/ ■ n. a long and distinct period of history. ▶ Geology a major division of time that is a subdivision of an aeon and is itself subdivided into periods.
– ORIGIN C17: from late Latin *aera*, denoting a number used as a basis of reckoning, an epoch from which time is reckoned, pl. of *aes, aer-* 'money, counter'.

eradicate /ɪˈradɪkeɪt/ ■ v. remove or destroy completely.
– DERIVATIVES **eradicable** adj. **eradicant** n. **eradication** n. **eradicator** n.
– ORIGIN Middle English: from Latin *eradicare* 'tear up by the roots'.

eradicated ■ adj. [postpos.] Heraldry (of a tree or plant) depicted with the roots exposed.

erase /ɪˈreɪz/ ■ v. rub out or obliterate; remove all traces of.
– DERIVATIVES **erasable** adj. **erasure** n.
– ORIGIN C16: from Latin *eradere* 'scrape away'.

erased ■ adj. [postpos.] Heraldry (of a head or limb) depicted as cut off in a jagged line.

eraser ■ n. a piece of rubber or plastic used to rub out something written.

erbium /'ə:bɪəm/ ■ n. the chemical element of atomic number 68, a soft silvery-white metal of the lanthanide series. (Symbol: **Er**)
– ORIGIN C19: modern Latin, from *Ytterby* (see **YTTERBIUM**).

ere /ɛː/ ■ prep. & conj. poetic/literary or archaic before (in time).
– ORIGIN Old English, of Germanic origin.

erect ■ adj. rigidly upright or straight. ▶ (of the penis, clitoris, or nipples) enlarged and rigid, especially in sexual excitement. ▶ (of hair) standing up from the skin. ■ v. construct (a building, wall, etc.). ▶ create or establish (a theory or system).
– DERIVATIVES **erectable** adj. **erectly** adv. **erectness** n. **erector** n.
– ORIGIN Middle English: from Latin *erect-, erigere* 'set up'.

erectile /ɪ'rɛktʌɪl/ ■ adj. able to become erect. ▶ denoting tissues which are capable of becoming temporarily engorged with blood, particularly those of the penis or other sexual organs. ▶ relating to this process.

erection ■ n. **1** the action of erecting. **2** a building or other upright structure. **3** an erect state of the penis.

eremite /'ɛrɪmʌɪt/ ■ n. a Christian hermit.
– DERIVATIVES **eremitic** adj. **eremitical** adj.
– ORIGIN Middle English: from Old French *eremite*, from late Latin *eremita* (see **HERMIT**).

erethism /'ɛrɪθɪz(ə)m/ ■ n. **1** excessive sensitivity to stimulation of a part of the body, especially the sexual organs. **2** a state of abnormal mental excitement or irritation.
– ORIGIN C19: from Greek *erethismos*, from *erethizein* 'irritate'.

erewhile /ɛː'wʌɪl/ ■ adv. archaic a while before; some time ago.
– ORIGIN Middle English: from ERE + WHILE.

erf /əːf/ ■ n. (pl. **-s** or **erven**) S. African a plot of land.
– ORIGIN from Dutch, orig. 'inheritance'.

erg[1] /əːɡ/ ■ n. Physics a unit of work or energy, equal to the work done by a force of one dyne when its point of application moves one centimetre in the direction of action of the force.
– ORIGIN C19: from Greek *ergon* 'work'.

erg[2] /əːɡ/ ■ n. (pl. **ergs**) an area of shifting sand dunes in the Sahara.
– ORIGIN C19: from French, from Arabic *'irk*, *'erg*.

ergative /'əːɡətɪv/ Grammar ■ adj. **1** (in some languages, e.g. Basque) relating to or denoting a case of nouns that identifies the doer of an action as the object rather than the subject of a verb. **2** (in English) denoting verbs which can be used both transitively and intransitively to describe the same action, with the object in the former case being the subject in the latter, as in *I boiled the kettle* and *the kettle boiled*. ■ n. an ergative word or the ergative case.
– DERIVATIVES **ergativity** n.
– ORIGIN 1950s: from Greek *ergatēs* 'worker', from *ergon* 'work'.

ergo /'əːɡəʊ/ ■ adv. therefore.
– ORIGIN from Latin.

ergometer /əː'ɡɒmɪtə/ ■ n. an apparatus which measures work or energy expended during a period of physical exercise.

ergonomics /ˌəːɡə'nɒmɪks/ ■ pl. n. [treated as sing.] the study of people's efficiency in their working environment.
– DERIVATIVES **ergonomic** adj. **ergonomist** n.
– ORIGIN 1950s: from Greek *ergon* 'work', on the pattern of *economics*.

ergot /'əːɡɒt/ ■ n. **1** a fungal disease of rye and other cereals, forming black elongated fruiting bodies which are a source of various medicinal alkaloids. **2** a small horny protuberance on the back of a horse's fetlock.
– ORIGIN C17: from French, from Old French *argot* 'cock's spur' (because of the appearance produced by the disease).

ergotamine /əː'ɡɒtəmiːn/ ■ n. Medicine an ergot alkaloid that causes constriction of blood vessels and is used to treat migraine.

ergotism /'əːɡətɪz(ə)m/ ■ n. poisoning produced by eating food affected by ergot, typically resulting in headache, vomiting, diarrhoea, and gangrene of the fingers and toes.

erica /'ɛrɪkə/ ■ n. a plant of a large genus including the heaths. [Genus *Erica*.]
– ORIGIN from Greek *ereikē*.

ericaceous /ˌɛrɪ'keɪʃəs/ ■ adj. Botany **1** relating to or denoting plants of the heather family (Ericaceae). **2** (of compost) suitable for heathers and other lime-hating plants.
– ORIGIN C19: from the genus name *Erica* (see **ERICA**).

erigeron /ɪ'rɪdʒərɒn, ɛ-/ ■ n. a herbaceous plant of the daisy family. [Genus *Erigeron*.]
– ORIGIN from Latin, 'groundsel' (the original sense in English), from Greek *ērigerōn*, from *ēri* 'early' + *gerōn* 'old man' (because the plant flowers early in the year in the northern hemisphere, and some species bear grey down).

Erin /'ɛrɪn, 'ɪərɪn/ ■ n. archaic or poetic/literary Ireland.
– ORIGIN from Irish *Ériu, Éirinn*.

eristic /ɛ'rɪstɪk/ formal ■ adj. of or characterized by debate or argument. ▶ (of an argument or arguer) aiming at winning rather than at reaching the truth. ■ n. a person given to debate or argument. ▶ the art or practice or debate or argument.
– DERIVATIVES **eristically** adv.
– ORIGIN C17: from Greek *eristikos*, from *erizein* 'to wrangle', from *eris* 'strife'.

Eritrean /ˌɛrɪ'treɪən/ ■ n. a native or inhabitant of the independent state of Eritrea in NE Africa. ■ adj. of or relating to Eritrea or its inhabitants.

Erlenmeyer flask /'əːlənˌmʌɪə/ ■ n. a conical flat-bottomed laboratory flask with a narrow neck.
– ORIGIN C19: named after the German chemist Emil *Erlenmeyer*.

erl-king /'əːlkɪŋ/ ■ n. (in Germanic mythology) a bearded giant or goblin believed to lure little children to the land of death.
– ORIGIN C18: from German *Erlkönig* 'alder-king', a mistranslation of Danish *ellerkonge* 'king of the elves'.

ERM ■ abbrev. Exchange Rate Mechanism.

ermine /'əːmɪn/ ■ n. (pl. same or **ermines**) **1** a stoat. ▶ the white winter fur of the stoat, used for trimming the ceremonial robes of judges or peers. ▶ Heraldry fur represented as black spots on a white ground, as a heraldic tincture. **2** a stout-bodied moth that has cream or white wings with black spots, and a very hairy caterpillar. [Genus *Spilosoma*: several species.]
– DERIVATIVES **ermined** adj.
– ORIGIN Middle English: from Old French *hermine*, prob. from medieval Latin (*mus*) *Armenius* 'Armenian (mouse)'.

-ern ■ suffix forming adjectives such as *northern*.
– ORIGIN Old English, of Germanic origin.

erode /ɪ'rəʊd/ ■ v. (with reference to the action of wind, water, etc. on the land) gradually wear or be worn away. ▶ gradually destroy (an abstract quality or state). ▶ Medicine (of a disease) gradually destroy (bodily tissue).
– DERIVATIVES **erodible** adj.
– ORIGIN C17: from Latin *erodere*, from *e-* (var. of *ex-*) 'out, away' + *rodere* 'gnaw'.

erogenous /ɪ'rɒdʒɪnəs, ɛ-/ ■ adj. (of a part of the body) sensitive to sexual stimulation.
– ORIGIN C19: from **EROS** + **-GENOUS**.

Eros /'ɪərɒs/ ■ n. **1** sexual love or desire. **2** (in Freudian theory) the life instinct. Often contrasted with **THANATOS**. **3** (in Jungian psychology) the principle of personal relatedness in human activities, associated with the anima. Often contrasted with **LOGOS**.
– ORIGIN from Greek *erōs* 'sexual love' (also the name of the god of love in Greek mythology).

erosion /ɪ'rəʊʒ(ə)n/ ■ n. **1** the process or result of eroding or being eroded. **2** Medicine a place where surface tissue has been gradually destroyed.
– DERIVATIVES **erosional** adj. **erosive** adj.

erotic /ɪ'rɒtɪk/ ■ adj. of, relating to, or tending to arouse sexual desire or excitement.
– DERIVATIVES **erotically** adv.
– ORIGIN C17: from Greek *erōtikos*, from *erōs, erōt-* 'sexual love'.

erotica ■ pl. n. [treated as sing. or pl.] erotic literature or art.

– ORIGIN C19: from Greek *erōtika*, from *erōtikos* (see EROTIC).

eroticism ▪ n. **1** the quality or character or being erotic. **2** sexual desire or excitement.

eroticize (also **-ise**) ▪ v. give erotic qualities to.
– DERIVATIVES **eroticization** (also **-isation**) n.

erotism /ˈɛrətɪz(ə)m/ ▪ n. sexual desire or excitement.
– ORIGIN C19: from Greek *erōs*, *erōt-* 'sexual love'.

eroto- /ɪˈrɒtəʊ/ ▪ comb. form relating to eroticism: *erotomania*.
– ORIGIN from Greek *erōs*, *erōt-* 'sexual love'.

erotology /ˌɛrəˈtɒlədʒi/ ▪ n. the study of sexual love and behaviour.

erotomania /ɪˌrɒtə(ʊ)ˈmeɪnɪə/ ▪ n. excessive sexual desire.
– DERIVATIVES **erotomaniac** n.

err /əː/ ▪ v. be mistaken or incorrect. ▸ [often as adj. **erring**] do wrong.
– PHRASES **err on the right side** act so that the least harmful of possible errors is the most likely to occur. **err on the side of** display more rather than less of (a specified quality) in one's actions.
– ORIGIN Middle English: from Latin *errare* 'to stray'.

errand ▪ n. a short journey made to deliver or collect something, especially on someone else's behalf.
– PHRASES **errand of mercy** a journey or mission carried out to help someone in difficulty or danger.
– ORIGIN Old English *ǣrende* 'message, mission', of Germanic origin.

errant /ˈɛr(ə)nt/ ▪ adj. **1** chiefly formal or humorous erring or straying from the accepted course or standards. **2** archaic or poetic/literary travelling in search of adventure. See also KNIGHT ERRANT.
– DERIVATIVES **errancy** n. **errantry** n.
– ORIGIN Middle English: sense 1 from Latin *errare* 'err'; sense 2 from Old French *errant* 'travelling', from *errer*, from late Latin *iterare* 'go on a journey', from *iter* 'journey'.

erratic /ɪˈratɪk/ ▪ adj. not even or regular in pattern or movement. ▪ n. (also **erratic block** or **boulder**) Geology a large rock that differs from the surrounding rock, brought from a distance by glacial action.
– DERIVATIVES **erratically** adv. **erraticism** n.
– ORIGIN Middle English: from Latin *erraticus*, from *errare* 'to stray, err'.

erratum /eˈrɑːtəm, -reɪt-/ ▪ n. (pl. **errata**) an error in printing or writing. ▸ (**errata**) a list of corrected errors appended to a publication.
– ORIGIN C16: from Latin, 'error', from *errare* 'err'.

erroneous /ɪˈrəʊnɪəs, ɛ-/ ▪ adj. wrong; incorrect.
– DERIVATIVES **erroneously** adv. **erroneousness** n.
– ORIGIN Middle English: from Latin *erroneus*, from *erro(n-)* 'vagabond', from *errare* 'to stray, err'.

error ▪ n. **1** a mistake. **2** the state of being wrong in conduct or judgement. **3** technical a measure of the estimated difference between the observed or calculated value of a quantity and its true value.
– PHRASES **see the error of one's ways** acknowledge one's wrongdoing.
– DERIVATIVES **errorless** adj.
– ORIGIN Middle English: from Latin *error*, from *errare* 'to stray, err'.

error bar ▪ n. Mathematics a line through a point on a graph, parallel to one of the axes, which represents the uncertainty or error of the corresponding coordinate of the point.

ersatz /ˈəːsats, ˈɛː-/ ▪ adj. (of a product) made or used as an inferior substitute for something else. ▸ not real or genuine: *ersatz emotion*.
– ORIGIN C19: from German, 'replacement'.

Erse /əːs/ ▪ n. the Scottish or Irish Gaelic language.
– ORIGIN early Scots form of IRISH.

erst /əːst/ ▪ adv. archaic long ago; formerly.
– ORIGIN Old English, of Germanic origin.

erstwhile ▪ adj. former. ▪ adv. archaic formerly.

eructation /ˌiːrʌkˈteɪʃ(ə)n, ɪ-, ɛ-/ ▪ n. formal a belch.
– ORIGIN Middle English: from Latin *eructatio(n-)*, from *eructare*, from *e-* (var. of *ex-*) 'out' + *ructare* 'belch'.

erudite /ˈɛrʊdʌɪt/ ▪ adj. having or showing knowledge or learning.
– DERIVATIVES **eruditely** adv. **erudition** n.
– ORIGIN Middle English: from Latin *eruditus*, *erudire* 'instruct, train', from *rudis* 'rude, untrained'.

erupt ▪ v. **1** (of a volcano) forcefully eject lava, rocks, ash, or gases. **2** break out suddenly: *fierce fighting erupted*. **3** (**erupt in**) give vent to (feelings) in a sudden and noisy way: *they erupted in fits of laughter*. **4** (of a spot, rash, etc.) suddenly appear on the skin. ▸ (of the skin) suddenly develop spots, a rash, etc. **5** (of a tooth) break through the gums.
– DERIVATIVES **eruptive** adj.
– ORIGIN C17: from Latin *erupt-*, *erumpere* 'break out'.

eruption ▪ n. an act or instance or erupting. ▸ a spot or rash appearing suddenly on the skin.

erven /ˈəːvən/ plural form of ERF.

-ery (also **-ry**) ▪ suffix forming nouns: **1** denoting a class or kind: *greenery*. **2** denoting an occupation, a state or condition, or behaviour: *archery* | *bravery*. ▸ with depreciatory reference: *tomfoolery*. **3** denoting a place set aside for an activity or a grouping of things, animals, etc.: *rookery*.
– ORIGIN from French *-erie*, from Latin *-arius*, *-ator*.

eryngium /ɪˈrɪndʒɪəm/ ▪ n. (pl. **eryngiums**) sea holly or a related plant. [Genus *Eryngium*.]
– ORIGIN C16: from Latin *eryngion*, from a diminutive of Greek *ērungos*.

eryngo /ɪˈrɪŋɡəʊ/ ▪ n. (pl. **-os** or **-oes**) another term for SEA HOLLY or ERYNGIUM.
– ORIGIN C16: from Italian and Spanish *eringio*, from Latin *eryngion* (see ERYNGIUM).

erysipelas /ˌɛrɪˈsɪpɪləs/ ▪ n. Medicine a skin disease caused by a streptococcus and characterized by large raised red patches on the face and legs.
– ORIGIN Middle English: from Greek *erusipelas*; perhaps rel. to *eruthros* 'red' and *pella* 'skin'.

erysipeloid /ˌɛrɪˈsɪpɪlɔɪd/ ▪ n. Medicine a bacterial dermatitis of the hands, occurring mainly among handlers of meat and fish products.

erythema /ˌɛrɪˈθiːmə/ ▪ n. Medicine superficial reddening of the skin caused by dilatation of the blood capillaries, as a result of injury or irritation.
– DERIVATIVES **erythemal** adj. **erythematous** adj.
– ORIGIN C18: from Greek *eruthēma*, from *eruthainein* 'be red', from *eruthros* 'red'.

erythrism /ˈɛrɪθrɪz(ə)m/ ▪ n. Zoology a congenital condition of abnormal redness in an animal's fur, plumage, or skin.
– ORIGIN C19: from Greek *eruthros* 'red'.

erythro- ▪ comb. form red (used commonly in zoological and medical terms): *erythrocyte*.
– ORIGIN from Greek *eruthros* 'red'.

erythroblast /ɪˈrɪθrə(ʊ)blast/ ▪ n. Physiology an immature erythrocyte, containing a nucleus.
– DERIVATIVES **erythroblastic** adj.

erythroblastosis /ɪˌrɪθrə(ʊ)blasˈtəʊsɪs/ ▪ n. Medicine the abnormal presence of erythroblasts in the blood.

erythrocyte /ɪˈrɪθrə(ʊ)sʌɪt/ ▪ n. a red blood cell (typically a biconcave disc without a nucleus) that contains the pigment haemoglobin and transports oxygen and carbon dioxide to and from the tissues.
– DERIVATIVES **erythrocytic** adj.

erythrogenic /ɪˌrɪθrə(ʊ)ˈdʒɛnɪk/ ▪ adj. Medicine (of a bacterial toxin) causing inflammation and reddening of the skin.

erythromycin /ɪˌrɪθrə(ʊ)ˈmʌɪsɪn/ ▪ n. Medicine an antibiotic obtained from a streptomycete bacterium (*Streptomyces erythreus*).
– ORIGIN 1950s: from elements of the modern Latin taxonomic name.

erythropoiesis /ɪˌrɪθrə(ʊ)pɔɪˈiːsɪs/ ▪ n. Physiology the production of red blood cells.
– DERIVATIVES **erythropoietic** adj.

erythropoietin /ɪˌrɪθrə(ʊ)pɔɪˈɛtɪn/ ▪ n. Biochemistry a hormone secreted by the kidneys that increases the rate of production of red blood cells in response to falling levels of oxygen in the tissues.

Es ■ symb. the chemical element einsteinium.

-es¹ ■ suffix 1 forming plurals of nouns ending in sibilant sounds: *kisses*. 2 forming plurals of certain nouns ending in *-o*: *potatoes*.
– ORIGIN var. of **-s¹**.

-es² ■ suffix forming the third person singular of the present tense: 1 in verbs ending in sibilant sounds: *pushes*. 2 in verbs ending in *-o* (but not *-oo*): *goes*.
– ORIGIN var. of **-s²**.

escalate /ˈɛskəleɪt/ ■ v. 1 increase rapidly. 2 become or cause to become more intense or serious.
– DERIVATIVES **escalation** n.
– ORIGIN 1920s ('travel on an escalator'): back-formation from **ESCALATOR**.

escalator ■ n. a moving staircase consisting of a circulating belt of steps driven by a motor.
– ORIGIN C20 (orig. US, as a trade name): from obsolete *escalade* 'climb a wall by ladder', on the pattern of *elevator*.

escalator clause (also **escalation clause**) ■ n. a clause in a contract that allows for a rise in wages or prices under certain conditions.

escallonia /ˌɛskəˈləʊnɪə/ ■ n. an evergreen South American shrub with pink or white flowers. [Genus *Escallonia*.]
– ORIGIN named after the C18 Spanish traveller *Escallon*, who discovered the plants.

escallop /ɪˈskaləp, ɛ-, -ˈskɒl-/ ■ n. 1 variant spelling of **ESCALOPE**. 2 another term for **SCALLOP** (in sense 2). ■ v. (**escalloped**, **escalloping**) another term for **SCALLOP** (in sense 3).
– ORIGIN C15: from Old French *escalope* 'shell'.

escalope /ɪˈskaləp, ɛ-, -ˈskɒl-, ˈɛskəlǝʊp/ ■ n. a thin slice of coated and fried meat, especially veal.
– ORIGIN French.

escapade /ˈɛskəpeɪd, ˌɛskəˈpeɪd/ ■ n. an incident involving daring and adventure.
– ORIGIN C17: from French, from Provençal or Spanish, from *escapar* 'to escape'.

escape ■ v. 1 break free from confinement or control. ▸ (of a gas, liquid, or heat) leak from a container. 2 elude or get free from (someone). 3 succeed in eluding (something dangerous or undesirable): *the baby narrowly escaped death*. ■ n. 1 an act of escaping. 2 a means of escaping. 3 (also **escape key**) Computing a key on a computer keyboard which interrupts the current operation or converts subsequent characters to a control sequence. 4 a garden plant or pet animal that has gone wild and (in plants) become naturalized.
– DERIVATIVES **escapable** adj. **escapee** n. **escaper** n.
– ORIGIN Middle English: from Old French *eschaper*, from medieval Latin *ex-* 'out' + *cappa* 'cloak'.

escape clause ■ n. a clause in a contract which specifies the conditions under which one party can be freed from an obligation.

escapement /ɪˈskeɪpm(ə)nt, ɛ-/ ■ n. 1 a mechanism in a clock or watch that connects and regulates the motive power. 2 the part of the mechanism in a piano that enables the hammer to fall back as soon as it has struck the string.
– ORIGIN C18: from French *échappement*, from *échapper* 'to escape'.

escape road ■ n. chiefly Brit. a slip road on a bend in a racing circuit or on a steep hill, into which a driver can turn if unable to negotiate a bend or slope safely.

escape velocity ■ n. the lowest velocity which a body must have in order to escape the gravitational attraction of a particular planet or other object.

escapism ■ n. the process of seeking distraction from reality by engaging in entertainment or fantasy.
– DERIVATIVES **escapist** n. & adj.

escapologist /ˌɛskəˈpɒlədʒɪst/ ■ n. an entertainer who specializes in breaking free from ropes, handcuffs, and chains.
– DERIVATIVES **escapology** n.

escargot /ɛˈskɑːɡəʊ, ɪ-/ ■ n. an edible snail.
– ORIGIN French: from Provençal *escaragol*.

escarpment /ɪˈskɑːpm(ə)nt, ɛ-/ ■ n. a long, steep slope at the edge of a plateau or separating areas of land at different heights.
– ORIGIN C19: from French *escarpement*, *escarpe* 'scarp', from Italian *scarpa* 'slope'.

-esce ■ suffix forming verbs, often denoting the initiation of action: *effervesce*.
– ORIGIN from Latin verbs ending in *-escere*.

-escent ■ suffix forming adjectives denoting a developing state or action: *coalescent*.
– DERIVATIVES **-escence** suffix forming corresponding nouns.
– ORIGIN from French, or from Latin stem *-escent-*.

eschar /ˈɛskɑː/ ■ n. Medicine a dry, dark scab caused by a burn, bite, etc.
– ORIGIN Middle English: from late Latin *eschara* 'scar, scab', from Greek (see also **SCAR**).

eschatology /ˌɛskəˈtɒlədʒi/ ■ n. the part of theology concerned with death, judgement, and destiny.
– DERIVATIVES **eschatological** adj. **eschatologist** n.
– ORIGIN C19: from Greek *eskhatos* 'last' + **-LOGY**.

eschaton /ˈɛskətɒn/ ■ n. Theology the final event in the divine plan; the end of the world.
– ORIGIN 1930s: from Greek *eskhaton*, neuter of *eskhatos* 'last'.

eschew /ɪsˈtʃuː, ɛs-/ ■ v. abstain from.
– DERIVATIVES **eschewal** n.
– ORIGIN Middle English: from Old French *eschiver*, of Germanic origin.

eschscholzia /ɪsˈʃɒlzɪə, ɛʃˈʃɒlzɪə/ (also **eschscholtzia** /-tsɪə/) ■ n. a North American poppy with bright yellow, orange, or red flowers. [Genus *Eschscholzia*: several species, in particular the California poppy.]
– ORIGIN named in honour of the Russian-born botanist Johann Friedrich von *Eschscholtz*.

escolar /ˌɛskəˈlɑː/ ■ n. a large, elongated predatory marine fish. [Family Gempylidae: several species.]
– ORIGIN C19: from Spanish, 'scholar', so named because the ringed markings around the eyes resemble spectacles.

escort ■ n. /ˈɛskɔːt/ 1 a person or vehicle (or group of these) accompanying another to provide protection or as a mark of rank. 2 a person who is hired or formally requested to accompany a member of the opposite sex to a social event. ■ v. /ɪˈskɔːt, ɛ-/ accompany as an escort.
– ORIGIN C16: from French *escorte* (n.), *escorter* (v.), from Italian *scorta*, from *scorgere* 'to conduct, guide', from Latin *ex-* 'out of' + *corrigere* (see **CORRECT**).

escritoire /ˌɛskriːˈtwɑː/ ■ n. a small writing desk with drawers and compartments.
– ORIGIN C16: from French, from medieval Latin *scriptorium* (see **SCRIPTORIUM**).

escrow /ˈɛskrəʊ, ɛ-/ ■ n. a bond, deed, deposit, etc. kept in the custody of a third party, taking effect or made available only when a specified condition has been fulfilled. ▸ the state of being kept in this way.
– ORIGIN C16: from Old French *escroe* 'scrap, scroll', from medieval Latin *scroda*, of Germanic origin; rel. to **SHRED**.

escudo /ɛˈsk(j)uːdəʊ, ɛˈʃk-/ ■ n. (pl. **-os**) the former monetary unit of Portugal and Cape Verde.
– ORIGIN Spanish and Portuguese, from Latin *scutum* 'shield'.

escutcheon /ɪˈskʌtʃ(ə)n, ɛ-/ ■ n. 1 a shield or emblem bearing a coat of arms. 2 (also **escutcheon plate**) a flat piece of metal framing a keyhole, door handle, or light switch.
– PHRASES **a blot on one's escutcheon** a stain on one's reputation or character.
– DERIVATIVES **escutcheoned** adj.
– ORIGIN C15: from Anglo-Norman French *escuchon*, from Latin *scutum* 'shield'.

ESE ■ abbrev. east-south-east.

-ese ■ suffix forming adjectives and nouns: 1 denoting an inhabitant or language of a country or city: *Taiwanese*. 2 often derogatory (especially with reference to language) denoting character or style: *journalese*.
– ORIGIN from Old French *-eis*, based on Latin *-ensis*.

esker /ˈɛskə/ ■ n. Geology a long winding ridge of gravel and other sediment, deposited by meltwater from a retreating glacier or ice sheet.
– ORIGIN C19: from Irish *eiscir*.

Eskimo ■ n. (pl. same or **-os**) **1** a member of an indigenous people inhabiting northern Canada, Alaska, Greenland, and eastern Siberia. **2** either of the two main languages of this people (Inuit and Yupik). ■ adj. of or relating to the Eskimos or their languages.
– ORIGIN an Algonquian word, perhaps in the sense 'people speaking a different language'.

USAGE
In recent years, the word **Eskimo** has come to be regarded by some as offensive: the peoples inhabiting the regions from NW Canada to western Greenland prefer to call themselves **Inuit**. The term **Eskimo**, however, continues to be the only term which can be properly understood as applying to the people as a whole and is still widely used in anthropological and archaeological contexts.

Eskimo roll ■ n. a complete rollover in canoeing, from upright to capsized to upright.

Eskom /ˈɛskɒm/ ■ abbrev. (in South Africa) a statutory company controlling the public electricity supply.
– ORIGIN 1950s: blend of *Electricity Supply* and Afrikaans *Kommissie* 'Commission'.

ESL ■ abbrev. English as a second language.

ESN ■ abbrev. electronic serial number.

ESOL ■ abbrev. English for speakers of other languages.

esophagus etc. ■ n. US spelling of **OESOPHAGUS** etc.

esoteric /ˌɛsəˈtɛrɪk, ˌiːsə-/ ■ adj. intended for or understood by only a small number of people with a specialized knowledge or interest. The opposite of **EXOTERIC**.
– DERIVATIVES **esoterically** adv. **esotericism** n. **esotericist** n.
– ORIGIN C17: from Greek *esōterikos*, from *esōterō*, from *esō* 'within', from *es*, *eis* 'into'.

esoterica /ˌɛsəˈtɛrɪkə, ˌiːsə-/ ■ pl. n. [treated as sing. or pl.] esoteric subjects or publications.
– ORIGIN C20: from Greek *esōterika*, from *esōterikos* 'esoteric'.

ESP ■ abbrev. extrasensory perception.

esp. ■ abbrev. especially.

espadrille /ˈɛspədrɪl, ˌɛspəˈdrɪl/ ■ n. a light canvas shoe with a plaited fibre sole.
– ORIGIN C19: from Provençal *espardi(l)hos*, from *espart* 'esparto', from Latin *spartum* (see **ESPARTO**).

espalier /ɪˈspaljə, ɛ-/ ■ n. a fruit tree or ornamental shrub whose branches are trained to grow flat against a wall. ■ v. train (a tree or shrub) in such a way.
– ORIGIN C17: from Italian *spalliera*, from *spalla* 'shoulder', from Latin *spatula* (see **SPATULA**), in late Latin 'shoulder blade'.

esparto /ɛˈspɑːtəʊ, ɪ-/ (also **esparto grass**) ■ n. (pl. **-os**) a coarse grass native to Spain and North Africa, used to make ropes, wickerwork, and paper. [*Stipa tenacissima*.]
– ORIGIN C19: from Spanish, via Latin from Greek *sparton* 'rope'.

especial /ɪˈspɛʃ(ə)l, ɛ-/ ■ adj. **1** notable; special. **2** for or belonging chiefly to one person or thing.
– ORIGIN Middle English: from Latin *specialis* 'special', from *species* (see **SPECIES**).

especially ■ adv. **1** in particular. **2** to a great extent; very much.

Esperanto /ˌɛspəˈrantəʊ/ ■ n. an artificial language devised in 1887 as an international medium of communication, based on roots from the chief European languages.
– DERIVATIVES **Esperantist** n.
– ORIGIN from the name *Dr Esperanto*, used as a pen name by the inventor of the language, Polish physician Ludwik Latin Zamenhof; the literal sense is 'one who hopes', from Latin *sperare* 'to hope'.

espionage /ˈɛspɪənɑːʒ, -ɪdʒ/ ■ n. the practice of spying or of using spies.
– ORIGIN C18: from French, from *espionner* 'to spy', from *espion* 'a spy'.

esplanade /ˌɛspləˈneɪd, -ˈnɑːd/ ■ n. a long, open, level area, typically beside the sea, along which people may promenade. ▶ an open, level space separating a fortress from a town.
– ORIGIN C16: from Italian *spianata*, from Latin *explanatus* 'levelled', from *explanare* (see **EXPLAIN**).

espousal /ɪˈspaʊz(ə)l, ɛ-/ ■ n. **1** the action of espousing. **2** archaic a marriage or engagement.

espouse /ɪˈspaʊz, ɛ-/ ■ v. **1** adopt or support (a cause, belief, or way of life). **2** archaic marry. ▶ (**be espoused to**) be engaged to.
– DERIVATIVES **espouser** n.
– ORIGIN Middle English: from Old French *espouser*, from Latin *sponsare*, from *sponsus* 'betrothed', from *spondere*.

espresso /ɛˈsprɛsəʊ/ (also **expresso**) ■ n. (pl. **-os**) strong black coffee made by forcing steam through ground coffee beans.
– ORIGIN 1940s: from Italian (*caffè*) *espresso* 'pressed out (coffee)'.

esprit /ɛˈspriː/ ■ n. liveliness.
– ORIGIN French: from Latin *spiritus* 'spirit'.

esprit de corps /ɛˌspriː də ˈkɔː/ ■ n. a feeling of pride, fellowship, and loyalty uniting the members of a particular group.
– ORIGIN French, 'spirit of the body'.

espy /ɪˈspʌɪ, ɛ-/ ■ v. (**-ies**, **-ied**) poetic/literary catch sight of.
– ORIGIN Middle English: from Old French *espier*, of Germanic origin.

Esq. ■ abbrev. Esquire.

-esque ■ suffix (forming adjectives) in the style of; resembling: *Dantesque*.
– ORIGIN from French, via Italian *-esco* from medieval Latin *-iscus*.

Esquimau ■ n. (pl. **Esquimaux**) archaic spelling of **ESKIMO**.

esquire /ɪˈskwʌɪə, ɛ-/ (abbrev.: **esq.**) ■ n. **1** (**Esquire**) Brit. a polite title appended to a man's name when no other title is used, especially in a letter. ▶ N. Amer. a title appended to a lawyer's surname. **2** historical a young nobleman who, in training for knighthood, acted as an attendant to a knight. ▶ an officer in the service of a king or nobleman. ▶ a landed proprietor or country squire.
– ORIGIN Middle English: from Old French *esquier*, from Latin *scutarius* 'shield-bearer', from *scutum* 'shield'.

ESR ■ abbrev. Physics electron spin resonance.

-ess¹ ■ suffix forming nouns denoting female gender: *abbess*.
– ORIGIN from French *-esse*, from Greek *-issa*.

USAGE
In modern English, there are few new words coined with the suffix **-ess**. Many existing feminine forms (e.g. **poetess, authoress**) are likely to be regarded as old-fashioned or sexist and avoided in favour of the 'neutral' base form (e.g. **poet, author**).

-ess² ■ suffix forming abstract nouns from adjectives, such as *largess*.
– ORIGIN Middle English: via French *-esse* from Latin *-itia*.

essay ■ n. /ˈɛseɪ/ **1** a piece of writing on a particular subject. **2** formal an attempt or effort. **3** a trial design of a postage stamp. ■ v. /ɛˈseɪ/ formal attempt.
– DERIVATIVES **essayist** n. **essayistic** adj.
– ORIGIN C15: alteration of **ASSAY**, by association with Old French *essayer*, from late Latin *exagium* 'weighing'; the noun (C16) is from Old French *essai* 'trial'.

esse /ˈɛsi/ ■ n. Philosophy essential nature or essence.
– ORIGIN Latin, 'to be'.

essence ■ n. **1** the intrinsic nature of something; the quality which determines something's character. ▶ Philosophy a property or group of properties of something without which it would not exist or be what it is. **2** an extract or concentrate obtained from a plant or other substance and used for flavouring or scent.
– PHRASES **in essence** basically; fundamentally. **of the essence** critically important.
– ORIGIN Middle English: from Latin *essentia*, from *esse* 'be'.

essential /ɪˈsɛnʃ(ə)l/ ■ adj. **1** fundamental; central. **2** absolutely necessary; extremely important. **3** (of an amino acid or fatty acid) required for normal growth but

essentialism

not synthesized in the body and therefore necessary in the diet. **4** Medicine (of a disease) with no known external stimulus or cause; idiopathic. ■ n. (**essentials**) **1** the fundamental elements. **2** things that are absolutely necessary.
– DERIVATIVES **essentiality** n. **essentially** adv. **essentialness** n.
– ORIGIN Middle English: from late Latin *essentialis*, from Latin *essentia* (see ESSENCE).

essentialism ■ n. Philosophy a belief that things have a set of characteristics which make them what they are; the doctrine that essence is prior to existence.
– DERIVATIVES **essentialist** n. & adj.

essential oil ■ n. a natural oil extracted from a plant, used especially in aromatherapy or in making perfume.

EST ■ abbrev. Eastern Standard Time.

est /ɛst/ ■ n. a system aimed at developing a person's potential through intensive group awareness and training sessions.
– ORIGIN 1970s: acronym from *Erhard Seminars Training*, from the name of Werner *Erhard*, the American businessman who devised the technique.

-est[1] ■ suffix forming the superlative of adjectives (such as *shortest*) and of adverbs (such as *soonest*).
– ORIGIN Old English *-ost-*, *-ust-*, *-ast-*.

-est[2] (also **-st**) ■ suffix archaic forming the second person singular of verbs: *goest*.
– ORIGIN Old English *-est*, *-ast*, *-st*.

est. ■ abbrev. **1** established. **2** estimated.

establish ■ v. **1** set up on a firm or permanent basis. **2** initiate or bring about. **3** (**be established**) be settled or accepted in a particular place or role. **4** (of a plant) take root and grow. **5** show to be true or certain by determining the facts. **6** Bridge ensure that one's remaining cards in (a suit) will be winners (if not trumped) by playing off the high cards in that suit. **7** [as adj. **established**] recognized by the state as the national Church or religion.
– DERIVATIVES **establisher** n.
– ORIGIN Middle English: from Old French *establiss-*, *establir*, from Latin *stabilire* 'make firm', from *stabilis* (adj.) 'stable'.

establishment ■ n. **1** the action of establishing or being established. **2** a business organization, public institution, or household. **3** (**the Establishment**) a group in a society exercising power and influence over matters of policy, opinion, or taste, and seen as resisting change.

estate ■ n. **1** a property consisting of a large house and extensive grounds. **2** an area of land and modern buildings developed for residential, industrial, or commercial purposes. **3** a property where crops such as coffee or rubber are cultivated or where wine is produced. ▶ S. African a registered vineyard producing wines made exclusively from its own grapes. **4** a person's money and property in its entirety at the time of their death. **5** (also **estate of the realm**) a class or order forming part of the body politic, in particular (in Britain) one of the three groups constituting Parliament, now the Lords spiritual (the heads of the Church), the Lords temporal (the peerage), and the Commons (known as the three estates). **6** archaic or poetic/literary a particular state, period, or condition in life. **7** short for ESTATE CAR.
– ORIGIN Middle English: from Old French *estat*, from Latin *status* 'state, condition', from *stare* 'to stand'.

estate agency ■ n. a business that sells and rents out buildings and land for clients.
– DERIVATIVES **estate agent** n.

estate car ■ n. a car incorporating a large carrying area behind the seats, accessed by a door at the rear.

estate duty ■ n. a death duty.

estate wine ■ n. S. African wine produced on a vineyard legally registered as an estate.

esteem ■ n. respect and admiration. ■ v. **1** (usu. **be esteemed**) respect and admire. **2** formal consider; deem.
– ORIGIN Middle English: from Old French *estime* (n.), *estimer* (v.), from Latin *aestimare* 'to estimate'.

ester /'ɛstə/ ■ n. Chemistry an organic compound made by replacing the hydrogen of an acid by an alkyl or other organic group.
– DERIVATIVES **esterify** /ɛ'stɛrɪfʌɪ/ v. (**-ies**, **-ied**).
– ORIGIN C19: from German, prob. from a blend of *Essig* 'vinegar' and *Äther* 'ether'.

esterase /'ɛstəreɪz/ ■ n. Biochemistry an enzyme which breaks down particular esters into acids and alcohols or phenols.

esthetic etc. ■ adj. US spelling of AESTHETIC etc.

estimable /'ɛstɪməb(ə)l/ ■ adj. worthy of great respect.
– DERIVATIVES **estimably** adv.

estimate ■ n. /'ɛstɪmət/ **1** an approximate calculation or judgement. ▶ a written statement indicating the likely price that will be charged for specified work. **2** a judgement or appraisal. ■ v. /'ɛstɪmeɪt/ form an estimate of.
– DERIVATIVES **estimation** n. **estimative** /-mətɪv/ adj. **estimator** n.
– ORIGIN Middle English: from Latin *aestimare* 'determine, appraise'.

estivation ■ n. US spelling of AESTIVATION.

estoile /ɪ'stɔɪl, ɛ-/ ■ n. Heraldry a star with (usually six) wavy points or rays.
– ORIGIN C16: from Latin *stella* 'star'.

Estonian ■ n. **1** a native or national of Estonia, or a person of Estonian descent. **2** the language of Estonia. ■ adj. of or relating to Estonia or its people or language.

estop /ɪ'stɒp/ ■ v. (**estopped**, **estopping**) Law bar or preclude by estoppel.
– ORIGIN Middle English: from Old French *estopper* 'stop up, impede'.

estoppel /ɪ'stɒp(ə)l/ ■ n. Law the principle which precludes a person from asserting something contrary to what is implied by a previous action or statement of that person or by a previous pertinent judicial determination.
– ORIGIN C16: from Old French *estouppail* 'bung', from *estopper* (see ESTOP).

estradiol ■ n. US spelling of OESTRADIOL.

estrange /ɪ'streɪn(d)ʒ, ɛ-/ ■ v. **1** cause to feel less close or friendly; alienate. **2** [as adj. **estranged**] (of a husband or wife) no longer living with their spouse.
– DERIVATIVES **estrangement** n.
– ORIGIN C15: from Old French *estranger*, from Latin *extraneare* 'treat as a stranger'.

estrogen etc. ■ n. US spelling of OESTROGEN etc.

estrus etc. ■ n. US spelling of OESTRUS etc.

estuary /'ɛstjʊ(ə)ri/ ■ n. (pl. **-ies**) the tidal mouth of a large river.
– DERIVATIVES **estuarial** adj. **estuarine** /-rʌɪn/ adj.
– ORIGIN C16: from Latin *aestuarium* 'tidal part of a shore', from *aestus* 'tide'.

Estuary English ■ n. (in the UK) a type of accent identified as spreading outwards from London and containing features of both received pronunciation and London speech.

-et[1] ■ suffix forming nouns which were originally diminutives: *baronet*.
– ORIGIN from Old French *-et*, *-ete*.

-et[2] (also **-ete**) ■ suffix forming nouns such as *comet*, and often denoting people: *athlete*.
– ORIGIN from Greek *-ētēs*.

ETA /ˌiːtiː'eɪ/ ■ abbrev. estimated time of arrival.

eta /'iːtə/ ■ n. the seventh letter of the Greek alphabet (Η, η), transliterated as 'e' or 'ē'.
– ORIGIN from Greek *ēta*.

etagere /ˌɛtɑ'ʒɛː/ ■ n. (pl. same or **etageres**) a piece of furniture with a number of open shelves.
– ORIGIN French *étagère*, from *étage* 'shelf'.

et al. /ɛt 'al/ ■ abbrev. and others.
– ORIGIN from Latin *et alii*.

etalon /'ɛtəlɒn/ ■ n. Physics a device consisting of two reflecting plates, for producing interfering light beams.
– ORIGIN C20: from French *étalon* 'standard of measurement'.

etc. ■ abbrev. et cetera.

et cetera /ɛt'sɛt(ə)rə, ɪt-/ (also **etcetera**) ■ adv. and other similar things; and so on. ■ n. (**et ceteras**) unspecified extra items.

—ORIGIN Latin: from *et* 'and' + *cetera* 'the rest', from *ceterus* 'left over'.

etch ■ v. **1** engrave (metal, glass, or stone) by coating it with a protective layer, drawing on it with a needle, and then covering it with acid to attack the parts the needle has exposed. **2** (of an acid or other solvent) corrode or eat away the surface of. **3** cut or carve (a text or design) on a surface. ▶ carve with a text or design. **4** cause to be clearly defined: *the outline of the town was etched against the sky*.
—DERIVATIVES **etcher** n.
—ORIGIN C17: from Dutch *etsen*, from German *ätzen*.

etchant /ˈɛtʃ(ə)nt/ ■ n. an acid or corrosive chemical used in etching; a mordant.

etching ■ n. **1** the art or process of etching. **2** a print produced by the process of etching.

-ete ■ suffix variant spelling of -ET² (as in *athlete*).

eternal /ɪˈtɜːn(ə)l, iː-/ ■ adj. **1** lasting or existing forever. ▶ informal tediously lengthy or persistent. **2** valid for all time; essentially unchanging: *eternal truths*. **3** (**the Eternal**) used to refer to an everlasting or universal spirit, as represented by God.
—PHRASES **the Eternal City** the city of Rome. **eternal triangle** a relationship between three people involving sexual rivalry.
—DERIVATIVES **eternality** /ˌɪtɜːˈnalɪti, iː-/ n. **eternalize** (also **-ise**) v. **eternally** adv. **eternalness** n.
—ORIGIN Middle English: from late Latin *aeternalis*, from Latin *aeternus*, from *aevum* 'age'.

eternity ■ n. (pl. **-ies**) infinite or unending time. ▶ Theology endless life after death. ▶ (**an eternity**) informal an undesirably long period of time.

eternity ring ■ n. a ring given as a symbol of lasting affection, typically set with an unbroken circle of gems.

eth /ɛð/ (also **edh**) ■ n. an Old English letter, ð or Ð, eventually superseded by the digraph *th*.
—ORIGIN from Danish *edh*, perhaps representing the sound of the letter.

-eth¹ ■ suffix variant spelling of -TH¹ (as in *fiftieth*).

-eth² (also **-th**) ■ suffix archaic forming the third person singular of the present tense of verbs: *doeth*.
—ORIGIN Old English *-eth*, *-ath*, *-th*.

ethanal /ˈɛθ(ə)nal/ ■ n. systematic chemical name for ACETALDEHYDE.
—ORIGIN C19: blend of ETHANE and ALDEHYDE.

ethanamide /ɪˈθanəmʌɪd/ ■ n. systematic chemical name for ACETAMIDE.

ethane /ˈiːθeɪn, ˈɛθ-/ ■ n. Chemistry a flammable hydrocarbon gas of the alkane series, present in petroleum and natural gas. [C_2H_6.]
—ORIGIN C19: from ETHER + -ANE².

ethanediol /ˈiːθeɪnˌdʌɪɒl, ˈɛθ-/ ■ n. systematic chemical name for ETHYLENE GLYCOL.

ethanoic acid /ˌɛθəˈnəʊɪk/ ■ n. systematic chemical name for ACETIC ACID.
—DERIVATIVES **ethanoate** n.

ethanol /ˈɛθənɒl/ ■ n. systematic chemical name for ETHYL ALCOHOL (see ALCOHOL).

ethene /ˈɛθiːn/ ■ n. systematic chemical name for ETHYLENE.
—ORIGIN C19: from ETHER + -ENE.

ether /ˈiːθə/ ■ n. **1** (also **diethyl ether**) a pleasant-smelling, volatile, highly flammable liquid used as an anaesthetic and as a solvent. **2** Chemistry any organic compound with an oxygen atom linking two alkyl groups. **3** (also **aether**) chiefly poetic/literary the clear sky; the upper regions of air beyond the clouds. **4** (also **aether**) Physics, historical a substance formerly postulated to permeate all space and to transmit light.
—DERIVATIVES **etheric** /iːˈθɛrɪk, ˈiːθ(ə)rɪk/ adj.
—ORIGIN Middle English: from Greek *aithēr* 'upper air', from the base of *aithein* 'burn, shine'.

ethereal /ɪˈθɪərɪəl/ (also **etherial**) ■ adj. **1** extremely delicate and light in a way that seems not to be of this world. **2** Chemistry (of a solution) having diethyl ether as a solvent.
—DERIVATIVES **ethereality** n. **etherealize** (also **-ise**) v. **ethereally** adv.
—ORIGIN C16: from Greek *aitherios*, from *aithēr* 'ether'.

Ethernet /ˈiːθənɛt/ ■ n. Computing a system for connecting a number of computer systems to form a local area network.
—ORIGIN 1970s: blend of ETHER and NETWORK.

ethic /ˈɛθɪk/ ■ n. a set of moral principles.
—ORIGIN Middle English: from Latin *ethice*, from Greek (*hē*) *ēthikē* (*teknē*) '(the science of) morals', from *ēthos* (see ETHOS).

ethical ■ adj. **1** of or relating to moral principles or the branch of knowledge concerned with these. **2** morally correct. **3** (of a medicine) available only on prescription.
—DERIVATIVES **ethicality** n. **ethically** adv.

ethics ■ pl. n. **1** [usu. treated as pl.] the moral principles governing or influencing conduct. **2** [usu. treated as sing.] the branch of knowledge concerned with moral principles.
—DERIVATIVES **ethicist** n.

Ethiopian ■ n. a native or national of Ethiopia, or a person of Ethiopian descent. ■ adj. **1** of or relating to Ethiopia or its people. **2** Zoology relating to or denoting a zoogeographical region comprising sub-Saharan Africa, the Arabian peninsula, and (usually) Madagascar.

Ethiopic /ˌiːθɪˈɒpɪk/ ■ n. another term for GE'EZ.

ethmoid /ˈɛθmɔɪd/ ■ n. Anatomy a square bone at the root of the nose, forming part of the cranium, and having many perforations through which the olfactory nerves pass to the nose.
—DERIVATIVES **ethmoidal** adj.
—ORIGIN C18: from Greek *ēthmoeidēs*, from *ēthmos* 'a sieve'.

ethnic ■ adj. **1** of or relating to a group of people having a common national or cultural tradition. **2** denoting origin by birth or descent rather than by present nationality: *ethnic Albanians*. **3** characteristic of or belonging to a non-Western cultural tradition: *ethnic dresses*. ■ n. chiefly N. Amer. a member of an ethnic minority.
—DERIVATIVES **ethnically** adv. **ethnicity** n.
—ORIGIN Middle English: from Greek *ethnikos* 'heathen', from *ethnos* 'nation'.

ethnic cleansing ■ n. the mass expulsion or killing of members of one ethnic or religious group in an area by those of another.

ethnic minority ■ n. a subgroup within a community which differs ethnically from the main population.

ethno- /ˈɛθnəʊ/ ■ comb. form ethnic; ethnological: *ethnocentric*.
—ORIGIN from Greek *ethnos* 'nation'.

ethnocentric ■ adj. evaluating other cultures according to preconceptions originating in one's own culture.
—DERIVATIVES **ethnocentrically** adv. **ethnocentricity** n. **ethnocentrism** n.

ethnocultural ■ adj. of or relating to a particular ethnic group.

ethnography /ɛθˈnɒɡrəfi/ ■ n. the scientific description of peoples and cultures with reference to their particular customs and characteristics.
—DERIVATIVES **ethnographer** n. **ethnographic** adj. **ethnographical** adj. **ethnographically** adv.

ethnology /ɛθˈnɒlədʒi/ ■ n. the study of the characteristics of different peoples and the differences and relationships between them.
—DERIVATIVES **ethnologic** /-nəˈlɒdʒɪk/ adj. **ethnological** adj. **ethnologically** adv. **ethnologist** n.

ethnomusicology ■ n. the study of the music of different cultures.
—DERIVATIVES **ethnomusicologic** adj. **ethnomusicological** adj. **ethnomusicologist** n.

ethology /iːˈθɒlədʒi/ ■ n. **1** the science of animal behaviour. **2** the study of human behaviour and social organization from a biological perspective.
—DERIVATIVES **ethological** adj. **ethologist** n.
—ORIGIN C19: from Greek *ēthologia*, from *ēthos* (see ETHOS).

ethos /ˈiːθɒs/ ■ n. the characteristic spirit of a culture, era, or community as manifested in its attitudes and aspirations.
—ORIGIN C19: from modern Latin, from Greek *ēthos* 'nature, disposition', (pl.) 'customs'.

ethyl

ethyl /ˈɛθʌɪl, -θɪl, ˈiː-/ ■ n. [as modifier] Chemistry of or denoting the alkyl radical -C$_2$H$_5$, derived from ethane.
– ORIGIN C19: from German, from *Äther* 'ether'.

ethyl acetate ■ n. Chemistry a colourless volatile liquid with a fruity smell, used as a plastics solvent and in flavourings and perfumes.

ethyl alcohol ■ n. another term for ALCOHOL (in sense 1).

ethylene /ˈɛθɪliːn, -θ(ə)l-/ ■ n. Chemistry a flammable hydrocarbon gas of the alkene series, occurring in natural gas and coal gas. [C$_2$H$_4$.]

ethylene glycol ■ n. Chemistry a colourless viscous hygroscopic liquid used in antifreeze and in wood preservatives.

ethyne /ˈiːθʌɪn, ˈɛθ-/ ■ n. systematic chemical name for ACETYLENE.

-etic ■ suffix forming adjectives and nouns, such as *pathetic, peripatetic*.
– ORIGIN from Greek *-ētikos* or *-ētikos*.

etiolated /ˈiːtɪəˌleɪtɪd/ ■ adj. (of a plant) pale and weak due to a lack of light.
– DERIVATIVES **etiolation** n.
– ORIGIN C18: from *etiolate*, from Norman French *étieuler* 'grow into haulm'.

etiology ■ n. US spelling of AETIOLOGY.

etiquette /ˈɛtɪkɛt, ɛtɪˈkɛt/ ■ n. the customary code of polite behaviour in a society.
– ORIGIN C18: from French *étiquette* 'list of ceremonial observances of a court', also 'label, etiquette', from Old French *estiquette*, from *estiquier* 'to fix'.

Etonian /iːˈtəʊnɪən/ ■ n. a pupil of Eton College, a boys' private school in southern England. ■ adj. relating to or typical of Eton College.

etrier /ˈɛtrɪeɪ/ ■ n. Climbing a short rope ladder with a few rungs of wood or metal.
– ORIGIN 1950s: from French *étrier* 'stirrup'.

Etruscan /ɪˈtrʌsk(ə)n/ ■ adj. of or relating to Etruria, an ancient state of western Italy that was at its height *c.*500 BC.
– ORIGIN from Latin *Etruscus*.

et seq. (also **et seqq.**) ■ adv. and what follows (used in page references).
– ORIGIN from Latin *et sequens* 'and the following'.

-ette ■ suffix forming nouns: **1** denoting small size: *kitchenette*. **2** denoting an imitation or substitute: *leatherette*. **3** denoting female gender: *suffragette*.
– ORIGIN from Old French *-ette*, feminine of -ET^1.

étude /ˈeɪtjuːd, eɪˈtjuːd/ ■ n. a short musical composition or exercise.
– ORIGIN C19: from French, 'study'.

etymology /ˌɛtɪˈmɒlədʒi/ ■ n. (pl. **-ies**) an account of the origins and the developments in meaning of a word.
– DERIVATIVES **etymological** adj. **etymologically** adv. **etymologist** n. **etymologize** (also **-ise**) v.
– ORIGIN Middle English: from Greek *etumologia*, from *etumologos* 'student of etymology', from *etumon*, from *etumos* 'true'.

EU ■ abbrev. European Union.

Eu ■ symb. the chemical element europium.

eu- ■ comb. form well; easily:
– ORIGIN from Greek *eu* 'well', from *eus* 'good'.

eubacteria /ˌjuːbakˈtɪərɪə/ ■ pl. n. Biology a large group of bacteria with simple cells and rigid cell walls, comprising the 'true' bacteria and cyanobacteria as distinct from archaea.
– DERIVATIVES **eubacterial** adj.
– ORIGIN C20: from EU- (in sense 'normal') + BACTERIUM.

eucalyptus /ˌjuːkəˈlɪptəs/ (also **eucalypt**) ■ n. (pl. **eucalyptuses** or **eucalypti** /-tʌɪ/) a fast-growing evergreen Australasian tree valued for its wood, oil, gum, and resin. [Genus *Eucalyptus*: numerous species.] ▸ the oil from eucalyptus leaves, chiefly used for its medicinal properties.
– ORIGIN from Greek *eu* 'well' + *kaluptos* 'covered', because the unopened flower is protected by a cap.

eucaryote ■ n. variant spelling of EUKARYOTE.

Eucharist /ˈjuːk(ə)rɪst/ ■ n. the Christian service, ceremony, or sacrament commemorating the Last Supper, in which bread and wine are consecrated and consumed. ▸ the consecrated elements, especially the bread.
– DERIVATIVES **Eucharistic** adj. **Eucharistical** adj.
– ORIGIN Middle English: from eccles. Greek *eukharistia* 'thanksgiving', from Greek *eukharistos* 'grateful', from *eu* 'well' + *kharizesthai* 'offer graciously', from *kharis* 'grace'.

Euclidean /juːˈklɪdɪən/ ■ adj. of or relating to the ancient Greek mathematician Euclid and his system of geometry.

eudaemonism /juːˈdiːmənɪz(ə)m/ (also **eudemonism**) ■ n. a system of ethics that bases moral value on the likelihood of actions producing happiness.
– DERIVATIVES **eudaemonist** n. **eudaemonistic** adj.
– ORIGIN C19: from Greek *eudaimonismos* 'system of happiness', from *eudaimōn*, from *eu* 'well' + *daimōn* 'guardian spirit'.

eudiometer /ˌjuːdɪˈɒmɪtə/ ■ n. Chemistry a graduated glass tube in which mixtures of gases can be made to react by an electric spark, used to measure changes in volume during chemical reactions.
– DERIVATIVES **eudiometric** adj. **eudiometrical** adj. **eudiometry** n.
– ORIGIN C18 (denoting an instrument used to measure amounts of oxygen, thought to be greater in fine weather): from Greek *eudios* 'clear, fine' (weather), from *eu* 'well' + *dios* 'heavenly'.

eugenics /juːˈdʒɛnɪks/ ■ pl. n. [treated as sing.] the science of using controlled breeding to increase the occurrence of desirable heritable characteristics in a population.
– DERIVATIVES **eugenic** adj. **eugenically** adv. **eugenicist** n. & adj. **eugenist** n. & adj.
– ORIGIN C19: from EU- + -GEN- + -ICS.

euglena /juːˈgliːnə/ ■ n. Biology a single-celled freshwater flagellate organism, sometimes forming a green scum on stagnant water. [Genus *Euglena*.]
– DERIVATIVES **euglenoid** n. & adj.
– ORIGIN from EU- + Greek *glēnē* 'eyeball, socket of joint'.

euhedral /juːˈhiːdr(ə)l/ ■ adj. Geology (of a mineral crystal) having faces corresponding to its regular crystal form, not constrained by adjacent minerals.

eukaryote /juːˈkarɪəʊt/ (also **eucaryote**) ■ n. Biology an organism consisting of a cell or cells in which the genetic material is DNA in the form of chromosomes contained within a distinct nucleus (that is, all living organisms other than the eubacteria and archaea). Compare with PROKARYOTE.
– DERIVATIVES **eukaryotic** adj.
– ORIGIN 1960s: from EU- + KARYO- + -*ote* as in *zygote*.

eulogium /juːˈləʊdʒɪəm/ ■ n. (pl. **eulogia** /-dʒɪə/ or **eulogiums**) another term for EULOGY.
– ORIGIN C17: from medieval Latin, 'praise'.

eulogize /ˈjuːlədʒʌɪz/ (also **-ise**) ■ v. praise highly.
– DERIVATIVES **eulogist** n. **eulogistic** adj. **eulogistically** adv.

eulogy /ˈjuːlədʒi/ ■ n. (pl. **-ies**) a speech or piece of writing that praises someone highly.
– ORIGIN Middle English: from Greek *eulogia* 'praise', apparently influenced by Latin *elogium* 'inscription on a tomb', from Greek *elegia* 'elegy'.

eunuch /ˈjuːnək/ ■ n. a man who has been castrated.
– ORIGIN Old English: from Greek *eunoukhos* 'bedroom guard', from *eunē* 'bed' + a second element rel. to *ekhein* 'to hold'.

euonymus /juːˈɒnɪməs/ ■ n. a shrub or small tree noted for its autumn colours and bright fruit. [Genus *Euonymus*: numerous species.]
– ORIGIN from Latin *euonymos*, from Greek *euōnumos*, from *eus* 'good' + *onoma* 'name'.

euphausiid /juːˈfɔːzɪɪd/ ■ n. Zoology a shrimp-like planktonic crustacean of an order (Euphausiaceae) which includes krill.
– ORIGIN C19: from *Euphausia* (genus name), from Greek *eu* 'well' + *phainein* 'to show' + *ousia* 'substance'.

euphemism /ˈjuːfəmɪz(ə)m/ ■ n. a mild or less direct word substituted for one that is harsh or blunt when referring to something unpleasant or embarrassing.
– DERIVATIVES **euphemistic** adj. **euphemistically** adv. **euphemize** (also **-ise**) v.
– ORIGIN C16: from Greek *euphēmismos*, from *euphēmizein* 'use auspicious words', from *eu* 'well' + *phēmē* 'speaking'.

euphonious /juːˈfəʊnɪəs/ ■ adj. sounding pleasant.
– DERIVATIVES **euphoniously** adv.

euphonium /juːˈfəʊnɪəm/ ■ n. a valved brass musical instrument of tenor pitch, resembling a small tuba.
– ORIGIN C19: from Greek *euphōnos* 'having a pleasing sound'.

euphony /ˈjuːf(ə)ni/ ■ n. (pl. **-ies**) **1** the quality of being pleasing to the ear. **2** the tendency to make phonetic change for ease of pronunciation.
– DERIVATIVES **euphonic** adj. **euphonize** (also **-ise**) v.
– ORIGIN Middle English: from Greek *euphōnia*, from *euphōnos* 'well sounding', from *phōnē* 'sound'.

euphorbia /juːˈfɔːbɪə/ ■ n. a plant of a genus that comprises the spurges. [Genus *Euphorbia*.]
– ORIGIN Middle English: from Latin *euphorbea*, named after *Euphorbus*, Greek physician to the reputed discoverer of the plant, Juba II of Mauretania.

euphoria /juːˈfɔːrɪə/ ■ n. a feeling of intense happiness.
– DERIVATIVES **euphoric** adj. **euphorically** adv.
– ORIGIN C17: modern Latin, from Greek, from *euphoros*, from *eu* 'well' + *pherein* 'to bear'.

euphrasia /juːˈfreɪzɪə/ ■ n. eyebright or a related plant, especially as a herbal or homeopathic remedy for eye problems. [Genus *Euphrasia*.]
– ORIGIN C18: from Greek, 'cheerfulness'.

Eurasian ■ adj. **1** of mixed European (or European-American) and Asian parentage. **2** of or relating to Eurasia. ■ n. a person of Eurasian parentage.

eureka /jʊ(ə)ˈriːkə/ ■ exclam. a cry of joy or satisfaction when one finds or discovers something. ■ n. an alloy of copper and nickel used for electrical filament and resistance wire.
– ORIGIN C17: from Greek *heurēka* 'I have found it', said to have been uttered by Archimedes when he hit upon a method of determining the purity of gold.

eurhythmics (also **eurhythmy**; US also **eurythmics**, **eurythmy**) ■ pl. n. [treated as sing.] a system of rhythmical physical movements to music used to teach musical understanding or for therapeutic purposes.
– ORIGIN C20: from **EU-** + **RHYTHM** + **-ICS**.

Euro /ˈjʊərəʊ/ ■ adj. informal European, especially concerned with the European Union.

Euro- ■ comb. form European; European and ... ▶ relating to Europe or the European Union: *a Euro-MP*.

euro ■ n. (pl. **euros** or **euro**) the single European currency, introduced in the European Union in 1999.

Eurobond ■ n. an international bond issued in Europe or elsewhere outside the country in whose currency its value is stated.

Eurocentric ■ adj. implicitly regarding European culture as pre-eminent.
– DERIVATIVES **Eurocentricity** n. **Eurocentrism** n.

Eurocommunism ■ n. a European form of communism which advocates the preservation of many elements of Western liberal democracy.
– DERIVATIVES **Eurocommunist** adj. & n.

Eurocrat ■ n. informal, chiefly derogatory a bureaucrat in the administration of the European Union.

Eurocurrency ■ n. **1** a form of money held or traded outside the country in whose currency its value is stated. **2** a single currency for use by the member states of the European Union.

Eurodollar ■ n. a US dollar held in Europe or elsewhere outside the US.

Euromarket ■ n. **1** a financial market which deals with Eurocurrencies. **2** the European Union regarded as a single commercial or financial market.

Euro-MP ■ n. a member of the European Parliament.

European ■ n. a native or inhabitant of Europe. ▶ a person who is white or of European parentage. ■ adj. of or relating to Europe or the European Union.
– DERIVATIVES **Europeanism** n. **Europeanization** (also **-isation**) n. **Europeanize** (also **-ise**) v.

European Union ■ n. an economic and political association of certain European countries as a unit with internal free trade and common external tariffs.

europium /jʊ(ə)ˈrəʊpɪəm/ ■ n. the chemical element of atomic number 63, a soft silvery-white metal of the lanthanide series. (Symbol: **Eu**)

– ORIGIN C20: modern Latin, from *Europe*.

Euro-sceptic ■ n. a person who is opposed to increasing the powers of the European Union.
– DERIVATIVES **Euro-scepticism** n.

Eurostar ■ n. trademark the high-speed passenger rail service that links London with various European cities via the Channel Tunnel.

Eurotrash ■ n. informal rich European socialites, especially those living or working in the United States.

eurozone ■ n. the area comprising those European Union countries which have adopted the euro as their principal monetary unit.

eury- ■ comb. form denoting a wide variety or range of something specified: *eurytopic*.
– ORIGIN from Greek *eurus* 'wide'.

euryhaline /jʊərɪˈheɪlaɪn, -ˈheɪliːn/ ■ adj. Ecology able to tolerate a wide range of salinity. Often contrasted with **STENOHALINE**.
– ORIGIN C19: from Greek *eurus* 'wide' + *halinos* 'of salt'.

eurypterid /jʊ(ə)ˈrɪptərɪd/ ■ n. a giant fossil marine arthropod of a group occurring in the Palaeozoic era, resembling large scorpions.
– ORIGIN C19: from *Eurypterus* (genus name), from **EURY-** + Greek *pteron* 'wing'.

eurythermal /jʊərɪˈθəːm(ə)l/ ■ adj. Ecology able to tolerate a wide range of temperature. Often contrasted with **STENOTHERMAL**.

eurythmics (also **eurythmy**) ■ pl. n. US spelling of **EURHYTHMICS**.

Euskara /ˈjuːskərə/ ■ n. the Basque language.
– ORIGIN the name in Basque.

eusocial /juːˈsəʊʃ(ə)l/ ■ adj. Zoology denoting social organisms (e.g. the honeybee) in which a single female or caste produces the offspring and non-reproductive individuals cooperate in caring for the young.
– DERIVATIVES **eusociality** n.

Eustachian tube /juːˈsteɪʃ(ə)n/ ■ n. Anatomy a narrow passage leading from the pharynx to the cavity of the middle ear, permitting the equalization of pressure on each side of the eardrum.
– ORIGIN C18: named after the C16 Italian anatomist Bartolomeo *Eustachio*.

eustasy /ˈjuːstəsi/ ■ n. a change of sea level throughout the world, caused typically by movements of parts of the earth's crust or melting of glaciers.
– DERIVATIVES **eustatic** adj.
– ORIGIN 1940s: back-formation from *eustatic*, coined in German from Greek *eu* 'well' + *statikos* 'static'.

eutectic /juːˈtɛktɪk/ ■ adj. Chemistry relating to or denoting a mixture of two substances that melts and solidifies at a single temperature lower than the melting points of the separate constituents or of any other mixture of them.
– ORIGIN C19: from Greek *eutēktos* 'easily melting'.

eutectic point ■ n. Chemistry the temperature at which a particular eutectic mixture freezes or melts.

euthanasia /juːθəˈneɪzɪə/ ■ n. the painless killing of a patient suffering from an incurable disease or in an irreversible coma.
– ORIGIN C17: from Greek, from *eu* 'well' + *thanatos* 'death'.

euthanize /ˈjuːθənʌɪz/ (also **-ise**) ■ v. N. Amer. put (an animal) to death humanely.

Eutheria /juːˈθɪərɪə/ ■ pl. n. Zoology a major group of mammals that comprises the placentals. Compare with **METATHERIA**.
– DERIVATIVES **eutherian** n. & adj.
– ORIGIN from **EU-** + Greek *thēria*, pl. of *thērion* 'wild beast'.

euthyroid /juːˈθʌɪrɔɪd/ ■ adj. Medicine having a normally functioning thyroid gland.

eutrophic /juːˈtrəʊfɪk, -ˈtrɒfɪk/ ■ adj. Ecology (of a body of water) rich in nutrients and so supporting a dense plant population, the decomposition of which kills animal life

by depriving it of oxygen.
- DERIVATIVES **eutrophicate** v. **eutrophication** n.
- ORIGIN C18: from Greek *eutrophia*, from *eu* 'well' + *trephein* 'nourish'.

eV ■ abbrev. electronvolt(s).

evacuant /ɪˈvakjʊənt/ ■ adj. (of a medicine or treatment) acting to induce some kind of bodily discharge. ■ n. an evacuant medicine.

evacuate /ɪˈvakjʊeɪt/ ■ v. 1 remove from a place of danger to a safer place. ▸ leave (a dangerous place). 2 technical remove air, water, or other contents from (a container). ▸ empty (the bowels or another bodily organ).
- DERIVATIVES **evacuation** n.
- ORIGIN Middle English: from Latin *evacuare*, from *e-* (var. of *ex-*) 'out of' + *vacuus* 'empty'.

evacuee ■ n. a person evacuated from a place of danger.

evade ■ v. 1 escape or avoid, especially by guile or trickery. ▸ avoid giving a direct answer to (a question). 2 escape paying (tax or duty), especially by illegitimate presentation of one's finances. ▸ defeat the intention of (a law or rule), especially while complying with its letter.
- DERIVATIVES **evader** n.
- ORIGIN C15: from Latin *evadere* from *e-* (var. of *ex-*) 'out of' + *vadere* 'go'.

evaginate /ɪˈvadʒɪneɪt/ ■ v. Biology & Physiology turn (a tubular or pouch-shaped organ or structure) inside out.
- DERIVATIVES **evagination** n.
- ORIGIN C17: from Latin *evaginare* 'unsheath'.

evaluate ■ v. 1 form an idea of the amount, number, or value of; assess. 2 Mathematics find a numerical expression or equivalent for (an equation, formula, or function).
- DERIVATIVES **evaluation** n. **evaluative** adj. **evaluator** n.
- ORIGIN C19: back-formation from *evaluation*, from French *évaluer*, from *es-* (from Latin *ex-*) 'out, from' + Old French *value* 'value'.

evanescent ■ adj. 1 chiefly poetic/literary quickly fading from sight, memory, or existence. 2 Physics denoting a field or wave which extends into a region where it cannot propagate and whose amplitude therefore decreases with distance.
- DERIVATIVES **evanesce** v. **evanescence** n. **evanescently** adv.
- ORIGIN C18: from Latin *evanescere* 'disappear'.

evangelical ■ adj. 1 of or according to the teaching of the gospel or the Christian religion. ▸ of or denoting a tradition within Protestant Christianity emphasizing the authority of the Bible, personal conversion, and the doctrine of salvation by faith in the Atonement. 2 fervent in advocating something. ■ n. a member of the evangelical tradition in the Christian Church.
- DERIVATIVES **evangelic** adj. **evangelicalism** n. **evangelically** adv.

evangelist ■ n. 1 a person who seeks to convert others to the Christian faith, especially by public preaching. 2 Christian Church the writer of one of the four Gospels (Matthew, Mark, Luke, or John). 3 a zealous advocate of something.
- DERIVATIVES **evangelism** n. **evangelistic** adj.

evangelize (also **-ise**) ■ v. convert or seek to convert (someone) to Christianity. ▸ preach the gospel.
- DERIVATIVES **evangelization** (also **-isation**) n. **evangelizer** (also **-iser**) n.

evaporate /ɪˈvapəreɪt/ ■ v. 1 turn from liquid into vapour. 2 (of something abstract) cease to exist.
- DERIVATIVES **evaporable** adj. **evaporation** n. **evaporative** adj. **evaporator** n.
- ORIGIN Middle English: from Latin *evaporare*, from *e-* (var. of *ex-*) 'out of' + *vapor* 'steam, vapour'.

evaporated milk ■ n. thick sweetened milk that has had some of the liquid removed by evaporation.

evaporating dish ■ n. Chemistry a small ceramic dish in which liquids are heated over a flame so that they evaporate, leaving a solid residue.

evaporite /ɪˈvapəraɪt/ ■ n. Geology a natural salt or mineral deposit left after the evaporation of a body of water.

evapotranspiration /ɪˌvapəʊtranspɪˈreɪʃ(ə)n/ ■ n. the process by which water is transferred from the land to the atmosphere by evaporation from the soil and other surfaces and by transpiration from plants.

evasion ■ n. the action or an instance of evading.

evasive ■ adj. tending to avoid commitment or self-revelation, especially by responding only indirectly. ▸ directed towards avoidance or escape: *evasive action*.
- DERIVATIVES **evasively** adv. **evasiveness** n.

eve ■ n. 1 the day or period of time immediately before an event or occasion. ▸ the evening or day before a religious festival. 2 chiefly poetic/literary evening.
- ORIGIN Middle English: short form of EVEN².

evection /ɪˈvɛkʃ(ə)n/ ■ n. Astronomy regular variation in the eccentricity of the moon's orbit around the earth, caused mainly by the sun's attraction.
- ORIGIN C17: from Latin *evectio(n-)*, from *evehere* 'carry out or up'.

even¹ ■ adj. 1 flat and smooth; level. ▸ having little variation in quality; regular. 2 equal in number, amount, or value. 3 equally balanced: *the match was fairly even*. 4 (of a person's temper or disposition) equable; calm. 5 (of a number) divisible by two without a remainder. ■ v. (often **even out/up**) make or become even. ■ adv. used to emphasize something surprising or extreme, or in comparisons.
- PHRASES **even as** at the very same time as. **an even break** informal a fair chance. **even if** despite the possibility or fact that. **even now** (or **then**) 1 now (or then) as well as before. 2 in spite of what has (or had) happened. 3 at this (or that) very moment. **even so** nevertheless. **even though** despite the fact that. **of even date** Law or formal of the same date. **on an even keel** not listing or tilting to one side.
- DERIVATIVES **evenly** adv. **evenness** n.
- ORIGIN Old English, of Germanic origin.

even² ■ n. archaic or poetic/literary evening.
- ORIGIN Old English, of Germanic origin.

even-handed ■ adj. fair and impartial.
- DERIVATIVES **even-handedly** adv. **even-handedness** n.

evening ■ n. the period of time at the end of the day, between late afternoon and bedtime. ■ adv. (**evenings**) informal in the evening; every evening.
- ORIGIN Old English *ǣfnung*, from *ǣfnian* 'approach evening', from *ǣfen* (see EVEN²).

evening primrose ■ n. a plant with pale yellow flowers that open in the evening, yielding seeds from which a medicinal oil is extracted. [Genus *Oenothera*: numerous species.]

evening star ■ n. (**the evening star**) the planet Venus, seen shining in the western sky after sunset.

even money ■ n. (in betting) odds offering an equal chance of winning or losing, with the amount won being the same as the stake.

evens ■ pl. n. another term for EVEN MONEY.

evensong ■ n. (especially in the Anglican Church) a service of evening prayers, psalms, and canticles.

even-steven (also **even-stevens**) ■ adj. & adv. informal fair and equal in competition or distribution of resources.

event ■ n. 1 a thing that happens or takes place. ▸ a public or social occasion. 2 each of several contests making up a sports competition. 3 Physics a single occurrence of a process, e.g. the ionization of one atom.
- PHRASES **in any event** (or **at all events**) whatever happens or may have happened. **in the event** 1 as it turned out. 2 (**in the event of/that**) if the specified thing happens.
- DERIVATIVES **eventless** adj.
- ORIGIN C16: from Latin *eventus*, from *evenire* 'result, happen'.

eventful ■ adj. marked by interesting or exciting events.
- DERIVATIVES **eventfully** adv. **eventfulness** n.

event horizon ■ n. Astronomy a notional boundary around a black hole beyond which no light or other radiation can escape.

eventide ■ n. archaic or poetic/literary evening.

eventing ■ n. an equestrian sport in which competitors must take part in each of several contests, usually cross-country, dressage, and showjumping.

eventual /ɪˈvɛn(t)ʃʊəl/ ■ adj. occurring at the end of or resulting from a process or period of time.

– DERIVATIVES **eventually** adv.
– ORIGIN C17 (in the sense 'relating to an event or events'): from Latin *eventus* (see EVENT), on the pattern of *actual*.

eventuality ■ n. (pl. -ies) a possible event or outcome.

eventuate /ɪ'vɛn(t)ʃʊeɪt, -tjʊ-/ ■ v. formal occur as a result. ▶ (**eventuate in**) lead to as a result.
– DERIVATIVES **eventuation** n.
– ORIGIN C18 (orig. US): from EVENT, on the pattern of *actuate*.

ever ■ adv. **1** [usu. with neg. or in questions] at any time. ▶ used in comparisons for emphasis. **2** always. **3** increasingly; constantly. **4** used for emphasis in questions expressing astonishment or outrage.
– PHRASES **ever and anon** archaic occasionally. **ever since** throughout the period since.
– ORIGIN Old English.

evergreen ■ adj. **1** (of a plant) retaining green leaves throughout the year. Often contrasted with DECIDUOUS. **2** having an enduring freshness, success, or popularity. ■ n. an evergreen plant.

everlasting ■ adj. lasting forever or a very long time. ■ n. a helichrysum or similar flower that retains its shape and colour after being dried.
– DERIVATIVES **everlastingly** adv. **everlastingness** n.

evermore ■ adv. archaic or poetic/literary always; forever.

evert /ɪ'vɜːt/ ■ v. Biology & Physiology turn (a structure or organ) outwards or inside out.
– DERIVATIVES **eversible** adj. **eversion** n.
– ORIGIN C16: from Latin *evertere*, from *e-* (var. of *ex-*) 'out' + *vertere* 'to turn'.

every ■ det. **1** used to refer to all the individual members of a set without exception. ▶ all possible; the utmost. **2** used to indicate something happening at specified intervals.
– PHRASES **every bit as** (in comparisons) quite as. **every now and again** (or **every so often**) occasionally. **every other** each alternate in a series. **every which way** informal in all directions. ▶ by all available means.
– ORIGIN Old English.

everybody ■ pron. every person.

everyday ■ adj. **1** daily. **2** commonplace.

Everyman ■ n. an ordinary or typical human being.

everyone ■ pron. every person.

every one ■ pron. each one.

everything ■ pron. **1** all things, or all the things of a group or class. ▶ all things of importance. ▶ the most important thing or aspect: *money isn't everything*. **2** the current situation; life in general.

everywhere ■ adv. in or to all places. ▶ very common or widely distributed.

evict ■ v. expel (someone) from a property, especially with the support of the law.
– DERIVATIVES **eviction** n. **evictor** n.
– ORIGIN Middle English ('recover property by legal process'): from Latin *evict-*, *evincere* 'overcome, defeat'.

evidence ■ n. information indicating whether a belief or proposition is true or valid. ▶ Law information used to establish facts in a legal investigation or admissible as testimony in a law court. ▶ signs; indications. ■ v. be or show evidence of.
– PHRASES **in evidence** noticeable; conspicuous. **turn state's** (or Brit. **King's** or **Queen's**) **evidence** Law (of a criminal) give information in court against one's partners in order to receive a less severe punishment.
– ORIGIN Middle English: from Latin *evidentia*, from *evident-* (see EVIDENT).

evident ■ adj. plain or obvious; clear.
– DERIVATIVES **evidently** adv.
– ORIGIN Middle English: from Latin *evidens, evident-* 'obvious to the eye or mind', from *e-* (var. of *ex-*) 'out' + *videre* 'to see'.

evidential /ˌɛvɪ'dɛnʃl/ ■ adj. formal of or providing evidence.
– DERIVATIVES **evidentiality** n. **evidentially** adv.

evidentiary /ˌɛvɪ'dɛnʃ(ə)ri/ ■ adj. another term for EVIDENTIAL.

evil ■ adj. **1** profoundly immoral and malevolent. ▶ embodying or associated with the forces of the devil.

405

▶ harmful or tending to harm. **2** extremely unpleasant: *an evil smell*. ■ n. profound wickedness and depravity, especially when regarded as a supernatural force. ▶ something harmful or undesirable: *social evils*.
– PHRASES **the evil eye** a gaze or stare superstitiously believed to cause material harm. **the Evil One** archaic the Devil. **speak evil of** slander.
– DERIVATIVES **evilly** adv. **evilness** n.
– ORIGIN Old English, of Germanic origin.

evil-doer ■ n. a person who commits evil deeds.
– DERIVATIVES **evil-doing** n.

evince /ɪ'vɪns/ ■ v. formal reveal the presence of; indicate (a quality or feeling).
– ORIGIN C16: from Latin *evincere* (see EVICT).

eviscerate /ɪ'vɪsəreɪt/ ■ v. formal disembowel.
– DERIVATIVES **evisceration** n.
– ORIGIN C16: from Latin *eviscerare*, from *e-* (var. of *ex-*) 'out' + *viscera* 'internal organs'.

evocative /ɪ'vɒkətɪv/ ■ adj. evoking strong images, memories, or feelings.
– DERIVATIVES **evocatively** adv. **evocativeness** n.

evoke /ɪ'vəʊk/ ■ v. **1** bring or recall to the conscious mind. **2** elicit (a response). **3** invoke (a spirit or deity).
– DERIVATIVES **evocation** n. **evoker** n.
– ORIGIN C17 (*evocation* Middle English): from Latin *evocare*, from *e-* (var. of *ex-*) 'out of, from' + *vocare* 'to call'.

evolution /ˌiːvə'luːʃ(ə)n, ˌɛv-/ ■ n. **1** the process by which different kinds of living organism are believed to have developed from earlier forms, especially by natural selection. **2** gradual development. **3** Chemistry the giving off of a gaseous product, or of heat. **4** a pattern of movements or manoeuvres.
– DERIVATIVES **evolutional** adj. **evolutionally** adv. **evolutionarily** adv. **evolutionary** adj. **evolutive** adj.
– ORIGIN C17: from Latin *evolutio(n-)* 'unrolling', from *evolvere* (see EVOLVE).

evolutionist ■ n. a person who believes in the theories of evolution and natural selection.
– DERIVATIVES **evolutionism** n.

evolve ■ v. **1** develop gradually. **2** (of an organism or biological feature) develop over successive generations by evolution. **3** Chemistry give off (gas or heat).
– DERIVATIVES **evolvable** adj. **evolvement** n.
– ORIGIN C17 ('make more complex, develop'): from Latin *evolvere*, from *e-* (var. of *ex-*) 'out of' + *volvere* 'to roll'.

Ewe /'eɪweɪ/ ■ n. (pl. same) **1** a member of a West African people of Ghana, Togo, and Benin. **2** the Kwa language of this people.
– ORIGIN the name in Ewe.

ewe /juː/ ■ n. a female sheep.
– ORIGIN Old English, of Germanic origin.

ewer /'juːə/ ■ n. a large jug with a wide mouth.
– ORIGIN Middle English: from Anglo-Norman French *ewer*, var. of Old French *aiguiere*, from Latin *aquarius* 'of water'.

ex[1] ■ prep. **1** (of goods) sold direct from. **2** without; excluding.
– ORIGIN C19: from Latin, 'out of'.

ex[2] ■ n. informal a former husband, wife, or partner in a relationship.

ex-[1] (also **e-**; **ef-** before *f*) ■ prefix **1** out: *exclude*. **2** upward: *extol*. **3** denoting removal or release: *excommunicate*. **4** forming verbs which denote inducement of a state: *exasperate*. **5** denoting a former state: *ex-husband*.
– ORIGIN from Latin *ex* 'out of'.

ex-[2] ■ prefix out: *exodus*.
– ORIGIN from Greek *ex* 'out of'.

exa- ■ comb. form denoting a factor of 10^{18}: *exajoule*.
– ORIGIN from (*h*)*exa-* (see HEXA-), based on the supposed analogy of *tera-* and *tetra-*.

exacerbate /ɪg'zasəbeɪt, ɛk'sas-/ ■ v. make (something bad) worse.
– DERIVATIVES **exacerbation** n.
– ORIGIN C17 (*exacerbation* Middle English): from Latin *exacerbare* 'make harsh'.

exact ■ adj. not approximated in any way; precise. ▶ accurate or correct in all details: *an exact replica*. ▶ tending to be accurate and careful about minor details. ■ v. 1 demand and obtain (something) from someone. 2 inflict (revenge) on someone.
– DERIVATIVES **exactable** adj. **exactitude** n. **exactness** n.
– ORIGIN Middle English: from Latin *exact-, exigere* 'complete, ascertain, enforce'; the adj. reflects Latin *exactus* 'precise'.

exacting ■ adj. making great demands on one's endurance or skill.
– DERIVATIVES **exactingly** adv. **exactingness** n.

exaction ■ n. formal the action or an act of exacting something, especially a payment. ▶ a sum of money exacted.

exactly ■ adv. 1 in exact terms. 2 used to confirm or agree with what has just been said.

exaggerate /ɪɡˈzadʒəreɪt, ɛɡ-/ ■ v. represent (something) as being larger or better than it really is. ▶ [as adj. **exaggerated**] enlarged or altered beyond normal proportions.
– DERIVATIVES **exaggeratedly** adv. **exaggeration** n. **exaggerative** adj. **exaggerator** n.
– ORIGIN C16: from Latin *exaggerare* 'heap up'.

exalt /ɪɡˈzɔːlt, ɛɡ-/ ■ v. 1 praise or regard highly. 2 raise to a higher rank or position. ▶ make noble in character; dignify.
– ORIGIN Middle English: from Latin *exaltare*, from *ex-* 'out, upward' + *altus* 'high'.

exaltation ■ n. 1 extreme happiness. 2 the action of exalting.

exalted ■ adj. 1 at a high level. 2 (of an idea) noble; lofty. 3 extremely happy.
– DERIVATIVES **exaltedly** adv. **exaltedness** n.

exam ■ n. 1 short for EXAMINATION (in sense 2). 2 N. Amer. a medical test of a specified kind.

examination ■ n. 1 a detailed inspection or investigation. ▶ the action of examining. 2 a formal test of knowledge or proficiency in a subject or skill. 3 Law the formal questioning of a defendant or witness in court.

examination-in-chief ■ n. Law the questioning of a witness by the party which has called that witness to give evidence, in order to support their case.

examine ■ v. 1 inspect closely to determine the nature or condition of; investigate thoroughly. 2 test the knowledge or proficiency of. 3 Law formally question (a defendant or witness) in court.
– DERIVATIVES **examinable** adj. **examinee** n. **examiner** n.
– ORIGIN Middle English: from Latin *examinare* 'weigh, test', from *examen* 'test, examination'.

example ■ n. 1 a thing characteristic of its kind or illustrating a general rule. ▶ a written problem or exercise designed to illustrate a rule. 2 a person or thing regarded in terms of their fitness to be imitated: *parents should set an example*. ■ v. (**be exampled**) be exemplified.
– PHRASES **for example** by way of illustration. **make an example of** punish as a warning or deterrent to others.
– ORIGIN Middle English: from Latin *exemplum*, from *eximere* 'take out'.

ex ante /ɛks ˈanti/ ■ adj. & adv. based on forecasts rather than actual results.
– ORIGIN modern Latin: from Latin *ex* 'from, out of' + *ante* 'before'.

exanthema /ɪkˈsanθɪmə, ˌɛksanˈθiːmə/ ■ n. (pl. **exanthemata**) Medicine a skin rash accompanying a disease or fever.
– DERIVATIVES **exanthematic** adj. **exanthematous** adj.
– ORIGIN C17: from Greek *exanthēma* 'eruption', from *ex-* 'out' + *antheein* 'to blossom'.

exasperate /ɪɡˈzasp(ə)reɪt, ɛɡ-/ ■ v. irritate intensely.
– DERIVATIVES **exasperated** adj. **exasperatedly** adv. **exasperating** adj. **exasperatingly** adv. **exasperation** n.
– ORIGIN C16: from Latin *exasperare* 'irritate to anger'.

ex cathedra /ˌɛks kəˈθiːdrə/ ■ adv. & adj. with the full authority of office.
– ORIGIN Latin, 'from the (teacher's) chair'.

excavate /ˈɛkskəveɪt/ ■ v. 1 make (a hole or channel) by digging. ▶ extract (material) from the ground by digging. 2 carefully remove earth from (an area) in order to find buried remains.
– DERIVATIVES **excavation** n. **excavator** n.
– ORIGIN C16: from Latin *excavare* 'hollow out'.

exceed ■ v. be greater in number or size than. ▶ go beyond what is allowed or stipulated by (a set limit, especially of one's authority). ▶ surpass.
– ORIGIN Middle English ('go over (a boundary or point)'): from Latin *excedere*, from *ex-* 'out' + *cedere* 'go'.

exceeding archaic or poetic/literary ■ adj. very great.
■ adv. exceedingly.

exceedingly ■ adv. extremely.

excel /ɪkˈsɛl, ɛk-/ ■ v. (**excelled**, **excelling**) be exceptionally good at an activity or subject. ▶ (**excel oneself**) perform exceptionally well.
– ORIGIN Middle English: from Latin *excellere*, from *ex-* 'out, beyond' + *celsus* 'lofty'.

excellence ■ n. the quality of being excellent.

excellency ■ n. (pl. **-ies**) 1 (**His/Your**) etc. **Excellency** a title or form of address for certain high officials of state, especially ambassadors, or of the Roman Catholic Church. 2 archaic an outstanding feature or quality.

excellent ■ adj. extremely good; outstanding.
– DERIVATIVES **excellently** adv.
– ORIGIN Middle English: from Latin *excellere* (see EXCEL).

except ■ prep. not including; other than. ■ conj. 1 used before a statement that forms an exception to one just made. 2 archaic unless. ■ v. [often as postpos. adj. **excepted**] specify as not included: *present company excepted*.
– ORIGIN Middle English: from Latin *except-, excipere* 'take out'.

excepting ■ prep. except for; apart from.

exception ■ n. a person or thing that is excepted or that does not follow a rule. ▶ the action or state of excepting or being excepted.
– PHRASES **take exception to** object strongly to; be offended by.

exceptionable ■ adj. formal open to objection; causing disapproval or offence.

exceptional ■ adj. unusual; not typical. ▶ unusually good. ■ n. an item in a company's accounts arising from its normal activity but much larger or smaller than usual.
– DERIVATIVES **exceptionality** n. **exceptionally** adv.

excerpt ■ n. /ˈɛksəːpt/ a short extract from a film or piece of music or writing. ■ v. /ɪkˈsəːpt, ɛk-/ take (a short extract) from a text.
– DERIVATIVES **excerption** n.
– ORIGIN C16: from Latin *excerpere* 'pluck out'.

excess /ɪkˈsɛs, ɛk-, ˈɛksɛs/ ■ n. 1 an amount that is more than necessary, permitted, or desirable. ▶ (often in phr. **in/to excess**) the action of exceeding a permitted or proper limit. ▶ the amount by which one quantity or number exceeds another. 2 lack of moderation, especially in eating or drinking. ▶ (**excesses**) outrageous or immoderate behaviour. 3 a part of an insurance claim to be paid by the insured. ■ adj. /usu. ˈɛksɛs/ exceeding a prescribed or desirable amount.
– PHRASES **in excess of** more than; exceeding.
– ORIGIN Middle English: from Latin *excessus*, from *excedere* (see EXCEED).

excess baggage ■ n. luggage weighing more than the limit allowed on an aircraft, liable to an extra charge.

excessive ■ adj. more than is necessary, normal, or desirable.
– DERIVATIVES **excessively** adv. **excessiveness** n.

exchange ■ v. give something and receive something else, especially of the same kind, in return. ■ n. 1 an act or the action of exchanging. 2 a short conversation or argument. 3 the giving of money for its equivalent in the currency of another country. ▶ a system or market in which commercial transactions involving currency, shares, etc. can be carried out within or between countries. 4 a building or institution used for the trading of commodities. 5 Chess a move or short sequence of moves in which both players capture material of comparable value. 6 a set of equipment that connects telephone lines

during a call.
– DERIVATIVES **exchangeability** n. **exchangeable** adj. **exchanger** n.
– ORIGIN Middle English: from Old French *eschange* (n.), *eschangier* (v.), from *changer* (see **CHANGE**).

exchange rate ■ n. the value of one currency for the purpose of conversion to another.

exchequer /ɪksˈtʃɛkə, ɛks-/ ■ n. 1 a royal or national treasury. 2 (**Exchequer**) Brit. the account at the Bank of England into which tax receipts and other public monies are paid. ► historical the former government office in charge of national revenue.
– ORIGIN Middle English: from Old French *eschequier*, from medieval Latin *scaccarium* 'chessboard', from *scaccus* (see **CHECK**[1]); modern senses derive from the chequered tablecloth on which accounts were kept by means of counters.

excimer /ˈɛksɪmə/ ■ n. Chemistry an unstable excited molecule which is formed by the combination of two smaller molecules and rapidly dissociates with emission of radiation.
– ORIGIN 1960s: blend of *excited* and **DIMER**.

excipient /ɛkˈsɪpɪənt/ ■ n. an inactive substance that serves as the vehicle or medium for a drug or other active substance.
– ORIGIN C18 (as adj. in the sense 'that takes exception'): from Latin *excipient-*, *excipere* 'take out'.

excise[1] /ˈɛksaɪz/ ■ n. a tax levied on certain goods and commodities and on licences granted for certain activities. ■ v. [usu. as adj. **excised**] charge excise on (goods).
– ORIGIN C15: from Middle Dutch *excijs, accijs*, perhaps from Latin *accensare* 'to tax'; rel. to **CENSUS**.

excise[2] /ɪkˈsaɪz, ɛk-/ ■ v. 1 cut out surgically. 2 remove (a section) from a text or piece of music.
– DERIVATIVES **excision** n.
– ORIGIN C16: from Latin *excis-, excidere* 'cut out'.

exciseman ■ n. (pl. **-men**) Brit. historical an official who collected excise duty and prevented smuggling.

excitable ■ adj. 1 easily excited. 2 (of tissue or a cell) responsive to stimulation.
– DERIVATIVES **excitability** n. **excitably** adv.

excite ■ v. 1 cause strong feelings of enthusiasm and eagerness in. ► arouse (someone) sexually. 2 bring out or give rise to (a feeling or reaction). 3 produce a state of increased energy or activity in (a physical or biological system).
– DERIVATIVES **excitation** n. (chiefly technical). **excited** adj. **excitedly** adv. **exciter** n.
– ORIGIN Middle English: from Latin *excitare*, from *exciere* 'call out'.

excitement ■ n. a feeling of great enthusiasm and eagerness. ► something exciting. ► sexual arousal.

exciting ■ adj. causing great enthusiasm and eagerness.
– DERIVATIVES **excitingly** adv. **excitingness** n.

exciton /ˈɛksɪtɒn, ɪkˈsʌɪ-, ɛk-/ ■ n. Physics a mobile concentration of energy in a crystal formed by an excited electron and an associated hole.

exclaim ■ v. cry out suddenly, especially in surprise, anger, or pain.
– DERIVATIVES **exclamatory** adj.
– ORIGIN C16 (*exclamation* Middle English): from Latin *exclamare*, from *ex-* 'out' + *clamare* 'to shout'.

exclamation ■ n. a sudden cry or remark expressing surprise, strong emotion, or pain.

exclamation mark (N. Amer. **exclamation point**) ■ n. a punctuation mark (!) indicating an exclamation.

exclave /ˈɛkskleɪv/ ■ n. a portion of territory of one state completely surrounded by territory of another or others. Compare with **ENCLAVE**.
– ORIGIN C19: from **EX-**[1] + **ENCLAVE**.

exclude ■ v. deny access to; keep out. ► rule out. ► prevent the occurrence of. ► expel (a pupil) from a school.
– PHRASES **law** (or **principle**) **of the excluded middle** Logic the principle that one (and one only) of two contradictory propositions must be true.
– DERIVATIVES **excludable** adj. **excluder** n.
– ORIGIN Middle English: from Latin *excludere*, from *ex-* 'out' + *claudere* 'to shut'.

excluding ■ prep. not taking into account; except.

excursion

exclusion ■ n. 1 the process or state of excluding or being excluded. 2 an item or eventuality specifically not covered by an insurance policy or other contract.
– DERIVATIVES **exclusionary** adj.

exclusionist ■ adj. acting to exclude someone from a place, group, or privilege. ■ n. a person favouring the exclusion of another person or group.

exclusive ■ adj. 1 excluding or not admitting other things. ► unable to exist or be true if something else exists or is true: *mutually exclusive options*. ► (of terms) excluding all but what is specified. 2 restricted to the person, group, or area concerned. ► not published or broadcast elsewhere. 3 high-class and expensive; select. 4 (**exclusive of**) not including. ■ n. an exclusive story or broadcast.
– DERIVATIVES **exclusively** adv. **exclusiveness** n. **exclusivity** n.
– ORIGIN C15: from medieval Latin *exclusivus*, from Latin *excludere* (see **EXCLUDE**).

exclusive economic zone (also **economic exclusion zone**) ■ n. an internationally recognized area of up to 200 nautical miles off a country's coast in which it has the rights to the economic resources.

exclusivism ■ n. the action or policy of excluding a person or group from a place, group, or privilege.
– DERIVATIVES **exclusivist** adj. & n.

excommunicate ■ v. /ˌɛkskəˈmjuːnɪkeɪt/ officially exclude from participation in the sacraments and services of the Christian Church. ■ adj. /ˌɛkskəˈmjuːnɪkət/ excommunicated. ■ n. /ˌɛkskəˈmjuːnɪkət/ an excommunicated person.
– DERIVATIVES **excommunication** n. **excommunicative** adj. **excommunicator** n. **excommunicatory** adj.
– ORIGIN Middle English: from eccles. Latin *excommunicare*, from *ex-* 'out' + Latin *communis* 'common to all'.

ex-con ■ n. informal an ex-convict.

excoriate /ɪkˈskɔːrɪeɪt, ɛks-/ ■ v. 1 chiefly Medicine damage or remove part of the surface of (the skin). 2 formal censure or criticize severely.
– DERIVATIVES **excoriation** n.
– ORIGIN Middle English: from Latin *excoriare* 'to skin', from *ex-* 'out, from' + *corium* 'skin, hide'.

excrement /ˈɛkskrɪm(ə)nt/ ■ n. faeces.
– DERIVATIVES **excremental** adj.
– ORIGIN C16: from Latin *excrementum*, from *excernere* (see **EXCRETE**).

excrescence /ɪkˈskrɛs(ə)ns, ɛks-/ ■ n. an abnormal outgrowth on a body or plant. ► an unattractive or superfluous addition or feature.
– DERIVATIVES **excrescent** adj.
– ORIGIN Middle English: from Latin *excrescentia*, from *excrescere* 'grow out'.

excreta /ɪkˈskriːtə, ɛk-/ ■ n. [treated as sing. or pl.] waste discharged from the body, especially faeces and urine.
– ORIGIN C19: from Latin, from *excretus*, from *excernere* (see **EXCRETE**).

excrete /ɪkˈskriːt, ɛk-/ ■ v. (of a living organism) separate and expel as waste (a substance, especially a product of metabolism).
– DERIVATIVES **excreter** n. **excretion** n. **excretive** adj. **excretory** adj.
– ORIGIN C17: from Latin *excret-, excernere* 'sift out'.

excruciating ■ adj. 1 intensely painful. 2 very embarrassing, awkward, or tedious.
– DERIVATIVES **excruciatingly** adv.

exculpate /ˈɛkskʌlpeɪt/ ■ v. formal show or declare to be not guilty of wrongdoing.
– DERIVATIVES **exculpation** n. **exculpatory** adj.
– ORIGIN C17: from medieval Latin *exculpare* 'free from blame', from *ex-* 'out, from' + Latin *culpa* 'blame'.

excursion ■ n. 1 a short journey or trip, especially one taken for leisure. 2 technical a movement along a path or through an angle. ► a deviation from a regular pattern, path, or level of operation. 3 archaic a digression.
– DERIVATIVES **excursionist** n.
– ORIGIN C16: from Latin *excursio(n-)*, from *excurrere* 'run out'.

excursus /ɪkˈskəːsəs, ɛk-/ ■ n. (pl. same or **excursuses**) a detailed discussion of a particular point in a book, usually in an appendix. ▸ a digression in a written text.
– ORIGIN C19: from Latin, 'excursion', from *excurrere* 'run out'.

excuse ■ v. /ɪkˈskjuːz, ɛk-/ **1** seek or serve to justify (a fault or offence); mitigate. ▸ forgive (a fault or offence, or a person committing one). **2** release from a duty or requirement. ▸ (used in polite formulas) allow (someone) to leave a room or gathering. ▸ (**excuse oneself**) say politely that one is leaving. ■ n. /ɪkˈskjuːs, ɛk-/ **1** a defence or justification of a fault or offence. **2** something said to conceal the real reason for an action. **3** (**an excuse for**) informal a poor or inadequate example of.
– PHRASES **excuse me** a polite apology for an interruption, lack of ceremony, etc. ▸ chiefly N. Amer. used to ask someone to repeat what they have just said.
– DERIVATIVES **excusable** adj. **excusably** adv. **excusatory** adj.
– ORIGIN Middle English: from Latin *excusare* 'to free from blame', from *ex-* 'out' + *causa* 'accusation, cause'.

ex-directory ■ adj. Brit. (of a telephone number) not listed in a telephone directory at the wish of the subscriber.

ex dividend ■ adj. & adv. (of stocks or shares) not including the next dividend.

execrable /ˈɛksɪkrəb(ə)l/ ■ adj. extremely bad or unpleasant.
– DERIVATIVES **execrably** adv.
– ORIGIN Middle English: from Latin *execrabilis*, from *exsecrari* (see EXECRATE).

execrate /ˈɛksɪkreɪt/ ■ v. **1** feel or express great loathing for. **2** archaic curse; swear.
– DERIVATIVES **execration** n. **execrative** adj. **execratory** adj.
– ORIGIN C16 (*execration* Middle English): from Latin *exsecrari* 'curse'.

executant /ɪɡˈzɛkjʊt(ə)nt, ɛɡ-/ ■ n. formal **1** a person who puts something into effect. **2** an artist or performer.

execute /ˈɛksɪkjuːt/ ■ v. **1** carry out or put into effect (a plan, order, etc.). ▸ perform (an activity or manoeuvre). ▸ Law make (a legal instrument) valid by signing or sealing it. ▸ Law carry out (a judicial sentence, the terms of a will, or other order). ▸ Computing run (a file or program). **2** carry out a sentence of death on (a condemned person).
– DERIVATIVES **executable** adj. (Computing).
– ORIGIN Middle English: from medieval Latin *executare*, from Latin *exsequi* 'follow up, carry out, punish'.

execution ■ n. **1** the action of executing a plan, order, legal instrument, etc. ▸ the technique or style with which an artistic work is produced or performed: *the film is entirely professional in its execution*. **2** an act of executing a condemned person.
– DERIVATIVES **executioner** n.

executive /ɪɡˈzɛkjʊtɪv, ɛɡ-/ ■ adj. having the power to execute plans, actions, or laws. ■ n. **1** a person with senior managerial responsibility in a business organization. ▸ an executive committee within an organization. **2** (**the executive**) the branch of a government responsible for executing plans, actions, or laws.
– DERIVATIVES **executively** adv.
– ORIGIN Middle English: from medieval Latin *executivus*, from *exsequi* (see EXECUTE).

executor /ɪɡˈzɛkjʊtə, ɛɡ-/ ■ n. (fem. **executrix** /ɪɡˈzɛkjʊtrɪks, ɛɡ-/; pl. **executrices** /-trɪsiːz/ or **executrixes**) Law a person appointed by a testator to carry out the terms of their will.
– DERIVATIVES **executorship** n. **executory** adj.

exegesis /ˌɛksɪˈdʒiːsɪs/ ■ n. (pl. **exegeses** /-siːz/) critical explanation or interpretation of a text, especially of scripture.
– DERIVATIVES **exegetic** /-ˈdʒɛtɪk/ adj. **exegetical** adj.
– ORIGIN C17: from Greek *exēgēsis*, from *exēgeisthai* 'interpret'.

exemplar /ɪɡˈzɛmplə, ɛɡ-/ ■ n. a person or thing serving as a typical example or appropriate model.
– ORIGIN Middle English: from late Latin *exemplarium*, from Latin *exemplum* (see EXAMPLE).

exemplary ■ adj. **1** serving as a desirable model; very good. **2** (of a punishment) serving as a warning or deterrent. ▸ Law (of damages) exceeding the amount needed for simple compensation.
– DERIVATIVES **exemplarily** adv. **exemplariness** n. **exemplarity** n.

exemplify /ɪɡˈzɛmplɪfʌɪ, ɛɡ-/ ■ v. (**-ies**, **-ied**) be or give a typical example of.
– DERIVATIVES **exemplification** /-fɪˈkeɪʃ(ə)n/ n.

exempt /ɪɡˈzɛm(p)t, ɛɡ-/ ■ adj. free from an obligation or liability imposed on others. ■ v. make exempt. ■ n. a person who is exempt from something, especially the payment of tax.
– DERIVATIVES **exemption** n.
– ORIGIN Middle English: from Latin *exempt-*, *eximere* 'take out, free'.

exequies /ˈɛksɪkwi/ ■ pl. n. (sing. **exequy**) formal funeral rites.
– ORIGIN Middle English: from Latin *exsequiae* 'funeral ceremonies', from *exsequi* 'follow after'.

exercise ■ n. **1** activity requiring physical effort carried out for the sake of health and fitness. **2** a task set to practise or test a skill. **3** an activity carried out for a specific purpose: *an exercise in public relations*. **4** a military drill or training manoeuvre. **5** the application of a faculty, right, or process: *the exercise of authority*. ■ v. **1** use or apply (a faculty, right, or process). **2** take or subject to exercise. **3** worry or perplex.
– DERIVATIVES **exercisable** adj. **exerciser** n.
– ORIGIN Middle English: from Latin *exercitium*, from *exercere* 'keep busy, practise'.

exercise bike ■ n. a stationary piece of exercise equipment resembling an ordinary bicycle.

exercise book ■ n. a booklet with blank pages for students to write in.

exercise price ■ n. Stock Exchange the price per share at which the owner of a traded option is entitled to buy or sell the underlying security.

exercise yard ■ n. an enclosed area used for physical exercise in a prison.

exert /ɪɡˈzəːt, ɛɡ-/ ■ v. **1** apply or bring to bear (a force, influence, or quality). **2** (**exert oneself**) make a physical or mental effort.
– DERIVATIVES **exertion** n.
– ORIGIN C17: from Latin *exserere* 'put forth'.

exeunt /ˈɛksɪʌnt/ ■ v. (as a stage direction) (actors) leave the stage.
– ORIGIN C15: Latin, 'they go out'.

exfoliant ■ n. a cosmetic for exfoliating the skin.

exfoliate /ɪksˈfəʊlɪeɪt, ɛks-/ ■ v. **1** shed or be shed from a surface in scales or layers. **2** wash or rub (the skin) with a granular substance to remove dead cells.
– DERIVATIVES **exfoliation** n. **exfoliative** adj. **exfoliator** n.
– ORIGIN C17: from late Latin *exfoliare* 'strip off leaves', from *ex-* 'out, from' + *folium* 'leaf'.

ex gratia /ˌɛks ˈɡreɪʃə/ ■ adv. & adj. (with reference to payment) done from a sense of moral obligation rather than because of any legal requirement.
– ORIGIN Latin, 'from favour', from *ex* 'from' + *gratia* (see GRACE).

exhale /ɪksˈheɪl, ɛks-/ ■ v. **1** breathe out. **2** give off (vapour or fumes).
– DERIVATIVES **exhalation** n.
– ORIGIN Middle English: from Old French *exhaler*, from Latin *exhalare*, from *ex-* 'out' + *halare* 'breathe'.

exhaust /ɪɡˈzɔːst, ɛɡ-/ ■ v. **1** [often as adj. **exhausted** or **exhausting**] tire out completely. **2** use up (resources or reserves) completely. ▸ explore (a subject) thoroughly. **3** expel (gas or steam) from an engine or other machine. ■ n. waste gases or air expelled from an engine or other machine. ▸ the system through which such gases are expelled.
– DERIVATIVES **exhaustedly** adv. **exhaustibility** /-ˈbɪlɪti/ n. **exhaustible** adj. **exhaustingly** adv.
– ORIGIN C16: from Latin *exhaust-*, *exhaurire* 'drain out'.

exhaustion ■ n. **1** the action or state of exhausting something or of being exhausted. **2** Logic the process of establishing a conclusion by eliminating all the alternatives.

exhaustive ■ adj. fully comprehensive.
– DERIVATIVES **exhaustively** adv. **exhaustiveness** n.

exhibit /ɪgˈzɪbɪt, ɛg-/ ■ v. **1** publicly display (an item) in an art gallery or museum. **2** manifest one's possession of (a quality). ▸ show as a sign or symptom. ■ n. **1** an object or collection of objects on display in an art gallery or museum. **2** Law a document or other object produced in a court as evidence. **3** N. Amer. an exhibition.
– DERIVATIVES **exhibitor** n.
– ORIGIN Middle English: from Latin *exhibere* 'hold out'.

exhibition ■ n. **1** a public display of items in an art gallery or museum. **2** a display or demonstration of a particular skill or quality.
– PHRASES **make an exhibition of oneself** behave very foolishly in public.

exhibitionism ■ n. **1** extravagant behaviour that is intended to attract attention to oneself. **2** Psychiatry a mental condition characterized by the compulsion to display one's genitals in public.
– DERIVATIVES **exhibitionist** n. **exhibitionistic** adj. **exhibitionistically** adv.

exhilarate /ɪgˈzɪləreɪt, ɛg-/ ■ v. [often as adj. **exhilarated** or **exhilarating**] cause to feel very happy or animated.
– DERIVATIVES **exhilaratingly** adv. **exhilaration** n.
– ORIGIN C16: from Latin *exhilarare* 'make cheerful', from *ex-* + *hilaris* 'cheerful'.

exhort /ɪgˈzɔːt, ɛg-/ ■ v. strongly encourage or urge (someone) to do something.
– DERIVATIVES **exhortation** n. **exhortative** adj. **exhortatory** /-tət(ə)ri/ adj. **exhorter** n.
– ORIGIN Middle English: from Latin *exhortari*, from *ex-* 'thoroughly' + *hortari* 'encourage'.

exhume /ɛksˈ(h)juːm, ɪgˈzjuːm/ ■ v. dig out (something buried, especially a corpse) from the ground.
– DERIVATIVES **exhumation** n.
– ORIGIN Middle English: from medieval Latin *exhumare*, from *ex-* 'out of' + *humus* 'ground'.

exigency /ˈɛksɪdʒ(ə)nsi, ˈɛgzɪ-, ɪgˈzɪ-, ɛgˈzɪ-/ (also **exigence**) ■ n. (pl. **-ies**) urgent need or demand.
– ORIGIN C16: from late Latin *exigentia*, from Latin *exigere* (see EXACT).

exigent /ˈɛksɪdʒ(ə)nt, ˈɛgzɪ-/ ■ adj. formal pressing; demanding.
– ORIGIN C17: from Latin *exigere* (see EXACT).

exigible /ˈɛksɪdʒɪb(ə)l, ˈɛgzɪ-/ ■ adj. (of a tax or duty) able to be charged or levied.
– ORIGIN C17: from French, from *exiger*, from Latin *exigere* (see EXACT).

exiguous /ɪgˈzɪgjʊəs, ɛg-/ ■ adj. formal very small.
– DERIVATIVES **exiguity** /-ˈgjuːɪti/ n. **exiguously** adv. **exiguousness** n.
– ORIGIN C17: from Latin *exiguus* 'scanty', from *exigere* 'weigh exactly'.

exile ■ n. **1** (often in phr. **in exile**) the state of being barred from one's native country. **2** a person who lives in exile. ■ v. expel and bar (someone) from their native country.
– ORIGIN Middle English: noun from Old French *exil* 'banishment', *exile* 'banished person'; verb from Old French *exiler*; all from Latin *exilium* 'banishment'.

exine /ˈɛksɪn, -ʌɪn/ ■ n. Botany the decay-resistant outer coating of a pollen grain or spore.
– ORIGIN C19: perhaps from EX-[2] + Greek *is, in-* 'fibre'.

exist ■ v. **1** have objective reality or being. ▸ be found: *two conflicting stereotypes exist.* **2** live, especially under adverse conditions.
– ORIGIN C17: prob. a back-formation from EXISTENCE.

existence ■ n. the fact or state of existing. ▸ a way of living.
– ORIGIN Middle English: from late Latin *existentia*, from Latin *exsistere* 'come into being'.

existent ■ adj. existing.

existential /ˌɛgzɪˈstɛnʃ(ə)l/ ■ adj. **1** of or relating to existence. ▸ Logic (of a proposition) affirming or implying the existence of a thing. **2** Philosophy concerned with existentialism.
– DERIVATIVES **existentially** adv.

existentialism ■ n. a philosophical theory which emphasizes the existence of the individual person as a free and responsible agent determining their own development through acts of the will.
– DERIVATIVES **existentialist** n. & adj.

exophthalmos

exit ■ n. **1** a way out of a building, room, or passenger vehicle. ▸ a place for traffic to leave a major road or traffic circle. **2** an act of leaving. ▸ a departure of an actor from the stage. **3** poetic/literary a person's death. ■ v. (**exited, exiting**) **1** go out of or leave a place. ▸ (of an actor) leave the stage. ▸ (**exit**) (as a stage direction) indicating that a character leaves the stage: *exit Pamela.* **2** poetic/literary die. **3** Computing terminate a process or program. **4** Bridge relinquish the lead.
– ORIGIN C16 (as a stage direction): from Latin *exit* 'he or she goes out', from *exire*, from *ex-* 'out' + *ire* 'go'.

exit poll ■ n. an opinion poll of people leaving a polling station, asking how they voted.

ex libris /ɛks ˈlɪbrɪs, ˈliː-b-, ˈlʌɪb-, ˈliːbriːs/ ■ adv. used as an inscription on a bookplate to show the name of the book's owner.
– ORIGIN Latin, 'out of the books or library (of someone)'.

exo- ■ prefix external; from outside: *exoskeleton.*
– ORIGIN from Greek *exō* 'outside'.

exocarp /ˈɛksəʊkɑːp/ ■ n. Botany the outer layer of the pericarp of a fruit.

exocentric /ˌɛksəʊˈsɛntrɪk/ ■ adj. Linguistics denoting or being a construction which has no explicit head, for example *John slept*. Contrasted with ENDOCENTRIC.

exocrine /ˈɛksə(ʊ)krʌɪn, -krɪn/ ■ adj. Physiology relating to or denoting glands which secrete their products through ducts opening on to an epithelium rather than directly into the bloodstream.
– ORIGIN C20: from EXO- + Greek *krinein* 'sift'.

exocytosis /ˌɛksəʊsʌɪˈtəʊsɪs/ ■ n. Biology the release of the contents of a cell vacuole to the exterior.
– DERIVATIVES **exocytotic** adj.

exodus /ˈɛksədəs/ ■ n. **1** a mass departure of people, especially emigrants. **2** (**Exodus**) the second book of the Bible, recounting the departure of the Israelites from Egypt.
– ORIGIN Old English: from Greek *exodos*, from *ex-* 'out of' + *hodos* 'way'.

exoenzyme ■ n. Biochemistry an enzyme which acts outside the cell that produces it.

ex officio /ˌɛks əˈfɪʃɪəʊ/ ■ adv. & adj. by virtue of one's position or status.
– ORIGIN Latin, from *ex* 'out of, from' + *officium* 'duty'.

exogamy /ɪkˈsɒgəmi, ɛk-/ ■ n. **1** Anthropology the custom of marrying outside a community, clan, or tribe. Compare with ENDOGAMY. **2** Biology outbreeding or cross-pollination.
– DERIVATIVES **exogamous** adj.
– ORIGIN C19: from EXO- + Greek *gamos* 'marriage'.

exogenic /ˌɛksə(ʊ)ˈdʒɛnɪk/ ■ adj. Geology formed or occurring on the surface of the earth. Often contrasted with ENDOGENIC.

exogenous /ɪkˈsɒdʒɪnəs, ɛk-/ ■ adj. of, relating to, or developing from external factors. Often contrasted with ENDOGENOUS.
– DERIVATIVES **exogenously** adv.

exon /ˈɛksɒn/ ■ n. Biochemistry a segment of a DNA or RNA molecule containing information coding for a protein or peptide sequence. Compare with INTRON.
– ORIGIN C20: from *expressed* (see EXPRESS[1]) + -ON.

exonerate /ɪgˈzɒnəreɪt, ɛg-/ ■ v. **1** officially absolve from blame. **2** (**exonerate someone from**) release someone from (a duty or obligation).
– DERIVATIVES **exoneration** n. **exonerative** adj.
– ORIGIN Middle English: from Latin *exonerare* 'free from a burden', from *onus, oner-* 'a burden'.

exonuclease /ˌɛksəʊˈnjuːklɪeɪz/ ■ n. Biochemistry an enzyme which removes successive nucleotides from the end of a polynucleotide molecule.

exophthalmos /ˌɛksɒfˈθalmɒs/ ■ n. Medicine abnormal protrusion of the eyeball or eyeballs.
– DERIVATIVES **exophthalmic** adj.
– ORIGIN C17: from modern Latin *exophthalmus*, from Greek *exophthalmos* 'having prominent eyes'.

exorbitant

exorbitant /ɪgˈzɔːbɪt(ə)nt/ ■ adj. (of a price or amount charged) unreasonably high.
– DERIVATIVES **exorbitance** n. **exorbitantly** adv.
– ORIGIN Middle English: from late Latin *exorbitare* 'go off the track'.

exorcize /ˈɛksɔːsʌɪz/ (also **-ise**) ■ v. drive out (a supposed evil spirit) from a person or place.
– DERIVATIVES **exorcism** n. **exorcist** n.
– ORIGIN Middle English ('conjure up (an evil spirit)'): from eccles. Latin *exorcizare*, from Greek *exorkizein*, from *ex-* 'out' + *horkos* 'oath'.

exoskeleton ■ n. Zoology a rigid external covering for the body in some invertebrate animals, especially arthropods. Compare with ENDOSKELETON.
– DERIVATIVES **exoskeletal** adj.

exostosis /ˌɛksɒsˈtəʊsɪs/ ■ n. (pl. **exostoses** /-siːz/) Medicine a benign outgrowth of cartilaginous tissue on a bone.
– ORIGIN C16: from Greek, from *ex-* 'out' + *osteon* 'bone'.

exoteric /ˌɛksə(ʊ)ˈtɛrɪk/ ■ adj. formal intended for or likely to be understood by the general public. The opposite of ESOTERIC.
– ORIGIN C17: from Greek *exōterikos*, from *exōterō* 'outer'.

exothermic /ˌɛksə(ʊ)ˈθəːmɪk/ ■ adj. Chemistry (of a reaction) accompanied by the release of heat. The opposite of ENDOTHERMIC.
– DERIVATIVES **exothermically** adv.

exotic /ɪgˈzɒtɪk, ɛg-/ ■ adj. **1** originating in or characteristic of a distant foreign country. **2** strikingly colourful or unusual. ■ n. an exotic plant or animal.
– DERIVATIVES **exotically** adv. **exoticism** n.
– ORIGIN C16: via Latin from Greek *exōtikos* 'foreign', from *exō* 'outside'.

exotica /ɪgˈzɒtɪkə, ɛg-/ ■ pl. n. objects considered exotic.
– ORIGIN C19: from Latin, from *exoticus* (see EXOTIC).

exotoxin ■ n. Microbiology a toxin released by a living bacterial cell into its surroundings. Compare with ENDOTOXIN.

exp ■ abbrev. **1** experience. **2** experimental. **3** expiry. **4** Mathematics the exponential function raising *e* to the power of the given quantity. **5** Photography exposures.

expand /ɪkˈspand, ɛk-/ ■ v. **1** make or become larger or more extensive. **2** (often **expand on**) give a fuller version or account of. **3** become less reserved.
– DERIVATIVES **expandable** adj. **expander** n. **expansibility** n. **expansible** adj.
– ORIGIN Middle English: from Latin *expandere* 'to spread out'.

expanded ■ adj. **1** denoting materials which have a light cellular structure. **2** denoting sheet metal slit and stretched into a mesh, used to reinforce concrete and other brittle materials. **3** relatively broad in shape.

expanse ■ n. **1** a wide continuous area of something, typically land or sea. **2** the distance to which something expands or can be expanded.

expansion ■ n. **1** the action or an instance of expanding. **2** the increase in the volume of fuel on combustion in the cylinder of an engine, or the piston stroke in which this occurs.
– DERIVATIVES **expansionary** adj.

expansionism ■ n. the policy of territorial or economic expansion.
– DERIVATIVES **expansionist** n. & adj. **expansionistic** adj.

expansion joint ■ n. a joint that makes allowance for thermal expansion of the parts joined without distortion.

expansive ■ adj. **1** covering a wide area; extensive. **2** relaxed, genial, and communicative. **3** tending towards economic or territorial expansion.
– DERIVATIVES **expansively** adv. **expansiveness** n.

expansivity ■ n. Physics the amount a material expands or contracts per unit length due to a one-degree change in temperature.

ex parte /ˌɛks ˈpɑːteɪ/ ■ adj. & adv. Law with respect to or in the interests of one side only.
– ORIGIN Latin, 'from a side'.

expat ■ n. & adj. informal short for EXPATRIATE.

expatiate /ɪkˈspeɪʃɪeɪt, ɛk-/ ■ v. speak or write at length or in detail.
– DERIVATIVES **expatiation** n.
– ORIGIN C16: from Latin *exspatiari* 'move beyond one's usual bounds', from *spatium* 'space'.

expatriate ■ n. /ɪksˈpatrɪət, -ˈpeɪtrɪət, ɛks-/ a person who lives outside their native country. ■ adj. /ɪksˈpatrɪət, -ˈpeɪtrɪət, ɛks-/ living outside one's native country. ■ v. /ɪksˈpatrɪeɪt, -ˈpeɪtrɪeɪt, ɛks-/ settle abroad.
– DERIVATIVES **expatriation** n.
– ORIGIN C18: from medieval Latin *expatriare*, from *ex-* 'out' + *patria* 'native country'.

expect ■ v. **1** regard as likely to happen, do, or be the case. ▸ suppose or assume: *I expect I'll be late.* **2** believe that (someone) will arrive soon. ▸ (**be expecting**) informal be pregnant. **3** require as appropriate or rightfully due.
– DERIVATIVES **expectable** adj.
– ORIGIN C16: from Latin *exspectare* 'look out for'.

expectancy ■ n. (pl. **-ies**) **1** hope or anticipation that something, especially something pleasant, will happen. **2** a future prospect: *life expectancy.*

expectant ■ adj. **1** hoping or anticipating that something, especially something pleasant, is about to happen. **2** (of a woman) pregnant. ■ n. archaic a person who anticipates receiving something, especially high office.
– DERIVATIVES **expectantly** adv.

expectation ■ n. **1** belief that something will happen or be the case. **2** (**expectations**) archaic prospects of inheritance. **3** Mathematics another term for EXPECTED VALUE.

expected value ■ n. Mathematics a predicted value of a variable, calculated as the sum of all possible values each multiplied by the probability of its occurrence.

expectorant ■ n. a medicine which promotes the secretion of sputum by the air passages, used especially to treat coughs.
– ORIGIN C17: from Latin *expectorare* 'expel from the chest', from *pectus* 'breast'.

expectorate /ɪkˈspɛktəreɪt, ɛk-/ ■ v. cough or spit out (phlegm) from the throat or lungs.
– DERIVATIVES **expectoration** n.

expedient /ɪkˈspiːdɪənt, ɛk-/ ■ adj. **1** convenient and practical although possibly improper or immoral. **2** suitable or appropriate. ■ n. a means of attaining an end, especially one that is convenient but possibly improper.
– DERIVATIVES **expedience** n. **expediency** n. **expediently** adv.
– ORIGIN Middle English: from Latin *expedire* (see EXPEDITE).

expedite /ˈɛkspɪdʌɪt/ ■ v. cause to happen sooner or be accomplished more quickly.
– DERIVATIVES **expediter** (also **expeditor**) n.
– ORIGIN C15: from Latin *expedire* 'extricate (orig. by freeing the feet), put in order', from *ex-* 'out' + *pes, ped-* 'foot'.

expedition ■ n. **1** a journey undertaken by a group of people with a particular purpose. **2** formal promptness or speed in doing something.
– DERIVATIVES **expeditionary** adj.
– ORIGIN Middle English: from Latin *expeditio(n-)*, from *expedire* (see EXPEDITE).

expeditious /ˌɛkspɪˈdɪʃəs/ ■ adj. quick and efficient.
– DERIVATIVES **expeditiously** adv. **expeditiousness** n.

expel ■ v. (**expelled**, **expelling**) **1** force or drive out. **2** force (a pupil) to leave a school.
– DERIVATIVES **expellable** adj. **expellee** n. **expeller** n.
– ORIGIN Middle English: from Latin *expellere*, from *ex-* 'out' + *pellere* 'to drive'.

expend ■ v. spend or use up (a resource).
– ORIGIN Middle English: from Latin *expendere*, from *ex-* 'out' + *pendere* 'weigh, pay'.

expendable ■ adj. not worth preserving after use; able to be sacrificed or abandoned.
– DERIVATIVES **expendability** n. **expendably** adv.

expenditure /ɪkˈspɛndɪtʃə, ɛk-/ ■ n. **1** the action of spending funds. ▸ the amount of money spent. **2** the use of energy or other resources.

expense ■ n. **1** cost incurred or required. ▸ (**expenses**)

costs incurred in the performance of a job or task. **2** something on which money must be spent.
– PHRASES **at the expense of 1** paid for by. **2** to the detriment of.
– ORIGIN Middle English: from late Latin *expensa (pecunia)* '(money) spent', from Latin *expendere* (see EXPEND).

expense account ■ n. an arrangement under which money spent in the course of business is later reimbursed by one's employer.

expensive ■ adj. costing a lot of money.
– DERIVATIVES **expensively** adv. **expensiveness** n.

experience ■ n. **1** practical contact with and observation of facts or events. **2** knowledge or skill acquired over time. **3** an event or occurrence which leaves an impression on one. ■ v. encounter or undergo (an event or occurrence). ▶ feel (an emotion).
– ORIGIN Middle English: from Latin *experientia*, from *experiri* 'try'.

experienced ■ adj. having knowledge or skill in a particular field gained over time.

experiential /ɪkˌspɪərɪˈɛnʃ(ə)l, ɛk-/ ■ adj. involving or based on experience and observation.
– DERIVATIVES **experientially** adv.

experiment ■ n. **1** a scientific procedure undertaken to make a discovery, test a hypothesis, or demonstrate a known fact. **2** a course of action tentatively adopted without being sure of the eventual outcome. ■ v. **1** perform a scientific experiment. **2** try out new things.
– DERIVATIVES **experimentation** n. **experimenter** n.
– ORIGIN Middle English: from Latin *experimentum*, from *experiri* 'try'.

experimental ■ adj. **1** based on untested ideas or techniques and not yet established or finalized. ▶ of or relating to scientific experiments. **2** (of art) radically new and innovative.
– DERIVATIVES **experimentalism** n. **experimentalist** n. **experimentally** adv.

experimental psychology ■ n. the branch of psychology concerned with the scientific investigation of responses to stimuli in controlled situations.

expert ■ n. a person who is very knowledgeable about or skilful in a particular area. ■ adj. having or involving such knowledge or skill.
– DERIVATIVES **expertly** adv. **expertness** n.
– ORIGIN Middle English: from French, from Latin *expertus*, from *experiri* 'try'.

expertise /ˌɛkspəːˈtiːz/ ■ n. great skill or knowledge in a particular field.

expert system ■ n. Computing a piece of software which uses databases of expert knowledge to offer advice or make decisions.

expiate /ˈɛkspɪeɪt/ ■ v. atone for (guilt or sin).
– DERIVATIVES **expiable** adj. **expiation** n. **expiator** n. **expiatory** /ˈɛkspɪət(ə)ri, ˌɛkspɪˈeɪt(ə)ri/ adj.
– ORIGIN C16 (*expiation* Middle English): from Latin *expiare* 'appease by sacrifice', from *pius* 'pious'.

expire /ɪkˈspʌɪə, ɛk-/ ■ v. **1** (of a document or agreement) come to the end of the period of validity. ▶ (of a period of time) come to an end. **2** (of a person) die. **3** technical exhale (air) from the lung.
– DERIVATIVES **expiration** n. **expiratory** adj.
– ORIGIN Middle English: from Latin *exspirare* 'breathe out'.

expiry ■ n. the time when something expires.

explain ■ v. **1** make (something) clear by describing it in more detail. **2** (**explain oneself**) excuse or justify one's motives or conduct. ▶ (**explain something away**) minimize the significance of something embarrassing by giving an excuse or justification. **3** give a reason or justification for.
– DERIVATIVES **explainable** adj. **explainer** n.
– ORIGIN Middle English: from Latin *explanare*, from *planus* 'plain'.

explanation ■ n. an explanatory statement. ▶ a reason or justification for an action or belief.

explanatory /ɪkˈsplanəˌt(ə)ri, ɛk-/ ■ adj. serving to explain something.
– DERIVATIVES **explanatorily** adv.

expletive /ɪkˈspliːtɪv, ɛk-/ ■ n. **1** an oath or swear word.

exponentiation

2 Grammar a word or phrase used to fill out a sentence or a line of verse without adding to the sense. ■ adj. Grammar (of a word or phrase) serving to fill out a sentence or line of verse.
– ORIGIN Middle English: from late Latin *expletivus*, from *explere* 'fill out'.

explicable /ɪkˈsplɪkəb(ə)l, ɛk-, ˈɛksplɪˌkəb(ə)l/ ■ adj. able to be explained or accounted for.
– ORIGIN C16: from Latin *explicabilis*, from *explicare* (see EXPLICATE).

explicate /ˈɛksplɪkeɪt/ ■ v. analyse and develop (an idea or principle) in detail. ▶ analyse (a literary work) in order to reveal its meaning.
– DERIVATIVES **explication** n. **explicative** /ɛkˈsplɪkətɪv, ˈɛksplɪkeɪtɪv/ adj. **explicator** n. **explicatory** /ɛkˈsplɪkət(ə)ri, ˈɛksplɪkeɪt(ə)ri/ adj.
– ORIGIN C16: from Latin *explicare* 'unfold'.

explicit /ɪkˈsplɪsɪt, ɛk-/ ■ adj. **1** clear and detailed, with no room for confusion or doubt. **2** graphically describing or representing sexual activity.
– DERIVATIVES **explicitly** adv. **explicitness** n.
– ORIGIN C17: from Latin *explicit-*, *explicare* (see EXPLICATE).

explode ■ v. **1** burst or shatter violently, especially as a result of rapid combustion or excessive internal pressure. **2** suddenly give expression to violent emotion, especially anger. **3** show (a belief or theory) to be false or unfounded. **4** [as adj. **exploded**] (of a diagram) showing the components of a mechanism in the normal relative positions but slightly separated from each other. **5** increase suddenly in number or extent.
– DERIVATIVES **exploder** n.
– ORIGIN C16: from Latin *explodere* 'drive out by clapping, hiss off the stage', from *ex-* 'out' + *plaudere* 'to clap'.

exploit ■ v. /ɪkˈsplɔɪt, ɛk-/ **1** make use of and derive benefit from (a resource). **2** make use of unfairly; benefit unjustly from the work or actions of. ■ n. /ˈɛksplɔɪt/ a bold or daring feat.
– DERIVATIVES **exploitable** adj. **exploitation** n. **exploitative** adj. **exploiter** n. **exploitive** adj.
– ORIGIN Middle English (as n. in sense 'success, progress'): from Old French *esploit*, from Latin *explicare* (see EXPLICATE); verb from modern French *exploiter*.

explore ■ v. **1** travel through (an unfamiliar area) in order to learn about it. **2** inquire into or discuss in detail. ▶ evaluate (a new option or possibility). **3** examine by touch.
– DERIVATIVES **exploration** n. **explorational** adj. **explorative** adj. **exploratory** adj. **explorer** n.
– ORIGIN C16 (*exploratory* Middle English): from French *explorer*, from Latin *explorare* 'search out', from *ex-* 'out' + *plorare* 'utter a cry'.

explosion ■ n. an act or instance of exploding.

explosive ■ adj. **1** able or likely to explode. **2** likely to cause an eruption of anger or controversy. **3** (of an increase) sudden and dramatic. **4** Phonetics (of a vocal sound) produced with a sharp release of air. ■ n. a substance which can be made to explode.
– DERIVATIVES **explosively** adv. **explosiveness** n.

expo ■ n. short for EXPOSITION (in sense 2).

exponent /ɪkˈspəʊnənt, ɛk-/ ■ n. **1** a promoter of an idea or theory. **2** a person who does a particular thing skilfully. **3** Mathematics the power to which a given number or expression is raised (e.g. 3 in $2^3 = 2 \times 2 \times 2$). **4** Linguistics a linguistic unit that realizes another, more abstract unit.
– ORIGIN C16: from Latin *exponere* (see EXPOUND).

exponential /ˌɛkspəˈnɛnʃ(ə)l/ ■ adj. **1** (of an increase) becoming more and more rapid. **2** Mathematics of or expressed by a mathematical exponent.
– DERIVATIVES **exponentially** adv.

exponential function ■ n. Mathematics a function whose value is a constant raised to the power of the argument, especially the function where the constant is *e*.

exponentiation /ˌɛkspənɛnʃɪˈeɪʃ(ə)n/ ■ n. Mathematics the operation of raising one quantity to the power of another.
– DERIVATIVES **exponentiate** v.

export ■ v. /ɪkˈspɔːt, ɛk-, ˈɛkspɔːt/ **1** send (goods or services) to another country for sale. ▶ spread or introduce (ideas or customs) to another country. **2** Computing transfer (data) in a format that can be used by other programs.
■ n. /ˈɛkspɔːt/ **1** an exported commodity, article, or service. **2** the exporting of goods or services. ▶ [as modifier] of a high standard suitable for export: *export ales*.
– DERIVATIVES **exportability** n. **exportable** adj. **exportation** n. **exporter** n.
– ORIGIN C15: from Latin *exportare*, from *ex-* 'out' + *portare* 'carry'.

expose ■ v. **1** make (something) visible by uncovering it. ▶ (**expose oneself**) publicly and indecently display one's genitals. **2** [as adj. **exposed**] unprotected from the weather. **3** (often **expose someone to**) cause (someone) to be vulnerable or at risk. **4** reveal the true, objectionable nature of. **5** subject (photographic film) to light. **6** leave (a child) in the open to die.
– DERIVATIVES **exposer** n.
– ORIGIN Middle English: from Old French *exposer*, from Latin *exponere* (see EXPOUND), but influenced by Latin *expositus* 'put or set out' and Old French *poser* 'to place'.

exposé /ɪkˈspəʊzeɪ, ɛk-/ ■ n. a report in the media that reveals something discreditable.
– ORIGIN C19: from French, from *exposer* (see EXPOSE).

exposition ■ n. **1** a comprehensive description and explanation of a theory. **2** a large public exhibition of art or trade goods. ▶ a participatory exhibition, often related to education. **3** Music the part of a movement, especially in sonata form, in which the principal themes are first presented.
– DERIVATIVES **expositional** adj.
– ORIGIN Middle English: from Latin *expositio(n-)*, from *exponere* (see EXPOUND).

expositor /ɪkˈspɒzɪtə, ɛk-/ ■ n. a person or thing that explains complicated ideas or theories.
– DERIVATIVES **expository** adj.

ex post /ɛks ˈpəʊst/ ■ adj. & adv. based on actual results rather than forecasts.
– ORIGIN modern Latin: from *ex* 'from' + *post* 'after'.

ex post facto /ˌɛks pəʊst ˈfaktəʊ/ ■ adj. & adv. with retrospective action or force.
– ORIGIN erroneous division of Latin *ex postfacto* 'in the light of subsequent events'.

expostulate /ɪkˈspɒstjʊleɪt, ɛk-/ ■ v. express strong disapproval or disagreement.
– DERIVATIVES **expostulation** n. **expostulatory** /-lət(ə)ri/ adj.
– ORIGIN C16: from Latin *expostulare* 'demand'.

exposure ■ n. **1** the state of being exposed to something harmful. ▶ a physical condition resulting from being exposed to severe weather conditions. **2** the action of exposing a photographic film. ▶ the quantity of light reaching a photographic film, as determined by shutter speed and lens aperture. **3** the revelation of something secret. ▶ the publicizing of information or an event. **4** the direction in which a building faces.
– ORIGIN C17: from EXPOSE, on the pattern of words such as *enclosure*.

exposure meter ■ n. Photography a device for measuring the strength of light, giving the correct exposure to use with a given film.

expound ■ v. present and explain (a theory or idea) systematically.
– DERIVATIVES **expounder** n.
– ORIGIN Middle English *expoune*: from Old French *espondre*, from Latin *exponere* 'explain, publish', from *ex-* 'out' + *ponere* 'put'.

express¹ /ɪkˈsprɛs, ɛk-/ ■ v. **1** convey (a thought or feeling) in words or by gestures and conduct. **2** squeeze out (liquid or air). **3** chiefly Mathematics represent by a figure, symbol, or formula.
– DERIVATIVES **expresser** n. **expressible** adj.
– ORIGIN Middle English: from Old French *ex-* 'out' + *pressare* 'to press'.

express² /ɪkˈsprɛs, ɛk-/ ■ adj. operating at high speed. ▶ denoting a service in which deliveries are made by a special messenger. ■ adv. by express train or delivery service. ■ n. **1** (also **express train**) a train that stops at few stations and so travels quickly. **2** a special delivery service. ■ v. send by express messenger or delivery.
– ORIGIN C18: extension of EXPRESS³; the adjective is from *express train*, reflecting an earlier sense of *express* 'done or made for a special purpose', later interpreted in the sense 'rapid'.

express³ /ɪkˈsprɛs, ɛk-, ˈɛksprɛs/ ■ adj. stated explicitly. ▶ specific.
– DERIVATIVES **expressly** adv.
– ORIGIN Middle English: from Latin *expressus* 'distinctly presented', from *exprimere* 'press out, express'.

expression ■ n. **1** the action of expressing something. **2** the look on someone's face, seen as conveying a particular emotion. **3** a word or phrase expressing an idea. **4** Mathematics a collection of symbols that jointly express a quantity.
– DERIVATIVES **expressional** adj. **expressionless** adj. **expressionlessly** adv. **expressionlessness** n.

expressionism ■ n. a style of painting, music, or drama in which the artist or writer seeks to express the inner world of emotion rather than external reality.
– DERIVATIVES **expressionist** n. & adj. **expressionistic** adj. **expressionistically** adv.

expressive ■ adj. effectively conveying thought or feeling. ▶ (**expressive of**) conveying (a specified quality or idea).
– DERIVATIVES **expressively** adv. **expressiveness** n. **expressivity** n.
– ORIGIN Middle English: from medieval Latin *expressivus*, from *exprimere* (see EXPRESS³).

expresso /ɛkˈsprɛsəʊ/ ■ n. variant spelling of ESPRESSO.

expressway ■ n. chiefly N. Amer. an urban freeway.

expropriate /ɪksˈprəʊprɪeɪt, ɛks-/ ■ v. (of the state) take (property) from its owner for public use or benefit.
– DERIVATIVES **expropriation** n. **expropriator** n.
– ORIGIN C16 (*expropriation* Middle English): from medieval Latin *expropriare* 'take from the owner', from *ex-* 'out, from' + *proprium* 'property'.

expulsion ■ n. the action of expelling.
– DERIVATIVES **expulsive** adj.
– ORIGIN Middle English: from Latin *expulsio(n-)*, from *expellere* (see EXPEL).

expunge /ɪkˈspʌn(d)ʒ, ɛk-/ ■ v. obliterate or remove completely.
– DERIVATIVES **expungement** n. **expunger** n.
– ORIGIN C17: from Latin *expungere* 'mark for deletion by means of points', from *ex-* 'out' + *pungere* 'to prick'.

expurgate /ˈɛkspəːɡeɪt/ ■ v. [often as adj. **expurgated**] remove matter regarded as obscene or unsuitable from (a text or account).
– DERIVATIVES **expurgation** n. **expurgatory** /ɛkˈspəːɡət(ə)ri/ adj.
– ORIGIN C17 (*expurgation* Middle English): from Latin *expurgare* 'cleanse thoroughly'.

exquisite /ˈɛkskwɪzɪt, ɪkˈskwɪzɪt, ɛk-/ ■ adj. **1** of great beauty and delicacy. **2** acute: *the exquisite pain of love*. ▶ highly sensitive: *exquisite taste*.
– DERIVATIVES **exquisitely** adv. **exquisiteness** n.
– ORIGIN Middle English ('precise'): from Latin *exquisit-*, *exquirere* 'seek out'.

ex-serviceman (or **ex-servicewoman**) ■ n. (pl. **-men** or **-women**) chiefly Brit. a former member of the armed forces.

exsolve /ɪkˈsɒlv, ɛk-/ ■ v. [usu. as adj. **exsolved**] Geology (with reference to minerals) separate out from solid solution in a rock.
– DERIVATIVES **exsolution** n.
– ORIGIN C20: orig. as *exsolution*, from EX-¹ + SOLUTION.

ext. ■ abbrev. **1** extension (in a telephone number). **2** exterior. **3** external.

extant /ɪkˈstant, ɛk-, ˈɛkst(ə)nt/ ■ adj. still in existence.
– ORIGIN C16: from Latin *exstare* 'be visible or prominent, exist'.

extemporaneous /ɪkˌstɛmpəˈreɪnɪəs, ɛk-/ ■ adj. another term for EXTEMPORARY.
– DERIVATIVES **extemporaneously** adv. **extemporaneousness** n.

extemporary /ɪkˈstɛmp(ə)(r)əri, ɛk-/ ■ adj. spoken or done

without preparation.
-DERIVATIVES **extemporarily** adv. **extemporariness** n.
-ORIGIN C16: from **EXTEMPORE**, on the pattern of *temporary*.

extempore /ɪkˈstɛmp(ə)ri, ɛk-/ ■ adj. & adv. spoken or done without preparation.
-ORIGIN C16: from Latin *ex tempore* 'on the spur of the moment', literally 'out of the time'.

extemporize /ɪkˈstɛmpəraɪz, ɛk-/ (also **-ise**) ■ v. improvise.
-DERIVATIVES **extemporization** (also **-isation**) n.

extend ■ v. **1** make larger or longer in space or time. ▸ occupy a specified area or continue for a specified distance. **2** hold out towards someone. ▸ offer. **3** (**extend to**) be applicable to.
-DERIVATIVES **extendability** n. **extendable** adj. **extendibility** n. **extendible** adj. **extensibility** n. **extensible** adj.
-ORIGIN Middle English: from Latin *extendere* 'stretch out'.

extended family ■ n. a family which extends beyond the nuclear family to include relatives, who live nearby or in the one household.

extender ■ n. a person or thing that extends something. ▸ a substance added to a product such as paint or glue to dilute its colour or increase its bulk.

extension ■ n. **1** a part added to a structure or building to enlarge it. ▸ the action or process of enlarging or extending something. ▸ an additional period of time given to someone to hold office or fulfil an obligation. **2** (also **extension lead** or **cable**) a length of electric cable which permits the use of appliances at some distance from a fixed socket. **3** a subsidiary telephone, especially one with its own additional number on a line leading from a main switchboard. **4** [chiefly as modifier] denoting community education or training, especially in agriculture, provided by academic or government institutions. **5** the extending of a limb from a bent to a straight position. **6** Logic the range of a term or concept as measured by the objects which it denotes or contains. Often contrasted with **INTENSION**. **7** Physics & Philosophy the property of occupying space.
-DERIVATIVES **extensional** adj.
-ORIGIN Middle English: from late Latin *extensio(n-)*, from *extendere* (see **EXTEND**).

extensive ■ adj. **1** covering a large area. ▸ large in amount or scale. **2** (of agriculture) obtaining a relatively small crop from a large area with a minimum of capital and labour. Often contrasted with **INTENSIVE**.
-DERIVATIVES **extensively** adv. **extensiveness** n.
-ORIGIN Middle English: from late Latin *extensivus*, from *extendere* (see **EXTEND**).

extensor /ɪkˈstɛnsə, ɛk-/ ■ n. Anatomy a muscle whose contraction extends a limb or other part of the body. Often contrasted with **FLEXOR**.

extent ■ n. **1** the area covered by something. ▸ the size or scale of something. **2** the particular degree to which something is the case: *everyone has to compromise to some extent*.
-ORIGIN Middle English: from medieval Latin *extenta*, from Latin *extendere* (see **EXTEND**).

extenuate /ɪkˈstɛnjʊeɪt, ɛk-/ ■ v. [usu. as adj. **extenuating**] lessen the seriousness of (guilt or an offence) by reference to a mitigating factor.
-DERIVATIVES **extenuation** n. **extenuatory** /-jʊət(ə)ri/ adj.
-ORIGIN Middle English: from Latin *extenuare* 'make thin', from *tenuis* 'thin'.

exterior ■ adj. forming, situated on, or relating to the outside. ■ n. the outer surface or structure of something. ▸ a person's apparent behaviour or demeanour.
-DERIVATIVES **exteriority** n. **exteriorize** (also **-ise**) v. **exteriorly** adv.
-ORIGIN C16: from Latin, from *exter* 'outer'.

exterior angle ■ n. Geometry the angle between a side of a rectilinear figure and an adjacent side extended outward.

exterminate /ɪkˈstəːmɪneɪt, ɛk-/ ■ v. destroy completely; eradicate.
-DERIVATIVES **extermination** n. **exterminator** n. **exterminatory** /-nət(ə)ri/ adj.
-ORIGIN Middle English ('drive out'): from Latin *exterminare*, from *ex-* 'out' + *terminus* 'boundary'.

external ■ adj. **1** belonging to, situated on, or forming the

413

extract

outside. **2** coming or derived from a source outside the subject affected. ▸ coming from or relating to a country or institution other than the main subject. **3** for or concerning students registered with and taking the examinations of a university but not resident there. ■ n. (**externals**) outward features.
-DERIVATIVES **externally** adv.
-ORIGIN Middle English: from medieval Latin, from Latin *exter* 'outer'.

external ear ■ n. the parts of the ear outside the eardrum, especially the pinna.

externality /ˌɛkstəːˈnalɪti/ ■ n. (pl. **-ies**) Economics a consequence of an economic activity which affects other parties without this being reflected in market prices.

externalize (also **-ise**) ■ v. give external existence or form to. ▸ Psychology project (a mental image or process) on to a figure outside oneself.
-DERIVATIVES **externalization** (also **-isation**) n.

extinct ■ adj. (of a species, family, or other larger group) having no living members. ▸ no longer in existence. ▸ (of a volcano) not having erupted in recorded history.
-ORIGIN Middle English ('no longer alight'): from Latin *exstinct-*, *exstinguere* (see **EXTINGUISH**).

extinction ■ n. **1** the state or process of being or becoming extinct. **2** Physics reduction to zero of the intensity of light or other radiation passing through a medium, due to absorption, reflection, or scattering.

extinguish ■ v. **1** put out (a fire or light). **2** put an end to. **3** cancel (a debt) by full payment. ▸ Law render (a right or obligation) void.
-DERIVATIVES **extinguishable** adj. **extinguisher** n. **extinguishment** n. (Law).
-ORIGIN C16: from Latin *exstinguere*, from *ex-* 'out' + *stinguere* 'quench'.

extirpate /ˈɛkstəːpeɪt/ ■ v. search out and destroy completely.
-DERIVATIVES **extirpation** n. **extirpator** n.
-ORIGIN Middle English: from Latin *exstirpare*, from *ex-* 'out' + *stirps* 'a stem'.

extol /ɪkˈstəʊl, ɛk-/ ■ v. (**extolled**, **extolling**) praise enthusiastically.
-DERIVATIVES **extoller** n. **extolment** n.
-ORIGIN Middle English: from Latin *extollere*, from *ex-* 'out, upward' + *tollere* 'raise'.

extort /ɪkˈstɔːt, ɛk-/ ■ v. obtain by force, threats, or other unfair means.
-DERIVATIVES **extortion** n. **extortioner** n. **extortionist** n.
-ORIGIN C16 (*extortion* Middle English): from Latin *extort-*, *extorquere* 'wrest', from *torquere* 'twist'.

extortionate /ɪkˈstɔːʃ(ə)nət, ɛk-/ ■ adj. **1** (of a price) much too high. **2** using or given to extortion.
-DERIVATIVES **extortionately** adv.

extra ■ adj. added to an existing or usual amount or number. ■ adv. **1** to a greater extent than usual. **2** in addition. ■ n. **1** an item for which an extra charge is made. **2** an extra item. **3** a person engaged temporarily to fill out a crowd scene in a film or play. **4** Cricket a run scored other than from a hit with the bat, credited to the batting side rather than to a batsman.
-ORIGIN C17: prob. a shortening of **EXTRAORDINARY**, suggested by similar forms in French and German.

extra- ■ prefix outside; beyond: *extragalactic*. ▸ beyond the scope of: *extra-curricular*.
-ORIGIN from Latin *extra* 'outside'.

extracellular ■ adj. Biology situated or taking place outside a cell or cells.

extra cover ■ n. Cricket a fielding position between cover point and mid-off but further from the wicket.

extract ■ v. /ɪkˈstrakt, ɛk-/ remove, especially by effort or force. ▸ obtain (money, information, etc.) from someone unwilling to give it. ▸ obtain (a substance or resource) from something by a special method. ▸ select (a passage from a text, film, or piece of music) for quotation, performance, or reproduction. ■ n. /ˈɛkstrakt/ **1** a short passage taken from a text, film, or piece of music. **2** a preparation containing the active ingredient of a

extraction

substance in concentrated form: *vanilla extract.*
– DERIVATIVES **extractability** n. **extractable** adj. **extractive** adj.
– ORIGIN Middle English: from Latin *extract-*, *extrahere* 'draw out'.

extraction ■ n. **1** the action of extracting. **2** the ethnic origin of someone's family: *a worker of Polish extraction.*

extractor ■ n. a machine or device used to extract something. ▸ [as modifier] denoting a fan or other device for extracting odours and stale air.

extra-curricular ■ adj. (of an activity at a school or college) pursued in addition to the normal curriculum.
– DERIVATIVES **extra-curricularly** adv.

extradite /'ɛkstrədʌɪt/ ■ v. hand over (a person accused or convicted of a crime) to the jurisdiction of the foreign state in which the crime was committed.
– DERIVATIVES **extraditable** adj. **extradition** n.
– ORIGIN C19 (as *extradition*): from French, from *ex-* 'out, from' + *tradition* 'delivery'.

extrados /ɪk'streɪdɒs, ɛk-/ ■ n. Architecture the upper or outer curve of an arch. Often contrasted with INTRADOS.
– ORIGIN C18: from Latin *extra* 'outside' + French *dos* 'back'.

extragalactic /ˌɛkstrəɡə'laktɪk/ ■ adj. Astronomy occurring or originating outside the Milky Way galaxy.

extrajudicial ■ adj. Law (of a sentence) not legally authorized. ▸ (of a settlement or statement) out-of-court.
– DERIVATIVES **extrajudicially** adv.

extramarital /ˌɛkstrə'marɪt(ə)l/ ■ adj. (especially of sexual relations) occurring outside marriage.
– DERIVATIVES **extramaritally** adv.

extramural /ˌɛkstrə'mjʊər(ə)l/ ■ adj. (of a course of study) arranged for people who are not full-time members of a university or other educational establishment. ▸ additional to one's studies.
– DERIVATIVES **extramurally** adv.
– ORIGIN C19: from Latin *extra muros* 'outside the walls'.

extraneous /ɪk'streɪnɪəs, ɛk-/ ■ adj. **1** irrelevant or unrelated to the subject. **2** of external origin.
– DERIVATIVES **extraneously** adv. **extraneousness** n.
– ORIGIN C17: from Latin *extraneus*.

extraordinary /ɪk'strɔː(r)d(ə)n(ə)ri, ɛk-, ˌɛkstrə'ɔːdɪn(ə)ri/ ■ adj. **1** very unusual or remarkable. **2** (of a meeting) specially convened. ▸ [postpos.] (of an official) specially employed: *Ambassador Extraordinary.*
– DERIVATIVES **extraordinarily** adv. **extraordinariness** n.
– ORIGIN Middle English: from Latin *extraordinarius*, from *extra ordinem* 'outside the normal course of events'.

extraordinary rendition ■ n. another term for RENDITION (in sense 3).

extrapolate /ɪk'strapəleɪt, ɛk-/ ■ v. **1** extend (a graph) by inferring unknown values from trends in the known data. **2** extend the application of (a method, conclusion, etc.) to different or larger groups.
– DERIVATIVES **extrapolation** n. **extrapolative** adj. **extrapolator** n.
– ORIGIN C19: from EXTRA- + a shortened form of INTERPOLATE.

extraposition /ˌɛkstrəpə'zɪʃ(ə)n/ ■ n. Grammar the placing of a word or group of words outside or at the end of a clause, while retaining the sense (e.g. *it's no use crying over spilt milk*).

extrapyramidal /ˌɛkstrəpɪ'ramɪd(ə)l/ ■ adj. Anatomy & Medicine relating to or denoting motor nerves descending from the cortex to the spine but not part of the pyramidal system.

extrasensory perception /ˌɛkstrə'sɛns(ə)ri/ ■ n. the supposed faculty of perceiving things by means other than the known senses, e.g. by telepathy.

extraterrestrial /ˌɛkstrətə'rɛstrɪəl/ ■ adj. of or from outside the earth or its atmosphere. ■ n. a hypothetical or fictional being from outer space.

extraterritorial /ˌɛkstrətɛrɪ'tɔːrɪəl/ ■ adj. **1** situated or valid outside a country's territory. **2** denoting the freedom of embassy staff from the jurisdiction of the territory of residence.
– DERIVATIVES **extraterritoriality** n.

extravagant /ɪk'stravəɡ(ə)nt, ɛk-/ ■ adj. **1** lacking restraint in spending money or using resources. ▸ resulting from or showing this: *extravagant gifts.* **2** exceeding what is reasonable or appropriate: *extravagant claims.*
– DERIVATIVES **extravagance** n. **extravagancy** n. **extravagantly** adv.
– ORIGIN Middle English: from medieval Latin *extravagari* 'diverge greatly', from Latin *extra-* 'outside' + *vagari* 'wander'.

extravaganza /ɪkˌstravə'ɡanzə, ɛk-/ ■ n. an elaborate and spectacular entertainment.
– ORIGIN C18: from Italian *estravaganza* 'extravagance'.

extravascular /ˌɛkstrə'vaskjʊlə/ ■ adj. Medicine situated or occurring outside the vascular system.

extravert ■ n. variant spelling of EXTROVERT.

extra virgin ■ adj. denoting a particularly fine grade of olive oil made from the first pressing of the olives.

extrema plural form of EXTREMUM.

extreme ■ adj. **1** very great. ▸ exceptional. ▸ very severe or serious. **2** far from moderate, especially politically. ▸ denoting or relating to a sport performed in a hazardous environment. **3** furthest from the centre or a given point. ■ n. either of two abstract things that are as different from each other as possible. ▸ the most extreme degree of something.
– DERIVATIVES **extremely** adv. **extremeness** n.
– ORIGIN Middle English: from Latin *extremus* 'outermost, utmost', superlative of *exterus* 'outer'.

extreme unction ■ n. (in the Roman Catholic Church) a former name for the sacrament of anointing of the sick, especially when administered to the dying.

extremist ■ n. chiefly derogatory a person who holds extreme political or religious views.
– DERIVATIVES **extremism** n.

extremity /ɪk'strɛmɪti, ɛk-/ ■ n. (pl. **-ies**) **1** the furthest point or limit. ▸ (**extremities**) the hands and feet. **2** severity or seriousness. ▸ extreme adversity.

extremum /ɪk'striːməm, ɛk-/ ■ n. (pl. **extremums** or **extrema**) Mathematics the maximum or minimum value of a function.
– ORIGIN C20: from Latin, neuter of *extremus* (see EXTREME).

extricate /'ɛkstrɪkeɪt/ ■ v. free from a constraint or difficulty.
– DERIVATIVES **extricable** adj. **extrication** n.
– ORIGIN C17: from Latin *extricare* 'unravel', from *ex-* 'out' + *tricae* 'perplexities'.

extrinsic /ɛk'strɪnsɪk, -zɪk/ ■ adj. not essential or inherent.
– DERIVATIVES **extrinsically** adv.
– ORIGIN C16: from late Latin *extrinsecus* 'outward', from *exter* 'outer'.

extrovert /'ɛkstrəvəːt/ (also technical **extravert**) ■ n. an outgoing, socially confident person. ▸ Psychology a person predominantly concerned with external things or objective considerations. Compare with INTROVERT. ■ adj. of, denoting, or typical of an extrovert.
– DERIVATIVES **extroversion** n. **extroverted** adj.
– ORIGIN C20 (*extroversion* C17): from *extro-* (var. of EXTRA-) + Latin *vertere* 'to turn'.

extrude /ɪk'struːd, ɛk-/ ■ v. thrust or force out. ▸ shape (a material such as metal or plastic) by forcing it through a die.
– DERIVATIVES **extrudable** adj. **extrusion** n.
– ORIGIN C16: from Latin *extrudere*, from *ex-* 'out' + *trudere* 'to thrust'.

extrusive ■ adj. Geology relating to or denoting rock that has been extruded at the earth's surface as lava or other volcanic deposits.

exuberant /ɪɡ'zjuːb(ə)r(ə)nt, ɛɡ-/ ■ adj. **1** lively and cheerful. **2** chiefly poetic/literary growing profusely.
– DERIVATIVES **exuberance** n. **exuberantly** adv.
– ORIGIN Middle English ('overflowing'): from French *exubérant*, from Latin *exuberare* 'be abundantly fruitful', from *uber* 'fertile'.

exude /ɪɡ'zjuːd, ɛɡ-/ ■ v. **1** (with reference to moisture or a smell) discharge or be discharged slowly and steadily. **2** display (an emotion or quality) strongly and openly.
– DERIVATIVES **exudate** n. **exudation** n.

exudative /ɪɡˈzjuːdətɪv, ɛɡ-/ adj.
–ORIGIN C16: from Latin *exsudare*, from *ex-* 'out' + *sudare* 'to sweat'.

exult ■ v. show or feel triumphant elation.
–DERIVATIVES **exultancy** n. **exultant** adj. **exultantly** adv. **exultation** n. **exulting** adj. **exultingly** adv.
–ORIGIN C16 (*exultation* Middle English): from Latin *exsultare*, from *exsilire* 'leap up'.

exuviae /ɪɡˈzjuːviː, ɛɡ-/ ■ pl. n. [also treated as sing.] Zoology the cast or sloughed skin of an animal, especially of an insect larva.
–DERIVATIVES **exuvial** adj.
–ORIGIN C17: from Latin, 'animal skins'.

ex-works ■ adj. & adv. Brit. direct from the factory or place of manufacture.

-ey ■ suffix variant spelling of -Y² (as in *Charley*).

eyas /ˈʌɪəs/ ■ n. (pl. **eyasses**) a young hawk, especially (in falconry) an unfledged nestling taken from the nest for training.
–ORIGIN C15 (orig. *nyas*): from French *niais*, from Latin *nidus* 'nest'; the initial *n* was lost by wrong division of *a nyas*.

eye ■ n. 1 the organ of sight in humans or other animals. ▸ a person's attitude or feelings: *to European eyes, it may seem that the city is overcrowded*. 2 a rounded eye-like marking on an animal, such as those on the tail of a peacock. ▸ a round, dark spot on a potato from which a new shoot can grow. 3 the small hole in a needle through which the thread is passed. ▸ a small metal loop into which a hook is fitted as a fastener on a garment. ▸ Nautical a loop at the end of a rope, especially one at the top end of a shroud or stay. 4 S. African the source of a spring. 5 (**eyes**) Nautical the extreme forward part of a ship. ■ v. (**eyeing** or **eying**) look at closely or with interest. ▸ (**eye someone up**) informal look at someone in a way that reveals a sexual interest.
–PHRASES **be all eyes** be watching eagerly and attentively. **close** (or **shut**) **one's eyes to** refuse to acknowledge (something unpleasant). **an eye for an eye and a tooth for a tooth** retaliation in kind is the appropriate way to deal with an offence or crime. [with biblical allusion to Exodus 21:24.] **the eye of the storm** the calm region at the centre of a storm. **the eye of the wind** the direction from which the wind is blowing. **eyes front** (or **left** or **right**) a military command to turn the head in the direction stated. **get one's eye in** Brit. improve one's judgement or skill through experience. **give someone the eye** informal look at someone with sexual interest. **half an eye** a partial degree of attention. **have an eye for** be able to recognize and make good judgements about. **have** (or **keep**) **one's eye on** keep under careful observation. ▸ (**have one's eye on**) aim to acquire. **have** (or **with**) **an eye to** have (or having) as one's objective. (**only**) **have eyes for** be (exclusively) interested in. **have eyes in the back of one's head** know what is going on around one even when one cannot see it. **keep an eye on** keep under careful observation. **keep an eye out** (or **open**) look out for something. **keep one's eyes open** (or **peeled** or Brit. **skinned**) watch out for something. **make eyes at** look at in a way that indicates one's sexual interest. **one in the eye for** a disappointment or setback for. **open someone's eyes** cause someone to realize something. **see eye to eye** be in full agreement. **a twinkle** (or **gleam**) **in someone's eye** something that is as yet no more than an idea or dream. **up to the** (or **one's**) **eyes** (**in**) informal extremely busy. **with one's eyes open** fully aware of possible difficulties.
–DERIVATIVES **-eyed** adj. **eyeless** adj.
–ORIGIN Old English, of Germanic origin.

eyeball ■ n. the round part of the eye of a vertebrate, within the eyelids and socket. ■ v. informal stare at closely.
–PHRASES **eyeball to eyeball** face to face with someone, especially in an aggressive way. **up to one's eyeballs in** informal extremely busy.

eyebath ■ n. a small container used for applying cleansing solutions to the eye.

eye bolt ■ n. a bolt or bar with an eye at the end for attaching a hook or ring to.

eyebright ■ n. a small white-flowered plant, traditionally used as a remedy for eye problems. [*Euphrasia officinalis* and other species.]

eyebrow ■ n. the strip of hair growing on the ridge above a person's eye socket.
–PHRASES **raise one's eyebrows** (or **an eyebrow**) show surprise or mild disapproval.

eye candy ■ n. informal visual images that are superficially entertaining but intellectually undemanding.

eye-catching ■ adj. immediately appealing or noticeable.
–DERIVATIVES **eye-catcher** n. **eye-catchingly** adv.

eyeful ■ n. informal 1 a long steady look. 2 an eye-catching person or thing.

eyeglass ■ n. 1 a single lens for correcting or assisting defective eyesight, especially a monocle. 2 (**eyeglasses**) chiefly N. Amer. another term for GLASSES. 3 another term for EYEPIECE.

eyehole ■ n. a hole to look through.

eyelash ■ n. each of the short hairs growing on the edges of the eyelids.

eyelet ■ n. a small round hole in leather or cloth for threading a lace, string, or rope through. ▸ a metal ring used to reinforce such a hole. ▸ a small hole with stitching around its edge, used as a form of decoration in embroidery. ■ v. (**eyeleted**, **eyeleting**) make eyelets in (fabric).
–ORIGIN Middle English *oilet*, from Old French *oillet*, diminutive of *oil* 'eye', from Latin *oculus*.

eye level ■ n. the level of the eyes looking straight ahead.

eyelid ■ n. each of the upper and lower folds of skin which cover the eye when closed.

eyeliner ■ n. a cosmetic applied as a line round the eyes.

eye-opener ■ n. informal 1 an unexpected revelation. 2 N. Amer. an alcoholic drink taken early in the day.
–DERIVATIVES **eye-opening** adj.

eyepatch ■ n. a patch worn to protect an injured eye.

eyepiece ■ n. the lens or group of lenses that is closest to the eye in a microscope or other optical instrument.

eye-popping ■ adj. informal astonishingly large or blatant.

eye rhyme ■ n. a similarity between words in spelling but not in pronunciation, for example *love* and *move*.

eyeshade ■ n. a translucent visor used to protect the eyes from strong light.

eyeshadow ■ n. a coloured cosmetic applied to the eyelids or to the skin around the eyes.

eyeshot ■ n. the distance for which one can see.

eyesight ■ n. a person's ability to see.

eye socket ■ n. the cavity in the skull which encloses an eyeball with its surrounding muscles.

eyesore ■ n. a thing that is very ugly, especially a building.

eyespot ■ n. 1 a rounded eye-like marking, especially on a butterfly or moth. 2 a fungal disease of cereals and other grasses, characterized by yellowish oval spots.

eyestripe ■ n. a stripe on a bird's head which encloses or appears to run through the eye.

eye tooth ■ n. a canine tooth, especially one in the upper jaw.
–PHRASES **give one's eye teeth for** (or **to be**) do anything in order to have or be.

eyewash ■ n. 1 cleansing lotion for a person's eye. 2 informal nonsense.

eyewitness ■ n. a person who has personally seen something happen and so can give a first-hand description of it.

eye worm ■ n. 1 a filarial worm of equatorial Africa, affecting the eyes. [*Loa loa*.] 2 a nematode worm that occurs in the region of the eyelid and tear duct, found chiefly in hoofed mammals. [Genus *Thelazia*.]

eyrie /ˈɪəri, ˈʌɪri, ˈɛːri/ (US also **aerie**) ■ n. a large nest of an eagle or other bird of prey, typically built high in a tree or on a cliff.
–ORIGIN C15: from medieval Latin *aerea*, *eyria*, prob. from Latin *area* 'level piece of ground', in late Latin, 'nest of a bird of prey'.

Ff

F¹ (also **f**) ■ *n.* (pl. **Fs** or **F's**) **1** the sixth letter of the alphabet. **2** denoting the next after E in a set of items, categories, etc. **3** *Music* the fourth note of the diatonic scale of C major.

F² ■ *abbrev.* **1** Fahrenheit. **2** farad(s). **3** *Chemistry* faraday(s). **4** (in racing results) favourite. **5** female. **6** fighter (in designations of US aircraft types). **7** (in motor racing) formula. **8** Franc(s). **9** (in tables of sports results) goals or points for. ■ *symb.* **1** the chemical element fluorine. **2** *Physics* force.

f ■ *abbrev.* **1** femto- (10⁻¹⁵). **2** (in textual references) folio. **3** (in horse racing results) furlong(s). **4** *Chemistry* denoting electrons and orbitals possessing three units of angular momentum. [*f* from *fundamental*, orig. applied to lines in atomic spectra.] ■ *symb.* **1** focal length. **2** *Mathematics* a function of a specified variable.

FA ■ *abbrev.* **1** Fanny Adams. **2** Football Association.

fa ■ *n.* variant spelling of **FAH**.

fab ■ *adj.* informal fabulous; wonderful.

faba bean /'fɑːbə/ ■ *n.* variant spelling of **FAVA BEAN**.

Fabian /'feɪbɪən/ ■ *n.* a member or supporter of the Fabian Society, an organization of socialists aiming to achieve socialism by non-revolutionary methods. ■ *adj.* **1** relating to or characteristic of the Fabians. **2** employing a cautiously persistent and dilatory strategy to wear out an enemy.
– DERIVATIVES **Fabianism** *n.* **Fabianist** *n.*
– ORIGIN C18: from the name of the Roman general Quintus *Fabius* Maximus Verrucosus, known for his delaying tactics.

fable /'feɪb(ə)l/ ■ *n.* a short story, typically with animals as characters, conveying a moral. ▸ a supernatural story incorporating elements of myth and legend. ▸ myth and legend.
– ORIGIN Middle English: from Old French *fable*, from Latin *fabula* 'story', from *fari* 'speak'.

fabled ■ *adj.* **1** famous. **2** mythical or imaginary.

fabric ■ *n.* **1** material produced by weaving or knitting textile fibres; cloth. **2** a structure or framework, especially the walls, floor, and roof of a building. ▸ the essential structure of something abstract: *the fabric of society.*
– ORIGIN C15 (orig. 'something made'): from French *fabrique*, from Latin *fabrica* 'something skilfully produced'.

fabricate ■ *v.* **1** invent, typically with deceitful intent. **2** construct or manufacture (an industrial product), especially from prepared components.
– DERIVATIVES **fabrication** *n.* **fabricator** *n.*
– ORIGIN Middle English: from Latin *fabricare* 'manufacture', from *fabrica* (see **FABRIC**).

fabulate /'fabjʊleɪt/ ■ *v.* tell invented stories.
– DERIVATIVES **fabulation** *n.*
– ORIGIN C17: from Latin *fabulari* 'narrate as a fable'.

fabulous ■ *adj.* **1** extraordinary, especially extraordinarily large. ▸ informal wonderful. **2** mythical.
– DERIVATIVES **fabulously** *adv.* **fabulousness** *n.*
– ORIGIN Middle English: from Latin *fabulosus* 'celebrated in fable', from *fabula* (see **FABLE**).

facade /fə'sɑːd/ ■ *n.* **1** the face of a building, especially its principal front. **2** a deceptive outward appearance.
– ORIGIN C17: from French *façade*, from *face* 'face', on the pattern of Italian *facciata*.

face ■ *n.* **1** the front part of a person's head from the forehead to the chin, or the corresponding part in an animal. ▸ an aspect of something: *the unacceptable face of social drinking.* **2** an expression on someone's face. **3** the surface of a thing, especially one that is presented to the view or has a particular function. ▸ *Geometry* each of the surfaces of a solid. ▸ a vertical or sloping side of a mountain or cliff. ■ *v.* **1** be positioned with the face or front towards or in a specified direction. **2** confront and deal with. ▸ have (a difficult event or situation) in prospect. ▸ (**face off**) *chiefly N. Amer.* take up an attitude of confrontation, especially at the start of a fight or game. **3** (*usu.* **be faced with**) cover the surface of (something) with a layer of a different material.
– PHRASES **be in someone's face** *informal* be blatantly aggressive or critical. **someone's face fits** *Brit.* someone has the necessary qualities for something. **face the music** be confronted with the unpleasant consequences of one's actions. **face to face** close together and looking directly at one another. **in face** (or **the face**) **of** when confronted with. ▸ despite. **lose** (or **save**) **face** incur (or avoid) humiliation. **on the face of it** apparently. **set one's face against** resist with determination. **to one's face** openly in one's presence.
– DERIVATIVES **-faced** *adj.*
– ORIGIN Middle English: from Old French, from Latin *facies* 'form, appearance, face'.

facebook ■ *n.* trademark (**Facebook**) a social networking website allowing people to interact with others by publishing or viewing personal information. ▸ [as modifier] of or relating to the networking environment provided by this service: *Facebook friend, Facebook app* ▸ *N. Amer.* informal a directory of names with accompanying photographs, typically as provided to university students to help introduce them to each other. ■ *v.* (**facebooked**, **facebooking**) use the social networking website of the same name.

face card ■ *n. chiefly N. Amer.* another term for **COURT CARD**.

facecloth ■ *n.* **1** a small towelling cloth for washing one's face. **2** smooth-surfaced woollen cloth.

faceless ■ *adj.* remote and impersonal: *faceless bureaucrats.*
– DERIVATIVES **facelessness** *n.*

facelift ■ *n.* a cosmetic surgical operation to remove unwanted wrinkles by tightening the skin of the face.

face mask ■ *n.* **1** a protective mask covering the nose and mouth or nose and eyes. **2** another term for **FACE PACK**.

face-off ■ *n.* **1** *chiefly N. Amer.* a direct confrontation. **2** *Ice Hockey* the start of play.

face pack ■ *n. chiefly Brit.* a cosmetic preparation spread over the face to improve the skin.

face paint ■ *n.* bold-coloured paint used to decorate the face.
– DERIVATIVES **face-painter** *n.* **face-painting** *n.*

faceplate ■ *n.* **1** an enlarged end or attachment on the end of the mandrel on a lathe, on which work can be mounted. **2** the transparent window of a diver's or astronaut's helmet. **3** the part of a cathode ray tube that carries the phosphor screen.

face-saving ■ *adj.* preserving one's reputation or dignity.
– DERIVATIVES **face-saver** *n.*

facet /'fasɪt, -ɛt/ ■ *n.* **1** one side of something many-sided, especially of a cut gem. ▸ *Zoology* any of the individual units that make up the compound eye of an insect or crustacean. **2** a particular aspect of something.
– DERIVATIVES **-faceted** *adj.*
– ORIGIN C17: from French *facette*, diminutive of *face* (see **FACE**).

facetious /fə'siːʃəs/ ■ *adj.* trying but failing to be amusing, or using inappropriate humour.
– DERIVATIVES **facetiously** *adv.* **facetiousness** *n.*
– ORIGIN C16: from Latin *facetia* 'jest'.

face value ■ *n.* **1** the value printed or depicted on a coin,

---

VOWELS   a cat   ɑː arm   ɛ bed   ɛː hair   ə ago   əː her   ɪ sit   i cosy   iː see   ɒ hot   ɔː saw   ʌ run

postage stamp, etc., especially when less than the actual value. **2** apparent worth or implication.

faceworker ■ *n.* a miner who works at the coalface.

facia ■ *n.* chiefly Brit. variant spelling of FASCIA.

facial /ˈfeɪʃ(ə)l/ ■ *adj.* of or affecting the face. ■ *n.* a beauty treatment for the face.
–DERIVATIVES **facially** *adv.*

facial nerves ■ *pl. n.* Anatomy the pair of cranial nerves supplying the facial muscles and the tongue.

facies /ˈfeɪʃiːz/ ■ *n.* (pl. same) **1** Medicine the facial expression of an individual that is typical of a particular disease or condition. **2** Geology the character of a rock expressed by its formation, composition, and fossil content.
–ORIGIN C17: from Latin, 'appearance, face'.

facile /ˈfasʌɪl, -sɪl/ ■ *adj.* **1** appearing comprehensive only by ignoring the complexities of an issue; superficial. **2** (of success, especially in sport) effortless.
–DERIVATIVES **facilely** *adv.* **facileness** *n.*
–ORIGIN C15: from Latin *facilis* 'easy'.

facilitate /fəˈsɪlɪteɪt/ ■ *v.* make easy or easier.
–DERIVATIVES **facilitation** *n.* **facilitative** *adj.* **facilitator** *n.* **facilitatory** *adj.*
–ORIGIN C17: from French *faciliter*.

facility ■ *n.* (pl. **-ies**) **1** a building, service, or piece of equipment provided for a particular purpose. ▸ an additional feature of a service or machine. **2** a natural aptitude. ▸ absence of difficulty or effort.
–ORIGIN C16: from Latin *facilitas*.

facing ■ *n.* **1** a piece of material sewn on the inside of a garment, especially at the neck and armholes, to strengthen it. **2** an outer layer covering the surface of a wall. ■ *adj.* positioned so as to face.

facsimile /fakˈsɪmɪli/ ■ *n.* an exact copy, especially of written or printed material.
–ORIGIN C16 (orig. as *fac simile*): modern Latin, from Latin *fac!* (from *facere* 'make') + *simile* (from *similis* 'like').

fact ■ *n.* a thing that is indisputably the case. ▸ (**facts**) information used as evidence or as part of a report.
–PHRASES **before** (or **after**) **the fact** Law before (or after) the committing of a crime. **a fact of life** something that must be accepted, even if unpalatable. **the facts of life** information about sexual matters, especially as given to children. **in** (**point of**) **fact** in reality.
–ORIGIN C15 (orig. 'an act', later 'a crime'): from Latin *factum*, from *facere* 'do'.

faction[1] ■ *n.* a small dissentient group within a larger one.
–DERIVATIVES **factional** *adj.* **factionalism** *n.* **factionally** *adv.*
–ORIGIN C15: from Latin *factio(n-)*, from *facere* 'do, make'.

faction[2] ■ *n.* a literary and cinematic genre in which real events are used as a basis for a fictional narrative or dramatization.
–ORIGIN 1960s: blend of FACT and FICTION.

factionalize (also **-ise**) ■ *v.* (of an organized group) split into factions.

faction fight ■ *n.* S. African a violent conflict between opposing groups of people or clans, typically over a prolonged period of time.
–DERIVATIVES **faction fighting** *n.*

factious /ˈfakʃəs/ ■ *adj.* relating or inclined to dissension.
–DERIVATIVES **factiously** *adv.* **factiousness** *n.*
–ORIGIN C16: from Latin *factiosus*, from *factio* (see FACTION[1]).

factitious /fakˈtɪʃəs/ ■ *adj.* artificial; contrived.
–DERIVATIVES **factitiously** *adv.* **factitiousness** *n.*
–ORIGIN C17: from Latin *facticius* 'made by art'.

factoid ■ *n.* **1** an item of unreliable information that is repeated so often that it becomes accepted as fact. **2** N. Amer. a brief or trivial item of information.

factor ■ *n.* **1** a circumstance, fact, or influence that contributes to a result. **2** Mathematics a number or quantity that when multiplied with another produces a given number or expression. **3** Physiology any of a number of substances in the blood which are involved in coagulation. **4** a business agent. ▸ a company that buys a manufacturer's invoices at a discount and takes responsibility for collecting the payments due on them.

▸ chiefly Scottish a land agent or steward. ■ *v.* **1** Mathematics another term for FACTORIZE. **2** sell (one's receivable debts) to a factor. **3** (**factor something in/out**) include (or exclude) something as a relevant element when making a decision.
–DERIVATIVES **factorable** *adj.*
–ORIGIN Middle English (meaning 'doer', also in the Scots sense 'agent'): from Latin *factor*, from *facere* 'do'.

factor analysis ■ *n.* Statistics a process in which the values of observed data are expressed as functions of a number of possible causes to determine which are most important.

factorial Mathematics ■ *n.* the product of an integer and all the integers below it; e.g. factorial four (4!) is equal to 24. (Symbol: !) ▸ the product of a series of factors in an arithmetical progression. ■ *adj.* relating to a factor or factorial.
–DERIVATIVES **factorially** *adv.*

factorize (also **-ise**) ■ *v.* Mathematics resolve or be resolvable into factors.
–DERIVATIVES **factorization** (also **-isation**) *n.*

factor VIII (also **factor eight**) ■ *n.* Physiology a blood protein involved in clotting, a deficiency of which causes one of the main forms of haemophilia.

factory ■ *n.* (pl. **-ies**) a building or buildings where goods are manufactured or assembled chiefly by machine.
–ORIGIN C16: from late Latin *factorium* 'oil press', and Portuguese *feitoria*.

factory farming ■ *n.* a system of rearing poultry, pigs, or cattle indoors under strictly controlled conditions.
–DERIVATIVES **factory farm** *n.*

factory floor ■ *n.* the workers in a company or industry, rather than the management.

factory ship ■ *n.* a fishing or whaling ship with facilities for immediate processing of the catch.

factory shop (chiefly N. Amer. also **factory outlet**) ■ *n.* a shop in which goods, especially surplus stock, are sold directly by the manufacturers at a discount.

factotum /fakˈtəʊtəm/ ■ *n.* (pl. **factotums**) an employee who does all kinds of work.
–ORIGIN C16 (orig. in the phrs *dominum* (or *magister*) *factotum* 'master of everything' and *Johannes factotum* 'Jack of all trades'): from Latin *fac!* 'do!' (from *facere*) + *totum* 'the whole thing' (neuter of *totus*).

factual /ˈfaktʃʊəl, -tjʊəl/ ■ *adj.* based on or concerned with fact or facts.
–DERIVATIVES **factuality** *n.* **factually** *adv.* **factualness** *n.*

factum /ˈfaktəm/ ■ *n.* (pl. **factums** or **facta**) Law a statement of the facts of a case.
–ORIGIN C18: from Latin, 'something done or made'.

facture /ˈfaktʃə/ ■ *n.* an artist's characteristic handling of paint.
–ORIGIN Middle English: Latin *factura* 'manufacture', from *facere* 'do, make'.

facultative /ˈfak(ə)lˌtətɪv/ ■ *adj.* **1** occurring optionally in response to circumstances rather than by nature. **2** Biology capable of but not restricted to a particular function or mode of life: *a facultative parasite*.
–DERIVATIVES **facultatively** *adv.*
–ORIGIN C19: from French *facultatif*, *-ive*, from *faculté* (see FACULTY).

faculty ■ *n.* (pl. **-ies**) **1** an inherent mental or physical power. ▸ an aptitude or talent. **2** a group of university departments concerned with a major division of knowledge. ▸ N. Amer. the teaching or research staff of a university or college.
–ORIGIN Middle English: from Latin *facultas*, from *facilis* 'easy', from *facere* 'make, do'.

fad ■ *n.* **1** a craze. **2** an idiosyncrasy or arbitrary like or dislike.
–DERIVATIVES **faddish** *adj.* **faddishly** *adv.* **faddishness** *n.* **faddism** *n.* **faddist** *n.*
–ORIGIN C19 (orig. dialect): prob. the second element of *fidfad*, contraction of FIDDLE-FADDLE.

fade ■ *v.* **1** gradually grow faint and disappear. ▸ lose or cause to lose colour. ▸ (of a vehicle brake) become temporarily less efficient as a result of frictional heating.

fado

2 (with reference to film and television images) come or cause to come gradually into or out of view, or to merge into another shot. ▶ (with reference to recorded sound) increase or decrease in volume or merge into another recording. **3** Golf (of the ball) deviate to the right (or, for a left-handed golfer, the left), typically as a result of spin. ■ n. **1** an act or instance of fading. **2** Golf a shot causing the ball to fade.
– ORIGIN Middle English: from Old French *fader*, from *fade* 'dull, insipid', prob. from a blend of Latin *fatuus* 'silly' and *vapidus* 'vapid'.

fado /ˈfɑːdəʊ/ ■ n. (pl. **-os**) a type of popular Portuguese song, usually with a melancholy theme.
– ORIGIN Portuguese, 'fate'.

faeces /ˈfiːsiːz/ (US **feces**) ■ pl. n. waste matter remaining after food has been digested, discharged from the bowels.
– DERIVATIVES **faecal** /ˈfiːk(ə)l/ adj.
– ORIGIN Middle English: from Latin, pl. of *faex* 'dregs'.

faff informal, chiefly Brit. ■ v. bustle ineffectually. ■ n. ineffectual activity.
– ORIGIN C18 (orig. dialect 'blow in puffs', describing the wind): imitative.

fag[1] informal, chiefly Brit. ■ n. **1** a tiring or unwelcome task. **2** a junior pupil at a private school who does minor chores for a senior pupil. ■ v. (**fagged**, **fagging**) **1** (of a private-school pupil) act as a fag. **2** [as adj. **fagged out**] exhausted.
– ORIGIN C16 (in the sense 'grow weary').

fag[2] ■ n. N. Amer. informal, derogatory a male homosexual.
– ORIGIN 1920s: short for FAGGOT (in sense 3).

fag[3] ■ n. informal a cigarette.
– ORIGIN C19: elliptically from FAG END.

fag end ■ n. informal, chiefly Brit. a cigarette end. ▶ a useless remnant.
– ORIGIN C17: from C15 *fag* 'a flap'.

faggot /ˈfagət/ ■ n. **1** Brit. a ball of seasoned chopped liver, baked or fried. **2** (US **fagot**) a bundle of sticks bound together as fuel. ▶ a bundle of iron rods bound together for reheating, welding, and hammering into bars. **3** N. Amer. informal, derogatory a male homosexual. **4** Brit. informal, dated an unpleasant or contemptible woman.
– ORIGIN Middle English: from Old French *fagot*, from Italian *fagotto*, from Greek *phakelos* 'bundle'.

fag hag ■ n. N. Amer. informal, derogatory a heterosexual woman who spends much of her time with homosexual men.

fah (also **fa**) ■ n. Music (in tonic sol-fa) the fourth note of a major scale. ▶ the note F in the fixed-doh system.
– ORIGIN Middle English: representing (as an arbitrary name for the note) the first syllable of *famuli*, taken from a Latin hymn.

fah-fee /ˈfɑːfiː/ ■ n. S. African an illegal gambling game resembling a lottery with thirty-six numbers, the winning number being selected in advance of betting.
– ORIGIN 1900s: perhaps from Chinese.

Fahr. ■ abbrev. Fahrenheit.

Fahrenheit /ˈfar(ə)nhʌɪt, ˈfɑː-/ (abbrev.: **F**) ■ adj. [postpos. when used with a numeral] of or denoting a scale of temperature on which water freezes at 32° and boils at 212°. ■ n. (also **Fahrenheit scale**) this scale of temperature.
– ORIGIN C18: named after the German physicist Gabriel Daniel *Fahrenheit*.

faience /fʌɪˈɒ̃s, fɛɪ-, -ˈɑːns/ ■ n. glazed ceramic ware, in particular decorated tin-glazed earthenware of the type which includes delftware.
– ORIGIN C17 (orig. denoting pottery made at Faenza): from French *faïence*, from *Faïence*, the French name for *Faenza*, a city in Italy.

fail ■ v. **1** be unsuccessful in an undertaking. ▶ be unable to meet the standards set by (a test). ▶ judge (a candidate in an examination or test) not to have passed. **2** neglect to do something. ▶ disappoint expectations: *commuter chaos has failed to materialize.* **3** stop working properly. ▶ become weaker or less good. ▶ go out of business. **4** desert or let down: *her nerve failed her.* ■ n. a mark which is not high enough to pass an examination or test.
– PHRASES **without fail** whatever happens.
– ORIGIN Middle English: from Old French *faillir* (v.), from Latin *fallere* 'deceive'.

failing ■ n. a weakness, especially in someone's character. ■ prep. if not.

faille /feɪl/ ■ n. a soft, light-woven fabric with a ribbed texture.
– ORIGIN C16 (denoting a kind of hood or veil worn by women): from Old French.

fail-safe ■ adj. **1** causing a piece of machinery to revert to a safe condition in the event of a breakdown. **2** unlikely or unable to fail.

failure ■ n. **1** lack of success. ▶ an unsuccessful person or thing. **2** the omission of expected or required action. **3** the action or state of not functioning. ▶ a sudden cessation of power. ▶ the collapse of a business.

fain archaic ■ adj. pleased or willing under the circumstances. ■ adv. gladly.
– ORIGIN Old English *fægen* 'happy', of Germanic origin.

faint ■ adj. **1** (of a sight, smell, or sound) barely perceptible. ▶ (of a hope, chance, or idea) slight. **2** close to losing consciousness. ■ v. briefly lose consciousness because of a temporarily insufficient supply of oxygen to the brain. ■ n. a sudden loss of consciousness.
– DERIVATIVES **faintly** adv. **faintness** n.
– ORIGIN Middle English: from Old French *feint*, from *feindre* (see FEIGN).

faint heart ■ n. a person who has a timid or reserved nature.
– DERIVATIVES **faint-hearted** adj. **faint-heartedly** adv. **faint-heartedness** n.

fair[1] ■ adj. **1** treating people equally. ▶ just or appropriate in the circumstances. **2** (of hair or complexion) light; blonde. **3** considerable in size or amount. ▶ moderately good. **4** (of weather) fine and dry. **5** archaic beautiful. ■ adv. in a fair manner.
– PHRASES **fair and square 1** with absolute accuracy. **2** honestly and straightforwardly. **fair dinkum** see DINKUM. **fair dos** Brit. informal a request for just treatment or an acceptance that it has been given. **fair enough** informal that is reasonable or acceptable. **the fair sex** (also **the fairer sex**) dated or humorous women. **fair's fair** informal a request for just treatment or an assertion that an arrangement is just. **it's a fair cop** informal an admission that the speaker has been caught doing wrong and deserves punishment.
– DERIVATIVES **fairish** adj. **fairness** n.
– ORIGIN Old English *fæger* 'pleasing, attractive', of Germanic origin.

fair[2] ■ n. **1** a gathering of stalls and amusements for public entertainment. **2** a periodic gathering for the sale of goods. ▶ an exhibition, especially to promote particular products.
– ORIGIN Middle English: from late Latin *feria*, sing. of Latin *feriae* 'holy days' (on which such fairs were often held).

fair[3] ■ v. [usu. as adj. **faired**] streamline (a vehicle, boat, or aircraft) by adding fairings.
– ORIGIN Old English in the senses 'beautify' and 'appear or become clean'.

fair copy ■ n. written or printed matter transcribed or reproduced after final correction.

fair game ■ n. a person or thing that is considered a reasonable target for criticism or exploitation.

fairground ■ n. an outdoor area where a fair is held.

fair-haired ■ adj. N. Amer. favourite; cherished.

fairing ■ n. an external metal or plastic structure added to increase streamlining on a high-performance vehicle, boat, or aircraft.

Fair Isle ■ n. a traditional multicoloured geometric design used in woollen knitwear.
– ORIGIN *Fair Isle* in the Shetland Islands, north of Scotland where the design was first devised.

fairly ■ adv. **1** with justice. **2** moderately. **3** actually; positively: *he fairly snarled at her.*
– PHRASES **fairly and squarely** another term for fair and square (see FAIR[1]).

fair-minded ■ adj. impartial; just.
– DERIVATIVES **fair-mindedly** adv. **fair-mindedness** n.

fair play ■ n. respect for the rules or equal treatment of all concerned.

fair trade ■ n. trade in which fair prices are paid to producers in developing countries.

fairway ■ n. 1 the part of a golf course between a tee and the corresponding green, where the grass is kept short. 2 a navigable channel in a river or harbour. ▸ a regular course followed by ships.

fair-weather friend ■ n. a person who stops being a friend in times of difficulty.

fairy ■ n. (pl. **-ies**) 1 a small imaginary being of human form that has magical powers. 2 informal, derogatory a male homosexual.
– DERIVATIVES **fairylike** adj.
– ORIGIN Middle English (denoting fairyland): from Old French *faerie*, from *fae* 'a fairy', from Latin *fata* 'the Fates', pl. of *fatum* (see **FATE**).

fairy cake ■ n. chiefly Brit. a small individual sponge cake, usually with icing.

fairy godmother ■ n. a female character in some fairy stories who brings unexpected good fortune to the hero or heroine.

fairyland ■ n. the imaginary home of fairies.

fairy lights ▸ pl. n. small coloured electric lights used for decoration, especially on a Christmas tree.

fairy ring ■ n. a ring of grass that is darker in colour than the surrounding grass due to the growth of certain fungi, popularly believed to have been caused by fairies dancing.

fairy shrimp ■ n. a small transparent crustacean which typically swims on its back, using its legs to filter food particles from the water. [Order Anostraca: many species.]

fairy story ■ n. a children's tale about magical and imaginary beings and lands. ▸ an untrue account.

fairy tale ■ n. a fairy story. ▸ [as modifier] denoting something regarded as resembling a fairy story in being magical or idealized: *a fairy-tale romance*.

fait accompli /ˌfeɪt əˈkɒmpliː/ ■ n. a thing that has been done or decided, leaving those affected with no option but to accept.
– ORIGIN C19: from French, 'accomplished fact'.

faith ■ n. 1 complete trust or confidence. 2 strong belief in a religion, based on spiritual apprehension rather than proof. 3 a system of religious belief.
– ORIGIN Middle English: from Old French *feid*, from Latin *fides*.

faithful ■ adj. 1 remaining loyal and steadfast. ▸ remaining sexually loyal to a lover or spouse. 2 true to the facts or the original. ■ n. (**the faithful**) the believers in a particular religion, especially Islam.
– DERIVATIVES **faithfulness** n.

faithfully ■ adv. in a faithful manner.
– PHRASES **yours faithfully** a formula for ending a formal letter in which the recipient is not addressed by name.

faith healing ■ n. healing achieved by religious faith and prayer, rather than by medical treatment.
– DERIVATIVES **faith healer** n.

faithless ■ adj. 1 disloyal, especially to a spouse or lover. 2 without religious faith.
– DERIVATIVES **faithlessly** adv. **faithlessness** n.

fajitas /fəˈhiːtəz, fəˈdʒiːtəz/ ▸ pl. n. a dish of Mexican origin consisting of strips of spiced meat, chopped vegetables, and grated cheese, wrapped in a soft tortilla.
– ORIGIN Mexican Spanish, 'little strips'.

fake ■ adj. not genuine. ■ n. a person or thing that is not genuine. ■ v. forge or counterfeit. ▸ pretend to feel or suffer from (an emotion or illness).
– DERIVATIVES **faker** n.
– ORIGIN C18: origin uncertain, perhaps ultimately rel. to German *fegen* 'sweep, thrash'.

fakir /ˈfeɪkɪə, ˈfɑː-/ ■ n. a Muslim (or, loosely, a Hindu) religious ascetic who lives solely on alms.
– ORIGIN C17: from Arabic *faḳīr* 'needy man'.

falafel /fəˈlæf(ə)l, -ˈlɑː-/ (also **felafel**) ■ n. a Middle Eastern dish of spiced mashed chickpeas formed into balls and deep-fried.
– ORIGIN from colloquial Egyptian Arabic *falāfil*, pl. of Arabic *filfil* 'pepper'.

Falasha /fəˈlɑːʃə/ ■ n. (pl. same or **Falashas**) a member of a group of people in Ethiopia who hold the Jewish faith.
– ORIGIN Amharic, 'exile, immigrant'.

falcate /ˈfalkeɪt/ ■ adj. Biology curved like a sickle; hooked.
– ORIGIN C19: from Latin *falcatus*, from *falx* 'sickle'.

falchion /ˈfɔːl(t)ʃ(ə)n/ ■ n. historical a broad, slightly curved sword with the cutting edge on the convex side.
– ORIGIN Middle English *fauchon*, from Latin *falx, falc-* 'sickle'.

falciparum /falˈsɪpərəm/ (also **falciparum malaria**) ■ n. the most severe form of malaria, caused by *Plasmodium falciparum*.
– ORIGIN 1930s: modern Latin, from Latin *falx, falc-* 'sickle' + *-parum* 'bearing'.

falcon /ˈfɔː(l)k(ə)n, ˈfɒlk(ə)n/ ■ n. a fast-flying bird of prey with long pointed wings. [Genus *Falco*: many species.] ▸ Falconry the female of such a bird, especially a peregrine. Compare with **TIERCEL**.
– ORIGIN Middle English *faucon*: from late Latin *falco*, from Latin *falx* 'scythe', or of Germanic origin.

falconer ■ n. a person who keeps, trains, or hunts with falcons or other birds of prey.

falconry ■ n. the keeping and training of falcons or other birds of prey; the sport of hunting with such birds.

fall ■ v. (past **fell**; past part. **fallen**) 1 move from a higher to a lower level, typically rapidly and without control. ▸ (**fall off**) become detached and drop to the ground. ▸ hang down. ▸ slope downwards. ▸ (of someone's face) show dismay or disappointment by appearing to droop. 2 lose one's balance and collapse. ▸ be captured or defeated. ▸ archaic yield to temptation. 3 decrease in number, amount, intensity, or quality. 4 pass into a specified state. ▸ (**fall to doing something**) begin to do something. ▸ (usu. **fall on**) occur. ▸ be classified in the way specified: *Tulbagh falls within the winter rainfall area*. ■ n. 1 an act of falling. ▸ Wrestling a move which pins the opponent's shoulders on the ground for a count of three. ▸ a downward difference in height between parts of a surface. ▸ a sudden onset or arrival. 2 a thing which falls or has fallen. ▸ a waterfall or cascade. 3 a decline. 4 a defeat or downfall. ▸ (**the Fall of Man**) the lapse of humankind into a state of sin, ascribed in Jewish and Christian theology to the disobedience of Adam and Eve. 5 N. Amer. autumn.
– PHRASES **fall foul** (or rarely N. Amer. **afoul**) **of** come into conflict with. **fall in** (or **into**) **line** conform. [with ref. to military formation.] **fall into place** begin to make sense. **fall over oneself to do something** informal be excessively eager to do something. **fall short** (**of**) 1 (of a missile) fail to reach its target. 2 be deficient or inadequate. **take the fall** N. Amer. informal receive blame or punishment, typically in the place of another.
– PHRASAL VERBS **fall about** informal laugh uncontrollably. **fall apart** (or **to pieces**) informal lose one's capacity to cope. **fall away** S. African cease to apply; be waived or removed. **fall back** retreat. **fall back on** have recourse to when in difficulty. **fall down** fail. **fall for** informal 1 fall in love with. 2 be deceived by. **fall in** take one's place in a military formation. **fall in with** 1 meet by chance and become involved with. 2 agree to. **fall on** (or **upon**) 1 attack fiercely or unexpectedly. 2 (of someone's eyes or gaze) be directed towards. 3 (of a burden or duty) be borne or incurred by. **fall out** 1 have an argument. 2 leave one's place in a military formation. 3 happen. **fall through** fail. **fall to** become the duty of. ▸ (of property) revert to the ownership of.
– ORIGIN Old English *fallan, feallan*, of Germanic origin; the noun is partly from Old Norse *fall* 'downfall, sin'.

fallacy /ˈfaləsi/ ■ n. (pl. **-ies**) 1 a mistaken belief. 2 Logic a failure in reasoning which renders an argument invalid.
– DERIVATIVES **fallacious** adj. **fallaciously** adv. **fallaciousness** /fəˈleɪʃəsnɪs/ n.
– ORIGIN C15: from Latin *fallacia*, from *fallax* 'deceiving'.

fallback ■ n. 1 an alternative plan for use in an emergency. 2 a reduction.

fallen past participle of **FALL**. ■ adj. 1 dated (of a woman) regarded as having lost her honour through engaging in an extramarital sexual relationship. 2 killed in battle.
– DERIVATIVES **fallenness** n.

fallen angel

fallen angel ■ n. (in Christian, Jewish, and Muslim tradition) an angel who rebelled against God and was cast out of heaven.

faller ■ n. chiefly Brit. a person or thing that falls, especially a horse that falls during a race.

fall guy ■ n. informal a scapegoat.

fallible /ˈfalɪb(ə)l/ ■ adj. capable of making mistakes or being erroneous.
–DERIVATIVES **fallibility** n.
–ORIGIN Middle English: from medieval Latin *fallibilis*, from Latin *fallere* 'deceive'.

falling-out ■ n. a quarrel.

falling star ■ n. a meteor or shooting star.

fall line ■ n. **1** (**the fall line**) Skiing the route leading straight down any particular part of a slope. **2** a narrow zone marking the geological boundary between an upland region and a plain, distinguished by the occurrence of falls where rivers cross it.

fall-off ■ n. a decrease.

Fallopian tube /fəˈləʊpɪən/ ■ n. Anatomy (in a female mammal) either of a pair of tubes along which eggs travel from the ovaries to the uterus.
–ORIGIN C18: from *Fallopius*, Latinized form of the name of Gabriello *Fallopio*, the Italian anatomist who first described them.

fallout ■ n. **1** radioactive particles carried into the atmosphere by a nuclear explosion and gradually falling to the ground over a wide area. **2** the adverse results of a situation.

fallow[1] ■ adj. **1** (of farmland) ploughed and harrowed but left for a period without being sown. **2** inactive: *a fallow period*. **3** (of a sow) not pregnant. ■ n. a piece of fallow land.
–ORIGIN Old English *fealgian* 'to break up land for sowing', of Germanic origin.

fallow[2] ■ n. a pale brown or reddish yellow colour.
–ORIGIN Old English, of Germanic origin.

fallow deer ■ n. a deer with branched palmate antlers, typically having a white-spotted reddish-brown coat in summer. [*Cervus dama*.]

false ■ adj. **1** not according with truth or fact. ▸ invalid or illegal: *false imprisonment*. **2** deliberately intended to deceive. ▸ artificial. **3** illusory. ▸ used in names of plants, animals, and gems that superficially resemble the thing properly so called, e.g. false scorpion. **4** disloyal.
–PHRASES **play someone false** deceive or cheat someone.
–DERIVATIVES **falsely** adv. **falseness** n. **falsity** n.
–ORIGIN Old English *fals* 'fraud', from Latin *falsum*, from *fallere* 'deceive'; reinforced or re-formed in Middle English from Old French *fals*, *faus* 'false'.

false alarm ■ n. a warning given about something that fails to happen.

false card ■ n. Bridge a card played to give one's opponents a misleading impression of one's strength in the suit led.

false colour ■ n. colour added during the processing of a photographic or computer image to aid interpretation of the subject.

false economy ■ n. an apparent financial saving that in fact leads to greater expenditure.

false friend ■ n. a word or expression having a similar form to one in a person's native language, but a different meaning (e.g. English *magazine* and French *magasin* 'shop').

falsehood ■ n. the state of being untrue. ▸ a lie.

false memory ■ n. Psychology an apparent recollection of an event which did not actually occur, especially one of childhood sexual abuse arising from suggestion during psychoanalysis.

false move ■ n. an unwise action with potentially dangerous consequences.

false pretences ■ pl. n. behaviour intended to deceive.

false rib ■ n. another term for **FLOATING RIB**.

false scorpion ■ n. a minute arachnid with pincers but no long abdomen or sting. [Order Pseudoscorpiones.]

false start ■ n. an invalid start to a race.

false step ■ n. a slip or stumble. ▸ a mistake.

falsetto /fɔːlˈsɛtəʊ, fɒl-/ ■ n. (pl. **-os**) Music a method of voice production used by male singers, especially tenors, to sing notes higher than their normal range.
–ORIGIN C18: from Italian, diminutive of *falso* 'false'.

falsify /ˈfɔːlsɪfʌɪ, ˈfɒls-/ ■ v. (**-ies**, **-ied**) **1** alter (information or evidence) so as to mislead. **2** prove (a statement or theory) to be false.
–DERIVATIVES **falsifiable** adj. **falsification** n.
–ORIGIN Middle English: from medieval Latin *falsificare*, from Latin *falsificus* 'making false', from *falsus* 'false'.

Falstaffian /fɔːlˈstɑːfɪən, fɒl-/ ■ adj. of or resembling Shakespeare's character Sir John Falstaff in being fat, jolly, and debauched.

falter /ˈfɔːltə, ˈfɒl-/ ■ v. lose strength or momentum.
▸ move or speak hesitantly.
–DERIVATIVES **faltering** adj. **falteringly** adv.
–ORIGIN Middle English: perhaps from **FOLD**[1] (which was occasionally used of the faltering of the legs or tongue) + *-ter* as in *totter*.

fame ■ n. the state of being famous.
–ORIGIN Middle English: from Latin *fama*.

famed ■ adj. famous; well known.
–ORIGIN Middle English: from archaic *fame* (v.), from Latin *fama*.

familiar ■ adj. **1** well known. ▸ common; usual. **2** (**familiar with**) having a good knowledge of. **3** in close friendship. ▸ inappropriately intimate or informal. ■ n. **1** (also **familiar spirit**) a demon supposedly attending and obeying a witch. **2** (in the Roman Catholic Church) a person rendering certain services in a pope's or bishop's household. **3** a close friend or associate.
–DERIVATIVES **familiarity** n. (pl. **-ies**). **familiarly** adv.
–ORIGIN Middle English: from Latin *familiaris*, from *familia* 'household servants, family'.

familiarize (also **-ise**) ■ v. (usu. **familiarize someone with**) make (someone) familiar with something.
–DERIVATIVES **familiarization** (also **-isation**) n.

family ■ n. (pl. **-ies**) **1** [treated as sing. or pl.] a group consisting of two parents and their children living together as a unit. ▸ a group of people related by blood or marriage. ▸ the children of a person or couple. **2** all the descendants of a common ancestor. ▸ all the languages ultimately derived from a particular early language, regarded as a group. **3** a group united by a significant shared characteristic. ▸ Biology a principal taxonomic category ranking above genus and below order. ■ adj. designed to be suitable for children as well as adults.
–PHRASES **in the family way** informal pregnant.
–DERIVATIVES **familial** /fəˈmɪlɪəl/ adj.
–ORIGIN Middle English: from Latin *familia* 'household servants, family', from *famulus* 'servant'.

Family Day ■ n. S. African a public holiday on the first Monday after Easter.

family name ■ n. a surname.

family planning ■ n. the practice of controlling the number of children in a family and the intervals between their births, particularly by means of contraception.

family tree ■ n. a diagram showing the relationship between people in several generations of a family.

family values ■ pl. n. values supposedly characteristic of a traditional family unit, typically those of high moral standards and discipline.

famine /ˈfamɪn/ ■ n. extreme scarcity of food. ▸ a shortage.
–ORIGIN Middle English: from Old French, from *faim* 'hunger', from Latin *fames*.

famished /ˈfamɪʃd/ ■ adj. informal extremely hungry.

famous ■ adj. **1** known about by many people. **2** informal magnificent.
–DERIVATIVES **famously** adv.
–ORIGIN Middle English: from Latin *famosus* 'famed', from *fama* (see **FAME**).

famulus /ˈfamjʊləs/ ■ n. (pl. **famuli** /-lʌɪ, -liː/) historical an assistant or servant, especially one working for a magician or scholar.
–ORIGIN C19: from Latin, 'servant'.

fan¹ ■ n. **1** an apparatus with rotating blades that creates a current of air for cooling or ventilation. **2** a hand-held device, typically folding and shaped like a segment of a circle when spread out, that is waved so as to cool the user. **3** a fan-shaped alluvial or talus deposit at the foot of a slope. ■ v. (**fanned**, **fanning**) **1** cool by waving something to create a current of air. ▸ drive away with a waving movement. **2** (of an air current) increase the strength of (a fire). ▸ cause (a belief or emotion) to become stronger. **3** (**fan out**) spread out from a central point to cover a wide area.
– DERIVATIVES **fan-like** adj.
– ORIGIN Old English *fann* (as a noun denoting a device for winnowing grain), *fannian* (v.), from Latin *vannus* 'winnowing fan'.

fan² ■ n. a person who has a strong interest in or admiration for a particular sport, art form, or famous person.
– DERIVATIVES **fandom** n.
– ORIGIN C19 (orig. US): abbrev. of FANATIC.

Fanagalo /ˌfanagaˈlɪɒ, ˈfanagalɒ/ (also **Fanakalo**) ■ n. S. African a language with elements taken from the Nguni languages, English, and Afrikaans, used as a lingua franca, especially in the mines.
– ORIGIN 1940s: from Nguni *fana ka lo*, from *fana* 'be like' + the possessive suffix *-ka* + *lo* 'this'.

fanatic /fəˈnatɪk/ ■ n. a person filled with excessive zeal, especially for an extreme religious or political cause. ▸ informal a person with an obsessive enthusiasm for a pastime or hobby. ■ adj. filled with or expressing excessive zeal.
– DERIVATIVES **fanatical** adj. **fanatically** adv. **fanaticism** n.

> **HISTORY**
> The word **fanatic** derives from Latin *fanaticus*, meaning 'of a temple' or 'inspired by a god', from *fanum* 'temple'. It was first used in the 16th century, as an adjective describing behaviour or speech that might result from possession by a god or demon; hence the earliest sense of the noun 'a religious maniac'. Another English word deriving ultimately from *fanum* is **profane**, which comes from Latin *profanus*, meaning 'outside the temple'.

fan belt ■ n. (in a motor-vehicle engine) a belt that transmits motion from the driveshaft to the radiator fan and the dynamo or alternator.

fanboy ■ n. informal a male fan, especially one who is obsessive about comics, music, film, or science fiction.

fancier ■ n. a person who has a special interest in or breeds a particular animal.

fanciful ■ adj. **1** over-imaginative and unrealistic. ▸ existing only in the imagination. **2** highly ornamental or imaginative in design.
– DERIVATIVES **fancifully** adv. **fancifulness** n.

fan club ■ n. an organized group of fans of a famous person or team.

fancy ■ v. (**-ies, -ied**) **1** informal, chiefly Brit. feel a desire for. ▸ find sexually attractive. **2** regard as a likely winner. **3** imagine. ▸ used to express surprise: *fancy that!* ■ adj. (**-ier, -iest**) elaborate or highly decorated. ▸ chiefly N. Amer. (especially of foodstuffs) of high quality. ▸ (of an animal) bred to develop particular points of appearance. ■ n. (pl. **-ies**) **1** a superficial or transient feeling of liking or attraction. **2** the faculty of imagination. ▸ an unfounded or tentative belief or idea. **3** (also **fancy cake**) a small iced cake or biscuit.
– PHRASES **take** (or **catch**) **someone's fancy** appeal to someone. **take a fancy to** become fond of, especially without an obvious reason.
– DERIVATIVES **fanciable** adj. (informal). **fanciness** n.
– ORIGIN Middle English: contraction of FANTASY.

fancy dress ■ n. a costume worn to make someone look like a famous person, fictional character, or an animal.

fancy-free ■ adj. without emotional commitments.

fancy goods ■ pl. n. items for sale that are purely or chiefly ornamental.

fancy man ■ n. informal, often derogatory a woman's lover.

fancy woman ■ n. informal, often derogatory a married man's mistress.

fancy-work ■ n. ornamental needlework, crochet, or knitting.

fan dance ■ n. a dance in which the female performer is apparently nude and remains partly concealed throughout by large fans.

fandango /fanˈdaŋɡəʊ/ ■ n. (pl. **-oes** or **-os**) **1** a lively Spanish dance for two people, typically accompanied by castanets or tambourine. **2** foolish nonsense. ▸ a useless or purely ornamental thing.
– ORIGIN C18: Spanish.

fanfare ■ n. **1** a short ceremonial tune or flourish played on brass instruments, especially to introduce something. **2** an elaborate welcome or introduction.
– ORIGIN C18: from French, of imitative origin.

Fang /faŋ/ ■ n. (pl. same or **Fangs**) **1** a member of a people inhabiting parts of Cameroon, Equatorial Guinea, and Gabon. **2** the Bantu language of this people.
– ORIGIN French: prob. from Fang *Pangwe*.

fang ■ n. a large sharp tooth, especially a canine tooth of a dog or wolf. ▸ a tooth with which a snake injects poison. ▸ the biting mouthpart of a spider.
– DERIVATIVES **fanged** adj. **fangless** adj.
– ORIGIN Old English (denoting booty or spoils): from Old Norse *fang* 'capture, grasp'.

fanlight ■ n. a small window, typically semicircular, over a door or another window. ▸ another term for SKYLIGHT.

fanny ■ n. (pl. **-ies**) **1** vulgar slang a woman's genitals. **2** informal, chiefly N. Amer. a person's buttocks. ■ v. (**fanny about/around**) Brit. informal mess around and waste time.
– ORIGIN C19.

Fanny Adams (also **sweet Fanny Adams**) ■ n. Brit. informal nothing at all.
– ORIGIN C19: orig. a nautical term for tinned meat or stew (darkly humorous ref. to the name of a murder victim c.1870), now often understood as a euphemism for *fuck all*.

fanny pack ■ n. North American term for MOONBAG.

fan palm ■ n. a palm with large lobed fan-shaped leaves. [*Chamaerops* and other genera: many species.]

fantabulous /fanˈtabjʊləs/ ■ adj. informal excellent; wonderful.
– ORIGIN 1950s: blend of FANTASTIC and FABULOUS.

fantail ■ n. **1** a fan-shaped tail or end. **2** chiefly N. Amer. the overhanging part of the stern of a warship. **3** a domestic pigeon of a broad-tailed variety. **4** (also **fantail flycatcher**) a SE Asian and Australasian flycatcher with a long tapering tail, often fanned out. [Genus *Rhipidura*: numerous species.]
– DERIVATIVES **fan-tailed** adj.

fan-tan /ˈfantan/ ■ n. **1** a Chinese gambling game in which players try to guess the remainder after the banker has divided a number of hidden objects into four groups. **2** a card game in which players build on sequences of sevens.
– ORIGIN C19: from Chinese *fān tān* 'repeated divisions'.

fantasia /fanˈteɪzɪə, ˌfantəˈziːə/ ■ n. a musical or other composition with a free form and often an improvisatory style.
– ORIGIN C18: from Italian, 'fantasy'.

fantasize (also **-ise**) ■ v. indulge in daydreaming or speculation about something desired.
– DERIVATIVES **fantasist** n.

fantastic ■ adj. **1** imaginative or fanciful; remote from reality. **2** informal extraordinarily good or attractive.
– DERIVATIVES **fantastical** adj. **fantastically** adv.
– ORIGIN Middle English: from Greek *phantastikos*, from *phantazein* 'make visible', *phantazesthai* 'have visions', from *phantos* 'visible'.

fantasy ■ n. (pl. **-ies**) **1** the faculty or activity of imagining improbable or impossible things. ▸ a fanciful mental image, especially one on which a person often dwells and which reflects their wishes. ▸ an idea with no basis in reality. **2** a genre of imaginative fiction involving magic and adventure. **3** a fantasia.
– ORIGIN Middle English: from Latin *phantasia*, from Greek, 'imagination, appearance', later 'phantom', from *phantazein* (see FANTASTIC).

Fante

Fante /'fanti/ (also **Fanti**) ■ n. (pl. same or **Fantis**) **1** a member of a people of southern Ghana. **2** the dialect of Akan spoken by this people.
– ORIGIN the name in Akan.

fan worm ■ n. a tube-dwelling marine bristle worm which bears a fan-like crown of filaments for filtering the water for food. [Families Sabellidae and Serpulidae: many species.]

fanzine /'fanzi:n/ ■ n. a magazine for fans of a particular team, performer, or genre.
– ORIGIN 1940s: blend of FAN² and MAGAZINE.

FAO ■ abbrev. Food and Agriculture Organization.

FAQ ■ abbrev. Computing frequently asked questions.

far ■ adv. (**further**, **furthest** or **farther**, **farthest**) **1** at, to, or by a great distance. **2** a long way in space or time. **3** by a great deal. ■ adj. **1** situated at a great distance in space or time. ▸ more distant than another object of the same kind. **2** distant from the centre; extreme.
– PHRASES **as far as 1** for as great a distance as. **2** to the extent that. **be a far cry from** be very different to. **by far** by a great amount. **far and away** by a very large amount. **far and wide** over a large area. **far be it from** (or **for**) **me to** used to express reluctance. **far from** very different from being; tending to the opposite of. **far gone 1** in a bad or worsening state. **2** advanced in time. **go far 1** achieve a great deal. **2** be worth or amount to much. **go so far as to do something** do something regarded as extreme. **go too far** exceed the limits of what is reasonable or acceptable. **so far 1** to a certain limited extent. **2** up to this time. (**in**) **so far as** (or **that**) to the extent that.
– ORIGIN Old English, of Germanic origin.

farad /'farad/ (abbrev.: **F**) ■ n. the SI unit of electrical capacitance, equal to a capacitance in which one coulomb of charge causes a potential difference of one volt.
– ORIGIN C19: shortening of FARADAY.

faradaic /,farə'deɪɪk/ ■ adj. produced by or associated with electrical induction.

faraday /'farədeɪ/ (abbrev.: **F**) ■ n. Chemistry a unit of electric charge equal to Faraday's constant.
– ORIGIN C20: from the name of the C19 English physicist Michael *Faraday*.

Faraday's constant ■ n. Chemistry the quantity of electric charge carried by one mole of electrons (equal to roughly 96 490 coulombs).

faraway ■ adj. **1** distant in space or time. **2** seeming remote; dreamy: *a strange faraway look*.

farce ■ n. **1** a comic dramatic work or genre using buffoonery and horseplay and typically including ludicrously improbable situations. **2** an absurd event: *the debate turned into a drunken farce*.
– ORIGIN C16: from French, 'stuffing' (used metaphorically for comic interludes 'stuffed' into religious plays), from *farcir* 'to stuff'.

farceur /fɑː'sə:/ ■ n. a writer of or performer in farces. ▸ a joker or comedian.
– ORIGIN C17: French.

farcical ■ adj. resembling farce; absurd or ridiculous.
– DERIVATIVES **farcicality** n. **farcically** adv.

fare ■ n. **1** the money a passenger on public transport has to pay. **2** a range of food: *traditional Scottish fare*. ■ v. **1** perform in a specified way in a particular situation or period: *the party fared badly in the elections*. **2** archaic travel.
– ORIGIN Old English *fær*, *faru* 'travelling, a journey', *faran* 'to travel', also 'get on (well or badly)', of Germanic origin.

Far East ■ n. China, Japan, and other countries of east Asia.
– DERIVATIVES **Far Eastern** adj.

farewell ■ exclam. used to express good wishes on parting. ■ n. an act of parting or of marking someone's departure.
– ORIGIN Middle English: from FARE + the adv. WELL¹.

farfalle /fɑː'faleɪ, -li/ ■ pl. n. small pieces of pasta shaped like bows or butterflies' wings.
– ORIGIN Italian, pl. of *farfalla* 'butterfly'.

far-fetched ■ adj. unconvincing; implausible.

far-flung ■ adj. distant or remote. ▸ widely distributed.

farina /fə'rʌɪnə, fə'ri:nə/ ■ n. flour or meal made of cereal grains, nuts, or starchy roots.
– ORIGIN Middle English: from Latin, from *far* 'corn'.

farm ■ n. an area of land and its buildings used for growing crops and rearing animals. ▸ a farmhouse. ▸ an establishment for breeding or growing something, or devoted to a particular thing: *a fish farm* | *a wind farm*. ■ v. **1** make one's living by growing crops or keeping livestock. ▸ use (land) for this purpose. ▸ (S. African also **farm with**) breed or grow (a specified type of livestock or crop) commercially. **2** (**farm someone/thing out**) send out or subcontract work to others. ▸ arrange for a child to be looked after by someone.
– DERIVATIVES **farmable** adj. **farming** n.
– ORIGIN Middle English (orig. denoting a fixed annual amount payable as rent or tax): from Old French *ferme*, from medieval Latin *firma* 'fixed payment', from Latin *firmare* 'fix, settle'.

farmer ■ n. a person who owns or manages a farm.

farmhand ■ n. a worker on a farm.

farmhouse ■ n. a house attached to a farm, especially the main house in which the farmer lives.

farm school ■ n. S. African a school providing education for children in a rural community, usually at primary level.

farm stall ■ n. chiefly S. African a rural roadside stall that sells farm produce and crafts.

farmstead ■ n. a farm and its buildings.

farmyard ■ n. a yard or enclosure attached to a farmhouse. ■ adj. (of manners or language) coarse.

faro /'fɛːrəʊ/ ■ n. a gambling card game in which players bet on the order in which the cards will appear.
– ORIGIN C18: from French *pharaon* 'pharaoh', said to have been the name of the king of hearts.

far-off ■ adj. remote in time or space.

far out ■ adj. **1** unconventional or avant-garde. **2** informal, dated excellent.

farrago /fə'rɑːgəʊ, fə'reɪgəʊ/ ■ n. (pl. **-os** or US **-oes**) a confused mixture.
– ORIGIN C17: from Latin, 'mixed fodder', from *far* 'corn'.

far-reaching ■ adj. having important and extensive effects or implications.

farrier /'farɪə/ ■ n. a smith who shoes horses.
– DERIVATIVES **farriery** n.
– ORIGIN C16: from Old French *ferrier*, from Latin *ferrarius*, from *ferrum* 'iron, horseshoe'.

farrow ■ n. a litter of pigs. ■ v. (of a sow) give birth to (piglets).
– ORIGIN Old English *fearh*, *færh* 'young pig', of West Germanic origin.

far-seeing ■ adj. having shrewd judgement and foresight.

Farsi /'fɑːsɪ/ ■ n. the modern form of the Persian language, spoken in Iran.
– ORIGIN from Arabic *fārsī*, from *Fārs*, from Persian *Pārs* 'Persia'.

far sight ■ n. the abnormal inability to see things clearly if they are relatively close to the eyes.

far-sighted ■ adj. **1** far-seeing. **2** having far sight.
– DERIVATIVES **far-sightedly** adv. **far-sightedness** n.

fart informal ■ v. **1** emit wind from the anus. **2** (**fart about/around**) waste time on silly or trivial things. ■ n. **1** an emission of wind from the anus. **2** a boring or contemptible person: *an old fart*.
– ORIGIN Old English, of Germanic origin.

farther ■ adv. & adj. variant form of FURTHER.

farthermost ■ adj. variant form of FURTHERMOST.

farthest ■ adj. & adv. variant form of FURTHEST.

farthing ■ n. **1** a former monetary unit and coin of the UK, equal to a quarter of an old penny. **2** [usu. with neg.] the least possible amount.
– ORIGIN Old English *fēorthing*, from *fēortha* 'fourth', perhaps on the pattern of Old Norse *fjórthungr* 'quarter'.

fartlek /'fɑːtlɛk/ ■ n. a system of training for distance runners in which the terrain and pace are continually varied.
– ORIGIN 1940s: from Swedish, from *fart* 'speed' + *lek* 'play'.

FAS ■ abbrev. fetal alcohol syndrome.

fascia /ˈfeɪʃɪə, -ʃə/ (also **facia** except in sense 4) ■ n. **1** a board covering the ends of rafters or other fittings. **2** a signboard on a shopfront. **3** chiefly Brit. the dashboard of a motor vehicle. **4** /ˈfaʃə/ (pl. **fasciae** /-ʃiː/) Anatomy a thin sheath of fibrous tissue enclosing a muscle or other organ.
– ORIGIN C16: from Latin, 'band, door frame'.

fasciated /ˈfaʃɪeɪtɪd, -ɪətɪd/ ■ adj. Botany showing abnormal fusion of parts, resulting in a flattened ribbon-like structure.
– DERIVATIVES **fasciation** n.
– ORIGIN C18 ('striped, banded'): from Latin *fasciare* 'swathe'.

fascicle /ˈfasɪk(ə)l/ ■ n. **1** (also **fascicule** /-kjuːl/) a separately published instalment of a book. **2** Anatomy & Biology a bundle of structures, such as nerves or muscle fibres.
– DERIVATIVES **fascicular** adj. **fasciculate** /-ˈsɪkjʊlət/ adj.
– ORIGIN C15: from Latin *fasciculus*, diminutive of *fascis* 'bundle'.

fasciculation /faˌsɪkjʊˈleɪʃ(ə)n/ ■ n. **1** Medicine a brief spontaneous contraction affecting a small number of muscle fibres. **2** chiefly Biology arrangement in bundles.

fasciitis /ˌfasɪˈʌɪtɪs, ˌfaʃɪ-/ ■ n. Medicine inflammation of the fascia of a muscle or organ.

fascinate ■ v. irresistibly attract the interest of.
– DERIVATIVES **fascinating** adj. **fascinatingly** adv. **fascination** n.
– ORIGIN C16: from Latin *fascinare* 'bewitch', from *fascinum* 'spell, witchcraft'.

fascism /ˈfaʃɪz(ə)m, -sɪz(ə)m/ ■ n. an authoritarian and nationalist right-wing system of government.
– DERIVATIVES **fascist** n. & adj. **fascistic** adj.
– ORIGIN 1920s (with ref. to Mussolini's regime in Italy): from Italian *fascismo*, from *fascio* 'bundle, political group', from Latin *fascis* 'bundle'.

fashion ■ n. **1** a popular trend, especially in dress or manners of behaviour. ▸ the production and marketing of new styles of clothing and cosmetics. **2** a manner of doing something. ■ v. make into a particular form or article.
– PHRASES **after a fashion** to a certain extent but not perfectly. **after** (or **in**) **the fashion of** in a manner similar to. **in** (or **out of**) **fashion** fashionable (or unfashionable).
– ORIGIN Middle English: from Old French *façon*, from Latin *factio(n-)*, from *facere* 'do, make'.

fashionable ■ adj. characteristic of or influenced by a current popular trend or style.
– DERIVATIVES **fashionably** adv.

fashion victim ■ n. informal a person who follows popular fashions slavishly.

fast¹ ■ adj. **1** moving or capable of moving at high speed. ▸ taking place or acting rapidly. **2** (of a clock or watch) showing a time ahead of the correct time. **3** firmly fixed or attached. ▸ (of friends) close and loyal. ▸ (of a dye) not fading in light or when washed. **4** Photography needing only a short exposure. **5** involving or engaging in exciting or shocking activities: *the fast life she led in London*. ■ adv. **1** at high speed. ▸ within a short time. **2** so as to be hard to move; firmly or securely. **3** so as to be hard to wake: *fast asleep*.
– PHRASES **pull a fast one** informal try to gain an unfair advantage.
– ORIGIN Old English *fæst* 'firmly fixed, steadfast' and *fæste* 'firmly, securely', of Germanic origin.

fast² ■ v. abstain from food or drink, especially as a religious observance. ■ n. an act or period of fasting.
– ORIGIN Old English, of Germanic origin.

fastback ■ n. a car with a rear that slopes continuously down to the bumper.

fast breeder ■ n. a breeder reactor in which the neutrons causing fission are not slowed by any moderator.

fasten ■ v. **1** close or do up securely. ▸ fix or hold in place. ▸ (**fasten something off**) secure the end of a thread with stitches or a knot. **2** (**fasten on/upon**) single out (something) and concentrate on it obsessively: *critics fastened on two sections of the report*.
– DERIVATIVES **fastener** n.
– ORIGIN Old English *fæstnian* 'make sure, confirm', also 'immobilize', of West Germanic origin.

fastening ■ n. a device that closes or secures something. ▸ the way in which something is fastened.

fast food ■ n. cooked food sold in snack bars and restaurants as a quick meal or to be taken away.

fast forward ■ n. a control on a tape or video player for advancing the tape rapidly. ■ v. (**fast-forward**) advance (a tape) rapidly with such a control.

fastidious /faˈstɪdɪəs/ ■ adj. **1** very attentive to accuracy and detail. **2** very concerned about matters of cleanliness.
– DERIVATIVES **fastidiously** adv. **fastidiousness** n.
– ORIGIN Middle English: from Latin *fastidiosus*, from *fastidium* 'loathing'.

fastness ■ n. **1** a secure place well protected by natural features. **2** the ability of a dye to maintain its colour without fading or washing away.

fast-talk ■ v. informal, chiefly N. Amer. pressurize into doing something using rapid or misleading speech.

fast track ■ n. a rapid route or method. ■ v. (**fast-track**) accelerate the development or progress of.

fat ■ n. **1** a natural oily substance in animal bodies, especially when deposited under the skin or around certain organs. ▸ such a substance, or a similar one made from plants, used in cooking. **2** the presence of excess fat in a person or animal: *he was running to fat*. **3** Chemistry any of a group of natural esters of glycerol and various fatty acids, which are solid at room temperature and are the main constituents of animal and vegetable fat. Compare with OIL. ■ adj. (**fatter**, **fattest**) **1** (of a person or animal) having much excess fat; corpulent. **2** (of food) containing much fat. **3** informal substantial: *fat profits*.
– PHRASES **kill the fatted calf** produce one's best food to celebrate, especially at a prodigal's return. **live off** (or **on**) **the fat of the land** have the best of everything.
– DERIVATIVES **fatness** n. **fattish** adj.
– ORIGIN Old English, of West Germanic origin.

fatal /ˈfeɪt(ə)l/ ■ adj. causing death. ▸ leading to failure or disaster.
– DERIVATIVES **fatally** adv.
– ORIGIN Middle English ('destined by fate, ominous'): from Latin *fatalis*, from *fatum* (see FATE).

fatalism ■ n. the belief that all events are predetermined and therefore inevitable. ▸ a submissive attitude to events.
– DERIVATIVES **fatalist** n. **fatalistic** adj. **fatalistically** adv.

fatality /fəˈtalɪti, feɪ-/ ■ n. (pl. **-ies**) **1** an occurrence of death by accident, in war, or from disease. **2** helplessness in the face of fate.

fatcake ■ n. S. African another term for VETKOEK.

fat cat ■ n. derogatory a wealthy and powerful businessman or politician.

fate ■ n. **1** the development of events outside a person's control, regarded as predetermined by a supernatural power. **2** the outcome of a particular situation for someone or something, especially the end of a person's life. **3** (**the Fates**) Greek & Roman Mythology the three goddesses (Clotho, Lachesis, and Atropos) who preside over the birth and life of humans. ■ v. (**be fated**) be destined to happen, turn out, or act in a particular way.
– PHRASES **seal someone's fate** make it inevitable that something unpleasant will happen to someone.
– ORIGIN Middle English: from Latin *fatum* 'that which has been spoken', from *fari* 'speak'.

fateful ■ adj. having far-reaching, especially disastrous consequences or implications.
– DERIVATIVES **fatefully** adv.

fat farm ■ n. informal, chiefly N. Amer. a health farm for people who are overweight.

fathead ■ n. informal a stupid person.

fat hen ■ n. a herbaceous weed with mealy edible leaves. [*Chenopodium alba*.]
– ORIGIN C18: said to be so named because the seeds were eaten by poultry.

father ■ n. **1** a man in relation to his natural child or children. ▸ a male animal in relation to its offspring. ▸ an important figure in the origin and early history of something. ▸ a man who gives care and protection. ▸ the oldest member or doyen of a society or other body. ▸ (**the**

Father) (in Christian belief) the first person of the Trinity; God. ▸ (**Father**) used in proper names to suggest an old and venerable character: *Father Time.* **2** (often as a title or form of address) a priest. **3** (**Fathers** or **Fathers of the Church**) early Christian theologians who are regarded as especially authoritative. ■ v. be the father of. ▸ [usu. as noun **fathering**] treat with fatherly protective care. ▸ be the source or originator of.
– PHRASES **how's your father** Brit. informal, dated used humorously to refer to sexual intercourse.
– DERIVATIVES **fatherhood** n. **fatherless** adj. **fatherlike** adj. & adv.
– ORIGIN Old English *fæder*, of Germanic origin.

Father Christmas ■ n. an imaginary being said to bring presents for children on the night before Christmas Day.

father-in-law ■ n. (pl. **fathers-in-law**) the father of one's husband or wife.

fatherland ■ n. a person's native country. ▸ (**the Fatherland**) Germany during the period of Hitler's control.

fatherly ■ adj. of, resembling, or characteristic of a father, especially in being protective and affectionate.
– DERIVATIVES **fatherliness** n.

Father's Day ■ n. a day of the year on which fathers are honoured with gifts and greetings cards (usually the third Sunday in June).

fathom ■ n. a unit of length equal to 1.8 metres (six feet), chiefly used in reference to the depth of water. ■ v. **1** [usu. with neg.] understand (something) after much thought. **2** measure the depth of.
– DERIVATIVES **fathomless** adj.

fatigue ■ n. **1** extreme tiredness, especially resulting from mental or physical exertion or illness. **2** weakness in metal or other materials caused by repeated variations of stress. **3** (**fatigues**) menial non-military tasks performed by a soldier. ▸ a group of soldiers ordered to do such a task. ▸ (**fatigues**) loose-fitting clothing of a sort worn by soldiers. ■ v. (**fatigues**, **fatigued**, **fatiguing**) (often **be fatigued**) cause to suffer fatigue.
– ORIGIN C17: from French *fatigue* (n.), *fatiguer* (v.), from Latin *fatigare* 'tire out', from *ad fatim, affatim* 'to satiety or surfeit, to bursting'.

fatso ■ n. (pl. **-oes**) informal, derogatory a fat person.

fat tackies (also **fat takkies**) ■ n. S. African informal large or broad tyres.

fatten ■ v. make or become fat or fatter.

fatty ■ adj. (**-ier**, **-iest**) **1** containing a large amount of fat. **2** Medicine involving abnormal deposition of fat: *fatty degeneration*. ■ n. (pl. **-ies**) informal a fat person.
– DERIVATIVES **fattiness** n.

fatty acid ■ n. Chemistry an organic acid consisting of a hydrocarbon chain and a terminal carboxyl group.

fatuous /ˈfatjʊəs/ ■ adj. silly and pointless.
– DERIVATIVES **fatuously** adv. **fatuousness** n.
– ORIGIN C17: from Latin *fatuus* 'foolish'.

fatwa /ˈfatwɑː/ ■ n. an authoritative ruling on a point of Islamic law.
– ORIGIN C17: from Arabic *fatwā*, from *'aftā* 'decide a point of law'.

fauces /ˈfɔːsiːz/ ■ pl. n. Anatomy the arched opening at the back of the mouth leading to the pharynx.
– ORIGIN Middle English: from Latin, 'throat'.

faucet /ˈfɔːsɪt/ ■ n. chiefly N. Amer. a tap.
– ORIGIN Middle English: from Old French *fausset*, from Provençal *falset*, from *falsar* 'to bore'.

faugh /fɔː/ ■ exclam. expressing disgust.

fault /fɔːlt, fɒlt/ ■ n. **1** an unattractive or unsatisfactory feature; a defect or mistake. ▸ (in tennis and similar games) a service of the ball not in accordance with the rules. **2** responsibility for an accident or misfortune. **3** Geology an extended break in a rock formation, marked by the relative displacement and discontinuity of strata. ■ v. **1** criticize for inadequacy or mistakes. **2** (**be faulted**) Geology be broken by a fault or faults.
– PHRASES **at fault 1** in the wrong. **2** mistaken or defective. **find fault** make an adverse criticism or objection, sometimes unfairly or destructively. **—— to a fault** displaying the specified commendable quality to an excessive extent.
– DERIVATIVES **faultless** adj. **faultlessly** adv.
– ORIGIN Middle English *faut(e)* 'lack, failing', from Old French, from Latin *fallere* 'deceive'.

faulty ■ adj. (**-ier**, **-iest**) having or displaying faults.

faun /fɔːn/ ■ n. Greek & Roman Mythology a lustful rural god represented as a man with a goat's horns, ears, legs, and tail.
– ORIGIN Middle English: from the name of the Roman pastoral god *Faunus*.

fauna /ˈfɔːnə/ ■ n. the animals of a particular region, habitat, or geological period. Compare with **FLORA**.
– DERIVATIVES **faunal** adj. **faunistic** adj.
– ORIGIN C18: modern Latin *Fauna*, the name of a Roman rural goddess, sister of *Faunus* (see **FAUN**).

Fauntleroy /ˈfɔːntlərɔɪ/ (also **Little Lord Fauntleroy**) ■ n. an excessively well-mannered or elaborately dressed young boy.
– ORIGIN from the name of the boy hero of Frances Hodgson Burnett's novel *Little Lord Fauntleroy* (1886).

Faustian /ˈfaʊstɪən/ ■ adj. relating to or characteristic of the 16th-century German astronomer and necromancer Johann Faust, reputed to have sold his soul to the Devil.

faute de mieux /fəʊt də ˈmjəː/ ■ adv. for want of a better alternative.
– ORIGIN from French.

Fauve /fəʊv/ ■ n. a member of a group of early 20th-century French painters who favoured a vivid expressionistic and non-naturalistic use of colour.
– DERIVATIVES **fauvism** n. **fauvist** n. & adj.
– ORIGIN French, 'wild beast', with ref. to a remark by the art critic Louis Vauxcelles.

faux /fəʊ/ ■ adj. made in imitation; artificial.
– ORIGIN French, 'false'.

faux pas /fəʊ ˈpɑː/ ■ n. (pl. same) a social blunder.
– ORIGIN French, 'false step'.

fava bean /ˈfɑːvə/ (also **faba bean**) ■ n. chiefly N. Amer. another term for **BROAD BEAN**.
– ORIGIN Italian *fava*, from Latin *faba* 'bean'.

fave ■ n. & adj. informal short for **FAVOURITE**.

favour (US **favor**) ■ n. **1** approval or liking. ▸ over-generous preferential treatment. **2** an act of kindness beyond what is due or usual. ▸ (**one's favours**) dated a woman's consent to a man having sexual intercourse with her. ■ v. **1** regard or treat with favour. ▸ work to the advantage of. **2** (**favour someone with**) give someone (something that they want).
– PHRASES **in** (or **out of**) **favour** meeting with (or having lost) approval. **in favour of 1** to be replaced by. **2** in support or to the advantage of.
– ORIGIN Middle English: from Latin *favor*, from *favere* 'show kindness to'.

favourable (US **favorable**) ■ adj. **1** expressing approval or consent. **2** to the advantage of someone or something. ▸ auspicious.
– DERIVATIVES **favourably** adv.

favourite (US **favorite**) ■ adj. preferred to all others of the same kind. ■ n. **1** a favourite person or thing. **2** the competitor thought most likely to win.
– PHRASES **favourite son** a famous man who is particularly popular in his native area.
– ORIGIN C16: from Italian *favorito*, from *favorire* 'to favour'.

favouritism (US **favoritism**) ■ n. the unfair favouring of one person or group at the expense of another.

fawn[1] ■ n. **1** a young deer in its first year. **2** a light brown colour. ■ v. (of a deer) produce young.
– ORIGIN Middle English: from Old French *faon*, from Latin *fetus* 'offspring'.

fawn[2] ■ v. give a servile display of exaggerated flattery or affection. ▸ (of an animal, especially a dog) show slavish devotion, especially by rubbing against someone.
– DERIVATIVES **fawning** adj.
– ORIGIN Old English *fagnian* 'make or be glad', of Germanic origin.

fax ■ n. an exact copy of a document made by electronic scanning and transmitted as data by telecommunications

links. ► the production or transmission of documents in this way. ► (also **fax machine**) a machine for transmitting and receiving such documents. ■ v. send (a document) by fax. ► contact by fax.
– ORIGIN 1940s: abbrev. of FACSIMILE.

fay ■ n. poetic/literary a fairy.
– ORIGIN Middle English: from Old French *fae, faie*, from Latin *fata* 'the Fates', pl. of *fatum* (see FATE).

fayre ■ n. pseudo-archaic spelling of FAIR².

faze ■ v. [usu. with neg.] (usu. **be fazed**) informal disturb or disconcert.
– ORIGIN C19 (orig. US): var. of dialect *feeze* 'drive off', from Old English *fēsian*.

FBI ■ abbrev. (in the US) Federal Bureau of Investigation.

FC ■ abbrev. Football Club.

FDA ■ abbrev. (in the US) Food and Drug Administration.

FDDI ■ abbrev. fibre distributed data interface, an industry standard for high-speed optical-fibre networks.

FDI ■ abbrev. foreign direct investment, investment by a company in a country other than that in which the company is based.

Fe ■ symb. the chemical element iron.
– ORIGIN from Latin *ferrum*.

fealty /ˈfiːəlti/ ■ n. historical a feudal tenant's or vassal's sworn loyalty to a lord.
– ORIGIN Middle English: from Old French *fealte*, from Latin *fidelitas* (see FIDELITY).

fear ■ n. 1 an unpleasant emotion caused by the threat of danger, pain, or harm. ► (**fear for**) a feeling of anxiety concerning the outcome of something or the safety of someone. ► the likelihood of something unwelcome happening. 2 archaic a mixed feeling of dread and reverence. ■ v. 1 be afraid of. ► (**fear for**) feel anxiety on behalf of. ► used to express regret or apology. 2 archaic regard (God) with reverence and awe.
– PHRASES **for fear of** (or **that**) to avoid the risk of (or that). **never fear** used to reassure someone. **no fear** informal, chiefly Brit. used as an emphatic expression of denial or refusal. **put the fear of God in** (or **into**) **someone** cause someone to be very frightened. **without fear or favour** impartially.
– DERIVATIVES **fearless** adj. **fearlessly** adv. **fearlessness** n.
– ORIGIN Old English *fǣr* 'danger', *fǣran* 'frighten', also 'revere', of Germanic origin.

fearful ■ adj. 1 showing or causing fear. 2 informal very great.
– DERIVATIVES **fearfully** adv. **fearfulness** n.

fearsome ■ adj. frightening, especially in appearance.
– DERIVATIVES **fearsomely** adv.

feasible /ˈfiːzɪb(ə)l/ ■ adj. 1 possible and practical to achieve easily or conveniently. 2 informal likely.
– DERIVATIVES **feasibility** n. **feasibly** adv.
– ORIGIN Middle English: from Old French *faisible*, from *fais-, faire* 'do, make', from Latin *facere*.

feast ■ n. 1 a large meal, especially a celebratory one. ► a plentiful supply of something enjoyable. 2 an annual religious celebration. ► a day dedicated to a particular saint. ■ v. eat and drink sumptuously. ► give a sumptuous meal to.
– PHRASES **ghost** (or **skeleton**) **at the feast** a person or thing that brings gloom to an otherwise pleasant occasion. **feast one's eyes on** gaze at with pleasure.
– ORIGIN Middle English: from Old French *feste* (n.), *fester* (v.), from Latin *festa*, from *festus* 'joyous'.

feast day ■ n. a day on which an annual Christian celebration is held.

feat ■ n. an achievement requiring great courage, skill, or strength.
– ORIGIN Middle English: from Old French *fait*, from Latin *factum* (see FACT).

feather ■ n. 1 any of the flat appendages growing from a bird's skin, consisting of a partly hollow horny shaft fringed with vanes of barbs. 2 (**feathers**) a fringe of long hair on the legs of a dog, horse, or other animal. ■ v. 1 rotate the blades of (a propeller) about their own axes in such a way as to lessen the air or water resistance. ► Rowing turn (an oar) so that it passes through the air edgeways. 2 [as adj. **feathered**] covered or decorated with feathers. 3 float or move like a feather.

425

– PHRASES **a feather in one's cap** an achievement to be proud of. **feather one's** (**own**) **nest** make money illicitly and at someone else's expense.
– DERIVATIVES **featherless** adj. **feathery** adj.
– ORIGIN Old English, of Germanic origin.

feather bed ■ n. a bed with a mattress stuffed with feathers. ■ v. (**feather-bed**) provide with excessively favourable economic or working conditions.

feather-brain ■ n. a silly or absent-minded person.
– DERIVATIVES **feather-brained** adj.

feather edge ■ n. a fine edge produced by tapering a board, plank, or other object.

feathering ■ n. 1 a bird's plumage. ► the feathers of an arrow. ► fringes of hairs on a dog. 2 feather-like markings or structure. ► Architecture cusping in tracery.

feather palace ■ n. S. African historical one of a number of luxurious houses built in the Oudtshoorn district in the 19th century during the boom in the ostrich feather industry.

feather star ■ n. an echinoderm with a small disc-like body and long feathery arms. [Order Comatulida: many species.]

feather stitch ■ n. ornamental zigzag sewing. ■ v. (**feather-stitch**) [usu. as noun **feather-stitching**] sew with such a stitch.

featherweight ■ n. 1 a weight in boxing and other sports intermediate between bantamweight and lightweight. 2 a person or thing not worth serious consideration.

feature ■ n. 1 a distinctive attribute or aspect of something. ► a part of the face, such as the mouth, making a significant contribution to its overall appearance. 2 a newspaper or magazine article or a broadcast programme devoted to a particular topic. ► (also **feature film**) a full-length film intended as the main item in a cinema programme. ■ v. have as a feature. ► have as an important actor or participant. ► be a feature of or take an important part in.
– DERIVATIVES **-featured** adj. **featureless** adj.
– ORIGIN Middle English: from Old French *faiture* 'form', from Latin *factura* (see FACTURE).

Feb. ■ abbrev. February.

febrifuge /ˈfɛbrɪfjuːdʒ/ ■ n. a medicine used to reduce fever.
– DERIVATIVES **febrifugal** /fɪˈbrɪfjʊg(ə)l, ˌfɛbrɪˈfjuːg(ə)l/ adj.
– ORIGIN C17: from French *fébrifuge*, from Latin *febris* 'fever' + *fugare* 'drive away'.

febrile /ˈfiːbrʌɪl/ ■ adj. 1 having or showing the symptoms of a fever. 2 having or showing a great deal of nervous excitement.
– ORIGIN C17: from medieval Latin *febrilis*, from *febris* 'fever'.

February /ˈfɛbrʊəri, ˈfɛbjʊəri/ ■ n. (pl. **-ies**) the second month of the year.
– ORIGIN Middle English: from Latin *februarius*, from *februa*, name of a purification feast held in this month.

feces ■ n. US spelling of FAECES.

feckless ■ adj. 1 ineffectual; feeble. 2 unthinking and irresponsible.
– DERIVATIVES **fecklessness** n.
– ORIGIN C16: from Scots and northern English dialect *feck*, from *effeck*, var. of EFFECT.

feculent /ˈfɛkjʊl(ə)nt/ ■ adj. of or containing dirt, sediment, or waste matter.
– ORIGIN C15: from Latin *faeculentus*, from *faex, faec-* 'dregs'.

fecund /ˈfɛk(ə)nd, ˈfiːk-/ ■ adj. highly fertile; able to produce offspring.
– DERIVATIVES **fecundity** /fɪˈkʌndɪti/ n.
– ORIGIN Middle English: from Latin *fecundus*.

Fed ■ n. US informal 1 a member of the FBI or other federal agent or official. 2 (usu. **the Fed**) short for FEDERAL RESERVE.

fed past and past participle of FEED.

federal ■ adj. 1 having or relating to a system of

federal

Federal Reserve

government in which several states form a unity but remain independent in internal affairs. **2** relating to or denoting the central government as distinguished from the separate units constituting a federation. ▸ **(Federal)** US historical of the Northern States in the Civil War.
– DERIVATIVES **federalism** n. **federalist** n. & adj. **federalization** (also **-isation**) n. **federalize** (also **-ise**) v. **federally** adv.
– ORIGIN C17: from Latin *foedus, foeder-* 'league, covenant'.

Federal Reserve ■ n. (in the US) the banking authority that performs the functions of a central bank.

federate ■ v. /ˈfɛdəreɪt/ (of a number of states or organizations) organize or be organized on a federal basis. ■ adj. /ˈfɛd(ə)rət/ of or relating to such an arrangement.
– ORIGIN C18: from late Latin *foederatus*, from *foedus, foeder-* (see **FEDERAL**).

federation ■ n. **1** a federal group of states. ▸ an organization within which smaller divisions have some degree of internal autonomy. **2** the action of federating.
– DERIVATIVES **federationist** n.

fedora /fɪˈdɔːrə/ ■ n. a low, soft felt hat with a curled brim and the crown creased lengthways.
– ORIGIN C19: from *Fédora*, the title of a drama written by the French dramatist Victorien Sardou.

fed up ■ adj. (often **fed up with**) informal annoyed or bored.

fee ■ n. **1** a payment made to a professional person or to a professional or public body in exchange for advice or services. ▸ a charge made for a privilege such as admission. **2** Law, historical an estate of land, especially one held on condition of feudal service.
– ORIGIN Middle English: from an Anglo-Norman French var. of Old French *feu, fief*, from medieval Latin *feodum, feudum*, of Germanic origin.

feeble ■ adj. (**-er**, **-est**) lacking physical strength. ▸ lacking strength of character. ▸ failing to convince or impress: *a feeble excuse*.
– DERIVATIVES **feebleness** n. **feebly** adv.
– ORIGIN Middle English: from Old French *fieble*, earlier *fleible*, from Latin *flebilis* 'lamentable', from *flere* 'weep'.

feeble-minded ■ adj. foolish; stupid. ▸ dated having less than average intelligence.
– DERIVATIVES **feeble-mindedly** adv. **feeble-mindedness** n.

feed ■ v. (past and past part. **fed** /fɛd/) **1** give food to. ▸ provide an adequate supply of food for. **2** eat. ▸ (**feed on/off**) derive regular nourishment from (a particular substance). **3** supply with material, power, water, etc. ▸ prompt (an actor) with (a line). ▸ (in ball games) pass (the ball) to a player. **4** pass gradually through a confined space. **5** (**feed back**) (of an electrical or other system) produce feedback. ■ n. **1** an act of feeding or of being fed. ▸ food for domestic animals. **2** a device or pipe for supplying material to a machine. ▸ the supply of raw material to a machine or device. **3** a prompt given to an actor on stage.
– ORIGIN Old English, of Germanic origin.

feedback ■ n. **1** information given in response to a product, a person's performance of a task, etc., used as a basis for improvement. **2** the modification or control of a process or system by its results or effects. **3** the return of a fraction of the output of an amplifier, microphone, or other device to the input, causing distortion or a whistling sound.

feeder ■ n. **1** a person or animal that eats a particular food or in a particular manner: *filter-feeders*. **2** a container filled with food for birds or mammals. **3** a thing that supplies something. ▸ a road or rail route linking outlying districts with a main system.

feedforward ■ n. the modification or control of a process using its anticipated results or effects.

feeding frenzy ■ n. **1** an aggressive and competitive group attack on prey by a number of sharks or piranhas. **2** an episode of frantic competition for something.

feedlot ■ n. an area or building where livestock are fed or fattened up.

feedstock ■ n. raw material to supply a machine or industrial process.

feedstuff ■ n. fodder.

feel ■ v. (past and past part. **felt**) **1** perceive, examine, or search by touch. ▸ be aware of (something happening) through physical sensation. ▸ give a sensation of a particular physical quality when touched: *the wool feels soft*. ▸ (**feel someone up**) informal fondle someone for one's own sexual stimulation. **2** experience (an emotion or sensation). ▸ consider oneself: *he doesn't feel obliged to visit*. ▸ (**feel up to**) have the strength and energy to. ▸ be emotionally affected by. ▸ have a specified reaction or attitude towards something. **3** have a belief or impression, especially without an identifiable reason. ■ n. **1** an act of feeling. ▸ the sense of touch. **2** a sensation given by an object or material when touched. **3** the impression given by something.
– PHRASES **feel for** informal have concern for or sympathy with. **get a** (or **the**) **feel for** (or **of**) become accustomed to. **have a feel for** have a sensitive appreciation or understanding of. **make oneself** (or **one's presence**) **felt** have a noticeable effect.
– ORIGIN Old English, of West Germanic origin.

feeler ■ n. **1** an animal organ such as an antenna that is used for testing things by touch or for searching for food. **2** a tentative proposal intended to ascertain someone's attitude or opinion.

feeler gauge ■ n. a gauge consisting of a number of thin blades for measuring narrow gaps or clearances.

feel-good ■ adj. informal causing a feeling of happiness and well-being: *a feel-good movie*.
– DERIVATIVES **feel-goodism** n.

feeling ■ n. **1** an emotional state or reaction. ▸ (**feelings**) emotional responses or tendencies to respond. ▸ strong emotion. **2** a belief or opinion. **3** the capacity to feel. ▸ the sensation of touching or being touched. **4** (**feeling for**) a sensitivity to or intuitive understanding of. ■ adj. showing emotion or sensitivity.
– PHRASES **one's better feelings** one's conscience.
– DERIVATIVES **feelingless** adj. **feelingly** adv.

feet plural form of **FOOT**.

feign ■ v. **1** pretend to be affected by (a feeling, state, or injury). **2** archaic invent (a story or excuse).
– ORIGIN Middle English: from Old French *feign-, feindre*, from Latin *fingere* 'mould, contrive'.

feint¹ /feɪnt/ ■ n. a deceptive or pretended blow, thrust, or other attacking movement, especially in boxing or fencing. ■ v. make a feint.
– ORIGIN C17: from French *feinte*, from *feindre* 'feign'.

feint² /feɪnt/ ■ adj. denoting paper printed with faint lines as a guide for handwriting.
– ORIGIN C19: var. of **FAINT**.

feisty /ˈfʌɪsti/ ■ adj. (**-ier**, **-iest**) informal **1** spirited and exuberant. **2** touchy and aggressive.
– DERIVATIVES **feistily** adv. **feistiness** n.
– ORIGIN C19: from earlier *feist, fist* 'small dog', from *fisting cur* or *hound*, a derogatory term for a lapdog, from Middle English *fist* 'break wind'.

felafel /fəˈlaf(ə)l, -ˈlɑː-/ ■ n. variant spelling of **FALAFEL**.

Feldenkrais method /ˈfɛld(ə)nkrʌɪs/ ■ n. a system designed to promote bodily and mental well-being by analysis of neuromuscular activity via exercises which improve flexibility and coordination.
– ORIGIN 1930s: named after the Russian-born physicist and mechanical engineer Moshe *Feldenkrais*.

feldspar /ˈfɛldspɑː/ (also **felspar**) ■ n. an abundant rock-forming aluminosilicate mineral, typically colourless or pale-coloured.
– DERIVATIVES **feldspathic** adj.
– ORIGIN C18: alteration of German *Feldspat, Feldspath*, from *Feld* 'field' + *Spat, Spath* (see **SPAR³**); the form *felspar* is by mistaken association with German *Fels* 'rock'.

felicitations ■ pl. n. congratulations.

felicitous /fɪˈlɪsɪtəs/ ■ adj. well chosen or appropriate: *a felicitous phrase*. ▸ pleasing.
– DERIVATIVES **felicitously** adv. **felicitousness** n.

felicity ■ n. (pl. **-ies**) **1** complete happiness. **2** the ability to express oneself appropriately. ▸ a felicitous feature of a work of literature or art.

CONSONANTS **b** but **d** dog **f** few **g** get **h** he **j** yes **k** cat **l** leg **m** man **n** no **p** pen **r** red

– ORIGIN Middle English: from Latin *felicitas*, from *felix* 'happy'.

felid /ˈfiːlɪd/ ■ n. Zoology a mammal of the cat family (Felidae).
– ORIGIN C19: from Latin *feles* 'cat'.

feline /ˈfiːlaɪn/ ■ adj. of, relating to, or resembling a cat. ■ n. a cat or other animal of the cat family.
– ORIGIN C17: from Latin *felinus*, from *feles* 'cat'.

fell[1] past of FALL.

fell[2] ■ v. 1 cut down (a tree). ▶ knock down. 2 stitch down (the edge of a seam) to lie flat. ■ n. an amount of wood cut.
– DERIVATIVES **feller** n.
– ORIGIN Old English, of Germanic origin.

fell[3] ■ n. a hill or stretch of high moorland, especially in northern England.
– ORIGIN Middle English: from Old Norse *fjall*, *fell* 'hill'.

fell[4] ■ adj. poetic/literary of terrible evil or ferocity.
– PHRASES **in** (or **at**) **one fell swoop** all in one go. [from Shakespeare's *Macbeth* (IV. iii. 219).]
– ORIGIN Middle English: from Old French *fel*, from *felon* (see FELON).

fellah /ˈfɛlə/ ■ n. (pl. **fellahin** /-ˈhiːn/) an Egyptian peasant.
– ORIGIN from Arabic *fallāḥ* 'tiller of the soil'.

fellatio /fɛˈleɪʃɪəʊ, -ˈlɑːt-/ ■ n. oral stimulation of a man's penis.
– DERIVATIVES **fellate** v. **fellator** /fɛˈleɪtə/ n.
– ORIGIN C19: from Latin *fellare* 'to suck'.

fellow ■ n. 1 informal a man or boy. 2 a person in the same position or otherwise associated with another. ▶ a thing of the same kind as or otherwise associated with another. 3 a member of a learned society. ▶ Brit. an incorporated senior member of a college. ▶ (also **research fellow**) an elected graduate receiving a stipend for a period of research. ▶ a member of the governing body in some universities. ■ adj. sharing a particular activity, quality, or condition: *a fellow sufferer*.
– ORIGIN Old English *fēolaga* 'a colleague' (literally 'one who lays down money in a joint enterprise'), from Old Norse *félagi*, from *fé* 'property, money' + the Germanic base of LAY[1].

fellow feeling ■ n. sympathy based on shared experiences.

fellowship ■ n. 1 friendliness and companionship based on shared interests. 2 a group of people meeting to pursue a shared interest or aim. ▶ a guild or corporation. 3 the status of a fellow of a college or society.

fellow-traveller ■ n. a sympathizer with, but non-member of, the Communist Party.
– DERIVATIVES **fellow-travelling** adj.

felon /ˈfɛlən/ ■ n. a person who has committed a felony. ■ adj. archaic cruel; wicked.
– ORIGIN Middle English: from Old French, 'wicked, a wicked person', from medieval Latin *fello, fellon-*.

felony ■ n. (pl. **-ies**) a crime, typically one involving violence, regarded in the US and other judicial systems as more serious than a misdemeanour.
– DERIVATIVES **feloniously** adv.

felsic /ˈfɛlsɪk/ ■ adj. Geology relating to or denoting a group of light-coloured minerals including feldspar, quartz, and muscovite. Often contrasted with MAFIC.
– ORIGIN C20: from FELDSPAR + a contraction of SILICA.

felspar /ˈfɛlspɑː/ ■ n. variant spelling of FELDSPAR.

felt[1] ■ n. cloth made by rolling and pressing wool or another suitable textile accompanied by the application of moisture or heat, which causes the fibres to mat together. ■ v. 1 mat together or become matted. 2 cover with felt.
– DERIVATIVES **felty** adj.
– ORIGIN Old English, of West Germanic origin; rel. to FILTER.

felt[2] past and past participle of FEEL.

felt-tip pen (also **felt-tipped pen**) ■ n. a pen with a writing point made of felt or tightly packed fibres.

felucca /fɛˈlʌkə/ ■ n. a small boat propelled by oars or lateen sails or both, used on the Nile and formerly more widely in the Mediterranean region.
– ORIGIN C17: from Italian *feluc(c)a*, of Arabic origin.

fender

female ■ adj. 1 of or denoting the sex that can bear offspring or produce eggs. ▶ relating to or characteristic of women or female animals. ▶ (of a plant or flower) having a pistil but no stamens. 2 (of a fitting) manufactured hollow so that a corresponding male part can be inserted. ■ n. a female person, animal, or plant.
– DERIVATIVES **femaleness** n.
– ORIGIN Middle English: from Latin *femella*, diminutive of *femina* 'a woman'; the change in the ending was due to association with MALE.

female circumcision ■ n. (among some peoples) the action or traditional practice of cutting off the clitoris and sometimes the labia of girls or young women.

female condom ■ n. a contraceptive device made of thin rubber, inserted into a woman's vagina before sexual intercourse.

feminine ■ adj. 1 having qualities traditionally associated with women, especially delicacy and prettiness. ▶ female. 2 Grammar of or denoting a gender of nouns and adjectives, conventionally regarded as female. ■ n. (**the feminine**) the female sex or gender.
– DERIVATIVES **femininely** adv. **feminineness** n. **femininity** n.
– ORIGIN Middle English: from Latin *femininus*, from *femina* 'woman'.

feminine rhyme ■ n. Prosody a rhyme between stressed syllables followed by one or more unstressed syllables (e.g. *stocking/shocking*).

feminism ■ n. the advocacy of women's rights on the grounds of sexual equality.
– DERIVATIVES **feminist** n. & adj.
– ORIGIN C19: from French *féminisme*.

feminize (also **-ise**) ■ v. make more feminine or female.
– DERIVATIVES **feminization** (also **-isation**) n.

femme /fem/ (also **fem**) ■ n. informal a lesbian who takes a traditionally feminine sexual role.
– ORIGIN 1960s: French, 'woman'.

femme fatale /ˌfam fəˈtɑːl/ ■ n. (pl. **femmes fatales** pronunc. same) an attractive and seductive woman.
– ORIGIN C20: French, 'disastrous woman'.

femto- /ˈfɛmtəʊ/ ■ comb. form denoting a factor of 10^{-15}: *femtosecond*.
– ORIGIN from Danish or Norwegian *femten* 'fifteen'.

femur /ˈfiːmə/ ■ n. (pl. **femurs** or **femora** /ˈfɛm(ə)rə/) 1 Anatomy the bone of the thigh or upper hindlimb. 2 Zoology the third segment of the leg in insects and some other arthropods.
– DERIVATIVES **femoral** /ˈfɛm(ə)r(ə)l/ adj.
– ORIGIN C15: from Latin *femur, femor-* 'thigh'.

fen ■ n. a low and marshy or frequently flooded area of land.
– ORIGIN Old English, of Germanic origin.

fence ■ n. 1 a barrier enclosing an area, typically consisting of posts connected by wire, wood, etc. ▶ a large upright obstacle in steeplechasing, showjumping, or cross-country. 2 a guard or guide on a plane or other tool. 3 informal a dealer in stolen goods. ■ v. 1 surround or protect with a fence. ▶ (**fence something in/off**) enclose or separate an area with a fence. 2 informal deal in (stolen goods). 3 practise the sport of fencing. ▶ conduct a discussion or argument in an evasive way.
– PHRASES **sit on the fence** avoid making a decision or commitment.
– DERIVATIVES **fenceless** adj. **fencer** n.
– ORIGIN Middle English: shortening of DEFENCE.

fencing ■ n. 1 the sport of fighting with blunted swords according to a set of rules in order to score points. 2 a series of fences. ▶ material for making fences.

fend ■ v. 1 (**fend for oneself**) look after and provide for oneself. 2 (**fend someone/thing off**) defend oneself from an attack or attacker.
– ORIGIN Middle English: shortening of DEFEND.

fender ■ n. 1 a low frame bordering a fireplace to keep in falling coals. 2 a tyre or other cushioning device hung over a ship's side to protect it against impact. 3 N. Amer. the mudguard or area around the wheel well of a vehicle.

fender bender

fender bender ■ n. N. Amer. informal a minor collision between motor vehicles.

fenestra /fɪˈnɛstrə/ ■ n. (pl. **fenestrae** /-triː/) **1** Anatomy & Zoology a small hole or opening in a bone, especially either of two in the middle ear (fenestra ovalis, fenestra rotunda). **2** a perforation in a forceps blade.
– ORIGIN C19: from Latin, 'window'.

fenestrated /ˈfɛnəˌstreɪtɪd, fɪˈnɛstreɪtɪd/ ■ adj. **1** provided with a window or windows. **2** chiefly Anatomy having fenestrae.

fenestration /ˌfɛnɪˈstreɪʃ(ə)n/ ■ n. Architecture the arrangement of windows in a building.

feng shui /ˌfɛŋ ˈʃuːi, ˌfʌŋ ˈʃweɪ/ ■ n. (in Chinese thought) a system of laws considered to govern spatial arrangement and orientation in relation to the flow of energy, and whose effects are taken into account when siting and designing buildings.
– ORIGIN Chinese: from *fēng* 'wind' and *shuǐ* 'water'.

Fenian /ˈfiːnɪən/ ■ n. **1** a member of the Irish Republican Brotherhood, a 19th-century revolutionary nationalist organization among the Irish in the US and Ireland. **2** informal, offensive (chiefly in Northern Ireland) a Protestant name for a Catholic.
– ORIGIN from Old Irish *féne*, the name of an ancient Irish people, confused with *fianna, fianna* 'band of warriors', in particular the soldiers of the legendary king Finn MacCool.

fennec /ˈfɛnɛk/ ■ n. a small pale fox of North African and Arabian deserts, with large pointed ears. [*Vulpes zerda*.]
– ORIGIN C18: from Persian *fanak, fanaj*.

fennel /ˈfɛn(ə)l/ ■ n. an aromatic yellow-flowered plant of the parsley family, with feathery leaves used as culinary herbs or eaten as a vegetable. [*Foeniculum vulgare, Ferula communis* (giant fennel), and other species.]
– ORIGIN Old English *finule, fenol*, from Latin *faeniculum*, diminutive of *faenum* 'hay'.

fentanyl /ˈfɛntənɪl/ ■ n. Medicine a synthetic opiate drug which is a powerful painkiller and tranquillizer.
– ORIGIN 1960s: apparently from *fen* (representing **PHEN-**) + *-t-* + *an* + **-YL**.

fenugreek /ˈfɛnjʊɡriːk/ ■ n. a white-flowered leguminous plant with aromatic leaves and seeds that are used as a spice. [*Trigonella foenum-graecum*.]
– ORIGIN Old English *fenogrecum*, from Latin, from *faenum graecum* 'Greek hay' (the Romans used the dried plant as fodder).

feral /ˈfɛr(ə)l, ˈfɪə-/ ■ adj. **1** (of an animal or plant) in a wild state, especially after having been domesticated or cultivated. **2** resembling a wild animal: *a feral snarl*.
– ORIGIN C17: from Latin *fera* 'wild animal'.

feral pigeon ■ n. another term for **ROCK DOVE**.

fer de lance /ˌfɛː də ˈlɑːns/ ■ n. (pl. **fers de lance** pronunc. same or **fer de lances**) a large and dangerous pit viper native to Central and South America. [*Bothrops atrox* and related species.]
– ORIGIN C19: from French, 'iron (head) of a lance'.

ferial /ˈfɪərɪəl, ˈfɛ-/ ■ adj. Christian Church denoting an ordinary weekday, as opposed to one appointed for a festival or fast.
– ORIGIN Middle English: from Latin *feria* 'holiday', in late Latin, 'day of the week'.

Fermat's last theorem ■ n. Mathematics the theorem (proved in 1995) that if n is an integer greater than 2, the equation $x^n + y^n = z^n$ has no positive integral solutions.
– ORIGIN C19: named after the C17 French mathematician Pierre de *Fermat*.

ferment ■ v. /fəˈmɛnt/ **1** undergo or cause to undergo fermentation. **2** stir up (disorder). ■ n. /ˈfəːmɛnt/ agitation and social unrest.
– DERIVATIVES **fermentable** adj. **fermenter** (US also **fermentor**) n.
– ORIGIN Middle English: from Latin *fermentum* 'yeast', from *fervere* 'to boil'.

fermentation ■ n. the chemical breakdown of a substance by bacteria, yeasts, or other micro-organisms, especially that involved in the making of beers, wines, and spirits in which sugars are converted to ethyl alcohol.

– DERIVATIVES **fermentative** adj.

fermion /ˈfəːmɪɒn/ ■ n. Physics a subatomic particle, such as a nucleon, which has half-integral spin.
– ORIGIN 1940s: named after the Italian physicist Enrico *Fermi*.

fermium /ˈfəːmɪəm/ ■ n. the chemical element of atomic number 100, an artificially made radioactive metal of the actinide series. (Symbol: **Fm**)

fern ■ n. (pl. same or **ferns**) a flowerless vascular plant which has feathery or leafy fronds and reproduces by spores released from the undersides of the fronds. [Class Filicopsida.]
– DERIVATIVES **fernery** n. (pl. **-ies**). **ferny** adj.
– ORIGIN Old English, of West Germanic origin.

ferocious ■ adj. **1** savagely fierce, cruel, or violent. **2** informal very great; extreme.
– DERIVATIVES **ferociously** adv. **ferociousness** n. **ferocity** n.
– ORIGIN C17 (*ferocity* C16): from Latin *ferox, feroc-* 'fierce'.

-ferous (usu. **-iferous**) ■ comb. form having, bearing, or containing (a specified thing): *Carboniferous*.
– DERIVATIVES **-ferously** comb. form. **-ferousness** comb. form.
– ORIGIN from Latin *-fer* 'producing', from *ferre* 'to bear'.

ferrate /ˈfɛreɪt/ ■ n. Chemistry a salt in which the anion contains both iron and oxygen: *sodium ferrate*.
– ORIGIN C19: from Latin *ferrum* 'iron'.

ferret /ˈfɛrɪt/ ■ n. **1** a domesticated albino or brown polecat, used for catching rabbits. [*Mustela furo*.] **2** an assiduous search. ■ v. (**ferreted**, **ferreting**) **1** hunt with ferrets. **2** search for something in a place or container. ▶ (**ferret something out**) investigate something assiduously.
– DERIVATIVES **ferreter** n. **ferrety** adj.
– ORIGIN Middle English: from Old French *fuiret*, alteration of *fuiron*, from late Latin *furo* 'thief, ferret', from Latin *fur* 'thief'.

ferri- /ˈfɛri/ ■ comb. form Chemistry of iron with a valency of three; ferric. Compare with **FERRO-**.
– ORIGIN from Latin *ferrum* 'iron'.

ferric /ˈfɛrɪk/ ■ adj. Chemistry of iron with a valency of three; of iron(III).
– ORIGIN C18: from Latin *ferrum* 'iron'.

ferrimagnetic ■ adj. Physics denoting or exhibiting a weak form of ferromagnetism associated with parallel but opposite alignment of adjacent electron spins.
– DERIVATIVES **ferrimagnetism** n.

Ferris wheel /ˈfɛrɪs/ ■ n. a fairground ride consisting of a giant vertical revolving wheel with passenger cars suspended on its outer edge.
– ORIGIN C19: named after George W. G. *Ferris*, the American engineer who invented it.

ferrite /ˈfɛrʌɪt/ ■ n. **1** a ceramic ferrimagnetic oxide of iron and one or more other metals, used in high-frequency electrical components such as aerials. **2** Metallurgy a form of pure iron occurring in low-carbon steel.
– DERIVATIVES **ferritic** /fɛˈrɪtɪk/ adj.
– ORIGIN C19: from Latin *ferrum* 'iron'.

ferro- /ˈfɛrəʊ/ ■ comb. form **1** containing iron: *ferroconcrete*. **2** Chemistry of iron with a valency of two; ferrous. Compare with **FERRI-**.
– ORIGIN from Latin *ferrum* 'iron'.

ferroconcrete ■ n. concrete reinforced with steel.

ferroelectric ■ adj. Physics displaying or denoting permanent electric polarization which varies in strength with the applied electric field.
– DERIVATIVES **ferroelectricity** n.

ferromagnetic ■ adj. Physics displaying or denoting the strong, persistent magnetism displayed by iron, associated with parallel magnetic alignment of neighbouring atoms.
– DERIVATIVES **ferromagnetism** n.

ferrous /ˈfɛrəs/ ■ adj. **1** (chiefly of metals) containing or consisting of iron. **2** Chemistry of iron with a valency of two; of iron(II).
– ORIGIN C19: from Latin *ferrum* 'iron'.

ferruginous /fɛˈruːdʒɪnəs/ ■ adj. **1** containing iron oxides or rust. **2** rust-coloured.
– ORIGIN C17: from Latin *ferrugo, ferrugin-* 'rust, dark red'.

ferrule /'fɛruːl, 'fɛr(ə)l/ ■ n. a ring or cap which strengthens the end of a handle, stick, or tube. ▸ a metal band strengthening or forming a joint.
– ORIGIN C17: alteration (prob. by association with Latin *ferrum* 'iron') of obsolete *verrel*, from Old French *virelle*, from Latin *viriola*, diminutive of *viriae* 'bracelets'.

ferry ■ n. (pl. **-ies**) a boat or ship for conveying passengers and goods, especially as a regular service. ■ v. (**-ies, -ied**) convey by ferry or other transport, especially on short, regular trips.
– DERIVATIVES **ferryman** n. (pl. **-men**)
– ORIGIN Middle English: from Old Norse *ferja* 'ferry boat', of Germanic origin and rel. to FARE.

fertile /'fəːtʌɪl/ ■ adj. **1** (of soil or land) producing or capable of producing abundant vegetation or crops. **2** (of a person, animal, or plant) able to conceive young or produce seed. ▸ (of a seed or egg) capable of becoming a new individual. **3** productive in generating new ideas; inventive.
– DERIVATIVES **fertility** n.
– ORIGIN Middle English: from Latin *fertilis*, from *ferre* 'to bear'.

fertility cult ■ n. a religious system of some agricultural societies in which seasonal rites are performed to ensure good harvests and the well-being of the community.

fertilize (also **-ise**) ■ v. **1** cause (an egg, female animal, or plant) to develop a new individual by introducing male reproductive material. **2** make (soil or land) more fertile by adding fertilizer.
– DERIVATIVES **fertilization** (also **-isation**) n.

fertilizer (also **-iser**) ■ n. a chemical or natural substance added to soil to increase its fertility.

fervent /'fəːv(ə)nt/ ■ adj. **1** intensely passionate. **2** archaic hot or glowing.
– DERIVATIVES **fervency** n. **fervently** adv.
– ORIGIN Middle English: from Latin *fervent-, fervere* 'boil'.

fervid /'fəːvɪd/ ■ adj. **1** intensely enthusiastic, especially to an excessive degree. **2** poetic/literary hot or glowing.
– DERIVATIVES **fervidly** adv.
– ORIGIN C16: from Latin *fervidus*, from *fervere* 'to boil'.

fervour /'fəːvə/ (US **fervor**) ■ n. **1** intense and passionate feeling. **2** archaic intense heat.
– ORIGIN Middle English: from Latin *fervor*, from *fervere* 'to boil'.

fescue /'fɛskjuː/ ■ n. a narrow-leaved grass, some kinds of which are valuable for pasture and fodder. [Genera *Festuca* and *Vulpia*.]
– ORIGIN Middle English *festue* 'straw, twig', from Latin *festuca* 'stalk, straw'.

fess[1] /fɛs/ (also **fesse**) ■ n. Heraldry an ordinary in the form of a broad horizontal stripe across the middle of the shield.
– ORIGIN C15: from Old French *fesse*, alteration of *faisse*, from Latin *fascia* 'band'.

fess[2] /fɛs/ ■ v. (**fess up**) informal confess.

fess point ■ n. Heraldry a point at the centre of a shield.

-fest ■ comb. form informal in nouns denoting a festival or large gathering of a specified kind: *a media-fest*.
– ORIGIN from German *Fest* 'festival'.

festal ■ adj. relating to a festival; festive.
– ORIGIN C15: from late Latin *festalis*, from Latin *festum*, (pl.) *festa* 'feast'.

fester ■ v. [often as adj. **festering**] **1** (of a wound or sore) become septic. ▸ (of food or rubbish) become rotten. **2** (of a negative feeling or a problem) intensify, especially through neglect. **3** deteriorate physically and mentally in isolated inactivity.
– ORIGIN Middle English: from *fester* 'fistula', later 'festering sore', from Old French *festre*, from Latin *fistula* 'reed, fistula'.

festival ■ n. **1** a day or period of celebration, typically for religious reasons. **2** an organized series of concerts, films, etc., typically one held annually in the same place.
– ORIGIN Middle English: from medieval Latin *festivalis*, from Latin *festivus*, from *festum*, (pl.) *festa* 'feast'.

festival of lights ■ n. **1** another term for DIWALI. **2** another term for HANUKKAH.

festive ■ adj. **1** of or relating to a festival. **2** jovially celebratory.
– DERIVATIVES **festively** adv. **festiveness** n.
– ORIGIN C17: from Latin *festivus* (see FESTIVAL).

fetter

festivity ■ n. (pl. **-ies**) joyful and exuberant celebration. ▸ (**festivities**) celebratory activities or events.
– ORIGIN Middle English: from Latin *festivitas*, from *festivus* (see FESTIVAL).

festoon /fɛ'stuːn/ ■ n. an ornamental chain or garland of flowers, leaves, or ribbons, hung in a curve. ▸ a carved or moulded ornament representing this. ■ v. (often **be festooned with**) adorn with festoons or other decorations.
– ORIGIN C17: from French *feston*, from Italian *festone* 'festal ornament'.

Festschrift /'fɛst,ʃrɪft/ ■ n. (pl. **Festschriften** or **Festschrifts**) a collection of writings published in honour of a scholar.
– ORIGIN C19: from German, from *Fest* 'celebration' + *Schrift* 'writing'.

FET ■ abbrev. **1** (in South Africa) further education and training, comprising grades 10 to 12 or equivalent levels of qualification. Compare with GET and HET. **2** field-effect transistor.

feta /'fɛtə/ (also **feta cheese** or **fetta**) ■ n. a white salty Greek cheese made from the milk of ewes or goats.
– ORIGIN from modern Greek *pheta*.

fetal /'fiːt(ə)l/ ■ adj. of or relating to a fetus. ▸ denoting a posture characteristic of a fetus, with the back curved forwards and the limbs folded in front of the body.

fetal alcohol syndrome ■ n. a congenital condition causing growth and developmental abnormalities, resulting from excessive consumption of alcohol by the pregnant mother.

fetch ■ v. **1** go for and bring back. ▸ cause to come to a place. **2** achieve (a particular price) when sold. **3** archaic bring forth (blood or tears). ▸ take (a breath). **4** informal inflict (a blow) on (someone). **5** (**fetch up**) informal arrive or come to rest. ■ n. **1** the distance travelled by wind or waves across open water. ▸ the distance a vessel must sail to reach open water. **2** an act of fetching.
– PHRASES **fetch and carry** run backwards and forwards bringing things to someone in a servile fashion.
– DERIVATIVES **fetcher** n.
– ORIGIN Old English *fecc(e)an*, var. of *fetian*, prob. rel. to *fatian* 'grasp', of Germanic origin.

fetching ■ adj. attractive: *a fetching little garment*.
– DERIVATIVES **fetchingly** adv.

fête /feɪt/ ■ n. **1** an outdoor public function to raise funds for a charity or institution, typically involving entertainment and the sale of goods. **2** chiefly N. Amer. a celebration or festival. ■ v. (usu. **be fêted**) honour or entertain lavishly.
– ORIGIN Middle English ('festival, fair'): from French, from Old French *feste* (see FEAST).

feticide /'fiːtɪsʌɪd/ ■ n. destruction or abortion of a fetus.

fetid /'fɛtɪd, 'fiːt-/ (also **foetid**) ■ adj. smelling unpleasant.
– ORIGIN Middle English: from Latin *fetidus*, from *fetere* 'to stink'.

fetish /'fɛtɪʃ/ ■ n. **1** an inanimate object worshipped for its supposed magical powers or because it is considered to be inhabited by a spirit. **2** a form of sexual desire in which gratification is linked to an abnormal degree to a particular object, part of the body, or activity. **3** a course of action to which one has an excessive and irrational commitment.
– DERIVATIVES **fetishism** n. **fetishist** n. **fetishistic** adj. **fetishization** (also **-isation**) n. **fetishize** (also **-ise**) v.
– ORIGIN C17: from French *fétiche*, from Portuguese *feitiço* 'charm, sorcery'.

fetlock /'fɛtlɒk/ ■ n. the joint of a horse's or other quadruped's leg between the cannon bone and the pastern.
– ORIGIN Middle English: of Germanic origin; rel. to FOOT.

fetor /'fiːtə/ ■ n. a strong, foul smell.
– ORIGIN C15: from Latin, from *fetere* 'to stink'.

fetta ■ n. variant spelling of FETA.

fetter ■ n. a chain or shackle placed around a prisoner's ankles. ▸ a restraint or check. ■ v. restrain with fetters. ▸ (often **be fettered**) restrict.
– ORIGIN Old English, of Germanic origin.

fettle

fettle ■ n. condition: *the horse remains in fine fettle.* ■ v. trim or clean the rough edges of (a metal casting or a piece of pottery) before firing.
– ORIGIN Middle English ('to prepare'): from dialect *fettle* 'strip of material', from Old English *fetel*, of Germanic origin.

fettuccine /ˌfetuˈtʃiːneɪ, -ni/ (also **fettucini**) ■ pl. n. pasta made in ribbons.
– ORIGIN from Italian: pl. of *fettucina*, diminutive of *fetta* 'ribbon'.

fetus /ˈfiːtəs/ (Brit. (in non-technical use) also **foetus**) ■ n. (pl. **fetuses**) an unborn or unhatched offspring of a mammal, in particular an unborn human more than eight weeks after conception.
– ORIGIN Middle English: from Latin *fetus* 'pregnancy, childbirth, offspring'.

feud ■ n. a prolonged and bitter quarrel or dispute. ▸ a state of prolonged mutual hostility, typically between two families or communities. ■ v. take part in a feud.
– ORIGIN Middle English *fede* 'hostility', from Old French *feide*, from Middle Dutch, Middle Low German *vēde*, of Germanic origin; rel. to FOE.

feudal /ˈfjuːd(ə)l/ ■ adj. according to, resembling, or denoting the system of feudalism.
– DERIVATIVES **feudalization** /-ˈzeɪʃ(ə)n/ (also **-isation**) n. **feudalize** (also **-ise**) v. **feudally** adv.
– ORIGIN C17: from medieval Latin *feudalis*, from *feudum* (see FEE).

feudalism ■ n. the dominant social system in medieval Europe, in which the nobility held lands from the Crown in exchange for military service, and vassals were tenants of and protected by the nobles, giving their lords homage, labour, and a share of the produce.
– DERIVATIVES **feudalist** n. **feudalistic** adj.

feudatory /ˈfjuːdət(ə)ri/ historical ■ adj. owing feudal allegiance to. ■ n. (pl. **-ies**) a person who held land under the feudal system.
– ORIGIN C16: from medieval Latin *feudatorius*, from *feudare* 'give freehold property in exchange for service', from *feudum* (see FEE).

fever ■ n. 1 an abnormally high body temperature, usually accompanied by shivering, headache, and in severe instances, delirium. 2 a state of nervous excitement or agitation. ■ v. [as adj. **fevered**] 1 having or showing the symptoms of fever. 2 nervously excited or agitated.
– DERIVATIVES **feverish** adj. **feverishly** adv. **feverishness** n.
– ORIGIN Old English, from Latin *febris*; reinforced in Middle English by Old French *fievre*, also from *febris*.

feverfew /ˈfiːvəfjuː/ ■ n. a small bushy aromatic Eurasian plant of the daisy family, with feathery leaves and daisy-like flowers, used as a herbal remedy for headaches. [*Tanacetum parthenium*.]
– ORIGIN Old English *feferfuge*, from Latin *febrifuga*, from *febris* 'fever' + *fugare* 'drive away'.

feverous ■ adj. archaic feverish.

fever pitch ■ n. a state of extreme excitement.

fever tree ■ n. 1 a southern African tree formerly believed to cause malaria. [*Acacia xanthophloea*.] 2 a North American tree used in the treatment of malaria during the Civil War. [*Pinckneya pubens*.]

few ■ det., pron., & adj. 1 (**a few**) a small number of. 2 not many. ■ n. [as pl. n. **the few**] a select minority.
– PHRASES **few and far between** scarce. **a good few** a fairly large number of. **no fewer than** a surprisingly large number of. **not a few** a considerable number. **quite a few** a fairly large number. **some few** some but not many.
– ORIGIN Old English, of Germanic origin.

> **USAGE**
> **Fewer**, the comparative form of **few**, is correctly used with words denoting people or countable things, while **less** is used with mass nouns, denoting things which cannot be counted. In addition, **less** is normally used with numbers and expressions of measurement or time. The use of **less** with a count noun (*less people*) is incorrect in standard English.

fey /feɪ/ ■ adj. 1 unworldly and vague. 2 having clairvoyant powers.
– DERIVATIVES **feyness** n.
– ORIGIN Old English, of Germanic origin.

fez /fez/ ■ n. (pl. **fezzes**) a flat-topped conical red hat with a black tassel on top, worn by men in some Muslim countries.
– DERIVATIVES **fezzed** adj.
– ORIGIN C19: from Turkish *fes*, named after *Fez*, a city in Morocco, once the chief place of manufacture.

ff. ■ abbrev. 1 folios. 2 following pages.

f-hole ■ n. either of a pair of soundholes resembling an *f* and a reversed *f* in shape, cut in the front of musical instruments of the violin family, and some other stringed instruments such as mandolins.

fiacre /fɪˈɑːkrə, -kə/ ■ n. historical a small four-wheeled carriage for public hire.
– ORIGIN C17: from French, named after the Hôtel de St Fiacre in Paris, where such vehicles were first hired out.

fiancé /fɪˈɒnseɪ, -ˈɑːns-, -ˈɒ̃s-/ ■ n. (fem. **fiancée** pronunc. same) a person to whom another is engaged to be married.
– ORIGIN C19: from French, from *fiancer* 'betroth'.

fianchetto /ˌfɪənˈtʃetəʊ, -ˈketəʊ/ Chess ■ n. (pl. **-oes**) the development of a bishop by moving it one square to a long diagonal of the board. ■ v. (**-oes**, **-oed**) develop (a bishop) in such a way.
– ORIGIN C19: from Italian, diminutive of *fianco* 'flank'.

fiasco /fɪˈaskəʊ/ ■ n. (pl. **-os**) a ludicrous or humiliating failure.

fiat /ˈfʌɪat/ ■ n. an official order or authorization.
– ORIGIN Middle English: from Latin, 'let it be done', from *fieri* 'be done'.

fib ■ n. a trivial lie. ■ v. (**fibbed**, **fibbing**) tell a fib.
– DERIVATIVES **fibber** n.
– ORIGIN C16: perhaps a shortening of obsolete *fible-fable* 'nonsense', reduplication of FABLE.

fiber etc. ■ n. US spelling of FIBRE etc.

Fibonacci series ■ n. Mathematics a series of numbers in which each number (Fibonacci number) is the sum of the two preceding numbers (e.g. the series 1, 1, 2, 3, 5, 8, etc.).
– ORIGIN C19: named after the Italian mathematician Leonardo *Fibonacci* (c.1170–c.1250), who discovered it.

fibre (US **fiber**) ■ n. 1 a thread or filament from which a plant or animal tissue, mineral substance, or textile is formed. 2 a substance formed of fibres. 3 dietary material containing substances such as cellulose, that are resistant to the action of digestive enzymes. 4 strength of character: *a weak person with no moral fibre.*
– DERIVATIVES **-fibred** adj. **fibreless** adj.
– ORIGIN Middle English: from Latin *fibra* 'fibre, entrails'.

fibreboard (US **fiberboard**) ■ n. a building material made of wood or other plant fibres compressed into boards.

fibrefill ■ n. synthetic material used for padding and insulation in garments and soft furnishings such as duvets.

fibreglass (US **fiberglass**) ■ n. 1 a reinforced plastic material composed of glass fibres embedded in a resin matrix. 2 a textile fabric made from woven glass filaments.

fibre optics ■ pl. n. [treated as sing.] the use of thin flexible transparent fibres to transmit light signals, chiefly for telecommunications or for internal inspection of the body.
– DERIVATIVES **fibre-optic** adj.

fibrescope (US **fiberscope**) ■ n. a fibre-optic device for viewing inaccessible internal structures, especially in the human body.

fibril /ˈfʌɪbrɪl/ ■ n. technical a small or slender fibre.
– DERIVATIVES **fibrillar** adj.
– ORIGIN C17: from modern Latin *fibrilla*, diminutive of Latin *fibra* (see FIBRE).

fibrillate /ˈfʌɪbrɪleɪt, ˈfɪb-/ ■ v. 1 (of a muscle, especially in the heart) make a quivering movement due to uncoordinated contraction of the individual fibrils. 2 (with reference to a fibre) split up or break into fibrils.
– DERIVATIVES **fibrillation** n.

fibrin /ˈfʌɪbrɪn, ˈfɪb-/ ■ n. Biochemistry an insoluble protein formed as a fibrous mesh during the clotting of blood.
– DERIVATIVES **fibrinoid** adj. **fibrinous** adj.

fibrinogen /fʌɪˈbrɪnədʒ(ə)n, fɪ-/ ■ n. Biochemistry a soluble protein present in blood plasma, from which fibrin is produced by the enzyme thrombin.

fibrinolysis /ˌfʌɪbrɪˈnɒlɪsɪs, ˌfɪb-/ ■ n. Physiology the enzymatic breakdown of the fibrin in blood clots.
– DERIVATIVES **fibrinolytic** adj.

fibroblast /ˈfʌɪbrə(ʊ)blɑːst/ ■ n. Physiology a cell in connective tissue which produces collagen and other fibres.

fibroid /ˈfʌɪbrɔɪd/ ■ adj. of or characterized by fibres or fibrous tissue. ■ n. Medicine a benign tumour of muscular and fibrous tissues, typically developing in the wall of the womb.

fibroin /ˈfʌɪbrəʊɪn/ ■ n. a protein which is the chief constituent of silk.

fibroma /fʌɪˈbrəʊmə/ ■ n. (pl. **fibromas** or **fibromata** /-mətə/) Medicine a benign fibrous tumour of connective tissue.
– ORIGIN C19: from Latin *fibra* (see FIBRE).

fibromyalgia /ˌfʌɪbrəʊmʌɪˈaldʒɪə/ ■ n. a rheumatic condition characterized by muscular or musculoskeletal pain with stiffness and tenderness at specific points on the body.

fibrosis /fʌɪˈbrəʊsɪs/ ■ n. Medicine the thickening and scarring of connective tissue, usually as a result of injury.
– DERIVATIVES **fibrotic** adj.

fibrositis /ˌfʌɪbrəˈsʌɪtɪs/ ■ n. Medicine inflammation of fibrous connective tissue, typically affecting the back and causing stiffness and pain.
– DERIVATIVES **fibrositic** adj.

fibrous ■ adj. consisting of or characterized by fibres.
– DERIVATIVES **fibrously** adv. **fibrousness** n.

fibula /ˈfɪbjʊlə/ ■ n. (pl. **fibulae** /-liː/ or **fibulas**) **1** Anatomy the outer and usually smaller of the two bones between the knee and the ankle, parallel with the tibia. **2** Archaeology a brooch or clasp.
– DERIVATIVES **fibular** adj.
– ORIGIN C16: from Latin, 'brooch' (because the shape it makes with the tibia resembles a clasp).

-fic (usu. as **-ific**) ■ suffix (forming adjectives) producing; making: *prolific*.
– ORIGIN from French *-fique* or Latin *-ficus*, from *facere* 'do, make'.

FICA S. African ■ abbrev. Financial Intelligence Centre Act, passed in 2001 to combat money-laundering.

-fication (usu. as **-ification**) ■ suffix forming nouns of action from verbs ending in *-fy* (such as *simplification* from *simplify*).
– ORIGIN from French, or from Latin *-fication-*, from verbs ending in *-ficare*.

fiche ■ n. short for MICROFICHE.

fichu /ˈfiːʃuː/ ■ n. a small triangular shawl, worn round a woman's shoulders and neck.
– ORIGIN C18: from French, from *ficher* 'to fix, pin'.

fickle ■ adj. changeable, especially as regards one's loyalties.
– DERIVATIVES **fickleness** n. **fickly** adv.
– ORIGIN Old English *ficol* 'deceitful', of Germanic origin.

fiction ■ n. **1** prose literature, especially novels, describing imaginary events and people. **2** invention as opposed to fact. ▸ a false belief or statement, accepted as true because such acceptance is considered expedient.
– DERIVATIVES **fictional** adj. **fictionality** n. **fictionalization** (also **-isation**) n. **fictionalize** (also **-ise**) v. **fictionally** adv.
– ORIGIN Middle English: from Latin *fictio(n-)*, from *fingere* 'form, contrive'.

fictitious /fɪkˈtɪʃəs/ ■ adj. **1** not real or true, being imaginary or invented. **2** relating to or denoting the characters and events found in fiction.
– DERIVATIVES **fictitiously** adv. **fictitiousness** n.
– ORIGIN C17: from Latin *ficticius*, from *fingere* 'contrive, form'.

fictive ■ adj. creating or created by imagination.

ficus /ˈfiːkəs, ˈfʌɪkəs/ ■ n. (pl. same) a tree, shrub, or climber of warm and tropical climates belonging to a large genus that includes the figs and the rubber plant. [Genus *Ficus*.]
– ORIGIN C19: from Latin, 'fig (tree)'.

fiddle ■ n. **1** informal a violin. **2** informal, chiefly Brit. an act of fraud or cheating. **3** informal an unnecessarily intricate or awkward task. **4** Nautical a raised rim that prevents things from falling off a table in rough seas. ■ v. informal **1** touch or fidget with something restlessly or nervously. **2** chiefly Brit. falsify (figures, data, or records).
– PHRASES **fiddle while Rome burns** be concerned with relatively trivial matters while ignoring the serious events going on around one. (**as**) **fit as a fiddle** in very good health. **on the fiddle** informal engaged in fraud or cheating. **play second fiddle to** take a subordinate role to.
– DERIVATIVES **fiddler** n. (informal).
– ORIGIN Old English *fithele*, from Latin *vitulari* 'celebrate a festival'.

fiddle-back ■ n. a thing shaped like the back of a violin, especially the back of a chair or the front of a chasuble.

fiddle-de-dee ■ n. dated nonsense.
– ORIGIN C18: from FIDDLE + a reduplication without meaning.

fiddle-faddle ■ n. trivial matters; nonsense. ■ v. fuss.
– ORIGIN C16: reduplication of FIDDLE.

fiddlehead ■ n. **1** (also **fiddlehead greens**) the young, curled, edible frond of certain ferns. **2** a scroll-like carving at a ship's bows.

fiddler crab ■ n. a small amphibious crab, the males of which have one greatly enlarged claw. [Genus *Uca*.]

fiddlestick informal ■ exclam. (**fiddlesticks**) nonsense. ■ n. a violin bow.

fiddling ■ adj. informal **1** annoyingly trivial. **2** involved in fraud.

fiddly ■ adj. (**-ier, -iest**) informal complicated and awkward to do or use.

fideism /ˈfʌɪdiːɪz(ə)m/ ■ n. the doctrine that knowledge depends on faith or revelation.
– DERIVATIVES **fideist** n. **fideistic** adj.
– ORIGIN C19: from Latin *fides* 'faith'.

fidelity /fɪˈdɛlɪti/ ■ n. **1** continuing loyalty to a person, cause, or belief. **2** the degree of exactness with which something is copied or reproduced.
– ORIGIN Middle English: from Latin *fidelitas*, from *fidelis* 'faithful', from *fides* 'faith'.

fidelity insurance ■ n. insurance taken out by an employer against losses incurred through dishonesty by employees.

fidget /ˈfɪdʒɪt/ ■ v. (**fidgeted, fidgeting**) make small movements through nervousness or impatience. ■ n. a person who fidgets. ▸ an act of fidgeting. ▸ (**fidgets**) mental or physical restlessness.
– DERIVATIVES **fidgeter** n. **fidgetiness** n. **fidgety** adj.
– ORIGIN C17: from obsolete or dialect *fidge* 'to twitch'.

fiduciary /fɪˈdjuːʃ(ə)ri/ ■ adj. **1** Law involving trust, especially with regard to the relationship between a trustee and a beneficiary. **2** Finance (of a paper currency) depending for its value on securities or the reputation of the issuer. ■ n. (pl. **-ies**) a trustee.
– ORIGIN C16: from Latin *fiduciarius*, from *fiducia* 'trust'.

fie /fʌɪ/ ■ exclam. archaic or humorous used to express disgust or outrage.
– ORIGIN Middle English: from Latin *fi*, an exclamation of disgust at a stench.

fief /fiːf/ ■ n. **1** historical another term for FEE (in sense 2). **2** a person's sphere of operation or control.
– DERIVATIVES **fiefdom** n.
– ORIGIN C17: from French (see FEE).

field ■ n. **1** an area of open land, especially one planted with crops or pasture. ▸ a piece of land used for a sport or game. ▸ a large area of land or water completely covered in snow or ice. ▸ an area rich in a natural product, typically oil or gas. **2** a particular branch of study or sphere of activity. ▸ Computing a part of a record, representing an item of data. **3** a space or range within which objects are visible from a particular viewpoint or through a piece of apparatus. **4** (**the field**) all the participants in a contest or sport. ▸ Cricket fielders collectively. ▸ a fielder of specified ability. **5** Heraldry the surface of an escutcheon or of one of its divisions. **6** Physics the region in which a force such as gravity or magnetism is effective, regardless of the presence or absence of a material medium. ■ v. **1** chiefly Cricket & Baseball attempt to catch or stop the ball and return it after it has been hit. ▸ catch or stop (the ball) and return it. **2** select for a

field cornet 432

particular game or to stand in an election. **3** deal with (a difficult question, telephone call, etc.). ■ adj. carried out or working in the natural environment, rather than in a laboratory or office. ▶ (of military equipment) light and mobile for use on campaign. ▶ used in names of animals or plants found in the open country, e.g. field mouse.
–PHRASES **hold the field** remain the most important. **in the field 1** engaged in combat or manoeuvres. **2** engaged in fieldwork. **play the field** informal indulge in a series of casual sexual relationships. **take the field 1** (of a team) go on to a field to begin a game. **2** start a military campaign.
–ORIGIN Old English, of West Germanic origin.

field cornet ■ n. S. African historical an unpaid civil officer appointed to preserve law and order in outlying areas.

fieldcraft ■ n. the techniques involved in living or making military or scientific observations in the field.

field day ■ n. **1** an opportunity for action or success, especially at the expense of others. **2** Military a review or an exercise, especially in manoeuvring. **3** chiefly N. Amer. a day devoted to athletics or other sporting events.

field-effect transistor ■ n. Electronics a transistor in which most current is carried along a channel whose effective resistance can be controlled by a transverse electric field.

fielder ■ n. chiefly Cricket & Baseball a player on the fielding team, especially one other than the bowler or pitcher.

field events ■ pl. n. athletic sports other than races, such as throwing and jumping events. Compare with TRACK EVENTS.

field glasses ■ pl. n. binoculars for outdoor use.

field goal ■ n. **1** American Football a goal scored by a place kick. **2** Basketball a goal scored while the clock is running and the ball is in play.

field hockey ■ n. hockey played on grass or a hard pitch, as opposed to ice hockey.

field hospital ■ n. a temporary hospital set up near a battlefield.

field mark ■ n. a visible mark used in identifying a bird or other animal in the field.

field marshal ■ n. the highest rank of military officer in the British army.

field mouse ■ n. a common dark brown mouse with a long tail and large eyes. [*Apodemus sylvaticus* and related species.]

field mushroom ■ n. the common edible mushroom. [*Agaricus campestris*.]

field officer ■ n. a major, lieutenant colonel, or colonel.

fieldsman ■ n. (pl. -**men**) **1** Cricket a fielder. **2** an agent or salesman working for a company.

field sports ■ pl. n. outdoor sports, especially hunting, shooting, and fishing.

fieldstone ■ n. stone used in its natural form.

field test ■ n. (also **field trial**) a test carried out in the environment in which a product or device is to be used. ■ v. (**field-test**) test in such a way.

fieldwork ■ n. practical work conducted by a researcher in the field.
–DERIVATIVES **fieldworker** n.

fiend /fiːnd/ ■ n. **1** an evil spirit or demon. ▶ a very wicked or cruel person. **2** informal an enthusiast or devotee: *a jazz fiend*.
–DERIVATIVES **fiendlike** adj.
–ORIGIN Old English *feond* 'an enemy, the devil', of Germanic origin.

fiendish ■ adj. **1** extremely cruel or unpleasant. **2** extremely difficult.
–DERIVATIVES **fiendishly** adv. **fiendishness** n.

fierce ■ adj. violent or aggressive; ferocious. ▶ intense: *fierce opposition*.
–DERIVATIVES **fiercely** adv. **fierceness** n.
–ORIGIN Middle English: from Old French *fiers* 'fierce, brave', from Latin *ferus* 'untamed'.

fiery ■ adj. (-**ier**, -**iest**) **1** resembling or consisting of fire. **2** quick-tempered or passionate.

–DERIVATIVES **fierily** adv. **fieriness** n.

fiesta /fɪˈɛstə/ ■ n. **1** (in Spanish-speaking countries) a religious festival. **2** a festive event.
–ORIGIN Spanish: from Latin *festum*, (pl.) *festa* (see FEAST).

FIFA /ˈfiːfə/ ■ abbrev. Fédération Internationale de Football Association, the international governing body of soccer.

fife ■ n. a kind of small shrill flute used with the drum in military bands.
–DERIVATIVES **fifer** n.
–ORIGIN C16: from German *Pfeife* 'pipe', or from French *fifre* from Swiss German *Pfifer* 'piper'.

FIFO /ˈfaɪfəʊ/ ■ abbrev. first in, first out (chiefly with reference to methods of stock valuation and data storage).

fifteen ■ cardinal number **1** equivalent to the product of three and five; one more than fourteen; 15. (Roman numeral: **xv** or **XV**.) **2** a team of fifteen players, especially in rugby.
–DERIVATIVES **fifteenth** ordinal number.
–ORIGIN Old English, of Germanic origin.

fifth ■ ordinal number **1** constituting number five in a sequence; 5th. **2** (**a fifth/one fifth**) each of five equal parts into which something is or may be divided. **3** Music an interval spanning five consecutive notes in a diatonic scale, in particular (also **perfect fifth**) an interval of three tones and a semitone. ▶ the note which is higher by such an interval than the root of a diatonic scale.
–PHRASES **take the fifth** (in the US) exercise the right guaranteed by the Fifth Amendment to the Constitution of refusing to answer questions in order to avoid incriminating oneself.
–DERIVATIVES **fifthly** adv.

fifth column ■ n. a group within a country at war who are working for its enemies.
–DERIVATIVES **fifth columnist** n.
–ORIGIN from the Spanish Civil War, when General Mola, leading four columns of troops towards Madrid, declared that he had a fifth column inside the city.

fifth-generation ■ adj. denoting a proposed new class of computer or programming language employing artificial intelligence.

fifth wheel ■ n. **1** chiefly N. Amer. a spare wheel for a four-wheeled vehicle. ▶ informal a superfluous person or thing. **2** a coupling between a vehicle used for towing and a trailer.

fifty ■ cardinal number (pl. -**ies**) the number equivalent to the product of five and ten; half of one hundred; 50. (Roman numeral: **l** or **L**.)
–DERIVATIVES **fiftieth** ordinal number. **fiftyfold** adj. & adv.
–ORIGIN Old English.

fifty-fifty ■ adj. & adv. with equal shares or chances.

fig ■ n. **1** a soft pear-shaped fruit with sweet dark flesh and many small seeds. **2** (also **fig tree**) the deciduous tree or shrub bearing this fruit. [*Ficus carica*.] ▶ used in names of related plants, e.g. strangling fig.
–PHRASES **not give** (or **care**) **a fig** not care at all.
–ORIGIN Middle English: from Old French *figue*, from Provençal *fig(u)a*; from Latin *ficus*.

fig. ■ abbrev. figure.

fight ■ v. (past and past part. **fought**) **1** take part in a violent struggle involving physical force or weapons. ▶ engage in (a war or contest). ▶ quarrel or argue. ▶ (**fight someone/thing off**) defend oneself against an attack by someone or something. **2** struggle to overcome, eliminate, or prevent. ▶ (**fight for**) try very hard to obtain or do. **3** (**fight one's way**) move forward with difficulty. ■ n. an act of fighting. ▶ the inclination or ability to fight or struggle.
–PHRASES **fight fire with fire** use the weapons or tactics of one's opponent, even if one finds them distasteful. **fight shy of** avoid through unwillingness. **fight or flight** the instinctive physiological response to a threatening situation, which readies one either to resist forcibly or to run away.
–ORIGIN Old English, of West Germanic origin.

fightback ■ n. a rally or recovery.

fighter ■ n. **1** a person or animal that fights. **2** a fast military aircraft designed for attacking other aircraft.

fighting chance ■ n. a possibility of success if great effort is made.

fighting fish (also **Siamese fighting fish**) ■ n. a small labyrinth fish native to Thailand, the males of which fight vigorously. [*Betta splendens*.]

fighting fit ■ adj. in excellent health.

fighting fund ■ n. money raised to finance a campaign.

fighting stick ■ n. a stick, especially one of a pair, used in stick fighting.

fighting words (also **fighting talk**) ■ pl. n. **1** informal words indicating a willingness to fight. **2** US insulting language, especially of an ethnic, racial, or sexist nature, considered unacceptable or illegal.

fig leaf ■ n. a leaf of a fig tree, often used for concealing the genitals in paintings and sculpture.
– ORIGIN C16: with ref. to the story of Adam and Eve (Genesis 3:7).

figment /'fɪgm(ə)nt/ ■ n. a thing believed to be real but existing only in the imagination.
– ORIGIN Middle English: from Latin *figmentum*, rel. to *fingere* 'form, contrive'.

figural /'fɪgjʊr(ə)l/ ■ adj. another term for FIGURATIVE.

figuration /ˌfɪgə'reɪʃ(ə)n, -gjʊ-/ ■ n. **1** ornamentation by means of figures. **2** allegorical representation.

figurative ■ adj. **1** departing from a literal use of words; metaphorical. **2** Art representing forms that are recognizably derived from life.
– DERIVATIVES **figuratively** adv. **figurativeness** n.

figure /'fɪgə/ ■ n. **1** a number or a numerical symbol. ▸ an amount of money. ▸ (**figures**) arithmetical calculations. **2** a person's bodily shape, especially that of a woman. ▸ a person seen indistinctly. ▸ a person of a particular kind: *a public figure*. ▸ an artistic representation of a human or animal form. **3** a shape defined by one or more lines in two dimensions, or one or more surfaces in three dimensions. ▸ a diagram or illustrative drawing. ▸ (in skating) a movement or series of movements following a prescribed pattern. ▸ a pattern formed by the movements of a group of people, for example in country dancing, as part of a longer dance or display. ▸ archaic external form or shape. ■ v. **1** be a significant part of or contributor to something. **2** calculate arithmetically. **3** informal, chiefly N. Amer. think; consider. ▸ be perfectly understandable: *she supposed that figured*. ▸ (**figure someone/thing out**) informal reach an understanding of someone or something. **4** (**figure on**) N. Amer. informal count or rely on something happening or being the case. **5** represent in a diagram or picture. ▸ [usu. as adj. **figured**] embellish with a pattern.
– DERIVATIVES **figureless** adj.
– ORIGIN Middle English: from Latin *figura* 'figure, form'; rel. to *fingere* 'form, contrive'.

figured bass ■ n. Music a bass line with the intended harmonies indicated by figures rather than written out as chords, typical of continuo parts.

figurehead ■ n. **1** a carved bust or full-length figure set at the prow of an old-fashioned sailing ship. **2** a nominal leader without real power.

figure of eight (N. Amer. **figure eight**) ■ n. an object or movement having the shape of the number eight.

figure of speech ■ n. a word or phrase used in a non-literal sense for rhetorical or vivid effect.

figure skating ■ n. the sport of skating in prescribed patterns from a stationary position.
– DERIVATIVES **figure skater** n.

figurine /'fɪgəriːn, -gjʊ-/ ■ n. a small statue of a human form.
– ORIGIN C19: from Italian *figurina*, diminutive of *figura*, from Latin *figura* (see FIGURE).

figwort ■ n. a herbaceous plant of the northern hemisphere with purplish-brown two-lobed flowers. [Genus *Scrophularia*: several species.]
– ORIGIN C16 (orig. denoting pilewort, used as a treatment for piles): from obsolete *fig* 'piles' + WORT.

Fijian /fiː'dʒiːən/ ■ n. **1** a native or national of Fiji, or a person of Fijian descent. **2** the Austronesian language of the indigenous people of Fiji. ■ adj. of or relating to Fiji, its people, or language.

filagree /'fɪləgriː/ ■ n. variant spelling of FILIGREE.

filament /'fɪləm(ə)nt/ ■ n. **1** a slender thread-like object or fibre, especially one found in animal or plant structures. **2** a metal wire in an electric light bulb, made incandescent by an electric current. **3** Botany the slender part of a stamen that supports the anther.
– DERIVATIVES **filamentary** adj. **filamentous** adj.
– ORIGIN C16: from modern Latin *filamentum*, from late Latin *filare* 'to spin'.

filaria /fɪ'lɛːrɪə/ ■ n. (pl. **filariae** /-riiː/) a thread-like parasitic nematode worm which is transmitted by biting flies and mosquitoes in the tropics, causing disease. [Super-family Filarioidea.]
– DERIVATIVES **filarial** adj.
– ORIGIN C19: former genus name, from Latin *filum* 'thread'.

filariasis /ˌfɪlə'raɪəsɪs, fɪlə'raɪəsɪs/ ■ n. Medicine a tropical disease caused by the presence of filarial worms, especially in the lymph vessels.

filbert ■ n. **1** a cultivated oval hazelnut. **2** the tree that bears these nuts. [*Corylus maxima* and other species.] **3** (also **filbert brush**) a brush with bristles forming a flattened oval head, used in oil painting.
– ORIGIN Middle English: from Anglo-Norman French *philbert*, from dialect French *noix de filbert* (so named because it is ripe about 20 August, the feast day of St *Philibert*).

filch /fɪltʃ/ ■ v. informal pilfer; steal.
– DERIVATIVES **filcher** n.
– ORIGIN Middle English.

file[1] ■ n. **1** a folder or box for keeping loose papers together and in order. **2** Computing a collection of data or programs stored under a single identifying name. ■ v. **1** place (a document) in a file. ▸ submit (a legal document, application, or charge) to be officially placed on record. **2** (of a reporter) send (a story) to a newspaper or news organization.
– DERIVATIVES **filer** n. **filing** n.
– ORIGIN Middle English ('string documents on a thread or wire'): from French *filer* 'to string', *fil* 'a thread', both from Latin *filum* 'a thread'.

file[2] ■ n. **1** a line of people or things one behind another. **2** Military a small detachment of men. **3** Chess each of the eight rows of eight squares on a chessboard running away from the player towards the opponent. Compare with RANK[1] (in sense 6). ■ v. walk one behind the other.
– ORIGIN C16: from French *file*, from *filer* 'to string'.

file[3] ■ n. a tool with a roughened surface or surfaces, used for smoothing or shaping a hard material. ■ v. smooth or shape with a file.
– DERIVATIVES **filer** n.
– ORIGIN Old English, of West Germanic origin.

file 13 ■ n. informal, humorous the waste-paper bin.
– ORIGIN with ref. to the superstition that the number thirteen is unlucky because there were thirteen people at the Last Supper.

filefish ■ n. (pl. same or **-fishes**) a fish with a dorsal spine and rough scales, occurring chiefly in tropical seas. [Family Balistidae: many species.]
– ORIGIN C18: from FILE[3] (because of its rough skin).

file snake ■ n. a non-venomous nocturnal African snake which kills its prey by constriction. [Genus *Mehelya*: several species.]

filet /'fiːleɪ, 'fɪlɪt/ ■ n. **1** French spelling of FILLET, used in the names of French or French-sounding dishes: *filet de boeuf*. **2** a kind of net or lace with a square mesh.
– ORIGIN C19: from French, 'net'.

filet mignon /ˌfiːleɪ 'miːnjɒ̃/ ■ n. a small tender piece of beef from the end of the undercut.
– ORIGIN French, 'dainty fillet'.

filial /'fɪlɪəl/ ■ adj. of, relating to, or due from a son or daughter.
– DERIVATIVES **filially** adv.
– ORIGIN Middle English: from eccles. Latin *filialis*, from Latin *filius* 'son', *filia* 'daughter'.

filibuster /'fɪlɪbʌstə/ ■ n. **1** prolonged speaking or other action which obstructs progress in a legislative assembly while not technically contravening the required procedures. **2** historical a person engaging in unauthorized warfare against a foreign state. ■ v. [often as noun

filicide 434

filibustering] obstruct legislation with a filibuster.
– ORIGIN C18: from French *flibustier*, first applied to pirates who pillaged the Spanish colonies in the West Indies, influenced by Spanish *filibustero*, denoting American adventurers who incited revolution in Latin America; ultimately from Dutch *vrijbuiter* 'freebooter'.

filicide /ˈfɪlɪsʌɪd/ ■ n. the killing of one's son or daughter. ▸ a person who does this.
– ORIGIN C17 from Latin *filius* 'son', *filia* 'daughter' + -CIDE.

filiform /ˈfʌɪlɪfɔːm/ ■ adj. Biology thread-like.
– ORIGIN C18: from Latin *filum* 'thread' + -IFORM.

filigree /ˈfɪlɪgriː/ (also **filagree**) ■ n. delicate ornamental work of fine gold, silver, or copper wire.
– DERIVATIVES **filigreed** adj.
– ORIGIN C17: from French *filigrane*, from Italian *filigrana*, from Latin *filum* 'thread' + *granum* 'seed'.

filing cabinet ■ n. a large piece of office furniture with deep drawers for storing files.

filings ■ pl. n. small particles rubbed off by a file.

Filipino /ˌfɪlɪˈpiːnəʊ/ (also **Pilipino**) ■ n. (fem. **Filipina** /-nə/, pl. **-os** or **-as**) 1 a native or national of the Philippines, or a person of Filipino descent. 2 the national language of the Philippines, a standardized form of Tagalog. ■ adj. of or relating to the Philippines, the Filipinos, or their language.
– ORIGIN Spanish: from *las Islas Filipinas* 'the Philippine Islands'.

fill ■ v. 1 make or become full. ▸ block up (a hole, gap, etc.). ▸ pervade with an emotion or feeling. ▸ (of a sail) curve out tautly from its supports as the wind blows into it. 2 appoint a person to hold (a vacant post). ▸ hold and perform the duties of (a position or role). 3 occupy (a period of time). 4 chiefly N. Amer. be supplied with the items described in (a prescription or order). ■ n. 1 (**one's fill**) as much as one wants or can bear. 2 material which fills a space, especially in building or engineering work. 3 (in popular music) a short interjected instrumental phrase.
– PHRASES **fill someone's shoes** (or **boots**) informal take over someone's role and fulfil it satisfactorily.
– PHRASAL VERBS **fill in** act as a substitute. **fill someone in** inform someone more fully of a matter. **fill something in** 1 add information to complete a form or document. 2 complete a drawing by adding colour or shade to the spaces within an outline. **fill out** put on weight. **fill something out** add information to complete a form or document. ▸ give more details about something.
– ORIGIN Old English, of Germanic origin; rel. to FULL¹.

filler /ˈfɪlə/ ■ n. 1 something used to fill a gap or cavity, or to increase bulk. ▸ an item serving only to fill space or time in a newspaper, broadcast, or recording. ▸ a word or sound filling a pause in an utterance or conversation (e.g. *er*). 2 a person or thing that fills a space or container: *a shelf-filler*.

filler cap ■ n. a cap closing the pipe leading to the petrol tank of a motor vehicle.

fillet ■ n. 1 a fleshy boneless piece of meat from near the loins or the ribs of an animal. ▸ (also **fillet steak**) a beef steak cut from the lower part of a sirloin. ▸ a boned side of a fish. 2 a band or ribbon binding the hair. 3 Architecture a narrow flat band separating two mouldings. ▸ a small band between the flutes of a column. 4 a roughly triangular strip of material which rounds off an interior angle between two surfaces. 5 a plain line impressed on the cover of a book. ■ v. (**filleted**, **filleting**) remove the bones from (a fish). ▸ cut (fish or meat) into fillets.
– DERIVATIVES **filleter** n.
– ORIGIN Middle English: from Old French *filet* 'thread', from Latin *filum* 'thread'.

filling ■ n. a quantity or piece of material that fills or is used to fill something. ■ adj. (of food) leaving one with a pleasantly satiated feeling.

filling station ■ n. a petrol station.

fillip /ˈfɪlɪp/ ■ n. 1 a stimulus or boost. 2 archaic a movement made by bending the last joint of the finger against the thumb and suddenly releasing it. ■ v. (**filliped**, **filliping**) archaic propel (a small object) with a flick of the fingers.
– ORIGIN Middle English: symbolic.

filly ■ n. (pl. **-ies**) 1 a young female horse, especially one less than four years old. 2 humorous a lively girl or young woman.
– ORIGIN Middle English: from Old Norse *fylja*, of Germanic origin.

film ■ n. 1 a thin flexible strip of plastic or other material coated with light-sensitive emulsion for exposure in a camera. 2 material in the form of a very thin flexible sheet. ▸ a thin layer covering a surface. 3 a story or event recorded by a camera as a series of moving images and shown in a cinema or on television. ■ v. 1 make a film of; record on film. 2 become or appear to become covered with a thin film.
– ORIGIN Old English *filmen* 'membrane', of West Germanic origin.

filmic ■ adj. of or relating to films or cinematography.

film noir /fɪlm ˈnwɑː/ ■ n. a style or genre of cinematographic film marked by a mood of pessimism, fatalism, and menace.
– ORIGIN French, 'black film'.

filmography ■ n. (pl. **-ies**) a list of films by one director or actor, or on one subject.
– ORIGIN 1960s: from FILM + -GRAPHY, on the pattern of *bibliography*.

filmsetting ■ n. Printing the setting of material to be printed by projecting it on to photographic film from which the printing surface is prepared.
– DERIVATIVES **filmset** v. **filmsetter** n.

filmstrip ■ n. a series of transparencies in a strip for projection.

filmy ■ adj. (**-ier**, **-iest**) 1 (especially of fabric) thin and translucent. 2 covered with or as with a thin film.
– DERIVATIVES **filmily** adv. **filminess** n.

filo /ˈfiːləʊ/ (also **phyllo**) ■ n. a kind of flaky pastry stretched into very thin sheets, used especially in eastern Mediterranean cookery.
– ORIGIN 1950s: from modern Greek *phullo* 'leaf'.

Filofax /ˈfʌɪlə(ʊ)faks/ ■ n. trademark a loose-leaf notebook for recording appointments, addresses, and notes.
– ORIGIN 1930s: representing a colloquial pronunciation of *file of facts*.

filovirus /ˈfiːləʊˌvʌɪrəs/ ■ n. a filamentous RNA virus of a group which causes severe haemorrhagic fevers.

filter ■ n. 1 a porous device for removing impurities or solid particles from a liquid or gas passed through it. ▸ a screen, plate, or layer which absorbs some of the light passing through it. ▸ a device for suppressing electrical or sound waves of frequencies not required. 2 Brit. an arrangement whereby vehicles may turn left (or right) while other traffic waiting to go straight ahead or turn right (or left) is stopped by a red light. 3 Computing a piece of software that processes text, e.g. by removing unwanted spaces. ■ v. 1 pass through a filter. 2 (often **filter in/out/through**) move gradually through something or in a specified direction. ▸ (of information) gradually become known.
– DERIVATIVES **filterable** (also **filtrable**) adj.
– ORIGIN Middle English: from French *filtre*, from medieval Latin *filtrum* 'felt used as a filter', of West Germanic origin.

filter bed ■ n. a tank or pond containing a layer of sand or gravel, used for filtering large quantities of liquid.

filter-feeding ■ adj. Zoology (of an aquatic animal) feeding by filtering out plankton or nutrients suspended in the water.
– DERIVATIVES **filter-feeder** n.

filter tip ■ n. a filter attached to a cigarette for removing impurities from the inhaled smoke.
– DERIVATIVES **filter-tipped** adj.

filth ■ n. disgusting dirt. ▸ obscene and offensive language or printed material. ▸ corrupt behaviour.
– ORIGIN Old English *fylth* 'rotting matter', also 'corruption, obscenity', of Germanic origin.

filthy ■ adj. (**-ier**, **-iest**) disgustingly dirty. ▸ obscene and offensive. ▸ Brit. informal (of weather) very unpleasant. ▸ informal (of a mood) very disagreeable. ■ adv. informal extremely: *filthy rich*.
– DERIVATIVES **filthily** adv. **filthiness** n.

filtrate /ˈfɪltreɪt/ ■ n. a liquid which has passed through a filter.

CONSONANTS   b but   d dog   f few   g get   h he   j yes   k cat   l leg   m man   n no   p pen   r red

– DERIVATIVES **filtration** n.
– ORIGIN C17: from modern Latin *filtrare* 'filter'.

fimbriated /ˈfɪmbrɪeɪtɪd/ (also **fimbriate**) ■ adj. **1** Biology having a structure which forms or resembles a fringe. **2** Heraldry having a narrow border.

fin ■ n. **1** a flattened appendage on the body of a fish or other aquatic animal, used for propelling, steering, and balancing. ▸ an underwater swimmer's flipper. **2** a small flattened projecting surface or attachment on an aircraft, rocket, or motor car, for providing aerodynamic stability. **3** a flattened projection for increasing heat transfer from an object. ■ v. (**finned**, **finning**) swim under water by means of flippers.
– DERIVATIVES **finless** adj. **-finned** adj.
– ORIGIN Old English, of Germanic origin.

finagle /fɪˈneɪɡ(ə)l/ ■ v. informal obtain or act dishonestly or deviously.
– ORIGIN 1920s (orig. US): from dialect *fainaigue* 'cheat'.

final ■ adj. **1** coming at the end of a series. ▸ reached as the outcome of a process: *the final cost will run into six figures*. **2** allowing no further doubt or dispute. ■ n. **1** the last game in a sports tournament or other competition, which will decide the overall winner. ▸ (**finals**) a series of games constituting the final stage of a competition. **2** (**finals**) Brit. a series of examinations at the end of a degree course. ▸ (**final**) an examination at the end of a term, school year, or particular class.
– DERIVATIVES **finality** n. **finally** adv.
– ORIGIN Middle English: from Latin *finalis*, from *finis* 'end'.

final cause ■ n. Philosophy the purpose of an action or the end towards which a thing naturally develops.

final clause ■ n. Grammar a clause expressing purpose or intention (e.g. one introduced by *in order that*).

finale /fɪˈnɑːli, -leɪ/ ■ n. the last part of a piece of music, an entertainment, or a public event.
– ORIGIN C18: from Italian.

finalist ■ n. **1** a participant in the final or finals of a competition. **2** a student taking finals.

finalize (also **-ise**) ■ v. **1** complete (a transaction) after discussion of the terms. **2** produce or agree on a finished version of.
– DERIVATIVES **finalization** (also **-isation**) n.

finance /ˈfaɪnans, fɪ-, ˈfaɪnans/ ■ n. the management of large amounts of money, especially by governments or large companies. ▸ monetary support for an enterprise. ▸ (**finances**) the monetary resources and affairs of a state, organization, or person. ■ v. provide funding for.
– ORIGIN Middle English: from Old French, from *finer* 'settle a debt', from *fin* (see FINE²).

finance company (also **finance house**) ■ n. a company concerned primarily with providing money, e.g. for hire-purchase transactions.

financial /faɪˈnanʃ(ə)l, fɪ-/ ■ adj. of or relating to finance. ■ n. (**financials**) the financial situation of an organization or individual.
– DERIVATIVES **financially** adv.

financial year ■ n. a year as reckoned for taxing or accounting purposes (e.g. the South African tax year, reckoned from 1 March).

financier /faɪˈnansɪə, fɪ-/ ■ n. a person engaged in managing the finances of governments or other large organizations.
– ORIGIN C17: from French, from *finance* (see FINANCE).

finback ■ n. another term for FIN WHALE.

finch ■ n. a seed-eating songbird of a large group including the chaffinch, goldfinch, linnet, etc., typically with a stout bill and colourful plumage. [Many species, especially in the family Fringillidae.]
– ORIGIN Old English, of West Germanic origin.

find ■ v. (past and past part. **found**) **1** discover by chance or deliberately. ▸ (**find something out**) or **find out about something**) discover information or a fact. ▸ succeed in obtaining: *she also found the time to raise a family*. ▸ (**find someone out**) detect someone in a crime or lie. **2** recognize or discover to be present: *vitamin B12 is found in dairy products*. ▸ discover or perceive to be the case. ▸ ascertain by research or calculation. ▸ Law (of a court) officially declare to be the case. ▸ (**find against**) or **for** Law (of a court) make a decision against (or in favour of); judge to be guilty (or innocent). **3** reach or arrive at by a natural or normal process: *water finds its own level*.
▸ (**find one's way**) reach one's destination without knowing or having been told in advance how to get there. ■ n. a discovery of something valuable or interesting, typically an archaeological one. ▸ a person who is found to be useful or interesting.
– PHRASES **all found** Brit. dated (of an employee's wages) with board and lodging provided free. **find one's feet** stand up and become able to walk. ▸ establish oneself in a particular field. **find it in one's heart to do** [usu. with neg.] allow or force oneself to do.
– ORIGIN Old English, of Germanic origin.

finder ■ n. **1** a person that finds someone or something. **2** a small telescope attached to a large one to locate an object for observation. ▸ a viewfinder.
– PHRASES **finders keepers** (**losers weepers**) informal whoever finds something is entitled to keep it.

fin de siècle /ˌfã də ˈsjɛkl(ə)/ ■ adj. relating to or characteristic of the end of a century, especially the 19th century.
– ORIGIN French, 'end of century'.

finding ■ n. a conclusion reached as a result of an inquiry, investigation, or trial.

fine¹ /faɪn/ ■ adj. **1** of very high quality. ▸ satisfactory. ▸ in good health and feeling well. ▸ (of speech or writing) sounding impressive but ultimately insincere: *fine words*.
▸ (of gold or silver) containing a specified high proportion of pure metal. **2** (of the weather) bright and clear. **3** (of a thread, filament, or hair) thin. ▸ consisting of small particles. ▸ of delicate or intricate workmanship. ▸ subtle and therefore perceptible with difficulty: *a fine distinction*. ▸ (of feelings) refined; elevated. **4** Cricket behind the wicket and close to the line of flight of the bowling. ■ n. (**fines**) very small particles found in mining or milling. ■ adv. **1** informal in a satisfactory or pleasing manner. **2** Cricket to a fine position. ■ v. **1** clarify (beer or wine) by causing the precipitation of sediment. **2** (usu. **fine something down**) or **fine down** make or become thinner.
– PHRASES **cut it** (or **things**) **fine** allow a very small margin of time. **one's finest hour** the time of one's greatest success. **not to put too fine a point on it** to speak bluntly. **one fine day** at some unspecified time.
– DERIVATIVES **finely** adv. **fineness** n.
– ORIGIN Middle English: from Old French *fin*, from Latin *finire* (see FINISH).

fine² /faɪn/ ■ n. a sum of money exacted as a penalty by a court of law or other authority. ■ v. punish by a fine.
– DERIVATIVES **fineable** adj.
– ORIGIN Middle English: from Old French *fin* 'end, payment', from Latin *finis* 'end' (in medieval Latin denoting a sum paid on settling a lawsuit).

fine art (also **fine arts**) ■ n. art intended to be appreciated primarily or solely for its aesthetic content.
– PHRASES **have** (or **get**) **something down to a fine art** achieve a high level of skill in something through experience.

fine chemicals ■ pl. n. highly pure chemicals prepared for use in research and industry.

fine ounce ■ n. (of gold) a troy ounce (approximately 31 grams) that is 995 per 1 000 parts pure.

fine print ■ n. another term for SMALL PRINT.

finery /ˈfaɪn(ə)ri/ ■ n. ostentatious clothes or decoration.
– ORIGIN C17: from FINE¹, on the pattern of *bravery*.

fines herbes /fiːnz ˈɛːb/ ■ pl. n. mixed herbs used in cooking.
– ORIGIN French, 'fine herbs'.

fine-spun ■ adj. (especially of fabric) fine or delicate in texture.

finesse ■ n. **1** refinement and delicacy. ▸ subtle skill in handling or manipulating people or situations. **2** (in bridge and whist) an attempt to win a trick with a card that is not a certain winner. ■ v. **1** do in a subtle and delicate manner. ▸ slyly attempt to avoid blame when dealing with (a situation). **2** (in bridge and whist) play (a card) as a finesse.
– ORIGIN Middle English: from French, rel. to FINE¹.

fine-tooth comb

fine-tooth comb (also **fine-toothed comb**) ■ n. (in phr. **with a fine-tooth comb**) with a very thorough search or analysis.

fine-tune ■ v. make small adjustments to in order to achieve the best performance.

finfoot ■ n. (pl. **finfoots**) a grebe-like waterbird with a long bill, neck, and tail, and lobed feet. [Family Heliornithidae: three species.]

finger ■ n. each of the four slender jointed parts attached to either hand (or five, if the thumb is included). ▸ a measure of liquor in a glass, based on the breadth of a finger. ■ v. 1 touch or feel with the fingers. 2 (usu. **finger someone for**) informal, chiefly N. Amer. inform on to the police. ▸ identify or choose (someone) for a particular purpose.
– PHRASES **be all fingers and thumbs** Brit. informal be clumsy. **pull one's finger out** informal cease prevaricating and start to act. **get one's fingers burned** (or **burnt**) (or **burn one's fingers**) suffer unpleasant consequences as a result of one's actions. **give someone the finger** informal, chiefly N. Amer. make a gesture with the middle finger raised as an obscene sign of contempt. **have a finger in the pie** be involved in a matter. **have** (or **keep**) **one's finger on the pulse** be aware of the latest trends. **lay a finger on** touch (someone), especially with the intention of harming them. **put the finger on** informal inform on. **put one's finger on** identify (something) exactly. **snap** (or **click**) **one's fingers** make a sharp clicking sound by bending the last joint of the middle finger against the thumb and suddenly releasing it.
– DERIVATIVES **-fingered** adj. **fingerless** adj.
– ORIGIN Old English, of Germanic origin.

finger alphabet ■ n. a form of sign language using the fingers to spell out words.

fingerboard ■ n. a flat strip on the neck of a stringed instrument, against which the strings are pressed to shorten the vibrating length and produce notes of higher pitches.

finger bowl ■ n. a small bowl holding water for rinsing the fingers during or after a meal.

finger-dry ■ v. dry and style (hair) by repeatedly running one's fingers through it.

finger food ■ n. food served in a form that can conveniently be eaten with the fingers.

fingering ■ n. a manner or technique of using the fingers to play a musical instrument.

fingerling ■ n. a very young fish, especially the parr of salmon or trout.
– ORIGIN C18: from FINGER (with ref. to its transverse dusky bars).

fingernail ■ n. the nail on the upper surface of the tip of each finger.

finger-paint ■ n. thick paint designed to be applied with the fingers, used especially by young children.
– DERIVATIVES **finger-painting** n.

fingerpick ■ v. play (a guitar or similar instrument) using the fingernails or plectrums worn on the fingertips. ■ n. a plectrum worn on a fingertip.
– DERIVATIVES **fingerpicker** n.

fingerplate ■ n. a piece of metal or porcelain fixed to a door above the handle to prevent fingermarks on the door itself.

fingerpost ■ n. a post at a road junction from which signs project in the direction of the place indicated.

fingerprint ■ n. a mark made on a surface by a person's fingertip, especially as consisting of a unique pattern used for purposes of identification. ■ v. record the fingerprints of.

fingertip ■ adj. using or operated by the fingers.
– PHRASES **at one's fingertips** (especially of information) readily available. **to one's fingertips** completely.

finger wave ■ n. a wave set in wet hair using the fingers.

Fingo ■ n. (pl. same or **Fingos**) another term for MFENGU.
– ORIGIN C19: from isiXhosa *fenguza* (see MFENGU).

finial /ˈfɪnɪəl, ˈfaɪn-/ ■ n. a distinctive section or ornament at the apex of a roof, pinnacle, or similar structure in a building. ▸ an ornament at the top, end, or corner of an object.
– ORIGIN Middle English: from Latin *finis* 'end'.

finicky ■ adj. 1 fussy. 2 excessively detailed or elaborate.
– DERIVATIVES **finickiness** n.

fining ■ n. a substance used for clarifying beer or wine.

finish ■ v. 1 bring or come to an end. ▸ consume or get through the whole or the remainder of (food or drink). ▸ (**finish with**) have nothing more to do with. ▸ reach the end of a race or other sporting competition. ▸ (**finish up**) chiefly Brit. end by doing something or being in a particular position. ▸ (**finish someone off**) kill or comprehensively defeat someone. 2 complete the manufacture or decoration of (something) by giving it an attractive surface appearance. ▸ complete the fattening of (livestock) before slaughter. 3 dated prepare (a girl) for entry into fashionable society. ■ n. 1 an end or final stage. ▸ the place at which a race or competition ends. 2 the manner in which a manufactured article is finished. ▸ the surface appearance of a manufactured article. ▸ the final taste impression of a wine or beer.
– PHRASES **a fight to the finish** a fight or contest which ends only with the complete defeat of one of the participants.
– ORIGIN Middle English: from Latin *finire*, from *finis* 'end'.

finisher ■ n. 1 a person or thing that finishes something. 2 an animal that has been fattened for slaughter.

finishing school ■ n. 1 a private college where girls are prepared for entry into fashionable society. 2 S. African a school where pupils seek to improve on their final year examination results.

finishing touch ■ n. a final detail completing and enhancing a piece of work.

finite /ˈfaɪnaɪt/ ■ adj. 1 limited in size or extent. 2 Grammar (of a verb form) having a specific tense, number, and person.
– DERIVATIVES **finitely** adv. **finiteness** n. **finitude** /ˈfɪnɪtjuːd/ n.
– ORIGIN Middle English: from Latin *finitus*, *finire* (see FINISH).

finitism /ˈfaɪnaɪtɪz(ə)m/ ■ n. Philosophy rejection of the belief that anything can be infinite.

finito /fɪˈniːtəʊ/ ■ adj. informal finished.
– ORIGIN from Italian.

fink ■ n. N. Amer. informal 1 an unpleasant or contemptible person. 2 an informer.
– ORIGIN C19: perhaps from German, literally 'finch', but also a pejorative term.

Finn ■ n. a native or national of Finland or a person of Finnish descent.
– ORIGIN Old English.

Finnish ■ n. the language of the Finns. ■ adj. of or relating to the Finns or their language.

finny ■ adj. poetic/literary or humorous of, relating to, or resembling a fish.

fino /ˈfiːnəʊ/ ■ n. (pl. **-os**) a light-coloured dry sherry.
– ORIGIN Spanish, 'fine'.

fin whale ■ n. a large rorqual with a small dorsal fin and white underparts. [*Balaenoptera physalus*.]

fiord ■ n. variant spelling of FJORD.

fir ■ n. an evergreen coniferous tree with upright cones and flat needle-shaped leaves. [Genus *Abies*: many species.]
– ORIGIN Middle English: prob. from Old Norse *fyri-*.

fir cone ■ n. chiefly Brit. the dry fruit of a fir tree or other conifer.

fire ■ n. 1 the state of burning, in which substances combine chemically with oxygen from the air and give out bright light, heat, and smoke. ▸ a destructive burning. 2 a collection of fuel burnt in a hearth or stove for heating or cooking. ▸ Brit. (also **electric fire** or **gas fire**) a domestic heating appliance that uses electricity (or gas) as fuel. 3 a burning sensation. ▸ passionate emotion or enthusiasm. 4 the firing of guns. ▸ strong criticism. ■ v. 1 propel (a bullet or projectile) from a gun or other weapon. ▸ discharge (a gun or other weapon). ▸ direct a rapid succession of (questions or statements) towards someone. 2 informal dismiss from a job. 3 supply (a furnace, power

station, etc.) with fuel. ▶ (of an internal-combustion engine) undergo ignition of its fuel. ▶ set fire to. **4** stimulate (the imagination or an emotion). ▶ fill with enthusiasm: *he was fired up for the Cup final.* **5** bake or dry (pottery, bricks, etc.) in a kiln.
– PHRASES **catch fire** begin to burn. **fire and brimstone** the supposed torments of hell. **fire away** informal go ahead. **firing on all (four)** cylinders functioning at a peak level. **go through fire (and water)** face any peril. **on fire 1** burning. **2** very excited. **set fire to** (or **set something on fire**) cause to burn. **set the world** (or Brit. **Thames**) **on fire** do something remarkable or sensational. **take fire** start to burn. **under fire 1** being shot at. **2** being rigorously criticized.
– DERIVATIVES **fireless** adj. **firer** n. **firing** n.
– ORIGIN Old English *fȳr* (n.), *fȳrian* 'supply with material for a fire', of West Germanic origin.

fire alarm ■ n. a device making a loud noise that gives warning of a fire.

fire ant ■ n. a tropical American ant with a painful sting. [*Solenopsis invicta* and other species.]

firearm ■ n. a rifle, pistol, or other portable gun.

fireball ■ n. **1** a ball of flame or fire. ▶ a large bright meteor. **2** an energetic or hot-tempered person.

fireballer ■ n. Baseball a pitcher known for throwing pitches at maximum speed.
– DERIVATIVES **fireballing** adj.

fire blanket ■ n. a sheet of flexible material, typically woven fibreglass, used to smother a fire.

fireblight ■ n. a serious bacterial disease of fruit trees and other plants, giving the leaves a scorched appearance.

firebomb ■ n. a bomb designed to cause a fire. ■ v. attack with a firebomb.

firebox ■ n. the chamber of a steam engine or boiler in which the fuel is burnt.

firebrand ■ n. a fervent supporter of a particular cause, especially one who incites unrest.

firebreak ■ n. an obstacle to the spread of fire, e.g. a strip of open space in a forest.

firebrick ■ n. a brick capable of withstanding intense heat, used especially to line furnaces and fireplaces.

fire brigade ■ n. an organized body of people trained and employed to extinguish fires.

fireclay ■ n. clay capable of withstanding high temperatures, chiefly used for making firebricks.

firecracker ■ n. a loud, explosive firework.

firedamp ■ n. methane, especially as forming an explosive mixture with air in coal mines.

fire department ■ n. the department of a local or municipal authority in charge of preventing and fighting fires.

firedog ■ n. each of a pair of decorative metal supports for wood burning in a fireplace.

fire door ■ n. **1** a fire-resistant door to prevent the spread of fire. **2** a door to the outside of a building used only as an emergency exit.

firedrake ■ n. a dragon in Germanic mythology.
– ORIGIN Old English *fȳr-draca*, from *fȳr* (see FIRE) + *draca* 'dragon', from Latin *draco*.

fire drill ■ n. a practice of the emergency procedures to be used in case of fire.

fire-eater ■ n. **1** an entertainer who appears to eat fire. **2** dated an aggressive or quarrelsome person.

fire engine ■ n. a vehicle carrying firefighters and their equipment.

fire escape ■ n. a staircase or other apparatus used for escaping from a building on fire.

fire extinguisher ■ n. a portable device that discharges a jet of liquid, foam, or gas to extinguish a fire.

firefight ■ n. Military a battle using guns rather than bombs or other weapons.

firefighter ■ n. a person whose job is to extinguish fires.
– DERIVATIVES **firefighting** n.

firefish ■ n. (pl. same or **-fishes**) a typically red-and-white striped marine fish of the scorpionfish family with venomous dorsal spines. [Genus *Pterois*.]

firefly ■ n. (pl. **-flies**) a soft-bodied beetle related to the glow-worm, the winged male and flightless female of which both have luminescent organs. [Family Lampyridae: numerous species.]

fireguard ■ n. **1** a protective screen or grid placed in front of an open fire. **2** N. Amer. a firebreak in a forest.

fire irons ■ pl. n. tongs, a poker, and a shovel for tending a domestic fire.

firelighter ■ n. a piece of flammable material used to help start a fire.

fire lily ■ n. a scarlet-flowered South African lily that usually blooms after fire. [Genus *Cyrtanthus*: several species.]

fireman ■ n. (pl. **-men**) **1** a male firefighter. **2** a person who tends a furnace or the fire of a steam engine or steamship.

fire opal ■ n. another term for GIRASOL (in sense 1).

fireplace ■ n. a partially enclosed space at the base of a chimney for a domestic fire.

firepower ■ n. the destructive capacity of guns, missiles, or a military force.

fire practice ■ n. Brit. a fire drill.

fireproof ■ adj. able to withstand fire or great heat. ■ v. make fireproof.

fire-raiser ■ n. Brit. an arsonist.
– DERIVATIVES **fire-raising** n.

fire salamander ■ n. a short-tailed nocturnal salamander with black skin and bright red, orange, and yellow markings. [*Salamandra salamandra*.]

fire sale ■ n. a sale of goods remaining after a fire. ▶ a sale of goods or assets at a very low price.

fire screen ■ n. a fireguard. ▶ an ornamental screen placed in front of a fireplace when the fire is unlit.

fireship ■ n. historical a ship loaded with burning material and explosives and set adrift to burn an enemy's ships.

fireside ■ n. the area round a fireplace, especially as considered to be the focus of domestic life.

fireside chat ■ n. an informal and intimate conversation.

fire station ■ n. the headquarters of a fire brigade.

fire stone ■ n. stone that can withstand fire and great heat, used especially for lining furnaces and ovens.

firestorm ■ n. a very intense and destructive fire (typically one caused by bombing) in which the blaze is fanned by strong currents of air drawn in from the surrounding area.

firethorn ■ n. another term for PYRACANTHA.

fire trap ■ n. a building without proper provision for escape in case of fire.

fire-walking ■ n. the practice of walking barefoot over hot stones or wood ashes, especially as a religious rite.
– DERIVATIVES **fire-walker** n.

firewall ■ n. **1** a wall or partition designed to inhibit or prevent the spread of fire. **2** Computing a part of a computer system or network which is designed to block unauthorized access while permitting outward communication. ■ v. Computing protect (a network or system) from unauthorized access with a firewall.

firewater ■ n. informal strong alcoholic liquor.

fireweed ■ n. a plant that springs up on burnt land, especially the rosebay willowherb.

firewood ■ n. wood that is burnt as fuel.

firework ■ n. **1** a device containing gunpowder and other combustible chemicals which causes spectacular effects and explosions when ignited. **2** (**fireworks**) an outburst of anger or a display of brilliance.

firing line ■ n. **1** the front line of troops in a battle. **2** a position where one is subject to criticism or blame.

firing party ■ n. **1** a group of soldiers detailed to fire the salute at a military funeral. **2** another term for FIRING SQUAD.

firing squad ■ n. a group of soldiers detailed to shoot a condemned person.

firkin

firkin /'fə:kin/ ■ n. chiefly historical a small cask used chiefly for liquids, butter, or fish.
– ORIGIN Middle English *ferdekyn*, prob. from the Middle Dutch diminutive of *vierde* 'fourth' (a firkin orig. contained a quarter of a barrel).

firm¹ ■ adj. 1 having an unyielding surface or structure. 2 solidly in place and stable. 3 having steady power or strength: *a firm grip*. ▸ steadfast and enduring. 4 showing resolute determination. 5 (of a currency, a commodity, or shares) having a steady value or price which is more likely to rise than fall. ■ v. 1 make stable or unyielding. 2 (of a price) rise to reach a level considered secure. 3 (often **firm something up**) make (an agreement or plan) explicit and definite. ■ adv. in a resolute and determined manner: *she will stand firm*.
– PHRASES **be on firm ground** be sure of one's facts or secure in one's position. **a firm hand** strict discipline or control.
– DERIVATIVES **firmly** adv. **firmness** n.
– ORIGIN Middle English: from Latin *firmus*.

firm² ■ n. a company or business partnership.
– ORIGIN C16 (orig. denoting a signature, later the name under which the business of a firm was transacted): from Spanish and Italian *firma*, from Latin *firmare* 'fix, settle' (in late Latin 'confirm by signature'), from *firmus* 'firm'.

firmament /'fə:məm(ə)nt/ ■ n. poetic/literary the heavens; the sky.
– DERIVATIVES **firmamental** adj.
– ORIGIN Middle English: from Latin *firmamentum*, from *firmare* 'fix, settle'.

firmware ■ n. Computing permanent software programmed into a read-only memory.

first ■ ordinal number 1 coming before all others in time or order; earliest; 1st. ▸ before doing something else specified or implied. ▸ for the first time. ▸ with a specified part or person in a leading position: *it plunged nose first into the river*. 2 foremost in position, rank, or importance. 3 informal something never previously achieved or occurring. 4 a place in the top grade in an examination for a degree.
– PHRASES **at first** at the beginning. **first and foremost** most importantly; more than anything else. **first and last** fundamentally; on the whole. **first of all** before doing anything else; at the beginning. ▸ most importantly. **first off** informal, chiefly N. Amer. as a first point; first of all. **first past the post** winning a race by being the first to reach the finishing line. ▸ Brit. denoting an electoral system in which a candidate or party is selected by achievement of a simple majority. **first thing** early in the morning; before anything else. **first things first** important matters should be dealt with before other things. **first up** informal first of all. **in the first place** as the first consideration or point. ▸ at the beginning; to begin with. **of the first order** (or **magnitude**) excellent or considerable of its kind.
– ORIGIN Old English, of Germanic origin.

first aid ■ n. help given to a sick or injured person until full medical treatment is available.
– DERIVATIVES **first-aider** n.

firstborn ■ adj. denoting the first child to be born to someone. ■ n. a firstborn child.

First Cause ■ n. Philosophy a supposed ultimate cause of all events, which does not itself have a cause, identified with God.

first class ■ n. 1 a set of people or things grouped together as the best. 2 the best accommodation in an aircraft, train, or ship. 3 the highest division in the results of the examinations for a university degree. ■ adj. & adv. (**first-class**) of or relating to the first class.

first-day cover ■ n. an envelope bearing a stamp or set of stamps postmarked on their day of issue.

first-degree ■ adj. 1 Medicine denoting burns that affect only the surface of the skin and cause reddening. 2 Law, chiefly N. Amer. denoting the most serious category of a crime, especially murder.
– PHRASES **first-degree relative** a person's parent, sibling, or child.

first finger ■ n. the index finger.

first-foot ■ v. [usu. as noun **first-footing**] be the first person to cross someone's threshold in the New Year. ■ n. the first person to cross a threshold in such a way.
– DERIVATIVES **first-footer** n.

first fruits ■ pl. n. 1 the first agricultural produce of a season. 2 the initial results of an enterprise or endeavour.

first-hand ■ adj. & adv. (of information or experience) from the original source or personal experience; direct.
– PHRASES **at first hand** directly or from personal experience.

first lady ■ n. the wife of the President or other head of state.

first lieutenant ■ n. 1 a naval officer with executive responsibility for a ship or other command. 2 a rank of officer in the US army or air force, above second lieutenant and below captain.

firstly ■ adv. in the first place; first.

first mate ■ n. the officer second in command to the master of a merchant ship.

first name ■ n. a personal name given to someone at birth or baptism and used before a family name.
– PHRASES **on first-name terms** having a friendly and informal relationship.

first night ■ n. the first public performance of a play or show.

first offender ■ n. a person who is convicted of a criminal offence for the first time.

first officer ■ n. 1 the first mate on a merchant ship. 2 the second in command to the captain on an aircraft.

first-order ■ adj. 1 of the first order. 2 having an order of one, especially denoting mathematical equations involving only the first power of the independent variable or only the first derivative of a function.

first person ■ n. see PERSON (sense 5).

first position ■ n. 1 Ballet a standing position in which the feet are turned outwards with the heels touching. 2 Music the position of the hand on the fingerboard of a stringed instrument furthest from the bridge.

first principles ■ pl. n. the fundamental concepts or assumptions on which a theory, system, or method is based.

first-rate ■ adj. of the best class, quality, or condition; excellent.

first reading ■ n. the first presentation of a bill to a legislative assembly, to permit its introduction.

first refusal ■ n. the privilege of deciding whether to accept or reject something before it is offered to others.

first strike ■ n. an opening attack with nuclear weapons.

First World ■ n. the industrialized capitalist countries of western Europe, North America, Japan, Australia, and New Zealand.

firth ■ n. a narrow inlet of the sea.
– ORIGIN Middle English: from Old Norse *fjǫrthr* (see FJORD).

fiscal /'fɪsk(ə)l/ ■ adj. 1 of or relating to government revenue, especially taxes. 2 chiefly N. Amer. of or relating to financial matters. ▸ N. Amer. denoting a particular financial year: *the deficit for fiscal 1996*.
– DERIVATIVES **fiscally** adv.
– ORIGIN C16: from Latin *fiscalis*, from *fiscus* 'purse, treasury'.

fiscal shrike ■ n. another term for COMMON FISCAL.

fiscal year ■ n. North American term for FINANCIAL YEAR.

fish ■ n. (pl. same or **fishes**) 1 a limbless cold-blooded vertebrate animal with gills and fins, living wholly in water. ▸ the flesh of fish as food. 2 used in names of invertebrate animals living wholly in water, e.g. shellfish, jellyfish. 3 informal a person who is strange in a specified way: *he's a cold fish*. ■ v. 1 catch fish with a net or hook and line. ▸ fish in (a particular body of water). 2 (**fish something out**) pull or take something out of water or a receptacle. 3 grope or feel for something concealed. 4 try subtly or deviously to elicit a response or information.
– PHRASES **a big fish** an important person. **a big fish in a small pond** a person who is important only within a small community. **a fish out of water** a person who feels out of place in their surroundings. **have other** (or **bigger**) **fish to fry** have more important matters to attend to.

- DERIVATIVES **fishable** adj. **fishing** n.
- ORIGIN Old English *fisc* (as a noun denoting any animal living exclusively in water), *fiscian* (v.), of Germanic origin.

fishbowl ▪ n. a round glass bowl for keeping pet fish in.

fish cake ▪ n. a patty of shredded fish and mashed potato.

fish eagle ▪ n. an eagle that preys largely on fish. [*Haliaeetus vocifer* (Africa) and other species.]

fisherfolk ▪ pl. n. people who catch fish for a living.

fisherman ▪ n. (pl. **-men**) a person who catches fish for a living or for sport.

fisherman's bend ▪ n. a knot tied by making a full turn round something, a half hitch through the turn, and a half hitch round the standing part of the rope.

fisherman's knot ▪ n. a knot used to join two small ropes by tying an overhand knot in the end of each around the opposite standing part.

fishery ▪ n. (pl. **-ies**) **1** a place where fish are reared, or caught in numbers. **2** the occupation or industry of catching or rearing fish.

fisheye ▪ n. **1** a very wide-angle lens with a field of vision covering up to 180°, the scale being reduced towards the edges. **2** US informal a suspicious or unfriendly look. **3** a defect in metal causing a spot to stand out brightly against its surroundings.

fish finger ▪ n. a small oblong piece of flaked or minced fish coated in batter or breadcrumbs.

fish hawk ▪ n. another term for OSPREY.

fishing fly ▪ n. a natural or artificial flying insect used as bait in fishing.

fishing line ▪ n. a long thread of silk or nylon attached to a baited hook, with a sinker or float, and used for catching fish.

fishing pole ▪ n. N. Amer. a simple fishing rod with no reel.

fishing rod ▪ n. a long, tapering rod to which a fishing line is attached.

fish kettle ▪ n. an oval pan for boiling fish.

fish knife ▪ n. a blunt knife with a broad blade used for eating or serving fish.

fish louse ▪ n. a parasitic crustacean which attaches itself to the skin or gills of fish. [Many species in classes Branchiura and Copepoda.]

fishmeal ▪ n. ground dried fish used as fertilizer or animal feed.

fishmonger ▪ n. a person or shop that sells fish for food.

fishmoth ▪ n. another term for SILVERFISH.

fishnet ▪ n. a fabric with an open mesh resembling a fishing net.

fishplate ▪ n. **1** a flat piece of metal used to connect adjacent rails in a railway track. **2** a flat piece of metal with ends like a fish's tail, used to position masonry.

fish slice ▪ n. Brit. a kitchen utensil with a broad flat blade for lifting fish and fried foods.

fishtail ▪ n. a thing resembling a fish's tail in shape or movement. ▪ v. make or cause to make a fishtail movement.

fishwife ▪ n. (pl. **-wives**) **1** a coarse-mannered woman who is prone to shouting. **2** archaic a woman who sells fish.

fishy ▪ adj. (**-ier**, **-iest**) **1** of, relating to, or resembling fish or a fish. **2** informal arousing feelings of doubt or suspicion.
- DERIVATIVES **fishily** adv. **fishiness** n.

fissile /ˈfɪsaɪl/ ▪ adj. **1** (of an atom or element) able to undergo nuclear fission. **2** (chiefly of rock) easily split.
- DERIVATIVES **fissility** /-ˈsɪlɪti/ n.
- ORIGIN C17: from Latin *fissilis*, from *fiss-*, *findere* 'split, crack'.

fission /ˈfɪʃ(ə)n/ ▪ n. **1** the action of splitting or being split into two or more parts. **2** a reaction in which a heavy atomic nucleus splits in two, releasing much energy. **3** Biology reproduction by means of a cell or organism dividing into two or more new cells or organisms. ▪ v. (chiefly of atoms) undergo fission.
- DERIVATIVES **fissionable** adj.
- ORIGIN C17: from Latin *fissio(n-)*, from *findere* 'to split'.

fission bomb ▪ n. another term for ATOM BOMB.

fissiparous /fɪˈsɪp(ə)rəs/ ▪ adj. **1** inclined to cause or undergo fission. **2** Biology (of an organism) reproducing by fission.
- ORIGIN C19: from Latin *fissus*, from *findere* 'split', on the pattern of *viviparous*.

fissure /ˈfɪʃə/ ▪ n. **1** a long, narrow crack. **2** a state of division or disagreement. ▪ v. [usu. as adj. **fissured**] split; crack.
- ORIGIN Middle English: from Latin *fissura*, from *fiss-*, *findere* 'to split'.

fist ▪ n. a person's hand when the fingers are bent in towards the palm and held there tightly. ▪ v. (of a goalkeeper) strike (a ball or shot) with the fist.
- PHRASES **make a —— fist of** (or **at**) informal do something to the specified degree of success.
- DERIVATIVES **-fisted** adj. **fistful** n. (pl. **-fuls**).
- ORIGIN Old English, of West Germanic origin.

fisticuffs ▪ pl. n. fighting with the fists.
- ORIGIN C17: prob. from obsolete *fisty* 'relating to the fists or to fist fighting' + CUFF².

fistula /ˈfɪstjʊlə/ ▪ n. (pl. **fistulas** or **fistulae** /-liː/) Medicine an abnormal or surgically made passage between a hollow or tubular organ and the body surface, or between two hollow or tubular organs.
- DERIVATIVES **fistular** adj. **fistulous** adj.
- ORIGIN Middle English: from Latin, 'pipe, flute, fistula'.

fit¹ ▪ adj. (**fitter**, **fittest**) **1** of a suitable quality, standard, or type. ▸ socially acceptable: *a fit subject*. ▸ (**fit to do something**) informal having reached such an extreme condition as to be on the point of doing the thing specified: *they were fit to kill him*. **2** in good health, especially because of regular physical exercise. ▪ v. (**fitted** (US also **fit**), **fitting**) **1** be of the right shape and size for. ▸ (usu. **be fitted for**) try clothing on (someone) in order to make or alter it to the correct size. **2** be or make able to occupy a particular position, place, or period of time. **3** fix into place. ▸ (often **be fitted with**) provide with a particular component or article. ▸ join or cause to join together to form a whole. **4** be or make suitable for. ▪ n. the particular way in which something fits.
- PHRASES **fit to be tied** informal very angry. **fit to bust** with excessive energy. **see** (or **think**) **fit** consider it correct or acceptable.
- PHRASAL VERBS **fit in 1** be compatible; be in harmony. **2** (also **fit into**) constitute part of a particular situation or larger structure. **fit someone/thing out** (or **up**) provide someone or something with necessary items. **fit someone up** Brit. informal incriminate someone by falsifying evidence against them.
- DERIVATIVES **fitly** adv. **fitter** n.
- ORIGIN Middle English.

fit² ▪ n. **1** a sudden attack of convulsions. ▸ a sudden attack of coughing, fainting, etc. **2** a sudden burst of intense feeling or activity.
- PHRASES **in** (or **by**) **fits and starts** with irregular bursts of activity.
- ORIGIN Old English *fitt* 'conflict', in Middle English also 'position of danger' and 'short period'.

fitful ▪ adj. active or occurring intermittently; not regular or steady.
- DERIVATIVES **fitfully** adv. **fitfulness** n.

fitment ▪ n. chiefly Brit. a fixed item of furniture or piece of equipment.

fitness ▪ n. the state of being fit.

fitted ▪ adj. **1** made to fill a space or to cover something closely. ▸ (of a room) equipped with matching units of furniture. **2** attached to or provided with a particular component or article. **3** (**fitted for/to do**) being fit for or to do: *the type best fitted for the job*.

fitting ▪ n. **1** an attachment. **2** (**fittings**) items which are fixed in a building but can be removed when the owner moves. Compare with FIXTURE (in sense 1). **3** the action of fitting or being fitted. ▪ adj. **1** appropriate; right or proper. **2** [in combination] fitted in a specified way: *loose-fitting trousers*.
- DERIVATIVES **fittingly** adv. **fittingness** n.

fitting room ▪ n. a room in a shop in which one can try on clothes before purchase.

fitting shop

fitting shop ■ n. a part of a factory where machine parts are put together.

five ■ cardinal number equivalent to the sum of two and three; one more than four, or half of ten; 5. (Roman numeral: **v** or **V**.)
– DERIVATIVES **fivefold** adj. & adv.
– ORIGIN Old English, of Germanic origin.

five-and-dime (also **five-and-dime store** or **five-and-ten**) ■ n. N. Amer. a shop selling a wide variety of inexpensive goods.

five-a-side ■ n. a form of soccer with five players in each team.

five o'clock shadow ■ n. a slight growth of beard visible on a man's chin several hours after he has shaved.

fiver ■ n. 1 Brit. informal a five-pound note. 2 N. Amer. a five-dollar bill.

five-spice ■ n. a blend of five powdered spices, typically fennel seeds, cinnamon, cloves, star anise, and peppercorns, used in Chinese cuisine.

fix ■ v. 1 attach or position securely. ▶ (**fix on**) direct or be directed unwaveringly toward: *her gaze fixed on Jess.* ▶ discover the exact location of (something) by using radar, visual bearings, or astronomical observation. 2 decide or settle on. ▶ (**be fixing to do something**) N. Amer. informal be intending or planning to do something. ▶ assign or determine (a person's liability or responsibility) for legal purposes. 3 repair or restore. 4 make arrangements for. ▶ informal, chiefly N. Amer. provide with food or drink. ▶ (**fix someone up**) informal provide someone with something. 5 make unchanging or constant. ▶ make (a dye, photographic image, or drawing) permanent. ▶ (of a plant or micro-organism) assimilate (nitrogen or carbon dioxide) by forming a non-gaseous compound. 6 informal deviously influence the outcome of. 7 informal take an injection of a narcotic drug. 8 castrate or spay (an animal). ■ n. 1 an act of fixing. 2 informal a difficult or awkward situation. 3 informal a dose of a narcotic drug to which one is addicted. 4 a position determined by visual or radio bearings or astronomical observations.
– PHRASES **get a fix on** determine the position of. ▶ informal determine the nature or facts of.
– DERIVATIVES **fixable** adj. **fixed** adj. **fixedly** adv. **fixedness** n. **fixer** n.
– ORIGIN Middle English: from Latin *fixus*, from *figere* 'fix, fasten'.

fixate /ˈfɪkseɪt/ ■ v. 1 (often **be fixated on**) cause to be obsessively interested in something or someone. 2 direct one's eyes towards.
– ORIGIN C19: from Latin *fixus*, from *figere* (see FIX).

fixation ■ n. 1 the action or condition of fixating or being fixated. 2 the action or process of fixing or being fixed, especially chemically or biologically.
– ORIGIN Middle English: from medieval Latin *fixatio(n-)*, from *fixare* (see FIX).

fixative /ˈfɪksətɪv/ ■ n. a substance used to fix, protect, or stabilize something. ■ adj. (of a substance) used in such a way.

fixed assets ■ pl. n. assets which are purchased for long-term use and are not likely to be converted quickly into cash, such as land, buildings, and equipment. Compare with CURRENT ASSETS.

fixed capital ■ n. capital invested in fixed assets.

fixed costs ■ pl. n. business costs, such as rent, that are constant whatever the amount of goods produced.

fixed-doh ■ adj. denoting a system of solmization in which C is called 'doh', D is called 'ray', etc., irrespective of the key in which they occur. Compare with MOVABLE-DOH.

fixed income ■ n. an income from a pension or investment that is set at a particular figure and does not vary like a dividend or rise with the rate of inflation.

fixed odds ■ pl. n. odds in betting (especially on soccer results) that are predetermined, as opposed to a pool system or a starting price.

fixed point ■ n. Physics a well-defined reproducible temperature which can be used as a reference point, e.g. one defined by a change of phase.

fixed-wing ■ adj. denoting aircraft of the conventional type as opposed to those with rotating wings, such as helicopters.

fixing ■ n. 1 the action of fixing something. 2 (**fixings**) Brit. screws, bolts, etc. used to fix or assemble building material, furniture, or equipment. 3 (**fixings**) N. Amer. ingredients, apparatus, or equipment required for a meal or other purpose.

fixity ■ n. the state of being unchanging or permanent.
– ORIGIN C17: partly from obsolete *fix* 'fixed', partly from French *fixité*.

fixture /ˈfɪkstʃə, -tjə/ ■ n. 1 a piece of equipment or furniture which is fixed in position in a building or vehicle. ▶ (**fixtures**) articles attached to a house or land and considered legally part of it so that they normally remain in place when an owner moves. Compare with FITTING (in sense 2). 2 informal a person or thing that has become established in a particular place. 3 a sporting event which takes place on a particular date.
– ORIGIN C16: alteration of obsolete *fixure* (from late Latin *fixura*, from Latin *figere* 'to fix'), with *t* inserted on the pattern of *mixture*.

fizz ■ v. 1 (of a liquid) produce bubbles of gas and make a hissing sound. 2 make a buzzing or crackling sound. ■ n. 1 the action or sound of fizzing. 2 informal an effervescent drink, especially sparkling wine. 3 exuberance.
– ORIGIN C17: imitative.

fizzle ■ v. 1 make a feeble hissing or spluttering sound. 2 (usu. **fizzle out**) end or fail in a weak or disappointing way. ■ n. an instance of fizzling.
– ORIGIN Middle English ('break wind quietly'): prob. imitative, perhaps rel. to Middle English *fist* (see FEISTY).

fizzy ■ adj. (**-ier**, **-iest**) 1 (of a drink) effervescent. 2 exuberant.
– DERIVATIVES **fizzily** adv. **fizziness** n.

fjord /fjɔːd, fiˈɔːd/ (also **fiord**) ■ n. a long, narrow, deep inlet of the sea between high cliffs, typically formed by submergence of a glaciated valley and found predominantly in Norway.
– ORIGIN C17: Norwegian, from Old Norse *fjorthr*.

fl. ■ abbrev. 1 floor. 2 floruit. 3 fluid.

Flaaitaal /ˈflʌɪtɑːl/ (also **Flytaal**) ■ n. S. African another term for TSOTSITAAL.
– ORIGIN from *fly* 'clever' + Afrikaans *taal* 'language'.

flab ■ n. informal soft, loose flesh on a person's body; fat.
– ORIGIN 1950s: back-formation from FLABBY.

flabbergast /ˈflabəɡɑːst/ ■ v. (usu. as adj. **flabbergasted**) informal surprise greatly.
– ORIGIN C18.

flabby ■ adj. (**-ier**, **-iest**) 1 (of a part of a person's body) soft, loose, and fleshy. 2 not tightly controlled and therefore ineffective.
– DERIVATIVES **flabbily** adv. **flabbiness** n.
– ORIGIN C17: alteration of earlier *flappy*.

flaccid /ˈflasɪd, ˈflaksɪd/ ■ adj. soft and limp.
– DERIVATIVES **flaccidity** /flakˈsɪdɪti, flaˈsɪdɪti/ n. **flaccidly** adv.
– ORIGIN C17: from Latin *flaccidus*, from *flaccus* 'flabby'.

flack ■ n. variant spelling of FLAK.

flag¹ ■ n. 1 an oblong piece of cloth that is raised on a pole and used as an emblem, especially of nationality. 2 a ship's ensign. 3 a device or symbol resembling a flag, used as a marker. 4 a small paper badge given to people who donate to a charity appeal. ■ v. (**flagged**, **flagging**) 1 mark for attention. 2 direct or alert by waving a flag or using hand signals. ▶ (**flag someone down**) signal to a driver to stop. ▶ (**flag someone off**) wave a flag at someone as a starting signal. 3 provide or decorate with a flag or flags.
– PHRASES **fly the flag** (of a ship) be registered in a particular country and sail under its flag. ▶ (also **show** or **carry** or **wave the flag**) represent one's country or demonstrate one's affiliation with a party or organization. **put the flags** (or **flag**) **out** celebrate. **wrap oneself in the flag** chiefly N. Amer. make an excessive show of one's patriotism.
– ORIGIN C16: perhaps from obsolete *flag* 'drooping'.

flag² ■ n. a flat rectangular or square stone slab, used for paving.
– DERIVATIVES **flagged** adj.
– ORIGIN Middle English: prob. of Scandinavian origin and rel. to Icelandic *flag* 'spot from which a sod has been cut' and Old Norse *flaga* 'slab of stone'.

flag³ ■ n. a waterside plant with long sword-shaped leaves. [*Iris pseudacorus* (yellow flag, native to Europe) and other species.]
– ORIGIN Middle English.

flag⁴ ■ v. (**flagged, flagging**) become tired or less enthusiastic.
– ORIGIN C16: rel. to obsolete *flag* 'hanging down'.

flag boat ■ n. a boat serving as a mark in sailing matches.

flag captain ■ n. the captain of a flagship.

flag day ■ n. Brit. a day on which money is collected in the street for a charity and contributors are given flags to wear.

flagellant /ˈflædʒ(ə)l(ə)nt, fləˈdʒel(ə)nt/ ■ n. a person who subjects themselves to flagellation.

flagellate¹ /ˈflædʒəleɪt/ ■ v. flog, either as a religious discipline or for sexual gratification.
– DERIVATIVES **flagellation** n. **flagellator** n. **flagellatory** /-lət(ə)ri/ adj.
– ORIGIN C17: from Latin *flagellare* 'whip'.

flagellate² /ˈflædʒ(ə)lət, -eɪt/ Zoology ■ n. any of a large group of protozoans that have one or more flagella used for swimming. ■ adj. bearing one or more flagella.
– ORIGIN C19: from FLAGELLUM.

flagellum /fləˈdʒeləm/ ■ n. (pl. **flagella**) Biology a slender thread-like structure, especially a microscopic whip-like appendage which enables many protozoans, bacteria, spermatozoa, etc. to swim.
– DERIVATIVES **flagellar** adj.
– ORIGIN C19: from Latin, diminutive of *flagrum* 'scourge'.

flageolet¹ /ˌflædʒəˈlet, ˈflædʒəlɪt, ˈfla(d)ʒəleɪ/ (also French **flageolet**) ■ n. 1 a very small flute-like instrument resembling a recorder but with four finger holes on top and two thumb holes below. 2 a tin whistle.
– ORIGIN C17: from French, diminutive of Old French *flageol*, from Provençal *flaujol*.

flageolet² /ˈfla(d)ʒəleɪ, ˌflædʒəˈlet/ ■ n. a French kidney bean of a small variety used in cooking.
– ORIGIN C19: from French, from Latin *phaseolus* 'bean'.

flagitious /fləˈdʒɪʃəs/ ■ adj. archaic extremely and criminally wicked.
– DERIVATIVES **flagitiously** adv. **flagitiousness** n.
– ORIGIN Middle English: from Latin *flagitiosus*, from *flagitium* 'importunity, shameful crime', from *flagitare* 'demand earnestly'.

flagman ■ n. (pl. **-men**) a person who gives signals with a flag.

flag of convenience ■ n. a flag of a country under which a ship is registered in order to avoid financial charges or restrictive regulations in the owner's country.

flag officer ■ n. an admiral, vice admiral, or rear admiral, or the commodore of a yacht club.

flag of truce ■ n. a white flag indicating a desire for a truce.

flagon /ˈflæɡ(ə)n/ ■ n. a large container for serving or consuming drinks. ▸ a large bottle in which wine or cider is sold, typically holding 1.13 litres.
– ORIGIN Middle English: from Old French *flacon*, from late Latin *flasco, flascon-*.

flagpole ■ n. a pole used for flying a flag.

flag rank ■ n. the rank attained by flag officers.

flagrant /ˈfleɪɡr(ə)nt/ ■ adj. conspicuous; blatant.
– DERIVATIVES **flagrancy** n. **flagrantly** adv.
– ORIGIN C15: from Latin *flagrare* 'blaze'.

flagship ■ n. 1 the ship in a fleet which carries the commanding admiral. 2 the best or most important thing owned or produced by an organization.

flagstaff /ˈflæɡstɑːf/ ■ n. a flagpole.

flagstone ■ n. another term for FLAG².
– DERIVATIVES **flagstoned** adj.

flail /fleɪl/ ■ n. a threshing tool consisting of a wooden staff with a short heavy stick swinging from it. ▸ a similar device used as a weapon or for flogging. ▸ a machine having a similar action. ■ v. 1 swing or cause to swing wildly. 2 (**flail around/about**) flounder; struggle. 3 beat; flog.
– ORIGIN Old English, of West Germanic origin, from Latin *flagellum* (see FLAGELLUM).

flair ■ n. 1 a natural ability or talent. 2 stylishness.
– ORIGIN C19: from French, from *flairer* 'to smell', from Latin *fragrare* 'smell sweet'.

flak (also **flack**) ■ n. 1 anti-aircraft fire. 2 strong criticism.
– ORIGIN 1930s: from German, abbrev. of *Fliegerabwehrkanone* 'aviator-defence gun'.

flake¹ ■ n. 1 a small, flat, very thin piece of something. 2 a snowflake. 3 Archaeology a piece of hard stone chipped off for use as a tool. 4 thin pieces of crushed dried food or bait for fish. 5 N. Amer. informal a crazy or eccentric person. ■ v. 1 come away from a surface in flakes. 2 split or cause to split into flakes.
– DERIVATIVES **flaked** adj.
– ORIGIN Middle English: the immediate source is unknown, the senses perhaps deriving from different words; prob. of Germanic origin and rel. to FLAG² and FLAW.

flake² ■ n. a rack for storing or drying food such as fish.
– ORIGIN Middle English (denoting a wicker hurdle): perhaps of Scandinavian origin.

flake³ ■ v. (**flake out**) informal fall asleep; drop from exhaustion.
– ORIGIN C15: var. of obsolete *flack* and FLAG⁴.

flake⁴ Nautical ■ n. a single turn of a coiled rope or hawser. ■ v. lay (a rope) in loose coils in order to prevent it tangling. ▸ lay (a sail) down in folds either side of the boom.
– ORIGIN C17.

flake white ■ n. a pure white pigment made from flakes of white lead.

flak jacket ■ n. a sleeveless jacket made of heavy fabric reinforced with metal, worn as protection against bullets and shrapnel.

flaky ■ adj. (**-ier, -iest**) 1 breaking or separating easily into flakes. 2 informal chiefly N. Amer. unconventional or eccentric. 3 informal unreliable.
– DERIVATIVES **flakily** adv. **flakiness** n.

flaky pastry ■ n. pastry consisting of a number of thin layers.

flambé /ˈflɒmbeɪ/ ■ adj. 1 [postpos.] (of food) covered with spirits and set alight briefly: *steak flambé*. 2 denoting or characterized by a lustrous red copper-based porcelain glaze with purple streaks. ■ v. (**flambés, flambéed, flambéing**) cover (food) with spirits and set it alight briefly.
– ORIGIN C19: French, 'singed', from *flamber*, from *flambe* 'a flame'.

flambeau /ˈflæmbəʊ/ ■ n. (pl. **flambeaus** or **flambeaux** /-əʊz/) 1 a flaming torch. 2 a branched candlestick.
– ORIGIN C17: from French, from *flambe* 'a flame'.

flamboyant /flæmˈbɔɪənt/ ■ adj. 1 conspicuously and confidently exuberant. 2 brightly coloured and showy. 3 Architecture of or denoting a style of French Gothic architecture marked by wavy flamelike tracery and ornate decoration. ■ n. a Madagascan tree with bright red flowers, planted as a street tree in the tropics. [*Delonix regia*.]
– DERIVATIVES **flamboyance** n. **flamboyancy** n. **flamboyantly** adv.
– ORIGIN C19: from French, 'flaming, blazing', *flamboyer*, from *flambe* 'a flame'.

flame ■ n. 1 a hot glowing body of ignited gas that is generated by something on fire. 2 a thing compared to a flame's ability to burn fiercely or be extinguished: *the flame of hope*. 3 a brilliant orange-red colour. 4 Computing, informal a vitriolic or abusive message distributed electronically through a computer network. ■ v. 1 give off flames. ▸ apply a flame to; set alight. 2 (of an intense emotion) appear suddenly and fiercely. 3 (of a person's face) become red with embarrassment or anger. 4 Computing, informal send a flame. 5 (**flame out**) (of a jet

flame gun

engine) lose power through the extinction of the flame in the combustion chamber. **6** informal, chiefly N. Amer. fail conspicuously.
– PHRASES **old flame** informal a former lover.
– DERIVATIVES **flameless** adj. **flamer** n. (Computing, informal) **flamy** adj.
– ORIGIN Middle English: from Old French *flame* (n.), *flamer* (v.), from Latin *flamma* 'a flame'.

flame gun ■ n. a device for producing a jet of flame.

flame lily ■ n. a tuberous climbing plant which bears yellow or yellow and red flowers with undulating petals, native to southern Africa. [Genus *Gloriosa*.]

flamenco /fləˈmɛŋkəʊ/ ■ n. a spirited style of Spanish guitar music accompanied by singing and dancing.
– ORIGIN C19: Spanish, 'like a gypsy', literally 'Fleming'.

flameout ■ n. **1** an instance of the flame in the combustion chamber of a jet engine being extinguished, with a resultant loss of power. **2** informal, chiefly N. Amer. a conspicuous failure.

flameproof ■ adj. **1** (of fabric) treated so as to be non-flammable. **2** (of cookware) able to be used either in an oven or on a hob. ■ v. make flameproof.

flame-thrower ■ n. a weapon that sprays out burning fuel.

flame tree ■ n. any of several trees with brilliant red flowers. [*Spathodea campanulata* (Africa), *Brachychiton acerifolius* (Australia), and other species.]

flaming ■ adj. **1** emitting flames. **2** very hot: *flaming June*. **3** of a flame colour. **4** (especially of an argument) passionate. **5** informal expressing annoyance: *that flaming dog*.

flamingo /fləˈmɪŋɡəʊ/ ■ n. (pl. -os or -oes) a tall wading bird with mainly pink or scarlet plumage, long legs and neck, and a crooked bill. [Family Phoenicopteridae: several species.]
– ORIGIN C16: from Spanish *flamengo*, earlier form of *flamenco* (see FLAMENCO); associated, because of its colour, with Latin *flamma* 'a flame'.

flammable /ˈflaməb(ə)l/ ■ adj. easily set on fire.
– DERIVATIVES **flammability** n.
– ORIGIN C19: from Latin *flammare*, from *flamma* 'a flame'.

USAGE
The words **flammable** and **inflammable** have the same meaning: see INFLAMMABLE.

flan ■ n. **1** a baked dish consisting of an open-topped pastry case with a savoury or sweet filling. **2** a disc of metal such as one from which a coin is made.
– ORIGIN C19: from French, from Old French *flaon*, from medieval Latin *flado*, *fladon-*, of West Germanic origin.

flange /flan(d)ʒ/ ■ n. a projecting rim or piece.
– DERIVATIVES **flanged** adj. **flangeless** adj.
– ORIGIN C17: perhaps from Old French *flanchir* 'to bend'.

flanger /ˈflan(d)ʒə/ ■ n. an electronic device which alters a sound signal by introducing a cyclically varying phase shift into one of two identical copies of the signal and recombining them, used especially in popular music.

flanging /ˈflandʒɪŋ/ ■ n. **1** the provision of a flange on an object. **2** the alteration of sound using a flanger.

flank ■ n. **1** the side of a person's or animal's body between the ribs and the hip. **2** the side of something such as a building or mountain. **3** the left or right side of a body of people. **4** (also **flank forward**) Rugby another term for FLANKER. ■ v. be situated on each or on one side of.
– ORIGIN Old English, from Old French *flanc*, of Germanic origin.

flanker ■ n. **1** Rugby a forward who forms part of a scrum to gain possession of the ball. **2** American Football an offensive back who is positioned to the outside of an end. **3** Military a fortification to the side of a force or position.

flannel ■ n. **1** a kind of soft-woven woollen or cotton fabric that is slightly milled and raised. **2** (**flannels**) men's trousers made of woollen flannel. **3** Brit. a small piece of towelling used for washing oneself. **4** Brit. informal bland, fluent talk used to gloss over a difficult subject. ■ v. (**flannelled, flannelling**; US also **flaneled, flaneling**)

informal, chiefly Brit. use such talk.
– ORIGIN Middle English: prob. from Welsh *gwlanen* 'woollen article', from *gwlân* 'wool'.

flannelette /ˌflanəˈlɛt/ ■ n. a napped cotton fabric resembling flannel.

flannelled (US also **flaneled**) ■ adj. wearing flannel trousers.

flap ■ v. (**flapped, flapping**) **1** move or be moved up and down or from side to side. **2** (**flap at**) strike at loosely. **3** informal be agitated. ■ n. **1** a piece of something that is attached on one side only. **2** a hinged or sliding section of an aircraft wing used to control lift. **3** a single flapping movement. **4** informal a state of agitation. **5** a large broad mushroom.
– DERIVATIVES **flappy** adj.
– ORIGIN Middle English: prob. imitative.

flapjack ■ n. **1** Brit. a soft, thick biscuit made from oats and butter. **2** chiefly N. Amer. a pancake.
– ORIGIN C17: from FLAP (in the dialect sense 'toss a pancake') + JACK.

flapper ■ n. informal (in the 1920s) a young woman who wore fashionable clothing and flouted convention.

flare ■ n. **1** a sudden brief burst of flame or light. **2** a device producing a very bright flame as a signal or marker. **3** a sudden burst of intense emotion. **4** Photography extraneous illumination on film caused by internal reflection in the camera. **5** a gradual widening towards the hem of a garment. ▶ (**flares**) trousers of which the legs widen from the knees down. **6** an upward and outward curve of a ship's bows. ■ v. **1** burn, shine, or be revealed with a sudden intensity. **2** (**flare up**) suddenly become intense, angry, or violent. **3** gradually become wider at one end. **4** (with reference to the nostrils) dilate or cause to dilate.
– DERIVATIVES **flared** adj.
– ORIGIN C16 (in the sense 'spread out (one's hair)').

flarepath ■ n. an area illuminated to enable an aircraft to land or take off.

flare star ■ n. Astronomy a dwarf star which displays spasmodic outbursts of radiation, believed to be due to extremely intense flares.

flash ■ v. **1** shine or cause to shine in a bright but brief, sudden, or intermittent way. **2** move, pass, or send very quickly in a particular direction. **3** display or be displayed briefly or repeatedly. ▶ informal display conspicuously so as to impress: *they flash their money about*. ▶ informal (of a man) show one's genitals in public. **4** (**flash over**) make an electric circuit by sparking across a gap. ■ n. **1** a sudden brief burst of bright light. **2** a camera attachment that produces a flash of light, for taking photographs in poor light. **3** a sudden or brief manifestation or occurrence. **4** a bright patch of colour. ▶ an emblem or coloured patch of cloth worn on a uniform. **5** a rush of water, especially down a weir to take a boat over shallows. ■ adj. informal ostentatiously stylish or expensive.
– PHRASES **flash in the pan** a sudden but brief success. [with allusion to the priming of a firearm, the flash arising from an explosion of gunpowder within the lock.]
– DERIVATIVES **flasher** n.
– ORIGIN Middle English: prob. imitative.

flashback ■ n. **1** a scene in a film, novel, etc. set in a time earlier than the main story. **2** a sudden vivid memory of an event in the past. **3** a flame moving rapidly back through a combustible vapour.

flashbulb ■ n. a bulb for a flashgun.

flash burn ■ n. a burn caused by brief exposure to intense radiant heat.

flashcard ■ n. a card containing a clear display of a word or words, used in teaching reading.

flash drive ■ n. Computing a small data storage device which uses flash memory and connects to a computer or to other electronic equipment via USB.

flash flood ■ n. a sudden case of local flooding resulting from extreme rainfall.

flash-freeze ■ v. freeze (food or other material) very rapidly so as to prevent the formation of ice crystals.
– DERIVATIVES **flash-freezer** n.

flashgun ■ n. a device which gives a brief flash of intense light, used for taking photographs in poor light.

flashing ■ n. a strip of metal used to seal the junction of a roof with another surface.

flash lamp ■ n. a flashgun.

flashlight ■ n. **1** an electric torch with a strong beam. **2** a flashing light used for signals. **3** a flashgun.

flash memory ■ n. Computing memory that retains data in the absence of a power supply.

flash mob ■ n. a public gathering of complete strangers, organized via the Internet or cellphone, who perform a pointless act and then disperse again.
– DERIVATIVES **flash mobber** n. **flash mobbing** n.

flashpoint ■ n. **1** a point or place at which anger or violence flares up. **2** Chemistry the temperature at which a particular organic compound gives off sufficient vapour to ignite in air.

flash stick ■ n. Computing another term for FLASH DRIVE.

flashy ■ adj. (**-ier**, **-iest**) ostentatiously stylish.
– DERIVATIVES **flashily** adv. **flashiness** n.

flask ■ n. **1** a narrow-necked conical or spherical bottle. **2** S. African & Brit. a vacuum flask. **3** a hip flask. **4** (also **nuclear flask**) a lead-lined container for radioactive nuclear waste.
– ORIGIN Middle English ('cask'): from medieval Latin *flasca*.

flat[1] ■ adj. (**flatter**, **flattest**) **1** having a level surface; without raised areas or indentations. ▸ not sloping.
▸ having a broad level surface but little height or depth: *a flat box*. **2** (of shoes) without high heels. **3** dull; lifeless: *a flat voice*. ▸ showing little or no activity: *sales were flat*. **4** (of a sparkling drink) having lost its effervescence. **5** (of a battery) having exhausted its charge. **6** (of something kept inflated) having lost some or all of its air. **7** (of a photograph) lacking contrast. **8** (of a fee, charge, or price) unvarying; fixed. **9** (of a negative statement) definite and firm: *a flat denial*. **10** (of musical sound) below true or normal pitch. ▸ [postpos.] (of a key) having a flat or flats in the signature. ▸ [postpos.] (of a note) a semitone lower than a specified note. ■ adv. **1** in or to a horizontal position. ▸ lying in close juxtaposition to a surface. ▸ so as to become level and even. **2** informal completely; absolutely: *I'm turning you down flat*. **3** emphasizing the speed of an action or task: *in ten minutes flat*. **4** below the true or normal pitch of musical sound. ■ n. **1** the flat part of something. **2** an upright section of stage scenery. **3** informal a flat tyre. **4** (**flats**) chiefly N. Amer. shoes with a very low heel or no heel. **5** (**flats**) an area of low level ground, especially near water. **6** (**the Flat**) Brit. flat racing. **7** a musical note lowered a semitone below natural pitch.
▸ the sign (♭) indicating this.
– PHRASES **fall flat** fail to produce the intended effect. **flat out 1** as fast or as hard as possible. **2** informal, chiefly N. Amer. unequivocally. **3** lying down in a state of exhaustion. **on the flat 1** on level ground as opposed to uphill. **2** (**on the Flat**) (of a horse race) on a course without jumps.
– DERIVATIVES **flatly** adv. **flatness** n. **flattish** adj.
– ORIGIN Middle English: from Old Norse *flatr*.

flat[2] ■ n. a set of rooms comprising an individual place of residence within a larger building.
– DERIVATIVES **flatlet** n.
– ORIGIN C19: alteration of obsolete *flet* 'floor, dwelling', of Germanic origin and rel. to FLAT[1].

flatbed ■ n. **1** a long flat area or structure. **2** [as modifier] denoting a vehicle with a flat load-carrying area. **3** Computing a scanner, plotter, or other device which keeps paper flat during use.

flatboat ■ n. a boat with a flat bottom for use in shallow water.

flatfish ■ n. (pl. same or **-fishes**) a flounder, plaice, dab, sole, or other marine fish that swims on its side with both eyes on the upper side of its flattened body. [Order Pleuronectiformes.]

flatfoot ■ n. (pl. **flatfoots** or **flatfeet**) informal, dated a police officer.

flat foot ■ n. a foot with an arch that is lower than usual.

flat-footed ■ adj. **1** having flat feet. **2** informal clumsy.
– DERIVATIVES **flat-footedly** adv. **flat-footedness** n.

flathead ■ n. an edible tropical marine fish that has a pointed flattened head with the eyes on the top. [Family Platycephalidae: several species.]

443

flavour

flatline ■ v. informal (of a person) die.
– DERIVATIVES **flatliner** n.
– ORIGIN 1980s: with ref. to the continuous straight line displayed on a heart monitor.

flatmate ■ n. a person with whom one shares a flat.

flat-pack ■ n. **1** [as modifier] denoting furniture or other equipment that is sold in pieces and assembled by the buyer. **2** Electronics a package for an integrated circuit consisting of a rectangular sealed unit with a number of horizontal metal pins protruding from its sides.
– DERIVATIVES **flat-packed** adj.

flat race ■ n. a horse race over a course with no jumps, as opposed to a steeplechase or hurdles.
– DERIVATIVES **flat racing** n.

flatten ■ v. **1** make or become flat or flatter. **2** press (oneself) against a surface. **3** raze to the ground. **4** informal strike (someone) so as to make them fall down.
– DERIVATIVES **flattened** adj. **flattener** n.

flatter ■ v. **1** lavish compliments on, especially in order to further one's own interests. **2** (usu. **be flattered**) cause to feel honoured and pleased. **3** (**flatter oneself**) please, congratulate, or delude oneself. **4** (of clothing or a colour) enhance; make attractive. **5** give an unrealistically favourable impression of.
– DERIVATIVES **flatterer** n. **flattering** adj. **flatteringly** adv. **flattery** n.
– ORIGIN Middle English (as *flattery*): from Old French *flaterie*, from *flater* 'stroke, flatter', prob. of Germanic origin.

flattie (also **flatty**) ■ n. (pl. **-ies**) informal **1** S. African a brownish fast-moving wall crab spider with a flattened oval body, commonly found in houses. [Family Selenopidae.] **2** a flat-heeled shoe.

flatulent /'flatjʊl(ə)nt/ ■ adj. suffering from or marked by an accumulation of gas in the alimentary canal.
– DERIVATIVES **flatulence** n. **flatulency** n. **flatulently** adv.
– ORIGIN C16: from modern Latin *flatulentus*, from Latin *flatus* 'blowing', from *flare* 'to blow'.

flatware ■ n. **1** items of crockery such as plates and saucers. **2** N. Amer. domestic cutlery.

flatworm ■ n. a worm of a phylum (Platyhelminthes) which includes the planarians, parasitic flukes, and tapeworms, distinguished by a simple flattened body lacking blood vessels.

flat-woven ■ adj. (of a carpet or rug) woven so as not to form a projecting pile.
– DERIVATIVES **flat-weave** n.

flaunt ■ v. display ostentatiously.
– DERIVATIVES **flaunter** n. **flaunty** adj.
– ORIGIN C16.

USAGE
It is a common error to use **flaunt** when **flout** is intended. **Flaunt** means 'display ostentatiously', while **flout** means 'openly disregard (a rule or convention)'.

flautist /'flɔːtɪst/ ■ n. a flute player.
– ORIGIN C19: from Italian *flautista*, from *flauto* 'flute'.

flavin /'fleɪvɪn/ ■ n. Biochemistry any of a group of naturally occurring pigments including riboflavin, having a tricyclic aromatic molecular structure.
– ORIGIN C19: from Latin *flavus* 'yellow'.

flavoprotein /ˌfleɪvə(ʊ)'prəʊtiːn/ ■ n. Biochemistry any of a class of conjugated proteins that contain flavins and are involved in oxidation reactions in cells.
– ORIGIN 1930s: blend of FLAVIN and PROTEIN.

flavour (US **flavor**) ■ n. **1** the distinctive taste of a food or drink. **2** a quality reminiscent of something specified: *an African flavour*. **3** a sample of the distinctive quality of something: *a flavour of the content of the conversation*. **4** Physics a quantized property of quarks with values designated up, down, charmed, strange, top, and bottom. ■ v. give flavour to.
– PHRASES **flavour of the month** a person or thing that is currently popular.
– DERIVATIVES **flavoured** adj. **flavourful** adj. **flavourless** adj. **flavoursome** adj.
– ORIGIN Middle English ('fragrance, aroma'): from Old

flavouring

French *flaor*, perhaps from a blend of Latin *flatus* 'blowing' and *foetor* 'stench'; the *-v-* appears to have been introduced by association with **SAVOUR**.

flavouring (US **flavoring**) ■ n. a substance used to enhance the flavour of a food or drink.

flaw ■ n. 1 a blemish; an imperfection. 2 a fundamental weakness. ■ v. (usu. **be flawed**) mar or weaken.
–DERIVATIVES **flawed** adj. **flawless** adj. **flawlessly** adv. **flawlessness** n.
–ORIGIN Middle English (orig. 'a flake of snow', later, 'a fragment or splinter'): perhaps from Old Norse *flaga* 'slab'.

flax ■ n. 1 a blue-flowered herbaceous plant that is cultivated for its seed (linseed) and for textile fibre made from its stalks. [*Linum usitatissimum.*] ▶ textile fibre obtained from this plant. 2 (also **New Zealand flax**) another term for **FLAX-LILY**.
–ORIGIN Old English, of West Germanic origin.

flaxen ■ adj. 1 of flax. 2 poetic/literary (especially of hair) of the pale yellow colour of dressed flax.

flax-lily ■ n. a New Zealand plant that yields fibre and is also grown as an ornamental. [*Phormium tenax.*]

flaxseed ■ n. another term for **LINSEED**.

flay ■ v. 1 strip the skin from (a body or carcass). 2 whip or beat harshly. 3 criticize harshly.
–DERIVATIVES **flayer** n.
–ORIGIN Old English, of Germanic origin.

F-layer ■ n. the highest and most strongly ionized region of the ionosphere.
–ORIGIN 1920s: arbitrary use of *F* + **LAYER**.

flea ■ n. a small wingless jumping insect which feeds on the blood of mammals and birds. [*Pulex irritans* (human flea) and other species, order Siphonaptera.]
–PHRASES (**as**) **fit as a flea** in very good health. **a flea in one's ear** a sharp reproof.
–ORIGIN Old English, of Germanic origin.

flea beetle ■ n. a small jumping beetle that can be a pest of plants such as crucifers. [*Phyllotreta* and other genera.]

flea-bitten ■ adj. 1 bitten by or infested with fleas. 2 dilapidated or disreputable.

flea collar ■ n. a collar for a cat or dog that is impregnated with insecticide to kill or deter fleas.

flea market ■ n. a street market selling second-hand goods.

fleapit ■ n. chiefly Brit. a dingy, dirty place, especially a run-down cinema.

fleck ■ n. 1 a very small patch of colour or light. 2 a speck. ■ v. (usu. **be flecked**) mark or dot with flecks.
–ORIGIN Middle English: perhaps from Old Norse *flekkr* (n.), *flekka* (v.), or from Middle Low German, Middle Dutch *vlecke*.

fled past and past participle of **FLEE**.

fledge /flɛdʒ/ ■ v. (with reference to a young bird) develop or allow to develop wing feathers that are large enough for flight.
–DERIVATIVES **fledged** adj.
–ORIGIN late C16: from the obsolete adj. *fledge* 'ready to fly', from Old English, of Germanic origin.

fledgling (also **fledgeling**) ■ n. 1 a young bird that has just fledged. 2 [as modifier] denoting an inexperienced person or emergent system: *fledgling democracies.*
–ORIGIN C19: from the obsolete adj. *fledge* (see **FLEDGE**), on the pattern of *nestling.*

flee ■ v. (**flees**, **fleeing**; past and past part. **fled**) run away.
–ORIGIN Old English, of Germanic origin.

fleece ■ n. 1 the wool coat of a sheep. 2 a soft, warm fabric with a texture similar to sheep's wool, or a garment made from this. ■ v. informal obtain an unfair amount of money from.
–DERIVATIVES **fleeced** adj. **fleecy** adj. **fleeciness** n.
–ORIGIN Old English, of West Germanic origin.

fleer /flɪə/ ■ v. poetic/literary laugh impudently or jeeringly. ■ n. archaic an impudent or jeering look or speech.
–ORIGIN Middle English: prob. of Scandinavian origin and rel. to Norwegian and Swedish dialect *flira* 'to grin'.

fleet[1] ■ n. 1 a group of ships sailing together. 2 (**the fleet**) a country's navy: *the US fleet.* 3 a number of vehicles or aircraft operating together.
–ORIGIN Old English *flēot* 'ship, shipping', from *flēotan* 'float, swim', of Germanic origin.

fleet[2] ■ adj. fast and nimble: *fleet of foot.*
–DERIVATIVES **fleetly** adv. **fleetness** n.
–ORIGIN C16: prob. from Old Norse *fljótr*, of Germanic origin.

Fleet Admiral ■ n. the highest rank of admiral in the US navy.

fleeting ■ adj. lasting for a very short time.
–DERIVATIVES **fleetingly** adv.

Fleming /'flɛmɪŋ/ ■ n. 1 a native of Flanders. 2 a member of the Flemish-speaking people inhabiting northern and western Belgium. Compare with **WALLOON**.
–ORIGIN Old English *Flǣmingi*, from Old Norse, reinforced by Middle Dutch *Vlāming*, rel. to *Vlaanderen* 'Flanders'.

Flemish /'flɛmɪʃ/ ■ n. 1 (**the Flemish**) the people of Flanders, a region divided between Belgium, France, and the Netherlands. 2 the Dutch language as spoken in Flanders. ■ adj. of or relating to the Flemish people or language.
–ORIGIN Middle English: from Middle Dutch *Vlāmisch*, rel. to *Vlaanderen* 'Flanders'.

flense /flɛns/ (also **flench** /flɛn(t)ʃ/) ■ v. slice the skin or fat from (a carcass, especially that of a whale).
–ORIGIN C19: from Danish *flensa*.

flesh ■ n. 1 the soft substance in the body consisting of muscle tissue and fat. 2 the edible pulpy part of a fruit or vegetable. 3 the surface of the human body (with reference to its appearance or sensory properties). 4 (**the flesh**) the physicality of the human body as contrasted with the mind or the soul. ■ v. 1 (**flesh out**) make more substantial. 2 remove the flesh from (a hide).
–PHRASES **all flesh** all human and animal life. **in the flesh** in person or (of a thing) in its actual state. **make someone's flesh creep** (or **crawl**) cause someone to feel fear, horror, or disgust. **put flesh on** (**the bones of**) **something** flesh something out.
–DERIVATIVES **-fleshed** adj. **fleshless** adj.
–ORIGIN Old English, of Germanic origin.

flesh fly ■ n. a fly that breeds in carrion. [Family Sarcophagidae: many species.]

fleshly ■ adj. (**-ier**, **-iest**) 1 of or relating to the body; sensual. 2 having an actual physical presence.
–ORIGIN Old English, of Germanic origin.

fleshpots ■ pl. n. places providing a hedonistic experience.
–ORIGIN C16: with biblical allusion to the *fleshpots of Egypt* (Exodus 16:3).

flesh wound ■ n. a wound that breaks the skin but does not damage bones or vital organs.

fleshy ■ adj. (**-ier**, **-iest**) 1 having a substantial amount of flesh; plump. 2 (of plant or fruit tissue) soft and thick. 3 resembling flesh.
–DERIVATIVES **fleshiness** n.

fletch /flɛtʃ/ ■ v. provide (an arrow) with feathers.
–ORIGIN C17: alteration of **FLEDGE**, prob. influenced by *fletcher*.

fletcher ■ n. chiefly historical a person who makes and sells arrows.
–ORIGIN Middle English: from Old French *flechier*, from *fleche* 'arrow'.

fletching ■ n. the feathers of an arrow.

fleur-de-lis /ˌflɜːdəˈliː/ (also **fleur-de-lys**) ■ n. (pl. **fleurs-de-lis** pronunc. same) 1 Art & Heraldry a stylized lily composed of three petals bound together near their bases. 2 a variety of iris.
–ORIGIN Middle English: from Old French *flour de lys* 'flower of the lily'.

fleury /ˈflʊəri/ ■ adj. variant spelling of **FLORY**.

flew past of **FLY**[1].

flews /fluːz/ ■ pl. n. the thick hanging lips of a bloodhound or similar dog.
–ORIGIN C16.

flex¹ ■ v. **1** bend (a limb or joint). **2** contract or tense (a muscle). **3** warp or bend and then revert to shape. **4** [usu. as adj. **flexed**] Archaeology place (a corpse) with the legs drawn up under the chin.
– ORIGIN C16: from Latin *flex-, flectere* 'bend'.

flex² ■ n. a flexible insulated cable used for carrying electric current to an appliance.
– ORIGIN C20: abbrev. of FLEXIBLE.

flexible ■ adj. **1** capable of bending easily without breaking. **2** readily adaptable.
– DERIVATIVES **flexibility** n. **flexibly** adv.
– ORIGIN Middle English: from Latin *flexibilis*, from *flectere* 'to bend'.

flexion /ˈflɛkʃ(ə)n/ (also **flection**) ■ n. the action of bending or the condition of being bent.
– ORIGIN C17: from Latin *flexio(n-)*, from *flectere* 'to bend'.

flexitime (N. Amer. also **flextime**) ■ n. a system allowing some flexibility in when workers put in their allotted hours.

flexography /flɛkˈsɒɡrəfi/ ■ n. a rotary relief printing method using rubber or plastic plates and fluid inks or dyes, for printing on impervious materials such as plastics, as well as on fabrics and paper.
– DERIVATIVES **flexographic** adj.

flexor /ˈflɛksə/ ■ n. Anatomy a muscle whose contraction bends a limb or other part of the body.

flexure /ˈflɛkʃə/ ■ n. chiefly Anatomy & Geology **1** the action of bending or curving, or the condition of being bent or curved. **2** a bent or curved part.
– DERIVATIVES **flexural** adj.
– ORIGIN C16: from Latin *flexura*, from *flectere* 'to bend'.

flibbertigibbet /ˌflɪbətɪˈdʒɪbɪt/ ■ n. a frivolous and restless person.
– ORIGIN Middle English: prob. imitative of idle chatter.

flick ■ n. **1** a sudden smart movement up and down or from side to side. **2** the sudden release of a finger or thumb held bent against another finger. **3** informal a cinema film. ▸ (**the flicks**) the cinema. ■ v. **1** make or cause to make a sudden sharp movement. **2** propel with a flick of the fingers. **3** (**flick through**) look quickly through (a volume or a collection of papers).
– ORIGIN Middle English: symbolic, *fl-* freq. beginning words denoting sudden movement.

flicker ■ v. **1** shine or burn unsteadily and fitfully. **2** (of a feeling) be briefly perceptible. **3** make small, quick movements. ■ n. an instance of flickering.
– DERIVATIVES **flickering** adj. & n.
– ORIGIN Old English *flicorian, flycerian* 'to flutter', prob. of Germanic origin.

flick knife ■ n. a knife with a blade that springs out from the handle when a button is pressed.

flier ■ n. variant spelling of FLYER.

flight ■ n. **1** the action or process of flying. ▸ a journey made in an aircraft or in space. ▸ the movement or trajectory of a projectile through the air. **2** a flock of birds or body of insects flying in the air. **3** a group of aircraft operating together. **4** the action of fleeing. **5** a series of steps between floors or levels. ▸ a series of locks by which a canal ascends an incline. ▸ a series of hurdles across a racetrack. **6** an uninhibited mental journey: *a flight of fancy*. **7** the tail of an arrow or dart. ■ v. **1** Brit. (in soccer, cricket, etc.) deliver (a ball) with well-judged trajectory and pace. **2** provide (an arrow or dart) with a flight. **3** shoot (wildfowl) in flight.
– PHRASES **in full flight** having gained optimum momentum. **take flight 1** (of a bird) take off and fly. **2** flee.
– ORIGIN Old English, of Germanic origin; rel. to FLY¹.

flight capital ■ n. capital which has been moved from an area in economic difficulties to a more stable region.

flight deck ■ n. **1** the cockpit of a large aircraft. **2** the deck of an aircraft carrier, used for take-off and landing.

flight envelope ■ n. the range of combinations of speed, altitude, angle of attack, etc., within which a flying object is aerodynamically stable.

flight feather ■ n. any of the large primary or secondary feathers in a bird's wing, supporting it in flight.

flightless ■ adj. (of a bird or insect) naturally unable to fly.
– DERIVATIVES **flightlessness** n.

445

flippant

flight lieutenant ■ n. a rank of officer in the RAF, above flying officer and below squadron leader.

flight path ■ n. the course of an aircraft or spacecraft.

flight recorder ■ n. a device in an aircraft to record technical details during a flight, used in the event of an accident to discover its cause.

flight sergeant ■ n. a rank of non-commissioned officer in the air force, above sergeant and below warrant officer.

flight simulator ■ n. a machine resembling a cockpit and simulating the conditions of an aircraft in flight, used for training pilots.

flighty ■ adj. (**-ier, -iest**) fickle; erratic; restlessly flirtatious.
– DERIVATIVES **flightily** adv. **flightiness** n.

flimflam ■ n. informal **1** insincere and unconvincing talk. **2** a confidence trick.
– DERIVATIVES **flimflammer** n. **flimflammery** n.
– ORIGIN C16: symbolic reduplication.

flimsy ■ adj. (**-ier, -iest**) **1** weak and insubstantial. **2** light and thin. **3** (of a pretext or account) weak; unconvincing. ■ n. (pl. **-ies**) Brit. **1** very thin paper. **2** a copy of a document, produced on very thin paper.
– DERIVATIVES **flimsily** adv. **flimsiness** n.
– ORIGIN C18: prob. from FLIMFLAM.

flinch ■ v. **1** make a quick, nervous movement as an instinctive reaction to fear or pain. **2** (**flinch from**) avoid through fear or anxiety. ■ n. an act of flinching.
– DERIVATIVES **flincher** n. **flinching** adj. **flinchingly** adv.
– ORIGIN C16: from Old French *flenchir* 'turn aside', of West Germanic origin.

flinders ■ pl. n. small fragments or splinters.
– ORIGIN Middle English: prob. of Scandinavian origin.

fling ■ v. (past and past part. **flung**) **1** throw forcefully; hurl. **2** (**fling oneself into**) wholeheartedly engage in (an activity or enterprise). **3** move with speed: *he flung away to his study*. ■ n. **1** a short period of enjoyment or wild behaviour: *a final fling*. ▸ a short sexual relationship. **2** short for HIGHLAND FLING.
– DERIVATIVES **flinger** n.
– ORIGIN Middle English: perhaps rel. to Old Norse *flengja* 'flog'.

flint ■ n. **1** a hard grey rock consisting of nearly pure silica (chert), occurring chiefly as nodules in chalk. **2** a piece of flint, especially one shaped to form a primitive tool or weapon. **3** a piece of flint used with steel to produce an igniting spark.
– ORIGIN Old English; rel. to Middle Dutch *vlint* and Old High German *flins*.

flint glass ■ n. a pure lustrous kind of glass originally made with flint.

flintlock ■ n. an old-fashioned type of gun fired by a spark from a flint, or the lock producing the spark.

flinty ■ adj. (**-ier, -iest**) **1** of, containing, or reminiscent of flint. **2** (of a person or their expression) very hard and unyielding.
– DERIVATIVES **flintily** adv. **flintiness** n.

flip ■ v. (**flipped, flipping**) **1** turn over or cause to turn over with a quick, smooth movement. **2** toss (something) into the air so that it turns over. **3** (**flip through**) flick through. **4** informal suddenly become deranged or very angry. ■ n. a flipping action or movement. ■ adj. flippant.
– PHRASES **flip one's lid** (or chiefly N. Amer. **one's wig**) informal suddenly become deranged or lose one's self-control.
– ORIGIN C16: prob. a contraction of FILLIP.

flip chart ■ n. a very large pad of paper bound so that pages can be turned over at the top, used on a stand at presentations.

flip-flop ■ n. **1** a light sandal with a thong that passes between the big and second toes. **2** N. Amer. a backward somersault or handspring. **3** Electronics a switching circuit which works by changing between two stable states. ■ v. move with a flapping sound or motion.

flippant ■ adj. not showing a serious or respectful attitude.
– DERIVATIVES **flippancy** n. **flippantly** adv.
– ORIGIN C17 (earlier 'nimble, talkative', later 'playful'): from FLIP.

flipper

flipper ■ n. **1** a broad, flat limb without fingers, used for swimming by sea animals such as seals, whales, and turtles. **2** a flat rubber attachment worn on the foot for underwater swimming. **3** a pivoted arm in a pinball machine.

flipping ■ adj. informal, chiefly Brit. used for emphasis or to express mild annoyance.
– ORIGIN C20: from **FLIP**.

flip side ■ n. informal **1** the less important side of a pop single. **2** the reverse aspect or unwelcome concomitant of something.

flip-top ■ adj. denoting or having a lid that can be easily flipped open.

flirt ■ v. **1** behave playfully in a sexually enticing manner. **2** (**flirt with**) experiment casually with (an idea or activity). **3** (**flirt with**) deliberately risk (danger or death). **4** (of a bird) flap or wave (its wings or tail) with a quick flicking motion. ■ n. a person who habitually flirts.
– DERIVATIVES **flirtation** n. **flirtatious** adj. **flirtatiously** adv. **flirtatiousness** n. **flirty** adj. (**-ier**, **-iest**).
– ORIGIN C16 (orig. 'give someone a sharp blow'; the earliest noun senses were 'joke, gibe' and 'flighty girl'): apparently symbolic, the elements *fl-* and *-irt* both suggesting sudden movement.

flit ■ v. (**flitted**, **flitting**) **1** move swiftly and lightly. **2** chiefly Scottish & N. English move house or leave one's home, especially in secrecy. ■ n. Brit. informal an act of leaving one's home in secrecy.
– ORIGIN Middle English: from Old Norse *flytja*.

flitch /flɪtʃ/ ■ n. **1** a slab of wood cut from a tree trunk. **2** (also **flitch plate**) the strengthening plate in a flitch beam.
– ORIGIN Old English *flicce*, orig. denoting the cured side of any meat, of Germanic origin.

flitch beam ■ n. a compound beam made of an iron plate between two slabs of wood.

flitter ■ v. move quickly in a random manner. ■ n. a flittering movement.
– ORIGIN Middle English: from **FLIT**.

flittermouse ■ n. (pl. **-mice**) old-fashioned term for **BAT**[2] (in sense 1).
– ORIGIN C16: on the pattern of Dutch *vledermuis* or German *Fledermaus*.

float ■ v. **1** rest or cause to rest on the surface of a liquid without sinking. **2** be suspended freely in a liquid or gas. **3** move slowly or hover in a liquid or the air. **4** (in sport) make (the ball) travel lightly and effortlessly through the air. **5** put forward (an idea) as a suggestion or test of reactions. **6** offer the shares of (a company) for sale on the stock market for the first time. **7** (with reference to a currency) fluctuate or allow to fluctuate freely in value. ■ n. **1** any hollow or lightweight object or device used to achieve buoyancy in water. **2** a small floating object attached to a fishing line signalling the bite of a fish. **3** a floating device which forms part of a valve apparatus controlling a flow of water. **4** Brit. a small vehicle or cart powered by electricity. **5** a platform mounted on a truck and carrying a display in a procession. **6** a sum of money used for change at the beginning of a period of selling in a shop or stall. **7** a hand tool with a rectangular blade used for smoothing plaster. **8** a soft drink with a scoop of ice cream floating in it. **9** (in critical path analysis) the period of time by which the duration of an activity may be extended without affecting the overall time for the process.
– PHRASES **float someone's boat** informal appeal to or excite someone.
– DERIVATIVES **floatable** adj.
– ORIGIN Old English, of Germanic origin.

floatation ■ n. variant spelling of **FLOTATION**.

float chamber ■ n. the cavity in a carburettor containing a device which floats on the surface of the fuel and seals off the flow as the level rises.

floater ■ n. a person or thing that floats. ▸ a loose particle within the eyeball which is apparent in one's field of vision.

floating ■ adj. not settled or fixed permanently; fluctuating or variable: *floating exchange rates*.

floating-point ■ n. [as modifier] Computing denoting a mode of representing numbers as two sequences of bits, one representing the digits in the number and the other an exponent which determines the position of the radix point.

floating rib ■ n. any of the lower ribs which are not attached directly to the breastbone.

floating voter ■ n. a person who has not decided which way to vote in an election, or one who does not consistently vote for the same party.

floatplane ■ n. a seaplane.

float stone ■ n. light, porous stone that floats, e.g. pumice.

float valve ■ n. a ball valve.

floaty ■ adj. chiefly Brit. (especially of a woman's garment or a fabric) light and flimsy.

floccinaucinihilipilification /ˌflɒksɪˌnɔːsɪˌnɪhɪlɪˌpɪlɪfɪˈkeɪʃ(ə)n/ ■ n. the action or habit of estimating something as worthless.
– ORIGIN C18: from Latin *flocci, nauci, nihili, pili* (words meaning 'at little value').

floccose /ˈflɒkəʊs/ ■ adj. chiefly Botany covered with or consisting of woolly tufts.
– ORIGIN C18: from late Latin *floccosus*, from Latin *floccus* 'flock'.

flocculant /ˈflɒkjʊl(ə)nt/ ■ n. a substance which promotes the clumping of particles, especially one used in treating waste water.

flock[1] ■ n. **1** a number of birds moving or resting together. ▸ a number of domestic animals, especially sheep, goats, or geese, that are kept together. **2** (**a flock/flocks**) a large number or crowd. **3** a Christian congregation under the charge of a particular minister. ■ v. congregate or move in a flock.
– ORIGIN Old English *flocc*, in the sense 'a band or body of people'.

flock[2] ■ n. **1** a soft material for stuffing cushions and quilts, made of wool refuse or torn-up cloth. ▸ powdered wool or cloth, used in making flock wallpaper. **2** a lock or tuft of wool or cotton.
– DERIVATIVES **flocky** adj.
– ORIGIN Middle English: from Latin *floccus* 'lock or tuft of wool'.

flock wallpaper ■ n. wallpaper sized and sprinkled with powdered wool to make a raised pattern.

floe /fləʊ/ ■ n. a sheet of floating ice.
– ORIGIN C19: prob. from Norwegian *flo*, from Old Norse *fló* 'layer'.

flog ■ v. (**flogged**, **flogging**) **1** beat with a whip or stick as a punishment. **2** informal work at or promote repetitively or at excessive length. **3** informal sell or offer for sale. **4** Brit. informal make one's way with strenuous effort.
– PHRASES **flog a dead horse** waste energy on a lost cause or unalterable situation.
– DERIVATIVES **flogger** n.
– ORIGIN C17: perhaps imitative, or from Latin *flagellare* 'to whip'.

flokati /flɒˈkɑːti/ ■ n. (pl. **flokatis**) a Greek woven woollen rug with a thick loose pile.
– ORIGIN C20: from modern Greek *phlokatē* 'peasant's blanket'.

flood ■ n. **1** an overflow of a large amount of water over dry land. ▸ (**the Flood**) the biblical flood brought by God upon the earth because of the wickedness of the human race. **2** the inflow of the tide. ▸ poetic/literary a river, stream, or sea. **3** an outpouring of tears or emotion. **4** an overwhelming quantity of things or people appearing at once. **5** short for **FLOODLIGHT**. ■ v. **1** cover or become covered with water in a flood. ▸ (of a river) become swollen and overflow its banks. **2** arrive in or overwhelm with very large numbers. ▸ fill or suffuse completely: *she flooded the room with light*. **3** overfill the carburettor of (an engine) with petrol.
– DERIVATIVES **flooding** n.
– ORIGIN Old English *flōd*, of Germanic origin; rel. to **FLOW**.

floodgate ■ n. **1** a gate that can be opened or closed to admit or exclude water, especially the lower gate of a lock. **2** (**the floodgates**) last restraints holding back a powerful outpouring.

floodlight ■ n. a large, powerful light used to illuminate a stage or sports ground. ■ v. (past and past part. **-lit**) [usu. as adj. **floodlit**] illuminate with floodlights.

flood plain ■ n. an area of low-lying ground adjacent to a river that is subject to flooding.

flood tide ■ n. an incoming tide.

floor ■ n. **1** the lower surface of a room, on which one may walk. ▸ the bottom of the sea, a cave, etc.: *the ocean floor*. **2** a storey of a building. **3** (**the floor**) the part of a legislative assembly in which members sit and from which they speak. ▸ the right to speak in an assembly. **4** a minimum level of prices or wages. ■ v. **1** provide with a floor. **2** informal knock or punch to the ground. ▸ baffle or confound completely.
– DERIVATIVES **flooring** n.
– ORIGIN Old English, of Germanic origin.

floorboard ■ n. a long plank making up part of a wooden floor.

floor lamp ■ n. chiefly N. Amer. a standard lamp.

floor manager ■ n. **1** the stage manager of a television production. **2** a supervisor of shop assistants in a large store.

floor show ■ n. an entertainment presented on the floor of a nightclub or restaurant.

floozy (also **floozie**) ■ n. (pl. **-ies**) informal a disreputable or promiscuous girl or woman.
– ORIGIN C20: perhaps rel. to FLOSSY or to dialect *floosy* 'fluffy'.

flop ■ v. (**flopped**, **flopping**) **1** fall, hang, or collapse in a heavy, loose, and ungainly way. **2** informal (of a performer or show) fail totally. **3** informal rest or sleep in an improvised place. ■ n. **1** a heavy, loose, and ungainly fall. **2** informal a total failure. **3** informal, chiefly US a cheap place to sleep.
– ORIGIN C17: var. of FLAP.

-flop ■ comb. form Computing floating-point operations per second: *a gigaflop computer*.

flophouse ■ n. informal, chiefly N. Amer. a dosshouse.

floppy ■ adj. (**-ier**, **-iest**) tending to flop or hang loosely. ■ n. (pl. **-ies**) (also **floppy disk**) Computing a flexible removable magnetic disk used for storing data.
– DERIVATIVES **floppily** adv. **floppiness** n.

flora ■ n. (pl. **floras** or **florae** /-riː/) **1** the plants of a particular region, habitat, or geological period. Compare with FAUNA. **2** [with modifier] the symbiotic bacteria occurring naturally in the intestines: *the gut flora*.
– ORIGIN C18: from Latin *flos, flor-* 'flower'.

floral /ˈflɔːr(ə)l, ˈflɒ-/ ■ adj. **1** of or decorated with flowers. **2** Botany of flora or floras.
– DERIVATIVES **florally** adv.

Florentine /ˈflɒr(ə)ntʌɪn/ ■ adj. **1** of or relating to Florence in Italy. **2** (**florentine** /-tiːn/) [postpos.] (of a dish) served on a bed of spinach: *eggs florentine*. ■ n. **1** a native or citizen of Florence. **2** a biscuit consisting mainly of nuts and preserved fruit, coated on one side with chocolate.

florescence /flɔːˈrɛs(ə)ns, flə-/ ■ n. the process of flowering.
– ORIGIN C18: from Latin *florescere* 'begin to flower', from *flos* 'flower'.

floret /ˈflɒrɪt, ˈflɔː-/ ■ n. **1** Botany one of the small flowers making up a composite flower head. ▸ a small flower. **2** one of the flowering stems making up a head of cauliflower or broccoli.
– ORIGIN C17: from Latin *flos, flor-* 'flower'.

floribunda /ˌflɒrɪˈbʌndə, ˌflɔː-/ ■ n. a plant, especially a rose, which bears dense clusters of flowers.
– ORIGIN C19: modern Latin, from *floribundus* 'freely flowering'.

floriculture /ˈflɒrɪˌkʌltʃə, ˈflɔː-/ ■ n. the cultivation of flowers.
– DERIVATIVES **floricultural** adj. **floriculturist** n.

florid /ˈflɒrɪd/ ■ adj. **1** having a red or flushed complexion. **2** elaborately or excessively intricate or complicated. **3** Medicine (of a disease or its manifestations) occurring in a fully developed form.

447

– DERIVATIVES **floridity** n. **floridly** adv. **floridness** n.
– ORIGIN C17: from Latin *floridus*, from *flos, flor-* 'flower'.

floriferous /flɒˈrɪf(ə)rəs, flɔː-/ ■ adj. (of a plant) producing many flowers.

florin /ˈflɒrɪn/ ■ n. **1** a former British coin and monetary unit worth two shillings. **2** an English gold coin of the 14th century. **3** a foreign coin of gold or silver, especially a Dutch guilder.
– ORIGIN from Italian *fiorino*, diminutive of *fiore* 'flower' (orig. referring to a Florentine coin bearing a fleur-de-lis).

florist ■ n. a person who sells and arranges cut flowers.
– DERIVATIVES **floristry** n.

floristic /fləˈrɪstɪk/ ■ adj. Botany relating to the study of the distribution of plants.
– DERIVATIVES **floristically** adv.

floristics ■ pl. n. [treated as sing.] Botany the branch of phytogeography concerned with the study of plant species present in an area.

flory /ˈflɔːri/ (also **fleury**) ■ adj. Heraldry **1** decorated with fleurs-de-lis. **2** (of a cross) having the end of each limb splayed out into three pointed lobes.
– ORIGIN Middle English: from Old French *floure*, from *flour* 'flower'.

floss ■ n. **1** the rough silk enveloping a silkworm's cocoon. **2** untwisted silk fibres used in embroidery. **3** (also **dental floss**) a soft thread used to clean between the teeth. **4** the silky down in maize and other plants. ■ v. clean between (one's teeth) with dental floss.
– ORIGIN C18: from French (*soie*) *floche*, from Old French *flosche* 'down, nap of velvet'.

flossy ■ adj. (**-ier**, **-iest**) of or like floss.

flotation /fləʊˈteɪʃ(ə)n/ (also **floatation**) ■ n. **1** the action of floating or capacity to float. **2** the separation of small particles of a solid by their different capacities to float. **3** the process of offering a company's shares for sale on the stock market for the first time.

flotation tank ■ n. a lightproof, soundproof tank of salt water in which a person floats as a form of deep relaxation.

flotilla /fləˈtɪlə/ ■ n. a small fleet of ships or boats.
– ORIGIN C18: from Spanish, diminutive of *flota* 'fleet'.

flotsam /ˈflɒts(ə)m/ ■ n. wreckage found floating on the sea. Compare with JETSAM.
– PHRASES **flotsam and jetsam** useless or discarded objects.
– ORIGIN C17: from Anglo-Norman French *floteson*, from *floter* 'to float'.

flounce[1] ■ v. move in an exaggeratedly impatient or angry manner. ■ n. an exaggerated action expressing annoyance or impatience.
– ORIGIN C16: perhaps of Scandinavian origin and rel. to Norwegian *flunsa* 'hurry', or perhaps symbolic, like *bounce*.

flounce[2] ■ n. a wide ornamental strip of material gathered and sewn to a skirt or dress; a frill.
– DERIVATIVES **flounced** adj. **flouncy** adj.
– ORIGIN C18: from an alteration of obsolete *frounce* 'a fold or pleat', from Old French *fronce*.

flounder[1] ■ n. a small flatfish that typically occurs in shallow coastal water. [Families Bothidae and Pleuronectidae: numerous species.]
– ORIGIN Middle English: from Old French *flondre*, prob. of Scandinavian origin.

flounder[2] ■ v. **1** stagger clumsily in mud or water. **2** have trouble doing or understanding something.
– ORIGIN C16: perhaps a blend of FOUNDER[3] and BLUNDER, or perhaps symbolic.

USAGE
On the confusion of **flounder** with **founder**, see FOUNDER[3].

flour ■ n. a powder obtained by grinding grain, used to make bread, cakes, and pastry. ■ v. sprinkle with flour.
– ORIGIN Middle English: a specific use of FLOWER in the sense 'the best part', used orig. to mean 'the finest quality of ground wheat'.

flourish

flourish ■ v. **1** grow or develop in a healthy or vigorous way. ▸ be working or at the height of one's career during a specified period. **2** wave (something) about dramatically. ■ n. **1** a bold or extravagant gesture or action. **2** an ornamental flowing curve in handwriting or scrollwork.
– DERIVATIVES **flourisher** n.
– ORIGIN Middle English: from Old French *floriss-*, *florir*, from Latin *florere*, from *flos*, *flor-* 'a flower'.

floury ■ adj. **1** covered with flour. ▸ of or resembling flour. **2** (of a potato) having a soft, fluffy texture when cooked.
– DERIVATIVES **flouriness** n.

flout /flaʊt/ ■ v. **1** openly disregard (a rule, law, or convention). **2** archaic mock; scoff.
– ORIGIN C16: perhaps from Dutch *fluiten* 'whistle, play the flute, hiss'.

USAGE
On the confusion of **flout** with **flaunt**, see **FLAUNT**.

flow ■ v. **1** move steadily and continuously in a current or stream. **2** (of the sea or a tidal river) move towards the land; rise. Compare with **EBB**. **3** move or issue forth steadily and freely. ▸ [often as adj. **flowing**] hang loosely in a graceful manner: *a long flowing gown*. **4** (of a solid) undergo a permanent change of shape under stress, without melting. ■ n. **1** the action or process of flowing. **2** the rise of a tide or a river. **3** a steady, continuous stream: *the flow of traffic*.
– PHRASES **go with the flow** informal be relaxed and accept a situation. **in full flow** talking or performing fluently and enthusiastically.
– DERIVATIVES **flowingly** adv.
– ORIGIN Old English, of Germanic origin; rel. to **FLOOD**.

flow chart (also **flow diagram**) ■ n. **1** a diagram of a sequence of movements or actions making up a complex system. **2** a graphical representation of a computer program in relation to its sequence of functions.

flower ■ n. **1** the seed-bearing part of a plant, consisting of reproductive organs (stamens and carpels) typically surrounded by brightly coloured petals (the corolla) and green sepals (the calyx). **2** (often in phr. **in flower**) the state or period in which a plant's flowers have developed and opened. **3** (**the flower of**) the finest individuals out of a number of people or things. ■ v. **1** [often as adj. **flowering**] (of a plant) produce flowers. **2** be in or reach an optimum stage of development.
– DERIVATIVES **flowerer** n. **flowerless** adj. **flower-like** adj.
– ORIGIN Middle English: from Old French *flour*, *flor*, from Latin *flos*, *flor-*.

flowered ■ adj. **1** having a floral design. **2** [in combination] bearing flowers: *yellow-flowered japonica*.

floweret /ˈflaʊərɪt/ ■ n. a floret, especially of cauliflower or broccoli.

flower head ■ n. a compact mass of flowers at the top of a stem, especially a capitulum.

flowering plant ■ n. an angiosperm.

flowerpot ■ n. a small, typically earthenware container in which to grow a plant.

flower power ■ n. the promotion by hippies of peace and love as means of changing the world.

flowery ■ adj. **1** filled with or resembling flowers. **2** (of speech or writing) elaborate.
– DERIVATIVES **floweriness** n.

flown past participle of **FLY**[1].

flowsheet ■ n. another term for **FLOW CHART**.

flowstone ■ n. Geology rock deposited as a thin sheet by precipitation from flowing water.

Flt Lt ■ abbrev. Flight Lieutenant.

Flt Sgt ■ abbrev. Flight Sergeant.

flu ■ n. influenza or any similar, milder infection.

flub informal, chiefly N. Amer. ■ v. (**flubbed**, **flubbing**) botch or bungle. ■ n. something done badly or clumsily; a blunder.
– ORIGIN 1920s.

fluconazole /fluˈkɒnəzəʊl, flə-/ ■ n. Medicine a drug used to treat candidiasis and other fungal diseases often associated with HIV.

fluctuate /ˈflʌktʃʊeɪt, -tjʊ-/ ■ v. rise and fall irregularly in number or amount.
– DERIVATIVES **fluctuation** n.
– ORIGIN C17 (*fluctuation* Middle English): from Latin *fluctuare* 'undulate', from *fluere* 'to flow'.

flue /fluː/ ■ n. a duct in a chimney for smoke and waste gases. ▸ a channel for conveying heat.
– ORIGIN Middle English (denoting the mouthpiece of a hunting horn).

fluence /ˈfluːəns/ ■ n. Brit. informal magical or hypnotic power.
– ORIGIN C20: shortening of **INFLUENCE**.

fluent /ˈfluːənt/ ■ adj. **1** speaking or writing easily and accurately, especially in a foreign language. ▸ (of a language) used easily and accurately. **2** smoothly graceful and easy. **3** able to flow freely; fluid.
– DERIVATIVES **fluency** n. **fluently** adv.
– ORIGIN C16: from Latin *fluere* 'flow'.

flue pipe ■ n. **1** a pipe acting as a flue. **2** an organ pipe into which the air enters directly without striking a reed.

fluff ■ n. **1** soft fibres accumulated in small light clumps. ▸ the fur or feathers of a young mammal or bird. **2** trivial or superficial entertainment or writing. **3** informal a mistake, especially in speech, sport, or music. ■ v. **1** (usu. **fluff something up**) make something fuller and softer by shaking or patting it. **2** informal fail to accomplish (something) properly.
– ORIGIN C18: prob. a dialect alteration of C16 *flue* 'down, nap, fluff', apparently from Flemish *vluwe*.

fluffy ■ adj. (**-ier**, **-iest**) **1** of, like, or covered with fluff. **2** (of food) light in texture. **3** informal frivolous, silly, or vague.
– DERIVATIVES **fluffily** adv. **fluffiness** n.

flugelhorn /ˈfluːɡ(ə)lhɔːn/ ■ n. a valved brass musical instrument like a cornet but with a broader tone.
– ORIGIN C19: from German *Flügelhorn*, from *Flügel* 'wing' + *Horn* 'horn'.

fluid ■ n. a substance that has no fixed shape and yields easily to external pressure; a gas or (especially) a liquid. ■ adj. **1** able to flow easily. **2** (of a clutch or coupling) using a liquid to transmit power. **3** not settled or stable. **4** smoothly elegant or graceful.
– DERIVATIVES **fluidity** n. **fluidly** adv.
– ORIGIN Middle English: from Latin *fluidus*, from *fluere* 'to flow'.

fluid mechanics ■ pl. n. [treated as sing.] the study of forces and motion within fluids.

fluid ounce ■ n. **1** Brit. a unit of capacity equal to one twentieth of a pint (approximately 0.028 litre). **2** (also **fluidounce**) US a unit of capacity equal to one sixteenth of a US pint (approximately 0.03 litre).

fluke[1] ■ n. an unlikely chance occurrence, especially a stroke of luck. ■ v. achieve by luck rather than skill.
– DERIVATIVES **flukily** adv. **flukiness** n.
fluky (also **flukey**) adj.
– ORIGIN C19 (orig. a term in games such as billiards): perhaps a dialect word.

fluke[2] ■ n. a parasitic flatworm which typically has suckers and hooks for attachment to the host. [Classes Trematoda and Monogenea.]
– ORIGIN Old English.

fluke[3] ■ n. **1** a broad triangular plate on the arm of an anchor. **2** either of the lobes of a whale's tail.
– ORIGIN C16: perhaps from **FLUKE**[2] (because of the shape).

flume /fluːm/ ■ n. **1** an artificial channel conveying water, typically used for transporting logs. **2** a water slide or chute at a swimming pool or amusement park.
– ORIGIN Middle English: from Latin *flumen* 'river', from *fluere* 'to flow'.

flummery /ˈflʌm(ə)ri/ ■ n. (pl. **-ies**) **1** empty compliments; nonsense. **2** a sweet dish made with beaten eggs and sugar.
– ORIGIN C17: from Welsh *llymru*; perhaps rel. to *llymrig* 'soft, slippery'.

flummox /ˈflʌməks/ ■ v. informal perplex; bewilder.
– ORIGIN C19: prob. of dialect origin.

| VOWELS | a cat | ɑː arm | ɛ bed | ɛː hair | ə ago | əː her | ɪ sit | i cosy | iː see | ɒ hot | ɔː saw | ʌ run |

flung past and past participle of **FLING**.

flunk ■ v. informal fail to reach the required standard in (an examination). ▸ (**flunk out**) be dismissed from school or college for failing examinations.
– ORIGIN C19: perhaps rel. to **FUNK**¹, or perhaps a var. of **FLINCH**.

flunkey (also **flunky**) ■ n. (pl. **-eys** or **-ies**) chiefly derogatory a liveried manservant or footman. ▸ a person who performs menial tasks.
– DERIVATIVES **flunkeyism** n.
– ORIGIN C18: perhaps from **FLANK** in the sense 'a person who stands at one's flank'.

fluoresce /flʊəˈrɛs, flɔː-/ ■ v. shine or glow brightly due to fluorescence.

fluorescein /ˌflʊəˈrɛsiːn, -sɪn, ˌflɔː-/ ■ n. Chemistry an orange dye with a yellowish-green fluorescence, used as an indicator and tracer.

fluorescence /flʊəˈrɛs(ə)ns, flɔː-/ ■ n. light or other radiation emitted by a substance when it is exposed to incident radiation of a shorter wavelength such as X-rays or ultraviolet light. ▸ the property of emitting light in this way.
– ORIGIN C19: from **FLUORSPAR** (which fluoresces), on the pattern of *opalescence*.

fluorescent ■ adj. **1** having or showing fluorescence. ▸ denoting lighting based on fluorescence from phosphor illuminated by ultraviolet light from mercury vapour inside a glass tube. **2** vividly colourful.

fluorescent screen ■ n. a transparent screen coated with fluorescent material to show images from X-rays.

fluoridate /ˈflʊərɪdeɪt, ˈflɔː-/ ■ v. add traces of fluorides to (something, especially a water supply).
– DERIVATIVES **fluoridation** n.

fluoride /ˈflʊəraɪd, ˈflɔː-/ ■ n. **1** Chemistry a compound of fluorine with another element or group: *calcium fluoride*. **2** sodium fluoride or another fluorine-containing salt added to water supplies or toothpaste in order to reduce tooth decay.

fluorinate /ˈflʊərɪneɪt, ˈflɔː-/ ■ v. **1** Chemistry introduce fluorine into (a compound). **2** another term for **FLUORIDATE**.
– DERIVATIVES **fluorination** n.

fluorine /ˈflʊəriːn, ˈflɔː-/ ■ n. the chemical element of atomic number 9, a poisonous pale yellow gas of the halogen series. (Symbol: **F**)
– ORIGIN C19: from *fluor* (see **FLUORSPAR**).

fluorite /ˈflʊəraɪt, ˈflɔː-/ ■ n. a mineral consisting of calcium fluoride which typically occurs as cubic crystals, colourless when pure but often coloured by impurities.

fluoro- /ˈflʊərəʊ, ˈflɔː-/ ■ comb. form **1** representing **FLUORINE**. **2** representing **FLUORESCENCE**.

fluorocarbon ■ n. Chemistry a compound formed by replacing one or more of the hydrogen atoms in a hydrocarbon with fluorine atoms.

fluorochrome ■ n. a chemical that fluoresces, especially one used as a label in biological research.

fluorosis /flʊəˈrəʊsɪs, flɔː-/ ■ n. Medicine a chronic condition caused by excessive intake of fluorine compounds, marked by mottling of the teeth and, if severe, calcification of the ligaments.

fluorspar /ˈflʊəspɑː, ˈflɔː-/ ■ n. another term for **FLUORITE**.
– ORIGIN C18: from *fluor* 'a flow, a mineral used as a flux, fluorspar' (from Latin *fluere* 'to flow') + **SPAR**³.

fluoxetine /fluːˈɒksɪtiːn/ ■ n. Medicine a synthetic compound which inhibits the uptake of serotonin in the brain and is taken to treat depression. Also called **PROZAC** (trademark).
– ORIGIN 1970s: from *fluo(rine)* + *ox(y)* + *-etine* (perhaps from *e* + a blend of **TOLUENE** and **AMINE**).

flurried ■ adj. agitated, nervous, or anxious.

flurry ■ n. (pl. **-ies**) **1** a small swirling mass of snow, leaves, etc. moved by sudden gusts of wind. **2** a sudden short period of commotion or excitement. ▸ a number of things arriving suddenly and simultaneously. ■ v. (**-ies, -ied**) move in flurries; swirl.
– ORIGIN C17: from obsolete *flurr* 'fly up, flutter, whirr' (imitative).

flush¹ ■ v. **1** (of a person's skin or face) become red and hot, typically through illness or emotion. ▸ glow or cause to glow with warm colour or light. ▸ (**be flushed with**) be excited or elated by. **2** cleanse (something, especially a toilet) by passing large quantities of water through it. ▸ remove or dispose of in such a way. **3** drive (a bird or animal, especially a game bird) from cover. **4** (of a plant) send out fresh shoots. ■ n. **1** a reddening of the face or skin. ▸ an area of warm colour or light. **2** a sudden rush of intense emotion. ▸ a period of freshness and vigour: *the first flush of youth*. **3** an act of flushing. **4** a fresh growth of leaves, flowers, or fruit.
– DERIVATIVES **flusher** n.
– ORIGIN Middle English ('move rapidly, spring or fly up'): symbolic; perhaps influenced by **FLASH** and **BLUSH**.

flush² ■ adj. **1** completely level or even with another surface. **2** informal having plenty of money. ■ v. fill in (a joint) level with a surface.
– DERIVATIVES **flushness** n.
– ORIGIN C16 ('perfect, lacking nothing'): prob. rel. to **FLUSH**¹.

flush³ ■ n. (in poker or brag) a hand of cards all of the same suit.
– ORIGIN C16: from French *flux* (formerly *flus*), from Latin *fluxus* (see **FLUX**).

flush⁴ ■ n. Ecology a piece of wet ground over which water flows without being confined to a definite channel.
– ORIGIN Middle English ('marshy place'): rel. to Old French *flache* and Dutch *vlacke*.

fluster ■ v. [often as adj. **flustered**] make (someone) agitated or confused. ■ n. a flustered state.
– ORIGIN C17 ('make slightly drunk'): perhaps of Scandinavian origin and rel. to Icelandic *flaustra* 'hurry, bustle'.

flute ■ n. **1** a high-pitched wind instrument consisting of a tube with holes along it, usually held horizontally so that the breath can be directed against a fixed edge. **2** Architecture an ornamental vertical groove in a column. ▸ a trumpet-shaped frill on a garment. **3** a tall, narrow wine glass. ■ v. **1** speak in a melodious way. ▸ poetic/literary play a flute or pipe. **2** [often as adj. **fluted**] make flutes or grooves in.
– DERIVATIVES **fluting** n. **fluty** (also **flutey**) adj.
– ORIGIN Middle English: from Old French *flahute*, prob. from Provençal *flaüt*, perhaps a blend of *flaujol* 'flageolet' + *laüt* 'lute'.

flutist ■ n. US term for **FLAUTIST**.

flutter ■ v. **1** fly unsteadily by flapping the wings quickly and lightly. **2** move or fall with a light irregular motion. **3** (of a pulse or heartbeat) beat feebly or irregularly. ■ n. **1** an act or instance of fluttering. **2** a state or sensation of tremulous excitement. **3** Brit. informal a small bet. **4** Electronics rapid variation in the pitch or amplitude of a signal, especially of recorded sound. Compare with **WOW**². **5** Aeronautics undesired oscillation in a part of an aircraft under stress.
– DERIVATIVES **flutterer** n. **fluttering** adj. **flutteringly** adv. **fluttery** adj.
– ORIGIN Old English.

fluvial /ˈfluːvɪəl/ ■ adj. chiefly Geology of or found in a river.
– ORIGIN Middle English: from Latin *fluvialis*, from *fluvius* 'river', from *fluere* 'to flow'.

fluvio- /ˈfluːvɪəʊ/ ■ comb. form river; relating to rivers: *fluvioglacial*.
– ORIGIN from Latin *fluvius* 'river'.

fluvioglacial ■ adj. Geology relating to or denoting erosion or deposition caused by flowing meltwater from glaciers or ice sheets.

fluvoxamine /fluːˈvɒksəmiːn/ ■ n. Medicine a synthetic antidepressant drug which acts by prolonging the effect of the neurotransmitter serotonin on the brain.

flux /flʌks/ ■ n. **1** the action or process of flowing. **2** Medicine an abnormal discharge of blood or other matter from or within the body. ▸ archaic diarrhoea or dysentery. **3** continuous change. **4** Physics the amount of radiation, particles, etc. incident on or passing through an area in a given time. ▸ the total electric or magnetic field passing through a surface. **5** a substance mixed with a solid to lower the melting point, especially in soldering or

fly

smelting. ▪v. treat (a metal object) with a flux to promote melting.
– ORIGIN Middle English: from Latin *fluxus*, from *fluere* 'to flow'.

fly¹ ▪v. (**flies**; past **flew**; past part. **flown**) **1** (of a winged creature or aircraft) move through the air under control. ▸ control the flight of (an aircraft). **2** move or be hurled quickly through the air. ▸ Baseball hit a ball high into the air. **3** go or move quickly. ▸ informal depart hastily. ▸ (of time) pass swiftly. ▸ [as of.] **flying**] hasty; brief: *a flying visit*. ▸ (**fly into**) suddenly go into (a rage or other strong emotion). ▸ (**fly at**) attack verbally or physically. **4** wave or flutter in the wind. ▸ (of a flag) be displayed on a flagpole. **5** archaic flee. ▪n. (pl. **flies**) **1** (Brit. also **flies**) an opening at the crotch of a pair of trousers, closed with a zip or buttons. **2** a flap of material covering the opening of a tent. **3** (**the flies**) the space over the stage in a theatre. **4** (pl. usu. **flys**) Brit. historical a one-horse hackney carriage.
– PHRASES **fly in the face of** be openly at variance with (what is usual or expected). **fly a kite** informal try something out to test public opinion. **fly off the handle** informal lose one's temper suddenly. **on the fly** while in motion or progress. **with flying colours** with distinction.
– DERIVATIVES **flyable** adj.
– ORIGIN Old English *flēogan*, of Germanic origin; rel. to **FLY²**.

fly² ▪n. (pl. **flies**) a flying insect of a large order characterized by a single pair of transparent wings and sucking or piercing mouthparts. [Order Diptera.] ▸ used in names of other flying insects, e.g. dragonfly, firefly. ▸ a fishing bait consisting of a mayfly or other natural or artificial flying insect.
– PHRASES **drop like flies** die or collapse in large numbers. **a fly in the ointment** a minor irritation that spoils the enjoyment of something. **fly on the wall** an unnoticed observer. **there are no flies on** —— the person specified is quick and astute.
– ORIGIN Old English *flyge, flēoge*, of West Germanic origin; rel. to **FLY¹**.

fly³ ▪adj. (**flyer, flyest**) informal **1** Brit. knowing and clever; worldly-wise. **2** N. Amer. stylish and fashionable.
– DERIVATIVES **flyness** n.
– ORIGIN C19.

fly agaric ▪n. a poisonous toadstool which has a red cap with fluffy white spots. [*Amanita muscaria*.]

fly ash ▪n. ash produced in small dark flecks and carried into the air.

flyaway ▪adj. (of hair) fine and difficult to control.

fly ball ▪n. Baseball a ball batted high into the air.

flyblown ▪adj. contaminated by contact with flies and their eggs and larvae.

fly boy ▪n. N. Amer. informal a pilot, especially one in the air force.

flybridge ▪n. an open deck above the main bridge of a vessel, typically equipped with duplicate controls.

fly-by-night ▪adj. unreliable or untrustworthy, especially in business or financial matters.

fly-by-wire ▪n. a semi-automatic, usually computer-regulated system for controlling an aircraft or spacecraft.

flycatcher ▪n. a bird that catches flying insects, especially in short agile flights from a perch. [Muscicapidae and other families: many species.]

flyer (also **flier**) ▪n. **1** a person or thing that flies. ▸ informal a fast-moving person or thing. **2** a small handbill advertising an event or product. **3** a flying start. **4** informal, chiefly N. Amer. a speculative action or investment.

fly-fishing ▪n. the sport of fishing using a rod and an artificial fly as bait.
– DERIVATIVES **fly-fish** v.

fly half ▪n. Rugby a halfback who forms a link between the scrum half and the three-quarters.

flying boat ▪n. a large seaplane that floats with its fuselage in the water.

flying bomb ▪n. a small pilotless aircraft with an explosive warhead.

flying bridge ▪n. another term for **FLYBRIDGE**.

flying buttress ▪n. Architecture a buttress slanting from a separate column, typically forming an arch with the wall it supports.

flying doctor ▪n. (in Australia) a doctor who travels by aircraft to visit patients in remote areas of the country.

flying fish ▪n. a fish of warm seas which leaps out of the water and uses its wing-like pectoral fins to glide for some distance. [*Exocoetus volitans* and other species.]

flying fox ▪n. a large fruit bat with a foxlike face, found in Madagascar, SE Asia, and northern Australia. [*Pteropus* and two other genera: numerous species.]

flying jacket ▪n. a short leather jacket with a warm lining or collar.

flying lizard (also **flying dragon**) ▪n. an arboreal SE Asian lizard with expanding membranes along its body, used for gliding between trees. [Genus *Draco*: several species.]

flying officer ▪n. a rank of commissioned officer in the RAF, above pilot officer and below flight lieutenant.

flying picket ▪n. Brit. a person who travels to picket a workplace where there is an industrial dispute.

flying saucer ▪n. a disc-shaped flying craft supposedly piloted by aliens.

flying squad ▪n. a division of a police force which is capable of reaching an incident quickly.

flying squirrel ▪n. a squirrel that has skin joining the fore- and hindlimbs for gliding from tree to tree. [Many species, chiefly in subfamily Pteromyinae.]

flying start ▪n. a good beginning, especially one giving an advantage over competitors.

flying suit ▪n. a one-piece garment worn by the pilot and crew of a military or light aircraft.

flyleaf ▪n. (pl. **-leaves**) a blank page at the beginning or end of a book.

flyover ▪n. a bridge carrying one road or railway line over another.

flypaper ▪n. sticky, poison-treated strips of paper that are hung indoors to catch and kill flies.

fly-past ▪n. a ceremonial flight of aircraft past a person or a place.

flysheet ▪n. **1** a fabric cover pitched over a tent to give extra protection against bad weather. **2** a tract or circular of two or four pages.

Flytaal /ˈflaɪtɑːl/ ▪n. variant spelling of **FLAAITAAL**.

flyway ▪n. Ornithology a route regularly used by large numbers of migrating birds.

flyweight ▪n. a weight in boxing and other sports intermediate between light flyweight and bantamweight.

flywheel ▪n. a heavy revolving wheel in a machine which is used to increase momentum and thereby provide greater stability or a reserve of available power.

FM ▪abbrev. frequency modulation.

Fm ▪symb. the chemical element fermium.

f-number ▪n. Photography the ratio of the focal length of a camera lens to the diameter of the aperture being used for a particular shot.

foal ▪n. a young horse or related animal. ▪v. (of a mare) give birth to a foal.
– ORIGIN Old English, of Germanic origin; rel. to **FILLY**.

foam ▪n. **1** a mass of small bubbles formed on or in liquid. ▸ a liquid preparation containing many small bubbles. **2** a lightweight form of rubber or plastic made by solidifying foam. ▪v. form or produce foam.
– DERIVATIVES **foamless** adj. **foamy** adj.
– ORIGIN Old English, of West Germanic origin.

fob¹ ▪n. a chain attached to a watch for carrying in a waistcoat or waistband pocket. ▸ a small ornament attached to a watch chain. ▸ (**fob pocket**) a small pocket for carrying a watch. ▸ a tab on a key ring.
– ORIGIN C17: origin uncertain; prob. rel. to German dialect *Fuppe* 'pocket'.

fob² ▪v. (**fobbed, fobbing**) (**fob someone off**) deceitfully attempt to satisfy someone by making excuses or giving them something inferior. ▸ (**fob something off on**) give something inferior to.

–ORIGIN Middle English: origin uncertain; perhaps rel. to German *foppen* 'deceive, banter', or to **FOP**.

f.o.b. ■ abbrev. free on board.

fob watch ■ n. a pocket watch.

focaccia /fəˈkatʃə/ ■ n. a type of flat Italian bread made with olive oil and flavoured with herbs.
–ORIGIN from Italian.

focal /ˈfəʊk(ə)l/ ■ adj. **1** of or relating to a focus, in particular the focus of a lens. **2** (of a disease or medical condition) occurring in one particular site in the body.
–DERIVATIVES **focalization** (also **-isation**) n. **focalize** (also **-ise**) v.

focal length ■ n. the distance between the centre of a lens or curved mirror and its focus. ▸ the equivalent distance in a compound lens or telescope.

focal point ■ n. **1** the point at which rays or waves meet after reflection or refraction, or the point from which diverging rays or waves appear to proceed. **2** the centre of interest or activity.

fo'c's'le /ˈfəʊks(ə)l/ ■ n. variant spelling of **FORECASTLE**.

focus ■ n. (pl. **focuses** or **foci** /ˈfəʊsʌɪ/) **1** the centre of interest or activity. ▸ an act of focusing on something. **2** Geology the point of origin of an earthquake. Compare with **EPICENTRE**. **3** Medicine the principal site of an infection or other disease. **4** the state or quality of having or producing clear visual definition. ▸ another term for **FOCAL POINT**. ▸ the point at which an object must be situated with respect to a lens or mirror for an image of it to be well defined. **5** Geometry one of the fixed points from which the distances to any point of an ellipse, parabola, or other curve are connected by a linear relation. **6** Linguistics another term for **RHEME**. ■ v. (**focused**, **focusing** or **focussed**, **focussing**) **1** adapt to the prevailing level of light and become able to see clearly. ▸ adjust the focus of (a telescope, camera, etc.). ▸ (of rays or waves) meet at a single point. ▸ (of light, radio waves, or other energy) become concentrated into a sharp beam of light or energy. **2** (**focus on**) pay particular attention to. **3** Linguistics place the focus on (a part of a sentence).
–DERIVATIVES **focuser** n.
–ORIGIN C17: from Latin, 'domestic hearth'.

focus group ■ n. a group of people assembled to assess a new product, political campaign, television series, etc.

fodder ■ n. **1** food for cattle and other livestock. **2** a person or thing regarded only as material for a specific use: *young people ending up as factory fodder*. ■ v. give fodder to (cattle or other livestock).
–ORIGIN Old English, of Germanic origin; rel. to **FOOD**.

fody /ˈfəʊdi/ ■ n. (pl. **-ies**) a songbird of the weaver family native to Madagascar and other islands in the Indian Ocean, the male of which is mainly red. [Genus *Foudia*: several species.]
–ORIGIN a local word.

foe ■ n. formal or poetic/literary an enemy or opponent.
–ORIGIN Old English *fāh* 'hostile' and *gefā* 'enemy', of West Germanic origin.

foefie slide /ˈfufi slʌɪd/ ■ n. S. African a rope or cable with a handle or pulley attached, typically suspended over a body of water, used as a means of crossing or for sliding.
–ORIGIN *foefie*: 1970s, from Afrikaans, 'stunt, trick'.

foehn ■ n. variant spelling of **FÖHN**.

foetid ■ adj. variant spelling of **FETID**.

foetus ■ n. variant spelling of **FETUS**.
–DERIVATIVES **foetal** adj. **foeticide** n.

fog ■ n. **1** a thick cloud of tiny water droplets suspended in the atmosphere at or near the earth's surface which obscures or restricts visibility. ▸ Photography cloudiness obscuring the image on a developed negative or print. **2** a state or cause of perplexity or confusion. ■ v. (**fogged**, **fogging**) **1** cover or become covered with steam. ▸ Photography make (a film, negative, or print) obscure or cloudy. **2** bewilder or puzzle. **3** treat with something, especially an insecticide, in the form of a spray.
–ORIGIN C16: perhaps a back-formation from **FOGGY**.

fog bank ■ n. a dense mass of fog, especially at sea.

fogey /ˈfəʊgi/ (also **fogy**) ■ n. (pl. **-eys** or **-ies**) a very old-fashioned or conservative person.
–DERIVATIVES **fogeydom** n. **fogeyish** adj. **fogeyism** n.
–ORIGIN C18: rel. to earlier slang *fogram*.

foliage

foggy ■ adj. (**-ier**, **-iest**) **1** full of or accompanied by fog. **2** confused.
–PHRASES **not have the foggiest** (**idea** or **notion**) informal have no idea at all.
–DERIVATIVES **foggily** adv. **fogginess** n.
–ORIGIN C15: perhaps from rare *fog*, denoting the grass growing in a field after it has been harvested for hay.

foghorn ■ n. a device making a loud, deep sound as a warning to ships in fog.

föhn /fəːn/ (also **foehn**) ■ n. a hot southerly wind on the northern slopes of the Alps.
–ORIGIN C19: from German, from Latin (*ventus*) *Favonius* 'mild west wind', *Favonius* being the Roman personification of the west or west wind.

foible /ˈfɔɪb(ə)l/ ■ n. **1** a minor weakness or eccentricity. **2** Fencing the part of a sword blade from the middle to the point. Compare with **FORTE**.
–ORIGIN C16: from obsolete French, in Old French *fieble* (see **FEEBLE**).

foie gras /fwɑː ˈɡrɑː/ ■ n. short for **PÂTÉ DE FOIE GRAS**.

foil[1] ■ v. prevent the success of.
–ORIGIN Middle English: perhaps from Old French *fouler* 'to full cloth, trample', from Latin *fullo* 'fuller'.

foil[2] ■ n. **1** metal hammered or rolled into a thin flexible sheet. ▸ a thin leaf of metal placed under a precious stone to increase its brilliance. **2** a person or thing that contrasts with and so enhances the qualities of another. **3** Architecture a leaf-shaped curve formed by the cusping of an arch or circle.
–ORIGIN Middle English: from Latin *folium* 'leaf'.

foil[3] ■ n. a light, blunt-edged fencing sword with a button on its point.
–DERIVATIVES **foilist** n.
–ORIGIN C16.

foist /fɔɪst/ ■ v. (**foist someone/thing on**) impose an unwelcome or unnecessary person or thing on.
–ORIGIN C16 ('dishonestly manipulate a dice'): from Dutch dialect *vuisten* 'take in the hand', from *vuist* 'fist'.

fold[1] ■ v. **1** bend (something) over on itself so that one part of it covers another. ▸ [often as adj. **folding**] be able to be folded into a flatter shape. **2** use (a soft or flexible material) to cover or wrap something in. ▸ affectionately clasp in one's arms. **3** informal (of a company) cease trading as a result of financial problems. ▸ (of a sports player or team) suddenly stop performing well. **4** (**fold something in/into**) mix an ingredient gently with (another ingredient). **5** (in poker and other card games) drop out of a hand. **6** Geology cause (rock strata) to undergo bending or curvature. ■ n. **1** a form produced by the gentle draping of a garment or piece of cloth. ▸ an area of skin that sags or hangs loosely. **2** chiefly Brit. a slight hill or hollow. **3** Geology a bend or curvature of strata. **4** a line or crease produced by folding.
–PHRASES **fold one's arms** bring one's arms together and cross them over one's chest.
–DERIVATIVES **foldable** adj.
–ORIGIN Old English *falden*, *fealden*, of Germanic origin.

fold[2] ■ n. **1** a pen or enclosure for livestock, especially sheep. **2** (**the fold**) a group or community with shared aims and values. ■ v. shut (livestock) in a fold.
–ORIGIN Old English *fald*, of Germanic origin.

-fold ■ suffix forming adjectives and adverbs from cardinal numbers: **1** in an amount multiplied by: *threefold*. **2** consisting of so many parts or facets: *twofold*.
–ORIGIN Old English *-fald*, *-feald*; rel. to **FOLD**[1].

foldaway ■ adj. designed to be folded up for ease of storage or transport.

folder ■ n. **1** a folding cover or wallet for storing loose papers. **2** N. Amer. a leaflet or booklet made of folded sheets of paper. **3** Computing a directory containing related files or documents.

folderol /ˈfɒldərɒl/ ■ n. **1** trivial or nonsensical fuss. **2** dated a showy but useless item.
–ORIGIN from a meaningless refrain in old songs.

foliage /ˈfəʊlɪdʒ/ ■ n. plant leaves, collectively.
–ORIGIN Middle English *foilage*: from Old French, from *feuille* 'leaf', from Latin *folium*.

foliar

foliar /ˈfəʊlɪə/ ▪ adj. technical of or relating to leaves.
foliar feed ▪ n. nutrients supplied to plant leaves.
– DERIVATIVES **foliar feeding** n.

foliated ▪ adj. **1** decorated with leaves or leaf-like motifs. ▸ Architecture decorated with foils. **2** chiefly Geology consisting of thin sheets or laminae.

folic acid /ˈfəʊlɪk, ˈfɒl-/ ▪ n. Biochemistry a vitamin of the B complex found especially in leafy green vegetables, liver, and kidney.
– DERIVATIVES **folate** n.
– ORIGIN 1940s: *folic* from Latin *folium* 'leaf'.

folie à deux /ˌfɒli a ˈdɜː/ ▪ n. (pl. **folies à deux**) delusion or mental illness shared by two people in close association.
– ORIGIN French, 'shared madness'.

folie de grandeur /ˌfɒli də grɒ̃ˈdɜː/ ▪ n. delusions of grandeur.
– ORIGIN from French.

folio /ˈfəʊlɪəʊ/ ▪ n. (pl. **-os**) **1** a sheet of paper folded once to form two leaves (four pages) of a book. ▸ a book made up of such sheets. **2** an individual leaf of paper or parchment numbered on the recto or front side only. ▸ the page number in a printed book.
– ORIGIN Middle English: from Latin, from *folium* 'leaf', in medieval Latin used to mean 'on leaf so-and-so'.

foliose /ˈfəʊlɪəʊs, -z/ ▪ adj. Botany (of a lichen) having a lobed, leaf-like shape.

folk /fəʊk/ ▪ pl. n. **1** (also **folks**) informal people in general. ▸ (**one's folks**) one's family, especially one's parents. **2** (also **folk music**) traditional music of unknown authorship, transmitted orally. **3** [as modifier] originating from the beliefs and customs of ordinary people: *folk wisdom*.
– ORIGIN Old English, of Germanic origin.

folk dance ▪ n. a traditional dance associated with a particular people or area.
– DERIVATIVES **folk dancer** n. **folk dancing** n.

folk devil ▪ n. a person or thing held to be a bad influence on society.

folk etymology ▪ n. **1** a popular but mistaken account of the origin of a word or phrase. **2** the process by which the form of an unfamiliar or foreign word is adapted to a more familiar form through popular usage.

folkie ▪ n. informal a singer, player, or fan of folk music.

folkish ▪ adj. **1** characteristic of ordinary people or traditional culture. **2** resembling folk music.

folklore ▪ n. the traditional beliefs and customs of a community, passed on by word of mouth.
– DERIVATIVES **folkloric** adj. **folklorist** n. **folkloristic** adj.

folk memory ▪ n. a body of recollections or legends that persists among a people.

folk rock ▪ n. popular music derived from folk music but having a stronger beat and using electric instruments.

folksy ▪ adj. (**-ier**, **-iest**) traditional and unpretentious, especially in a contrived or artificial way.
– DERIVATIVES **folksiness** n.

folk tale ▪ n. a traditional story originally transmitted orally.

folky ▪ adj. (**-ier**, **-iest**) resembling or characteristic of folk music.
– DERIVATIVES **folkiness** n.

follicle /ˈfɒlɪk(ə)l/ ▪ n. **1** the sheath of cells and connective tissue which surrounds the root of a hair. **2** short for **GRAAFIAN FOLLICLE**. **3** Botany a dry fruit derived from a single carpel and opening on one side only to release its seeds.
– DERIVATIVES **follicular** /fɒˈlɪkjʊlə/ adj. **folliculate** /-lət/ adj.
– ORIGIN Middle English: from Latin *folliculus* 'little bag', diminutive of *follis* 'bellows'.

follicle-stimulating hormone ▪ n. Biochemistry a hormone secreted by the anterior pituitary gland which promotes the formation of ova or sperm.

folliculitis /fəˌlɪkjʊˈlʌɪtɪs/ ▪ n. Medicine inflammation of the hair follicles.

follow ▪ v. **1** move or travel behind. ▸ go after (someone) in order to observe or monitor them. ▸ go along (a route or path). **2** (**follow through**) (in sport) continue the movement of a stroke after the ball has been struck. ▸ (**follow something through**) continue an action or task to its conclusion. ▸ (**follow something up**) pursue or investigate something further. **3** come after in time or order. ▸ (also **follow on from**) occur as a consequence or result of. **4** be a logical consequence: *it thus follows that the value must be negative*. **5** act according to (an instruction or precept). ▸ act according to the lead or example of. **6** pay close attention to the movement, course, or progress of. ▸ be a supporter or fan of. **7** understand the meaning of: *I still don't follow you*. **8** practise (a trade or profession). ▸ undertake or carry out (a course of action or study). **9** archaic strive after; aim at.
– PHRASES **follow on** (of a cricket team) be required to bat again immediately after failing to reach a certain score in their first innings. **follow one's nose 1** trust to one's instincts. **2** go straight ahead. **follow suit 1** conform to another's actions. **2** (in bridge, whist, and other card games) play a card of the suit led.
– ORIGIN Old English, of Germanic origin.

follower ▪ n. **1** a person who follows. **2** a supporter, fan, or disciple.

following ▪ prep. coming after or as a result of. ▪ n. a body of supporters or admirers. ▪ adj. **1** next in time or order. ▸ about to be mentioned: *the following information*. **2** (of a wind) blowing in the same direction as the course of a vessel.

follow-the-leader (also **follow-my-leader**) ▪ n. a children's game in which the participants must copy the actions and words of a person acting as leader.

follow-through ▪ n. the continuing of an action or task to its conclusion. ▸ a continuation of a stroke after a ball has been struck.

follow-up ▪ n. **1** a study carried out to monitor or further develop earlier work. **2** a work that follows or builds on an earlier work.

folly ▪ n. (pl. **-ies**) **1** foolishness. **2** (especially in the UK) an ornamental building with no practical purpose, especially a tower or mock-Gothic ruin in a large garden or park. **3** (**Follies**) a theatrical revue with glamorous female performers.
– ORIGIN Middle English: from Old French *folie* 'madness', from *fol* 'fool'.

Folsom /ˈfəʊlsəm/ ▪ n. [as modifier] Archaeology denoting a Palaeo-Indian culture of Central and North America, dated to about 10 500–8 000 years ago.
– ORIGIN named after *Folsom* in New Mexico.

foment /fə(ʊ)ˈmɛnt/ ▪ v. instigate or stir up (revolution or strife).
– DERIVATIVES **fomentation** n. **fomenter** n.
– ORIGIN Middle English: from late Latin *fomentare*, from Latin *fomentum* 'poultice, lotion'.

fomites /ˈfəʊmɪtiːz/ ▪ pl. n. Medicine objects or materials which are likely to carry infection.
– ORIGIN C19: from Latin, pl. of *fomes* 'touchwood, tinder'.

Fon /fɒn/ ▪ n. (pl. same or **Fons**) **1** a member of a people inhabiting the southern part of Benin. **2** the Kwa language of this people.
– ORIGIN the name in Fon.

fond ▪ adj. **1** (**fond of**) having an affection or liking for. ▸ affectionate; loving: *fond memories*. **2** (of a hope or belief) foolishly optimistic; naive.
– DERIVATIVES **fondly** adv. **fondness** n.
– ORIGIN Middle English: from obsolete *fon* 'a fool, be foolish'.

fondant /ˈfɒnd(ə)nt/ ▪ n. a thick paste made of sugar and water, used in making sweets and icing cakes. ▸ a sweet made of such a paste.
– ORIGIN C19: from French, 'melting', from *fondre*.

fondle ▪ v. stroke or caress lovingly or erotically. ▪ n. an act of fondling.
– DERIVATIVES **fondler** n.
– ORIGIN C17: back-formation from obsolete *fondling* 'much-loved or petted person', from **FOND**.

fondue /ˈfɒnd(j)uː/ ▪ n. a dish in which small pieces of food are dipped into a hot sauce or a hot cooking medium such as oil or broth.
– ORIGIN French: from *fondre* 'to melt'.

fong kong S. African informal ■ adj. (of a product) made as an inferior copy; fake: *fong kong Diesel jeans*. ■ n. such a product.
– ORIGIN prob. from *Hong Kong*, perceived to be a source of imitation goods.

font¹ ■ n. **1** a receptacle in a church for the water used in baptism. **2** a reservoir for oil in an oil lamp.
– ORIGIN Old English: from Latin *fons, font-* 'spring, fountain'.

font² (Brit. also **fount**) ■ n. Printing a set of type of a particular face and size.
– ORIGIN C16 (denoting the action or process of casting or founding): from French *fonte*, from *fondre* 'to melt'.

fontanelle /ˌfɒntəˈnɛl/ (US **fontanel**) ■ n. a soft area between the bones of the cranium in an infant or fetus, where the sutures are not yet fully formed.
– ORIGIN C16: from modern Latin *fontanella*, from an Old French diminutive of *fontaine* (see **FOUNTAIN**).

food ■ n. any nutritious substance that people or animals eat or drink or that plants absorb in order to maintain life and growth.
– PHRASES **food for thought** something that warrants serious consideration.
– ORIGIN Old English, of Germanic origin; rel. to **FODDER**.

food chain ■ n. a series of organisms each dependent on the next as a source of food.

foodie (also **foody**) ■ n. (pl. **-ies**) informal a person with a particular interest in food; a gourmet.

food poisoning ■ n. illness caused by bacteria or other toxins in food, typically with vomiting and diarrhoea.

foodstuff ■ n. a substance suitable for consumption as food.

food value ■ n. the nutritional value of a foodstuff.

food web ■ n. Ecology a system of interlocking and interdependent food chains.

foo-foo ■ n. variant spelling of **FUFU**.

fool¹ ■ n. **1** a person who acts unwisely. ▶ archaic a person who is duped or imposed on. **2** historical a jester or clown, especially one retained in a great household. ■ v. **1** trick, deceive, or dupe. **2** (usu. **fool about/around**) act in a joking or frivolous way. ▶ (**fool around**) engage in casual or extramarital sexual activity. ■ adj. informal, chiefly N. Amer. foolish or silly.
– PHRASES **be no** (or **nobody's**) **fool** be shrewd or prudent. **make a fool of** trick or deceive (someone) so that they look foolish. ▶ (**make a fool of oneself**) appear foolish through incompetent or inappropriate behaviour. **more fool** —— the specified person is behaving unwisely.
– DERIVATIVES **foolery** n.
– ORIGIN Middle English: from Old French *fol* 'fool, foolish', from Latin *follis* 'bellows, windbag', by extension 'empty-headed person'.

fool² ■ n. a cold dessert made of puréed fruit mixed or served with cream or custard.
– ORIGIN C16: perhaps from **FOOL¹**.

foolhardy ■ adj. (**-ier**, **-iest**) recklessly bold or rash.
– DERIVATIVES **foolhardily** adv. **foolhardiness** n.
– ORIGIN Middle English: from Old French *folhardi*, from *fol* 'foolish' + *hardi* (see **HARDY**).

foolish ■ adj. lacking good sense or judgement; silly or unwise.
– DERIVATIVES **foolishly** adv. **foolishness** n.

foolproof ■ adj. incapable of going wrong or being misused.

foolscap /ˈfuːlzkap, ˈfuːls-/ ■ n. a size of paper, about 330 × 200 (or 400) mm.
– ORIGIN C17: said to be named from a former watermark representing a fool's cap.

fool's errand ■ n. a task or activity that has no hope of success.

fool's gold ■ n. a brassy yellow mineral that can be mistaken for gold, especially pyrite.

fool's paradise ■ n. a state of happiness based on not knowing about or ignoring potential trouble.

foot ■ n. (pl. **feet** /fiːt/) **1** the lower extremity of the leg below the ankle, on which a person or animal stands or walks. **2** poetic/literary manner or speed of walking or running: *fleet of foot*. **3** [treated as pl.] Brit. historical infantry; foot soldiers. **4** the lower or lowest part of something vertical; the base or bottom. ▶ the end of a table furthest from the host. ▶ the end of a bed where the occupant's feet normally rest. **5** a unit of linear measure equal to 12 inches (30.48 cm). **6** Prosody a group of syllables constituting a metrical unit. **7** a device on a sewing machine for holding the material steady as it is sewn. ■ v. **1** informal pay (a bill, especially a large or unreasonable one). **2** (**foot it**) cover a distance, especially a long one, on foot. ▶ archaic dance.
– PHRASES **feet of clay** a fundamental flaw or weakness in a person otherwise revered. **get** (or **start**) **off on the right** (or **wrong**) **foot** make a good (or bad) start at something. **have** (or **keep**) **one's feet on the ground** be (or remain) practical and sensible. **have** (or **get**) **a foot in the door** have (or gain) a first introduction to a profession or organization. **have one foot in the grave** humorous be very old or ill. **my foot!** informal said to express strong contradiction. **on** (or **by**) **foot** walking rather than travelling by car or using other transport. **put one's best foot forward** begin with as much effort and determination as possible. **put one's foot down** informal **1** adopt a firm policy when faced with opposition or disobedience. **2** accelerate a motor vehicle by pressing the accelerator pedal. **put one's foot in it** informal say or do something tactless or embarrassing. **put a foot wrong** [usu. with neg.] make a mistake. **under one's feet** in one's way. **under foot** on the ground.
– DERIVATIVES **footless** adj.
– ORIGIN Old English, of Germanic origin.

footage ■ n. **1** a length of film made for cinema or television. **2** size or length measured in feet.

foot-and-mouth disease ■ n. a contagious viral disease of cloven-hoofed animals such as cattle and sheep, causing ulceration of the hoofs and around the mouth.

football ■ n. **1** any of a number of forms of team game involving kicking a ball, in particular (in the UK) soccer or (in the US) American football. **2** a large inflated ball used in such a game. **3** a topical issue that arouses controversy: *the use of education as a political football*.
– DERIVATIVES **footballer** n. **footballing** adj.

footboard ■ n. **1** an upright panel forming the foot of a bed. **2** a board serving as a step up to a vehicle such as a carriage or train.

footbrake ■ n. a foot-operated brake lever in a motor vehicle.

footbridge ■ n. a bridge for pedestrians.

-footed ■ comb. form **1** of or involving a specified number of feet: *four-footed locomotion*. **2** using the foot specified: *right-footed*. **3** having feet of a specified kind.

footer /ˈfʊtə/ ■ n. **1** [in combination] a person or thing of a specified number of feet in length or height: *a six-footer*. ▶ a kick of a football performed with a specified foot: *a low left-footer*. **2** variant of **FOOTY**. **3** a line or block of text appearing at the foot of each page of a book or document.

footfall ■ n. the sound of a footstep or footsteps.

foot fault ■ n. (in tennis, squash, etc.) an infringement of the rules made by overstepping the baseline when serving. ■ v. (**foot-fault**) make a foot fault.

foothill ■ n. a low hill at the base of a mountain or mountain range.

foothold ■ n. **1** a place where one can lodge a foot to give secure support while climbing. **2** a secure position from which further progress may be made: *a foothold in the Russian market*.

footie ■ n. variant spelling of **FOOTY**.

footing ■ n. **1** (**one's footing**) a secure grip with one's feet. **2** the basis on which something is established or operates. **3** the foundations of a wall, usually with a course of brickwork wider than the base of the wall.

footle /ˈfuːt(ə)l/ ■ v. chiefly Brit. engage in fruitless activity; mess about.
– ORIGIN C19: perhaps from dialect *footer* 'idle, potter about', from C16 *foutre* 'worthless thing', from Old French, 'have sexual intercourse with'.

footlights ■ pl. n. a row of spotlights along the front of a stage at the level of the actors' feet.

footling

footling /ˈfuːtlɪŋ/ ▪ adj. trivial and irritating.

footlocker ▪ n. N. Amer. a small trunk or storage chest.

footloose ▪ adj. free to go where one likes and do as one pleases.

footman ▪ n. (pl. **-men**) **1** a liveried servant whose duties include admitting visitors and waiting at table. **2** historical a soldier in the infantry.

footmark ▪ n. a footprint.

footnote ▪ n. an additional piece of information at the bottom of a page. ▪ v. add a footnote or footnotes to.

footpad ▪ n. historical a highwayman operating on foot rather than riding a horse.

footpath ▪ n. a path for people to walk along, especially in the countryside.

footplate ▪ n. the platform for the crew in the cab of a locomotive.

foot-pound-second system ▪ n. a system of measurement with the foot, pound, and second as basic units.

footprint ▪ n. **1** the impression left by a foot or shoe on the ground. **2** the impact of human activity on the natural environment through pollution or the depletion of its resources, often due to a specified practice: *environmental footprint | carbon footprint*. **3** the area in which a broadcast signal can be received. **4** the area beneath an aircraft or a land vehicle which is affected by its noise or weight.

foot rot ▪ n. **1** a bacterial disease of the feet in sheep and other hoofed animals. **2** a fungal disease of plants in which the base of the stem rots.

footsie /ˈfutsi/ (S. African also **footsie-footsie**) ▪ n. (usu. in phr. **play footsie**) informal the action of touching someone's feet lightly with one's own feet as a playful expression of romantic interest.
– ORIGIN 1940s: humorous diminutive of **FOOT**.

footslog ▪ v. (**-slogged**, **-slogging**) laboriously walk or march for a long distance. ▪ n. a long and exhausting walk or march.
– DERIVATIVES **footslogger** n.

foot soldier ▪ n. **1** a soldier who fights on foot. **2** a low-ranking person who nevertheless does valuable work.

footsore ▪ adj. having sore feet from much walking.

footstep ▪ n. a step taken in walking, especially as heard by another person.
– PHRASES **follow** (or **tread**) **in someone's footsteps** do as another person did before.

footstool ▪ n. a low stool for resting the feet on when sitting.

footwall ▪ n. Geology the block of rock which lies on the underside of an inclined fault or mineral vein.

footwear ▪ n. shoes, boots, and other coverings for the feet.

footwell ▪ n. a space for the feet in front of a seat in a vehicle.

footwork ▪ n. the manner in which one moves one's feet in dancing and sport.

footy (also **footie** or **footer**) ▪ n. Brit. informal term for **FOOTBALL** (in sense 1).

foo yong /fuːˈjɒŋ/ ▪ n. a Chinese dish or sauce made with egg as a main ingredient.
– ORIGIN from Chinese *foo yung* 'hibiscus'.

fop ▪ n. a man who is excessively concerned with his clothes and appearance.
– DERIVATIVES **foppery** n. **foppish** adj. **foppishly** adv. **foppishness** n.
– ORIGIN Middle English ('fool'): perhaps rel. to **FOB**[2].

for ▪ prep. **1** in favour of. **2** affecting or with regard to. **3** on behalf of or to the benefit of. **4** having as a purpose or function. **5** having as a reason or cause. **6** having as a destination. **7** representing. **8** in exchange for. ▸ charged as (a price). **9** in relation to the expected norm of. **10** indicating the extent of (a distance) or the length of (a period of time). **11** indicating an occasion in a series. ▪ conj. poetic/literary because; since.

– PHRASES **be for it** Brit. informal be about to be punished or get into trouble. —— **for Africa** S. African informal —— in huge numbers; —— in plenty. **oh for** —— I long for ——.
– ORIGIN Old English, prob. a reduction of a Germanic preposition meaning 'before' (in place or time); rel. to German *für*.

for- ▪ prefix **1** denoting prohibition: *forbid*. **2** denoting abstention, neglect, or renunciation: *forgive*. **3** used as an intensifier: *forlorn*.
– ORIGIN Old English.

fora plural form of **FORUM** (in sense 3).

forage /ˈfɒrɪdʒ/ ▪ v. search widely for food or provisions. ▸ obtain (food) by searching. ▸ search (a place) so as to obtain food. ▪ n. **1** food for horses and cattle. **2** an act of foraging.
– DERIVATIVES **forager** n.
– ORIGIN Middle English: from Old French *fourrage* (n.), *fourrager* (v.), from *fuerre* 'straw', of Germanic origin.

forage cap ▪ n. a soldier's peaked cap.

forage fish ▪ n. a species of fish which is the prey of more valuable game fish.

foramen /fəˈreɪmɛn/ ▪ n. (pl. **foramina** /-ˈrammə/) Anatomy an opening, hole, or passage, especially in a bone.
– ORIGIN C17: from Latin.

foramen magnum /ˈmaɡnəm/ ▪ n. Anatomy the hole in the base of the skull through which the spinal cord passes.
– ORIGIN Latin, 'large opening'.

foraminifer /ˌfɒrəˈmɪnɪfə/ ▪ n. (pl. **foraminifers** or **foraminifera** /ˌfɒrəmɪˈnɪf(ə)rə/) Zoology a single-celled planktonic animal with a perforated chalky shell through which slender protrusions of protoplasm extend. [Order Foraminiferida.]
– DERIVATIVES **foraminiferal** /ˌfɒrəmɪˈnɪf(ə)rəl/ adj. **foraminiferan** n. & adj. **foraminiferous** adj.
– ORIGIN C19: from Latin *foramen* (see **FORAMEN**) + *-fer* 'bearing'.

forasmuch as ▪ conj. archaic because; since.
– ORIGIN Middle English *for as much*, translating Old French *por tant que* 'for so much as'.

foray /ˈfɒreɪ/ ▪ n. **1** a sudden attack or incursion into enemy territory. **2** a brief but spirited attempt to become involved in a new activity. ▪ v. make or go on a foray.
– ORIGIN Middle English: back-formation from *forayer* 'a person who forays', from Old French *forrier* 'forager', from *fuerre* (see **FORAGE**).

forb /fɔːb/ ▪ n. Botany a herbaceous flowering plant other than a grass.
– ORIGIN 1920s: from Greek *phorbē* 'fodder'.

forbade (also **forbad**) past of **FORBID**.

forbear[1] /fɔːˈbɛː/ ▪ v. (past **forbore**; past part. **forborne**) refrain from doing something.
– ORIGIN Old English *forberan* (see **FOR-**, **BEAR**[1]).

forbear[2] /ˈfɔːbɛː/ ▪ n. variant spelling of **FOREBEAR**.

forbearance ▪ n. patient self-control.

forbearing ▪ adj. patient and restrained.

forbid ▪ v. (**forbidding**; past **forbade** /-ˈbad, -ˈbeɪd/ or **forbad**; past part. **forbidden**) **1** refuse to allow. ▸ order not to do. **2** [as adj. **forbidden**] Physics denoting or relating to a quantum transition that does not conform to a particular selection rule.
– PHRASES **the forbidden degrees** the number of steps of descent from the same ancestor that bar two related people from marrying. **forbidden fruit** a thing that is desired all the more because it is not allowed. [with biblical allusion to Genesis 2:17.] **God** (or **Heaven**) **forbid** expressing a fervent wish that something does not happen.
– ORIGIN Old English *forbēodan* (see **FOR-**, **BID**[2]).

forbidding ▪ adj. unfriendly or threatening.
– DERIVATIVES **forbiddingly** adv.

forbore past of **FORBEAR**[1].

forborne past participle of **FORBEAR**[1].

forbye /fəˈbʌɪ, fɔː-/ (also **forby**) ▪ adv. & prep. archaic or Scottish in addition; besides.

force ▪ n. **1** physical strength or energy as an attribute of action or movement. ▸ Physics an influence tending to change the motion of a body or produce motion or stress in a stationary body. **2** coercion backed by the use or threat of violence. **3** mental or moral power; influence. ▸ a

person or thing exerting this. **4** an organized body of military personnel, police, or workers. ▶ (**forces**) troops and weaponry. ▶ (**the forces**) Brit. informal the army, navy, and air force. ■ v. **1** make a way through or into by force. ▶ push into a specified position using force. ▶ achieve by effort. **2** artificially hasten the development or maturity of (a plant). **3** make (someone) do something against their will. ▶ (**force something on/upon**) impose something on. **4** Baseball put out (a runner) by a force-out.
– PHRASES **by force of** by means of. **force the bidding** (at an auction) make bids to raise the price rapidly. **force someone's hand** make someone do something. **force the issue** compel the making of an immediate decision. **in force 1** in great strength or numbers. **2** (**in/into force**) in or into effect.
– DERIVATIVES **forceable** adj. **forcer** n.
– ORIGIN Middle English: from Old French *force* (n.), *forcer* (v.), from Latin *fortis* 'strong'.

forced landing ■ n. an act of abruptly landing an aircraft in an emergency.
– DERIVATIVES **force-land** v.

forced march ■ n. a fast march by soldiers, typically over a long distance.

forced removal ■ n. S. African historical (under apartheid) the forcible resettlement of black people to officially designated areas.

force-feed ■ v. force to eat food.

force field ■ n. (chiefly in science fiction) an invisible barrier of force.

forceful ■ adj. powerful, assertive, or vigorous.
– DERIVATIVES **forcefully** adv. **forcefulness** n.

force majeure /ˌfɔːs maˈʒɜː/ ■ n. **1** Law another term for VIS MAJOR. **2** superior strength.
– ORIGIN French, 'superior strength'.

forcemeat ■ n. a mixture of meat or vegetables chopped and seasoned for use as a stuffing or garnish.
– ORIGIN C17: from obsolete *force* 'to stuff', alteration (influenced by the verb FORCE) of *farce* (see FARCE).

force-out ■ n. Baseball a play in which a runner is put out after being forced (by another runner) to advance to a base at which a fielder is holding the ball.

forceps /ˈfɔːsɛps, -sɪps/ (also **a pair of forceps**) ■ pl. n. a pair of pincers used in surgery or in a laboratory. ▶ a large instrument of such a type with broad blades, used to assist in the delivery of a baby.
– ORIGIN C16: from Latin, 'tongs, pincers'.

force pump ■ n. a pump used to move liquid under greater than ambient pressure.

forcible ■ adj. done by force.
– DERIVATIVES **forcibly** adv.

forcing ■ adj. Bridge (of a bid) requiring by convention a response from one's partner, no matter how weak their hand may be.

ford ■ n. a shallow place in a river or stream that can be crossed on foot or in a vehicle. ■ v. cross at a ford.
– DERIVATIVES **fordable** adj. **fordless** adj.
– ORIGIN Old English, of West Germanic origin; rel. to FARE.

fore ■ adj. situated or placed in front. ■ n. the front part of something, especially a ship. ■ exclam. called out as a warning to people in the path of a golf ball.
– PHRASES **to the fore** in or to a conspicuous or leading position.
– ORIGIN Old English: of Germanic origin.

fore- comb. form **1** (added to verbs) in front: *foreshorten*. ▶ in advance: *forebode*. **2** (added to nouns) situated in front of: *forecourt*. ▶ the front part of: *forebrain*. ▶ preceding: *forefather*.
– ORIGIN Old English (see FORE).

fore and aft ■ adv. at the front and rear. ▶ backwards and forwards. ■ adj. **1** backwards and forwards. **2** (of a sail or rigging) set lengthwise, not on the yards.
– ORIGIN C17: perhaps translating a phr. of Low German origin.

forearm[1] /ˈfɔːrɑːm/ ■ n. the part of a person's arm extending from the elbow to the wrist or the fingertips.

forearm[2] /fɔːrˈɑːm/ ■ v. (usu. **be forearmed**) prepare in advance for danger or attack.

forebear (also **forbear**) ■ n. an ancestor.

– ORIGIN C15: from FORE + *bear*, var. of obsolete *beer* 'someone who exists'.

forebode ■ v. archaic or poetic/literary act as an advance warning of (something bad).

foreboding ■ n. fearful apprehension. ■ adj. ominous.
– DERIVATIVES **forebodingly** adv.

forebrain ■ n. Anatomy the anterior part of the brain, including the cerebral hemispheres, the thalamus, and the hypothalamus.

forecast ■ v. (past and past part. **-cast** or **-casted**) predict or estimate (a future event or trend). ■ n. a prediction or estimate, especially of the weather or a financial trend.
– DERIVATIVES **forecaster** n.

forecastle /ˈfəʊks(ə)l/ (also **fo'c'sle**) ■ n. the forward part of a ship below the deck, traditionally used as the crew's living quarters.

forecheck ■ v. Ice Hockey play an aggressive style of defence, checking opponents before they can attack.
– DERIVATIVES **forechecker** n.

foreclose ■ v. **1** take possession of a mortgaged property as a result of defaults in loan or mortgage payments. **2** rule out or prevent.
– DERIVATIVES **foreclosure** n.
– ORIGIN Middle English (orig. 'bar from escaping, shut out'): from Old French *forclos, forclore*, from *for-* 'out' + *clore* 'to close'.

forecourt ■ n. **1** an open area in front of a large building or petrol station. **2** Tennis the part of the court between the service line and the net.

foredoom ■ v. (usu. **be foredoomed**) condemn beforehand to certain failure.

fore-edge ■ n. technical the outer vertical edge of the pages of a book.

forefather (or **foremother**) ■ n. an ancestor.

forefinger ■ n. the finger next to the thumb.

forefoot ■ n. (pl. **forefeet**) each of the front feet of a four-footed animal.

forefront ■ n. the leading position or place.

foregather (also **forgather**) ■ v. formal assemble or gather together.
– ORIGIN C15 (orig. Scots *forgadder*): from Dutch *vergaderen*.

forego[1] ■ v. variant spelling of FORGO.

forego[2] ■ v. (**-goes**; past **-went**; past part. **-gone**) archaic precede in place or time.
– DERIVATIVES **foregoer** n.

foregoing ■ adj. previously mentioned.

foregone past participle of FOREGO[2]. ■ adj. [often postpos.] archaic past.
– PHRASES **a foregone conclusion** an easily predictable result.

foreground ■ n. **1** the part of a view or image nearest to the observer. **2** the most prominent or important position. ■ v. place in the foreground.
– ORIGIN C17: from FORE- + GROUND[1], on the pattern of Dutch *voorgrond*.

foregut ■ n. Anatomy & Zoology the anterior part of the gut, towards the mouth.

forehand ■ n. (in tennis and other racket sports) a stroke played with the palm of the hand facing in the direction of the stroke.

forehanded ■ adv. (in tennis and other racket sports) with a forehand stroke.

forehead /ˈfɒrɪd, ˈfɔːhɛd/ ■ n. the part of the face above the eyebrows.
– ORIGIN Old English (see FORE-, HEAD).

foreign /ˈfɒrɪn/ ■ adj. **1** of, from, in, or characteristic of a country or language other than one's own. ▶ dealing with or relating to other countries. **2** coming or introduced from outside. **3** (usu. **foreign to**) unfamiliar or uncharacteristic.
– DERIVATIVES **foreignness** /ˈfɒr(ə)nnɪs/ n.
– ORIGIN Middle English: from Old French *forein, forain*, from Latin *foras, foris* 'outside', from *fores* 'door'.

foreign body

foreign body ■ n. an object or piece of extraneous matter that has entered the body by accident or design.

foreigner ■ n. a person born in or coming from a foreign country. ▸ informal a stranger or outsider.

foreign exchange ■ n. the currency of other countries.

Foreign Legion ■ n. a military formation of the French army composed chiefly of non-Frenchmen and originally founded to fight France's colonial wars.

foreign service ■ n. the government department concerned with the representation of a country abroad.

foreknowledge ■ n. awareness of something before it happens or exists.

foreland ■ n. 1 an area of land in front of a particular feature. 2 a cape or promontory.

foreleg ■ n. either of the front legs of a four-footed animal or of an insect.

forelimb ■ n. either of the front limbs of an animal.

Forelle ■ n. a dessert pear of a small yellow and red variety.
– ORIGIN C19: from German, 'trout' (because of its speckled skin).

forelock ■ n. a lock of hair growing just above the forehead.
– PHRASES **touch** (or **tug**) **one's forelock** raise a hand to one's forehead in deference to a person of higher social rank.

foreman (or **forewoman**) ■ n. (pl. **-men** or **-women**) 1 a worker who supervises other workers. 2 (in a law court) a person who presides over a jury and speaks on its behalf.
– ORIGIN Middle English: perhaps suggested by Dutch *voorman*.

foremast ■ n. the mast of a ship nearest the bow.

foremost ■ adj. the most prominent in rank, importance, or position. ■ adv. in the first place.
– ORIGIN Old English *formest, fyrmest*, from *forma* 'first' + -EST¹.

forename ■ n. another term for FIRST NAME.

forenoon ■ n. N. Amer or Nautical the morning.

forensic /fəˈrɛnsɪk/ ■ adj. 1 relating to or denoting the application of scientific methods and techniques to the investigation of crime. 2 of or relating to courts of law. ■ n. (**forensics**) forensic tests or techniques.
– DERIVATIVES **forensically** adv.
– ORIGIN C17: from Latin *forensis* 'in open court, public', from *forum* (see FORUM).

forensic medicine ■ n. the application of medical knowledge to the investigation of crime, particularly in establishing the causes of injury or death.

foreordain /ˌfɔːrɔːˈdeɪn/ ■ v. (of God or fate) appoint or decree beforehand.
– DERIVATIVES **foreordination** n.

forepart ■ n. the foremost part.

forepeak ■ n. the front end of the hold in the angle of the bows of a ship.

foreplay ■ n. sexual activity that precedes intercourse.

forequarters ■ pl. n. the front legs and adjoining parts of a quadruped.

forerun ■ v. (**-running**; past **-ran**; past part. **-run**) poetic/literary go before or indicate the coming of.

forerunner ■ n. a precursor.

foresail /ˈfɔːseɪl, -s(ə)l/ ■ n. the principal sail on a foremast.

foresee ■ v. (**-sees, -seeing**; past **-saw**; past part. **-seen**) be aware of beforehand; predict.
– DERIVATIVES **foreseeability** n. **foreseeable** adj. **foreseeably** adv. **foreseer** /-ˈsiːə/ n.
– ORIGIN Old English *foresēon* (see FORE-, SEE¹).

foreshadow ■ v. be a warning or indication of.

foresheet ■ n. Nautical 1 a rope by which the lee corner of a foresail is kept in place. 2 (**foresheets**) the inner part of the bows.

foreshock ■ n. a mild tremor preceding a larger earthquake.

foreshore ■ n. the part of a shore between high- and low-water marks, or between the water and cultivated or developed land.

foreshorten ■ v. 1 represent as having less depth or distance than in reality, so as to convey an effect of perspective. 2 shorten or reduce in time or scale.

foreshow ■ v. (past part. **-shown**) archaic give warning or promise of.

foresight ■ n. 1 the ability to predict or action of predicting the future. 2 the front sight of a gun. 3 Surveying a sight taken forwards.
– DERIVATIVES **foresighted** adj. **foresightedly** adv. **foresightedness** n.
– ORIGIN Middle English: from FORE- + SIGHT, prob. suggested by Old Norse *forsjá, forsjó*.

foreskin ■ n. the retractable roll of skin covering the end of the penis.

forest ■ n. 1 a large area covered chiefly with trees and undergrowth. ▸ Brit. historical an area, typically owned by the sovereign and partly wooded, kept for hunting and having its own laws. 2 a dense mass of vertical or tangled objects. ■ v. [usu. as adj. **forested**] plant with trees.
– DERIVATIVES **forestation** n.
– ORIGIN Middle English: from late Latin *forestis (silva)* '(wood) outside', from Latin *foris* (see FOREIGN).

forestall /fɔːˈstɔːl/ ■ v. prevent or obstruct (something anticipated) by taking advance action. ▸ anticipate and prevent the action of.
– DERIVATIVES **forestalment** n.
– ORIGIN Old English *foresteall* 'an ambush' (see FORE- and STALL).

forestay /ˈfɔːsteɪ/ ■ n. a rope supporting a ship's foremast, running from its top to the deck at the bow.

forester ■ n. a person in charge of a forest or skilled in forestry.

forestry ■ n. 1 the science or practice of planting, managing, and caring for forests. 2 forests.

foretaste ■ n. a sample or suggestion of something that lies ahead.

foretell ■ v. (past and past part. **-told**) predict.
– DERIVATIVES **foreteller** n.

forethought ■ n. careful consideration of what will be necessary or may happen in the future.

foretold past and past participle of FORETELL.

forever ■ adv. 1 (also **for ever**) for all future time. ▸ a very long time (used hyperbolically). 2 continually.

for evermore (N. Amer. **forevermore**) ■ adv. forever.

forewarn ■ v. warn in advance.

forewent past of FOREGO¹, FOREGO².

forewing ■ n. either of the two front wings of a four-winged insect.

foreword ■ n. a short introduction to a book, typically by a person other than the author.
– ORIGIN C19: from FORE- + WORD, on the pattern of German *Vorwort*.

forex ■ abbrev. foreign exchange.

forfeit /ˈfɔːfɪt/ ■ v. (**forfeited, forfeiting**) lose or be deprived of (property or a right or privilege) as a penalty for wrongdoing. ▸ lose or give up as a necessary consequence. ■ n. a fine or penalty for wrongdoing. ▸ Law a forfeited item of property, right, or privilege. ▸ (**forfeits**) a game in which trivial penalties are exacted for minor misdemeanours. ■ adj. lost or surrendered as a forfeit.
– DERIVATIVES **forfeitable** adj. **forfeiter** n. **forfeiture** n.
– ORIGIN Middle English (orig. denoting a crime or transgression): from Old French *forfait, forfaire* 'transgress', from *for-* 'out' + *faire* 'do'.

forfend /fɔːˈfɛnd/ ■ v. archaic avert or prevent (something evil or unpleasant).
– PHRASES **God** (or **Heaven**) **forfend** archaic or humorous used to express dismay at the thought of another.

forgather ■ v. variant spelling of FOREGATHER.

forgave past of FORGIVE.

forge¹ /fɔːdʒ/ ■ v. 1 make or shape (a metal object) by heating it and beating or hammering it. 2 create: *the two women forged a close bond*. 3 produce a fraudulent copy or imitation of (a banknote, work of art, etc.). ■ n. a

blacksmith's workshop. ▶ a furnace or hearth for melting or refining metal.
– DERIVATIVES **forgeable** adj. **forger** n. **forgery** n.
– ORIGIN Middle English: from Old French *forger*, from Latin *fabricare* 'fabricate', from *fabrica* 'manufactured object, workshop'.

forge² /fɔːdʒ/ ■ v. move forward gradually or steadily. ▶ (**forge ahead**) take the lead or make progress.
– ORIGIN C18: perhaps an aberrant pronunciation of FORCE.

forget ■ v. (**forgetting**; past **forgot**; past part. **forgotten** or chiefly US **forgot**) fail to remember. ▶ inadvertently neglect to do. ▶ S. African inadvertently leave behind. ▶ cease to think of. ▶ (**forget oneself**) neglect to behave appropriately.
– DERIVATIVES **forgetful** adj. **forgetfully** adv. **forgetfulness** n. **forgetter** n.
– ORIGIN Old English, of West Germanic origin; ultimately rel. to FOR- and GET.

forget-me-not ■ n. a low-growing plant of the borage family with bright blue flowers. [*Myosotis scorpioides* and other species.]
– ORIGIN C16: translating the Old French name *ne m'oubliez mye*; said to ensure that the wearer of the flower would never be forgotten by a lover.

forgettable ■ adj. not interesting or remarkable and therefore easily forgotten.

forgive ■ v. (past **forgave**; past part. **forgiven**) stop feeling angry or resentful towards (someone) for an offence or mistake. ▶ excuse (an offence, flaw, or mistake).
– DERIVATIVES **forgivable** adj. **forgivably** adv. **forgiveness** n. **forgiver** n. **forgiving** adj. **forgivingly** adv.
– ORIGIN Old English, of Germanic origin, ultimately rel. to FOR- and GIVE.

forgo (also **forego**) ■ v. (**-goes**; past **-went**; past part. **-gone**) go without (something desirable).
– ORIGIN Old English (see FOR-, GO¹).

forgot past of FORGET.

forgotten past participle of FORGET.

fork ■ n. **1** an implement with two or more prongs used for lifting or holding food. ▶ a farm or garden tool of larger but similar form used for digging or lifting. **2** each of a pair of supports in which a bicycle or motorcycle wheel revolves. **3** the point where something, especially a road or river, divides into two parts. ▶ either of two such parts. **4** Chess a simultaneous attack on two or more pieces by one. ■ v. **1** divide into two parts. ▶ take one road or the other at a fork. **2** dig or lift with a fork. **3** (**fork out/up**) (or N. Amer. **fork over**) informal pay money for something, especially reluctantly. **4** Chess attack (two pieces) simultaneously with one.
– DERIVATIVES **forkful** n. (pl. **-fuls**).
– ORIGIN Old English: from Latin *furca* 'pitchfork, forked stick'; reinforced in Middle English by Anglo-Norman French *furke*.

forkball ■ n. Baseball a pitch released from between the widely spread index finger and middle finger.

forked ■ adj. having a divided or pronged end.

forked lightning ■ n. lightning that is visible in the form of a zigzag or branching line across the sky.

forklift truck ■ n. a vehicle with a pronged device in front for lifting and carrying heavy loads.

forlorn /fəˈlɔːn/ ■ adj. **1** pitifully sad and lonely. **2** unlikely to succeed or be fulfilled.
– PHRASES **forlorn hope** a persistent or desperate hope that is unlikely to be fulfilled. [C16: from Dutch *verloren hoop* 'lost troop', orig. denoting a band of soldiers picked to begin an attack, many of whom would not survive.]
– DERIVATIVES **forlornly** adv. **forlornness** n.
– ORIGIN Old English *forlēoren* 'depraved', from *forlēosan* 'lose', of Germanic origin; ultimately rel. to FOR- and LOSE.

form ■ n. **1** visible shape or configuration. ▶ style, design, and arrangement in an artistic work as distinct from its content. **2** a way in which a thing exists or appears. ▶ any of the ways in which a word may be spelled, pronounced, or inflected. ▶ Philosophy the essential nature of a species or thing, especially (in Plato's thought) regarded as an abstract ideal which real things imitate or participate in. **3** a type or variety of something. **4** the customary or correct method or procedure. ▶ a ritual or convention. **5** a printed document with blank spaces for information to be inserted. **6** chiefly Brit. a class or year in a school. **7** the state of a sports player with regard to their current standard of play. ▶ details of previous performances by a racehorse or greyhound. ▶ a person's mood and state of health. ▶ Brit. informal a criminal record. **8** Brit. a long bench without a back. **9** Brit. a hare's lair. **10** a temporary wooden structure used to hold concrete during setting. ■ v. **1** bring together parts to create. ▶ go to make up. ▶ establish or develop. ▶ (**form people/things up**) or **form up** bring or be brought into a certain formation. ▶ articulate (a word or other linguistic unit). **2** (often **form something into**) or **form into** make or be made into a certain form.
– PHRASES **in** (or **on**) **form** playing or performing well. **off** (or **out of**) **form** not playing or performing well.
– DERIVATIVES **formable** adj. **formless** adj. **formlessly** adv. **formlessness** n.
– ORIGIN Middle English: from Latin *forma* 'a mould or form'.

-form (usu. as **-iform**) ■ comb. form **1** having the form of: *cruciform*. **2** having a particular number of: *multiform*.
– ORIGIN from Latin *-formis*, from *forma* 'form'.

forma /ˈfɔːmə/ ■ n. (pl. **formas** or **formae** /-miː/) Botany a taxonomic category that ranks below variety, representing e.g. a colour variant.
– ORIGIN C20: Latin, 'form'.

formal ■ adj. **1** done in accordance with rules of convention or etiquette. ▶ having a conventionally recognized structure or set of rules: *a formal education*. ▶ of or denoting a style of writing or public speaking characterized by more elaborate grammatical structures and more conservative and technical vocabulary. ▶ (especially of a garden) arranged in a precise or symmetrical manner. **2** officially recognized: *a formal complaint*. **3** of or concerned with outward form rather than content. ▶ having the form without the spirit. ▶ of or relating to linguistic or logical form as opposed to function or meaning. ■ n. chiefly N. Amer. an evening dress.
– DERIVATIVES **formally** adv.
– ORIGIN Middle English: from Latin *formalis*, from *forma* (see FORM).

formaldehyde /fɔːˈmaldɪhʌɪd/ ■ n. Chemistry a colourless pungent gas made by oxidizing methanol, and used in solution as a preservative for biological specimens.
– ORIGIN C19: blend of FORMIC ACID and ALDEHYDE.

formalin /ˈfɔːm(ə)lɪn/ ■ n. a solution of formaldehyde in water.

formalism ■ n. **1** excessive adherence to prescribed forms. **2** concern or excessive concern with form rather than content in artistic creation. **3** a description in formal mathematical or logical terms.
– DERIVATIVES **formalist** n. **formalistic** adj.

formality ■ n. (pl. **-ies**) the rigid observance of rules or convention. ▶ a thing that is done simply to comply with convention, regulations, or custom. ▶ (**a formality**) something done or happening as a matter of course.

formalize (also **-ise**) ■ v. **1** give legal or formal status to. **2** give a definite form to.
– DERIVATIVES **formalization** (also **-isation**) n.

formal sector ■ n. the part of the economy represented by business activities regulated by taxation and labour legislation.

formant /ˈfɔːm(ə)nt/ ■ n. Phonetics any of the three characteristic pitch constituents of a vowel.
– ORIGIN C20: German, from Latin *formare* 'form'.

format ■ n. the way in which something is arranged or presented. ▶ Computing a defined structure for the processing, storage, or display of data. ■ v. (**formatted**, **formatting**) (especially in computing) arrange or put into a format. ▶ prepare (a storage medium) to receive data.
– ORIGIN C19: from Latin *formatus* (*liber*) 'shaped (book)'.

formation ■ n. **1** the action of forming or the process of being formed. **2** a structure or arrangement. ▶ a formal arrangement of aircraft in flight or troops.
– DERIVATIVES **formational** adj.

formation dancing ■ n. a variety of competitive ballroom dancing in which a team of couples dance a prepared routine.

formative

formative ■ adj. serving to form something, especially having a profound influence on a person's development. ▶ Linguistics denoting or relating to any of the smallest meaningful units that are used to form words in a language, typically combining forms and inflections.
– DERIVATIVES **formatively** adv.
– ORIGIN C15: from medieval Latin *formativus*, from Latin *formare* (see FORM).

form class ■ n. Linguistics a part of speech or subset of a part of speech.

form drag ■ n. Aeronautics that part of the drag on an aerofoil which arises from its shape.

former[1] ■ adj. **1** having been previously. ▶ of or occurring in the past. **2** (**the former**) denoting the first or first-mentioned of two people or things.
– ORIGIN Middle English: from Old English *forma* 'first'.

former[2] ■ n. **1** a person or thing that forms something. **2** [in combination] chiefly Brit. a person in a particular school year: *a fifth-former*.

formerly ■ adv. in the past.

Formica /fɔːˈmʌɪkə/ ■ n. trademark a hard durable plastic laminate used for worktops, cupboard doors, etc.
– ORIGIN 1920s (orig. US).

formic acid /ˈfɔːmɪk/ ■ n. Chemistry an irritant volatile organic acid present in the fluid emitted by some ants. [HCOOH.]
– DERIVATIVES **formate** n.
– ORIGIN C18: *formic* from Latin *formica* 'ant'.

formication /ˌfɔːmɪˈkeɪʃ(ə)n/ ■ n. a sensation like insects crawling over the skin.
– ORIGIN C18: from Latin *formicatio(n-)*, from *formicare* 'crawl like an ant'.

formidable /ˈfɔːmɪdəb(ə)l, fɔːˈmɪd-/ ■ adj. inspiring fear or respect through being impressively large, powerful, or capable.
– DERIVATIVES **formidableness** n. **formidably** adv.
– ORIGIN Middle English: from Latin *formidabilis*, from *formidare* 'to fear'.

form letter ■ n. a standardized letter to deal with frequently occurring matters.

formol /ˈfɔːmɒl/ ■ n. another term for FORMALIN.

formula /ˈfɔːmjʊlə/ ■ n. **1** (pl. **formulae** /-liː/) a mathematical relationship or rule expressed in symbols. ▶ (also **chemical formula**) a set of chemical symbols showing the elements present in a compound and their relative proportions. **2** (pl. **formulas**) a fixed form of words, especially one used in particular contexts or as a conventional usage. ▶ a rule or style unintelligently followed. **3** (pl. **formulas**) a method or procedure for achieving something. ▶ a list of ingredients with which something is made. ▶ an infant's liquid food preparation based on cow's milk or soya protein. **4** (usually followed by a numeral) a classification of racing car, especially by the engine capacity.
– DERIVATIVES **formularize** (also **-ise**) v.
– ORIGIN C17: from Latin, diminutive of *forma* 'shape, mould'.

formulable ■ adj. capable of being formulated.

formulaic /ˌfɔːmjʊˈleɪɪk/ ■ adj. constituting or containing a set form of words. ▶ produced in accordance with a mechanically followed rule or style: *formulaic, disposable pop*.
– DERIVATIVES **formulaically** adv.

formulate /ˈfɔːmjʊleɪt/ ■ v. create or prepare methodically. ▶ express (an idea) in a concise or systematic way.
– DERIVATIVES **formulator** n.

formulation ■ n. **1** the action of formulating. **2** a material or mixture prepared according to a formula.

formwork ■ n. another term for FORM (in sense 10).

fornicate ■ v. formal or humorous have sexual intercourse with someone one is not married to.
– DERIVATIVES **fornication** n. **fornicator** n.
– ORIGIN C16 (*fornication* Middle English): from eccles. Latin *fornicari* 'to arch', from *fornix* 'vaulted chamber', later 'brothel'.

forsake ■ v. (past **forsook**; past part. **forsaken**) chiefly poetic/literary abandon. ▶ renounce or give up.
– DERIVATIVES **forsakenness** n. **forsaker** n.
– ORIGIN Old English *forsacan* 'renounce, refuse', of West Germanic origin.

forsooth /fəˈsuːθ/ ■ adv. archaic or humorous indeed.
– ORIGIN Old English (see FOR, SOOTH).

forswear ■ v. (past **forswore**; past part. **forsworn**) formal **1** agree to give up or do without. **2** (**forswear oneself/be forsworn**) commit perjury.
– ORIGIN Old English (see FOR-, SWEAR).

forsythia /fɔːˈsʌɪθɪə, fə-/ ■ n. an ornamental Eurasian shrub whose bright yellow flowers appear in early spring before its leaves. [Genus *Forsythia*: several species.]
– ORIGIN named after the C18 Scottish botanist William *Forsyth*.

fort ■ n. a fortified building or strategic position.
– ORIGIN Middle English: from Latin *fortis* 'strong'.

forte[1] /ˈfɔːteɪ, ˈfɔːti, fɔːt/ ■ n. **1** a thing at which someone excels. **2** Fencing the part of a sword blade from the hilt to the middle. Compare with FOIBLE.
– ORIGIN C17: from French *fort* (masculine), *forte* (feminine) 'strong'.

forte[2] /ˈfɔːteɪ/ ■ adv. & adj. Music loud or loudly.
– ORIGIN Italian, 'strong, loud'.

fortepiano /ˌfɔːteɪˈpjɑːnəʊ, -ˈpjanəʊ/ ■ n. (pl. **-os**) Music a piano, especially of the kind made in the 18th and early 19th centuries.
– ORIGIN C18: from FORTE[2] + PIANO[2].

forth ■ adv. chiefly archaic **1** out from a starting point and forwards or into view. **2** onwards in time.
– PHRASES **and so forth** and so on.
– ORIGIN Old English, of Germanic origin; rel. to FORE-.

forthcoming ■ adj. **1** about to happen or appear. **2** [often with neg.] ready or made available when required. **3** willing to divulge information.
– DERIVATIVES **forthcomingness** n.

forthright ■ adj. direct and outspoken.
– DERIVATIVES **forthrightly** adv. **forthrightness** n.
– ORIGIN Old English *forthriht* 'straight forward, directly' (see FORTH, RIGHT).

forthwith /fɔːθˈwɪθ, -ð/ ■ adv. without delay.
– ORIGIN Middle English ('at the same time'): partly from earlier *forthwithal*, partly representing *forth with* used alone without a following noun.

fortify /ˈfɔːtɪfʌɪ/ ■ v. (**-ies, -ied**) **1** provide with defensive works as protection against attack. **2** invigorate or encourage. **3** [often as adj. **fortified**] add spirits to (wine) to make port, sherry, etc. **4** increase the nutritive value of (food) by adding vitamins.
– DERIVATIVES **fortifiable** adj. **fortification** n. **fortifier** n.
– ORIGIN Middle English: from late Latin *fortificare*, from Latin *fortis* 'strong'.

fortis /ˈfɔːtɪs/ ■ adj. Phonetics (of a consonant) strongly articulated, especially more so than another consonant articulated in the same place. The opposite of LENIS.
– ORIGIN C20: from Latin, 'strong'.

fortitude /ˈfɔːtɪtjuːd/ ■ n. courage in adversity.
– ORIGIN Middle English: from Latin *fortitudo*, from *fortis* 'strong'.

fortnight ■ n. a period of two weeks.
– ORIGIN Old English *fēowertīene niht* 'fourteen nights'.

fortnightly ■ adj. happening or produced every two weeks. ■ adv. every two weeks.

Fortran /ˈfɔːtran/ ■ n. a high-level computer programming language used especially for scientific calculations.
– ORIGIN 1950s: contraction of *formula translation*.

fortress ■ n. a military stronghold, especially a strongly fortified town fit for a large garrison.
– ORIGIN Middle English: from Old French *forteresse* 'strong place', from Latin *fortis* 'strong'.

fortuitous /fɔːˈtjuːɪtəs/ ■ adj. happening by chance rather than design. ▶ informal happening by a lucky chance.
– DERIVATIVES **fortuitously** adv. **fortuitousness** n. **fortuity** n. (pl. **-ies**).
– ORIGIN C17: from Latin *fortuitus*, from *forte* 'by chance'.

CONSONANTS   b *but*   d *dog*   f *few*   g *get*   h *he*   j *yes*   k *cat*   l *leg*   m *man*   n *no*   p *pen*   r *red*

fortunate ■ adj. favoured by or involving good luck. ▶ auspicious or favourable.

fortunately ■ adv. it is fortunate that.

Fortune 500 ■ n. (trademark in the US) an annual list of the five hundred most profitable US industrial corporations.

fortune ■ n. **1** chance as an arbitrary force affecting human affairs. ▶ luck, especially good luck. ▶ (**fortunes**) the success or failure of a person or enterprise. **2** a large amount of money or assets.
– PHRASES **a small fortune** informal a large amount of money. **tell someone's fortune** make predictions about a person's future by palmistry or similar divining methods.
– ORIGIN Middle English: from Latin *Fortuna*, the name of a Roman goddess personifying luck or chance.

fortune cookie ■ n. N. Amer. a small biscuit containing a slip of paper bearing a prediction or motto, served in Chinese restaurants.

fortune-hunter ■ n. a person seeking wealth by marriage.
– DERIVATIVES **fortune-hunting** n.

fortune-teller ■ n. a person who tells people's fortunes.
– DERIVATIVES **fortune-telling** n.

forty ■ cardinal number (pl. **-ies**) the number equivalent to the product of four and ten; ten less than fifty; 40. (Roman numeral: **xl** or **XL**.)
– PHRASES **forty winks** informal a short daytime sleep.
– DERIVATIVES **fortieth** ordinal number. **fortyfold** adj. & adv.
– ORIGIN Old English.

forum /ˈfɔːrəm/ ■ n. (pl. **forums**) **1** a meeting or medium for an exchange of views. **2** chiefly N. Amer. a court or tribunal. **3** (pl. **fora**) (in an ancient Roman city) a public square or marketplace used for judicial and other business.
– ORIGIN Middle English: from Latin, 'what is out of doors'.

forward ■ adv. (also **forwards**) **1** in the direction that one is facing or travelling. ▶ in or near the front of a ship or aircraft. **2** onward so as to make progress. **3** in the normal order or sequence. **4** ahead in time. ■ adj. **1** towards the direction that one is facing or travelling. ▶ situated in or near the front of a ship or aircraft. **2** relating to the future. **3** bold or over-familiar in manner. **4** further advanced than expected or required. ■ n. **1** an attacking player in soccer, hockey, or other sports. **2** (**forwards**) agreements to trade specified assets at a specified price at a certain future date. Compare with FUTURE (in sense 4). ■ v. **1** send (a letter) on to a further destination. ▶ dispatch; send. **2** promote.
– DERIVATIVES **forwarder** n. **forwardly** adv. **forwardness** n.
– ORIGIN Old English (see FORTH, -WARD).

forward-looking ■ adj. progressive.

forwent past of FORGO.

fosse /fɒs/ ■ n. Archaeology a long narrow trench or ditch, especially in a fortification.
– ORIGIN Old English: from Latin *fossa* 'ditch'.

fossick /ˈfɒsɪk/ ■ v. informal, chiefly Austral./NZ rummage; search. ▶ search for gold in abandoned workings.
– DERIVATIVES **fossicker** n.
– ORIGIN C19: prob. from the English dialect sense 'obtain by asking'.

fossil /ˈfɒs(ə)l, -sɪl/ ■ n. **1** the remains or impression of a prehistoric plant or animal embedded in rock and preserved in petrified form. **2** humorous an antiquated person or thing. **3** a word or phrase that has become obsolete except in set phrases or forms, e.g. *hue* in *hue and cry*.
– DERIVATIVES **fossiliferous** adj. **fossilization** (also **-isation**) n. **fossilize** (also **-ise**) v.
– ORIGIN C16: from Latin *fossilis* 'dug up'.

fossil fuel ■ n. a natural fuel such as coal or gas, formed in the geological past from the remains of living organisms.

fossil ivory ■ n. ivory from the tusks of a mammoth.

fossorial /fɒˈsɔːrɪəl/ ■ adj. Zoology (of an animal) burrowing. ▶ (of limbs) adapted for use in burrowing.
– ORIGIN C19: from medieval Latin *fossorius*, from Latin *fossor* 'digger'.

foster ■ v. **1** promote the development of. **2** bring up (a child that is not one's own by birth).
– DERIVATIVES **fosterer** n.
– ORIGIN Old English *fōstrian*, from *fōster* 'food, nourishment', of Germanic origin.

foster- ■ comb. form denoting someone having a specified family connection through fostering: *foster-parent*. ▶ concerned with fostering: *foster care*.
– ORIGIN Old English.

fought past and past participle of FIGHT.

foul ■ adj. **1** offensive to the senses. ▶ informal very disagreeable or unpleasant. ▶ (of the weather) wet and stormy. **2** morally offensive; wicked or obscene. ▶ done contrary to the rules of a sport. **3** polluted or contaminated. ▶ (**foul with**) clogged or choked with. ▶ Nautical (of a rope or anchor) entangled. ■ n. (in sport) an unfair or invalid stroke or piece of play. ▶ a collision or entanglement in riding, rowing, or running. ■ v. **1** make foul; pollute. ▶ (of an animal) dirty with excrement. **2** (in sport) commit a foul against. **3** (**foul something up**) or **foul up** make a mistake with or spoil something. **4** (of a ship) collide with or interfere with the passage of (another). ▶ cause (a cable, anchor, etc.) to become entangled or jammed.
– DERIVATIVES **foully** adv. **foulness** n.
– ORIGIN Old English, of Germanic origin.

Foulah /ˈfuːlə/ ■ n. variant spelling of FULA.

foulard /ˈfuːlɑː(d)/ ■ n. a thin, soft material of silk or silk and cotton.
– ORIGIN C19: from French.

foul line ■ n. Baseball either of the straight lines extending from home plate and marking the limit of the playing area within which a ball is deemed to be fair.

foul mouth ■ n. a tendency to use bad language.
– DERIVATIVES **foul-mouthed** adj.

foul play ■ n. **1** unfair play in a game or sport. **2** criminal or violent activity, especially murder.

found[1] past and past participle of FIND. ■ adj. **1** (of an object or sound) collected in its natural state and presented in a new context as part of a work of art or piece of music. **2** (of a ship) equipped.

found[2] ■ v. **1** establish (an institution or organization). ▶ plan and begin the building of (a settlement). **2** (usu. **be founded on/upon**) base on a particular principle or concept. ▶ serve as a basis for.
– ORIGIN Middle English: from Old French *fonder*, from Latin *fundare*, from *fundus* 'bottom, base'.

found[3] ■ v. **1** melt and mould (metal). ▶ fuse (materials) to make glass. ▶ make by founding.
– ORIGIN C16: from French *fondre*, from Latin *fundere* 'melt, pour'.

foundation ■ n. **1** the lowest load-bearing part of a building, typically below ground level. **2** an underlying basis or principle. ▶ [often with neg.] justification or reason. **3** the action of founding an institution or organization. ▶ an institution so established. **4** a cream or powder applied to the face as a base for other make-up.
– DERIVATIVES **foundational** adj.

foundation course ■ n. Brit. a preparatory course taken at some colleges and universities, either in a wide range of subjects or in one subject at a basic level.

foundation garment ■ n. a woman's supportive undergarment, such as a corset.

foundation phase ■ n. S. African the period of primary school education comprising grades R–3.

foundation stone ■ n. a stone laid with ceremony to celebrate the founding of a building.

founder[1] ■ n. a person who founds an institution or settlement.
– DERIVATIVES **foundress** n.

founder[2] ■ n. the owner or operator of a foundry.
– ORIGIN Middle English: prob. from Old French *fondeur*, from *fondre* (see FOUND[3]).

founder[3] ■ v. **1** (of a ship) fill with water and sink. ▶ (of a plan or undertaking) fail. **2** (of a horse) stumble or fall.
– ORIGIN Middle English: from Old French *fondrer*,

founding father 460

esfondrer 'submerge, collapse', from Latin *fundus* 'bottom, base'.

> **USAGE**
> The words **founder** and **flounder** are often confused. **Founder** means, in its general and extended use, 'fail or come to nothing', while **flounder** means 'struggle; be in a state of confusion'.

founding father ■ n. a founder. ▶ (**Founding Father**) a member of the convention that drew up the constitution of the US in 1787.

foundling ■ n. an infant that has been abandoned by its parents and is discovered and cared for by others.
–ORIGIN Middle English: from FOUND¹.

foundry ■ n. (pl. **-ies**) a workshop or factory for casting metal.

fount¹ ■ n. 1 a source of a desirable quality. 2 poetic/literary a spring or fountain.
–ORIGIN C16: back-formation from FOUNTAIN, on the pattern of the pair *mountain*, *mount*.

fount² ■ n. Brit. variant spelling of FONT².

fountain ■ n. 1 an ornamental structure in a pool or lake from which one or more jets of water are pumped into the air. 2 S. African or poetic/literary a natural spring of water. 3 a source of a desirable quality. 4 Heraldry a circle with wavy horizontal stripes of blue and white. ■ v. spurt or cascade like a fountain.
–ORIGIN Middle English: from Old French *fontaine*, from late Latin *fontana*, feminine of Latin *fontanus*, from *fons* 'a spring'.

fountain bush ■ n. S. African a southern African shrub or small tree with blue or mauve pea-shaped flowers, growing near springs and wetlands. [*Psoralea pinnata*.]

fountainhead ■ n. an original source.

fountain pen ■ n. a pen with a reservoir or cartridge from which ink flows continuously to the nib.

four ■ cardinal number 1 equivalent to the product of two and two; one more than three, or six less than ten; 4. (Roman numeral: **iv** or **IV**, archaic **iiii** or **IIII**.) 2 Cricket a hit that reaches the boundary after first striking the ground, scoring four runs. 3 a four-oared rowing boat or its crew.
–DERIVATIVES **fourfold** adj. & adv.
–ORIGIN Old English, of Germanic origin.

4x4 /ˌfɔː baɪ ˈfɔː/ (also **four-by-four**) ■ n. informal a vehicle with four-wheel drive.

four-dimensional ■ adj. having four dimensions, typically the three dimensions of space (length, breadth, and depth) plus time.

four-eyes ■ n. informal, derogatory a person who wears glasses.
–DERIVATIVES **four-eyed** adj.

four-leaf clover (also **four-leaved clover**) ■ n. a clover leaf with four lobes, thought to bring good luck.

four-letter word ■ n. any of several short words referring to sexual or excretory functions, regarded as coarse or offensive.

419 (also **four-one-nine**) ■ n. [often as modifier] a fraudulent scheme in which a person is asked to help secure the release of a sum of money by paying an advance fee in return for a percentage of the total amount.
–ORIGIN 1990s: named after Section 419 of the Nigerian Criminal Code, which describes fraudulent activities.

four-poster (also **four-poster bed**) ■ n. a bed with a post at each corner supporting a canopy.

fours ■ pl. n. 1 a race for four-oared rowing boats. 2 a competition for teams of four players, especially in bowls.

fourscore ■ cardinal number archaic eighty.

foursome ■ n. 1 a group of four people. 2 a golf match between two pairs of players, with partners playing the same ball.

four-square ■ adj. 1 (of a building) having a square shape and solid appearance. 2 firm and resolute. ■ adv. 1 squarely and solidly. 2 firmly and resolutely.

four-stroke ■ adj. denoting an internal-combustion engine having a cycle of four strokes (intake, compression, combustion, and exhaust).

fourteen ■ cardinal number equivalent to the product of seven and two; one more than thirteen, or six less than twenty; 14. (Roman numeral: **xiv** or **XIV**.)
–DERIVATIVES **fourteenth** ordinal number.
–ORIGIN Old English, of Germanic origin.

fourth ■ ordinal number 1 constituting number four in a sequence; 4th. 2 (**a fourth/one fourth**) chiefly N. Amer. a quarter. 3 Music an interval spanning four consecutive notes in a diatonic scale, in particular (also **perfect fourth**) an interval of two tones and a semitone. ▶ Music the note which is higher by this interval than the tonic of a diatonic scale or root of a chord.
–PHRASES **the fourth estate** the press; journalism.
–DERIVATIVES **fourthly** adv.

fourth dimension ■ n. 1 a postulated spatial dimension additional to those determining length, area, and volume. 2 time regarded as analogous to linear dimensions.

Fourth World ■ n. those countries and communities considered to be the poorest and most underdeveloped of the Third World.

4WD ■ abbrev. four-wheel drive.

four-wheel drive ■ n. a transmission system which provides power directly to all four wheels of a vehicle.

fovea /ˈfəʊvɪə/ ■ n. (pl. **foveae** /-viːiː/) Anatomy a small depression in the retina of the eye where visual acuity is highest.
–DERIVATIVES **foveal** adj.
–ORIGIN C17: from Latin, 'small pit'.

fowl ■ n. (pl. same or **fowls**) 1 (also **domestic fowl**) a domesticated bird derived from a junglefowl and kept for its eggs or flesh; a cock or hen. ▶ any domesticated bird, e.g. a turkey or duck. ▶ used in the names of birds that resemble the domestic fowl, e.g. spurfowl. 2 birds collectively, especially as the quarry of hunters.
–DERIVATIVES **fowler** n. **fowling** n.
–ORIGIN Old English, of Germanic origin.

fowl plague ■ n. a serious infectious disease of poultry caused by an influenza virus.

fox ■ n. 1 a carnivorous mammal of the dog family with a pointed muzzle, bushy tail, and typically a reddish coat. [*Vulpes vulpes* (red fox) and other species.] 2 informal a cunning or sly person. 3 N. Amer. informal a sexually attractive woman. ■ v. informal baffle or deceive.
–DERIVATIVES **foxlike** adj.
–ORIGIN Old English, of Germanic origin.

foxed ■ adj. (of the paper of old books or prints) discoloured with brown spots.
–DERIVATIVES **foxing** n.

foxglove ■ n. a tall Eurasian plant with erect spikes of typically pinkish-purple flowers shaped like the fingers of gloves. [*Digitalis purpurea* and related species.]

foxhole ■ n. a hole in the ground used by troops as a shelter against enemy fire or as a firing point.

fox-hunting ■ n. the sport of hunting a fox across country with a pack of hounds by a group of people on foot and horseback.
–DERIVATIVES **fox-hunter** n.

foxtail ■ n. a common meadow grass with soft brush-like flowering spikes. [*Alopecurus pratensis* (Eurasia) and related species.]

fox terrier ■ n. a terrier of a short-haired or wire-haired breed originally used for unearthing foxes.

foxtrot ■ n. 1 a ballroom dance having an uneven rhythm with alternation of slow and quick steps. ▶ music for the foxtrot. 2 a code word representing the letter F, used in radio communication. ■ v. (**-trotted**, **-trotting**) dance the foxtrot.

foxy ■ adj. (**-ier**, **-iest**) 1 resembling or likened to a fox. 2 informal cunning or sly. 3 N. Amer. informal (of a woman) sexually attractive. 4 (of paper or other material) foxed.
–DERIVATIVES **foxily** adv. **foxiness** n.

foyer /ˈfɔɪeɪ/ ■ n. an entrance hall or other open area in a public building, especially a hotel or theatre.
–ORIGIN C18: from French, 'hearth, home'.

f.p. ■ abbrev. freezing point.

VOWELS   a cat   ɑː arm   ɛ bed   ɛː hair   ə ago   əː her   ɪ sit   i cosy   iː see   ɒ hot   ɔː saw   ʌ run

fps (also **f.p.s.**) ▪ abbrev. **1** feet per second. **2** frames per second.

Fr ▪ abbrev. Father (as a courtesy title of priests). [from French *frère*, literally 'brother'.] ▪ symb. the chemical element francium.

fr. ▪ abbrev. franc(s).

Fra /frɑː/ ▪ n. a prefixed title given to an Italian monk or friar.
– ORIGIN Italian: abbrev. of *frate* 'brother'.

fracas /ˈfrakɑː/ ▪ n. (pl. same /-kɑːz/ or US **fracases**) a noisy disturbance or quarrel.
– ORIGIN C18: French, from Italian *fracassare* 'make an uproar'.

fractal /ˈfrakt(ə)l/ Mathematics ▪ n. a curve or geometrical figure each part of which has the same statistical character as the whole. ▪ adj. relating to or of the nature of a fractal or fractals.
– ORIGIN 1970s: from Latin *fract-, frangere* 'break'.

fraction /ˈfrakʃ(ə)n/ ▪ n. **1** a numerical quantity that is not a whole number (e.g. ½, 0.5). **2** a small or tiny part, amount, or proportion. ▸ a dissenting group within a larger one. **3** Chemistry each of the portions into which a mixture may be separated according to a physical property such as boiling point or solubility.
– ORIGIN Middle English: from eccles. Latin *fractio(n-)* 'breaking (bread)', from Latin *frangere* 'to break'.

fractional ▪ adj. **1** of, relating to, or expressed as a fraction. **2** small or tiny in amount. **3** Chemistry relating to or denoting the separation of a mixture into fractions.
– DERIVATIVES **fractionally** adv.

fractionalize (also **-ise**) ▪ v. [usu. as adj. **fractionalized** (also **-ised**)] divide into separate groups or parts.
– DERIVATIVES **fractionalization** (also **-isation**) n.

fractionate /ˈfrakʃ(ə)neɪt/ ▪ v. chiefly Chemistry divide into fractions or components.

fractious /ˈfrakʃəs/ ▪ adj. **1** easily irritated. **2** difficult to control.
– DERIVATIVES **fractiousness** n.
– ORIGIN C17: from FRACTION, prob. on the pattern of *faction, factious*.

fracture ▪ n. the cracking or breaking of a hard object or material. ▸ a crack or break, especially in a bone or a rock stratum. ▸ the shape of the surface formed by a freshly broken rock or mineral. ▪ v. break or cause to break. ▸ (of a group or organization) break up or fragment.
– ORIGIN Middle English: from Latin *fractura*, from *frangere* 'to break'.

fragile /ˈfradʒʌɪl/ ▪ adj. **1** easily broken or damaged. **2** delicate and vulnerable.
– DERIVATIVES **fragilely** adv. **fragility** n.
– ORIGIN C15 ('morally weak'): from Latin *fragilis*, from *frangere* 'to break'.

fragment ▪ n. /ˈfragmənt/ a small part broken off or detached. ▸ an isolated or incomplete part. ▪ v. /fragˈmɛnt/ break or cause to break into fragments.
– DERIVATIVES **fragmental** adj. (chiefly Geology). **fragmentary** adj. **fragmentation** n.
– ORIGIN Middle English: from Latin *fragmentum*, from *frangere* 'to break'.

fragmentation bomb (or **fragmentation grenade**) ▪ n. a bomb (or grenade) designed to break into small fragments as it explodes.

fragrance /ˈfreɪɡr(ə)ns/ ▪ n. a pleasant, sweet smell. ▸ a perfume or aftershave.
– DERIVATIVES **fragranced** adj.

fragrant ▪ adj. having a pleasant or sweet smell.
– DERIVATIVES **fragrantly** adv.
– ORIGIN Middle English: from Latin *fragrare* 'smell sweet'.

frail ▪ adj. **1** weak and delicate. **2** easily damaged or broken.
– ORIGIN Middle English: from Old French *fraile*, from Latin *fragilis* (see FRAGILE).

frail care ▪ n. chiefly S. African nursing and medical care provided for elderly people, usually in an institution or home.

frailty ▪ n. (pl. **-ies**) the condition of being frail. ▸ weakness in character or morals.

framboise /frɒmˈbwɑːz/ ▪ n. **1** (in cookery) a raspberry. **2** a white brandy distilled from raspberries.
– ORIGIN from French.

frame ▪ n. **1** a rigid structure surrounding a picture, door, etc. ▸ (**frames**) a metal or plastic structure holding the lenses of a pair of glasses. ▸ the rigid supporting structure of a vehicle, aircraft, or other object. ▸ a person's body with reference to its size or build. ▸ a box-like structure of glass or plastic in which seeds or young plants are grown. **2** a basic underlying or supporting structure of a system, concept, or text. **3** Linguistics a structural environment within which a class of words or other linguistic units can be correctly used (e.g. *I —— him* is a frame for a large class of transitive verbs). **4** a single complete picture in a series forming a cinema, television, or video film. ▸ Computing a graphic panel in an Internet browser which encloses a self-contained section of data and permits multiple independent document viewing. **5** the triangular structure for positioning the red balls in snooker. ▸ a single game of snooker. ▪ v. **1** place (a picture or photograph) in a frame. ▸ surround so as to create a sharp or attractive image. **2** formulate. **3** informal produce false incriminating evidence against (an innocent person).
– PHRASES **be in** (or **out of**) **the frame** be (or not be) eligible. ▸ be wanted (or not wanted) by the police. **frame of mind** a particular mood.
– DERIVATIVES **framed** adj. **frameless** adj. **framer** n. **framing** n.
– ORIGIN Old English *framian* 'be useful', later 'prepare timber for building, make the wooden parts of a building': of Germanic origin.

frame of reference ▪ n. **1** a set of criteria in relation to which judgements can be made. **2** a system of geometrical axes in relation to which size, position, or motion can be defined.

frame tent ▪ n. a tent supported by a tall frame, giving it nearly perpendicular sides and standing headroom throughout.

frame-up ▪ n. informal a conspiracy to incriminate someone falsely.

framework ▪ n. an essential supporting or underlying structure.

franc /fraŋk/ ▪ n. the former monetary unit of France, Belgium, and Luxembourg. ▸ the basic monetary unit of Switzerland and some other countries, equal to 100 centimes.
– ORIGIN from Latin *Francorum Rex* 'king of the Franks', the legend on gold coins struck in the 14th century.

franchise /ˈfran(t)ʃʌɪz/ ▪ n. **1** an authorization granted by a government or company to an individual or group enabling them to carry out specified commercial activities. ▸ a business or service granted such authorization. ▸ N. Amer. an authorization given by a professional league to own a sports team. **2** the right to vote in public elections, especially for members of parliament. ▪ v. grant a franchise to. ▸ grant a franchise for the sale of (goods) or the operation of (a service).
– DERIVATIVES **franchisee** n. **franchiser** (also **franchisor**) n.
– ORIGIN Middle English (denoting a grant of legal immunity): from Old French, from *franc, franche* (see FRANK¹).

Franciscan /franˈsɪsk(ə)n/ ▪ n. a monk, nun, or lay member of a Christian religious order following the rule of St Francis of Assisi. ▪ adj. of St Francis or the Franciscans.

francium /ˈfransɪəm/ ▪ n. the chemical element of atomic number 87, an unstable radioactive member of the alkali metal group. (Symbol: **Fr**)
– ORIGIN 1940s: from the country *France*.

Franco- (also **franco-**) ▪ comb. form French; French and ...: *francophone*. ▸ relating to France: *Francophile*.
– ORIGIN from medieval Latin *Francus* 'Frank'.

Francoist ▪ n. a supporter of the Spanish dictator General Francisco Franco (1892–1975) or his policies. ▪ adj. of or relating to Franco's regime or policies.
– DERIVATIVES **Francoism** n.

francolin /ˈfraŋkə(ʊ)lɪn/ ▪ n. a large game bird resembling a partridge, found in Africa and South Asia. [Genus *Francolinus*: many species.]
– ORIGIN C17: from French, from Italian *francolino*.

Francophile ▪ n. a person who is fond of or greatly admires France or the French.

ʊ put   uː too   ʌɪ my   aʊ how   eɪ day   əʊ no   ɪə near   ɔɪ boy   ʊə poor   ʌɪə fire   aʊə sour

francophone

francophone /ˈfraŋkə(ʊ)fəʊn/ ■ adj. French-speaking. ■ n. a French-speaking person.

frangipani /ˌfran(d)ʒɪˈpani, -ˈpɑːni/ ■ n. (pl. **frangipanis**) a tropical American tree or shrub with clusters of fragrant white, pink, or yellow flowers. [*Plumeria rubra* and related species.] ▸ perfume obtained from this plant.
– ORIGIN C19: named after the Marquis Muzio *Frangipani*, a C16 Italian nobleman who invented a perfume for scenting gloves.

franglais /ˈfrɒŋɡleɪ/ ■ n. a blend of French and English, either French that makes excessive use of English expressions, or unidiomatic French spoken by an English person.
– ORIGIN 1960s: coined in French, from a blend of *français* 'French' and *anglais* 'English'.

Frank ■ n. a member of a Germanic people that conquered Gaul in the 6th century.
– DERIVATIVES **Frankish** adj. & n.
– ORIGIN Old English *Franca*, of Germanic origin; perhaps from the name of a weapon and rel. to Old English *franca* 'javelin'; reinforced in Middle English by medieval Latin *Francus* and Old French *Franc*, of the same origin.

frank[1] ■ adj. 1 candid and honest. ▸ sincere or undisguised. 2 Medicine unmistakable.
– DERIVATIVES **frankness** n.
– ORIGIN Middle English: from Old French *franc*, from medieval Latin *francus* 'free', from *Francus* (see **FRANK**: only Franks had full freedom in Frankish Gaul).

frank[2] ■ v. stamp an official mark on (a letter or parcel) to indicate that postage has been paid or does not need to be paid. ▸ historical sign (a letter or parcel) to ensure delivery free of charge. ■ n. a franking mark or signature on a letter or parcel.
– DERIVATIVES **franking** n.
– ORIGIN C18: from **FRANK**[1], an early sense being 'free of obligation'.

Frankenstein /ˈfraŋk(ə)nstʌɪn/ (also **Frankenstein's monster**) ■ n. a thing that becomes terrifying or destructive to its maker.
– ORIGIN Baron *Frankenstein*, a character in a novel (1818) by Mary Shelley, who creates a manlike monster which eventually destroys him.

frankfurter ■ n. a seasoned smoked sausage made of beef and pork.
– ORIGIN from German *Frankfurter Wurst* 'Frankfurt sausage'.

frankincense /ˈfraŋkɪnsens/ ■ n. an aromatic gum resin obtained from an African tree (*Boswellia sacra*) and burnt as incense.
– ORIGIN Middle English: from Old French *franc encens* 'high-quality incense', from *franc* (see **FRANK**[1]) in an obsolete sense 'of high quality' + *encens* 'incense'.

frankly ■ adv. in a frank manner. ▸ to be frank.

frantic ■ adj. 1 distraught with fear, anxiety, etc. 2 conducted in a hurried and chaotic way.
– DERIVATIVES **frantically** adv. **franticness** n.
– ORIGIN Middle English *frentik* 'violently mad', from Old French *frenetique* (see **FRENETIC**).

frappé[1] /ˈfrapeɪ/ ■ adj. [postpos.] (of a drink) iced or chilled. ■ n. a drink served with ice or frozen to a slushy consistency.
– ORIGIN from French.

frappé[2] /ˈfrapeɪ/ ■ adj. [postpos.] Ballet (of a position) involving a beating action of the toe of one foot against the ankle of the supporting leg.
– ORIGIN French, 'struck'.

Frascati /fraˈskɑːti/ ■ n. a wine, typically white, produced in the region of Frascati, Italy.

frat ■ n. N. Amer. informal a students' fraternity.

fraternal /frəˈtəːn(ə)l/ ■ adj. 1 of or like a brother or brothers. 2 of or denoting a fraternity. 3 (of twins) developed from separate ova and therefore not identical.
– DERIVATIVES **fraternalism** n. **fraternally** adv.
– ORIGIN Middle English: from Latin *fraternus*, from *frater* 'brother'.

fraternity /frəˈtəːnɪti/ ■ n. (pl. **-ies**) 1 [treated as sing. or pl.] a group of people sharing a common profession or interests. ▸ N. Amer. a male students' society in a university or college. ▸ a religious or masonic society or guild. 2 friendship and mutual support within a group.
– ORIGIN Middle English: from Latin *fraternitas*, from *fraternus* (see **FRATERNAL**).

fraternize /ˈfratənʌɪz/ (also **-ise**) ■ v. (usu. **fraternize with**) be on friendly terms.
– DERIVATIVES **fraternization** (also **-isation**) n.
– ORIGIN C17: from medieval Latin *fraternizare*, from Latin *fraternus* (see **FRATERNAL**).

fratricide /ˈfratrɪsʌɪd/ ■ n. 1 the killing of one's brother or sister. ▸ a person who does this. 2 the accidental killing of one's own forces in war.
– DERIVATIVES **fratricidal** adj.
– ORIGIN C15: from late Latin *fratricidium*, from *frater* 'brother' + *-cidium* (see **-CIDE**).

Frau /fraʊ/ ■ n. a title or form of address for a married or widowed German-speaking woman.
– ORIGIN from German.

fraud /frɔːd/ ■ n. 1 wrongful or criminal deception intended to result in financial or personal gain. 2 a person or thing intended to deceive.
– DERIVATIVES **fraudster** n.
– ORIGIN Middle English: from Latin *fraus*, *fraud-* 'deceit, injury'.

fraudulent /ˈfrɔːdjʊl(ə)nt/ ■ adj. done by or involving fraud. ▸ deceitful or dishonest.
– DERIVATIVES **fraudulence** n. **fraudulently** adv.

fraught /frɔːt/ ■ adj. 1 (**fraught with**) filled with (something undesirable). 2 causing or affected by anxiety or stress.
– ORIGIN Middle English: from obsolete *fraught* 'load with cargo', from Middle Dutch *vrachten*, from *vracht* 'ship's cargo'.

Fräulein /ˈfrɔɪlʌɪn/ ■ n. a title or form of address for an unmarried German-speaking woman, especially a young woman.
– ORIGIN German: diminutive of **FRAU**.

fray[1] ■ v. 1 (of a fabric, rope, or cord) unravel or become worn at the edge. 2 (of a person's nerves or temper) show the effects of strain.
– ORIGIN Middle English: from Old French *freiier*, from Latin *fricare* 'to rub'.

fray[2] ■ n. (**the fray**) a situation of intense competitive activity. ▸ a battle or fight.
– ORIGIN Middle English: from archaic *fray* 'to quarrel', from *affray*, from Anglo-Norman French *afrayer* 'disturb, startle'.

frazzle informal ■ v. 1 [usu. as adj. **frazzled**] cause to feel completely exhausted. 2 cause to shrivel up with burning. ■ n. (**a frazzle**) 1 an exhausted state. 2 a charred or burnt state.
– ORIGIN C19: perhaps a blend of **FRAY**[1] and obsolete *fazle* 'ravel out', of Germanic origin.

freak ■ n. 1 (also **freak of nature**) a person, animal, or plant which is abnormal or deformed. 2 [often as modifier] a very unusual and unexpected event or situation: *a freak storm*. 3 informal a person who is obsessed with a particular activity or interest: *a fitness freak*. ■ v. (usu. **freak out**) informal behave or cause to behave in a wild and irrational way.
– DERIVATIVES **freakish** adj. **freakishly** adv. **freakishness** n.
– ORIGIN C16: prob. from a dialect word.

freaky ■ adj. (**-ier**, **-iest**) informal very odd or strange.
– DERIVATIVES **freakiness** n.

freckle ■ n. a small light brown spot on the skin, often becoming more pronounced through exposure to the sun. ■ v. cover or become covered with freckles.
– DERIVATIVES **freckly** adj.
– ORIGIN Middle English: alteration of dialect *frecken*, from Old Norse *freknur* (pl.).

free ■ adj. (**freer**, **freest**) 1 not under the control or in the power of another. ▸ subject neither to foreign domination nor despotic government: *a free press*. ▸ permitted to take a specified action. 2 not or no longer confined, obstructed, or fixed: *the researchers set the birds free*. ▸ Physics (of power or energy) disengaged or available. ▸ Physics & Chemistry not bound in an atom, molecule, or compound: *free oxygen*. 3 not subject to engagements or obligations. ▸ not occupied or in use. 4 (**free of/from**) not

subject to or affected by: *an area free from weeds.* **5** available without charge. **6** generous or lavish: *she was always free with her money.* ▸ frank or unrestrained. **7** not subject to the normal conventions; improvised: *free jazz.* ▸ (of a translation) conveying only the broad sense; not literal. **8** Nautical (of the wind) blowing from a favourable direction to the side or aft of a vessel. ■ adv. **1** without cost or payment. **2** Nautical with the sheets eased. ■ v. (**frees**, **freed**, **freeing**) **1** make free; release. **2** make available.
–PHRASES **free and easy** informal and relaxed. **a free hand** freedom to act completely at one's own discretion. **free on board** (or **rail**) including delivery without charge to a ship or railway wagon. **a free ride** a situation in which someone benefits without having to make a fair contribution. **the free world** the non-communist countries of the world, as formerly opposed to the Soviet bloc. **make free with** treat without ceremony or proper respect.
–ORIGIN Old English, of Germanic origin.

-free ■ comb. form free of or from: *tax-free.*

free association ■ n. Psychology a psychoanalytic technique for investigation of the unconscious mind, in which words and thoughts are elicited from the subject as they occur, especially in response to key words or images put forward by the analyst.

freebase ■ n. cocaine that has been purified by heating with ether, taken by inhaling the fumes or smoking the residue. ■ v. take (cocaine) in such a way.

freebie ■ n. informal a thing given free of charge.
–ORIGIN 1940S: an arbitrary form from FREE.

freeboard ■ n. the height of a ship's side between the waterline and the deck.

freebooter ■ n. a pirate or lawless adventurer.
–ORIGIN C16: from Dutch *vrijbuiter*, from *vrij* 'free' + *buit* 'booty'.

freeborn ■ adj. not born in slavery.

Free Burgher ■ n. S. African historical an employee of the Dutch East India Company who was released from its service to take up farming. ▸ (also **burgher**) a white male citizen of the Cape, who was not in the service of the Dutch East India Company.

Free Church ■ n. a Christian Church which has dissented or seceded from an established Church.

free climbing ■ n. rock climbing without the use of devices such as pegs placed in the rock, but occasionally using ropes and belays. Compare with AID CLIMBING.
–DERIVATIVES **free climb** n. & v.

freedman ■ n. (pl. **-men**) historical an emancipated slave.

freedom ■ n. **1** the power or right to act, speak, or think freely. **2** the state of being free. ▸ unrestricted use of something. **3** (**freedom from**) exemption or immunity from. **4** the power of self-determination attributed to the will; the quality of being independent of fate or necessity. **5** a special privilege or right of access, especially that of full citizenship of a particular city given to a public figure as an honour: *he accepted the freedom of the City of Durban.*
–ORIGIN Old English.

Freedom Charter ■ n. historical a document drawn up in 1955 setting out guidelines for human rights and the duties of the state in a future democratic South Africa.

Freedom Day ■ n. S. African 27 April, a public holiday commemorating the first democratic election held in South Africa in 1994.

freedom fighter ■ n. a person who takes part in a revolutionary struggle.

freedom song ■ n. a song or chant sung at rallies or demonstrations.

free enterprise ■ n. an economic system in which private business operates in competition and largely free of state control.

free fall ■ n. downward movement under the force of gravity only. ▸ rapid descent or decline without means of stopping. ■ v. (**free-fall**) move under the force of gravity only; fall rapidly.

free flight ■ n. the flight of a spacecraft, rocket, or missile when the engine is not producing thrust.

free state

free-floating ■ adj. **1** not attached to anything and able to move or act freely. **2** Psychiatry (of anxiety) chronic and generalized, without an obvious cause.

free-for-all ■ n. a disorganized or unrestricted situation or event in which everyone may take part, especially a fight or discussion.

free-form ■ adj. not conforming to a regular or formal structure.

freehand ■ adj. & adv. done manually without the aid of instruments such as rulers.

free-handed ■ adj. generous, especially with money.

freehold ■ n. permanent and absolute tenure of land or property with freedom to dispose of it at will. ▸ a piece of land or property held by such tenure.
–DERIVATIVES **freeholder** n.

free kick ■ n. (in soccer and rugby) an unimpeded kick of the stationary ball awarded for a foul or infringement.

freelance /ˈfriːlɑːns/ ■ adj. self-employed and hired to work for different companies on particular assignments. ■ adv. earning one's living in such a way. ■ n. a freelance worker. ■ v. earn one's living as a freelance.
–DERIVATIVES **freelancer** n.
–ORIGIN C19 (orig. denoting a mercenary): from FREE + LANCE.

free-living ■ adj. Biology living freely and independently, not as a parasite or attached to a substrate.

freeloader ■ n. informal a person who takes advantage of others' generosity without giving anything in return.
–DERIVATIVES **freeload** v.

free love ■ n. the idea or practice of having sexual relations without fidelity to one partner.

freely ■ adv. **1** not under the control of another. **2** without restriction or interference. **3** in copious or generous amounts: *she drank freely.* **4** openly and honestly. ▸ willingly and readily.

freeman ■ n. (pl. **-men**) historical a person who is not a slave or serf.

free market ■ n. an economic system in which prices are determined by unrestricted competition between privately owned businesses.
–DERIVATIVES **free marketeer** n.

Freemason ■ n. a member of an international order established for mutual help and fellowship, which holds elaborate secret ceremonies.

freemasonry ■ n. **1** the system and institutions of the Freemasons. **2** instinctive sympathy or fellow feeling between people with something in common.

free pardon ■ n. an unconditional remission of the legal consequences of an offence or conviction.

free port ■ n. **1** a port open to all traders. **2** a port area where goods in transit are exempt from customs duty.

Freepost ■ n. a postal service whereby the cost of postage is paid by the business that receives the letter.

free radical ■ n. Chemistry an uncharged molecule (typically highly reactive) having an unpaired valency electron.

free-range ■ adj. (of livestock or their produce) kept or produced in natural conditions, where the animals have freedom of movement.

free safety ■ n. American Football a defensive back who is usually free from an assignment to cover a particular player on the opposing team.

freesia /ˈfriːzɪə/ ■ n. a small plant with fragrant, colourful, tubular flowers, native to southern Africa. [Genus *Freesia*.]
–ORIGIN named after the German physician Friedrich H. T. Freese (died 1876).

free skating ■ n. a type of figure skating performed to music, in which the skater has some choice of type and sequence of figures.

free-standing ■ adj. not attached to or supported by another structure.

free state ■ n. historical a state of the US in which slavery did not exist.

freestone ■ n. **1** a fine-grained stone which can be cut easily in any direction, in particular a type of sandstone or limestone. **2** a fruit in which the stone is easily separated from the flesh when the fruit is ripe. Contrasted with **CLINGSTONE**.

freestyle ■ n. [often as modifier] a contest, race, or type of sport in which there are few restrictions on the style or technique that competitors employ: *freestyle wrestling.*

free-tailed bat ■ n. a fast-flying insectivorous bat with a projecting tail. [Family Molossidae: many species.]

freethinker ■ n. a person who rejects accepted opinions, especially those concerning religious belief.
– DERIVATIVES **freethinking** n. & adj.

free throw ■ n. Basketball an unimpeded attempt at a goal awarded following a foul or other infringement.

free-to-air ■ adj. denoting television programmes broadcast on standard public or commercial networks, as opposed to satellite, cable, or digital programmes available only to fee-paying viewers.

free trade ■ n. international trade left to its natural course without tariffs, quotas, or other restrictions.

free verse ■ n. poetry that does not rhyme or have a regular rhythm.

free vote ■ n. a parliamentary division in which members vote according to their own beliefs rather than following a party policy.

freeware ■ n. software that is available free of charge.

freeway ■ n. a dual-carriageway main road.

freewheel ■ v. **1** coast on a bicycle, in a car, etc. without applying power through the driving mechanism. **2** [as adj. **freewheeling**] cheerily unconcerned: *the freewheeling drug scene of the sixties.*

free will ■ n. the power of acting without the constraint of necessity or fate; the ability to act at one's own discretion.

freeze ■ v. (past **froze**; past part. **frozen**) **1** (with reference to a liquid) turn or be turned into ice or another solid as a result of extreme cold. ▶ become or cause to become blocked or rigid with ice. **2** be or cause to be very cold. ▶ store at a very low temperature as a means of preservation. **3** become suddenly motionless or paralysed with fear or shock. ▶ (of a computer screen) suddenly become locked. **4** keep or stop at a fixed level or in a fixed state. ▶ prevent (assets) from being used for a period of time. **5** (**freeze someone out**) informal behave in a hostile or obstructive way so as to exclude someone. ■ n. **1** an act of freezing: *a pay freeze.* **2** informal a period of very cold weather: *the big freeze.*
– DERIVATIVES **freezable** adj.
– ORIGIN Old English, of Germanic origin.

freeze-dry ■ v. preserve by rapid freezing followed by subjection to a high vacuum which removes ice by sublimation.

freeze-frame ■ n. **1** a single frame forming a motionless image from a film or videotape. **2** the facility or process of stopping a film or videotape to obtain such a frame.

freezer ■ n. a refrigerated cabinet or room for preserving food at very low temperatures.

freezing ■ adj. **1** below 0°C. ▶ informal very cold. **2** (of fog or rain) consisting of droplets which freeze rapidly on contact with a surface. ■ n. the freezing point of water (0°C).

freezing point ■ n. the temperature at which a liquid turns into a solid when cooled.

freight /freɪt/ ■ n. **1** transport of goods in bulk, especially by truck, train, or ship. ▶ goods transported by freight. ▶ a charge for such transport. ■ v. **1** transport by freight. **2** (**be freighted with**) be laden or burdened with: *each word was freighted with anger.*
– ORIGIN Middle English: from Middle Dutch, Middle Low German *vrecht*, var. of *vracht* 'ship's cargo'.

freightage ■ n. the carrying of goods in bulk. ▶ freight.

freighter ■ n. **1** a large ship or aircraft designed to carry freight. **2** a person who loads, receives, or forwards goods for transport.

French ■ adj. of or relating to France or its people or language. ■ n. the language of France, also used in parts of Belgium, Switzerland, Canada, and some African countries.
– PHRASES (**if you'll**) **excuse** (or **pardon**) **my French** informal used to apologize for swearing.
– DERIVATIVES **Frenchness** n.
– ORIGIN Old English, of Germanic origin, from the base of **FRANK**.

French bean ■ n. chiefly Brit. a tropical American bean plant of which many varieties are commercially cultivated for food. [*Phaseolus vulgaris*.]

French bread ■ n. white bread in a long, crisp loaf.

French Canadian ■ n. a Canadian whose native language is French. ■ adj. of or relating to French Canadians or their language.

French chalk ■ n. a kind of steatite used for marking cloth and removing grease and as a dry lubricant.

French door ■ n. each of a pair of glazed doors in an outside wall, opening on to a garden or balcony.

French dressing ■ n. a salad dressing of vinegar, oil, and seasonings.

French fries ■ pl. n. chiefly N. Amer. potatoes deep-fried in thin strips; chips.

French horn ■ n. a brass instrument with a coiled tube, valves, and a wide bell, played with the right hand in the bell to soften the tone and increase the range of harmonics.

Frenchie ■ n. (pl. **-ies**) variant spelling of **FRENCHY**.

Frenchify ■ v. (**-ies, -ied**) often derogatory make French in form or character.

French kiss ■ n. a kiss with contact between tongues.
– DERIVATIVES **French kissing** n.

French knickers ■ pl. n. women's loose-fitting, wide-legged underpants.

French letter ■ n. Brit. informal, dated a condom.

Frenchman ■ n. (pl. **-men**) a man who is French by birth or descent.

French mustard ■ n. mild mustard mixed with vinegar.

French plait ■ n. a type of plait in which all the hair is gathered tightly and pulled back from the forehead and down the back of the head.

French polish ■ n. shellac polish that produces a high gloss on wood.

French roll ■ n. a hairstyle in which the hair is tucked into a vertical roll down the back of the head.

French seam ■ n. a seam with the raw edges enclosed.

French stick ■ n. a loaf of French bread.

French tickler ■ n. informal a ribbed condom.

French toast ■ n. bread coated in egg and milk and fried.

French window ■ n. a French door.

Frenchwoman ■ n. (pl. **-women**) a woman who is French by birth or descent.

Frenchy (also **Frenchie**) informal, chiefly derogatory ■ adj. French in character. ■ n. (pl. **-ies**) a French person.

frenetic /frəˈnɛtɪk/ ■ adj. fast and energetic in a rather wild and uncontrolled way.
– DERIVATIVES **frenetically** adv. **freneticism** n.
– ORIGIN Middle English: from Greek *phrenitikos*, from *phrenitis* 'delirium'.

frenulum /ˈfriːnjʊləm/ ■ n. Anatomy a small fold or ridge of tissue, in particular a fold of skin beneath the tongue or between the lip and the gum.
– ORIGIN C18: modern Latin, diminutive of Latin *frenum* 'bridle'.

frenum /ˈfriːnəm/ (also **fraenum**) ■ n. another term for **FRENULUM**.
– ORIGIN C18: from Latin, 'bridle'.

frenzy ■ n. (pl. **-ies**) a state or period of uncontrolled excitement or wild behaviour.
– DERIVATIVES **frenzied** adj. **frenziedly** adv.
– ORIGIN Middle English: from medieval Latin *phrenesia*, from Latin *phrenesis*, from Greek *phrēn* 'mind'.

Freon /ˈfriːɒn/ ■ n. trademark an aerosol propellant, refrigerant, or organic solvent consisting of one or more

of a group of chlorofluorocarbons and related compounds.
– ORIGIN 1930s.

frequency ■ n. (pl. **-ies**) **1** the rate at which something occurs over a particular period or in a given sample. **2** the fact or state of being frequent. **3** the rate per second of a vibration constituting a wave, e.g. sound, light, or radio waves. ▸ the particular waveband at which radio signals are broadcast or transmitted.

frequency distribution ■ n. Statistics a mathematical function showing the number of instances in which a variable takes each of its possible values.

frequency modulation (abbrev.: **FM**) ■ n. the modulation of a radio or other wave by variation of its frequency, especially to carry an audio signal.

frequency response ■ n. Electronics the dependence on signal frequency of the output–input ratio of an amplifier or other device.

frequent ■ adj. /ˈfriːkw(ə)nt/ **1** occurring or done many times at short intervals. **2** habitual. ■ v. /frɪˈkwɛnt/ visit (a place) often or habitually.
– DERIVATIVES **frequenter** n. **frequently** adv.
– ORIGIN Middle English ('profuse'): from Latin *frequens* 'crowded, frequent'.

frequentative /frɪˈkwɛntətɪv/ Grammar ■ adj. (of a verb or verbal form) expressing frequent repetition or intensity of action. ■ n. a frequentative form.

fresco /ˈfrɛskəʊ/ ■ n. (pl. **-oes** or **-os**) a type of painting done in watercolour on wet plaster on a wall or ceiling, in which the colours penetrate the plaster and become fixed as it dries.
– DERIVATIVES **frescoed** adj.
– ORIGIN C16: Italian, 'cool, fresh'; first recorded in the phr. *in fresco*, representing Italian *affresco*, *al fresco* 'on the fresh (plaster)'.

fresh ■ adj. **1** not previously known or used; new or different. **2** (of food) recently made or obtained; not tinned, frozen, or otherwise preserved. **3** full of energy and vigour. ▸ (of a colour or a person's complexion) bright or healthy in appearance. **4** (of water) not salty. **5** (of the wind) cool and fairly strong. ▸ pleasantly clean, invigorating, and cool: *fresh air*. **6** (**fresh from/out of**) newly come from; having just had (a particular experience): *we were fresh out of art school*. **7** informal presumptuous or impudent, especially sexually. **8** attractively youthful and inexperienced. ■ adv. newly; recently.
– PHRASES **be fresh out of** informal have just run out of.
– DERIVATIVES **freshly** adv. **freshness** n.
– ORIGIN Old English *fersc* 'not salt, fit for drinking', superseded in Middle English by forms from Old French *freis*, *fresche*; both of Germanic origin.

freshen ■ v. **1** make or become fresh. ▸ (**freshen up**) refresh oneself by washing oneself or changing one's clothes. **2** (of wind) become stronger and colder.

fresher ■ n. informal, chiefly Brit. a first-year student at college or university.

freshet /ˈfrɛʃɪt/ ■ n. the flood of a river from heavy rain or melted snow. ▸ a rush of fresh water flowing into the sea.
– ORIGIN C16: prob. from Old French *freschete*, diminutive of *freis* 'fresh'.

freshman ■ n. (pl. **-men**) a first-year student at university or (N. Amer.) at high school.

freshwater ■ adj. of or found in fresh water; not of the sea.

fresnel lens /ˈfreɪnɛl/ ■ n. Photography a flat lens made of a number of concentric rings, to reduce spherical aberration.
– ORIGIN C19: named after the French physicist and civil engineer Augustin J. Fresnel.

fret¹ ■ v. (**fretted**, **fretting**) **1** be constantly or visibly anxious. **2** gradually wear away by rubbing or gnawing. **3** flow or move in small waves. ■ n. a state of anxiety.
– ORIGIN Old English *fretan* 'devour, consume', of Germanic origin.

fret² ■ n. **1** Architecture a repeating ornamental design of vertical and horizontal lines. **2** Heraldry a device of narrow diagonal bands interlaced through a diamond.
■ v. (**fretted**, **fretting**) [usu. as adj. **fretted**] decorate with fretwork.

465

– ORIGIN Middle English: from Old French *frete* 'trelliswork' and *freter* (v.).

fret³ ■ n. each of a sequence of ridges on the fingerboard of some stringed instruments such as the guitar, used for fixing the positions of the fingers to produce the desired notes. ■ v. (**fretted**, **fretting**) [often as adj. **fretted**] **1** provide with frets. **2** play (a note) while pressing against a fret.
– ORIGIN C16.

fretful ■ adj. anxious or irritated.
– DERIVATIVES **fretfully** adv. **fretfulness** n.

fretsaw ■ n. a saw with a narrow blade stretched vertically on a frame, for cutting designs in thin wood or metal.

fretwork ■ n. ornamental design, typically openwork, done with a fretsaw.

Freudian ■ adj. relating to or influenced by Sigmund Freud (1856–1939) and his methods of psychoanalysis, especially with reference to the importance of sexuality in human behaviour. ▸ susceptible to analysis in terms of unconscious thoughts or desires: *a Freudian slip*. ■ n. a follower of Freud or his methods.
– DERIVATIVES **Freudianism** n.

Fri. ■ abbrev. Friday.

friable /ˈfrʌɪəb(ə)l/ ■ adj. easily crumbled.
– DERIVATIVES **friability** n. **friableness** n.
– ORIGIN C16: from Latin *friabilis*, from *friare* 'to crumble'.

friar ■ n. a member of any of certain religious orders of men, especially the Augustinians, Carmelites, Dominicans, and Franciscans.
– ORIGIN Middle English: from Old French *frere*, from Latin *frater* 'brother'.

friar's balsam ■ n. a solution containing benzoin in alcohol, used chiefly as an inhalant.

friary ■ n. (pl. **-ies**) a building or community occupied by friars.

fricassée /ˈfrɪkəsiː, ˌfrɪkəˈsiː/ ■ n. a dish of stewed or fried pieces of meat served in a thick white sauce.
– ORIGIN French: from *fricasser* 'cut up and cook in a sauce'.

fricative /ˈfrɪkətɪv/ Phonetics ■ adj. denoting a type of consonant (e.g. *f* and *th*) made by the friction of breath in a narrow opening. ■ n. a fricative consonant.
– ORIGIN C19: from modern Latin *fricativus*, from Latin *fricare* 'to rub'.

friction ■ n. **1** the resistance that one surface or object encounters when moving over another. ▸ the action of one surface or object rubbing against another. **2** conflict or disagreement.
– DERIVATIVES **frictional** adj. **frictionless** adj.
– ORIGIN C16: from Latin *frictio(n-)*, from *fricare* 'to rub'.

frictional unemployment ■ n. Economics unemployment due to people being in the process of moving between jobs.

Friday ■ n. the day of the week before Saturday and following Thursday. ■ adv. on Friday: *we'll go Friday*. ▸ (**Fridays**) on Fridays; each Friday.
– ORIGIN Old English *Frīgedæg*, named after the Germanic goddess *Frigga*; translation of late Latin *Veneris dies* 'day of the planet Venus'.

fridge ■ n. short for REFRIGERATOR.

fridge-freezer ■ n. an upright unit comprising a separate refrigerator and freezer.

fridge tart ■ n. chiefly S. African a sweet tart, made without pastry, that has to set in a refrigerator.

fried past and past participle of FRY¹. ■ adj. (of food) cooked in hot fat or oil.

friend ■ n. **1** a person with whom one has a bond of mutual affection, typically one exclusive of sexual or family relations. ▸ used in polite address to an acquaintance or stranger. **2** a familiar or helpful thing. **3** a person who supports a particular cause or organization: *the Friends of the Library raise money for new books*. **4** (in battle) an ally. **5** (**Friend**) a member of the Religious Society of Friends; a Quaker.
– PHRASES **be** (or **make**) **friends with** be (or become) on friendly terms with. **a friend at court** a person in a

friendly

position to use their influence on one's behalf.
- DERIVATIVES **friendless** adj. **friendship** n.
- ORIGIN Old English, of Germanic origin.

friendly ■ adj. (**-ier**, **-iest**) **1** kind and pleasant; of or like a friend. **2** Military of, belonging to, or allied with one's own forces. **3** favourable or serviceable. **4** [in combination] not harmful to a specified thing: *an environment-friendly policy*. ■ n. (pl. **-ies**) a game or match not forming part of a serious competition.
- DERIVATIVES **friendlily** adv. **friendliness** n.

friendly fire ■ n. Military weapon fire coming from one's own side that causes accidental injury or death to one's own forces.

friendly society ■ n. a mutual association providing sickness benefits, life assurance, and pensions.

frier ■ n. variant spelling of FRYER.

Friesian /ˈfriːʒ(ə)n/ ■ n. British term for FRIESLAND.

Friesland ■ n. an animal of a black-and-white breed of dairy cattle originally from Friesland in the Netherlands.

frieze /friːz/ ■ n. **1** a broad horizontal band of sculpted or painted decoration. **2** Architecture the part of an entablature between the architrave and the cornice.
- ORIGIN C16: from French *frise*, from medieval Latin *frisium*, var. of *frigium*, from Latin *Phrygium (opus)* '(work) of Phrygia'.

frig ■ v. (**frigged**, **frigging**) vulgar slang have sexual intercourse with. ▶ masturbate.
- ORIGIN Middle English (orig. 'move restlessly', later 'rub, chafe').

frigate /ˈfrɪɡət/ ■ n. a warship with a mixed armament, generally lighter than a destroyer. ▶ historical a sailing warship of a size and armament just below that of a ship of the line.
- ORIGIN C16: from French *frégate*, from Italian *fregata*.

frigate bird ■ n. a predatory tropical seabird with dark plumage, long narrow wings, a deeply forked tail, and a long hooked bill. [Genus *Fregata*: five species.]

fright ■ n. a sudden intense feeling of fear. ▶ an experience causing fright; a shock.
- PHRASES **look a fright** informal look ridiculous or grotesque. **take fright** suddenly become frightened.
- ORIGIN Old English, of Germanic origin.

frighten ■ v. cause to be afraid. ▶ (**frighten someone off**) drive someone away by fear.
- DERIVATIVES **frightened** adj. **frightening** adj. **frighteningly** adv.

frightener ■ n. a frightening person or thing.
- PHRASES **put the frighteners on** Brit. informal threaten or intimidate (someone).

frightful ■ adj. **1** very unpleasant, serious, or shocking. **2** informal terrible; awful: *her hair was a frightful mess*.
- DERIVATIVES **frightfully** adv.

frigid /ˈfrɪdʒɪd/ ■ adj. **1** very cold. **2** (of a woman) unable to be sexually responsive or aroused. **3** stiff or formal in behaviour or style.
- DERIVATIVES **frigidity** n. **frigidly** adv.
- ORIGIN Middle English: from Latin *frigidus*, from *frigere* 'be cold'.

frigid zone ■ n. each of the two areas of the earth respectively north of the Arctic Circle and south of the Antarctic Circle.

frikkadel ■ n. S. African a meatball.
- ORIGIN Afrikaans: from French *fricandeau*, denoting sliced meat fried and served with a sauce.

frill ■ n. **1** a strip of gathered or pleated material sewn by one side only on to a garment or piece of material as a decorative edging or ornament. **2** a frill-like fringe of feathers, hair, skin, etc. on a bird, reptile, or other animal. **3** (**frills**) unnecessary extra features or embellishments: *a comfortable flat with no frills*.
- DERIVATIVES **frilled** adj. **frilliness** n. **frilly** adj.
- ORIGIN C16: from or rel. to Flemish *frul*.

fringe ■ n. **1** a border of threads, tassels, or twists, used to edge clothing or material. **2** the front part of someone's hair, cut so as to hang over the forehead. ▶ a natural border of hair or fibres in an animal or plant. **3** the outer or marginal part of something. ▶ [as modifier] not part of the mainstream; unconventional: *fringe theatre*. **4** a band of contrasting brightness or darkness produced by diffraction or interference of light. ▶ a strip of false colour in an optical image. ■ v. provide with or form a fringe.
- DERIVATIVES **fringeless** adj. **fringing** n.
- ORIGIN Middle English: from Old French *frenge*, from late Latin *fimbria*, earlier a pl. noun meaning 'fibres, shreds'.

fringe benefit ■ n. an additional benefit, especially a benefit given to an employee, such as a company car or private health care.

fringing reef ■ n. a coral reef that lies close to the shore.

frippery /ˈfrɪp(ə)ri/ ■ n. (pl. **-ies**) showy or unnecessary ornament.
- ORIGIN C16 (denoting second-hand clothes): from Old French *freperie*, from *frepe* 'rag'.

frisbee /ˈfrɪzbi/ ■ n. trademark a concave plastic disc designed for skimming through the air as an outdoor game.
- ORIGIN 1950s: said to be named after the pie tins of the *Frisbie* bakery (Bridgeport, Connecticut).

frisée /ˈfriːzeɪ/ ■ n. a kind of endive with curled leaves.
- ORIGIN French: from *chicorée frisée* 'curly endive'.

Frisian /ˈfriːzɪən, ˈfriːʒ(ə)n, ˈfrɪ-/ ■ n. **1** a native or inhabitant of Frisia or Friesland in the Netherlands. **2** the Germanic language spoken in northern parts of the Netherlands and adjacent islands.

frisk ■ v. **1** (of a police officer or official) pass the hands over (someone) in a search for hidden weapons or drugs. **2** (of an animal or person) skip or move playfully; frolic.
- DERIVATIVES **frisker** n.
- ORIGIN C16: from obsolete *frisk* 'lively', from Old French *frisque* 'alert, lively'.

frisky ■ adj. (**-ier**, **-iest**) playful and full of energy.
- DERIVATIVES **friskily** adv. **friskiness** n.

frisson /ˈfriːsɔ̃, ˈfrɪsɒn/ ■ n. a strong feeling of excitement or fear; a thrill.
- ORIGIN C18: French.

frit ■ n. a mixture of silica and fluxes which is fused at high temperature to make glass. ▶ a similar calcined and pulverized mixture used to make soft-paste porcelain or ceramic glazes. ■ v. (**fritted**, **fritting**) make into frit.
- ORIGIN C17: from Italian *fritta*, from *friggere* 'to fry'.

fritter[1] ■ v. (often **fritter something away**) waste time, money, or energy on trifling matters.
- ORIGIN C18: based on obsolete *fitter* 'break into fragments'.

fritter[2] ■ n. a piece of fruit, vegetable, or meat that is coated in batter and deep-fried.
- ORIGIN Middle English: from Old French *friture*, from Latin *frigere* (see FRY[1]).

fritto misto /ˌfriːtəʊ ˈmiːstəʊ/ ■ n. a dish of various foods, typically seafood, deep-fried in batter.
- ORIGIN Italian, 'mixed fry'.

Fritz ■ n. Brit. informal, dated a German or the German people collectively, especially a soldier in the First World War.
- ORIGIN abbrev. of the German given name *Friedrich*.

frivolous ■ adj. not having any serious purpose or value. ▶ (of a person) carefree and superficial.
- DERIVATIVES **frivolity** n. **frivolously** adv. **frivolousness** n.
- ORIGIN Middle English: from Latin *frivolus* 'silly, trifling'.

frizz /frɪz/ ■ v. (of hair) form into a mass of small, tight curls. ■ n. a mass of tightly curled hair.
- ORIGIN Middle English: from French *friser*.

frizzle[1] ■ v. fry until crisp or burnt.
- ORIGIN C18: from FRY[1], prob. influenced by SIZZLE.

frizzle[2] ■ v. form (hair) into tight curls. ■ n. a tight curl in hair.
- DERIVATIVES **frizzly** adj.
- ORIGIN C16: from FRIZZ.

frizzy ■ adj. (**-ier**, **-iest**) formed of a mass of small, tight, wiry curls.
- DERIVATIVES **frizziness** n.

fro ■ adv. see TO AND FRO.
- ORIGIN Middle English: from Old Norse *frá* (see FROM).

frock ■ n. **1** a woman's or girl's dress. **2** a loose outer garment, in particular a long gown with flowing sleeves worn by monks, priests, or clergy.

- DERIVATIVES **frocked** adj.
- ORIGIN Middle English: from Old French *froc*, of Germanic origin.

frock coat ■ n. a man's double-breasted, long-skirted coat, now worn chiefly on formal occasions.

frog[1] ■ n. **1** a tailless amphibian with a short squat body, moist smooth skin, and very long hind legs for leaping. [Many species, chiefly in the family Ranidae.] **2** (**Frog**) derogatory a French person.
- PHRASES **have a frog in one's throat** informal lose one's voice or find it hard to speak because of hoarseness.
- DERIVATIVES **froggy** adj.
- ORIGIN Old English, of Germanic origin. Its application to the French (late 18th century) is partly alliterative, partly from the reputation of the French for eating frogs' legs.

frog[2] ■ n. **1** a thing used to hold or fasten something. **2** an ornamental coat fastener consisting of a spindle-shaped button and a loop. **3** an attachment to a belt for holding a sword or bayonet. **4** a perforated or spiked device for holding the stems of flowers in an arrangement.
- DERIVATIVES **frogged** adj. **frogging** n.
- ORIGIN C18: perhaps a use of **FROG**[1], influenced by Italian *forchetta* or French *fourchette* 'small fork', because of the shape.

frog[3] ■ n. an elastic horny pad growing in the sole of a horse's hoof, helping to absorb the shock when the hoof hits the ground.
- ORIGIN C17: perhaps from **FROG**[1]; perhaps also influenced by Italian *forchetta* or French *fourchette* (see **FROG**[2]).

frogfish ■ n. (pl. same or **-fishes**) an anglerfish that typically lives on the seabed, where its warty skin provides camouflage. [*Antennaria* and other genera.]

froghopper ■ n. a jumping, plant-sucking bug, the larva of which produces a whitish froth on leaves and plant stems. [Family Cercopidae: many species.]

frogman ■ n. (pl. **-men**) a diver equipped with a rubber suit, flippers, and breathing equipment for working under water.

frogmarch ■ v. force (someone) to walk forward by holding and pinning their arms from behind.

frogspawn ■ n. a mass of frogs' eggs surrounded by transparent jelly.

frolic ■ v. (**frolicked**, **frolicking**) play or move about in a cheerful and lively way. ■ n. a playful action or movement.
- ORIGIN C16: from Dutch *vrolijk* 'merry, cheerful'.

frolicsome ■ adj. lively and playful.
- DERIVATIVES **frolicsomeness** n.

from ■ prep. **1** indicating the point in space or time at which a journey, process, or action starts. **2** indicating source or provenance. ▸ indicating the raw material of manufacture. **3** indicating the starting point of a specified range. **4** indicating separation, removal, or prevention. **5** indicating a cause. **6** indicating a distinction.
- PHRASES **from day to day** (or **hour to hour** etc.) daily (or hourly etc.). **from time to time** occasionally.
- ORIGIN Old English, of Germanic origin; rel. to Old Norse *frá* (see **FRO**).

fromage blanc /ˌfrɒmɑːʒ ˈblɒ̃/ ■ n. a type of soft French cheese having a creamy sour taste.
- ORIGIN French, 'white cheese'.

fromage frais /ˌfrɒmɑːʒ ˈfreɪ/ ■ n. a type of smooth soft fresh cheese.
- ORIGIN French, 'fresh cheese'.

frond ■ n. the leaf or leaf-like part of a palm, fern, or similar plant.
- DERIVATIVES **frondage** n. **fronded** adj.
- ORIGIN C18: from Latin *frons, frond-* 'leaf'.

frons /frɒnz/ ■ n. (pl. **frontes**) Zoology the forehead or equivalent part of an animal, especially the middle part of an insect's face between the eyes and above the clypeus.
- ORIGIN C19: from Latin, 'front, forehead'.

front ■ n. **1** the side or part of an object that presents itself to view or that is normally seen or used first. ▸ the position directly ahead. ▸ the forward-facing part of a person's body. **2** the foremost line or part of an armed force; the furthest position that an army has reached. ▸ [often in names] an organized political group: *the Patriotic Front*. **3** Meteorology the boundary of an advancing mass of air, in particular the leading edge (warm front) or trailing edge (cold front) of the warm sector of a low-pressure system. **4** a particular situation or sphere of operation: *good news on the jobs front*. **5** a deceptive appearance or mode of behaviour assumed by someone to conceal truth or genuine feelings. ▸ a person or organization serving as a cover for subversive or deceptive activities. **6** boldness and confidence of manner. ■ adj. **1** of or at the front. **2** Phonetics (of a vowel sound) formed by raising the tongue towards the hard palate. ■ v. **1** have the front facing towards. ▸ place or be placed at the front of. **2** (usu. **be fronted**) provide with a front or facing. **3** lead or be at the forefront of. ▸ present or host (a television or radio programme). **4** act as a front for. **5** Phonetics articulate (a vowel sound) with the tongue further forward.
- PHRASES **front of house** the parts of a theatre in front of the proscenium arch. ▸ the business of a theatre that concerns the audience, such as ticket sales. **in front 1** in a position just ahead or further forward. **2** on the front part or side. **3** (**in front of**) in the presence of. **out front** chiefly N. Amer. at or to the front; in front.
- DERIVATIVES **frontless** adj. **frontmost** adj.
- ORIGIN Middle English: from Latin *frons, front-* 'forehead, front'.

frontage ■ n. **1** the facade of a building. **2** a strip or extent of land abutting on a street or waterway.

frontal ■ adj. **1** of or at the front. **2** of or relating to the forehead or front part of the skull: *the frontal sinuses*. ■ n. a decorative cloth for covering the front of an altar.
- DERIVATIVES **frontally** adv.

frontal bone ■ n. the bone which forms the front part of the skull and the upper part of the eye sockets.

frontal lobe ■ n. each of the paired lobes of the brain lying immediately behind the forehead, including areas concerned with behaviour, learning, personality, and voluntary movement.

front bench ■ n. the foremost seats in the South African parliament, the British House of Commons, or a similar legislative chamber, occupied by the members of the cabinet and shadow cabinet.
- DERIVATIVES **frontbencher** n.

front-end ■ adj. **1** of or relating to the front, especially of a vehicle. **2** informal (of money) paid or charged at the beginning of a transaction. **3** Computing (of a device or program) directly accessed by the user and allowing access to further devices or programs. ■ n. Computing the front-end part of a computer or program.

front-fanged ■ adj. denoting a snake (such as a cobra or viper) in which the front pair of teeth have grooves to conduct the venom. Compare with **BACK-FANGED**.

frontier /ˈfrʌntɪə, frʌnˈtɪə/ ■ n. **1** a border separating two countries. **2** the extreme limit of settled land beyond which lies wilderness. ▸ (**the Frontier**) S. African historical the eastern districts of the Cape Colony which marked the boundary between the area controlled by Xhosa people and that under colonial rule. **3** the extreme limit of understanding or achievement in a particular area.
- DERIVATIVES **frontierless** adj.
- ORIGIN Middle English: from Old French *frontiere*, from Latin *frons* 'front'.

frontiersman (or **frontierswoman**) ■ n. (pl. **-men** or **-women**) a man (or woman) living in the region of a frontier, especially that between settled and unsettled country.

frontier war ■ n. **1** a war fought on the boundary between two regions, especially one prompted by colonization. **2** (**Frontier War** or **Cape Frontier War**) any of nine wars (1779–1878) fought in the eastern areas of the Cape Colony between its forces and the (mainly Xhosa) local inhabitants.

fronting ■ n. S. African the practice of misrepresenting the level of inclusion of black people in the ownership or management of a business in order to give the appearance of compliance with black economic empowerment legislation.

frontispiece /ˈfrʌntɪspiːs/ ■ n. **1** an illustration facing the title page of a book. **2** Architecture the principal face of a building. ▸ a decorated entrance. ▸ a pediment over a door or window.
- ORIGIN C16: from late Latin *frontispicium* 'facade', from

front line

Latin *frons* 'front' + *specere* 'to look'.

front line ■ n. the military line or part of an army that is closest to the enemy.

frontline state ■ n. historical any country sharing a border with South Africa or actively supporting liberation movements in their struggle against apartheid.

frontman ■ n. (pl. **-men**) a person who acts as a front, in particular the leader of a band or the representative of an illegal organization.

front office ■ n. chiefly N. Amer. the main administrative office of a business or other organization.

front-runner ■ n. the contestant that is leading in a race or other competition. ▸ an athlete or horse that runs best when in the front of the field.

front-running ■ n. Stock Exchange the practice by market-makers of dealing on advance information provided by their brokers and investment analysts, before their clients have been given the information.

front-wheel drive ■ n. a transmission system that provides power to the front wheels of a motor vehicle.

frost ■ n. **1** a deposit of small white ice crystals formed on the ground or other surfaces when the temperature falls below freezing. **2** a period of cold weather when frost forms. ■ v. **1** cover or be covered with or as if with frost; freeze. **2** N. Amer. decorate with icing.
– PHRASES **degrees of frost** chiefly Brit. degrees below freezing point.
– ORIGIN Old English, of Germanic origin.

frostbite ■ n. injury to body tissues, especially the nose, fingers, or toes, caused by exposure to extreme cold.

frosted ■ adj. **1** covered with or as if with frost. **2** (of glass) having a translucent textured surface so that it is difficult to see through.

frost heave ■ n. the uplift of soil or other surface deposits due to expansion of groundwater on freezing.
– DERIVATIVES **frost heaving** n.

frosting ■ n. **1** N. Amer. icing. **2** a roughened matt finish on otherwise shiny material such as glass or steel.

frosty ■ adj. (**-ier**, **-iest**) **1** (of the weather) very cold with frost forming on surfaces. **2** cold and unfriendly.
– DERIVATIVES **frostily** adv. **frostiness** n.

froth ■ n. **1** a mass of small bubbles in liquid caused by agitation, fermentation, or salivating. ▸ impure matter that rises to the surface of liquid. **2** worthless or insubstantial talk, ideas, or activities. ■ v. form, produce, or contain froth.
– DERIVATIVES **frothily** adv. **frothy** adj.
– ORIGIN Middle English: from Old Norse *frotha*, *frauth*.

frothy ■ n. (pl. **-ies**) S. African informal a fit of temper; a tizzy.
– PHRASES **have** (**or throw**) **a frothy** have a tantrum.

frottage /ˈfrɒtɑːʒ/ ■ n. **1** Art the technique or process of taking a rubbing from an uneven surface to form the basis of a work of art. **2** the practice of rubbing against the clothed body of another person in a crowd as a means of obtaining sexual gratification.
– DERIVATIVES **frotteur** n. (pl. same). **frotteurism** n.
– ORIGIN 1930s: French, 'rubbing, friction', from *frotter* 'to rub'.

Froude number /fruːd/ ■ n. a dimensionless number used in hydrodynamics to indicate how well a particular model works in relation to a real system.
– ORIGIN C19: named after the English civil engineer William Froude (1810–79).

frou-frou /ˈfruːfruː/ ■ n. [often as modifier] frills or other ornamentation, particularly on women's clothes: *a little frou-frou skirt*.
– ORIGIN C19: from French, imitative.

froward /ˈfrəʊəd/ ■ adj. archaic (of a person) difficult to deal with; contrary.
– DERIVATIVES **frowardly** adv. **frowardness** n.
– ORIGIN Old English *frāward* 'leading away from, away', from Old Norse *frá* (see **FRO**, **FROM**).

frown ■ v. furrow one's brows in an expression indicating disapproval, displeasure, or concentration. ▸ (**frown on/upon**) disapprove of. ■ n. an expression of this type.

– DERIVATIVES **frowning** adj. **frowningly** adv.
– ORIGIN Middle English: from Old French, from *froigne* 'surly look', of Celtic origin.

frowst /fraʊst/ informal, chiefly Brit. ■ n. a warm stuffy atmosphere in a room. ■ v. lounge about in such an atmosphere.

frowsty ■ adj. (**-ier**, **-iest**) Brit. having a stale, warm, and stuffy atmosphere.
– DERIVATIVES **frowstiness** n.
– ORIGIN C19 (orig. dialect): var. of **FROWZY**.

frowzy /ˈfraʊzi/ (also **frowsy**) ■ adj. (**-ier**, **-iest**) scruffy, dingy, and neglected in appearance.
– DERIVATIVES **frowziness** n.
– ORIGIN C17 (orig. dialect).

froze past of **FREEZE**.

frozen past participle of **FREEZE**.

frozen shoulder ■ n. Medicine chronic painful stiffness of the shoulder joint.

fructification /ˌfrʌktɪfɪˈkeɪʃ(ə)n/ ■ n. **1** the process of fructifying. **2** Botany a spore-bearing or fruiting structure, especially in a fungus.

fructify /ˈfrʌktɪfʌɪ/ ■ v. (**-ies**, **-ied**) **1** formal make or become fruitful. **2** bear fruit.
– ORIGIN Middle English: from Latin *fructificare*, from *fructus* 'fruit'.

fructose /ˈfrʌktəʊz, -s/ ■ n. Chemistry a sugar of the hexose class found especially in honey and fruit.
– ORIGIN C19: from Latin *fructus* 'fruit'.

fructuous /ˈfrʌktjʊəs/ ■ adj. formal full of or producing a great deal of fruit.
– ORIGIN Middle English: from Latin *fructuosus*, from *fructus* 'fruit'.

frug ■ n. a vigorous dance to pop music, popular in the mid 1960s. ■ v. (**frugged**, **frugging**) perform such a dance.

frugal /ˈfruːɡ(ə)l/ ■ adj. sparing or economical as regards money or food.
– DERIVATIVES **frugality** n. **frugally** adv.
– ORIGIN C16: from Latin *frugalis*, from *frugi* 'economical, thrifty', from *frux* 'fruit'.

frugivore /ˈfruːdʒɪvɔː/ ■ n. Zoology an animal that feeds on fruit.
– DERIVATIVES **frugivorous** adj.
– ORIGIN C20: from Latin *frux*, *frug-* 'fruit' + *-vore* (see **-VOROUS**).

fruit ■ n. **1** the sweet and fleshy product of a tree or other plant that contains seed and can be eaten as food. ▸ Botany the seed-bearing structure of a plant, e.g. an acorn.
▸ archaic or poetic/literary natural produce that can be used for food: *the fruits of the earth*. **2** the result or reward of work or activity. **3** archaic offspring. **4** informal, derogatory, chiefly N. Amer. a male homosexual. ■ v. produce fruit.
– PHRASES **bear fruit** have good results. **in fruit** at the stage of producing fruit.
– ORIGIN Middle English: from Latin *fructus* 'enjoyment of produce, harvest', from *frui* 'enjoy', rel. to *fruges* 'fruits of the earth', pl. of *frux* 'fruit'.

fruitarian ■ n. a person who eats only fruit.
– DERIVATIVES **fruitarianism** n.

fruit bat ■ n. a large bat which feeds chiefly on fruit or nectar, found mainly in the Old World tropics. [Family Pteropodidae: numerous species.]

fruit body ■ n. another term for **FRUITING BODY**.

fruitcake ■ n. **1** a cake containing dried fruit and nuts. **2** informal an eccentric or mad person.

fruit cocktail ■ n. a finely chopped fruit salad, commercially produced in tins.

fruit cup ■ n. **1** chiefly Brit. a drink consisting of a mixture of fruit juices. **2** N. Amer. a fruit salad.

fruit drop ■ n. the shedding of unripe fruit from a tree.

fruiterer ■ n. a retailer of fruit.
– ORIGIN Middle English: from *fruiter*.

fruit fly ■ n. a small fly which feeds on fruit in both its adult and larval stages. [Families Drosophilidae and Tephritidae: many species.]

fruitful ■ adj. **1** producing much fruit; fertile. **2** producing good results; productive.
– DERIVATIVES **fruitfully** adv. **fruitfulness** n.

fruiting body ■ n. Botany the spore-producing organ of a fungus, often seen as a toadstool.

fruition /fruˈɪʃ(ə)n/ ■ n. **1** the realization or fulfilment of a plan or project. **2** poetic/literary the state or action of producing fruit.
– ORIGIN Middle English ('enjoyment'): from late Latin *fruitio(n-)*, from *frui* (see FRUIT).

fruitless ■ adj. **1** failing to achieve the desired results; unproductive. **2** not producing fruit.
– DERIVATIVES **fruitlessly** adv. **fruitlessness** n.

fruitlet ■ n. an immature or small fruit.

fruit machine ■ n. another term for SLOT MACHINE (in sense 1).

fruit salad ■ n. a mixture of different types of chopped fruit served in syrup or juice.

fruit sugar ■ n. another term for FRUCTOSE.

fruity ■ adj. (**-ier**, **-iest**) **1** of, resembling, or containing fruit. **2** (of a voice) mellow, deep, and rich. ▸ informal, chiefly Brit. sexually suggestive. **3** informal, chiefly US eccentric or crazy. **4** informal, derogatory, chiefly N. Amer. relating to or associated with homosexuals.
– DERIVATIVES **fruitily** adv. **fruitiness** n.

frump ■ n. an unattractive woman who wears dowdy old-fashioned clothes.
– DERIVATIVES **frumpily** adv. **frumpiness** n. **frumpish** adj. **frumpishly** adv. **frumpy** adj.
– ORIGIN C16: prob. a contraction of Middle English *frumple* 'wrinkle', from Middle Dutch *verrompelen*.

frusemide /ˈfruːsəmʌɪd/ (chiefly US also **furosemide**) ■ n. Medicine a synthetic compound with a strong diuretic action, used especially in the treatment of oedema.
– ORIGIN 1960s: from *fru-* (alteration of *fur(yl)*, denoting a radical derived from furan) + *sem-* (of unknown origin) + -IDE.

frustrate ■ v. **1** prevent (a plan or action) from progressing, succeeding, or being fulfilled. ▸ prevent (someone) from doing or achieving something. **2** cause to feel dissatisfied or unfulfilled.
– DERIVATIVES **frustrating** adj. **frustratingly** adv. **frustration** n.
– ORIGIN Middle English: from Latin *frustrare* 'disappoint', from *frustra* 'in vain'.

frustrated ■ adj. **1** feeling dissatisfaction and a lack of fulfilment. **2** prevented from progressing, succeeding, or being fulfilled: *a frustrated attempt*.
– DERIVATIVES **frustratedly** adv.

fruticose /ˈfruːtɪkəʊz, -s/ ■ adj. Botany (of a lichen) having upright or pendulous branches.
– ORIGIN C17: from Latin *fruticosus*, from *frutex* 'bush, shrub'.

fry[1] ■ v. (**-ies**, **-ied**) **1** cook or be cooked in hot fat or oil. **2** informal (of a person) burn or overheat. ■ n. (pl. **-ies**) a fried dish or meal. ▸ (**fries**) N. Amer. short for FRENCH FRIES.
– ORIGIN Middle English: from Old French *frire*, from Latin *frigere*.

fry[2] ■ pl. n. young fish, especially when newly hatched. ▸ the young of other animals produced in large numbers, such as frogs.
– ORIGIN Middle English: from Old Norse *frjó*.

fryer (also **frier**) ■ n. a large, deep container for frying food.

frying pan (N. Amer. also **frypan**) ■ n. a shallow pan with a long handle, used for frying food.
– PHRASES **out of the frying pan into the fire** from a bad situation to one that is worse.

fry-up ■ n. Brit. informal a dish or meal of fried food.

FSH ■ abbrev. follicle-stimulating hormone.

f-stop ■ n. Photography a camera setting corresponding to a particular f-number.

Ft ■ abbrev. Fort.

ft ■ abbrev. foot or feet.

FTC ■ abbrev. (in the US) Federal Trade Commission.

FTP ■ abbrev. Computing file transfer protocol, a standard for the exchange of program and data files across a network.

FTSE index (also **FT index**) ■ n. a figure (published by the *Financial Times*) indicating the relative prices of shares on the London Stock Exchange.
– ORIGIN abbrev. of *Financial Times Stock Exchange*.

fugal

fubsy /ˈfʌbzi/ ■ adj. (**-ier**, **-iest**) Brit. informal fat and squat.
– ORIGIN C18: from dialect *fubs* 'small fat person', perhaps a blend of FAT and CHUB.

fuchsia /ˈfjuːʃə/ ■ n. **1** an ornamental shrub native to America and New Zealand, with drooping tubular flowers that are typically of two contrasting colours. [Genus *Fuchsia*.] **2** a vivid purplish-red colour like that of a typical fuchsia flower.
– ORIGIN named in honour of the C16 German botanist Leonhard *Fuchs*.

fuchsin /ˈfuːksiːn/ (also **fuchsine**) ■ n. a deep red synthetic dye used as a biological stain and disinfectant.
– ORIGIN C19: from German *Fuchs* 'fox', translating French *Renard* (the name of the chemical company which first produced fuchsin commercially).

fuck vulgar slang ■ v. **1** have sexual intercourse with. **2** damage or ruin. ■ n. an act of sexual intercourse. ■ exclam. a strong expression of annoyance, contempt, or impatience.
– PHRASES **fuck all** absolutely nothing.
– PHRASAL VERBS **fuck about** (or **around**) spend time doing unimportant or trivial things. **fuck someone around** (or **about**) waste someone's time. **fuck off** go away. **fuck someone up** damage or confuse someone emotionally. **fuck something up** (or **fuck up**) do something badly or ineptly.
– DERIVATIVES **fuckable** adj. **fucker** n.
– ORIGIN C16: of Germanic origin.

fucus /ˈfjuːkəs/ ■ n. (pl. **fuci** /ˈfjuːsʌɪ/) a seaweed of a large genus of brown algae having flat leathery fronds. [Genus *Fucus*.]
– DERIVATIVES **fucoid** adj. & n.
– ORIGIN C17: from Latin, 'rock lichen, red dye, rouge', from Greek *phukos* 'seaweed', of Semitic origin.

fuddle /ˈfʌd(ə)l/ ■ v. [usu. as adj. **fuddled**] confuse or stupefy, especially with alcohol. ■ n. a state of confusion or intoxication.
– ORIGIN C16 ('go on a drinking bout').

fuddy-duddy ■ n. (pl. **-ies**) informal a person who is very old-fashioned and pompous.
– ORIGIN C20 (orig. dialect).

fudge ■ n. **1** a soft crumbly or chewy sweet made from sugar, butter, and milk or cream. **2** [as modifier] chiefly N. Amer. rich chocolate, used as a sauce or a filling for cakes. **3** an attempt to fudge an issue. ▸ archaic nonsense. **4** a piece of late news inserted in a newspaper page. ■ v. present in a vague or inadequate way, especially to mislead. ▸ adjust or manipulate (facts or figures) so as to present a desired picture.
– ORIGIN C17: prob. an alteration of obsolete *fadge* 'to fit'; the sense in confectionery prob. arose from early verb usage 'merge together'.

fuehrer ■ n. variant spelling of FÜHRER.

fuel ■ n. **1** material such as coal, gas, or oil that is burned to produce heat or power. ▸ food, drink, or drugs as a source of energy. **2** something that acts to sustain or inflame passion, argument, or other intense emotion. ■ v. (**fuelled**, **fuelling**; US **fueled**, **fueling**) **1** supply or power with fuel. **2** sustain or inflame: *their anger is fuelled by bitterness over the regrading*.
– ORIGIN Middle English: from Old French *fouaille*, from Latin *focus* 'hearth', in late Latin, 'fire'.

fuel cell ■ n. a cell producing an electric current direct from a chemical reaction.

fuel injection ■ n. the direct introduction of fuel under pressure into the combustion units of an internal-combustion engine.
– DERIVATIVES **fuel-injected** adj.

fuel oil ■ n. oil used as fuel in an engine or furnace.

fufu /ˈfuːfuː/ (also **foo-foo**) ■ n. dough made from boiled and ground plantain or cassava, used as a staple food in parts of West and central Africa.
– ORIGIN C18: from Twi *fufuu*.

fug ■ n. Brit. informal a warm, stuffy atmosphere.
– DERIVATIVES **fuggy** adj.
– ORIGIN C19 (orig. dialect and schoolchildren's slang).

fugal /ˈfjuːg(ə)l/ ■ adj. of or relating to a fugue.

fugitive

fugitive ■ n. a person who has escaped from captivity or is in hiding. ■ adj. quick to disappear; fleeting.
– ORIGIN Middle English: from Old French *fugitif, -ive*, from Latin *fugitivus*, from *fugere* 'flee'.

fugue /fjuːg/ ■ n. **1** Music a contrapuntal composition in which a short melody or phrase (the subject) is introduced by one part and successively taken up by others. **2** Psychiatry a state or period of loss of awareness of one's identity, often coupled with flight from one's usual environment, associated with certain forms of hysteria and epilepsy.
– ORIGIN C16: from Italian *fuga*, from Latin *fuga* 'flight'.

führer /ˈfjʊərə/ (also **fuehrer**) ■ n. the title assumed by Hitler as leader of Germany.
– ORIGIN from German *Führer* 'leader'.

-ful ■ suffix **1** (forming adjectives from nouns) full of; having the qualities of: *sorrowful*. **2** forming adjectives from adjectives or from Latin stems with little change of sense: *grateful*. **3** (forming adjectives from verbs) apt to; able to; accustomed to: *forgetful*. **4** (pl. **-fuls**) forming nouns denoting the amount needed to fill the specified container: *bucketful*.

Fula /ˈfuːlə/ (also **Foulah**) ■ n. the language of the Fulani people, belonging to the Benue-Congo language family and widely used in West Africa as a lingua franca.
– ORIGIN from Fula *pulo* 'Fula person'.

Fulani /fuːˈlɑːni/ ■ n. (pl. same) **1** a member of a mainly Muslim people living in regions of West Africa. **2** another term for FULA.
– ORIGIN the name in Hausa.

fulcrum /ˈfʊlkrəm, ˈfʌl-/ ■ n. (pl. **fulcra** /-rə/ or **fulcrums**) the point against which a lever is placed to get a firm hold, or on which it turns or is supported.
– ORIGIN C17: from Latin, 'post of a couch', from *fulcire* 'to prop up'.

fulfil (US **fulfill**) ■ v. (**fulfilled**, **fulfilling**) **1** achieve or realize (something desired, promised, or predicted). ▸ (**fulfil oneself**) gain happiness or satisfaction by fully achieving one's potential. **2** satisfy or meet (a requirement or condition).
– DERIVATIVES **fulfilled** adj. **fulfiller** n. **fulfilling** adj. **fulfilment** (US **fulfillment**) n.
– ORIGIN Old English *fullfyllan* 'fill up, make full' (see FULL[1], FILL).

fulguration /ˌfʌlɡjʊˈreɪʃ(ə)n/ ■ n. Medicine the destruction of small growths or areas of tissue using diathermy.
– ORIGIN C17: from Latin *fulguratio(n-)* 'sheet lightning'.

fulgurite /ˈfʌlɡjʊraɪt/ ■ n. Geology vitreous material formed of sand or other sediment fused by lightning.
– ORIGIN C19: from Latin *fulgur* 'lightning'.

full[1] ■ adj. **1** containing or holding as much or as many as possible; having no empty space. ▸ (**full of**) having a large number or quantity of. **2** not lacking or omitting anything; complete. ▸ (of a covering material in bookbinding) used for the entire cover. **3** plump or rounded: *the fuller figure*. ▸ (of the hair) having body. ▸ (of a garment) made using much material. ▸ (of a sound or colour) strong and rich. **4** (**full of**) unable to stop talking or thinking about: *they had their photographs taken and he was full of it*. ▸ filled with intense emotion. **5** involving a lot of activities: *he lived a full life*. **6** informal, chiefly Austral./NZ & Scottish drunk. ■ adv. **1** straight; directly. **2** very: *he knew full well she was too polite to barge in*. ▸ archaic entirely. ■ v. **1** gather or pleat so as to make a garment full. **2** dialect or US (of the moon or tide) become full.
– PHRASES **full and by** Nautical close-hauled but with sails filling. **full of oneself** very self-satisfied and with an exaggerated sense of self-worth. **full on 1** running at or providing maximum power or capacity. **2** so as to make a direct or significant impact. ▸ (**full-on**) informal not diluted in nature or effect; intense or uncompromising: *full-on boogie*. **full out 1** with maximum effort or power. **2** Printing flush with the margin. **full steam** (or **speed**) **ahead** proceeding with as much speed or energy as possible. **full up** filled to capacity. **in full 1** with nothing omitted. **2** to the full amount due. **3** to the utmost; completely. **to the full** to the greatest possible extent.
– ORIGIN Old English, of Germanic origin.

full[2] ■ v. [often as noun **fulling**] clean, shrink, and felt (cloth) by heat, pressure, and moisture.
– ORIGIN Middle English: prob. a back-formation from *fuller*, influenced by Old French *fouler* 'press hard upon' or medieval Latin *fullare*, from Latin *fullo* 'fuller'.

fullback ■ n. a player in a defensive position near the goal in a ball game such as soccer, rugby, or field hockey.

full beam ■ n. the brightest setting of a vehicle's headlights.

full-blooded ■ adj. **1** of unmixed ancestry. **2** vigorous and whole-hearted.

full-blown ■ adj. **1** fully developed; complete. **2** (of a flower) in full bloom.

full board ■ n. provision of accommodation and all meals at a hotel or guest house.

full-bodied ■ adj. rich and satisfying in flavour or sound.

full bore chiefly N. Amer. ■ adv. at full speed or maximum capacity. ■ adj. **1** denoting firearms of relatively large calibre. **2** complete; thoroughgoing: *a full-bore leftist*.

full-court press ■ n. Basketball an aggressive tactic in which members of a team cover their opponents throughout the court and not just in the region near their own basket.

full-cream ■ adj. (of milk) unskimmed.

full dress ■ n. clothes worn on ceremonial or very formal occasions. ■ adj. formal and serious: *a full-dress conference*.

fuller[1] ■ n. a person whose occupation is fulling cloth.

fuller[2] ■ n. a grooved or rounded tool on which iron is shaped. ■ v. stamp (iron) using a fuller.
– ORIGIN C19.

fullerene /ˈfʊlərɪːn/ ■ n. Chemistry a form of carbon having a molecule consisting of a large spheroidal cage of atoms, produced chiefly by the action of arc discharges between carbon electrodes.
– ORIGIN C20: contraction of BUCKMINSTERFULLERENE (the first known example).

fuller's earth ■ n. a type of clay used in fulling cloth and as an adsorbent.

full face ■ adv. with all the face visible; facing directly at someone or something. ■ adj. **1** showing all of the face. **2** covering all of the face.

full-fledged ■ adj. another term for FULLY FLEDGED.

full flood ■ n. the tide at its highest.
– PHRASES **in full flood** speaking enthusiastically and volubly.

full forward ■ n. Australian Rules the centrally positioned player in front of the goal on the forward line of the attacking team.

full-frontal ■ adj. with full exposure of the front of the body.

full-grown ■ adj. having reached maturity.

full house ■ n. **1** a theatre or meeting that is filled to capacity. **2** a poker hand with three of a kind and a pair, which beats a flush and loses to four of a kind. **3** a winning card at bingo.

full marks ■ pl. n. the maximum award in an examination or assessment.

full moon ■ n. the phase of the moon in which its whole disc is illuminated.

full-motion video ■ n. digital video data that is transmitted or stored on video discs for real-time reproduction at a rate of not less than 25 frames per second.

full-mouthed ■ adj. (of cattle, sheep, etc.) having a full set of adult teeth.

full nelson ■ n. see NELSON.

fullness (also **fulness**) ■ n. **1** the state of being full. **2** richness or abundance.
– PHRASES **in the fullness of time** after a due length of time has elapsed; eventually.

full note ■ n. Music a semibreve.

full point ■ n. another term for FULL STOP (as a punctuation mark).

full professor ■ n. chiefly N. Amer. a professor of the highest grade in a university.

full-rigged ■ adj. (of a sailing ship) having three or more masts that all carry square sails.

full-scale ■ adj. **1** (of a model or representation) of the same size as the thing represented. **2** unrestricted in extent or intensity: *a full-scale invasion*.

full score ■ n. a score of a musical composition giving the parts for all performers on separate staves.

full stop ■ n. a punctuation mark (.) used at the end of a sentence or an abbreviation.

full-time ■ adj. occupying the whole of the time available. ■ adv. on a full-time basis. ■ n. (**full time**) the end of a sports match.
– DERIVATIVES **full-timer** n.

full toss Cricket ■ n. a ball pitched right up to the batsman. ■ adv. without the ball having touched the ground.

fully ■ adv. **1** completely or entirely; to the fullest extent. **2** no less or fewer than: *fully 65 per cent*.

-fully ■ suffix forming adverbs corresponding to adjectives ending in *-ful* (such as *sorrowfully* corresponding to *sorrowful*).

fully fashioned ■ adj. (of women's clothing) shaped and seamed to fit the body.

fully fledged ■ adj. **1** with fully developed wing feathers and able to fly. **2** completely developed or established; of full status.

fulmar /'fʊlmə/ ■ n. a gull-sized grey and white seabird of the petrel family. [Genus *Fulmarus*: two species.]
– ORIGIN C17: from Hebridean Norn dialect, from Old Norse *fúll* 'stinking, foul' (because of its habit of regurgitating its stomach contents when disturbed) + *már* 'gull'.

fulminant /'fʊlmɪnənt, 'fʌl-/ ■ adj. Medicine (of a disease or symptom) severe and sudden in onset.
– ORIGIN C17: from Latin *fulminare* (see **FULMINATE**).

fulminate /'fʊlmɪneɪt, 'fʌl-/ ■ v. **1** express vehement protest. **2** poetic/literary explode violently or flash like lightning. **3** [usu. as adj. **fulminating**] Medicine (of a disease or symptom) develop suddenly and severely.
– ORIGIN Middle English: from medieval Latin *fulminare*, from Latin *fulminat-* 'struck by lightning', from *fulmen* 'lightning'.

fulmination ■ n. **1** an expression of vehement protest. **2** a violent explosion or a flash like lightning.

fulness ■ n. variant spelling of FULLNESS.

fulsome ■ adj. **1** flattering to an excessive degree. **2** of large size or quantity.
– DERIVATIVES **fulsomely** adv. **fulsomeness** n.
– ORIGIN Middle English: from FULL[1].

fumarole /'fjuːmərəʊl/ ■ n. an opening in or near a volcano, through which hot sulphurous gases emerge.
– DERIVATIVES **fumarolic** adj.
– ORIGIN C19: from obsolete Italian *fumaruolo*, from late Latin *fumariolum* 'vent, hole for smoke'.

fumble ■ v. **1** use the hands clumsily while doing or handling something. ▸ (of the hands) do or handle something clumsily. ▸ (**fumble about/around**) move about clumsily using the hands to find one's way. ▸ (in ball games) fail to catch or field (the ball) cleanly. **2** express oneself or deal with something clumsily or nervously. ■ n. an act of fumbling. ▸ informal an act of fondling someone for sexual pleasure.
– DERIVATIVES **fumbler** n. **fumbling** adj.
– ORIGIN Middle English: from Low German *fommeln* or Dutch *fommelen*.

fume ■ n. **1** a gas or vapour that smells strongly or is dangerous to inhale. **2** poetic/literary a watery vapour rising from the earth or sea. ■ v. **1** emit fumes. **2** [usu. as adj. **fumed**] expose (something, especially wood) to ammonia fumes in order to produce dark tints. **3** feel great anger.
– DERIVATIVES **fuming** adj. **fumy** adj.
– ORIGIN Middle English: from Latin *fumare* 'to smoke'.

fume cupboard (US **fume hood**) ■ n. a ventilated enclosure in a chemistry laboratory, in which harmful volatile chemicals can be used or kept.

fumigate ■ v. disinfect or purify with the fumes of certain chemicals.
– DERIVATIVES **fumigant** n. **fumigation** n. **fumigator** n.
– ORIGIN C16 ('to perfume'): from Latin *fumigare*, from *fumus* 'smoke'.

fumitory /'fjuːmɪt(ə)ri/ ■ n. a plant with spikes of small tubular pink or white flowers and finely divided greyish leaves. [Genus *Fumaria*.]
– ORIGIN Middle English: from Old French *fumeterre*, from medieval Latin *fumus terrae* 'smoke of the earth' (because of its greyish leaves).

fun ■ n. **1** light-hearted pleasure or amusement. **2** a source of this. **3** playfulness or good humour: *she's full of fun*. ■ adj. informal enjoyable.
– PHRASES **in fun** not intended seriously. **make fun of** tease or laugh at in a mocking or unkind way.
– ORIGIN C17: from obsolete *fun* 'to cheat or hoax', dialect var. of Middle English *fon* 'make a fool of, be a fool', rel. to *fon* 'a fool'.

funboard ■ n. a type of windsurfing board that is less stable but faster than a standard board.

function ■ n. **1** an activity that is natural to or the purpose of a person or thing. ▸ a computer operation corresponding to a single instruction from the user. **2** a large or formal social event or ceremony. **3** Mathematics a relation or expression involving one or more variables. ▸ a variable quantity regarded as depending on another variable; a consequence: *depreciation is a function of time*. **4** Chemistry a functional group. ■ v. work or operate in a proper or particular way. ▸ (**function as**) fulfil the purpose or task of (a specified thing).
– DERIVATIVES **functionless** adj.
– ORIGIN C16: from Latin *functio(n-)*, from *fungi* 'perform'.

functional ■ adj. **1** of, relating to, or having a function: *a functional role*. ▸ relating to the way in which something functions: *there are functional differences between the left and right brain*. **2** designed to be practical and useful, rather than attractive. **3** working or operating. **4** (of a disease) affecting the operation rather than the structure of an organ. **5** (of a mental illness) having no discernible organic cause.
– DERIVATIVES **functionally** adv.

functional food ■ n. a food containing health-giving additives.

functional group ■ n. Chemistry a group of atoms responsible for the characteristic reactions of a particular compound.

functionalism ■ n. **1** the theory that the design of an object should be determined by its function rather than by aesthetic considerations. **2** (in social sciences) the study or interpretation of phenomena in terms of the functions which they fulfil within an overall system.
– DERIVATIVES **functionalist** n. & adj.

functionality ■ n. **1** the quality of being functional. **2** the range of operations that can be run on a computer or other electronic system.

functionary /'fʌŋkʃ(ə)n(ə)ri/ ■ n. (pl. **-ies**) an official.

function key ■ n. Computing a key on a computer keyboard to which software can assign a particular function.

function word ■ n. Linguistics a word whose purpose is to contribute to the syntax rather than the meaning of a sentence, for example *do* in *we do not live here*.

fund ■ n. **1** a sum of money saved or made available for a particular purpose. **2** (**funds**) financial resources. **3** a large stock. ■ v. provide with a fund.
– PHRASES **in funds** Brit. having money to spend.
– DERIVATIVES **funding** n.
– ORIGIN C17: from Latin *fundus* 'bottom, piece of landed property'.

fundal /'fʌnd(ə)l/ ■ adj. Medicine of or relating to a fundus.

fundament /'fʌndəm(ə)nt/ ■ n. **1** the foundation or basis of something. **2** humorous a person's buttocks or anus.
– ORIGIN Middle English: from Latin *fundamentum*, from *fundare* 'to found'.

fundamental /fʌndə'mɛnt(ə)l/ ■ adj. of or serving as a foundation or core; of central importance. ■ n. **1** a central or primary rule or principle. **2** Music a fundamental note,

fundamental frequency

tone, or frequency.
– DERIVATIVES **fundamentally** adv.

fundamental frequency ■ n. **1** Physics the lowest frequency produced by the oscillation of the whole of an object, as distinct from harmonics. **2** Music the principal frequency in a harmonic series.

fundamentalism ■ n. **1** a form of Protestant Christianity which upholds belief in the strict and literal interpretation of the Bible. **2** the strict maintenance of the ancient or fundamental doctrines of any religion or ideology.
– DERIVATIVES **fundamentalist** n. & adj.

fundamental note ■ n. Music the lowest note of a chord in its original (uninverted) form.

fundamental tone ■ n. Music the tone which represents the fundamental frequency of a vibrating object such as a string or bell.

fundamental unit ■ n. each of a set of unrelated units of measurement from which other units are derived, for example (in the SI system) the metre, kilogram, and second.

fundi¹ /ˈfʊndi/ ■ n. (pl. **fundis**) chiefly S. African an expert in a particular field. ▸ an enthusiast for an activity or pastime.
– ORIGIN perhaps from isiNdebele *umfundi* 'learner', from *funda* 'to read'.

fundi² plural form of FUNDUS.

fund-raiser ■ n. **1** a person engaged in seeking financial support for an organization or cause. **2** an event held to generate such financial support.
– DERIVATIVES **fund-raising** n.

fundus /ˈfʌndəs/ ■ n. (pl. **fundi** /-dʌɪ/) Anatomy **1** the part of a hollow organ (such as the uterus or the gall bladder) that is furthest from the opening. **2** the part of the eyeball opposite the pupil.
– ORIGIN C18: from Latin, 'bottom'.

funeral ■ n. a ceremony in which a dead person is buried or cremated. ▸ archaic or poetic/literary a procession of mourners at a burial.
– PHRASES **it's one's funeral** informal it is one's own responsibility (used to imply that an undesirable outcome is possible).
– ORIGIN Middle English: from late Latin *funeralis*, from Latin *funus, funer-* 'funeral, death, corpse'.

funeral director ■ n. an undertaker.

funeral parlour (also **funeral home**) ■ n. an establishment where the dead are prepared for burial or cremation.

funeral pyre (also **funeral pile**) ■ n. a pile of wood on which a corpse is burnt as part of a funeral ceremony.

funeral urn ■ n. an urn holding the ashes of a cremated body.

funerary /ˈfjuːn(ə)(rə)ri/ ■ adj. relating to a funeral or the commemoration of the dead.

funereal /fjuːˈnɪərɪəl/ ■ adj. having the sombre character appropriate to a funeral.
– DERIVATIVES **funereally** adv.

funfair ■ n. a fair consisting of rides, sideshows, and other amusements.

fungi plural form of FUNGUS.

fungible /ˈfʌn(d)ʒɪb(ə)l/ ■ adj. Law (of goods contracted for without an individual specimen being specified) interchangeable with other identical items.
– DERIVATIVES **fungibility** n.
– ORIGIN C17: from medieval Latin *fungibilis*, from *fungi* 'perform, enjoy'.

fungicide /ˈfʌn(d)ʒɪsʌɪd, ˈfʌŋgɪ-/ ■ n. a chemical that destroys fungus.
– DERIVATIVES **fungicidal** adj.

fungivorous /fʌŋˈdʒɪv(ə)rəs/ ■ adj. feeding on fungi or mushrooms.

fungus /ˈfʌŋgəs/ ■ n. (pl. **fungi** /-gʌɪ, -(d)ʒʌɪ/ or **funguses**) any of a large group of spore-producing organisms which live on organic matter and include moulds, yeast, mushrooms, and toadstools.
– DERIVATIVES **fungal** adj. **fungoid** adj.

– ORIGIN Middle English: from Latin, perhaps from Greek *spongos* (see SPONGE).

funicular /fjʊˈnɪkjʊlə, fəˈnɪk-/ ■ adj. (of a railway on a steep slope) operated by cable with ascending and descending cars counterbalanced. ■ n. a funicular railway.
– ORIGIN C17: from Latin *funiculus* (see FUNICULUS).

funiculus /fjʊˈnɪkjʊləs/ ■ n. (pl. **funiculi** /-lʌɪ, -liː/) Anatomy a bundle of nerve fibres, especially forming one of the main tracts of white matter in the spinal cord.
– ORIGIN C17: from Latin, diminutive of *funis* 'rope'.

funk¹ informal ■ n. (also **blue funk**) a state of panic or depression. ■ v. avoid out of fear.
– ORIGIN C18: perhaps from FUNK² in the dated sense 'tobacco smoke', or from obsolete Flemish *fonck* 'disturbance, agitation'.

funk² ■ n. a style of popular dance music of US origin, having a strong rhythm that typically accentuates the first beat in the bar. ■ v. (**funk something up**) give music elements of funk.
– ORIGIN C17: perhaps from French dialect *funkier* 'blow smoke on'.

funkster ■ n. informal a performer or fan of funk music.

funky ■ adj. (-ier, -iest) informal **1** (of music) having a strong dance rhythm. **2** unconventionally modern and stylish. **3** N. Amer. strongly musty.
– DERIVATIVES **funkily** adv. **funkiness** n.

funnel ■ n. **1** a utensil that is wide at the top and narrow at the bottom, used for guiding liquid or powder into a small opening. **2** a metal chimney on a ship or steam engine. ■ v. (**funnelled, funnelling**; US **funneled, funneling**) guide or move through or as if through a funnel.
– ORIGIN Middle English: apparently from Provençal *fonilh*, from late Latin *fundibulum*, from Latin *infundibulum*, from *infundere* 'pour into'.

funny ■ adj. (-ier, -iest) **1** causing laughter or amusement. **2** strange; peculiar. **3** arousing suspicion: *there was something funny going on*. **4** informal slightly unwell; out of sorts. **5** eccentric or slightly deranged. ■ n. (**funnies**) informal **1** amusing jokes. **2** chiefly N. Amer. the comic strips in newspapers.
– PHRASES **funny ha-ha** (or **funny peculiar**) funny in its sense 'amusing' rather than 'peculiar' (or vice versa). [coined by Ian Hay in his novel *Housemaster* (1936).]
– DERIVATIVES **funnily** adv. **funniness** n.

funny bone ■ n. informal the part of the elbow over which passes the ulnar nerve, which may cause numbness and pain along the forearm and hand if knocked.

funny farm ■ n. informal a psychiatric hospital.

funny man ■ n. a professional clown or comedian.

funny money ■ n. informal currency that is forged or otherwise worthless.

funny paper ■ n. N. Amer. a section of a newspaper containing cartoons and humorous matter.

fun run ■ n. informal an uncompetitive run for sponsored runners, held in support of a charity.

funster ■ n. informal a joker.

Fur /fʊə, fəː/ ■ n. (pl. same) **1** a member of a Muslim people of the mountainous and desert regions of SW Sudan. **2** the Nilo-Saharan language of the Fur.

fur ■ n. **1** the short, fine, soft hair of certain animals. **2** the skin of an animal with fur on it, used in making or trimming garments. **3** a coat made from fur. **4** Heraldry any of several heraldic tinctures representing animal skins in stylized form (e.g. ermine, vair). **5** a coating formed on the tongue as a symptom of sickness. ■ v. (**furred, furring**) level (floor or wall timbers) by inserting strips of wood.
– PHRASES **the fur will fly** informal there will be a dramatic argument.
– DERIVATIVES **furless** adj. **-furred** adj.
– ORIGIN Middle English: from Old French *forrer* 'to line, sheathe', from *forre* 'sheath', of Germanic origin.

furbelow /ˈfəːbɪləʊ/ ■ n. **1** a flounce on a skirt or petticoat. **2** (**furbelows**) showy trimmings.
– ORIGIN C17: from French *falbala* 'trimming, flounce'.

furbish /ˈfəːbɪʃ/ ■ v. **1** give a fresh look to; renovate. **2** archaic polish (a weapon).
– ORIGIN Middle English: from Old French *forbiss-, forbir*, of Germanic origin.

furcate ■ v. /ˈfəːkeɪt, fəːˈkeɪt/ divide into two or more branches; fork. ■ adj. /ˈfəːkeɪt, -kət/ furcated; forked.
– ORIGIN C19: from late Latin *furcatus* 'cloven', from Latin *furca* 'fork'.

furcula /ˈfəːkjʊlə/ ■ n. (pl. **furculae** /-liː/) Zoology the wishbone of a bird.
– ORIGIN C19: from Latin, diminutive of *furca* 'fork'.

furious ■ adj. **1** extremely angry. **2** full of energy or intensity.
– DERIVATIVES **furiously** adv. **furiousness** n.
– ORIGIN Middle English: from Latin *furiosus*, from *furia* 'fury'.

furl ■ v. roll or fold up neatly and securely.
– DERIVATIVES **furled** adj.
– ORIGIN C16: from French *ferler*.

furling ■ n. equipment for furling sails around their yards or booms.

furlong ■ n. an eighth of a mile, 220 yards (201 metres).
– ORIGIN Old English *furlang*, from *furh* 'furrow' + *lang* 'long' (orig. denoting the length of a furrow in a common field).

furlough /ˈfəːləʊ/ ■ n. leave of absence, especially from military duty. ■ v. US grant furlough to.
– ORIGIN C17: from Dutch *verlof*, of West Germanic origin.

furnace ■ n. **1** an enclosed chamber in which material can be heated to very high temperatures. **2** chiefly N. Amer. a boiler serving a central heating system. **3** a very hot place.
– ORIGIN Middle English: from Old French *fornais(e)*, from Latin *fornax*, *fornac-*, from *fornus* 'oven'.

furnish ■ v. **1** provide (a room or building) with furniture and fittings. **2** supply with equipment or information. **3** be a source of; provide.
– DERIVATIVES **furnished** adj. **furnisher** n.
– ORIGIN Middle English: from Old French *furniss-*, *furnir*, of West Germanic origin.

furnishing ■ n. **1** (**furnishings**) furniture and fittings in a room or building. **2** [as modifier] denoting fabrics used for curtains or upholstery.

furniture ■ n. **1** the movable articles that are used to make a room or building suitable for living or working in, such as tables, chairs, or desks. **2** the small accessories or fittings that are required for a particular task or function.
– PHRASES **a part of the furniture** informal a person or thing that has become so familiar as to be unquestioned or unnoticed.
– ORIGIN C16: from French *fourniture*, from *fournir* 'to furnish'.

furniture beetle ■ n. a small brown beetle, the larva of which (the woodworm) bores holes in dead wood. [*Anobium punctatum*.]

furore /ˌfjʊə(ə)ˈrɔːri, ˌfjʊ(ə)ˈrɔː/ (US **furor** /ˈfjʊərɔː/) ■ n. an outbreak of public anger or excitement.
– ORIGIN C18: from Italian.

furosemide /ˌfjʊəˈrɒsəmʌɪd/ ■ n. variant spelling of FRUSEMIDE.

furrier /ˈfʌrɪə/ ■ n. a person who prepares or deals in furs.
– ORIGIN Middle English: from Old French *forreor*, from *forrer* (see FUR).

furring strip ■ n. a length of wood tapering to nothing, used in roofing and other construction work.

furrow ■ n. **1** a long, narrow trench made in the ground by a plough. **2** a rut or groove. **3** S. African a watercourse constructed for irrigation. **4** a deep wrinkle on a person's face. ■ v. **1** make a furrow in. **2** mark or be marked with furrows.
– ORIGIN Old English, of Germanic origin.

furry ■ adj. (**-ier**, **-iest**) covered with or resembling fur.
– DERIVATIVES **furriness** n.

fur seal ■ n. a gregarious eared seal of the Pacific and southern oceans, whose thick underside fur is used commercially as sealskin. [Family Otariidae: several species.]

further used as comparative of FAR. ■ adv. (also **farther**) **1** at, to, or by a greater distance. **2** over a greater expanse of space or time. ▶ beyond the point already reached. **3** at or to a more advanced, successful, or desirable stage. **4** in addition; also. ■ adj. **1** (also **farther**) more distant in space. ▶ more remote from a central point. **2** additional: *a further ten minutes*. ■ v. help the progress or development of.
– PHRASES **further to** formal following on from (used especially at the beginning of a letter): *further to our telephone conversation, I enclose an order for a new printer*. **until further notice** until another announcement is made.
– ORIGIN Old English *furthor*, of Germanic origin; rel. to FORTH.

furtherance ■ n. the advancement of a scheme or interest.

further education ■ n. education below degree level for people above school age.

furthermore ■ adv. in addition; besides.

furthermost (also **farthermost**) ■ adj. at the greatest distance from a central point or implicit standpoint.

furthest (also **farthest**) used as superlative of FAR. ■ adj. situated at the greatest distance. ▶ covering the greatest area or distance. ■ adv. **1** at or by the greatest distance. **2** over the greatest distance or area. ▶ indicating the most distant point reached in a specified direction: *it was the furthest north I had ever travelled*. **3** to the most extreme or advanced point.
– PHRASES **at the furthest** at most.
– ORIGIN Middle English: formed as a superlative of FURTHER.

furtive /ˈfəːtɪv/ ■ adj. characterized by guilty or evasive secrecy; stealthy.
– DERIVATIVES **furtively** adv. **furtiveness** n.
– ORIGIN C17: from Latin *furtivus*, from *furtum* 'theft'.

fury ■ n. (pl. **-ies**) **1** extreme anger. **2** extreme strength or violence in an action or a natural phenomenon. **3** (**Fury**) Greek & Roman Mythology a spirit of punishment, often represented as one of three goddesses (identified at an early date with the Eumenides).
– PHRASES **like fury** informal with great energy or effort.
– ORIGIN Middle English: from Latin *furia*, from *furiosus* 'furious', from *furere* 'be mad, rage'.

furze /fəːz/ ■ n. another term for GORSE.
– ORIGIN Old English.

fusarium /fjʊˈzɛːrɪəm/ ■ n. a mould that causes diseases of plants, especially wilting. [Genus *Fusarium*.]
– ORIGIN C20: Latin *fusus* 'spindle'.

fuse¹ ■ v. **1** join, blend, or coalesce to form a single entity. **2** melt (a material or object) with intense heat, so as to join it with something else. **3** Brit. (with reference to an electrical appliance) stop or cause to stop working when a fuse melts. **4** provide (a circuit or electrical appliance) with a fuse. ■ n. a safety device consisting of a strip of wire that melts and breaks an electric circuit if the current exceeds a safe level.
– ORIGIN C16: from Latin *fus-*, *fundere* 'pour, melt'.

fuse² (also **fuze**) ■ n. a length of material along which a small flame moves to explode a bomb or firework. ▶ a device in a bomb that controls the timing of the explosion. ■ v. fit a fuse to (a bomb).
– DERIVATIVES **fuseless** adj.
– ORIGIN C17: from Latin *fusus* 'spindle'.

fuse box (or **fuse board**) ■ n. a box or board housing the fuses for circuits in a building.

fusee /fjuːˈziː/ (US **fuzee**) ■ n. a conical pulley or wheel in a watch or clock.
– ORIGIN C16: from French *fusée* 'spindleful', from Latin *fusus* 'spindle'.

fuselage /ˈfjuːzəlɑːʒ, -lɪdʒ/ ■ n. the main body of an aircraft.
– ORIGIN C20: from French, from *fuseler* 'shape into a spindle'.

fuse wire ■ n. thin wire used in an electric fuse.

fusible /ˈfjuːzɪb(ə)l/ ■ adj. able to be fused or melted easily.
– DERIVATIVES **fusibility** n.

fusiform /ˈfjuːzɪfɔːm/ ■ adj. Botany & Zoology tapering at both ends; spindle-shaped.
– ORIGIN C18: from Latin *fusus* 'spindle' + -IFORM.

fusil¹ /ˈfjuːzɪl/ ■ n. historical a light musket.
– ORIGIN C16 (denoting a flint in a tinderbox): from French, from Latin *focus* 'hearth, fire'.

fusil² /ˈfjuːzɪl/ ■ n. Heraldry an elongated lozenge.
– ORIGIN Middle English: from Old French *fusel*, from a diminutive of Latin *fusus* 'spindle'.

fusilier /ˌfjuːzɪˈlɪə/ (US also **fusileer**) ■ n. **1** (**Fusilier**) a member of any of several British regiments formerly armed with fusils. **2** historical a soldier armed with a fusil.

fusillade /ˌfjuːzɪˈleɪd, -ˈlɑːd/ ■ n. a series of shots fired at the same time or in rapid succession.
– ORIGIN C19: from French.

fusilli /f(j)ʊˈziːli/ ■ pl. n. pasta pieces in the form of short spirals.
– ORIGIN Italian, 'little spindles'.

fusion ■ n. **1** the process or result of fusing. **2** a reaction in which light atomic nuclei fuse to form a heavier nucleus, releasing much energy. **3** music that is a mixture of different styles, especially jazz and rock.
– DERIVATIVES **fusional** adj.
– ORIGIN C16: from Latin *fusio(n-)*, from *fundere* 'pour, melt'.

fusion bomb ■ n. a bomb deriving its energy from nuclear fusion, especially a hydrogen bomb.

fuss ■ n. **1** a display of unnecessary or excessive excitement, activity, or interest. **2** a protest or complaint. ■ v. **1** show unnecessary or excessive concern about something. **2** Brit. disturb or bother. **3** treat with excessive attention or affection.
– PHRASES **not be fussed** Brit. informal not have strong feelings about something.
– DERIVATIVES **fusser** n.
– ORIGIN C18: perhaps Anglo-Irish.

fusspot ■ n. informal a fussy person.

fussy ■ adj. (**-ier**, **-iest**) **1** fastidious about one's requirements and hard to please. **2** full of unnecessary detail or decoration.
– DERIVATIVES **fussily** adv. **fussiness** n.

fustian /ˈfʌstɪən/ ■ n. a thick, hard-wearing twilled cloth with a short nap.
– ORIGIN Middle English: from medieval Latin *fustaneum*, from (*pannus*) *fustaneus* 'cloth from *Fostat*', a suburb of Cairo.

fusty ■ adj. (**-ier**, **-iest**) **1** smelling stale, damp, or stuffy. **2** old-fashioned.
– DERIVATIVES **fustily** adv. **fustiness** n.
– ORIGIN C15: from Old French *fuste* 'smelling of the cask'.

futhark /ˈfuːθɑːk/ (also **futhorc** /ˈfuːθɔːk/, **futhork**) ■ n. the runic alphabet.
– ORIGIN C19: from its first six letters: *f, u, th, a* (or *o*), *r, k*.

futile ■ adj. producing no useful result; pointless.
– DERIVATIVES **futilely** adv. **futility** n.
– ORIGIN C16: from Latin *futilis* 'leaky, futile', apparently from *fundere* 'pour'.

futon /ˈfuːtɒn/ ■ n. a padded unsprung mattress originating in Japan, that can be rolled up or folded in two.
– ORIGIN C19: Japanese.

future ■ n. **1** (**the future**) time that is still to come. ▸ events or conditions occurring or existing in that time. **2** a prospect of success or happiness: *I might have a future as an artist.* **3** Grammar a tense of verbs expressing events that have not yet happened. **4** (**futures**) contracts for assets (especially commodities or shares) bought at agreed prices but delivered and paid for later. Compare with FORWARD (in sense 2). ■ adj. **1** existing or occurring in the future. ▸ (of a person) planned or destined to hold a specified position: *his future wife.* **2** Grammar (of a tense) expressing an event yet to happen.
– PHRASES **in future** from now onwards.
– DERIVATIVES **futureless** adj.
– ORIGIN Middle English: from Latin *futurus*, future participle of *esse* 'be' (from the stem *fu-*, ultimately from a base meaning 'grow, become').

future history ■ n. (in science fiction) a narration of imagined future events.

future perfect ■ n. Grammar a tense of verbs expressing expected completion in the future, in English exemplified by *will have done*.

future-proof ■ adj. (of a product) unlikely to become obsolete.
– DERIVATIVES **future-proofed** adj. **future-proofing** n.

future shock ■ n. a state of distress or disorientation due to rapid social or technological change.

Futurism ■ n. an artistic movement launched in Italy in 1909, which strongly rejected traditional forms and embraced the dynamism of modern technology.
– ORIGIN from Italian *futurismo*.

futurist ■ n. **1** (**Futurist**) an adherent of Futurism. **2** a person who studies the future and makes predictions about it based on current trends. **3** Theology a person who believes that eschatological prophecies are still to be fulfilled. ■ adj. **1** (**Futurist**) of or relating to Futurism or the Futurists. **2** relating to a vision of the future.

futuristic ■ adj. **1** having or involving very modern technology or design. **2** (of a film or book) set in the future, typically in a world of highly advanced technology. **3** dated of or characteristic of Futurism.
– DERIVATIVES **futuristically** adv.

futurity /fjuːˈtjʊərɪti, -tʃ-/ ■ n. (pl. **-ies**) **1** the future time. **2** a future event. **3** renewed or continuing existence. **4** short for FUTURITY RACE.

futurity race (also **futurity stakes**) ■ n. chiefly US a race for young horses for which entries may be made before the horses are born.

futurology /ˌfjuːtʃəˈrɒlədʒi/ ■ n. systematic forecasting of the future based on present trends.
– DERIVATIVES **futurological** adj. **futurologist** n.

fuze ■ n. variant spelling of FUSE².

fuzee ■ n. US spelling of FUSEE.

fuzz¹ ■ n. **1** a frizzy mass of hair or fibre. **2** a blurred image. **3** a buzzing or distorted sound. ▸ such a sound deliberately produced on an electric guitar. ■ v. **1** make or become fuzzy. **2** make a distorted buzzing sound with (a guitar).
– DERIVATIVES **fuzzed** adj.
– ORIGIN C16: prob. of Low German or Dutch origin.

fuzz² ■ n. (**the fuzz**) informal the police.
– ORIGIN 1920s (orig. US).

fuzzbox ■ n. a device which adds fuzz to an electric guitar.

fuzzy ■ adj. (**-ier**, **-iest**) **1** having a frizzy texture or appearance. **2** indistinct or vague. ▸ (of an electric guitar) having a distorted, buzzing sound; fuzzed. **3** Computing & Logic of or relating to a form of set theory and logic in which predicates may have degrees of applicability, rather than simply being true or false.
– PHRASES **warm and fuzzy** N. Amer. informal sentimentally emotional.
– DERIVATIVES **fuzzily** adv. **fuzziness** n.

fwd ■ abbrev. forward.

f.w.d. ■ abbrev. **1** four-wheel drive. **2** front-wheel drive.

F-word ■ n. euphemistic the word 'fuck'.

FX ■ abbrev. visual or sound effects.
– ORIGIN from the pronunciation of the two syllables of *effects*.

FY ■ abbrev. financial, or fiscal year.

-fy ■ suffix **1** (added to nouns) forming verbs denoting making or producing: *speechify*. ▸ denoting transformation or the process of making into: *petrify*. **2** forming verbs denoting the making of a state defined by an adjective: *falsify*. **3** forming verbs expressing a causative sense: *horrify*.
– ORIGIN from French *-fier*, from Latin *-ficare*, *-facere*, from *facere* 'do, make'.

FYI ■ abbrev. for your information.

fynbos /ˈfeɪnbɒs, ˈfeɪnbɔs/ ■ n. fine-leaved shrub-like vegetation characterizing the Cape Floral Kingdom, including proteas, heathers, and restios.
– ORIGIN Afrikaans, 'fine bush'.

Gg

G[1] (also **g**) ▪ n. (pl. **Gs** or **G's**) **1** the seventh letter of the alphabet. **2** denoting the next after F in a set of items, categories, etc. **3** Music the fifth note in the diatonic scale of C major.

G[2] ▪ abbrev. **1** Physics gauss. **2** giga- (10^9). **3** N. Amer. informal grand (a thousand dollars). **4** the force exerted by the earth's gravitational field. **5** group of: **G7** | **G8**. ▪ symb. **1** Chemistry Gibbs free energy. **2** Physics the gravitational constant (6.67×10^{-11} N m² kg⁻²).

g ▪ abbrev. **1** Chemistry gas. **2** gram(s). ▪ symb. Physics the acceleration due to gravity (9.81 m s⁻²).

G7 ▪ abbrev. Group of Seven: a group of seven leading industrial nations outside the former communist bloc, consisting of the US, Japan, Germany, France, the UK, Italy, and Canada.

G8 ▪ abbrev. Group of Eight: the G7 countries plus Russia.

Ga ▪ symb. the chemical element gallium.

gaan /xɑːn/ ▪ v. (in phr. **gaan aan**) S. African informal complain persistently.
– ORIGIN prob. from Afrikaans *aangaan* 'to storm, rave, carry on'.

GAAP ▪ abbrev. generally accepted accounting principles.

gab informal ▪ v. (**gabbed**, **gabbing**) talk at length. ▪ n. talk; chatter.
– PHRASES **the gift of the gab** the ability to speak with eloquence and fluency.
– DERIVATIVES **gabby** adj. (**-ier**, **-iest**).
– ORIGIN C18: var. of **GOB**[1].

GABA ▪ abbrev. gamma-aminobutyric acid.

gabardine ▪ n. variant spelling of **GABERDINE**.

gabble ▪ v. talk rapidly and unintelligibly. ▪ n. rapid, unintelligible talk.
– DERIVATIVES **gabbler** n.
– ORIGIN C16: from Dutch *gabbelen*, of imitative origin.

gabbro /'gabrəʊ/ ▪ n. (pl. **-os**) Geology a dark, coarse-grained plutonic rock consisting mainly of pyroxene, plagioclase feldspar, and often olivine.
– DERIVATIVES **gabbroic** adj. **gabbroid** adj.
– ORIGIN C19: from Latin *glaber*, *glabr-* 'smooth'.

gaberdine /ˌgabə'diːn, 'gabədiːn/ (also **gabardine**) ▪ n. **1** a smooth, durable twill-woven worsted or cotton cloth. **2** Brit. a raincoat made of gaberdine. **3** historical a loose, long upper garment worn particularly by Jews.
– ORIGIN C16: from Old French *gauvardine*, earlier *gallevardine*, perhaps from Middle High German *wallevart* 'pilgrimage' and orig. 'a garment worn by a pilgrim'.

gabion /'ɡeɪbɪən/ ▪ n. a cylindrical basket or container filled with earth, stones, or other material and used as a component of civil engineering works.
– ORIGIN C16: from Italian *gabbione*, from *gabbia* 'cage'.

gable ▪ n. **1** the triangular upper part of a wall at the end of a ridged roof. **2** a gable-shaped canopy over a window or door.
– DERIVATIVES **gabled** adj.
– ORIGIN Middle English: from Old Norse *gafl*, of Germanic origin.

Gabonese /ˌɡabə'niːz/ ▪ n. (pl. same) a native or inhabitant of Gabon, a country in West Africa. ▪ adj. of or relating to Gabon or its people.

gad[1] ▪ v. (**gadded**, **gadding**) (**gad about/around**) informal go around from one place to another in the pursuit of pleasure.
– ORIGIN Middle English: back-formation from obsolete *gadling* 'wanderer, vagabond', (earlier) 'companion', of Germanic origin.

gad[2] (also **by gad**) ▪ exclam. archaic expressing surprise or emphatic assertion.
– ORIGIN C15: euphemistic alteration of **GOD**.

gadabout ▪ n. informal a person who gads about.

gadfly ▪ n. (pl. **-flies**) **1** a fly that bites livestock, especially a horsefly, warble fly, or botfly. **2** an annoying and provocative person.
– ORIGIN C16: from **GAD**[1], or obsolete *gad* 'goad, spike', from Old Norse *gaddr*, of Germanic origin.

gadget ▪ n. a small mechanical device or tool.
– DERIVATIVES **gadgeteer** n. **gadgetry** n. **gadgety** adj.
– ORIGIN C19: prob. from French *gâchette* 'lock mechanism' or from French dialect *gagée* 'tool'.

gadoid /'ɡeɪdɔɪd, 'ɡa-/ ▪ n. Zoology a bony fish of an order (Gadiformes) that comprises cod, hake, and related fish.
– ORIGIN C19: from modern Latin *gadus*, from Greek *gados* 'cod'.

gadolinite /'ɡad(ə)lɪnʌɪt, ɡə'dəʊlɪnʌɪt/ ▪ n. a rare dark brown or black mineral, consisting of a silicate of iron, beryllium, and rare earths.
– ORIGIN C19: named after the Finnish mineralogist Johan Gadolin.

gadolinium /ˌɡadə'lɪnɪəm/ ▪ n. the chemical element of atomic number 64, a soft silvery-white metal of the lanthanide series. (Symbol: **Gd**)
– ORIGIN C19: from **GADOLINITE**.

gadwall /'ɡadwɔːl/ ▪ n. (pl. same or **gadwalls**) a brownish-grey freshwater duck. [*Anas strepera*.]
– ORIGIN C17.

gadzooks /ɡad'zuːks/ ▪ exclam. archaic expressing surprise or annoyance.
– ORIGIN C17: alteration of *God's hooks*, i.e. the nails by which Christ was fastened to the cross.

Gael /ɡeɪl/ ▪ n. a Gaelic-speaking person.
– DERIVATIVES **Gaeldom** n.
– ORIGIN from Scottish Gaelic *Gaidheal*.

Gaelic /'ɡeɪlɪk, 'ɡalɪk/ ▪ n. **1** (also **Scottish Gaelic**) a Celtic language spoken in western Scotland, brought from Ireland in the 5th and 6th centuries AD. **2** (also **Irish Gaelic**) another term for **IRISH** (the language). ▪ adj. of or relating to the Goidelic group of Celtic languages, particularly Scottish Gaelic, and the speakers of these languages and their culture.

Gaelic coffee ▪ n. coffee served with cream and whisky.

gaff[1] ▪ n. **1** a stick with a hook or barbed spear, for landing large fish. **2** Nautical a spar to which the head of a fore-and-aft sail is bent. ▪ v. seize or impale with a gaff.
– ORIGIN Middle English: from Provençal *gaf* 'hook'; rel. to **GAFFE**.

gaff[2] ▪ n. (in phr. **blow the gaff**) Brit. informal reveal a plot or secret.
– ORIGIN C19.

gaffe /ɡaf/ (also **gaff**) ▪ n. an embarrassing blunder.
– ORIGIN C20: from French, 'boathook', in colloquial use 'blunder'.

gaffer ▪ n. Brit. **1** informal an old man. **2** informal a boss. **3** the chief electrician in a film or television production unit.
– ORIGIN C16: prob. a contraction of **GODFATHER**.

gaffer tape ▪ n. strong cloth-backed waterproof adhesive tape.

gag[1] ▪ n. **1** a piece of cloth put in or over a person's mouth to prevent them from speaking. **2** a device for keeping the patient's mouth open during a dental or surgical operation. **3** a restriction on free speech. ▪ v. (**gagged**, **gagging**) **1** put a gag on. **2** choke or retch.
– ORIGIN Middle English: perhaps rel. to Old Norse *gagháls* 'with the neck thrown back', or imitative of a person choking.

s sit　t top　v voice　w we　z zoo　ʃ she　ʒ decision　θ thin　ð this　ŋ ring　x loch　tʃ chip　dʒ jar

gag² ■ n. a joke or funny story, especially one forming part of a comedian's act. ■ v. tell jokes.
– ORIGIN C19 (orig. theatrical slang).

gaga /ˈgɑːgɑː, ˈgɑgə/ ■ adj. informal slightly mad, especially as a result of old age.
– ORIGIN C20: from French, 'senile, a senile person'.

gage¹ /geɪdʒ/ archaic ■ n. **1** a valued object deposited as a guarantee of good faith. **2** a pledge, especially a glove, thrown down as a challenge to fight.
– ORIGIN Middle English: from Old French *gage* (n.), *gager* (v.), of Germanic origin.

gage² ■ n. & v. variant spelling of GAUGE.

gaggle ■ n. **1** a flock of geese. **2** informal a disorderly group of people.
– ORIGIN Middle English: imitative of the noise that a goose makes.

gagster ■ n. a writer or performer of gags.

Gaia /ˈgaɪə/ ■ n. the earth viewed as a vast self-regulating organism.
– ORIGIN 1970s: coined by the English scientist James Lovelock from the name of the Greek goddess *Gaia*.

gaiety (US also **gayety**) ■ n. (pl. **-ies**) **1** the state or quality of being light-hearted and cheerful. **2** merrymaking; festivity.
– ORIGIN C17: from French *gaieté*.

gaily ■ adv. **1** in a light-hearted and cheerful manner. **2** without thinking of the consequences. **3** with a bright appearance.

gain ■ v. **1** obtain or secure (something favourable). **2** reach or arrive at (a destination). **3** (**gain on**) come closer to (a person or thing pursued). **4** increase the amount or rate of (weight, speed, etc.). **5** increase in value. **6** (**gain in**) improve or advance in some respect: *canoeing is gaining in popularity.* **7** (of a clock or watch) become fast. ■ n. **1** a thing that is gained. **2** an increase in wealth or resources: *personal gain.* **3** the factor by which power or voltage is increased in an amplifier or other electronic device, usually expressed as a logarithm.
– DERIVATIVES **gainable** adj. **gainer** n.
– ORIGIN C15 (orig. 'booty'): from Old French *gaigne* (n.), *gaignier* (v.), of Germanic origin.

gainful ■ adj. serving to increase wealth or resources.
– DERIVATIVES **gainfully** adv.

gainsay /geɪnˈseɪ/ ■ v. (past and past part. **-said**) formal deny or contradict; speak against.
– DERIVATIVES **gainsayer** n.
– ORIGIN Middle English: from obsolete *gain-* 'against' + SAY.

'gainst ■ prep. poetic/literary short for AGAINST.

gait /geɪt/ ■ n. **1** a person's manner of walking. **2** the paces of a horse or dog.
– ORIGIN Middle English: var. of dialect *gate*, denoting a street in place names, from Old Norse *gata*.

gaiter ■ n. **1** a covering of cloth or leather for the ankle and lower leg. **2** chiefly US a shoe or overshoe extending to the ankle or above.
– DERIVATIVES **gaitered** adj.
– ORIGIN C18: from French *guêtre*, prob. of Germanic origin.

gal ■ n. informal, chiefly N. Amer. a girl or young woman.
– ORIGIN C18: representing a pronunciation.

gal. ■ abbrev. gallon(s).

gala /ˈgɑːlə, ˈgeɪlə/ ■ n. **1** a festive entertainment or performance. **2** S. African & Brit. a special sports meeting, especially a swimming competition.
– ORIGIN C17 ('showy dress'): from Old French *gale* 'rejoicing'.

galactic /gəˈlaktɪk/ ■ adj. **1** of or relating to a galaxy or galaxies. **2** Astronomy measured relative to the galactic equator.
– ORIGIN C19: from Greek *galaktias*.

galactic equator ■ n. Astronomy the great circle of the celestial sphere passing as closely as possible through the densest parts of the Milky Way.

galactose /gəˈlaktəʊz, -s/ ■ n. Chemistry a sugar of the hexose class which is a constituent of lactose and many polysaccharides.
– ORIGIN from Greek *gala, galaktos* 'milk'.

galago /gəˈleɪgəʊ/ ■ n. (pl. **-os**) another term for BUSHBABY.
– ORIGIN modern Latin (genus name).

galah /gəˈlɑː/ ■ n. a small Australian cockatoo with a grey back and rosy pink head and underparts, regarded as a pest. [*Eulophus roseicapillus*.]
– ORIGIN C19: from Yuwaalaraay (an Aboriginal language).

Galahad /ˈgaləhad/ (also **Sir Galahad**) ■ n. a person of great nobility and integrity.
– ORIGIN C19: the name of one of King Arthur's knights.

galangal /ˈgal(ə)ŋgal/ ■ n. an Asian plant of the ginger family, the rhizome of which is used in cookery and herbal medicine. [Genera *Alpinia* and *Kaempferia*.]
– ORIGIN Middle English *galingale*, from Arabic *kalanjān*, perhaps from Chinese *gāoliángjiāng*, from *gāoliáng* (the name of a district in Guangdong Province, China) + *jiāng* 'ginger'.

galantine /ˈgal(ə)ntiːn/ ■ n. a dish of cooked meat or fish served cold in aspic.
– ORIGIN Middle English ('sauce for fish'): from Old French, alteration of *galatine*, from medieval Latin *galatina*.

galaxy ■ n. (pl. **-ies**) **1** a system of millions or billions of stars, together with gas and dust, held together by gravitational attraction. ▶ (**the Galaxy**) the galaxy of which the solar system is a part; the Milky Way. **2** a large and impressive group of people or things.
– ORIGIN Middle English (orig. referring to the Milky Way): from medieval Latin *galaxia*, from Greek *galaxias* (*kuklos*) 'milky (vault)', from *gala, galakt-* 'milk'.

gale ■ n. **1** a very strong wind. **2** an outburst of laughter.
– ORIGIN C16: perhaps rel. to Old Norse *galinn* 'mad, frantic'.

galena /gəˈliːnə/ ■ n. a metallic grey or black mineral consisting of lead sulphide.
– ORIGIN C17: from Latin, 'lead ore'.

galette /gəˈlɛt/ ■ n. a savoury pancake made from grated potatoes or a buckwheat batter.
– ORIGIN from French.

Galician ■ n. **1** a native or inhabitant of Galicia in NW Spain. **2** the language of Galicia in NW Spain, a Romance language closely related to Portuguese. **3** a native or inhabitant of Galicia in east central Europe. ■ adj. **1** of or relating to Galicia in NW Spain, its people, or their language. **2** of or relating to Galicia in east central Europe.

Galilean¹ /ˌgalɪˈleɪən/ ■ adj. of or relating to the Italian astronomer and physicist Galileo Galilei (1564–1642) or his methods.

Galilean² /ˌgalɪˈliːən/ ■ n. a native or inhabitant of Galilee. ■ adj. of or relating to Galilee or its people.

Galilean telescope ■ n. an astronomical telescope of the earliest type, with a biconvex objective and biconcave eyepiece.

galjoen /xalˈjʊn/ ■ n. S. African an edible deep-bodied fish endemic to southern African coastal waters. [*Coracinus capensis* and the banded galjoen *C. multifasciatus*.]
– ORIGIN C19: from Afrikaans, from Dutch, 'galleon'.

gall¹ /gɔːl/ ■ n. **1** bold and impudent behaviour. **2** archaic the contents of the gall bladder; bile. **3** an animal's gall bladder. **4** bitterness or cruelty: *life's gall*.
– ORIGIN Old English *gealla* (denoting bile), of Germanic origin.

gall² /gɔːl/ ■ n. **1** annoyance; humiliation. **2** a sore on the skin made by chafing. ■ v. annoy; humiliate.
– DERIVATIVES **galling** adj. **gallingly** adv.
– ORIGIN Old English *gealle* 'sore on a horse', perhaps rel. to GALL¹.

gall³ /gɔːl/ ■ n. **1** an abnormal growth formed in response to the presence of insect larvae, mites, or fungi on plants and trees, especially oaks. **2** [as modifier] denoting insects or mites that produce galls.
– ORIGIN Middle English: from Latin *galla*.

gall. ■ abbrev. gallon(s).

Galla /ˈgalə/ ■ n. & adj. another term for OROMO.

gallant /ˈgal(ə)nt/ ■ adj. **1** brave; heroic. **2** /also gəˈlant/ (of a man) charming; chivalrous. ■ n. /also gəˈlant/ **1** a man who is charmingly attentive to women. **2** archaic a dashing gentleman.

– DERIVATIVES **gallantly** adv.
– ORIGIN Middle English ('finely dressed'): from Old French *galant*, from *galer* 'have fun, make a show', from *gale* 'pleasure, rejoicing'.

gallantry ■ n. (pl. **-ies**) **1** courageous behaviour, especially in battle. **2** polite attention or respect given by men to women. ▶ (**gallantries**) actions or words used when paying such attention.

gall bladder ■ n. a small sac-shaped organ beneath the liver, in which bile is stored.

galleon ■ n. a large sailing ship in use from the 15th to the 18th centuries, typically square-rigged and with three or more decks and masts.
– ORIGIN C16: either from French *galion*, from *galie* 'galley', or from Spanish *galeón*.

galleria /ˌgaləˈriːə/ ■ n. an arcade of small shops.
– ORIGIN Italian (see **GALLERY**).

gallery ■ n. (pl. **-ies**) **1** a room or building for the display or sale of works of art. **2** a balcony or upper floor projecting from a back or side wall inside a hall or church. **3** the highest balcony in a theatre, having the cheapest seats. **4** (**the gallery**) a group of spectators, especially those at a golf tournament. **5** a long room or passage forming a portico or colonnade. **6** a horizontal underground passage in a mine.
– PHRASES **play to the gallery** aim to attract popular attention.
– DERIVATIVES **galleried** adj.
– ORIGIN Middle English: from Italian *galleria* 'gallery', formerly also 'church porch', from medieval Latin *galeria*.

gallery forest ■ n. a forest restricted to the banks of a river or stream.

galley ■ n. (pl. **-eys**) **1** historical a low, flat ship with one or more sails and up to three banks of oars, chiefly used for warfare or piracy and often manned by slaves or criminals. **2** the kitchen in a ship or aircraft. **3** (also **galley proof**) a printer's proof in the form of long single-column strips.
– ORIGIN Middle English: from medieval Latin *galea*, from medieval Greek *galaia*.

Galliano /ˌgalɪˈɑːnəʊ/ ■ n. a golden-yellow Italian liqueur flavoured with herbs.
– ORIGIN named after Major Giuseppe *Galliáno*, a noted C19 military officer.

galliard /ˈgalɪɑːd, -əd/ ■ n. historical a lively dance in triple time for two people.
– ORIGIN Middle English (as adj. meaning 'valiant, sturdy' and 'lively, brisk'): from Old French *gaillard* 'valiant', of Celtic origin.

Gallic /ˈgalɪk/ ■ adj. **1** of or characteristic of France or the French. **2** of or relating to the Gauls.
– DERIVATIVES **Gallicize** (also **-ise**) v.
– ORIGIN C17: from Latin *Gallicus*, from *Gallus* 'a Gaul'.

Gallicism /ˈgalɪsɪz(ə)m/ ■ n. a French word or idiom adopted in another language.

gallimaufry /ˌgalɪˈmɔːfri/ ■ n. a jumble or medley of things.
– ORIGIN C16: from archaic French *galimafrée* 'unappetizing dish'.

gallimimus /ˌgalɪˈmʌɪməs/ ■ n. an ostrich dinosaur of the late Cretaceous period.
– ORIGIN from Latin *galli* 'of a cockerel' + *mimus* 'mime, pretence'.

gallinaceous /ˌgalɪˈneɪʃəs/ ■ adj. of or relating to birds of an order (Galliformes) which includes domestic poultry and game birds.
– ORIGIN C18: from Latin *gallinaceus*.

gallinule /ˈgalɪnjuːl/ ■ n. a marshbird of the rail family, with mainly black or dark plumage and a red bill. [*Porphyrula porphyrio* (purple gallinule) and other species.]
– ORIGIN C18: from modern Latin *Gallinula* (genus term).

gallium /ˈgalɪəm/ ■ n. the chemical element of atomic number 31, a soft, silvery-white metal which melts at about 30°C. (Symbol: **Ga**)
– ORIGIN C19: modern Latin, from Latin *Gallia* 'France' or *gallus* 'cock'; named by the French chemist Paul-Émile Lecoq de Boisbaudran.

gallivant /ˈgalɪvant, ˌgalɪˈvant/ ■ v. informal go from place to place in pursuit of pleasure.

– ORIGIN C19: perhaps an alteration of **GALLANT**.

gall midge ■ n. a small fly which induces gall formation in plants. [Family Cecidomyiidae: many species.]

Gallo- /ˈgaləʊ/ ■ comb. form French; French and ...: *Gallo-German*. ▶ relating to France.
– ORIGIN from Latin *Gallus* 'a Gaul'.

gallon /ˈgalən/ ■ n. **1** a unit of volume for liquid measure equal to eight pints: in Britain (also **imperial gallon**), equivalent to 4.55 litres; in the US, equivalent to 3.79 litres. **2** informal (**gallons**) informal large quantities.
– DERIVATIVES **gallonage** n.
– ORIGIN Middle English: from Anglo-Norman French *galon*, from the base of medieval Latin *galleta*, *galletum* 'pail, liquid measure', perhaps of Celtic origin.

gallop ■ n. **1** the fastest pace of a horse or other quadruped, with all the feet off the ground together in each stride. **2** a ride on a horse at a gallop. **3** Brit. a track where horses are exercised at a gallop. ■ v. (**galloped**, **galloping**) **1** go or cause to go at the pace of a gallop. **2** proceed at great speed: *he galloped through the service*.
– DERIVATIVES **galloper** n. **galloping** adj.
– ORIGIN C16: from Old French *galop* (n.), *galoper* (v.), vars of Old Northern French *walop*, *waloper* (see **WALLOP**).

galloway /ˈgaləweɪ/ ■ n. an animal of a black hornless breed of cattle which originated in Galloway in Scotland.

gallows ■ pl. n. [usu. treated as sing.] a structure, typically consisting of two uprights and a crosspiece, used for hanging a person. ▶ (**the gallows**) execution by hanging.
– ORIGIN Old English, of Germanic origin.

gallows humour ■ n. grim and ironical humour in a desperate or hopeless situation.

gallows tree ■ n. another term for **GALLOWS**.

gallstone /ˈgɔːlstəʊn/ ■ n. a small, hard crystalline mass formed abnormally in the gall bladder or bile ducts from bile pigments, cholesterol, and calcium salts.

Gallup poll /ˈgaləp/ ■ n. trademark an assessment of public opinion by the questioning of a representative sample, used in forecasting voting results in an election.
– ORIGIN 1940s: named after the American statistician George H. *Gallup*.

galoot /ɡəˈluːt/ ■ n. N. Amer. & Scottish informal a clumsy or stupid person.
– ORIGIN C19 (orig. in nautical use meaning 'an inexperienced marine').

galore ■ adj. [postpos.] in abundance: *there were prizes galore*.
– ORIGIN C17: from Irish *go leor* 'to sufficiency'.

galosh /ɡəˈlɒʃ/ ■ n. a waterproof rubber overshoe.
– ORIGIN Middle English (denoting a type of clog): from late Latin *gallicula*, diminutive of Latin *gallica* (*solea*) 'Gallic (shoe)'.

galumph /ɡəˈlʌmf/ ■ v. informal move in a clumsy, ponderous, or noisy manner.
– DERIVATIVES **galumphing** adj.
– ORIGIN 1871: coined by Lewis Carroll in *Through the Looking Glass*; perhaps a blend of **GALLOP** and **TRIUMPH**.

galvanic /galˈvanɪk/ ■ adj. **1** relating to or involving electric currents produced by chemical action. **2** sudden and dramatic.
– DERIVATIVES **galvanically** adv.
– ORIGIN C18: from French *galvanique*, from the name of the Italian physiologist Luigi *Galvani*, known for his discovery of the twitching of frogs' legs in an electric field.

galvanic skin response (also **galvanic skin reflex**) ■ n. a change in the electrical resistance of the skin caused by emotional stress.

galvanize /ˈgalvənʌɪz/ (also **-ise**) ■ v. **1** shock or excite into action. **2** [often as adj. **galvanized** (also **-ised**)] coat (iron or steel) with a protective layer of zinc.
– DERIVATIVES **galvanization** (also **-isation**) n. **galvanizer** (also **-iser**) n.
– ORIGIN C19 ('stimulate by electricity'): from French *galvaniser* (see **GALVANIC**).

galvanometer /ˌgalvəˈnɒmɪtə/ ■ n. an instrument for detecting and measuring small electric currents.
– DERIVATIVES **galvanometric** adj.

gam

gam ▪ n. informal a leg.
– ORIGIN C18: prob. a var. of the heraldic term *gamb*, denoting a charge representing an animal's leg.

Gamay /'gameɪ/ ▪ n. a variety of black wine grape native to the Beaujolais district of France. ▸ a red wine made from this grape.
– ORIGIN from the name of a hamlet in Burgundy, eastern France.

gamba /'gambə/ ▪ n. short for VIOLA DA GAMBA.

Gambian /'gambɪən/ ▪ n. a native or national of Gambia, a country in West Africa. ▪ adj. of or relating to Gambia or its people.

gambit ▪ n. **1** an action or remark that is calculated to gain an advantage. **2** (in chess) an opening move in which a player makes a sacrifice, typically of a pawn, for the sake of some compensating advantage.
– ORIGIN C17: orig. *gambett*, from Italian *gambetto* 'tripping up'.

gamble ▪ v. **1** play games of chance for money; bet. ▸ bet (a sum of money). **2** take risky action in the hope of a desired result. ▪ n. **1** an act of gambling. **2** a risky undertaking or enterprise.
– DERIVATIVES **gambler** n.
– ORIGIN C18: from obsolete *gamel* 'play games', or from the verb GAME¹.

gambol ▪ v. (**gambolled**, **gambolling**; US **gamboled**, **gamboling**) run or jump about playfully. ▪ n. an act of gambolling.
– ORIGIN C16: from Italian *gambata* 'trip up'.

game¹ ▪ n. **1** an activity engaged in for amusement. **2** a form of competitive activity or sport played according to rules. **3** a complete episode or period of play, ending in a final result. **4** a single portion of play, forming a scoring unit within a game. **5** (**games**) a meeting for sporting contests. **6** (**games**) Brit. athletics or sports as a period of activity and instruction in a school. **7** the equipment used in playing a board game, computer game, etc. **8** a type of activity or business regarded as a game. **9** a secret plan or trick: *I was on to his little game.* **10** wild mammals or birds hunted for sport or food. ▸ the flesh of these, as food. ▪ adj. eager and willing to do something new or challenging: *they were game for anything.* ▪ v. **1** [as noun **gaming**] playing at games of chance for money. **2** play video or computer games.
– PHRASES **ahead of the game** ahead of one's competitors or peers. **beat someone at their own game** use someone's own methods to outdo them. **the game is up** the deception or crime is revealed or foiled. **on the game** Brit. informal working as a prostitute. **play the game** behave in a fair or honourable way; abide by the rules.
– DERIVATIVES **gamely** adv. **gameness** n. **gamester** n.
– ORIGIN Old English *gamen* 'amusement, fun', *gamenian* 'play, amuse oneself', of Germanic origin.

game² ▪ adj. (of a person's leg) lame.
– ORIGIN C18: orig. dialect.

game bird ▪ n. **1** a bird shot for sport or food. **2** a bird of a large group that includes pheasants, grouse, quails, guineafowl, etc. [Order Galliformes.]

gamecock (also **gamefowl**) ▪ n. a cock bred and trained for cockfighting.

game farm ▪ n. (especially in southern Africa) a farm stocked with a variety of wild animals, usually with facilities for visitors to observe or hunt the animals.

game fish ▪ n. (pl. same) a fish caught by anglers for sport, especially (in fresh water) salmon and trout and (in the sea) billfishes, sharks, bass, and mackerel. Compare with COARSE FISH.

gamekeeper ▪ n. a person employed to breed and protect game for a large estate.
– DERIVATIVES **gamekeeping** n.

gamelan /'gamələn/ ▪ n. a traditional instrumental ensemble in Java and Bali, including many bronze percussion instruments.
– ORIGIN C19: from Javanese.

gamepad ▪ n. a hand-held controller for video games.

game plan ▪ n. a strategy worked out in advance, especially in sport, politics, or business.

gameplay ▪ n. (in a computer game) the plot and the way the game is played, as distinct from the graphics and sound effects.

game point ▪ n. (in tennis and other sports) a point which if won by a player or side will also win them the game.

gamer ▪ n. a person who plays a game or games, especially a participant in a computer or role-playing game.

game ranch ▪ n. another term for GAME FARM.

game show ▪ n. a programme on television in which people compete to win prizes.

gamesmanship ▪ n. the art of winning games by using various ploys and tactics to gain a psychological advantage.
– DERIVATIVES **gamesman** n. (pl. -**men**).

gametangium /ˌgamɪ'tan(d)ʒɪəm/ ▪ n. (pl. **gametangia**) Botany a specialized organ in which gametes are formed in algae, ferns, and some other plants.
– ORIGIN C19: from modern Latin *gameta* (see GAMETE) + Greek *angeion* 'vessel'.

gamete /'gamiːt/ ▪ n. Biology a mature haploid male or female germ cell which is able to unite with another of the opposite sex in sexual reproduction to form a zygote.
– DERIVATIVES **gametic** /gə'mɛtɪk/ adj.
– ORIGIN C19: from modern Latin *gameta*, from Greek *gametē* 'wife', *gametēs* 'husband', from *gamos* 'marriage'.

game theory ▪ n. the mathematical study of strategies for dealing with competitive situations where the outcome of a participant's choice of action depends critically on the actions of other participants. Compare with DECISION THEORY.

gameto- /gə'miːtəʊ/ ▪ comb. form Biology representing GAMETE.

gametocyte /gə'miːtə(ʊ)sʌɪt/ ▪ n. Biology a cell that divides (by meiosis) to form gametes.

gametogenesis /gəˌmiːtə(ʊ)'dʒɛnɪsɪs/ ▪ n. Biology the process in which cells undergo meiosis to form gametes.

gametophyte /gə'miːtə(ʊ)fʌɪt/ ▪ n. Botany (in the life cycle of plants with alternating generations, e.g. ferns) the gamete-producing phase (typically haploid), which produces the zygote from which the sporophyte arises.
– DERIVATIVES **gametophytic** adj.

gamey ▪ adj. variant spelling of GAMY.

gamine /ga'miːn/ ▪ n. a girl with a mischievous, boyish charm. ▪ adj. characteristic of a gamine.
– ORIGIN C19: French.

gamma /'gamə/ ▪ n. **1** the third letter of the Greek alphabet (Γ, γ), transliterated as 'g'. ▸ [as modifier] denoting the third in a series of items or categories. **2** [as modifier] relating to gamma rays. **3** (pl. same) Physics a unit of magnetic field strength equal to 10^{-5} oersted.
– ORIGIN from Greek.

gamma-aminobutyric acid /ˌgaməəˌmiːnəʊbjuː'tɪrɪk, -əˌmʌɪnəʊ-, -'amɪnəʊ-/ ▪ n. Biochemistry an amino acid which acts to inhibit the transmission of nerve impulses.
– ORIGIN C20: *gamma* indicating the position of amino on the third carbon away from the acid group.

gamma globulin ▪ n. Biochemistry a mixture of blood plasma proteins, mainly immunoglobulins, with relatively low mobility under electrophoresis.

gamma rays (also **gamma radiation**) ▪ pl. n. penetrating electromagnetic radiation of shorter wavelength than X-rays.

gammon¹ ▪ n. **1** ham which has been cured like bacon. **2** the bottom piece of a side of bacon, including a hind leg.
– ORIGIN C15: from Old Northern French *gambon*, from *gambe* 'leg'.

gammon² ▪ n. a victory in backgammon (carrying a double score) in which the winner removes all his or her pieces before the loser has removed any. ▪ v. defeat with a gammon.
– ORIGIN C18: apparently from Old English *gamen* or *gamenian* (see GAME¹).

gammy ▪ adj. informal (especially of a leg) unable to function normally because of injury or chronic pain.
– ORIGIN C19 (in the sense 'bad, false'): dialect form of GAME².

gamut /ˈgamət/ ■ n. **1** the complete range or scope of something. **2** Music a complete scale of musical notes; the compass or range of a voice or instrument. **3** a scale consisting of seven overlapping hexachords, containing all the recognized notes used in medieval music, covering almost three octaves from bass G to treble E. ▸ the lowest note in this scale.
– PHRASES **run the gamut** experience, display, or perform the complete range of something.
– ORIGIN Middle English: from medieval Latin *gamma ut*: the Greek letter Γ (gamma) was used for bass G, with *ut* indicating that it was the first note in the lowest of the hexachords or six-note scales.

gamy (also **gamey**) ■ adj. (**-ier**, **-iest**) **1** (of meat) having the strong flavour or smell of game, especially when it is high. **2** chiefly N. Amer. racy or risqué.
– DERIVATIVES **gamily** adv. **gaminess** n.

ganache /ɡəˈnaʃ/ ■ n. a whipped filling of chocolate and cream, used in cakes and confectionery.
– ORIGIN from French.

gander /ˈɡandə/ ■ n. **1** a male goose. **2** informal a look or glance.
– ORIGIN Old English, of Germanic origin; sense 2 was orig. criminals' slang.

gang ■ n. an organized group of criminals or disorderly young people. ▸ informal a group of people who regularly associate together. ▸ an organized group of people doing manual work. ■ v. **1** (**gang together**) form a group or gang. ▸ (**gang up**) join together, typically in order to intimidate someone. **2** arrange (electrical devices or machines) together to work in coordination.
– ORIGIN Old English, from Old Norse *gangr*, *ganga* 'gait, course, going', of Germanic origin.

gang bang ■ n. informal a gang rape. ▸ a sexual orgy.
– DERIVATIVES **gang-bang** v. **gang banger** n.

gangboard ■ n. another term for GANGPLANK.

gangbuster ■ n. informal a police officer engaged in breaking up criminal gangs.

gangling (also **gangly**) ■ adj. tall, thin, and awkward.
– ORIGIN C19: from dialect *gang* 'go'.

ganglion /ˈɡaŋɡlɪən/ ■ n. (pl. **ganglia** or **ganglions**)
1 Anatomy a structure containing a number of nerve cells, often forming a swelling on a nerve fibre. ▸ a well-defined mass of grey matter within the central nervous system. **2** Medicine an abnormal benign swelling on a tendon sheath.
– DERIVATIVES **ganglionic** adj.
– ORIGIN C17: from Greek *ganglion* 'tumour on or near sinews or tendons'.

ganglioside /ˈɡaŋɡlɪə(ʊ)sʌɪd/ ■ n. Biochemistry any of a group of complex lipids present in the grey matter of the human brain.
– ORIGIN 1940s: from GANGLION.

gangplank ■ n. a movable plank used to board or disembark from a ship or boat.

gang rape ■ n. the rape of one person by a group of other people.
– DERIVATIVES **gang-rape** v.

gangrene /ˈɡaŋɡriːn/ ■ n. Medicine localized death and decomposition of body tissue, resulting from either obstructed circulation or bacterial infection. ■ v. become affected with gangrene.
– DERIVATIVES **gangrenous** /ˈɡaŋɡrɪnəs/ adj.
– ORIGIN C16: from Greek *gangraina*.

gangsta ■ n. **1** chiefly N. Amer. a gang member. **2** (also **gangsta rap**) a type of rap music featuring aggressive macho lyrics, often with reference to gang warfare.

gangster ■ n. a member of an organized gang of violent criminals.
– DERIVATIVES **gangsterism** n.

gangue /ɡaŋ/ ■ n. the commercially valueless material in which ore is found.
– ORIGIN C19: from French, from German *Gang* 'course, lode'.

gangway ■ n. **1** a raised platform or walkway providing a passage. **2** a movable bridge linking a ship to the shore. ▸ an opening in the bulwarks by which a ship is entered or left. **3** Brit. a passage between rows of seats, especially in a theatre or aircraft. ■ exclam. make way!

ganja /ˈɡan(d)ʒə, ˈɡɑː-/ ■ n. cannabis.
– ORIGIN C19: from Hindi *gāṁjā*.

ganna /ˈxana/ ■ n. chiefly S. African any of several desert shrubs, the ashes of which were formerly used in soap-making. [Genus *Salsola*, in particular *S. aphylla*.]
– ORIGIN perhaps from Khoikhoi.

gannet /ˈɡanɪt/ ■ n. a large seabird with mainly white plumage, catching fish by plunge-diving. [*Morus capensis* (Cape gannet) and other species.]
– ORIGIN Old English, of Germanic origin.

gannetry ■ n. (pl. **-ies**) a breeding colony of gannets, usually on an isolated rock.

ganoid /ˈɡanɔɪd/ ■ adj. Zoology (of fish scales) hard and bony with a shiny enamelled surface. Compare with CTENOID and PLACOID.
– ORIGIN C19: from French *ganoïde*, from Greek *ganos* 'brightness'.

gantlet /ˈɡantlɪt/ ■ n. US spelling of GAUNTLET².

gantry ■ n. (pl. **-ies**) **1** a bridge-like overhead structure supporting equipment such as a crane or railway signals. ▸ a tall framework supporting a space rocket prior to launching. **2** a collection of inverted bottles with optics for serving measures in a bar.
– ORIGIN Middle English (denoting a wooden stand for barrels): prob. from dialect *gawn* (contraction of GALLON) + TREE.

Gantt chart /ɡant/ ■ n. a chart in which a series of horizontal lines shows the amount of work done in certain periods of time in relation to the amount planned for those periods.
– ORIGIN early C20: named after the American management consultant Henry L. *Gantt*.

gaol ■ n. variant spelling of JAIL.

gap ■ n. **1** a break or hole in an object or between two objects. **2** a space, interval, or break.
– PHRASES **take the gap** S. African informal seize an opportunity or opening. ▸ relocate to another country.
– DERIVATIVES **gapped** adj. **gappy** adj.
– ORIGIN Middle English: from Old Norse, 'chasm'; rel. to GAPE.

gape ■ v. **1** be or become wide open. **2** stare with one's mouth open wide in amazement or wonder. ■ n. a wide opening. ▸ an open-mouthed stare. ▸ a widely open mouth or beak.
– DERIVATIVES **gaping** adj. **gapingly** adv.
– ORIGIN Middle English: from Old Norse *gapa*; rel. to GAP.

gap year ■ n. a year off from formal education, often taken between leaving school and going to university, spent working, travelling, or doing community service.

garage /ˈɡarɑː(d)ʒ, -ɪdʒ, ɡəˈrɑːʒ/ ■ n. **1** a building for housing a motor vehicle or vehicles. **2** an establishment which sells fuel or which repairs and sells motor vehicles. **3** a style of unpolished energetic rock music. [from the idea of amateur bands practising in garages.] **4** a variety of house music influenced by soul music. [from *Paradise Garage*, the name of a Manhattan dance club.] ■ v. put or keep (a motor vehicle) in a garage.
– ORIGIN C20: from French, from *garer* 'to shelter'.

garage sale ■ n. a sale of unwanted goods held in a garage or front garden.

garam masala /ˌɡʌrəm məˈsɑːlə/ ■ n. a spice mixture used in Indian cookery.
– ORIGIN from Urdu *garam maṣālaḥ*, from *garam* 'hot, pungent' + *maṣālaḥ* 'spice'.

garb¹ ■ n. clothing or dress, especially of a distinctive or special kind. ■ v. dress in distinctive clothes.
– ORIGIN C16: from Italian *garbo* 'elegance', of Germanic origin.

garb² ■ n. Heraldry a sheaf of wheat.
– ORIGIN C16: from Old Northern French *garbe*.

garbage ■ n. chiefly N. Amer. **1** rubbish or waste, especially domestic refuse. **2** something worthless or meaningless.
– PHRASES **garbage in, garbage out** Computing, informal incorrect or poor-quality input will always produce faulty output.
– ORIGIN Middle English ('offal'): from Anglo-Norman French.

garbage collector

garbage collector ■ n. 1 N. Amer. a dustman. 2 Computing a program that automatically removes unwanted data held temporarily in memory during processing.

garbanzo /gɑːˈbænzəʊ/ ■ n. (pl. -os) N. Amer. a chickpea.
– ORIGIN C18: from Spanish.

garble ■ v. [often as adj. **garbled**] reproduce (a message or transmission) in a confused and distorted way. ■ n. a garbled account or transmission.
– ORIGIN Middle English: from Anglo-Latin and Italian *garbellare*, from Arabic *ġarbala* 'sift', perhaps from late Latin *cribellare* 'to sieve'.

garçon /ˈɡɑːsɒn, ɡɑːˈsɔ̃/ ■ n. a waiter in a French restaurant.
– ORIGIN French, 'boy'.

Garda /ˈɡɑːdə/ ■ n. [treated as sing. or pl.] the state police force of the Irish Republic. ▶ (pl. **Gardai** /-diː/) a member of the Irish police force.
– ORIGIN from Irish *Garda Siochá* 'Civic Guard'.

garden ■ n. 1 a piece of ground adjoining a house, used for growing flowers, fruit, or vegetables. 2 (**gardens**) ornamental grounds laid out for public enjoyment. ■ v. cultivate or work in a garden.
– DERIVATIVES **gardener** n. **gardening** n.
– ORIGIN Middle English: from Old Northern French *gardin*, var. of Old French *jardin*, of Germanic origin.

garden centre ■ n. an establishment where plants and gardening equipment are sold.

garden city ■ n. a new town designed as a whole with much open space and greenery.

garden cress ■ n. a type of cress that is grown as a sprouting vegetable, often mixed with sprouting mustard, and used in salads. [*Lepidium sativum*.]

gardenia /ɡɑːˈdiːnɪə/ ■ n. a tree or shrub of warm climates, with large fragrant white or yellow flowers. [Genus *Gardenia*: many species.]
– ORIGIN named in honour of the Scottish naturalist Dr Alexander *Garden* (1730–91).

garden party ■ n. a social event held on a lawn in a garden.

garden pea ■ n. a variety of pea grown for food.

garden suburb ■ n. S. African & Brit. a suburb set in rural surroundings or incorporating much landscaping.

garden-variety ■ adj. of the usual or ordinary type; commonplace.

garden warbler ■ n. a migratory Eurasian songbird with drab plumage, frequenting woodland. [*Sylvia borin*.]

garderobe /ˈɡɑːdrəʊb/ ■ n. 1 a toilet in a medieval building. 2 a wardrobe or storeroom in a medieval building.
– ORIGIN Middle English: French, from *garder* 'to keep' + *robe* 'robe, dress'.

garfish ■ n. (pl. same or -**fishes**) 1 a long, slender marine fish with beak-like jaws containing sharp teeth. [Family Belonidae: several species.] 2 N. Amer. a similar freshwater fish. [Genus *Lepisosteus*.]
– ORIGIN Middle English: apparently from Old English *gār* 'spear' + FISH.

garganey /ˈɡɑːɡ(ə)ni/ ■ n. (pl. same or -**eys**) a small duck, the male of which has a brown head with a white stripe from the eye to the neck. [*Anas querquedula*.]
– ORIGIN C17: from Italian dialect *garganei*, of imitative origin.

gargantuan /ɡɑːˈɡantjʊən/ ■ adj. enormous.
– ORIGIN C16: from *Gargantua*, the name of a voracious giant in Rabelais's book of the same name.

gargle ■ v. wash one's mouth and throat with a liquid that is kept in motion by breathing through it with a gurgling sound. ■ n. an act of gargling. ▶ a liquid used for gargling.
– ORIGIN C16: from French *gargouiller* 'gurgle, bubble', from *gargouille* (see GARGOYLE).

gargoyle /ˈɡɑːɡɔɪl/ ■ n. a grotesque carved human or animal face or figure projecting from the gutter of a building, usually as a spout to carry water clear of a wall.
– ORIGIN Middle English: from Old French *gargouille* 'throat', also 'gargoyle', rel. to Greek *gargarizein* 'to gargle' (of imitative origin).

garibaldi /ˌɡarɪˈbɔːldi, -ˈbaldi/ ■ n. (pl. **garibaldis**) Brit. a thin biscuit containing a compressed layer of currants.
– ORIGIN C19: named after the Italian patriot Giuseppe *Garibaldi*.

garingboom /ˈxɑːrɪŋbʊəm/ ■ n. S. African another term for CENTURY PLANT.
– ORIGIN from Afrikaans *garing* 'thread' + *boom* 'tree'.

garish /ˈɡɛːrɪʃ/ ■ adj. obtrusively bright and showy; lurid.
– DERIVATIVES **garishly** adv. **garishness** n.
– ORIGIN C16.

garland ■ n. 1 a wreath of flowers and leaves, worn on the head or hung as a decoration. 2 a prize or distinction. 3 archaic a literary anthology. ■ v. adorn or crown with a garland.
– ORIGIN Middle English: from Old French *garlande*.

garlic ■ n. 1 a strong-smelling pungent-tasting bulb, used as a flavouring in cookery. 2 the central Asian plant, closely related to the onion, which produces this bulb. [*Allium sativum*.] ▶ used in names of plants with a similar smell or flavour, e.g. wild garlic.
– DERIVATIVES **garlicky** adj.
– ORIGIN Old English *gārlēac*, from *gār* 'spear' (because the shape of a clove resembles the head of a spear) + *lēac* 'leek'.

garment ■ n. an item of clothing.
– ORIGIN Middle English: from Old French *garnement* 'equipment', from *garnir* (see GARNISH).

garner ■ v. 1 gather or collect (something, especially information or approval). 2 archaic store; deposit. ■ n. archaic a storehouse for corn; a granary.
– ORIGIN Middle English: from Old French *gernier*, from Latin *granarium* 'granary'.

garnet /ˈɡɑːnɪt/ ■ n. a vitreous silicate mineral, in particular a deep red form used as a gem.
– ORIGIN Middle English: prob. from Old French *grenat*, from medieval Latin *granatus*, perhaps from *granatum* (see POMEGRANATE), because the garnet is similar in colour to the pulp of the fruit.

garnish ■ v. 1 decorate or embellish (something, especially food). 2 Law serve notice on (a third party) for the purpose of legally seizing money belonging to a debtor or defendant. ▶ seize (money, especially part of a person's salary) to settle a debt or claim. ■ n. a decoration or embellishment, especially for food.
– DERIVATIVES **garnishment** n.
– ORIGIN Middle English: from Old French *garnir*, prob. of Germanic origin.

garnishee /ˌɡɑːnɪˈʃiː/ Law ■ n. a third party who is garnished. ■ v. (**garnishees, garnisheed**) another term for GARNISH (in sense 2).

garotte ■ v. & n. variant spelling of GARROTTE.

garret ■ n. a top-floor or attic room, especially a small dismal one.
– ORIGIN Middle English ('watchtower'): from Old French *garite*, from *garir* (see GARRISON).

garrick ■ n. a large game fish with a leathery skin, found from the Mediterranean southwards along the western and southern African coast. [*Lichia amia*.]

garrison ■ n. a body of troops stationed in a fortress or town to defend it. ■ v. provide (a place) with a garrison.
– ORIGIN Middle English: from Old French *garison*, from *garir* 'defend, provide', of Germanic origin.

garrotte /ɡəˈrɒt/ (also **garotte**; US **garrote**) ■ v. kill by strangulation, especially with an iron collar or a length of wire or cord. ■ n. a wire, cord, or apparatus used for garrotting.
– ORIGIN C17: from Spanish *garrote* 'a cudgel, a garrotte', perhaps of Celtic origin.

garrulous /ˈɡar(j)ʊləs/ ■ adj. excessively talkative, especially on trivial matters.
– DERIVATIVES **garrulity** /ɡəˈruːlɪti/ n. **garrulously** adv. **garrulousness** n.
– ORIGIN C17: from Latin *garrulus*, from *garrire* 'to chatter, prattle'.

garryowen /ˌɡarɪˈəʊɪn/ ■ n. Rugby an up-and-under.

–ORIGIN 1960s: named after a rugby club in Limerick, Republic of Ireland.

garter ■ n. a band worn around the leg to keep up a stocking or sock. ► N. Amer. a suspender for a sock or stocking.
–DERIVATIVES **gartered** adj.
–ORIGIN Middle English: from Old French *gartier*, from *garet* 'bend of the knee, calf of the leg', prob. of Celtic origin.

garter belt ■ n. N. Amer. a suspender belt.

garter snake ■ n. 1 a nocturnal burrowing African snake, typically dark with lighter bands. [Genus *Elapsoidea*.] 2 a common, harmless North American snake with well-defined longitudinal stripes. [*Thamnophis sirtalis* and related species.]

garter stitch ■ n. knitting in which all of the rows are knitted in plain stitch, rather than alternating with purl rows.

gas ■ n. (pl. **gases** or chiefly US **gasses**) 1 an air-like fluid substance which expands freely to fill any space available, irrespective of its quantity. ► Physics a substance of this type that cannot be liquefied by pressure alone. Compare with VAPOUR. ► a flammable substance of this type used as a fuel. 2 a gaseous anaesthetic such as nitrous oxide, used in dentistry. 3 chiefly N. Amer. flatulence. 4 Mining an explosive mixture of firedamp with air. 5 N. Amer. informal short for GASOLINE. 6 (**a gas**) informal an entertaining or amusing person or thing. ■ v. (**gases**, **gassed**, **gassing**) 1 attack with, expose to, or kill with gas. ► (of a storage battery or dry cell) give off gas. 2 informal talk idly; chatter.
–DERIVATIVES **gasification** n. **gasify** v. **gasser** n.
–ORIGIN C17: invented by the Belgian chemist J. B. van Helmont to denote an occult principle which he believed to exist in all matter; suggested by Greek *khaos* 'chaos'.

gasbag ■ n. informal a person who talks idly and excessively.

gas chamber ■ n. an airtight room that can be filled with poisonous gas to kill people or animals.

gas chromatography ■ n. chromatography employing a gas as the moving carrier medium.

gas constant ■ n. Chemistry the constant of proportionality in the gas equation, equal to 8.314 joule kelvin^{-1} mole^{-1}.

gaseous /ˈɡasɪəs, ˈɡeɪsɪəs/ ■ adj. relating to or having the characteristics of a gas.
–DERIVATIVES **gaseousness** n.

gas equation ■ n. Chemistry the equation of state of an ideal gas, $PV = nRT$, where P = pressure, V = volume, T = absolute temperature, R = the gas constant, and n = the number of moles of gas.

gas guzzler ■ n. informal, chiefly N. Amer. a large motor car with a high fuel consumption.

gash ■ n. a long, deep slash, cut, or wound. ■ v. make a gash in.
–ORIGIN Middle English *garse*, from Old French *garcer* 'to chap, crack', perhaps from Greek *kharassein* 'sharpen, scratch'.

gasket /ˈɡaskɪt/ ■ n. a sheet or ring of rubber or other material sealing the junction between two surfaces in an engine or other device.
–ORIGIN C17: perhaps from French *garcette* 'thin rope', orig. 'little girl'.

gaskin /ˈɡaskɪn/ ■ n. the muscular part of the hind leg of a horse between the stifle and the hock.
–ORIGIN C16: perhaps from obsolete *galligaskins* 'breeches'.

gas laws ■ pl. n. Chemistry the physical laws that describe the properties of gases, including Boyle's and Charles's laws.

gaslight ■ n. light from lamps in which an incandescent mantle is heated by a jet of burning gas.
–DERIVATIVES **gaslit** adj.

gas mask ■ n. a protective mask used to cover the face as a defence against poison gas.

gas–liquid chromatography ■ n. chromatography employing a gas as the moving carrier medium and a liquid as the stationary medium.

gas oil ■ n. a type of fuel oil distilled from petroleum and heavier than paraffin oil.

gasoline (also **gasolene**) ■ n. North American term for PETROL.

gasometer ■ n. a large tank in which gas for use as fuel is stored before being distributed to consumers.

gasp ■ v. 1 catch one's breath with an open mouth, owing to pain or astonishment. ► (**gasp for**) strain to obtain (air) by gasping. 2 (**be gasping for**) informal be desperate to obtain or consume; crave: *I'm gasping for a drink!* ■ n. a convulsive catching of breath.
–PHRASES **the last gasp** the point of exhaustion, death, or completion.
–ORIGIN Middle English: from Old Norse *geispa* 'to yawn'.

gasper ■ n. Brit. informal, dated a cigarette.

gas-permeable ■ adj. (of a contact lens) allowing the diffusion of gases into and out of the cornea.

gassy ■ adj. (**-ier**, **-iest**) 1 resembling or full of gas. 2 informal verbose; idly chattering.
–DERIVATIVES **gassiness** n.

gasteria ■ n. a plant of a genus of aloe-like succulents native to southern Africa, with fleshy leaves and tubular flowers. [Genus *Gasteria*.]

gastrectomy /ɡaˈstrɛktəmi/ ■ n. (pl. **-ies**) surgical removal of a part or the whole of the stomach.

gastric ■ adj. of the stomach.
–ORIGIN C17: from modern Latin *gastricus*, from Greek *gastēr*, *gastr-* 'stomach'.

gastric flu ■ n. a short-lived stomach disorder of unknown cause, popularly attributed to a virus.

gastric juice ■ n. an acid fluid secreted by the stomach glands and active in promoting digestion.

gastrin ■ n. Biochemistry a hormone which stimulates secretion of gastric juice, and is secreted into the bloodstream by the stomach wall in response to the presence of food.

gastritis /ɡaˈstrʌɪtɪs/ ■ n. Medicine inflammation of the lining of the stomach.

gastro- /ˈɡastrəʊ/ ■ comb. form of or relating to the stomach: *gastro-enteritis*.
–ORIGIN from Greek *gastēr*, *gastr-* 'stomach'.

gastrocnemius /ˌɡastrə(ʊ)ˈkniːmɪəs/ (also **gastrocnemius muscle**) ■ n. (pl. **gastrocnemii** /-mɪʌɪ/) Anatomy the chief muscle of the calf of the leg, which flexes the knee and foot.
–ORIGIN C17: modern Latin, from Greek *gastroknēmia* 'calf of the leg', from *gaster* 'stomach' + *knēmē* 'leg' (from the bulging shape of the calf).

gastro-enteritis ■ n. inflammation of the stomach and intestines, typically resulting from bacterial toxins or viral infection and causing vomiting and diarrhoea.

gastroenterology /ˌɡastrəʊɛntəˈrɒlədʒi/ ■ n. the branch of medicine which deals with disorders of the stomach and intestines.
–DERIVATIVES **gastroenterological** adj. **gastroenterologist** n.

gastrointestinal /ˌɡastrəʊɪnˈtɛstɪn(ə)l, -ɪntɛsˈtʌɪn(ə)l/ ■ adj. of or relating to the stomach and the intestines.

gastrolith /ˈɡastrə(ʊ)lɪθ/ ■ n. 1 Zoology a small stone swallowed by a bird, reptile, or fish to aid digestion in the gizzard. 2 Medicine a hard concretion in the stomach.

gastronome /ˈɡastrənəʊm/ ■ n. a gourmet.

gastronomy /ɡaˈstrɒnəmi/ ■ n. the practice or art of choosing, cooking, and eating good food.
–DERIVATIVES **gastronomic** adj. **gastronomical** adj. **gastronomically** adv.
–ORIGIN C19: from Greek *gastronomia*, alteration of *gastrologia* (see GASTRO-, -LOGY).

Gastropoda /ˌɡastrəˈpəʊdə, ɡaˈstrɒpədə/ ■ pl. n. Zoology a large class of molluscs which includes snails, slugs, and whelks.
–DERIVATIVES **gastropod** n.
–ORIGIN from Greek *gastēr*, *gastr-* 'stomach' + *pous*, *pod-* 'foot'.

gastroscope

gastroscope ▪ n. an optical instrument used for inspecting the interior of the stomach.
– DERIVATIVES **gastroscopic** adj. **gastroscopy** n.

gastrula /ˈgastrʊlə/ ▪ n. (pl. **gastrulae** /-liː/) Embryology an embryo at the stage following the blastula, when it is a hollow cup-shaped structure having three layers of cells.
– DERIVATIVES **gastrulation** n.
– ORIGIN C19: modern Latin, from Greek *gastēr, gastr-* 'stomach' + the Latin diminutive ending *-ula*.

gas turbine ▪ n. a turbine driven by expanding hot gases produced by burning fuel, as in a jet engine.

gasworks ▪ pl. n. [treated as sing.] a place where gas is manufactured and processed.

gate ▪ n. 1 a hinged barrier used to close an opening in a wall, fence, or hedge. ▸ an exit from an airport building to an aircraft. ▸ a hinged or sliding barrier for controlling the flow of water: *a sluice gate*. 2 the number of people who pay to enter a sports ground for an event. 3 an arrangement of slots into which the gear lever of a motor vehicle moves to engage each gear. 4 an electric circuit with an output which depends on the combination of several inputs. ▪ v. Brit. confine (a pupil or student) to school or college.
– DERIVATIVES **gated** adj.
– ORIGIN Old English, of Germanic origin.

-gate ▪ comb. form in nouns denoting a scandal, especially one involving a cover-up: *Hansiegate*.
– ORIGIN 1970s: suggested by the *Watergate* scandal in the US, 1972.

gateau /ˈgatəʊ/ ▪ n. (pl. **gateaus** or **gateaux** /-əʊz/) chiefly Brit. a rich cake, typically one containing layers of cream or fruit.
– ORIGIN C19: from French *gâteau* 'cake'.

gatecrash ▪ v. enter (a party) without an invitation or ticket.
– DERIVATIVES **gatecrasher** n.

gated community ▪ n. 1 S. African an existing neighbourhood that has been fenced off, with controlled access. 2 a security complex.

gatefold ▪ n. an oversized page in a book or magazine folded to the same size as the other pages but intended to be opened out for reading.

gatehouse ▪ n. 1 a house standing by a gateway. 2 historical a room over a city or palace gate, often used as a prison.

gatekeeper ▪ n. an attendant at a gate. ▸ a person or thing that controls access to something.

gateleg table ▪ n. a table with hinged legs that may be swung out from the centre to support folding leaves.
– DERIVATIVES **gatelegged** adj.

gatepost ▪ n. a post on which a gate is hinged, or against which it shuts.

gateway ▪ n. 1 an opening that can be closed by a gate. ▸ a frame or arch built around or over a gate. 2 Computing a device used to connect two different networks, especially a connection to the Internet.

gather ▪ v. 1 come or bring together; assemble or accumulate. ▸ harvest (a crop). ▸ collect plants, fruits, etc., for food: *hunting and gathering*. ▸ draw together or towards oneself. 2 summon up (a mental or physical attribute): *he gathered his thoughts together*. 3 develop a higher degree of: *the Green movement is gathering pace*. 4 infer; understand. 5 draw and hold together (fabric or a part of a garment) by running thread through it. ▪ n. (**gathers**) a part of a garment that is gathered or drawn in.
– PHRASES **gather way** (of a ship) begin to move.
– DERIVATIVES **gatherer** n.
– ORIGIN Old English, of West Germanic origin.

gathering ▪ n. an assembly or meeting, especially a social one.

Gatling gun ▪ n. an early type of machine gun, with clustered barrels.
– ORIGIN C19: named after the American inventor Richard J. *Gatling*.

gatsby ▪ n. (pl. **-ies**) S. African a long loaf or roll filled with salad, fried chips, and meat or fish.

gatvol /ˈxʌtfɔl/ ▪ adj. S. African informal extremely fed up or disgusted.
– ORIGIN from Afrikaans *gat* 'anus, arse' + *vol* 'full'.

gauche /ɡəʊʃ/ ▪ adj. unsophisticated and socially awkward.
– DERIVATIVES **gauchely** adv. **gaucheness** n.
– ORIGIN C18: French, 'left'.

gaucherie /ˈɡəʊʃ(ə)ri/ ▪ n. awkward or unsophisticated ways.

gaucho /ˈɡaʊtʃəʊ, ˈɡɔː-/ ▪ n. (pl. **-os**) a cowboy from the South American pampas.
– ORIGIN Latin American Spanish, prob. from Araucanian *kauču* 'friend'.

gaud /ɡɔːd/ ▪ n. archaic a showy and purely ornamental thing.
– ORIGIN Middle English (denoting a trick or pretence): perhaps from Old French *gaudir* 'rejoice', from Latin *gaudere*.

gaudy ▪ adj. (**-ier, -iest**) extravagantly or tastelessly bright or showy.
– DERIVATIVES **gaudily** adv. **gaudiness** n.
– ORIGIN C15: prob. from GAUD.

gauge /ɡeɪdʒ/ (chiefly US also **gage**) ▪ n. 1 an instrument that measures and gives a visual display of the amount, level, or contents of something. 2 the thickness, size, or capacity of a wire, sheet, tube, bullet, etc., especially as a standard measure. 3 the distance between the rails of a line of railway track. ▪ v. 1 estimate or determine the amount or level of. ▸ judge or assess (a situation, mood, etc.). 2 measure the dimensions of with a gauge. ▸ [as adj. **gauged**] made in standard dimensions.
– DERIVATIVES **gauger** n.
– ORIGIN Middle English: from Old French *gauge* (n.), *gauger* (v.), var. of Old Northern French *jauge, jauger*.

gauge pressure ▪ n. Engineering the amount by which the pressure measured in a fluid exceeds that of the atmosphere.

Gaul /ɡɔːl/ ▪ n. a native or inhabitant of the ancient European region of Gaul.
– ORIGIN from Latin *Gallus*, prob. of Celtic origin.

Gauleiter /ˈɡaʊlʌɪtə/ ▪ n. 1 historical a political official governing a district under Nazi rule. 2 an overbearing official.
– ORIGIN 1930s: German, from *Gau* 'administrative district' + *Leiter* 'leader'.

Gaulish ▪ n. the Celtic language of the ancient Gauls. ▪ adj. relating to or denoting the ancient Gauls.

Gaullism /ˈɡəʊlɪz(ə)m/ ▪ n. the principles and policies of the French statesman Charles de Gaulle (1890–1970), characterized by conservatism, nationalism, and advocacy of centralized government.
– DERIVATIVES **Gaullist** n. & adj.

gaunt ▪ adj. 1 lean and haggard, especially through suffering, hunger, or age. 2 (of a place) grim or desolate in appearance.
– DERIVATIVES **gauntly** adv. **gauntness** n.
– ORIGIN Middle English.

gauntlet[1] ▪ n. a stout glove with a long loose wrist. ▸ historical an armoured glove.
– PHRASES **take up** (or **throw down**) **the gauntlet** accept (or issue) a challenge.
– ORIGIN Middle English: from Old French *gantelet*, diminutive of *gant* 'glove', of Germanic origin.

gauntlet[2] (US also **gantlet**) ▪ n. (in phr. **run the gauntlet**) 1 go through an intimidating crowd or experience in order to reach a goal. 2 historical undergo the military punishment of receiving blows while running between two rows of men with sticks.
– ORIGIN C17: alteration of *gantlope* (from Swedish *gatlopp*, from *gata* 'lane' + *lopp* 'course'), associated with GAUNTLET[1].

gauss /ɡaʊs/ ▪ n. (pl. same or **gausses**) Physics a unit of magnetic induction, equal to one ten-thousandth of a tesla.
– ORIGIN C19: named after the German mathematician K. *Gauss*.

Gaussian distribution /ˈɡaʊsɪən/ ▪ n. another term for NORMAL DISTRIBUTION.

gauze /ɡɔːz/ ▪ n. 1 a thin transparent fabric. ▸ Medicine

thin, loosely woven cloth used for dressing and swabs. **2** (also **wire gauze**) a very fine wire mesh.
– DERIVATIVES **gauzy** adj.
– ORIGIN C16: from French *gaze*, perhaps from *Gaza*, the name of a town in Palestine.

gave past of GIVE.

gavel /ˈgav(ə)l/ ■ n. a small hammer with which an auctioneer, judge, etc., hits a surface to call for attention or order. ■ v. (**gavelled**, **gavelling**; US **gaveled**, **gaveling**) bring to order by use of a gavel.
– ORIGIN C19 'stonemason's mallet'.

gavial /ˈgeɪvɪəl/ ■ n. variant spelling of GHARIAL.

gavotte /gəˈvɒt/ ■ n. a medium-paced French dance, popular in the 18th century.
– ORIGIN French: from Provençal *gavoto* 'dance of the mountain people', from *Gavot* 'a native of the Alps'.

gawk ■ v. stare openly and stupidly. ■ n. an awkward or shy person.
– DERIVATIVES **gawker** n. **gawkish** adj.
– ORIGIN C17: perhaps rel. to obsolete *gaw* 'to gaze', from Old Norse *gá* 'heed'.

gawky ■ adj. (**-ier**, **-iest**) nervously awkward and ungainly.
– DERIVATIVES **gawkily** adv. **gawkiness** n.

gawp ■ v. Brit. informal stare openly in a stupid or rude manner.
– DERIVATIVES **gawper** n.
– ORIGIN C17: perhaps an alteration of GAPE.

gay ■ adj. (**-er**, **-est**) **1** (especially of a man) homosexual. ▶ relating to or used by homosexuals. **2** dated light-hearted and carefree. **3** dated brightly coloured; showy. ■ n. a homosexual person, especially a man.
– DERIVATIVES **gayness** n.
– ORIGIN Middle English: from Old French *gai*.

gayety ■ n. US variant spelling of GAIETY.

Gay-Lussac's law /geɪˈluːsaks/ ■ n. Chemistry a law stating that the volumes of gases undergoing a reaction at constant pressure and temperature are in a simple ratio to each other and to that of the product.
– ORIGIN C19: named after the French scientist Joseph L. Gay-Lussac.

gazania /gəˈzeɪnɪə/ ■ n. a tropical herbaceous plant of the daisy family, with showy orange or yellow flowers. [Genus *Gazania*.]
– ORIGIN named after the C15 Greek scholar Theodore of Gaza.

gaze ■ v. look steadily and intently. ■ n. a steady intent look.
– DERIVATIVES **gazer** n.
– ORIGIN Middle English: perhaps rel. to obsolete *gaw* (see GAWK).

gazebo /gəˈziːbəʊ/ ■ n. (pl. **-os** or **-oes**) a small building, especially one in the garden of a house, that gives a wide view of the surrounding area.
– ORIGIN C18: perhaps humorously from GAZE, in imitation of Latin future tenses ending in *-ebo*.

gazelle ■ n. a small slender African or Asian antelope, typically having curved horns and fawn-coloured with white underparts. [*Gazella* and other genera: several species.]
– ORIGIN C17: from French, prob. from Arabic *ghazāl*.

gazette ■ n. **1** a journal or newspaper, especially the official one of an organization or institution. ▶ (**the Gazette**) (in South Africa) the Government Gazette. **2** historical a news-sheet. ■ v. announce or publish in an official gazette: *the National Plan was gazetted on 9 March 2001.* ▶ publish the fact of the appointment of (someone) to a military or other official post.
– ORIGIN C17: from Italian *gazzetta*, orig. Venetian *gazeta de la novità* 'a halfpennyworth of news' (with ref. to a news-sheet sold for a *gazeta*, a Venetian coin of small value).

gazetteer /ˌgazəˈtɪə/ ■ n. a geographical index or dictionary.
– ORIGIN C17: from Italian *gazzettiere*, from *gazzetta* (see GAZETTE); current sense is from a gazetteer called *The Gazetteer's: or, Newsman's Interpreter*.

gazpacho /gasˈpatʃəʊ/ ■ n. (pl. **-os**) a cold Spanish soup made from tomatoes, peppers, and other salad vegetables.
– ORIGIN from Spanish.

GB ■ abbrev. **1** Great Britain. **2** (also **Gb**) Computing gigabyte(s) or gigabit(s).

GBH ■ abbrev. grievous bodily harm.

Gbyte ■ abbrev. gigabyte(s).

GC ■ abbrev. George Cross.

GCE ■ abbrev. General Certificate of Education, an examination taken by secondary school pupils, chiefly in the UK (except Scotland), at advanced level and, formerly, at ordinary level.

GCIS ■ abbrev. (in South Africa) Government Communication and Information System.

GCSE ■ abbrev. General Certificate of Secondary Education, an examination taken chiefly in the UK (except Scotland) by secondary school pupils at age 15 or 16.

Gd ■ symb. the chemical element gadolinium.

Gdns ■ abbrev. Gardens (as part of an address).

GDP ■ abbrev. gross domestic product.

GDR ■ abbrev. historical German Democratic Republic.

Ge ■ symb. the chemical element germanium.

GEAR ■ abbrev. (in South Africa) Growth, Employment, and Redistribution: *the GEAR strategy*.

gear ■ n. **1** a toothed wheel that works with others to alter the relation between the speed of an engine and the speed of the driven parts (e.g. wheels). ▶ a particular setting of engaged gears: *in fifth gear*. **2** informal apparatus or equipment. ▶ clothing: *designer gear*. ■ v. **1** design or adjust gears to give a specified speed or power output. **2** (often **gear something up**) make ready; prepare. ▶ equip or adapt for a particular purpose. **3** (**gear down**) or **up** change to a lower (or higher) gear.
– PHRASES **in** (or **out of**) **gear** with a gear (or no gear) engaged.
– ORIGIN Middle English: of Scandinavian origin.

gearbox ■ n. a set of gears with its casing, especially in a motor vehicle; the transmission.

geared ■ adj. **1** fitted with gears. **2** (of a company) having a specified ratio of loan capital (debt) to the value of its ordinary shares (equity).

gearing ■ n. **1** the set or arrangement of gears in a machine. **2** the ratio of a company's loan capital (debt) to the value of its ordinary shares (equity).

gear lever (also **gearstick**) ■ n. a lever used to engage or change gear in a motor vehicle.

gear shift ■ n. chiefly N. Amer. a gear lever.

gear train ■ n. a system of gears which transmits motion from one shaft to another.

gearwheel ■ n. a toothed wheel in a set of gears. ▶ (on a bicycle) a cogwheel driven directly by the chain.

gecko /ˈgɛkəʊ/ ■ n. (pl. **-os** or **-oes**) a lizard found in warm regions, many of which are nocturnal and have adhesive pads on the feet. [Gekkonidae and related families: many species.]
– ORIGIN C18: from Malay dialect *geko*, *gekok*, imitative of its cry.

gee[1] (also **gee whiz**) ■ exclam. informal, chiefly N. Amer. a mild expression of surprise, enthusiasm, or sympathy.
– ORIGIN C19: perhaps an abbrev. of JESUS.

gee[2] ■ exclam. (**gee up**) a command to a horse to go faster. ■ v. (**gees**, **geed**, **geeing**) (**gee someone/thing up**) command a horse to go faster. ▶ encourage someone to work more quickly.
– ORIGIN C17.

gee-gee ■ n. Brit. informal a child's word for a horse.
– ORIGIN C19: reduplication of GEE[2].

geek /giːk/ ■ n. informal, chiefly N. Amer. an unfashionable or socially inept person. ▶ a knowledgeable and obsessive enthusiast: *a computer geek*.
– DERIVATIVES **geeky** adj.
– ORIGIN C19: from the rel. English dialect word *geck* 'fool', of Germanic origin.

geelbek /ˈxɪəlbɛk/ ■ n. S. African an edible marine fish with distinctive yellow edges to its jaws and gill covers. [*Atractoscion aequidens*.]
– ORIGIN C19: from S. African Dutch *geel* 'yellow' + *bek* 'mouth'.

geel dikkop /ˈxɪel dɪkəp/ ■ n. S. African poisoning in sheep and goats caused by a plant (usually *Tribulus*), characterized by jaundice and swelling of the head.
– ORIGIN Afrikaans: from *geel* 'yellow' + DIKKOP.

geese plural form of GOOSE.

gee-string ■ n. variant spelling of G-STRING.

gee whiz ■ exclam. another term for GEE[1].

Geez ■ exclam. variant spelling of JEEZ.

Ge'ez /ˈgiːɛz/ ■ n. an ancient Semitic language of Ethiopia, which survives as the liturgical language of the Ethiopian Orthodox Church.
– ORIGIN of Ethiopic origin.

geezer /ˈgiːzə/ ■ n. informal a man.
– ORIGIN C19: representing a dialect pronunciation of earlier *guiser* 'mummer'.

gefilte fish /gəˈfɪltə/ ■ n. a dish of stewed or baked stuffed fish, or of fish cakes boiled in a fish or vegetable broth.
– ORIGIN Yiddish, 'stuffed fish', from *filn* 'to fill' + FISH.

gegenschein /ˈgeɪgənˌʃaɪn/ ■ n. Astronomy a patch of very faint reflected light sometimes seen in the night sky opposite the position of the sun.
– ORIGIN C19: German *Gegenschein*, from *gegen* 'opposite' + *Schein* 'glow, shine'.

Gehenna /gəˈhɛnə/ ■ n. a name for hell.
– ORIGIN via eccles. Latin from Greek *geenna*, from Hebrew *gē' hinnōm* 'hell', literally 'valley of Hinnom', a place near Jerusalem where children were sacrificed to Baal.

Geiger counter ■ n. a device for measuring radioactivity by detecting and counting ionizing particles.
– ORIGIN C20: named after the German physicist Hans Geiger.

geisha /ˈgeɪʃə/ ■ n. (pl. same or **geishas**) a Japanese hostess trained to entertain men with conversation, dance, and song.
– ORIGIN Japanese, 'entertainer'.

gel[1] /dʒɛl/ ■ n. a jelly-like substance containing a cosmetic, medicinal, or other preparation. ▸ Chemistry a semi-solid colloidal suspension of a solid dispersed in a liquid. ■ v. (**gelled**, **gelling**) 1 Chemistry form into a gel. 2 smooth (one's hair) with gel.
– ORIGIN C19: abbrev. of GELATIN.

gel[2] /dʒɛl/ ■ v. variant spelling of JELL.

gelati plural form of GELATO.

gelatin /ˈdʒɛlətɪn/ (also **gelatine** /-tiːn/) ■ n. 1 a virtually colourless and tasteless water-soluble protein prepared from collagen and used in food preparation, in photographic processing, and for making glue. 2 a high explosive consisting chiefly of a gel of nitroglycerine with added cellulose nitrate.
– DERIVATIVES **gelatinization** (also **-isation**) n. **gelatinize** (also **-ise**) v.
– ORIGIN C19: from Italian *gelatina*, from *gelata*, from Latin (see JELLY).

gelatinous ■ adj. having a jelly-like consistency. ▸ of or like the protein gelatin.

gelatin paper ■ n. Brit. paper coated with sensitized gelatin for photographic use.

gelation[1] ■ n. technical solidification by freezing.
– ORIGIN C19: from Latin *gelatio(n-)*, from *gelare* 'freeze'.

gelation[2] ■ n. Chemistry the process of forming a gel.

gelato /dʒəˈlɑːtəʊ/ ■ n. (pl. **gelati** /dʒəˈlɑːti/) an Italian or Italian-style ice cream.
– ORIGIN from Italian.

geld ■ v. castrate (a male animal).
– ORIGIN Middle English: from Old Norse *gelda*, from *geldr* 'barren'.

gelding ■ n. a castrated animal, especially a male horse.

gelid /ˈdʒɛlɪd/ ■ adj. icy; extremely cold.
– ORIGIN C17: from Latin *gelidus*, from *gelu* 'frost, intense cold'.

gelignite /ˈdʒɛlɪgnʌɪt/ ■ n. a high explosive made from a gel of nitroglycerine and nitrocellulose in a base of wood pulp and sodium or potassium nitrate, used particularly for blasting rock.

– ORIGIN C19: prob. from GELATIN + Latin *(l)ignis* 'wood'.

gelsemium /dʒɛlˈsiːmɪəm/ ■ n. a preparation of the rhizome of yellow jasmine, used in homeopathy to treat flu-like symptoms.
– ORIGIN C19: modern Latin, from Italian *gelsomino* 'jasmine'.

gem ■ n. 1 a precious or semi-precious stone, especially when cut and polished or engraved. 2 an outstanding person or thing.
– DERIVATIVES **gem-like** adj. **gemmed** adj.
– ORIGIN Old English *gim*, from Latin *gemma* 'bud, jewel'; influenced in Middle English by Old French *gemme*.

Gemara /gəˈmɑːrə/ ■ n. (**the Gemara**) a rabbinical commentary on the Mishnah, forming the second part of the Talmud.
– ORIGIN from Aramaic *gĕmārā* 'completion'.

gematria /gɪˈmeɪtrɪə/ ■ n. a Kabbalistic method of interpreting the Hebrew scriptures by computing the numerical value of words, based on those of their constituent letters.
– ORIGIN C17: from Aramaic *gīmaṭrĕyā*, from Greek *gēometria* (see GEOMETRY).

Gemeinschaft /gəˈmʌɪnʃaft/ ■ n. social relations based on close personal and family ties. Contrasted with GESELLSCHAFT.
– ORIGIN German, from *gemein* 'common' + *-schaft* (see -SHIP).

geminal /ˈdʒɛmɪn(ə)l/ ■ adj. Chemistry denoting substituent atoms or groups, especially protons, attached to the same atom in a molecule.
– ORIGIN C20: from Latin *geminus* 'twin'.

Gemini ■ n. 1 Astronomy a northern constellation (the Twins), said to represent the twins Castor and Pollux. 2 Astrology the third sign of the zodiac, which the sun enters about 21 May.
– DERIVATIVES **Geminian** /dʒɛmɪˈniːən/ n. & adj.
– ORIGIN Latin, pl. of *geminus* 'twin'.

gemma /ˈdʒɛmə/ ■ n. (pl. **gemmae** /-miː/) Biology a small cellular body or bud that can separate to form a new organism.
– ORIGIN C18: from Latin, 'bud, jewel'.

gemmation /dʒɛˈmeɪʃ(ə)n/ ■ n. Biology asexual reproduction by the production of gemmae; budding.
– ORIGIN C18: from French *gemmer* 'to bud', from *gemme* 'bud', from Latin *gemma*.

gemmiparous /dʒɛˈmɪp(ə)rəs/ ■ adj. Biology reproducing by gemmation.

gemmology ■ n. the study of precious stones.
– DERIVATIVES **gemmological** adj. **gemmologist** n.

gemmule /ˈdʒɛmjuːl/ ■ n. Zoology a tough-coated dormant cluster of embryonic cells produced by a freshwater sponge for development in more favourable conditions.
– DERIVATIVES **gemmulation** n.
– ORIGIN C19: from Latin *gemmula*, diminutive of *gemma* 'bud, jewel'.

gemsbok /ˈxɛmzbɒk, ˈxɛms-/ (also **gemsbuck**) ■ n. a large antelope with distinctive black-and-white head markings and long straight horns, native to SW and East Africa. [*Oryx gazella*.]
– ORIGIN C18: from Dutch, 'chamois'.

gem squash ■ n. S. African an edible squash of a small round variety with a hard dark green rind and yellow flesh.

gemstone ■ n. a precious or semi-precious stone, especially one cut, polished, and used in a piece of jewellery.

Gemütlichkeit /gəˈmuːtlɪxkʌɪt/ ■ n. geniality; friendliness.
– ORIGIN from German.

Gen. ■ abbrev. General.

gen /dʒɛn/ Brit. informal ■ n. information. ■ v. (**genned**, **genning**) (**gen someone up**) provide someone with information. ▸ (**gen up on**) find out about; learn about.
– ORIGIN SECOND WORLD WAR: perhaps from *general information*.

-gen ■ comb. form Chemistry denoting a substance that produces something: *allergen*.

VOWELS a cat ɑː arm ɛ bed ɛː hair ə ago əː her ɪ sit i cosy iː see ɒ hot ɔː saw ʌ run

–ORIGIN from Greek *genēs* '-born, of a specified kind', from *gignomai* 'be born, become'.

gendarme /'ʒɒndɑːm/ ■ n. **1** a paramilitary police officer in French-speaking countries. **2** a rock pinnacle on a mountain, occupying and blocking an arête.
–ORIGIN C16: French, from *gens d'armes* 'men of arms'.

gendarmerie /ʒɒn'dɑːməri/ ■ n. a force of gendarmes. ▶ the headquarters of such a force.

gender ■ n. **1** Grammar a class (usually masculine, feminine, common, or neuter) into which nouns and pronouns are placed in some languages, distinguished by a particular inflection. ▶ the property of belonging to such a class. **2** the state of being male or female (chiefly in cultural or social contexts). ▶ the members of one or other sex: *differences between the genders*.
–DERIVATIVES **gendered** adj.
–ORIGIN Middle English: from Old French *gendre* (modern *genre*), from Latin *genus* 'birth, family, nation'.

gender bender ■ n. informal a person who dresses and behaves in a way characteristic of the opposite sex.

gender dysphoria ■ n. Medicine the condition of feeling one's emotional and psychological identity as male or female to be opposite to one's biological sex.

gene /dʒiːn/ ■ n. Biology a unit of heredity which is transferred from a parent to offspring and is held to determine some characteristic of the offspring; in particular, a distinct sequence of DNA forming part of a chromosome.
–ORIGIN C20: from German *Gen*, from *Pangen*, a supposed ultimate unit of heredity (from Greek *pan-* 'all' + *genos* 'race, kind, offspring').

genealogical tree ■ n. a chart like an inverted branching tree showing the lines of descent of a family or of an animal species.

genealogy /dʒiːnɪ'alədʒi, dʒɛn-/ ■ n. (pl. **-ies**) **1** a line of descent traced continuously from an ancestor. **2** the study of lines of descent.
–DERIVATIVES **genealogical** /ˌdʒiːnɪə'lɒdʒɪk(ə)l, ˌdʒɛn-/ adj. **genealogically** adv. **genealogist** n.
–ORIGIN Middle English: from Greek *genealogia*, from *genea* 'race, generation' + *-logia* (see **-LOGY**).

gene pool ■ n. the stock of different genes in an interbreeding population.

genera plural form of **GENUS**.

general ■ adj. **1** affecting or concerning all or most people or things; not specialized or limited. ▶ normal or usual. **2** involving only the main features or elements and disregarding exceptions; overall. **3** chief or principal: *the general manager*. ■ n. a commander of an army, or an army or air force officer ranking above lieutenant general. ▶ short for **LIEUTENANT GENERAL** or **MAJOR GENERAL**.
–PHRASES **in general 1** usually; mainly. **2** as a whole.
–DERIVATIVES **generalship** n.
–ORIGIN Middle English: from Latin *generalis*, from *genus*, *gener-* 'class, race, kind'.

general anaesthetic ■ n. an anaesthetic that affects the whole body and causes a loss of consciousness.

general average ■ n. Law the apportionment of financial liability for the loss arising from the jettisoning of cargo among all those whose property has been preserved by the action.

general dealer ■ n. (in South Africa) a rural, village, or township store selling a variety of items.

general election ■ n. the election of representatives to a legislature from constituencies throughout the country.

general headquarters ■ n. [treated as sing. or pl.] the headquarters of a military commander.

generalissimo /ˌdʒɛn(ə)rə'lɪsɪməʊ/ ■ n. (pl. **-os**) the commander of a combined military force consisting of army, navy, and air force units.
–ORIGIN C17: Italian, 'having greatest authority', superlative of *generale* (see **GENERAL**).

generalist ■ n. a person competent in several different fields or activities.

generality ■ n. (pl. **-ies**) **1** a statement or principle having general rather than specific validity or force. ▶ the quality or state of being general. **2** (**the generality**) the majority.

generalize (also **-ise**) ■ v. **1** make a general or broad

485

genet

statement by inferring from specific cases. **2** make more common or more widely applicable. **3** [as adj. **generalized** (also **-ised**)] Medicine (of a disease) affecting much or all of the body; not localized.
–DERIVATIVES **generalizability** (also **-isability**) n. **generalizable** (also **-isable**) adj. **generalization** (also **-isation**) n.

generally ■ adv. **1** in most cases. **2** without regard to particulars or exceptions. **3** widely.

general meeting ■ n. a meeting open to all members of an organization.

general practitioner ■ n. a community doctor who treats patients with minor or chronic illnesses.
–DERIVATIVES **general practice** n.

general-purpose ■ adj. having a range of potential uses or functions.

general staff ■ n. [treated as sing. or pl.] the staff assisting a military commander.

general strike ■ n. a strike of workers in all or most industries.

generate ■ v. **1** cause to arise or come about. **2** produce (energy, especially electricity). **3** Mathematics & Linguistics produce (a set or sequence of items) by performing mathematical or logical operations on an initial set. **4** Mathematics form (a line, surface, or solid) by notionally moving a point, line, or surface.
–DERIVATIVES **generable** adj.
–ORIGIN C16 (*generation* Middle English): from Latin *generare* 'create', from *genus*, *gener-* 'stock, race'.

generation ■ n. **1** all of the people born and living at about the same time, regarded collectively. ▶ the average period in which children grow up and have children of their own (usually reckoned as about thirty years). **2** a set of members of a family regarded as a single step or stage in descent. **3** the action of producing or generating. ▶ the propagation of living organisms; procreation.
–DERIVATIVES **generational** adj.

generation gap ■ n. a difference in attitudes between people of different generations, leading to lack of understanding.

Generation X ■ n. the generation born between the mid 1960s and the mid 1970s, perceived as being disaffected and directionless.
–DERIVATIVES **Generation Xer** n.

generative /'dʒɛn(ə)rətɪv/ ■ adj. **1** relating to or capable of production or reproduction. **2** Linguistics relating to the application of a set of rules in order to produce all and only the well-formed items of a language.

generative grammar ■ n. grammar which describes a language in terms of a set of logical rules whereby the infinite number of possible sentences of that language can be generated.

generator ■ n. **1** a person or thing that generates. **2** a dynamo or similar machine for converting mechanical energy into electricity.

generic /dʒɪ'nɛrɪk/ ■ adj. **1** characteristic of or relating to a class or group; not specific. **2** (of goods, especially medicinal drugs) having no brand name. **3** Biology of or relating to a genus. ■ n. a generic drug or other product.
–DERIVATIVES **generically** adv.
–ORIGIN C17: from Latin *genus*, *gener-* 'stock, race'.

generous ■ adj. **1** freely giving more of something, especially money, than is strictly necessary or expected. ▶ kind towards others. **2** larger or more plentiful than is usual.
–DERIVATIVES **generosity** n. **generously** adv. **generousness** n.
–ORIGIN C16 (*generosity* Middle English): from Latin *generosus* 'noble, magnanimous'.

genesis /'dʒɛnɪsɪs/ ■ n. the origin or mode of formation of something. ▶ (**Genesis**) the first book of the Bible, which includes the story of the creation of the world.
–ORIGIN Old English, from Greek, 'generation, creation', from the base of *gignesthai* 'be born or produced'.

genet /'dʒɛnɪt/ ■ n. a nocturnal catlike mammal with short legs and a long bushy ringed tail, found in Africa, SW

gene therapy

Europe, and Arabia. [*Genetta genetta* and related species.]
– ORIGIN Middle English: from Old French *genete*, prob. from Arabic *jarnait*.

gene therapy ■ n. the introduction of normal genes into cells in place of missing or defective ones in order to correct genetic disorders.

genetic /dʒɪˈnetɪk/ ■ adj. **1** of or relating to genes or heredity. ► of or relating to genetics. **2** of or relating to origin, or arising from a common origin.
– DERIVATIVES **genetical** adj. **genetically** adv.
– ORIGIN C19: from GENESIS.

genetically modified ■ adj. (of an organism) containing genetic material that has been artificially altered so as to produce a desired characteristic.

genetic code ■ n. the means by which DNA and RNA molecules carry genetic information in living cells.

genetic engineering ■ n. the deliberate modification of the characteristics of an organism by manipulating its genetic material.

genetic fingerprinting (also **genetic profiling**) ■ n. the analysis of DNA from samples of body tissues or fluids in order to identify individuals.

genetics ■ pl. n. **1** [treated as sing.] the study of heredity and the variation of inherited characteristics. **2** [treated as sing. or pl.] the genetic properties or features of an organism.
– DERIVATIVES **geneticist** n.

genetic screening ■ n. the study of a person's DNA in order to identify susceptibility to particular diseases or abnormalities.

genever /dʒɪˈniːvə/ ■ n. Dutch gin.
– ORIGIN C18: from Dutch, from Old French *genevre*, from an alteration of Latin *juniperus* (gin being flavoured with juniper berries).

genial /ˈdʒiːnɪəl/ ■ adj. **1** friendly and cheerful. **2** poetic/literary (of weather) pleasantly mild and warm.
– DERIVATIVES **geniality** n. **genially** adv.
– ORIGIN C16: from Latin *genialis* 'nuptial, productive', from *genius* (see GENIUS).

-genic ■ comb. form **1** producing or produced by: *carcinogenic*. **2** well suited to: *mediagenic*.
– DERIVATIVES **-genically** suffix forming corresponding adverbs.
– ORIGIN from -GEN + -IC.

genie ■ n. (pl. **genii** /ˈdʒiːnɪaɪ/ or **genies**) (in Arabian folklore) a jinn or spirit, especially one imprisoned within a bottle or oil lamp and capable of granting wishes when summoned.
– ORIGIN C17 (denoting a guardian or protective spirit): from French *génie*, from Latin *genius* (see GENIUS), adopted in current sense because of its resemblance to Arabic *jinnī* 'jinn'.

genii plural form of GENIE, GENIUS.

genital ■ adj. of or relating to the human or animal reproductive organs. ■ n. (**genitals**) a person or animal's external organs of reproduction.
– ORIGIN Middle English: from Latin *genitalis*, from *genit-*, *gignere* 'beget'.

genitalia /ˌdʒɛnɪˈteɪlɪə/ ■ pl. n. formal or technical the genitals.

genitive /ˈdʒɛnɪtɪv/ Grammar ■ adj. denoting a case indicating possession or close association. ■ n. a word in the genitive case.
– DERIVATIVES **genitival** /-ˈtaɪv(ə)l/ adj.
– ORIGIN Middle English: from Latin *genitivus (casus)* '(case) of production or origin', from *gignere* 'beget'.

genitor /ˈdʒɛnɪtə/ ■ n. Anthropology a person's biological father. Often contrasted with PATER.
– ORIGIN Middle English: from Latin *genitor*, from the root of *gignere* 'beget'.

genito-urinary /ˌdʒɛnɪtəʊˈjʊərɪn(ə)ri/ ■ adj. chiefly Medicine of or relating to the genital and urinary organs.

genius ■ n. (pl. **geniuses**) **1** exceptional intellectual or creative power or other natural ability. **2** an exceptionally intelligent or able person. **3** (pl. **genii** /-nɪaɪ/) (in some mythologies) a spirit associated with a person, place, or institution. **4** the prevalent character or spirit of a nation, period, etc.
– ORIGIN Middle English: from Latin, from the root of *gignere* 'beget'.

genius loci /ˈləʊsaɪ, ˈlɒkiː/ ■ n. the prevailing character or atmosphere of a place.
– ORIGIN Latin, 'spirit of the place'.

genlock /ˈdʒɛnlɒk/ ■ n. a device for maintaining synchronization between two different video signals, or between a video signal and a computer or audio signal, enabling video images and computer graphics to be mixed.
– ORIGIN 1960s: from GENERATOR + LOCK¹.

genoa /ˈdʒɛnəʊə, dʒɛˈnəʊə/ (also **genoa jib**) ■ n. Nautical a large jib or foresail whose foot extends aft of the mast, used especially on racing yachts.
– ORIGIN *Genoa*, a city in Italy.

Genoa cake ■ n. a rich fruit cake with almonds on top.

genocide /ˈdʒɛnəsaɪd/ ■ n. the deliberate killing of a very large number of people from a particular ethnic group or nation.
– DERIVATIVES **genocidal** adj.
– ORIGIN 1940s: from Greek *genos* 'race' + -CIDE.

genome /ˈdʒiːnəʊm/ ■ n. Biology **1** the haploid set of chromosomes of an organism. **2** the complete set of genetic material of an organism.
– DERIVATIVES **genomic** adj.
– ORIGIN 1930s: blend of GENE and CHROMOSOME.

genotype /ˈdʒɛnətaɪp, ˈdʒiː-/ Biology ■ n. the genetic constitution of an individual organism. Often contrasted with PHENOTYPE. ■ v. investigate the genotype of.
– DERIVATIVES **genotypic** /-ˈtɪpɪk/ adj.

-genous ■ comb. form **1** producing; inducing: *erogenous*. **2** originating in: *endogenous*.
– ORIGIN from -GEN + -OUS.

genre /ˈʒɒ̃rə, ˈ(d)ʒɒnrə/ ■ n. **1** a style or category of art or literature. **2** [as modifier] denoting a style of painting depicting scenes from ordinary life.
– ORIGIN C19: French, 'a kind' (see GENDER).

gent ■ n. informal a gentleman. ► (**the Gents**) a men's public toilet.

genteel ■ adj. affectedly polite and refined.
– DERIVATIVES **genteelism** n. **genteelly** adv. **genteelness** n.
– ORIGIN C16 ('fashionable, stylish'): from French *gentil* 'well-born'.

gentian /ˈdʒɛnʃ(ə)n/ ■ n. a plant of temperate and mountainous regions with violet or blue trumpet-shaped flowers. [Genera *Gentiana* and *Gentianella*.]
– ORIGIN Middle English: from Latin *gentiana*, allegedly named after *Gentius*, king of Illyria, who discovered the plant's medicinal properties.

gentian violet ■ n. a synthetic violet dye used as an antiseptic.

Gentile /ˈdʒɛntaɪl/ ■ adj. not Jewish. ■ n. a person who is not Jewish.
– ORIGIN Middle English: from Latin *gentilis* 'of a family or nation, of the same clan', from *gens* 'family, race'.

gentility /dʒɛnˈtɪlɪti/ ■ n. socially superior or genteel character or behaviour.
– ORIGIN Middle English ('honourable birth'): from Old French *gentilite*, from *gentil* (see GENTLE).

gentle ■ adj. (**-er**, **-est**) **1** mild or kind; not rough or violent. **2** moderate; not harsh or severe: *a gentle breeze*. **3** archaic noble or courteous. ■ v. make or become gentle; calm or pacify. ► touch gently.
– DERIVATIVES **gentleness** n. **gently** adv.
– ORIGIN Middle English: from Old French *gentil* 'high-born, noble', from Latin *gentilis* (see GENTILE).

gentlefolk ■ pl. n. archaic people of noble birth or good social position.

gentleman ■ n. (pl. **-men**) **1** a courteous or honourable man. **2** a man of good social position, especially one of wealth and leisure. **3** (in polite or formal use) a man.
– DERIVATIVES **gentlemanliness** n. **gentlemanly** adj.

gentleman-at-arms ■ n. one of the bodyguards of the British monarch on ceremonial occasions.

gentleman farmer ■ n. (pl. **gentlemen farmers**) a country gentleman who has a farm as part of his estate.

gentleman's agreement ■ n. an arrangement or understanding which is based on trust rather than being legally binding.

gentleman's gentleman ■ n. a valet.

gentlewoman ■ n. (pl. **-women**) archaic a woman of noble birth or good social standing.

gentoo /dʒɛnˈtuː/ ■ n. a tall penguin with a white triangular patch above the eye. [*Pygoscelis papua*.]
– ORIGIN C19: perhaps from Anglo-Indian *Gentoo* 'a Hindu', from Portuguese *gentio* 'gentile'.

gentrify ■ v. (**-ies**, **-ied**) renovate and improve (a house or district) so that it conforms to middle-class taste.
– DERIVATIVES **gentrification** n. **gentrifier** n.

gentry /ˈdʒɛntri/ ■ n. **1** (**the gentry**) people of good social position, specifically the class next below the nobility. **2** derogatory or humorous people of a specified kind: *devices beyond the comprehension of all but the bespectacled gentry who invented them.*
– ORIGIN Middle English ('superiority of birth or rank'): from Anglo-Norman French *genterie*, based on *gentil* (see **GENTLE**).

genuflect /ˈdʒɛnjʊflɛkt/ ■ v. lower one's body briefly by bending one knee to the ground in worship or as a sign of respect.
– DERIVATIVES **genuflection** (also **genuflexion**) n. **genuflector** n.
– ORIGIN C17 (*genuflection* Middle English): from eccles. Latin *genuflectere*, from Latin *genu* 'knee' + *flectere* 'to bend'.

genuine ■ adj. **1** truly what it is said to be; authentic. **2** sincere; honest.
– DERIVATIVES **genuinely** adv. **genuineness** n.
– ORIGIN C16: from Latin *genuinus*, from *genu* 'knee' (with ref. to the Roman custom of a father acknowledging paternity of a newborn child by placing it on his knee); later associated with *genus* 'birth, race, stock'.

genus /ˈdʒiːnəs, ˈdʒɛnəs/ ■ n. (pl. **genera** /ˈdʒɛn(ə)rə/) **1** Biology a principal taxonomic category that ranks above species and below family, denoted by a capitalized Latin name, e.g. *Leo*. **2** a class of things which have common characteristics and which can be divided into subordinate kinds.
– ORIGIN C16: from Latin, 'birth, race, stock'.

-geny ■ comb. form denoting the mode by which something develops or is produced: *orogeny*.
– ORIGIN from Greek *-geneia*, from *gen-* (root of *gignomai* 'be born, become' and *genos* 'a kind').

geo- /ˈdʒiːəʊ/ ■ comb. form of or relating to the earth: *geocentric*.
– ORIGIN from Greek *gē* 'earth'.

geobotany ■ n. another term for **PHYTOGEOGRAPHY**.
– DERIVATIVES **geobotanical** adj. **geobotanist** n.

geocaching /ˈdʒiːəʊkaʃɪŋ/ ■ n. a form of treasure hunt in which an item is hidden somewhere in the world and its coordinates posted on the Internet, so that GPS users can locate it.
– DERIVATIVES **geocacher** n.
– ORIGIN early C21: from **GEO-** + **CACHE**.

geocentric ■ adj. **1** having or representing the earth as the centre, as in former astronomical systems. Compare with **HELIOCENTRIC**. **2** Astronomy measured from or considered in relation to the centre of the earth.
– DERIVATIVES **geocentrically** adv. **geocentrism** n.

geochemistry ■ n. the study of the chemical composition of the earth and its rocks and minerals.
– DERIVATIVES **geochemical** adj. **geochemist** n.

geochronology ■ n. the branch of geology concerned with the dating of rock formations and geological events.
– DERIVATIVES **geochronological** adj. **geochronologist** n.

geochronometric /ˌdʒiːə(ʊ)ˌkrɒnəˈmɛtrɪk/ ■ adj. of or relating to geochronological measurement.
– DERIVATIVES **geochronometry** n.

geode /ˈdʒiːəʊd/ ■ n. a small cavity in rock lined with crystals or other mineral matter. ▸ a rock containing such a cavity.
– DERIVATIVES **geodic** /ˈdʒiːˈɒdɪk/ adj.
– ORIGIN C17: from Greek *geōdēs* 'earthy'.

geodesic /ˌdʒiːə(ʊ)ˈdɛsɪk, -ˈdiːsɪk/ ■ adj. **1** relating to or denoting the shortest possible line between two points on a sphere or other curved surface. **2** (of a dome) constructed from struts which follow geodesic lines and form an open framework of triangles and polygons. **3** another term for **GEODETIC**.

geodesy /dʒɪˈɒdɪsi/ ■ n. the branch of mathematics concerned with the shape and area of the earth or large portions of it.
– DERIVATIVES **geodesist** n.
– ORIGIN C16: from Greek *geōdaisia*, from *gē* 'earth' + *daiein* 'to divide'.

geodetic /ˌdʒiːəˈdɛtɪk/ ■ adj. of or relating to geodesy, especially as applied to land surveying.

geographical ■ adj. of or relating to geography.
– DERIVATIVES **geographic** adj. **geographically** adv.

geographical latitude ■ n. the angle made with the plane of the equator by a perpendicular to the earth's surface at any point.

geographical mile ■ n. a distance equal to one minute of longitude or latitude at the equator (about 1 850 metres).

geography ■ n. **1** the study of the physical features of the earth and of human activity as it relates to these. **2** the relative arrangement of places and physical features.
– DERIVATIVES **geographer** n.
– ORIGIN C15: from Greek *geōgraphia*, from *gē* 'earth' + *-graphia* 'writing'.

geoid /ˈdʒiːɔɪd/ ■ n. (**the geoid**) the shape of the earth taken as mean sea level and its imagined extension under (or over) land areas.
– ORIGIN C19: from Greek *geoeidēs*, from *gē* 'earth' + *-oeidēs*, rel. to *eides* 'form'.

geology ■ n. **1** the science which deals with the physical structure and substance of the earth. **2** the geological features of a district.
– DERIVATIVES **geologic** adj. **geological** adj. **geologically** adv. **geologist** n.
– ORIGIN C18: from modern Latin *geologia*, from Greek *gē* 'earth' + *-logia* (see **-LOGY**).

geomagnetism ■ n. the branch of geology concerned with the magnetic properties of the earth.
– DERIVATIVES **geomagnetic** adj. **geomagnetically** adv.

geomancy /ˈdʒiːə(ʊ)mansi/ ■ n. **1** the art of siting buildings auspiciously. **2** divination from the configuration of a handful of earth or random dots.
– DERIVATIVES **geomantic** adj.

geomatics ■ n. the branch of science and technology concerned with landscape surveying and with the manipulation and presentation of spatial data.
– DERIVATIVES **geomatician** n.

geometric /ˌdʒɪəˈmɛtrɪk/ ■ adj. **1** of or relating to geometry. **2** (of a design) characterized by or decorated with regular lines and shapes. ▸ (**Geometric**) Archaeology of or denoting a period of Greek culture (c. 900–700 BC) characterized by geometrically decorated pottery.
– DERIVATIVES **geometrical** adj. **geometrically** adv.

geometric tortoise ■ n. a small tortoise with geometric starlike markings on its carapace, endemic to south-western parts of South Africa. [*Psammobates geometricus*.]

geometrid /dʒɪˈɒmɪtrɪd/ ■ n. Entomology a moth of a large family (Geometridae), distinguished by having twig-like caterpillars that move by looping and straightening the body.
– ORIGIN C19: from the genus name *Geometra*, from Latin *geometres* 'geometer'.

geometry /dʒɪˈɒmɪtri/ ■ n. (pl. **-ies**) **1** the branch of mathematics concerned with the properties and relations of points, lines, surfaces, solids, and higher dimensional analogues. **2** the shape and relative arrangement of the parts of something.
– DERIVATIVES **geometrician** /ˌdʒɪəmɪˈtrɪʃ(ə)n/ n.
– ORIGIN Middle English: from Latin *geometria*, from Greek, from *gē* 'earth' + *metria* (see **-METRY**).

geomorphic /ˌdʒiːə(ʊ)ˈmɔːfɪk/ ■ adj. of or relating to the form of the landscape and other natural features of the earth's surface.

geomorphology /ˌdʒiːə(ʊ)mɔːˈfɒlədʒi/ ■ n. the study of the physical features of the surface of the earth and their relation to its geological structures.
– DERIVATIVES **geomorphological** adj. **geomorphologist** n.

geophysics ■ pl. n. [treated as sing.] the physics of the earth.
– DERIVATIVES **geophysical** adj. **geophysicist** n.

geopolitics ■ pl. n. [treated as sing. or pl.] politics, especially international relations, as influenced by geographical factors.
– DERIVATIVES **geopolitical** adj. **geopolitically** adv. **geopolitician** n.

Geordie ■ n. Brit. informal a person from Tyneside.
– ORIGIN C19: diminutive of the given name *George*.

George lily ■ n. a South African lily with trumpet-shaped scarlet or pink flowers and sword-shaped glossy green leaves. [*Cyrtanthus elatus*.]
– ORIGIN 1910s: named after the town of *George* in the Western Cape.

georgette /dʒɔːˈdʒɛt/ ■ n. a thin silk or crêpe dress material.
– ORIGIN C20: named after the French dressmaker *Georgette de la Plante*.

Georgian[1] ■ adj. of or characteristic of the reigns of the British Kings George I–IV (1714–1830). ▸ relating to British architecture of this period, characterized by restrained elegance and the use of neoclassical styles.

Georgian[2] ■ n. 1 a native or national of the country of Georgia. 2 the official language of Georgia. ■ adj. of or relating to Georgia, its people, or their language.

georgic /ˈdʒɔːdʒɪk/ ■ n. a poem or book concerned with agriculture or rural topics. ■ adj. poetic/literary rustic; pastoral.
– ORIGIN C16: from Greek *geōrgikos*, from *geōrgos* 'farmer'.

geoscience (also **geosciences**) ■ n. earth sciences, especially geology.
– DERIVATIVES **geoscientist** n.

geostationary ■ adj. (of an artificial satellite) moving in a circular geosynchronous orbit so that it appears to be stationary above a fixed point on the surface.

geostrophic /ˌdʒiːə(ʊ)ˈstrɒfɪk, -ˈstrəʊf-/ ■ adj. Meteorology & Oceanography denoting the component of a wind or current that arises from the balance between pressure gradients and coriolis forces.
– ORIGIN C20: from GEO- + Greek *strophē* 'a turn'.

geosynchronous /ˌdʒiːə(ʊ)ˈsɪŋkrənəs/ ■ adj. of or denoting a satellite which revolves in its orbit in exactly the same time as the primary body rotates on its axis.

geotechnics ■ pl. n. [treated as sing.] the branch of civil engineering concerned with the study and modification of soil and rocks.
– DERIVATIVES **geotechnic** adj. **geotechnical** adj.

geothermal ■ adj. relating to or produced by the internal heat of the earth.

geotropism /ˌdʒiːə(ʊ)ˈtrəʊpɪz(ə)m/ ■ n. Botany the growth of the parts of plants in response to the force of gravity.
– DERIVATIVES **geotropic** adj.
– ORIGIN C19: from GEO- + Greek *tropē* 'turning'.

geranium /dʒɪˈreɪnɪəm/ ■ n. a herbaceous plant or small shrub of a genus that comprises the cranesbills and their relatives. [Genus *Geranium*.] ▸ (in general use) a cultivated pelargonium.
– ORIGIN from Greek *geranion*, from *geranos* 'crane'.

gerbera /ˈdʒɜːb(ə)rə, ˈɡɜː-/ ■ n. a tropical plant of the daisy family, with large brightly coloured flowers. [Genus *Gerbera*: many species.]
– ORIGIN named after the German naturalist Traugott Gerber (died 1743).

gerbil /ˈdʒɜːbɪl/ ■ n. a burrowing mouse-like rodent found in arid regions of Africa and Asia. [*Gerbillus* and other genera: many species.]
– ORIGIN C19: from modern Latin *gerbillus*, diminutive of *gerboa* (see JERBOA).

geriatric /ˌdʒɛrɪˈatrɪk/ ■ adj. 1 of or relating to old people. 2 informal decrepit or out of date. ■ n. an old person, especially one receiving special care.
– ORIGIN 1920s: from Greek *gēras* 'old age' + *iatros* 'doctor', on the pattern of *paediatric*.

geriatrics ■ pl. n. [treated as sing. or pl.] the branch of medicine or social science concerned with the health and care of old people.
– DERIVATIVES **geriatrician** n.

germ ■ n. 1 a micro-organism, especially one which causes disease. 2 a portion of an organism capable of developing into a new one or part of one. ▸ the embryo in a cereal grain or other plant seed. 3 an initial stage from which something may develop: *the germ of a brilliant idea*.
– DERIVATIVES **germy** adj. (informal).
– ORIGIN Middle English: from Latin *germen* 'seed, sprout'.

German ■ n. 1 a native or national of Germany, or a person of German descent. 2 the West Germanic language of Germany, Austria, and parts of Switzerland. ■ adj. of or relating to Germany, its people, or their language.

germander /dʒəˈmandə/ ■ n. a plant of the mint family, some kinds of which are cultivated as ornamentals. [Genus *Teucrium*: many species.]
– ORIGIN Middle English: from medieval Latin *germandra*, from Greek *khamaidrus* 'ground oak' (because the leaves of some species were thought to resemble those of the oak).

germane /dʒəˈmeɪn/ ■ adj. relevant to a subject under consideration.
– DERIVATIVES **germanely** adv. **germaneness** n.
– ORIGIN C17: var. of archaic *german*, from Latin *germanus* 'genuine, of the same parents'.

Germanic ■ adj. 1 relating to or denoting the branch of the Indo-European language family that includes English, German, Dutch, Frisian, and the Scandinavian languages. ▸ relating to or denoting the peoples of ancient northern and western Europe speaking such languages. 2 characteristic of Germans or Germany. ■ n. the Germanic languages collectively.

germanium /dʒəˈmeɪnɪəm/ ■ n. the chemical element of atomic number 32, a shiny grey semimetal. (Symbol: **Ge**)
– ORIGIN C19: from Latin *Germanus* 'German'.

German measles ■ pl. n. [usu. treated as sing.] another term for RUBELLA.

German print ■ n. S. African another term for SHWESHWE.
– ORIGIN from its introduction to South Africa by German settlers.

German shepherd ■ n. a large dog of a breed often used as guard dogs or for police work; an Alsatian.

germ cell ■ n. Biology a gamete, or an embryonic cell with the potential of developing into one.

germicide ■ n. a substance or other agent which destroys harmful micro-organisms.
– DERIVATIVES **germicidal** adj.

germinal ■ adj. 1 of or relating to the nature of a germ cell or embryo. 2 in the earliest stage of development. ▸ providing material for future development.
– DERIVATIVES **germinally** adv.
– ORIGIN C19: from Latin *germen* 'sprout, seed'.

germinate /ˈdʒɜːmɪneɪt/ ■ v. (of a seed or spore) begin to grow and put out shoots after a period of dormancy.
– DERIVATIVES **germination** n. **germinative** adj. **germinator** n.
– ORIGIN C16: from Latin *germinare* 'sprout forth, bud', from *germen* 'sprout, seed'.

germ layer ■ n. Embryology each of the three layers of cells (ectoderm, mesoderm, and endoderm) that are formed in the early embryo.

germ line ■ n. Biology a series of germ cells each descended or developed from earlier cells in the series, regarded as continuing through successive generations of an organism.

germ warfare ■ n. the use of disease-spreading micro-organisms as a military weapon.

Geronimo /dʒəˈrɒnɪməʊ/ ■ exclam. used to express exhilaration when leaping or moving quickly.
– ORIGIN SECOND WORLD WAR: adopted as a slogan by American paratroopers, by association with the Apache chief *Geronimo*.

gerontocracy /ˌdʒɛrənˈtɒkrəsi/ ■ n. a state, society, or group governed by old people. ▸ government based on rule by old people.
– DERIVATIVES **gerontocrat** n. **gerontocratic** adj.

gerontology /ˌdʒɛrənˈtɒlədʒi/ ■ n. the scientific study of old age and old people.
– DERIVATIVES **gerontological** adj. **gerontologist** n.

gerrymander /ˈdʒɛrɪˌmandə/ ■ v. [often as noun **gerrymandering**] manipulate the boundaries of (an electoral constituency) so as to favour one party or class.
– ORIGIN C19: from the name of Governor Elbridge *Gerry* of Massachusetts + SALAMANDER, from the supposed similarity between a salamander and the shape of a new voting district created when he was in office, which was felt to favour his party.

gerund /ˈdʒɛrʌnd/ ■ n. Grammar a verb form which functions as a noun, in Latin ending in *-ndum* (declinable), in English ending in *-ing* (e.g. *asking* in *do you mind my asking you?*).
– ORIGIN C16: from late Latin *gerundum*, var. of *gerendum*, the gerund of Latin *gerere* 'do'.

gerundive /dʒəˈrʌndɪv/ ■ n. Grammar a form of a Latin verb, ending in *-ndus* (declinable) and functioning as an adjective meaning 'that should or must be done'.
– ORIGIN Middle English: from late Latin *gerundivus (modus)* 'gerundive (mood)', from *gerundium* (see GERUND).

Gesellschaft /ɡəˈzɛlʃaft/ ■ n. social relations based on impersonal ties, as duty to a society or organization. Often contrasted with GEMEINSCHAFT.
– ORIGIN German: from *Gesell(e)* 'companion' + *-schaft* (see -SHIP).

gesso /ˈdʒɛsəʊ/ ■ n. (pl. **-oes**) a hard compound of plaster of Paris or whiting in glue, used in sculpture or as a base for gilding or painting on wood.
– ORIGIN C16: Italian, from Latin *gypsum* (see GYPSUM).

gestalt /ɡəˈʃtɑːlt, -ˈʃtalt/ ■ n. Psychology an organized whole that is perceived as more than the sum of its parts.
– DERIVATIVES **gestaltism** n. **gestaltist** n.
– ORIGIN 1920s: from German *Gestalt* 'form, shape'.

gestalt therapy ■ n. a psychotherapeutic approach focusing on insight into gestalts in patients and often using role playing.

Gestapo /ɡəˈstɑːpəʊ/ ■ n. the German secret police under Nazi rule.
– ORIGIN German, from *Geheime Staatspolizei* 'secret state police'.

gestation ■ n. 1 the process of carrying or being carried in the womb between conception and birth. 2 the development of a plan or idea over a period of time.
– DERIVATIVES **gestate** v.
– ORIGIN C16: from Latin *gestatio(n-)*, from *gestare* 'carry (in the womb)'.

gesticulate /dʒɛˈstɪkjʊleɪt/ ■ v. gesture dramatically in place of or to emphasize speech.
– DERIVATIVES **gesticulation** n. **gesticulator** n.
– ORIGIN C17 (*gesticulation* Middle English): from Latin *gesticulari*, from *gesticulus*, diminutive of *gestus* 'action'.

gesture ■ n. 1 a movement of part of the body, especially a hand or the head, to express an idea or meaning. 2 an action performed to convey one's feelings or intentions: *a kind gesture.* ▸ an action performed for show in the knowledge that it will have no effect. ■ v. make a gesture.
– DERIVATIVES **gestural** adj.
– ORIGIN Middle English: from medieval Latin *gestura*, from *gerere* 'bear, wield, perform'.

GET ■ abbrev. (in South Africa) general education and training, comprising grades R to 9. Compare with FET and HET.

get ■ v. (**getting**; past **got**; past part. **got**, N. Amer. or archaic **gotten**) 1 come to have or hold; receive. ▸ experience, suffer, or be afflicted with (something bad). 2 succeed in attaining, achieving, or experiencing; obtain. 3 move in order to pick up, deal with, or bring. ▸ tend to meet with or find. ▸ travel by or catch (a form of transport). 4 bring or come into a specified state or condition. ▸ used with past participle to form the passive mood: *the cat got drowned.* ▸ begin to be or do something, especially gradually or by chance: *we got talking.* 5 come or go eventually or with some difficulty: *I got to the airport.* ▸ move or come into a specified position or state: *she got into the car.* 6 (**have got**) see HAVE. 7 catch, apprehend, or thwart. ▸ strike or wound with a blow or missile. ▸ informal punish, injure, or kill, especially as retribution. ▸ (**get one's**) informal be killed or suffer retribution. 8 informal understand (an argument or the person making it). 9 archaic acquire (knowledge) by study. ■ n. 1 dated an animal's offspring. 2 Brit. informal or dialect an unpleasant or stupid person.
– PHRASES **get one's own back** informal have one's revenge. **get over oneself** informal stop being conceited or pretentious. **getting on for** chiefly Brit. almost (a specified time, age, or amount). **get someone with child** archaic make a woman pregnant.
– PHRASAL VERBS **get something across** manage to communicate an idea clearly. **get ahead** become successful in one's life or career. **get along 1** chiefly N. Amer. another way of saying get on (in sense 2). **2** manage to live or survive. **get at 1** reach or gain access to. ▸ bribe or unfairly influence. **2** informal imply. **3** Brit. informal criticize subtly and repeatedly. **get away 1** escape. **2** informal said to express disbelief or scepticism. **get away with** escape blame or punishment for. **get back at** take revenge on. **get by** manage with difficulty to live or accomplish something. **get down** N. Amer. informal dance energetically. **get down to** begin to do or give serious attention to. **get off 1** informal escape a punishment; be acquitted. **2** go to sleep. **3** informal chiefly Brit. (usu. **get off with**) have a sexual encounter. **4** (often **get off on**) informal be excited or aroused. **get on 1** manage or make progress with a task. ▸ chiefly Brit. be successful in one's life or career. **2** have a harmonious or friendly relationship. **3** (**be getting on**) informal be old or comparatively old. **get out of** contrive to avoid or escape. **get over 1** recover from (an ailment or an unpleasant experience). **2** overcome (a difficulty). **get something over 1** manage to communicate an idea or theory. **2** promptly complete an unpleasant or tedious but necessary task. **get round** (or **around**) **1** coax or persuade (someone) to do or allow something. **2** deal successfully with (a problem). ▸ evade (a regulation or restriction) without contravening it. **get round to** (or **around to**) deal with (a task) in due course. **get through 1** pass or endure (a difficult experience or period). **2** chiefly Brit. use up (a large amount or number of something). **3** make contact by telephone. ▸ succeed in communicating with someone. **get to 1** informal annoy or upset by persistent action. **2** another way of saying get round to. **get together** gather or assemble socially or to cooperate. **get up 1** rise from bed after sleeping. **2** (of wind or the sea) become strong or agitated. **get someone up** (usu. **be got up**) dress someone in a specified manner, elaborate, or unusual way. **get something up** prepare or organize a project or piece of work. **get up to** informal be involved in (something illicit or surprising).
– DERIVATIVES **gettable** adj.
– ORIGIN Middle English: from Old Norse *geta* 'obtain, beget, guess'; rel. to Old English *gietan*.

getaway ■ n. 1 an escape or quick departure, especially after committing a crime. 2 informal a short holiday.

get-go ■ n. informal, chiefly N. Amer. the very beginning: *the quintet experienced difficulties from the get-go.*

get-out ■ n. Brit. a means of avoiding something.
– PHRASES **as —— as all get-out** N. Amer. informal as —— as is possible.

getter ■ n. 1 [in combination] a person or thing that gets a specified desirable thing: *an attention-getter.* 2 Physics a substance used to remove residual gas from a vacuum tube, or impurities or defects from a semiconductor crystal.

get-together ■ n. an informal gathering.

get-up ■ n. informal a style or arrangement of dress, especially an elaborate or unusual one.

geum /ˈdʒiːəm/ ■ n. a plant of a genus which comprises the avens. [Genus *Geum*.]
– ORIGIN var. of Latin *gaeum*.

gewgaw /ˈɡjuːɡɔː/ ■ n. a showy thing, especially one that is useless or worthless.
– ORIGIN Middle English.

Gewürztraminer /ɡəˈvʊətstrəˌmiːnə/ ■ n. a variety of white grape grown mainly in Alsace, Austria, and the Rhine valley. ▸ a wine made from this grape.
– ORIGIN German: from *Gewürz* 'spice' + *Traminer*, denoting a variety of white grape.

geyser

geyser ▪ n. **1** /ˈɡiːzə, ˈɡʌɪ-/ a hot spring in which water intermittently boils, sending a tall column of water and steam into the air. **2** /ˈɡiːzə/ Brit. a heater which heats water very rapidly as it flows through. ▸ S. African a hot-water storage tank with an electric heating element.
– ORIGIN C18: from Icelandic *Geysir*, the name of a particular spring in Iceland; rel. to *geysa* 'to gush'.

Ghanaian /ɡɑːˈneɪən/ ▪ n. a native or inhabitant of Ghana. ▪ adj. of or relating to Ghana.

gharana /ɡʌˈrɑːnə/ ▪ n. a school or method of Indian classical music or dance.
– ORIGIN from Hindi *gharānā* 'family'.

gharial /ˈɡɑrɪəl, ˌɡʌrɪˈɑːl, ˈɡəːrɪəl/ (also **gavial**) ▪ n. a large fish-eating crocodile with a long narrow snout that widens at the nostrils, native to the Indian subcontinent. [*Gavialis gangeticus*.]
– ORIGIN C19: from Hindi *gharịyāl*.

ghastly ▪ adj. (-**ier**, -**iest**) **1** causing great horror or fear; macabre. **2** deathly white or pallid. **3** informal very objectionable or unpleasant.
– DERIVATIVES **ghastliness** n.
– ORIGIN Middle English: from obsolete *gast* 'terrify', from Old English *gǣstan*, of Germanic origin; rel. to (and influenced in spelling by) GHOST.

ghat /ɡɑːt/ ▪ n. **1** (in the Indian subcontinent) a flight of steps leading down to a river. ▸ a level place on the edge of a river where Hindus cremate their dead. **2** (in the Indian subcontinent) a mountain pass.
– ORIGIN from Hindi *ghāṭ*.

GHB ▪ abbrev. (sodium) gamma-hydroxybutyrate, a designer drug with anaesthetic properties.

ghee /ɡiː/ ▪ n. clarified butter used in Indian cooking.
– ORIGIN from Hindi *ghī*, from Sanskrit *ghṛtá* 'sprinkled'.

gherkin /ˈɡəːkɪn/ ▪ n. a small variety of cucumber, or a young green cucumber, used for pickling.
– ORIGIN C17: from Dutch *augurkje*, *gurkje*, diminutive of *augurk*, *gurk*, from medieval Greek *angourion* 'cucumber'.

ghetto /ˈɡɛtəʊ/ ▪ n. (pl. **-os** or **-oes**) **1** a part of a city, especially a slum area, occupied by a minority group. **2** historical the Jewish quarter in a city.
– DERIVATIVES **ghettoization** (also **-isation**) n. **ghettoize** (also **-ise**) v.
– ORIGIN C17: perhaps from Italian *getto* 'foundry' (because the first ghetto was established on the site of a foundry in Venice), or from Italian *borghetto*, diminutive of *borgo* 'borough'.

ghetto blaster ▪ n. informal a large portable radio and cassette or CD player.

ghillie ▪ n. variant spelling of GILLIE.

ghomma ▪ n. variant spelling of GOEMA (in sense 2).

ghost ▪ n. **1** an apparition of a dead person which is believed to appear to the living, typically as a nebulous image. ▸ archaic a spirit or soul. **2** a faint trace: *the ghost of a smile*. **3** a faint secondary image produced by a fault in an optical system or on a cathode ray screen. ▪ v. **1** act as ghost writer of. **2** glide smoothly and effortlessly.
– PHRASES **give up the ghost** die or stop functioning.
– DERIVATIVES **ghostlike** adj.
– ORIGIN Old English, of Germanic origin.

ghosting ▪ n. the appearance of a secondary image on a television or other display screen.

ghostly ▪ adj. (-**ier**, -**iest**) of or like a ghost; eerie and unnatural.
– DERIVATIVES **ghostliness** n.

ghost town ▪ n. a town with few or no remaining inhabitants.

ghost train ▪ n. a miniature train at a funfair that travels through a dark tunnel in which there are eerie effects.

ghostwriter ▪ n. a person employed to write material for another person, who is the named author.
– DERIVATIVES **ghostwrite** v.

ghoul /ɡuːl/ ▪ n. **1** an evil spirit or phantom, especially one supposed to rob graves and feed on dead bodies. **2** a person morbidly interested in death or disaster.
– DERIVATIVES **ghoulish** adj. **ghoulishly** adv. **ghoulishness** n.
– ORIGIN C18: from Arabic *ġūl*, a desert demon believed to rob graves and devour corpses.

GHQ ▪ abbrev. General Headquarters.

ghyll ▪ n. variant spelling of GILL[3].

GHz (also **gHz**) ▪ abbrev. gigahertz.

GI[1] ▪ n. (pl. **GIs**) a private soldier in the US army.
– ORIGIN 1930s (orig. denoting equipment supplied to US forces): abbrev. of *government* (or *general*) *issue*.

GI[2] ▪ abbrev. glycaemic index.

giant ▪ n. **1** an imaginary or mythical being of human form but superhuman size. **2** an abnormally tall or large person, animal, or plant. **3** Astronomy a star of relatively great size and luminosity. ▪ adj. of very great size or force; gigantic.
– DERIVATIVES **giantess** n. **giantlike** adj.
– ORIGIN Middle English: from Greek *gigas*, *gigant-*.

giant-killer ▪ n. a person or team that defeats a seemingly much more powerful opponent.
– DERIVATIVES **giant-killing** n.

giant protea ▪ n. another term for KING PROTEA.

giant squid ▪ n. a deep-sea squid which is the largest known invertebrate, reaching a length of 18 m (59 ft) or more. [Genus *Architeuthis*.]

giant toad ▪ n. another term for CANE TOAD.

giardiasis /ˌdʒiːɑːˈdʌɪəsɪs/ ▪ n. infection of the intestine with a flagellate protozoan.
– ORIGIN C20: from modern Latin *Giardia*, from the name of the French biologist Alfred M. *Giard*.

gibber /ˈdʒɪbə, ˈɡɪbə/ ▪ v. speak rapidly and unintelligibly, typically through fear or shock.
– DERIVATIVES **gibbering** adj.
– ORIGIN C17: imitative.

gibberish /ˈdʒɪb(ə)rɪʃ, ˈɡɪb-/ ▪ n. unintelligible or meaningless speech or writing; nonsense.
– ORIGIN C16: perhaps from GIBBER (but recorded earlier).

gibbet historical ▪ n. **1** a gallows. **2** an upright post with an arm on which the bodies of executed criminals were left hanging as a warning or deterrent to others.
▪ v. (**gibbeted**, **gibbeting**) hang up on a gibbet or execute by hanging.
– ORIGIN Middle English: from Old French *gibet* 'staff, cudgel, gallows', diminutive of *gibe* 'club, staff', prob. of Germanic origin.

gibbon ▪ n. a small, slender tree-dwelling ape with long, powerful arms, native to the forests of SE Asia. [Genus *Hylobates*: several species.]
– ORIGIN C18: from French, from an Indian dialect word.

gibbous /ˈɡɪbəs/ ▪ adj. **1** (of the moon) having the illuminated part greater than a semicircle and less than a circle. **2** convex or protuberant.
– DERIVATIVES **gibbosity** /-ˈbɒsɪti/ n.
– ORIGIN Middle English: from late Latin *gibbosus*, from Latin *gibbus* 'hump'.

Gibbs free energy ▪ n. Chemistry a thermodynamic quantity equal to enthalpy minus the product of the entropy and the absolute temperature.
– ORIGIN C20: named after the American chemist J. W. *Gibbs*.

gibe /dʒʌɪb/ ▪ n. & v. variant spelling of JIBE[1].

giblets /ˈdʒɪblɪts/ ▪ pl. n. the liver, heart, gizzard, and neck of a chicken or other fowl, usually removed before the bird is cooked.
– ORIGIN Middle English ('an inessential appendage', later 'offal'): from Old French *gibelet* 'game bird stew', prob. from *gibier* 'birds or mammals hunted for sport'.

Gibraltarian /ˌdʒɪbrɔːlˈtɛːrɪən/ ▪ n. a native or inhabitant of Gibraltar. ▪ adj. of or relating to Gibraltar.

Gibson girl ▪ n. a girl typifying the fashionable ideal of the late 19th and early 20th centuries.
– ORIGIN represented in the work of the American artist and illustrator Charles D. *Gibson*.

gid /ɡɪd/ ▪ n. a fatal disease of sheep and goats, marked by loss of balance and caused by larvae of the dog tapeworm encysted in the brain.
– ORIGIN C17: back-formation from GIDDY.

giddy ▪ adj. (-**ier**, -**iest**) **1** having or causing a sensation of whirling and a tendency to fall or stagger; dizzy.

2 excitable and frivolous. ■ v. (-ies, -ied) make (someone) feel excited to the point of disorientation.
– PHRASES **play the giddy goat** dated act irresponsibly; fool around.
– DERIVATIVES **giddily** adv. **giddiness** n.
– ORIGIN Old English *gidig* 'insane', 'possessed by a god', from the base of GOD.

giddy-up ■ exclam. said to induce a horse to start moving or go faster.
– ORIGIN 1920s: reproducing a pronunciation of *get up*.

GIF ■ n. Computing a popular format for image files, with built-in data compression. ▸ (also **gif**) a file in this format.
– ORIGIN C20: acronym from *graphic interchange format*.

GIFT ■ n. Medicine gamete intrafallopian transfer.

gift ■ n. **1** a thing given willingly to someone without payment; a present. ▸ informal a very easy task or unmissable opportunity. **2** a natural ability or talent. ■ v. **1** give as a gift, especially formally. ▸ informal inadvertently allow (an opponent) to have something. **2** (**gift someone with**) endow someone with (an ability or talent). ▸ [as adj. **gifted**] having exceptional talent or ability.
– PHRASES **in the gift of** (of a Church living or official appointment) in the power of (someone) to award.
– DERIVATIVES **giftedness** adj.
– ORIGIN Middle English: from Old Norse *gipt*; rel. to GIVE.

gift certificate ■ n. N. Amer. a gift token.

gift token (also **gift voucher**) ■ n. a voucher given as a gift which is exchangeable for goods.

giftware ■ n. goods sold as being suitable as gifts.

gift wrap ■ n. decorative paper for wrapping gifts. ■ v. (**gift-wrap**) [usu. as adj. **gift-wrapped**] wrap (a gift) in decorative paper.

gig¹ /gɪg/ ■ n. **1** chiefly historical a light two-wheeled carriage pulled by one horse. **2** a light, fast, narrow boat adapted for rowing or sailing.
– ORIGIN C18: apparently a transferred sense of obsolete *gig* 'a flighty girl'.

gig² /gɪg/ informal ■ n. a live performance by a musician or other performer. ■ v. (**gigged, gigging**) perform a gig or gigs.
– ORIGIN 1920s.

gig³ /gɪg/ ■ n. a harpoon-like weapon used for catching fish. ■ v. (**gigged, gigging**) fish using such a weapon.
– ORIGIN C18: shortening of earlier *fizgig*, prob. from Spanish *fisga* 'harpoon'.

gig⁴ /gɪg, dʒɪg/ ■ n. Computing, informal short for GIGABYTE.

giga- /ˈgɪgə, ˈdʒɪgə/ ■ comb. form **1** denoting a factor of 10⁹: *gigahertz*. **2** Computing denoting a factor of 2³⁰.
– ORIGIN from Greek *gigas* 'giant'.

gigabyte /ˈgɪgəbʌɪt, ˈdʒ-/ ■ n. Computing a unit of information equal to one thousand million (10⁹) or (strictly) 2³⁰ bytes.

gigaflop /ˈgɪgəflɒp, ˈdʒ-/ ■ n. Computing a unit of computing speed equal to one thousand million floating-point operations per second.
– ORIGIN 1970s: back-formation from *gigaflops* (see GIGA-, -FLOP).

gigahertz (abbrev.: **GHz** or **gHz**) ■ n. a measure of frequency equivalent to one thousand million (10⁹) cycles per second.

gigantic ■ adj. of very great size or extent.
– DERIVATIVES **gigantically** adv.
– ORIGIN C17: from Greek *gigas*, *gigant-*.

gigantism /ˈdʒʌɪgantɪz(ə)m, dʒʌɪˈgantɪz(ə)m/ ■ n. chiefly Biology unusual or abnormal largeness.

giggle ■ v. laugh lightly in a nervous, affected, or silly manner. ■ n. **1** a laugh of such a kind. **2** informal an amusing person or thing.
– DERIVATIVES **giggler** n. **giggly** adj. (**-ier, -iest**).
– ORIGIN C16: imitative.

GIGO /ˈgʌɪgəʊ/ ■ abbrev. chiefly Computing garbage in, garbage out.

gigolo /ˈ(d)ʒɪgələʊ/ ■ n. (pl. **-os**) **1** a young man paid or financially supported by an older woman to be her escort or lover. **2** a professional male dancing partner.
– ORIGIN 1920s: from French, formed as the masculine of *gigole* 'dance hall woman', from colloquial *gigue* 'leg'.

gigot /ˈdʒɪgət/ ■ n. a leg of mutton or lamb.
– ORIGIN French: diminutive of colloquial *gigue* 'leg'.

491

gimme

Gila monster /ˈhiːlə/ ■ n. a large, slow-moving venomous lizard native to the south-western US and Mexico. [*Heloderma suspectum*.]
– ORIGIN C19: named after *Gila*, a river in New Mexico and Arizona.

gild ■ v. **1** cover thinly with gold. **2** [as adj. **gilded**] wealthy and privileged: *gilded youth*.
– PHRASES **gild the lily** try to improve what is already beautiful or excellent.
– DERIVATIVES **gilder** n. **gilding** n.
– ORIGIN Old English, of Germanic origin.

gilded cage ■ n. a luxurious but restrictive environment.

gilet /ˈʒɪleɪ, ˈʒiːleɪ/ ■ n. (pl. **gilets** pronunc. same) a light sleeveless padded jacket.
– ORIGIN C19: French, 'waistcoat', from Spanish *jileco*, from Turkish *yelek*.

gill¹ /gɪl/ ■ n. **1** the paired respiratory organ of fishes and some amphibians, by which oxygen is extracted from water flowing over surfaces within or attached to the walls of the pharynx. **2** the vertical plates arranged radially on the underside of mushrooms and many toadstools. **3** (**gills**) the wattles or dewlap of a fowl. ■ v. **1** gut or clean (a fish). **2** catch (a fish) in a gill net.
– PHRASES **green about** (or **around**) **the gills** sickly-looking. **to the gills** until completely full.
– DERIVATIVES **-gilled** adj.
– ORIGIN Middle English: from Old Norse.

gill² /dʒɪl/ ■ n. a unit of liquid measure, equal to a quarter of a pint.
– ORIGIN Middle English: from Old French *gille* 'measure for wine', from late Latin *gillo* 'water pot'.

gill³ /gɪl/ (also **ghyll**) ■ n. chiefly N. English **1** a deep ravine, especially a wooded one. **2** a narrow mountain stream.
– ORIGIN Middle English: from Old Norse *gil* 'deep glen'.

gillie /ˈgɪli/ (also **ghillie**) ■ n. **1** S. African & Scottish an attendant on a hunting or fishing expedition. **2** historical a Highland chief's attendant.
– ORIGIN C16: from Scottish Gaelic *gille* 'lad, servant'.

gill net ■ n. a fishing net which is hung vertically so that fish get trapped in it by their gills.
– DERIVATIVES **gill-netter** n.

gillyflower /ˈdʒɪlɪˌflaʊə/ (also **gilliflower**) ■ n. any of a number of fragrant flowers, such as the wallflower or white stock.
– ORIGIN Middle English: from Old French *gilofre*, *girofle*, from Greek *karuophullon*, from *karuon* 'nut' + *phullon* 'leaf'.

gilt¹ ■ adj. covered thinly with gold leaf or gold paint. ■ n. **1** gold leaf or gold paint applied in a thin layer to a surface. **2** (**gilts**) Finance a bond or security issued by a government, with a fixed or variable rate of interest.
– ORIGIN Middle English: archaic past participle of GILD.

gilt² ■ n. a young sow.
– ORIGIN Middle English: from Old Norse *gyltr*.

gilt-edged ■ adj. relating to or denoting stocks or securities (such as gilts) that are regarded as extremely reliable investments.

gimbal /ˈdʒɪmb(ə)l/ (also **gimbals**) ■ n. a contrivance for keeping an instrument such as a compass or chronometer horizontal in a moving vessel or aircraft.
– DERIVATIVES **gimballed** adj.
– ORIGIN C16: var. of earlier *gimmal*, itself a var. of Middle English *gemel* 'twin, hinge', from Old French *gemel* 'twin'.

gimcrack /ˈdʒɪmkrak/ ■ adj. showy but flimsy or poorly made. ■ n. a cheap and showy ornament.
– ORIGIN Middle English.

gimlet /ˈgɪmlɪt/ ■ n. **1** a small T-shaped tool with a screw-tip for boring holes. **2** a cocktail of gin or vodka and lime juice.
– ORIGIN Middle English: from Old French *guimbelet*, diminutive of *guimble* 'drill', of Germanic origin.

gimlet eye ■ n. an eye with a piercing stare.
– DERIVATIVES **gimlet-eyed** adj.

gimme informal ■ contr. give me. ■ n. chiefly N. Amer. something very easy to perform or obtain.

gimmick

gimmick ■ n. a trick or device intended to attract attention rather than fulfil a useful purpose.
– DERIVATIVES **gimmickry** n. **gimmicky** adj.
– ORIGIN 1920s ('piece of magicians' apparatus'): perhaps an approximate anagram of *magic*.

gimp /gɪmp/ ■ n. **1** twisted, reinforced material used as upholstery trimming. **2** (in lacemaking) coarser thread forming the outline of the design. **3** fishing line made of silk bound with wire.
– ORIGIN C17: from Dutch.

gin[1] ■ n. **1** a clear alcoholic spirit distilled from grain or malt and flavoured with juniper berries. **2** (also **gin rummy**) a form of the card game rummy.
– ORIGIN C18: abbrev. of GENEVER.

gin[2] ■ n. **1** a machine for separating cotton from its seeds. **2** a machine for raising and moving heavy weights. **3** a trap for catching small game. ■ v. (**ginned**, **ginning**) treat (cotton) in a gin.
– DERIVATIVES **ginner** n. **ginnery** n.
– ORIGIN Middle English ('a tool or device, a trick'): from Old French *engin* (see ENGINE).

ginger ■ n. **1** a hot, fragrant spice made from the rhizome of a plant. **2** a SE Asian plant, resembling bamboo in appearance, from which ginger is taken. [*Zingiber officinale*.] **3** a light reddish-yellow colour. **4** spirit; mettle. ■ v. **1** [usu. as adj. **gingered**] flavour with ginger. **2** (**ginger someone/thing up**) stimulate or enliven someone or something.
– DERIVATIVES **gingery** adj.
– ORIGIN Old English: from medieval Latin *gingiber*, from Greek *zingiberis*, from Pali *siṅgivera*, of Dravidian origin.

ginger ale (also **ginger beer**) ■ n. an effervescent, sometimes alcoholic drink flavoured with ginger.

gingerbread ■ n. **1** cake made with treacle or syrup and flavoured with ginger. **2** informal fancy decoration on a building.
– PHRASES **take the gilt off the gingerbread** make something no longer attractive or desirable.
– ORIGIN Middle English: from Old French *gingembrat*, from medieval Latin *gingibratum*, from *gingiber* (see GINGER).

gingerly ■ adv. in a careful or cautious manner. ■ adj. showing great care or caution.
– DERIVATIVES **gingerliness** n.
– ORIGIN C16: perhaps from Old French *gensor* 'delicate', from *gent* 'graceful', from Latin *genitus* '(well-) born'.

ginger nut ■ n. a hard ginger-flavoured biscuit.

gingham /ˈɡɪŋəm/ ■ n. lightweight plain-woven cotton cloth, typically checked.
– ORIGIN C17: from Dutch *gingang*, from Malay *genggang*, orig. an adj. meaning 'striped'.

gingival /dʒɪnˈdʒaɪv(ə)l/ ■ adj. Medicine concerned with the gums.
– ORIGIN C17: from Latin *gingiva* 'gum'.

gingivitis /ˌdʒɪndʒɪˈvaɪtɪs/ ■ n. Medicine inflammation of the gums.

ginkgo /ˈɡɪŋkɡəʊ, ˈɡɪŋkəʊ/ (also **gingko**) ■ n. (pl. **-os** or **-oes**) a deciduous Chinese tree related to the conifers, with fan-shaped leaves and yellow flowers. [*Ginkgo biloba*.]
– ORIGIN C18: from Japanese *ginkyō*, from Chinese *yinxing*.

ginormous ■ adj. informal extremely large.
– ORIGIN 1940s: blend of GIANT and ENORMOUS.

ginseng /ˈdʒɪnsɛŋ/ ■ n. **1** a plant tuber credited with various tonic and medicinal properties. **2** the plant from which this tuber is obtained, native to east Asia and North America. [Genus *Panax*: several species.]
– ORIGIN C17: from Chinese *rénshēn*, from *rén* 'man' + *shēn*, a kind of herb (because of the supposed resemblance of the forked root to a person).

gip ■ n. variant spelling of GYP[1].

gippo guts ■ pl. n. variant spelling of GYPPO GUTS.

gippy tummy /ˈdʒɪpɪ/ ■ n. informal British term for GYPPO GUTS.
– ORIGIN 1940s: *gippy*, abbrev. of EGYPTIAN.

gipsy ■ n. variant spelling of GYPSY.

giraffe ■ n. (pl. same or **giraffes**) a large African mammal with a very long neck and forelegs, the tallest living animal. [*Giraffa camelopardalis*.]
– ORIGIN C16: from French *girafe*, Italian *giraffa*, or Spanish and Portuguese *girafa*, from Arabic *zarāfa*.

girandole /ˈdʒɪr(ə)ndəʊl/ ■ n. a branched support for candles or other lights.
– ORIGIN C17: from French, from Italian *girandola*, from *girare* 'gyrate, turn'.

girasol /ˈdʒɪrəsɒl, -səʊl/ (also **girasole** /-səʊl/) ■ n. **1** a kind of opal reflecting a reddish glow. **2** North American term for JERUSALEM ARTICHOKE.
– ORIGIN C16 ('sunflower'): from Italian *girasole*, from *girare* 'to turn' + *sole* 'sun'.

gird ■ v. (past and past part. **girded** or **girt**) poetic/literary **1** encircle or secure with a belt or band. **2** (often in phr. **gird one's loins**) prepare and strengthen oneself for what is to come.
– ORIGIN Old English, of Germanic origin.

girder ■ n. a large metal beam used in building bridges and large buildings.
– ORIGIN C17: from GIRD in the archaic sense 'brace, strengthen'.

girdle ■ n. **1** a belt or cord worn round the waist. **2** a woman's elasticated corset extending from waist to thigh. **3** the part of a cut gem dividing the crown from the base and embraced by the setting. **4** a ring made around a tree by removing bark. ■ v. **1** encircle with a girdle or belt. ▶ surround; encircle. **2** kill (a tree or branch) by cutting through the bark all the way round.
– DERIVATIVES **girdler** n.
– ORIGIN Old English, of Germanic origin.

girl ■ n. **1** a female child. **2** a young or relatively young woman. ▶ (**girls**) informal women who mix socially or belong to a group or team. ▶ a person's girlfriend. **3** dated a female servant. ▶ S. African offensive a black woman.
– DERIVATIVES **girlhood** n. **girlish** adj. **girlishly** adv. **girlishness** n.
– ORIGIN Middle English (denoting a child or young person of either sex): perhaps rel. to Low German *gör* 'child'.

girlfriend ■ n. a person's regular female companion in a romantic or sexual relationship. ▶ a woman's female friend.

Girl Guide ■ n. a member of the Girl Guides Association.

girlie ■ n. (also **girly**) (pl. **-ies**) informal a girl or young woman. ■ adj. **1** (usu. **girly**) often derogatory like or characteristic of a girl. **2** depicting nude or partially nude young women in erotic poses: *girlie magazines*.

Girl Scout ■ n. a girl belonging to the Scout Association.

giro /ˈdʒaɪrəʊ/ ■ n. (pl. **-os**) **1** a system of electronic credit transfer used in Europe and Japan, involving banks, post offices, and public utilities. **2** a cheque or payment by giro, especially a social security payment.
– ORIGIN C19: from Italian, 'circulation (of money)'.

girt past participle of GIRD.

girth ■ n. **1** the measurement around the middle of something, especially a person's waist. **2** a band attached to a saddle and fastened around a horse's belly. ■ v. archaic surround; encircle.
– ORIGIN Middle English: from Old Norse *gjǫrth*.

GIS ■ abbrev. geographic information system.

gismo ■ n. variant spelling of GIZMO.

gist /dʒɪst/ ■ n. **1** the substance or essence of a speech or text. **2** Law the real point of an action.
– ORIGIN C18: from Old French, third person sing. present tense of *gesir* 'to lie', in Anglo-French legal phr. *cest action gist* 'this action lies', denoting that there were sufficient grounds to proceed.

git ■ n. Brit. informal an unpleasant or contemptible person.
– ORIGIN 1940s: var. of the noun GET.

Gita /ˈɡiːtə/ ■ n. short for BHAGAVADGITA.

gîte /ʒiːt/ ■ n. a small furnished holiday house in France.
– ORIGIN French: from Old French *giste*; rel. to *gésir* 'to lie'.

give ■ v. (past **gave**; past part. **given**) (usu. **give something to**) give someone something **1** freely transfer the possession of; cause to receive or have. ▶ communicate or impart (a message). ▶ commit, consign, or entrust. ▶ cause to experience or suffer: *you gave me a fright*. ▶ allot (a score) to. **2** yield as a product or result. ▶ (**give something**

off/out) emit odour, vapour, etc. **3** carry out (an action). ▶ produce (a sound). ▶ provide (a party or meal) as host or hostess. **4** state or put forward (information or argument). ▶ pledge or assign as a guarantee. ▶ deliver (a judgement) authoritatively. **5** present (an appearance or impression): *he gave no sign of life*. **6** alter in shape under pressure rather than resist or break. ▶ yield or give way to pressure. ▶ N. Amer. informal concede defeat; surrender. **7** (of an umpire or referee) declare whether or not (a player) is out or offside. ▶ adjudicate that (a goal) has been legitimately scored. **8** concede or yield (something) as valid or deserved in respect of (someone). ■ n. capacity to bend or alter in shape under pressure.

– PHRASES **give oneself airs** act pretentiously or snobbishly. **give and take** mutual concessions and compromises. **give the game (or show) away** inadvertently reveal something secret or concealed. **give or take ——** informal **1** to within a specified amount. **2** apart from. **give rise to** cause or induce to happen. **give someone to understand** inform someone in a formal and rather indirect way. **give someone what for** informal, chiefly Brit. punish or scold someone severely. **not give a damn (or hoot** etc.) informal not care at all. **what gives?** informal what's the news?

– PHRASAL VERBS **give someone away 1** reveal incriminating or hidden information about someone. **2** hand over a bride ceremonially to her bridegroom. **give something away 1** reveal something secret or concealed. **2** (in sport) concede a goal or advantage to the opposition. **give in** cease fighting or arguing. **give on to (or into)** Brit. overlook or lead into. **give out** be completely used up. ▶ stop functioning. **give over** Brit. informal stop doing something. **give up** cease making an effort; resign oneself to failure. **give someone up** deliver a wanted person to authority. **give something up 1** part with something that one would prefer to keep. **2** stop doing something. **give up on** stop having faith or belief in.

– DERIVATIVES **giver** n.
– ORIGIN Old English, of Germanic origin.

giveaway ■ n. informal **1** something given free, especially for promotional purposes. **2** something that makes an inadvertent revelation.

given past participle of GIVE. ■ adj. **1** specified or stated. **2 (given to)** inclined or disposed to. ■ prep. taking into account. ■ n. a known or established fact or situation.

given name ■ n. another term for FIRST NAME.

gizmo /ˈgɪzməʊ/ (also **gismo**) ■ n. (pl. **-os**) informal a gadget, especially one whose name the speaker does not know or cannot recall.
– ORIGIN 1940s (orig. US).

gizzard /ˈgɪzəd/ ■ n. a muscular, thick-walled part of a bird's stomach for grinding food, typically with grit. ▶ a muscular stomach of some fish, insects, molluscs, and other invertebrates.
– ORIGIN Middle English *giser*: from Old French, from Latin *gigeria* 'cooked entrails of fowl'.

GLA ■ abbrev. gamma linolenic acid.

glabella /gləˈbɛlə/ ■ n. (pl. **glabellae** /-liː/) Anatomy the smooth part of the forehead above and between the eyebrows.
– DERIVATIVES **glabellar** adj.
– ORIGIN C19: modern Latin, from Latin *glabellus* (adj.), diminutive of *glaber* 'smooth'.

glabrous /ˈɡleɪbrəs/ ■ adj. technical free from hair or down; smooth.
– ORIGIN C17: from Latin *glaber, glabr-* 'hairless, smooth'.

glacé /ˈɡlaseɪ/ ■ adj. **1** (of fruit) having a glossy surface due to preservation in sugar. **2** (of cloth or leather) smooth and highly polished.
– ORIGIN C19: French, 'iced', from *glace* 'ice'.

glacé icing ■ n. icing made with icing sugar and water.

glacial /ˈɡleɪʃ(ə)l, -sɪəl/ ■ adj. **1** relating to ice, especially in the form of glaciers or ice sheets. **2** extremely cold or unfriendly; icy. **3** Chemistry denoting pure organic acids (especially acetic acid) which form ice-like crystals on freezing. ■ n. Geology a glacial period.
– DERIVATIVES **glacially** adv.
– ORIGIN C17: from Latin *glacialis* 'icy'.

glaciated /ˈɡleɪsɪeɪtɪd, ˈɡlas-/ ■ adj. covered or having been covered by glaciers or ice sheets.
– ORIGIN C19: from obsolete *glaciate*, from Latin *glaciare* 'freeze'.

glaciation /ˌɡleɪsɪˈeɪʃ(ə)n/ ■ n. Geology **1** the condition or result of being glaciated. **2** a period in the earth's history when ice sheets were extensive; an ice age.

glacier /ˈɡlasɪə, ˈɡleɪs-/ ■ n. a slowly moving mass of ice formed by the accumulation and compaction of snow on mountains or near the poles.
– ORIGIN C18: from French, from *glace* 'ice'.

glaciology /ˌɡleɪsɪˈɒlədʒi/ ■ n. the study of glaciers.
– DERIVATIVES **glaciological** adj. **glaciologist** n.

glad ■ adj. (**gladder**, **gladdest**) **1** pleased; delighted. ▶ causing happiness: *glad tidings*. **2** (often **glad of**) grateful.
– PHRASES **give someone the glad eye** informal, dated look flirtatiously at someone.
– DERIVATIVES **gladly** adv. **gladness** n. **gladsome** adj. (poetic/literary).
– ORIGIN Old English *glæd* (orig. in the sense 'bright, shining'), of Germanic origin; rel. to Latin *glaber* 'smooth, hairless'.

gladden ■ v. make glad.

glade ■ n. an open space in a wood or forest.
– ORIGIN Middle English: perhaps rel. to GLAD or GLEAM, with ref. to the comparative brightness of a clearing.

glad-hand chiefly N. Amer. ■ v. (especially of a politician) greet or welcome warmly. ■ n. (**glad hand**) a warm and hearty greeting or welcome.
– DERIVATIVES **glad-hander** n.

gladiator /ˈɡladɪeɪtə/ ■ n. (in ancient Rome) a man trained to fight with weapons against other men or wild animals in an arena.
– DERIVATIVES **gladiatorial** adj.
– ORIGIN Middle English: from Latin, from *gladius* 'sword'.

gladiolus /ˌɡladɪˈəʊləs/ ■ n. (pl. **gladioli** /-lʌɪ/ or **gladioluses**) a plant of the iris family with sword-shaped leaves and spikes of brightly coloured flowers. [Genus *Gladiolus*.]
– ORIGIN Old English: from Latin, diminutive of *gladius* 'sword'.

glad rags ■ pl. n. informal clothes for a party or special occasion.

Gladstone bag ■ n. a bag like a briefcase having two equal compartments joined by a hinge.
– ORIGIN C19: named after the British statesman W. E. Gladstone.

glam informal ■ adj. glamorous. ■ n. glamour. ■ v. (**glammed**, **glamming**) (**glam up**) make oneself look glamorous.

glamorize (also **glamourize** or **-ise**) ■ v. make (something) seem glamorous or desirable, especially spuriously so.
– DERIVATIVES **glamorization** (also **-isation**) n.

glamour (US also **glamor**) ■ n. **1** an attractive and exciting quality, especially sexual allure. **2** archaic enchantment; magic.
– DERIVATIVES **glamorous** adj. **glamorously** adv.
– ORIGIN C18: alteration of GRAMMAR, with ref. to the occult practices associated with learning in medieval times.

glam rock ■ n. a style of rock music characterized by male performers wearing exaggeratedly flamboyant clothes and make-up.

glance ■ v. **1** take a brief or hurried look. **2** (often **glance off**) strike at an angle and bounce off obliquely. ■ n. **1** a brief or hurried look. **2** poetic/literary a flash or gleam of light.
– DERIVATIVES **glancing** adj. **glancingly** adv.
– ORIGIN Middle English: prob. a nasalized form of obsolete *glace*, from Old French *glacier* 'to slip', from *glace* 'ice'.

gland[1] ■ n. an organ of the body which secretes particular chemical substances. ▶ a lymph node.
– ORIGIN C17: from French *glande*, alteration of Old French *glandre*, from Latin *glandulae* 'throat glands'.

gland[2] ■ n. a sleeve used to produce a seal round a piston rod or other shaft.
– ORIGIN C19: prob. a var. of Scots *glam* 'a vice or clamp'.

glanders /ˈɡlandəz/ ■ pl. n. [usu. treated as sing.] a rare contagious disease that mainly affects horses,

glandular

characterized by swellings below the jaw and mucous discharge from the nostrils.
– ORIGIN C15: from Old French *glandre* (see **GLAND**¹).

glandular /ˈglandjʊlə, ˈɡlan(d)ʒʊlə/ ■ adj. relating to or affecting a gland or glands.

glandular fever ■ n. an infectious viral disease characterized by swelling of the lymph glands and prolonged lassitude.

glans /glanz/ ■ n. (pl. **glandes** /ˈglandiːz/) Anatomy the rounded part forming the end of the penis or clitoris.
– ORIGIN C17: from Latin, 'acorn'.

glare ■ v. 1 stare in an angry or fierce way. 2 shine with a strong or dazzling light. 3 [as adj. **glaring**] highly obvious or conspicuous. ■ n. 1 a fierce or angry stare. 2 strong and dazzling light.
– DERIVATIVES **glaringly** adv. **glary** adj.
– ORIGIN Middle English: from Middle Dutch and Middle Low German *glaren* 'to gleam or glare'.

glasnost /ˈglaznɒst, ˈɡlɑːs-/ ■ n. (in the former Soviet Union) the policy or practice of more open government and wider dissemination of information.
– ORIGIN from Russian *glasnost'* 'the fact of being public, openness'.

glass ■ n. 1 a hard, brittle, usually transparent or translucent substance made by fusing sand with soda and lime. ▸ ornaments and other articles made from glass. ▸ greenhouses or cold frames considered collectively. 2 a drinking container made of glass. 3 a lens or optical instrument, in particular a monocle or a magnifying lens. 4 chiefly Brit. a mirror. ■ v. cover or enclose with glass.
– DERIVATIVES **glassful** n. (pl. **-fuls**). **glassless** adj. **glass-like** adj. **glassware** n.
– ORIGIN Old English, of Germanic origin.

glass-blowing ■ n. the craft of making glassware by blowing semi-molten glass through a long tube.
– DERIVATIVES **glass-blower** n.

glass ceiling ■ n. an unacknowledged barrier to advancement in a profession, especially affecting women and members of minorities.

glass cloth ■ n. 1 chiefly Brit. a cloth covered with powdered glass or other abrasive, used for smoothing and polishing. 2 woven fabric of fine-spun glass thread.

glass eel ■ n. an elver at the time that it first enters brackish or fresh water, when it is translucent.

glasses ■ pl. n. a pair of lenses set in a frame that rests on the nose and ears, used to correct or assist defective eyesight.

glass fibre ■ n. chiefly Brit. a strong plastic, textile, or other material containing embedded glass filaments for reinforcement.

glasshouse ■ n. Brit. 1 a greenhouse. 2 military slang a place of detention.

glassine /ˈglɑːsiːn/ ■ n. a glossy transparent paper.

glass lizard (also **glass snake**) ■ n. a legless burrowing lizard of snake-like appearance. [Genus *Ophisaurus*: several species.]

glasspaper ■ n. paper covered with powdered glass, used for smoothing and polishing.

glass wool ■ n. glass in the form of fine fibres used for packing and insulation.

glassy ■ adj. (**-ier**, **-iest**) 1 of or resembling glass. ▸ (of water) having a smooth surface. 2 (of a person's eyes or expression) showing no interest or animation.
– DERIVATIVES **glassily** adv. **glassiness** n.

Glaswegian /glazˈwiːdʒ(ə)n, glas-, glɑːz-, glɑːs-/ ■ n. a native of Glasgow. ■ adj. of or relating to Glasgow.

Glauber's salt /ˈglaʊbəz, ˈglɔː-/ ■ n. a crystalline hydrated form of sodium sulphate, used chiefly as a laxative.
– ORIGIN C18: named after the German chemist Johann R. Glauber (1604–1668).

glaucoma /glɔːˈkəʊmə/ ■ n. Medicine a condition of increased pressure within the eyeball, causing gradual loss of sight.
– DERIVATIVES **glaucomatous** adj.

– ORIGIN C17: from Greek *glaukōma*, from *glaukos* 'bluish green or grey' (because of the grey-green haze in the pupil).

glaucous /ˈglɔːkəs/ ■ adj. technical or poetic/literary 1 of a dull greyish-green or blue colour. 2 covered with a powdery bloom like that on grapes.
– ORIGIN C17: from Greek *glaukos*.

glaze ■ v. 1 fit panes of glass into (a window frame or similar structure). ▸ enclose or cover with glass. 2 cover with a glaze. 3 (often **glaze over**) lose brightness and animation. ■ n. 1 a vitreous substance fused on to the surface of pottery to form a hard, impervious decorative coating. 2 a thin topcoat of transparent paint used to modify the tone of an underlying colour. 3 a liquid such as milk or beaten egg, used to form a smooth shiny coating on food. 4 N. Amer. a thin, glassy coating of ice on the ground or water.
– DERIVATIVES **glazer** n. **glazing** n.
– ORIGIN Middle English *glase*, from **GLASS**.

glazier /ˈgleɪzɪə/ ■ n. a person whose trade is fitting glass into windows and doors.

GLC ■ abbrev. Chemistry gas–liquid chromatography.

gleam ■ v. shine brightly, especially with reflected light. ■ n. 1 a faint or brief light. 2 a brief or faint show of a quality or emotion.
– PHRASES **a gleam in someone's eye** see **EYE**.
– DERIVATIVES **gleaming** adj. **gleamingly** adv.
– ORIGIN Old English *glǣm* 'brilliant light', of Germanic origin.

glean /gliːn/ ■ v. 1 collect gradually from various sources. 2 historical gather (leftover grain) after a harvest.
– DERIVATIVES **gleaner** n.
– ORIGIN Middle English: from late Latin *glennare*, prob. of Celtic origin.

gleanings ■ pl. n. things gleaned from various sources rather than acquired as a whole.

glebe /gliːb/ ■ n. 1 historical a piece of land serving as part of a clergyman's benefice and providing income. 2 archaic land; fields.
– ORIGIN Middle English: from Latin *gleba*, *glaeba* 'clod, land, soil'.

glee ■ n. 1 great delight. 2 a song for men's voices in three or more parts, usually unaccompanied.
– DERIVATIVES **gleesome** adj. (archaic).
– ORIGIN Old English *glēo* 'entertainment, music, fun', of Germanic origin.

glee club ■ n. a society for singing part songs.

gleeful ■ adj. exuberantly or triumphantly joyful.
– DERIVATIVES **gleefully** adv. **gleefulness** n.

glen ■ n. a narrow valley, especially in Scotland or Ireland.
– ORIGIN Middle English: from Scottish Gaelic and Irish *gleann* (earlier *glenn*).

glenoid cavity /ˈgliːnɔɪd/ (also **glenoid fossa**) ■ n. Anatomy a shallow depression on a bone into which another bone fits to form a joint, especially on the scapula into which the head of the humerus fits.
– ORIGIN C18: *glenoid* from Greek *glēnoeidēs*, from *glēnē* 'socket'.

gley /gleɪ/ ■ n. Soil Science a sticky waterlogged soil lacking in oxygen, typically grey to blue in colour.
– ORIGIN 1920s: from Ukrainian, 'sticky blue clay'.

glia /ˈglʌɪə, ˈgliːə/ ■ n. Anatomy the connective tissue of the nervous system, consisting of several different types of cell associated with neurons.
– DERIVATIVES **glial** adj.
– ORIGIN C19: from Greek, 'glue'.

glib ■ adj. (**glibber**, **glibbest**) articulate and voluble but insincere and shallow.
– DERIVATIVES **glibly** adv. **glibness** n.
– ORIGIN C16: of Germanic origin.

glide ■ v. 1 move with a smooth, quiet, continuous motion. 2 fly without power or in a glider. ■ n. 1 an instance of gliding. 2 Phonetics a sound produced as the vocal organs move towards or away from articulation of a vowel or consonant, for example /j/ in *duke* /djuːk/.
– DERIVATIVES **gliding** n.
– ORIGIN Old English, of Germanic origin.

glider ■ n. 1 a light aircraft designed to fly without using an engine. **2** a person or thing that glides. **3** US a long swinging seat suspended from a frame in a porch.

glimmer ■ v. shine faintly with a wavering light. ■ n. **1** a faint or wavering light. **2** a faint sign of a feeling or quality, especially a desirable one: *a glimmer of hope*.
– DERIVATIVES **glimmering** adj. & n. **glimmeringly** adv.
– ORIGIN Middle English: prob. of Scandinavian origin; rel. to Swedish *glimra* and Danish *glimre*.

glimpse ■ n. a momentary or partial view. ■ v. see briefly or partially.
– ORIGIN Middle English ('shine faintly'): prob. of Germanic origin; rel. to GLIMMER.

glint ■ v. give out or reflect small flashes of light. ■ n. a small flash of light, especially a reflected one.
– ORIGIN Middle English: var. of dialect *glent*, prob. of Scandinavian origin and rel. to Swedish dialect *glinta* 'to slip, slide, gleam'.

glioma /glʌɪˈəʊmə/ ■ n. (pl. **gliomas** or **gliomata** /-mətə/) Medicine a malignant tumour of the glial tissue of the nervous system.
– ORIGIN C19: from Greek *glia* 'glue'.

glissade /glɪˈsɑːd, -ˈseɪd/ ■ n. **1** a slide down a steep slope of snow or ice, typically on the feet with the support of an ice axe. **2** Ballet a movement in which one leg is brushed outwards from the body and then takes the weight while the second leg is brushed in to meet it. ■ v. perform or move by means of a glissade.
– ORIGIN C19: French, from *glisser* 'to slip, slide'.

glissando /glɪˈsandəʊ/ ■ n. (pl. **glissandi** /-di/ or **glissandos**) Music a continuous slide upwards or downwards between two notes.
– ORIGIN Italian: from French *glisser* 'to slip, slide'.

glissé /gliːˈseɪ/ ■ n. (pl. pronounced same) Ballet a movement in which one foot is slid outward from the body and briefly extended off the ground and the other is brought to meet it.
– ORIGIN French, 'slipped, glided', from *glisser*.

glisten ■ v. (of something wet or greasy) shine or sparkle. ■ n. a sparkling light reflected from something wet.
– ORIGIN Old English, of Germanic origin.

glister /ˈglɪstə/ poetic/literary ■ v. sparkle; glitter. ■ n. a sparkle.
– ORIGIN Middle English: prob. from Middle Low German *glistern* or Middle Dutch *glisteren*.

glitch ■ n. informal **1** a sudden, usually temporary malfunction or irregularity of equipment. ▸ an unexpected setback in a plan. **2** Astronomy a brief irregularity in the rotation of a pulsar.
– DERIVATIVES **glitchy** adj.
– ORIGIN 1960s (orig. US).

glitter ■ v. **1** shine with a bright, shimmering reflected light. **2** [as adj. **glittering**] impressively successful or glamorous: *a glittering career*. ■ n. **1** bright, shimmering reflected light. **2** tiny pieces of sparkling material used for decoration. **3** an attractive and exciting but superficial quality.
– DERIVATIVES **glitteringly** adv. **glittery** adj.
– ORIGIN Middle English: from Old Norse *glitra*.

glitterati /ˌglɪtəˈrɑːti/ ■ pl. n. informal fashionable people involved in show business or some other glamorous activity.
– ORIGIN 1950s: blend of GLITTER and LITERATI.

glitz ■ n. informal extravagant but superficial display.
– DERIVATIVES **glitziness** n. **glitzy** adj.
– ORIGIN 1960s (as *glitzy*): from GLITTER, suggested by RITZY.

gloaming ■ n. (**the gloaming**) poetic/literary twilight; dusk.
– ORIGIN Old English *glōmung*, from *glōm* 'twilight', of Germanic origin.

gloat ■ v. contemplate one's own success or another's misfortune with smugness or malignant pleasure. ■ n. an act of gloating.
– DERIVATIVES **gloater** n. **gloating** adj. & n. **gloatingly** adv.
– ORIGIN C16: perhaps rel. to Old Norse *glotta* 'to grin' and Middle High German *glotzen* 'to stare'.

glob ■ n. informal a lump of a semi-liquid substance.
– ORIGIN C20: perhaps a blend of BLOB and GOB².

global /ˈgləʊb(ə)l/ ■ adj. **1** of or relating to the whole world; worldwide. **2** relating to or embracing the whole of something, or of a group of things. ▸ Computing operating or applying through the whole of a file or program.
– DERIVATIVES **globalist** n. **globalize** (also **-ise**) v. **globally** adv.

globalization (also **-isation**) ■ n. international integration, especially with reference to world trade and financial markets.

global village ■ n. the world considered as a single community linked by telecommunications.

global warming ■ n. the gradual increase in the overall temperature of the earth's atmosphere due to the greenhouse effect caused by increased levels of carbon dioxide, CFCs, and other pollutants.

globe ■ n. **1** a spherical or rounded object. **2** S. African & Austral./NZ an electric light bulb. **3** a spherical representation of the earth with a map on the surface. **4** (**the globe**) the earth.
– DERIVATIVES **globe-like** adj. **globoid** adj. & n. **globose** adj.
– ORIGIN Middle English: from Latin *globus*.

globetrotter ■ n. informal a person who travels widely.
– DERIVATIVES **globetrot** v. **globetrotting** n. & adj.

globular /ˈglɒbjʊlə/ ■ adj. **1** globe-shaped; spherical. **2** composed of globules.

globular cluster ■ n. Astronomy a large compact spherical star cluster, typically of old stars in the outer regions of a galaxy.

globule /ˈglɒbjuːl/ ■ n. **1** a small round particle of a substance; a drop. **2** Astronomy a small dark cloud of gas and dust seen against a brighter background such as a luminous nebula.
– ORIGIN C17: from Latin *globulus*, diminutive of *globus* 'spherical object, globe'.

globulin /ˈglɒbjʊlɪn/ ■ n. Biochemistry any of a group of simple proteins soluble in salt solutions and forming a large fraction of blood serum protein.

glockenspiel /ˈglɒk(ə)nspiːl, -ʃpiːl/ ■ n. a musical percussion instrument consisting of a set of tuned metal pieces mounted in a frame and struck with small hammers.
– ORIGIN C19: from German *Glockenspiel* 'bell play'.

glomerulonephritis /glɒˌmɛrjʊləʊnɪˈfrʌɪtɪs/ ■ n. Medicine acute inflammation of the kidney, typically caused by an immune response.

glomerulus /glɒˈmɛr(j)ʊləs/ ■ n. (pl. **glomeruli** /-lʌɪ, -liː/) Anatomy & Biology a cluster of nerve endings, spores, or small blood vessels, especially of capillaries around the end of a kidney tubule.
– DERIVATIVES **glomerular** adj.
– ORIGIN C19: modern Latin, diminutive of Latin *glomus*, *glomer-* 'ball of thread'.

gloom ■ n. **1** partial or total darkness. **2** a state of depression or despondency. ■ v. appear gloomy.
– ORIGIN Middle English (as v.).

gloomy ■ adj. (**-ier**, **-iest**) **1** poorly lit, especially so as to cause fear or depression. **2** causing or feeling depression or despondency.
– DERIVATIVES **gloomily** adv. **gloominess** n.

gloop ■ n. informal sloppy or sticky semi-fluid matter.
– DERIVATIVES **gloopy** adj.
– ORIGIN C20: symbolic.

Gloria ■ n. Christian Church a hymn beginning *Gloria in excelsis Deo* (Glory be to God in the highest), forming a set part of the Mass.

glorify ■ v. (**-ies**, **-ied**) **1** praise and worship (God). **2** describe or represent as admirable, especially unjustifiably or undeservedly. **3** [as adj. **glorified**] represented as or appearing more elevated or special than is the case: *the word processor is not merely a glorified typewriter*.
– DERIVATIVES **glorification** n. **glorifier** n.

glorious ■ adj. **1** having or bringing glory. **2** strikingly beautiful or impressive.
– DERIVATIVES **gloriously** adv. **gloriousness** n.

glory ■ n. (pl. **-ies**) **1** high renown or honour won by notable achievements. **2** praise and worship offered to

glory hole

God. **3** magnificence; great beauty. ▸ the splendour and bliss of heaven. **4** a luminous ring or halo, especially as depicted around the head of Christ or a saint. ■ v. (**glory in**) take great pride or pleasure in. ▸ exult in unpleasantly or boastfully.
– PHRASES **glory be!** expressing enthusiastic piety. ▸ (**Glory Be**) the liturgical formula beginning 'Glory be to the Father'. **glory days** the most successful period of a person's past life. **go to glory** die. **in one's glory** informal in a state of extreme joy or exaltation.
– ORIGIN Middle English: from Latin *gloria*.

glory hole ■ n. informal an untidy room or cupboard used for storage.

gloss[1] ■ n. **1** shine or lustre on a smooth surface. **2** a superficially attractive appearance or impression: *beneath the gloss of success*. ■ v. **1** give a glossy appearance to. **2** (**gloss something over**) try to conceal or pass over something embarrassing or unfavourable.
– ORIGIN C16.

gloss[2] ■ n. a translation or explanation of a word, phrase, or passage. ■ v. provide a gloss for (a text, word, etc.).
– ORIGIN C16: alteration of archaic *gloze* 'make excuses for, comment', from Old French *glose* 'a gloss, comment', from medieval Latin *glossa* 'explanation of a difficult word'.

glossary ■ n. (pl. **-ies**) an alphabetical list of words relating to a specific subject, text, or dialect, with explanations.
– DERIVATIVES **glossarial** adj. **glossarist** n.
– ORIGIN Middle English: from Latin *glossarium*, from *glossa* (see GLOSS[2]).

glossitis /glɒˈsʌɪtɪs/ ■ n. Medicine inflammation of the tongue.

glossopharyngeal nerves /ˌglɒsə(ʊ)fəˈrɪn(d)ʒɪəl, -ˌfar(ə)nˈdʒiːəl/ ■ pl. n. Anatomy the pair of cranial nerves supplying the tongue and pharynx.

glossy ■ adj. (**-ier**, **-iest**) **1** shiny and smooth. **2** superficially attractive and stylish. ■ n. (pl. **-ies**) informal a magazine printed on glossy paper with many colour photographs.
– DERIVATIVES **glossily** adv. **glossiness** n.

glottal ■ adj. of or produced by the glottis.

glottal stop ■ n. a consonant formed by the audible release of the airstream after complete closure of the glottis.

glottis /ˈglɒtɪs/ ■ n. the part of the larynx consisting of the vocal cords and the slit-like opening between them.
– DERIVATIVES **glottic** adj.
– ORIGIN C16: modern Latin, from Greek *glōttis*, from *glōtta*, var. of *glōssa* 'tongue'.

glove ■ n. a covering for the hand having separate parts for each finger and the thumb. ▸ a padded protective covering for the hand used in boxing and other sports.
– PHRASES **fit like a glove** (of clothes) fit exactly.
– DERIVATIVES **gloved** adj. **gloveless** adj.
– ORIGIN Old English, of Germanic origin.

glovebox ■ n. **1** a glove compartment. **2** a closed chamber with sealed-in gloves for handling radioactive or other hazardous material.

glove compartment ■ n. a recess with a flap in the dashboard of a motor vehicle, used for storing small items.

glove puppet ■ n. a cloth puppet fitted on the hand and worked by the fingers.

glover ■ n. a maker of gloves.

glow ■ v. **1** give out steady light without flame. ▸ have an intense colour and a slight shine. **2** convey deep pleasure through one's expression and bearing. ▸ [as adj. **glowing**] expressing great praise. ■ n. **1** a steady radiance of light or heat. ▸ a feeling or appearance of warmth. **2** a strong feeling of pleasure or well-being: *a glow of pride*.
– DERIVATIVES **glowingly** adv.
– ORIGIN Old English, of Germanic origin.

glower /ˈglaʊə/ ■ v. have an angry or sullen look on one's face; scowl. ■ n. an angry or sullen look.
– DERIVATIVES **glowering** adj. **gloweringly** adv.
– ORIGIN C15: perhaps a Scots var. of dialect *glore*, or from obsolete *glow* 'to stare', both possibly of Scandinavian origin.

glow-worm ■ n. a soft-bodied beetle whose larvalike wingless female emits light to attract males. [Family Lampyridae: numerous species.]

gloxinia /glɒkˈsɪnɪə/ ■ n. a tropical American plant with large, velvety, bell-shaped flowers. [Genera *Gloxinia* and *Sinningia*: several species.]
– ORIGIN named after the C18 German botanist Benjamin P. *Gloxin*.

glucagon /ˈgluːkəg(ə)n, -gɒn/ ■ n. Biochemistry a hormone formed in the pancreas which promotes the breakdown of glycogen to glucose in the liver.
– ORIGIN 1920s: from Greek *glukus* 'sweet' + *agōn* 'leading, bringing'.

glucose /ˈgluːkəʊs, -z/ ■ n. a simple sugar which is an important energy source in living organisms and is a component of many carbohydrates. ▸ a syrup containing glucose and other sugars, made by hydrolysis of starch and used in the food industry.
– ORIGIN C19: from Greek *gleukos* 'sweet wine'.

glucoside /ˈgluːkəsʌɪd/ ■ n. Biochemistry a glycoside derived from glucose.
– DERIVATIVES **glucosidic** adj.

glue ■ n. an adhesive substance used for sticking objects or materials together. ■ v. (**glues**, **glued**, **gluing** or **glueing**) **1** fasten or join with glue. **2** (**be glued to**) informal be paying very close attention to.
– DERIVATIVES **glue-like** adj. **gluey** adj.
– ORIGIN Middle English: from Old French *glu* (n.), *gluer* (v.), from late Latin *glus*, from Latin *gluten*.

glue ear ■ n. blocking of the Eustachian tube by mucus occurring especially in children, and causing impaired hearing.

glue-sniffing ■ n. the practice of inhaling intoxicating fumes from the solvents in adhesives.
– DERIVATIVES **glue-sniffer** n.

glug informal ■ v. (**glugged**, **glugging**) pour or drink (liquid) with a hollow gurgling sound. ■ n. a hollow gurgling sound as of liquid being poured from a bottle.
– DERIVATIVES **gluggable** adj.
– ORIGIN C17: imitative.

Glühwein /ˈgluːvʌɪn/ ■ n. mulled wine.
– ORIGIN German: from *glühen* 'to mull' + *Wein* 'wine'.

glum ■ adj. (**glummer**, **glummest**) dejected; morose.
– DERIVATIVES **glumly** adv. **glumness** n.
– ORIGIN C16: rel. to dialect *glum* 'to frown', var. of GLOOM.

glume /gluːm/ ■ n. Botany each of two membranous bracts surrounding the spikelet of a grass (forming the husk of a cereal grain) or one surrounding the florets of a sedge.
– ORIGIN C18: from Latin *gluma* 'husk'.

gluon /ˈgluːɒn/ ■ n. Physics a hypothetical massless subatomic particle believed to transmit the force binding quarks together in hadrons.
– ORIGIN 1970s: from GLUE.

glut ■ n. an excessively abundant supply of something. ■ v. (**glutted**, **glutting**) supply or fill to excess. ▸ archaic satisfy fully.
– ORIGIN Middle English: prob. from Latin *gluttire* 'to swallow'; rel. to GLUTTON.

glutamate /ˈgluːtəmeɪt/ ■ n. Biochemistry a salt or ester of glutamic acid. ▸ short for MONOSODIUM GLUTAMATE.

glutamic acid /gluːˈtamɪk/ ■ n. Biochemistry an acidic amino acid which is a constituent of many proteins.
– ORIGIN C19: from GLUTEN + AMINE.

glutamine /ˈgluːtəmiːn/ ■ n. Biochemistry a hydrophilic amino acid which is a constituent of most proteins.
– ORIGIN C19: blend of GLUTAMIC ACID and AMINE.

glute (also **glutes**) ■ n. informal short for GLUTEUS.

gluten /ˈgluːt(ə)n/ ■ n. a substance present in cereal grains, especially wheat, which is responsible for the elastic texture of dough.
– ORIGIN C16: from Latin, 'glue'.

gluteus /ˈgluːtɪəs, gluːˈtiːəs/ ■ n. (pl. **glutei** /-tɪʌɪ, -ˈtiːʌɪ/) any of three muscles in each buttock which move the thigh, the largest of which is the gluteus maximus.
– DERIVATIVES **gluteal** adj.
– ORIGIN C17: modern Latin, from Greek *gloutos* 'buttock'.

glutinous /ˈgluːtɪnəs/ ■ adj. like glue in texture; sticky.
– DERIVATIVES **glutinously** adv. **glutinousness** n.

–ORIGIN Middle English: from Latin *glutinosus*, from *gluten* 'glue'.

glutton ■ n. an excessively greedy eater. ► a person who is very fond of something: *he is a glutton for poetry.*
–PHRASES **a glutton for punishment** a person who is always eager to undertake hard or unpleasant tasks.
–DERIVATIVES **gluttonize** (also **-ise**) v. **gluttonous** adj. **gluttonously** adv.
–ORIGIN Middle English: from Latin *glutto(n-)*, rel. to *gluttire* 'to swallow' and *gluttus* 'greedy'.

gluttony ■ n. habitual greed or excess in eating.

glycaemic index /glʌɪˈsiːmɪk/ (US also **glycemic index**) ■ n. a figure representing the relative ability of a carbohydrate food to increase the level of glucose in the blood.

glyceride /ˈglɪs(ə)rʌɪd/ ■ n. a fatty acid ester of glycerol.

glycerine /ˈglɪs(ə)riːn, -ɪn/ (US **glycerin**) ■ n. another term for GLYCEROL.
–ORIGIN C19: from French *glycerin*, from Greek *glukeros* 'sweet'.

glycerol /ˈglɪs(ə)rɒl/ ■ n. a colourless, sweet, viscous liquid formed as a by-product in soap manufacture, used as an emollient and laxative and for making explosives and antifreeze.

glycine /ˈglʌɪsiːn/ ■ n. Biochemistry the simplest naturally occurring amino acid, a constituent of most proteins.
–ORIGIN C19: from Greek *glukus* 'sweet'.

glyco- ■ comb. form of, relating to, or producing sugar: *glycoside.*
–ORIGIN from Greek *glukus* 'sweet'.

glycogen /ˈglʌɪkəd͡ʒ(ə)n/ ■ n. Biochemistry a polysaccharide deposited in bodily tissues as a store of carbohydrates.
–DERIVATIVES **glycogenic** /-ˈd͡ʒɛnɪk/ adj.

glycogenesis /ˌglʌɪkə(ʊ)ˈd͡ʒɛnɪsɪs/ ■ n. Biochemistry the formation of glycogen from sugar.

glycol /ˈglʌɪkɒl/ ■ n. 1 short for ETHYLENE GLYCOL. 2 another term for DIOL.
–ORIGIN C19: from GLYCERINE + -OL.

glycolysis /glʌɪˈkɒlɪsɪs/ ■ n. Biochemistry the breakdown of glucose by enzymes, releasing energy and pyruvic acid.
–DERIVATIVES **glycolytic** /ˌglʌɪkəˈlɪtɪk/ adj.

glycoprotein /ˌglʌɪkə(ʊ)ˈprəʊtiːn/ ■ n. Biochemistry any of a class of proteins which have carbohydrate groups attached to the polypeptide chain.

glycoside /ˈglʌɪkə(ʊ)sʌɪd/ ■ n. Biochemistry a compound formed from a simple sugar and another compound by replacement of a hydroxyl group in the sugar molecule.
–DERIVATIVES **glycosidic** adj.
–ORIGIN C19: from GLYCO-, on the pattern of *glucoside*.

glycosuria /ˌglʌɪkə(ʊ)ˈsjʊərɪə/ ■ n. Medicine a condition characterized by an excess of sugar in the urine, typically associated with diabetes or kidney disease.
–DERIVATIVES **glycosuric** adj.
–ORIGIN C19: from French *glycosurie*, from *glucos* 'glucose'.

glyph /glɪf/ ■ n. 1 a hieroglyphic character; a pictograph or sculptured symbol. 2 Architecture an ornamental carved groove or channel, as on a Greek frieze.
–DERIVATIVES **glyphic** adj.
–ORIGIN C18: from Greek *gluphē* 'carving'.

glyphosate /ˈglʌɪfə(ʊ)seɪt/ ■ n. a synthetic compound which is a non-selective systemic herbicide.
–ORIGIN 1970s: from GLYCINE + PHOSPHO-.

GM ■ abbrev. 1 general manager. 2 General Motors. 3 genetically modified. 4 George Medal. 5 Chess grandmaster.

gm ■ abbrev. gram(s).

G-man ■ n. US informal an FBI agent.
–ORIGIN C20: prob. an abbrev. of *Government man*.

GMO ■ abbrev. genetically modified organism.

GMT ■ abbrev. Greenwich Mean Time.

gnarl /nɑːl/ ■ n. a rough, knotty protuberance, especially on a tree.
–ORIGIN C19: back-formation from GNARLED.

gnarled ■ adj. knobbly, rough, and twisted, especially with age.
–ORIGIN C17: var. of *knarled*, from archaic *knar*, denoting a knot or protuberance on a tree trunk, from Middle English *knarre*, denoting a rugged rock or stone.

gnarly ■ adj. (**-ier**, **-iest**) 1 gnarled. 2 N. Amer. informal difficult, dangerous, or challenging. ► unpleasant or unattractive.

gnash /naʃ/ ■ v. grind (one's teeth) together, especially as a sign of anger.
–ORIGIN Middle English: perhaps rel. to Old Norse *gnastan* 'a gnashing of teeth'.

gnashers ■ pl. n. Brit. informal teeth.

gnat /nat/ ■ n. a small two-winged fly resembling a mosquito, typically forming large swarms. [*Culex pipiens* and many other species, especially in the family Culicidae.]
–ORIGIN Old English, of Germanic origin.

gnaw /nɔː/ ■ v. 1 bite at or nibble persistently. 2 [often as adj. **gnawing**] cause persistent anxiety or distress.
–DERIVATIVES **gnawingly** adv.
–ORIGIN Old English, of Germanic origin; ultimately imitative.

gneiss /nʌɪs/ ■ n. a typically coarse-grained metamorphic rock with a banded or foliated structure.
–DERIVATIVES **gneissic** adj. **gneissose** adj.
–ORIGIN C18: from German, from Old High German *gneisto* 'spark' (because of the rock's sheen).

gnocchi /ˈn(j)ɒki, ˈgnɒki/ ■ pl. n. (in Italian cooking) small dumplings made from potato, semolina, or flour.
–ORIGIN Italian: pl. of *gnocco*, alteration of *nocchio* 'knot in wood'.

gnome /nəʊm/ ■ n. 1 a legendary dwarfish creature supposed to guard the earth's treasures underground. 2 a small garden ornament in the form of a bearded man with a pointed hat. 3 informal a person having secret or sinister influence, especially in financial matters: *the gnomes of Zurich.*
–DERIVATIVES **gnomish** adj.
–ORIGIN C17: from modern Latin *gnomus*, a word used by the C16 Swiss physician Paracelsus as a synonym of *Pygmaeus* (see PYGMY).

gnomic /ˈnəʊmɪk/ ■ adj. 1 in the form of short, pithy maxims or aphorisms. 2 enigmatic; ambiguous.
–DERIVATIVES **gnomically** adv.

gnomon /ˈnəʊmɒn/ ■ n. 1 the projecting piece on a sundial that shows the time by its shadow. 2 Geometry the part of a parallelogram left when a similar parallelogram has been taken from its corner. 3 Astronomy a structure used in observing the sun's meridian altitude.
–DERIVATIVES **gnomonic** /-ˈmɒnɪk/ adj.
–ORIGIN C16: from Greek *gnōmōn* 'indicator, carpenter's square'.

gnostic /ˈnɒstɪk/ ■ adj. 1 of or relating to knowledge, especially esoteric mystical knowledge. 2 (**Gnostic**) of or relating to Gnosticism. ■ n. (**Gnostic**) an adherent of Gnosticism.
–ORIGIN C16: from Greek *gnōstikos*, from *gnōstos* 'known'.

Gnosticism /ˈnɒstɪˌsɪz(ə)m/ ■ n. a heretical movement of the 2nd-century Christian Church, teaching that knowledge of spiritual mysteries (gnosis) of the supreme divine being enabled the redemption of the human spirit.

GNP ■ abbrev. gross national product.

Gnr ■ abbrev. Gunner.

gnu /(g)nuː, (g)njuː/ ■ n. another term for WILDEBEEST.
–ORIGIN C18: from Khoikhoi and San, perhaps imitative of the sound made by the animal when alarmed.

go[1] ■ v. (**goes**, **going**; past **went**; past part. **gone**) 1 move from one place to another; travel. ► engage in a specified activity: *she used to go swimming*. ► (**go to**) attend or visit for a particular purpose. ► pass time in a particular way: *they went for two months without talking*. ► lie or extend in a certain direction. 2 leave; depart. ► (of time) pass or elapse. ► come to an end; cease to exist. ► disappear or be used up. 3 (**be going to be/do something**) used to express a future tense: *I'm going to be late*. 4 pass into or be in a specified state, especially an undesirable one: *her mind went blank*. ► (**go to/into**) enter into a specified state or course of action: *she went back to sleep*. ► make a sound of a specified kind. ► (**go by/under**) be known or called by (a specified name). 5 turn out in a specified way.

go

▸ be acceptable or permitted: *anything goes.* **6** be harmonious, complementary, or matching. **7** (of a machine or device) function. ▸ continue in operation or existence. **8** fit into or be regularly kept in a particular place. **9** informal use a toilet; urinate or defecate. **10** informal say. ■ *n.* (pl. **goes**) informal **1** an attempt or trial. ▸ chiefly Brit. a state of affairs. ▸ chiefly Brit. an attack of illness. **2** a person's turn to do or use something. **3** spirit, animation, or energy. ▸ vigorous activity: *it's all go.*
– PHRASES **from the word go** informal from the very beginning. **go figure!** N. Amer. informal said to express the belief that something is amazing or incredible. **go halves** (or **shares**) share something equally. **going!, gone!** an auctioneer's announcement that bidding is closing or closed. **going on** —— (also **going on for** ——) approaching a specified time, age, or amount. **go to show** (or **prove**) serve as evidence or proof. **go well** S. African said to a person departing to express one's good wishes. **have a go at** attack or criticize. **have** —— **going for one** informal be in one's favour or to one's advantage. **make a go of** informal be successful in. **no go** informal impossible, hopeless, or forbidden. **on the go** informal very active or busy. **to be going on with** Brit. to start with; for the time being. **to go** chiefly N. Amer. (of food or drink from a restaurant or café) to be eaten or drunk off the premises. **who goes there?** said by a sentry as a challenge.
– PHRASAL VERBS **go about 1** begin or carry on work at: *you went about it in the wrong way.* **2** Nautical in sailing, change to an opposite tack. **go against** oppose or resist. ▸ be contrary to or unfavourable for. **go ahead** proceed or be carried out. **go along with** consent or agree to. **go at** energetically attack or tackle. **go back on** fail to keep (a promise). **go down 1** be defeated in a contest. **2** be recorded or remembered in a particular way. **3** elicit a specified reaction. **4** N. Amer. informal happen. **5** Brit. informal be sent to prison. **go for 1** decide on; choose. **2** attempt to gain or attain. **3** launch oneself at; attack. **4** end up having a specified value or effect. **5** apply to; have relevance for. **go in for 1** enter (a contest) as a competitor. **2** like or habitually take part in. **go into 1** investigate or enquire into. **2** (of a whole number) be capable of dividing another, typically without a remainder. **go off 1** (of a gun or bomb) explode or fire. ▸ (of an alarm) begin to sound. **2** (of food) begin to decompose. **3** informal, chiefly Brit. begin to dislike. **4** go to sleep. **go on 1** continue or persevere. ▸ talk at great or excessive length. ▸ continue speaking or doing something after a short pause. ▸ informal said when encouraging someone or expressing disbelief. **2** happen; take place. **3** proceed to do. **4** [usu. with neg.] informal have a specified amount of care or liking for. **go out 1** (of a fire or light) be extinguished. **2** (of the tide) ebb; recede to low tide. **3** leave home to go to an entertainment or social event. ▸ carry on a regular romantic relationship with someone. **4** (in some card games) be the first to dispose of one's cards. **go over 1** examine or check the details of. **2** change one's allegiance or religion. **3** be received in a specified way. **go round** (chiefly US also **go around**) **1** spin; revolve. **2** be sufficient to supply everybody present. **go through 1** undergo (a difficult or painful period or experience). **2** search through or examine carefully. **3** be officially approved or completed. **4** informal use up or spend. **go to!** archaic said to express disbelief, impatience, or admonition. **go under** (of a business) become bankrupt. **go up** explode or suddenly burst into flames. **go with 1** give one's consent or agreement to. **2** have a romantic or sexual relationship with. **go without** suffer lack or deprivation.
– ORIGIN Old English, of Germanic origin; the form *went* was orig. the past tense of WEND.

go² ■ *n.* a Japanese board game of territorial possession and capture.
– ORIGIN C19: Japanese.

goad /gəʊd/ ■ *n.* **1** a spiked stick used for driving cattle. **2** a thing that stimulates someone into action. ■ *v.* **1** provoke to action or reaction. **2** drive or urge on with a goad.
– ORIGIN Old English, of Germanic origin.

go-ahead informal ■ *n.* (usu. **the go-ahead**) permission to proceed. ■ *adj.* enthusiastic about new projects; enterprising.

goal ■ *n.* **1** (in soccer, rugby, etc.) a pair of posts linked by a crossbar and forming a space into or over which the ball has to be sent in order to score. **2** an instance of sending the ball into or over a goal. **3** an aim or desired result. ▸ the destination of a journey.
– PHRASES **in goal** in the position of goalkeeper.
– DERIVATIVES **goalless** *adj.*
– ORIGIN Middle English ('limit, boundary').

goal area ■ *n.* Soccer a rectangular area in front of the goal from within which goal kicks must be taken.

goal average ■ *n.* Soccer the ratio of the numbers of goals scored for and against a team in a series of matches.

goal difference ■ *n.* Soccer the difference between the number of goals scored for and against a team in a series of matches.

goalie ■ *n.* informal a goalkeeper or goaltender.

goalkeeper ■ *n.* a player in soccer or field hockey whose special role is to stop the ball from entering the goal.
– DERIVATIVES **goalkeeping** *n.*

goal kick ■ *n.* **1** Soccer a free kick taken by the defending side from within their goal area after attackers send the ball over the byline. **2** Rugby an attempt to kick a goal.
– DERIVATIVES **goal-kicker** *n.* (Rugby). **goal-kicking** *n.* (Rugby).

goal line ■ *n.* a line across a soccer, rugby, or hockey field on which the goal is placed or which acts as the boundary beyond which a try or touchdown is scored.

goalmouth ■ *n.* the area just in front of a goal in soccer or hockey.

goalpost ■ *n.* either of the two upright posts of a goal.
– PHRASES **move the goalposts** unfairly alter the conditions or rules of a procedure during its course.

goaltender ■ *n.* chiefly N. Amer. a goalkeeper, especially in ice hockey.
– DERIVATIVES **goaltending** *n.*

Goan /'gəʊən/ (also **Goanese** /ˌgəʊə'niːz/) ■ *n.* a native or inhabitant of the Indian state of Goa. ■ *adj.* of or relating to Goa.

goat ■ *n.* **1** a hardy domesticated ruminant mammal that has backward-curving horns and (in the male) a beard. [*Capra hircus.*] ▸ a wild mammal related to this, such as the ibex. **2** informal a lecherous man. **3** Brit. informal a stupid person; a fool.
– PHRASES **get someone's goat** informal irritate someone.
– DERIVATIVES **goatish** *adj.* **goaty** *adj.*
– ORIGIN Old English *gāt* 'nanny goat', of Germanic origin.

goat-antelope ■ *n.* a ruminant mammal of a group including the chamois and musk ox, with characteristics of both goats and antelopes. [Subfamily Caprinae.]

goatee /gəʊ'tiː/ ■ *n.* a small pointed beard like that of a goat.
– DERIVATIVES **goateed** *adj.*

goatfish ■ *n.* (pl. same or **-fishes**) a bottom-dwelling marine fish with two long barbels on the chin. [Family Mullidae: many species.]

goatherd ■ *n.* a person who tends goats.
– ORIGIN Old English, from GOAT + obsolete *herd* 'herdsman'.

goat moth ■ *n.* a large greyish moth, the caterpillar of which bores into wood and has a goat-like smell. [Several genera, in particular *Cossus*.]

goatskin ■ *n.* the skin of a goat. ▸ leather made from such a skin. ▸ a garment or object made out of goatskin.

goatsucker ■ *n.* another term for NIGHTJAR.

go-away bird ■ *n.* a mainly grey, crested, long-tailed African bird with a call that resembles the words 'go away'. [*Corythaixoides concolor* and other species.]

gob¹ ■ *n.* informal, chiefly Brit. a person's mouth.
– ORIGIN C16: perhaps from Scottish Gaelic *gob* 'beak, mouth'.

gob² informal ■ *n.* **1** Brit. a lump or clot of a slimy or viscous substance. ▸ N. Amer. a small lump. **2** (**gobs of**) N. Amer. a lot of. ■ *v.* (**gobbed, gobbing**) chiefly Brit. spit.
– ORIGIN Middle English: from Old French *gobe* 'mouthful, lump', from *gober* 'to swallow, gulp', perhaps of Celtic origin.

gobbet /'gɒbɪt/ ■ *n.* **1** a piece or lump of flesh, food, or

other matter. **2** an extract from a text set for translation or comment in an examination.
–ORIGIN Middle English: from Old French *gobet*, diminutive of *gobe* (see GOB²).

gobble¹ ■ v. (often **gobble something up**) eat hurriedly and noisily. ▸ use a large amount of very quickly.
–DERIVATIVES **gobbler** n.
–ORIGIN C17: prob. from GOB².

gobble² ■ v. (of a turkeycock) make a characteristic swallowing sound in the throat.
–DERIVATIVES **gobbler** n.
–ORIGIN C17: imitative, perhaps influenced by GOBBLE¹.

gobbledegook /ˈgɒb(ə)ldɪˌguːk, -ˌgʊk/ (also **gobbledygook**) ■ n. informal meaningless or unintelligible language, especially when over-technical or pompous.
–ORIGIN 1940s: prob. imitating a turkey's gobble.

go-between ■ n. an intermediary or negotiator.

goblet ■ n. **1** a drinking glass with a foot and a stem. ▸ archaic a bowl-shaped metal or glass drinking cup. **2** Brit. a receptacle forming part of a liquidizer.
–ORIGIN Middle English: from Old French *gobelet*, diminutive of *gobel* 'cup'.

goblet cell ■ n. Anatomy a column-shaped cell found in the respiratory and intestinal tracts, which secretes the main component of mucus.

goblin ■ n. a mischievous, ugly, dwarf-like creature of folklore.
–ORIGIN Middle English: from Old French *gobelin*, possibly rel. to German *Kobold*, denoting a spirit who haunts houses, or to Greek *kobalos* 'mischievous goblin'.

gobsmacked ■ adj. informal, chiefly Brit. utterly astonished.
–DERIVATIVES **gobsmacking** adj.

gobstopper ■ n. chiefly Brit. a large, hard spherical sweet.

goby /ˈgəʊbi/ ■ n. (pl. **-ies**) a small marine fish, typically with a sucker on the underside. [Family Gobiidae: many species.]
–ORIGIN C18: from Latin *gobius*, from Greek *kōbios*.

GOC ■ abbrev. General Officer Commanding.

go-cart ■ n. variant spelling of GO-KART.

God ■ n. **1** (in Christianity and other monotheistic religions) the creator and ruler of the universe; the supreme being. **2** (**god**) a superhuman being or spirit worshipped as having power over nature or human fortunes; a deity. ▸ an image of a god; an idol. **3** (**god**) a greatly admired or influential person. **4** (**the gods**) informal the gallery in a theatre. ■ exclam. used to express surprise, anger, distress, etc. or for emphasis.
–PHRASES **God's acre** archaic a churchyard. **God the Father** (in Christian doctrine) the first person of the Trinity, God as creator and supreme authority. **God the Son** (in Christian doctrine) Christ regarded as the second person of the Trinity; God as incarnate and resurrected saviour. **play God** behave as if all-powerful or supremely important. **with God** dead and in heaven.
–DERIVATIVES **godhood** n. **godlike** adj. **godship** n. **godward** adj. & adv. **godwards** adv.
–ORIGIN Old English, of Germanic origin.

God-awful ■ adj. informal extremely bad or unpleasant.

godchild ■ n. (pl. **-children**) a person in relation to a godparent.

goddam (also **goddamn**, **goddamned**) ■ adj. & adv. informal, chiefly N. Amer. used for emphasis, especially to express anger or frustration.

god-daughter ■ n. a female godchild.

goddess ■ n. **1** a female deity. **2** a woman who is adored, especially for her beauty.

godet /gəʊˈdɛt, ˈgəʊdeɪ/ ■ n. a triangular piece of material inserted in a garment to make it flared or for ornamentation.
–ORIGIN C19: from French.

godetia /gəˈ(ʊ)diːʃə/ ■ n. a North American plant with showy lilac to red flowers. [Genus *Clarkia* (or *Godetia*).]
–ORIGIN named after the Swiss botanist Charles H. *Godet*.

godfather ■ n. **1** a male godparent. **2** a man who is influential or pioneering in a movement or organization. **3** a person directing an illegal organization, especially a leader of the American Mafia.

God-fearing ■ adj. earnestly religious.

499

goggle

godforsaken ■ adj. lacking any merit or attraction.

godhead ■ n. **1** (usu. **the Godhead**) God. ▸ divine nature. **2** informal an adored, admired, or influential person.

godless ■ adj. lacking or not recognizing God. ▸ profane; wicked.
–DERIVATIVES **godlessness** n.

godly ■ adj. (**-ier**, **-iest**) devoutly religious; pious.
–DERIVATIVES **godliness** n.

godmother ■ n. a female godparent.

godown /ˈgəʊdaʊn, gəʊˈdaʊn/ ■ n. (in east Asia, especially India) a warehouse.
–ORIGIN C16: from Portuguese *gudão*, from Tamil *kiṭaṅku*, Malayalam *kiṭaṅṅu*, or Kannada *gadaṅgu* (all Dravidian languages).

godparent ■ n. a person nominated to present a child at baptism and promising to take responsibility for their religious education.

God Save the Queen (or **King**) ■ n. the British national anthem.

godsend ■ n. something very helpful or opportune.

God's gift ■ n. chiefly ironic the ideal or best possible person or thing.

godson ■ n. a male godchild.

Godspeed ■ exclam. dated an expression of good wishes to a person starting a journey.

God's truth ■ n. the absolute truth.

godwit ■ n. a large, long-legged wader with a long straight or slightly upcurved bill. [Genus *Limosa*: four species.]
–ORIGIN C16.

goema /ˈguma/ ■ n. S. African **1** a style of music fusing traditional Cape Malay folk elements with jazz and rock. **2** (also **ghomma** /ˈgɒma/) a single-headed drum used in traditional Cape Malay music.
–ORIGIN 1930s: prob. from a Malay dialect word rel. to *gong* 'gong'.

goer ■ n. **1** a person who attends a specified place or event: *a theatre-goer*. **2** informal a person or thing that goes. **3** informal a sexually unrestrained woman.

goes third person singular present of GO¹.

goest /ˈgəʊɪst/ archaic second person singular present of GO¹.

goeth /ˈgəʊɪθ/ archaic third person singular present of GO¹.

Goethean /ˈgəːtɪən/ (also **Goethian**) ■ adj. of or relating to the German poet and dramatist Johann Wolfgang von Goethe (1749–1832).

goethite /ˈgəːtʌɪt/ ■ n. a dark or yellowish-brown mineral consisting of hydrated iron oxide.
–ORIGIN C19: from *Goethe* (see GOETHEAN).

gofer /ˈgəʊfə/ (also **gopher**) ■ n. informal, chiefly N. Amer. a person who runs errands, especially on a film set or in an office; a dogsbody.
–ORIGIN 1960s: from *go for* (i.e. go and fetch).

goffer /ˈgɒfə/ ■ v. **1** [usu. as adj. **goffered**] crimp or flute (a lace edge or frill) with heated irons. **2** [as adj. **goffered**] (of the gilt edges of a book) embossed with a repeating design. ■ n. an iron used to crimp or flute lace.
–ORIGIN C16: from French, from *gaufre* 'honeycomb', from Middle Low German *wāfel* (see WAFFLE²).

go-getter ■ n. informal an aggressively enterprising person.
–DERIVATIVES **go-getting** adj.

gogga /ˈxɔxə/ (also **goggo** /ˈxɔxɒ/) ■ n. S. African informal a creepy-crawly.
–ORIGIN Afrikaans, from Khoikhoi *xo-xon*, a collective term for creeping things.

goggle ■ v. look with wide open eyes, typically in amazement or wonder. ▸ (of the eyes) protrude or open wide. ■ adj. (of the eyes) protuberant or rolling. ■ n. (**goggles**) **1** close-fitting protective glasses with side shields. **2** the staggers (a disease of sheep).
–DERIVATIVES **goggled** adj.
–ORIGIN Middle English: prob. from a base symbolic of oscillating movement.

s sit   t top   v voice   w we   z zoo   ʃ she   ʒ decision   θ thin   ð this   ŋ ring   x loch   tʃ chip   dʒ jar

goggle-box

goggle-box ■ n. Brit. informal a television set.

goggle-eyed ■ adj. having goggle eyes, especially through astonishment.

gogo /'gɒgəʊ/ ■ n. S. African informal granny. ▶ used as a respectful form of address for an elderly person, usually a woman.
– ORIGIN from isiZulu *ugogo* 'elderly person'.

go-go ■ adj. **1** denoting an unrestrained and erotic style of dancing to popular music. **2** assertively dynamic. ■ n. a style of popular music with an incessant funk beat.
– ORIGIN 1960s: reduplication of GO¹, perhaps influenced by dated *a gogo* 'in abundance'.

going ■ n. **1** the condition of the ground viewed in terms of suitability for horse racing or travel. **2** conditions for, or progress in, an endeavour: *when the going gets tough, the tough get going*. ■ adj. **1** chiefly Brit. existing or available; to be had. **2** (of a price) fair or correct; current: *the going rate*.

going concern ■ n. a business that is operating and making a profit.

going-over ■ n. informal **1** a thorough cleaning or inspection. **2** a beating.

goings-on ■ pl. n. events or behaviour, especially of an unusual or suspect nature.

goitre /'gɔɪtə/ (US **goiter**) ■ n. a swelling of the neck resulting from enlargement of the thyroid gland.
– DERIVATIVES **goitrous** adj.
– ORIGIN C17: from French, a back-formation from *goitreux* 'having a goitre', from Latin *guttur* 'throat'.

go-kart (also **go-cart**) ■ n. a small racing car with a lightweight or skeleton body.
– DERIVATIVES **go-karting** n.

gold ■ n. **1** a yellow precious metal, the chemical element of atomic number 79, used in jewellery and decoration and as a monetary medium. (Symbol: **Au**) **2** a deep lustrous yellow or yellow-brown colour. **3** coins or articles made of gold. ▶ money in large sums; wealth. **4** the bullseye of an archery target.
– PHRASES **pot** (or **crock**) **of gold** a large but distant or imaginary reward. [with allusion to the story of a crock of gold supposedly to be found at the end of a rainbow.]
– ORIGIN Old English, of Germanic origin.

goldcrest ■ n. a very small Eurasian warbler with a black-bordered yellow or orange crest. [*Regulus regulus*].

gold-digger ■ n. informal a woman who forms relationships with men purely to extract money from them.
– DERIVATIVES **gold-digging** adj.

gold disc ■ n. a framed golden disc awarded to a recording artist or group for sales exceeding a specified figure.

gold dust ■ n. **1** fine particles of gold. **2** something very valuable.

golden ■ adj. **1** made of, coloured like, or shining like gold. **2** (of a period) very happy and prosperous. **3** (of an opportunity) very favourable.
– DERIVATIVES **goldenly** adv.

golden age ■ n. **1** an idyllic, often imaginary past time of peace, prosperity, and happiness. **2** the period when a specified art or activity is at its peak.

golden boy (or **golden girl**) ■ n. informal a very popular or successful young man or woman.

Golden Delicious ■ n. a widely grown dessert apple of a greenish-yellow, soft-fleshed variety.

golden eagle ■ n. a large northern-hemisphere eagle with yellow-tipped head feathers in the mature adult. [*Aquila chrysaetos*].

goldeneye ■ n. (pl. same or **goldeneyes**) a migratory northern diving duck, the male of which has a dark head with a white cheek patch and yellow eyes. [Genus *Bucephala*: two species.]

golden goal ■ n. (in some soccer competitions) the first goal scored during extra time, which ends the match and gives victory to the scoring side.

golden goose ■ n. a continuing source of wealth or profit that may be exhausted if it is misused. See also kill the goose that lays the golden eggs at EGG¹.

golden handcuffs ■ pl. n. informal benefits provided by an employer to discourage an employee from taking employment elsewhere.

golden handshake ■ n. informal a payment given to someone who is made redundant or retires early.

golden jubilee ■ n. the fiftieth anniversary of a significant event.

golden mean ■ n. **1** the ideal moderate position between two extremes. **2** another term for GOLDEN SECTION.

golden oldie ■ n. informal **1** an old song of enduring popularity. **2** a person who is no longer young but is still successful.

golden parachute ■ n. informal a payment guaranteed to a company executive should they be dismissed as a result of a merger or takeover.

golden plover ■ n. a northern plover with a gold-speckled back and black face and underparts in the breeding season. [*Pluvialis apricaria* and related species.]

golden retriever ■ n. a retriever of a breed with a thick golden-coloured coat.

goldenrod ■ n. a plant of the daisy family, with tall spikes of small bright yellow flowers. [Genus *Solidago*.]

golden rule ■ n. a basic principle which should always be followed.

golden section ■ n. the division of a line so that the whole is to the greater part as that part is to the smaller part (i.e. in a ratio of 1 to ½ (5 + 1)), a proportion which is considered to be particularly pleasing to the eye.

golden share ■ n. Brit. a share in a company that gives control of at least 51 per cent of the voting rights, especially when held by the government.

golden syrup ■ n. a pale treacle.

golden wedding ■ n. the fiftieth anniversary of a wedding.

goldfield ■ n. a district in which gold is found as a mineral.

goldfinch ■ n. a brightly coloured finch with yellow feathers in the plumage. [*Carduelis carduelis* (Eurasia), *C. tristis* (American goldfinch), and related species.]

goldfish ■ n. (pl. same or **-fishes**) a small reddish-golden carp popular in ponds and aquaria. [*Carassius auratus*.]

goldfish bowl ■ n. **1** a spherical glass container for goldfish. **2** a place or situation lacking privacy.

goldilocks ■ n. informal a person with golden hair.

gold leaf ■ n. gold that has been beaten into a very thin sheet, used in gilding.

gold medal ■ n. a medal made of or coloured gold, customarily awarded for first place in a race or competition.

gold mine ■ n. **1** a place where gold is mined. **2** a source of great wealth or valuable resources.
– DERIVATIVES **gold miner** n.

gold plate ■ n. **1** a thin layer of gold applied as a coating to another metal. **2** plates, dishes, etc. made of or plated with gold. ■ v. (**gold-plate**) cover with gold plate.

gold reserve ■ n. a quantity of gold held by a central bank.

gold rush ■ n. a rapid movement of people to a newly discovered goldfield.

goldsmith ■ n. a person who makes gold articles.

gold standard ■ n. historical the system by which the value of a currency was defined in terms of gold, for which the currency could be exchanged.

golem /'gəʊləm, 'gɒɪl-/ ■ n. **1** (in Jewish legend) a clay figure brought to life by magic. **2** an automaton or robot.
– ORIGIN C19: from Yiddish *goylem*, from Hebrew *gōlem* 'shapeless mass'.

golf ■ n. **1** a game played on a large open-air course, the aim of which is to strike a small, hard ball with a club into a series of small holes with the fewest possible strokes. **2** a code word representing the letter G, used in radio communication. ■ v. [often as noun **golfing**] play golf.
– DERIVATIVES **golfer** n.

VOWELS   a cat   ɑː arm   ɛ bed   eː hair   ə ago   əː her   ɪ sit   i cosy   iː see   ɒ hot   ɔː saw   ʌ run

–ORIGIN Middle English: perhaps rel. to Dutch *kolf* 'club, bat'.

golf ball ■ n. **1** a small, hard ball used in the game of golf. **2** (**golfball**) a small metal globe used in some electric typewriters to carry the type.

golf club ■ n. see CLUB² (sense 2).

golf course ■ n. a course on which golf is played.

golf estate ■ n. chiefly S. African an upmarket housing development built around a golf course.

golf shirt ■ n. a light, short-sleeved shirt with a collar, typically of a knitted fabric and with buttons at the neck only.

Golgi body /ˈgɒldʒi, -gi/ (also **Golgi apparatus**) ■ n. Biology a complex of vesicles and folded membranes within the cytoplasm of a cell, involved in secretion and intracellular transport.
–ORIGIN named after the Italian scientist Camillo *Golgi*.

goliath beetle ■ n. a very large tropical beetle, the male of which has a forked horn on the head. [*Goliathus giganteus* (Africa, the largest known beetle) and related species.]
–ORIGIN named after the Philistine giant *Goliath* in the Bible.

goliath frog ■ n. a giant frog of West Central Africa. [*Rana goliath*.]

golliwog ■ n. a soft doll with a black face and fuzzy hair.
–ORIGIN C19: from *Golliwogg*, the name of a doll character in books by Bertha Upton.

golly¹ ■ exclam. informal used to express surprise or delight.
–ORIGIN C18: euphemism for GOD.

golly² ■ n. (pl. **-ies**) Brit. informal short for GOLLIWOG.

gombeen /gɒmˈbiːn/ ■ n. [as modifier] Irish involved in the practice of usury: *a gombeen man*.
–ORIGIN C19: from Irish *gaimbín*, perhaps from the same Celtic source as medieval Latin *cambire* 'to change'.

-gon ■ comb. form in nouns denoting plane figures with a specified number of angles and sides: *hexagon*.
–ORIGIN from Greek *-gōnos* '-angled'.

gonad /ˈgəʊnad/ ■ n. Physiology & Zoology an organ that produces gametes; a testis or ovary.
–DERIVATIVES **gonadal** /gə(ʊ)ˈneɪd(ə)l/ adj.
–ORIGIN C19: from modern Latin *gonades*, pl. of *gonas*, from Greek *gonē* 'generation, seed'.

gonadotrophin /ˌgəʊnədə(ʊ)ˈtrəʊfɪn/ (also **gonadotropin** /-ˈtrəʊpɪn, -ˈtrɒpɪn/) ■ n. Biochemistry any of a group of hormones secreted by the pituitary which stimulate the activity of the gonads.
–DERIVATIVES **gonadotrophic** adj.

Gond /gɒnd, gəʊnd/ (also **Gondi** /ˈgɒndi/) ■ n. (pl. same) **1** a member of an indigenous people living in the hill forests of central India. **2** the Dravidian language of this people.
–ORIGIN from Sanskrit *goṇḍa*.

gondola /ˈgɒndələ/ ■ n. **1** a light flat-bottomed boat used on Venetian canals, having a high point at each end and worked by one oar at the stern. **2** a cabin on a ski lift, or suspended from an airship or balloon. **3** (also **gondola car**) N. Amer. an open railway freight wagon. **4** a free-standing block of shelves used to display goods in a shop.
–ORIGIN C16: from Venetian Italian, from Rhaeto-Romance *gondolà* 'to rock, roll'.

gondolier /ˌgɒndəˈlɪə/ ■ n. a person who propels and steers a gondola.

gone past participle of GO¹. ■ adj. **1** no longer present; departed. ▶ no longer in existence; dead or extinct. **2** informal in a trance or stupor, especially through exhaustion, drink, or drugs. **3** informal having reached a specified time in a pregnancy. ■ prep. Brit. **1** (of time) past: *it's gone half past eleven*. **2** (of age) older than.
–PHRASES **be gone on** informal be infatuated with.

goner /ˈgɒnə/ ■ n. informal a person or thing that is doomed or cannot be saved.

gong ■ n. **1** a metal disc with a turned rim, giving a resonant note when struck. **2** Brit. informal a medal or decoration. ■ v. sound a gong or make a sound like that of a gong.
–ORIGIN C17: from Malay *gong, gung*, of imitative origin.

gonna ■ contr. informal going to.

gonococcus /ˌgɒnəˈkɒkəs/ ■ n. (pl. **gonococci** /-k(s)ʌɪ,

-k(s)iː/) a bacterium which causes gonorrhoea. [*Neisseria gonorrhoeae*.]
–DERIVATIVES **gonococcal** adj.

gonorrhoea /ˌgɒnəˈrɪə/ (US **gonorrhea**) ■ n. a venereal disease involving inflammatory discharge from the urethra or vagina.
–DERIVATIVES **gonorrhoeal** adj.
–ORIGIN C16: from Greek *gonorrhoia*, from *gonos* 'semen' + *rhoia* 'flux'.

gonzo ■ adj. informal, chiefly N. Amer. **1** of or denoting journalism of an exaggerated, subjective, and fictionalized style. **2** bizarre or crazy.
–ORIGIN 1970s: perhaps from Italian *gonzo* 'foolish' or Spanish *ganso* 'goose, fool'.

goo ■ n. informal **1** a sticky or slimy substance. **2** sickly sentiment.
–ORIGIN C20: perhaps from *burgoo*, a nautical slang term for porridge, from Persian *bulġūr* 'bruised grain'.

good ■ adj. (**better**, **best**) **1** to be desired or approved of; welcome; pleasant. ▶ (**good for**) beneficial to. ▶ expressing good wishes on meeting: *good morning*. **2** having the required qualities; of a high standard. ▶ appropriate. ▶ (of language) with correct grammar and pronunciation. ▶ strictly adhering to the principles of a religion or cause: *a good Catholic girl*. **3** morally right; virtuous. ▶ (of a child) obedient; well behaved. **4** enjoyable or satisfying: *a good time*. ▶ (of clothes) smart and formal. **5** thorough: *a good look around*. ▶ at least; no less than: *a good twenty years*. **6** chiefly N. Amer. (of a ticket) valid. ■ n. **1** that which is morally right; righteousness. **2** benefit or advantage. **3** (**goods**) merchandise or possessions. ▶ [often as modifier] freight: *a goods train*.
–PHRASES **as good as** —— very nearly or inevitably ——. **be any** (or **no** or **much**) **good** have some (or none or a lot of) merit. **be to the good** have a net profit or advantage. **come up with** (or **deliver**) **the goods** informal do what is expected or required. **do good 1** act virtuously, especially by helping others. **2** make a helpful contribution. **do someone good** be beneficial, especially to health. **for good** forever. (**as**) **good as gold** (of a child) extremely well behaved. **the Good Book** the Bible. **good for** (or **on**) **you!** well done! **the Good Shepherd** a name for Jesus. **a good word** words in recommendation or defence of a person. **in good time 1** with no risk of being late. **2** (also **all in good time**) in due course but without haste. **make good** be successful. **make something good 1** compensate for loss, damage, or expense. **2** fulfil a promise or claim. **take something in good part** not be offended. **up to no good** doing something wrong.
–ORIGIN Old English, of Germanic origin.

goodbye (US also **goodby**) ■ exclam. used to express good wishes when parting or ending a conversation.
■ n. (pl. **goodbyes**; US also **goodbys**) an instance of saying 'goodbye'; a parting.
–ORIGIN C16: contraction of *God be with you!*

good faith ■ n. honesty or sincerity of intention.

good form ■ n. behaviour complying with social conventions.

good-for-nothing ■ adj. (of a person) worthless.
■ n. a worthless person.

Good Friday ■ n. the Friday before Easter Sunday, on which the Crucifixion of Christ is commemorated in the Christian Church.

good-hearted ■ adj. kind and well meaning.
–DERIVATIVES **good-heartedness** n.

good-humoured ■ adj. genial; cheerful.
–DERIVATIVES **good-humouredly** adv.

goodie ■ n. variant spelling of GOODY¹.

goodish ■ adj. fairly good. ▶ fairly large.

good-looking ■ adj. (of a person) attractive.
–DERIVATIVES **good-looker** n.

goodly ■ adj. (**-ier**, **-iest**) **1** considerable in size or quantity. **2** archaic attractive, excellent, or virtuous.
–DERIVATIVES **goodliness** n.

good nature ■ n. a kind and unselfish disposition.
–DERIVATIVES **good-natured** adj. **good-naturedly** adv.

goodness

goodness ■ n. **1** the quality of being good. **2** the beneficial or nourishing element of food. ■ exclam. (as a substitution for 'God') expressing surprise, anger, etc.
– PHRASES **goodness of fit** Statistics the extent to which observed data match the values expected by theory.

goodnight ■ exclam. expressing good wishes on parting at night or before going to bed.

goods and chattels ■ pl. n. chiefly Law all kinds of personal possessions.

good-tempered ■ adj. not easily irritated or made angry.
– DERIVATIVES **good-temperedly** adv.

good-time ■ adj. (of a person) recklessly pursuing pleasure. ▶ (of music) intended purely to entertain.
– DERIVATIVES **good-timer** n.

goodwill ■ n. **1** friendly or helpful feelings or attitude. **2** the established reputation of a business regarded as a quantifiable asset.

good works ■ pl. n. charitable acts.

goody[1] ■ n. (also **goodie**) (pl. **-ies**) informal **1** a good or favoured person, especially a hero in a story or film. **2** (usu. **goodies**) something tasty to eat. ■ exclam. expressing childish delight.

goody[2] ■ n. (pl. **-ies**) archaic (with a name) an elderly woman of humble position: *Goody Blake*.
– ORIGIN C16: familiar form of archaic *goodwife*, denoting the female head of a household.

goody-goody informal ■ n. a smug or obtrusively virtuous person. ■ adj. smug or obtrusively virtuous.

gooey ■ adj. (**-ier**, **-iest**) informal **1** soft and sticky. **2** mawkishly sentimental.
– DERIVATIVES **gooeyness** n.

goof informal, chiefly N. Amer. ■ n. **1** a mistake. **2** a foolish or stupid person. ■ v. **1** fool around. ▶ (**goof off**) evade a duty; idle or shirk. **2** make a mistake; blunder.
– ORIGIN C20.

goofball ■ n. informal, chiefly N. Amer. **1** a naive or stupid person. **2** a narcotic drug in pill form, especially a barbiturate.

goofy ■ adj. (**-ier**, **-iest**) informal **1** chiefly N. Amer. foolish; harmlessly eccentric. **2** having protruding or crooked front teeth.
– DERIVATIVES **goofily** adv. **goofiness** n.

google ■ v. informal search for information about (someone or something) on the Internet.
– ORIGIN 1990s: from *Google*, the proprietary name of an Internet search engine.

googly ■ n. (pl. **-ies**) Cricket an off break bowled with an apparent leg-break action.
– ORIGIN C20.

googol /'guːgɒl/ ■ cardinal number equivalent to ten raised to the power of a hundred (10[100]).
– ORIGIN 1940s: said to have been coined by the young nephew of the American mathematician E. Kasner.

goo-goo ■ adj. informal **1** amorously adoring: *making goo-goo eyes*. **2** (of speech or vocal sounds) childish or meaningless.
– ORIGIN C20: possibly rel. to **GOGGLE**.

gook[1] /guːk, gʊk/ ■ n. offensive, chiefly N. Amer. a foreigner, especially a person of SE Asian descent.
– ORIGIN 1930s.

gook[2] /guːk, gʊk/ ■ n. informal a sloppy wet or viscous substance.
– ORIGIN 1970s: var. of rare *guck*.

goolie /'guːli/ (also **gooly**) ■ n. (pl. **-ies**) (often **goolies**) informal a testicle.
– ORIGIN 1930s: apparently of Indian origin; cf. Hindi *golī* 'bullet, ball, pill'.

goon ■ n. informal **1** a foolish or eccentric person. **2** chiefly N. Amer. a bully or thug, especially a member of an armed force.
– ORIGIN C19: perhaps from dialect *gooney* 'booby'; later influenced by the American cartoon character 'Alice the Goon'.

goosander /guː'sændə/ ■ n. (pl. same or **goosanders**) a large merganser, the male of which has a dark green head and whitish underparts. [*Mergus merganser*.]
– ORIGIN C17: prob. from **GOOSE** + *-ander* as in dialect *bergander* 'shelduck'.

goose /guːs/ ■ n. (pl. **geese** /giːs/) **1** a large waterbird with a long neck, short legs, webbed feet, and a short, broad bill. [Several genera in the family Anatidae.] ▶ the female of such a bird. **2** informal a foolish person. ■ v. informal **1** poke (someone) in the bottom. **2** N. Amer. give a boost to; invigorate.
– ORIGIN Old English, of Germanic origin.

goose barnacle ■ n. a stalked barnacle which hangs from floating objects, catching passing prey with its feathery legs. [Genus *Lepas*.]

gooseberry ■ n. (pl. **-ies**) **1** a round edible yellowish-green or reddish berry with a thin translucent hairy skin. **2** the thorny European shrub which bears this fruit. [*Ribes grossularia*.] **3** S. African another term for **CAPE GOOSEBERRY**. **4** informal a third person in the company of two people, especially lovers, who would prefer to be alone.
– ORIGIN C16: the first element perhaps from **GOOSE**, or perhaps from Old French *groseille*.

goosebumps ■ pl. n. chiefly N. Amer. another term for **GOOSE PIMPLES**.

gooseflesh ■ n. a pimply state of the skin with the hairs erect, produced by cold or fright.

goosefoot ■ n. (pl. **goosefoots**) a plant with divided leaves which are said to resemble the foot of a goose. [Genus *Chenopodium*.]

goosegrass ■ n. **1** an Indian grass with an extensive root system, naturalized as a weed in other countries. [*Eleusine indica*.] **2** a widely distributed scrambling plant with hooked bristles on the stem, leaves, and seeds. [*Galium aparine*.]

gooseneck ■ n. a support or pipe curved like a goose's neck.

goose pimples ■ pl. n. the pimples that form gooseflesh.

goose step ■ n. a military marching step in which the legs are not bent at the knee. ■ v. (**goose-step**) march with such a step.

GOP ■ abbrev. informal Grand Old Party (a name for the US Republican Party).

gopher /'gəʊfə/ ■ n. **1** (also **pocket gopher**) a burrowing American rodent with fur-lined pouches on its cheeks. [Family Geomyidae: many species.] ▶ informal North American term for **GROUND SQUIRREL** (in sense 2). ▶ [as modifier] in names of various burrowing reptiles: *gopher tortoise*. **2** variant spelling of **GOFER**.
– ORIGIN C18: perhaps from Canadian French *gaufre* 'honeycomb' (because the gopher 'honeycombs' the ground with its burrows).

Gordian knot /'gɔːdɪən/ ■ n. (in phr. **cut the Gordian knot**) solve a difficult problem in a direct or forceful way.
– ORIGIN C16: from the legendary knot tied by *Gordius*, king of Gordium, and cut through by Alexander the Great in response to the prophecy that whoever untied it would rule Asia.

gore[1] ■ n. blood that has been shed, especially as a result of violence.
– ORIGIN Old English *gor* 'dung, dirt', of Germanic origin.

gore[2] ■ v. (of an animal such as a bull) pierce or stab with a horn or tusk.
– ORIGIN Middle English.

gore[3] ■ n. a triangular or tapering piece of material used in making a garment, sail, or umbrella. ■ v. shape with a gore or gores.
– ORIGIN Old English, of Germanic origin; prob. rel. to Old English *gār* 'spear'.

Gore-tex /'gɔːtɛks/ ■ n. trademark a breathable waterproof fabric used in outdoor clothing.

gorge ■ n. **1** a steep, narrow valley or ravine. **2** (usu. phr. **one's gorge rises**) the contents of the stomach. **3** Architecture the narrow rear entrance to a fortification. ■ v. eat a large amount greedily.
– ORIGIN Middle English: from Old French, from *gorge* 'throat', from Latin *gurges* 'whirlpool'.

gorged ■ adj. [postpos.] Heraldry having the neck encircled by a coronet or collar.

gorgeous ■ adj. **1** beautiful; very attractive. **2** informal very pleasant.
– DERIVATIVES **gorgeously** adv. **gorgeousness** n.
– ORIGIN C15: from Old French *gorgias* 'fine, elegant'.

gorget /'gɔːdʒɪt/ ■ n. **1** historical an article of clothing or piece of armour covering the throat. **2** a patch of colour on the throat of a bird or other animal.
– ORIGIN Middle English: from Old French *gorgete*, from *gorge* (see **GORGE**).

gorgon /'gɔːg(ə)n/ ■ n. **1** Greek & Roman Mythology each of three sisters with snakes for hair, who had the power to turn anyone who looked at them to stone. **2** a fierce, frightening, or repulsive woman.
– ORIGIN from Greek *Gorgō*, from *gorgos* 'terrible'.

gorgonian /gɔː'gəʊnɪən/ ■ n. Zoology a colonial coral of an order (Gorgonacea) having a horny tree-like skeleton, including the sea fans and precious red coral.
– ORIGIN C19: from Latin *Gorgo* (see **GORGON**).

Gorgonzola /ˌgɔːg(ə)n'zəʊlə/ ■ n. a rich, strong-flavoured Italian cheese with bluish-green veins.
– ORIGIN named after *Gorgonzola*, a village in northern Italy.

gorilla ■ n. **1** a powerfully built great ape of central Africa, the largest living primate. [*Gorilla gorilla*.] **2** informal a heavily built aggressive-looking man.
– ORIGIN C19: from Greek, representing an alleged African word for a wild or hairy person.

gormandize /'gɔːm(ə)ndʌɪz/ (also **-ise**) ■ v. variant spelling of **GOURMANDIZE**.

gormless ■ adj. informal, chiefly Brit. lacking sense or initiative; foolish.
– DERIVATIVES **gormlessly** adv. **gormlessness** n.
– ORIGIN C18 (orig. as *gaumless*): from dialect *gaum* 'understanding' (from Old Norse *gaumr* 'care, heed').

gorse ■ n. a yellow-flowered shrub of the pea family, the leaves of which have the form of spines. [*Ulex europaeus* (Europe) and related species.]
– DERIVATIVES **gorsy** adj.
– ORIGIN Old English *gors*, from an Indo-European root meaning 'rough, prickly'.

gory ■ adj. (**-ier**, **-iest**) **1** involving or showing violence and bloodshed. **2** covered in blood.
– PHRASES **the gory details** humorous the explicit details of something.
– DERIVATIVES **gorily** adv. **goriness** n.

gosh ■ exclam. informal used to express surprise or give emphasis.
– ORIGIN C18: euphemism for **GOD**.

goshawk /'gɒshɔːk/ ■ n. a short-winged hawk resembling a large sparrowhawk. [Genera *Accipiter*, *Melierax* (chanting goshawk), and *Micronisus* (gabar goshawk).]
– ORIGIN Old English *gōshafoc*, from *gōs* 'goose' + *hafoc* 'hawk'.

gosling /'gɒzlɪŋ/ ■ n. a young goose.
– ORIGIN Middle English: from Old Norse *gæslingr*, from *gás* 'goose' + **-LING**.

go-slow ■ n. a form of industrial action in which work is delayed or slowed down.

gospel ■ n. **1** the teaching or revelation of Christ. **2** (**Gospel**) the record of Christ's life and teaching in the first four books of the New Testament. ▸ each of these books. **3** (also **gospel truth**) something absolutely true. **4** (also **gospel music**) a fervent style of black American evangelical religious singing.
– ORIGIN Old English *gōdspel*, from *gōd* 'good' + *spel* 'news, a story', translating eccles. Latin *bona annuntiatio* or *bonus nuntius*, used to gloss eccles. Latin *evangelium*, from Greek *euangelion* 'good news'.

gospeller (US **gospeler**) ■ n. a zealous preacher.

gossamer ■ n. a fine, filmy substance consisting of cobwebs spun by small spiders, seen especially in autumn. ■ adj. very fine and insubstantial: *gossamer wings*.
– ORIGIN Middle English: apparently from **GOOSE** + **SUMMER**, perhaps from the time of year around St Martin's day (11 November, in late autumn in the northern hemisphere), when geese were eaten.

gossan /'gɒs(ə)n/ ■ n. Geology & Mining an iron-containing secondary deposit of oxides, typically yellowish or reddish, occurring above an ore deposit.
– ORIGIN C18: prob. of Cornish origin.

gossip ■ n. **1** casual conversation or unsubstantiated reports about other people. **2** chiefly derogatory a person who likes talking about other people's private lives. ■ v. (**gossiped**, **gossiping**) engage in gossip.
– DERIVATIVES **gossiper** n. **gossipy** adj.

HISTORY
A **gossip** was originally a rather more serious and worthy person than they are now. In Old English the word was spelled *godsibb* and meant 'godfather or godmother', literally 'a person related to one in God'; it came from *sibb* 'a relative', the source of **sibling**. In medieval times a **gossip** was 'a close friend, a person with whom one gossips', hence 'a person who gossips', later (early 19th century) 'casual conversation about other people'.

gossip column ■ n. a section of a newspaper devoted to gossip about well-known people.
– DERIVATIVES **gossip columnist** n.

got past and past participle of **GET**.

gotcha (also **gotcher**) ■ exclam. informal I have got you.

Goth /gɒθ/ ■ n. **1** a member of a Germanic people that invaded the Roman Empire between the 3rd and 5th centuries. **2** (**goth**) a style of rock music typically having apocalyptic or mystical lyrics. ▸ a member of a subculture favouring black clothing and goth music.
– ORIGIN Old English *Gota*, superseded in Middle English by the adoption of late Latin *Gothi*, from Greek *Gothoi*, from Gothic *Gutthiuda* 'the Gothic people'.

Gothic ■ adj. **1** of or relating to the ancient Goths or their East Germanic language. **2** of or in the style of architecture prevalent in western Europe in the 12th–16th centuries (and revived in the 18th and 19th centuries), characterized by pointed arches. **3** (also pseudo-archaic **Gothick**) portentously gloomy or horrifying. **4** (of lettering) derived from the angular style of handwriting with broad vertical downstrokes used in medieval western Europe. **5** (**gothic**) of or relating to goths or their rock music. ■ n. **1** the language of the Goths. **2** the Gothic style of architecture. **3** Gothic type.
– DERIVATIVES **Gothicism** n.

gothic novel ■ n. an English genre of fiction popular in the 18th to early 19th centuries, characterized by an atmosphere of mystery and horror.

gotta ■ contr. informal **1** have got a. **2** have got to.

gotten past participle of **GET**.

USAGE
The form **gotten** is commonly used in South African, Australian, and North American English, though it is often regarded as non-standard.

gouache /guːˈɑːʃ, gwaːʃ/ ■ n. a method of painting using opaque pigments ground in water and thickened with a glue-like substance. ▸ paint of this kind; opaque watercolour.
– ORIGIN C19: French, from Italian *guazzo*.

Gouda /'gaʊdə/ ■ n. a flat round Dutch cheese with a yellow rind.
– ORIGIN orig. made in *Gouda* in the Netherlands.

gouge /gaʊdʒ, guːdʒ/ ■ v. **1** make (a rough hole or indentation) in a surface. **2** (**gouge something out**) cut or force something out roughly or brutally. ■ n. **1** a chisel with a concave blade. **2** an indentation or groove made by gouging.
– ORIGIN Middle English: from late Latin *gubia*, *gulbia*, perhaps of Celtic origin; cf. Old Irish *gulba* 'beak' and Welsh *gylf* 'beak, pointed instrument'.

goujons /'guː(d)ʒənz/ ■ pl. n. deep-fried strips of chicken or fish.
– ORIGIN from French *goujon* 'gudgeon'.

goulash /'guːlaʃ/ ■ n. **1** a highly seasoned Hungarian soup or stew of meat and vegetables, flavoured with paprika. **2** (in informal bridge) a redealing of the cards, unshuffled and several at a time, after no player has bid.
– ORIGIN from Hungarian *gulyás-hús*, from *gulyás* 'herdsman' + *hús* 'meat'.

gourami /gʊ(ə)ˈrɑːmi, ˈgʊərəmi/ ■ n. (pl. same or **gouramis**) an Asian labyrinth fish of a large group including many kinds popular in aquaria. [Osphronemidae (the giant gouramis), Belontiidae, and other families.]
– ORIGIN C19: from Malay *gurami*.

gourd /gʊəd, gɔːd/ ■ n. **1** a large fleshy fruit with a hard skin. ▸ a drinking vessel or water container made from the hollowed and dried skin of a gourd. **2** a climbing or trailing plant which bears this fruit. [*Cucurbita* and other genera.]
– DERIVATIVES **gourdful** n. (pl. **-fuls**).
– ORIGIN Middle English: from Old French *gourde*, from Latin *cucurbita*.

gourmand /ˈgʊəmənd, ˈgɔː-/ ■ n. **1** a person who enjoys eating, sometimes to excess. **2** a connoisseur of good food; a gourmet.
– DERIVATIVES **gourmandism** n.
– ORIGIN Middle English: from Old French.

gourmandize /ˌgʊəm(ə)nˈdiːz, ˈgɔː-/ (also **-ise**, **gormandize**) ■ v. indulge in good eating; eat greedily. ■ n. appreciation or consumption of good food.

gourmet /ˈgʊəmeɪ, ˈgɔː-/ ■ n. a connoisseur of good food. ▸ [as modifier] suitable for a gourmet: *a gourmet meal*.
– ORIGIN C19: French, orig. 'wine taster', influenced by GOURMAND.

gousblom /ˈxəʊsblɒm/ ■ n. (pl. **-blomme**) S. African a herbaceous plant of the daisy family with showy yellow, white, orange, or red flowers. [Genera *Arctotis* and *Gazania*.]
– ORIGIN Afrikaans: from Dutch *goudsbloem* 'marigold.'

gout /gaʊt/ ■ n. a disease in which defective metabolism of uric acid causes arthritis, especially in the smaller bones of the feet.
– DERIVATIVES **gouty** adj.
– ORIGIN Middle English: from Old French *goute*, from medieval Latin *gutta* 'drop' (because gout was believed to be caused by the dropping of diseased matter from the blood into the joints).

gov. ■ abbrev. **1** government. **2** governor.

govern /ˈgʌv(ə)n/ ■ v. **1** conduct the policy and affairs of (a state, organization, or people). ▸ control or influence. **2** constitute a rule, standard, or principle for. ▸ serve to decide (a legal case). **3** Grammar (of a word) require that (another word or group of words) be in a particular case.
– DERIVATIVES **governability** n. **governable** adj.
– ORIGIN Middle English: from Old French *governer*, from Latin *gubernare* 'to steer, rule', from Greek *kubernan* 'to steer'.

governance ■ n. the action or manner of governing. ▸ archaic control.

governess ■ n. a woman employed to teach children in a private household.
– DERIVATIVES **governessy** adj.
– ORIGIN Middle English: from Old French *governeresse*, feminine of *governeour* (see GOVERNOR).

governing body ■ n. a group of people who govern an institution in partnership with the managers.

government /ˈgʌv(ə)n,m(ə)nt, ˈgʌvəm(ə)nt/ ■ n. **1** [treated as sing. or pl.] the governing body of a state. ▸ the system by which a state or community is governed. ▸ the action or manner of governing a state, organization, or people. **2** Grammar the relation between a governed and a governing word.
– DERIVATIVES **governmental** adj. **governmentally** adv.

Government House ■ n. the official residence of a governor.

government paper ■ n. bonds or other promissory certificates issued by the government.

government securities ■ pl. n. another term for GOVERNMENT PAPER.

government surplus ■ n. unused equipment sold by the government.

governor ■ n. **1** an official appointed to govern a town or region. ▸ the elected executive head of a state of the US. ▸ the representative of the British Crown in a colony or in a Commonwealth state that regards the monarch as head of state. **2** the head of a public institution. ▸ a member of a governing body. **3** Brit. informal the person in authority. **4** a device automatically regulating the supply of fuel, steam, or water to a machine.
– DERIVATIVES **governorship** n.
– ORIGIN Middle English: from Old French *governeour*, from Latin *gubernator*, from *gubernare* (see GOVERN).

Governor General ■ n. (pl. **Governors General**) the chief representative of the Crown in a Commonwealth country of which the British monarch is head of state.

govt ■ abbrev. government.

gown ■ n. a long dress worn on formal occasions. ▸ a protective garment worn in hospital, either by a staff member during surgery or by a patient. ▸ S. African a dressing gown. ▸ a loose cloak indicating one's profession or status, worn by a lawyer, teacher, academic, or university student. ▸ the members of a university as distinct from the residents of a town. Often contrasted with TOWN. ■ v. (**be gowned**) be dressed in a gown.
– ORIGIN Middle English: from Old French *goune*, from late Latin *gunna* 'fur garment'.

goy /gɔɪ/ ■ n. (pl. **goyim** /ˈgɔɪɪm/ or **goys**) informal, offensive a Jewish name for a non-Jew.
– ORIGIN from Hebrew *gôy* 'people, nation'.

GP ■ abbrev. **1** general practitioner. **2** Grand Prix.

gph ■ abbrev. gallons per hour.

gpm ■ abbrev. gallons per minute.

GPO ■ abbrev. chiefly historical General Post Office.

GPS ■ abbrev. Global Positioning System (a satellite navigational system).

gr. ■ abbrev. **1** grain(s). **2** gram(s). **3** gross.

Graafian follicle /ˈgrɑːfɪən/ ■ n. Physiology a fluid-filled structure in the ovary within which an ovum develops prior to ovulation.
– ORIGIN C19: named after the C17 Dutch anatomist R. de *Graaf*.

grab ■ v. (**grabbed**, **grabbing**) **1** seize suddenly and roughly. ▸ informal obtain quickly or opportunistically. ▸ (of a brake on a vehicle) grip the wheel harshly or jerkily. **2** [usu. with neg. or in questions] informal impress: *how does that grab you?* ■ n. **1** a quick sudden clutch or attempt to seize. ▸ [as modifier] denoting a bar or strap to hold on to for support or in a moving vehicle. **2** a mechanical device for clutching, lifting, and moving loads.
– PHRASES **up for grabs** informal available.
– DERIVATIVES **grabber** n.
– ORIGIN C16: from Middle Low German and Middle Dutch *grabben*; perhaps rel. to GRIP and GROPE.

grab bag ■ n. chiefly N. Amer. a lucky dip in which wrapped items are chosen blindly from a bag. ▸ a lucky packet.

graben /ˈgrɑːb(ə)n/ ■ n. (pl. same or **grabens**) Geology an elongated block of the earth's crust lying between two faults and displaced downwards, as in a rift valley.
– ORIGIN C19: from German *Graben* 'a ditch'.

grace ■ n. **1** elegance of movement. **2** courteous good will. ▸ (**graces**) an attractively polite manner of behaving. **3** (in Christian belief) the free and unearned favour of God. ▸ a divinely given talent or blessing. ▸ a person's favour. **4** a period officially allowed for fulfilment of an obligation. **5** a short prayer of thanks said before or after a meal. **6** (**His**), **Her, or Your Grace** used as forms of description or address for a duke, duchess, or archbishop. ■ v. lend honour to by one's presence. ▸ be an attractive presence in or on.
– PHRASES **be in someone's good** (or **bad**) **graces** be regarded by someone with favour (or disfavour). **the (Three) Graces** Greek & Roman Mythology three beautiful goddesses, daughters of Zeus, believed to personify and bestow charm, grace, and beauty. **with good** (or **bad**) **grace** in a willing (or reluctant) manner.
– ORIGIN Middle English: from Latin *gratia*, from *gratus* 'pleasing, thankful'; rel. to GRATEFUL.

graceful ■ adj. having or showing grace or elegance.
– DERIVATIVES **gracefully** adv. **gracefulness** n.

graceless ■ adj. lacking grace, elegance, or charm.
– DERIVATIVES **gracelessly** adv. **gracelessness** n.

grace note ■ n. Music an extra note added as an embellishment and not essential to the harmony or melody.

gracilaria ■ pl. n. a group of red algae cultivated for food and the production of agar. [Phylum Rhodophyta.]

gracile /ˈɡrasɪl, ˈɡrasʌɪl/ ■ adj. Anthropology (of a hominid species) of slender build.
– ORIGIN C17: from Latin *gracilis* 'slender'.

gracious ■ adj. **1** courteous, kind, and pleasant. **2** showing the elegance and comfort brought by wealth. ■ exclam. expressing polite surprise.
– DERIVATIVES **graciously** adv. **graciousness** n.
– ORIGIN Middle English: from Latin *gratiosus*, from *gratia* (see GRACE).

grad[1] ■ n. informal term for GRADUATE.

grad[2] ■ abbrev. gradient.

gradable ■ adj. Grammar denoting an adjective that can be used in the comparative and superlative and take a submodifier.
– DERIVATIVES **gradability** n.

gradation ■ n. **1** a scale of successive changes, stages, or degrees. **2** a stage in a such a scale. **3** a minute change from one shade, tone, or colour to another.
– DERIVATIVES **gradate** v. **gradational** adj.
– ORIGIN C16: from Latin *gradatio(n-)*, from *gradus* 'step'.

grade ■ n. **1** a particular level of rank, quality, proficiency, or value. **2** a mark indicating the quality of a student's work. **3** (with specifying ordinal number) a class or division in a school in which pupils are grouped by age or ability for teaching at a particular level for a year. **4** chiefly N. Amer. a gradient or slope. **5** a variety of cattle produced by crossing with a superior breed. ■ v. **1** arrange in or allocate to grades. **2** chiefly N. Amer. give a mark to. **3** pass gradually from one level to another. **4** reduce (a road) to an easy gradient. **5** cross (livestock) with a superior breed.
– PHRASES **make the grade** informal succeed.
– ORIGIN C16: from Latin *gradus* 'step'.

grade R ■ n. (in South Africa) the reception year at school, before grade 1.

grader ■ n. **1** a person or thing that grades. **2** a wheeled machine for levelling the ground, especially in making roads. **3** [in combination] N. Amer. a pupil of a specified grade in a school: *first-grader*.

grade school ■ n. N. Amer. elementary school.

gradient /ˈɡreɪdɪənt/ ■ n. **1** a sloping part of a road or railway. **2** the degree of such a slope, expressed as change of height divided by distance travelled. ▶ Mathematics the degree of steepness of a graph. **3** Physics a change in the magnitude of a property (e.g. temperature) observed in passing from one point or moment to another.
– ORIGIN C19: from GRADE, on the pattern of *salient*.

gradiometer /ˌɡreɪdɪˈɒmɪtə/ ■ n. **1** a surveying instrument for setting out or measuring a gradient. **2** Physics an instrument for measuring the gradient of a gravitational, magnetic, or other field.

gradual /ˈɡradʒʊəl/ ■ adj. **1** taking place in stages over an extended period. **2** (of a slope) not steep or abrupt.
– DERIVATIVES **gradually** adv. **gradualness** n.
– ORIGIN Middle English: from medieval Latin *gradualis*, from Latin *gradus* 'step'.

gradualism ■ n. a policy or theory of gradual rather than sudden change.
– DERIVATIVES **gradualist** n. **gradualistic** adj.

graduand /ˈɡradʒʊand, -dj-, -ənd/ ■ n. a person who is about to receive an academic degree.
– ORIGIN C19: from medieval Latin *graduandus*, gerundive of *graduare* (see GRADUATE).

graduate ■ n. /ˈɡradʒʊət, -djʊət/ a person who has successfully completed a period of study or training, especially a first academic degree or (N. Amer.) a high-school diploma. ■ v. /ˈɡradʒʊeɪt, -djʊeɪt/ **1** successfully complete a degree, course, or (N. Amer.) high school. ▶ N. Amer. confer a degree or other academic qualification on. **2** (**graduate to**) move up to (something more advanced). **3** arrange or mark out in gradations. **4** change gradually.
– DERIVATIVES **graduation** n.
– ORIGIN Middle English: from medieval Latin *graduat-* 'graduated', from *graduare* 'take a degree', from Latin *gradus* 'degree, step'.

505

graduate school ■ n. a department of a university for advanced work by graduates.

Graeco- /ˈɡriːkəʊ, ˈɡrʌɪ-/ (also **Greco-**) ■ comb. form Greek; Greek and ...: *Graecophile*.
– ORIGIN from Latin *Graecus* (see GREEK).

Graeco-Roman ■ adj. **1** of or relating to the ancient Greeks and Romans. **2** denoting a style of wrestling in which holds below the waist are prohibited.

graffiti /ɡrəˈfiːti/ ■ pl. n. (sing. **graffito** /-təʊ/) [treated as sing. or pl.] unauthorized writing or drawings on a surface in a public place. ■ v. write or draw graffiti on.
– DERIVATIVES **graffitist** n.
– ORIGIN C19: from Italian, from *graffio* 'a scratch'.

USAGE
In Italian the word **graffiti** is a plural noun and its singular form is **graffito**. In modern English, **graffiti** is used as a plural in some specialist fields such as archaeology but in normal general use it is treated as if it were a mass noun (with a singular verb), similar to a word like **writing**. This use is now widely accepted as standard.

graft[1] ■ n. **1** Horticulture a shoot or scion inserted into a slit of stock, from which it receives sap. **2** Medicine a piece of living tissue that is transplanted surgically. ▶ an operation in which tissue is transplanted. ■ v. **1** insert or transplant as a graft. **2** integrate in or attach to something else, especially inappropriately.
– ORIGIN Middle English *graff*, from Greek *graphion* 'writing implement' (with ref. to the tapered tip of the scion), from *graphein* 'write'.

graft[2] informal ■ n. hard work. ■ v. work hard.
– DERIVATIVES **grafter** n.
– ORIGIN C19: perhaps rel. to the phr. *spade's graft* 'the amount of earth that one stroke of a spade will move'.

graft[3] ■ n. informal bribery and other corrupt measures pursued for gain in politics or business. ■ v. make money by graft.
– DERIVATIVES **grafter** n.
– ORIGIN C19.

graham ■ adj. N. Amer. denoting wholewheat flour, or biscuits or bread made from this.
– ORIGIN C19: named after the American advocate of dietary reform Sylvester *Graham*.

Graham's law ■ n. Chemistry a law stating that the rates of diffusion and effusion of a gas are inversely proportional to the square root of its density.
– ORIGIN C19: named after the Scottish chemist Thomas *Graham*.

Grail (also **Holy Grail**) ■ n. (in medieval legend) the cup or platter used by Christ at the Last Supper and in which Joseph of Arimathea received Christ's blood, especially as the object of quests by knights.
– ORIGIN from Old French *graal*, from medieval Latin *gradalis* 'dish'.

grain ■ n. **1** wheat or other cultivated cereal used as food. ▶ a single seed or fruit of a cereal. **2** a small, hard particle of a substance such as sand. ▶ a discrete particle or crystal in a metal, igneous rock, etc. **3** the smallest unit of weight in the troy and avoirdupois systems, equal to 1/5760 of a pound troy and 1/7000 of a pound avoirdupois (approximately 0.0648 grams). ▶ the smallest possible amount: *there wasn't a grain of truth in what he said*. **4** the longitudinal arrangement of fibres in wood, paper, etc. ▶ the texture of wood, stone, etc. **5** the rough or wrinkled outer surface of leather. **6** Photography a grainy appearance of a photograph or negative. ■ v. **1** give a rough surface or texture to. **2** form into grains. **3** [usu. as noun **graining**] paint in imitation of the grain of wood or marble.
– PHRASES **against the grain** contrary to one's nature or instinct.
– DERIVATIVES **-grained** adj. **grainless** adj.
– ORIGIN Middle English: from Old French *grain*, from Latin *granum*; sense 3 arose because the weight was orig. equivalent to that of a grain of wheat.

grains of Paradise ▪ pl. n. the seeds of a West African plant (*Aframomum melegueta*), used as a spice and in herbal medicine.

grain whisky ▪ n. whisky made mainly from unmalted wheat or maize.

grainy ▪ adj. (**-ier, -iest**) **1** granular. ▸ (of a photograph) showing visible grains of emulsion. **2** (of wood) having prominent grain.
–DERIVATIVES **graininess** n.

gram¹ (Brit. also **gramme**) (abbrev.: **g**) ▪ n. a metric unit of mass equal to one thousandth of a kilogram.
–ORIGIN C18: from late Latin *gramma* 'a small weight'.

gram² ▪ n. chickpeas or other pulses used as food.
–ORIGIN C18: from Latin *granum* 'grain'.

-gram¹ ▪ comb. form forming nouns denoting something written or recorded: *cryptogram*.
–DERIVATIVES **-grammatic** comb. form in corresponding adjectives.
–ORIGIN from Greek *gramma* 'thing written, letter of the alphabet'.

-gram² ▪ comb. form forming nouns denoting a person paid to deliver a novelty greeting or message: *kissogram*.
–ORIGIN on the pattern of *telegram*.

gramadoelas /ˌxrɑməˈduːləs/ ▪ n. S. African informal remote or wild country.
–ORIGIN from Afrikaans, perhaps rel. to isiXhosa and isiZulu *induli* 'hillock'.

graminaceous /ˌɡrɑmɪˈneɪʃəs/ ▪ adj. Botany relating to or denoting plants of the grass family (Gramineae).
–ORIGIN C19: from Latin *gramen* 'grass'.

grammar ▪ n. **1** the whole system and structure of a language or of languages in general, usually taken as consisting of syntax and morphology. ▸ a particular analysis of this. **2** a book on grammar. **3** a set of prescriptive notions about correct use of a language. **4** the basic elements of an area of knowledge or skill.

> **HISTORY**
> Although the two concepts are rarely associated with each other, **grammar** and **glamour** are linked. Recorded in Middle English, the word **grammar** came via French *gramaire* and Latin *grammatica* from Greek *grammatikē* (*tekhnē*) '(art) of letters'. In the Middle Ages, Latin *grammatica* was often used to mean 'learning', and because many people associated scholarship with magic, **grammar** seems to have taken on the meaning 'enchantment, magic'. It was in Scottish English in the 18th century that the spelling change from **grammar** to **glamour** occurred, and the form **glamour** became fixed in the meaning 'magic' and later 'an attractive and exciting quality'. Similarly, **grimoire** 'a book of spells' derives from an alternative spelling of French *grammaire* 'grammar'.

grammarian /ɡrəˈmɛːrɪən/ ▪ n. a person who studies and writes about grammar.

grammar school ▪ n. **1** (in the UK, especially formerly) a state secondary school to which pupils are admitted on the basis of ability. ▸ historical a school founded in or before the 16th century for teaching Latin, later becoming a secondary school teaching academic subjects. **2** US dated another term for ELEMENTARY SCHOOL.

grammatical /ɡrəˈmatɪk(ə)l/ ▪ adj. **1** of or relating to grammar. **2** in accordance with the rules of grammar.
–DERIVATIVES **grammaticality** n. **grammatically** adv.
–ORIGIN C16: from Greek *grammatikos*, from *gramma, grammatos* 'letter of the alphabet'.

grammaticalize (also **-ise**) ▪ v. Linguistics change (an element with lexical meaning) into one having a largely grammatical function.
–DERIVATIVES **grammaticalization** (also **-isation**) n.

gramme ▪ n. variant spelling of GRAM¹.

Grammy ▪ n. (pl. **Grammys** or **Grammies**) each of a number of annual awards given by the American National Academy of Recording Arts and Sciences for achievement in the recording industry.
–ORIGIN 1950s: blend of GRAMOPHONE and EMMY.

Gram-negative ▪ adj. see GRAM STAIN.

gramophone ▪ n. chiefly Brit. old-fashioned term for RECORD PLAYER.
–ORIGIN C19: formed by inversion of elements of *phonogram* 'sound recording'.

gramophone record ▪ n. fuller form of RECORD (in sense 4).

gramp (also **gramps, grampy**) ▪ n. dialect or informal one's grandfather.

Gram-positive ▪ adj. see GRAM STAIN.

grampus /ˈɡrampəs/ ▪ n. (pl. **grampuses**) a killer whale or other cetacean of the dolphin family.
–ORIGIN C16: alteration (by association with GRAND) of Old French *grapois*, from medieval Latin *craspiscis*, from Latin *crassus piscis* 'fat fish'.

Gram stain ▪ n. Medicine a staining technique for the preliminary distinction of bacteria between two categories (Gram-positive and Gram-negative).
–ORIGIN C19: named after the Danish physician Hans C. J. Gram.

gran ▪ n. informal one's grandmother.

granadilla /ɡran-/ (also **grenadilla**) ▪ n. a passion fruit.
–ORIGIN C16: Spanish, diminutive of *granada* 'pomegranate'.

granary ▪ n. (pl. **-ies**) **1** a storehouse for threshed grain. **2** a region supplying large quantities of corn: *Egypt was the granary of Rome*.
–ORIGIN C16: from Latin *granarium*.

grand ▪ adj. **1** magnificent and imposing. ▸ large, ambitious, or impressive in scope or scale. ▸ dignified, noble, or proud. **2** of chief importance. ▸ of the highest rank (used especially in official titles). ▸ Law (of a crime) serious. Compare with PETTY (in sense 3). **3** informal excellent. **4** [in combination] (in names of family relationships) denoting one generation removed in ascent or descent. ▪ n. **1** (pl. same) informal a thousand dollars or pounds. **2** a grand piano.
–DERIVATIVES **grandly** adv. **grandness** n.
–ORIGIN Middle English: from Latin *grandis* 'full-grown, great'.

grandad (also **granddad**) ▪ n. informal one's grandfather.

grandam /ˈɡrandam/ (also **grandame**) ▪ n. archaic term for GRANDMOTHER.
–ORIGIN Middle English: from Anglo-Norman French *graund dame* (see GRAND, DAME).

grand apartheid ▪ n. historical (during the 1960s and 1970s) the principles and policies that dealt with the broader political and economic aspects of the apartheid system in South Africa, such as the creation of homelands.

grandchild ▪ n. (pl. **-children**) a child of one's son or daughter.

grand cru /ɡrɒ̃ ˈkruː/ ▪ n. (pl. **grands crus** pronunc. same) **1** (chiefly in France) a wine of the most superior grade. Compare with PREMIER CRU. **2** short for PREMIER GRAND CRU.
–ORIGIN French, 'great growth'.

granddad ▪ n. variant spelling of GRANDAD.

granddaughter ▪ n. a daughter of one's son or daughter.

grand duchess ▪ n. **1** the wife or widow of a grand duke. **2** a woman holding the rank of grand duke in her own right.

grand duke ▪ n. **1** a prince or nobleman ruling over a territory in certain European countries. **2** historical a son (or son's son) of a Russian tsar.
–DERIVATIVES **grand duchy** n.

grande dame /ɡrɒ̃d ˈdam/ ▪ n. an influential woman within a particular sphere.
–ORIGIN French, 'grand lady'.

grandee /ɡranˈdiː/ ▪ n. a Spanish or Portuguese nobleman of the highest rank. ▸ a man of high rank or eminence.
–ORIGIN C16: from Spanish and Portuguese *grande* 'grand', used as n.

grandeur /ˈɡrandjə, -(d)ʒə/ ▪ n. splendour and impressiveness. ▸ high rank or social importance.
–ORIGIN C16 (denoting tall stature): from French, from Latin *grandis* (see GRAND).

grandfather ▪ n. **1** the father of one's father or mother. **2** a founder or originator.
–DERIVATIVES **grandfatherly** adj.

grandfather clock ■ n. a clock in a tall free-standing wooden case, driven by weights.

Grand Guignol /ˌɡrɒ̃ ɡiːˈnjɒl/ ■ n. a dramatic entertainment of a sensational or horrific nature.
– ORIGIN French, 'Great Punch'.

grandiflora /ˌɡrandɪˈflɔːrə/ ■ adj. denoting cultivated plant varieties with large flowers.
– ORIGIN C20: modern Latin, from Latin *grandis* 'great' + *flos* 'flower'.

grandiloquent /ɡranˈdɪləkwənt/ ■ adj. pompous or extravagant in language, style, or manner.
– DERIVATIVES **grandiloquence** n. **grandiloquently** adv.
– ORIGIN C16: from Latin *grandiloquus* 'grand-speaking'; ending altered by association with ELOQUENT.

Grand Inquisitor ■ n. historical the director of the court of Inquisition, especially in Spain and Portugal.

grandiose /ˈɡrandɪəʊs/ ■ adj. **1** impressive or magnificent, especially pretentiously so. **2** conceived on a very ambitious scale.
– DERIVATIVES **grandiosely** adv. **grandiosity** n.
– ORIGIN C19: from Italian *grandioso*, from *grande* 'grand'.

grand jeté /ɡrɒ̃ ˈʒəteɪ, ʒəˈteɪ/ ■ n. Ballet a jump in which a dancer springs from one foot to land on the other with one leg forward of their body and the other stretched backwards while in the air.

grand jury ■ n. US Law a jury selected to examine the validity of an accusation prior to trial.

grand larceny ■ n. Law (in many US states and formerly in Britain) theft of personal property having a value above a legally specified amount.

grandma ■ n. informal one's grandmother.

grand mal /ɡrɒ̃ ˈmal/ ■ n. a serious form of epilepsy with muscle spasms and prolonged loss of consciousness. Compare with PETIT MAL.
– ORIGIN C19: from French, 'great sickness'.

grandmama (also **grandmamma**) ■ n. archaic form of GRANDMA.

Grand Marnier /ɡrɒ̃ ˈmɑːnɪeɪ/ ■ n. trademark an orange-flavoured cognac-based liqueur.
– ORIGIN from French.

grand master ■ n. **1** (usu. **grandmaster**) a chess player of the highest class, especially one who has won an international tournament. **2** (**Grand Master**) the head of an order of chivalry or of Freemasons.

grandmother ■ n. the mother of one's father or mother.
– PHRASES **teach one's grandmother to suck eggs** presume to advise a more experienced person.
– DERIVATIVES **grandmotherly** adj.

grandmother clock ■ n. a clock similar to a grandfather clock but about two thirds the size.

grand opera ■ n. an opera on a serious theme in which the entire libretto (including dialogue) is sung.

grandpa ■ n. informal one's grandfather.

grandpapa ■ n. old-fashioned term for GRANDFATHER.

grandparent ■ n. a grandmother or grandfather.
– DERIVATIVES **grandparental** adj. **grandparenthood** n.

grand piano ■ n. a large, full-toned piano which has the body, strings, and soundboard arranged horizontally and in line with the keys and is supported by three legs.

Grand Prix /ɡrɒ̃ ˈpriː/ ■ n. (pl. **Grands Prix** pronunc. same) any of a world championship series of international motor-racing or motorcycling contests.
– ORIGIN C19: French, 'great or chief prize'.

grandsire ■ n. archaic term for GRANDFATHER.

grand slam ■ n. **1** the winning of each of a group of major championships or matches in a particular sport in the same year. **2** Bridge the bidding and winning of all thirteen tricks. **3** Baseball a home run hit when each of the three bases is occupied by a runner.

grandson ■ n. the son of one's son or daughter.

grandstand ■ n. the main stand commanding the best view for spectators at racecourses or sports grounds. ■ v. [usu. as noun **grandstanding**] derogatory seek to attract fa-vourable public or media attention.

grandstand finish ■ n. a close or exciting finish to a race or competition.

grand total ■ n. the final amount after everything is added up.

grand tour ■ n. historical a cultural tour of Europe conventionally undertaken by a young man of the upper classes.

grange ■ n. Brit. a country house with farm buildings attached.
– ORIGIN Middle English: from medieval Latin *granica (villa)* 'grain house or farm', from Latin *granum* 'grain'.

granite /ˈɡranɪt/ ■ n. a very hard, granular, crystalline igneous rock consisting mainly of quartz, mica, and feldspar.
– DERIVATIVES **granitic** adj. **granitoid** adj. & n.
– ORIGIN C17: from Italian *granito* 'grained'.

granny (also **grannie**) ■ n. (pl. **-ies**) informal one's grandmother.
– ORIGIN C17: from *grannam* (representing a colloquial pronunciation of GRANDAM).

granny flat ■ n. informal a part of a house made into self-contained accommodation suitable for an elderly relative.

granny glasses ■ pl. n. informal round metal-rimmed glasses.

granny knot ■ n. a reef knot with the ends crossed the wrong way and therefore liable to slip.

Granny Smith ■ n. a dessert apple of a bright green variety with crisp sharp-flavoured flesh, originating in Australia.
– ORIGIN C19: named after Maria Ann (*Granny*) *Smith*.

granodiorite /ˌɡranə(ʊ)ˈdʌɪərʌɪt/ ■ n. Geology a coarse-grained plutonic rock between granite and diorite in composition.

granola /ɡraˈnəʊlə/ ■ n. N. Amer. a kind of breakfast cereal resembling muesli.
– ORIGIN C19: from *gran-* (representing GRANULAR or GRAIN) + *-ola* (suffix chiefly in US usage).

granophyre /ˈɡranə(ʊ)ˌfʌɪə/ ■ n. Geology a granitic rock containing intergrown feldspar and quartz crystals.
– ORIGIN C19: from German *Granophyr*, from *Granit* 'granite' + *Porphyr* (see PORPHYRY).

grant ■ v. **1** agree to give or allow (something requested) to. ▶ give (a right, property, etc.) formally or legally to. **2** agree or admit to (someone) that (something) is true. ■ n. **1** a sum of money given by a government or public body for a particular purpose. **2** formal the action of granting something. **3** Law a legal conveyance or formal conferment.
– PHRASES **take for granted 1** fail to appreciate through over-familiarity. **2** (**take something for granted**) assume that something is true.
– DERIVATIVES **grantee** n. (chiefly Law). **granter** n. **grantor** n. (chiefly Law).
– ORIGIN Middle English: from Old French *granter* 'consent to support', var. of *creanter* 'to guarantee', from Latin *credere* 'entrust'.

granted ■ adv. admittedly; it is true. ■ conj. (**granted that**) even assuming that.

grant-in-aid ■ n. (pl. **grants-in-aid**) a grant given to local government, an institution, or a particular scholar.

granular ■ adj. **1** resembling or consisting of granules. **2** having a roughened surface or structure.
– DERIVATIVES **granularity** n.

granulate ■ v. **1** [usu. as adj. **granulated**] form into or take the form of granules. **2** [often as adj. **granulating**] Medicine (of a wound or lesion) form multiple small prominences as part of the healing process. **3** [as adj. **granulated**] chiefly Biology having a roughened surface.
– DERIVATIVES **granulation** n.

granule /ˈɡranjuːl/ ■ n. a small compact particle.
– ORIGIN C17: from late Latin *granulum*, diminutive of Latin *granum* 'grain'.

granulite ■ n. Geology a fine-grained granular metamorphic rock consisting mainly of feldspars and quartz.

granulocyte

granulocyte /ˈgranjʊlə(ʊ)ˌsʌɪt/ ■ n. Physiology a white blood cell with secretory granules in its cytoplasm.
– DERIVATIVES **granulocytic** adj.

granuloma /ˌgranjʊˈləʊmə/ ■ n. (pl. **granulomas** or **granulomata** /-mətə/) Medicine a mass of granulated connective tissue, typically produced in response to infection, inflammation, or a foreign substance.
– DERIVATIVES **granulomatous** adj.

grape ■ n. a green, purple, or black berry growing in clusters on a vine, eaten as fruit and used in making wine. ▶ (**the grape**) informal wine.
– DERIVATIVES **grapey** (also **grapy**) adj.
– ORIGIN Middle English: from Old French, 'bunch of grapes', prob. from *graper* 'gather (grapes)', from *grap* 'hook' (used in harvesting grapes), of Germanic origin.

grapefruit ■ n. (pl. same) **1** a large round yellow citrus fruit with an acid juicy pulp. **2** the tree bearing this fruit. [*Citrus paradisi.*]
– ORIGIN C19: from GRAPE + FRUIT (prob. because the fruits grow in clusters).

grape hyacinth ■ n. a small plant of the lily family, with clusters of small globular blue flowers, cultivated as an ornamental or for use in perfume. [Genus *Muscari*.]

grapeseed oil ■ n. oil extracted from the residue of grapes which have been juiced.

grapeshot ■ n. historical ammunition consisting of a number of small iron balls fired together from a cannon.

grape sugar ■ n. dextrose present in or derived from grapes.

grapevine ■ n. **1** a vine bearing grapes. [*Vitis vinifera* and related species.] **2** (**the grapevine**) informal the circulation of rumours and unofficial information.

graph¹ /grɑːf, graf/ ■ n. **1** a diagram showing the relation between variable quantities, typically of two variables measured along a pair of axes at right angles. **2** Mathematics a collection of points whose coordinates satisfy a given relation. ■ v. plot or trace on a graph.
– ORIGIN C19: abbrev. of *graphic formula*.

graph² /grɑːf, graf/ ■ n. Linguistics a visual symbol representing a unit of sound or other feature of speech.
– ORIGIN 1930s: from Greek *graphē* 'writing'.

-graph ■ comb. form **1** in nouns denoting something written or drawn in a specified way: *autograph*. **2** in nouns denoting an instrument that records: *seismograph*.
– ORIGIN from French *-graphe*, from Greek *graphos* 'written, writing'.

grapheme /ˈgrafiːm/ ■ n. Linguistics the smallest meaningful contrastive unit in a writing system.
– DERIVATIVES **graphemic** adj.

-grapher ■ comb. form indicating a person concerned with a subject denoted by a noun ending in *-graphy*.
– ORIGIN from Greek *-graphos* 'writer'.

graphic ■ adj. **1** of or relating to visual art, especially involving drawing, engraving, or lettering. **2** giving vividly explicit detail. **3** Computing relating to or denoting a visual image. **4** of or in the form of a graph. **5** Geology of or denoting rocks having a surface texture resembling cuneiform writing. ■ n. Computing a graphical item displayed on a screen or stored as data.
– DERIVATIVES **graphically** adv.
– ORIGIN C17: from Greek *graphikos*, from *graphē* 'writing, drawing'.

-graphic ■ comb. form in adjectives corresponding to nouns ending in *-graphy*.
– DERIVATIVES **-graphically** comb. form in corresponding adverbs.
– ORIGIN suggested by Greek *-graphikos*, from *graphē* 'writing, drawing'; partly from -GRAPHY or -GRAPH + -IC.

graphicacy /ˈgrafɪkəsi/ ■ n. the ability to understand maps or graphs.
– ORIGIN 1960s: from GRAPHIC, on the pattern of *literacy*.

graphical ■ adj. **1** of or in the form of a graph. **2** of or relating to visual art or computer graphics.
– DERIVATIVES **graphically** adv.

-graphical ■ comb. form equivalent to -GRAPHIC.

graphical user interface ■ n. Computing a visual way of interacting with a computer using items such as windows and icons.

graphic arts ■ pl. n. the visual arts based on the use of line and tone rather than three-dimensional work or the use of colour.
– DERIVATIVES **graphic artist** n.

graphic design ■ n. the art or skill of combining text and pictures in advertisements, magazines, or books.
– DERIVATIVES **graphic designer** n.

graphic equalizer ■ n. an electronic device or computer program which allows the separate control of the strength and quality of selected frequency bands.

graphic novel ■ n. a novel in comic-strip format.

graphics ■ pl. n. [usu. treated as sing.] **1** the products of the graphic arts, especially commercial design or illustration. **2** the use of diagrams in calculation and design. **3** [treated as pl.] (also **computer graphics**) visual images produced or manipulated by computer processing. ▶ [treated as sing.] the use of computers to generate and manipulate visual images.

graphics tablet ■ n. Computing an input device which the user draws on or points at with a special stylus, to guide a pointer displayed on the screen.

graphite ■ n. a grey, crystalline, electrically conducting form of carbon which is used as a solid lubricant, as pencil lead, and as a moderator in nuclear reactors.
– DERIVATIVES **graphitic** adj. **graphitization** (also **-isation**) n.
– ORIGIN C18: from German *Graphit*, from Greek *graphein* 'write' (because of its use in pencils).

graphology ■ n. **1** the study of handwriting, especially as used to infer a person's character. **2** Linguistics the study of written and printed symbols and of writing systems.
– DERIVATIVES **graphological** adj. **graphologist** n.
– ORIGIN C19: from Greek *graphē* 'writing' + -LOGY.

graph paper ■ n. paper printed with a network of small squares to assist the drawing of graphs or other diagrams.

-graphy ■ comb. form in nouns denoting: **1** a descriptive science: *geography*. **2** a technique of producing images: *radiography*. **3** a style or method of writing or drawing: *calligraphy*. **4** writing about (a specified subject): *hagiography*. **5** a written or printed list: *filmography*.
– ORIGIN from or suggested by Greek *-graphia* 'writing'.

grapnel /ˈgrapn(ə)l/ ■ n. **1** a grappling hook. **2** a small anchor with several flukes.
– ORIGIN Middle English: from an Anglo-Norman French diminutive of Old French *grapon*, of Germanic origin.

grappa /ˈgrapə/ ■ n. a brandy distilled from the fermented residue of grapes after they have been pressed in winemaking.
– ORIGIN Italian, 'grape stalk'.

grapple ■ v. engage in a close fight or struggle without weapons. ▶ (**grapple with**) struggle to deal with. ■ n. an act of grappling.
– DERIVATIVES **grappler** n.
– ORIGIN Middle English: from Old French *grapil*, from Provençal, diminutive of *grapa* 'hook', of Germanic origin.

grappling hook (also **grappling iron**) ■ n. a device with iron claws, attached to a rope and used for dragging or grasping.

grasp /grɑːsp/ ■ v. **1** seize and hold firmly. **2** comprehend fully. ■ n. **1** a firm grip. **2** a person's capacity to attain something. **2** a person's understanding.
– DERIVATIVES **graspable** adj.
– ORIGIN Middle English: perhaps rel. to GROPE.

grasping ■ adj. greedy.
– DERIVATIVES **graspingness** n. **graspingly** adv.

grass ■ n. **1** vegetation consisting of short plants with long narrow leaves, growing wild or cultivated on lawns and pasture. ▶ ground covered with this. **2** a plant with jointed stems and spikes of small wind-pollinated flowers, predominant in such vegetation. [Family Gramineae: many species.] **3** informal cannabis. **4** informal police informer. ■ v. **1** cover with grass. **2** (often **grass on**) informal, chiefly Brit. inform the police of criminal activity or plans.
– PHRASES **at grass** grazing. **not let the grass grow under one's feet** not delay in taking action. **put out to grass** put

(an animal) out to graze. ▶ **(put someone out to grass)** informal force someone to retire.
– DERIVATIVES **grassless** adj. **grass-like** adj.
– ORIGIN Old English, of Germanic origin; ultimately rel. to GREEN and GROW. The sense 'police informer' is perhaps rel. to C19 rhyming slang *grasshopper* 'copper'.

grassbird ■ n. a brown streaked warbler frequenting long grass and reed beds. [Genus *Megalurus* (Australasia and Asia) and *Sphenoeacus afer* (southern Africa).]

grassbox ■ n. a receptacle on a lawnmower for collecting the cut grass.

grasshopper ■ n. a plant-eating insect with long hind legs which are used for jumping and for producing a chirping sound. [Family Acrididae: many species.]

grassland ■ n. **1** (also **grasslands**) a large area of grass-covered land, especially one used for grazing. **2** another term for GRASSVELD.

grass roots ■ pl. n. the most basic level of an activity or organization. ▶ ordinary people regarded as the main body of an organization's membership.

grass skirt ■ n. a skirt made of long grass and leaves fastened to a waistband, associated especially with female dancers from some Pacific islands.

grass snake ■ n. **1** a common harmless Eurasian snake, typically grey-green with a yellowish band around the neck. [*Natrix natrix*.] **2** a harmless African grassland snake, typically brown in colour. [Genus *Psammophis*.]

grassveld /'grasfɛlt/ ■ n. S. African uncultivated land covered with indigenous grass species.
– ORIGIN C19: partial translation of Afrikaans *grasveld* 'grassland'.

grassy ■ adj. (**-ier**, **-iest**) **1** of or covered with grass. **2** characteristic of or resembling grass.
– DERIVATIVES **grassiness** n.

grate[1] ■ v. **1** reduce (food) to small shreds by rubbing it on a grater. **2** make an unpleasant rasping sound. **3** have an irritating effect.
– ORIGIN Middle English: from Old French *grater*, of Germanic origin.

grate[2] ■ n. the recess of a fireplace or furnace. ▶ a metal frame confining fuel in a fireplace or furnace.
– ORIGIN Middle English: from Old French, from Latin *cratis* 'hurdle'.

grateful ■ adj. **1** feeling or showing gratitude. **2** archaic received with gratitude.
– DERIVATIVES **gratefully** adv. **gratefulness** n.
– ORIGIN C16: from obsolete *grate* 'pleasing, thankful', from Latin *gratus*.

grater ■ n. a device having a surface covered with sharp-edged holes, used for grating food.

graticule /'gratɪkjuːl/ ■ n. **1** a network of lines representing meridians and parallels, on which a map or plan can be represented. **2** a series of fine lines in an eyepiece or oscilloscope screen, used as a measuring scale or an aid in locating objects.
– ORIGIN C19: from medieval Latin *graticula* 'a little grating'.

gratify ■ v. (**-ies**, **-ied**) **1** give pleasure or satisfaction. **2** indulge or satisfy (a desire).
– DERIVATIVES **gratification** n. **gratifying** adj. **gratifyingly** adv.
– ORIGIN Middle English: from Latin *gratificari* 'give or do as a favour', from *gratus* 'pleasing, thankful'.

gratin /'gratã, 'gratan/ ■ n. a dish cooked au gratin.
– ORIGIN French: from *gratter*, earlier *grater* 'to grate'.

grating[1] ■ adj. **1** sounding harsh and unpleasant. **2** irritating.
– DERIVATIVES **gratingly** adv.

grating[2] ■ n. **1** a framework of parallel or crossed bars, typically preventing access through an opening. **2** (also **diffraction grating**) Optics a set of equally spaced parallel wires or ruled lines, used to produce spectra by diffraction.

gratis /'gratɪs, 'grɑː-, 'greɪ-/ ■ adv. & adj. free of charge.
– ORIGIN Middle English: from Latin, contraction of *gratiis* 'as a kindness', from *gratia* 'grace, kindness'.

gratitude ■ n. thankfulness; appreciation of kindness.

– ORIGIN Middle English: from medieval Latin *gratitudo*, from Latin *gratus* 'pleasing, thankful'.

gratuitous /grə'tjuːɪtəs/ ■ adj. **1** uncalled for. **2** free of charge.
– DERIVATIVES **gratuitously** adv. **gratuitousness** n.
– ORIGIN C17: from Latin *gratuitus* 'given freely, spontaneous'.

gratuity /grə'tjuːɪti/ ■ n. (pl. **-ies**) **1** formal a tip given to a waiter, porter, etc. **2** a sum of money paid to an employee at the end of a period of employment.
– ORIGIN C15: from medieval Latin *gratuitas* 'gift'.

graunch /grɔːn(t)ʃ/ ■ v. informal make a crunching or grinding noise.
– ORIGIN C19 (orig. dialect): imitative.

gravadlax /'gravəd,laks/ ■ n. variant spelling of GRAVLAX.

gravamen /grə'veɪmɛn/ ■ n. (pl. **gravamina** /-mɪnə/) chiefly Law the essence or most serious part of a complaint or accusation.
– ORIGIN C17: from late Latin, 'physical inconvenience'.

grave[1] ■ n. a hole dug in the ground to receive a coffin or corpse. ▶ **(the grave)** death.
– PHRASES **dig one's own grave** do something foolish which causes one's downfall. **turn** (N. Amer. also **turn over**) **in one's grave** (of a dead person) be thought of as angry or distressed about something had they been alive.
– ORIGIN Old English, of Germanic origin.

grave[2] ■ adj. **1** giving cause for alarm. **2** solemn.
– DERIVATIVES **gravely** adv. **graveness** n.
– ORIGIN C15: from Latin *gravis* 'heavy, serious'.

grave[3] ■ v. (past part. **graven** or **graved**) **1** archaic engrave (an inscription or image) on a surface. **2** poetic/literary fix indelibly in the mind.
– ORIGIN Old English *grafan* 'dig', of Germanic origin; rel. to GRAVE[1].

grave accent /grɑːv/ ■ n. a mark (`) placed over a vowel in some languages to indicate a feature such as altered sound quality.
– ORIGIN C17: French *grave* (see GRAVE[2]).

gravel ■ n. **1** a loose aggregation of small stones and coarse sand, often used for paths and roads. **2** Medicine aggregations of crystals formed in the urinary tract.
■ v. (**gravelled**, **gravelling**; US **graveled**, **graveling**) cover with gravel.
– ORIGIN Middle English: from Old French, diminutive of *grave* 'gravel, coarse sand'.

gravelly ■ adj. **1** resembling, containing, or consisting of gravel. **2** (of a voice) deep and rough-sounding.

graven past participle of GRAVE[3].

graven image ■ n. a carved figure of a god used as an idol.
– ORIGIN with biblical allusion to Exodus 20:4.

graver ■ n. **1** a burin or other engraving tool. **2** archaic an engraver.

Graves' disease ■ n. a swelling of the neck and protrusion of the eyes resulting from an overactive thyroid gland.
– ORIGIN C19: named after the Irish physician Robert J. Graves.

gravestone ■ n. an inscribed headstone marking a grave.

Gravettian /grə'vɛtɪən/ ■ adj. Archaeology relating to or denoting an Upper Palaeolithic culture in Europe following the Aurignacian, dated to about 28 000–19 000 years ago.
– ORIGIN 1930s: from *la Gravette* in SW France, where objects from this culture were found.

graveyard ■ n. a burial ground, especially one beside a church.

graveyard shift ■ n. chiefly N. Amer. a work shift that runs from midnight to 8 a.m.

gravid /'gravɪd/ ■ adj. technical pregnant.
– ORIGIN C16: from Latin *gravidus* 'laden, pregnant'.

gravimeter /grə'vɪmɪtə/ ■ n. an instrument for measuring the force of gravity at different places.
– ORIGIN C18: from French *gravimètre*, from *grave* 'heavy' + *-mètre* '(instrument) measuring'.

gravimetric

gravimetric /ˌgravɪˈmɛtrɪk/ ■ adj. **1** of or relating to the measurement of weight. **2** of or relating to the measurement of gravity.
– DERIVATIVES **gravimetry** /grəˈvɪmɪtri/ n.

gravitas /ˈgravɪtas, -tɑːs/ ■ n. dignity or solemnity of manner.
– ORIGIN Latin: from *gravis* 'serious'.

gravitate /ˈgravɪteɪt/ ■ v. **1** be drawn towards to a place, person, or thing. **2** Physics move, or tend to move, towards a centre of gravity.
– ORIGIN C17: from modern Latin *gravitare*, from Latin *gravitas* 'weight'.

gravitation ■ n. **1** movement, or a tendency to move, towards a centre of gravity. **2** Physics the force responsible for this; gravity.
– DERIVATIVES **gravitational** adj. **gravitationally** adv.

gravitational constant (abbrev.: **G**) ■ n. Physics the constant in Newton's law of gravitation relating gravity to the masses and separation of particles, equal to 6.67×10^{-11} N m^2 kg^{-2}.

gravitational lens ■ n. Astronomy a massive object whose gravitational field distorts light passing through it, producing a multiple image of a more remote object.

graviton /ˈgravɪtɒn/ ■ n. Physics a hypothetical particle representing a quantum of gravitational energy.

gravity ■ n. **1** Physics the force that attracts a body towards the centre of the earth, or towards any other physical body having mass. ▸ the degree of intensity of this, measured by acceleration. **2** extreme importance; seriousness. ▸ solemnity of manner.
– ORIGIN C15: from Latin *gravitas* 'weight, seriousness'.

gravity feed ■ n. a supply system making use of gravity to maintain the flow of material.
– DERIVATIVES **gravity-fed** adj.

gravity wave ■ n. Physics **1** a hypothetical wave carrying gravitational energy. **2** a wave propagated on a liquid surface or in a fluid through the effects of gravity.

gravlax /ˈgravlaks/ (also **gravadlax**) ■ n. a Scandinavian dish of dry-cured salmon marinated in herbs.
– ORIGIN Swedish, from *grav* 'trench' + *lax* 'salmon' (from the former practice of burying the salmon in salt in a hole in the ground).

gravure /grəˈvjʊə/ ■ n. short for PHOTOGRAVURE.

gravy ■ n. (pl. **-ies**) **1** the fat and juices exuding from meat during cooking. ▸ a sauce made from these juices together with stock and other ingredients. **2** informal unearned or unexpected money.
– ORIGIN Middle English: perhaps from a misreading (as *gravé*) of Old French *grané*, prob. from *grain* 'spice', from Latin *granum* 'grain'.

gravy boat ■ n. a long narrow jug used for serving gravy.

gravy train ■ n. informal a situation in which someone can easily make a lot of money.

gray[1] (abbrev.: **Gy**) ■ n. Physics the SI unit of the absorbed dose of ionizing radiation, corresponding to one joule per kilogram.
– ORIGIN 1970s: named after the English radiobiologist Louis H. *Gray*.

gray[2] ■ adj. US spelling of GREY.

graybeard etc. ■ n. US spelling of GREYBEARD ETC.

grayling ■ n. an edible silvery-grey freshwater fish with horizontal violet stripes and a long high dorsal fin, found in Eurasia and North America. [Genus *Thymallus*: several species.]
– ORIGIN Middle English: from *gray* (var. of GREY) + rare *ling*, denoting a fish of the cod family.

grayscale ■ n. US spelling of GREYSCALE.

graze[1] ■ v. **1** (of cattle, sheep, etc.) eat grass in a field. ▸ feed on (grass or grassland). **2** informal eat frequent snacks at irregular intervals. **3** informal, chiefly N. Amer. casually sample something. ■ n. S. African informal food.
– DERIVATIVES **grazer** n.
– ORIGIN Old English *grasian*, from *græs* 'grass'.

graze[2] ■ v. **1** scrape and break the skin on (part of the body). **2** touch or scrape lightly in passing. ■ n. a superficial injury caused by grazing the skin.
– ORIGIN C16: perhaps a specific use of GRAZE[1].

grazier /ˈgreɪzɪə/ ■ n. a person who rears or fattens cattle or sheep for market.
– ORIGIN Middle English: from GRASS.

grazing ■ n. grassland suitable for pasturage.

grease ■ n. **1** a thick oily substance, especially as used as a lubricant. **2** animal fat used or produced in cooking. ■ v. smear or lubricate with grease.
– PHRASES **grease the palm of** informal bribe. **like greased lightning** informal extremely rapidly.
– DERIVATIVES **greaseless** adj.
– ORIGIN Middle English: from Old French *graisse*, from Latin *crassus* 'thick, fat'.

grease gun ■ n. a device for pumping grease under pressure to a particular point.

grease monkey ■ n. informal a mechanic.

greasepaint ■ n. a waxy substance used as make-up by actors.

greaseproof ■ adj. (especially of paper used in cooking) impermeable to grease.

greaser ■ n. **1** a motor mechanic or unskilled engineer on a ship. **2** informal a young man with long hair belonging to a motorcycle gang.

greasy ■ adj. (**-ier**, **-iest**) **1** covered with or resembling grease. ▸ producing more body oils than average. ▸ containing or cooked with too much oil or fat. **2** effusively polite in a repellently insincere way.
– DERIVATIVES **greasily** adv. **greasiness** n.

greasy pole ■ n. informal a pole covered with grease, especially as climbed or walked along for entertainment. ▸ the difficult route to the top of a profession.

greasy spoon ■ n. informal a cheap, run-down café or restaurant serving fried foods.

great ■ adj. **1** of an extent, amount, or intensity considerably above average. ▸ (**Greater**) (of a city) including adjacent urban areas. **2** of ability, quality, or eminence considerably above average. ▸ (**the Great**) a title denoting the most important person of the name: *Alexander the Great.* ▸ informal excellent. **3** denoting the most important element of something. ▸ particularly deserving a specified description: *I was a great fan of Hank's.* **4** [in combination] (in names of family relationships) denoting one degree further removed upwards or downwards. ■ n. a distinguished person. ■ adv. informal very well.
– PHRASES **the great and the good** often ironic distinguished and worthy people collectively. **great and small** of all sizes, classes, or types. **Great Scott!** expressing surprise or amazement.
– DERIVATIVES **greatness** n.
– ORIGIN Old English *grēat* 'big', of West Germanic origin.

great ape ■ n. a large ape of a family closely related to humans, including the gorilla and chimpanzees. [Family Pongidae.]

great-aunt ■ n. an aunt of one's father or mother.

great circle ■ n. a circle on the surface of a sphere which lies in a plane passing through the sphere's centre, especially as representing the shortest path between two given points on the sphere.

greatcoat ■ n. a long heavy overcoat.

Great Dane ■ n. a dog of a very large, powerful, short-haired breed.

great divide ■ n. **1** the boundary between two contrasting groups, cultures, etc., that is very difficult to overcome. **2** the boundary between life and death.

great-hearted ■ adj. dated having a noble and generous spirit.
– DERIVATIVES **great-heartedness** n.

greatly ■ adv. very much.

great-nephew ■ n. a son of one's nephew or niece.

great-niece ■ n. a daughter of one's nephew or niece.

great organ ■ n. the chief keyboard in a large organ and its related pipes and mechanism.

Great Place ■ n. S. African the official residence of an African king or traditional leader.

Great Russian ■ adj. & n. former term for RUSSIAN (language and people), as distinguished from other peoples and languages of the old Russian Empire.

Great Seal ■ n. a seal used for the authentication of state documents of the highest importance.

great tit ■ n. a titmouse common in Eurasia and NW Africa with a black and white head, grey back, and yellow breast. [*Parus major*.]

Great Trek ■ n. historical the migration by Boers in 1836–37 from the Cape Colony to the interior of South Africa. ▶ (usu. **great trek**) any long and arduous journey.

great-uncle ■ n. an uncle of one's mother or father.

great white shark ■ n. a very large predatory shark with a brownish or grey back and white underparts. [*Carcharodon carcharias*.]

grebe /griːb/ ■ n. a diving waterbird with a long neck, lobed toes, and a very short tail. [Family Podicipedidae: several species.]
– ORIGIN C18: from French *grèbe*.

Grecian ■ adj. of or relating to ancient Greece, especially its architecture.
– ORIGIN Middle English: from Latin *Graecia* 'Greece'.

Grecian nose ■ n. a straight nose that continues the line of the forehead without a dip.

Greco- ■ comb. form variant spelling of GRAECO-.

greed ■ n. intense and selfish desire for wealth, power, or food.
– ORIGIN C16: back-formation from GREEDY.

greedy ■ adj. (-ier, -iest) having or showing greed.
– DERIVATIVES **greedily** adv. **greediness** n.
– ORIGIN Old English, of Germanic origin.

Greek ■ n. 1 a native or national of Greece, or a person of Greek descent. ▶ a Greek-speaking native of one of the ancient city states of Greece and the eastern Mediterranean. 2 the ancient or modern Indo-European language of Greece. ■ adj. of or relating to Greece, its people, or their language.
– PHRASES **it's (all) Greek to me** informal I can't understand it at all.
– DERIVATIVES **Greekness** n.
– ORIGIN Old English *Grēcas* 'the Greeks', from Latin *Graeci*, from Greek *Graikoi*, which according to Aristotle was the prehistoric name of the Hellenes.

Greek coffee ■ n. very strong black coffee served with the fine grounds in it.

Greek cross ■ n. a cross of which all four arms are of equal length.

Greek fire ■ n. historical a combustible composition, probably based on naptha and quicklime, first used by the Greeks in Constantinople (673–8) to set fire to enemy ships.

Greek key ■ n. a pattern of interlocking right-angled spirals.

Greek Orthodox Church (also **Greek Church**) ■ n. the Eastern Orthodox Church which uses the Byzantine rite in Greek, in particular the national Church of Greece.

green ■ adj. 1 of the colour between blue and yellow in the spectrum; coloured like grass. 2 covered with grass or other vegetation. 3 (of a plant or fruit) young or unripe. ▶ (of food, wood, pottery, or leather) in its untreated or original state; not cured, seasoned, fired, etc. 4 inexperienced or naive. 5 pale and sickly-looking. 6 (usu. **Green**) concerned with or supporting protection of the environment as a political principle. 7 (of a ski run) of the lowest level of difficulty. ■ n. 1 green colour, pigment, or material. ▶ green foliage or growing plants. 2 a piece of common grassy land, especially in the centre of a village. ▶ an area of smooth, very short grass immediately surrounding a hole on a golf course. 3 (**greens**) green vegetables. 4 (usu. **Green**) a member or supporter of an environmentalist group or party. ■ v. 1 make or become green. 2 make less harmful to the environment.
– DERIVATIVES **greenish** adj. **greenly** adv. **greenness** n. **greeny** adj.
– ORIGIN Old English, of Germanic origin; rel. to GRASS and GROW.

green algae ■ pl. n. algae which contain chlorophyll and store starch in discrete chloroplasts. [Division Chlorophyta.]

green revolution

green and gold ■ n. (**the green and gold**) the colours worn by South African national sports teams.

greenback ■ n. US informal a dollar.

green belt ■ n. 1 an area of open land around a city, on which building is restricted. 2 a green belt marking a level of proficiency below that of a brown belt in judo, karate, or other martial arts.

Green Beret ■ n. informal a British commando or a member of the US Army Special Forces.

greenbottle ■ n. a metallic green fly which sometimes lays eggs in wounds on sheep or other animals. [*Lucilia caesar* and related species.]

green card ■ n. 1 (in the US) a permit allowing a foreign national to live and work permanently in the US. 2 (in the UK) an international insurance document for motorists.

greenery ■ n. green foliage or vegetation.

green-eyed monster ■ n. (**the green-eyed monster**) informal, humorous jealousy personified.
– ORIGIN from Shakespeare's *Othello* (III. 3. 166).

greenfeed ■ n. S. African & Austral./NZ forage grown to be fed fresh to livestock.

greenfield ■ adj. relating to or denoting previously undeveloped sites for commercial development.

greenfinch ■ n. a large Eurasian finch with green and yellow plumage. [*Carduelis chloris*.]

green fingers ■ pl. n. informal natural ability in growing plants.
– DERIVATIVES **green-fingered** adj.

greenfly ■ n. (pl. same or **-flies**) chiefly Brit. a green aphid.

greengage ■ n. 1 a sweet greenish fruit resembling a small plum. 2 the tree bearing this fruit. [*Prunus domestica*.]
– ORIGIN C18: named after the English botanist Sir William Gage.

greengrocer ■ n. a retailer of fruit and vegetables.
– DERIVATIVES **greengrocery** n.

greenhorn ■ n. informal, chiefly N. Amer. an inexperienced or naive person.

greenhouse ■ n. a glass building in which plants that need protection from cold weather are grown.

greenhouse effect ■ n. the trapping of the sun's warmth in a planet's lower atmosphere, due to the greater transparency of the atmosphere to visible radiation from the sun than to infrared radiation emitted from the planet's surface.

greenhouse gas ■ n. a gas, such as carbon dioxide, that contributes to the greenhouse effect by absorbing infrared.

greenie ■ n. informal, often derogatory a campaigner for Green issues.

green jersey ■ n. (in a cycling race involving stages) a green jersey worn each day by the rider accumulating the highest number of points, and presented at the end of the race to the rider with the highest overall points total.

Greenlander ■ n. an inhabitant of Greenland.

green light ■ n. a green traffic light giving permission to proceed. ▶ permission to go ahead with a project. ■ v. (**green-light**) give permission to go ahead with.

greenmail ■ n. Stock Exchange the practice of buying enough shares in a company to threaten a takeover, forcing the owners to buy them back at a higher price in order to retain control.
– DERIVATIVES **greenmailer** n.
– ORIGIN 1980s: blend of GREEN and BLACKMAIL.

green manure ■ n. growing plants ploughed back into the soil as fertilizer.

green mealies ■ n. chiefly S. African a variety of maize grown for human consumption, usually sold on the cob.

Green Paper ■ n. a preliminary report of government proposals published to stimulate discussion.

green pepper ■ n. the mild-flavoured unripe fruit of a sweet pepper.

green revolution ■ n. a large increase in crop

green room

production in developing countries achieved by the use of artificial fertilizers, pesticides, and high-yield crop varieties.

green room ■ n. a room in a theatre or studio in which performers can relax when they are not performing.

greensand ■ n. Geology a greenish kind of sandstone, often loosely consolidated.

greenshank ■ n. a large grey and white sandpiper with long greenish legs. [*Tringa nebularia*.]

greenstick fracture ■ n. a fracture of the bone, occurring typically in children, in which one side of the bone is broken and the other only bent.

greenstone ■ n. a greenish igneous rock containing feldspar and hornblende.

greensward /'griːnˌswɔːd/ ■ n. archaic or poetic/literary grass-covered ground.

green tea ■ n. tea made from unfermented leaves, produced mainly in China and Japan.

green thumb ■ n. North American term for GREEN FINGERS.

greenwash ■ n. disinformation disseminated by an organization so as to present an environmentally responsible public image.
– DERIVATIVES **greenwashing** n.
– ORIGIN from GREEN, on the pattern of *whitewash*.

greenway ■ n. N. Amer. a strip of undeveloped land near an urban area, set aside for recreational use or environmental protection.

Greenwich Mean Time ■ n. the mean solar time at the Greenwich meridian, adopted as the standard time in a zone that includes the British Isles.
– ORIGIN *Greenwich* in London, former site of the Royal Observatory.

Greenwich meridian ■ n. the meridian of zero longitude, passing through Greenwich.

greenwood ■ n. archaic a wood or forest in leaf, especially as a refuge for outlaws.

green woodpecker ■ n. a large Eurasian green and yellow woodpecker with a red crown and a laughing call. [*Picus viridis*.]

greet ■ v. 1 give a word or sign of welcome when meeting (someone). 2 receive or acknowledge in a specified way: *the idea was warmly greeted*. 3 (of a sight or sound) become apparent to (a person arriving somewhere).
– DERIVATIVES **greeter** n.
– ORIGIN Old English *grētan* 'approach, attack, or salute', of West Germanic origin.

greeting ■ n. 1 a word or sign of welcome or recognition. ▶ the action of greeting. 2 (usu. **greetings**) a formal expression of goodwill.

greeting card (Brit. **greetings card**) ■ n. a decorative card sent to convey good wishes.

gregarious /grɪˈɡɛːrɪəs/ ■ adj. 1 fond of company; sociable. 2 (of animals) living in flocks or colonies. 3 (of plants) growing in clusters.
– DERIVATIVES **gregariously** adv. **gregariousness** n.
– ORIGIN C17: from Latin *gregarius*, from *grex, greg-* 'a flock'.

Gregorian calendar /grɪˈɡɔːrɪən/ ■ n. the modified form of the Julian calendar introduced in 1582 by Pope Gregory XIII, and still used today.

Gregorian chant ■ n. medieval church plainsong.
– ORIGIN C18: named after St *Gregory* the Great (c.540–604).

greisen /ˈɡraɪz(ə)n/ ■ n. Geology a light-coloured rock resulting from the alteration of granite by hot vapour from magma.
– ORIGIN C19: from German, prob. a dialect word, from *greis* 'grey with age'.

gremlin ■ n. a mischievous sprite regarded as responsible for unexplained mechanical or electrical faults.
– ORIGIN 1940s: perhaps suggested by GOBLIN.

Grenache /ɡrəˈnaʃ/ ■ n. a variety of black wine grape native to the Languedoc-Roussillon region of France. ▶ a sweet red dessert wine made from this grape.
– ORIGIN from French.

grenade /ɡrəˈneɪd/ ■ n. 1 a small bomb thrown by hand or launched mechanically. 2 a glass receptacle containing chemicals which are released on impact, used for testing drains and extinguishing fires.
– ORIGIN C16 ('pomegranate', which the bomb supposedly resembled in shape): from French, alteration of Old French (*pome*) *grenate* (see POMEGRANATE), on the pattern of Spanish *granada*.

Grenadian /ɡrɪˈneɪdɪən/ ■ n. a native or inhabitant of the Caribbean country of Grenada. ■ adj. of or relating to Grenada.

grenadier /ˌɡrɛnəˈdɪə/ ■ n. 1 historical a soldier armed with grenades. 2 a common bottom-dwelling fish with a large head, a long tapering tail, and typically a luminous gland on the belly. [Family Macrouridae: numerous species.] 3 a reddish-brown African waxbill with a red bill and a bright blue rump. [Genus *Uraeginthus*: two species.]

grenadilla /ˌɡrɛnəˈdɪlə/ ■ n. variant spelling of GRANADILLA.

grenadine /ˈɡrɛnədiːn/ ■ n. a sweet cordial made in France from pomegranates.
– ORIGIN French: from *grenade* (see GRENADE).

Gresham's law ■ n. Economics the tendency for money of lower intrinsic value to circulate more freely than money of higher intrinsic and equal nominal value (often expressed as 'Bad money drives out good').
– ORIGIN from the name of the C16 English financier Sir Thomas *Gresham*.

grew past of GROW.

grewia /ˈɡruːɪə/ ■ n. a shrub or small tree of a genus that occurs in Africa, Asia, and Australia. [Genus *Grewia*: numerous species.]

grey (US **gray**) ■ adj. 1 of a colour intermediate between black and white, as of ashes or lead. 2 (of hair) turning grey or white with age. ▶ informal, chiefly N. Amer. relating to old people as a group: *grey power*. 3 (of the weather) cloudy and dull; without sun. 4 dull and nondescript: *grey, faceless men*. 5 (of financial or trading activity) not accounted for in official statistics: *the grey economy*. ■ n. grey colour or pigment. ■ v. (especially of hair) become grey with age.
– DERIVATIVES **greyish** adj. **greyly** adv. **greyness** n.
– ORIGIN Old English, of Germanic origin.

grey area ■ n. 1 an ill-defined area of activity not readily conforming to an existing category or set of rules. 2 S. African historical (under apartheid) a residential or business area in which racial segregation was not strictly enforced.

greybeard (US **graybeard**) ■ n. humorous or derogatory an old man.

grey eminence ■ n. another term for ÉMINENCE GRISE.

grey goods ■ pl. n. 1 computing equipment. Compare with BROWN GOODS, WHITE GOODS. 2 another term for PARALLEL IMPORTS.

greyhound ■ n. a dog of a swift, slender, keen-sighted breed, used in racing and coursing.
– ORIGIN Old English *grīghund*; the first element is rel. to Old Norse *grey* 'bitch'.

greylag ■ n. a large Eurasian goose with mainly grey plumage, the ancestor of the domestic goose. [*Anser anser*.]
– ORIGIN C18: prob. from GREY + dialect *lag* 'goose'.

grey matter ■ n. 1 the darker tissue of the brain and spinal cord, consisting mainly of nerve cell bodies and branching dendrites. 2 informal intelligence.

grey mullet ■ n. a thick-bodied, blunt-headed food fish of inshore or estuarine waters. [Family Mugilidae: several species.]

greyscale (US **grayscale**) ■ n. Computing a range of grey shades from white to black, as used in a monochrome display or printout.

grey seal ■ n. a large North Atlantic seal with a spotted greyish coat. [*Halichoerus grypus*.]

grey squirrel ■ n. a tree squirrel with mainly grey fur, native to eastern North America and introduced to South Africa and elsewhere. [*Sciurus carolinensis*.]

greywacke /ˈɡreɪwakə/ (US **graywacke**) ■ n. Geology a dark

coarse-grained sandstone containing more than 15 per cent clay.
– ORIGIN C18: from German *Grauwacke*, from *grau* 'grey' + WACKE.

grey water ■ n. technical the relatively clean waste water from baths, sinks, and washing machines. Compare with BLACK WATER.

grid ■ n. 1 a framework of spaced bars that are parallel to or cross each other. 2 a network of lines that cross each other to form a series of squares or rectangles. ▸ a numbered grid on a map that enables a place to be precisely located. 3 a network of cables or pipes for distributing power, especially high-voltage electricity. 4 a pattern of lines marking the starting places on a motor-racing track. ■ v. [usu. as adj. **gridded**] put into or set out as a grid.
– ORIGIN C19: back-formation from GRIDIRON.

griddle ■ n. 1 a circular iron plate that is heated and used for cooking food. 2 historical a miner's wire-bottomed sieve. ■ v. cook on a griddle.
– ORIGIN Middle English: from Old French *gredil*, from Latin *craticula*, diminutive of *cratis* 'hurdle'.

gridiron /ˈɡrɪdaɪən/ ■ n. 1 a frame of parallel metal bars used for grilling meat or fish over an open fire. 2 a frame of parallel beams for supporting a ship in dock. 3 a field for American football, marked with regularly spaced parallel lines. ▸ N. Amer. the game of American football. 4 a grid pattern, especially of streets.
– ORIGIN Middle English *gredire*, alteration of *gredile* 'griddle' by association with IRON.

gridlock ■ n. a traffic jam affecting a whole network of intersecting streets.
– DERIVATIVES **gridlocked** adj.

grief ■ n. 1 intense sorrow, especially caused by someone's death. 2 informal trouble or annoyance.
– PHRASES **come to grief** have an accident; meet with disaster. **good grief!** an exclamation of surprise or alarm.
– ORIGIN Middle English: from Old French *grief*, from *grever* (see GRIEVE).

grievance ■ n. a real or imagined cause for complaint.
– ORIGIN Middle English: from Old French *grevance*, from *grever* (see GRIEVE).

grieve ■ v. 1 suffer grief. 2 cause great distress to.
– ORIGIN Middle English: from Old French *grever* 'burden', from Latin *gravare*, from *gravis* 'heavy, serious'.

grievous ■ adj. formal (of something bad) very severe or serious.
– DERIVATIVES **grievously** adv. **grievousness** n.
– ORIGIN Middle English: from Old French *greveus*, from *grever* (see GRIEVE).

grievous bodily harm ■ n. Law serious physical injury inflicted on a person by the deliberate action of another, considered more serious than actual bodily harm.

griffin (also **gryphon** or **griffon**) ■ n. a mythical creature with the head and wings of an eagle and the body of a lion.
– ORIGIN Middle English: from late Latin *gryphus*, from Greek *grups*.

griffon /ˈɡrɪf(ə)n/ ■ n. 1 a dog of a small terrier-like breed. 2 (also **griffon vulture**) a large Old World vulture with predominantly pale brown plumage. [*Gyps fulvus* and related species.] 3 variant spelling of GRIFFIN.
– ORIGIN Middle English: var. of GRIFFIN.

grill[1] ■ n. 1 a device on a cooker that radiates heat downwards for cooking food. 2 a gridiron used for cooking food on an open fire. 3 a dish of food, especially meat, cooked using a grill. 4 a restaurant serving grilled food. ■ v. 1 cook with a grill. 2 informal subject to intense questioning or interrogation.
– DERIVATIVES **griller** n.
– ORIGIN C17: from French *gril* (n.), *griller* (v.), from Old French *graille* 'grille'.

grill[2] ■ n. variant spelling of GRILLE.

grille (also **grill**) ■ n. a grating or screen of metal bars or wires.
– ORIGIN C17: from French, from medieval Latin *craticula*, diminutive of *cratis* 'hurdle'; rel. to GRATE[2] and GRIDDLE.

grim ■ adj. (**grimmer**, **grimmest**) 1 very serious or gloomy; forbidding. ▸ (of humour) black or ironic. 2 unappealing, unattractive, or depressing.
– PHRASES **like** (or **for**) **grim death** with great determination.
– DERIVATIVES **grimly** adv. **grimness** n.
– ORIGIN Old English, of Germanic origin.

grimace /ˈɡrɪmeɪs, ɡrɪˈmeɪs/ ■ n. an ugly, twisted expression on a person's face, typically expressing disgust, pain, or wry amusement. ■ v. make a grimace.
– DERIVATIVES **grimacer** n.
– ORIGIN C17: from Spanish *grimazo* 'caricature', from *grima* 'fright'.

grimalkin /ɡrɪˈmalkɪn, -ˈmɔːl-/ ■ n. archaic 1 a cat. 2 a spiteful old woman.
– ORIGIN C16: from GREY + *Malkin* (familiar form of the given name *Matilda*).

grime ■ n. dirt ingrained on a surface. ■ v. blacken or make dirty with grime.
– DERIVATIVES **grimily** adv. **griminess** n. **grimy** adj. (-**ier**, -**iest**).
– ORIGIN Middle English: from Middle Low German and Middle Dutch.

Grimm's law ■ n. Linguistics the observation that certain consonants undergo regular changes in the Germanic languages which are not seen in others such as Greek or Latin.
– ORIGIN from the name of the German philologist and folklorist Jacob *Grimm*.

grimoire /ɡrɪmˈwɑː/ ■ n. a book of magic spells and invocations.
– ORIGIN C19: French, alteration of *grammaire* 'grammar'.

grin ■ v. (**grinned**, **grinning**) 1 smile broadly. 2 grimace grotesquely in a way that reveals the teeth. ■ n. a smile or grimace produced by grinning.
– PHRASES **grin and bear it** suffer pain or misfortune in a stoical manner.
– DERIVATIVES **grinner** n. **grinning** adj. **grinningly** adv.
– ORIGIN Old English *grennian* 'bare the teeth in pain or anger', of Germanic origin.

grind ■ v. (past and past part. **ground**) 1 reduce to small particles or powder by crushing. 2 sharpen, smooth, or produce by crushing or friction. ▸ operate (a mill or machine) by turning the handle. 3 (**grind someone down**) wear someone down with harsh treatment. ▸ (**grind something out**) produce something slowly and laboriously. ▸ [as adj. **grinding**] oppressive and seemingly endless: *grinding poverty*. 4 rub together gratingly. ▸ move noisily and laboriously. 5 (often **grind away**) work or study hard. 6 informal (of a dancer) rotate the hips. ■ n. 1 an act or process of grinding. 2 hard dull work: *the daily grind*.
– PHRASES **grind to a halt** (or **come to a grinding halt**) slow down gradually and then stop completely.
– DERIVATIVES **grinder** n. **grindingly** adv.
– ORIGIN Old English, prob. of Germanic origin.

grindstone ■ n. 1 a thick revolving disc of abrasive material used for sharpening or polishing metal objects. 2 a millstone.
– PHRASES **keep one's nose to the grindstone** work hard and continuously.

gringo /ˈɡrɪŋɡəʊ/ ■ n. (pl. -**os**) informal (in Latin America) a white English-speaking person.
– ORIGIN Spanish, 'foreign, foreigner, or gibberish'.

griot /ˈɡriːəʊ/ ■ n. a West African travelling poet, musician, and storyteller.
– ORIGIN French, earlier *guiriot*, perhaps from Portuguese *criado*.

grip ■ v. (**gripped**, **gripping**) 1 take and keep a firm hold of; grasp tightly. 2 deeply affect or afflict. ▸ [often as adj. **gripping**] compel the attention or interest of. ■ n. 1 a firm hold; a tight grasp or clasp. ▸ effective control. ▸ intellectual understanding. 2 a part or attachment by which something is held in the hand. ▸ a hairgrip. 3 a travelling bag. 4 a stage hand in a theatre. ▸ a member of a camera crew responsible for moving and setting up equipment.
– PHRASES **come** (or **get**) **to grips with** 1 engage in combat with. 2 begin to deal with or understand. **get** (or **take**) **a grip on** take control of. **lose one's grip** become unable to understand or control one's situation.
– DERIVATIVES **gripper** n. **grippingly** adv. **grippy** adj.
– ORIGIN Old English *grippa* (v.), *gripe* 'grasp, clutch' (n.), *gripa* 'handful, sheath'.

gripe

gripe ▪ v. **1** informal express a trivial complaint; grumble. **2** affect with gastric or intestinal pain. **3** archaic grasp tightly; clutch. ▪ n. **1** informal a trivial complaint. **2** gastric or intestinal pain; colic.
– DERIVATIVES **griper** n.
– ORIGIN Old English *grīpan* 'grasp, clutch', of Germanic origin; rel. to GRIP and GROPE.

gripe water ▪ n. S. African & Brit. trademark a solution given to babies for the relief of colic, wind, and indigestion.

grippe /grɪp/ ▪ n. dated influenza.
– ORIGIN C18: French, from *gripper* 'seize'.

Griqua /ˈgriːkwə/ ▪ n. (pl. same or **Griquas**) a member of a South African people of mixed European and Khoikhoi origin.
– ORIGIN the name in Nama.

griseofulvin /ˌgrɪziːə(ʊ)ˈfʊlvɪn/ ▪ n. Medicine an antibiotic used against fungal infections of the hair and skin.
– ORIGIN 1930s: from modern Latin (*Penicillium*) *griseofulvum* (the source bacterium), from medieval Latin *griseus* 'greyish' + Latin *fulvus* 'reddish yellow'.

gris-gris /ˈgriːgriː/ ▪ n. (pl. same) **1** an African or Caribbean charm or amulet. **2** the use of such charms, especially in voodoo.
– ORIGIN C17: from French *grisgris*, of West African origin.

grisly /ˈgrɪzli/ ▪ adj. (**-ier**, **-iest**) causing horror or revulsion.
– DERIVATIVES **grisliness** n.
– ORIGIN Old English *grislic* 'terrifying', of Germanic origin.

grissini /grɪˈsiːni/ ▪ pl. n. thin, crisp breadsticks.
– ORIGIN from Italian.

grist ▪ n. **1** corn that is ground to make flour. **2** malt crushed to make mash for brewing.
– PHRASES **grist to the mill** useful experience or knowledge.
– ORIGIN Old English, 'grinding', of Germanic origin; rel. to GRIND.

gristle /ˈgrɪs(ə)l/ ▪ n. cartilage, especially when found as tough inedible tissue in meat.
– DERIVATIVES **gristly** adj.
– ORIGIN Old English.

grit ▪ n. **1** small loose particles of stone or sand. **2** (also **gritstone**) a coarse sandstone. **3** courage and resolve. ▪ v. (**gritted**, **gritting**) **1** clench (the teeth), especially in order to keep one's resolve. **2** spread grit on (an icy road). **3** move with or make a grating sound.
– DERIVATIVES **gritter** n.
– ORIGIN Old English, of Germanic origin.

grits ▪ pl. n. US coarsely ground maize kernels, served boiled with water or milk.
– ORIGIN Old English *grytt*, *grytte* 'bran, mill dust', of Germanic origin.

gritty ▪ adj. (**-ier**, **-iest**) **1** containing or covered with grit. **2** showing courage and resolve. ▸ tough and uncompromising: *a gritty look at urban life*.
– DERIVATIVES **grittily** adv. **grittiness** n.

grivet monkey /ˈgrɪvɪt/ ▪ n. another term for VERVET MONKEY.
– ORIGIN C19: from French.

grizzle[1] ▪ v. informal (of a child) cry or whimper fretfully.
– DERIVATIVES **grizzler** n.
– ORIGIN C18 ('show the teeth, grin').

grizzle[2] ▪ n. a mixture of dark and white hairs.
– ORIGIN Middle English: from Old French *grisel*, from *gris* 'grey'.

grizzled ▪ adj. having grey or grey-streaked hair.

grizzly bear ▪ n. a brown bear of a large race often with white-tipped fur, native to western North America.
– ORIGIN C19: *grizzly* from GRIZZLE[2].

groan ▪ v. **1** make a deep inarticulate sound in response to pain or despair. **2** make a low creaking sound when pressure or weight is applied. ▪ (**groan beneath/under**) be oppressed by. ▪ n. a groaning sound.
– DERIVATIVES **groaner** n. **groaning** adj. **groaningly** adv.
– ORIGIN Old English, of Germanic origin.

groat ▪ n. historical an English silver coin worth four old pence.

– ORIGIN from Middle Dutch *groot* or Middle Low German *grōte* 'great, thick', hence 'thick penny'.

groats ▪ pl. n. hulled or crushed grain, especially oats.
– ORIGIN Old English: rel. to GRIT and GRITS.

grocer ▪ n. a person who sells food and small household goods.
– ORIGIN Middle English (orig. 'a person who sold things by the gross'): from Old French *grossier*, from medieval Latin *grossarius*, from late Latin *grossus* 'gross'.

grocery ▪ n. (pl. **-ies**) **1** a grocer's shop or business. **2** (**groceries**) items of food sold in a grocer's shop or supermarket.

grog ▪ n. spirits (originally rum) mixed with water. ▸ informal alcoholic drink.
– ORIGIN C18: said to be from *Old Grog*, the reputed nickname of Admiral Vernon (because of his grogram (coarse fabric) cloak), who ordered diluted (instead of neat) rum to be served out to sailors.

groggy ▪ adj. (**-ier**, **-iest**) dazed and unsteady after intoxication, sleep, etc.
– DERIVATIVES **groggily** adv. **grogginess** n.

groin[1] ▪ n. **1** the area between the abdomen and the thigh on either side of the body. ▸ informal the region of the genitals. **2** Architecture a curved edge formed by two intersecting vaults.
– DERIVATIVES **groined** adj. (Architecture).
– ORIGIN Middle English, perhaps from Old English *grynde* 'depression, abyss'.

groin[2] ▪ n. US spelling of GROYNE.

grommet /ˈgrɒmɪt/ ▪ n. **1** a protective eyelet in a hole that a rope or cable passes through. **2** Medicine a tube surgically implanted in the eardrum to drain fluid from the middle ear.
– ORIGIN C17 ('a circle of rope used as a fastening'): from obsolete French *grommette*, from *gourmer* 'to curb'.

groom ▪ v. **1** brush and clean the coat of (a horse or dog). ▸ give a neat and tidy appearance to. **2** prepare or train for a particular purpose or activity. ▪ n. **1** a person employed to take care of horses. **2** a bridegroom.
– ORIGIN Middle English ('boy', later 'man, male servant').

groomsman ▪ n. (pl. **-men**) a male friend officially attending the bridegroom at a wedding.

groove ▪ n. **1** a long, narrow cut or depression in a hard material. ▸ a spiral track cut in a gramophone record, into which the stylus fits. **2** an established routine or habit. **3** informal a rhythmic pattern in popular or jazz music. ▪ v. **1** make a groove or grooves in. **2** informal dance to or play popular or jazz music. ▸ enjoy oneself.
– PHRASES **in** (or **into**) **the groove** informal **1** performing confidently. **2** enjoying oneself, especially by dancing.
– DERIVATIVES **grooved** adj.
– ORIGIN Middle English: from Dutch *groeve* 'furrow, pit'; rel. to GRAVE[1].

groovy ▪ adj. (**-ier**, **-iest**) informal, dated or humorous fashionable and exciting.
– DERIVATIVES **groovily** adv. **grooviness** n.

grope ▪ v. **1** feel about or search blindly or uncertainly with the hands. **2** informal feel or fondle (someone) for sexual pleasure, especially against their will. ▪ n. informal an act of groping someone.
– DERIVATIVES **groper** n. **groping** adj. **gropingly** adv.
– ORIGIN Old English, of West Germanic origin; rel. to GRIPE.

grosbeak /ˈgrəʊsbiːk/ ▪ n. a finch or related songbird with a stout conical bill and brightly coloured plumage. [Several species in the families Fringillidae and Emberizidae.]
– ORIGIN C17: from French *grosbec*, from *gros* 'big, fat' + *bec* 'beak'.

grosgrain /ˈgrəʊɡreɪn/ ▪ n. a heavy ribbed fabric, typically of silk or rayon.
– ORIGIN C19: French, 'coarse grain'.

gros point /ɡrəʊ ˈpwɑ̃/ ▪ n. a type of needlepoint embroidery consisting of stitches crossing two or more threads of the canvas in each direction.
– ORIGIN C19: French, 'large stitch', from *gros point de Venise*, a type of lace orig. from Venice.

gross ▪ adj. **1** unattractively large or bloated. **2** vulgar; unrefined. ▸ informal very unpleasant; repulsive. **3** complete; blatant: *a gross exaggeration*. **4** (of income,

profit, or interest) without deduction of tax or other contributions; total. Often contrasted with NET². ▸ (of weight) including contents or other variable items; overall. ■ adv. without tax or other contributions having been deducted. ■ v. 1 produce or earn (an amount of money) as gross profit or income. ▸ (**gross something up**) add deductions such as tax to a net amount. 2 (**gross someone out**) informal, chiefly N. Amer. disgust someone with repulsive behaviour or appearance. ■ n. 1 (pl. same) an amount equal to twelve dozen; 144. 2 (pl. **grosses**) a gross profit or income.
– DERIVATIVES **grossly** adv. **grossness** n.
– ORIGIN Middle English: from Old French *gros, grosse* 'large', from late Latin *grossus*; sense 1 of noun from French *grosse douzaine* 'large dozen'.

gross domestic product ■ n. the total value of goods produced and services provided within a country during one year.

gross national income ■ n. another term for GROSS NATIONAL PRODUCT.

gross national product ■ n. the total value of goods produced and services provided by a country during one year, equal to the gross domestic product plus the net income from foreign investments.

grot¹ ■ n. Brit. informal something unpleasant, dirty, or of poor quality; rubbish.
– ORIGIN 1960s: back-formation from GROTTY.

grot² ■ n. poetic/literary a grotto.
– ORIGIN C16: from Italian *grotta*, from Greek *kruptē* 'vault, crypt'.

grotesque /grə(ʊ)ˈtɛsk/ ■ adj. 1 comically or repulsively ugly or distorted. 2 shockingly incongruous or inappropriate. ■ n. 1 a grotesque figure or image. 2 a style of decorative painting or sculpture consisting of the interweaving of human and animal forms with flowers and foliage.
– DERIVATIVES **grotesquely** adv. **grotesqueness** n.
– ORIGIN C16: from Italian *grottesca*, from *opera* or *pittura grottesca* 'work or painting resembling that found in a grotto'.

grotesquerie /grəʊˈtɛskəri/ ■ n. (pl. **-ies**) grotesque quality or things.

grotto ■ n. (pl. **-oes** or **-os**) a small picturesque cave, especially an artificial one in a park or garden.
– DERIVATIVES **grottoed** adj.
– ORIGIN C17: from Italian *grotta*, from Greek *kruptē* (see CRYPT).

grotty ■ adj. (**-ier, -iest**) informal 1 unpleasant and of poor quality. 2 unwell.
– DERIVATIVES **grottiness** n.
– ORIGIN 1960s: from GROTESQUE.

grouch /ɡraʊtʃ/ informal ■ n. 1 a habitually grumpy person. 2 a complaint or grumble. ■ v. complain ill-temperedly; grumble.
– ORIGIN C19: var. of obsolete *grutch*, from Old French *grouchier* 'to grumble, murmur'.

grouchy ■ adj. (**-ier, -iest**) irritable and bad-tempered; grumpy.
– DERIVATIVES **grouchily** adv. **grouchiness** n.

ground¹ ■ n. 1 the solid surface of the earth. ▸ a limited or defined extent of land: *15 hectares of adjoining ground*. ▸ land of a specified kind: *marshy ground*. ▸ an area of land or sea with a specified use: *fishing grounds*. ▸ (**grounds**) an area of enclosed land surrounding a large house. ▸ Brit. the floor of a room. 2 (**grounds**) factors forming a basis for action or the justification for a belief. 3 a prepared surface to which paint or other decoration is applied. ▸ a substance used to prepare a surface for painting. ▸ a piece of wood fixed to a wall as a base for boards, plaster, or joinery. 4 (**grounds**) solid particles, especially of coffee, which form a residue. 5 N. Amer. electrical connection to the earth. ■ v. 1 prohibit or prevent (a pilot or aircraft) from flying. ▸ informal, chiefly N. Amer. (of a parent) refuse to allow (a child) to go out socially, as a punishment. 2 run (a ship) aground. 3 (usu. **be grounded in**) give a firm theoretical or practical basis to. ▸ [as adj. **grounded**] well balanced and sensible. 4 place on the ground or touch the ground with. 5 N. Amer. connect (an electrical device) with the ground.
– PHRASES **be thick** (or **thin**) **on the ground** exist in large (or small) numbers or amounts. **break new ground** be innovative. **gain ground 1** become more popular or accepted. **2** (usu. **gain ground on**) get closer to someone being pursued. **get off the ground** start happening or functioning successfully. **give** (or **lose**) **ground** retreat or lose one's advantage. **go to ground** (of a fox or other animal) enter its earth or burrow. **hold** (or **stand**) **one's ground** not retreat or lose one's advantage. **on the ground** in a place where real, practical work is done. **on one's own ground** in one's own territory or area of knowledge. **work** (or **run**) **oneself into the ground** exhaust oneself by working or running very hard.
– ORIGIN Old English, of Germanic origin.

ground² past and past participle of GRIND.

groundbait ■ n. bait thrown into the water while fishing.
– DERIVATIVES **groundbaiting** n.

ground ball ■ n. Baseball a ball hit along the ground.

ground bass ■ n. Music a short bass theme which is constantly repeated as the other parts of the music vary.

ground-breaking ■ adj. innovative; pioneering.
– DERIVATIVES **ground-breaker** n.

ground control ■ n. [treated as sing. or pl.] the personnel and equipment that monitor and direct the flight and landing of aircraft or spacecraft.
– DERIVATIVES **ground controller** n.

ground cover ■ n. low-growing, spreading plants that help to stop weeds growing.

ground effect ■ n. the aerodynamic buoyancy produced by a cushion of air below a vehicle moving close to the ground.

grounder ■ n. Baseball a ground ball.

ground floor ■ n. the floor of a building at ground level.

ground frost ■ n. Brit. frost formed on the surface of the ground or in the top layer of soil.

ground glass ■ n. 1 glass with a smooth ground surface that renders it non-transparent. 2 glass ground into an abrasive powder.

groundhog ■ n. North American term for WOODCHUCK.

grounding ■ n. basic training or instruction in a subject.

ground ivy ■ n. a creeping plant of the mint family, with bluish-purple flowers. [*Glechoma hederacea.*]

groundless ■ adj. not based on any good reason.
– DERIVATIVES **groundlessly** adv. **groundlessness** n.

groundling /ˈɡraʊn(d)lɪŋ/ ■ n. a fish that lives at the bottom of lakes and streams, especially a gudgeon or loach.

groundmass ■ n. Geology the compact, finer-grained material in which the crystals are embedded in a porphyritic rock.

groundnut ■ n. 1 another term for PEANUT. 2 a North American plant of the pea family with a sweet edible tuber. [*Apios tuberosa.*]

ground rule ■ n. a basic principle established to regulate action or facilitate cooperation.

groundsel /ˈɡraʊn(d)s(ə)l/ ■ n. a plant of the daisy family with small yellow rayless flowers. [*Senecio vulgaris* and related species.]
– ORIGIN Old English *gundæswelgiæ*, prob. from *gund* 'pus' + *swelgan* 'to swallow' (with ref. to its use in poultices).

groundsheet ■ n. a waterproof sheet spread on the ground under a tent.

groundskeeper ■ n. North American term for GROUNDSMAN.

ground sloth ■ n. a very large extinct terrestrial edentate mammal of the Cenozoic era in America.

groundsman ■ n. (pl. **-men**) a person who maintains a sports ground or the grounds of a large building.

ground speed ■ n. an aircraft's speed relative to the ground.

ground squirrel ■ n. 1 an African burrowing squirrel, which lives in colonies. [Genus *Xerus*: several species.] 2 a burrowing northern squirrel of a large group including the sousliks and chipmunks. [*Spermophilus* and other genera.]

ground state ■ n. Physics the lowest energy state of an atom or other particle.

groundstroke ■ n. Tennis a stroke played after the ball has bounced, as opposed to a volley.

groundswell /ˈɡraʊn(d)ˌswɛl/ ■ n. **1** a build-up of opinion in a large section of the population. **2** a large or extensive swell in the sea.

groundwater ■ n. water held underground in the soil or in pores and crevices in rock.

ground wave ■ n. a radio wave which reaches a receiver from a transmitter directly, without reflection from the ionosphere.

groundwork ■ n. preliminary or basic work.

ground zero ■ n. the point on the earth's surface directly above or below an exploding nuclear bomb.

group ■ n. [treated as sing. or pl.] **1** a number of people or things located, gathered, or classed together. **2** a number of musicians who play popular music together. **3** Chemistry a set of elements occupying a column in the periodic table and having broadly similar properties. **4** Chemistry a combination of atoms having a recognizable identity in a number of compounds. **5** a division of an air force, usually consisting of two or more stations. ■ v. place in or form a group or groups.
– DERIVATIVES **grouping** n.
– ORIGIN C17: from French *groupe*, from Italian *gruppo*, of Germanic origin; rel. to CROP.

group area ■ n. S. African historical (under apartheid) a residential area demarcated for occupation by a particular ethnic group.

group captain ■ n. a rank of officer in the RAF, above wing commander and below air commodore.

group dynamics ■ pl. n. Psychology the processes involved when people in a group interact with each other.

grouper ■ n. a large heavy-bodied fish of the sea bass family, found in warm seas. [*Epinephelus*, *Mycteroperca*, and other genera.]
– ORIGIN C17: from Portuguese *garoupa*, prob. from a local term in South America.

groupie ■ n. informal a person who devotedly follows a pop group or celebrity, especially in the hope of a sexual relationship with them.

group therapy ■ n. a form of psychiatric therapy in which patients meet to discuss their problems.

groupthink ■ n. chiefly N. Amer. unchallenged, poor-quality decision-making by a group.

group velocity ■ n. Physics the speed at which the energy of a wave travels.

groupware ■ n. Computing software designed to facilitate collective working by a number of different users.

grouse[1] ■ n. (pl. same) a medium-sized game bird with a plump body and feathered legs. [*Lagopus lagopus* (red or willow grouse) and other species.]
– ORIGIN C16: perhaps rel. to medieval Latin *gruta* or to Old French *grue* 'crane'.

grouse[2] ■ v. complain pettily; grumble. ■ n. a grumble or complaint.
– DERIVATIVES **grouser** n.
– ORIGIN C19: cf. GROUCH.

grout /ɡraʊt/ ■ n. a mortar or paste for filling crevices, especially the gaps between wall or floor tiles. ■ v. fill in with grout.
– DERIVATIVES **grouter** n. **grouting** n.
– ORIGIN C17: perhaps from obsolete *grouts* 'sediment, dregs, grounds' or rel. to French dialect *grouter* 'grout a wall'.

grove ■ n. a small wood, orchard, or group of trees.
– ORIGIN Old English, of Germanic origin.

grovel ■ v. (grovelled, grovelling; US groveled, groveling) **1** crouch or crawl abjectly on the ground. **2** act obsequiously to obtain forgiveness or favour.
– DERIVATIVES **groveller** n. **grovelling** adj. **grovellingly** adv.
– ORIGIN Middle English: back-formation from the obsolete adv. *grovelling*, from obsolete *groof*, *grufe* 'the face or front', from Old Norse *á grúfu* 'face downwards'.

grow /ɡrəʊ/ ■ v. (past **grew** /ɡruː/ ; past part. **grown** /ɡrəʊn/) **1** (of a living thing) undergo natural development by increasing in size and changing physically. ▸ (**grow up**) advance to maturity; become an adult. ▸ (**grow out of**) or **into** become too large (or large enough) to wear. **2** (of a plant) germinate and develop. ▸ produce by cultivation. **3** become larger or greater over a period of time; increase. **4** become gradually or increasingly: *we grew braver*. **5** (**grow on**) become gradually more appealing to.
– DERIVATIVES **growable** adj. **grower** n.
– ORIGIN Old English, of Germanic origin.

growing pains ■ pl. n. **1** neuralgic pains occurring in the limbs of young children. **2** difficulties experienced in the early stages of an enterprise.

growl ■ v. **1** (especially of a dog) make a low guttural sound of hostility in the throat. **2** say something in a low grating voice. **3** make a low or harsh rumbling sound. ■ n. a growling sound.
– DERIVATIVES **growling** n. & adj. **growlingly** adv.
– ORIGIN C17: prob. imitative.

growler ■ n. **1** a person or thing that growls. **2** a small iceberg.

grown past participle of GROW.

grown-up ■ adj. adult. ■ n. informal an adult.

growth ■ n. **1** the process of growing. **2** something that has grown or is growing. ▸ Medicine & Biology a tumour or other abnormal formation. **3** a vineyard or crop of grapes of a specified classification of quality.

growth factor ■ n. Biology a substance, such as a vitamin or hormone, which is required for the stimulation of growth in living cells.

growth hormone ■ n. a hormone which stimulates growth in animal or plant cells.

growth industry ■ n. an industry that is developing particularly rapidly.

growth ring ■ n. a concentric layer of wood, shell, or bone developed during an annual or other regular period of growth.

growth stock ■ n. a company stock that tends to increase in capital value rather than yield high income.

groyne (US **groin**) ■ n. a low wall or barrier built out into the sea from a beach to check erosion and drifting.
– ORIGIN C16: from dialect *groin* 'snout', from Old French *groign*, from late Latin *grunium* 'pig's snout'.

GRP ■ abbrev. glass-reinforced plastic.

grt ■ abbrev. gross registered tonnage.

grub ■ n. **1** the larva of an insect, especially a beetle. ▸ a maggot or small caterpillar. **2** informal food. ■ v. (**grubbed**, **grubbing**) **1** dig shallowly in soil. ▸ (**grub something up**) dig something up. **2** search clumsily and unmethodically; rummage. **3** do demeaning or humiliating work in order to achieve something.
– ORIGIN Middle English: perhaps rel. to Dutch *grobbelen*, also to GRAVE[1].

grubber ■ n. **1** a person who is determined to amass something, especially in an unscrupulous manner: *a money-grubber*. **2** an implement for digging up plants. **3** (in ball games) a ball that runs closely along the ground.

grubby ■ adj. (**-ier**, **-iest**) **1** dirty; grimy. **2** disreputable; sordid.
– DERIVATIVES **grubbily** adv. **grubbiness** n.

grub screw ■ n. a small headless screw, used typically to attach a handle to a spindle.

grudge ■ n. a persistent feeling of ill will or resentment resulting from a past insult or injury. ■ v. **1** be resentfully unwilling to grant or allow (something). **2** feel resentful that (someone) has achieved (something).
– DERIVATIVES **grudger** n. **grudging** adj. **grudgingly** adv. **grudgingness** n.
– ORIGIN Middle English: var. of obsolete *grutch* 'complain, murmur, grumble', from Old French *grouchier*.

gruel ■ n. a thin liquid food of oatmeal or other meal boiled in milk or water.
– ORIGIN Middle English: from Old French, of Germanic origin.

gruelling (US **grueling**) ■ adj. extremely tiring and demanding.
– DERIVATIVES **gruellingly** adv.

−ORIGIN C19: from *gruel* 'exhaust, punish', from an old phr. *get one's gruel* 'receive one's punishment'.

gruesome ■ adj. causing repulsion or horror; grisly.
▸ informal extremely unpleasant.
−DERIVATIVES **gruesomely** adv. **gruesomeness** n.
−ORIGIN C16: from Scottish *grue* 'to feel horror, shudder', of Scandinavian origin.

gruff ■ adj. **1** (of a voice) rough and low in pitch. **2** abrupt or taciturn in manner.
−DERIVATIVES **gruffly** adv. **gruffness** n.
−ORIGIN C15: from Flemish and Dutch *grof* 'coarse, rude', of West Germanic origin.

grumble ■ v. **1** complain or protest in a bad-tempered but muted way. **2** make a low rumbling sound. **3** [as adj. **grumbling**] (of an internal organ) giving intermittent discomfort. ■ n. an instance of grumbling; a complaint.
−DERIVATIVES **grumbler** n. **grumblingly** adv. **grumbly** adj.
−ORIGIN C16: from obsolete *grumme*, prob. of Germanic origin.

grump informal ■ n. **1** a grumpy person. **2** a fit of sulking. ■ v. act in a sulky, grumbling manner.
−DERIVATIVES **grumpish** adj. **grumpishly** adv.
−ORIGIN C18: imitating inarticulate sounds expressing displeasure.

grumpy ■ adj. (**-ier**, **-iest**) bad-tempered and sulky.
−DERIVATIVES **grumpily** adv. **grumpiness** n.

grunge ■ n. **1** chiefly N. Amer. grime; dirt. **2** a style of rock music characterized by a raucous guitar sound and lazy vocal delivery. **3** a casual style of fashion including loose, layered clothing and ripped jeans.
−DERIVATIVES **grunginess** n. **grungy** adj.
−ORIGIN 1970s: back-formation from *grungy*, perhaps suggested by **GRUBBY** and **DINGY**.

grunt ■ v. **1** (of an animal, especially a pig) make a low, short guttural sound. **2** make a low inarticulate sound to express effort or indicate assent. ■ n. **1** a grunting sound. **2** informal, chiefly N. Amer. a low-ranking soldier or other worker. **3** informal power, especially in a motor vehicle. **4** another term for **GRUNTER**.
−ORIGIN Old English, of Germanic origin; prob. orig. imitative.

grunter ■ n. an important food fish of tropical coasts and reefs that makes a loud grunting noise when captured. [Family Haemulidae: many species.]

gruntled ■ adj. humorous pleased; satisfied.
−ORIGIN 1930s: back-formation from **DISGRUNTLED**.

Gruyère /ˈɡruːjeː/ ■ n. a firm, tangy Swiss cheese.
−ORIGIN named after *Gruyère*, a district in Switzerland.

gryphon ■ n. variant spelling of **GRIFFIN**.

grysbok /ˈɡrʌɪsbɒk, ˈxreɪs-/ ■ n. a small mainly nocturnal southern African antelope, the males of which have small vertical horns. [Genus *Raphicerus*: two species.]
−ORIGIN C18: from Afrikaans, from Dutch *grijs* 'grey' + *bok* 'buck'.

GSM ■ abbrev. Global System for Mobile.

gsm ■ abbrev. grams per square metre.

GSOH ■ abbrev. good sense of humour.

G-spot ■ n. a sensitive area of the anterior wall of the vagina believed by some to be highly erogenous.
−ORIGIN 1944 (as *Gräfenberg spot*): G from *Gräfenberg* and Dickinson, who first described it.

GSR ■ abbrev. galvanic skin response.

G-string (also **gee-string**) ■ n. a skimpy undergarment covering the genitals, consisting of a narrow strip of cloth attached to a waistband.

G-suit ■ n. a garment with inflatable pressurized pouches, worn by fighter pilots and astronauts to enable them to withstand high gravitational forces.
−ORIGIN 1940s: from *g* (symbol of *gravity*) + **SUIT**.

GT ■ n. a high-performance car.
−ORIGIN 1960s: abbrev. of Italian *gran turismo* 'great touring'.

Gt ■ abbrev. Great.

GTi ■ n. a GT car with a fuel-injected engine.

guacamole /ˌɡwɑːkəˈməʊleɪ, -li/ ■ n. a dish of mashed avocado mixed with chilli peppers, tomatoes, etc.
−ORIGIN Latin American Spanish: from Nahuatl *ahuacamolli*, from *ahuacatl* 'avocado' + *molli* 'sauce'.

guard cell

Guadeloupian /ˌɡwɑːdəˈluːpɪən/ ■ n. a native or inhabitant of Guadeloupe, a group of islands in the Lesser Antilles. ■ adj. of or relating to Guadeloupe.

guanaco /ɡwəˈnɑːkəʊ/ ■ n. (pl. **-os**) a wild Andean mammal similar to the domestic llama, with a valuable pale brown pelt. [*Lama guanicoe*.]
−ORIGIN C17: from Quechua *huanacu*.

guanine /ˈɡwɑːniːn/ ■ n. Biochemistry a compound that occurs in guano and fish scales, and is one of the four constituent bases of nucleic acids.

guano /ˈɡwɑːnəʊ/ ■ n. (pl. **-os**) **1** the excrement of seabirds. **2** an artificial fertilizer resembling natural guano, especially one made from fish.
−ORIGIN C17: from Spanish, or from Latin American Spanish *huano*, from Quechua *huanu* 'dung'.

guanosine /ˈɡwɑːnəsiːn/ ■ n. Biochemistry a nucleoside consisting of guanine combined with ribose.

guar /ɡwɑː/ ■ n. a drought-resistant African and Asian plant grown as a vegetable and for gum used in the food and paper industries. [*Cyamopsis tetragonoloba*.]
−ORIGIN C19: from Hindi *guār*.

Guarani /ˌɡwɑːrəˈniː/ ■ n. (pl. same) **1** a member of an American Indian people of Paraguay and adjacent regions. **2** the Tupi-Guarani language of this people.
−ORIGIN from Spanish.

guarantee ■ n. **1** a formal assurance that certain conditions will be fulfilled, especially that restitution will be made if a product is not of a specified quality. **2** something that gives a certainty of outcome. **3** variant spelling of **GUARANTY**. **4** less common term for **GUARANTOR**. ■ v. (**guarantees**, **guaranteed**, **guaranteeing**) **1** provide a guarantee: *the company guarantees to refund your money.* ▸ provide a guarantee for (a product). ▸ provide financial security for; underwrite. **2** promise with certainty.
−ORIGIN C17: perhaps from Spanish *garante*, corresponding to French *garant* (see **WARRANT**), later influenced by French *garantie* 'guaranty'.

guarantee fund ■ n. a sum of money pledged as a contingent indemnity for loss.

guarantor /ˌɡar(ə)nˈtɔː/ ■ n. a person or organization that gives or acts as a guarantee.

guaranty /ˈɡar(ə)nti/ (also **guarantee**) ■ n. (pl. **-ies**) an undertaking to answer for the payment of a debt or for the performance of an obligation by another person liable in the first instance. ▸ a thing serving as security for such an undertaking.
−ORIGIN C16: from Old French *garantie*, from *garantir*; rel. to **WARRANT**.

guard ■ v. **1** watch over in order to keep safe; protect.
▸ watch over in order to control or restrict. **2** (**guard against**) take precautions against. **3** Basketball stay close to (an opponent) to prevent them getting or passing the ball. ■ n. **1** a person, especially a soldier, who guards or keeps watch. ▸ N. Amer. a prison warder. **2** [treated as sing. or pl.] a body of soldiers serving to protect a place or person.
▸ (**Guards**) the household troops of the British army. **3** a device worn or fitted to prevent injury or damage. **4** (often in phr. **on** (or **off**) **guard**) a defensive posture adopted in a fight. ▸ a state of vigilance against adverse circumstances: *he let his guard slip.* **5** Brit. an official who rides on and is in general charge of a train. **6** Basketball each of two players chiefly responsible for marking opposing players.
7 American Football each of two players either side of the centre.
−PHRASES **guard of honour** a group of soldiers ceremonially welcoming an important visitor. **take guard** Cricket (of a batsman) stand in position ready to receive the ball.
−ORIGIN Middle English: from Old French *garde* (n.), *garder* (v.), of West Germanic origin.

guardant /ˈɡɑːd(ə)nt/ ■ adj. Heraldry (of an animal) depicted with the body sideways and the face towards the viewer.

guard cell ■ n. Botany each of a pair of curved cells that surround a stoma.

guarded ■ adj. cautious and having possible reservations: *he gave a guarded welcome to the idea.*
– DERIVATIVES **guardedly** adv. **guardedness** n.

guard hair ■ n. long, coarse hair forming an animal's outer fur.

guardhouse ■ n. a building used to accommodate a military guard or to detain military prisoners.

guardian ■ n. **1** a defender, protector, or keeper. **2** a person legally responsible for someone unable to manage their own affairs, especially a child whose parents have died.
– DERIVATIVES **guardianship** n.
– ORIGIN Middle English: from Old French *garden*, of Germanic origin; cf. WARDEN.

guardian angel ■ n. a spirit that is thought to watch over and protect a person or place.

guard rail ■ n. a rail that prevents people from falling off or being hit by something.

guardroom ■ n. a room in a military base used to accommodate a guard or detain prisoners.

guardsman ■ n. (pl. -**men**) **1** (in the UK) a soldier of a regiment of Guards. **2** (in the US) a member of the National Guard.

guard's van ■ n. Brit. a carriage or wagon occupied by the guard on a train.

guarri /'gwari/ (also **guarrie**) ■ n. a shrub or small tree with berry-like fruits that occurs in Africa and Arabia. [Genus *Euclea*: several species.]
– ORIGIN from Khoikhoi.

Guatemalan /,gwɑːtəˈmɑːlən/ ■ n. a native or inhabitant of Guatemala in Central America. ■ adj. of or relating to Guatemala.

guava /'gwɑːvə/ ■ n. **1** a tropical American fruit with pink juicy flesh and a strong, sweet aroma. **2** the small tree which bears this fruit. [*Psidium guajava* and related species.]
– ORIGIN C16: from Spanish *guayaba*, prob. from Taino (an extinct Caribbean language).

gubbins ■ pl. n. informal, chiefly Brit. **1** [treated as sing. or pl.] miscellaneous items; paraphernalia; rubbish. **2** [treated as sing.] a gadget.
– ORIGIN C16: from obsolete *gobbon* 'piece, slice, gob', from Old French.

gubernatorial /,g(j)uːbənəˈtɔːrɪəl/ ■ adj. of or relating to a governor, particularly that of a state in the US.
– ORIGIN C18: from Latin *gubernator* 'governor'.

gudgeon /'gʌdʒ(ə)n/ ■ n. **1** a small freshwater fish often used as bait by anglers. [*Gobio gobio*.] **2** archaic a credulous or easily fooled person.
– ORIGIN Middle English: from Old French *goujon*, from Latin *gobio(n-)*, from *gobius* 'goby'.

gudgeon pin ■ n. a pin holding a piston rod and a connecting rod together.

guelder rose /'gɛldə/ ■ n. a deciduous shrub with flattened heads of fragrant creamy-white flowers, followed by translucent red berries. [*Viburnum opulus*.]
– ORIGIN C16: from Dutch *geldersche roos* 'rose of Gelderland' (a province of the Netherlands).

guenon /ɡəˈnɒn/ ■ n. a long-tailed African monkey of a group including the vervet and patas monkeys. [Genus *Cercopithecus*: several species.]
– ORIGIN C19: from French.

guerdon /'ɡəːd(ə)n/ archaic ■ n. a reward or recompense. ■ v. give a reward to.
– ORIGIN Middle English: from medieval Latin *widerdonum*, alteration (by association with Latin *donum* 'gift') of a West Germanic compound represented by Old High German *widarlōn* 'repayment'.

Guernsey /'ɡəːnzɪ/ ■ n. (pl. -**eys**) **1** an animal of a breed of dairy cattle from Guernsey, noted for producing rich, creamy milk. **2** (**guernsey**) a thick sweater made with oiled wool, originally worn by fishermen.

Guernsey lily ■ n. a nerine with large heads of pink lily-like flowers. [*Nerine sarniensis*.]

guerrilla /ɡəˈrɪlə/ (also **guerilla**) ■ n. a member of a small independent group taking part in irregular warfare, typically against larger regular forces.
– ORIGIN C19: from Spanish, diminutive of *guerra* 'war'.

guess ■ v. **1** estimate or suppose (something) without sufficient information to be sure of being correct. **2** correctly conjecture or perceive. **3** (**I guess**) informal I suppose. ■ n. an estimate or conjecture.
– PHRASES **be anybody's** (or **anyone's**) **guess** be very difficult or impossible to determine.
– DERIVATIVES **guessable** adj. **guesser** n.
– ORIGIN Middle English: perhaps from Dutch *gissen*, and prob. rel. to GET.

guesstimate (also **guestimate**) informal ■ n. /'ɡɛstɪmət/ an estimate based on a mixture of guesswork and calculation. ■ v. /'ɡɛstɪmeɪt/ form such an estimate of.

guesswork ■ n. the process or results of guessing.

guest ■ n. **1** a person who is invited to visit someone's home or take part in a function. ▸ a visiting performer invited to take part in an entertainment. ▸ a person lodging at a hotel or boarding house. ■ v. informal appear as a guest.
– PHRASES **be my guest** informal please do! **guest of honour** the most important guest at an occasion.
– ORIGIN Middle English: from Old Norse *gestr*, of Germanic origin.

guest beer ■ n. Brit. a draught beer offered temporarily or in addition to those produced by the parent brewery.

guest farm ■ n. chiefly S. African a farm offering accommodation to paying guests.

guest house ■ n. a private house offering accommodation to paying guests.

guestimate ■ n. & v. variant spelling of GUESSTIMATE.

guff ■ n. informal trivial or worthless talk or ideas.
– ORIGIN C19 ('puff, whiff of a bad smell'): imitative.

guffaw /ɡəˈfɔː/ ■ n. a loud and boisterous laugh. ■ v. laugh in such a way.
– ORIGIN C18 (orig. Scots): imitative.

GUI ■ abbrev. Computing graphical user interface.

guidance ■ n. **1** advice or information aimed at resolving a problem or difficulty. **2** the directing of the motion or position of something.

guide ■ n. **1** a person who advises or shows the way to others. ▸ a professional mountain climber in charge of a group. **2** a directing principle or standard. ▸ a book providing information on a subject. **3** a structure or marking which directs the motion or positioning of something. **4** (**Guide**) a member of the Girl Guides Association, a girls' organization corresponding to the Scouts. ■ v. **1** show or indicate the way to. **2** direct the motion, positioning, or course of. ▸ [as adj. **guided**] directed by remote control or internal equipment: *a guided missile.*
– DERIVATIVES **guidable** adj. **guider** n.
– ORIGIN Middle English: from Old French *guide* (n.), *guider* (v.), of Germanic origin.

guidebook ■ n. a book of information about a place for visitors or tourists.

guide dog ■ n. a dog that has been trained to lead a blind person.

guideline ■ n. a general rule, principle, or piece of advice.

guidepost ■ n. archaic term for SIGNPOST.

Guider ■ n. an adult leader in the Girl Guides Association or the Scout Association.

guidon /'ɡʌɪd(ə)n/ ■ n. a pennant that narrows to a point or fork.
– ORIGIN C16: from Italian *guidone*, from *guida* 'a guide'.

guild ■ n. **1** a medieval association of craftsmen or merchants. **2** an association of people for mutual aid or the pursuit of a common goal. **3** Ecology a group of species with similar roles within a community.
– ORIGIN Old English: prob. from Middle Low German and Middle Dutch *gilde*, of Germanic origin; rel. to YIELD.

guilder /'ɡɪldə/ ■ n. (pl. same or **guilders**) **1** the former monetary unit of the Netherlands. **2** historical a gold or silver coin formerly used in the Netherlands, Germany, and Austria.
– ORIGIN alteration of Dutch *gulden* 'golden'.

guildhall ■ n. a building used as the meeting place of a guild or corporation. ▶ Brit. a town hall.

guile /gaɪl/ ■ n. sly or cunning intelligence.
– DERIVATIVES **guileful** adj. **guilefully** adv.
– ORIGIN Middle English: from Old French, prob. from Old Norse.

guileless ■ adj. innocent and without deception.
– DERIVATIVES **guilelessly** adv. **guilelessness** n.

Guillain–Barré syndrome /ˌgɪjæ̃ˈbæreɪ/ ■ n. Medicine an acute disorder of the peripheral nerves causing weakness and often paralysis of the limbs.
– ORIGIN 1916: named after the French physicians Georges *Guillain* and Jean *Barré*, who described the syndrome.

guillemot /ˈgɪlɪmɒt/ ■ n. an auk with a narrow pointed bill, typically nesting on cliff ledges. [*Uria aalge* and other species.]
– ORIGIN C17: from French, diminutive of *Guillaume* 'William'.

guillotine /ˈgɪlətiːn, ˌgɪləˈtiːn/ ■ n. 1 a machine with a heavy blade sliding vertically in grooves, used for beheading people. 2 a device with a descending or sliding blade used for cutting paper or sheet metal. 3 a surgical instrument with a sliding blade typically for the removal of the tonsils. 4 Brit. (in parliament) a procedure used to limit discussion of a legislative bill by fixing times at which various parts of it must be voted on. ■ v. 1 execute by guillotine. 2 cut with a guillotine. 3 Brit. (in parliament) apply a guillotine to (a bill or debate).
– ORIGIN C18: from French, named after the French physician Joseph-Ignace *Guillotin*.

guilt ■ n. 1 the fact of having committed an offence or crime. 2 a feeling of having committed wrong or failed in an obligation.
– DERIVATIVES **guiltless** adj. **guiltlessly** adv. **guiltlessness** n.
– ORIGIN Old English.

guilt trip informal ■ n. a feeling of guilt, especially when self-indulgent or unjustified. ■ v. (**guilt-trip**) make (someone) feel guilty, especially in order to induce them to do something.

guilty ■ adj. (**-ier**, **-iest**) 1 (often **guilty of**) culpable of a specified wrongdoing. ▶ justly chargeable with a particular fault or error. 2 having or showing a feeling of guilt: *a guilty conscience*.
– DERIVATIVES **guiltily** adv. **guiltiness** n.

guinea /ˈgɪni/ ■ n. Brit. 1 the sum of £1.05 (21 shillings in pre-decimal currency), used mainly for determining professional fees and auction prices. 2 a former British gold coin with a value of 21 shillings.
– ORIGIN named after *Guinea* in West Africa (the source of the gold from which the first guineas were minted).

guineafowl ■ n. (pl. same) a large African game bird with slate-coloured, white-spotted plumage. [*Numida meleagris* (helmeted guineafowl) and other species.]

Guinean /ˈgɪniən/ ■ n. a native or inhabitant of Guinea, a country on the west coast of Africa. ■ adj. of or relating to Guinea.

guinea pig ■ n. 1 a tailless South American cavy, now completely domesticated as a pet or laboratory animal. [*Cavia porcellus*.] 2 a person or thing used as a subject for experiment.

Guinea worm ■ n. a very long parasitic nematode worm which lives under the skin of infected humans and other mammals in rural Africa and Asia. [*Dracunculus medinensis*.]

guipure /gɪˈpjʊə/ ■ n. heavy lace consisting of embroidered motifs held together by large connecting stitches.
– ORIGIN C19: from French, from *guiper* 'cover with silk'.

guiro /ˈgwɪərəʊ/ ■ n. (pl. **-os**) a musical instrument with a serrated surface which gives a rasping sound when scraped with a stick.
– ORIGIN Spanish, 'gourd'.

guise /gaɪz/ ■ n. an external form, appearance, or manner of presentation.
– ORIGIN Middle English: from Old French, of Germanic origin.

guitar ■ n. a stringed musical instrument with a fretted fingerboard and six or twelve strings, played by plucking or strumming with the fingers or a plectrum.

519

gulp

– DERIVATIVES **guitarist** n.
– ORIGIN C17: from Spanish *guitarra*, from Greek *kithara*, denoting an instrument similar to the lyre.

guitarfish ■ n. (pl. same or **-fishes**) a fish related to the rays, with a guitar-like body shape. [Genus *Rhinobatus*.]

Gujarati /ˌguːdʒəˈrɑːti, ˌgʊ-/ (also **Gujerati**) ■ n. (pl. **Gujaratis**) 1 a native or inhabitant of the Indian state of Gujarat. 2 the Indic language of the Gujaratis. ■ adj. of or relating to the Gujaratis or their language.

gulab jamun /ˌgʊˌlɑːb ˈjɑːmʌn/ ■ n. an Indian sweet consisting of a ball of deep-fried paneer boiled in a sugar syrup.
– ORIGIN from Hindi *gulāb* 'rose water' and *jāmun* 'fruit'.

Gulag /ˈguːlag/ ■ n. (**the Gulag**) a system of harsh labour camps maintained in the Soviet Union 1930–1955.
– ORIGIN Russian, from G(*lavnoe*) u(*pravlenie ispra-vitel'no-trudovykh*) lag(*ereĭ*) 'Chief Administration for Corrective Labour Camps'.

gular /ˈgjuːlə/ ■ adj. Zoology of or relating to the throat, especially of a reptile, fish, or bird.
– ORIGIN C19: from Latin *gula* 'throat'.

gulch /gʌltʃ/ ■ n. N. Amer. a narrow, steep-sided ravine marking the course of a fast stream.
– ORIGIN C19: perhaps from dialect *gulch* 'to swallow'.

gules /gjuːlz/ ■ n. red, as a heraldic tincture.
– ORIGIN Middle English: from Old French *goles* (pl. of *gole* 'throat', from Latin *gula*), used to denote pieces of red-dyed fur used as a neck ornament.

gulf ■ n. 1 a deep inlet of the sea almost surrounded by land, with a narrow mouth. 2 a deep ravine, chasm, or abyss. 3 a substantial difference between two people, concepts, or situations.
– ORIGIN Middle English: from Old French *golfe*, from Greek *kolpos* 'bosom, gulf'.

Gulf War syndrome ■ n. an unexplained medical condition affecting some veterans of the 1991 Gulf War, causing fatigue, chronic headaches, and skin and respiratory disorders.

gulfweed ■ n. another term for **SARGASSUM**.

gull[1] ■ n. a long-winged, web-footed seabird typically having white plumage with a grey or black mantle. [Family Laridae: many species.]
– ORIGIN Middle English: of Celtic origin; rel. to Welsh *gwylan* and Breton *gwelan*.

gull[2] ■ v. fool or deceive (someone). ■ n. a person who is fooled or deceived.
– ORIGIN C16.

Gullah /ˈgʌlə/ ■ n. 1 a member of a black people living on the coast of South Carolina and nearby islands. 2 the Creole language of this people, having an English base with West African elements.
– ORIGIN perhaps a shortening of *Angola*, or from *Gola*, the name of a people of Liberia and Sierra Leone.

gullet ■ n. the passage by which food passes from the mouth to the stomach; the oesophagus.
– ORIGIN Middle English: from Old French *goulet*, diminutive of *goule* 'throat', from Latin *gula*.

gulley ■ n. (pl. **-eys**) variant spelling of **GULLY**.

gullible ■ adj. easily persuaded to believe something; credulous.
– DERIVATIVES **gullibility** n. **gullibly** adv.
– ORIGIN C19: from **GULL**[2].

gull-wing ■ n. [as modifier] (of a door on a car or aircraft) opening upwards.

gully ■ n. (pl. **-ies**) 1 (also **gulley**) a water-worn ravine. ▶ a gutter or drain. 2 Cricket a fielding position on the off side between point and the slips. ■ v. (also **gulley**) [usu. as adj. **gullied**] erode gullies into (land) by water action.
– ORIGIN C16: from French *goulet* (see **GULLET**).

gulp ■ v. 1 swallow (drink or food) quickly or in large mouthfuls, often audibly. 2 make an effortful swallowing motion, typically in response to strong emotion. ■ n. 1 an act of gulping food or drink. ▶ a large mouthful of liquid hastily drunk. 2 an effortful swallowing motion.
– DERIVATIVES **gulpy** adj.
– ORIGIN Middle English: prob. from Middle Dutch *gulpen*, of imitative origin.

gum

gum¹ ▪ n. **1** a viscous secretion of some trees and shrubs that hardens on drying but is soluble in water. ▸ a sticky secretion collecting in the corner of the eye. **2** glue used for sticking paper or other light materials together. **3** chewing gum or bubble gum. **4** a firm, jelly-like sweet made with gelatin or gum arabic. **5** a gum tree, especially a eucalyptus. ▪ v. (**gummed, gumming**) cover or fasten with gum or glue. ▸ (**gum something up**) clog up a mechanism and prevent it from working properly.
– ORIGIN Middle English: from Old French *gomme*, from Greek *kommi*, from Egyptian *kemai*.

gum² ▪ n. the firm area of flesh around the roots of the teeth in the upper or lower jaw.
– ORIGIN Old English *gōma* 'inside of the mouth or throat', of Germanic origin.

gum³ ▪ n. (in phr. **by gum!**) chiefly N. English an exclamation used for emphasis.
– ORIGIN C19: euphemistic alteration of *God*.

gum arabic ▪ n. a gum exuded by some kinds of acacia and used as glue and in incense.

gumba /ˈɡʊmbə/ (also **gumba-gumba**) ▪ n. S. African informal a party, typically involving music and the sale of liquor.
– ORIGIN 1970s.

gumbo ▪ n. (pl. **-os**) N. Amer. **1** okra, especially the gelatinous pods used in cooking. ▸ (in Cajun cooking) a spicy chicken or seafood soup thickened with okra or rice. **2** a type of Cajun music consisting of a lively blend of styles and sounds.
– ORIGIN C19: from the Angolan word *kingombo* 'okra'.

gumboil ▪ n. a small swelling formed on the gum over an abscess at the root of a tooth.

gumboot ▪ n. a long rubber boot; a wellington.

gumboot dance ▪ n. S. African a dance originally developed by mine workers, performed wearing gumboots.
– DERIVATIVES **gumboot dancer** n. **gumboot dancing** n.

gumdrop ▪ n. a firm, jelly-like sweet made with gelatin or gum arabic.

gummy¹ ▪ adj. (**-ier, -iest**) viscous; sticky.
– DERIVATIVES **gumminess** n.

gummy² ▪ adj. (**-ier, -iest**) toothless: *a gummy grin*.
– DERIVATIVES **gummily** adv.

gum olibanum ▪ n. another term for FRANKINCENSE.

gumption /ˈɡʌm(p)ʃ(ə)n/ ▪ n. informal shrewd or spirited initiative and resourcefulness.
– ORIGIN C18 (orig. Scots).

gum resin ▪ n. a plant secretion consisting of resin mixed with gum.

gumshield ▪ n. a pad or plate held in the mouth by a sports player to protect the teeth and gums.

gumshoe ▪ n. N. Amer. informal a detective.
– ORIGIN C20: from *gumshoes* in the sense 'sneakers', suggesting stealth.

gum tree ▪ n. a tree that exudes gum, especially a eucalyptus.
– PHRASES **up a gum tree** Brit. informal in or into a predicament.

gun ▪ n. **1** a weapon incorporating a metal tube from which bullets or shells are propelled by explosive force. ▸ N. Amer. a gunman: *a hired gun*. **2** a device for discharging something (e.g. grease) in a required direction. ▪ v. (**gunned, gunning**) **1** (**gun someone down**) shoot someone with a gun. **2** (**gun for**) aggressively pursue or act against. ▸ strive for determinedly. **3** informal cause (an engine) to race. ▸ accelerate (a vehicle).
– PHRASES **go great guns** informal proceed forcefully, vigorously, or successfully. **jump the gun** informal act before the proper or appropriate time. **stick to one's guns** informal refuse to compromise or change, despite criticism. **top gun** a (or the) most important person. **under the gun** N. Amer. informal under great pressure.
– DERIVATIVES **gunless** adj. **-gunned** adj.
– ORIGIN Middle English *gunne, gonne*, perhaps from a familiar form of the Scandinavian name *Gunnhildr*, from *gunnr* + *hildr*, both meaning 'war'.

gunboat ▪ n. a small ship mounting guns, for use in shallow coastal waters and rivers.

gunboat diplomacy ▪ n. foreign policy supported by the use or threat of military force.

gun carriage ▪ n. a wheeled support for a piece of artillery.

guncotton ▪ n. a highly nitrated form of nitrocellulose, used as an explosive.

gun deck ▪ n. a deck on a ship on which guns are placed. ▸ historical the lowest such deck on a ship of the line.

gun dog ▪ n. a dog trained to retrieve game for a gamekeeper or the members of a shoot.

gunfight ▪ n. a fight involving an exchange of fire with guns.
– DERIVATIVES **gunfighter** n.

gunfire ▪ n. the repeated firing of a gun or guns.

gunge informal ▪ n. a sticky, viscous, and unpleasantly messy material. ▪ v. (**gunged, gungeing**) (**gunge something up**) clog or obstruct something with gunge.
– DERIVATIVES **gungy** adj.
– ORIGIN 1960s: perhaps suggested by GOO and GUNK.

gung-ho /ɡʌŋˈhəʊ/ ▪ adj. unthinkingly enthusiastic and eager, especially about taking part in fighting or warfare.
– ORIGIN SECOND WORLD WAR: from Chinese *gōnghé*, taken to mean 'work together' and adopted as a slogan by US Marines.

gunk ▪ n. informal unpleasantly sticky or messy matter.
– ORIGIN 1930s (orig. US): the proprietary name of a detergent.

gunman ▪ n. (pl. **-men**) a man who uses a gun to commit a crime or terrorist act.

gunmetal ▪ n. **1** a grey corrosion-resistant form of bronze containing zinc. **2** a dull bluish-grey colour.

gun microphone ▪ n. a microphone with an elongated barrel which can be directed from a distance at a localized sound source.

gunnel ▪ n. variant spelling of GUNWALE.

gunner ▪ n. **1** a person who operates a gun. ▸ a soldier in the artillery corps. **2** historical a naval warrant officer in charge of a ship's guns and ordnance stores.

gunnera /ˈɡʌn(ə)rə, ɡʌˈnɪərə/ ▪ n. a South American plant with extremely large leaves, grown as a waterside ornamental. [Genus *Gunnera*.]
– ORIGIN named after the C18 Norwegian botanist Johann E. *Gunnerus*.

gunnery ▪ n. the design, manufacture, or firing of heavy guns.

gunny /ˈɡʌni/ ▪ n. chiefly N. Amer. coarse sacking, typically made of jute fibre.
– ORIGIN C18: from Marathi *gōnī*, from Sanskrit *goṇī* 'sack'.

gunplay ▪ n. chiefly N. Amer. the use of guns.

gunpoint ▪ n. (in phr. **at gunpoint**) while threatening someone or being threatened with a gun.

gunpowder ▪ n. **1** an explosive consisting of a powdered mixture of saltpetre, sulphur, and charcoal. **2** a fine green China tea of granular appearance.

gunroom ▪ n. **1** a room for storing guns. **2** Brit. dated a set of quarters for midshipmen or other junior officers in a warship.

gunrunner ▪ n. a person engaged in the illegal sale or importing of firearms.
– DERIVATIVES **gunrunning** n.

gunship ▪ n. a heavily armed helicopter.

gunshot ▪ n. a shot fired from a gun.

gun-shy ▪ adj. (especially of a hunting dog) alarmed at the sound of a gun.

gunsight ▪ n. a device on a gun enabling it to be aimed accurately.

gunslinger ▪ n. informal a man who carries a gun.
– DERIVATIVES **gunslinging** adj.

gunsmith ▪ n. a person who makes and sells small firearms.

gunstock ▪ n. the wooden support to which the barrel of a gun is attached.

gunwale /ˈɡʌn(ə)l/ (also **gunnel**) ▪ n. the upper edge or

planking of the side of a boat.
- ORIGIN Middle English: from **GUN** + **WALE** (because it was formerly used to support guns).

guppy /ˈgʌpi/ ■ n. (pl. **-ies**) a small live-bearing freshwater fish, native to tropical America and widely kept in aquaria. [*Poecilia reticulata*.]
- ORIGIN 1920s: named after the Trinidadian clergyman R. J. Lechmere *Guppy*, who sent the first specimen to the British Museum.

Gur /gəː/ ■ n. a branch of the Niger–Congo family of languages, spoken in parts of West Africa.

gurgle ■ v. make a hollow bubbling sound. ■ n. a gurgling sound.
- ORIGIN Middle English: imitative, or from Dutch *gorgelen*, German *gurgeln*, or medieval Latin *gurgulare*, all from Latin *gurgulio* 'gullet'.

Gurkha /ˈgəːkə, ˈgʊəkə/ ■ n. **1** a member of any of several Nepalese peoples noted for their military prowess. **2** a member of a regiment in the British army established for Nepalese recruits.
- ORIGIN name of a locality, from Sanskrit *gorakṣa* 'cowherd' (from *go* 'cow' + *rakṣ-* 'protect'), used as an epithet of their patron deity.

Gurmukhi /ˈgʊəmʊki/ ■ n. the script used by Sikhs for writing Punjabi.
- ORIGIN Punjabi: from Sanskrit *guru* (see **GURU**) + *mukha* 'mouth'.

gurnard /ˈgəːnəd/ ■ n. a small coastal fish with three finger-like pectoral rays with which it searches for food and walks on the seabed. [Family Triglidae.]
- ORIGIN Middle English: from Old French *gornart*, from *grondir* 'to grunt', from Latin *grundire*.

gurney /ˈgəːni/ ■ n. (pl. **-eys**) chiefly N. Amer. a wheeled stretcher for transporting hospital patients.
- ORIGIN C19: apparently named after the patentee of a new cab design, J. T. *Gurney*.

guru /ˈgʊruː, ˈgʊːruː/ ■ n. **1** a Hindu spiritual teacher. **2** each of the ten first leaders of the Sikh religion. **3** an influential teacher: *a management guru*.
- ORIGIN from Sanskrit *guru* 'weighty, grave', hence 'elder, teacher'.

gush ■ v. **1** send out or flow in a rapid and plentiful stream. **2** speak or write effusively. ■ n. **1** a rapid and plentiful stream. **2** effusiveness.
- DERIVATIVES **gushing** adj. **gushingly** adv.
- ORIGIN Middle English: prob. imitative.

gusher ■ n. **1** an oil well from which oil flows profusely without being pumped. **2** an effusive person.

gushy ■ adj. (**-ier**, **-iest**) excessively effusive.
- DERIVATIVES **gushily** adv. **gushiness** n.

gusset /ˈgʌsɪt/ ■ n. **1** a piece of material sewn into a garment to strengthen or enlarge a part of it, e.g. the crotch of an undergarment. **2** a bracket strengthening an angle of a structure.
- DERIVATIVES **gusseted** adj.
- ORIGIN Middle English: from Old French *gousset*, diminutive of *gousse* 'pod, shell'.

gussy ■ v. (**-ies**, **-ied**) (**gussy someone/thing up**) informal, chiefly N. Amer. make someone or something more attractive, especially in a showy way.
- ORIGIN 1940s: perhaps from *Gussie*, familiar form of the given name *Augustus*.

gust ■ n. **1** a brief, strong rush of wind. **2** a burst of rain, sound, emotion, etc. ■ v. blow in gusts.
- ORIGIN C16: from Old Norse *gustr*, rel. to *gjósa* 'to gush'.

gustation ■ n. formal the action or faculty of tasting.
- DERIVATIVES **gustative** adj. **gustatory** /gʌˈsteɪt(ə)ri, ˈgʌstət(ə)ri/ adj.
- ORIGIN C16: from Latin *gustatio(n-)*, from *gustare* 'to taste', from *gustus* 'taste'.

gusto ■ n. enjoyment or vigour.
- ORIGIN C17: from Italian, from Latin *gustus* 'taste'.

gusty ■ adj. (**-ier**, **-iest**) **1** characterized by or blowing in gusts. **2** showing gusto.
- DERIVATIVES **gustily** adv. **gustiness** n.

gut ■ n. **1** the stomach or belly. ▶ Medicine & Biology the intestine. ▶ (**guts**) entrails that have been removed or exposed. **2** (**guts**) the internal parts or essence of something. **3** (**guts**) used in names attributing negative characteristics: *greedy guts*. **4** (**guts**) informal personal courage and determination. **5** [as modifier] informal (of a feeling or reaction) instinctive. **6** fibre from the intestines of animals, used especially for violin or racket strings.
■ v. (**gutted**, **gutting**) **1** take out the internal organs of (a fish or other animal) before cooking. **2** remove or destroy the internal parts of.
- PHRASES **bust a gut** informal make a strenuous effort. **hate someone's guts** informal dislike someone intensely. **have someone's guts for garters** informal, humorous used as a threat of punishment. **sweat** (or **work**) **one's guts out** informal work extremely hard.
- ORIGIN Old English *guttas* (pl.), prob. rel. to *gēotan* 'pour'.

gutless ■ adj. informal lacking courage or determination.
- DERIVATIVES **gutlessly** adv. **gutlessness** n.

gutsy ■ adj. (**-ier**, **-iest**) informal **1** showing courage and determination. **2** strongly flavoursome. **3** greedy.
- DERIVATIVES **gutsily** adv. **gutsiness** n.

gutta-percha /ˌgʌtəˈpəːtʃə/ ■ n. the hard tough coagulated latex of certain Malaysian trees, resembling rubber.
- ORIGIN C19: from Malay *getah perca*, from *getah* 'gum' + *perca* 'strips of cloth' (which it resembles), altered by association with obsolete *gutta* 'gum'.

guttation /gʌˈteɪʃ(ə)n/ ■ n. the secretion of droplets of water from the pores of plants.
- ORIGIN C19: from Latin *gutta* 'drop'.

gutted ■ adj. informal bitterly disappointed or upset.

gutter ■ n. **1** a shallow trough beneath the edge of a roof, or a channel at the side of a street, for carrying off rainwater. ▶ technical a groove or channel for flowing liquid. **2** (**the gutter**) a poor or squalid environment. **3** the blank space between facing pages of a book or between adjacent columns of type or stamps in a sheet. ■ v. (of a flame) flicker and burn unsteadily.
- ORIGIN Middle English: from Old French *gotiere*, from Latin *gutta* 'a drop'.

guttering ■ n. the gutters of a building.

gutter press ■ n. chiefly Brit. newspapers engaging in sensational journalism.

guttersnipe ■ n. a street urchin.

guttural /ˈgʌt(ə)r(ə)l/ ■ adj. **1** (of a speech sound) produced in the throat. **2** (of speech) characterized by guttural sounds. ■ n. a guttural consonant (e.g. *k*, *g*).
- DERIVATIVES **gutturally** adv.
- ORIGIN C16: from medieval Latin *gutturalis*, from Latin *guttur* 'throat'.

gut-wrenching ■ adj. informal extremely unpleasant or upsetting.

guv ■ n. Brit. informal (as a form of address) sir.

guy[1] ■ n. **1** informal a man. ▶ (**guys**) people of either sex. **2** a figure representing the Catholic conspirator Guy Fawkes, burnt on a bonfire on 5 November to commemorate a plot to blow up the British Parliament in 1605.

guy[2] ■ n. a rope or line fixed to the ground to secure a tent. ■ v. secure with a guy or guys.
- ORIGIN Middle English: prob. of Low German origin; rel. to Dutch *gei* 'brail' and German *Geitaue* 'brails'.

Guyanese /ˌgaɪəˈniːz/ ■ n. (pl. same) a native or inhabitant of Guyana, a country on the NE coast of South America. ■ adj. of or relating to Guyana.

Guy Fawkes Night ■ n. (in the UK and South Africa) 5 November, on which fireworks are set off and effigies of Guy Fawkes are burnt in memory of the Gunpowder Plot of 1605.

guzzle ■ v. eat or drink greedily.
- DERIVATIVES **guzzler** n.
- ORIGIN C16: from Old French *gosillier* 'chatter, vomit', from *gosier* 'throat', from late Latin *geusiae* 'cheeks'.

Gy ■ abbrev. Physics gray(s).

gybe /dʒaɪb/ (US **jibe**) Nautical ■ v. change course by swinging the sail across a following wind. ▶ (of a sail or boom) swing across the wind. ■ n. an act of gybing.
- ORIGIN C17: from obsolete Dutch *gijben*.

gym ■ n. **1** a gymnasium. ▶ a private club providing a

gymkhana

range of facilities designed to improve and maintain physical fitness. **2** gymnastics. ■ v. (**gymmed**, **gymming**) informal exercise at a gym.

gymkhana /dʒɪmˈkɑːnə/ ■ n. **1** an event comprising competitions on horseback, typically for children. **2** chiefly S. African an event in which cars negotiate obstacles round a course, testing driver skill and vehicle performance.
– ORIGIN C19: from Urdu *gendkānah* 'racket court', from Hindi *geṁd* 'ball' + Persian *kānah* 'house'.

gymnasium /dʒɪmˈneɪzɪəm/ ■ n. (pl. **gymnasiums** or **gymnasia** /-zɪə/) **1** a hall or building equipped for gymnastics and other physical exercise. **2** /ɡɪmˈnɑːzɪəm/ a school in Germany, Scandinavia, or central Europe that prepares pupils for university.
– ORIGIN C16: from Greek *gumnasion*, from *gumnazein* 'exercise naked', from *gumnos* 'naked'.

gymnast ■ n. a person trained in gymnastics.
– ORIGIN C16: from French *gymnaste* or Greek *gumnastēs* 'trainer of athletes', from *gumnazein* (see GYMNASIUM).

gymnastics ■ pl. n. [also treated as sing.] **1** exercises involving physical agility, flexibility, and coordination, especially tumbling and acrobatic feats. **2** physical or mental agility of a specified kind: *vocal gymnastics.*
– DERIVATIVES **gymnastic** adj. **gymnastically** adv.

gymno- /ˈdʒɪmnəʊ/ ■ comb. form bare; naked: *gymnosperm*.
– ORIGIN from Greek *gumnos* 'naked'.

gymnogene /ˈdʒɪmnə(ʊ)dʒiːn/ ■ n. Another term for AFRICAN HARRIER HAWK.
– ORIGIN C19: from Greek *gumnos* 'naked' + *genus* 'chin'.

gymnosperm /ˈdʒɪmnə(ʊ)spəːm/ ■ n. Botany a plant of a group (subdivision Gymnospermae) that comprises those that have seeds unprotected by an ovary or fruit, including conifers and cycads. Compare with ANGIOSPERM.
– DERIVATIVES **gymnospermous** /-ˈspəːməs/ adj.

gymslip ■ n. S. African & Brit. dated a sleeveless belted tunic reaching from the shoulder to the knee, worn by schoolgirls doing physical education.

gynaeco- /ˈɡaɪnɪkɒ, ɡaɪˈniːkəʊ, dʒ-/ (US **gyneco-**) ■ comb. form relating to women; female: *gynaecology*.
– ORIGIN from Greek *gunē*, *gunaik-* 'woman, female'.

gynaecology /ˌɡaɪnɪˈkɒlədʒi, dʒ-/ (US **gynecology**) ■ n. the branch of physiology and medicine concerned with the functions and diseases specific to women and girls, especially those affecting the reproductive system.
– DERIVATIVES **gynaecologic** adj. **gynaecological** adj. **gynaecologically** adv. **gynaecologist** n.

gynaecomastia /ˌɡaɪnɪkə(ʊ)ˈmastɪə, ɡaɪˈniːkəʊ-, dʒ-/ (US **gynecomastia**) ■ n. Medicine enlargement of a man's breasts, due to hormone imbalance or hormone therapy.

gynarchy /ˈɡaɪnɑːki, ˈdʒaɪ-/ ■ n. (pl. **-ies**) rule by women or a woman.

gyneco- ■ comb. form US spelling of GYNAECO-.

gynocentric /ˌɡaɪnə(ʊ)ˈsɛntrɪk, ˌdʒaɪ-/ ■ adj. concerned exclusively with women; taking a female (or feminist) point of view.

gynoecium /ɡaɪˈniːsɪəm, dʒ-/ ■ n. (pl. **gynoecia** /-sɪə/) Botany the female part of a flower, consisting of one or more carpels.
– ORIGIN C19: from Greek *gunaikeion* 'women's apartments', from *gunē* 'woman, female' + *oikos* 'house'.

gynophobia /ˌɡaɪnə(ʊ)ˈfəʊbɪə, ˌdʒaɪ-/ ■ n. extreme or irrational fear of women.
– DERIVATIVES **gynophobic** adj.

gyp¹ /dʒɪp/ (also **gip**) ■ n. Brit. informal pain or discomfort.
– ORIGIN C19: perhaps from *gee-up* (see GEE²).

gyp² /dʒɪp/ informal ■ v. (**gypped**, **gypping**) cheat or swindle (someone). ■ n. a swindle.
– ORIGIN C19.

gyppo guts (also **gippo guts**) ■ n. S. African informal diarrhoea.

gypsophila /dʒɪpˈsɒfɪlə/ ■ n. a plant of a genus which includes baby's breath. [Genus *Gypsophila*.]
– ORIGIN modern Latin: from Greek *gupsos* 'chalk, gypsum' + *philos* 'loving'.

gypsum /ˈdʒɪpsəm/ ■ n. a soft white or grey mineral consisting of hydrated calcium sulphate, used to make plaster of Paris and in the building industry.
– DERIVATIVES **gypsiferous** /-ˈsɪf(ə)rəs/ adj.
– ORIGIN Middle English: from Greek *gupsos*.

gypsy (also **gipsy**) ■ n. (pl. **-ies**) a member of a travelling people with dark skin and hair, speaking a language (Romany) related to Hindi, and traditionally living by itinerant trade and fortune telling.
– ORIGIN C16: orig. *gipcyan*, short for EGYPTIAN (because gypsies were believed to have come from Egypt).

gypsy moth ■ n. a tussock moth having a brown male and larger white flightless female. [*Lymantria dispar*.]

gyral /ˈdʒaɪr(ə)l/ ■ adj. chiefly Anatomy of or relating to a gyrus or gyri.

gyrate ■ v. move or cause to move in a circle or spiral.
– DERIVATIVES **gyration** n. **gyrator** n.
– ORIGIN C19 (*gyration* C17): from Latin *gyrare* 'revolve', from Greek *guros* 'a ring'.

gyratory /ˈdʒaɪrət(ə)ri, ˈdʒaɪrət-/ ■ adj. of or involving circular or spiral motion. ■ n. (pl. **-ies**) a traffic system requiring the circular movement of traffic.

gyre /ˈdʒaɪə, ˈɡaɪə/ ■ v. poetic/literary whirl; gyrate. ■ n. **1** a spiral; a vortex. **2** Geography a circular pattern of currents in an ocean basin.
– ORIGIN Middle English: from late Latin *gyrare*, from Latin *gyrus* 'a ring', from Greek *guros*.

gyrfalcon /ˈdʒəː.fɔː(l)k(ə)n, -ˌfɒlk(ə)n/ ■ n. a large arctic falcon, occurring in several colour forms including a mainly white one. [*Falco rusticolus*.]
– ORIGIN Middle English: from Old French *gerfaucon*, of Germanic origin, prob. rel. to Old High German *gēr* 'spear'.

gyri plural form of GYRUS.

gyro¹ /ˈdʒaɪrəʊ/ ■ n. (pl. **-os**) short for GYROSCOPE or GYROCOMPASS.

gyro² /ˈdʒaɪrəʊ/ ■ n. (pl. **-os**) N. Amer. a sandwich of spiced meat cooked on a spit, served in pitta bread.
– ORIGIN 1970s: from modern Greek *guros* 'turning'.

gyro- /ˈdʒaɪrəʊ/ ■ comb. form **1** relating to rotation: *gyromagnetic*. **2** gyroscopic: *gyrostabilizer*.
– ORIGIN from Greek *guros* 'a ring'.

gyrocompass ■ n. a compass in which the direction of true north is maintained by a gyroscope rather than magnetism.

gyrocopter ■ n. a small single-seater autogiro.

gyromagnetic ■ adj. combining a gyroscope and a magnetic compass.

gyron /ˈdʒaɪr(ə)n/ ■ n. Heraldry a triangular ordinary formed by two lines from the edge of the shield meeting at the fess point at 45 degrees.
– ORIGIN C16: from Old French *giron* 'gusset'.

gyronny /dʒaɪˈrɒni/ ■ adj. Heraldry (of a shield) divided into eight gyrons.
– ORIGIN Middle English: from French *gironné*, from *giron* (see GYRON).

gyropilot ■ n. a gyrocompass providing automatic steering for a ship or aircraft.

gyroplane ■ n. an autogiro or similar aircraft.

gyroscope ■ n. a device, used to provide stability or maintain a fixed orientation, consisting of a wheel or disc spinning rapidly about an axis which is itself free to alter in direction.
– DERIVATIVES **gyroscopic** adj. **gyroscopically** adv.
– ORIGIN C19: from Greek *guros* 'a ring' + modern Latin *scopium* (see -SCOPE).

gyrostabilizer ■ n. a gyroscopic device for maintaining the equilibrium of a ship, aircraft, platform etc.

gyrus /ˈdʒaɪrəs/ ■ n. (pl. **gyri** /-raɪ/) Anatomy a ridge or fold on the cerebral surface in the brain.
– ORIGIN C19: from Greek *guros* 'a ring'.

gyve /dʒaɪv, ɡaɪv/ ■ n. archaic a fetter or shackle.
– DERIVATIVES **gyved** adj.
– ORIGIN Middle English.

Hh

H¹ (also **h**) ■ n. (pl. **Hs** or **H's**) **1** the eighth letter of the alphabet. **2** denoting the next after G in a set of items, categories, etc. **3** (**H**) Music (in the German system) the note B natural.

H² ■ abbrev. **1** (of a pencil lead) hard. **2** height. **3** Physics henry(s). **4** informal heroin. ■ symb. **1** Physics enthalpy. **2** the chemical element hydrogen. **3** Physics magnetic field strength.

h ■ abbrev. **1** (in measuring the height of horses) hand(s). **2** hecto-. **3** Brit. (with reference to sporting fixtures) home. **4** horse. **5** hot. **6** hour(s). ■ symb. Physics Planck's constant.

ha¹ (also **hah**) ■ exclam. expressing surprise, suspicion, triumph, etc.
– ORIGIN natural utterance: first recorded in Middle English.

ha² ■ abbrev. hectare(s).

haai /hʌɪ/ ■ exclam. S. African expressing mild dismay, disbelief, etc.
– ORIGIN from isiXhosa *hayi* 'no!'.

HAART ■ abbrev. Medicine highly active antiretroviral therapy, a form of drug treatment for HIV infection consisting of a regimen of at least three antiretroviral drugs.

habanera /ˌhabəˈnɛːrə, ˌɑːbə-/ ■ n. a Cuban dance in slow duple time.
– ORIGIN C19: Spanish, short for *danza habanera* 'dance of Havana'.

Habanero /ˌabəˈnɛːrəʊ/ ■ n. a small very hot chilli pepper.
– ORIGIN Spanish, 'of Havana'.

Habdalah /havˈdɑːlə/ (also **Havdalah**) ■ n. a Jewish ceremony or prayer marking the end of the Sabbath.
– ORIGIN from Hebrew *haḇdālāh* 'separation, division'.

habeas corpus /ˌheɪbɪəs ˈkɔːpəs/ (S. African also **interdict de homine libero exhibendo**) ■ n. Law a writ requiring a person to be brought before a judge or into court, especially to investigate the lawfulness of their detention.
– ORIGIN Middle English: Latin, 'thou shalt have the body (in court)'.

haberdasher /ˈhabəˌdaʃə/ ■ n. **1** a dealer in dressmaking and sewing goods. **2** N. Amer. a dealer in men's clothing.
– DERIVATIVES **haberdashery** n. (pl. **-ies**).
– ORIGIN Middle English: prob. from Anglo-Norman French *hapertas*, perhaps the name of a fabric.

habit ■ n. **1** a settled or regular tendency or practice. **2** general shape or mode of growth, especially of a plant or a mineral. **3** a long, loose garment worn by a member of a religious order. ▸ archaic dress; attire. ■ v. (usu. **be habited**) archaic dress.
– PHRASES **break** (or informal **kick**) **the habit** stop engaging in a habitual practice.
– ORIGIN Middle English: from Latin *habitus* 'condition, appearance', from *habere* 'have, consist of'.

habitable ■ adj. suitable to live in.
– DERIVATIVES **habitability** n.
– ORIGIN Middle English: from Latin *habitabilis*, from *habitare* 'possess, inhabit'.

habitat ■ n. the natural home or environment of an organism.
– ORIGIN C18: from Latin, 'it dwells', from *habitare* (see HABITABLE).

habitation ■ n. **1** the state or process of inhabiting. **2** formal a house or home.
– ORIGIN Middle English: from Latin *habitatio(n-)*, from *habitare* 'inhabit'.

habit-forming ■ adj. addictive.

habitual /həˈbɪtʃʊəl, -tjʊəl/ ■ adj. **1** done constantly or as a habit. **2** regular; usual: *his habitual dress*.
– DERIVATIVES **habitually** adv.

– ORIGIN Middle English ('part of one's character'): from medieval Latin *habitualis*, from *habitus* (see HABIT).

habituate ■ v. chiefly Zoology make or become accustomed to something.
– DERIVATIVES **habituation** n.
– ORIGIN C15 (*habituation* Middle English): from late Latin *habituare* 'accustom', from *habitus* (see HABIT).

habitué /(h)əˈbɪtjʊeɪ/ ■ n. a resident of or frequent visitor to a place.
– ORIGIN C19: French, 'accustomed', from *habituer*.

haboob /həˈbuːb/ ■ n. (especially in Sudan) a violent and oppressive summer wind bringing sand from the desert.
– ORIGIN C19: from Arabic *habūb* 'blowing furiously'.

hachures /haˈʃʊəz/ ■ pl. n. parallel lines used in hill-shading on maps, their closeness indicating steepness of gradient.
– DERIVATIVES **hachured** adj.
– ORIGIN C19: from French, from *hacher* (see HATCH³).

hack¹ ■ v. **1** cut with rough or heavy blows. **2** kick wildly or roughly. **3** use a computer to gain unauthorized access to data. **4** [usu. with neg.] (**hack it**) informal manage; cope. **5** (**hack someone off**) informal annoy someone. **6** (**hack around**) N. Amer. pass one's time idly. ■ n. **1** a rough cut or blow. ▸ archaic a gash or wound. **2** informal an instance of computer hacking.
– PHRASES **hacking cough** a dry, frequent cough.
– DERIVATIVES **hacker** n.
– ORIGIN Old English *haccian* 'cut in pieces', of West Germanic origin.

hack² ■ n. **1** a writer producing dull, unoriginal work. ▸ a person who does dull routine work. **2** a horse for ordinary riding. ▸ an inferior or worn-out horse. ▸ a horse let out for hire. ▸ a ride on a horse. ■ v. [usu. as noun **hacking**] ride a horse.
– ORIGIN Middle English: abbrev. of HACKNEY.

hack³ ■ n. **1** Falconry a board on which a hawk's meat is laid. **2** a wooden frame for drying bricks, cheeses, etc.
– PHRASES **at hack** (of a young hawk) not yet allowed to hunt for itself.
– ORIGIN Middle English (denoting the lower half of a divided door): var. of HATCH¹.

hackberry ■ n. (pl. **-ies**) **1** a tree with leaves that resemble those of nettles. [*Celtis occidentalis* (N. America) and other species.] **2** the purple berry of this tree.
– ORIGIN C18: var. of northern English dialect *hagberry*, of Scandinavian origin.

hackle ■ n. **1** (**hackles**) erectile hairs along an animal's back, which rise when it is angry or alarmed. **2** a long, narrow feather on the neck or saddle of a domestic cock or other bird. **3** Fishing a feather wound around a fishing fly so that its filaments are splayed out. **4** a bunch of feathers in a military headdress.
– PHRASES **make someone's hackles rise** make someone angry or indignant.
– ORIGIN Middle English: var. of obsolete *hatchel*, of West Germanic origin.

hackney ■ n. (pl. **-eys**) chiefly historical **1** a light horse with a high-stepping trot, used in harness. **2** a horse-drawn vehicle kept for hire.
– ORIGIN Middle English: prob. from *Hackney* in East London, England where horses were pastured.

hackney carriage ■ n. Brit. the official term for a taxi.

hackneyed ■ adj. (of a phrase or idea) unoriginal and trite.
– ORIGIN from the obsolete verb *hackney* 'use (a horse) for general purposes', later 'make commonplace by overuse'.

hacksaw

hacksaw ▪ n. a saw with a narrow blade set in a frame, used for cutting metal. ▪ v. (past part. **-sawn** or **-sawed**) cut with a hacksaw.

had past and past participle of HAVE.

haddock ▪ n. (pl. same) a silvery-grey bottom-dwelling fish of North Atlantic coastal waters, popular as a food fish. [*Melanogrammus aeglefinus*.]
– ORIGIN Middle English: from Anglo-Norman French *hadoc*, from Old French *hadot*.

hade /heɪd/ Geology ▪ n. the inclination of a mineral vein or fault from the vertical. ▪ v. incline from the vertical.
– ORIGIN C17: perhaps a dialect form of HEAD (v.).

hadeda /ˈhɑːdɪdɑː/ (also **hadeda ibis**, **hadedah**) ▪ n. a large grey-brown African ibis with a long decurved bill, iridescent patches on the wings, and a raucous call. [*Bostrychia hagedash*.]
– ORIGIN C18: imitative of its call.

Hades /ˈheɪdiːz/ ▪ n. **1** Greek & Roman Mythology the underworld; the abode of the spirits of the dead. **2** informal hell.
– ORIGIN from Greek *Haidēs* (a name of Pluto, the god of the dead).

Hadith /haˈdiːθ/ ▪ n. (pl. same or **Hadiths**) a collection of Islamic traditions containing sayings of the prophet Muhammad.
– ORIGIN from Arabic *ḥadīṯ* 'tradition'.

Hadley cell ▪ n. Meteorology a large-scale atmospheric convection cell in which air rises at the equator and sinks at medium latitudes.
– ORIGIN 1950s: named after the C18 English scientific writer George *Hadley*.

hadn't ▪ contr. had not.

hadron /ˈhadrɒn/ ▪ n. Physics a subatomic particle that can take part in the strong interaction, such as a baryon or meson.
– DERIVATIVES **hadronic** adj.
– ORIGIN 1960s: from Greek *hadros* 'bulky'.

hadrosaur /ˈhadrəsɔː/ ▪ n. a large herbivorous mainly bipedal dinosaur with jaws flattened like the bill of a duck.
– ORIGIN C19: from *Hadrosaurus* (genus name), from Greek *hadros* 'thick, stout' + *sauros* 'lizard'.

hadst archaic second person singular past of HAVE.

háček /ˈhɑːtʃɛk, ˈha-/ ▪ n. a diacritic mark (ˇ) placed over a letter to modify the sound in Slavic and other languages.
– ORIGIN Czech, diminutive of *hák* 'hook'.

haem /hiːm/ (US **heme**) ▪ n. Biochemistry an iron-containing compound of the porphyrin class which forms the non-protein part of haemoglobin.
– ORIGIN 1920s: back-formation from HAEMOGLOBIN.

haemal /ˈhiːm(ə)l/ (US **hemal**) ▪ adj. **1** Physiology of or concerning the blood. **2** Zoology situated on the same side of the body as the heart and major blood vessels (i.e. in chordates, ventral).
– ORIGIN C19: from Greek *haima* 'blood'.

haematin /ˈhiːmətɪn/ (US **hematin**) ▪ n. Biochemistry a bluish-black compound derived from haemoglobin by removal of the protein part and oxidation of the iron atom.
– ORIGIN C19: from Greek *haima*, *haimat-* 'blood'.

haematite /ˈhiːmətʌɪt/ (US **hematite**) ▪ n. a reddish-black mineral consisting of ferric oxide.
– ORIGIN Middle English: from Greek *haimatitēs* (*lithos*) 'blood-like (stone)', from *haima* 'blood'.

haemato- (US **hemato-**) ▪ comb. form of or relating to the blood: *haematology*.
– ORIGIN from Greek *haima*, *haimat-* 'blood'.

haematocele /ˈhiːmətə(ʊ)siːl/ (US **hematocele**) ▪ n. Medicine a swelling caused by blood collecting in a body cavity.

haematogenous /ˌhiːməˈtɒdʒɪnəs/ (US **hematogenous**) ▪ adj. Medicine originating in or carried by the blood.

haematology /ˌhiːməˈtɒlədʒi/ (US **hematology**) ▪ n. the study of the physiology of the blood.
– DERIVATIVES **haematologic** adj. **haematological** adj. **haematologist** n.

haematoma /ˌhiːməˈtəʊmə/ (US **hematoma**) ▪ n. (pl. **haematomas** or **haematomata** /-mətə/) Medicine a solid swelling of clotted blood within the tissues.

haematophagous /ˌhiːməˈtɒfəɡəs/ (US **hematophagous**) ▪ adj. Zoology feeding on blood.

haematuria /ˌhiːməˈtjʊəriə/ (US **hematuria**) ▪ n. Medicine the presence of blood in the urine.

-haemia ▪ comb. form variant spelling of -AEMIA.

haemo- (US **hemo-**) ▪ comb. form equivalent to HAEMATO-.
– ORIGIN from Greek *haima* 'blood'.

haemochromatosis /ˌhiːmə(ʊ)ˌkrəʊməˈtəʊsɪs/ (US **hemochromatosis**) ▪ n. Medicine a hereditary liver disorder in which iron salts are deposited in the tissues.

haemocoel /ˈhiːməsiːl/ (US **hemocoel**) ▪ n. Zoology the primary body cavity of most invertebrates, containing circulatory fluid.
– ORIGIN C19: from HAEMO- + Greek *koilos* 'hollow, cavity'.

haemodialysis /ˌhiːmə(ʊ)dʌɪˈalɪsɪs/ (US **hemodialysis**) ▪ n. (pl. **haemodialyses** /-siːz/) Medicine kidney dialysis.

haemodynamic (US **hemodynamic**) ▪ adj. Physiology of or relating to the flow of blood within the body.
– DERIVATIVES **haemodynamically** adv. **haemodynamics** pl. n.

haemoglobin /ˌhiːməˈɡləʊbɪn/ (US **hemoglobin**) ▪ n. Biochemistry a red protein containing iron, responsible for transporting oxygen in the blood of vertebrates.
– ORIGIN C19: a contracted form of *haematoglobulin*, in the same sense.

haemolymph /ˈhiːmə(ʊ)lɪmf/ (US **hemolymph**) ▪ n. a fluid equivalent to blood in most invertebrates.

haemolysis /hiːˈmɒlɪsɪs/ (US **hemolysis**) ▪ n. the rupture or destruction of red blood cells.
– DERIVATIVES **haemolytic** /ˌhiːməˈlɪtɪk/ adj.

haemolytic disease of the newborn ▪ n. Medicine a severe form of anaemia caused in a fetus or newborn infant by incompatibility with the mother's blood type.

haemophilia /ˌhiːməˈfɪliə/ (US **hemophilia**) ▪ n. a medical condition in which the ability of the blood to clot is severely reduced, causing severe bleeding from even a slight injury.
– DERIVATIVES **haemophiliac** n. **haemophilic** adj.

haemopoiesis /ˌhiːmə(ʊ)pɔɪˈiːsɪs/ (US **hemopoiesis**) ▪ n. the production of blood cells and platelets in the bone marrow.
– DERIVATIVES **haemopoietic** adj.
– ORIGIN C20: from HAEMO- + Greek *poiēsis* 'making'.

haemoptysis /hiːˈmɒptɪsɪs/ (US **hemoptysis**) ▪ n. the coughing up of blood.
– ORIGIN C17: from HAEMO- + Greek *ptusis* 'spitting'.

haemorrhage /ˈhɛmərɪdʒ/ (US **hemorrhage**) ▪ n. **1** an escape of blood from a ruptured blood vessel. **2** a damaging loss of something valuable: *a haemorrhage of highly qualified teachers*. ▪ v. **1** suffer a haemorrhage. **2** expend in large amounts, seemingly uncontrollably.
– DERIVATIVES **haemorrhagic** /ˌhɛməˈradʒɪk/ adj.
– ORIGIN C17: alteration of obsolete *haemorrhagy*, from Greek *haimorrhagia*, from *haima* 'blood' + the stem of *rhēgnunai* 'burst'.

haemorrhoid /ˈhɛmərɔɪd/ (US **hemorrhoid**) ▪ n. (usu. **haemorrhoids**) a swollen vein or group of veins (piles) in the region of the anus.
– DERIVATIVES **haemorrhoidal** adj.
– ORIGIN Middle English: from Greek *haimorrhoides* (*phlebes*) 'bleeding (veins)', from *haima* 'blood' + an element rel. to *rhein* 'to flow'.

haemostasis /ˌhiːmə(ʊ)ˈsteɪsɪs/ (US **hemostasis**) ▪ n. Medicine the stopping of a flow of blood.
– DERIVATIVES **haemostatic** adj.

hafiz /ˈhɑːfɪz/ ▪ n. a Muslim who knows the Koran by heart.
– ORIGIN from Arabic *ḥāfiẓ* 'guardian', from *ḥāfiẓa* 'guard, know by heart'.

hafnium /ˈhafnɪəm/ ▪ n. the chemical element of atomic number 72, a hard silver-grey metal resembling zirconium. (Symbol: **Hf**)
– ORIGIN 1920s: from *Hafnia*, Latinized form of Danish *Havn*, former name of Copenhagen.

haft /hɑːft/ ▪ n. the handle of a knife, axe, or spear.

■ v. [often as adj. **hafted**] provide with a haft.
–ORIGIN Old English, of Germanic origin: rel. to HEAVE.

Haftorah /hɑːfˈtəʊrɑː/ (also **Haphtarah**, **Haphtorah**)
■ n. (pl. **Haftoroth** /-rəʊt/) Judaism a short reading from the Prophets following the reading from the Law in a synagogue.
–ORIGIN from Hebrew *hapṭārāh* 'dismissal'.

hag¹ ■ n. a witch. ▶ an ugly old woman.
–DERIVATIVES **haggish** adj.
–ORIGIN Middle English: perhaps from Old English.

hag² ■ n. an overhang of peat.
–ORIGIN Middle English: from Old Norse *hǫgg* 'gap', from *hǫggva* 'hack, hew'.

hagfish ■ n. (pl. same or **-fishes**) a primitive jawless marine fish with a slimy eel-like body, a slit-like mouth, and a rasping tongue used for feeding on dead or dying fish. [*Myxine* and other genera, family Myxinidae.]

Haggadah /həˈɡɑːdə, haɡaˈdɑː/ ■ n. (pl. **Haggadoth** or **Haggadot** /-dəʊt/) Judaism **1** the text recited at the Seder on the first two nights of the Passover. **2** a legend or anecdote used to illustrate a point of the Law in the Talmud. ▶ this (non-legal) element of the Talmud.
–DERIVATIVES **Haggadic** /-ˈɡadɪk, -ˈɡɑːdɪk/ adj. **Haggadist** n.
–ORIGIN from Hebrew *Haggāḏāh* 'tale, parable', from *higgīḏ* 'tell, expound'.

haggard ■ adj. looking exhausted and unwell.
–DERIVATIVES **haggardly** adv. **haggardness** n.
–ORIGIN C16: from French *hagard*; perhaps rel. to HEDGE.

haggis ■ n. (pl. same) a Scottish dish consisting of seasoned sheep's or calf's offal mixed with suet and oatmeal, boiled in a bag traditionally made from the animal's stomach.
–ORIGIN Middle English: prob. from earlier *hag* 'hack, hew', from Old Norse *hǫggva*.

haggle ■ v. dispute or bargain persistently, especially over a price. ■ n. a period of haggling.
–DERIVATIVES **haggler** n.
–ORIGIN C16 ('hack, mangle'): from Old Norse *hǫggva* 'hew'.

hagio- ■ comb. form relating to saints or holiness: *hagiographer*.
–ORIGIN from Greek *hagios* 'holy'.

hagiographer /ˌhaɡɪˈɒɡrəfə/ ■ n. a writer of the lives of the saints.

hagiography /ˌhaɡɪˈɒɡrəfi/ ■ n. **1** the writing of the lives of saints. **2** a biography idealizing its subject.
–DERIVATIVES **hagiographic** adj. **hagiographical** adj.

hagiolatry /ˌhaɡɪˈɒlətri/ ■ n. the worship of saints.

hagiology /ˌhaɡɪˈɒlədʒi/ ■ n. literature concerned with the lives and legends of saints.

hag-ridden ■ adj. afflicted by nightmares or anxieties.

hah ■ exclam. variant spelling of HA¹.

ha ha ■ exclam. used to represent laughter.
–ORIGIN natural utterance: first recorded in Old English.

ha-ha ■ n. a ditch with a wall on its inner side below ground level, forming a boundary to a park or garden without interrupting the view.
–ORIGIN C18: from French, said to be from the cry of surprise on encountering such an obstacle.

haikona ■ exclam. variant spelling of AIKONA.

haiku /ˈhʌɪkuː/ ■ n. (pl. same or **haikus**) a Japanese poem of seventeen syllables, in three lines of five, seven, and five.
–ORIGIN Japanese, contraction of *haikai no ku* 'light verse'.

hail¹ ■ n. **1** pellets of frozen rain falling in showers from cumulonimbus clouds. **2** a large number of things hurled forcefully through the air. ■ v. (**it hails,**) it is hailing, etc. hail falls.
–ORIGIN Old English, of Germanic origin.

hail² ■ v. **1** call out to (someone) to attract attention. ▶ signal for (a taxi). **2** acclaim enthusiastically as something: *he has been hailed as the new James Dean*. **3** (**hail from**) have one's home or origins in. ■ exclam. archaic expressing greeting or acclaim. ■ n. a call to attract attention.
–PHRASES **within hail** within earshot.
–DERIVATIVES **hailer** n.
–ORIGIN Middle English: from the obsolete adj. *hail* 'healthy' (used in greetings and toasts), from Old Norse *heill*, rel. to HALE.

hail-fellow-well-met ■ adj. showing excessive familiarity.

Hail Mary ■ n. (pl. **Hail Marys**) a prayer to the Virgin Mary used chiefly by Roman Catholics.

hailstone ■ n. a pellet of hail.

hair ■ n. **1** any of the fine thread-like strands growing from the skin of mammals and other animals, or from the epidermis of a plant. ▶ such strands collectively, especially those on a person's head. **2** a very small quantity or extent.
–PHRASES **hair of the dog** informal an alcoholic drink taken to cure a hangover. [from *hair of the dog that bit you*, formerly recommended as an efficacious remedy for the bite of a mad dog.] **a hair's breadth** a very small margin. **in** (or **out of**) **someone's hair** informal burdening (or ceasing to burden) someone. **keep your hair on!** Brit. informal stay calm. **let one's hair down** informal behave wildly or uninhibitedly. **make someone's hair stand on end** alarm someone. **not turn a hair** remain apparently unmoved. **split hairs** make overfine distinctions.
–DERIVATIVES **-haired** adj. **hairless** adj.
–ORIGIN Old English, of Germanic origin.

hairball ■ n. a ball of hair which collects in the stomach of a cat or similar animal as a result of the animal licking its coat.

hairband ■ n. a band for securing or tying back one's hair.

hairbrush ■ n. a brush for smoothing one's hair.

haircloth ■ n. stiff cloth with a cotton or linen warp and horsehair weft.

haircut ■ n. **1** the style in which someone's hair is cut. **2** an act of cutting someone's hair.

hairdo ■ n. (pl. **-os**) informal the style of a woman's hair.

hairdresser ■ n. a person who cuts and styles hair.
–DERIVATIVES **hairdressing** n.

hairdryer (also **hairdrier**) ■ n. an electrical device for drying the hair with warm air.

hairgrip ■ n. Brit. a flat hairpin with the ends close together.

hairline ■ n. **1** the edge of a person's hair. **2** [as modifier] very thin or fine: *a hairline fracture*.

hairnet ■ n. a fine mesh for confining the hair.

hairpiece ■ n. a patch or bunch of false hair used to augment a person's natural hair.

hairpin ■ n. a U-shaped pin for fastening the hair.

hairpin bend ■ n. a sharp U-shaped bend in a road.

hair-raising ■ adj. terrifying.

hair shirt ■ n. a shirt of haircloth, formerly worn by penitents and ascetics.
–DERIVATIVES **hair-shirted** adj.

hairslide ■ n. Brit. a clip for keeping a woman's hair in position.

hair-splitting ■ n. the action of making overfine distinctions.
–DERIVATIVES **hair-splitter** n.

hairspray ■ n. a solution sprayed on to hair to keep it in place.

hairspring ■ n. a slender flat coiled spring regulating the movement of the balance wheel in a watch.

hairstreak ■ n. a butterfly with narrow streaks or a row of dots on the underside of the hindwing. [Subfamily Theclinae: many species.]

hairstyle ■ n. a way in which someone's hair is cut or arranged.
–DERIVATIVES **hairstyling** n. **hairstylist** n.

hair trigger ■ n. a trigger of a firearm set for release at the slightest pressure.

hairy ■ adj. (**-ier**, **-iest**) **1** covered with hair. ▶ having the feel of hair. **2** informal alarming and difficult.
–DERIVATIVES **hairily** adv. **hairiness** n.

Haitian

Haitian /ˈheɪʃən, -ʃ(ə)n/ ■ n. **1** a native or inhabitant of Haiti. **2** (also **Haitian Creole**) the French-based Creole language spoken in Haiti. ■ adj. of or relating to Haiti, its inhabitants, or their language.

haji /ˈhadʒiː/ (also **hajji**) ■ n. (pl. **hajis**) a Muslim who has been to Mecca as a pilgrim.
– ORIGIN from Persian and Turkish *hājī*, *hājī*, from Arabic *ḥajj* (see **HAJJ**).

hajj /hadʒ/ (also **haj**) ■ n. the pilgrimage to Mecca which all Muslims are expected to make at least once.
– ORIGIN from Arabic (*al-*) *ḥajj* '(the Great) Pilgrimage'.

haka /ˈhɑːkə/ ■ n. a Maori ceremonial war dance involving chanting.
– ORIGIN from Maori.

hake ■ n. a large-headed elongated food fish with long jaws and strong teeth. [Genus *Merluccius*.]
– ORIGIN Middle English: perhaps from Old English *haca* 'hook'.

hakea ■ n. an Australian shrub with hard woody fruit, naturalized in South Africa. [Genus *Hakea*, family Proteaceae.]

halaal /həˈlɑːl/ (also **halal**) ■ adj. denoting or relating to meat prepared as prescribed by Muslim law. ■ n. halaal meat.
– ORIGIN C19: from Arabic *ḥalāl* 'according to religious law'.

Halacha /ˌhalɑːˈxɑː, həˈlɑːkə/ (also **Halakah**) ■ n. Jewish law and jurisprudence, based on the Talmud.
– DERIVATIVES **Halachic** adj.
– ORIGIN from Hebrew *hălākāh* 'law'.

halala /ˈhʌlʌlʌ, hʌˈlɑːlʌ/ ■ exclam. S. African **1** used to congratulate someone, honour or praise someone or something, or to express joy. **2** used to welcome or greet someone.
– ORIGIN from isiXhosa and isiZulu.

halberd /ˈhalbəːd/ (also **halbert**) ■ n. historical a combined spear and battleaxe.
– ORIGIN C15: from French *hallebarde*, from Middle High German *helmbarde*, from *helm* 'handle' + *barde* 'hatchet'.

halcyon /ˈhalsɪən, -ʃ(ə)n/ ■ adj. denoting a past time that was idyllically happy and peaceful. ■ n. **1** a tropical Asian and African kingfisher with brightly coloured plumage. [Genus *Halcyon*: many species.] **2** a mythical bird said to breed in a nest floating at sea, charming the wind and waves into calm.
– ORIGIN Middle English: from Greek *alkuōn* 'kingfisher' (also *halkuōn*, by association with *hals* 'sea' and *kuōn* 'conceiving').

haldi /ˈhʌldi/ ■ n. Indian term for **TURMERIC**.
– ORIGIN from Sanskrit *haridrā*.

hale ■ adj. (of an old person) strong and healthy.
– ORIGIN Old English, northern var. of *hāl* 'whole'.

half ■ n. (pl. **halves**) **1** either of two equal or corresponding parts into which something is or can be divided. ▶ either of two equal periods into which a sports game or performance is divided. **2** Brit. informal half a pint of beer. **3** Brit. informal a half-price fare or ticket. **4** Golf a score for a hole that is the same as one's opponent's. **5** a halfback. ■ predet. & pron. an amount equal to a half. ■ adj. forming a half. ■ adv. to the extent of half.
▶ partly: *half-cooked*.
– PHRASES **half a chance** informal the slightest opportunity. **the half of it** [usu. with neg.] informal the most important part or aspect. **half one** (**two**, etc.) informal way of saying half past one (two, etc.). **half past one** (**two**, etc.) thirty minutes after one (two, etc.) o'clock. **not do things by halves** do things thoroughly or extravagantly. **not half 1** not nearly: *he is not half such a fool as they thought*. **2** informal not at all: *the players are not half bad*. **3** Brit. informal to an extreme degree: *she didn't half flare up!* **too —— by half** excessively ——: *too superstitious by half*.
– ORIGIN Old English, of Germanic origin.

half a crown ■ n. another term for **HALF-CROWN**.

half a dozen ■ n. another term for **HALF-DOZEN**.

half-and-half ■ adv. & adj. in equal parts. ■ n. N. Amer. a mixture of milk and cream.

half-arsed (US **half-assed**) ■ adj. vulgar slang incompetent; inadequate.

halfback ■ n. a player in a ball game whose position is between the forwards and fullbacks.

half-baked ■ adj. incompetently planned or considered.

half blood ■ n. **1** the relationship between people having one parent in common. ▶ a person related to another in this way. **2** offensive another term for **HALF-BREED**.
– DERIVATIVES **half-blooded** adj.

half board ■ n. chiefly Brit. provision of bed, breakfast, and a main meal at a hotel or guest house.

half-boot ■ n. a boot reaching up to the calf.

half-breed ■ n. offensive a person of mixed race.

half-brother (or **half-sister**) ■ n. a brother (or sister) with whom one has only one parent in common.

half-caste ■ n. offensive a person of mixed race.

half-century ■ n. **1** a period of fifty years. **2** a score of fifty in a sporting event, especially cricket.

half-cock ■ n. the partly raised position of the cock of a gun.
– PHRASES **at half-cock 1** (of a gun) with the cock partly raised. **2** when only partly ready.
– DERIVATIVES **half-cocked** adj.

half-crown (also **half a crown**) ■ n. a former British coin equal to two shillings and sixpence (12½p.).

half-cut ■ adj. informal drunk.

half-dozen (also **half a dozen**) ■ n. a group of six.

half-duplex ■ adj. (of a communications system or computer circuit) allowing the transmission of signals in both directions but not simultaneously.

half-hardy ■ adj. (of a plant) able to grow outdoors except in severe frost.

half-hearted ■ adj. without enthusiasm or energy.
– DERIVATIVES **half-heartedly** adv. **half-heartedness** n.

half hitch ■ n. a knot formed by passing the end of a rope round its standing part and then through the loop.

half holiday ■ n. a half day taken as a holiday, especially at school.

half-hour ■ n. **1** (also **half an hour**) a period of thirty minutes. **2** a point in time thirty minutes after a full hour of the clock.
– DERIVATIVES **half-hourly** adj. & adv.

half-inch ■ n. a unit of length half as large as an inch.

half-jack ■ n. S. African informal a small flat bottle of spirit, holding 375 millilitres.

half-life ■ n. **1** the time taken for the radioactivity of an isotope to fall to half its original value. **2** the time required for any specified property to decrease by half.

half-light ■ n. dim light, as at dusk.

half mast ■ n. **1** a position of a flag halfway down its mast, as a mark of respect for a person who has died. **2** humorous a position lower than normal, especially for clothes.

half measure ■ n. an inadequate action or policy.

halfmens /ˈhɑːfmɛns/ ■ n. S. African a succulent with an unbranched spiny trunk and a crown of oblong-shaped leaves. [*Pachypodium namaquanum*.]
– ORIGIN Afrikaans, from *half* 'half' + *mens* 'person'.

half-moon ■ n. **1** the moon when only half its surface is visible from the earth. **2** a semicircular or crescent-shaped object.

half nelson ■ n. see **NELSON**.

half note ■ n. Music **1** chiefly N. Amer. a minim. **2** (in tonic sol-fa) a quaver.

halfpenny /ˈheɪpni/ (also **ha'penny**) ■ n. (pl. **-pennies** (for separate coins); **-pence** (for a sum of money) /ˈheɪp(ə)ns/) a former British coin equal to half an old or new penny.

halfpennyworth /ˈheɪpəθ, ˈheɪpnɪˌwəθ/ (also **ha'p'orth**) ■ n. Brit. **1** as much as could be bought for a halfpenny. **2** [usu. with neg.] (**ha'p'orth**) informal a negligible amount.

half relief ■ n. a method of moulding, carving, or stamping a design in which figures project to half their true proportions.

half-sovereign ■ n. a former British gold coin worth ten shillings (50p).

half-term ■ n. a short holiday halfway through a school term.

half-tester ■ n. historical a canopy extending over half the length of a bed.

half-timbered ■ adj. having walls with a timber frame and a brick or plaster filling.
– DERIVATIVES **half-timbering** n.

half-time ■ n. a short interval between two halves of a game.

half-title ■ n. the title of a book, printed on the right-hand page before the title page.

half-tone ■ n. a reproduction of an image in which the tones of grey or colour are produced by variously sized dots.

half-truth ■ n. a statement conveying only part of the truth.

half-volley ■ n. (chiefly in tennis and soccer) a strike or kick of the ball immediately after it bounces.

halfway ■ adv. & adj. **1** at or to a point equidistant between two others. **2** [as adv.] to some extent: *halfway decent*.

halfway house ■ n. **1** the halfway point in a progression. **2** a compromise. **3** a centre for rehabilitating former prisoners, psychiatric patients, or others used to institutional life.

halfwit ■ n. informal a stupid person.
– DERIVATIVES **half-witted** adj.

half-yearly ■ adj. & adv. at intervals of six months.

halibut /ˈhalɪbət/ ■ n. (pl. same) a large marine flatfish, used as food. [*Hippoglossus hippoglossus* (N. Atlantic), *H. stenolepis* (N. Pacific), and other species.]
– ORIGIN Middle English: from *haly* 'holy' + obsolete *butt* 'flatfish' (because it was often eaten on holy days).

halide /ˈheɪlʌɪd/ ■ n. Chemistry a binary compound of a halogen with another element or group.

halite /ˈhalʌɪt/ ■ n. sodium chloride as a mineral; rock salt.
– ORIGIN C19: from Greek *hals* 'salt'.

halitosis /ˌhalɪˈtəʊsɪs/ ■ n. unpleasant-smelling breath.
– ORIGIN C19: from Latin *halitus* 'breath'.

hall ■ n. **1** the room or space just inside the front entrance of a house. ▶ N. Amer. a corridor or passage in a building. **2** a large room for meetings, concerts, etc. ▶ the dining room of a college, university, or school. **3** (also **hall of residence**) a university building in which students live. **4** a large country house: *Toadbury Hall*.
– ORIGIN Old English, of Germanic origin.

Hall effect ■ n. Physics the production of a potential difference across an electrical conductor when a magnetic field is applied perpendicular to the current direction.
– ORIGIN C20: named after the American physicist Edwin H. *Hall*.

hallelujah /ˌhalɪˈluːjə/ (also **alleluia**) ■ exclam. God be praised. ■ n. an utterance of the word 'hallelujah'.
– ORIGIN Old English, from Greek *allēlouia*, or from Hebrew *hallĕlūyāh* 'praise ye the Lord'.

hallmark ■ n. **1** a mark stamped on articles of gold, silver, or platinum by the British assay offices, certifying purity. **2** a distinctive feature, especially of excellence. ■ v. **1** stamp with a hallmark. **2** designate as distinctive.
– ORIGIN C18: from *Goldsmiths' Hall* in London, where articles were tested and stamped.

hallo ■ exclam. variant spelling of **HELLO**.

Hall of Fame ■ n. the group of people who have excelled in a particular sphere.

halloo ■ exclam. used to incite dogs to the chase during a hunt. ▶ used to attract someone's attention. ■ n. a cry of 'halloo'. ■ v. (**halloos**, **hallooed**) cry or shout 'halloo'.
– ORIGIN C16: prob. from the rare v. *hallow* 'pursue or urge on with shouts', from imitative Old French *haloer*.

hallow /ˈhaləʊ/ ■ v. **1** make holy; consecrate. **2** honour as holy. ▶ [as adj. **hallowed**] greatly revered.
– ORIGIN Old English, of Germanic origin; rel. to **HOLY**.

Halloween (also **Hallowe'en**) ■ n. the night of 31 October, the eve of All Saints' Day.

527   **halter**

– ORIGIN C18: contraction of *All Hallow Even* (see **HALLOW**, **EVEN**²).

hall porter ■ n. chiefly Brit. a concierge or person who carries guests' luggage in a hotel.

hallstand ■ n. a coat stand in the hall of a house.

hallucinate /həˈluːsɪneɪt/ ■ v. experience a seemingly real perception of something not actually present.
– DERIVATIVES **hallucination** n.
– ORIGIN C17: from Latin *hallucinari* 'go astray in thought', from Greek *alussein* 'be uneasy or distraught'.

hallucinatory /həˈluːsɪnəˌt(ə)ri/ ■ adj. of or resembling a hallucination. ▶ causing hallucinations.

hallucinogen /həˈluːsɪnədʒ(ə)n/ ■ n. a drug causing hallucinations.
– DERIVATIVES **hallucinogenic** adj.

hallway ■ n. another term for **HALL** (in sense 1).

halo /ˈheɪləʊ/ ■ n. (pl. **-oes** or **-os**) **1** (in a painting) a circle of light surrounding the head of a holy person. **2** a circle of light round the sun or moon caused by refraction through ice crystals in the atmosphere. ■ v. (**-oes**, **-oed**) surround with or as if with a halo.
– ORIGIN C16: from Latin *halos*, from Greek *halōs* 'disc of the sun or moon'.

halo- /ˈheɪləʊ/ ■ comb. form **1** relating to salinity: *halophile*. [from Greek *hals*, *halo* 'salt'.] **2** representing **HALOGEN**.

halocarbon ■ n. Chemistry a compound in which the hydrogen of a hydrocarbon is replaced by halogens.

halo effect ■ n. the tendency for an impression created in one area to influence opinion in another area.

halogen /ˈhalədʒ(ə)n, ˈheɪl-/ ■ n. **1** Chemistry any of the group of reactive, non-metallic elements fluorine, chlorine, bromine, iodine, and astatine. **2** [as modifier] denoting lamps and radiant heat sources using a filament surrounded by halogen vapour.
– DERIVATIVES **halogenic** adj.
– ORIGIN C19: from Greek *hals*, *halo-* 'salt' + **-GEN**.

halogenate /həˈlɒdʒɪneɪt/ ■ v. [usu. as adj. **halogenated**] Chemistry introduce one or more halogen atoms into (a compound or molecule).
– DERIVATIVES **halogenation** n.

halon /ˈheɪlɒn/ ■ n. any of a number of unreactive gaseous compounds of carbon with halogens, used in fire extinguishers.
– ORIGIN 1960s: from **HALOGEN**.

haloperidol /ˌhalə(ʊ)ˈpɛrɪdɒl, ˌheɪlə(ʊ)-/ ■ n. Medicine a synthetic antidepressant used chiefly in the treatment of psychotic conditions.
– ORIGIN 1960s: blend of **HALOGEN** and *piperidine* (denoting a liquid derived from pyridine).

halophile /ˈhalə(ʊ)fʌɪl, ˈheɪl-/ ■ n. Ecology an organism that grows in or can tolerate saline conditions.
– DERIVATIVES **halophilic** adj.

halophyte /ˈhaləfʌɪt, ˈheɪlə-/ ■ n. Botany a plant adapted to growing in saline conditions.

halothane /ˈhalə(ʊ)θeɪn/ ■ n. Medicine a volatile synthetic organic compound used as a general anaesthetic.
– ORIGIN 1950s: blend of **HALOGEN** and **ETHANE**.

halt¹ ■ v. bring or come to an abrupt stop. ■ n. **1** a suspension of movement or activity. **2** a minor stopping place on a local railway line.
– PHRASES **call a halt** order a stop.
– ORIGIN C16: orig. in the phr. *make halt*, from German *haltmachen*, from *halten* 'to hold'.

halt² archaic ■ adj. lame. ■ v. walk with a limp.
– ORIGIN Old English, of Germanic origin.

halter ■ n. **1** a rope or strap placed around the head of an animal and used to lead or tether it. **2** archaic a noose for hanging a person. **3** a strap passing behind the neck by which the bodice of a sleeveless dress or top is held in place. ■ v. put a halter on (an animal). ▶ archaic hang (someone).
– ORIGIN Old English *hælftre*, of Germanic origin, meaning 'something to hold things by'.

halteres /halˈtɪə/ ■ pl. n. Entomology a pair of knobbed filaments that replace the hindwings of a two-winged fly and act as balancing organs during flight.
– ORIGIN C16 (orig. denoting weights held to give impetus when jumping): from Greek *haltēres*, from *hallesthai* 'to leap'.

halter neck ■ n. a style of neckline incorporating a halter.

halting ■ adj. slow and hesitant.
– DERIVATIVES **haltingly** adv.

halva /ˈhalvɑː, -və/ (also **halvah**) ■ n. a Middle Eastern sweet made of sesame flour and honey.
– ORIGIN from Arabic and Persian *ḥalwā* 'sweetmeat'.

halve /hɑːv/ ■ v. 1 divide into two parts of equal size. ▸ share (something) equally with another person. 2 reduce or be reduced by half. 3 Golf use the same number of strokes as an opponent and thus draw (a hole or match). 4 [usu. as noun **halving**] fit (crossing timbers) together by cutting out half the thickness of each.
– ORIGIN Middle English: from HALF.

halves plural form of HALF.

halwa /ˈhalwɑː/ (also **halwah**) ■ n. a sweet Indian dish with carrots or semolina, almonds, and cardamom.
– ORIGIN from Arabic, 'sweetmeat'.

halyard /ˈhaljəd/ ■ n. a rope used for raising and lowering a sail, yard, or flag on a ship.
– ORIGIN Middle English *halier*, from obsolete *hale* 'haul'; the change in the ending was due to association with YARD[1].

ham[1] ■ n. 1 meat from the upper part of a pig's leg salted and dried or smoked. 2 (**hams**) the back of the thigh or the thighs and buttocks.
– ORIGIN Old English *ham*, *hom* (denoting the back of the knee), from a Germanic base meaning 'be crooked'.

ham[2] ■ n. 1 an inexpert or unsubtle actor or piece of acting. 2 (also **radio ham**) informal an amateur radio operator. ■ v. (**hammed**, **hamming**) (usu. **ham it up**) informal overact.
– ORIGIN C19: perhaps from the first syllable of AMATEUR.

hamadryad /ˌhaməˈdrʌɪad, -ad/ ■ n. 1 Greek & Roman Mythology a nymph who lives in a tree and dies when it dies. 2 another term for KING COBRA.
– ORIGIN from Greek *Hamadruas*, from *hama* 'together' + *drus* 'tree'.

hamadryas /ˌhaməˈdrʌɪəs, -as/ ■ n. a large Arabian and NE African baboon, the male of which has a silvery-grey coat of hair and a naked red face and rump. [*Papio hamadryas*.]
– ORIGIN 1930s: (see HAMADRYAD).

hamburger ■ n. a round patty of minced beef, fried or grilled and typically served in a bread roll.
– ORIGIN C19: from German, from *Hamburg*, a city in northern Germany.

hamel /ˈhɑːməl/ ■ n. S. African a castrated ram; a wether.
– ORIGIN Afrikaans, from Dutch.

hamerkop ■ n. variant spelling of HAMMERKOP.

ham-fisted ■ adj. informal clumsy; awkward.
– DERIVATIVES **ham-fistedly** adv. **ham-fistedness** n.

ham-handed ■ adj. another term for HAM-FISTED.
– DERIVATIVES **ham-handedly** adv. **ham-handedness** n.

Hamitic /həˈmɪtɪk/ ■ adj. of or denoting a hypothetical language family including Berber and ancient Egyptian.

hamlet ■ n. a small village, especially (in Britain) one without a church.
– ORIGIN Middle English: from Old French *hamelet*, diminutive of *hamel* 'little village'; rel. to HOME.

hammer ■ n. 1 a tool consisting of a heavy metal head mounted at the end of a handle, used for breaking things and driving in nails. ▸ an auctioneer's mallet, tapped to indicate a sale. 2 a part of a mechanism that hits another, e.g. one exploding the charge in a gun or striking piano strings. 3 a heavy metal ball attached to a wire for throwing in an athletic contest. 4 another term for MALLEUS. ■ v. 1 hit or beat repeatedly with or as with a hammer. 2 (**hammer away**) work hard and persistently. 3 (**hammer something in/into**) inculcate something forcefully or repeatedly. 4 (**hammer something out**) laboriously work out the details of a plan or agreement. 5 (**hammer something out**) play a tune loudly and unskilfully, especially on the piano. 6 informal utterly defeat.
– PHRASES **come** (or **go**) **under the hammer** be sold at an auction. **hammer and tongs** informal enthusiastically or vehemently: *they fought hammer and tongs*.
– DERIVATIVES **hammering** n.
– ORIGIN Old English, of Germanic origin.

hammer and sickle ■ n. the symbols of the industrial worker and the peasant used as the emblem of the former USSR and of international communism.

hammer drill ■ n. a power drill that delivers a rapid succession of blows.

hammerhead ■ n. 1 a shark with flattened blade-like extensions on either side of the head. [Genus *Sphyrna*: several species.] 2 another term for HAMMERKOP.

hammerkop /ˈhaməkɒp/ (also **hamerkop**) ■ n. a brown African marshbird related to the storks, with a crest that looks like a backward projection of the head. [*Scopus umbretta*.]
– ORIGIN C19: from Afrikaans, from *hamer* 'hammer' + *kop* 'head'.

hammock ■ n. a wide strip of canvas or rope mesh suspended by two ends, used as a bed.
– ORIGIN C16: from Taino (an extinct Caribbean language) *hamaka*.

Hammond organ ■ n. trademark a type of electronic organ.
– ORIGIN 1930s: named after the American mechanical engineer Laurens *Hammond*.

hammy ■ adj. (**-ier**, **-iest**) 1 informal (of acting or an actor) exaggerated or over-theatrical. 2 (of a hand or thigh) thick and solid.

hamper[1] ■ n. a basket with a carrying handle and a hinged lid, used for food, cutlery, etc. on a picnic. ▸ a box containing special items of food and drink, sometimes offered as a prize.
– ORIGIN Middle English: from Anglo-Norman French *hanaper* 'case for a goblet', from Old French *hanap* 'goblet', of Germanic origin.

hamper[2] ■ v. hinder or impede the movement or progress of.
– ORIGIN Middle English: perhaps rel. to German *hemmen* 'restrain'.

hamster ■ n. a burrowing rodent with a short tail and large cheek pouches, native to Europe and North Asia. [*Mesocricetus auratus* (**golden hamster**, often kept as a pet), *Cricetus cricetus* (**common hamster**), and other species.]
– ORIGIN C17: from Old High German *hamustro* 'corn-weevil'.

hamstring ■ n. any of five tendons at the back of a person's knee. ▸ the great tendon at the back of a quadruped's hock. ■ v. (past and past part. **hamstrung**) 1 cripple by cutting the hamstrings. 2 severely restrict; thwart: *we were hamstring by a total lack of knowledge*.
– ORIGIN C16: from HAM[1] + STRING.

Han /han/ ■ n. 1 the Chinese dynasty that ruled almost continuously from 206 BC until AD 220. 2 the dominant ethnic group in China.

hand ■ n. 1 the end part of the arm beyond the wrist, including the palm, fingers, and thumb. ▸ [as modifier] operated by or held in the hand: *hand tool*. ▸ [as modifier or in combination] done or made manually: *hand wash* | *hand-carved*. 2 a pointer on a clock or watch indicating the passing of units of time. 3 (**hands**) with reference to someone's power or control: *taking the law into their own hands*. ▸ (usu. **a hand**) an active role: *he had a big hand in organizing the event*. ▸ (usu. **a hand**) help in doing something. 4 a person engaging in manual labour, especially in a factory, on a farm, or on board a ship. 5 informal a round of applause: *his fans gave him a big hand*. 6 the set of cards dealt to a player in a card game. ▸ a round or short spell of play in a card game. 7 a person's handwriting. 8 a unit of measurement of a horse's height, equal to 4 inches (10.16 cm). [denoting the breadth of a hand.] 9 a pledge of marriage by a woman. ■ v. 1 pick (something) up and give it to (someone). 2 dated hold the hand of, in order to guide or assist: *he handed*

him into a carriage. **3** Nautical take in or furl (a sail).
- PHRASES **all hands on deck** a cry or signal used on board ship to indicate that all crew members are to go on deck. **at hand 1** close by; readily accessible. **2** close in time; about to happen. **at** (or **by**) **the hands** (or **hand**) **of** through the agency of. **by hand** by a person and not a machine. **get** (or **keep**) **one's hand in** become (or remain) practised in something. **give** (or **lend**) **a hand** assist. **hand in glove** in close association: *they were working hand in glove with our enemies*. **hand in hand** closely associated; together. (**from**) **hand to mouth** satisfying only one's immediate needs because of lack of money. **hands down** easily and decisively. **hands-off** not involving or requiring direct intervention: *a hands-off management style*. **hands-on** involving or offering active participation. **have one's hands tied** informal be unable to act freely. **have to hand it to someone** informal used to acknowledge the merit or achievement of someone. **in hand 1** in progress; requiring immediate attention. **2** ready for use if required; in reserve. **3** under one's control. **in safe hands** protected by someone trustworthy from harm or damage. **make** (or **lose** or **spend**) **money hand over fist** informal make (or lose or spend) money very rapidly. **off someone's hands** not having to be dealt with by the person specified. **on every hand** all around. **on hand 1** present and available. **2** needing to be dealt with. **on someone's hands 1** under the responsibility of the person specified. **2** at someone's disposal. **on the one** (or **the other**) **hand** used to present factors for (and against). **out of hand 1** not under control. **2** without taking time to think: *they rejected negotiations out of hand*. **a safe pair of hands** denoting someone who is capable, reliable, or trustworthy in a situation. **set** (or **put**) **one's hand to** start work on. **stay someone's hand** restrain someone from acting. **take a hand** become influential; intervene: *fate was about to take a hand in the outcome of the championship*. **to hand** within easy reach. **turn one's hand to** undertake (an activity different from one's usual occupation). **wait on someone hand and foot** attend to all someone's needs or requests, especially when unreasonable.
- PHRASAL VERBS **hand something down 1** pass something on to a successor. **2** announce something formally or publicly. **hand someone off** Rugby push away a tackling opponent with one's hand. **hand something on** pass something to the next person. **hand something out 1** distribute something among a group of people. **2** impose a penalty or misfortune on someone. **hand over** pass to someone else. **hand something round** (or **around**) offer something to each of a number of people in turn.
- DERIVATIVES **handless** adj.
- ORIGIN Old English, of Germanic origin.

handbag ▪ n. a small bag used by a woman to carry everyday personal items.

handball ▪ n. **1** a game in which the ball is hit with the hand in a walled court. **2** Soccer touching of the ball with the hand or arm, constituting a foul.

handbell ▪ n. a small bell with a handle or strap, especially one of a set tuned to a range of notes and played by a group of people.

handbill ▪ n. a small printed advertisement or other notice distributed by hand.

handbook ▪ n. a book giving brief information such as basic facts on a particular subject or instructions for operating a machine.

handbrake ▪ n. a brake operated by hand, used to hold an already stationary vehicle.

handcart ▪ n. a small cart pushed or drawn by hand.

handcraft ▪ v. [usu. as adj. **handcrafted**] make skilfully by hand. ▪ n. another term for HANDICRAFT.

handcuff ▪ n. (**handcuffs**) a pair of lockable linked metal rings for securing a prisoner's wrists. ▪ v. put handcuffs on.

-handed ▪ comb. form **1** for or involving a specified number of hands: *a two-handed back-hand*. **2** using the hand specified: *right-handed*. **3** having hands as specified: *empty-handed*.
- DERIVATIVES **-handedly** adv. **-handedness** n.

handful ▪ n. (pl. **-fuls**) **1** a quantity that fills the hand. ▸ a small number or amount. **2** informal a person who is difficult to deal with or control.

hand grenade ▪ n. a hand-thrown grenade.

handgrip ▪ n. a handle for holding something by.

handgun ▪ n. a gun designed for use by one hand, chiefly either a pistol or a revolver.

hand-held ▪ adj. (of equipment) designed to be held in the hand when being used.

handhold ▪ n. something for a hand to grip on.

handicap ▪ n. **1** a condition that markedly restricts a person's ability to function physically, mentally, or socially. **2** a disadvantage imposed on a superior competitor in sports such as golf and horse racing in order to make the chances more equal. ▸ the extra weight given as a handicap to a racehorse or other competitor. ▸ the number of strokes by which a golfer normally exceeds par for a course. ▪ v. (**handicapped**, **handicapping**) act as a handicap to; place at a disadvantage.
- ORIGIN C17: from the phr. *hand in cap*, a game in which players showed acceptance or rejection of a disputed object's valuation by bringing their hands either full or empty out of a cap in which forfeit money had been deposited. In the 18th century a similar practice was used to signify agreement or disagreement with an allocation of additional weight to be carried in horse races.

handicapped ▪ adj. having a handicap.

handicapper ▪ n. **1** a person appointed to assess a competitor's handicap. **2** a person or horse having a specified handicap.

handicraft ▪ n. (often **handicrafts**) **1** a particular skill of making decorative domestic or other objects by hand. **2** an object made using a skill of this kind.
- ORIGIN Middle English: alteration of HANDCRAFT, on the pattern of *handiwork*.

handiwork ▪ n. **1** (**one's handiwork**) something that one has made or done. **2** the making of things by hand.
- ORIGIN Old English *handgeweorc*, from HAND + *geweorc* 'something made', interpreted as *handy* + *work*.

handkerchief /ˈhaŋkətʃɪf/ ▪ n. (pl. **handkerchiefs** or **handkerchieves** /-tʃiːvz/) a square of cotton or other material for wiping one's nose.

handlanger /ˈhantlaŋə/ ▪ n. S. African an assistant, especially to an artisan.
- ORIGIN Afrikaans, from *hand* 'hand' + *lang(s)* 'alongside'.

handle ▪ v. **1** feel or manipulate with the hands. ▸ (of a vehicle) respond or behave in a specified way when being driven: *the new model does not handle well*. **2** manage or cope with (a situation, person, or problem). ▸ control or manage commercially. **3** deal with. ▸ receive or deal in (stolen goods). **4** (**handle oneself**) conduct oneself. ▪ n. **1** the part by which a thing is held, carried, or controlled. **2** a means of understanding, controlling, or approaching a person or situation: *it'll give people some kind of handle on these issues*. **3** informal the name of a person or place: *that's some handle for a baby*. **4** the feel of goods, especially textiles, when handled.
- DERIVATIVES **-handled** adj. **handleless** adj. **handling** n.
- ORIGIN Old English, from HAND.

handlebar (also **handlebars**) ▪ n. the steering bar of a bicycle, motorbike, or other similar vehicle.

handlebar moustache ▪ n. a wide, thick moustache with the ends curving slightly upwards.

handler ▪ n. **1** a person who handles a particular type of article or commodity. **2** a person who trains or has charge of an animal. **3** a person who trains or manages another person. ▸ a person who trains and acts as second to a boxer.

handmade ▪ adj. made by hand rather than machine.

handmaid ▪ n. **1** archaic a female servant. **2** a subservient partner or element.

handmaiden ▪ n. another term for HANDMAID.

hand-me-down ▪ n. a garment or other item that has been passed on from another person.

handoff ▪ n. **1** Rugby the act of pushing away an opponent with the hand in a tackle. **2** American Football an exchange made by handing the ball to a teammate.

handout ▪ n. **1** an amount of money or other aid given to a needy person or organization. **2** a piece of printed

handover

information provided free of charge, especially to accompany a lecture or advertise something.

handover ■ n. an act or instance of handing something over.

hand-pick ■ v. [usu. as adj. **hand-picked**] select carefully.

handprint ■ n. the mark left by the impression of a hand.

handrail ■ n. a rail fixed to posts or a wall for people to hold on to for support.

handset ■ n. 1 the part of a telephone that is held up to speak into and listen to. 2 a hand-held control device for a piece of electronic equipment.

hands-free ■ adj. (especially of a telephone) designed to be operated without the use of the hands.

handshake ■ n. an act of shaking a person's hand.
– DERIVATIVES **handshaking** n.

handsome ■ adj. (**-er**, **-est**) 1 (of a man) good-looking. ▶ (of a woman) striking and imposing rather than conventionally pretty. 2 (of a thing) well made, imposing, and of obvious quality. 3 (of an amount) substantial; sizeable.
– DERIVATIVES **handsomely** adv. **handsomeness** n.
– ORIGIN Middle English: from HAND + -SOME¹; the original sense was 'easy to handle or use', hence 'apt, clever'.

handspring ■ n. a jump through the air on to one's hands followed by another on to one's feet.

handstand ■ n. an act of balancing upside down on one's hands.

hand-to-hand ■ adj. (of fighting) at close quarters.

handwriting ■ n. writing with a pen or pencil rather than by typing or printing. ▶ a person's particular style of writing.

handwritten ■ adj. written with a pen, pencil, or other hand-held implement.

handy ■ adj. (**-ier**, **-iest**) 1 convenient to handle or use; useful. 2 ready to hand. ▶ placed or occurring conveniently. 3 skilful.
– PHRASES **come in handy** informal turn out to be useful.
– DERIVATIVES **handily** adv.

handyman ■ n. (pl. **-men**) a person employed to do general decorating or domestic repairs.

hanepoot /'ha:nəpuət/ ■ n. a variety of muscat grape used as a table grape, and for raisins and wine-making. ▶ sweet wine made from this grape, unfortified for table use or fortified as a muscatel wine.
– ORIGIN C19: S. African Dutch, from Dutch *haan* 'cock' + *poot* 'claw'.

hang ■ v. (past and past part. **hung** except in sense 2) 1 suspend or be suspended from above with the lower part not attached. ▶ attach or be attached so as to allow free movement about the point of attachment: *hanging a door*. ▶ (of fabric or a garment) fall or drape in a specified way. ▶ paste (wallpaper) to a wall. 2 (past and past part. **hanged**) kill or be killed by tying a rope attached from above around the neck and removing the support from beneath the feet (used as a form of capital punishment). 3 attach (meat or game) to a hook and leave it until dry, tender, or high. 4 remain static in the air. ▶ be present or imminent, especially oppressively or threateningly. 5 Computing come unexpectedly to a state in which no further operations can be carried out. ■ n. a downward droop or bend. ▶ the way in which something hangs or is hung. ■ exclam. dated used in expressions as a mild oath: *well, hang it all!*
– PHRASES **get the hang of** informal learn how to operate or do. **hang fire** delay or be delayed in taking action. (a) **hang of** S. African informal very great; extremely. **hang one's hat** be resident. **hang a left** (or **right**) informal make a left (or right) turn. **hang someone out to dry** informal, chiefly N. Amer. leave someone in a difficult or vulnerable situation. **hang tough** N. Amer. be or remain inflexible or firmly resolved. **let it all hang out** informal be very relaxed or uninhibited. **not care** (or **give**) **a hang** informal not care at all.
– PHRASAL VERBS **hang around** (or **round** or Brit. **about**) 1 loiter; wait around. 2 (**hang around with**) associate with. **hang back** remain behind. ▶ show reluctance to act or move. **hang in** informal remain persistent and

determined in difficult circumstances. **hang on 1** hold tightly. ▶ informal remain firm or resolved. 2 informal wait for a short time. 3 be contingent or dependent on. 4 listen closely to. **hang out** informal spend time relaxing or enjoying oneself. **hang together 1** make sense; be consistent. 2 (of people) help or support one another. **hang up** end a telephone conversation by cutting the connection.
– ORIGIN Old English, of West Germanic origin, reinforced by Old Norse *hanga*.

hangar /'haŋə/ ■ n. a large building with extensive floor area, typically for housing aircraft.
– DERIVATIVES **hangarage** n.
– ORIGIN C17: from French; prob. from Germanic bases meaning 'hamlet' and 'enclosure'.

hangdog ■ adj. having a dejected or guilty appearance; shamefaced.

hanger¹ ■ n. 1 a person who hangs something. 2 (also **coat hanger**) a shaped piece of wood, plastic, or metal with a hook at the top, for hanging clothes from a rail.

hanger² ■ n. Brit. a wood on the side of a steep hill.
– ORIGIN Old English *hangra*, from *hangian* 'hang'.

hanger-on ■ n. (pl. **hangers-on**) a person who associates sycophantically with another person.

hang-glider ■ n. an unpowered flying apparatus for a single person, consisting of a frame with a fabric aerofoil stretched over it from which the operator is suspended in a harness, controlling flight by body movement.
– DERIVATIVES **hang-glide** v. **hang-gliding** n.

hanging ■ n. 1 the practice of hanging condemned people as a form of capital punishment. 2 a decorative piece of fabric hung on the wall of a room or around a bed. ■ adj. 1 suspended in the air. 2 situated or designed so as to appear to hang down.

hanging valley ■ n. a valley which is cut across by a deeper valley or a cliff.

hangman ■ n. (pl. **-men**) an executioner who hangs condemned people.

hangnail ■ n. a piece of torn skin at the root of a fingernail.
– ORIGIN C17: alteration of *agnail* 'painful swelling around a nail', influenced by HANG.

hang-out ■ n. informal a place one lives in or frequently visits.

hangover ■ n. 1 a severe headache or other after-effects caused by drinking an excess of alcohol. 2 a thing that has survived from the past.

hang-up ■ n. informal an emotional problem or inhibition.

hank ■ n. 1 a coil or skein of wool, hair, or other material. 2 a measurement of the length per unit mass of cloth or yarn (equal to 840 yards (768 metres) for cotton yarn and 560 yards (512 metres) for worsted). 3 Nautical a ring for securing a staysail to the stay.
– ORIGIN Middle English: from Old Norse *hǫnk*; cf. Swedish *hank* 'string' and Danish *hank* 'handle'.

hanker ■ v. (**hanker after/for/to do something**) feel a strong desire for or to do something.
– ORIGIN C17: prob. rel. to HANG.

hanky (also **hankie**) ■ n. (pl. **-ies**) informal a handkerchief.

hanky-panky ■ n. informal, humorous behaviour considered improper but not seriously so.
– ORIGIN C19: perhaps an alteration of *hokey-pokey* (see HOKEY-COKEY).

Hansard /'hansɑ:d, -səd/ ■ n. the official verbatim record of debates in the South African, British, and some other parliaments.
– ORIGIN C19: named after the English printer Thomas C. Hansard.

hansom /'hans(ə)m/ (also **hansom cab**) ■ n. historical a two-wheeled horse-drawn cab with space for two inside, with the driver seated behind.
– ORIGIN C19: named after the English architect Joseph A. Hansom, who patented it.

Hanukkah /'hanʊkə, x-/ (also **Chanukkah**) ■ n. an eight-day Jewish festival of lights held in December, commemorating the rededication of the Jewish Temple in Jerusalem in 165 BC after its desecration.
– ORIGIN from Hebrew *ḥănukkāh* 'consecration'.

hap ■ n. S. African informal a bite or chunk of something.
– ORIGIN Afrikaans.

ha'penny ■ n. variant spelling of HALFPENNY.

haphazard /ˈhapˌhazəd/ ■ adj. lacking order or organization.
– DERIVATIVES **haphazardly** adv.
– ORIGIN C16: from archaic *hap* 'luck, fortune' + HAZARD.

hapless ■ adj. unlucky; unfortunate.
– DERIVATIVES **haplessly** adv.
– ORIGIN Middle English: from the noun *hap* (see HAPHAZARD).

haplodiploid /ˌhaplə(ʊ)ˈdɪplɔɪd/ ■ adj. Biology denoting or possessing a genetic system in which females develop from fertilized (diploid) eggs and males from unfertilized (haploid) ones.

haploid /ˈhaplɔɪd/ ■ adj. Genetics (of a cell or nucleus) having a single set of unpaired chromosomes. Compare with DIPLOID.
– DERIVATIVES **haploidy** n.

happen ■ v. 1 take place; occur. 2 come about by chance. ▶ chance to do something or come about. ▶ **(happen on)** come across by chance. ▶ used as a polite formula in questions: *do you happen to know who her doctor is?* 3 **(happen to)** be experienced by; befall. ▶ become of. ■ adv. N. English perhaps; maybe.
– PHRASES **as it happens** actually; as a matter of fact.
– ORIGIN Middle English (superseding the verb *hap* 'come about by chance'): from the noun *hap* (see HAPHAZARD).

happening ■ n. 1 an event or occurrence. 2 a partly improvised or spontaneous performance, typically involving audience participation. ■ adj. informal fashionable; trendy.

happenstance /ˈhap(ə)nˌstans/ ■ n. chiefly N. Amer. coincidence.
– ORIGIN C19: blend of HAPPEN and CIRCUMSTANCE.

happy ■ adj. (-ier, -iest) 1 feeling or showing pleasure or contentment. ▶ willing to do something. 2 fortunate and convenient: *a happy coincidence.* 3 [in combination] informal inclined to use a specified thing excessively or at random: *trigger-happy.*
– DERIVATIVES **happily** adv. **happiness** n.
– ORIGIN Middle English: from the noun *hap* (see HAPHAZARD).

happy-go-lucky ■ adj. cheerfully unconcerned about the future.

happy hour ■ n. a period of the day when drinks are sold at reduced prices in a bar or other establishment.

happy hunting ground ■ n. a place where success or enjoyment is obtained.
– ORIGIN orig. referring to the optimistic hope of American Indians for good hunting grounds in the afterlife.

happy letter ■ n. S. African a certificate approving the completed work of a building contractor, signed by a customer or beneficiary of a house in a low-cost development programme before legal transfer of ownership may take place.

hapten /ˈhaptən/ ■ n. Physiology a small molecule which, when combined with a protein, can elicit the production of antibodies.
– ORIGIN C20: from Greek *haptein* 'fasten'.

haptic /ˈhaptɪk/ ■ adj. technical of or relating to the sense of touch.
– ORIGIN C19: from Greek *haptikos* 'able to touch or grasp', from *haptein* 'fasten'.

haptoglobin /ˌhaptə(ʊ)ˈɡləʊbɪn/ ■ n. Biochemistry a protein present in blood serum which binds to and removes free haemoglobin from the bloodstream.
– ORIGIN 1940s: from Greek *haptein* 'fasten' + (*haemo*)*globin*.

haraam /hɑːˈrɑːm/ (also **haram**) ■ adj. forbidden or proscribed by Islamic law.
– ORIGIN from Arabic *ḥarām* 'forbidden'.

hara-kiri /ˌharəˈkɪri/ ■ n. ritual suicide by disembowelment with a sword, formerly practised in Japan by samurai as an honourable alternative to disgrace or execution.
– ORIGIN C19: colloquial Japanese, from *hara* 'belly' + *kiri* 'cutting'.

harangue /həˈraŋ/ ■ v. criticize at length in an aggressive and hectoring manner. ■ n. a forceful and aggressive speech.
– ORIGIN Middle English: from medieval Latin *harenga*, perhaps of Germanic origin; altered to conform with French *harangue* (n.), *haranguer* (v.).

harass /ˈharəs, həˈras/ ■ v. torment by subjecting to constant interference or intimidation.
– DERIVATIVES **harassed** adj. **harasser** n. **harassing** adj. **harassment** n.
– ORIGIN C17: from French *harasser*, from *harer* 'set a dog on', from Germanic *hare*, a cry urging a dog to attack.

USAGE
The word **harass** is pronounced either with the stress on the **har-** or with the stress on the **-rass**. The former pronunciation is the older and is regarded by some as the only correct one.

harbinger /ˈhɑːbɪn(d)ʒə/ ■ n. a person or thing that announces or signals the approach of something.
– ORIGIN Middle English (orig. 'a person who provides or goes ahead to find lodging'): from Old French, from *herbergier* 'provide lodging for', from *herberge* 'lodging', from Old Saxon *heriberga* 'shelter for an army, lodging'.

harbour (US **harbor**) ■ n. a place on the coast where ships may moor in shelter, either naturally formed or artificially created. ■ v. 1 keep (a thought or feeling) secretly in one's mind. 2 give a refuge or shelter to. ▶ carry the germs of (a disease).
– ORIGIN Old English *herebeorg* 'shelter', *herebeorgian* 'occupy shelter', of Germanic origin.

harbourage (US **harborage**) ■ n. a harbour or other place of shelter.

harbour master (US **harbormaster**) ■ n. an official in charge of a harbour.

hard ■ adj. 1 solid, firm, and rigid; not easily broken, bent, or pierced. ▶ (of a person) not showing any signs of weakness; tough. ▶ (of prices of shares, commodities, etc.) high and stable; firm. 2 requiring or demonstrating a great deal of endurance or effort; difficult. ▶ strict and demanding: *a hard taskmaster.* 3 (of information or a subject of study) concerned with precise and verifiable facts: *hard science.* 4 harsh or unpleasant to the senses. ▶ (of a season or the weather) severe. ▶ (of wine) harsh or sharp to the taste, especially because of tannin. 5 done with a great deal of force or strength: *a hard whack.* 6 very potent, strong, or intense. ▶ (of liquor) strongly alcoholic; spirit rather than beer or wine. ▶ (of a drug) potent and addictive. ▶ (of radiation) highly penetrating. ▶ (of pornography) highly obscene and explicit. 7 denoting an extreme or dogmatic faction within a political party: *the hard left.* 8 (of water) containing mineral salts. 9 (of a consonant) pronounced as a velar plosive (as *c* in *cat, g* in *go*). ■ adv. 1 with a great deal of effort. ▶ with a great deal of force; violently. 2 so as to be solid or firm. 3 to the fullest extent possible: *put the wheel hard over to starboard.*
– PHRASES **be hard put (to it)** find it very difficult. **go hard with** dated turn out to (someone's) disadvantage. **hard and fast** [usu. with neg.] (of a rule or distinction) fixed and definitive. **hard at it** informal busily working. **hard by** close to. **hard done by** harshly or unfairly treated. **hard feelings** [usu. with neg.] feelings of resentment. **hard going** difficult to understand or enjoy. **hard luck** informal used to express sympathy or commiserations. **hard of hearing** not able to hear well. **hard on** (or **upon**) close to; following soon after. **hard up** informal short of money. **play hard to get** informal deliberately adopt an aloof or uninterested attitude.
– DERIVATIVES **hardness** n.
– ORIGIN Old English, of Germanic origin.

hardback ■ n. a book bound in stiff covers.

hardball ■ n. 1 baseball, especially as contrasted with softball. 2 informal (often in phr. **play hardball**) uncompromising and ruthless behaviour.

hardbitten ■ adj. tough and cynical.

hardboard ■ n. stiff board made of compressed and treated wood pulp.

hard-boiled ■ adj. **1** (of an egg) boiled until solid. **2** (of a person) tough and cynical. ▸ denoting a tough, realistic style of detective fiction.

hard cash ■ n. negotiable coins and banknotes as opposed to other forms of payment.

hard coal ■ n. another term for ANTHRACITE.

hard-code ■ v. Computing fix (data or parameters) in a program in such a way that they cannot easily be altered.

hard copy ■ n. a printed version on paper of data held in a computer.

hard core ■ n. **1** the most active, committed, or doctrinaire members of a group. **2** popular music that is experimental in nature and typically characterized by high volume and aggressive presentation. **3** pornography of a very explicit kind. **4** broken bricks and rubble used as a filling or foundation in building.

hardcover ■ adj. & n. another term for HARDBACK.

hard disk (also **hard drive**) ■ n. Computing a rigid non-removable magnetic disk with a large data storage capacity.

hardegat /ˈhɑːdəxat/ ■ adj. S. African informal stubborn; arrogant.
– ORIGIN Afrikaans, from *hard* 'hard' + *gat* 'anus'.

harden ■ v. **1** make or become hard or harder. **2** (of prices of shares, commodities, etc.) rise and remain steady at a higher level. **3** (**harden something off**) accustom a plant to cold by gradually increasing its exposure to the outside.
– DERIVATIVES **hardener** n.

hardened ■ adj. **1** having become or been made hard or harder. **2** experienced, tough, and cynical: *hardened police officers*. ▸ fixed in a bad habit or way of life: *hardened criminals*.

harder ■ n. S. African a commercially important mullet of southern African coastal waters. [*Liza richardsonii* and other species.]
– ORIGIN Dutch, 'mullet'.

hard hat ■ n. a rigid protective helmet, as worn by factory and building workers.

hard-headed ■ adj. tough and realistic.
– DERIVATIVES **hard-headedly** adv. **hard-headedness** n.

hard-hearted ■ adj. unfeeling.
– DERIVATIVES **hard-heartedly** adv. **hard-heartedness** n.

hard labour ■ n. heavy manual work as a punishment.

hard line ■ n. an uncompromising adherence to a firm policy.
– DERIVATIVES **hardliner** n.

hardly ■ adv. scarcely; barely. ▸ only with great difficulty. ▸ no or not (suggesting surprise at or disagreement with a statement).

hard-nosed ■ adj. informal realistic and tough-minded.

hard-on ■ n. vulgar slang an erection of the penis.

hard palate ■ n. the bony front part of the palate.

hardpan ■ n. a hardened impervious layer, typically of clay, occurring in or below the soil.

hard-paste ■ adj. denoting true porcelain made of fusible and infusible materials fired at a high temperature.

hard pear ■ n. an evergreen tree of southern and eastern Africa which bears small red berries and yields hard, heavy wood. [Genus *Olinia*, in particular *O. ventosa*.]

hard power ■ n. a coercive approach to international political relations, especially one that involves the use of military power. Compare with SOFT POWER.

hard-pressed ■ adj. **1** closely pursued. **2** in difficulties.

hard rock ■ n. highly amplified rock music with a heavy beat.

hard sauce ■ n. a sauce of butter and sugar, typically with brandy, rum, or vanilla added.

hard sell ■ n. a policy or technique of aggressive selling or advertising.

hardship ■ n. severe suffering or privation.

hard shoulder ■ n. a hardened strip alongside a highway for use in an emergency.

hardstone ■ n. precious or semi-precious stone used for intaglio, mosaic work, etc.

hard tack ■ n. archaic hard dry bread or biscuit, especially as rations for sailors or soldiers.

hardtop ■ n. a motor vehicle with a rigid roof which in some cases is detachable.

hardware ■ n. **1** heavy military equipment such as tanks and missiles. **2** the machines, wiring, and other physical components of a computer. Compare with SOFTWARE. **3** tools, implements, and other items used in the home and in activities such as gardening.

hard-wired ■ adj. Electronics involving or achieved by permanently connected circuits rather than software.
– DERIVATIVES **hard-wire** v. & adj.

hardwood ■ n. **1** the wood from a broadleaved tree as distinguished from that of conifers. **2** (in gardening) mature growth on shrubs from which cuttings may be taken.

hardy ■ adj. (**-ier**, **-iest**) capable of enduring difficult conditions; robust. ▸ (of a plant) able to survive drought conditions, the cold of winter, etc.
– DERIVATIVES **hardiness** n.
– ORIGIN Middle English: from Old French *hardi*, from *hardir* 'become bold', of Germanic origin; rel. to HARD.

hare ■ n. a fast-running, long-eared mammal resembling a large rabbit, with very long hind legs. [*Lepus* and other genera.] ■ v. run with great speed.
– ORIGIN Old English, of Germanic origin.

harebell ■ n. a bellflower with slender stems and pale blue flowers in late summer. [*Campanula rotundifolia*.]

hare-brained ■ adj. rash; ill-judged.

Hare Krishna /ˌhari ˈkrɪʃnə, ˌhaːreɪ/ ■ n. a member of the International Society for Krishna Consciousness, a religious sect based on the worship of the Hindu god Krishna.
– ORIGIN 1960s: Sanskrit, 'O Vishnu Krishna'.

harelip ■ n. another term for CLEFT LIP.
– ORIGIN C16: from a perceived resemblance to the mouth of a hare.

harem /ˈhɑːriːm, hɑːˈriːm, ˈhɛːrəm/ ■ n. **1** the separate part of a Muslim household reserved for wives, concubines, and female servants. **2** the wives (or concubines) of a polygamous man. ▸ a group of female animals sharing a single mate.
– ORIGIN C17: from Arabic *ḥaram*, *ḥarīm* 'prohibited place', from *ḥarama* 'be prohibited'.

haricot /ˈharɪkəʊ/ ■ n. a French bean of a variety with small white seeds, which can be dried and used as a vegetable.
– ORIGIN C17: perhaps from Aztec *ayacotli*.

Harijan /ˈhʌrɪdʒ(ə)n, ˈharɪdʒan/ ■ n. a member of a hereditary Hindu group of the lowest social and ritual status. See UNTOUCHABLE.
– ORIGIN from Sanskrit *harijana* 'a person dedicated to Vishnu', from *Hari* 'Vishnu' + *jana* 'person'.

harissa /ˈarɪsə/ ■ n. a hot sauce or paste used in North African cuisine, made from chilli peppers, paprika, and olive oil.
– ORIGIN from Arabic.

hark ■ v. **1** poetic/literary listen. **2** (**hark at**) informal used to draw attention to an ill-advised or foolish remark or action: *just hark at you!* **3** (**hark back**) recall an earlier period.
– ORIGIN Middle English: of Germanic origin.

harken ■ v. variant spelling of HEARKEN.

harlequin /ˈhɑːlɪkwɪn/ ■ n. (**Harlequin**) a mute character in traditional pantomime, typically masked and dressed in a diamond-patterned costume. ■ adj. in varied colours; variegated.
– ORIGIN C16: from obsolete French, from earlier *Herlequin*, the leader of a legendary troop of demon horsemen.

harlot /ˈhɑːlət/ ■ n. archaic a prostitute or promiscuous woman.
– DERIVATIVES **harlotry** n.

harvest

−ORIGIN Middle English (denoting a vagabond, later a lecherous person): from Old French *herlot* 'young man, knave'.

harm ■ n. physical injury, especially that which is deliberately inflicted. ▸ material damage. ▸ actual or potential ill effect. ■ v. physically injure. ▸ have an adverse effect on.
−PHRASES **out of harm's way** in a safe place.
−ORIGIN Old English, of Germanic origin.

harmattan /hɑːˈmat(ə)n/ ■ n. a very dry, dusty easterly or north-easterly wind on the West African coast, occurring from December to February.
−ORIGIN C17: from Twi *haramata*.

harmful ■ adj. causing or likely to cause harm.
−DERIVATIVES **harmfully** adv. **harmfulness** n.

harmless ■ adj. not able or likely to cause harm.
−DERIVATIVES **harmlessly** adv. **harmlessness** n.

harmonic /hɑːˈmɒnɪk/ ■ adj. **1** of, relating to, or characterized by harmony. **2** Music relating to or denoting a harmonic or harmonics. **3** Physics of or denoting components of a complex oscillation or wave whose frequencies are exact multiples of the basic frequency. ■ n. **1** Music an overtone accompanying a fundamental tone at a fixed interval, produced by vibration of a string, column of air, etc. in an exact fraction of its length. ▸ a note produced on a musical instrument as an overtone, e.g. by lightly touching a string while sounding it. **2** Physics a harmonic component of a complex oscillation or wave.
−DERIVATIVES **harmonically** adv.

harmonica /hɑːˈmɒnɪkə/ ■ n. a small rectangular wind instrument with a row of metal reeds along its length, held against the lips and moved from side to side to produce different notes by blowing or sucking.
−ORIGIN C18: from Greek *harmonikos*, from *harmonia* (see HARMONY).

harmonic minor ■ n. Music a scale containing a minor third, minor sixth, and major seventh, forming the basis of conventional harmony in minor keys.

harmonic progression ■ n. Music a series of chord changes forming the underlying harmony of a piece of music.

harmonic series ■ n. a set of frequencies consisting of a fundamental and the harmonics related to it by an exact fraction.

harmonious ■ adj. **1** tuneful; not discordant. **2** free from conflict.
−DERIVATIVES **harmoniously** adv. **harmoniousness** n.

harmonist ■ n. a person skilled in musical harmony.

harmonium /hɑːˈməʊnɪəm/ ■ n. a keyboard instrument in which the notes are produced by air driven through metal reeds by foot-operated bellows.
−ORIGIN C19: from Latin *harmonia* (see HARMONY) or Greek *harmonios* 'harmonious'.

harmonize (also **-ise**) ■ v. **1** Music provide harmony for. ▸ sing or play in harmony. **2** make or be harmonious. **3** make consistent: *plans to harmonize the railways of Europe*.
−DERIVATIVES **harmonization** (also **-isation**) n.

harmony ■ n. (pl. **-ies**) **1** the combination of simultaneously sounded musical notes to produce chords and chord progressions having a pleasing effect. **2** agreement or concord.
−ORIGIN Middle English: from Latin *harmonia* 'joining, concord', from Greek, from *harmos* 'joint'.

harness ■ n. **1** a set of straps and fittings by which a horse or other draught animal is fastened to a cart, plough, etc. and is controlled by its driver. **2** a similar arrangement of straps, as for fastening a parachute to a person's body or for restraining a young child. ■ v. **1** fit with a harness. **2** control and make use of (resources).
−PHRASES **in harness 1** (of an animal) used for draught work. **2** in the routine of daily work: *an ordinary man who died in harness*. **3** in close partnership.
−ORIGIN Middle English: from Old French *harneis* 'military equipment', from Old Norse, from *herr* 'army' + *nest* 'provisions'.

harness racing ■ n. another term for TROTTING.

harp ■ n. a musical instrument, roughly triangular in shape, consisting of a frame supporting a graduated series of parallel strings, played by plucking with the fingers. ■ v. (**harp on**) talk or write persistently and tediously on a particular topic.
−DERIVATIVES **harper** n. **harpist** n.
−ORIGIN Old English, of Germanic origin.

harpoon ■ n. a barbed spear-like missile attached to a long rope and thrown by hand or fired from a gun, used for catching whales and other large sea creatures. ■ v. spear with a harpoon.
−DERIVATIVES **harpooner** n.
−ORIGIN C17: from French *harpon*, from *harpe* 'dog's claw, clamp'.

harpsichord /ˈhɑːpsɪkɔːd/ ■ n. a keyboard instrument similar in shape to a grand piano, with horizontal strings plucked by points operated by depressing the keys.
−DERIVATIVES **harpsichordist** n.
−ORIGIN C17: from obsolete French *harpechorde*, from late Latin *harpa* 'harp' + *chorda* 'string'.

harpy ■ n. (pl. **-ies**) Greek & Roman Mythology a rapacious monster usually depicted with a woman's head and body and a bird's wings and claws.
−ORIGIN Middle English: from Greek *harpuiai* 'snatchers'.

harquebus /ˈhɑːkwɪbəs/ (also **arquebus**) ■ n. historical an early type of portable gun supported on a tripod or a forked rest.
−ORIGIN C16: from French *harquebuse*, from Middle Low German *hakebusse*, from *hake* 'hook' + *busse* 'gun'.

harridan /ˈharɪd(ə)n/ ■ n. a strict, bossy, or belligerent old woman.
−ORIGIN C17: perhaps from French *haridelle* 'old horse'.

harrier[1] ■ n. a person who harries others.

harrier[2] ■ n. a hound of a breed used for hunting hares.
−ORIGIN Middle English *hayrer*, from HARE.

harrier[3] ■ n. a long-winged, slender-bodied bird of prey with low quartering flight. [Genus *Circus*: several species.]
−ORIGIN C16 (as *harrower*): from *harrow* 'harry, rob' (var. of HARRY); spelling influenced by HARRIER[1].

Harris tweed ■ n. trademark handwoven tweed made traditionally on the island of Lewis and Harris in Scotland.

harrow ■ n. an implement consisting of a heavy frame set with teeth or tines which is dragged over ploughed land to break up or spread the soil. ■ v. **1** draw a harrow over. **2** [usu. as adj. **harrowing**] cause distress to: *a harrowing film about racism*.
−DERIVATIVES **harrowingly** adv.
−ORIGIN Middle English: from Old Norse *herfi*.

harrumph /həˈrʌmf/ ■ v. **1** clear the throat noisily. **2** grumpily express dissatisfaction: *sceptics tend to harrumph at case histories like this*.
−ORIGIN 1930s: imitative.

harry ■ v. (**-ies**, **-ied**) **1** persistently carry out attacks on (an enemy). **2** persistently harass.
−ORIGIN Old English, of Germanic origin.

harsh ■ adj. **1** unpleasantly rough or jarring to the senses. **2** cruel or severe. ▸ (of reality or a fact) grim and unpalatable.
−DERIVATIVES **harshen** v. **harshly** adv. **harshness** n.
−ORIGIN Middle English: from Middle Low German *harsch* 'rough, hairy', from *haer* 'hair'.

hart ■ n. an adult male deer, especially a red deer over five years old.
−ORIGIN Old English, of Germanic origin.

hartebeest /ˈhɑːtɪbiːst/ ■ n. a large African antelope with a long head and sloping back. [*Alcelaphus buselaphus* (**red hartebeest**) and other species.]
−ORIGIN C18: from S. African Dutch, from Dutch *hert* 'hart' + *beest* 'beast'.

hartshorn /ˈhɑːtsˌhɔːn/ ■ n. archaic aqueous ammonia solution used as smelling salts, formerly prepared from the horns of deer.

harum-scarum /ˌhɛːrəmˈskɛːrəm/ ■ adj. reckless; impetuous.
−ORIGIN C17: reduplication based on HARE and SCARE.

harvest ■ n. the process or period of gathering in crops. ▸ the season's yield or crop. ■ v. **1** gather as a harvest.

harvest home

2 remove (cells or tissue) from a person or animal for experimental or transplantation purposes.
– DERIVATIVES **harvestable** adj. **harvester** n.
– ORIGIN Old English *hærfest* 'autumn', of Germanic origin.

harvest home ■ n. the gathering in of the final part of the year's harvest. ▶ a festival marking the end of the harvest period.

harvestman ■ n. (pl. **-men**) an arachnid with a globular body and very long thin legs. [Order Opiliones: many species.]

harvest moon ■ n. the full moon that is seen closest to the time of the autumn equinox.

harvest mouse ■ n. **1** a small North Eurasian mouse with a prehensile tail, nesting among the stalks of growing cereals. [*Micromys minutus*.] **2** a nocturnal mouse found in North and Central America. [Genus *Reithrodontomys*: several species.]

Harvey Wallbanger ■ n. a cocktail made from vodka or gin, orange juice, and Galliano.

has third person singular present of HAVE.

has-been ■ n. informal a person or thing that is outmoded or no longer of any significance.

hash¹ ■ n. **1** a dish of diced cooked meat reheated with potatoes. ▶ N. Amer. a finely chopped mixture. **2** a jumble; a mess. ■ v. **1** make or chop into a hash. **2** (**hash something out**) come to agreement after lengthy and vigorous discussion.
– PHRASES **make a hash of** informal make a mess of. **settle someone's hash** informal, dated deal with and subdue someone in no uncertain manner.
– ORIGIN C16: from French *hacher*, from *hache* (see HATCHET).

hash² ■ n. informal short for HASHISH.

hash³ ■ n. the symbol #.
– ORIGIN 1980s: prob. from HATCH³, alteration by folk etymology.

hash browns (also **hashed browns**) ■ pl. n. chiefly N. Amer. a dish of chopped and fried cooked potatoes.

Hashemite /ˈhaʃɪmʌɪt/ ■ n. a member of an Arab princely family claiming descent from Hashim, great-grandfather of Muhammad.

hashish /ˈhaʃiːʃ, -ʃɪʃ, haˈʃiːʃ/ ■ n. cannabis.
– ORIGIN C16: from Arabic *ḥašīš* 'dry herb, powdered hemp leaves'.

Hasidism /ˈhasɪˌdɪz(ə)m/ (also **Chasidism**, **Chassidism**, or **Hassidism**) ■ n. a mystical Jewish movement founded in Poland in the 18th century, represented today by fundamentalist communities in Israel and New York.
– DERIVATIVES **Hasidic** /-ˈsɪdɪk/ adj.

hasn't ■ contr. has not.

hasp /hɑːsp/ ■ n. a slotted hinged metal plate that forms part of a fastening for a door or lid and is fitted over a metal loop and secured by a pin or padlock.
– ORIGIN Old English, of Germanic origin.

hassium /ˈhasɪəm/ ■ n. the chemical element of atomic number 108, a very unstable element made by high-energy atomic collisions. (Symbol: **Hs**)
– ORIGIN 1990s: modern Latin, from Latin *Hassias* 'Hesse', the German state where it was discovered.

hassle informal ■ n. irritating inconvenience. ▶ deliberate harassment. ■ v. harass; pester.
– ORIGIN C19 (orig. dialect, 'hack or saw at').

hassock /ˈhasək/ ■ n. **1** chiefly Brit. a cushion for kneeling on in church. ▶ N. Amer. a footstool. **2** a firm clump of grass or vegetation in marshy ground.
– ORIGIN Old English.

hast archaic second person singular present of HAVE.

haste ■ n. excessive speed or urgency of action. ■ v. archaic term for HASTEN: *haste ye back!*
– ORIGIN Middle English: from Old French *haste*, of Germanic origin.

hasten ■ v. **1** be quick to do something; move quickly. **2** cause to happen sooner than anticipated.

hasty ■ adj. (**-ier**, **-iest**) **1** done or acting with haste; hurried. **2** archaic quick-tempered.

– DERIVATIVES **hastily** adv. **hastiness** n.

hat ■ n. a shaped covering for the head, typically with a brim and a crown.
– PHRASES **hat in hand** see CAP IN HAND at CAP. **keep something under one's hat** keep something a secret. **pass the hat round** (or N. Amer. **pass the hat**) collect contributions of money. **pick something out of a hat** select something at random. **take one's hat off to** used to express admiration or praise for. **talk through one's hat** informal talk foolishly or ignorantly. **throw one's hat into the ring** express willingness to take up a challenge.
– DERIVATIVES **hatful** n. (pl. **-fuls**). **hatless** adj. **hatted** adj.
– ORIGIN Old English, of Germanic origin.

hatband ■ n. a decorative ribbon encircling a hat, held in position above the brim.

hatbox ■ n. a large cylindrical box used to store hats.

hatch¹ ■ n. **1** a small opening in a floor, wall, or roof allowing access from one area to another, in particular that in the deck of a boat leading to the cabin or lower level. ▶ a door in an aircraft, spacecraft, or submarine. **2** short for HATCHBACK.
– PHRASES **down the hatch** informal used as a toast.
– ORIGIN Old English *hæcc* (denoting the lower half of a divided door), of Germanic origin.

hatch² ■ v. **1** (of a young bird, fish, or reptile) emerge from its egg. ▶ (of an egg) open and produce a young animal. ▶ cause (a young animal) to emerge from its egg. **2** conspire to devise (a plot or plan). ■ n. a newly hatched brood.
– ORIGIN Middle English *hacche*, rel. to Swedish *häcka* and Danish *hække*.

hatch³ ■ v. (in technical drawing) shade with closely drawn parallel lines.
– DERIVATIVES **hatching** n.
– ORIGIN C15 ('inlay with strips of metal'): from Old French *hacher*, from *hache* (see HATCHET).

hatchback ■ n. a car with a door across the full width at the back end that opens upwards to provide easy access for loading.

hatchery ■ n. (pl. **-ies**) an establishment where fish or poultry eggs are hatched.

hatchet ■ n. a small axe with a short handle for use in one hand.
– PHRASES **bury the hatchet** end a quarrel or conflict.
– ORIGIN Middle English: from Old French *hachette*, diminutive of *hache* 'axe'.

hatchet-faced ■ adj. informal sharp-featured and grim-looking.

hatchet job ■ n. informal a fierce verbal or written attack.

hatchet man ■ n. informal **1** a person employed to carry out controversial or disagreeable tasks. **2** a harsh critic.

hatchling ■ n. a newly hatched young animal.

hatchment ■ n. a large diamond-shaped tablet bearing the coat of arms of someone who has died, displayed in their honour.
– ORIGIN C16: prob. from obsolete French *hachement*, from Old French *acesmement* 'adornment'.

hatchway ■ n. an opening or hatch, especially in a ship's deck.

hate ■ v. feel intense dislike for or a strong aversion towards. ■ n. **1** intense dislike; strong aversion. **2** informal a disliked person or thing: *Richard's pet hate is filling in tax forms.*
– DERIVATIVES **hatable** (also **hateable**) adj. **hater** n.
– ORIGIN Old English, of Germanic origin.

hate crime ■ n. a crime motivated by racial, sexual, or other prejudice, typically one involving violence.

hateful ■ adj. arousing or deserving of hatred.
– DERIVATIVES **hatefully** adv. **hatefulness** n.

hath archaic third person singular present of HAVE.

hatha yoga /ˈhʌtə, ˈhaθə/ ■ n. a system of physical exercises and breathing control used in yoga.
– ORIGIN from Sanskrit *haṭha* 'force'.

hatred ■ n. intense dislike.
– ORIGIN Middle English: from HATE + *-red* (from Old English *rǣden* 'condition').

hatstand ■ n. a tall free-standing post fitted with large hooks for hanging hats on.

hatter ■ n. a person who makes and sells hats.
– PHRASES **(as) mad as a hatter** informal completely crazy. [with allusion to the effects of mercury poisoning from the use of mercurous nitrate in the manufacture of felt hats.]

hat-trick ■ n. three successes of the same kind, especially (in soccer) the scoring of three goals in a game by one player or (in cricket) the taking of three wickets by the same bowler with successive balls.
– ORIGIN C19: orig. referring to the club presentation of a new hat to a bowler taking three wickets successively.

hauberk /'hɔːbəːk/ ■ n. historical a full-length coat of mail.
– ORIGIN Middle English: from Old French, of Germanic origin.

haughty ■ adj. (-ier, -iest) arrogantly superior and disdainful.
– DERIVATIVES **haughtily** adv. **haughtiness** n.
– ORIGIN C16: from obsolete *haught*, earlier *haut*, from Old French, from Latin *altus* 'high'.

haul ■ v. 1 pull or drag with effort or force. 2 transport in a truck or cart. 3 (especially of a sailing ship) make an abrupt change of course. ■ n. 1 a quantity of something obtained, especially illegally: *they escaped with a haul of antiques*. 2 a number of fish caught at one time. 3 a distance to be travelled.
– PHRASES **haul someone over the coals** see COAL.
– DERIVATIVES **hauler** n.
– ORIGIN C16: var. of obsolete *hale*, from Old French, from Old Norse *hala*.

haulage ■ n. the commercial transport of goods.

haulier /'hɔːlɪə/ ■ n. 1 a person or company employed in the commercial transport of goods by road. 2 a miner who is responsible for transporting coal within a mine.

haulm /hɔːm/ ■ n. a stalk or stem. ▸ the stalks or stems of peas, beans, or potatoes collectively, as used for bedding.
– ORIGIN Old English, of Germanic origin.

haunch ■ n. 1 the buttock and thigh considered together, in a human or animal. ▸ the leg and loin of an animal, as food. 2 Architecture the side of an arch, between the crown and the pier.
– ORIGIN Middle English: from Old French *hanche*, of Germanic origin.

haunt ■ v. 1 (of a ghost) manifest itself regularly at (a place). ▸ (of a person) frequent (a place). 2 be persistently and disturbingly present in the mind: *cities haunted by the shadow of cholera*. ■ n. a place frequented by a specified person: *a favourite haunt of pickpockets*.
– DERIVATIVES **haunter** n.
– ORIGIN Middle English: from Old French *hanter*, of Germanic origin.

haunted ■ adj. 1 (of a place) frequented by a ghost. 2 having or showing signs of mental anguish: *the hollow cheeks, the haunted eyes*.

haunting ■ adj. poignant; evocative.
– DERIVATIVES **hauntingly** adv.

haurient /'hɔːrɪənt/ ■ adj. [postpos.] Heraldry (of a fish or marine creature) depicted swimming vertically.
– ORIGIN C16: from Latin *haurient-* 'drawing in (air, water, etc.)', from *haurire*.

Hausa /'haʊsə/ ■ n. (pl. same or **Hausas**) 1 a member of a people of northern Nigeria and adjacent regions. 2 the Chadic language of this people, used as a lingua franca in parts of West Africa.
– ORIGIN the name in Hausa.

haustorium /hɔːˈstɔːrɪəm/ ■ n. (pl. **haustoria** /-rɪə/) Botany a slender projection from the root of a parasitic plant or from the hyphae of a parasitic fungus, enabling the parasite to penetrate the tissues of its host.
– ORIGIN C19: from Latin *haustor* 'thing that draws in', from *haurire*.

hautboy /'(h)əʊbɔɪ/ ■ n. archaic form of OBOE.
– ORIGIN C16: from French *hautbois*, from *haut* 'high' + *bois* 'wood'.

haute couture /ˌəʊt kuːˈtjʊə/ ■ n. the designing and making of high-quality fashionable clothes by leading fashion houses.
– ORIGIN French, 'high dressmaking'.

haute cuisine /ˌəʊt kwɪˈziːn/ ■ n. high-quality cooking following the style of traditional French cuisine.
– ORIGIN French, 'high cookery'.

hauteur /əʊˈtəː/ ■ n. proud haughtiness of manner.
– ORIGIN French, from *haut* 'high'.

haut monde /əʊ ˈmɒd/ ■ n. fashionable society.
– ORIGIN French, literally 'high world'.

Havana /həˈvanə/ ■ n. a cigar made in Cuba or from Cuban tobacco.
– ORIGIN named after *Havana*, the capital of Cuba.

Havdalah ■ n. variant spelling of HABDALAH.

have ■ v. (**has**; past and past part. **had**) 1 (also **have got**) possess, own, or hold. ▸ be made up of; comprise. ▸ be able to make use of. ▸ know (a language or subject): *I had only a little French*. 2 experience; undergo. ▸ (also **have got**) suffer from (an illness or disability). ▸ cause to be in a particular state. ▸ cause to be done for one by someone else. 3 (**have to**) or **have got to** be obliged to; must. ▸ be strongly recommended to. 4 perform the action indicated by the noun specified: *he had a look round*. ▸ eat or drink. ▸ give birth to or be due to give birth to. 5 (also **have got**) demonstrate (a personal attribute): *he had little patience*. ▸ [with neg.] refuse to tolerate. 6 (also **have got**) place, hold, or keep in a particular position. 7 be the recipient or host of. 8 (usu. **be had**) informal cheat or deceive: *I realized I'd been had*. 9 (also **have got**) informal have put (someone) at a disadvantage in an argument: *you've got me there*. ■ aux. v. used with a past participle to form the perfect, pluperfect, and future perfect tenses, and the conditional mood: ■ n. (usu. in phr. **the haves and the have-nots**) informal people with plenty of money.
– PHRASES **have had it** informal 1 be beyond repair or revival: *the car has had it*. 2 be unable to tolerate any longer. **have (got) it in for** informal behave in a hostile way towards. **have (got) it in one (to do something)** informal have the capacity or potential (to do something). **have it off** (or Brit. **away**) vulgar slang have sexual intercourse. **have it out** informal attempt to resolve a contentious matter by open confrontation. **have (got) nothing on** informal be not nearly as good as. **have nothing** (or **something**) **on someone** informal know nothing (or something) discreditable or incriminating about someone.
– PHRASAL VERBS **have someone on** informal try to make someone believe something that is untrue, especially as a joke. **have something out** undergo an operation to extract a part of one's body. **have someone up** (usu. **be had up**) informal bring someone before a court of justice to answer for an alleged offence.
– ORIGIN Old English, of Germanic origin.

> **USAGE**
> Be careful not to write the word **of** when you mean **have** or **'ve**: *I could have* (or *could've*) *told you that* not *I could of told you that*. The mistake arises from the fact that the pronunciation of **have** in unstressed contexts is the same as that of **of**, and the two words are confused when writing them down.

haven ■ n. 1 a place of safety or refuge. 2 a harbour or small port.
– ORIGIN Old English, from Old Norse *hǫfn*.

have-nots ■ pl. n. informal economically disadvantaged people.

haven't ■ contr. have not.

haver /'heɪvə/ ■ v. 1 Scottish talk foolishly; babble. 2 Brit. act in an indecisive manner.
– ORIGIN C18.

haversack /'havəsak/ ■ n. a small, stout bag carried on the back or over the shoulder, used especially by soldiers and walkers.
– ORIGIN C18: from French *havresac*, from obsolete German *Habersack*, denoting a bag used to carry oats as horse feed, from dialect *Haber* 'oats' + *Sack* 'sack, bag'.

havoc ■ n. 1 widespread destruction. 2 great confusion or disorder.
– PHRASES **play havoc with** completely disrupt.
– ORIGIN Middle English: from Anglo-Norman French *havok*, alteration of Old French *havot*; the word was orig. used in the phr. **cry havoc** 'to give an army the order *havoc*', which was the signal for plundering.

haw[1] ■ n. the red fruit of the hawthorn.
– ORIGIN Old English, of Germanic origin.

haw

haw² ■ n. the third eyelid or nictitating membrane in certain mammals, especially dogs and cats.
– ORIGIN Middle English (denoting a discharge from the eye).

Hawaiian ■ n. 1 a native or inhabitant of Hawaii. 2 the Austronesian language of Hawaii. ■ adj. of or relating to Hawaii or its people or language.

Hawaiian guitar ■ n. a steel-stringed guitar in which a characteristic glissando effect is produced by sliding a metal bar along the strings as they are plucked.

hawk¹ ■ n. 1 a fast-flying bird of prey with broad rounded wings and a long tail, such as a sparrowhawk. [*Accipiter* and other genera: many species.] ▶ N. Amer. a buzzard or similar large bird of prey. ▶ any bird used in falconry. 2 a person who advocates an aggressive or warlike foreign policy. 3 used in names of hawkmoths, e.g. eyed hawk. ■ v. 1 hunt game with a trained hawk. 2 (of a bird or dragonfly) hunt on the wing for food.
– DERIVATIVES **hawkish** adj. **hawkishly** adv. **hawkishness** n.
– ORIGIN Old English, of Germanic origin.

hawk² ■ v. carry about and offer (goods) for sale in the street.
– ORIGIN C15: prob. a back-formation from HAWKER.

hawk³ ■ v. clear the throat noisily. ▶ bring (phlegm) up from the throat.
– ORIGIN C16: prob. imitative.

hawk⁴ ■ n. a plasterer's square board with a handle underneath for carrying plaster or mortar.
– ORIGIN Middle English.

hawk eagle ■ n. a small tropical eagle with broad wings and a long tail. [Genera *Spizaetus, Spizastur, Hieraaetus,* and *Lophaetus*.]

hawker ■ n. a person who travels about selling goods. ▶ S. African a street vendor.
– ORIGIN C16: prob. from Low German or Dutch and rel. to HUCKSTER.

hawkmoth ■ n. a large swift-flying moth with a stout body and narrow forewings, typically feeding on nectar while hovering. [Family Sphingidae: many species.]

hawk-nosed ■ adj. (of a person) having a nose which is curved like a hawk's beak.

hawksbill turtle ■ n. a small tropical sea turtle with hooked jaws and overlapping horny plates on the shell, hunted as the traditional source of tortoiseshell. [*Eretmochelys imbricata*.]

haworthia /heɪˈwʊəθɪə/ ■ n. a small southern African succulent plant, typically with rosettes of leaves and small white flowers. [Genus *Haworthia*: numerous species.]
– ORIGIN C19: named after the English botanist Adrian Haworth (1768–1833).

hawse /hɔːz/ ■ n. the part of a ship's bows through which the anchor cables pass. ▶ the space between the head of an anchored vessel and the anchors.
– ORIGIN Middle English *halse*, prob. from Old Norse *há* 'neck, ship's bow'.

hawser /ˈhɔːzə/ ■ n. a thick rope or cable for mooring or towing a ship.
– ORIGIN Middle English: from Anglo-Norman French *haucer*, from Old French *haucier* 'to hoist', from Latin *altus* 'high'.

hawthorn ■ n. a thorny shrub or tree with white, pink, or red blossom and small dark red fruits (haws). [*Crataegus monogyna* and related species.]
– ORIGIN Old English *hagathorn*, prob. 'hedge thorn' (see HAW¹, THORN).

hay ■ n. grass that has been mown and dried for use as fodder.
– PHRASES **hit the hay** informal go to bed. **make hay (while the sun shines)** make good use of an opportunity while it lasts.
– DERIVATIVES **haying** n.
– ORIGIN Old English, of Germanic origin; rel. to HEW.

haybox ■ n. chiefly historical a box stuffed with hay in which heated food was left to continue cooking.

haycock ■ n. a conical heap of hay left in the field to dry.

hay fever ■ n. an allergy caused by pollen or dust in which the mucous membranes of the eyes and nose are inflamed, causing sneezing and watery eyes.

haylage /ˈheɪlɪdʒ/ ■ n. silage made from grass which has been partially dried.
– ORIGIN 1960s: blend of HAY and SILAGE.

hayloft ■ n. a loft over a stable used for storing hay or straw.

haymaker ■ n. 1 a person who is involved in making hay. 2 an apparatus for shaking and drying hay. 3 informal a forceful blow.
– DERIVATIVES **haymaking** n.

hayrick ■ n. another term for HAYSTACK.

hayride ■ n. chiefly N. Amer. a ride taken for pleasure in a wagon carrying hay.

hayseed ■ n. 1 grass seed obtained from hay. 2 informal, chiefly N. Amer. a simple, unsophisticated country person.

haystack ■ n. a large packed pile of hay.

haywire ■ adj. informal erratic; out of control.
– ORIGIN C20: from HAY + WIRE, from the use of hay-baling wire in makeshift repairs.

hazard /ˈhazəd/ ■ n. 1 a danger or risk. 2 a permanent feature of a golf course which presents an obstruction to playing a shot. 3 poetic/literary chance; probability: *the laws of hazard*. 4 a gambling game using two dice. 5 Billiards a stroke with which a ball is pocketed. ▶ (**losing hazard**) the pocketing of the cue ball off another ball. ▶ (**winning hazard**) the pocketing of the object ball. ■ v. 1 venture to say: *he hazarded a guess*. 2 risk to chance.
– ORIGIN Middle English: from Old French *hasard*, from Arabic *az-zahr* 'chance', from Persian *zār* or Turkish *zar* 'dice'.

hazard lights ■ pl. n. flashing right and left indicator lights on a vehicle, used to warn that the vehicle is stationary or unexpectedly slow.

hazardous ■ adj. risky; dangerous.
– DERIVATIVES **hazardously** adv. **hazardousness** n.

haze¹ ■ n. 1 a slight obscuration of the lower atmosphere, typically caused by fine suspended particles. 2 a state of obscurity or confusion: *through an alcoholic haze*.
– ORIGIN C18: prob. a back-formation from HAZY.

haze² ■ v. N. Amer. torment or harass (a new student or recruit) by subjection to strenuous, humiliating, or dangerous tasks.
– ORIGIN C17 (orig. Scots and dialect in the sense 'frighten, scold, or beat'): perhaps rel. to obsolete French *haser* 'tease or insult'.

hazel ■ n. 1 a shrub or small tree bearing prominent catkins in spring and edible nuts in autumn. [*Corylus avellana* and related species.] 2 a rich reddish-brown colour.
– ORIGIN Old English, of Germanic origin.

hazelnut ■ n. the round brown edible hard-shelled nut of the hazel.

hazy ■ adj. (**-ier, -iest**) 1 covered by a haze. 2 vague, indistinct, or ill-defined.
– DERIVATIVES **hazily** adv. **haziness** n.
– ORIGIN C17.

HB ■ abbrev. 1 half board. 2 (also **hb**) hardback. 3 hard black (as a medium grade of pencil lead).

Hb ■ symb. haemoglobin.

H-bomb ■ n. short for HYDROGEN BOMB.

HC ■ abbrev. 1 (in the UK) House of Commons. 2 hydrocarbon.

HCF ■ abbrev. Mathematics highest common factor.

HCFC ■ n. Chemistry hydrochlorofluorocarbon, any of a class of inert compounds of carbon, hydrogen, hydrocarbons, chlorine, and fluorine.

HDD ■ abbrev. Computing hard disk drive.

HDI ■ abbrev. 1 Human Development Index. 2 (in South Africa) historically disadvantaged individual.

HDL ■ abbrev. Biochemistry high-density lipoprotein.

HDSA ■ abbrev. historically disadvantaged South African(s).

HDTV ■ abbrev. high-definition television.

HE ■ abbrev. 1 higher education. 2 high explosive. 3 His Eminence. 4 His or Her Excellency.

He ▪ symb. the chemical element helium.

he ▪ pron. [third person sing.] **1** used to refer to a man, boy, or male animal previously mentioned or easily identified. **2** used to refer to a person or animal of unspecified sex (in modern use, now largely replaced by 'he or she' or 'they'). **3** any person (in modern use, now largely replaced by 'anyone' or 'the person'). ▪ n. a male; a man.
– ORIGIN Old English, of Germanic origin.

head ▪ n. **1** the upper part of the human body, or the front or upper part of the body of an animal, typically separated from the rest of the body by a neck, and containing the brain, mouth, and sense organs. **2** the front, forward, or upper part or end of something. ▸ the source of a river or stream. ▸ the end of a lake or inlet at which a river enters. ▸ [usu. in place names] a promontory: *Beachy Head*. ▸ the top of a ship's mast. ▸ the bows of a ship. ▸ the foam on top of a glass of beer, or the cream on the top of milk. **3** the cutting or operational end of a tool or mechanism. ▸ the flattened or knobbed end of a nail, pin, screw, or match. **4** a compact mass of leaves or flowers at the top of a stem, especially a capitulum. ▸ the edible leafy part at the top of the stem of vegetables such as cabbage and lettuce. ▸ one saleable unit of certain vegetables such as cabbage or celery. **5** a person in charge; a director or leader. **6** a person considered as a numerical unit: *they paid fifty pounds a head*. ▸ [treated as pl.] a number of cattle or game as specified: *seventy head of dairy cattle*. **7** a component in an audio, video, or information system by which information is transferred from an electrical signal to the recording medium, or vice versa. ▸ the part of a record player that holds the playing cartridge and stylus. **8** a body of water kept at a particular height in order to provide a supply at sufficient pressure: *an 8 m head of water in the shafts*. ▸ the pressure exerted by such water. **9** informal a toilet on a ship or boat. **10** (**heads**) the side of a coin bearing the image of a head (used when tossing a coin to determine a winner). **11** Grammar the word that governs all the other words in a phrase in which it is used. ▪ adj. chief; principal. ▪ v. **1** be at or act as the head of. **2** give a title or heading to. **3** move in a specified direction: *he was heading for the exit*. **4** (**head someone/thing off**) intercept and turn aside someone or something; forestall something. **5** Soccer shoot or pass (the ball) with the head. **6** lop off the upper part or branches of (a plant or tree). **7** (of a lettuce or cabbage) form a head. **8** Nautical (**head up**) steer towards the wind. ▸ Nautical steer towards the wind.
– PHRASES **be banging one's head against a brick wall** be doggedly attempting the impossible. **bang** (or **knock**) **people's heads together** reprimand people in an attempt to stop them arguing. **be hanging over someone's head** threaten to affect someone at any moment. **be on someone's (own) head** be someone's sole responsibility. **by the head** Nautical (of a boat or ship) deeper in the water forward than astern. **come to a head** reach a crisis. **do someone's head in** informal, chiefly Brit. cause someone to feel annoyed, confused, or frustrated. **get one's head down** informal **1** sleep. **2** concentrate on the task in hand. **get one's head round** (or **around**) informal understand or come to terms with. **give someone his** (or **her**) **head** allow someone complete freedom of action. **give someone head** vulgar slang perform oral sex on someone. **go to someone's head 1** (of alcohol) make someone slightly drunk. **2** (of success) make someone conceited. **a head for** an aptitude for or tolerance of: *a head for heights*. **——'s head off** informal talk, laugh, shout, etc. unrestrainedly: *he was laughing his head off*. **head over heels 1** turning over completely in forward motion, as in a somersault. **2** madly in love. **a head start** an advantage granted or gained at the beginning. **heads will roll** people will be dismissed or forced to resign. **in one's head** by mental process without use of physical aids. **keep one's head** remain calm. **keep one's head above water** avoid succumbing to difficulties. **knock something on the head** dismiss an idea or rumour once and for all. **lose one's head** lose self-control; panic. **make head or tail of** [usu. with neg.] understand at all. **off** (or **out of**) **one's head** informal crazy. **off the top of one's head** without careful thought or investigation. **over someone's head 1** (also **above someone's head**) beyond someone's ability to understand. **2** without consultation or involvement. **put their** (or **our** or **your**) **heads together** consult and work together. **stand** (or **turn**) **something on its head** completely reverse an idea or argument. **turn someone's head** make someone conceited. **turn heads** attract a great deal of attention.
– DERIVATIVES **-headed** adj. **headless** adj. **headward** adj. & adv.
– ORIGIN Old English, of Germanic origin.

-head ▪ comb. form **1** denoting the head or end of a specified thing: *spearhead*. **2** in nouns used informally to express disparagement of a person: *airhead*. **3** in nouns used informally to denote an addict of a specified drug: *crackhead*.

headache ▪ n. **1** a continuous pain in the head. **2** informal something that causes worry or trouble.
– DERIVATIVES **headachy** adj.

headage ▪ n. the number of animals held as stock on a farm.

headband ▪ n. **1** a band of fabric worn around the head as a decoration or to keep the hair off the face. **2** an ornamental strip of coloured silk fastened to the top of the spine of a book.

headbanger ▪ n. informal **1** a fan or performer of heavy metal music. **2** a mad or eccentric person.

headbanging ▪ n. violent rhythmic shaking of the head by fans of heavy metal music.

headboard ▪ n. **1** an upright panel at the head of a bed. **2** a board or sign, especially on the front of a train. **3** Nautical a reinforcement at the top of a triangular sail such as a mainsail.

headbutt ▪ v. attack (someone) using a forceful and aggressive thrust with the head. ▪ n. an act of headbutting.

head case ▪ n. informal a mentally ill or unstable person.

headcount ▪ n. a count of the number of people present or available.

headdress ▪ n. an ornamental covering for the head, especially one worn on ceremonial occasions.

header ▪ n. **1** Soccer a shot or pass made with the head. **2** informal a headlong fall or dive. **3** a brick or stone laid at right angles to the face of a wall. Compare with **STRETCHER** (in sense 5). **4** (also **header tank**) a raised tank of water maintaining pressure in a plumbing system. **5** a line or block of text appearing at the top of each page of a book or document.

head first ▪ adj. & adv. **1** with the head in front of the rest of the body. **2** without sufficient forethought.

head gasket ▪ n. the gasket which fits between the cylinder head and the cylinders or cylinder block in an internal-combustion engine.

headgear ▪ n. hats, helmets, and other items worn on the head.

headhunt ▪ v. **1** [as noun **headhunting**] the practice among some peoples of collecting the heads of dead enemies as trophies. **2** identify and approach (someone employed elsewhere) to fill a business position.
– DERIVATIVES **headhunter** n.

heading ▪ n. **1** a title at the head of a page or section of a book. **2** a direction or bearing. **3** the top of a curtain extending above the hooks or wire by which it is suspended. **4** a horizontal passage made in preparation for building a tunnel. ▸ Mining another term for **DRIFT**.

headland ▪ n. **1** a narrow piece of land projecting into the sea. **2** a strip of land left unploughed at the end of a field.

headlight (also **headlamp**) ▪ n. a powerful light at the front of a motor vehicle or railway engine.

headline ▪ n. a heading at the top of an article or page in a newspaper or magazine. ▸ (**the headlines**) a summary of the most important items of news. ▪ v. **1** provide with a headline. **2** appear as the star performer at (a concert).

headliner ▪ n. the performer or act promoted as the star attraction on a bill.

headlock ▪ n. a method of restraining someone by holding an arm firmly around their head.

headlong ▪ adv. & adj. **1** with the head foremost. **2** in a rush; with reckless haste.
– ORIGIN Middle English *headling*, from **HEAD** + the adverbial suffix *-ling*.

head louse ■ n. a louse which infests the hair of the human head. [*Pediculus humanus capitis*.]

headman ■ n. (pl. **-men**) the chief or leader of a village, community, or tribe.

headmaster ■ n. a male head teacher.
–DERIVATIVES **headmasterly** adj.

headmistress ■ n. a female head teacher.
–DERIVATIVES **headmistressy** adj.

headnote ■ n. 1 a note at the head of an article or document. 2 Law a summary of a decided case prefixed to the case report.

head of state ■ n. the chief public representative of a country, who may also be the head of government.

head-on ■ adj. & adv. 1 with or involving the front of a vehicle. 2 with or involving direct confrontation.

headphones ■ pl. n. a pair of earphones joined by a band placed over the head.

headpiece ■ n. 1 a device worn on the head. 2 an illustration or ornamental motif at the head of a chapter in a book.

headquarter ■ v. (**be headquartered**) have headquarters at a specified place.

headquarters ■ n. [treated as sing. or pl.] the managerial and administrative centre of an organization. ▸ the premises of a military commander and their staff.

headrest ■ n. a padded support for the head on the back of a seat or chair.

headroom ■ n. the space between the top of a person's head and the ceiling or other structure above.

headsail /'hedseɪl, -s(ə)l/ ■ n. a sail on a ship's foremast or bowsprit.

headscarf (also **headsquare**) ■ n. (pl. **-scarves**) a square of fabric worn as a covering for the head, often folded into a triangle and knotted under the chin.

headset ■ n. 1 a set of headphones with a microphone attached. 2 the bearing assembly which links the front fork of a bicycle to its frame.

headship ■ n. the position of leader or chief. ▸ the position of head teacher in a school.

headsman ■ n. (pl. **-men**) historical an executioner who beheaded prisoners.

headstock ■ n. 1 a set of bearings in a machine, supporting a revolving part. 2 the piece at the end of a guitar neck to which the tuning pegs are fixed.

headstone ■ n. an inscribed stone slab set up at the head of a grave.

headstrong ■ adj. energetically wilful and determined.

heads-up ■ n. an advance warning.

head teacher ■ n. the teacher in charge of a school.

head-to-head ■ adj. & adv. involving two parties confronting each other. ■ n. a conversation or confrontation between two parties.

head-turning ■ adj. extremely noticeable or attractive.
–DERIVATIVES **head-turner** n.

head-up display ■ n. a display of instrument readings in an aircraft or vehicle that can be seen without lowering the eyes, typically through being projected on to the windscreen or visor.

headwater ■ n. a tributary stream of a river close to or forming part of its source.

headway ■ n. 1 forward movement or progress. 2 the average interval between trains or buses on a regular service.

headwind ■ n. a wind blowing from directly in front.

headword ■ n. a word which begins a separate entry in a reference work.

headwork ■ n. 1 activities taxing the mind; mental work. 2 (**headworks**) apparatus for controlling the flow of water in a river or canal.

heady ■ adj. (**-ier**, **-iest**) 1 (of liquor) potent; intoxicating. 2 having a strong or exhilarating effect.
–DERIVATIVES **headily** adv. **headiness** n.

heal ■ v. 1 make or become sound or healthy again. 2 correct or put right (an undesirable situation).
–DERIVATIVES **healable** adj. **healer** n.
–ORIGIN Old English, of Germanic origin; rel. to WHOLE.

heal-all ■ n. 1 a universal remedy; a panacea. 2 any of a number of medicinal plants.

health ■ n. the state of being free from illness or injury. ▸ a person's mental or physical condition.
–ORIGIN Old English, of Germanic origin; rel. to WHOLE.

health care ■ n. the organized provision of medical care to individuals or a community.

health centre ■ n. an establishment housing local medical services or the practice of a group of doctors.

health farm ■ n. a residential establishment where people seek improved health by a regimen of dieting, exercise, and treatment.

health food ■ n. natural food that is thought to have health-giving qualities.

healthful ■ adj. having or conducive to good health.
–DERIVATIVES **healthfully** adv. **healthfulness** n.

health physics ■ pl. n. [treated as sing.] the branch of radiology concerned with the health of people working with radioactive materials.

health service ■ n. a public service providing medical care.

health visitor ■ n. Brit. a nurse who visits the homes of the chronically ill or parents with very young children.

healthy ■ adj. (**-ier**, **-iest**) 1 in good health; not unwell or diseased. ▸ promoting good health: *a healthy diet*. 2 normal, natural, or desirable: *a healthy attitude*. ▸ of a very satisfactory size or amount: *a healthy profit*.
–DERIVATIVES **healthily** adv. **healthiness** n.

heap ■ n. 1 a mound or pile of a substance. ▸ an untidy collection of objects piled up haphazardly. 2 informal a large amount or number: *we have heaps of room*. 3 informal an untidy or dilapidated place or vehicle. ■ v. put in or form a heap. ▸ load copiously with. ▸ [as adj. **heaped**] (of a spoon) with the contents piled above the brim or edge.
–ORIGIN Old English, of Germanic origin.

hear ■ v. (past and past part. **heard**) 1 perceive (a sound) with the ear. 2 be told or informed of. ▸ (**have heard of**) be aware of the existence of. ▸ (**hear from**) receive a letter or phone call from. ▸ (**hear someone out**) listen to all that someone has to say. 3 Law listen to and judge (a case or plaintiff). 4 listen to and grant (a prayer).
–PHRASES **hear! hear!** used to express wholehearted agreement with something said in a speech. **will** (or **would**) **not hear of** will (or would) not allow or agree to.
–DERIVATIVES **hearer** n.
–ORIGIN Old English, of Germanic origin.

hearing ■ n. 1 the faculty of perceiving sounds. ▸ the range within which sounds may be heard; earshot. 2 an opportunity to state one's case. 3 Law an act of listening to evidence, especially a trial before a judge without a jury.

hearing aid ■ n. a small amplifying device worn on the ear by a partially deaf person.

hearken /'hɑːk(ə)n/ (also **harken**) ■ v. (usu. **hearken to**) archaic listen.
–ORIGIN Old English; prob. rel. to HARK.

hearsay ■ n. information which cannot be adequately substantiated; rumour.

hearsay evidence ■ n. Law evidence given by a witness based on information received from others rather than personal knowledge.

hearse /hɜːs/ ■ n. a vehicle for conveying the coffin at a funeral.

heart ■ n. 1 a hollow muscular organ that pumps the blood through the circulatory system by rhythmic contraction and dilation. 2 the central, innermost, or vital part of something. 3 a conventional representation of a heart with two equal curves meeting at a point at the bottom and a cusp at the top. 4 (**hearts**) one of the four suits in a conventional pack of playing cards, denoted by a red figure of such a shape. ▸ a card of this suit. 5 a person's feeling of or capacity for love or compassion.

mood or feeling: *they had a change of heart.* ▸ courage or enthusiasm: *they may lose heart as the work mounts up.* **6** the close compact head of a cabbage or lettuce.
–PHRASES **after one's own heart** sharing one's tastes. **at heart** in one's real nature, in contrast to how one may appear. **break someone's heart** overwhelm someone with sadness. **by heart** from memory. **close** (or **dear**) **to one's heart** of deep interest and concern to one. **from the** (or **the bottom of one's**) **heart** with sincere feeling. **have a heart** be merciful; show pity. **have a heart of gold** have a generous or compassionate nature. **have one's heart in one's mouth** be greatly alarmed or apprehensive. **have one's heart in the right place** be sincere or well intentioned. **one's heart's desire** something that one greatly wishes for. **one's heart-strings** used in reference to one's deepest feelings of love or compassion. **in one's heart of hearts** in one's innermost feelings. **take something to heart** take criticism seriously and be affected by it. **wear one's heart on one's sleeve** make one's feelings apparent.
–DERIVATIVES **-hearted** adj.
–ORIGIN Old English, of Germanic origin.

heartache ■ n. emotional anguish or grief.

heart attack ■ n. a sudden occurrence of coronary thrombosis, typically resulting in the death of part of a heart muscle.

heartbeat ■ n. **1** a pulsation of the heart. **2** an animating force or influence.
–PHRASES **a heartbeat away** very close.

heartbreak ■ n. overwhelming distress.
–DERIVATIVES **heartbreaker** n.

heartbreaking ■ adj. causing overwhelming distress.
–DERIVATIVES **heartbreakingly** adv.

heartbroken ■ adj. suffering from overwhelming distress; very upset.

heartburn ■ n. a form of indigestion felt as a burning sensation in the chest, caused by acid regurgitation into the oesophagus.

hearten ■ v. make more cheerful or confident.
–DERIVATIVES **heartening** adj. **hearteningly** adv.

heart failure ■ n. severe failure of the heart to function properly, especially as a cause of death.

heartfelt ■ adj. sincere; deeply and strongly felt.

hearth /hɑːθ/ ■ n. **1** the floor or surround of a fireplace (often used as a symbol of home). **2** the base or lower part of a furnace, where molten metal collects.
–ORIGIN Old English, of West Germanic origin.

hearthrug ■ n. a rug laid in front of a fireplace.

hearthstone ■ n. a flat stone forming a hearth.

heartily ■ adv. **1** in a hearty manner. **2** very; to a great degree: *they were heartily sick of the subject.*

heartland ■ n. the central or most important part of a country or area.

heartless ■ adj. completely lacking in feeling or consideration.
–DERIVATIVES **heartlessly** adv. **heartlessness** n.

heart-lung machine ■ n. a machine that temporarily takes over the functions of the heart and lungs, especially during heart surgery.

heart-rending ■ adj. causing great sadness or distress.
–DERIVATIVES **heart-rendingly** adv.

heart-searching ■ n. thorough examination of one's feelings and motives.

heartsease /ˈhɑːtsiːz/ ■ n. a wild pansy with purple and yellow flowers, source of most garden varieties. [*Viola tricolor.*]

heartsick (also **heartsore**) ■ adj. chiefly poetic/literary despondent from grief or loss of love.

heart-stopping ■ adj. thrilling; full of suspense.
–DERIVATIVES **heart-stopper** n. **heart-stoppingly** adv.

heart-throb ■ n. informal a man whose good looks excite romantic feelings in women.

heart-to-heart ■ adj. (of a conversation) intimate and personal. ■ n. an intimate and personal conversation.

heart-warming ■ adj. emotionally rewarding or uplifting.

heartwater ■ n. S. African a viral disease affecting livestock and antelope, transmitted by the bont tick.

heartwater tick ■ n. another term for BONT TICK.

heartwood ■ n. the dense inner part of a tree trunk, yielding the hardest wood.

heartworm ■ n. a parasitic nematode worm which infests the hearts of dogs and other animals. [*Dirofilaria immitis.*]

hearty ■ adj. (**-ier, -iest**) **1** loudly vigorous and cheerful. ▸ (of a feeling or opinion) heartfelt. **2** strong and healthy. **3** (of a person's appetite) robust and healthy. ▸ (of food) wholesome and substantial. ■ n. Brit. informal (**me hearties**) a form of address ascribed to sailors.
–DERIVATIVES **heartiness** n.

heat ■ n. **1** the quality of being hot; high temperature. ▸ Physics heat seen as a form of energy arising from the random motion of the molecules of bodies. ▸ technical the amount of heat needed for or evolved in a specific process. ▸ a source or level of heat for cooking. **2** intensity of feeling, especially of anger or excitement. ▸ (**the heat**) informal intensive and unwelcome pressure or criticism: *the heat is on.* **3** a preliminary round in a race or contest. ■ v. **1** make or become hot or warm. **2** (**heat up**) become more intense and exciting. ▸ [as adj. **heated**] inflamed with passion or conviction: *a heated argument.*
–PHRASES **in the heat of the moment** while temporarily angry or excited and without stopping for thought. **on** (or N. Amer. **in**) **heat** (of a female mammal) in the receptive period of the sexual cycle; in oestrus.
–DERIVATIVES **heatedly** adv.
–ORIGIN Old English, of Germanic origin; rel. to HOT.

heat capacity ■ n. another term for THERMAL CAPACITY.

heat death ■ n. Physics a state of uniform distribution of energy, especially viewed as a possible fate of the universe.

heater ■ n. **1** a device for heating something, especially a room. **2** Baseball a fast ball.

heat-exchanger ■ n. a device for transferring heat from one medium to another.

heath ■ n. **1** chiefly Brit. an area of open uncultivated land, typically on acid sandy soil and covered with heather, gorse, and coarse grasses. **2** a dwarf shrub with small leathery leaves and small pink or purple flowers, characteristic of heathland and moorland. [*Erica* and related genera.]
–ORIGIN Old English, of Germanic origin.

heathen /ˈhiːð(ə)n/ ■ n. derogatory **1** a person who does not belong to a widely held religion (especially Christianity, Judaism, or Islam) as regarded by those who do. **2** informal a person lacking culture or moral principles. ■ adj. of or relating to heathens.
–DERIVATIVES **heathendom** n. **heathenish** adj. **heathenism** n.
–ORIGIN Old English *hæthen*, prob. from a Germanic adj. meaning 'inhabiting open country, savage', from the base of HEATH.

heather ■ n. a purple-flowered heath typical of moorland and heathland. [*Calluna vulgaris.*] ▸ informal any plant of this family (Ericaceae); a heath.
–DERIVATIVES **heathery** adj.
–ORIGIN Old English.

heathland ■ n. (also **heathlands**) an extensive area of heath.

Heath Robinson ■ adj. Brit. ingeniously or ridiculously over-complicated in design or construction.
–ORIGIN C20: named after the English cartoonist William *Heath Robinson.*

heating ■ n. equipment or devices used to provide heat, especially to a building.

heat pump ■ n. a device that transfers heat from a colder area to a hotter area by using mechanical energy, as in a refrigerator.

heat-seeking ■ adj. (of a missile) able to detect and home in on infrared radiation emitted by a target, such as the exhaust vent of a jet aircraft.

heat shield ■ n. a device or coating for protection from excessive heat, in particular an outer covering on a

heatstroke

spacecraft to protect it from the heat generated during re-entry into the earth's atmosphere.

heatstroke ■ n. a feverish condition caused by failure of the body's temperature-regulating mechanism when exposed to excessively high temperatures.

heat treatment ■ n. the use of heat for therapeutic purposes in medicine or to modify the properties of a material, especially in metallurgy.
– DERIVATIVES **heat-treat** v.

heatwave ■ n. a prolonged period of abnormally hot weather.

heave /hiːv/ ■ v. (past and past part. **heaved** or chiefly Nautical **hove**) **1** lift or haul (a heavy thing) with great effort. ▸ informal throw (something heavy). **2** produce (a sigh). **3** rise and fall rhythmically or spasmodically. **4** make an effort to vomit; retch. **5** (**heave to**) Nautical come to a stop, especially by turning across the wind leaving the headsail backed. ▸ (**heave in sight**) or **into view** come into view. ■ n. **1** an act of heaving. **2** (**heaves**) another term for COPD in horses. **3** Geology a sideways displacement in a fault.
– DERIVATIVES **heaver** n.
– ORIGIN Old English, of Germanic origin.

heave-ho ■ exclam. a cry emitted with an action that requires physical effort. ■ n. (**the heave-ho**) informal dismissal.

heaven ■ n. **1** a place regarded in various religions as the abode of God or the gods and of the good after death, often depicted as being above the sky. **2** (**the heavens**) poetic/literary the sky. **3** informal a place or state of supreme bliss. **4** (also **heavens**) used in exclamations as a substitute for 'God': *heaven knows!*
– PHRASES **the heavens open** it suddenly starts to rain very heavily. **in seventh heaven** in a state of ecstasy. **move heaven and earth to do something** make extraordinary efforts to do a thing. **stink** (or **smell**) **to high heaven** informal smell very bad.
– DERIVATIVES **heavenward** adj. & adv. **heavenwards** adv.
– ORIGIN Old English, of Germanic origin.

heavenly ■ adj. **1** of heaven; divine. **2** of or relating to the sky. **3** informal very pleasing; wonderful.
– DERIVATIVES **heavenliness** n.

heavenly body ■ n. a planet, star, or other celestial body.

heavenly host ■ n. a literary or biblical term for the angels.

heaven-sent ■ adj. (of an event or opportunity) occurring at a very favourable time.

heaving ■ adj. Brit. informal (of a place) extremely crowded.

heavy ■ adj. (**-ier**, **-iest**) **1** of great weight; difficult to lift or move. **2** of great density; thick or substantial. ▸ (of food) hard to digest; too filling. ▸ (of ground) muddy or full of clay. ▸ not delicate or graceful; coarse or slow-moving. ▸ (of a smell) overpowering. **3** of more than the usual size, amount, or force: *a heavy cold*. ▸ (**heavy on**) using a lot of. ▸ doing something to excess: *a heavy smoker*. **4** striking or falling with force. **5** needing much physical effort. ▸ mentally oppressive; hard to endure. ▸ very important or serious. **6** (of music, especially rock) having a strong bass component and a forceful rhythm. **7** informal strict, harsh, or difficult to deal with. **8** Physics containing atoms of an isotope of greater than the usual mass: *heavy water*. ■ n. (pl. **-ies**) **1** something large or heavy of its kind. ▸ informal a large, strong man, especially one hired for protection. ▸ informal an important person. **2** chiefly Scottish strong beer, especially bitter.
– PHRASES **heavy going** a person or situation that is difficult or boring to deal with.
– DERIVATIVES **heavily** adv. **heaviness** n. **heavyish** adj.
– ORIGIN Old English, of Germanic origin; rel. to HEAVE.

heavy breathing ■ n. breathing that is audible through being deep or laboured.

heavy chemicals ■ pl. n. bulk chemicals used in industry and agriculture.

heavy cream ■ n. North American term for DOUBLE CREAM.

heavy-duty ■ adj. **1** designed to withstand the stresses of demanding use. **2** informal intense, important, or abundant.

heavy-handed ■ adj. clumsy, insensitive, or overly forceful.
– DERIVATIVES **heavy-handedly** adv. **heavy-handedness** n.

heavy-hearted ■ adj. feeling depressed or melancholy.

heavy hydrogen ■ n. another term for DEUTERIUM.

heavy industry ■ n. the manufacture of large, heavy articles and materials in bulk.

heavy metal ■ n. **1** a metal of relatively high density, or of high relative atomic weight. **2** a type of highly amplified harsh-sounding rock music with a strong beat.

heavy oil ■ n. any of the relatively dense hydrocarbons (denser than water) derived from petroleum, coal tar, and similar materials.

heavy petting ■ n. erotic contact between two people involving stimulation of the genitals but stopping short of intercourse.

heavy water ■ n. water in which the hydrogen in the molecules is partly or wholly replaced by the isotope deuterium, used especially as a moderator in nuclear reactors.

heavyweight ■ n. **1** a weight in boxing and other sports, typically the heaviest category. **2** informal a person of influence or importance. ■ adj. **1** of above-average weight. **2** informal serious, important, or influential.

hebdomadal /hɛbˈdɒməd(ə)l/ ■ adj. formal weekly.
– ORIGIN C17: from Greek *hebdomas*, *hebdomad-* 'the number seven, seven days', from *hepta* 'seven'.

hebe /ˈhiːbi/ ■ n. an evergreen flowering shrub with spikes of mauve, pink, or white flowers, native to New Zealand. [Genus *Hebe*.]
– ORIGIN named after the Greek goddess *Hebe*.

Hebraic /hɪˈbreɪɪk/ ■ adj. of Hebrew or the Hebrews.
– DERIVATIVES **Hebraically** adv.

Hebraism /ˈhiːbreɪɪz(ə)m/ ■ n. **1** a Hebrew idiom or expression. **2** the Jewish religion, culture, or character.

Hebraist /ˈhiːbreɪɪst/ ■ n. a scholar of the Hebrew language.

Hebrew /ˈhiːbruː/ ■ n. **1** a member of an ancient people living in what is now Israel and Palestine, who established the kingdoms of Israel and Judah. **2** old-fashioned and sometimes offensive term for JEW. **3** the Semitic language of the Hebrews, in its ancient or modern form.
– ORIGIN from late Greek *Hebraios*, from Aramaic 'ibray, from Hebrew 'ibrî understood to mean 'one from the other side (of the river)'.

Hebrew Bible ■ n. the sacred writings of Judaism, called by Christians the Old Testament.

Hebridean /ˈhɛbrɪdiːən/ ■ n. a native or inhabitant of the Hebrides off the NW coast of Scotland. ■ adj. of or relating to the Hebrides.

hecatomb /ˈhɛkətuːm/ ■ n. (in ancient Greece or Rome) a great public sacrifice, originally of a hundred oxen.
– ORIGIN C16: from Greek *hekatombē*, from *hekaton* 'hundred' + *bous* 'ox'.

heck ■ exclam. expressing surprise, frustration, or dismay. ▸ (**the heck**) or **a heck of a** —— used for emphasis.
– ORIGIN C19: euphemistic alteration of HELL.

heckle ■ v. **1** interrupt (a public speaker) with derisive comments or abuse. **2** dress (flax or hemp) to split and straighten the fibres for spinning. ■ n. a heckling comment.
– DERIVATIVES **heckler** n.
– ORIGIN Middle English: from *heckle* 'flax comb', a dialect form of HACKLE.

hectare /ˈhɛktɛː, -ɑː/ (abbrev.: **ha**) ■ n. a metric unit of square measure, equal to 10 000 square metres (2.471 acres).
– DERIVATIVES **hectarage** n.
– ORIGIN C19: from French, from Greek *hekaton* 'hundred'.

hectic ■ adj. **1** full of incessant or frantic activity. **2** Medicine, archaic affected by or denoting a recurrent fever typically accompanying tuberculosis, with flushed cheeks and hot, dry skin.
– DERIVATIVES **hectically** adv.

–ORIGIN Middle English: from late Latin *hecticus*, from Greek *hektikos* 'habitual'.

hecto- ■ comb. form a hundred: *hectometre*.
–ORIGIN from Greek *hekaton* 'hundred'.

hectogram (also **hectogramme**) (abbrev.: **hg**) ■ n. a metric unit of mass equal to one hundred grams.

hectolitre /ˈhɛktə(ʊ)ˌliːtə/ (US **hectoliter**) (abbrev.: **hl**) ■ n. a metric unit of capacity equal to one hundred litres.

hectometre /ˈhɛktəˌmiːtə/ (US **hectometer**) (abbrev.: **hm**) ■ n. a metric unit of length equal to one hundred metres.

hector /ˈhɛktə/ ■ v. talk to (someone) in a bullying way.
–DERIVATIVES **hectoring** adj. **hectoringly** adv.
–ORIGIN Middle English: from the Trojan warrior *Hector* in Homer's *Iliad*.

he'd ■ contr. **1** he had. **2** he would.

hedge ■ n. **1** a fence or boundary formed by closely growing bushes or shrubs. **2** a contract entered into or asset held as a protection against possible financial loss. **3** a word or phrase used to allow for additional possibilities or to avoid over-precise commitment, for example *etc.* or *usually*. ■ v. **1** surround or bound with a hedge. **2** limit or qualify by conditions or exceptions. ▸ avoid making a definite statement or commitment. **3** protect (one's investment or an investor) against loss by making balancing or compensating contracts or transactions.
–PHRASES **hedge one's bets** avoid committing oneself when faced with a difficult choice.
–DERIVATIVES **hedger** n. **hedging** n.
–ORIGIN Old English, of Germanic origin.

hedge fund ■ n. an offshore investment fund that engages in speculation using credit or borrowed capital.

hedgehog ■ n. **1** a nocturnal insectivorous mammal with a spiny coat and short legs, able to roll itself into a ball for defence. [*Atelerix frontalis* (southern Africa), *Erinaceus europaeus*, and other species, family Erinaceidae.] **2** [as modifier] used in names of plants or fruits having spines, e.g. *hedgehog cactus*.

hedge-hop ■ v. fly an aircraft at a very low altitude.
–DERIVATIVES **hedge-hopper** n.

hedgerow ■ n. a hedge of wild shrubs and occasional trees bordering a field.
–ORIGIN Old English: from HEDGE + obsolete *rew* 'hedgerow'.

hedge sparrow ■ n. another term for DUNNOCK.

hedonism /ˈhiːd(ə)nɪz(ə)m, ˈhɛ-/ ■ n. **1** the pursuit of pleasure; sensual self-indulgence. **2** Philosophy the ethical theory that pleasure (in the sense of the satisfaction of desires) is the highest good and proper aim of human life.
–DERIVATIVES **hedonist** n. **hedonistic** adj. **hedonistically** adv.
–ORIGIN C19: from Greek *hēdonē* 'pleasure'.

-hedron ■ comb. form (pl. **-hedra** or **-hedrons**) in nouns denoting geometrical solids having a specified number of plane faces: *decahedron*. ▸ denoting geometrical solids having faces of a specified shape: *rhombohedron*.
–DERIVATIVES **-hedral** comb. form in corresponding adjectives.
–ORIGIN from Greek *hedra* 'seat, base'.

heebie-jeebies ■ pl. n. (**the heebie-jeebies**) informal a state of nervous fear or anxiety.
–ORIGIN 1920s (orig. US).

heed ■ v. pay attention to; take notice of. ■ n. (usu. in phr. **pay** (or **take**) **heed**) careful attention.
–DERIVATIVES **heedful** adj. **heedfully** adv. **heedfulness** n.
–ORIGIN Old English, of West Germanic origin.

heedless ■ adj. showing a reckless lack of care or attention.
–DERIVATIVES **heedlessly** adv. **heedlessness** n.

hee-haw ■ n. the loud, harsh cry of a donkey or mule. ■ v. make such a cry.

heel[1] ■ n. **1** the back part of the foot below the ankle. ▸ the part of the palm of the hand next to the wrist. **2** the part of a shoe or boot supporting the heel. **3** informal, dated an inconsiderate or untrustworthy person. **4** the end of a violin bow at which it is held. **5** the part of the head of a golf club nearest the shaft. **6** a crusty end of a loaf of bread. **7** a piece of the main stem of a plant left attached to the base of a cutting. ■ exclam. a command to a dog to walk close behind its owner. ■ v. **1** fit or renew a heel on (a shoe or boot). **2** Rugby push or kick (the ball) out of the back of the scrum with one's heel. **3** Golf strike (the ball) with the heel of the club. **4** touch the ground with the heel when dancing.
–PHRASES **at** (or **on**) **the heels of** following closely after. **bring someone to heel** bring someone under control. **cool** (or Brit. **kick**) **one's heels** be kept waiting. **kick up one's heels** chiefly N. Amer. have a lively, enjoyable time. **take to one's heels** run away. **turn** (**on one's**) **heel** turn sharply.
–DERIVATIVES **-heeled** adj. **heelless** adj.
–ORIGIN Old English *hēla*, *hǣla*, of Germanic origin.

heel[2] ■ v. (of a ship) lean over owing to the pressure of wind or an uneven load. ■ n. an instance of heeling, or the amount that a ship heels.
–ORIGIN C16: from obsolete *heeld*, *hield* 'incline', of Germanic origin.

heel[3] ■ v. (**heel something in**) set a plant in the ground and cover its roots; plant something temporarily.
–ORIGIN Old English *helian* 'cover, hide', of Germanic origin.

heel bar ■ n. a small shop or stall where shoes are repaired.

heel bone ■ n. the calcaneus.

heft ■ v. **1** lift or carry (something heavy). **2** lift or hold (something) to test its weight. ■ n. chiefly N. Amer. **1** weight. **2** ability or influence.
–ORIGIN Middle English: prob. from HEAVE, on the pattern of *cleft*.

hefty ■ adj. (**-ier**, **-iest**) large, heavy, and powerful.
–DERIVATIVES **heftily** adv. **heftiness** n.

Hegelian /heɪˈɡiːlɪən, hɪ-, -ˈɡeɪl-/ ■ adj. of or relating to the German philosopher Georg Hegel (1770–1831) or his philosophy of objective idealism. ■ n. a follower of Hegel.
–DERIVATIVES **Hegelianism** n.

hegemony /hɪˈdʒɛməni, -ˈɡɛ-/ ■ n. leadership or dominance, especially by one state or social group over others.
–DERIVATIVES **hegemonic** adj.
–ORIGIN C16: from Greek, from *hēgemōn* 'leader', from *hēgeisthai* 'to lead'.

Hegira /ˈhɛdʒɪrə/ (also **Hejira** or **Hijra**) ■ n. **1** Muhammad's departure from Mecca to Medina in AD 622, marking the consolidation of the first Muslim community. ▸ the Muslim era reckoned from this date. **2** (**hegira**) an exodus or migration.
–ORIGIN from Arabic *hijra* 'departure'.

heifer /ˈhɛfə/ ■ n. a cow that has not borne a calf, or has borne only one calf. Compare with COW[1].
–ORIGIN Old English.

heigh-ho /heɪˈhəʊ/ ■ exclam. informal expressing boredom, resignation, or jollity.

height ■ n. **1** the measurement of someone or something from head to foot or from base to top. ▸ the quality of being tall or high. **2** elevation above ground or a recognized level (typically sea level). ▸ a high place or area. **3** the most intense part or period of something. ▸ an extreme instance or example of something: *the height of bad manners*.
–ORIGIN Old English, of Germanic origin; rel. to HIGH.

heighten ■ v. **1** make higher. **2** make or become more intense.

Heimlich procedure /ˈhaɪmlɪx/ (also **Heimlich manoeuvre**) ■ n. a first-aid procedure for dislodging an obstruction from a person's windpipe, in which a sudden strong pressure is applied on the abdomen between the navel and the ribcage.
–ORIGIN 1970s: named after the American physician Henry J. Heimlich.

heinous /ˈheɪnəs, ˈhiːnəs/ ■ adj. utterly odious or wicked: *a heinous crime*.
–DERIVATIVES **heinously** adv. **heinousness** n.
–ORIGIN Middle English: from Old French *haineus*, from *hair* 'to hate', of Germanic origin.

heir /ɛː/ ■ n. **1** a person legally entitled to the property or

rank of another on that person's death. **2** a person who continues the work of a predecessor.
– DERIVATIVES **heirdom** n. **heirless** adj. **heirship** n.
– ORIGIN Middle English: from Latin *heres*.

heir apparent ▪ n. (pl. **heirs apparent**) **1** an heir whose claim cannot be set aside by the birth of another heir. Compare with HEIR PRESUMPTIVE. **2** a person who is most likely to succeed to the place of another.

heiress ▪ n. a female heir, especially to vast wealth.

heirloom ▪ n. a valuable object that has belonged to a family for several generations.
– ORIGIN Middle English: from HEIR + LOOM¹ (which formerly had the senses 'tool, heirloom').

heir presumptive ▪ n. (pl. **heirs presumptive**) an heir whose claim may be set aside by the birth of another heir. Compare with HEIR APPARENT.

heish ▪ n. variant spelling of EISH.

heist /haɪst/ informal ▪ n. a robbery. ▪ v. chiefly N. Amer. steal.
– ORIGIN C19: representing a local pronunciation of HOIST.

heita /ˈeɪtə, ˈheɪtə/ ▪ exclam. S. African informal used mainly by urban black people as a friendly greeting.
– ORIGIN 1970s: from Tsotsitaal.

Hejira ▪ n. variant spelling of HEGIRA.

HeLa cells /ˈhiːlə/ ▪ pl. n. human epithelial cells of a strain maintained in tissue culture since 1951 and used in research, especially in virology.
– ORIGIN 1950s: from the name of *Henrietta La*cks, whose cervical carcinoma provided the original cells.

held past and past participle of HOLD¹.

heliacal /hɪˈlaɪək(ə)l/ ▪ adj. Astronomy denoting the first rising (or last setting) of a star or planet which occurs at the same time as the rising of the sun.
– ORIGIN C17: from Greek *hēliakos*, from *hēlios* 'sun'.

helianthemum /ˌhiːlɪˈanθɪməm/ ▪ n. a low evergreen shrub with saucer-shaped flowers, grown as an ornamental. [Genus *Helianthemum*.]
– ORIGIN from Greek *hēlios* 'sun' + *anthemon* 'flower'.

helical /ˈhɛlɪk(ə)l, ˈhiː-/ ▪ adj. having the shape or form of a helix; spiral.
– DERIVATIVES **helically** adv.

helices plural form of HELIX.

helichrysum /ˌhɛlɪˈkraɪsəm/ ▪ n. a plant of the daisy family, with flowers retaining their shape and colour when dried. [Genus *Helichrysum*.]
– ORIGIN from Greek *helikhrusos*, from *helix* 'spiral' + *khrusos* 'gold'.

helicity /hiːˈlɪsɪti/ ▪ n. **1** chiefly Biochemistry helical character, especially of DNA. **2** Physics a combination of the spin and the linear motion of a subatomic particle.

helicopter ▪ n. a type of aircraft deriving both lift and propulsion from one or two sets of horizontally revolving rotors and capable of moving vertically and horizontally. ▪ v. transport or fly by helicopter.
– ORIGIN C19: from French *hélicoptère*, from Greek *helix* 'spiral' + *pteron* 'wing'.

helio- /ˈhiːlɪəʊ/ ▪ comb. form of or relating to the sun: *heliograph*.
– ORIGIN from Greek *hēlios* 'sun'.

heliocentric ▪ adj. **1** having or representing the sun as the centre, as in the accepted astronomical model of the solar system. Compare with GEOCENTRIC. **2** Astronomy measured from or considered in relation to the centre of the sun.
– DERIVATIVES **heliocentrically** adv.

heliograph ▪ n. **1** a signalling device by which sunlight is reflected in flashes from a movable mirror. ▶ a message sent in such a way. **2** a telescopic apparatus for photographing the sun. **3** historical a type of early photographic engraving made using a sensitized silver plate and an asphalt or bitumen varnish. ▪ v. **1** send (a message) by heliograph. **2** take a heliographic photograph of.
– DERIVATIVES **heliographic** adj. **heliography** n.

heliometer /ˌhiːlɪˈɒmɪtə/ ▪ n. Astronomy a refracting telescope with a split objective lens, used for finding the angular distance between two stars.

heliosphere ▪ n. Astronomy the region of space, encompassing the solar system, in which the solar wind has a significant influence.
– DERIVATIVES **heliospheric** adj.

heliotrope /ˈhiːlɪətrəʊp, ˈhɛl-/ ▪ n. a plant of the borage family, cultivated for its fragrant purple or blue flowers. [Genus *Heliotropium*.]
– ORIGIN Old English: from Greek *hēliotropion*, from *hēlios* 'sun' + *trepein* 'to turn'.

heliotropism /ˌhiːlɪə(ʊ)ˈtrəʊpɪz(ə)m/ ▪ n. Biology growth or movement of a plant or other organism in response to sunlight.
– DERIVATIVES **heliotropic** adj.

helipad ▪ n. a landing and take-off area for helicopters.

heliport ▪ n. an airport or landing place for helicopters.

heli-skiing ▪ n. skiing in which the skier is taken up the mountain by helicopter.
– DERIVATIVES **heli-ski** v. **heli-skier** n.

helium /ˈhiːlɪəm/ ▪ n. the chemical element of atomic number 2, an inert gas which is the lightest member of the noble gas series. (Symbol: **He**)
– ORIGIN C19: modern Latin, from Greek *hēlios* 'sun', because its existence was inferred from an emission line in the sun's spectrum.

helix /ˈhiːlɪks/ ▪ n. (pl. **helices** /ˈhiːlɪsiːz, ˈhɛl-/) **1** an object having a three-dimensional shape like that of a wire wound uniformly in a single layer around a cylinder or cone, as in a corkscrew or spiral staircase. **2** Architecture a spiral ornament. **3** Anatomy the rim of the external ear.
– ORIGIN C16: from Greek.

hell ▪ n. **1** a place regarded in various religions as a spiritual realm of evil and suffering, often depicted as a place of perpetual fire beneath the earth to which the wicked are consigned after death. **2** a state or place of great suffering. ▪ exclam. used to express annoyance or surprise or for emphasis.
– PHRASES **all hell breaks** (or **is let**) **loose** informal suddenly there is pandemonium. **come hell or high water** whatever difficulties may occur. **for the hell of it** informal just for fun. **get hell** informal be severely reprimanded. **give someone hell** informal severely reprimand or make things very unpleasant for someone. **go to hell in a handbasket** (or **handcart**) N. Amer. informal deteriorate rapidly. **hell for leather** as fast as possible. **the hell in** S. African informal extremely angry. **hell of a —** informal used for emphasis. **hell's bells** informal an exclamation of annoyance or anger. **like hell** informal **1** very fast, much, hard, etc. **2** used in ironic expressions of scorn or disagreement. **not a hope in hell** informal no chance at all. **play hell** (or **merry hell**) informal create havoc or cause damage. **there will be hell to pay** informal serious trouble will result. **until hell freezes over** forever.
– DERIVATIVES **hellward** adv. & adj.
– ORIGIN Old English, of Germanic origin.

he'll ▪ contr. he shall or he will.

Helladic /hɛˈladɪk/ ▪ adj. Archaeology relating to or denoting the Bronze Age cultures of mainland Greece (*c*.3000–1050 BC).
– ORIGIN C19: from Greek, from *Hellas*, *Hellad-* 'Greece'.

hell-bent ▪ adj. determined to achieve something at all costs.

hellcat ▪ n. a spiteful, violent woman.

hellebore /ˈhɛlɪbɔː/ ▪ n. a poisonous winter-flowering Eurasian plant with coarse divided leaves and large white, green, or purplish flowers. [Genus *Helleborus*: several species.]
– ORIGIN Old English, from medieval Latin *eleborus*, from Greek *helleboros*.

Hellene /ˈhɛliːn/ ▪ n. a Greek.
– ORIGIN from Greek *Hellēn* 'a Greek'.

Hellenic /hɛˈlɛnɪk, -ˈliːnɪk/ ▪ adj. **1** Greek. **2** Archaeology relating to or denoting Iron Age and Classical Greek culture (between Helladic and Hellenistic). ▪ n. the branch of the Indo-European language family comprising classical and modern Greek. ▶ the Greek language.
– DERIVATIVES **Hellenism** n. **Hellenist** n. **Hellenization** (also **-isation**) n. **Hellenize** (also **-ise**) v. **Hellenizer** n.

Hellenistic ■ adj. of or relating to Greek culture in the Mediterranean and Near East from the death of Alexander the Great (323 BC) to the defeat of Cleopatra and Mark Antony by Octavian in 31 BC.

hellfire ■ n. the fire regarded as existing in hell.

hellhole ■ n. an oppressive or unbearable place.

hellhound ■ n. a demon in the form of a dog.

hellion /ˈheljən/ ■ n. N. Amer. informal a rowdy or mischievous person, especially a child.
– ORIGIN C19: perhaps from dialect *hallion* 'a worthless fellow', altered by association with HELL.

hellish ■ adj. **1** of or like hell. **2** informal extremely difficult or unpleasant. ■ adv. Brit. informal very; extremely.
– DERIVATIVES **hellishly** adv. **hellishness** n.

hello (also **hallo** or **hullo**) ■ exclam. **1** used as a greeting or to begin a telephone conversation. **2** Brit. used to express surprise or as a cry to attract someone's attention.
– ORIGIN C19: var. of earlier *hollo*; rel. to HOLLA.

hellraiser ■ n. a person who causes trouble by violent, drunken, or outrageous behaviour.
– DERIVATIVES **hellraising** adj. & n.

Hell's Angel ■ n. a member of a gang of male motorcycle enthusiasts notorious for lawless behaviour.

helluva ■ contr. a hell of a (representing a non-standard pronunciation).

helm¹ ■ n. **1** a tiller or wheel for steering a ship or boat. **2** (**the helm**) a position of leadership. ■ v. **1** steer (a boat or ship). **2** manage the running of.
– ORIGIN Old English *helma*.

helm² ■ n. archaic a helmet.
– DERIVATIVES **helmed** adj.
– ORIGIN Old English, of Germanic origin; rel. to HELMET.

helmet ■ n. **1** a hard or padded protective hat. **2** (also **helmet shell**) a predatory mollusc with a squat heavy shell, living in tropical and temperate seas. [Family Cassidae.]
– DERIVATIVES **helmeted** adj.
– ORIGIN Middle English: from Old French, diminutive of *helme*, of Germanic origin.

helminth /ˈhelmɪnθ/ ■ n. a parasitic worm; a fluke, tapeworm, or nematode.
– DERIVATIVES **helminthic** adj. **helminthological** adj. **helminthology** n.
– ORIGIN C19: from Greek *helmins*, *helminth-* 'intestinal worm'.

helminthiasis /ˌhelmɪnˈθaɪəsɪs/ ■ n. Medicine infestation with parasitic worms.

helmsman ■ n. (pl. **-men**) a person who steers a boat.

help ■ v. **1** make it easier for (someone) to do something. ▸ improve (a situation or problem); be of benefit to. ▸ assist (someone) to move in a specified direction. **2** (**help someone to**) serve someone with (food or drink). ▸ (**help oneself**) take something without permission. **3** (**can/could not help**) cannot or could not avoid. ▸ (**can/could not help oneself**) cannot or could not stop oneself from acting in a certain way. ■ n. **1** assistance or a source of assistance. **2** [as modifier] Computing giving assistance to a user in the form of displayed instructions: *a help menu*. **3** a domestic servant or employee. ■ exclam. used as an appeal for urgent assistance.
– PHRASES **so help me** (**God**) used to emphasize that one means what one is saying. **there is no help for it** there is no way of avoiding or remedying a situation.
– DERIVATIVES **helper** n.
– ORIGIN Old English, of Germanic origin.

helper cell ■ n. Physiology a T-lymphocyte that influences or controls the differentiation or activity of other cells of the immune system.

helpful ■ adj. **1** giving or ready to give help. **2** useful.
– DERIVATIVES **helpfully** adv. **helpfulness** n.

helping ■ n. a portion of food served to one person at one time.

helpless ■ adj. **1** unable to defend oneself or to act without help. **2** uncontrollable: *helpless laughter*.
– DERIVATIVES **helplessly** adv. **helplessness** n.

helpline ■ n. a telephone service providing help with problems.

helpmate (also **helpmeet**) ■ n. a helpful companion or partner.

– ORIGIN C17 (as *helpmeet*): from an erroneous reading of Genesis 2:18, 20, where Adam's future wife is described as 'an help meet for him' (i.e. a suitable helper for him).

helter-skelter ■ adj. & adv. in disorderly haste or confusion. ■ n. Brit. a tall spiral slide winding around a tower at a fair.
– ORIGIN C16: a rhyming jingle perhaps symbolic of running feet, or from Middle English *skelte* 'hasten'.

Helvetian (also **Helvetic**) ■ adj. Swiss. ■ n. a native of Switzerland.
– ORIGIN from Latin *Helvetia* 'Switzerland'.

hem¹ ■ n. the edge of a piece of cloth or clothing which has been turned under and sewn. ■ v. (**hemmed**, **hemming**) **1** turn under and sew the edge of (a piece of cloth). **2** (**hem someone/thing in**) surround and restrict the space or movement of someone or something.
– ORIGIN Old English, 'the border of a piece of cloth', of West Germanic origin.

hem² ■ exclam. expressing the sound made when coughing or clearing the throat to attract someone's attention or show hesitation. ■ v. (**hemmed**, **hemming**) archaic make such a sound.
– PHRASES **hem and haw** another way of saying hum and haw (see HUM¹).
– ORIGIN C15: imitative.

hemal ■ adj. US spelling of HAEMAL.

he-man ■ n. informal a very well-built, masculine man.

hemato- ■ comb. form US spelling of HAEMATO-.

heme ■ n. US spelling of HAEM.

hemerocallis /ˌhem(ə)rə(ʊ)ˈkalɪs/ ■ n. (pl. same) a plant of a genus that comprises the day lilies. [Genus *Hemerocallis*.]
– ORIGIN from Greek *hēmerokallis* 'a lily that flowers for a day'.

hemi- ■ prefix half.
– ORIGIN from Greek *hēmi-*; rel. to Latin *semi-*.

-hemia ■ comb. form US spelling of -AEMIA.

hemicellulose ■ n. Biochemistry a constituent of the cell walls of plants, consisting of polysaccharides of simpler structure than cellulose.

Hemichordata /ˌhemɪkɔːˈdeɪtə/ ■ pl. n. Zoology a small phylum of marine invertebrates that comprises the acorn worms.
– DERIVATIVES **hemichordate** n. & adj.

hemicycle ■ n. a semicircular shape or structure.

hemihydrate /ˌhemɪˈhaɪdreɪt/ ■ n. Chemistry a crystalline hydrate containing one molecule of water for every two molecules of the compound in question.

hemimetabolous /ˌhemɪməˈtabələs/ ■ adj. Entomology (of an insect) having no pupal stage in the transition from larva to adult.
– DERIVATIVES **hemimetabolic** adj.

hemiparasite ■ n. Botany a plant which obtains part of its food by parasitism but also photosynthesizes, e.g. mistletoe.

hemiparesis /ˌhemɪpəˈriːsɪs/ ■ n. another term for HEMIPLEGIA.

hemipenis /ˈhemɪpiːnɪs/ ■ n. (pl. **hemipenes**) Zoology each of the paired male reproductive organs in snakes and lizards.

hemiplegia /ˌhemɪˈpliːdʒə/ ■ n. Medicine paralysis of one side of the body.
– DERIVATIVES **hemiplegic** n. & adj.

Hemiptera /həˈmɪpt(ə)rə/ ■ pl. n. Entomology a large order of insects comprising the bugs, which include aphids, cicadas, and leafhoppers.
– DERIVATIVES **hemipteran** n. & adj. **hemipterous** adj.
– ORIGIN from Greek *hemi-* 'half' + *pteron* 'wing' (because of the forewing structure, partly hardened at the base and partly membranous).

hemisphere ■ n. **1** a half of a sphere. **2** a half of the earth, usually as divided into northern and southern halves by the equator, or into western and eastern halves by an imaginary line passing through the poles. ▸ a half of the celestial sphere. **3** (also **cerebral hemisphere**) each of the two parts of the cerebrum (left and right) in the brain

hemline

of a vertebrate.
- DERIVATIVES **hemispheric** adj. **hemispherical** adj. **hemispherically** adv.
- ORIGIN Middle English: from Greek *hēmisphairion*, from *hēmi-* 'half' + *sphaira* 'sphere'.

hemline ■ n. the level of the lower edge of a garment such as a skirt, dress, or coat.

hemlock ■ n. **1** a highly poisonous plant of the parsley family, with fern-like leaves, small white flowers, and an unpleasant smell. [*Conium maculatum*.] ▸ a sedative or poisonous potion obtained from this plant. **2** (also **hemlock fir** or **spruce**) a North American conifer with dark green foliage which is said to smell like hemlock when crushed. [Genus *Tsuga*: several species.]
- ORIGIN Old English.

hemo- ■ comb. form US spelling of HAEMO-.

hemp ■ n. **1** (also **Indian hemp**) the cannabis plant. ▸ the fibre of this plant, extracted from the stem and used to make rope, stout fabrics, fibreboard, and paper. ▸ used in names of other plants that yield fibre, e.g. Manila hemp. **2** the drug cannabis.
- DERIVATIVES **hempen** adj. (archaic).
- ORIGIN Old English, of Germanic origin; rel. to Greek *kannabis*.

hemp agrimony ■ n. a Eurasian plant of the daisy family resembling a valerian, with clusters of pale purple flowers and hairy stems. [*Eupatorium cannabinum*.]

hemstitch ■ n. a decorative stitch used especially alongside a hem, in which several adjacent threads are pulled out and the crossing threads are tied into bunches, making a row of small openings. ■ v. incorporate such a decoration in the hem of.

hen ■ n. a female bird, especially of a domestic fowl. ▸ (**hens**) domestic fowls of either sex. ▸ used in names of various birds, e.g. rails. ▸ a female lobster, crab, or salmon.
- PHRASES **as rare** (or **scarce**) **as hen's teeth** extremely rare.
- ORIGIN Old English, of Germanic origin.

hen and chickens ■ n. **1** a houseleek or other plant producing additional small flower heads or offshoots. [*Sempervivum tectorum* and other species.] **2** S. African a plant of the lily family having long narrow leaves with a central yellow stripe, popular as a house plant. [*Chlorophytum comosum*.]

henbane /'hɛnbeɪn/ ■ n. a poisonous Eurasian plant of the nightshade family, with sticky hairy leaves and an unpleasant smell. [*Hyoscyamus niger*.]

hence ■ adv. **1** as a consequence; for this reason. **2** from now; in the future. **3** (also **from hence**) archaic from here.
- ORIGIN Middle English *hennes*: from earlier *henne*, from Old English *heonan*, of Germanic origin.

henceforth (also **henceforward**) ■ adv. from this or that time on.

henchman ■ n. (pl. **-men**) **1** chiefly derogatory a faithful follower or political supporter, especially one prepared to engage in crime or dishonest practices. **2** historical a squire or page of honour to a person of rank. ▸ (in Scotland) the principal attendant of a Highland chief.
- ORIGIN Middle English, from Old English *hengest* 'male horse' + MAN, the original sense being prob. 'groom'.

hendeca- /'hɛndɛkə, hɛn'dɛkə/ ■ comb. form eleven; having eleven: *hendecasyllable*.
- ORIGIN from Greek *hendeka* 'eleven'.

hendecagon /hɛn'dɛkəɡ(ə)n/ ■ n. a plane figure with eleven straight sides and angles.
- DERIVATIVES **hendecagonal** /ˌhɛndɪˈkaɡ(ə)n(ə)l/ adj.

hendecasyllable /ˌhɛndɛkəˈsɪləbəl/ ■ n. Prosody a line of verse containing eleven syllables.
- DERIVATIVES **hendecasyllabic** adj.

hendiadys /hɛnˈdʌɪədɪs/ ■ n. the expression of a single idea by two words connected with 'and', e.g. *nice and warm*, when one could be used to modify the other, as in *nicely warm*.
- ORIGIN C16: from Greek *hen dia duoin* 'one thing by two'.

henequen /'hɛnɪkɛn/ ■ n. **1** a fibre resembling sisal, used for binder twine and paper pulp. **2** a Central American agave from which such fibre is obtained. [*Agave fourcroydes*.]

- ORIGIN C17: from Spanish *jeniquen*, from a local word.

henge /hɛn(d)ʒ/ ■ n. a prehistoric monument consisting of a circle of stone or wooden uprights.
- ORIGIN C18: back-formation from the megalithic monument *Stonehenge* in Wiltshire, England, from Old English *stān* 'stone' + an element rel. to *hengan* 'to hang'.

hen harrier ■ n. a northern-hemisphere harrier of open country, the male of which is mainly pale grey and the female brown. [*Circus cyaneus*.]

Henle's loop ■ n. another term for LOOP OF HENLE.

henna ■ n. **1** the powdered leaves of a tropical shrub, used as a reddish-brown dye to colour the hair and decorate the body. **2** the shrub which produces these leaves, with small pink, red, or white flowers. [*Lawsonia inermis*] ■ v. (**hennas, hennaed, hennaing**) dye with henna.
- ORIGIN C17: from Arabic *ḥinnā'*.

hen night ■ n. Brit. informal a celebration held for a woman who is about to get married, attended only by women.

hen party ■ n. informal a social gathering of women.

henpeck ■ v. [usu. as adj. **henpecked**] (of a woman) continually criticize and order about (her husband).

henry (abbrev.: **H**) ■ n. (pl. **henries** or **henrys**) Physics the SI unit of inductance, equal to an electromotive force of one volt in a closed circuit with a uniform rate of change of current of one ampere per second.
- ORIGIN C19: named after the American physicist Joseph Henry.

Henry's law ■ n. Chemistry a law stating that the mass of a dissolved gas in a given volume of solvent at equilibrium is proportional to the partial pressure of the gas.
- ORIGIN C19: named after the English chemist William Henry.

hensopper /'hɛnsɔpə/ ■ n. S. African historical, derogatory a term used by the Boers of Boers who surrendered to the British forces during the Anglo-Boer War of 1899–1902. Often contrasted with BITTERENDER (in sense 2).
- ORIGIN C20: Afrikaans, from an alteration of English *hands up!* (the command to and gesture of surrender).

heparin /'hɛpərɪn/ ■ n. Biochemistry a compound occurring in the liver and other tissues which inhibits blood coagulation, used as an anticoagulant in the treatment of thrombosis.
- DERIVATIVES **heparinization** (also **-isation**) n. **heparinize** (also **-ise**) v.
- ORIGIN C20: from Greek *hēpar* 'liver'.

hepatic /hɪ'patɪk/ ■ adj. of or relating to the liver.
- ORIGIN Middle English: from Greek *hēpatikos*, from *hēpar* 'liver'.

hepatitis /ˌhɛpə'tʌɪtɪs/ ■ n. a disease characterized by inflammation of the liver.
- ORIGIN C18: modern Latin, from Greek *hēpar, hēpat-* 'liver'.

hepatitis A ■ n. a form of viral hepatitis transmitted in food, causing fever and jaundice.

hepatitis B ■ n. a severe form of viral hepatitis transmitted in infected blood, causing fever, debility, and jaundice.

hepatitis C ■ n. a form of viral hepatitis transmitted in infected blood, causing chronic liver disease.

hepato- /'hɛpətəʊ, hɛ'patə(ʊ)-/ ■ comb. form of or relating to the liver.
- ORIGIN from Greek *hēpar, hēpat-* 'liver'.

hepatocyte /'hɛpətəʊsʌɪt, hɛ'patə(ʊ)-/ ■ n. Physiology a liver cell.

hepatoma /ˌhɛpə'təʊmə/ ■ n. (pl. **hepatomas** or **hepatomata** /-mətə/) Medicine a cancer of the cells of the liver.

hepatomegaly /ˌhɛpətəʊˈmɛɡəli, hɛˌpatəʊ-/ ■ n. Medicine abnormal enlargement of the liver.

hepatotoxic /ˌhɛpətəʊˈtɒksɪk, hɛˌpatəʊ-/ ■ adj. damaging or destructive to liver cells.
- DERIVATIVES **hepatotoxicity** n. **hepatotoxin** n.

hepta- ■ comb. form seven; having seven: *heptathlon*.
- ORIGIN from Greek *hepta* 'seven'.

heptad /'hɛptad/ ■ n. technical a group or set of seven.
- ORIGIN C17: from Greek *heptas, heptad-*, from *hepta* 'seven'.

heptagon /ˈhɛptəɡ(ə)n/ ■ n. a plane figure with seven straight sides and angles.
– DERIVATIVES **heptagonal** adj.
– ORIGIN C16: from Greek *heptagonos* 'seven-angled'.

heptahedron /ˌhɛptəˈhiːdrən, -ˈhɛd-/ ■ n. (pl. **heptahedra** or **heptahedrons**) a solid figure with seven plane faces.
– DERIVATIVES **heptahedral** adj.

heptamerous /hɛpˈtamərəs/ ■ adj. Botany & Zoology having parts arranged in groups of seven. ▸ consisting of seven joints or parts.

heptameter /hɛpˈtamɪtə/ ■ n. Prosody a line of verse consisting of seven metrical feet.

heptane /ˈhɛpteɪn/ ■ n. Chemistry a colourless liquid hydrocarbon of the alkane series, present in petroleum spirit.
– ORIGIN C19: from HEPTA- 'seven' (denoting seven carbon atoms) + -ANE[2].

heptathlon /hɛpˈtaθlɒn, -lən/ ■ n. an athletic contest for women that consists of seven separate events.
– DERIVATIVES **heptathlete** n.
– ORIGIN 1970s: from HEPTA- + Greek *athlon* 'contest', on the pattern of *decathlon*.

heptavalent /ˌhɛptəˈveɪl(ə)nt/ ■ adj. Chemistry having a valency of seven.

her ■ pron. [third person sing.] **1** used as the object of a verb or preposition to refer to a female person or animal previously mentioned. ▸ referring to a ship, country, or other inanimate thing regarded as female. **2** archaic or N. Amer. dialect herself. ■ possess. det. **1** belonging to or associated with a female person or animal previously mentioned. **2** (**Her**) used in titles.
– ORIGIN Old English *hire*, genitive and dative of *hīo*, *hēo* 'she'.

herald ■ n. **1** historical a person who carried official messages, made proclamations, and oversaw tournaments. **2** a person or thing viewed as a sign that something is about to happen. **3** an official employed to oversee state ceremonial, precedence, and the use of armorial bearings. ▸ (in the UK) an official of the College of Arms ranking below a pursuivant. ■ v. **1** signal the imminence of. **2** acclaim.
– ORIGIN Middle English: from Old French *herault* (n.), *herauder* (v.), of Germanic origin.

heraldic /hɛˈraldɪk/ ■ adj. of or relating to heraldry.
– DERIVATIVES **heraldically** adv.

heraldry ■ n. the system by which coats of arms and other armorial bearings are devised, described, and regulated. ▸ armorial bearings or other heraldic symbols.
– DERIVATIVES **heraldist** n.

herald snake ■ n. a back-fanged African snake, olive-brown in colour, usually with red or yellow lips, which has a venomous but not fatal bite. [*Crotaphopeltis hotamboeia* and other species.]

herb ■ n. **1** any plant with leaves, seeds, or flowers used for flavouring, food, medicine, or perfume. **2** Botany any seed-bearing plant which does not have a woody stem and dies down to the ground after flowering.
– DERIVATIVES **herby** adj. (**-ier**, **-iest**).
– ORIGIN Middle English: from Latin *herba* 'grass, green crops, herb'.

herbaceous /həˈbeɪʃəs/ ■ adj. denoting or relating to herbs (in the botanical sense).

herbaceous border ■ n. a garden border containing flowering plants, typically herbaceous perennials.

herbaceous perennial ■ n. a plant whose growth dies down annually but whose roots or other underground parts survive.

herbage ■ n. **1** herbaceous vegetation. ▸ the succulent part of this vegetation, used as pasture. **2** historical the right of pasture on another person's land.

herbal ■ adj. relating to or made from herbs, especially those used in cooking and medicine. ■ n. a book that describes herbs and their culinary and medicinal properties.

herbalism ■ n. the study or practice of the medicinal and therapeutic use of plants.

herbalist ■ n. **1** a practitioner of herbalism or dealer in herbs. **2** an early botanical writer.

545

heredity

herbarium /həˈbɛːrɪəm/ ■ n. (pl. **herbaria** /-rɪə/) a systematically arranged collection of dried plants.

herbary ■ n. (pl. **-ies**) archaic a herb garden.

herbed ■ adj. (of food) cooked or flavoured with herbs.

herbicide /ˈhəːbɪsʌɪd/ ■ n. a toxic substance used to destroy unwanted vegetation.

herbivore /ˈhəːbɪvɔː/ ■ n. an animal that feeds on plants.
– DERIVATIVES **herbivorous** /-ˈbɪv(ə)rəs/ adj.
– ORIGIN C19: from Latin *herba* 'herb' + *-vore* (see -VOROUS).

herb Robert ■ n. a common cranesbill with pungent-smelling red-stemmed leaves and pink flowers. [*Geranium robertianum*.]
– ORIGIN translating medieval Latin *herba Roberti*, variously supposed to refer to Robert Duke of Normandy, St *Robert*, or St Rupert.

Herculean /ˌhəːkjʊˈliːən, həːˈkjuːlɪən/ ■ adj. requiring or having great strength or effort: *a Herculean task*.
– ORIGIN C16: from the name of the Greek mythological hero *Hercules* (famed for his strength).

Hercynian /həːˈsɪnɪən/ ■ adj. Geology denoting a major mountain-forming period in western Europe, eastern North America, and the Andes, in the Upper Palaeozoic era.
– ORIGIN C16: from Latin *Hercynia silva*, the ancient name of an area of forested mountains in central Germany.

herd ■ n. **1** a large group of animals, especially hoofed mammals, that live or are kept together. **2** derogatory a large group or class of people. ■ v. **1** move in a large group. **2** keep or look after (livestock).
– DERIVATIVES **herder** n.
– ORIGIN Old English, of Germanic origin.

herd book ■ n. a book recording the pedigrees of cattle, goats, or other livestock.

herd instinct ■ n. an inclination in people or animals to behave or think like the majority.

herdsman ■ n. (pl. **-men**) the owner or keeper of a herd of domesticated animals.

Herdwick /ˈhəːdwɪk/ ■ n. a sheep of a hardy mountain breed from the north of England.
– ORIGIN C19: from obsolete *herdwick* 'pasture ground'.

here ■ adv. **1** in, at, or to this place or position. **2** (usu. **here is/are**) used when introducing or handing over something or someone. **3** used when indicating a time, point, or situation that has arrived or is happening. ■ exclam. used to attract someone's attention.
– PHRASES **here and now** at the present time. **here and there** in various places. **here goes** said to indicate that one is about to start something difficult or exciting. **here's to** used to wish health or success before drinking. **here we go again** said to indicate that the same events, typically undesirable ones, are recurring. **neither here nor there** of no importance or relevance.
– ORIGIN Old English, of Germanic origin; rel. to HE.

hereabouts (also **hereabout**) ■ adv. near this place.

hereafter ■ adv. formal from now on or at some time in the future. ▸ after death. ■ n. (**the hereafter**) life after death.

hereat ■ adv. archaic as a result of this.

hereby ■ adv. formal as a result of this document or utterance.

hereditary /hɪˈrɛdɪt(ə)ri/ ■ adj. **1** conferred by, based on, or relating to inheritance. ▸ (of a characteristic or disease) able to be passed on from parents to their offspring or descendants. **2** Mathematics (of a set) defined such that every element which has a given relation to a member of the set is also a member of the set.
– DERIVATIVES **hereditarily** adv. **hereditariness** n.
– ORIGIN Middle English: from Latin *hereditarius*, from *hereditas* (see HEREDITY).

heredity /hɪˈrɛdɪti/ ■ n. **1** the passing on of physical or mental characteristics genetically from one generation to another. ▸ a person's ancestry. **2** inheritance of title, office, or right.
– ORIGIN C18: from Latin *hereditas* 'heirship', from *heres* 'heir'.

Hereford

Hereford /ˈhɛrɪfəd/ ■ n. an animal of a breed of red and white beef cattle.
– ORIGIN from *Hereford* in west central England.

herein ■ adv. formal in this document, book, or matter.

hereinafter ■ adv. formal further on in this document.

hereinbefore ■ adv. formal before this point in this document.

hereof ■ adv. formal of this document.

Herero /həˈrɛːrəʊ, -ˈrɪərəʊ/ ■ n. (pl. same or **-os**) **1** a member of a people living in Namibia, Angola, and Botswana. **2** the Bantu language of this people.
– ORIGIN Herero, from *Otshi-Herero*, the Herero word for the language.

heresy /ˈhɛrɪsi/ ■ n. (pl. **-ies**) **1** belief or opinion contrary to orthodox religious (especially Christian) doctrine. **2** opinion profoundly at odds with what is generally accepted.
– ORIGIN Middle English: from Latin *haeresis*, from Greek *hairesis* 'choice', in eccles. Greek, 'heretical sect'.

heretic /ˈhɛrɪtɪk/ ■ n. a person believing in or practising heresy.
– DERIVATIVES **heretical** /hɪˈrɛtɪk(ə)l/ adj. **heretically** adv.

hereto ■ adv. formal to this matter or document.

heretofore ■ adv. formal before now.

hereunder ■ adv. formal as provided for under the terms of this document. ▶ further on in this document.

hereunto ■ adv. archaic or formal to this document.

hereupon ■ adv. archaic after or as a result of this.

herewith ■ adv. formal with this letter.

heritable ■ adj. able to be inherited.
– DERIVATIVES **heritability** n. **heritably** adv.

heritage ■ n. **1** property that is or may be inherited; an inheritance. **2** valued things such as historic buildings that have been passed down from previous generations. ▶ [as modifier] of special value and worthy of preservation. **3** archaic a special or individual possession; an allotted portion. ▶ God's chosen people (the people of Israel, or the Christian Church).

Heritage Day ■ n. S. African 24 September, a public holiday instituted in 1995.

hermaphrodite /həˈmafrədʌɪt/ ■ n. **1** a person or animal having both male and female sex organs or other sexual characteristics. **2** Botany a plant having stamens and pistils in the same flower. **3** archaic a person or thing combining opposite qualities or characteristics. ■ adj. of or denoting a person, animal, or plant of this kind.
– DERIVATIVES **hermaphroditic** adj. **hermaphroditical** adj. **hermaphroditism** n.
– ORIGIN Middle English: from Greek *hermaphroditos*, orig. the name of the son of Hermes and Aphrodite who became joined in one body with the nymph Salmacis.

hermeneutic /ˌhəːmɪˈnjuːtɪk/ ■ adj. concerning interpretation, especially of the Bible or literary texts.
– DERIVATIVES **hermeneutical** adj. **hermeneutically** adv. **hermeneutics** pl. n.
– ORIGIN C17: from Greek *hermēneutikos*, from *hermēneuein* 'interpret'.

hermetic /həːˈmɛtɪk/ ■ adj. **1** (of a seal or closure) complete and airtight. **2** insulated or protected from outside influences. **3** (also **Hermetic**) of or denoting an ancient occult tradition encompassing alchemy, astrology, and theosophy. ▶ esoteric; cryptic.
– DERIVATIVES **hermetically** adv. **hermeticism** n.
– ORIGIN C17: from modern Latin *hermeticus*, from *Hermes Trismegistus*, the legendary founder of alchemy and astrology identified with the Greek god Hermes.

hermit ■ n. a person living in solitude as a religious discipline. ▶ a reclusive or solitary person.
– DERIVATIVES **hermitage** n. **hermitic** adj.
– ORIGIN Middle English: from Old French *hermite*, from Greek *erēmitēs*, from *erēmos* 'solitary'.

hermit crab ■ n. a crab with a soft abdomen, which lives in a cast-off mollusc shell for protection. [Super-family Paguroidea: many species.]

Hernhutter ■ n. variant spelling of **HERRNHUTER** (in sense 2).

hernia /ˈhəːnɪə/ ■ n. (pl. **hernias** or **herniae** /-niː/) a condition in which part of an organ (most commonly, the intestine) is displaced and protrudes through the wall of the cavity containing it.
– DERIVATIVES **hernial** adj.
– ORIGIN Middle English: from Latin.

herniate ■ v. [usu. as adj. **herniated**] (of an organ) suffer a hernia: *a herniated disc*.
– DERIVATIVES **herniation** n.

hero ■ n. (pl. **-oes**) **1** a person, typically a man, who is admired for their courage or outstanding achievements. ▶ (in mythology and folklore) a person of superhuman qualities, in particular one of those whose exploits were the subject of ancient Greek legends. **2** the chief male character in a book, play, or film. **3** (also **hero sandwich**) chiefly N. Amer. another term for **HOAGIE**.
– DERIVATIVES **heroism** n. **heroize** (also **-ise**) v.
– ORIGIN Middle English: from Greek *hērōs*.

heroic ■ adj. **1** having the characteristics of a hero or heroine; very brave. ▶ of or representing heroes or heroines. **2** (of language or a work of art) grand or grandiose in scale or intention. ■ n. (**heroics**) **1** behaviour or talk that is bold or dramatic. **2** short for **HEROIC VERSE**.
– DERIVATIVES **heroically** adv.

heroic age ■ n. the period in Greek history and legend before the Trojan War and its aftermath, in which the legends of the heroes were set.

heroic couplet ■ n. (in verse) a pair of rhyming iambic pentameters.

heroic verse ■ n. a type of verse used for epic or heroic subjects, such as the iambic pentameter.

heroin ■ n. a highly addictive analgesic drug derived from morphine, often used illicitly as a narcotic.
– ORIGIN C19: from German *Heroin*, from Latin *heros* 'hero' (because of its effects on the user's self-esteem).

heroine ■ n. **1** a woman admired for her courage or outstanding achievements. ▶ (in mythology and folklore) a woman of superhuman qualities, in particular one whose dealings with the gods were the subject of ancient Greek legends. **2** the chief female character in a book, play, or film.

heron ■ n. a large fish-eating wading bird with long legs, a long S-shaped neck, and a long pointed bill. [*Ardea cinerea* (grey heron) and other species, family Ardeidae.]
– ORIGIN Middle English: from Old French, of Germanic origin.

heronry ■ n. (pl. **-ies**) a breeding colony of herons, typically in a group of trees.

hero worship ■ n. excessive admiration for someone. ■ v. (**hero-worship**) admire excessively.
– DERIVATIVES **hero-worshipper** n.

herpes /ˈhəːpiːz/ ■ n. a disease caused by a herpesvirus, affecting the skin (often with blisters) or the nervous system.
– DERIVATIVES **herpetic** adj.
– ORIGIN Middle English: from Greek *herpēs* 'shingles', literally 'creeping', from *herpein* 'to creep'.

herpes simplex ■ n. a form of herpes which can produce cold sores, genital inflammation, or conjunctivitis.

herpesvirus /ˈhəːpiːzˌvʌɪrəs/ ■ n. Medicine any of a group of DNA viruses causing herpes and other diseases.

herpes zoster /ˈzɒstə/ ■ n. medical name for **SHINGLES**.
– ORIGIN Middle English: from **HERPES** and Latin *zoster*, from Greek *zōstēr* 'girdle, shingles'.

herpetology /ˌhəːpɪˈtɒlədʒi/ ■ n. the branch of zoology concerned with reptiles and amphibians.
– DERIVATIVES **herpetological** adj. **herpetologist** n.
– ORIGIN C19: from Greek *herpeton* 'creeping thing' (from *herpein* 'to creep') + **-LOGY**.

Herr /hɛː/ ■ n. (pl. **Herren** /ˈhɛr(ə)n/) a title or form of address used of or to a German-speaking man, corresponding to *Mr* and also used before a rank or occupation.
– ORIGIN German, from Old High German *hērro*, comparative of *hēr* 'exalted'.

herring ■ n. a silvery fish which is most abundant in coastal waters and is an important food fish. [*Clupea*

harengus (N. Atlantic) and other species, family Clupeidae.]
– ORIGIN Old English, of West Germanic origin.

herringbone ■ n. **1** a pattern consisting of short parallel lines, with all the lines in one column sloping one way and all the lines in the next column sloping the other way. ▸ a cross stitch with a pattern resembling this. **2** Skiing a method of ascending a slope by walking with the skis pointing outwards. ■ v. **1** mark with a herringbone pattern. ▸ work with a herringbone stitch. **2** Skiing ascend a slope using the herringbone technique.

herring gull ■ n. a common northern gull with grey black-tipped wings. [*Larus argentatus*.]

Herrnhuter /'hɛːnhuːtə, 'hɛːr(ə)n-/ ■ n. **1** a member of a Moravian Church. **2** (also **Hernhutter**) S. African historical a type of sheath-knife.
– ORIGIN C18: German, from *Herrnhut* 'the Lord's keeping', the name of the first German settlement of the Moravian Church.

hers ■ possess. pron. used to refer to a thing or things belonging to or associated with a female person or animal previously mentioned.

herself ■ pron. [third person sing.] **1** [reflexive] used as the object of a verb or preposition to refer to a female person or animal previously mentioned as the subject of the clause. **2** [emphatic] she or her personally.

hertz /hɜːts/ (abbrev.: **Hz**) ■ n. (pl. same) the SI unit of frequency, equal to one cycle per second.
– ORIGIN C19: named after the German physicist H. R. *Hertz*.

Hertzog cookie /'hɛːtspg kʊki/ ■ n. S. African a small jam tart with a coconut topping.
– ORIGIN 1940s: named after the former South African prime minister J. B. M. *Hertzog*.

he's ■ contr. **1** he is. **2** he has.

hesitant ■ adj. slow to act or speak through indecision or reluctance.
– DERIVATIVES **hesitance** n. **hesitancy** n. **hesitantly** adv.
– ORIGIN Middle English: from Latin *haesitare* (see HESITATE).

hesitate ■ v. pause in indecision. ▸ be reluctant to do something.
– DERIVATIVES **hesitater** n. **hesitating** adj. **hesitatingly** adv. **hesitation** n.
– ORIGIN C17: from Latin *haesitare* 'stick fast, leave undecided'.

Hesperus /'hɛspərəs/ ■ n. poetic/literary the planet Venus.
– ORIGIN Latin, from Greek *hesperos* 'western', (as n.) 'the evening star'.

hessian ■ n. a strong, coarse fabric made from hemp or jute, used especially for sacks and in upholstery.
– ORIGIN C19: from *Hesse*, a state of western Germany.

Hessian fly ■ n. a gall midge whose larvae are a pest of cereal crops. [*Mayetiola destructor*.]
– ORIGIN C18: so named because it was supposed (erroneously) to have been carried to America by troops from Hesse in Germany during the War of Independence.

hest ■ n. archaic form of BEHEST.
– ORIGIN Old English, of Germanic origin.

HET ■ abbrev. (in South Africa) higher education and training, comprising tertiary education. Compare with GET and FET.

hetaera /hɪˈtɪərə/ (also **hetaira** /-ˈtʌɪrə/) ■ n. (pl. **hetaeras** or **hetaerae** /-ˈtɪəriː/ or **hetairas** or **hetairai** /-ˈtʌɪrʌɪ/) a courtesan or mistress, especially an educated one in ancient Greece.
– ORIGIN from Greek *hetaira*, feminine of *hetairos* 'companion'.

hetero- ■ comb. form other; different: *heterosexual*.
– ORIGIN from Greek *heteros* 'other'.

heterochromatic /ˌhɛt(ə)rəʊkrəˈmatɪk/ ■ adj. of several different colours or (in physics) wavelengths.

heterocyclic /ˌhɛt(ə)rə(ʊ)ˈsʌɪklɪk, -ˈsɪklɪk/ ■ adj. Chemistry denoting a compound whose molecule contains a ring of atoms of at least two elements (one of which is generally carbon).

heterodox /'hɛt(ə)rə(ʊ)dɒks/ ■ adj. not conforming with orthodox standards or beliefs.
– DERIVATIVES **heterodoxy** n.
– ORIGIN C17: from Greek *heterodoxos*, from *heteros* 'other' + *doxa* 'opinion'.

heterogametic /ˌhɛt(ə)rə(ʊ)gəˈmɛtɪk/ ■ adj. Biology denoting the sex which has sex chromosomes that differ in morphology, e.g. (in mammals) the male and (in birds) the female.

heterogamy /ˌhɛtəˈrɒgəmi/ ■ n. **1** chiefly Zoology alternation of generations, especially between sexual and parthenogenetic generations. **2** Botany a state in which the flowers of a plant are of two or more types. **3** marriage between people from different backgrounds.
– DERIVATIVES **heterogamous** adj.
– ORIGIN C19: from HETERO- + Greek *gamos* 'marriage'.

heterogeneous /ˌhɛt(ə)rə(ʊ)ˈdʒiːnɪəs, -ˈdʒɛn-/ ■ adj. **1** diverse in character or content. **2** Chemistry denoting a process involving substances in different phases (solid, liquid, or gaseous): *heterogeneous catalysis*.
– DERIVATIVES **heterogeneity** /-dʒɪˈniːɪti, -ˈnɛɪti/ n. **heterogeneously** adv. **heterogeneousness** n.
– ORIGIN C17: from Greek *heterogenēs*, from *heteros* 'other' + *genos* 'a kind'.

USAGE
Heterogeneous is commonly misspelled as **heterogenous**. **Heterogenous** is a different word, meaning 'originating outside the organism'.

heterograft ■ n. another term for XENOGRAFT.

heterologous /ˌhɛtəˈrɒləgəs/ ■ adj. chiefly Medicine & Biology not homologous.
– DERIVATIVES **heterology** n.

heteromorphic /ˌhɛt(ə)rə(ʊ)ˈmɔːfɪk/ ■ adj. Biology occurring in two or more different forms, especially at different stages in the life cycle.
– DERIVATIVES **heteromorph** n. **heteromorphism** n. **heteromorphy** n.

heteronomous /ˌhɛtəˈrɒnəməs/ ■ adj. subject to a law or standard external to itself.
– DERIVATIVES **heteronomy** n.

heteronym /'hɛtərə(ʊ)nɪm/ ■ n. Linguistics **1** each of two or more words which are spelled identically but have different sounds and meanings (e.g. TEAR[1] and TEAR[2]). **2** each of two or more words which are used to refer to the identical thing in different geographical areas of a speech community, e.g. *nappy* and *diaper*.
– DERIVATIVES **heteronymic** adj. **heteronymous** adj.

heteropolar /ˌhɛtərəʊˈpəʊlə/ ■ adj. chiefly Physics characterized by opposite or alternating polarity.

Heteroptera /ˌhɛtəˈrɒpt(ə)rə/ ■ pl. n. Entomology a group of bugs comprising those, such as the predatory and water bugs, in which the forewings are non-uniform, having a thickened base and membranous tip. Compare with HOMOPTERA.
– DERIVATIVES **heteropteran** n. & adj. **heteropterous** adj.
– ORIGIN from Greek *heteros* 'other' + *pteron* 'wing'.

heterosexism ■ n. discrimination or prejudice against homosexuals on the assumption that heterosexuality is the norm.
– DERIVATIVES **heterosexist** adj.

heterosexual ■ adj. sexually attracted to the opposite sex. ▸ involving or characterized by such sexual attraction. ■ n. a heterosexual person.
– DERIVATIVES **heterosexuality** n. **heterosexually** adv.

heterotransplant ■ n. another term for XENOGRAFT.

heterotroph /'hɛt(ə)rə(ʊ)trəʊf, -ˈtrɒf/ ■ n. Biology an organism that derives nutrients from complex organic substances. Compare with AUTOTROPH.
– DERIVATIVES **heterotrophic** adj. **heterotrophy** n.

heterozygote /ˌhɛt(ə)rə(ʊ)ˈzʌɪgəʊt/ ■ n. Genetics an individual having two different alleles of a particular gene or genes, and so giving rise to varying offspring. Compare with HOMOZYGOTE.
– DERIVATIVES **heterozygosity** n. **heterozygous** adj.

het up ■ adj. informal angry and agitated.
– ORIGIN C19: from dialect *het* 'heated, hot'.

heuchera /'hɔɪkərə, 'hjuːk-/ ■ n. a North American plant

heuristic

with dark green round or heart-shaped leaves and slender stems of tiny flowers. [Genus *Heuchera*: many species.]
– ORIGIN named after the C18 German botanist Johann H. von Heucher.

heuristic /hjʊ(ə)ˈrɪstɪk/ ■ adj. **1** enabling a person to discover or learn something for themselves. **2** Computing proceeding to a solution by trial and error or by rules that are only loosely defined. ■ n. a heuristic process or method. ▸ (**heuristics**) [usu. treated as sing.] the study and use of heuristic techniques.
– DERIVATIVES **heuristically** adv.
– ORIGIN C19: from Greek *heuriskein* 'find'.

hew /hjuː/ ■ v. (past part. **hewn** or **hewed**) **1** chop or cut (wood, coal, etc.) with an axe, pick, or other tool. ▸ (usu. **be hewn**) make or shape by cutting or chopping a hard material. **2** (**hew to**) N. Amer. conform to.
– ORIGIN Old English, of Germanic origin.

hewer ■ n. dated a person who hews something, especially a miner who cuts coal from a seam.
– PHRASES **hewers of wood and drawers of water** menial drudges. [with biblical allusion to Joshua 9:21.]

hex[1] chiefly N. Amer. ■ v. cast a spell on. ■ n. **1** a magic spell. **2** a witch.
– ORIGIN C19: from Pennsylvania German, from German *hexen* (v.), *Hexe* (n.).

hex[2] ■ adj. short for **HEXADECIMAL**.

hexa- (also **hex-** before a vowel) ■ comb. form six; having six.
– ORIGIN from Greek *hex* 'six'.

hexad /ˈhɛksad/ ■ n. technical a group or set of six.
– ORIGIN C17: from Greek *hexas*, *hexad-*, from *hex* 'six'.

hexadecimal /ˌhɛksəˈdɛsɪm(ə)l/ ■ adj. Computing relating to or using a system of numerical notation that has 16 rather than 10 as its base.
– DERIVATIVES **hexadecimally** adv.

hexagon /ˈhɛksəɡ(ə)n/ ■ n. a plane figure with six straight sides and angles.
– DERIVATIVES **hexagonal** adj.
– ORIGIN C16: from Greek *hexagōnon*, neuter of *hexagōnos* 'six-angled'.

hexagram ■ n. **1** a star-shaped figure formed by two intersecting equilateral triangles. **2** any of a set of sixty-four figures made up of six parallel whole or broken lines, occurring in the ancient Chinese I Ching.
– ORIGIN C19: from **HEXA-** + Greek *gramma* 'line'.

hexahedron /ˌhɛksəˈhiːdrən, -ˈhɛd-/ ■ n. (pl. **hexahedra** or **hexahedrons**) a solid figure with six plane faces.
– DERIVATIVES **hexahedral** adj.
– ORIGIN C16: from Greek *hexaedron*, neuter of *hexaedros* 'six-faced'.

hexamerous /hɛkˈsam(ə)rəs/ ■ n. Botany & Zoology having parts arranged in groups of six.

hexameter /hɛkˈsamɪtə/ ■ n. Prosody a line of verse consisting of six metrical feet.

hexane /ˈhɛkseɪn/ ■ n. Chemistry a colourless liquid hydrocarbon of the alkane series, present in petroleum spirit. [C_6H_{14}.]
– ORIGIN C19: from **HEXA-** 'six' (denoting six carbon atoms) + **-ANE**[2].

hexaploid /ˈhɛksəplɔɪd/ ■ adj. Genetics having or denoting cells or nuclei containing six homologous sets of chromosomes.
– DERIVATIVES **hexaploidy** n.

Hexapoda /ˌhɛksəˈpəʊdə/ ■ pl. n. Entomology a class of six-legged arthropods that comprises the insects (especially when distinguished from the primitive Apterygota).
– DERIVATIVES **hexapod** n.
– ORIGIN from Greek *hexapous*, *hexapod-*, from **HEXA-** + *pous* 'foot'.

hexavalent /ˌhɛksəˈveɪl(ə)nt/ ■ adj. Chemistry having a valency of six.

hexose /ˈhɛksəʊz, -s/ ■ n. Chemistry any of the class of simple sugars whose molecules contain six carbon atoms (e.g. glucose).

hey ■ exclam. **1** used to attract attention or to express surprise, interest, etc. **2** S. African used to ask for something to be repeated or explained, or to elicit agreement.

heyday ■ n. (**one's heyday**) the period of one's greatest success, activity, or vigour.
– ORIGIN C16: from archaic *heyday!*, an exclam. of joy or surprise.

hey presto ■ exclam. see **PRESTO**.

HF ■ abbrev. Physics high frequency.

Hf ■ symb. the chemical element hafnium.

HFC ■ abbrev. hydrofluorocarbon.

Hg ■ symb. the chemical element mercury.
– ORIGIN abbrev. of modern Latin *hydrargyrum*.

hg ■ abbrev. hectogram(s).

HGH ■ abbrev. human growth hormone.

HGV ■ abbrev. Brit. heavy goods vehicle.

HH ■ abbrev. **1** Brit. Her or His Highness. **2** His Holiness. **3** extra hard (as a grade of pencil lead).

hh. ■ abbrev. hands (as a unit of measurement of a horse's height).

hi ■ exclam. informal used as a friendly greeting.

hiatus /hʌɪˈeɪtəs/ ■ n. (pl. **hiatuses**) a pause or gap in continuity. ▸ Prosody & Grammar a break between two vowels coming together but not in the same syllable, as in *the ear*.
– DERIVATIVES **hiatal** adj.
– ORIGIN C16: from Latin, 'gaping'.

hiatus hernia (also **hiatal hernia**) ■ n. Medicine the protrusion of an organ (usually the stomach) through the oesophageal opening in the diaphragm.

hibachi /hɪˈbatʃi, ˈhɪbətʃi/ ■ n. (pl. **hibachis**) a portable cooking apparatus similar to a small barbecue. ▸ (in Japan) a large earthenware pan or brazier in which charcoal is burnt to provide indoor heating.
– ORIGIN C19: Japanese *hibachi*, *hi-hachi*, from *hi* 'fire' + *hachi* 'bowl, pot'.

hibernate ■ v. (of an animal or plant) spend the winter in a dormant state.
– DERIVATIVES **hibernation** n. **hibernator** n.
– ORIGIN C19 (*hibernation* C17): from Latin *hibernare*, from *hiberna* 'winter quarters'.

Hibernian /hʌɪˈbəːnɪən/ ■ adj. of or concerning Ireland (now chiefly used in names). ■ n. a native of Ireland (now chiefly used in names).
– ORIGIN from Latin *Hibernia* (alteration of *Iverna*), from Greek *I(w)ernē*, of Celtic origin.

hibiscus /hɪˈbɪskəs/ ■ n. a plant of the mallow family with large brightly coloured flowers. [Genus *Hibiscus*: many species.]
– ORIGIN from Greek *hibiskos* 'marsh mallow'.

hic ■ exclam. used in writing to express the sound of a hiccup.
– ORIGIN C19: imitative.

hiccup (also **hiccough** pronunc. same)) ■ n. **1** an involuntary spasm of the diaphragm and respiratory organs, with a sudden closure of the glottis and a characteristic gulping sound. **2** a minor difficulty or setback. ■ v. (**hiccuped**, **hiccuping**) make the sound of a hiccup or series of hiccups.
– DERIVATIVES **hiccupy** adj.
– ORIGIN C16: imitative; the form *hiccough* arose by association with **COUGH**.

hick ■ n. informal, chiefly N. Amer. a country-dweller, regarded as unintelligent or parochial.
– ORIGIN C16: familiar form of the given name *Richard*.

hickory ■ n. **1** a chiefly North American tree which yields tough, heavy wood and bears edible nuts. [Genus *Carya*: several species.] **2** a stick made of hickory wood.
– ORIGIN C17: abbrev. of *pohickery*, the local Virginian name, from Algonquian *pawcohiccora*.

hid past of **HIDE**[1].

hidden past participle of **HIDE**[1].
– DERIVATIVES **hiddenness** n.

hidden agenda ■ n. a secret or ulterior motive.

hide[1] ■ v. (past **hid**; past part. **hidden**) put or keep out of sight. ▸ keep secret. ▸ conceal oneself. ■ n. a camouflaged shelter used to observe wildlife at close quarters.
– PHRASES **hide one's light under a bushel** keep quiet about one's talents or accomplishments. [with biblical allusion to Matthew 15.]

- DERIVATIVES **hider** n.
- ORIGIN Old English *hȳdan*, of West Germanic origin.

hide² ■ n. the skin of an animal, especially when tanned or dressed.
- PHRASES **hide or hair of** [with neg.] the slightest trace of. **save one's hide** escape from difficulty. **tan** (or **whip**) **someone's hide** beat or flog someone.
- DERIVATIVES **hided** adj.
- ORIGIN Old English *hȳd*, of Germanic origin.

hide-and-seek ■ n. a children's game in which one or more players hide and the other or others have to look for them.

hideaway ■ n. a hiding place, especially as a retreat from others.

hidebound ■ adj. constrained by tradition or convention; narrow-minded.
- ORIGIN C16 (orig. referring to malnourished cattle, later extended to emaciated human beings, hence the sense 'narrow in outlook'): from HIDE² + BOUND⁴.

hideous ■ adj. extremely ugly. ► extremely unpleasant.
- DERIVATIVES **hideously** adv. **hideousness** n.
- ORIGIN Middle English: from Old French *hideus*, from *hide, hisde* 'fear'.

hideout ■ n. a hiding place, especially one used by someone who has broken the law.

hidey-hole (also **hidy-hole**) ■ n. informal a hiding place.

hiding¹ ■ n. 1 a physical beating. 2 informal a severe defeat.
- PHRASES **be on a hiding to nothing** Brit. be unlikely to succeed.
- ORIGIN C19: from HIDE².

hiding² ■ n. the action of hiding or the state of being hidden.
- ORIGIN Middle English: from HIDE¹.

hie /hʌɪ/ ■ v. (**hies**, **hied**, **hieing** or **hying**) archaic go quickly.
- ORIGIN Middle English: from Old English *hīgian* 'strive, pant'.

hierarchy /ˈhʌɪərɑːki/ ■ n. (pl. **-ies**) 1 a ranking system ordered according to status or authority. ► (**the hierarchy**) the upper echelons of a hierarchical system. ► an arrangement according to relative importance or inclusiveness. 2 Theology the traditional system of orders of angels and other heavenly beings.
- DERIVATIVES **hierarchic** adj. **hierarchical** adj. **hierarchically** adv. **hierarchization** (also **-isation**) n. **hierarchize** (also **-ise**) v.
- ORIGIN Middle English: from Greek *hierarkhia*, from *hierarkhēs*, from *hieros* 'sacred' + *arkhēs* 'ruler'.

hieratic /ˌhʌɪəˈratɪk/ ■ adj. 1 of or concerning priests. 2 of or in the ancient Egyptian writing of abridged hieroglyphics used by priests. Compare with DEMOTIC. 3 of or concerning Egyptian or Greek styles of art adhering to early methods as laid down by religious tradition.
- DERIVATIVES **hieratically** adv.
- ORIGIN C17 (orig. as *hieratical*): from Greek *hieratikos*, from *hierasthai* 'be a priest'.

hieroglyph /ˈhʌɪərəɡlɪf/ ■ n. a stylized picture of an object representing a word, syllable, or sound, as found in ancient Egyptian and certain other writing systems.
- ORIGIN C16: back-formation from HIEROGLYPHIC.

hieroglyphic ■ n. (**hieroglyphics**) writing consisting of hieroglyphs. ■ adj. of or written in hieroglyphs.
- DERIVATIVES **hieroglyphical** adj. **hieroglyphically** adv.
- ORIGIN C16: from Greek *hierogluphikos*, from *hieros* 'sacred' + *gluphē* 'carving'.

hi-fi informal ■ adj. of or relating to the reproduction of high fidelity sound. ■ n. (pl. **hi-fis**) a set of equipment for high-fidelity sound reproduction.

higgledy-piggledy ■ adv. & adj. in confusion or disorder.
- ORIGIN C16: rhyming jingle, prob. with ref. to the irregular herding together of pigs.

high ■ adj. 1 of great vertical extent. ► of a specified height. ► far above ground or sea level. ► extending above the normal level. ► (of latitude) near the North or South Pole. 2 great in amount, value, size, or intensity. ► (of a period or movement) at its peak. 3 great in rank or status. ► morally or culturally superior. 4 (of a sound or note) having a frequency at the upper end of the auditory range.

highfalutin

5 informal euphoric, especially from the effects of drugs or alcohol. **6** (of food) strong-smelling because beginning to go bad. ► (of game) slightly decomposed and so ready to cook. **7** Phonetics (of a vowel) produced with the tongue relatively near the palate. ■ n. **1** a high point, level, or figure. **2** an anticyclone. **3** informal a state of euphoria. ■ adv. **1** at or to a considerable or specified height. **2** highly. ► at a high price. **3** (of a sound) at or to a high pitch.
- PHRASES **ace** (or **king** or **queen** etc.) **high** (in card games) having the ace (or another specified card) as the highest-ranking. **from on high** from remote high authority or heaven. **high and dry 1** stranded by the sea as it retreats. **2** without resources. **high and low** in many different places. **high and mighty** informal arrogant. **the high ground** a position of superiority. **a high old time** informal a most enjoyable time. **it is high time that** —— it is past the time when something should have happened or been done. **on one's high horse** informal behaving arrogantly or pompously. **run high 1** (of a river) be full and close to overflowing, with a strong current. **2** (of feeling) be intense.
- ORIGIN Old English, of Germanic origin.

high altar ■ n. the chief altar of a church.

highball ■ n. N. Amer. a long drink consisting of a spirit and a mixer such as soda, served with ice.

highbrow ■ adj. often derogatory intellectual or rarefied in taste.

high chair ■ n. a small chair with long legs for a baby or small child, fitted with a tray and used at mealtimes.

High Church ■ n. a tradition within the Anglican Church emphasizing ritual, priestly authority, sacraments, and historical continuity with Catholic Chris-tianity.
- DERIVATIVES **High Churchman** n. (pl. **-men**).

high-class ■ adj. of a high standard, quality, or social class.

high colour ■ n. a flushed complexion.

high command ■ n. the commander-in-chief and associated senior staff of an army, navy, or air force.

high commission ■ n. an embassy of one Commonwealth country in another.
- DERIVATIVES **high commissioner** n.

high court ■ n. a supreme court of justice.

high day ■ n. Brit. the day of a religious festival.
- PHRASES **high days and holidays** informal special occasions.

high-density lipoprotein ■ n. a kind of lipoprotein in blood plasma that promotes the transfer of cholesterol to the liver for excretion or reuse.

Higher ■ n. (in Scotland) the more advanced of the two main levels of the Scottish Certificate of Education. Compare with ORDINARY GRADE.

higher animals ■ pl. n. mammals and other vertebrates, regarded as having relatively advanced characteristics.

higher court ■ n. Law a court that can overrule the decision of another.

higher education ■ n. education at universities or similar educational establishments, especially to degree level.

Higher Grade ■ n. (in South Africa) the more advanced of the two levels at which subjects could be studied for matriculation. Compare with STANDARD GRADE.

higher mathematics ■ pl. n. [usu. treated as sing.] the more advanced aspects of mathematics, such as number theory and topology.

higher plants ■ pl. n. vascular plants, regarded as having relatively advanced characteristics.

highest common factor ■ n. the highest number that can be divided exactly into each of two or more numbers.

high explosive ■ n. a powerful chemical explosive of the kind used in shells and bombs.

highfalutin /ˌhʌɪfəˈluːtɪn/ (also **highfaluting** /-tɪŋ/) ■ adj. informal pompous or pretentious.
- ORIGIN C19: perhaps from HIGH + *fluting* (present participle of FLUTE).

high fashion

high fashion ■ n. another term for HAUTE COUTURE.

high fidelity ■ n. the reproduction of sound with little distortion.

high finance ■ n. financial transactions involving large sums.

high five ■ n. informal, chiefly N. Amer. a gesture of celebration or greeting in which two people slap each other's palms with their arms raised.

high-flown ■ adj. (especially of language) extravagant or grandiose.

high-flyer (also **high flier**) ■ n. 1 a person or thing that is or has the potential to be very successful. ▶ a person indulging in an extravagant lifestyle. 2 S. African a high-ranking member of a criminal gang.
–DERIVATIVES **high-flying** adj.

high frequency ■ n. (in radio) a frequency of 3–30 megahertz.

high gear ■ n. a gear that causes a wheeled vehicle to move fast.

High German ■ n. the standard literary and spoken form of German, originally used in the highlands in the south of Germany.

high-handed ■ adj. domineering or inconsiderate.
–DERIVATIVES **high-handedly** adv. **high-handedness** n.

high hat ■ n. 1 a top hat. 2 N. Amer. informal a snobbish or supercilious person. ■ adj. (**high-hat**) N. Amer. informal snobbish. ■ v. (**high-hat**) (**-hatted, -hatting**) N. Amer. informal treat superciliously.

High Holidays (also **High Holy Days**) ■ pl. n. the Jewish festivals of Yom Kippur and Rosh Hashana.

high-impact ■ adj. 1 (of plastic or a similar substance) able to withstand great impact without breaking. 2 denoting extremely strenuous aerobic exercises.

high jinks ■ pl. n. boisterous fun.
–ORIGIN C17: see JINK.

high jump ■ n. (**the high jump**) an athletic event in which competitors jump as high as possible over a bar of adjustable height.
–PHRASES **be for the high jump** Brit. informal be about to be severely reprimanded.
–DERIVATIVES **high jumper** n.

high-key (also **high-keyed**) ■ adj. Art & Photography having a predominance of light or bright tones.

highland ■ n. (also **highlands**) an area of high or mountainous land. ▶ (**the Highlands**) the mountainous northern part of Scotland.
–DERIVATIVES **highlander** n. **highlandman** n. (pl. **-men**).
–ORIGIN Old English *hēahland* 'a high promontory' (see HIGH, LAND).

Highland cattle ■ pl. n. animals of a shaggy-haired breed of cattle with long, curved, widely spaced horns.

Highland dress ■ n. the kilt and other clothing in the traditional style of the Scottish Highlands, now worn chiefly on formal occasions.

Highland fling ■ n. a vigorous solo Scottish dance consisting of a series of complex steps.

Highland Games ■ pl. n. a meeting for athletic events, playing of the bagpipes, and dancing, held in the Scottish Highlands or by Scots elsewhere.

high-level ■ adj. 1 of relatively high importance. 2 Computing denoting a programming language (e.g. BASIC) that has instructions resembling an existing language such as English. 3 (of nuclear waste) highly radioactive and requiring long-term storage in isolation.

high life ■ n. 1 (also **high living**) an extravagant social life as enjoyed by the wealthy. 2 (usu. **highlife**) a style of dance music of West African origin, influenced by rock and jazz.

highlight ■ n. 1 an outstanding part of an event or period of time. 2 a bright or reflective area in a painting, picture, or design. ▶ (usu. **highlights**) a bright tint in the hair, produced by bleaching or dyeing. ■ v. 1 draw attention to. ▶ mark with a highlighter. 2 create highlights in (hair).

highlighter ■ n. 1 a broad marker pen used to overlay transparent fluorescent colour on text or a part of an illustration. 2 a cosmetic that is lighter than the wearer's foundation or skin, used to emphasize the cheekbones or other features.

highly ■ adv. 1 to a high degree or level. 2 favourably.

highly strung ■ adj. very nervous and easily upset.

High Mass ■ n. a Roman Catholic or Anglo-Catholic mass with full ceremonial, including music and incense.

high-minded ■ adj. having strong moral principles.
–DERIVATIVES **high-mindedly** adv. **high-mindedness** n.

highness ■ n. (**His/Your etc.**) **Highness** a title given to a person of royal rank, or used in addressing them.

high-octane ■ adj. 1 denoting petrol having a high octane number and thus good anti-knock properties. 2 powerful or dynamic.

high-powered ■ adj. informal (of a person) dynamic and capable.

high priest ■ n. a chief priest of a non-Christian religion, especially of historic Judaism. ▶ (or **high priestess**) the leader of a cult or movement.

high relief ■ n. see RELIEF (sense 6).

high-rise ■ adj. (of a building) having many storeys.

high road ■ n. 1 a main road. 2 N. Amer. a morally superior approach.

high roller ■ n. informal, chiefly N. Amer. a person who gambles or spends large sums of money.
–DERIVATIVES **high-rolling** adj.
–ORIGIN with ref. to rolling dice.

high school ■ n. S. African & N. Amer. a secondary school.

high seas ■ pl. n. (**the high seas**) the open ocean, especially that not within any country's jurisdiction.

high season ■ n. the most popular time of year for a holiday, when prices are highest.

high spirits ■ pl. n. lively and cheerful behaviour or mood.
–DERIVATIVES **high-spirited** adj. **high-spiritedness** n.

high spot ■ n. the most enjoyable or significant part of an experience or period of time.
–PHRASES **hit the high spots** informal visit the most exciting places in town.

high-stick ■ v. [often as noun **high-sticking**] Ice Hockey strike (an opponent) on or above the shoulders with one's stick, for which a penalty may be assessed.

high street ■ n. Brit. the main street and often the principal shopping area of a town. ▶ [as modifier] (of retail goods) catering to the needs of the ordinary public.

high table ■ n. Brit. a table in a dining hall at which high-ranking people, such as the fellows of a college, sit.

hightail ■ v. informal, chiefly N. Amer. move or travel fast.

high tea ■ n. Brit. a meal eaten in the late afternoon or early evening, typically consisting of a cooked dish and tea.

high-tech (also **hi-tech**) ■ adj. 1 employing, requiring, or involved in high technology. 2 (of architecture and interior design) employing a functional style and industrial materials, such as steel and plastic. ■ n. (**high tech**) short for HIGH TECHNOLOGY.

high technology ■ n. advanced technological development, especially in electronics.

high-tensile ■ adj. (of metal) very strong under tension.

high tide ■ n. the state of the tide when at its highest level.

high-top ■ adj. denoting a soft-soled sports shoe with a laced upper that extends above the ankle. ■ n. (**high-tops**) a pair of such shoes.

high treason ■ n. see TREASON.

highveld /ˈhʌɪfɛlt/ ■ n. S. African 1 (also **Highveld**) the inland plateau of southern Africa, lying mostly between 1 200 and 1 800 metres above sea level. ▶ the grasslands of this region. 2 (**Highveld**) Johannesburg, Pretoria, and the surrounding areas.
–DERIVATIVES **Highvelder** n.
–ORIGIN C19: partial translation of Afrikaans *hoëveld* 'high land'.

high water ■ n. high tide.

high-water mark ■ n. the level reached by the sea at

CONSONANTS **b** but **d** dog **f** few **g** get **h** he **j** yes **k** cat **l** leg **m** man **n** no **p** pen **r** red

high tide, or by a lake or river in time of flood. ▸ a maximum recorded level or value.

highway ■ n. S. African & N. Amer. a main road. ▸ (chiefly in official use) a public road.

highwayman ■ n. (pl. **-men**) historical a man, typically on horseback, who held up and robbed travellers.

high wire ■ n. a high tightrope.

hi-hat (also **high-hat**) ■ n. a pair of foot-operated cymbals forming part of a drum kit.

hijab /ˈhidʒab/ ■ n. a head covering worn in public by some Muslim women. ▸ the religious code which governs the wearing of such clothing.
– DERIVATIVES **hijabi** n.
– ORIGIN Persian from Arabic *hajaba* 'to veil'.

hijack ■ v. illegally seize control of (an aircraft, ship, or vehicle) while in transit. ▸ S. African stop and steal a motor vehicle. ■ n. an instance of hijacking.
– DERIVATIVES **hijacker** n.
– ORIGIN 1920s (orig. US).

Hijra /ˈhidʒrə/ ■ n. variant spelling of **HEGIRA**.

hike ■ n. 1 a long walk or walking tour. 2 a sharp increase, especially in price. ■ v. 1 go on a hike. ▸ informal go on foot. 2 pull or lift up (clothing). 3 increase (a price) sharply.
– PHRASES **take a hike** informal, chiefly N. Amer. go away.
– DERIVATIVES **hiker** n.
– ORIGIN C19 (orig. dialect).

hila plural form of **HILUM**.

hilar /ˈhaɪlə/ ■ adj. Anatomy & Botany of or relating to a hilus or hilum.

hilarious /hɪˈlɛːrɪəs/ ■ adj. extremely funny or merry.
– DERIVATIVES **hilariously** adv. **hilarity** n.
– ORIGIN C19 (*hilarity* Middle English): from Latin *hilaris*, from Greek *hilaros* 'cheerful'.

Hilary term ■ n. Brit. (in some universities) the university term beginning in January.
– ORIGIN Middle English: named after the 4th century French bishop St *Hilary*.

hili plural form of **HILUS**.

hill ■ n. a naturally raised area of land, not as high or craggy as a mountain. ▸ a heap or mound. ■ v. form into a heap. ▸ bank up (a plant) with soil.
– PHRASES **a hill of beans** [with neg.] N. Amer. informal an insignificant amount. **over the hill** informal old and past one's best.
– ORIGIN Old English, of Germanic origin.

hillbilly ■ n. (pl. **-ies**) N. Amer. informal, chiefly derogatory an unsophisticated country person, originally one from the Appalachians.
– ORIGIN C20: from **HILL** + *Billy* (familiar form of the given name *William*).

hill climb ■ n. a race for vehicles up a steep hill.
– DERIVATIVES **hill-climber** n. **hill-climbing** n.

hill figure ■ n. an outline of a horse, human, or other design cut into the turf of a hill, especially in the chalk downs of southern England.

hill fort ■ n. a fort built on a hill, in particular an Iron Age system of defensive banks and ditches.

hillock ■ n. a small hill or mound.
– DERIVATIVES **hillocky** adj.

hill station ■ n. a town in the low mountains of the Indian subcontinent, popular as a holiday resort during the hot season.

hillwalking ■ n. the pastime of walking in hilly country.
– DERIVATIVES **hillwalker** n.

hilly ■ adj. (**-ier**, **-iest**) having many hills.
– DERIVATIVES **hilliness** n.

hilt ■ n. the handle of a sword, dagger, or knife.
– PHRASES **(up) to the hilt** completely.
– DERIVATIVES **hilted** adj.
– ORIGIN Old English, of Germanic origin.

hilum /ˈhaɪləm/ ■ n. (pl. **hila** /-lə/) 1 Botany the scar on a seed marking the point of attachment to its seed vessel. 2 Anatomy another term for **HILUS**.
– ORIGIN C17: from Latin, 'little thing, trifle', once thought to mean 'that which sticks to a bean', hence the botanical sense.

hilus /ˈhaɪləs/ ■ n. (pl. **hili** /ˈhaɪlaɪ/) Anatomy an indentation in the surface of a kidney or other organ, where blood vessels, nerve fibres, etc. enter or leave it.
– ORIGIN C19: modern Latin, alteration of **HILUM**.

him ■ pron. [third person sing.] 1 used as the object of a verb or preposition to refer to a male person or animal previously mentioned. 2 referring to a person or animal of unspecified sex (now largely replaced by 'him or her' or 'they'). 3 archaic or N. Amer. dialect himself.
– ORIGIN Old English, dative sing. form of *he*, *hē* 'he' and *hit* 'it'.

Himalayan ■ adj. of or relating to the Himalayas.

Himba ■ n. a member of an isolated pastoral people living in northern Namibia and southern Angola.

himself ■ pron. [third person sing.] 1 [reflexive] used as the object of a verb or preposition to refer to a male person or animal previously mentioned as the subject of the clause. 2 [emphatic] he or him personally. ▸ chiefly Irish an important male third party, especially the master of the house.

hind¹ ■ adj. (especially of a bodily part) situated at the back.
– ORIGIN Middle English: perhaps shortened from Old English *behindan* (see **BEHIND**).

hind² ■ n. a female deer, especially a red deer or sika in and after the third year.
– ORIGIN Old English, of Germanic origin.

hind- ■ comb. form (added to nouns) posterior: *hindquarters*.

hindbrain ■ n. the lower part of the brainstem, comprising the cerebellum, pons, and medulla oblongata.

hinder¹ /ˈhɪndə/ ■ v. delay or impede.
– ORIGIN Old English *hindrian* 'damage', of Germanic origin.

hinder² /ˈhaɪndə/ ■ adj. (especially of a bodily part) hind.
– ORIGIN Middle English: perhaps from Old English *hinderweard* 'backward'.

Hindi /ˈhɪndi/ ■ n. an Indic language of northern India derived from Sanskrit, an official language of India. ■ adj. of or relating to Hindi.
– ORIGIN from Urdu *hindī*, from *Hind* 'India'.

hindmost ■ adj. furthest back.

hindquarters ■ pl. n. the hind legs and adjoining parts of a quadruped.

hindrance /ˈhɪndr(ə)ns/ ■ n. a thing that hinders.

hindsight ■ n. understanding of a situation or event only after it has happened.

Hindu /ˈhɪndu:, hɪnˈdu:/ ■ n. (pl. **Hindus**) a follower of Hinduism. ■ adj. of or relating to Hindus or Hinduism.
– ORIGIN from Persian *hindū*, from *Hind* 'India'.

Hinduism ■ n. a major religious and cultural tradition of the Indian subcontinent, including belief in reincarnation and the worship of a large pantheon of deities.
– DERIVATIVES **Hinduize** (also **-ise**) v.

Hindustani /ˌhɪnduˈstɑːni/ ■ n. a group of mutually intelligible languages and dialects spoken in NW India, principally Hindi and Urdu. ▸ the Delhi dialect of Hindi, widely used throughout India as a lingua franca. ■ adj. of or relating to the culture of NW India.

hindwing ■ n. either of the two back wings of a four-winged insect.

hinge ■ n. a movable joint or mechanism by which a door, gate, or lid opens and closes or which connects linked objects. ■ v. (**hingeing** or **hinging**) 1 attach or join with or as if with a hinge. 2 (**hinge on**) depend entirely on.
– DERIVATIVES **hingeless** adj.
– ORIGIN Middle English *henge*; rel. to **HANG**.

hinny ■ n. (pl. **-ies**) the offspring of a female donkey and a male horse. Compare with **MULE**.
– ORIGIN C17: from Greek *hinnos*.

hint ■ n. 1 a slight or indirect indication. ▸ a very small trace. 2 a small piece of practical information. ■ v. indicate indirectly. ▸ (**hint at**) be a slight indication of.
– ORIGIN C17: apparently from obsolete *hent* 'grasp', from Old English, of Germanic origin.

hinterland

hinterland /ˈhɪntəland/ ■ n. **1** the remote areas of a country away from the coast or the banks of major rivers. ▸ the area around or beyond a major town or port. **2** an area lying beyond what is visible or known.
– ORIGIN C19: from German, from *hinter* 'behind' + *Land* 'land'.

hip¹ ■ n. **1** a projection of the pelvis and upper thigh bone on each side of the body. ▸ (**hips**) the circumference of the body at the buttocks. **2** the edge formed where two sloping sides of a roof meet.
– ORIGIN Old English *hype*, of Germanic origin.

hip² (also **rose hip**) ■ n. the fruit of a rose, especially a wild kind.
– ORIGIN Old English *hēope, hīope*, of West Germanic origin.

hip³ ■ adj. (**hipper, hippest**) informal, dated **1** fashionable. **2** (**hip to**) aware of or informed about.
– DERIVATIVES **hipness** n.
– ORIGIN C20 (orig. US).

hip⁴ ■ exclam. introducing a communal cheer.
– ORIGIN C18.

hip bath ■ n. a portable bath large enough to sit rather than lie down in.

hip bone ■ n. a large bone forming the main part of the pelvis on each side of the body and consisting of the fused ilium, ischium, and pubis.

hip flask ■ n. a small flask for spirits, of a kind intended to be carried in a hip pocket.

hip hop ■ n. a style of popular music of US black and Hispanic origin, featuring rap with an electronic backing.
– ORIGIN 1980s: reduplication prob. from HIP³.

hipped ■ adj. **1** [in combination] having hips of a specified kind. **2** (of a roof) having a hip or hips.

hippie ■ n. variant spelling of HIPPY¹.

hippo ■ n. (pl. same or **-os**) informal term for HIPPOPOTAMUS.

hippocampus /ˌhɪpə(ʊ)ˈkampəs/ ■ n. (pl. **hippocampi** /-pi, -paɪ/) Anatomy the system of elongated ridges on the floor of the lateral ventricles of the brain, thought to be the centre of emotion, memory, and the autonomic nervous system.
– ORIGIN C16: from Greek *hippokampos*, from *hippos* 'horse' + *kampos* 'sea monster'.

Hippocratic oath /ˌhɪpəˈkratɪk/ ■ n. a former oath taken by those beginning medical practice, affirming their obligations and proper conduct, parts of which are still used in some medical schools.
– ORIGIN C18: *Hippocratic* from medieval Latin *Hippocraticus* 'relating to *Hippocrates*', a Greek physician of the 5th century BC.

Hippocrene /ˈhɪpəkriːn/ ■ n. poetic/literary poetic or literary inspiration.
– ORIGIN C17: from Greek *Hippokrēnē, Hippou krēnē* 'fountain of the horse', the name of a fountain on Mount Helicon sacred to the Muses, which according to Greek legend was produced by a stroke of Pegasus' hoof.

hippodrome /ˈhɪpədrəʊm/ ■ n. **1** [in names] a theatre or concert hall. **2** (in ancient Greece or Rome) a course for chariot or horse races.
– ORIGIN C16: from Greek *hippodromos*, from *hippos* 'horse' + *dromos* 'race, course'.

hippogriff /ˈhɪpə(ʊ)ɡrɪf/ (also **hippogryph**) ■ n. a mythical creature with the body of a horse and a griffin's wings and head.
– ORIGIN C17: from Greek *hippos* 'horse' + Italian *grifo* 'griffin'.

hippopotamus /ˌhɪpəˈpɒtəməs/ ■ n. (pl. **hippopotamuses** or **hippopotami** /-maɪ/) a large thick-skinned semiaquatic African mammal, with massive jaws. [*Hippopotamus amphibius* and *Choeropsis liberiensis* (**pygmy hippopotamus**).]
– ORIGIN Middle English: from Greek *hippopotamos*, earlier *hippos ho potamios* 'river horse'.

hippuric acid /hɪˈpjʊərɪk/ ■ n. Biochemistry an organic acid present in the urine of herbivores and other mammals.
– DERIVATIVES **hippurate** n.

– ORIGIN C19: from Greek *hippos* 'horse' + *ouron* 'urine'.

hippy¹ (also **hippie**) ■ n. (pl. **-ies**) (especially in the 1960s) a young person associated with a subculture which rejected traditional social values, advocated peace and free love, and adopted an unconventional appearance.
– DERIVATIVES **hippiedom** n. **hippiness** n. **hippyish** adj.
– ORIGIN 1950s: from HIP³.

hippy² ■ adj. (of a woman) having large hips.

hipster¹ ■ adj. (of a garment) having the waistline at the hips rather than the waist. ■ n. (**hipsters**) trousers with such a waistline.

hipster² ■ n. informal, dated a person who follows the latest trends and fashions.
– ORIGIN 1940s: from HIP³.

hire ■ v. **1** obtain the temporary use of in return for payment. ▸ (**hire something out**) grant the temporary use of something in return for payment. **2** employ for wages. ▸ obtain the services of (someone) to do a particular job. ■ n. the action of hiring.
– PHRASES **for** (or **on**) **hire** available to be hired.
– DERIVATIVES **hireable** (US also **hirable**) adj. **hirer** n.
– ORIGIN Old English *hȳrian* 'employ for wages', *hȳr* 'payment for the use of something', of West Germanic origin.

hired gun ■ n. informal, chiefly N. Amer. **1** an expert brought in to resolve complex legal or financial problems, disputes, etc. ▸ a lobbyist or similar person able to attain power or influence for others quickly and efficiently. **2** a bodyguard, mercenary, or other person hired to protect or fight for another. ▸ a hired assassin.

hireling ■ n. chiefly derogatory a person who is hired, especially for morally dubious or illegal work.

hire purchase ■ n. a system by which someone pays for a thing in regular instalments while having the use of it.

hirsute /ˈhəːsjuːt/ ■ adj. formal, often humorous hairy: *their hirsute chests*.
– DERIVATIVES **hirsuteness** n.
– ORIGIN C17: from Latin *hirsutus*.

hirsutism /ˈhəːsjuːtɪz(ə)m/ ■ n. Medicine abnormal growth of hair on a woman's face and body.

hirundine /ˈhɪrʌndʌɪn, hɪˈrʌndʌɪn/ ■ n. Ornithology a bird of the swallow family (Hirundinidae).
– ORIGIN C19: from Latin *hirundo* 'swallow'.

his ■ possess. det. **1** belonging to or associated with a male person or animal previously mentioned. ▸ belonging to or associated with a person or animal of unspecified sex (in modern use chiefly replaced by 'his or her' or 'their'). **2** (**His**) used in titles. ■ possess. pron. used to refer to a thing or things belonging to or associated with a male person or animal previously mentioned.
– ORIGIN Old English, genitive sing. form of *he, hē* 'he' and *hit* 'it'.

Hispanic /hɪˈspanɪk/ ■ adj. of or relating to Spain or to Spanish-speaking countries, especially those of Central and South America. ▸ of or relating to Spanish-speaking people or their culture, especially in the US. ■ n. a Spanish-speaking person, especially one of Latin American descent, living in the US.
– ORIGIN from Latin *Hispanicus*, from *Hispania* 'Spain'.

Hispano- /hɪˈspanəʊ/ ■ comb. form Spanish; Spanish and ...: *Hispano-Argentine*.
– ORIGIN from Latin *Hispanus* 'Spanish'.

hispid /ˈhɪspɪd/ ■ adj. Botany & Zoology covered with stiff hair or bristles.
– ORIGIN C17: from Latin *hispidus*.

hiss ■ v. make a sharp sibilant sound as of the letter *s*, often as a sign of disapproval or derision. ▸ whisper something in an urgent or angry way. ■ n. a hissing sound. ▸ electrical interference at audio frequencies.
– ORIGIN Middle English: imitative.

hissy fit ■ n. informal an angry outburst; a temper tantrum.
– ORIGIN 1930s (as *hissy*): perhaps from hysterics (see HYSTERIC).

hist ■ exclam. archaic used to attract attention or call for silence.
– ORIGIN C16: natural exclam.

hist- ■ comb. form variant spelling of HISTO- shortened before a vowel (as in *histidine*).

histamine /ˈhɪstəmiːn/ ■ n. Biochemistry a compound which is released by cells in response to injury and in allergic and inflammatory reactions, causing muscle contraction and capillary dilation.
– DERIVATIVES **histaminic** adj.
– ORIGIN C20: blend of **HISTIDINE** and **AMINE**.

histidine /ˈhɪstɪdiːn/ ■ n. Biochemistry an amino acid which is a constituent of most proteins and is essential in the human diet.
– ORIGIN C19: from Greek *histos* 'web, tissue' + -IDE + -INE[4].

histo- /ˈhɪstəʊ/ (also **hist-** before a vowel) ■ comb. form Biology relating to organic tissue: *histochemistry*.
– ORIGIN from Greek *histos* 'web, tissue'.

histochemistry ■ n. the branch of science concerned with the chemical constituents of tissues and their study using stains, indicators, and microscopy.
– DERIVATIVES **histochemical** adj.

histocompatibility ■ n. Medicine compatibility between the tissues of different individuals.

histogram ■ n. Statistics a diagram consisting of rectangles whose positions and dimensions represent the values of a variable quantity.
– ORIGIN C19: from Greek *histos* 'mast, web' + -GRAM[1].

histology /hɪˈstɒlədʒi/ ■ n. the branch of biology concerned with the microscopic structure of tissues.
– DERIVATIVES **histological** adj. **histologist** n.

histolysis /hɪˈstɒlɪsɪs/ ■ n. Biology the breaking down of tissues (e.g. during animal metamorphosis).
– DERIVATIVES **histolytic** adj.

histone /ˈhɪstəʊn/ ■ n. Biochemistry any of a group of basic proteins found in chromatin.
– ORIGIN C19: German *Histon*, perhaps from Greek *histanai* 'arrest' or from *histos* 'web, tissue'.

histopathology ■ n. the branch of medicine concerned with the changes in tissues caused by disease.
– DERIVATIVES **histopathological** adj. **histopathologist** n.

histoplasmosis /ˌhɪstəʊplazˈməʊsɪs/ ■ n. Medicine infection by a fungus found in the droppings of birds and bats in humid areas.
– ORIGIN C20: from modern Latin *Histoplasma* (genus name of the fungus).

historian ■ n. an expert in or student of history.

historiated /hɪˈstɔːrɪeɪtɪd/ ■ adj. (of an initial letter in an illuminated manuscript) decorated with designs representing scenes from the text.
– ORIGIN C19: from French, from *historier* in an obsolete sense 'illustrate', from medieval Latin *historiare*, from *historia* (see **HISTORY**).

historic ■ adj. 1 famous or important in history, or potentially so. ▶ archaic of the past. 2 Grammar (of a tense) used in the narration of past events, especially Latin and Greek imperfect and pluperfect.

historical ■ adj. of or concerning history. ▶ belonging to or set in the past. ▶ (of the study of a subject) based on an analysis of its development over a period.
– DERIVATIVES **historically** adv.

historically disadvantaged ■ adj. another term for **PREVIOUSLY DISADVANTAGED**.

historical materialism ■ n. another term for **DIALECTICAL MATERIALISM**.

historicism ■ n. 1 the theory that social and cultural phenomena are determined by history. ▶ the belief that historical events are governed by natural laws. 2 the tendency to regard historical development as the most basic aspect of human existence. 3 (in art and architecture) excessive regard for past styles.
– DERIVATIVES **historicist** n. **historicization** (also **-isation**) n. **historicize** (also **-ise**) v.

historicity /ˌhɪstəˈrɪsɪti/ ■ n. historical authenticity.

historic present ■ n. Grammar the present tense used instead of the past in vivid narrative.

historiography /hɪˌstɔːrɪˈɒɡrəfi, -ˌstɒrɪ-/ ■ n. the study of the writing of history and of written histories. ▶ the writing of history.
– DERIVATIVES **historiographer** n. **historiographic** adj. **historiographical** adj.
– ORIGIN C16: from Greek *historiographia*, from *historia* 'history' + -*graphia* 'writing'.

hitherto

history ■ n. (pl. **-ies**) 1 the study of past events. 2 the past considered as a whole. ▶ the whole series of past events connected with someone or something. ▶ an eventful past. 3 a continuous, typically chronological, record of past events or trends.
– PHRASES **be history** informal used to indicate imminent departure, dismissal, or death. **the rest is history** the events succeeding those already related are so well known that they need not be recounted again.
– ORIGIN Middle English: from Greek *historia* 'narrative, history', from *histōr* 'learned, wise man'.

histosol /ˈhɪstəsɒl/ ■ n. Soil Science a peaty soil with a deep surface layer of purely organic material.

histrionic /ˌhɪstrɪˈɒnɪk/ ■ adj. 1 overly theatrical or melodramatic. 2 formal of or concerning actors or acting. ■ n. (**histrionics**) exaggerated dramatic behaviour designed to attract attention.
– DERIVATIVES **histrionically** adv.
– ORIGIN C17: from late Latin *histrionicus*, from Latin *histrio(n-)* 'actor'.

hit ■ v. (**hitting**; past and past part. **hit**) 1 direct a blow at with one's hand or a tool or weapon. ▶ accidentally strike (part of one's body) against something. ▶ (of a moving object or body) come into contact with (someone or something stationary) quickly and forcefully. 2 strike (a target). 3 cause harm or distress to. ▶ (**hit out**) make a strongly worded criticism or attack. ▶ informal, chiefly N. Amer. attack and rob or kill. 4 informal reach or arrive at. ▶ take effect. ▶ be suddenly and vividly realized by: *it hit her that I wanted to settle down here.* ▶ (**hit on**) discover or think of, especially by chance. ▶ (**hit on**) N. Amer. informal make sexual advances towards. 5 propel (a ball) with a bat, racket, etc. ▶ score (runs or points) in this way. ■ n. 1 an instance of hitting or being hit. 2 informal, chiefly N. Amer. a murder carried out by a criminal organization. 3 Baseball short for **BASE HIT**. 4 Computing an instance of identifying an item of data which matches the requirements of a search. ▶ an instance of a particular website being accessed by a user. 5 a successful and popular film, pop record, person, etc. 6 informal a dose of a narcotic drug.
– PHRASES **hit-and-miss** done or occurring at random. **hit-and-run** 1 denoting a road accident from which the perpetrator escapes before being discovered and without lending assistance. 2 denoting an attack or aggressive enterprise from which the aggressor withdraws rapidly on achieving their goal. **hit someone below the belt** 1 Boxing give one's opponent an illegal low blow. 2 behave unfairly towards someone. **hit someone for six** Brit. affect someone very severely. [with allusion to a forceful hit that scores six runs in cricket.] **hit the ground running** informal proceed at a fast pace with enthusiasm. **hit it off** informal be naturally friendly or well suited. **hit the nail on the head** find exactly the right answer. **hit-or-miss** as likely to be unsuccessful as successful. **hit the road** (or N. Amer. **trail**) informal set out on a journey. **hit wicket** Cricket the action of a batsman stepping on or knocking over their own wicket, resulting in their dismissal.
– DERIVATIVES **hitter** n.
– ORIGIN Old English *hittan*, from Old Norse *hitta* 'come upon, meet with'.

hitch ■ v. 1 move (something) into a different position with a jerk. 2 informal travel or obtain (a lift) by hitch-hiking. 3 fasten or tether with a rope. ▶ harness (a draught animal or team). ■ n. 1 a temporary difficulty. 2 a knot of a kind used to fasten one thing temporarily to another: *an overhand hitch.* 3 informal an act of hitch-hiking.
– PHRASES **get hitched** informal marry.
– ORIGIN Middle English.

hitcher ■ n. a hitch-hiker.

hitch-hike ■ v. travel by getting free lifts in passing vehicles. ■ n. a journey made by hitch-hiking.
– DERIVATIVES **hitch-hiker** n.

hither ■ adv. archaic or poetic/literary to or towards this place. ■ adj. archaic situated on this side.
– ORIGIN Old English, of Germanic origin.

hither and thither (also **hither and yon**) ■ adv. to and fro.

hitherto ■ adv. until the point in time under discussion.

hitherward

hitherward ■ adv. archaic to or towards this place.

Hitler ■ n. 1 an authoritarian or tyrannical person. 2 [as modifier] used with reference to Hitler's rule or personal characteristics: *a Hitler moustache*.
– DERIVATIVES **Hitlerian** adj. **Hitlerism** n. **Hitlerite** n. & adj.
– ORIGIN from Adolf *Hitler* (1889–1945), Austrian-born Nazi leader, Chancellor of Germany 1933–45.

hit list ■ n. a list of people to be killed for criminal or political reasons.

hit man ■ n. informal a hired assassin.

hit parade ■ n. dated a weekly listing of the current best-selling pop records.

Hittite /ˈhɪtʌɪt/ ■ n. 1 a member of an ancient people who established an empire in Asia Minor and Syria *c.*1700–1200 BC. ▸ a member of a Canaanite or Syrian people mentioned in the Bible (11th to 8th century BC). 2 the language of the Hittites, the oldest attested Indo-European language. ■ adj. of or relating to the Hittites, their empire, or their language.
– ORIGIN from Hebrew *Ḥittīm*, ultimately from Hittite *Ḥatti*.

HIV ■ abbrev. human immunodeficiency virus, a retrovirus which causes Aids.

hive ■ n. 1 a beehive. 2 a busy swarming place. ■ v. place (bees) in a hive.
– PHRASAL VERBS **hive something off** separate something from a larger group or organization.
– ORIGIN Old English, of Germanic origin.

hives ■ pl. n. [treated as sing. or pl.] another term for URTICARIA.
– ORIGIN C16 (orig. Scots).

HIV-positive ■ adj. having had a positive result in a blood test for HIV.

hiya ■ exclam. an informal greeting.
– ORIGIN 1940s: alteration of *how are you?*

HK ■ abbrev. Hong Kong.

hl ■ abbrev. hectolitre(s).

hlonipha /xlɒˈniːpə/ S. African ■ n. the traditional practice among Xhosa and Zulu women of avoiding use of the names of male relatives by marriage and other similar-sounding words. ■ v. 1 pay respect (to someone) by avoiding a sound, word, or name regarded as taboo. 2 practise ritual avoidance of certain words or sounds.
– ORIGIN from the Nguni languages.

hm ■ abbrev. hectometre(s).

hmm ■ exclam. & n. variant spelling of HEM², HUM².

HMS ■ abbrev. Her or His Majesty's Ship.

H1N1 ■ n. Medicine a subtype of influenza virus. ▸ (also H1N1 flu) another term for SWINE FLU.

Ho ■ symb. the chemical element holmium.

ho ■ exclam. 1 an expression of surprise, triumph, or derision. 2 used to call for attention. ▸ Nautical used to draw attention to something: *land ho!*
– ORIGIN Middle English: natural exclam.

hoagie /ˈhəʊgi/ ■ n. (pl. **-ies**) a long roll of bread.

hoar /hɔː/ archaic or poetic/literary ■ adj. grey or grey-haired with age. ■ n. hoar frost.
– ORIGIN Old English, of Germanic origin.

hoard ■ n. a store of money or valued objects. ▸ an amassed store of useful information. ■ v. amass and hide or store away.
– DERIVATIVES **hoarder** n.
– ORIGIN Old English, of Germanic origin.

USAGE
The words **hoard** and **horde** are sometimes confused. A **hoard** is 'a secret stock or store', as in *a hoard of treasure*, while a **horde** is a disparaging word for 'a large group of people', as in *hordes of greedy shareholders*.

hoarding ■ n. chiefly Brit. 1 a large board used to display advertisements. 2 a temporary board fence around a building site.
– ORIGIN C19: from obsolete *hoard* in the same sense.

hoar frost ■ n. frozen water vapour deposited in clear still weather on vegetation, fences, etc.

hoarhound ■ n. variant spelling of HOREHOUND.

hoarse ■ adj. (of a voice) rough and harsh.
– DERIVATIVES **hoarsely** adv. **hoarsen** v. **hoarseness** n.
– ORIGIN Old English, of Germanic origin.

hoary ■ adj. (**-ier**, **-iest**) 1 greyish-white. ▸ having grey hair; aged. 2 old and trite.
– DERIVATIVES **hoarily** adv. **hoariness** n.

hoax ■ n. a humorous or malicious deception. ■ v. deceive with a hoax.
– DERIVATIVES **hoaxer** n.
– ORIGIN C18: prob. a contraction of obsolete *hocus* 'trickery'.

hob ■ n. 1 a cooking appliance, or the flat top part of a cooker, with hotplates or burners. ▸ a flat metal shelf at the side of a fireplace, used for heating pans. 2 a machine tool for cutting gears or screw threads.
– ORIGIN C16: alteration of HUB.

Hobbesian /ˈhɒbzɪən/ ■ adj. of or relating to the English political philosopher Thomas Hobbes (1588–1679) or his philosophy.

hobbit ■ n. a member of an imaginary race similar to humans, of small size and with hairy feet, in stories by J. R. R. Tolkien.
– ORIGIN 1937: invented by Tolkien in his book *The Hobbit*, and said by him to mean 'hole-dweller'.

hobble ■ v. 1 walk awkwardly, typically because of pain. 2 strap together the legs of (a horse) to prevent straying. ▸ cause to limp. 3 be or cause a problem for. ■ n. 1 an awkward way of walking. 2 a rope or strap for hobbling a horse.
– ORIGIN Middle English: prob. of Dutch or Low German origin and rel. to Dutch *hobbelen* 'rock from side to side'.

hobbledehoy /ˈhɒb(ə)ldɪˌhɔɪ/ ■ n. informal, dated a clumsy or awkward youth.
– ORIGIN C16.

hobby¹ ■ n. (pl. **-ies**) 1 an activity done regularly for pleasure. 2 archaic a small horse or pony. 3 historical an early type of velocipede.
– ORIGIN Middle English ('small horse', later 'toy horse') *hobyn*, *hoby*, from familiar forms of the given name *Robin*.

hobby² ■ n. (pl. **-ies**) a small migratory falcon which hunts birds and insects on the wing. [*Falco subbuteo*.]
– ORIGIN Middle English: from Old French *hobet*, diminutive of *hobe* 'falcon'.

hobby horse ■ n. 1 a child's toy consisting of a stick with a model of a horse's head at one end. ▸ a rocking horse. ▸ a model of a horse used in morris dancing. 2 a favourite topic.

hobbyist ■ n. a person with a particular hobby.

hobgoblin ■ n. a mischievous imp; a bogey.
– ORIGIN C16: from archaic *hob* 'sprite, elf' + GOBLIN.

hobnail ■ n. 1 a short heavy-headed nail used to reinforce the soles of boots. 2 a blunt projection, especially in cut or moulded glassware.
– DERIVATIVES **hobnailed** adj.
– ORIGIN C16: from HOB + NAIL.

hobnob ■ v. (**hobnobbed**, **hobnobbing**) informal mix socially, especially with those of higher social status.
– ORIGIN C19 ('drink together, drink each other's health'): from archaic *hob or nob*, *hob and nob*, prob. meaning 'give and take'.

hobo ■ n. (pl. **-oes** or **-os**) a vagrant.
– ORIGIN C19.

Hobson's choice ■ n. a choice of taking what is offered or nothing at all.
– ORIGIN C17: named after Thomas *Hobson*, who hired out horses, making the customer take the one nearest the door or none at all.

hock¹ ■ n. 1 the joint in a quadruped's hind leg between the knee and the fetlock. 2 a knuckle of meat, especially pork or ham.
– ORIGIN Middle English: var. of rare *hough*, from Old English *hōh* 'heel', of Germanic origin.

hock² ■ n. a dry white wine from the German Rhineland.
– ORIGIN abbrev. of obsolete *hockamore*, alteration of German *Hochheimer* (*Wein*) '(wine) from Hochheim'.

hock³ ■ v. informal pawn (an object).
– PHRASES **in hock** having been pawned. ▸ in debt.
– ORIGIN C19: from Dutch *hok* 'hutch, prison, debt'.

hocket ■ n. Music a spasmodic or interrupted effect, produced by dividing a melody between two parts, notes in one part coinciding with rests in the other.
– DERIVATIVES **hocketing** n.
– ORIGIN C18: from French *hoquet* 'hiccup'.

hockey /'hɒki/ ■ n. a game played between two teams of eleven players each, using hooked sticks to drive a small hard ball towards a goal.
– ORIGIN C16.

hocus-pocus ■ n. **1** meaningless talk used for trickery. **2** a form of words used by a conjuror.
– ORIGIN C17: from *hax pax max Deus adimax*, a pseudo-Latin phr. used as a magic formula by conjurors.

HoD ■ abbrev. Head of Department.

hod ■ n. **1** a builder's V-shaped open trough on a pole, used for carrying bricks. **2** a coal scuttle.
– ORIGIN C16: from northern English dialect *hot* 'basket for carrying earth', from Old French *hotte* 'pannier'.

hodgepodge ■ n. N. Amer. variant of HOTCHPOTCH.
– ORIGIN Middle English: changed by association with archaic *Hodge*, denoting a typical English farm labourer, from the familiar form of the given name *Roger*.

Hodgkin's disease ■ n. a malignant disease of lymphatic tissues typically causing enlargement of the lymph nodes, liver, and spleen.
– ORIGIN C19: named after the English physician Thomas *Hodgkin*.

hoe ■ n. a long-handled gardening tool with a small metal blade, often used for weeding. ▸ a farm implement with a large rectangular blade, used for turning over the ground. ■ v. (-oes, -oed, -oeing) use a hoe to dig up (earth or plants).
– DERIVATIVES **hoer** n.
– ORIGIN Middle English: from Old French *houe*, of Germanic origin.

hoedown ■ n. N. Amer. a lively folk dance.

Hoffmansdruppels /'hɒfmənzdrəpəlz/ ■ pl. n. S. African a mixture of ether, alcohol, and ethereal oil, traditionally used as a remedy for heart complaints, nervous tension, and headaches.
– ORIGIN Afrikaans, 'Hoffman's drops', named after the German physician F. *Hoffman* (1660–1742).

hog ■ n. **1** a pig, especially a castrated male reared for slaughter. **2** informal a greedy person. ■ v. (**hogged, hogging**) **1** informal take or hoard selfishly. **2** distort (a ship) by supporting the centre and allowing the bow and stern to droop.
– PHRASES **go the whole hog** informal do something completely or thoroughly. **live high on** (or **off**) **the hog** N. Amer. informal have a luxurious lifestyle.
– DERIVATIVES **hogger** n. **hoggery** n. **hoggish** adj. **hoggishly** adv. **hog-like** adj.
– ORIGIN Old English, perhaps of Celtic origin.

hogback (also **hog's back**) ■ n. a long steep hill or mountain ridge.

hogfish ■ n. (pl. same or **-fishes**) a robust and colourful wrasse with sharp canine teeth and a hog-like snout. [Genera *Bodianus* and *Lachnolaimus*.]

Hogmanay /'hɒɡməneɪ, ˌhɒɡməˈneɪ/ ■ n. (in Scotland) New Year's Eve.
– ORIGIN C17: perhaps from *hoguinané*, Norman French form of Old French *aguillanneuf* 'last day of the year, new year's gift'.

hogshead ■ n. **1** a large cask. **2** a measure of liquid volume equal to 238.7 litres for wine or 245.5 litres for beer.
– ORIGIN Middle English: from HOG + HEAD.

hog-tie ■ v. N. Amer. **1** secure (a person or animal) by fastening the hands and feet or all four feet together. **2** impede.

hogwash ■ n. informal nonsense.
– ORIGIN C15 ('kitchen swill for pigs'): from HOG + WASH.

ho ho ■ exclam. **1** used to represent deep laughter. **2** used to express triumph.

ho-hum ■ exclam. used to express boredom or resignation.

555

– ORIGIN 1920s: imitative of a yawn.

hoick Brit. informal ■ v. lift or pull with a jerk. ■ n. a jerky pull.
– ORIGIN C19: perhaps a var. of HIKE.

hoi polloi /ˌhɔɪ pɒˈlɔɪ/ ■ pl. n. derogatory the common people.
– ORIGIN C17: Greek, 'the many'.

USAGE
Hoi polloi is sometimes used incorrectly to mean 'upper class', i.e. the exact opposite of its normal meaning. The confusion probably arose by association with the similar-sounding but otherwise unrelated word **hoity-toity**.

hoisin sauce /'hɔɪzɪn/ ■ n. a sweet, spicy dark red sauce made from soya beans, used in Chinese cooking.
– ORIGIN Cantonese *hoisin* 'seafood', from *hoi* 'sea' + *sin* 'fresh'.

hoist ■ v. raise by means of ropes and pulleys. ▸ haul up. ■ n. **1** an act of hoisting. **2** an apparatus for hoisting something. **3** the part of a flag nearest the staff. **4** a group of flags raised as a signal.
– PHRASES **hoist one's flag** (of an admiral) take up command. **hoist the flag** stake one's claim to territory by displaying a flag.
– ORIGIN C15: alteration of dialect *hoise*, prob. from Dutch *hijsen* or Low German *hiesen*.

hoity-toity ■ adj. haughty.
– ORIGIN C17: from obsolete *hoit* 'indulge in riotous mirth'.

hok ■ n. (pl. **hoks** or **hokke**) S. African **1** an enclosure for domestic animals. **2** a shack.
– ORIGIN from S. African Dutch.

Hokan /'həʊkən/ ■ n. a group of American Indian languages of California and western Mexico. ■ adj. relating to this hypothetical language family.
– ORIGIN from Hokan *hok* 'about two'.

hokey ■ adj. (**-ier, -iest**) N. Amer. informal excessively sentimental or contrived.
– DERIVATIVES **hokeyness** (also **hokiness**) n.
– ORIGIN 1940s: from HOKUM.

hokey-cokey (US also **hokey-pokey**) ■ n. a communal song and dance performed in a circle with synchronized shaking of the limbs in turn.
– ORIGIN 1940s: perhaps from HOCUS-POCUS.

hokkie ■ n. S. African **1** another term for HOK. **2** a small, restricted space.

hokku /'hɒkuː/ ■ n. (pl. same) another term for HAIKU.
– ORIGIN Japanese, 'opening verse'.

hokum /'həʊkəm/ ■ n. informal **1** nonsense. **2** sentimental or unrealistic situations and dialogue in a film or other work.
– ORIGIN C20.

Holarctic /hə(ʊ)ˈlɑːktɪk/ ■ adj. Zoology relating to or denoting a zoogeographical region comprising the Nearctic and Palaearctic regions combined.
– ORIGIN C19: from HOLO- + ARCTIC.

hold¹ ■ v. (past and past part. **held**) **1** grasp, carry, or support. **2** keep or detain. ▸ keep possession of. ▸ keep in a specified position. ▸ continue to follow (a course). ▸ stay or cause to stay at a certain value or level. ▸ (in sport) manage to achieve a draw against. **3** remain secure or intact. ▸ be or remain valid or available. ▸ (**hold to**) refuse to abandon or change (a principle). ▸ (**hold someone to**) cause someone to adhere to (a commitment). **4** contain or be capable of containing. ▸ be able to drink (a reasonable amount of alcohol) without suffering ill effects. **5** have in one's possession. ▸ have or occupy (a job or position). ▸ have in store: *I don't know what the future holds*. ▸ have (a belief or opinion). ▸ consider to be responsible for a situation. ▸ (**hold someone/thing in**) regard someone or something with (a specified feeling): *the speed limit is held in contempt*. ▸ (of a judge or court) rule. **6** reserve. ▸ maintain (a telephone connection). **7** N. Amer. informal refrain from adding or using. ▸ (**hold it**) informal wait or stop doing something. **8** arrange and take part in (a

hold

hold

meeting or conversation). ■ n. **1** a grip. **2** a handhold. **3** a degree of power or control.
– PHRASES **be left holding the baby** (or N. Amer. **bag**) informal be left with an unwelcome responsibility. **get hold of** grasp. ▸ informal find or contact. **hold court** be the centre of attention. **hold something dear** value something greatly. **hold fast** remain tightly secured. ▸ continue to adhere to a principle. **hold the fort** take responsibility for something temporarily. **hold good** (or **true**) remain true or valid. **hold hard** Brit. stop or wait. **hold someone/thing harmless** Law indemnify someone or something. **hold one's horses** informal wait a moment. **hold the line** not yield to pressure. **hold thumbs** S. African hope for good luck. **hold someone to bail** Law bind someone by bail. **hold one's tongue** informal remain silent. **hold water** (of a theory) appear sound. **no holds barred 1** (in wrestling) with no restrictions on the kinds of holds that are used. **2** without rules or restrictions. **on hold 1** waiting to be connected by telephone. **2** pending. **take hold** start to have an effect.
– PHRASAL VERBS **hold something against** allow past events to have a negative influence on one's present attitude towards. **hold back** hesitate. **hold something down** informal succeed in keeping a job. **hold forth** talk at length or tediously. **hold off** (of bad weather) fail to occur. **hold someone/thing off** resist an attacker or challenge. ▸ postpone an action or decision. **hold on 1** wait; stop. **2** keep going in difficult circumstances. **hold out 1** resist difficult circumstances. **2** continue to be sufficient. **hold out for** continue to demand. **hold out on** informal refuse to give something to. **hold something over 1** postpone something. **2** use information to threaten. **hold up** remain strong or vigorous. **hold someone/thing up 1** delay the progress of someone or something. **2** rob someone using the threat of violence. **3** present someone or something as an example. **hold with** [with neg.] informal approve of.
– DERIVATIVES **holdable** adj. **holder** n.
– ORIGIN Old English, of Germanic origin.

hold² ■ n. a storage space in the lower part of a ship or aircraft.
– ORIGIN C16: from obsolete *holl*, from Old English *hol* (see **HOLE**); the -*d* was added by association with **HOLD¹**.

holdall ■ n. a large bag with handles and a shoulder strap.

holdfast ■ n. **1** a staple or clamp securing an object. **2** Biology a stalked organ by which a simple aquatic organism attaches itself to a substrate.

holding ■ n. **1** an area of land held by lease. **2** (**holdings**) financial assets.

holding company ■ n. a company created to buy shares in other companies, which it then controls.

holding pattern ■ n. the flight path maintained by an aircraft awaiting permission to land.

hold-up ■ n. **1** a cause of delay. **2** a robbery conducted with the threat of violence. **3** a stocking held up by an elasticated top.

hole ■ n. **1** an empty space in a solid body or surface. ▸ an aperture. ▸ a cavity on a golf course into which the ball must be hit. **2** Physics a position from which an electron is absent, regarded as a mobile carrier of positive charge in a semiconductor. **3** informal a small or unpleasant place. ▸ an awkward situation. ■ v. **1** make a hole or holes in. **2** Golf hit (the ball) into a hole. **3** (**hole up**) informal hide oneself.
– PHRASES **blow a hole in** ruin the effectiveness of. **in the hole** N. Amer. informal in debt. **in holes** worn so much that holes have formed. **make a hole in** use a large amount of.
– DERIVATIVES **holey** adj.
– ORIGIN Old English, of Germanic origin.

hole-and-corner ■ adj. secret.

hole-in-one ■ n. (pl. **holes-in-one**) Golf a shot that enters the hole from the tee.

hole in the heart ■ n. Medicine a congenital defect in the heart septum, resulting in inadequate circulation of oxygenated blood.

hole saw ■ n. a tool for making circular holes, consisting of a metal cylinder with a toothed edge.

Holi /ˈhəʊliː/ ■ n. a Hindu spring festival celebrated in honour of Krishna.
– ORIGIN from Sanskrit *holī*.

holiday ■ n. **1** an extended period of recreation, especially away from home. **2** a day of festivity or recreation when no work is done. ■ v. spend a holiday.
– ORIGIN Old English *hāligdæg* 'holy day'.

holiday camp ■ n. Brit. a site for holidaymakers with accommodation and entertainments.

holidaymaker ■ n. a tourist.

holier-than-thou ■ adj. self-righteous.

holiness ■ n. **1** the state of being holy. **2** (**His/Your Holiness**) the title of the Pope, Orthodox patriarchs, and the Dalai Lama.

holism /ˈhəʊlɪz(ə)m, ˈhɒl-/ ■ n. **1** chiefly Philosophy the theory that certain wholes are greater than the sum of their parts. **2** Medicine the treating of the whole person, rather than just the symptoms of a disease.
– DERIVATIVES **holist** adj. & n.
– ORIGIN 1920s: from **HOLO-**.

holistic /həʊˈlɪstɪk/ ■ adj. **1** chiefly Philosophy characterized by the belief that the parts of something are explicable only by reference to the whole. **2** Medicine treating the whole person rather than just the physical symptoms of a disease.
– DERIVATIVES **holistically** adv.

holla /ˈhɒlə/ ■ exclam. archaic used to call attention to something.
– ORIGIN C16: from French *holà*, from *ho* 'ho!' + *là* 'there'.

hollandaise sauce /ˌhɒlənˈdeɪz, ˈhɒlənˌdeɪz/ ■ n. a creamy sauce for fish, made of butter, egg yolks, and vinegar.
– ORIGIN French *hollandaise*, feminine of *hollandais* 'Dutch'.

Hollander ■ n. dated **1** a native of the Netherlands. **2** S. African a Dutch-speaking immigrant from the Netherlands, contrasted with a Dutch- or Afrikaans-speaking South African.

Hollands ■ n. **1** archaic Dutch gin. **2** S. African dated the Dutch language.
– ORIGIN sense 1 from archaic Dutch *hollandsch genever* 'Dutch gin'; sense 2 from Afrikaans *Hollands* 'Dutch'.

holler informal ■ v. give a loud shout. ■ n. a loud shout.
– ORIGIN C17: var. of the rare verb *hollo*; rel. to **HALLOO**.

hollow ■ adj. **1** having a hole or empty space inside. ▸ concave. **2** (of a sound) echoing. **3** insincere: *a hollow promise.* ■ n. **1** a hole or depression. **2** a small valley. ■ v. (usu. **hollow something out**) make hollow. ▸ form by hollowing.
– PHRASES **beat someone hollow** defeat someone thoroughly.
– DERIVATIVES **hollowly** adv. **hollowness** n.
– ORIGIN Old English *holh* 'cave'.

hollowware ■ n. hollow cookware, tableware, etc., such as pots and jugs.

holly ■ n. an evergreen shrub, with prickly dark green leaves, small white flowers, and red berries. [*Ilex aquifolium* and other species.]
– ORIGIN Middle English *holi*, shortened form of Old English *holegn*, *holen*, of Germanic origin.

hollyhock ■ n. a tall plant of the mallow family, with large showy flowers. [*Alcea rosea.*]
– ORIGIN Middle English: from **HOLY** + obsolete *hock* 'mallow'.

Hollywood ■ n. [often as modifier] the commercial film industry of the United States, largely based in Hollywood, a district in Los Angeles.

holmium /ˈhəʊlmɪəm/ ■ n. the chemical element of atomic number 67, a soft silvery-white metal of the lanthanide series. (Symbol: **Ho**)
– ORIGIN C19: modern Latin, from *Holmia*, Latinized form of *Stockholm*, the capital of Sweden (because holmium and related minerals are found there).

holm oak ■ n. an evergreen oak with dark green glossy leaves. [*Quercus ilex.*]
– ORIGIN Middle English: alteration of dialect *hollin*, from Old English *holen* 'holly'.

holo- ■ comb. form whole; complete: *holocaust* | *holophytic*.

–ORIGIN from Greek *holos* 'whole'.

holocaust /ˈhɒləkɔːst/ ■ n. **1** destruction or slaughter on a mass scale: *a nuclear holocaust.* ▶ (**the Holocaust**) the mass murder of Jews under the German Nazi regime in World War II. **2** *historical* a Jewish sacrificial offering burnt on an altar.
–ORIGIN Middle English: from Greek *holokauston*, from *holos* 'whole' + *kaustos* 'burnt'.

Holocene /ˈhɒləsiːn/ ■ adj. *Geology* relating to or denoting the present epoch (from about 10 000 years ago, following the Pleistocene).
–ORIGIN C19: coined in French from HOLO- + Greek *kainos* 'new'.

holoenzyme /ˌhɒləʊˈɛnzʌɪm/ ■ n. *Biochemistry* a biochemically active compound of an enzyme combined with a coenzyme.

hologram /ˈhɒləɡram/ ■ n. **1** a three-dimensional image formed by the interference of light beams from a laser or other coherent light source. **2** a photograph of an interference pattern which, when suitably illuminated, produces a three-dimensional image.

holograph /ˈhɒləɡrɑːf/ ■ n. a manuscript handwritten by its author.

holography /hɒˈlɒɡrəfi/ ■ n. the study or production of holograms.
–DERIVATIVES **holographic** adj. **holographically** adv.

holometabolous /ˌhɒlə(ʊ)mɛˈtabələs/ ■ adj. *Entomology* (of an insect) having a pupal stage in the transition from larva to adult.
–DERIVATIVES **holometabolic** adj.

holophytic /ˌhɒlə(ʊ)ˈfɪtɪk/ ■ adj. *Biology* able to photosynthesize.

holothurian /ˌhɒlə(ʊ)ˈθjʊərɪən/ ■ n. *Zoology* a sea cucumber.
–ORIGIN C19: from the genus name *Holothuria*, from Greek *holothourion*, denoting a kind of zoophyte.

holotype /ˈhɒlətʌɪp/ ■ n. *Botany & Zoology* a single type specimen upon which the description and name of a new species is based.

hols ■ pl. n. *informal*, chiefly *Brit.* holidays.

Holstein /ˈhɒlstʌɪn, -iːn/ ■ n. an animal of a typically black-and-white breed of large dairy cattle.
–ORIGIN from *Holstein* in NW Germany.

holster /ˈhəʊlstə, ˈhɒl-/ ■ n. a holder for carrying a handgun, typically worn on a belt or under the arm. ■ v. put (a gun) into its holster.
–ORIGIN C17: rel. to Dutch *holster*.

holt /həʊlt/ ■ n. the den of an otter.
–ORIGIN Middle English: var. of HOLD¹.

holus-bolus /ˌhəʊləsˈbəʊləs/ ■ adv. *S. African & Canadian* all at once.
–ORIGIN C19: perhaps pseudo-Latin for 'whole bolus, whole lump'.

holy ■ adj. (**-ier**, **-iest**) **1** dedicated to God or a religious purpose. **2** morally and spiritually excellent and to be revered.
–ORIGIN Old English, of Germanic origin.

Holy City ■ n. **1** a city held sacred by the adherents of a religion, especially Jerusalem. **2** heaven.

holy day ■ n. a religious festival.

Holy Family ■ n. Christ as a child with Mary and Joseph (and often John the Baptist or St Anne), as a subject for a painting.

Holy Father ■ n. the Pope.

Holy Ghost ■ n. another term for HOLY SPIRIT.

Holy Joe ■ n. *informal* a pious man. ▶ a clergyman.
–ORIGIN C19: orig. nautical slang.

Holy Office ■ n. the former judicial body of the Catholic Church, founded to succeed the suppressed Inquisition.

holy of holies ■ n. **1** *historical* the inner chamber of the sanctuary in the Jewish Temple in Jerusalem. **2** a place regarded as most sacred or special.

holy orders ■ pl. n. the sacrament or rite of ordination as a member of the clergy.

Holy Roman Empire ■ n. the western part of the Roman empire, as revived by Charlemagne in 800 AD.

Holy Scripture ■ n. the Bible.

Holy See ■ n. the papacy or the papal court.

Holy Spirit ■ n. (in Christianity) the third person of the Trinity; God as spiritually active in the world.

holy war ■ n. a war waged in support of a religious cause.

holy water ■ n. water blessed by a priest and used in religious ceremonies.

Holy Week ■ n. the week before Easter.

Holy Writ ■ n. sacred writings collectively, especially the Bible.

homage /ˈhɒmɪdʒ/ ■ n. **1** honour or respect shown publicly. **2** formal public acknowledgement of feudal allegiance.
–ORIGIN Middle English: from medieval Latin *hominaticum*, from Latin *homo* 'man'.

hombre /ˈɒmbreɪ/ ■ n. *informal*, chiefly N. Amer. a man.
–ORIGIN C19: Spanish, 'man'.

homburg /ˈhɒmbəːɡ/ ■ n. a man's felt hat having a narrow curled brim and a lengthwise indentation in the crown.
–ORIGIN C19: named after *Homburg*, a town in western Germany, where such hats were first worn.

home ■ n. **1** the place where one lives permanently. ▶ a house or flat. **2** an institution for people needing professional care. **3** a place where something flourishes or from which it originated. **4** the finishing point in a race. **5** (in games) the place where a player is free from attack. **6** (in lacrosse) each of the three players nearest their opponents' goal. ■ adj. **1** of or relating to one's home. ▶ made, done, or intended for use in the home. **2** relating to one's own country. **3** (of a team or player) belonging to the place in which a sporting event occurs. ▶ played on a team's own ground. ■ adv. **1** to or at one's home. **2** to the end or conclusion of something. **3** to the intended or correct position. ■ v. **1** (of an animal) return by instinct to its territory. **2** (**home in on**) move or be aimed towards. **3** provide (a pet) with a home.
–PHRASES **at home 1** comfortable and at ease. **2** ready to receive visitors. **bring something home to** make (someone) realize the significance of something. **close** (or **near**) **to home** (of a remark) accurate to the point that one feels uncomfortable. **come home** Golf play the last nine holes in a round of eighteen. **drive** (or **hammer**) **something home** stress a point forcefully. **hit** (or **strike**) **home** (of words) have the intended effect. ▶ (of the significance of a situation) be fully realized. **home and dry** (N. Amer. **home free**, Austral./NZ **home and hosed**) having achieved one's objective.
–DERIVATIVES **homeless** adj. **homelessness** n. **homelike** adj.
–ORIGIN Old English, of Germanic origin.

home bird ■ n. *Brit.* another term for HOMEBODY.

homebody ■ n. (pl. **-ies**) *informal* a person who likes to stay at home.

homeboy (or **homegirl**) ■ n. *S. African & US informal* a person from one's own town or neighbourhood. ▶ *S. African* a person belonging to one's own clan.

home brew ■ n. beer or other alcoholic drink brewed at home.
–DERIVATIVES **home-brewed** adj.

homecoming ■ n. **1** an instance of returning home. **2** N. Amer. a reunion of former students of a college or high school.

home economics ■ pl. n. [often treated as sing.] the study of cookery and household management.

home farm ■ n. *S. African & Brit.* a farm on an estate that provides produce for the estate owner.

home-grown ■ adj. grown or produced in one's own garden or country.

Home Guard ■ n. the British citizen army organized in 1940 to defend the UK against invasion.

home help ■ n. *Brit.* a person employed to help in another's home.

home key ■ n. **1** *Music* the basic key in which a work is written. **2** a key on a keyboard acting as the base position for one's fingers in touch-typing.

homeland

homeland ▪ n. **1** a person's native land. **2** an autonomous state occupied by a particular people. ▸ S. African historical (under apartheid) any of ten partially self-governing areas in South Africa designated as regions where black people might claim citizenship and permanent residence.

home language ▪ n. the language spoken in one's home.

homely ▪ adj. (-ier, -iest) **1** simple but comfortable. ▸ unsophisticated. **2** chiefly N. Amer. unattractive.
– DERIVATIVES **homeliness** n.

home-made ▪ adj. made at home.

homemaker ▪ n. a person who manages a home.
– DERIVATIVES **homemaking** n.

home movie ▪ n. a film made at home or without professional equipment.

Home Office ▪ n. the British government department dealing with law and order, immigration, etc. in England and Wales.

homeopath /ˈhəʊmɪəpaθ, ˈhɒm-/ (also **homoeopath**) ▪ n. a person who practises homeopathy.

homeopathy /ˌhəʊmɪˈɒpəθi, hɒm-/ (also **homoeopathy**) ▪ n. a system of complementary medicine in which disease is treated by minute doses of natural substances that in a healthy person would produce symptoms of disease. Often contrasted with ALLOPATHY.
– DERIVATIVES **homeopathic** adj. **homeopathically** adv. **homeopathist** n.
– ORIGIN C19: coined in German from Greek *homoios* 'like' + *patheia* (see -PATHY).

homeosis /ˌhɒmɪˈəʊsɪs/ (also **homoeosis**) ▪ n. (pl. **homeoses** /-siːz/) Biology the replacement of part of one segment of an insect or other segmented animal by a structure characteristic of a different segment, especially through mutation.
– DERIVATIVES **homeotic** adj.
– ORIGIN C19: from Greek *homoiōsis* 'becoming like'.

homeostasis /ˌhɒmɪə(ʊ)ˈsteɪsɪs, ˌhəʊm-/ (also **homoeostasis**) ▪ n. (pl. **homeostases** /-siːz/) the maintenance of a stable equilibrium, especially through physiological processes.
– DERIVATIVES **homeostatic** adj.
– ORIGIN 1920s: modern Latin, from Greek *homoios* 'like' + -STASIS.

homeotherm /ˈhɒmɪə(ʊ)ˌθəːm/ (also **homoiotherm**) ▪ n. Zoology an organism that maintains its body temperature at a constant level by its metabolic activity. Often contrasted with POIKILOTHERM.
– DERIVATIVES **homeothermal** adj. **homeothermic** adj. **homeothermy** n.
– ORIGIN C19: modern Latin, from Greek *homoios* 'like' + *thermē* 'heat'.

home page ▪ n. Computing a person's or organization's introductory document on the World Wide Web.

home plate ▪ n. Baseball the five-sided flat white rubber base which must be touched in scoring a run.

homer ▪ n. **1** Baseball a home run. **2** a homing pigeon.

Homeric /həʊˈmɛrɪk/ ▪ adj. **1** of, or in the style of, the ancient Greek poet Homer (8th century BC) or the epic poems ascribed to him. **2** of Bronze Age Greece as described in these poems.

homeroom ▪ n. N. Amer. a classroom in which a group of students assembles daily with the same teacher for announcements, opening exercises, etc. before dispersing to other classes.

home rule ▪ n. the government of a place by its own citizens.

home run ▪ n. Baseball a hit that allows the batter to make a complete circuit of the bases.

homesick ▪ adj. upset due to absence from one's home.
– DERIVATIVES **homesickness** n.

homespun ▪ adj. **1** simple and unsophisticated. **2** (of cloth or yarn) made or spun at home. ▪ n. cloth of this type.

homestead ▪ n. **1** a house, especially a farmhouse, and outbuildings. **2** S. African a cluster of huts or houses in a rural area, occupied by one family or clan.
– DERIVATIVES **homesteader** n. **homesteading** n.
– ORIGIN Old English *hāmstede* 'a settlement' (see HOME, STEAD).

home straight (also **home stretch**) ▪ n. the concluding stretch of a racecourse, athletics track, or other sports circuit.

homestyle ▪ adj. chiefly N. Amer. simple and unpretentious.

home truth ▪ n. an unpleasant fact about oneself.

homeward ▪ adv. (also **homewards**) towards home. ▪ adj. going or leading towards home.

homework ▪ n. **1** school work that a pupil is required to do at home. **2** preparation. **3** paid work done in one's own home.

homeworker ▪ n. a person who works from home.
– DERIVATIVES **homeworking** n.

homey (also **homy**) ▪ adj. (-ier, -iest) **1** comfortable and cosy. **2** unsophisticated. ▪ n. variant spelling of HOMIE.

homicide ▪ n. murder.
– DERIVATIVES **homicidal** adj.
– ORIGIN Middle English: from Latin *homicidium*, from *homo* 'man'.

homie (also **homey**) ▪ n. (pl. **-ies**) informal, chiefly US a homeboy or homegirl.

homily /ˈhɒmɪli/ ▪ n. (pl. **-ies**) **1** a religious discourse intended for spiritual edification rather than instruction. **2** a tedious moralizing discourse.
– ORIGIN Middle English: from eccles. Latin *homilia*, from Greek, 'discourse' (in eccles. use, 'sermon'), from *homilos* 'crowd'.

homing ▪ adj. **1** (of a pigeon or other animal) able to return home from a great distance. **2** (of a weapon) able to find and hit a target electronically.

hominid /ˈhɒmɪnɪd/ ▪ n. Zoology a primate of a family (Hominidae) which includes humans and their fossil ancestors.
– ORIGIN C19: from *Hominidae* (pl.), from Latin *homo*, *homin-* 'man'.

hominoid /ˈhɒmɪnɔɪd/ ▪ n. Zoology a primate of a group (superfamily Hominoidea) that includes humans, their fossil ancestors, and the great apes.

hominy /ˈhɒmɪni/ ▪ n. US coarsely ground corn (maize) used to make grits.
– ORIGIN shortened from Virginia Algonquian *uskatahomen*.

Homo /ˈhəʊməʊ, ˈhɒməʊ/ ▪ n. the genus of primates of which modern humans (*Homo sapiens*) are the present-day representatives.
– ORIGIN Latin, 'man'.

homo /ˈhəʊməʊ/ informal, chiefly derogatory ▪ n. (pl. **-os**) a homosexual man. ▪ adj. homosexual.

homo- comb. form **1** same: *homogametic*. **2** relating to homosexual love: *homoerotic*.
– ORIGIN from Greek *homos* 'same'.

homocentric[1] ▪ adj. having the same centre.

homocentric[2] ▪ adj. another term for ANTHROPOCENTRIC.

homoeopath ▪ n. variant spelling of HOMEOPATH.

homoeopathy ▪ n. variant spelling of HOMEOPATHY.

homoeosis ▪ n. variant spelling of HOMEOSIS.

homoeostasis ▪ n. variant spelling of HOMEOSTASIS.

homoerotic /ˌhəʊməʊɪˈrɒtɪk, ˌhɒməʊ-/ ▪ adj. concerning or arousing sexual desire centred on a person of the same sex.
– DERIVATIVES **homoeroticism** n.

homogametic /ˌhɒmə(ʊ)gəˈmɛtɪk, -ˈmiːtɪk, ˌhəʊm-/ ▪ adj. Biology denoting the sex which has sex chromosomes that do not differ in morphology, e.g. (in mammals) the female and (in birds) the male.

homogamy /hɒˈmɒgəmi/ ▪ n. **1** Biology inbreeding. **2** marriage between people from similar backgrounds.
– DERIVATIVES **homogamous** adj.
– ORIGIN C19: from HOMO- + Greek *gamos* 'marriage'.

homogenate /həˈmɒdʒɪneɪt/ ▪ n. Biology a suspension of cell fragments and constituents obtained when tissue is homogenized.

homogeneous /ˌhɒmə(ʊ)ˈdʒiːnɪəs, -ˈdʒɛn-, ˌhəʊm-/ ■ adj. **1** of the same kind. ▶ consisting of parts all of the same kind. **2** Chemistry denoting a process involving substances in the same phase (solid, liquid, or gaseous): *homogeneous catalysis.*
– DERIVATIVES **homogeneity** /-dʒɪˈniːɪti, -dʒɪˈneɪɪti/ n. **homogeneously** adv. **homogeneousness** n.
– ORIGIN C17 (as *homogeneity*): from Greek *homogenēs*, from *homos* 'same' + *genos* 'race, kind'.

> **USAGE**
> **Homogeneous** is commonly misspelled as **homogenous**. **Homogenous** is a different word, a rather dated term used in biology.

homogenize (also **-ise**) ■ v. **1** make homogeneous. **2** [often as adj. **homogenized** (also **-ised**)] subject (milk) to a process in which the fat droplets are emulsified and the cream does not separate.
– DERIVATIVES **homogenization** /-ˈzeɪʃ(ə)n/ (also **-isation**) n. **homogenizer** (also **-iser**) n.

homograft /ˈhɒməɡrɑːft, ˈhəʊm-/ ■ n. a tissue graft from a donor of the same species.

homograph ■ n. each of two or more words spelled the same but having different meanings and origins.
– DERIVATIVES **homographic** adj.

homoiotherm /hɒmɔɪə(ʊ)ˌθəːm/ ■ n. variant spelling of **HOMEOTHERM**.

homologous /hɒˈmɒləɡəs/ ■ adj. **1** having the same relation, relative position, or structure. **2** Biology (of organs) similar in position, structure, and evolutionary origin. Often contrasted with **ANALOGOUS**. **3** Biology (of chromosomes) pairing at meiosis and having the same structure and pattern of genes. **4** Chemistry (of a series of chemical compounds) similar in properties but differing in composition by a fixed group of atoms.
– DERIVATIVES **homologize** (also **-ise**) v. **homology** /hɒˈmɒlədʒi/ n.
– ORIGIN C17: from Greek *homologos* 'agreeing, consistent', from *homos* 'same' + *logos* 'ratio, proportion'.

homomorphic ■ adj. technical of the same or similar form.
– DERIVATIVES **homomorphically** adv.

homonym /ˈhɒmənɪm/ ■ n. **1** each of two or more words having the same spelling and pronunciation but different meanings and origins (e.g. POLE¹ and POLE²). **2** Biology a Latin name which is identical to that of a different organism, the newer name being invalid.
– DERIVATIVES **homonymic** adj. **homonymous** adj. **homonymy** /həˈmɒnɪmi/ n.
– ORIGIN C17: from Greek, from *homōnumos*, from *homos* 'same' + *onoma* 'name'.

homophobia /ˌhɒməˈfəʊbɪə, ˌhəʊmə-/ ■ n. an extreme and irrational aversion to homosexuality and homosexuals.
– DERIVATIVES **homophobe** n. **homophobic** adj.

homophone /ˈhɒməfəʊn, ˈhəʊm-/ ■ n. **1** each of two or more words having the same pronunciation but different meanings, origins, or spelling (e.g. *new* and *knew*). **2** a symbol denoting the same sound as another.
– DERIVATIVES **homophonous** /həˈmɒf(ə)nəs/ adj. **homophony** /həˈmɒf(ə)ni/ n.

homopolar ■ adj. having equal or unchanging polarity.

Homoptera /hɒˈmɒpt(ə)rə/ ■ pl. n. Entomology a group of bugs comprising those with uniform forewings, such as the plant bugs, aphids, and cicadas. Compare with **HETEROPTERA**.
– DERIVATIVES **homopteran** n. & adj. **homopterous** adj.
– ORIGIN from HOMO- + Greek *pteron* 'wing'.

Homo sapiens /ˌhəʊməʊ ˈsapɪɛnz, ˌhɒməʊ-/ ■ n. the primate species to which modern humans belong.
– ORIGIN Latin, 'wise man'.

homosexual /ˌhɒmə(ʊ)ˈsɛksjʊəl, ˌhəʊm-, -ʃʊəl/ ■ adj. feeling or involving sexual attraction to people of one's own sex. ■ n. a homosexual person.
– DERIVATIVES **homosexuality** n. **homosexually** adv.
– ORIGIN C19: from HOMO- + SEXUAL.

homosocial ■ adj. of or relating to social interaction between members of the same sex.

homozygote /ˌhɒmə(ʊ)ˈzʌɪɡəʊt, ˌhəʊm-/ ■ n. Genetics an individual having two identical alleles of a particular gene or genes and so breeding true for the corresponding characteristic. Compare with **HETEROZYGOTE**.
– DERIVATIVES **homozygosity** n. **homozygous** adj.

homunculus /hɒˈmʌŋkjʊləs/ (also **homuncule** /-kjuːl/) ■ n. (pl. **homunculi** /-lʌɪ/ or **homuncules**) a very small human or humanoid creature.
– ORIGIN C17: from Latin, diminutive of *homo* 'man'.

homy ■ adj. variant spelling of **HOMEY**.

Hon ■ abbrev. **1** (in official job titles) Honorary. **2** (in titles, especially of the British nobility and US judges) Honourable.

honcho /ˈhɒn(t)ʃəʊ/ informal ■ n. (pl. **-os**) a leader. ■ v. (**-oes**, **-oed**) chiefly N. Amer. be in charge of.
– ORIGIN 1940s: from Japanese *hanchō* 'group leader'.

Honduran /hɒnˈdjʊər(ə)n/ ■ n. a native or inhabitant of Honduras, a country in Central America. ■ adj. of or relating to Honduras.

hone ■ v. sharpen with a whetstone. ▶ (usu. **be honed**) make sharper or more focused or efficient. ■ n. a whetstone, especially one used to sharpen razors.
– ORIGIN Middle English: from Old English *hān* 'stone', of Germanic origin.

honest ■ adj. **1** free of deceit; truthful and sincere. **2** fairly earned: *an honest living.* **3** (of an action) well intentioned even if misguided. **4** simple and unpretentious: *good honest food with no gimmicks.* ■ adv. informal genuinely; really.
– PHRASES **earn** (or **turn**) **an honest penny/buck** earn money fairly. **make an honest woman of** dated or humorous marry a woman, especially to avoid scandal if she is pregnant.
– ORIGIN Middle English: from Latin *honestus*, from *honos* (see HONOUR).

honest broker ■ n. an impartial mediator.

honestly ■ adv. **1** in an honest way. **2** really: *honestly, that man is the limit!*

honest-to-God informal ■ adj. genuine; real. ■ adv. genuinely; really.

honest-to-goodness ■ adj. genuine and straight-forward.

honesty ■ n. **1** the quality of being honest. **2** a plant with purple or white flowers and round, flat, translucent seed pods. [Genus *Lunaria*.]
– ORIGIN Middle English: from Latin *honestas*, from *honestus* (see HONEST); the plant is so named from its seed pods, translucency symbolizing lack of deceit.

honey ■ n. (pl. **-eys**) **1** a sweet, sticky yellowish-brown fluid made by bees and other insects from flower nectar. **2** informal an excellent example of something. **3** chiefly N. Amer. darling; sweetheart.
– ORIGIN Old English, of Germanic origin.

honey ant ■ n. an ant that stores large amounts of honeydew and nectar in its elastic abdomen, regurgitating it to feed nest mates. [*Myrmecocystus* and other genera.]

honey badger ■ n. a short, thickset mammal with a white or grey back, black underparts, and a short bushy tail, native to Africa and Asia. [*Mellivora capensis*.]

honeybee ■ n. see BEE (sense 1).

honey beer ■ n. an alcoholic drink made from honey fermented with leaven and, occasionally, the larvae of bees; mead.

honeybird ■ n. a small, drab African bird of the honeyguide family. [Genus *Prodotiscus*: three species.]

honeybush (also **honeybush tea**) ■ n. **1** a South African shrub of the pea family with bright yellow flowers and fragrant three-lobed leaves. [*Cyclopia genistoides* and other species.] **2** a sweet-tasting infusion of the leaves of this plant drunk as tea.

honey buzzard ■ n. a large broad-winged bird of prey feeding chiefly on bees and wasps and their nests. [*Pernis apivorus* and related species.]

honeycomb ■ n. **1** a structure of hexagonal cells of wax, made by bees to store honey and eggs. **2** a structure of linked cavities. **3** a raised hexagonal or cellular pattern on fabric. **4** tripe from the second stomach of a ruminant. ■ v. fill with cavities or tunnels.

honeydew ■ n. **1** a sweet, sticky substance excreted by aphids. **2** poetic/literary an ideally sweet substance. **3** (also **honeydew melon**) a melon of a variety with smooth pale skin and sweet green flesh.

honeyed (also **honied**) ■ adj. **1** containing or coated with honey. **2** having a warm yellow colour. **3** (of words or a tone of voice) soothing and soft.

honey fungus (also **honey mushroom**) ■ n. a parasitic fungus producing honey-coloured toadstools at the base of trees. [*Armillaria mellea*.]

honeyguide ■ n. **1** a small, drab tropical songbird, feeding chiefly on beeswax and bee grubs. [Family Indicatoridae: several species.] **2** Botany a marking on a flower petal thought to guide insects to nectar.

honey locust ■ n. a spiny leguminous tree grown for its fern-like foliage. [*Gleditsia triacanthos* (from N. America) and related species.]

honeymoon ■ n. **1** a holiday taken by a newly married couple. **2** an initial period of enthusiasm or goodwill. ■ v. spend a honeymoon.
– DERIVATIVES **honeymooner** n.
– ORIGIN C16: from HONEY + MOON (orig. referring to affection waning like the moon, later denoting the first month after marriage).

honeypot ■ n. **1** a container for honey. **2** a place to which many people are attracted.

honeysuckle ■ n. a climbing shrub with fragrant tubular flowers, typically yellow and pink. [Genus *Lonicera*: many species.]
– ORIGIN Middle English *honysoukil*, extension of *honysouke*, from Old English *hunigsūce* (see HONEY, SUCK).

honey tea ■ n. S. African another term for HONEYBUSH.

hongi /ˈhɒŋi/ ■ n. NZ the traditional Maori greeting in which people press their noses together.
– ORIGIN from Maori.

honied ■ adj. variant spelling of HONEYED.

Honiton lace /ˈhɒnɪt(ə)n, ˈhʌn-/ ■ n. lace consisting of floral sprigs hand sewn to fine net or joined by lacework.
– ORIGIN C19: from *Honiton*, a town in Devon, England.

honk ■ n. **1** the cry of a goose. **2** the sound of a car horn. ■ v. emit or cause to emit a honk.
– DERIVATIVES **honker** n.
– ORIGIN C19: imitative.

honky ■ n. (pl. **-ies**) N. Amer. informal, derogatory a white person or white people collectively.
– ORIGIN 1960s.

honky-tonk ■ n. informal **1** chiefly N. Amer. a cheap or disreputable bar or club. **2** ragtime piano music.
– ORIGIN C19.

honor ■ n. & v. US spelling of HONOUR.

honorable ■ adj. US spelling of HONOURABLE.

honorand /ˈɒnərand/ ■ n. a person to be honoured, especially with an honorary degree.
– ORIGIN 1950s: from Latin *honorandus* 'to be honoured', from *honorare* 'to honour'.

honorarium /ˌɒnəˈrɛːrɪəm/ ■ n. (pl. **honorariums** or **honoraria** /-rɪə/) a payment for professional services that are rendered nominally without charge.
– ORIGIN C17: from Latin, denoting a gift made on being admitted to public office, from *honorarius* (see HONORARY).

honorary ■ adj. **1** (of a title or position) conferred as an honour. ▶ holding such a title or position. **2** (of an office or its holder) unpaid.
– ORIGIN C17: from Latin *honorarius*, from *honor* 'honour'.

Honorary White ■ n. S. African historical (under apartheid) a person, usually of Japanese or Chinese descent, not registered as a white person but given privileges normally reserved for white people.

honorific ■ adj. given as a mark of respect. ■ n. a title or word expressing respect.
– DERIVATIVES **honorifically** adv.
– ORIGIN C17: from Latin *honorificus*, from *honor* 'honour'.

honoris causa /ɒˌnɔːrɪs ˈkauzə/ ■ adv. (especially of a degree awarded without examination) as a mark of esteem.
– ORIGIN Latin, 'for the sake of honour'.

honour (US **honor**) ■ n. **1** high respect. ▶ a feeling of pride and pleasure from being shown respect. ▶ a person or thing that brings credit. **2** a clear sense of what is morally right. **3** a thing conferred as a distinction. ▶ (**honours**) a special distinction for proficiency in an examination.
▶ (**honours**) a course of degree studies more specialized than for an ordinary pass. **4** (**His/Your**) etc. **Honour** a title of respect, especially for a judge or (in the US) a mayor. **5** Golf the right of driving off first, having won the previous hole. **6** dated a woman's chastity. **7** Bridge an ace, king, queen, jack, or ten. ▶ (**honours**) possession of at least four of these cards, or of all four aces in no trumps, for which a bonus is scored. ▶ (in whist) an ace, king, queen, or jack of trumps. ■ v. **1** regard with great respect. ▶ pay public respect to. **2** grace; privilege. **3** fulfil (an obligation) or keep (an agreement). ▶ accept (a bill) or pay (a cheque) when due.
– PHRASES **do the honours** informal perform a social duty for others, especially serve food or drink. **honours are even** there is equality in the contest. **in honour of** as an expression of respect for. **on one's honour** under a moral obligation. **on** (or **upon**) **my honour** used to express sincerity.
– ORIGIN Middle English: from Latin *honor*.

honourable (US **honorable**) ■ adj. **1** bringing or worthy of honour. ▶ formal or humorous (of the intentions of a man courting a woman) directed towards marriage.
2 (**Honourable**) a title given to certain high officials, members of parliament, and (in Britain) the children of some ranks of the nobility.
– DERIVATIVES **honourableness** n. **honourably** adv.

honourable mention ■ n. a commendation for a candidate in an examination or competition not awarded a prize.

honours list ■ n. (especially in Britain) a list of people to be awarded honours.

honours of war ■ pl. n. privileges granted to a capitulating force, e.g. that of marching out with colours flying.

honour system ■ n. a system of payment or examinations relying on the honesty of those concerned.

Hon. Sec. ■ abbrev. honorary secretary.

hooch /huːtʃ/ (also **hootch**) ■ n. informal alcoholic liquor, especially inferior or illicit whisky.
– ORIGIN C19: abbrev. of *Hoochinoo*, an Alaskan Indian people who made liquor.

hood¹ ■ n. **1** a covering for the head and neck with an opening for the face, typically part of a coat or cloak. ▶ a similar garment worn over a university gown or surplice to indicate the wearer's degree. ▶ Falconry a leather covering for a hawk's head. **2** a folding waterproof cover of a vehicle or pram. **3** N. Amer. the bonnet of a vehicle. **4** a canopy to protect users of machinery or to remove fumes from it. **5** a hood-like structure or marking on the head or neck of an animal. **6** the upper part of a flower such as a dead-nettle. ■ v. put a hood on or over.
– DERIVATIVES **hoodless** adj. **hood-like** adj.
– ORIGIN Old English *hōd*, of West Germanic origin.

hood² ■ n. informal, chiefly N. Amer. a gangster or violent criminal.
– ORIGIN 1930s: abbrev. of HOODLUM.

hood³ ■ n. S. African & N. Amer. informal a neighbourhood.

-hood ■ suffix forming nouns: **1** denoting a condition or quality: *womanhood*. **2** denoting a collection or group: *brotherhood*.
– ORIGIN Old English *-hād*.

hooded ■ adj. **1** having or wearing a hood. **2** (of eyes) having drooping upper eyelids.

hoodia ■ n. **1** a plant of a genus of cactus-like succulents native to southern Africa. [Genus *Hoodia*, in particular *H. gordonii*.] **2** the appetite suppressant drug made from some species.

hoodie ■ n. variant spelling of HOODY.

hoodlum /ˈhuːdləm/ ■ n. a hooligan or gangster.
– ORIGIN C19 (orig. US).

hood mould (also **hood moulding**) ■ n. Architecture a dripstone.

hoodoo ■ n. **1** voodoo. **2** bad luck. ▸ a cause of bad luck. ■ v. (**hoodoos**, **hoodooed**) bewitch.
–ORIGIN C19: apparently an alteration of VOODOO.

hoodwink ■ v. deceive or trick.
–ORIGIN C16 (orig. 'to blindfold'): from HOOD¹ + an obsolete sense of WINK 'close the eyes'.

hoody (also **hoodie**) ■ n. (pl. **hoodies**) a hooded sweatshirt, jacket, or other top. ▸ chiefly Brit. informal a person, especially a youth, wearing a hooded top.

hooey ■ n. informal nonsense.
–ORIGIN 1920s (orig. US).

hoof ■ n. (pl. **hoofs** or **hooves**) the horny part of the foot of an ungulate, especially a horse. ■ v. informal **1** kick (a ball) powerfully. **2** (**hoof it**) go on foot. ▸ dance.
–PHRASES **on the hoof 1** (of livestock) not yet slaughtered. **2** informal without great thought or preparation.
–DERIVATIVES **hoofed** adj.
–ORIGIN Old English, of Germanic origin.

hoo-ha ■ n. informal a commotion.
–ORIGIN 1930s.

hook ■ n. **1** a piece of curved metal or other material for catching hold of things or hanging things on. ▸ (also **fish hook**) a bent piece of metal, typically barbed and baited, for catching fish. **2** a thing designed to catch people's attention. ▸ a catchy chorus or repeated passage in a pop or rock song. **3** a curved cutting instrument. **4** a short swinging punch made with the elbow bent and rigid. **5** a hooking stroke in sport. **6** a curved promontory or sand spit. ■ v. **1** be or become attached or fastened with a hook. **2** (**hook up**) link or be linked to electronic equipment. **3** bend or be bent into the shape of a hook. **4** Rugby secure (the ball) and pass it backward with the foot in the scrum. **5** catch with a hook. ▸ archaic, informal steal. **6** (**be hooked**) informal be captivated or addicted. **7** Cricket hit (the ball) round to the on side with a slightly upward swing of the bat at shoulder height. ▸ (in sport) strike (the ball) so that it deviates in the direction of the follow-through. **8** Boxing punch one's opponent with the elbow bent and rigid.
–PHRASES **by hook or by crook** by any possible means. **get one's hooks into** informal get hold of. **hook, line, and sinker** entirely: *he fell for the story hook, line, and sinker*. **off the hook 1** informal no longer in difficulty or trouble. **2** (of a telephone receiver) not on its rest. **sling one's hook** Brit. informal leave.
–DERIVATIVES **hookless** adj. **hooklet** n. **hook-like** adj.
–ORIGIN Old English, of Germanic origin.

hookah /ˈhʊkə/ ■ n. an oriental tobacco pipe with a long, flexible tube which draws the smoke through water in a bowl.
–ORIGIN C18: from Arabic *ḥuḳḳa* 'casket, jar'.

hook and eye ■ n. a small metal hook and loop used to fasten a garment.

hooked ■ adj. **1** having or resembling a hook or hooks. **2** (of a rug) made by pulling woollen yarn through canvas with a hook.

hooker¹ ■ n. **1** Rugby the player in the middle of the front row of the scrum, who tries to hook the ball. **2** informal, chiefly N. Amer. a prostitute.

hooker² ■ n. N. Amer. informal a drink of undiluted brandy, whisky, or other spirit.
–ORIGIN C19.

hookey (also **hooky**) ■ n. (in phr. **play hookey**) N. Amer. informal play truant.
–ORIGIN C19.

hook nose ■ n. an aquiline nose.
–DERIVATIVES **hook-nosed** adj.

hooktip ■ n. a slender moth with hooked tips to the forewings. [Family Drepanidae.]

hook-up ■ n. a connection, especially to mains electricity or a communications system.

hookworm ■ n. a parasitic nematode worm inhabiting the intestines and feeding by attaching itself to the wall of the gut with hook-like mouthparts. [*Ancylostoma*, *Uncinaria*, *Necator*, and other genera.]

hooky¹ ■ adj. (of a tune) catchy.

hooky² ■ n. variant spelling of HOOKEY.

561

hope

hooley ■ n. (pl. **-eys**) informal, chiefly Irish a wild or noisy party.
–ORIGIN C19.

hooligan ■ n. a violent young troublemaker.
–DERIVATIVES **hooliganism** n.
–ORIGIN C19: perhaps from *Hooligan*, the surname of a fictional rowdy Irish family in a music-hall song.

hoop ■ n. **1** a rigid circular band, especially one used for binding the staves of barrels or forming a framework. ▸ a large ring used as a toy or for circus performers to jump through. ▸ historical a circle of flexible material used to expand a woman's petticoat. **2** a metal arch through which the balls are hit in croquet. **3** a contrasting horizontal band on a sports shirt or cap. ■ v. bind or encircle with or as with hoops.
–PHRASES **put someone** (or **go**) **through the hoops** make someone undergo (or be made to undergo) a gruelling test.
–DERIVATIVES **hooped** adj.
–ORIGIN Old English, of West Germanic origin.

hoopla /ˈhuːplɑː/ ■ n. **1** Brit. a game in which rings are thrown in an attempt to encircle a prize. **2** informal unnecessary fuss.
–ORIGIN 1909: from HOOP + *la!*, used to direct attention or as an exclamation of surprise.

hoopoe /ˈhuːpuː, -pəʊ/ ■ n. a salmon-pink bird with a long downcurved bill, a large crest, and black-and-white wings and tail. [*Upupa epops*.]
–ORIGIN C17: alteration of obsolete *hoop*, from Old French *huppe*, from Latin *upupa*, imitative of the bird's call.

hooray ■ exclam. hurrah.

hoot ■ n. **1** a low musical sound made by many kinds of owl. ▸ a similar sound made by a horn, siren, etc. **2** a shout expressing scorn or disapproval. **3** an outburst of laughter. ▸ (**a hoot**) informal an amusing person or thing. ■ v. **1** make or cause to make a hoot. **2** (**hoot something down**) express loud scornful disapproval of something.
–PHRASES **not care** (or **give**) **a hoot** (or **two hoots**) informal not care at all.
–ORIGIN Middle English: perhaps imitative.

hootch ■ n. variant spelling of HOOCH.

hooter ■ n. **1** a siren, steam whistle, or horn. **2** informal a nose.

Hoover ■ n. trademark a vacuum cleaner. ■ v. (**hoover**) clean with a vacuum cleaner.
–ORIGIN 1920s: named after the American industrialist William H. *Hoover*.

hooves plural form of HOOF.

hop¹ ■ v. (**hopped**, **hopping**) **1** move by jumping on one foot. ▸ (of a bird or animal) move by jumping with two or all feet at once. ▸ jump over. ▸ informal jump on to (a vehicle). **2** informal move or go quickly. ▸ (**hop it**) Brit. go away. ▸ [usu. as noun **hopping**] pass quickly from one place to another: *island-hopping*. ■ n. **1** a hopping movement. **2** a short journey or distance. **3** an informal dance.
–PHRASES **hop, skip** (or **step**), **and jump 1** old-fashioned term for TRIPLE JUMP. **2** informal a short distance. **on the hop** Brit. informal **1** unprepared. **2** busy.
–ORIGIN Old English *hoppian*, of Germanic origin.

hop² ■ n. **1** (**hops**) the dried cone-like flowers of a twining climbing plant, used in brewing to give a bitter flavour and as a mild sterilant. ▸ Austral./NZ informal beer. **2** the plant from which hops are obtained. [*Humulus lupulus*.] ■ v. (**hopped**, **hopping**) flavour with hops.
–DERIVATIVES **hoppy** adj.
–ORIGIN Middle English *hoppe*, from Middle Low German or Middle Dutch.

hop bine ■ n. the climbing stem of the hop.

hope ■ n. **1** a feeling of expectation and desire. ▸ a person or thing that gives cause for hope. ▸ grounds for hoping. **2** archaic a feeling of trust. ■ v. expect and desire. ▸ intend if possible to do something.
–PHRASES **hope against hope** cling to a mere possibility. **not a** (or **some**) **hope** informal no chance at all.
–DERIVATIVES **hoper** n.
–ORIGIN Old English, of Germanic origin.

hopeful

hopeful ▪ adj. feeling or inspiring hope. ▪ n. a person likely or hoping to succeed.
– DERIVATIVES **hopefulness** n.

hopefully ▪ adv. **1** in a hopeful manner. **2** it is to be hoped that: *hopefully it should be finished by next year.*

USAGE
The traditional sense of **hopefully**, 'in a hopeful manner', has been used since the 17th century. In the 20th century a new use arose, with the meaning 'it is to be hoped that'. This sense is regarded by some traditionalists as incorrect, despite the fact that it is now the dominant use.

hopeless ▪ adj. **1** feeling or causing despair. **2** inadequate; incompetent.
– DERIVATIVES **hopelessly** adv. **hopelessness** n.

Hopi /ˈhoʊpi/ ▪ n. (pl. same or **Hopis**) **1** a member of a Pueblo Indian people living chiefly in NE Arizona. **2** the language of this people.
– ORIGIN the name in Hopi.

hoplite /ˈhɒplʌɪt/ ▪ n. a heavily armed foot soldier of ancient Greece.
– ORIGIN from Greek *hoplitēs*, from *hoplon* 'weapon'.

hopper ▪ n. **1** a container for grain, rock, or rubbish, typically one that tapers downward and discharges its contents at the bottom. ▶ a tapering container, working with a hopping motion, through which grain passes into a mill. **2** a railway wagon able to discharge bulk material through its floor. **3** a person or thing that hops. ▶ a hopping insect, especially a young locust.

hopping ▪ adj. informal very active or lively.
– PHRASES **hopping mad** informal extremely angry.

hopscotch ▪ n. a children's game of hopping into and over squares marked on the ground to retrieve a marker.
– ORIGIN C19: from HOP[1] + SCOTCH.

horde ▪ n. **1** chiefly derogatory a large group of people. **2** an army or tribe of nomadic warriors.
– ORIGIN C16: from Polish *horda*, from Turkish *ordu* '(royal) camp'.

horehound /ˈhɔːhaʊnd/ (also **hoarhound**) ▪ n. a strong-smelling hairy plant of the mint family, traditionally used as a medicinal herb. [*Marrubium vulgare* (**white horehound**) and *Ballota nigra* (**black horehound**).]
– ORIGIN Old English *hāre hūne*, from *hār* (see HOAR) + *hūne*, the name of the white horehound.

horizon ▪ n. **1** the line at which the earth's surface and the sky appear to meet. ▶ (also **apparent horizon**) this line represented as a circle, ignoring irregularities and obstructions. ▶ (also **true horizon**) Astronomy a great circle of the celestial sphere, the plane of which passes through the centre of the earth and is parallel to that of the apparent horizon. **2** the limit of a person's mental perception, experience, or interest. **3** Geology & Archaeology a layer or level with particular characteristics or representing a particular period.
– PHRASES **on the horizon** imminent.
– ORIGIN Middle English: from Greek *horizōn (kuklos)* 'limiting (circle)'.

horizontal ▪ adj. **1** parallel to the plane of the horizon. **2** uniform; based on uniformity. ▶ combining firms engaged in the same stage or type of production: *a horizontal merger.* **3** of or at the horizon. ▪ n. **1** a horizontal line or plane. **2** a horizontal structure.
– DERIVATIVES **horizontality** n. **horizontally** adv.

hormonal ▪ adj. /hɔːˈməʊn(ə)l/ relating to or containing a hormone or hormones. ▶ informal affected by one's sex hormones.
– DERIVATIVES **hormonally** adv.

hormone ▪ n. Physiology a regulatory substance produced by a living organism and transported in tissue fluids to stimulate specific cells or tissues into action.
– ORIGIN C20: from Greek *hormōn*, from *horman* 'set in motion'.

hormone replacement therapy ▪ n. treatment with oestrogens to alleviate menopausal symptoms or osteoporosis.

horn ▪ n. **1** a hard permanent outgrowth of bone encased in hardened skin, often curved and pointed and found in pairs on the heads of cattle and other animals. ▶ a projection of similar appearance on the head of another animal, e.g. a snail's tentacle. ▶ (**horns**) archaic a pair of horns as an emblem of a cuckold. **2** the substance of which horns are composed. ▶ a receptacle or instrument made of horn, such as a drinking container. **3** a sharp promontory or mountain peak. ▶ (**the Horn**) Cape Horn. ▶ an arm or branch of a river or bay. ▶ the extremity of the moon or other crescent. **4** a wind instrument, conical in shape or wound into a spiral, originally made of horn (now typically brass). **5** an instrument sounding a warning or other signal. ▪ v. **1** butt or gore with the horns. **2** (**horn in**) informal interfere.
– PHRASES **blow** (or **toot**) **one's own horn** N. Amer. informal boast about oneself or one's achievements. **draw** (or **pull**) **in one's horns** become less assertive or ambitious. **on the horn** N. Amer. informal on the telephone. **on the horns of a dilemma** faced with a decision involving equally unfavourable alternatives.
– DERIVATIVES **horned** adj. **hornist** n. **hornless** adj. **horn-like** adj.
– ORIGIN Old English, of Germanic origin.

hornbeam ▪ n. a deciduous tree of Eurasia and North America with oval serrated leaves, tough winged nuts, and hard pale wood. [Genus *Carpinus*: several species.]
– ORIGIN Middle English: so named because of the tree's hard wood.

hornbill ▪ n. a medium to large tropical bird with a very large curved bill that typically has a large horny or bony casque. [Family Bucerotidae: numerous species.]

hornblende /ˈhɔːnblɛnd/ ▪ n. a dark brown, black, or green mineral consisting of a silicate of calcium, magnesium, and iron and present in many rocks.
– ORIGIN C18: from German, from *Horn* 'horn' + *blende* 'sphalerite'.

horned owl (also **great horned owl**) ▪ n. a large owl found throughout North and South America, with horn-like ear tufts. [*Bubo virginianus*.]

horned poppy ▪ n. a Eurasian poppy with greyish-green lobed leaves, large flowers, and a long curved seed capsule. [*Glaucium flavum* and related species.]

horned toad ▪ n. **1** an American lizard with spiny skin and large spines on the head. [*Phrynosoma cornutum* and other species.] **2** a large toad with horn-shaped projections of skin over the eyes. [*Megophrys* (SE Asia), *Ceratophrys* (S. America), and other genera.]

hornet ▪ n. a large wasp which is typically red and yellow or red and black and usually nests in hollow trees. [*Vespa crabro* (Europe) and other species.]
– PHRASES **stir up a hornets' nest** provoke opposition or difficulties.
– ORIGIN Old English, of Germanic origin.

hornfels /ˈhɔːnfɛlz/ ▪ n. a dark, fine-grained metamorphic rock consisting largely of quartz, mica, and feldspars.
– ORIGIN C19: from German, 'horn rock'.

horn of plenty ▪ n. a cornucopia.

hornpipe ▪ n. a lively solo dance traditionally performed by sailors. ▶ a piece of music for such a dance.
– ORIGIN Middle English (denoting a wind instrument made of horn, played to accompany dancing): from HORN + PIPE.

horn-rimmed ▪ adj. (of glasses) having rims made of horn or a similar substance.

hornworm ▪ n. chiefly N. Amer. a hawkmoth caterpillar with a spike on its tail, some kinds of which are pests of tobacco and other crops.

horny ▪ adj. (**-ier**, **-iest**) **1** of or resembling horn. ▶ hard and rough. **2** informal sexually aroused or arousing.
– DERIVATIVES **horniness** n.

horology /hɒˈrɒlədʒi/ ▪ n. **1** the study and measurement of time. **2** the art of making clocks and watches.
– DERIVATIVES **horologer** n. **horologic** adj. **horological** adj. **horologist** n.
– ORIGIN C19: from Greek *hōra* 'time' + -LOGY.

horoscope ■ n. a forecast of a person's future based on the relative positions of the stars and planets at the time of their birth.
– DERIVATIVES **horoscopic** /-'skɒpɪk/ adj. **horoscopy** /hɒ'rɒskəpi/ n.
– ORIGIN Old English: from Greek *hōroskopos*, from *hōra* 'time' + *skopos* 'observer'.

horrendous /hɒ'rɛndəs/ ■ adj. extremely unpleasant or horrifying.
– DERIVATIVES **horrendously** adv.
– ORIGIN C17: from Latin *horrendus*, from *horrere* (see HORRID).

horrible ■ adj. **1** causing or likely to cause horror. **2** informal very unpleasant.
– DERIVATIVES **horribleness** n. **horribly** adv.
– ORIGIN Middle English: from Latin *horribilis*, from *horrere* (see HORRID).

horrid ■ adj. **1** causing horror. **2** informal very unpleasant. **3** poetic/literary rough; bristling.
– DERIVATIVES **horridly** adv. **horridness** n.
– ORIGIN C16: from Latin *horridus*, from *horrere* 'shudder, (of hair) stand on end'.

horries ■ pl. n. (**the horries**) S. African informal delirium tremens.
– ORIGIN var. of *horrors*, perhaps via Afrikaans.

horrific ■ adj. causing horror.
– DERIVATIVES **horrifically** adv.
– ORIGIN C17: from Latin *horrificus*, from *horrere* (see HORRID).

horrify ■ v. (**-ies, -ied**) fill with horror.
– DERIVATIVES **horrification** n. **horrified** adj. **horrifiedly** adv. **horrifying** adj. **horrifyingly** adv.
– ORIGIN C18: from Latin *horrificare*, from *horrificus* (see HORRIFIC).

horror ■ n. **1** an intense feeling of fear, shock, or disgust. ▶ a thing causing such a feeling. ▶ intense dismay. **2** informal a bad or mischievous person, especially a child.
– ORIGIN Middle English: from Latin *horror*, from *horrere* (see HORRID).

hors de combat /ˌɔː də 'kɒbɑː/ ■ adj. out of action due to injury or damage.
– ORIGIN French, 'out of the fight'.

hors d'oeuvre /ɔː 'dɜːv, 'dɜːvr(ə)/ ■ n. (pl. same or **hors d'oeuvres** pronunc. same or /'dɜːvz/) a savoury appetizer.
– ORIGIN French, 'outside the work'.

horse ■ n. **1** a solid-hoofed plant-eating quadruped with a flowing mane and tail, domesticated for riding and as a draught animal. [*Equus caballus* and other species, family Equidae.] ▶ an adult male horse, as opposed to a mare or colt. ▶ [treated as sing. or pl.] historical cavalry. **2** a frame or structure on which something is mounted or supported. **3** informal a unit of horsepower. **4** Mining an obstruction in a vein. ■ v. **1** provide with a horse or horses. **2** (**horse around/about**) informal fool about.
– PHRASES **from the horse's mouth** (of information) from an authoritative source. **to horse** (as a command) mount your horses!
– DERIVATIVES **horseless** adj. **horse-like** adj.
– ORIGIN Old English, of Germanic origin.

horseback ■ adj. & adv. mounted on a horse.

horsebean ■ n. a field bean of a variety with relatively large seeds, used as fodder.

horsebox ■ n. a motorized vehicle or a trailer for transporting one or more horses.

horse chestnut ■ n. **1** a deciduous Eurasian tree with large leaves of five leaflets, upright conical clusters of white, pink, or red flowers, and nuts enclosed in a spiny case. [*Aesculus hippocastanum* and related species.] **2** the nut of this tree; a conker.
– ORIGIN C16: translating (now obsolete) botanical Latin *Castanea equina*; its fruit is said to have been an Eastern remedy for chest diseases in horses.

horseflesh ■ n. horses considered collectively.

horsefly ■ n. (pl. **-flies**) a stoutly built fly, the female of which is a bloodsucker and inflicts painful bites on horses and other large mammals. [*Haematopota pluvialis* and other species, family Tabanidae.]

Horse Guards ■ pl. n. (in the UK) the mounted squadrons provided from the Household Cavalry for ceremonial duties.

horsehair ■ n. hair from the mane or tail of a horse, used in furniture for padding.

horse latitudes ■ pl. n. a belt of calm air and sea occurring in both the northern and southern hemispheres between the trade winds and the westerlies.
– ORIGIN C18.

horse laugh ■ n. a loud, coarse laugh.

horseleech ■ n. a large predatory leech of freshwater and terrestrial habitats which feeds on carrion and small invertebrates. [Genus *Haemopis*.]

horse mackerel ■ n. another term for MAASBANKER.

horseman (or **horsewoman**) ■ n. (pl. **-men** or **-women**) a rider on horseback, especially a skilled one.
– DERIVATIVES **horsemanship** n.

horse mushroom ■ n. a large edible mushroom with a creamy-white cap. [*Agaricus arvensis*.]

horse opera ■ n. N. Amer. informal a western film.

horseplay ■ n. rough, boisterous play.

horsepower (abbrev.: **h.p.**) ■ n. (pl. same) an imperial unit of power equal to 550 foot-pounds per second (about 750 watts). ▶ engine power measured in terms of this.

horse racing ■ n. a sport in which horses and their riders take part in races, either on a flat course or over hurdles or fences.

horseradish ■ n. a plant of the cabbage family with long broad leaves, grown for its pungent root which is often made into a sauce. [*Armoracia rusticana*.]

horse sense ■ n. informal common sense.

horseshoe ■ n. a shoe for a horse formed of a narrow band of iron in the form of an extended circular arc. ▶ (**horseshoes**) [treated as sing.] chiefly N. Amer. a game resembling quoits in which horseshoes are thrown at a peg.

horseshoe bat ■ n. an insectivorous bat with a horseshoe-shaped ridge on the nose. [Genus *Rhinolophus*: many species.]

horseshoe crab ■ n. a large marine arthropod with a domed horseshoe-shaped shell and a long tail spine. [*Limulus polyphemus* (N. America) and other species.]

horse sickness ■ n. short for AFRICAN HORSE SICKNESS.

horsetail ■ n. a flowerless spore-producing plant with a hollow jointed stem bearing whorls of narrow leaves. [Genus *Equisetum*, class Sphenopsida.]

horse-trading ■ n. informal hard and shrewd bargaining.
– DERIVATIVES **horse-trade** v. **horse-trader** n.

horsewhip ■ n. a long whip used for driving and controlling horses. ■ v. (**-whipped, -whipping**) beat with such a whip.

horsey (also **horsy**) ■ adj. (**-ier, -iest**) **1** of or resembling a horse. **2** concerned with or devoted to horses or horse racing.
– DERIVATIVES **horsily** adv. **horsiness** n.

horst /hɔːst/ ■ n. Geology a raised elongated block of the earth's crust lying between two faults.
– ORIGIN C19: from German *Horst* 'heap'.

hortatory /'hɔːtət(ə)ri/ ■ adj. formal tending or aiming to exhort.
– DERIVATIVES **hortation** n. **hortative** adj.
– ORIGIN C16: from Latin *hortatorius*, from *hortari* 'exhort'.

horticulture /'hɔːtɪˌkʌltʃə/ ■ n. the art or practice of garden cultivation and management.
– DERIVATIVES **horticultural** adj. **horticulturalist** n. **horticulturist** n.
– ORIGIN C17: from Latin *hortus* 'garden' + CULTURE.

hosanna (also **hosannah**) ■ n. & exclam. (especially in biblical use) a cry of praise or joy.
– ORIGIN Old English, from Greek *hōsanna*, from Rabbinical Hebrew *hōšaʿnā*, abbrev. of biblical *hōšīʿā-nnā* 'save, we pray' (Psalms 118:25).

hose ■ n. **1** a flexible tube conveying water, used chiefly

hosel

for watering plants and in firefighting. **2** [treated as pl.] stockings, socks, and tights. ▸ historical breeches. ■ v. water or spray with a hose.
– ORIGIN Old English, of Germanic origin.

hosel /ˈhəʊz(ə)l/ ■ n. the socket of a golf club head which the shaft fits into.
– ORIGIN C16: diminutive of HOSE, in the dialect sense 'sheathing'.

hosepipe ■ n. another term for HOSE (in sense 1).

hosier /ˈhəʊzɪə/ ■ n. a manufacturer or seller of hosiery.

hosiery ■ n. stockings, socks, and tights collectively.

hospice ■ n. **1** a home providing care for the sick or terminally ill. **2** archaic a lodging for travellers, especially one run by a religious order.
– ORIGIN C19: from Latin *hospitium*, from *hospes* (see HOST[1]).

hospitable /hɒˈspɪtəb(ə)l, ˈhɒspɪt-/ ■ adj. **1** showing or inclined to show hospitality. **2** (of an environment) pleasant and favourable for living in.
– DERIVATIVES **hospitably** adv.
– ORIGIN C16: from French, from obsolete *hospiter* 'receive a guest', from Latin *hospes, hospit-* (see HOST[1]).

hospital ■ n. **1** an institution providing medical and surgical treatment and nursing care for sick or injured people. **2** historical a hospice.
– DERIVATIVES **hospitalization** (also **-isation**) n. **hospitalize** (also **-ise**) v.
– ORIGIN Middle English: from Latin *hospitalis* 'hospitable', from *hospes, hospit-* (see HOST[1]).

hospital corners ■ pl. n. overlapping folds used to tuck sheets neatly and securely under the mattress at the corners, in a manner used in hospitals.

hospital fever ■ n. historical louse-borne typhus acquired in overcrowded, insanitary conditions in an old-fashioned hospital.

hospitality ■ n. the friendly and generous reception and entertainment of guests or strangers. ▸ [as modifier] relating to or denoting the business of entertaining tourists, clients or official visitors.
– ORIGIN Middle English: from Latin *hospitalitas*, from *hospitalis* (see HOSPITAL).

hospitaller /ˈhɒspɪt(ə)lə/ (US **hospitaler**) ■ n. a member of a charitable religious order.
– ORIGIN Middle English: from medieval Latin *hospitalarius*, from *hospitale* (see HOSPITAL).

hospital ship ■ n. a ship which functions as a hospital, especially to receive or take home sick or wounded military personnel.

host[1] ■ n. **1** a person who receives or entertains other people as guests. ▸ the presenter of a television or radio programme. **2** Biology an animal or plant on or in which a parasite or commensal organism lives. **3** the recipient of transplanted tissue or a transplanted organ. **4** a computer which mediates multiple access to databases or provides other services to a network. ■ v. act as host at (an event) or for (a television or radio programme).
– ORIGIN Middle English: from Old French *hoste*, from Latin *hospes, hospit-* 'host, guest'.

host[2] ■ n. **1** (**a host/hosts of**) a large number of. **2** archaic an army.
– ORIGIN Middle English: from Old French *ost, hoost*, from Latin *hostis* 'stranger, enemy', in medieval Latin, 'army'.

host[3] ■ n. (**the Host**) Christian Church the bread consecrated in the Eucharist.
– ORIGIN Middle English: from Latin *hostia* 'victim'.

hosta /ˈhɒstə/ ■ n. an East Asian plant cultivated chiefly for its shade-tolerant ornamental foliage. [Genus *Hosta*.]
– ORIGIN named after the Austrian physician Nicolaus T. Host.

hostage ■ n. a person seized or held as security for the fulfilment of a condition.
– PHRASES **a hostage to fortune** an act or remark regarded as unwise because it invites trouble.
– ORIGIN Middle English: based on late Latin *obsidatus* 'the state of being a hostage', from Latin *obses* 'hostage'.

hostel ■ n. **1** an establishment which provides cheap food and lodging for a specific group of people. ▸ S. African a boarding house for black mineworkers or migrants to urban areas. ▸ S. African a boarding house for pupils attending a school or for students at a university. **2** archaic an inn providing accommodation.
– ORIGIN Middle English: from Old French, from medieval Latin *hospitale* (see HOSPITAL).

hostelling (US **hosteling**) ■ n. the practice of staying in youth hostels when travelling.
– DERIVATIVES **hosteller** n.

hostelry ■ n. (pl. **-ies**) archaic or humorous an inn or pub.
– ORIGIN Middle English: from Old French, from *hostelier* 'innkeeper', from *hostel* (see HOSTEL).

hostess ■ n. a female host. ▸ a woman employed to welcome and entertain customers at a nightclub or bar. ▸ a stewardess on an aircraft, train, etc.

hostile ■ adj. antagonistic; opposed. ▸ of or belonging to a military enemy. ▸ (of a takeover bid) opposed by the company to be bought.
– DERIVATIVES **hostilely** adv.
– ORIGIN Middle English (as *hostility*): from Latin *hostilis*, from *hostis* 'stranger, enemy'.

hostile witness ■ n. Law a witness who is antagonistic to the party calling them.

hostility ■ n. (pl. **-ties**) hostile behaviour. ▸ (**hostilities**) acts of warfare: *a cessation of hostilities.*

hostler ■ n. variant spelling of OSTLER.

hot ■ adj. (**hotter, hottest**) **1** having a high temperature. ▸ feeling or producing an uncomfortable sensation of heat. ▸ causing a burning sensation in the mouth. ▸ informal at a high voltage; live. ▸ informal radioactive. **2** feeling or showing intense excitement, anger, lust, or other emotion. **3** currently popular, fashionable, or interesting. ▸ Hunting (of the scent) fresh and strong. ▸ (in children's games) very close to finding or guessing something. ▸ informal (of goods) stolen and difficult to dispose of because easily identifiable. **4** (often **hot on**) informal very knowledgeable or skilful. ▸ [usu. with neg.] good; promising. **5** (**hot on**) informal strict about. ■ v. (**hotted, hotting**) **1** (**hot up**) or **hot something up** informal become or make more intense or exciting. **2** (**hot up**) informal become hot.
– PHRASES **go hot and cold** experience a sudden feeling of fear or shock. **have the hots for** informal be sexually attracted to. **hot under the collar** informal angry or resentful. **in hot water** informal in trouble or disgrace. **make** (or **things**) **hot for** informal stir up trouble for (someone).
– DERIVATIVES **hotly** adv. **hotness** n. **hottish** adj.
– ORIGIN Old English, of Germanic origin.

hot air ■ n. informal empty or boastful talk.

hotbed ■ n. **1** a bed of earth heated by fermenting manure, for raising or forcing plants. **2** an environment promoting the growth of an activity or trend.

hot-blooded ■ adj. lustful; passionate.

hot box ■ n. another term for WONDERBOX.

hotchpotch (N. Amer. **hodgepodge**) ■ n. a confused mixture.
– ORIGIN Middle English: var. of obsolete *hotchpot*, from Anglo-Norman French and Old French *hochepot*, from *hocher* 'to shake' + *pot* 'pot'.

hot cross bun ■ n. a bun marked with a cross and containing dried fruit, traditionally eaten on Good Friday.

hot-desking ■ n. the allocation of desks to office workers when they are required or on a rota system.

hot dog ■ n. **1** a hot sausage served in a long, soft roll. **2** N. Amer. informal a person, especially a skier or surfer, who performs clever moves. ■ exclam. N. Amer. informal used to express enthusiastic approval. ■ v. (**hotdog**) N. Amer. informal perform clever moves.
– DERIVATIVES **hotdogger** n.

hotel ■ n. **1** an establishment providing accommodation and meals for travellers and tourists. ▸ chiefly Austral./NZ a public house. **2** a code word representing the letter H, used in radio communication.
– ORIGIN C18: from French *hôtel*, from Old French *hostel* (see HOSTEL).

hotelier ■ n. a person who owns or manages a hotel.
– ORIGIN C20: from French *hôtelier*.

hot flush (also **hot flash**) ■ n. a sudden feeling of feverish heat, typically as a symptom of the menopause.

hotfoot ■ adv. in eager haste. ■ v. (**hotfoot it**) hurry eagerly.

hot gospel ■ n. informal zealous evangelism.
– DERIVATIVES **hot gospeller** n.

hothead ■ n. an impetuous or quick-tempered person.
– DERIVATIVES **hot-headed** adj. **hot-headedly** adv. **hot-headedness** n.

hothouse ■ n. 1 a heated greenhouse. 2 an environment that encourages rapid growth or development. ■ v. educate (a child) to a higher level than is usual for their age.

hot key ■ n. Computing a key or combination of keys providing quick access to a function within a program.

hotline ■ n. a direct telephone line set up for a specific purpose, especially for use in emergencies or for communication between heads of government.

hot metal ■ n. a typesetting technique in which type is newly made each time from molten metal.

hot money ■ n. capital which is frequently transferred between financial institutions in an attempt to maximize interest or capital gain.

hot pants ■ pl. n. women's very tight, brief shorts.

hotplate ■ n. a flat heated metal or ceramic surface on an electric cooker.

hotpot ■ n. Brit. a casserole of meat and vegetables with a covering layer of sliced potato.

hot potato ■ n. informal a controversial and awkward issue or situation.

hot rod ■ n. a motor vehicle that has been specially modified to give it extra power and speed. ■ v. (**hot-rod**) 1 modify (a vehicle or other device) to make it faster or more powerful. 2 drive a hot rod.
– DERIVATIVES **hot-rodder** n.

hot seat ■ n. (**the hot seat**) informal 1 the position of a person who carries full responsibility for something. 2 chiefly N. Amer. the electric chair.

hot shoe ■ n. Photography a socket on a camera with direct electrical contacts for an attached flashgun or other accessory.

hotshot ■ n. informal an important or exceptionally able person. ▸ a sports player with a good aim.

hot spot ■ n. 1 a small area with a relatively high temperature. 2 a place of significant activity or danger. 3 a place in a public building that is equipped with a device enabling computer users to make a wireless connection to the Internet.

hot spring ■ n. a spring of naturally hot water, typically heated by subterranean volcanic activity.

hotspur /'hɒtspə:, -spə/ ■ n. archaic a rash, impetuous person.
– ORIGIN Middle English, 'a person whose spur is hot from rash or constant riding'.

hot stuff ■ n. informal a person or thing of outstanding talent or interest. ▸ a sexually exciting person, book, etc.

hot-swap ■ v. informal fit or replace (a computer part) with the power still connected.
– DERIVATIVES **hot-swappable** adj.

hot-tempered ■ adj. easily angered.

Hottentot /'hɒt(ə)ntɒt/ ■ n. 1 historical the Khoikhoi people. 2 (also **hottentot**) an edible marine fish of southern African coastal waters with a bronzy-brown body. [*Pachymetopon blochi* and *P. aeneum*.] ■ adj. historical used to refer to Khoikhoi peoples.
– ORIGIN Dutch, perhaps a repetitive formula in a Nama dancing song, transferred by European travellers to the people themselves.

USAGE
The word **Hottentot** is now regarded as offensive with reference to people (where **Khoikhoi** is the standard term) but is still standard when used in the names of some animals and plants.

Hottentot fig ■ n. a succulent mat-forming plant with bright yellow or lilac daisy-like flowers and edible fruit, native to South Africa and naturalized elsewhere. [*Carpobrotus edulis*.]

Hottentot's cabbage ■ n. a low-growing plant with edible asparagus-like inflorescences which bear star-shaped pink and white flowers, native to southern Africa. [Genus *Trachyandra*: several species.]

hot ticket ■ n. informal a person or thing that is much in demand.

hottie (also **hotty**) ■ n. (pl. **-ies**) informal 1 a hot-water bottle. 2 a sexually attractive person.

hot tub ■ n. a large tub filled with hot aerated water used for recreation or physical therapy.

hot war ■ n. a war with active military hostilities.

hot-water bottle (US also **hot-water bag**) ■ n. a flat, oblong rubber container that is filled with hot water and used for warming a bed or part of the body.

hot-wire ■ v. informal start the engine of (a vehicle) by bypassing the ignition switch.

Houdini /huːˈdiːni/ ■ n. a person skilled at escaping.
– ORIGIN C20: from the name of Harry *Houdini* (Erik Weisz), American magician and escape artist.

hoummos ■ n. variant spelling of HUMMUS.

hound ■ n. 1 a dog of a breed used for hunting, especially one able to track by scent. 2 a person keen in pursuit of something: *a publicity hound*. ■ v. harass or pursue relentlessly.
– ORIGIN Old English, of Germanic origin.

hound's tongue ■ n. a tall plant with small purplish flowers, tongue-shaped leaves, and a mousy smell. [*Cynoglossum officinale* and other species.]

houndstooth ■ n. a large dog-tooth pattern.

houngan /'huːŋɡ(ə)n/ ■ n. a voodoo priest.
– ORIGIN C20: from Fon, from *hun*, a deity represented by a fetish, + *ga* 'chief'.

hour ■ n. 1 a period of time equal to a twenty-fourth part of a day and night and divided into 60 minutes. 2 a time of day specified as an exact number of hours from midnight or midday. ▸ (**hours**) [with preceding numeral] a time so specified on the 24-hour clock. 3 a period set aside for a particular purpose or marked by a specific activity: *leisure hours*. ▸ a point in time: *the shop is half-full even at this hour*. 4 (**hours**) (in the Western (Latin) Church) a short service of psalms and prayers to be said at a particular time of day. 5 Astronomy 15° of longitude or right ascension (one twenty-fourth part of a circle).
– PHRASES **on the hour 1** at an exact hour, or on each hour, of the day or night. **2** after a period of one hour.
– ORIGIN Middle English: from Greek *hōra* 'season, hour'.

hourglass ■ n. an invertible device with two connected glass bulbs containing sand that takes an hour to pass from the upper to the lower bulb.

houri /'hʊəri/ ■ n. (pl. **houris**) one of the virgin companions of the faithful in the Muslim Paradise.
– ORIGIN C18: from Persian *ḥūrī*, from Arabic *ḥūr*, pl. of *'aḥwar* 'having eyes with a marked contrast of black and white'.

hourly ■ adj. 1 done or occurring every hour. 2 reckoned hour by hour. ■ adv. 1 every hour. 2 by the hour.

house ■ n. /haʊs/ 1 a building for human habitation. ▸ a building in which animals live or in which things are kept. 2 a building in which people meet for a particular activity. ▸ a firm or institution: *a fashion house*. ▸ (**the House**) Brit. informal the Stock Exchange. ▸ a restaurant or inn. 3 a religious community that occupies a particular building. ▸ a body of pupils living in the same building at a boarding school. ▸ Brit. formal a college of a university. 4 a legislative or deliberative assembly. ▸ (**the House**) (in the UK) the House of Commons or Lords; (in the US) the House of Representatives. 5 a dynasty. 6 (also **house music**) a style of fast popular dance music typically using drum machines and synthesized bass lines. 7 Astrology a twelfth division of the celestial sphere. ■ adj. 1 (of an animal or plant) kept in, frequenting, or infesting buildings. 2 of or relating to medical staff resident at a hospital. 3 of or relating to a firm, institution, or society. ■ v. /haʊz/

house arrest

1 provide with shelter or accommodation. **2** provide space for. ▶ enclose or encase.
– PHRASES **get on** (or **along**) **like a house on fire** informal have a very good and friendly relationship. **go (all) round the houses** take a circuitous route. **keep house** run a household. **on the house** (of a drink or meal in a bar or restaurant) at the management's expense. **put** (or **set** or **get**) **one's house in order** make necessary reforms.
– DERIVATIVES **houseful** n. (pl. **-fuls**). **houseless** adj.
– ORIGIN Old English, of Germanic origin.

house arrest ■ n. the state of being kept as a prisoner in one's own house.

houseboat ■ n. a boat which is fitted for use as a dwelling.

housebound ■ adj. unable to leave one's house, typically due to illness or old age.

houseboy ■ n. dated, offensive a boy or man employed to undertake domestic duties.

housebreak ■ v. chiefly N. Amer. another term for HOUSE-TRAIN.

housebreaking ■ n. the action of breaking into a building to commit a crime.
– DERIVATIVES **housebreaker** n.

housecoat ■ n. a woman's long, loose, lightweight robe for informal wear around the house.

house cricket ■ n. a cricket with a birdlike warble, native to North Africa and SW Asia and found in warm buildings elsewhere. [*Acheta domesticus*.]

housefather (or **housemother**) ■ n. a person in charge of and living in a boarding school house or children's home.

housefly ■ n. (pl. **-flies**) a common small fly occurring in and around human habitation and laying its eggs in decaying material. [*Musca domestica*.]

household ■ n. a house and its occupants regarded as a unit.

Household Cavalry ■ n. (in the British army) the two cavalry regiments with responsibility for guarding the monarch.

householder ■ n. a person who owns or rents a house.

household name (also **household word**) ■ n. a famous person or thing.

house-hunting ■ n. the process of seeking a house to buy or rent.
– DERIVATIVES **house-hunter** n.

house husband ■ n. a man who lives with a partner and carries out the household duties traditionally done by a housewife.

housekeeper ■ n. a person, typically a woman, employed to manage a household.
– DERIVATIVES **housekeep** v. (dated).

housekeeping ■ n. **1** the management of household affairs. ▶ money set aside for this. **2** non-productive but necessary routine operations such as record-keeping or administration in a computer or other system.

houseleek /ˈhaʊsliːk/ ■ n. a succulent Eurasian plant, cultivated elsewhere, with rosettes of fleshy leaves and small pink flowers, growing naturally on walls and roofs. [*Sempervivum tectorum* and other species.]

house lights ■ pl. n. the lights in the auditorium of a theatre.

housemaid ■ n. a female domestic employee who cleans rooms.

housemaid's knee ■ n. inflammation of the fluid-filled cavity covering the kneecap, often due to excessive kneeling.

houseman ■ n. (pl. **-men**) another term for HOUSE OFFICER.
– DERIVATIVES **housemanship** n. (S. African).

house martin ■ n. a black-and-white bird of the swallow family which builds mud nests on the walls of buildings. [*Delichon urbica*.]

housemaster (or **housemistress**) ■ n. a teacher in charge of a house at a boarding school.

house mouse ■ n. a greyish-brown mouse found abundantly as a scavenger in human dwellings. [*Mus musculus*.]

House of Commons ■ n. (in the UK) the elected chamber of Parliament.

house of correction ■ n. historical an institution where vagrants and minor offenders were confined and set to work.

house officer ■ n. Brit. a recent medical graduate receiving supervised training in a hospital and acting as an assistant physician or surgeon.

house of God ■ n. a place of religious worship, especially a church.

house of ill fame (also **house of ill repute**) ■ n. archaic or humorous a brothel.

House of Lords ■ n. (in the UK) the chamber of Parliament composed of peers and bishops. ▶ a committee of specially qualified members of this, appointed as the ultimate judicial appeal court of England and Wales.

House of Representatives ■ n. the lower house of the US Congress and other legislatures.

house plant ■ n. a plant which is grown indoors.

house-proud ■ adj. attentive to, or preoccupied with, the care and appearance of one's home.

houseroom ■ n. space or accommodation in one's house.
– PHRASES **not give something houseroom** Brit. be unwilling to have or consider something.

house-sit ■ v. live in and look after a house while its owner is away.
– DERIVATIVES **house-sitter** n.

Houses of Parliament ■ pl. n. (in the UK) the Houses of Lords and Commons regarded together.

house sparrow ■ n. a common brown and grey sparrow that nests in the eaves and roofs of houses. [*Passer domesticus*.]

house-to-house ■ adj. & adv. performed at or taken to each house in turn.

house-train ■ v. train (a pet) to excrete outside the house.

house-warming ■ n. a party celebrating a move to a new home.

housewife ■ n. (pl. **-wives**) **1** a married woman whose main occupation is caring for her family and running the household. **2** /ˈhʌzɪf/ a small case for needles, thread, and other small sewing items.
– DERIVATIVES **housewifely** adj. **housewifery** n.

housework ■ n. regular work done in housekeeping, such as cleaning and cooking.

housing ■ n. **1** houses and flats considered collectively. ▶ the provision of accommodation. **2** a rigid casing that houses a piece of moving or delicate equipment.

housing estate ■ n. a residential area planned and built as a unit.

hove chiefly Nautical past of HEAVE.

hovel ■ n. a small squalid or poorly constructed dwelling.
– ORIGIN Middle English.

hover ■ v. remain in one place in the air. ▶ linger close at hand in an uncertain manner. ▶ remain at or near a particular level. ■ n. an act of hovering.
– DERIVATIVES **hoverer** n.
– ORIGIN Middle English: from archaic *hove* 'hover, linger'.

hovercraft ■ n. (pl. same) a vehicle or craft that travels over land or water on a cushion of air provided by a downward blast.

hoverfly ■ n. (pl. **-flies**) a fly, typically black and yellow, which frequently hovers in the air and feeds on the nectar of flowers. [Family Syrphidae: many species.]

hoverport ■ n. a terminal for hovercraft.

how[1] ■ adv. **1** in what way or by what means. **2** in what condition or health. **3** to what extent or degree. **4** that. ▶ however.
– PHRASES **and how!** informal very much so. **how about?** would you like? **the how and why** the methods and reasons for doing something. **how do you do?** a formal greeting. **how many** what number. **how much** what amount or price. **how now?** archaic what is the meaning of

hugger-mugger

this? **how's that?** Cricket is the batsman out or not? (said by an umpire).
– ORIGIN Old English, of West Germanic origin; rel. to WHO and WHAT.

how² ■ exclam. a greeting attributed to North American Indians.
– ORIGIN C19: perhaps from Sioux *háo* or Omaha *hou*.

howbeit ■ adv. archaic nevertheless.

howdah /ˈhaʊdə/ ■ n. (in the Indian subcontinent) a seat for riding on the back of an elephant, usually having a canopy.
– ORIGIN from Urdu *haudah*, from Arabic *hawdaj* 'litter'.

how-do-you-do (also **how-de-do** or **how-d'ye-do**) ■ n. informal an awkward or annoying situation.

howdy ■ exclam. N. Amer. an informal friendly greeting.
– ORIGIN C19: alteration of *how d'ye*.

however ■ adv. **1** used to introduce a statement contrasting with a previous one. **2** in whatever way. ▸ to whatever extent.

howitzer /ˈhaʊtsə/ ■ n. a short gun for firing shells on high trajectories at low velocities.
– ORIGIN C17: from Dutch *houwitser*, from German *Haubitze*, from Czech *houfnice* 'catapult'.

howl ■ n. a long doleful cry uttered by an animal such as a dog. ▸ a loud cry of pain, amusement, etc. ■ v. make a howling sound.
– ORIGIN Middle English *houle*, prob. imitative.

howler ■ n. **1** informal a ludicrous mistake. **2** (also **howler monkey**) a fruit-eating monkey with a loud howling call, native to the forests of tropical America. [Genus *Alouatta*: several species.]

howling ■ adj. informal great: *a howling success*.

howsoever formal or archaic ■ adv. to whatever extent. ■ conj. in whatever way.

howzat ■ exclam. Cricket shortened form of how's that, (see HOW¹).

howzit ■ exclam. S. African an informal friendly greeting.
– ORIGIN 1970s: contracted form of *how is it?*

hoy ■ exclam. used to attract someone's attention.
– ORIGIN Middle English: natural exclam.

hoya /ˈhɔɪə/ ■ n. an evergreen climbing shrub with ornamental foliage and waxy flowers, native to SE Asia and the Pacific. [Genus *Hoya*.]
– ORIGIN C19: named after the English gardener Thomas Hoy.

hoyden /ˈhɔɪd(ə)n/ ■ n. dated a boisterous girl.
– DERIVATIVES **hoydenish** adj.
– ORIGIN C16: prob. from Middle Dutch *heiden* (see HEATHEN).

h.p. (also **HP**) ■ abbrev. **1** high pressure. **2** hire purchase. **3** horsepower.

HQ ■ abbrev. headquarters.

hr ■ abbrev. hour.

HRC ■ abbrev. (in South Africa) Human Rights Commission.

HRH ■ abbrev. Brit. Her or His Royal Highness (as a title).

hrs ■ abbrev. hours.

HRT ■ abbrev. hormone replacement therapy.

Hs ■ symb. the chemical element hassium.

HSRC ■ abbrev. (in South Africa) Human Sciences Research Council.

HT ■ abbrev. (electrical) high tension.

HTML ■ n. Computing Hypertext Mark-up Language.

HTTP ■ abbrev. Computing Hypertext Transport (or Transfer) Protocol.

hub ■ n. **1** the central part of a wheel, rotating on or with the axle, and from which the spokes radiate. **2** the centre of an activity, region, or network.
– ORIGIN C16 (denoting a shelf at the side of a fireplace used for heating pans): cf. HOB.

Hubbard squash ■ n. a very large winter squash with a warty green or bluish rind and yellow flesh. [*Cucurbita maxima*.]
– ORIGIN C19: named after Mrs Elizabeth *Hubbard*, who brought it to the attention of a seedsman in the US state of Massachusetts.

hubble-bubble (S. African also **hubbly-bubbly** or **hubbly**) ■ n. a hookah.
– ORIGIN C17: imitative repetition of BUBBLE.

Hubble's law ■ n. Astronomy a law stating that the speed of recession of a galaxy (due to the expansion of the universe) is related to its distance by a constant factor (Hubble's constant).
– ORIGIN 1930s: named after the American astronomer Edwin P. *Hubble*.

hubbub ■ n. a chaotic din caused by a crowd. ▸ a busy, noisy situation.
– ORIGIN C16: perhaps of Irish origin.

hubby ■ n. (pl. **-ies**) informal a husband.

hubcap ■ n. a cover for the hub of a motor vehicle's wheel.

hubris /ˈhjuːbrɪs/ ■ n. excessive pride or self-confidence. ▸ (in Greek tragedy) excessive pride or presumption towards the gods, leading to nemesis.
– DERIVATIVES **hubristic** adj.
– ORIGIN from Greek.

huckleberry ■ n. **1** a soft edible blue-black fruit resembling a currant. **2** the low-growing North American plant of the heath family which bears this fruit. [Genus *Gaylussacia*.]
– ORIGIN C16: prob. orig. a dialect name for the bilberry, from dialect *huckle* 'hip, haunch' (because of the plant's jointed stems).

huckster ■ n. **1** a person who sells small items, either door-to-door or from a stall. **2** N. Amer. a person who uses aggressive selling techniques. ■ v. chiefly N. Amer. **1** promote or sell aggressively. **2** bargain.
– DERIVATIVES **hucksterism** n.
– ORIGIN Middle English: prob. of Low German origin.

huddle ■ v. crowd together. ▸ curl one's body into a small space. ■ n. a number of people or things crowded together. ▸ a brief gathering of players during a game to receive instructions, especially in American football.
– ORIGIN C16 ('conceal'): perhaps of Low German origin.

hue ■ n. **1** a colour or shade. ▸ technical the attribute of a colour, dependent on its dominant wavelength, by virtue of which it is discernible as red, green, etc. **2** aspect.
– DERIVATIVES **-hued** adj. **hueless** adj.
– ORIGIN Old English, of Germanic origin.

hue and cry ■ n. **1** a loud clamour or public outcry. **2** historical a loud cry calling for the pursuit and capture of a criminal.
– ORIGIN Middle English: from the Anglo-Norman French legal phr. *hu e cri* 'outcry and cry'.

huff ■ v. **1** (often **huff and puff**) blow out noisily. ▸ show (one's annoyance) in an obvious way. **2** (in draughts) remove (an opponent's piece that could have made a capture) from the board as a forfeit. [from the former practice of blowing on the piece.] ■ n. a fit of petty annoyance.
– DERIVATIVES **huffish** adj.
– ORIGIN C16: imitative of the sound of blowing.

huffy ■ adj. (**-ier**, **-iest**) easily offended.
– DERIVATIVES **huffily** adv. **huffiness** n.

hug ■ v. (**hugged**, **hugging**) **1** squeeze or hold tightly in one's arms. **2** keep close to: *a few craft hugged the shore*. ■ n. an act of hugging. ▸ a squeezing grip in wrestling.
– DERIVATIVES **huggable** adj.
– ORIGIN C16: prob. of Scandinavian origin.

huge ■ adj. (**huger**, **hugest**) extremely large.
– DERIVATIVES **hugeness** n.
– ORIGIN Middle English: shortening of Old French *ahuge*.

hugely ■ adv. very much; to a very great extent.

hugger-mugger ■ adj. **1** confused. **2** secret. ■ n. **1** confusion. **2** secrecy.
– ORIGIN C16: prob. rel. to HUDDLE and to dialect *mucker* 'hoard money, conceal'.

Huguenot

Huguenot /'hju:gənəʊ, -nɒt/ ■ n. a French Protestant of the 16th–17th centuries.
– ORIGIN French, alteration (by association with the name of a Geneva burgomaster, Besançon *Hugues*) of *eiguenot*, from Dutch *eedgenot*, from Swiss German *Eidgenoss* 'confederate'.

huh ■ exclam. used to express scorn or surprise, or in questions to invite agreement.

hula /'hu:lə/ (also **hula-hula**) ■ n. a dance performed by Hawaiian women, characterized by six basic steps, undulating hips, and symbolic gestures.
– ORIGIN C19: Hawaiian.

hula hoop (also US trademark **Hula-Hoop**) ■ n. a large hoop spun round the body by gyrating the hips.

hula skirt ■ n. a long grass skirt as worn by a hula dancer.

hulk ■ n. 1 an old ship stripped of fittings and permanently moored, especially for use as storage or (formerly) as a prison. 2 a large or clumsy boat, object, or person.
– ORIGIN Old English *hulc* 'fast ship'; prob. of Mediterranean origin and rel. to Greek *holkas* 'cargo ship'.

hulking ■ adj. informal very large or clumsy.

hull[1] ■ n. the main body of a ship or other vessel, including the bottom, sides, and deck but not the superstructure, engines, and other fittings. ■ v. hit and pierce the hull of.
– DERIVATIVES **-hulled** adj.
– ORIGIN Middle English: perhaps from **HULL**[2], or rel. to **HOLD**[2].

hull[2] ■ n. 1 the outer covering of a fruit or seed. 2 the green calyx of a strawberry or raspberry. ■ v. [usu. as adj. **hulled**] remove the hulls from.
– ORIGIN Old English, of Germanic origin; rel. to **HEEL**[3].

hullabaloo ■ n. informal a commotion or uproar.
– ORIGIN C18: reduplication of *hallo*, *hullo*, etc.

hullo ■ exclam. variant spelling of **HELLO**.

hum[1] ■ v. (**hummed**, **humming**) 1 make a low, steady continuous sound like that of a bee. ▶ sing with closed lips. 2 informal be in a state of great activity. 3 Brit. informal smell unpleasant. ■ n. a low, steady continuous sound. ▶ an unwanted low-frequency noise in an amplifier.
– PHRASES **hum and haw** (or **ha**) be indecisive.
– DERIVATIVES **hummable** adj. **hummer** n.
– ORIGIN Middle English: imitative.

hum[2] ■ exclam. used to express hesitation or dissent.
– ORIGIN C16: imitative; rel. to **HUM**[1].

human ■ adj. of, relating to, or characteristic of humankind. ▶ of or characteristic of people as opposed to God or animals or machines: *human error*. ▶ showing the better qualities of humankind, such as sensitivity. ■ n. a human being.
– DERIVATIVES **humanness** n.
– ORIGIN Middle English: from Latin *humanus*, from *homo* 'man, human being'.

human being ■ n. a man, woman, or child of the species *Homo sapiens*.

human chain ■ n. a line of people formed for passing things quickly from one site to another.

Human Development Index ■ n. an index which measures a nation's wealth by evaluating the standard of living, health care, and education available to an individual.

humane /hju'meɪn/ ■ adj. 1 compassionate or benevolent. ▶ inflicting the minimum of pain. 2 formal (of a branch of learning) intended to have a civilizing effect.
– DERIVATIVES **humanely** adv. **humaneness** n.
– ORIGIN Middle English: the earlier form of **HUMAN**, restricted to the senses above in the 18th century.

human geography ■ n. the branch of geography concerned with how human activity affects or is influenced by the earth's surface.

human interest ■ n. the aspect of a news story concerned with the experiences or emotions of individuals.

humanism ■ n. 1 a rationalistic outlook or system of thought attaching prime importance to human rather than divine or supernatural matters. 2 a Renaissance cultural movement which turned away from medieval scholasticism and revived interest in ancient Greek and Roman thought.
– DERIVATIVES **humanist** n. & adj. **humanistic** adj. **humanistically** adv.

humanitarian /hju,mænɪ'tɛːrɪən/ ■ adj. concerned with or seeking to promote human welfare. ■ n. a humanitarian person.
– DERIVATIVES **humanitarianism** n.

humanity ■ n. (pl. **-ies**) 1 the human race. ▶ human nature. 2 compassion or benevolence. 3 (**humanities**) learning or literature concerned with human culture, especially literature, history, art, music, and philosophy.

humanize (also **-ise**) ■ v. 1 make more humane. 2 give a human character to.
– DERIVATIVES **humanization** (also **-isation**) n.

humankind ■ n. human beings considered collectively.

humanly ■ adv. from a human point of view; in a human manner. ▶ within human ability.

human nature ■ n. the general psychological characteristics, feelings, and behavioural traits of humankind.

humanoid /'hju:mənɔɪd/ ■ adj. having an appearance or character resembling that of a human. ■ n. (especially in science fiction) a humanoid being.

human right ■ n. (usu. **human rights**) a right which is believed to belong justifiably to every person.

Human Rights Day ■ n. S. African 21 March, a public holiday.

humble ■ adj. (**-er**, **-est**) 1 having or showing a modest or low estimate of one's own importance. 2 of low rank. 3 of modest pretensions or dimensions. ■ v. lower in dignity or importance. ▶ decisively defeat (a sporting opponent previously thought to be superior).
– PHRASES **eat humble pie** make a humble apology and accept humiliation. [from a pun based on archaic *umbles* 'offal', considered inferior food.]
– DERIVATIVES **humbleness** n. **humbly** adv.
– ORIGIN Middle English: from Latin *humilis* 'low, lowly', from *humus* 'ground'.

humble-bee ■ n. another term for **BUMBLEBEE**.
– ORIGIN Middle English: prob. from Middle Low German *hummelbē*, from *hummel* 'to buzz' + *bē* 'bee'.

humbug ■ n. 1 deceptive or false talk or behaviour. ▶ a hypocrite. 2 a boiled peppermint sweet. ■ v. (**humbugged**, **humbugging**) deceive; trick.
– ORIGIN C18.

humdinger /hʌm'dɪŋə/ ■ n. informal a remarkable or outstanding person or thing of its kind.
– ORIGIN C20 (orig. US).

humdrum ■ adj. dull or monotonous. ■ n. monotonous routine.
– ORIGIN C16: prob. a reduplication of **HUM**[1].

humectant /hju'mɛkt(ə)nt/ ■ adj. retaining or preserving moisture. ■ n. a substance, especially a skin lotion or a food additive, used to reduce the loss of moisture.
– ORIGIN C19: from Latin *humectant*-. *humectare* 'moisten'.

humerus /'hju:m(ə)rəs/ ■ n. (pl. **humeri** /-rʌɪ/) Anatomy the bone of the upper arm or forelimb, between the shoulder and the elbow.
– ORIGIN Middle English: from Latin, 'shoulder'.

humic /'hju:mɪk/ ■ adj. relating to or consisting of humus.

humid /'hju:mɪd/ ■ adj. marked by a relatively high level of water vapour in the atmosphere.
– ORIGIN Middle English: from Latin *humidus*, from *humere* 'be moist'.

humidify ■ v. (**-ies**, **-ied**) [often as adj. **humidified**] increase the level of moisture in (air).
– DERIVATIVES **humidification** n. **humidifier** n.

humidity ■ n. (pl. **-ies**) the state or quality of being humid. ▶ a quantity representing the amount of water vapour in the atmosphere or a gas.

humidor /'hju:mɪdɔː/ ■ n. an airtight container for keeping cigars or tobacco moist.
– ORIGIN C20: from **HUMID**.

humiliate ■ v. injure the dignity and self-respect of.
– DERIVATIVES **humiliating** adj. **humiliatingly** adv. **humiliation** n. **humiliator** n.
– ORIGIN C16 (*humiliation* Middle English): from late Latin *humiliare* 'make humble' from *humilis* (see HUMBLE).

humility ■ n. a humble view of one's own importance.
– ORIGIN Middle English: from Latin *humilitas*, from *humilis* (see HUMBLE).

hummingbird ■ n. a small long-billed nectar-feeding American bird, typically with colourful iridescent plumage, that is able to hover by beating its wings extremely fast. [Family Trochilidae: many species.]

hummock ■ n. a hillock or knoll.
– DERIVATIVES **hummocky** adj.
– ORIGIN C16.

hummus /ˈhʊməs/ (also **hoummos** or **houmous**) ■ n. a thick dip of Middle Eastern origin, made from ground chickpeas and sesame seeds, olive oil, lemon, and garlic.
– ORIGIN from Arabic *ḥummuṣ*.

humongous /hjuːˈmʌŋɡəs/ (also **humungous**) ■ adj. informal enormous.
– ORIGIN 1970s (orig. US): perhaps based on HUGE and MONSTROUS, influenced by the stress pattern of *stupendous*.

humor ■ n. US spelling of HUMOUR.

humoral /ˈhjuːm(ə)r(ə)l/ ■ adj. Physiology of or relating to the body fluids, in particular (of immunity) involving the action of circulating antibodies. Often contrasted with CELL-MEDIATED.
– ORIGIN Middle English: from medieval Latin *humoralis*, from Latin *humor* (see HUMOUR).

humoresque /ˌhjuːməˈrɛsk/ ■ n. a short, lively piece of music.
– ORIGIN C19: from German *Humoreske*, from *Humor* 'humour'.

humorist ■ n. a humorous writer, performer, or artist.

humorous ■ adj. causing amusement. ▸ having or showing a sense of humour.
– DERIVATIVES **humorously** adv. **humorousness** n.

humour (US **humor**) ■ n. 1 the quality of being amusing or comic, especially as expressed in literature or speech. ▸ the ability to appreciate or express humour. 2 a state of mind: *her good humour vanished*. 3 historical each of four fluids of the body (blood, phlegm, yellow bile or choler, and black bile or melancholy), formerly held to determine a person's physical and mental qualities. ■ v. comply with the wishes or whims of.
– PHRASES **out of humour** in a bad mood.
– DERIVATIVES **humourless** adj. **humourlessly** adv. **humourlessness** n.

HISTORY
The word **humour** entered English from Old French in the 14th century. Ultimately it comes from Latin *humor* 'moisture', from *humere* 'be moist' (**humid** is from the same root). The original sense in English was 'bodily fluid', surviving today in the medical terms **aqueous humour** and **vitreous humour**, fluids present in the eyeball. In the Middle Ages it was believed that the relative proportions of the four bodily fluids known as the **cardinal humours**, namely blood, phlegm, choler, and melancholy, affected a person's general physical and mental health. This idea led, in the 16th century, to the use of **humour** in the senses 'mood' and 'whim', with the current primary sense becoming established by the end of that century.

hump ■ n. 1 a rounded protuberance found on the back of a camel or other animal or as an abnormality on a person's back. 2 a rounded raised mass of earth or land. ■ v. 1 informal lift or carry (a heavy object) with difficulty. 2 make hump-shaped. 3 vulgar slang have sexual intercourse with.
– PHRASES **get** (or **have**) **the hump** Brit. informal become or be annoyed or sulky. **over the hump** informal past the most difficult part of something.
– DERIVATIVES **humped** adj. **humpless** adj. **humpy** adj. (**-ier**, **-iest**).
– ORIGIN C18: prob. rel. to Low German *humpe* 'hump'.

humpback ■ n. another term for HUNCHBACK.
– DERIVATIVES **humpbacked** adj.

humpback bridge ■ n. Brit. a small road bridge with a steep ascent and descent.

humpback whale ■ n. a baleen whale which has a hump (instead of a dorsal fin) and long white flippers. [*Megaptera novaeangliae*.]

humph ■ exclam. used to express doubt or dissatisfaction.

humungous ■ adj. variant spelling of HUMONGOUS.

humus /ˈhjuːməs/ ■ n. the organic component of soil, formed by the decomposition of leaves and other plant material by soil micro-organisms.
– ORIGIN C18: from Latin, 'soil'.

Humvee /ˈhʌmviː/ ■ n. trademark, chiefly N. Amer. a modern military jeep.
– ORIGIN C20: alteration from the initials of *high-mobility multi-purpose vehicle*.

Hun ■ n. 1 a member of a warlike Asiatic nomadic people who invaded and ravaged Europe in the 4th–5th centuries. 2 informal, derogatory a German (especially in military contexts during the First and Second World Wars).
– DERIVATIVES **Hunnish** adj.
– ORIGIN Old English: from late Latin *Hunni*, from Greek *Hounnoi*, of Middle Iranian origin.

hunch ■ v. raise (one's shoulders) and bend the top of one's body forward. ▸ sit or stand in such a position. ■ n. a feeling or guess based on intuition.
– ORIGIN C15 (orig. 'push, shove' (n. and v.)).

hunchback ■ n. a back deformed by a sharp forward angle, forming a hump, typically caused by collapse of a vertebra. ▸ often offensive a person with such a deformity.
– DERIVATIVES **hunchbacked** adj.

hundred ■ cardinal number (pl. **hundreds** or (with numeral or quantifying word) **hundred**) 1 (**a/one hundred**) the number equivalent to the product of ten and ten; ten more than ninety; 100. (Roman numeral: **c** or **C**.) 2 (**hundreds**) informal an unspecified large number. 3 used to express whole hours in the twenty-four-hour system.
– PHRASES **a** (or **one**) **hundred per cent** entirely. ▸ [usu. with neg.] informal completely fit and healthy. ▸ informal maximum effort and commitment.
– DERIVATIVES **hundredfold** adj. & adv. **hundredth** ordinal number.
– ORIGIN Old English, from *hund* 'hundred' + a second element meaning 'number', of Germanic origin.

hundreds and thousands ■ pl. n. tiny sugar beads of varying colours used for decorating cakes and desserts.

hundredweight (abbrev.: **cwt.**) ■ n. (pl. same or **-weights**) 1 (also **long hundredweight**) Brit. a unit of weight equal to 112 lb avoirdupois (about 50.8 kg). 2 (also **short hundredweight**) US a unit of weight equal to 100 lb (about 45.4 kg). 3 (also **metric hundredweight**) a unit of weight equal to 50 kg.

hung past and past participle of HANG. ■ adj. 1 (of an elected body) having no political party with an overall majority. ▸ (of a jury) unable to agree on a verdict. 2 (**hung up**) informal emotionally confused or disturbed.

Hungarian /hʌŋˈɡɛːrɪən/ ■ n. a native or national of Hungary, or a person of Hungarian descent. ■ adj. of or relating to Hungary, its people, or their language.

hunger ■ n. 1 a feeling of discomfort or weakness caused by lack of food, coupled with the desire to eat. 2 a strong desire. ■ v. 1 (**hunger after/for**) have a strong desire for. 2 archaic feel or suffer hunger.
– ORIGIN Old English, of Germanic origin.

hunger strike ■ n. a prolonged refusal to eat, carried out as a protest by a prisoner.
– DERIVATIVES **hunger striker** n.

hung-over ■ adj. suffering from a hangover.

hungry ■ adj. (**-ier**, **-iest**) 1 feeling, showing, or causing hunger. 2 (often **hungry for**) having a strong desire.
– DERIVATIVES **hungrily** adv. **hungriness** n.
– ORIGIN Old English, of West Germanic origin; rel. to HUNGER.

hunk

hunk ■ n. **1** a large piece cut or broken from something larger. **2** informal a large, strong, sexually attractive man.
– DERIVATIVES **hunky** adj. (**-ier**, **-iest**)
– ORIGIN C19: prob. of Dutch or Low German origin.

hunker ■ v. **1** squat or crouch down low. **2** (**hunker down**) apply oneself seriously to a task.
– ORIGIN C18: prob. rel. to German *hocken*.

hunky-dory ■ adj. informal excellent.
– ORIGIN C19 (orig. US): *hunky* from Dutch *honk* 'home' (in games).

hunt ■ v. **1** pursue and kill (a wild animal) for sport or food. ▸ (of an animal) chase and kill (its prey). ▸ (of the police) pursue (a criminal). ▸ (**hunt someone down**) pursue and capture someone. ▸ [as adj. **hunted**] appearing alarmed or harassed as if being hunted. **2** search diligently for. **3** (of a device or system) oscillate about a desired speed, position, or state. **4** (**hunt down/up**) (in change-ringing) move the place of a bell in a simple progression. ■ n. an act or the process of hunting. ▸ an association of people who meet regularly to hunt, especially with hounds. ▸ an area where hunting takes place.
– ORIGIN Old English, of Germanic origin.

hunter ■ n. a person or animal that hunts. ▸ a horse of a breed developed for stamina in fox-hunting.
– DERIVATIVES **huntress** n.

hunter-gatherer ■ n. a member of a nomadic people who live chiefly by hunting and fishing, and harvesting wild food.

hunter's moon ■ n. the first full moon after a harvest moon.

hunting ■ n. **1** the activity of hunting wild animals or game, especially for food or sport. ▸ chiefly Brit. the pursuit of a wild animal with a pack of trained hounds, especially a fox or hare. **2** [in combination] the activity of searching for something: *bargain-hunting*. **3** (also **plain hunting**) Bell-ringing a simple system of changes in which bells move through the order in a regular progression.

hunting crop (also **hunting whip**) ■ n. a short rigid riding whip with a handle at right angles to the stock and a long leather thong, used chiefly in hunting with hounds.

hunting dog (also **Cape hunting dog**) ■ n. another term for WILD DOG (in sense 2).

hunting ground ■ n. a place likely to be a fruitful source of something desired or sought.

hunting horn ■ n. a straight horn blown to give signals while hunting with hounds.

Huntington's chorea ■ n. a hereditary disease marked by degeneration of brain cells, causing chorea and progressive dementia.
– ORIGIN C19: named after the American neurologist George *Huntington*.

huntsman ■ n. (pl. **-men**) a person who hunts. ▸ a hunt official in charge of hounds.

hurdle ■ n. **1** one of a series of upright frames which athletes in a race must jump over. ▸ (**hurdles**) a hurdle race. **2** an obstacle or difficulty. **3** a portable rectangular frame strengthened with withies or wooden bars, used as a temporary fence. ▸ a horse race over a series of such frames. ■ v. **1** [often as noun **hurdling**] run in a hurdle race. ▸ jump over (a hurdle or other obstacle) while running. **2** enclose or fence off with hurdles.
– DERIVATIVES **hurdler** n.
– ORIGIN Old English *hyrdel* 'temporary fence', of Germanic origin.

hurdy-gurdy /ˈhəːdɪˌɡəːdi/ ■ n. (pl. **-ies**) a musical instrument with a droning sound produced by turning a handle, which is typically attached to a rosined wheel sounding a series of drone strings, with keys worked by the left hand. ▸ informal a barrel organ.
– ORIGIN C18: prob. imitative of the instrument's sound.

hurl ■ v. throw or impel with great force. ▸ utter (abuse) vehemently. ▸ informal vomit.
– ORIGIN Middle English: prob. imitative.

hurling ■ n. an Irish game resembling hockey, played with a shorter stick with a broader oval blade.

hurly-burly ■ n. busy, boisterous activity.
– ORIGIN Middle English: reduplication based on HURL.

Huron /ˈhjʊərɒn/ ■ n. (pl. same or **Hurons**) a member of a confederation of native North American peoples formerly living in the region east of Lake Huron.
– ORIGIN French, 'having hair standing in bristles', from Old French *hure* 'head of a wild boar'.

hurrah (also **hooray**, **hurray**) ■ exclam. used to express joy or approval.
– ORIGIN C17: alteration of HUZZA; perhaps orig. a sailors' cry when hauling.

hurricane /ˈhʌrɪkən, -keɪn/ ■ n. a storm with a violent wind, in particular a tropical cyclone in the Caribbean.
– ORIGIN C16: prob. from Taino (an extinct Caribbean language) *hurakán* 'god of the storm'.

hurricane deck ■ n. a covered deck at or near the top of a ship's superstructure.

hurricane lamp ■ n. an oil lamp with a glass chimney, designed to protect the flame even in high winds.

hurry ■ v. (**-ies**, **-ied**) move or act quickly or more quickly. ▸ do or finish (something) quickly. ■ n. great haste. ▸ [with neg. and in questions] a need for haste; urgency.
– PHRASES **in a hurry 1** rushed; in a rushed manner. **2** [usu. with neg.] informal easily; readily.
– DERIVATIVES **hurried** adj. **hurriedly** adv. **hurriedness** n.
– ORIGIN C16: imitative.

hurt ■ v. (past and past part. **hurt**) **1** cause physical pain or injury to. ▸ (of a part of the body) suffer pain. **2** cause mental pain or distress to. ▸ feel mental pain or distress: *he was hurting badly*. ■ n. injury or pain; harm.
– ORIGIN Middle English (orig. 'to strike, a blow'): from Old French *hurter* (v.), *hurt* (n.), perhaps ultimately of Germanic origin.

hurtful ■ adj. causing mental pain or distress.
– DERIVATIVES **hurtfully** adv. **hurtfulness** n.

hurtle ■ v. move or cause to move at great speed, typically in a wildly uncontrolled manner.
– ORIGIN Middle English ('collide with'): from HURT.

husband ■ n. a married man considered in relation to his wife. ■ v. use (resources) economically.
– DERIVATIVES **husbandless** adj. **husbandly** adj.
– ORIGIN Old English: from Old Norse *húsbóndi* 'master of a house', from *hús* 'house' + *bóndi* 'occupier and tiller of the soil'.

husbandry ■ n. **1** the care, cultivation, and breeding of crops and animals. **2** management and conservation of resources.
– ORIGIN Middle English: from HUSBAND in the obsolete sense 'farmer'.

hush ■ v. **1** make or become quiet. **2** (**hush something up**) suppress public mention of something. ■ n. a silence.
– ORIGIN C16: back-formation from obsolete *husht* 'silent', from an interjection *husht* 'quiet!'

hushaby (also **hushabye**) ■ exclam. archaic used to lull a child.
– ORIGIN C18: from HUSH + *-by* as in BYE-BYE.

hush-hush ■ adj. informal highly secret or confidential.

hush money ■ n. informal money paid to someone to prevent them from disclosing embarrassing or discreditable information.

husk¹ ■ n. **1** the dry outer covering of some fruits or seeds. **2** a dry or rough discarded outer layer. ■ v. remove the husk from.
– ORIGIN Middle English: prob. from Low German *hūske* 'sheath', literally 'little house'.

husk² ■ n. **1** bronchitis in cattle, sheep, or pigs caused by parasitic infestation, typically marked by a husky cough. **2** huskiness.
– ORIGIN C18: partly from HUSKY¹, partly from the earlier verb *husk* 'cough'.

husky¹ ■ adj. (**-ier**, **-iest**) **1** (of a voice) sounding low-pitched and slightly hoarse. **2** strong; hefty. **3** like or consisting of husks.
– DERIVATIVES **huskily** adv. **huskiness** n.

husky² ■ n. (pl. **-ies**) a powerful dog of a breed with a thick double coat, used in the Arctic for pulling sledges.
– ORIGIN C19 (orig. denoting the Eskimo language or an Eskimo): abbrev. of obsolete *Ehuskemay* or Newfoundland dialect *Huskemaw* 'Eskimo'.

hydrochloric acid

hussar /hʊˈzɑː/ ■ n. historical (except in titles) **1** a soldier in a light cavalry regiment which adopted a dress uniform modelled on that of the Hungarian hussars. **2** a Hungarian light horseman of the 15th century.
– ORIGIN from Old Serbian *husar*, from Italian *corsaro* (see CORSAIR).

hussy ■ n. (pl. **-ies**) dated or humorous a promiscuous or immoral girl or woman.
– ORIGIN Middle English: contraction of HOUSEWIFE.

hustings ■ n. [treated as pl. or sing.] a meeting at which candidates in an election address potential voters.
– ORIGIN Old English *husting* 'deliberative assembly, council', from Old Norse *hústhing*, from *hús* 'house' + *thing* 'assembly, parliament'.

hustle ■ v. **1** push roughly; jostle. ▸ force to move hurriedly or unceremoniously: *I was hustled away.* **2** informal, chiefly N. Amer. obtain illicitly or by forceful action or persuasion. ▸ (**hustle someone into**) coerce or pressure someone into doing something. ▸ sell aggressively. **3** N. Amer. informal engage in prostitution. ■ n. **1** busy movement and activity. **2** N. Amer. informal a fraud or swindle.
– ORIGIN C17: from Middle Dutch *hutselen*.

hustler ■ n. informal, chiefly N. Amer. **1** a person adept at aggressive selling or illicit dealing. **2** a prostitute.

hut ■ n. a small single-storey building of simple or crude construction. ■ v. (**hutted**, **hutting**) provide with huts.
– ORIGIN C16 ('wooden shelter for troops'): from French *hutte*, from Middle High German *hütte*.

hutch ■ n. **1** a box or cage for keeping rabbits or other small domesticated animals. **2** N. Amer. a storage chest. ▸ a cupboard or dresser.
– ORIGIN Middle English ('storage chest'): from Old French *huche*, from medieval Latin *hutica*.

hutment ■ n. Military an encampment of huts.

Hutu /ˈhuːtuː/ ■ n. (pl. same or **Hutus**) a member of a Bantu-speaking people forming the majority population in Rwanda and Burundi.
– ORIGIN a local name.

huzza /hʊˈzɑː/ (also **huzzah**) ■ exclam. archaic used to express approval or delight.
– ORIGIN C16: perhaps used orig. as a sailor's cry when hauling.

hyacinth /ˈhaɪəsɪnθ/ ■ n. **1** a bulbous plant of the lily family with a spike of bell-shaped fragrant flowers. [Genus *Hyacinthus*: several species.] **2** another term for JACINTH.
– DERIVATIVES **hyacinthine** /-ˈsɪnθiːn, -θʌɪn/ adj.
– ORIGIN C16: from French *hyacinthe*, from Greek *huakinthos*, with ref. to the Greek mythological story of Hyacinthus, a youth loved by Apollo but accidentally killed by him, from whose blood Apollo caused a flower to grow.

hyaena ■ n. variant spelling of HYENA.

hyalin /ˈhaɪəlɪn/ ■ n. Physiology a clear substance produced especially by the degeneration of epithelial or connective tissues.
– ORIGIN C19: from Greek *hualinos*, from *hualos* 'glass'.

hyaline /ˈhaɪəlɪn, -iːn, -ʌɪn/ ■ adj. Anatomy & Zoology **1** (chiefly of cartilage) glassy and translucent in appearance. **2** relating to or consisting of hyalin.

hyaloid /ˈhaɪəlɔɪd/ ■ adj. Anatomy glassy; transparent.
– ORIGIN C19: from Greek *hualoeidēs* 'like glass', from *hualos* 'glass'.

hyaluronic acid /ˌhaɪəljʊəˈrɒnɪk/ ■ n. Biochemistry a viscous fluid carbohydrate present in connective tissue, synovial fluid, and the humours of the eye.
– DERIVATIVES **hyaluronate** n.
– ORIGIN 1930s: from a blend of HYALOID and *uronic acid* (an oxidized sugar, from URO-1 'urine').

hybrid /ˈhaɪbrɪd/ ■ n. **1** Biology the offspring of two plants or animals of different species or varieties, such as a mule. **2** a thing made by combining two different elements. ▸ a word formed from elements taken from different languages.
– DERIVATIVES **hybridism** n. **hybridity** n.
– ORIGIN C17: from Latin *hybrida* 'offspring of a tame sow and wild boar, child of a freeman and slave, etc.'.

hybridize (also **-ise**) ■ v. cross-breed to produce hybrids.
– DERIVATIVES **hybridizable** (also **-isable**) adj. **hybridization** (also **-isation**) n.

hybrid vigour ■ n. Genetics the tendency of a cross-bred individual to show qualities superior to those of both parents.

hydathode /ˈhaɪdəθəʊd/ ■ n. Botany a modified pore, especially on a leaf, which exudes drops of water.
– ORIGIN C19: from Greek *hudōr, hudat-* 'water' + *hodos* 'way'.

hydr- ■ comb. form variant spelling of HYDRO- shortened before a vowel (as in *hydraulic*).

hydra ■ n. a minute freshwater coelenterate with a stalk-like tubular body and a ring of tentacles around the mouth. [Genus *Hydra*.]
– ORIGIN named after the *Hydra* of Greek mythology, a many-headed snake whose heads regrew as they were cut off: so named because, if cut into pieces, each section can grow into a whole animal.

hydrangea /haɪˈdreɪn(d)ʒə/ ■ n. a shrub with flowering heads of white, blue, or pink florets, native to Asia and America. [*Hydrangea macrophylla* and related species.]
– ORIGIN from Greek *hudro-* 'water' + *angeion* 'vessel' (from the cup shape of its seed capsule).

hydrant /ˈhaɪdr(ə)nt/ ■ n. a water pipe with a nozzle to which a fire hose can be attached.
– ORIGIN C19: formed from HYDRO-.

hydrate ■ n. /ˈhaɪdreɪt/ Chemistry a compound in which water molecules are chemically bound to another compound or an element. ■ v. /haɪˈdreɪt/ cause to absorb or combine with water.
– DERIVATIVES **hydratable** adj. **hydration** n. **hydrator** n.
– ORIGIN C19: from Greek *hudōr* 'water'.

hydraulic /haɪˈdrɔːlɪk, haɪˈdrɒlɪk/ ■ adj. **1** denoting or relating to a liquid moving in a confined space under pressure. **2** of or relating to the science of hydraulics. **3** (of cement) hardening under water.
– DERIVATIVES **hydraulically** adv.
– ORIGIN C17: from Greek *hudraulikos*, from *hudro-* 'water' + *aulos* 'pipe'.

hydraulic ram ■ n. an automatic pump in which a large volume of water flows through a valve which it periodically forces shut, the sudden pressure change being used to raise a smaller volume of water to a higher level.

hydraulics ■ pl. n. [usu. treated as sing.] the branch of science and technology concerned with the conveyance of liquids through pipes and channels.

hydric /ˈhaɪdrɪk/ ■ adj. Ecology containing plenty of moisture; very wet. Compare with MESIC and XERIC.
– ORIGIN C20: from HYDRO-.

hydride /ˈhaɪdrʌɪd/ ■ n. Chemistry a binary compound of hydrogen with a metal.

hydriodic acid /ˌhaɪdrɪˈɒdɪk, -ʌɪˈɒdɪk/ ■ n. Chemistry a strongly acidic solution of the gas hydrogen iodide. [HI.]

hydro ■ n. (pl. **-os**) **1** a hotel or clinic originally providing hydropathic treatment. **2** a hydroelectric power plant. ▸ hydroelectricity.

hydro- (also **hydr-**) ■ comb. form **1** water; relating to water: *hydraulic.* ▸ Medicine affected with an accumulation of serous fluid: *hydrocephalus.* **2** Chemistry combined with hydrogen: *hydrocarbon.*
– ORIGIN from Greek *hudōr* 'water'.

hydrobromic acid /ˌhaɪdrə(ʊ)ˈbrəʊmɪk/ ■ n. Chemistry a strongly acidic solution of the gas hydrogen bromide. [HBr.]

hydrocarbon ■ n. Chemistry a compound of hydrogen and carbon, such as any of those which are the chief components of petroleum and natural gas.

hydrocele /ˈhaɪdrə(ʊ)siːl/ ■ n. Medicine abnormal accumulation of serous fluid in a sac in the body.

hydrocephalus /ˌhaɪdrəˈsɛf(ə)ləs, -ˈkɛf-/ ■ n. Medicine a condition in which fluid accumulates in the brain.
– DERIVATIVES **hydrocephalic** adj. **hydrocephaly** n.
– ORIGIN C17: modern Latin, from Greek *hudrokephalon*, from *hudro-* 'water' + *kephalē* 'head'.

hydrochloric acid ■ n. Chemistry a strongly acidic solution of the gas hydrogen chloride. [HCl.]

hydrochloride

hydrochloride ■ n. Chemistry a compound of an organic base with hydrochloric acid.

hydrocolloid /ˌhaɪdrə(ʊ)ˈkɒlɔɪd/ ■ n. a substance which forms a gel in the presence of water.

hydrocortisone ■ n. Biochemistry a steroid hormone produced by the adrenal cortex, used medicinally to treat inflammation and rheumatism.

hydrocyanic acid /ˌhaɪdrə(ʊ)saɪˈanɪk/ ■ n. Chemistry a highly poisonous acidic solution of hydrogen cyanide.

hydrodynamics ■ pl. n. [treated as sing.] the branch of science concerned with forces acting on or exerted by fluids (especially liquids).
– DERIVATIVES **hydrodynamic** adj. **hydrodynamical** adj. **hydrodynamicist** n.

hydroelectric ■ adj. relating to or denoting the generation of electricity using flowing water to drive a turbine which powers a generator.
– DERIVATIVES **hydroelectricity** n.

hydrofluoric acid /ˌhaɪdrə(ʊ)ˈflʊərɪk/ ■ n. Chemistry an acidic, extremely corrosive solution of the liquid hydrogen fluoride. [HF.]

hydrofoil ■ n. a boat fitted underneath with shaped vanes (foils) which lift the hull clear of the water at speed. ▸ each of the foils of such a craft.
– ORIGIN 1920s: from HYDRO-, on the pattern of *aerofoil*.

hydrogel ■ n. a gel in which the liquid component is water.

hydrogen /ˈhaɪdrədʒ(ə)n/ ■ n. a colourless, odourless, highly flammable gas, the chemical element of atomic number 1. (Symbol: **H**)
– DERIVATIVES **hydrogenous** /-ˈdrɒdʒɪnəs/ adj.
– ORIGIN C18: from Greek *hudro-* 'water' + *-genēs* (see -GEN).

hydrogenase /haɪˈdrɒdʒəneɪz/ ■ n. Biochemistry an enzyme which promotes the reduction of a particular substance by hydrogen.

hydrogenate /haɪˈdrɒdʒəneɪt, ˈhaɪdrədʒəneɪt/ ■ v. [often as adj. **hydrogenated**] charge with or cause to combine with hydrogen.
– DERIVATIVES **hydrogenation** n.

hydrogen bomb ■ n. a nuclear bomb whose destructive power comes from the fusion of isotopes of hydrogen (deuterium and tritium).

hydrogen bond ■ n. Chemistry a weak chemical bond resulting from electrostatic attraction between a proton in one molecule and an electronegative atom in another.

hydrogen cyanide ■ n. Chemistry a highly poisonous gas or volatile liquid with an odour of bitter almonds, made by the action of acids on cyanides. [HCN.]

hydrogen peroxide ■ n. Chemistry a colourless viscous liquid with strong oxidizing properties, used in some disinfectants and bleaches. [H_2O_2.]

hydrogen sulphide ■ n. Chemistry a colourless poisonous gas with a smell of bad eggs, made by the action of acids on sulphides. [H_2S.]

hydrogeology ■ n. the branch of geology concerned with underground or surface water.
– DERIVATIVES **hydrogeological** adj. **hydrogeologist** n.

hydrography /haɪˈdrɒɡrəfi/ ■ n. the science of surveying and charting bodies of water.
– DERIVATIVES **hydrographer** n. **hydrographic** adj. **hydrographical** adj. **hydrographically** adv.

hydroid /ˈhaɪdrɔɪd/ ■ n. Zoology a coelenterate of an order (Hydroida) which includes the hydras.

hydrolase /ˈhaɪdrəleɪz/ ■ n. Biochemistry an enzyme that promotes the hydrolysis of a particular substrate.

hydrology ■ n. the branch of science concerned with the properties and distribution of water on the earth's surface.
– DERIVATIVES **hydrologic** adj. **hydrological** adj. **hydrologically** adv. **hydrologist** n.

hydrolyse /ˈhaɪdrəlaɪz/ (also **hydrolyze**) ■ v. Chemistry break down (a compound) by chemical reaction with water.

hydrolysis /haɪˈdrɒlɪsɪs/ ■ n. Chemistry the chemical breakdown of a compound due to reaction with water.
– DERIVATIVES **hydrolytic** adj.

hydromagnetics ■ pl. n. another term for MAGNETOHYDRODYNAMICS.
– DERIVATIVES **hydromagnetic** adj.

hydromassage ■ n. massage using jets of water.

hydromechanics ■ pl. n. [treated as sing.] the mechanics of liquids; hydrodynamics.
– DERIVATIVES **hydromechanical** adj.

hydrometer /haɪˈdrɒmɪtə/ ■ n. an instrument for measuring the density of liquids.
– DERIVATIVES **hydrometric** adj. **hydrometry** n.

hydronium ion /haɪˈdrəʊnɪəm/ ■ n. another term for HYDROXONIUM ION.

hydropathy /haɪˈdrɒpəθi/ ■ n. the treatment of illness through the use of water, either internally or externally.
– DERIVATIVES **hydropathic** adj. **hydropathist** n.

hydrophilic /ˌhaɪdrə(ʊ)ˈfɪlɪk/ ■ adj. having a tendency to mix with, dissolve in, or be wetted by water.
– DERIVATIVES **hydrophilicity** n.

hydrophobia /ˌhaɪdrə(ʊ)ˈfəʊbɪə/ ■ n. **1** extreme or irrational fear of water, especially as a symptom of rabies. **2** rabies.

hydrophobic ■ adj. **1** tending to repel or fail to mix with water. **2** of or suffering from hydrophobia.
– DERIVATIVES **hydrophobicity** n.

hydrophone ■ n. a microphone which detects sound waves under water.

hydrophyte ■ n. Botany a plant which grows only in or on water.
– DERIVATIVES **hydrophytic** adj.

hydroplane ■ n. **1** a light, fast motor boat. **2** a fin-like attachment which enables a moving submarine to rise or fall in the water. **3** US a seaplane. ■ v. chiefly N. Amer. another term for AQUAPLANE.

hydroponics /ˌhaɪdrə(ʊ)ˈpɒnɪks/ ■ pl. n. [treated as sing.] the process of growing plants in sand, gravel, or liquid, with added nutrients but without soil.
– DERIVATIVES **hydroponic** adj. **hydroponically** adv.
– ORIGIN 1930s: from HYDRO- + Greek *ponos* 'labour'.

hydropower ■ n. hydroelectric power.

hydrospeed (also **hydrospeeding**) ■ n. a sport that involves jumping into fast-flowing white water and being carried along at high speed while buoyed up by a float.

hydrosphere ■ n. the seas, lakes, and other waters of the earth's surface, considered collectively.

hydrostatic ■ adj. relating to or denoting the equilibrium of liquids and the pressure exerted by liquid at rest.
– DERIVATIVES **hydrostatical** adj. **hydrostatically** adv. **hydrostatics** pl. n.
– ORIGIN C17: prob. from Greek *hudrostatēs* 'hydrostatic balance', from *hudro-* 'water' + *statikos* (see STATIC).

hydrotherapy ■ n. **1** the therapeutic use of exercises in a pool. **2** another term for HYDROPATHY.
– DERIVATIVES **hydrotherapist** n.

hydrothermal ■ adj. relating to or denoting the action of heated water in the earth's crust.
– DERIVATIVES **hydrothermally** adv.

hydrothermal vent ■ n. an opening in the sea floor out of which heated mineral-rich water flows.

hydrothorax ■ n. Medicine the condition of having fluid in the pleural cavity.

hydrotropism /haɪˈdrɒtrəpɪz(ə)m/ ■ n. Botany the growth or turning of plant roots towards moisture.

hydrous ■ adj. chiefly Chemistry & Geology containing water as a constituent.
– ORIGIN C19: from Greek *hudro-* 'water'.

hydroxide ■ n. Chemistry a compound containing the hydroxide ion OH⁻ or the group -OH.

hydroxonium ion /ˌhaɪdrɒkˈsəʊnɪəm/ ■ n. Chemistry the ion H_3O^+, present in all aqueous acids.
– ORIGIN 1920s: from HYDRO- (relating to hydrogen) + OXY-² + the suffix *-onium* (from AMMONIUM).

hydroxyl /haɪˈdrɒksʌɪl, -sɪl/ ■ n. [as modifier] Chemistry of or denoting the radical -OH, present in alcohols and many other organic compounds.

Hydrozoa /ˌhaɪdrə(ʊ)ˈzəʊə/ ■ pl. n. Zoology a class of coelenterates which includes hydras and Portuguese men-of-war.

– DERIVATIVES **hydrozoan** n. & adj.
– ORIGIN from HYDRO- + Greek *zōion* 'animal'.

hyena (also **hyaena**) ■ n. a doglike carnivorous African mammal with shoulders higher than the rump. [Family Hyaenidae: three species.]
– ORIGIN Middle English: from Greek *huaina*, feminine of *hus* 'pig' (prob. because of the resemblance of the mane to a hog's bristles).

hygiene ■ n. conditions or practices conducive to maintaining health and preventing disease, especially cleanliness.
– ORIGIN C16: from modern Latin *hygieina*, from Greek *hugieinē (tekhnē)* '(art) of health', from *hugiēs* 'healthy'.

hygienic ■ adj. promoting or conducive to hygiene; sanitary.
– DERIVATIVES **hygienically** adv.

hygienist ■ n. a specialist in the promotion of hygiene.

hygro- ■ comb. form relating to moisture: *hygrometer*.
– ORIGIN from Greek *hugros* 'wet'.

hygrometer /hʌɪˈgrɒmɪtə/ ■ n. an instrument for measuring humidity.
– DERIVATIVES **hygrometric** adj. **hygrometry** n.

hygrophilous /hʌɪˈgrɒfɪləs/ ■ adj. Botany (of a plant) growing in damp conditions.

hygrophyte /ˈhʌɪgrəfʌɪt/ ■ n. Botany a plant which grows in wet conditions.

hygroscope /ˈhʌɪgrə(ʊ)skəʊp/ ■ n. an instrument which gives an indication (though not necessarily a measurement) of the humidity of the air.

hygroscopic ■ adj. (of a substance) tending to absorb moisture from the air.
– DERIVATIVES **hygroscopically** adv.

hying present participle of HIE.

hylomorphism /ˌhʌɪlə(ʊ)ˈmɔːfɪz(ə)m/ ■ n. Philosophy the doctrine that matter is the first cause of the universe and that physical objects result from the combination of matter and form.
– DERIVATIVES **hylomorphic** adj.
– ORIGIN C19: from Greek *hulē* 'matter' + *morphē* 'form'.

hymen /ˈhʌɪmən/ ■ n. a membrane which partially closes the opening of the vagina and whose presence is traditionally taken to be a mark of virginity.
– DERIVATIVES **hymenal** adj.
– ORIGIN C16: from Greek *humēn* 'membrane'.

hymeneal /ˌhʌɪmɪˈniːəl/ ■ adj. poetic/literary of or concerning marriage.
– ORIGIN C17: from Latin *hymenaeus*, from *Hymen* (from Greek *Humēn*), the name of the god of marriage.

Hymenoptera /ˌhʌɪməˈnɒpt(ə)rə/ ■ pl. n. Entomology a large order of insects including the bees, wasps, ants, and sawflies, having four transparent wings.
– DERIVATIVES **hymenopteran** n. & adj. **hymenopterous** adj.
– ORIGIN from Greek *humenopteros* 'membrane-winged'.

hymn ■ n. a religious song of praise, typically a Christian song in praise of God. ■ v. praise or celebrate with or as if with a hymn.
– DERIVATIVES **hymnic** /ˈhɪmnɪk/ adj.
– ORIGIN Old English: from Greek *humnos* 'ode or song in praise'.

hymnal /ˈhɪmn(ə)l/ ■ n. a book of hymns. ■ adj. of or relating to hymns.

hymnody /ˈhɪmnədi/ ■ n. the singing or composition of hymns.
– DERIVATIVES **hymnodist** n.
– ORIGIN C18: from Greek *humnōidia*, from *humnos* 'hymn'.

hyoid /ˈhʌɪɔɪd/ Anatomy & Zoology ■ n. a U-shaped bone in the neck which supports the tongue. ■ adj. relating to or denoting this bone.
– ORIGIN C19: from modern Latin *hyoïdes*, from Greek *huoeidēs* 'shaped like the letter upsilon (υ)'.

hyp- ■ comb. form variant spelling of HYPO- shortened before a vowel or *h*.

hype[1] informal ■ n. extravagant or intensive publicity or promotion. ▸ a deception or hoax. ■ v. promote or publicize intensively or extravagantly.
– ORIGIN 1920s (orig. US 'short-change, cheat').

hype[2] informal ■ n. a hypodermic needle or injection. ▸ a drug addict. ■ v. (usu. **be hyped up**) stimulate or excite.
– ORIGIN 1920s: abbrev. of HYPODERMIC.

hyper ■ adj. informal hyperactive or unusually energetic.

hyper- ■ prefix **1** over; beyond; above: *hypersonic*.
▸ excessively; above normal: *hyperthyroidism*. **2** relating to hypertext: *hyperlink*.
– ORIGIN from Greek *huper* 'over, beyond'.

hyperactive ■ adj. abnormally or extremely active.
– DERIVATIVES **hyperactivity** n.

hyperaemia /ˌhʌɪpərˈiːmɪə/ (US **hyperemia**) ■ n. Medicine an excess of blood in an organ or other part of the body.
– DERIVATIVES **hyperaemic** adj.

hyperalgesia /ˌhʌɪpəralˈdʒiːzɪə/ ■ n. Medicine abnormally heightened sensitivity to pain.
– DERIVATIVES **hyperalgesic** adj.
– ORIGIN from Greek *huperalgein* 'to be in great pain', from *algos* 'pain'.

hyperalimentation ■ n. Medicine artificial supply of nutrients, typically intravenously.

hyperbaric /ˌhʌɪpəˈbarɪk/ ■ adj. relating to or denoting a gas at a pressure greater than normal.
– ORIGIN 1960s: from HYPER- + Greek *baros* 'heavy'.

hyperbola /hʌɪˈpəːbələ/ ■ n. (pl. **hyperbolas** or **hyperbolae** /-liː/) Mathematics a symmetrical open curve (or pair of curves) formed by the intersection of a cone (or pair of oppositely directed cones) with a plane at a smaller angle with its axis than the side of the cone.
– ORIGIN C17: from modern Latin, from Greek *huperbolē* 'excess', from *huper* 'above' + *ballein* 'to throw'.

hyperbole /hʌɪˈpəːbəli/ ■ n. deliberate exaggeration, not meant to be taken literally.
– DERIVATIVES **hyperbolical** adj. **hyperbolically** adv. **hyperbolism** n.
– ORIGIN Middle English: from Greek *huperbolē* (see HYPERBOLA).

hyperbolic /ˌhʌɪpəˈbɒlɪk/ ■ adj. **1** of or relating to a hyperbola. ▸ Mathematics denoting trigonometrical functions defined with reference to a hyperbola rather than a circle. **2** (of language) deliberately exaggerated.

hyperboloid /hʌɪˈpəːbəlɔɪd/ ■ n. a solid or surface having plane sections that are hyperbolas, ellipses, or circles.
– DERIVATIVES **hyperboloidal** adj.

hyperborean /ˌhʌɪpəbɔːˈriːən, -ˈbɔːrɪən/ poetic/literary ■ n. **1** an inhabitant of the extreme north. **2** (**Hyperborean**) Greek & Roman Mythology a member of a race worshipping Apollo and living in a land of sunshine beyond the north wind. ■ adj. of or relating to the extreme north.
– ORIGIN Middle English: from Greek *huperboreos*, from *huper* 'beyond' + *boreas* 'north wind'.

hypercholesterolaemia /ˌhʌɪpəkəˌlestərɒˈliːmɪə/ (US **hypercholesterolemia**) ■ n. Medicine an excess of cholesterol in the bloodstream.

hypercorrection ■ n. the use of an erroneous word form or pronunciation based on a false analogy with a correct or prestigious form, such as the use of *I* in *he invited my husband and I to lunch*.
– DERIVATIVES **hypercorrect** adj.

hypercritical ■ adj. excessively and unreasonably critical.
– DERIVATIVES **hypercritically** adv.

hyperdrive ■ n. (in science fiction) a supposed propulsion system for travel in hyperspace.

hyperemia ■ n. US spelling of HYPERAEMIA.

hyperextend ■ v. forcefully extend a limb or joint beyond its normal limits.
– DERIVATIVES **hyperextension** n.

hyperfocal distance ■ n. the distance between a camera lens and the closest object which is in focus when the lens is focused at infinity.

hyperglycaemia /ˌhʌɪpəglʌɪˈsiːmɪə/ (US **hyperglycemia**) ■ n. Medicine an excess of glucose in the bloodstream, often associated with diabetes mellitus.
– DERIVATIVES **hyperglycaemic** adj.
– ORIGIN C19: from HYPER- + GLYCO- + -AEMIA.

hypericum /hʌɪˈpɛrɪkəm/ ■ n. a yellow-flowered plant of a

hyperimmune

genus that includes the St John's worts and rose of Sharon. [Genus *Hypericum*.]
– ORIGIN from Greek *hupereikon*, from *huper* 'over' + *ereikē* 'heath'.

hyperimmune ▪ adj. Medicine having a high concentration of antibodies produced in reaction to repeated injections of an antigen.
– DERIVATIVES **hyperimmunized** (also **-ised**) adj.

hyperinflation ▪ n. monetary inflation occurring at a very high rate.

hyperkeratosis /ˌhaɪpəkɛrə'təʊsɪs/ ▪ n. Medicine abnormal thickening of the outer layer of the skin.

hyperkinesis /ˌhaɪpəkɪ'niːsɪs, -kʌɪ-/ (also **hyperkinesia**) ▪ n. 1 Medicine muscle spasm. 2 Psychiatry a disorder of children marked by hyperactivity and inability to concentrate.
– DERIVATIVES **hyperkinetic** adj.
– ORIGIN C19: from HYPER- + Greek *kinēsis* 'motion'.

hyperlink ▪ n. Computing a link from a hypertext document to another location, activated by clicking on a highlighted word or image.

hyperlipaemia /ˌhaɪpəlɪ'piːmɪə/ (US **hyperlipemia**) ▪ n. Medicine an abnormally high concentration of fats or lipids in the blood.
– DERIVATIVES **hyperlipaemic** adj.

hyperlipidaemia /ˌhaɪpəˌlɪpɪ'diːmɪə/ (US **hyperlipidemia**) ▪ n. another term for HYPERLIPAEMIA.
– DERIVATIVES **hyperlipidaemic** adj.

hypermarket ▪ n. a very large supermarket.
– ORIGIN 1970s: translation of French *hypermarché*, from HYPER- + *marché* 'market'.

hypermedia ▪ n. Computing an extension to hypertext providing multimedia facilities, such as sound and video.

hypermetropia /ˌhaɪpəmɪ'trəʊpɪə/ ▪ n. far-sightedness (in sense 2).
– DERIVATIVES **hypermetropic** adj.
– ORIGIN C19: from Greek *hupermetros* 'beyond measure' + *ōps* 'eye'.

hypermnesia /ˌhaɪpəm'niːzɪə/ ▪ n. unusual power of memory, typically under abnormal conditions such as trauma or narcosis.
– ORIGIN C19: from HYPER- + Greek *mnēsia* 'memory'.

hyperopia /ˌhaɪpər'əʊpɪə/ ▪ n. another term for HYPERMETROPIA.
– DERIVATIVES **hyperopic** adj.
– ORIGIN C19: from HYPER- + Greek *ōps* 'eye'.

hyperparasite ▪ n. Biology a parasite whose host is itself a parasite.
– DERIVATIVES **hyperparasitic** adj. **hyperparasitism** n.

hyperparathyroidism /ˌhaɪpəˌparə'θaɪrɔɪdɪz(ə)m/ ▪ n. Medicine an abnormally high concentration of parathyroid hormone in the blood, resulting in weakening of the bones through loss of calcium.
– DERIVATIVES **hyperparathyroid** adj.

hyperplasia /ˌhaɪpə'pleɪzɪə/ ▪ n. Medicine & Biology the enlargement of an organ or tissue caused by an increase in the reproduction rate of its cells, often as an initial stage in the development of cancer.
– ORIGIN C19: from HYPER- + Greek *plasis* 'formation'.

hyperreal ▪ adj. 1 exaggerated in comparison to reality. 2 (of art) extremely realistic in detail.
– DERIVATIVES **hyperrealism** n. **hyperrealist** adj. **hyperrealistic** adj. **hyperreality** n.

hypersensitive ▪ adj. abnormally or excessively sensitive, either emotionally or in physical response.
– DERIVATIVES **hypersensitiveness** n. **hypersensitivity** n.

hypersonic ▪ adj. 1 relating to speeds of more than five times the speed of sound (Mach 5). 2 relating to sound frequencies above about a thousand million hertz.
– DERIVATIVES **hypersonically** adv.

hyperspace ▪ n. 1 space of more than three dimensions. 2 (in science fiction) a notional space–time continuum in which it is possible to travel faster than light.
– DERIVATIVES **hyperspatial** adj.

hypertension ▪ n. Medicine abnormally high blood pressure.

hypertensive Medicine ▪ adj. exhibiting hypertension. ▪ n. a person with high blood pressure.

hypertext ▪ n. Computing a system allowing extensive cross-referencing between related sections of text.

hyperthermia /ˌhaɪpə'θəːmɪə/ ▪ n. Medicine the condition of having a body temperature greatly above normal.
– DERIVATIVES **hyperthermic** adj.
– ORIGIN C19: from HYPER- + Greek *thermē* 'heat'.

hyperthyroidism /ˌhaɪpə'θaɪrɔɪdɪz(ə)m/ ▪ n. Medicine overactivity of the thyroid gland, resulting in a rapid heartbeat and an increased rate of metabolism.
– DERIVATIVES **hyperthyroid** adj. **hyperthyroidic** adj.

hypertonic /ˌhaɪpə'tɒnɪk/ ▪ adj. 1 Biology having a higher osmotic pressure than a particular fluid. 2 Physiology of or in a state of abnormally high muscle tone.
– DERIVATIVES **hypertonia** n. **hypertonicity** n.

hyperventilate ▪ v. 1 breathe at an abnormally rapid rate, increasing the rate of loss of carbon dioxide. 2 be or become overexcited.
– DERIVATIVES **hyperventilation** n.

hypha /'haɪfə/ ▪ n. (pl. **hyphae** /-fiː/) Botany each of the branching filaments that make up the mycelium of a fungus.
– DERIVATIVES **hyphal** adj.
– ORIGIN C19: modern Latin, from Greek *huphē* 'web'.

hyphen /'haɪf(ə)n/ ▪ n. the sign (-) used to join words to indicate that they have a combined meaning or that they are grammatically linked, or to indicate word division at the end of a line.
– ORIGIN C17: from Greek *huphen* 'together'.

> **USAGE**
> In modern English the use of hyphens is decreasing, especially in compound nouns: **website** is preferred to **web-site** and **air raid** to **air-raid**. Hyphens are still often used to clarify meaning where a compound expression precedes a noun, as in *twenty-odd people*. Phrasal verbs are not usually hyphenated (*we must build up the pressure*) except when they are used as a noun (*a build-up of pressure*). For more information see **Hyphens** in *Guide to Good English* p. SP 22.

hyphenate ▪ v. write or separate with a hyphen.
– DERIVATIVES **hyphenation** n.

hypno- ▪ comb. form 1 relating to sleep: *hypnopaedia*. 2 relating to hypnosis: *hypnotherapy*.
– ORIGIN from Greek *hupnos* 'sleep'.

hypnopaedia /ˌhɪpnəʊ'piːdɪə/ (US **hypnopedia**) ▪ n. learning by hearing while asleep or under hypnosis.
– ORIGIN C20: from HYPNO- + Greek *paideia* 'learning'.

hypnosis ▪ n. the induction of a state of consciousness in which a person loses the power of voluntary action and is highly responsive to suggestion or direction.
– ORIGIN C19: from Greek *hupnos* 'sleep'.

hypnotherapy ▪ n. the use of hypnosis as a therapeutic technique.
– DERIVATIVES **hypnotherapist** n.

hypnotic ▪ adj. 1 of, producing, or relating to hypnosis. 2 having a compelling or soporific effect: *her voice had a hypnotic quality*. 3 Medicine (of a drug) sleep-inducing. ▪ n. 1 Medicine a sleep-inducing drug. 2 a person under or open to hypnosis.
– DERIVATIVES **hypnotically** adv.
– ORIGIN C17: from Greek *hupnōtikos* 'causing sleep', from *hupnoun* 'put to sleep'.

hypnotism ▪ n. the study or practice of hypnosis.
– DERIVATIVES **hypnotist** n.

hypnotize (also **-ise**) ▪ v. produce a state of hypnosis in.
– DERIVATIVES **hypnotizable** (also **-isable**) adj.

hypo¹ ▪ n. Photography the chemical sodium thiosulphate (formerly called hyposulphite) used as a photographic fixer.

hypo² ▪ n. (pl. **-os**) informal an attack of hypoglycaemia.

hypo- (also **hyp-**) ▪ prefix 1 under: *hypodermic*. ▸ below normal: *hypoglycaemia*. 2 slightly: *hypomanic*. 3 Chemistry containing an element with an unusually low valency: *hypochlorous*.
– ORIGIN from Greek *hupo* 'under'.

hypo-allergenic ■ adj. (especially of cosmetics and textiles) unlikely to cause an allergic reaction.

hypocalcaemia /ˌhʌɪpəʊkalˈsiːmɪə/ (US **hypocalcemia**) ■ n. Medicine deficiency of calcium in the bloodstream.

hypochlorous acid /ˌhʌɪpə(ʊ)ˈklɔːrəs/ ■ n. Chemistry a weak acid with oxidizing and bleaching properties, formed when chlorine dissolves in cold water. [HOCl.]
– DERIVATIVES **hypochlorite** n.
– ORIGIN C19: from HYPO- + CHLORINE.

hypochondria /ˌhʌɪpəˈkɒndrɪə/ ■ n. abnormal chronic anxiety about one's health.
– ORIGIN Middle English: from Greek *hupokhondria*, denoting the soft body area below the ribs, orig. thought to be the seat of melancholy.

hypochondriac ■ n. a person who is abnormally anxious about their health. ■ adj. (also **hypochon-driacal**) related to or affected by hypochondria.

hypochondriasis /ˌhʌɪpə(ʊ)kɒnˈdrʌɪəsɪs/ ■ n. technical term for HYPOCHONDRIA.

hypocotyl /ˌhʌɪpə(ʊ)ˈkɒtɪl/ ■ n. Botany the part of the stem of an embryo plant between the stalks of the cotyledons and the root.
– ORIGIN C19: from HYPO- + COTYLEDON.

hypocrisy ■ n. (pl. **-ies**) the practice of claiming to have higher standards or beliefs than is the case.
– ORIGIN Middle English: from Greek *hupokrisis* 'acting of a theatrical part', from *hupokrinesthai* 'play a part, pretend'.

hypocrite ■ n. a person who indulges in hypocrisy.
– DERIVATIVES **hypocritical** adj. **hypocritically** adv.

hypodermic ■ adj. 1 Medicine of or relating to the region immediately beneath the skin. 2 (of a needle or syringe) used to inject beneath the skin. ▶ (of a drug) injected beneath the skin. ■ n. a hypodermic syringe or injection.
– DERIVATIVES **hypodermically** adv.
– ORIGIN C19: from HYPO- + Greek *derma* 'skin'.

hypogastrium /ˌhʌɪpə(ʊ)ˈgastrɪəm/ ■ n. (pl. **hypogastria** /-rɪə/) Anatomy the front central region of the abdomen.
– DERIVATIVES **hypogastric** adj.
– ORIGIN C17: from Greek *hupogastrion*, from *hupo* 'under' + *gastēr* 'belly'.

hypogeal /ˌhʌɪpə(ʊ)ˈdʒiːəl/ (also **hypogean**) ■ adj. Botany remaining or occurring underground. Compare with EPIGEAL.
– ORIGIN C17: from Greek *hupogeios*, from *hupo* 'under' + *gē* 'earth'.

hypogene /ˈhʌɪpə(ʊ)dʒiːn/ ■ adj. Geology produced or occurring under the surface of the earth.
– DERIVATIVES **hypogenic** adj.
– ORIGIN C19: from HYPO- + Greek *genēs* '-born'.

hypoglossal nerves /ˌhʌɪpə(ʊ)ˈglɒs(ə)l/ ■ pl. n. Anatomy the pair of cranial nerves supplying the muscles of the tongue.
– ORIGIN C19: *hypoglossal* from HYPO- + Greek *glōssa* 'tongue'.

hypoglycaemia /ˌhʌɪpəʊglʌɪˈsiːmɪə/ (US **hypoglycemia**) ■ n. Medicine deficiency of glucose in the bloodstream.
– DERIVATIVES **hypoglycaemic** adj.
– ORIGIN C19: from HYPO- + GLYCO- + -AEMIA.

hypogonadism /ˌhʌɪpə(ʊ)ˈgəʊnadɪz(ə)m/ ■ n. Medicine reduction or absence of hormone secretion or other physiological activity of the gonads (testes or ovaries).
– DERIVATIVES **hypogonadal** adj. **hypogonadic** n. & adj.

hypogynous /hʌɪˈpɒdʒɪnəs/ ■ adj. Botany (of a plant or flower) having the stamens situated below the carpels (or gynoecium). Compare with EPIGYNOUS and PERIGYNOUS.
– DERIVATIVES **hypogyny** n.

hypoid /ˈhʌɪpɔɪd/ (also **hypoid gear**) ■ n. a bevel wheel with teeth engaging with a spiral pinion mounted at right angles to the wheel's axis, used to connect non-intersecting shafts in vehicle transmissions.
– ORIGIN 1920s: perhaps a contraction of HYPERBOLOID.

hypomania ■ n. Psychiatry a mild form of mania, marked by elation and hyperactivity.
– DERIVATIVES **hypomanic** adj.

hypoparathyroidism /ˌhʌɪpəʊˌparəˈθʌɪrɔɪdɪz(ə)m/ ■ n. Medicine diminished concentration of parathyroid hormone in the blood, causing deficiencies of calcium and phosphorus compounds.
– DERIVATIVES **hypoparathyroid** adj.

hypophysis /hʌɪˈpɒfɪsɪs/ ■ n. (pl. **hypophyses** /-siːz/) Anatomy technical term for PITUITARY.
– DERIVATIVES **hypophyseal** /ˌhʌɪpə(ʊ)ˈfɪzɪəl/ (also **hypophysial**) adj.
– ORIGIN C17: modern Latin, from Greek *hupophusis* 'offshoot'.

hypopituitarism /ˌhʌɪpəʊpɪˈtjuːɪt(ə)rɪz(ə)m/ ■ n. Medicine diminished hormone secretion by the pituitary gland, causing dwarfism and premature ageing.
– DERIVATIVES **hypopituitary** adj.

hypospadias /ˌhʌɪpəʊˈspeɪdɪəs/ ■ n. Medicine a congenital condition in males in which the opening of the urethra is on the underside of the penis.
– ORIGIN C19: from Greek *hupospadias* 'person having hypospadias'.

hypostasis /hʌɪˈpɒstəsɪs/ ■ n. (pl. **hypostases** /-siːz/)
1 Medicine the accumulation of fluid or blood in parts of the body or organs, as occurs in cases of poor circulation or after death. 2 Philosophy an underlying reality or substance. 3 Theology each of the three persons of the Trinity. ▶ the single person of Christ, as contrasted with his dual human and divine nature.
– ORIGIN C16: from Greek *hupostasis* 'essence'.

hypostatic /ˌhʌɪpə(ʊ)ˈstatɪk/ ■ adj. Theology relating to the persons of the Trinity.
– DERIVATIVES **hypostatical** adj.

hypostyle /ˈhʌɪpə(ʊ)stʌɪl/ ■ adj. Architecture having a roof supported by pillars. ■ n. a building having such a roof.
– ORIGIN C19: from Greek *hupostulos*, from *hupo* 'under' + *stulos* 'column'.

hypotension ■ n. Medicine abnormally low blood pressure.
– DERIVATIVES **hypotensive** adj.

hypotenuse /hʌɪˈpɒtənjuːz, -s/ ■ n. the longest side of a right-angled triangle, opposite the right angle.
– ORIGIN C16: via Latin *hypotenusa* from Greek *hupoteinousa (grammē)* 'subtending (line)', from *hupo* 'under' + *teinein* 'stretch'.

hypothalamus /ˌhʌɪpə(ʊ)ˈθaləməs/ ■ n. (pl. **hypothalami** /-mʌɪ/) Anatomy a region of the forebrain below the thalamus, controlling body temperature, thirst, and hunger, and involved in sleep and emotional activity.
– DERIVATIVES **hypothalamic** adj.

hypothermia /ˌhʌɪpə(ʊ)ˈθəːmɪə/ ■ n. Medicine the condition of having an abnormally (typically dangerously) low body temperature.
– ORIGIN C19: from HYPO- + Greek *thermē* 'heat'.

hypothesis /hʌɪˈpɒθɪsɪs/ ■ n. (pl. **hypotheses** /-siːz/) a supposition or proposed explanation made on the basis of limited evidence as a starting point for further investigation. ▶ Philosophy a proposition made as a basis for reasoning.
– DERIVATIVES **hypothesize** (also **-ise**) v.
– ORIGIN C16: from Greek *hupothesis* 'foundation'.

hypothetical /ˌhʌɪpəˈθɛtɪk(ə)l/ ■ adj. 1 of, based on, or serving as a hypothesis. ▶ supposed but not necessarily real or true. 2 Logic denoting or containing a proposition of the logical form *if p then q*. ■ n. a hypothetical proposition or statement.
– DERIVATIVES **hypothetically** adv.

hypothyroidism /ˌhʌɪpəʊˈθʌɪrɔɪdɪz(ə)m/ ■ n. Medicine abnormally low activity of the thyroid gland, resulting in retardation of growth and mental development.
– DERIVATIVES **hypothyroid** n. & adj.

hypotonic /ˌhʌɪpə(ʊ)ˈtɒnɪk/ ■ adj. 1 Biology having a lower osmotic pressure than a particular fluid. 2 Physiology of or in a state of abnormally low muscle tone.
– DERIVATIVES **hypotonia** n. **hypotonicity** n.

hypoventilation ■ n. Medicine breathing at an abnormally slow rate, resulting in an increased amount of carbon dioxide in the blood.

hypovolaemia

hypovolaemia /ˌhaɪpə(ʊ)vəˈliːmɪə/ (US **hypovolemia**) ■ n. Medicine a decreased volume of circulating blood in the body.
– DERIVATIVES **hypovolaemic** adj.
– ORIGIN C20: from HYPO- + VOLUME + Greek *haima* 'blood'.

hypoxaemia /ˌhaɪpɒkˈsiːmɪə/ (US **hypoxemia**) ■ n. Medicine an abnormally low concentration of oxygen in the blood.
– ORIGIN C19: from HYPO- + OXYGEN + -AEMIA.

hypoxia /haɪˈpɒksɪə/ ■ n. Medicine deficiency in the amount of oxygen reaching the tissues.
– DERIVATIVES **hypoxic** adj.
– ORIGIN 1940s: from HYPO- + OXYGEN.

hypsometer /hɪpˈsɒmɪtə/ ■ n. a device for measuring the boiling point of water, especially in order to determine height above sea level.
– DERIVATIVES **hypsometric** adj.
– ORIGIN from Greek *hupsos* 'height' + -METER

hyracotherium /ˌhaɪrəkə(ʊ)ˈθɪərɪəm/ ■ n. the earliest fossil ancestor of the horse, a small forest animal of the Eocene epoch with four toes on the front feet and three on the back.
– ORIGIN modern Latin: from *hyraco-* (combining form from HYRAX) + Greek *thērion* 'wild animal'.

hyrax /ˈhaɪraks/ ■ n. a small short-tailed herbivorous mammal, found in Africa and Arabia. [Family Procaviidae: several species.]
– ORIGIN C19: modern Latin, from Greek *hurax* 'shrew-mouse'.

hyssop /ˈhɪsəp/ ■ n. **1** a small bushy aromatic plant of the mint family, the leaves of which are used in cookery and herbal medicine. [*Hyssopus officinalis*.] **2** (in biblical use) a wild shrub whose twigs were used for sprinkling in ancient Jewish rites of purification.
– ORIGIN Old English: from Greek *hyssōpos*, of Semitic origin.

hysterectomy /ˌhɪstəˈrɛktəmɪ/ ■ n. (pl. **-ies**) a surgical operation to remove all or part of the womb.
– ORIGIN C19: from Greek *hustera* 'womb' + -ECTOMY.

hysteresis /ˌhɪstəˈriːsɪs/ ■ n. Physics the phenomenon in which the value of a physical property lags behind changes in the effect causing it, especially that involving magnetic induction and a magnetizing force.
– ORIGIN C19: from Greek *husterēsis* 'shortcoming'.

hysteria ■ n. **1** Psychiatry a psychological disorder whose symptoms include selective amnesia, volatile emotions, and attention-seeking behaviour. **2** exaggerated or uncontrollable emotion or excitement.
– ORIGIN C19: from Latin *hystericus* (see HYSTERIC).

hysteric ■ n. **1** (**hysterics**) informal wildly emotional behaviour. ▶ uncontrollable laughter. **2** a person suffering from hysteria. ■ adj. another term for HYSTERICAL.
– ORIGIN C17: from Greek *husterikos* 'of the womb', from *hustera* 'womb' (hysteria being thought to be associated with the womb).

hysterical ■ adj. wildly uncontrolled: *the band were mobbed by hysterical fans.* ▶ informal extremely funny.
– DERIVATIVES **hysterically** adv.

hysteron proteron /ˌhɪstərɒn ˈprɒtərɒn/ ■ n. Rhetoric a figure of speech in which the natural order of elements is reversed.
– ORIGIN C16: from Greek *husteron proteron* 'the latter (put in place of) the former'.

Hz ■ abbrev. hertz.

Ii

I¹ (also **i**) ■ n. (pl. **Is** or **I's**) **1** the ninth letter of the alphabet. **2** denoting the next after H in a set of items, categories, etc. **3** the Roman numeral for one.

I² ■ pron. [first person sing.] used by a speaker to refer to himself or herself.
– ORIGIN Old English, of Germanic origin.

I³ ■ abbrev. (**I.**) Island(s) or Isle(s) (chiefly on maps). ■ symb. **1** electric current. **2** the chemical element iodine.

i ■ symb. (*i*) Mathematics the imaginary quantity equal to the square root of minus one. Compare with **J**.

-i¹ ■ suffix forming the plural: **1** of nouns adopted from Latin ending in *-us*: *foci*. **2** of nouns adopted from Italian ending in *-e* or *-o*: *dilettanti*.

-i² ■ suffix forming adjectives from place names in the Near or Middle East: *Azerbaijani*.
– ORIGIN from Semitic and Indo-Iranian adj. endings.

-ia¹ ■ suffix **1** forming nouns adopted from Latin or Greek (such as *mania*), and modern Latin terms (such as *utopia*). **2** forming names of: ▶ Medicine states and disorders: *anaemia*. ▶ Botany & Zoology genera and higher groups: *dahlia*. **3** forming place names: *India*.
– ORIGIN representing Latin or Greek endings.

-ia² ■ suffix forming noun plurals: **1** from Greek neuter nouns ending in *-ion* or from those in Latin ending in *-ium* or *-e*: *paraphernalia*. **2** Zoology in the names of classes: *Reptilia*.

IAEA ■ abbrev. International Atomic Energy Agency.

-ial ■ suffix forming adjectives such as *celestial*.
– ORIGIN from French *-iel* or Latin *-ialis*.

iamb /ˈaɪam(b)/ ■ n. another term for **IAMBUS**.

iambic /aɪˈambɪk/ ■ adj. Prosody of or using iambuses. ■ n. (**iambics**) verse using iambuses.

iambus /aɪˈambəs/ ■ n. (pl. **iambuses** or **iambi** /-bʌɪ/) Prosody a metrical foot consisting of one short (or unstressed) syllable followed by one long (or stressed) syllable.
– ORIGIN C16: from Greek *iambos* 'iambus, lampoon', from *iaptein* 'attack verbally' (because the iambic trimeter was first used by Greek satirists).

-ian ■ suffix forming adjectives and nouns such as *antediluvian* and *Jordanian*.
– ORIGIN from French *-ien* or Latin *-ianus*.

-iasis ■ suffix a common form of **-ASIS**.

IATA /aɪˈɑːtə/ ■ abbrev. International Air Transport Association.

IB ■ abbrev. International Baccalaureate.

IBA ■ abbrev. Independent Broadcasting Authority.

Iberian ■ n. a native of Iberia (the Iberian peninsula), especially in ancient times. ■ adj. relating to or denoting Iberia.

ibex /ˈʌɪbɛks/ ■ n. (pl. **ibexes**) a wild mountain goat with long, thick ridged horns and a beard. [*Capra ibex* (Eurasia and NE Africa), and *C. pyrenaica* (Pyrenees).]
– ORIGIN C17: from Latin.

IBF ■ abbrev. International Boxing Federation.

Ibibio /ˌɪbɪˈbiːəʊ/ ■ n. (pl. same or **-os**) a member of a people of southern Nigeria.
– ORIGIN the name in Ibibio.

ibid. /ˈɪbɪd/ ■ adv. in the same source (referring to a previously cited work).
– ORIGIN abbrev. of Latin *ibidem* 'in the same place'.

-ibility ■ suffix forming nouns corresponding to adjectives ending in *-ible* (such as *accessibility* corresponding to *accessible*).
– ORIGIN from French *-ibilité* or Latin *-ibilitas*.

ibis /ˈʌɪbɪs/ ■ n. (pl. **ibises**) a large wading bird with a long downcurved bill, long neck, and long legs. [*Threskiornis*, *Plegadis*, and other genera: numerous species.]
– ORIGIN Middle English: from Greek.

-ible ■ suffix forming adjectives: **1** able to be: *defensible*. **2** suitable for being: *edible*. **3** causing: *horrible*.
– ORIGIN from French *-ible* or Latin *-ibilis*.

-ibly ■ suffix forming adverbs corresponding to adjectives ending in *-ible* (such as *audibly* corresponding to *audible*).

IBM ■ abbrev. International Business Machines.

Ibo /ˈiːbəʊ/ ■ n. & adj. variant form of **IGBO**.

ibogaine /ɪˈbəʊɡəˌiːn/ ■ n. a hallucinogenic compound from the roots of a West African shrub, sometimes used to treat heroin or cocaine addiction.
– ORIGIN C20: from a blend of *iboga* (local name for the compound) and **COCAINE**.

IBRD ■ abbrev. International Bank for Reconstruction and Development.

IBSA ■ abbrev. India Brazil South Africa, a trilateral political and economic cooperation group formed by the governments of these countries.

ibuprofen /ˌʌɪbjuːˈprəʊf(ə)n/ ■ n. a synthetic compound used as an analgesic and anti-inflammatory drug.
– ORIGIN 1960s: from elements of the chemical name 2-(4-isobutylphenyl) propionic acid.

IC ■ abbrev. **1** integrated circuit. **2** internal-combustion.

-ic ■ suffix **1** forming adjectives such as *Islamic*, *terrific*. **2** forming nouns such as *lyric*, *mechanic*. **3** Chemistry denoting an element in a higher valency: *ferric*. Compare with **-OUS**.
– ORIGIN from French *-ique*, Latin *-icus*, or Greek *-ikos*.

i/c ■ abbrev. **1** in charge of. **2** in command.

-ical ■ suffix forming adjectives: **1** corresponding to nouns or adjectives usually ending in *-ic* (such as *comical* corresponding to *comic*). **2** corresponding to nouns ending in *-y* (such as *pathological* corresponding to *pathology*).
– DERIVATIVES **-ically** suffix forming corresponding adverbs.

ICBM ■ abbrev. intercontinental ballistic missile.

ICC ■ abbrev. **1** International Chamber of Commerce. **2** International Cricket Council. **3** International Criminal Court.

ice ■ n. **1** frozen water, a brittle transparent crystalline solid. ▶ chiefly Brit. an ice cream or water ice. **2** informal diamonds. ■ v. **1** decorate with icing. **2** (usu. **ice up/over**) become covered or blocked with ice. **3** N. Amer. informal kill.
– PHRASES **break the ice** relieve tension or get conversation going at the start of a party or between strangers. **on ice 1** (of wine or food) kept chilled using ice. **2** suspended; on hold. **on thin ice** in a precarious or risky situation.
– DERIVATIVES **iced** adj.
– ORIGIN Old English, of Germanic origin.

-ice ■ suffix forming nouns such as *service*, *police*, and abstract nouns such as *justice*.
– ORIGIN from Old French *-ice*, from Latin *-itia*, *-itius*, *-itium*.

ice age ■ n. a period or series of periods when ice sheets were unusually extensive across the earth's surface, in particular during the Pleistocene period.

ice axe ■ n. a small axe used by climbers for cutting footholds in ice.

ice beer ■ n. a type of strong lager matured at a low temperature after the main fermentation is complete.

iceberg ■ n. a large mass of ice floating in the sea.
– PHRASES **the tip of an** (or **the**) **iceberg** the small perceptible part of a much larger situation or problem.
– ORIGIN C18: from Dutch *ijsberg*, from *ijs* 'ice' + *berg* 'hill'.

ʊ put   uː too   ʌɪ my   aʊ how   eɪ day   əʊ no   ɪə near   ɔɪ boy   ʊə poor   ʌɪə fire   aʊə sour

iceberg lettuce ■ n. a lettuce of a variety having a dense round head of crisp pale leaves.

icebox ■ n. a chilled container for keeping food cold. ▶ Brit. a compartment in a refrigerator for making and storing ice. ▶ US dated a refrigerator.

ice-breaker ■ n. a ship designed for breaking a channel through ice.

ice cap ■ n. a permanent covering of ice over a large area, especially in the polar region of a planet.

ice cream ■ n. a semi-soft frozen dessert made with sweetened and flavoured milk fat.

ice cube ■ n. a small block of ice made in a freezer, used for adding to drinks.

ice dancing ■ n. a form of ice skating incorporating choreographed dance moves based on ballroom dances.
– DERIVATIVES **ice dance** n. & v. **ice dancer** n.

iced tea (also **ice tea**) ■ n. a chilled drink of sweetened black tea.

icefall ■ n. **1** a steep part of a glacier like a frozen waterfall. **2** an avalanche of ice.

ice field ■ n. a large permanent expanse of ice, especially in polar regions.

ice-fish ■ v. fish through holes in the ice on a lake or river.
– DERIVATIVES **ice-fishing** n.

ice hockey ■ n. a fast contact sport developed from field hockey, played on an ice rink between two teams of six skaters, who attempt to drive a small rubber disc or puck into the opposing goal with hooked sticks.

ice house ■ n. a building for storing ice.

Icelander ■ n. a native or inhabitant of Iceland.

Icelandic /aɪsˈlandɪk/ ■ n. the language of Iceland. ■ adj. of or relating to Iceland, its people, or its language.

Iceland poppy ■ n. a tall poppy with colourful flowers, native to arctic and north temperate regions. [*Papaver nudicaule*.]

ice lolly (also **iced lolly**) ■ n. S. African & Brit. a piece of flavoured water ice or ice cream on a stick.

ice pack ■ n. **1** a bag or piece of cloth filled with ice and applied to the body to reduce swelling or lower temperature. **2** an expanse of large pieces of floating ice forming a nearly continuous mass, as occurs in polar seas.

ice pick ■ n. a small pick as used by climbers or for breaking ice.

ice plant ■ n. **1** a southern African succulent which has leaves covered with glistening fluid-filled protuberances that resemble ice crystals. [Genera *Mesembryanthemum* and *Dorotheanthus*.] **2** an Asian stonecrop which bears domed heads of tiny pink flowers. [*Sedum spectabile*.]

ice shelf ■ n. a floating sheet of ice permanently attached to a land mass.

ice skate ■ n. a boot with a blade attached to the sole, used for skating on ice. ■ v. (**ice-skate**) skate on ice as a sport or pastime.
– DERIVATIVES **ice skater** n. **ice skating** n.

I Ching /iː ˈtʃɪŋ/ ■ n. an ancient Chinese manual of divination based on eight symbolic trigrams and sixty-four hexagrams, interpreted in terms of the principles of yin and yang.
– ORIGIN from Chinese *yijing* 'book of changes'.

ichneumon /ɪkˈnjuːmən/ ■ n. **1** (also **ichneumon wasp** or **ichneumon fly**) a slender parasitic wasp with long antennae, which deposits its eggs in or on the larvae of other insects. [Family Ichneumonidae: many species.] **2** the large grey mongoose. [*Herpestes ichneumon*.]
– ORIGIN C15: from Greek *ikhneumōn* 'tracker', from *ikhneuein* 'to track'.

ichthyo- /ˈɪkθɪəʊ/ ■ comb. form relating to fish; fishlike: *ichthyosaur*.
– ORIGIN from Greek *ikhthus* 'fish'.

ichthyology /ˌɪkθɪˈɒlədʒi/ ■ n. the branch of zoology concerned with fishes.
– DERIVATIVES **ichthyological** adj. **ichthyologist** n.

ichthyosaur /ˈɪkθɪəsɔː/ (also **ichthyosaurus** /ˌɪkθɪəˈsɔːrəs/) ■ n. a fossil marine reptile of the Mesozoic era, resembling a dolphin with a long pointed head, four flippers, and a vertical tail.

ichthyosis /ˌɪkθɪˈəʊsɪs/ ■ n. Medicine a congenital skin condition which causes the epidermis to become dry and horny like fish scales.
– DERIVATIVES **ichthyotic** adj.

-ician ■ suffix (forming nouns) denoting a person involved in a particular subject: *statistician*.
– ORIGIN from French *-icien*.

icicle ■ n. a hanging, tapering piece of ice formed by the freezing of dripping water.
– ORIGIN Middle English: from ICE + dialect *ickle* 'icicle' (from Old English *gicel*).

icing ■ n. **1** a mixture of sugar with liquid or fat, used as a coating for cakes or biscuits. **2** the formation of ice on a vehicle or in an engine.
– PHRASES **the icing on the cake** an attractive but inessential addition or enhancement.

icing sugar ■ n. finely powdered sugar used to make icing.

-icity ■ suffix forming abstract nouns especially from adjectives ending in *-ic* (such as *authenticity* from *authentic*).

ick informal, chiefly N. Amer. ■ n. a sticky or congealed substance. ■ exclam. an expression of disgust.
– DERIVATIVES **ickiness** n. **icky** adj.
– ORIGIN 1940s: prob. imitative.

-icle ■ suffix forming nouns which were originally diminutives: *particle*.
– ORIGIN from French *-cule* or Latin *-culus, -cula, -culum*.

icon /ˈaɪkɒn, -k(ə)n/ ■ n. **1** (also **ikon**) a devotional painting of Christ or another holy figure, typically on wood, venerated in the Byzantine and other Eastern Churches. **2** a person or thing regarded as a representative symbol or as worthy of veneration. **3** Computing a symbol or graphic representation on a VDU screen of a program, option, or window. **4** Linguistics a sign which has a characteristic in common with the thing it signifies, for example the word *snarl* pronounced in a snarling way.
– ORIGIN C16: from Greek *eikōn* 'image'.

iconic ■ adj. of, relating to, or of the nature of an icon.
– DERIVATIVES **iconically** adv. **iconicity** n. (chiefly Linguistics).

iconoclast /aɪˈkɒnəklast/ ■ n. **1** a person who attacks cherished beliefs or institutions. **2** a person who destroys images used in religious worship, especially one belonging to a movement opposing such images in the Byzantine Church during the 8th and 9th century.
– DERIVATIVES **iconoclasm** n. **iconoclastic** adj. **iconoclastically** adv.
– ORIGIN C17: from eccles. Greek *eikonoklastēs*, from *eikōn* 'likeness' + *klan* 'to break'.

iconography /ˌaɪkəˈnɒɡrəfi/ ■ n. (pl. **-ies**) **1** the use or study of images or symbols in visual arts. ▶ the visual images, symbols, or modes of representation collectively associated with a person or movement. **2** the illustration of a subject by drawings or figures.
– DERIVATIVES **iconographer** n. **iconographic** adj. **iconographical** adj. **iconographically** adv.

iconology /ˌaɪkəˈnɒlədʒi/ ■ n. the study of visual imagery and its symbolism. ▶ symbolism.
– DERIVATIVES **iconological** adj.

iconostasis /ˌaɪkəˈnɒstəsɪs/ ■ n. (pl. **iconostases** /-siːz/) a screen bearing icons, separating the sanctuary of many Eastern churches from the nave.
– ORIGIN C19: from modern Greek *eikonostasis*, from *eikōn* 'likeness' + *stasis* 'standing'.

icosahedron /ˌaɪkɒsəˈhiːdrən, -ˈhɛd-/ ■ n. (pl. **icosahedra** or **icosahedrons**) a three-dimensional shape having twenty plane faces, in particular a regular solid figure with twelve equal triangular faces.
– DERIVATIVES **icosahedral** adj.
– ORIGIN C16: from Greek *eikosaedron*, from *eikosaedros* 'twenty-faced'.

-ics ■ suffix (forming nouns) denoting a subject of study or branch of knowledge, or a field of activity: *politics*.
– ORIGIN from French *-iques*, Latin *-ica*, or Greek *-ika*, pl. forms.

ICT ■ abbrev. information and computing technology.

icterine warbler /ˈɪkt(ə)rʌɪn/ ■ n. a Eurasian warbler with bright yellow underparts. [*Hippolais icterina*.]
– ORIGIN C19: *icterine* from ICTERUS.

icterus /ˈɪkt(ə)rəs/ ■ n. Medicine technical term for JAUNDICE.
– DERIVATIVES **icteric** /ɪkˈtɛrɪk/ adj.
– ORIGIN C18: from Greek *ikteros*.

ictus /ˈɪktəs/ ■ n. (pl. same or **ictuses**) **1** Prosody a rhythmical or metrical stress. **2** Medicine a stroke or seizure.
– DERIVATIVES **ictal** adj. (Medicine).
– ORIGIN C18: from Latin, 'a blow'.

icy ■ adj. (**-ier**, **-iest**) **1** covered with or consisting of ice. ▸ very cold. **2** very unfriendly or hostile.
– DERIVATIVES **icily** adv. **iciness** n.

ID ■ abbrev. identification or identity.

Id ■ n. variant spelling of EID.

I'd ■ contr. **1** I had. **2** I should or I would.

id /ɪd/ ■ n. Psychoanalysis the part of the mind in which innate instinctive impulses and primary processes are manifest. Compare with EGO and SUPEREGO.
– ORIGIN 1920s: from Latin, 'that', translating German *es*.

-id[1] ■ suffix forming adjectives such as *putrid*.
– ORIGIN from French *-ide*, from Latin *-idus*.

-id[2] ■ suffix **1** forming nouns such as *pyramid*. **2** Biology forming names of structural constituents: *plastid*.
– ORIGIN from or suggested by French *-ide*, from Greek *-is*, *-id-*.

-id[3] ■ suffix forming nouns: **1** Zoology denoting an animal belonging to a family with a name ending in *-idae* or to a class with a name ending in *-ida*: *arachnid*. **2** denoting a member of a specified dynasty or family.
– ORIGIN from or suggested by Latin *-ides* (pl. *-idae*, *-ida*), from Greek.

id. ■ abbrev. idem.

Idasa /ɪˈdɑːsə/ ■ abbrev. Institute for Democracy in South Africa (formerly Institute for a Democratic Alternative for South Africa).

IDC ■ abbrev. (in South Africa) Industrial Development Corporation.

IDE ■ abbrev. Computing Integrated Drive Electronics.

-ide ■ suffix Chemistry forming nouns: ▸ denoting binary compounds of a non-metallic element or group: *chloride*. ▸ denoting other compounds: *peptide*. ▸ denoting elements of a series in the periodic table: *lanthanide*.
– ORIGIN orig. used in *oxide*.

idea ■ n. **1** a thought or suggestion as to a possible course of action. ▸ a mental impression. ▸ a belief. **2** (**the idea**) the aim. **3** Philosophy (in Platonic thought) an eternally existing pattern of which individual things in any class are imperfect copies. ▸ (in Kantian thought) a concept of pure reason, not empirically based in experience.
– PHRASES **get** (or **give someone**) **ideas** informal become (or make someone) ambitious, conceited, or tempted to do something. **have no idea** informal not know at all. **that's the idea** informal that's right. **the very idea!** informal an exclamation of disapproval or disagreement.
– ORIGIN Middle English: from Greek *idea* 'form, pattern', from the base of *idein* 'to see'.

ideal ■ adj. **1** most suitable; perfect. **2** desirable or perfect but existing only in the imagination: *in an ideal world*. ▸ representing an abstract or hypothetical optimum. ■ n. a perfect type. ▸ a standard of perfection.
– DERIVATIVES **ideally** adv.
– ORIGIN Middle English (as a term in Platonic philosophy, in the sense 'existing as an archetype'): from late Latin *idealis*, from Latin *idea* (see IDEA).

ideal gas ■ n. Chemistry a hypothetical gas whose molecules occupy negligible space and have no interactions, and which consequently obeys the gas laws exactly.

idealism ■ n. **1** the practice of forming or pursuing ideals, especially unrealistically. **2** (in art or literature) the representation of things in ideal form. **3** Philosophy any of various systems of thought in which the objects of knowledge are held to be in some way dependent on the activity of mind.
– DERIVATIVES **idealist** n. **idealistic** adj. **idealistically** adv.

idealize (also **-ise**) ■ v. [often as adj. **idealized** (or **-ised**)]

579 **ides**

regard or represent as perfect or better than in reality.
– DERIVATIVES **idealization** (also **-isation**) n. **idealizer** (also **-iser**) n.

idée fixe /ˌiːdeɪ ˈfiːks/ ■ n. (pl. **idées fixes** pronunc. same) an obsession.
– ORIGIN French, 'fixed idea'.

idem /ˈʌɪdɛm, ˈɪdɛm/ ■ adv. used in citations to indicate an author or word that has just been mentioned.
– ORIGIN Latin, 'the same'.

identical ■ adj. **1** exactly alike. ▸ (of twins) developed from a single fertilized ovum, and therefore of the same sex and usually very similar in appearance. Compare with FRATERNAL (in sense 3). **2** Logic & Mathematics expressing an identity.
– DERIVATIVES **identically** adv.
– ORIGIN C16: from medieval Latin *identicus*, from late Latin *identitas* (see IDENTITY).

identification ■ n. the action or process of identifying or the fact of being identified. ▸ an official document or other proof of a person's identity.

identify ■ v. (**-ies**, **-ied**) **1** establish the identity of. **2** recognize or select by analysis. **3** (**identify someone/thing with**) associate someone or something closely with. ▸ (**identify with**) regard oneself as sharing the same characteristics or thinking as (someone else).
– DERIVATIVES **identifiable** adj. **identifiably** adv. **identifier** n.
– ORIGIN C17: from medieval Latin *identificare*, from late Latin *identitas* (see IDENTITY) + Latin *-ficare*, from *facere* 'make'.

identikit /ʌɪˈdɛntɪkɪt/ ■ n. trademark a picture of a person sought by the police, reconstructed from typical facial features according to witnesses' descriptions. ■ adj. often derogatory having typical features and few unique ones; formulaic.

identity ■ n. (pl. **-ies**) **1** the fact of being who or what a person or thing is. ▸ the characteristics determining this. ▸ [as modifier] serving to establish the identity of the owner: *an identity card*. **2** a close similarity or affinity. **3** Mathematics (also **identity operation**) a transformation that leaves an object unchanged. ▸ (also **identity element**) an element of a set which, if combined with another element, leaves that element unchanged. **4** Mathematics an equation expressing the equality of two expressions for all values of the variables, e.g. $(x + 1)^2 = x^2 + 2x + 1$.
– ORIGIN C16: from late Latin *identitas*, from Latin *idem* 'same'.

identity parade ■ n. S. African & Brit. a group of people assembled for the purpose of having an eyewitness identify a suspect for a crime from among them.

identity theft ■ n. the fraudulent practice of using another person's name and personal information in order to obtain credit, loans, etc.

ideogram /ˈɪdɪə(ʊ)gram, ˈʌɪd-/ ■ n. a character symbolizing the idea of a thing without indicating the sounds used to say it (e.g. a numeral).
– ORIGIN C19: from Greek *idea* 'form' + -GRAM[1].

ideograph /ˈɪdɪə(ʊ)grɑːf, ˈʌɪd-/ ■ n. another term for IDEOGRAM.
– DERIVATIVES **ideographic** adj. **ideography** n.

ideologue /ˈʌɪdɪəlɒg, ˈɪd-/ ■ n. a dogmatic or uncompromising adherent of an ideology.

ideology /ˌʌɪdɪˈɒlədʒi, ɪd-/ ■ n. (pl. **-ies**) a system of ideas and ideals forming the basis of an economic or political theory. ▸ the set of beliefs characteristic of a social group or individual.
– DERIVATIVES **ideological** adj. **ideologically** adv. **ideologist** n.
– ORIGIN C18: from Greek *idea* 'form' + *-logos* (denoting discourse or compilation).

ideophone ■ n. **1** Linguistics a word or lexical item which symbolizes a sensual perception, such as sound, movement, duration, etc. **2** variant spelling of IDIOPHONE.

ides /ʌɪdz/ ■ pl. n. (in the ancient Roman calendar) a day falling roughly in the middle of each month (the 15th day of March, May, July, and October, and the 13th of other months) from which other dates were calculated.
– ORIGIN Old English: from Latin *idus* (pl.).

idio-

idio- /ˈɪdɪəʊ/ ■ comb. form personal; own: *idiotype*.
– ORIGIN from Greek *idios* 'own, distinct'.

idiocy ■ n. (pl. **-ies**) extremely stupid behaviour.
– ORIGIN C16: from IDIOT.

idiolect /ˈɪdɪəlɛkt/ ■ n. the speech habits peculiar to a particular person.
– ORIGIN 1940s: from IDIO- + *-lect* as in *dialect*.

idiom ■ n. 1 a group of words established by usage as having a meaning not deducible from those of the individual words (e.g. *over the moon*). ▸ a form of expression natural to a language, person, or group. 2 a characteristic mode of expression in music or art.
– DERIVATIVES **idiomatic** adj. **idiomatically** adv.
– ORIGIN C16: from Greek *idiōma* 'private property'.

idiopathy /ˌɪdɪˈɒpəθi/ ■ n. (pl. **-ies**) Medicine a disease or condition which arises spontaneously or for which the cause is unknown.
– DERIVATIVES **idiopathic** adj.
– ORIGIN C17: from Greek *idiopatheia*, from *idios* 'own' + *-patheia* 'suffering'.

idiophone (also **ideophone**) ■ n. Music an instrument in which sound is produced by making the body of the instrument itself vibrate, for example by striking, shaking, or scraping it.

idiosyncrasy /ˌɪdɪə(ʊ)ˈsɪŋkrəsi/ ■ n. (pl. **-ies**) 1 a mode of behaviour or way of thought peculiar to an individual. ▸ a distinctive characteristic of a thing. 2 Medicine an abnormal physical reaction by an individual to a food or drug.
– DERIVATIVES **idiosyncratic** adj. **idiosyncratically** adv.
– ORIGIN C17: from Greek *idiosunkrasia*, from *idios* 'own' + *sun* 'with' + *krasis* 'mixture'.

idiot ■ n. 1 informal a stupid person. 2 archaic a mentally handicapped person.
– DERIVATIVES **idiotic** adj. **idiotically** adv.
– ORIGIN Middle English: from Greek *idiōtēs* 'layman, ignorant person', from *idios* 'own'.

idiot savant /ˌiːdjəʊ saˈvɒ̃, ˌɪdɪəʊ/ ■ n. (pl. **idiot savants** or **idiots savants** pronunc. same) a person considered to be mentally handicapped but who displays brilliance in a specific area, especially one involving memory.
– ORIGIN French, 'knowledgeable idiot'.

idiotype /ˈɪdɪə(ʊ)tʌɪp/ ■ n. Biology the set of genetic determinants of an individual.

idle ■ adj. (**idler**, **idlest**) 1 avoiding work; lazy. ▸ not working or in use. ▸ (of money) held in cash or in accounts paying no interest. 2 having no purpose or basis: *idle threats*. ■ v. 1 spend time doing nothing. ▸ move aimlessly. 2 (of an engine) run slowly while disconnected from a load or out of gear.
– DERIVATIVES **idleness** n. **idly** adv.
– ORIGIN Old English *īdel* 'empty, useless', of West Germanic origin.

idler ■ n. 1 a person who idles. 2 a pulley that transmits no power but guides or tensions a belt or rope. 3 an idle wheel.

idle wheel ■ n. an intermediate wheel between two geared wheels, to allow them to rotate in the same direction.

idol ■ n. 1 an image or representation of a god used as an object of worship. 2 an object of adulation: *a soccer idol*.
– ORIGIN Middle English: from Latin *idolum* 'image', from Greek *eidōlon*, from *eidos* 'form'.

idolatry ■ n. 1 worship of idols. 2 adulation.
– DERIVATIVES **idolater** n. **idolatrous** adj.
– ORIGIN Middle English: from Old French *idolatrie*, from Greek *eidōlolatreia*, from *eidōlon* (see IDOL) + *-latreia* 'worship'.

idolize (also **-ise**) ■ v. revere or love greatly or excessively.
– DERIVATIVES **idolization** (also **-isation**) n. **idolizer** (also **-iser**) n.

idyll /ˈɪdɪl/ (also **idyl**) ■ n. 1 a blissful or peaceful period or situation. 2 a short description in verse or prose of a picturesque pastoral scene or incident.
– DERIVATIVES **idyllic** adj. **idyllically** adv.
– ORIGIN C16: from Latin *idyllium*, from Greek *eidullion*, diminutive of *eidos* 'form'.

-ie ■ suffix variant spelling of -Y² (as in *auntie*).
– ORIGIN earlier form of *-y*.

i.e. ■ abbrev. that is to say.
– ORIGIN from Latin *id est* 'that is'.

IEC ■ abbrev. (in South Africa) Independent Electoral Commission.

-ier ■ suffix forming personal nouns denoting an occupation or interest: 1 pronounced with stress on the preceding element: *grazier*. 2 pronounced with stress on the final element: *brigadier*.
– ORIGIN sense 1 from Middle English: var. of -ER¹; sense 2 from French *-ier*, from Latin *-arius*.

IF ■ abbrev. intermediate frequency.

if ■ conj. 1 introducing a conditional clause: ▸ on the condition or supposition that. ▸ (with past tense) introducing a hypothetical situation. ▸ every time. 2 despite the possibility that. ▸ despite being. 3 whether. 4 expressing a polite request or tentative opinion. 5 expressing surprise or regret. ■ n. a condition or supposition.
– PHRASES **if and only if** used to introduce a condition which is necessary as well as sufficient. **if anything** used to suggest tentatively that something may be the case. **if not** perhaps even (used to introduce a more extreme term than one first mentioned). **if only** even if for no other reason than. **if so** if that is the case.
– ORIGIN Old English, of Germanic origin.

-iferous ■ comb. form common form of -FEROUS.

iff ■ conj. Logic & Mathematics if and only if.
– ORIGIN 1950s: arbitrary extension of *if*.

iffy ■ adj. (**-ier**, **-iest**) informal doubtful. ▸ of doubtful quality or legality.

-ific ■ suffix common form of -FIC.

-ification ■ suffix common form of -FICATION.

-iform ■ comb. form common form of -FORM.

IFP ■ abbrev. S. African Inkatha Freedom Party.

Igbo /ˈiːbəʊ/ (also **Ibo**) ■ n. (pl. same or **-os**) 1 a member of a people of SE Nigeria. 2 the language of this people.
– ORIGIN a local name.

igloo ■ n. a dome-shaped Eskimo house, typically built from blocks of solid snow.
– ORIGIN C19: from Inuit *iglu* 'house'.

igneous /ˈɪɡnɪəs/ ■ adj. Geology 1 (of rock) having solidified from lava or magma. 2 relating to or involving volcanic or plutonic processes.
– ORIGIN C17: from Latin *igneus*, from *ignis* 'fire'.

ignimbrite /ˈɪɡnɪmbrʌɪt/ ■ n. Geology a volcanic rock formed by the consolidation of material deposited by pyroclastic flows.
– ORIGIN 1930s: from Latin *ignis* 'fire' + *imber* 'shower of rain, storm cloud'.

ignite /ɪɡˈnʌɪt/ ■ v. 1 catch fire or cause to catch fire. 2 provoke or inflame (an emotion or situation).
– DERIVATIVES **ignitability** n. **ignitable** adj.
– ORIGIN C17: from Latin *ignire* 'set on fire', from *ignis* 'fire'.

igniter ■ n. 1 a device for igniting a fuel mixture in an engine. 2 a device for causing an electric arc.

ignition ■ n. 1 the action of igniting or the state of being ignited. 2 the process of starting the combustion of fuel in the cylinders of an internal-combustion engine. ▸ the mechanism used to bring about ignition.

ignitron /ɪɡˈnʌɪtrɒn/ ■ n. a kind of rectifier with a mercury cathode, able to carry large electric currents.
– ORIGIN 1930s: from IGNITE or IGNITION + -TRON.

ignoble ■ adj. (**-er**, **-est**) 1 not honourable; base. 2 of humble origin or social status.
– DERIVATIVES **ignobility** n. **ignobly** adv.
– ORIGIN Middle English: from Latin *ignobilis*, from *in-* 'not' + *gnobilis*, older form of *nobilis* 'noble'.

ignominious /ˌɪɡnəˈmɪnɪəs/ ■ adj. deserving or causing public disgrace or shame.
– DERIVATIVES **ignominiously** adv. **ignominiousness** n. **ignominy** n.
– ORIGIN Middle English: from Latin *ignominiosus*, from *ignominia*, from *in-* 'not' + a var. of *nomen* 'name'.

ignoramus /ˌɪgnəˈreɪməs/ ■ n. (pl. **ignoramuses**) an ignorant or stupid person.
– ORIGIN C16 (as the endorsement made by a grand jury on an indictment backed by insufficient evidence to bring before a petty jury): Latin, 'we do not know' (in legal use 'we take no notice of it').

ignorant ■ adj. **1** lacking knowledge or awareness in general. ▸ (often **ignorant of**) uninformed about or unaware of a specific subject or fact. **2** informal discourteous.
– DERIVATIVES **ignorance** n. **ignorantly** adv.
– ORIGIN Middle English: from Latin *ignorare* (see IGNORE).

ignoratio elenchi /ˌɪgnəˈreɪʃɪəʊ ɪˈlɛŋkʌɪ/ ■ n. (pl. **ignorationes elenchi** /-ˈəʊniːzɪ/) Philosophy a logical fallacy which consists in apparently refuting an opponent while actually disproving something not asserted.
– ORIGIN Latin, 'ignorance of the elenchus'.

ignore ■ v. disregard intentionally. ▸ fail to consider (something significant).
– DERIVATIVES **ignorable** adj. **ignorer** n.
– ORIGIN C15 ('be ignorant of'): from Latin *ignorare* 'not know'.

iguana /ɪˈgwɑːnə/ ■ n. a large lizard with a spiny crest along the back. [*Iguana iguana* (green iguana, tropical America) and other species, family Iguanidae.]
– DERIVATIVES **iguanid** n.
– ORIGIN C16: from Spanish, from Arawak *iwana*.

iguanodon /ɪˈgwɑːnədɒn/ ■ n. a large partly bipedal herbivorous dinosaur of the early to mid Cretaceous period, with a broad stiff tail and the thumb developed into a spike.
– ORIGIN modern Latin, from IGUANA + Greek *odous, odont-* 'tooth' (because its teeth resemble those of the iguana).

ikat /ˈiːkat, ɪˈkat/ ■ n. fabric made using an Indonesian decorative technique in which warp or weft threads, or both, are tie-dyed before weaving.
– ORIGIN 1930s: Malay, 'fasten, tie'.

ikebana /ˌɪkɪˈbɑːnə/ ■ n. the art of Japanese flower arrangement, with formal display according to strict rules.
– ORIGIN Japanese, 'living flowers'.

ikon ■ n. variant spelling of ICON (in sense 1).

ikowe /ɪˈkɔːwɛ/ ■ n. S. African a large edible mushroom which grows on termite mounds. [*Termitomyces umkowaanii*.]
– ORIGIN isiZulu.

-il ■ suffix forming adjectives and nouns such as *civil*.
– ORIGIN from Old French, from Latin *-ilis*.

il- ■ prefix variant spelling of IN-¹, IN-² assimilated before *l* (as in *illustrate*).

ilala palm ■ n. an African fan palm producing fibres, vegetable ivory, and sap that is used to make palm wine. [*Hyphaene coriacea*.]
– ORIGIN *ilala*: from isiZulu *lala* 'sleep'.

-ile ■ suffix forming adjectives and nouns such as *agile*.
– ORIGIN var. of -IL especially in adoptions from French.

ileitis /ˌɪlɪˈʌɪtɪs/ ■ n. Medicine inflammation of the ileum.

ileostomy /ˌɪlɪˈɒstəmi/ ■ n. (pl. **-ies**) a surgical operation in which a damaged part is removed from the ileum and the end diverted to an artificial opening.
– ORIGIN C19: from ILEUM + Greek *stoma* 'mouth'.

ileum /ˈɪlɪəm/ ■ n. (pl. **ilea**) Anatomy the third portion of the small intestine, between the jejunum and the caecum.
– DERIVATIVES **ileac** adj. **ileal** adj.
– ORIGIN C17: from medieval Latin, var. of ILIUM.

ileus /ˈɪlɪəs/ ■ n. Medicine a painful obstruction of the ileum or other part of the intestine.
– ORIGIN C17: from Latin, from Greek *eileos, ilios* 'colic'.

ilex /ˈʌɪlɛks/ ■ n. **1** the holm oak. **2** a tree or shrub of a genus that includes holly. [Genus *Ilex*.]
– ORIGIN Middle English: from Latin.

ilium /ˈɪlɪəm/ ■ n. (pl. **ilia**) the large broad bone forming the upper part of each half of the pelvis.
– ORIGIN Middle English (orig. denoting the ileum): from Latin, sing. of *ilia* 'flanks, entrails'.

ilk ■ n. **1** a type: *fascists, racists, and others of that ilk*. **2** (**of that ilk**) Scottish, chiefly archaic of the place or estate of the same name.
– ORIGIN Old English *ilca* 'same', of Germanic origin.

I'll ■ contr. I shall; I will.

ill ■ adj. **1** not in full health; unwell. **2** poor in quality. ▸ harmful or hostile. ▸ unfavourable. ■ adv. **1** badly, wrongly, or imperfectly: *ill-chosen*. ▸ unfavourably. **2** only with difficulty. ■ n. a problem or misfortune. ▸ evil or harm.
– PHRASES **ill at ease** uncomfortable or embarrassed. **speak** (or **think**) **ill of** say (or think) something critical about.
– ORIGIN Middle English: from Old Norse *illr* 'evil, difficult'.

ill-advised ■ adj. unwise. ▸ badly thought out.
– DERIVATIVES **ill-advisedly** adv.

ill-assorted ■ adj. not well matched.

illative /ɪˈleɪtɪv/ ■ adj. **1** of the nature of or stating an inference. ▸ proceeding by inference. **2** Grammar relating to or denoting a case of nouns in some languages used to express motion into something.
– DERIVATIVES **illatively** adv.
– ORIGIN C16: from Latin *illativus*, from *illat-, inferre* (see INFER).

ill-bred ■ adj. badly brought up or rude.
– DERIVATIVES **ill breeding** n.

ill-disposed ■ adj. unfriendly or unsympathetic.

illegal ■ adj. contrary to or forbidden by law. ■ n. **1** S. African historical (under apartheid) a black person resident or present in an urban area in contravention of the law. **2** an illegal immigrant.
– DERIVATIVES **illegality** n. (pl. **-ies**). **illegally** adv.

USAGE
Illegal and **unlawful** have slightly different meanings. Something that is **illegal** is against the law, whereas an **unlawful** act merely contravenes the rules that apply in a particular context. Thus handball in soccer is **unlawful**, but not **illegal**. A third word with a similar meaning is **illicit**: this tends to encompass things that are forbidden by custom or society, as in *an illicit love affair*.

illegible /ɪˈlɛdʒɪb(ə)l/ ■ adj. not clear enough to be read.
– DERIVATIVES **illegibility** n. **illegibly** adv.

illegitimate /ˌɪlɪˈdʒɪtɪmət/ ■ adj. **1** not in accordance with the law or accepted standards. **2** (of a child) born of parents not lawfully married to each other.
– DERIVATIVES **illegitimacy** n. **illegitimately** adv.

ill fame ■ n. dated disrepute.

ill-fated ■ adj. destined to fail or have bad luck.

ill-favoured (US **ill-favored**) ■ adj. unattractive or offensive.

ill-gotten ■ adj. acquired by illegal or unfair means.

ill humour ■ n. irritability or bad temper.
– DERIVATIVES **ill-humoured** adj.

illiberal ■ adj. opposed to liberal principles.
– DERIVATIVES **illiberality** n. **illiberally** adv.

illicit ■ adj. forbidden by law, rules, or custom.
– DERIVATIVES **illicitly** adv. **illicitness** n.
– ORIGIN C16: from Latin *illicitus*, from *in-* 'not' + *licitus, licere* 'allow'.

USAGE
On the distinctions between **illicit**, **illegal**, and **unlawful**, see usage at ILLEGAL.

illimitable ■ adj. limitless.
– DERIVATIVES **illimitability** n. **illimitably** adv.

illiquid /ɪˈlɪkwɪd/ ■ adj. **1** (of assets) not easily converted into cash. **2** (of a market) with a low volume of activity.
– DERIVATIVES **illiquidity** n.

illiterate /ɪˈlɪt(ə)rət/ ■ adj. **1** unable to read or write. **2** ignorant in a particular subject or activity: *politically illiterate*. ■ n. a person who is unable to read or write.
– PHRASES **functionally illiterate** lacking the literacy necessary for coping with most jobs and daily situations.
– DERIVATIVES **illiteracy** n. **illiterately** adv. **illiterateness** n.

ill-natured ■ adj. bad-tempered and churlish.
– DERIVATIVES **ill-naturedly** adv.

illness

illness ■ n. a disease or period of sickness.

illogical ■ adj. lacking sense or sound reasoning.
— DERIVATIVES **illogic** n. **illogicality** n. (pl. **-ies**). **illogically** adv.

ill-omened ■ adj. attended by bad omens.

ill-starred ■ adj. unlucky.

ill-tempered ■ adj. irritable or morose.

ill-treat ■ v. act cruelly towards.
— DERIVATIVES **ill-treatment** n.

illuminance /ɪˈl(j)uːmɪnəns/ ■ n. Physics the amount of luminous flux per unit area.

illuminant ■ n. technical a means of lighting or source of light. ■ adj. giving off light.

illuminate /ɪˈl(j)uːmɪneɪt/ ■ v. 1 light up. 2 [usu. as adj. **illuminating**] help to clarify or explain. 3 [often as adj. **illuminated**] decorate (a page or initial letter in a manuscript) with gold, silver, or coloured designs.
— DERIVATIVES **illuminatingly** adv. **illuminative** adj. **illuminator** n.
— ORIGIN Middle English: from Latin *illuminare* 'illuminate', from *in-* 'upon' + *lumen* 'light'.

illuminati /ɪˌl(j)uːmɪˈnɑːti/ ■ pl. n. people claiming to possess special enlightenment or knowledge.
— DERIVATIVES **illuminism** n. **illuminist** n.
— ORIGIN C16: pl. of Latin *illuminatus* 'enlightened', from *illuminare* (see ILLUMINATE).

illumination ■ n. 1 lighting or light. ▶ (**illuminations**) lights used in decorating a building or other structure. 2 the action or process of illuminating.

illumine ■ v. poetic/literary light up; illuminate.
— ORIGIN Middle English: from Latin *illuminare* (see ILLUMINATE).

ill-use ■ v. ill-treat. ■ n. (**ill use**) ill-treatment.

illusion /ɪˈl(j)uːʒ(ə)n/ ■ n. a false or unreal perception. ▶ a deceptive appearance or impression. ▶ a false idea or belief.
— PHRASES **be under the illusion that** believe mistakenly that.
— DERIVATIVES **illusional** adj.
— ORIGIN Middle English: from Latin *illusio(n-)*, from *illudere* 'to mock'.

illusionist ■ n. a person who performs tricks that deceive the eye; a magician.

illusive /ɪˈl(j)uːsɪv/ ■ adj. chiefly poetic/literary deceptive; illusory.
— ORIGIN C17: from medieval Latin *illusivus*, from Latin *illudere* (see ILLUSION).

illusory /ɪˈl(j)uːs(ə)ri/ ■ adj. based on illusion; not real.
— DERIVATIVES **illusorily** adv. **illusoriness** n.

illustrate ■ v. 1 provide (a book or periodical) with pictures. 2 elucidate by using examples, charts, etc. ▶ serve as an example of.
— DERIVATIVES **illustrator** n.
— ORIGIN C16 (*illustration* Middle English): from Latin *illustrare* 'light up'.

illustration ■ n. 1 a picture illustrating a book or periodical. 2 the action or fact of illustrating. ▶ an illustrative example.
— DERIVATIVES **illustrational** adj.

illustrative ■ adj. serving as an example or explanation.
— DERIVATIVES **illustratively** adv.

illustrious /ɪˈlʌstrɪəs/ ■ adj. well known and admired for past achievements.
— DERIVATIVES **illustriously** adv. **illustriousness** n.
— ORIGIN C16: from Latin *illustris* 'clear, bright'.

ill will ■ n. animosity.

ilmenite /ˈɪlmənʌɪt/ ■ n. a black mineral consisting of oxides of iron and titanium.
— ORIGIN C19: named after the *Ilmen* mountains in the Urals, in western Russia.

ILO ■ abbrev. International Labour Organization.

-ily ■ suffix forming adverbs corresponding to adjectives ending in *-y* (such as *happily* corresponding to *happy*).
— ORIGIN see -Y[1], -LY[2].

I'm ■ contr. I am.

im- ■ prefix variant spelling of IN-[1], IN-[2] assimilated before *b*, *m*, *p* (as in *imbibe*, *impart*).

image ■ n. 1 a representation of the external form of a person or thing in art. ▶ a visible impression obtained by a camera, telescope, or other device, or displayed on a video screen. ▶ an optical appearance produced by light from an object reflected in a mirror or refracted through a lens. ▶ a mental representation. 2 the general impression that a person, organization, or product presents to the public. 3 a simile or metaphor. 4 a person or thing closely resembling another. ▶ likeness. ▶ (in biblical use) an idol. 5 Mathematics a point or set formed by mapping from another point or set. ■ v. make or form an image of.
— DERIVATIVES **imageless** adj.
— ORIGIN Middle English: from Latin *imago*; rel. to IMITATE.

image intensifier ■ n. a device used to make a brighter version of an image on a photoelectric screen.

imager ■ n. an electronic or other device which records images.

imagery ■ n. 1 figurative language, especially in a literary work. ▶ visual symbolism. 2 visual images collectively.

imagesetter ■ n. Computing a very high-quality type of colour printer.

imaginable ■ adj. possible to be thought of or believed.
— DERIVATIVES **imaginably** adv.

imaginal /ɪˈmadʒɪn(ə)l/ ■ adj. Entomology of or relating to an adult insect or imago.
— ORIGIN C19: from Latin *imago*, *imagin-* 'image'.

imaginary ■ adj. 1 existing only in the imagination. 2 Mathematics (of a number or quantity) expressed in terms of the square root of −1 (represented by *i* or *j*).
— DERIVATIVES **imaginarily** adv.
— ORIGIN Middle English: from Latin *imaginarius*, from *imago* 'image'.

imagination ■ n. the faculty or action of forming ideas or mental images. ▶ the ability of the mind to be creative or resourceful.
— ORIGIN Middle English: from Latin *imaginatio(n-)*, from *imaginari* 'picture to oneself', from *imago* 'image'.

imaginative ■ adj. having or showing creativity or inventiveness.
— DERIVATIVES **imaginatively** adv. **imaginativeness** n.

imagine ■ v. 1 form a mental image or concept of. ▶ [often as adj. **imagined**] believe (something unreal) to exist. 2 suppose or assume.
— DERIVATIVES **imaginer** n.
— ORIGIN Middle English: from Latin *imaginare* 'form an image of' and *imaginari* 'picture to oneself', both from *imago* 'image'.

imagines plural form of IMAGO.

imaginings ■ pl. n. thoughts or fantasies.

imagism /ˈɪmɪdʒɪz(ə)m/ ■ n. a movement in early 20th-century English and American poetry which sought clarity of expression through the use of precise images.
— DERIVATIVES **imagist** n. **imagistic** adj.

imago /ɪˈmeɪɡəʊ/ ■ n. (pl. **imagos** or **imagines** /ɪˈmeɪdʒɪniːz/) Entomology the final and fully developed adult stage of an insect.
— ORIGIN C18: modern Latin use of Latin *imago* 'image'.

imam /ɪˈmɑːm/ ■ n. 1 the person who leads prayers in a mosque. 2 (**Imam**) a title of various Muslim leaders, especially of one succeeding Muhammad as leader of Shiite Islam.
— DERIVATIVES **imamate** n.
— ORIGIN from Arabic *'imām* 'leader'.

Imari /ɪˈmɑːri/ ■ n. a type of richly decorated Japanese porcelain.
— ORIGIN C19: from the name of a port in NW Kyushu, Japan, from which it was shipped.

IMAX /ˈʌɪmaks/ ■ n. trademark a cinematographic technique which produces an image approximately ten times larger than that from standard 35 mm film.
— ORIGIN 1960s: from *i-* (prob. representing a pronunciation of EYE) + *max* (short for MAXIMUM).

imbalance ■ n. a lack of proportion or balance.

imbecile /ˈɪmbɪsiːl/ ■ n. informal a stupid person. ■ adj. stupid.

–DERIVATIVES **imbecilic** adj. **imbecility** n. (pl. **-ies**).
–ORIGIN C16 (as adj., 'physically weak'): from Latin *imbecillus* 'without a supporting staff'.

imbed ■ v. variant spelling of **EMBED**.

imbibe /ɪmˈbaɪb/ ■ v. formal or humorous drink (alcohol). ▸ absorb (ideas or knowledge).
–DERIVATIVES **imbiber** n.
–ORIGIN Middle English: from Latin *imbibere*, from *in-* 'in' + *bibere* 'to drink'.

imbizo /ɪmˈbiːzəʊ/ ■ n. S. African a gathering called by a traditional leader. ▸ a meeting or workshop.
–ORIGIN isiZulu, from *biza* 'call, summon'.

imbongi /ɪmˈbɒŋɡi/ ■ n. S. African a praise singer.
–ORIGIN isiXhosa and isiZulu, 'praise poet'.

imbroglio /ɪmˈbrəʊliəʊ/ ■ n. (pl. **-os**) an extremely confused or complicated situation.
–ORIGIN C18: Italian, from *imbrogliare* 'confuse'.

imbue /ɪmˈbjuː/ ■ v. (**imbues**, **imbued**, **imbuing**) (often **be imbued with**) fill with a feeling or quality.
–ORIGIN Middle English: from French *imbu* 'moistened', from Latin *imbuere* 'moisten'.

imbuia /ɪmˈbuːjə, ɪmˈbwiːjə/ ■ n. **1** a hard decorative wood, used chiefly for making fine furniture, panelling, and flooring. **2** the large tree, native to Brazil, which yields this wood. [*Phoebe porosa*, also called *Ocotea porosa*.]
–ORIGIN 1910s: from Portuguese *imbuia*, the name for the tree in Brazil.

IMEI ■ abbrev. international mobile equipment identity, a number within an international coding system assigned to each cellphone, which provides information such as the serial number and manufacturer.

IMF ■ abbrev. International Monetary Fund.

imide /ˈɪmaɪd/ ■ n. Chemistry an organic compound containing the group -CONHCO-.
–ORIGIN C19: from French, arbitrary alteration of AMIDE.

imifino /ɪmɪˈfiːnɔː/ (also **imfino**) S. African ■ n. another term for MOROGO.
–ORIGIN from isiXhosa.

imipramine /ɪˈmɪprəmiːn/ ■ n. Medicine a synthetic compound used to treat depression.
–ORIGIN 1950s: from *imi(ne)* + *pr(opyl)* + AMINE.

imitate ■ v. follow as a model. ▸ copy (a person's speech or mannerisms), especially for comic effect. ▸ copy or simulate.
–DERIVATIVES **imitable** adj. **imitator** n.
–ORIGIN C16 (*imitation* Middle English): from Latin *imitari* 'copy'; rel. to *imago* 'image'.

imitation ■ n. the action of imitating. ▸ a copy.

imitative /ˈɪmɪtətɪv/ ■ adj. **1** following a model. **2** (of a word) reproducing a natural sound (e.g. *fizz*) or pronounced in a way thought to correspond to the appearance or character of the object or action described (e.g. *blob*).
–DERIVATIVES **imitatively** adv. **imitativeness** n.

immaculate ■ adj. **1** perfectly clean, neat, or tidy. **2** free from flaws or mistakes.
–DERIVATIVES **immaculacy** n. **immaculately** adv. **immaculateness** n.
–ORIGIN Middle English: from Latin *immaculatus*, from *in-* 'not' + *maculatus* 'stained'.

Immaculate Conception ■ n. (in Catholic theology) the doctrine that God preserved the Virgin Mary from the taint of original sin from the moment she was conceived.

immanent /ˈɪmənənt/ ■ adj. existing or operating within. ▸ (of God) permanently pervading the universe. Often contrasted with TRANSCENDENT.
–DERIVATIVES **immanence** n. **immanency** n. **immanentism** n. **immanentist** n.
–ORIGIN C16: from late Latin *immanere* 'remain within'.

immaterial ■ adj. **1** irrelevant. **2** Philosophy spiritual rather than physical.
–DERIVATIVES **immateriality** n. **immaterially** adv.

immature ■ adj. not fully developed. ▸ having or showing emotional or intellectual development appropriate to someone younger.
–DERIVATIVES **immaturely** adv. **immaturity** n.

immeasurable ■ adj. too large, extensive, or extreme to measure.
–DERIVATIVES **immeasurability** n. **immeasurably** adv.

immoral

immediacy ■ n. the quality of providing direct and instant involvement: *the power and immediacy of television images.* ▸ lack of delay; speed.

immediate ■ adj. **1** occurring or done at once. ▸ most urgent; current. **2** nearest in time, space, or relationship. ▸ (of a relation or action) direct. **3** Philosophy (of knowledge or reaction) intuitive.
–DERIVATIVES **immediateness** n.
–ORIGIN Middle English: from late Latin *immediatus*, from *in-* 'not' + *mediatus* 'intervening', from *mediare* (see MEDIATE).

immediately ■ adv. **1** at once. **2** very close or adjacent in time or space. ▸ in direct or very close relation. ■ conj. chiefly Brit. as soon as.

immemorial ■ adj. very old or long past: *from time immemorial.*
–DERIVATIVES **immemorially** adv.
–ORIGIN C17: from medieval Latin *immemorialis*, from *in-* 'not' + *memorialis* 'relating to the memory'.

immense ■ adj. extremely large or great.
–DERIVATIVES **immensity** n.
–ORIGIN Middle English: from Latin *immensus*, from *in-* 'not' + *mensus* 'measured'.

immensely ■ adv. to a great extent; extremely.

immerse ■ v. **1** dip or submerge in a liquid. **2** (**immerse oneself**) or **be immersed** involve oneself deeply in a particular activity or interest.
–ORIGIN C17 (*immersion* C15): from Latin *immergere* 'dip into'.

immersion ■ n. **1** the action of immersing or the state of being immersed. **2** chiefly N. Amer. a method of teaching a foreign language by the exclusive use of that language.

immersion heater ■ n. an electric heating element that is positioned in the liquid to be heated, typically in a domestic hot-water tank.

immigrant ■ n. a person who comes to live permanently in a foreign country.

immigrate ■ v. come to live permanently in a foreign country.
–DERIVATIVES **immigration** n.
–ORIGIN C17: from Latin *immigrare*, from *in-* 'into' + *migrare* 'migrate'.

imminent ■ adj. **1** about to happen. **2** archaic overhanging.
–DERIVATIVES **imminence** n. **imminently** adv.
–ORIGIN Middle English: from Latin *imminere* 'overhang, impend', from *in-* 'upon, towards' + *minere* 'to project'.

immiscible /ɪˈmɪsɪb(ə)l/ ■ adj. (of liquids) not forming a homogeneous mixture when added together.
–DERIVATIVES **immiscibility** n. **immiscibly** adv.

immiseration /ɪˌmɪzəˈreɪʃ(ə)n/ ■ n. economic impoverishment.
–DERIVATIVES **immiserate** v.
–ORIGIN 1940s: translating German *Verelendung*.

immobile ■ adj. not moving. ▸ incapable of moving or being moved.
–DERIVATIVES **immobility** n.

immobilize (also **-ise**) ■ v. prevent from moving or operating as normal. ▸ restrict the movements of (a limb or patient) to allow healing.
–DERIVATIVES **immobilization** (also **-isation**) n. **immobilizer** (also **-iser**) n.

immoderate ■ adj. lacking moderation; excessive.
–DERIVATIVES **immoderately** adv. **immoderation** n.

immodest ■ adj. not humble, decent, or decorous.
–DERIVATIVES **immodestly** adv. **immodesty** n.

immolate /ˈɪməleɪt/ ■ v. kill or offer as a sacrifice, especially by burning.
–DERIVATIVES **immolation** n. **immolator** n.
–ORIGIN C16 (*immolation* Middle English): from Latin *immolare* 'sprinkle with sacrificial meal', from *mola* 'meal'.

immoral ■ adj. not conforming to accepted standards of morality.
–DERIVATIVES **immorality** n. (pl. **-ies**). **immorally** adv.

immoral earnings

immoral earnings ■ pl. n. earnings from prostitution.

immortal /ɪˈmɔːt(ə)l/ ■ adj. living forever. ▸ deserving to be remembered forever. ■ n. an immortal being, especially a god of ancient Greece or Rome. ▸ a person of enduring fame.
– DERIVATIVES **immortality** /ɪmɔːˈtalɪti/ n. **immortalization** (also **-isation**) n. **immortalize** (also **-ise**) v. **immortally** adv.

immovable (also **immoveable**) ■ adj. not able to be moved or changed. ▸ Law (of property) consisting of land, buildings, or other permanent items. ■ n. (**immovables**) Law immovable property.
– DERIVATIVES **immovability** n. **immovably** adv.

immune ■ adj. **1** resistant to a particular infection owing to the presence of specific antibodies or sensitized white blood cells. **2** exempt from an obligation or penalty. **3** (often **immune to**) not susceptible.
– ORIGIN Middle English: from Latin *immunis* 'exempt from public service or charge', from *in-* 'not' + *munis* 'ready for service'.

immune response ■ n. the reaction of the cells and fluids of the body to the presence of an antigen.

immune system ■ n. the organs and processes of the body that provide resistance to infection and toxins.

immunity ■ n. (pl. **-ies**) **1** the ability of an organism to resist an infection by activating an immune response. **2** exemption or protection from an obligation or penalty. ▸ Law officially exempted from legal proceedings or liability.

immunize (also **-ise**) ■ v. make immune to infection, typically by inoculation.
– DERIVATIVES **immunization** (also **-isation**) n. **immunizer** (also **-iser**) n.

immuno- /ˈɪmjʊnəʊ, ɪˈmjuːnəʊ/ ■ comb. form Medicine representing IMMUNE, immunity (see IMMUNE), or IMMUNOLOGY.

immunoassay /ˌɪmjʊnəʊˈaseɪ, ɪˌmjuːnəʊ-/ ■ n. Biochemistry a procedure for detecting or measuring substances through their properties as antigens or antibodies.

immunochemistry ■ n. the branch of biochemistry concerned with immune responses and systems.

immunocompromised ■ adj. Medicine having an impaired immune system.

immunodeficiency ■ n. Medicine reduced ability of the immune system to protect the body from infection.

immunogenic /ˌɪmjʊnəʊˈdʒɛnɪk, ɪˌmjuːnəʊ-/ ■ adj. (of a substance) able to produce an immune response.
– DERIVATIVES **immunogenicity** n.

immunoglobulin /ˌɪmjʊnəʊˈglɒbjʊlɪn, ɪˌmjuːnəʊ-/ ■ n. Biochemistry any of a class of blood proteins which function as antibodies.

immunology ■ n. the branch of medicine and biology concerned with immunity.
– DERIVATIVES **immunologic** adj. **immunological** adj. **immunologically** adv. **immunologist** n.

immunosuppression ■ n. Medicine suppression of an immune response, especially as induced to help the survival of an organ after a transplant operation.
– DERIVATIVES **immunosuppressant** n. **immunosuppressed** adj.

immunosuppressive ■ adj. Medicine (chiefly of drugs) partially or completely suppressing the immune response of an individual. ■ n. a drug of this kind.

immunotherapy ■ n. Medicine the prevention or treatment of disease with substances that stimulate the immune response.

immure /ɪˈmjʊə/ ■ v. (usu. **be immured**) confine or imprison.
– DERIVATIVES **immurement** n.
– ORIGIN C16: from medieval Latin *immurare*, from *in-* 'in' + *murus* 'wall'.

immutable /ɪˈmjuːtəb(ə)l/ ■ adj. unchanging or unchangeable.
– DERIVATIVES **immutability** n. **immutably** adv.

imp ■ n. a mischievous child. ▸ a small, mischievous devil or sprite.
– ORIGIN Old English (in Middle English denoting a child of the devil or an evil person): *impa*, *impe* 'young shoot', from *impian* 'to graft', from Greek *emphuein* 'to implant'.

impact ■ n. /ˈɪmpakt/ **1** the action of one object coming forcibly into contact with another. **2** a marked effect or influence. ■ v. /ɪmˈpakt/ **1** come into forcible contact with another object. **2** (often **impact on**) have a strong effect. **3** press firmly.
– DERIVATIVES **impactive** adj. **impactor** n.
– ORIGIN C17: from Latin *impact-*, *impingere* (see IMPINGE).

impacted ■ adj. Medicine **1** (of a tooth) wedged between another tooth and the jaw. **2** (of a fractured bone) having the parts crushed together. **3** (of faeces) lodged in the intestine.
– DERIVATIVES **impaction** n.

impair ■ v. weaken or damage.
– DERIVATIVES **impairment** n.
– ORIGIN Middle English: from Old French *empeirier*, based on late Latin *pejorare*, from Latin *pejor* 'worse'.

impaired ■ adj. [often in combination] having a disability of a specified kind: *hearing-impaired*.

impala /ɪmˈpɑːlə, -ˈpalə/ ■ n. (pl. same or **impalas**) a graceful antelope of southern and East Africa, the male of which has lyre-shaped horns. [*Aepyceros melampus*.]
– ORIGIN C19: from isiZulu *i-mpala*.

impala lily ■ n. a succulent shrub with showy pink or white flowers and toxic milky sap, native to southern Africa and widely grown as an ornamental. [Genus *Adenium*, in particular *A. multiflorum* and *A. obesum*.]

impale ■ v. **1** transfix or pierce with a sharp instrument. **2** Heraldry display (a coat of arms) side by side with another on the same shield, separated by a vertical line.
– DERIVATIVES **impalement** n. **impaler** n.
– ORIGIN C16: from medieval Latin *impalare*, from Latin *in-* 'in' + *palus* 'a stake'.

impalpable ■ adj. **1** unable to be felt by touch. **2** not easily comprehended.
– DERIVATIVES **impalpability** n. **impalpably** adv.

impart ■ v. communicate (information). ▸ bestow (a quality).
– ORIGIN Middle English ('give a share of'): from Latin *impartire*, from *in-* 'in' + *pars* 'part'.

impartial ■ adj. treating all rivals or disputants equally.
– DERIVATIVES **impartiality** n. **impartially** adv.

impassable ■ adj. impossible to travel along or over.
– DERIVATIVES **impassability** n. **impassableness** n. **impassably** adv.

impasse /amˈpɑːs, ˈampɑːs/ ■ n. a deadlock.
– ORIGIN C19: from French, from *im-* (expressing negation) + the stem of *passer* 'to pass'.

impassioned ■ adj. filled with or showing great emotion.

impassive ■ adj. not feeling or showing emotion.
– DERIVATIVES **impassively** adv. **impassiveness** n. **impassivity** n.

impasto /ɪmˈpastəʊ/ ■ n. Art the process or technique of laying on paint or pigment thickly so that it stands out from a surface.
– ORIGIN C18: from Italian, from *impastare*, from *im-* 'upon' + *pasta* 'a paste'.

impatiens /ɪmˈpatɪɛnz/ ■ n. a plant of a genus that includes busy Lizzie and its many hybrids. [Genus *Impatiens*.]
– ORIGIN from Latin, 'impatient' (because the capsules of the plant readily burst open when touched).

impatient ■ adj. **1** having or showing a lack of patience or tolerance. **2** restlessly eager.
– DERIVATIVES **impatience** n. **impatiently** adv.

impeach ■ v. **1** call into question the integrity or validity of (a practice). **2** Brit. charge with treason or another crime against the state. ▸ chiefly US charge (the holder of a public office) with misconduct.
– DERIVATIVES **impeachable** adj. **impeachment** n.
– ORIGIN Middle English: from Old French *empecher* 'impede', from late Latin *impedicare* 'entangle', from Latin *pes*, *ped-* 'foot'.

impeccable /ɪmˈpɛkəb(ə)l/ ■ adj. in accordance with the highest standards.

– DERIVATIVES **impeccability** n. **impeccably** adv.
– ORIGIN C16: from Latin *impeccabilis*, from *in-* 'not' + *peccare* 'to sin'.

impecunious /ˌɪmpɪˈkjuːnɪəs/ ■ adj. having little or no money.
– DERIVATIVES **impecuniosity** n. **impecuniousness** n.
– ORIGIN C16: from IN-¹ + obsolete *pecunious* 'wealthy', from Latin *pecuniosus*, from *pecunia* 'money'.

impedance /ɪmˈpiːd(ə)ns/ ■ n. the effective resistance to an alternating electric current arising from the combined effects of ohmic resistance and reactance.

impede /ɪmˈpiːd/ ■ v. delay or block the progress or action of.
– ORIGIN C16 (*impediment* Middle English): from Latin *impedire* 'shackle the feet of', from *pes, ped-* 'foot'.

impediment /ɪmˈpɛdɪm(ə)nt/ ■ n. **1** a hindrance or obstruction. **2** (also **speech impediment**) a defect in a person's speech, such as a lisp or stammer.

impedimenta /ɪmˌpɛdɪˈmɛntə/ ■ pl. n. equipment for an activity or expedition, especially when an encumbrance.
– ORIGIN C17: from Latin, pl. of *impedimentum* 'impediment', from *impedire* (see IMPEDE).

impel /ɪmˈpɛl/ ■ v. (**impelled**, **impelling**) drive, force, or urge to do something. ▸ drive forward.
– ORIGIN Middle English: from Latin *impellere*, from *in-* 'towards' + *pellere* 'to drive'.

impeller (also **impellor**) ■ n. the rotating part of a centrifugal pump, compressor, etc. designed to move a fluid. ▸ a similar device used to measure speed or distance travelled through water.

impend /ɪmˈpɛnd/ ■ v. [usu. as adj. **impending**] be about to happen. ▸ (of something bad) loom.
– ORIGIN C16: from Latin *impendere*, from *in-* 'towards, upon' + *pendere* 'hang'.

impenetrable /ɪmˈpɛnɪtrəb(ə)l/ ■ adj. **1** impossible to pass through or enter. ▸ impervious to new ideas or influences. **2** impossible to understand. **3** Physics (of matter) incapable of occupying the same space as other matter at the same time.
– DERIVATIVES **impenetrability** n. **impenetrably** adv.
– ORIGIN Middle English: from Latin *impenetrabilis*, from *in-* 'not' + *penetrabilis* 'able to be pierced', from *penetrare* 'go into'.

impenitent ■ adj. not feeling shame or regret.
– DERIVATIVES **impenitence** n. **impenitently** adv.

impepho ■ n. (pl. same) variant spelling of IMPHEPHO.

imperative ■ adj. **1** of vital importance. **2** giving an authoritative command. ▸ Grammar denoting the mood of a verb that expresses a command or exhortation, as in *come here!* ■ n. an essential or urgent thing. ▸ a factor or influence making something necessary.
– DERIVATIVES **imperatively** adv. **imperativeness** n.
– ORIGIN Middle English: from late Latin *imperativus* 'specially ordered', from *imperare* 'to command', from *in-* 'towards' + *parare* 'make ready'.

imperceptible ■ adj. so slight, gradual, or subtle as not to be perceived.
– DERIVATIVES **imperceptibility** n. **imperceptibly** adv.

imperceptive ■ adj. lacking in perception or insight.

imperfect ■ adj. **1** faulty or incomplete. **2** Grammar (of a tense) denoting a past action in progress but not completed at the time in question. **3** Law (of a gift, title, etc.) transferred without all the necessary conditions or requirements being met.
– DERIVATIVES **imperfection** n. **imperfectly** adv.

imperforate /ɪmˈpəːf(ə)rət/ ■ adj. **1** (of a postage stamp or a block or sheet of stamps) lacking perforations, especially as an error. **2** Anatomy & Zoology lacking the normal opening.

imperial ■ adj. **1** of or relating to an empire or an emperor. ▸ characteristic of an emperor; majestic or magnificent. **2** relating to or denoting the system of non-metric weights and measures formerly used for all measures in the UK, and still used for some.
– DERIVATIVES **imperially** adv.
– ORIGIN Middle English: from Latin *imperialis*, from *imperium* 'command, empire'.

imperial gallon ■ n. see GALLON (sense 1).

imperialism ■ n. **1** a policy of extending a country's power and influence through colonization, use of military force, or other means. **2** chiefly historical rule by an emperor.
– DERIVATIVES **imperialist** n. & adj. **imperialistic** adj. **imperialistically** adv.

imperil ■ v. (**imperilled**, **imperilling**; US **imperiled**, **imperiling**) put into danger.
– ORIGIN Middle English: from PERIL, prob. on the pattern of *endanger*.

imperious /ɪmˈpɪərɪəs/ ■ adj. arrogant and domineering.
– DERIVATIVES **imperiously** adv. **imperiousness** n.
– ORIGIN C16: from Latin *imperiosus*, from *imperium* (see IMPERIUM).

imperishable ■ adj. enduring forever.
– DERIVATIVES **imperishability** /-ˈbɪlɪti/ n. **imperishably** adv.

imperium /ɪmˈpɪərɪəm/ ■ n. absolute power.
– ORIGIN C17: from Latin, 'command, empire'.

impermanent ■ adj. not permanent.
– DERIVATIVES **impermanence** n. **impermanency** n. **impermanently** adv.

impermeable /ɪmˈpəːmɪəb(ə)l/ ■ adj. not allowing fluid to pass through.
– DERIVATIVES **impermeability** n.

impersonal ■ adj. **1** not influenced by or involving personal feelings. ▸ featureless and anonymous. **2** not existing as a person: *an impersonal God.* **3** Grammar (of a verb) used only with a formal subject (in English usually *it*) and expressing an action not attributable to a definite subject (as in *it is snowing*).
– DERIVATIVES **impersonality** n. **impersonally** adv.

impersonal pronoun ■ n. the pronoun *it* when used without definite reference or antecedent, as in *it was snowing.*

impersonate ■ v. pretend to be (another person) for entertainment or fraud.
– DERIVATIVES **impersonation** n. **impersonator** n.
– ORIGIN C17: from IN-² + Latin *persona* 'person', on the pattern of *incorporate*.

impertinent ■ adj. **1** not showing proper respect. **2** formal not pertinent.
– DERIVATIVES **impertinence** n. **impertinently** adv.
– ORIGIN Middle English: from late Latin *impertinent-*, from *in-* 'not' + *pertinere* 'pertain'.

imperturbable /ˌɪmpəˈtəːbəb(ə)l/ ■ adj. unable to be upset or excited.
– DERIVATIVES **imperturbability** n. **imperturbably** adv.
– ORIGIN Middle English: from late Latin *imperturbabilis*, from *in-* 'not' + *perturbare* (see PERTURB).

impervious /ɪmˈpəːvɪəs/ ■ adj. **1** not allowing fluid to pass through. **2** (**impervious to**) unable to be affected by.
– DERIVATIVES **imperviously** adv. **imperviousness** n.

impetigo /ˌɪmpɪˈtaɪɡəʊ/ ■ n. a contagious bacterial skin infection forming pustules and yellow crusty sores.
– ORIGIN Middle English: from Latin, from *impetere* 'to attack'.

impetuous ■ adj. **1** acting or done quickly and rashly. **2** moving forcefully or rapidly.
– DERIVATIVES **impetuosity** n. **impetuously** adv. **impetuousness** n.
– ORIGIN Middle English: from late Latin *impetuosus*, from *impetere* 'to attack'.

impetus ■ n. the force or energy with which a body moves. ▸ a driving force.
– ORIGIN C17: from Latin, 'assault, force'.

imphepho /ɪmˈpɛːpɔː/ (also **impepho**) ■ n. (pl. same) S. African **1** any of several species of everlasting. [Genus *Helichrysum*: several species.] **2** the dried leaves and twigs of this plant, used in herbal medicine or burnt in divination.
– ORIGIN from isiXhosa *impepho*.

impi /ˈɪmpi/ ■ n. (pl. **impis**) a body of Zulu warriors. ▸ a group of armed Zulu men involved in urban or rural conflict.
– ORIGIN isiZulu, 'regiment, armed band'.

impiety /ɪmˈpaɪɪti/ ■ n. (pl. **-ies**) lack of piety or reverence.

impimpi /ɪmˈpiːmpi/ ■ n. (pl. same or **impimpis**) S. African

impinge

informal an informer.
– ORIGIN isiXhosa, 'informer'.

impinge ■ v. (**impinging**) (usu. **impinge on**) have an effect. ▸ come into contact; encroach.
– DERIVATIVES **impingement** n. **impinger** n.
– ORIGIN C16: from Latin *impingere* 'drive something in or at'.

impious /ˈɪmpɪəs, ɪmˈpʌɪəs/ ■ adj. not showing respect or reverence. ▸ wicked.
– DERIVATIVES **impiously** adv. **impiousness** n.

impish ■ adj. mischievous.
– DERIVATIVES **impishly** adv. **impishness** n.

implacable ■ adj. unable to be appeased. ▸ relentless.
– DERIVATIVES **implacability** n. **implacably** adv.

implant ■ v. /ɪmˈplɑːnt/ **1** insert or fix (tissue or an artificial object) into the body. ▸ (of a fertilized egg) become attached to the wall of the uterus. **2** establish (an idea) in the mind. ■ n. /ˈɪmplɑːnt/ a thing implanted.
– DERIVATIVES **implantation** n.
– ORIGIN Middle English: from late Latin *implantare* 'engraft'.

implausible ■ adj. not seeming reasonable or probable.
– DERIVATIVES **implausibility** n. **implausibly** adv.

implement ■ n. /ˈɪmplɪm(ə)nt/ a tool, utensil, or other piece of equipment, used for a particular purpose. ■ v. /ˈɪmplɪmɛnt/ put into effect.
– DERIVATIVES **implementation** n. **implementer** n.
– ORIGIN Middle English: from medieval Latin *implementa* (pl.) and late Latin *implementum*, from Latin *implere* 'fill up', later 'employ'.

implicate ■ v. /ˈɪmplɪkeɪt/ **1** show to be involved in a crime. ▸ (**be implicated in**) bear some of the responsibility for (an action or process). **2** convey (a meaning or intention) indirectly; imply. ■ n. /ˈɪmplɪkət/ chiefly Logic a thing implied.
– DERIVATIVES **implicative** /ɪmˈplɪkətɪv/ adj. **implicatively** adv.
– ORIGIN Middle English (orig. 'entwine'): from Latin *implicatus* 'folded in', from *implicare* (see IMPLY).

implication ■ n. **1** the implicit conclusion that can be drawn from something. ▸ a likely consequence. **2** the action of implicating or the state of being implicated.
– DERIVATIVES **implicational** adj.

implicit /ɪmˈplɪsɪt/ ■ adj. **1** implied though not directly expressed. **2** (**implicit in**) always to be found in. **3** with no qualification or question: *an implicit faith in God*. **4** Mathematics (of a function) not expressed directly in terms of independent variables.
– DERIVATIVES **implicitly** adv. **implicitness** n.
– ORIGIN C16: from Latin *implicitus*, later form of *implicatus* 'entwined', from *implicare* (see IMPLY).

implode /ɪmˈpləʊd/ ■ v. collapse or cause to collapse violently inwards.
– DERIVATIVES **implosion** n. **implosive** adj.
– ORIGIN C19: from IN-² + Latin *plodere*, *plaudere* 'to clap', on the pattern of *explode*.

implore ■ v. beg earnestly or desperately.
– DERIVATIVES **imploring** adj. **imploringly** adv.
– ORIGIN C16: from Latin *implorare* 'invoke with tears'.

imply ■ v. (**-ies**, **-ied**) indicate by suggestion rather than explicit reference. ▸ (of a fact or occurrence) suggest as a logical consequence.
– DERIVATIVES **implied** adj. **impliedly** adv.
– ORIGIN Middle English (orig. 'entangle'): from Latin *implicare*, from *in-* 'in' + *plicare* 'to fold'.

impolite ■ adj. not having or showing good manners.
– DERIVATIVES **impolitely** adv. **impoliteness** n.

impolitic /ɪmˈpɒlɪtɪk/ ■ adj. failing to possess or display prudence.

imponderable ■ adj. difficult or impossible to estimate or assess. ■ n. an imponderable factor.
– DERIVATIVES **imponderability** /-ˈbɪlɪti/ n. **imponderably** adv.

import ■ v. **1** bring (goods or services) into a country from abroad. **2** Computing transfer (data) into a file or document. **3** archaic indicate or signify. ■ n. **1** an imported commodity, article, or service. ▸ the action or process of importing. **2** the implied meaning of something. ▸ importance.
– DERIVATIVES **importable** adj. **importation** n. **importer** n.
– ORIGIN Middle English: from medieval Latin *importare* 'bring in' (in medieval Latin, 'imply, be of consequence').

important ■ adj. **1** of great significance or value. **2** having high rank or status.
– DERIVATIVES **importance** n. **importantly** adv.
– ORIGIN Middle English: from medieval Latin *important-*, *importare* (see IMPORT).

importunate /ɪmˈpɔːtjʊnət/ ■ adj. persistent or pressing.
– DERIVATIVES **importunately** adv. **importunity** n. (pl. **-ies**)
– ORIGIN C16: from Latin *importunus* 'inconvenient', from *Portunus*, the name of the god who protected harbours.

importune /ˌɪmpɔːˈtjuːn/ ■ v. **1** harass with persistent requests. **2** [usu. as noun **importuning**] approach to offer one's services as a prostitute.
– ORIGIN C16: from medieval Latin *importunari*, from Latin *importunus* (see IMPORTUNATE).

impose ■ v. **1** force to be accepted, undertaken, or complied with. **2** (often **impose on**) take advantage of someone. **3** Printing arrange (pages of type) so as to be in the correct order after printing and folding.
– ORIGIN C15 (*imposition* Middle English): from French *imposer*, from Latin *imponere* 'inflict, deceive', but influenced by *impositus* 'inflicted' and Old French *poser* 'to place'.

imposing ■ adj. grand and impressive.
– DERIVATIVES **imposingly** adv.

imposition ■ n. **1** the action of imposing or of being imposed. **2** an unwelcome demand or burden.

impossible ■ adj. not able to occur, exist, or be done. ▸ very difficult to deal with.
– DERIVATIVES **impossibility** n. (pl. **-ies**). **impossibly** adv.

impost¹ /ˈɪmpəʊst/ ■ n. **1** a tax or similar compulsory payment. **2** Horse Racing the weight carried by a horse as a handicap.
– ORIGIN C16: from medieval Latin *impostus*, from Latin *impositus*, from *imponere* (see IMPOSE).

impost² /ˈɪmpəʊst/ ■ n. Architecture the top course of a pillar that supports an arch.
– ORIGIN C15: from Italian *imposta*, from *imporre*, from Latin *imponere* (see IMPOSE).

impostor (also **imposter**) ■ n. a person who assumes a false identity in order to deceive or defraud.
– ORIGIN C16: from late Latin *impostor*, contraction of *impositor*, from Latin *imponere* (see IMPOSE).

imposture ■ n. an instance of assuming a false identity.

impotent /ˈɪmpət(ə)nt/ ■ adj. **1** helpless or powerless. **2** (of a man) abnormally unable to achieve an erection or orgasm.
– DERIVATIVES **impotence** n. **impotency** n. **impotently** adv.

impound ■ v. **1** seize and take legal custody of. **2** shut up (domestic animals) in a pound. **3** (of a dam) hold back or confine (water).
– DERIVATIVES **impoundable** adj. **impounder** n. **impoundment** n.

impoverish ■ v. **1** make poor. **2** exhaust the strength or natural fertility of.
– DERIVATIVES **impoverishment** n.
– ORIGIN Middle English: from Old French *empoveriss-*, *empoverir*, from *povre* 'poor'.

impracticable ■ adj. impossible in practice to do or carry out.
– DERIVATIVES **impracticability** n. **impracticably** adv.

impractical ■ adj. **1** not adapted for use or action; not sensible. **2** chiefly N. Amer. impracticable.
– DERIVATIVES **impracticality** n. **impractically** adv.

imprecation ■ n. formal a spoken curse.
– DERIVATIVES **imprecatory** adj.
– ORIGIN Middle English: from Latin *imprecatio(n-)*, from *imprecari* 'invoke (evil)', from *in-* 'towards' + *precari* 'pray'.

imprecise ■ adj. lacking exactness.
– DERIVATIVES **imprecisely** adv. **impreciseness** n. **imprecision** n.

impregnable ■ adj. unable to be captured or broken into. ▸ unable to be overcome.

– DERIVATIVES **impregnability** n. **impregnably** adv.

impregnate /ˈɪmprɛgneɪt/ ■ v. 1 (usu. **be impregnated with**) soak or saturate with a substance. ▶ fill with a feeling or quality. 2 make pregnant; fertilize.
– DERIVATIVES **impregnation** n.
– ORIGIN C17 (*impregnation* Middle English): from late Latin *impregnare* 'make pregnant'.

impresario /ˌɪmprɪˈsɑːrɪəʊ/ ■ n. (pl. **-os**) a person who organizes and often finances theatrical or musical productions. ▶ chiefly historical the manager of a musical, theatrical, or operatic company.
– ORIGIN C18: from Italian, from *impresa* 'undertaking'.

impress[1] ■ v. 1 make (someone) feel admiration and respect. 2 make a mark or design on using a stamp or seal. 3 (**impress something on**) emphasize an idea in the mind of. 4 apply (an electric current or potential) from an external source. ■ n. 1 an act of making an impression. ▶ a mark made by a seal or stamp. 2 a person's characteristic mark or quality.
– DERIVATIVES **impressible** adj.
– ORIGIN Middle English: from Old French *empresser*, from *em-* 'in' + *presser* 'to press', influenced by Latin *imprimere* (see IMPRINT).

impress[2] ■ v. historical force to serve in an army or navy. ▶ commandeer (goods or equipment) for public service.
– DERIVATIVES **impressment** n.
– ORIGIN C16: from IN-[2] + PRESS[2].

impression ■ n. 1 an idea, feeling, or opinion. ▶ an effect produced on someone: *her quick wit made a good impression*. 2 an imitation of a person or thing, done to entertain. 3 a mark impressed on a surface. ▶ Dentistry a negative copy of the teeth or mouth made by pressing them into a soft substance. 4 the printing of a number of copies of a publication for issue at one time. ▶ a particular printed version of a book, especially one reprinted with no or only minor alteration. ▶ a print taken from an engraving.
– DERIVATIVES **impressional** adj.

impressionable ■ adj. easily influenced.
– DERIVATIVES **impressionability** n. **impressionably** adv.

Impressionism ■ n. 1 a style or movement in painting characterized by a concern with depicting the visual impression of the moment, especially in terms of the shifting effect of light. 2 a literary or artistic style that seeks to capture a feeling or experience rather than to achieve accurate depiction.
– DERIVATIVES **Impressionist** n. & adj.
– ORIGIN from French *impressionnisme*, from *impressionniste*, orig. applied unfavourably with ref. to a painting done by Monet.

impressionist ■ n. an entertainer who impersonates famous people.

impressionistic ■ adj. 1 based on subjective impressions presented unsystematically. 2 (**Impressionistic**) in the style of Impressionism.
– DERIVATIVES **impressionistically** adv.

impressive ■ adj. evoking admiration through size, quality, or skill.
– DERIVATIVES **impressively** adv. **impressiveness** n.

imprest ■ n. a fund used by a business for small items of expenditure and restored to a fixed amount periodically. ▶ a sum of money advanced to a person for a particular purpose.
– ORIGIN C16: from the earlier phr. *in prest* 'as a loan', influenced by Italian or medieval Latin *imprestare* 'lend'.

imprimatur /ˌɪmprɪˈmeɪtə, -ˈmɑːtə, -ˈmɑːtʊə/ ■ n. an official licence issued by the Roman Catholic Church to print an ecclesiastical or religious book. ▶ authority or approval.
– ORIGIN C17: from Latin, 'let it be printed'.

imprint ■ v. 1 (usu. **be imprinted**) impress or stamp (a mark or outline) on a surface or body. 2 make an impression or mark on. ▶ fix (an idea) firmly in someone's mind. 3 (**imprint on**) Zoology (of a young animal) come to recognize (another animal, person, or thing) as a parent or object of habitual trust. ■ n. 1 an impressed mark or outline. 2 a printer's or publisher's name and other details in a book or other publication. ▶ a brand name under which books are published, typically the name of a former publishing house now part of a larger group.

– ORIGIN Middle English: from Old French *empreinter*, from Latin *imprimere*, from *in-* 'into' + *premere* 'to press'.

imprison ■ v. put or keep in prison.
– DERIVATIVES **imprisonment** n.
– ORIGIN Middle English *emprison*, from Old French *emprisoner*.

improbable ■ adj. not likely to be true or to happen. ▶ unexpected and apparently inauthentic.
– DERIVATIVES **improbability** n. (pl. **-ies**). **improbably** adv.

impromptu /ɪmˈprɒm(p)tjuː/ ■ adj. & adv. unplanned or unrehearsed. ■ n. (pl. **impromptus**) a short piece of instrumental music, especially a solo, reminiscent of an improvisation.
– ORIGIN C17: from Latin *in promptu* 'in readiness', from *promptus* (see PROMPT).

improper ■ adj. not in accordance with accepted standards of behaviour. ▶ unseemly or indecent.
– DERIVATIVES **improperly** adv.

impropriety /ˌɪmprəˈpraɪətɪ/ ■ n. (pl. **-ies**) improper behaviour or character.

improve ■ v. 1 make or become better. ▶ (**improve on/upon**) achieve or produce something better than. 2 [as adj. **improving**] giving moral or intellectual benefit.
– DERIVATIVES **improvability** n. **improvable** adj. **improvement** n. **improver** n.
– ORIGIN C16: from Anglo-Norman French *emprower*, from Old French *prou* 'profit'.

improvident ■ adj. lacking foresight; thoughtless.
– DERIVATIVES **improvidence** n. **improvidently** adv.

improvise ■ v. 1 create and perform (music, drama, or verse) spontaneously or without preparation. 2 produce or make (something) from whatever is available.
– DERIVATIVES **improvisation** n. **improvisational** adj. **improvisatorial** adj. **improvisatory** adj. **improviser** n.
– ORIGIN C19 (*improvisation* C18): from French *improviser* or Italian *improvvisare*, from *improvviso* 'extempore'.

imprudent ■ adj. not showing care for the consequences of an action; rash.
– DERIVATIVES **imprudence** n. **imprudently** adv.

impudent /ˈɪmpjʊd(ə)nt/ ■ adj. not showing due respect for another person; impertinent.
– DERIVATIVES **impudence** n. **impudently** adv.
– ORIGIN Middle English: from Latin *impudent-*, from *in-* 'not' + *pudent-* 'ashamed, modest'.

impugn /ɪmˈpjuːn/ ■ v. dispute the truth, validity, or honesty of (a statement or motive).
– DERIVATIVES **impugnable** adj. **impugnment** n.
– ORIGIN Middle English: from Latin *impugnare* 'assail'.

impulse ■ n. 1 a sudden strong and unreflective urge or desire to act. 2 a driving or motivating force; an impetus. 3 a pulse of electrical energy; a brief current. 4 Physics a force acting briefly on a body and producing a change of momentum.
– ORIGIN C17 (*impulsion* Middle English, as a verb meaning 'give an impulse to'): from Latin *impuls-*, *impellere* (see IMPEL).

impulsion ■ n. 1 a strong urge to do something. 2 the force or motive behind an action or process.

impulsive ■ adj. 1 acting or done without forethought. 2 Physics acting as an impulse.
– DERIVATIVES **impulsively** adv. **impulsiveness** n. **impulsivity** n.

impunity /ɪmˈpjuːnɪtɪ/ ■ n. (usu. in phr. **with impunity**) exemption from punishment or freedom from the injurious consequences of an action.
– ORIGIN C16: from Latin *impunitas*, from *impunis* 'unpunished'.

impure ■ adj. 1 mixed with foreign matter; adulterated or tainted. 2 morally wrong, especially in sexual matters. ▶ defiled or contaminated according to ritual prescriptions.
– DERIVATIVES **impurely** adv. **impureness** n.

impurity ■ n. (pl. **-ies**) 1 the quality or condition of being impure. 2 a constituent which impairs the purity of something.

impute /ɪmˈpjuːt/ ■ v. 1 (usu. **impute something to**)

attribute (something, especially something bad) to someone. **2** Theology ascribe (righteousness, guilt, etc.) to someone by virtue of a similar quality in another. **3** Finance assign (a value) to something by inference from the value of the products or processes to which it contributes.
– DERIVATIVES **imputable** adj. **imputation** n.
– ORIGIN Middle English: from Latin *imputare* 'enter in the account'.

In ■ symb. the chemical element indium.

in ■ prep. **1** expressing the situation of being enclosed or surrounded by something. **2** expressing motion that results in being within or surrounded by something. **3** expressing a period of time during which an event takes place or a situation remains the case. **4** expressing the length of time before a future event is expected to take place. **5** expressing a state, condition, or quality. **6** expressing inclusion or involvement. **7** indicating someone's occupation or profession. **8** indicating the language or medium used. **9** expressing a value as a proportion of (a whole). ■ adv. **1** expressing movement that results in being enclosed or surrounded by something. **2** expressing the situation of being enclosed or surrounded by something. ▶ present at one's home or office. ▶ Cricket batting. **3** expressing arrival at a destination. **4** (of the tide) rising or at its highest level. ■ adj. informal fashionable.
– PHRASES **be in for** have good reason to expect (something, typically something unpleasant). **be in for it** have good reason to expect trouble or retribution. **in on** privy to (a secret). **in that** for the reason that. **in with** informal enjoying friendly relations with. **the ins and outs** informal all the details of something.
– ORIGIN Old English, of Germanic origin.

-in[1] ■ suffix Chemistry forming names of organic compounds, pharmaceutical products, proteins, etc.: *insulin*.
– ORIGIN alteration of -INE[4].

-in[2] ■ comb. form denoting a gathering of people for a common purpose, typically as a form of protest: *sit-in*.

in-[1] (also **il-** before *l*; **im-** before *b*, *m*, *p*; **ir-** before *r*) ■ prefix **1** (added to adjectives) not: *infertile*. **2** (added to nouns) without; a lack of: *inexperience*.
– ORIGIN from Latin.

in-[2] (also **il-** before *l*; **im-** before *b*, *m*, *p*; **ir-** before *r*) ■ prefix in; into; towards; within: *influx*.
– ORIGIN representing IN or the Latin preposition *in*.

in. ■ abbrev. inch(es).

-ina ■ suffix **1** denoting feminine names and titles: *tsarina*. **2** denoting names of musical instruments: *concertina*. **3** denoting names of plant and animal groups: *globigerina*.
– ORIGIN from Italian, Spanish, or Latin.

inability ■ n. the state of being unable to do something.

in absentia /ˌɪn abˈsɛntɪə/ ■ adv. while not present.
– ORIGIN Latin, 'in absence'.

inaccessible ■ adj. **1** unable to be reached. ▶ unable to be seen or used. **2** difficult to understand or appreciate. **3** not open to advances or influence; unapproachable.
– DERIVATIVES **inaccessibility** n. **inaccessibly** adv.

inaccurate ■ adj. not accurate.
– DERIVATIVES **inaccuracy** n. **inaccurately** adv.

inaction ■ n. lack of action where some is expected or appropriate.

inactivate ■ v. make inactive or inoperative.
– DERIVATIVES **inactivation** n. **inactivator** n.

inactive ■ adj. not active, working, or energetic.
– DERIVATIVES **inactively** adv. **inactivity** n.

inadequate ■ adj. **1** lacking the quality or quantity required; insufficient for a purpose. **2** (of a person) unable to deal with a situation or with life.
– DERIVATIVES **inadequacy** n. (pl. **-ies**). **inadequately** adv.

inadmissible ■ adj. **1** (especially of evidence in court) not accepted as valid. **2** not to be allowed or tolerated.
– DERIVATIVES **inadmissibility** n. **inadmissibly** adv.

inadvertent ■ adj. not resulting from or achieved through deliberate planning.
– DERIVATIVES **inadvertence** n. **inadvertency** n.

inadvertently adv.
– ORIGIN C17: from IN-[1] + Latin *advertere* 'turn the mind to'.

inadvisable ■ adj. likely to have unfortunate consequences; unwise.
– DERIVATIVES **inadvisability** n.

inalienable ■ adj. unable to be taken away from or given away by the possessor.
– DERIVATIVES **inalienability** n. **inalienably** adv.

inalterable ■ adj. unable to be changed.
– DERIVATIVES **inalterability** n. **inalterably** adv.

inane ■ adj. lacking sense or meaning; silly.
– DERIVATIVES **inanely** adv. **inaneness** n. **inanity** n. (pl. **-ies**).
– ORIGIN C16: from Latin *inanis* 'empty, vain'.

inanimate ■ adj. **1** not alive, especially not in the manner of animals and humans. **2** showing no sign of life; lifeless.
– DERIVATIVES **inanimately** adv.

inanition /ˌɪnəˈnɪʃ(ə)n/ ■ n. **1** exhaustion caused by lack of nourishment. **2** lack of vigour and enthusiasm.
– ORIGIN Middle English: from late Latin *inanitio(n-)*, from Latin *inanire* 'make empty', from *inanis* 'empty, vain'.

inapplicable ■ adj. not relevant or appropriate.
– DERIVATIVES **inapplicability** n. **inapplicably** adv.

inapposite /ɪnˈapəzɪt/ ■ adj. out of place; inappropriate.
– DERIVATIVES **inappositely** adv. **inappositeness** n.

inappreciable ■ adj. **1** too small or insignificant to be valued or perceived. **2** archaic too valuable to be properly estimated.
– DERIVATIVES **inappreciably** adv.

inappropriate ■ adj. not suitable or appropriate.
– DERIVATIVES **inappropriately** adv. **inappropriateness** n.

inapt ■ adj. not suitable or appropriate.
– DERIVATIVES **inaptitude** n. **inaptly** adv.

inarguable ■ adj. another term for UNARGUABLE.
– DERIVATIVES **inarguably** adv.

inarticulate /ˌɪnɑːˈtɪkjʊlət/ ■ adj. **1** unable to speak distinctly or express oneself clearly. ▶ unspoken or not expressed in words. **2** without joints or articulations.
– DERIVATIVES **inarticulacy** n. **inarticulately** adv. **inarticulateness** n.

inartistic ■ adj. having or showing a lack of skill or talent in art.
– DERIVATIVES **inartistically** adv.

inasmuch ■ adv. (in phr. **inasmuch as**) **1** to the extent that; in so far as. **2** considering that; since.

inattentive ■ adj. not paying attention. ▶ failing to attend to the comfort or wishes of others.
– DERIVATIVES **inattention** n. **inattentively** adv. **inattentiveness** n.

inaudible ■ adj. unable to be heard.
– DERIVATIVES **inaudibility** n. **inaudibly** adv.

inaugural /ɪˈnɔːɡjʊr(ə)l/ ■ adj. marking the beginning of an institution, activity, or period of office: *the President's inaugural address*. ■ n. an inaugural speech, especially one made by an incoming US president.

inaugurate /ɪˈnɔːɡjʊreɪt/ ■ v. **1** begin or introduce (a system, period, project, etc.). **2** admit formally to office.
– DERIVATIVES **inauguration** n. **inaugurator** n. **inauguratory** adj.
– ORIGIN C16: from Latin *inaugurat-* 'interpreted as omens (from the flight of birds)', from *augurare* 'to augur'.

inauspicious ■ adj. not conducive to success; unpromising.
– DERIVATIVES **inauspiciously** adv. **inauspiciousness** n.

inauthentic ■ n. not authentic, genuine, or sincere.
– DERIVATIVES **inauthentically** adv. **inauthenticity** n.

in-between ■ adj. informal situated somewhere between two extremes; intermediate.

inboard ■ adv. & adj. within or towards the centre of a ship, aircraft, or vehicle.

inborn ■ adj. existing from birth. ▶ natural to a person or animal.

inbound ■ adj. & adv. travelling towards a particular place, especially when returning to the original point of departure.

inbox ■ n. **1** an in tray. **2** Computing the window in which a user's received emails and similar electronic communications are displayed.

inbred ■ adj. **1** produced by inbreeding. **2** existing in a person or animal from birth; congenital.

inbreed ■ v. (past and past part. **inbred**) [often as noun **inbreeding**] breed from closely related people or animals, especially over many generations.

inbuilt ■ adj. existing as an original or essential part.

Inc. ■ abbrev. Incorporated.

Inca ■ n. **1** a member of a South American Indian people living in the central Andes before the Spanish conquest. **2** the supreme ruler of this people.
– DERIVATIVES **Incan** adj.
– ORIGIN the name in Quechua, 'lord, royal person'.

incalculable ■ adj. **1** too great to be calculated or estimated. **2** not able to be calculated, estimated, or predicted.
– DERIVATIVES **incalculably** adv.

Inca lily ■ n. another term for ALSTROEMERIA.

in camera ■ adv. see CAMERA².

incandesce /ˌɪnkanˈdɛs/ ■ v. glow with heat.

incandescent ■ adj. **1** emitting light as a result of being heated. ▸ (of an electric light) containing a filament which glows white-hot when heated by a current passed through it. **2** informal extremely angry.
– DERIVATIVES **incandescence** n. **incandescently** adv.
– ORIGIN C18: from Latin *incandescere* 'glow'.

incant /ɪnˈkant/ ■ v. chant or intone.

incantation ■ n. a series of words said as a magic spell or charm.
– DERIVATIVES **incantatory** adj.
– ORIGIN Middle English: from late Latin *incantatio(n-)*, from Latin *incantare* 'chant, bewitch', from *cantare* 'sing'.

incapable ■ adj. **1** (**incapable of**) unable to do or achieve. ▸ not able to be treated in a certain way. **2** unable to behave rationally or manage one's own affairs.
– DERIVATIVES **incapability** n. **incapably** adv.

incapacitant ■ n. a substance capable of temporarily incapacitating a person without wounding or killing them.

incapacitate /ˌɪnkəˈpasɪteɪt/ ■ v. **1** prevent from functioning in a normal way. **2** Law deprive (someone) of their legal capacity.
– DERIVATIVES **incapacitation** n.

incapacity ■ n. (pl. **-ies**) **1** physical or mental inability to do something or to manage one's affairs. **2** legal disqualification.

incarcerate /ɪnˈkɑːsəreɪt/ ■ v. imprison or confine.
– DERIVATIVES **incarceration** n.
– ORIGIN C16 (*incarceration* Middle English): from medieval Latin *incarcerare*, from Latin *carcer* 'prison'.

incarnadine /ɪnˈkɑːnədʌɪn/ poetic/literary ■ v. colour (something) a bright crimson or pinkish-red. ■ n. a bright crimson or pinkish-red colour.
– ORIGIN C16: from French *incarnadin(e)*, from Italian *incarnadino*, var. of *incarnatino* 'flesh colour', based on Latin *incarnare* (see INCARNATE).

incarnate ■ adj. /ɪnˈkɑːnət/ [often postpos.] **1** (of a deity or spirit) embodied in flesh; in human form. **2** represented in the ultimate or most extreme form: *capitalism incarnate*. ■ v. /ˈɪnkɑːneɪt, -ˈkɑːneɪt/ **1** embody or represent (a deity or spirit) in human form. **2** be the living embodiment of (a quality).
– ORIGIN Middle English: from eccles. Latin *incarnare* 'make flesh', from Latin *in-* 'into' + *caro, carn-* 'flesh'.

incarnation ■ n. **1** a living embodiment of a deity, spirit, or abstract quality. **2** (**the Incarnation**) (in Christian theology) the embodiment of God the Son in human flesh as Jesus Christ. **3** (with reference to reincarnation) each of a series of earthly lifetimes or forms.

incase ■ v. variant spelling of ENCASE.

incautious ■ adj. heedless of potential problems or risks.
– DERIVATIVES **incaution** n. **incautiously** adv. **incautiousness** n.

incendiary /ɪnˈsɛndɪəri/ ■ adj. **1** (of a device or attack) designed to cause fires. **2** tending to stir up conflict or excitement. ■ n. (pl. **-ies**) an incendiary bomb or device.
– DERIVATIVES **incendiarism** n.

– ORIGIN Middle English: from Latin *incendiarius*, from *incendium* 'conflagration', from *incendere* 'set fire to'.

incense¹ /ˈɪnsɛns/ ■ n. a gum, spice, or other substance that is burned for the sweet smell it produces. ■ v. perfume with incense or a similar fragrance.
– ORIGIN Middle English: from eccles. Latin *incensum* 'something burnt, incense', from *incendere* 'set fire to'.

incense² /ɪnˈsɛns/ ■ v. make very angry.
– ORIGIN Middle English: from Latin *incendere* 'set fire to'.

incentive ■ n. a thing that motivates or encourages someone to do something. ▸ a payment or concession to stimulate greater output or investment.
– DERIVATIVES **incentivize** (also **-ise**) v.
– ORIGIN Middle English: from Latin *incentivum* 'something that sets the tune or incites', from *incantare* 'to chant or charm'.

incentre (US **incenter**) ■ n. Geometry the centre of the incircle of a triangle or other figure.

inception ■ n. the establishment or starting point of an institution or activity.
– ORIGIN Middle English: from Latin *inceptio(n-)*, from *incipere* 'begin'.

incertitude ■ n. a state of uncertainty or hesitation.

incessant ■ adj. (especially of something unpleasant) continuing without pause or interruption.
– DERIVATIVES **incessancy** n. **incessantly** adv. **incessantness** n.
– ORIGIN Middle English: from late Latin *incessant-*, from Latin *in-* 'not' + *cessant-, cessare* 'cease'.

incest ■ n. sexual relations between people classed as being too closely related to marry each other.
– ORIGIN Middle English: from Latin *incestus, incestum* 'unchastity, incest', from *in-* 'not' + *castus* 'chaste'.

incestuous /ɪnˈsɛstjʊəs/ ■ adj. **1** involving or guilty of incest. **2** (of human relations) excessively close and resistant to outside influence.
– DERIVATIVES **incestuously** adv. **incestuousness** n.

inch ■ n. **1** a unit of linear measure equal to one twelfth of a foot (2.54 cm). ▸ (**inches**) informal a person's height or waist measurement. ▸ a very small amount or distance. **2** (also **inch of mercury**) a unit of atmospheric pressure able to support a column of mercury one-inch high in a barometer. ■ v. move along slowly and carefully.
– PHRASES **every inch 1** the whole surface, distance, or area. **2** entirely; very much so. (**to**) **within an inch of one's life** almost to the point of death.
– ORIGIN Old English: from Latin *uncia* 'twelfth part', from *unus* 'one' (prob. denoting a unit).

-in-chief ■ comb. form supreme: *commander-in-chief*.

inchoate ■ adj. /ɪnˈkəʊeɪt, ˈɪnk-, -ət/ **1** not fully formed or developed; rudimentary. ▸ confused or incoherent. **2** Law (of an offence, such as incitement or conspiracy) anticipating a further criminal act.
– DERIVATIVES **inchoately** adv. **inchoateness** n.
– ORIGIN C16: from Latin *inchoare*, var. of *incohare* 'begin'.

incidence ■ n. **1** the occurrence, rate, or frequency of a disease, crime, or other undesirable thing. **2** Physics the intersection of a line, or something moving in a straight line, such as a beam of light, with a surface. **3** the way in which the burden of a tax falls upon the population.
– ORIGIN Middle English: from medieval Latin *incidentia*, from Latin *incidere* (see INCIDENT).

incident ■ n. **1** an event or occurrence; an instance of something happening. ▸ a violent event, such as an assault or skirmish. **2** Law a privilege, burden, or right attaching to an office, estate, or other holding. ■ adj. **1** (**incident to**) liable to happen because of; resulting from. **2** (especially of light or other radiation) falling on or striking something. ▸ of or relating to incidence. **3** (**incident to**) Law attaching to.
– ORIGIN Middle English: from Latin *incidere* 'to fall upon, happen to'.

incidental ■ adj. **1** occurring as a minor accompaniment. ▸ occurring by chance in connection with something else. **2** (**incidental to**) liable to happen as a consequence of. ■ n. an incidental detail, expense, event, etc.

incidentally

incidentally ■ adv. **1** as an incidental comment; by the way. **2** in an incidental manner.

incidental music ■ n. music used in a film or play as a background.

incinerate /ɪnˈsɪnəreɪt/ ■ v. destroy (something, especially waste material) by burning.
– DERIVATIVES **incineration** n.
– ORIGIN C15: from medieval Latin *incinerare* 'burn to ashes'.

incinerator ■ n. an apparatus for incinerating waste material, especially industrial waste.

incipient /ɪnˈsɪpɪənt/ ■ adj. in an initial stage; beginning to happen or develop.
– DERIVATIVES **incipience** n. **incipiency** n. **incipiently** adv.
– ORIGIN C16: from Latin *incipere* 'undertake, begin'.

incipit /ˈɪnsɪpɪt/ ■ n. the opening of a manuscript, early printed book, or chanted liturgical text.
– ORIGIN Latin, '(here) begins'.

incircle ■ n. Geometry a circle inscribed in a triangle or other figure so as to touch (but not cross) each side.

incise ■ v. make a cut or cuts in (a surface). ▶ cut (a mark or decoration) into a surface.
– ORIGIN C16 (*incision* Middle English): from French *inciser*, from Latin *incidere* 'cut into'.

incision ■ n. **1** a surgical cut made in skin or flesh. **2** the action or process of cutting into something.

incisive ■ adj. **1** intelligently analytical and concise. **2** (of an action) quick and direct.
– DERIVATIVES **incisively** adv. **incisiveness** n.

incisor ■ n. a narrow-edged tooth at the front of the mouth, adapted for cutting.

incite ■ v. encourage or stir up (violent or unlawful behaviour). ▶ urge or persuade to act in a violent or unlawful way.
– DERIVATIVES **incitation** n. **inciteful** adj. **incitement** n. **inciter** n.
– ORIGIN C15 (*incitation* Middle English): from Latin *in-citare*, from *in-* 'towards' + *citare* 'rouse'.

incivility ■ n. (pl. -ies) rude or unsociable speech or behaviour.

incl. ■ abbrev. including.

inclement /ɪnˈklɛm(ə)nt/ ■ adj. (of the weather) unpleasantly cold or wet.
– DERIVATIVES **inclemency** n. (pl. -ies).

inclination ■ n. **1** a natural tendency or urge to act or feel in a particular way. ▶ (**inclination for/to/towards**) an interest in or liking for. **2** a slope or slant. **3** the angle at which a straight line or plane is inclined to another.

incline ■ v. **1** (usu. **be inclined to/towards/to do something**) be favourably disposed towards or willing to do. **2** (usu. **be inclined to/to do something**) have a specified tendency, disposition, or talent. **3** lean or turn away from a given plane or direction, especially the vertical or horizontal. ▶ bend (one's head) forwards and downwards. ■ n. an inclined surface, slope, or plane.
– ORIGIN Middle English: from Latin *inclinare* 'to bend towards'.

inclined plane ■ n. a plane inclined at an angle to the horizontal.

inclinometer /ˌɪnklɪˈnɒmɪtə/ ■ n. a device for measuring the angle of inclination of something, especially from the horizontal.

inclose ■ v. variant spelling of ENCLOSE.

inclosure ■ n. variant spelling of ENCLOSURE.

include ■ v. **1** comprise or contain as part of a whole. **2** make part of a whole or set. ▶ allow (someone) to share in an activity or privilege.
– ORIGIN Middle English: from Latin *includere*, from *in-* 'into' + *claudere* 'to shut'.

including ■ prep. containing as part of the whole being considered.

inclusion ■ n. **1** the action or state of including or of being included. ▶ a person or thing that is included. **2** chiefly Geology a body or particle of distinct composition embedded in a rock or other material.

inclusive ■ adj. **1** (**inclusive of**) containing (a specified element) as part of a whole. ▶ including all the expected or required services or items. ▶ [postpos.] between the extreme limits stated: *the ages of 55 to 59 inclusive*. **2** not excluding any section of society or any party. ▶ (of language) deliberately non-sexist, especially avoiding the use of masculine pronouns to cover both men and women.
– DERIVATIVES **inclusively** adv. **inclusiveness** n. **inclusivism** n.

inclusive fitness ■ n. Genetics the ability of an individual organism to pass on its genes to the next generation, taking into account the shared genes passed on by the organism's close relatives.

incognito /ˌɪnkɒɡˈniːtəʊ, ɪnˈkɒɡnɪtəʊ/ ■ adj. & adv. having one's true identity concealed. ■ n. (pl. -os) an assumed or false identity.
– ORIGIN C17: from Italian, 'unknown'.

incoherent ■ adj. **1** incomprehensible or confusing in speech or writing. ▶ internally inconsistent; illogical. **2** Physics (of waves) having no definite or stable phase relationship.
– DERIVATIVES **incoherence** n. **incoherency** n. (pl. -ies). **incoherently** adv.

incohesion ■ n. lack of social cohesion.

incombustible ■ adj. (especially of a building material) not inflammable.
– DERIVATIVES **incombustibility** n.

income ■ n. money received, especially on a regular basis, for work or through investments.
– ORIGIN Middle English ('entrance, arrival'): in early use from Old Norse *innkoma*, later from IN + COME.

incomer ■ n. chiefly Brit. a person who has come to live in an area in which they have not grown up.

income support ■ n. (in the UK and Canada) payment made by the state to people on a low income.

income tax ■ n. tax levied directly on personal income.

incoming ■ adj. in the process of coming in. ▶ (of a message) being received rather than sent. ▶ (of an official or administration) having just been elected or appointed to succeed another. ■ n. (**incomings**) revenue; income.

incommensurable /ˌɪnkəˈmɛnʃ(ə)rəb(ə)l, -sjə-/ ■ adj. **1** not able to be judged or measured by the same standards; having no common standard. **2** Mathematics (of numbers) in a ratio that cannot be expressed as a ratio of integers. ■ n. an incommensurable quantity.
– DERIVATIVES **incommensurability** n. **incommensurably** adv.

incommensurate /ˌɪnkəˈmɛnʃ(ə)rət, -sjə-/ ■ adj. **1** (**incommensurate with**) out of keeping or proportion with. **2** another term for INCOMMENSURABLE (in sense 1).
– DERIVATIVES **incommensurately** adv. **incommensurateness** n.

incommode ■ v. formal cause inconvenience to.
– ORIGIN C16: from Latin *incommodare*, from *in-* 'not' + *commodus* 'convenient'.

incommodious ■ adj. formal or dated causing inconvenience or discomfort.
– DERIVATIVES **incommodiously** adv. **incommodiousness** n.

incommunicable ■ adj. not able to be communicated to others.
– DERIVATIVES **incommunicability** n. **incommunicableness** n. **incommunicably** adv.

incommunicado /ˌɪnkəmjuːnɪˈkɑːdəʊ/ ■ adj. & adv. not able to communicate with other people.
– ORIGIN C19: from Spanish *incomunicado*, from *incomunicar* 'deprive of communication'.

incommunicative ■ adj. another term for UNCOMMUNICATIVE.

incomparable /ɪnˈkɒmp(ə)rəb(ə)l/ ■ adj. **1** without an equal in quality or extent; matchless. **2** unable to be compared; totally different.
– DERIVATIVES **incomparability** n. **incomparably** adv.

incompatible ■ adj. (of two things) not able to exist or be used together. ▶ (of two people) unable to live together harmoniously.
– DERIVATIVES **incompatibility** n. **incompatibly** adv.

incompetent ■ adj. **1** not sufficiently skilful to do

something successfully. **2** Law not qualified to act in a particular capacity. ■ n. an incompetent person.
– DERIVATIVES **incompetence** n. **incompetency** n. **incompetently** adv.

incomplete ■ adj. not complete.
– DERIVATIVES **incompletely** adv. **incompleteness** n. **incompletion** n.

incomprehensible ■ adj. not able to be understood.
– DERIVATIVES **incomprehensibility** n. **incomprehensibleness** n. **incomprehensibly** adv. **incomprehension** n.

incompressible ■ adj. not able to be compressed.
– DERIVATIVES **incompressibility** n.

inconceivable ■ adj. not capable of being imagined or grasped mentally; unbelievable.
– DERIVATIVES **inconceivability** n. **inconceivableness** n. **inconceivably** adv.

inconclusive ■ adj. not conclusive.
– DERIVATIVES **inconclusively** adv. **inconclusiveness** n.

incongruent /ɪnˈkɒŋɡrʊənt/ ■ adj. **1** incongruous. **2** Chemistry affecting the components of an alloy or other substance differently: *incongruent melting*.
– DERIVATIVES **incongruence** n. **incongruently** adv.

incongruous /ɪnˈkɒŋɡrʊəs/ ■ adj. not in keeping with the surroundings or other elements; out of place.
– DERIVATIVES **incongruity** n. (pl. **-ies**). **incongruously** adv.

inconnu /ˈãkɒnuː, ˌãkɒˈn(j)uː/ ■ n. an unknown person or thing.
– ORIGIN C19: French, 'unknown'.

inconsequent ■ adj. **1** not connected or following logically; irrelevant. **2** inconsequential.
– DERIVATIVES **inconsequence** n. **inconsequently** adv.

inconsequential ■ adj. not important or significant.
– DERIVATIVES **inconsequentiality** n. (pl. **-ies**). **inconsequentially** adv. **inconsequentialness** n.

inconsiderable ■ adj. [usu. with neg.] of small size, amount, or extent. ▶ unimportant or insignificant.

inconsiderate ■ adj. thoughtlessly causing hurt or inconvenience to others.
– DERIVATIVES **inconsiderately** adv. **inconsiderateness** n. **inconsideration** n.

inconsistent ■ adj. not consistent.
– DERIVATIVES **inconsistency** n. **inconsistently** adv.

inconsolable ■ adj. not able to be comforted or consoled.
– DERIVATIVES **inconsolability** n. **inconsolably** adv.

inconspicuous ■ adj. not clearly visible or attracting attention.
– DERIVATIVES **inconspicuously** adv. **inconspicuousness** n.

inconstant ■ adj. frequently changing; variable or irregular.
– DERIVATIVES **inconstancy** n. (pl. **-ies**). **inconstantly** adv.

incontestable ■ adj. not able to be disputed.
– DERIVATIVES **incontestability** n. **incontestably** adv.

incontinent ■ adj. **1** lacking voluntary control over urination or defecation. **2** lacking self-restraint; uncontrolled.
– DERIVATIVES **incontinence** n. **incontinently** adv.

incontrovertible ■ adj. not able to be denied or disputed.
– DERIVATIVES **incontrovertibility** n. **incontrovertibly** adv.

inconvenience ■ n. the state or fact of being slightly troublesome or difficult. ■ v. cause inconvenience to.
– DERIVATIVES **inconvenient** adj. **inconveniently** adv.

inconvertible ■ adj. not able to be converted.
– DERIVATIVES **inconvertibility** n. **inconvertibly** adv.

incorporate ■ v. **1** take in or include as part of a whole. **2** constitute (a company, city, or other organization) as a legal corporation. ■ adj. **1** constituted as a legal corporation; incorporated. **2** poetic/literary having a bodily form; embodied.
– DERIVATIVES **incorporation** n. **incorporative** adj.
– ORIGIN Middle English: from late Latin *incorporare* 'embody', from Latin *corpus* 'body'.

incorporeal /ˌɪnkɔːˈpɔːrɪəl/ ■ adj. **1** not composed of matter; having no material existence. **2** Law having no physical existence, as in shares or patent rights.

incorrect ■ adj. not in accordance with fact or particular standards; wrong.
– DERIVATIVES **incorrectly** adv. **incorrectness** n.

incorrigible ■ adj. not able to be corrected or reformed: *she's an incorrigible flirt*.
– DERIVATIVES **incorrigibility** n. **incorrigibly** adv.

incorruptible ■ adj. **1** not susceptible to corruption, especially by bribery. **2** not subject to death or decay; everlasting.
– DERIVATIVES **incorruptibility** n. **incorruptibly** adv.

increase ■ v. make or become greater in size, amount, or degree. ■ n. an instance of increasing.
– DERIVATIVES **increasable** adj. **increasing** adj. **increasingly** adv.
– ORIGIN Middle English: from Old French *encreistre*, from Latin *increscere*, from *in-* 'into' + *crescere* 'grow'.

incredible ■ adj. **1** impossible to believe. **2** difficult to believe; extraordinary. ▶ informal amazingly good.
– DERIVATIVES **incredibility** n. **incredibly** adv.

incredulous ■ adj. unwilling or unable to believe something.
– DERIVATIVES **incredulity** n. **incredulously** adv. **incredulousness** n.

increment /ˈɪŋkrɪm(ə)nt/ ■ n. **1** an increase or addition, especially one of a series on a fixed scale. ▶ a regular increase in salary on such a scale. **2** Mathematics a small positive or negative change in a variable quantity or function.
– DERIVATIVES **incremental** adj. **incrementally** adv.
– ORIGIN Middle English: from Latin *incrementum*, from the stem of *increscere* (see **INCREASE**).

incrementalism ■ n. belief in or advocacy of change by degrees.
– DERIVATIVES **incrementalist** n. & adj.

incriminate /ɪnˈkrɪmɪneɪt/ ■ v. make (someone) appear guilty of a crime or wrongdoing.
– DERIVATIVES **incrimination** n. **incriminatory** adj.
– ORIGIN C18 (*incrimination* C17): from late Latin *incriminare* 'accuse', from Latin *crimen* 'crime'.

in-crowd ■ n. (**the in-crowd**) informal a small group of people that are particularly fashionable or popular.

incubate /ˈɪŋkjʊbeɪt/ ■ v. **1** (of a bird) sit on (eggs) in order to keep them warm and bring them to hatching. **2** develop (something, especially an infectious disease) slowly without outward or perceptible signs.
– DERIVATIVES **incubation** n.
– ORIGIN C17: from Latin *incubare* 'lie on'.

incubator ■ n. **1** an apparatus used to hatch eggs or grow micro-organisms under controlled conditions. **2** an enclosed apparatus providing a controlled and protective environment for the care of premature babies.

incubus /ˈɪŋkjʊbəs/ ■ n. (pl. **incubi** /-bʌɪ/) a male demon believed to have sexual intercourse with sleeping women.
– ORIGIN Middle English: late Latin form of Latin *incubo* 'nightmare', from *incubare* (see **INCUBATE**).

incudes plural form of **INCUS**.

inculcate /ˈɪnkʌlkeɪt/ ■ v. instil (an idea or habit) by persistent instruction.
– DERIVATIVES **inculcation** n. **inculcator** n.
– ORIGIN C16: from Latin *inculcare* 'press in'.

incumbency ■ n. (pl. **-ies**) the period during which an office is held.

incumbent /ɪnˈkʌmb(ə)nt/ ■ adj. **1** (**incumbent on/upon**) necessary for (someone) as a duty or responsibility. **2** (of an official or regime) currently holding office. ■ n. the holder of an office or post.
– ORIGIN Middle English: from Latin *incumbere* 'lie or lean on'.

incur ■ v. (**incurred**, **incurring**) become subject to (something unwelcome or unpleasant) as a result of one's actions.
– DERIVATIVES **incurrence** n.
– ORIGIN Middle English: from Latin *incurrere*, from *in-* 'towards' + *currere* 'run'.

incurable ■ adj. not able to be cured.
– DERIVATIVES **incurability** n. **incurably** adv.

incurious ■ adj. not eager to know something; lacking curiosity.
– DERIVATIVES **incuriosity** n. **incuriously** adv. **incuriousness** n.

incursion /ɪnˈkəːʃ(ə)n/ ■ n. an invasion or attack, especially a sudden or brief one.
– DERIVATIVES **incursive** adj.
– ORIGIN Middle English: from Latin *incursio(n-)*, from *incurrere* (see INCUR).

incurve ■ v. [usu. as adj. **incurved**] curve inwards.

incus /ˈɪŋkəs/ ■ n. (pl. **incudes** /ˈɪŋkjʊdiːz, ɪŋˈkjuːdiːz/) Anatomy a small anvil-shaped bone in the middle ear, transmitting vibrations between the malleus and stapes.
– ORIGIN C17: from Latin, 'anvil'.

Ind. ■ abbrev. **1** Independent. **2** India.

indaba /ɪnˈdɑːbə/ ■ n. S. African **1** a meeting or discussion. **2** informal a problem or concern: *that's his indaba*.
– ORIGIN isiXhosa and isiZulu, 'matter, business'.

indebted ■ adj. owing money or gratitude.
– DERIVATIVES **indebtedness** n.
– ORIGIN Middle English: from Old French *endetter* 'involve in debt', associated with medieval Latin *indebitare*.

indecent ■ adj. not conforming with generally accepted standards of behaviour or propriety.
– DERIVATIVES **indecency** n. **indecently** adv.

indecent assault ■ n. sexual assault that does not involve rape.

indecent exposure ■ n. the crime of intentionally showing one's sexual organs in public.

indecipherable /ˌɪndɪˈsʌɪf(ə)rəb(ə)l/ ■ adj. not able to be read or understood.

indecisive ■ adj. **1** not able to make decisions quickly and effectively. **2** not settling an issue.
– DERIVATIVES **indecision** n. **indecisively** adv. **indecisiveness** n.

indecorous ■ adj. not in keeping with good taste and propriety; improper.
– DERIVATIVES **indecorously** adv. **indecorousness** n.

indecorum /ˌɪndɪˈkɔːrəm/ ■ n. failure to conform to good taste, propriety, or etiquette.

indeed ■ adv. **1** used to emphasize a statement, description, or response. **2** used to introduce a further and stronger or more surprising point. **3** used in a response to express interest, incredulity, or contempt.
– ORIGIN Middle English: orig. as *in deed*.

indefatigable /ˌɪndɪˈfatɪɡəb(ə)l/ ■ adj. persisting tirelessly; unflagging.
– DERIVATIVES **indefatigability** n. **indefatigably** adv.
– ORIGIN C17: from Latin *indefatigabilis*, from *in-* 'not' + *de-* 'away, completely' + *fatigare* 'wear out'.

indefeasible /ˌɪndɪˈfiːzɪb(ə)l/ ■ adj. chiefly Law & Philosophy not able to be lost, annulled, or overturned.
– DERIVATIVES **indefeasibility** n. **indefeasibly** adv.

indefensible ■ adj. **1** not justifiable by argument. **2** not able to be protected against attack.
– DERIVATIVES **indefensibly** adv. **indefensibility** n.

indefinable ■ adj. not able to be defined or described exactly.
– DERIVATIVES **indefinably** adv.

indefinite ■ adj. not clearly expressed or defined; vague. ▸ lasting for an unknown or unstated length of time.
– DERIVATIVES **indefinitely** adv. **indefiniteness** n.

indefinite article ■ n. Grammar a determiner (*a* and *an* in English) that introduces a noun phrase and implies that the thing referred to is non-specific.

indefinite integral ■ n. Mathematics an integral expressed without limits, and so containing an arbitrary constant.

indefinite pronoun ■ n. Grammar a pronoun that does not refer to any person or thing in particular, e.g. *anything, something, anyone, everyone*.

indehiscent /ˌɪndɪˈhɪs(ə)nt/ ■ adj. Botany (of a pod or fruit) not splitting open to release the seeds when ripe.
– DERIVATIVES **indehiscence** n.

indelible /ɪnˈdɛlɪb(ə)l/ ■ adj. **1** (of ink or a mark) unable to be removed. **2** unable to be forgotten.
– DERIVATIVES **indelibility** n. **indelibly** adv.
– ORIGIN C15: from Latin *indelebilis*, from *in-* 'not' + *delebilis*, from *delere* 'efface, delete'.

indelicate ■ adj. **1** lacking sensitive understanding or tact. **2** slightly indecent.
– DERIVATIVES **indelicacy** n. (pl. *-ies*) **indelicately** adv.

indemnify /ɪnˈdɛmnɪfʌɪ/ ■ v. (*-ies, -ied*) **1** compensate in respect of harm or loss. **2** secure (someone) against legal responsibility for their actions.
– DERIVATIVES **indemnification** n. **indemnifier** n.

indemnity /ɪnˈdɛmnɪti/ ■ n. (pl. *-ies*) **1** security or protection against a loss or other financial burden. ▸ security against or exemption from legal responsibility for one's actions. **2** a sum of money paid as compensation, especially by a country defeated in war.
– ORIGIN Middle English: from late Latin *indemnitas*, from Latin *indemnis* 'unhurt, free from loss', from *damnum* 'loss, damage'.

indemonstrable /ˌɪndɪˈmɒnstrəb(ə)l, ɪnˈdɛmən-/ ■ adj. not able to be proved or demonstrated. ▸ Philosophy (of a truth) axiomatic and hence not provable.

indent¹ ■ v. /ɪnˈdɛnt/ **1** form deep recesses or notches in. **2** position or begin (a line or block of text) further from the margin than the main part of the text. **3** make a requisition or written order for something. **4** historical divide (a document drawn up in duplicate) into its two copies with a zigzag line, thus ensuring identification. ▸ draw up (a legal document) in exact duplicate. **5** [as adj. **indented**] Heraldry divided or edged with a zigzag line. ■ n. /ˈɪndɛnt/ **1** Brit. an official order or requisition for goods or stores. **2** a space left by indenting text. **3** a deep recess or notch. **4** an indenture.
– DERIVATIVES **indentation** n.
– ORIGIN Middle English: from medieval Latin *indentare*, from *en-, in-* 'into' + Latin *dens, dent-* 'tooth'.

indent² /ɪnˈdɛnt/ ■ v. make a dent or depression in.

indenture /ɪnˈdɛntʃə/ ■ n. **1** a formal agreement, contract, or list, formerly one of which copies with indented edges were made for the contracting parties. **2** an agreement binding an apprentice to a master. **3** historical a contract by which a person agreed to work for a set period for a colonial landowner in exchange for passage to the colony. ■ v. chiefly historical bind by an indenture.
– DERIVATIVES **indentureship** n.

independent ■ adj. **1** free from outside control; not subject to another's authority. ▸ (of a country) self-governing. **2** not depending on another for livelihood or subsistence. **3** not connected with another; separate. ■ n. an independent person or body.
– DERIVATIVES **independence** n. **independency** n. **independently** adv.

independent variable ■ n. Mathematics a variable (often denoted by x) whose variation does not depend on that of another.

in-depth ■ adj. comprehensive and thorough.

indescribable ■ adj. too unusual, extreme, or indefinite to be adequately described.
– DERIVATIVES **indescribability** n. **indescribably** adv.

indestructible ■ adj. not able to be destroyed.
– DERIVATIVES **indestructibility** n. **indestructibly** adv.

indeterminable ■ adj. **1** not able to be determined. **2** Law (of a dispute or difficulty) not able to be resolved.
– DERIVATIVES **indeterminably** adv.

indeterminate /ˌɪndɪˈtəːmɪnət/ ■ adj. **1** not exactly known, established, or defined. ▸ Mathematics (of a quantity) having no definite or definable value. ▸ Medicine (of a condition) from which a diagnosis of the underlying cause cannot be made. **2** Botany (of a shoot) not having all the axes terminating in flower buds and so potentially of indefinite length.
– DERIVATIVES **indeterminacy** n. **indeterminately** adv. **indeterminateness** n.

indetermination ■ n. the state of being uncertain or undecided.

index /ˈɪndɛks/ ■ n. (pl. **indexes** or especially in technical use **indices** /ˈɪndɪsiːz/) **1** an alphabetical list of names, subjects, etc., with references to the places in a book where they occur. ▸ an alphabetical list or catalogue of books or

documents. **2** an indicator, sign, or measure of something. ▶ a number representing the relative value or magnitude of something in terms of a standard: *a price index.* **3** Mathematics an exponent or other superscript or subscript number appended to a quantity. **4** Printing a symbol shaped like a pointing hand used to draw attention to a note. ■ v. **1** record in or provide with an index. **2** link the value of (prices, wages, etc.) automatically to the value of a price index. **3** [often as noun **indexing**] (of a machine or part) move from one predetermined position to another to carry out a sequence of operations.
– DERIVATIVES **indexable** adj. **indexation** n. **indexer** n. **indexible** adj.
– ORIGIN Middle English: from Latin *index, indic-* 'forefinger, informer, sign', from *in-* 'towards' + a second element rel. to *dicere* 'say' or *dicare* 'make known'.

index finger ■ n. the forefinger.

index futures ■ pl. n. contracts to buy a range of shares at an agreed price but delivered and paid for later.

indexical /ɪnˈdɛksɪk(ə)l/ ■ adj. Linguistics another term for DEICTIC.

index-linked ■ adj. adjusted according to the changes in the index of the cost of living.
– DERIVATIVES **index-linking** n.

India ■ n. a code word representing the letter I, used in radio communication.

India ink ■ n. another term for INDIAN INK.

Indiaman ■ n. (pl. **-men**) historical a ship engaged in trade with India or the East or West Indies, especially an East Indiaman.

Indian ■ n. **1** a native or national of India, or a person of Indian descent. **2** an American Indian. ■ adj. **1** of or relating to India. **2** of or relating to the indigenous peoples of America.
– DERIVATIVES **Indianism** n. **Indianization** (also **-isation**) n. **Indianize** (also **-ise**) v. **Indianness** n.
– ORIGIN American native peoples were called 'Indian' as a result of Christopher Columbus and others believing that, when they reached the east coast of America, they had reached part of India by a new route.

> USAGE
> The terms **Indian** and **Red Indian** are today regarded as old-fashioned, recalling, as they do, the stereotypical portraits of the Wild West. The term **American Indian**, however, is well established.

Indian club ■ n. each of a pair of bottle-shaped clubs swung to exercise the arms in gymnastics.

Indian corn ■ n. another term for MAIZE.

Indian file ■ n. another term for SINGLE FILE.

Indian ink (also **India ink**) ■ n. deep black ink containing dispersed carbon particles, used especially in drawing and technical graphics.
– ORIGIN C17: orig. applied to Chinese and Japanese pigments prepared in solid blocks and imported to Europe via India.

Indian red ■ n. a red ferric oxide pigment made typically by roasting ferrous salts.

Indian summer ■ n. a period of dry, warm weather occurring in late autumn.

India paper ■ n. very thin, tough, opaque printing paper, used especially for Bibles.

India rubber ■ n. natural rubber.

Indic /ˈɪndɪk/ ■ n. the group of Indo-European languages comprising Sanskrit and the modern Indian languages which are its descendants. ■ adj. relating to or denoting this language group.

indicate ■ v. **1** point out; show. ▶ be a sign or symptom of; strongly imply. ▶ state briefly or indirectly. ▶ (of a gauge or meter) register a reading of. **2** suggest as a desirable or necessary course of action: *treatment for shock may be indicated.* **3** (of a driver) use an indicator to signal an intention to change lanes or turn.
– DERIVATIVES **indicant** n. **indication** n.
– ORIGIN C17 (*indication* Middle English): from Latin *indicare* 'point out'.

indicative /ɪnˈdɪkətɪv/ ■ adj. **1** serving as a sign or indication. **2** Grammar denoting a mood of verbs expressing simple statement of a fact. Compare with SUBJUNCTIVE. ■ n. Grammar a verb in the indicative mood.
– DERIVATIVES **indicatively** adv.

indicator ■ n. **1** a thing that indicates a state or level. **2** a gauge or meter of a specified kind. **3** a flashing light on a vehicle to show that it is about to change lanes or turn. **4** Brit. an information board or screen in a railway station, airport, etc. **5** Chemistry a compound which changes colour at a specific pH value or in the presence of a particular substance, and can be used to monitor a chemical change.

indices plural form of INDEX.

indicia /ɪnˈdɪʃɪə, -sɪə/ ■ pl. n. formal signs, indications, or distinguishing marks.
– ORIGIN C17: pl. of Latin *indicium*, from *index, indic-* 'informer, sign'.

indict /ɪnˈdaɪt/ ■ v. formally accuse or charge with a serious crime.
– DERIVATIVES **indictee** n. **indicter** n.
– ORIGIN Middle English *endite, indite*, from Anglo-Norman French *enditer*, from Latin *indicere* 'proclaim, appoint'.

indictable ■ adj. (of an offence) rendering a person who commits it liable to be charged with a serious crime that warrants a trial in a court of law.

indictment /ɪnˈdaɪtm(ə)nt/ ■ n. **1** Law a formal charge or accusation of a serious crime. **2** an indication that a system or situation is bad and deserves to be condemned.

indie informal ■ adj. (of a pop group or record label) not belonging or affiliated to a major record company. ■ n. **1** a pop group or record label of this type. **2** an independent film company.

indifferent ■ adj. **1** having no particular interest or sympathy; unconcerned. **2** neither good nor bad; mediocre. ▶ not especially good; fairly bad.
– DERIVATIVES **indifference** n. **indifferently** adv.
– ORIGIN Middle English: from Latin *indifferent-* 'making no difference', from *in-* 'not' + *differre* (see DIFFER).

indigenize /ɪnˈdɪdʒɪnaɪz/ (also **-ise**) ■ v. bring under the control of native people.
– DERIVATIVES **indigenization** (also **-isation**) n.

indigenous ■ adj. originating or occurring naturally in a particular place; native.
– DERIVATIVES **indigenously** adv. **indigenousness** n.

indigent /ˈɪndɪdʒ(ə)nt/ ■ adj. poor; needy. ■ n. a needy person.
– DERIVATIVES **indigence** n.
– ORIGIN Middle English: from late Latin *indigere* 'to lack'.

indigestible ■ adj. **1** (of food) difficult or impossible to digest. **2** difficult to read or understand.
– DERIVATIVES **indigestibility** n. **indigestibly** adv.

indigestion ■ n. pain or discomfort in the stomach associated with difficulty in digesting food.
– DERIVATIVES **indigestive** adj.

indignant /ɪnˈdɪɡnənt/ ■ adj. feeling or showing annoyance at what is perceived as unfair treatment.
– DERIVATIVES **indignantly** adv.

indignation ■ n. annoyance provoked by what is perceived as unfair treatment.
– ORIGIN Middle English: from Latin *indignatio(n-)*, from *indignari* 'regard as unworthy'.

indignity ■ n. (pl. **-ies**) treatment or circumstances that cause one to feel shame or to lose one's dignity.

indigo /ˈɪndɪɡəʊ/ ■ n. (pl. **-os** or **-oes**) **1** a tropical plant formerly widely cultivated as a source of dark blue dye. [*Indigofera tinctoria* and related species.] **2** the dark blue dye obtained from this plant. ▶ a colour between blue and violet in the spectrum.
– ORIGIN C16: from Portuguese *índigo*, from Greek *indikon*, from *indikos* 'Indian (dye)'.

indirect ■ adj. **1** not direct. ▶ Soccer denoting a free kick from which a goal may not be scored directly. **2** (of costs) deriving from overhead charges or subsidiary work. **3** (of taxation) levied on goods and services rather than income or profits.
– DERIVATIVES **indirection** n. **indirectly** adv. **indirectness** n.

indirect object ■ n. Grammar a noun phrase referring to a person or thing that is affected by the action of a transitive verb but is not the primary object (e.g. *him* in *give him the book*).

indirect question ■ n. Grammar a question in reported speech (e.g. *they asked who I was*).

indirect speech ■ n. another term for REPORTED SPEECH.

indiscernible /ˌɪndɪˈsəːnɪb(ə)l/ ■ adj. impossible to see or clearly distinguish.
– DERIVATIVES **indiscernibility** n. **indiscernibly** adv.

indiscipline ■ n. lack of discipline.

indiscreet ■ adj. too ready to reveal things that should remain secret or private.
– DERIVATIVES **indiscreetly** adv. **indiscretion** n.

indiscriminate /ˌɪndɪˈskrɪmɪnət/ ■ adj. done or acting at random or without careful judgement.
– DERIVATIVES **indiscriminately** adv. **indiscriminateness** n. **indiscrimination** n.
– ORIGIN C16: from IN-1 + Latin *discriminare* (see DISCRIMINATE).

indispensable ■ adj. absolutely necessary.
– DERIVATIVES **indispensability** n. **indispensableness** n. **indispensably** adv.

indisposed ■ adj. 1 slightly unwell. 2 averse; unwilling.
– DERIVATIVES **indisposition** n.

indisputable ■ adj. unable to be challenged or denied.
– DERIVATIVES **indisputability** n. **indisputably** adv.

indissoluble /ˌɪndɪˈsɒljʊb(ə)l/ ■ adj. unable to be destroyed; lasting.
– DERIVATIVES **indissolubility** n. **indissolubly** adv.

indistinct ■ adj. not clear or sharply defined.
– DERIVATIVES **indistinctly** adv. **indistinctness** n.

indistinguishable ■ adj. not able to be identified as different or distinct.
– DERIVATIVES **indistinguishably** adv.

indium /ˈɪndɪəm/ ■ n. the chemical element of atomic number 49, a soft, silvery-white metal occurring naturally in association with zinc and some other metals. (Symbol: **In**)
– ORIGIN C19: from INDIGO (because there are two characteristic indigo lines in its spectrum).

individual ■ adj. 1 single; separate. 2 of or for a particular person. ▸ designed for use by one person. 3 striking or unusual; original. ■ n. 1 a single human being or item as distinct from a group. ▸ informal a person of a specified kind: *a most selfish, egotistical individual*. 2 a distinctive or original person.
– DERIVATIVES **individualization** (also **-isation**) n. **individualize** (also **-ise**) v. **individually** adv.
– ORIGIN Middle English ('indivisible'): from medieval Latin *individualis*, from Latin *individuus*, from *dividere* 'to divide'.

individualism ■ n. 1 independence and self-reliance. ▸ self-centred feeling or conduct; egoism. 2 a social theory favouring freedom of action for individuals over collective or state control.
– DERIVATIVES **individualist** n. & adj. **individualistic** adj. **individualistically** adv.

individuality ■ n. 1 distinctive quality or character. 2 separate existence.

individuate ■ v. distinguish from others of the same kind; single out.
– DERIVATIVES **individuation** n.

indivisible ■ adj. unable to be divided or separated. ▸ (of a number) unable to be divided by another number exactly without leaving a remainder.
– DERIVATIVES **indivisibility** n. **indivisibly** adv.

indlamu /ɪnˈdlɑːmʊ/ ■ n. S. African an energetic traditional dance of the Nguni peoples which involves raising and stamping the feet.
– ORIGIN isiZulu.

Indo- /ˈɪndəʊ/ ■ comb. form (especially in linguistic and ethnological terms) Indian; Indian and ...: *Indo-Chinese*. ▸ relating to India.

Indo-Aryan ■ adj. another term for INDIC.

Indo-Chinese ■ adj. of or relating to the peninsula of Indo-China, which contains Burma (Myanmar), Thailand, Malaya, Laos, Cambodia, and Vietnam.

indoctrinate /ɪnˈdɒktrɪneɪt/ ■ v. cause to accept a set of beliefs uncritically through repeated instruction.
– DERIVATIVES **indoctrination** n. **indoctrinator** n. **indoctrinatory** adj.
– ORIGIN C17: from IN-2 + DOCTRINE + -ATE3, or from obsolete *indoctrine* (v.), from French *endoctriner*.

indoda /ɪnˈdɔːdə/ ■ n. (pl. **amadoda**) S. African a man, especially one who has undergone traditional initiation.
– ORIGIN isiXhosa and isiZulu.

Indo-European ■ n. the family of languages spoken over the greater part of Europe and Asia as far as northern India. ■ adj. relating to or denoting Indo-European.

indolent /ˈɪnd(ə)l(ə)nt/ ■ adj. 1 wanting to avoid activity or exertion; lazy. 2 Medicine (of an ulcer or other disease condition) slow to develop or heal.
– DERIVATIVES **indolence** n. **indolently** adv.
– ORIGIN C17: from late Latin *indolent-*, from *in-* 'not' + *dolere* 'suffer or give pain'.

Indo-Malaysian (also **Indo-Malayan**) ■ adj. of or relating to both the Indian subcontinent and Malaysia or the Malay Peninsula. ▸ Botany & Zoology denoting a biogeographical region comprising the Indian subcontinent, Malaysia, Indonesia, East and SE Asia.

indomitable /ɪnˈdɒmɪtəb(ə)l/ ■ adj. impossible to subdue or defeat.
– DERIVATIVES **indomitability** n. **indomitableness** n. **indomitably** adv.
– ORIGIN C17: from late Latin *indomitabilis*, from *in-* 'not' + Latin *domitare* 'to tame'.

Indonesian ■ n. 1 a native or national of Indonesia, or a person of Indonesian descent. 2 the group of Austronesian languages spoken in Indonesia. ■ adj. of or relating to Indonesia, Indonesians, or their languages.

indoor ■ adj. situated, conducted, or used within a building or under cover.

indoors ■ adv. into or within a building. ■ n. the area or space inside a building.

Indo-Pacific ■ adj. 1 of or relating to the Indian Ocean and the adjacent parts of the Pacific. 2 another term for AUSTRONESIAN.

indorse ■ v. variant spelling of ENDORSE.

indrawn ■ adj. (of breath) taken in.

indri /ˈɪndri/ ■ n. (pl. **indris**) a large, short-tailed Madagascan lemur. [*Indri indri*.]
– ORIGIN C19: from Malagasy *indry!* 'behold!' or *indry izy!* 'there he is!', mistaken for its name.

indubitable /ɪnˈdjuːbɪtəb(ə)l/ ■ adj. impossible to doubt; unquestionable.
– DERIVATIVES **indubitably** adv.
– ORIGIN Middle English: from Latin *indubitabilis*, from *in-* 'not' + *dubitabilis*, from *dubitare* 'to doubt'.

induce /ɪnˈdjuːs/ ■ v. 1 succeed in persuading or leading (someone) to do something. 2 bring about or give rise to. ▸ produce (an electric charge or current or a magnetic state) by induction. 3 Medicine bring on (childbirth or abortion) artificially, typically by the use of drugs. 4 Logic derive by inductive reasoning.
– DERIVATIVES **inducer** n. **inducible** adj.
– ORIGIN Middle English: from Latin *inducere* 'lead in'.

inducement ■ n. a thing that persuades or leads someone to do something. ▸ a bribe.

induct /ɪnˈdʌkt/ ■ v. admit formally to a post or organization. ▸ formally introduce (a member of the clergy) into possession of a benefice. ▸ US enlist (someone) for military service.
– ORIGIN Middle English: from Latin *inducere* (see INDUCE).

inductance ■ n. Physics the property of an electric conductor or circuit that causes an electromotive force to be generated by a change in the current flowing.

induction ■ n. 1 the action or process of inducting someone to a post, organization, etc. 2 the action or process of inducing something. 3 Logic the inference of a general law from particular instances. Often contrasted with DEDUCTION. ▸ the production of facts to prove a general statement. 4 Mathematics the proof of a theorem by showing that if it is true of any particular case it is true of the next case in a series, and then showing that it is indeed true in one particular case. **5** the production of an electric or magnetic state by the proximity (without contact) of an electrified or magnetized body. ▸ the production of an electric current in a conductor by varying an applied magnetic field. **6** the drawing of the fuel mixture into the cylinders of an internal-combustion engine.

induction coil ■ n. a coil for generating intermittent high voltage from a direct current.

induction heating ■ n. heating of a material by inducing an electric current within it.

induction loop ■ n. a sound system in which a loop of wire around an area in a building produces an electromagnetic signal received directly by hearing aids.

inductive ■ adj. **1** Logic characterized by the inference of general laws from particular instances. **2** of or relating to electric or magnetic induction. ▸ possessing inductance.
– DERIVATIVES **inductively** adv. **inductivism** n. **inductivist** n. & adj.

inductor ■ n. **1** a component in an electric or electronic circuit which possesses inductance. **2** a substance that promotes an equilibrium reaction by reacting with one of the substances produced.

indulge ■ v. **1** (**indulge in**) allow oneself to enjoy the pleasure of. ▸ become involved in (an activity that is undesirable or disapproved of). **2** satisfy or yield freely to (a desire or interest). ▸ allow (someone) to enjoy a desired pleasure.
– ORIGIN C17 (*indulgence* Middle English): from Latin *indulgere* 'give free rein to'.

indulgence ■ n. **1** the action or fact of indulging. ▸ a thing that is indulged in; a luxury. **2** the state or attitude of being indulgent or tolerant. **3** an extension of the time in which a bill or debt has to be paid. **4** chiefly historical (**in the Roman Catholic Church**) a grant by the Pope of remission of the temporal punishment in purgatory still due for sins after absolution.

indulgent ■ adj. **1** readily indulging someone or overlooking their faults; tolerant or lenient. **2** self-indulgent.
– DERIVATIVES **indulgently** adv.

indumentum /ˌɪndjʊˈmɛntəm/ ■ n. (pl. **indumenta**) Botany & Zoology a covering of hairs (or feathers) on an animal or plant.
– ORIGIN C19: from Latin, 'garment'.

induna /ɪnˈduːnə/ ■ n. S. African **1** a tribal councillor or headman. **2** dated a black foreman, head servant, or overseer.
– ORIGIN isiXhosa and isiZulu, 'captain, councillor'.

indurate /ˈɪndjʊreɪt/ ■ v. [usu. as adj. **indurated**] harden.
– DERIVATIVES **induration** n.
– ORIGIN C16 (*induration* Middle English): from Latin *indurare* 'make hard'.

industrial ■ adj. **1** of, used in, or characterized by industry. **2** relating to or denoting a type of harsh, uncompromising rock music incorporating sounds resembling those produced by industrial machinery. ■ n. (**industrials**) shares in industrial companies.
– DERIVATIVES **industrially** adv.

industrial action ■ n. action taken by employees of a company as a protest, especially striking or working to rule.

industrial archaeology ■ n. the study of equipment and buildings formerly used in industry.

industrial diamond ■ n. a small diamond, not of gem quality, used in abrasives and in cutting and drilling tools.

industrial estate ■ n. another term for **INDUSTRIAL PARK**.

industrialism ■ n. a social or economic system in which manufacturing industries are prevalent.

industrialist ■ n. a person involved in the ownership and management of industry.

industrialize (also -**ise**) ■ v. [often as adj. **industrialized** (also -**ised**)] develop industries in (a country or region) on a wide scale.
– DERIVATIVES **industrialization** (also -**isation**) n.

industrial park ■ n. an area of land developed as a site for factories and other industrial uses.

industrial relations ■ pl. n. the relations between management and workers in industry.

industrial-strength ■ adj. very strong or powerful.

industrious ■ adj. diligent and hard-working.
– DERIVATIVES **industriously** adv. **industriousness** n.

industry ■ n. (pl. -**ies**) **1** economic activity concerned with the processing of raw materials and manufacture of goods in factories. ▸ a particular branch of economic or commercial activity: *the tourist industry*. **2** hard work: *the kitchen became a hive of industry*.
– ORIGIN Middle English: from Latin *industria* 'diligence'.

indwell ■ v. (past and past part. **indwelt**) **1** be permanently present or living in. **2** [as adj. **indwelling**] Medicine (of a catheter, needle, etc.) fixed in a person's body for a long period of time.
– ORIGIN Middle English: translating Latin *inhabitare*.

Indy ■ n. a form of motor racing in which cars are driven round a banked, regular oval circuit.
– ORIGIN 1950s: named after the US city of *Indianapolis*, where the principal race is held.

-ine¹ /ʌɪn, ɪn, iːn/ ■ suffix **1** (forming adjectives) belonging to; resembling: *canine*. **2** forming adjectives from the names of genera or subfamilies (such as *bovine* from the genus *Bos*).
– ORIGIN from French -*in*, -*ine*, or from Latin -*inus*.

-ine² /ʌɪn/ ■ suffix forming adjectives from the names of minerals, plants, etc.: *crystalline*.
– ORIGIN from Latin -*inus*, from Greek -*inos*.

-ine³ /ɪn, iːn/ ■ suffix forming feminine nouns such as *heroine*.
– ORIGIN from French, from Greek -*inē*, or from German -*in*.

-ine⁴ /iːn, ɪn/ ■ suffix **1** forming chiefly abstract nouns and diminutives such as *doctrine*, *medicine*. **2** Chemistry forming names of alkaloids, halogens, amino acids, and other substances: *cocaine*.
– ORIGIN from French, from the Latin feminine form -*ina*.

inebriate ■ v. /ɪˈniːbrɪeɪt/ [usu. as adj. **inebriated**] make drunk; intoxicate. ■ adj. /ɪˈniːbrɪət/ drunk; intoxicated.
– DERIVATIVES **inebriation** n. **inebriety** n.
– ORIGIN Middle English: from Latin *inebriatus*, from *inebriare* 'intoxicate'.

inedible ■ adj. not fit for eating.
– DERIVATIVES **inedibility** n.

ineducable /ɪnˈɛdjʊkəb(ə)l/ ■ adj. considered incapable of being educated.
– DERIVATIVES **ineducability** n.

ineffable /ɪnˈɛfəb(ə)l/ ■ adj. **1** too great or extreme to be expressed in words: *the ineffable natural beauty of the Everglades*. **2** too sacred to be uttered.
– DERIVATIVES **ineffability** n. **ineffably** adv.

ineffaceable /ˌɪnɪˈfeɪsəb(ə)l/ ■ adj. unable to be erased or forgotten.

ineffective ■ adj. not producing any or the desired effect.
– DERIVATIVES **ineffectively** adv. **ineffectiveness** n.

ineffectual ■ adj. not producing any or the desired effect. ▸ lacking ability to cope with a role or situation: *she was ineffectual as a parent*.
– DERIVATIVES **ineffectuality** n. **ineffectually** adv. **ineffectualness** n.

inefficacious /ˌɪnɛfɪˈkeɪʃəs/ ■ adj. not producing the desired effect.
– DERIVATIVES **inefficacy** n.

inefficient ■ adj. not achieving maximum productivity; failing to make the best use of time or resources.
– DERIVATIVES **inefficiency** n. **inefficiently** adv.

inegalitarian /ˌɪnɪgalɪˈtɛːrɪən/ ■ adj. characterized by or promoting inequality.

inelastic ■ adj. **1** (of a material) not elastic. **2** Economics (of demand or supply) insensitive to changes in price or income. **3** Physics (of a collision) involving an overall loss of translational kinetic energy.
– DERIVATIVES **inelastically** adv. **inelasticity** n.

inelegant ■ adj. lacking elegance or refinement.
– DERIVATIVES **inelegance** n. **inelegantly** adv.

ineligible

ineligible ■ adj. not eligible.
– DERIVATIVES **ineligibility** n. **ineligibly** adv.

ineluctable /ˌɪnɪˈlʌktəb(ə)l/ ■ adj. unable to be resisted or avoided; inescapable.
– DERIVATIVES **ineluctability** /-ˈbɪlɪti/ n. **ineluctably** adv.
– ORIGIN C17: from Latin *ineluctabilis*, from *in-* 'not' + *eluctari* 'struggle out'.

inept ■ adj. incompetent; awkward or clumsy.
– DERIVATIVES **ineptitude** n. **ineptly** adv. **ineptness** n.
– ORIGIN C16 ('unsuitable'): from Latin *ineptus*, from *in-* 'not' + *aptus* (see APT).

inequality ■ n. (pl. **-ies**) **1** lack of equality. **2** Mathematics a symbolic expression of the fact that two quantities are not equal, employing a sign such as ≠ 'not equal to', > 'greater than', or < 'less than'.

inequitable ■ adj. unfair; unjust.
– DERIVATIVES **inequitably** adv.

inequity ■ n. (pl. **-ies**) lack of fairness or justice.

ineradicable /ˌɪnɪˈradɪkəb(ə)l/ ■ adj. unable to be destroyed or removed.
– DERIVATIVES **ineradicably** adv.

inert ■ adj. **1** lacking the ability or strength to move. ▸ lacking vigour. **2** chemically inactive.
– DERIVATIVES **inertly** adv. **inertness** n.
– ORIGIN C17: from Latin *iners, inert-* 'unskilled, inactive', from *in-* + *ars, art-* 'skill, art'.

inert gas ■ n. another term for NOBLE GAS.

inertia /ɪˈnəːʃə/ ■ n. **1** a tendency to do nothing or to remain unchanged. **2** Physics a property of matter by which it continues in its existing state of rest or uniform motion in a straight line, unless changed by an external force. ▸ resistance to change in some other physical property: *the thermal inertia of the oceans*.
– ORIGIN C18: from Latin, from *iners, inert-* (see INERT).

inertial ■ adj. **1** chiefly Physics of, relating to, or arising from inertia. **2** (of navigation) depending on internal instruments which measure a craft's acceleration and compare the calculated position with stored data.

inertia reel ■ n. a reel device which allows a vehicle seat belt to unwind freely but which locks under force of impact or rapid deceleration.

inescapable ■ adj. unable to be avoided or denied.
– DERIVATIVES **inescapability** n. **inescapably** adv.

inescutcheon /ˌɪnɪˈskʌtʃ(ə)n, ˌɪnɛ-/ ■ n. Heraldry a small shield placed within a larger one.

inessential ■ adj. not absolutely necessary. ■ n. an inessential thing.

inestimable ■ adj. not able to be measured; very great.
– DERIVATIVES **inestimably** adv.

inevitable ■ adj. certain to happen; unavoidable. ■ n. (**the inevitable**) a situation that is unavoidable.
– DERIVATIVES **inevitability** n. **inevitably** adv.
– ORIGIN Middle English: from Latin *inevitabilis*, from *in-* 'not' + *evitabilis* 'avoidable'.

inexact ■ adj. not quite accurate.
– DERIVATIVES **inexactitude** n. **inexactly** adv. **inexactness** n.

inexcusable ■ adj. too bad to be justified or tolerated.
– DERIVATIVES **inexcusably** adv.

inexhaustible ■ adj. **1** (of a supply) never ending; incapable of being used up. **2** tireless.
– DERIVATIVES **inexhaustibility** n. **inexhaustibly** adv.

inexorable /ɪnˈɛks(ə)rəb(ə)l/ ■ adj. **1** impossible to stop or prevent: *the inexorable march of new technology*. **2** impossible to persuade by request or entreaty.
– DERIVATIVES **inexorability** n. **inexorably** adv.
– ORIGIN C16: from Latin *inexorabilis*, from *in-* 'not' + *exorabilis*, from *exorare* 'entreat'.

inexpedient ■ adj. not practical, suitable, or advisable.
– DERIVATIVES **inexpediency** n.

inexpensive ■ adj. not costing a great deal; cheap.
– DERIVATIVES **inexpensively** adv. **inexpensiveness** n.

inexperience ■ n. lack of experience.
– DERIVATIVES **inexperienced** adj.

inexpert ■ adj. lacking skill or knowledge.
– DERIVATIVES **inexpertly** adv.

inexpertise ■ n. lack of expertise.

inexpiable /ɪnˈɛkspɪəb(ə)l/ ■ adj. (of an offence) not able to be expiated.
– DERIVATIVES **inexpiably** adv.

inexplicable /ˌɪnɪkˈsplɪkəb(ə)l, ˌɪnɛk-, ɪnˈɛksplɪ-/ ■ adj. unable to be explained or accounted for.
– DERIVATIVES **inexplicability** n. **inexplicably** adv.

inexplicit ■ adj. not clearly expressed or explained.

inexpressible ■ adj. not able to be expressed.
– DERIVATIVES **inexpressibly** adv.

inexpressive ■ adj. showing no expression.
– DERIVATIVES **inexpressively** adv.

in extenso /ˌɪn ɛkˈstɛnsəʊ/ ■ adv. in full.
– ORIGIN Latin, from *in* 'in' + *extensus*, from *extendere* 'stretch out'.

inextinguishable ■ adj. unable to be extinguished.

in extremis /ˌɪn ɛkˈstriːmɪs/ ■ adv. **1** in an extremely difficult situation. **2** at the point of death.
– ORIGIN Latin, from *in* 'in' + *extremis*, from *extremus* 'outermost'.

inextricable /ɪnˈɛkstrɪkəb(ə)l, ˌɪnɪkˈstrɪk-, ˌɪnɛk-/ ■ adj. **1** impossible to disentangle or separate. **2** impossible to escape from.
– DERIVATIVES **inextricability** n. **inextricably** adv.

infallibility ■ n. **1** the quality of being infallible. **2** (**papal infallibility**) (in the Roman Catholic Church) the doctrine that in specified circumstances the Pope is incapable of error in pronouncing dogma.

infallible /ɪnˈfalɪb(ə)l/ ■ adj. **1** incapable of making mistakes or being wrong. **2** never failing; always effective: *infallible cures*.
– DERIVATIVES **infallibly** adv.

infamous /ˈɪnfəməs/ ■ adj. **1** well known for some bad quality or deed: *an infamous war criminal*. **2** morally bad; shocking: *infamous misconduct*.
– DERIVATIVES **infamously** adv. **infamy** /ˈɪnfəmi/ n. (pl. **-ies**).

infancy ■ n. **1** the state or period of early childhood or babyhood. **2** the early stage in the development or growth of something. **3** Law the condition of being a minor.

infant ■ n. **1** a very young child or baby. **2** [as modifier] denoting something in an early stage of development: *the infant universe*. **3** Law a person who has not attained legal majority. ▸ S. African Law a child under the age of seven.
– ORIGIN Middle English: from Latin *infant-* 'unable to speak', from *in-* 'not' + *fari* 'speak'.

infanta /ɪnˈfantə/ ■ n. historical a daughter of the ruling monarch of Spain or Portugal, especially the eldest daughter who was not heir to the throne.
– ORIGIN C16: Spanish and Portuguese, feminine of *infante*, from Latin *infant-* (see INFANT).

infanticide /ɪnˈfantɪsʌɪd/ ■ n. the killing of an infant.
– DERIVATIVES **infanticidal** adj.

infantile /ˈɪnf(ə)ntʌɪl/ ■ adj. **1** of or occurring among infants. **2** derogatory childish.
– DERIVATIVES **infantility** n. (pl. **-ies**).

infantile paralysis ■ n. dated poliomyelitis.

infantilism /ɪnˈfantɪlɪz(ə)m/ ■ n. childish behaviour.

infant mortality ■ n. the death of children under the age of one year.

infantry ■ n. foot soldiers collectively.
– DERIVATIVES **infantryman** n. (pl. **-men**).
– ORIGIN C16: from Italian *infanteria*, from *infante* 'youth, infantryman', from Latin *infant-* (see INFANT).

infarct /ˈɪnfɑːkt, ɪnˈfɑːkt/ ■ n. Medicine a small localized area of dead tissue resulting from failure of blood supply.
– ORIGIN C19: from modern Latin *infarctus*, from *infarcire* 'stuff into or with'.

infarction /ɪnˈfɑːkʃ(ə)n/ ■ n. the obstruction of the blood supply, typically by a thrombus or embolus, causing local death of the tissue.

infatuate ■ v. (**be infatuated with**) be inspired with an intense but short-lived passion for.
– DERIVATIVES **infatuation** n.
– ORIGIN C16: from Latin *infatuare* 'make foolish'.

infauna /ˈɪnfɔːnə/ ■ n. Ecology animals living in the

sediments of the ocean floor or river or lake beds. Compare with EPIFAUNA.
– DERIVATIVES **infaunal** adj.

infeasible ■ adj. inconvenient or impracticable.
– DERIVATIVES **infeasibility** n.

infect ■ v. **1** affect (a person, organism, cell, etc.) with a disease-causing organism. **2** Computing affect with a virus. **3** contaminate; affect adversely.
– DERIVATIVES **infector** n.
– ORIGIN Middle English: from Latin *infect-*, *inficere* 'taint', from *in-* 'into' + *facere* 'put, do'.

infection ■ n. **1** the process of infecting or the state of being infected. **2** an infectious disease.

infectious ■ adj. **1** (of a disease or disease-causing organism) liable to be transmitted through the environment. ▸ liable to spread infection. **2** likely to spread to or influence others: *her enthusiasm is infectious.*
– DERIVATIVES **infectiously** adv. **infectiousness** n.

infective ■ adj. capable of causing infection.
– DERIVATIVES **infectiveness** n.

infelicitous ■ adj. unfortunate; inappropriate.

infelicity ■ n. (pl. **-ies**) **1** an act or thing that is inapt or inappropriate, especially a remark or expression. **2** archaic unhappiness; misfortune.
– DERIVATIVES **infelicitously** adv.

infer ■ v. (**inferred, inferring**) deduce from evidence and reasoning rather than from explicit statements.
– DERIVATIVES **inferable** (also **inferrable**) adj.
– ORIGIN C15: from Latin *inferre* 'bring in, bring about'.

USAGE
Do not confuse the words **infer** and **imply**. They can describe the same situation, but from different points of view. If a speaker or writer **implies** something, as in *he implied that the General was a traitor*, it means that the person is suggesting something though not saying it directly. If you **infer** something from what has been said, as in *we inferred from his words that the General was a traitor*, this means that something in the speaker's words enabled you to deduce that the General was a traitor.

inference /'ɪnf(ə)r(ə)ns/ ■ n. **1** a conclusion reached on the basis of evidence and reasoning. **2** the process of reaching a conclusion by inferring.
– DERIVATIVES **inferential** adj. **inferentially** adv.

inferior ■ adj. **1** lower in rank, status, or quality. ▸ of low standard or quality. **2** Law (of a court or tribunal) able to have its decisions overturned by a higher court. **3** chiefly Anatomy low or lower in position. ▸ Botany (of the ovary of a flower) situated below the sepals. **4** (of a letter or symbol) written or printed below the line. ■ n. **1** a person lower than another in rank, status, or ability. **2** Printing an inferior letter, figure, or symbol.
– DERIVATIVES **inferiority** n. **inferiorly** adv. (Anatomy).
– ORIGIN Middle English: from Latin, from *inferus* 'low'.

inferior goods ■ pl. n. Economics goods or services which are in greater demand during a recession, e.g. second-hand clothes.

inferiority complex ■ n. a feeling of general inadequacy caused by actual or supposed inferiority, marked by aggressive behaviour or withdrawal.

inferior planet ■ n. Astronomy either of the two planets Mercury and Venus, whose orbits are closer to the sun than the earth's.

infernal ■ adj. **1** of or relating to hell or the underworld. **2** informal terrible; awful: *you're an infernal nuisance.*
– DERIVATIVES **infernally** adv.
– ORIGIN Middle English: from Christian Latin *infernalis*, from Latin *infernus* 'below, underground', used in Christianity to mean 'hell'.

inferno ■ n. (pl. **-os**) **1** a large fire that is dangerously out of control. **2** (**Inferno**) hell (with reference to Dante's *Divine Comedy*).
– ORIGIN C19: from Italian, from Christian Latin *infernus* (see INFERNAL).

infertile ■ adj. **1** unable to reproduce. **2** (of land) unable to sustain crops or vegetation.
– DERIVATIVES **infertility** n.

in flagrante delicto

infest ■ v. (of insects or organisms) be present in large numbers, typically so as to cause damage or disease.
– DERIVATIVES **infestation** n.
– ORIGIN Middle English ('torment, harass'): from Latin *infestare* 'assail', from *infestus* 'hostile'.

infibulation ■ n. the practice in some societies of removing the clitoris and labia of a girl or woman and stitching together the edges of the vulva to prevent sexual intercourse.
– DERIVATIVES **infibulate** v.
– ORIGIN C17: from Latin *infibulare* 'fasten with a clasp'.

infidel /'ɪnfɪd(ə)l/ ■ n. chiefly archaic a person who has no religion or whose religion is not that of the majority.
– ORIGIN C15: from Latin *infidelis*, from *in-* 'not' + *fidelis* 'faithful'.

infidelity ■ n. (pl. **-ies**) **1** the action or state of being sexually unfaithful. **2** lack of religious faith.

infield ■ n. **1** Cricket the part of the field closer to the wicket. **2** Baseball the area within and near the four bases. ■ adv. into or towards the infield.
– DERIVATIVES **infielder** n.

infighting ■ n. hidden conflict within a group or organization.
– DERIVATIVES **infighter** n.

infill ■ n. (also **infilling**) material or buildings used to fill a space or hole. ■ v. fill or block up (a space or hole).

infiltrate /'ɪnfɪltreɪt/ ■ v. **1** surreptitiously and gradually enter or gain access to (an organization, place, etc.). **2** permeate or cause to permeate by filtration. ■ n. Medicine an infiltrating substance or group of cells.
– DERIVATIVES **infiltration** n. **infiltrator** n.

infinite /'ɪnfɪnɪt/ ■ adj. **1** limitless in space, extent, or size. ▸ very great in amount or degree. **2** Mathematics greater than any assignable quantity or countable number.
– DERIVATIVES **infinitely** adv. **infiniteness** n. **infinitude** /ɪn'fɪnɪtjuːd/ n.
– ORIGIN Middle English: from Latin *infinitus*, from *in-* 'not' + *finitus* 'finished, finite'.

infinitesimal /ˌɪnfɪnɪ'tɛsɪm(ə)l/ ■ adj. extremely small. ■ n. Mathematics an indefinitely small quantity; a value approaching zero.
– DERIVATIVES **infinitesimally** adv.
– ORIGIN C17: from modern Latin *infinitesimus*, from Latin *infinitus* (see INFINITE), on the pattern of *centesimal*.

infinitesimal calculus ■ n. see CALCULUS.

infinitive /ɪn'fɪnɪtɪv/ ■ n. the basic form of a verb, without an inflection binding it to a particular subject or tense (normally occurring in English with the word *to*, as in *to see, to ask*).
– DERIVATIVES **infinitival** /-'tʌɪv(ə)l/ adj. **infinitivally** adv.
– ORIGIN Middle English: from Latin *infinitivus*, from *infinitus* (see INFINITE).

infinity ■ n. (pl. **-ies**) **1** the state or quality of being infinite. ▸ a very great number or amount. **2** Mathematics a number greater than any assignable quantity or countable number (symbol ∞). **3** a point in space or time that is or seems infinitely distant: *the lawns stretched into infinity.*

infinity pool ■ n. a swimming pool constructed to give the impression that it merges into the surrounding landscape, especially the sea.

infirm ■ adj. not physically strong, especially through age.
– DERIVATIVES **infirmly** adv.
– ORIGIN Middle English: from Latin *infirmus*, from *in-* 'not' + *firmus* 'firm'.

infirmary ■ n. (pl. **-ies**) a place for the care of those who are ill or injured; a hospital.

infirmity ■ n. (pl. **-ies**) physical or mental weakness.

infix ■ v. /ɪn'fɪks/ **1** implant or insert firmly in something. **2** Grammar insert (a formative element) into the body of a word. ■ n. /'ɪnfɪks/ Grammar a formative element inserted in a word.
– DERIVATIVES **infixation** n.

in flagrante delicto /ɪn fləˌgrantɛ dɪ'lɪktəʊ, fləˌgrantiː/ ■ adv. in the very act of wrongdoing, especially in an act of sexual misconduct.
– ORIGIN Latin, 'in the heat of the crime'.

inflame

inflame ■ v. **1** intensify or aggravate: *high fines further inflamed public feelings.* ▸ provoke (someone) to strong feelings. **2** (usu. **be inflamed**) cause inflammation in. **3** poetic/literary light up with or as if with flames.

inflammable ■ adj. easily set on fire. ■ n. a substance which is easily set on fire.
– DERIVATIVES **inflammability** n. **inflammableness** n. **inflammably** adv.

USAGE
The words **inflammable** and **flammable** both mean 'easily set on fire'. **Inflammable** is formed using the Latin prefix **in-** which here has the meaning 'into' (rather than the more common use of **in-** to indicate negation), and here has the effect of intensifying the meaning of the word in English.

inflammation ■ n. a localized physical condition in which part of the body becomes reddened, swollen, hot, and often painful, especially as a reaction to injury or infection.

inflammatory ■ adj. **1** relating to or causing inflammation. **2** arousing or intended to arouse angry or violent feelings: *inflammatory language.*

inflatable ■ adj. capable of being inflated. ■ n. a plastic or rubber object that must be inflated before use.

inflate ■ v. **1** expand or cause to expand by filling with air or gas. **2** [usu. as adj. **inflated**] increase by a large or excessive amount. ▸ exaggerate. **3** bring about inflation of (a currency) or in (an economy).
– DERIVATIVES **inflatedly** adv. **inflater** (also **inflator**) n.
– ORIGIN Middle English: from Latin *inflare* 'blow into', from *in-* 'into' + *flare* 'to blow'.

inflation ■ n. **1** the action of inflating or the condition of being inflated. **2** Economics a general increase in prices and fall in the purchasing value of money. **3** Astronomy (in some theories of cosmology) a very brief exponential expansion of the early universe, interrupting the standard linear expansion.
– DERIVATIVES **inflationary** adj. **inflationism** n. **inflationist** n. & adj.

inflect ■ v. **1** Grammar change or be changed by inflection. **2** vary the intonation or pitch of (the voice), especially to express mood or feeling. **3** technical bend or deflect from a straight course, especially inwards.
– DERIVATIVES **inflective** adj.
– ORIGIN Middle English: from Latin *inflectere*, from *in-* 'into' + *flectere* 'to bend'.

inflection (chiefly Brit. also **inflexion**) ■ n. **1** Grammar a change in the form of a word (typically the ending) to express a grammatical function or attribute such as tense, mood, person, number, case, and gender. **2** the modulation of intonation or pitch. **3** chiefly Mathematics a change of curvature from convex to concave.
– DERIVATIVES **inflectional** adj. **inflectionally** adv. **inflectionless** adj.

inflexible ■ adj. **1** unwilling to change; not able to be changed or adapted. **2** not able to be bent; stiff.
– DERIVATIVES **inflexibility** n. **inflexibly** adv.

inflict ■ v. cause (something unpleasant or painful) to be suffered by someone else.
– DERIVATIVES **infliction** n.
– ORIGIN C16 ('afflict'): from Latin *infligere* 'strike against'.

in-flight ■ adj. occurring or provided during an aircraft flight.

inflorescence /ˌɪnflɔːˈrɛs(ə)ns, -flə-/ ■ n. Botany **1** the complete flower head of a plant including stems, stalks, bracts, and flowers. **2** the process of flowering.
– ORIGIN C18: from modern Latin *inflorescentia*, from late Latin *inflorescere* 'come into flower'.

inflow ■ n. **1** the action of flowing or moving in; influx: *monitoring the inflow and outflow of traffic.* **2** something, such as water, money, etc., that flows or moves in.
– DERIVATIVES **inflowing** n. & adj.

influence ■ n. **1** the capacity to have an effect on the character or behaviour of someone or something, or the effect itself. **2** the power arising out of status, contacts, or wealth: *members of the clergy in positions of influence.* **3** a person or thing with such a capacity or power: *Fiona was a good influence on her.* ■ v. have an influence on.
– PHRASES **under the influence** informal affected by alcoholic drink.
– DERIVATIVES **influencer** n.
– ORIGIN Middle English: from medieval Latin *influentia* 'inflow', from Latin *influere*, from *in-* 'into' + *fluere* 'to flow'.

influential ■ adj. having great influence.
– DERIVATIVES **influentially** adv.

influenza ■ n. a highly contagious viral infection of the respiratory passages causing fever, severe aching, and catarrh.
– DERIVATIVES **influenzal** adj.

influx /ˈɪnflʌks/ ■ n. **1** the arrival or entry of large numbers of people or things. **2** an inflow of water into a river, lake, or the sea.
– ORIGIN C16: from late Latin *influxus*, from *influere* (see INFLUENCE).

influx control ■ n. S. African historical (under apartheid) the strict limitation and control imposed on the movement of black people into urban areas.

info ■ n. informal short for INFORMATION.

infomercial /ˌɪnfə(ʊ)ˈmɜːʃ(ə)l/ ■ n. an advertising film which promotes a product in an informative and supposedly objective style.
– ORIGIN 1980s: blend of INFORMATION and COMMERCIAL.

inform ■ v. **1** give facts or information to. **2** (**inform on**) give incriminating information about (someone) to the police or other authority. **3** give an essential or formative principle or quality to: *my perspective is informed by a child-centred approach.*
– ORIGIN Middle English *enforme, informe* 'give form or shape to', from Latin *informare* 'shape, describe'.

informal ■ adj. **1** relaxed and unofficial; not formal. ▸ (of dress) casual; suitable for everyday wear. **2** of or denoting the grammatical structures, vocabulary, and idiom suitable to everyday language and conversation rather than to official or formal contexts. **3** (of economic activity) carried on by self-employed or independent people on a small scale, especially unofficially or illegally.
– DERIVATIVES **informality** n. **informally** adv.

informal economy ■ n. the part of an economy represented by people involved in trading on a small scale and not covered by normal business legislation, e.g. street vendors.

informal settlement ■ n. S. African an area of previously unoccupied land situated in or close to a town, where people live in improvised buildings or shelters.

informant ■ n. **1** a person who gives information to another. **2** another term for INFORMER.

informatics /ˌɪnfəˈmatɪks/ ■ pl. n. [treated as sing.] Computing the science of processing data for storage and retrieval.

information ■ n. **1** facts or knowledge provided or learned as a result of research or study. **2** what is conveyed or represented by a particular sequence of symbols, impulses, etc.: *genetically transmitted information.*
– DERIVATIVES **informational** adj.

information retrieval ■ n. Computing the tracing and recovery of information from stored data.

information science ■ n. Computing the study of processes for storing and retrieving information.

information superhighway ■ n. an extensive electronic network such as the Internet, used for the rapid transfer of information in digital form.

information technology ■ n. the study or use of systems (especially computers and telecommunications) for storing, retrieving, and sending information.

information theory ■ n. the mathematical study of the coding of information in the form of sequences of symbols, impulses, etc. and of how rapidly such information can be transmitted.

informative ■ adj. providing useful information.
– DERIVATIVES **informatively** adv. **informativeness** n.

informed ■ adj. having or showing knowledge. ▸ (of a judgement) based on a sound understanding of the facts.

CONSONANTS   b but   d dog   f few   g get   h he   j yes   k cat   l leg   m man   n no   p pen   r red

–DERIVATIVES **informedly** /ɪnˈfɔːmɪdli/ adv. **informedness** /ɪnˈfɔːmɪdnɪs/ n.

informer ■ n. a person who informs on another person to the police or other authority.

infotainment ■ n. broadcast material which is intended both to entertain and to inform.
–ORIGIN 1980s (orig. US): blend of **INFORMATION** and *entertainment* (see **ENTERTAIN**).

infotech ■ n. short for **INFORMATION TECHNOLOGY**.

infra- /ˈɪnfrə/ ■ prefix below: *infrasonic.*
–ORIGIN from Latin *infra* 'below'.

infraclass ■ n. Biology a taxonomic category that ranks below a subclass.

infraction ■ n. chiefly Law a violation or infringement of a law or agreement.
–DERIVATIVES **infractor** n.
–ORIGIN Middle English: from Latin *infractio(n-)*, from *infringere* (see **INFRINGE**).

infra dig /ˌɪnfrə ˈdɪɡ/ ■ adj. informal beneath one; demeaning.
–ORIGIN C19: abbrev. of Latin *infra dignitatem* 'beneath (one's) dignity'.

infraorder ■ n. Biology a taxonomic category that ranks below a suborder.

infrared ■ n. electromagnetic radiation having a wavelength just greater than that of red light but less than that of microwaves, emitted particularly by heated objects. ■ adj. of or denoting such radiation.

infrasonic ■ adj. relating to or denoting sound waves with a frequency below the lower limit of human audibility.

infrasound ■ n. infrasonic sound waves.

infrastructure ■ n. the basic physical and organizational structures (e.g. buildings, roads, power supplies) needed for the operation of a society or enterprise.
–DERIVATIVES **infrastructural** adj.

infrequent ■ adj. not occurring often; rare.
–DERIVATIVES **infrequency** n. **infrequently** adv.

infringe ■ v. 1 violate (a law, agreement, etc.). 2 encroach on (a right or privilege).
–DERIVATIVES **infringement** n. **infringer** n.
–ORIGIN C16: from Latin *infringere*, from *in-* 'into' + *frangere* 'to break'.

infuriate /ɪnˈfjʊərɪeɪt/ ■ v. make irritated or angry.
–DERIVATIVES **infuriating** adj. **infuriatingly** adv.
–ORIGIN C17: from medieval Latin *infuriare* 'make angry'.

infuse ■ v. 1 pervade; fill. 2 instil (a quality) in someone or something. ▸ Medicine allow (a liquid) to flow into a patient, vein, etc. 3 soak (tea, herbs, etc.) to extract the flavour or healing properties.
–DERIVATIVES **infuser** n.
–ORIGIN Middle English: from Latin *infus-, infundere* 'pour in'.

infusion ■ n. 1 a drink, remedy, or extract prepared by infusing. 2 the action or process of infusing.

-ing[1] ■ suffix 1 denoting a verbal action, activity, or result: *building.* 2 denoting material used for or associated with a process: *piping.* 3 forming the gerund of verbs (such as *painting* as in *I love painting*).
–ORIGIN Old English *-ung, -ing,* of Germanic origin.

-ing[2] ■ suffix 1 forming the present participle of verbs: *calling.* 2 forming adjectives from nouns: *hulking.*
–ORIGIN Middle English: alteration of earlier *-ende,* later *-inde.*

ingcibi /ɪnˈsiːbɪ, ˈɪŋˌkiːbɪ/ ■ n. (pl. **iingcibi** or **ingcibis**) S. African (in traditional Xhosa society) a man responsible for circumcizing young men at an initiation school.
–ORIGIN isiXhosa, 'skilled worker'.

ingenious /ɪnˈdʒiːnɪəs/ ■ adj. clever, original, and inventive.
–DERIVATIVES **ingeniously** adv. **ingeniousness** n.
–ORIGIN Middle English: from Latin *ingeniosus,* from *ingenium* 'mind, intellect'.

ingénue /ˈãʒeɪn(j)uː/ ■ n. an innocent or unsophisticated young woman.
–ORIGIN French, feminine of *ingénu* 'ingenuous'.

ingenuity /ˌɪndʒɪˈnjuːɪti/ ■ n. the quality of being ingenious.

inhalant

–ORIGIN C16: from Latin *ingenuitas* 'ingenuousness', from *ingenuus* 'inborn'; the current meaning arose by confusion of *ingenuous* with *ingenious.*

ingenuous /ɪnˈdʒɛnjʊəs/ ■ adj. innocent, artless, and unsuspecting.
–DERIVATIVES **ingenuously** adv. **ingenuousness** n.
–ORIGIN C16: from Latin *ingenuus* 'native, inborn'.

ingest ■ v. take (food or drink) into the body by swallowing or absorbing it.
–DERIVATIVES **ingestion** n.
–ORIGIN C17: from Latin *ingest-, ingerere* 'bring in'.

inglenook ■ n. a space on either side of a large fireplace.
–ORIGIN *ingle* from Scottish Gaelic *aingeal* 'light, fire', Irish *aingeal* 'live ember'.

inglorious ■ adj. 1 not worthy of honour. 2 not famous or renowned.
–DERIVATIVES **ingloriously** adv. **ingloriousness** n.

ingoing ■ adj. going towards or into.

ingoma /ɪnˈɡɔːmə/ ■ n. S. African a traditional Zulu dance style accompanied by chanting, later popular with migrant workers.
–ORIGIN isiZulu, 'royal song, hymn'.

ingot /ˈɪŋɡət/ ■ n. a rectangular block of steel, gold, or other metal.
–ORIGIN Middle English (denoting a mould): perhaps from **IN** + Old English *goten,* from *geotan* 'pour, cast'.

ingrain (also **engrain**) ■ v. firmly fix or establish (a habit, belief, or attitude) in a person.
–ORIGIN Middle English: from **EN-[1], IN-[2]** + **GRAIN**.

ingrained (also **engrained**) ■ adj. 1 (of a habit or attitude) firmly established. 2 (of dirt) deeply embedded.

ingrate /ˈɪnɡreɪt, ɪnˈɡreɪt/ formal or poetic/literary ■ n. an ungrateful person. ■ adj. ungrateful.
–ORIGIN Middle English: from Latin *ingratus,* from *in-* 'not' + *gratus* 'grateful'.

ingratiate /ɪnˈɡreɪʃɪeɪt/ ■ v. (**ingratiate oneself**) bring oneself into favour with someone by flattering or trying to please them.
–DERIVATIVES **ingratiating** adj. **ingratiatingly** adv. **ingratiation** n.
–ORIGIN C17: from Latin *in gratiam* 'into favour'.

ingratitude ■ n. a discreditable lack of gratitude.

ingredient ■ n. 1 any of the foods or substances that are combined to make a particular dish. 2 a component part or element.
–ORIGIN Middle English: from Latin *ingredient-, ingredi* 'enter', from *in-* 'into' + *gradi* 'walk'.

ingress /ˈɪnɡrɛs/ ■ n. 1 the action or fact of entering or coming in: *the sides are sealed against the ingress of water.* 2 a place or means of access. 3 Astronomy & Astrology the arrival of the sun, moon, or a planet in a specified constellation or part of the sky.
–DERIVATIVES **ingression** n.
–ORIGIN Middle English: from Latin *ingressus,* from *ingredi* 'enter'.

in-group ■ n. an exclusive group of people with a shared interest or identity.

ingrown ■ adj. 1 growing or having grown within; innate: *ingrown habit.* 2 inward-looking. 3 (of a toenail) having grown into the flesh.
–DERIVATIVES **ingrowing** adj. **ingrowth** n.

inguinal /ˈɪŋɡwɪn(ə)l/ ■ adj. Anatomy of the groin.
–ORIGIN Middle English: from Latin *inguinalis,* from *inguen* 'groin'.

inhabit ■ v. (**inhabited, inhabiting**) live in or occupy.
–DERIVATIVES **inhabitable** adj. **inhabitation** n.
–ORIGIN Middle English, from Latin *inhabitare,* from *in-* 'in' + *habitare* 'dwell'.

inhabitant ■ n. a person or animal that lives in or occupies a place.

inhalant ■ n. a medicinal preparation for inhaling. ▸ a solvent or other material producing vapour that is inhaled by drug abusers. ■ adj. chiefly Zoology serving for inhalation.
–DERIVATIVES **inhalator** n.

---

s sit   t top   v voice   w we   z zoo   ʃ she   ʒ decision   θ thin   ð this   ŋ ring   x loch   tʃ chip   dʒ jar

inhale

inhale /ɪnˈheɪl/ ■ v. breathe in (air, gas, smoke, etc.).
– DERIVATIVES **inhalation** n.
– ORIGIN C18 (*inhalation* C17): from Latin *inhalare* 'breathe in'.

inhaler ■ n. a portable device for administering a drug which is to be inhaled.

inhere /ɪnˈhɪə/ ■ v. (**inhere in/within**) formal exist essentially or permanently in.
– ORIGIN C16: from Latin *inhaerere* 'stick to'.

inherent /ɪnˈhɪər(ə)nt, -ˈhɛr(ə)nt/ ■ adj. existing in something as a permanent or essential attribute.
– DERIVATIVES **inherently** adv.

inherit ■ v. (**inherited**, **inheriting**) 1 receive (money, property, or a title) as an heir at the death of the previous holder. 2 derive (a quality or characteristic) from one's parents or ancestors. ▸ receive or be left with (a situation, object, etc.) from a predecessor or former owner.
– DERIVATIVES **inheritable** adj. **inheritor** n.
– ORIGIN Middle English *enherite* 'receive as a right', from late Latin *inhereditare* 'appoint as heir'.

inheritance ■ n. 1 a thing that is inherited. 2 the action of inheriting.

inheritance tax ■ n. (in the UK) tax levied on property and money acquired by gift or inheritance.

inhibit ■ v. (**inhibited**, **inhibiting**) 1 hinder, restrain, or prevent (an action or process). 2 make (someone) unable to act in a relaxed and natural way.
– DERIVATIVES **inhibited** adj. **inhibitive** adj.
– ORIGIN Middle English: from Latin *inhibere* 'hinder', from *in-* 'in' + *habere* 'hold'.

inhibition ■ n. 1 the action or process of inhibiting or being inhibited. 2 a feeling that makes one unable to act in a relaxed and natural way. ▸ Psychology a restraint on the direct expression of an instinct.

inhibitor ■ n. a substance which slows down or prevents a particular chemical reaction or other process.
– DERIVATIVES **inhibitory** adj.

inhospitable /ˌɪnhɒˈspɪtəb(ə)l, ɪnˈhɒspɪt-/ ■ adj. not hospitable.
– DERIVATIVES **inhospitableness** n. **inhospitably** adv. **inhospitality** n.

in-house ■ adj. & adv. within an organization.

inhuman ■ adj. 1 lacking positive human qualities; cruel and barbaric. 2 not human in nature or character.
– DERIVATIVES **inhumanly** adv.

inhumane ■ adj. without compassion for misery or suffering; cruel.
– DERIVATIVES **inhumanely** adv.

inhumanity ■ n. (pl. **-ies**) cruel and brutal behaviour.

inhumation /ˌɪnhjʊˈmeɪʃ(ə)n/ ■ n. chiefly Archaeology 1 the action or practice of burying the dead. 2 a burial or buried corpse.
– ORIGIN from rare *inhume* 'bury', from Latin *inhumare*, from *in-* 'into' + *humus* 'ground'.

inimical /ɪˈnɪmɪk(ə)l/ ■ adj. tending to obstruct or harm; hostile.
– DERIVATIVES **inimically** adv.
– ORIGIN C16: from late Latin *inimicalis*, from Latin *inimicus* (see ENEMY).

inimitable /ɪˈnɪmɪtəb(ə)l/ ■ adj. impossible to imitate; unique.
– DERIVATIVES **inimitability** n. **inimitably** adv.

iniquity /ɪˈnɪkwɪti/ ■ n. (pl. **-ies**) injustice or immoral behaviour.
– DERIVATIVES **iniquitous** adj. **iniquitously** adv. **iniquitousness** n.
– ORIGIN Middle English: from Latin *iniquitas*, from *iniquus*, from *in-* 'not' + *aequus* 'equal, just'.

initial ■ adj. existing or occurring at the beginning. ■ n. the first letter of a name or word, especially that of a person's given name. ■ v. (**initialled**, **initialling**; N. Amer. **initialed**, **initialing**) mark or sign with one's initials as a sign of approval or endorsement.
– DERIVATIVES **initially** adv.
– ORIGIN C16: from Latin *initialis*, from *initium* 'beginning'.

initialism ■ n. an abbreviation consisting of initial letters pronounced separately (e.g. *SABC*).

initialize (also **-ise**) ■ v. Computing set to the appropriate starting value or condition.
– DERIVATIVES **initialization** (also **-isation**) n.

initiate ■ v. /ɪˈnɪʃɪeɪt/ 1 cause (a process or action) to begin. 2 admit formally into a society or group, typically with a ritual. 3 (**initiate someone into**) introduce someone to (a new activity or skill). ■ n. /ɪˈnɪʃɪət/ a person who has been initiated.
– DERIVATIVES **initiation** n. **initiatory** adj.
– ORIGIN C16: from Latin *initiare* 'begin'.

initiation school ■ n. (in some traditional societies) a place of seclusion where adolescent boys or girls undergo the customary rites of passage to adulthood, often including ritual circumcision.

initiative ■ n. 1 the ability to initiate. ▸ the power or opportunity to act before others do: *we have lost the initiative*. 2 a fresh approach.
– PHRASES **on one's own initiative** without being prompted by others.

initiator ■ n. 1 a person or thing that initiates. 2 Chemistry a substance which starts a chain reaction. 3 an explosive or device used to detonate the main charge.

inject ■ v. 1 introduce (a liquid, especially a drug or vaccine) into the body with a syringe. ▸ administer a drug or medicine to (a person or animal) in this way. 2 introduce or feed (something) under pressure into another substance. 3 introduce (a new or different element): *she tried to inject scorn into her tone*.
– DERIVATIVES **injectable** adj. & n. **injector** n.
– ORIGIN C16: from Latin *inject-, incere* 'throw in'.

injection ■ n. 1 an act of injecting or being injected. 2 a substance that is injected.

injection moulding ■ n. the shaping of rubber or plastic articles by injecting heated material into a mould.
– DERIVATIVES **injection-moulded** adj.

in-joke ■ n. a joke that is shared exclusively by a small group.

injudicious ■ adj. showing poor judgement; unwise.
– DERIVATIVES **injudiciously** adv. **injudiciousness** n.

injunction ■ n. 1 Law a judicial order restraining a person from an action, or compelling a person to carry out a certain act. 2 an authoritative warning.
– DERIVATIVES **injunctive** adj.

injure ■ v. 1 do or undergo physical harm to; wound. 2 archaic do injustice or wrong to.
– ORIGIN Middle English: back-formation from INJURY.

injured ■ adj. 1 physically harmed or wounded. 2 offended; wronged: *the injured party*.

injuria ■ n. S. African Law an unlawful act or omission.
– ORIGIN Latin, 'a wrong, an injustice'.

injurious /ɪnˈdʒʊərɪəs/ ■ adj. causing or likely to cause injury. 2 (of language) maliciously insulting; libellous.
– DERIVATIVES **injuriously** adv.

injury ■ n. (pl. **-ies**) 1 an instance of being injured. 2 the fact of being injured; harm or damage.
– ORIGIN Middle English: from Latin *injuria* 'a wrong'.

injury time ■ n. (in rugby, soccer, and other sports) extra playing time allowed to compensate for time lost as a result of injuries.

injustice ■ n. 1 lack of justice. 2 an unjust act or occurrence.

ink ■ n. 1 a coloured fluid used for writing, drawing, or printing. 2 a black liquid ejected by a cuttlefish, octopus, or squid to confuse a predator. ■ v. write or mark with ink. ▸ cover (type or a stamp) with ink before printing.
– ORIGIN Middle English: from Old French *enque*, from Greek *enkauston*, denoting the purple ink used by Roman emperors for signatures, from *enkaiein* 'burn in'.

ink-blot test ■ n. another term for RORSCHACH TEST.

inkhorn ■ n. historical a small portable container for ink, originally made from a horn.

ink-jet printer ■ n. a printer in which the characters are formed by minute jets of ink.

inkling ■ n. a slight suspicion; a hint.
– ORIGIN Middle English: from *inkle* 'utter in an undertone'.

VOWELS a cat ɑː arm ɛ bed ɛː hair ə ago əː her ɪ sit i cosy iː see ɒ hot ɔː saw ʌ run

inkstand ■ n. a stand for ink bottles, pens, and other stationery items.

inkwell ■ n. a container for ink, normally housed in a hole in a desk.

inky ■ adj. (-ier, -iest) 1 as dark as ink. 2 stained with ink.
– DERIVATIVES **inkiness** n.

inlaid past and past participle of INLAY.

inland ■ adj. & adv. 1 in or into the interior of a country. 2 [as adj.] carried on within the limits of a country; domestic. ■ n. the interior of a country or region.

inland revenue ■ n. public revenue consisting of income tax and some other direct taxes.

inland sea ■ n. an entirely landlocked large body of salt or fresh water.

in-law ■ n. a relative by marriage. ■ comb. form related by marriage: *father-in-law*.

inlay ■ v. (past and past part. **inlaid**) ornament by embedding pieces of a different material in a surface. ■ n. 1 an inlaid design or piece of material. ▸ a material or substance used for inlaying. ▸ inlaid work or decoration. 2 a filling shaped to fit a tooth cavity. 3 a printed insert supplied with a CD, video, etc.
– DERIVATIVES **inlaying** n.

inlet ■ n. 1 a small arm of the sea, a lake, or a river. 2 a place or means of entry: *an air inlet*. 3 (in tailoring and dressmaking) an inserted piece of material.

inlier /'ɪnlʌɪə/ ■ n. Geology an older rock formation isolated among newer rocks.

in-line ■ adj. 1 having parts arranged in a line. 2 constituting an integral part of a continuous sequence of operations or machines.

in-line skate ■ n. a type of roller skate in which the wheels are fixed in a single line along the sole.
– DERIVATIVES **in-line skater** n. **in-line skating** n.

in loco parentis /ɪn ˌlɒkəʊ pəˈrɛntɪs/ ■ adv. & adj. (of a teacher or other adult) in the place of a parent.
– ORIGIN from Latin.

inly /'ɪnli/ ■ adv. poetic/literary inwardly.

inlying /'ɪnlʌɪɪŋ/ ■ adj. within or near a centre.

inmate ■ n. a person living in an institution such as a prison or hospital.
– ORIGIN C16 (denoting a lodger or subtenant): prob. orig. from INN + MATE¹, later associated with IN.

in medias res /ɪn ˌmiːdɪɑːs ˈreɪz/ ■ adv. in or into the midst or middle; without preamble.
– ORIGIN from Latin.

in memoriam /ˌɪn mɪˈmɔːrɪam/ ■ prep. in memory of (a dead person).
– ORIGIN from Latin.

inmost ■ adj. innermost.

inn ■ n. a public house, traditionally an establishment also providing food and lodging.
– ORIGIN Old English: of Germanic origin; rel. to IN.

innards ■ pl. n. informal 1 internal organs; entrails. 2 the internal workings of a device or machine.
– ORIGIN C19: representing a dialect pronunciation of INWARDS.

innate /ɪˈneɪt, 'ɪneɪt/ ■ adj. 1 inborn; natural. 2 Philosophy originating in the mind.
– DERIVATIVES **innately** adv. **innateness** n.
– ORIGIN Middle English: from Latin *innatus*, from *innasci*, from *in-* 'into' + *nasci* 'be born'.

inner ■ adj. 1 situated inside; close to the centre. 2 mental or spiritual; not visible: *inner strength*. ▸ private; not expressed. ■ n. 1 an inner part. 2 (in archery and shooting) a division of the target next to the bullseye.

inner city ■ n. the area near the centre of a city, especially when associated with social and economic problems.

inner ear ■ n. the part of the ear embedded in the temporal bone, consisting of the semicircular canals and cochlea.

innermost ■ adj. 1 furthest in; closest to the centre. 2 (of thoughts) most private and deeply felt.

inner space ■ n. 1 the region between the earth and outer space, or below the surface of the sea. 2 the part of the mind not normally accessible to consciousness.

601

inordinate

inner tube ■ n. a separate inflatable tube inside a pneumatic tyre casing.

innervate /'ɪnəveɪt, ɪˈnɜːveɪt/ ■ v. Anatomy & Zoology supply (an organ or other body part) with nerves.
– DERIVATIVES **innervation** n.
– ORIGIN C19: from IN-² + NERVE.

inning ■ n. Baseball each division of a game during which both sides have a turn at batting.
– ORIGIN Old English *innung* 'a putting or getting in', rel. to IN.

innings ■ n. (pl. same) [treated as sing.] Cricket each of the divisions of a game during which one side has a turn at batting. ▸ a player's turn at batting.
– PHRASES **have had a good innings** informal have had a long and fulfilling life or career.

innkeeper ■ n. chiefly archaic a person who runs an inn.

innocent ■ adj. 1 not guilty of a crime or offence. ▸ not responsible or directly involved: *an innocent bystander*. 2 free from moral wrong; not corrupted. 3 not intended to cause offence; harmless. 4 (**innocent of**) without experience or knowledge of: *a man innocent of war's cruelties*. ▸ without; lacking. ■ n. an innocent person.
– DERIVATIVES **innocence** n. **innocency** n. (archaic). **innocently** adv.
– ORIGIN Middle English: from Latin *innocent-* 'not harming', from *in-* 'not' + *nocere* 'to hurt'.

innocuous /ɪˈnɒkjʊəs/ ■ adj. not harmful or offensive.
– DERIVATIVES **innocuously** adv. **innocuousness** n.
– ORIGIN C16: from Latin *innocuus*, from *in-* 'not' + *nocuus* (see NOCUOUS).

Inn of Court ■ n. (in the UK) each of the four legal societies having the exclusive right of admitting people to the English bar.

innominate /ɪˈnɒmɪnət/ ■ adj. not named or classified.
– ORIGIN C17: from late Latin *innominatus*, from *in-* 'not' + *nominatus* 'named'.

innovate /'ɪnəveɪt/ ■ v. make changes in something already existing, as by introducing new methods, ideas, or products.
– DERIVATIVES **innovation** n. **innovational** adj. **innovator** n. **innovatory** adj.
– ORIGIN C16 (*innovation* Middle English): from Latin *innovare* 'renew, alter', from *in-* 'into' + *novare* 'make new'.

innovative /'ɪnəvətɪv/ ■ adj. featuring new methods or original ideas. ▸ creative in thinking.

innuendo /ˌɪnjʊˈɛndəʊ/ ■ n. (pl. **-oes** or **-os**) an allusive or oblique remark, typically a suggestive or disparaging one.
– ORIGIN C16: Latin, 'by nodding at, by pointing to', from *innuere*, from *in-* 'towards' + *nuere* 'to nod'.

innumerable ■ adj. too many to be counted.
– DERIVATIVES **innumerably** adv.

innumerate ■ adj. without a basic knowledge of mathematics and arithmetic. ■ n. an innumerate person.
– DERIVATIVES **innumeracy** n.

inoculant ■ n. a substance used for inoculation.

inoculate /ɪˈnɒkjʊleɪt/ ■ v. 1 another term for VACCINATE. ▸ introduce (an infective agent) into an organism. 2 introduce (cells or organisms) into a culture medium.
– DERIVATIVES **inoculable** adj. **inoculation** n. **inoculator** n.
– ORIGIN Middle English ('graft a bud or shoot'): from Latin *inoculare* 'engraft', from *in-* 'into' + *oculus* 'eye, bud'.

in-off ■ n. Billiards & Snooker the pocketing of the cue ball (a scoring stroke in billiards, a foul in snooker) by bouncing it off another ball.

inoffensive ■ adj. not objectionable or harmful.
– DERIVATIVES **inoffensively** adv. **inoffensiveness** n.

inoperable ■ adj. 1 Medicine not able to be suitably operated on. 2 not able to be used or operated. 3 impractical; unworkable.
– DERIVATIVES **inoperability** n. **inoperably** adv.

inoperative ■ adj. not working or taking effect.

inopportune ■ adj. occurring at an inconvenient time.
– DERIVATIVES **inopportunely** adv. **inopportuneness** n.

inordinate /ɪˈnɔːdɪnət/ ■ adj. 1 unusually large; excessive

inorganic

2 archaic unrestrained in feelings or behaviour; disorderly.
– DERIVATIVES **inordinately** adv.
– ORIGIN Middle English: from Latin *inordinatus*, from *in-* 'not' + *ordinatus* 'set in order'.

inorganic ■ adj. **1** not arising from natural growth. **2** Chemistry relating to or denoting compounds which are not organic (broadly, compounds not containing carbon). Compare with ORGANIC. **3** without organized physical structure.
– DERIVATIVES **inorganically** adv.

inositol /ʌɪˈnəʊsɪtɒl/ ■ n. Biochemistry a simple carbohydrate which occurs in animal and plant tissue and is a vitamin of the B group.
– ORIGIN C19: from the earlier name *inosite*.

inpatient ■ n. a patient who lives in hospital while under treatment.

in personam /ˌɪn pəˈsəʊnam/ ■ adj. & adv. Law made against or affecting a specific person only. Compare with IN REM.
– ORIGIN Latin, 'against a person'.

in-phase ■ adj. of or relating to electrical signals that are in phase.

in propria persona /ɪn ˌprəʊprɪə pəˈsəʊnə/ ■ adv. in his or her own person.
– ORIGIN from Latin.

input ■ n. **1** what is put in, taken in, or operated on by any process or system. ▸ a person's contribution: *her input on issues was appreciated*. **2** the action or process of putting or feeding something in. **3** energy supplied to a device or system; an electrical signal. **4** Electronics a place or device from which energy or information enters a system. ■ v. (**inputting**; past and past part. **input** or **inputted**) put (data) into a computer.
– DERIVATIVES **inputter** n.

inquest ■ n. Law a judicial inquiry to ascertain the facts relating to an incident. ▸ an inquiry by a magistrate (in South Africa) or coroner (in the UK) into the cause of a death.
– ORIGIN Middle English from Old French *enqueste*, from Latin *inquirere*, from *quaerere* 'seek'.

inquietude /ɪnˈkwʌɪətjuːd/ ■ n. physical or mental unease.

inquire ■ v. another term for ENQUIRE.
– DERIVATIVES **inquirer** n.

inquiry ■ n. (pl. **-ies**) another term for ENQUIRY.

inquisition ■ n. **1** a period of prolonged and intensive questioning or investigation. **2** (**the Inquisition**) an ecclesiastical tribunal established *c*.1232 for the suppression of heresy, notorious for its use of torture.
– DERIVATIVES **inquisitional** adj.
– ORIGIN Middle English: from Latin *inquisitio(n-)* 'examination', from *inquirere*, from *quaerere* 'seek'.

inquisitive ■ adj. curious or enquiring. ▸ unduly curious; prying.
– DERIVATIVES **inquisitively** adv. **inquisitiveness** n.

inquisitor /ɪnˈkwɪzɪtə/ ■ n. a person making an inquiry or conducting an inquisition, especially when regarded as harsh or very searching.

inquisitorial ■ adj. **1** of or like an inquisitor. **2** Law (of a trial) in which the judge has an examining role. Compare with ACCUSATORIAL, ADVERSARIAL.
– DERIVATIVES **inquisitorially** adv.

inquorate /ɪnˈkwɔːrət, -eɪt/ ■ adj. S. African & Brit. (of an assembly) not having a quorum.

in re /ɪn ˈriː, ˈreɪ/ ■ prep. in the legal case of; with regard to.
– ORIGIN Latin, 'in the matter of'.

in rem /ɪn ˈrɛm/ ■ adj. Law made against or affecting a thing, and therefore other people generally. Compare with IN PERSONAM.
– ORIGIN Latin, 'against a thing'.

INRI ■ abbrev. Jesus of Nazareth, King of the Jews (the inscription over Christ's head at the Crucifixion).
– ORIGIN from the initials of Latin *Iesus Nazarenus Rex Iudaeorum*.

inroad ■ n. **1** an instance of something being encroached or intruded upon. **2** a hostile attack.

inrush ■ n. a sudden inward rush or flow.
– DERIVATIVES **inrushing** adj. & n.

insalubrious /ˌɪnsəˈluːbrɪəs/ ■ adj. seedy; unwholesome.
– DERIVATIVES **insalubrity** n.

insane ■ adj. **1** in or relating to an unsound state of mind; seriously mentally ill. **2** extremely foolish; irrational.
– DERIVATIVES **insanely** adv. **insanity** n.
– ORIGIN C16: from Latin *insanus*, from *in-* 'not' + *sanus* 'healthy'.

insangu /ɪnˈsangu:/ (also **intsangu**) ■ n. S. African informal cannabis.
– ORIGIN from isiZulu *insangu* and isiXhosa *intsangu*.

insanitary ■ adj. so dirty or germ-ridden as to be a danger to health.

insatiable /ɪnˈseɪʃəb(ə)l/ ■ adj. impossible to satisfy.
– DERIVATIVES **insatiability** n. **insatiably** adv.

inscribe ■ v. (usu. **be inscribed**) **1** write or carve (words or symbols) on a surface, especially as a formal or permanent record. **2** write a dedication to someone in (a book). **3** Geometry draw (a figure) within another so that their boundaries touch but do not intersect. Compare with CIRCUMSCRIBE. **4** archaic enter the name of (someone) on a list; enrol.
– DERIVATIVES **inscribable** adj. **inscriber** n.
– ORIGIN Middle English: from Latin *inscribere*, from *in-* 'into' + *scribere* 'write'.

inscription ■ n. **1** a thing inscribed, as on a monument or in a book. **2** the action of inscribing.
– DERIVATIVES **inscriptional** adj. **inscriptive** adj.
– ORIGIN Middle English: from Latin *inscriptio(n-)*, from *inscribere* (see INSCRIBE).

inscrutable /ɪnˈskruːtəb(ə)l/ ■ adj. impossible to understand or interpret.
– DERIVATIVES **inscrutability** n. **inscrutably** adv.
– ORIGIN Middle English: from eccles. Latin *inscrutabilis*, from *in-* 'not' + *scrutari* 'search, examine'.

inseam ■ n. N. Amer. another term for INSIDE LEG.

insect ■ n. an arthropod animal of a large class (Insecta) having a head, thorax, and abdomen, six legs, two antennae, and one or two pairs of wings. ▸ informal any small invertebrate animal such as a spider or tick.
– ORIGIN C17: from Latin *(animal) insectum* 'segmented (animal)' (translating Greek *zōion entomon*), from *insecare* 'cut up or into'.

insectary /ɪnˈsɛktəri/ (also **insectarium** /ˌɪnsɛkˈtɛːrɪəm/) ■ n. (pl. **insectaries** or **insectariums**) a place where insects are kept, exhibited, and studied.

insecticide ■ n. a substance used for killing insects.
– DERIVATIVES **insecticidal** adj.

Insectivora /ˌɪnsɛkˈtɪvərə/ ■ pl. n. Zoology an order of small mammals that includes the shrews, moles, hedgehogs, and tenrecs.

insectivore /ɪnˈsɛktɪvɔː/ ■ n. **1** an animal that feeds on insects and other invertebrates. **2** Zoology a mammal of the order Insectivora.
– DERIVATIVES **insectivorous** adj.

insecure ■ adj. **1** not confident or assured. **2** (of a thing) not firm or firmly fixed. ▸ not permanent: *insecure employment*. **3** easily broken into; not protected.
– DERIVATIVES **insecurely** adv. **insecurity** n.

inselberg /ˈɪns(ə)lbəːɡ, -z-/ ■ n. Geology an isolated hill rising abruptly from a plain.
– ORIGIN C20: from German, from *Insel* 'island' + *Berg* 'mountain'.

inseminate /ɪnˈsɛmɪneɪt/ ■ v. introduce semen into (a woman or a female animal).
– DERIVATIVES **insemination** n. **inseminator** n.
– ORIGIN C17: from Latin *inseminare* 'sow', from *in-* 'into' + *seminare* 'sow'.

insensate ■ adj. **1** lacking physical sensation. **2** lacking sympathy; unfeeling. **3** completely lacking sense or reason.
– DERIVATIVES **insensately** adv.

insensible ■ adj. **1** without one's mental faculties; unconscious. ▸ numb; without feeling. **2** (**insensible of/to**) unaware of; indifferent to. **3** too small or gradual to

be perceived: *varying by insensible degrees.*
– DERIVATIVES **insensibly** adv. **insensibleness** n.

insensitive ■ adj. **1** showing or feeling no concern for others' feelings. **2** not sensitive to physical sensation. **3** not appreciative of or able to respond to something.
– DERIVATIVES **insensitively** adv. **insensitiveness** n. **insensitivity** n.

insentient ■ adj. incapable of feeling; inanimate.

inseparable ■ adj. unable to be separated or treated separately.
– DERIVATIVES **inseparability** n. **inseparably** adv.

insert ■ v. /ɪnˈsəːt/ place, fit, or incorporate (something) in something else. ▸ include (text) in a piece of writing. ■ n. /ˈɪnsəːt/ **1** a loose page or section in a magazine, typically one carrying an advertisement. **2** an ornamental section of cloth inserted into a garment. **3** a shot inserted in a film or video.
– DERIVATIVES **insertable** adj. **inserter** n.
– ORIGIN C15: from Latin *insert-*, *inserere* 'put in', from *in-* 'into' + *serere* 'to join'.

insertion ■ n. **1** the action of inserting. **2** an amendment or addition inserted in a text. ▸ each appearance of an advertisement in a newspaper or periodical. **3** an insert in a garment. **4** Anatomy & Zoology the manner or place of attachment of an organ or muscle.

in-service ■ adj. (of training) intended to take place during the course of employment.

inset ■ n. /ˈɪnsɛt/ a thing inserted; an insert. ▸ a small picture or map inserted within the border of a larger one. ■ v. /ɪnˈsɛt/ (**insetting**; past and past part. **inset** or **insetted**) **1** put in as an inset. **2** decorate with an inset.

inshallah /ɪnˈʃalə/ ■ exclam. if Allah wills it.
– ORIGIN from Arabic *in šāʾ Allāh.*

inshore ■ adj. at sea but close to the shore; operating near the coast: *an inshore lifeboat.* ■ adv. towards or closer to the shore.

inside ■ n. /ɪnˈsʌɪd/ **1** the inner side or surface of a thing. ▸ S. African & N. Amer. the part of the road nearest to the centre, closest to vehicles going in the opposite direction. ▸ Brit. the part of a road furthest from the centre. ▸ the side of a bend where the edge is shorter. **2** the inner part; the interior. ▸ (**insides**) informal the stomach and bowels. **3** (**the inside**) informal a position affording private information: *they must have a spy on the inside.* ■ adj. /ˈɪnsʌɪd/ **1** situated on or in, or derived from, the inside. **2** (in hockey, soccer, and other sports) denoting positions nearer to the centre of the field. ■ prep. & adv. /ɪnˈsʌɪd/ **1** situated or moving within. ▸ within (the body or mind of a person). **2** informal in prison. **3** (in soccer, rugby, and other sports) closer to the centre of the field than. **4** in less than (the period of time specified).
– PHRASES **inside of** informal **1** within. **2** in less than (the period of time specified).

inside job ■ n. informal a crime committed by or with the assistance of a person associated with the premises where it occurred.

inside leg ■ n. the length of a person's leg or trouser leg from crotch to ankle.

inside out ■ adv. with the inner surface turned outwards.
– PHRASES **know something inside out** know something very thoroughly.

insider ■ n. a person within an organization, especially someone privy to information unavailable to others.

insider dealing (also **insider trading**) ■ n. the illegal practice of trading on the stock exchange to one's own advantage through having access to confidential information.

insidious /ɪnˈsɪdɪəs/ ■ adj. proceeding in a gradual, subtle way, but with harmful effects.
– DERIVATIVES **insidiously** adv. **insidiousness** n.
– ORIGIN C16: from Latin *insidiosus* 'cunning'.

insight ■ n. **1** the capacity to gain an accurate and deep intuitive understanding of something. ▸ an understanding of this kind. **2** Psychiatry awareness by a mentally ill person that their mental experiences are not based in external reality.
– DERIVATIVES **insightful** adj. **insightfully** adv.
– ORIGIN Middle English: prob. of Scandinavian and Low German origin.

inspector

insignia /ɪnˈsɪɡnɪə/ ■ n. (pl. same) a badge or distinguishing mark of military rank, office, or membership.
– ORIGIN C17: from Latin, pl. of *insigne* 'sign, badge', neuter of *insignis* 'distinguished'.

insignificant ■ adj. too small or unimportant to be worth consideration.
– DERIVATIVES **insignificance** n. **insignificancy** n. **insignificantly** adv.

insincere ■ adj. not expressing genuine feelings.
– DERIVATIVES **insincerely** adv. **insincerity** n. (pl. **-ies**).

insinuate /ɪnˈsɪnjʊeɪt/ ■ v. **1** suggest or hint (something bad) in an indirect and unpleasant way. **2** (**insinuate oneself into**) manoeuvre oneself gradually into (a favourable position).
– DERIVATIVES **insinuating** adj. **insinuatingly** adv. **insinuator** n.
– ORIGIN C16: from Latin *insinuare* 'introduce tortuously', from *in-* 'in' + *sinuare* 'to curve'.

insinuation ■ n. an unpleasant hint or suggestion.

insipid /ɪnˈsɪpɪd/ ■ adj. **1** lacking flavour. **2** lacking vigour or interest.
– DERIVATIVES **insipidity** n. **insipidly** adv. **insipidness** n.
– ORIGIN C17: from late Latin *insipidus*, from *in-* 'not' + *sapidus*, from *sapere* 'to taste'.

insist ■ v. demand or state forcefully, without accepting refusal or contradiction. ▸ (**insist on**) persist in (doing).
– ORIGIN C16: from Latin *insistere* 'persist', from *in-* 'upon' + *sistere* 'stand'.

insistent ■ adj. **1** insisting or very demanding. **2** repeated and demanding attention: *a telephone started ringing, loud and insistent.*
– DERIVATIVES **insistence** n. **insistency** n. **insistently** adv.

in situ /ɪn ˈsɪtjuː/ ■ adv. & adj. in the original or appropriate position.
– ORIGIN from Latin.

insobriety ■ n. drunkenness.

insofar ■ adv. variant spelling of in so far (see **FAR**).

insolation /ˌɪnsəˈleɪʃ(ə)n/ ■ n. technical exposure to the sun's rays. ▸ the amount of solar radiation reaching a given area.
– ORIGIN C17: from Latin *insolatio(n-)*, from *insolare*, from *in-* 'towards' + *sol* 'sun'.

insole ■ n. a removable sole worn in a shoe for warmth or to improve the fit. ▸ the fixed inner sole of a boot or shoe.

insolent ■ adj. rude and disrespectful.
– DERIVATIVES **insolence** n. **insolently** adv.
– ORIGIN Middle English: from Latin *insolent-* 'immoderate, arrogant'.

insoluble ■ adj. **1** impossible to solve. **2** (of a substance) incapable of being dissolved.
– DERIVATIVES **insolubility** n. **insolubly** adv.

insolvent ■ adj. **1** unable to pay debts owed. **2** of or relating to bankruptcy. ■ n. an insolvent person.
– DERIVATIVES **insolvency** n.

insomnia ■ n. habitual sleeplessness.
– DERIVATIVES **insomniac** n. & adj.
– ORIGIN C17: from Latin, from *insomnis* 'sleepless'.

insomuch ■ adv. (**insomuch that/as**) to the extent that.

insouciant /ɪnˈsuːsɪənt/ ■ adj. casually unconcerned.
– DERIVATIVES **insouciance** n. **insouciantly** adv.
– ORIGIN C18: French, from *insouciant*, from *in-* 'not' + *souciant* 'worrying'.

inspan /ˈɪnspan/ ■ v. (**inspanned**, **inspanning**) S. African **1** yoke (draught animals) to a vehicle. **2** use for a particular purpose.
– ORIGIN C19: from Dutch *inspannen* 'to stretch'.

inspect ■ v. look at closely. ▸ examine officially.
– DERIVATIVES **inspection** n.
– ORIGIN C17 (*inspection* Middle English): from Latin *inspect-*, *inspicere* 'look into, examine'.

inspector ■ n. **1** an official who ensures that regulations are obeyed. ▸ Brit. an official who examines bus or train

inspector general

tickets for validity. **2** a police officer ranking below a chief inspector.
– DERIVATIVES **inspectorate** n. **inspectorial** adj. **inspectorship** n.

inspector general ■ n. **1** the head of a body of inspectors. **2** Military a staff officer who conducts inspections and investigations. ▶ S. African the highest rank of officer in the intelligence service.

inspector of taxes (also **tax inspector**) ■ n. (in the UK) an official of the Inland Revenue responsible for collecting taxes.

inspiration ■ n. **1** the process or quality of being inspired. ▶ a person or thing that inspires. ▶ a sudden brilliant or timely idea. ▶ the divine influence supposed to have led to the writing of the Bible. **2** inhalation.
– DERIVATIVES **inspirational** adj.

inspiratory /ɪnˈspʌɪrət(ə)ri/ ■ adj. Physiology relating to inhalation.

inspire ■ v. **1** fill with the urge or ability to do or feel something. ▶ create (a feeling) in a person. ▶ (**inspire someone with**) animate someone with (a feeling). **2** give rise to. **3** inhale.
– DERIVATIVES **inspirer** n. **inspiring** adj. **inspiringly** adv.
– ORIGIN Middle English: from Latin *inspirare* 'breathe or blow into'.

inspired ■ adj. **1** showing or characterized by inspiration: *an inspired contribution to the debate.* **2** (of air or another substance) having been inhaled.
– DERIVATIVES **inspiredly** adv.

inst. ■ abbrev. **1** dated (in business letters) instant. **2** institute; institution.

instability ■ n. (pl. **-ies**) lack of stability.

install (also **instal**) ■ v. (**installed, installing**) **1** place or fix (equipment) in position ready for use. **2** establish in a new place, condition, or role.
– DERIVATIVES **installer** n.
– ORIGIN Middle English: from medieval Latin *installare*, from *in-* 'into' + *stallum* 'place, stall'.

installation ■ n. **1** the action or process of installing or being installed. **2** a large piece of equipment installed for use. **3** a military or industrial establishment. **4** an art exhibit constructed within a gallery.

instalment (US also **installment**) ■ n. **1** a sum of money due as one of several equal payments for something, spread over an agreed period of time. **2** one of several parts of something which are published or broadcast in sequence at intervals.
– ORIGIN C18: alteration of obsolete *estalment* (prob. by association with INSTALLATION), from Anglo-Norman French *estalement*, from Old French *estaler* 'to fix'.

instance ■ n. an example or single occurrence of something. ▶ a particular case. ■ v. cite as an example.
– PHRASES **at first instance** Law at the first court hearing concerning a case. **at the instance of** formal at the request or instigation of. **for instance** as an example. **in the first** (or **second** etc.) **instance** in the first (or second etc.) place or stage of a proceeding.
– ORIGIN Middle English: from Latin *instantia* 'presence, urgency', from *instare* 'be present, press upon', from *in-* 'upon' + *stare* 'to stand'.

instant ■ adj. **1** immediate. ▶ (of food) processed to allow quick preparation. **2** urgent; pressing. **3** [postpos.] dated (in business letters) of the current month: *your letter of the 6th instant.* **4** archaic of the present. ■ n. **1** a precise moment of time. **2** a very short time.
– DERIVATIVES **instantly** adv.
– ORIGIN Middle English: from Latin *instare* 'be at hand', from *in-* 'in, at' + *stare* 'to stand'.

instantaneous /ˌɪnst(ə)nˈteɪnɪəs/ ■ adj. **1** occurring or done instantly. **2** Physics existing or measured at a particular instant.
– DERIVATIVES **instantaneity** n. **instantaneously** adv. **instantaneousness** n.
– ORIGIN C17: from medieval Latin *instantaneus*, from Latin *instant-*, from *instare* 'be at hand'.

instantiate /ɪnˈstanʃɪeɪt/ ■ v. represent as or by an instance. ▶ (**be instantiated**) Philosophy (of a universal or abstract concept) be represented by an actual example.
– DERIVATIVES **instantiation** n.
– ORIGIN 1940s: from Latin *instantia* (see INSTANCE).

instar /ˈɪnstɑː/ ■ n. Zoology a phase between two periods of moulting in the development of an insect larva or other invertebrate.
– ORIGIN C19: from Latin, 'form, likeness'.

instate ■ v. install or establish.
– ORIGIN C17: from IN-² + STATE.

instead ■ adv. as an alternative or substitute. ▶ (**instead of**) in place of.
– ORIGIN Middle English: from IN + STEAD.

instep ■ n. the part of a person's foot between the ball and the ankle. ▶ the part of a shoe which fits over or under this.
– ORIGIN Middle English; cf. West Frisian *ynstap* 'opening in a shoe for insertion of the foot'.

instigate /ˈɪnstɪɡeɪt/ ■ v. bring about or initiate. ▶ (**instigate someone to/to do something**) incite someone to do something.
– DERIVATIVES **instigation** n. **instigator** n.
– ORIGIN C16 (*instigation* Middle English): from Latin *instigare* 'urge, incite'.

instil /ɪnˈstɪl/ (also **instill**) ■ v. (**instilled, instilling**) **1** gradually but firmly establish in someone's mind. **2** put (a liquid) into something in drops.
– DERIVATIVES **instillation** n. **instilment** n.
– ORIGIN Middle English: from Latin *instillare*, from *in-* 'into' + *stillare* 'to drop'.

instinct ■ n. **1** an innate pattern of behaviour in animals in response to certain stimuli. ▶ a natural or intuitive way of acting or thinking. **2** a natural propensity or skill. ■ adj. (**instinct with**) formal imbued or filled with (a quality).
– DERIVATIVES **instinctual** adj. **instinctually** adv.
– ORIGIN Middle English: from Latin *instinctus* 'impulse', from *instinguere*, from *in-* 'towards' + *stinguere* 'to prick'.

instinctive ■ adj. relating to or prompted by instinct. ▶ apparently natural or automatic.
– DERIVATIVES **instinctively** adv.

institute ■ n. **1** an organization for the promotion of science, education, etc. **2** archaic a treatise or summary of principles, especially of law. ■ v. **1** set in motion or establish. ▶ begin (legal proceedings). **2** appoint to a position, especially as a cleric.
– ORIGIN Middle English: from Latin *instituere* 'establish'.

institution ■ n. **1** an organization founded for a religious, educational, or social purpose. ▶ an organization providing residential care for people with special needs. ▶ an official organization with an important role in a country. **2** an established law or custom. ▶ informal a well-established and familiar person or thing: *he became a national institution*. **3** the action of instituting.

institutional ■ adj. of, in, or like an institution. ▶ regimented or unimaginative. ▶ expressed or organized through institutions: *institutional religion*. **2** (of advertising) intended to create prestige.
– DERIVATIVES **institutionalism** n. **institutionally** adv.

institutionalize (also **-ise**) ■ v. **1** establish as a convention in an organization or culture. **2** place in a residential institution. ▶ (**be/become institutionalized**) suffer the deleterious effects of long-term residence in an institution.
– DERIVATIVES **institutionalization** (also **-isation**) n.

instruct ■ v. **1** direct or command. **2** teach. **3** authorize (a lawyer or attorney) to act on one's behalf. ▶ (of an attorney) inform (an advocate) about a case. ▶ (of a judge) inform (a jury) about the legal principles of a case. **4** inform of a fact or situation.
– ORIGIN Middle English: from Latin *instruct-*, *instruere* 'construct, equip, teach', from *in-* 'upon, towards' + *struere* 'pile up'.

instruction ■ n. **1** a direction or order. ▶ (**instructions**) Law directions to a lawyer, advocate, or jury. **2** Computing a code in a program which defines and carries out an operation. **3** education.
– DERIVATIVES **instructional** adj.

instruction set ■ n. Computing the complete set of instructions in machine code that can be recognized by a central processing unit.

instructive ■ adj. useful and informative.
– DERIVATIVES **instructively** adv. **instructiveness** n.

instructor (or **instructress**) ■ n. a teacher.
—DERIVATIVES **instructorship** n.

instrument ■ n. **1** a tool or implement, especially for precision work. **2** a measuring device, especially in a vehicle or aircraft. **3** (also **musical instrument**) a device for producing musical sounds. **4** a means of pursuing an aim. **5** a person who is made use of. **6** a formal or legal document. ■ v. equip with measuring instruments.
—ORIGIN Middle English: from Latin *instrumentum* 'equipment, implement', from *instruere* 'construct, equip'.

instrumental ■ adj. **1** serving as a means of pursuing an aim. **2** (of music) performed on instruments. **3** of or relating to an implement or measuring device. **4** Grammar denoting or relating to a case of nouns and pronouns indicating a means or instrument. ■ n. a piece of music performed by instruments, with no vocals.
—DERIVATIVES **instrumentality** n. **instrumentally** adv.

instrumentalism ■ n. a pragmatic philosophical approach which regards an activity (e.g. science, law, or education) chiefly as an instrument for some practical purpose.

instrumentalist ■ n. **1** a player of a musical instrument. **2** an adherent of instrumentalism. ■ adj. of or in terms of instrumentalism.

instrumentation ■ n. **1** the instruments used in a piece of music. ▸ the arrangement of a piece of music for particular instruments. **2** measuring instruments collectively. ▸ the design or use of such instruments.

insubordinate ■ adj. disobedient.
—DERIVATIVES **insubordinately** adv. **insubordination** n.

insubstantial ■ adj. lacking strength and solidity. ▸ imaginary.
—DERIVATIVES **insubstantiality** n. **insubstantially** adv.

insufferable ■ adj. intolerable. ▸ unbearably arrogant or conceited.
—DERIVATIVES **insufferableness** n. **insufferably** adv.
—ORIGIN Middle English: perhaps via French *insouffrable*, from Latin *sufferre* (see SUFFER).

insufficiency ■ n. the condition of being insufficient.

insufficient ■ adj. not enough.
—DERIVATIVES **insufficiently** adv.

insulant ■ n. an insulating material.

insular ■ adj. **1** lacking contact with other people. ▸ narrow-minded. **2** of, relating to, or from an island. **3** of or relating to the art of Britain and Ireland in the early Middle Ages. **4** (of climate) equable because of the influence of the sea.
—DERIVATIVES **insularity** n. **insularly** adv.
—ORIGIN C16: from late Latin *insularis*, from *insula* 'island'.

insulate ■ v. **1** protect by interposing material to prevent loss of heat or intrusion of sound. ▸ cover with non-conducting material to prevent the passage of electricity. **2** protect from something unpleasant.
—ORIGIN C16: from Latin *insula* 'island'.

insulating tape (also **insulation tape**) ■ n. adhesive tape used to cover exposed electric wires.

insulation ■ n. **1** the action of insulating or state of being insulated. **2** material used to insulate something.

insulator ■ n. a substance which does not readily allow the passage of heat, sound, or electricity. ▸ a block of glass, ceramic, or other insulating material enclosing an electric wire where it crosses a support.

insulin ■ n. Biochemistry a pancreatic hormone which regulates glucose levels in the blood, a lack of which causes diabetes.
—ORIGIN C20: from Latin *insula* 'island' (with ref. to the islets of Langerhans in the pancreas).

insulin shock ■ n. Medicine an acute condition resulting from excess insulin in the blood, involving weakness, convulsions, and potentially coma.

insult ■ v. /ɪnˈsʌlt/ speak to or treat with disrespect or abuse. ■ n. /ˈɪnsʌlt/ **1** an insulting remark or action. ▸ a thing so worthless or contemptible as to be offensive: *the pay offer is an absolute insult*. **2** Medicine an event which causes damage to a tissue or organ.
—DERIVATIVES **insulter** n. **insulting** adj. **insultingly** adv.
—ORIGIN C16: from Latin *insultare* 'jump or trample on'; noun from eccles. Latin *insultus*.

insuperable /ɪnˈs(j)uːp(ə)rəb(ə)l/ ■ adj. impossible to overcome.
—DERIVATIVES **insuperability** n. **insuperably** adv.
—ORIGIN Middle English: from Latin *insuperabilis*, from *in-* 'not' + *superabilis*, from *superare* 'overcome'.

insupportable ■ adj. **1** unable to be supported or justified. **2** intolerable.
—DERIVATIVES **insupportably** adv.

insurance ■ n. **1** the action of insuring someone or something. ▸ the business of providing insurance policies. ▸ money paid for this, or as compensation under an insurance policy. **2** a thing providing protection against a possible eventuality.

insurance broker ■ n. an agent selling insurance.

insurance carrier ■ n. chiefly N. Amer. an insurance company.

insurance policy ■ n. a contract of insurance.

insure /ɪnˈʃʊə/ ■ v. **1** arrange for compensation in the event of damage to or loss of (property, life, or a person), in exchange for regular payments to a company. ▸ secure the payment of (a sum) in this way. ▸ (**insure someone against**) protect someone against (a possible contingency). **2** another term for ENSURE.
—DERIVATIVES **insurability** n. **insurable** adj. **insurer** n.
—ORIGIN Middle English: alteration of ENSURE.

insured ■ adj. covered by insurance. ■ n. (**the insured**) (pl. same) a person covered by insurance.

insurgent /ɪnˈsɜːdʒ(ə)nt/ ■ adj. rising in active revolt. ■ n. a rebel or revolutionary.
—DERIVATIVES **insurgence** n. **insurgency** n. (pl. **-ies**).
—ORIGIN C18: from Latin *insurgere* 'arise'.

insurmountable /ˌɪnsəˈmaʊntəb(ə)l/ ■ adj. too great to be overcome.
—DERIVATIVES **insurmountably** adv.

insurrection /ˌɪnsəˈrɛkʃ(ə)n/ ■ n. a violent uprising against authority.
—DERIVATIVES **insurrectionary** adj. **insurrectionist** n. & adj.
—ORIGIN Middle English: from late Latin *insurrectio(n-)*, from *insurgere* 'rise up'.

insusceptible ■ adj. not susceptible.
—DERIVATIVES **insusceptibility** n.

inswinger ■ n. Cricket a ball bowled with a swing from the off to the leg side.

int. ■ abbrev. **1** interior. **2** internal. **3** international.

intact ■ adj. not damaged or impaired.
—DERIVATIVES **intactness** n.
—ORIGIN Middle English: from Latin *intactus*, from *in-* 'not' + *tactus*, from *tangere* 'touch'.

intaglio /ɪnˈtaljəʊ, -ˈtɑːl-/ ■ n. (pl. **-os**) an incised or engraved design. ▸ a gem with an incised design. ▸ a printing process in which the type or design is engraved.
—ORIGIN C17: Italian, from *intagliare* 'engrave'.

intake ■ n. **1** an amount or quantity taken in. ▸ an act of taking someone or something in. **2** a location or structure through which something is taken in.

intangible ■ adj. unable to be touched; not solid or real. ▸ vague and abstract. ■ n. an intangible thing.
—DERIVATIVES **intangibility** n. **intangibly** adv.

integer /ˈɪntɪdʒə/ ■ n. **1** a whole number. **2** a thing complete in itself.
—ORIGIN C16: from Latin, 'intact, whole', from *in-* (expressing negation) + the root of *tangere* 'to touch'.

integral ■ adj. /ˈɪntɪɡr(ə)l, ɪnˈtɛɡr(ə)l/ **1** necessary to make a whole complete; fundamental. ▸ included as part of a whole. ▸ having all the parts necessary to be complete. **2** Mathematics of or denoted by an integer or integers. ■ n. /ˈɪntɪɡr(ə)l/ Mathematics a function of which a given function is the derivative, and which may express the area under the curve of a graph of the function.
—DERIVATIVES **integrality** n. **integrally** adv.
—ORIGIN C16: from late Latin *integralis*, from *integer* (see INTEGER).

integral calculus ■ n. Mathematics the part of calculus concerned with the integrals of functions.

integrand /ˈɪntɪɡrand/ ■ n. Mathematics a function that is to

integrate

be integrated.
– ORIGIN C19: from Latin *integrandus*, from *integrare* (see INTEGRATE).

integrate /ˈɪntɪgreɪt/ ■ v. **1** combine or be combined to form a whole. **2** bring or come into equal participation in an institution or body. **3** Mathematics find the integral of. ▸ [usu. as adj. **integrated**] find the mean value or total sum of (a variable quantity or property).
– DERIVATIVES **integrable** /ˈɪntɪgrəb(ə)l/ adj. **integrative** /ˈɪntɪgrətɪv/ adj. **integrator** n.
– ORIGIN C17: from Latin *integrare* 'make whole', from *integer* (see INTEGER).

integrated circuit ■ n. an electronic circuit on a small piece of semi-conducting material, performing the same function as a larger circuit of discrete components.

integrated services digital network (abbrev.: ISDN) ■ n. a telecommunications network through which sound, images, and data can be transmitted as digitized signals.

integration ■ n. **1** the action or process of integrating. **2** Mathematics the finding of an integral or integrals. **3** Psychology the coordination of processes in the nervous system.
– DERIVATIVES **integrationist** n.

integrity /ɪnˈtɛgrɪti/ ■ n. **1** the quality of having strong moral principles. **2** the state of being whole. ▸ the condition of being unified or sound in construction. ▸ internal consistency or lack of corruption in electronic data.
– ORIGIN Middle English: from Latin *integritas*, from *integer* (see INTEGER).

integument /ɪnˈtɛgjʊm(ə)nt/ ■ n. a tough outer protective layer, especially of an animal or plant.
– DERIVATIVES **integumental** adj. **integumentary** adj.
– ORIGIN C17: from Latin *integumentum*, from *integere*, from *in-* 'in' + *tegere* 'to cover'.

intellect ■ n. **1** the faculty of reasoning and understanding objectively. ▸ one's mental powers. **2** a clever person.
– ORIGIN Middle English: from Latin *intellectus* 'understanding', from *intellegere* (see INTELLIGENCE).

intellectual /ˌɪntəˈlɛktʃʊəl, -tjʊəl/ ■ adj. of, relating to, or appealing to the intellect. ▸ having a highly developed intellect. ■ n. a person with a highly developed intellect.
– DERIVATIVES **intellectuality** n. **intellectually** adv.

intellectualism ■ n. the exercise of the intellect at the expense of the emotions.
– DERIVATIVES **intellectualist** n.

intellectualize (also **-ise**) ■ v. **1** give an intellectual character to. **2** talk or write intellectually.
– DERIVATIVES **intellectualization** (also **-isation**) n.

intellectual property ■ n. Law intangible property that is the result of creativity, e.g. patents or copyrights.

intelligence ■ n. **1** the ability to acquire and apply knowledge and skills. **2** a person with this ability. **3** the gathering of information of military or political value. ▸ information gathered in this way. **4** archaic news.
– ORIGIN Middle English: from Latin *intelligentia*, from *intelligere*, var. of *intellegere* 'understand', from *inter* 'between' + *legere* 'choose'.

intelligence quotient (abbrev.: IQ) ■ n. a number representing a person's reasoning ability, compared to the statistical norm, 100 being average.

intelligent ■ adj. **1** having intelligence, especially of a high level. **2** (of a device) able to vary its state or action in response to varying situations and past experience. ▸ (of a computer terminal) having its own processing capability.
– DERIVATIVES **intelligently** adv.

intelligentsia /ɪnˌtɛlɪˈdʒɛntsɪə/ ■ n. [treated as sing. or pl.] intellectuals or highly educated people, regarded as possessing culture and political influence.
– ORIGIN C20: from Russian *intelligentsiya*, from Polish *inteligencja*, from Latin *intelligentia* (see INTELLIGENCE).

intelligible /ɪnˈtɛlɪdʒɪb(ə)l/ ■ adj. able to be understood. ▸ Philosophy able to be understood only by the intellect.
– DERIVATIVES **intelligibility** n. **intelligibly** adv.

– ORIGIN Middle English: from Latin *intelligibilis*, from *intelligere* (see INTELLIGENCE).

intemperate ■ adj. showing a lack of self-control. ▸ characterized by excessive indulgence, especially in alcohol.
– DERIVATIVES **intemperance** n. **intemperately** adv. **intemperateness** n.

intend ■ v. **1** have as one's aim or plan. ▸ (**intend something as/to do something**) plan that something should be or act as something. ▸ plan that speech should have (a particular meaning). **2** (**intend for/to do something**) design or destine for a particular purpose. ▸ (**be intended for**) be meant for the use of.
– DERIVATIVES **intender** n.
– ORIGIN Middle English *entend* ('direct the attention to'), from Latin *intendere* 'intend, extend, direct'.

intended ■ adj. planned or meant. ■ n. (**one's intended**) informal one's fiancé(e).
– DERIVATIVES **intendedly** adv.

intense ■ adj. (**-er**, **-est**) **1** of extreme force, degree, or strength: *intense concentration.* **2** extremely earnest or serious: *an intense young woman.*
– DERIVATIVES **intensely** adv. **intenseness** n.
– ORIGIN Middle English: from Latin *intensus* 'stretched tightly, strained', from *intendere* (see INTEND).

intensifier ■ n. **1** Photography a chemical used to intensify a negative. **2** Grammar an adverb used to give force or emphasis.

intensify ■ v. (**-ies**, **-ied**) **1** make or become more intense. **2** Photography increase the opacity of (a negative) using a chemical.
– DERIVATIVES **intensification** n.
– ORIGIN C19: coined by the English poet Samuel Taylor Coleridge.

intension ■ n. Logic the internal content of a concept. Often contrasted with EXTENSION.
– DERIVATIVES **intensional** adj. **intensionally** adv.
– ORIGIN C17: from Latin *intensio(n-)*, from *intendere* (see INTEND).

intensity ■ n. (pl. **-ies**) **1** the quality of being intense. **2** chiefly Physics the measurable amount of a property.

intensive ■ adj. **1** very thorough or vigorous. **2** (of agriculture) aiming to achieve maximum production within a limited area. Often contrasted with EXTENSIVE. **3** [in combination] concentrating on or making much use of something: *computer-intensive methods.*
– DERIVATIVES **intensively** adv. **intensiveness** n.
– ORIGIN Middle English: from medieval Latin *intensivus*, from *intendere* (see INTEND).

intensive care ■ n. special medical treatment of a dangerously ill patient.

intent ■ n. intention or purpose. ■ adj. **1** (**intent on/upon**) resolved or determined to do. ▸ attentively occupied with. **2** showing earnest and eager attention.
– PHRASES **to all intents and purposes** in all important respects. **with intent** Law with the intention of committing a crime.
– DERIVATIVES **intently** adv. **intentness** n.
– ORIGIN Middle English: from Old French *entent, entente,* from Latin *intendere* (see INTEND).

intention ■ n. **1** an aim or plan. ▸ the action or fact of intending. ▸ (**one's intentions**) a person's, especially a man's, designs in respect to marriage. **2** Medicine the healing process of a wound. **3** (**intentions**) Logic conceptions formed by directing the mind towards an object.
– DERIVATIVES **-intentioned** adj.

intentional ■ adj. deliberate.
– DERIVATIVES **intentionality** n. **intentionally** adv.

inter /ɪnˈtəː/ ■ v. (**interred, interring**) (usu. **be interred**) place (a corpse) in a grave or tomb.
– ORIGIN Middle English: from Old French *enterrer*, based on Latin *in-* 'into' + *terra* 'earth'.

inter- prefix **1** between; among: *interbreed.* **2** mutually; reciprocally: *interatomic.*
– ORIGIN from Old French *entre-* or Latin *inter* 'between, among'.

interact ■ v. act in such a way as to have an effect on another.
– DERIVATIVES **interactant** adj. & n.

interaction ■ n. reciprocal action or influence.
– DERIVATIVES **interactional** adj.

interactionism (also **symbolic interactionism**) ■ n. Sociology a view of social behaviour that emphasizes the role of linguistic communication and its subjective understanding.
– DERIVATIVES **interactionist** n. & adj.

interactive ■ adj. **1** (of two people or things) influencing each other. **2** (of a computer or other electronic device) allowing a two-way flow of information between it and a user, responding to the user's input.
– DERIVATIVES **interactively** adv. **interactivity** n.

inter alia /ˌɪntər 'eɪlɪə, 'ɑːlɪə/ ■ adv. among other things.
– ORIGIN from Latin.

inter-allied ■ adj. of or relating to two or more states cooperating for military purposes.

interatomic ■ adj. Physics existing or acting between atoms.

interbreed ■ v. (past and past part. **-bred**) breed or cause to breed with an animal of a different race or species.

intercalary /ɪn'tɜːkəl(ə)ri, ˌɪntə'kal(ə)ri/ ■ adj. **1** (of a day or month) inserted in the calendar to harmonize it with the solar year, e.g. 29 February. **2** (of an academic period) additional to the standard course and taken at a different institution. **3** Botany denoting meristem tissue located between its daughter cells.
– ORIGIN C17: from Latin *intercalarius*, from *intercalare* (see INTERCALATE).

intercalate /ɪn'tɜːkəleɪt/ ■ v. **1** insert (an intercalary period) in a calendar. **2** (usu. **be intercalated**) insert between layers in a crystal lattice or other structure.
– DERIVATIVES **intercalation** n.
– ORIGIN C17: from Latin *intercalare* 'proclaim as inserted in the calendar'.

intercede /ˌɪntə'siːd/ ■ v. intervene on behalf of another.
– DERIVATIVES **interceder** n.
– ORIGIN C16: Latin *intercedere* 'intervene', from *inter-* 'between' + *cedere* 'go'.

intercellular ■ adj. Biology located or occurring between cells.

intercept ■ v. /ˌɪntə'sɛpt/ **1** obstruct and prevent from continuing to a destination. **2** Mathematics mark or cut off (part of a space, line, or surface). ■ n. /'ɪntəsɛpt/ **1** an act of intercepting. **2** Mathematics the point at which a given line cuts a coordinate axis.
– DERIVATIVES **interception** n. **interceptive** adj.
– ORIGIN Middle English: from Latin *intercept-, intercipere* 'catch between'.

interceptor ■ n. **1** a person or thing that intercepts another. **2** a fast aircraft for stopping or repelling hostile aircraft.

intercession /ˌɪntə'sɛʃ(ə)n/ ■ n. the action of intervening on behalf of another. ▸ the action of saying a prayer on behalf of another person.
– DERIVATIVES **intercessor** n. **intercessory** adj.
– ORIGIN Middle English: from Latin *intercessio(n-)*, from *intercedere* (see INTERCEDE).

interchange ■ v. /ˌɪntə'tʃeɪn(d)ʒ/ (of two people) exchange (things) with each other. ▸ put each of (two things) in the other's place. ■ n. /'ɪntətʃeɪn(d)ʒ/ **1** the action of interchanging. ▸ an exchange of words. **2** alternation. **3** a road junction on several levels so that traffic streams do not intersect. **4** a station where passengers may change from one railway line or bus service to another.
– DERIVATIVES **interchangeability** n. **interchangeable** adj. **interchangeableness** n. **interchangeably** adv.

intercity ■ adj. existing or travelling between cities.

intercollegiate ■ adj. existing or conducted between colleges or universities.

intercolumniation /ˌɪntəkəlʌmnɪ'eɪʃ(ə)n/ ■ n. Architecture the distance between adjacent columns.
– DERIVATIVES **intercolumnar** adj.

intercom ■ n. an electrical device allowing one-way or two-way communication.
– ORIGIN SECOND WORLD WAR: abbrev. of *intercommunication* (see INTERCOMMUNICATE).

intercommunicate ■ v. **1** engage in two-way communication. **2** (of rooms) have a common connecting door.

– DERIVATIVES **intercommunication** n.

interconnect ■ v. connect with each other.
– DERIVATIVES **interconnection** n.

intercontinental ■ adj. relating to or travelling between continents.
– DERIVATIVES **intercontinentally** adv.

interconvert ■ v. (usu. **be interconverted**) cause to be converted into each other.
– DERIVATIVES **interconversion** n. **interconvertible** adj.

intercooler ■ n. an apparatus for cooling gas between successive compressions, especially in a supercharged engine.
– DERIVATIVES **intercool** v.

intercorrelation /ˌɪntəkɒrə'leɪʃ(ə)n/ ■ n. a mutual connection between two or more things.
– DERIVATIVES **intercorrelate** v.

intercostal /ˌɪntə'kɒst(ə)l/ Anatomy ■ adj. situated between the ribs. ■ n. an intercostal muscle.
– DERIVATIVES **intercostally** adv.

intercourse ■ n. **1** communication or dealings between people. **2** short for SEXUAL INTERCOURSE.
– ORIGIN Middle English: from Latin *intercursus*, from *intercurrere* 'intervene', from *inter-* 'between' + *currere* 'run'.

intercrop ■ v. (**-cropped**, **-cropping**) [often as noun **intercropping**] grow (a crop) among plants of a different kind.

intercurrent ■ adj. Medicine (of a disease) occurring during the progress of another.
– ORIGIN C17: from Latin *intercurrere* 'intervene'.

intercut ■ v. (**-cutting**; past and past part. **-cut**) alternate (scenes) with contrasting scenes in a film.

interdenominational /ˌɪntədɪnɒmɪ'neɪʃ(ə)n(ə)l/ ■ adj. of or relating to more than one religious denomination.
– DERIVATIVES **interdenominationally** adv.

interdepartmental ■ adj. of or relating to more than one department.
– DERIVATIVES **interdepartmentally** adv.

interdependent ■ adj. dependent on each other.
– DERIVATIVES **interdepend** v. **interdependence** n. **interdependency** n.

interdict ■ n. /'ɪntədɪkt/ **1** Law a court order forbidding an act. **2** (in the Roman Catholic Church) a sentence debarring a person or place from ecclesiastical functions and privileges. ■ v. /ˌɪntə'dɪkt/ chiefly N. Amer. **1** prohibit or forbid. **2** intercept (a prohibited commodity).
– DERIVATIVES **interdiction** n.
– ORIGIN Middle English: from Latin *interdictum*, from *interdicere* 'interpose, forbid by decree'.

interdict de homine libero exhibendo ■ n. S. African Law another term for HABEAS CORPUS.
– ORIGIN from Latin.

interdigital ■ adj. between the fingers or toes.

interdisciplinary ■ adj. of or relating to more than one branch of knowledge.

interest ■ n. **1** the state of wanting to know about something or someone. ▸ a quality exciting curiosity or holding the attention: *a tale full of interest*. ▸ a subject in which one is concerned. **2** money paid for the use of money lent, or for delaying the repayment of a debt. **3** the advantage or benefit of someone. ▸ archaic self-interest. **4** a share or involvement in an undertaking. ▸ a legal concern, title, or right in property. **5** a group having a common concern, especially in politics or business. ■ v. **1** excite the curiosity or attention of. ▸ (**interest someone in**) persuade someone to undertake or acquire. **2** [as adj. **interested**] having an interest or involvement; not impartial: *seeking views from interested parties*.
– PHRASES **at interest** (of money borrowed) on the condition that interest is payable. **declare an** (or **one's**) **interest** make known one's financial interests in an undertaking before it is discussed. **in the interests** (or **interest**) **of something** for the benefit of.
– DERIVATIVES **interestedly** adv. **interestedness** n.
– ORIGIN Middle English: from Latin *interesse* 'differ, be

interest-free

important', from *inter-* 'between' + *esse* 'be'; the *-t* was added by association with Old French *interest* 'damage, loss'.

interest-free ■ adj. & adv. with no interest charged.

interesting ■ adj. arousing curiosity or interest.
– DERIVATIVES **interestingly** adv. **interestingness** n.

interface ■ n. 1 a point where two things meet and interact. ▶ chiefly Physics a surface forming a boundary between two portions of matter or space. 2 Computing a device or program enabling a user to communicate with a computer, or for connecting two items of hardware or software. ■ v. (**interface with**) 1 interact with. 2 Computing connect with (something) by an interface.

interfacial ■ adj. 1 included between two faces of a crystal or other solid. 2 relating to or denoting an interface.

interfacing ■ n. an extra layer of material or an adhesive stiffener, applied to the facing of a garment to add support.

interfaith ■ adj. of, relating to, or between different religions.

interfere ■ v. 1 (**interfere with**) prevent from continuing or being carried out properly. ▶ get in the way of. ▶ handle or adjust without permission. ▶ Law attempt to bribe or intimidate (a witness). 2 intervene without invitation or necessity. 3 (**interfere with**) euphemistic sexually molest. 4 Physics interact to produce interference.
– DERIVATIVES **interferer** n. **interfering** adj. **interferingly** adv.
– ORIGIN Middle English: from Old French *s'entreferir* 'strike each other', from *entre-* 'between' + *ferir*, from Latin *ferire* 'to strike'.

interference ■ n. 1 the action of interfering or process of being interfered with. 2 Physics the combination of two or more waveforms to form a resultant wave in which the displacement is either reinforced or cancelled. ▶ disturbance to radio signals caused by unwanted signals from other sources.
– DERIVATIVES **interferential** adj.

interferometer /ˌɪntəˈfɒrəmɪtə/ ■ n. Physics an instrument in which wave interference is employed to make precise measurements in terms of the wavelength.
– DERIVATIVES **interferometric** adj. **interferometrically** adv. **interferometry** n.

interferon /ˌɪntəˈfɪərɒn/ ■ n. Biochemistry a protein released by animal cells which inhibits virus replication.
– ORIGIN 1950s: from INTERFERE.

interfile ■ v. file together or into an existing sequence.

interfuse ■ v. poetic/literary join or mix together.
– DERIVATIVES **interfusion** n.

intergalactic ■ adj. of, relating to, or situated between galaxies.
– DERIVATIVES **intergalactically** adv.

intergeneric /ˌɪntədʒɪˈnɛrɪk/ ■ adj. Biology existing between or obtained from different genera.

interglacial Geology ■ adj. relating to or denoting a period of milder climate between two glacial periods. ■ n. an interglacial period.

intergovernmental ■ adj. of, relating to, or conducted between governments.
– DERIVATIVES **intergovernmentally** adv.

interim /ˈɪnt(ə)rɪm/ ■ n. the intervening time. ■ adj. 1 provisional. 2 relating to less than a full year's business activity: *interim profits*.
– ORIGIN C16: from Latin, 'meanwhile'.

interior ■ adj. 1 situated within or inside; inner. ▶ (**interior to**) chiefly technical situated further in or within. 2 inland. 3 relating to a country's internal or domestic affairs. ■ n. 1 the interior part of something. 2 the internal affairs of a country.
– DERIVATIVES **interiorize** (also **-ise**) v. **interiorly** adv.
– ORIGIN C15: from Latin, 'inner', from *inter* 'within'.

interior angle ■ n. the angle between adjacent sides of a rectilinear figure.

interior decoration ■ n. the decoration of the interior of a building or room, especially with regard for colour combination and artistic effect.
– DERIVATIVES **interior decorator** n.

interior design ■ n. the design or decoration of the interior of a room or building.
– DERIVATIVES **interior designer** n.

interiority ■ n. the quality of being interior or inward.

interior monologue ■ n. a piece of writing expressing a character's thoughts.

interject /ˌɪntəˈdʒɛkt/ ■ v. say abruptly, especially as an interruption.
– DERIVATIVES **interjectory** adj.
– ORIGIN C16 (*interjection* Middle English): from Latin *interject-*, *interjicere* 'interpose', from *inter-* 'between' + *jacere* 'to throw'.

interjection ■ n. an exclamation, especially as a part of speech (e.g. *ah!*, *dear me!*).
– DERIVATIVES **interjectional** adj.

interlace ■ v. 1 interweave. ▶ (**interlace something with**) mingle or intersperse something with. 2 Electronics scan (a video image) in such a way that alternate lines form one sequence which is followed by the other lines in a second sequence.
– DERIVATIVES **interlacement** n.

interlanguage ■ n. a language or form of language having features of two others, e.g. a pidgin.

interlard ■ v. (**interlard something with**) intersperse or embellish something with (different material).
– ORIGIN Middle English ('mix with alternate layers of fat'): from French *entrelarder*, from *entre-* 'between' + *larder* 'to lard'.

interlay ■ v. (past and past part. **-laid**) interpose. ■ n. an inserted layer.

interlead ■ v. chiefly S. African [often as adj. **interleading**] connect (a room or building) to another by means of a door or passageway.

interleave ■ v. 1 insert extra pages, typically blank, between the pages of (a book). ▶ place something between the layers of. 2 Telecommunications mix (digital signals) by alternating between them. 3 Computing divide (memory or processing power) between a number of tasks by allocating successive segments of it to each task in turn.

interleukin /ˌɪntəˈluːkɪn/ ■ n. Biochemistry any of a class of glycoproteins produced by leucocytes for regulating immune responses.
– ORIGIN 1970s: from INTER- + *leukocyte*, var. of LEUCOCYTE.

interline ■ v. put an extra lining in (a garment, curtain, etc.).

interlinear ■ adj. written between the lines of a text.

interlingual ■ adj. between or relating to two languages.

interlining ■ n. material used to interline a garment, curtain, etc.

interlink ■ v. join or connect together.
– DERIVATIVES **interlinkage** n.

interlobular /ˌɪntəˈlɒbjʊlə/ ■ adj. Anatomy situated between lobes.

interlock ■ v. 1 (of two or more things) engage with each other by overlapping or fitting together. 2 Music space notes in such a way that each performer or group of performers follows a beat falling between the beat of others. ■ n. 1 a device or mechanism for connecting or coordinating the function of components. 2 (also **interlock fabric**) a fabric with closely interlocking stitches allowing it to stretch.
– DERIVATIVES **interlocker** n.

interlocutor /ˌɪntəˈlɒkjʊtə/ ■ n. formal a person who takes part in a dialogue.
– DERIVATIVES **interlocution** n.
– ORIGIN C16: modern Latin, from Latin *interlocut-*, *interloqui* 'interrupt (with speech)', from *inter-* 'between' + *loqui* 'speak'.

interlocutory /ˌɪntəˈlɒkjʊt(ə)ri/ ■ adj. Law (of a decree or judgement) given provisionally during the course of a legal action.

interloper /ˈɪntələʊpə/ ■ n. a person who interferes in another's affairs; an intruder.
– DERIVATIVES **interlope** v.

– ORIGIN C16: from **INTER-** + *-loper* as in archaic *landloper* 'vagabond', from Middle Dutch *landlooper*.

interlude ■ n. **1** an intervening period of time. ▸ a pause between the acts of a play. **2** a thing occurring or done during an interval. ▸ a piece of music played between other pieces or between the verses of a hymn. **3** a temporary amusement or diversion: *a romantic interlude*.
– ORIGIN Middle English: from medieval Latin *interludium*, from *inter-* 'between' + *ludus* 'play'.

intermarriage ■ n. **1** marriage between people of different races, castes, or religions. **2** marriage between close relations.
– DERIVATIVES **intermarry** v.

intermediary /ˌɪntəˈmiːdɪəri/ ■ n. (pl. **-ies**) a mediator. ■ adj. intermediate.
– ORIGIN C18: from Italian *intermediario*, from Latin *intermedius* (see **INTERMEDIATE**).

intermediate /ˌɪntəˈmiːdɪət/ ■ adj. **1** coming between two things in time, place, character, etc. **2** having more than basic knowledge or skills but not yet advanced. ■ n. **1** an intermediate person or thing. **2** a chemical compound formed by one reaction and then taking part in another. ■ v. /ˌɪntəˈmiːdɪeɪt/ mediate.
– DERIVATIVES **intermediacy** n. **intermediately** adv. **intermediateness** n. **intermediation** n. **intermediator** n.
– ORIGIN Middle English: from medieval Latin *intermediatus*, from Latin *intermedius*, from *inter-* 'between' + *medius* 'middle'.

intermediate phase ■ n. S. African the phase of primary school education comprising grades 4–6.

intermediate technology ■ n. technology suitable for developing countries, typically using local resources.

interment /ɪnˈtəːm(ə)nt/ ■ n. the burial of a corpse in a grave or tomb.

intermesh ■ v. mesh together.

intermezzo /ˌɪntəˈmɛtsəʊ/ ■ n. (pl. **intermezzi** /-ˈmɛtsi/ or **intermezzos**) **1** a short connecting instrumental movement in an opera or other musical work. ▸ a short piece for a solo instrument. **2** a light dramatic or other performance between the acts of a play.
– ORIGIN C18: from Italian, from Latin *intermedium* 'interval'.

interminable ■ adj. endless.
– DERIVATIVES **interminableness** n. **interminably** adv.
– ORIGIN Middle English: from late Latin *interminabilis*, from *in-* 'not' + *terminare* (see **TERMINATE**).

intermingle ■ v. mix or mingle together.

intermission ■ n. a pause or break. ▸ an interval between parts of a play or film.
– ORIGIN Middle English: from Latin *intermissio(n-)*, from *intermittere* (see **INTERMIT**).

intermit /ˌɪntəˈmɪt/ ■ v. (**intermitted**, **intermitting**) suspend or discontinue for a time. ▸ (especially of a fever or pulse) stop for a time.
– ORIGIN C16: from Latin *intermittere*, from *inter-* 'between' + *mittere* 'let go'.

intermittent ■ adj. occurring at irregular intervals.
– DERIVATIVES **intermittence** n. **intermittency** n. **intermittently** adv.

intermix ■ v. mix together.
– DERIVATIVES **intermixture** n.

intermodal ■ adj. involving two or more different modes of transport.

intermolecular ■ adj. existing or occurring between molecules.

intern ■ n. /ˈɪntəːn/ a recent medical graduate receiving supervised training in a hospital and acting as an assistant physician or surgeon. ▸ a student or trainee who does a job to gain work experience or for a qualification. ■ v. **1** /ɪnˈtəːn/ confine as a prisoner. **2** /ˈɪntəːn/ serve as an intern.
– DERIVATIVES **internment** n. **internship** n.
– ORIGIN C16: from Latin *internus* 'inward, internal'.

internal ■ adj. **1** of or situated on the inside. ▸ inside the body. ▸ existing within an organization. ▸ relating to affairs and activities within a country. **2** experienced in one's mind. **3** intrinsic. ■ n. (**internals**) inner parts or features.
– DERIVATIVES **internality** n. **internally** adv.

– ORIGIN C16: from modern Latin *internalis*, from Latin *internus* 'inward, internal'.

internal-combustion engine ■ n. an engine in which petrol or other fuel is burned with air and the hot gases produced are used to do work such as driving a piston.

internal evidence ■ n. evidence derived from the contents of the thing discussed.

internal exile ■ n. penal banishment from a part of one's own country.

internalize (also **-ise**) ■ v. **1** Psychology make (attitudes or behaviour) part of one's nature by learning or unconscious assimilation. ▸ acquire knowledge of (the rules of a language). **2** Economics incorporate (costs) as part of a pricing structure.
– DERIVATIVES **internalization** (also **-isation**) n.

internal market ■ n. another term for **SINGLE MARKET**.

international ■ adj. existing or occurring between nations. ▸ agreed on by all or many nations. ▸ used by people of many nations. ■ n. a game or contest between teams representing different countries. ▸ a player who has taken part in such a contest.
– DERIVATIVES **internationality** n. **internationally** adv.

International Baccalaureate ■ n. a set of examinations qualifying candidates for higher education in any of several countries.

international candle ■ n. see **CANDLE**.

International Date Line ■ n. see **DATE LINE**.

Internationale /ˌɪntənæʃəˈnɑːl/ ■ n. (**the Internationale**) a revolutionary song composed in France and adopted by socialists.
– ORIGIN French, feminine of *international* 'international'.

internationalism ■ n. **1** the advocacy of cooperation and understanding between nations. **2** the state or process of being international.
– DERIVATIVES **internationalist** n.

internationalize (also **-ise**) ■ v. **1** make international. **2** bring under the protection or control of two or more nations.
– DERIVATIVES **internationalization** (also **-isation**) n.

international law ■ n. a body of rules established by custom or treaty and recognized by nations as binding in their relations with one another.

International Phonetic Alphabet ■ n. an internationally recognized set of phonetic symbols.

international style ■ n. a functional style of 20th-century architecture characterized by the use of steel and reinforced concrete, wide windows, uninterrupted interior spaces, simple lines, and strict geometric forms.

international system of units ■ n. the SI system of units.

internecine /ˌɪntəˈniːsʌɪn/ ■ adj. destructive to both sides in a conflict. ▸ of or relating to conflict within a group.
– ORIGIN C17: from Latin *internecinus*, from *inter-* 'among' + *necare* 'to kill'.

internee /ˌɪntəːˈniː/ ■ n. a prisoner.

Internet ■ n. an international information network linking computers, accessible to the public via modem links.
– ORIGIN C20: from **INTER-** + **NETWORK**.

internist ■ n. Medicine, chiefly N. Amer. a specialist in internal diseases.

internode /ˈɪntənəʊd/ ■ n. **1** Botany a part of a plant stem between nodes. **2** Anatomy a stretch of a nerve, sheathed with myelin, between two nodes of Ranvier.

internuclear ■ adj. between nuclei.

interoceanic ■ adj. between or connecting two oceans.

interpersonal ■ adj. of or relating to relationships or communication between people.
– DERIVATIVES **interpersonally** adv.

interphase ■ n. Biology the resting phase between successive mitotic divisions of a cell, or between the first and second divisions of meiosis.

interplanetary ■ adj. situated or travelling between planets.

interplant

interplant ■ v. plant (a crop or plant) together with another. ▸ plant with a mixture of crops.

interplay ■ n. the way in which two or more things affect each other.

interpleader ■ n. Law a suit pleaded between two parties to determine a matter of right to property held by a third party.

Interpol /ˈɪntəpɒl/ ■ n. an organization based in France that coordinates investigations made by the police forces of member countries into international crimes.
– ORIGIN from *Inter*(*national*) *pol*(*ice*).

interpolate /ɪnˈtɜːpəleɪt/ ■ v. **1** insert (words) in a book, especially to give a false impression as to its date. ▸ make such insertions in (a book). **2** interject (a remark) in a conversation. **3** Mathematics insert (an intermediate term) into a series by estimating or calculating it from surrounding known values.
– DERIVATIVES **interpolation** n. **interpolative** adj. **interpolator** n.
– ORIGIN C17: from Latin *interpolare* 'refurbish, alter', from *inter-* 'between' + *-polare*, rel. to *polire* 'to polish'.

interpose ■ v. **1** insert between one thing and another. **2** intervene between parties. **3** say as an interruption. **4** exercise or advance (a veto or objection).
– DERIVATIVES **interposition** n.
– ORIGIN C16: from Latin *interponere* 'put in' (from *inter-* 'between' + *ponere* 'put'), but influenced by *interpositus* 'inserted' and Old French *poser* 'to place'.

interpret ■ v. (**interpreted**, **interpreting**) **1** explain the meaning of (words, actions, etc.). ▸ translate orally the words of a person speaking a different language. **2** perform (a creative work) in a way that conveys one's understanding of the creator's ideas. ▸ understand as having a particular meaning or significance.
– DERIVATIVES **interpretability** n. **interpretable** adj. **interpretation** n. **interpretational** adj. **interpretative** adj. **interpretatively** adv. **interpretive** adj. **interpretively** adv.
– ORIGIN Middle English: from Latin *interpretari* 'explain, translate', from *interpres* 'translator, interpreter'.

interpreter ■ n. **1** a person who interprets foreign speech orally. **2** Computing a program that can analyse and execute a program line by line.

interprovincial ■ adj. existing or carried on between provinces of the same country.

interracial ■ adj. existing between or involving different races.
– DERIVATIVES **interracially** adv.

interregnum /ˌɪntəˈrɛgnəm/ ■ n. (pl. **interregnums** or **interregna** /-nə/) a period when normal government is suspended, especially between successive reigns or regimes.
– ORIGIN C16: from Latin, from *inter-* 'between' + *regnum* 'reign'.

interrelate ■ v. relate or connect to one other.
– DERIVATIVES **interrelatedness** n. **interrelation** n. **interrelationship** n.

interrogate ■ v. **1** ask questions of (someone) closely, aggressively, or formally. **2** obtain data or information automatically from (a device, database, etc.).
– DERIVATIVES **interrogation** n. **interrogational** adj. **interrogator** n.
– ORIGIN C15 (*interrogation* Middle English): from Latin *interrogare* 'question', from *inter-* 'between' + *rogare* 'ask'.

interrogation point (also **interrogation mark**) ■ n. another term for QUESTION MARK.

interrogative /ˌɪntəˈrɒgətɪv/ ■ adj. having the force of a question. ▸ Grammar used in questions. Contrasted with AFFIRMATIVE and NEGATIVE. ■ n. an interrogative word, e.g. *how* or *what*.
– DERIVATIVES **interrogatively** adv.

interrogatory /ˌɪntəˈrɒgət(ə)ri/ ■ adj. questioning. ■ n. (pl. **-ies**) Law a written question which is formally put to one party in a case by another party and which must be answered.

interrupt ■ v. **1** stop the continuous progress of. ▸ stop (a person who is speaking) by saying or doing something. **2** break the continuity of (a line, surface, or view): *a sunken fence which doesn't interrupt the view across the fields.*
– DERIVATIVES **interruptible** adj. **interruptive** adj.
– ORIGIN Middle English: from Latin *interrupt-, interrumpere*, from *inter-* 'between' + *rumpere* 'to break'.

interrupter (also **interruptor**) ■ n. **1** a person or thing that interrupts. **2** a device that automatically breaks an electric circuit if a fault develops.

interruption ■ n. the action of interrupting or the fact of being interrupted. ▸ an act, utterance, or period that interrupts.

intersect ■ v. divide (something) by passing or lying across it. ▸ (of lines, roads, etc.) cross or cut each other.
– ORIGIN C17 (*intersection* C16): from Latin *intersecare* 'cut, intersect'.

intersection ■ n. a point or line common to lines or surfaces that intersect. ▸ a point at which two or more things, especially roads, intersect.

interseptal /ˌɪntəˈsɛpt(ə)l/ ■ adj. Anatomy & Zoology situated between septa or partitions.

intersexual ■ adj. existing or occurring between the sexes.

interspace ■ n. a space between objects. ■ v. (usu. **be interspaced**) put or occupy a space between.

interspecific /ˌɪntəspəˈsɪfɪk/ ■ adj. Biology existing or occurring between different species.

intersperse ■ v. (usu. **be interspersed**) scatter among or between other things. ▸ diversify with other things at intervals.
– DERIVATIVES **interspersion** n.
– ORIGIN C16: from Latin *interspers-, interspergere* 'scatter between'.

interstadial /ˌɪntəˈsteɪdɪəl/ Geology ■ adj. relating to or denoting a minor period of less cold climate during a glacial period. ■ n. an interstadial period.
– ORIGIN C20: from INTER- + *stadial*, from Latin *stadialis*, from *stadium* 'stage'.

interstate ■ adj. existing or carried on between states, especially of the US. ■ n. one of a system of motorways running between US states.

interstellar /ˌɪntəˈstɛlə/ ■ adj. occurring or situated between stars.

interstice /ɪnˈtəːstɪs/ ■ n. a small intervening space.
– ORIGIN Middle English: from Latin *interstitium*, from *intersistere* 'stand between'.

interstitial /ˌɪntəˈstɪʃ(ə)l/ ■ adj. of, forming, or occupying interstices.
– DERIVATIVES **interstitially** adv.

intersubjective ■ adj. Philosophy existing between conscious minds.
– DERIVATIVES **intersubjectively** adv. **intersubjectivity** n.

intertextuality /ˌɪntətɛkstjuˈalɪti/ ■ n. the relationship between texts.
– DERIVATIVES **intertextual** adj. **intertextually** adv.

intertidal ■ adj. Ecology of or denoting the area of a seashore which is covered at high tide and uncovered at low tide.

intertribal ■ adj. existing or occurring between different tribes.

intertwine ■ v. twist or twine together.
– DERIVATIVES **intertwinement** n.

interval ■ n. **1** an intervening time or space. **2** a pause or break. ▸ a period of time separating parts of a theatrical or musical performance. **3** a gap. **4** the difference in pitch between two sounds.
– PHRASES **at intervals** with time or spaces between, not continuously.
– DERIVATIVES **intervallic** adj.
– ORIGIN Middle English: from Latin *intervallum* 'space between ramparts, interval'.

intervalometer /ˌɪntəvəˈlɒmɪtə/ ■ n. Photography a device on a camera that operates the shutter regularly at set intervals over a period.

intervene ■ v. **1** come between so as to prevent or alter something. ▸ occur as a delay or obstacle to something being done. ▸ interrupt verbally. ▸ Law interpose in a lawsuit as a third party. **2** [usu. as adj. **intervening**] occur in

time between events. ► be situated between things.
- DERIVATIVES **intervener** (also **intervenor**) n.
- ORIGIN C16 (*intervention* Middle English): from Latin *intervenire*, from *inter-* 'between' + *venire* 'come'.

intervention ■ n. **1** the action or process of intervening. ► interference by a state in another's affairs. **2** action taken to improve a medical disorder.
- DERIVATIVES **interventional** adj.

interventionist ■ adj. favouring intervention, especially by a government in its domestic economy or by one state in the affairs of another. ■ n. an interventionist person.
- DERIVATIVES **interventionism** n.

intervertebral /ˌɪntəˈvəːtɪbr(ə)l/ ■ adj. situated between vertebrae.

interview ■ n. **1** a conversation between a journalist or broadcaster and a person of public interest. **2** an oral examination of an applicant for a job or college place. ► a session of formal questioning of a person by the police. ■ v. hold an interview with.
- DERIVATIVES **interviewee** n. **interviewer** n.
- ORIGIN C16: from French *entrevue*, from *s'entrevoir* 'see each other', from *voir* 'to see', on the pattern of *vue* 'a view'.

inter vivos /ˌɪntə ˈviːvəʊs/ ■ adv. & adj. (especially of a gift as opposed to a legacy) between living people.
- ORIGIN from Latin.

interweave ■ v. (past -**wove**; past part. -**woven**) weave or become woven together.

intestate /ɪnˈtesteɪt/ ■ adj. not having made a will before one dies. ■ n. a person who has died intestate.
- DERIVATIVES **intestacy** /-təsi/ n.
- ORIGIN Middle English: from Latin *intestatus*, from *in-* 'not' + *testatus* (see TESTATE).

intestine (also **intestines**) ■ n. the lower part of the alimentary canal from the end of the stomach to the anus. ► (in invertebrates) the whole alimentary canal.
- DERIVATIVES **intestinal** adj.
- ORIGIN Middle English: from Latin, from *intestinus*, from *intus* 'within'.

intifada /ˌɪntɪˈfɑːdə/ ■ n. the Palestinian uprising against Israeli occupation of the West Bank and Gaza Strip, beginning in 1987.
- ORIGIN from Arabic *intifāḍa* 'an uprising', from *intifaḍa* 'be shaken, shake oneself'.

intimacy ■ n. (pl. -**ies**) **1** close familiarity or friendship. **2** an intimate act, especially sexual intercourse. ► an intimate remark.

intimate¹ /ˈɪntɪmət/ ■ adj. **1** closely acquainted; familiar. ► having an informal friendly atmosphere. **2** private and personal. ► euphemistic having a sexual relationship. **3** involving very close connection. **4** (of knowledge) detailed. ■ n. a very close friend.
- DERIVATIVES **intimately** adv.
- ORIGIN C17: from late Latin *intimatus*, from Latin *intimare* 'impress, make familiar', from *intimus* 'inmost'.

intimate² /ˈɪntɪmeɪt/ ■ v. state or make known. ► imply or hint.
- DERIVATIVES **intimation** n.
- ORIGIN C16 (*intimation* Middle English): from late Latin *intimare* (see INTIMATE¹).

intimidate ■ v. frighten or overawe.
- DERIVATIVES **intimidating** adj. **intimidatingly** adv. **intimidation** n. **intimidator** n. **intimidatory** adj.
- ORIGIN C17: from medieval Latin *intimidare* 'make timid', from *timidus* 'timid'.

into ■ prep. **1** expressing motion or direction to a point on or within. **2** indicating a route to a destination. **3** indicating the direction towards which someone or something is turned. **4** indicating an object of interest. **5** expressing a change of state. **6** expressing the result of an action. **7** expressing division. **8** informal taking a lively and active interest in.
- ORIGIN Old English (see IN, TO).

intolerable ■ adj. unable to be endured.
- DERIVATIVES **intolerably** adv.

intolerant ■ adj. not tolerant.
- DERIVATIVES **intolerance** n. **intolerantly** adv.

intonation ■ n. **1** the rise and fall of the voice in speaking. ► the action of intoning. **2** accuracy of pitch.

611

in tray

- DERIVATIVES **intonational** adj.

intone /ɪnˈtəʊn/ ■ v. say or recite with little rise and fall of the pitch of the voice.
- DERIVATIVES **intoner** n.
- ORIGIN C15: from medieval Latin *intonare*, from *in-* 'into' + Latin *tonus* 'tone'.

in toto /ɪn ˈtəʊtəʊ/ ■ adv. as a whole.
- ORIGIN from Latin.

intoxicant ■ n. an intoxicating substance.

intoxicate ■ v. [usu. as adj. **intoxicated**] **1** (of alcoholic drink or a drug) cause (someone) to lose control of their faculties. **2** poison. **3** excite or exhilarate.
- DERIVATIVES **intoxicating** adj. **intoxicatingly** adv. **intoxication** n.
- ORIGIN Middle English: from medieval Latin *intoxicare*, from *in-* 'into' + *toxicare* 'to poison', from Latin *toxicum* 'poison'.

intra- /ˈɪntrə/ ■ prefix (added to adjectives) on the inside; within: *intramural*.
- ORIGIN from Latin *intra* 'inside'.

intracellular ■ adj. Biology located or occurring within a cell or cells.
- DERIVATIVES **intracellularly** adv.

intracranial ■ adj. within the skull.
- DERIVATIVES **intracranially** adv.

intractable /ɪnˈtraktəb(ə)l/ ■ adj. hard to control or deal with. ► stubborn.
- DERIVATIVES **intractability** n. **intractableness** n. **intractably** adv.

intrados /ɪnˈtreɪdɒs/ ■ n. Architecture the lower or inner curve of an arch. Often contrasted with EXTRADOS.
- ORIGIN C18: from French, from *intra-* 'on the inside' + *dos* 'the back', from Latin *dorsum*.

intramolecular ■ adj. existing or occurring within a molecule.

intramural /ˌɪntrəˈmjʊər(ə)l/ ■ adj. **1** situated or done within a building. ► chiefly N. Amer. within a single educational institution. ► forming part of normal university or college studies. **2** situated or done within a community.
- ORIGIN C19: from INTRA- + Latin *murus* 'wall'.

intramuscular ■ adj. situated or taking place within, or administered into, a muscle.
- DERIVATIVES **intramuscularly** adv.

Intranet /ˈɪntrənɛt/ ■ n. Computing a private communications network created using World Wide Web software.

intransigent /ɪnˈtransɪdʒ(ə)nt, -ˈtrɑː-, -nz-/ ■ adj. unwilling to change one's views or to agree. ■ n. an intransigent person.
- DERIVATIVES **intransigence** n. **intransigency** n. **intransigently** adv.
- ORIGIN C19: from French *intransigeant*, from Spanish *los intransigentes* (a name adopted by the extreme republicans in the Cortes); from Latin *in-* 'not' + *transigere* 'come to an understanding'.

intransitive /ɪnˈtransɪtɪv, -ˈtrɑː-, -nz-/ ■ adj. (of a verb or a sense or use of a verb) not taking a direct object, e.g. *look* in *look at the sky*. The opposite of TRANSITIVE.
- DERIVATIVES **intransitively** adv. **intransitivity** n.

intraspecific ■ adj. Biology occurring or existing within a species.

intrauterine /ˌɪntrəˈjuːtərʌɪn, -rɪn/ ■ adj. within the uterus.

intrauterine device (abbrev.: **IUD**) ■ n. a contraceptive device fitted inside the uterus and physically preventing the implantation of fertilized ova.

intravascular /ˌɪntrəˈvaskjʊlə/ ■ adj. Medicine & Biology situated or occurring within the vascular system.
- DERIVATIVES **intravascularly** adv.

intravenous /ˌɪntrəˈviːnəs/ (abbrev.: **IV**) ■ adj. existing or taking place within, or administered into, a vein or veins.
- DERIVATIVES **intravenously** adv.

in tray ■ n. a tray on a desk for letters and documents that have to be dealt with.

intrench

intrench ■ v. variant spelling of ENTRENCH.
intrepid ■ adj. fearless; adventurous.
– DERIVATIVES **intrepidity** n. **intrepidly** adv.
– ORIGIN C17: from Latin *intrepidus*, from *in-* 'not' + *trepidus* 'alarmed'.
intricacy /'ɪntrɪkəsi/ ■ n. (pl. **-ies**) **1** the quality of being intricate. **2** (**intricacies**) details.
intricate ■ adj. very complicated or detailed.
– DERIVATIVES **intricately** adv.
– ORIGIN Middle English: from Latin *intricare* 'entangle', from *in-* 'into' + *tricae* 'tricks, perplexities'.
intrigue ■ v. /ɪn'triːg/ (**intrigues**, **intrigued**, **intriguing**) **1** arouse the curiosity or interest of. **2** plot something illicit or harmful. ■ n. /ɪn'triːg, 'ɪn-/ **1** the plotting of something illicit or harmful. ▸ a secret love affair. **2** a mysterious or fascinating quality.
– DERIVATIVES **intriguer** n. **intriguing** adj. **intriguingly** adv.
– ORIGIN C17: from French *intrigue* 'plot', *intriguer* 'to tangle, to plot', from Latin *intricare* (see INTRICATE).
intrinsic /ɪn'trɪnsɪk/ ■ adj. belonging naturally; essential.
– DERIVATIVES **intrinsically** adv.
– ORIGIN C15 ('interior, inner'): from late Latin *intrinsecus*, from the earlier adv. *intrinsecus* 'inwardly, inwards'.
intro ■ n. (pl. **-os**) informal an introduction.
intro- ■ prefix into; inwards: *introvert*.
– ORIGIN from Latin *intro* 'to the inside'.
introduce ■ v. **1** bring into use or operation for the first time. ▸ bring (a plant, animal, or disease) to a place for the first time. ▸ (**introduce something to**) bring a subject to the attention of (someone) for the first time. ▸ present (new legislation) for debate in a legislative assembly. **2** present (someone) by name to another. **3** insert or bring into something. **4** occur at the start of. ▸ provide an opening announcement for.
– DERIVATIVES **introducer** n.
– ORIGIN Middle English: from Latin *introducere*, from *intro-* 'to the inside' + *ducere* 'to lead'.
introduction ■ n. **1** the action of introducing or being introduced. ▸ a thing, such as a product, plant, etc., newly brought in. **2** a formal presentation of one person to another. **3** a preliminary thing, such as an explanatory section at the beginning of a book, report, etc. ▸ a preliminary section in a piece of music. **4** a book or course of study intended to introduce a subject to a person. ▸ a person's first experience of a subject or thing.
introductory ■ adj. serving as an introduction; basic or preliminary.
introgression /ˌɪntrə(ʊ)'grɛʃ(ə)n/ ■ n. Biology the transfer of genetic information from one species to another through hybridization and repeated backcrossing.
– ORIGIN C17: from Latin *intro-* 'to the inside' on the pattern of *ingression*.
introit /'ɪntrɔɪt, ɪn'trəʊɪt/ ■ n. Christian Church a psalm or antiphon sung or said while the priest approaches the altar for the Eucharist.
– ORIGIN Middle English: from Latin *introitus*, from *introire* 'enter', from *intro-* 'to the inside' + *ire* 'go'.
introjection /ˌɪntrə(ʊ)'dʒɛkʃ(ə)n/ ■ n. Psychoanalysis the unconscious adoption of the ideas or attitudes of others.
– DERIVATIVES **introject** v.
– ORIGIN C19: from INTRO-, on the pattern of *projection*.
intromittent organ /ˌɪntrə(ʊ)'mɪt(ə)nt/ ■ n. Zoology the male copulatory organ of an animal, especially a hermaphrodite.
– ORIGIN C19: from Latin *intromittere* 'introduce', from *intro-* 'to the inside' + *mittere* 'send'.
intron /'ɪntrɒn/ ■ n. Biochemistry a segment of a DNA or RNA molecule which does not code for proteins and interrupts the sequence of genes. Compare with EXON.
– DERIVATIVES **intronic** adj.
– ORIGIN 1970s: from INTRA-.
introspect /ˌɪntrə(ʊ)'spɛkt/ ■ v. examine one's own thoughts or feelings.
– ORIGIN C17: from Latin *introspicere* 'look into', or from *introspectare* 'keep looking into'.
introspection ■ n. the examination of one's own thoughts or feelings.
– DERIVATIVES **introspective** adj. **introspectively** adv. **introspectiveness** n.
introvert ■ n. a shy, reticent person. ▸ Psychology a person predominantly concerned with their own thoughts and feelings rather than with external things. Compare with EXTROVERT. ■ adj. of, denoting, or typical of an introvert.
– DERIVATIVES **introversion** n. **introversive** /-'vəːsɪv/ adj.
– ORIGIN C17: from modern Latin *introvertere*, from *intro-* 'to the inside' + *vertere* 'to turn'.
introverted ■ adj. **1** of, denoting, or typical of an introvert. **2** Anatomy & Zoology (of an organ etc.) turned or pushed inward on itself.
intrude ■ v. **1** come into a place or situation where one is unwelcome or uninvited. ▸ introduce into or enter with adverse effect. **2** Geology (of igneous rock) be forced or thrust into (a pre-existing formation).
– ORIGIN C16: from Latin *intrudere*, from *in-* 'into' + *trudere* 'to thrust'.
intruder ■ n. a person who intrudes, especially into a building with criminal intent.
intrusion ■ n. the action of intruding. ▸ a thing that intrudes.
– ORIGIN Middle English: from medieval Latin *intrusio(n-)*, from Latin *intrudere* (see INTRUDE).
intrusive ■ adj. **1** intruding or tending to intrude. **2** Phonetics (of a sound) added between words or syllables to facilitate pronunciation, e.g. an *r* in *saw a film*. **3** Geology relating to or formed by the intrusion of igneous rock.
– DERIVATIVES **intrusively** adv. **intrusiveness** n.
intrust ■ v. archaic spelling of ENTRUST.
intubate /'ɪntjʊbeɪt/ ■ v. Medicine insert a tube into.
– DERIVATIVES **intubation** n.
– ORIGIN C19: from IN-[2] + Latin *tuba* 'tube' + -ATE[3].
intuit /ɪn'tjuːɪt/ ■ v. understand or work out by instinct.
– ORIGIN C18 (*intuition* Middle English): from Latin *intueri* 'contemplate', from *in-* 'upon' + *tueri* 'to look'.
intuition ■ n. the ability to understand something immediately, without the need for conscious reasoning.
– DERIVATIVES **intuitional** adj.
intuitionism ■ n. Philosophy the theory that primary truths and principles are known by intuition.
– DERIVATIVES **intuitionist** n. & adj.
intuitive ■ adj. **1** instinctive. **2** (chiefly of computer software) easy to use and understand.
– DERIVATIVES **intuitively** adv. **intuitiveness** n.
Inuit /'ɪnjʊɪt, 'ɪnʊɪt/ ■ n. **1** the members of an indigenous people of northern Canada and parts of Greenland and Alaska. Compare with ESKIMO. **2** the language of this people.
– ORIGIN Inuit, pl. of *inuk* 'person'.
inulin /'ɪnjʊlɪn/ ■ n. Biochemistry a substance derived from fructose, present in the roots of various plants.
– ORIGIN C19: from Latin *inula* 'elecampane'.
inundate /'ɪnʌndeɪt/ ■ v. (usu. **be inundated**) **1** flood. **2** overwhelm with things to be dealt with.
– DERIVATIVES **inundation** n.
– ORIGIN C16 (*inundation* Middle English): from Latin *inundare* 'flood', from *in-* 'into, upon' + *undare* 'to flow', from *unda* 'a wave'.
inure /ɪ'njʊə/ ■ v. **1** (usu. **be inured to**) accustom to something, especially something unpleasant. **2** Law variant spelling of ENURE.
– DERIVATIVES **inurement** n.
– ORIGIN Middle English: from an Anglo-Norman French phr. meaning 'in use or practice', from *en* 'in' + Old French *euvre* 'work', from Latin *opera*.
in utero /ɪn 'juːtərəʊ/ ■ adv. & adj. in a woman's uterus; before birth.
– ORIGIN from Latin.
invade ■ v. **1** enter (a country) as or with an army so as to subjugate or occupy it. ▸ enter in large numbers, especially intrusively. ▸ (of a parasite or disease) attack and spread into (an organism or bodily part). **2** intrude on: *he felt his privacy was being invaded*.
– DERIVATIVES **invader** n.
– ORIGIN Middle English: from Latin *invadere*, from *in-* 'into' + *vadere* 'go'.
invagination ■ n. chiefly Anatomy & Biology the action or

process of being turned inside out or folded back on itself to form a cavity or pouch. ▸ a cavity or pouch so formed.
– DERIVATIVES **invaginate** v.
– ORIGIN C17: from modern Latin *invaginatio(n-)*, from IN-² + Latin *vagina* 'sheath'.

invalid¹ /ˈɪnvəliːd, -lɪd/ ▪ n. a person made weak or disabled by illness or injury. ▪ v. (**invalided**, **invaliding**) (usu. **be invalided**) remove from active service in the armed forces because of injury or illness. ▸ disable by injury or illness.
– DERIVATIVES **invalidism** n.
– ORIGIN C17 (as adj. 'infirm, disabled'): a special sense of INVALID², with a change of pronunciation.

invalid² /ɪnˈvalɪd/ ▪ adj. **1** not legally recognized because contravening a regulation or law. **2** not true because based on erroneous information or unsound reasoning.
– DERIVATIVES **invalidly** adv.
– ORIGIN C16 (earlier than *valid*): from Latin *invalidus*, from *in-* 'not' + *validus* 'strong'.

invalidate /ɪnˈvalɪdeɪt/ ▪ v. **1** make or prove (an argument, theory, etc.) unsound or erroneous. **2** make (an official document or procedure) no longer legally valid.
– DERIVATIVES **invalidation** n.

invalidity ▪ n. **1** the condition of being an invalid. **2** the fact of being invalid.

invaluable ▪ adj. extremely useful.
– DERIVATIVES **invaluably** adv.

invariable ▪ adj. never changing.
– DERIVATIVES **invariability** n. **invariableness** n.

invariably ▪ adv. always.

invariant ▪ adj. never changing. ▪ n. Mathematics a function which remains unchanged when a specified transformation is applied.
– DERIVATIVES **invariance** n.

invasion ▪ n. an instance of invading. ▸ the action or process of being invaded.

invasive ▪ adj. tending to invade or intrude. ▸ (of medical procedures) involving the introduction of instruments or other objects into the body or body cavities.
– ORIGIN Middle English: from medieval Latin *invasivus*, from Latin *invadere* (see INVADE).

invected ▪ adj. Heraldry having convex semicircular projections along the edge. Compare with ENGRAILED.
– ORIGIN C17: from Latin *invehect-*, *invehere* 'carry in'.

invective ▪ n. strongly abusive or critical language.
– ORIGIN Middle English (orig. as adj. 'abusive'): from late Latin *invectivus* 'attacking', from *invehere* (see INVEIGH).

inveigh /ɪnˈveɪ/ ▪ v. (**inveigh against**) speak or write about with great hostility.
– ORIGIN C15 ('carry in'): from Latin *invehere* 'carry in', *invehi* 'be carried into, assail'.

inveigle /ɪnˈviːɡ(ə)l, ɪnˈveɪɡ(ə)l/ ▪ v. (usu. **inveigle someone into**) persuade by deception or flattery.
– DERIVATIVES **inveiglement** n.
– ORIGIN C15: from Anglo-Norman French *envegler*, alteration of Old French *aveugler* 'to blind'.

invent ▪ v. create or design (a new device, process, etc.). ▸ make up (a name, story, etc.), especially so as to deceive.
– DERIVATIVES **inventor** n. **inventress** n.
– ORIGIN C15 (*invention* Middle English): from Latin *invent-*, *invenire* 'contrive, discover'.

invention ▪ n. **1** the action of inventing. ▸ something invented. ▸ a fabricated story. **2** creative ability.

inventive ▪ adj. having or showing creativity or original thought.
– DERIVATIVES **inventively** adv. **inventiveness** n.

inventory /ˈɪnv(ə)nt(ə)ri/ ▪ n. (pl. **-ies**) a complete list of items such as goods in stock or the contents of a building. ▸ a quantity of goods in stock. ▸ (in accounting) the entire stock of a business, including materials and finished product. ▪ v. (**-ies**, **-ied**) make an inventory of.
– ORIGIN Middle English: from medieval Latin *inventorium*, alteration of late Latin *inventarium* 'a list of what is found', from Latin *invenire* 'come upon'.

inverse /ˈɪnvəːs, ɪnˈvəːs/ ▪ adj. opposite in position, direction, order, or effect. ▪ n. **1** a thing that is the opposite or reverse of another. **2** Mathematics a reciprocal quantity.
– DERIVATIVES **inversely** adv.

– ORIGIN Middle English: from Latin *inversus*, from *invertere* (see INVERT).

inverse proportion (also **inverse ratio**) ▪ n. a relation between two quantities such that one increases in proportion as the other decreases.

inversion ▪ n. **1** the action of inverting or the state of being inverted. ▸ reversal of the normal order of words, typically for rhetorical effect. ▸ Music an inverted interval, chord, or phrase. **2** (also **temperature** or **thermal inversion**) a reversal of the normal decrease of air temperature with altitude, or of water temperature with depth. **3** Mathematics the process of finding an inverse or reciprocal quantity from a given one. **4** Chemistry a reaction causing a change from one optically active configuration to the opposite configuration.
– DERIVATIVES **inversive** adj.

invert ▪ v. /ɪnˈvəːt/ put upside down or in the opposite position, order, or arrangement.
– DERIVATIVES **invertibility** n. **invertible** adj.
– ORIGIN C16: from Latin *invertere* 'turn inside out'.

invertase /ˈɪnvəːteɪz, ɪnˈvəːt-/ ▪ n. Biochemistry an enzyme produced by yeast which promotes the hydrolysis of sucrose, forming invert sugar.

invertebrate /ɪnˈvəːtɪbrət/ ▪ n. an animal lacking a backbone, such as an arthropod, mollusc, annelid, etc. Compare with VERTEBRATE. ▪ adj. of or relating to this division of animals.
– ORIGIN C19: from modern Latin *invertebrata* (pl.) (former taxonomic group), from French, from *in-* 'without' + Latin *vertebra* (see VERTEBRA).

inverted comma ▪ n. another term for QUOTATION MARK.

inverted snobbery ▪ n. derogatory the attitude of disdaining anything associated with wealth and high social status, while elevating those things associated with lack of wealth and social position.
– DERIVATIVES **inverted snob** n.

inverter ▪ n. **1** an apparatus which converts direct current into alternating current. **2** Electronics a device that converts either of the two binary digits or signals into the other.

invert sugar ▪ n. a mixture of glucose and fructose obtained by the hydrolysis of sucrose.
– ORIGIN C19: from *inverted* with ref. to inversion of optical activity.

invest ▪ v. **1** put money into financial schemes, shares, or property with the expectation of achieving a profit. ▸ devote (one's time or energy) to an undertaking with the expectation of a worthwhile result. ▸ (**invest in**) informal buy (something) whose usefulness will repay the cost. **2** (**invest someone/thing with**) endow someone or something with (a particular quality or attribute). ▸ endow someone with (a rank or office). ▸ (**invest something in**) establish a right or power in.
– DERIVATIVES **investable** adj. **investible** adj. **investor** n.
– ORIGIN C16: from Latin *investire*, from *in-* 'into, upon' + *vestire* 'clothe'; sense 1 is influenced by Italian *investire*.

investigate ▪ v. carry out a systematic or formal inquiry into (an incident or allegation) so as to establish the truth. ▸ carry out research into (a subject). ▸ make a search or systematic inquiry.
– DERIVATIVES **investigable** adj. **investigation** n. **investigator** n. **investigatory** adj.
– ORIGIN C16 (*investigation* Middle English): from Latin *investigare* 'trace out'.

investigative /ɪnˈvɛstɪɡətɪv, -ɡeɪtɪv/ ▪ adj. of or concerned with investigating. ▸ (of journalism or a journalist) investigating and seeking to expose malpractice or the miscarriage of justice.

investiture /ɪnˈvɛstɪtʃə, -tʃə/ ▪ n. the action of formally investing a person with honours or rank. ▸ a ceremony at which this takes place.
– ORIGIN Middle English: from medieval Latin *investitura*, from *investire* (see INVEST).

investment ▪ n. the action or process of investing. ▸ a thing worth buying because it may be profitable or useful in the future.

inveterate

inveterate /ɪnˈvɛt(ə)rət/ ■ adj. having a long-standing and firmly established habit or activity. ▸ (of a feeling or habit) firmly established.
– DERIVATIVES **inveteracy** n. **inveterately** adv.
– ORIGIN Middle English ('chronic' (referring to disease)): from Latin *inveteratus* 'made old', from *inveterare*.

invidious /ɪnˈvɪdɪəs/ ■ adj. unacceptable, unfair, and likely to arouse resentment or anger in others.
– DERIVATIVES **invidiously** adv. **invidiousness** n.
– ORIGIN C17: from Latin *invidiosus*, from *invidia* (see ENVY).

invigilate /ɪnˈvɪdʒɪleɪt/ ■ v. supervise candidates during an examination.
– DERIVATIVES **invigilation** n. **invigilator** n.
– ORIGIN C16: from Latin *invigilare* 'watch over'.

invigorate /ɪnˈvɪɡəreɪt/ ■ v. give strength or energy to.
– DERIVATIVES **invigorating** adj. **invigoratingly** adv. **invigoration** n. **invigorator** n.
– ORIGIN C17: from medieval Latin *invigorare* 'make strong'.

invincible /ɪnˈvɪnsɪb(ə)l/ ■ adj. too powerful to be defeated or overcome.
– DERIVATIVES **invincibility** n. **invincibly** adv.
– ORIGIN Middle English: from Latin *invincibilis*, from *in-* 'not' + *vincibilis* (see VINCIBLE).

in vino veritas /ɪn ˌviːnəʊ ˈvɛrɪtɑːs/ ■ exclam. under the influence of alcohol, a person tells the truth.
– ORIGIN Latin, 'truth in wine'.

inviolable /ɪnˈvʌɪələb(ə)l/ ■ adj. never to be infringed or dishonoured.
– DERIVATIVES **inviolability** n. **inviolably** adv.

inviolate /ɪnˈvʌɪələt/ ■ adj. free from injury or violation.
– DERIVATIVES **inviolacy** n. **inviolately** adv.
– ORIGIN Middle English: from Latin *inviolatus*, from *in-* 'not' + *violare* 'violate'.

inviscid /ɪnˈvɪsɪd/ ■ adj. Physics having no or negligible viscosity.

invisible ■ adj. 1 unable to be seen, either by nature or because concealed. ▸ treated as if unable to be seen; ignored. 2 Economics relating to or denoting earnings which a country makes from the sale of services or other items not constituting tangible commodities. ■ n. (**invisibles**) invisible exports and imports.
– DERIVATIVES **invisibility** n. **invisibly** adv.

invisible ink ■ n. a type of ink used to produce writing that cannot be seen until the paper is heated or otherwise treated.

invitation ■ n. 1 a written or verbal request inviting someone to go somewhere or to do something. ▸ the action of inviting. 2 a situation or action inviting a particular outcome or response.

invitational ■ adj. (especially of a competition) open only to those invited.

invite ■ v. 1 ask in a friendly or formal way to go somewhere or to do something. 2 request (something) formally or politely from someone. 3 (of an action or situation) tend to elicit (a particular outcome or response). ■ n. informal an invitation.
– DERIVATIVES **invitee** n. **inviter** n.
– ORIGIN C16 (*invitation* Middle English): from Latin *invitare*.

inviting ■ adj. tempting or attractive.
– DERIVATIVES **invitingly** adv.

in vitro /ɪn ˈviːtrəʊ/ ■ adj. & adv. Biology (of processes) taking place in a test tube, culture dish, or elsewhere outside a living organism.
– ORIGIN Latin, 'in glass'.

in vivo /ɪn ˈviːvəʊ/ ■ adv. & adj. Biology (of processes) taking place in a living organism.
– ORIGIN Latin, 'in a living thing'.

invocation ■ n. the action of invoking. ▸ an incantation used to invoke a deity or the supernatural. ▸ (in the Christian Church) a form of words introducing a prayer, sermon, etc.
– DERIVATIVES **invocatory** /ɪnˈvɒkət(ə)ri/ adj.

invoice ■ n. a list of goods sent or services provided, with a statement of the sum due. ■ v. send an invoice to. ▸ send an invoice for (goods or services provided).
– ORIGIN C16: orig. the pl. of obsolete *invoy*, from obsolete French *envoy*, from *envoyer* 'send'.

invoke /ɪnˈvəʊk/ ■ v. 1 appeal to as an authority or in support of an argument. ▸ call on (a deity or spirit) in prayer or as a witness. ▸ call earnestly for. ▸ summon (a spirit) by charms or incantation. 2 Computing cause (a procedure) to be carried out.
– DERIVATIVES **invoker** n.
– ORIGIN C15 (*invocation* Middle English): from Latin *invocare*.

involucre /ˈɪnvəl(j)uːkə/ ■ n. Botany a whorl of bracts surrounding an inflorescence or at the base of an umbel.
– ORIGIN C16: from Latin *involucrum*, from *involvere* (see INVOLVE).

involuntary ■ adj. 1 done without conscious control. ▸ (especially of muscles or nerves) concerned in bodily processes that are not under the control of the will. 2 done against someone's will.
– DERIVATIVES **involuntarily** adv. **involuntariness** n.

involuted ■ adj. complicated; abstruse.

involution ■ n. Physiology the shrinkage of an organ in old age or when inactive.
– DERIVATIVES **involutional** adj.
– ORIGIN Middle English ('(part) curling inwards'): from Latin *involutio(n-)*, from *involvere* (see INVOLVE).

involve ■ v. 1 include as a necessary part or result. ▸ cause to experience or participate in an activity or situation. 2 [as adj. **involved**] connected, typically on an emotional or personal level. 3 [as adj. **involved**] complicated.
– DERIVATIVES **involvement** n.
– ORIGIN Middle English ('enfold, entangle'): from Latin *involvere*, from *in-* 'into' + *volvere* 'to roll'.

invulnerable ■ adj. impossible to harm or damage.
– DERIVATIVES **invulnerability** n. **invulnerably** adv.
– ORIGIN C16 (earlier than *vulnerable*): from Latin *invulnerabilis*, from *in-* 'not' + *vulnerabilis* (see VULNERABLE).

-in-waiting ■ comb. form 1 denoting a position as attendant to a royal personage: *lady-in-waiting*. 2 awaiting a turn or about to happen: *a political administration-in-waiting*.

inward ■ adj. directed or proceeding towards the inside. ▸ mental or spiritual. ■ adv. variant of INWARDS.
– DERIVATIVES **inwardly** adv. **inwardness** n.

inward investment ■ n. investment made within a country from outside.

inward-looking ■ adj. self-absorbed or insular.

inwards (also **inward**) ■ adv. towards the inside. ▸ into or towards the mind, spirit, or soul.

inyanga /ɪnˈjaŋɡə/ ■ n. S. African a traditional healer who uses herbal remedies. Compare with SANGOMA.
– ORIGIN isiZulu, 'herbalist, doctor'.

in-your-face ■ adj. informal blatantly aggressive or provocative.
– ORIGIN 1970s: from *in your face*, used as a derisive insult.

I/O ■ abbrev. Electronics input-output.

IOC ■ abbrev. International Olympic Committee.

iodic acid /ʌɪˈɒdɪk/ ■ n. Chemistry a crystalline acid with strong oxidizing properties, made by oxidation of iodine. [HIO_3.]
– DERIVATIVES **iodate** n.

iodide /ˈʌɪədʌɪd/ ■ n. Chemistry a compound of iodine with another element or group: *sodium iodide*.

iodine /ˈʌɪədiːn, -ʌɪn, -ɪn/ ■ n. the chemical element of atomic number 53, a halogen forming black crystals and a violet vapour. (Symbol: **I**) ▸ an antiseptic solution of this in alcohol.
– DERIVATIVES **iodinate** v. **iodination** n.
– ORIGIN C19: from French *iode*, from Greek *iōdēs* 'violet-coloured'.

iodism /ˈʌɪədɪz(ə)m/ ■ n. Medicine iodine poisoning.

iodo- (usu. **iod-** before a vowel) ■ comb. form Chemistry representing IODINE.

ion /ˈʌɪən/ ■ n. an atom or molecule with a net electric charge through loss or gain of electrons, either positive (a

cation) or negative (an anion).
– ORIGIN C19: from Greek, from *ienai* 'go'.

-ion ▪ suffix **1** forming nouns denoting verbal action or an instance of this: *communion*. **2** denoting a resulting state or product: *oblivion*.
– ORIGIN via French from Latin *-ion-*.

ion exchange ▪ n. the exchange of ions of the same charge between an insoluble solid and a solution in contact with it, used in purification and separation processes.
– DERIVATIVES **ion exchanger** n.

Ionian ▪ n. **1** a member of an ancient Hellenic people inhabiting Attica, parts of western Asia Minor, and the Aegean islands in pre-classical times. **2** a native or inhabitant of the Ionian Islands, a chain of islands off the western coast of mainland Greece. ▪ adj. of or relating to the Ionians, Ionia, or the Ionian Islands.
– ORIGIN C16: from Greek, from *Iōnia* 'Ionia', an ancient region on the west coast of Asia Minor.

Ionic /ʌɪˈɒnɪk/ ▪ adj. **1** relating to or denoting a classical order of architecture characterized by a column with scroll shapes on either side of the capital. **2** another term for IONIAN. ▪ n. **1** the Ionic order of architecture. **2** the ancient Greek dialect used in Ionia.

ionic /ʌɪˈɒnɪk/ ▪ adj. of or relating to ions. ▸ denoting chemical bonds formed by the electrostatic attraction of oppositely charged ions. Often contrasted with COVALENT.
– DERIVATIVES **ionically** adv.

ionize /ˈʌɪənʌɪz/ (also **-ise**) ▪ v. convert (an atom, molecule, or substance) into an ion or ions, typically by removing one or more electrons.
– DERIVATIVES **ionizable** (also **-isable**) adj. **ionization** (also **-isation**) n.

ionizer (also **-iser**) ▪ n. a device which produces ions, especially one used to improve the quality of the air in a room.

ionizing radiation (also **-ising**) ▪ n. radiation consisting of particles, X-rays, or gamma rays which produce ions in the medium through which it passes.

ionophore /ʌɪˈɒnə(ʊ)fɔː/ ▪ n. Biochemistry a substance which is able to transport particular ions through a lipid membrane in a cell.

ionosphere /ʌɪˈɒnəsfɪə/ ▪ n. the layer of the atmosphere above the mesosphere, which contains a high concentration of ions and electrons and is able to reflect radio waves.
– DERIVATIVES **ionospheric** adj.

iota /ʌɪˈəʊtə/ ▪ n. **1** the ninth letter of the Greek alphabet (Ι, ι), transliterated as 'i'. **2** [usu. with neg.] an extremely small amount.
– ORIGIN from Greek *iōta*; sense 2 derives from *iota* being the smallest letter of the Greek alphabet.

IOU ▪ n. a signed document acknowledging a debt.
– ORIGIN C18: representing the pronunciation of *I owe you*.

-ious ▪ suffix (forming adjectives) characterized by; full of: *cautious*.
– ORIGIN from French *-ieux*, from Latin *-iosus*.

IP ▪ abbrev. Computing Internet Protocol.

IPA ▪ abbrev. International Phonetic Alphabet.

IPO ▪ abbrev. Finance initial public offer(ing).

IPR ▪ abbrev. intellectual property rights.

ipso facto /ˌɪpsəʊ ˈfaktəʊ/ ▪ adv. by that very fact or act.
– ORIGIN from Latin.

IQ ▪ abbrev. intelligence quotient.

IR ▪ abbrev. infrared.

Ir ▪ symb. the chemical element iridium.

ir- ▪ prefix variant spelling of IN-[1], IN-[2] assimilated before *r* (as in *irradiate*).

IRA ▪ abbrev. Irish Republican Army.

Iranian ▪ n. a native or national of Iran, or a person of Iranian descent. ▪ adj. **1** of or relating to Iran or its people. **2** relating to or denoting the group of Indo-European languages that includes Persian (Farsi), Pashto, Avestan, and Kurdish.

Iraqi ▪ n. (pl. **Iraqis**) **1** a native or national of Iraq, or a person of Iraqi descent. **2** the form of Arabic spoken in Iraq. ▪ adj. of or relating to Iraq, its people, or their language.

irascible /ɪˈrasɪb(ə)l/ ▪ adj. hot-tempered; irritable.
– DERIVATIVES **irascibility** n. **irascibly** adv.
– ORIGIN Middle English: from late Latin *irascibilis*, from Latin *irasci* 'grow angry', from *ira* 'anger'.

irate /ʌɪˈreɪt/ ▪ adj. extremely angry.
– DERIVATIVES **irately** adv. **irateness** n.
– ORIGIN C19: from Latin *iratus*, from *ira* 'anger'.

IRBM ▪ abbrev. intermediate-range ballistic missile.

IRC ▪ abbrev. Computing Internet Relay Chat.

ire /ʌɪə/ ▪ n. chiefly poetic/literary anger.
– DERIVATIVES **ireful** adj.
– ORIGIN Middle English: from Latin *ira*.

irenic ▪ adj. variant spelling of EIRENIC.

irid ▪ n. a plant of a family (Iridaceae) which includes gladiolus, freesia, and ixia.
– ORIGIN C19: from Greek *iris irid-* 'iris'.

iridescent /ˌɪrɪˈdɛs(ə)nt/ ▪ adj. showing luminous colours that seem to change when seen from different angles.
– DERIVATIVES **iridescence** n. **iridescently** adv.
– ORIGIN C18: from Latin *iris, irid-* 'rainbow'.

iridium /ɪˈrɪdɪəm, ʌɪ-/ ▪ n. the chemical element of atomic number 77, a hard, dense silvery-white metal. (Symbol: **Ir**)
– ORIGIN C19: from Latin *iris, irid-* 'rainbow' (so named because it forms compounds of various colours).

iridology /ˌʌɪrɪˈdɒlədʒi, ˌɪrɪ-/ ▪ n. (in alternative medicine) diagnosis by examination of the iris of the eye.
– DERIVATIVES **iridologist** n.
– ORIGIN C20: from Greek *iris, irid-* 'iris' + -LOGY.

irie /ˈʌɪriː/ informal ▪ adj. nice, good, or pleasing. ▪ exclam. used by Rastafarians as a friendly greeting.
– ORIGIN perhaps representing a pronunciation of *all right*.

iris ▪ n. **1** a flat, coloured, ring-shaped membrane behind the cornea of the eye, with an adjustable circular opening (pupil) in the centre. **2** a plant with showy flowers, typically purple or yellow, and sword-shaped leaves. [Genus *Iris*: many species.] **3** (also **iris diaphragm**) an adjustable diaphragm of thin overlapping plates for regulating the size of a central aperture. ▪ v. open or close in the manner of an iris.
– ORIGIN from Greek *iris* 'rainbow, iris'.

Irish ▪ adj. **1** of or relating to Ireland, its people, or the Celtic language traditionally and historically spoken there. **2** offensive illogical or apparently so.
– DERIVATIVES **Irishman** n. (pl. **-men**). **Irishness** n. **Irishwoman** n. (pl. **-women**).
– ORIGIN Middle English: from Old English *Īr-*, stem of *Īras* 'the Irish' and *Īrland* 'Ireland'.

Irish coffee ▪ n. coffee mixed with a dash of Irish whiskey and served with cream on top.

Irish setter ▪ n. a dog of a breed of setter with a long, silky dark red coat and a long feathered tail.

Irish stew ▪ n. a stew made with mutton, potatoes, and onions.

Irish terrier ▪ n. a terrier of a rough-haired light reddish-brown breed.

Irish wolfhound ▪ n. a large, typically greyish hound of a rough-coated breed.

iritis /ʌɪˈrʌɪtɪs/ ▪ n. Medicine inflammation of the iris of the eye.

irk /əːk/ ▪ v. irritate; annoy.
– DERIVATIVES **irksome** adj. **irksomely** adv.
– ORIGIN Middle English: perhaps from Old Norse *yrkja* 'to work'.

iroko /ɪˈrəʊkəʊ, iː-/ ▪ n. (pl. **-os**) a tropical African hardwood tree producing pale wood. [*Chlorophora excelsa* and related species.]
– ORIGIN C19: from Yoruba.

iron ▪ n. **1** a strong, hard magnetic silvery-grey metal, the chemical element of atomic number 26, used in construction and manufacturing (especially as steel). (Symbol: **Fe**) **2** a tool or implement made of iron. ▸ (**irons**) fetters or handcuffs. **3** a hand-held implement with a

heated flat steel base, used to smooth clothes and linen. **4** a golf club with an angled metal head used for lofting the ball. ■ v. **1** smooth (clothes) with an iron. **2 (iron something out)** settle a difficulty or problem.
– PHRASES **have many** (or **other**) **irons in the fire** have a range of options or interests. **in irons 1** having the feet or hands fettered. **2** Nautical stalled head to wind and unable to come about or tack either way. **an iron hand** (or **fist**) **in a velvet glove** firmness or ruthlessness cloaked in outward gentleness.
– DERIVATIVES **ironer** n. **ironware** n.
– ORIGIN Old English, of Germanic origin.

Iron Age ■ n. a prehistoric period that followed the Bronze Age, when weapons and tools came to be made of iron.

ironclad ■ adj. **1** covered or protected with iron. **2** impossible to weaken or change. ■ n. a 19th-century warship with armour plating.

Iron Curtain ■ n. (**the Iron Curtain**) a notional barrier separating the former Soviet bloc and the West prior to the decline of communism in eastern Europe in 1989.

iron horse ■ n. archaic a steam railway locomotive.

ironic /ʌɪˈrɒnɪk/ ■ adj. using or characterized by irony.
▸ happening in the opposite way to what is expected.
– DERIVATIVES **ironical** adj. **ironically** adv.
– ORIGIN C17: from late Latin *ironicus*, from Greek *eirōnikos* 'dissembling', from *eirōneia* (see **IRONY**[1]).

ironing ■ n. clothes and linen that need to be or have just been ironed.

ironing board ■ n. a long, narrow board having folding legs, on which clothes are ironed.

ironist /ˈʌɪr(ə)nɪst/ ■ n. a person who uses irony.
– DERIVATIVES **ironize** (also **-ise**) v.

iron lung ■ n. a rigid case fitted over a patient's body, used for administering prolonged artificial respiration by means of mechanical pumps.

iron maiden ■ n. a former instrument of torture consisting of a coffin-shaped box lined with iron spikes.

iron man ■ n. an exceptionally strong or robust man, especially a sportsman. ▸ a multi-event sporting contest demanding stamina, in particular a consecutive triathlon of swimming, cycling, and running.

ironmonger ■ n. Brit. a retailer of tools and other hardware.
– DERIVATIVES **ironmongery** n. (pl. **-ies**).

iron rations ■ pl. n. a small emergency supply of food.

ironstone ■ n. **1** sedimentary rock containing a substantial proportion of iron compounds. **2** a kind of dense, opaque stoneware.

ironwood ■ n. a tree that produces very hard wood. [*Vepris lanceolata* (white ironwood) and other species.]

ironworks ■ n. [treated as sing. or pl.] a place where iron is smelted or iron goods are made.

irony[1] /ˈʌɪrəni/ ■ n. (pl. **-ies**) the expression of meaning through the use of language signifying the opposite, typically for humorous effect. ▸ a state of affairs that appears perversely contrary to what one expects. ▸ (also **dramatic** or **tragic irony**) a literary technique, originally used in Greek tragedy, by which the significance of a character's words or actions are clear to the audience or reader although unknown to the character.
– ORIGIN C16: from Greek *eirōneia* 'simulated ignorance', from *eirōn* 'dissembler'.

irony[2] /ˈʌɪəni/ ■ adj. of or like iron.

Iroquoian ■ n. a language family of eastern North America, including Cherokee and Mohawk. ■ adj. of or relating to the Iroquois people or the Iroquoian language family.

Iroquois /ˈɪrəkwɔɪ, -kɔɪ/ ■ n. (pl. same) a member of a former confederacy of six American Indian peoples who lived mainly in southern Ontario and Quebec and northern New York State.
– ORIGIN French, from an Algonquian language.

irradiance ■ n. **1** Physics the flux of radiant energy per unit area. **2** poetic/literary the fact of shining brightly.

irradiate ■ v. **1** (often **be irradiated**) expose to radiation. **2** shine light on.
– ORIGIN C16: from Latin *irradiare* 'shine upon'.

irradiation ■ n. **1** the process or fact of irradiating or being irradiated. **2** Optics the apparent extension of the edges of an illuminated object seen against a dark background.

irrational ■ adj. **1** not logical or reasonable. **2** Mathematics (of a number or quantity) not expressible as a ratio of two integers (e.g. π).
– DERIVATIVES **irrationality** n. **irrationalize** (also **-ise**) v. **irrationally** adv.

irrationalism ■ n. a system of belief or action that disregards rational principles.
– DERIVATIVES **irrationalist** n. & adj.

irrebuttable /ˌɪrɪˈbʌtəb(ə)l/ ■ adj. unable to be rebutted.

irreclaimable ■ adj. not able to be reclaimed or reformed.

irreconcilable ■ adj. **1** (of ideas, facts, etc.) incompatible. **2** mutually and implacably hostile. ■ n. any of two or more irreconcilable ideas, facts, etc.
– DERIVATIVES **irreconcilability** n. **irreconcilably** adv.

irrecoverable ■ adj. not able to be recovered or remedied.
– DERIVATIVES **irrecoverably** adv.

irredeemable ■ adj. **1** not able to be saved, improved, or corrected. **2** (of securities) on which no date is given for repayment of the capital sum.
– DERIVATIVES **irredeemability** /-ˈbɪlɪti/ n. **irredeemably** adv.

irredentist /ˌɪrɪˈdɛntɪst/ ■ n. a person advocating the restoration to their country of any territory formerly belonging to it.
– DERIVATIVES **irredentism** n.
– ORIGIN from Italian *irredentista*, from (*Italia*) *irredenta* 'unredeemed (Italy)'.

irreducible ■ adj. not able to be reduced or simplified.
– DERIVATIVES **irreducibility** n. **irreducibly** adv.

irrefragable /ɪˈrɛfrəɡəb(ə)l/ ■ adj. indisputable.
– ORIGIN C16: from late Latin *irrefragabilis*, from *in-* 'not' + *refragari* 'oppose'.

irrefutable /ɪˈrɛfjʊtəb(ə)l, ˌɪrɪˈfjuː-/ ■ adj. impossible to deny or disprove.
– DERIVATIVES **irrefutability** n. **irrefutably** adv.

irregular ■ adj. **1** not regular in shape, arrangement, or occurrence. **2** contrary to a rule, standard, or convention. **3** Grammar (of a word) having inflections that do not conform to the usual rules. ■ n. a member of an irregular military force.
– DERIVATIVES **irregularity** n. (pl. **-ies**). **irregularly** adv.

irrelevant ■ adj. not relevant.
– DERIVATIVES **irrelevance** n. **irrelevancy** n. (pl. **-ies**). **irrelevantly** adv.

irreligious ■ adj. indifferent or hostile to religion.
– DERIVATIVES **irreligion** n. **irreligiousness** n.

irremediable /ˌɪrɪˈmiːdɪəb(ə)l/ ■ adj. impossible to remedy.
– DERIVATIVES **irremediably** adv.

irremovable ■ adj. incapable of being removed.
– DERIVATIVES **irremovability** n. **irremovably** adv.

irreparable /ɪˈrɛp(ə)rəb(ə)l/ ■ adj. impossible to rectify or repair.
– DERIVATIVES **irreparability** /-ˈbɪlɪti/ n. **irreparably** adv.

irreplaceable ■ adj. impossible to replace if lost or damaged.
– DERIVATIVES **irreplaceably** adv.

irrepressible ■ adj. not able to be restrained.
– DERIVATIVES **irrepressibility** n. **irrepressibly** adv.

irreproachable ■ adj. beyond criticism.
– DERIVATIVES **irreproachably** adv.

irresistible ■ adj. too tempting or powerful to be resisted.
– DERIVATIVES **irresistibility** n. **irresistibly** adv.

irresolute ■ adj. uncertain.
– DERIVATIVES **irresolutely** adv. **irresoluteness** n. **irresolution** n.

irresolvable ■ adj. (of a problem) impossible to solve.

irrespective ■ adj. (**irrespective of**) regardless of.

– DERIVATIVES **irrespectively** adv.

irresponsible ■ adj. not showing a proper sense of responsibility.
– DERIVATIVES **irresponsibility** n. **irresponsibly** adv.

irretrievable ■ adj. not able to be retrieved.
– DERIVATIVES **irretrievability** n. **irretrievably** adv.

irreverent /ɪˈrɛv(ə)r(ə)nt/ ■ adj. disrespectful.
– DERIVATIVES **irreverence** n. **irreverential** adj. **irreverently** adv.

irreversible ■ adj. impossible to be reversed or altered.
– DERIVATIVES **irreversibility** n. **irreversibly** adv.

irrevocable /ɪˈrɛvəkəb(ə)l/ ■ adj. not able to be changed, reversed, or recovered.
– DERIVATIVES **irrevocability** n. **irrevocably** adv.
– ORIGIN Middle English: from Latin *irrevocabilis*.

irrigate /ˈɪrɪɡeɪt/ ■ v. 1 supply water to (land or crops) by means of channels or pipes. ▶ (of a river or stream) supply (land) with water. 2 Medicine apply a flow of water or medication to (an organ or wound).
– DERIVATIVES **irrigable** adj. **irrigation** n. **irrigator** n.
– ORIGIN C17: from Latin *irrigare* 'moisten'.

irritable ■ adj. 1 easily annoyed or angered. 2 Medicine characterized by abnormal sensitivity. 3 Biology able to respond actively to physical stimuli.
– DERIVATIVES **irritability** n. **irritableness** n. **irritably** adv.

irritable bowel syndrome ■ n. a condition involving recurrent abdominal pain and diarrhoea or constipation, often associated with stress or previous infection.

irritant ■ n. a substance that irritates part of the body. ▶ a source of continual annoyance. ■ adj. causing irritation to the body.
– DERIVATIVES **irritancy** n.

irritate ■ v. 1 make annoyed or angry. 2 cause inflammation in (a part of the body).
– DERIVATIVES **irritated** adj. **irritatedly** adv. **irritating** adj. **irritatingly** adv. **irritation** n. **irritative** adj. **irritator** n.
– ORIGIN C16 (*irritation* Middle English): from Latin *irritare* 'irritate'.

irrupt /ɪˈrʌpt/ ■ v. 1 enter forcibly or suddenly. 2 (chiefly of a bird) migrate into an area in abnormally large numbers.
– DERIVATIVES **irruption** n. **irruptive** adj.
– ORIGIN C19 (*irruption* C16): from Latin *irrupt-*, *irrumpere* 'break into'.

IRS ■ abbrev. US Internal Revenue Service.

Is. ■ abbrev. 1 Island(s). 2 Isle(s).

is third person singular present of BE.

ISBN ■ abbrev. international standard book number.

Iscamtho /ɪsˈkʌmtəʊ, ɪsˈ|ʌmtəʊ/ ■ n. variant of ISICAMTHO.

ischaemia /ɪˈskiːmɪə/ (US **ischemia**) ■ n. Medicine an inadequate blood supply to a part of the body, especially the heart muscles.
– DERIVATIVES **ischaemic** adj.
– ORIGIN C19: modern Latin, from Greek *iskhaimos* 'stopping blood'.

ischium /ˈɪskɪəm/ ■ n. (pl. **ischia** /-kɪə/) Anatomy the curved bone forming the base of each half of the pelvis.
– DERIVATIVES **ischial** adj.
– ORIGIN C17: from Greek *iskhion* 'hip joint', later 'ischium'.

ISDN ■ abbrev. integrated services digital network.

-ise[1] ■ suffix variant spelling of -IZE.

> **USAGE**
> The forms **-ise** and **-ize** are, in many cases, straightforward spelling variants. The **-ise** form is often preferred in traditional British and South African usage, though the **-ize** form is found universally. The **-ise** is obligatory where it is part of a larger word element, such as **-mise** in **compromise**, and in verbs corresponding to nouns with **-s-** in the stem, such as **advertise** and **televise**.

-ise[2] ■ suffix forming nouns of quality, state, or function: *expertise*.
– ORIGIN from Old French *-ise*, from Latin *-itia*, *-itium*.

isentropic /ˌʌɪsɛnˈtrɒpɪk/ ■ adj. Physics having equal entropy.
– ORIGIN from ISO- + ENTROPY.

617

-ish[1] ■ suffix forming adjectives: 1 (from nouns) having the qualities or characteristics of: *girlish*. ▶ of the nationality of: *Swedish*. 2 (from adjectives) somewhat: *yellowish*. ▶ informal denoting an approximate age or time of day: *sixish*.
– ORIGIN Old English *-isc*, of Germanic origin.

-ish[2] ■ suffix forming verbs such as *abolish*.
– ORIGIN from French *-iss-*, from Latin *-isc-*.

Isicamtho /ɪsɪˈkʌmtəʊ, ɪsɪˈ|ʌmtəʊ/ (also **Iscamtho** /ɪsˈ|ʌmtəʊ/) ■ n. S. African a widely-spoken township patois largely influenced by the Nguni languages.
– ORIGIN the name in Isicamtho, from isiZulu *camto* 'speak'.

isicathamiya /ɪsɪˌkataˈmiːjə, ɪsɪˌataˈmiːjə/ ■ n. S. African a type of a cappella choral music, accompanied by rhythmic movements.
– ORIGIN isiZulu, 'stalking movement'.

isigodi /ɪsɪˈɡɒdi/ ■ n. (pl. same or **isigodis**) S. African a rural or semi-rural administrative ward of a customarily defined Zulu community that is governed by a traditional leader.
– ORIGIN from isiZulu *isigodi* 'district, division of territory'.

isiNdebele /ˌɪsɪ(ə)ndɛˈbeɪle/ ■ n. (especially in South Africa) the Bantu language of the Ndebele people.
– ORIGIN the name in isiNdebele.

isinglass /ˈʌɪzɪŋˌɡlɑːs/ ■ n. 1 a kind of gelatin obtained from fish, especially sturgeon. 2 chiefly US mica or a similar material in thin transparent sheets.
– ORIGIN C16: alteration (by association with GLASS) of obsolete Dutch *huysenblas* 'sturgeon's bladder'.

isit (also **izzit**) ■ exclam. S. African informal really?; is that so?
– ORIGIN partly translating Afrikaans *is dit?* 'is that so?', partly from the English tag question *is it?*

isiXhosa /ɪsɪˈkɔsa, ɪsɪˈ|ɔsə/ ■ n. the Bantu language of the Xhosa people.
– ORIGIN the name in isiXhosa.

isiZulu /ɪsɪˈzuːluː/ ■ n. the Bantu language of the Zulu people.
– ORIGIN the name in isiZulu.

Islam /ˈɪzlɑːm, ɪzˈlɑːm, -lam/ ■ n. the religion of the Muslims, a monotheistic faith regarded as revealed through Muhammad as the Prophet of Allah. ▶ the Muslim world.
– DERIVATIVES **Islamization** (also **-isation**) n. **Islamize** (also **-ise**) v.
– ORIGIN from Arabic *'islām* 'submission', from *'aslama* 'submit (to God)'.

Islamic /ɪzˈlamɪk, ɪzˈlɑːmɪk/ ■ adj. of or relating to Islam.
– DERIVATIVES **Islamicization** (also **-isation**) n. **Islamicize** (also **-ise**) v.

Islamism /ˈɪzləmɪz(ə)m, 's-/ ■ n. Islamic militancy or fundamentalism.
– DERIVATIVES **Islamist** (also **-icist**) n. & adj.

island ■ n. 1 a piece of land surrounded by water. 2 a thing that is isolated, detached, or surrounded. ▶ Anatomy a detached portion of tissue or group of cells. Compare with ISLET.
– DERIVATIVES **islander** n.
– ORIGIN Old English *iegland*, from *ieg* 'island' (from a base meaning 'watery') + LAND; spelling influenced by ISLE.

isle ■ n. poetic/literary (except in place names) an island.
– ORIGIN Middle English *ile*, from Old French, from Latin *insula*.

islet /ˈʌɪlɪt/ ■ n. 1 a small island. 2 Anatomy a portion of tissue structurally distinct from its surroundings. Compare with ISLAND.
– ORIGIN C16: from Old French, diminutive of *isle* (see ISLE).

islets of Langerhans /ˈlaŋəhanz/ ■ pl. n. groups of pancreatic cells secreting insulin and glucagon.
– ORIGIN C19: named after the German anatomist Paul Langerhans.

ism /ˈɪz(ə)m/ ■ n. informal, chiefly derogatory an unspecified system, philosophy, or ideological movement.
– ORIGIN C17: independent usage of -ISM.

-ism ■ suffix forming nouns: 1 denoting an action or its result: *baptism*. ▶ denoting a state or quality: *barbarism*. 2 denoting a system, principle, or ideological movement:

Ismaili

Anglicanism. ▶ denoting a basis for prejudice or discrimination: *racism.* **3** denoting a peculiarity in language: *colloquialism.* **4** denoting a pathological condition: *alcoholism.*
– ORIGIN from French *-isme,* from Greek *-ismos, -isma.*

Ismaili /ˌɪsmʌˈiːli, ˌɪsmɑː-/ ■ n. (pl. **Ismailis**) a member of a Shiite Muslim sect believing that Ismail, the son of the sixth Shiite imam, should have become the seventh imam.

isn't ■ contr. is not.

ISO ■ abbrev. International Organization for Standardization.
– ORIGIN from Greek *isos* 'equal'.

iso- ■ comb. form **1** equal: *isosceles.* **2** Chemistry (chiefly of hydrocarbons) isomeric: *isooctane.*
– ORIGIN from Greek *isos* 'equal'.

isobar /ˈʌɪsə(ʊ)bɑː/ ■ n. **1** Meteorology a line on a map connecting points having the same atmospheric pressure. **2** Physics each of two or more isotopes of different elements, with the same atomic weight.
– DERIVATIVES **isobaric** adj.
– ORIGIN C19: from Greek *isobaros* 'of equal weight'.

isobutylene ■ n. Chemistry an easily liquefied hydrocarbon gas used in the making of butyl rubber. [C_4H_8.]

isochron /ˈʌɪsə(ʊ)krɒn/ ■ n. chiefly Geology a line on a diagram or map connecting points relating to the same time or equal times.

isoclinal /ˌʌɪsə(ʊ)ˈklʌɪm(ə)l/ ■ adj. Geology denoting a fold in which the two limbs are parallel.
– ORIGIN C19: from **ISO-** + Greek *klinein* 'to lean'.

isoclinic /ˌʌɪsə(ʊ)ˈklɪnɪk/ ■ adj. Geography denoting a line on a map connecting points where the dip of the earth's magnetic field is the same.

isodynamic ■ adj. Geography denoting a line on a map connecting points where the intensity of the magnetic force is the same.

isoelectronic ■ adj. Chemistry having the same numbers of electrons or the same electronic structure.

isogamy /ʌɪˈsɒɡəmi/ ■ n. Biology sexual reproduction by the fusion of similar gametes. Compare with **ANISOGAMY**.
– DERIVATIVES **isogamete** n. **isogamous** adj.
– ORIGIN C19: from **ISO-** + Greek *gamos* 'marriage'.

isogeotherm /ˌʌɪsə(ʊ)ˈdʒiːə(ʊ)θəːm/ ■ n. Geography a line or surface on a diagram of the earth's interior connecting points having the same temperature.
– DERIVATIVES **isogeothermal** adj.
– ORIGIN C19: from **ISO-** + **GEO-** + Greek *thermē* 'heat'.

isogloss /ˈʌɪsə(ʊ)ɡlɒs/ ■ n. Linguistics a line on a map marking an area having a distinct linguistic feature.
– ORIGIN C20: from **ISO-** + Greek *glōssa* 'tongue, word'.

isogonic /ˌʌɪsə(ʊ)ˈɡɒnɪk/ ■ adj. Geography denoting a line on a map connecting points at which the magnetic declination is the same.
– ORIGIN C19: from Greek *isogōnios* 'equiangular'.

isohel /ˈʌɪsə(ʊ)hɛl/ ■ n. Meteorology a line on a map connecting points having the same duration of sunshine.
– ORIGIN C20: from **ISO-** + Greek *hēlios* 'sun'.

isohyet /ˌʌɪsə(ʊ)ˈhʌɪɪt/ ■ n. Meteorology a line on a map connecting points having the same amount of rainfall.
– ORIGIN C19: from **ISO-** + Greek *huetos* 'rain'.

isolate ■ v. **1** place apart or alone; cut off. ▶ place in quarantine. **2** Chemistry obtain or extract (a compound, etc.) in a pure form. **3** cut off the electrical or other connection to (a part of a network). ■ n. a person or thing that has become isolated.
– DERIVATIVES **isolable** adj. **isolatable** adj. **isolator** n.
– ORIGIN C19: back-formation from **ISOLATED**.

isolated ■ adj. **1** remote; lonely. **2** single; exceptional.
– ORIGIN C18: from Italian *isolato,* from late Latin *insulatus* 'made into an island', from Latin *insula* 'island'.

isolation ■ n. the process or fact of isolating or being isolated.
– PHRASES **in isolation** without relation to others; separately.

isolationism ■ n. a policy of remaining apart from the political affairs of other countries.
– DERIVATIVES **isolationist** n.

isomer /ˈʌɪsəmə/ ■ n. **1** Chemistry each of two or more compounds with the same formula but a different arrangement of atoms in the molecule and different properties. **2** Physics each of two or more atomic nuclei with the same atomic number and mass number but different energy states.
– DERIVATIVES **isomeric** adj. **isomerism** n. **isomerize** (also **-ise**) v.
– ORIGIN C19: from Greek *isomerēs* 'sharing equally', from *isos* 'equal' + *meros* 'a share'.

isomerous /ʌɪˈsɒm(ə)rəs/ ■ adj. Biology having parts that are similar in number or position.

isometric ■ adj. **1** of or having equal dimensions. **2** Physiology (of muscular action) in which tension is developed without contraction. **3** denoting a method of perspective drawing in which the three principal dimensions are represented by three axes 120° apart. **4** Mathematics (of a transformation) without change of shape or size.
– DERIVATIVES **isometrically** adv. **isometry** n.
– ORIGIN C19: from Greek *isometria* 'equality of measure', from *isos* 'equal' + *-metria* 'measuring'.

isometrics ■ pl. n. a system of physical exercises in which muscles are caused to act against each other or against a fixed object.

isomorphic /ˌʌɪsə(ʊ)ˈmɔːfɪk/ ■ adj. corresponding or similar in form and relations.
– DERIVATIVES **isomorphism** n. **isomorphous** adj.

-ison ■ suffix (forming nouns) equivalent to **-ATION** (as in *comparison*).
– ORIGIN from Old French *-aison, -eison,* from Latin *-atio(n)-.*

isoniazid /ˌʌɪsə(ʊ)ˈnʌɪəzɪd/ ■ n. Medicine a synthetic compound used as a bacteriostatic drug, chiefly to treat tuberculosis.
– ORIGIN 1950s: from **ISO-** + *ni(cotinic acid)* + *(hydr)azine* + **-IDE**.

isooctane /ˌʌɪsəʊˈɒkteɪn/ ■ n. Chemistry a liquid hydrocarbon present in petroleum, used as a standard in the system of octane numbers.

isopleth /ˈʌɪsə(ʊ)plɛθ/ ■ n. Meteorology a line on a map connecting points having equal incidence of a specified feature.
– ORIGIN C20: from Greek *isoplēthēs,* from Greek *isos* 'equal' + *plēthos* 'multitude, quantity'.

Isopoda /ˌʌɪsəˈpəʊdə/ ■ pl. n. Zoology an order of crustaceans that includes the woodlice and many aquatic forms.
– DERIVATIVES **isopod** n.
– ORIGIN from Greek *isos* 'equal' + *pous, pod-* 'foot'.

isoprene /ˈʌɪsə(ʊ)priːn/ ■ n. Chemistry a volatile liquid hydrocarbon whose molecule forms the basic structural unit of rubber.
– ORIGIN C19: apparently from **ISO-** + *pr(opyl)ene.*

isoproterenol /ˌʌɪsə(ʊ)prəʊtəˈriːnɒl/ ■ n. Medicine a synthetic derivative of adrenalin, used for the relief of bronchial asthma and pulmonary emphysema.
– ORIGIN 1950s: from elements of the semi-systematic name *N-isopropylarterenol.*

isosceles /ʌɪˈsɒsɪliːz/ ■ adj. (of a triangle) having two sides of equal length.
– ORIGIN C16: from Greek *isoskelēs,* from *isos* 'equal' + *skelos* 'leg'.

isostasy /ʌɪˈsɒstəsi/ ■ n. Geology the equilibrium that exists between parts of the earth's crust, which rise if material (such as an ice cap) is removed and sink if material is deposited.
– DERIVATIVES **isostatic** adj.
– ORIGIN C19: from **ISO-** + Greek *stasis* 'station'.

isotherm /ˈʌɪsə(ʊ)θəːm/ ■ n. a line on a map or diagram connecting points having the same temperature.
– DERIVATIVES **isothermal** adj. & n. **isothermally** adv.
– ORIGIN C19: from Greek *isos* 'equal' + *thermē* 'heat'.

isotonic /ˌʌɪsə(ʊ)ˈtɒnɪk/ ■ adj. **1** Physiology (of muscle action) taking place with normal contraction. **2** Physiology having the same osmotic pressure. **3** (of a drink) containing essential salts and minerals in the same concentration as in the body.

– DERIVATIVES **isotonically** adv. **isotonicity** n.
– ORIGIN C19: from Greek *isotonos*, from *isos* 'equal' + *tonos* 'tone'.

isotope /ˈʌɪsətəʊp/ ■ n. Chemistry each of two or more forms of the same element that contain equal numbers of protons but different numbers of neutrons in their nuclei.
– DERIVATIVES **isotopic** adj. **isotopically** adv. **isotopy** n.
– ORIGIN 1913: from ISO- + Greek *topos* 'place' (because the isotopes occupy the same place in the periodic table).

isotropic /ˌʌɪsə(ʊ)ˈtrɒpɪk/ ■ adj. Physics having the same magnitude or properties when measured in different directions.
– DERIVATIVES **isotropically** adv. **isotropy** /ʌɪˈsɒtrəpi/ n.
– ORIGIN C19: from ISO- + Greek *tropos* 'a turn'.

ISP ■ abbrev. Internet service provider.

Israeli /ɪzˈreɪli/ ■ n. (pl. **Israelis**) a native or national of Israel, or a person of Israeli descent. ■ adj. of or relating to the modern country of Israel.

Israelite /ˈɪzrəlʌɪt/ ■ n. a member of the ancient Hebrew nation. ▶ old-fashioned and sometimes offensive term for JEW. ■ adj. of or relating to the Israelites.

Issa /ˈiːsɑː/ ■ n. (pl. same or **Issas**) a member of a Somali people living in the Republic of Djibouti.
– ORIGIN the name in Somali.

issei /ˈiːseɪ/ ■ n. (pl. same) N. Amer. a Japanese immigrant to North America. Compare with NISEI and SANSEI.
– ORIGIN Japanese, 'generation'.

ISSN ■ abbrev. international standard serial number.

issuant /ˈɪʃ(j)ʊənt, ˈɪsjuː-/ ■ adj. Heraldry (of the upper part of an animal) shown rising up or out from another bearing.

issue /ˈɪʃ(j)uː, ˈɪsjuː/ ■ n. 1 an important topic for debate or resolution. 2 the action of issuing. 3 each of a regular series of publications. ▶ a number or set of items issued at one time. 4 formal or Law children of one's own. 5 dated a result or outcome. ■ v. (**issues**, **issued**, **issuing**) 1 supply or distribute for use or sale. ▶ (**issue someone with**) supply someone with. ▶ formally send out or make known. 2 (**issue from**) come, go, or flow out from.
– PHRASES **at issue** under discussion. **make an issue of** treat too seriously or as a problem. **take issue with** challenge.
– DERIVATIVES **issuable** adj. **issuance** n. **issueless** adj. **issuer** n.
– ORIGIN Middle English ('outflowing'): from Latin *exit-*, *exire* 'go out'.

issue of fact ■ n. Law a dispute in court in which the significance of a fact or facts is denied.

issue of law ■ n. Law a dispute in court in which the application of the law is contested.

-ist ■ suffix forming personal nouns and some related adjectives: 1 denoting an adherent of a system of beliefs expressed by nouns ending in *-ism*: *hedonist*. ▶ denoting a person who subscribes to a prejudice or practises discrimination: *sexist*. 2 denoting a member of a profession or business activity: *dentist*. ▶ denoting a person who uses something: *flautist*. ▶ denoting a person who does something expressed by a verb ending in *-ize*: *plagiarist*.
– ORIGIN from Old French *-iste*, Latin *-ista*, from Greek *-istēs*.

isthmian /ˈɪsθmɪən, ˈɪstm-, ˈɪsm-/ ■ adj. of or relating to an isthmus.

isthmus /ˈɪsθməs, ˈɪstməs, ˈɪsməs/ ■ n. 1 (pl. **isthmuses**) a narrow strip of land with sea on either side, linking two larger areas of land. 2 (pl. **isthmi**) Anatomy a narrow organ, passage, or piece of tissue connecting two larger parts.
– ORIGIN C16: from Greek *isthmos*.

IT ■ abbrev. information technology.

it[1] ■ pron. [third person sing.] 1 used to refer to a thing previously mentioned or easily identified. ▶ referring to an animal or child of unspecified sex. 2 used to identify a person. 3 used in the normal subject position in statements about time, distance, or weather. 4 used in the normal subject or object position when a more specific subject or object is given later in the sentence. 5 used to emphasize a following part of a sentence. 6 the situation or circumstances. 7 exactly what is needed or desired. 8 informal sexual attractiveness or sex appeal. 9 (in children's games) the player who has to catch the others.
– PHRASES **that's it** 1 that is the main point or difficulty. 2 that is enough. **this is it** the expected event is about to happen.
– ORIGIN Old English *hit*, neuter of HE, of Germanic origin.

it[2] ■ n. Brit. informal, dated Italian vermouth.

ITA ■ abbrev. initial teaching alphabet.

ital. ■ abbrev. italic.

Italian ■ n. 1 a native or national of Italy, or a person of Italian descent. 2 the Romance language of Italy, descended from Latin. ■ adj. of or relating to Italy, its people, or their language.
– DERIVATIVES **Italianize** (also **-ise**) v.

Italianate ■ adj. Italian in character or appearance.
– ORIGIN C16: from Italian *italianato*.

Italianism ■ n. 1 an Italian characteristic, expression, or custom. 2 attachment to Italy or Italian ideas or practices.

Italian vermouth ■ n. a type of bitter-sweet vermouth made in Italy.

Italic /ɪˈtalɪk/ ■ n. the branch of Indo-European languages that includes Latin and the Romance languages. ■ adj. relating to or denoting the Italic group of languages.
– ORIGIN C19: from Greek *Italikos* (see ITALIC).

italic /ɪˈtalɪk/ ■ adj. Printing of the sloping kind of typeface used especially for emphasis and in foreign words. ▶ (of handwriting) cursive and sloping and with elliptical or pointed letters, in the style of 16th-century Italian handwriting. ■ n. (also **italics**) an italic typeface or letter.
– DERIVATIVES **italicization** (also **-isation**) n. **italicize** (also **-ise**) v.
– ORIGIN Middle English ('Italian'): from Greek *Italikos*, from *Italia* 'Italy'.

Italo- /ˈɪtələʊ, ɪˈtɑːləʊ/ ■ comb. form Italian; Italian and …: *Italophile*.

itch ■ n. 1 an uncomfortable sensation or condition that causes a desire to scratch the skin. 2 informal an impatient desire. ■ v. 1 be the site of or experience an itch. 2 informal feel an impatient desire to do something.
– PHRASES **an itching palm** an avaricious nature.
– ORIGIN Old English, of West Germanic origin.

itching powder ■ n. a powder used to make someone's skin itch, typically as a practical joke.

itch mite ■ n. a parasitic mite which burrows under the skin, causing scabies or (in animals) sarcoptic mange. [*Sarcoptes scabiei*.]

itchy ■ adj. (**-ier**, **-iest**) having or causing an itch.
– PHRASES **get** (or **have**) **itchy feet** informal have or develop a strong urge to travel.
– DERIVATIVES **itchiness** n.

it'd ■ contr. 1 it had. 2 it would.

-ite[1] ■ suffix 1 forming names denoting natives of a country: *Israelite*. ▶ often derogatory denoting followers of a movement: *Luddite*. 2 used in scientific and technical terms: ▶ forming names of minerals or fossil organisms: *ammonite*. ▶ forming names of constituent parts of a body or organ: *somite*. ▶ forming names of explosives and other commercial products: *dynamite*. ▶ Chemistry forming names of salts or esters of acids ending in *-ous*: *sulphite*.
– ORIGIN from French *-ite*, from Greek *-ites*.

-ite[2] ■ suffix 1 forming adjectives such as *composite*. 2 forming nouns such as *appetite*. 3 forming verbs such as *unite*.
– ORIGIN from Latin *-itus*.

item ■ n. an individual article or unit. ▶ a piece of news or information. ▶ an entry in an account. ■ adv. archaic (used to introduce each item in a list) also.
– PHRASES **be an item** informal (of a couple) be in a romantic or sexual relationship.
– ORIGIN Middle English: from Latin, 'in like manner, also'.

itemize (also **-ise**) ■ v. present as a list of individual items or parts.
– DERIVATIVES **itemization** /-ˈzeɪʃ(ə)n/ (also **-isation**) n. **itemizer** (also **-iser**) n.

iterate /ˈɪtəreɪt/ ■ v. 1 perform or utter repeatedly. 2 make repeated use of a mathematical or computational procedure, applying it each time to the result of the

iterative

previous application.
- DERIVATIVES **iteration** n.
- ORIGIN C16 (*iteration* Middle English): from Latin *iterare* 'repeat'.

iterative ■ adj. **1** relating to or involving iteration, especially of a mathematical or computational process. **2** Grammar (of a verb or verbal form) expressing frequent repetition or intensity of action.
- DERIVATIVES **iteratively** adv.

-itic ■ suffix forming adjectives and nouns corresponding to nouns ending in *-ite* (such as *Semitic* corresponding to *Semite*). ▸ corresponding to nouns ending in *-itis* (such as *arthritic* corresponding to *arthritis*). ▸ from other bases: *syphilitic*.
- ORIGIN from French *-itique*, from Greek *-itikos*.

itinerant /ɪˈtɪn(ə)r(ə)nt, ʌɪ-/ ■ adj. travelling from place to place. ■ n. an itinerant person.
- DERIVATIVES **itinerancy** n.
- ORIGIN C16: from late Latin *itinerari* 'travel'.

itinerary /ʌɪˈtɪn(ə)(ə)ri, ɪ-/ ■ n. (pl. **-ies**) a planned route or journey. ▸ a travel document recording this.
- ORIGIN Middle English: from late Latin, from *itinerarius* 'of a journey or roads', from Latin *iter, itiner-* 'journey, road'.

itinerate /ɪˈtɪnəreɪt, ʌɪ-/ ■ v. (especially of a Church minister or a magistrate) travel from place to place to perform one's professional duty.
- DERIVATIVES **itineration** n.
- ORIGIN C17: from late Latin *itinerari* 'travel'.

-ition ■ suffix (forming nouns) equivalent to -ATION (as in *audition*).
- ORIGIN from Latin *-itio(n)-*.

-itious¹ ■ suffix forming adjectives corresponding to nouns ending in *-ition* (such as *ambitious* corresponding to *ambition*).
- ORIGIN from Latin *-itiosus*.

-itious² ■ suffix (forming adjectives) related to; having the nature of: *fictitious*.
- ORIGIN from late Latin *-itius*, alteration of Latin *-icius*.

-itis ■ suffix forming names of inflammatory diseases: *cystitis*.
- ORIGIN from Greek feminine form of adjectives ending in *-itēs* (combined with *nosos* 'disease' implied).

-itive ■ suffix (forming adjectives) equivalent to -ATIVE (as in *positive*).
- ORIGIN from French *-itif, -itive* or Latin *-itivus*.

it'll ■ contr. **1** it shall. **2** it will.

-itous ■ suffix forming adjectives corresponding to nouns ending in *-ity* (such as *calamitous* corresponding to *calamity*).
- ORIGIN from French *-iteux*, from Latin *-itosus*.

its ■ possess. det. belonging to or associated with a thing previously mentioned or easily identified. ▸ belonging to or associated with a child or animal of unspecified sex.

USAGE
In writing, be careful not to confuse the possessive **its** (as in *turn the camera on its side*) with the contraction **it's** (short for either **it is** or **it has**), as in *it's my fault*.

it's ■ contr. **1** it is. **2** it has.

itself ■ pron. [third person sing.] **1** [reflexive] used as the object of a verb or preposition to refer to a thing or animal previously mentioned as the subject of the clause. **2** [emphatic] used to emphasize a particular thing or animal mentioned. ▸ used to emphasize what a perfect example of a particular quality someone or something is.
- PHRASES **in itself** viewed in its essential qualities.

itsy-bitsy (also **itty-bitty**) ■ adj. informal very small.
- ORIGIN 1930s: from a child's form of LITTLE + *bitsy*, from BIT¹.

ITU ■ abbrev. International Telecommunication Union.

-ity ■ suffix forming nouns denoting quality or condition:

humility. ▸ denoting an instance or degree of this: *a profanity*.
- ORIGIN from French *-ité*, from Latin *-itas, -itatis*.

IUD ■ abbrev. **1** intrauterine death (of the fetus before birth). **2** intrauterine device.

-ium ■ suffix **1** forming nouns adopted unchanged from Latin (such as *alluvium*) or based on Latin or Greek words (such as *euphonium*). **2** (also **-um**) forming names of metallic elements: *cadmium*. **3** denoting a region of the body: *pericardium*. **4** denoting a biological structure: *mycelium*.
- ORIGIN modern Latin in senses 2, 3, and 4, via Latin from Greek *-ion*.

IV ■ abbrev. intravenous or intravenously.

I've ■ contr. I have.

-ive ■ suffix (forming adjectives, also nouns derived from them) tending to; having the nature of: *palliative*.
- DERIVATIVES **-ively** suffix forming corresponding adverbs. **-iveness** suffix forming corresponding nouns.
- ORIGIN from French *-if, -ive*, from Latin *-ivus*.

ivermectin /ˌʌɪvəˈmɛktɪn/ ■ n. a macrocyclic compound used as an anthelmintic in veterinary medicine and as a treatment for river blindness.
- ORIGIN 1980s: from *i* + *avermectin*, denoting a similar compound, from modern Latin (*Streptomyces*) *averm*(*itilis*), the name of the source bacterium.

IVF ■ abbrev. in vitro fertilization.

ivied ■ adj. **1** covered in ivy. **2** US of or relating to the academic institutions of the Ivy League.

ivory ■ n. (pl. **-ies**) **1** a hard creamy-white substance composing the main part of the tusks of an elephant, walrus, or narwhal. **2** the creamy-white colour of ivory. **3** (**the ivories**) informal the keys of a piano. **4** (**ivories**) informal a person's teeth.
- DERIVATIVES **ivoried** adj.
- ORIGIN Middle English: from Anglo-Norman French *ivurie*, from Latin *ebur*.

ivory black ■ n. a black carbon pigment made from charred ivory or bone, used in drawing and painting.

ivory tower ■ n. a state of privileged seclusion or separation from the facts and practicalities of the real world.
- ORIGIN C20: translating French *tour d'ivoire*, used by the C19 French writer Charles Augustin Sainte-Beuve.

ivy ■ n. a woody evergreen climbing plant, typically with shiny five-pointed leaves. [*Hedera helix* and related species.] ▸ used in names of other climbing plants, e.g. poison ivy.
- ORIGIN Old English, of Germanic origin.

Ivy League ■ n. a group of long-established and prestigious universities in the eastern US.
- ORIGIN with ref. to the ivy traditionally growing over their walls.

IWC ■ abbrev. International Whaling Commission.

ixia /ˈɪksɪə/ ■ n. a South African plant of the iris family, bearing showy six-petalled starlike flowers. [Genus *Ixia*: many cultivars.]
- ORIGIN modern Latin, from Latin, denoting a kind of thistle.

-ize (also **-ise**) ■ suffix forming verbs meaning: **1** make or become: *privatize*. ▸ cause to resemble: *Americanize*. **2** treat in a specified way: *pasteurize*. ▸ treat or cause to combine with a specified substance: *carbonize*. **3** follow a specified practice: *agonize*. ▸ subject to a practice: *hospitalize*.
- DERIVATIVES **-ization** (also **-isation**) suffix forming corresponding nouns. **-izer** (also **-iser**) suffix forming agent nouns.
- ORIGIN from French *-iser*, via late Latin *-izare* from Greek verbs ending in *-izein*.

USAGE
On the use of the forms **-ize** and **-ise**, see -ISE.

Iznik /ˈɪznɪk/ ■ adj. denoting ceramics produced during the 16th and 17th centuries in Iznik (ancient Nicaea), a town in NW Turkey.

izzit ■ exclam. variant spelling of ISIT.

Jj

J¹ (also **j**) ■ n. (pl. **Js** or **J's**) **1** the tenth letter of the alphabet. **2** denoting the next after I in a set of items, categories, etc.

J² ■ abbrev. **1** (in card games) jack. **2** Physics joule(s). **3** (in titles) Journal (of).

j ■ symb. (*j*) (in electrical engineering and electronics) the imaginary quantity equal to the square root of minus one. Compare with I.

ja /jɑː/ (also **yah**) ■ exclam. S. African informal yes.
– ORIGIN from Dutch.

jab ■ v. (**jabbed**, **jabbing**) poke roughly or quickly with something sharp or pointed. ■ n. **1** a quick, sharp poke or blow. **2** informal a hypodermic injection, especially a vaccination.
– ORIGIN C19 (orig. Scots): var. of archaic *job* 'prod, stab'.

jabber ■ v. talk rapidly and excitedly but with little sense. ■ n. such talk.
– ORIGIN C15: imitative.

jabberwocky /ˈdʒabəˌwɒki/ ■ n. (pl. **-ies**) invented or meaningless language.
– ORIGIN C20: from the title of a nonsense poem in Lewis Carroll's *Through the Looking Glass* (1871).

jabot /ˈʒabəʊ/ ■ n. an ornamental ruffle on the front of a shirt or blouse.
– ORIGIN C19: French, orig. 'crop of a bird'.

jacana /ˈdʒakənə/ (also **jaçana** /ˌdʒasəˈnɑː/) ■ n. a small tropical wading bird with greatly elongated toes and claws that enable it to walk on floating vegetation. [Family Jacanidae: several species.]
– ORIGIN C18: from Portuguese *jaçanã*, from Tupi-Guarani *jasanã*.

jacaranda /ˌdʒakəˈrandə/ ■ n. a tropical American tree which has blue trumpet-shaped flowers, fern-like leaves, and fragrant wood. [Genus *Jacaranda*.]
– ORIGIN C18: from Portuguese, from Tupi-Guarani *jakara'nda*.

jacinth /ˈdʒasɪnθ, ˈdʒeɪ-/ ■ n. a reddish-orange gem variety of zircon.
– ORIGIN Middle English: from medieval Latin *iacintus*, alteration of Latin *hyacinthus* (see HYACINTH).

jack ■ n. **1** a device for lifting heavy objects, especially one for raising the axle of a motor vehicle. **2** a playing card bearing a representation of a soldier, page, or knave, normally ranking next below a queen. **3** (also **jack socket**) a socket designed to receive a jack plug. **4** (in bowls) a small white ball at which the players aim. **5** a small round pebble or star-shaped piece of metal or plastic used in tossing and catching games. ▶ (**jacks**) a game played by tossing and catching jacks. **6** a small version of a national flag flown at the bow of a vessel in harbour. **7** US informal money. **8** a device for turning a spit. **9** a part of the mechanism in a spinet or harpsichord that connects a key to its corresponding string. **10** a perch-like marine fish, typically with a row of large spiky scales along each side. [Family Carangidae: numerous species.] **11** the male of various animals, especially a merlin or (N. Amer.) an ass. ■ v. **1** (**jack something up**) raise something with a jack. **2** (**jack something up**) informal increase something by a considerable amount. **3** (**jack in/into**) log into or connect up (a computer or electronic device).
– PHRASES **every man jack** informal every single person. **jack of all trades** (**and master of none**) a person who can do many different types of work (but has special skill in none).
– PHRASAL VERBS **jack someone around** N. Amer. informal cause someone inconvenience or problems. **jack something in** Brit. informal give something up. **jack off** vulgar slang masturbate. **jack up** informal inject oneself with a narcotic drug.
– ORIGIN Middle English: from *Jack*, familiar form of the given name *John*, used orig. to denote an ordinary man, hence the 'knave' in cards and 'male animal', also denoting various devices saving human labour.

jackal /ˈdʒakəl, -kɔːl/ ■ n. a slender, long-legged wild dog that often hunts or scavenges in packs, found in Africa and southern Asia. [Genus *Canis*: four species.]
– ORIGIN C17: from Turkish *çakal*.

jackal-berry ■ n. an African tree which bears edible yellow-orange fruits often eaten by jackals. [Genus *Diospyros*: several species.]

jackal buzzard ■ n. a southern African buzzard, with slate-grey head and back, yellow legs, and a chestnut breast with a white band. [*Buteo rufofuscus*.]
– ORIGIN so named because its cry is like that of a jackal.

jackanapes /ˈdʒakəneɪps/ ■ n. **1** dated an impertinent person. **2** archaic a tame monkey.
– ORIGIN C16 (orig. *Jack Napes*): perhaps from a playful name for a tame ape, the initial *n-* by elision of *an ape*.

jackaroo /ˌdʒakəˈruː/ informal Austral. ■ n. a young, inexperienced worker on a sheep or cattle station. ■ v. work as a jackaroo.
– ORIGIN C19: alteration of an Aboriginal term *dhugai-iu* 'wandering white man'.

jackass ■ n. **1** a stupid person. **2** a male ass or donkey.

jackass penguin ■ n. former term for AFRICAN PENGUIN.

jackboot ■ n. a large leather military boot reaching to the knee.
– DERIVATIVES **jackbooted** adj.

jackdaw ■ n. a small grey-headed crow, noted for its inquisitiveness. [Genus *Corvus*: two species, in particular the Eurasian *C. monedula*.]
– ORIGIN from JACK + earlier *daw* (of Germanic origin).

jacket ■ n. **1** an outer garment extending to the waist or hips, with sleeves and a fastening down the front. **2** an outer covering placed around something for protection or insulation. **3** the skin of a potato. **4** a steel frame fixed to the seabed to support an oil production platform. ■ v. (**jacketed**, **jacketing**) cover with a jacket.
– DERIVATIVES **-jacketed** adj.
– ORIGIN Middle English: from Old French *jaquet*, diminutive of *jaque*, perhaps from Arabic.

jacket potato ■ n. chiefly Brit. a baked potato served with the skin on.

Jack Frost ■ n. a personification of frost.

jackfruit ■ n. the very large edible fruit of a fast-growing tropical Asian tree (*Artocarpus heterophyllus*), resembling a breadfruit.
– ORIGIN C16: from Portuguese *jaca* (from Malayalam *chakka*) + FRUIT.

jackhammer ■ n. a portable pneumatic hammer or drill. ■ v. beat or hammer heavily or loudly and repeatedly.

jackie hangman (also **jacky hangman**) ■ n. South African term for COMMON FISCAL.
– ORIGIN C20: so named because of its habit of impaling its prey on thorns.

jack-in-the-box ■ n. a toy consisting of a box containing a figure on a spring which pops up when the lid is opened.

Jack-in-the-pulpit ■ n. **1** another term for CUCKOO PINT. **2** a North American arum with a green or purple-brown spathe. [*Arisaema triphyllum*.]
– ORIGIN C19: so named because the erect spadix overarched by the spathe resembles a person in a pulpit.

jackknife ■ n. (pl. **-knives**) **1** a large knife with a folding blade. **2** a dive in which the body is bent at the waist and then straightened. ■ v. (**-knifed**, **-knifing**) **1** move (one's body) into a bent or doubled-up position. **2** (of an

ʊ put   uː too   ʌɪ my   aʊ how   eɪ day   əʊ no   ɪə near   ɔɪ boy   ʊə poor   ʌɪə fire   aʊə sour

jack-o'-lantern

articulated vehicle) bend into a V-shape in an uncontrolled skidding movement. **3** (of a diver) perform a jackknife.

jack-o'-lantern ■ n. **1** a lantern made from a hollowed-out pumpkin or turnip in which holes are cut to represent facial features. **2** archaic a will-o'-the-wisp.

jack plane ■ n. a medium-sized plane for use in rough joinery.

jack plug ■ n. a plug consisting of a single shaft used to make a connection which transmits a signal, typically used in sound equipment.

jackpot ■ n. a large cash prize or accumulated stake in a game or lottery.
– PHRASES **hit the jackpot** informal **1** win a jackpot. **2** have great or unexpected success.
– ORIGIN C19 (orig. used in a form of poker): from JACK + POT¹.

jackrabbit ■ n. a hare found on the prairies and steppes of North America. [Genus *Lepus*: several species.]
– ORIGIN C19: abbrev. of *jackass-rabbit*, because of its long ears.

jackroll ■ v. S. African informal abduct and gang-rape (a girl or woman).
– DERIVATIVES **jackroller** n.
– ORIGIN orig. US slang *jackroll* 'rob, mug', prob. from *jack*, a shortening of LUMBERJACK, + *roll* 'rob'.

Jack Russell (also **Jack Russell terrier**) ■ n. a terrier of a small working breed with short legs.
– ORIGIN C20: named after the English clergyman Revd John (*Jack*) *Russell*, a breeder of such terriers.

jack screw ■ n. **1** a screw which can be turned to adjust the position of an object into which it fits. **2** another term for SCREW JACK.

jackstaff ■ n. a short staff at a ship's bow, on which a jack is hoisted.

Jack tar ■ n. Brit. informal, dated a sailor.

Jack the Lad ■ n. informal a brash, cocky young man.
– ORIGIN nickname of *Jack* Sheppard, C18 thief.

jacky hangman ■ n. variant spelling of JACKIE HANGMAN.

Jacobean /ˌdʒakəˈbiːən/ ■ adj. of or relating to the reign of James I of England (1603–1625). ▸ denoting the architectural style prevalent at this time, consisting of a blend of Gothic and classical features. ▸ (of furniture) made in the style prevalent at this time, characterized by the use of dark oak. ■ n. a person who lived in the Jacobean period.
– ORIGIN C19: from modern Latin *Jacobaeus*, from eccles. Latin *Jacobus* 'James'.

Jacobin /ˈdʒakəbɪn/ ■ n. **1** historical a member of a radical democratic club established in Paris in 1789, in the wake of the French Revolution. **2** an extreme political radical. **3** chiefly historical a Dominican friar. **4** (**jacobin**) a pigeon of a breed with reversed feathers on the back of its neck like a cowl.
– DERIVATIVES **Jacobinic** adj. **Jacobinical** adj. **Jacobinism** n.
– ORIGIN Middle English (denoting the Dominican friars): from Old French, from eccles. Latin *Jacobus* 'James', after the church in Paris, St Jacques, near which the friars built their first convent; the latter eventually became the headquarters of the French revolutionary group.

Jacobite /ˈdʒakəbʌɪt/ ■ n. historical a supporter of the deposed James II and his descendants in their claim to the British throne after the Revolution of 1688.
– DERIVATIVES **Jacobitical** adj. **Jacobitism** n.
– ORIGIN from Latin *Jacobus* 'James'.

Jacobson's organ ■ n. Zoology a scent organ situated in the mouth of snakes, lizards, and some other vertebrates.
– ORIGIN C19: named after the Dutch anatomist Ludwig L. *Jacobson*.

jaconet /ˈdʒakənɪt/ ■ n. a lightweight cotton cloth with a smooth and slightly stiff finish.
– ORIGIN C18: from Hindi *Jagannāth(purī)* (now *Puri*) in India, its place of origin.

jacquard /ˈdʒakɑːd, -kəd/ ■ n. **1** an apparatus consisting of perforated cards, fitted to a loom to facilitate the weaving of figured and brocaded fabrics. ▸ [as modifier] denoting a loom fitted with a jacquard. **2** a fabric made on a jacquard loom.
– ORIGIN C19: named after the French weaver Joseph M. *Jacquard*.

jacuzzi /dʒəˈkuːzi/ ■ n. (pl. **jacuzzis**) trademark a large bath incorporating jets of water to massage the body.
– ORIGIN 1960s: named after the Italian-born American inventor Candido *Jacuzzi*.

jade ■ n. **1** a hard, typically green, stone consisting of the minerals jadeite or nephrite, used for ornaments and jewellery. **2** the light bluish green colour of jade.
– ORIGIN C16: from French *le jade*, from Spanish *piedra de ijada* 'stone of the flank', i.e. stone for colic, which it was believed to cure.

jaded ■ adj. tired or lacking enthusiasm after having had a surfeit of something.
– DERIVATIVES **jadedly** adv. **jadedness** n.
– ORIGIN C16 ('disreputable'): from archaic *jade* 'disreputable woman, worn-out horse'.

jadeite /ˈdʒeɪdʌɪt/ ■ n. a green, blue, or white silicate mineral which is one of the forms of jade.

j'adoube /ʒɑːˈduːb/ ■ exclam. Chess a declaration by a player intending to adjust the placing of a chessman without making a move with it.
– ORIGIN French, 'I adjust'.

Jaffa /ˈdʒafə/ ■ n. Brit. a large oval orange of a thick-skinned variety.
– ORIGIN from the city of *Jaffa* in Israel.

jaffle ■ n. S. African & Austral. a sealed toasted sandwich with a savoury or sweet filling. ■ v. prepare a jaffle.

jaffle iron ■ n. a device for cooking jaffles, with a long handle and two metal pans hinged together.

jag¹ ■ v. (**jagged**, **jagging**) stab, pierce, or prick. ■ n. a sharp projection.
– ORIGIN Middle English: perhaps symbolic of sudden movement or unevenness.

jag² ■ n. informal a bout of unrestrained activity or emotion.
– ORIGIN C16 ('a load of hay or wood', later 'as much alcohol as one can hold').

jagged /ˈdʒagɪd/ ■ adj. with rough, sharp points protruding.
– DERIVATIVES **jaggedly** adv. **jaggedness** n.
– ORIGIN Middle English: from JAG¹.

jaggery /ˈdʒag(ə)ri/ ■ n. a coarse brown sugar made in India from the sap of palm trees.
– ORIGIN C16: from Portuguese *jag(a)ra*, from Malayalam *cakkarā*, from Sanskrit *śarkarā* 'sugar'.

jaguar /ˈdʒagjʊə/ ■ n. a large, heavily built cat that has a yellowish-brown coat with black spots, found mainly in the dense forests of Central and South America. [*Panthera onca*.]
– ORIGIN C17: from Portuguese, from Tupi-Guarani *yaguára*.

jaguarundi /ˌdʒagwəˈrʌndi/ ■ n. (pl. **jaguarundis**) a small American wild cat with a uniform red or grey coat, slender body, and short legs, found from Arizona to Argentina. [*Felis yagouaroundi*.]
– ORIGIN C19: from Portuguese, from Tupi-Guarani, from *yaguára* 'jaguar' + *undi* 'dark'.

Jah /dʒɑː, jɑː/ ■ n. the Rastafarian name of God.
– ORIGIN representing Hebrew *Yāh*, abbrev. of YAHWEH.

jail (Brit. also **gaol**) ■ n. a place for the confinement of people accused or convicted of a crime. ■ v. put (someone) in jail.
– DERIVATIVES **jailer** (also **gaoler**) n.
– ORIGIN Middle English: from Latin *cavea* (see CAGE); the word came into English in two forms, *jaiole* from Old French and *gayole* from Anglo-Norman French *gaole* (surviving in the spelling *gaol*).

jailbait ■ n. [treated as sing. or pl.] informal a young woman, or young women collectively, considered in sexual terms but under the age of consent.

jailbird ■ n. informal a person who is or has repeatedly been in prison.

jailbreak ■ n. an escape from jail.

jailhouse ■ n. chiefly N. Amer. a prison.

Jain /dʒeɪn/ ■ n. an adherent of Jainism. ■ adj. of or relating to Jainism.
– ORIGIN from Sanskrit *jaina* 'of or concerning a *Jina* (a great teacher)'.

Jainism ■ n. a non-theistic religion founded in India in the 6th century BC, in opposition to Brahmanism.
– DERIVATIVES **Jainist** n.

jakes /dʒeɪks/ ■ n. archaic an outdoor toilet.
– ORIGIN C16: perhaps from the given name *Jacques*, or from the pet name *Jack* (see JACK).

jalapeño /ˌhaləˈpeɪnjəʊ, -ˈpiːnəʊ/ ■ n. (pl. -os) a very hot green chilli pepper.
– ORIGIN 1940s: from Mexican Spanish (*chile*) *jalapeño*, from the name of the Mexican city *Jalapa*.

jalebi /dʒəˈleɪbi/ ■ n. (pl. jalebis) an Indian sweet made of a coil of batter fried and steeped in syrup.
– ORIGIN from Hindi *jalebī*.

jalfrezi /dʒalˈfreɪzi/ ■ n. a medium-hot Indian dish consisting of chicken or lamb with fresh chillies, tomatoes, and onions.
– ORIGIN from Bengali *jalfrezi*, from *jal* 'hot'.

jalopy /dʒəˈlɒpi/ ■ n. (pl. -ies) informal an old car in a dilapidated condition.
– ORIGIN 1920s (orig. US).

jalousie /ˈʒaluːzi/ ■ n. a blind or shutter made of a row of angled slats.
– ORIGIN C18: French, 'jealousy', from Italian *geloso* 'jealous', also (by extension) 'screen', associated with the screening of women from view in the Middle East.

jam[1] ■ v. (**jammed**, **jamming**) **1** squeeze or pack tightly into a space. ▸ push roughly and forcibly into a position. ▸ crowd so as to block (a road, telephone line, etc.). **2** become or make unable to move or work due to a part becoming stuck. **3** (**jam something on**) apply something forcibly: *he jammed on the brakes*. **4** make (a radio transmission) unintelligible by causing interference. **5** informal (in jazz or blues) improvise with other musicians. ■ n. **1** an instance of jamming. **2** informal an awkward situation or predicament: *I'm in a jam*. **3** Climbing a handhold obtained by jamming a part of the body into a crack in the rock. **4** informal (in jazz or blues) an improvised performance by a group of musicians.
– DERIVATIVES **jammer** n.
– ORIGIN C18: prob. symbolic; cf. JAG[1].

jam[2] ■ n. a conserve and spread made from fruit and sugar.
– PHRASES **jam tomorrow** a desirable thing that is promised but rarely materializes. [phr. from Lewis Carroll's *Through the Looking Glass* (1871).]
– ORIGIN C18: perhaps from JAM[1].

Jamaican /dʒəˈmeɪkən/ ■ n. a native or inhabitant of Jamaica. ■ adj. of or relating to Jamaica or its people.

Jamaica pepper ■ n. another term for ALLSPICE (in senses 1 and 2).

jamb /dʒam/ ■ n. a side post of a doorway, window, or fireplace.
– ORIGIN Middle English: from Old French *jambe* 'leg, vertical support', based on Greek *kampē* 'joint'.

jambalaya /ˌdʒambəˈlʌɪə/ ■ n. a Cajun dish of rice with shrimps, chicken, and vegetables.
– ORIGIN Louisiana French, from Provençal *jambalaia*.

jamboree /ˌdʒambəˈriː/ ■ n. **1** a lavish or boisterous celebration or party. **2** a large rally of Scouts or Guides.
– ORIGIN C19 (orig. US slang).

jammy ■ adj. (**-ier, -iest**) **1** covered, filled with, or resembling jam. **2** Brit. informal lucky.

jam-packed ■ adj. informal extremely crowded or full to capacity.

Jan. ■ abbrev. January.

janbruin /janˈbreɪn/ ■ n. another term for JOHN BROWN.

jane ■ n. informal, chiefly US a woman.
– PHRASES **plain Jane** an unattractive girl or woman.
– ORIGIN C20: from the given name *Jane*.

ja-nee /jɑːˈnɪə/ ■ exclam. S. African informal, often ironic used to express vague approval or resigned acceptance. ▸ indicating emphatic agreement or affirmation.
– ORIGIN from Afrikaans *ja* 'yes' + *nee* 'no'.

jangle ■ v. **1** make or cause to make a ringing metallic sound. **2** (of one's nerves) be set on edge. ■ n. an instance of jangling.
– DERIVATIVES **jangly** adj.
– ORIGIN Middle English ('talk excessively or noisily, squabble'): from Old French *jangler*.

janissary /ˈdʒanɪs(ə)ri/ (also **janizary** /-z(ə)ri/) ■ n. (pl. -ies) historical a Turkish infantryman in the Sultan's guard.
– ORIGIN C16: from Turkish *yeniçeri*, from *yeni* 'new' + *çeri* 'troops'.

janitor /ˈdʒanɪtə/ ■ n. a caretaker of a building.
– DERIVATIVES **janitorial** adj.
– ORIGIN C16: from Latin, from *janua* 'door'.

January /ˈdʒanjʊ(ə)ri/ ■ n. (pl. -ies) the first month of the year.
– ORIGIN Old English, from Latin *Januarius* (*mensis*) '(month) of *Janus*' (the Roman god who presided over doors and beginnings).

Jap ■ n. & adj. informal, offensive short for JAPANESE.

japan ■ n. a black glossy varnish of a type originating in Japan. ■ v. (**japanned**, **japanning**) cover with japan.
– DERIVATIVES **japanned** adj. **japanning** n.

Japanese ■ n. (pl. same) **1** a native or national of Japan, or a person of Japanese descent. **2** the language of Japan. ■ adj. of or relating to Japan, its people, or their language.

Japanese cedar ■ n. another term for CRYPTOMERIA.

Japanese lantern ■ n. another term for CHINESE LANTERN (in sense 1).

jape ■ n. a practical joke. ■ v. say or do something in jest or mockery.
– DERIVATIVES **japery** n.
– ORIGIN Middle English: apparently combining the form of Old French *japer* 'to yelp, yap' with the sense of Old French *gaber* 'to mock'.

japonica /dʒəˈpɒnɪkə/ ■ n. an Asian shrub of the rose family, with bright red flowers followed by edible fruits. [*Chaenomeles speciosa* (Japanese quince) and related species.]
– ORIGIN C19: modern Latin, feminine of *japonicus* 'Japanese'.

jar[1] ■ n. **1** a wide-mouthed cylindrical container made of glass or pottery. **2** Brit. informal a glass of beer.
– ORIGIN C16: from Arabic *jarra*.

jar[2] ■ v. (**jarred, jarring**) **1** send a painful or uncomfortable shock through (a part of the body). ▸ strike against something with an unpleasant vibration or jolt. **2** have a disturbing or incongruous effect. ■ n. an instance of jarring.
– DERIVATIVES **jarring** adj. **jarringly** adv.
– ORIGIN C15 ('disagreement, dispute'): prob. imitative.

jardinière /ˌʒɑːdɪnˈjɛː/ ■ n. an ornamental pot or stand for displaying plants.
– ORIGIN C19: French, 'female gardener'.

jargon[1] /ˈdʒɑːg(ə)n/ ■ n. words or expressions used by a particular profession or group that are difficult for others to understand.
– DERIVATIVES **jargonistic** adj. **jargonize** (also **-ise**) v.
– ORIGIN Middle English (orig. 'chattering', later 'gibberish'): from Old French *jargoun*.

jargon[2] /ˈdʒɑːg(ə)n/ ■ n. a translucent, colourless, or smoky gem variety of zircon.
– ORIGIN C18: from French; prob. ultimately rel. to ZIRCON.

jarrah /ˈdʒarə/ ■ n. a eucalyptus tree native to western Australia. [*Eucalyptus marginata*.]
– ORIGIN C19: from Nyungar (an extinct Aboriginal language) *djarryl, jerrhyl*.

jasmine /ˈdʒazmɪn, ˈdʒas-/ (also **jessamine**) ■ n. a shrub or climbing plant with fragrant flowers, often yellow. [Genus *Jasminum*: many species.] ▸ used in names of other shrubs or climbers with fragrant flowers, e.g. yellow jasmine.
– ORIGIN C16: from French *jasmin* and obsolete French *jessemin*.

jasmine tea ■ n. a tea perfumed with dried jasmine flowers.

jasper ■ n. an opaque reddish-brown variety of chalcedony.

jati

−ORIGIN Middle English: from Old French *jasp(r)e*, from Latin *iaspis*, from Greek, of oriental origin.

jati /ˈdʒɑːti/ ■ n. (pl. same or **jatis**) Indian a caste or subcaste.
−ORIGIN from Sanskrit *jāti* 'birth'.

JATO /ˈdʒeɪtəʊ/ ■ abbrev. Aeronautics jet-assisted take-off.

jaundice /ˈdʒɔːndɪs/ ■ n. **1** Medicine yellowing of the skin due to an excess of bile pigments in the blood. **2** bitterness or resentment.
−DERIVATIVES **jaundiced** adj.
−ORIGIN Middle English: from Old French *jaunice* 'yellowness', from *jaune* 'yellow'.

jaunt ■ n. a short excursion for pleasure. ■ v. go on a jaunt.
−ORIGIN C16.

jaunty ■ adj. (**-ier, -iest**) having a lively and self-confident manner.
−DERIVATIVES **jauntily** adv. **jauntiness** n.
−ORIGIN C17 ('well-bred, genteel'): from French *gentil* (see **GENTLE, GENTEEL**).

Java /ˈdʒɑːvə/ ■ n. trademark a computer programming language designed to work across different computer systems.

java /ˈdʒɑːvə/ ■ n. N. Amer. informal coffee.

Javan /ˈdʒɑːvən/ ■ n. a native or inhabitant of the Indonesian island of Java. ■ adj. of or relating to Java.

Javanese ■ n. (pl. same) **1** a native or national of Java, or a person of Javanese descent. **2** the Indonesian language of central Java. ■ adj. of or relating to Java.

javelin /ˈdʒav(ə)lɪn/ ■ n. a long, light spear thrown in a competitive sport or as a weapon.
−ORIGIN Middle English: from Old French *javeline*, of Celtic origin.

jaw ■ n. **1** each of the upper and lower bony structures in vertebrates forming the framework of the mouth and containing the teeth. ▸ (**jaws**) the grasping, biting, or crushing mouthparts of an invertebrate. **2** (**jaws**) the gripping parts of a wrench, vice, etc. **3** (**jaws**) the grasping or destructive power of something: *the jaws of death*. **4** informal tedious talk or gossip. ■ v. informal talk or gossip at length.
−DERIVATIVES **-jawed** adj. **jawless** adj.
−ORIGIN Middle English: from Old French *joe* 'cheek, jaw'.

jawbone ■ n. a bone of the jaw, especially that of the lower jaw (the mandible).

jawbreaker ■ n. **1** informal a word that is very long or hard to pronounce. **2** chiefly N. Amer. a large gobstopper.

jaw-dropping ■ adj. informal amazing.
−DERIVATIVES **jaw-droppingly** adv.

ja well no fine /jɑː ˌwɛl nəʊ ˈfʌɪn/ ■ exclam. S. African informal, often humorous used as a non-committal response.
−ORIGIN 1970s: coined as 'Jarwellknowfine' in 1978 by R. J. B. Wilson as the title for an SABC radio series.

jaw-jaw informal ■ n. lengthy or pointless talk. ■ v. talk pointlessly or at length.
−ORIGIN C19: reduplication of **JAW**.

jawline ■ n. the contour of the lower edge of a person's jaw.

Jaws of Life ■ n. trademark a hydraulic apparatus used to pry apart the wreckage of crashed vehicles in order to free people trapped inside.

jay ■ n. **1** a bird of the crow family with boldly patterned plumage, typically with blue feathers in the wings or tail and a harsh chattering call. [*Garrulus glandarius* (Eurasia) and other species.] **2** informal, dated a prattler.
−ORIGIN C15: from late Latin *gaius, gaia*, perhaps from the Latin given name *Gaius*.

jaywalk ■ v. walk in or across a road without regard for approaching traffic.
−DERIVATIVES **jaywalker** n.
−ORIGIN C20: from **JAY** in the colloquial sense 'silly person' + **WALK**.

jazz ■ n. a type of music of black American origin characterized by improvisation, syncopation, and a regular rhythm, typically played on brass and woodwind instruments. ■ v. **1** dated play or dance to jazz. **2** (**jazz something up**) make something more lively.
−PHRASES **and all that jazz** informal and such similar things.
−DERIVATIVES **jazzer** n.
−ORIGIN C20.

jazzy ■ adj. (**-ier, -iest**) **1** of or in the style of jazz. **2** bright, colourful, and showy.
−DERIVATIVES **jazzily** adv. **jazziness** n.

JCB ■ n. Brit. trademark a type of mechanical excavator with a shovel at the front and a digging arm at the rear.
−ORIGIN 1960s: the initials of *J. C. Bamford*, the makers.

JCL ■ abbrev. Computing job control language.

jealous ■ adj. **1** envious of someone else's possessions, achievements, or advantages. ▸ suspicious or resentful of a perceived sexual rival. **2** fiercely protective or vigilant of one's rights or possessions. **3** (of God) demanding faithfulness and exclusive worship.
−DERIVATIVES **jealously** adv. **jealousy** n.
−ORIGIN Middle English: from Old French *gelos*, from Latin *zelus* 'zeal, jealousy'.

jean ■ n. **1** heavy twilled cotton cloth, especially denim. **2** (in commercial use) a pair of jeans: *a button-fly jean*.
−ORIGIN C15: from Old French *Janne* (now *Gênes*), from medieval Latin *Janua* 'Genoa', the place of original production.

jeans ■ pl. n. hard-wearing trousers made of denim or other cotton fabric.
−ORIGIN C19: pl. of **JEAN**.

jeep ■ n. trademark a small, sturdy motor vehicle with four-wheel drive, especially one used by the army.
−ORIGIN SECOND WORLD WAR: from the initials *GP*, standing for *general purpose*, influenced by 'Eugene the Jeep', a creature in the *Popeye* comic strip.

jeepers (also **jeepers creepers**) ■ exclam. informal, chiefly N. Amer. expressing surprise or alarm.
−ORIGIN 1920s: alteration of **JESUS**.

jeer ■ v. make rude and mocking remarks at someone. ■ n. a rude and mocking remark.
−DERIVATIVES **jeering** adj. & n. **jeeringly** adv.
−ORIGIN C16.

jeera /ˈdʒiːrə/ (also **zeera** /ˈzɪːrə/) ■ n. Indian term for CUMIN.
−ORIGIN from Hindi *jīrā*.

Jeez (also **Geez**) ■ exclam. informal expressing surprise or annoyance.
−ORIGIN 1920s: abbrev. of **JESUS**.

jehad ■ n. variant spelling of **JIHAD**.

Jehovah /dʒɪˈhəʊvə/ ■ n. a form of the Hebrew name of God used in some translations of the Bible.
−ORIGIN from medieval Latin *Iehouah, Iehoua*, from Hebrew *YHWH* or *JHVH*, the consonants of the name of God, with the inclusion of vowels taken from *'ăḏōnāy* 'my lord'; cf. **YAHWEH**.

Jehovah's Witness ■ n. a member of a fundamentalist Christian sect that denies many traditional Christian doctrines (including the divinity of Christ) and preaches the Second Coming.

jejune /dʒɪˈdʒuːn/ ■ adj. **1** naive and simplistic. **2** (of ideas or writings) dull.
−DERIVATIVES **jejunely** adv. **jejuneness** n.
−ORIGIN C17: from Latin *jejunus* 'fasting, barren'.

jejunum /dʒɪˈdʒuːnəm/ ■ n. Anatomy the part of the small intestine between the duodenum and ileum.
−DERIVATIVES **jejunal** adj.
−ORIGIN C16: from medieval Latin, neuter of *jejunus* 'fasting' (because it is usu. found to be empty after death).

Jekyll /ˈdʒɛk(ə)l/ ■ n. (in phr. **a Jekyll and Hyde**) a person displaying alternately good and evil personalities.
−ORIGIN after the central character in Robert Louis Stevenson's story *The Strange Case of Dr Jekyll and Mr Hyde* (1886).

jell (also **gel**) ■ v. (**jelled, jelling**) **1** (of jelly or a similar substance) set or become firmer. **2** take definite form or begin to work well.

jellaba ■ n. variant spelling of **DJELLABA**.

jello (also trademark **Jell-O**) ■ n. N. Amer. a fruit-flavoured gelatin dessert made up from a commercially prepared powder.

jelly ■ n. (pl. **-ies**) **1** a dessert consisting of a sweet, fruit-flavoured liquid set with gelatin to form a semi-solid mass. ▸ a small sweet made with gelatin. **2** a similar preparation made with fruit or other ingredients as a condiment. ▸ a savoury preparation made from gelatin and meat stock. **3** any substance of a similar semi-solid consistency. **4** Brit. informal term for **GELIGNITE**. ■ v. (**-ies**, **-ied**) [usu. as adj. **jellied**] set (food) as or in a jelly.
–DERIVATIVES **jellification** n. **jellify** v.
–ORIGIN Middle English: from Old French *gelee* 'frost, jelly', from Latin *gelata* 'frozen'.

jelly baby ■ n. a jelly sweet in the stylized shape of a baby.

jelly bean ■ n. a jelly sweet in the shape of a bean.

jellyfish ■ n. (pl. same or **-fishes**) **1** a free-swimming marine coelenterate with a jelly-like bell- or saucer-shaped body that has stinging tentacles around the edge. [Classes Scyphozoa and Cubozoa.] **2** informal a feeble person.

jelly roll ■ n. N. Amer. a Swiss roll.

jembe ■ n. variant spelling of **DJEMBE**.

jemmy (N. Amer. **jimmy**) ■ n. (pl. **-ies**) a short crowbar. ■ v. (**-ies**, **-ied**) informal force open (a window or door) with a jemmy.
–ORIGIN C19: familiar form of the given name *James*.

je ne sais quoi /ˌʒə nə seɪ ˈkwɑː/ ■ n. a quality that cannot be easily identified.
–ORIGIN French, 'I do not know what'.

jenny ■ n. (pl. **-ies**) **1** a female donkey or ass. **2** short for **SPINNING JENNY**.
–ORIGIN C17: familiar form of the given name *Janet*, used as a feminine prefix and in names of machines (cf. **JACK**).

jeopardize /ˈdʒɛpədʌɪz/ (also **-ise**) ■ v. put into a situation in which there is a danger of loss, harm, or failure.

jeopardy /ˈdʒɛpədi/ ■ n. **1** danger of loss, harm, or failure. **2** Law danger arising from being on trial for a criminal offence.
–ORIGIN Middle English *iuparti*, from Old French *ieu parti* '(evenly) divided game', orig. used in chess to denote a position in which the chances of winning or losing were evenly balanced.

jerboa /dʒəːˈbəʊə, ˈdʒɜːbəʊə/ ■ n. a desert-dwelling rodent with very long hind legs that enable it to perform long jumps, found from North Africa to central Asia. [Family Dipodidae: several species.]
–ORIGIN C17: modern Latin, from Arabic *yarbū*ʿ.

jeremiad /ˌdʒɛrɪˈmʌɪəd/ ■ n. a long, mournful complaint or lamentation; a list of woes.
–ORIGIN C18: from French, with ref. to the Lamentations of Jeremiah in the Old Testament.

Jeremiah /ˌdʒɛrɪˈmʌɪə/ ■ n. a person who complains continually or foretells disaster.
–ORIGIN C18: from *Jeremiah* (see **JEREMIAD**).

Jerepigo /ˌdʒɛrəˈpiːɡəʊ/ (also **Jeripigo**) ■ n. S. African a red or white fortified dessert wine.
–ORIGIN from Portuguese *jeropiga*, from Greek *hieros* 'sacred' + *pikros* 'bitter'.

jerk[1] ■ n. **1** a quick, sharp, sudden movement. **2** Weightlifting the raising of a barbell above the head from shoulder level by an abrupt straightening of the arms and legs. **3** informal a contemptibly foolish person. ■ v. **1** move or cause to move with a jerk. **2** Weightlifting raise (a barbell) with a jerk. **3** (**jerk someone around**) N. Amer. informal deal with someone dishonestly or unfairly. **4** (**jerk off**) vulgar slang, chiefly N. Amer. masturbate.
–DERIVATIVES **jerker** n.
–ORIGIN C16 (denoting a stroke with a whip): prob. imitative.

jerk[2] ■ v. (usu. as adj. **jerked**) **1** cure (meat) by cutting it into strips and drying it (originally in the sun). **2** prepare (pork or chicken) by marinating it in spices and barbecuing it over a wood fire. ■ n. jerked meat.
–ORIGIN C18: from Latin American Spanish, from *charqui*, from Quechua *echarqui* 'dried flesh'.

jerkin ■ n. **1** a sleeveless jacket. **2** historical a man's close-fitting skirted jacket, typically of leather.
–ORIGIN C16.

jerky[1] ■ adj. (**-ier**, **-iest**) characterized by abrupt stops and starts.
–DERIVATIVES **jerkily** adv. **jerkiness** n.

jerky[2] ■ n. strips of meat that has been cured by drying; jerked meat.

jeroboam /ˌdʒɛrəˈbəʊəm/ ■ n. a wine bottle with a capacity four times larger than that of an ordinary bottle.
–ORIGIN C19: named after *Jeroboam*, a king of Israel.

Jerry ■ n. (pl. **-ies**) Brit. informal, dated a German or Germans collectively (especially in military contexts).
–ORIGIN FIRST WORLD WAR: prob. an alteration of **GERMAN**.

jerry-built ■ adj. badly or hastily built.
–DERIVATIVES **jerry-builder** n. **jerry-building** n.
–ORIGIN C19: sometimes said to be from the name of a firm of builders in Liverpool, or to allude to the walls of Jericho, which fell down at the sound of Joshua's trumpets (Joshua 6:20).

jerrycan (also **jerrican**) ■ n. a large flat-sided metal container for storing or transporting liquids.
–ORIGIN SECOND WORLD WAR: from **JERRY** + **CAN**[2], because such containers were first used in Germany.

jersey ■ n. (pl. **-eys**) **1** a knitted garment with long sleeves, worn over the upper body. **2** a distinctive shirt worn by a player or competitor in certain sports. **3** a soft knitted fabric. **4** (**Jersey**) an animal of a breed of light brown dairy cattle from Jersey.
–ORIGIN C16 (denoting woollen worsted fabric): from *Jersey*, one of the Channel Islands off the NW coast of France, where the fabric was made.

Jerusalem artichoke ■ n. **1** a knobbly tuber with white flesh, eaten as a vegetable. **2** the tall North American plant, closely related to the sunflower, which produces this tuber. [*Helianthus tuberosus*.]
–ORIGIN C17: *Jerusalem*, alteration of Italian *girasole* 'sunflower'.

jess Falconry ■ n. a short leather strap that is fastened round each leg of a hawk, to which a leash may be attached. ■ v. put a jess or jesses on (a hawk).
–ORIGIN Middle English: from Old French *ges*, from Latin *jactus* 'a throw'.

jessamine /ˈdʒɛsəmɪn/ ■ n. variant spelling of **JASMINE**.

jest ■ n. a joke. ■ v. speak or act in a joking manner.
–ORIGIN Middle English (orig. 'heroic deed', later 'a narrative of such deeds'): from earlier *gest*, from Latin *gesta* 'actions, exploits'.

jester ■ n. historical a professional joker or 'fool' at a medieval court.

Jesuit /ˈdʒɛz(j)ʊɪt/ ■ n. a member of a Roman Catholic order of priests founded by St Ignatius Loyola and others in 1534.
–ORIGIN from modern Latin *Jesuita*, from Christian Latin *Iesus* 'Jesus'.

Jesuitical ■ adj. **1** of or concerning the Jesuits. **2** dissembling or equivocating, in a manner once associated with Jesuits.
–DERIVATIVES **Jesuitically** adv.

Jesus (also **Jesus Christ**) ■ n. the central figure of the Christian religion, considered by Christians to be the Christ or Messiah and the Son of God. ■ exclam. informal expressing irritation, dismay, or surprise.

Jesus freak ■ n. informal, derogatory a fervent evangelical Christian.

jet[1] ■ n. **1** a rapid stream of liquid or gas forced out of a small opening. **2** a jet engine. ▸ an aircraft powered by jet engines. ■ v. (**jetted**, **jetting**) **1** spurt out in a jet. **2** travel by jet aircraft.
–ORIGIN C16: from French *jeter* 'to throw', from Latin *jactare*, from *jacere* 'to throw'.

jet[2] ■ n. **1** a hard black semi-precious variety of lignite. **2** a glossy black colour.
–ORIGIN Middle English: from Old French *jaiet*, from Latin *Gagates*, from Greek *gagatēs* 'from Gagai', a town in Asia Minor.

jeté /ˈʒɛteɪ, ʒəˈteɪ/ ■ n. Ballet a spring from one foot to the other, with the following leg extended backwards while in the air.
–ORIGIN French, from *jeter* 'to throw'.

jet engine

jet engine ■ n. an engine using jet propulsion for forward thrust.

jet lag ■ n. extreme tiredness and other effects felt by a person after a long flight across different time zones.
– DERIVATIVES **jet-lagged** adj.

jetliner ■ n. a large jet aircraft carrying passengers.

jetsam /'dʒets(ə)m/ ■ n. unwanted material or goods that have been thrown overboard from a ship and washed ashore. Compare with FLOTSAM.
– ORIGIN C16 (as *jetson*): contraction of JETTISON.

jet set ■ n. (**the jet set**) informal wealthy people who travel widely and frequently for pleasure.
– DERIVATIVES **jet-setter** n. **jet-setting** adj.

jet ski ■ n. trademark a small jet-propelled vehicle which skims across the surface of water and is ridden in a similar way to a motorcycle. ■ v. (**jet-ski**) ride on a jet ski.
– DERIVATIVES **jet-skier** n. **jet-skiing** n.

jet stream ■ n. 1 any of several narrow variable bands of very strong predominantly westerly air currents encircling the globe several miles above the earth. 2 a flow of exhaust gases from a jet engine.

jettison /'dʒetɪs(ə)n, -z(ə)n/ ■ v. 1 throw or drop from an aircraft or ship. 2 abandon or discard. ■ n. the action of jettisoning.
– ORIGIN Middle English: from Old French *getaison*, from Latin *jactatio(n-)*, from *jactare* (see JET¹).

jetty ■ n. (pl. **-ies**) 1 a landing stage or small pier. 2 a bridge or staircase used by passengers boarding an aircraft. 3 a construction built out into the water to protect a harbour, stretch of coast, or riverbank.
– ORIGIN Middle English: from Old French *jetee*, from *jeter* (see JET¹).

jeu d'esprit /ˌʒɜː dɛˈspriː/ ■ n. (pl. **jeux d'esprit** pronunc. same) a light-hearted display of wit.
– ORIGIN French, 'game of the mind'.

jeunesse dorée /ˌʒɜːnɛs ˈdɔːreɪ/ ■ n. young people of wealth, fashion, and flair.
– ORIGIN C19: French, literally 'gilded youth'.

Jew ■ n. a member of the people whose traditional religion is Judaism and who trace their origins to the ancient Hebrew people of Israel.
– ORIGIN Middle English: from Old French *juiu*, from Greek *Ioudaios*, via Aramaic from Hebrew *yĕhūḏī*, from *yĕhūḏāh* 'Judah'.

jewel ■ n. 1 a precious stone, especially a single crystal or a cut and polished piece of a lustrous or translucent mineral. ▸ (**jewels**) pieces of jewellery. ▸ a hard precious stone used as a bearing in a watch, compass, etc. 2 a highly valued person or thing.
– PHRASES **the jewel in the** (or **one's**) **crown** the most valuable or successful part of something.
– DERIVATIVES **jewelled** (US **jeweled**) adj.
– ORIGIN Middle English: from Old French *joel*, from *jeu* 'game, play', from Latin *jocus* 'jest'.

jewel beetle ■ n. a chiefly tropical beetle that has bold metallic colours and patterns, the larvae of which are mainly wood-borers and may be serious pests of wood. [Family Buprestidae.]

jewel box ■ n. 1 a box for the storage of jewellery. 2 (also **jewel case**) a storage box for a compact disc.

jewelfish ■ n. (pl. same or **-fishes**) a brightly coloured African freshwater cichlid. [Genus *Hemichromis*: several species.]

jeweller (US **jeweler**) ■ n. a person or company that makes or sells jewels or jewellery.

jewellery (US also **jewelry**) ■ n. personal ornaments, such as necklaces, rings, or bracelets, that are made from or contain jewels and precious metal.

Jewess ■ n. a Jewish woman or girl.

jewfish ■ n. (pl. same or **-fishes**) a large sporting or food fish of warm coastal waters. [*Epinephelus itajara* (N. America) and other species elsewhere.]

Jewish¹ ■ adj. relating to, associated with, or denoting Jews or Judaism.
– DERIVATIVES **Jewishly** adv. **Jewishness** n.

Jewish² ■ adj. S. African informal elegantly dressed.
– ORIGIN from Isicamtho *iJuwish* 'stylish, excellent', from *Jewish*.

Jewish New Year ■ n. another term for ROSH HASHANA.

Jewry /'dʒʊəri/ ■ n. (pl. **-ies**) 1 Jews collectively. 2 historical a Jewish quarter in a town or city.

Jew's harp ■ n. a small lyre-shaped musical instrument held between the teeth and struck with a finger.

Jezebel /'dʒɛzəbɛl/ ■ n. a shameless or immoral woman.
– ORIGIN C16: *Jezebel*, wife of Ahab in the Bible.

jib¹ ■ n. 1 Nautical a triangular staysail set forward of the mast. 2 the projecting arm of a crane.
– ORIGIN C17.

jib² ■ v. (**jibbed, jibbing**) 1 (usu. **jib at**) (of a person) be unwilling to do or accept something. 2 (of a horse) stop and refuse to go on.
– DERIVATIVES **jibber** n.
– ORIGIN C19: perhaps rel. to French *regimber* (earlier *regiber*) 'to buck, rear'; cf. JIBE¹.

jib boom ■ n. Nautical a spar run out forward as an extension of the bowsprit.

jibe¹ (also **gibe**) ■ n. an insulting or mocking remark. ■ v. make jibes.
– ORIGIN C16: perhaps from Old French *giber* 'handle roughly' (in modern dialect 'kick').

jibe² ■ v.& n. US variant of GYBE.

jibe³ ■ v. informal, chiefly N. Amer. be in accordance; agree.
– ORIGIN C19.

jib sheet ■ n. Nautical a rope by which a jib is trimmed.

jiffy (also **jiff**) ■ n. informal a moment.
– ORIGIN C18.

Jiffy bag ■ n. 1 S. African a clear plastic bag used to store or freeze food. 2 trademark a padded envelope for protecting fragile items in the post.

jig ■ n. 1 a lively dance with leaping movements. ▸ a piece of music for a jig, typically in compound time. 2 a device that guides tools and holds materials or parts securely. 3 Fishing a type of artificial bait that is jerked up and down through the water. ■ v. (**jigged, jigging**) 1 dance a jig. 2 move up and down with a quick jerky motion. 3 equip (a workshop) with a jig or jigs. 4 fish with a jig.
– ORIGIN C16.

jigger¹ ■ n. 1 a machine or vehicle with a part that rocks or moves to and fro. 2 a person who dances a jig. 3 a small sail set at the stern of a ship. 4 a small tackle consisting of a double and single block with a rope. 5 a measure or small glass of spirits or wine. 6 informal a rest for a billiard cue. 7 Golf, dated a metal golf club with a narrow face. ■ v. informal rearrange or tamper with.

jigger² ■ n. variant spelling of CHIGGER.

jiggered ■ adj. Brit. informal damaged, broken, or exhausted.
– PHRASES **I'll be jiggered** expressing astonishment.
– ORIGIN C19: from JIGGER¹; prob. euphemism for *buggered*.

jiggery-pokery ■ n. informal, chiefly Brit. deceitful or dishonest behaviour.
– ORIGIN C19: prob. a var. of Scots *joukery-pawkery*, from *jouk* 'dodge, skulk'.

jiggle ■ v. move or cause to move lightly and quickly from side to side or up and down. ■ n. an instance of jiggling.
– DERIVATIVES **jiggly** adj.
– ORIGIN C19: partly an alteration of JOGGLE¹, reinforced by JIG.

jigsaw ■ n. 1 a puzzle consisting of a picture printed on cardboard or wood and cut into numerous interlocking shapes that have to be fitted together. 2 a machine saw with a fine blade enabling it to cut curved lines in a sheet of wood, metal, etc.

jihad /dʒɪˈhɑːd, -ˈhad/ (also **jehad**) ■ n. a holy war undertaken by Muslims against unbelievers.
– DERIVATIVES **jihadist** n.
– ORIGIN from Arabic *jihād* 'effort'.

jihadi /dʒɪˈhɑːdi/ (also **jehadi**) ■ n. (pl. **jihadis**) a person involved in a jihad; an Islamic militant.
– ORIGIN from Arabic *jihādi*, from *jihād* (see JIHAD).

jilt ■ v. abruptly break a relationship with (a lover). ■ n. archaic a person, especially a woman, who capriciously rejects a lover.
– ORIGIN C17 ('deceive, trick').

Jim Crow ■ n. US **1** the former practice of segregating black people in the US. **2** offensive a black person. **3** an implement for straightening iron bars or bending rails by screw pressure.
– DERIVATIVES **Jim Crowism** n.
– ORIGIN C19: the name of a black character in a plantation song.

jim-jams[1] ■ pl. n. informal a fit of depression or nervousness.
– ORIGIN C16: fanciful reduplication.

jim-jams[2] ■ pl. n. Brit. informal pyjamas.
– ORIGIN C20: abbrev. of *pie-jim-jams*, alteration of PYJAMAS.

jimmy ■ n. & v. North American spelling of JEMMY.

jingle ■ n. **1** a light, loose ringing sound such as that made by metal objects being shaken together. **2** a short easily remembered slogan, verse, or tune. ■ v. **1** make or cause to make a jingle. **2** (of writing) be full of alliteration or rhymes.
– DERIVATIVES **jingler** n. **jingly** adj.
– ORIGIN Middle English: imitative.

jingo /ˈdʒɪŋɡəʊ/ ■ n. (pl. -oes) dated, chiefly derogatory a vociferous supporter of a patriotic war policy.
– PHRASES **by jingo!** an exclamation of surprise.
– ORIGIN C17: from a popular song adopted by those supporting the sending of a British fleet into Turkish waters to resist Russia in 1878.

jingoism ■ n. chiefly derogatory extreme patriotism, especially in the form of aggressive foreign policy.
– DERIVATIVES **jingoist** n. **jingoistic** adj.

jink /dʒɪŋk/ ■ v. change direction suddenly and nimbly. ■ n. a sudden quick change of direction.
– ORIGIN C17 (orig. Scots as *high jinks*, denoting antics at drinking parties): prob. symbolic of nimble motion.

jinn /dʒɪn/ (also **djinn**) ■ n. (pl. same or **jinns**) (in Arabian and Muslim mythology) an intelligent spirit able to appear in human and animal form.
– ORIGIN from Arabic *jinnī*, pl. *jinn*.

jinx ■ n. a person or thing that brings bad luck. ■ v. (usu. **be jinxed**) bring bad luck to.
– ORIGIN C20: prob. a var. of *jynx* 'wryneck' (because the bird was used in witchcraft).

jislaaik /ˈjɪslʌɪk/ ■ exclam. S. African informal expressing surprise, admiration, or consternation.
– ORIGIN Afrikaans.

JIT ■ abbrev. (of manufacturing systems) just-in-time.

jit /dʒɪt/ (also **jit jive**) ■ n. a style of dance music popular in Zimbabwe.
– ORIGIN Shona, from *jit* 'to dance'.

jitney /ˈdʒɪtni/ ■ n. (pl. **-eys**) N. Amer. informal a small bus carrying passengers for a low fare.
– ORIGIN C20 (orig. denoting a five-cent piece).

jitter informal ■ n. **1** (**the jitters**) a feeling of extreme nervousness. **2** slight, irregular movement, variation, or unsteadiness in an electrical signal or electronic device. ■ v. **1** act nervously. **2** (of a signal or device) suffer from jitter.
– DERIVATIVES **jitteriness** n. **jittery** adj.
– ORIGIN 1920S.

jitterbug ■ n. a fast dance performed to swing music, popular in the 1940s. ■ v. (**-bugged**, **-bugging**) dance the jitterbug.

jiu-jitsu ■ n. variant spelling of JU-JITSU.

jive ■ n. **1** a style of lively dance popular in the 1940s and 1950s, performed to swing music or rock and roll. **2** (also **township jive**) a style of dance music popular in South Africa. **3** (also **jive talk**) a form of slang associated with black American jazz musicians. **4** informal, chiefly N. Amer. deceptive or worthless talk. ■ v. **1** dance the jive. **2** N. Amer. informal taunt or sneer at. **3** informal, chiefly N. Amer. talk nonsense. ■ adj. N. Amer. informal deceitful or worthless.
– DERIVATIVES **jiver** n. **jivey** adj.
– ORIGIN 1920S (orig. US): the musical sense 'jazz' gave rise to 'dance performed to jazz' (1940s).

jizz ■ n. informal (among birdwatchers and naturalists) the characteristic impression given by a particular species of animal or plant.
– ORIGIN 1920S.

Jnr ■ abbrev. Junior (in names).

job ■ n. **1** a paid position of regular employment. **2** a task or piece of work. ▶ a responsibility or duty. ▶ informal a crime, especially a robbery. **3** informal a procedure to improve the appearance of something: *a nose job*. **4** informal a thing of a specified nature: *the car was a fast job*. ■ v. (**jobbed**, **jobbing**) **1** [usu. as adj. **jobbing**] do casual or occasional work. **2** buy and sell (stocks) as a broker-dealer, especially on a small scale. **3** N. Amer. informal cheat; betray. **4** archaic turn a public office or a position of trust to private advantage.
– PHRASES **be** (or **have**) **a job** to have or have a difficult task. **a good job** informal a fortunate fact or circumstance. **jobs for the boys** the practice of giving paid employment to one's friends, supporters, or relations. **just the job** informal exactly what is needed. **on the job 1** while working; at work. **2** Brit. informal engaged in sexual intercourse.
– DERIVATIVES **jobless** adj. **joblessness** n.
– ORIGIN C16.

jobber ■ n. **1** (in the UK) a principal or wholesaler dealing only on the Stock Exchange with brokers, not directly with the public (term officially replaced by broker-dealer in 1986). **2** N. Amer. a wholesaler. **3** a person who does casual or occasional work.

jobbery ■ n. the practice of using a public office or position of trust for one's own gain or advantage.

jobbie ■ n. informal **1** an object or product of a specified kind: *these computer jobbies*. **2** a piece of excrement.

jobcentre ■ n. (in the UK) a government office in a local area, giving information about available jobs and administering benefits to unemployed people.

job club ■ n. (in the UK) an organization providing support and practical help for the long-term unemployed in seeking work.

job control language ■ n. Computing a language enabling the user to define the tasks to be undertaken by the operating system.

job lot ■ n. a batch of articles sold or bought at one time, especially at a discount.

job reservation ■ n. S. African historical the official policy of protecting skilled positions for a particular ethnic group, especially white people.

Job's comforter /dʒəʊbz/ ■ n. a person who aggravates distress under the guise of giving comfort.
– ORIGIN C18: alluding to the biblical story (Job 16:2) of the patriarch *Job*.

job-share ■ v. (of two part-time employees) jointly do a full-time job. ■ n. an arrangement of such a kind.
– DERIVATIVES **job-sharer** n.

Job's tears /dʒəʊbz/ ■ pl. n. a SE Asian grass which bears its seeds inside shiny pear-shaped receptacles, which are sometimes used as beads. [*Coix lacryma-jobi*.]
– ORIGIN C16: named after the biblical patriarch *Job*.

jobsworth ■ n. Brit. informal an official who mindlessly upholds petty rules.
– ORIGIN 1970S: from 'it's more than my *job's worth* (not) to...'.

Jock ■ n. informal, often offensive a Scotsman.
– ORIGIN C16: Scots form of the given name *Jack* (see JACK).

jock[1] ■ n. informal **1** a disc jockey. **2** N. Amer. an enthusiast or participant in a specified activity: *a computer jock*.
– ORIGIN C18 (denoting a jockey): abbrev.

jock[2] ■ n. informal **1** N. Amer. another term for JOCKSTRAP. **2** an enthusiastic male athlete or sports fan.
– DERIVATIVES **jockish** adj.

jockey ■ n. (pl. **-eys**) a professional rider in horse races. ■ v. (**-eys**, **-eyed**) **1** struggle to gain or achieve something. **2** handle or manipulate in a skilful manner.
– DERIVATIVES **jockeyship** n.
– ORIGIN C16: diminutive of JOCK, orig. denoting an ordinary man, later 'mounted courier' and 'horse dealer'.

jockey cap ■ n. a strengthened cap with a long peak of a kind worn by jockeys.

jock itch

jock itch ■ n. N. Amer. informal a fungal infection of the groin area.
– ORIGIN 1970s: *jock* from **JOCKSTRAP**.

jockstrap ■ n. a support or protection for the male genitals, worn especially by sportsmen.
– ORIGIN C19: from slang *jock* 'genitals' + **STRAP**.

jocose /dʒəˈkəʊs/ ■ adj. formal playful or humorous.
– DERIVATIVES **jocosely** adv. **jocoseness** n. **jocosity** /-ˈkɒsɪti/ n. (pl. **-ies**).
– ORIGIN C17: from Latin *jocosus*, from *jocus* 'joke, wordplay'.

jocular /ˈdʒɒkjʊlə/ ■ adj. fond of or characterized by joking; humorous.
– DERIVATIVES **jocularity** n. **jocularly** adv.
– ORIGIN C17: from Latin *jocularis*, from *joculus*, diminutive of *jocus* (see **JOCOSE**).

jocund /ˈdʒɒk(ə)nd, ˈdʒəʊk-/ ■ adj. formal cheerful and light-hearted.
– DERIVATIVES **jocundity** n. (pl. **-ies**). **jocundly** adv.
– ORIGIN Middle English: from Latin *jocundus*, var. (influenced by *jocus* 'joke') of *jucundus* 'pleasant, agreeable'.

jodhpurs /ˈdʒɒdpəz/ ■ pl. n. trousers worn for horse riding that are close-fitting below the knee and have reinforced patches on the inside of the leg.
– ORIGIN C19: named after the Indian city of *Jodhpur*.

joe ■ n. an ordinary man.
– ORIGIN C19: familiar form of the given name *Joseph*.

Joe Bloggs (N. Amer. **Joe Blow**) ■ n. informal a name used to represent the average person.

Joe Public ■ n. Brit. informal a name used to represent the general public.

joey ■ n. (pl. **-eys**) Austral. 1 a young kangaroo, wallaby, or possum. 2 informal a baby or young child.
– ORIGIN from Aboriginal *joè*.

jog ■ v. (**jogged**, **jogging**) 1 run at a steady, gentle pace, especially as a form of exercise. ▸ (of a horse) move at a slow trot. ▸ (**jog along/on**) continue in a steady, uneventful way. 2 nudge or knock slightly. ▸ trigger; stimulate. ■ n. 1 a spell of jogging. 2 a gentle running pace. 3 a slight push or nudge.
– ORIGIN Middle English ('stab, pierce'): var. of **JAG**[1].

jogger ■ n. 1 a person who jogs. 2 (**joggers**) tracksuit trousers worn for jogging.

joggle[1] ■ v. move or cause to move with repeated small bobs or jerks. ■ n. a joggling movement.
– ORIGIN C16: from **JOG**.

joggle[2] ■ n. a joint between two pieces of stone, concrete, or timber, consisting of a projection in one of the pieces fitting into a notch in the other, or a small piece let in between the two. ■ v. join with a joggle.
– ORIGIN C18: perhaps rel. to **JAG**[1].

jog-shuttle ■ n. a facility on some video recorders which allows the speed at which the tape is played to be varied.

jogtrot ■ n. a slow trot.

john ■ n. informal 1 chiefly N. Amer. a toilet. 2 a prostitute's client.
– ORIGIN C20: from the given name *John*.

John Brown ■ n. a deep-bodied edible marine fish with a conspicuous blue eye that occurs along the south-eastern coast of South Africa. [*Gymnocrotaphus curvidens*.]
– ORIGIN 1900s: translation of Afrikaans *jan bruin*, perhaps orig. from Dutch *tambrijn* and Malay *tambera* 'bronze', from the colour of the fish.

John Bull ■ n. a personification of England or the typical Englishman.
– ORIGIN C18: from the name of a character in the satire by the Scottish writer John Arbuthnot, *Law is a Bottomless Pit; or, the History of John Bull* (1712).

John Doe ■ n. 1 Law, chiefly N. Amer. an anonymous party in a legal action. 2 N. Amer. informal a hypothetical average man.
– ORIGIN C18: orig. in legal use as a name for a fictitious plaintiff, corresponding to *Richard Roe*, a fictitious defendant.

John Dory ■ n. (pl. **-ies**) an edible dory (fish) of the eastern Atlantic and Mediterranean, with a black oval mark on each side and yellow spines. [*Zeus faber*.]
– ORIGIN C18: adaptation of the orig. name **DORY** influenced by the name of the privateer *John Dory*, the subject of a popular song.

Johne's disease /ˈjəʊnəz/ ■ n. a form of chronic enteritis in cattle and sheep, caused by a mycobacterium.
– ORIGIN C20: named after the German veterinary surgeon Heinrich A. *Johne*.

johnny ■ n. (pl. **-ies**) Brit. informal 1 a man. 2 a condom.
– ORIGIN C17: familiar form of the given name *John*.

johnny-come-lately ■ n. informal a newcomer or late starter.

John Q. Public ■ n. North American term for **JOE PUBLIC**.

joie de vivre /ˌʒwɑː də ˈviːvr(ə)/ ■ n. exuberant enjoyment of life.
– ORIGIN French, 'joy of living'.

join ■ v. 1 link or become linked or connected to. ▸ unite. 2 become a member or employee of. ▸ take part in. ▸ (**join up**) become a member of the armed forces. ▸ come into the company of. ▸ support in an activity. ■ n. a place where two or more things are joined.
– PHRASES **join battle** formal begin fighting. **join forces** combine efforts.
– DERIVATIVES **joinable** adj.
– ORIGIN Middle English: from Old French *joindre*, from Latin *jungere* 'to join'.

joinder /ˈdʒɔɪndə/ ■ n. Law the action of bringing together.
– ORIGIN Middle English: from Anglo-Norman French, from Old French *joindre* 'to join'.

joiner ■ n. 1 a person who constructs the wooden components of a building. 2 informal a person who readily joins groups. ▸ S. African historical, derogatory a term used by the Boers of Afrikaners who joined the British forces during the Anglo-Boer War of 1899–1902.

joinery ■ n. the wooden components of a building collectively.

joint ■ n. 1 a point at which parts are joined. ▸ Geology a break or fracture in a mass of rock. ▸ a piece of flexible material forming the hinge of a book cover. 2 a structure in a body by which two bones are fitted together. ▸ a section of a body or limb between connecting places. ▸ a large piece of meat. ▸ the part of a plant stem from which a leaf or branch grows. ▸ a section of a plant stem between such parts. 3 informal an establishment of a specified kind: *a burger joint*. ▸ (**the joint**) N. Amer. prison. 4 informal a cannabis cigarette. ■ adj. shared, held, or made by two or more people. ▸ sharing in an achievement or activity. ■ v. 1 provide or fasten with joints. ▸ prepare (a board) to be joined to another by planing its edge. 2 point (masonry or brickwork). 3 cut (the body of an animal) into joints.
– PHRASES **out of joint** (of a joint of the body) dislocated. ▸ in a state of disorder or disorientation.
– DERIVATIVES **jointless** adj. **jointly** adv.
– ORIGIN Middle English: from Old French *joindre* (see **JOIN**).

joint and several ■ adj. (of a legal obligation) undertaken by two or more people, each having liability for the whole.

jointed cactus ■ n. a low-growing South American cactus with jointed stems and long sharp spines, an invasive weed in South Africa. [*Opuntia aurantiaca*.]

jointer ■ n. 1 a plane for preparing a wooden edge for joining to another. 2 a tool for pointing masonry or brickwork. 3 a person who joints pipes or wires.

joint-stock company ■ n. Finance a company whose stock is owned jointly by the shareholders.

joist /dʒɔɪst/ ■ n. a length of timber or steel supporting part of the structure of a building.
– DERIVATIVES **joisted** adj.
– ORIGIN Middle English *giste*, from Old French, 'beam supporting a bridge', from Latin *jacere* 'lie down'.

jojoba /həˈhəʊbə, həʊ-/ ■ n. (also **jojoba oil**) an oil extracted from the seeds of a North American shrub, widely used in cosmetics. ▸ the leathery-leaved evergreen shrub that produces these seeds. [*Simmondsia chinensis*.]
– ORIGIN C20: from Mexican Spanish.

joke ■ n. **1** a thing said to cause amusement. ▸ a trick played for fun. **2** informal a ridiculously inadequate person or thing. ■ v. make jokes.
– PHRASES **be no joke** informal be a serious or difficult matter. **be beyond a joke** informal be serious or worrying.
– DERIVATIVES **jokey** (also **joky**) adj. **jokily** adv. **jokiness** n. **joking** adj. **jokingly** adv.
– ORIGIN C17: perhaps from Latin *jocus* 'jest, wordplay'.

joker ■ n. **1** a person who is fond of joking. ▸ informal a foolish or inept person. **2** a playing card with the figure of a jester, used as a wild card.
– PHRASES **the joker in the pack** an unpredictable person or factor.

jol S. African informal ■ n. a celebratory event or party. ▸ a good time. ■ v. (**jolled**, **jolling**) **1** have a good time; party. ▸ engage in a love affair. **2** go; hurry.
– DERIVATIVES **joller** n.
– ORIGIN from Afrikaans, 'dance, party'.

jollification ■ n. merrymaking.

jollity ■ n. (pl. **-ies**) lively and cheerful activity. ▸ the quality of being jolly.

jolly[1] ■ adj. (**-ier**, **-iest**) happy and cheerful. ▸ informal, dated lively and entertaining. ■ v. (**-ies**, **-ied**) informal encourage in a friendly way. ▸ (**jolly someone/thing up**) make someone or something more jolly. ■ adv. Brit. informal very. ■ n. (pl. **-ies**) Brit. informal a party or celebration.
– PHRASES **get one's jollies** informal have fun. **jolly well** Brit. informal used for emphasis: *I should jolly well hope so!*
– DERIVATIVES **jollily** adv. **jolliness** n.
– ORIGIN Middle English: from Old French *jolif*, an earlier form of *joli* 'pretty', perhaps from Old Norse *jól* (see YULE).

jolly[2] (also **jolly boat**) ■ n. (pl. **-ies**) a clinker-built ship's boat that is smaller than a cutter.
– ORIGIN C18: perhaps rel. to YAWL.

Jolly Roger ■ n. a pirate's flag with a white skull and crossbones on a black background.
– ORIGIN C18.

jolt /dʒəʊlt, dʒɒlt/ ■ v. **1** push or shake abruptly and roughly. **2** shock (someone) in order to make them act or change. ■ n. **1** an act of jolting. **2** a surprise or shock.
– DERIVATIVES **jolty** adj.
– ORIGIN C16.

jondolo ■ n. variant spelling of MJONDOLO.

Joneses ■ n. (in phr. **keep up with the Joneses**) strive not be outdone by one's neighbours.
– ORIGIN C20: from the surname *Jones*.

jong /jɒŋ/ S. African ■ n. chiefly historical a young black male servant. ▸ offensive a black man. ■ exclam. informal expressing surprise, delight, or frustration.
– ORIGIN Afrikaans, from earlier S. African Dutch *jongen* 'lad'.

jongleur /dʒɒ̃ˈɡlə:/ ■ n. historical an itinerant minstrel.
– ORIGIN French, var. of *jougleur* 'juggler', earlier *jogleor* 'pleasant, smiling', from Latin *joculator* 'joker'.

jonquil /ˈdʒɒŋkwɪl, ˈdʒɒn-/ ■ n. a narcissus with small fragrant yellow flowers and cylindrical leaves. [*Narcissus jonquilla*.]
– ORIGIN C17: from modern Latin *jonquilla*, from Spanish *junquillo*, diminutive of *junco*, from Latin *juncus* 'rush, reed'.

Jordanian ■ n. a native or inhabitant of Jordan. ■ adj. of or relating to Jordan or the River Jordan in the Middle East.

josh ■ v. informal tease playfully; banter.
– ORIGIN C19.

Joshua tree ■ n. a tall branching yucca of SW North America, with clusters of spiky leaves. [*Yucca brevifolia*.]
– ORIGIN C19: apparently from *Joshua* (Joshua 8:18), the plant being likened to a man with a spear.

joss ■ n. a Chinese idol.
– ORIGIN C18: from Javanese *dejos*, from obsolete Portuguese *deos*, from Latin *deus* 'god'.

joss stick ■ n. a thin stick of a fragrant substance, burnt as incense.

jostle ■ v. push or bump against roughly. ▸ (**jostle for**) struggle or compete forcefully for. ■ n. the action of jostling.
– ORIGIN Middle English *justle*, from *just*, an earlier form of JOUST.

jot ■ v. (**jotted**, **jotting**) write quickly. ■ n. [usu. with neg.] a very small amount.
– ORIGIN C15: from Greek *iōta*, the smallest letter of the Greek alphabet (see IOTA).

jotter ■ n. a small notebook.

jotting ■ n. a brief note.

joule /dʒuːl/ (abbrev.: **J**) ■ n. the SI unit of work or energy, equal to the work done by a force of one newton when its point of application moves one metre in the direction of action of the force.
– ORIGIN C19: named after the English physicist James P. Joule.

journal /ˈdʒəːn(ə)l/ ■ n. **1** a newspaper or magazine dealing with a particular subject. **2** a diary. ▸ Nautical a log-book. ▸ (**the Journals**) a record of the daily proceedings in the British Houses of Parliament. ▸ (in bookkeeping) a daily record of business transactions. **3** the part of a shaft or axle that rests on bearings.
– ORIGIN Middle English: from Old French *jurnal*, from late Latin *diurnalis* (see DIURNAL).

journalese ■ n. informal a hackneyed writing style supposedly characteristic of journalists.

journalism ■ n. the activity or profession of being a journalist.

journalist ■ n. a person who writes for newspapers or magazines or prepares news to be broadcast on radio or television.
– DERIVATIVES **journalistic** adj. **journalistically** adv.

journalize (also **-ise**) ■ v. dated enter (information) in a journal.

journey ■ n. (pl. **-eys**) an act of travelling from one place to another. ■ v. (**-eys**, **-eyed**) travel.
– DERIVATIVES **journeyer** n.
– ORIGIN Middle English: from Old French *jornee* 'day, a day's travel, a day's work', from Latin *diurnum* 'daily portion', from *diurnus* (see DIURNAL).

journeyman ■ n. (pl. **-men**) **1** a skilled worker who is employed by another. **2** a worker who is reliable but not outstanding.
– ORIGIN Middle English: from JOURNEY (in the obsolete sense 'day's work') + MAN; so named because the journeyman was paid by the day.

journo ■ n. (pl. **-os**) informal a journalist.

joust /dʒaʊst/ ■ v. **1** [often as noun **jousting**] (of a medieval knight) engage in a contest in which two opponents on horseback fight with lances. **2** compete for superiority. ■ n. a jousting contest.
– DERIVATIVES **jouster** n.
– ORIGIN Middle English: from Old French *jouster* 'bring together', from Latin *juxta* 'near'.

Jove /dʒəʊv/ ■ n. (in phr. **by Jove**) dated used for emphasis or to indicate surprise.
– ORIGIN from *Jove*, the chief of the Roman gods, equivalent to Jupiter.

jovial /ˈdʒəʊvɪəl, -vj(ə)l/ ■ adj. cheerful and friendly.
– DERIVATIVES **joviality** n. **jovially** adv.
– ORIGIN C16: from late Latin *jovialis* 'of Jupiter', with ref. to the supposed influence of the planet Jupiter on those born under it.

Jovian /ˈdʒəʊvɪən/ ■ adj. **1** (in Roman mythology) of or like the god Jove (or Jupiter). **2** of, relating to, or resembling the planet Jupiter.

jowl ■ n. the lower part of a cheek, especially when fleshy or drooping. ▸ N. Amer. the cheek of a pig as meat. ▸ the dewlap of cattle or wattle of birds.
– DERIVATIVES **-jowled** adj. **jowly** adj.
– ORIGIN Old English *ceole*, partly merged with Old English *ceafl* 'jaw'.

joy ■ n. **1** a feeling of great pleasure and happiness. ▸ a cause of joy. **2** [usu. with neg.] informal success or satisfaction. ■ v. poetic/literary rejoice.
– PHRASES **be full of the joys of spring** be lively and cheerful. **wish someone joy** Brit., chiefly ironic congratulate someone.
– DERIVATIVES **joyless** adj. **joylessly** adv.
– ORIGIN Middle English: from Old French *joie*, from Latin *gaudium*, from *gaudere* 'rejoice'.

joyful

joyful ■ adj. feeling or causing joy.
– DERIVATIVES **joyfully** adv. **joyfulness** n.

joyous ■ adj. chiefly poetic/literary full of happiness and joy.
– DERIVATIVES **joyously** adv. **joyousness** n.

joypad ■ n. a device for a computer games console which uses buttons to control an image on the screen.
– ORIGIN C20: blend of **JOYSTICK** and **KEYPAD**.

joyride ■ n. informal **1** a fast ride in a stolen vehicle. **2** a ride for enjoyment.
– DERIVATIVES **joyrider** n. **joyriding** n.

joystick ■ n. informal **1** the control column of an aircraft. **2** a lever for controlling the movement of an image on a computer screen.

JP ■ abbrev. Justice of the Peace.

JPEG /ˈdʒeɪpɛg/ ■ n. Computing a format for compressing images.
– ORIGIN 1990s: abbrev. of *Joint Photographic Experts Group*.

Jr ■ abbrev. (in names) junior.

JSC ■ abbrev. Judicial Service Commission.

JSE ■ abbrev. **1** JSE Securities Exchange South Africa. **2** historical Johannesburg Stock Exchange.

jubilant ■ adj. happy and triumphant.
– DERIVATIVES **jubilance** n. **jubilantly** adv.
– ORIGIN C17: from Latin *jubilare* (see **JUBILATION**).

Jubilate /ˌdʒuːbɪˈlɑːteɪ/ ■ n. Psalm 100, beginning *Jubilate deo*, especially as used as a canticle.
– ORIGIN Latin, 'shout for joy!', imperative of *jubilare* (see **JUBILATION**).

jubilation /ˌdʒuːbɪˈleɪʃ(ə)n/ ■ n. a feeling of great happiness and triumph.
– ORIGIN Middle English: from Latin *jubilare* 'shout for joy'.

jubilee ■ n. **1** a special anniversary, especially one celebrating twenty-five or fifty years of something. **2** Judaism a year of emancipation and restoration, kept every fifty years. **3** a period of remission from the penal consequences of sin, granted by the Roman Catholic Church under certain conditions for a year, at intervals of twenty-five years.
– ORIGIN Middle English: from late Latin *jubilaeus (annus)* '(year) of jubilee', from Hebrew *yōbēl*, orig. 'ram's-horn trumpet', with which the jubilee was proclaimed.

Judaean /dʒuːˈdiːən/ ■ n. a native or inhabitant of Judea, the southern part of ancient Palestine. ■ adj. of or relating to Judea.

Judaeo- /dʒuːˈdiːəʊ/ (US **Judeo-**) ■ comb. form **1** Jewish; Jewish and ...: *Judaeo-Christian*. **2** relating to Judaea.
– ORIGIN from Latin *Judaeus* 'Jewish'.

Judaic /dʒuːˈdeɪɪk/ ■ adj. of or relating to Judaism or the ancient Jews.

Judaism /ˈdʒuːdeɪɪz(ə)m/ ■ n. **1** the monotheistic religion of the Jews, based on the Old Testament and the Talmud. **2** Jews collectively.
– DERIVATIVES **Judaist** n.
– ORIGIN Middle English: from late Latin *Judaismus*, from Greek *Ioudaïsmos*, from *Ioudaios* (see **JEW**).

Judaize /ˈdʒuːdeɪʌɪz/ (also **-ise**) ■ v. **1** make Jewish. **2** follow Jewish customs or religious rites.
– DERIVATIVES **Judaization** (also **-isation**) n.

Judas /ˈdʒuːdəs/ ■ n. a person who betrays a friend.
– ORIGIN from the name of *Judas* Iscariot, the disciple who betrayed Christ.

Judas tree ■ n. a Mediterranean tree of the pea family, with purple flowers that appear before the rounded leaves. [*Cercis siliquastrum*.]

judder ■ v. shake and vibrate rapidly and forcefully. ■ n. an instance of juddering.
– DERIVATIVES **juddery** adj.
– ORIGIN 1930s: imitative; cf. **SHUDDER**.

judenrein /ˈjuːd(ə)nrʌɪn/ ■ adj. (chiefly in Nazi Germany) denoting a place from which Jews are excluded.
– ORIGIN German, 'free of Jews'.

Judeo- ■ comb. form US spelling of **JUDAEO-**.

judge ■ n. a public officer appointed to decide cases in a law court. ▶ a person who decides the results of a competition. ▶ a person able or qualified to give an opinion: *a good judge of character*. ■ v. form an opinion about. ▶ give a verdict on in a law court. ▶ decide the results of.
– DERIVATIVES **judgeship** n.
– ORIGIN Middle English: from Old French *juge* (n.), *juger* (v.), from Latin *judex*, from *jus* 'law' + *dicere* 'to say'.

judgement (also **judgment**) ■ n. **1** the ability to make considered decisions or form sensible opinions. ▶ an opinion or conclusion. ▶ a decision of a law court or judge. **2** formal or humorous a misfortune viewed as a divine punishment.
– PHRASES **against one's better judgement** contrary to what one feels to be wise. **sit in judgement** assume the right to judge someone, especially critically.

> **USAGE**
> The normal spelling in general contexts is **judgement**. However, the spelling **judgment** is conventional in legal contexts, and in North American English.

judgemental (also **judgmental**) ■ adj. **1** of or concerning the use of judgement. **2** having an excessively critical point of view.
– DERIVATIVES **judgementally** adv.

Judgement Day ■ n. the time of the Last Judgement.

judgement in default ■ n. Law judgement awarded to the plaintiff on the defendant's failure to plead.

Judges' Rules ■ pl. n. English Law rules regarding the admissibility of an accused's statements as evidence.

judicature /ˈdʒuːdɪkəˌtʃə, dʒʊˈdɪk-/ ■ n. **1** the administration of justice. **2** (**the judicature**) the judiciary.
– DERIVATIVES **judicatory** adj.
– ORIGIN C16: from medieval Latin *judicatura*, from Latin *judicare* 'to judge'.

judicial /dʒuːˈdɪʃ(ə)l/ ■ adj. of, by, or appropriate to a law court or judge.
– DERIVATIVES **judicially** adv.
– ORIGIN Middle English: from Latin *judicialis*, from *judicium* 'judgement', from *judex* (see **JUDGE**).

judicial review ■ n. **1** (in the UK and South Africa) a procedure by which a court can pronounce on an administrative action by a public body. **2** (in the US) review by the Supreme Court of the constitutional validity of a legislative act.

judicial separation ■ n. another term for **LEGAL SEPARATION** (in sense 1).

judiciary /dʒuːˈdɪʃ(ə)ri/ ■ n. (pl. **-ies**) (usu. **the judiciary**) the judicial authorities of a country.

judicious /dʒuːˈdɪʃəs/ ■ adj. having or done with good judgement.
– DERIVATIVES **judiciously** adv. **judiciousness** n.
– ORIGIN C16: from Latin *judicium* (see **JUDICIAL**).

judo ■ n. a sport of unarmed combat derived from ju-jitsu, using holds and leverage to unbalance the opponent.
– DERIVATIVES **judoist** n.
– ORIGIN C19: Japanese, from *jū* 'gentle' + *dō* 'way'.

judoka /ˈdʒuːdəʊˌkə/ ■ n. a person who practises judo.
– ORIGIN Japanese, from **JUDO** + *-ka* 'person, profession'.

jug ■ n. **1** a cylindrical container with a handle and a lip, for holding and pouring liquids. ▶ N. Amer. a large container for liquids, with a narrow mouth. **2** (**the jug**) informal prison. **3** (**jugs**) vulgar slang a woman's breasts. ■ v. (**jugged**, **jugging**) [usu. as adj. **jugged**] stew or boil (a hare or rabbit) in a covered container.
– DERIVATIVES **jugful** n. (pl. **-fuls**).
– ORIGIN C16: perhaps from *Jug*, familiar form of the given names *Joan*, *Joanna*, and *Jenny*.

jug band ■ n. a group of jazz, blues, or folk musicians using simple or improvised instruments such as jugs and washboards.

juggernaut /ˈdʒʌɡənɔːt/ ■ n. **1** Brit. a large heavy vehicle, especially an articulated truck. **2** a huge and overwhelming force.
– ORIGIN C19: from Sanskrit *Jagannātha* 'Lord of the world', the name of an image of the Hindu god Krishna carried in procession on a heavy chariot.

juggle ▪ v. **1** continuously toss into the air and catch a number of objects so as to keep at least one in the air at any time. **2** cope with by adroitly balancing (several activities). **3** misrepresent (facts). ▪ n. an act of juggling.
– DERIVATIVES **juggler** n. **jugglery** n.
– ORIGIN Middle English: back-formation from *juggler*, or from Old French *jogler*, from Latin *joculari*, from *joculus*, diminutive of *jocus* 'jest'.

Jugoslav ▪ n. & adj. old-fashioned spelling of **YUGOSLAV**.

jugular /ˈdʒʌɡjʊlə/ ▪ adj. **1** of the neck or throat. **2** Zoology (of fish's pelvic fins) located in front of the pectoral fins. ▪ n. short for **JUGULAR VEIN**.
– ORIGIN C16: from late Latin *jugularis*, from Latin *jugulum* 'collarbone, throat', diminutive of *jugum* 'yoke'.

jugular vein ▪ n. any of several large veins in the neck, carrying blood from the head.

juice ▪ n. **1** the liquid present in fruit or vegetables. ▸ a drink made from this. **2** (**juices**) fluid secreted by the body, especially in the stomach. **3** (**juices**) liquid coming from meat or other food in cooking. **4** informal electrical energy. ▸ petrol. **5** (**juices**) one's vitality or creative faculties. **6** N. Amer. informal alcoholic drink. ▪ v. **1** extract the juice from. **2** (**juice something up**) informal, chiefly N. Amer. liven something up. **3** [as adj. **juiced**] N. Amer. informal drunk.
– DERIVATIVES **juiceless** adj.
– ORIGIN Middle English: from Latin *jus* 'broth, vegetable juice'.

juicer ▪ n. an appliance for extracting juice from fruit and vegetables.

juicy ▪ adj. (**-ier**, **-iest**) **1** full of juice. **2** informal interestingly scandalous. **3** informal profitable.
– DERIVATIVES **juicily** adv. **juiciness** n.

ju-jitsu /dʒuːˈdʒɪtsuː/ (also **jiu-jitsu** or **ju-jutsu** /-ˈjʌtsuː/) ▪ n. a Japanese system of unarmed combat and physical training.
– ORIGIN Japanese *jūjutsu*, from *jū* 'gentle' + *jutsu* 'skill'.

juju[1] /ˈdʒuːdʒuː/ ▪ n. a style of Nigerian music characterized by the use of guitars and variable-pitch drums.
– ORIGIN perhaps from Yoruba *jo jo* 'dance'.

juju[2] /ˈdʒuːdʒuː/ ▪ n. a charm or fetish, especially as used by some West African peoples. ▸ supernatural power.
– ORIGIN C17: of West African origin, perhaps from French *joujou* 'toy'.

jujube /ˈdʒuːdʒuːb/ ▪ n. **1** the edible berry-like fruit of the jujube bush, formerly taken as a cough cure. ▸ chiefly N. Amer. a jujube-flavoured lozenge or sweet. **2** (also **jujube bush**) the Eurasian shrub that produces this fruit. [*Ziziphus jujuba*.]
– ORIGIN Middle English: from medieval Latin *jujuba*, from Greek *zizuphos*.

jukebox ▪ n. a machine that automatically plays a selected musical recording when a coin is inserted.

jukskei /ˈjʊkskeɪ/ ▪ n. S. African a game similar to quoits, in which a bottle-shaped peg, originally part of an ox yoke, is thrown at a stake planted in a sand pit.
– ORIGIN S. African Dutch, from Dutch *juk* 'yoke' + *schei* 'crossbar, tie piece'.

Jul. ▪ abbrev. July.

julep /ˈdʒuːlɛp/ ▪ n. a sweet drink made from sugar syrup, sometimes containing alcohol or medicine.
– ORIGIN Middle English: from medieval Latin *julapium*, from Persian *gulāb*, from *gul* 'rose' + *āb* 'water'.

Julian calendar ▪ n. a calendar introduced by Julius Caesar, in which the year consisted of 365 days, every fourth year having 366, replaced by the Gregorian calendar.

julienne /ˌdʒuːliˈɛn/ ▪ n. a portion of food cut into short, thin strips.
– ORIGIN C18: French, from the male given names *Jules* or *Julien*.

Juliet /ˈdʒuːlɪet/ ▪ n. a code word representing the letter J, used in radio communication.

Juliet cap ▪ n. a small ornamental cap of lace or net, typically worn by brides.
– ORIGIN C20: so named because it is part of the usual costume of Juliet in Shakespeare's *Romeo and Juliet*.

July ▪ n. (pl. **Julys**) **1** the seventh month of the year. **2** (**the July, the Durban July**) S. African a horse race held annually on the first Saturday in July in Durban.
– ORIGIN Middle English: from Latin *Julius* (*mensis*) '(month) of July', named after the Roman general Julius Caesar.

jumar /ˈdʒuːmə/ Climbing ▪ n. a clamp attached to a fixed rope that tightens when weight is applied and relaxes when it is removed. ▪ v. (**jumared**, **jumaring**) climb using a jumar.
– ORIGIN 1960s: orig. in Swiss use.

jumble ▪ n. **1** an untidy collection of things. **2** Brit. articles collected for a jumble sale. ▪ v. mix up in a confused way.
– ORIGIN C16: prob. symbolic.

jumble sale ▪ n. a sale of miscellaneous second-hand goods, typically for charity.

jumbo informal ▪ n. (pl. **-os**) a very large person or thing. ▸ (also **jumbo jet**) a very large airliner (specifically a Boeing 747). ▪ adj. very large.
– ORIGIN C19: prob. the second element of **MUMBO-JUMBO**.

jump ▪ v. **1** push oneself off the ground using the muscles in one's legs and feet. ▸ pass over by jumping. ▸ get on or off (a vehicle) quickly. **2** move suddenly and quickly. ▸ make a sudden involuntary movement in surprise. ▸ informal attack suddenly and unexpectedly. ▸ (**jump on**) informal attack or criticize suddenly. ▸ pass abruptly from one subject or state to another. ▸ rise or increase suddenly. **3** informal fail to stop at (a red traffic light). **4** informal (of a place) be very lively. **5** (**jump at/on**) accept eagerly. **6** vulgar slang, chiefly N. Amer. have sexual intercourse with. **7** Bridge make a bid that is higher than necessary, in order to signal a strong hand. **8** N. Amer. take summary possession of (land) after alleged abandonment or forfeiture by the former occupant. ▪ n. **1** an act of jumping. ▸ a sudden dramatic increase. ▸ a large or sudden change. **2** a sudden startled movement. ▸ (**the jumps**) informal extreme nervousness. **3** an obstacle to be jumped, especially by a horse in a competition. **4** Bridge a bid that is higher than necessary.
– PHRASES **get** (or **have**) **the jump on** informal, chiefly N. Amer. get (or have) an advantage over (someone) due to prompt action. **jump down someone's throat** informal respond in a sudden and angry way. **jump out of one's skin** informal be startled. **jump the queue** (or N. Amer. **jump in line**) push into a queue of people. ▸ take unfair precedence over others. **jump the rails** (or **track**) (of a train) become dislodged from the track. **jump rope** N. Amer. skip with a rope. **jump ship** (of a sailor) leave a ship without permission. **jump through hoops** be made to go through a complicated procedure. **jump** (or **leap**) **to conclusions** (or **the conclusion**) form an opinion hastily without considering all the facts. **jump to it!** informal act promptly. **one jump ahead** one stage ahead of a rival.
– DERIVATIVES **jumpable** adj.
– ORIGIN C16: prob. imitative of the sound of feet landing on the ground.

jump ball ▪ n. Basketball a ball put in play by the referee, who throws it up between two opposing players.

jumped-up ▪ adj. informal considering oneself to be more important than one really is.

jumper[1] ▪ n. **1** Brit. a pullover or sweater. **2** N. Amer. a pinafore dress.
– ORIGIN C19: prob. from dialect *jump* 'short coat'.

jumper[2] ▪ n. **1** a person or animal that jumps. **2** (also **jumper wire**) a short wire used to shorten or close an electric circuit. **3** a heavy chisel-ended iron bar for drilling blast holes.

jumper cable ▪ n. either of a pair of cables for recharging a battery in a motor vehicle by connecting it to a battery in another.

jumping bean ▪ n. a plant seed or leaf gall that jumps due to the movement of a moth larva developing inside it.

jumping castle ▪ n. a large inflatable structure on which children can jump and play.

jumping jack ▪ n. **1** Brit. dated a small firework producing repeated explosions. **2** a toy figure of a man, with movable limbs. **3** a jump done from a standing position with the arms and legs pointing outwards.

jumping-off place

jumping-off place (also **jumping-off point**) ■ n. a starting place.

jump jet ■ n. a jet aircraft that can take off and land vertically.

jump lead ■ n. another term for JUMPER CABLE.

jump-off ■ n. a deciding round in a showjumping competition.

jump rope ■ n. N. Amer. a skipping rope.

jump seat ■ n. an extra seat in a car or aircraft that folds back when not in use.

jump-start ■ v. start (a car with a flat battery) with jumper cables or by a sudden release of the clutch while it is being pushed. ■ n. an act of jump-starting a car.

jumpsuit ■ n. a garment incorporating trousers and a sleeved top in one piece.
– ORIGIN 1940s: so named because it was first used to denote a parachutist's garment.

jumpy ■ adj. (-ier, -iest) informal **1** anxious and uneasy. **2** stopping and starting abruptly.
– DERIVATIVES **jumpily** adv. **jumpiness** n.

Jun. ■ abbrev. **1** June. **2** (in names) junior.

junction ■ n. **1** a point where two or more things, especially roads or railway lines, meet or are joined. **2** Electronics a region of transition in a semiconductor between a part where conduction is mainly by electrons and a part where it is mainly by holes. **3** the action of joining or being joined.
– ORIGIN C18: from Latin *junctio(n-)*, from *jungere* 'to join'.

junction box ■ n. a box containing a junction of electric wires or cables.

juncture /'dʒʌŋ(k)tʃə/ ■ n. **1** a particular point in time. **2** a place where things join. **3** Phonetics the features in speech that enable a hearer to detect a word boundary (e.g. distinguishing *I scream* from *ice cream*).
– ORIGIN Middle English: from Latin *junctura* 'joint', from *jungere* 'to join'.

June ■ n. the sixth month of the year.
– ORIGIN Middle English: from Latin *Junius* (*mensis*) '(month) of June', var. of *Junonius* 'sacred to the goddess Juno'.

June bug ■ n. chiefly N. Amer. a chafer or similar beetle which often flies in June.

Jungian /'jʊŋɪən/ ■ adj. of or relating to the Swiss psychologist Carl Jung (1875–1961) or his system of analytical psychology. ■ n. a follower of Jung or his system.

jungle ■ n. **1** an area of land with dense forest and tangled vegetation, typically in the tropics. ▸ a tangled mass, especially of vegetation. **2** a very bewildering or competitive place. **3** (also **jungle music**) a style of dance music with very fast electronic drum tracks and slower synthesized bass lines.
– PHRASES **the law of the jungle** the principle that those who are strongest and most selfish will be most successful.
– DERIVATIVES **jungled** adj. **jungly** adj.
– ORIGIN C18: from Sanskrit *jāṅgala* 'rough and arid (terrain)'.

junglefowl ■ n. (pl. same) a southern Asian game bird related to the domestic fowl. [*Gallus gallus* and other species.]

jungle gym ■ n. S. African & N. Amer. an extensive apparatus in a park or playground for children to climb on.

jungle juice ■ n. informal powerful or roughly prepared alcoholic liquor.

junior ■ adj. **1** of, for, or denoting young or younger people. ▸ N. Amer. of or for students in the third year of a four-year course at college or high school. **2** [postpos.] denoting the younger of two with the same name in a family. **3** low or lower in rank or status. ■ n. **1** a person who is a specified amount younger than someone else: *he's five years her junior.* **2** Brit. a child at a junior school. ▸ N. Amer. a student in the third year at college or high school. ▸ (in sport) a young competitor, typically under 16 or 18. **3** N. Amer. informal a nickname for one's son. **4** a person with low rank or status.

– DERIVATIVES **juniority** /-'ɒrɪti/ n.
– ORIGIN Middle English: from Latin, from *juvenis* 'young'.

junior college ■ n. (in the US) a college offering courses for two years beyond high school.

junior common room ■ n. Brit. a room used for social purposes by the undergraduates of a college.

junior high school ■ n. (in the US and Canada) a school intermediate between an elementary school and a high school.

junior lightweight ■ n. a weight in boxing of 57.1–59 kilograms.

junior middleweight ■ n. a weight in boxing of 66.7–69.8 kilograms.

junior school ■ n. a school for young children, especially for those aged 7–11.

junior welterweight ■ n. a weight in boxing of 61.2–63.5 kilograms.

juniper /'dʒuːnɪpə/ ■ n. an evergreen shrub or small tree bearing berry-like cones, many kinds having aromatic cones or foliage. [*Juniperus communis* and related species.]
– ORIGIN Middle English: from Latin *juniperus*.

junk[1] ■ n. **1** informal useless or worthless articles. ▸ nonsense. **2** Finance junk bonds. **3** informal heroin. ■ v. informal discard unceremoniously.
– ORIGIN Middle English (denoting an old or inferior rope).

junk[2] ■ n. a flat-bottomed sailing vessel used in China and the East Indies, with a prominent stem and lugsails.
– ORIGIN C16: from Portuguese *junco*, from Malay *jong*, reinforced by Dutch *jonk*.

junk bond ■ n. a high-yielding high-risk security, typically issued to finance a takeover.

Junker /'jʊŋkə/ ■ n. historical a German nobleman or aristocrat, especially one of the Prussian aristocracy.
– DERIVATIVES **junkerdom** n.
– ORIGIN German, earlier *Junkher*, from Middle High German *junc* 'young' + *herre* 'lord'.

junket /'dʒʌŋkɪt/ ■ n. **1** a dish of sweetened and flavoured curds of milk, often served with fruit. **2** informal an extravagant trip, especially one by an official at public expense. ■ v. (**junketed**, **junketing**) [often as noun **junketing**] informal go on such a trip.
– ORIGIN Middle English (denoting cream cheese, formerly made in a rush basket): from Old French *jonquette* 'rush basket', from *jonc* 'rush', from Latin *juncus*.

junk food ■ n. food with little nutritional value.

junkie (also **junky**) ■ n. informal a drug addict.
– ORIGIN 1920s (orig. US): from JUNK[1].

junk mail ■ n. informal unsolicited advertising material sent by post.

junk shop ■ n. informal a shop selling second-hand goods or inexpensive antiques.

junky informal ■ adj. regarded as junk. ■ n. (pl. **-ies**) variant spelling of JUNKIE.

junkyard ■ n. a scrapyard.

Junoesque /ˌdʒuːnəʊ'ɛsk/ ■ adj. (of a woman) tall and shapely.
– ORIGIN C19: from the name of *Juno*, goddess of ancient Rome and wife of Jupiter.

Junr ■ abbrev. (in names) Junior.

junta /'dʒʌntə, 'hʊ-/ ■ n. a military or political group ruling a country after taking power by force.
– ORIGIN C17: from Latin *juncta*, from *jungere* 'to join'.

Jurassic /dʒʊ'rasɪk/ ■ adj. Geology relating to or denoting the second period of the Mesozoic era (between the Triassic and Cretaceous periods, about 208 to 146 million years ago), a time when large reptiles were dominant and the first birds appeared.
– ORIGIN C19: from French *jurassique*; named after the *Jura* Mountains on the border of France and Switzerland.

juridical /dʒʊ'rɪdɪk(ə)l/ ■ adj. Law of or relating to judicial proceedings and the law.
– DERIVATIVES **juridically** adv.
– ORIGIN C16: from Latin *juridicus*, from *jus*, *jur-* 'law' + *dicere* 'say'.

jurisdiction /ˌdʒʊərɪs'dɪkʃ(ə)n/ ■ n. **1** the official power to make legal decisions and judgements. ▸ the territory or

sphere over which the legal authority of a court or other institution extends. **2** a system of law courts.
– DERIVATIVES **jurisdictional** adj.
– ORIGIN Middle English: from Latin *jurisdictio(n-)*, from *jus, jur-* 'law' + *dictio* 'saying', from *dicere* 'say'.

jurisprudence /ˌdʒʊərɪsˈpruːd(ə)ns/ ■ n. **1** the theory or philosophy of law. **2** a legal system.
– DERIVATIVES **jurisprudent** adj. & n. **jurisprudential** adj.
– ORIGIN C17: from late Latin *jurisprudentia*, from Latin *jus, jur-* 'law' + *prudentia* 'knowledge'.

jurist /ˈdʒʊərɪst/ ■ n. **1** an expert in law. **2** N. Amer. a lawyer or a judge.
– DERIVATIVES **juristic** adj.
– ORIGIN C15: from medieval Latin *jurista*, from *jus, jur-* 'law'.

juror ■ n. **1** a member of a jury. **2** historical a person taking an oath.
– ORIGIN Middle English: from Old French *jureor*, from Latin *jurator*, from *jurare* 'swear', from *jus, jur-* 'law'.

jury[1] ■ n. (pl. **-ies**) a body of people (typically twelve) sworn to give a verdict on the basis of evidence submitted in court. ▸ a body of people judging a competition. ■ v. (**-ies, -ied**) [usu. as adj. **juried**] judge (an art or craft exhibit).
– PHRASES **the jury is out** a decision has not been reached.
– ORIGIN Middle English: from Old French *juree* 'oath, inquiry', from Latin *jurata*, from *jurare* (see **JUROR**).

jury[2] ■ adj. Nautical denoting improvised or temporary fittings: *a jury rudder*.
– ORIGIN C17: perhaps from Old French *ajurie* 'aid'.

jury box ■ n. a segregated area for the jury in a court of law.

jury-rigged ■ adj. **1** (of a ship) having makeshift rigging. **2** chiefly N. Amer. makeshift; improvised.

jus /ʒuː/ ■ n. (especially in French cuisine) a sauce.
– ORIGIN from French.

just ■ adj. morally right and fair. ▸ appropriate or deserved. ▸ (of an opinion or appraisal) well founded. ■ adv. **1** exactly. ▸ exactly or nearly at this or that moment. **2** very recently. **3** barely; by a little. **4** simply; only. ▸ really: *they're just great.* **5** expressing agreement.
– PHRASES **just in case** as a precaution. **just now** S. African informal in a while. **just so 1** arranged or done very carefully. **2** formal expressing agreement.
– DERIVATIVES **justly** adv. **justness** n.
– ORIGIN Middle English: from Latin *justus*, from *jus* 'law, right'.

justice ■ n. **1** just behaviour or treatment. ▸ the quality of being just. **2** the administration of the law or authority in maintaining this. **3** a judge or magistrate.
– PHRASES **bring someone to justice** arrest and try someone in court for a crime. **do oneself justice** perform as well as one is able. **do someone/thing justice** treat or represent with due fairness. **Mr** (or **Mrs**) **Justice** a form of address to a judge of the supreme court.
– DERIVATIVES **justiceship** n.
– ORIGIN Old English *iustise* 'administration of the law', from Latin *justitia*, from *justus* (see **JUST**).

Justice of the Peace ■ n. **1** (in South Africa) a person authorized to take down confessions, issue warrants of arrest, etc. **2** (in the UK) a lay magistrate appointed to hear minor cases, grant licences, etc., in a town or county.

justiciable /dʒʌˈstɪʃəb(ə)l/ ■ adj. Law subject to trial in a court of law.
– ORIGIN Middle English: from Old French, from *justicier* 'bring to trial', from Latin *justitia* 'equity', from *justus* (see **JUST**).

juxtapose

justifiable ■ adj. able to be justified.
– DERIVATIVES **justifiability** n. **justifiableness** n. **justifiably** adv.

justification ■ n. **1** the action of justifying something. **2** good reason for something that exists or has been done: *there's no justification for the job losses.*

justify /ˈdʒʌstɪfʌɪ/ ■ v. (**-ies, -ied**) **1** prove to be right or reasonable. ▸ be a good reason for. **2** Theology declare or make righteous in the sight of God. **3** Printing [often as adj. **justified**] adjust (text or a line of type) so that the print fills a space evenly or forms a straight edge.
– DERIVATIVES **justificatory** adj. **justifier** n.
– ORIGIN Middle English: from Christian Latin *justificare* 'do justice to', from Latin *justus* (see **JUST**).

just-in-time ■ adj. denoting a manufacturing system in which materials are delivered immediately before use in order to minimize storage costs.

jut ■ v. (**jutted, jutting**) extend out, over, or beyond the main body or line of something. ■ n. a point that sticks out.
– ORIGIN C16: var. of **JET**[1].

Jute /dʒuːt/ ■ n. a member of a Germanic people, possibly from Jutland, that settled in southern Britain in the 5th century.
– DERIVATIVES **Jutish** adj.
– ORIGIN Old English *Eotas, Iotas*, influenced by medieval Latin *Jutae, Juti*.

jute /dʒuːt/ ■ n. rough fibre made from the stems of a tropical plant (*Corchorus capsularis* (China) and *C. olitorius* (India)), used for making rope or woven into sacking.
– ORIGIN C18: from Bengali *jhuṭo*, from Prakrit *juṭṭi*.

juvenescence /ˌdʒuːvəˈnɛs(ə)ns/ ■ n. formal youth.
– DERIVATIVES **juvenescent** adj.
– ORIGIN C19: from Latin *juvenescere* 'reach the age of youth', from *juvenis* 'young'.

juvenile /ˈdʒuːvənʌɪl/ ■ adj. of, for, or relating to young people, birds, or animals. ▸ childish. ■ n. a young person, bird, or animal. ▸ Law a person below the age at which ordinary criminal prosecution is possible (18 in most countries).
– DERIVATIVES **juvenility** /-ˈnɪlɪti/ n.
– ORIGIN C17: from Latin *juvenilis*, from *juvenis* 'young, a young person'.

juvenile court ■ n. a court for the trial or legal supervision of juveniles.

juvenile delinquency ■ n. the habitual committing of criminal acts by a juvenile.
– DERIVATIVES **juvenile deliquent** n.

juvenile hormone ■ n. Entomology a hormone regulating larval development in insects.

juvenilia /ˌdʒuːvəˈnɪlɪə/ ■ pl. n. works produced by an author or artist when young.
– ORIGIN C17: from Latin, from *juvenilis* (see **JUVENILE**).

juxtapose /ˌdʒʌkstəˈpəʊz/ ■ v. place close together.
– DERIVATIVES **juxtaposition** n. **juxtapositional** adj.
– ORIGIN C19 (*juxtaposition* Middle English): from French *juxtaposer*, from Latin *juxta* 'next' + French *poser* 'to place'.

Kk

K¹ (also **k**) ■ n. (pl. **Ks** or **K's**) **1** the eleventh letter of the alphabet. **2** denoting the next after J in a set of items, categories, etc.

K² ■ abbrev. **1** Physics kelvin(s). **2** Computing kilobyte(s). **3** kilometre(s). **4** king (in card games and chess). **5** Köchel (catalogue of Mozart's works). **6** informal thousand. [from KILO-.] ■ symb. the chemical element potassium. [from modern Latin *kalium*.]

k ■ abbrev. kilo-. ■ symb. **1** a constant in a formula or equation. **2** Chemistry Boltzmann's constant.

ka /kɑː/ ■ n. (in ancient Egypt) the supposed spiritual part of an individual, which survived after death.
–ORIGIN from Egyptian.

Kaaba /ˈkɑːəbə/ (also **Caaba**) ■ n. a square building in Mecca, the site most holy to Muslims, containing a sacred black stone.
–ORIGIN from Arabic (*al-*)*kaʿba* '(the) square house'.

kaalgat /ˈkɑːlxat/ ■ adj. S. African informal, chiefly humorous naked.
–ORIGIN from Afrikaans *kaal* 'naked' + *gat* 'arse'.

kaalvoet /ˈkɑːlfut/ ■ adj. & adv. S. African informal barefoot.
–ORIGIN from Afrikaans *kaal* 'naked' + *voet* 'foot'.

Kaapenaar /ˈkɑːpɑnɑː/ ■ n. S. African informal a native or inhabitant of Cape Town or of the Western Cape province.
–ORIGIN Afrikaans, from *Kaap* 'Cape' + noun-forming suffix *-enaar*.

Kabbalah /kəˈbɑːlə, ˈkabələ/ (also **Kabbala**, **Cabbala**, **Cabala**, or **Qabalah**) ■ n. the ancient Jewish tradition of mystical interpretation of the Bible.
–DERIVATIVES **Kabbalism** n. **Kabbalist** n. **Kabbalistic** adj.
–ORIGIN from medieval Latin *cabbala*, from Rabbinical Hebrew *qabbālāh* 'tradition', from *qibbēl* 'receive, accept'.

kabeljou /ˌkab(ə)lˈjəu/ ■ n. S. African another term for KOB¹.
–ORIGIN C18: from Afrikaans, from Dutch, 'cod'.

Kabinett /ˌkabɪˈnɛt/ ■ n. a wine of German origin or style of superior quality.
–ORIGIN from German *Kabinettwein* 'chamber wine'.

kabob /kəˈbɒb/ ■ n. US spelling of KEBAB.

kabuki /kəˈbuːki/ ■ n. a form of traditional Japanese drama performed by men, with highly stylized song, mime, and dance.
–ORIGIN Japanese, orig. as a verb meaning 'act dissolutely', later interpreted as if from *ka* 'song' + *bu* 'dance' + *ki* 'art'.

Kaddish /ˈkadɪʃ/ ■ n. an ancient Jewish prayer sequence recited in the synagogue service. ▸ a form of this recited for the dead.
–ORIGIN from Aramaic *qaddīš* 'holy'.

Kaffir /ˈkafə/ ■ n. offensive, chiefly S. African a black African.
–ORIGIN from Arabic *kāfir* 'infidel', from *kafara* 'not believe'.

> **USAGE**
> The word **Kaffir** was originally a descriptive term for a particular ethnic group. Now it is a racially abusive and offensive term, and in South Africa its use is actionable.

Kaffir lily ■ n. former term for RIVER LILY.

kaffiyeh ■ n. variant spelling of KEFFIYEH.

kafir /ˈkafɪə/ ■ n. (among Muslims) a person who is not a Muslim.
–ORIGIN from Arabic *kāfir* 'infidel, unbeliever'; cf. KAFFIR.

Kafkaesque /ˌkafkəˈɛsk/ ■ adj. of or relating to the Czech novelist Franz Kafka (1883–1924) or his nightmarish fictional world.

kaftan /ˈkaftan/ (also **caftan**) ■ n. a man's long belted tunic, worn in the Near East. ▸ a woman's long loose dress. ▸ a loose shirt or top.
–ORIGIN C16: from Turkish, from Persian *kaftān*, partly influenced by French *cafetan*.

kagoul ■ n. variant spelling of CAGOULE.

kahuna /kəˈhuːnə/ ■ n. N. Amer. informal an important person.
–ORIGIN from Hawaiian.

kaiser /ˈkaɪzə/ ■ n. historical the German Emperor, the Emperor of Austria, or the head of the Holy Roman Empire.
–DERIVATIVES **kaisership** n.
–ORIGIN Middle English, from Old Norse *keisari*, from Latin *Caesar* (see CAESAR).

kaizen /kaɪˈzɛn/ ■ n. a Japanese business philosophy of continuous improvement.
–ORIGIN Japanese, 'improvement'.

kak /kʌk/ S. African vulgar slang ■ n., v., & exclam. shit. ■ adj. bad; worthless.
–ORIGIN Afrikaans, from Dutch, 'excrement'.

kakapo /ˈkɑːkəpəʊ/ ■ n. (pl. **-os**) an endangered nocturnal flightless New Zealand parrot, with greenish plumage. [*Strigops habroptilus*.]
–ORIGIN C19: from Maori, 'night parrot'.

Kalahari truffle (also **Kalahari desert truffle**) ■ n. a southern African desert truffle, considered a culinary delicacy. [*Terfezia pfeilii*.]

kalanchoe /ˌkalənˈkəʊi/ ■ n. a tropical succulent plant with clusters of tubular flowers, sometimes producing miniature plants along the edges of the leaves. [Genus *Kalanchoe*.]
–ORIGIN C19: from French, from Chinese *gāláncài*.

Kalashnikov /kəˈlaʃnɪkɒf, -ˈlɑːʃ-/ ■ n. a type of rifle or sub-machine gun made in Russia.
–ORIGIN 1970s: named after the Russian designer Mikhail T. *Kalashnikov*.

kale /keɪl/ ■ n. a hardy cabbage of a variety which produces erect stems with large leaves and no compact head.
–ORIGIN Middle English: northern English form of archaic *cole*, from Old English, from Latin *caulis* 'stem, cabbage'.

kaleidoscope /kəˈlaɪdəskəʊp/ ■ n. **1** a toy consisting of a tube containing mirrors and pieces of coloured glass or paper, whose reflections produce changing patterns when the tube is rotated. **2** a constantly changing pattern or sequence.
–DERIVATIVES **kaleidoscopic** adj. **kaleidoscopically** adv.
–ORIGIN C19: from Greek *kalos* 'beautiful' + *eidos* 'form' + -SCOPE.

kalends ■ pl. n. variant spelling of CALENDS.

kalimba /kəˈlɪmbə/ ■ n. a type of African thumb piano.
–ORIGIN 1950s: a local word; rel. to MARIMBA.

Kama Sutra /ˌkɑːmə ˈsuːtrə/ ■ n. an ancient Sanskrit treatise on the art of love and sexual technique.
–ORIGIN Sanskrit, from *kāma* 'love' + *sūtra* 'thread'.

Kamba /ˈkambə/ ■ n. (pl. same, **Kambas**, or **Wakamba**) **1** a member of a people of central Kenya. **2** the Bantu language of this people.
–ORIGIN the name in Kamba.

kambro (also **kambroo**) ■ n. an African milkweed plant with a succulent edible tuber. [Genus *Fockea*: several species.]
–ORIGIN C18: from Nama *cama-re-*(*bi*), perhaps from //*gami* (or Khoikhoi *kama*) 'water' + //*hoe-* or //*ho-* 'container' + diminutive element *-ro-*.

kame /keɪm/ ■ n. Geology a steep mound of sand and gravel deposited by a melting ice sheet.
–ORIGIN C18: Scots form of COMB.

CONSONANTS **b** but **d** dog **f** few **g** get **h** he **j** yes **k** cat **l** leg **m** man **n** no **p** pen **r** red

kameez /kəˈmiːz/ ▪ n. (pl. same or **kameezes**) a long tunic worn by people from the Indian subcontinent.
– ORIGIN from Arabic *ḳamīṣ*, perhaps from late Latin *camisia* (see CHEMISE).

kamikaze /ˌkamɪˈkɑːzi/ ▪ n. (in the Second World War) a Japanese aircraft loaded with explosives and making a deliberate suicidal crash on an enemy target. ▪ adj. reckless or potentially self-destructive.
– ORIGIN Japanese, from *kami* 'divinity' + *kaze* 'wind'.

kampong /kamˈpɒŋ, ˈkampɒŋ/ ▪ n. a Malaysian enclosure or village.
– ORIGIN Malay; cf. COMPOUND².

Kampuchean /ˌkampʊˈtʃiːən/ ▪ n. & adj. another term for CAMBODIAN.

kana /ˈkɑːnə/ ▪ n. the system of syllabic writing used for Japanese.
– ORIGIN from Japanese.

kanban /ˈkanban/ ▪ n. a Japanese manufacturing system in which the supply of components is regulated by way of an instruction card sent along the production line.
– ORIGIN C20: Japanese, 'billboard, sign'.

kanga¹ /ˈkaŋɡə/ ▪ n. Austral. informal a kangaroo.

kanga² /ˈkaŋɡə/ (also **khanga**) ▪ n. a garment consisting of a long piece of colourful cloth wrapped round the chest or waist, traditionally worn in East Africa.
– ORIGIN from Kiswahili.

kangaroo ▪ n. a large plant-eating marsupial with a long powerful tail and strongly developed hindlimbs that enable it to travel by leaping, found only in Australia and New Guinea. [Genus *Macropus*: several species.]
– ORIGIN C18: the name of a specific kind of kangaroo in an extinct Aboriginal language.

kangaroo court ▪ n. an unofficial court formed by a group of people to settle disputes among themselves.

kangaroo rat ▪ n. a seed-eating hopping rodent with large cheek pouches and long hind legs, found from Canada to Mexico. [Genus *Dipodomys*: several species.]

kangaroo vine ▪ n. an Australian evergreen vine, grown as a house plant. [*Cissus antarctica*.]

kanji /ˈkandʒi, ˈkɑːn-/ ▪ n. a system of Japanese writing using Chinese characters.
– ORIGIN Japanese, from *kan* 'Chinese' + *ji* 'character'.

kanna ▪ n. a South African succulent plant, parts of which are sometimes used for their narcotic effects. [*Sceletium tortuosum*.]
– ORIGIN from Khoikhoi.

Kantian /ˈkantɪən/ ▪ adj. of or relating to the German philosopher Immanuel Kant (1724–1804) or his philosophy. ▪ n. an adherent of Kant's philosophy.
– DERIVATIVES **Kantianism** n.

KANU /ˈkɑːnuː/ ▪ abbrev. Kenya African National Union.

kaolin /ˈkeɪəlɪn/ ▪ n. a fine soft white clay, used for making porcelain and china and in medicinal absorbents.
– DERIVATIVES **kaolinize** (also **-ise**) v.
– ORIGIN C18: from Chinese *gāolǐng* 'high hill', the name of a mountain in Jiangxi province where the clay is found.

kaolinite /ˈkeɪəlɪnʌɪt/ ▪ n. a clay mineral which is the chief constituent of kaolin.

kaon /ˈkeɪɒn/ ▪ n. Physics a meson with a mass several times that of a pion.
– ORIGIN 1950s: from *ka* representing the letter *K* (as a symbol for the particle).

kapok /ˈkeɪpɒk/ ▪ n. a fine fibrous substance which grows around the seeds of a ceiba or silk-cotton tree, used as stuffing for cushions.
– ORIGIN C18: from Malay *kapuk*.

Kaposi's sarcoma /kəˈpəʊsɪz/ ▪ n. Medicine a form of cancer involving multiple tumours of the lymph nodes or skin, occurring chiefly as a result of Aids.
– ORIGIN C19: named after the Hungarian dermatologist Moritz K. *Kaposi*.

kappa /ˈkapə/ ▪ n. the tenth letter of the Greek alphabet (Κ, κ), transliterated as 'k'.
– ORIGIN from Greek.

kappie /ˈkapi/ ▪ n. S. African historical a large cloth sun bonnet with a deep brim and a frill or flap protecting the neck, traditionally worn by rural Afrikaner women.
– ORIGIN Afrikaans, from Dutch, 'little hood'.

kaput /kəˈpʊt/ ▪ adj. informal broken and useless.
– ORIGIN C19: from German *kaputt*, from French (*être*) *capot* '(be) without tricks in a card game'.

karabiner /ˌkarəˈbiːnə/ (also **carabiner**) ▪ n. a coupling link with a safety closure, used by rock climbers.
– ORIGIN 1930s: from German *Karabiner-haken* 'spring hook'.

karakul /ˈkarəkʊl/ (also **caracul**) ▪ n. **1** a sheep of an Asian breed with a dark curled fleece when young. **2** cloth or fur made from or resembling this fleece.
– ORIGIN C19: from Russian.

karaoke /ˌkarəˈəʊki, ˌkarɪ-/ ▪ n. a form of entertainment in which people sing popular songs over pre-recorded backing tracks.
– ORIGIN 1970s: from Japanese, 'empty orchestra'.

karat ▪ n. US spelling of CARAT (in sense 2).

karate /kəˈrɑːti/ ▪ n. an oriental system of unarmed combat using the hands and feet to deliver and block blows.
– ORIGIN Japanese, from *kara* 'empty' + *te* 'hand'.

karateka /kəˈrɑːtɪkɑː/ ▪ n. (pl. same or **karatekas**) a practitioner of karate.
– ORIGIN from Japanese.

karee /kəˈriː, kəˈrɪə/ (also **karree**) ▪ n. a hardy evergreen tree of southern Africa with lance-shaped leaves, small berries, and a gnarled trunk. [*Rhus lancea* and related species.]
– ORIGIN from Khoikhoi.

Karelian /kəˈriːlɪən/ ▪ n. a native or inhabitant of Karelia, a region on the border between Russia and Finland. ▪ adj. of or relating to Karelia.

Karen /kəˈrɛn/ ▪ n. (pl. same or **Karens**) a member of a people of eastern Burma (Myanmar) and western Thailand.
– ORIGIN from Burmese *ka-reng* 'wild unclean man'.

karma /ˈkɑːmə, ˈkəːmə/ ▪ n. (in Hinduism and Buddhism) the sum of a person's actions in this and previous states of existence, viewed as affecting their future fate. ▸ informal the sum of good or bad luck, viewed as resulting from one's actions.
– DERIVATIVES **karmic** adj. **karmically** adv.
– ORIGIN from Sanskrit *karman* 'action, effect, fate'.

Karoo /kəˈruː/ ▪ n. (**the Karoo**) a vast arid inland plateau extending from the Western to the Eastern Cape and north to the Free State.
– ORIGIN C18: from Khoikhoi *karo-* 'dry, hard'.

Karoo cottage ▪ n. S. African a small house built in an architectural style typical of the Karoo region, characterized by natural stone walls, reed ceilings, and flat roofs.

Karoo oyster ▪ n. S. African informal lamb's liver wrapped in caul fat or bacon and grilled, usually over charcoal.

Karoo thorn ▪ n. another term for SWEET THORN.

Karoo veld /ˈkɑːruː fɛlt/ ▪ n. S. African semi-desert land typical of the Karoo. ▸ drought-resistant vegetation that grows on this land.

kaross /kəˈrɒs/ ▪ n. (pl. **-es**) S. African a cape or blanket of animal skins stitched together, traditionally used by the indigenous peoples of southern Africa.
– ORIGIN from Khoikhoi *caro-s* 'skin blanket'.

karpenter ▪ n. variant spelling of CARPENTER².

karree ▪ n. variant spelling of KAREE.

karretjie people /ˈkʌrəkiː/ (also **karretjiemense**) ▪ pl. n. S. African nomadic people living in the Karoo who travel by donkey cart taking seasonal employment on farms.
– ORIGIN from Afrikaans *karretjie* 'little cart'.

karri /ˈkari/ ▪ n. (pl. **karris**) a tall Australian eucalyptus with hard red wood. [*Eucalyptus diversicolor*.]
– ORIGIN C19: from an extinct Aboriginal language.

karroid ▪ adj. S. African, chiefly technical of or characteristic of the Karoo.

karst /kɑːst/ ▪ n. Geology landscape underlain by limestone which has been eroded by dissolution, producing towers,

kart

fissures, sinkholes, etc.
– DERIVATIVES **karstic** adj. **karstification** n. **karstify** v. (**-ies, -ied**).
– ORIGIN C19: from German *Karst*, the name of a limestone region in Slovenia.

kart ■ n. a small unsprung motor-racing vehicle with a tubular frame and a rear-mounted engine.
– DERIVATIVES **karting** n.
– ORIGIN C20: shortening of GO-KART.

karyo- ■ comb. form Biology denoting the nucleus of a cell: *karyotype*.
– ORIGIN from Greek *karuon* 'kernel'.

karyokinesis /ˌkarɪəʊkɪˈniːsɪs, -kaɪ-/ ■ n. Biology division of a cell nucleus during mitosis.

karyotype /ˈkarɪə(ʊ)tʌɪp/ ■ n. Biology & Medicine the number and visual appearance of the chromosomes in the cell nuclei of an organism.
– DERIVATIVES **karyotypic** adj.

kasbah /ˈkazbɑː/ (also **casbah**) ■ n. a North African citadel. ► the area surrounding a citadel.
– ORIGIN C18: from Arabic *ḳaṣaba* 'citadel'.

kasha /ˈkaʃə/ ■ n. (in Russia and Poland) porridge made from cooked buckwheat or similar grain.
– ORIGIN from Russian.

Kashmir goat ■ n. a goat of a Himalayan breed yielding fine, soft wool, which is used to make cashmere.

Kashmiri /kaʃˈmɪəri/ ■ n. **1** a native or inhabitant of Kashmir, a region on the border of India and Pakistan. **2** the Indic language of Kashmir. ■ adj. of or relating to Kashmir, its people, or their language.

kashrut /kaʃˈruːt/ (also **kashruth**) ■ n. the body of Jewish religious laws concerning the suitability of food, the use of ritual objects, etc.
– ORIGIN Hebrew, 'legitimacy (in religion)'.

kasi /ˈkɑːsi/ (also **kasie**) ■ n. S. African informal a township. ► [as modifier] denoting or relating to life in a township.
– ORIGIN from Tsotsitaal, abbrev. of Afrikaans *lokasie* 'location'.

kassler ■ n. a type of smoked pork.
– ORIGIN prob. named after the town of *Kassel* in Germany.

kata /ˈkɑːtɑː/ ■ n. a system of individual training exercises in karate and other martial arts.
– ORIGIN from Japanese.

katabatic /ˌkatəˈbatɪk/ ■ adj. Meteorology (of a wind) caused by local downward motion of cool air.
– ORIGIN C19: from Greek *katabatikos*, from *katabainein* 'go down'.

katabolism ■ n. variant spelling of CATABOLISM.

katana /kəˈtɑːnə/ ■ n. a long, single-edged sword used by Japanese samurai.
– ORIGIN C17: from Japanese.

Kathak /ˈkʌtək/ ■ n. **1** a type of northern Indian classical dance with passages of mime. **2** (pl. same or **Kathaks**) a member of an Indian caste of storytellers and musicians.
– ORIGIN from Sanskrit *kathaka* 'professional storyteller', from *kathā* 'story'.

Kathakali /ˌkɑːtəˈkɑːli, ˌkʌtəˈkɑːli/ ■ n. a type of dramatic dance from southern India, based on Hindu literature.
– ORIGIN from Sanskrit *kathā* 'story' + Malayalam *kaḷi* 'play'.

katharevousa /ˌkaθəˈrɛvuːsə/ ■ n. a heavily archaized form of modern Greek used in traditional literary writing. Compare with DEMOTIC.
– ORIGIN C20: modern Greek, 'purified'.

katydid /ˈkeɪtɪdɪd/ ■ n. a tropical green bush cricket with long antennae, the male of which makes a characteristic sound from which it derives its name. [Family Tettigoniidae: numerous species.]

kauri /ˈkaʊri/ (also **kauri pine**) ■ n. (pl. **kauris**) a tall coniferous forest tree native to New Zealand, which produces valuable resin and wood. [*Agathis australis*.]
– ORIGIN C19: from Maori.

kava /ˈkɑːvə/ ■ n. **1** a narcotic drink made in Polynesia from the crushed roots of a plant of the pepper family. ► (also **kava kava**) a herbal remedy prepared from this root, used in alternative medicine to relieve anxiety and insomnia. **2** the Polynesian shrub from which this root is obtained. [*Piper methysticum*.]
– ORIGIN C18: from Tongan.

Kavango ■ n. a member of a people of NE Namibia, originally from East Africa.

kay ■ n. S. African informal a kilometre.

kayak /ˈkʌɪak/ ■ n. a canoe of a type used originally by the Inuit, made of a light frame with a watertight covering having a small opening for the seat. ■ v. (**kayaked, kayaking**) [usu. as noun **kayaking**] travel in or use a kayak.
– ORIGIN C18: from Inuit *qayaq*.

kayo /keɪˈəʊ/ informal Boxing. ■ n. (pl. **-os**) a knockout. ■ v. (**-oes, -oed**) knock (someone) out.
– ORIGIN 1920s: representing the pronunciation of *KO*.

Kazakh /kəˈzak, ˈkazak/ ■ n. **1** a member of a people living chiefly in Kazakhstan. **2** the Turkic language of this people.
– ORIGIN Russian, from Turkic (see COSSACK).

kazoo /kəˈzuː/ ■ n. a simple musical instrument consisting of a pipe with a hole in it, over which is a membrane that vibrates and adds a buzzing sound when the player hums into the pipe.
– ORIGIN C19: apparently imitative of the sound produced.

KB (also **Kb**) ■ abbrev. kilobyte(s).

KBE ■ abbrev. (in the UK) Knight Commander of the Order of the British Empire.

Kbps ■ abbrev. kilobits per second.

kbyte ■ abbrev. kilobyte(s).

KC ■ abbrev. Law King's Counsel.

kc ■ abbrev. kilocycle(s).

kcal ■ abbrev. kilocalorie(s).

KCB ■ abbrev. (in the UK) Knight Commander of the Order of the Bath.

KCMG ■ abbrev. (in the UK) Knight Commander of the Order of St Michael and St George.

kc/s ■ abbrev. kilocycles per second.

KCVO ■ abbrev. (in the UK) Knight Commander of the Royal Victorian Order.

kea /ˈkiːə/ ■ n. a New Zealand mountain parrot with a long, narrow bill and mainly olive-green plumage, sometimes feeding on carrion. [*Nestor notabilis*.]
– ORIGIN C19: from Maori, imitative of its call.

kebab /kɪˈbab, kəˈbaːb/ (N. Amer. also **kabob**) ■ n. a dish of pieces of meat, fish, or vegetables roasted or grilled on a skewer or spit.
– ORIGIN C17: from Arabic *kabāb*.

ked (also **sheep ked**) ■ n. a wingless louse fly that parasitizes sheep. [*Melophagus ovinus*.]
– ORIGIN C16.

kedge /kɛdʒ/ ■ v. move (a boat) by hauling in a hawser attached at a distance to an anchor. ■ n. (also **kedge anchor**) a small anchor used for such a purpose.
– ORIGIN C15: perhaps a specific use of dialect *cadge* 'bind, tie'.

kedgeree /ˈkɛdʒəriː/ ■ n. **1** an Indian dish consisting chiefly of rice, split pulses, onions, and eggs. **2** a European dish consisting chiefly of smoked fish, rice, and hard-boiled eggs.
– ORIGIN from Hindi *khichṛī*, from Sanskrit *khiccā*.

keek Scottish ■ v. peep surreptitiously. ■ n. a surreptitious peep.
– ORIGIN Middle English: perhaps rel. to Dutch *kijken* 'have a look'.

keel ■ n. **1** a lengthwise structure along the base of a ship, in some vessels extended downwards as a ridge to increase stability. **2** Botany a prow-shaped pair of petals, such as present in the flowers of the pea family. ■ v. (**keel over**) **1** (of a boat or ship) turn over on its side; capsize. **2** informal fall over; collapse.
– DERIVATIVES **keeled** adj. **keelless** adj.
– ORIGIN Middle English: from Old Norse *kjǫlr*, of Germanic origin.

keelboat ■ n. **1** a yacht built with a permanent keel rather than a centreboard. **2** a large, flat freight boat used on American rivers.

keelhaul ■ v. **1** historical punish (someone) by dragging them through the water from one side of a boat to the other, under the keel. **2** humorous punish or reprimand severely.

keelson /'ki:ls(ə)n/ (also **kelson**) ▪ n. a structure running the length of a ship, that fastens the timbers or plates of the floor to the keel.
–ORIGIN Middle English *kelswayn*, from *kiel* 'keel of a ship' + *swīn* 'swine' (used as the name of a timber).

keen¹ ▪ adj. **1** eager; enthusiastic. ▸ (**keen on**) interested in or attracted by. **2** (of the edge or point of a blade) sharp. ▸ (of a sense or mental faculty) acute or quick. ▸ (of the air or wind) cold and biting.
–DERIVATIVES **keenly** adv. **keenness** n.
–ORIGIN Old English *cēne* 'wise, clever', also 'brave, daring', of Germanic origin.

keen² ▪ v. wail in grief for a dead person. ▸ make an eerie wailing sound.
–DERIVATIVES **keener** n.
–ORIGIN C19: from Irish *caoinim* 'I wail'.

keep ▪ v. (past and past part. **kept** /kɛpt/) **1** have or retain possession of. ▸ retain or reserve for use in the future. ▸ put or store in a regular place. ▸ (of a perishable commodity) remain in good condition. **2** continue or cause to continue in a specified condition, position, or activity: *she kept quiet about it.* ▸ (**keep something from**) cause something to stay out of. ▸ (**keep something from**) cause something to remain a secret from. ▸ (**keep from**) avoid doing something. ▸ (**keep someone from**) guard or protect someone from. **3** provide for the sustenance of. ▸ own and look after (an animal). ▸ [as adj. **kept**] supported financially in return for sexual favours. **4** delay or detain; cause to be late. **5** honour or fulfil (a commitment or undertaking). ▸ observe or pay due regard to (a law, custom, or religious occasion). **6** record or regularly maintain (a note or diary). ▪ n. **1** food, clothes, and other essentials for living. **2** archaic charge; control. **3** the strongest or central tower of a castle.
–PHRASES **for keeps** informal permanently; indefinitely.
–PHRASAL VERBS **keep something in** restrain oneself from expressing a feeling. **keep off** (of bad weather) fail to occur. **keep on** continue to do something. **keep on about** speak about (something) repeatedly. **keep on at** harass with constant requests. **keep someone/thing on** continue to use or employ someone or something. **keep to 1** avoid leaving (a path, road, or place). **2** adhere to (a schedule). **3** observe (a promise). **4** confine or restrict oneself to. **keep up** move or progress at the same rate as someone or something else. **keep up with 1** learn about or be aware of (current events or developments). **2** continue to be in contact with (someone). **3** meet a regular commitment to pay or do (something). **keep someone up** prevent someone from going to bed or to sleep. **keep something up** continue a course of action.
–DERIVATIVES **keepable** adj.
–ORIGIN Old English *cēpan* 'seize, take in', also 'care for, attend to'.

keeper ▪ n. **1** a person who manages or looks after something or someone. **2** short for GOALKEEPER or WICKETKEEPER. **3** an object which protects or secures another.
–DERIVATIVES **keepership** n.

keep-fit ▪ n. chiefly Brit. regular exercises to improve personal fitness and health.

keeping ▪ n. the action of keeping something.
–PHRASES **in someone's keeping** in someone's care or custody. **in** (or **out of**) **keeping with** in (or out of) harmony or conformity with.

keepnet ▪ n. Fishing a net secured in the water and keeping alive the fish that have been caught.

keepsake ▪ n. a small item kept in memory of the person who gave it or originally owned it.

keeshond /'keɪshɒnd/ ▪ n. a dog of a Dutch breed with long thick grey hair, resembling a large Pomeranian.
–ORIGIN 1920s: Dutch, from *Kees* (familiar form of the given name *Cornelius*) + *hond* 'dog'.

kef /kɛf/ ▪ n. & adj. variant spelling of KIF.

keffiyeh /kə'fi:(j)ə/ (also **kaffiyeh**) ▪ n. a Bedouin Arab's kerchief worn as a headdress.
–ORIGIN C19: from Arabic *keffiyya, kūfiyya*.

keftedes /kɛf'tɛðiːz/ ▪ pl. n. (in Greek cookery) small meatballs made with herbs and onions.

637

–ORIGIN from Greek *kephtedes*, pl. of *kephtes*, from Persian *koftah* (see KOFTA).

keg ▪ n. **1** a small barrel, especially one of less than 10 gallons or (in the US) 30 gallons. **2** short for KEG BEER.
–ORIGIN C17: var. of Scots and US dialect *cag*, from Old Norse *kaggi*.

keg beer ▪ n. Brit. beer supplied in a keg, to which carbon dioxide has been added.

Kei apple /kaɪ/ ▪ n. S. African a dense spiny shrub with edible apricot-coloured fruits. [*Dovyalis caffra*.]

kelim ▪ n. variant spelling of KILIM.

kelp ▪ n. **1** a very large brown seaweed that typically has a long, tough stalk with a broad frond divided into strips. [*Laminaria* and other genera, family Laminariaceae.] **2** the calcined ashes of seaweed, used as a source of various salts.
–ORIGIN Middle English.

kelpie /'kɛlpi/ ▪ n. **1** a water spirit of Scottish folklore, typically taking the form of a horse. **2** a sheepdog of an Australian breed with a smooth coat, originally bred from a Scottish collie.
–ORIGIN C17: perhaps from Scottish Gaelic *cailpeach*, *colpach* 'bullock, colt'.

kelson /'kɛls(ə)n/ ▪ n. variant spelling of KEELSON.

kelvin (abbrev.: **K**) ▪ n. the SI base unit of thermodynamic temperature, equal in magnitude to the degree Celsius.
–ORIGIN C19: named after the British physicist William T. *Kelvin*.

Kelvin scale ▪ n. a scale of temperature with absolute zero as zero, and the triple point of water as exactly 273.16 degrees.

kemp ▪ n. a coarse hair or fibre in wool.
–DERIVATIVES **kempy** adj.
–ORIGIN Middle English: from Old Norse *kampr* 'beard, whisker'.

kempt ▪ adj. maintained in a neat and clean condition.
–ORIGIN Old English *cemd-*, from *cemban* 'to comb', of Germanic origin; rel. to COMB.

ken ▪ n. (**one's ken**) one's range of knowledge or sight. ▪ v. (**kenning**; past and past part. **kenned** or **kent**) Scottish & N. English **1** know. **2** recognize; identify.
–ORIGIN Old English *cennan* 'tell, make known', of Germanic origin.

kenaf /kə'naf/ ▪ n. a brown plant fibre similar to jute, used to make ropes and coarse cloth.
–ORIGIN C19: from Persian, var. of *kanab* 'hemp'.

Kendal Green /'kɛnd(ə)l/ ▪ n. **1** a kind of rough green woollen cloth. **2** the green colour of this cloth.
–ORIGIN from the name of *Kendal* in Cumbria, NW England.

Kendal mint cake ▪ n. a hard peppermint-flavoured sweet produced in flat rectangular blocks.

kendo /'kɛndəʊ/ ▪ n. a Japanese form of fencing with two-handed bamboo swords.
–DERIVATIVES **kendoist** n.
–ORIGIN Japanese, from *ken* 'sword' + *dō* 'way'.

kennel ▪ n. **1** a small shelter for a dog. **2** (**kennels**) [treated as sing. or pl.] a boarding or breeding establishment for dogs. ▪ v. (**kennelled, kennelling**; US **kenneled, kenneling**) put or keep (a dog) in a kennel or kennels.
–ORIGIN Middle English: from Old French *chenil*, from Latin *canis* 'dog'.

keno /'ki:nəʊ/ ▪ n. a game of chance similar to bingo, based on the drawing of numbers and covering of corresponding numbers on cards.
–ORIGIN C19: from French *kine*, denoting a set of five winning lottery numbers.

kenosis /kɪ'nəʊsɪs/ ▪ n. (in Christian theology) the full or partial renunciation of his divine nature by Christ in the Incarnation.
–DERIVATIVES **kenotic** adj.
–ORIGIN C19: from Greek *kenōsis* 'an emptying', from *kenoein*, with biblical allusion (Philippians 2:7) to Greek *heauton ekenōse* 'emptied himself'.

kent past and past participle of KEN.

kent

K

kente /ˈkɛntə/ ■ n. a brightly coloured material consisting of separate strips sewn together, made in Ghana.
– ORIGIN C20: from Twi, 'cloth'.

kentia palm /ˈkɛntɪə/ ■ n. an Australasian palm tree popular as a house plant. [*Howeia* (formerly *Kentia*) *forsteriana*.]
– ORIGIN C19: named after the botanical collector William Kent.

Kenyan /ˈkɛnjən/ ■ n. a native or inhabitant of Kenya. ■ adj. of or relating to Kenya.

kepi /ˈkɛpi, ˈkeɪpi/ ■ n. (pl. **kepis**) a French military cap with a horizontal peak.
– ORIGIN C19: from French *képi*, from Swiss German *Käppi*, diminutive of *Kappe* 'cap'.

kept past and past participle of **KEEP**.

kerat- ■ comb. form variant spelling of **KERATO-** shortened before a vowel (as in *keratectomy*).

keratectomy /ˌkɛrəˈtɛktəmi/ ■ n. surgical removal of a section or layer of the cornea, usually performed using a laser to correct myopia.

keratin /ˈkɛrətɪn/ ■ n. a fibrous protein forming the main structural constituent of hair, feathers, hoofs, claws, and horns.
– DERIVATIVES **keratinous** adj.
– ORIGIN C19: from Greek *keras*, *kerat-* 'horn'.

keratinize /ˈkɛrətɪnaɪz, kəˈrat-/ (also **-ise**) ■ v. Biology change or become changed into a form containing keratin.
– DERIVATIVES **keratinization** (also **-isation**) n.

keratinocyte /ˌkɛrəˈtɪnə(ʊ)saɪt/ ■ n. Biology an epidermal cell which produces keratin.

kerato- (also **kerat-**) ■ comb. form **1** relating to keratin or horny tissue. **2** relating to the cornea.
– ORIGIN from Greek *keras*, *kerat-* 'horn'.

keratoplasty /ˈkɛrətə(ʊ)ˌplasti/ ■ n. Medicine surgery carried out on the cornea, especially corneal transplantation.

keratosis /ˌkɛrəˈtəʊsɪs/ ■ n. (pl. **keratoses**) Medicine a horny growth, especially on the skin.

keratotomy /ˌkɛrəˈtɒtəmi/ ■ n. a surgical operation involving cutting into the cornea of the eye, especially (radial keratotomy) performed to correct myopia.

kerb (US **curb**) ■ n. a stone edging to a pavement or raised path.
– ORIGIN C17 (denoting a raised border or frame): var. of **CURB**.

kerb-crawling ■ n. the action of driving slowly along the edge of the road in search of a prostitute or in an attempt to entice a passer-by.
– DERIVATIVES **kerb-crawler** n.

kerb drill ■ n. Brit. a set of precautions taken before crossing the road, as taught to children.

kerbing ■ n. the stones collectively forming a kerb.

kerbstone (US **curbstone**) ■ n. a long, narrow stone or concrete block, laid end to end with others to form a kerb.

kerb weight ■ n. the weight of a motor car without occupants or baggage.

kerchief /ˈkəːtʃɪf/ ■ n. **1** a piece of fabric used to cover the head. **2** a handkerchief.
– DERIVATIVES **kerchiefed** adj.
– ORIGIN Middle English *kerchef*, from Old French *cuevrechief*, from *couvrir* 'to cover' + *chief* 'head'.

kerf /kəːf/ ■ n. **1** a slit made by cutting with a saw. **2** the cut end of a felled tree.
– DERIVATIVES **kerfed** adj.
– ORIGIN Old English *cyrf* 'cutting, a cut', of West Germanic origin.

kerfuffle /kəˈfʌf(ə)l/ ■ n. informal a commotion or fuss.
– ORIGIN C19: perhaps from Scots *curfuffle*, prob. from Scottish Gaelic *car* 'twist, bend' + imitative Scots *fuffle* 'to disorder'.

kermes /ˈkəːmɪz/ ■ n. a red dye obtained from the dried bodies of a scale insect (*Kermes illicis*).
– ORIGIN C16: from French *kermès*, from Arabic *kirmiz*; rel. to **CRIMSON**.

kermis /ˈkəːmɪs/ ■ n. **1** a summer fair held in towns and villages in the Netherlands. **2** US a fair or carnival, especially one held to raise money for a charity.
– ORIGIN C16: Dutch, orig. denoting a mass on the anniversary of the dedication of a church, when a fair was held, from *kerk* 'church' + *mis* 'Mass'.

kern Printing ■ n. a part of a metal type projecting beyond the body or shank, or a part of a printed character that overlaps its neighbours. ■ v. **1** provide (metal type or a printed character) with a kern. **2** [usu. as noun **kerning**] adjust the spacing between (characters).
– ORIGIN C17: perhaps from French *carne* 'corner', from Latin *cardo*, *cardin-* 'hinge'.

kernel /ˈkəːn(ə)l/ ■ n. **1** a softer part of a nut, seed, or fruit stone contained within its hard shell. ▸ the seed and hard husk of a cereal, especially wheat. **2** the central or most important part of something. ▸ Computing the most basic level or core of an operating system.
– ORIGIN Old English *cyrnel*, diminutive of **CORN**[1].

kerosene /ˈkɛrəsiːn/ (also **kerosine**) ■ n. a light fuel oil obtained by distilling petroleum; paraffin oil.
– ORIGIN C19: from Greek *kēros* 'wax'.

kerria /ˈkɛrɪə/ ■ n. an East Asian shrub of the rose family, cultivated for its yellow flowers. [*Kerria japonica*.]
– ORIGIN C19: named after the English botanical collector William Ker(r).

Kerry blue ■ n. a terrier of a breed with a silky blue-grey coat.
– ORIGIN from *Kerry* in Ireland.

kersey /ˈkəːzi/ ■ n. a kind of coarse, ribbed cloth with a short nap, woven from short-stapled wool.
– ORIGIN Middle English: prob. from *Kersey*, a town in Suffolk, England where woollen cloth was made.

kestrel ■ n. a small falcon that hunts by hovering with rapidly beating wings. [*Falco tinnunculus* (Eurasia and Africa), *F. sparverius* (N. America), and other species.]
– ORIGIN Middle English *castrel*, perhaps from *casserelle*, dialect var. of Old French *crecerelle*, perhaps imitative of its call.

ketamine /ˈkiːtəmiːn/ ■ n. a synthetic compound used as an anaesthetic and analgesic drug and also illicitly as a hallucinogen.
– ORIGIN C20: blend of **KETONE** and **AMINE**.

ketch ■ n. a two-masted, fore-and-aft rigged sailing boat with a mizzenmast stepped forward of the rudder and smaller than its foremast.
– ORIGIN C17: later form of obsolete *catch*, prob. from **CATCH**.

ketchup /ˈkɛtʃəp, -ʌp/ (also **catchup**, US also **catsup**) ■ n. a spicy sauce made chiefly from tomatoes and vinegar, used as a relish.
– ORIGIN C17: perhaps from Chinese (Cantonese dialect) *k'ē chap* 'tomato juice'.

keto- /ˈkiːtəʊ/ ■ comb. form Chemistry denoting ketones or the carbonyl group characteristic of them.

ketonaemia /ˌkiːtə(ʊ)ˈniːmɪə/ (US **ketonemia**) ■ n. Medicine the presence of an abnormally high concentration of ketone bodies in the blood.

ketone /ˈkiːtəʊn/ ■ n. Chemistry an organic compound containing a carbonyl group =C=O bonded to two alkyl groups, e.g. acetone.
– DERIVATIVES **ketonic** /kɪˈtɒnɪk/ adj.
– ORIGIN C19: from German *Keton*, alteration of *Aketon* 'acetone'.

ketone bodies ■ pl. n. Biochemistry three related compounds (one of which is acetone) produced during the metabolism of fats.

ketonuria /ˌkiːtə(ʊ)ˈnjʊərɪə/ ■ n. Medicine the excretion of abnormally large amounts of ketone bodies in the urine, characteristic of diabetes mellitus, starvation, or other medical conditions.

ketosis /kɪˈtəʊsɪs/ ■ n. Medicine a condition characterized by raised levels of ketone bodies in the body, associated with abnormal fat metabolism and diabetes mellitus.
– DERIVATIVES **ketotic** adj.

kettle ■ n. a metal or plastic container with a lid, spout, and handle, used for boiling water.
– PHRASES **a different kettle of fish** informal a person or matter that is altogether different from the one just

mentioned. **the pot calling the kettle black** the criticisms a person is aiming at someone could equally well apply to themselves. **a pretty** (or **fine**) **kettle of fish** informal an awkward state of affairs.
– ORIGIN Old English *cetel*, *cietel*, of Germanic origin, based on Latin *catillus*, diminutive of *catinus* 'deep container for cooking or serving food'.

kettledrum ■ n. a large drum shaped like a bowl, with a membrane adjustable for tension (and so pitch) stretched across.
– DERIVATIVES **kettledrummer** n.

kettle hole ■ n. Geology a hollow, typically filled by a lake, resulting from the melting of a mass of ice trapped in glacial deposits.

keurboom /ˈkɪəbʊəm/ ■ n. an evergreen South African tree with profuse pink or mauve scented blossoms. [*Virgilia oroboides* and *V. divaricata*.]
– ORIGIN from Afrikaans *keur* 'choice' + *boom* 'tree'.

keV ■ abbrev. kilo-electronvolt(s).

Kevlar /ˈkɛvlɑː/ ■ n. trademark a synthetic fibre of high tensile strength used especially as a reinforcing agent in the manufacture of tyres and other rubber products.
– ORIGIN 1970s: an arbitrary formation.

kewpie /ˈkjuːpi/ (also **kewpie doll**) ■ n. (trademark in the US) a type of doll characterized by a large head, big eyes, chubby cheeks, and a curl or topknot on top of its head.
– ORIGIN C20: from *Cupid*, the name of the Roman god of love (represented as a naked winged boy).

key[1] ■ n. (pl. **-eys**) **1** a small piece of shaped metal with incisions cut to fit the wards of a particular lock, which is inserted into the lock and rotated to open or close it or to operate a switch. ▸ an instrument for grasping and turning a screw, peg, or nut. ▸ a pin, bolt, or wedge inserted into a hole or between parts so as to lock the parts together. **2** a lever depressed by the finger in playing an instrument such as the organ, piano, flute, or concertina. **3** each of several buttons on a panel for operating a typewriter, word processor, or computer terminal. **4** a lever operating a mechanical device for making or breaking an electric circuit. **5** a thing that provides access to or understanding of something: *a key to success*. ▸ an explanatory list of symbols used in a map or table. ▸ a structured comparison of the significant characteristics of a group of birds, plants, etc., to aid identification. ▸ a set of answers to exercises or problems. ▸ a word or system for solving a cipher or code. ▸ the first move in the solution of a chess problem. **6** Music a group of notes based on a particular note and comprising a scale, regarded as forming the tonal basis of a passage of music. ▸ the tone or pitch of someone's voice. **7** the dry winged fruit of an ash, maple, or sycamore. **8** roughness on a surface, provided to assist adhesion of plaster or other material. **9** Basketball the keyhole-shaped area marked on the court near each basket. ■ adj. of crucial importance: *a key figure*. ■ v. (**-eys**, **-eyed**) **1** enter or operate on (data) by means of a computer keyboard. **2** fasten into position with a pin, wedge, or bolt. **3** (**key to**) link with. ▸ (**key into/in with**) be connected or in harmony with. **4** (**be keyed up**) be nervous, tense, or excited. **5** roughen (a surface) to provide a key.
– PHRASES **in** (or **out of**) **key** in (or out of) harmony.
– DERIVATIVES **keyed** adj. **keyless** adj.
– ORIGIN Old English.

key[2] ■ n. a low-lying island or reef (especially in the Caribbean).
– ORIGIN C17: from Spanish *cayo* 'reef', influenced by QUAY.

keyboard ■ n. **1** a panel of keys for use with a computer or typewriter. **2** a set of keys on a piano or similar musical instrument. **3** an electronic musical instrument with keys arranged as on a piano. ■ v. enter (data) by means of a keyboard.
– DERIVATIVES **keyboarder** n. **keyboardist** n.

key card ■ n. a small plastic card bearing magnetically encoded data that can be read by an electronic device, used instead of a door key.

keyholder ■ n. a person who is entrusted with keeping a key to commercial or industrial premises.

keyhole ■ n. a hole in a lock into which the key is inserted.

keyhole surgery ■ n. minimally invasive surgery carried out through a very small incision, with special instruments and techniques including fibre optics.

key industry ■ n. an industry that is essential to the functioning of others, such as the manufacture of machine tools.

key light ■ n. the main source of light in a photograph or film.

Key lime ■ n. a small yellowish lime with a sharp flavour.
– ORIGIN named after the Florida *Keys*.

keylogger ■ n. a computer program that records every keystroke made by a computer user, especially in order to gain fraudulent access to passwords and other confidential information.
– DERIVATIVES **keylogging** n.

key map ■ n. a map in bare outline, to simplify the use of a full map.

key money ■ n. a payment required from a new tenant in exchange for the provision of a key to the premises.

Keynesian /ˈkeɪnzɪən/ ■ adj. of or relating to the theories of the English economist John Maynard Keynes (1883–1946). ■ n. an adherent of Keynesian theories.
– DERIVATIVES **Keynesianism** n.

keynote ■ n. **1** a prevailing tone or central theme. ▸ [as modifier] (of a speech) setting out the central theme of a conference. **2** Music the note on which a key is based.

keypad ■ n. a miniature keyboard or set of buttons for operating a portable electronic device, telephone, or other equipment.

keypunch ■ n. a device for transferring data by means of punched holes or notches on a series of cards or paper tape. ■ v. transfer (data) to a keypunch.
– DERIVATIVES **keypuncher** n.

key ring ■ n. a metal ring for holding keys together in a bunch.

key signature ■ n. Music any of several combinations of sharps or flats after the clef at the beginning of each stave, indicating the key of a composition.

keystone ■ n. **1** a central stone at the summit of an arch, locking the whole together. **2** the central principle or part of a policy or system.

keystroke ■ n. a single depression of a key on a keyboard.

keyword ■ n. **1** a word which acts as the key to a cipher or code. **2** a word or concept of great significance. ▸ a word used in an information retrieval system to indicate the content of a document. ▸ a significant word mentioned in an index.

kg ■ abbrev. kilogram(s).

kgotla /ˈxɒtlə, ˈkɒtlə/ ■ n. S. African a meeting place of a chief and his tribe or the people of a village. ▸ an assembly of villagers to discuss local affairs. ▸ a tribal court.
– ORIGIN Sesotho and Setswana, 'courtyard, meeting place'.

khaki /ˈkɑːki/ ■ n. (pl. **khakis**) **1** a cotton or wool fabric of a dull brownish-yellow colour, used especially in military clothing. ▸ (**khakis**) clothing made of khaki. ▸ S. African historical a British soldier. **2** a dull brownish-yellow colour.
– ORIGIN C19: from Urdu *k̲h̲ākī* 'dust-coloured', from *k̲h̲āk* 'dust', from Persian.

khaki weed ■ n. S. African **1** a creeping roadside or garden weed with hairy branches and clusters of small pungent straw-coloured flowers, originally from South America. [*Alternanthera pungens*.] **2** (also **khaki bush**) a sticky aromatic shrub with dark green leaves and white flowers followed by seeds with downy tufts, native to the Mediterranean. [*Inula graveolens*.]

Khalsa /ˈkʌlsə/ ■ n. the company of fully initiated Sikhs to which devout orthodox Sikhs are ritually admitted at puberty.
– ORIGIN from Persian, from the feminine form of Arabic *k̲h̲āliṣ* 'pure, belonging to'.

khan /kɑːn, kan/ ■ n. **1** a title given to rulers and officials in central Asia, Afghanistan, and certain other Muslim countries. **2** any of the successors of Genghis Khan, supreme rulers of the Turkish, Tartar, and Mongol peoples and emperors of China in the Middle Ages.
– DERIVATIVES **khanate** n.
– ORIGIN Middle English: from Turkic *k̲h̲ān* 'lord, prince'.

khanga ■ n. variant spelling of KANGA[2].

khat

khat /kɑːt/ ■ n. **1** the leaves of an Arabian shrub, which are chewed (or drunk as an infusion) as a stimulant. **2** the shrub that produces these leaves. [*Catha edulis*.]
– ORIGIN C19: from Arabic *ḳāt*.

Khmer /kmɛː/ ■ n. **1** a native or inhabitant of the ancient kingdom of Khmer in SE Asia. **2** a native or inhabitant of Cambodia. **3** the language of the Khmers, the official language of Cambodia.
– ORIGIN the name in Khmer.

Khoe-khoe /ˈkɔɪkɔɪ/ ■ n. variant spelling of KHOIKHOI.

Khoikhoi /ˈkɔɪkɔɪ/ (also **Khoe-khoe**, **Khoi**) ■ n. (pl. same) **1** a member of a group of indigenous peoples of South Africa and Namibia, including the Nama. **2** any of the group of languages spoken by these peoples.
– ORIGIN Nama, 'men of men'.

Khoisan /ˈkɔɪsɑːn/ ■ n. **1** [usu. treated as pl.] a collective term for the Khoikhoi and San peoples of southern Africa. **2** a language family of southern Africa, including the languages of the Khoikhoi and San, notable for the use of clicks as additional consonants.
– ORIGIN blend of KHOIKHOI and SAN.

kHz ■ abbrev. kilohertz.

ki ■ n. variant spelling of CHI².

kiaat /kɪˈɑːt/ ■ n. a tree with sweetly-scented yellow flowers followed by round, creamy-winged pods. [*Pterocarpus angolensis*.] ▸ the brown, conspicuously grained wood of this tree, used for making furniture.
– ORIGIN from Dutch *kiaat*, from Javanese and Malay *kayu jati*, from *kayu* 'wood' + *jati* 'teak'.

kibble¹ /ˈkɪb(ə)l/ ■ v. [usu. as adj. **kibbled**] grind or chop (beans, grain, etc.) coarsely. ■ n. N. Amer. ground meal shaped into pellets, especially for pet food.
– ORIGIN C18.

kibble² /ˈkɪb(ə)l/ ■ n. an iron hoisting bucket used in mines.
– ORIGIN Middle English: from Middle High German *kübel*, from medieval Latin *cupellus* 'corn measure', diminutive of *cuppa* 'cup'.

kibbutz /kɪˈbʊts/ ■ n. (pl. **kibbutzim** /-ˈtsiːm/) a communal farming settlement in Israel.
– ORIGIN 1930s: from modern Hebrew *qibbūṣ* 'gathering'.

kibbutznik /kɪˈbʊtsnɪk/ ■ n. a member of a kibbutz.

kibe /kaɪb/ ■ n. archaic an ulcerated chilblain.
– ORIGIN Middle English.

kibitz /ˈkɪbɪts/ ■ v. informal, chiefly N. Amer. **1** look on and offer unwelcome advice, especially at a card game. **2** speak informally; chat.
– DERIVATIVES **kibitzer** n.
– ORIGIN 1920s: Yiddish, from German *Kiebitz* 'interfering onlooker'.

kiblah /ˈkɪblə/ (also **qibla**) ■ n. the direction of the Kaaba in Mecca, to which Muslims turn when at prayer.
– ORIGIN C17: from Arabic *ḳibla* 'that which is opposite'.

kibosh /ˈkʌɪbɒʃ/ (also **kybosh**) ■ n. (in phr. **put the kibosh on**) informal put a decisive end to.
– ORIGIN C19.

kick¹ ■ v. **1** strike or propel forcibly with the foot. ▸ strike out with the foot or feet. ▸ (chiefly in rugby) score (a goal) by a kick. ▸ (**kick oneself**) be annoyed with oneself. ▸ (**kick against**) express disagreement or frustration with. ▸ (**kick someone/thing out**) informal expel or dismiss someone or something. **2** informal succeed in giving up (a habit or addiction). **3** (of a gun) recoil when fired. ■ n. **1** an instance of kicking. **2** informal a sharp stimulant effect. ▸ a thrill of pleasurable excitement. **3** Billiards & Snooker an irregular movement of the ball caused by dust.
– PHRASES **kick the bucket** informal die. **a kick in the teeth** informal a grave setback or disappointment. **kick someone upstairs** informal remove someone from an influential position in a business by giving them an ostensible promotion.
– PHRASAL VERBS **kick around** (or **about**) (of a thing) lie unwanted or unexploited. ▸ (of a person) drift idly from place to place. **kick someone around** (or **about**) treat someone roughly or without respect. **kick something around** (or **about**) discuss an idea casually or experimentally. **kick back** N. Amer. informal be at leisure; relax. **kick in** become activated; come into effect. **kick something in** N. Amer. informal contribute something, especially money. **kick off 1** (of a soccer match) be started or resumed by a player kicking the ball from the centre spot. ▸ (also **kick something off**) begin or cause something to begin. **2** become angry. **kick someone out** informal expel or dismiss someone.
– DERIVATIVES **kickable** adj.
– ORIGIN Middle English.

kick² ■ n. archaic an indentation in the bottom of a glass bottle, diminishing the internal capacity.
– ORIGIN C19.

kick-ass ■ adj. informal, chiefly N. Amer. forceful, vigorous, and aggressive.

kickback ■ n. **1** a sudden forceful recoil. **2** informal a payment made to someone who has facilitated a transaction or appointment, especially illicitly.

kickball ■ n. N. Amer. an informal game combining elements of baseball and soccer.

kick-boxing ■ n. a form of martial art which combines boxing with elements of karate, in particular kicking with bare feet.
– DERIVATIVES **kick-boxer** n.

kick-down ■ n. a device for changing gear in a motor vehicle with automatic transmission by full depression of the accelerator.

kick drum ■ n. informal a bass drum played using a pedal.

kicker ■ n. **1** a person or animal that kicks. **2** a player in a team who scores or gains positional advantage by kicking. **3** an extra clause in a contract. **4** informal a small outboard motor. **5** (in poker) a high third card retained in the hand with a pair at the draw.

kicking ■ adj. informal (especially of music) lively and exciting.

kicking strap ■ n. **1** a strap used to prevent a horse from kicking. **2** Nautical a rope lanyard fixed to a boom to prevent it from rising.

kick-off ■ n. the start or resumption of a football match, in which a player kicks the ball from the centre spot.

kick plate ■ n. a metal plate at the base of a door or panel to protect it from damage or wear.

kick-pleat ■ n. an inverted pleat in a narrow skirt to allow freedom of movement.

kickstand ■ n. a metal rod attached to a bicycle or motorcycle that may be kicked into a vertical position to support the vehicle when it is stationary.

kick-start ■ v. **1** start (an engine on a motorcycle) with a downward thrust of a pedal. **2** provide an impetus to start or restart (a process). ■ n. **1** an act or instance of kick-starting. **2** a device to kick-start an engine.

kick-turn ■ n. **1** (in skiing) a turn carried out while stationary by lifting first one and then the other ski through 180°. **2** (in skateboarding) a turn performed with the front wheels lifted off the ground.

kid¹ ■ n. **1** a young goat. ▸ leather made from a young goat's skin. **2** informal a child or young person. ■ v. (**kidded**, **kidding**) (of a goat) give birth.
– PHRASES **handle** (or **treat**) **someone/thing with kid gloves** deal with someone or something very carefully. **kids' stuff** informal something that is easy or simple to do.
– ORIGIN Middle English: from Old Norse *kith*, of Germanic origin.

kid² ■ v. (**kidded**, **kidding**) informal **1** deceive playfully; tease. **2** fool into believing something.
– DERIVATIVES **kidder** n. **kidding** adj. **kiddingly** adv.
– ORIGIN C19: perhaps from KID¹, expressing the notion 'make a child or goat of'.

kid brother ■ n. informal a younger brother.

kiddie (also **kiddy**) ■ n. (pl. **-ies**) informal a young child.

kiddush /ˈkɪdʊʃ/ ■ n. a Jewish ceremony of prayer and blessing over wine, performed at a meal preceding the Sabbath or a holy day.
– ORIGIN C18: from Hebrew *qiddūš* 'sanctification'.

kidnap ■ v. (**kidnapped**, **kidnapping**; US also **kidnaped**, **kidnaping**) abduct and hold captive, typically to obtain a ransom. ■ n. an instance of kidnapping.
– DERIVATIVES **kidnapper** n.

– ORIGIN C17: back-formation from *kidnapper*, from **KID**[1] + slang *nap* 'nab, seize'.

kidney ■ n. (pl. **-eys**) each of a pair of organs in the abdominal cavity, with one concave and one convex side, that excrete urine. ▶ the kidney of a sheep, ox, or pig as food.
– ORIGIN Middle English.

kidney bean ■ n. a kidney-shaped bean, especially a dark red one from a dwarf French bean plant.

kidney dish ■ n. (in medicine) a kidney-shaped receptacle.

kidney machine ■ n. an artificial kidney or dialysis machine.

kidney stone ■ n. a hard mass formed in the kidneys, typically consisting of insoluble calcium compounds; a renal calculus.

kidney vetch ■ n. a yellow- or orange-flowered leguminous Mediterranean grassland plant, sometimes grown as a fodder crop. [*Anthyllis vulneraria*.]

kidology /kɪˈdɒlədʒi/ ■ n. informal, chiefly Brit. the art or practice of deliberately deceiving or teasing people.

kid sister ■ n. informal a younger sister.

kiepersol /ˈkɪpəsɒl/ ■ n. S. African another term for **CABBAGE TREE**.
– ORIGIN Afrikaans, prob. from obsolete Indian English *kittisol* 'parasol'.

kierie /ˈkɪri/ ■ n. S. African another term for **KNOBKERRIE**.
– ORIGIN Afrikaans.

kif /kɪf/ (also **kef**) ■ n. a substance, especially cannabis, smoked to produce a drowsy state. ■ adj. S. African informal fashionably attractive; cool.
– ORIGIN C19: from Arabic *kayf* 'enjoyment, well-being'.

kikoi /kɪˈkɔɪ/ ■ n. (pl. **kikois**) a distinctive striped cloth with an end fringe, used as a wrap-around.
– ORIGIN C20: from Kiswahili.

Kikongo /kɪˈkɒŋɡəʊ/ ■ n. either of two similar Bantu languages spoken in the Congo, the Democratic Republic of Congo, and adjacent areas.
– ORIGIN the name in Kikongo.

Kikuyu /kɪˈkuːjuː/ ■ n. (pl. same or **Kikuyus**) **1** a member of a people forming the largest ethnic group in Kenya. **2** the Bantu language of this people. **3** (**kikuyu**, **kikuyu grass**) a creeping perennial grass which is native to Kenya and cultivated elsewhere as a lawn and fodder grass. [*Pennisetum clandestinum*.]
– ORIGIN the name in Kikuyu.

kilim /kɪˈliːm, ˈkiːlɪm/ (also **kelim**) ■ n. a flat-woven carpet or rug made in Turkey, Kurdistan, and neighbouring areas.
– ORIGIN C19: from Persian *gelīm*.

kill ■ v. **1** cause the death of. ▶ put an end to. ▶ stop (a computing process). ▶ (**kill oneself**) overexert oneself. **2** informal overwhelm with an emotion: *the suspense is killing me.* ▶ cause pain or anguish to. **3** pass (the time). **4** (in soccer and other ball games) make (the ball) stop. ▶ Tennis hit (the ball) so that it cannot be returned. ■ n. **1** an act of killing, especially of one animal by another: *a lion has made a kill.* ▶ an animal or animals killed by a hunter or another animal. **2** informal an act of destroying or disabling an enemy aircraft, submarine, etc.
– PHRASES **be in at the kill** be present at or benefit from the successful conclusion of an enterprise. **go for the kill** take ruthless or decisive action to secure an advantage. **kill someone with kindness** spoil someone through overindulgence.
– ORIGIN Middle English ('strike, beat', also 'put to death'): prob. of Germanic origin.

killer ■ n. **1** a person or thing that kills. **2** informal a formidable person or thing. **3** informal a hilarious joke.

killer bee ■ n. informal, chiefly US an Africanized honeybee.

killer cell ■ n. Physiology a white blood cell (a type of lymphocyte) which destroys infected or cancerous cells.

killer instinct ■ n. a ruthless determination to succeed or win.

killer whale ■ n. a large, toothed whale with distinctive black-and-white markings and a prominent dorsal fin, living in groups that hunt fish, seals, and penguins cooperatively. [*Orcinus orca*.]

killifish /ˈkɪlɪfɪʃ/ ■ n. (pl. same or **-fishes**) a small, typically brightly coloured fish of fresh or brackish water. [Families Aplocheilidae (Africa and SE Asia) and Cyprinodontidae (America and Africa): many species.]
– ORIGIN C19: apparently from **KILL** + **FISH**.

killing ■ n. an act of causing death. ■ adj. **1** [in combination] causing the death of a specified thing: *weed-killing*. **2** informal overwhelming or unbearable.
– PHRASES **make a killing** have a great financial success.
– DERIVATIVES **killingly** adv.

killing field ■ n. (usu. **killing fields**) a place where many people have been massacred or killed.

killing zone (also **kill zone**) ■ n. **1** the area of a military engagement with a high concentration of deaths. **2** an area of the body where entry of a bullet, arrow, etc. would kill.

killjoy ■ n. a person who deliberately spoils the enjoyment of others through resentful or overly sober behaviour.

kiln ■ n. a furnace or oven for burning, baking, or drying, especially one for calcining lime or firing pottery.
– ORIGIN Old English, from Latin *culina* 'kitchen, cooking stove'.

kiln-dry ■ v. [usu. as adj. **kiln-dried**] dry in a kiln.

Kilner jar /ˈkɪlnə/ ■ n. trademark a glass jar with a lid which forms an airtight seal, used to bottle fruit and vegetables.
– ORIGIN C20: from the name of the manufacturing company.

kilo ■ n. (pl. **-os**) **1** a kilogram. **2** a code word representing the letter K, used in radio communication.
– ORIGIN C19: from French, abbrev. of *kilogramme*.

kilo- /ˈkɪləʊ, ˈkiːləʊ/ ■ comb. form denoting a factor of 1 000: *kilolitre*.
– ORIGIN via French from Greek *khilioi* 'thousand'.

kilobase (abbrev.: **kb**) ■ n. Biochemistry (in expressing the lengths of nucleic acid molecules) one thousand bases.

kilobit ■ n. Computing a unit of memory or data equal to 1 024 bits.

kilobyte (abbrev.: **Kb** or **KB**) ■ n. Computing a unit of memory or data equal to 1 024 bytes.

kilocalorie ■ n. a unit of energy of one thousand calories (equal to one large calorie).

kilocycle (abbrev.: **kc**) ■ n. a former measure of frequency, equivalent to 1 kilohertz.

kilogram (also **kilogramme**) (abbrev.: **kg**) ■ n. the SI unit of mass, equal to 1 000 grams (approximately 2.205 lb) and equivalent to the international standard kept at Sèvres near Paris.
– ORIGIN C18: from French *kilogramme* (see **KILO-**, **GRAM**[1]).

kilohertz (abbrev.: **kHz**) ■ n. a measure of frequency equivalent to 1 000 cycles per second.

kilojoule (abbrev.: **kJ**) ■ n. 1 000 joules, especially as a measure of the energy value of foods.

kilolitre (US **kiloliter**) (abbrev.: **kl**) ■ n. 1 000 litres (equivalent to 220 imperial gallons).

kilometre /ˈkɪləˌmiːtə, kɪˈlɒmɪtə/ (US **kilometer**) (abbrev.: **km**) ■ n. a metric unit of measurement equal to 1 000 metres (approximately 0.62 miles).
– DERIVATIVES **kilometric** adj.
– ORIGIN C18: from French *kilomètre* (see **KILO-**, **METRE**[1]).

kiloton (also **kilotonne**) ■ n. a unit of explosive power equivalent to 1 000 tons of TNT.

kilovolt (abbrev.: **kV**) ■ n. 1 000 volts.

kilowatt (abbrev.: **kW**) ■ n. 1 000 watts.

kilowatt-hour (abbrev.: **kWh**) ■ n. a measure of electrical energy equivalent to a power consumption of one thousand watts for one hour.

kilt ■ n. a knee-length skirt of pleated tartan cloth, traditionally worn by men as part of Scottish Highland dress and also worn by women and girls. ■ v. arrange (a garment or material) in vertical pleats.
– DERIVATIVES **kilted** adj.
– ORIGIN Middle English (as v. 'tuck up around the body'): of Scandinavian origin.

kilter

kilter ▪ n. (in phr. **out of kilter**) out of harmony or balance.
– ORIGIN C17.

kimberlite /ˈkɪmbəlʌɪt/ ▪ n. Geology a rare, blue-tinged, coarse-grained intrusive igneous rock sometimes containing diamonds, found in South Africa and Siberia.
– ORIGIN C19: from *Kimberley*, a city and diamond-mining centre in the Northern Cape.

kimono /kɪˈməʊnəʊ/ ▪ n. (pl. **-os**) a long, loose robe having wide sleeves and tied with a sash, originally worn as a formal garment in Japan.
– DERIVATIVES **kimonoed** adj.
– ORIGIN C17: Japanese, from *ki* 'wearing' + *mono* 'thing'.

kin ▪ n. [treated as pl.] one's family and relations. ▪ adj. (of a person) related.
– DERIVATIVES **kinless** adj.
– ORIGIN Old English, of Germanic origin.

-kin ▪ suffix forming diminutive nouns such as *catkin*.
– ORIGIN from Middle Dutch *-kijn*, *-ken*, Middle Low German *-kin*.

kind[1] ▪ n. 1 a class or type of people or things having similar characteristics. 2 character; nature: *the trials were different in kind from any that preceded them*. 3 each of the elements (bread and wine) of the Eucharist.
– PHRASES **in kind** 1 in the same way. 2 (of payment) in goods or services as opposed to money. **kind of** informal rather. **nothing of the kind** not at all like the thing in question. ▸ expressing emphatic denial: *he did nothing of the kind*. **of its kind** within the limitations of its class. **of a kind** hardly or only partly deserving the name: *there is tribute, of a kind, in such popularity*. **one of a kind** unique. **two** (or **three, four,** etc.) **of a kind** the same or very similar. 2 (of cards) having the same face value but of a different suit.
– ORIGIN Old English, of Germanic origin; rel. to KIN.

kind[2] ▪ adj. 1 considerate and generous. 2 (**kind to**) (of a product) not harmful to. 3 archaic affectionate; loving.
– ORIGIN Old English *gecynde* 'natural, native', in Middle English 'well-born', whence 'courteous, gentle'.

kinda ▪ contr. informal kind of.

kindergarten /ˈkɪndəˌɡɑːt(ə)n/ ▪ n. a nursery school.
– DERIVATIVES **kindergartener** n.
– ORIGIN C19: from German, 'children's garden'.

kind-hearted ▪ adj. kind and sympathetic.
– DERIVATIVES **kind-heartedly** adv. **kind-heartedness** n.

kindle[1] /ˈkɪnd(ə)l/ ▪ v. 1 light (a flame); set on fire. 2 (with reference to an emotion) arouse or be aroused.
– DERIVATIVES **kindler** n.
– ORIGIN Middle English: from Old Norse *kynda*, influenced by Old Norse *kindill* 'candle, torch'.

kindle[2] /ˈkɪnd(ə)l/ ▪ v. (of a hare or rabbit) give birth.
– ORIGIN Middle English: apparently from KIND[1].

kindling ▪ n. small sticks or twigs used for lighting fires.

kindly[1] ▪ adv. 1 in a kind manner. 2 please (used in a polite request): *will you kindly sign this letter*.
– PHRASES **look kindly on** regard sympathetically. **not take kindly to** not welcome or be pleased by. **take something kindly** like or be pleased by something. **thank someone kindly** thank someone very much.
– ORIGIN Old English *gecyndelīce* 'naturally, characteristically (see KIND[2]).

kindly[2] ▪ adj. (**-ier, -iest**) kind; warm-hearted.
– DERIVATIVES **kindliness** n.

kindness ▪ n. 1 the quality of being kind. 2 a kind act.

kindred /ˈkɪndrɪd/ ▪ n. 1 [treated as pl.] one's family and relations. 2 relationship by blood. ▪ adj. similar in kind; related.
– ORIGIN Middle English: from KIN + *-red* (from Old English *rǣden* 'condition'), with insertion of *-d-* in the modern spelling through phonetic development (as in *thunder*).

kindred spirit ▪ n. a person whose interests or attitudes are similar to one's own.

kine /kʌɪn/ ▪ pl. n. archaic cows collectively.

kinematics /ˌkɪnɪˈmatɪks, ˌkʌɪn-/ ▪ pl. n. [treated as sing.] the branch of mechanics concerned with the motion of objects without reference to the forces which cause the motion. Compare with DYNAMICS.
– DERIVATIVES **kinematic** adj. **kinematically** adv.
– ORIGIN C19: from Greek *kinēma* 'motion'.

kinematograph /ˌkɪnɪˈmatəɡrɑːf/ ▪ n. variant spelling of CINEMATOGRAPH.

kinesics /kɪˈniːsɪks, kʌɪ-/ ▪ pl. n. [treated as sing.] the study of the way in which certain gestures and movements of the body serve for non-verbal communication.
– ORIGIN 1950s: from Greek *kinēsis* 'motion'.

kinesiology /kɪˌniːsɪˈɒlədʒi, kʌɪ-/ ▪ n. the study of the mechanics of body movements.
– DERIVATIVES **kinesiological** adj. **kinesiologist** n.
– ORIGIN C19: from Greek *kinēsis* 'movement' + -LOGY.

kinesis /kɪˈniːsɪs, kʌɪ-/ ▪ n. (pl. **kineses**) 1 movement; motion. 2 Biology an undirected movement of a cell, organism, or part in response to an external stimulus. Compare with TAXIS. 3 Zoology mobility of the bones of the skull, as in some birds and reptiles.
– ORIGIN C17: from Greek *kinēsis* 'movement'.

kinetic /kɪˈnɛtɪk, kʌɪ-/ ▪ adj. 1 of, relating to, or resulting from motion. 2 (of a work of art) depending on movement for its effect.
– DERIVATIVES **kinetically** adv.
– ORIGIN C19: from Greek *kinētikos*, from *kinein* 'to move'.

kinetic energy ▪ n. Physics energy which a body possesses by virtue of being in motion. Compare with POTENTIAL ENERGY.

kinetics /kɪˈnɛtɪks, kʌɪ-/ ▪ pl. n. [treated as sing.] 1 the branch of chemistry concerned with the rates of chemical reactions. 2 Physics another term for DYNAMICS (in sense 1).

kinetic theory ▪ n. the body of theory which explains the physical properties of matter in terms of the motions of its constituent particles.

kinetin /ˈkʌɪnɪtɪn/ ▪ n. a synthetic compound, used to stimulate cell division in plants.
– ORIGIN 1950s: from Greek *kinetos* 'movable'.

kinetochore /kɪˈniːtəʊkɔː, kʌɪ-/ ▪ n. another term for CENTROMERE.
– ORIGIN C20: from Greek *kinetos* 'movable' + *khōros* 'place'.

kinfolk ▪ pl. n. another term for KINSFOLK.

king ▪ n. 1 the male ruler of an independent state, especially one who inherits the position by right of birth. 2 a person or thing regarded as the finest or most important in its sphere or group. 3 used in names of animals and plants that are particularly large, e.g. king cobra. 4 the most important chess piece, which the opponent has to checkmate in order to win. 5 a piece in draughts with extra capacity for moving, made by crowning an ordinary piece that has reached the opponent's baseline. 6 a playing card bearing a representation of a king, ranking next below an ace.
– DERIVATIVES **kinghood** n. **kingless** adj. **kingliness** n. **kingly** adj. **kingship** n.
– ORIGIN Old English, of Germanic origin; rel. to KIN.

kingbolt ▪ n. a kingpin.

King Charles spaniel ▪ n. a spaniel of a small breed, typically with a white, black, and tan coat.

king cobra ▪ n. a brownish cobra native to the Indian subcontinent, the largest of all venomous snakes. [*Ophiophagus hannah*.]

king crab ▪ n. 1 another term for HORSESHOE CRAB. 2 N. Amer. an edible crab of the North Pacific, resembling a spider crab. [Genus *Paralithodes*.]

kingdom ▪ n. 1 a country, state, or territory ruled by a king or queen. 2 a realm associated with a particular person or thing. 3 the spiritual reign or authority of God. ▸ heaven as the abode of God and of the faithful after death. 4 each of the three divisions (animal, vegetable, and mineral) in which natural objects have conventionally been classified. ▸ Biology the highest category in taxonomic classification.
– PHRASES **till** (or **until**) **kingdom come** informal forever. **to kingdom come** informal into the next world: *the truck was blown to kingdom come*.
– ORIGIN Old English *cyningdōm* 'kingship' (see KING, -DOM).

King Edward ▪ n. an oval potato of a variety with a white skin mottled with red.

– ORIGIN 1920s: named after the British monarch *King Edward* VII.

kingfish ■ n. (pl. same or **-fishes**) a large sea fish, generally valued for food or sport. [Family Carangidae: many species.]

kingfisher ■ n. a colourful bird with a large head and long sharp beak which dives to catch fish in streams, ponds, etc. [Genera include *Alcedo* and *Halcyon*, family Alcedinidae.]

kingfisher blue ■ n. a brilliant turquoise-blue colour.

King James Bible (also **King James Version**) ■ n. another name for AUTHORIZED VERSION.

kingklip /'kɪŋklɪp/ ■ n. a cusk-eel of South African waters, important as a food fish. [*Genypterus capensis*.]
– ORIGIN C19: abbrev. of *kingklipfish*, partly translating Afrikaans *koningklipvis* 'king rock fish'.

kinglet ■ n. chiefly derogatory a minor king.

kingmaker ■ n. a person who brings leaders to power through the exercise of political influence.
– ORIGIN used orig. with ref. to the Earl of Warwick (1428–71), the English statesman known as Warwick the *Kingmaker*.

King of the Castle ■ n. Brit. a children's game in which the object is to beat one's rivals to an elevated position at the top of a mound or other high place.

kingpin ■ n. 1 a main or large bolt in a central position. ▶ a vertical bolt used as a pivot. 2 a person or thing that is essential to the success of an organization or opera-tion.

king prawn ■ n. a large edible prawn. [Genus *Penaeus*.]

king protea ■ n. a southern African plant of the protea family with large pink cone-shaped flowers, the national flower of South Africa. [*Protea cynaroides*.]

kin group ■ n. another term for KINSHIP GROUP.

King's Bench ■ n. Brit. in the reign of a king, the term for QUEEN'S BENCH.

king's bishop ■ n. Chess each player's bishop on the kingside at the start of a game.

King's Counsel ■ n. Brit. in the reign of a king, the term for QUEEN'S COUNSEL.

King's English ■ n. Brit. in the reign of a king, the term for QUEEN'S ENGLISH.

kingside ■ n. Chess the half of the board on which each king stands at the start of a game.

king-sized (also **king-size**) ■ adj. of a larger size than the standard; very large.

king's knight ■ n. Chess each player's knight on the kingside at the start of a game.

king's pawn ■ n. Chess the pawn immediately in front of each player's king at the start of a game.

king's rook ■ n. Chess each player's rook on the kingside at the start of a game.

King's speech ■ n. Brit. in the reign of a king, the term for QUEEN'S SPEECH.

kink ■ n. 1 a sharp twist or curve in something linear. 2 a flaw or obstacle in a plan or project. 3 a quirk of character or behaviour. ■ v. form or cause to form a kink.
– ORIGIN C17: from Middle Low German *kinke*, prob. from Dutch *kinken* 'to kink'.

kinky ■ adj. (**-ier**, **-iest**) 1 having kinks or twists. 2 informal involving or given to unusual sexual behaviour. ▶ (of clothing) sexually provocative.
– DERIVATIVES **kinkily** adv. **kinkiness** n.
– ORIGIN C19: from KINK.

kino /'kiːnəʊ/ ■ n. a gum obtained from certain tropical trees, used as an astringent and in tanning.
– ORIGIN C18: apparently from a West African language.

-kins ■ suffix equivalent to -KIN, typically expressing endearment.

kin selection ■ n. Zoology natural selection in favour of behaviour by individuals which may decrease their own chance of survival but increases that of their kin.

kinsfolk (also **kinfolk**) ■ pl. n. 1 (in anthropological or formal use) a person's blood relations, regarded collectively. 2 a group of people related by blood.

kinship ■ n. 1 blood relationship. 2 a sharing of characteristics or origins: *they felt a kinship with the oppressed*.

kinship group ■ n. Anthropology a family, clan, or other group based on blood relationship.

kinsman (or **kinswoman**) ■ n. (pl. **-men** or **-women**) (in anthropological or formal use) one of a person's blood relations.

kiosk /'kiːɒsk/ ■ n. 1 a small open-fronted hut or cubicle from which newspapers, refreshments, tickets, etc. are sold. 2 (usu. **telephone kiosk**) Brit. a public telephone booth.
– ORIGIN C17: from French *kiosque*, from Turkish *köşk* 'pavilion'.

kip informal ■ n. a sleep; a nap. ■ v. (**kipped**, **kipping**) sleep.
– ORIGIN C18 ('brothel'): perhaps rel. to Danish *kippe* 'hovel, tavern'.

kipper ■ n. a herring that has been split open, salted, and dried or smoked. ■ v. [usu. as adj. **kippered**] cure (a herring) in such a way.
– ORIGIN Old English, of Germanic origin.

kipper tie ■ n. a brightly coloured and very wide tie.

Kir /kɪə/ ■ n. trademark a drink made from dry white wine and crème de cassis.
– ORIGIN 1960s: named after Canon Félix *Kir*, a mayor of Dijon, France said to have invented the recipe.

kirby grip /'kəːbi/ (also trademark **Kirbigrip**) ■ n. Brit. a hairgrip consisting of a thin folded and sprung metal strip.
– ORIGIN 1920s: named after *Kirby*, Beard & Co. Ltd, the original manufacturers.

Kirghiz ■ n. variant spelling of KYRGYZ.

kirk /kəːk/ ■ n. Scottish & N. English 1 a church. 2 (**the Kirk** or **the Kirk of Scotland**) the Church of Scotland.
– ORIGIN Middle English: from Old Norse *kirkja*, from Old English *cirice* (see CHURCH).

kirpan /kəːˈpɑːn/ ■ n. a short curved sword, worn as one of the five distinguishing signs of the Sikh Khalsa.
– ORIGIN from Sanskrit *kṛpāṇa* 'sword'.

kirsch /kɪəʃ/ (also **kirschwasser** /'kɪəʃvasə/) ■ n. brandy distilled from the fermented juice of cherries.
– ORIGIN German, abbrev. of *Kirschenwasser*, from *Kirsche* 'cherry' + *Wasser* 'water'.

kirtle /'kəːt(ə)l/ ■ n. archaic 1 a woman's gown or outer petticoat. 2 a man's tunic or coat.
– ORIGIN Old English *cyrtel*, of Germanic origin, prob. from Latin *curtus* 'short'.

kismet /'kɪzmɛt, -mɪt, -s-/ ■ n. destiny; fate.
– ORIGIN C19: from Arabic *ḳismat* 'division, portion, lot', from *ḳasama* 'to divide'.

kiss ■ v. 1 touch or caress with the lips as a sign of love, affection, or greeting. 2 Billiards & Snooker (of a ball) lightly touch (another ball). 3 (**kiss someone/thing off**) N. Amer. informal dismiss someone rudely; end a relationship abruptly. 4 (**kiss up to**) N. Amer. informal behave obsequiously towards. ■ n. 1 a touch or caress with the lips. 2 Billiards & Snooker a slight touch of a ball against another ball. 3 N. Amer. a small cake, biscuit, or sweet.
– PHRASES **kiss and tell** chiefly derogatory recount one's sexual exploits concerning a famous person. **kiss someone's arse** (or N. Amer. **ass**) vulgar slang behave obsequiously towards someone. **kiss of death** an action that ensures failure, especially when apparently benign. **kiss of life** 1 mouth-to-mouth resuscitation. 2 something that revives a failing enterprise. **kiss of peace** a ceremonial kiss signifying unity, especially during the Eucharist.
– DERIVATIVES **kissable** adj.
– ORIGIN Old English, of Germanic origin.

kiss curl ■ n. a small curl of hair on the forehead, at the nape of the neck, or in front of the ear.

kisser ■ n. 1 a person who kisses someone. 2 informal a person's mouth.

kissing bug ■ n. a bloodsucking North American bug which inflicts a painful bite, often on the face. [*Melanolestes picipes*.]

kissing cousin ■ n. a relative known well enough to greet with a kiss.

kissing gate ■ n. Brit. a small gate hung in a U- or V-shaped enclosure, letting one person through at a time.

kiss-off ■ n. informal, chiefly N. Amer. a rude or abrupt dismissal.

kissogram ■ n. a novelty greeting delivered by a man or woman who accompanies it with a kiss.

kissy ■ adj. informal characterized by or given to kissing.

kist ■ n. 1 S. African a storage chest. [S. African Dutch, from Dutch.] 2 variant spelling of CIST.

Kiswahili /ˌkiːswɑːˈhiːli, ˌkɪswɑː-/ ■ n. another term for SWAHILI (the language).
– ORIGIN from the Bantu prefix ki- (used in names of languages) + SWAHILI.

kit¹ ■ n. 1 a set of articles or equipment for a specific purpose. 2 the clothing and other items needed for an activity. 3 a set of all the parts needed to assemble something. ■ v. (**kit someone/thing out/up**) provide someone or something with appropriate clothing or equipment.
– PHRASES **get one's kit off** Brit. informal take off one's clothes.
– ORIGIN Middle English: from Middle Dutch *kitte* 'wooden vessel'.

kit² ■ n. Brit. historical a small violin, especially one used by a dancing master.
– ORIGIN C16: perhaps from Latin *cithara* (see CITTERN).

kitbag ■ n. a long, cylindrical canvas bag.

kitchen ■ n. 1 a room where food is prepared and cooked. 2 [as modifier] (of a language) in an uneducated or domestic form.
– ORIGIN Old English *cycene*, of West Germanic origin, based on Latin *coquere* 'to cook'.

kitchen cabinet ■ n. informal a group of unofficial advisers considered to be unduly influential.

kitchener ■ n. historical a kitchen range.

kitchenette ■ n. a small kitchen or part of a room equipped as a kitchen.

kitchen garden ■ n. a garden where vegetables, fruit, etc. are grown for domestic use.

kitchen paper ■ n. absorbent paper used for drying and cleaning in a kitchen.

kitchen roll ■ n. Brit. kitchen paper.

kitchen-sink ■ adj. (chiefly of drama) realistic in the depiction of drab or sordid subjects.

kitchen tea ■ n. S. African & Austral./NZ a party before a wedding to which female guests bring kitchen equipment for the bride-to-be.

kitchenware ■ n. kitchen utensils.

kite ■ n. 1 a toy consisting of a light frame with thin material stretched over it, flown in the wind at the end of a long string. 2 Nautical, informal a spinnaker. 3 a long-winged bird of prey with a forked tail, frequently soaring. [*Milvus migrans parasiticus* (yellow-billed kite) and other species.] 4 informal a fraudulent cheque, bill, or receipt. 5 Geometry a quadrilateral figure having two pairs of equal adjacent sides, symmetrical only about one diagonal. ■ v. 1 [usu. as noun **kiting**) fly a kite. ▸ fly; move quickly. 2 informal, chiefly N. Amer. write or use (a fraudulent cheque, bill, or receipt).
– PHRASES (**as**) **high as a kite** informal intoxicated with drugs or alcohol.
– ORIGIN Old English *cȳta* (in sense 3); prob. of imitative origin.

kite-flying ■ n. 1 the action of trying something out to test public opinion. 2 informal the using of a fraudulent cheque, bill, or receipt.

Kitemark ■ n. trademark (in the UK) an official kite-shaped mark on goods approved by the British Standards Institution.

kitesurfing (also **kiteboarding**) ■ n. the sport or pastime of riding on a modified surfboard while holding on to a specially designed kite, using the wind for propulsion.
– DERIVATIVES **kitesurfer** n.

kith /kɪθ/ ■ n. (in phr. **kith and kin**) one's relations.
– ORIGIN Old English *cȳthth* ('knowledge', 'one's native land', and 'friends and neighbours'), of Germanic origin.

kitke /ˈkɪtkə/ ■ n. S. African a plaited loaf of white leavened bread, traditionally baked to celebrate the Jewish sabbath.
– ORIGIN perhaps from Hebrew *kikkar* 'loaf'.

kitsch /kɪtʃ/ ■ n. garish, tasteless, or sentimental art, objects, or design.
– DERIVATIVES **kitschiness** n. **kitschy** adj.
– ORIGIN 1920s: German.

kitten ■ n. a young cat. ▸ the young of certain other animals, such as the rabbit and beaver. ■ v. give birth to kittens.
– PHRASES **have kittens** Brit. informal be extremely nervous or upset.
– ORIGIN Middle English *kitoun, ketoun*, from Old French *chitoun*, diminutive of *chat* 'cat'.

kitten heel ■ n. a type of low stiletto heel.

kittenish ■ adj. playful, lively, or flirtatious.
– DERIVATIVES **kittenishly** adv. **kittenishness** n.

kittiwake /ˈkɪtɪweɪk/ ■ n. a small gull that nests in colonies on sea cliffs and has a loud call that resembles its name. [*Rissa tridactyla*.]

kittle /ˈkɪt(ə)l/ ■ adj. archaic difficult to deal with.
– ORIGIN C16: from *kittle* 'to tickle' (now Scots and dialect), prob. from Old Norse *kitla*.

kitty¹ ■ n. (pl. **-ies**) 1 a fund of money for communal use. 2 a pool of money in some card games. 3 (in bowls) the jack.
– ORIGIN C19 (denoting a jail).

kitty² ■ n. (pl. **-ies**) a pet name for a cat.

kitty-corner ■ adj. & adv. N. Amer. another term for CATER-CORNERED.

Kiwanian /kɪˈwɑːniən/ ■ n. a member of the Kiwanis Club, a North American society of business and professional people which supports local communities. ■ adj. of or relating to the Kiwanis Club.
– ORIGIN C20.

kiwi ■ n. (pl. **kiwis**) 1 a flightless, tailless New Zealand bird with hair-like feathers and a long downcurved bill. [Genus *Apteryx*: three species.] 2 (**Kiwi**) informal a New Zealander.
– ORIGIN C19: from Maori.

kiwi fruit ■ n. (pl. same) the fruit of an East Asian climbing plant (*Actinidia chinensis*), with a thin hairy skin, green flesh, and black seeds.

kJ ■ abbrev. kilojoule(s).

KKK ■ abbrev. Ku Klux Klan.

kl ■ abbrev. kilolitre(s).

klaar /klɑː/ ■ adj. (in phr. **finished and/en klaar** (also **finish and/en klaar**)) S. African informal over and done with; nothing more to be said.
– ORIGIN Afrikaans, 'done, ready'.

klaberjas /ˈklɑːbəjʌs/ (also **klabejas**) ■ n. S. African a card game, similar to piquet, in which the jack of clubs is the highest card.
– ORIGIN Afrikaans, from Dutch *klaverjas*, from *klaver* 'club' + *jas* 'jack of trumps'.

Klansman (or **Klanswoman**) ■ n. (pl. **-men** or **-women**) a member of the Ku Klux Klan.

klap /klʌp/ (also **clap**) S. African informal ■ v. (**klapped**, **klapping**) hit; strike. ■ n. a blow.
– ORIGIN Afrikaans.

klapper ■ n. S. African another term for MONKEY ORANGE.
– ORIGIN from Malay *kelapa* 'coconut', from the similarity in the fruit's casing to the coconut shell.

klaxon /ˈklaks(ə)n/ ■ n. trademark a vehicle horn or warning hooter.
– ORIGIN 1910: the name of the manufacturers.

Kleenex ■ n. (pl. same or **Kleenexes**) trademark a paper tissue.

kleptomania /ˌklɛptə(ʊ)ˈmeɪnɪə/ ■ n. a recurrent urge to steal.
– DERIVATIVES **kleptomaniac** n. & adj.
– ORIGIN C19: from Greek *kleptēs* 'thief' + -MANIA.

kleptoparasite ■ n. Zoology a bird, insect, or other animal which habitually robs another species of food.
– DERIVATIVES **kleptoparasitic** adj. **kleptoparasitism** n.

klezmer /ˈklɛzmə/ ■ n. (pl. **klezmorim** /-rɪm/) **1** traditional eastern European Jewish music. **2** a musician who plays this.
– ORIGIN C20: Yiddish, contraction of Hebrew *kĕlē zemer* 'musical instruments'.

klick ■ n. informal a kilometre.
– ORIGIN C20 (orig. used in the Vietnam War).

klieg light /kliːg/ ■ n. a powerful electric lamp used in filming.
– ORIGIN 1920s: named after the American brothers, Anton T. *Kliegl* and John H. *Kliegl*, who invented it.

Klinefelter's syndrome /ˈklʌɪnˌfɛltəz/ ■ n. Medicine a syndrome affecting males in which the cells have an extra X chromosome, characterized by a tall thin physique, small infertile testes, and enlarged breasts.
– ORIGIN C20: named after the American physician Harry F. *Klinefelter*.

klinker ■ n. S. African variant spelling of **CLINKER**.

klipfish ■ n. (pl. same or **-fishes**) a small variegated viviparous sea fish, found in shallow water or rock pools. [Family Clinidae: many species.]
– ORIGIN partial translation of S. African Dutch *klipvisch*, from Dutch *klip* 'rock' + *visch* 'fish'.

klipspringer /ˈklɪpˌsprɪŋə/ ■ n. a small rock-dwelling African antelope with a yellowish-grey coat. [*Oreotragus oreotragus.*]
– ORIGIN C18: from Afrikaans, from Dutch *klip* 'rock' + *springer* 'jumper'.

kloof /kluːf/ S. African ■ n. a ravine or valley.
– ORIGIN Afrikaans, from Middle Dutch *clove* 'cleft'.

kloofing ■ n. the sport of exploring kloofs, which may involve scrambling up and down cliffs, swimming, and jumping from a height into a stream.

klutz /klʌts/ ■ n. informal, chiefly N. Amer. a clumsy, awkward, or foolish person.
– DERIVATIVES **klutzy** adj.
– ORIGIN 1960s: from Yiddish *klots* 'wooden block'.

klystron /ˈklʌɪstrɒn/ ■ n. Physics an electron tube that generates or amplifies microwaves by velocity modulation.
– ORIGIN 1930s: from Greek *kluzein, klus-* 'wash over'.

km ■ abbrev. kilometre(s).

K-meson ■ n. another term for **KAON**.
– ORIGIN 1950s: from *K* (for **KAON**) + **MESON**.

kn. ■ abbrev. knot(s).

knack ■ n. an acquired or natural skill at performing a task. ▸ a tendency to do something.
– ORIGIN Middle English: prob. rel. to obsolete *knack* 'sharp blow or sound', of imitative origin.

knacker ■ n. **1** Brit., chiefly historical a person who disposes of dead or unwanted animals. **2** (**knackers**) vulgar slang testicles. ■ v. (often as adj. **knackered**) informal exhaust; wear out.
– ORIGIN C16: possibly from obsolete *knack* 'trinket'; sense 2 may be from dialect *knacker* 'castanet'.

knacker's yard ■ n. Brit. a place where old or injured animals are slaughtered.

knap /nap/ ■ v. (**knapped, knapping**) **1** Architecture & Archaeology shape (a stone) by striking it, so as to make a tool or a flat stone for building walls. **2** archaic knock.
– DERIVATIVES **knapper** n.
– ORIGIN Middle English: imitative.

knapsack ■ n. a soldier's or hiker's bag with shoulder straps, carried on the back.
– ORIGIN C17: from Middle Low German, from Dutch *knapzack*, prob. from German *knappen* 'to bite' + *zak* 'sack'.

knapweed ■ n. a tough-stemmed Eurasian plant with purple thistle-like flower heads. [*Centaurea nigra* and related species.]
– ORIGIN Middle English (orig. *knopweed*): from rare *knop* 'knob', from Middle Low German and Middle Dutch *knoppe* (because of its rounded flower heads) + **WEED**.

knave ■ n. **1** archaic a scoundrel. **2** (in cards) a jack.
– DERIVATIVES **knavery** n. (pl. **-ies**) **knavish** adj. **knavishly** adv. **knavishness** n.
– ORIGIN Old English *cnafa* 'boy, servant', of West Germanic origin.

knawel /ˈnɔːɪl/ ■ n. a low-growing inconspicuous plant of the pink family. [Genus *Scleranthus*.]
– ORIGIN C16: from German *Knäuel* 'knotgrass'.

knead ■ v. **1** work (dough or clay) with the hands. **2** massage as if kneading.
– DERIVATIVES **kneadable** adj. **kneader** n.
– ORIGIN Old English, of Germanic origin.

knee ■ n. **1** the joint between the thigh and the lower leg. ▸ a person's lap. **2** an angled piece of wood or metal supporting the beams of a wooden ship. **3** an abrupt obtuse or right-angled bend in a graph. ■ v. (**knees, kneed, kneeing**) hit with the knee.
– PHRASES **at one's mother's** (or **father's**) **knee** at an early age. **bend** (or **bow**) **the** (or **one's**) **knee** (**to**) submit. **bring someone** (or **something**) **to their** (or **its**) **knees** reduce someone or something to a state of weakness or submission. **on bended knee**(**s**) kneeling.
– ORIGIN Old English, of Germanic origin.

kneeboard ■ n. a short board for surfing or waterskiing in a kneeling position.
– DERIVATIVES **kneeboarder** n. **kneeboarding** n.

knee breeches ■ pl. n. archaic short trousers fastened at or just below the knee.

kneecap ■ n. the convex bone in front of the knee joint; the patella. ■ v. (**-capped, -capping**) shoot in the knee or leg as a punishment.

knee-deep ■ adj. **1** immersed up to the knees. ▸ deeply involved in something. **2** so deep as to reach the knees.

knee-halter ■ v. S. African tie a horse's bridle to the knee to prevent it from straying.

knee-high ■ adj. & adv. so high as to reach the knees. ■ n. a stocking with an elasticated top reaching to the knee.
– PHRASES **knee-high to a grasshopper** informal very small or young.

kneehole ■ n. a space for the knees, especially under a desk.

knee-jerk ■ n. an involuntary reflex kick caused by a blow on the tendon just below the knee. ■ adj. automatic and unthinking.

kneel ■ v. (past and past part. **knelt** or chiefly N. Amer. also **kneeled**) fall or rest on a knee or the knees.
– ORIGIN Old English: rel. to **KNEE**.

knee-length ■ adj. reaching up or down to the knees.

kneeler ■ n. **1** a person who kneels. **2** a cushion or bench for kneeling on.

knees-up ■ n. Brit. informal a lively party.

knee-trembler ■ n. informal an act of sexual intercourse between people in a standing position.

knell /nɛl/ poetic/literary ■ n. the sound of a bell, especially when rung solemnly for a death or funeral. ▸ something regarded as a warning of disaster. ■ v. (of a bell) ring solemnly. ▸ proclaim by or as if by a knell.
– ORIGIN Old English, of West Germanic origin; the spelling is perhaps influenced by **BELL**[1].

knelt past and past participle of **KNEEL**.

knew past of **KNOW**.

knickerbocker ■ n. **1** (**knickerbockers**) loose-fitting breeches gathered at the knee or calf. **2** (**Knickerbocker**) informal a New Yorker.
– DERIVATIVES **knickerbockered** adj.
– ORIGIN C19: named after Diedrich *Knickerbocker*, pretended author of W. Irving's *History of New York* (1809); sense 1 is said to be from the knee breeches worn by Dutch settlers in Irving's book.

Knickerbocker Glory ■ n. Brit. a dessert consisting of ice cream, fruit, and cream in a tall glass.

knickers ■ pl. n. **1** Brit. a woman's or girl's undergarment, covering the body from the waist or hips to the top of the thighs and having two holes for the legs. **2** N. Amer. knickerbockers.
– PHRASES **get one's knickers in a knot** (or Brit. **twist**) informal become upset or angry.
– DERIVATIVES **knickered** adj. **knickerless** adj.
– ORIGIN C19: abbrev. of *knickerbockers* (see **KNICKERBOCKER**).

knick-knack

knick-knack (also **nick-nack**) ■ n. a small worthless object, especially an ornament.
– DERIVATIVES **knick-knackery** n.
– ORIGIN C16 ('a petty trick'): reduplication of KNACK.

knick point /nɪk/ ■ n. Geology an abrupt change of gradient in the profile of a stream or river.
– ORIGIN C20: partial translation of German *Knickpunkt*, from *Knick* 'bend'.

knife ■ n. (pl. **knives**) 1 a cutting instrument consisting of a blade fixed into a handle. 2 a cutting blade on a machine. ■ v. 1 stab with a knife. 2 cut like a knife.
– PHRASES **before you can say knife** informal very quickly. **that one could cut with a knife** (of an accent or atmosphere) very obvious. **get** (or **stick**) **the knife into** (or **in**) informal treat in a hostile or aggressive manner. **go** (or **be**) **under the knife** informal have surgery.
– DERIVATIVES **knife-like** adj. **knifer** n.
– ORIGIN Old English, from Old Norse *knífr*, of Germanic origin.

knife block ■ n. a block of wood with long hollow grooves into which kitchen knives can be inserted.

knife-edge ■ n. 1 the cutting edge of a knife. 2 a very tense or dangerous situation. 3 [as modifier] (of creases or pleats) very fine. 4 a steel wedge on which a pendulum or other device oscillates or is balanced. 5 an arête.

knifeman ■ n. (pl. **-men**) a man who uses a knife as a weapon.

knife pleat ■ n. a sharp, narrow pleat on a skirt.

knifepoint ■ n. the pointed end of a knife.
– PHRASES **at knifepoint** under threat of injury from a knife.

knight ■ n. 1 (in England and Wales in the Middle Ages) a man raised to honourable military rank after service as a page and squire. ▶ (also **knight of the shire**) historical a gentleman representing a shire or county in the British Parliament. ▶ poetic/literary a man devoted to a cause or the service of a woman. 2 (in the UK) a man awarded a non-hereditary title by the sovereign and entitled to use the honorific 'Sir' in front of his name. 3 a chess piece, typically shaped like a horse's head, that moves by jumping to the opposite corner of a rectangle two squares by three. ■ v. invest with the title of knight.
– PHRASES **knight in shining armour** (or **knight on a white charger**) an idealized chivalrous man.
– DERIVATIVES **knighthood** n. **knightliness** n. **knightly** adj.
– ORIGIN Old English *cniht* 'boy, servant', of West Germanic origin.

knight bachelor ■ n. (pl. **knights bachelor**) (in the UK) a knight not belonging to any particular order of knighthood.

knight commander ■ n. a very high class in some orders of knighthood.

knight errant ■ n. a medieval knight wandering in search of chivalrous adventures.
– DERIVATIVES **knight-errantry** n.

knight service ■ n. (in the Middle Ages) the tenure of land by a knight on condition of performing military service.

kniphofia /nɪˈfəʊfɪə, nʌɪ-, nɪpˈhəʊfɪə/ ■ n. a plant of a genus comprising the red-hot pokers. [Genus *Kniphofia*.]
– ORIGIN named after the C18 German botanist Johann H. *Kniphof*.

knit ■ v. (**knitting**; past and past part. **knitted** or (especially in sense 2) **knit**) 1 make by interlocking loops of yarn with knitting needles or on a machine. ▶ make (a plain stitch) in knitting. 2 unite or cause to unite. ▶ (of parts of a broken bone) become joined. 3 tighten (one's eyebrows) in a frown. ■ n. (**knits**) knitted garments.
– DERIVATIVES **knitter** n.
– ORIGIN Old English, of West Germanic origin; rel. to KNOT[1].

knitting ■ n. the craft or action of knitting.

knitting needle ■ n. a long, thin, pointed rod used as part of a pair for hand knitting.

knitwear ■ n. knitted garments.

knives plural form of KNIFE.

knob ■ n. 1 a rounded lump or ball, especially at the end or on the surface of something. 2 a ball-shaped handle on a door or drawer. 3 a round button on a machine. 4 a small lump of something. 5 chiefly N. Amer. a prominent round hill. 6 vulgar slang a man's penis.
– PHRASES **with** (**brass**) **knobs on** Brit. informal and something more, used especially for returning an insult.
– DERIVATIVES **knobbed** adj. **knobby** adj. **knob-like** adj.
– ORIGIN Middle English: from Middle Low German *knobbe* 'knot, knob, bud'.

knobble ■ n. Brit. a small lump on something.
– DERIVATIVES **knobbly** adj. (**-ier, -iest**).
– ORIGIN Middle English: diminutive of KNOB.

knobkerrie /ˈnɒbˌkɛri/ (also **knobkierie**) ■ n. S. African a short stick with a knobbed head, used as a weapon.
– ORIGIN C19: from KNOB + *-kerrie* (from Nama *kieri* 'knobkerrie'), suggested by Afrikaans *knopkierie*.

knobstick ■ n. another term for KNOBKERRIE.

knobthorn ■ n. a southern African tree with hooked thorns borne on knobby protuberances on the trunk and branches, bearing spikes of cream, sweet-smelling flowers. [*Acacia nigrescens*.]

knobwood ■ n. a southern African tree with spine-tipped knobs on the trunk, citrus-smelling leaves, cream flowers, and clusters of round reddish-orange fruits. [Genus *Zanthoxylum*: several species.]

knock ■ v. 1 strike a surface noisily to attract attention. ▶ strike or thump together or against something. ▶ (of a motor) make a thumping or rattling noise. 2 collide forcefully with. ▶ force to move or fall with a blow or collision. ▶ damage by striking. 3 make (a hole, dent, etc.) in something by striking it. ▶ bring into a specified condition: *two rooms had been knocked into one.* 4 informal criticize. ■ n. 1 a sudden short sound caused by a blow. ▶ a continual thumping or rattling made by an engine. 2 a blow or collision. 3 a setback. ▶ informal a critical comment. 4 Cricket, informal an innings.
– PHRASES **knock it off** informal stop doing something. **knock someone on the head** euphemistic kill someone. **knock something on the head** Brit. informal put an end to an idea, plan, etc. **knock spots off** Brit. informal easily outdo. **the school of hard knocks** painful or difficult but useful life experiences.
– PHRASAL VERBS **knock about** (or **around**) informal 1 spend time or travel without a specific purpose. 2 happen to be present. **knock something back** informal consume a drink quickly. **knock something down** 1 (at an auction) confirm a sale by a knock with a hammer. ▶ informal reduce the price of an article. 2 US informal earn a specified sum as a wage. **knock off** informal stop work. **knock someone off** 1 informal kill someone. 2 Brit. vulgar slang have sexual intercourse with a woman. **knock something off** 1 informal produce a piece of work quickly and easily. 2 informal deduct an amount from a total. 3 Brit. informal steal something. **knock on** 1 informal grow old. 2 (also **knock the ball on**) Rugby illegally drive the ball with the hand or arm towards the opponents' goal line. **knock someone out** 1 make someone unconscious. ▶ knock down (a boxer) for a count of ten. ▶ informal astonish or greatly impress someone. 2 eliminate a competitor from a knockout competition. **knock something out** 1 destroy or disable equipment. 2 informal produce work at a steady fast rate. **knock someone sideways** informal astonish someone. **knock something together** assemble something roughly and hastily. **knock up** informal (in a racket game) practise before play begins. **knock someone up** 1 Brit. awaken someone by knocking at their door. 2 informal, chiefly N. Amer. make a woman pregnant. **knock something up** 1 make something hurriedly. 2 Cricket score runs rapidly.
– ORIGIN Old English, of imitative origin.

knockabout ■ adj. 1 denoting rough, slapstick comedy. 2 (of clothes) suitable for rough use. ■ n. US & Austral. a tramp.

knock and drop ■ n. [as modifier] denoting or relating to the door-to-door delivery of free leaflets or publications.

knock-back ■ n. informal a refusal or setback.

knock-down ■ adj. 1 informal (of a price) very low. 2 capable of knocking someone or something down. ▶ (of furniture) easily dismantled. ■ n. Boxing an act of knocking an opponent down.

CONSONANTS b but d dog f few g get h he j yes k cat l leg m man n no p pen r red

knocker ■ n. **1** an object hinged to a door and rapped by visitors to attract attention. **2** informal a person who buys or sells from door to door. **3** informal a person who continually finds fault. **4** (**knockers**) informal a woman's breasts.

knock-for-knock agreement ■ n. S. African & Brit. an agreement between insurance companies by which each pays its own policyholders regardless of liability.

knocking shop ■ n. Brit. informal a brothel.

knock knees ■ pl. n. a condition in which the legs curve inwards at the knee.
– DERIVATIVES **knock-kneed** adj.

knock-off ■ n. informal a copy or imitation.

knock-on ■ n. **1** a secondary, indirect, or cumulative effect. **2** Rugby an act of knocking on.

knockout ■ n. **1** an act of knocking someone out. **2** a tournament in which the loser in each round is eliminated. **3** informal an extremely attractive or impressive person or thing.

knockout drops ■ pl. n. a liquid drug added to a drink to cause unconsciousness.

knock-up ■ n. Brit. (in racket sports) a period of practice play before a game.

knoll¹ /nəʊl/ ■ n. a small hill or mound.
– ORIGIN Old English, of Germanic origin.

knoll² /nəʊl/ ■ v. & n. archaic form of KNELL.
– ORIGIN Middle English: prob. an imitative alteration of KNELL.

knot¹ ■ n. **1** a fastening made by looping a piece of string, rope, etc. on itself and tightening it. ▸ a tangled mass in hair, wool, etc. ▸ an ornamental ribbon. **2** a protuberance or node in a stem, branch, or root. ▸ a hard mass in wood at the intersection of a trunk with a branch. ▸ a hard lump of bodily tissue. **3** a small group of people. **4** a unit of speed equivalent to one nautical mile per hour, used of ships, aircraft, or winds. ■ v. (**knotted**, **knotting**) **1** fasten with a knot. ▸ make (a carpet) with knots. ▸ tangle. **2** cause (a muscle) to become tense and hard. ▸ (of the stomach) tighten as a result of tension.
– PHRASES **at a rate of knots** Brit. informal very fast. **get knotted** Brit. informal go away. **tie someone (up) in knots** informal confuse someone completely. **tie the knot** informal get married.
– DERIVATIVES **knotless** adj. **knotter** n.

> **HISTORY**
> Knot is first recorded in Old English in the sense 'a fastening made in string or rope'. The link with the later (17th-century) usage as a unit of speed for ships and aircraft is made through the knotted line of the nautical device called a *log* (see LOG¹). The number of **knots**, or length of line, that was run out in a certain time gave an estimate of the vessel's speed. There is no foundation for the attractive story that relates it to King Canute (Danish *Knut*), who tried to stop the tide.

knot² ■ n. (pl. same or **knots**) a short-billed northern sandpiper. [*Calidris canutus*.]
– ORIGIN Middle English.

knot garden ■ n. an intricately designed formal garden.

knotgrass ■ n. a common plant of the dock family, with jointed creeping stems and small pink flowers. [*Polygonum aviculare* and related species.]

knothole ■ n. a hole in a piece of wood where a knot has fallen out.

knotting ■ n. the action or craft of tying knots in yarn to make carpets or other decorative items. ▸ the knots in such an item.

knotty ■ adj. (-ier, -iest) **1** full of knots. **2** extremely difficult or intricate.
– DERIVATIVES **knottily** adv. **knottiness** n.

know ■ v. (past **knew**; past part. **known**) **1** be aware of through observation, inquiry, or information. ▸ have knowledge or information concerning. ▸ be absolutely sure of something. **2** be familiar or friendly with. ▸ have a good command of (a subject or language). ▸ have personal experience of. ▸ (usu. **be known as**) regard as having a specified characteristic or title. **3** archaic have sexual intercourse with.
– PHRASES **be in the know** be aware of something known only to a few people. **God** (or **goodness** or **heaven**) **knows** I have no idea. **I know** (**what**) I have a new idea. **know better than** be wise enough to avoid doing something. **know someone by sight** recognize someone without knowing their name or being well acquainted with them. **know no bounds** have no limits. **know one's own mind** be decisive and certain. **know the ropes** have experience of the appropriate procedures. **know what's what** informal be experienced and competent in a particular area. **not want to know** informal refuse to react or take notice. **what do you know** (**about that**)? N. Amer. informal used as an expression of surprise. **you know** informal implying something generally known or known by the listener. ▸ used as a gap-filler in conversation.
– DERIVATIVES **knowable** adj. **knower** n.
– ORIGIN Old English *cnāwan* 'recognize, identify', of Germanic origin; rel. to CAN¹ and KEN.

know-all (also **know-it-all**) ■ n. informal a person who behaves as if they know everything.

know-how ■ n. expertise.

knowing ■ adj. **1** suggesting that one has secret knowledge. **2** chiefly derogatory experienced or shrewd, especially excessively or prematurely so. ■ n. the state of being aware or informed.
– PHRASES **there is no knowing** no one can tell.
– DERIVATIVES **knowingly** adv. **knowingness** n.

knowledge ■ n. **1** information and skills acquired through experience or education. ▸ the sum of what is known. ▸ Philosophy true, justified belief, as opposed to opinion. **2** awareness or familiarity gained by experience.
– PHRASES **come to one's knowledge** become known to one. **to** (**the best of**) **my knowledge 1** so far as I know. **2** as I know for certain.
– ORIGIN Middle English (orig. as v. 'acknowledge, recognize'): from an Old English compound based on *cnāwan* (see KNOW).

knowledgeable (also **knowledgable**) ■ adj. intelligent and well informed.
– DERIVATIVES **knowledgeability** n. **knowledgeably** adv.

knowledge economy ■ n. an economy in which growth is dependent on the quantity, quality, and accessibility of the information available, rather than the means of production.

knowledge worker ■ n. a person whose job involves handling or using information.

known past participle of KNOW. ■ adj. **1** recognized, familiar, or within the scope of knowledge. **2** publicly acknowledged to be. **3** Mathematics (of a quantity or variable) having a value that can be stated.

knuckle ■ n. **1** a part of a finger at a joint where the bone is near the surface. **2** a projection of the carpal or tarsal joint of a quadruped. ▸ a joint of meat consisting of such a projection together with the adjoining parts. ■ v. rub or press with the knuckles.
– PHRASES **near the knuckle** Brit. informal verging on the indecent or offensive. **rap someone on** (or **over**) **the knuckles** rebuke or criticize someone.
– PHRASAL VERBS **knuckle down 1** apply oneself seriously to a task. **2** (also **knuckle under**) submit.
– DERIVATIVES **knuckly** adj.
– ORIGIN Middle English, from Middle Low German, Middle Dutch *knökel*, diminutive of *knoke* 'bone'; the verb *knuckle* (*down*) expressed setting the knuckles down to start a game of marbles.

knuckleball ■ n. Baseball a slow pitch made by releasing the ball from the knuckles of the index and middle finger.
– DERIVATIVES **knuckleballer** n.

knuckle bone ■ n. a bone forming or corresponding to a knuckle. ▸ a knuckle of meat.

knuckleduster ■ n. a metal guard worn over the knuckles in fighting to increase the effect of blows.

knucklehead ■ n. informal a stupid person.

knuckle joint ■ n. a hinged joint in which a projection in one part fits into a recess in the other.

knuckle sandwich ■ n. informal a punch in the mouth.

knurl

knurl /nəːl/ ■ n. a small projecting knob or ridge.
– DERIVATIVES **knurled** adj.
– ORIGIN C17: apparently a derivative of Middle English *knur*, var. of *knarre*, denoting a rugged rock or stone.

Knysna lily /ˈnaɪznə/ ■ n. another term for GEORGE LILY.
– ORIGIN named after the town of *Knysna* in the Western Cape.

Knysna turaco /ˈnaɪznə/ (also **Knysna lourie**) ■ n. a large southern African turaco that is mainly green with a white-tipped crest and crimson underwing. [*Tauraco corythaix*.]

KO[1] ■ abbrev. kick-off.

KO[2] Boxing ■ n. a knockout in a boxing match. ■ v. (**KO's, KO'd, KO'ing**) knock out in a boxing match.
– ORIGIN 1920s: abbrev.

koala /kəʊˈɑːlə/ ■ n. a bear-like arboreal Australian marsupial that has thick grey fur and feeds on eucalyptus leaves. [*Phascolarctos cinereus*.]
– ORIGIN C19: from an extinct Aboriginal language.

koan /ˈkəʊɑːn, ˈkəʊan/ ■ n. a paradoxical anecdote or riddle, used in Zen Buddhism to show the inadequacy of logical reasoning and provoke enlightenment.
– ORIGIN Japanese, 'matter for public thought', from Chinese *gōngàn* 'official business'.

kob[1] (also **cob**) ■ n. (pl. same or **kobs**) a large edible marine fish that inhabits tropical and temperate waters. [Genus *Argyrosomus*: several species.]
– ORIGIN C20: abbrev. of KABELJOU, with anglicization of the vowel.

kob[2] ■ n. (pl. same) a southern African antelope with a reddish coat and lyre-shaped horns. [*Kobus kob*.]
– ORIGIN C18: from Wolof *kooba*.

Kodiak bear /ˈkəʊdɪak/ ■ n. a large brown bear of a race found on Kodiak and other Alaskan islands.

koekoek /ˈkʊkkʊk/ ■ n. S. African short for POTCHEFSTROOM KOEKOEK.
– ORIGIN Afrikaans, prob. from isiXhosa and isiZulu *inkuku* 'chicken'.

koeksister /ˈkʊksɪstə/ (also **koeksuster**) ■ n. S. African a plaited fried doughnut dipped in syrup.
– ORIGIN Afrikaans, prob. from Dutch *koek* 'cake' + *sister*, perhaps from *sissen* 'sizzle'.

kofta /ˈkɒftə, ˈkəʊftə/ ■ n. (pl. same or **koftas**) (in Middle Eastern and Indian cookery) a savoury ball of minced meat, paneer, or vegetables.
– ORIGIN from Urdu and Persian *koftah* 'pounded meat'.

kohen /ˈkɒhɛn, kɔɪn/ (also **cohen**) ■ n. (pl. **kohanim** /-nɪm/ or **cohens**) Judaism a member of the priestly caste.
– ORIGIN from Hebrew, 'priest'.

kohl /kəʊl/ ■ n. a black powder, usually antimony sulphide or lead sulphide, used as eye make-up, especially in Eastern countries.
– ORIGIN C18: from Arabic *kuḥl*.

kohlrabi /kəʊlˈrɑːbi/ ■ n. (pl. **kohlrabies**) a cabbage of a variety with an edible turnip-like swollen stem.
– ORIGIN C19: from Italian *cavoli rape*, pl. of *cavola rapa*, from medieval Latin *caulorapa*, from Latin *caulis* 'stem, cabbage' + *rapum* 'turnip'.

koi /kɔɪ/ ■ n. (pl. same) a large common carp of a Japanese ornamental variety.
– ORIGIN C18: from Japanese, 'carp'.

koine /ˈkɔɪniː/ ■ n. **1** the common language of the Greeks from the close of the classical period to the Byzantine era. **2** a lingua franca.
– ORIGIN C19: from Greek *koinē* (*dialektos*) 'common (language)'.

koinonia /kɔɪˈnəʊnɪə/ ■ n. Theology Christian fellowship.
– ORIGIN C20: from Greek *koinōnia* 'fellowship'.

kokerboom /ˈkʊəkəbʊəm/ ■ n. another term for QUIVER TREE.
– ORIGIN from S. African Dutch *koker* 'sheath, quiver' + *boom* 'tree'.

Koki /ˈkəʊki/ (also **koki pen**) ■ n. S. African trademark a coloured felt-tipped pen.

kola ■ n. variant spelling of COLA (in sense 2).

kolkhoz /ˈkɒlkɒz, kʌlkˈhɔːz/ ■ n. (pl. same or **kolkhozes** or **kolkhozy**) a collective farm in the former USSR.
– ORIGIN 1920s: Russian, from *kol*(*lektivnoe*) *khoz*(*yaĭstvo*) 'collective farm'.

kombi /ˈkɒmbi/ (also **combi**) ■ n. S. African a minibus, especially one used as a taxi.
– ORIGIN from Volkswagen's proprietary name *Kombi*, abbrev. of German *Kombiwagen*, from *Kombination* 'combination' + *Wagen* 'car'.

Komodo dragon ■ n. a very large monitor lizard native to Komodo and neighbouring Indonesian islands. [*Varanus komodoensis*.]

konfyt /kɒnˈfeɪt/ ■ n. S. African a preserve containing whole fruits or pieces of fruit.
– ORIGIN Afrikaans, from Dutch *konfijt*.

Kongo /ˈkɒŋɡəʊ/ ■ n. (pl. same or **-os**) **1** a member of an indigenous people inhabiting the region of the River Congo in west central Africa. **2** Kikongo, the Bantu language of this people.
– ORIGIN the name in Kikongo.

kooboo-berry ■ n. an evergreen African shrub or small tree which bears small edible reddish-purple fruits. [*Mystroxylon aethiopicum*.]
– ORIGIN partial translation of Afrikaans *koeboebessie*, *kububessie*, perhaps from Khoikhoi *kubu* 'round' + BERRY.

kooigoed /ˈkɔɪxʊt/ S. African ■ n. **1** a South African sedge, the dried culms of which are used as straw or for weaving mats or baskets. [*Cyperus textilis* and other species.] **2** any of several species of southern African everlasting with aromatic leaves and flowers traditionally used in pillows and other bedding. [Genus *Helichrysum*.]
– ORIGIN Afrikaans, 'bedding'.

kook ■ n. N. Amer. informal a mad or eccentric person.
– ORIGIN 1960s: prob. from CUCKOO.

kookaburra /ˈkʊkəˌbʌrə/ ■ n. a very large Australasian kingfisher that feeds on reptiles and birds and has a loud cackling call. [*Dacelo novaeguineae*.]
– ORIGIN C19: from Wiradhuri (an extinct Aboriginal language) *gugubarra*.

kooky ■ adj. (**-ier, -iest**) informal strange or eccentric.
– DERIVATIVES **kookily** adv. **kookiness** n.

kop ■ n. S. African (especially in place names) a hill or peak.
– ORIGIN Afrikaans, from Dutch, 'head'.

kopek /ˈkəʊpɛk, ˈkɒpɛk/ (also **copeck** or **kopeck**) ■ n. a monetary unit of Russia and some other countries of the former USSR, equal to one hundredth of a rouble.
– ORIGIN from Russian *kopeĭka*, diminutive of *kop'ë* 'lance' (from the figure on the coin (1535) of Tsar Ivan IV, bearing a lance).

koppie /ˈkɒpi/ (also **kopje**) ■ n. S. African a small hill.
– ORIGIN Afrikaans, from Dutch *kopje*, diminutive of *kop* 'head'.

kora /ˈkɔːrə/ ■ n. a West African musical instrument shaped like a lute and played like a harp.
– ORIGIN C18: a local word.

Koran /kɔːˈrɑːn, kə-/ (also **Quran** or **Qur'an** /kʊ-/) ■ n. the Islamic sacred book, believed to be the word of God as dictated to Muhammad and written down in Arabic.
– DERIVATIVES **Koranic** /-ˈranɪk, -ˈrɑːnɪk/ adj.
– ORIGIN from Arabic *ḳurʾān* 'recitation', from *ḳaraʾa* 'read, recite'.

Korean ■ adj. of or relating to North or South Korea or its people or language. ■ n. **1** a native or national of North or South Korea, or a person of Korean descent. **2** the language of Korea, distantly related to Japanese.

korfball /ˈkɔːfbɔːl/ ■ n. a game similar to basketball, played by teams each consisting of six men and six women.
– ORIGIN C20: from Dutch *korfbal*, from *korf* 'basket' + *bal* 'ball'.

korhaan /ˈkɔːrɑːn/ ■ n. a long-necked, long-legged African bird of open country, the males of which are boldly marked. [Genera *Afrotis*, *Eupodotis* and *Lophotis*: several species.]
– ORIGIN imitative of its call; transferred use of Dutch *korhaan*, denoting the male black grouse, from *korren* 'to coo' + *haan* 'cock'.

Kori bustard ■ n. a very large grey and brown bustard with a small crest, occurring in open country in southern and eastern Africa. [*Ardeotis kori*.]

korma /ˈkɔːmə/ ■ n. a mild Indian curry of meat or fish marinaded in yogurt or curds.
– ORIGIN from Urdu ḵormā, from Turkish kavurma.

Korsakoff's syndrome /ˈkɔːsəkɒfs/ ■ n. Psychiatry a serious mental illness with loss of recent memory, typically the result of chronic alcoholism.
– ORIGIN C20: named after the C19 Russian psychiatrist Sergei S. Korsakoff.

kosher /ˈkəʊʃə/ ■ adj. 1 satisfying the requirements of Jewish law with regards to the preparation of food. 2 informal genuine and legitimate. ■ v. prepare (food) according to Jewish law.
– ORIGIN C19: from Hebrew kāšēr 'proper'.

Kosovar /ˈkɒsəvɑː/ ■ n. a native or inhabitant of Kosovo, a former province of Serbia whose population is largely of Albanian descent.
– DERIVATIVES **Kosovan** n. & adj.

koumiss /ˈkuːmɪs/ ■ n. a fermented liquor prepared from mare's milk, used as a drink and medicine by Asian nomads.
– ORIGIN C16: from Tartar kumiz.

kowtow /kaʊˈtaʊ/ ■ v. 1 historical kneel and touch the ground with the forehead in submission as part of Chinese custom. 2 be excessively subservient towards someone. ■ n. historical an act of kowtowing.
– DERIVATIVES **kowtower** n.
– ORIGIN C19: from Chinese kētóu, from kē 'knock' + tóu 'head'.

kph ■ abbrev. kilometres per hour.

Kr ■ symb. the chemical element krypton.

kraal /krɑːl/ S. African ■ n. 1 a traditional rural settlement of huts and houses; a village. 2 another term for **HOMESTEAD** (in sense 3). 3 an animal enclosure. ■ v. drive (animals) into a kraal.
– ORIGIN Dutch, from Portuguese curral, perhaps from Latin currere 'to run'.

kraft /krɑːft/ (also **kraft paper**) ■ n. a kind of strong, smooth brown wrapping paper.
– ORIGIN C20: from Swedish, 'strength'.

kragdadigheid /krax'dɑːdəxheɪt/ ■ n. S. African forceful and uncompromising tactics, especially in politics or policing.
– ORIGIN from Afrikaans kragdadig 'autocratic, heavy-handed' + suffix -heid '-ness'.

krait /kraɪt/ ■ n. a highly venomous Asian cobra. [Genus Bungarus: several species.]
– ORIGIN C19: from Hindi karait.

kraken /ˈkrɑːk(ə)n/ ■ n. a mythical sea monster said to appear off the coast of Norway.
– ORIGIN from Norwegian.

kramat /krɑˈmɑt/ ■ n. S. African an Islamic shrine, especially the tomb of a holy man.
– ORIGIN from Malay keramat 'holy person or place', from Arabic karama 'miracle performed by a holy man'.

krantz /krɑːns/ (also **krans**) ■ n. S. African a precipitous or overhanging wall of rocks.
– ORIGIN S. African Dutch, from Dutch krans 'coronet'.

Kraut /kraʊt/ ■ n. informal, offensive a German.
– ORIGIN FIRST WORLD WAR: shortening of **SAUERKRAUT**.

Krebs cycle /krɛbz/ ■ n. Biochemistry the sequence of reactions by which living cells generate energy during aerobic respiration.
– ORIGIN 1940s: named after the German-born British biochemist Sir Hans Krebs.

kremlin /ˈkrɛmlɪn/ ■ n. a citadel within a Russian town. ▸ (**the Kremlin**) the citadel in Moscow, housing the Russian government.
– ORIGIN C17: from Russian kreml' 'citadel'.

kriegspiel /ˈkriːgspiːl/ ■ n. 1 a war game in which blocks representing armies are moved about on maps. 2 a form of chess with an umpire, in which each player has only limited information about the opponent's moves.
– ORIGIN C19: from German, from Krieg 'war' + Spiel 'game'.

kriging /ˈkriːgɪŋ, ˈkrɪxɪŋ/ ■ n. a statistical technique for evaluating the economic potential of a mineral deposit.
– ORIGIN 1960s: named after D.G. Krige of Johannesburg, who developed the procedure.

kukri

krill ■ pl. n. small shrimp-like planktonic crustaceans which are the principal food of baleen whales. [Meganyctiphanes norvegica and other species, order Euphausiacea.]
– ORIGIN C20: from Norwegian kril 'small fish fry'.

kris /kriːs/ ■ n. a Malay or Indonesian dagger with a wavy-edged blade.
– ORIGIN C16: from Malay keris.

Krishnaism /ˈkrɪʃnaɪz(ə)m/ ■ n. Hinduism the worship of Krishna as an incarnation of the supreme deity Vishnu.

krona /ˈkrəʊnə/ ■ n. 1 (pl. **kronor** pronunc. same) the basic monetary unit of Sweden. 2 (pl. **kronur** pronunc. same) the basic monetary unit of Iceland.
– ORIGIN Swedish and Icelandic, 'crown'.

krone /ˈkrəʊnə/ ■ n. (pl. **kroner** pronunc. same) the basic monetary unit of Denmark and Norway.
– ORIGIN Danish and Norwegian, 'crown'.

krugerrand /ˈkruːgərand/ (also **Kruger**) ■ n. a South African gold coin with a portrait of President Kruger on the obverse.
– ORIGIN 1967: from the name of Paul Kruger, President of Transvaal 1883–99, + **RAND**.

krummhorn /ˈkrʌmhɔːn, ˈkrʊm-/ (also **crumhorn**) ■ n. a medieval wind instrument with an enclosed double reed and an upward-curving end.
– ORIGIN from German, from krumm 'crooked' + Horn 'horn'.

krypton /ˈkrɪptɒn/ ■ n. the chemical element of atomic number 36, a member of the noble gas group. (Symbol: **Kr**)
– ORIGIN C19: from Greek krupton, neuter of kruptos 'hidden'.

Kt ■ abbrev. Knight.

kt ■ abbrev. knot(s).

K/T boundary ■ n. Geology the boundary between the Cretaceous and Tertiary periods, about 65 million years ago, marked by the extinction of dinosaurs and many other groups of animals.
– ORIGIN from symbols for Cretaceous and Tertiary.

kudos /ˈkjuːdɒs/ ■ n. praise and honour.
– ORIGIN C18: Greek.

USAGE
Despite appearances, **kudos** is not a plural form. This means that the use of **kudos** as a plural, as in the following sentence, is incorrect: he received many kudos for his work (correct use is he received much kudos for his work).

kudu /ˈkuːduː, ˈkʊdʊ/ ■ n. (pl. same or **kudus**) a striped African antelope, the male of which has long spirally curved horns. [Tragelaphus strepsiceros and T. imberbis.]
– ORIGIN C18: from Afrikaans koedoe, from isiXhosa i-qudu.

kudzu /ˈkʊdzuː/ ■ n. a quick-growing East Asian climbing plant with reddish-purple flowers. [Pueraria lobata.]
– ORIGIN from Japanese kuzu.

Kufic /ˈkjuːfɪk/ (also **Cufic**) ■ n. an early angular form of the Arabic alphabet found chiefly in decorative inscriptions. ■ adj. of or in this type of script.
– ORIGIN C18: from the name Kufa, a city south of Baghdad, Iraq (because it was attributed to the city's scholars).

kugel /ˈkuːg(ə)l/ ■ n. 1 (in Jewish cookery) a baked pudding made with potatoes or noodles. 2 S. African informal a wealthy urban woman, often Jewish, typically ostentatiously dressed and speaking with a nasal drawl.
– DERIVATIVES **kugelism** n.
– ORIGIN Yiddish, 'ball'.

Ku Klux Klan /ˌkuː klʌks ˈklan/ ■ n. an extreme white supremacist secret society in the US.
– DERIVATIVES **Ku Kluxer** n.
– ORIGIN perhaps from Greek kuklos 'circle' + **CLAN**.

kukri /ˈkʊkri/ ■ n. (pl. **kukris**) a curved knife broadening towards the point, used by Gurkhas.
– ORIGIN C19: from Nepalese khukuri.

kulfi /ˈkʊlfi/ ▪ n. a type of Indian ice cream, typically served in the shape of a cone.
– ORIGIN from Hindi *kulfī*.

Kumbh Mela /kʊm ˈmeɪlɑː/ ▪ n. a Hindu festival, held once every twelve years, at which pilgrims bathe in the Ganges and Jumna Rivers.
– ORIGIN from Sanskrit, 'pitcher festival', from *kumbh* 'pitcher' + *melā* 'assembly'.

kumkum /ˈkʊmkʊm/ ▪ n. a red pigment used by Hindu women to make a mark on the forehead.
– ORIGIN C20: from Sanskrit *kuṅkuma* 'saffron'.

kümmel /ˈkʊm(ə)l/ ▪ n. a sweet liqueur flavoured with caraway and cumin seeds.
– ORIGIN from German, from Old High German *kumil*, var. of *kumîn* 'cumin'.

kumquat /ˈkʌmkwɒt/ (also **cumquat**) ▪ n. **1** an East Asian citrus-like fruit with an edible sweet rind and acid pulp. **2** the tree which yields this fruit. [Genus *Fortunella*.]
– ORIGIN C17: from Chinese *kamkwat* 'little orange'.

kundalini /ˌkʊndəˈliːni/ ▪ n. (in yoga) latent female energy believed to lie coiled at the base of the spine.
– ORIGIN Sanskrit, 'snake'.

Kung /kʊŋ/ ▪ n. **1** (pl. same) a member of a San (Bushman) people of the Kalahari Desert in southern Africa. **2** the Khoisan language of this people.
– ORIGIN Khoikhoi *!Kung* 'people'.

kung fu /kʊŋ ˈfuː, kʌŋ/ ▪ n. a Chinese martial art resembling karate.
– ORIGIN from Chinese *gongfu*, from *gong* 'merit' + *fu* 'master'.

Kupffer cell /ˈkʊpfə/ ▪ n. Anatomy a phagocytic liver cell, involved in the breakdown of red blood cells.
– ORIGIN C20: named after the Bavarian anatomist Karl Wilhelm von *Kupffer*.

Kurd /kəːd/ ▪ n. a member of a mainly pastoral Islamic people living in Kurdistan.
– ORIGIN the name in Kurdish.

Kurdish /ˈkəːdɪʃ/ ▪ n. the Iranian language of the Kurds. ▪ adj. of or relating to the Kurds or their language.

kurper /ˈkəːpə/ ▪ n. S. African **1** an African freshwater tilapia. [Genera *Tilapia* and *Oreochromis*.] **2** a freshwater labyrinth fish. [*Sandelia capensis* (**Cape kurper**) and other species.]
– ORIGIN Afrikaans, from Dutch *karper* 'carp'.

kurta /ˈkəːtə/ ▪ n. a loose collarless shirt worn by people from the Indian subcontinent.
– ORIGIN from Urdu and Persian *kurtah*.

kurtosis /kəːˈtəʊsɪs/ ▪ n. Statistics the sharpness of the peak of a frequency-distribution curve.
– ORIGIN C20: from Greek *kurtōsis* 'a bulging', from *kurtos* 'bulging, convex'.

kuru /ˈkʊruː/ ▪ n. Medicine a fatal brain disease occurring in New Guinea, spread by cannibalism and believed to be caused by a prion.
– ORIGIN 1950s: a local word.

Kuwaiti /kʊˈweɪti/ ▪ n. a native or inhabitant of Kuwait. ▪ adj. of or relating to Kuwait.

kV ▪ abbrev. kilovolt(s).

kvetch /kvɛtʃ/ N. Amer. informal ▪ n. **1** a person who complains a great deal. **2** a complaint. ▪ v. complain.
– ORIGIN 1960s: from Yiddish *kvetsh* (n.), *kvetshn* (v.), from Middle High German *quetschen* 'crush'.

kW ▪ abbrev. kilowatt(s).

Kwa /kwɑː/ ▪ n. a major branch of the Niger–Congo family of languages, spoken from the Ivory Coast to Nigeria.
– ORIGIN the name in Kwa.

kwacha /ˈkwɑːtʃə/ ▪ n. the basic monetary unit of Zambia and Malawi.
– ORIGIN from a Bantu word meaning 'dawn', used as a Zambian nationalist slogan calling for a new 'dawn' of freedom.

kwaito /ˈkwaɪtəʊ/ ▪ n. S. African a style of popular dance music featuring rhythmically recited vocals over an instrumental backing with strong bass lines.
– ORIGIN named after the *Amakwaito*, a group of 1950s gangsters in Sophiatown, from Afrikaans *kwaai* 'angry, vicious'.

kwanza /ˈkwanzə/ ▪ n. (pl. same or **kwanzas**) the basic monetary unit of Angola.
– ORIGIN perhaps from a Kiswahili word meaning 'first'.

Kwanzaa /ˈkwanzɑː/ ▪ n. N. Amer. a secular festival observed by many African Americans from 26 December to 1 January as a celebration of their cultural heritage.
– ORIGIN from Kiswahili *matunda ya kwanza* 'first fruits (of the harvest)', from *kwanza* 'first'.

kwasa kwasa /ˌkwasa ˈkwasa/ ▪ n. a lively, erotic dance originating in central Africa. ▸ a genre of popular contemporary African music to which this dance is performed.

kwashiorkor /ˌkwɒʃɪˈɔːkɔː, ˌkwa-/ ▪ n. malnutrition caused by protein deficiency.
– ORIGIN 1930s: a local word in Ghana.

kwela /ˈkweɪlə/ ▪ n. a style of popular music developed in South Africa in the 1950s, in which the lead part is played on a penny whistle.
– ORIGIN C20: Afrikaans, perhaps from isiZulu *khwela* 'mount, climb'.

kwela-kwela /ˌkweɪləˈkweɪlə/ ▪ n. S. African informal **1** a police van. **2** a minibus taxi.
– ORIGIN from isiXhosa and isiZulu *khwela* 'climb on'.

kWh ▪ abbrev. kilowatt-hour(s).

KWIC ▪ abbrev. Computing keyword in context.

K-word (also **'K' word**) ▪ n. S. African euphemistic the word 'Kaffir'.

kyanite /ˈkaɪənaɪt/ ▪ n. a blue or green mineral consisting of aluminium silicate, used in heat-resistant ceramics.
– ORIGIN C18: from Greek *kuaneos* 'dark blue'.

kybosh ▪ n. variant spelling of **KIBOSH**.

kyle /kaɪl/ ▪ n. Scottish a narrow sea channel.
– ORIGIN C16: from Scottish Gaelic *caol* 'strait', (as adj.) 'narrow'.

kymograph /ˈkaɪmə(ʊ)grɑːf/ ▪ n. an instrument for recording variations in pressure, e.g. in sound waves or in circulating blood.
– DERIVATIVES **kymographic** adj.
– ORIGIN C19: from Greek *kuma* 'wave' + -GRAPH.

kyphosis /kaɪˈfəʊsɪs/ ▪ n. Medicine excessive forward curvature of the spine, causing a hunched back. Compare with LORDOSIS.
– DERIVATIVES **kyphotic** adj.
– ORIGIN C19: from Greek *kuphōsis*, from *kuphos* 'bent, hunchbacked'.

Kyrgyz /kɪəˈgiːz, ˈkəːgɪz/ (also **Kirghiz**) ▪ n. (pl. same) **1** a member of a people of central Asia, living chiefly in Kyrgyzstan. **2** the Turkic language of this people.
– ORIGIN the name in Kyrgyz.

Kyrie /ˈkɪrieɪ/ (also **Kyrie eleison** /ɪˈleɪɪzɒn, -sɒn, ɛˈleɪ-/) ▪ n. a short repeated invocation (in Greek or in translation) used in many Christian liturgies.
– ORIGIN from Greek *Kurie eleēson* 'Lord, have mercy'.

kyu /kjuː/ ▪ n. a grade of the less advanced level of proficiency in martial arts.
– ORIGIN from Japanese *kyū* 'class'.

Ll

L¹ (also **l**) ■ n. (pl. **Ls** or **L's**) **1** the twelfth letter of the alphabet. **2** denoting the next after K in a set of items, categories, etc. **3** the Roman numeral for 50.

L² ■ abbrev. **1** Chemistry laevorotatory. **2** (**Latin**) Lake, Loch, or Lough. **3** large (as a clothes size). **4** learner driver. **5** (**L.**) Linnaeus (as the source of names of animal and plant species). **6** lire. **7** (in tables of sports results) lost.

l ■ abbrev. **1** left. **2** (in horse racing) length(s). **3** (**l.**) line. **4** Chemistry liquid. **5** litre(s). **6** (**l.**) archaic pound(s). ■ symb. (in mathematical formulae) length.

LA ■ abbrev. Los Angeles.

La ■ symb. the chemical element lanthanum.

la ■ n. Music variant spelling of **LAH**.

laager /ˈlɑːgə/ S. African ■ n. **1** historical an encampment formed by a circle of wagons. **2** an entrenched position or viewpoint. ■ v. historical form or enclose with a laager.
– ORIGIN S. African Dutch, from Dutch *leger*, *lager* 'camp'; cf. **LAGER** and **LAIR**.

laaitie /ˈlʌɪti/ ■ n. variant spelling of **LIGHTY**.

laatlammetjie /ˈlɑːtlaməki/ ■ n. S. African a child born many years after his or her siblings.
– ORIGIN Afrikaans, from *laat* 'late' + *lam* 'lamb' + diminutive suffix.

Lab ■ abbrev. **1** Brit. Labour. **2** Labrador.

lab ■ n. informal a laboratory.

Labarang /ləˈbaraŋ/ ■ n. S. African (among Cape Muslims) Eid.
– ORIGIN from Malay *lebaran* 'religious feast'.

labdanum /ˈlabdənəm/ ■ n. variant spelling of **LADANUM**.

label ■ n. **1** a small piece of paper, fabric, etc. attached to an object and giving information about it. ▸ a piece of fabric sewn inside a garment and bearing the brand name, size, or care instructions. **2** the name or trademark of a fashion company. ▸ a company that produces recorded music. **3** a classifying name applied to a person or thing, especially inaccurately. ▸ (in a dictionary entry) a word or words used to specify the subject area, register, or geographical origin of the word being defined. ▸ Computing a string of characters used to refer to a particular instruction in a program. **4** Biology & Chemistry a radioactive isotope, fluorescent dye, or enzyme used to make something identifiable. **5** Heraldry a narrow horizontal strip superimposed on a coat of arms by an eldest son during the life of his father. **6** Architecture another term for **DRIPSTONE**. ■ v. (**labelled**, **labelling**; US **labeled**, **labeling**) **1** attach a label to. **2** assign to a category, especially inaccurately. **3** Biology & Chemistry make (a substance, cell, etc.) identifiable using a label.
– DERIVATIVES **labeller** n.
– ORIGIN Middle English: from Old French, 'ribbon', prob. of Germanic origin.

labellum /ləˈbɛləm/ ■ n. (pl. **labella**) Entomology a lobe at the tip of the proboscis in some insects.
– ORIGIN C19: from Latin, diminutive of *labrum* 'lip'.

labia plural form of **LABIUM**.

labial /ˈleɪbɪəl/ ■ adj. **1** chiefly Anatomy & Biology of or relating to the lips or a labium. **2** Phonetics (of a consonant) requiring partial or complete closure of the lips (e.g. *p* or *w*), or (of a vowel) requiring rounded lips (e.g. *oo*).
– DERIVATIVES **labialize** (also **-ise**) v. **labially** adv.
– ORIGIN C16: from medieval Latin *labialis*, from Latin *labium* 'lip'.

labia majora /məˈdʒɔːrə/ ■ pl. n. Anatomy the larger outer folds of the vulva.

labia minora /mɪˈnɔːrə/ ■ pl. n. Anatomy the smaller inner folds of the vulva.

labiate /ˈleɪbɪət/ ■ adj. **1** Botany of or relating to the mint family (Labiatae), plants of which have distinctive two-lobed flowers. **2** Botany & Zoology resembling or possessing a lip or labium.
– ORIGIN C18: from modern Latin *labiatus*, from *labium* 'lip'.

labile /ˈleɪbɪl, -ʌɪl/ ■ adj. **1** technical liable to change; easily altered. **2** Chemistry easily broken down or displaced.
– DERIVATIVES **lability** /ləˈbɪlɪti/ n.
– ORIGIN Middle English ('liable to err or sin'): from late Latin *labilis*, from *labi* 'to fall'.

labio- /ˈleɪbɪəʊ/ ■ comb. form of or relating to the lips: *labiodental*.
– ORIGIN from Latin *labium* 'lip'.

labiodental ■ adj. Phonetics (of a sound) made with the lips and teeth, e.g. *f* and *v*.

labiovelar ■ adj. Phonetics (of a sound) made with the lips and soft palate, e.g. *w*.

labium /ˈleɪbɪəm/ ■ n. (pl. **labia** /-bɪə/) **1** Entomology a fused mouthpart forming the floor of the mouth of an insect. **2** (**labia**) Anatomy the labia majora or minora.
– ORIGIN C16: from Latin, 'lip'; rel. to **LABRUM**.

lablab /ˈlablab/ ■ n. a tropical Asian plant of the pea family, grown for its edible seeds and pods. [*Lablab purpureus*.]
– ORIGIN C19: from Arabic *lablāb*.

labor ■ n. US and Australian spelling of **LABOUR** etc.

laboratory /ləˈbɒrə,t(ə)ri, ˈlab(ə)rə,t(ə)ri/ ■ n. (pl. **-ies**) a room or building for scientific experiments, research, or teaching, or for the manufacture of drugs or chemicals.
– ORIGIN C17: from medieval Latin *laboratorium*, from Latin *laborare* 'to labour'.

labored ■ adj. US spelling of **LABOURED**.

laborer ■ n. US spelling of **LABOURER**.

laborious /ləˈbɔːrɪəs/ ■ adj. requiring considerable time and effort. ▸ (especially of speech or writing) showing obvious signs of effort.
– DERIVATIVES **laboriously** adv. **laboriousness** n.
– ORIGIN Middle English: from Latin *laboriosus*, from *labor* 'labour'.

labour (US & Austral. **labor**) ■ n. **1** work, especially hard physical work. **2** workers, especially manual workers, collectively. **3** (**Labour**) [treated as sing. or pl.] the Labour Party. **4** the process of childbirth from the start of uterine contractions to delivery. ■ v. **1** work hard. ▸ work at an unskilled manual job. ▸ archaic till (the ground). **2** have difficulty despite working hard. ▸ (of an engine) work noisily and with difficulty. ▸ move with difficulty. ▸ (of a ship) roll or pitch heavily. **3** (**labour under**) be misled by (a mistaken belief).
– PHRASES **a labour of love** a task done for pleasure, not reward. **labour the point** explain or discuss something at excessive length.
– ORIGIN Middle English: from Old French *labour* (n.), *labourer* (v.), both from Latin *labor* 'toil, trouble'.

labour camp ■ n. a prison camp with a regime of hard labour.

Labour Day ■ n. a public holiday held in honour of working people in some countries on 1 May, or (in the US and Canada) on the first Monday in September.

laboured (US **labored**) ■ adj. **1** done with great difficulty. **2** not spontaneous or fluent.

labourer (US **laborer**) ■ n. a person doing unskilled manual work.

labour force ■ n. the members of a population who are able to work.

labour-intensive ■ adj. needing a large workforce or a large amount of work in relation to output.

labour-saving ▪ adj. (of an appliance) designed to reduce or eliminate work.

labour tenant ▪ n. S. African historical a person who worked without pay for a farmer for part of the year in return for the use of land for crops and grazing.
– DERIVATIVES **labour tenancy** n.

labour union ▪ n. chiefly N. Amer. a trade union.

labra plural form of **LABRUM**.

Labrador /'labrədɔː/ (also **Labrador retriever**) ▪ n. a retriever of a breed typically having a black or yellow coat, widely used as a gun dog or guide dog.
– ORIGIN C20: named after the *Labrador* Peninsula of eastern Canada, where the breed was developed.

labradorite /ˌlabrə'dɔːrʌɪt/ ▪ n. a mineral of the plagioclase feldspar group, found in many igneous rocks.

labrum /'leɪbrəm/ ▪ n. (pl. **labra** /-brə/) Zoology a structure corresponding to a lip, especially the upper border of the mouthparts of a crustacean or insect.
– DERIVATIVES **labral** adj.
– ORIGIN C18: from Latin, 'lip'; rel. to **LABIUM**.

laburnum /lə'bəːnəm/ ▪ n. a small hardwood tree with hanging clusters of yellow flowers followed by pods of poisonous seeds. [Genus *Laburnum*.]
– ORIGIN from Latin.

labyrinth /'lab(ə)rɪnθ/ ▪ n. 1 a complicated irregular network of passages or paths. ▶ an intricate and confusing arrangement. 2 Anatomy a complex fluid-filled bony structure in the inner ear which contains the organs of hearing and balance.
– DERIVATIVES **labyrinthian** adj.
– ORIGIN Middle English (referring to the maze constructed by Daedalus in Greek mythology to house the Minotaur): from Latin *labyrinthus*, from Greek *laburinthos*.

labyrinth fish ▪ n. a freshwater fish of a large group including gouramis, with poorly developed gills and a labyrinthine accessory breathing organ. [Suborder Anabantoidei.]

labyrinthine /ˌlabə'rɪnθʌɪn/ ▪ adj. like a labyrinth, especially in being complicated or twisted.

labyrinthodont /ˌlabə'rɪnθədɒnt/ Zoology & Palaeontology ▪ adj. (of teeth) having the enamel deeply folded to form a labyrinthine structure. ▪ n. a fossil amphibian of a large group having such teeth.
– ORIGIN C19: from *Labyrinthodontia* (pl. n.), from Greek *laburinthos* 'labyrinth' + *odous, odont-* 'tooth'.

lac ▪ n. a resinous substance secreted as a protective covering by the lac insect, used to make varnish, shellac, etc.
– ORIGIN Middle English: from medieval Latin *lac, lac(c)a*, from Portuguese *laca*, from Hindi *lākh* or Persian *lāk*.

laccolith /'lakəlɪθ/ ▪ n. Geology a lens-shaped mass of igneous rock intruded between rock strata, causing doming.
– ORIGIN C19: from Greek *lakkos* 'reservoir' + **-LITH**.

lace ▪ n. 1 a fine open fabric of cotton or silk made by looping, twisting, or knitting thread in patterns, used especially as a trimming. ▶ braid used for trimming, especially on military dress uniforms. 2 a cord or leather strip passed through eyelets or hooks to fasten a shoe or garment. ▪ v. 1 fasten or be fastened with a lace or laces. ▶ tighten a laced corset around the waist of. ▶ [as adj. **laced**] trimmed or fitted with a lace or laces. 2 entwine. 3 (often **be laced with**) add an ingredient, especially alcohol, to (a drink or dish) to enhance its flavour or strength.
– ORIGIN Middle English: from Old French *laz, las* (n.), *lacier* (v.), from Latin *laqueus* 'noose'.

lace bug ▪ n. a small plant-eating bug with a patterned upper surface. [Family Tingidae.]

lace pillow ▪ n. a cushion placed on the lap to provide support in lacemaking.

lacerate /'lasəreɪt/ ▪ v. tear or deeply cut (the flesh or skin).
– DERIVATIVES **laceration** n.
– ORIGIN Middle English: from Latin *lacerare* 'mangle', from *lacer* 'torn'.

Lacertilia /ˌlasə'tɪlɪə/ ▪ pl. n. Zoology a suborder of reptiles that comprises the lizards.
– DERIVATIVES **lacertilian** n. & adj.
– ORIGIN from Latin *lacerta* 'lizard'.

lacewing ▪ n. a slender delicate insect with large clear membranous wings, predatory on aphids. [Chrysopidae (green lacewings) and other families.]

lacewood ▪ n. the wood of the plane tree.

lachrymal /'lakrɪm(ə)l/ (also **lacrimal** or **lacrymal**) ▪ adj. 1 formal or poetic/literary connected with weeping or tears. 2 (**lacrimal**) Physiology & Anatomy concerned with the secretion of tears. ▪ n. (**lacrimal** or **lacrimal bone**) Anatomy a small bone forming part of the eye socket.
– ORIGIN Middle English: from medieval Latin *lachrymalis*, from Latin *lacrima* 'tear'.

lachrymation /ˌlakrɪ'meɪʃ(ə)n/ (also **lacrimation** or **lacrymation**) ▪ n. poetic/literary or Medicine the flow of tears.
– ORIGIN C16: from Latin *lacrimatio(n-)*, from *lacrimare* 'weep'.

lachrymose /'lakrɪməʊs, -z/ ▪ adj. formal or poetic/literary 1 tearful. 2 inducing tears; sad.
– DERIVATIVES **lachrymosely** adv. **lachrymosity** n.
– ORIGIN C17 ('like tears'): from Latin *lacrimosus*, from *lacrima* 'tear'.

lacing ▪ n. 1 a laced fastening of a shoe or garment. 2 a dash of spirits added to a drink.

lacing course ▪ n. a strengthening course of bricks built into an arch or wall.

lac insect ▪ n. an Asian scale insect which lives on croton trees and produces lac. [*Laccifer lacca*.]

lack ▪ n. absence or deficiency of something. ▪ v. (also **lack for**) be without or deficient in.
– ORIGIN Middle English: corresponding to, and perhaps partly from, Middle Dutch and Middle Low German *lak* 'deficiency', Middle Dutch *laken* 'lack'.

lackadaisical /ˌlakə'deɪzɪk(ə)l/ ▪ adj. lacking enthusiasm and thoroughness.
– DERIVATIVES **lackadaisically** adv.
– ORIGIN C18: from the archaic interjection *lackaday*, *lackadaisy*, obsolete var. of **ALACK**.

lackey ▪ n. (pl. **-eys**) 1 a servant, especially a liveried footman or manservant. 2 a servile or obsequious person. 3 a brownish moth whose caterpillars live in groups in a silken shelter. [*Malacosoma neustria*.] ▪ v. (**-eys, -eyed**) archaic behave servilely towards.
– ORIGIN C16: from French *laquais*, perhaps from Arabic *al-kā'id* 'the chief'. Sense 3 derives from the resemblance of the coloured stripes of the caterpillars to a footman's livery.

lacking ▪ adj. absent or deficient.

lacklustre (US **lackluster**) ▪ adj. 1 lacking in vitality, force, or conviction. 2 not shining; dull.

laconic /lə'kɒnɪk/ ▪ adj. using very few words; terse.
– DERIVATIVES **laconically** adv. **laconicism** n.
– ORIGIN C16 ('Laconian'): from Greek *Lakōnikos*, from *Lakōn* 'Laconia, Sparta', the Spartans being known for their terse speech.

lacquer /'lakə/ ▪ n. 1 a liquid made of shellac dissolved in alcohol, or of synthetic substances, that dries to form a hard protective coating for wood, metal, etc. 2 the sap of the lacquer tree used to varnish wood or other materials. 3 decorative wooden ware coated with lacquer. 4 Brit. a chemical substance sprayed on hair to keep it in place. ▪ v. [often as adj. **lacquered**] coat with lacquer.
– DERIVATIVES **lacquerer** n.
– ORIGIN C16: from obsolete French *lacre* 'sealing wax', from Portuguese *laca* (see **LAC**).

lacquer tree ▪ n. an East Asian tree with a sap used as a hard-wearing varnish. [*Rhus verniciflua*.]

lacrimal ▪ adj. & n. variant spelling of **LACHRYMAL**.

lacrimation ▪ n. variant spelling of **LACHRYMATION**.

lacrosse /lə'krɒs/ ▪ n. a team game in which a ball is thrown, carried, and caught with a long-handled stick having a curved L-shaped or triangular frame at one end with a piece of netting in the angle.
– ORIGIN C19: from French (*le jeu de*) *la crosse* '(the game of) the hooked stick'.

lacrymal ▪ adj. & n. variant spelling of **LACHRYMAL**.

lacrymation ▪ n. variant spelling of **LACHRYMATION**.

lactam /ˈlaktam/ ■ n. Chemistry an organic compound containing an amide group -NHCO- as part of a ring.
–ORIGIN C19: blend of LACTONE and AMIDE.

lactase /ˈlakteɪz/ ■ n. Biochemistry an enzyme which converts lactose to glucose and galactose.
–ORIGIN C19: from LACTOSE.

lactate /lakˈteɪt/ ■ v. (of a female mammal) secrete milk.
–ORIGIN C19: back-formation from LACTATION.

lactation ■ n. 1 the secretion of milk by the mammary glands. 2 the suckling of young.
–DERIVATIVES **lactational** adj.
–ORIGIN C17: from Latin *lactatio(n-)*, from *lactare* 'suckle'.

lacteal /ˈlaktɪəl/ ■ adj. 1 of milk. 2 Anatomy conveying chyle or other milky fluid. ■ n. (**lacteals**) Anatomy the lymphatic vessels of the small intestine which absorb digested fats.
–ORIGIN C17: from Latin *lacteus*, from *lac, lact-* 'milk'.

lactic /ˈlaktɪk/ ■ adj. of, relating to, or obtained from milk.
–ORIGIN C18: from Latin *lac, lact-* 'milk'.

lactic acid ■ n. Biochemistry a syrupy organic acid present in sour milk, and produced in the muscles during strenuous exercise.

lacto- ■ comb. form 1 of or relating to milk: *lacto-vegetarian*. 2 of or relating to lactic acid or lactose: *lactobacillus*.
–ORIGIN from Latin *lac, lact-* 'milk'.

lactobacillus /ˌlaktəʊbəˈsɪləs/ ■ n. (pl. **lactobacilli** /-lʌɪ/) Biology a rod-shaped bacterium which produces lactic acid from the fermentation of carbohydrates. [Genus *Lactobacillus*.]

lactone /ˈlaktəʊn/ ■ n. Chemistry an organic compound containing an ester group -OCO- as part of a ring.

lactoprotein ■ n. the protein component of milk.

lactose /ˈlaktəʊs, -s/ ■ n. Chemistry a compound sugar present in milk, containing glucose and galactose units.

lacto-vegetarian ■ n. a person who eats only dairy products and vegetables.

lacuna /ləˈkjuːnə/ ■ n. (pl. **lacunae** /-niː/ or **lacunas**) 1 a gap or missing portion. 2 Anatomy a cavity or depression, especially in bone.
–DERIVATIVES **lacunal** adj. **lacunar** adj. **lacunary** adj. **lacunate** adj. **lacunose** adj.
–ORIGIN C17: from Latin, 'pool'.

lacustrine /ləˈkʌstrʌɪn, -trɪn/ ■ adj. technical or poetic/literary of or relating to lakes.
–ORIGIN C19: from Latin *lacus* 'lake', the stem *lacustr-* influenced by Latin *palustris* 'marshy'.

lacy ■ adj. (-ier, -iest) made of, resembling, or trimmed with lace.
–DERIVATIVES **lacily** adv. **laciness** n.

lad ■ n. 1 informal a boy or young man. ▶ (**lads**) chiefly Brit. a group of men sharing recreational or working interests. ▶ Brit. a boisterously macho or high-spirited man. 2 Brit. a stable worker (regardless of age or sex).
–DERIVATIVES **laddish** adj. **laddishness** n.
–ORIGIN Middle English.

Ladakhi /ləˈdɑːki/ ■ n. (pl. **Ladakhis**) 1 a native or inhabitant of Ladakh, a region of NW India, Pakistan, and China. 2 the language of Ladakh, a dialect of Tibetan. ■ adj. of or relating to Ladakh, the Ladakhis, or their language.
–ORIGIN the name in Ladakhi.

ladanum /ˈlad(ə)nəm/ (also **labdanum**) ■ n. a gum resin obtained from a rock rose, used in perfumery and for fumigation.
–ORIGIN C16: from Greek *ladanon, lēdanon*, from *lēdon* 'mastic'.

ladder ■ n. 1 a structure consisting of a series of bars or steps between two upright lengths of wood, metal, or rope, used for climbing up or down. 2 a hierarchical structure, especially as providing a means of advancement. 3 a vertical strip of unravelled fabric in tights or stockings. ■ v. (with reference to tights or stockings) develop or cause to develop a ladder.
–ORIGIN Old English, of West Germanic origin.

ladder-back ■ n. an upright chair with a back resembling a ladder.

ladder stitch ■ n. a stitch in embroidery consisting of transverse bars.

laddie ■ n. informal, chiefly Scottish a boy or young man.

laddu /ˈlʌduː/ ■ n. (pl. **laddus**) an Indian sweet made from flour, sugar, and shortening, which is fried and then shaped into a ball.
–ORIGIN from Hindi *laḍḍū*.

lade /leɪd/ ■ v. (past part. **laden**) archaic put cargo on board (a ship). ▶ ship (goods) as cargo.
–DERIVATIVES **lading** n.
–ORIGIN Old English, of West Germanic origin; rel. to LADLE.

laden ■ adj. heavily loaded or weighed down.
–ORIGIN C16: from LADE.

la-di-da (also **lah-di-dah**) ■ adj. informal pretentious or snobbish.
–ORIGIN C19: imitative of an affected manner of speech.

ladies plural form of LADY.

ladies' bar ■ n. S. African a licensed bar, especially a comfortably furnished one in a hotel.

ladies' fingers ■ pl. n. another term for OKRA.

ladies' man (also **lady's man**) ■ n. informal a man who enjoys spending time and flirting with women.

ladies' night ■ n. a function at a men's institution or club to which women are invited.

ladies' room ■ n. a toilet for women in a public or institutional building.

Ladino /ləˈdiːnəʊ/ ■ n. (pl. -os) 1 the language of some Sephardic Jews, especially formerly in Mediterranean countries, based on medieval Spanish with some Hebrew, Greek, and Turkish words. 2 a mestizo or Spanish-speaking white person in Central America.
–ORIGIN Spanish, from Latin *Latinus* (see LATIN).

ladino /ləˈdiːnəʊ/ ■ n. (pl. -os) a white clover of a large variety native to Italy and cultivated for fodder.
–ORIGIN 1920s: from Italian.

ladle ■ n. 1 a large long-handled spoon with a cup-shaped bowl, used for serving soup or sauce. 2 a container for transporting molten metal in a foundry. ■ v. 1 serve or transfer with a ladle. 2 (**ladle something out**) distribute something in large amounts.
–DERIVATIVES **ladleful** n. (pl. -fuls). **ladler** n.
–ORIGIN Old English: rel. to LADE.

lady ■ n. (pl. -ies) 1 (in polite or formal use) a woman. 2 a woman of superior social position, especially one of noble birth. ▶ (**Lady**) a title used by peeresses, female relatives of peers, the wives and widows of knights, etc. ▶ a courteous or genteel woman. 3 (**one's lady**) dated a man's wife. ▶ historical a woman to whom a knight is chivalrously devoted. 4 (**the Ladies**) a women's public toilet.
–PHRASES **it isn't over till the fat lady sings** there is still time for a situation to change. [by association with the final aria in tragic opera.] **My Lady** a polite form of address to female judges and certain noblewomen.

HISTORY
The forerunner of the word **lady** in Old English was *hlǣfdīge*, meaning the female head of a household, or a woman to whom homage or obedience was due, such as the wife of a lord or, specifically, the Virgin Mary. The word came from *hlāf* 'loaf' and a Germanic base meaning 'knead' which is related to **dough** and **dairy**; thus a lady was a 'loaf kneader'. The word **lord** developed in a similar way; in Old English it literally meant 'bread keeper'.

ladybird ■ n. a small beetle with a domed back, typically red or yellow with black spots. [Family Coccinellidae: many species.]

ladybug ■ n. North American term for LADYBIRD.

Lady chapel ■ n. a chapel dedicated to the Virgin Mary in a church or cathedral.

Lady Day ■ n. the feast of the Annunciation, 25 March.

ladyfinger ■ n. 1 another term for LADY'S FINGER (in sense 2). 2 a type of small short banana.

ladyfish ■ n. an elongated silvery marine fish, popular with anglers. [*Elops machnata*.]

lady-in-waiting ■ n. (pl. **ladies-in-waiting**) a woman who attends a queen or princess.

ladykiller ■ n. informal a charming man who habitually seduces women.

ladylike ■ adj. appropriate for or typical of a well-mannered, decorous woman or girl.
– DERIVATIVES **ladylikeness** n.

lady of the night ■ n. euphemistic a prostitute.

lady's finger ■ n. **1** another term for KIDNEY VETCH. **2** a finger-shaped sponge cake with a sugar topping.

ladyship ■ n. (**Her/Your Ladyship**) a respectful form of reference or address to a Lady.

lady's maid ■ n. chiefly historical a maid who attended to the personal needs of her mistress.

lady's man ■ n. variant spelling of LADIES' MAN.

lady's mantle ■ n. a plant with inconspicuous greenish flowers, formerly valued in herbal medicine. [*Alchemilla vulgaris*.]

lady's slipper ■ n. an orchid whose flower has a conspicuous pouch- or slipper-shaped lip. [Genus *Cypripedium*.]

Lady Superior ■ n. the head of a convent or nunnery in certain orders.

laevo- /ˈliːvəʊ/ (also **levo-**) ■ comb. form on or to the left: *laevorotatory*.
– ORIGIN from Latin *laevus* 'left'.

laevorotatory /ˌliːvəʊˈrəʊtət(ə)ri/ (US **levorotatory**) ■ adj. Chemistry (of a compound) having the property of rotating the plane of a polarized light ray to the left, i.e. anticlockwise facing the oncoming radiation. The opposite of DEXTROROTATORY.
– DERIVATIVES **laevorotation** n.

Laffer curve /ˈlafə/ ■ n. Economics a supposed relationship between economic activity and the rate of taxation which suggests that there is an optimum tax rate which maximizes revenue.
– ORIGIN 1970s: named after the American economist Arthur *Laffer*.

lag[1] ■ v. (**lagged**, **lagging**) enclose or cover (a boiler, pipes, etc.) with insulating material.
– DERIVATIVES **lagger** n.
– ORIGIN C19: from earlier *lag* 'piece of insulating cover'.

lag[2] ■ v. (**lagged**, **lagging**) **1** fall behind; follow after a delay. **2** N. Amer. another term for STRING (in sense 6). ■ n. (also **time lag**) a period of time between two events; a delay.
– DERIVATIVES **lagger** n.
– ORIGIN C16: rel. to the dialect adj. *lag* (perhaps from a fanciful distortion of LAST[1], or of Scandinavian origin).

lager ■ n. an effervescent beer, light in colour and body.
– ORIGIN C19: from German *Lagerbier* 'beer brewed for keeping', from *Lager* 'storehouse'; cf. LAAGER and LAIR.

lager lout ■ n. Brit. informal a young man who behaves offensively as a result of excessive drinking.

laggard /ˈlagəd/ ■ n. a person who falls behind others. ■ adj. slower than desired or expected.
– DERIVATIVES **laggardly** adj. & adv. **laggardness** n.
– ORIGIN C18: from LAG[1].

lagging ■ n. material providing heat insulation for a boiler, pipes, etc.
– ORIGIN C19: from LAG[2].

Lagomorpha /ˌlagəˈmɔːfə/ ■ pl. n. Zoology an order of mammals that comprises the hares, rabbits, and pikas, distinguished by the possession of double incisor teeth.
– DERIVATIVES **lagomorph** n. & adj.
– ORIGIN from Greek *lagōs* 'hare' + *morphē* 'form'.

lagoon ■ n. **1** a stretch of salt water separated from the sea by a low sandbank or coral reef. **2** N. Amer. & Austral./NZ a small freshwater lake near a larger lake or river. **3** an artificial pool for the treatment of effluent or to accommodate an overspill from surface drains.
– DERIVATIVES **lagoonal** adj.
– ORIGIN C17: from Italian and Spanish *laguna*, from Latin *lacuna* (see LACUNA).

Lagrangian point /ləˈgrɒʒɪən/ ■ n. Astronomy each of five points in the plane of orbit of one body around another at which a small third body can remain stationary with respect to the others.
– ORIGIN C19: named after the Italian-born French mathematician Joseph Louis *Lagrange*.

lah (also **la**) ■ n. Music (in tonic sol-fa) the sixth note of a major scale. ▸ the note A in the fixed-doh system.
– ORIGIN Middle English: representing (as an arbitrary name for the note) the first syllable of Latin *labii*, taken from a Latin hymn.

lahar /ˈlɑːhɑː/ ■ n. Geology a destructive flow of mud on the slopes of a volcano.
– ORIGIN 1920s: from Javanese.

lah-di-dah ■ n. variant spelling of LA-DI-DA.

laic /ˈleɪɪk/ ■ adj. formal of the laity; secular.
– ORIGIN C16: from late Latin *laicus* (see LAY[2]).

laicize /ˈleɪɪsʌɪz/ (also **-ise**) ■ v. formal withdraw clerical character, control, or status from.
– DERIVATIVES **laicism** n. **laicization** (also **-isation**) n.

laid past and past participle of LAY[1].

laid-back ■ adj. informal relaxed and easy-going.

laid paper ■ n. paper that has a finely ribbed appearance. Compare with WOVE PAPER.

lain past participle of LIE[1].

lair ■ n. **1** a wild animal's resting place. **2** a person's hiding place or den.
– ORIGIN Old English *leger* 'resting place, bed', of Germanic origin; rel. to LIE[1].

laird /lɛːd/ ■ n. (in Scotland) a person who owns a large estate.
– DERIVATIVES **lairdship** n.
– ORIGIN Middle English: Scots form of LORD.

laissez-faire /ˌlɛseɪˈfɛː/ ■ n. a policy of non-interference, especially abstention by governments from interfering in the workings of the free market.
– DERIVATIVES **laisser-faireism** n.
– ORIGIN French, 'allow to do'.

laissez-passer /ˌlɛseɪˈpɑːseɪ/ ■ n. a permit allowing the holder to go somewhere.
– ORIGIN French, 'allow to pass'.

laity /ˈleɪɪti/ ■ n. (**the laity**) [usu. treated as pl.] lay people.
– ORIGIN Middle English: from LAY[2].

lake[1] ■ n. a large area of water surrounded by land.
– ORIGIN Old English, from Old French *lac*, from Latin *lacus* 'pool, lake'.

lake[2] ■ n. **1** an insoluble pigment made by combining a soluble organic dye and an insoluble mordant. **2** a purplish-red pigment of this kind, originally one made with lac.
– ORIGIN C17: var. of LAC.

Lake District ■ n. a region of lakes and mountains in Cumbria, England.

la-la land ■ n. N. Amer. informal **1** Los Angeles or Hollywood, especially with regard to the film and television industry. **2** a dreamworld.
– ORIGIN *la-la*: reduplication of LA (i.e. Los Angeles).

Lallans /ˈlalənz/ ■ n. a distinctive Scottish literary form of English, based on standard older Scots.
– ORIGIN C18: Scots var. of *Lowlands*, with ref. to a central Lowlands dialect.

lallation /laˈleɪʃ(ə)n/ ■ n. imperfect speech, especially the pronunciation of *r* as *l*.
– ORIGIN C17: from Latin *lallatio(n-)*, from *lallare* 'sing a lullaby'.

lam[1] ■ v. (**lammed**, **lamming**) (often **lam into**) informal hit hard or repeatedly.
– ORIGIN C16: perhaps of Scandinavian origin.

lam[2] ■ n. (in phr. **on the lam**) N. Amer. informal in flight, especially from the police.
– ORIGIN C19: from LAM[1].

lama /ˈlɑːmə/ ■ n. **1** an honorific title applied to a spiritual leader in Tibetan Buddhism. **2** a Tibetan or Mongolian Buddhist monk.
– DERIVATIVES **Lamaism** n. **Lamaist** n. & adj.
– ORIGIN C17: from Tibetan *bla-ma* (with silent *b*) 'superior one'.

Lamarckism /ləˈmɑːkɪz(ə)m/ ■ n. the theory of evolution based on the supposed inheritance of acquired characteristics, devised by the French naturalist Jean Baptiste de Lamarck (1744–1829).
– DERIVATIVES **Lamarckian** n. & adj.

lamasery /ˈlɑːməs(ə)ri, ləˈmɑːs(ə)ri/ ■ n. (pl. **-ies**) a monastery of lamas.

lamb ■ n. **1** a young sheep. **2** a mild-mannered, gentle, or innocent person. ■ v. (of a ewe) give birth to lambs. ► **tend (ewes)** at lambing time.
– PHRASES **in lamb** pregnant.
– DERIVATIVES **lambing** n. **lambkin** n. **lamblike** adj.
– ORIGIN Old English, of Germanic origin.

lambada /lamˈbɑːdə/ ■ n. a fast erotic Brazilian dance which couples perform in close physical contact.
– ORIGIN 1980s: Portuguese, 'a beating'.

lambaste /lamˈbeɪst/ (also **lambast** /-ˈbast/) ■ v. criticize harshly.
– DERIVATIVES **lambasting** n.
– ORIGIN C17 ('beat'): from LAM[1] + BASTE[3].

lambda /ˈlamdə/ ■ n. **1** the eleventh letter of the Greek alphabet (Λ, λ), transliterated as 'l'. **2** Anatomy the point at the back of the skull where the parietal bones and the occipital bone meet. ■ symb. (λ) **1** wavelength. **2** Astronomy celestial longitude.
– ORIGIN from Greek.

lambent /ˈlamb(ə)nt/ ■ adj. poetic/literary glowing or flickering with a soft radiance.
– DERIVATIVES **lambency** n. **lambently** adv.
– ORIGIN C17: from Latin *lambent-, lambere* 'to lick'.

lambert /ˈlambət/ ■ n. a former unit of luminance, equal to the emission or reflection of one lumen per square centimetre.
– ORIGIN C20: named after the C18 German physicist Johann H. *Lambert*.

Lamb of God ■ n. a title of Jesus Christ (see John 1:29).

Lambrusco /lamˈbrʊskəʊ/ ■ n. a variety of wine grape grown in the Emilia-Romagna region of North Italy. ► a sparkling red or white wine made from this grape.
– ORIGIN Italian, 'grape of the wild vine'.

lamb's ears ■ pl. n. [usu. treated as sing.] a SW Asian ornamental plant of the mint family, with grey-green woolly leaves. [*Stachys byzantina*.]

lamb's fry ■ n. chiefly Brit. lamb's testicles or other offal as food.

lamb's lettuce ■ n. a small blue-flowered herbaceous plant, used in salad. [*Valerianella locusta*.]

lame ■ adj. **1** disabled in the leg or foot. **2** (of an explanation or excuse) unconvincingly feeble. **3** informal naive or socially inept. ■ v. make lame.
– DERIVATIVES **lamely** adv. **lameness** n.
– ORIGIN Old English, of Germanic origin.

lamé /ˈlɑːmeɪ/ ■ n. fabric with interwoven gold or silver threads.
– ORIGIN 1920s: French, from Latin *lamina* 'thin plate'.

lame duck ■ n. **1** an ineffectual or unsuccessful person or thing. **2** N. Amer. a President or administration in the final period of office, after the election of a successor.

lamella /ləˈmɛlə/ ■ n. (pl. **lamellae** /-liː/) **1** a thin layer, membrane, or plate of tissue, especially in bone. **2** Botany a membranous fold in a chloroplast.
– DERIVATIVES **lamellar** adj. **lamellate** adj. **lamellose** adj.
– ORIGIN C17: from Latin, diminutive of *lamina* 'thin plate'.

lamellibranch /ləˈmɛlɪbraŋk/ ■ n. another term for BIVALVE.
– ORIGIN C19: from Latin LAMELLA + Greek *brankhia* 'gills'.

lament ■ n. **1** a passionate expression of grief. **2** a song, piece of music, or poem expressing grief or regret. ■ v. **1** mourn (a person's death). ► [as adj. **lamented**] (usu. **late lamented**) a conventional way of referring to a dead person. **2** express regret or disappointment about.
– DERIVATIVES **lamentation** n. **lamenter** n.
– ORIGIN Middle English: from Latin *lamentari*, from *lamenta* (pl.) 'weeping'.

lamentable /ˈlaməntəb(ə)l/ ■ adj. **1** deplorable or regrettable. **2** archaic sorrowful.
– DERIVATIVES **lamentably** adv.

lamia /ˈleɪmɪə/ ■ n. (pl. **lamias** or **lamiae** /-ɪiː/) a mythical monster with the body of a woman, supposed to prey on human beings and suck the blood of children.
– ORIGIN from Greek, denoting a carnivorous fish or mythical monster.

lamina /ˈlamɪnə/ ■ n. (pl. **laminae** /-niː/) technical a thin layer, plate, or scale of sedimentary rock, organic tissue, or other material.
– ORIGIN C17: from Latin.

laminar /ˈlamɪnə/ ■ adj. **1** consisting of laminae. **2** Physics denoting flow that takes place along constant streamlines, without turbulence.

laminate ■ v. /ˈlamɪneɪt/ [often as adj. **laminated**] **1** overlay (a flat surface) with a layer of protective material. **2** manufacture by placing layer on layer. **3** split into layers or leaves. **4** beat or roll (metal) into thin plates. ■ n. /ˈlamɪnət/ a laminated structure or material. ■ adj. /ˈlamɪnət/ in the form of a lamina or laminae.
– DERIVATIVES **lamination** n. **laminator** n.
– ORIGIN C17: from LAMINA.

laminectomy /ˌlamɪˈnɛktəmi/ ■ n. (pl. **-ies**) a surgical operation to remove the back of one or more vertebrae.

lamington /ˈlamɪŋtən/ ■ n. S. African & Austral./NZ a square of sponge cake dipped in melted chocolate and grated coconut.
– ORIGIN apparently from the name of Lord *Lamington*, Governor of Queensland, Australia (1895–1901).

laminitis /ˌlamɪˈnʌɪtɪs/ ■ n. inflammation of sensitive layers of tissue inside the hoof in horses and other animals.

Lammas /ˈlaməs/ (also **Lammas Day**) ■ n. the first day of August, formerly observed in the UK as harvest festival.
– ORIGIN Old English *hlāfmæsse* (see LOAF[1], MASS), later interpreted as if from LAMB + MASS.

lammergeier /ˈlaməˌgʌɪə/ (also **lammergeyer**) ■ n. another term for BEARDED VULTURE.
– ORIGIN C19: from German *Lämmergeier*, from *Lämmer* 'lambs' + *Geier* 'vulture'.

lamp ■ n. **1** an electric, oil, or gas device for giving light. **2** an electrical device producing ultraviolet or other radiation, especially for therapeutic purposes. ■ v. **1** supply with lamps; illuminate. **2** (usu. as noun **lamping**) hunt at night for rabbits using lamps.
– DERIVATIVES **lamper** n. **lampless** adj.
– ORIGIN Middle English: from late Latin *lampada*, from Latin *lampas* 'torch', from Greek.

lampblack ■ n. a black pigment made from soot.

lamp chimney ■ n. a glass cylinder encircling the wick of an oil lamp and providing a draught for the flame.

lamplighter ■ n. historical a person employed to light street gaslights by hand.

lampoon /lamˈpuːn/ ■ v. publicly satirize or ridicule. ■ n. a satirical attack.
– DERIVATIVES **lampooner** n. **lampoonist** n.
– ORIGIN C17: from French *lampon*, said to be from *lampons* 'let us drink'.

lamprey /ˈlampri/ ■ n. (pl. **-eys**) an eel-like jawless fish, often parasitic, that has a sucker mouth with horny teeth and a rasping tongue. [Family Petromyzonidae: several species.]
– ORIGIN Middle English: from medieval Latin *lampreda*, prob. from Latin *lambere* 'to lick' + *petra* 'stone' (because the lamprey attaches itself to stones by its mouth).

lamprophyre /ˈlamprəˌfʌɪə/ ■ n. Geology an igneous rock containing biotite crystals in a fine-grained feldspathic groundmass.
– ORIGIN C19: from Greek *lampros* 'bright' + *porphureos* 'purple'.

lamp shell ■ n. a marine invertebrate resembling a bivalve mollusc, with arms of ciliated tentacles used for filter-feeding. [Phylum Brachiopoda.]
– ORIGIN C19: from its resemblance to an ancient oil lamp.

lamsiekte /ˈlamsɪktə/ ■ n. S. African a type of botulism affecting mainly cattle.
– ORIGIN Afrikaans, from *lam* 'paralyzed' + *siekte* 'disease'.

LAN ■ abbrev. **1** limestone ammonium nitrate, used as fertilizer. **2** local area network.

Lancashire

Lancashire /ˈlaŋkəʃə/ ■ n. a mild crumbly white cheese, originally made in Lancashire, England.

Lancashire hotpot ■ n. a stew of meat and vegetables, covered with a layer of sliced potato.

Lancastrian /lanˈkastrɪən/ ■ n. 1 a native of Lancashire or Lancaster. 2 a follower of the House of Lancaster in the Wars of the Roses. ■ adj. of or relating to Lancashire or Lancaster, or the House of Lancaster.

lance ■ n. 1 a long weapon with a wooden shaft and a pointed steel head, formerly used by a horseman in charging. 2 a similar weapon used in hunting fish or whales. 3 a metal pipe supplying a jet of oxygen to a furnace or to make a very hot flame for cutting. ■ v. 1 Medicine prick or cut open with a lancet or other sharp instrument. 2 pierce with or as if with a lance. 3 move suddenly and quickly.
– ORIGIN Middle English: from Old French *lance* (n.), *lancier* (v.), from Latin *lancea* (n.).

lance bombardier ■ n. the lowest non-commissioned rank in the artillery, corresponding to lance corporal in the infantry.

lance corporal ■ n. the lowest non-commissioned rank in the army and air force, below corporal.
– ORIGIN C18: on the analogy of obsolete *lancepesade*, the lowest grade of non-commissioned officer, based on Italian *lancia spezzata* 'broken lance'.

lancelet /ˈlɑːnslɪt/ ■ n. a jawless fish-like marine animal that possesses a notochord and typically burrows in sand. [Family Branchiostomidae.]

lanceolate /ˈlɑːnsɪələt/ ■ adj. technical of a narrow oval shape tapering to a point at each end.
– ORIGIN C18: from Latin *lanceola*, diminutive of *lancea* 'a lance'.

lancer ■ n. 1 a cavalry soldier armed with a lance. ▶ (**Lancer**) a soldier of a regiment originally armed with lances. 2 (**lancers**) [treated as sing.] a quadrille for eight or sixteen pairs.

lancet /ˈlɑːnsɪt/ ■ n. a small, broad two-edged surgical knife or blade with a sharp point.
– ORIGIN Middle English: from Old French *lancette*, diminutive of *lance* 'a lance'.

lancet window ■ n. a narrow window with an acutely pointed head.

lancewood ■ n. a tree with tough elastic wood. [*Oxandra lanceolata* (Caribbean) and *Pseudopanax crassifolius* (New Zealand).]

land ■ n. 1 the part of the earth's surface that is not covered by water. ▶ an area of ground, especially in terms of its ownership or use. ▶ S. African a field planted with crops. 2 a country or state. 3 the space between the rifling-grooves in a gun. ■ v. 1 put or go ashore. ▶ unload (goods) from a ship. ▶ bring (a fish) to land with a net or rod. ▶ informal succeed in obtaining or achieving (something desirable). 2 (with reference to aircraft, birds, etc.) come or bring down to the ground. ▶ come to rest after falling or being thrown. 3 (**land up**) reach a place or destination. ▶ (**land up with**) end up with (an unwelcome situation). 4 (**land someone in**) informal cause someone to be in (a difficult situation). ▶ (**land someone with**) inflict (an unwelcome task or a difficult situation) on someone. 5 informal inflict (a blow) on someone.
– PHRASES **how the land lies** what the state of affairs is. **in the land of the living** humorous alive or awake. **the land of Nod** humorous a state of sleep. [punningly, with biblical allusion to the place name *Nod* (Genesis 4:16).] **land** (or **fall**) **on one's feet** have good luck or success.
– DERIVATIVES **landless** adj. **landlessness** n.
– ORIGIN Old English, of Germanic origin.

land agent ■ n. Brit. 1 a person employed to manage an estate on behalf of its owners. 2 a person who deals with the sale of land.
– DERIVATIVES **land agency** n.

landau /ˈlandɔː, -aʊ/ ■ n. a four-wheeled enclosed horse-drawn carriage with a removable front cover and a back cover that can be raised and lowered.
– ORIGIN C18: named after *Landau* in Germany, where it was first made.

land bank ■ n. 1 a large body of land held in trust for future development or disposal. 2 a bank providing loans for land purchase.

land breeze ■ n. a breeze blowing towards the sea from the land.

land bridge ■ n. an area of land formerly connecting two land masses which are now separate.

land claim ■ n. a legally registered claim for the restitution of rights over an area of land.

land crab ■ n. a crab that lives in burrows on land and migrates to the sea to breed. [Family Gecarcinidae.]

land drain ■ n. a drain made of porous or perforated piping and placed in a gravel-filled trench, used for subsoil drainage.

landdrost /ˈlandrɒst/ ■ n. S. African historical the chief administrator of a district; a magistrate.
– ORIGIN from S. African Dutch, from *land* 'country' + *drost* 'bailiff'.

landed ■ adj. owning much land, especially through inheritance. ▶ consisting of or relating to such land.

lander ■ n. a spacecraft designed to land on the surface of a planet or moon.

landfall ■ n. 1 an arrival at land on a sea or air journey. 2 a collapse of a mass of land.

landfill ■ n. 1 the disposal of waste material by burying it, especially as a method of filling in and reclaiming excavated pits. 2 waste material used in this way.

landform ■ n. a natural feature of the earth's surface.

land girl ■ n. (in the UK) a woman doing farm work during the Second World War.

landholder ■ n. a landowner, especially one who either makes their living from it or rents it out.
– DERIVATIVES **landholding** n.

landing ■ n. 1 the process of coming to or bringing something to land. 2 a place where people and goods can be landed from a boat. 3 a level area at the top of a staircase or between flights of stairs.

landing craft ■ n. a boat specially designed for putting troops and military equipment ashore on a beach.

landing gear ■ n. the undercarriage of an aircraft.

landing stage ■ n. a platform on to which passengers or cargo can be landed from a boat.

landlady ■ n. (pl. **-ies**) 1 a woman who leases land or property. 2 a woman who keeps lodgings, a boarding house, or (Brit.) a public house.

ländler /ˈlɛndlə/ ■ n. an Austrian folk dance in triple time, a precursor of the waltz.
– ORIGIN C19: German, from *Landl* 'Upper Austria'.

landline ■ n. a conventional telecommunications connection by cable laid across land.

landlocked ■ adj. almost or entirely surrounded by land.

landlord ■ n. 1 a man (in legal use also a woman) who leases land or property. 2 a man who keeps lodgings, a boarding house, or (Brit.) a public house.

landlordism ■ n. the system whereby land (or property) is owned by landlords to whom tenants pay a fixed rent.

landlubber ■ n. informal a person unfamiliar with the sea or sailing.

landmark ■ n. 1 an object or feature of a landscape or town that is easily seen and recognized from a distance. ▶ historical the boundary of an area of land, or an object marking this. 2 an event, discovery, or change marking an important stage or turning point.

land mass ■ n. a continent or other large body of land.

landmine ■ n. an explosive mine laid on or just under the surface of the ground.

land office ■ n. chiefly N. Amer. a government office recording dealings in public land.
– PHRASES **do a land-office business** N. Amer. informal do a lot of successful trading.

landowner ■ n. a person who owns land.
– DERIVATIVES **landownership** n. **landowning** adj. & n.

landrace ■ n. a pig of a large white breed, originally developed in Denmark.
– ORIGIN 1930s: from Danish.

landrail ■ n. another term for CORNCRAKE.

landscape ■ n. **1** all the visible features of an area of land. **2** a picture representing an area of countryside. **3** the distinctive features of a sphere of intellectual activity: *the political landscape.* **4** [as modifier] denoting a format of printed matter which is wider than it is high. Compare with PORTRAIT. ■ v. improve the aesthetic appearance of (a piece of land) by changing its contours, planting trees and shrubs, etc.
– DERIVATIVES **landscaper** n. **landscapist** n.
– ORIGIN C16: from Middle Dutch *lantscap*, from *land* 'land' + *scap* (equivalent of -SHIP).

landscape architecture ■ n. the art and practice of designing the outdoor environment, especially designing parks or gardens to harmonize with buildings or roads.
– DERIVATIVES **landscape architect** n.

landscape gardening ■ n. the art and practice of laying out grounds in a way which is ornamental or which imitates natural scenery.
– DERIVATIVES **landscape gardener** n.

landside ■ n. the side of an airport terminal to which the general public has unrestricted access.

landslide ■ n. **1** (chiefly Brit. also **landslip**) the sliding down of a mass of earth or rock from a mountain or cliff. **2** an overwhelming majority of votes for one party in an election.

landsman ■ n. (pl. **-men**) a person unfamiliar with the sea or sailing.

land tax ■ n. tax levied on the ownership of land.

landward ■ adv. (also **landwards**) towards land. ■ adj. facing towards land as opposed to sea.

land yacht ■ n. a wind-powered wheeled vehicle with sails, used for recreation and sport.

lane ■ n. **1** a narrow road, especially in a rural area. ▸ [in place names] an urban street. **2** a division of a road intended to separate single lines of traffic according to speed or direction. **3** each of a number of parallel strips of track or water for runners, rowers, or swimmers in a race. **4** a path or course prescribed for or regularly followed by ships or aircraft.
– ORIGIN Old English.

langarm /ˈlaŋɑːm/ ■ adj. & adv. S. African of or relating to a style of ballroom dancing in which partners raise their leading arms and move rapidly across the dance floor.
– ORIGIN Afrikaans, from *lang* 'long' + *arm* 'arm'.

langlauf /ˈlaŋlaʊf/ ■ n. cross-country skiing.
– ORIGIN 1920s: from German, 'long run'.

langouste /lɒŋˈɡuːst/ ■ n. a spiny lobster, especially when prepared and cooked.
– ORIGIN from Old Provençal *lagosta*, from Latin *locusta* 'locust, crustacean'.

langoustine /ˈlɒŋɡustiːn/ ■ n. a Norway lobster.
– ORIGIN French, from *langouste* (see LANGOUSTE).

language ■ n. **1** the method of human communication, either spoken or written, consisting of the use of words in a structured and conventional way. ▸ any method of expression or communication: *body language.* **2** the system of communication used by a particular community or country. ▸ the phraseology and vocabulary of a particular group. ▸ Computing a system of symbols and rules for writing programs or algorithms. **3** the manner or style of a piece of writing or speech. ▸ (usu. **bad/foul/strong language**) coarse or offensive language.
– PHRASES **speak the same language** understand one another as a result of shared opinions or values.
– ORIGIN Middle English: from Old French *langage*, from Latin *lingua* 'tongue'.

language engineering ■ n. the use of computers to process language for purposes such as speech recognition, speech synthesis, and machine translation.

language laboratory ■ n. a room equipped with audio and visual equipment for learning a foreign language.

langue /lɒ̃ɡ/ ■ n. (pl. pronounced same) Linguistics a language viewed as an abstract system used by a speech community. Contrasted with PAROLE.
– ORIGIN 1920s: French.

langued /ˈlaŋɡd/ ■ adj. Heraldry having the tongue of a specified tincture.
– ORIGIN Middle English: from French *langué* 'tongued'.

languid ■ adj. **1** having or showing a disinclination for physical exertion. **2** weak or faint from illness or fatigue.
– DERIVATIVES **languidly** adv.
– ORIGIN C16: from Latin *languidus*, from *languere* (see LANGUISH).

languish ■ v. **1** grow weak or feeble. ▸ archaic pine with love or grief. **2** be kept in an unpleasant place or situation: *he was languishing in jail.*
– DERIVATIVES **languishment** n. (archaic).
– ORIGIN Middle English: from a var. of Latin *languere*, rel. to *laxus* 'lax'.

languor /ˈlaŋɡə/ ■ n. **1** tiredness or inactivity, especially when pleasurable. **2** an oppressive stillness of the air.
– DERIVATIVES **languorous** adj. **languorously** adv.
– ORIGIN Middle English (orig. 'illness', later 'faintness, lassitude'): from Latin, from *languere* (see LANGUISH).

langur /ˈlaŋɡə, lanˈɡʊə/ ■ n. a long-tailed Asian monkey with a characteristic loud call. [*Presbytis* and other genera: several species.]
– ORIGIN C19: from Sanskrit *lāṅgūla*.

La Niña /la ˈniːnjə/ ■ n. (pl. **-as**) an irregularly occurring and complex series of climatic changes characterized by the cooling of the eastern Pacific ocean region, which affect world weather patterns.
– ORIGIN Spanish, 'the little girl', perhaps in contrast to EL NIÑO.

lanie ■ adj. & n. variant spelling of LARNEY.

lank[1] ■ adj. **1** (of hair) long, limp, and straight. **2** lanky.
– DERIVATIVES **lankly** adv. **lankness** n.
– ORIGIN Old English *hlanc* 'thin', of Germanic origin.

lank[2] ■ adj. S. African informal **1** very numerous or plentiful. **2** very good.
– ORIGIN sense 1 is perhaps from Afrikaans *geld lank* 'money galore'; sense 2 is perhaps rel. to Afrikaans *lank nie sleg nie* 'not at all bad'.

lanky ■ adj. (**-ier**, **-iest**) ungracefully thin and tall.
– DERIVATIVES **lankily** adv. **lankiness** n.

lanner /ˈlanə/ ■ n. a falcon with a dark brown back and buff cap, found in SE Europe, the Middle East, and Africa. [*Falco biarmicus.*]
– ORIGIN Middle English: from Old French *lanier*.

lanolin ■ n. a fatty substance found naturally on sheep's wool and used as a base for ointments.
– ORIGIN C19: coined in German from Latin *lana* 'wool' + *oleum* 'oil'.

lantana /lanˈtɑːnə, -ˈteɪnə/ ■ n. a tropical evergreen flowering shrub which bears pink-red or orange-yellow flowers and poisonous black berries, often cultivated as an ornamental. [*Lantana camara* (S. America) and related species.]
– ORIGIN from the name of the wayfaring tree *Viburnum lantana*, which it resembles superficially.

lantern ■ n. **1** a lamp with a transparent case protecting the flame or electric bulb. ▸ the light chamber at the top of a lighthouse. **2** a square, curved, or polygonal structure on the top of a dome or a room, with glazed or open sides.
– ORIGIN Middle English: from Latin *lanterna*, from Greek *lamptēr* 'lamp', from *lampein* 'to shine'.

lanternfish ■ n. (pl. same or **-fishes**) a deep-sea fish with light-emitting organs on its body. [Family Myctophidae.]

lantern fly ■ n. a brightly coloured tropical bug which typically has a bizarrely shaped head and was formerly thought to be luminescent. [Family Fulgoridae.]

lantern jaw ■ n. a long, thin jaw and prominent chin.
– DERIVATIVES **lantern-jawed** adj.

lantern slide ■ n. historical a mounted photographic transparency for projection by a magic lantern.

lanthanide /ˈlanθənaɪd/ ■ n. Chemistry any of the series of fifteen metallic elements from lanthanum (atomic number 57) to lutetium (atomic number 71) in the periodic table. See also RARE EARTH.

lanthanum /ˈlanθənəm/ ■ n. the chemical element of atomic number 57, a silvery-white rare-earth metal. (Symbol: **La**)
– ORIGIN C19: from Greek *lanthanein* 'escape notice' (because it was long undetected in cerium oxide).

lanugo

lanugo /lə'nju:gəʊ/ ■ n. fine, soft hair, especially that which covers the body and limbs of a human fetus.
– ORIGIN C17: from Latin, 'down', from *lana* 'wool'.

lanyard /'lanjəd/ ■ n. **1** a rope used to secure or raise and lower something such as a ship's sails. **2** a cord passed round the neck, shoulder, or wrist for holding a whistle or similar object.
– ORIGIN Middle English, from Old French *laniere*, altered by association with YARD[1].

Lao /laʊ/ ■ n. (pl. same or **Laos**) **1** a member of an indigenous people of Laos and NE Thailand. **2** the language of this people.
– ORIGIN the name in Lao.

laogai /laʊ'gʌɪ/ ■ n. (**the laogai**) (in China) a system of labour camps, many of whose inmates are political dissidents.
– ORIGIN Chinese, 'reform through labour'.

Laotian /laʊʃ(ə)n/ ■ n. a native or inhabitant of the country of Laos in SE Asia. ■ adj. of or relating to Laos.

lap[1] ■ n. **1** the flat area between the waist and knees of a seated person. **2** archaic a hanging flap on a garment or a saddle.
– PHRASES **fall** (or **drop**) **into someone's lap** be acquired by or happen to someone without any effort. **in the lap of the gods** open to chance. **in the lap of luxury** in conditions of great comfort and wealth.
– ORIGIN Old English *læppa* (orig. 'fold, flap', later meaning the front of a skirt when held up to carry something), of Germanic origin.

lap[2] ■ n. **1** one circuit of a track or racetrack. **2** a part of a journey. **3** an overlapping or projecting part. **4** a single turn of rope, thread, or cable round a drum or reel. **5** a rotating abrasive disc for polishing gems, metal, and optical glass. ■ v. (**lapped**, **lapping**) **1** overtake (a competitor in a race) to become one or more laps ahead. **2** (**lap someone/thing in**) poetic/literary enfold someone or something protectively in. **3** project beyond or overlap. **4** polish with a lap.
– ORIGIN Middle English: from LAP[1].

lap[3] ■ v. (**lapped**, **lapping**) **1** (of an animal) take up (liquid) with the tongue. **2** (**lap something up**) accept something with obvious pleasure. **3** (of water) wash against with a gentle rippling sound. ■ n. the action of water lapping.
– ORIGIN Old English, of Germanic origin.

lapa /'lɑ:pə, 'lapə/ ■ n. S. African a walled, often roofed enclosure used as an outdoor entertainment area.
– ORIGIN from Sesotho *lelapa* 'homestead, courtyard'.

laparoscopy /ˌlapə'rɒskəpi/ ■ n. (pl. **-ies**) a surgical procedure in which a fibre-optic instrument is inserted through the abdominal wall to view the organs in or permit small-scale surgery.
– DERIVATIVES **laparoscope** n. **laparoscopic** adj. **laparoscopically** adv.
– ORIGIN C19: from Greek *lapara* 'flank' + -SCOPY.

laparotomy /ˌlapə'rɒtəmi/ ■ n. (pl. **-ies**) a surgical incision into the abdominal cavity, for diagnosis or in preparation for major surgery.

lap dance ■ n. an erotic dance or striptease performed near to or on the lap of a person watching.
– DERIVATIVES **lap dancer** n. **lap dancing** n.

lapdog ■ n. **1** a small pampered pet dog. **2** a person who is completely under the influence of another.

lapel ■ n. the part on each side of a coat or jacket immediately below the collar which is folded back against the front opening.
– DERIVATIVES **-lapelled** adj.
– ORIGIN C17: diminutive of LAP[1].

lapidary /'lapɪd(ə)ri/ ■ adj. **1** of or relating to the engraving, cutting, or polishing of stones and gems. **2** (of language) elegant and concise, suitable for engraving on stone. ■ n. (pl. **-ies**) a person who cuts, polishes, or engraves stones and gems.
– ORIGIN Middle English: from Latin *lapidarius* (in late Latin 'stonecutter'), from *lapis* 'stone'.

lapilli /lə'pɪlʌɪ/ ■ pl. n. Geology rock fragments ejected from a volcano.
– ORIGIN C18: from Latin, pl. of *lapillus*, diminutive of *lapis* 'stone'.

lapis lazuli /ˌlapɪs 'lazjʊlʌɪ, -li/ (also **lapis**) ■ n. **1** a bright blue metamorphic rock consisting largely of lazurite, used in jewellery. **2** ultramarine, originally made by crushing this rock.
– ORIGIN Middle English: from Latin *lapis* 'stone' and medieval Latin *lazuli*, from *lazulum*, from Persian *lāžward* 'lapis lazuli'.

lap joint ■ n. a joint made by halving the thickness of each member at the joint and fitting them together.

Laplander /'laplandə/ ■ n. a native or inhabitant of Lapland in northern Europe.

lap of honour ■ n. a celebratory circuit of a sports field, track, etc. by the victorious person or team.

Lapp ■ n. **1** a member of an indigenous people of the extreme north of Scandinavia. **2** the language of this people.
– ORIGIN Swedish, perhaps orig. a term of contempt and rel. to Middle High German *lappe* 'simpleton'.

USAGE
Although the term **Lapp** is still widely used and is the most familiar term to many people, the people themselves prefer to be called **Sami**.

lappet /'lapɪt/ ■ n. **1** a fold or hanging piece of flesh in some animals. **2** a loose or overlapping part of a garment.
– ORIGIN Middle English (denoting a lobe of the ear, liver, etc.): diminutive of LAP[1].

lappie ■ n. S. African a cloth or rag.
– ORIGIN from Dutch *lap* 'rag, cloth'.

Lappish ■ n. the Lapp language. ■ adj. of or relating to the Lapps (Sami) or their language.

lapsang souchong /ˌlapsaŋ ˌsu:'ʃɒŋ/ ■ n. a fine black variety of China tea with a smoky flavour.
– ORIGIN C19: from an invented first element + *souchong*, from Chinese *siú* 'small' + *chúng* 'sort'.

lapse ■ n. **1** a brief failure of concentration, memory, or judgement. ▶ a decline from previously high standards. **2** an interval of time. **3** Law the termination of a right or privilege through disuse or failure to follow appropriate procedures. ■ v. **1** (of a right, privilege, or agreement) become invalid because it is not used, claimed, or renewed. **2** cease to follow the rules and practices of a religion or doctrine. **3** (**lapse into**) pass gradually into (a different, often worse, state or condition).
– ORIGIN Middle English: from Latin *lapsus*, from *labi* 'to slip or fall'.

lapse rate ■ n. the rate at which air temperature falls with increasing altitude.

laptop ■ n. a portable microcomputer suitable for use while travelling.

lapwing ■ n. a large crested plover with a dark green back, black-and-white head and underparts, and a loud call. [Genus *Vanellus*, family Charadriidae.]
– ORIGIN Old English *hlēapewince*, from *hlēapan* 'to leap' and a base meaning 'move from side to side' (because of the way it flies); the spelling was changed by association with LAP[2] and WING.

larceny /'lɑ:s(ə)ni/ ■ n. (pl. **-ies**) theft of personal property.
– DERIVATIVES **larcenous** adj.
– ORIGIN C15: from Old French *larcin*, from Latin *latrocinium*, from *latro(n-)* 'robber'.

larch ■ n. a northern coniferous tree with bunches of deciduous bright green needles and tough wood. [*Larix decidua* and related species.]
– ORIGIN C16: from Middle High German *larche*, from Latin *larix*.

lard ■ n. fat from the abdomen of a pig, rendered and clarified for use in cooking. ■ v. **1** insert strips of fat or bacon in (meat) before cooking. **2** (usu. **be larded with**) embellish (talk or writing) excessively with esoteric or technical expressions.
– DERIVATIVES **lardy** adj.
– ORIGIN Middle English: from Old French, 'bacon', from Latin *lardum*, *laridum*, rel. to Greek *larinos* 'fat'.

lardass /'lɑ:dɑ:s, 'lɑ:das/ ■ n. N. Amer. informal, derogatory a fat person.

larder ■ n. a room or large cupboard for storing food.
– ORIGIN Middle English (denoting a store of meat): from Old French *lardier*, from medieval Latin *lardarium*, from *laridum* (see LARD).

lardon /'lɑːdən/ (also **lardoon** /-'duːn/) ■ n. a chunk or strip of bacon used to lard meat.
– ORIGIN Middle English: from French, from *lard* (see LARD).

large ■ adj. **1** of considerable or relatively great size, extent, or capacity. **2** pursuing an occupation or activity on a significant scale. **3** of wide range or scope.
– PHRASES **at large 1** escaped or not yet captured. **2** as a whole: *society at large*. **in large measure** (or **part**) to a great extent.
– DERIVATIVES **largeness** n. **largish** adj.
– ORIGIN Middle English: from Latin *larga*, feminine of *largus* 'copious'.

large-hearted ■ adj. sympathetic and generous.

large intestine ■ n. Anatomy the caecum, colon, and rectum collectively.

largely ■ adv. on the whole; mostly.

large-scale ■ adj. extensive.

largesse /lɑː'(d)ʒes/ (also **largess**) ■ n. **1** generosity. **2** money or gifts given generously.
– ORIGIN Middle English: from Latin *largus* 'copious'.

Lariam ■ n. trademark for MEFLOQUINE.

lark¹ ■ n. a songbird with brown streaky plumage, elongated hind claws, and a song that is delivered on the wing. [Family Alaudidae: many species.] ► used in names of similar birds of other families, e.g. meadowlark.
– PHRASES **be up with the lark** get out of bed very early in the morning.
– ORIGIN Old English.

lark² informal ■ n. **1** an amusing adventure or escapade. **2** Brit. an activity regarded as foolish or a waste of time: *he's serious about this music lark*. ■ v. behave in a playful and mischievous way.
– DERIVATIVES **larky** adj.
– ORIGIN C19: perhaps from dialect *lake* 'play', but cf. SKYLARK in the same sense, which is recorded earlier.

larkspur ■ n. a Mediterranean plant resembling a delphinium, with spikes of spurred flowers. [Genus *Consolida*.]

larney /'lɑːni/ (also **larnie**, **lanie**) S. African ■ adj. informal wealthy and of high status; smart. ■ n. (pl. **-eys** or **-ies**) derogatory a white person. ► a boss or employer.

HISTORY
The origins of the word **larney** are uncertain. Although it appeared in Tsotsitaal in the 1950s, no one is quite sure where it came from before that. Some researchers thought it originated in an Indian language, but a more recent opinion is that it may derive from a 19th century vernacular Cape Afrikaans pronunciation of the term *Hollander*, used originally of wealthier, higher status Dutch people in the Cape, but later extended to denote any upper class white person.

larva /'lɑːvə/ ■ n. (pl. **larvae** /-viː/) an active immature form of an insect or other animal that undergoes metamorphosis, e.g. a caterpillar or tadpole.
– DERIVATIVES **larval** adj. **larvicide** n.
– ORIGIN C17: from Latin, 'ghost, mask'.

laryngeal /lə'rɪn(d)ʒɪəl/ ■ adj. **1** of or relating to the larynx. **2** Phonetics (of a speech sound) made in the larynx with the vocal cords partly closed and partly vibrating.

laryngitis /ˌlarɪn'dʒʌɪtɪs/ ■ n. inflammation of the larynx.
– DERIVATIVES **laryngitic** /-'dʒɪtɪk/ adj.

laryngology /ˌlarɪŋ'ɡɒlədʒi/ ■ n. the branch of medicine concerned with the larynx and its diseases.

laryngoscope /lə'rɪŋɡəskəʊp/ ■ n. an instrument for examining the larynx, or for inserting a tube through it.
– DERIVATIVES **laryngoscopy** n.

larynx /'larɪŋks/ ■ n. (pl. **larynges** /lə'rɪn(d)ʒiːz/) Anatomy the hollow muscular organ forming an air passage to the lungs and containing the vocal cords.
– ORIGIN C16: modern Latin, from Greek *larunx*.

lasagne /lə'zanjə, -'san-, -'sɑːn-, -'zɑːn-/ ■ n. **1** pasta in the form of sheets or wide strips. **2** an Italian dish consisting of this baked with meat or vegetables and a cheese sauce.
– ORIGIN Italian, pl. of *lasagna*, from Latin *lasanum* 'chamber pot', perhaps also 'cooking pot'.

Lascar /'laskə/ ■ n. dated a sailor from India or SE Asia.
– ORIGIN C17: from Urdu and Persian *laškarī* 'soldier'.

lascivious /lə'sɪvɪəs/ ■ adj. feeling or revealing an overt or offensive sexual desire.
– DERIVATIVES **lasciviously** adv. **lasciviousness** n.
– ORIGIN Middle English: from late Latin *lasciviosus*, from Latin *lascivia* 'lustfulness'.

laser ■ n. a device that generates an intense narrow beam of coherent monochromatic light by stimulating the emission of photons from excited atoms or molecules.
– ORIGIN 1960s: acronym from *light amplification by stimulated emission of radiation*, based on the earlier MASER.

laserdisc ■ n. a disc that resembles a compact disc but is the size of a long-playing record, used for high-quality video and for interactive multimedia.

laser printer ■ n. a computer printer in which a laser is used to form a pattern of electrostatically charged dots on a light-sensitive drum, which attracts toner.

lash ■ v. **1** strike or beat with a whip or stick. ► beat forcefully against: *waves lashed the coast*. ► (**lash out**) hit or kick out. ► (**lash out**) launch a verbal attack. **2** (of an animal) move (a part of the body, especially the tail) quickly and violently. **3** fasten securely with a cord or rope. **4** (**lash out**) Brit. spend money extravagantly. ■ n. **1** a sharp blow or stroke with a whip or stick. **2** the flexible leather part of a whip. **3** an eyelash.
– DERIVATIVES **-lashed** adj. **lasher** n.
– ORIGIN Middle English ('make a sudden movement'): prob. imitative.

lashing ■ n. **1** a whipping or beating. **2** a cord used to fasten something securely.

lashings ■ pl. n. informal a copious amount of something, especially food or drink.

lass (also **lassie**) ■ n. chiefly Scottish & N. English a girl or young woman.
– ORIGIN Middle English: from Old Norse *laskura* 'unmarried'.

Lassa fever /'lasə/ ■ n. an acute and often fatal viral disease occurring chiefly in West Africa.
– ORIGIN 1970s: named after the village of *Lassa*, in NW Nigeria, where it was first reported.

lassi /'lasi/ ■ n. a sweet or savoury Indian drink made from a yogurt or buttermilk base with water.
– ORIGIN from Hindi *lassī*.

lassitude /'lasɪtjuːd/ ■ n. physical or mental weariness; lack of energy.
– ORIGIN Middle English: from Latin *lassitudo*, from *lassus* 'tired'.

lasso /lə'suː, 'lasəʊ/ ■ n. (pl. **-os** or **-oes**) a rope with a noose at one end, used especially in North America for catching cattle. ■ v. (**-oes**, **-oed**) catch with a lasso.
– DERIVATIVES **lassoer** n.
– ORIGIN C18: representing an American Spanish pronunciation of Spanish *lazo*, from Latin *laqueus* 'noose'.

last¹ ■ adj. **1** coming after all others in time or order; final. ► lowest in importance or rank. ► (**the last**) the least likely or suitable. **2** most recent in time; latest. **3** immediately preceding in order; previous in a sequence or enumeration. **4** only remaining. ■ adv. **1** on the last occasion before the present; previously. **2** [in combination] after all others in order or sequence: *the last-named film*. **3** (in enumerating points) lastly. ■ n. (pl. same) the last person or thing. ► (**the last of**) the only remaining part. ► (**the last**) the end or last moment, especially death.
– PHRASES **at last** (or **at long last**) in the end; after much delay. **last thing** late in the evening, especially immediately before going to bed.
– ORIGIN Old English *latost*, of Germanic origin; rel. to LATE.

last² ■ v. **1** continue for a specified period of time. **2** remain operating or usable for a considerable or specified length of time. **3** (of provisions or resources) be

last 660

adequate or sufficient for a specified length of time.
– ORIGIN Old English *lǣstan*, of Germanic origin, rel. to LAST³.

last³ ■ n. a shoemaker's model for shaping or repairing a shoe or boot.
– ORIGIN Old English *lǣste*, of Germanic origin, from a base meaning 'follow'.

last-ditch ■ adj. denoting a final desperate attempt to achieve something.

last-gasp ■ adj. informal at the last possible moment.

last hurrah ■ n. chiefly N. Amer. a final act, performance, or effort.

lasting ■ adj. enduring or able to endure over a long period of time.

Last Judgement ■ n. the judgement of humankind expected in some religious traditions to take place at the end of the world.

lastly ■ adv. in the last place; last.

last minute (also **last moment**) ■ n. the latest possible time before an event.

last name ■ n. one's surname.

last offices ■ pl. n. the preparation of a corpse for burial; laying out.

last post ■ n. a bugle call giving notice of the hour of retiring at night, also played at military funerals and acts of remembrance.

last rites ■ pl. n. (in the Christian Church) rites administered to a person who is about to die.

Last Supper ■ n. the supper eaten by Jesus and his disciples on the night before the Crucifixion.

last word ■ n. 1 a final or definitive pronouncement on a subject. 2 the most modern or advanced example of something.

lat /lat/ ■ n. informal (in bodybuilding) a latissimus muscle.

lat. ■ abbrev. latitude.

latch ■ n. 1 a bar with a catch and lever used for fastening a door or gate. 2 a spring lock for an outer door, which catches when the door is closed and can only be opened from the outside with a key. 3 Electronics a circuit which retains whatever output state results from a momentary input signal until reset by another signal. ■ v. 1 fasten with a latch. 2 Electronics (of a device) become fixed in a particular state. 3 (**latch on**) understand the meaning of something. 4 (usu. **latch on to something**) become attached. ▸ associate oneself enthusiastically with something.
– PHRASES **on the latch** (of a door or gate) closed but not locked.
– ORIGIN Old English *læccan* 'take hold of, grasp', of Germanic origin.

latchkey ■ n. (pl. **-eys**) a key of an outer door of a house.

latchkey child ■ n. a child who is alone at home after school until a parent returns from work.

late ■ adj. 1 acting, arriving, or happening after the expected or usual time. 2 belonging or taking place far on in a particular time or period. 3 far on in the day or night. 4 (**the/one's late**) (of a specified person) no longer alive. ▸ no longer having the specified status; former. 5 (**latest**) of most recent date or origin. ■ adv. 1 after the expected or usual time. 2 towards the end of a period. 3 far on in the day or night. 4 (**later**) at a time in the near future; afterwards. 5 (**late of**) formerly but not now living or working in a specified place or institution. ■ n. (**the latest**) the most recent news or fashion.
– PHRASES **at the latest** no later than the time specified. **late in the day** (or N. Amer. **game**) at a late stage in proceedings. **of late** recently.
– DERIVATIVES **lateness** n.
– ORIGIN Old English, of Germanic origin.

USAGE
In standard English **late** is used attributively to mean 'deceased', as in *my late grandfather*. In South African English the predicative use is common among Bantu language speakers, as in *my grandfather is late*.

latecomer ■ n. a person who arrives late.

lateen sail /laˈtiːn/ ■ n. a triangular sail on a long yard at an angle of 45° to the mast.
– ORIGIN C16: from French (*voile*) *Latine* 'Latin (sail)', so named because it was common in the Mediterranean.

late harvest ■ n. sweet wine made from grapes picked later than normal, when their sugar content is higher.

late Latin ■ n. Latin of about AD 200–600.

lately ■ adv. recently; not long ago.

latent ■ adj. existing but not yet developed, manifest, or active: *her latent talent*.
– DERIVATIVES **latency** n. **latently** adv.
– ORIGIN Middle English: from Latin *latent-*, *latere* 'be hidden'.

latent heat ■ n. Physics the heat required to convert a solid into a liquid or vapour, or a liquid into a vapour, without change of temperature.

latent image ■ n. Photography an image on film that has not yet been made visible by developing.

latent period ■ n. Medicine the period between infection and the onset of symptoms.

lateral ■ adj. 1 of, at, towards, or from the side or sides. 2 Phonetics (of a consonant, especially the English clear *l*) pronounced with partial closure of the air passage by the tongue, which allows the breath to flow on one or both sides of the point of contact. ■ n. 1 a side part of something, especially a shoot or branch growing out from the side of a stem. 2 Phonetics a lateral consonant. 3 American Football a pass thrown sideways or back.
– DERIVATIVES **laterally** adv.
– ORIGIN Middle English: from Latin *lateralis*, from *latus*, *later-* 'side'.

laterality ■ n. dominance of one side of the brain in controlling particular activities or functions, or of one of a pair of organs such as the eyes or hands.

lateralize (also **-ise**) ■ v. (**be lateralized**) (also **-ised**) Physiology & Medicine be localized to one or other side of the brain.
– DERIVATIVES **lateralization** (also **-isation**) n.

lateral line ■ n. Zoology a visible line along the side of a fish, consisting of a series of sense organs which detect pressure and vibration.

lateral thinking ■ n. the solving of problems by an indirect and creative approach.

lateral ventricle ■ n. Anatomy each of the first and second ventricles in the centre of each cerebral hemisphere of the brain.

laterite /ˈlatərʌɪt/ ■ n. a reddish clayey material, hard when dry, forming a topsoil in some tropical regions and sometimes used for building.
– DERIVATIVES **lateritic** adj.
– ORIGIN C19: from Latin *later* 'brick'.

latex /ˈleɪtɛks/ ■ n. (pl. **latexes** or **latices** /-tɪsiːz/) 1 a milky fluid found in many plants, notably the rubber tree, which coagulates on exposure to the air. 2 a synthetic product resembling this, used to make paints, coatings, etc.
– ORIGIN C17 (denoting various bodily fluids): from Latin, 'liquid, fluid'.

lath /lɑːθ, lɑːð/ ■ n. (pl. **laths** /lɑːθs, lɑːðz, lɑːθs/) a thin, flat strip of wood, especially one of a series forming a foundation for the plaster of a wall.
– ORIGIN Old English, of Germanic origin; rel. to LATTICE.

lathe /leɪð/ ■ n. a machine for shaping wood or metal by means of a rotating drive which turns the piece being worked on against changeable cutting tools.
– ORIGIN Middle English: prob. from Old Danish *lad* 'structure, frame', perhaps from Old Norse *hlath* 'pile, heap'.

lather /ˈlɑːðə, ˈlaðə/ ■ n. 1 a frothy white mass of bubbles produced by soap when mixed with water. 2 heavy sweat visible on a horse's coat as a white foam. 3 (**a lather**) informal a state of agitation or nervous excitement. ■ v. 1 form or cause to form a lather. ▸ rub with soap until a lather is produced. 2 cover or spread liberally with (a substance).
– ORIGIN Old English, of Germanic origin.

latices plural form of LATEX.

latifundia /ˌlatɪˈfʌndɪə, ˌlatɪ-/ ■ pl. n. (sing. **latifundium**)

large landed estates or ranches worked by peasants or slaves, especially in Spain or Latin America.
– ORIGIN C17: from Latin, from *latus* 'broad' + *fundus* 'landed estate'.

Latin ■ n. **1** the language of ancient Rome and its empire. **2** a native or inhabitant of a country whose language developed from Latin, e.g. a Latin American. ■ adj. **1** of or relating to the Latin language. **2** relating to or denoting countries using languages that developed from Latin, especially Latin America. **3** relating to or denoting the Western or Roman Catholic Church.
– DERIVATIVES
– ORIGIN from Latin *Latinus* 'of Latium'.

Latina /ləˈtiːnə/ ■ n. fem. of **LATINO**.

Latin American ■ adj. of or relating to the parts of the American continent where Spanish or Portuguese is the main national language. ■ n. a native or inhabitant of this region.

Latinate /ˈlatɪneɪt/ ■ adj. (of language) having the character of Latin.

Latin Church ■ n. the Roman Catholic Church as distinguished from Orthodox and Uniate Churches.

Latin cross ■ n. a plain cross in which the vertical part below the horizontal is longer than the other three parts.

Latinize (also **-ise**) ■ v. give a Latin or Latinate form to (a word).

Latino /ləˈtiːnəʊ/ ■ n. (fem. **Latina**), (pl. **-os** or **-as**) chiefly N. Amer. a Latin American inhabitant of the United States.
– ORIGIN from Latin American Spanish.

Latin square ■ n. an arrangement of letters in a square array of n^2 compartments, each letter appearing n times but never twice in the same row or column.

latissimus /ləˈtɪsɪməs/ (also **latissimus dorsi** /ˈdɔːsaɪ, -siː/) ■ n. (pl. **latissimi** /ləˈtɪsɪmaɪ, -miː/) Anatomy either of a pair of large, roughly triangular muscles covering the lower part of the back.
– ORIGIN C17: modern Latin, from *musculus latissimus dorsi* 'broadest muscle of the back'.

latitude /ˈlatɪtjuːd/ ■ n. **1** the angular distance of a place north or south of the equator. **2** (**latitudes**) regions of reference to their temperature and distance from the equator: *northern latitudes*. **3** scope for freedom of action or thought.

latitudinarian /ˌlatɪtjuːdɪˈnɛːrɪən/ ■ adj. liberal, especially in religious views. ■ n. a person with a latitudinarian attitude.

latke /ˈlʌtkə/ ■ n. (in Jewish cookery) a pancake, especially one made with grated potato.
– ORIGIN from Yiddish.

latrine /ləˈtriːn/ ■ n. a toilet, especially a communal one in a camp or barracks.
– ORIGIN Middle English: from Latin *latrina*, contraction of *lavatrina*, from *lavare* 'to wash'.

-latry ■ comb. form denoting worship of a specified thing: *idolatry*.
– ORIGIN from Greek *-latria* 'worship'.

latte /ˈlɑːteɪ, ˈlateɪ/ ■ n. short for **CAFFÈ LATTE**.

latter ■ adj. **1** nearer to the end of something than to the beginning. ▶ belonging to the final stages of something, especially of a person's life. ▶ recent: *in latter years*. **2** (**the latter**) denoting the second or second-mentioned of two people or things.
– ORIGIN Old English *lætra* 'slower', from *læt* (see **LATE**).

latter-day ■ adj. modern or contemporary, especially when mirroring some person or thing of the past: *a latter-day Noah*.

Latter-Day Saints ■ pl. n. the Mormons' name for themselves.

latterly ■ adv. **1** recently. **2** in the later stages of a period of time.

lattice ■ n. **1** a structure or pattern consisting of strips crossing each other with square or diamond-shaped spaces left between. **2** Physics a regular repeated three-dimensional arrangement of atoms, ions, or molecules in a metal or other crystalline solid.
– DERIVATIVES **latticed** adj. **latticework** n.
– ORIGIN Middle English: from Old French *lattis*, from *latte* 'lath', of Germanic origin.

lattice window ■ n. a window with small panes set in diagonally crossing strips of lead.

Latvian ■ n. **1** a native or citizen of Latvia, or a person of Latvian descent. **2** the Baltic language of Latvia. ■ adj. of or relating to Latvia, its people, or their language.

laud /lɔːd/ ■ v. formal praise highly, especially in a public context. ■ n. archaic praise.
– ORIGIN Middle English: from Latin *laus, laud-* 'praise'.

laudable ■ adj. deserving praise and commendation.
– DERIVATIVES **laudably** adv.

laudanum /ˈlɔːd(ə)nəm, ˈlɒd-/ ■ n. an alcoholic solution containing morphine, prepared from opium and formerly used as a narcotic painkiller.
– ORIGIN C16: modern Latin, perhaps a var. of Latin *ladanum* (see **LADANUM**).

laudatory /ˈlɔːdət(ə)ri/ ■ adj. expressing praise and commendation.

laugh ■ v. **1** make the sounds and movements that express lively amusement and sometimes also derision. ▶ (**laugh at**) ridicule; scorn. **2** (**laugh something off**) dismiss something by treating it in a light-hearted way. **3** (**be laughing**) informal be in a fortunate or successful position. ■ n. **1** an act of laughing. **2** (**a laugh**) informal a person or thing that causes laughter.
– PHRASES **have the last laugh** be finally vindicated. **a laugh a minute** very funny. **laugh out of court** dismiss with contempt as being obviously ridiculous. **laugh up one's sleeve** be secretly or inwardly amused. **no laughing matter** something serious that should not be joked about.
– DERIVATIVES **laugher** n. **laughing** adj. **laughingly** adv.
– ORIGIN Old English, of Germanic origin.

laughable ■ adj. so ludicrous as to be amusing.
– DERIVATIVES **laughably** adv.

laughing gas ■ n. non-technical term for **NITROUS OXIDE**.

laughing hyena ■ n. another term for **SPOTTED HYENA**.

laughing stock ■ n. a person subjected to general mockery or ridicule.

laughter ■ n. the action or sound of laughing.
– ORIGIN Old English, of Germanic origin.

launch[1] ■ v. **1** set (a boat or ship) afloat, especially by sliding it into the water. **2** send out or hurl forcefully (a rocket or other missile). **3** begin (an enterprise) or introduce (a new product). ▶ (**launch into**) begin (something) energetically and enthusiastically. ■ n. an act or instance of launching something.
– ORIGIN Middle English: from Anglo-Norman French *launcher*, var. of Old French *lancier* (see **LANCE**).

launch[2] ■ n. **1** a large motor boat. **2** historical the largest boat carried on a man-of-war.
– ORIGIN C17: from Spanish *lancha* 'pinnace', perhaps from Malay, from *lanchar* 'swift, nimble'.

launcher ■ n. a structure that holds a rocket or missile during launching.

launch pad (also **launching pad**) ■ n. the area on which a rocket stands for launching.

launder ■ v. **1** wash and iron (clothes or linen). **2** informal transfer (illegally obtained money) to conceal its origins. ■ n. **1** a trough for holding or conveying water, especially (in mining) one used for washing ore. **2** a channel for conveying molten metal to a ladle or mould.
– DERIVATIVES **launderer** n.
– ORIGIN Middle English (as n. denoting a person who washes linen): contraction of *lavender*, from Old French *lavandier*, from Latin *lavanda* 'things to be washed', from *lavare* 'to wash'.

launderette (also **laundrette**) ■ n. an establishment with coin-operated washing machines and dryers for public use.

laundress ■ n. a woman employed to launder clothes and linen.

laundromat ■ n. (trademark in the US) a launderette.

laundry ■ n. (pl. **-ies**) **1** clothes and linen that need to be washed or that have been newly washed. **2** a room or

laureate /ˈlɒrɪət, ˈlɔː-/ ■ n. **1** a person given an award for outstanding creative or intellectual achievement: *a Nobel laureate*. **2** short for **POET LAUREATE**.
– DERIVATIVES **laureateship** n.
– ORIGIN Middle English: from Latin *laureatus*, from *laurea* 'laurel wreath'.

laurel ■ n. **1** an aromatic evergreen shrub or small tree with dark green glossy leaves. [*Laurus* and other genera, family Lauraceae.] **2** (**laurels**) a crown woven from the foliage of the bay tree and awarded as an emblem of victory or mark of honour in classical times. ▶ honour or praise. ■ v. (**laurelled**, **laurelling**; US **laureled**, **laureling**) adorn with or as if with a laurel.
– PHRASES **look to one's laurels** be careful not to lose one's superior position to a rival. **rest on one's laurels** be so satisfied with what one has already achieved that one makes no further effort.
– ORIGIN Middle English, from Provençal *laurier*, from earlier *laur*, from Latin *laurus*.

lav ■ n. informal a lavatory.

lava ■ n. hot molten or semi-fluid rock erupted from a volcano or fissure, or solid rock resulting from cooling of this.
– ORIGIN C18: from Italian (orig. denoting a stream caused by sudden rain), from *lavare* 'to wash', from Latin.

lavage /ˈlævɪdʒ, ləˈvɑːʒ/ ■ n. Medicine washing out of a body cavity, such as the colon or stomach, with water or a medicated solution.
– ORIGIN C18: from French, from *laver* 'to wash'.

lava lamp ■ n. a transparent electric lamp containing a viscous liquid in which a suspended waxy substance rises and falls in constantly changing shapes.

lavatorial ■ adj. **1** of, relating to, or resembling lavatories. **2** (of conversation or humour) characterized by undue reference to lavatories and their use.

lavatory ■ n. (pl. **-ies**) a toilet.
– ORIGIN Middle English: from late Latin *lavatorium* 'place for washing', from Latin *lavare* 'to wash'.

lavender ■ n. **1** a small aromatic evergreen shrub of the mint family, with narrow leaves and bluish-purple flowers. [Genus *Lavandula*.] ▶ (also **lavender oil**) a scented oil distilled from lavender flowers. ▶ used in names of similar plants, e.g. sea lavender. **2** a pale blue colour with a trace of mauve.
– ORIGIN Middle English: from Anglo-Norman French *lavendre*, from medieval Latin *lavandula*.

lavender water ■ n. a perfume made from distilled lavender, alcohol, and ambergris.

laver[1] /ˈlɑːvə, ˈleɪvə/ (also **purple laver**) ■ n. an edible seaweed with thin reddish-purple and green sheet-like fronds. [*Porphyra umbilicalis*.]
– ORIGIN Old English, from Latin.

laver[2] /ˈleɪvə/ ■ n. **1** archaic or poetic/literary a basin or similar container used for washing oneself. **2** (in biblical use) a large brass bowl for Jewish priests' ritual ablutions.
– ORIGIN Middle English: from Old French *laveoir*, from late Latin *lavatorium* (see **LAVATORY**).

lavish ■ adj. **1** sumptuously rich, elaborate, or luxurious. **2** giving or given in profusion. ■ v. (usu. **lavish something on**) bestow or cover in generous or extravagant quantities.
– DERIVATIVES **lavishly** adv. **lavishness** n.
– ORIGIN Middle English (as n. denoting profusion): from Old French *lavasse* 'deluge of rain', from *laver* 'to wash', from Latin *lavare*.

law ■ n. **1** a rule or system of rules recognized by a country or community as regulating the actions of its members and enforced by the imposition of penalties. ▶ such rules as a subject of study or as the basis of the legal profession. ▶ statute law and the common law. ▶ something regarded as having binding force or effect: *his word was law*. ▶ (**the law**) informal the police. **2** a statement of fact, deduced from observation, to the effect that a particular natural or scientific phenomenon always occurs if certain conditions are present. **3** a rule defining correct procedure or behaviour in a sport. **4** the body of divine commandments as expressed in the Bible or other religious texts. ▶ (**the Law**) the Pentateuch.
– PHRASES **be a law unto oneself** behave in an unconventional or unpredictable manner. **lay down the law** issue instructions in an authoritative or dogmatic way. **take the law into one's own hands** illegally or violently punish someone according to one's own ideas of justice.
– ORIGIN Old English, from Old Norse *lag* 'something laid down or fixed', of Germanic origin.

law-abiding ■ adj. obedient to the laws of society.

lawbreaker ■ n. a person who breaks the law.
– DERIVATIVES **lawbreaking** n. & adj.

law court ■ n. a court of law.

lawful ■ adj. conforming to, permitted by, or recognized by law or rules.
– DERIVATIVES **lawfully** adv. **lawfulness** n.

lawgiver ■ n. a person who draws up and enacts laws.

lawless ■ adj. not governed by or obedient to laws.
– DERIVATIVES **lawlessly** adv. **lawlessness** n.

law lord ■ n. (in the UK) a member of the House of Lords qualified to perform its legal work.

lawmaker ■ n. a legislator.
– DERIVATIVES **law-making** adj. & n.

lawman ■ n. (pl. **-men**) (in the US) a law-enforcement officer, especially a sheriff.

lawn[1] ■ n. an area of mown grass in a garden or park.
– DERIVATIVES **lawned** adj.
– ORIGIN C16: alteration of dialect *laund* 'glade, pasture', from Old French *launde* 'wooded district, heath', of Celtic origin.

lawn[2] ■ n. a fine linen or cotton fabric used for making clothes.
– ORIGIN Middle English: prob. from *Laon*, the name of a city in France important for linen manufacture.

lawnmower ■ n. a machine for cutting the grass on a lawn.

lawn tennis ■ n. dated or formal tennis.

law of averages ■ n. the supposed principle that future events are likely to turn out so that they balance any past deviation from a presumed average.

law office ■ n. a lawyer's office.

law of mass action ■ n. Chemistry the principle that the rate of a chemical reaction is proportional to the masses of the reacting substances.

law of nations ■ n. Law international law.

law of nature ■ n. another term for **NATURAL LAW**.

law of succession ■ n. the law regulating the inheritance of property.

lawrencium /lɒˈrɛnsɪəm/ ■ n. the chemical element of atomic number 103, an artificially made radioactive metal. (Symbol: **Lr**)
– ORIGIN 1960s: named after the American physicist Ernest O. *Lawrence*.

lawsuit ■ n. a claim or dispute brought to a law court for adjudication.

lawyer ■ n. a person who practises or studies law, especially (in South Africa) an attorney or advocate or (in the UK) a solicitor or barrister.
– DERIVATIVES **lawyering** n. **lawyerly** adj.

lax ■ adj. **1** not sufficiently strict, severe, or careful. **2** (of the limbs or muscles) relaxed. **3** Phonetics (of a speech sound, especially a vowel) pronounced with the vocal muscles relaxed. The opposite of **TENSE**[1].
– DERIVATIVES **laxity** n. **laxly** adv. **laxness** n.
– ORIGIN Middle English: from Latin *laxus*.

laxative ■ adj. tending to stimulate or facilitate evacuation of the bowels. ■ n. a laxative drug or medicine.
– ORIGIN Middle English: from late Latin *laxativus*, from Latin *laxare* 'loosen'.

lay[1] ■ v. (past and past part. **laid**) **1** put down, especially gently or carefully. **2** put down and set in position for use. ▶ set cutlery on (a table) in preparation for a meal. ▶ put the material for (a fire) in place. ▶ make ready (a trap). ▶ (**lay something before**) present material for consideration and action to (someone). **3** (with an abstract noun) put or place: *lay the blame*. **4** (of a female bird, reptile, etc.) produce (an egg) from inside the body. **5** stake

(an amount of money) in a wager. **6** cause (a ghost) to stop appearing; exorcize. **7** vulgar slang have sexual intercourse with. **8** Nautical follow (a specified course). ▶ **n. 1** the general appearance of an area of land. ▶ the position or direction in which something lies: *roll the carpet against the lay of the nap.* **2** vulgar slang a sexual partner or act of sexual intercourse. **3** the laying of eggs or the period during which they are laid.
– PHRASES **lay claim to** assert one's right to or possession of. **lay hands on** find and take possession of or acquire. **lay hold of** (or **on**) catch at or gain possession of. **lay someone low** reduce someone to inactivity, illness, or lowly position. **lay something on thick** (or **with a trowel**) informal grossly exaggerate or overemphasize something. **lay someone open to** expose someone to the risk of. **lay someone/thing to rest 1** bury a body in a grave. **2** soothe and dispel fear, anxiety, etc.
– PHRASAL VERBS **lay about** beat or attack violently. **lay something down 1** formulate and enact a rule or principle. **2** begin to construct a ship or railway. **3** build up a deposit of a substance. **4** store wine in a cellar. **5** pay or wager money. **lay something in/up** build up a stock of something in case of need. **lay into** informal attack violently. **lay off** informal give up. **lay someone off** discharge a worker temporarily or permanently because of a shortage of work. **lay someone out 1** prepare someone for burial after death. **2** informal knock someone unconscious. **lay something out 1** spread something out to its full extent. **2** construct or arrange buildings or gardens according to a plan. ▶ arrange and present material for printing and publication. **3** informal spend a sum of money. **lay someone up** put someone out of action through illness or injury. **lay something up 1** see *lay something in.* **2** take a ship or other vehicle out of service.
– ORIGIN Old English, of Germanic origin; rel. to LIE¹.

> USAGE
> The words **lay** and **lie** are often used incorrectly. **Lay** means, broadly, 'put something down', as in *they are going to lay the carpet*, whereas **lie** means 'be in a horizontal position to rest', as in *why don't you lie down?* The past tense and the past participle of **lay** is **laid** (*they laid the carpet*); the past tense of **lie** is **lay** (*he lay on the floor*) and the past participle is **lain** (*she had lain awake for hours*).

lay² ■ adj. **1** not ordained into or belonging to the clergy. **2** not having professional qualifications or expert knowledge.
– ORIGIN Middle English: from Old French *lai*, from Greek *laïkos*, from *laos* 'people'.

lay³ ■ n. **1** a short lyric or narrative poem meant to be sung. **2** poetic/literary a song.
– ORIGIN Middle English: from Old French *lai*, corresponding to Provençal *lais*.

lay⁴ past of LIE¹.

layabout ■ n. derogatory a person who habitually does little or no work.

layaway ■ n. chiefly N. Amer. another term for LAY-BY.

lay brother (or **lay sister**) ■ n. a person who has taken the vows of a religious order but is not ordained and is employed in ancillary or manual work.

lay-by ■ n. (pl. **lay-bys**) **1** an area at the side of a road where vehicles may pull off the road and stop. **2** (also **lay-bye**) S. African & Austral./NZ a system of paying a deposit to secure an article for later purchase.

layer ■ n. **1** a sheet or thickness of material, typically one of several, covering a surface or body. **2** a person or thing that lays something. **3** a shoot fastened down to take root while attached to the parent plant. ■ v. [often as adj. **layered**] **1** arrange or cut in a layer or layers. **2** propagate (a plant) as a layer.
– ORIGIN Middle English (denoting a mason): from LAY¹.

layer cake ■ n. a cake of two or more layers with jam, cream, or icing between.

layette ■ n. a set of clothing and bedclothes for a newborn child.
– ORIGIN C19: from French, diminutive of Old French *laie* 'drawer'.

leach

layman (or **layperson**) ■ n. (pl. **-men**) **1** a non-ordained member of a Church. **2** a person without professional or specialized knowledge.

lay-off ■ n. **1** a temporary or permanent discharge of a worker or workers. **2** a period during which someone is unable to take part in a sport or other activity due to injury or illness.

layout ■ n. **1** the way in which something, especially a page, is laid out. **2** a thing set out in a particular way: *a model railway layout.*

layover ■ n. chiefly N. Amer. a period of rest or waiting before a further stage in a journey.

lay reader ■ n. (in the Anglican Church) a layperson licensed to preach and to conduct some services but not to celebrate the Eucharist.

laywoman ■ n. (pl. **-women**) a non-ordained female member of a Church.

lazarette /ˌlazəˈrɛt/ (also **lazaret**) ■ n. the after part of a ship's hold, used for stores.
– ORIGIN C17: from obsolete *lazaretto*, denoting an isolation hospital for people with infectious diseases, from Italian, diminutive of *lazzaro* 'beggar', from medieval Latin *lazarus*, with biblical allusion to *Lazarus*, a beggar covered in sores (Luke 16:20).

laze ■ v. spend time in a relaxed, lazy manner. ■ n. a spell of lazing.

lazurite /ˈlazjʊrʌɪt/ ■ n. a bright blue mineral which is the chief constituent of lapis lazuli and consists chiefly of a silicate and sulphate of sodium and aluminium.

lazy ■ adj. (**-ier**, **-iest**) **1** unwilling to work or use energy. **2** showing a lack of effort or care. **3** (of a river) slow-moving.
– DERIVATIVES **lazily** adv. **laziness** n.
– ORIGIN C16: perhaps rel. to Low German *lasich* 'languid, idle'.

lazybones ■ n. (pl. same) informal a lazy person.

lazy eye ■ n. an eye with poor vision due to underuse, especially the unused eye in a squint.

lazy Susan ■ n. a revolving stand or tray on a table, used especially for holding condiments.

lb ■ abbrev. pound(s) (in weight).
– ORIGIN from Latin *libra*.

LBO ■ abbrev. leveraged buyout.

lbw ■ abbrev. Cricket leg before wicket.

l.c. ■ abbrev. **1** letter of credit. **2** lower case.

LCD ■ abbrev. **1** Electronics & Computing liquid crystal display. **2** Mathematics lowest (or least) common denominator.

LCM ■ abbrev. Mathematics lowest (or least) common multiple.

LD ■ abbrev. **1** learning disability (or disabled). **2** lethal dose (of a toxic compound, drug, or pathogen).

LDC ■ abbrev. less-developed country.

LDL ■ abbrev. Biochemistry low-density lipoprotein.

LDV ■ abbrev. light delivery vehicle.

-le¹ ■ suffix **1** forming names of appliances or instruments: *bridle.* **2** forming names of animals and plants: *beetle.*
– ORIGIN Old English, of Germanic origin.

-le² (also **-el**) ■ suffix forming nouns having or originally having a diminutive sense: *mantle.*
– ORIGIN Middle English *-el*, *-elle*, partly from Old English and partly from Old French (based on Latin forms).

-le³ ■ suffix (forming adjectives from an original verb) apt to; liable to: *brittle.*
– ORIGIN Middle English: from *-el*, of Germanic origin.

-le⁴ ■ suffix forming verbs, chiefly expressing repeated action or movement (as in *babble*, *dazzle*), or having diminutive sense (as in *nestle*).
– ORIGIN Old English *-lian*, of Germanic origin.

lea ■ n. poetic/literary an open area of grassy or arable land.
– ORIGIN Old English, of Germanic origin.

leach ■ v. remove (a soluble substance) from soil or other material by the action of percolating liquid, especially

leachate

rainwater.
– ORIGIN Old English *leccan* 'to water', of West Germanic origin.

leachate ■ n. technical water that has percolated through a solid and leached out some of the constituents.

lead¹ /liːd/ ■ v. (past and past part. **led** /led/) **1** cause (a person or animal) to go with one by drawing them along. ▸ show (someone) the way to a destination by preceding or accompanying them. ▸ (**lead someone on**) deceive someone into believing that one is attracted to them. **2** (usu. **lead to**) be a route or means of access to a particular place. ▸ culminate or result in. ▸ (**lead someone to/to do something**) be someone's reason or motive for. ▸ (**lead up to**) precede or provide an introduction to. ▸ (often **lead** (**off**) with) begin a report or text with a particular item. ▸ Law present (evidence). **3** be in charge or command of. **4** have the advantage in a race or game. ▸ be superior to (a competitor). **5** have or experience (a particular way of life). **6** channel or direct (water, rope, etc.). **7** (**lead with**) Boxing make an attack with (a particular punch or fist). **8** (in card games) play (the first card) in a trick or round of play. ■ n. **1** the initiative in an action: *women in Zambia take the lead*. **2** a clue to be followed in the resolution of a problem. **3** (**the lead**) a position of advantage in a contest; first place. ▸ an amount by which a competitor is ahead of the others. **4** the chief part in a play or film. ▸ [as modifier] playing the chief part in a musical group: *the lead singer*. ▸ [as modifier] denoting the principal item in a report or text: *the lead article*. **5** a strap or cord for restraining and guiding a dog. **6** a wire conveying electric current from a source to an appliance, or connecting two points of a circuit together. **7** the distance advanced by a screw in one turn.
– PHRASES **lead someone astray** cause someone to act or think foolishly or wrongly. **lead someone up** (or **down**) **the garden path** informal give someone misleading clues or signals.
– ORIGIN Old English *lǣdan*, of Germanic origin; rel. to **LOAD**.

lead² /led/ ■ n. **1** a heavy bluish-grey soft ductile metal, the chemical element of atomic number 82. (Symbol: **Pb**) **2** graphite used as the part of a pencil that makes a mark. **3** Printing a blank space between lines of print (originally created by a metal strip). **4** Nautical a lump of lead suspended on a line to determine the depth of water. **5** (**leads**) Brit. sheets or strips of lead covering a roof. **6** (**leads**) lead frames holding the glass of a lattice or stained-glass window.
– PHRASES **go down** (or N. Amer. **over**) **like a lead balloon** (of a speech, proposal, or joke) be poorly received.
– ORIGIN Old English *lēad*, of West Germanic origin.

lead crystal ■ n. another term for **LEAD GLASS**.

leaded ■ adj. **1** framed, covered, or weighted with lead. **2** (of petrol) containing tetraethyl lead.

leaden ■ adj. **1** dull, heavy, or slow. **2** of the colour of lead; dull grey. **3** archaic made of lead.
– DERIVATIVES **leadenly** adv. **leadenness** n.

leader ■ n. **1** the person who leads, commands, or precedes a group, organization, or country. ▸ (also **Leader of the House**) (in some countries) a member of the government officially responsible for initiating business in Parliament. **2** the principal player in a music group. **3** Brit. a leading article in a newspaper. **4** a short strip of non-functional material at each end of a reel of film or recording tape for connection to the spool. **5** a length of filament attached to the end of a fishing line to carry the hook or fly. **6** a shoot of a plant at the apex of a stem or main branch. **7** (**leaders**) Printing a series of dots or dashes across the page to guide the eye, especially in tabulated material.
– DERIVATIVES **leaderless** adj. **leadership** n.

leader board ■ n. a scoreboard showing the names and current scores of the leading competitors, especially in a golf match.

lead-free ■ adj. (of petrol) without added tetraethyl lead.

lead glass ■ n. glass containing a substantial proportion of lead oxide, making it more refractive.

lead-in ■ n. **1** an introduction or preamble. **2** a wire leading in from outside, especially from an aerial to a receiver or transmitter.

leading¹ /ˈliːdɪŋ/ ■ adj. most important or in first place.

leading² /ˈledɪŋ/ ■ n. the amount of blank space between lines of print.

leading article ■ n. a newspaper article giving the editorial opinion.

leading counsel ■ n. the senior advocate of the team which represents either party in a legal case.

leading edge ■ n. **1** Aeronautics the foremost edge of an aerofoil, especially a wing or propeller blade. **2** the forefront or vanguard, especially of technological development. **3** Electronics the part of a pulse in which the amplitude increases.

leading light ■ n. a person who is prominent or influential in a particular field or organization.

leading man (or **leading lady**) ■ n. the actor playing the principal part in a play, film, or television show.

leading note ■ n. Music the note below the tonic, the seventh note of the diatonic scale of any key.

leading question ■ n. a question that prompts or encourages the answer wanted.

leading seaman ■ n. a rank in the navy, above able seaman and below petty officer.

lead tetraethyl ■ n. Chemistry another term for **TETRAETHYL LEAD**.

lead time ■ n. the time between the initiation and completion of a production process.

lead-up ■ n. an event or sequence that leads up to something else.

leadwood ■ n. a southern African tree with very hard wood. [*Combretum imberbe*.]

leaf ■ n. (pl. **leaves**) **1** a flattened structure of a plant, typically green and blade-like, in which photosynthesis and transpiration mainly take place. ▸ (often in phr. **in/into leaf**) the state of having leaves. **2** a single thickness of paper, especially in a book. **3** gold, silver, or other metal in the form of very thin foil. **4** the part of a door, shutter, or table that is hinged or may be inserted. ■ v. **1** (of a plant) put out new leaves. **2** (**leaf through**) turn over (pages or papers), reading them quickly or casually.
– PHRASES **turn over a new leaf** start to act or behave in a better way.
– DERIVATIVES **leafage** n. **-leafed** adj. **leafless** adj. **leaf-like** adj.
– ORIGIN Old English, of Germanic origin.

leaf beetle ■ n. a small beetle of a large group that are typically metallic in appearance and include some serious crop pests. [Family Chrysomelidae.]

leafcutter ant ■ n. a tropical ant which cuts pieces from leaves and uses them to cultivate fungi for food. [Genus *Atta*.]

leaf green ■ n. a bright, deep green colour.

leafhopper ■ n. a small plant bug which leaps when disturbed. [Family Cicadellidae.]

leaf insect ■ n. a large slow-moving tropical insect with a flattened leaf-like body. [Family Phylliidae.]

leaflet ■ n. **1** a printed sheet of paper containing information or advertising and usually distributed free. **2** a small leaf, especially a component of a compound leaf. ■ v. (**leafleted**, **leafleting**) distribute leaflets to.

leaf miner ■ n. a small fly, moth, or sawfly whose larvae burrow between the two surfaces of a leaf.

leaf mould ■ n. **1** soil consisting chiefly of decayed leaves. **2** a fungal disease of tomatoes in which mould develops on the leaves.

leaf spot ■ n. a fungal, bacterial, or viral plant disease which causes leaves to develop discoloured spots.

leaf spring ■ n. a spring made of a number of strips of metal curved slightly upwards and clamped together one above the other.

leafy ■ adj. (**-ier**, **-iest**) having many leaves or much foliage.
– DERIVATIVES **leafiness** n.

league¹ ■ n. **1** a collection of people, countries, or groups that combine for mutual protection or cooperation.

VOWELS a cat ɑː arm ɛ bed ɛː hair ə ago əː her ɪ sit i cosy iː see ɒ hot ɔː saw ʌ run

2 a group of sports clubs which play each other over a period for a championship. **3** a class or category of quality or excellence: *the two men were not in the same league*. ■ v. (**leagues, leagued, leaguing**) join in a league or alliance.
– PHRASES **in league** conspiring with another or others.
– ORIGIN Middle English: from Italian *lega*, from *legare* 'to bind', from Latin *ligare*.

league² ■ n. a former measure of distance by land, usually about three miles.
– ORIGIN Middle English: from late Latin *leuga, leuca*, late Greek *leugē*, or Provençal *lega*.

leaguer¹ ■ n. a member of a particular league, especially a sports player.

leaguer² ■ n. historical (in South Africa) a large wine cask. ▶ a former measure of wine equal to 127 gallons (about 577 litres).
– ORIGIN from Dutch *legger*.

league table ■ n. a list of the competitors in a league ranked according to performance. ▶ a comparison of achievement or merit in a competitive area.

leak ■ v. **1** (of a container or covering) accidentally lose or admit contents through a hole or crack. ▶ (of liquid, gas, etc.) pass in or out through a hole or crack in such a way. **2** (of secret information) become known. ▶ intentionally disclose (secret information). ■ n. **1** a hole in a container or covering through which contents leak. ▶ an instance of leaking in such a way. **2** an intentional disclosure of secret information.
– PHRASES **have** (or **take**) **a leak** informal urinate.
– DERIVATIVES **leakage** n. **leakiness** n. **leaky** adj.
– ORIGIN Middle English: prob. of Low German or Dutch origin and rel. to **LACK**.

lean¹ ■ v. (past and past part. **leaned** or **leant**) **1** be in or move into a sloping position. ▶ (**lean against/on**) incline from the perpendicular and rest against. **2** (**lean on**) rely on or derive support from. **3** (**lean on**) informal put pressure on (someone) to act in a certain way. **4** (**lean to/towards**) incline or be partial to (a view or position). ▶ [as noun **leaning**] a tendency or partiality. ■ n. a deviation from the perpendicular; an inclination.
– ORIGIN Old English *hleonian, hlinian*, of Germanic origin.

lean² ■ adj. **1** (of a person) thin, especially healthily so. ▶ (of meat) containing little fat. ▶ informal (of an industry or company) efficient and with no wastage. **2** offering little reward, substance, or nourishment: *the lean years*. **3** (of a vaporized fuel mixture) having a high proportion of air.
– DERIVATIVES **leanly** adv. **leanness** n.
– ORIGIN Old English *hlǣne*, of Germanic origin.

lean-burn ■ adj. (of an internal-combustion engine) designed to run on a lean mixture to reduce pollution.

lean-to ■ n. (pl. -os) a building sharing a wall with a larger building and having a roof that leans against that wall.

leap ■ v. (past or past part. **leaped** or **leapt**) **1** jump or spring a long way. ▶ jump across. **2** move quickly and suddenly. ▶ (**leap at**) accept (an opportunity) eagerly. ▶ (**leap out**) (especially of writing) be conspicuous; stand out. **3** (of a price or figure) increase dramatically. ■ n. **1** an instance of leaping; a forceful jump or quick movement. **2** a sudden abrupt change or transition.
– PHRASES **a leap in the dark** a daring step or enterprise with unpredictable consequences. **by** (or **in**) **leaps and bounds** with startlingly rapid progress. **leap to the eye** (especially of writing) be immediately apparent.
– DERIVATIVES **leaper** n.
– ORIGIN Old English, of Germanic origin.

leapfrog ■ n. a game in which players in turn vault with parted legs over others who are bending down. ■ v. (**-frogged, -frogging**) **1** perform such a vault. **2** surpass or overtake a competitor or obstacle to move into a leading position.

leap second ■ n. a second which is occasionally inserted into the atomic scale of reckoning time in order to bring it into line with solar time.

leap year ■ n. a year, occurring once every four years, which has 366 days including 29 February as an intercalary day.
– ORIGIN Middle English: prob. from the fact that feast days after February in such a year fell two days later than in the previous year, rather than one day later as in other years, and could be said to have 'leaped' a day.

learn ■ v. (past and past part. **learned** or **learnt**) **1** acquire knowledge of or skill in (something) through study or experience or by being taught. ▶ commit to memory. ▶ S. African study or revise for an examination or test. ▶ become aware of by information or from observation. **2** archaic or dialect teach.
– DERIVATIVES **learnability** n. **learnable** adj.
– ORIGIN Old English, of West Germanic origin; rel. to **LORE¹**.

learned /ˈlɜːnɪd/ ■ adj. having or characterized by much knowledge acquired by study.
– DERIVATIVES **learnedly** adv. **learnedness** n.

learned helplessness ■ n. Psychiatry a condition characterized by a sense of powerlessness, arising from a traumatic event or persistent failure to succeed.

learner ■ n. **1** a person who is taught by another, especially a school pupil. **2** a person who learns to do something: *learner driver*.

learnership ■ n. S. African a vocational training programme that combines theory and work experience, and leads to an officially recognised qualification.

learning ■ n. knowledge or skills acquired through experience or study or by being taught.

learning area ■ n. a field of study within an outcomes-based education curriculum, e.g. mathematics, technology, or arts and culture.

learning curve ■ n. the rate of a person's progress in gaining experience or new skills.

learning difficulties ■ pl. n. difficulties in acquiring knowledge and skills to the normal level expected of those of the same age, especially because of mental disability or cognitive disorder.

learning disability ■ n. a condition giving rise to learning difficulties, especially when not associated with physical handicap.

lease ■ n. a contract by which one party conveys land, property, services, etc. to another for a specified time. ■ v. **1** grant (property) on lease; let. **2** take (property) on lease; rent.
– PHRASES **a new lease of** (or **on**) **life** a substantially improved prospect of life or use after rejuvenation or repair.
– ORIGIN Middle English: from Old French, from *lesser, laissier* 'let, leave', from Latin *laxare* 'make loose', from *laxus* 'loose'.

leaseback ■ n. the leasing of a property back to the vendor.

leasehold ■ n. the holding of property by lease. ▶ a piece of land or property held by lease.
– DERIVATIVES **leaseholder** n.

leash ■ n. **1** a dog's lead. **2** Falconry a thong or string attached to the jesses of a hawk, used for tying it to a perch or creance. ■ v. put a leash on (a dog).
– ORIGIN Middle English: from Old French *lesse, laisse*, from *laissier* in the specific sense 'let run on a slack lead' (see **LEASE**).

least ■ det. & pron. (usu. **the least**) smallest in amount, extent, or significance. ■ adj. used in names of very small animals and plants: *least shrew*. ■ adv. to the smallest extent or degree.
– PHRASES **at least 1** not less than; at the minimum. **2** if nothing else. **3** anyway. **at the least** (or **very least**) **1** not less than; at the minimum. **2** taking the most pessimistic or unfavourable view. **not in the least** not in the smallest degree; not at all. **not least** in particular; notably. **to say the least** using moderate terms; to put it mildly.
– ORIGIN Old English, of Germanic origin; rel. to **LESS**.

least common denominator ■ n. another term for **LOWEST COMMON DENOMINATOR**.

least common multiple ■ n. another term for **LOWEST COMMON MULTIPLE**.

least significant bit ■ n. Computing the bit in a binary number which is of the lowest numerical value.

least squares ■ n. a method of estimating a quantity or

leastways

fitting a graph to data so as to minimize the sum of the squares of the differences between the observed values and the estimated values.

leastways (also **leastwise**) ■ adv. dialect or informal at least.

leat /liːt/ ■ n. Brit. an open watercourse conducting water to a mill.
– ORIGIN C16: from Old English -gelǣt in wætergelǣt 'water channel', rel. to lǣtan 'to let'.

leather ■ n. 1 a material made from the skin of an animal by tanning or a similar process. 2 a piece of leather as a polishing cloth. 3 (**leathers**) leather clothes worn by a motorcyclist. ■ v. [usu. as adj. **leathered**] cover with leather.
– ORIGIN Old English, of Germanic origin.

leatherback turtle ■ n. a very large black turtle with a thick leathery shell, living chiefly in tropical seas. [Dermochelys coriacea.]

leatherette ■ n. imitation leather.

leathern ■ adj. archaic made of leather.

leathery ■ adj. having a tough, hard texture like leather.

leave[1] ■ v. (past and past part. **left**) 1 go away from. ▶ depart from permanently: *he left home at 16*. ▶ cease attending or working for (an organization, school, etc.). ▶ abandon (a spouse or partner). 2 allow or cause to remain. ▶ deposit (something) to be collected or attended to. ▶ have as (a surviving relative) after one's death. ▶ (**leave off**) discontinue (an activity). ▶ (**leave something off**) omit to add or put on something. ▶ (**leave someone/thing out**) fail to include someone or something. 3 (**be left**) remain to be used or dealt with. 4 cause to be in a particular state or position. ▶ let (someone) do or deal with something without offering help or assistance. ▶ (**leave something to**) entrust a decision, choice, or action to. 5 bequeath. ■ n. (in snooker, croquet, and other games) the position in which a player leaves the balls for the next player.
– PHRASES **be left for dead** be abandoned as being almost dead or certain to die. **be left to oneself** be left alone or allowed to do what one wants. **leave someone be** informal refrain from disturbing or interfering with someone. **leave go** informal remove one's hold or grip. **leave hold of** cease holding. **leave much** (or **a lot**) **to be desired** be highly unsatisfactory.
– DERIVATIVES **leaver** n.
– ORIGIN Old English lǣfan, of Germanic origin.

leave[2] ■ n. 1 (also **leave of absence**) time when one has permission to be absent from work or duty. 2 (often in phr. **by your leave**) formal permission.
– PHRASES **take one's leave** formal say goodbye. **take leave to do something** formal venture or presume to do something.
– ORIGIN Old English lēaf 'permission', of West Germanic origin.

leaved ■ adj. having a leaf or leaves of a particular kind or number.

leaven /ˈlɛv(ə)n/ ■ n. 1 a substance, typically yeast, added to dough to make it ferment and rise. 2 a pervasive influence that modifies something or transforms it for the better. ■ v. 1 [usu. as adj. **leavened**] cause (dough or bread) to ferment and rise by adding leaven. 2 permeate and modify or transform for the better.
– ORIGIN Middle English: from Old French levain, from Latin levamen 'relief' (literally 'means of raising'), from levare 'to lift'.

leaves plural form of LEAF.

leave-taking ■ n. an act of saying goodbye.

leavings ■ pl. n. things that have been left as worthless.

Lebanese /lɛbəˈniːz/ ■ n. (pl. same) a native or inhabitant of Lebanon. ■ adj. of or relating to Lebanon.

Lebensraum /ˈleɪb(ə)nzˌraʊm/ ■ n. territory which a state or nation believes is needed for its natural development.
– ORIGIN German, 'living space'.

lech /lɛtʃ/ informal, derogatory ■ n. 1 a lecher. 2 a lecherous urge or desire. ■ v. act in a lecherous or lustful manner.

Le Chatelier's principle /lə ʃaˈtɛljeɪ/ ■ n. Chemistry a principle stating that if a constraint is applied to a system in equilibrium, the equilibrium will shift so as to tend to counteract the effect of the constraint.
– ORIGIN C20: named after the French chemist Henry le Chatelier.

lecher /ˈlɛtʃə/ ■ n. a lecherous man.
– DERIVATIVES **lechery** n.

lecherous ■ adj. having or showing excessive or offensive sexual desire.
– DERIVATIVES **lecherously** adv. **lecherousness** n.
– ORIGIN Middle English: from Old French lecheros, from lecheor, from lechier 'live in debauchery or gluttony', of West Germanic origin.

lechwe /ˈlɛːtʃwi/ ■ n. (pl. same) an African antelope with a reddish-brown coat and white underparts, inhabiting swampy areas. [Genus Kobus: two species.]
– ORIGIN C19: from Setswana.

lecithin /ˈlɛsɪθɪn/ ■ n. Biochemistry a substance found in egg yolk and other animal and plant tissues, consisting of phospholipids linked to choline.
– ORIGIN C19: from Greek lekithos 'egg yolk'.

lectern /ˈlɛkt(ə)n, -təːn/ ■ n. a tall stand with a sloping top from which a speaker can read while standing up.
– ORIGIN Middle English: from medieval Latin lectrum, from legere 'to read'.

lectin ■ n. Biochemistry a protein which binds specifically to a sugar and causes agglutination of particular cell types.
– ORIGIN 1950s: from Latin lect-, legere 'choose'.

lectionary /ˈlɛkʃ(ə)n(ə)ri/ ■ n. (pl. **-ies**) a list or book of portions of the Bible appointed to be read at divine service.

lector /ˈlɛktɔː/ ■ n. 1 a reader, especially someone who reads lessons in a church service. 2 (fem. **lectrice** /lɛkˈtriːs/) a person employed in a foreign university to teach in their native language.
– ORIGIN Middle English: from Latin, from lect-, legere 'read, choose'.

lecture ■ n. 1 an educational talk to an audience, especially one of students in a university. 2 a long serious speech, especially one given as a scolding or reprimand. ■ v. 1 deliver an educational lecture or lectures. 2 talk seriously or reprovingly to.
– ORIGIN Middle English ('reading, a text to read'): from medieval Latin lectura, from Latin lect-, legere 'read, choose'.

lecturer ■ n. a person who gives lectures, especially as a teacher in higher education.

lectureship ■ n. a post as a lecturer.

LED ■ abbrev. light-emitting diode, a semiconductor diode which glows when a voltage is applied.

led past and past participle of LEAD[1].

lederhosen /ˈleɪdəˌhəʊz(ə)n/ ■ pl. n. leather shorts with H-shaped braces, traditionally worn by men in Alpine regions such as Bavaria.
– ORIGIN from German, from Leder 'leather' + Hosen 'trousers'.

ledge ■ n. 1 a narrow horizontal surface projecting from a wall, cliff, etc. 2 an underwater ridge, especially one of rocks near the seashore. 3 Mining a stratum of metal-bearing rock.
– DERIVATIVES **ledged** adj.
– ORIGIN Middle English (denoting a strip of wood or other material fixed across a door or gate): perhaps from an early form of LAY[1].

ledger ■ n. 1 a book or other collection of financial accounts. 2 a flat stone slab covering a grave. 3 a horizontal scaffolding pole, parallel to the face of the building. 4 a weight used on a fishing line to anchor the bait in a particular place.
– ORIGIN Middle English legger, ligger (denoting a large bible or breviary), prob. from vars of LAY[1] and LIE[1], influenced by Dutch legger and ligger.

ledger line ■ n. Music variant spelling of LEGER LINE.

lee ■ n. 1 shelter from wind or weather given by an object. 2 (also **lee side**) the sheltered side; the side away from the wind. Contrasted with WEATHER.
– PHRASES **lee ho** Nautical a helmsman's command or warning indicating the moment of going about.
– ORIGIN Old English hlēo, hlēow 'shelter', of Germanic origin.

CONSONANTS **b** but   **d** dog   **f** few   **g** get   **h** he   **j** yes   **k** cat   **l** leg   **m** man   **n** no   **p** pen   **r** red

leech¹ ■ n. **1** a parasitic or predatory annelid worm with suckers at both ends, examples of which were formerly used in medicine for bloodletting. [*Hirudo medicinalis* and other species, class Hirudinea.] **2** a person who extorts profit from or lives off others. ■ v. (**leech on/off**) habitually exploit or rely on.
– PHRASES **like a leech** persistently or clingingly.
– ORIGIN Old English *lǣce*, *lȳce*.

leech² ■ n. archaic a doctor or healer.
– ORIGIN Old English *lǣce*, of Germanic origin.

leech³ ■ n. Nautical the after or leeward edge of a fore-and-aft sail, the leeward edge of a spinnaker, or a vertical edge of a square sail.
– ORIGIN C15: prob. of Scandinavian origin and rel. to Swedish *lik* and Danish *lig*.

lee helm ■ n. Nautical the tendency of a ship to turn its bow to the leeward side.

leek ■ n. a plant related to the onion, with flat overlapping leaves forming an elongated cylindrical bulb which together with the leaf bases is eaten as a vegetable. [*Allium porrum*.]
– ORIGIN Old English, of Germanic origin.

leer ■ v. look or gaze in a lascivious or unpleasant way. ■ n. a lascivious or unpleasant look.
– DERIVATIVES **leering** adj.
– ORIGIN C16 ('look sideways'): perhaps from obsolete *leer* 'cheek', from Old English.

leervis /'lɪəfɪs/ ■ n. S. African another term for GARRICK.
– ORIGIN from S. African Dutch *leervisch*, from *leer* 'leather' + *visch*, *vis* 'fish'.

leery ■ adj. (-ier, -iest) cautious or wary due to realistic suspicions.
– ORIGIN C17: from obsolete *leer* 'looking askance', from LEER.

lees ■ pl. n. the sediment of wine in the barrel; dregs.
– ORIGIN Middle English: pl. of obsolete *lee* in the same sense, from medieval Latin *liae* (pl.), of Gaulish origin.

lee shore ■ n. a shore lying on the leeward side of a ship (and on to which the ship could be blown).

leeward /'liːwəd, 'luːəd/ ■ adj. & adv. on or towards the side sheltered from the wind or towards which the wind is blowing; downwind. Contrasted with WINDWARD. ■ n. the leeward side.

leeway ■ n. **1** the amount of freedom to move or act that is available. ▸ margin of safety. **2** the sideways drift of a ship to leeward of the desired course.

left¹ ■ adj. **1** on, towards, or relating to the side of a human body or of a thing which is to the west when the person or thing is facing north. **2** of or relating to a left-wing person or group. ■ adv. on or to the left side. ■ n. **1** (**the left**) the left-hand part, side, or direction. ▸ a left turn. ▸ a person's left fist, or a blow given with it. **2** (often **the Left**) [treated as sing. or pl.] a group or party favouring radical, reforming, or socialist views.
– PHRASES **have two left feet** be clumsy or awkward. **left, right, and centre** (also **left and right** or **right and left**) on all sides.
– DERIVATIVES **leftish** adj. **leftmost** adj. **leftward** adj. & adv. **leftwards** adv.
– ORIGIN Old English *lyft*, *left* 'weak', of West Germanic origin.

left² past and past participle of LEAVE¹.

left back ■ n. a defender in soccer or field hockey who plays primarily on the left of the field.

left bank ■ n. the bank of a river on the left as one faces downstream.

left brain ■ n. the left-hand side of the human brain, which is believed to be associated with linear and analytical thought.

left field ■ n. Baseball the part of the outfield to the left of the batter when facing the pitcher. ■ adj. (**left-field**) unconventional or unusual.
– DERIVATIVES **left fielder** n.

left hand ■ n. **1** the hand of a person's left side. **2** the region or direction on the left side. ■ adj. **1** on or towards the left side. **2** done with or using the left hand.

left-hand drive ■ n. a motor-vehicle steering system with the steering wheel and other controls fitted on the left side, for use in countries where vehicles drive on the right-hand side of the road.

left-handed ■ adj. **1** using or done with the left hand. **2** turning to the left; towards the left. ▸ (of a screw) advanced by turning anticlockwise. **3** perverse or ambiguous.
– DERIVATIVES **left-handedly** adv. **left-handedness** n.

left-hander ■ n. **1** a left-handed person. **2** a blow struck with a person's left hand.

leftie ■ n. variant spelling of LEFTY.

leftism ■ n. the political views or policies of the left.
– DERIVATIVES **leftist** n. & adj.

left luggage ■ n. S. African & Brit. travellers' luggage left in temporary storage at a railway station, bus station, or airport.

leftover ■ n. something, especially food, remaining after the rest has been used. ■ adj. remaining; surplus.

left wing ■ n. **1** the radical, reforming, or socialist section of a political party or system. [with ref. to the National Assembly in France (1789–91), where the nobles sat to the president's right and the commons to the left.] **2** the left side of a sports team on the field or of an army.
– DERIVATIVES **left-winger** n.

lefty (also **leftie**) ■ n. (pl. **-ies**) informal **1** a left-wing person. **2** a left-handed person.

leg ■ n. **1** each of the limbs on which a person or animal walks and stands. ▸ a leg of an animal or bird as food. ▸ a part of a garment covering a leg or part of a leg. ▸ (**legs**) informal sustained momentum or success. **2** a long, thin support or prop, especially of a chair or table. **3** a section or stage of a journey or process. ▸ (in sport) each of two or more games or stages constituting a round or match. ▸ Nautical a run made on a single tack. **4** a branch of a forked object. **5** (also **leg side**) Cricket the half of the field away from which the batsman's feet are pointed when standing to receive the ball. The opposite of OFF. **6** archaic an obeisance made by drawing back one leg and bending it while keeping the front leg straight. ■ v. (**legged**, **legging**) **1** (**leg it**) informal travel by foot; walk. ▸ run away. **2** chiefly historical propel (a boat) through a canal tunnel by pushing with one's legs against the tunnel roof or sides.
– PHRASES **feel** (or **find**) **one's legs** become able to stand or walk. **get one's leg over** vulgar slang (of a man) have sexual intercourse. **not have a leg to stand on** have no sound justification for one's arguments or actions. **on one's last legs** near the end of life, usefulness, or existence.
– DERIVATIVES **-legged** adj. **-legger** n.
– ORIGIN Middle English: from Old Norse *leggr*, of Germanic origin.

legacy ■ n. (pl. **-ies**) **1** an amount of money or property left to someone in a will. **2** something handed down by a predecessor. ■ adj. Computing denoting hardware or software that has been superseded but is difficult to replace because of its wide use.
– ORIGIN Middle English: from Old French *legacie*, from medieval Latin, from *legare* (see LEGATE).

legal ■ adj. **1** of, based on, or required by the law. **2** permitted by law.
– DERIVATIVES **legally** adv.
– ORIGIN Middle English: from Latin *legalis*, from *lex* 'law'.

legal aid ■ n. payment from public funds allowed, in cases of need, to help pay for legal advice or proceedings.

legal clinic (also **legal aid clinic**) ■ n. S. African & N. Amer. a place where one can obtain legal advice and assistance, paid for by legal aid.

legal eagle (also **legal beagle**) ■ n. informal a lawyer.

legalese /ˌliːgə'liːz/ ■ n. informal the formal and technical language of legal documents.

legal fiction ■ n. an assumption of the truth of something, though unproven or unfounded, for legal purposes.

legalism ■ n. excessive adherence to the details of law.
– DERIVATIVES **legalist** n. & adj. **legalistic** adj. **legalistically** adv.

legality ■ n. (pl. **-ies**) **1** the quality or state of being legal. **2** (**legalities**) obligations imposed by law.

legalize (also **-ise**) ■ v. make legal.
– DERIVATIVES **legalization** (also **-isation**) n.

legal person ■ n. Law an individual, company, or other entity which has legal rights and is subject to obligations.

legal separation ■ n. **1** an arrangement by which a husband and wife remain married but live apart, following a court order. **2** an arrangement by which a child lives apart from a natural parent and with another natural or foster-parent of their choice, following a court decree.

legal tender ■ n. coins or banknotes that must be accepted if offered in payment of a debt.

legate /ˈlɛgət/ ■ n. **1** a member of the clergy who represents the Pope. **2** archaic an ambassador or messenger.
– DERIVATIVES **legateship** n. **legatine** /-tɪn/ adj.
– ORIGIN Old English, from Old French *legat*, from Latin *legare* 'depute, bequeath'.

legatee /ˌlɛgəˈtiː/ ■ n. a person who receives a legacy.
– ORIGIN C17: from *legate* 'bequeath', from Latin *legare* 'delegate, bequeath'.

legation ■ n. **1** a diplomatic mission. **2** the official residence of a diplomat. **3** archaic the sending of a papal legate on a mission. ▶ a legateship.
– ORIGIN Middle English: from Latin *legatio(n-)*, from *legare* 'depute, bequeath'.

legator /lɪˈgeɪtə/ ■ n. a person leaving a legacy.

leg before wicket (also **leg before**) ■ adv. & adj. Cricket (of a batsman) adjudged to be out through obstructing the ball with the leg (or other part of the body) when the ball would otherwise have hit the wicket.

leg break ■ n. Cricket a ball which spins from the leg side towards the off side after pitching.

leg bye ■ n. Cricket a run scored from a ball that has touched the batsman's body without touching the bat, the batsman having made an attempt to hit it.

leg-cutter ■ n. Cricket a fast leg break.

legend ■ n. **1** a traditional story popularly regarded as historical but which is not authenticated. **2** an extremely famous or notorious person: *a screen legend*. **3** an inscription, caption, or key. **4** historical the written account of a saint's life. ■ adj. very well known.
– ORIGIN Middle English: from Old French *legende*, from medieval Latin *legenda* 'things to be read', from Latin *legere* 'read'.

legendary ■ adj. **1** of, described in, or based on legends. **2** remarkable enough to be famous; very well known.
– DERIVATIVES **legendarily** adv.
– ORIGIN C16: from medieval Latin *legendarius*, from *legenda* (see LEGEND).

legerdemain /ˌlɛdʒədɪˈmeɪn/ ■ n. **1** skilful use of one's hands when performing conjuring tricks. **2** deception; trickery.
– ORIGIN Middle English: from French *léger de main* 'dexterous, light of hand'.

leger line /ˈlɛdʒə/ (also **ledger line**) ■ n. Music a short line added for notes above or below the range of a stave.
– ORIGIN C19: *leger*, var. of LEDGER.

leggings ■ pl. n. **1** a woman's tight-fitting stretchy garment covering the legs, hips, and bottom. **2** stout protective overgarments for the legs.

leggy ■ adj. (**-ier**, **-iest**) **1** long-legged. ▶ (of a woman) having attractively long legs. **2** (of a plant) having a long and straggly stem or stems.
– DERIVATIVES **legginess** n.

leghorn /ˈlɛgɔːn, ˈlɛghɔːn/ ■ n. **1** fine plaited straw. ▶ a hat made of this. **2** (**Leghorn**) a chicken of a small hardy breed.
– ORIGIN C18: anglicized from the Italian name *Leghorno* (now *Livorno*), from where the straw and fowls were imported.

legible ■ adj. (of handwriting or print) clear enough to read.
– DERIVATIVES **legibility** n. **legibly** adv.

– ORIGIN Middle English: from late Latin *legibilis*, from *legere* 'to read'.

legion ■ n. **1** a division of 3000–6000 men in the ancient Roman army. **2** a national association of former servicemen and servicewomen, such as the South African Legion. **3** (**a legion/legions of**) a vast number of people or things. ■ adj. great in number: *her fans are legion*.
– DERIVATIVES **legioned** adj.
– ORIGIN Middle English: from Latin *legio(n-)*, from *legere* 'choose, levy'.

legionary ■ n. (pl. **-ies**) a soldier in a Roman legion. ■ adj. of or relating to a Roman legion.

legionnaire /ˌliːdʒəˈnɛː/ ■ n. a member of a legion.

legionnaires' disease ■ n. a form of bacterial pneumonia caused by the bacterium *Legionella pneumophila*, spread chiefly in water droplets through air conditioning and similar systems.
– ORIGIN 1976 (identified after an outbreak at an American Legion meeting).

leg iron ■ n. a metal band or chain placed around a prisoner's ankle as a restraint.

legislate /ˈlɛdʒɪsleɪt/ ■ v. **1** make or enact laws. **2** effect by making or enacting laws.
– ORIGIN C18: back-formation from LEGISLATION.

legislation ■ n. laws, considered collectively.
– ORIGIN C17: from late Latin *legis latio(n-)* 'proposing of a law'.

legislative /ˈlɛdʒɪslətɪv/ ■ adj. **1** of or having the power to make laws. **2** of or relating to laws or a legislature.
– DERIVATIVES **legislatively** adv.

legislator ■ n. a person who makes laws; a member of a legislative body.
– ORIGIN C15: from Latin *legis lator* 'proposer of a law', from *lex* 'law' + *lator* 'proposer, mover'.

legislature /ˈlɛdʒɪslətʃə/ ■ n. the legislative body of a state.

legit /lɪˈdʒɪt/ ■ adj. informal legitimate.

legitimate ■ adj. /lɪˈdʒɪtɪmət/ **1** conforming to the law or to rules. **2** able to be defended with logic or justification. **3** (of a child) born of parents lawfully married to each other. **4** (of a sovereign) having a title based on strict hereditary right. ■ v. /lɪˈdʒɪtɪmeɪt/ make legitimate.
– DERIVATIVES **legitimacy** n. **legitimately** adv. **legitimation** n. **legitimatization** (also **-isation**) n. **legitimatize** (also **-ise**) v.
– ORIGIN Middle English: from medieval Latin *legitimare* 'make legal'.

legitimize (also **-ise**) ■ v. make legitimate.
– DERIVATIVES **legitimization** (also **-isation**) n.

legless ■ adj. **1** having no legs. **2** informal extremely drunk.

Lego ■ n. trademark a toy consisting of interlocking plastic building blocks.
– ORIGIN 1950s: from Danish *leg godt* 'play well'.

leg-of-mutton sleeve ■ n. a sleeve which is full on the upper arm but close-fitting on the forearm and wrist.

legroom ■ n. space in which a seated person can put their legs.

leg slip ■ n. Cricket a fielding position just behind the batsman on the leg side.

leg spin ■ n. Cricket bowling of leg breaks.
– DERIVATIVES **leg-spinner** n.

leguan /ˈlɛgjʊən, ˈlɛgwɑːn/ (also **leguaan**) ■ n. S. African an African monitor lizard. [*Varanus niloticus* (**water leguan**) and *V. exanthematicus* (**rock leguan**).]
– ORIGIN C18: from Dutch, prob. from French *l'iguane* 'the iguana'.

legume /ˈlɛgjuːm/ ■ n. **1** a leguminous plant grown as a crop. **2** a seed, pod, or other edible part of a leguminous plant, used as food. **3** Botany the long seed pod of a leguminous plant.
– ORIGIN C17: from French *légume*, from Latin *legumen*, *legere* 'to pick'.

leguminous /lɪˈgjuːmɪnəs/ ■ adj. Botany relating to or denoting plants of the pea family (Leguminosae), typically having seeds in pods, distinctive flowers, and root nodules containing nitrogen-fixing bacteria.
– ORIGIN Middle English: from medieval Latin *leguminosus*, from *legumen* (see LEGUME).

leg-up ■ n. **1** an act of helping someone to mount a horse or high object. **2** a boost to improve one's position.

leg warmers ■ pl. n. a pair of tubular knitted garments covering the legs from ankle to knee or thigh.

legwork ■ n. work that involves tiring or tedious movement from place to place.

Leicester /ˈlɛstə/ ■ n. **1** (also **Red Leicester**) a kind of mild, firm orange-coloured cheese originally made in Leicestershire. **2** (also **Border Leicester**) a sheep of a breed often crossed with other breeds to produce lambs for the meat industry.

leishmania /liːʃˈmeɪnɪə/ ■ n. (pl. same or **leishmanias** or **leishmaniae** /-ˈmeɪnɪʌɪ/) a single-celled parasitic protozoan which is transmitted to vertebrates by the bite of sandflies. [Genus *Leishmania*.]
– ORIGIN from the name of William B. *Leishman*, a British pathologist.

leishmaniasis /ˌliːʃməˈnʌɪəsɪs/ ■ n. a tropical and subtropical disease caused by leishmania and transmitted by the bite of sandflies.

leisure /ˈlɛʒə/ ■ n. time spent in or free for relaxation or enjoyment.
– PHRASES **at leisure 1** not occupied; free. **2** in an unhurried manner. **at one's leisure** at one's convenience. **lady** (or **man** or **gentleman**) **of leisure** a person who does not need to earn money.
– DERIVATIVES **leisured** adj.
– ORIGIN Middle English: from Old French *leisir*, from Latin *licere* 'be allowed'.

leisure centre (also **leisure complex**) ■ n. a public building or complex offering facilities for sport and recreation.

leisurely ■ adj. relaxed and unhurried. ■ adv. without hurry.
– DERIVATIVES **leisureliness** n.

leisurewear ■ n. casual clothes worn for leisure activities.

leitmotif /ˈlʌɪtməʊˌtiːf/ (also **leitmotiv**) ■ n. a recurring theme in a musical or literary composition.
– ORIGIN C19: from German *Leitmotiv*, from *leit-* 'leading' + *Motiv* 'motive'.

leiwater /ˈleɪvɑːtə/ ■ n. S. African [often as modifier] water that is conveyed sequentially to a number of properties through an irrigation system consisting of channels and sluices, with each property being entitled to a regular allocation.
– ORIGIN Afrikaans, 'irrigation water'.

lekgotla /lɛˈxɔtlə/ ■ n. S. African a strategy planning meeting, especially one convened by government or the executive committee of an organization.
– ORIGIN Sesotho, 'assembly, council'.

lekker /ˈlɛkə, ˈlakə/ S. African informal ■ adj. good; pleasant. ▸ delicious. ▸ tipsy. ■ adv. **1** well. **2** extremely.
– PHRASES **local is lekker** a slogan expressing pride in South African music, products, etc.
– ORIGIN Afrikaans, from Dutch, 'delicious'.

leman /ˈlɛmən, ˈliː-/ ■ n. (pl. **lemans**) archaic a lover or sweetheart.
– ORIGIN Middle English *lēofman*, from *lēof* (see **LIEF**) + **MAN**.

Lemba ■ n. (pl. same or **Balemba**) a member of a people, said to be of mixed Semitic and black African origin, living mainly among the Venda in the Limpopo province of South Africa and in southern Zimbabwe.

lemma /ˈlɛmə/ ■ n. (pl. **lemmas** or **lemmata** /-mətə/) **1** a subsidiary or intermediate theorem in an argument or proof. **2** a heading indicating the subject of a literary composition, annotation, or dictionary entry.
– ORIGIN C16: from Greek *lēmma* 'something assumed'.

lemme ■ contr. informal let me.

lemming ■ n. **1** a short-tailed, thickset Arctic rodent, noted for fluctuating populations and periodic mass migrations. [*Lemmus lemmus* and other species.] **2** a person who unthinkingly joins a mass movement, especially a headlong rush to destruction.
– ORIGIN C18: from Norwegian and Danish; rel. to Old Norse *lómundr*.

lemon ■ n. **1** a pale yellow oval citrus fruit with thick skin and fragrant, acidic juice. ▸ a drink made from or flavoured with lemon juice. **2** the evergreen citrus tree which produces this fruit. [*Citrus limon*.] **3** a pale yellow colour. **4** informal a feeble or unsatisfactory person or thing.
– DERIVATIVES **lemony** adj.
– ORIGIN Middle English: via Old French *limon* from Arabic *līmūn*.

lemonade ■ n. a sweetened drink made from lemon juice or lemon flavouring and still or carbonated water.
– ORIGIN C17: from French *limonade*, from *limon* 'lemon'.

lemon balm ■ n. a bushy lemon-scented herb of the mint family. [*Melissa officinalis*.]

lemon curd (Brit. also **lemon cheese**) ■ n. conserve made from lemons, butter, eggs, and sugar.

lemon grass ■ n. a fragrant tropical grass which yields an oil that smells of lemon, used in Asian cooking and in perfumery and medicine. [*Cymbopogon citratus*.]

lemon sole ■ n. a common European flatfish of the plaice family. [*Microstomus kitt*.]
– ORIGIN C19: *lemon* from French *limande*.

lemon thyme ■ n. thyme of a hybrid variety with lemon-scented leaves. [*Thymus × citriodorus*.]

lemon verbena ■ n. a South American shrub with lemon-scented leaves used as flavouring and to make a sedative tea. [*Aloysia triphylla*.]

lemur /ˈliːmə/ ■ n. an arboreal primate with a pointed snout and typically a long tail, found only in Madagascar. [Lemuridae and other families: several species.]
– ORIGIN C18: from Latin *lemures* 'spirits of the dead' (from their spectre-like faces).

lend ■ v. (past and past part. **lent**) **1** grant to (someone) the use of (something) on the understanding that it shall be returned. **2** allow (a person) the use of (a sum of money) under an agreement to pay it back later, typically with interest. **3** contribute or add (a quality) to. **4** (**lend oneself to**) accommodate or adapt oneself to. ▸ (**lend itself to**) (of a thing) be suitable for.
– DERIVATIVES **lendable** adj. **lender** n.
– ORIGIN Old English, of Germanic origin.

USAGE
On the confusion of **lend** and **borrow**, which have reciprocal meanings, see **BORROW**.

lending library ■ n. a public library from which books may be borrowed and taken away for a limited time.

length /lɛŋθ, lɛŋkθ/ ■ n. **1** the measurement or extent of something from end to end; the greater or greatest of two or more dimensions of a body. ▸ the length of a horse, boat, etc., as a measure of the lead in a race. **2** the amount of time occupied by something. **3** the quality of being long. **4** the full distance that a thing extends for: *the muscles running the length of my spine*. **5** the extent of a garment in a vertical direction when worn. **6** (in bridge or whist) the number of cards of a suit held in one's hand. **7** a stretch or piece of something. **8** a degree or extreme to which a course of action is taken.
– PHRASES **at length 1** in detail; fully. **2** after a long time. **the length and breadth of** the whole extent of.
– ORIGIN Old English, of Germanic origin.

-length ■ comb. form **1** reaching up or down to the place specified: *knee-length*. **2** of the size, duration, or extent specified: *full-length*.

lengthen ■ v. make or become longer.

lengthways ■ adv. in a direction parallel with a thing's length.

lengthwise ■ adv. lengthways. ■ adj. lying or moving lengthways.

lengthy ■ adj. (**-ier**, **-iest**) of considerable or unusual duration.
– DERIVATIVES **lengthily** adv. **lengthiness** n.

lenient /ˈliːnɪənt/ ■ adj. merciful or tolerant.
– DERIVATIVES **lenience** n. **leniency** n. **leniently** adv.
– ORIGIN C17: from Latin *lenire* 'soothe', from *lenis* 'mild, gentle'.

Leninism

Leninism ■ n. Marxism as interpreted and applied by the Soviet premier Lenin (1870–1924).
– DERIVATIVES **Leninist** n. & adj. **Leninite** n. & adj.

lenis /ˈlɛnɪs, ˈleɪnɪs, ˈliːnɪs/ ■ adj. Phonetics (of a consonant) weakly articulated, especially the less or least strongly articulated of two or more similar consonants. The opposite of FORTIS.
– ORIGIN C20: from Latin, 'mild, gentle'.

lenity /ˈlɛnɪti/ ■ n. poetic/literary kindness; gentleness.
– ORIGIN Middle English: from Latin *lenitas*, from *lenis* 'gentle'.

lens ■ n. **1** a piece of glass or other transparent material with one or both sides curved for concentrating or dispersing light rays. ▶ Anatomy the transparent elastic structure behind the iris by which light is focused on to the retina of the eye. ▶ short for CONTACT LENS. **2** the light-gathering device of a camera, containing a group of compound lenses. **3** Physics an object or device which focuses or otherwise modifies a beam of radiation, sound, electrons, etc.
– DERIVATIVES **lensed** adj. **lensless** adj.
– ORIGIN C17: from Latin, 'lentil' (because of the similarity in shape).

lensman ■ n. (pl. **-men**) a professional photographer or cameraman.

Lent ■ n. (in the Christian Church) the period preceding Easter (in the Western Church from Ash Wednesday to Holy Saturday), which is devoted to fasting, abstinence, and penitence in commemoration of Christ's fasting in the wilderness.
– ORIGIN Middle English: abbrev. of LENTEN.

lent past and past participle of LEND.

Lenten ■ adj. of, in, or appropriate to Lent.
– ORIGIN Old English *lencten* 'spring, Lent', of Germanic origin.

lentic /ˈlɛntɪk/ ■ adj. Ecology inhabiting or situated in still fresh water. Compare with LOTIC.
– ORIGIN C20: from Latin *lentus* 'calm, slow'.

lenticel /ˈlɛntɪsɛl/ ■ n. Botany one of many raised pores in the stem of a woody plant allowing gas exchange between the atmosphere and the internal tissues.
– ORIGIN C19: from *lenticella*, diminutive of Latin *lens* 'lentil'.

lenticular /lɛnˈtɪkjʊlə/ ■ adj. **1** shaped like a lentil; biconvex. **2** of or relating to the lens of the eye.
– ORIGIN Middle English: from Latin *lenticularis*, from *lenticula*, diminutive of *lens* 'lentil'.

lentiform nucleus ■ n. Anatomy the lower of the two grey nuclei of the corpus striatum.
– ORIGIN C18: *lentiform* from Latin *lens*.

lentil ■ n. **1** a high-protein pulse which is dried and then soaked and cooked prior to eating. **2** the plant which yields this pulse, native to the Mediterranean and Africa. [*Lens culinaris*.]
– ORIGIN Middle English: from Old French *lentille*, from Latin *lenticula*, diminutive of *lens* 'lentil'.

lentivirus /ˈlɛntɪˌvʌɪrəs/ ■ n. Medicine any of a group of retroviruses producing illnesses characterized by a delay in the onset of symptoms after infection.
– ORIGIN 1970S: from Latin *lentus* 'slow' + VIRUS.

lentoid /ˈlɛntɔɪd/ ■ adj. another term for LENTICULAR (in sense 1).
– ORIGIN C19: from Latin *lens* 'lentil'.

Leo ■ n. **1** Astronomy a large constellation (the Lion), said to represent the lion slain by Hercules. **2** Astrology the fifth sign of the zodiac, which the sun enters about 23 July.
– DERIVATIVES **Leonian** n. & adj.
– ORIGIN from Latin.

leonine /ˈliːənʌɪn/ ■ adj. of or resembling a lion or lions.
– ORIGIN Middle English: from Latin *leoninus*, from *leo* 'lion'.

leopard ■ n. (fem. **leopardess**) a large solitary cat that has a fawn or brown coat with black spots, found in the forests of Africa and southern Asia. [*Panthera pardus*.] ▶ Heraldry the spotted leopard as a heraldic device; also, a lion passant guardant as in the arms of England. ▶ [as modifier] spotted like a leopard.
– ORIGIN Middle English: from late Greek *leopardos*, from *leōn* 'lion' + *pardos* 'panther, leopard'.

leopard-crawl ■ v. move carefully along the ground, using the knees and elbows to drag the body along.

leopard seal ■ n. a large grey Antarctic seal which has leopard-like spots and preys on penguins and other seals. [*Hydrurga leptonyx*.]

leopard tortoise ■ n. a large African tortoise with a blotchy yellow and dark brown carapace. [*Geochelone pardalis*.]

leotard /ˈliːətɑːd/ ■ n. a close-fitting, stretchy one-piece garment covering the body to the top of the thighs, worn for dance, gymnastics, and exercise.
– ORIGIN C20: named after the French trapeze artist Jules Léotard.

leper ■ n. **1** a person suffering from leprosy. **2** a person who is shunned by others.
– ORIGIN Middle English: from Old French *lepre*, from Greek *lepros* 'scaly'.

Lepidoptera /ˌlɛpɪˈdɒpt(ə)rə/ ■ pl. n. Entomology an order of insects comprising the butterflies and moths.
– DERIVATIVES **lepidopteran** adj. & n. **lepidopterous** adj.
– ORIGIN from Greek *lepis* 'scale' + *pteron* 'wing'.

lepidopterist ■ n. a person who collects or studies butterflies and moths.
– DERIVATIVES **lepidoptery** n.

leprechaun /ˈlɛprəkɔːn/ ■ n. (in Irish folklore) a small, mischievous sprite.
– ORIGIN C17: from Irish *leipreachán*, from Old Irish *luchorpán*, from *lu* 'small' + *corp* 'body'.

lepromatous /lɛˈprəʊmətəs/ ■ adj. Medicine relating to or denoting the more severe of the two principal forms of leprosy. Compare with TUBERCULOID.

leprosarium /ˌlɛprəˈsɛːrɪəm/ ■ n. a hospital for people with leprosy.

leprosy ■ n. a contagious bacterial disease that affects the skin, mucous membranes, and nerves, causing discoloration and lumps on the skin and, in severe cases, disfigurement and deformities.
– ORIGIN C16 (in Middle English *lepry*): from LEPROUS.

leprous ■ adj. relating to, resembling, or suffering from leprosy.
– ORIGIN Middle English: from late Latin *leprosus*, from Greek *lepros* 'scaly'.

leptin ■ n. Biochemistry a protein produced by fatty tissue which is believed to regulate fat storage in the body.
– ORIGIN 1990S: from Greek *leptos* 'fine, thin'.

leptocephalic /ˌlɛptə(ʊ)sɪˈfalɪk, -kɛˈfalɪk-/ (also **leptocephalous** /-ˈsɛf(ə)ləs, -ˈkɛf-/) ■ adj. narrow-skulled.

leptomeninges /ˌlɛptəʊmɪˈnɪndʒiːz/ ■ pl. n. Anatomy the inner two meninges, the arachnoid and the pia mater, between which circulates the cerebrospinal fluid.
– DERIVATIVES **leptomeningeal** adj.

lepton /ˈlɛptɒn/ ■ n. Physics a subatomic particle that does not take part in the strong interaction, such as an electron, muon, or neutrino.
– DERIVATIVES **leptonic** adj.
– ORIGIN 1940S: from Greek *leptos* 'small'.

leptospirosis /ˌlɛptə(ʊ)spʌɪˈrəʊsɪs/ ■ n. an infectious bacterial disease of rodents, dogs, and other mammals, transmissible to humans.
– ORIGIN 1920S: from *Leptospira*, genus name of the bacteria, from Greek *leptos* 'fine, delicate' + *speira* 'coil'.

leptotene /ˈlɛptə(ʊ)tiːn/ ■ n. Biology the first stage of the prophase of meiosis, during which each chromosome becomes visible as two fine threads (chromatids).
– ORIGIN C20: from Greek *leptos* 'fine, delicate' + *tainia* 'band, ribbon'.

lesbian ■ n. a homosexual woman. ■ adj. of or relating to lesbians or lesbianism.
– DERIVATIVES **lesbianism** n.
– ORIGIN C19: from Greek *Lesbios*, from *Lesbos*, Greek island and home of Sappho, who expressed affection for women in her poetry.

lese-majesty /liːzˈmadʒɪsti/ ■ n. the insulting of a sovereign; treason.

–ORIGIN Middle English: from French *lèse-majesté*, from Latin *laesa majestas* 'injured sovereignty'.

lesiba /lɛˈsiːbə, lɛˈsɪːbʌ/ ■ n. a Basotho mouth bow, played by breathing across a piece of quill attached to one end of its string.
–ORIGIN from Sesotho.

lesion /ˈliːʒ(ə)n/ ■ n. chiefly Medicine a region in an organ or tissue which has suffered damage through injury or disease.
–ORIGIN Middle English: from Latin *laesio(n-)*, from *laedere* 'injure'.

less ■ det. & pron. **1** a smaller amount of; not as much. **2** fewer in number. ■ adv. to a smaller extent; not so much. ■ prep. minus.
–ORIGIN Old English, of Germanic origin.

USAGE
On the difference in use between **less** and **fewer**, see FEW.

-less ■ suffix forming adjectives and adverbs: **1** (from nouns) not having; without; free from: *flavourless*. **2** (from verbs) not affected by or not carrying out the action of the verb: *tireless*.
–DERIVATIVES **-lessly** suffix forming corresponding adverbs. **-lessness** suffix forming corresponding nouns.
–ORIGIN Old English, from *léas* 'devoid of'.

less-developed country ■ n. another term for DEVELOPING COUNTRY.

lessee /lɛˈsiː/ ■ n. a person who holds the lease of a property.
–DERIVATIVES **lesseeship** n.
–ORIGIN C15: from Old French *lesser* 'to let, leave'.

lessen ■ v. make or become less.

lesser ■ adj. not so great or important as the other or the rest.
–ORIGIN Middle English: from LESS.

lesson ■ n. **1** a period of learning or teaching. ▸ a thing learned. ▸ a thing that serves as a warning or encouragement. **2** a passage from the Bible read aloud during a church service.
–ORIGIN Middle English: from Old French *leçon*, from Latin *lectio*, from *legere* 'to read'.

lessor /lɛˈsɔː, ˈlɛsɔː/ ■ n. a person who leases or lets a property to another.
–ORIGIN Middle English: from Old French *lesser* 'let, leave'.

lest ■ conj. formal **1** with the intention of preventing; to avoid the risk of. **2** because of the possibility of.
–ORIGIN Old English *thý læs the* 'whereby less that', later *the læste*.

let[1] ■ v. (**letting**; past and past part. **let**) **1** not prevent or forbid; allow. **2** used in the imperative to express an intention, proposal, or instruction: *let's have a drink*. **3** used to express an assumption upon which a theory or calculation is to be based: *let A and B stand for X and Y*. **4** allow someone to have the use of (a room or property) in return for payment. **5** award (a contract for a project) to an applicant. ■ n. Brit. a period during which a room or property is rented: *a short let*.
–PHRASES **let alone** not to mention. **let someone/thing be** stop interfering with someone or something. **let fly** attack physically or verbally. **let oneself go 1** act in an uninhibited way. **2** become careless or untidy in one's habits or appearance. **let someone/thing go 1** allow someone or something to go free. **2** dismiss or retrench an employee. **3** (also **let go** or **let go of**) relinquish one's grip on someone or something. **let someone have it** informal attack someone. **to let** available for rent.
–PHRASAL VERBS **let down** (of an aircraft) descend prior to making a landing. **let someone down** fail to support or help someone. ▸ (**let someone/thing down**) have a detrimental effect on someone or something. **let oneself in for** informal involve oneself in (something difficult or unpleasant). **let someone in on/into** allow someone to know or share (something secret). **let something into** set something back into (a surface). **let someone off 1** refrain from punishing someone. **2** excuse someone a task or obligation. **let something off** cause a gun, firework, or bomb to fire or explode. **let on** informal **1** divulge information. **2** pretend. **let someone out** release someone from obligation or suspicion. **let something out** **1** utter a sound or cry. **2** make a garment looser or larger. **3** reveal a piece of information. **let up** informal become less intense. ▸ relax one's efforts.
–DERIVATIVES **letting** n.
–ORIGIN Old English *lǣtan* 'leave behind, leave out', of Germanic origin.

let[2] ■ n. (in racket sports) a circumstance under which a service is nullified and has to be retaken, especially (in tennis) when the ball clips the top of the net and falls within bounds. ■ v. (**letting**; past and past part. **letted** or **let**) archaic hinder.
–PHRASES **let or hindrance** formal obstruction or impediment. **play a let** (in racket sports) play a point again because the ball or one of the players has been obstructed.
–ORIGIN Old English *lettan* 'hinder', of Germanic origin.

-let ■ suffix **1** (forming nouns) denoting a smaller or lesser kind: *booklet*. **2** denoting articles of ornament or dress: *anklet*.
–ORIGIN orig. corresponding to French *-ette* added to nouns ending in *-el*.

let-down ■ n. **1** a disappointment. **2** the release of milk in a nursing mother or lactating animal as a reflex response to suckling or massage.

lethal ■ adj. **1** sufficient to cause death. **2** very harmful or destructive.
–DERIVATIVES **lethality** n. **lethally** adv.
–ORIGIN C16: from Latin *lethalis*, from *lethum*, a var. (influenced by Greek *lēthē* 'forgetfulness'), of *letum* 'death'.

lethargy /ˈlɛθədʒi/ ■ n. **1** a lack of energy and enthusiasm. **2** Medicine a pathological state of sleepiness or deep unresponsiveness.
–DERIVATIVES **lethargic** adj. **lethargically** adv.
–ORIGIN Middle English: from Greek *lēthargia*, from *lēthargos* 'forgetful'.

Lethean /liːˈθiːən/ ■ adj. poetic/literary causing forgetfulness and oblivion.
–ORIGIN from *Lethe*, a river of the underworld in Greek mythology whose water when drunk made the souls of the dead forget their life on earth.

let-off ■ n. informal an instance of unexpectedly escaping or avoiding something.

let-out ■ n. Brit. informal an opportunity to escape from or avoid a difficult situation.

let-out clause ■ n. informal a clause specifying a circumstance in which the terms of an agreement shall not apply.

let's ■ contr. let us.

letsema /lɛˈtsɛːmʌ, lɛˈtsɛːmə/ ■ n. S. African (in some rural communities) a traditional communal endeavour in which people work voluntarily to accomplish a specific task. ▸ a public project involving community volunteer work: *a housing letsema*.
–ORIGIN Setswana *letseme* 'seed-time'.

letter ■ n. **1** a character representing one or more of the sounds used in speech; any of the symbols of an alphabet. **2** a written, typed, or printed communication, sent by post or messenger. **3** the precise terms of a statement or requirement: *adherence to the letter of the law*. **4** (**letters**) literature: *the world of letters*. **5** (**letters**) archaic erudition: *a man of letters*. ■ v. inscribe or provide with letters.
–PHRASES **to the letter** with adherence to every detail.
–DERIVATIVES **lettering** n.
–ORIGIN Middle English: from Old French *lettre*, from Latin *litera* 'letter of the alphabet', (pl.) 'epistle, literature, culture'.

letter bomb ■ n. an explosive device hidden in a small package and detonated when the package is opened.

letter box ■ n. **1** a box or similar container outside a house into which mail is delivered. **2** chiefly Brit. a slot in a door through which mail is put. **3** another term for POSTBOX (in sense 1). **4** (**letterbox**) a format for presenting widescreen films on a standard television screen, in which the image fills the width but not the height of the screen. ■ v. (**letterbox**) record on to video in letterbox format.

letter-carrier ■ n. N. Amer. a postman or postwoman.
lettered ■ adj. dated formally educated.
letterhead ■ n. a printed heading on stationery, stating the sender's name and address. ▸ stationery with a printed heading.
letter of comfort ■ n. an assurance about a debt, short of a legal guarantee, given to a bank by a third party.
letter of credence ■ n. a letter of introduction, especially of an ambassador.
letter of credit ■ n. a letter issued by one bank to another to serve as a guarantee for payments made to a specified person.
letterpress ■ n. **1** printing from a hard, raised image under pressure, using viscous ink. **2** Brit. printed text as opposed to illustrations.
letterset ■ n. a method of printing in which ink is transferred from a raised surface to a cylinder and from that to the paper.
– ORIGIN 1960s: blend of **LETTERPRESS** and **OFFSET**.
letters of administration ■ pl. n. Law authority to administer the estate of someone who has died without making a will.
letters patent ■ pl. n. an open document issued by a monarch or government conferring a patent or other right.
– ORIGIN Middle English: from medieval Latin *litterae patentes* 'letters lying open'.
lettuce ■ n. a cultivated plant of the daisy family, with edible leaves that are eaten in salads. [*Lactuca sativa*.] **2** used in names of other plants with edible green leaves.
– ORIGIN Middle English: from Old French *laitues*, pl. of *laitue*, from Latin *lactuca*, from *lac* 'milk' (because of its milky juice).
let-up ■ n. informal a pause or reduction in the intensity of something dangerous, difficult, or tiring.
leucadendron /ˌl(j)uːkəˈdɛndrən/ ■ n. a South African shrub or small tree of the protea family with flower heads that have prominent, colourful bracts. [Genus *Leucadendron*.]
leucine /ˈluːsiːn/ ■ n. Biochemistry a hydrophobic amino acid which is an essential nutrient in the diet of vertebrates.
– ORIGIN C19: coined in French from Greek *leukos* 'white'.
leuco- (also **leuko-**) ■ comb. form **1** white: *leucoma*. **2** representing **LEUCOCYTE**.
– ORIGIN from Greek *leukos* 'white'.
leucocyte /ˈluːkə(ʊ)sʌɪt/ (also **leukocyte**) ■ n. Physiology a colourless cell which circulates in the blood and body fluids and is involved in counteracting foreign substances and disease; a white (blood) cell.
– DERIVATIVES **leucocytic** adj.
leucocytosis /ˌluːkə(ʊ)sʌɪˈtəʊsɪs/ (also **leukocytosis**) ■ n. Medicine an increase in the number of white cells in the blood, especially during an infection.
– DERIVATIVES **leucocytotic** adj.
leucoderma /ˌluːkə(ʊ)ˈdəːmə/ (also **leukoderma**) ■ n. another term for **VITILIGO**.
leucopenia /ˌluːkə(ʊ)ˈpiːnɪə/ (also **leukopenia**) ■ n. Medicine a reduction in the number of white cells in the blood.
– DERIVATIVES **leucopenic** adj.
– ORIGIN C19: from Greek *leukos* 'white' + *penia* 'poverty'.
leucoplast /ˈluːkə(ʊ)plast, -plɑːst/ ■ n. Botany a colourless organelle found in plant cells, used for the storage of starch or oil.
leucosis /luːˈkəʊsɪs/ (also **leukosis**) ■ n. a leukaemic disease of animals, especially one of a group of malignant viral diseases of poultry or cattle.
– DERIVATIVES **leucotic** adj.
leucospermum /ˌl(j)uːkəʊˈspəːməm/ ■ n. a southern African shrub of a genus of the protea family that comprises the pincushions. [Genus *Leucospermum*.]
leukaemia /luːˈkiːmɪə/ (US **leukemia**) ■ n. a malignant progressive disease in which the bone marrow and other blood-forming organs produce increased numbers of immature or abnormal leucocytes, suppressing the production of normal blood cells.
– DERIVATIVES **leukaemic** adj.
– ORIGIN C19: coined in German from Greek *leukos* 'white' + *haima* 'blood'.
leuko- ■ comb. form variant spelling of **LEUCO-**.
Levant /lɪˈvant/ ■ n. (**the Levant**) archaic the eastern part of the Mediterranean.
– DERIVATIVES **Levantine** n. & adj.
– ORIGIN C15: from French, 'rising', from *lever* 'to lift' used as a noun in the sense 'point of sunrise, east'.
levator /lɪˈveɪtə/ ■ n. Anatomy a muscle whose contraction causes the raising of a part of the body.
– ORIGIN C17: from Latin, 'a person who lifts', from *levare* 'raise, lift'.
levee[1] /ˈlɛvi, ˈlɛveɪ/ ■ n. a reception or assembly of people.
– ORIGIN C17: from French *levé*, var. of *lever* 'rising', from the verb *lever*.
levee[2] /ˈlɛvi, lɪˈviː/ ■ n. **1** an embankment built to prevent the overflow of a river. ▸ a ridge of sediment deposited naturally alongside a river. **2** chiefly N. Amer. a landing place; a quay.
– ORIGIN C18 (orig. US): from French *levée*, from *lever* 'to lift'.
level ■ n. **1** a horizontal plane or line with respect to the distance above or below of a given point. **2** a height or distance from the ground or another base. ▸ a floor within a multi-storey building. **3** a position or stage on a scale of quantity, extent, rank, or quality. **4** a flat tract of land. **5** an instrument giving a line parallel to the plane of the horizon for testing whether things are horizontal. ▸ Surveying an instrument for giving a horizontal line of sight. ■ adj. **1** having a flat, horizontal surface. ▸ (of a quantity of a dry substance) with the contents not rising above the brim of the measure: *a level teaspoon*. **2** at the same height as someone or something else. **3** having the same relative position; not in front or behind. **4** calm and steady: *a level voice*. ■ v. (**levelled**, **levelling**; US **leveled**, **leveling**) **1** make or become level. ▸ demolish (a building or town). **2** make or become equal or similar. **3** aim or direct (a weapon, criticism, or accusation). **4** (**level with**) informal be frank or honest with. **5** Surveying ascertain differences in the height of (land).
– PHRASES **do one's level best** make all possible efforts. **be level pegging** be equal in score or achievement during a contest. **a level playing field** a situation in which everyone has an equal chance of succeeding. **on the level** informal honest; truthful.
– DERIVATIVES **levelly** adv. **levelness** n.
– ORIGIN Middle English: from Old French *livel*, from Latin *libella*, diminutive of *libra* 'scales, balance'.
level crossing ■ n. a place where a railway and a road cross at the same level.
level-headed ■ adj. calm and sensible.
– DERIVATIVES **level-headedly** adv. **level-headedness** n.
leveller (US **leveler**) ■ n. a person or thing that levels something.
lever /ˈliːvə/ ■ n. a rigid bar resting on a pivot, used to move a load with one end when pressure is applied to the other. ▸ a projecting arm or handle that is moved to operate a mechanism. ■ v. **1** lift or move with a lever. **2** cause to move with a concerted physical effort: *she levered herself up*.
– ORIGIN Middle English: from Old French *levier*, from *lever* 'to lift'.
leverage ■ n. **1** the exertion of force by means of a lever. **2** the power to influence: *political leverage*. **3** Finance another term for **GEARING** (in sense 2). ■ v. [usu. as adj. **leveraged**] use borrowed capital for (an investment), expecting the profits made to be greater than the interest payable.
leveraged buyout ■ n. the purchase of a controlling share in a company by its management using outside capital.
leveret /ˈlɛv(ə)rɪt/ ■ n. a young hare in its first year.
– ORIGIN Middle English: from Anglo-Norman French, diminutive of *levre*, from Latin *lepus, lepor-* 'hare'.
leviathan /lɪˈvʌɪəθ(ə)n/ ■ n. **1** (in biblical use) a sea monster. ▸ a very large aquatic creature, especially a whale. ▸ something very large or powerful. **2** an autocratic

monarch or state. [with allusion to the English philosopher Thomas Hobbes' *Leviathan* (1651).]
– ORIGIN from Hebrew *liwyāṯān*.

levirate /'liːvɪrət, 'lɛv-/ ■ n. (usu. **the levirate**) a custom of the ancient Hebrews and some other peoples by which a man may be obliged to marry his brother's widow.
– ORIGIN C18: from Latin *levir* 'brother-in-law'.

levitate /'lɛvɪteɪt/ ■ v. rise or cause to rise and hover in the air.
– DERIVATIVES **levitation** n. **levitator** n.
– ORIGIN C17: from Latin *levis* 'light', on the pattern of *gravitate*.

Levite /'liːvʌɪt/ ■ n. a member of the Hebrew tribe of Levi, in particular an assistant to the priests in the Jewish temple.
– ORIGIN Middle English: from Greek *leuitēs*, from Hebrew *Lēwī* 'Levi'.

levity /'lɛvɪti/ ■ n. the treatment of a serious matter with humour or lack of respect.
– ORIGIN C16: from Latin *levitas*, from *levis* 'light'.

levo- ■ comb. form US spelling of **LAEVO-**.

levonorgestrel /ˌliːvəʊnɔːˈdʒɛstr(ə)l/ ■ n. Biochemistry a synthetic steroid hormone which has a similar effect to progesterone and is used in some contraceptive pills.
– ORIGIN 1970s: from **LEVO-** (it being a laevorotatory isomer) + *norgestrel*, a synthetic steroid hormone.

levy /'lɛvi/ ■ n. **1** the imposition of a tax, fee, fine, or subscription. ▸ a sum of money raised by such a levy. **2** an item or set of items of property seized to satisfy a legal judgement. **3** a body of enlisted troops. ■ v. (**-ies**, **-ied**) **1** impose or seize as a levy. **2** archaic enlist for military service.
– DERIVATIVES **leviable** adj.
– ORIGIN Middle English: from Old French *levee*, from *lever* 'raise', from Latin *levare*, from *levis* 'light'.

lewd ■ adj. crude and offensive in a sexual way.
– DERIVATIVES **lewdly** adv. **lewdness** n.
– ORIGIN Old English *lǣwede* ('belonging to the laity', later 'belonging to the common people, vulgar').

lewensessens /'lɪəvənsɛsəns/ ■ n. S. African a herbal remedy used as a laxative, prepared from aloe, gentian, rhubarb, and other plants.
– ORIGIN Afrikaans, 'essence of life', from *lewe* 'life' + *essens* 'essence'.

lewis ■ n. a steel device for lifting heavy blocks of stone or concrete, consisting of three pieces arranged to form a dovetail.
– ORIGIN Middle English: prob. from Old French *lou(p)* 'wolf', the name of a kind of siege engine.

Lewis acid ■ n. Chemistry a compound or ionic species which can accept an electron pair from a donor compound.
– ORIGIN 1940s: named after the American chemist Gilbert N. Lewis.

Lewis base ■ n. Chemistry a compound or ionic species which can donate an electron pair to an acceptor compound.
– ORIGIN 1960s: see **LEWIS ACID**.

lexeme /'lɛksiːm/ ■ n. Linguistics a basic lexical unit of a language consisting of one or several words, the elements of which do not separately convey the meaning of the whole.
– ORIGIN 1940s: from **LEXICON**.

lex fori /lɛks 'fɔːrʌɪ/ ■ n. Law the law of the country in which an action is brought.
– ORIGIN Latin, 'law of the court'.

lexical /'lɛksɪk(ə)l/ ■ adj. **1** of or relating to the words or vocabulary of a language. **2** relating to or of the nature of a lexicon or dictionary.
– DERIVATIVES **lexically** adv.
– ORIGIN C19: from Greek *lexikos* 'of words'.

lexicography /ˌlɛksɪ'kɒɡrəfi/ ■ n. the practice of compiling dictionaries.
– DERIVATIVES **lexicographer** n. **lexicographic** adj. **lexicographical** /-kə'ɡrafɪk(ə)l/ adj. **lexicographically** adv.

lexicology ■ n. the study of the form, meaning, and behaviour of words.
– DERIVATIVES **lexicological** adj. **lexicologically** adv.

lexicon /'lɛksɪk(ə)n/ ■ n. **1** the vocabulary of a person, language, or branch of knowledge. **2** a dictionary.
– ORIGIN C17: from Greek *lexikon* (*biblion*) '(book) of words', from *lexis* 'word'.

lexis /'lɛksɪs/ ■ n. the total stock of words in a language.
– ORIGIN 1950s: from Greek, 'word'.

lex loci /lɛks 'ləʊsʌɪ/ ■ n. Law the law of the country in which a transaction is performed, a tort is committed, or a property is situated.
– ORIGIN Latin, 'law of the place'.

lex talionis /lɛks ˌtalɪ'əʊnɪs/ ■ n. Law the law of retaliation, whereby a punishment resembles the offence committed in kind and degree.
– ORIGIN Latin, from *lex* 'law' and *talio(n-)* 'retaliation' (from *talis* 'such').

ley[1] /leɪ/ ■ n. a piece of land temporarily put down to grass, clover, etc., in contrast to permanent pasture.
– ORIGIN Old English *lǣge* 'fallow'.

ley[2] /leɪ, liː/ (also **ley line**) ■ n. a supposed straight line connecting three or more ancient sites, sometimes regarded as the line of a former track and associated by some with lines of energy and other paranormal phenomena.
– ORIGIN 1920s: var. of **LEA**.

Leyden jar /'lʌɪd(ə)n/ ■ n. an early form of capacitor consisting of a glass jar with layers of metal foil on the outside and inside.
– ORIGIN C18: named after *Leyden* (or *Leiden*), the city in the Netherlands where it was invented (1745).

LF ■ abbrev. low frequency.

LH ■ abbrev. Biochemistry luteinizing hormone.

l.h. ■ abbrev. left hand.

LHD ■ abbrev. left-hand drive.

Li ■ symb. the chemical element lithium.

liability ■ n. (pl. **-ies**) **1** the state of being liable. **2** a thing for which someone is liable, especially a financial obligation. **3** a person or thing likely to cause one embarrassment or put one at a disadvantage.

liable ■ adj. **1** responsible by law; legally answerable. ▸ (**liable to**) subject by law to. **2** (**liable to do something**) likely to do something. **3** (**liable to**) likely to experience (something undesirable): *areas liable to flooding*.
– ORIGIN Middle English: from French *lier* 'to bind', from Latin *ligare*.

liaise /lɪ'eɪz/ ■ v. **1** cooperate on a matter of mutual concern. **2** (**liaise between**) act as a link to assist communication between.
– ORIGIN 1920s: back-formation from **LIAISON**.

liaison ■ n. **1** communication or cooperation between people or organizations. **2** a sexual relationship, especially one that is secret. **3** the binding or thickening agent of a sauce. **4** Phonetics the sounding of a consonant that is normally silent at the end of a word, because the next word begins with a vowel.
– ORIGIN C17 (as a cookery term): from French, from *lier* 'to bind'.

liana /lɪ'ɑːnə/ (also **liane** /-'ɑːn/) ■ n. a woody climbing plant that hangs from trees, especially in tropical rain-forests. ▸ the free-hanging stem of such a plant.
– ORIGIN C18: from French *liane* 'clematis, liana'.

liar ■ n. a person who tells lies.
– ORIGIN Old English *lēogere* (see **LIE**[2]).

liar dice ■ n. a gambling game resembling poker dice, in which the thrower conceals the dice thrown and sometimes declares a false score.

liatris /lɪ'atrɪs/ ■ n. (pl. same) a plant native to North America, sometimes cultivated as a border plant. [Genus *Liatris*.]

lib ■ n. informal (in the names of political movements) the liberation of a specified group: *women's lib*.
– DERIVATIVES **libber** n.

libation /lʌɪ'beɪʃ(ə)n/ ■ n. **1** the pouring out of a drink as an offering to a deity. ▸ such a drink. **2** humorous an alcoholic drink.
– ORIGIN Middle English: from Latin *libatio(n-)*, from *libare* 'pour as an offering'.

Lib Dem ■ n. informal (in the UK) Liberal Democrat.

libel ■ n. 1 defamation. ▶ UK Law written defamation. Com-pare with SLANDER. ▶ a defamatory statement; a written defamation. 2 (in admiralty and ecclesiastical law) a plaintiff's written declaration. ■ v. (**libelled**, **libelling**; US **libeled**, **libeling**) 1 Law defame by publishing a libel. 2 (in admiralty and ecclesiastical law) bring a suit against.
– DERIVATIVES **libeller** n. **libellous** (US also **libelous**) adj. **libellously** (US also **libelously**) adv.
– ORIGIN Middle English: from Latin *libellus*, diminutive of *liber* 'book'.

liberal ■ adj. 1 respectful and accepting of behaviour or opinions different from one's own; open to new ideas. ▶ (of a society, law, etc.) favourable to individual rights and freedoms. 2 (in a political context) favouring individual liberty, free trade, and moderate political and social reform. 3 (of education) concerned with broadening general knowledge and experience. 4 (especially of an interpretation of a law) broadly construed; not strictly literal. 5 given, used, or giving in generous amounts. ■ n. a person of liberal views.
– DERIVATIVES **liberalism** n. **liberalist** n. **liberalistic** adj. **liberality** n. **liberally** adv. **liberalness** n.
– ORIGIN Middle English ('suitable for a free man' hence 'suitable for a gentleman'): from Latin *liberalis*, from *liber* 'free (man)'.

liberal arts ■ pl. n. chiefly N. Amer. arts subjects such as literature and history, as distinct from science and technology.

liberalize (also **-ise**) ■ v. remove or loosen restrictions on (something, typically an economic or political system).
– DERIVATIVES **liberalization** (also **-isation**) n. **liberalizer** (also **-iser**) n.

liberal studies ■ pl. n. [usu. treated as sing.] Brit. an additional course in arts subjects taken by students studying for a qualification in science, technology, or the humanities.

liberate ■ v. 1 set free, especially from imprisonment or oppression. ▶ [as adj. **liberated**] free from social conventions, especially with regard to sexual roles. 2 Chemistry & Physics release (gas, energy, etc.) as a result of chemical reaction or physical decomposition.
– DERIVATIVES **liberated** adj. **liberating** adj. **liberation** n. **liberationist** n. **liberator** n.
– ORIGIN C16 (*liberation* Middle English): from Latin *liberare* 'to free', from *liber* 'free'.

liberation theology ■ n. a movement in Christian theology which attempts to address the problems of poverty and social injustice as well as spiritual matters.

Liberian /lʌɪˈbɪərɪən/ ■ n. a native or inhabitant of Liberia, a country in West Africa. ■ adj. of or relating to Liberia or Liberians.

libero /ˈliːbərəʊ/ ■ n. (pl. **-os**) Soccer another term for SWEEPER (in sense 2).
– ORIGIN 1960s: from Italian, abbrev. of *battitore libero* 'free defender', literally 'free beater'.

libertarian /ˌlɪbəˈtɛːrɪən/ ■ n. 1 an adherent of libertarianism. 2 a person who advocates civil liberty. 3 a person who believes in free will.
– ORIGIN C18: from LIBERTY, on the pattern of *unitarian*.

libertarianism ■ n. an extreme laissez-faire political philosophy advocating only minimal state intervention in the lives of citizens.

libertine /ˈlɪbətiːn, -tɪn, -tʌɪn/ ■ n. 1 a person who is freely indulgent in sensual pleasures. 2 a freethinker in matters of religion. ■ adj. 1 characterized by free indulgence in sensual pleasures. 2 freethinking.
– DERIVATIVES **libertinage** n. **libertinism** n.
– ORIGIN Middle English: from Latin *libertinus* 'freedman', from *liber* 'free', influenced by French *libertin*.

liberty ■ n. (pl. **-ies**) 1 the state of being free from oppression or imprisonment. 2 a right or privilege, especially a statutory one. 3 the power or scope to act as one pleases. 4 informal a presumptuous remark or action. 5 Nautical shore leave granted to a sailor.
– PHRASES **at liberty** 1 not imprisoned. 2 allowed or entitled to do something. **take liberties** 1 behave in an unduly familiar manner towards a person. 2 treat something freely, without strict faithfulness to the facts or to an original. **take the liberty** venture to do something without first asking permission.
– ORIGIN Middle English: from Old French *liberte*, from Latin *libertas*, from *liber* 'free'.

liberty bodice ■ n. Brit. trademark a girl's or woman's bodice made from thick or quilted cotton, formerly worn as an undergarment.

Liberty Hall ■ n. a place where one may do as one likes.

libidinous /lɪˈbɪdɪnəs/ ■ adj. having or showing excessive sexual drive.
– DERIVATIVES **libidinously** adv. **libidinousness** n.
– ORIGIN Middle English: from Latin *libidinosus*, from *libido* 'desire, lust'.

libido /lɪˈbiːdəʊ, lɪˈbʌɪdəʊ/ ■ n. (pl. **-os**) 1 sexual desire. 2 Psychoanalysis the energy of the sexual drive as a component of the life instinct.
– DERIVATIVES **libidinal** adj. **libidinally** adv.
– ORIGIN C20: from Latin, 'desire, lust'.

Libra /ˈliːbrə, ˈlɪb-, ˈlʌɪb-/ ■ n. 1 Astronomy a small constellation (the Scales or Balance), said to represent a pair of scales symbolizing justice. 2 Astrology the seventh sign of the zodiac, which the sun enters at the northern autumnal equinox (about 23 September).
– DERIVATIVES **Libran** n. & adj.
– ORIGIN from Latin.

librarian ■ n. a person in charge of or assisting in a library.
– DERIVATIVES **librarianship** n.
– ORIGIN C17: from Latin *librarius* 'relating to books'.

library ■ n. (pl. **-ies**) 1 a building or room containing a collection of books and periodicals for use by the public or the members of an institution. 2 a private collection of books. ▶ a series of books or recordings issued by a company as a set. ▶ (also **software library**) Computing a collection of programs and software packages made generally available.
– ORIGIN Middle English: from Latin *libraria* 'bookshop', from *liber* 'book'.

libration /lʌɪˈbreɪʃ(ə)n/ ■ n. Astronomy an apparent or real oscillation of the moon, by which parts near the edge of the disc that are often not visible from the earth sometimes come into view.
– DERIVATIVES **librate** v.
– ORIGIN C17: from Latin *libratio(n-)*, from *librare* 'weigh', from *libra* 'a balance'.

libretto /lɪˈbrɛtəʊ/ ■ n. (pl. **libretti** /-ti/ or **librettos**) the text of an opera or other long vocal work.
– DERIVATIVES **librettist** n.
– ORIGIN C18: from Italian, diminutive of *libro* 'book'.

Librium /ˈlɪbrɪəm/ ■ n. trademark for CHLORDIAZEPOXIDE.
– ORIGIN 1960s.

Libyan /ˈlɪbɪən/ ■ n. a native or inhabitant of Libya. ■ adj. of or relating to Libya or Libyans.

lice plural form of LOUSE.

licence (US **license**) ■ n. 1 a permit from an authority to own or use something, do a particular thing, or carry on a trade (especially in alcoholic liquor). ▶ formal or official permission. 2 a writer's or artist's conventional freedom to deviate from facts or accepted rules. 3 freedom to behave without restraint.
– ORIGIN Middle English: from Latin *licentia* 'freedom, licentiousness' (medieval Latin, 'authority, permission'), from *licere* 'be lawful or permitted'.

license (also **licence**) ■ v. 1 grant a licence to. 2 authorize.
– DERIVATIVES **licensable** adj. **licenser** n. **licensing** adj. **licensor** n.
– ORIGIN Middle English: from LICENCE; the spelling *-se* arose by analogy with pairs such as *practice*, *practise*.

licensed (also **licenced**) ■ adj. having an official licence. ▶ (of premises) having a licence for the sale of alcoholic drinks.

licensee ■ n. the holder of a licence, especially to sell alcoholic drinks.

license plate ■ n. North American term for NUMBER PLATE.

licentiate /lʌɪˈsɛnʃɪət/ ■ n. 1 the holder of a certificate of competence to practise a particular profession. 2 (in some foreign universities) a degree between that of bachelor and

master or doctor. **3** a licensed preacher not yet having an appointment, especially in a Presbyterian Church.
– DERIVATIVES **licentiateship** n.
– ORIGIN C15: from medieval Latin, from *licentiatus* 'having freedom', from *licentia* 'freedom'.

licentious /laɪˈsɛnʃəs/ ■ adj. **1** promiscuous and unprincipled in sexual matters. **2** archaic disregarding accepted rules or conventions, especially in grammar or literary style.
– DERIVATIVES **licentiously** adv. **licentiousness** n.
– ORIGIN Middle English: from Latin *licentiosus*, from *licentia* 'freedom'.

lichen /ˈlaɪk(ə)n, ˈlɪtʃ(ə)n/ ■ n. **1** a simple composite plant consisting of a fungus in association with an alga, typically growing on rocks, walls, and trees. **2** a skin disease in which small, round, hard lesions occur close together.
– DERIVATIVES **lichened** adj. **lichenology** n. **lichenous** adj.
– ORIGIN C17: from Greek *leikhēn*.

licit /ˈlɪsɪt/ ■ adj. not forbidden; lawful.
– DERIVATIVES **licitly** adv.
– ORIGIN C15: from Latin *licere* 'allow'.

lick ■ v. **1** pass the tongue over (something), typically in order to taste, moisten, or clean it. **2** move lightly and quickly like a tongue. **3** informal defeat comprehensively. ■ n. **1** an act of licking. ▸ a place where animals come to lick salt. **2** informal a small amount or quick application of something. **3** informal a short phrase or solo in jazz or popular music. **4** informal a smart blow.
– PHRASES **a lick and a promise** informal a hasty wash. **lick someone's boots** (or vulgar slang **arse**) be excessively obsequious towards someone.
– DERIVATIVES **-licker** n. **licking** n.
– ORIGIN Old English, of West Germanic origin.

lickety-split ■ adv. informal, chiefly N. Amer. at full speed.
– ORIGIN C19 (in the phr. *as fast as lickety* 'at full speed'): from a fanciful extension of LICK + SPLIT.

lickspittle ■ n. a person who behaves obsequiously to those in power.

licorice ■ n. US spelling of LIQUORICE.

lid ■ n. **1** a removable or hinged cover for the top of a container. **2** an eyelid. **3** the top crust of a pie.
– DERIVATIVES **lidded** adj. **lidless** adj.
– ORIGIN Old English, of Germanic origin.

lidar /ˈlaɪdɑː/ ■ n. a detection system which works on the principle of radar, but uses light from a laser.
– ORIGIN 1960s: blend of LIGHT[1] and RADAR.

lido /ˈliːdəʊ, ˈlaɪ-/ ■ n. (pl. **-os**) a public open-air swimming pool or bathing beach.
– ORIGIN C17: from Italian *Lido*, the name of a bathing beach near Venice, from *lido* 'shore'.

lidocaine /ˈlɪdə(ʊ)keɪn/ ■ n. another term for LIGNOCAINE.
– ORIGIN 1940s: from (*acetani*)*lid*(*e*) + -*caine* (from COCAINE).

lie[1] ■ v. (**lying**; past **lay**; past part. **lain**) **1** be in or assume a horizontal or resting position on a supporting surface. ▸ be buried in a particular place. **2** be or remain in a specified state. **3** reside or be found: *the solution lies in a return to traditional values.* ▸ be situated in a specified position or direction. **4** Law (of an action, charge, or claim) be admissible or sustainable. ■ n. **1** the way, direction, or position in which something lies or comes to rest. **2** the place of cover of an animal or a bird.
– PHRASES **let something lie** take no action regarding a sensitive matter. **lie low** keep out of sight; avoid attention. **the lie** (N. Amer. **lay**) **of the land 1** the features or characteristics of an area. **2** the current situation or state of affairs. **take something lying down** accept an insult, setback, or rebuke without protest.
– PHRASAL VERBS **lie behind** be the real reason for. **lie in 1** remain in bed after the normal time for getting up. **2** archaic (of a pregnant woman) go to bed to give birth. **lie off** Nautical (of a ship) stand some distance from shore or from another ship. **lie up** (of a ship) go into dock or be out of commission. **lie with** archaic have sexual intercourse with.
– ORIGIN Old English *licgan*, of Germanic origin.

USAGE
On the distinction between **lie** and **lay**, see usage at LAY[1].

life

lie[2] ■ n. an intentionally false statement. ▸ a situation involving deception or founded on a mistaken impression: *she had been living a lie.* ■ v. (**lies**, **lied**, **lying**) tell a lie or lies. ▸ (of a thing) present a false impression.
– PHRASES **give the lie to** serve to show that (something assumed to be true) is not true. **lie through one's teeth** informal tell an outright lie.
– ORIGIN Old English *lyge* (n.), *lēogan* (v.), of Germanic origin.

Liebfraumilch /ˈliːbfraʊˌmɪlʃ/ ■ n. a light white wine from the Rhine region of Germany.
– ORIGIN German, from *lieb* 'dear' + *Frau* 'lady' (referring to the Virgin Mary, patroness of the convent where it was first made) + *Milch* 'milk'.

lied /liːd, -t/ ■ n. (pl. **lieder** /ˈliːdə/) a type of German song, especially of the Romantic period, typically for solo voice with piano accompaniment.
– ORIGIN from German *Lied*.

lie detector ■ n. an instrument for determining whether a person is telling the truth by testing for physiological changes considered to be associated with lying.

lie-down ■ n. chiefly Brit. a short rest on a bed or sofa.

lief /liːf/ ■ adv. (**as lief**) archaic as happily; as gladly.
– ORIGIN Old English *lēof* 'dear, pleasant', of Germanic origin.

liege /liːdʒ/ historical ■ adj. concerned with or relating to the relationship between a feudal superior and a vassal. ■ n. **1** (also **liege lord**) a feudal superior or sovereign. **2** a vassal or subject.
– ORIGIN Middle English: via Old French *lige*, *liege* from medieval Latin *laeticus*, prob. of Germanic origin.

liegeman ■ n. (pl. **-men**) historical a vassal who owes feudal service or allegiance to a nobleman.

lie-in ■ n. a prolonged stay in bed in the morning.

lien /liːn, ˈliːən, ˈlaɪən/ ■ n. Law a right to keep possession of property belonging to another person until a debt owed by that person is discharged.
– ORIGIN C16: via Old French *loien* from Latin *ligamen* 'bond'.

lieu /ljuː, luː/ ■ n. (in phr. **in lieu**or) **in lieu of** instead (of).
– ORIGIN Middle English: via French from Latin *locus* 'place'.

Lieut. ■ abbrev. Lieutenant.

lieutenant /lɛfˈtɛnənt/ ■ n. **1** a deputy or substitute acting for a superior. **2** a rank of officer in the army and air force, above second lieutenant and below captain. **3** a rank of officer in the navy, above sub lieutenant and below lieutenant commander. **4** (in the US) a police officer next in rank below captain.
– DERIVATIVES **lieutenancy** n. (pl. **-ies**).
– ORIGIN Middle English: from Old French (see LIEU, TENANT).

lieutenant colonel ■ n. a rank of officer in the army and the air force, above major and below colonel.

lieutenant commander ■ n. a rank of officer in the navy, above lieutenant and below commander.

lieutenant general ■ n. a high rank of officer in the army, above major general and below general.

lieutenant governor ■ n. an acting or deputy governor (especially of US states or Canadian provinces).

life ■ n. (pl. **lives**) **1** the condition that distinguishes animals and plants from inorganic matter, including the capacity for growth, functional activity, and continual change preceding death. ▸ living things and their activity. ▸ a particular type or aspect of people's existence: *school life*. **2** the existence of an individual human being or animal. ▸ a biography. ▸ (in various games) each of a specified number of chances each player has before being put out. **3** informal a sentence of imprisonment for life. **4** vitality, vigour, or energy. **5** [as modifier] (in art) based on a living rather than an imagined form: *a life drawing*.
– PHRASES **come** (or **bring**) **to life 1** regain or cause to regain consciousness. **2** become or cause to become active, lively, or interesting. **for dear** (or **one's**) **life** as if or in order to escape death. **for the life of me** informal however hard I try. **as large as** (or **larger than**) **life** informal

life-affirming

conspicuously present. **the life and soul of the party** a vivacious and sociable person. **a matter of life and death** a matter of vital importance. **not on your life** informal emphatically not. **see life** gain a wide experience of the world. **take one's life in one's hands** risk being killed.
– ORIGIN Old English, of Germanic origin.

life-affirming ■ adj. having an emotionally or spiritually uplifting effect.

life assurance ■ n. another term for LIFE INSURANCE.

lifebelt ■ n. a ring of buoyant or inflatable material used to help a person who has fallen into water to stay afloat.

lifeblood ■ n. **1** poetic/literary blood, as being necessary to life. **2** an indispensable factor or force giving something its strength and vitality.

lifeboat ■ n. **1** a specially constructed boat launched from land to rescue people in distress at sea. **2** a small boat kept on a ship for use in an emergency. **3** an emergency loan or fund set up to rescue a commercial bank or business that is in danger of becoming insolvent.
– DERIVATIVES **lifeboatman** n. (pl. **-men**).

lifebuoy ■ n. a buoyant support such as a lifebelt for keeping a person afloat in water.

life coach ■ n. a person employed to help people attain their goals in life.

life cycle ■ n. the series of changes in the life of an organism including reproduction.

life expectancy ■ n. the period that a person may expect to live.

life force ■ n. the force that gives something its life, vitality, or strength.

life form ■ n. any living thing.

lifeguard ■ n. a person employed to rescue bathers who get into difficulty at a beach or swimming pool.

life imprisonment ■ n. a long term of imprisonment (rarely the whole of a person's life).

life insurance ■ n. insurance that pays out a sum of money either on the death of the insured person or after a set period.

life jacket ■ n. a sleeveless buoyant or inflatable jacket for keeping a person afloat in water.

lifeless ■ adj. **1** dead or apparently dead. ▸ devoid of living things. **2** lacking vigour, vitality, or excitement.
– DERIVATIVES **lifelessly** adv. **lifelessness** n.

lifelike ■ adj. accurate in its representation of a living person or thing.

lifeline ■ n. **1** a rope or line used for life-saving, typically one thrown to rescue someone in difficulties in water or one used by sailors to secure themselves to a boat. ▸ a line used by a diver for sending signals to the surface. **2** a thing which is essential for the continued existence of someone or something or which provides a means of escape from a difficult situation. **3** (in palmistry) a line on the palm of a person's hand, regarded as indicating how long they will live.

lifelong ■ adj. lasting or remaining in a particular state throughout a person's life.

life member ■ n. a person who has lifelong membership of a society.
– DERIVATIVES **life membership** n.

life office ■ n. an office or company dealing in life insurance.

life peer (or **life peeress**) ■ n. (in the UK) a peer (or peeress) whose title cannot be inherited.
– DERIVATIVES **life peerage** n.

life preserver ■ n. **1** a life jacket or lifebelt. **2** Brit. a short truncheon with a heavily loaded end.

lifer ■ n. **1** informal a person serving a life sentence. **2** N. Amer. a person who spends their life in a particular career, especially in the armed forces.

life raft ■ n. an inflatable raft for use in an emergency at sea.

lifesaver ■ n. informal a thing that saves one from serious difficulty. **2** S. African & Austral./NZ a lifeguard on a beach.

life sciences ■ pl. n. the sciences concerned with the study of living organisms, including biology, botany, zoology, and related subjects.
– DERIVATIVES **life scientist** n.

life sentence ■ n. a punishment of life imprisonment.

life-size (also **life-sized**) ■ adj. of the same size as the person or thing represented.

life skill ■ n. a skill that enables someone to deal effectively with the practical demands of everyday life.

lifespan ■ n. the length of time for which a person or animal lives or a thing functions.

lifestyle ■ n. the way in which one lives.

lifestyle drug ■ n. a pharmaceutical product characterized as improving the quality of life rather than alleviating or curing disease.

life support ■ n. Medicine maintenance of vital functions following disablement or in an adverse environment.

life table ■ n. a table of statistics relating to life expectancy and mortality.

life-threatening ■ adj. potentially fatal.

lifetime ■ n. **1** the duration of a person's life. ▸ the duration of a thing or its usefulness. **2** informal a very long time.

LIFO /ˈlaɪfəʊ/ ■ abbrev. last in, first out (chiefly with reference to methods of stock valuation and data storage).

lift ■ v. **1** raise or be raised to a higher position or level. ▸ raise (someone's spirits or confidence). ▸ dig up. **2** pick up and move to a different position. ▸ transport by air. ▸ (**lift off**) (of an aircraft, spacecraft, etc.) take off, especially vertically. **3** formally remove or end (a legal restriction, decision, etc.). **4** carry off or win (a prize or event). ▸ informal steal. **5** informal arrest. ■ n. **1** a platform or compartment housed in a shaft for raising and lowering people or things. ▸ a device for carrying people up or down a mountain. **2** a built-up heel or device in a boot or shoe. **3** an act or instance of lifting. ▸ upward force exerted by the air on an aerofoil or other structure, counteracting gravity. ▸ the maximum weight that an aircraft can raise. **4** a free ride in another person's vehicle. **5** a feeling of increased cheerfulness.
– PHRASES **lift a finger** (or **hand**) [usu. with neg.] make the slightest effort.
– DERIVATIVES **liftable** adj. **lifter** n.
– ORIGIN Middle English: from Old Norse *lypta*, of Germanic origin.

lift-off ■ n. the vertical take-off of a spacecraft, rocket, etc.

lig Brit. informal ■ v. (**ligged**, **ligging**) take advantage of free parties, shows, or travel offered by companies for publicity purposes. ■ n. a free party or show of this type.
– DERIVATIVES **ligger** n.
– ORIGIN 1960s: from a dialect var. of LIE¹, 'lie about, loaf', whence 'freeload'.

ligament /ˈlɪɡəm(ə)nt/ ■ n. Anatomy a short band of tough, flexible, fibrous connective tissue which connects two bones or cartilages or holds together a joint. ▸ a membranous fold that supports an organ and keeps it in position.
– DERIVATIVES **ligamentary** adj. **ligamentous** adj.
– ORIGIN Middle English: from Latin *ligamentum* 'bond', from *ligare* 'to bind'.

ligand /ˈlɪɡ(ə)nd/ ■ n. **1** Chemistry an ion or molecule attached to a metal atom by coordinate bonding. **2** Biochemistry a molecule that binds to another.
– ORIGIN 1950s: from Latin *ligandus* 'that can be tied'.

ligate /lɪˈɡeɪt/ ■ v. Surgery tie up (an artery or vessel).
– ORIGIN C16 (*ligation* Middle English): from Latin *ligare* 'to tie'.

ligation ■ n. **1** the surgical procedure of tying a ligature tightly around a blood vessel or other duct or tube in the body. **2** Biochemistry the joining of two DNA strands or other molecules by a phosphate ester linkage.

ligature /ˈlɪɡətʃə/ ■ n. **1** a thing used for tying something tightly. ▸ a cord used in surgery, especially to tie up a bleeding artery. **2** Printing a character consisting of two or more joined letters, e.g. æ. ■ v. bind or connect with a ligature.
– ORIGIN Middle English: via late Latin *ligatura* from Latin *ligare* 'to tie'.

liger /ˈlaɪɡə/ ■ n. the hybrid offspring of a male lion and a tigress.

light¹ ■ n. **1** the natural agent that stimulates sight and makes things visible; electromagnetic radiation from about 390 to 740 nm in wavelength. ▸ a source of illumination. ▸ (**lights**) traffic lights. ▸ Law the light falling on windows, the obstruction of which by a neighbour is illegal. **2** an expression in someone's eyes.
▸ enlightenment: *light dawned in her eyes*. ▸ (**lights**) a person's opinions, standards, and abilities. **3** an area that is brighter or paler than its surroundings. **4** a device producing a flame or spark. **5** a window or opening to let light in. ▸ a perpendicular division of a mullioned window. ▸ a pane of glass in a greenhouse or cold frame. **6** a person eminent in a particular sphere. ■ v. (past **lit**; past part. **lit** or **lighted**) **1** provide with light. ▸ (**light up**) become illuminated. ▸ (**light up**) (of the face or eyes) suddenly become animated with liveliness or joy. **2** ignite or be ignited. ▸ (**light up**) ignite a cigarette, cigar, or pipe and begin to smoke it. ■ adj. **1** having a considerable or sufficient amount of light. **2** (of a colour or object) reflecting a lot of light; pale.
–PHRASES **bring** (or **come**) **to light** make (or become) widely known or evident. **go out like a light** informal fall asleep or lose consciousness suddenly. **in a —— light** in the way specified: *the audit portrayed them in a favourable light*. **in** (**the**) **light of** taking (something) into consideration. **light at the end of the tunnel** an indication that a period of difficulty is ending. **the light of day** general public attention. **the light of someone's life** a much loved person. **lit up** informal, dated drunk. **punch someone's lights out** beat someone up. **see the light** understand or realize something. ▸ undergo religious conversion. **see the light of day** be born. ▸ come into existence. **throw** (or **cast** or **shed**) **light on** help to explain by providing further information.
–DERIVATIVES **lightish** adj. **lightless** adj. **lightness** n.
–ORIGIN Old English *lēoht*, *līht* (n. and adj.), *līhtan* (v.), of Germanic origin.

light² ■ adj. **1** of little weight. ▸ deficient in weight. ▸ carrying or suitable for small loads. ▸ carrying only light armaments. ▸ (of a vehicle, ship, etc.) unladen or with less than a full load. ▸ (of food or a meal) small in quantity and easy to digest. ▸ low in fat, cholesterol, sugar, or alcohol. ▸ (of soil) friable, porous, and workable. **2** not strongly or heavily built. **3** relatively low in density, amount, or intensity. ▸ (**light on**) rather short of. ▸ (of sleep or a sleeper) easily disturbed. ▸ easily borne or done: *some light housework*. **4** gentle or delicate. ▸ (of type) having thin strokes. **5** not profound or serious. ▸ free from worry: *I left with a light heart*. **6** Physics containing atoms of an isotope of relatively low mass. **7** archaic (of a woman) promiscuous.
–PHRASES **make light of** treat as unimportant. **make light work of** accomplish quickly and easily. **travel light** travel with a minimum load or little luggage.
–DERIVATIVES **lightish** adj. **lightly** adv. **lightness** n.
–ORIGIN Old English *lēoht*, *līht* (n.), *lēohte* (adv.), of Germanic origin.

light³ ■ v. (past and past part. **lit** or **lighted**) **1** (**light on/upon**) come upon or discover by chance. **2** archaic descend.
▸ (**light on**) fall or land on.
–ORIGIN Old English *līhtan*, from LIGHT².

light box ■ n. a box with a translucent top and containing an electric light, providing an evenly lighted flat surface for viewing transparencies.

light bulb ■ n. a glass bulb containing inert gas, fitted into a lamp or ceiling socket, which provides light when an electric current is passed through it.

light-emitting diode ■ n. see LED.

lighten¹ ■ v. **1** make or become lighter in weight. **2** make or become less serious.

lighten² ■ v. **1** make or become brighter. **2** archaic enlighten spiritually.

light engine ■ n. a railway locomotive with no vehicles attached.

lighter¹ ■ n. a device producing a small flame, used to light cigarettes.

lighter² ■ n. a flat-bottomed barge used to transfer goods to and from ships in harbour.

677

–ORIGIN Middle English: from LIGHT² (in the sense 'unload'), or from Middle Low German *luchter*.

lightfast ■ adj. (of a pigment) not prone to discolour when exposed to light.
–DERIVATIVES **lightfastness** n.

light-fingered ■ adj. prone to steal.

light flyweight ■ n. the lowest weight in amateur boxing.

light-footed ■ adj. fast, nimble, or stealthy on one's feet.
–DERIVATIVES **light-footedly** adv.

light-headed ■ adj. dizzy and slightly faint.
–DERIVATIVES **light-headedly** adv. **light-headedness** n.

light-hearted ■ adj. amusing and entertaining. ▸ cheerful or carefree.
–DERIVATIVES **light-heartedly** adv. **light-heartedness** n.

light heavyweight ■ n. a weight in boxing and other sports intermediate between middleweight and heavyweight.

lighthouse ■ n. a tower or other structure containing a beacon light to warn ships at sea.

lightie ■ n. variant spelling of LIGHTY.

light industry ■ n. the manufacture of small or light articles.

lighting ■ n. equipment for producing light. ▸ the arrangement or effect of lights.

light meter ■ n. an instrument measuring the intensity of light, used when taking photographs.

light middleweight ■ n. a weight in amateur boxing intermediate between welterweight and middleweight.

lightning ■ n. **1** the occurrence of a brief natural high-voltage electrical discharge between a cloud and the ground or within a cloud, accompanied by a bright flash and often thunder. **2** [as modifier] very quick: *lightning speed*.
–ORIGIN Middle English: special use of *lightening* (verbal noun from LIGHTEN²).

lightning conductor (also chiefly N. Amer. **lightning rod**) ■ n. a metal rod or wire fixed in a high and exposed place to divert lightning into the ground.

light pen ■ n. **1** Computing a hand-held pen-like photosensitive device held to a computer display screen for passing information to the computer. **2** a hand-held device for reading bar codes.

light pollution ■ n. excessive brightening of the night sky by street lights and other man-made sources.

lightproof ■ adj. able to block out light completely.

light railway ■ n. a railway for light traffic.

lights ■ pl. n. the lungs of sheep, pigs, or bullocks as food for pets.
–ORIGIN Middle English: use of LIGHT² as a noun (so named because of their lightness).

lightship (also **light vessel**) ■ n. an anchored boat with a beacon light to warn ships at sea.

lightsome ■ adj. chiefly poetic/literary **1** carefree. **2** gracefully nimble.
–DERIVATIVES **lightsomely** adv. **lightsomeness** n.

light water ■ n. water containing the normal proportion (or less) of deuterium oxide.

lightweight ■ n. **1** a weight in boxing and other sports intermediate between featherweight and welterweight. **2** informal a person of little importance or influence. ■ adj. **1** of thin material or build. **2** informal having little importance or influence.

light well ■ n. an open area or vertical shaft in the centre of a building, typically roofed with glass.

light welterweight ■ n. a weight in amateur boxing intermediate between lightweight and welterweight.

lighty (also **lightie**, **laaitie**) ■ n. S. African informal a male child or adolescent. ▸ (also **my lighty**) used as a form of address for a boy or man.
–ORIGIN prob. from LIGHT², in the sense 'light of heart, mind'.

light year ■ n. Astronomy a unit of distance equivalent to

ligneous

the distance that light travels in one year, 9.4607 × 10¹² km (nearly 6 million million miles).

ligneous /ˈlɪgnɪəs/ ■ adj. made, consisting of, or resembling wood.
– ORIGIN C17: from Latin *ligneus* 'relating to wood'.

ligni- ■ comb. form relating to wood: *lignify*.
– ORIGIN from Latin *lignum* 'wood'.

lignify /ˈlɪgnɪfʌɪ/ ■ v. (-ies, -ied) [usu. as adj. **lignified**] Botany make rigid and woody by the deposition of lignin in cell walls.
– DERIVATIVES **lignification** n.

lignin /ˈlɪgnɪn/ ■ n. Botany a complex organic polymer deposited in the cell walls of many plants, making them rigid and woody.
– ORIGIN C19: from LIGNI-.

lignite /ˈlɪgnʌɪt/ ■ n. soft brownish coal, intermediate between bituminous coal and peat.
– DERIVATIVES **lignitic** adj.
– ORIGIN C19: coined in French from Latin *lignum* 'wood'.

ligno- ■ comb. form **1** relating to wood. **2** representing LIGNIN.
– ORIGIN from Latin *lignum* 'wood'.

lignocaine /ˈlɪgnə(ʊ)keɪn/ ■ n. Medicine a synthetic compound used as a local anaesthetic, e.g. for dental surgery, and in treating abnormal heart rhythms.
– ORIGIN 1950s: from LIGNO- (Latin equivalent of XYLO-, used in the earlier name *xylocaine* and reflecting chemical similarity to XYLENE) + *-caine* (from COCAINE).

ligule /ˈlɪgjuːl/ ■ n. Botany a narrow strap-shaped part of a plant, especially a membranous scale on the inner side of the leaf sheath in grasses.
– DERIVATIVES **ligulate** adj.
– ORIGIN C19: from Latin *ligula* 'strap'.

likable ■ adj. variant spelling of LIKEABLE.

like¹ ■ prep. **1** similar to. ▸ in the manner of. ▸ in a way appropriate to. ▸ characteristic of. ▸ used to ask about someone's or something's characteristics. **2** in this manner. **3** such as. ■ conj. informal **1** in the same way that. **2** as though. ■ n. a similar person or thing. ▸ (**the like**) things of the same kind. ■ adj. having similar characteristics to another. ■ adv. **1** informal used in speech as a meaningless filler. **2** informal used to convey a person's reported attitude or feelings in the form of direct speech: *so she comes in and she's like 'Where is everybody?'* **3** (**like as/to**) archaic in the manner of.
– PHRASES **and the like** et cetera. (**as**) **like as not** probably. **like so** informal in this manner. **the likes of** informal a person such as.
– ORIGIN Middle English: from Old Norse *líkr*.

like² ■ v. **1** find agreeable, enjoyable, or satisfactory. **2** wish for; want. ▸ prefer. ▸ (in questions) feel about or regard. ■ n. (**likes**) the things one likes.
– ORIGIN Old English *līcian* 'be pleasing', of Germanic origin.

-like ■ comb. form (added to nouns) similar to; characteristic of: *crust-like*.

likeable (also **likable**) ■ adj. pleasant; easy to like.
– DERIVATIVES **likeability** n. **likeableness** n. **likeably** adv.

likelihood ■ n. the state or fact of being likely.

likely ■ adj. (-ier, -iest) **1** such as well might happen or be true. **2** promising. ■ adv. probably.
– PHRASES **a likely story!** used to express disbelief. **as likely as not** probably. **not likely!** informal certainly not.
– DERIVATIVES **likeliness** n.
– ORIGIN Middle English: from Old Norse *líkligr*, from *líkr* (see LIKE¹).

like-minded ■ adj. having similar tastes or opinions.
– DERIVATIVES **like-mindedness** n.

liken ■ v. (**liken someone/thing to**) point out the resemblance of someone or something to.

likeness ■ n. resemblance. ▸ the semblance or outward appearance of. ▸ a portrait or representation.
– ORIGIN Old English *gelīcnes*.

likewise ■ adv. **1** also; moreover. **2** similarly.
– ORIGIN Middle English: from the phr. *in like wise*.

liking ■ n. **1** a regard or fondness for something. **2** one's taste.

lilac ■ n. **1** a shrub or small tree with fragrant violet, pink, or white blossom. [Genus *Syringa*: several species.] **2** a pale pinkish-violet colour.
– ORIGIN C17: from Persian *līlak*, var. of *nīlak* 'bluish', from *nīl* 'blue'.

lilangeni /ˌliːlænˈɡeɪni/ ■ n. (pl. **emalangeni** /ˌɪˌmalænˈɡeɪni/) the basic monetary unit of Swaziland, equal to 100 cents.
– ORIGIN from the Bantu prefix *li-* (denote sing.) + *-langeni* 'member of a royal family'.

Lilliputian /ˌlɪlɪˈpjuːʃ(ə)n/ ■ adj. trivial or very small. ■ n. a Lilliputian person or thing.
– ORIGIN C18: from the imaginary country of *Lilliput* in Jonathan Swift's *Gulliver's Travels* (1726), inhabited by 6-inch high people.

lilo /ˈlʌɪləʊ/ (also trademark **Li-lo**) ■ n. (pl. **-os**) an inflatable mattress used as a bed or for floating on water.
– ORIGIN 1930s: alteration of *lie low*.

lilt ■ n. a pleasant gentle accent. ▸ a gentle rhythm in a tune. ▸ archaic, chiefly Scottish a cheerful tune. ■ v. [often as adj. **lilting**] speak, sing, or sound with a lilt.
– ORIGIN Middle English *lulte* 'sound (an alarm)' or 'lift up (the voice)'.

lily ■ n. **1** a bulbous plant with large trumpet-shaped, typically fragrant, flowers on a tall, slender stem. [Genus *Lilium*: many species.] ▸ used in names of other similar plants, e.g. arum lily. **2** a heraldic fleur-de-lis.
– DERIVATIVES **lilied** adj.
– ORIGIN Old English, from Latin *lilium*, from Greek *leirion*.

lily-livered ■ adj. cowardly.

lily of the valley ■ n. a plant of the lily family, with broad leaves and fragrant white bell-shaped flowers. [Genus *Convallaria*.]

lily pad ■ n. a leaf of a water lily.

lily-trotter ■ n. (especially in Africa) a jacana.

lily-white ■ adj. **1** pure white. **2** totally innocent or immaculate.

Lima ■ n. a code word representing the letter L, used in radio communication.

lima bean /ˈliːmə/ ■ n. **1** an edible flat whitish bean. **2** the tropical American plant which yields this bean. [*Phaseolus lunatus*.]
– ORIGIN C18: from the name of the Peruvian capital *Lima*.

limb¹ ■ n. **1** an arm, leg, or wing. **2** a large branch of a tree. ▸ a branch of a cross. ▸ a projecting landform such as a spur of a mountain range. ▸ a projecting section of a building.
– PHRASES **life and limb** life and bodily faculties. **out on a limb 1** isolated. **2** in a position not supported by anyone else. **tear someone limb from limb** violently dismember someone.
– DERIVATIVES **-limbed** adj. **limbless** adj.
– ORIGIN Old English *lim*, of Germanic origin.

limb² ■ n. **1** Astronomy a specified edge of the disc of the sun, moon, or other celestial object. **2** Botany the blade or broad part of a leaf or petal. ▸ the spreading upper part of a tube-shaped flower. **3** the graduated arc of a quadrant or other scientific instrument.
– ORIGIN Middle English: from French *limbe* or Latin *limbus* 'hem, border'.

limber /ˈlɪmbə/ ■ adj. supple; flexible. ■ v. (often **limber up**) warm up in preparation for exercise or activity.
– DERIVATIVES **limberness** n.

limbic system /ˈlɪmbɪk/ ■ n. a complex system of nerves and networks in the brain, controlling the basic emotions and drives.
– ORIGIN C19: *limbic* from French *limbique*, from Latin *limbus* 'edge, border'.

limbo¹ ■ n. **1** (in some Christian beliefs) the supposed abode of the souls of unbaptized infants, and of the just who died before Christ. **2** an uncertain period of awaiting a decision or resolution: *he was left in limbo*.
– ORIGIN Middle English: from the medieval Latin phr. *in limbo*, from *limbus* 'border, limbo'.

limbo² ■ n. (pl. **-os**) a West Indian dance in which the dancer bends backwards to pass under a horizontal bar

which is progressively lowered toward the ground. ■ v. dance the limbo.
– ORIGIN 1950s: from **LIMBER**.

lime¹ ■ n. 1 quicklime, slaked lime, or any salt or alkali containing calcium. 2 archaic birdlime. ■ v. 1 treat with lime. 2 archaic catch (a bird) with birdlime.
– DERIVATIVES **limy** adj. (**-ier**, **-iest**).
– ORIGIN Old English *līm*, of Germanic origin.

lime² ■ n. 1 a rounded green citrus fruit similar to a lemon. ▸ a drink made from lime juice. 2 (also **lime tree**) the evergreen citrus tree which produces this fruit. [*Citrus aurantifolia*.] 3 a bright light green colour.
– DERIVATIVES **limey** adj.
– ORIGIN C17: from modern Provençal *limo*, Spanish *lima*, from Arabic *līma*.

lime³ (also **lime tree**) ■ n. another term for **LINDEN**.
– ORIGIN C17: from Old English *lind* (see **LINDEN**).

limeade ■ n. a drink made from lime juice sweetened with sugar.

limekiln ■ n. a kiln in which quicklime is produced.

limelight ■ n. 1 (**the limelight**) the focus of public attention. 2 an intense white light produced by heating lime in an oxyhydrogen flame, formerly used in theatres.

limerick /ˈlɪm(ə)rɪk/ ■ n. a humorous five-line poem with a rhyme scheme *aabba*.
– ORIGIN C19: said to be from the chorus 'will you come up to Limerick?', sung between improvised verses at a gathering.

limestone ■ n. a hard sedimentary rock composed mainly of calcium carbonate, used as building material and in cement.

lime sulphur ■ n. an insecticide and fungicide containing calcium polysulphides.

limewash ■ n. a mixture of lime and water for coating walls. ■ v. apply limewash to.

lime water ■ n. Chemistry an alkaline solution of calcium hydroxide in water.

Limey ■ n. (pl. **-eys**) chiefly derogatory a British person.
– ORIGIN C19: from **LIME²**, because of the former enforced consumption of lime juice in the British navy.

liminal /ˈlɪmɪn(ə)l/ ■ adj. technical 1 of or relating to a transitional or initial stage. 2 at a boundary or threshold.
– DERIVATIVES **liminality** n.
– ORIGIN C19: from Latin *limen* 'threshold'.

limit ■ n. 1 a point beyond which something does not or may not pass. ▸ a terminal point or boundary. ▸ the furthest extent of one's endurance. 2 a restriction on the size or amount of something: *an age limit*. 3 Mathematics a value which a sequence, function, or sum can be made to approach progressively. ■ v. (**limited**, **limiting**) set or serve as a limit to.
– PHRASES **be the limit** informal be intolerable. **off limits** out of bounds. **within limits** up to a point.
– DERIVATIVES **limitative** adj. **limiter** n.
– ORIGIN Middle English: from Latin *limes*, *limit-* 'boundary, frontier'; verb from Latin *limitare*.

limitation ■ n. 1 a restriction. ▸ a defect or failing. 2 (also **limitation period**) Law a legally specified period beyond which an action may be defeated or a property right is not to continue.

limited ■ adj. 1 restricted in size, amount, or extent. ▸ not great in ability. 2 (of a monarchy or government) exercised under limitations of power prescribed by a constitution. 3 (**Limited**) denoting a limited company.
– DERIVATIVES **limitedness** n.

limited company (also **limited liability company**) ■ n. a private company whose owners are legally responsible for its debts only to the extent of the amount of capital they invested.

limited liability ■ n. the condition of being legally responsible for the debts of a company only to the extent of the nominal value of their shares.

limitless ■ adj. without a limit; very large or extensive.
– DERIVATIVES **limitlessly** adv. **limitlessness** n.

limn /lɪm/ ■ v. poetic/literary depict or describe in painting or words. ▸ suffuse or highlight with bright colour or light.
– DERIVATIVES **limner** n.
– ORIGIN Middle English (in the sense 'illuminate a manuscript'): alteration of obsolete *lumine* 'illuminate', from Latin *luminare* 'make light'.

limnology /lɪmˈnɒlədʒi/ ■ n. the study of lakes and other bodies of fresh water.
– DERIVATIVES **limnological** adj. **limnologist** n.
– ORIGIN C19: from Greek *limnē* 'lake' + **-LOGY**.

limo ■ n. (pl. **-os**) informal a limousine.

limonite /ˈlʌɪmənʌɪt/ ■ n. a form of iron ore consisting of a brownish mixture of hydrous ferric oxides.
– ORIGIN C19: from German *Limonit*, prob. from Greek *leimōn* 'meadow'.

Limousin /ˈlɪmʊzæ̃/ ■ n. an animal of a French breed of beef cattle.

limousine /ˈlɪməziːn, ˌlɪməˈziːn/ ■ n. a large, luxurious car, typically with a partition behind the driver. ▸ chiefly N. Amer. a passenger vehicle carrying people to and from an airport.

HISTORY
Limousine entered English from French in the early 20th century and is derived from *Limousin*, a region in central France. The car acquired its name from a type of caped cloak worn by cart drivers in Limousin: early limousines had an outside driving seat and an enclosed passenger compartment, the roof of which was likened to the cart driver's cloak.

limp¹ ■ v. walk with difficulty because of an injured leg or foot. ▸ (of a damaged ship or aircraft) proceed with difficulty. ■ n. a limping gait.
– ORIGIN Middle English: rel. to obsolete *limphalt* 'lame', prob. of Germanic origin.

limp² ■ adj. 1 not stiff or firm. ▸ (of a book cover) not stiffened with board. 2 without energy or will.
– DERIVATIVES **limply** adv. **limpness** n.
– ORIGIN C18: perhaps rel. to **LIMP¹**.

limpet ■ n. a marine mollusc with a shallow conical shell and a broad muscular foot for clinging tightly to rocks. [Family Patellidae.]
– ORIGIN Old English *lempedu*, from medieval Latin *lampreda* 'limpet, lamprey'.

limpet mine ■ n. a mine that attaches magnetically to a ship's hull and explodes after a certain time.

limpid ■ adj. (of a liquid or the eyes) clear. ▸ (especially of writing or music) clear and accessible or melodious.
– DERIVATIVES **limpidity** n. **limpidly** adv.
– ORIGIN Middle English: from Latin *limpidus*; perhaps rel. to **LYMPH**.

limp-wristed ■ adj. informal effeminate.

linage /ˈlʌɪnɪdʒ/ ■ n. the number of lines in printed or written matter.

linchpin (also **lynchpin**) ■ n. 1 a pin through the end of an axle keeping a wheel in position. 2 an indispensable person or thing.
– ORIGIN Middle English: from Old English *lynis* 'linchpin' + **PIN**.

linctus /ˈlɪŋktəs/ ■ n. thick liquid medicine, especially cough mixture.
– ORIGIN C17: from Latin, from *lingere* 'to lick'.

lindane /ˈlɪndeɪn/ ■ n. a synthetic insecticide, now restricted in use owing to its persistence in the environment.
– ORIGIN 1940s: named after the Dutch chemist Teunis van der *Linden*.

linden ■ n. a deciduous tree with heart-shaped leaves and fragrant yellowish blossom. [Genus *Tilia*: many species.]
– ORIGIN Old English: from *lind* 'lime tree'.

line¹ ■ n. 1 a long, narrow mark or band. ▸ Mathematics a straight or curved continuous extent of length without breadth. ▸ a wrinkle in the skin. ▸ a contour or outline as a feature of design. ▸ a curve connecting all points having a common property on a map or graph. ▸ the starting or finishing point in a race. ▸ (**the Line**) the equator. ▸ a notional limit or boundary. ▸ Physics a narrow range of the spectrum that is noticeably brighter or darker than the adjacent parts. ▸ [as modifier] Printing & Computing denoting an

line

image consisting of lines and solid areas, with no gradation of tone. ▸ informal a dose of cocaine laid out in a line ready to be taken. ▸ each of (usually five) horizontal lines forming a stave in musical notation. ▸ a sequence of notes or tones forming a melody. **2** a length of cord, wire, etc. serving a purpose. ▸ a telephone connection. ▸ a railway track or route. ▸ a company providing a form of passenger transport on particular routes: *a shipping line*. **3** a row of written or printed words. ▸ (**lines**) the words of an actor's part. ▸ (**lines**) a number of repetitions of a sentence written out as a school punishment. **4** a row or connected series of people or things. ▸ chiefly N. Amer. a queue. ▸ a range of commercial goods. **5** a sphere of activity. ▸ a direction, course, or channel. ▸ (**lines**) a way of doing something: *thinking along the same lines*. ▸ a policy. ▸ informal a false or exaggerated story. **6** a connected series of military defences facing an enemy force. ▸ (also **line of battle**) a disposition of troops for action in battle. ▸ (**the line**) regular army regiments. ■ v. **1** stand or be positioned at intervals along. **2** (**line someone/thing up**) arrange people or things in a row. **3** (**line someone/thing up**) have someone or something prepared. **4** [usu. as adj. **lined**] mark or cover with lines. –PHRASES **above** (or **below**) **the line** Finance denoting or relating to money spent on items of current (or capital) expenditure. **come** (or **bring**) **into line** conform (or cause to conform). **the end of the line** the point at which one can go no further. **get a line on** informal learn something about. **in line** under control. **in line for** likely to receive. **in the line of duty** while one is working or serving in a military force. **in** (or **out of**) **line with** (in or not in) alignment or accordance with. **lay** (or **put**) **it on the line** speak frankly. **line of credit** an amount of credit extended to a borrower. **line of fire** the expected path of gunfire or a missile. **line of force** an imaginary line representing the strength and direction of a magnetic, gravitational, or electric field at any point. **line of march** the route taken in marching. **line of scrimmage** American Football the imaginary line separating the teams at the beginning of a play. **line of sight** a straight line along which an observer has unobstructed vision. **line of vision** the straight line along which an observer looks. **on the line 1** at serious risk. **2** (of a picture) hung with its centre about level with the spectator's eye. **out of line** informal behaving inappropriately or incorrectly.
–ORIGIN Old English *līne* 'rope, series', prob. of Germanic origin, from Latin *linea* (*fibra*) 'flax (fibre)', from Latin *linum* 'flax', reinforced in Middle English by Old French *ligne*.

line² ■ v. cover the inner surface of (something) with a layer of different material. ▸ cover as if with a lining. ▸ informal fill (one's stomach).
–ORIGIN Middle English: from obsolete *line* 'flax', with ref. to the use of linen for linings.

lineage /ˈlɪnɪdʒ/ ■ n. ancestry or pedigree.
–ORIGIN Middle English: from Old French *lignage*, from Latin *linea* (see LINE¹).

lineal /ˈlɪnɪəl/ ■ adj. **1** in a direct line of descent or ancestry. **2** linear.
–DERIVATIVES **lineally** adv.
–ORIGIN Middle English: from late Latin *linealis*, from *linea* (see LINE¹).

lineament /ˈlɪnɪəm(ə)nt/ ■ n. **1** poetic/literary a distinctive feature, especially of the face. **2** Geology a linear feature on the earth's surface.
–ORIGIN Middle English: from Latin, from *lineare* 'make straight', from *linea* (see LINE¹).

linear /ˈlɪnɪə/ ■ adj. **1** arranged in or extending along a straight line. ▸ consisting of lines or outlines. ▸ involving one dimension only. **2** sequential. **3** Mathematics able to be represented by a straight line on a graph. ▸ involving directly proportional change in two related quantities.
–DERIVATIVES **linearity** n. **linearization** (also **-isation**) n. **linearize** (also **-ise**) v. **linearly** adv.
–ORIGIN C17: from Latin *linearis*, from *linea* (see LINE¹).

linear equation ■ n. an equation between two variables that gives a straight line when plotted on a graph.

linear programming ■ n. a mathematical technique for maximizing or minimizing a linear function of several variables.

lineation /ˌlɪnɪˈeɪʃ(ə)n/ ■ n. the action of drawing lines or marking with lines. ▸ a line or linear marking.

linebacker ■ n. American Football a defensive player positioned just behind the line of scrimmage.

line dancing ■ n. a type of country and western dancing in which a line of dancers follow a choreographed pattern of steps.
–DERIVATIVES **line-dance** v. **line dancer** n.

line drawing ■ n. a drawing consisting only of lines.

line drive ■ n. Baseball a powerfully struck shot that travels along or close to the ground.

linefeed ■ n. the advancing of paper in a printing machine by the space of one line. ▸ Computing the analogous movement of text on a VDU screen.

linefish ■ n. S. African a marine fish caught from the shore or with a line from a boat, to be eaten as food.

line function ■ n. each of a set of functions defining the managerial authority and responsibilities associated with specific tasks or jobs, used to control an organization's activities.

lineman ■ n. (pl. **-men**) **1** a person who lays and maintains railway tracks. ▸ North American term for LINESMAN (in sense 2). **2** American Football a player on the line of scrimmage.

line manager ■ n. a manager to whom an employee is directly responsible.
–DERIVATIVES **line management** n.

linen ■ n. cloth woven from flax. ▸ articles such as sheets or clothes made, or originally made, of linen.
–ORIGIN Old English *līnen* 'made of flax', of West Germanic origin.

linen basket ■ n. chiefly Brit. a basket for soiled clothing.

line-out ■ n. Rugby a formation of parallel lines of opposing forwards at right angles to the touchline when the ball is thrown in.

line printer ■ n. a machine that prints computer output a line at a time rather than character by character.

liner¹ ■ n. **1** a large passenger ship of a type formerly used on a regular line. **2** a fine paintbrush. ▸ a cosmetic for outlining or accentuating a facial feature. **3** a boat engaged in sea fishing with lines.

liner² ■ n. a lining of a garment, container, etc.

-liner ■ comb. form informal denoting a text of a specified number of lines: *two-liner*.

liner note ■ n. text printed on the paper insert of a compact disc or on the sleeve of a gramophone record.

linesman ■ n. (pl. **-men**) **1** (in games played on a field or court) an official who assists the referee or umpire, especially in deciding whether the ball is out of play. **2** a person who repairs and maintains telephone or electricity power lines.

line-up ■ n. **1** a group of people or things assembled for a particular purpose. **2** an identity parade.

ling ■ n. the common heather. [*Calluna vulgaris*.]
–ORIGIN Middle English: from Old Norse *lyng*.

-ling ■ suffix **1** forming nouns from nouns (e.g. *hireling*, *sapling*). **2** forming nouns from adjectives and adverbs (e.g. *darling*, *underling*). **3** forming diminutive nouns: *gosling*. ▸ with depreciatory reference: *princeling*.
–ORIGIN Old English; sense 3 from Old Norse.

Lingala /lɪŋˈɡɑːlə/ ■ n. a Bantu language used as a lingua franca in Congo and the Democratic Republic of Congo.
–ORIGIN the name in Lingala.

lingam /ˈlɪŋɡəm/ (also **linga** /ˈlɪŋɡə/) ■ n. Hinduism a phallus or phallic object as a symbol of Shiva.
–ORIGIN from Sanskrit *liṅga* 'mark, (sexual) characteristic'.

linger ■ v. be slow or reluctant to leave. ▸ (**linger over**) spend a long time over. ▸ be slow to disappear or die.
–DERIVATIVES **lingerer** n. **lingering** adj. **lingeringly** adv.
–ORIGIN Middle English: from obsolete *leng* 'prolong', of Germanic origin.

lingerie /ˈlãʒ(ə)ri/ ■ n. women's underwear and night-clothes.
–ORIGIN C19: from French, from *linge* 'linen'.

lingo ■ n. (pl. **-os** or **-oes**) informal, often humorous a foreign language. ▸ the jargon of a particular subject or group.
– ORIGIN C17: prob. via Portuguese *lingoa* from Latin *lingua* 'tongue'.

lingua franca /ˌlɪŋgwə ˈfraŋkə/ ■ n. (pl. **lingua francas**) **1** a language used as a common language between speakers whose native languages are different. **2** historical a mixture of Italian with French, Greek, Arabic, and Spanish, formerly used in the eastern Mediterranean.
– ORIGIN C17: from Italian, 'Frankish tongue'.

lingual /ˈlɪŋgw(ə)l/ ■ adj. technical **1** of, relating to, or near the tongue. ▸ (of a sound) formed by the tongue. **2** of or relating to speech or language.
– DERIVATIVES **lingually** adv.
– ORIGIN C17: from medieval Latin *lingualis*, from Latin *lingua* 'tongue, language'.

linguine /lɪŋˈgwiːneɪ, -ni/ ■ pl. n. small ribbons of pasta.
– ORIGIN Italian, pl. of *linguina*, diminutive of *lingua* 'tongue'.

linguist ■ n. **1** a person skilled in foreign languages. **2** a person who studies linguistics.
– ORIGIN C16: from Latin *lingua* 'language'.

linguistic ■ adj. of or relating to language or linguistics.
– DERIVATIVES **linguistically** adv.

linguistics /lɪŋˈgwɪstɪks/ ■ pl. n. [treated as sing.] the scientific study of language and its structure.

lingulate /ˈlɪŋɡjʊleɪt/ ■ adj. Botany & Zoology tongue-shaped.
– ORIGIN C19: from Latin *lingulatus*, from *lingua* 'tongue'.

liniment /ˈlɪnɪm(ə)nt/ ■ n. an embrocation, especially one made with oil.
– ORIGIN Middle English: from late Latin *linimentum*, from Latin *linire* 'to smear'.

lining ■ n. a layer of different material covering or attached to the inside of something.

link ■ n. **1** a relationship or connection between people or things. ▸ something that enables communication between people. ▸ a means of contact or transport between two places. ▸ Computing a code or instruction connecting one part of a program or an element in a list to another. **2** a loop in a chain. ▸ ■ v. make, form, or suggest a link with or between. ▸ join physically. ▸ clasp; intertwine.
– DERIVATIVES **linker** n.
– ORIGIN Middle English: from Old Norse *hlekkr*, of Germanic origin.

linkage ■ n. **1** the action of linking or the state of being linked. ▸ a system of links. **2** Genetics the tendency of groups of genes on the same chromosome to be inherited together.

linking ■ adj. connecting or joining two things. ▸ Phonetics denoting a consonant that is sounded at a boundary where two vowels would otherwise be adjacent, as in *law(r) and order*.

linkman ■ n. (pl. **-men**) **1** a person serving as a connection between others. **2** Brit. a person providing continuity between items on radio or television.

links (also **golf links**) ■ pl. n. [treated as sing. or pl.] a golf course, especially one on sandy ground near the sea.
– ORIGIN Old English *hlinc* 'rising ground'.

link-up ■ n. an instance of two or more people or things linking. ▸ a connection enabling people or machines to communicate with each other.

Linnaean /lɪˈniːən/ (also **Linnean**) ■ adj. of or relating to the Swedish botanist Linnaeus (Latinized name of Carl von Linné) (1707–78) or his system of binomial nomenclature in the classification of animals and plants. ■ n. a follower of Linnaeus.

linnet ■ n. a mainly brown and grey finch with a reddish breast and forehead. [Genus *Acanthis*: three species.]
– ORIGIN C16: from Old French *linette*, from *lin* 'flax' (because the bird feeds on flaxseeds).

lino ■ n. (pl. **-os**) informal linoleum.

linocut ■ n. a design carved in relief on a block of linoleum, used for printing.
– DERIVATIVES **linocutting** n.

linoleic acid /ˌlɪnə(ʊ)ˈliːɪk, -ˈleɪk/ ■ n. Chemistry a polyunsaturated fatty acid present in linseed oil and other oils and essential in the human diet.
– DERIVATIVES **linoleate** n.
– ORIGIN C19: from Latin *linum* 'flax' + *oleic acid*, denoting an unsaturated fatty acid found in fats and soaps, from Latin *oleum* 'oil'.

linoleum /lɪˈnəʊlɪəm/ ■ n. a material consisting of a canvas backing thickly coated with a preparation of linseed oil and powdered cork, used as a floor covering.
– DERIVATIVES **linoleumed** adj.
– ORIGIN C19: from Latin *linum* 'flax' + *oleum* 'oil'.

linseed ■ n. the seeds of the flax plant.
– ORIGIN Old English *līnsǣd*, from *līn* 'flax' + *sǣd* 'seed'.

linseed cake ■ n. pressed linseed used as cattle food.

linseed oil ■ n. oil extracted from linseed, used especially in paint and varnish.

lint ■ n. **1** short, fine fibres which separate from cloth or yarn during processing. ▸ the fibrous material of a cotton boll. **2** a fabric with a raised nap on one side, used for dressing wounds.
– DERIVATIVES **linty** adj.
– ORIGIN Middle English *lynnet* 'flax prepared for spinning', perhaps from Old French *linette* 'linseed', from *lin* 'flax'.

lintel ■ n. a horizontal support across the top of a door or window.
– DERIVATIVES **lintelled** (US **linteled**) adj.
– ORIGIN Middle English: from late Latin *liminare*, from Latin *limen* 'threshold'.

Linux /ˈlɪnʌks, ˈlaɪnʌks/ ■ n. Computing (trademark in the US) an operating system modelled on Unix, whose source code is publicly available at no charge.
– ORIGIN 1990s: from the name of the Finnish software engineer *Linus* Benedict Torvalds, who wrote the first version, + *-x*, as in *Unix*.

liny ■ adj. (**-ier**, **-iest**) informal marked with lines.

lion ■ n. **1** a large tawny-coloured cat of Africa and NW India, of which the male has a shaggy mane. [*Panthera leo*.] **2** a brave, strong, or fierce person.
– PHRASES **the lion's den** an intimidating or unpleasant place. **the lion's share** the largest part of something.
– DERIVATIVES **lioness** n. **lion-like** adj.
– ORIGIN Middle English: from Anglo-Norman French *liun*, from Latin *leo*, from Greek *leōn*.

lion-hearted ■ adj. brave and determined.

lionize /ˈlaɪənaɪz/ (also **-ise**) ■ v. treat as a celebrity.
– DERIVATIVES **lionization** (also **-isation**) n.

lip ■ n. **1** either of the two fleshy parts forming the edges of the mouth opening. ▸ another term for **LABIUM** (in sense 1). **2** the edge of a hollow container or an opening. **3** informal impudent talk. ■ v. (**lipped**, **lipping**) **1** (of water) lap against. **2** Golf (of the ball) hit the rim of (a hole) but fail to go in.
– PHRASES **bite one's lip** stifle laughter or a retort. **curl one's lip** sneer. **pass one's lips** be eaten, drunk, or spoken. **pay lip service to** express approval or support for insincerely.
– DERIVATIVES **lipless** adj. **lip-like** adj. **-lipped** adj.
– ORIGIN Old English *lippa*, of Germanic origin.

lipase /ˈlɪpeɪz, ˈlaɪp-/ ■ n. Biochemistry a pancreatic enzyme that promotes the breakdown of fats.
– ORIGIN C19: from Greek *lipos* 'fat'.

lipgloss ■ n. a glossy cosmetic applied to the lips.

lipid ■ n. Chemistry any of a class of fatty acids or their derivatives that are insoluble in water and include many natural oils, waxes, and steroids.
– ORIGIN C20: from French *lipide*, from Greek *lipos* 'fat'.

Lipizzaner /ˌlɪpɪˈtsɑːnə, ˌlɪpɪˈzeɪnə/ ■ n. a horse of a white breed used especially in dressage.
– ORIGIN C20: from German, from *Lippiza*, site of the former Austrian Imperial stud near Trieste.

lipline ■ n. the outline of the lips.

lipliner ■ n. a cosmetic applied to the outline of the lips.

lipo- /ˈlɪpəʊ, ˈlaɪpəʊ/ ■ comb. form relating to fat or other lipids: *liposuction*.
– ORIGIN from Greek *lipos* 'fat'.

lipogenesis /ˌlɪpə(ʊ)ˈdʒɛnɪsɪs, ˌlʌɪ-/ ■ n. Physiology the metabolic formation of fat.
– DERIVATIVES **lipogenic** adj.

lipolysis /lɪˈpɒlɪsɪs/ ■ n. Physiology the breakdown of lipids by hydrolysis.
– DERIVATIVES **lipolytic** adj.

lipoma /lɪˈpəʊmə/ ■ n. (pl. **lipomas** or **lipomata** /-mətə/) Medicine a benign tumour of fatty tissue.

lipoprotein ■ n. Biochemistry a soluble protein that combines with and transports lipids in the blood.

liposome /ˈlɪpəsəʊm, ˈlaɪ-/ ■ n. Biochemistry a minute artificial spherical sac of phospholipid molecules enclosing a water droplet, used to carry drugs or other substances into the tissues.

liposuction /ˈlɪpə(ʊ)ˌsʌkʃ(ə)n, ˈlaɪ-/ ■ n. a technique in cosmetic surgery for removing excess fat from under the skin by suction.

lippy informal ■ adj. (**-ier**, **-iest**) impertinent. ■ n. (also **lippie**) (pl. **-ies**) lipstick.

lip-read ■ v. understand speech from observing a speaker's lip movements.
– DERIVATIVES **lip-reader** n.

lipsalve ■ n. a preparation to prevent or relieve sore lips.

lipstick ■ n. coloured cosmetic applied to the lips from a small solid stick.

lip-sync (also **-synch**) ■ n. the movement of a performer's lips in synchronization with a pre-recorded soundtrack. ■ v. perform (a song or speech) in this way.
– DERIVATIVES **lip-syncer** n.

liquate /lɪˈkweɪt/ ■ v. Metallurgy separate or purify (a metal) by melting it.
– DERIVATIVES **liquation** n.
– ORIGIN C19: from Latin *liquare* 'make liquid'.

liquefy /ˈlɪkwɪfaɪ/ (also **liquify**) ■ v. (**-ies**, **-ied**) make or become liquid.
– DERIVATIVES **liquefaction** n. **liquefactive** adj. **liquefiable** adj. **liquefier** n.
– ORIGIN Middle English: from French *liquéfier* from Latin *liquefacere* 'make liquid', from *liquere* 'be liquid'.

liquescent /lɪˈkwɛs(ə)nt/ ■ adj. poetic/literary becoming or apt to become liquid.

liqueur /lɪˈkjʊə/ ■ n. a strong, sweet flavoured alcoholic spirit.
– ORIGIN C18: from French, 'liquor'.

liquid ■ adj. **1** having a consistency like that of water or oil, i.e. flowing freely but of constant volume. ▸ having the translucence of water. ▸ denoting a gas that has been liquefied. **2** not fixed or stable. **3** (of a sound) clear and flowing. **4** (of assets) held in or easily converted into cash. ▸ having ready cash or liquid assets. ■ n. a liquid substance.
– DERIVATIVES **liquidly** adv. **liquidness** n.
– ORIGIN Middle English: from Latin *liquidus*, from *liquere* 'be liquid'.

liquidambar /ˌlɪkwɪdˈambə/ ■ n. **1** a North American or Asian tree with maple-like leaves. [Genus *Liquidambar*: several species.] **2** liquid balsam obtained from such a tree, used medicinally and in perfume.
– ORIGIN C16: from Latin *liquidus* 'liquid' + medieval Latin *ambar* 'amber'.

liquidate ■ v. **1** wind up the affairs of (a company) by ascertaining liabilities and apportioning assets. ▸ convert (assets) into cash. ▸ pay off (a debt). **2** informal eliminate; kill.
– DERIVATIVES **liquidation** n. **liquidator** n.
– ORIGIN C16 (set out (accounts) clearly): from medieval Latin *liquidare* 'make clear', from Latin *liquidus* (see LIQUID).

liquid crystal ■ n. a liquid with some degree of ordering in the arrangement of its molecules.

liquid crystal display ■ n. an electronic visual display in which the application of an electric current to a liquid crystal layer makes it opaque.

liquidity /lɪˈkwɪdɪti/ ■ n. Finance the availability of liquid assets to a market or company. ▸ liquid assets.

liquidize (also **-ise**) ■ v. convert (solid food) into a liquid or purée.

liquidizer (also **-iser**) ■ n. a machine for liquidizing.

liquid measure ■ n. a unit for measuring the volume of liquids.

liquid paraffin ■ n. a colourless, odourless oily liquid obtained from petroleum, used as a laxative.

liquify ■ v. variant spelling of LIQUEFY.

liquor /ˈlɪkə/ ■ n. **1** alcoholic drink, especially spirits. **2** water used in brewing. **3** liquid that has been produced in or used for cooking. **4** the liquid from which a substance has been crystallized or extracted. ■ v. **1** dress (leather) with grease or oil. **2** steep in water.
– ORIGIN Middle English: from Latin *liquor*; rel. to *liquare* 'liquefy', *liquere* 'be fluid'.

liquorice /ˈlɪk(ə)rɪs, -rɪʃ/ (US **licorice**) ■ n. **1** a sweet, chewy, aromatic black substance made from the juice of a root and used as a sweet and in medicine. **2** a leguminous plant from which liquorice is obtained. [Genus *Glycyrrhiza*; many species.]
– ORIGIN Middle English: from Old French *licoresse*, from late Latin *liquiritia*, from Greek *glukurrhiza*, from *glukus* 'sweet' + *rhiza* 'root'.

lira /ˈlɪərə/ ■ n. (pl. **lire** /ˈlɪərə, ˈlɪəreɪ, ˈlɪəri/) the basic monetary unit of Turkey and formerly of Italy.
– ORIGIN Italian, from Provençal *liura*, from Latin *libra* 'pound'.

lisente plural form of SENTE.

lisle /laɪl/ ■ n. a fine, smooth cotton thread used for stockings.
– ORIGIN C16: from *Lisle*, former spelling of *Lille*, a city in northern France where lisle was orig. made.

lisp ■ n. a speech defect in which *s* is pronounced like *th* in *thick* and *z* is pronounced like *th* in *this*. ■ v. speak with a lisp.
– DERIVATIVES **lisper** n. **lisping** n. & adj. **lispingly** adv.
– ORIGIN Old English *wlispian*, from *wlisp* (adj.) 'lisping', of imitative origin.

lissom (also **lissome**) ■ adj. slim, supple, and graceful.
– DERIVATIVES **lissomness** n.
– ORIGIN C18: contraction from LITHE + -SOME¹.

list¹ ■ n. **1** a number of connected items or names written consecutively. **2** (**lists**) historical palisades enclosing an area for a tournament. ▸ the scene of a contest. ■ v. **1** make a list of. ▸ include in a list. **2** archaic enlist for military service.
– PHRASES **enter the lists** issue or accept a challenge.
– DERIVATIVES **listable** adj.
– ORIGIN Old English *liste* ' a border or edging', of Germanic origin; sense 2 from Old French *lisse*.

list² ■ v. (of a ship) lean over to one side. ■ n. an instance of listing.
– ORIGIN C17.

list³ archaic ■ v. want; like. ■ n. desire; inclination.
– ORIGIN Old English *lystan* (v.), of Germanic origin, from a base meaning 'pleasure'.

listed ■ adj. **1** denoting companies whose shares are quoted on the main market of a stock exchange. **2** (of a building in the UK) officially designated as being of historical importance and so protected.

listen ■ v. give one's attention to a sound. ▸ respond to advice or a request. ▸ make an effort to hear something. ▸ (**listen in**) listen to a private conversation. ▸ (**listen in**) listen to a radio broadcast. ■ n. an act of listening.
– DERIVATIVES **listener** n.
– ORIGIN Old English *hlysnan* 'pay attention to', of Germanic origin.

listenable ■ adj. easy or pleasant to listen to.
– DERIVATIVES **listenability** n.

listening post ■ n. a station for intercepting electronic communications. ▸ a point near enemy lines for detecting movements by sound.

listeria /lɪˈstɪərɪə/ ■ n. a type of bacterium which infects humans and other animals through contaminated food.
– ORIGIN 1940s: named after the English surgeon Joseph Lister.

listeriosis /lɪˌstɪərɪˈəʊsɪs/ ■ n. disease caused by infection with listeria, which can resemble influenza or meningitis and may cause miscarriage.

listing ■ n. a list or catalogue. ▸ an entry in a list.

listless ▪ adj. lacking energy or enthusiasm.
– DERIVATIVES **listlessly** adv. **listlessness** n.
– ORIGIN Middle English: from LIST³.

list price ▪ n. the price of an article as listed by the manufacturer.

LISTSERV ▪ n. trademark an electronic mailing list of people who wish to receive specified information from the Internet.

list system ▪ n. a system of voting in which votes are cast for a list of candidates to allow a degree of proportional representation.

lit past and past participle of LIGHT¹, LIGHT³.

litany /'lɪt(ə)ni/ ▪ n. (pl. **-ies**) **1** a series of petitions used in church services, usually recited by the clergy and responded to by the people. ▸ **(the Litany)** such petitions in the Book of Common Prayer. **2** a tedious recital.
– ORIGIN Middle English: from Old French *letanie*, from Greek *litaneia* 'prayer', from *litē* 'supplication'.

litchi ▪ n. variant spelling of LYCHEE.

lite ▪ adj. of or relating to low-fat or low-sugar versions of food or drink products.
– ORIGIN 1950s: a deliberate respelling of LIGHT².

-lite ▪ suffix forming names of rocks, minerals, and fossils: *rhyolite*.
– ORIGIN from Greek *lithos* 'stone'.

liter ▪ n. US spelling of LITRE.

literacy ▪ n. **1** the ability to read and write. **2** competence or knowledge in a specified area: *computer literacy*.
– ORIGIN C19: from LITERATE, on the pattern of *illiteracy*.

literal ▪ adj. **1** taking words in their usual or most basic sense without metaphor or allegory. ▸ free from distortion. ▸ informal absolute. **2** (of a translation) representing the exact words of the original text. **3** lacking imagination. **4** of, in, or expressed by a letter of the alphabet. ▪ n. Printing a misprint of a letter.
– DERIVATIVES **literality** n. **literalize** (also **-ise**) v. **literalness** n.
– ORIGIN Middle English: from late Latin *litteralis*, from Latin *littera* (see LETTER).

literalism ▪ n. the literal interpretation of words.
– DERIVATIVES **literalist** n. **literalistic** adj.

literally ▪ adv. in a literal manner or sense. ▸ informal used for emphasis while not being literally true: *we were literally killing ourselves laughing*.

literary ▪ adj. **1** concerning the writing, study, or content of literature, especially of the kind valued for quality of form. ▸ concerned with literature as a profession. **2** associated with literary works or formal writing.
– DERIVATIVES **literarily** adv. **literariness** n.
– ORIGIN C17: from Latin *litterarius*, from *littera* (see LETTER).

literary criticism ▪ n. the art or practice of judging the qualities and character of literary works.
– DERIVATIVES **literary critic** n.

literary executor ▪ n. a person entrusted with a dead writer's papers and works.

literary history ▪ n. the history of the treatment of a subject in literature.
– DERIVATIVES **literary historian** n.

literate ▪ adj. able to read and write. ▸ educated or knowledgeable: *politically literate*. ▪ n. a literate person.
– DERIVATIVES **literately** adv.
– ORIGIN Middle English: from Latin *litteratus*, from *littera* (see LETTER).

literati /ˌlɪtəˈrɑːti/ ▪ pl. n. educated people who are interested in literature.
– ORIGIN C17: from Latin, pl. of *literatus* 'acquainted with letters', from *littera* (see LETTER).

literature ▪ n. written works, especially those regarded as having artistic merit. ▸ books and writings on a particular subject. ▸ leaflets and other material used in advertising or to give advice.
– ORIGIN Middle English: from Latin *litteratura*, from *littera* (see LETTER).

-lith ▪ suffix denoting types of stone: *monolith*.
– ORIGIN from Greek *lithos* 'stone'.

lithe ▪ adj. slim, supple, and graceful.
– DERIVATIVES **lithely** adv. **litheness** n.

– ORIGIN Old English *līthe* 'gentle, meek', also 'mellow', of Germanic origin.

lithesome ▪ adj. poetic/literary lithe.

lithiasis /lɪˈθaɪəsɪs/ ▪ n. Medicine the formation of stones in an internal organ such as the kidney or gall bladder.
– ORIGIN C17: from Greek *lithos* 'stone'.

lithic /'lɪθɪk/ ▪ adj. chiefly Archaeology & Geology of, like, or relating to stone.
– ORIGIN C18: from Greek *lithikos*, from *lithos* 'stone'.

lithify /'lɪθɪfʌɪ/ ▪ v. (**-ies**, **-ied**) chiefly Geology transform into stone.
– DERIVATIVES **lithification** n.
– ORIGIN C19: from Greek *lithos* 'stone'.

lithium /'lɪθɪəm/ ▪ n. **1** the chemical element of atomic number 3, the lightest of the alkali metals. (Symbol: **Li**) **2** a lithium salt used as a mood-stabilizing drug.
– ORIGIN C19: from Greek *litheios*, from *lithos* 'stone'.

litho /'lʌɪθəʊ, 'lɪθ-/ ▪ n. (pl. **-os**) short for LITHOGRAPHY or LITHOGRAPH.

litho- ▪ comb. form **1** of or relating to stone: *lithosol*. **2** relating to a calculus: *lithotomy*.
– ORIGIN from Greek *lithos* 'stone'.

lithograph /'lɪθəɡrɑːf, 'lʌɪ-/ ▪ n. a print made by lithography. ▪ v. print by lithography.
– DERIVATIVES **lithographic** adj. **lithographically** adv.

lithography /lɪˈθɒɡrəfi/ ▪ n. **1** the process of printing from a flat metal, formerly stone, surface treated so as to repel the ink except where it is required for printing. **2** Electronics an analogous method for making printed circuits.
– DERIVATIVES **lithographer** n.

lithology /lɪˈθɒlədʒi/ ▪ n. the study of the physical characteristics of rocks.
– DERIVATIVES **lithological** adj.

lithophyte /'lɪθə(ʊ)fʌɪt, 'lʌɪ-/ ▪ n. Botany a plant that grows on bare rock or stone.

lithops /'lɪθɒps/ ▪ n. a plant of a genus of southern African succulents with two fleshy lobe-like leaves that resemble stones. [Genus *Lithops*.]
– ORIGIN C20: modern Latin, from Greek *lith-* 'stone' + *ops-* 'face'.

lithosphere /'lɪθəsfɪə/ ▪ n. Geology the rigid outer part of the earth, consisting of the crust and upper mantle.
– DERIVATIVES **lithospheric** adj.

lithotomy /lɪˈθɒtəmi/ ▪ n. surgical removal of a calculus (stone) from the bladder, kidney, or urinary tract.
– ORIGIN C17: from Greek *lithotomia* (see LITHO-, -TOMY).

lithotripsy /'lɪθəˌtrɪpsi/ ▪ n. Surgery a treatment using ultrasound to shatter a urinary calculus so that it can be passed out by the body.
– DERIVATIVES **lithotripter** (also **lithotriptor**) n. **lithotriptic** adj.
– ORIGIN C19: from LITHO- + Greek *tripsis* 'rubbing'.

Lithuanian ▪ n. **1** a native or citizen of Lithuania, or a person of Lithuanian descent. **2** the Baltic language of Lithuania. ▪ adj. of or relating to Lithuania, its people, or its language.

litigate /'lɪtɪɡeɪt/ ▪ v. go to law; be a party to a lawsuit. ▸ take (a dispute) to a law court.
– DERIVATIVES **litigant** n. **litigation** n. **litigator** n.
– ORIGIN C17 (*litigation* C16): from Latin *litigare* 'to dispute in a lawsuit', from *lis*, *lit-* 'lawsuit'.

litigious /lɪˈtɪdʒəs/ ▪ adj. tending to go to law to settle disputes. ▸ concerned with or disputable by litigation.
– DERIVATIVES **litigiously** adv. **litigiousness** n.
– ORIGIN Middle English: from Latin *litigiosus*, from *litigium* 'litigation', from *lis*, *lit-* 'lawsuit'.

litmus /'lɪtməs/ ▪ n. a dye obtained from certain lichens that is red under acid conditions and blue under alkaline conditions.
– ORIGIN Middle English: from Old Norse *lit-mosi*, from *litr* 'dye' + *mosi* 'moss'.

litmus paper ▪ n. paper stained with litmus, used as a test for acids or alkalis.

litmus test

litmus test ▪ n. **1** Chemistry a test using litmus. **2** a decisively indicative test.

litotes /laɪˈtəʊtiːz/ ▪ n. ironical understatement in which an affirmative is expressed by the negative of its contrary (e.g. *I shan't be sorry* for *I shall be glad*).
– ORIGIN C16: from Greek *litotēs*, from *litos* 'plain, meagre'.

litre (US **liter**) /ˈliːtə/ (abbrev.: **l**) ▪ n. a metric unit of capacity, formerly the volume of one kilogram of water under standard conditions, now equal to 1 000 cubic centimetres (about 1.75 pints).
– DERIVATIVES **litreage** /ˈliːt(ə)rɪdʒ/ n.
– ORIGIN C18: from French *litron* (an obsolete measure of capacity), from Greek *litra*, a Sicilian monetary unit.

LittD ▪ abbrev. Doctor of Letters.
– ORIGIN from Latin *Litterarum Doctor*.

litter ▪ n. **1** rubbish left in an open or public place. ▸ an untidy collection of things. **2** a number of young born to an animal at one time. **3** (also **cat litter**) granular absorbent material lining a tray for a cat to urinate and defecate in indoors. **4** straw or other plant matter used as animal bedding. **5** (also **leaf litter**) decomposing leaves and other matter forming a layer on top of soil. **6** historical a vehicle containing a bed or seat enclosed by curtains and carried by men or animals. ▸ a framework with a couch for transporting the sick. ▪ v. make untidy with discarded articles. ▸ (usu. **be littered with**) leave (rubbish or objects) lying about untidily.
– ORIGIN Middle English: from Old French *litiere*, from medieval Latin *lectaria*, from Latin *lectus* 'bed'.

litterbug (also **litter lout**) ▪ n. informal a person who carelessly drops litter.

little ▪ adj. small in size, amount, or degree. ▸ (of a person) young or younger: *my little brother*. ▸ denoting something that is the smaller or smallest of those so named. ▸ of short distance or duration. ▸ trivial, unimportant, or humble. ▪ det. & pron. **1** (**a little**) a small amount of. ▸ a short time or distance. **2** not much. ▪ adv. (**less**, **least**) **1** (**a little**) to a small extent. **2** hardly or not at all.
– PHRASES **little by little** gradually. **little or nothing** hardly anything. **no little** considerable. **not a little** a great deal (of). ▸ very.
– DERIVATIVES **littleness** n.
– ORIGIN Old English *lȳtel*, of Germanic origin.

little end ▪ n. Mechanics the smaller end of a connecting rod, attached to the piston.

Little Englander ▪ n. informal a person opposed to an international role or policy for Britain.

little finger ▪ n. the smallest finger, at the outer side of the hand.
– PHRASES **twist** (or **wind** or **wrap**) someone around one's little finger be able to make someone do whatever one wants.

little grebe ▪ n. a small grebe with a short neck and bill and a trilling call. [*Tachybaptus ruficollis*.]

little green man ▪ n. informal an imaginary being from outer space.

Little League ▪ n. organized baseball for children aged 8–12.

little ones ▪ pl. n. young children.

little people ▪ pl. n. **1** the ordinary people of a country or organization. **2** fairies or leprechauns.

little toe ▪ n. the smallest toe, on the outer side of the foot.

littoral /ˈlɪt(ə)r(ə)l/ ▪ adj. of, relating to, or on the shore of the sea or a lake. ▪ n. a littoral region.
– ORIGIN C17: from Latin *littoralis*, from *litus* 'shore'.

liturgical /lɪˈtəːdʒɪk(ə)l/ ▪ adj. of or related to liturgy or public worship.
– DERIVATIVES **liturgically** adv. **liturgist** /ˈlɪtədʒɪst/ n.

liturgy /ˈlɪtədʒi/ ▪ n. (pl. **-ies**) a form according to which public religious worship, especially Christian worship, is conducted. ▸ (**the Liturgy**) the Communion office of the Orthodox Church.
– ORIGIN C16: from Greek *leitourgia* 'public service, worship of the gods'.

livable ▪ adj. variant spelling of LIVEABLE.

live¹ /lɪv/ ▪ v. **1** remain alive. ▸ be alive at a specified time. ▸ spend one's life in a particular way. ▸ supply oneself with the means of subsistence. **2** make one's home in a particular place or with a particular person. **3** survive in someone's mind: *her name lived on*.
– PHRASES **live and breathe** be devoted to a subject or activity. **live in the past** have outdated ideas and attitudes. **live it up** informal lead a life of extravagance and exciting social activity. **live rough** live outdoors as a result of being homeless. **live with oneself** be able to retain one's self-respect as a consequence of one's actions. **long ——!** said to express loyalty or support for a specified person or thing.
– PHRASAL VERBS **live something down** [usu. with neg.] succeed in making others forget something embarrassing. **live for** regard as the most important aspect of one's life. **live in** (or **out**) (of an employee or student) reside at (or away from) the place where one works or studies. **live off** (or **on**) depend on as a source of income or support. ▸ have (a particular amount of money) with which to buy food and other necessities. **live something out 1** do in reality that which one has imagined. **2** spend the rest of one's life in a particular place or particular circumstances. **live through** survive (an unpleasant experience or period). **live together** (of a couple not married to each other) share a home and have a sexual relationship. **live up to** fulfil. **live with 1** share a home and have a sexual relationship with (someone to whom one is not married). **2** accept or tolerate (something unpleasant).
– ORIGIN Old English *libban*, *lifian*, of Germanic origin.

live² /lʌɪv/ ▪ adj. **1** living. ▸ (of yogurt) containing the living micro-organisms by which it is formed. **2** (of a musical performance) given in concert. ▸ (of a broadcast) transmitted at the time of occurrence. **3** (of a wire or device) connected to a source of electric current. ▸ of, containing, or using undetonated explosive. ▸ (of coals) burning. ▸ (of a wheel or axle in machinery) moving or imparting motion. **4** of current or continuing interest and importance. ▪ adv. as or at an actual event or performance.
– ORIGIN C16: shortening of ALIVE.

liveable (US also **livable**) ▪ adj. worth living. ▸ fit to live in. ▸ (**liveable with**) informal easy to live with.
– DERIVATIVES **liveability** n.

live action ▪ n. action in films involving real people or animals, as contrasted with animation or computer-generated effects.

live bait ▪ n. small living fish or worms used as bait.

live-bearing ▪ adj. bearing live young rather than laying eggs.
– DERIVATIVES **livebearer** n.

lived-in ▪ adj. **1** (of a room or building) showing comforting signs of wear and habitation. **2** informal (of a person's face) marked by experience.

live-in ▪ adj. (of a domestic employee) resident in an employer's house. ▸ (of a person) living with another in a sexual relationship. ▸ residential. ▪ n. informal a live-in sexual partner or employee.

livelihood ▪ n. a means of securing the necessities of life.
– ORIGIN Old English *līflād* 'way of life', from *līf* 'life' + *lād* 'course', associated with LIVELY and -HOOD.

livelong /ˈlɪvlɒŋ/ ▪ adj. poetic/literary (of a period of time) entire: *all this livelong day*.
– ORIGIN Middle English *leve longe* 'dear long'.

lively ▪ adj. (**-ier**, **-iest**) full of life, energy, or activity. ▸ intellectually stimulating or perceptive. ▸ ironic, chiefly Brit. difficult.
– PHRASES **look lively** informal move more quickly and energetically.
– DERIVATIVES **liveliness** n.
– ORIGIN Old English *līflic* 'living'.

liven ▪ v. (usu. **liven something up**) make or become more lively or interesting.

live oak ▪ n. a large, spreading, evergreen North American oak. [*Quercus virginiana*.]

liver¹ ▪ n. **1** a large lobed glandular organ in the abdomen, involved in processing digestive products, neutralizing toxins, secreting bile, and other metabolic processes. ▸ the flesh of an animal's liver as food. **2** (also **liver colour**) a dark reddish brown.
– ORIGIN Old English *lifer*, of Germanic origin.

liver² ■ n. a person who lives in a specified way: *a clean liver.*

liver chestnut ■ n. a horse of a dark chestnut colour.

liver fluke ■ n. a fluke of which the adult lives in the liver of a vertebrate and the larva in a secondary host such as a snail or fish. [*Fasciola hepatica* and other species.]

liverish ■ adj. slightly ill, as though having a disordered liver. ▸ unhappy and bad-tempered.
– DERIVATIVES **liverishly** adv. **liverishness** n.

Liverpudlian /ˌlɪvəˈpʌdlɪən/ ■ n. 1 a native or inhabitant of Liverpool. 2 the dialect or accent of people from Liverpool. ■ adj. of or relating to Liverpool.
– ORIGIN C19: humorous formation from *Liverpool* + PUDDLE.

liver salts ■ pl. n. chiefly Brit. salts taken in water to relieve indigestion or nausea.

liver sausage (also **liverwurst**) ■ n. a savoury meat paste in the form of a sausage containing cooked liver, or a mixture of liver and pork.

liver spot ■ n. a small brown spot on the skin.
– DERIVATIVES **liver-spotted** adj.

liverwort /ˈlɪvəwɜːt/ ■ n. a small flowerless green plant with leaf-like stems or lobed leaves, lacking true roots and reproducing by spores. [Class Hepaticae.]
– ORIGIN Old English, from LIVER¹ + WORT, translating medieval Latin *hepatica*.

livery¹ ■ n. (pl. **-ies**) 1 a special uniform worn by a servant or official. ▸ a distinctive design and colour scheme used on the vehicles, aircraft, or products of a company. 2 historical a provision of food or clothing for servants.
– PHRASES **at livery** (of a horse) kept for the owner and fed and cared for at a fixed charge.
– DERIVATIVES **liveried** adj.
– ORIGIN Middle English: from Old French *livree* 'delivered', from *livrer*, from Latin *liberare* 'liberate'.

livery² ■ adj. resembling liver in colour or consistency. ▸ informal liverish.

livery company ■ n. (in the UK) any of a number of Companies of the City of London descended from the medieval trade guilds.

livery stable (also **livery yard**) ■ n. a stable where horses are kept at livery or let out for hire.

lives plural form of LIFE.

livestock ■ n. farm animals regarded as an asset.

live wire ■ n. informal an energetic and lively person.

livid ■ adj. 1 informal furiously angry. 2 (of a colour or the skin) having a dark inflamed appearance.
– DERIVATIVES **lividity** n. **lividly** adv. **lividness** n.
– ORIGIN Middle English: from French *livide* or Latin *lividus*, from *livere* 'be bluish'.

living ■ n. an income sufficient to live on, or the means of earning it. ▸ Brit. (in church use) a position as a vicar or rector with an income or property. ■ adj. alive. ▸ (of a language) still spoken and used. ▸ poetic/literary (of water) perennially flowing.
– PHRASES **in** (or **within**) **living memory** within or during a time that is remembered by people still alive. **the living image of** an exact copy or likeness of.

living death ■ n. a state of existence characterized by total emptiness or misery.

living rock ■ n. rock that is not detached but still forms part of the earth.

living room ■ n. a room in a house for general everyday use.

living stone ■ n. another term for LITHOPS.

living wage ■ n. a wage which is high enough to maintain a normal standard of living.

living will ■ n. a written statement detailing a person's desires regarding their medical treatment in circumstances in which they are no longer able to express informed consent.

lizard ■ n. a reptile that typically has a long body and tail, four legs, movable eyelids, and a rough, scaly, or spiny skin. [Suborder Lacertilia: many species.]
– ORIGIN Middle English: from Old French *lesard(e)*, from Latin *lacertus* 'lizard, sea fish', also 'muscle'.

'll ■ contr. shall; will.

ll. ■ abbrev. (in textual references) lines.

llama /ˈlɑːmə/ ■ n. a domesticated pack animal of the camel family found in the Andes, valued for its soft woolly fleece. [*Lama glama*.] ▸ the wool of the llama.
– ORIGIN C17: from Spanish, prob. from Quechua.

LLB ■ abbrev. Bachelor of Laws.
– ORIGIN from Latin *legum baccalaureus*.

LLD ■ abbrev. Doctor of Laws.
– ORIGIN from Latin *legum doctor*.

LLM ■ abbrev. Master of Laws.
– ORIGIN from Latin *legum magister*.

Lloyd's ■ n. 1 an incorporated society of insurance underwriters in London, made up of private syndicates. 2 short for LLOYD'S REGISTER.
– ORIGIN named after the coffee house of Edward *Lloyd* (*fl.* 1688–1726), in which underwriters and merchants congregated and where *Lloyd's List* was started.

Lloyd's Register (in full **Lloyd's Register of Shipping**) ■ n. a classified list of merchant ships over a certain tonnage, published annually in London.

lm ■ abbrev. lumen(s).

ln ■ abbrev. Mathematics natural logarithm.
– ORIGIN from modern Latin *logarithmus naturalis*.

LNG ■ abbrev. liquefied natural gas.

lo ■ exclam. archaic used to draw attention to an interesting event.
– PHRASES **lo and behold** used to present a new scene or situation.
– ORIGIN first recorded as *lā* in Old English; reinforced in Middle English by a shortened form of *loke* 'look!'

loach /ləʊtʃ/ ■ n. a small, elongated freshwater fish with several barbels near the mouth. [Families Cobitidae and Homalopteridae: numerous species.]
– ORIGIN Middle English: from Old French *loche*.

load ■ n. 1 a heavy or bulky thing that is being carried or is about to be carried. ▸ [in combination] the total number or amount that can be carried in a vehicle or container: *a carload of people*. 2 a weight or source of pressure. ▸ the amount of work to be done by a person or machine. ▸ a burden of responsibility, worry, or grief. 3 (**a load of**) informal a lot of. ▸ (**a load/loads**) plenty. 4 the amount of power supplied by a source. ▸ the resistance of moving parts to be overcome by a motor. ▸ Electronics an impedance or circuit that receives or develops the output of a transistor or other device. ■ v. 1 put a load on or in (a vehicle, ship, etc.). ▸ (of a ship or vehicle) take on a load. 2 make (someone or something) carry or hold a large amount of heavy things. ▸ (**load someone/thing with**) supply someone or something in overwhelming abundance or to excess with. 3 insert (something) into a device so that it will operate. ▸ charge (a firearm) with ammunition. 4 bias towards a particular outcome.
– PHRASES **get a load of** informal used to draw attention to someone or something. **load the dice against** (or **in favour of**) put at a disadvantage (or advantage).
– ORIGIN Old English *lād* 'journey, conveyance', of Germanic origin.

loaded ■ adj. 1 carrying or bearing a load. ▸ informal wealthy. ▸ N. Amer. informal drunk. 2 weighted or biased towards a particular outcome. ▸ charged with an underlying meaning.

loader ■ n. 1 a machine or person that loads something. 2 [in combination] a gun, machine, or truck which is loaded in a specified way: *a front-loader*.

load factor ■ n. the ratio of the average or actual amount of some quantity and the maximum possible or permissible.

loading ■ n. 1 the application of a load to something. ▸ the amount of this. 2 an increase in an insurance premium due to a factor increasing the risk involved. 3 Austral. an increment added to a basic wage for special skills or qualifications.

load line ■ n. another term for PLIMSOLL LINE.

loadmaster ■ n. the member of an aircraft's crew responsible for the cargo.

load-shedding ■ n. action to reduce the load on something, especially the interruption of an electricity supply to avoid excessive load on the generating plant.

loadstone ■ n. variant spelling of **LODESTONE**.

loaf¹ ■ n. (pl. **loaves**) a quantity of bread that is shaped and baked in one piece.
– PHRASES **use one's loaf** Brit. informal use one's common sense. [prob. from *loaf of bread*, rhyming slang for 'head'.]
– ORIGIN Old English, of Germanic origin.

loaf² ■ v. idle one's time away in aimless loitering.
– ORIGIN C19: prob. a back-formation from **LOAFER**.

loafer ■ n. **1** a person who idles their time away. **2** trademark a leather shoe shaped like a moccasin, with a flat heel.
– ORIGIN C19: perhaps from German *Landläufer* 'tramp'.

loam ■ n. **1** a fertile soil of clay and sand containing humus. **2** a paste of clay and water with sand and chopped straw, used in making bricks and plastering walls.
– DERIVATIVES **loaminess** n. **loamy** adj.
– ORIGIN Old English *lām* 'clay', of West Germanic origin.

loan ■ n. a thing that is borrowed, especially a sum of money that is expected to be paid back with interest. ▸ the action of lending. ▸ short for **LOANWORD**. ■ v. give as a loan.
– PHRASES **on loan** being borrowed.
– DERIVATIVES **loanable** adj. **loanee** n. **loaner** n.
– ORIGIN Middle English: from Old Norse *lán*, of Germanic origin.

loan shark ■ n. informal a moneylender who charges exorbitant rates of interest, typically illicitly.

loan translation ■ n. an expression adopted by one language from another in a more or less literally translated form.

loanword ■ n. a word adopted from a foreign language with little or no modification.

loath /ləʊθ/ (also **loth**) ■ adj. reluctant; unwilling: *I was loath to leave.*
– ORIGIN Old English *lāth* 'hostile', of Germanic origin.

loathe /ləʊð/ ■ v. feel hatred or disgust for.
– DERIVATIVES **loather** n.
– ORIGIN Old English *lāthian*, of Germanic origin; rel. to **LOATH**.

loathsome ■ adj. causing hatred or disgust.
– ORIGIN Middle English: from archaic *loath* 'disgust'.

loaves plural form of **LOAF¹**.

lob ■ v. (**lobbed**, **lobbing**) throw or hit (a ball or missile) in a high arc. ▸ (in soccer or tennis) kick or hit the ball over (an opponent) in such a way. ■ n. a ball lobbed over an opponent or a stroke producing this result.
– ORIGIN C16: from the archaic noun *lob* 'lout, pendulous object', prob. from Low German or Dutch.

lobar /ˈləʊbə/ ■ adj. chiefly Anatomy & Medicine of or relating to a lobe, especially a lobe of a lung.

lobby ■ n. (pl. **-ies**) **1** a room out of which one or more other rooms or corridors lead, typically one near the entrance of a public building. ▸ (also **division lobby**) either of two corridors in the British Houses of Parliament to which MPs retire to vote. **2** a group of people seeking to influence legislators on a particular issue. ▸ an organized attempt by members of the public to influence legislators. ■ v. (**-ies**, **-ied**) seek to influence (a legislator or other person with power).
– DERIVATIVES **lobbyist** n.
– ORIGIN C16: from medieval Latin *lobia*, *lobium* 'covered walk'.

lobby correspondent ■ n. (in the UK) a senior political journalist of a group receiving direct but unattributable briefings from the government.

lobe ■ n. a roundish and flattish projecting or hanging part of something, often one of two or more such parts divided by a fissure.
– DERIVATIVES **lobed** adj. **lobeless** adj.
– ORIGIN Middle English: from Greek *lobos* 'lobe, pod'.

lobectomy ■ n. (pl. **-ies**) surgical removal of a lobe of an organ such as the lung or brain.

lobelia /ləˈbiːlɪə/ ■ n. a plant of the bellflower family, typically with blue or scarlet flowers. [Genus *Lobelia*: many species.]
– ORIGIN named after the Flemish botanist Matthias de Lobel (1538–1616).

lobola /ləˈbəʊlə/ (also **lobolo** /ləˈbəʊləʊ/) ■ n. (among southern African peoples) a bride price, formerly paid with cattle but now often with money. ■ v. offer cattle, etc. for a woman in order to marry her.
– ORIGIN from isiXhosa and isiZulu.

lobopodium /ˌləʊbə(ʊ)ˈpəʊdɪəm/ ■ n. (pl. **lobopodia** /-ɪə/) Zoology **1** the primitive leg of an onychophoran. **2** a lobe-like pseudopodium in an amoeba.
– ORIGIN C20: from modern Latin *lobosus* 'having many lobes' + **PODIUM**.

lobotomize (also **-ise**) ■ v. Surgery perform a lobotomy on. ▸ informal reduce the mental ability to function of.

lobotomy /ləˈbɒtəmi/ ■ n. (pl. **-ies**) a surgical operation involving incision into the prefrontal lobe of the brain, formerly used to treat mental illness.

lobster ■ n. a large marine crustacean with a cylindrical body, stalked eyes, and the first of its five pairs of limbs modified as pincers. [*Homarus* and other genera.] ▸ the flesh of this animal as food. ■ v. catch lobsters.
– ORIGIN Old English *lopustre*, alteration of Latin *locusta* 'crustacean, locust'.

lobster pot ■ n. a basket-like trap in which lobsters are caught.

lobster thermidor /ˈθəːmɪdɔː/ ■ n. a dish of lobster cooked in a cream sauce, returned to its shell, sprinkled with cheese, and browned under the grill.
– ORIGIN *thermidor* from *Thermidor*, the eleventh month of the French Republican calendar.

lobule /ˈlɒbjuːl/ ■ n. chiefly Anatomy a small lobe.
– DERIVATIVES **lobular** adj. **lobulated** adj.

lobworm ■ n. a large earthworm used as fishing bait.
– ORIGIN C17: from **LOB** in the obsolete sense 'pendulous object'.

local ■ adj. relating or restricted to a particular area or one's neighbourhood. ▸ (in technical use) relating to a particular region or part, or to each of any number of these: *a local infection.* ▸ Computing only available for use in one part of a program. ■ n. a local person or thing. ▸ Brit. informal a pub convenient to a person's home.
– DERIVATIVES **locally** adv. **localness** n.
– ORIGIN Middle English: from late Latin *localis*, from Latin *locus* 'place'.

local anaesthetic ■ n. an anaesthetic that affects a restricted area of the body.

local area network ■ n. a computer network that links devices within a building or group of adjacent buildings.

local authority ■ n. an administrative body in local government.

local colour ■ n. **1** the characteristic customs or other aspects of a place or period. **2** Art the actual colour of a thing in ordinary daylight, without the influence of other colours in proximity.

local derby ■ n. see **DERBY**.

locale /ləʊˈkɑːl/ ■ n. a place associated with particular events.
– ORIGIN C18: from French *local* (n.), respelled to indicate stress on the final syllable; cf. **MORALE**.

local government ■ n. the administration of a particular city, district, or county, with representatives elected by those who live there.

localism ■ n. **1** preference for one's own locality, particularly when this results in a limitation of outlook. **2** a characteristic of a particular locality, such as an idiom.
– DERIVATIVES **localist** n. & adj.

locality ■ n. (pl. **-ies**) the position or site of something. ▸ an area or neighbourhood.
– ORIGIN C17: from French *localité* or late Latin *localitas*, from *localis* (see **LOCAL**).

localize (also **-ise**) ■ v. **1** [often as adj. **localized** (also **-ised**)] restrict or assign to a particular place. **2** make local in character.
– DERIVATIVES **localizable** (also **-isable**) adj. **localization** (also **-isation**) n.

local time ■ n. time as reckoned in a particular region or time zone.

locate /lə(ʊ)'keɪt/ ■ v. **1** discover the exact place or position of. **2** (**be located**) be situated in a particular place. ▸ N. Amer. establish oneself or one's business in a specified place.
– DERIVATIVES **locatable** adj. **locator** n.
– ORIGIN C16: from Latin *locare* 'to place'.

location ■ n. **1** a particular place or position. ▸ the action or process of locating. **2** an actual place in which a film or broadcast is made, as distinct from a simulation in a studio. **3** S. African another term for TOWNSHIP (sense 1).
– DERIVATIVES **locational** adj.

locative /'lɒkətɪv/ ■ adj. Grammar relating to or denoting a case in some languages of nouns, pronouns, and adjectives, expressing location.

loc. cit. ■ abbrev. in the passage already cited.
– ORIGIN from Latin *loco citato*.

loch /lɒk, lɒx/ ■ n. Scottish a lake. ▸ (also **sea loch**) an arm of the sea, especially when narrow or partially land-locked.
– ORIGIN Middle English: from Scottish Gaelic.

lochan /'lɒk(ə)n, 'lɒx(ə)n/ ■ n. Scottish a small loch.
– ORIGIN C17: from Scottish Gaelic, diminutive of *loch*.

loci plural form of LOCUS.

lock[1] ■ n. **1** a mechanism for keeping a door, lid, or container fastened, typically operated by a key. ▸ a similar device used to prevent the operation of a vehicle or other machine. **2** a short section of a canal or river with gates and sluices at each end which can be opened or closed to change the water level, used for raising and lowering boats. **3** the turning of the front wheels of a vehicle to change its direction of motion. **4** (in wrestling and martial arts) a hold that prevents an opponent from moving a limb. **5** (also **lock forward**) Rugby a player in the second row of a scrum. **6** archaic a mechanism for exploding the charge of a gun. ■ v. **1** fasten or be fastened with a lock. ▸ enclose or secure by locking a door. ▸ (**lock someone up/away**) imprison someone. **2** make or become rigidly fixed or immovable. ▸ (**lock someone/thing in**) engage or entangle someone or something in (an embrace or struggle). ▸ (**lock on to**) locate (a target) by radar or similar means and then track.
– PHRASES **lock horns** engage in conflict. **lock, stock, and barrel** including everything. [referring to the complete mechanism of a firearm.]
– DERIVATIVES **lockable** adj.
– ORIGIN Old English *loc*, of Germanic origin.

lock[2] ■ n. **1** a piece of a person's hair that coils or hangs together. ▸ (**locks**) chiefly poetic/literary a person's hair. **2** a tuft of wool or cotton.
– DERIVATIVES **-locked** adj.
– ORIGIN Old English *locc*, of Germanic origin.

lockdown ■ n. N. Amer. the confining of prisoners to their cells, typically in order to regain control during a riot.

locker ■ n. **1** a small lockable cupboard or compartment, typically as one of a number placed together for public use. ▸ a chest or compartment on a ship or boat for clothes, stores, or ammunition. **2** a device that locks something.

locker room ■ n. a room containing lockers, especially a sports changing room. ▸ [as modifier] characteristic of a men's locker room, especially in being coarse or ribald.

locket ■ n. a small ornamental case worn round a person's neck on a chain and used to hold things of sentimental value.
– ORIGIN Middle English: from Old French *locquet*, diminutive of *loc* 'latch, lock', of Germanic origin.

lock forward ■ n. another term for LOCK[1] (in sense 5).

lock-in ■ n. **1** an arrangement according to which a person or company is obliged to negotiate or trade only with a specific company. **2** a period during which customers are locked into a bar or pub after closing time to continue drinking privately.

lockjaw ■ n. non-technical term for TRISMUS.

locknut ■ n. a nut screwed down on another to keep it tight. **2** a nut designed so that, once tightened, it cannot be accidentally loosened.

lockout ■ n. the exclusion of employees by their employer from their place of work until certain terms are agreed to.

locksmith ■ n. a person who makes and repairs locks.

lockstep ■ n. a way of marching with each person as close as possible to the one in front.

lock stitch ■ n. a stitch made by a sewing machine by firmly linking together two threads or stitches.

lock-up ■ n. **1** a jail, especially a temporary one. **2** non-residential premises that can be locked up, typically a garage. **3** an investment in assets which cannot readily be realized or sold on in the short term.

lock-up-and-go ■ n. S. African a small house or flat that requires little maintenance and can be safely and conveniently left unoccupied.

loco[1] ■ n. (pl. **-os**) informal a locomotive.

loco[2] ■ adj. informal crazy.
– ORIGIN C19: from Spanish, 'insane'.

locomotion ■ n. movement or the ability to move from one place to another.
– DERIVATIVES **locomotory** adj.
– ORIGIN C17: from Latin *locus* 'place' + *motio* (see MOTION).

locomotive ■ n. a powered railway vehicle used for pulling trains. ■ adj. of or relating to locomotion.
– ORIGIN C17: from Latin *locus* 'place' + late Latin *motivus* 'motive'.

locomotor ■ adj. chiefly Biology of or relating to locomotion.

locoweed ■ n. N. Amer. a plant which can cause a brain disorder if eaten by livestock. [Genera *Astragalus* and *Oxytropis*.]

locule /'lɒkjuːl/ ■ n. another term for LOCULUS.

loculus /'lɒkjʊləs/ ■ n. (pl. **loculi** /-lʌɪ, -liː/) chiefly Botany each of a number of small separate cavities, especially in an ovary.
– DERIVATIVES **locular** adj.
– ORIGIN C19: from Latin, 'compartment'.

locum /'ləʊkəm/ ■ n. informal short for LOCUM TENENS.

locum tenens /ˌləʊkəm 'tiːnɛnz, 'tɛn-/ ■ n. (pl. **locum tenentes** /tɪ'nɛntiːz, tɛ-/) a temporary deputy, especially one acting for a cleric or doctor.
– ORIGIN C17: from medieval Latin, 'one holding a place'.

locus /'ləʊkəs/ ■ n. (pl. **loci** /-sʌɪ, -kʌɪ, -kiː/) **1** technical a particular position, point, or place. **2** Mathematics a curve or other figure formed by all the points satisfying a particular condition.
– ORIGIN C18: from Latin, 'place'.

locus classicus /ˌləʊkəs 'klasɪkəs, ˌlɒkəs/ ■ n. (pl. **loci classici** /ˌləʊkʌɪ 'klasɪsʌɪ, ˌlɒkiː 'klasɪkiː/) the best known or most authoritative passage on a subject.
– ORIGIN Latin, 'classical place'.

locus standi /ˌləʊkəs 'standʌɪ, ˌlɒkəs/ ■ n. (pl. **loci standi** /ˌləʊsʌɪ 'standʌɪ, ˌlɒkiː 'standiː/) Law the right or capacity to bring an action or to appear in a court.
– ORIGIN Latin, 'place of standing'.

locust ■ n. **1** a large, mainly tropical grasshopper which migrates in vast swarms and is very destructive to vegetation. [*Locusta migratoria* and other species.] **2** (also **locust tree**) a carob tree, false acacia, or similar pod-bearing tree.
– ORIGIN Middle English: from Latin *locusta* 'locust, crustacean'.

locution /lə'kjuːʃ(ə)n/ ■ n. **1** a word or phrase, especially with regard to style or idiom. ▸ a person's style of speech. **2** an utterance regarded in terms of its intrinsic meaning or reference, as distinct from its function or purpose in context.
– DERIVATIVES **locutionary** adj.
– ORIGIN Middle English: from Latin *locutio(n-)*, from *loqui* 'speak'.

lode /ləʊd/ ■ n. a vein of metal ore in the earth.
– ORIGIN Old English *lād* 'way, course', var. of LOAD.

loden /'ləʊd(ə)n/ ■ n. **1** a thick waterproof woollen cloth. **2** the dark green colour in which such cloth is often made.
– ORIGIN C20: from German *Loden*.

lodestar ■ n. a star that is used to guide the course of a ship, especially the pole star.
– ORIGIN Middle English: from **LODE** in the obsolete sense 'way, course' + **STAR**.

lodestone (also **loadstone**) ■ n. a piece of magnetite or other naturally magnetized mineral, able to be used as a magnet.

lodge ■ n. **1** a small house at the gates of a park or in the grounds of a large house, occupied by a gatekeeper or other employee. ▶ a small country house occupied in season for sports such as hunting and shooting. ▶ [in names] a hotel or rest camp in a game reserve. ▶ a porter's quarters at the main entrance of a college or other large building. **2** an American Indian tent or other dwelling. **3** a beaver's den. **4** a branch or meeting place of an organization such as the Freemasons. ■ v. **1** present (a complaint, appeal, etc.) formally to the proper authorities. **2** make or become firmly fixed in a place. **3** rent accommodation in another person's house. **4** (**lodge something in/with**) leave money or a valuable item in (a place) or with (someone) for safe keeping.
– ORIGIN Middle English, via Old French *loge* 'arbour, hut' from medieval Latin *laubia*, *lobia* (see **LOBBY**), of Germanic origin.

lodgement ■ n. **1** chiefly poetic/literary a place in which a person or thing is lodged. **2** the depositing of money in a particular bank or account.

lodger ■ n. a person who pays rent to live in a property with the owner.

lodging ■ n. a temporary place of residence. ▶ (**lodgings**) a rented room or rooms, usually in the same residence as the owner.

lodging house ■ n. a private house providing rented accommodation.

loerie /'luəri/ ■ n. S. African **1** variant spelling of **LOURIE**. **2** (**Loerie**) an annual award given for achievement in the advertising industry.
– ORIGIN from Afrikaans (see **LOURIE**).

loess /'ləʊɪs, lɜːs/ ■ n. Geology a loosely compacted yellowish-grey deposit of wind-blown sediment.
– DERIVATIVES **loessial** adj.
– ORIGIN C19: from German *Löss*, from Swiss German *lösch* 'loose'.

lo-fi (also **low-fi**) ■ adj. of or employing sound reproduction of a lower quality than hi-fi.
– ORIGIN 1950s: from **LOW**[1] + *-fi* on the pattern of *hi-fi*.

loft ■ n. **1** a room or storage space directly under the roof of a house or other building. ▶ a gallery in a church or hall. ▶ a large, open area in a shop, warehouse, or other large building that has been converted into living space. ▶ a pigeon house. **2** Golf upward inclination given to the ball in a stroke. **3** the thickness of insulating matter in an object such as a sleeping bag. ■ v. kick, hit, or throw (a ball or missile) high up.
– ORIGIN Old English, from Old Norse *lopt* 'air, upper room', of Germanic origin.

lofty ■ adj. (**-ier**, **-iest**) **1** of imposing height. **2** noble; elevated. ▶ haughty and aloof. **3** (of wool and other textiles) thick and resilient.
– DERIVATIVES **loftily** adv. **loftiness** n.
– ORIGIN Middle English: from **LOFT**, influenced by **ALOFT**.

log[1] ■ n. **1** a part of the trunk or a large branch of a tree that has fallen or been cut off. **2** (also **logbook**) an official record of events during the voyage of a ship or aircraft. **3** an apparatus for determining the speed of a ship, originally one consisting of a float attached to a knotted line. ■ v. (**logged**, **logging**) **1** enter in a log. ▶ achieve (a certain distance, speed, or time). **2** (**log in/on**) or **off/out** go through the procedures to begin (or conclude) use of a computer system. **3** cut down (an area of forest) to exploit the wood commercially.
– DERIVATIVES **logger** n. **logging** n.

HISTORY
Log is a Middle English word of obscure origin. The link between the original sense of the noun, 'a part of a tree that has fallen or been cut off', and the verb 'enter something in a log' is found in sense 3 of the noun, 'an apparatus for determining the speed of a ship'. This originally consisted of a 'log' or wooden float attached to a very long knotted line; the log was tossed overboard and the length of line run out in a certain time was used as an estimate of the vessel's speed. From here came the notion of a ship's journal or **logbook**, in which a detailed daily record of a voyage was entered, and so the verb developed. See also **KNOT**[1].

log[2] ■ n. short for **LOGARITHM**.

-log ■ comb. form US spelling of **-LOGUE**.

loganberry /'ləʊg(ə)n,b(ə)ri, -,bɛri/ ■ n. **1** an edible dull-red soft fruit, considered to be a hybrid of a raspberry and an American dewberry. **2** the plant bearing this fruit. [*Rubus loganobaccus*.]
– ORIGIN C19: from the name of John H. *Logan*, an American horticulturalist.

logarithm /'lɒgərɪð(ə)m, -rɪθ-/ ■ n. a quantity representing the power to which a fixed number (the base) must be raised to produce a given number.
– DERIVATIVES **logarithmic** adj. **logarithmically** adv.
– ORIGIN C17: from Greek *logos* 'reckoning, ratio' + *arithmos* 'number'.

logbook ■ n. **1** another term for **LOG**[1] (in sense 2). **2** Brit. another term for **REGISTRATION DOCUMENT**.

loge /ləʊʒ/ ■ n. a private box or enclosure in a theatre.
– ORIGIN C18: from French.

-loger ■ comb. form equivalent to **-LOGIST**.
– ORIGIN on the pattern of words such as (*astro*)*loger*.

loge ■ symb. natural logarithm.

loggerhead (also **loggerhead turtle**) ■ n. a large-headed reddish-brown turtle of warm seas. [*Caretta caretta*.]
– PHRASES **at loggerheads** in violent dispute or disagreement. [perhaps a use of *loggerhead* in the C17 sense 'long-handled iron instrument for heating liquids' (when wielded as a weapon).]
– ORIGIN C16: from dialect *logger* 'block of wood for hobbling a horse' + **HEAD**.

loggia /'ləʊdʒə, 'lɒ-, -dʒɪə/ ■ n. a gallery or room with one or more open sides, especially one having one side open to a garden.
– ORIGIN C18: from Italian, 'lodge'.

logic ■ n. **1** reasoning conducted or assessed according to strict principles of validity. ▶ a particular system or codification of this. ▶ the ability to reason correctly. ▶ (**the logic of**) the course of action following as a necessary consequence of. **2** a system or set of principles underlying the arrangements of elements in a computer or electronic device so as to perform a specified task.
– DERIVATIVES **logician** n.
– ORIGIN Middle English: from late Latin *logica*, from Greek *logikē* (*tekhnē*) '(art) of reason'.

-logic ■ comb. form equivalent to **-LOGICAL** (as in *pharmacologic*).
– ORIGIN from Greek *-logikos*.

logical ■ adj. of or according to the rules of logic. ▶ capable of or showing rational thought. ▶ expected or reasonable under the circumstances.
– DERIVATIVES **logicality** /-'kalɪti/ n. **logically** adv.

-logical ■ comb. form in adjectives corresponding chiefly to nouns ending in *-logy* (such as *pharmacological* corresponding to *pharmacology*).

logical atomism ■ n. Philosophy the theory that all propositions can be analysed into simple independent elements of meaning corresponding to elements making up facts about the world.

logical necessity ■ n. that state of things which obliges something to be as it is because no alternative is logically possible.

logical positivism (also **logical empiricism**) ■ n. a form of positivism which considers that the only meaningful philosophical problems are those which can be solved by logical analysis.

logic bomb ■ n. Computing a set of instructions secretly

-logist ■ comb. form indicating a person skilled or involved in a branch of study denoted by a noun ending in *-logy* (such as *biologist* corresponding to *biology*).

logistic ■ adj. of or relating to logistics.
– DERIVATIVES **logistical** adj. **logistically** adv.

logistics /ləˈdʒɪstɪks/ ■ pl. n. [treated as sing. or pl.] the detailed coordination of a large and complex operation. ▸ the activity of organizing the movement, equipment, and accommodation of troops. ▸ the commercial activity of transporting goods to customers.
– ORIGIN C19 ('movement and supply of troops and equipment'): from French *logistique*, from *loger* 'lodge'.

logjam ■ n. 1 a crowded mass of logs blocking a river. 2 a deadlock. 3 a backlog.

log-normal ■ adj. Statistics of or denoting a set of data in which the logarithm of the variate follows a normal distribution.
– DERIVATIVES **log-normality** n.

logo /ˈlɒɡəʊ, ˈləʊɡəʊ/ ■ n. (pl. **-os**) an emblematic design adopted by an organization to identify its products.
– ORIGIN 1930s: abbrev. of LOGOGRAM or LOGOTYPE.

logocentric ■ adj. regarding words and language as a fundamental expression of an external reality.
– DERIVATIVES **logocentrism** n.
– ORIGIN 1930s: from Greek *logos* 'word, speech, reason' + -CENTRIC.

logogram ■ n. a sign or character representing a word or phrase, as used in shorthand and some ancient writing systems.
– ORIGIN C19: from Greek *logos* 'word' + -GRAM¹.

logograph ■ n. another term for LOGOGRAM.
– DERIVATIVES **logographic** adj.

Logos /ˈlɒɡɒs/ ■ n. 1 Theology the Word of God, or principle of divine reason and creative order, identified with the second person of the Trinity incarnate in Jesus Christ. 2 (in Jungian psychology) the principle of reason and judgement, associated with the animus. Often contrasted with EROS.
– ORIGIN Greek, 'word, reason'.

logotype ■ n. Printing a single piece of type that prints a word, a group of separate letters, or a logo.
– ORIGIN C19: from Greek *logos* 'word' + TYPE.

logrolling ■ n. N. Amer. 1 informal the exchange of favours between politicians by reciprocal voting for each other's proposed legislation. [from the phr. *you roll my log and I'll roll yours*.] 2 a sport in which two contestants stand on a floating log and spin it with their feet to try to dislodge their opponent.

-logue (US also **-log**) ■ comb. form 1 denoting discourse of a specified type: *dialogue*. 2 denoting compilation: *catalogue*. 3 equivalent to -LOGIST.,
– ORIGIN from French *-logue*, from Greek *-logos, -logon*.

-logy ■ comb. form 1 (usu. as **-ology**) denoting a subject of study or interest: *psychology*. 2 denoting a characteristic of speech or language: *eulogy*. ▸ denoting a type of discourse: *trilogy*.
– ORIGIN from French *-logie* or medieval Latin *-logia*, from Greek.

loin ■ n. 1 the part of the body on both sides of the spine between the lowest ribs and the hip bones. ▸ a joint of meat that includes the vertebrae of the loins. 2 (**loins**) poetic/literary the region of the sexual organs, regarded as the source of erotic or procreative power.
– ORIGIN Middle English: from Old French *loigne*, from Latin *lumbus*.

loincloth ■ n. a single piece of cloth wrapped round the hips, typically worn by men in some hot countries as their only garment.

loiter ■ v. stand around or move without apparent purpose.
– DERIVATIVES **loiterer** n.
– ORIGIN Middle English: perhaps from Middle Dutch *loteren* 'wag about'.

Lolita /lə(ʊ)ˈliːtə/ ■ n. a sexually precocious young girl.
– ORIGIN from the eponymous character in the novel *Lolita* (1958) by Vladimir Nabokov.

loll ■ v. 1 sit, lie, or stand in a lazy, relaxed way. 2 hang loosely.
– ORIGIN Middle English.

lollipop ■ n. a large, flat, rounded boiled sweet on the end of a stick. ▸ British term for ICE LOLLY.
– ORIGIN C18: perhaps from dialect *lolly* 'tongue' + POP¹.

lollipop lady (or **lollipop man**) ■ n. informal, chiefly Brit. a person employed to help children cross the road safely near a school by holding up a circular sign on a pole to stop the traffic.

lollop ■ v. (**lolloped, lolloping**) move in an ungainly way in a series of clumsy bounds.
– ORIGIN C18: prob. from LOLL, associated with TROLLOP.

lollo rosso /ˌlɒləʊ ˈrɒsəʊ/ ■ n. lettuce of a variety with deeply divided red-edged leaves.
– ORIGIN Italian, from *lolla* 'husk, chaff' + *rosso* 'red'.

lolly ■ n. (pl. **-ies**) informal 1 chiefly Brit. a lollipop. ▸ Austral./NZ a boiled sweet. 2 Brit. money.

Lombardy poplar ■ n. a black poplar of an Italian variety with a distinctive tall, slender columnar form. [*Populus nigra* var. *italica*.]

Londoner ■ n. a native or inhabitant of London.

London plane ■ n. a hybrid plane tree which is resistant to pollution and widely planted in towns. [*Platanus × hispanica*.]

lone ■ adj. having no companions; solitary. ▸ lacking the support of others. ▸ poetic/literary unfrequented and remote.
– ORIGIN Middle English: shortening of ALONE.

lone hand ■ n. (in phr. **play a lone hand**) act on one's own without help.

lonely ■ adj. (**-ier, -iest**) sad because one has no friends or company. ▸ solitary. ▸ unfrequented and remote.
– DERIVATIVES **loneliness** n.

lonely hearts ■ pl. n. people looking for a lover or friend by advertising in a newspaper.

loner ■ n. a person who prefers not to associate with others.

lonesome ■ adj. chiefly N. Amer. lonely.
– PHRASES **by** (or **on**) **one's lonesome** informal all alone.
– DERIVATIVES **lonesomeness** n.

lone wolf ■ n. a person who prefers to act alone.

long¹ ■ adj. (**-er, -est**) 1 of a great distance or duration. ▸ of a specified distance or duration. ▸ (of a ball in sport) travelling a great distance, or further than expected. 2 relatively great in extent. ▸ having a great extent. 3 Phonetics (of a vowel) categorized as long with regard to quality and length (e.g. in standard English the vowel /uː/ in *food*). ▸ Prosody (of a vowel or syllable) having the greater of the two recognized durations. 4 (of odds or a chance) reflecting or representing a low level of probability. 5 Finance (of shares or other assets) bought in advance, with the expectation of a rise in price. ▸ (of a security) maturing at a distant date. 6 (of a drink) large and refreshing, and in which alcohol, if present, is not concentrated. 7 (**long on**) informal well supplied with. ■ n. 1 a long time. 2 informal long trousers. 3 (**longs**) Finance long securities or assets. ■ adv. (**longer, longest**) 1 for a long time. ▸ at a distant time: *long ago*. ▸ throughout a specified period of time: *all day long*. 2 (with reference to the ball in sport) at, to, or over a great distance.
– PHRASES **as** (or **so**) **long as** 1 during the whole time that. 2 provided that. **be long** take a long time. **in the long run** (or **term**) eventually. **the long and the short of it** all that can or need be said. **long in the tooth** rather old. **with long teeth** S. African informal reluctantly.
– DERIVATIVES **longish** adj.
– ORIGIN Old English *lang, long* (adj.), *lange, longe* (adv.), of Germanic origin.

long² ■ v. (**long for/to do**) have a strong wish for or to do.
– ORIGIN Old English *langian* 'grow long', also 'yearn', of Germanic origin.

-long ■ comb. form (added to nouns) for the duration of: *lifelong*.

long. ■ abbrev. longitude.

longan /ˈlɒŋɡ(ə)n/ ■ n. an edible juicy fruit from a SE

longboard

Asian plant (*Dimocarpus longan*) related to the lychee.
– ORIGIN C18: from Chinese *lóngyǎn* 'dragon's eye'.

longboard ■ n. a type of long surfboard.

longboat ■ n. a large boat which may be launched from a sailing ship. ► another term for **LONGSHIP**.

longbow ■ n. a large bow drawn by hand and shooting a long feathered arrow.

long-case clock ■ n. another term for **GRANDFATHER CLOCK**.

long-dated ■ adj. (of securities) not due for early payment or redemption.

long distance ■ adj. 1 travelling or operating between distant places. 2 (in athletics) denoting or relating to a race distance of 6 miles or 10 000 metres, or longer. ■ adv. between distant places.

long division ■ n. division of numbers with details of intermediate calculations written down.

long-drawn (also **long-drawn-out**) ■ adj. prolonged, especially unduly.

long drop ■ n. a pit latrine.

longeron /ˈlɒn(d)ʒərɒn/ ■ n. a longitudinal structural component of an aircraft's fuselage.
– ORIGIN C20: from French, 'girder'.

longevity /lɒnˈdʒɛvɪti/ ■ n. long life.
– ORIGIN C17: from late Latin *longaevitas*, from Latin *longus* 'long' + *aevum* 'age'.

long face ■ n. an unhappy or disappointed expression.
– DERIVATIVES **long-faced** adj.

longhair ■ n. a cat of a long-haired breed.

longhand ■ n. ordinary handwriting (as opposed to shorthand, typing, or printing).

long haul ■ n. 1 a long distance (with reference to the transport of goods or passengers). 2 a lengthy and difficult task.
– PHRASES **over the long haul** chiefly N. Amer. over an extended period of time.

long-headed ■ adj. dated having or showing foresight and good judgement.

long hop ■ n. Cricket a short-pitched, easily hit ball.

longhorn ■ n. an animal of a breed of cattle with long horns.

longhorn beetle ■ n. an elongated beetle with long antennae, the larva of which typically bores in wood. [Family Cerambycidae.]

longhouse ■ n. (among the Iroquois and other North American Indians) a traditional dwelling shared by several nuclear families. ► a large communal village house in parts of Malaysia and Indonesia.

longing ■ n. a yearning desire. ■ adj. having or showing such desire.
– DERIVATIVES **longingly** adv.

longitude /ˈlɒn(d)ʒɪtjuːd, ˈlɒŋgɪ-/ ■ n. the angular distance of a place east or west of a standard meridian, especially the Greenwich meridian.
– ORIGIN Middle English: from Latin *longitudo*, from *longus* 'long'.

longitudinal /ˌlɒndʒɪˈtjuːdɪn(ə)l, ˌlɒŋgɪ-/ ■ adj. 1 running lengthwise. 2 of or relating to longitude. 3 involving information about an individual or group gathered over a prolonged period.
– DERIVATIVES **longitudinally** adv.

longitudinal wave ■ n. Physics a wave vibrating in the direction of propagation.

long johns ■ pl. n. informal underpants with closely fitted legs extending to the wearer's ankles.

long jump ■ n. (**the long jump**) an athletic event in which competitors jump as far as possible along the ground in one leap.
– DERIVATIVES **long jumper** n.

long leg ■ n. Cricket a fielding position far behind the batsman on the leg side.

long-life ■ adj. (of perishable goods) treated so as to stay fresh for longer than usual.

longline ■ n. a deep-sea fishing line with a large number of hooks attached to it.

longliner ■ n. a fishing vessel which uses longlines.

long metre ■ n. Prosody a quatrain of iambic tetrameters with alternate lines rhyming.

long off ■ n. Cricket a fielding position far behind the bowler and towards the off side.

long on ■ n. Cricket a fielding position far behind the bowler and towards the on side.

long-playing ■ adj. (of a gramophone record) about 30 cm in diameter and designed to rotate at 33⅓ revolutions per minute.
– DERIVATIVES **long-player** n.

long-range ■ adj. 1 able to be used or be effective over long distances. 2 relating to a period of time far into the future.

longship ■ n. a long, narrow warship, with oars and a sail, used by the Vikings and other ancient northern European peoples.

longshore ■ adj. of, relating to, or moving along the seashore.
– ORIGIN C19: from *along shore*.

longshore drift ■ n. the movement of material along a coast by waves which approach at an angle to the shore but recede directly away from it.

longshoreman ■ n. (pl. -**men**) N. Amer. a docker.

long shot ■ n. a venture or guess that has only the slightest chance of succeeding or being accurate.
– PHRASES (**not**) **by a long shot** informal (not) by far or at all.

long sight ■ n. British term for **FAR SIGHT**.

long-sighted ■ adj. British term for **FAR-SIGHTED** (in sense 2).
– DERIVATIVES **long-sightedness** n.

long-standing ■ adj. having existed for a long time.

long-suffering ■ adj. bearing problems or provocation with patience.
– DERIVATIVES **long-sufferingly** adv.

long suit ■ n. (in bridge or whist) a holding of several cards of one suit in a hand, typically 5 or more out of the 13.

longueur /lɔ̃(ŋ)ˈɡəː/ ■ n. a tedious passage or period.
– ORIGIN French, 'length'.

long vacation ■ n. a summer holiday of two or three months taken by universities.

long wave ■ n. a radio wave of a wavelength above one kilometre (and a frequency below 300 kHz). ► broadcasting using radio waves of 1 to 10 km wavelength.

longways (also **longwise**) ■ adv. lengthways.

long-winded ■ adj. tediously lengthy.
– DERIVATIVES **long-windedly** adv. **long-windedness** n.

Lonsdale belt ■ n. Boxing an ornate belt awarded to a professional boxer winning a British title fight.
– ORIGIN C20: named after the fifth Earl of *Lonsdale*.

loo¹ ■ n. informal a toilet.

> **HISTORY**
> **Loo** meaning 'toilet' was first recorded in the early 1930s; the origin of the word is uncertain, although various theories have been put forward. One suggests that the source is *Waterloo*, a trade name for iron cisterns in the early 20th century. Another idea is that it is from the former French euphemism for a latrine, *lieu d'aisances* (literally 'place of ease'), an expression which could have been picked up by British troops in France during the First World War. Yet another theory traces the term back to the cry *gardy loo*! (from French *gardez l'eau* 'beware of the water'), formerly uttered by people who were about to throw the contents of their chamber pots out of their windows.

loo² ■ n. a gambling card game in which a player who fails to win a trick must pay a sum to a pool.
– ORIGIN C17: abbrev. of obsolete *lanterloo* from French *lanturlu*, a meaningless song refrain.

loofah /ˈluːfə/ ■ n. 1 the fibrous matter of the fluid-transport system of a marrow-like fruit, which is used dried as a bath sponge. 2 the tropical climbing plant

of the gourd family which produces these fruits, which are also edible. [*Luffa cylindrica*.]
– ORIGIN C19: from Egyptian Arabic *lūfa*, denoting the plant.

look ■ v. 1 direct one's gaze in a specified direction. ▸ have an outlook in a specified direction. ▸ (**look through**) ignore by pretending not to see. ▸ (**look something over**) inspect something with a view to establishing its merits. ▸ (**look at/on**) regard in a specified way. ▸ (**look at**) examine (a matter) and consider what action to take. ▸ (**look into**) investigate. ▸ (**look for**) attempt to find. 2 have the appearance or give the impression of being. ▸ (**look like**) informal show a likelihood of. 3 (**look to**) rely on (someone) to do something. ▸ hope or expect to do. ▸ archaic make sure. ■ n. 1 an act of looking. ▸ an expression of a feeling or thought by such an act. 2 appearance, especially as expressing a particular quality. ▸ (**looks**) a person's facial appearance considered aesthetically. ▸ a style or fashion. ■ exclam. (also **look here!**) used to call attention to what one is going to say.
– PHRASES **look down one's nose at** another way of saying look down on. **look someone in the eye** (or **face**) look directly at someone without showing embarrassment, fear, or shame. **look lively** informal be quick; get moving. **look sharp** be quick.
– PHRASAL VERBS **look after** take care of. **look back** [with neg.] suffer a setback or interrupted progress. **look down on** regard with a feeling of superiority. **look in** make a short visit or call. **look on** watch without getting involved. **look out** be vigilant and take notice. **look something out** Brit. search for and produce something. **look up** improve. **look someone up** informal make social contact with someone. **look something up** search for and find a piece of information in a reference book. **look up to** have a great deal of respect for.
– ORIGIN Old English *lōcian* (v.), of West Germanic origin.

lookalike ■ n. a person or thing that closely resembles another.

look-and-say ■ n. [as modifier] denoting a method of teaching reading based on the visual recognition of words rather than the association of sounds and letters.

looker ■ n. a person with a specified appearance: *she's not a bad looker*. ▸ informal a very attractive person.

look-in ■ n. informal a chance of participation or success.

looking glass ■ n. a mirror. ▸ [as modifier] opposite to what is normal or expected.

lookout ■ n. 1 a place from which to keep watch or view landscape. ▸ a person stationed to keep watch. 2 informal, chiefly Brit. a good or bad prospect or outcome. 3 (**one's lookout**) informal, chiefly Brit. one's own concern.
– PHRASES **be on the lookout** (or **keep a lookout**) for be alert to. ▸ keep searching for.

look-see ■ n. informal a brief look or inspection.
– ORIGIN C19: from, or in imitation of, pidgin English.

loom¹ ■ n. an apparatus for making fabric by weaving yarn or thread.
– ORIGIN Old English *gelōma* 'tool', shortened to *lome* in Middle English.

loom² ■ v. appear as a vague form, especially one that is threatening. ▸ (of an event regarded as threatening) seem about to happen. ■ n. a vague first appearance of an object seen in darkness or fog, especially at sea.
– ORIGIN C16: prob. from Low German or Dutch.

loon¹ ■ n. informal a silly or foolish person.
– ORIGIN C19: from LOON² (referring to the bird's actions when escaping from danger), perhaps influenced by LOONY.

loon² ■ n. North American term for DIVER (in sense 2).
– ORIGIN C17: prob. an alteration of Shetland dialect *loom*, denoting especially a guillemot or a diver.

loons (also **loon pants**) ■ pl. n. Brit. dated close-fitting casual trousers widely flared from the knees downwards.
– ORIGIN 1970s.

loony informal ■ n. (pl. **-ies**) a mad or silly person. ■ adj. (**-ier**, **-iest**) mad or silly.
– DERIVATIVES **looniness** n.
– ORIGIN C19: abbrev. of LUNATIC.

loony bin ■ n. informal, derogatory an institution for people with mental illnesses.

loose-leaf

loop ■ n. 1 a shape produced by a curve that bends round and crosses itself. ▸ a length of thread or similar material forming such a shape, used as a fastening or handle. ▸ (also **loop line**) a length of railway track which is connected at either end to the main line and on to which trains can be diverted. ▸ (also **loop-the-loop**) a manoeuvre in which an aircraft describes a vertical circle in the air. 2 a structure, series, or process the end of which is connected to the beginning. ▸ an endless strip of tape or film allowing continuous repetition. ▸ a complete circuit for an electric current. ▸ Computing a programmed sequence of instructions that is repeated until or while a particular condition is satisfied. ■ v. form into a loop or loops; encircle. ▸ follow a course that forms a loop or loops. ▸ put into or execute a loop of tape, film, or computing instructions. ▸ (also **loop the loop**) circle an aircraft vertically in the air.
– PHRASES **in** (or **out of**) **the loop** informal aware (or unaware) of information known to only a privileged few. **throw** (or **knock**) **someone for a loop** informal surprise or astonish someone.
– ORIGIN Middle English: perhaps rel. to Scottish Gaelic *lùb* 'loop, bend'.

loop diuretic ■ n. Medicine a powerful diuretic which inhibits resorption of water and sodium from the loop of Henle.

looper ■ n. a caterpillar of a geometrid moth, which moves forward by arching itself into loops.

loophole ■ n. an ambiguity or inadequacy in the law or a set of rules.
– DERIVATIVES **loopholed** adj.
– ORIGIN C16: from obsolete *loop* 'embrasure' + HOLE.

loop of Henle /ˈhɛnli/ ■ n. Anatomy the part of a kidney tubule from which water and salts are resorbed into the blood.
– ORIGIN C19: named after the German anatomist Friedrich G. J. Henle.

loop stitch ■ n. a method of sewing or knitting in which each stitch incorporates a free loop of thread, for ornament or to give a thick pile.
– DERIVATIVES **loop-stitched** adj.

loopy ■ adj. (**-ier**, **-iest**) 1 informal mad or silly. 2 having many loops.
– DERIVATIVES **loopiness** n.

loose /luːs/ ■ adj. 1 not firmly or tightly fixed in place. ▸ not held, tied, or packaged together. ▸ not bound or tethered. ▸ (of the ball in a game) in play but not in any player's possession. 2 not fitting tightly or closely. 3 relaxed; physically slack. ▸ not strict or exact. ▸ careless and indiscreet: *loose talk*. ▸ dated promiscuous; immoral. 4 not dense or compact. ▸ (of play, especially in rugby) with the players far apart. ■ v. 1 set free. ▸ untie; unfasten. ▸ relax (one's grip). 2 (usu. **loose something off**) discharge; fire.
– PHRASES **hang** (or **stay**) **loose** informal, chiefly N. Amer. be relaxed. **on the loose** having escaped from confinement.
– DERIVATIVES **loosely** adv. **looseness** n.
– ORIGIN Middle English *loos* 'free from bonds', from Old Norse *lauss*, of Germanic origin.

loose box ■ n. a stable or stall in which a horse is kept without a tether.

loose cannon ■ n. an unpredictable person who is liable to cause unintentional damage.

loose cover ■ n. a removable fitted cloth cover for a chair or sofa.

loose end ■ n. a detail that is not yet settled or explained.
– PHRASES **be at a loose end** (or N. Amer. **at loose ends**) have nothing specific to do.

loose forward ■ n. Rugby a forward who plays at the back of the scrum.

loose head ■ n. Rugby the forward in the front row of a scrummage who is nearest to the scrum half as the ball is put in.

loose-leaf ■ adj. (of a notebook or folder) having each sheet of paper separate and removable.

loosen ■ v. make or become loose. ▶ make more lax. ▶ (**loosen up**) warm up in preparation for an activity. – PHRASES **loosen someone's tongue** make someone talk freely.

loose scrum ■ n. Rugby a scrum formed by the players round the ball during play, not ordered by the referee.

loosestrife /ˈluːsˌstraɪf/ ■ n. any of several waterside plants with a tall upright spike of flowers. [Genera *Lythrum* and *Lysimachia*.]
– ORIGIN C16: from LOOSE + STRIFE, taking the Greek name *lusimakheion* (actually from *Lusimakhos*, the name of its discoverer) to be from *luein* 'undo' + *makhē* 'battle'.

loot ■ n. **1** private property taken from an enemy in war or stolen by thieves. **2** informal money. ■ v. steal goods from, especially during a war or riot. ▶ steal (goods).
– DERIVATIVES **looter** n.
– ORIGIN C19: from Hindi *lūṭ*, from Sanskrit *luṇṭh-* 'rob'.

lop ■ v. (**lopped, lopping**) cut off (a branch or limb) from a tree or body. ▶ informal remove (something regarded as unnecessary or burdensome): *the new rail link lops an hour off journey times.*
– ORIGIN Middle English.

lope ■ v. run with a long bounding stride. ■ n. a long bounding stride.
– ORIGIN Middle English: var. of Scots *loup*, from Old Norse *hlaupa* 'leap'.

lop-eared ■ adj. (of an animal) having drooping ears.
– DERIVATIVES **lop ears** pl. n.

loperamide /ləʊˈpɛrəmaɪd/ ■ n. Medicine a synthetic drug of the opiate class used to treat diarrhoea.
– ORIGIN 1970s: prob. from (*ch*)*lo*(*ro*-) + (*pi*)*per*(*idine*) + AMIDE.

lopolith /ˈlɒpə(ʊ)lɪθ/ ■ n. Geology a large saucer-shaped intrusion of igneous rock.
– ORIGIN C20: from Greek *lopas* 'basin' + -LITH.

lopsided ■ adj. with one side lower or smaller than the other.
– DERIVATIVES **lopsidedly** adv. **lopsidedness** n.
– ORIGIN C18: from archaic *lop* 'hang limply' + SIDE.

loquacious /lɒˈkweɪʃəs/ ■ adj. talkative.
– DERIVATIVES **loquaciously** adv. **loquaciousness** n. **loquacity** n.
– ORIGIN C17 (*loquacity* Middle English): from Latin *loquax, loquac-* (from *loqui* 'talk').

loquat /ˈləʊkwɒt/ ■ n. a small yellow egg-shaped acidic fruit from an East Asian tree (*Eriobotrya japonica*).
– ORIGIN C19: from Chinese dialect *luh kwat* 'rush orange'.

lor ■ exclam. Brit. informal used to indicate surprise or dismay.
– ORIGIN C19: abbrev. of LORD.

Loran /ˈlɔːran, ˈlɒ-/ ■ n. a system of long-distance navigation in which position is determined from the intervals between signal pulses received from widely spaced radio transmitters.
– ORIGIN 1940s: from *lo*(*ng*-)*ra*(*nge*) *n*(*avigation*).

lord ■ n. a man of noble rank or high office. ▶ (**Lord**) a title given formally to a baron, and less formally to a marquess, earl, or viscount (prefixed to a family or territorial name). ▶ (**the Lords**) (in the UK) the House of Lords, or its members collectively. ▶ (**Lord**) a courtesy title given to a younger son of a duke or marquess (prefixed to a Christian name). ▶ a feudal superior, especially the owner of a manor house. ▶ (**Lord**) a name for God or Christ. ■ exclam. (**Lord**) used in exclamations expressing surprise or worry, or for emphasis. ■ v. (**lord it over**) act in a superior and domineering manner towards.
– PHRASES **the Lord's Day** Sunday. **the Lord's Prayer** the prayer taught by Christ to his disciples, beginning 'Our Father.' **My Lord** a polite form of address to judges, bishops, and certain noblemen.
– ORIGIN Old English *hlāford*, from *hlāfweard* 'bread-keeper', from a Germanic base.

Lord Bishop ■ n. the formal title of a bishop, in particular that of a diocesan bishop.

Lord Chamberlain (also **Lord Chamberlain of the Household**) ■ n. (in the UK) the official in charge of the royal household.

Lord Chancellor (also **Lord High Chancellor**) ■ n. (in the UK) the highest officer of the Crown, presiding in the House of Lords, the Chancery Division, or the Court of Appeal.

Lord Chief Justice ■ n. (in the UK) the officer presiding over the Queen's Bench Division and the Court of Appeal.

Lord Commissioner (also **Lord High Commissioner**) ■ n. (**Lords Commissioners**) (in the UK) the members of a board performing the duties of a high state office put in commission.

Lord Justice (also **Lord Justice of Appeal**) ■ n. (pl. **Lords Justices**) (in the UK) a judge in the Court of Appeal.

Lord Lieutenant ■ n. (in the UK) the chief executive authority and head of magistrates in each county.

lordling ■ n. archaic, chiefly derogatory a minor lord.

lordly ■ adj. (**-ier, -iest**) of, characteristic of, or suitable for a lord.
– DERIVATIVES **lordliness** n.

Lord Mayor ■ n. the title of the mayor in London and some other large cities.

lordosis /lɔːˈdəʊsɪs/ ■ n. Medicine excessive backward curvature of the spine, causing concavity of the back. Compare with KYPHOSIS.
– DERIVATIVES **lordotic** adj.
– ORIGIN C18: from Greek *lordōsis*, from *lordos* 'bent backwards'.

Lord Privy Seal ■ n. (in the UK) a senior cabinet minister without specified official duties.

lordship ■ n. **1** supreme power or rule. **2** (**His/Your**) etc. **Lordship** a form of address to a judge, bishop, or titled man.

Lords spiritual ■ pl. n. the bishops in the British House of Lords.

Lords temporal ■ pl. n. the members of the British House of Lords other than the bishops.

Lord Treasurer ■ n. see TREASURER.

Lordy ■ exclam. informal used to express surprise or dismay.

lore[1] ■ n. a body of traditions and knowledge on a subject: *farming lore.*
– ORIGIN Old English *lār* 'instruction', of Germanic origin.

lore[2] ■ n. Zoology the surface on each side of a bird's head between the eye and the upper base of the beak, or between the eye and nostril in snakes.
– ORIGIN C19: from Latin *lorum* 'strap'.

lorgnette /lɔːˈnjɛt/ (also **lorgnettes**) ■ n. a pair of glasses or opera glasses held by a long handle at one side.
– ORIGIN C19: from French, from *lorgner* 'to squint'.

lorica /ləˈraɪkə/ ■ n. (pl. **loricae** /-kiː/ or **loricas**) Zoology the rigid case or shell of some rotifers and protozoans.
– DERIVATIVES **loricate** adj.
– ORIGIN Latin, 'breastplate'.

lorikeet /ˈlɒrɪkiːt/ ■ n. a small bird of the lory family, found chiefly in New Guinea. [*Charmosyna* and other genera: several species.]
– ORIGIN C18: diminutive of LORY, on the pattern of *parakeet*.

loris /ˈlɔːrɪs/ ■ n. (pl. **lorises**) a small, slow-moving nocturnal primate living in dense vegetation in South Asia. [*Loris tardigradus* (**slender loris**) and genus *Nycticebus* (**slow loris**).]
– ORIGIN C18: from French, perhaps from obsolete Dutch *loeris* 'clown'.

lorn ■ adj. poetic/literary forlorn.
– ORIGIN Middle English: from obsolete *lese*, from Old English *lēosan* 'lose'.

lorry /ˈlɒri/ ■ n. (pl. **-ies**) a large, heavy motor vehicle for transporting goods or troops.
– PHRASES **fall off of the back a lorry** informal (of goods) be acquired in dubious circumstances.
– ORIGIN C19: perhaps from the given name *Laurie*.

lory /ˈlɔːri/ ■ n. (pl. **-ies**) a small Australasian or SE Asian parrot with a brush-tipped tongue. [Family Loridae: many species.]
– ORIGIN C17: from Malay *lūri*.

los ■ v. S. African informal leave (someone or something); let go.
– ORIGIN Afrikaans.

lose /luːz/ ▪ v. (past and past part. **lost**) **1** be deprived of or cease to have or retain. ▸ be deprived of (a relative or friend) through their death. ▸ (of a pregnant woman) miscarry (a baby). ▸ (**be lost**) be destroyed or killed. ▸ decrease in (body weight). ▸ (of a clock) become slow by (a specified amount of time). ▸ (**lose it**) informal lose control of one's temper or emotions. **2** become unable to find. ▸ evade or shake off (a pursuer). ▸ N. Amer. informal get rid of. ▸ (**lose oneself in/be lost in**) be or become deeply absorbed in. **3** fail to win. **4** earn less (money) than one is spending. **5** waste or fail to take advantage of: *he may have lost his chance.* **6** (**lose out**) be disadvantaged.
–PHRASES **lose face** lose one's credibility. **lose heart** become discouraged. **lose one's mind** (or **marbles**) informal go insane. **lose one's** (or **the**) **way** become lost.
–ORIGIN Old English *losian* 'perish, destroy', also 'become unable to find', from *los* 'loss'.

loser ▪ n. a person or thing that loses or has lost. ▸ informal a person who fails frequently.
–PHRASES **be on** (or **on to**) **a loser** informal be involved in something that is bound to fail.

losing battle ▪ n. a struggle in which failure seems certain.

loss ▪ n. the fact or process of losing something or someone. ▸ a defeat in sport. ▸ the feeling of grief after losing a valued person or thing. ▸ a person or thing that is badly missed when lost.
–PHRASES **at a loss 1** uncertain or puzzled. **2** making less money than is spent in operation or production.
–ORIGIN Old English *los* 'destruction', of Germanic origin.

loss adjuster ▪ n. an insurance agent who assesses the amount of compensation that should be paid to a claimant.

loss-leader ▪ n. a product sold at a loss to attract customers.

lossless ▪ adj. **1** without dissipation of electrical or electromagnetic energy. **2** Computing (of data compression) without loss of information.

lossy ▪ adj. **1** having or involving dissipation of electrical or electromagnetic energy. **2** Computing (of data compression) in which unnecessary information is discarded.

lost past and past participle of **LOSE**. ▪ adj. unable to find one's way; not knowing one's whereabouts.
–PHRASES **be lost for words** be so surprised or upset that one cannot think what to say. **be lost on** fail to be noticed or appreciated by. **get lost!** informal go away!

lost cause ▪ n. a person or thing that can no longer hope to succeed or be changed for the better.

lost generation ▪ n. **1** a generation with many of its men killed in war, especially the First World War. **2** an unfulfilled generation maturing during a period of instability.

lost wax ▪ n. a method of casting bronze using a clay core and a wax coating placed in a mould; the wax is melted in the mould and bronze poured into the space left, producing a hollow bronze figure when the core is discarded.

lot ▪ pron. (**a lot** or **lots**) informal a large number or amount; a great deal. ▸ (**the lot**) or **the whole lot** the whole number or quantity. ▪ adv. (**a lot** or **lots**) informal a great deal. ▪ n. **1** [treated as sing. or pl.] informal a particular group or set of people or things. **2** an item or set of items for sale at an auction. **3** a method of deciding something by random selection, especially by choosing one from a number of pieces of paper. ▸ the choice resulting from such a process. **4** a person's destiny, luck, or condition in life. **5** chiefly N. Amer. a plot of land. ▸ (also **parking lot**) a car park.
–PHRASES **draw** (or **cast**) **lots** decide by lot. **fall to someone's lot** become someone's task or responsibility. **throw in one's lot with** decide to share the fate of.
–ORIGIN Old English, of Germanic origin.

loth ▪ adj. variant spelling of **LOATH**.

Lothario /ləˈθɛːrɪəʊ, -ˈθɑː-/ ▪ n. (pl. **-os**) a womanizer.
–ORIGIN from a character in Nicholas Rowe's tragedy *The Fair Penitent* (1703).

loti /ˈlɒʊti, ˈluːti/ ▪ n. (pl. **maloti** /məˈlɒʊti, -ˈluːti/) the basic monetary unit of Lesotho, equal to 100 lisente.
–ORIGIN from Sesotho.

693

lotic /ˈləʊtɪk/ ▪ adj. Ecology inhabiting or situated in rapidly moving fresh water. Compare with **LENTIC**.
–ORIGIN C20: from Latin *lotus* 'washing'.

lotion ▪ n. a thick liquid preparation applied to the skin as a medicine or cosmetic.
–ORIGIN Middle English: from Latin *lotio(n-)*, from *lavare* 'wash'.

lottery ▪ n. (pl. **-ies**) a means of raising money by selling numbered tickets and giving prizes to the holders of numbers drawn at random. ▸ something whose success is governed by chance.
–ORIGIN C16: prob. from Dutch *loterij*, from *lot* 'lot'.

lotto ▪ n. **1** a children's game similar to bingo, using illustrated counters or cards. **2** a lottery.
–ORIGIN C18: from Italian.

lotus ▪ n. **1** a large water lily, now or formerly regarded as sacred. [*Nymphaea lotus* and *N. caerulea* (Egypt) and *Nelumbo nucifera* (sacred lotus, Asia).] **2** (in Greek mythology) a legendary plant whose fruit induces a dreamy forgetfulness and an unwillingness to leave.
–ORIGIN C15: from Greek *lōtos*, of Semitic origin.

lotus-eater ▪ n. a person given to indulgence in pleasure and luxury.
–DERIVATIVES **lotus-eating** adj.

lotus position ▪ n. a cross-legged position for meditation, with the feet resting on the thighs.

louche /luːʃ/ ▪ adj. disreputable; dubious.
–ORIGIN C19: from French, 'squinting'.

loud ▪ adj. **1** producing or capable of producing much noise. **2** strong in expression: *loud protests.* ▸ obtrusive; gaudy. ▪ adv. with a great deal of volume.
–PHRASES **out loud** audibly.
–DERIVATIVES **loudly** adv. **loudness** n.
–ORIGIN Old English *hlūd*, of West Germanic origin; from an Indo-European root meaning 'hear'.

loudhailer ▪ n. chiefly Brit. a megaphone.

loudmouth ▪ n. informal a person who talks too much, especially tactlessly.
–DERIVATIVES **loud-mouthed** adj.

loudspeaker ▪ n. an apparatus converting electrical impulses into sound, typically as part of a public address system.

Lou Gehrig's disease ▪ n. another term for **AMYOTROPHIC LATERAL SCLEROSIS**.

lough /lɒk, lɒx/ ▪ n. Anglo-Irish spelling of **LOCH**.
–ORIGIN Middle English: from Irish *loch*.

louis /ˈluːi/ (also **louis d'or** /-ˈdɔː/) ▪ n. (pl. same /ˈluːɪz/) a French gold coin issued between 1640 and 1793.
–ORIGIN from *Louis*, the name of many kings of France.

lounge ▪ v. recline or stand in a relaxed or lazy way. ▪ n. **1** a sitting room. ▸ a public sitting room in a hotel or theatre. ▸ a seating area in an airport for waiting passengers. **2** a spell of lounging.
–ORIGIN C16.

lounge bar ▪ n. a more comfortable bar in a pub or hotel.

lounge lizard ▪ n. informal an idle, pleasure-seeking man who spends his time in fashionable society.

lounger ▪ n. **1** a comfortable chair, especially an outdoor chair that reclines. **2** a person spending their time lazily or in a relaxed way.

lounge suit ▪ n. a man's suit for ordinary day wear.

loupe /luːp/ ▪ n. a small magnifying glass used by jewellers and watchmakers.
–ORIGIN C19: from French.

lour /ˈlaʊə/ (also **lower**) ▪ v. **1** scowl. **2** (of the sky) look dark and threatening. ▪ n. **1** a scowl. **2** a louring appearance of the sky.
–DERIVATIVES **louring** adj.
–ORIGIN Middle English.

lourie /ˈlʊəri/ (also **loerie**) ▪ n. S. African another term for **TURACO** and **GO-AWAY BIRD**.
–ORIGIN from Afrikaans *loerie*, from Malay *luri*, dialect form of *nuri* 'parrot'.

lourie

ʊ put uː too ʌɪ my aʊ how eɪ day əʊ no ɪə near ɔɪ boy ʊə poor ʌɪə fire aʊə sour

louse

louse ■ n. **1** (pl. **lice**) a small wingless parasitic insect which infests human skin and hair. [*Pediculus humanus* (see BODY LOUSE, HEAD LOUSE).] ▸ a related insect which lives on the skin of mammals or birds. [Orders Anoplura (sucking lice) and Mallophaga (biting lice).] ▸ used in names of small invertebrates that parasitize aquatic animals or infest plants, e.g. fish louse. **2** (pl. **louses**) informal a contemptible person. ■ v. **1** (**louse something up**) informal spoil something. **2** archaic remove lice from.
–ORIGIN Old English *lūs*, (pl.) *lȳs*, of Germanic origin.

louse fly ■ n. a flattened bloodsucking fly which typically spends much of its life on an individual host. [Family Hippoboscidae: many species.]

lousewort ■ n. a partially parasitic herbaceous plant of Eurasia and North America, typically favouring damp habitats and formerly reputed to harbour lice. [Genus *Pedicularis*: several species.]

lousy ■ adj. (**-ier**, **-iest**) **1** informal very poor or bad. **2** infested with lice. ▸ (**lousy with**) informal teeming with (something undesirable).
–DERIVATIVES **lousily** adv. **lousiness** n.

lout ■ n. an uncouth or aggressive man.
–DERIVATIVES **loutish** adj. **loutishly** adv. **loutishness** n.
–ORIGIN C16: perhaps from archaic *lout* 'to bow down', of Germanic origin.

louvre /ˈluːvə/ (US also **louver**) ■ n. **1** each of a set of angled slats fixed at regular intervals in a door, shutter, or cover to allow air or light through. **2** a domed structure on a roof, with side openings for ventilation.
–DERIVATIVES **louvred** adj.
–ORIGIN Middle English: from Old French *lover*, *lovier* 'skylight', prob. of Germanic origin.

lovable (also **loveable**) ■ adj. inspiring love or affection.
–DERIVATIVES **lovability** n. **lovableness** n. **lovably** adv.

lovage /ˈlʌvɪdʒ/ ■ n. a large edible white-flowered plant of the parsley family. [*Levisticum officinale* (Mediterranean) and other species.]
–ORIGIN Middle English *loveache*, alteration of Old French *luvesche*, via late Latin *levisticum* from Latin *ligusticum* 'Ligurian'.

lovat /ˈlʌvət/ (also **lovat green**) ■ n. a muted green used especially in tweed and woollen garments.
–ORIGIN C20: from *Lovat*, a place in Highland Scotland.

love ■ n. **1** an intense feeling of deep affection. ▸ a deep romantic or sexual attachment to someone. ▸ a great interest and pleasure in something. ▸ affectionate greetings. **2** (**Love**) love personified, often as the Roman god Cupid. **3** a person or thing that one loves. ▸ Brit. informal a friendly form of address. **4** (in tennis, squash, etc.) a score of zero. ■ v. feel a deep romantic or sexual attachment to. ▸ like very much. ▸ have deep affection for. ▸ [as adj. **loving**] showing love or great care.
–PHRASES **for love** for pleasure not profit. **for the love of God** used with an urgent request or to express annoyance. **make love 1** have sexual intercourse. **2** dated (**make love to**) pay amorous attention to. **not for love or money** informal not in any circumstances. **there's no love lost between** there is mutual dislike between.
–DERIVATIVES **loveless** adj. **lovelessness** n. **lovingly** adv. **lovingness** n.
–ORIGIN Old English, of Germanic origin.

loveable ■ adj. variant spelling of LOVABLE.

love affair ■ n. **1** a romantic or sexual relationship, especially outside marriage. **2** an intense enthusiasm for something.

love apple ■ n. archaic a tomato.

lovebird ■ n. **1** a very small mainly green African or Madagascan parrot, noted for the affectionate behaviour of mated birds. [Genus *Agapornis*: several species.] **2** (**lovebirds**) informal an affectionate couple.

love bite ■ n. a temporary red mark on the skin caused by biting or sucking during sexual play.

love child ■ n. a child born to parents who are not married to each other.

love game ■ n. (in tennis, squash, etc.) a game in which the loser does not score.

love handles ■ pl. n. informal deposits of excess fat at the waistline.

love-in ■ n. informal (especially among hippies in the 1960s) a gathering at which people are encouraged to express friendship and physical attraction.

love-in-a-mist ■ n. a European plant of the buttercup family whose blue flowers are surrounded by thread-like green bracts, giving them a hazy appearance. [*Nigella damascena*.]

love interest ■ n. an actor whose main role in a story or film is that of a lover of the central character.

love-lies-bleeding ■ n. a South American plant with long drooping tassels of crimson flowers. [*Amaranthus caudatus*.]

love life ■ n. the part of one's life concerning relationships with lovers.

lovelorn ■ adj. unhappy because of unrequited love.

lovely ■ adj. (**-ier**, **-iest**) exquisitely beautiful. ▸ informal very pleasant. ■ n. (pl. **-ies**) informal a beautiful woman or girl.
–DERIVATIVES **loveliness** n.
–ORIGIN Old English.

love match ■ n. a marriage based on love.

love nest ■ n. informal a secluded place where two lovers spend time together.

lover ■ n. **1** a person having a sexual or romantic relationship with another. **2** a person who enjoys a specified thing: *a music lover*.

love seat ■ n. a sofa designed in an S-shape so that two people can face each other.

lovesick ■ adj. pining or feeling weak due to being in love.
–DERIVATIVES **lovesickness** n.

lovey ■ n. (pl. **-eys**) informal used as an affectionate form of address.

lovey-dovey ■ adj. informal very affectionate or romantic.

loving ■ adj. feeling or showing love or great care. ▸ (**-loving**) [in combination] enjoying the specified thing: *a fun-loving child*
–DERIVATIVES **lovingly** adv. **lovingness** n.

loving cup ■ n. a two-handled cup passed round at banquets.

loving kindness ■ n. tenderness and consideration.

low[1] ■ adj. **1** of less than average height. ▸ situated not far above the ground, horizon, etc. ▸ (of latitude) near the equator. ▸ (of women's clothing) cut so as to reveal the upper part of the breasts. **2** (of a sound) deep. **3** below average in amount, extent, or intensity: *a low income*. ▸ (of a sound) not loud. **4** lacking importance, prestige, or quality; inferior: *training was given low priority*. ▸ unscrupulous or dishonest. ▸ unfavourable: *a low opinion*. **5** depressed or lacking energy. **6** Phonetics (of a vowel) open. ■ n. **1** a low point, level, or figure. **2** an area of low barometric pressure. ■ adv. **1** in or into a low position or state. **2** quietly. ▸ at or to a low pitch.
–DERIVATIVES **lowish** adj. **lowness** n.
–ORIGIN Middle English: from Old Norse *lágr*, of Germanic origin.

low[2] ■ v. (of a cow) moo. ■ n. a moo.
–ORIGIN Old English *hlōwan*, of Germanic origin.

lowball ■ n. Baseball a ball pitched so as to pass over the plate below knee-level. ▸ [as modifier] N. Amer. informal (of an estimate) unrealistically low.

lowboy ■ n. N. Amer. a low chest or table with drawers.

lowbrow ■ adj. informal, chiefly derogatory not highly intellectual or cultured.

Low Church ■ n. a tradition within the Anglican Church giving relatively little emphasis to ritual and sacraments.

low comedy ■ n. comedy bordering on farce.

low-density lipoprotein ■ n. the form of lipoprotein by which cholesterol is transported in the blood.

low-down informal ■ adj. mean and unfair. ■ n. (**the low-down**) the relevant information.

lower[1] ■ adj. comparative of LOW[1]. **1** less high. ▸ denoting the first of two numbered forms through which pupils pass in successive years. ▸ (often **Lower**) denoting an older (and hence typically deeper) part of an archaeological

division. **2** [in place names] situated to the south. ▪ adv. in or into a lower position.
– DERIVATIVES **lowermost** adj.

lower² ▪ v. **1** cause to move downward. ▸ reduce the height, pitch, or elevation of. **2** make or become less in amount, extent, or value. ▸ (**lower oneself**) demean oneself.

lower³ ▪ v.& n. variant spelling of LOUR.

lower animals ▪ pl. n. invertebrate animals, regarded as having relatively primitive characteristics.

lower case ▪ n. small letters.

lower chamber ▪ n. another term for LOWER HOUSE.

lower class ▪ n. [treated as sing. or pl.] the working class. ▪ adj. of or relating to the lower class.

lower court ▪ n. Law a court whose decisions may be overruled by another. ▸ (in South Africa) a magistrates' court or regional court.

lower deck ▪ n. **1** the deck of a ship immediately above the hold. **2** the petty officers and crew of a ship.

lower house ▪ n. the larger, typically elected, body of a bicameral parliament. ▸ (**the Lower House**) (in the UK) the House of Commons.

lower plants ▪ pl. n. plants without vascular systems, e.g. algae, mosses, and liverworts, regarded as having relatively primitive characteristics.

lower regions ▪ pl. n. archaic hell.

lowest common denominator ▪ n. **1** Mathematics the lowest common multiple of the denominators of several vulgar fractions. **2** the least desirable common feature of members of a group.

lowest common multiple ▪ n. Mathematics the lowest quantity that is a multiple of two or more given quantities.

low frequency ▪ n. (in radio) 30–300 kilohertz.

low gear ▪ n. a gear that causes a wheeled vehicle to move slowly.

Low German ▪ n. a German dialect spoken in much of northern Germany.

low-impact ▪ adj. **1** denoting exercises, especially aerobics, putting little stress on the body. **2** affecting or altering the environment as little as possible.

low-key ▪ adj. modest or restrained.

lowland /'ləʊlənd/ ▪ n. (also **lowlands**) low-lying country. ▸ (**the Lowlands**) the part of Scotland lying south and east of the Highlands.
– DERIVATIVES **lowlander** n.

Low Latin ▪ n. medieval and later forms of Latin.

low-level ▪ adj. **1** of relatively little importance. **2** Computing denoting a programming language that is close to machine code in form. **3** (of nuclear waste) having a small degree of radioactivity.

low life ▪ n. disreputable or criminal people or activities. ▸ (**lowlife**) informal a person of this type.
– DERIVATIVES **low-lifer** n.

lowlight ▪ n. **1** (**lowlights**) darker dyed streaks in the hair. **2** informal a disappointing or dull event or feature.
– ORIGIN C20: from LOW¹, suggested by HIGHLIGHT.

low-loader ▪ n. a truck with a low floor and no sides, for heavy loads.

lowly ▪ adj. (**-ier**, **-iest**) **1** low in status or importance. **2** (of an organism) primitive or simple. ▪ adv. to a low degree: *lowly paid workers*.
– DERIVATIVES **lowliness** n.

low-lying ▪ adj. at low altitude above sea level.

Low Mass ▪ n. (in the Catholic Church) Mass with no music and a minimum of ceremony.

low relief ▪ n. see RELIEF (sense 6).

low-rider ▪ n. US a customized vehicle with a chassis that can be lowered nearly to the road.

low-rise ▪ adj. (of a building) having few storeys.

low season ▪ n. the least popular time of year for a holiday, when prices are lowest.

low spirits ▪ pl. n. sadness and despondency.
– DERIVATIVES **low-spirited** adj.

Low Sunday ▪ n. the Sunday after Easter.

– ORIGIN perhaps in contrast to the high days of Holy Week and Easter.

low-tech ▪ adj. involved in or employing low technology.

low technology ▪ n. less advanced technological development or equipment.

low tide ▪ n. the state of the tide when at its lowest level.

lowveld /'laʊfɛlt/ (also **Lowveld**) ▪ n. S. African the subtropical region of north-eastern South Africa, lying mostly below 600 metres.
– DERIVATIVES **Lowvelder** n.
– ORIGIN partial translation of Afrikaans *laeveld* 'low land'.

low water ▪ n. low tide.

low-water mark ▪ n. **1** the level reached by the sea at low tide. **2** a minimum recorded level or value.

lox¹ /lɒks/ ▪ n. liquid oxygen.
– ORIGIN C20: acronym from *liquid oxygen explosive*, later interpreted as being from *liquid oxygen*.

lox² /lɒks/ ▪ n. N. Amer. smoked salmon.
– ORIGIN 1940s: from Yiddish *laks*.

loxion /'lɒkʃən/ (also **lokshin**) ▪ n. S. African informal another term for KASI.
– ORIGIN from Tsotsitaal, from LOCATION.

loyal ▪ adj. showing firm and constant support or allegiance to a person or institution.
– DERIVATIVES **loyally** adv.
– ORIGIN C16: via Old French *loial* from Latin *legalis* (see LEGAL).

loyalist ▪ n. a person who remains loyal to the established ruler or government, especially in the face of a revolt. ▸ (**Loyalist**) a supporter of union between Great Britain and Northern Ireland.
– DERIVATIVES **loyalism** n.

loyalty ▪ n. (pl. **-ies**) the state of being loyal. ▸ a strong feeling of support or allegiance.

loyalty card ▪ n. a card issued by a retailer to its customers, on which credits are accumulated for future discounts every time a transaction is recorded.

lozenge /'lɒzɪn(d)ʒ/ ▪ n. **1** a rhombus or diamond shape. ▸ Heraldry a charge in the shape of a solid diamond. **2** a small medicinal tablet, originally of this shape, for dissolving in the mouth.
– ORIGIN Middle English: from Old French *losenge*, prob. derived from Spanish *losa* 'slab', from late Latin *lausiae* (*lapides*) 'stone slabs'.

LP ▪ abbrev. **1** long-playing (gramophone record). **2** low pressure.

l.p. ▪ abbrev. low pressure.

LPG ▪ abbrev. liquefied petroleum gas.

L-plate ▪ n. a sign bearing the letter L, attached to a vehicle to indicate that the driver is a learner.

Lr ▪ symb. the chemical element lawrencium.

LRA ▪ abbrev. (in South Africa) Labour Relations Act.

LS ▪ abbrev. Lesotho (international vehicle registration).

LSB ▪ abbrev. Computing least significant bit.

LSD ▪ n. a synthetic crystalline compound, lysergic acid diethylamide, which is a powerful hallucinogenic drug.
– ORIGIN 1950s: abbrev.

LSE ▪ abbrev. London School of Economics.

LSM ▪ abbrev. S. African Living Standards Measure, a system for rating consumer expenditure patterns and standards of living.

Lt ▪ abbrev. Lieutenant.

Ltd ▪ abbrev. (after a company name) Limited.

Lu ▪ symb. the chemical element lutetium.

lubber ▪ n. archaic or dialect a big, clumsy person.
– ORIGIN Middle English: perhaps via Old French *lobeor* 'swindler, parasite' from *lober* 'deceive'.

lubber line ▪ n. a line on a compass, showing the direction straight ahead.

lube /luːb/ informal ▪ n. a lubricant. ▪ v. lubricate.

lubricant ▪ n. a substance, e.g. oil or grease, for lubricating an engine or component. ▪ adj. lubricating.

lubricate

lubricate /ˈluːbrɪkeɪt/ ■ v. **1** apply oil or grease to (an engine or component) to minimize friction. **2** informal make convivial with alcohol.
– DERIVATIVES **lubrication** n. **lubricator** n.
– ORIGIN C17: from Latin *lubricare* 'make slippery', from *lubricus* 'slippery'.

lubricious /luːˈbrɪʃəs/ (also **lubricous** /ˈluːbrɪkəs/) ■ adj. **1** lewd. **2** smooth and slippery with oil or grease.
– DERIVATIVES **lubriciously** adv. **lubricity** n.
– ORIGIN C16 (*lubricity* C15): from Latin *lubricus* 'slippery'.

lucerne /luːˈsɜːn/ ■ n. another term for ALFALFA.
– ORIGIN C17: from French *luzerne*, from modern Provençal *luzerno* 'glow-worm' (with ref. to its shiny seeds).

lucid /ˈluːsɪd/ ■ adj. **1** clear; easy to understand. ▸ showing an ability to think clearly. **2** poetic/literary bright or luminous.
– DERIVATIVES **lucidity** n. **lucidly** adv.
– ORIGIN C16: from Latin *lucidus*, from *lucere* 'shine', from *lux, luc-* 'light'.

Lucifer /ˈluːsɪfə/ ■ n. **1** the Devil. **2** poetic/literary the planet Venus in the morning.
– ORIGIN Old English, from Latin, 'light-bringing, morning star', from *lux, luc-* 'light' + *-fer* 'bearing'.

lucite /ˈluːsaɪt/ ■ n. trademark, chiefly N. Amer. a tough transparent plastic made of an acrylic resin, used as a substitute for glass.
– ORIGIN 1930s: from Latin *lux, luc-* 'light'.

luck ■ n. success or failure apparently brought by chance. ▸ chance considered as a force causing success or failure. ■ v. informal (**luck into/upon**) chance to find or acquire.
– PHRASES **one's luck is in** one is fortunate. **no such luck** informal unfortunately not. **try one's luck** attempt something risky. **worse luck** informal unfortunately.
– ORIGIN Middle English: from Middle Low German *lucke*, of West Germanic origin.

luckily ■ adv. it is fortunate that.

luckless ■ adj. unfortunate.

lucky ■ adj. (-**ier**, -**iest**) having, bringing, or resulting from good luck.

lucky bag ■ n. Brit. another term for LUCKY PACKET.

lucky bean ■ n. **1** a plant of the pea family producing poisonous shiny scarlet beans with a black eye, sometimes used as amulets. [*Abrus precatorius*.] **2** (**lucky bean tree**) S. African another term for CORAL TREE. ▸ the scarlet, black-eyed bean of the coral tree.

lucky dip ■ n. a game in which small prizes are concealed in a container and chosen at random by participants.

lucky packet ■ n. S. African an assortment of items in a sealed bag which one buys or is given without knowing the contents.

lucrative /ˈluːkrətɪv/ ■ adj. profitable.
– DERIVATIVES **lucratively** adv. **lucrativeness** n.
– ORIGIN Middle English: from Latin *lucrativus*, from *lucrari* 'to gain', from *lucrum* (see LUCRE).

lucre /ˈluːkə/ ■ n. poetic/literary money, especially when gained dishonourably.
– ORIGIN Middle English: from French *lucre* or Latin *lucrum*.

lucubration ■ n. formal study; meditation. ▸ a piece of writing, typically a pedantic or over-elaborate one.

lud ■ n. (**m'ludor**) **my lud** Brit. used to address a judge in court.
– ORIGIN C18: alteration of LORD.

Luddite /ˈlʌdaɪt/ ■ n. **1** a member of any of the bands of English workers who opposed mechanization and destroyed machinery in the early 19th century. **2** a person opposed to industrialization or new technology.
– DERIVATIVES **Luddism** n. **Ludditism** n.
– ORIGIN perhaps named after Ned *Lud*, a participant in the destruction of machinery.

ludicrous ■ adj. absurd; ridiculous.
– DERIVATIVES **ludicrously** adv. **ludicrousness** n.
– ORIGIN C17: from Latin *ludicrus*, prob. from *ludicrum* 'stage play'.

ludo ■ n. a board game in which players move counters according to throws of a dice.
– ORIGIN C19: from Latin, 'I play'.

luff chiefly Nautical ■ n. the edge of a fore-and-aft sail next to the mast or stay. ■ v. **1** steer (a yacht) nearer the wind. ▸ obstruct (an opponent in yacht racing) by sailing closer to the wind. **2** raise or lower (the jib of a crane).
– ORIGIN Middle English: from Old French *lof*, prob. from Low German.

Luftwaffe /ˈluftwafə/ ■ n. the German air force until the end of the Second World War.
– ORIGIN German, from *Luft* 'air' + *Waffe* 'weapon'.

lug[1] ■ v. (**lugged**, **lugging**) carry or drag with great effort. ■ n. a box for transporting fruit.
– ORIGIN Middle English: prob. of Scandinavian origin.

lug[2] ■ n. **1** a projection on an object by which it may be carried or fixed in place. **2** informal, chiefly N. Amer. a lout.
– ORIGIN C15 (denoting the ear flap of a hat): prob. of Scandinavian origin.

Luganda /luːˈɡandə/ ■ n. the Bantu language of the Baganda people.

luge /luːʒ/ ■ n. a light toboggan ridden in a sitting or supine position. ■ v. ride on a luge.
– ORIGIN C19: from Swiss French.

Luger /ˈluːɡə/ ■ n. (trademark in the US) a type of German automatic pistol.
– ORIGIN C20: named after the German firearms expert George *Luger*.

luggage ■ n. suitcases or other bags for a traveller's belongings.
– ORIGIN C16: from LUG[1].

lugger ■ n. a small ship with two or three masts and a lugsail on each.
– ORIGIN C18: from LUGSAIL.

lughole ■ n. Brit. informal an ear.

lugsail /ˈlʌɡseɪl, -s(ə)l/ ■ n. an asymmetrical four-sided sail, bent on and hoisted from a steeply inclined yard.
– ORIGIN C17: prob. from LUG[2] + SAIL.

lugubrious /luˈɡuːbrɪəs/ ■ adj. mournful; sad and dismal.
– DERIVATIVES **lugubriously** adv. **lugubriousness** n.
– ORIGIN C17: from Latin *lugubris*, from *lugere* 'mourn'.

lugworm ■ n. a bristle worm living in muddy sand and leaving characteristic worm casts, widely used as fishing bait. [Genus *Arenicola*: several species.]
– ORIGIN C19: from *lug* (of unknown origin) + WORM.

lukewarm ■ adj. **1** only moderately warm. **2** unenthusiastic.
– DERIVATIVES **lukewarmly** adv. **lukewarmness** n.
– ORIGIN Middle English: from dialect *luke*, prob. from *lew* 'lukewarm' + WARM.

lull ■ v. calm or send to sleep with soothing sounds or movements. ▸ cause to feel deceptively secure. ▸ allay (doubts, fears, etc.), typically by deception. ▸ (of noise or a storm) abate. ■ n. a temporary period of quiet or inactivity.
– ORIGIN Middle English: imitative of sounds used to quieten a child.

lullaby ■ n. (pl. -**ies**) a soothing song sung to send a child to sleep.
– ORIGIN C16: from LULL + *bye-bye*, a sound used as a refrain in lullabies.

lulu ■ n. informal an outstanding person or thing.
– ORIGIN C19: perhaps from *Lulu*, familiar form of the given name *Louise*.

lumbago /lʌmˈbeɪɡəʊ/ ■ n. pain in the lower back.
– ORIGIN C17: from Latin, from *lumbus* 'loin'.

lumbar /ˈlʌmbə/ ■ adj. relating to the lower back.
– ORIGIN C17: from medieval Latin *lumbaris*, from Latin *lumbus* 'loin'.

lumbar puncture ■ n. Medicine the withdrawal of spinal fluid from the lower back through a hollow needle, typically for diagnostic purposes.

lumber[1] ■ v. move in a slow, heavy, awkward way.
– ORIGIN Middle English *lomere*.

lumber[2] ■ n. partly prepared timber. ■ v. **1** (usu. be **lumbered with**) informal burden with an unwanted responsibility. **2** (usu. as noun **lumbering**) chiefly N. Amer. cut and prepare forest timber for transport and sale.

lumberjack (also **lumberman**) ■ n. a person who fells trees, cuts them into logs, or transports them.

lumberjacket ■ n. a thick jacket, typically with a bright check pattern, of the kind worn by lumberjacks.

lumber room ■ n. Brit. a room for storing disused or bulky things.

lumbersome ■ adj. unwieldy; awkward.

lumen¹ /ˈluːmen/ (abbrev.: **lm**) ■ n. Physics the SI unit of luminous flux, equal to the amount of light emitted per second in a unit solid angle of one steradian from a uniform source of one candela.
–ORIGIN C19: from Latin, 'light'.

lumen² /ˈluːmən/ ■ n. (pl. **lumina** /-mɪnə/) Anatomy the central cavity of a hollow structure in an organism or cell.
–DERIVATIVES **luminal** /ˈluːmɪn(ə)l/ adj.
–ORIGIN C19: from Latin, 'opening'.

luminaire /ˌluːmɪˈnɛː, ˌlʌmɪˈnɛː/ ■ n. a complete electric light unit.
–ORIGIN C20: from French.

luminance /ˈluːmɪn(ə)ns/ ■ n. **1** Physics the intensity of light emitted from a surface per unit area in a given direction. **2** the component of a television signal which carries information on the brightness of the image.
–ORIGIN C19: from Latin *luminare* 'illuminate'.

luminary /ˈluːmɪn(ə)ri/ ■ n. (pl. **-ies**) **1** a person who inspires or influences others. **2** poetic/literary a natural light-giving body, especially the sun or moon.
–ORIGIN Middle English: from late Latin *luminarium*, from Latin *lumen* 'light'.

luminesce /ˌluːmɪˈnɛs/ ■ v. emit light by luminescence.

luminescence /ˌluːmɪˈnɛs(ə)ns/ ■ n. the emission of light by a substance that has not been heated, as in fluorescence and phosphorescence.
–DERIVATIVES **luminescent** adj.
–ORIGIN C19: from Latin *lumen* 'light' + *-escence* (denoting a state).

luminosity ■ n. (pl. **-ies**) luminous quality. ▸ Astronomy the intrinsic brightness of an object (as distinct from its apparent brightness).

luminous /ˈluːmɪnəs/ ■ adj. **1** bright or shining, especially in the dark. **2** Physics of or relating to visible light.
–DERIVATIVES **luminously** adv. **luminousness** n.
–ORIGIN Middle English: from Old French *lumineux* or Latin *luminosus*, from *lumen* 'light'.

lumme /ˈlʌmi/ ■ exclam. Brit. informal, dated an expression of surprise.
–ORIGIN C19: from (*Lord*) *love me*.

lummox /ˈlʌməks/ ■ n. informal, chiefly N. Amer. a clumsy, stupid person.
–ORIGIN C19.

lump¹ ■ n. **1** a compact mass, especially one without a definite or regular shape. ▸ a swelling under the skin. **2** informal a heavy, ungainly, or slow-witted person. ■ v. **1** (often **lump things together**) put in an indiscriminate mass or group. **2** Brit. carry (a heavy load) somewhere with difficulty.
–PHRASES **a lump in the throat** a feeling of tightness in the throat caused by strong emotion.
–DERIVATIVES **lumper** n.
–ORIGIN Middle English: perhaps from a Germanic base meaning 'shapeless piece'.

lump² ■ v. (**lump it**) informal accept or tolerate something whether one likes it or not.
–ORIGIN C16: symbolic of displeasure; cf. *dump* and *grump*.

lumpectomy ■ n. (pl. **-ies**) a surgical operation in which a lump, typically a tumour, is removed from the breast.

lumpen ■ adj. **1** (in Marxist contexts) uninterested in revolutionary advancement. ▸ boorish and stupid. **2** lumpy and misshapen. ■ n. (**the lumpen**) the lumpen-proletariat.
–ORIGIN C20: back-formation from **LUMPENPROLETARIAT**; the sense 'misshapen' by association with **LUMPISH**.

lumpenproletariat /ˌlʌmpənˌprəʊlɪˈtɛːrɪət/ ■ n. [treated as sing. or pl.] (especially in Marxist terminology) the apolitical lower orders of society uninterested in revolutionary advancement.

697

–ORIGIN C20: from German, from *Lumpen* 'rag, rogue' + **PROLETARIAT**.

lumpfish ■ n. (pl. same or **-fishes**) a North Atlantic fish with edible roe, which is sometimes used as a substitute for caviar. [*Cyclopterus lumpus*.]
–ORIGIN C17: from Middle Low German *lumpen*, Middle Dutch *lompe* + **FISH**.

lumpish ■ adj. **1** roughly or clumsily formed. **2** stupid and lethargic.
–DERIVATIVES **lumpishly** adv. **lumpishness** n.

lump sum ■ n. a single payment made at one time, as opposed to many instalments.

lumpy ■ adj. (**-ier, -iest**) **1** full of or covered with lumps. **2** Nautical (of water) formed by the wind into small waves.
–DERIVATIVES **lumpily** adv. **lumpiness** n.

lunacy ■ n. (pl. **-ies**) insanity (not in technical use). ▸ extreme folly.
–ORIGIN C16 from **LUNATIC**.

lunar /ˈluːnə/ ■ adj. of, determined by, or resembling the moon.
–ORIGIN Middle English: from Latin *lunaris*, from *luna* 'moon'.

lunar cycle ■ n. another term for **METONIC CYCLE**.

lunar distance ■ n. the angular distance of the moon from the sun, a planet, or a star, used in finding longitude at sea.

lunar eclipse ■ n. an eclipse in which the moon passes into the earth's shadow.

lunar month ■ n. a month measured between successive new moons (roughly 29½ days). ▸ (in general use) four weeks.

lunar year ■ n. a period of twelve lunar months (approximately 354 days).

lunatic ■ n. a person who is mentally ill (not in technical use). ▸ an extremely foolish person.
–ORIGIN Middle English: from Old French *lunatique*, from late Latin *lunaticus*, from Latin *luna* 'moon' (from the belief that changes of the moon caused intermittent insanity).

lunatic asylum ■ n. dated an institution for the mentally ill.

lunatic fringe ■ n. an extreme or eccentric minority.

lunation /luːˈneɪʃ(ə)n/ ■ n. Astronomy another term for **LUNAR MONTH**.
–ORIGIN Middle English: from medieval Latin *lunatio(n-)*, from Latin *luna* 'moon'.

lunch ■ n. a meal eaten in the middle of the day. ■ v. eat lunch. ▸ take (someone) out for lunch.
–PHRASES **do lunch** informal meet for lunch. **out to lunch** informal unbalanced or stupid.
–DERIVATIVES **luncher** n.
–ORIGIN C19: abbrev. of **LUNCHEON**.

lunch box ■ n. **1** a container for a packed meal. **2** humorous a man's genitals.

luncheon ■ n. formal lunch.
–ORIGIN C16: perhaps from obsolete *lunch* 'thick piece, hunk', from Spanish *lonja* 'slice'.

luncheonette ■ n. N. Amer. a small restaurant serving light lunches.

luncheon meat ■ n. finely minced cooked pork mixed with cereal, often sold in a tin.

luncheon voucher ■ n. Brit. a voucher given to employees and exchangeable for food at restaurants and shops.

lunch hour ■ n. a break from work when lunch is eaten.

lune /luːn/ ■ n. a crescent-shaped figure formed on a sphere or plane by two arcs intersecting at two points.
–ORIGIN C18: from Latin *luna* 'moon'.

lunette /luːˈnɛt/ ■ n. **1** an arched aperture or window in a domed ceiling. **2** a crescent-shaped or semicircular alcove containing a painting or statue. **3** a fortification with two faces forming a projecting angle, and two flanks. **4** a ring on a vehicle, by which it can be towed.
–ORIGIN C16: from French, diminutive of *lune* 'moon', from Latin *luna*.

lung

lung ■ n. each of the pair of organs within the ribcage into which air is drawn in breathing, so that oxygen can pass into the blood and carbon dioxide be removed.
– DERIVATIVES **-lunged** adj. **lungful** n. (pl. **-fuls**). **lungless** adj.
– ORIGIN Old English *lungen*, of Germanic origin.

lunge¹ ■ n. a sudden forward movement of the body. ▸ a thrust in fencing, in which the leading leg is bent while the back leg remains straightened. ■ v. (**lunging** or **lungeing**) make a lunge. ▸ make a sudden forward thrust with.
– ORIGIN C18: from earlier *allonge*, from French *allonger* 'lengthen'.

lunge² ■ n. a long rein on which a horse is made to move in a circle round its trainer. ■ v. (**lungeing**) exercise (a horse or rider) on a lunge.
– ORIGIN C18: from French *longe*, from *allonge* 'lengthening out'.

lungfish ■ n. (pl. same or **-fishes**) an elongated freshwater fish with one or two sacs which function as lungs, enabling it to breathe in air and aestivate in mud to survive drought. [Subclass Dipnoi: several species.]

lungi /ˈlʊŋɡiː/ ■ n. (pl. **lungis**) a length of cotton cloth worn as a loincloth in India or as a skirt in Burma (Myanmar).
– ORIGIN from Urdu.

lungworm ■ n. a parasitic nematode worm found in the lungs of mammals. [*Dictyocaulus* and other genera.]

lungwort ■ n. 1 a bristly pink-flowered European plant with white-spotted leaves said to resemble a diseased lung. [*Pulmonaria officinalis* and related species.] 2 (also **tree lungwort**) a large lichen which grows on trees, formerly used to treat lung disease. [*Lobaria pulmonaria*.]

lunisolar /ˌluːnɪˈsəʊlə/ ■ adj. of or concerning the sun and moon.
– ORIGIN C17: from Latin *luna* 'moon' + SOLAR¹.

lunula /ˈluːnjʊlə/ ■ n. (pl. **lunulae** /-liː/) the white area at the base of a fingernail.
– DERIVATIVES **lunular** adj. **lunulate** adj.
– ORIGIN C16: from Latin, diminutive of *luna* 'moon'.

lunule /ˈluːnjuːl/ ■ n. another term for LUNULA.

Luo /ˈluːəʊ/ ■ n. (pl. same or **-os**) 1 a member of an East African people of Kenya and the upper Nile valley. 2 the Nilotic language of this people.
– ORIGIN the name in Luo.

lupin /ˈluːpɪn/ (also **lupine** /-pɪn/) ■ n. a plant of the pea family, with deeply divided leaves and tall colourful tapering spikes of flowers. [Genus *Lupinus*: several species.]
– ORIGIN Middle English: from Latin *lupinus* (see LUPINE).

lupine /ˈluːpʌɪn/ ■ adj. of or like a wolf or wolves.
– ORIGIN C17: from Latin *lupinus*, from *lupus* 'wolf'.

lupus /ˈluːpəs/ ■ n. Medicine an ulcerous skin condition, especially one due to direct infection with tuberculosis.
– DERIVATIVES **lupoid** adj. **lupous** adj.
– ORIGIN C16: from Latin, 'wolf'.

lurch¹ ■ n. a sudden unsteady movement. ■ v. make such a movement; stagger.
– ORIGIN C17.

lurch² ■ n. (in phr. **leave someone in the lurch**) leave someone in a difficult situation without assistance or support.
– ORIGIN C16: from French *lourche*, the name of a game resembling backgammon, used in the phr. *demeurer lourche* 'be discomfited'.

lurcher ■ n. 1 Brit. a cross-bred dog, typically a retriever, collie, or sheepdog crossed with a greyhound, originally used for hunting and by poachers. 2 archaic a prowler, swindler, or petty thief.
– ORIGIN C16: from obsolete *lurch*, var. of LURK.

lure /l(j)ʊə/ ■ v. tempt to do something or to go somewhere. ■ n. 1 a thing that lures a person or animal to do something. ▸ a type of bait used in fishing or hunting. ▸ Falconry a bunch of feathers with a piece of meat attached to a long string, swung around the head of a falconer to recall a hawk. 2 the attractive qualities of a person or thing.

– ORIGIN Middle English: from Old French *luere*, of Germanic origin.

lurex /ˈl(j)ʊəreks/ ■ n. trademark yarn or fabric incorporating a glittering metallic thread.
– ORIGIN 1940s.

lurgy /ˈləːɡi/ ■ n. (pl. **-ies**) humorous an unspecified illness.
– ORIGIN C20: used in the British radio series *The Goon Show*, of the 1950s and 1960s.

lurid /ˈl(j)ʊərɪd/ ■ adj. 1 unpleasantly vivid in colour. 2 (of a description) shocking or sensational.
– DERIVATIVES **luridly** adv. **luridness** n.
– ORIGIN C17: from Latin *luridus*; rel. to *luror* 'wan or yellow colour'.

lurk ■ v. 1 be or remain hidden so as to wait in ambush. 2 be present in a latent or barely discernible state.
– DERIVATIVES **lurker** n.
– ORIGIN Middle English: perhaps from LOUR.

luscious ■ adj. 1 having a pleasingly rich, sweet taste. 2 richly verdant or opulent. 3 (of a woman) sexually attractive.
– DERIVATIVES **lusciously** adv. **lusciousness** n.
– ORIGIN Middle English: perhaps from obsolete *licious*, shortened form of DELICIOUS.

lush¹ ■ adj. 1 (of vegetation) luxuriant. ▸ luxurious. ▸ (of colour or music) rich. 2 informal sexually attractive.
– DERIVATIVES **lushly** adv. **lushness** n.
– ORIGIN Middle English: perhaps from obsolete *lash* 'soft, lax', from Old French *lasche* 'lax'.

lush² informal, chiefly N. Amer. ■ n. a drunkard.
– ORIGIN C18: perhaps a humorous use of LUSH¹.

lusophone /ˈluːsəfəʊn/ ■ adj. Portuguese-speaking.
– ORIGIN 1970s: from *luso-* (representing *Lusitania*, a Roman province, now Portugal) + -PHONE.

lust ■ n. strong sexual desire. ▸ a passionate desire for something. ▸ chiefly Theology a sensuous appetite regarded as sinful. ■ v. (usu. **lust for/after**) feel lust for someone or something.
– DERIVATIVES **lustful** adj. **lustfully** adv. **lustfulness** n.
– ORIGIN Old English, of Germanic origin.

luster ■ n. US spelling of LUSTRE.

lusterware ■ n. US spelling of LUSTREWARE.

lustral /ˈlʌstr(ə)l/ ■ adj. relating to or used in ceremonial purification.
– ORIGIN C16: from Latin *lustralis*, from *lustrum*, orig. denoting a purificatory sacrifice after a quinquennial census.

lustre (US **luster**) ■ n. 1 a gentle sheen or soft glow. ▸ the manner in which the surface of a mineral reflects light. 2 a thin metallic coating giving an iridescent glaze to ceramics. ▸ lustreware. 3 glory or distinction. 4 a fabric or yarn with a sheen. 5 a prismatic glass pendant on a chandelier. ▸ a cut-glass chandelier or candelabra.
– DERIVATIVES **lustred** adj. **lustreless** adj. **lustrous** adj. **lustrously** adv. **lustrousness** n.
– ORIGIN C16: from Italian *lustro*, from Latin *lustrare* 'illuminate'.

lustreware (US **lusterware**) ■ n. ceramic articles with an iridescent metallic glaze.

lusty ■ adj. (**-ier**, **-iest**) healthy and strong; vigorous.
– DERIVATIVES **lustily** adv. **lustiness** n.
– ORIGIN Middle English: from LUST.

lutanist ■ n. variant spelling of LUTENIST.

lute¹ ■ n. a stringed instrument with a long neck and a rounded body with a flat front, played by plucking.
– ORIGIN Middle English: from Old French *lut*, *leut*, prob. from Arabic *al-'ūd*.

lute² ■ n. (also **luting**) liquid clay or cement used to seal a joint, coat a crucible, or protect a graft. ▸ a rubber seal for a jar. ■ v. seal, join, or coat with lute.
– ORIGIN Middle English: from Old French *lut* or medieval Latin *lutum*, from Latin *lutum* 'potter's clay'.

luteal /ˈluːtɪəl/ ■ adj. Physiology of or relating to the corpus luteum.

lutein /ˈluːtɪɪn/ ■ n. Biochemistry a deep yellow pigment found in plant leaves, egg yolk, and the corpus luteum.
– ORIGIN C19: from Latin *luteum* 'egg yolk'.

luteinizing hormone /ˈluːtənʌɪzɪŋ/ (also **-ising**) ■ n. Biochemistry a pituitary hormone that stimulates ovulation in females and the synthesis of androgen in males.

lutenist /ˈluːt(ə)nɪst/ (also **lutanist**) ■ n. a lute player.
– ORIGIN C17: from medieval Latin *lutanista*, from *lutana* 'lute'.

lutetium /luːˈtiːʃɪəm, -sɪəm/ ■ n. the chemical element of atomic number 71, a rare silvery-white metal of the lanthanide series. (Symbol: **Lu**)
– ORIGIN C20: from French *lutécium*, from Latin *Lutetia*, the ancient name of Paris.

Lutheran ■ n. a follower of the German protestant theologian Martin Luther (1483–1546). ▸ a member of the Lutheran Church. ■ adj. of or characterized by the theology of Martin Luther. ▸ of or relating to the Lutheran Church.
– DERIVATIVES **Lutheranism** n.

Lutheran Church ■ n. the Protestant Church founded on the doctrines of Martin Luther, with justification by faith alone as a cardinal doctrine.

luthier /ˈluːtɪə/ ■ n. a maker of stringed instruments.
– ORIGIN C19: from French, from *luth* 'lute'.

luting ■ n. see LUTE².

lutist ■ n. **1** a lute player. **2** a lute maker.

lutz /lʊts/ ■ n. a jump in skating from the backward outside edge of one skate to the backward outside edge of the other, with a full turn in the air.
– ORIGIN 1930s: prob. from the name of Gustave *Lussi*, who invented it.

luvvy (also **luvvie**) ■ n. (pl. **-ies**) Brit. informal **1** an effusive or affected actor or actress. **2** variant spelling of LOVEY.
– DERIVATIVES **luvviedom** n.

lux /lʌks/ (abbrev.: **lx**) ■ n. (pl. same) the SI unit of illuminance, equal to one lumen per square metre.
– ORIGIN C19: from Latin, 'light'.

luxe /lʌks, lʊks/ ■ n. luxury.
– ORIGIN C16: from Latin *luxus* 'abundance'.

Luxembourger /ˈlʌksəmbəːɡə/ ■ n. a native or inhabitant of Luxembourg.

luxuriant /lʌɡˈʒʊərɪənt, lʌɡˈzjʊə-, lʌkˈsjʊə-/ ■ adj. **1** (of vegetation) rich and profuse in growth. **2** (of hair) thick and healthy.
– DERIVATIVES **luxuriance** n. **luxuriantly** adv.
– ORIGIN C16: from Latin *luxuriare* 'grow rankly', from *luxuria* 'luxury, rankness'.

luxuriate /lʌɡˈʒʊərɪeɪt, lʌɡˈzjʊə-, lʌkˈsjʊə-/ ■ v. (**luxuriate in/over**) enjoy as a luxury.
– ORIGIN C17: from Latin *luxuriare* 'grow in abundance'.

luxurious ■ adj. characterized by luxury. ▸ giving self-indulgent pleasure.
– DERIVATIVES **luxuriously** adv. **luxuriousness** n.
– ORIGIN Middle English: from Old French *luxurios*, from Latin *luxuriosus*, from *luxuria* 'luxury'.

luxury ■ n. (pl. **-ies**) **1** the state of great comfort and extravagant living. **2** an inessential but desirable item. ■ adj. of the nature of a luxury.
– ORIGIN Middle English: from Latin *luxuria*, from *luxus* 'excess'.

lx ■ abbrev. Physics lux.

-ly¹ ■ suffix forming adjectives meaning: **1** having the qualities of: *brotherly*. **2** recurring at intervals of: *hourly*.
– ORIGIN Old English *-lic*, of Germanic origin.

-ly² ■ suffix forming adverbs from adjectives: *greatly*.
– ORIGIN Old English *-lice*, of Germanic origin.

lycanthrope /ˈlʌɪkən(ˌ)θrəʊp/ ■ n. a werewolf.
– ORIGIN C17: from Greek *lukanthrōpos* (see LYCANTHROPY).

lycanthropy /lʌɪˈkanθrəpi/ ■ n. the mythical transformation of a person into a wolf. ▸ archaic a form of madness involving the delusion of being an animal, usually a wolf.
– DERIVATIVES **lycanthropic** adj.
– ORIGIN C16: from Greek *lukanthrōpia*, from *lukos* 'wolf' + *anthrōpos* 'human being'.

lycée /ˈliːseɪ/ ■ n. (pl. pronounced same) a French secondary school funded by the state.
– ORIGIN French, from Latin *lyceum* (see LYCEUM).

Lyceum /lʌɪˈsiːəm/ ■ n. **1** the garden at Athens in which Aristotle taught philosophy. ▸ Aristotelian philosophy and its followers. **2** (**lyceum**) US archaic a literary institution, lecture hall, or teaching place.
– ORIGIN from Greek *Lukeion*, from *Lukeios*, epithet of Apollo, from whose neighbouring temple the Lyceum was named.

lychee /ˈlʌɪtʃiː, ˈlɪ-/ (also **litchi**) ■ n. **1** a small rounded fruit with sweet white scented flesh, a large stone, and thin rough skin. **2** the Chinese tree which bears this fruit. [*Nephelium litchi*.]
– ORIGIN C16: from Chinese *lìzhī*.

lychgate /ˈlɪtʃɡeɪt/ ■ n. a roofed gateway to a churchyard, formerly used at burials for sheltering a coffin until the clergyman's arrival.
– ORIGIN C15: from Old English *līc* 'body' + GATE.

lycopene /ˈlʌɪkə(ʊ)piːn/ ■ n. Biochemistry a red carotenoid pigment present in tomatoes and many berries and fruits.
– ORIGIN 1930s: from *lycopin* from *Lycopersicon*, genus name of plants including the tomato.

lycopodium /ˌlʌɪkə(ʊ)ˈpəʊdɪəm/ ■ n. **1** a plant of a genus that includes the common clubmosses. [Genus *Lycopodium*.] **2** a fine flammable powder consisting of clubmoss spores, formerly used as an absorbent in surgery and in making fireworks.
– DERIVATIVES **lycopod** n.
– ORIGIN from Greek *lukos* 'wolf' + *pous, pod-* 'foot' (because of the claw-like shape of the root).

Lycra /ˈlʌɪkrə/ ■ n. an elastic polyurethane fibre or fabric used especially for close-fitting sports clothing.
– ORIGIN C20.

Lydian mode ■ n. Music the mode represented by the natural diatonic scale F–F (containing an augmented 4th).

lye ■ n. a strongly alkaline solution, especially of potassium hydroxide, used for washing or cleansing.
– ORIGIN Old English, of Germanic origin.

lying¹ present participle of LIE¹.

lying² present participle of LIE². ■ adj. not telling the truth.
– DERIVATIVES **lyingly** adv.

lying-in ■ n. archaic seclusion before and after childbirth.

lying-in-state ■ n. the display of the corpse of a public figure for public tribute before it is buried or cremated.

Lyme disease /lʌɪm/ ■ n. a form of arthritis caused by bacteria that are transmitted by ticks.
– ORIGIN 1970s: named after *Lyme*, a town in Connecticut, US, where an outbreak occurred.

lymph /lɪmf/ ■ n. **1** Physiology a colourless fluid containing white blood cells, which bathes the tissues and drains through the lymphatic system into the bloodstream. ▸ fluid exuding from a sore or inflamed tissue. **2** poetic/literary pure water.
– DERIVATIVES **lymphous** adj.
– ORIGIN C16: from French *lymphe* or Latin *lympha, limpa* 'water'.

lymph- ■ comb. form variant spelling of LYMPHO- shortened before a vowel.

lymphadenitis /ˌlɪmfadɪˈnʌɪtɪs/ ■ n. Medicine inflammation of the lymph nodes.
– ORIGIN C19: from LYMPH- + Greek *adēn* 'gland'.

lymphadenopathy /ˌlɪmfadɪˈnɒpəθi/ ■ n. Medicine a disease affecting the lymph nodes.

lymphatic ■ adj. Physiology of or relating to lymph or its secretion. ■ n. Anatomy a vein-like vessel conveying lymph in the body.
– ORIGIN C17: from Latin *lymphaticus* 'mad', from Greek *numpholēptos* 'seized by nymphs'; now associated with LYMPH.

lymphatic system ■ n. the network of vessels through which lymph drains from the tissues into the blood.

lymph gland ■ n. less technical term for LYMPH NODE.

lymph node ■ n. Physiology each of a number of small swellings in the lymphatic system where lymph is filtered and lymphocytes are formed.

lympho- (also **lymph-** before a vowel) ■ comb. form representing LYMPH: *lymphocyte*.

lymphoblast

lymphoblast /ˈlɪmfə(ʊ)blast/ ■ n. Medicine an abnormal cell resembling a large lymphocyte, produced in large numbers in a form of leukaemia.
– DERIVATIVES **lymphoblastic** adj.

lymphocyte /ˈlɪmfə(ʊ)sʌɪt/ ■ n. Physiology a form of small leucocyte (white blood cell) with a single round nucleus, occurring especially in the lymphatic system.
– DERIVATIVES **lymphocytic** adj.

lymphoid /ˈlɪmfɔɪd/ ■ adj. Anatomy relating to or denoting tissue responsible for producing lymphocytes and antibodies.

lymphoma /lɪmˈfəʊmə/ ■ n. (pl. **lymphomas** or **lympho-mata** /-mətə/) Medicine cancer of the lymph nodes.

lymphoreticular /ˌlɪmfə(ʊ)rɪˈtɪkjʊlə/ ■ adj. another term for RETICULOENDOTHELIAL.

lynch ■ v. (of a group) kill (someone) for an alleged offence without a legal trial, especially by hanging.
– DERIVATIVES **lyncher** n.
– ORIGIN C19: from *Lynch's law*, named after Capt. William Lynch, head of a self-constituted judicial tribunal in Virginia c.1780.

lynchpin ■ n. variant spelling of LINCHPIN.

lynx ■ n. 1 a wild cat with a short tail and tufted ears. [*Lynx lynx* (northern Eurasia) and other species.] 2 (also **African lynx**) S. African another term for CARACAL.
– ORIGIN Middle English: from Greek *lunx*.

lynx-eyed ■ adj. keen-sighted.

lyonnaise /ˌliːəˈneɪz/ ■ adj. (of sliced potatoes) cooked with onions or with a white wine and onion sauce.
– ORIGIN French, 'characteristic of the city of Lyons'.

lyophilic /ˌlʌɪə(ʊ)ˈfɪlɪk/ ■ adj. Chemistry (of a colloid) readily dispersed by a solvent and not easily precipitated.
– ORIGIN C20: from Greek *luein* 'loosen, dissolve' + *philos* 'loving'.

lyophobic /ˌlʌɪəˈfəʊbɪk/ ■ adj. Chemistry (of a colloid) not lyophilic.

lyrate /ˈlʌɪreɪt/ ■ adj. Biology lyre-shaped.

lyre ■ n. a stringed instrument like a small U-shaped harp with strings fixed to a crossbar, used especially in ancient Greece.
– ORIGIN Middle English: via Old French *lire* and Latin *lyra* from Greek *lura*.

lyrebird ■ n. a large Australian songbird, the male of which has a long lyre-shaped tail. [Genus *Menura*.]

lyric ■ n. 1 (also **lyrics**) the words of a song. 2 a lyric poem or verse. ■ adj. 1 (of poetry) expressing the writer's emotions, usually briefly and in stanzas or recognized forms. 2 (of a singing voice) using a light register.
– ORIGIN C16: from Latin *lyricus*, from Greek *lurikos*, from *lura* 'lyre'.

lyrical ■ adj. 1 (of literature, art, or music) expressing the writer's emotions in an imaginative and beautiful way. ▶ (of poetry) lyric. 2 of or relating to the words of a popular song.
– PHRASES **wax lyrical** talk in a highly enthusiastic and effusive way.
– DERIVATIVES **lyrically** adv.

lyricism ■ n. an artist's expression of emotion in an imaginative and beautiful way; lyrical quality.

lyricist ■ n. a person who writes the words to popular songs.

lyrist ■ n. 1 /ˈlʌɪərɪst/ a person who plays the lyre. 2 /ˈlɪrɪst/ a lyric poet.

lysergic acid /lʌɪˈsəːdʒɪk/ ■ n. Chemistry a crystalline compound prepared from natural ergot alkaloids or synthetically, from which the drug LSD (**lysergic acid diethylamide**) can be made.
– ORIGIN 1930s: *lysergic* from (*hydro*)*lys*(*is*) + *erg*(*ot*).

lysine /ˈlʌɪsiːn/ ■ n. Biochemistry a basic amino acid which is a constituent of most proteins, an essential nutrient in the diet of vertebrates.

lysis /ˈlʌɪsɪs/ ■ n. Biology the disintegration of a cell by rupture of the cell wall or membrane.
– ORIGIN C19: from Greek *lusis* 'loosening', from *luein* 'loosen'.

-lysis ■ comb. form forming nouns denoting disintegration or decomposition: *hydrolysis* | *haemolysis*.
– ORIGIN from Greek *lusis* 'loosening'.

Lysol /ˈlʌɪsɒl/ ■ n. trademark a disinfectant consisting of a mixture of cresols and soft soap.
– ORIGIN C19: from -LYSIS.

lysosome /ˈlʌɪsəsəʊm/ ■ n. Biology an organelle in the cytoplasm of eukaryotic cells containing degradative enzymes enclosed in a membrane.
– DERIVATIVES **lysosomal** adj.

lysozyme /ˈlʌɪsəzʌɪm/ ■ n. Biochemistry an enzyme which catalyses the destruction of the cell walls of certain bacteria, found notably in tears and egg white.

-lytic ■ comb. form in adjectives corresponding to nouns ending in *-lysis* (such as *hydrolytic* corresponding to *hydrolysis*).

Supplementary Pages

Contents

1. A History of English — SP 2
2. South African English — SP 6
   Our national language statistics
3. English Uncovered — SP 8
4. Guide to Good English — SP 13
   1. Parts of speech
   2. Inflection
   3. Sentences
   4. Agreement
   5. Punctuation
5. Countries of the World — SP 24
   Independent countries
   Principal dependencies
6. Prime Ministers and Presidents — SP 28
   Prime Ministers and Presidents of South Africa
   Presidents of the United States of America
   Prime Ministers of Great Britain and the United Kingdom
7. Kings and Queens of England and the United Kingdom — SP 30
8. Chemical Elements — SP 31
9. Greek Alphabet — SP 31
10. Metric Measures and Notation — SP 32
    Metric measures
    The metric prefixes
    Power notation
    SI units
11. The Solar System — SP 34
    The sun and planets
    Principal planetary satellites

1 A History of English

Well before 4000 BC, people living in the region of the Black Sea spoke a language that was the ancestor of many later languages. We now call that early language Proto-Indo-European. Over the following centuries, the tribes who spoke it scattered and settled in different parts of Europe and Asia, and dialects and new forms of the language evolved. Twelve major families of languages descended from it:

Proto-Indo-European:
- **Indic** (including Sanskrit, and many Indian languages descended from it)
- **Iranian** (including Farsi, also called Iranian or Persian)
- **Anatolian** (including Hittite and other extinct languages)
- **Armenian**
- **Hellenic** (Greek)
- **Albanian**
- **Italic** or **Romance** languages (including Latin and languages descended from it, e.g. French, Italian, Portuguese, Spanish)
- **Celtic**
- **Tocharian** (an extinct Asian group)
- **Germanic** (including English, German, Dutch, Afrikaans, and Scandinavian languages, and older languages that these descended from)
- **Baltic**
- **Slavic** (including Russian, Polish, Czech, Bulgarian, Serbian and Croatian)

In the 5th century AD the Angles, Saxons, and Jutes, tribes who spoke Germanic languages and who lived where northern Germany, Denmark and the Netherlands are now, crossed the sea and invaded England. By the end of the 5th century they occupied most of England, and had killed or marginalized the native Celts.

England became known as 'Anglia', meaning 'the land of the Angles'. This word became 'Englaland' and then 'England'. The word 'English' has the same origin.

Old English

By AD 500 the invaders' Germanic language was dominant in England. We refer to it now as Old English or Anglo-Saxon. Its grammar and vocabulary were very different from the language we speak now; indeed, a modern English-speaker would understand almost nothing of it. However, earlier forms of about half the words we use most commonly in English now were in the language then. Examples are *cow, goat, ghost, gospel, man, milk, mouse, rain, woman, wife,* and *work*. (If an English word is similar to the Afrikaans word for the same thing, for example, *milk/melk*, this is often a clue that it comes from Old English; remember that Old English came from roughly the area where the Dutch nation developed. And Afrikaans evolved mainly from Dutch.)

The impact of Latin

In 43 BC (over four centuries before the Anglo-Saxon invasion), the Romans colonized Britain and then introduced literacy. During their 400-year occupation, the Roman language, Latin, had little influence on Celtic.

In AD 597, however, a new influx of Romans began to arrive. They were missionaries who had been sent by the Pope to re-establish Christianity in Britain. Many Latin words – especially words to do with the Church – were absorbed into Old English at this time. Examples include *abbot, altar, cap,* and *sack*.

The impact of Old Norse

In 787 the Vikings, who were pirates and traders from Scandinavia (and who included many

Danes), invaded Britain and continued to raid the country for 200 years. By 850 many Danes had settled in England, and they eventually controlled a large region. Many became assimilated in Anglo-Saxon communities. As a result, their Germanic language, which we refer to now as Old Norse, had a major influence on Old English. Many place names in England are of Old Norse origin, as are many personal names, such as *Jackson, Davidson*, and other surnames ending in *-son*. Old Norse influenced the grammar of English, and gave us hundreds of everyday words that we still use now. These include *cross, reindeer, steak*, and many words that have the *sk-* sound, such as *scuttle, skill, skin, skirt*, and *sky*.

The impact of Old French

In 1066 England suffered yet another invasion when William of Normandy (William the Conqueror) defeated the English king and took over the throne himself. Old Norman, a variety of Old French, and the language of the Norman conquerors, was soon established as the language of power. It became the language of the English parliament, the law courts, the church, and of literature. For over 200 years the kings of England spoke Old French and not English. Little written English has survived from the 150-year period following the Norman Conquest, but it thrived as a spoken vernacular language, and was strongly influenced by Old French; this is clear from later texts written in a more modern form of the language which we call Middle English.

Here is a line from the Lord's Prayer in Old English, followed by a modern equivalent:

> Fæder ure þu þe eart on heofonum, si þin nama gehalgod
> (Father of ours, thou who art in heaven, be thy name hallowed).

Middle English

From the early 1200s, there was a growing sense of pride in English culture and language, and French began to lose some of its status in England. More and more official records were written in English, and by the 1400s it was the language of government, the church, and the court. English texts from this time show us that about 10 000 French words had been absorbed into the language following the Norman Conquest; most are still in our language today. They include many words to do with law and government (for example, *parliament, reign, revenue, sergeant, sovereign*), food and cooking (for example, *beef, mutton, poultry, saffron, sage, salad, soup*), clothing and fashion (for example, *diamond, embroider, fashion, jacket*), and general words (*abandon, adventure, besiege, riff-raff* and many thousands more).

The influence of Latin and other languages

In the 14th century, a new wave of words came into English from Latin, especially words to do with religion, medicine and other sciences, literature, and the law. Examples are *equator, galaxy, secretary, sacrosanct*, and *sum*.

Other languages fed into English as well. For example, we got *deck, yacht, skipper*, and other words to do with shipping from the sea-faring Dutch, and *algebra, algorithm, alkali, nadir*, and other words to do with mathematics, science and astronomy from Arabic.

These are lines from the Prologue of Geoffrey Chaucer's *Canterbury Tales*, written in Middle English in the late 14th century:

> Whan that Aprill with his shoures soote
> The droghte of March hath perced to
>   the roote...
> (When April's sweet showers have pierced the drought of March to the root...)

Modern English

Most scholars date Modern English from the 15th century. Its development was linked to the climate of change brought by the Renaissance. Renaissance means 'rebirth' and it refers to a revival of interest in the classical culture of the ancient Greeks and Romans that took place in Europe and England between the 14th and the 17th centuries. It was a period of intense and rapid development in many fields of learning and invention: in art, literature, architecture, astronomy, medicine, and other branches of science and technology. But English lacked the vocabulary to name or describe the new ideas, discoveries, and inventions of the time – and many words were therefore borrowed or systematically created at this time from classical sources. Examples include *corpuscle*, *maximum*, *millennium*, *millipede*, *minimum*, and *pulmonary* from Latin, and *arachnid*, *haemorrhage*, and *skeleton* from Greek.

Exploration, colonization and trade in other parts of the world also resulted in many new words being absorbed into English. Examples are *maize* and *potato*, which came into English in the 16th century via Spanish from Taino, a now-extinct Caribbean language, and *bamboo* from Malay, *banana* from Mande, a West African language, *cheetah* and *chintz* from Hindi, and *tea* from Chinese.

These lines from Shakespeare's *Romeo and Juliet*, written in the 1590s, are an example of early Modern English:

> How cam'st thou hither, tell me, and wherefore?
> The orchard walls are high and hard to climb.
> (Act 2 scene 2 line 62)

The English of today

By the early 1800s, when Charles Dickens and Jane Austen were writing, English had become similar to the language we speak now. It has continued to acquire new words constantly – in particular, from contact with other people and languages, and from new inventions.

The first half of the 20th century brought a wealth of new technology, and new vocabulary to accommodate it. Most of the new words were still based on Latin and Greek, the classical languages of science. So *radio* (from Latin) took over from wireless *telegraphy* (from Greek), and *aeroplanes* (from Greek) and *helicopters* (also from Greek) entered everyday life. Other words for the century's new inventions were formed either from acronyms that described their functions, like *radar* (**ra**dio **d**etection **a**nd **r**anging) and, later, *laser* (**l**ight **a**mplification by the **s**timulated **e**mission of **r**adiation) or by blending component words, such as *transistor* (transfer + resistor).

But it was late in the 20th century, when electronic communications became a reality, that changes in the English language gained a new momentum. Instead of turning to 'old' languages to describe these new developments, English words were tailored to fit; the *Web* connecting information electronically world wide gave rise to compounds such as *websurfing*, *web site*, *webmaster*, *webcam*, and *weblog*. The last of these was soon abbreviated to *blog*, which in turn generated *blogging* and the *blogosphere*. The telephone, already abbreviated to *phone*, became portable as a *mobile-* or *cellphone*. And letter-writing has been largely overtaken by electronic mail, or *email*. All these advances have led to a profound change in the written language. In blogs and emails, for example, the formal 'rules' of spelling and grammar are often left to one side in favour of an informal, chatty style, more like spoken than written English. The language of cellphone communication – *SMSing* or *texting* – has taken this to a more extreme degree. Ingenious spellings and abbreviations such as *l8tr* (later), *BTW* (by the way) and *lol* (laugh out loud) have become commonplace shorthand in electronic communications, sometimes – to the frustration of many English teachers – straying into more formal writing domains like school essays. It is too soon to say how much it will influence the English of the future, but what seems certain is that, as a global language, spoken by millions of people as a first language and millions more as an additional language, English will continue to adapt and change as it has through the centuries.

English is now the chief language of Britain, the USA, Australia, and a number of other countries. Well over 300 million people speak it as their first or only language, and millions more in all parts of the world learn it as an additional language.

World Englishes

Although the forms of English that had evolved a separate identity from that of British English only began to be described as 'World Englishes' in the late 20th century, the first distinctive 'new' English began to be recognized in the 18th century. Following America's successful bid for independence from Britain in 1783, American speakers of English started to claim independence for 'their' English too. Among the leaders of this movement was the famous dictionary writer

Noah Webster, who proposed many of the spellings that still characterize the difference between British and American English, for example, *-or* not *-our* in words like *labor* and *color*, and *-er* instead of *-re* in *center* and *liter*. Another distinguishing feature is the simplification of some of spellings which use vowels derived from classical Greek and Latin, such as the *ae* in words like *arch**ae**ology* and ***ae**sthetics* which become *archeology* and *esthetics*, or the *oe* in words like *am**oe**ba* and ***oe**strogen*, which become *ameba* and *estrogen* in American spelling.

Words that represented different aspects of life in the 'New World' were also adopted into American English. The word *powwow*, for example, originated from a cultural practice of the indigenous peoples, while others like *canyon* (Spanish), *prairie* (French), *stoop* (Dutch), *wiener* (German) and *chutzpah* (Yiddish) represent the great mix of cultures that have helped form the nation. At the same time, as the continent's governance, business, and daily life developed their own specifically American character, words like *caucus*, *freeway*, *drugstore*, *movie*, and *popcorn* entered the vocabulary.

In the same way, countries in Australasia, Africa, and the Caribbean that had also come under British influence began to develop their own 'Englishes' with distinct characteristics that reflected their local environment and society. Among the best-known of these varieties are Indian English, Australian English, and South African English. However, Canada, New Zealand, and Singapore, among others, also have their own varieties of the language. Some words from these other Englishes are now generally recognized by most English speakers worldwide, for example *curry* and its accompaniment *chutney* from India, and *boomerang* and *walkabout* from Australia. From South African English, words like *trek* and *commando* are found in general English. But there are many words and expressions unique to each individual variety of English, that might not be recognized by other English speakers: words like *bach* (New Zealand, a weekend cottage), *dillybag* (Australia, a bag for carrying odds and ends), *panchayat* (India, a village council) and *hoser* (Canada, an unsophisticated person).

2 South African English

In South Africa, only about eight per cent of the population speak English as their first language. However, it is spoken as a second or additional language by many, many, more people. English is recognized as a common language which enables the diverse language groups that live in South Africa to communicate. But, like the English of other countries colonized by the British, South African English has developed a distinct vocabulary that separates it quite clearly from the language spoken by the original colonists.

Early influences

The earliest roots of the English we speak in South Africa, which is different in many ways from that spoken in the rest of the English-speaking world, lie in the newly-colonized Cape of the 17th and 18th centuries. Before that, explorers and sailors passing by the Cape on their way to Britain's other colonies had begun to note some of the names of local plants, animals and things or events in day-to-day life that English had no words for. But it was only after the British took over governance of the Cape Colony from the Dutch at the end of the 18th century that English really began to show the influence of life in this unfamiliar land. Words that appear in South African English from that time show the influence of the indigenous Khoikhoi, the Dutch, and even the Malays living in the Cape then. Examples include *dagga*, *kaross*, *stoep*, and *pondok*.

Settler English

The next, and perhaps most influential, development occurred with the arrival in 1820 of some 4 000 settlers, who had been encouraged by the British government to establish a new life for themselves on the eastern frontier of the Cape Colony. They were positioned to serve as a buffer in a zone between Dutch farmers and the Xhosa people, and the settlers were the first large group of English speakers to come into prolonged contact with the Nguni-speaking peoples of southern Africa. Increasingly, as new settlers arrived, and missionaries moved further into the interior, words were absorbed from the Nguni and, to a lesser extent, the Sotho languages. Many of these had to do with the culture and customs of these peoples, so words like *indaba*, *kgotla* (the origin of today's more widely known *lekgotla*), *muti*, and *sangoma* appear in English for the first time. At the same time, the settlers were in close contact with South African Dutch speakers, especially farmers and hunters, so new meanings were given to existing English words, as anglicizations of the Dutch. Examples of these are *land*, *camp*, and *zinc*.

Social change

The massive social change of the 20th century added yet another dimension to the English of South Africa. In towns and cities, black workers and their families had to live in *locations*, separated from white residential areas. Later to become the more neutral *townships*, these multicultural urban hubs generated many new English expressions, often reflecting the need for people dislocated from their homes to forge new bonds. *Shebeens* and *stokvels* brought people together in social gatherings. In the churches, women's associations known as *manyanos* provided urban churchgoing women with a space to meet and socialize. Disaffected young men became *tsotsis*, originally distinguished by their sharp dress-style, but soon to be associated with criminal activity. Their street language, *Tsotsitaal*, once a criminal slang, became a lingua franca of the townships and added words like *moegoe* and *larney* to South African English. At the same time, a rich musical culture developed, bringing *kwela* and *marabi* into English, for example. And, as the century moved into the dark days of apartheid, more words began to assume a special South African connotation: *pass* and *struggle*, for example.

In the 21st century, the language continues to reflect the changes in the country over the past decades. After the first democratic government was established in 1994, efforts were made to give equal status to the eleven main languages spoken in South Africa. As barriers between speakers of different languages have begun to break down, English is being enriched with increasing numbers of words from South Africa's other languages. Words like *letsema* and *mashonisa* have begun to appear in formal English, even though they may not be recognizable to many mother tongue English speakers in the country. At the less formal level, exclamations like *eish!* and adjectives like *makoya* show the influence of *kasi* culture and the rich language developed from the melting pot of peoples represented there.

The story of South African English has, in many ways, run parallel to the development of South Africa as a nation. And while globalization may be neutralizing many of the distinctive characteristics of the English we speak to each other across nations, it seems that South Africa can still depend on its rich cultural mix to keep adding to its own variety of English.

Our national language statistics

South Africa's eleven official languages are listed here. The table shows the numbers and percentages of people in South Africa who speak these languages as a home language or first language.

Note: Though Sepedi is often named as one of South Africa's official languages, rather than Sesotho sa Leboa (Northern Sotho), linguists argue that Sesotho sa Leboa is the chief language of the Basotho people of Limpopo province, and Sepedi is the main variation or dialect of it.

Language	Number	Percentage
Afrikaans	6 146 165	12.8
English	4 182 236	8.7
IsiNdebele	987 172	2.0
IsiXhosa	8 259 226	17.2
IsiZulu	12 024 624	25.0
Sesotho sa Leboa	4 567 992	9.5
Sesotho	3 574 174	7.4
Setswana	3 825 774	8.0
SiSwati	1 323 465	2.7
Tshivenda	981 375	2.0
Xitsonga	1 764 202	3.7
Other/unspecified	299 436	0.6
Total	47 935 841	100

Source: Statistics South Africa's Labour Force Survey, September 2007

3 English Uncovered

Introduction

English is a global language, spoken or used by an estimated one third of the world's population, from Manchester to Mumbai and Boston to Botswana. It is an adaptable, flexible, and ever-evolving language that has become the international medium of communication of the Internet, business, science, and popular culture.

Capturing and recording that language in all its variety is one of the greatest challenges faced by lexicographers today. In this section we consider how we make sense of this vastness and examine some of the more intriguing facts about English along the way.

How do we keep track of the language?

So where do Oxford's lexicographers get their information from? And how can you be sure that a dictionary entry is accurate? The answers to these questions lie in the *evidence* on which our dictionaries are based. Oxford Dictionaries runs the largest language research programme in the world, and its purpose is to examine what is happening in the language now and what happened in the past, together with the way in which we use it and how it is changing.

Clearly, language is all around us, all the time, every time we speak or listen to someone else speaking, every time we pick up a newspaper, look at a website, or read a novel. There is plenty of potential 'evidence'. But how do we access it, what form does it take, and how do we go about collecting it? There is no single answer to the question: there are different types of evidence, each useful in different ways, and it is important to look at a range in order to be able to give as full an account of the language as possible. The main types of evidence used in compiling Oxford dictionaries are explained here.

The evidence

The Oxford English Corpus

As part of our ongoing language research, we collect substantial pieces of text from a huge range of sources. These samples are drawn from all parts of the English-speaking world: not only from the United Kingdom, Ireland, and the United States but also from the Caribbean, Canada, India, Malaysia and Singapore, South Africa, and Australasia. The samples encompass all types of English, from academic journals and literary novels to newspapers and magazines, online and in print, and even the language of chat rooms, blogs, and speech.

Hundreds of thousands of such samples are then gathered together to form the Oxford English Corpus. This is an electronic collection of over two billion words of real 21st century English, the largest such corpus of its type. We do not, of course, mean two billion *different* words: a large proportion of the two billion words is taken up with many examples of the same words repeated in different contexts. By analysing the corpus and using special software, lexicographers see words in context and find out, for example, how words are used, how new words and senses are emerging, how many words there are in English, and what are the most common words.

The Oxford Reading Programme

Apart from the Oxford English Corpus, the other main resource is the Oxford Reading Programme. This is an electronic collection of sentences or short extracts drawn from a very wide range of sources, from song lyrics, TV scripts, and popular fiction to specialist periodicals and scientific textbooks. At present standing at over 100 million words, the database of the Oxford Reading Programme is growing by about 10 000 extracts a month.

The Oxford Reading Programme is based on the contributions of an international network of readers, who highlight instances of new words and meanings and other changes in the language and then record them within the short context in which they occur. These then form the extracts that make up the database as a whole. A similar, though very much smaller, programme is used by the Dictionary Unit for South African English to collect examples of English in South Africa.

The Oxford Reading Programme differs from the Oxford English Corpus in that it consists of short citations which have been manually selected: as a result it tells us more about new and unusual words and phrases. The Corpus, on the other hand collects whole documents, and is less selective in its approach, less focused on unusual and new words, and more likely to yield information about ordinary everyday words.

Together these resources give us a very accurate picture of the language today: they tell us not only about individual words but also about English as a whole.

How many words are there in English?

The full *Oxford English Dictionary* (*OED*) is the largest record of words used in English, past and present. It contains words that are now obsolete or rare (such as *xenagogue*, 'a person who guides strangers', and *vicine*, meaning 'neighbouring or adjacent') in addition to recent coinages such as *bling* and *podcasting*. The second edition of the *OED*, published in 1989 and consisting of twenty volumes, contains more than 615 000 entries, and the third, available online, is expanding all the time, with batches of 1 800 new and revised words and phrases being added in regular quarterly updates.

However, even the *OED* does not include every specialized technical term, or slang or dialect expression. New words are constantly being invented, developed from existing words, or adopted from other languages. Many of these will be used very rarely, or only by a small group of people. Hence an unlimited number of words may occur in speech and writing which will never be recorded in even the largest dictionary.

Furthermore, what exactly is a word? This dictionary has about 100 000 entries, meaning separate headwords such as *cat* and *dog*, and derived forms like *quickly* and *happiness* listed under other entries. This total includes compounds such as *walking stick*, which are made up of two or more existing words. Is *walking stick* to be counted as a word? There are almost unlimited numbers of such compounds, which cannot all be included in a dictionary.

The dictionary also contains abbreviations such as *SABC* and *CIA*, which again may be freely formed in limitless combinations. And what about proper names such as *Soweto*, *Madiba*, and *Harry Potter*? Are they words? As you can see, the question is not straightforward.

Although it may be impossible to know the number of words in English, the Oxford English Corpus can help us to make some observations about how many words are in current use. But instead of talking about words, it is more useful in this context to talk about 'lemmas'. A lemma is the base form of a word; for example, *climb*, *climbs*, *climbing*, and *climbed* are all examples of the one lemma, *climb*.

Just ten different lemmas (*the*, *be*, *to*, *of*, *and*, *a*, *in*, *that*, *have*, and *I*) account for a remarkable 25 per cent of all the two billion words used in the Oxford English Corpus. That means that if you were to read through the corpus, one word in four (ignoring proper names) would be an example of one of these ten lemmas.

Like all natural languages, English consists of a small number of very common words, a larger number of intermediate ones, and then an infinitely long 'tail' of very rare terms.

The long tail means that to account for 99 per cent of the Oxford English Corpus you would need a vocabulary of well over a million lemmas. This would include some words which may occur only once or twice in the whole corpus: highly technical terms like *chrondrogenesis* or *dicarboxylate* that most people would be unfamiliar with, and one-off coinages like *bootlickingly* or *unsurfworthy* that people would probably understand but be unlikely to use.

If we decide that about 90–95 per cent of the corpus gives a reasonable idea of an average vocabulary, we are left with a figure somewhere in the range of 7 000–50 000 lemmas: say, 25 000. What does a vocabulary of this size represent? It represents the set of most significant words in English: those which occur reasonably frequently and which account for all but a tiny part of everything we may encounter in speech or writing. It almost certainly includes all the words that we need to actively *use* in everyday life.

It is interesting to note that most reasonably-sized dictionaries contain far more than 25 000 lemmas. This dictionary lists more than 40 000 single-word lemmas, which means that most of its entries must belong to the long tail of rare words. But this makes good sense: such terms occur very infrequently, but when they do occur they are likely to be crucial to what is being said, and the reader might well want to look them up.

How many new words are created every year?

During the 20th century, the *OED* recorded around 90 000 neologisms (new words), about 900 per year. However, this figure represents only the tip of the iceberg in terms of the thousands of neologisms appearing in English every year, most of which either spring to brief prominence and then fade away almost as quickly or never gain currency outside a limited set of speakers (for instance, teenage slang terms), and are often never written down.

Oxford's lexicographers monitor in-house electronic databases (the Oxford English Corpus and the Oxford Reading Programme, described above) to track language change, noting hundreds of new items for possible inclusion in our dictionaries; a large proportion of these (possibly 70 per cent) may never appear in printed dictionaries. The breadth of coverage to be found in some online dictionaries and wordlists, which are less limited by considerations of space than printed dictionaries, gives some idea of the huge numbers of new coinages that occur.

Where do new words come from?

Neologisms enter English in a number of different ways:

■ **completely new terms:** perhaps surprisingly, these account for less than one per cent of new vocabulary. Many of these are or were originally trademarks (often named after their inventor, such as *Hoover* and *Jacuzzi*), some are technical coinages, and others are invented by writers such as Lewis Carroll (*chortle*) and J R R Tolkien (*hobbit*).

■ **from other languages:** it has been estimated that about half of all English words derive from languages other than Old English. Norman French was highly influential after the Norman Conquest in 1066, and in the 17th and 18th centuries a further large number of words came in from classical Latin and Greek. More recently, English has absorbed vocabulary from over 120 of the world's languages, from Italian (*casino*) and Japanese (*futon*) and Inuit (*kayak*). In all, around five per cent of the new words of the 20th century were borrowed in this way.

Loanwords recently added to this dictionary from African languages include *imifino* (isiXhosa), *leiwater* (Afrikaans), *letsema* (Setswana), *masonja* (Tshivenda), and *mjondolo* (isiZulu).

■ **from combinations of existing words:** over 50 per cent of new words are formed from words that already exist. These include compounds and 'blends', formed from existing words or parts of words (for example, *health centre*, *fanzine*, *website*, and *breathalyser*), and also words formed from suffixes and prefixes such as *un-*, *-able*, *-ly*, and *pre-* (for example, *customizable*, *unbeatably*, and *presoak*).

■ **from new senses of existing words:** this accounts for about 15 per cent of new coinages. The new meaning may take its place alongside existing senses of the word (for example, *issues* has recently developed the meaning 'personal problems'), or may eventually replace the original meaning of the word altogether (*hoodwink* originally meant 'to blindfold someone').

■ **by conversion:** this is the process by which a word begins as one part of speech, for example, a noun, and then becomes another part of speech, such as a verb. The noun *text* (in the sense 'a text message') quickly transformed into a verb (I *texted* her), while the adjective *organic* has recently developed a noun use meaning 'a food produced by organic farming' (as in *consumer interest in organics soared*).

■ **new abbreviations and acronyms:** although perhaps not strictly 'words', new abbreviations and acronyms are being coined in increasing numbers, driven partly by emails, chat rooms, and texting: situations in which speed and conciseness are paramount. Recent coinages include *CAL* (computer-assisted learning) and *FICA* (Financial Intelligence Centre Act).

How is English spelling changing?

Despite the existence of 'standard' or 'correct' spelling, which we learn at school, English spelling is not (and has never been) fixed. In fact alternative forms constantly arise. And in tracking the language, we are interested in spelling changes as much as changes in vocabulary and meaning. For example, corpus analysis shows a surprising fact about the adjective *minuscule*. This word derives from Latin *minuscula* (*littera*) meaning 'somewhat smaller (letter)'. However, because *minuscule* means 'very small', many people wrongly associate it with the well known prefix *mini-*, and spell it *miniscule* instead. By examining the Oxford English Corpus, we discovered that the spelling *miniscule* now accounts for about 52 per cent of all the instances of the word. We can see from the corpus that this includes examples in creditable printed sources such as newspapers and periodicals as well as in unedited personal blogs and similar informal contexts. In other words, according to the evidence, the non-standard form has now overtaken the accepted one in terms of usage.

What does this mean for dictionary editors? As everything we do is informed by the evidence on our databases, we need to consider when it is appropriate to add such an alternative spelling to the dictionary. You will see from the note given at the entry in this dictionary that the spelling *miniscule* is still regarded as an error to avoid. But what is controversial today may become acceptable in the future, in which case it could well be added to a future edition of the dictionary as a valid alternative spelling.

Reanalysing the language

Reinterpretation of spellings, in which a less familiar spelling is changed 'logically' to a more common one, is similar to the process known in linguistics as *reanalysis*, and it is one of the most interesting developments in spelling today. Reanalysis is the process by which an obscure word within a phrase is mistakenly replaced by a similar-sounding, more familiar word.

The phrase 'to curry favour' is well known today; what is less well known is that the original form of the phrase was 'curry favel'. Here, *curry* means 'to groom or rub down a horse', and *Favel* was a horse in a 14th century French romance, known for his cunning. So 'curry Favel' came to mean to use Favel's cunning, or to use cunning in general. In time, the name 'Favel' was forgotten, and replaced by the similar-sounding word 'favour', presumably because to later writers it made more sense than 'Favel'. If such an error seems to make sense, it may then recur among different writers, and eventually may become the standard form of the phrase.

The Oxford English Corpus enables us to examine this process in action today, by comparing the frequency of the older form of a phrase with the frequency of its reanalysis. Here are some examples:

Older form	Reanalysis (changed form)
moot point: 97%	3%: mute point
sleight of hand: 85%	15%: slight of hand
toe the line: 84%	16%: tow the line
fazed by: 71%	29%: phased by
home in on: 65%	35%: hone in on
a shoo-in: 65%	35%: a shoe-in
bated breath: 60%	40%: baited breath
free rein: 54%	46%: free reign
chaise longue: 54%	46%: chaise lounge
buck naked: 53%	47%: butt naked
vocal cords: 51%	49%: vocal chords
just deserts: 42%	58%: just desserts
fount of knowledge/wisdom: 41%	59%: font of knowledge/wisdom
strait-laced: 34%	66%: straight-laced

At the top of the list, *moot point* and *sleight of hand* still clearly predominate over *mute point* and *slight of hand*: the latter reanalyses are not well established in the language, and most people would regard them as incorrect. However, at the other end of the table there are cases like *strait-laced/straight-laced* where the reanalysis is becoming more common than the original, just as *miniscule* is overtaking *minuscule*. As the Oxford English Corpus develops, we will be able to track shifting balances over time: will *strait-laced* disappear from the language completely, or will *tow the line* ever become an acceptable alternative to *toe the line*?

Further information

If you are interested in the English language and want to explore further, you can find more information by visiting our websites:

www.AskOxford.com
www.oed.com
www.oup.com

4 Guide to Good English

1 Parts of speech

In this section the traditional names are used for parts of speech (*noun, verb, adjective, adverb, pronoun, conjunction,* and *preposition*). Two other terms are sometimes used in describing grammar. One is *modifier*, which means any word that adds to or qualifies the meaning of another word (usually a noun). It is broader in scope than 'adjective' and includes, for example, *table* in *table lamp* as well as *bright* in *a bright lamp* or *the lamp was bright*. The other is *determiner*, which means any word such as *a, the, this, those,* and *every* which you put before a noun to show how you are using the noun (as in *a fire, the fire, this fire, those fires,* and *every fire*).

Nouns

A noun is a word that names something: a person (*woman, boy, Frances*), a thing (*building, tree*), or an idea, event, or feeling (*birth, happiness*). A common noun names things generally, whereas a proper noun names a particular person, place, or thing. Collective nouns, such as *audience, family, generation, government, team,* are nouns which refer to groups of people or things. They can be treated as singular or plural: see 'Agreement' below.

Proper nouns

Proper nouns are normally spelled with a capital initial letter and refer to persons or things of which there is only one example (*Asia, Koran, Moses*). The term is sometimes understood more broadly to include geographical and ethnic designations such as *American* and *Zulu*, which behave like common nouns, for example in allowing the forms *an American* and *the Zulu*. Some genuinely proper names can also behave like common nouns in certain uses, for example *a fine Picasso* (= a painting by Picasso), *another Makeba* (= a singer comparable to Makeba).

In these uses it is usual to retain the capital initial letter.

Verbal nouns

A verbal noun (also called a gerund) is a form of a verb ending with *-ing* that acts as a noun, for example *smoking* in the phrase **no smoking** and in the sentence **Smoking annoys people**. It should be distinguished from *smoking* used as an adjective (**a smoking fire**) and as the present participle of the verb (**The man was smoking**).

Because a verbal noun is a part of a verb as well as being a noun, it keeps some of the characteristics of verbs in its grammatical behaviour; for example the forms **They objected to me swearing** (non-possessive) and **They objected to my swearing** (possessive) are both established in ordinary usage, although the second, in which *swearing* is treated as a full noun, is often preferred in more formal writing.

Verbs

A verb is a word that describes an action (*go, sit, put*) or state (*be, live*) and is normally an essential element in a clause or sentence. A verb is classified as transitive when the action affects a person or thing called the object (**We lit a fire**), and as intransitive when there is no object (**She smiled**).

Using the correct tense

Tense is the location in time of the state or action expressed by a verb. English verbs properly have only two tenses, the present (*I am*) and the past (*I was*). The future is formed with *shall* or *will*, other forms of the past are formed with auxiliary verbs (*I have been / I was being*), and the past perfect is formed with the past tense of *have* (*I had been*).

The tense used mostly corresponds to actual time, apart from conventional uses such as the so-called 'historic present', used for dramatic effect in narratives (as in **George gets up and walks over to the window**), and the future used in polite requests (as in **Will that be all for now?**).

However, choice of tense (called 'sequence of tenses') becomes more complex in reported speech. If a simple statement such as **I'm afraid I haven't finished** is put into indirect speech by means of a reporting verb such as *said*, *thought*, etc., the tense of the reported action changes in accordance with the time perspective of the speaker: **He said he was afraid he hadn't finished**.

The tense of the reported verb can stay the same if the time relative to the speaker is the same as that relative to the person reported: **She likes beans** can be converted either to **She said she liked beans** or to **She said she likes beans**, and **I won't be here tomorrow** can be converted either to **I said I wouldn't be here tomorrow** or to **I said I won't be here tomorrow**.

shall and will

The traditional view is that with *I* and *we*, *shall* should be used to form the simple future tense (expressing a prediction of a future action), while *will* is used to express determination to do something:

- ☑ **I shall be late for work.**
- ☑ **We will not tolerate this rudeness.**

With *you*, *he*, *she*, *it*, and *they*, the situation is reversed; simple future action is expressed with *will*, while *shall* expresses determination or a command:

- ☑ **He will be late for work.**
- ☑ **You shall join us or die!**

In practice, however, *shall* and *will* are used more or less interchangeably in statements (though not in questions) and this is acceptable in standard modern English. In speech, people are more likely to use intonation than syntax to express strong determination. Furthermore, the distinction between *shall* and *will* is often obscured by contractions like *I'll* and *she'll*.

should and would

The situation is similar with *should* and *would*. Strictly speaking, *should* is used with *I* and *we*, while *would* is used with *you*, *he*, *she*, *it*, and *they*:

- ☑ **I should be grateful if you would let me know.**
- ☑ **You didn't say you would be late.**

In practice, however, it is now normal to use *would* instead of *should* in reported speech and conditional clauses, such as **I said I would be late**.

Active and passive

Verbs can be either active, in which the subject is the person or thing performing the action (as in **France beat Brazil in the final**), or passive, in which the subject undergoes the action (**Brazil were beaten by France**). In the passive voice verbs are usually formed with *be* (and its other forms), and the subject is introduced by the preposition *by*.

The passive is also used for impersonal constructions with *it*:

It is believed that no action should be taken.

Other verbs besides *be* can be used to form so-called 'semi-passives' (as in **He got changed**, **They seem bothered**). Here *changed* and *bothered* are behaving more like adjectives.

Subjunctive

The subjunctive is a special form (or mood) of a verb expressing a wish or possibility instead of fact. It has a limited role in English:

It was suggested he wait till the next morning.

The law decrees that speeding drivers be fined.

In these sentences, the verbs *wait* (in the first) and *be* (in the second) are in the subjunctive; the ordinary forms (called the indicative) would be *waits* and *are*. There are other typical uses of the subjunctive:

- after *if* (or *as if*, *as though*, *unless*) in hypothetical conditions.

    ☑ **Each company was required to undertake that if it were given the contract it would place work locally.**

- *be* or *were* at the beginning of a clause with the subject following

    - ☑ Were I to get drunk, it would help me in the fight.

    - ☑ All books, be they fiction or non-fiction, should provide entertainment in some form or other.

- in certain fixed expressions and phrases, e.g. *be that as it may, come what may, perish the thought, so be it*, and others.

Participles

There are two kinds of participle in English: the present participle ending with *-ing* as in **We are going**, and the past participle ending with *-d* or *-ed* for many verbs and with *-t* or *-en* or some other form for others, as in **Have you decided?**, **New houses are being built**, and **It's not broken**.

Participles are often used to introduce subordinate clauses that are attached to other words in a sentence, e.g.

- ☑ Her mother, opening the door quietly, came into the room.

A stylistic error occurs with so-called 'unattached', 'misrelated', or 'dangling' participles, when the participle does not refer to the noun to which it is attached, normally the subject of the sentence:

- ☒ Recently converted into apartments, I passed by the house where I grew up.

Certain participles, such as *considering, assuming, excepting, given, provided, seeing, speaking (of)*, etc., have virtually become prepositions or conjunctions in their own right, and their use in a grammatically free role is now standard:

- ☑ Speaking of money, do you mind my asking what you did with yours?

Adjectives and adverbs

An adjective is a word used to describe a noun, such as *sweet, red*, or *technical*. An adverb is typically a word used to modify a verb, adjective, or other adverb, such as *gently, lazily*, or *very*.

Position

Most adjectives can be used in two positions: either before the noun they describe, where they are called 'attributive', as in **a black cat** and **a gloomy outlook**, or after a verb such as *be, become, grow, look*, or *seem*, where they are called 'predicative', as in **the cat was black** and **the prospect looks gloomy**.

Some adjectives are nearly always used in the predicative position and cannot stand before a noun (e.g. *afraid*), while others are only found in the attributive position (e.g. *main*).

Adjectives following a noun

In many fixed standard expressions, adjectives denoting status are placed immediately after the nouns they describe, e.g. in *court martial, heir apparent, poet laureate, president elect, situations vacant*, and *the village proper*. In other cases, an adjective follows a noun as a matter of sentence structure rather than peculiarity of expression:

> The waiter picked up our dirty glasses in his fingertips, his eyes impassive.

Position of adverbs

Adverbs normally come between the subject and its verb, or between an auxiliary verb and a main verb:

> She dutifully observes all its quaint rules.

> His policies were fiercely criticized.

But for emphasis, or when the adverb belongs closely to what follows the main verb, it comes after the verb and before a following adverbial phrase:

> There is little chance that the student will function effectively after he returns home.

Sentence adverbs

Some adverbs (such as *clearly, happily, hopefully, thankfully, unhappily*) refer to a whole statement, and form a comment associated more closely with the speaker or writer than with what is said. In this role they are called 'sentence adverbs'. Sentence adverbs often stand at the beginning of the sentence:

> Clearly, we will have to think again.

Sentence adverbs are well established in English, but some people consider the use of *thankfully* and (in particular) *hopefully* in this way as unsuitable in formal writing or speech.

[?] **Hopefully the road should be finished.**

Pronouns

A pronoun is a word such as *I, we, they, me, you, them*, etc., and other forms such as the possessive *hers* and *theirs* and the reflexive *myself* and *themselves*. They are used to refer to (and take the place of) a noun or noun phrase that has already been mentioned or is known, especially in order to avoid repetition, as in the sentence **When she saw her husband again, she wanted to hit him**.

Reflexive pronouns

Reflexive pronouns are the type formed with *-self*, e.g. *myself, herself,* and *ourselves*, used in sentences in which the subject of the verb and the object are the same person or thing, as in **We enjoyed ourselves** and **Make yourself at home**.

Conjunctions

A conjunction is a word such as *and, because, but, for, if, or,* and *when*, used to connect words, phrases, clauses, and sentences. On the use of *and* and *but* at the beginning of a sentence, see 'Sentences' below.

Prepositions

A preposition is a word such as *after, in, to,* and *with*, which usually stands before a noun or pronoun and establishes the way it relates to what has gone before (**The man on the platform**, and **They came after dinner**). It is sometimes stated that a preposition should always precede the word it governs and should not end a sentence. However, there are cases when it is either impossible or not natural to organize the sentence in a way that avoids a final preposition:

- in relative clauses and questions featuring verbs with linked adverbs or prepositions:

    What did Marion think she was up to?

    They must be convinced of the commitment they are taking on.

- in passive constructions:

    The dress had not even been paid for.

- in short sentences including an infinitive with *to* or a verbal noun:

    It was my dancing he objected to.

2 Inflection

Inflection is the process by which words (principally nouns, verbs, adjectives, and adverbs) change their form, especially their ending, in accordance with their grammatical role in a sentence.

Verbs

Verbs normally add *-s* or *-es* to form third-person present-tense forms (*changes, wants*), *-ed* to form past tenses and past participles (*changed, wanted*), and *-ing* to form present participles (*changing, wanting*). However, some verbs form tenses by changing their stem (*throw, threw, thrown*), and others are completely irregular (*have, had, had; go, went, gone*).

Verbs drop a final silent *-e* when the suffix begins with a vowel (as in *shave, shaving*). But a final *-e* is usually retained to preserve the soft sound of the *g* in *twingeing* and *whingeing*. It is also retained where it is needed to avoid confusion with similar words, for example in *dyeing* (from *dye*) as distinct from *dying* (from *die*).

Nouns

English nouns normally form their plurals by adding *-s*, or *-es* if the singular form ends in *-s, -x, -z, -sh*, or soft *-ch* (as in *church* but not *loch*).

Nouns ending in *-y* form plurals with *-ies* (*policy, policies*), unless the ending is *-ey*, in which case the plural form is normally *-eys* (*valley, valleys*).

Nouns ending in *-f* and *-fe*

Nouns ending in *-f* and *-fe* form plurals sometimes with *-fs* (*handkerchief, handkerchiefs; oaf, oafs; proof, proofs*), sometimes *-ves* (*calf, calves; half, halves; knife, knives; shelf, shelves*) and occasionally both *-fes* and *-ves* (*dwarf, dwarfs* or *dwarves; hoof, hoofs* or *hooves*).

Nouns ending in -o

Plurals of nouns ending in -o cause difficulty in English because there are few convenient rules for choosing between -os (as in *ratios*) and -oes (as in *heroes*).

As a guideline, the following typically form plurals with -os:

- words in which a vowel (usually *i* or *e*) precedes the final -o (*trios, videos*).
- words that are shortenings of other words (*demos, hippos*).
- words introduced from foreign languages (*boleros, placebos*).

Names of animals and plants normally form plurals with -oes (*buffaloes, tomatoes*).

A few nouns ending in -o have optional plurals (*cargoes* or *cargos*; *mangoes* or *mangos*).

Adjectives and adverbs: comparatives and superlatives

Adjectives

An adjective has three forms: a positive (*hot, splendid*), a comparative (*hotter, more splendid*), and a superlative (*hottest, most splendid*). Adjectives that form comparatives and superlatives using -er and -est in preference to (or as well as) *more* and *most* are:

- words of one syllable (e.g. *fast, hard, rich, wise*).
- words of two syllables ending in -y and -ly (e.g. *angry, early, happy, holy, likely, lively*) and corresponding *un-* forms when these exist (e.g. *unhappy, unlikely*). Words ending in -y change the *y* to *i* (e.g. *angrier, earliest*).
- words of two syllables ending in -le (e.g. *able, humble, noble, simple*), -ow (e.g. *mellow, narrow, shallow*), and some ending in -er (e.g. *clever, tender*).
- some words of two syllables pronounced with the stress on the second syllable (e.g. *polite, profound*, but not *antique, bizarre*, and others).
- other words of two syllables that do not belong to any classifiable group (e.g. *common, cruel, pleasant, quiet*).

Words of one syllable ending in a single consonant double the consonant when it is preceded by a single vowel (*glad, gladder,* *gladdest; hot, hotter, hottest*) but not when it is preceded by more than one vowel (*clean, cleaner, cleanest; loud, louder, loudest*). Words of two syllables ending in -l double the *l* (e.g. *cruel, crueller, cruellest*).

Adjectives of three or more syllables use forms with *more* and *most* (*more beautiful, most interesting*, etc.).

Adverbs

Adverbs that take -er and -est in preference to (or as well as) *more* and *most* are:

- adverbs that are not formed with -ly but are identical in form to corresponding adjectives (e.g. *runs faster, hits hardest, hold it tighter*).
- some independent adverbs (e.g. *often* and *soon*).

Adverbs ending in -ly formed from adjectives (e.g. *richly, softly, wisely*) generally do not have -er and -est forms but appear as *more softly, most wisely*, etc.

3 Sentences

A sentence is a group of words that makes a grammatically complete statement, question, or command. It contains a main verb, and begins with a capital letter and ends with a full stop (or the equivalent such as a question mark or an exclamation mark).

There are three basic kinds of sentence:

- a simple sentence normally contains one statement: **The train should be here soon.**
- a compound sentence contains more than one statement, normally joined by a conjunction such as *and* or *but*: **I have looked at the evidence and I have to say it is not sufficient.**
- a complex sentence contains a main clause and one or more subordinate clauses, such as a conditional clause beginning with *if* or a relative clause introduced by *which* or *who*: **The story would make headlines if it ever became public.**

Relative clauses: using words like *who* and *when*

A relative clause is one connected to a main clause by a relative pronoun or adjective such as *who* or *whom*, *which*, *whose*, or *that*, or by a relative adverb such as *when* and *where*. (These words, apart from *that*, are collectively called *wh-* words, and a *wh-* word means any of these.) Most problems with this kind of clause are to do with the choice between *that* and a *wh-* word, principally *which*, *who*, or *whom*. For much of the time *that* is interchangeable with any of these words, and it is the more usual choice in everyday writing and conversation.

There are two types of relative clause, called 'restrictive' and 'non-restrictive'. A restrictive clause gives essential information about a noun or noun phrase that comes before (**She held out the hand that was hurt**). A non-restrictive clause gives extra information that could be left out without affecting the structure or meaning of the sentence (**She held out her hand, which I clasped in both of mine**). A restrictive clause can be introduced by *that*, *which*, *who*, or *whose* and is not normally preceded by a comma, whereas a non-restrictive clause is normally introduced by *which*, *who*, or *whose* (and not usually *that*), and is preceded by a comma.

Sometimes *that* is more idiomatic and natural than *which*, for example when the construction is based on an impersonal *it* or an indefinite pronoun such as *anything*:

> There is something that I forgot to mention.
>
> Is there anything that you want?

That is also more usual when *which* already occurs earlier in the sentence in another role, for example as an interrogative word:

> Which is the one that you want?

Beginning sentences with *and* and *but*

It is not wrong to begin a sentence with a conjunction such as *and* or *but*. The practice is common in literature and can be effective. It is also used for other rhetorical purposes, especially to denote surprise (**And are you really going?**) and sometimes just to introduce an improvised afterthought (**I'm going to swim. And don't you dare watch**).

Negatives and double negatives

A repeated negative of the type **He never did no harm to no one** is incorrect. However, a double negative is acceptable when it is used with intentional cancelling effect as a figure of speech, as in **It has not gone unnoticed**.

Double negatives also occur, especially in speech, in uses of the type **You can't not go** (= you cannot consider not going, i.e. you have to go), in which *not go* is effectively a single idea expressed in a verb phrase.

4 Agreement

Agreement is the process of making words fit the context of sentences, for example ensuring that the singular form of a verb accompanies a singular subject. For most of the time we apply the rules of agreement instinctively, but problems can arise in sentences involving certain phrases and combinations.

Agreement within phrases

Awkward phrases

Some expressions can cause uncertainty because they are grammatically ambiguous or combine seemingly contradictory roles, for example phrases such as *more than one* and *either or both*:

> ✓ More than one dealer has shown an interest in the painting.

The meaning is clearly plural, but the grammar remains singular because *one* is closer to the verb as well as being the dominant word in its phrase (we could not say **More than one dealer have shown an interest in the painting**).

> ? The purchaser gets a licence to use either or both products.

Here there is a problem of agreement with the following noun, because *either* calls for the singular form *product* whereas *both* calls for the plural form *products*; *both* wins out because it is closer to the noun. Usually a better solution is to rephrase the sentence to avoid the problem altogether:

> ✓ The purchaser gets a licence to use either or both of the products.

Compound subjects

Two nouns joined by *and* are normally treated as plural:

> Speed and accuracy are top of the list.

But when the two nouns form a phrase that can be regarded as a single unit, they are sometimes treated as singular, even when one of them is plural:

> Fish and chips is my favourite meal.

When a singular noun forming the subject of a sentence is followed by an additional element tagged on by means of a phrase such as *as well as*, *accompanied by*, or *together with*, the following verb should be singular and not plural, since the singular noun is by itself the true subject:

> The little girl, together with her friend Kerry, was busy filling her bucket with sand.

Singular and plural nouns

Singular nouns treated as plural

Some nouns are singular in form but are used with a verb that can be either singular or plural, or in some cases only plural. The commonest of these are the collective nouns which stand for a group or collection of people or things, such as *audience*, *committee*, *crew*, *family*, *generation*, *government*, *group*, *jury*, *team*, and many others.

The general rule with words like these is to treat them as singular when the emphasis is on the group as a whole and as plural when the emphasis is on the individuals that form the group:

> A group of four young men in overalls was standing close to him. (singular)

> The committee met to consider their decision. (plural)

Some collective nouns are fully plural:

> By and large the police do a good job.

Plural nouns treated as singular

Other nouns are plural in form but are treated as singular, either always or in some meanings. Chief among these are the names of branches of knowledge or science, such as *acoustics* and *mathematics*, activities such as *billiards* and *gymnastics*, and diseases such as *measles*:

> Acoustics is taught as part of the course.

> The figures show that measles is on the increase.

Other plural nouns, such as *data*, *media*, and *agenda*, are now commonly treated as singular. Depending on their meaning, they are either countable nouns, which can be used with *a* or *an* and have plural forms, e.g. *agendas*, or mass nouns, which do not have a plural form but are used in the singular with words such as *this* and *much*:

> The media has lost interest in the subject.

> This data is incorrect.

Some plural words adopted unchanged from other languages, such as *spaghetti* and *graffiti*, develop singular meanings:

> Graffiti was daubed on the walls.

Subjects and objects

When the subject of the verb *be* is singular but the part that follows is plural, the verb should generally agree with its subject, regardless of what follows:

> The only traffic is ox carts and bicycles.

When the subject is a singular collective noun, the verb may be in the plural, following the usual pattern with such nouns:

> Its prey are other small animals.

Indefinite pronouns

Pronouns such as *each*, *either*, *neither*, and *none* are called indefinite pronouns. When used on their own like a noun, they can vary between singular and plural. They are treated as singular when the emphasis is on the individuals:

> Neither the chairman nor the chief executive is planning any dramatic gestures.

> None of them has had enough practical experience to run the company.

They are treated as plural when the emphasis is on the collection or group as a whole:

> Neither his mother nor his father earn much money now.
>
> None of the staff were aware of the ransom demand.

Plural pronouns used in the singular

There is often uncertainty about what possessive word (*his*, *her*, etc.) to use when referring to a subject whose gender is not specified. The safest option is to put *his or her*:

> Every student should hand in his or her assignment by Tuesday.

But this can be awkward, especially when the sentence continues for some time with repeated references back to the original subject. In cases like this it is now acceptable to use a plural form of pronoun:

> Every student should hand in their assignment by Tuesday.

Either ... or ... and neither ... nor ...

A problem arises when one of the alternatives in an *either ... or ...* or *neither ... nor ...* construction is singular and the other plural. Here, the normal choice is to make the verb agree with the one closer to it:

> ☑ Either the twins or their mother is responsible for this.

But often a better solution is to recast the sentence to avoid the problem:

> ☑ Either the twins are responsible for this or their mother is.

Personal pronouns

I, *we*, *he*, *she*, and *they* are subjective pronouns, which act as the subjects of verbs, while *me*, *us*, *him*, *her*, and *them* are objective, acting as the objects of verbs and prepositions:

> Melissa and I are leaving now.
>
> The boys are coming with Gavin and me.

After the verb *be* it is more natural and usual to use *me*, *us*, *him*, *her*, or *them* (the objective pronouns), although what follows *be* is not an object but a complement:

> I said it was only me.
>
> That's us sitting on the bench.

The subjective forms (*I*, *we*, *he*, *she*, or *they*) are not wrong but often sound stilted, especially the first-person forms *I* and *we*:

> [?] I said it was only I.

5 Punctuation

The purpose of punctuation is to make writing clear, by clarifying the structure of continuous writing and indicating how words relate to each other.

Full stop

The principal use of the full stop is to mark the end of a sentence that is a statement:

> Bernard wants to buy an atlas.

This applies to 'sentences' when, for stylistic effect, they are not complete statements or contain ellipsis:

> Cape Town. A wet and windy July.

If an abbreviation with a full stop comes at the end of a sentence, another full stop is not added:

> Bring your own pens, pencils, rulers, etc.

Comma

The role of the comma is to give detail to the structure of sentences and to make their meaning clear by marking off words that either do or do not belong together. It usually represents the natural breaks and pauses that you make in speech, and operates at phrase level and word level.

At phrase level

You should use a comma to mark off parts of a sentence that are separated by conjunctions (*and*, *but*, *yet*, etc.). This is especially important when there is a change or repetition of the subject, or when the sentence is a long one:

> Mokosh could foretell the future, and she could change herself into any form she pleased.

> Readings are taken at points on a grid marked out on the ground, and the results are usually plotted in the form of computer-drawn diagrams.

In formal writing, it is not correct to join the clauses of a compound sentence without a conjunction:

> ☒ His was the last house, the road ended with him.

Nor is it correct to separate a subject from its verb with a single comma:

> ☒ The man who was wearing no shoes, escaped through the window.
>
> ☑ The man who was wearing no shoes escaped through the window.

The following sentence uses commas correctly, but has a different meaning from the example above:

> The man, who was wearing no shoes, escaped through the window.

A comma also separates parts of a sentence that balance or complement each other, and can introduce direct speech, especially in continuation of dialogue:

> He was getting better, but not as fast as his doctor wished.
>
> Then Laura said, 'Do you mean that?'

An important function of the comma is to prevent ambiguity or momentary misunderstanding:

> Nick said that he had shot, himself, as a small boy.

Commas are used in pairs to separate elements in a sentence that are asides or not part of the main statement:

> All history, of course, is the history of wars.

Commas are also used to separate a relative clause that is non-restrictive (see 'Relative clauses' above):

> The money, which totals more than half a million, comes from three anonymous donors.

A single comma sometimes follows adverbs, phrases, and subordinate clauses that come at the beginning of a sentence:

> Moreover, they had lied about where they had been.
>
> When the sun began to sink, she could take the riverside walk to the hotel.

A comma is always needed with *however* when it means 'by contrast' or 'on the other hand':

> However, a good deal of discretion is needed.

At word level

A comma is used to separate adjectives having the same range of reference, that come before a noun:

> a cold, damp, badly heated room

The comma is omitted when the adjectives have a different range of reference (for example, size and colour) or when the last adjective has a closer relation to the noun:

> his baggy green jacket
>
> a distinguished foreign politician

Commas are used to separate items in a list or sequence:

> The visitors were given tea, scones, and cake.

(The final comma before *and* is regarded by many people as unnecessary and left out; this dictionary always includes one.)

Leave out the comma between nouns that occur together in the same grammatical role in a sentence (called apposition):

> My friend Judge Peters was not at home.

But use one when the noun is a piece of extra information that could be removed from the sentence without any noticeable effect on the meaning:

> His father, Max, was not so fortunate.

Semicolon

The main role of the semicolon is to mark a grammatical separation that is stronger in effect than a comma but less strong than a full stop. Normally the two parts of a sentence divided by a semicolon balance each other, rather than leading from one to the other:

> The sky grew bright with sunset; the earth glowed.

> Honey looked up and glared; the man scurried away.

You can also use a semicolon as a stronger division in a sentence that already contains commas:

> What has crippled me? Was it my grandmother, frowning on my childish affection and turning it to formality and cold courtesy; or my timid, fearful mother, in awe of everyone including, finally, me; or was it my wife's infidelities, or my own?

Colon

Whereas a semicolon links two balanced statements, a colon leads from the first statement to the second. Typically it links a general or introductory statement to an example, a cause to an effect, or a premise to a conclusion.

> He was being made to feel more part of the family: the children kissed him goodnight, like a third parent.

You also use a colon to introduce a list:

> The price includes the following: the flight to Venice, accommodation, and meals.

Apostrophe

The principal role of the apostrophe is to indicate a possessive, as in **Tessa's house** and **the town's mayor**.

Singular nouns form the possessive by adding *'s* (**the dog's tail** = one dog), and plural nouns ending in *-s* add an apostrophe after the *-s* (**the dogs' tails** = more than one dog). When a plural noun ends in a letter other than *s*, the possessive is formed by adding *'s*: **the children's games, the oxen's hoofs**, etc.

Beware of an apostrophe wrongly applied to an ordinary plural, particularly in words ending in *-o* but also in words such as *apples* and *pears* (e.g. ☒ **pear's R20 a kilo**).

Beware also of confusing the possessive *whose* with *who's*, which is a contraction of *who is*:

☒ Who's turn is it?

☑ Whose turn is it?

For names ending in *-s*, the best course is to add *'s* when you would pronounce the resulting form with an extra *s* in speech (e.g. *Charles's, Dickens's, Thomas's,*); and omit *'s* otherwise (e.g. *Bridges', Herodotus'*). With French names (and names of French origin) ending in silent *-s* or *-x*, add *'s* (e.g. *Du Plessis's, le Roux's*) and pronounce the modified word with a final *-z*.

An apostrophe should not be used in the pronouns *hers, its, ours, yours,* and *theirs*.

Be careful to distinguish *its* from *it's*. *Its* (no apostrophe) is a possessive meaning 'belonging to it', whereas *it's* (with an apostrophe) is a contraction meaning 'it is' or 'it has':

> Give the cat its dinner.

> It's hard to know where to start.

An apostrophe is not normally used in the plural of abbreviated forms (e.g. **several CEOs attended**), although it is used in the possessive (e.g. **the SABC's decision to go ahead with the broadcast**).

Another important use of the apostrophe is to mark contractions such as *I'll, they've, couldn't,* and *she's*.

Hyphens

In print a hyphen is half the length of a dash, but in writing there is often little noticeable difference. While the dash has the purpose of separating words and groups of words, the hyphen is meant to link words and parts of words. The use of hyphens is very variable in English, but the following guidelines reflect generally agreed principles.

The hyphen is used to join two or more words so as to form a single word (often called a compound word), e.g. *free-for-all, multi-ethnic, right-handed,* and *punch-drunk*. Straightforward noun compounds are now much more often spelled either as two words (*boiling point, credit card, focus group*) or as one (*database*), even when this involves a collision of consonants, which used to be a reason for putting in the hyphen (*earring, breaststroke*). In American English compound nouns generally written as two words in British English are often written as one word.

There are two cases in which a compound spelled as two words is made into a hyphenated form or a one-word form:

- when a verb phrase such as *hold up* or *back up* is made into a noun (*hold-up*, *backup*)
- when a noun compound is made into a verb (e.g. *a date stamp* but *to date-stamp*). Note that a normal phrasal verb should not be hyphenated: write **continue to build up your pension** not **continue to build-up your pension**.

A hyphen is often used:

- to join a prefix ending in a vowel (such as *co-* and *neo-*) to another word (e.g. *co-opt*, *neo-Impressionism*), although one-word forms are becoming more usual (*cooperate*, *neoclassical*).
- to avoid ambiguity by separating a prefix from the main word, e.g. to distinguish *re-cover* (= provide with a new cover) from *recover* and *re-sign* (= sign again) from *resign*.
- to join a prefix to a name or designation, e.g. *anti-Christian*, *ex-husband*.
- to stand for a common second element in all but the last word of a list, e.g. *two-, three-,* or *fourfold*.
- to clarify meanings in groups of words which might otherwise be unclear or ambiguous (e.g. **twenty-odd people came to the meeting**).
- to clarify the meaning of a compound that is normally spelled as separate words, when it is used attributively before a noun: write **an up-to-date record** but **the record is up to date**.

There is no need to insert a hyphen between an adverb ending in *-ly* and an adjective qualified by it, even when they come before the noun: **a highly competitive market**, **recently published material**. When the adverb does not end in *-ly*, however, a hyphen is normally required to make the meaning clear when the adverb precedes the noun: **a well-known woman** (but **the woman is well known**).

5 Countries of the World

Population figures are based on 2009 estimates.

Independent countries

Country	Capital	Area (km²)	Population	Currency unit
Afghanistan	Kabul	648 000	28 395 700	afghani = 100 puls
Albania	Tirana	28 700	3 639 500	lek = 100 qintars
Algeria	Algiers	2 319 000	34 178 200	dinar = 100 centimes
Andorra	Andorra la Vella	468	83 900	euro = 100 cents
Angola	Luanda	1 246 000	12 799 300	kwanza = 100 lwei
Antigua and Barbuda	St John's	442	85 600	dollar = 100 cents
Argentina	Buenos Aires	2 780 000	40 913 600	peso = 100 centavos
Armenia	Yerevan	29 800	2 967 000	dram = 100 luma
Australia	Canberra	7 692 000	21 262 600	dollar = 100 cents
Austria	Vienna	83 900	8 210 300	euro = 100 cents
Azerbaijan	Baku	86 600	8 238 700	manat = 100 gopik
Bahamas	Nassau	13 900	307 600	dollar = 100 cents
Bahrain	Manama	620	728 700	dinar = 1 000 fils
Bangladesh	Dhaka	144 000	156 050 900	taka = 100 poisha
Barbados	Bridgetown	431	284 600	dollar = 100 cents
Belarus	Minsk	208 000	9 648 500	rouble = 100 kopeks
Belgium	Brussels	30 500	10 414 300	euro = 100 cents
Belize	Belmopan	23 000	307 900	dollar = 100 cents
Benin	Porto Novo	113 000	8 791 800	franc = 100 centimes
Bhutan	Thimphu	46 600	691 100	ngultrum = 100 chetrum, Indian rupee
Bolivia	La Paz	1 099 000	9 775 200	boliviano = 100 centavos
Bosnia and Herzegovina	Sarajevo	51 100	4 613 400	mark = 100 fening
Botswana	Gaborone	600 000	1 990 900	pula = 100 thebe
Brazil	Brasilia	8 512 000	198 739 300	real = 100 centavos
Brunei	Bandar Seri Begawan	5 770	388 200	dollar = 100 sen
Bulgaria	Sofia	111 000	7 204 700	lev = 100 stotinki
Burkina Faso	Ouagadougou	274 000	15 746 200	franc = 100 centimes
Burma (Myanmar)	Naypyidaw	677 000	48 137 700	kyat = 100 pyas
Burundi	Bujumbura	27 800	9 511 300	franc = 100 centimes
Cambodia	Phnom Penh	181 000	14 494 300	riel = 100 sen
Cameroon	Yaoundé	475 000	18 879 300	franc = 100 centimes
Canada	Ottawa	9 976 000	33 487 200	dollar = 100 cents
Cape Verde Islands	Praia	4 030	429 500	escudo = 100 centavos
Central African Republic	Bangui	625 000	4 511 500	franc = 100 centimes
Chad	N'Djamena	1 284 000	10 329 200	franc = 100 centimes
Chile	Santiago	757 000	16 601 700	peso = 100 centavos
China	Beijing	9 561 000	1 338 613 000	yuan = 10 jiao or 100 fen
Colombia	Bogotá	1 140 000	43 677 400	peso = 100 centavos
Comoros	Moroni	1 790	752 400	franc = 100 centimes
Congo	Brazzaville	342 000	4 012 800	franc = 100 centimes
Congo, Democratic Republic of (Zaire)	Kinshasa	2 344 000	68 692 500	franc = 100 centimes
Costa Rica	San José	51 000	4 253 900	colón = 100 centimos
Côte d'Ivoire	Yamoussoukro	322 000	20 617 100	franc = 100 centimes
Croatia	Zagreb	56 500	4 489 400	kuna = 100 lipa
Cuba	Havana	111 000	11 451 700	peso = 100 centavos
Cyprus	Nicosia	9 250	1 084 700	euro = 100 cents
Czech Republic	Prague	78 900	10 211 900	koruna = 100 halers
Denmark	Copenhagen	43 100	5 500 500	krone = 100 øre
Djibouti	Djibouti	23 300	724 600	franc = 100 centimes
Dominica	Roseau	751	72 700	dollar = 100 cents

Country	Capital	Area (km²)	Population	Currency unit
Dominican Republic	Santo Domingo	48 400	9 650 100	peso = 100 centavos
East Timor	Dili	14 874	1 131 600	dollar = 100 centavos
Ecuador	Quito	271 000	14 573 100	dollar = 100 centavos
Egypt	Cairo	1 002 000	78 866 600	pound = 100 piastres or 1 000 milliemes
El Salvador	San Salvador	21 400	7 185 200	dollar = 100 cents
Equatorial Guinea	Malabo	28 100	633 400	franc = 100 centimes
Eritrea	Asmara	118 000	5 647 200	nakfa; Ethiopian birr
Estonia	Tallinn	45 100	1 299 400	kroon = 100 sents
Ethiopia	Addis Ababa	1 224 000	85 237 300	birr = 100 cents
Fiji	Suva	18 300	944 700	dollar = 100 cents
Finland	Helsinki	338 000	5 250 300	euro = 100 cents
France	Paris	547 000	64 420 100	euro = 100 cents
Gabon	Libreville	268 000	1 515 000	franc = 100 centimes
Gambia	Banjul	11 300	1 778 100	dalasi = 100 butut
Georgia	Tbilisi	69 700	4 615 800	lari = 100 tetri
Germany	Berlin	357 000	82 329 800	euro = 100 cents
Ghana	Accra	239 000	23 887 800	cedi = 100 pesewas
Greece	Athens	131 000	10 737 400	euro = 100 cents
Grenada	St George's	345	90 700	dollar = 100 cents
Guatemala	Guatemala City	109 000	13 276 500	quetzal = 100 centavos
Guinea	Conakry	246 000	10 058 000	franc = 100 centimes
Guinea-Bissau	Bissau	36 000	1 534 000	franc = 100 centimes
Guyana	Georgetown	215 000	752 900	dollar = 100 cents
Haiti	Port-au-Prince	27 800	9 035 500	gourde = 100 centimes
Honduras	Tegucigalpa	112 000	7 833 700	lempira = 100 centavos
Hungary	Budapest	93 000	9 905 600	forint = 100 filler
Iceland	Reykjavik	103 000	306 700	krona = 100 aurar
India	New Delhi	3 185 000	1 156 897 800	rupee = 100 paisa
Indonesia	Jakarta	1 905 000	240 271 500	rupiah = 100 sen
Iran	Tehran	1 648 000	66 429 300	rial = 100 dinars
Iraq	Baghdad	438 000	28 945 600	dinar = 1 000 fils
Ireland, Republic of	Dublin	70 300	4 203 200	euro = 100 cents
Israel	Jerusalem	20 800	7 233 700	shekel = 100 agora
Italy	Rome	301 000	58 126 200	euro = 100 cents
Ivory Coast (see Côte d'Ivoire)				
Jamaica	Kingston	11 000	2 825 900	dollar = 100 cents
Japan	Tokyo	378 000	127 078 700	yen
Jordan	Amman	97 700	6 269 300	dinar = 1 000 fils
Kazakhstan	Astana	2 717 000	15 399 400	tenge = 100 teins
Kenya	Nairobi	583 000	39 002 800	shilling = 100 cents
Kiribati	Bairiki	717	112 900	Australian dollar
Kuwait	Kuwait City	17 800	2 692 500	dinar = 1 000 fils
Kyrgyzstan	Bishkek	199 000	5 431 700	som = 100 tiyin
Laos	Vientiane	237 000	6 834 300	kip = 100 ats
Latvia	Riga	64 600	2 231 500	lat = 100 santims
Lebanon	Beirut	10 500	4 017 100	pound = 100 piastres
Lesotho	Maseru	30 300	2 130 800	loti = 100 lisente
Liberia	Monrovia	111 000	3 441 800	dollar = 100 cents
Libya	Tripoli	1 776 000	6 324 400	dinar = 1 000 dirhams
Liechtenstein	Vaduz	160	34 800	franc = 100 centimes
Lithuania	Vilnius	65 200	3 555 200	litas = 100 centas
Luxembourg	Luxembourg	2 590	491 800	euro = 100 cents
Macedonia	Skopje	25 700	2 066 700	denar = 100 deni
Madagascar	Antananarivo	587 000	20 653 600	ariary = 5 iraimbilanja
Malawi	Lilongwe	118 000	15 028 800	kwacha = 100 tambala
Malaysia	Kuala Lumpur	330 000	25 715 800	ringgit = 100 sen
Maldives	Male	298	396 300	rufiyaa = 100 laris
Mali	Bamako	1 240 000	13 443 200	franc = 100 centimes
Malta	Valletta	316	405 200	euro = 100 cents
Marshall Islands	Majuro	181	64 500	US dollar
Mauritania	Nouakchott	1 031 000	3 129 500	ouguiya = 5 khoums
Mauritius	Port Louis	2 040	1 284 300	rupee = 100 cents
Mexico	Mexico City	1 958 000	111 211 800	peso = 100 centavos
Micronesia	Palikir	701	107 400	US dollar

COUNTRIES OF THE WORLD

Country	Capital	Area (km^2)	Population	Currency unit
Moldova	Chișinău	33 700	4 320 700	leu = 100 bani
Monaco	Monaco	1.5	33 000	euro = 100 cents
Mongolia	Ulan Bator	1 565 000	3 041 100	tugrik = 100 mongos
Montenegro	Podgorica	13 812	672 200	euro = 100 cents
Morocco	Rabat	459 000	31 285 200	dirham = 100 centimes
Mozambique	Maputo	799 000	21 669 300	metical = 100 centavos
Myanmar (see Burma)				
Namibia	Windhoek	824 000	2 108 700	dollar = 100 cents
Nauru	–	21	14 000	Australian dollar
Nepal	Kathmandu	147 000	28 563 400	rupee = 100 paisa
Netherlands	Amsterdam	37 000	16 716 000	euro = 100 cents
New Zealand	Wellington	268 000	4 213 400	dollar = 100 cents
Nicaragua	Managua	120 000	5 891 200	cordoba = 100 centavos
Niger	Niamey	1 267 000	15 306 300	franc = 100 centimes
Nigeria	Abuja	924 000	149 229 100	naira = 100 kobo
North Korea	Pyongyang	121 000	22 665 300	won = 100 jun
Norway	Oslo	324 000	4 660 500	krone = 100 øre
Oman	Muscat	212 000	3 418 100	rial = 1 000 baiza
Pakistan	Islamabad	804 000	174 578 600	rupee = 100 paisa
Palau	Melekeok	459	20 800	dollar = 100 cents
Panama	Panama City	77 100	3 360 500	balboa = 100 centésimos
Papua New Guinea	Port Moresby	463 000	5 940 800	kina = 100 toea
Paraguay	Asunción	407 000	6 995 700	guarani = 100 centimos
Peru	Lima	1 285 000	29 547 000	sol = 100 cents
Philippines	Manila	300 000	97 976 600	peso = 100 centavos
Poland	Warsaw	304 000	38 482 900	zloty = 100 groszy
Portugal	Lisbon	92 000	10 707 900	euro = 100 cents
Qatar	Doha	11 400	833 300	riyal = 100 dirhams
Romania	Bucharest	229 000	22 215 400	leu = 100 bani
Russia	Moscow	17 075 000	140 041 200	rouble = 100 kopeks
Rwanda	Kigali	26 300	10 746 300	franc = 100 centimes
St Kitts and Nevis	Basseterre	261	40 100	dollar = 100 cents
St Lucia	Castries	616	160 300	dollar = 100 cents
St Vincent and the Grenadines	Kingstown	389	104 600	dollar = 100 cents
Samoa	Apia	2 840	220 000	tala = 100 sene
San Marino	San Marino	61	30 200	euro = 100 cents
São Tomé and Principe	São Tomé	964	212 700	dobra = 100 centavos
Saudi Arabia	Riyadh	2 150 000	28 686 600	riyal = 20 qursh or 100 halalas
Senegal	Dakar	197 000	13 711 600	franc = 100 centimes
Serbia	Belgrade	88 361	7 379 300	dinar = 100 paras
Seychelles	Victoria	453	87 500	rupee = 100 cents
Sierra Leone	Freetown	71 700	5 132 100	leone = 100 cents
Singapore	Singapore City	618	4 657 500	dollar = 100 cents
Slovakia	Bratislava	49 000	5 463 000	euro = 100 cents
Slovenia	Ljubljana	20 300	2 005 700	euro = 100 cents
Solomon Islands	Honiara	276 000	595 600	dollar = 100 cents
Somalia	Mogadishu	638 000	9 832 000	shilling = 100 cents
South Africa	Pretoria	1 221 000	49 052 500	rand = 100 cents
South Korea	Seoul	99 300	48 509 000	won = 100 jeon
Spain	Madrid	505 000	40 525 000	euro = 100 cents
Sri Lanka	Colombo	64 000	21 324 800	rupee = 100 cents
Sudan	Khartoum	2 506 000	41 087 800	pound = 100 piastres
Suriname	Paramaribo	163 000	481 300	dollar = 100 cents
Swaziland	Mbabane	17 000	1 337 200	lilangeni = 100 cents
Sweden	Stockholm	450 000	9 059 700	krona = 100 öre
Switzerland	Berne	41 000	7 604 500	franc = 100 centimes
Syria	Damascus	184 000	21 763 000	pound = 100 piastres
Taiwan	Taipei	36 000	22 974 300	dollar = 100 cents
Tajikistan	Dushanbe	143 000	7 349 100	somoni = 100 dirams
Tanzania	Dodoma	940 000	41 048 500	shilling = 100 cents
Thailand	Bangkok	513 000	65 998 400	baht = 100 satangs
Togo	Lomé	57 000	6 031 800	franc = 100 centimes
Tonga	Nuku'alofa	668	120 900	pa'anga = 100 seniti
Trinidad and Tobago	Port-of-Spain	5 130	1 230 000	dollar = 100 cents
Tunisia	Tunis	164 000	10 486 300	dinar = 1 000 milliemes

Country	Capital	Area (km²)	Population	Currency unit
Turkey	Ankara	779 000	76 805 500	lira = 100 kurus
Turkmenistan	Ashgabat	488 000	4 884 900	manat = 100 tenesi
Tuvalu	Funafuti	26	12 400	dollar = 100 cents
Uganda	Kampala	241 000	32 369 600	shilling = 100 cents
Ukraine	Kiev	604 000	45 700 400	hryvna = 100 kopiykas
United Arab Emirates	Abu Dhabi	77 770	4 798 500	dirham = 100 fils
United Kingdom	London	244 000	61 113 200	pound = 100 pence
United States	Washington DC	9 373 000	304 059 724	dollar = 100 cents
Uruguay	Montevideo	176 000	3 494 400	peso = 100 centésimos
Uzbekistan	Tashkent	447 000	27 606 000	som = 100 tiyin
Vanuatu	Port Vila	14 800	218 500	vatu = 100 centimes
Vatican City	Vatican City	0.44	800	euro = 100 cents
Venezuela	Caracas	912 000	26 814 800	bolivar = 100 centimos
Vietnam	Hanoi	330 000	88 576 800	dong = 100 xu
Yemen	Sana'a	540 000	22 858 200	riyal = 100 fils
Zambia	Lusaka	753 000	11 862 700	kwacha = 100 ngwee
Zimbabwe	Harare	391 000	11 392 600	dollar = 100 cents

Principal dependencies

Country	Capital	Area (km²)	Population	Currency unit
American Samoa (US)	Fagatogo	197	65 600	US dollar
Anguilla (UK)	The Valley	155	14 400	East Caribbean dollar
Aruba (Netherlands)	Oranjestad	193	103 100	florin
Bermuda (UK)	Hamilton	53	67 800	Bermudian dollar
Cayman Islands (UK)	George Town	259	49 000	Cayman Islands dollar
Christmas Island (Australia)	–	135	1 400	Australian dollar
Cocos Islands (Australia)	–	14	600	Australian dollar
Cook Islands (NZ)	Avarua	238	11 900	NZ dollar
Falkland Islands (UK)	Stanley	12 200	3 100	pound
Faroe Islands (Denmark)	Tórshavn	1 400	48 900	krone
French Guiana (France)	Cayenne	91 000	202 000	euro
French Polynesia (France)	Papeete	3 940	287 000	franc
Gibraltar (UK)	Gibraltar	5.9	28 800	pound
Greenland (Denmark)	Nuuk	2 186 100	57 600	Danish krone
Guadeloupe (France)	Basse-Terre	1 780	445 000	euro
Guam (US)	Agaña	541	178 400	US dollar
Martinique (France)	Fort-de-France	1 080	399 000	euro
Mayotte (France)	Mamoutzu	362	223 800	euro
Montserrat (UK)	Plymouth	102	5 100	East Caribbean dollar
Netherlands Antilles (Netherlands)	Willemstad	800	227 000	guilder
New Caledonia (France)	Nouméa	18 600	227 400	franc
Niue (NZ)	Alofi	263	1 400	NZ dollar
Norfolk Island (Australia)	–	35	2 100	Australian dollar
Northern Marianas (US)	Saipan	477	51 500	US dollar
Pitcairn Islands (UK)	–	4.6	50	NZ dollar
Puerto Rico (US)	San Juan	8 960	3 966 200	US dollar
Réunion (France)	Saint-Denis	2 510	807 000	euro
St Helena and dependencies (UK)	Jamestown	420	7 600	pound
St Pierre and Miquelon (France)	St-Pierre	242	7 100	euro
Svalbard (Norway)	Longyearbyen	62 000	2 100	Norwegian krone
Turks and Caicos Islands (UK)	Cockburn Town	430	22 900	US dollar
Virgin Islands (US)	Charlotte Amalie	342	109 800	US dollar
Virgin Islands, British (UK)	Road Town	153	24 500	US dollar
Wallis and Futuna Islands (France)	Mata-Utu	274	15 300	franc
Western Sahara (Morocco)	Laayoune	252 000	405 200	Moroccan dirham

6 Prime Ministers and Presidents

Prime Ministers and Presidents of South Africa

This list dates from the formation of the Union of South Africa in 1910. The Union became the Republic of South Africa in 1961. The head of government's title was Prime Minister until 1984, when it changed to President.

Prime Ministers

1910–1919	Louis Botha	South African Party
1919–1924	Jan C. Smuts	"
1924–1939	J. Barry Hertzog	National Party/ United Party
1939–1948	Jan C. Smuts	United Party
1948–1954	Daniel F. Malan	National Party
1954–1958	Johannes G. Strijdom	"
1958–1966	Hendrik F. Verwoerd	"
1966–1978	Balthazar J. Vorster	"
1978–1984	Pieter W. Botha	"

Presidents*

1984–1989	Pieter W. Botha	National Party
1989–1989	Chris Heunis (acting)	"
1989–1994	Frederik W. de Klerk	"
1994–1999	Nelson R. Mandela	African National Congress
1999–2008	Thabo M. Mbeki	"
2008–2009	Kgalema P. Motlanthe	"
2009–	Jacob G. Zuma	"

*The presidents listed here were or are the heads of government. Between 1961 and 1984, when prime ministers were the heads of government, South Africa also had 'State Presidents' whose role was ceremonial; the ceremonial presidents are not listed here.

Presidents of the United States of America

1789–1797	1.	George Washington	Federalist
1797–1801	2.	John Adams	"
1801–1809	3.	Thomas Jefferson	Democratic Republican
1809–1817	4.	James Madison	"
1817–1825	5.	James Monroe	"
1825–1829	6.	John Quincy Adams	Independent
1829–1837	7.	Andrew Jackson	Democrat
1837–1841	8.	Martin Van Buren	"
1841	9.	William H. Harrison	Whig
1841–1845	10.	John Tyler	Whig, then Democrat
1845–1849	11.	James K. Polk	Democrat
1849–1850	12.	Zachary Taylor	Whig
1850–1853	13.	Millard Fillmore	"
1853–1857	14.	Franklin Pierce	Democrat
1857–1861	15.	James Buchanan	"
1861–1865	16.	Abraham Lincoln	Republican
1865–1869	17.	Andrew Johnson	Democrat
1869–1877	18.	Ulysses S. Grant	Republican
1877–1881	19.	Rutherford B. Hayes	"
1881	20.	James A. Garfield	"
1881–1885	21.	Chester A. Arthur	"
1885–1889	22.	Grover Cleveland	Democrat
1889–1893	23.	Benjamin Harrison	Republican
1893–1897	24.	Grover Cleveland	Democrat
1897–1901	25.	William McKinley	Republican
1901–1909	26.	Theodore Roosevelt	"
1909–1913	27.	William H. Taft	"
1913–1921	28.	Woodrow Wilson	Democrat
1921–1923	29.	Warren G. Harding	Republican
1923–1929	30.	Calvin Coolidge	"
1929–1933	31.	Herbert Hoover	"
1933–1945	32.	Franklin D. Roosevelt	Democrat
1945–1953	33.	Harry S. Truman	"
1953–1961	34.	Dwight D. Eisenhower	Republican
1961–1963	35.	John F. Kennedy	Democrat
1963–1969	36.	Lyndon B. Johnson	"
1969–1974	37.	Richard Nixon	Republican
1974–1977	38.	Gerald Ford	"
1977–1981	39.	Jimmy Carter	Democrat
1981–1989	40.	Ronald Reagan	Republican
1989–1993	41.	George Bush	"
1993–2001	42.	Bill Clinton	Democrat
2001–2009	43.	George W. Bush	Republican
2009–	44.	Barack Obama	Democrat

Prime Ministers of Great Britain and the United Kingdom

[1721]–1742	Sir Robert Walpole	Whig	1866–1868	Earl of Derby	Conservative
1742–1743	Earl of Wilmington	"	1868	Benjamin Disraeli	"
1743–1754	Henry Pelham	"	1868–1874	William Ewart Gladstone	Liberal
1754–1756	Duke of Newcastle	"	1874–1880	Benjamin Disraeli	Conservative
1756–1757	Duke of Devonshire	"	1880–1885	William Ewart Gladstone	Liberal
1757–1762	Duke of Newcastle	"	1885–1886	Marquess of Salisbury	Conservative
1762–1763	Earl of Bute	Tory	1886	William Ewart Gladstone	Liberal
1763–1765	George Grenville	Whig	1886–1892	Marquess of Salisbury	Conservative
1765–1766	Marquess of Rockingham	"	1892–1894	William Ewart Gladstone	Liberal
1766–1768	William Pitt the Elder	"	1894–1895	Earl of Rosebery	"
1768–1770	Duke of Grafton	"	1895–1902	Marquess of Salisbury	Conservative
1770–1782	Lord North	Tory	1902–1905	Arthur James Balfour	"
1782	Marquess of Rockingham	Whig	1905–1908	Sir Henry Campbell-Bannerman	
1782–1783	Earl of Shelburne	"			Liberal
1783	Duke of Portland	coalition	1908–1916	Herbert Henry Asquith	"
1783–1801	William Pitt the Younger	Tory	1916–1922	David Lloyd George	coalition
1801–1804	Henry Addington	"	1922–1923	Andrew Bonar Law	Conservative
1804–1806	William Pitt the Younger	"	1923–1924	Stanley Baldwin	"
1806–1807	Lord William Grenville	Whig	1924	James Ramsay MacDonald	Labour
1807–1809	Duke of Portland	Tory	1924–1929	Stanley Baldwin	Conservative
1809–1812	Spencer Perceval	"	1929–1935	James Ramsay MacDonald	coalition
1812–1827	Earl of Liverpool	"	1935–1937	Stanley Baldwin	"
1827	George Canning	"	1937–1940	Neville Chamberlain	"
1827–1828	Viscount Goderich	"	1940–1945	Winston Churchill	"
1828–1830	Duke of Wellington	"	1945–1951	Clement Attlee	Labour
1830–1834	Earl Grey	Whig	1951–1955	Sir Winston Churchill	Conservative
1834	Viscount Melbourne	"	1955–1957	Sir Anthony Eden	"
1834	Duke of Wellington	Tory	1957–1963	Harold Macmillan	"
1834–1835	Sir Robert Peel	Conservative	1963–1964	Sir Alec Douglas-Home	"
1835–1841	Viscount Melbourne	Whig	1964–1970	Harold Wilson	Labour
1841–1846	Sir Robert Peel	Conservative	1970–1974	Edward Heath	Conservative
1846–1852	Lord John Russell	Whig	1974–1976	Harold Wilson	Labour
1852	Earl of Derby	Conservative	1976–1979	James Callaghan	"
1852–1855	Earl of Aberdeen	coalition	1979–1990	Margaret Thatcher	Conservative
1855–1858	Viscount Palmerston	Whig	1990–1997	John Major	"
1858–1859	Earl of Derby	Conservative	1997–2007	Tony Blair	Labour
1859–1865	Viscount Palmerston	Liberal	2007–2010	Gordon Brown	"
1865–1866	Earl Russell	Liberal	2010–	David Cameron	coalition

7 Kings and Queens of England and the United Kingdom

Ruler	Dates of reign	Life
Saxon line		
Edwy	955–957	died 959
Edgar	959–975	944–975
Edward the Martyr	975–978	c.963–978
Ethelred the Unready	978–1016	c.969–1016
Edmund Ironside	1016	c.980–1016
Danish line		
Canute (Cnut)	1017–1035	died 1035
Harold I	1037–1040	died 1040
Hardecanute	1040–1042	c.1019–1042
Saxon line		
Edward the Confessor	1042–1066	c.1003–1066
Harold II	1066	c.1019–1066
House of Normandy		
William I (the Conqueror)	1066–1087	c.1027–1087
William II	1087–1100	c.1060–1100
Henry I	1100–1135	1068–1135
Stephen	1135–1154	c.1097–1154
House of Plantagenet		
Henry II	1154–1189	1133–1189
Richard I	1189–1199	1157–1199
John	1199–1216	1165–1216
Henry III	1216–1272	1207–1272
Edward I	1272–1307	1239–1307
Edward II	1307–1327	1284–1327
Edward III	1327–1377	1312–1377
Richard II	1377–1399	1367–1400
House of Lancaster		
Henry IV	1399–1413	1367–1413
Henry V	1413–1422	1387–1422
Henry VI	1422–1461, 1470–1	1421–1471
House of York		
Edward IV	1461–1483	1442–1483
Edward V	1483	1470–c.1483
Richard III	1483–1485	1452–1485

Ruler	Dates of reign	Life
House of Tudor		
Henry VII	1485–1509	1457–1509
Henry VIII	1509–1547	1491–1547
Edward VI	1547–1553	1537–1553
Mary I	1553–1558	1516–1558
Elizabeth I	1558–1603	1533–1603
House of Stuart		
James I	1603–1625	1566–1625
Charles I	1625–1649	1600–1649
Commonwealth (declared 1649)		
Oliver Cromwell, Lord Protector	1653–1658	1599–1658
Richard Cromwell	1658–1659	1626–1712
House of Stuart		
Charles II	1660–1685	1630–1685
James II	1685–1688	1633–1701
William III and Mary II	1689–1702 (Mary died 1694)	William 1650–1702 Mary 1662–1694
Anne	1702–1714	1665–1714
House of Hanover		
George I	1714–1727	1660–1727
George II	1727–1760	1683–1760
George III	1760–1820	1738–1820
George IV	1820–1830	1762–1830
William IV	1830–1837	1765–1837
Victoria	1837–1901	1819–1901
House of Saxe-Coburg-Gotha		
Edward VII	1901–1910	1841–1910
House of Windsor		
George V	1910–1936	1865–1936
Edward VIII	1936	1894–1972
George VI	1936–1952	1895–1952
Elizabeth II	1952–	born 1926

8 Chemical Elements

Element	Symbol	Atomic no.	Element	Symbol	Atomic no.	Element	Symbol	Atomic no.
actinium	Ac	89	gold	Au	79	promethium	Pm	61
aluminium	Al	13	hafnium	Hf	72	protactinium	Pa	91
americium	Am	95	hassium	Hs	108	radium	Ra	88
antimony	Sb	51	helium	He	2	radon	Rn	86
argon	Ar	18	holmium	Ho	67	rhenium	Re	75
arsenic	As	33	hydrogen	H	1	rhodium	Rh	45
astatine	At	85	indium	In	49	roentgenium	Rg	111
barium	Ba	56	iodine	I	53	rubidium	Rb	37
berkelium	Bk	97	iridium	Ir	77	ruthenium	Ru	44
beryllium	Be	4	iron	Fe	26	rutherfordium	Rf	104
bismuth	Bi	83	krypton	Kr	36	samarium	Sm	62
bohrium	Bh	107	lanthanum	La	57	scandium	Sc	21
boron	B	5	lawrencium	Lr	103	seaborgium	Sg	106
bromine	Br	35	lead	Pb	82	selenium	Se	34
cadmium	Cd	48	lithium	Li	3	silicon	Si	14
caesium	Cs	55	lutetium	Lu	71	silver	Ag	47
calcium	Ca	20	magnesium	Mg	12	sodium	Na	11
californium	Cf	98	manganese	Mn	25	strontium	Sr	38
carbon	C	6	meitnerium	Mt	109	sulphur	S	16
cerium	Ce	58	mendelevium	Md	101	tantalum	Ta	73
chlorine	Cl	17	mercury	Hg	80	technetium	Tc	43
chromium	Cr	24	molybdenum	Mo	42	tellurium	Te	52
cobalt	Co	27	neodymium	Nd	60	terbium	Tb	65
copernicium	Cn	112	neon	Ne	10	thallium	Tl	81
copper	Cu	29	neptunium	Np	93	thorium	Th	90
curium	Cm	96	nickel	Ni	28	thulium	Tm	69
darmstadtium	Ds	110	niobium	Nb	41	tin	Sn	50
dubnium	Db	105	nitrogen	N	7	titanium	Ti	22
dysprosium	Dy	66	nobelium	No	102	tungsten	W	74
einsteinium	Es	99	osmium	Os	76	uranium	U	92
erbium	Er	68	oxygen	O	8	vanadium	V	23
europium	Eu	63	palladium	Pd	46	xenon	Xe	54
fermium	Fm	100	phosphorus	P	15	ytterbium	Yb	70
fluorine	F	9	platinum	Pt	78	yttrium	Y	39
francium	Fr	87	plutonium	Pu	94	zinc	Zn	30
gadolinium	Gd	64	polonium	Po	84	zirconium	Zr	40
gallium	Ga	31	potassium	K	19			
germanium	Ge	32	praseodymium	Pr	59			

9 Greek Alphabet

A	α	alpha	a	H	η	eta	ē	N	ν	nu	n	T	τ	tau	t
B	β	beta	b	Θ	θ	theta	th	Ξ	ξ	xi	x	Υ	υ	upsilon	u
Γ	γ	gamma	g	I	ι	iota	i	O	o	omicron	o	Φ	φ	phi	ph
Δ	δ	delta	d	K	κ	kappa	k	Π	π	pi	p	X	χ	chi	kh
E	ε	epsilon	e	Λ	λ	lambda	l	P	ρ	rho	r, rh	Ψ	ψ	psi	ps
Z	ζ	zeta	z	M	μ	mu	m	Σ	σ ς	sigma	s	Ω	ω	omega	ō

10 Metric Measures and Notation

Metric measures

Length
10 millimetres (mm)	= 1 centimetre (cm)
10 centimetres (cm)	= 1 decimetre (dm)
100 centimetres (cm)	= 1 metre (m)
10 metres (m)	= 1 decametre (dam)
10 decametres (dam)	= 1 hectometre (hm)
1 000 metres (m)	= 1 kilometre (km)

The basic unit of length is the metre.

Area
10 000 square centimetres (cm^2)	= 1 square metre (m^2)
100 square metres (m^2)	= 1 are
100 ares	= 1 hectare (ha)
100 hectares (ha)	= 1 square kilometre (km^2)

Mass
10 milligrams (mg)	= 1 centigram (cg)
100 milligrams (mg)	= 1 decigram (dg)
1 000 milligrams (mg)	= 1 gram (g)
100 grams (g)	= 1 hectogram (hg)
1 000 grams (g)	= 1 kilogram (kg)
1 000 kilograms (kg)	= 1 tonne (t)

The basic unit of mass is the kilogram.

Capacity
10 millilitres (ml)	= 1 centilitre (cl)
10 centilitres (cl)	= 1 decilitre (dl)
100 centilitres (cl)	= 1 litre (l)
1 000 millilitres (ml)	= 1 litre (l)
10 litres (l)	= 1 decalitre (dal)
100 litres (l)	= 1 hectolitre (hl)
1 000 litres (l)	= 1 kilolitre (kl)

The basic unit of capacity is the litre.

Temperature
Celsius or Centigrade: water boils at 100° and freezes at 0°.
Kelvin: water boils at 373.15 K and freezes at 273.15 K.
To convert Centigrade into Kelvin: add 273.15.

The metric prefixes

	Abbreviations	Factors
deca-	da	10
hecto-	h	10^2
kilo-	k	10^3
mega-	M	10^6
giga-	G	10^9
tera-	T	10^{12}
peta-	P	10^{15}
exa-	E	10^{18}
deci-	d	10^{-1}
centi-	c	10^{-2}
milli-	m	10^{-3}
micro-	µ	10^{-6}
nano-	n	10^{-9}
pico-	p	10^{-12}
femto-	f	10^{-15}
atto-	a	10^{-18}

Entries for the prefixes listed above are included at their alphabetical places in the dictionary. The prefixes may be applied to any units of the metric system, for example:

hectogram (abbr. hg) = 100 grams
kilowatt (abbr. kW) = 1 000 watts
megahertz (MHz) = 1 million hertz
centimetre (cm) = 1/100 metre
microvolt (µV) = one millionth of a volt
picofarad (pF) = 10^{-12} farad

They are sometimes applied to other units (for example, megabit).

Power notation

This expresses concisely any power of 10 (any number that is formed by multiplying or dividing ten by itself), and is sometimes used in the dictionary.
10^2 (ten squared) = 10 × 10 = 100
10^3 (ten cubed) = 10 × 10 × 10 = 1 000
10^4 = 10 × 10 × 10 × 10 = 10 000
10^{10} = 10 000 000 000 (1 followed by ten zeros)
10^{-2} = $1/10^2$ = 1/100 = 0.01
10^{-10} = $1/10^{10}$ = 1/10 000 000 000
6.2×10^3 = 6 200
4.7×10^{-2} = 0.047

SI units

1 Base units

Physical quantity	Name	Abbreviation or symbol
length	metre	m
mass	kilogram	kg
time	second	s
electric current	ampere	A
temperature	kelvin	K
amount of substance	mole	mol
luminous intensity	candela	cd

2 Supplementary units

Physical quantity	Name	Abbreviation or symbol
plane angle	radian	rad
solid angle	steradian	sr

3 Derived units with special names

Physical quantity	Name	Abbreviation or symbol
frequency	hertz	Hz
energy	joule	J
force	newton	N
power	watt	W
pressure	pascal	Pa
electric charge	coulomb	C
electromotive force	volt	V
electric resistance	ohm	Ω
electric conductance	siemens	S
electric capacitance	farad	F
magnetic flux	weber	Wb
inductance	henry	H
magnetic flux density	tesla	T
luminous flux	lumen	lm
illuminance	lux	lx

11 The Solar System

The sun and planets

Planet	Mean distance from sun (10⁶ km)	Equatorial diameter (km)	Mass (Earth = 1)	Volume (Earth = 1)	Orbital period or 'year'	Rotation period or 'day'
Sun	–	1 400 000	330 000	1 300 000	–	25d*
Mercury	57.9	4 878	0.06	0.06	87.97d	58.65d
Venus	108.2	12 102	0.81	0.86	224.7d	243.d(R)
Earth	149.6	12 756	1.00	1.00	365.3d	23.93h
Mars	227.9	6 786	0.11	0.15	687.0d	24.62h
Jupiter	778.3	142 980	318	1 323	11.86y	9.93h*
Saturn	1 427	120 540	95.2	752	29.46y	10.66h*
Uranus	2 871	51 120	14.5	64	84.01y	17.24h*(R)
Neptune	4 497	49 530	17.1	54	164.8y	16.11h*

Pluto was formerly regarded as the ninth planet, but in 2006 the International Astronomical Union declared it to be a dwarf planet rather than a planet proper.

*At equator. (R) retrograde.

Principal planetary satellites

Planet	Satellite	Year of discovery	Diameter (km)	Mean distance from centre of planet (10³km)	Orbital period (days)
Earth	Moon	–	3 476*	384.4	27.32
Mars	Phobos	1877	27*	9.4	0.319
	Deimos	1877	15*	23.5	1.262
Jupiter	Amalthea	1892	262*	181	0.498
	Io	1610	3 630*	422	1.769
	Europa	1610	3 138*	671	3.551
	Ganymede	1610	5 262*	1 070	7.155
	Callisto	1610	4 800*	1 883	16.69
Saturn	Mimas	1789	390*	199	0.942
	Enceladus	1789	500*	238	1.370
	Tethys	1684	1 050*	295	1.888
	Dione	1684	1 120*	377	2.737
	Rhea	1672	1 530*	527	4.518
	Titan	1655	5 150*	1 222	15.95
	Hyperion	1848	340*	1 481	21.28
	Iapetus	1671	1 440*	3 561	79.33
	Phoebe	1898	220*	12 952	550.5(R)
Uranus	Miranda	1948	480*	130	1.414
	Ariel	1851	1 160*	191	2.520
	Umbriel	1851	1 190*	266	4.144
	Titania	1787	1 600*	436	8.706
	Oberon	1787	1 550*	583	13.46
Neptune	Proteus	1989	400*	118	1.12
	Triton	1846	2 700*	354	5.877(R)
	Nereid	1949	340*	551	360.2

*Irregular: maximum dimension. (R) retrograde.
Many other small satellites are known for Jupiter, Saturn, Uranus, and Neptune.

Mm

M[1] (also **m**) ■ n. (pl. **Ms** or **M's**) **1** the thirteenth letter of the alphabet. **2** denoting the next after L in a set of items, categories, etc. **3** the Roman numeral for 1 000. [from Latin *mille*.]

M[2] ■ abbrev. **1** Cricket (on scorecards) maiden over(s). **2** male. **3** medium (as a clothes size). **4** mega-: 64*Mb*. **5** Chemistry (with reference to solutions) molar. **6** Economics used with following numeral in measures of money supply. **7** Monsieur. **8** (in UK road designations) motorway. ■ symb. Physics mutual inductance.

m ■ abbrev. **1** metre(s). **2** mile(s). **3** masculine. **4** (*m-*) Chemistry meta-. **5** milli-: *100 mA*. **6** million(s). **7** married. **8** minute(s). **9** mare. ■ symb. Physics mass.

m' ■ possess. det. Brit. short for **MY** (representing the pronunciation used by lawyers in court to refer to or address the judge or a fellow barrister on the same side).

m- ■ prefix denoting commercial activity conducted via cellphones: *m-commerce*.

MA ■ abbrev. Master of Arts.

ma ■ n. informal one's mother.

ma'am ■ n. a respectful form of address for a woman.

mañana /man'jɑːnə/ ■ adv. **1** tomorrow. **2** in the indefinite future.
– ORIGIN Spanish, 'tomorrow'.

maas /mɑːs/ (also **amasi**) ■ n. S. African milk that has been curdled naturally.
– ORIGIN perhaps via Afrikaans from isiXhosa and isiZulu *amasi*.

Maasai ■ n. & adj. variant spelling of **MASAI**.

maasbanker /'mɑːsbʌŋkə/ ■ n. S. African a commercially important shoaling fish of the eastern Atlantic. [*Trachurus trachurus*.]
– ORIGIN from Dutch *marsbanker*.

mabela /mə'beɪə/ ■ n. S. African sorghum. ▶ porridge made from sorghum meal.
– ORIGIN from Setswana.

Mac ■ n. informal, chiefly N. Amer. a form of address for a man whose name is unknown to the speaker.
– ORIGIN C17: from *Mac-*, a patronymic prefix in many Scots and Irish surnames.

mac (also **mack**) ■ n. Brit. informal a mackintosh.

macabre /mə'kɑːbr(ə)/ ■ adj. disturbing and horrifying because of involvement with or depiction of death and injury.
– ORIGIN C19: from French *macabre*, from *Danse Macabre* 'dance of death', perhaps from *Macabé* 'a Maccabee', with ref. to a miracle play depicting the slaughter of the Maccabees.

macadam /mə'kadəm/ ■ n. broken stone used in compacted layers for surfacing roads and paths, typically bound with tar or bitumen.
– DERIVATIVES **macadamed** adj. **macadamize** (also **-ise**) v.
– ORIGIN C19: named after the British surveyor John L. McAdam.

macadamia /makə'deɪmɪə/ ■ n. an Australian rainforest tree with slender, glossy evergreen leaves. [Genus *Macadamia*: several species.] ▶ the globular edible nut of this tree.
– ORIGIN named after the C19 Australian chemist John Macadam.

macaque /mə'kɑːk, -'kak/ ■ n. a medium-sized monkey with a long face and cheek pouches for holding food. [Genus *Macaca*: several species.]
– ORIGIN C17: via French and Portuguese, from Bantu *ma-* (denoting a pl.) + *kaku* 'monkey'.

macaroni /makə'rəʊni/ ■ n. (pl. **-ies**) **1** a variety of pasta formed in narrow tubes. **2** an 18th-century British dandy affecting Continental fashions.
– ORIGIN C16: from Italian *maccaroni*, pl. of *maccarone*, from late Greek *makaria* 'food made from barley'.

macaronic /makə'rɒnɪk/ ■ adj. denoting language, especially burlesque verse, containing words or inflections from one language introduced into the context of another. ■ n. (**macaronics**) macaronic verse.
– ORIGIN C17: from obsolete Italian *macaronico*, from *macaroni* (see **MACARONI**).

macaroni cheese ■ n. a savoury dish of macaroni in a cheese sauce.

macaroni penguin ■ n. a penguin with an orange crest, breeding on islands in the Antarctic. [*Eudyptes chrysolophus*.]
– ORIGIN C19: so named because the orange crest was thought to resemble the hairstyle of the *macaronies* (see **MACARONI** in sense 2).

macaroon /makə'ruːn/ ■ n. a light biscuit made with egg white, sugar, and ground almonds or sometimes coconut.
– ORIGIN C16: from French *macaron*, from Italian *maccarone* (see **MACARONI**).

Macassar /mə'kasə/ (also **Macassar oil**) ■ n. a kind of oil formerly used by men to make their hair shine and lie flat.
– ORIGIN C17: from *Makassar* (now Ujung Pandang) in Indonesia.

macaw /mə'kɔː/ ■ n. a large long-tailed parrot with brightly coloured plumage, native to Central and South America. [*Ara* and related genera: several species.]
– ORIGIN C17: from Portuguese *macau*.

Maccabees /'makəbiːz/ ■ pl. n. the followers or family of the 2nd-century Jewish leader Judas Maccabaeus.
– DERIVATIVES **Maccabean** /makə'biːən/ adj.

Mace ■ n. trademark an irritant chemical used in an aerosol to disable attackers.

mace[1] ■ n. **1** historical a heavy club with a metal head and spikes. **2** a staff of office.
– ORIGIN Middle English: from Old French *masse* 'large hammer'.

mace[2] ■ n. the reddish fleshy outer covering of the nutmeg, dried as a spice.
– ORIGIN Middle English *macis*, from Latin *macir*.

macédoine /'masɪdwɑːn/ ■ n. a mixture of vegetables or fruit cut into small pieces or in jelly.
– ORIGIN French, 'Macedonia', with ref. to the mixture of peoples in the Macedonian Empire of Alexander the Great.

Macedonian ■ n. **1** a native or inhabitant of the republic of Macedonia, of ancient Macedonia, or of the modern Greek region of Macedonia. **2** the Southern Slavic language of the republic of Macedonia and adjacent parts of Bulgaria. ■ adj. of or relating to Macedonia or Macedonian.

macerate /'masəreɪt/ ■ v. **1** soften or break up (food) by soaking in a liquid. **2** archaic cause to grow thinner or waste away.
– DERIVATIVES **maceration** n. **macerator** n.
– ORIGIN C16: from Latin *macerare* 'make soft, soak'.

Mach /mɑːk, mak/ (also **Mach number**) ■ n. the ratio of the speed of a body to the speed of sound in the surrounding medium, used with a numeral (as Mach 1, Mach 2, etc.) to indicate the speed of sound, twice the speed of sound, etc.
– ORIGIN 1930s: named after the Austrian physicist Ernst Mach.

machete /mə'tʃɛti, -'ʃɛti/ ■ n. a broad, heavy knife used as an implement or weapon.
– ORIGIN C16: from Spanish, from *macho* 'hammer'.

Machiavellian /makɪə'vɛlɪən/ ■ adj. cunning, scheming, and unscrupulous, especially in politics or business. ■ n.

machinable

(also **Machiavelli**) a Machiavellian person.
– DERIVATIVES **Machiavellianism** n.
– ORIGIN from the name of the Italian statesman and writer Niccolò *Machiavelli*, whose work *The Prince* (1532) advises that the acquisition and use of power may necessitate unethical methods.

machinable /məˈʃiːnəb(ə)l/ ■ adj. (of a material) able to be worked by a machine tool.
– DERIVATIVES **machinability** n.

machinate /ˈmakɪneɪt, ˈmaʃ-/ ■ v. engage in plots and intrigues; scheme.
– DERIVATIVES **machination** n. **machinator** n.
– ORIGIN C16 (*machination* Middle English): from Latin *machinari* 'contrive', from *machina* (see **MACHINE**).

machine ■ n. **1** an apparatus using or applying mechanical power and having several parts, each with a definite function and together performing a particular task. ▸ technical any device that transmits a force or directs its application. **2** an efficient and well-organized group of powerful people: *the party machine*. **3** a person who acts with the mechanical efficiency of a machine. ■ v. make or operate on with a machine. ▸ Brit. sew or make with a sewing machine.
– ORIGIN C16: from Doric Greek *makhana* (Greek *mēkhanē*, from *mēkhos* 'contrivance').

machine code (also **machine language**) ■ n. a computer programming language consisting of binary or hexadecimal instructions which a computer can respond to directly.

machine gun ■ n. an automatic gun that fires bullets in rapid succession for as long as the trigger is pressed. ■ v. (**machine-gun**) shoot with a machine gun.
– DERIVATIVES **machine-gunner** n.

machine head ■ n. each of the small pegs on the head of a guitar, used for tightening the strings.

machine-readable ■ adj. (of data or text) in a form that a computer can process.

machinery ■ n. **1** machines collectively, or the components of a machine. **2** the organization or structure of something: *the machinery of the state*.

machine screw ■ n. a fastening device similar to a bolt but having a socket in its head which allows it to be turned with a screwdriver.

machine tool ■ n. a non-portable powered tool for cutting or shaping metal, wood, etc.
– DERIVATIVES **machine-tooled** adj.

machine translation ■ n. translation carried out by a computer.

machinist ■ n. **1** a person who operates a machine, especially a machine tool or (Brit.) a sewing machine. **2** a person who makes machinery.

machismo /məˈtʃɪzməʊ, -ˈkɪz-/ ■ n. strong or aggressive masculine pride.
– ORIGIN 1940s: from Mexican Spanish, from *macho* 'male'.

macho /ˈmatʃəʊ/ ■ adj. showing aggressive pride in one's masculinity. ■ n. machismo.
– ORIGIN 1920s: from Mexican Spanish, 'masculine, vigorous'.

machonisa ■ n. variant spelling of **MASHONISA**.

Machtpolitik /ˈmɑːxtpɒlɪˌtiːk/ ■ n. power politics.
– ORIGIN from German.

macintosh ■ n. variant spelling of **MACKINTOSH**.

mack ■ n. variant spelling of **MAC**.

mackerel ■ n. (pl. same or **mackerels**) a surface-dwelling marine fish with a greenish-blue back, commercially important as a food fish. [*Scomber scombrus* (N. Atlantic) and other species.]
– ORIGIN Middle English: from Old French *maquerel*.

mackerel shark ■ n. another term for **PORBEAGLE**.

mackerel sky ■ n. a sky dappled with rows of small white fleecy (typically cirrocumulus) clouds, like the pattern on a mackerel's back.

mackinaw /ˈmakɪnɔː/ (also **mackinaw coat** or **jacket**) ■ n. chiefly N. Amer. a short coat or jacket made of a thick, heavy woollen cloth.
– ORIGIN C19: named after *Mackinaw* City, Michigan.

mackintosh (also **macintosh**) ■ n. Brit. a full-length waterproof coat.
– ORIGIN C19: named after the Scottish inventor Charles *Macintosh*.

mackle /ˈmak(ə)l/ ■ n. a blurred impression in printing.
– ORIGIN C16: from Latin *macula* 'stain'.

macramé /məˈkrɑːmi/ ■ n. the craft of knotting cord or string in patterns to make decorative articles.
– ORIGIN C19: from Turkish *makrama* 'tablecloth, towel', from Arabic *miḵrama* 'bedspread'.

macro ■ n. (pl. -os) **1** (also **macro instruction**) Computing a single instruction that expands automatically into a set of instructions to perform a particular task. **2** Photography a macro lens. ■ adj. large-scale; overall.

macro- ■ comb. form **1** long; over a long period: *macroevolution*. **2** large or large-scale: *macromolecule*.
– ORIGIN from Greek *makros* 'long, large'.

macrobiotic /ˌmakrə(ʊ)baɪˈɒtɪk/ ■ adj. relating to or denoting a diet of whole pure prepared foods which is based on Buddhist principles of the balance of yin and yang. ■ n. (**macrobiotics**) [treated as sing.] the use or theory of such a diet.

macrocarpa /ˌmakrə(ʊ)ˈkɑːpə/ ■ n. a Californian cypress tree with a large spreading crown of horizontal branches and leaves that smell of lemon when crushed. [*Cupressus macrocarpa*.]
– ORIGIN C20: from **MACRO-** + Greek *karpos* 'fruit'.

macrocephalic /ˌmakrə(ʊ)sɪˈfalɪk, -kɛˈfalɪk-/ (also **macrocephalous**) ■ adj. Anatomy having an unusually large head.
– DERIVATIVES **macrocephaly** n.

macrocosm /ˈmakrə(ʊ)kɒz(ə)m/ ■ n. **1** the universe; the cosmos. **2** the whole of a complex structure, especially as represented or epitomized in a small part of itself (a microcosm).
– DERIVATIVES **macrocosmic** adj. **macrocosmically** adv.

macrocyclic /ˌmakrə(ʊ)ˈsaɪklɪk, -ˈsɪk-/ ■ adj. Chemistry relating to or denoting a ring composed of a relatively large number of atoms.
– DERIVATIVES **macrocycle** n.

macroeconomics ■ pl. n. [treated as sing.] the part of economics concerned with large-scale or general economic factors, such as interest rates and national productivity.
– DERIVATIVES **macroeconomic** adj.

macroeconomy ■ n. a large-scale economic system.

macroevolution ■ n. Biology major evolutionary change, in particular the evolution of whole taxonomic groups over long periods of time.
– DERIVATIVES **macroevolutionary** adj.

macro lens ■ n. Photography a lens suitable for taking photographs unusually close to the subject.

macrolepidoptera /ˌmakrəʊlɛpɪˈdɒpt(ə)rə/ ■ pl. n. Entomology the butterflies and larger moths, comprising those of interest to the general collector.

macromolecule ■ n. Chemistry a molecule containing a very large number of atoms, such as a protein, nucleic acid, or synthetic polymer.
– DERIVATIVES **macromolecular** adj.

macron /ˈmakrɒn/ ■ n. a written or printed mark (ˉ) used to indicate a long vowel in some languages and phonetic transcription systems, or a stressed vowel in verse.
– ORIGIN C19: from Greek *makron*, neuter of *makros* 'long'.

macronutrient ■ n. Biology a substance required in relatively large amounts by living organisms.

macrophage /ˈmakrə(ʊ)feɪdʒ/ ■ n. Physiology a large phagocytic cell found in stationary form in the tissues or as a mobile white blood cell, especially at sites of infection.

macrophotography ■ n. the photography of small items larger than life size.

macrophyte /ˈmakrə(ʊ)faɪt/ ■ n. Botany a plant, especially an aquatic plant, large enough to be seen by the naked eye.

macroscopic /ˌmakrə(ʊ)ˈskɒpɪk/ ■ adj. **1** visible to the naked eye; not microscopic. **2** of or relating to large-scale or general analysis.
– DERIVATIVES **macroscopically** adv.

macrostructure ■ n. the large-scale or overall structure

of something, e.g. an organism, a mechanical construction, or a written text.
−DERIVATIVES **macrostructural** adj.

macula /ˈmakjʊlə/ (also **macula lutea** /ˈluːtɪə/) ■ n. (pl. **maculae** /-liː/ or **maculae luteae** /-triː/) Anatomy an oval yellowish area surrounding the fovea near the centre of the retina in the eye, which is the region of greatest visual acuity.
−DERIVATIVES **macular** adj.
−ORIGIN Middle English: from Latin, 'spot'.

macumba /məˈkʊmbə/ ■ n. a religious cult practised by black people in Brazil, using sorcery, ritual dance, and fetishes.
−ORIGIN from Portuguese.

mad ■ adj. (**madder**, **maddest**) 1 mentally ill; insane. ▸ extremely foolish or ill-advised. ▸ (of a dog) rabid. 2 informal frenzied. ▸ very enthusiastic about something: *he's soccer-mad.* 3 informal very angry.
−PHRASES **like mad** informal with great intensity, energy, or enthusiasm. **mad keen** informal extremely enthusiastic.
−DERIVATIVES **madly** adv. **madness** n.
−ORIGIN Old English, of Germanic origin.

Madagascan /ˌmadəˈgaskən/ ■ n. a native or inhabitant of Madagascar. ■ adj. of or relating to Madagascar.

madam ■ n. 1 a polite form of address for a woman. 2 S. African the mistress of a household, usually a white woman. ▸ humorous or derogatory an affluent urban white woman. 3 Brit. informal a conceited or precocious girl. 4 a female brothel-keeper.
−ORIGIN Middle English: from Old French *ma dame* 'my lady'.

Madame /məˈdɑːm, ˈmadəm/ ■ n. (pl. **Mesdames**) a title or form of address for a French-speaking woman.
−ORIGIN French; cf. MADAM.

madcap ■ adj. amusingly eccentric. ▸ crazy or reckless. ■ n. an eccentric person.

mad cow disease ■ n. informal term for BSE.

madden ■ v. 1 drive (someone) insane. 2 [often as adj. **maddening**] irritate or annoy greatly.
−DERIVATIVES **maddeningly** adv.

madder ■ n. a plant related to the bedstraws, with roots that yield a red dye. [*Rubia tinctorum* and other species.] ▸ a red dye or pigment obtained from this plant.
−ORIGIN Old English, of Germanic origin.

madding ■ adj. poetic/literary 1 acting madly; frenzied. 2 maddening.

made past and past participle of MAKE.

Madeira /məˈdɪərə/ ■ n. a fortified white wine from the island of Madeira.

Madeira cake ■ n. a close-textured, rich kind of sponge cake.

Madeiran /məˈdɪərən/ ■ n. a native or inhabitant of Madeira. ■ adj. of or relating to Madeira.

madeleine /ˈmadleɪn, ˈmad(ə)lɛn/ ■ n. a small rich sponge cake, often decorated with coconut and jam.
−ORIGIN French, prob. named after *Madeleine* Paulmier, a C19 French pastry cook.

Mademoiselle /ˌmadəmwəˈzɛl/ ■ n. (pl. **Mesdemoiselles**) 1 a title or form of address for an unmarried French-speaking woman. 2 (**mademoiselle**) a young Frenchwoman. ▸ dated a French governess.
−ORIGIN French, from *ma* 'my' + *demoiselle* 'damsel'.

made to measure ■ adj. (of clothes) specially made to fit a particular person. ▸ designed to fulfil a particular set of requirements.

made to order ■ adj. specially made according to a customer's specifications.

made-up ■ adj. 1 wearing make-up. 2 invented; untrue.

madhouse ■ n. 1 historical a mental institution. ▸ informal a psychiatric hospital. 2 informal a scene of extreme confusion or uproar.

Madiba shirt ■ n. a loose-fitting man's shirt with a button-down or mandarin collar, usually made from boldly patterned cotton or other fabric.

madman (or **madwoman**) ■ n. (pl. **-men** or **-women**) a person who is mentally ill. ▸ a foolish or reckless person.

Madonna ■ n. (**the Madonna**) the Virgin Mary.

−ORIGIN C16: Italian, from *ma* (old form of *mia* 'my') + *donna* 'lady' (from Latin *domina*).

madonna lily ■ n. a tall white-flowered lily with golden pollen, often depicted in paintings of the Madonna. [*Lilium candidum.*]

madras /məˈdrɑːs, -ˈdras/ ■ n. 1 a strong cotton fabric, typically patterned with colourful stripes or checks. 2 a hot spiced curry dish.
−ORIGIN C19: by association with the Indian city of *Madras*.

madrasa /məˈdrɑːsə/ (also **madrasah**, **medrese**, or S. African **madressa**) ■ n. a college for Islamic instruction.
−ORIGIN Arabic, from *darasa* 'to study'.

Madreporaria /ˌmadrɛpəˈrɛːrɪə/ ■ pl. n. Zoology another term for SCLERACTINIA.
−DERIVATIVES **madrepore** n. (dated).
−ORIGIN from *Madrepora* (genus name), from Italian, prob. from *madre* 'mother', with ref. to the prolific growth of the coral.

madrigal /ˈmadrɪg(ə)l/ ■ n. a 16th- or 17th-century part song for several voices, typically unaccompanied and arranged in elaborate counterpoint.
−DERIVATIVES **madrigalian** /-ˈgeɪlɪən/ adj. **madrigalist** n.
−ORIGIN from Italian *madrigale*, from medieval Latin *carmen matricale* 'simple song'.

madumbe /məˈdʊmbi/ (also **amadumbe**) ■ n. S. African the edible root of a plant cultivated chiefly in rural KwaZulu-Natal, similar to the sweet potato. [*Colocasia esculenta* and *C. antiquorum.*]
−ORIGIN from isiZulu *amadumbe*.

Madurese /ˌmadjʊˈriːz/ ■ n. (pl. same) 1 a native or inhabitant of the island of Madura in Indonesia. 2 the Indonesian language of Madura and nearby parts of Java. ■ adj. of or relating to the inhabitants of Madura or their language.

maelstrom /ˈmeɪlstrəm/ ■ n. 1 a powerful whirlpool. 2 a scene of confused movement or upheaval.
−ORIGIN C17: from early modern Dutch, from *maalen* 'grind, whirl' + *stroom* 'stream'.

maenad /ˈmiːnad/ ■ n. (in ancient Greece) a female follower of Bacchus, traditionally associated with divine possession and frenzied rites.
−DERIVATIVES **maenadic** adj.
−ORIGIN C16: from Greek *Mainas*, from *mainesthai* 'to rave'.

maestro /ˈmʌɪstrəʊ/ ■ n. (pl. **maestri** /-stri/ or **maestros**) 1 a distinguished conductor or performer of classical music. 2 a distinguished figure in any sphere.
−ORIGIN C18: Italian, 'master', from Latin *magister*.

Mae West ■ n. informal, dated an inflatable life jacket, originally as issued to RAF personnel during the Second World War.
−ORIGIN 1940s: from the name of the American film actress *Mae West*, noted for her large bust.

Mafia /ˈmafɪə/ ■ n. [treated as sing. or pl.] 1 (**the Mafia**) an organized international body of criminals originating in Sicily and having a complex and ruthless behavioural code. 2 (usu. **mafia**) a group exerting a hidden sinister influence: *the British literary mafia.*
−ORIGIN Italian (Sicilian dialect), orig. in the sense 'bragging'.

mafic /ˈmafɪk/ ■ adj. Geology relating to or denoting a group of dark-coloured, mainly ferromagnesian minerals such as pyroxene and olivine. Often contrasted with FELSIC.
−ORIGIN C20: blend of MAGNESIUM and FERRIC.

Mafioso /ˌmafɪˈəʊzəʊ, -səʊ/ ■ n. (pl. **Mafiosi** /-zi, -si/) a member of the Mafia.

mag ■ n. informal 1 a magazine. 2 magnesium or magnesium alloy. 3 a magneto. 4 magnitude (of stars or other celestial objects).

magazine ■ n. 1 a periodical publication containing articles and illustrations. ▸ a regular television or radio programme comprising a variety of items. 2 a chamber for holding a supply of cartridges to be fed automatically to the breech of a gun. 3 a store for arms, ammunition,

Magdalenian

and explosives.
- ORIGIN C16: from French *magasin*, from Italian *magazzino*, from Arabic *makzin* 'storehouse'.

Magdalenian /ˌmaɡdəˈliːnɪən/ ■ adj. Archaeology relating to or denoting the final Palaeolithic culture in Europe, following the Solutrean and dated to about 17 000–11 500 years ago.
- ORIGIN C19: from French *Magdalénien* 'from La Madeleine', a site in the Dordogne, France, where objects from this culture were found.

Magdeburg hemispheres ■ pl. n. a pair of copper or brass hemispheres joined to form a hollow globe from which the air can be extracted to demonstrate the pressure of the atmosphere, which then prevents them from being pulled apart.
- ORIGIN C19: named after the German city of *Magdeburg*, where they were invented.

mage /meɪdʒ/ ■ n. archaic or poetic/literary a magician or learned person.
- ORIGIN Middle English: anglicized form of Latin *magus* (see MAGUS).

Magen David /ˌmɑːɡen dɑːˈviːd/ ■ n. a hexagram used as a symbol of Judaism.
- ORIGIN C20: Hebrew, 'shield of David', with ref. to David, King of Israel.

magenta /məˈdʒɛntə/ ■ n. **1** a light mauvish-crimson which is one of the primary subtractive colours, complementary to green. **2** the dye fuchsin.
- ORIGIN C19: named after *Magenta* in northern Italy, site of a battle (1859) fought shortly before the dye (of blood-like colour) was discovered.

mageu /maˈxɛʊ/ ■ n. S. African a drink made from thin, slightly fermented maize-meal porridge.
- ORIGIN from isiXhosa *amarhewu*, isiZulu *amahewu*.

maggot ■ n. a soft-bodied legless larva, especially that of a fly or other insect and found in decaying matter.
- DERIVATIVES **maggoty** adj.
- ORIGIN Middle English: perhaps an alteration of dialect *maddock*, from Old Norse *mathkr*, of Germanic origin.

magi plural form of MAGUS. ■ pl. n. Christian Church (**the Magi**) the three wise men from the East who brought gifts to the infant Jesus (Matthew 2:1).
- DERIVATIVES **Magian** adj. & n.

magic ■ n. **1** the power of apparently influencing the course of events by using mysterious or supernatural forces. ▶ mysterious tricks performed as entertainment. **2** a mysterious and enchanting quality. ▶ informal exceptional skill or talent. ■ adj. **1** having or apparently having supernatural powers. **2** informal very exciting or good. ■ v. (**magicked, magicking**) move, change, or create by or as if by magic.
- DERIVATIVES **magical** adj. **magically** adv.
- ORIGIN Middle English: from Latin *magicus*, from Greek *magikē* (*tekhnē*) '(art of) a magus'.

magical realism ■ n. another term for MAGIC REALISM.

magic bullet ■ n. informal a medicine or other remedy, especially a hypothetical one, with advanced and highly specific properties.

magic carpet ■ n. a mythical carpet that is able to transport people through the air.

magic circle ■ n. a small group of people privileged to receive confidential information or make important decisions.

magic eye ■ n. **1** informal a photoelectric cell or similar electrical device used for identification, detection, or measurement. **2** a small cathode ray tube in some radio receivers that displays a pattern which enables the radio to be accurately tuned.

magician ■ n. a person with magical powers. ▶ a conjuror.

magick ■ n. archaic spelling of MAGIC.
- DERIVATIVES **magickal** adj.

magic lantern ■ n. historical a simple form of image projector used for showing photographic slides.

Magic Marker ■ n. trademark an indelible marker pen.

magic mushroom ■ n. informal a toadstool with hallucinogenic properties.

magic realism (also **magical realism**) ■ n. a literary or artistic genre in which realistic narrative and naturalistic technique are combined with surreal elements of dream or fantasy.
- DERIVATIVES **magic realist** n. & adj.

magic square ■ n. a square divided into smaller squares each containing a number, such that the figures in each vertical, horizontal, and diagonal row add up to the same value.

magisterial /ˌmadʒɪˈstɪərɪəl/ ■ adj. **1** having or showing great authority. ▶ domineering; dictatorial. **2** relating to or conducted by a magistrate.
- DERIVATIVES **magisterially** adv.

magistracy /ˈmadʒɪstrəsi/ ■ n. (pl. **-ies**) the office or authority of a magistrate. ▶ (**the magistracy**) magistrates collectively.

magistrate /ˈmadʒɪstrət, -streɪt/ ■ n. a civil officer or lay judge who administers the law, especially one who conducts a court concerned with minor offences and holds preliminary hearings for more serious ones.
- DERIVATIVES **magistrature** /-trətʃə/ n.
- ORIGIN Middle English: from Latin *magistratus* 'administrator', from *magister* 'master'.

Maglemosian /ˌmaɡləˈməʊsɪən, -z-/ ■ adj. Archaeology relating to or denoting a northern European Mesolithic culture, dated to about 9 500–7 700 years ago.
- ORIGIN C20: from *Maglemose*, the name of a town in Denmark where objects from this culture were found.

maglev /ˈmaɡlɛv/ ■ n. a transport system in which trains glide above a track, propelled by magnetic repulsion and propelled by a linear motor.
- ORIGIN C20: from *mag*(*netic*) *lev*(*itation*).

magma /ˈmaɡmə/ ■ n. hot fluid or semi-fluid material within the earth's crust from which lava and other igneous rock is formed by cooling.
- DERIVATIVES **magmatic** adj.
- ORIGIN Middle English: from Greek *magma*, from *massein* 'knead'.

magmatism ■ n. Geology the motion or activity of magma.

magna cum laude /ˌmaɡnə kʌm ˈlɔːdi, ˌmaɡnɑː kʊm ˈlaʊdeɪ/ ■ adv. & adj. chiefly N. Amer. with great distinction (with reference to university degrees and diplomas).
- ORIGIN Latin, 'with great praise'.

magnanimous /maɡˈnanɪməs/ ■ adj. very generous or forgiving, especially towards a rival or less powerful person.
- DERIVATIVES **magnanimity** /ˌmaɡnəˈnɪmɪti/ n. **magnanimously** adv.
- ORIGIN C16: from Latin, from *magnus* 'great' + *animus* 'soul'.

magnate /ˈmaɡneɪt/ ■ n. a wealthy and influential person, especially in business.
- ORIGIN Middle English: from late Latin *magnas, magnat-* 'great man', from Latin *magnus* 'great'.

magnesia /maɡˈniːʒə, -zɪə, -ʃə/ ■ n. Chemistry magnesium oxide. [MgO.] ▶ hydrated magnesium carbonate used as an antacid and laxative.
- DERIVATIVES **magnesian** adj.
- ORIGIN Middle English: from Greek *Magnēsia*, denoting a mineral from Magnesia in Asia Minor.

magnesite /ˈmaɡnɪsʌɪt/ ■ n. a whitish mineral consisting of magnesium carbonate, used as a refractory lining in furnaces.

magnesium /maɡˈniːzɪəm/ ■ n. the chemical element of atomic number 12, a silver-white metal of the alkaline earth series. (Symbol: **Mg**)

magnet ■ n. **1** a piece of iron or other material, typically in the form of a bar or horseshoe, that has the property of attracting similar objects or aligning itself in an external magnetic field. **2** a person or thing that has a powerful attraction.
- ORIGIN Middle English: from Latin *magnes, magnet-*, from Greek *magnēs lithos* 'lodestone', prob. influenced by Anglo-Norman French *magnete*.

magnetic ■ adj. **1** exhibiting magnetism. **2** (of a bearing in navigation) measured relative to magnetic north. **3** very attractive or alluring.

– DERIVATIVES **magnetically** adv.

magnetic equator ■ n. the irregular imaginary line, passing round the earth near the equator, on which a magnetic needle has no dip.

magnetic field ■ n. a region around a magnetic material or a moving electric charge within which the force of magnetism acts.

magnetic induction ■ n. **1** magnetic flux or flux density. **2** the process by which an object or material is magnetized by an external magnetic field.

magnetic moment ■ n. Physics the property of a magnet that interacts with an applied field to give a mechanical moment.

magnetic north ■ n. the direction in which the north end of a compass needle or other freely suspended magnet will point in response to the earth's magnetic field.

magnetic pole ■ n. **1** each of the points near the extremities of the axis of rotation of the earth where a magnetic needle dips vertically. **2** each of the two points or regions of a magnet to and from which the lines of magnetic force are directed.

magnetic resonance imaging ■ n. a technique for producing images of bodily organs by measuring the response of atomic nuclei to radio waves when placed in a strong magnetic field.

magnetic storm ■ n. a disturbance of the magnetic field of the earth.

magnetic tape ■ n. tape used in recording sound, pictures, or computer data.

magnetism ■ n. **1** a physical phenomenon produced by the motion of electric charge, which results in attractive and repulsive forces between objects. **2** the ability to attract and charm people.

magnetite /ˈmagnɪtʌɪt/ ■ n. a grey-black magnetic mineral which consists of an oxide of iron and is an important form of iron ore.

magnetize (also **-ise**) ■ v. make magnetic.
– DERIVATIVES **magnetizable** (also **-isable**) adj. **magnetization** (also **-isation**) n.

magneto ■ n. (pl. **-os**) a small electric generator containing a permanent magnet and used to provided high-voltage pulses, especially (formerly) in the ignition systems of internal-combustion engines.

magneto- /magˈniːtəʊ/ ■ comb. form relating to a magnet or magnetism: *magneto-electric*.

magneto-electric ■ adj. of or relating to electric currents generated in a material by its motion in a magnetic field.

magnetograph ■ n. an instrument for recording measurements of magnetic forces.

magnetohydrodynamics /magˌniːtəʊˌhʌɪdrə(ʊ)dʌɪˈnamɪks/ ■ pl. n. [treated as sing.] the branch of physics concerned with the behaviour of an electrically conducting fluid (such as plasma or molten metal) acted on by a magnetic field.
– DERIVATIVES **magnetohydrodynamic** adj.

magnetometer /ˌmagnɪˈtɒmɪtə/ ■ n. an instrument used for measuring magnetic forces, especially the earth's magnetism.
– DERIVATIVES **magnetometry** n.

magnetomotive force /magˌniːtə(ʊ)ˈməʊtɪv/ ■ n. Physics a quantity representing the sum of the magnetizing forces along a circuit.

magneton /ˈmagnɪtɒn/ ■ n. a unit of magnetic moment in atomic and nuclear physics.

magnetopause ■ n. the outer limit of a magnetosphere.

magnetoresistance ■ n. Physics the dependence of the electrical resistance of a body on an external magnetic field.
– DERIVATIVES **magnetoresistive** adj.

magnetosphere ■ n. the region surrounding the earth or another astronomical body in which its magnetic field is the predominant effective magnetic field.
– DERIVATIVES **magnetospheric** adj.

magnetron /ˈmagnɪtrɒn/ ■ n. an electron tube for amplifying or generating microwaves, with the flow of electrons controlled by an external magnetic field.

Magnificat /magˈnɪfɪkat/ ■ n. the hymn of the Virgin Mary (Luke 1:46–55) used as a canticle, especially at vespers and evensong.
– ORIGIN Middle English: Latin, 'magnifies', from the opening words, which translate as 'my soul magnifies the Lord'.

magnification ■ n. the action of magnifying or the process of being magnified. ▸ the degree to which something is or can be magnified. ▸ the magnifying power of an instrument. ▸ a magnified reproduction.

magnificence ■ n. **1** the quality of being magnificent. **2** (**His/Your**) etc. **Magnificence** a title or form of address for a monarch or other distinguished person.

magnificent ■ adj. **1** impressively beautiful, elaborate, or extravagant. **2** very good; excellent.
– DERIVATIVES **magnificently** adv.
– ORIGIN Middle English: from Latin *magnificent-* 'making great, serving to magnify', from *magnus* 'great'.

magnifico /magˈnɪfɪkəʊ/ informal ■ n. (pl. **-oes**) an eminent, powerful, or illustrious person. ■ adj. magnificent.
– ORIGIN C16: Italian, 'magnificent', orig. used to denote a Venetian magnate.

magnify ■ v. (**-ies**, **-ied**) **1** make (something) appear larger than it is, especially with a lens or microscope. ▸ intensify or exaggerate. **2** archaic extol; glorify.
– DERIVATIVES **magnifier** n.
– ORIGIN Middle English: from Old French *magnifier* or Latin *magnificare*, from Latin *magnus* 'great'.

magnifying glass ■ n. a lens that produces an enlarged image, used to examine small or finely detailed things.

magnitude /ˈmagnɪtjuːd/ ■ n. **1** great size, extent, or importance. **2** size. **3** Astronomy the brightness of a star, as represented by a number on a logarithmic scale.
– ORIGIN Middle English: from Latin *magnitudo*, from *magnus* 'great'.

magnolia /magˈnəʊlɪə/ ■ n. **1** a tree or shrub with large, typically creamy-pink, waxy flowers. [Genus *Magnolia*.] **2** a pale creamy-white colour like that of magnolia blossom.
– ORIGIN named after the C17 French botanist Pierre *Magnol*.

magnox /ˈmagnɒks/ ■ n. a magnesium-based alloy used to enclose uranium fuel elements in some nuclear reactors.
– ORIGIN 1950s: from the phr. *mag(nesium) n(o) ox(idation)*.

magnum /ˈmagnəm/ ■ n. (pl. **magnums**) **1** a wine bottle of twice the standard size, normally 1½ litres. **2** (trademark in the US) a gun designed to fire cartridges that are more powerful than its calibre would suggest.
– ORIGIN C18: from Latin, from *magnus* 'great'.

magnum opus /ˌmagnəm ˈəʊpəs, ˈɒpəs/ ■ n. (pl. **magnum opuses** or **magna opera** /ˌmagnə ˈəʊpərə, ˈɒpərə/) a large and important work of art, music, or literature, especially the most important work of an artist, writer, etc.
– ORIGIN C18: from Latin, 'great work'.

magpie ■ n. **1** a long-tailed bird of the crow family, typically with pied plumage and a raucous voice. [*Pica pica* and other species.] ▸ a black-and-white Australian butcher-bird with musical calls. [*Gymnorhina tibicen*.] **2** a person who obsessively collects things or who chatters idly.
– ORIGIN C16: prob. shortening of dialect *Magot* (Middle English familiar form of the given name *Marguerite*) + PIE[2].

maguey /ˈmagweɪ/ ■ n. an agave plant, especially one yielding pulque.
– ORIGIN C16: from Taino.

magus /ˈmeɪgəs/ ■ n. (pl. **magi** /ˈmeɪdʒʌɪ/) **1** a member of a priestly caste of ancient Persia. **2** a sorcerer.
– ORIGIN Middle English: from Old Persian *maguš*.

mag wheel ■ n. a motor-vehicle wheel made from lightweight magnesium steel, typically having a pattern of holes or spokes around the hub.

magwinya /mʌˈgwɪnjʌ, mʌˈgwɪnjə/ (also **magwenya**) ■ n. (pl. same or **magwinyas**) chiefly S. African another term for VETKOEK.
– ORIGIN from isiZulu *amagwinya*.

Magyar

Magyar /ˈmagjɑː/ ■ n. **1** a member of a people predominating in Hungary. **2** the Uralic language of this people; Hungarian.
– ORIGIN the name in Hungarian.

maharaja /ˌmɑː(h)əˈrɑːdʒə, məˌhɑː-/ (also **maharajah**) ■ n. historical an Indian prince.
– ORIGIN from Hindi *mahārājā*, from Sanskrit *mahā* 'great' + *rājan* 'raja'.

maharani /ˌmɑː(h)əˈrɑːni, məˌhɑː-/ (also **maharanee**) ■ n. a maharaja's wife or widow.
– ORIGIN from Hindi *mahārānī*, from Sanskrit *mahā* 'great' + *rājñī* 'ranee'.

Maharishi /ˌmɑː(h)əˈrɪʃi/ ■ n. a great Hindu sage or spiritual leader.
– ORIGIN alteration of Sanskrit *maharṣi*, from *mahā* 'great' + *ṛṣi* 'rishi'.

mahatma /məˈhatmə, məˈhɑː-/ ■ n. **1** (in the Indian subcontinent) a holy person or sage. **2** (in some forms of theosophy) a person in India or Tibet said to have preternatural powers.
– ORIGIN from Sanskrit *mahātman*, from *mahā* 'great' + *ātman* 'soul'.

Mahayana /ˌmɑː(h)əˈjɑːnə, ˌməhɑː-/ (also **Mahayana Buddhism**) ■ n. one of the two major traditions of Buddhism (the other being Theravada), practised especially in China, Tibet, Japan, and Korea.
– ORIGIN from Sanskrit, from *mahā* 'great' + *yāna* 'vehicle'.

Mahdi /ˈmɑːdi/ ■ n. (pl. **Mahdis**) **1** (in popular Muslim belief) a spiritual and temporal leader who will rule before the end of the world and restore religion and justice. **2** (in Shiite belief) the twelfth imam, who is expected to return and triumph over injustice.
– ORIGIN from Arabic *(al-)mahdī* 'he who is guided in the right way'.

Mahican /ˈmɑːhɪk(ə)n/ (also **Mohican**) ■ n. **1** a member of an American Indian people formerly inhabiting the Upper Hudson Valley. Compare with **MOHEGAN**. **2** the extinct Algonquian language of this people. ■ adj. of or relating to the Mahicans or their language.
– ORIGIN the name in Mahican, said to mean 'wolf'.

mah-jong /mɑːˈdʒɒŋ/ (also **mah-jongg**) ■ n. a Chinese game played, usually by four people, with 136 or 144 rectangular tiles.
– ORIGIN C20: from Chinese dialect *ma-tsiang* 'sparrows'.

mahogany /məˈhɒɡəni/ ■ n. **1** hard reddish-brown wood from a tropical tree, used for furniture. **2** the tree which produces this wood. [*Swietenia mahagoni* (tropical America) and other species.] **3** a rich reddish-brown colour.
– ORIGIN C17.

mahonia /məˈhəʊniə/ ■ n. an evergreen shrub of the barberry family, which produces clusters of small fragrant yellow flowers followed by purple or black berries. [Genus *Mahonia*.]
– ORIGIN named after the American botanist Bernard McMahon (c.1775–1816).

mahout /məˈhaʊt/ ■ n. (in the Indian subcontinent and SE Asia) a person who works with and rides an elephant.
– ORIGIN from Hindi *mahāvat*.

maid ■ n. **1** a female domestic servant. **2** archaic or poetic/literary a girl or young woman. ▸ a virgin.
– ORIGIN Middle English: abbrev. of **MAIDEN**.

maidan /mʌɪˈdɑːn/ ■ n. (in the Indian subcontinent) an open space in or near a town.
– ORIGIN from Urdu and Persian *maidān*, from Arabic *maydān*.

maiden ■ n. **1** archaic or poetic/literary a girl or young woman. ▸ a virgin. **2** (also **maiden over**) Cricket an over in which no runs are scored. ■ adj. **1** (of a woman, especially an older one) unmarried. ▸ (of a female animal) unmated. **2** being or involving the first attempt or act of its kind: *the Titanic's maiden voyage*. **3** denoting a horse that has never won a race, or a race intended for such horses.
– DERIVATIVES **maidenhood** n. **maidenly** adj.
– ORIGIN Old English, from a Germanic diminutive meaning 'maid, virgin'.

maidenhair (also **maidenhair fern**) ■ n. a fern having slender-stalked fronds with small round or wedge-shaped divided lobes. [*Adiantum capillus-veneris* and related species.]

maidenhair tree ■ n. the ginkgo, whose leaves resemble those of the maidenhair fern.

maidenhead ■ n. archaic virginity. ▸ the hymen.

maiden name ■ n. the surname that a married woman used before she was married.

maid of honour ■ n. **1** an unmarried noblewoman attending a queen or princess. **2** N. Amer. a principal bridesmaid. **3** Brit. a small tart filled with flavoured milk curds.

maidservant ■ n. dated a female domestic servant.

mail[1] ■ n. letters and parcels sent by post. ▸ (N. Amer. & W. Indian also **the mails**) the postal system. ▸ Computing email. ■ v. send (a letter or parcel) by post. ▸ Computing send (someone) email.
– DERIVATIVES **mailable** adj.
– ORIGIN Middle English: from Old French *male* 'wallet', of West Germanic origin.

mail[2] ■ n. **1** historical armour made of metal rings or plates joined together flexibly. **2** the protective shell or scales of certain animals. ■ v. [often as adj. **mailed**] clothe or cover with mail.
– ORIGIN Middle English: from Old French *maille*, from Latin *macula* 'spot or mesh'.

mailbag ■ n. **1** a large sack or bag for carrying mail. **2** the letters received by a person, especially a public figure.

mail bomb ■ n. **1** US a letter bomb. **2** an overwhelming quantity of email messages sent to one address.

mailbox ■ n. **1** chiefly N. Amer. another term for **POSTBOX**. **2** a computer file in which email messages are stored.

mail drop ■ n. **1** N. Amer. a receptacle for mail, especially one in which mail is kept until collected. **2** chiefly Brit. a delivery of mail.

mailer ■ n. **1** chiefly N. Amer. the sender of a letter or package by post. **2** a piece of advertising material sent out by post. **3** a container used for conveying items by post. **4** Computing a program that sends email messages.

mailing ■ n. something sent by mail, especially a piece of mass advertising.

mailing list ■ n. a list of the names and addresses of people to whom advertising matter or information may be mailed regularly.

maillot /mʌɪˈjəʊ/ ■ n. (pl. pronounced same) **1** a pair of tights worn for dancing or gymnastics. **2** chiefly N. Amer. a woman's tight-fitting one-piece swimsuit. **3** a jersey or top, especially one worn in sports such as cycling.
– ORIGIN from French.

mailman ■ n. (pl. -men) N. Amer. a postman.

mail merge ■ n. Computing the automatic addition of names and addresses from a database to letters and envelopes in order to facilitate sending mail to many addresses.

mail order ■ n. the ordering of goods by post.

mailshot ■ n. an item, especially a piece of advertising material, sent to a large number of addresses.

maim ■ v. wound or injure (someone) so that part of the body is permanently damaged.
– ORIGIN Middle English: from Old French *mahaignier*.

main ■ adj. chief in size or importance. ■ n. **1** a principal pipe carrying water or gas or a cable carrying electricity. ▸ (**the mains**) the source of public water, gas, or electricity supply through pipes or cables. **2** (**the main**) archaic or poetic/literary the open ocean. **3** Nautical short for **MAINSAIL** or **MAINMAST**.
– PHRASES **in the main** on the whole.
– ORIGIN Middle English: from Old English *mægen* 'physical force', reinforced by Old Norse *meginn*, *megn* 'strong, powerful', both from a Germanic base meaning 'have power'.

mainboard ■ n. another term for **MOTHERBOARD**.

main brace ■ n. the brace attached to the main yard of a sailing ship.

main clause ■ n. Grammar a clause that can form a complete sentence standing alone, having a subject and a predicate.

main course ■ n. **1** the most substantial course of a meal. **2** the mainsail of a square-rigged sailing ship.

main drag ■ n. informal, chiefly N. Amer. the main street of a town.

Maine Coon ■ n. a large, powerful cat of a long-haired breed, originally from America.
– ORIGIN 1970s: so named because of a resemblance to the raccoon.

mainframe ■ n. **1** a large high-speed computer, especially one supporting numerous workstations or peripherals. **2** the central processing unit and primary memory of a computer.

mainland ■ n. a large continuous extent of land that includes the greater part of a country or territory, as opposed to offshore islands and detached territories.
– DERIVATIVES **mainlander** n.

main line ■ n. **1** a chief railway line. **2** N. Amer. a chief road or street. **3** informal a principal vein as a site for a drug injection. ■ v. (**mainline**) informal inject (a drug) intravenously.
– DERIVATIVES **mainliner** n.

mainly ■ adv. more than anything else. ▶ for the most part.

main man ■ n. (pl. **men**) **1** informal a close and trusted friend. **2** a principal figure in an organization, team, etc. ▶ (pl. **manne** /'manə/) S. African informal a person who is successful or important in their field; a top dog.

mainmast ■ n. the principal mast of a ship.

mainsail /'meinseil, -s(ə)l/ ■ n. the principal sail of a ship. ▶ the sail set on the after part of the mainmast in a fore-and-aft rigged vessel.

main sequence ■ n. Astronomy a series of types to which most stars other than giants, supergiants, and white dwarfs belong.
– ORIGIN 1920s: so named because they occupy a broad band on a graph of magnitude against spectral type.

mainsheet ■ n. a sheet used for controlling and trimming the mainsail of a sailing boat.

mainspring ■ n. **1** the principal spring in a watch, clock, etc. **2** a prime source of motivation or support.

mainstay ■ n. **1** a stay which extends from the maintop to the foot of the foremast of a sailing ship. **2** the chief support or main part.

mainstream ■ n. (**the mainstream**) normal or conventional ideas, attitudes, or activities. ■ adj. belonging to or characteristic of the mainstream. ■ v. bring into the mainstream.

maintain ■ v. **1** cause or enable (a condition or state of affairs) to continue. ▶ keep at the same level or rate. **2** keep (a building, machine, etc.) in good condition by checking or repairing it regularly. **3** provide with necessities for life or existence. ▶ archaic give one's support to; uphold. **4** assert something to be the case.
– DERIVATIVES **maintainability** n. **maintainable** adj.
– ORIGIN Middle English: from Old French *maintenir*, from Latin *manu tenere* 'hold in the hand'.

maintainer ■ n. a person or thing that maintains.

maintenance ■ n. **1** the process or state of maintaining or being maintained. **2** a husband's or wife's provision for a spouse after separation or divorce.

maintop ■ n. a platform around the head of the lower section of a sailing ship's mainmast.

maiolica /mə'jɒlɪkə, mʌɪ'ɒlɪkə/ ■ n. fine earthenware with coloured decoration on an opaque white tin glaze, originating in Italy during the Renaissance.
– ORIGIN C16: from *Maiolica* 'Majorca'.

maisonette /ˌmeɪzə'nɛt/ ■ n. a set of rooms for living in, typically on two storeys of a larger building and having a separate entrance.
– ORIGIN C18: from French *maisonnette*, diminutive of *maison* 'house'.

mai tai /'mʌɪ tʌɪ/ ■ n. chiefly US a cocktail based on light rum, curaçao, and fruit juices.
– ORIGIN from Polynesian.

maître d'hôtel /ˌmɛtrə dəʊ'tɛl/ (also **maître d'** /ˌmɛtrə 'diː/) ■ n. (pl. **maîtres d'hôtel** (pronunc. same) or **maître d's**) **1** the head waiter of a restaurant. **2** the manager of a hotel.
– ORIGIN C16: French, 'master of (the) house'.

707

---

maize ■ n. a cereal plant originating in Central America and yielding large grains (corn or sweetcorn) set in rows on a cob. [*Zea mays*.]
– ORIGIN C16: from Spanish *maíz*, from Taino *mahiz*.

Maizena /meɪ'ziːnə, mʌɪ-/ ■ n. trademark, chiefly S. African cornflour.

Maj. ■ abbrev. Major.

majat /mə'dʒat/ ■ n. S. African informal cannabis of an inferior quality.
– ORIGIN 1950s: perhaps rel. to Malay *madat* 'opium'.

majestic ■ adj. having or showing impressive beauty or dignity.
– DERIVATIVES **majestically** adv.

majesty ■ n. (pl. **-ies**) **1** impressive stateliness, dignity, or beauty. **2** royal power. ▶ (**His/Your**) etc. **Majesty** a title given to a sovereign or a sovereign's wife or widow.
– ORIGIN Middle English: from Old French *majeste*, from Latin *majestas*, from a var. of *majus* (see MAJOR).

majlis /'madʒlɪs, madʒ'liːs/ ■ n. the parliament of various North African and Middle Eastern countries, especially Iran.
– ORIGIN Arabic, 'assembly'.

majolica /mə'jɒlɪkə, -'dʒɒl-/ ■ n. a kind of earthenware made in imitation of Italian maiolica, especially in England during the 19th century.
– ORIGIN var. of MAIOLICA.

major ■ adj. **1** important, serious, or significant. ▶ greater or more important; main. **2** Music (of a scale) having intervals of a semitone between the third and fourth, and seventh and eighth degrees. Contrasted with MINOR. ▶ (of an interval) equivalent to that between the tonic and another note of a major scale, and greater by a semitone than the corresponding minor interval. ▶ [postpos.] (of a key) based on a major scale: *Prelude in G Major*. **3** Brit. dated (appended to a surname in private schools) indicating the elder of two brothers. ■ n. **1** a rank of officer in the army and air force, above captain and below lieutenant colonel. ▶ an officer in charge of a section of band instruments: *a trumpet major*. **2** Music a major key, interval, or scale. **3** a major organization, company, or competition. **4** a student's principal subject or course. ▶ a student specializing in a specified subject: *a physics major*. ■ v. (**major in**) specialize in (a particular subject) at college or university.
– ORIGIN Middle English: from Latin, comparative of *magnus* 'great'; perhaps influenced by French *majeur*.

major axis ■ n. Geometry the longer axis of an ellipse, passing through its foci.

Majorcan /mə'jɔːkən/ ■ n. a native or inhabitant of Majorca. ■ adj. of or relating to Majorca.

major-domo /ˌmeɪdʒə'dəʊməʊ/ ■ n. (pl. **-os**) the chief steward of a large household.
– ORIGIN C16: from medieval Latin *major domus* 'highest official of the household'.

major general ■ n. a rank of officer in the army and air force, above brigadier general and below lieutenant general.

majoritarian /məˌdʒɒrɪ'tɛːrɪən/ ■ adj. governed by or believing in decision by a majority. ■ n. a majoritarian person.
– DERIVATIVES **majoritarianism** n.

majority ■ n. (pl. **-ies**) **1** the greater number. **2** the number by which the votes cast for one party or candidate exceed those for the next. ▶ US the number by which votes for one candidate are more than those for all other candidates together. **3** the age when a person is legally considered a full adult, usually 18 or 21.
– ORIGIN C16: from French *majorité*, from medieval Latin *majoritas*, from Latin *major* (see MAJOR).

majority rule ■ n. the principle that the greater number should exercise greater power.

majority verdict ■ n. English Law a verdict agreed by all but one or two of the members of a jury.

major league ■ n. N. Amer. the highest-ranking league in a particular professional sport, especially baseball.
– DERIVATIVES **major-leaguer** n.

majorly ▪ adv. informal very; extremely.

major planet ▪ n. any of the nine principal planets of the solar system, as distinct from an asteroid or moon.

major suit ▪ n. Bridge spades or hearts.

majuscule /ˈmadʒəskjuːl/ ▪ n. a large letter, either capital or uncial.
– DERIVATIVES **majuscular** /məˈdʒʌskjʊlə/ adj.
– ORIGIN C18: from Latin *majuscula* (*littera*) 'somewhat greater (letter)'.

makarapa /mʌkʌˈrʌpʌ, mʌkəˈrʌpə/ ▪ n. S. African **1** (also **makaraba**) an elaborately decorated hard hat or miner's helmet, worn as a headdress by supporters of a soccer or other sports team. **2** historical a mineworker or migrant labourer.
– ORIGIN from Sesotho sa Leboa, 'men who work in the cities'.

make ▪ v. (past and past part. **made**) **1** form by putting parts together or combining substances. ▸ (**make something into**) alter something so that it forms (something else). ▸ arrange bedclothes tidily on (a bed) ready for use. ▸ arrange and light materials for (a fire). **2** cause to exist or come about; bring about or perform. ▸ cause to be, become, or seem. ▸ appoint to a position. ▸ chiefly archaic enter into a contract of (marriage). **3** compel (someone) to do something. **4** constitute, amount to, or serve as. ▸ consider to be; estimate as. ▸ agree or decide on (a specified arrangement). **5** gain or earn (money or profit). ▸ Cricket score (a specified number of runs). ▸ (in sport) enable a teammate to score (a goal) by one's play. **6** manage to arrive at (a place) or catch (a train or other transport). ▸ (**make it**) become successful. ▸ achieve a place in. ▸ chiefly N. Amer. achieve the rank of. **7** prepare to go in a particular direction or do a particular thing. **8** informal, chiefly N. Amer. induce (someone) to have sexual intercourse with one. **9** (in bridge, whist, etc.) win (a trick). ▸ win the number of tricks that fulfils (a contract). ▪ n. the manufacturer or trade name of a product.
– PHRASES **be made of money** [usu. with neg.] informal be very rich. **have (got) it made** informal be in a position where success is certain. **make a day of it** devote a whole day to an activity. **make someone's day** make an otherwise ordinary day pleasingly memorable for someone. **make do** manage with the limited or inadequate means available. **make like** N. Amer. informal pretend to be. **make or break** be the factor which decides whether (something) will succeed or fail. **make a plan** S. African informal find a way of doing something, especially to overcome a difficulty. **make sail** Nautical spread a sail or sails. ▸ start a voyage. **make time** find an occasion when time is available to do something. **make a turn** S. African informal pay a brief visit. **make up one's mind** make a decision. **make way 1** allow room for someone or something else. **2** chiefly Nautical make progress; travel. **on the make** informal intent on gain. ▸ looking for a sexual partner.
– PHRASAL VERBS **make after** pursue. **make away with** another way of saying make off with. ▸ kill (someone) furtively and illicitly. **make for 1** move or head towards. ▸ approach (someone) to attack them. **2** tend to result in or be received as. **3** (**be made for**) be eminently suited for (a particular function or partnership). **make something of** give or ascribe a specified amount of attention or importance to. ▸ understand or derive advantage from. **make off** leave hurriedly. **make off with** carry away illicitly. **make out** informal **1** make progress; fare. **2** N. Amer. engage in sexual activity. **make someone/thing out 1** manage with some difficulty to see, hear, or understand. **2** represent as or pretend. **3** draw up or write out a list or document. **make someone over** give someone a new image with cosmetics, hairstyling, etc. **make something over** transfer the possession of. **make up** be reconciled after a quarrel. **make someone up** apply cosmetics to. **make something up 1** (also **make up for**) compensate for something lost, missed, or deficient. ▸ (**make it up to**) compensate (someone) for negligent or unfair treatment. **2** (**make up**) (of parts) compose or constitute (a whole). **3** put together or prepare something from parts or ingredients. ▸ Printing arrange type and illustrations into a page or pages. **4** concoct or invent a story. **make up to** informal attempt to win the favour of.

– DERIVATIVES **makable** (also **makeable**) adj.
– ORIGIN Old English *macian*, of West Germanic origin.

make-believe ▪ n. the action of pretending or imagining. ▪ adj. imitating something real. ▪ v. (**make believe**) pretend; imagine.

makeover ▪ n. a complete transformation of a person's appearance with cosmetics, hairstyling, etc.

maker ▪ n. **1** a person or thing that makes or produces something. **2** (**our**, **the**, etc. **Maker**) God.
– PHRASES **meet one's Maker** chiefly humorous die.

makeshift ▪ adj. interim and temporary. ▪ n. a temporary substitute or device.

make-up ▪ n. **1** cosmetics such as lipstick or powder applied to the face. **2** the composition or constitution of something. **3** Printing the arrangement of type, illustrations, etc. on a printed page.

makeweight ▪ n. **1** something put on a scale to make up the required weight. **2** an extra person or thing needed to complete something.

make-work chiefly N. Amer. ▪ adj. denoting an activity that serves to keep someone busy but is of little value in itself. ▪ n. work or activity of this kind.

making ▪ n. **1** the process of making or producing something. **2** (**makings**) informal earnings or profit. **3** (**makings**) the necessary qualities: *she had the makings of a great teacher.*
– PHRASES **be the making of someone** bring about someone's success or favourable development. **in the making** in the process of being made or being made. **of one's (own) making** (of a difficulty) caused by oneself.

mako /ˈmɑːkəʊ, ˈmeɪkəʊ/ ▪ n. (pl. **-os**) a large, fast-moving oceanic shark with a deep blue back and white underparts. [Genus *Isurus*: two species.]
– ORIGIN C19: from Maori.

Makonde /məˈkɒndeɪ/ ▪ n. (pl. same or **Makondes**) **1** a member of a people inhabiting southern Tanzania and NE Mozambique. **2** the Bantu language of this people.
– ORIGIN the name in Makonde.

makoro ▪ n. variant spelling of MOKORO.

makoti /maˈkɔːti/ ▪ n. S. African a young married woman; a bride.
– ORIGIN from isiZulu.

makoya /məˈkɔɪə, mʌˈkɔɪjə/ S. African informal ▪ n. (often in phr. **the real makoya**) the real thing; the genuine article. ▪ adj. real; actually existing.
– ORIGIN from English *the real McCoy* (see MCCOY).

Makua /ˈmakuːə/ ▪ n. (pl. same or **Makuas**) **1** a member of a people inhabiting the border regions of Mozambique, Malawi, and Tanzania. **2** the Bantu language of this people.
– ORIGIN the name in Makua.

makwerekwere /məˌkwɛrɛˈkwɛrɛ/ (also **amakwere-kwere**) ▪ pl. n. S. African informal, derogatory immigrants from other African countries.
– ORIGIN from isiXhosa *ikwerekwere* 'foreigner' (imitative of attempts to speak a foreign language).

mal /mʌl/ ▪ adj. S. African informal **1** mad; crazed. **2** angry.
– ORIGIN Afrikaans.

mal- ▪ comb. form **1** in an unpleasant degree: *malodorous*. **2** in a faulty manner: *malfunction*. ▸ in an improper manner: *malpractice*. ▸ in an inadequate manner: *malnourishment*. **3** not: *maladroit*.
– ORIGIN from French *mal*, from Latin *male* 'badly'.

malacca /məˈlakə/ ▪ n. brown cane (obtained from a Malaysian climbing palm *Calamus scipionum*) that is widely used for walking sticks and umbrella handles.
– ORIGIN C19: from the name *Malacca* (or *Melaka*), a state of Malaysia.

malachite /ˈmaləkʌɪt/ ▪ n. a bright green mineral consisting of hydrated basic copper carbonate.
– ORIGIN Middle English: from Old French *melochite*, from Greek *molokhitis*, from *molokhē*, var. of *malakhē* 'mallow'.

malaco- /ˈmaləkəʊ/ ▪ comb. form soft: *malacostracan*.
– ORIGIN from Greek *malakos* 'soft'.

malacology /ˌmaləˈkɒlədʒi/ ▪ n. the branch of zoology concerned with molluscs. Compare with CONCHOLOGY.
– DERIVATIVES **malacological** adj. **malacologist** n.

Malacostraca /ˌmaləˈkɒstrəkə/ ■ pl. n. Zoology a large class of crustaceans including crabs, shrimps, lobsters, isopods, and amphipods, having compound eyes that are typically on stalks.
– ORIGIN modern Latin, from **MALACO-** + Greek *ostrakon* 'shell'.

maladaptive ■ adj. not providing adequate or appropriate adjustment to the environment or situation.
– DERIVATIVES **maladaptation** n. **maladapted** adj.

maladjusted ■ adj. failing to cope with the demands of a normal social environment.
– DERIVATIVES **maladjustment** n.

maladminister ■ v. formal manage or administer badly or dishonestly.
– DERIVATIVES **maladministration** n.

maladroit /ˌmaləˈdrɔɪt/ ■ adj. inefficient or ineffective; clumsy.
– DERIVATIVES **maladroitly** adv. **maladroitness** n.
– ORIGIN C17: French.

malady ■ n. (pl. **-ies**) a disease or ailment.
– ORIGIN Middle English: from Old French *maladie*, from *malade* 'sick', from Latin *male* 'ill' + *habitus* 'having (as a condition)'.

Malagasy /ˌmaləˈgasi/ ■ n. (pl. same or **-ies**) 1 a native or national of Madagascar. 2 the Austronesian language of Madagascar.

malaise /maˈleɪz/ ■ n. a general feeling of discomfort, illness, or unease.
– ORIGIN C18: from Old French *mal* 'bad' (from Latin *malus*) + *aise* 'ease'.

malamute /ˈmaləmjuːt/ (also **malemute**) ■ n. a powerful dog of a breed with a thick, grey coat, bred by the Inuit and typically used to pull sledges.
– ORIGIN from Inuit *malimiut*, the name of a people of Kotzebue Sound, Alaska, who developed the breed.

malapropism /ˈmaləprɒˌpɪz(ə)m/ (US also **malaprop**) ■ n. the mistaken use of a word in place of a similar-sounding one (e.g. 'dance a *flamingo*' instead of *flamenco*).
– ORIGIN C19: from the name of the character Mrs *Malaprop* in Sheridan's play *The Rivals* (1775).

malapropos /ˌmaləprəˈpəʊ/ formal ■ adv. inopportunely; inappropriately. ■ adj. inopportune; inappropriate.
– ORIGIN C17: from French *mal à propos*, from *mal* 'ill' + *à* 'to' + *propos* 'purpose'.

malar /ˈmeɪlə/ ■ adj. Anatomy & Medicine of or relating to the cheek. ■ n. (also **malar bone**) another term for **ZYGOMATIC BONE**.
– ORIGIN C18: from modern Latin *malaris*, from Latin *mala* 'jaw'.

malaria ■ n. a mosquito-borne intermittent and remittent fever endemic to warmer regions and caused by a protozoan parasite (genus *Plasmodium*).
– DERIVATIVES **malarial** adj. **malarious** adj.
– ORIGIN C18: from Italian, from *mal'aria*, contracted form of *mala aria* 'bad air' (orig. denoting the unwholesome exhalations of marshes, to which the disease was formerly attributed).

malarkey /məˈlɑːki/ ■ n. informal nonsense.
– ORIGIN 1920S.

malathion /ˌmaləˈθaɪən/ ■ n. a synthetic organophosphorus compound which is used as an insecticide and is relatively harmless to plants and other animals.
– ORIGIN 1950S: from (*diethyl*) *mal*(*eate*) + **THIO-** + **-ON**.

Malawian /məˈlɑːwiən/ ■ n. a native or inhabitant of Malawi. ■ adj. of or relating to Malawi or Malawians.

Malay /məˈleɪ/ ■ n. 1 a member of a people inhabiting Malaysia and Indonesia. ▶ a person of Malay descent. ▶ short for **CAPE MALAY**. 2 the Austronesian language of the Malays. ■ adj. (in South Africa) of or relating to the Cape Malays.

Malayalam /ˌmaləˈjɑːləm/ ■ n. the Dravidian language of the Indian state of Kerala, closely related to Tamil.
– ORIGIN C19: from Malayalam, from *mala* 'mountain' + *āḷ* 'man'.

Malayan ■ n. another term for **MALAY**. ■ adj. of or relating to Malays, the Malay language, or Malaya (now part of Malaysia).

Malayo- ■ comb. form Malay; Malay and ...: *Malayo-Polynesian*.

Malayo-Polynesian ■ n. another term for **AUSTRONESIAN**.

Malaysian /məˈleɪziən, -ˈleɪʒən/ ■ n. a native or inhabitant of Malaysia. ■ adj. of or relating to Malaysia or Malaysians.

malcontent /ˈmalkəntɛnt/ ■ n. a discontented person. ■ adj. discontented; complaining.
– DERIVATIVES **malcontented** adj.
– ORIGIN C16: from French, from *mal* 'badly, ill' + *content* 'pleased'.

Maldivian /mɔːlˈdɪviən/ ■ n. 1 a native or inhabitant of the Maldives. 2 the Indic language spoken in the Maldives. ■ adj. of or relating to the Maldives, the Maldivians, or their language.

male ■ adj. 1 of or denoting the sex that can fertilize or inseminate the female to engender offspring. ▶ relating to or characteristic of men or male animals. ▶ (of a plant or flower) bearing stamens but lacking functional pistils. 2 (of a fitting) manufactured to fit inside a corresponding female part. ■ n. a male person, animal, or plant.
– DERIVATIVES **maleness** n.
– ORIGIN Middle English: from Old French *masle*, from Latin *masculus*, from *mas* 'a male'.

malediction /ˌmalɪˈdɪkʃ(ə)n/ ■ n. a curse.
– DERIVATIVES **maledictory** adj.
– ORIGIN Middle English: from Latin *maledictio*(*n-*), from *maledicere* 'speak evil of'.

malefactor /ˈmalɪˌfaktə/ ■ n. formal a person who commits a crime or some other wrong.
– DERIVATIVES **malefaction** n.
– ORIGIN Middle English: from Latin, from *malefacere* 'do wrong'.

malefic /məˈlɛfɪk/ ■ adj. 1 poetic/literary causing harm. 2 Astrology relating to the planets Saturn and Mars, traditionally considered to have an unfavourable influence.
– DERIVATIVES **maleficence** n. **maleficent** adj.
– ORIGIN C17: from Latin, from *male* 'ill' + *-ficus* 'doing'.

male menopause ■ n. a stage in a middle-aged man's life supposedly corresponding to the menopause of a woman, associated with loss of vigour and a crisis of identity (not in technical use).

malemute ■ n. variant spelling of **MALAMUTE**.

Malesian /məˈliːziən/ ■ adj. relating to the phytogeographical region of Malesia, comprising Malaysia, Indonesia, Brunei, the Philippines, and Papua New Guinea.

malevolent /məˈlɛv(ə)l(ə)nt/ ■ adj. wishing evil to others.
– DERIVATIVES **malevolence** n. **malevolently** adv.
– ORIGIN C16: from Latin *malevolent-* 'wishing evil', from *male* 'ill' + *velle* 'to wish'.

malfeasance /malˈfiːz(ə)ns/ ■ n. formal wrongdoing, especially (US) by a public official.
– ORIGIN C17: from Anglo-Norman French *malfaisance*, from *mal-* 'evil' + Old French *faisance* 'activity'.

malformation ■ n. abnormality of shape or form in a part of the body.
– DERIVATIVES **malformed** adj.

malfunction ■ v. (of a piece of equipment or machinery) fail to function normally. ■ n. a failure of this type.

Malian /ˈmɑːliən/ ■ n. a native or inhabitant of Mali, a country in West Africa. ■ adj. of or relating to Mali or Malians.

Malibu /ˈmalɪbuː/ (also **Malibu board**) ■ n. (pl. **Malibus**) a lightweight surfboard.
– ORIGIN 1960S: named after *Malibu* beach in southern California.

malice ■ n. 1 the desire to do harm to someone; ill will. 2 Law wrongful intention, especially as increasing the guilt of certain offences.
– ORIGIN Middle English: from Latin *malitia*, from *malus* 'bad'.

malice aforethought ■ n. Law or humorous the intention to kill or harm.

malicious

malicious ■ adj. characterized by malice; intending or intended to do harm.
– DERIVATIVES **maliciously** adv. **maliciousness** n.

malign /məˈlaɪn/ ■ adj. harmful or evil in nature or effect. ■ v. speak ill of.
– DERIVATIVES **maligner** n. **malignity** /məˈlɪɡnɪti/ n.
– ORIGIN Middle English: via Old French *maligne* (adj.), *malignier* (v.), from Latin *malignus* 'tending to evil', from *malus* 'bad'.

malignancy /məˈlɪɡnənsi/ ■ n. (pl. **-ies**) **1** the state or presence of a malignant tumour; cancer. ▸ a cancerous growth. ▸ a form of cancer. **2** the quality of being malign or malevolent.

malignant ■ adj. **1** harmful; malevolent. **2** (of a tumour) tending to invade normal tissue or to recur after removal; cancerous. Contrasted with **BENIGN**.
– DERIVATIVES **malignantly** adv.
– ORIGIN C16: from late Latin *malignare* 'contrive maliciously'.

malinger /məˈlɪŋɡə/ ■ v. exaggerate or feign illness in order to escape duty or work.
– DERIVATIVES **malingerer** n.
– ORIGIN C19: back-formation from *malingerer*, from French *malingre*, perhaps from *mal-* 'wrongly' + *haingre* 'weak', prob. of Germanic origin.

Malinke /məˈlɪŋkeɪ/ ■ n. (pl. same or **Malinkes**) **1** a member of a West African people living mainly in Senegal, Mali, and the Ivory Coast. **2** the Mande language of this people.
– ORIGIN the name in Malinke.

mall /mal, mɔːl, mɒl/ ■ n. **1** a large enclosed shopping area from which traffic is excluded. **2** a sheltered walk or promenade.
– ORIGIN C17: prob. a shortening of **PALL-MALL**; from *The Mall* in St James's Park, London, former site of a pall-mall alley.

mallam /ˈmaləm/ ■ n. (in parts of Africa) a learned man or scribe.
– ORIGIN from Hausa *mālam(i)*.

mallard ■ n. (pl. same or **mallards**) the commonest duck of the northern hemisphere, the male having a dark green head and white collar. [*Anas platyrhynchos*.]
– ORIGIN Middle English: from Old French, 'wild drake', from *masle* 'male'.

malleable /ˈmalɪəb(ə)l/ ■ adj. **1** (of a metal or other material) able to be hammered or pressed into shape without breaking or cracking. **2** easily influenced; pliable.
– DERIVATIVES **malleability** n. **malleably** adv.
– ORIGIN Middle English: from medieval Latin *malleabilis*, from Latin *malleus* 'a hammer'.

mallee /ˈmali/ ■ n. a low-growing bushy Australian eucalyptus. [*Eucalyptus dumosa* and other species.]
– ORIGIN C19: from Wuywurung (an Aboriginal language).

malleolus /maˈliːələs/ ■ n. (pl. **malleoli** /-lʌɪ/) Anatomy a bony projection with a shape likened to a hammer head, especially each of those on either side of the ankle.
– ORIGIN C17: from Latin, diminutive of *malleus* 'hammer'.

mallet ■ n. **1** a hammer with a large wooden head. **2** a long-handled wooden stick with a head like a hammer, used for hitting a croquet or polo ball.
– ORIGIN Middle English: from Old French *maillet*, from *mail* 'hammer', from Latin *malleus*.

malleus /ˈmalɪəs/ ■ n. (pl. **mallei** /ˈmalɪʌɪ/) Anatomy a small bone in the middle ear which transmits vibrations of the eardrum to the incus.
– ORIGIN C17: from Latin, 'hammer'.

malling /ˈmɔːlɪŋ/ ■ n. N. Amer. **1** the development of shopping malls. **2** the action of passing time in a shopping mall.

Mallophaga /məˈlɒfəɡə/ ■ pl. n. Entomology an order of insects that comprises the biting lice.
– ORIGIN from Greek *mallos* 'lock of wool' + *-phagos* 'eating'.

mallow ■ n. a herbaceous plant with hairy stems, pink or purple flowers, and disc-shaped fruit. [Genus *Malva*, family Malvaceae: many species.]
– ORIGIN Old English, from Latin *malva*.

malm /mɑːm/ ■ n. a soft, crumbly chalky rock, or the fertile loamy soil produced as it weathers.
– ORIGIN Old English, of Germanic origin.

malmsey /ˈmɑːmzi/ ■ n. a fortified Madeira wine of the sweetest type.
– ORIGIN Middle English: from Middle Dutch *malemeseye*, from *Monemvasia*, the name of a port in SE Greece.

malnourished ■ adj. suffering from malnutrition.
– DERIVATIVES **malnourishment** n.

malnutrition ■ n. lack of proper nutrition, caused by not having enough to eat, not eating enough of the right things, or being unable to use the food eaten.

malocclusion ■ n. Dentistry imperfect positioning of the teeth when the jaws are closed.

malodorous ■ adj. smelling very unpleasant.

malodour ■ n. a very unpleasant smell.

malolactic /ˌmalə(ʊ)ˈlaktɪk/ ■ adj. of or denoting bacterial fermentation which converts malic acid to lactic acid, especially as a secondary process used to reduce the acidity of some wines. ■ n. fermentation of this kind.

maloti plural form of **LOTI**.

Malpighi layer /malˈpɪɡɪən/ ■ n. Zoology & Anatomy a layer in the epidermis in which skin cells are continually formed by division.
– ORIGIN C19: named after the C17 Italian microscopist Marcello *Malpighi*.

Malpighian tubule ■ n. Zoology a tubular excretory organ, numbers of which open into the gut in insects and some other arthropods.

malpitte /ˈmalpɪtə/ ■ pl. n. S. African the poisonous and hallucinogenic seeds of the thorn apple.
– ORIGIN Afrikaans, from *mal* 'mad' + *pit* 'seed'.

malpractice ■ n. improper, illegal, or negligent professional activity or treatment.

malpresentation ■ n. Medicine abnormal positioning of a fetus at the time of delivery.

malt /mɔːlt, mɒlt/ ■ n. **1** barley or other grain that has been steeped, germinated, and dried, used especially for brewing or distilling and vinegar-making. **2** short for **MALT WHISKY**. ■ v. **1** convert (grain) into malt. **2** (of a seed) become malt when germination is checked by drought.
– DERIVATIVES **maltiness** n. **malty** adj.
– ORIGIN Old English, of Germanic origin.

Malta fever ■ n. another term for **UNDULANT FEVER**.
– ORIGIN C19: named after *Malta*, where it was once prevalent.

maltase /ˈmɒlteɪz, ˈmɔːl-/ ■ n. Biochemistry an enzyme, present in saliva and pancreatic juice, which catalyses the breakdown of maltose and similar sugars to form glucose.

malted ■ adj. mixed with malt or a malt extract.

malted milk ■ n. a hot drink made from dried milk and a malt preparation.

Maltese /mɔːlˈtiːz, mɒl-/ ■ n. (pl. same) **1** a native or national of Malta or a person of Maltese descent. **2** the national language of Malta. **3** short for **MALTESE POODLE** or **MALTESE DOG**. ■ adj. of or relating to Malta, its people, or their language.

Maltese cross ■ n. a cross with arms of equal length which broaden from the centre and have their ends indented in a shallow V-shape.
– ORIGIN so named because the cross was formerly worn by the Knights of Malta, a religious order.

Maltese dog (also **Maltese terrier**) ■ n. a dog of a very small long-haired breed, typically with white hair.

Maltese poodle ■ n. a small cross-breed dog believed to be bred mainly from the Maltese dog and the poodle.

malthouse ■ n. a building in which malt is prepared and stored.

Malthusian /malˈθjuːzɪən/ ■ adj. of or relating to the theory of the English economist Thomas Malthus (1766–1834), that without the practice of 'moral restraint' the population tends to increase at a greater rate than its means of subsistence, resulting in the population checks of war, famine, and epidemic.

maltings ■ n. a malthouse.

malt liquor ■ n. alcoholic liquor made from malt by fermentation rather than distillation, for example beer.

maltodextrin ■ n. dextrin containing maltose, used as a food additive.

maltose /'mɔːltəʊz, -s, mɒlt-/ ■ n. Chemistry a sugar produced by the breakdown of starch, e.g. by enzymes found in malt and saliva.
– ORIGIN C19: from MALT.

maltreat ■ v. treat cruelly or with violence.
– DERIVATIVES **maltreatment** n.
– ORIGIN C18: from French *maltraiter*.

maltster ■ n. chiefly Brit. a person who makes malt.

malt whisky ■ n. whisky made only from malted barley and not blended with grain whisky.

malva pudding ■ n. S. African a hot dessert consisting of a baked pudding topped with a sweet sauce.
– ORIGIN partial translation of Afrikaans *malvapoeding*, from *malva* 'marshmallow' + *poeding* 'pudding'.

mam ■ n. informal **1** one's mother. **2** a term of respectful address for a woman.
– ORIGIN sense 1 (C16) is perhaps imitative of a child's first syllables; sense 2 is a var. of MA'AM.

mama /'mamə, mə'mɑː/ ■ n. **1** (also **mamma**) dated or N. Amer. one's mother. **2** (also **mamma**) US informal a mature woman: *the ultimate tough blues mama*. ▶ S. African informal a black woman.
– ORIGIN C16: imitative of a child's first syllables *ma, ma*.

mamba /'mambə/ ■ n. a large, agile, highly venomous African snake. [*Dendroaspis polylepis* (black mamba), *D. angusticeps* (green mamba), and related species.]
– ORIGIN C19: from isiZulu *imamba*.

mambo /'mambəʊ/ ■ n. (pl. **-os**) **1** a Latin American dance similar in rhythm to the rumba. **2** a voodoo priestess. ■ v. (**-oes, -oed**) dance the mambo.
– ORIGIN 1940s: from American Spanish.

Mameluke /'maməluːk/ ■ n. a member of a regime descended from slaves, that formerly ruled parts of the Middle East.
– ORIGIN from French *mameluk*, from Arabic *mamlūk* 'slave', from *malaka* 'possess'.

mamilla /ma'mɪlə/ (also **mammilla**) ■ n. (pl. **mamillae** /-liː/) Anatomy a nipple.
– ORIGIN C17: from Latin, diminutive of *mamma* (see MAMMA[2]).

mamillary /'mamɪləri/ (also **mammillary**) ■ adj. **1** (of minerals) having several smoothly rounded convex surfaces. **2** Anatomy denoting two rounded bodies in the floor of the hypothalamus in the brain.
– ORIGIN C17: from modern Latin *mamillaris*, from *mamilla* (see MAMILLA).

mamma[1] /'mamə, mə'mɑː/ ■ n. variant spelling of MAMA.

mamma[2] /'mamə/ ■ n. (pl. **mammae** /-miː/) a milk-secreting organ of female mammals (in humans, the breast).
– ORIGIN Old English, from Latin, 'breast'.

mammal ■ n. a warm-blooded vertebrate animal of a class (Mammalia) that is distinguished by the possession of hair or fur, the secretion of milk, and (typically) the birth of live young.
– DERIVATIVES **mammalian** adj.
– ORIGIN C19: from Latin *mammalis* (adj.), from *mamma* (see MAMMA[2]).

mammalogy /ma'malədʒi/ ■ n. the branch of zoology concerned with mammals.

mammary /'maməri/ ■ adj. denoting or relating to the human female breasts or the milk-secreting organs of other mammals. ■ n. (pl. **-ies**) informal a breast.
– ORIGIN C17: from MAMMA[2].

mammary gland ■ n. the milk-producing gland of women or other female mammals.

mammilla ■ n. variant spelling of MAMILLA.

mammogram /'maməgram/ ■ n. an image obtained by mammography.

mammography /ma'mɒgrəfi/ ■ n. Medicine a technique using X-rays to diagnose and locate tumours of the breasts.
– ORIGIN 1930s: from MAMMA[2] + -GRAPHY.

Mammon /'mamən/ ■ n. wealth regarded as an evil influence or false object of worship (taken by medieval writers as the name of the devil of covetousness).

– ORIGIN Middle English: from New Testament Greek *mamōnas* (see Matthew 6:24, Luke 16:9–13), from Aramaic *māmôn* 'riches'.

mammoth ■ n. a large extinct elephant of the Pleistocene epoch, typically hairy and with long curved tusks. [*Mammuthus primigenius* (woolly mammoth) and related species.] ■ adj. huge.
– ORIGIN C18: from Russian *mamo(n)t*, prob. of Siberian origin.

mammy ■ n. (pl. **-ies**) informal **1** a child's name for their mother. **2** offensive (formerly in the southern United States) a black nursemaid or nanny in charge of white children.
– ORIGIN C16: from MAM.

mampara /mam'pɑːrə/ ■ n. S. African derogatory or humorous a stupid person.
– ORIGIN Fanagalo, 'a fool, waste material'.

mampoer /mam'pʊə/ ■ n. S. African a strong alcoholic spirit distilled from peaches or other fruit.
– ORIGIN perhaps from the name of the Pedi chief *Mampuru*.

man ■ n. (pl. **men**) **1** an adult human male. **2** a male member of a workforce, team, etc. **3** a husband or lover: *man and wife*. **4** a person. ▶ human beings in general; the human race. **5** (**the Man**) derogatory (used by black people) white people collectively regarded as a controlling group. **6** a figure or token used in a board game. ■ v. (**manned, manning**) provide (a place or machine) with the personnel to run, operate, or defend it. ■ exclam. informal, chiefly N. Amer. used for emphasis or to express surprise, admiration, or delight. ▶ S. African informal used for emphasis or to express irritation or frustration.
– PHRASES **be someone's (or the) man** be the person perfectly suited to a requirement or task. **be man enough** be brave enough. **man about town** a fashionable and sociable man. **man and boy** from childhood. **the man in (or chiefly US on) the street** the average man. **man of the cloth** a clergyman. **man of God** a clergyman. ▶ a holy man or saint. **man of the house** the male head of a household. **man of letters** a male scholar or author. **man to man 1** in a direct and frank way between two men. **2** denoting a defensive tactic in soccer or other sports in which each player is responsible for marking one opponent. **to a man** without exception.
– DERIVATIVES **manless** adj. **manlike** adj. **manned** adj.
– ORIGIN Old English *man(n)*, (pl.) *menn* (n.), of Germanic origin; rel. to Sanskrit *manu* 'mankind'.

USAGE
The generic use of **man** to refer to 'human beings in general' has become problematic in modern use; it is now widely regarded as old-fashioned or sexist. Alternative terms such as **the human race** or **humankind** may be used in some contexts, but elsewhere there are no established alternatives, for example for the term **manpower** or the verb **man**.

-man ■ comb. form **1** in nouns denoting a man of a specified nationality or origin: *Frenchman*. **2** in nouns denoting a person, especially a man, belonging to a specified group or having a specified occupation or role: *layman* | *oarsman*. **3** a ship of a specified kind: *merchantman*.

manacle /'manək(ə)l/ ■ n. a metal band, chain, or shackle for fastening someone's hands or ankles. ■ v. (usu. **be manacled**) fetter with a manacle or manacles.
– ORIGIN Middle English: from Old French *manicle* 'handcuff', from Latin *manicula*, diminutive of *manus* 'hand'.

manage ■ v. **1** be in charge of; run. **2** supervise (staff). **3** be the manager of (a sports team or a performer). **4** administer and regulate (resources under one's control). **5** maintain control or influence over (a person or animal). **6** control the use or exploitation of (land). **7** succeed in surviving or in attaining one's aims; cope. **8** succeed in achieving or producing (something difficult). **9** succeed in withstanding. **10** be free to attend to (at a certain time).
– DERIVATIVES **managing** adj. & n.
– ORIGIN C16: from Italian *maneggiare*, from Latin *manus* 'hand'.

manageable ■ adj. able to be controlled or dealt with without difficulty.
– DERIVATIVES **manageability** n. **manageableness** n. **manageably** adv.

managed care ■ n. a system of health care emphasizing preventative medicine and home treatment.

managed currency ■ n. a currency whose exchange rate is regulated or controlled by the government.

managed economy ■ n. an economy in which the framework and general policies are regulated or controlled by the government.

managed fund ■ n. an investment fund run on behalf of an investor by an agent (typically an insurance company).

management ■ n. **1** the process of managing. **2** [treated as sing. or pl.] the people managing an organization. **3** Medicine the treatment or control of diseases or disorders, or the care of patients who suffer them.

management accounting ■ n. the provision of financial data and advice to a company for use in the organization and development of its business.
– DERIVATIVES **management accountant** n.

management company ■ n. a company which is set up to manage a group of properties, a unit trust, an investment fund, etc.

manager ■ n. **1** a person who manages an organization or group of staff. **2** a person who controls the professional activities of a performer, sports player, etc. **3** a person in charge of the activities, tactics, and training of a sports team.
– DERIVATIVES **managerial** adj. **managerially** adv. **managership** n.

manageress ■ n. a female manager.

managerialism ■ n. belief in or reliance on the use of professional managers in administering or planning an activity.
– DERIVATIVES **managerialist** n. & adj.

manakin /'manəkın/ ■ n. a small brightly coloured tropical American bird with a large head and small bill. [Family Pipridae: many species.]
– ORIGIN C17: var. of MANIKIN.

man-at-arms ■ n. (pl. **men-at-arms**) archaic a soldier.

manatee /ˌmanə'tiː, 'manəti:/ ■ n. a sea cow of tropical Atlantic coasts and estuaries, with a rounded tail flipper. [Genus *Trichechus*: three species.]
– ORIGIN C16: from Carib *manáti*.

Manchester ■ n. S. African & Austral./NZ cotton textiles; household linen.
– ORIGIN from the name of the city of *Manchester* in NW England, historically a centre of cotton manufacture.

manchet /'mantʃɪt/ ■ n. archaic a fine wheaten loaf.
– ORIGIN Middle English: perhaps from obsolete *maine* 'flour of the finest quality' + obsolete *cheat*, denoting a kind of wheaten bread.

Manchu /man'tʃuː/ ■ n. **1** a member of a people originally living in Manchuria, who formed the last imperial dynasty of China (1644–1912). **2** the Tungusic language of the Manchus.
– ORIGIN the name in Manchu, 'pure'.

Mancunian /man'kjuːnɪən/ ■ n. a native or inhabitant of Manchester in NW England. ■ adj. of or relating to Manchester or Mancunians.
– ORIGIN C20: from *Mancunium*, the Latin name of Manchester.

-mancy ■ comb. form divination by a specified means: *geomancy*.
– DERIVATIVES **-mantic** comb. form in corresponding adjectives.
– ORIGIN from Old French *-mancie*, from Greek *manteia* 'divination'.

mandala /'mandələ, 'mʌn-/ ■ n. a circular figure representing the universe in Hindu and Buddhist symbolism.
– DERIVATIVES **mandalic** adj.
– ORIGIN from Sanskrit *maṇḍala* 'disc'.

mandamus /man'deɪməs/ ■ n. Law a judicial writ issued as a command to an inferior court or ordering a person to perform a public or statutory duty.
– ORIGIN C16: from Latin, 'we command'.

Mandan /'mand(ə)n/ ■ n. (pl. same or **Mandans**) **1** a member of an American Indian people formerly living along the northern reaches of the Missouri River. **2** the Siouan language of this people.
– ORIGIN from N. American French *Mandane*, prob. from Dakota Sioux *mawátāna*.

mandarin[1] /'mand(ə)rɪn/ ■ n. **1** (**Mandarin**) the standard literary and official form of Chinese. **2** an official in any of the nine top grades of the former imperial Chinese civil service. **3** porcelain decorated with figures representing Chinese mandarins. **4** a powerful official or senior bureaucrat.
– ORIGIN C16: from Portuguese *mandarim*, from Hindi *mantrī* 'counsellor'.

mandarin[2] /'mand(ə)rɪn/ (also **mandarine** /-riːn/) ■ n. **1** a small flattish citrus fruit with a loose yellow-orange skin. **2** the citrus tree that yields this fruit. [*Citrus reticulata*.]
– ORIGIN C18: from French *mandarine*; perhaps rel. to MANDARIN[1], the colour of the fruit being likened to the official's yellow robes.

mandarin collar ■ n. a small, close-fitting upright collar.

mandarin jacket ■ n. a plain jacket with a mandarin collar.

mandate ■ n. /'mandeɪt/ **1** an official order or commission to do something. **2** Law a commission by which a party is entrusted to perform a service, especially without payment and with indemnity against loss by that party. **3** a written authority enabling someone to carry out transactions on another's bank account. **4** the authority to carry out a policy or course of action, regarded as given by the electorate to a party or candidate that wins an election. ■ v. /man'deɪt/ **1** give (someone) authority to act in a certain way. **2** make mandatory.
– DERIVATIVES **mandated** adj.
– ORIGIN C16: from Latin *mandatum* 'something commanded', from *mandare*, from *manus* 'hand' + *dare* 'give'.

mandatory /'mandət(ə)ri/ ■ adj. required by law or mandate; compulsory.
– DERIVATIVES **mandatorily** adv.

man-day ■ n. a day regarded in terms of the amount of work that can be done by one person in this time.

Mande /'mɑːndeɪ/ ■ n. (pl. same or **Mandes**) **1** a member of any of a large group of peoples of West Africa. **2** the group of Niger–Congo languages spoken by these peoples.
– ORIGIN the name in Mande.

Mandela shirt ■ n. **1** another term for MADIBA SHIRT. **2** a T-shirt or short-sleeved shirt with a picture of Nelson Mandela on it.

Mandelbrot set ■ n. Mathematics a particular set of complex numbers which has a highly convoluted fractal boundary when plotted.
– ORIGIN 1980s: named after the Polish-born mathematician Benoit B. *Mandelbrot*.

mandible /'mandɪb(ə)l/ ■ n. Anatomy & Zoology **1** the jaw or a jawbone, especially the lower jawbone in mammals and fishes. **2** either of the upper and lower parts of a bird's beak. **3** either half of the crushing organ in an arthropod's mouthparts.
– DERIVATIVES **mandibular** adj. **mandibulate** adj.
– ORIGIN Middle English: from late Latin *mandibula*, from *mandere* 'to chew'.

mandola /man'dəʊlə/ ■ n. a large tenor or bass mandolin, used in ensembles and folk groups.
– ORIGIN C18: from Italian.

mandolin ■ n. **1** a musical instrument resembling a lute, having paired metal strings plucked with a plectrum. **2** (also **mandoline**) a kitchen utensil consisting of a flat frame with adjustable blades for slicing vegetables.
– DERIVATIVES **mandolinist** n.
– ORIGIN C18: from French *mandoline*, from Italian *mandolino*, diminutive of *mandola* (see MANDOLA).

mandragora /man'dragərə/ ■ n. poetic/literary the mandrake, especially when used as a narcotic.
– ORIGIN Old English, from Latin and Greek *mandragoras*.

mandrake ■ n. a Mediterranean plant of the nightshade

family, having a forked fleshy root which supposedly resembles the human form and was formerly alleged to shriek when pulled from the ground, widely used in medicine and magic. [*Mandragora officinarum*.]
– ORIGIN Middle English, from Middle Dutch *mandrag(r)e*, from medieval Latin *mandragora*; associated with MAN (because of the shape of its root) + *drake* in the Old English sense 'dragon'.

Mandrax /'mandraks/ ■ n. trademark a sedative drug containing methaqualone and diphenhydramine.
– ORIGIN 1960s.

mandrel /'mandr(ə)l/ ■ n. **1** a shaft or spindle in a lathe to which work is fixed while being turned. **2** a cylindrical rod round which metal or other material is forged or shaped.
– ORIGIN C16.

mandrill /'mandrɪl/ ■ n. a large West African baboon with a brightly coloured red and blue face, the male having a blue rump. [*Mandrillus sphinx*.]
– ORIGIN C18: prob. from MAN + DRILL[3].

mane ■ n. a growth of long hair on the neck of a horse, lion, or other animal. ▸ a person's long hair.
– DERIVATIVES **-maned** adj. **maneless** adj.
– ORIGIN Old English, of Germanic origin.

maneater ■ n. **1** an animal that has a propensity for killing and eating humans. **2** informal a dominant woman who has many sexual partners.
– DERIVATIVES **man-eating** adj.

manège /ma'nɛʒ/ ■ n. **1** an arena or enclosed area in which horses and riders are trained. **2** the movements of a trained horse. **3** horsemanship.
– ORIGIN C17: French, from Italian (see MANAGE).

maneuver ■ n. & v. US spelling of MANOEUVRE.

man Friday ■ n. a male helper or follower.
– ORIGIN from *Man Friday*, the name of a character in Defoe's novel *Robinson Crusoe* (1719).

manful ■ adj. resolute or brave, especially in the face of adversity.
– DERIVATIVES **manfully** adv. **manfulness** n.

manga /'maŋɡə/ ■ n. a Japanese genre of cartoons, comic books, and animated films, typically with a science-fiction or fantasy theme.
– ORIGIN Japanese, from *man* 'indiscriminate' + *ga* 'picture'.

mangabey /'maŋɡəbeɪ/ ■ n. a medium-sized long-tailed monkey native to the forests of West and central Africa. [Genus *Cercocebus*: several species.]
– ORIGIN C18: by erroneous association with *Mangabey*, a region of Madagascar.

manganate /'maŋɡənət, -neɪt/ ■ n. Chemistry a salt in which the anion contains both manganese and oxygen.

manganese /'maŋɡəniːz/ ■ n. the chemical element of atomic number 25, a hard grey metal used in special steels and magnetic alloys. (Symbol: **Mn**)
– DERIVATIVES **manganous** adj.
– ORIGIN C17: from Italian *manganese*, alteration of medieval Latin *magnesia* (see MAGNESIA).

manganite /'maŋɡənʌɪt/ ■ n. a steel-grey or black mineral consisting of a basic manganese oxide.

mange /meɪn(d)ʒ/ ■ n. a skin disease of mammals caused by parasitic mites and occasionally communicable to humans, typically causing severe itching and hair loss.
– ORIGIN Middle English: from Old French *mangeue*, from *mangier* 'eat', from Latin *manducare* 'to chew'.

mangel /'maŋɡ(ə)l/ (also **mangel-wurzel** /-,wəːz(ə)l/) ■ n. another term for MANGOLD.

manger ■ n. a long trough for feeding horses or cattle.
– ORIGIN Middle English: from Old French *mangeure*, from Latin *manducare* 'chew'.

mangetout /'mɒʒtuː, -'tuː/ ■ n. (pl. same or **mangetouts** pronunc. same) a pea of a variety with an edible pod, eaten when the pod is young and flat.
– ORIGIN C19: from French, 'eat all'.

mangey ■ adj. variant spelling of MANGY.

mangle[1] ■ n. **1** chiefly Brit. a machine having two or more cylinders turned by a handle, between which wet laundry is squeezed (to remove excess moisture) and pressed. **2** US a large machine for ironing sheets or other fabrics, using heated rollers. ■ v. press with a mangle.
– ORIGIN C17: from Dutch, from *mangelen* 'to mangle', from medieval Latin *mango*, from Greek *manganon* 'axis, engine'.

mangle[2] ■ v. severely mutilate or damage by tearing or crushing.
– DERIVATIVES **mangler** n.
– ORIGIN Middle English: from Anglo-Norman French *mahangler*, from *mahaignier* 'maim'.

mango ■ n. (pl. **-oes** or **-os**) a fleshy yellowish-red tropical fruit which is eaten ripe or used green for pickles or chutneys. ▸ the evergreen Indian tree which bears this fruit. [*Mangifera indica*.]
– ORIGIN C16: from Portuguese *manga*, from a Dravidian language.

mangold ■ n. a beet of a variety with a large root, cultivated as stockfeed. [*Beta vulgaris* subsp. *crassa*.]
– ORIGIN C19: from German *Mangoldwurzel*, from *Mangold* 'beet' + *Wurzel* 'root'.

mangosteen /'maŋɡəstiːn/ ■ n. **1** a tropical fruit with sweet juicy white segments of flesh inside a thick reddish-brown rind. **2** the slow-growing Malaysian tree which bears this fruit. [*Garcinia mangostana*.]
– ORIGIN C16: from Malay *manggustan*.

mangrove ■ n. a tree or shrub which grows in muddy, chiefly tropical, coastal swamps and has tangled roots that grow above ground and form dense thickets. [*Rhizophora*, *Avicennia*, and other genera.]
– ORIGIN C17: prob. from Portuguese *mangue*, Spanish *mangle*, from Taino; prob. also associated with GROVE.

mangy (also **mangey**) ■ adj. (**-ier**, **-iest**) **1** having mange. **2** in poor condition; shabby.
– DERIVATIVES **manginess** n.

manhandle ■ v. **1** move (a heavy object) with great effort. **2** handle roughly by dragging or pushing.

manhattan ■ n. a cocktail made of vermouth and a spirit.

manhole ■ n. a covered opening in a floor or pavement allowing access beneath, especially one leading to a sewer.

manhood ■ n. **1** the state or period of being a man rather than a child. **2** the men of a country or society regarded collectively. **3** archaic the condition of being human. **4** the qualities traditionally associated with men, such as strength and sexual potency. **5** (**one's manhood**) informal, euphemistic a man's penis.

man-hour ■ n. an hour regarded in terms of the amount of work that can be done by one person in this time.

manhunt ■ n. an organized search for a person, especially a criminal.

mania ■ n. **1** mental illness marked by periods of excitement, delusions, and overactivity. **2** an obsession.
– ORIGIN Middle English: from Greek, 'madness'.

-mania ■ comb. form Psychology **1** denoting a specified type of mental abnormality or obsession: *kleptomania*. **2** denoting extreme enthusiasm or admiration: *Beatlemania*.
– DERIVATIVES **-maniac** comb. form in corresponding nouns.

maniac /'meɪnɪak/ ■ n. **1** a person exhibiting extremely wild or violent behaviour. **2** informal an obsessive enthusiast. **3** Psychiatry, archaic a person suffering from mania.
– DERIVATIVES **maniacal** /mə'nʌɪək(ə)l/ adj. **maniacally** /mə'nʌɪək(ə)li/ adv.
– ORIGIN C16: from late Greek *maniakos*, from *mania* (see MANIA).

manic ■ adj. **1** Psychiatry relating to or affected by mania. **2** showing wild excitement and energy.
– DERIVATIVES **manically** adv.

manic depression ■ n. a mental disorder marked by alternating periods of elation and depression.
– DERIVATIVES **manic-depressive** adj. & n.

Manichaean /,manɪ'kiːən/ (also **Manichean**) ■ adj. **1** chiefly historical of or relating to Manichaeism. **2** of or characterized by dualistic contrast or conflict between opposites. ■ n. an adherent of Manichaeism.

Manichaeism /,manɪ'kiːɪz(ə)m/ (also **Manicheism**) ■ n. a dualistic religious system with Christian, Gnostic, and

manicure

pagan elements, founded in Persia in the 3rd century by Manes (c.216–c.276) and based on a supposed primeval conflict between light and darkness.
– ORIGIN C17: from late Latin *Manichaeus*, from the name *Manes*.

manicure ■ n. a cosmetic treatment of the hands and nails. ■ v. **1** give a manicure to. **2** [as adj. **manicured**] (of a lawn or garden) trimmed or neatly maintained.
– DERIVATIVES **manicurist** n.
– ORIGIN C19: from Latin *manus* 'hand' + *cura* 'care'.

manifest[1] ■ adj. clear or obvious to the eye or mind. ■ v. **1** make manifest; demonstrate. **2** become apparent. **3** (of a ghost) appear.
– DERIVATIVES **manifestly** adv.
– ORIGIN Middle English: from Latin *manifestus*.

manifest[2] ■ n. **1** a document detailing a ship's contents and cargo and listing passengers and crew, for the use of customs officers. **2** a list of passengers or cargo in an aircraft. **3** a list of the wagons forming a freight train. ■ v. record in a manifest.
– ORIGIN C16: from Italian *manifesto* (see **MANIFESTO**).

manifestation ■ n. **1** an event, object, or symptom that clearly shows or embodies something. **2** a symptom of an ailment. **3** a version or incarnation. **4** an appearance of a ghost or spirit.
– ORIGIN Middle English: from late Latin *manifestatio(n-)*, from *manifestare* 'make public'.

manifesto ■ n. (pl. **-os**) a public declaration of policy and aims.
– ORIGIN C17: from Italian, from Latin *manifestare* 'make public', from *manifestus* (see **MANIFEST**[1]).

manifold /ˈmanɪfəʊld/ ■ adj. formal or poetic/literary **1** many and various. **2** having many different forms. ■ n. **1** a pipe or chamber branching into several openings. **2** (in an internal-combustion engine) the part conveying air and fuel from the carburettor to the cylinders or that leading from the cylinders to the exhaust pipe.
– DERIVATIVES **manifoldly** adv. **manifoldness** n.
– ORIGIN Old English.

manikin (also **mannikin**) ■ n. **1** a very small person. **2** a jointed model of the human body.
– ORIGIN C16: from Dutch *manneken*, diminutive of *man* 'man'.

Manila /məˈnɪlə/ (also **Manilla**) ■ n. **1** (also **Manila hemp**) the strong fibre of a Philippine plant (*Musa textilis*), used for rope, matting, paper, etc. **2** strong brown paper, originally made from Manila hemp.
– ORIGIN C17: from *Manila*, capital of the Philippines.

manilla /məˈnɪlə/ ■ n. a metal bracelet used by some African peoples as a medium of exchange.
– ORIGIN C16: from Spanish, from Latin *manicula* (see **MANACLE**).

manioc /ˈmanɪɒk/ ■ n. another term for **CASSAVA**.
– ORIGIN C16: from Tupi *manioca*.

manipulate /məˈnɪpjʊleɪt/ ■ v. **1** handle or control with dexterity. **2** examine or treat (a part of the body) by feeling or moving it with the hand. **3** control or influence cleverly or unscrupulously. **4** alter or present (data) so as to mislead.
– DERIVATIVES **manipulability** n. **manipulable** adj. **manipulatable** adj. **manipulation** n. **manipulator** n. **manipulatory** adj.
– ORIGIN C19 (*manipulation* C18): from Latin *manipulus* 'handful'.

manipulative ■ adj. **1** tending to manipulate others cleverly or unscrupulously. **2** of or relating to manipulation of an object or part of the body.
– DERIVATIVES **manipulatively** adv. **manipulativeness** n.

mankind ■ n. **1** human beings collectively; the human race. **2** men, as distinct from women.

manky ■ adj. (**-ier**, **-iest**) Brit. informal **1** inferior; worthless. **2** grimy; dirty.
– ORIGIN 1950s: prob. from obsolete *mank* 'mutilated, defective', from Latin *mancus* 'maimed'.

manly ■ adj. (**-ier**, **-iest**) **1** having or denoting those good qualities traditionally associated with men, such as courage and strength. **2** (of an activity) befitting a man.
– DERIVATIVES **manliness** n.

man-made ■ adj. made or caused by human beings.

manna ■ n. **1** (in the Bible) the substance miraculously supplied as food to the Israelites in the wilderness (Exodus 16). **2** an unexpected or gratuitous benefit.
– ORIGIN Old English, from Aramaic *mannā*, from Hebrew *mān*, corresponding to Arabic *mann*, denoting an exudation of a tamarisk.

manne /ˈmʌnə/ ■ pl. n. S. African informal men belonging to a particular group and engaging in typically masculine activities.
– ORIGIN Afrikaans, 'men'.

mannequin /ˈmanɪkɪn, -kwɪn/ ■ n. a dummy used to display clothes in a shop window.
– ORIGIN C18: from French (see **MANIKIN**).

manner ■ n. **1** a way in which something is done or happens. **2** a style in literature or art. **3** (**manner of**) chiefly poetic/literary a kind or sort: **4** a person's outward bearing or way of behaving towards others. **5** (**manners**) polite or well-bred social behaviour. ▸ social behaviour or habits.
– PHRASES **all manner of** many different kinds of. **in a manner of speaking** in some sense; so to speak. **to the manner born** naturally at ease in a specified job or situation.
– ORIGIN Middle English: from Old French *maniere*, from Latin *manuarius* 'of the hand', from *manus* 'hand'.

mannered ■ adj. **1** [in combination] behaving in a specified way: *well-mannered*. **2** (of an artistic style) marked by idiosyncratic or exaggerated mannerisms.

mannerism ■ n. **1** a habitual gesture or way of speaking or behaving. **2** excessive or self-conscious use of a distinctive style in art, literature, or music. **3** (**Mannerism**) a style of 16th-century Italian art characterized by distortions in scale and perspective and the use of bright, often lurid colours.
– DERIVATIVES **mannerist** n. & adj.

mannerly ■ adj. well-mannered; polite.
– DERIVATIVES **mannerliness** n.

mannikin ■ n. **1** a small waxbill of the Old World tropics, typically brown, black, and white, popular as a cage bird. [Genera *Lonchura* and *Spermestes* (Africa): many species.] **2** variant spelling of **MANIKIN**.

mannish ■ adj. (of a woman) having an appearance and characteristics that are associated with men.
– DERIVATIVES **mannishly** adv. **mannishness** n.
– ORIGIN Old English *mennisc* 'human'; the current sense dates from Middle English.

manoeuvre /məˈnuːvə/ (US **maneuver**) ■ n. **1** a physical movement or series of moves requiring skill and care. **2** a carefully planned scheme or action. **3** (**manoeuvres**) a large-scale military exercise. ■ v. (**manoeuvred**, **manoeuvring**) **1** perform or carry out a manoeuvre. **2** carefully guide or manipulate (someone or something) in order to achieve an end.
– DERIVATIVES **manoeuvrability** n. **manoeuvrable** adj.
– ORIGIN C18: from French *manœuvre* (n.), *manœuvrer* (v.), from medieval Latin *manuoperare* from *manus* 'hand' + *operari* 'to work'.

man-of-war (also **man-o'-war**) ■ n. (pl. **men-of-war** or **men-o'-war**) historical an armed sailing ship.

manometer /məˈnɒmɪtə/ ■ n. an instrument for measuring the pressure acting on a column of fluid, especially one incorporating a U-shaped tube.
– DERIVATIVES **manometric** adj.
– ORIGIN C18: from French *manomètre*, from Greek *manos* 'thin' + -*mètre* '(instrument) measuring'.

manor ■ n. **1** a large country house with lands. **2** chiefly historical (especially in England and Wales) a unit of land, originally a feudal lordship, consisting of a lord's demesne and lands rented to tenants. **3** Brit. informal one's home territory or area of operation.
– DERIVATIVES **manorial** adj.
– ORIGIN Middle English: from Anglo-Norman French *maner* 'dwelling', from Latin *manere* 'remain'.

manpower ■ n. the number of people working or available for work or service.

manqué /ˈmɒŋkeɪ/ ■ adj. [postpos.] having failed to become what one might have been; unfulfilled: *an actor manqué*.
– ORIGIN C18: French, from *manquer* 'to lack'.

mansard /'mansɑːd, -səd/ ■ n. a roof having four sides, in each of which the lower part of the slope is steeper than the upper part.
– ORIGIN C18: from French *mansarde*, named after the C17 French architect François Mansart.

manse /mans/ ■ n. the house occupied by a minister, especially of a Presbyterian Church.
– ORIGIN C15: from medieval Latin *mansus* 'dwelling', from *manere* 'remain'.

manservant ■ n. (pl. **menservants**) a male servant.

-manship ■ suffix (forming nouns) denoting skill in a subject or activity: *marksmanship*.

mansion ■ n. 1 a large, impressive house. 2 (**mansion block**) Brit. a large block of flats. 3 (in names) a terrace or mansion block: *Carlyle Mansions*.
– ORIGIN Middle English: from Latin *mansio(n-)* 'place where someone stays', from *manere* 'remain'.

mansion house ■ n. Brit. 1 the house of a lord mayor or a landed proprietor. 2 (**the Mansion House**) the official residence of the Lord Mayor of London.

manslaughter ■ n. the crime of killing a human being without prior intention to do so, in circumstances not amounting to murder.

manta /'mantə/ ■ n. a devil ray that occurs in tropical seas and may reach very great size. [*Manta birostris*.]
– ORIGIN C17: from Latin American Spanish, 'large blanket'.

mantel (also **mantle**) ■ n. a mantelpiece or mantelshelf.
– ORIGIN C16: specialized use of MANTLE[1].

mantelpiece (also **mantlepiece**) ■ n. 1 a structure of wood, marble, or stone above and around a fireplace. 2 a mantelshelf.

mantelshelf (also **mantleshelf**) ■ n. 1 a shelf forming the top of a mantelpiece. 2 Climbing a projecting ledge of rock. ▶ a move for climbing on such a ledge from below by pressing down on it with the hands to raise the upper body. ■ v. Climbing perform such a move.

mantic /'mantɪk/ ■ adj. formal of or relating to divination or prophecy.
– ORIGIN C19: from Greek *mantikos*, from *mantis* 'prophet'.

mantid ■ n. another term for MANTIS.

mantilla /man'tɪlə/ ■ n. (in Spain) a lace or silk scarf worn by women over the hair and shoulders.
– ORIGIN Spanish, diminutive of *manta* 'mantle'.

mantis /'mantɪs/ ■ n. (also **praying mantis**) ■ n. (pl. same or **mantises**) a slender predatory insect with a triangular head, typically waiting motionless for prey with its forelegs folded like hands in prayer. [Suborder Mantodea: numerous species.]
– ORIGIN C17: from Greek, 'prophet'.

mantissa /man'tɪsə/ ■ n. Computing the part of a floating-point number which represents the significant digits of the number.
– ORIGIN C17: from Latin, 'makeweight', perhaps from Etruscan.

mantle[1] ■ n. 1 a woman's loose sleeveless cloak or shawl. 2 a covering: *a mantle of snow*. 3 (also **gas mantle**) a mesh cover fixed round a gas jet to give an incandescent light when heated. 4 Ornithology a bird's back, scapulars, and wing coverts. 5 Zoology an outer or enclosing layer of tissue, especially in molluscs, cirripedes, and brachiopods; a fold of skin enclosing the viscera and secreting the shell. 6 an important role or responsibility that passes from one person to another. 7 Geology the region of the earth's interior between the crust and the core, believed to consist of hot, dense silicate rocks (mainly peridotite). ■ v. 1 poetic/literary cloak or envelop. 2 (of the face) glow with a blush.
– ORIGIN Old English *mentel*, from Latin *mantellum* 'cloak'.

mantle[2] ■ n. variant spelling of MANTEL.

mantlepiece ■ n. variant spelling of MANTELPIECE.

mantleshelf ■ n. variant spelling of MANTELSHELF.

mantling ■ n. Heraldry a piece of ornamental drapery depicted issuing from a helmet and surrounding a shield.
– ORIGIN C16: from MANTLE[1].

Mantoux test /'mɒtuː, 'mantuː/ ■ n. Medicine a skin test for immunity to tuberculosis using injection of tuberculin.
– ORIGIN 1930s: named after the French physician Charles Mantoux.

mantra /'mantrə/ ■ n. 1 (originally in Hinduism and Buddhism) a word or sound repeated to aid concentration in meditation. 2 a Vedic hymn. 3 a statement or slogan repeated frequently.
– DERIVATIVES **mantric** adj.
– ORIGIN C18: Sanskrit, 'instrument of thought', from *man* 'think'.

mantrap ■ n. a trap for catching people.

manual ■ adj. 1 of, done, or worked with the hands. 2 using or working with the hands. ■ n. 1 a book giving instructions or information. 2 an organ keyboard played with the hands not the feet. 3 a vehicle with manual transmission.
– DERIVATIVES **manually** adv.
– ORIGIN Middle English: from Old French *manuel*, from Latin *manualis*, from *manus* 'hand'.

manual alphabet ■ n. another term for FINGER ALPHABET.

manufacture ■ v. 1 make (something) on a large scale using machinery. 2 (of a living thing) produce (a substance) naturally. 3 make or produce (something abstract) in a merely mechanical way. 4 invent or fabricate (evidence or a story). ■ n. the process of manufacturing.
– DERIVATIVES **manufacturable** adj. **manufacturer** n. **manufacturing** adj. & n.
– ORIGIN C16: from French (by association with Latin *manu factum* 'made by hand'), from Italian *manifattura*.

manumit /ˌmanjʊ'mɪt/ ■ v. (**manumitted**, **manumitting**) historical release from slavery; set free.
– DERIVATIVES **manumission** n.
– ORIGIN Middle English: from Latin *manumittere* 'send forth from the hand'.

manure ■ n. animal dung used for fertilizing land. ■ v. apply manure to.
– ORIGIN Middle English: from Anglo-Norman French *mainoverer*, Old French *manouvrer* (see MANOEUVRE).

manuscript ■ n. 1 a handwritten book, document, or piece of music. 2 a handwritten or typed text submitted for or awaiting printing and publication.
– ORIGIN C16: from medieval Latin *manuscriptus*, from *manu* 'by hand' + *scriptus* 'written'.

manuscript paper ■ n. paper printed with staves for writing music on.

Manx ■ n. the Celtic language formerly spoken in the Isle of Man, still used for some ceremonial purposes. ■ adj. of or relating to the Isle of Man or its people or language.
– ORIGIN from Old Norse, from Old Irish *Manu* 'Isle of Man' + *-skr* (equivalent of -ISH[1]).

Manx cat ■ n. a cat of a breed having no tail or an extremely short one.

many ■ det., pron., & adj. (**more**, **most**) a large number of. ■ n. [as pl. n. **the many**] the majority of people.
– PHRASES **a good** (or **great**) **many** a large number. **many a —** a large number of.
– ORIGIN Old English, of Germanic origin.

manzanilla /ˌmanzə'nɪlə, -'niːljə/ ■ n. a pale, very dry Spanish sherry.
– ORIGIN Spanish, 'chamomile' (because the flavour is said to be reminiscent of that of chamomile).

Mao /maʊ/ ■ n. [as modifier] denoting a jacket or suit of a plain style with a mandarin collar, associated with communist China.
– ORIGIN 1960s: by association with *Mao Zedong* (see MAOISM).

Maoism ■ n. the communist doctrines of Mao Zedong (1893–1976), Chinese head of state 1949–59, as formerly practised in China.
– DERIVATIVES **Maoist** n. & adj.

Maori /'maʊri/ ■ n. (pl. same or **Maoris**) 1 a member of the aboriginal people of New Zealand. 2 the Polynesian language of this people.
– ORIGIN the name in Maori.

map ■ n. 1 a diagrammatic representation of an area of land or sea showing physical features, cities, roads, etc. 2 a diagram or collection of data showing the spatial arrangement or distribution of something over an area. ■ v. (**mapped**, **mapping**) 1 represent or record on or

mapantsula

in a map. **2** (**map something out**) plan a route or course of action in detail. **3** Mathematics & Linguistics associate each element of (a set) with an element of another set. ▶ (**map on to**) be associated with or linked to.
– PHRASES **off the map** (of a place) very distant or remote. **put something on the map** bring something to prominence. **wipe something off the map** obliterate something totally.
– DERIVATIVES **mapless** adj. **mappable** adj. **mapper** n. **mapping** n.
– ORIGIN C16: from medieval Latin *mappa mundi* 'sheet of the world', from Latin *mappa* 'sheet, napkin'.

mapantsula ■ n. plural form of PANTSULA.

maple ■ n. a tree or shrub with lobed leaves, winged fruits, and a syrupy sap. [*Acer campestre* (field maple, Europe), *A. saccharum* (sugar maple, N. America), and related species.]
– ORIGIN Old English *mapel-* in *mapeltreow, mapulder* 'maple tree'.

maple leaf ■ n. the leaf of the maple, the emblem of Canada.

maple sugar ■ n. N. Amer. sugar produced by evaporating maple syrup.

maple syrup ■ n. syrup produced from the sap of certain maples, especially the sugar maple.

map reference ■ n. a set of numbers and letters specifying a location as represented on a map.

maquette /maˈket/ ■ n. a sculptor's small preliminary model or sketch.
– ORIGIN C20: from Italian *machietta*, diminutive of *macchia* 'spot'.

maquillage /ˌmakɪˈjɑːʒ/ ■ n. make-up; cosmetics.
– ORIGIN French, from *maquiller* 'to make up', from Old French *masquiller* 'to stain'.

maquis /maˈkiː/ ■ n. (pl. same) **1** (**the Maquis**) the French resistance movement during the German occupation (1940–5). ▶ a member of this movement. **2** dense scrub vegetation consisting of hardy evergreen shrubs and small trees, characteristic of coastal regions in the Mediterranean.
– ORIGIN C19: from French, 'brushwood', from Corsican Italian *macchia*.

Mar. ■ abbrev. March.

mar ■ v. (**marred**, **marring**) impair; spoil.
– ORIGIN Old English *merran* 'hinder, damage', of Germanic origin.

marabaraba ■ n. variant spelling of MORABARABA.

marabi /məˈrɑːbi/ ■ n. (in South Africa) a form of dance music common in the townships from the 1920s to 1940s, consisting of a blend of folk music styles and elements of American jazz.
– ORIGIN perhaps rel. to Sesotho *lerabi* (pl. *ma-*) 'gangster' or from *raba* 'fly around'.

marabou /ˈmarəbuː/ ■ n. **1** a large African stork with a massive bill and large neck pouch. [*Leptoptilos crumeniferus*.] **2** down from the wing or tail of the marabou used as a trimming for hats or clothing.
– ORIGIN C19: from Arabic *murābiṭ* 'holy man', the stork being regarded as holy.

maraca /məˈrakə/ ■ n. a hollow gourd or gourd-shaped container filled with small beans, stones, etc., forming one of a pair and shaken as a percussion instrument.
– ORIGIN C17: from Portuguese *maracá*, from Tupi.

maraschino /ˌmarəˈskiːnəʊ, -ˈʃiːnəʊ/ ■ n. (pl. **-os**) **1** a strong, sweet liqueur made from small black Dalmatian cherries. **2** (also **maraschino cherry**) a cherry preserved in maraschino.
– ORIGIN Italian, from *marasca* (the name of the cherry), from *amaro* 'bitter'.

marasmus /məˈrazməs/ ■ n. Medicine undernourishment causing a child's weight to be significantly low for their age.
– DERIVATIVES **marasmic** adj.
– ORIGIN C17: from Greek *marasmos* 'withering'.

Marathi /məˈrɑːti, -ˈrati/ (also **Mahratti**) ■ n. the Indic language of the Marathas, the princely and military castes of the former Hindu kingdom of Maharashtra in central India.

marathon ■ n. **1** a long-distance running race, strictly one of 26 miles and 385 yards (42.195 km). **2** a long-lasting and difficult task. ▶ [as modifier] of great duration or difficulty: *a marathon effort*.
– DERIVATIVES **marathoner** n.
– ORIGIN C19: from *Marathōn* in Greece, the scene of a victory over the Persians in 490 BC; the modern race is based on the tradition that a messenger ran from Marathon to Athens (22 miles) with the news.

maraud /məˈrɔːd/ ■ v. [often as adj. **marauding**] attack and steal; raid.
– DERIVATIVES **marauder** n.
– ORIGIN C17: from French *marauder*, from *maraud* 'rogue'.

marble ■ n. **1** a hard crystalline metamorphic form of limestone, typically variegated or mottled, which may be polished and is used in sculpture and building. **2** a small ball of coloured glass used as a toy. ▶ (**marbles**) [treated as sing.] a game in which marbles are rolled along the ground. **3** (**one's marbles**) informal one's mental faculties. ■ v. give (something) the appearance of marble.
– DERIVATIVES **marbled** adj. **marbleize** (also **-ise**) v.
– ORIGIN Middle English: via Old French (var. of *marbre*), from Latin *marmor*, from Greek *marmaros* 'shining stone'.

marble cake ■ n. a cake with a mottled appearance, made of light and dark sponge.

marbling ■ n. **1** colouring or marking that resembles marble. **2** streaks of fat in lean meat.

Marburg disease ■ n. an acute, often fatal, form of haemorrhagic fever caused by a filovirus (Marburg virus) which normally lives in African monkeys.

marc ■ n. **1** the refuse of grapes that have been pressed for winemaking. **2** an alcoholic spirit distilled from this.
– ORIGIN C17: from French, from *marcher* in the early sense 'to tread or trample'.

marcasite /ˈmɑːkəsʌɪt, -ziːt/ ■ n. **1** a semi-precious stone consisting of iron pyrites. **2** a bronze-yellow mineral consisting of iron disulphide but differing from pyrite in typically forming aggregates of tabular crystals. **3** a piece of polished steel or similar metal cut as a gem.
– ORIGIN Middle English: from medieval Latin *marcasita*, from Arabic *markaṣīta*, from Persian.

March ■ n. the third month of the year.
– ORIGIN Middle English: from an Old French var. of *marz*, from Latin *Martius* (*mensis*) '(month) of Mars'.

march[1] ■ v. **1** walk in a military manner with a regular measured tread. **2** walk or proceed quickly and with determination. ▶ force (someone) to walk somewhere quickly. **3** walk along public roads in an organized procession to make a protest. ■ n. **1** an act or instance of marching. **2** a piece of music composed to accompany or be suggestive of marching.
– PHRASES **on the march** engaged in marching or making progress.
– ORIGIN Middle English: from French *marcher* 'to walk'.

march[2] ■ n. (usu. **Marches**) an area of land on the border between two countries or territories. ■ v. (**march with**) have a common frontier with.
– ORIGIN Middle English: from Old French *marche* (n.), *marchir* (v.), of Germanic origin.

marcher[1] ■ n. a person taking part in a protest march.

marcher[2] ■ n. chiefly historical an inhabitant of a frontier or border district.

March hare ■ n. informal a brown hare in the breeding season, noted for its leaping, boxing, and chasing in circles.

marching orders ■ pl. n. **1** instructions from a superior officer for troops to depart. **2** informal a dismissal.

marchioness /ˌmɑːʃəˈnɛs, ˈmɑːʃ(ə)nɪs/ ■ n. **1** the wife or widow of a marquess. **2** a woman holding the rank of marquess in her own right.
– ORIGIN C16: from medieval Latin *marchionissa*, feminine of *marchio(n-)* 'ruler of a border territory'.

March lily ■ n. another term for BELLADONNA LILY.

marchpane /ˈmɑːtʃpeɪn/ ■ n. archaic marzipan.

march past ▪ n. a formal march by troops past a saluting point at a review.

Mardi Gras /ˌmɑːdi ˈɡrɑː/ ▪ n. a carnival, especially one held on Shrove Tuesday.
– ORIGIN French, 'fat Tuesday', alluding to the last day of feasting before the fast and penitence of Lent.

mardy ▪ adj. (**-ier, -iest**) N. English sulky and whining.
– ORIGIN C20: from dialect *mard* 'spoilt' (describing a child), alteration of *marred* (see MAR).

mare[1] /mɛː/ ▪ n. the female of a horse or other equine animal.
– ORIGIN Old English *mearh* 'horse', *mere* 'mare', from a Germanic base.

mare[2] /ˈmɑːreɪ, -ri/ ▪ n. (pl. **maria** /ˈmɑːrɪə/) Astronomy a large, level basalt plain on the surface of the moon, appearing dark by contrast with highland areas.
– ORIGIN C19: special use of Latin *mare* 'sea'; these areas were once thought to be seas.

mare's nest ▪ n. **1** a complex and difficult situation; a muddle. **2** an illusory discovery.
– ORIGIN C16: formerly in the phr. *to have found* (or *spied*) *a mare's nest* (i.e. something that does not exist), used in the sense 'to have discovered something amazing'.

mare's tail ▪ n. **1** a widely distributed water plant with whorls of narrow leaves around a tall stout stem. [*Hippuris vulgaris*.] **2** (**mare's tails**) long straight streaks of cirrus cloud.

Marfan's syndrome /ˈmɑːfɑ̃z/ ▪ n. Medicine a hereditary disorder of the connective tissue, resulting in abnormally long and thin digits and also frequently in optical and cardiovascular defects.
– ORIGIN 1930s: named after the French paediatrician Antonin B. J. *Marfan*.

margarine /ˌmɑːdʒəˈriːn, ˌmɑːɡəˈriːn/ ▪ n. a butter substitute made from vegetable oils or animal fats.
– ORIGIN C19: from Greek *margaron* 'pearl' (because of the lustre of the crystals of esters from which it was first made).

margarita /ˌmɑːɡəˈriːtə/ ▪ n. a cocktail made with tequila and citrus fruit juice.
– ORIGIN Spanish equivalent of the given name *Margaret*.

margate /ˈmɑːɡɪt/ ▪ n. a deep-bodied greyish fish which occurs in warm waters of the western Atlantic. [*Haemulon album* and *Anisotremus surinamesis* (black margate).]
– ORIGIN C18.

margay /ˈmɑːɡeɪ/ ▪ n. a small South American wild cat with large eyes and a yellowish coat with black spots and stripes. [*Felis wiedii*.]
– ORIGIN C18: from Tupi *marakaya*.

marge[1] ▪ n. informal short for MARGARINE.

marge[2] ▪ n. poetic/literary a margin.

margin ▪ n. **1** an edge or border. ▸ the blank border on each side of the print on a page. **2** the furthest reach or limit: *the margins of acceptability*. **3** an amount above (or below) an accepted or minimum point: *they won by a convincing 17-point margin*. ▸ Finance a sum deposited with a broker to cover the risk of loss on a transaction on account. ▸ Austral./NZ an increment to a basic wage. ▪ v. (**margined, margining**) provide with a margin: *its leaves are margined with yellow*.
– PHRASES **margin of error** a small amount allowed for in case of miscalculation or change of circumstances.
– DERIVATIVES **margined** adj.
– ORIGIN Middle English: from Latin *margo, margin-* 'edge'.

marginal ▪ adj. **1** of, relating to, or situated at the margin: *marginal notes*. ▸ of or relating to water adjacent to the land's edge or coast: *marginal aquatics*. **2** (of a decision or distinction) very narrow. ▸ (of costs or benefits) relating to or resulting from small or unit changes. ▸ chiefly Brit. (of a parliamentary seat) having a small majority. **3** of secondary or minor importance. ▪ n. **1** chiefly Brit. a marginal parliamentary seat. **2** a plant that grows in water close to the edge of land.
– DERIVATIVES **marginality** n.

marginalia /ˌmɑːdʒɪˈneɪlɪə/ ▪ pl. n. marginal notes.
– ORIGIN C19: from medieval Latin *marginalis*, from *margo* (see MARGIN).

marginalize (also **-ise**) ▪ v. treat as marginal or peripheral.
– DERIVATIVES **marginalization** (also **-isation**) n.

marginally ▪ adv. to only a limited extent; slightly.

marginate Biology ▪ v. /ˈmɑːdʒɪneɪt/ provide with a margin; form a margin to. ▪ adj. /ˈmɑːdʒɪnət/ having a distinct margin.
– DERIVATIVES **margination** n.

margin call ▪ n. Finance a demand by a broker that an investor deposit further cash or securities to cover possible losses.

margrave /ˈmɑːɡreɪv/ ▪ n. historical the hereditary title of some princes of the Holy Roman Empire.
– ORIGIN C16, from Middle Dutch *markgrave*, from *marke* 'boundary' + *grave* 'count'.

margravine /ˈmɑːɡrəviːn/ ▪ n. historical the wife of a margrave.

marguerite /ˌmɑːɡəˈriːt/ ▪ n. another term for OX-EYE DAISY.
– ORIGIN C17: French equivalent of the given name *Margaret*.

maria plural form of MARE[2].

mariachi /ˌmærɪˈɑːtʃi/ ▪ n. (pl. **mariachis**) [as modifier] denoting a traditional Mexican folk music performed by strolling musicians.
– ORIGIN Mexican Spanish, 'street singer'.

Marian /ˈmɛːrɪən/ ▪ adj. **1** of or relating to the Virgin Mary. **2** of or relating to Queen Mary I of England.

mariculture /ˈmarɪˌkʌltʃə/ ▪ n. the cultivation of fish or other marine life for food.
– ORIGIN C20: from Latin *mare, mari-* 'sea' + CULTURE.

Marie Rose ▪ n. a cold sauce made from mayonnaise and tomato purée and served with seafood.
– ORIGIN 1970s.

marigold ▪ n. a plant of the daisy family with yellow, orange, or copper-brown flowers, cultivated as an ornamental. [Genera *Calendula* and *Tagetes*.] ▸ used in names of other plants with yellow flowers, e.g. marsh marigold.
– ORIGIN Middle English: from the given name *Mary* + dialect *gold*, denoting the corn or garden marigold in Old English.

marijuana /ˌmærɪˈhwɑːnə/ (also **marihuana**) ▪ n. cannabis, especially as smoked in cigarettes.
– ORIGIN C19: from Latin American Spanish.

marimba /məˈrɪmbə/ ▪ n. a deep-toned xylophone of African origin.
– ORIGIN C18: from Kimbundu, a Bantu language of western Angola.

marina ▪ n. a specially designed harbour with moorings for pleasure boats, and often also restaurants, bars, and houses or flats.
– ORIGIN C19: from Latin *marinus* (see MARINE).

marinade ▪ n. /ˌmærɪˈneɪd, ˈmærɪneɪd/ a sauce, typically of oil, vinegar, and spices, in which meat, fish, or other food is soaked before cooking in order to flavour or soften it. ▪ v. /ˈmærɪneɪd/ another term for MARINATE.
– ORIGIN C17: from Spanish *marinada*, via *marinar* 'pickle in brine', from Latin *marinus* (see MARINE).

marinara /ˌmɑːrɪˈnɑːrə, 'mɑr-/ ▪ n. (in Italian cooking) a sauce made from tomatoes, onions, and herbs.
– ORIGIN from the Italian phr. *alla marinara* 'sailor-style'.

marinate /ˈmærɪneɪt/ ▪ v. soak in a marinade.
– DERIVATIVES **marination** n.
– ORIGIN C17: from Italian *marinare* 'pickle in brine', or from French *mariner* (from *marine* 'brine').

marine /məˈriːn/ ▪ adj. **1** of, relating to, or produced by the sea. **2** of or relating to shipping or naval matters. ▪ n. a member of a body of troops trained to serve on land or sea.
– PHRASES **tell that to the marines** a scornful expression of disbelief.
– ORIGIN Middle English: from Old French *marin*, from Latin *marinus*, from *mare* 'sea'.

mariner ▪ n. formal or poetic/literary a sailor.

Mariolatry /ˌmɛːrɪˈɒlətri/ ▪ n. idolatrous worship of the Virgin Mary.

Mariology /ˌmɛːrɪˈɒlədʒi/ ▪ n. the part of Christian

marionette

theology concerned with the Virgin Mary.
– DERIVATIVES **Mariological** adj.

marionette /ˌmarɪəˈnɛt/ ■ n. a puppet worked by strings.
– ORIGIN C17: from French *marionnette*, from *Marion*, diminutive of *Marie*.

Marist /ˈmɛːrɪst, ˈmarɪst/ ■ n. **1** a member of the Society of Mary, a Roman Catholic missionary and teaching order. **2** a member of the Little Brothers of Mary, a Roman Catholic teaching order.
– ORIGIN C19: from French *Mariste*, from *Marie*, equivalent of *Mary*.

marital ■ adj. of or relating to marriage or the relations between husband and wife.
– DERIVATIVES **maritally** adv.
– ORIGIN C16: from Latin *maritalis*, from *maritus* 'husband'.

maritime ■ adj. **1** connected with the sea, especially in relation to seafaring commercial or military activity. **2** living or found in or near the sea. **3** denoting a climate that is moist and temperate owing to the influence of the sea.
– ORIGIN C16: from Latin *maritimus*, from *mare* 'sea'.

maritime pine ■ n. a pine tree with long thick needles and clustered cones, native to the coasts of the Mediterranean and Iberia. [*Pinus pinaster*.]

marjoram /ˈmɑːdʒ(ə)rəm/ ■ n. **1** (also **sweet marjoram**) an aromatic southern European plant of the mint family, the leaves of which are used as a herb. [*Origanum majorana*.] **2** (also **wild marjoram**) another term for OREGANO.
– ORIGIN Middle English: from Old French *majorane*, from medieval Latin *majorana*.

mark¹ ■ n. **1** a small area on a surface having a different colour from its surroundings, typically one caused by accident or damage. **2** something that indicates position or acts as a pointer. ▸ a competitor's starting point in a race. ▸ Nautical a piece of material or a knot used to indicate a depth on a sounding line. ▸ Telecommunications one of two possible states of a signal in certain systems. The opposite of SPACE. **3** a sign or indication: *a mark of respect*. ▸ a written symbol made on a document in place of a signature by someone who cannot write. **4** a level or stage: *unemployment passed the two million mark*. **5** a point awarded for a correct answer or for proficiency in an examination. ▸ a figure or letter representing the total of such points. ▸ (also **handicap mark**) Horse Racing an official assessment of a horse's form, used as the basis for calculating the weight the horse has to carry in a race. **6** (followed by a numeral) a particular model or type of a vehicle or machine: *a Mark 10 Jaguar*. **7** a target. ▸ informal, chiefly US a person who is easily deceived or taken advantage of: *they figure I'm an easy mark*. **8** Rugby the act of cleanly catching the ball direct from a kick, knock-on, or forward throw by an opponent, on or behind one's own 22-metre line, and exclaiming 'Mark', after which a free kick can be taken by the catcher. **9** Australian Rules an act of catching a ball that has been kicked at least ten metres before it reaches the ground, or the spot from which the subsequent kick is taken. ■ v. **1** make a mark on. ▸ (**mark something up**) annotate or correct a text for printing, keying, or typesetting. ▸ become stained. **2** identify using a mark or by writing something down. ▸ separate or distinguish by means of a particular feature or characteristic. ▸ (**mark someone out for**) select or destine someone for (a particular role). ▸ (**mark someone down as**) judge someone to be. **3** indicate the position of. ▸ acknowledge or celebrate (an event) with a particular action. ▸ be an indication of (a significant event or phase). **4** (**mark something up** or **down**) (of a retailer) increase or reduce the indicated price of an item. **5** assess and give a mark to (written work). ▸ (**mark someone/thing down**) reduce the number of marks awarded to a candidate or their work. **6** notice or pay careful attention to. **7** (in team games) stay close to (an opponent) in order to prevent them getting or passing the ball. ▸ Australian Rules catch (the ball) from a kick of at least ten metres.
– PHRASES **be quick** (or **slow**) **off the mark** be fast (or slow) in responding. **get off the mark** get started. **leave** (or **make**) **its** (or **one's** or **a**) **mark** have a lasting or significant effect. **one's mark** Brit. something which is particularly typical of or suitable for someone: *'A motel! That's just about your mark!'* **mark time 1** (of troops) march on the spot without moving forward. **2** pass one's time in routine activities until a more favourable opportunity presents itself. **mark you** chiefly Brit. used to emphasize or draw attention. **near** (or **close**) **to the mark** almost accurate. **off** (or **wide of**) **the mark** incorrect or inaccurate. **on the mark** correct; accurate. **on your marks** used to instruct competitors in a race to prepare themselves in the correct starting position. **up to the mark** up to the required standard or normal level.
– ORIGIN Old English *mearc* (n.), *mearcian* (v.), of Germanic origin.

mark² ■ n. **1** the former basic monetary unit of Germany, equal to 100 pfennig. **2** a denomination of weight for gold and silver, formerly used throughout western Europe and typically equal to 8 ounces (226.8 grams).
– ORIGIN Old English *marc*, from Old Norse *mǫrk*.

markdown ■ n. a reduction in price.

marked ■ adj. **1** having a visible mark. ▸ (of playing cards) having distinctive marks on their backs to assist cheating. **2** Linguistics (of words or forms) distinguished by a particular feature. **3** clearly noticeable. **4** singled out, especially as a target for attack: *a marked man*.
– DERIVATIVES **markedly** adv. **markedness** n.

marker ■ n. **1** an object used to indicate a position, place, or route. ▸ a thing serving as a standard of comparison. **2** a felt-tip pen with a broad tip. **3** (in team games) a player who marks an opponent. **4** a person who marks a test or examination. ▸ a person who records the score in a game. **5** N. Amer. informal a promissory note; an IOU.

market ■ n. **1** a regular gathering of people for the purchase and sale of provisions, livestock, and other commodities. ▸ an open space or covered building where vendors convene to sell their goods. **2** an area or arena in which commercial dealings are conducted: *the labour market*. **3** a demand for a particular commodity or service. ▸ [often as modifier] the free market; the operation of supply and demand: *market forces*. **4** a stock market. ■ v. (**marketed**, **marketing**) advertise or promote.
– PHRASES **be in the market for** wish to buy. **make a market** Finance take part in active dealing in shares or other assets. **on the market** available for sale.
– DERIVATIVES **marketer** n.
– ORIGIN Middle English, from Latin *mercatus*, from *mercari* 'buy' (see MERCHANT).

marketable ■ adj. **1** able or fit to be sold or marketed. **2** in demand.
– DERIVATIVES **marketability** n.

marketeer ■ n. **1** a person who sells goods or services in a market. **2** a person who works in or advocates a particular type of market.

market garden ■ n. a place where vegetables and fruit are grown for sale.
– DERIVATIVES **market gardener** n. **market gardening** n.

marketing ■ n. the action or business of promoting and selling products or services.

market-maker ■ n. a dealer in securities or other assets who undertakes to buy or sell at specified prices at all times.

marketplace ■ n. **1** an open space where a market is held. **2** the arena of competitive or commercial dealings.

market research ■ n. the activity of gathering information about consumers' needs and preferences.
– DERIVATIVES **market researcher** n.

market share ■ n. the portion of a market controlled by a particular company or product.

market town ■ n. (in the UK) a town of moderate size where a regular market is held.

market value ■ n. the amount for which something can be sold on a given market. Often contrasted with BOOK VALUE.

marking ■ n. (usu. **markings**) an identification mark. ▸ a pattern of marks on an animal's fur, feathers, or skin.

Markov model /ˈmɑːkɒf/ (also **Markov chain**) ■ n. Statistics a stochastic model describing a sequence of possible events in which the probability of each event depends only on the state attained in the previous event.

–ORIGIN C20: named after the Russian mathematician Andrei A. *Markov*.

marksman ■ n. (pl. **-men**) a person skilled in shooting.
–DERIVATIVES **marksmanship** n.

mark-up ■ n. **1** the amount added to the cost price of goods to cover overheads and profit. **2** Computing a set of codes assigned to elements of a text to indicate their structural or logical relation to the rest of the text.

marl[1] ■ n. an unconsolidated sedimentary rock or soil consisting of clay and lime, formerly used as fertilizer.
–ORIGIN Middle English: from Old French *marle*, from medieval Latin *margila*, from Latin *marga*, of Celtic origin.

marl[2] ■ n. a mottled yarn or fabric.
–DERIVATIVES **marled** adj.
–ORIGIN C19: shortening of *marbled*.

marlin /'mɑ:lɪn/ ■ n. a large edible billfish of warm seas, which is a highly prized game fish. [Genera *Makaira* and *Tetrapterus*: several species.]
–ORIGIN C20: from **MARLINSPIKE** (with ref. to its pointed snout).

marline /'mɑ:lɪn/ ■ n. Nautical light rope made of two strands.
–ORIGIN Middle English: from Middle Low German *marling*.

marlinspike (also **marlinespike**) ■ n. a pointed metal tool used by sailors to separate strands of rope or wire.
–ORIGIN C17: from *marl* 'fasten with marline' (from Dutch *marlen* 'keep binding') + **SPIKE**[1].

marmalade ■ n. a preserve made from citrus fruit, especially bitter oranges.
–ORIGIN C15: from Portuguese *marmelada* 'quince jam', from *marmelo* 'quince', from Greek *melimēlon* (from *meli* 'honey' + *mēlon* 'apple').

Marmite /'mɑ:mʌɪt/ ■ n. trademark a dark savoury spread made from yeast extract and vegetable extract.

marmoreal /mɑ:'mɔ:rɪəl/ ■ adj. poetic/literary made of or likened to marble.
–DERIVATIVES **marmoreally** adv.
–ORIGIN C18: from Latin *marmoreus*, from *marmor* 'marble'.

marmoset /'mɑ:məzet/ ■ n. a small tropical American monkey with a silky coat and a long tail. [Genera *Callithrix* and *Cebuella*: four species.]
–ORIGIN Middle English: from Old French *marmouset* 'grotesque image'.

marmot /'mɑ:mət/ ■ n. a heavily built, gregarious burrowing rodent, typically living in mountainous country. [Genus *Marmota*: several species.]
–ORIGIN C17: from French *marmotte*, prob. via Romansh *murmont* from late Latin *mus montanus* 'mountain mouse'.

maroela /mə'rʊlə/ ■ n. variant spelling of **MARULA**.

marog /mə'rɒx/ ■ n. variant spelling of **MOROGO**.

Maronite /'marənʌɪt/ ■ n. a member of a Christian sect of Syrian origin, living chiefly in Lebanon and in communion with the Roman Catholic Church.
–ORIGIN C16: from medieval Latin *Maronita*, from the name of John *Maro*, a C7 Syrian religious leader.

maroon[1] ■ n. **1** a dark brownish-red colour. **2** chiefly Brit. a firework that makes a loud bang, used as a signal or warning.
–ORIGIN C17: from French *marron* 'chestnut'.

maroon[2] ■ v. (usu. **be marooned**) abandon (someone) alone in an inaccessible place, especially an island.
–ORIGIN C18: from *Maroon*, the name of a group of black people descended from runaway slaves and living in Suriname and the West Indies.

marque /mɑ:k/ ■ n. a make of car, as distinct from a specific model.
–ORIGIN C20: from French, from *marquer* 'to brand'.

marquee /mɑ:'ti:/ ■ n. **1** a large tent used for social or commercial functions. **2** N. Amer. a roof-like projection over the entrance to a theatre, hotel, or other building.
–ORIGIN C17: from **MARQUISE**.

Marquesan /mɑ:'keɪz(ə)n, -s(ə)n/ ■ n. **1** a native or inhabitant of the Marquesas Islands in the South Pacific. **2** the Polynesian language of this people.

marquess /'mɑ:kwɪs/ ■ n. a British nobleman ranking above an earl and below a duke. Compare with **MARQUIS**.
–ORIGIN C16: var. of **MARQUIS**.

marquetry /'mɑ:kɪtri/ (also **marquetery** or **marqueterie**) ■ n. inlaid work made from small pieces of variously coloured wood, used chiefly for the decoration of furniture.
–ORIGIN C16: from French *marqueterie*, from *marqueter* 'become variegated'.

marquis /'mɑ:kwɪs/ ■ n. **1** (in some European countries) a nobleman ranking above a count and below a duke. Compare with **MARQUESS**. **2** variant spelling of **MARQUESS**.
–DERIVATIVES **marquisate** (also **marquessate**) n.
–ORIGIN Middle English: from Old French *marchis*, rel. to **MARCH**[2].

marquise /mɑ:'ki:z/ ■ n. **1** the wife or widow of a marquis, or a woman holding the rank of marquis in her own right. **2** a finger ring set with a pointed oval gem or cluster of gems. **3** a chilled dessert similar to a chocolate mousse.
–ORIGIN C17: French, feminine of **MARQUIS**.

marram grass /'marəm/ ■ n. a coarse grass of coastal sand dunes. [*Ammophila arenaria*.]
–ORIGIN C17: from Old Norse *marálmr*, from *marr* 'sea' + *hálmr* 'haulm'.

marriage ■ n. **1** the formal union of a man and a woman, typically as recognized by law, by which they become husband and wife. **2** a combination of two or more elements.
–PHRASES **by marriage** as a result of a marriage. **in marriage** as husband or wife.
–ORIGIN Middle English: from Old French *mariage*, from *marier* 'marry'.

marriageable ■ adj. fit or suitable for marriage, especially in being wealthy or of the right age.
–DERIVATIVES **marriageability** n.

marriage guidance ■ n. counselling of married couples who have problems in their relationship.

marriage of convenience ■ n. a marriage concluded primarily to achieve a practical purpose.

married ■ adj. of, relating to, or united by marriage. ■ n. (**marrieds**) married people.

marron glacé /ˌmarɒ̃ 'glaseɪ/ ■ n. (pl. **marrons glacés** pronunc. same) a chestnut preserved in and coated with sugar.
–ORIGIN French, 'iced chestnut'.

marrow ■ n. **1** a long white-fleshed gourd with thin green skin, eaten as a vegetable. **2** the plant of the gourd family which produces this. [*Cucurbita pepo*.] **3** (also **bone marrow**) a soft fatty substance in the cavities of bones, in which blood cells are produced. **4** the vital part or essence.
–PHRASES **to the marrow** to one's innermost being.
–ORIGIN Old English, of Germanic origin.

marrowbone ■ n. a bone containing edible marrow.

marry ■ v. (**-ies, -ied**) **1** join in marriage. ▸ take as one's wife or husband in marriage. ▸ (**marry into**) become a member of (a family) by marriage. **2** join together; combine harmoniously. **3** Nautical splice (rope ends) together without increasing their girth.
–ORIGIN Middle English: from Old French *marier*, from Latin *maritare*, from *maritus* 'married, husband'.

Marsala /mɑ:'sɑ:lə/ ■ n. a dark, sweet fortified dessert wine produced in Sicily.
–ORIGIN named after *Marsala*, a town in Sicily.

marsh ■ n. an area of low-lying land which is flooded in wet seasons or at high tide, and typically remains waterlogged at all times.
–DERIVATIVES **marshiness** n. **marshy** adj.
–ORIGIN Old English, of West Germanic origin.

marshal ■ n. **1** an officer of the highest rank in the armed forces of some countries. ▸ chiefly historical a high-ranking officer of state. **2** US a federal or municipal law officer. ▸ the head of a police department. **3** an official responsible for supervising public events, especially sports events or parades. ■ v. (**marshalled, marshalling**; US **marshaled, marshaling**) **1** assemble (a group of people,

marshalling yard

e.g. soldiers) in order. ▶ (of an official) ensure order at a public event. **2** bring together or arrange in order (facts, information, etc.). **3** Heraldry combine (coats of arms), typically to indicate marriage, descent, or the bearing of office.
– DERIVATIVES **marshaller** n. **marshalship** n.
– ORIGIN Middle English: from Old French *mareschal* 'farrier, commander', from late Latin *mariscalcus*, from Germanic elements meaning 'horse' and 'servant'.

marshalling yard ■ n. a large railway yard in which freight wagons are organized into trains.

Marshal of the Royal Air Force ■ n. the highest rank of officer in the RAF.

Marsh Arab ■ n. a member of a semi-nomadic Arab people inhabiting marshland in southern Iraq.

marsh gas ■ n. methane, especially as generated by decaying matter in marshes.

marsh harrier ■ n. a large harrier that frequents marshes and reed beds. [*Circus ranivorus* (Africa) and *C. aeruginosus* (Eurasia).]

marshmallow ■ n. a spongy item of confectionery made from a mixture of sugar, albumen, and gelatin.

marsh rose ■ n. a rare South African plant of the protea family that has bright pink rose-shaped bracts. [*Orothamnus zeyheri*.]

marsupial /mɑːˈsuːpɪəl/ ■ n. a mammal of an order (Marsupialia) whose young are born incompletely developed and are carried and suckled in a pouch on the mother's belly.
– ORIGIN C17: from Greek *marsupion* (see **MARSUPIUM**).

marsupium /mɑːˈsuːpɪəm/ ■ n. (pl. **marsupia** /-pɪə/) Zoology a pouch that protects eggs, offspring, or reproductive structures, especially the pouch of a female marsupial mammal.
– ORIGIN C17: from Greek *marsupion*, diminutive of *marsipos* 'purse'.

mart ■ n. a trade centre or market.
– ORIGIN Middle English: from Middle Dutch *mart*, var. of *marct* 'market'.

marten /ˈmɑːtɪn/ ■ n. a weasel-like mammal of forests in Eurasia and North America, hunted for fur in some countries. [Genus *Martes*: several species.]
– ORIGIN Middle English: from Old French (*peau*) *martrine* 'marten (fur)', from *martre*, of West Germanic origin.

martensite /ˈmɑːtɪnzaɪt/ ■ n. Metallurgy a hard and very brittle solid solution of carbon in iron that is the main constituent of hardened steel.
– DERIVATIVES **martensitic** adj.
– ORIGIN C19: named after the German metallurgist Adolf Martens.

martial /ˈmɑːʃ(ə)l/ ■ adj. of or appropriate to war; war-like.
– DERIVATIVES **martially** adv.
– ORIGIN Middle English: from Latin *martialis*, from *Mars*, the name of the Roman god of war.

martial arts ■ pl. n. various sports or skills, mainly of Japanese origin, which originated as forms of self-defence or attack, such as judo, karate, and kendo.
– DERIVATIVES **martial artist** n.

martial eagle ■ n. a brown eagle with a brown-spotted white belly, the largest African eagle. [*Polmaetus bellicosus*.]

martial law ■ n. military government, involving the suspension of ordinary law.

Martian ■ adj. of or relating to the planet Mars or its supposed inhabitants. ■ n. a hypothetical or fictional inhabitant of Mars.
– ORIGIN Middle English, from Latin *Marti-*, *Mars*, the Roman god of war.

martin ■ n. used in names of small short-tailed swallows, e.g. house martin.
– ORIGIN Middle English: prob. a shortening of obsolete *martinet*, from French, prob. from the name of St Martin of Tours.

martinet /ˌmɑːtɪˈnɛt/ ■ n. a strict disciplinarian, especially in the armed forces.

– DERIVATIVES **martinettish** (also **martinetish**) adj.
– ORIGIN C17: named after Jean *Martinet*, C17 French drill master.

martingale /ˈmɑːtɪŋɡeɪl/ ■ n. a strap or set of straps running from the noseband or reins to the girth of a horse, used to prevent the horse from raising its head too high.
– ORIGIN C16: from Spanish *almártaga*, from Arabic *al-marta'a* 'the fastening', influenced by *martingale*, from Occitan *martegal* 'inhabitant of Martigues (in Provence)'.

Martini /mɑːˈtiːni/ ■ n. 1 trademark a type of vermouth produced in Italy. **2** a cocktail made from gin and dry vermouth.
– ORIGIN named after *Martini* and Rossi, an Italian firm selling vermouth.

martlet /ˈmɑːtlɪt/ ■ n. Heraldry a bird similar to a swallow but without feet, borne as a charge or a mark of cadency for a fourth son.
– ORIGIN Middle English: from Old French *merlet*, influenced by *martinet* (see **MARTIN**).

martyr ■ n. **1** a person who is killed because of their religious or other beliefs. **2** a person who displays or exaggerates their suffering or discomfort in order to obtain sympathy or admiration. ■ v. (usu. **be martyred**) kill as a martyr; make a martyr of.
– DERIVATIVES **martyrdom** n. **martyrization** (also **-isation**) n. **martyrize** (also **-ise**) v.
– ORIGIN Old English, from Greek *martur* 'witness' (in Christian use, 'martyr').

marula /məˈruːlə, məˈrʊlə/ (also **maroela**) ■ n. (also **marula tree**) a large southern African woodland tree. [*Sclerocarya birrea* subsp. *caffra*.] ▶ the edible yellow plum-like fruit of this tree.
– ORIGIN from Afrikaans *maroela*, from Sesotho sa Leboa *morula*.

marvel ■ v. (**marvelled**, **marvelling**; US **marveled**, **marveling**) be filled with wonder or astonishment. ■ n. a wonderful or astonishing person or thing.
– DERIVATIVES **marveller** n.
– ORIGIN Middle English: from Old French *merveille*, from Latin *mirabilis* 'wonderful', from *mirari* 'wonder at'.

marvellous (US **marvelous**) ■ adj. **1** causing great wonder; extraordinary. **2** extremely good or pleasing.
– DERIVATIVES **marvellously** adv. **marvellousness** n.

Marxism ■ n. the political and economic theories of Karl Marx and Friedrich Engels, later developed by their followers to form the basis for the theory and practice of communism.
– DERIVATIVES **Marxist** n. & adj.

Marxism–Leninism ■ n. the doctrines of Marx as interpreted and put into effect by Lenin in the Soviet Union and (at first) by Mao Zedong in China.
– DERIVATIVES **Marxist–Leninist** n. & adj.

Mary Jane ■ n. **1** a flat, round-toed shoe for women and girls, with a single strap across the top. **2** informal marijuana.

marzipan /ˈmɑːzɪpan, ˌmɑːzɪˈpan/ ■ n. a sweet yellowish paste of ground almonds, sugar, and egg whites, used to coat large cakes or to make confectionery.
– DERIVATIVES **marzipanned** adj.
– ORIGIN C15 (as *marchpane*): from Italian *marzapane*, perhaps from Arabic.

Masai /ˈmɑːsʌɪ, məˈsʌɪ, mɑːˈsʌɪ/ (also **Maasai**) ■ n. (pl. same or **Masais**) a member of a pastoral people living in Tanzania and Kenya.
– ORIGIN the name in Masai.

masala /məˈsɑːlə/ ■ n. a spice mixture ground into a paste or powder for use in Indian cookery.
– ORIGIN from Urdu *maṣālaḥ*, from Arabic *maṣāliḥ* 'ingredients, materials'.

mascara /maˈskɑːrə/ ■ n. a cosmetic for darkening and thickening the eyelashes.
– DERIVATIVES **mascaraed** adj.
– ORIGIN C19: from Italian, 'mask'.

mascarpone /ˌmaskəˈpəʊneɪ, -ˈpəʊni/ ■ n. a soft, mild Italian cream cheese.
– ORIGIN from Italian.

mascle /ˈmɑːsk(ə)l/ ■ n. Heraldry a lozenge voided, i.e. with a central lozenge-shaped aperture.

| VOWELS | a cat | ɑː arm | ɛ bed | ɛː hair | ə ago | əː her | ɪ sit | i cosy | iː see | ɒ hot | ɔː saw | ʌ run |

– ORIGIN Middle English: from Anglo-Latin *mascula* 'mesh'.

mascot ■ n. a person or thing that is supposed to bring good luck, especially one linked to a particular event or organization.
– ORIGIN C19: from French *mascotte*, from modern Provençal *mascotto*, diminutive of *masco* 'witch'.

masculine ■ adj. **1** having qualities or appearance traditionally associated with men. ▶ male. **2** Grammar of or denoting a gender of nouns and adjectives conventionally regarded as male. ■ n. (**the masculine**) the male sex or gender.
– DERIVATIVES **masculinist** adj. & n. **masculinity** n.
– ORIGIN Middle English: from Latin *masculinus*, from *masculus* 'male'.

masculine rhyme ■ n. Prosody a rhyme between final stressed syllables (e.g. *blow/flow, confess/redress*).

masculinize (also **-ise**) ■ v. induce male physiological characteristics in. ▶ cause to appear or seem masculine.
– DERIVATIVES **masculinization** (also **-isation**) n.

maser /ˈmeɪzə/ ■ n. a form of laser generating a beam of microwaves.
– ORIGIN 1950s: acronym from *microwave amplification by the stimulated emission of radiation*.

mash ■ n. **1** a soft mass made by crushing a substance into a pulp. **2** bran mixed with hot water, given as a warm food to horses. **3** informal boiled and mashed potatoes. ■ v. **1** reduce or beat to a mash. **2** (in brewing) mix (powdered malt) with hot water to form wort. **3** Brit. informal (with reference to tea) brew or infuse.
– DERIVATIVES **masher** n.
– ORIGIN Old English, of West Germanic origin.

Mashona /məˈʃəʊnə/ ■ n. the Shona people collectively, particularly those of Zimbabwe.
– ORIGIN the name in Shona.

mashonisa /ˌmʌʃəˈniːsʌ, ˌmʌʃɒˈniːsə/ (also **machonisa**) ■ n. (pl. same or **mashonisas**) S. African a loan shark or informal moneylender.
– ORIGIN isiZulu *umashonisa / omashonisa*.

mash-up ■ n. a mixture or fusion of disparate elements, especially a musical track comprising the vocals of one recording placed over the instrumental backing of another.

mask ■ n. **1** a covering for all or part of the face, worn as a disguise, for protection or hygiene, or for theatrical effect. **2** a likeness of a person's face moulded or sculpted in clay or wax. ▶ the face or head of an animal, especially of a fox, as a hunting trophy. **3** a disguise or pretence: *she let her mask of respectability slip*. **4** Photography a piece of material such as card used to cover part of an image that is not required when exposing a print. ▶ Electronics a patterned metal film used in the manufacture of microcircuits to allow selective modification of the underlying material. **5** a face pack. **6** a respirator used to filter inhaled air or to supply gas for inhalation. ■ v. **1** cover with a mask. **2** conceal from view; disguise: *brandy did not mask the bitter taste*. **3** cover so as to protect during a particular process, especially painting.
– DERIVATIVES **masked** adj. **masker** n.
– ORIGIN C16: from French *masque*, from Italian *maschera, mascara*, prob. from medieval Latin *masca* 'witch, spectre', but influenced by Arabic *maskara* 'buffoon'.

maskanda /masˈkandə/ ■ n. S. African a popular modernized form of traditional Zulu music.
– ORIGIN from isiZulu *umasikandi* 'conductor of a choir'.

masked ball ■ n. a ball at which participants wear masks to conceal their faces.

masking tape ■ n. adhesive tape used in painting to cover areas on which paint is not wanted.

masochism /ˈmasəkɪz(ə)m/ ■ n. the tendency to derive pleasure, especially sexual gratification, from one's own pain or humiliation.
– DERIVATIVES **masochist** n. **masochistic** adj. **masochistically** adv.
– ORIGIN C19: named after Leopold von Sacher-*Masoch*, the Austrian novelist who described it.

mason ■ n. **1** a builder and worker in stone. **2** (**Mason**) a Freemason. ■ v. build from or strengthen with stone.
– ORIGIN Middle English: from Old French *masson* (n.), *maçonner* (v.), prob. of Germanic origin.

Masonic /məˈsɒnɪk/ ■ adj. of or relating to Freemasons: *a Masonic lodge*.

Masonite ■ n. trademark fibreboard made from wood fibre pulped under steam at high pressure.
– ORIGIN 1920s: from the name of the *Mason* Fibre Co., Laurel, Mississippi.

masonja /mʌˈsɒndʒʌ/ ■ n. (pl. same or **masonjas**) S. African another term for **MOPANE WORM**.
– ORIGIN from Tshivenda *mashonzha*.

masonry ■ n. **1** stonework. ▶ the work of a mason. **2** (**Masonry**) Freemasonry.

masque /mɑːsk/ ■ n. a form of amateur dramatic entertainment, popular in 16th- and 17th-century England, which consisted of dancing and acting performed by masked players.
– DERIVATIVES **masquer** n.
– ORIGIN C16: prob. a back-formation (influenced by French *masque* 'mask') from *masker* 'person wearing a mask'.

masquerade /ˌmɑːskəˈreɪd, ˌmas-/ ■ n. **1** a false show or pretence. **2** a masked ball. ▶ the wearing of disguise. ■ v. pretend to be someone that one is not. ▶ be disguised or passed off as something else: *the idle gossip that masquerades as news*.
– DERIVATIVES **masquerader** n.
– ORIGIN C16: from French *mascarade*, from Italian, from *maschera* 'mask'.

Mass ■ n. the Christian Eucharist or Holy Communion, especially in the Roman Catholic Church. ▶ a musical setting of parts of the liturgy used in the Mass.
– ORIGIN Old English, from eccles. Latin *missa*, from Latin *mittere* 'dismiss', perhaps from the last words of the service, *Ite, missa est* 'Go, it is the dismissal'.

mass ■ n. **1** a coherent body of matter with no definite shape. ▶ any of the main portions in a painting that each have some unity in colour, lighting, etc. **2** a large number of people or objects gathered together. ▶ a large amount of material. **3** (**the mass of**) the majority of. ▶ (**the masses**) the ordinary people. **4** Physics the quantity of matter which a body contains, as measured by its acceleration under a given force or by the force exerted on it by a gravitational field. ▶ (in general use) weight. ■ adj. relating to, done by, or affecting large numbers of people or things: *a mass exodus of refugees*. ■ v. **1** assemble or cause to assemble into a single body or mass. **2** Law S. African consolidate the property of testators for disposition after the surviving testator's death.
– PHRASES **in mass** as a body. **in the mass** as a whole.
– DERIVATIVES **massy** adj. (poetic/literary).
– ORIGIN Middle English: from Old French *masse*, from Latin *massa*, from Greek *maza* 'barley cake'.

massacre ■ n. **1** an indiscriminate and brutal slaughter of people. **2** informal a very heavy defeat. ■ v. **1** deliberately and violently kill (a large number of people). **2** informal inflict a heavy defeat on.
– ORIGIN C16: from French.

mass action ■ n. widespread organized public protest.

massage /ˈmasɑːʒ, məˈsɑːʒ, -dʒ/ ■ n. the rubbing and kneading of muscles and joints of the body with the hands, especially to relieve tension or pain. ■ v. **1** give a massage to. ▶ (**massage something in/into**) rub a substance into (the skin or hair). **2** manipulate (figures) to give a more acceptable result. **3** gently flatter (someone's) ego).
– DERIVATIVES **massager** n.
– ORIGIN C19: from French, from *masser* 'knead, treat with massage', prob. from Portuguese *amassar* 'knead', from *massa* 'dough'.

massage parlour ■ n. an establishment providing massage. ▶ euphemistic a brothel.

mass defect ■ n. Physics the difference between the mass of an isotope and its mass number, representing binding energy.

mass energy ■ n. Physics a body's mass regarded as energy, according to the laws of relativity.

masseter /maˈsiːtə/ ■ n. Anatomy a muscle which runs through the rear part of the cheek and acts to close the

masseur

jaw in chewing.
- ORIGIN C16: from Greek *masētēr*, from *masasthai* 'to chew'.

masseur /ma'sə:/ ■ n. (fem. **masseuse** /ma'sə:z/) a person who provides massage professionally.
- ORIGIN French, from *masser* 'to massage'.

massif /'masıf, ma'si:f/ ■ n. a compact group of mountains.
- ORIGIN C16: French, 'massive', used as a noun.

massive ■ adj. **1** large and heavy or solid. **2** exceptionally large, intense, or severe. **3** Geology (of rocks or beds) having no discernible form or structure. ▶ (of a mineral) not visibly crystalline.
- DERIVATIVES **massively** adv. **massiveness** n.
- ORIGIN Middle English: from French *massif, -ive*, from Latin *massa* (see MASS).

mass market ■ n. the market for goods that are produced in large quantities.

mass noun ■ n. Grammar a noun denoting something which cannot be counted, in English usually a noun which lacks a plural in ordinary usage and is not used with the indefinite article, e.g. *luggage, happiness*. Contrasted with COUNT NOUN.

mass number ■ n. Physics the total number of protons and neutrons in a nucleus.

mass-produce ■ v. produce large quantities of (a standardized article) by an automated mechanical process.
- DERIVATIVES **mass-produced** adj. **mass-producer** n. **mass production** n.

mass spectrograph ■ n. a mass spectrometer in which the particles are detected photographically.

mass spectrometer ■ n. an apparatus for separating isotopes, molecules, and molecular fragments according to mass by ionizing them and making them move in different paths by means of electric and magnetic fields.

mast[1] ■ n. **1** a tall upright post, spar, or other structure on a boat, in sailing vessels generally carrying a sail or sails. **2** any tall upright post, especially a flagpole or a television or radio transmitter.
- PHRASES **before the mast** historical serving as an ordinary seaman. **nail** (or **pin**) **one's colours to the mast** declare openly and firmly what one believes.
- DERIVATIVES **-masted** adj.
- ORIGIN Old English, of West Germanic origin.

mast[2] ■ n. the fruit of beech, oak, chestnut, and other forest trees, especially as food for pigs.
- ORIGIN Old English, of West Germanic origin.

mast cell ■ n. Physiology a cell filled with basophil granules, found in connective tissue and releasing histamine and other substances during inflammatory and allergic reactions.
- ORIGIN C19: *mast* from German *Mast* 'fattening, feeding'.

mastectomy /ma'stɛktəmi/ ■ n. (pl. **-ies**) a surgical operation to remove a breast.
- ORIGIN 1920s: from Greek *mastos* 'breast' + -ECTOMY.

master ■ n. **1** chiefly historical a man who has people working for him, especially servants or slaves. ▶ dated a male head of a household. ▶ the male owner of a dog, cat, etc. **2** a skilled practitioner of a particular art or activity. ▶ a great artist, especially one belonging to the accepted canon. ▶ a very strong chess player. ▶ (**Masters**) [treated as sing.] (in some sports) a class for competitors over the usual age for the highest level of competition. **3** a person who has complete control of something: *he was master of the situation*. **4** a man in charge of an organization or group. ▶ chiefly Brit. a male schoolteacher, especially at a private school. ▶ the head of a college or school. ▶ the presiding officer of a livery company or Masonic lodge. ▶ the captain of a merchant ship. ▶ (in South Africa, England, and Wales) an official of the Supreme Court. **5** [usu. in titles] a person who holds a second or further degree: *a master's degree*. **6** a machine or device directly controlling another. Compare with SLAVE. **7** a title prefixed to the name of a boy. **8** an original film, recording, or document from which copies can be made. ■ adj. **1** having or showing very great skill or proficiency. ▶ denoting a person skilled in a particular trade and able to teach others: *a master builder*. **2** main; principal. ■ v. **1** acquire complete knowledge or skill in. **2** gain control of; overcome. **3** make a master copy of (a film or record).
- DERIVATIVES **masterdom** n. **masterhood** n. **masterless** adj. **mastership** n.
- ORIGIN Old English *mæg(i)ster*, from Latin *magister*.

master-at-arms ■ n. (pl. **masters-at-arms**) a warrant officer appointed to carry out or supervise police duties on board a ship.

masterclass ■ n. a class, especially in music, given by an expert to highly talented students.

masterful ■ adj. **1** powerful and able to control others. **2** performed or performing very skilfully.
- DERIVATIVES **masterfully** adv. **masterfulness** n.

master key ■ n. a key that opens several locks, each of which also has its own key.

masterly ■ adj. performed or performing very skilfully.

mastermind ■ n. a person with outstanding intellect. ▶ a person who plans and directs a complex scheme or enterprise. ■ v. be the mastermind of.

master of ceremonies ■ n. a person in charge of procedure at a state occasion, formal event, or entertainment, introducing the speakers or performers.

masterpiece ■ n. a work of outstanding artistry, skill, or workmanship.

master sergeant ■ n. a high rank of non-commissioned officer in the US armed forces.

masterwork ■ n. a masterpiece.

mastery ■ n. **1** comprehensive knowledge or skill in a particular field. **2** the mastering of a subject or skill. **3** control or superiority over someone or something.

masthead ■ n. **1** the highest part of a ship's mast or of the lower section of a mast. **2** the name of a newspaper or magazine printed at the top of the first or editorial page.

mastic /'mastık/ ■ n. **1** an aromatic gum or resin exuded from the bark of a Mediterranean tree (*Pistacia lentiscus*), used in making varnish and chewing gum and as a flavouring. **2** a putty-like waterproof filler and sealant used in building.
- ORIGIN Middle English: from Greek *mastikhē*, perhaps from *mastikhan* 'masticate'.

masticate /'mastıkeɪt/ ■ v. chew (food).
- DERIVATIVES **mastication** n. **masticator** n. **masticatory** adj.
- ORIGIN C17 (*mastication* Middle English): from late Latin *masticare* 'chew', from Greek *mastikhan* 'grind the teeth'.

mastiff /'mastıf, 'mɑː-/ ■ n. a dog of a large, strong breed with drooping ears and pendulous lips.
- ORIGIN Middle English: from Old French *mastin*, from Latin *mansuetus* 'tame'.

mastitis /ma'staɪtɪs/ ■ n. inflammation of the mammary gland in the breast or udder.
- ORIGIN C19: from Greek *mastos* 'breast'.

mastodon /'mastədɒn/ ■ n. a large extinct elephant-like mammal of the Miocene to Pleistocene epochs.
- ORIGIN C19: from Greek *mastos* 'breast' + *odous, odont-* 'tooth' (with ref. to nipple-shaped tubercles on the crowns of its molar teeth).

mastoid /'mastɔɪd/ ■ adj. Anatomy of or relating to the mastoid process. ■ n. Anatomy the mastoid process. ▶ (**mast-oids**) [treated as sing.] informal mastoiditis.
- ORIGIN C18: from Greek *mastoeidēs* 'breast-shaped', from *mastos* 'breast'.

mastoiditis /ˌmastɔɪˈdʌɪtɪs/ ■ n. Medicine inflammation of the mastoid process.

mastoid process ■ n. a conical prominence of the temporal bone behind the ear, to which neck muscles are attached, and which has air spaces linked to the middle ear.

masturbate /'mastəbeɪt/ ■ v. stimulate one's genitals with one's hand for sexual pleasure.
- DERIVATIVES **masturbation** n. **masturbator** n. **masturbatory** adj.
- ORIGIN C19: from Latin *masturbari* 'masturbate'.

mat[1] ■ n. **1** a thick piece of material placed on the floor and used as protection from dirt, for people to wipe their feet on, or as a decorative rug. ▶ a piece of resilient material for landing on in gymnastics, wrestling, or similar sports. **2** a small piece of cork, card, or similar material

placed on a surface to protect it from the heat or moisture of an object placed on it. **3** (also **mouse mat**) a small piece of rigid or resilient material on which a computer mouse is moved. **4** a thick, untidy layer of hairy or woolly material. ■ v. (**matted, matting**) [usu. as adj. **matted**] tangle in a thick mass: *matted hair*.
– PHRASES **go to the mat** informal vigorously engage in an argument, especially on behalf of another. **on the mat** informal being reprimanded by someone in authority. [with military ref., in which an accused would stand on the orderly room mat.]
– ORIGIN Old English, of West Germanic origin.

mat² ■ adj., n., & v. variant spelling of **MATT**.

Matabele /ˌmatəˈbiːli/ ■ n. the Ndebele people collectively, particularly those of Zimbabwe.
– ORIGIN from Sesotho *matebele*, sing. *letebele*, the name given to this people.

matador /ˈmatədɔː/ ■ n. a bullfighter whose task is to kill the bull.
– ORIGIN Spanish, 'killer', from *matar* 'to kill', from Persian *māt* 'dead'.

match¹ ■ n. **1** a contest in which people or teams compete against each other. **2** a person or thing able to contend with another as an equal. **3** a person or thing that resembles or corresponds to another. ▸ Computing a string that fulfils the specified conditions of a computer search. ▸ a pair that corresponds or is very similar. **4** a person viewed in regard to their eligibility for marriage. ▸ a marriage. ■ v. **1** correspond or cause to correspond in some essential respect; make or be harmonious. **2** be equal to in quality or strength. **3** place in contest or competition with another.
– DERIVATIVES **matchable** adj. **matching** adj.
– ORIGIN Old English *gemæcca* 'mate, companion', of West Germanic origin.

match² ■ n. **1** a short, thin piece of wood or cardboard used to light a fire, being tipped with a composition that ignites when rubbed against a rough surface. **2** historical a piece of wick or cord designed to burn at a uniform rate, used for firing a cannon or lighting gunpowder.
– ORIGIN Middle English: from Old French *meche*, perhaps from Latin *myxa* 'spout of a lamp, lamp wick'.

matchboard ■ n. interlocking boards joined together by tongue and groove.

matchbook ■ n. chiefly N. Amer. a small cardboard folder of matches.

matchbox ■ n. **1** a small box in which matches are sold. **2** [as modifier] very small: *her matchbox apartment*.

matchless ■ adj. unequalled; incomparable.
– DERIVATIVES **matchlessly** adv.

matchlock ■ n. historical a type of gun with a lock in which a piece of wick was used for igniting the powder.

matchmaker ■ n. a person who arranges marriages or initiates relationships between others.
– DERIVATIVES **matchmaking** n.

match play ■ n. play in golf in which the score is reckoned by counting the holes won by each side. Compare with STROKE PLAY.
– DERIVATIVES **match player** n.

match point ■ n. **1** (in tennis and other sports) a point which if won by one of the players will also win them the match. **2** (in duplicate bridge) a unit of scoring in matches and tournaments.

matchstick ■ n. **1** the stem of a match. **2** a long thin piece: *cut the vegetables into matchsticks*. ▸ [as modifier] (of a figure) drawn using thin straight lines.

matchwood ■ n. **1** very small pieces or splinters of wood. **2** light poor-quality wood.

mate¹ ■ n. **1** informal a friend or companion. **2** [in combination] a fellow member or joint occupant: *his table-mates*. **3** the sexual partner of a bird or other animal. **4** an assistant or deputy in some trades: *a plumber's mate*. **5** an officer on a merchant ship subordinate to the master. See also FIRST MATE. ■ v. **1** (with reference to animals or birds) come or bring together for breeding; copulate. **2** join or connect mechanically.
– DERIVATIVES **mateless** adj.
– ORIGIN Middle English: from Middle Low German *māt(e)* 'comrade', of West Germanic origin.

mate² ■ n. & v. Chess short for CHECKMATE.
– ORIGIN Middle English: from Anglo-Norman French *mat*, from the phr. *eschec mat* (see CHECKMATE).

maté /ˈmateɪ/ (also **yerba maté** or **maté tea**) ■ n. a bitter infusion made from the leaves of a South American shrub, which is high in caffeine.
– ORIGIN C18: from Spanish *mate* 'calabash', from Quechua *mati*.

matelassé /ˌmat(ə)ˈlaseɪ/ ■ n. a fabric having a raised design like quilting.
– ORIGIN C19: French, from *matelasser* 'to quilt', from *matelas* 'mattress'.

matelot /ˈmatləʊ/ ■ n. Brit. informal a sailor.
– ORIGIN C19: from French, var. of *matenot*, from Middle Dutch *mattenoot* 'bed companion', because sailors had to share hammocks.

mater /ˈmeɪtə/ ■ n. Brit. informal, dated mother.
– ORIGIN from Latin.

materfamilias /ˌmeɪtəfəˈmɪlɪas/ ■ n. (pl. **matresfamilias**) the female head of a family or household.
– ORIGIN Latin, from *mater* 'mother' + *familias*, from *familia* 'family'.

material ■ n. **1** the matter from which a thing is or can be made. **2** items needed for an activity. **3** information or ideas for use in creating a book, performance, or other work. **3** cloth or fabric. **4** a person of a specified quality or suitability: *he's not really Olympic material*. ■ adj. **1** denoting or consisting of physical objects rather than the mind or spirit: *the material world*. **2** important; essential; relevant: *the insects did not do any material damage*. **3** Philosophy concerned with the matter of reasoning, not its form.
– DERIVATIVES **materiality** n.
– ORIGIN Middle English: from late Latin *materialis*, from Latin *materia* 'matter'.

materialism ■ n. **1** a tendency to consider material possessions and physical comfort as more important than spiritual values. **2** Philosophy the doctrine that nothing exists except matter and its movements and modifications.
– DERIVATIVES **materialist** n. & adj. **materialistic** adj. **materialistically** adv.

materialize (also **-ise**) ■ v. **1** become actual fact; happen. ▸ appear or be present: *the train failed to materialize*. **2** (of a ghost or spirit) appear in bodily form.
– DERIVATIVES **materialization** (also **-isation**) n.

materially ■ adv. **1** substantially; considerably. **2** in terms of material possessions.

materiel /məˌtɪərɪˈɛl/ ■ n. military materials and equipment.
– ORIGIN C19: from French *matériel*.

maternal ■ adj. **1** of or relating to a mother. ▸ denoting feelings associated with or typical of a mother; motherly. **2** related through the mother's side of the family: *maternal grandparents*.
– DERIVATIVES **maternalism** n. **maternalist** adj. **maternalistic** adj. **maternally** adv.
– ORIGIN C15: from French *maternel*, from Latin *maternus*, from *mater* 'mother'.

maternity ■ n. **1** motherhood. **2** [usu. as modifier] the period during pregnancy and shortly after childbirth: *maternity clothes*.

matey (also **maty**) informal ■ adj. (**-ier, -iest**) familiar and friendly: *a matey grin*. ■ n. a familiar form of address to a male.
– DERIVATIVES **mateyness** (also **matiness**) n. **matily** adv.

math ■ n. N. Amer. short for MATHEMATICS.

mathematical ■ adj. **1** of or relating to mathematics. **2** (of a proof or analysis) rigorously precise.
– DERIVATIVES **mathematically** adv.
– ORIGIN Middle English: from Latin *mathematicalis*, from Greek *mathēmatikos*, from *mathēma* 'science', from *manthanein* 'learn'.

mathematics ■ pl. n. [usu. treated as sing.] the branch of science concerned with number, quantity, and space, either as abstract concepts (pure mathematics) or as applied to physics, engineering, and other subjects

maths

(applied mathematics).
- DERIVATIVES **mathematician** n.

maths ■ pl. n. short for MATHEMATICS.

Maties /'mɑːtiz/ ■ n. S. African informal **1** a nickname for the University of Stellenbosch. **2** (also **Matie**) [often as modifier] relating to or associated with the University of Stellenbosch.
- ORIGIN prob. an abbrev. of Afrikaans *tamatie* 'tomato' (because of the colour of Stellenbosch University's rugby jersey).

matinee /'matɪneɪ/ ■ n. an afternoon performance in a theatre or cinema.
- ORIGIN C19: from French *matinée*, 'morning (as a period of activity)', from *matin* 'morning': performances were formerly also in the morning.

matinee coat (also **matinee jacket**) ■ n. Brit. a baby's short coat.

matinee idol ■ n. informal, dated a handsome actor admired chiefly by women.

matins (also **mattins**) ■ n. a service of morning prayer, especially in the Anglican Church. ▶ a service forming part of the traditional Divine Office of the Western Christian Church, originally said (or chanted) at or after midnight.
- ORIGIN Middle English: from Old French *matines*, pl. of *matin* 'morning', from Latin *matutinus* 'early in the morning', from *Matuta*, the name of the dawn goddess.

matjieshuis /'maɪkɪsˌheɪs/ (also **matjies hut**) ■ n. (pl. **matjieshuise**) S. African a traditional Khoikhoi or Nama dwelling consisting of a dome-shaped frame of branches covered by layers of mats.
- ORIGIN from Afrikaans *matjie* 'little mat' + *huis* 'house'.

matriarch /'meɪtrɪɑːk/ ■ n. **1** a woman who is the head of a family or tribe. **2** an older woman who is powerful within a family or organization.
- DERIVATIVES **matriarchal** /-'ɑːk(ə)l/ adj. **matriarchate** n.
- ORIGIN C17: from Latin *mater* 'mother', on the false analogy of *patriarch*.

matriarchy ■ n. (pl. **-ies**) **1** a system of society or government ruled by women. **2** a form of social organization in which descent and relationship are reckoned through the female line.

matric /mə'trɪk/ ■ n. S. African **1** (also **matric exam**) an examination formerly taken in the final year of high school. **2** the certificate obtained by passing this examination. **3** short for MATRICULANT.

matrices plural form of MATRIX.

matric exemption ■ n. S. African a matric examination pass good enough to allow a student to study at university.

matricide /'matrɪsaɪd, 'meɪtrɪ-/ ■ n. the killing of one's mother. ▶ a person who kills their mother.
- DERIVATIVES **matricidal** adj.
- ORIGIN C16: from Latin *matricidium*, from *mater, matr-* 'mother' + *-cidium* (see -CIDE).

matriculant ■ n. **1** S. African a pupil studying for or having passed matric. **2** a person enrolled at a university or college.

matriculate /mə'trɪkjʊleɪt/ ■ v. **1** S. African leave school after passing matric. **2** enrol or be enrolled at a college or university.
- ORIGIN C16: from medieval Latin *matriculare* 'enrol', from late Latin *matricula* 'register', diminutive of Latin *matrix*.

matriculation ■ n. **1** S. African full form of MATRIC. **2** enrolment at a college or university.

matrilineal ■ adj. of or based on kinship with the mother or the female line.
- DERIVATIVES **matrilineally** adv.

matrimony /'matrɪməni/ ■ n. the state or ceremony of being married; marriage.
- DERIVATIVES **matrimonial** adj. **matrimonially** adv.
- ORIGIN Middle English: from Latin *matrimonium*, from *mater, matr-* 'mother'.

matrix /'meɪtrɪks/ ■ n. (pl. **matrices** /-siːz/ or **matrixes**) **1** an environment or material in which something develops. ▶ Biology the substance between cells or in which structures are embedded. **2** a mould in which something is cast or shaped. **3** Mathematics a rectangular array of quantities or expressions in rows and columns that is treated as a single entity and manipulated according to particular rules. ▶ a grid-like array of elements, especially of data items; a lattice. ▶ an organizational structure in which two or more lines of command, responsibility, or communication may run through the same individual. **4** a mass of fine-grained rock in which gems, crystals, or fossils are embedded. **5** fine material.
- ORIGIN Middle English: from Latin, 'breeding female', later 'womb', from *mater* 'mother'.

matron ■ n. **1** a woman in charge of domestic and medical arrangements at a boarding school or other establishment. **2** the woman in charge of the nursing in a hospital. **3** a married woman, typically one who is dignified or staid.
- DERIVATIVES **matronhood** n. **matronly** adj.
- ORIGIN Middle English: from Latin *matrona*, from *mater* 'mother'.

matron of honour ■ n. a married woman attending the bride at a wedding.

matronymic /ˌmatrə'nɪmɪk/ (also **metronymic**) ■ n. a name derived from the name of a mother or female ancestor.
- ORIGIN C18: from Latin *mater, matr-* 'mother', on the pattern of *patronymic*.

matt (also **matte** or **mat**) ■ adj. (of a colour or surface) dull and flat, without a shine. ■ n. **1** a matt colour, paint, or finish. **2** a sheet of cardboard placed on the back of a picture, as a mount to or form a border. ■ v. (**matted, matting**) give a matt appearance to.
- ORIGIN C17: from French *mat*.

matte[1] /mat/ ■ n. an impure product of the smelting of sulphide ores, especially those of copper or nickel.
- ORIGIN C19: from French (in Old French meaning 'curds', from *mat* 'matt'.

matte[2] ■ adj., n., & v. variant spelling of MATT.

matter ■ n. **1** physical substance or material in general, as distinct from mind and spirit; (in physics) that which occupies space and possesses mass, especially as distinct from energy. **2** an affair or situation under consideration; a topic. ▶ (**matters**) the present state of affairs. **3** [usu. with neg. or in questions] (**the matter**) the reason for a problem: *what's the matter?* **4** written or printed material. **5** Logic the particular content of a proposition, as distinct from its form. **6** Law something which is to be tried or proved in court; a case. ■ v. be important or significant.
- PHRASES **for that matter** used to indicate that a subject, though mentioned second, is as relevant as the first. **in the matter of** as regards. **a matter of 1** (of time) no more than: *they were shown the door in a matter of minutes*. **2** a question of. **a matter of course** the natural or expected thing. **a matter of record** a thing that is established as a fact through being officially recorded. **no matter 1** regardless of. **2** it is of no importance.
- ORIGIN Middle English: from Latin *materia* 'timber, substance', also 'subject of discourse', from *mater* 'mother'.

matter of fact ■ n. **1** a fact as distinct from an opinion or conjecture. **2** Law the part of a judicial inquiry concerned with the truth of alleged facts. Often contrasted with MATTER OF LAW. ■ adj. (**matter-of-fact**) **1** concerned only with factual content. **2** unemotional and practical.
- PHRASES **as a matter of fact** in reality; in fact.
- DERIVATIVES **matter-of-factly** adv. **matter-of-factness** n.

matter of law ■ n. Law the part of a judicial inquiry concerned with the interpretation of the law. Often contrasted with MATTER OF FACT.

matting ■ n. material used for mats, especially coarse fabric woven from a natural fibre.

mattins ■ n. variant spelling of MATINS.

mattock ■ n. an agricultural tool similar to a pickaxe, but with one arm of the head curved like an adze and the other like a chisel edge, used for breaking up hard ground, digging up roots, etc.
- ORIGIN Old English *mattuc*.

mattress ■ n. **1** a fabric case filled with soft, firm, or springy material used for sleeping on. **2** Engineering a flat structure of brushwood, concrete, or other material used as strengthening for foundations, embankments, etc.
- ORIGIN Middle English: from Arabic *maṭraḥ* 'carpet or cushion'.

VOWELS **a** cat **ɑː** arm **ɛ** bed **ɛː** hair **ə** ago **əː** her **ɪ** sit **i** cosy **iː** see **ɒ** hot **ɔː** saw **ʌ** run

maturation ■ n. the action or process of maturing.
– DERIVATIVES **maturational** adj. **maturative** adj.

mature ■ adj. (**-er**, **-est**) **1** fully developed physically; full-grown. **2** having reached a stage of mental or emotional development characteristic of an adult; grown-up. **3** having reached the most fully developed stage in a process. ▶ denoting an economy or industry that has developed to a point where substantial expansion no longer takes place. **4** (of certain foodstuffs or drinks) ready for consumption; ripe. **5** (of thought or planning) careful and thorough. **6** (of a bill) due for payment. ■ v. **1** become mature. **2** (of an insurance policy, security, etc.) reach the end of its term and hence become payable.
– DERIVATIVES **maturely** adv.
– ORIGIN Middle English: from Latin *maturus* 'timely, ripe'.

mature student ■ n. an adult student who is older than most other students, especially one who is over 25.

maturity ■ n. **1** the state, fact, or period of being mature. **2** the time when an insurance policy, security, etc. matures.

maty ■ adj. & n. variant spelling of MATEY.

matzo /'matsə, 'matsəʊ/ ■ n. a crisp biscuit of unleavened bread, traditionally eaten by Jews during Passover.
– ORIGIN Yiddish, from Hebrew *maṣṣāh*.

maudlin /'mɔːdlɪn/ ■ adj. self-pityingly or tearfully sentimental.
– ORIGIN Middle English: from Old French *Madeleine*, from eccles. Latin *Magdalena*; the current sense derives from images of Mary Magdalen weeping.

maul ■ v. **1** (of an animal) wound by scratching and tearing. **2** handle or treat savagely or roughly. **3** Rugby take part in a maul. ■ n. Rugby a loose scrum formed around a player with the ball off the ground. Compare with RUCK[1].
– DERIVATIVES **mauler** n.
– ORIGIN Middle English: from Old French *mail*, from Latin *malleus* 'hammer'.

maunder /'mɔːndə/ ■ v. move, talk, or act in a rambling or aimless manner.
– ORIGIN C17: perhaps from obsolete *maunder* 'to beg'.

Mauritanian /ˌmɒrɪ'teɪnɪən/ ■ n. a native or inhabitant of Mauritania, a country in West Africa. ■ adj. of or relating to Mauritania.

Mauritian /mə'rɪʃ(ə)n/ ■ n. a native or inhabitant of the island of Mauritius in the Indian Ocean. ■ adj. of or relating to Mauritius.

Mauritius thorn ■ n. chiefly S. African an evergreen Eurasian shrub which bears clusters of pale yellow flowers. [*Caesalpinia decapetala*.]

mausoleum /ˌmɔːsə'lɪəm, -z-/ ■ n. (pl. **mausolea** /-'lɪə/ or **mausoleums**) a building, especially a large and stately one, housing a tomb or tombs.
– ORIGIN C15: from Greek *Mausōleion*, from *Mausōlos*, the name of a king of Caria (4th century BC), to whose tomb in Halicarnassus the name was orig. applied.

mauve /məʊv/ ■ n. a pale purple colour.
– DERIVATIVES **mauvish** adj.
– ORIGIN C19: from French, 'mallow', from Latin *malva*.

maven /'meɪv(ə)n/ ■ n. N. Amer. informal an expert or connoisseur.
– ORIGIN 1960s: Yiddish.

maverick ■ n. [often as modifier] an unorthodox or independent-minded person: *a maverick politician*.
– ORIGIN C19: from the name of Samuel A. *Maverick*, a Texas rancher who did not brand his cattle.

maw ■ n. the jaws or throat, especially of a voracious animal.
– ORIGIN Old English *maga* (in the sense 'stomach'), of Germanic origin.

mawkish ■ adj. sentimental in a feeble or sickly way.
– DERIVATIVES **mawkishly** adv. **mawkishness** n.
– ORIGIN C17: from obsolete *mawk* 'maggot', from Old Norse *mathkr*, of Germanic origin.

max ■ abbrev. maximum. ■ v. N. Amer. informal reach or cause to reach a limit: *job growth will max out*.

maxi ■ n. (pl. **maxis**) **1** a racing yacht of between approximately 15 and 20 metres in length. **2** [in combination] large or long: *a maxi-skirt*.
– ORIGIN 1960s: abbrev. of MAXIMUM.

maxilla /mak'sɪlə/ ■ n. (pl. **maxillae** /-liː/) Anatomy & Zoology **1** the jaw or jawbone, specifically the upper jaw in most vertebrates. **2** (in many arthropods) each of a pair of mouthparts used in chewing.
– DERIVATIVES **maxillary** adj.
– ORIGIN Middle English: from Latin, 'jaw'.

maxim ■ n. a short, pithy statement expressing a general truth or rule of conduct.
– ORIGIN Middle English: from French *maxime*, from medieval Latin (*propositio*) *maxima* 'most important (proposition)'.

maxima plural form of MAXIMUM.

maximal ■ adj. of or constituting a maximum.
– DERIVATIVES **maximally** adv.

maximize (also **-ise**) ■ v. **1** make as large or great as possible. **2** make the best use of.
– DERIVATIVES **maximization** (also **-isation**) n. **maximizer** (also **-iser**) n.

maximum ■ n. (pl. **maxima** /-mə/ or **maximums**) the greatest amount, extent, or intensity possible or recorded. ■ adj. greatest in amount, extent, or intensity.
– ORIGIN C17: from Latin *maximus* 'greatest'.

maxwell (abbrev.: **Mx**) ■ n. Physics a unit of magnetic flux in the cgs system, equal to that induced through one square centimetre by a perpendicular magnetic field of one gauss.
– ORIGIN C20: named after the Scottish physicist J. C. *Maxwell* (1831–79).

May ■ n. the fifth month of the year.
– ORIGIN Old English, from Old French *mai*, from Latin *Maius* (*mensis*) '(month) of the goddess Maia'.

may[1] ■ modal v. (3rd sing. present **may**; past **might** /maɪt/) **1** expressing possibility. **2** expressing permission. **3** expressing a wish or hope.
– PHRASES **be that as it may** nevertheless. **that is as may be** that may or may not be so.
– ORIGIN Old English *mæg*, of Germanic origin, from a base meaning 'have power'.

may[2] ■ n. the hawthorn or its blossom.
– ORIGIN Middle English: from MAY.

Maya /'maɪ(j)ə, 'meɪ(j)ə/ ■ n. (pl. same or **Mayas**) **1** a member of an American Indian people of Yucatán and other parts of Central America. **2** the language of this people.
– ORIGIN the name in Maya.

maya /'mɑːjə/ ■ n. Hinduism & Buddhism the power by which the universe becomes manifest; the illusion or appearance of the phenomenal world.
– ORIGIN from Sanskrit *māyā*, from *mā* 'create'.

Mayan /'maɪ(j)ən, 'meɪ(j)ən/ ■ adj. denoting or relating to the Maya people or their language.

maybe ■ adv. perhaps; possibly. ■ n. a mere possibility or probability.

May Day ■ n. 1 May, celebrated in many countries as a traditional springtime festival or as an international day honouring workers.

Mayday ■ n. an international radio distress signal used by ships and aircraft.
– ORIGIN 1920s: representing a pronunciation of French *m'aider*, from *venez m'aider* 'come and help me'.

mayest /'meɪɪst/ archaic second person singular present of MAY[1].

mayfly ■ n. (pl. **-flies**) a short-lived slender insect with delicate transparent wings which lives close to water in which its larvae develop. [Order Ephemeroptera: many species.]

mayhap ■ adv. archaic perhaps; possibly.
– ORIGIN C16: from *it may hap*.

mayhem ■ n. violent or damaging disorder; chaos.
– ORIGIN C16: from Old French *mayhem* (see MAIM).

mayn't ■ contr. may not.

mayonnaise ■ n. a thick creamy dressing consisting of egg yolks beaten with oil and vinegar.
– ORIGIN French, prob. from *mahonnais* 'of or from Port Mahon', the capital of Minorca.

mayor

mayor ■ n. the elected head of a municipal administration.
– DERIVATIVES **mayoral** adj. **mayorship** n.
– ORIGIN Middle English: from Old French *maire*, from Latin *major* 'greater'.

mayoralty /'mɛːr(ə)lti/ ■ n. (pl. **-ies**) **1** the office of mayor. **2** the period of office of a mayor.

mayoress /'mɛːrɪs, ˌmɛːˈrɛs/ ■ n. **1** a woman holding the office of mayor. **2** the wife of a mayor.

maypole ■ n. a decorated pole round which people traditionally dance on May Day holding long ribbons attached to the top.

May queen ■ n. a pretty girl chosen and crowned in traditional celebrations of May Day.

mayst archaic second person singular present of **MAY**[1].

maze ■ n. **1** a network of paths and hedges designed as a puzzle through which one has to find a way. **2** a confusing mass of information. ■ v. (**be mazed**) archaic or dialect be dazed and confused.
– DERIVATIVES **mazy** adj. (**-ier**, **-iest**)
– ORIGIN Middle English: prob. from the base of **AMAZE**.

mazel tov /'maz(ə)l ˌtɒːv, ˌtɒf/ ■ exclam. (among Jews) congratulations; good luck.
– ORIGIN from modern Hebrew *mazzāl ṭōḇ* 'good star'.

mazurka /məˈzəːkə, məˈzʊəkə/ ■ n. a lively Polish dance.
– ORIGIN C19: from Polish *mazurka*, denoting a woman of the province Mazovia.

MB ■ abbrev. **1** Bachelor of Medicine. [from Latin *Medicinae Baccalaureus*.] **2** (also **Mb**) Computing megabyte(s).

MBA ■ abbrev. Master of Business Administration.

mbaqanga /ˌ(ə)mbaˈkɑːŋɡa, ˌ(ə)mbaˈlɑːŋɡa/ ■ n. a style of popular music developed in South Africa in the 1950s in which the lead part was originally played on brass instruments.
– ORIGIN from isiZulu *umbaqanga* 'steamed maize bread', with ref. to the notion of basic cultural sustenance.

MBE ■ abbrev. (in the UK) Member of the Order of the British Empire.

mbira /(ə)mˈbɪərə/ ■ n. another term for **THUMB PIANO**.
– ORIGIN C19: from Shona, prob. an alteration of *rimba* 'a note'.

mbube /(ə)mˈbuːbɛ/ ■ n. S. African another term for **ISICATHAMIYA**.

Mbuti /(ə)mˈbuːti/ ■ n. (pl. same or **Mbutis**) a member of a pygmy people of western Uganda and parts of the Democratic Republic of Congo.
– ORIGIN the name in local languages.

Mbyte ■ abbrev. megabyte(s).

MC ■ abbrev. **1** Master of Ceremonies. **2** (in the US) Member of Congress. **3** (in the UK) Military Cross.

Mc ■ abbrev. megacycle(s).

MCC ■ abbrev. Marylebone Cricket Club.

McCarthyism ■ n. a campaign against alleged communists in the US government and other institutions carried out under Senator Joseph McCarthy from 1950–4.
– DERIVATIVES **McCarthyist** adj. & n. **McCarthyite** adj. & n.

McCoy ■ n. (in phr. **the real McCoy**) informal the real thing; the genuine article.
– ORIGIN C19: perhaps from *the real Mackay*, an advertising slogan used by the whisky distillers G. Mackay and Co.; the form *McCoy* may come from the name of an American inventor Elijah McCoy.

mcg ■ abbrev. microgram.

McGuffin ■ n. an object or device in a film or a book which serves merely as a trigger for the plot.
– ORIGIN C20: a Scottish surname, said to have been borrowed by the English film director Alfred Hitchcock.

MCh (also **M Chir**) ■ abbrev. Master of Surgery.
– ORIGIN from Latin *Magister Chirurgiae*.

McJob /məkˈdʒɒb/ ■ n. a low-paid job with few prospects, typically one taken by an overqualified person.

MCom ■ abbrev. Master of Commerce.

MD ■ abbrev. **1** Doctor of Medicine. [from Latin *Medicinae Doctor*.] **2** Managing Director.

Md ■ symb. the chemical element mendelevium.

MDF ■ abbrev. medium density fibreboard.

MDMA ■ abbrev. methylenedioxymethamphetamine, the drug Ecstasy.

ME ■ abbrev. **1** Middle English. **2** Medicine myalgic encephalomyelitis.

me[1] ■ pron. [first person sing.] used by a speaker to refer to himself or herself as the object of a verb or preposition. ► used after the verb 'to be' and after 'than' or 'as'.
– PHRASES **me and mine** my relatives.
– ORIGIN Old English *mē*, accusative and dative of I[2], of Germanic origin.

me[2] (also **mi**) ■ n. Music (in tonic sol-fa) the third note of a major scale. ► the note E in the fixed-doh system.
– ORIGIN Middle English *mi*, representing (as an arbitrary name for the note) the first syllable of *mira*, taken from a Latin hymn.

mea culpa /ˌmeɪə ˈkʊlpə, ˌmiːə ˈkʌlpə/ ■ n. an acknowledgement of one's fault or error.
– ORIGIN Latin, 'by my fault'.

mead[1] ■ n. an alcoholic drink of fermented honey and water.
– ORIGIN Old English *me(o)du*, of Germanic origin.

mead[2] ■ n. poetic/literary a meadow.
– ORIGIN Old English *mǣd*, of Germanic origin.

meadow ■ n. **1** an area of grassland, especially one used for hay. **2** a piece of low ground near a river.
– DERIVATIVES **meadowy** adj.
– ORIGIN Old English *mǣdwe*, from *mǣd* (see **MEAD**[2]).

meadowsweet ■ n. a tall Eurasian plant with heads of creamy-white fragrant flowers, growing typically in damp meadows. [*Filipendula ulmaria*].

meagre (US **meager**) ■ adj. **1** lacking in quantity or quality. **2** lean; thin.
– DERIVATIVES **meagrely** adv. **meagreness** n.
– ORIGIN Middle English: from Old French *maigre*, from Latin *macer*.

meal[1] ■ n. any of the regular daily occasions when food is eaten. ► the food eaten on such an occasion.
– PHRASES **make a meal of** informal carry out (a task) with unnecessary effort or thoroughness. **meals on wheels** meals delivered to old people or invalids who cannot cook for themselves.
– ORIGIN Old English *mǣl*, of Germanic origin.

meal[2] ■ n. **1** the edible part of any grain or pulse ground to powder. **2** any powdery substance made by grinding: *herring meal*.
– ORIGIN Old English *melu, meolo*, of Germanic origin.

meal beetle ■ n. a dark brown beetle which is a pest of stored grain and cereal products. [*Tenebrio molitor*.]

mealie (also **mielie**) ■ n. chiefly S. African a maize plant or cob.
– ORIGIN C19: from Afrikaans *mielie*, from Portuguese *milho* 'maize, millet'.

mealiemeal ■ n. coarse or finely-ground maize meal.

mealie pap ■ n. S. African porridge made from ground maize meal.

mealie rice ■ n. S. African crushed maize kernels, often used as an inexpensive substitute for rice.

meal ticket ■ n. a person or thing that is exploited as a source of regular income.

mealtime ■ n. the time at which a meal is eaten.

mealworm ■ n. the larva of the meal beetle, used as food for cage birds and other insectivorous animals.

mealy ■ adj. (**-ier**, **-iest**) **1** of, like, or containing meal. **2** pale in colour.
– DERIVATIVES **mealiness** n.

mealy bug ■ n. a small sap-sucking scale insect which is coated with a white powdery wax resembling meal and which can be a serious pest. [*Pseudococcus* and other genera.]

mealy-mouthed ■ adj. reluctant to speak frankly.
– ORIGIN C16: perhaps from German *Mehl im Maule behalten* 'carry meal in the mouth', i.e. be unstraightforward in speech, or rel. to Latin *mel* 'honey'.

mean¹ ■ v. (past and past part. **meant**) **1** intend to convey or refer to. ▶ (of a word) have as its signification in the same language or its equivalent in another language. ▶ (**mean something to**) be of a specified degree of importance to. **2** intend to occur or be the case. ▶ (often **be meant for**) design or destine for a particular purpose. ▶ (**mean something by**) have as a motive or excuse in explanation. **3** have as a consequence or result.
– PHRASES **mean business** be in earnest. **mean well** have good intentions, but not always the ability to carry them out.
– ORIGIN Old English *mænan*, of West Germanic origin.

mean² ■ adj. **1** unwilling to give or share money. **2** unkind or unfair. ▶ vicious or aggressive. **3** poor in quality and appearance. ▶ (of a person's mental ability) inferior. **4** dated of low birth or social class. **5** informal excellent.
– PHRASES **no mean —** very good of its kind: *it was no mean feat*.
– DERIVATIVES **meanly** adv. **meanness** n.
– ORIGIN Middle English, shortening of Old English *gemæne*, of Germanic origin.

mean³ ■ n. **1** (also **arithmetic mean**) the average of a set of quantities. **2** a condition, quality, or course of action equally removed from two opposite extremes. ■ adj. **1** calculated as a mean. **2** equally far from two extremes.
– ORIGIN Middle English: from Old French *meien*, from Latin *medianus* (see MEDIAN).

meander /mɪˈandə, miː-/ ■ v. **1** (of a river or road) follow a winding course. **2** wander aimlessly. ■ n. **1** a winding curve or bend. **2** a circuitous journey.
– ORIGIN C16: from Latin *maeander*, from Greek *Maiandros, Menderes*, the name of a river of SW Turkey.

meaning ■ n. **1** what is meant by a word, text, concept, or action. **2** worthwhile quality; purpose. ■ adj. expressive: *she gave him a meaning look*.
– DERIVATIVES **meaningless** adj. **meaninglessly** adv. **meaninglessness** n. **meaningly** adv.

meaningful ■ adj. **1** having meaning. ▶ Logic having a recognizable function in a logical language or other sign system. **2** worthwhile. **3** expressive.
– DERIVATIVES **meaningfully** adv. **meaningfulness** n.

means ■ pl. n. **1** [treated as sing. or pl.] an action or system by which a result is achieved. **2** financial resources; income. ▶ substantial resources; wealth.
– PHRASES **by all means** of course. **by any means** [with neg.] at all. **by means of** by using. **by no means** (or **by no manner of means**) certainly not. **a means to an end** a thing that is not valued in itself but is useful in achieving an aim.
– ORIGIN Middle English: pl. of MEAN³, the early sense being 'intermediary'.

mean sea level ■ n. the sea level halfway between the mean levels of high and low water.

means test ■ n. an official investigation into a person's financial circumstances to determine their eligibility for state assistance. ■ v. (**means-test**) [usu. as adj. **means-tested**] make conditional on a means test.

meant past and past participle of MEAN¹.

meantime ■ adv. (also **in the meantime**) meanwhile.

meanwhile ■ adv. **1** (also **in the meanwhile**) in the intervening period of time. **2** at the same time.

measles ■ pl. n. [treated as sing.] an infectious viral disease causing fever and a red rash, typically occurring in childhood.
– ORIGIN Middle English, prob. from Middle Dutch *masel* 'pustule'.

measly ■ adj. (**-ier, -iest**) informal contemptibly small or few.
– ORIGIN C16: from MEASLES.

measurable ■ adj. able or large enough to be measured.
– DERIVATIVES **measurability** n. **measurably** adv.

measure ■ v. ascertain the size, amount, or degree of (something) by comparison with a standard unit or with an object of known size. ▶ be of (a specified size or degree). ▶ (**measure something out**) take an exact quantity of something. ▶ assess the extent, quality, value, or effect of. ▶ (**measure up**) reach the required or expected standard. ■ n. **1** a means of achieving a purpose: *cost-cutting measures*. ▶ a legislative bill. **2** standard

mechanical engineering

unit used to express size, amount, or degree. ▶ an instrument such as a container, rod, or tape marked with standard units and used for measuring. **3** (**a measure of**) a certain amount or degree of. ▶ an indication of extent or quality. **4** the rhythm of a piece of poetry or a piece of music. ▶ a particular metrical unit or group. ▶ N. Amer. a bar of music or the time of a piece of music. **5** archaic a dance. **6** (**measures**) Geology a group of rock strata. **7** Printing the width of a full line of type or print, typically expressed in picas.
– PHRASES **beyond measure** to a very great extent. **for good measure** as an amount or item beyond that which is strictly required. **get** (or **take** or **have**) **the measure of** assess or have assessed the character or abilities of. **in — measure** to the degree specified.
– ORIGIN Middle English: from Old French *mesure*, from Latin *mensura*, from *metiri* 'measure'.

measured ■ adj. **1** having a slow, regular rhythm. **2** (of speech or writing) deliberate and restrained.
– DERIVATIVES **measuredly** adv.

measureless ■ adj. having no limits.

measurement ■ n. the action of measuring. ▶ an amount, size, or extent as established by measuring. ▶ a unit or system of measuring.

meat ■ n. **1** the flesh of an animal (especially a mammal) as food. ▶ chiefly US the edible part of fruits, nuts, or eggs. ▶ archaic food of any kind. **2** (**the meat of**) the essence or chief part of.
– PHRASES **be meat and drink to** Brit. **1** be a source of great pleasure to. **2** be a routine matter for. **easy meat** informal a person or animal that is easily overcome or outwitted. **meat and potatoes** chiefly N. Amer. ordinary but fundamental things.
– DERIVATIVES **meatless** adj.
– ORIGIN Old English *mete* 'food', of Germanic origin.

meatball ■ n. a ball of minced or chopped meat.

meat loaf ■ n. minced or chopped meat moulded into the shape of a loaf and baked.

meatus /mɪˈeɪtəs/ ■ n. (pl. same or **meatuses**) Anatomy a passage or opening leading to the interior of the body.
– ORIGIN Middle English: from Latin, 'passage' from *meare* 'to flow, run'.

meaty ■ adj. (**-ier, -iest**) **1** resembling or full of meat. **2** brawny. **3** full of substance.
– DERIVATIVES **meatily** adv. **meatiness** n.

mebos /ˈmɪbɒs/ ■ n. S. African a kind of confectionery made from pulped apricots or other fruit, sun-dried, sugared, and formed into a slab or roll.
– ORIGIN from S. African Dutch, prob. from Japanese *umeboshi* 'pickled and dried plums'.

MEC ■ abbrev. (in South Africa) Member of the Executive Committee (of a provincial government).

Mecca ■ n. (**a Mecca**) a place which attracts people of a particular group or with a particular interest.
– ORIGIN from the city of *Mecca* in Saudi Arabia, considered by Muslims to be the holiest city of Islam.

mechanic ■ n. a skilled worker who repairs and maintains machinery.
– ORIGIN Middle English: from Greek *mēkhanikos*, from *mēkhanē* (see MACHINE).

mechanical ■ adj. **1** working or produced by machines or machinery. ▶ of or relating to machines or machinery. **2** lacking thought or spontaneity. **3** relating to physical forces or motion. ▶ (of a theory) explaining phenomena in terms only of physical processes. ■ n. (**mechanicals**) the working parts of a machine, especially a car.
– DERIVATIVES **mechanically** adv.

mechanical advantage ■ n. the ratio of the force produced by a machine to the force applied to it.

mechanical drawing ■ n. a scale drawing of a mechanical or architectural structure done with precision instruments.

mechanical engineering ■ n. the branch of engineering concerned with the design, construction, and use of machines.
– DERIVATIVES **mechanical engineer** n.

mechanician

mechanician ■ n. a person skilled in the design or construction of machinery.

mechanics ■ pl. n. 1 [treated as sing.] the branch of applied mathematics concerned with motion and forces producing motion. ▶ machinery as a subject. 2 the machinery or working parts of something. ▶ the practicalities or details of something.

mechanism ■ n. 1 a piece of machinery. 2 a process by which something takes place or is brought about. 3 Philosophy the doctrine that all natural phenomena allow mechanical explanation by physics and chemistry.
– DERIVATIVES **mechanist** n.
– ORIGIN C17: from Greek *mēkhanē* (see MACHINE).

mechanistic ■ adj. Philosophy of or relating to mechanism.
– DERIVATIVES **mechanistically** adv.

mechanize (also **-ise**) ■ v. introduce machines or automatic devices into. ▶ equip (a military force) with modern weapons and vehicles.
– DERIVATIVES **mechanization** (also **-isation**) n. **mechanizer** (also **-iser**) n.

mechanoreceptor ■ n. Zoology a sense organ or cell that responds to mechanical stimuli such as touch or sound.
– DERIVATIVES **mechanoreceptive** adj.

mechatronics ■ pl. n. [treated as sing.] technology combining electronics and mechanical engineering.
– ORIGIN 1980s: blend of MECHANICS and ELECTRONICS.

MEcon ■ abbrev. Master of Economics.

meconium /mɪˈkəʊnɪəm/ ■ n. Medicine the dark green substance forming the first faeces of a newborn infant.
– ORIGIN C18: from Latin, 'poppy juice'.

MEd ■ abbrev. Master of Education.

Med ■ n. (**the Med**) informal the Mediterranean Sea.

med. ■ abbrev. medium.

médaillon /ˌmeɪdʌɪˈjɒ̃/ ■ n. (pl. pronounced same) a small flat round or oval cut of meat or fish.
– ORIGIN French, 'medallion'.

medal ■ n. a metal disc with an inscription or design, awarded to acknowledge distinctive achievement or made to commemorate an event.
– DERIVATIVES **medalled** adj. **medallic** adj.
– ORIGIN C16: from French *médaille*, from medieval Latin *medalia* 'half a denarius'.

medallion ■ n. 1 a piece of jewellery in the shape of a medal, worn as a pendant. 2 an oval or circular painting, panel, or design used to decorate a building or textile.
– ORIGIN C17: from French *médaillon*, from Italian *medaglione*, from *medaglia* (see MEDAL).

medallist (US **medalist**) ■ n. 1 an athlete or other person awarded a medal. 2 an engraver or designer of medals.

medal play ■ n. Golf another term for STROKE PLAY.

meddle ■ v. (usu. **meddle in/with**) interfere in something that is not one's concern.
– DERIVATIVES **meddler** n. **meddlesome** adj. **meddlesomeness** n.
– ORIGIN Middle English: from Old French *medler*, var. of *mesler*, from Latin *miscere* 'to mix'.

Mede /miːd/ ■ n. a member of an Indo-European people who inhabited ancient Media (present-day Azerbaijan, NW Iran, and NE Iraq), establishing an extensive empire during the 7th century BC.
– DERIVATIVES **Median** adj.

medevac /ˈmɛdɪvak/ (also **medivac**) ■ n. the evacuation of military or other casualties to hospital by air. ■ v. (**medevacked**, **medevacking**) transport to hospital in this way.
– ORIGIN 1960s: blend of MEDICAL and *evacuation* (see EVACUATE).

medfly ■ n. (pl. **-flies**) another term for MEDITERRANEAN FRUIT FLY.

media[1] /ˈmiːdɪə/ ■ n. 1 plural form of MEDIUM. 2 [treated as sing. or pl.] the main means of mass communication (especially television, radio, and newspapers) regarded collectively.

> **USAGE**
> The word **media** comes from the Latin plural of **medium**. The traditional view is that it should therefore be treated as a plural noun in all its senses in English. In practice, in the sense 'television, radio, and the press collectively', it behaves as a collective noun (like **staff** or **clergy**, for example), which means that it is acceptable in standard English for it to take either a singular or a plural verb.

media[2] /ˈmiːdɪə/ ■ n. (pl. **mediae** /-diː/) Anatomy an intermediate layer, especially in the wall of a blood vessel.
– ORIGIN C19: shortening of modern Latin *tunica* (or *membrana*) *media* 'middle sheath (or layer)'.

mediaeval ■ adj. variant spelling of MEDIEVAL.

media event ■ n. an event intended primarily to attract publicity.

medial ■ adj. 1 situated in the middle. 2 Phonetics pronounced in the middle of the mouth.
– DERIVATIVES **medially** adv.
– ORIGIN C16: from late Latin *medialis*, from Latin *medius* 'middle'.

median /ˈmiːdɪən/ ■ adj. 1 technical, chiefly Anatomy situated in the middle, especially of the body. 2 denoting or relating to a value or quantity lying at the mid point of a frequency distribution of observed values or quantities, such that there is an equal probability of falling above or below it. ▶ denoting the middle term (or mean of the middle two terms) of a series arranged in order of magnitude. ■ n. 1 a median value. 2 (also **median strip**) the strip of land between the carriageways of a highway or other major road. 3 Geometry a straight line drawn from any vertex of a triangle to the middle of the opposite side.
– DERIVATIVES **medianly** adv.
– ORIGIN Middle English: from medieval Latin *medianus*, from *medius* 'mid'.

mediant /ˈmiːdɪənt/ ■ n. Music the third note of the diatonic scale of any key.
– ORIGIN C18: from French *médiante*, from Italian *mediante* 'coming between'.

mediastinum /ˌmiːdɪəˈstʌɪnəm/ ■ n. (pl. **mediastina** /-nə/) Anatomy a membranous partition, especially that between the lungs.
– DERIVATIVES **mediastinal** adj.
– ORIGIN Middle English: from medieval Latin *mediastinus* 'medial', from Latin *medius* 'middle'.

mediate ■ v. /ˈmiːdɪeɪt/ 1 intervene in a dispute to bring about an agreement or reconciliation. 2 technical be a medium for (a process or effect). ■ adj. /ˈmiːdɪət/ involving an intermediate agency.
– DERIVATIVES **mediately** adv. **mediation** n. **mediator** n. **mediatory** /ˈmiːdɪət(ə)ri/ adj.
– ORIGIN Middle English: from late Latin *mediare* 'place in the middle', from Latin *medius* 'middle'.

medic /ˈmɛdɪk/ ■ n. informal a medical practitioner or student.
– ORIGIN C17: from Latin *medicus* 'physician'.

Medicaid ■ n. (in the US) a federal system of health insurance for those requiring financial assistance.
– ORIGIN 1960s: from MEDICAL + AID.

medical ■ adj. of or relating to the science or practice of medicine. ■ n. an examination to assess a person's state of physical health or fitness.
– DERIVATIVES **medically** adv.
– ORIGIN C17: from medieval Latin *medicalis*, from Latin *medicus* 'physician'.

medical aid ■ n. S. African private health insurance.

medical certificate ■ n. a doctor's certificate giving the state of a person's health with regard to their fitness or unfitness to work.

medical officer ■ n. a doctor in charge of the health services of a civilian or military authority or other organization.

medical practitioner ■ n. a physician or surgeon.

medicament /mɪˈdɪkəm(ə)nt, ˈmɛdɪk-/ ■ n. a medicinal substance.

–ORIGIN Middle English: from Latin *medicamentum*, from *medicari* (see MEDICATE).

medicate ■ v. administer medicine or a drug to. ▸ add a medicinal substance to.
–DERIVATIVES **medicative** adj.
–ORIGIN C17 (*medication* Middle English): from Latin *medicari* 'administer remedies to'.

medication ■ n. a medicine or drug. ▸ treatment using drugs.

medicinal ■ adj. having healing properties. ▸ relating to medicines or drugs. ■ n. a medicinal substance.
–DERIVATIVES **medicinally** adv.

medicine ■ n. **1** the science or practice of the diagnosis, treatment, and prevention of disease (in technical use often taken to exclude surgery). **2** a drug or other preparation for the treatment or prevention of disease. **3** (in some traditional societies) a spell, charm, or fetish believed to have healing or magical power.
–PHRASES **give someone a dose** (or **taste**) **of their own medicine** give someone the same bad treatment that they have given to others. **take one's medicine** submit to punishment as being deserved.
–ORIGIN Middle English: from Latin *medicina*, from *medicus* 'physician'.

medicine ball ■ n. a large, heavy solid ball thrown and caught for exercise.

medicine man ■ n. (among North American Indians and some other peoples) a shaman. ▸ S. African another term for INYANGA or SANGOMA.

medico ■ n. (pl. **-os**) informal a medical practitioner or student.
–ORIGIN C17: from Latin *medicus* 'physician'.

medico- ■ comb. form relating to the field of medicine: *medico-social*.
–ORIGIN from Latin *medicus* 'physician'.

medieval /ˌmɛdɪˈiːv(ə)l, miː-/ (also **mediaeval**) ■ adj. of or relating to the Middle Ages. ▸ informal very old-fashioned or outdated.
–DERIVATIVES **medievalism** n. **medievalist** n. **medievally** adv.
–ORIGIN C19: from modern Latin *medium aevum* 'middle age'.

medieval Latin ■ n. Latin of about AD 600–1500.

medina /mɛˈdiːnə/ ■ n. the old quarter of a North African town.
–ORIGIN Arabic, 'town'.

mediocre /ˌmiːdɪˈəʊkə/ ■ adj. of only moderate or average quality.
–DERIVATIVES **mediocrely** adv. **mediocrity** n. (pl. **-ies**).
–ORIGIN C16: from French *médiocre*, from Latin *mediocris* 'of middle height or degree', literally 'somewhat mountainous'.

meditate ■ v. **1** focus one's mind for a period of time for spiritual purposes or as a method of relaxation. **2** (often **meditate on/upon**) think carefully about.
–DERIVATIVES **meditative** adj. **meditatively** adv. **meditativeness** n. **meditator** n.
–ORIGIN C16 (*meditation* Middle English): from Latin *meditari* 'contemplate', from a base meaning 'measure'.

meditation ■ n. **1** the action or practice of meditating. **2** a discourse expressing considered thoughts on a subject.

Mediterranean /ˌmɛdɪtəˈreɪnɪən/ ■ adj. of or characteristic of the Mediterranean Sea, the countries bordering it, or their inhabitants. ■ n. a native of a Mediterranean country.
–ORIGIN C16: from Latin *mediterraneus* 'inland', from *medius* 'middle' + *terra* 'land'.

Mediterranean climate ■ n. a climate distinguished by warm, wet winters under prevailing westerly winds and calm, hot, dry summers.

Mediterranean fruit fly ■ n. a fruit fly whose larvae are a pest of citrus fruit in many parts of the world. [*Ceratitis capitata*.]

medium ■ n. (pl. **media** or **mediums**) **1** an agency or means of doing something. ▸ the material or form used by an artist, composer, or writer. **2** a substance through which sensory impressions are conveyed or physical forces are transmitted. **3** a liquid (e.g. oil) with which pigments are mixed to make paint. **4** (pl. **mediums**) a person claiming to be able to communicate between the dead and the living. **5** the middle quality or state between two extremes. **6** the substance in which an organism lives or is cultured. ■ adj. between two extremes; average.
–DERIVATIVES **mediumistic** adj. **mediumship** n.
–ORIGIN C16: from Latin, 'middle'.

medium wave ■ n. a radio wave of a frequency between 300 kHz and 3 MHz. ▸ broadcasting using such radio waves.

medivac ■ n. & v. variant spelling of MEDEVAC.

medlar ■ n. **1** a small bushy European tree of the rose family. [*Mespilus germanica*.] **2** the small brown apple-like fruit of this tree, edible once it has begun to decay.
–ORIGIN Middle English: from Old French *medler*, from *medle* 'medlar fruit', from Greek *mespilē*.

medley ■ n. (pl. **-eys**) a varied mixture. ▸ a collection of songs or other musical items performed as a continuous piece. ▸ a swimming race in which contestants swim sections in different strokes.
–ORIGIN Middle English: from Old French *medlee*, var. of *meslee* 'melee', from medieval Latin *misculare* 'to mix'.

Médoc /ˈmeɪdɒk/ ■ n. (pl. same) a red wine produced in the Médoc area of SW France.

medrese /mɛˈdrɛseɪ/ ■ n. variant spelling of MADRASA.

medulla /mɛˈdʌlə/ ■ n. Anatomy **1** a distinct inner region of an organ or tissue, especially a kidney, the adrenal gland, or hair. **2** Botany the soft internal tissue or pith of a plant.
–DERIVATIVES **medullary** adj.
–ORIGIN Middle English: from Latin, 'pith or marrow'.

medulla oblongata /ˌɒblɒŋˈɡɑːtə/ ■ n. the continuation of the spinal cord within the skull, forming the lowest part of the brainstem.
–ORIGIN C17: modern Latin, 'elongated medulla'.

medusa /mɪˈdjuːzə, -sə/ ■ n. (pl. **medusae** /-ziː, -siː/ or **medusas**) Zoology the free-swimming sexual form of a jellyfish or other coelenterate, typically umbrella-shaped with stinging tentacles around the edge. Compare with POLYP.
–DERIVATIVES **medusoid** adj. & n.
–ORIGIN C18: named after *Medusa*, the name of a gorgon in Greek mythology with snakes in her hair.

meek ■ adj. quiet, gentle, and submissive.
–DERIVATIVES **meekly** adv. **meekness** n.
–ORIGIN Middle English, from Old Norse *mjúkr* 'soft, gentle'.

meerkat /ˈmɪəkat/ (also **meercat**) ■ n. a small southern African mammal with a long body and tail, especially the suricate (*Suricata suricatta*) and some species of mongoose.
–ORIGIN C18: from S. African Dutch, from Dutch, from *meer* 'sea' + *kat* 'cat'.

meerschaum /ˈmɪəʃɔːm, -ʃəm/ ■ n. a soft white clay-like material consisting of hydrated magnesium silicate, found chiefly in Turkey. ▸ a tobacco pipe with a bowl made from this.
–ORIGIN C18: from German, 'sea-foam', translation of Persian *kef-i-daryā* (alluding to its frothy appearance).

meet[1] ■ v. (past and past part. **met**) **1** arrange or happen to come into the presence or company of. ▸ make the acquaintance of for the first time. ▸ come together as opponents in a contest. ▸ experience (a particular situation or attitude). ▸ (**meet something with**) have (a particular reaction) to something: *the announcement was met with silence.* ▸ (**meet with**) receive (a particular reaction). **2** touch; join. **3** fulfil or satisfy (a requirement or condition). ▸ pay (a required amount). ■ n. **1** a gathering of riders and hounds before a hunt begins. **2** an organized event at which a number of races or other sporting contests are held.
–PHRASES **meet the case** Brit. be adequate. **meet someone's eye** (or **eyes** or **ear**) be visible (or audible). **meet someone's eye** (or **eyes** or **gaze**) look directly at someone. **meet someone halfway** make a compromise with someone.
–ORIGIN Old English *mētan* 'come upon', of Germanic origin.

meet

meet² ■ adj. archaic suitable or proper.
– DERIVATIVES **meetly** adv. **meetness** n.
– ORIGIN Middle English: shortening of Old English *gemǣte*, of Germanic origin.

meeting ■ n. **1** an assembly of people for a particular purpose, especially for formal discussion. ▶ an organized event at which a number of races or other sporting contests are held. **2** an instance of two or more people meeting.

meeting ground ■ n. a common area of knowledge or interest.

meeting house ■ n. a Quaker place of worship.

mefloquine /ˈmɛfləkwiːn/ ■ n. Medicine an antimalarial drug consisting of a fluorinated derivative of quinoline.
– ORIGIN 1970s: from *me(thyl)* + *fl(uor)o* + *quin(olin)e*.

mega informal ■ adj. **1** huge. **2** excellent. ■ adv. extremely.
– ORIGIN 1980s: independent usage of MEGA-.

mega- ■ comb. form **1** large: *megalith*. **2** denoting a factor of one million (10^6): *megahertz*. **3** Computing denoting a factor of 2^{20}.
– ORIGIN from Greek *megas* 'great'.

megabit ■ n. Computing a unit of data size or network speed, equal to one million or (strictly) 1 048 576 bits (per second).

megabuck ■ n. (**megabucks**) informal a huge sum of money.

megabyte (abbrev.: **Mb** or **MB**) ■ n. Computing a unit of information equal to one million or (strictly) 1 048 576 bytes.

megacity ■ n. **1** a city with a population of more than 10 million. **2** S. African another term for UNICITY.

megacycle ■ n. a unit of frequency equal to one million cycles.

megadeath ■ n. a unit used in quantifying the casualties of nuclear war, equal to the deaths of one million people.

megafauna ■ n. Zoology the large animals of a particular region, habitat, or geological period.
– DERIVATIVES **megafaunal** adj.

megaflop ■ n. Computing a unit of computing speed equal to one million or (strictly) 1 048 576 floating-point operations per second.

megahertz (abbrev.: **MHz**) ■ n. (pl. same) a unit of frequency equal to one million hertz.

megalith ■ n. Archaeology a large stone that forms a prehistoric monument or part of one.
– ORIGIN C19: back-formation from MEGALITHIC.

megalithic ■ adj. Archaeology made of, denoting, or marked by the use of megaliths.
– ORIGIN C19: from MEGA- + Greek *lithos* 'stone'.

megalo- /ˈmɛɡələʊ/ ■ comb. form great: *megalopolis*.
– ORIGIN from Greek *megas*, *megal-* 'great'.

megalomania ■ n. obsession with the exercise of power. ▶ delusion about one's own power or importance (typically as a symptom of manic or paranoid disorder).
– DERIVATIVES **megalomaniac** n. & adj. **megalomaniacal** adj. **megalomanic** adj.

megalopolis /ˌmɛɡəˈlɒp(ə)lɪs/ ■ n. a very large, heavily populated city or urban complex.
– DERIVATIVES **megalopolitan** n. & adj.
– ORIGIN C19 (*megalopolitan* C17): from MEGALO- + Greek *polis* 'city'.

megalosaurus /ˌmɛɡ(ə)ləˈsɔːrəs/ ■ n. a large carnivorous bipedal dinosaur of the mid Jurassic period.

megaphone ■ n. a large funnel-shaped device for amplifying and directing the voice.
– DERIVATIVES **megaphonic** adj.

megapixel ■ n. Computing a unit of graphic resolution equivalent to 2^{20} or (strictly) 1 048 576 pixels.

megastar ■ n. informal a very famous person in the world of entertainment or sport.
– DERIVATIVES **megastardom** n.

megastore ■ n. a very large shop, typically one specializing in a particular type of product.

megaton ■ n. a unit of explosive power equivalent to one million tons of TNT.

megavolt (abbrev.: **MV**) ■ n. a unit of electromotive force equal to one million volts.

megawatt (abbrev.: **MW**) ■ n. a unit of electrical or other power equal to one million watts.

me generation ■ n. a generation of people characterized by selfish materialism.

Megger /ˈmɛɡə/ ■ n. trademark an instrument for measuring the resistance of electrical insulation.
– ORIGIN C20: perhaps from MEGOHM.

Megillah /məˈɡɪlə/ ■ n. each of the books of the Hebrew scriptures (the Song of Solomon, Ruth, Lamentations, Ecclesiastes, and Esther) appointed to be read on certain Jewish notable days.
– ORIGIN from Hebrew *měgillāh* 'scroll'.

megohm /ˈmɛɡəʊm/ ■ n. a unit of electrical resistance equal to one million ohms.

megrim /ˈmiːɡrɪm/ ■ n. archaic **1** (**megrims**) low spirits. **2** a whim or fancy.
– ORIGIN Middle English: var. of MIGRAINE.

meibomian /maɪˈbəʊmɪən/ ■ adj. Anatomy relating to or denoting large sebaceous glands of the human eyelid, whose infection results in inflammation and swelling.
– ORIGIN C19: from the name of the C18 German anatomist Heinrich *Meibom*.

meiosis /maɪˈəʊsɪs/ ■ n. (pl. **meioses** /-siːz/) **1** Biology a type of cell division that results in daughter cells each with half the number of chromosomes of the parent cell. Compare with MITOSIS. **2** another term for LITOTES.
– DERIVATIVES **meiotic** adj. **meiotically** adv.
– ORIGIN C16: from Greek *meiōsis*, from *meioun* 'lessen'.

meisie /ˈmaɪsi/ ■ n. S. African informal a girl or young woman, especially an Afrikaner. ▶ a person's girlfriend.
– ORIGIN Afrikaans, from Dutch *meisje* 'girl'.

Meissen /ˈmaɪs(ə)n/ ■ n. fine hard-paste porcelain produced at Meissen in Germany since 1710.

meitnerium /maɪtˈnɪərɪəm/ ■ n. the chemical element of atomic number 109, a very unstable element made by high-energy atomic collisions. (Symbol: **Mt**)
– ORIGIN 1990s: from the name of the Swedish physicist Lise *Meitner*.

melamine /ˈmɛləmiːn/ ■ n. **1** Chemistry a white crystalline compound made by heating cyanamide. **2** a plastic made by polymerizing this with formaldehyde.
– ORIGIN C19: from German *melam* (an arbitrary formation), denoting an insoluble amorphous organic substance.

melancholia /ˌmɛlənˈkəʊlɪə/ ■ n. melancholy. ▶ dated a mental condition marked by persistent depression and ill-founded fears.
– ORIGIN Middle English: from late Latin (see MELANCHOLY).

melancholy ■ n. **1** a deep and long-lasting sadness. ▶ another term for MELANCHOLIA (as a mental condition). **2** historical another term for BLACK BILE. ■ adj. depressed or depressing.
– DERIVATIVES **melancholic** adj. **melancholically** adv.
– ORIGIN Middle English: from Old French *melancolie*, from Greek *melankholia*, from *melas*, *melan-* 'black' + *kholē* 'bile', an excess of which was formerly believed to cause depression.

Melanesian /ˌmɛləˈniːzɪən, -ʒ(ə)n/ ■ n. a native or inhabitant of any of the islands of Melanesia in the western Pacific. ■ adj. of or relating to Melanesia, its peoples, or their languages.

melange /meɪˈlɒ̃ʒ/ ■ n. a varied mixture.
– ORIGIN from French *mélange*, from *mêler* 'to mix'.

melanin /ˈmɛlənɪn/ ■ n. a dark brown to black pigment occurring in the hair, skin, and iris of the eye, responsible for tanning of skin exposed to sunlight.
– ORIGIN C19: from Greek *melas*, *melan-* 'black'.

melanism /ˈmɛlənɪz(ə)m/ ■ n. chiefly Zoology darkening of body tissues due to excessive production of melanin, especially as a form of colour variation in animals.
– DERIVATIVES **melanic** /mɪˈlanɪk/ adj.

melanocyte /ˈmɛlənə(ʊ)ˌsaɪt, mɪˈlanə(ʊ)-/ ■ n. Physiology a mature melanin-forming cell, especially in the skin.

melanoma /ˌmɛləˈnəʊmə/ ■ n. Medicine a tumour of

melanin-forming cells, especially a malignant tumour associated with skin cancer.
– ORIGIN C19: from Greek *melas, melan-* 'black'.

melanosis /ˌmɛləˈnəʊsɪs/ ■ n. Medicine excessive production of melanin in the skin or other tissue.
– DERIVATIVES **melanotic** adj.
– ORIGIN C19: from Greek *melas, melan-* 'black'.

melatonin /ˌmɛləˈtəʊnɪn/ ■ n. Biochemistry a hormone secreted by the pineal gland which inhibits melanin formation.
– ORIGIN 1950s: from Greek *melas* 'black' + SEROTONIN.

Melba sauce ■ n. a sauce made from puréed raspberries thickened with icing sugar.
– ORIGIN from the name of the Australian soprano Dame Nellie *Melba* (1861–1931).

Melba toast ■ n. very thin crisp toast.

meld[1] ■ v. blend; combine. ■ n. a thing formed by melding.
– ORIGIN 1930s: perhaps a blend of MELT and WELD.

meld[2] ■ v. (in rummy, canasta, and other card games) lay down or declare (a combination of cards) in order to score points. ■ n. a completed set or run of cards in any of these games.
– ORIGIN C19 (orig. US): from German *melden* 'announce'.

melee /ˈmɛleɪ/ ■ n. a confused crowd or scuffle.
– ORIGIN C17: from French *mêlée*, from an Old French var. of *meslee* (see MEDLEY).

melktert /ˈmɛlktɛːt/ ■ n. another term for MILK TART.
– ORIGIN Afrikaans.

melliferous /mɛˈlɪf(ə)rəs/ ■ adj. yielding or producing honey.
– ORIGIN C17: from Latin *mellifer*, from *mel* 'honey' + *-fer* 'bearing'.

mellifluous /mɛˈlɪflʊəs/ ■ adj. pleasingly smooth and musical to hear.
– DERIVATIVES **mellifluence** n. **mellifluent** adj. **mellifluously** adv. **mellifluousness** n.
– ORIGIN C15: from late Latin *mellifluus*, from Latin *mel* 'honey' + *fluere* 'to flow'.

mellow ■ adj. 1 (especially of sound, taste, and colour) pleasantly smooth or soft. ▸ archaic (of fruit) ripe, soft, sweet, and juicy. 2 (of a person's character) softened by maturity or experience. ▸ relaxed and good-humoured. 3 (of earth) rich and loamy. ■ v. make or become mellow.
– DERIVATIVES **mellowly** adv. **mellowness** n.
– ORIGIN Middle English: perhaps from Old English *melu, melw-*.

melodeon /mɪˈləʊdɪən/ (also **melodion**) ■ n. a small accordion of German origin, played especially by folk musicians.
– ORIGIN C19: prob. from MELODY, on the pattern of *accordion*.

melodic ■ adj. of, having, or producing melody. ▸ pleasant-sounding.
– DERIVATIVES **melodically** adv.

melodica /məˈlɒdɪkə/ ■ n. a wind instrument with a small keyboard controlling a row of reeds, and a mouthpiece at one end.
– ORIGIN 1960s: from MELODY, on the pattern of *harmonica*.

melodic minor ■ n. Music a minor scale with the sixth and seventh degrees raised when ascending and lowered when descending.

melodious ■ adj. pleasant-sounding; tuneful. ▸ relating to melody.
– DERIVATIVES **melodiously** adv. **melodiousness** n.

melodrama ■ n. a sensational dramatic piece with exaggerated characters and exciting events. ▸ language, behaviour, or events resembling such drama.
– ORIGIN C19: from French *mélodrame*, from Greek *melos* 'music' + French *drame* 'drama'.

melodramatic ■ adj. of, relating to, or characteristic of melodrama. ▸ exaggerated or overemotional.
– DERIVATIVES **melodramatically** adv. **melodramatics** pl. n.

melody ■ n. (pl. **-ies**) a sequence of single notes that is musically satisfying. ▸ the principal part in harmonized music.
– ORIGIN Middle English: from Old French *melodie*, from Greek *melōidia*, from *melos* 'song'.

melon ■ n. 1 the large round fruit of a plant of the gourd family, with sweet pulpy flesh and many seeds. 2 the plant which yields this fruit. [*Cucumis melo* subsp. *melo*.]
– ORIGIN Middle English: from late Latin *melo, melon-*, from Latin *melopepo*, from Greek, from *mēlon* 'apple' + *pepōn* 'gourd'.

melt ■ v. 1 make or become liquefied by heating. ▸ (**melt something down**) melt something, especially a metal article, so as to reuse the raw material. ▸ dissolve in liquid. 2 become or make more tender or loving. 3 (often **melt away**) disappear or disperse. ▸ (**melt into**) change or merge imperceptibly into (another form or state). ■ n. 1 an act of melting. ▸ metal or other material in a melted condition. ▸ an amount melted at any one time. 2 chiefly N. Amer. a sandwich, hamburger, or other dish containing or topped with melted cheese.
– DERIVATIVES **meltable** adj. **melter** n. **melting** adj. **meltingly** adv.
– ORIGIN Old English, of Germanic origin.

meltdown ■ n. 1 an accident in a nuclear reactor in which the fuel overheats and melts the reactor core or shielding. 2 a disastrous collapse or breakdown.

melting point ■ n. the temperature at which a given solid will melt.

melting pot ■ n. 1 a pot in which metals or other materials are melted and mixed. ▸ a place where different peoples, styles, etc., are mixed together. 2 a situation of constant change and uncertain outcome: *the railway's future is in the melting pot*.

melton ■ n. heavy woollen cloth with a close-cut nap, used for overcoats and jackets.
– ORIGIN C19: named after *Melton* Mowbray, a town in central England.

meltwater (also **meltwaters**) ■ n. water formed by the melting of snow and ice, especially from a glacier.

member ■ n. 1 a person, country, or organization belonging to a group, society, or team. ▸ (**Member**) a person formally elected to certain legislative bodies. 2 a constituent piece of a complex structure. ▸ a part of a sentence, equation, etc. 3 archaic a part of the body, especially a limb. ▸ (also **male member**) a man's penis.
– DERIVATIVES **-membered** adj. (chiefly Chemistry). **membership** n.
– ORIGIN Middle English: from Latin *membrum* 'limb'.

membrane ■ n. 1 Anatomy & Zoology a pliable sheet-like structure acting as a boundary, lining, or partition in an organism or cell. 2 a thin pliable sheet of material.
– DERIVATIVES **membranaceous** adj. **membraneous** adj. **membranous** adj.
– ORIGIN Middle English: from Latin *membrana*, from *membrum* 'limb'.

membranophone /mɛmˈbrɑːnəfəʊn/ ■ n. Music a musical instrument in which sound is produced by the vibration of a stretched membrane, for example a drum or tambourine.

meme /miːm/ ■ n. Biology a cultural or behavioural element passed on by imitation or other non-genetic means.
– DERIVATIVES **memetic** adj.
– ORIGIN 1970s: from Greek *mimēma* 'that which is imitated'.

memento /mɪˈmɛntəʊ/ ■ n. (pl. **-os** or **-oes**) an object kept as a reminder or souvenir.
– ORIGIN Middle English: from Latin, 'remember!', from *meminisse*.

memento mori /mɪˌmɛntəʊ ˈmɔːri, -rʌɪ/ ■ n. (pl. same) an object kept as a reminder that death is inevitable.
– ORIGIN Latin, 'remember (that you have) to die'.

memo ■ n. (pl. **-os**) informal a memorandum.

memoir ■ n. 1 a historical account or biography written from personal knowledge. ▸ (**memoirs**) an account written by a public figure of their life and experiences. 2 an essay on a learned subject. ▸ (**memoirs**) the proceedings of a learned society.
– DERIVATIVES **memoirist** n.
– ORIGIN C15: from French, a special use of *mémoire* 'memory'.

memorabilia

memorabilia /ˌmem(ə)rəˈbɪlɪə/ ■ pl. n. objects kept or collected because of their associations with memorable people or events.
– ORIGIN C18: from Latin, from *memorabilis* 'memorable'.

memorable ■ adj. worth remembering or easily remembered.
– DERIVATIVES **memorability** n. **memorably** adv.
– ORIGIN C15: from Latin *memorabilis*, from *memorare* 'bring to mind'.

memorandum ■ n. (pl. **memoranda** or **memorandums**) a written message in business or diplomacy. ▸ a note recording something. ▸ Law a document recording the terms of a transaction.
– ORIGIN Middle English: from Latin, 'something to be brought to mind', from *memorare*.

memorial ■ n. 1 a structure or object established in memory of a person or event. ▸ [as modifier] intended to commemorate someone or something. 2 chiefly historical a statement of facts, especially as the basis of a petition. ▸ a written record.
– DERIVATIVES **memorialist** n. **memorialize** (also **-ise**) v.
– ORIGIN Middle English: from late Latin *memoriale* 'record, memory', from Latin *memorialis* 'serving as a reminder'.

Memorial Day ■ n. (in the US) a day on which those who died on active service are remembered, usually the last Monday in May.

memorize (also **-ise**) ■ v. learn by heart.
– DERIVATIVES **memorizable** (also **-isable**) adj. **memorization** (also **-isation**) n. **memorizer** (also **-iser**) n.

memory ■ n. (pl. **-ies**) 1 the faculty by which the mind stores and remembers information. 2 something remembered. ▸ the remembering or commemoration of a dead person. ▸ the length of time over which a person or event continues to be remembered. 3 a computer's equipment or capacity for storing data or program instructions for retrieval.
– PHRASES **from memory** without reading or referring to notes. **in memory of** intended to remind people of. **take a trip** (or **walk**) **down memory lane** indulge in pleasant or sentimental memories.
– ORIGIN Middle English: from Old French *memorie*, from Latin *memoria* 'memory', from *memor* 'mindful, remembering'.

memsahib /ˈmemsɑːhiːb, ˈmemsɑːb/ ■ n. Indian dated a married white woman (used as a respectful form of address).
– ORIGIN from *mem* (representing an Indian pronunciation of MA'AM) + SAHIB.

men plural form of MAN.

menace ■ n. a threat or danger. ▸ a threatening quality. ■ v. threaten (someone).
– DERIVATIVES **menacer** n. **menacing** adj. **menacingly** adv.
– ORIGIN Middle English: from late Latin *minacia*, from Latin *minax* 'threatening', from *minae* 'threats'.

ménage /meɪˈnɑːʒ/ ■ n. the members of a household.
– ORIGIN Middle English: from Old French *menage*, from *mainer* 'to stay', from Latin *manere* 'remain'.

ménage à trois /meɪˌnɑːʒ ɑː ˈtrwɑ/ ■ n. (pl. **ménages à trois** pronunc. same) an arrangement in which a married couple and the lover of one of them live together.
– ORIGIN French, 'household of three'.

menagerie /məˈnadʒ(ə)ri/ ■ n. a collection of wild animals kept in captivity for exhibition.
– ORIGIN C17: from French *ménagerie*, from *ménage* (see MÉNAGE).

menaquinone /ˌmenəˈkwɪnəʊn/ ■ n. Biochemistry vitamin K, a compound produced by intestinal bacteria and essential for the blood-clotting process.
– ORIGIN 1940s: from the chemical name *me(thyl)-na(phtho)quinone*.

menarche /mɛˈnɑːki/ ■ n. the first occurrence of menstruation.
– ORIGIN C19: from Greek *mēn* 'month' + *arkhē* 'beginning'.

mend ■ v. 1 restore to a sound condition. ▸ return to health. ▸ improve: *mend your ways*. 2 add fuel to (a fire). ■ n. a repair in a material.
– PHRASES **mend (one's) fences** make peace with a person. **on the mend** improving in health or condition.
– DERIVATIVES **mendable** adj. **mender** n.
– ORIGIN Middle English: shortening of AMEND.

mendacious /mɛnˈdeɪʃəs/ ■ adj. untruthful.
– DERIVATIVES **mendaciously** adv. **mendacity** n.
– ORIGIN C17: from Latin *mendax, mendac-* 'lying'.

mendelevium /ˌmɛndəˈliːvɪəm, -ˈleɪvɪəm/ ■ n. the chemical element of atomic number 101, an artificially made radioactive metal of the actinide series. (Symbol: **Md**)
– ORIGIN 1950s: from the name of the Russian chemist Dimitri *Mendeleev* (1834–1907).

Mendelism /ˈmɛnd(ə)lɪz(ə)m/ ■ n. Biology the theory of heredity based on the recurrence of characteristics transmitted as genes, as formulated by the 19th-century Moravian botanist Gregor Johann Mendel.
– DERIVATIVES **Mendelian** adj. & n.

mendicant /ˈmɛndɪk(ə)nt/ ■ adj. given to begging. ▸ of or denoting a religious order originally dependent on alms. ■ n. a beggar. ▸ a member of a mendicant order.
– DERIVATIVES **mendicancy** n. **mendicity** n.
– ORIGIN Middle English: from Latin *mendicare* 'beg', from *mendicus* 'beggar', from *mendum* 'fault'.

mending ■ n. things to be repaired by sewing or darning.

meneer /məˈnɪə/ ■ n. S. African a polite form of address to a man.
– ORIGIN Afrikaans, from Dutch *mijnheer*, from *mijn* 'my' + *heer* 'master, lord'.

menfolk (US also **menfolks**) ■ pl. n. a group of men considered collectively.

menhir /ˈmɛnhɪə/ ■ n. Archaeology a tall upright stone of a kind erected in prehistoric times in western Europe.
– ORIGIN C19: from Breton *men* 'stone' + *hir* 'long'.

menial /ˈmiːnɪəl/ ■ adj. (of work) requiring little skill and lacking prestige. ▸ dated (of a servant) domestic. ■ n. a person with a menial job.
– DERIVATIVES **menially** adv.
– ORIGIN Middle English: from Old French, from *mesnee* 'household'.

Ménière's disease /mɛnˈjɛː/ ■ n. a disease of the inner ear causing progressive deafness, tinnitus, and vertigo.
– ORIGIN C19: named after the French physician Prosper *Ménière*.

meninges /mɪˈnɪndʒiːz/ ■ pl. n. (sing. **meninx**) Anatomy the three membranes (the dura mater, arachnoid, and pia mater) that line the skull and vertebral canal and enclose the brain and spinal cord.
– DERIVATIVES **meningeal** adj.
– ORIGIN from Greek *mēninx, mēning-* 'membrane'.

meningitis /ˌmɛnɪnˈdʒʌɪtɪs/ ■ n. a disease in which there is inflammation of the meninges, caused by viral or bacterial infection.
– DERIVATIVES **meningitic** adj.

meningococcus /mɪˌnɪŋɡəʊˈkɒkəs, -ˌnɪndʒəʊ-/ ■ n. (pl. **meningococci** /-ˈkɒk(s)ʌɪ, -ˈkɒk(s)iː/) a bacterium involved in some forms of meningitis. [*Neisseria meningitidis*.]
– DERIVATIVES **meningococcal** adj.

meninx /ˈmiːnɪŋks/ singular form of MENINGES.

meniscus /mɪˈnɪskəs/ ■ n. (pl. **menisci** /-sʌɪ/) 1 Physics the curved upper surface of a liquid in a tube. 2 a thin lens convex on one side and concave on the other. 3 Anatomy a thin fibrous cartilage between the surfaces of some joints.
– ORIGIN C17: from Greek *mēniskos* 'crescent'.

Mennonite /ˈmɛnənʌɪt/ ■ n. a member of a Protestant sect originating in Friesland in the 16th century, emphasizing adult baptism and rejecting Church organization, military service, and public office.
– ORIGIN from the name of its founder, *Menno* Simons (1496–1561).

meno- ■ comb. form relating to menstruation: *menopause*.
– ORIGIN from Greek *mēn* 'month'.

menopause /ˈmɛnəpɔːz/ ■ n. the ceasing of menstruation or the period in a woman's life (typically between 45 and 50) when this occurs.
– DERIVATIVES **menopausal** adj.
– ORIGIN C19: from MENO- + PAUSE.

menorah /mɪˈnɔːrə/ ■ n. 1 a holy candelabrum with seven branches, used in the ancient temple at Jerusalem. 2 a

candelabrum used in Jewish worship, typically with eight branches.
– ORIGIN from Hebrew.

menorrhagia /ˌmenəˈreɪdʒɪə/ ■ n. Medicine abnormally heavy bleeding at menstruation.
– ORIGIN C18: from MENO- + -rrhag-, stem of Greek *rhēgnunai* 'to burst'.

menorrhoea /ˌmenəˈriːə/ ■ n. Medicine the flow of blood at menstruation.
– ORIGIN C19: back-formation from AMENORRHOEA.

mensch /menʃ/ ■ n. informal, chiefly N. Amer. a person of integrity and honour.
– ORIGIN 1930s: Yiddish *mensh*, from German *Mensch* 'person'.

menses /ˈmensiːz/ ■ pl. n. 1 blood and other matter discharged from the uterus at menstruation. 2 [treated as sing.] the time of menstruation.
– ORIGIN C16: from Latin, pl. of *mensis* 'month'.

men's movement ■ n. (chiefly in the US) a movement aimed at liberating men from traditional views about their character and role in society.

mens rea /ˌmenz ˈriːə/ ■ n. Law the intention or knowledge of wrongdoing that constitutes part of a crime. Compare with ACTUS REUS.
– ORIGIN Latin, 'guilty mind'.

menstrual ■ adj. of or relating to the menses or menstruation.
– ORIGIN Middle English: from Latin *menstrualis*, from *menstruum* 'menses', from *mensis* 'month'.

menstrual cycle ■ n. the process of ovulation and menstruation in women and other female primates.

menstruate /ˈmenstrʊeɪt/ ■ v. (of a non-pregnant woman) discharge blood and other material from the lining of the uterus at intervals of about one lunar month.
– DERIVATIVES **menstruation** n.
– ORIGIN C17 (*menstruous* Middle English): from late Latin *menstruare* 'menstruate', from *menstrua* 'menses'.

menstruous ■ adj. of, relating to, or in the process of menstruation.

mensuration ■ n. measurement. ▸ the part of geometry concerned with ascertaining lengths, areas, and volumes.
– ORIGIN C16: from late Latin *mensuratio(n-)*, from *mensurare* 'to measure'.

-ment ■ suffix 1 forming nouns expressing the means or result of an action: *curtailment*. 2 forming nouns from adjectives (such as *merriment* from *merry*).
– ORIGIN from Latin *-mentum*.

mental ■ adj. 1 of, done by, or occurring in the mind. 2 of or relating to disorders or illnesses of the mind. ▸ informal mad.
– DERIVATIVES **mentally** adv.
– ORIGIN Middle English: from late Latin *mentalis*, from Latin *mens* 'mind'.

mental age ■ n. a person's mental ability expressed as the age at which an average person reaches the same ability.

mental block ■ n. an inability to recall something or to perform a mental action.

mental deficiency ■ n. dated the condition of having a mental handicap.

mental handicap ■ n. a condition in which the intellectual capacity of a person is permanently lowered or underdeveloped to an extent which prevents normal function in society.

mentalism ■ n. Philosophy the theory that physical and psychological phenomena are ultimately explicable only in terms of a creative and interpretative mind.
– DERIVATIVES **mentalist** n. & **mentalistic** adj.

mentality ■ n. (pl. -ies) 1 often derogatory a characteristic way of thinking. 2 the capacity for intelligent thought.

mentally handicapped ■ adj. having very limited intellectual functions.

menthol ■ n. a crystalline alcohol with a minty taste and odour, found in peppermint and other natural oils.
– DERIVATIVES **mentholated** adj.
– ORIGIN C19: from Latin *mentha* 'mint'.

mention ■ v. refer to briefly. ▸ refer to (someone) by name. ■ n. a reference to someone or something. ▸ a

---

733

merchandise

formal acknowledgement of something noteworthy.
– PHRASES **be mentioned in dispatches** Brit. be commended for one's actions by name in an official military report. **mention someone in one's will** leave a legacy to someone.
– DERIVATIVES **mentionable** adj.
– ORIGIN Middle English: from Latin *mentio(n-)*.

mentor ■ n. an experienced and trusted adviser. ▸ an experienced person who trains and counsels new employees or students. ■ v. be a mentor to.
– ORIGIN C18: from Greek *Mentōr*, the name of the adviser of the young Telemachus in Homer's *Odyssey*.

menu ■ n. 1 a list of dishes available in a restaurant. ▸ the food available or to be served in a restaurant or at a meal. 2 Computing a list of commands or facilities, especially one displayed on screen.
– ORIGIN C19: from French, 'detailed list' (noun use of *menu* 'small, detailed').

meow ■ n. & v. variant spelling of MIAOW.

MEP ■ abbrev. Member of the European Parliament.

meperidine /mɛˈperɪdiːn/ ■ n. another term for PETHIDINE.
– ORIGIN 1940s: blend of METHYL and (*pi*)*peridine*.

Mephistopheles /ˌmefɪˈstɒfɪliːz/ ■ n. an evil spirit to whom Faust, in the German legend, sold his soul.
– DERIVATIVES **Mephistophelean** /-ˈfiːlɪən, -fɪˈliːən/ (also **Mephistophelian**) adj.

mephitic /mɪˈfɪtɪk/ ■ adj. (especially of a gas or vapour) foul-smelling; noxious.
– ORIGIN C17: from late Latin *mephiticus*, from *mephitis* 'noxious exhalation'.

-mer ■ comb. form denoting polymers and related kinds of molecule: *elastomer*.
– ORIGIN from Greek *meros* 'part'.

meranti /məˈrantɪ/ ■ n. white, red, or yellow hardwood from a SE Asian tree. [Genus *Shorea*.]
– ORIGIN C18: from Malay.

mercantile /ˈmɜːk(ə)ntʌɪl/ ■ adj. 1 of or relating to trade or commerce. 2 of or relating to mercantilism.
– ORIGIN C17: from Italian, from *mercante* 'merchant'.

mercantile marine ■ n. another term for MERCHANT NAVY.

mercantilism /ˈmɜːk(ə)ntʌɪlɪz(ə)m/ ■ n. chiefly historical the economic theory that trade generates wealth and is stimulated by the accumulation of profitable balances, which a government should encourage by means of protectionism.
– DERIVATIVES **mercantilist** n. & adj.

mercaptan /məˈkapt(ə)n/ ■ n. Chemistry another term for THIOL.
– ORIGIN C19: from modern Latin *mercurium captans*, 'capturing mercury'.

Mercator projection ■ n. a world map projection made on to a cylinder in such a way that all parallels of latitude have the same length as the equator.
– ORIGIN from *Mercator*, Latinized name of the C16 Flemish geographer Gerhard Kremer.

mercenary /ˈmɜːsɪn(ə)ri/ ■ adj. motivated primarily by the desire for gain. ■ n. (pl. -ies) a professional soldier hired to serve in a foreign army.
– DERIVATIVES **mercenariness** n.
– ORIGIN Middle English: from Latin *mercenarius* 'hireling', from *merces* 'reward'.

mercer ■ n. Brit., chiefly historical a dealer in textile fabrics, especially silk and other fine materials.
– DERIVATIVES **mercery** n.
– ORIGIN Middle English: from Old French *mercier*, from Latin *merx* 'goods'.

mercerize (also **-ise**) ■ v. [often as adj. **mercerized** (also **-ised**)] treat (cotton fabric or thread) under tension with caustic alkali to impart strength and lustre.
– ORIGIN C19: from the name of John *Mercer*, said to have invented the process.

merchandise ■ n. /ˈmɜːtʃ(ə)ndʌɪs, -z/ goods for sale. ▸ products used to promote a film, pop group, etc. ■ v. /ˈmɜːtʃ(ə)ndʌɪz/ (also **-ize**) promote the sale of (goods).

merchant

advertise or publicize (an idea or person).
– DERIVATIVES **merchandisable** adj. **merchandiser** n. **merchandising** n.
– ORIGIN Middle English: from Old French *marchandise*, from *marchand* 'merchant'.

merchant ■ n. **1** a person involved in wholesale trade. ▶ chiefly N. Amer. a retail trader. **2** informal, chiefly derogatory a person with a partiality for a particular activity or view-point: *a speed merchant*. ■ adj. (of ships, sailors, or shipping activity) involved with commerce.
– ORIGIN Middle English: from Old French *marchant*, from Latin *mercari* 'to trade', from *merx* 'merchandise'.

merchantable ■ adj. saleable.
– ORIGIN C15: from *merchant* 'haggle, trade as a merchant', from Old French, from *marchand* 'merchant'.

merchant bank ■ n. a bank dealing in commercial loans and investment.
– DERIVATIVES **merchant banker** n.

merchantman ■ n. (pl. **-men**) a ship conveying merchandise.

merchant marine ■ n. chiefly US another term for MERCHANT NAVY.

merchant navy ■ n. a country's commercial shipping.

merchant prince ■ n. a merchant whose wealth is sufficient to confer political influence.

merciful ■ adj. showing mercy. ▶ coming as a mercy.
– DERIVATIVES **mercifulness** n.

mercifully ■ adv. **1** in a merciful manner. **2** to one's great relief.

merciless ■ adj. showing no mercy.
– DERIVATIVES **mercilessly** adv. **mercilessness** n.

Mercosur /ˌmɜːkəʊˈsʊər, ˈmɜːkəʊsʊər/ ■ n. an economic association of some South American countries having coordinated trade and commerce policies.
– ORIGIN C20: translation of Spanish *el Mercado Común del Sur* 'the Common Market of the South'.

mercurial /məːˈkjʊərɪəl/ ■ adj. **1** subject to sudden changes of mood or mind. **2** of or containing the element mercury. **3** (**Mercurial**) of the planet Mercury. ■ n. a drug containing mercury.
– DERIVATIVES **mercuriality** /-ˈalɪti/ n. **mercurially** adv.
– ORIGIN Middle English: from Latin *mercurialis* 'relating to the god Mercury', from *Mercurius* 'Mercury'.

Mercurian ■ adj. of or relating to the planet Mercury.

mercury ■ n. the chemical element of atomic number 80, a heavy silvery-white liquid metal used in some thermometers and barometers. (Symbol: **Hg**)
– DERIVATIVES **mercuric** adj. **mercurous** adj.
– ORIGIN Middle English: from Latin *Mercurius*, the name of the Roman god of trading and messenger of the gods.

mercury vapour lamp ■ n. a lamp in which light is produced by an electrical discharge through mercury vapour.

mercy ■ n. (pl. **-ies**) **1** compassion or forgiveness shown towards an enemy or offender in one's power. **2** something to be grateful for. **3** [as modifier] (especially of a journey or mission) motivated by compassion. ■ exclam. archaic used to express surprise or fear.
– PHRASES **at the mercy of** completely in the power of.
– ORIGIN Middle English: from Old French *merci* 'pity, thanks', from Latin *merces* 'reward', in Christian Latin 'pity, heavenly reward'.

mercy killing ■ n. the killing of someone suffering from an incurable and painful disease.

mere[1] /mɪə/ ■ adj. **1** that is solely or no more or better than what is specified: *mere mortals*. **2** (**the merest**) the smallest or slightest: *the merest hint*.
– ORIGIN Middle English: from Latin *merus* 'undiluted'.

mere[2] /mɪə/ ■ n. chiefly poetic/literary a lake or pond.
– ORIGIN Old English, of Germanic origin.

merely ■ adv. just; only.

merengue /məˈrɛŋɡeɪ/ (also **meringue**) ■ n. a Caribbean style of dance music typically in duple and triple time. ▶ a dance style associated with such music, with alternating long and short stiff-legged steps.

– ORIGIN C19: prob. American Spanish.

meretricious /ˌmɛrɪˈtrɪʃəs/ ■ adj. **1** showily but falsely attractive. **2** archaic characteristic of a prostitute.
– DERIVATIVES **meretriciously** adv. **meretriciousness** n.
– ORIGIN C17: from Latin *meretricius*, from *meretrix* 'prostitute', from *mereri* 'be hired'.

merganser /məːˈɡanzə, -sə/ ■ n. a fish-eating diving duck with a long, thin serrated and hooked bill. [*Mergus serrator* (red-breasted merganser) and related species.]
– ORIGIN C17: from Latin *mergus* 'diver' + *anser* 'goose'.

merge ■ v. combine or be combined to form one. ▶ blend or cause to blend gradually into something else.
– ORIGIN C17: from Latin *mergere* 'to dip, plunge'.

merger ■ n. the combining of two things, especially companies, into one.
– ORIGIN C18: from Anglo-Norman French *merger* (v. used as n.): see MERGE.

meridian /məˈrɪdɪən/ ■ n. **1** a circle of constant longitude passing through a given place on the earth's surface and the poles. ▶ Astronomy a circle passing through the celestial poles and the zenith of a given place on the earth's surface. **2** (in acupuncture and Chinese medicine) a pathway in the body along which vital energy is said to flow.
– ORIGIN Middle English: from Old French *meridien*, from Latin *meridianum* 'noon', from *medius* 'middle' + *dies* 'day'.

meridian circle ■ n. Astronomy a telescope mounted so as to move only on a North–South line, for observing the transit of celestial objects across the meridian.

meridional /məˈrɪdɪən(ə)l/ ■ adj. **1** southern. ▶ relating to or characteristic of the people of southern Europe. **2** of or relating to a meridian. ■ n. an inhabitant of the south, especially of France.
– ORIGIN Middle English: from late Latin *meridionalis*, from Latin *meridies* 'midday, south' (because in the northern hemisphere the sun is to the south at midday).

meringue[1] /məˈraŋ/ ■ n. an item of sweet food made from egg whites and sugar and baked until crisp.
– ORIGIN from French.

meringue[2] /məˈraŋ/ ■ n. variant spelling of MERENGUE.

merino /məˈriːnəʊ/ ■ n. (pl. **-os**) **1** a sheep of a breed with long, fine wool. **2** a soft woollen or wool-and-cotton material, originally of merino wool.
– ORIGIN C18: from Spanish.

meristem /ˈmɛrɪstɛm/ ■ n. Botany a region of plant tissue consisting of actively dividing cells.
– DERIVATIVES **meristematic** /-stəˈmatɪk/ adj.
– ORIGIN C19: from Greek *meristos* 'divisible' + *-em* on the pattern of *xylem*.

merit ■ n. **1** excellence; worth. ▶ an examination grade denoting above-average performance. **2** (usu. **merits**) a good point or feature. ▶ (**merits**) Theology good deeds entitling someone to a future reward. ▶ (**merits**) chiefly Law the intrinsic rights and wrongs of a case. ■ v. (**merited**, **meriting**) deserve or be worthy of.
– ORIGIN Middle English: from Latin *meritum* 'due reward', from *mereri* 'earn, deserve'.

meritocracy /ˌmɛrɪˈtɒkrəsi/ ■ n. (pl. **-ies**) government by people selected according to merit. ▶ a society governed by meritocracy. ▶ a ruling or influential class of educated people.
– DERIVATIVES **meritocratic** /-təˈkratɪk/ adj.

meritorious /ˌmɛrɪˈtɔːrɪəs/ ■ adj. **1** deserving reward or praise. **2** Law, chiefly N. Amer. (of an action) likely to succeed on the merits of the case.
– DERIVATIVES **meritoriously** adv. **meritoriousness** n.
– ORIGIN Middle English: from late Latin *meritorius*, from *mereri* 'earn'.

merle /məːl/ ■ n. Scottish or archaic a blackbird.
– ORIGIN Middle English: from Latin *merula*.

merlin ■ n. a small dark falcon that hunts small birds. [*Falco columbarius*.]
– ORIGIN Middle English: from Anglo-Norman French *merilun*, from Old French, from *esmeril*, of Germanic origin.

Merlot /ˈməːləʊ, -lɒt/ ■ n. a variety of black wine grape originally from the Bordeaux region of France.
– ORIGIN from French.

mermaid ■ n. a mythical sea creature with the head and trunk of a woman and the tail of a fish.
- DERIVATIVES **merman** n. (pl. **-men**).
- ORIGIN Middle English: from MERE² (in obsolete sense 'sea') + MAID.

mermaid's purse ■ n. the horny egg case of a skate, ray, or small shark.

-merous ■ comb. form Biology having a specified number of parts: *pentamerous*.

merriment ■ n. gaiety and fun.

merry ■ adj. (**-ier**, **-iest**) **1** cheerful and lively. ▶ characterized by festivity. **2** Brit. informal slightly drunk.
- PHRASES **make merry** indulge in merriment.
- DERIVATIVES **merrily** adv. **merriness** n.
- ORIGIN Old English *myrige* 'pleasing, delightful', of Germanic origin.

merry-go-round ■ n. **1** a revolving machine with model horses or cars on which people ride for amusement. **2** a continuous cycle of activities or events.

merrymaking ■ n. fun; festivity.
- DERIVATIVES **merrymaker** n.

mesa /'meɪsə/ ■ n. an isolated flat-topped hill with steep sides, found in landscapes with horizontal strata.
- ORIGIN C18: Spanish, 'table', from Latin *mensa*.

mésalliance /mɛ'zalɪəns/ ■ n. a marriage to a person thought to be unsuitable.
- ORIGIN French, from *més-* 'wrong, misdirected' + *alliance* (see ALLIANCE).

mescal /'mɛskal, mɛ'skal/ ■ n. **1** another term for MAGUEY. ▶ an intoxicating liquor distilled from the sap of an agave. **2** another term for PEYOTE.
- ORIGIN C18: from Spanish *mezcal*, from Nahuatl *mexcalli*.

mescaline /'mɛskəlɪn, -liːn/ (also **mescalin** /-lɪn/) ■ n. a hallucinogenic compound present in the peyote cactus.

Mesdames /meɪ'dɑːm, -'dam/ plural form of MADAME.

Mesdemoiselles /meɪd-/ plural form of MADEMOISELLE.

mesembryanthemum /mɪˌzɛmbrɪ'anθɪməm/ ■ n. a succulent South African plant with brightly coloured daisy-like flowers. [Family Mesembryanthemaceae.]
- ORIGIN from Greek *mesēmbria* 'noon' + *anthemon* 'flower'.

mesenchyme /'mɛsəŋkʌɪm, 'miːz-/ ■ n. Embryology embryonic tissue which develops into connective and skeletal tissues.
- DERIVATIVES **mesenchymal** adj.
- ORIGIN C19: from Greek *mesos* 'middle' + *enkhuma* 'infusion'.

mesenteron /mɪ'sɛntərɒn/ ■ n. Zoology the middle section of the intestine, especially in an embryo or arthropod.
- ORIGIN C19: from Greek *mesos* 'middle' + *enteron* 'intestine'.

mesentery /'mɛs(ə)nt(ə)ri/ ■ n. (pl. **-ies**) Anatomy a fold of the peritoneum attaching the stomach, small intestine, and other organs to the posterior wall of the abdomen.
- DERIVATIVES **mesenteric** adj.
- ORIGIN Middle English: from Greek *mesenterion*, from *mesos* 'middle' + *enteron* 'intestine'.

mesh ■ n. **1** material made of a network of wire or thread. **2** an interlaced structure. **3** a complex or constricting situation. ■ v. (of a gearwheel) lock together with another. ▶ make or become entangled or entwined. ▶ be or bring into harmony.
- PHRASES **in mesh** (of gearwheels) engaged.
- DERIVATIVES **meshed** adj.
- ORIGIN Middle English: prob. rel. to Middle Dutch *maesche*, of Germanic origin.

mesial /'miːzɪəl, 'mɛsɪəl/ ■ adj. Anatomy of, in, or directed towards the midline of a body.
- DERIVATIVES **mesially** adv.
- ORIGIN C19: from Greek *mesos* 'middle'.

mesic /'miːzɪk, 'mɛzɪk/ ■ adj. Ecology containing a moderate amount of moisture. Compare with HYDRIC and XERIC.
- ORIGIN 1920s: from Greek *mesos* 'middle'.

mesmeric /mɛz'mɛrɪk/ ■ adj. causing one to become transfixed and unaware of one's surroundings; hypnotic. ▶ archaic relating to or produced by mesmerism.
- DERIVATIVES **mesmerically** adv.

mesmerism ■ n. historical a therapeutic technique involving hypnotism.
- DERIVATIVES **mesmerist** n.
- ORIGIN C18: named after the Austrian physician Franz A. Mesmer.

mesmerize (also **-ise**) ■ v. capture the whole attention of; fascinate or transfix. ▶ archaic hypnotize.
- DERIVATIVES **mesmerization** (also **-isation**) n. **mesmerizer** (also **-iser**) n. **mesmerizing** (also **-ising**) adj. **mesmerizingly** (also **-isingly**) adv.

meso- /'mɛsəʊ, 'mɛzəʊ, 'miːsəʊ, 'miːzəʊ/ ■ comb. form middle; intermediate: *mesomorph*.
- ORIGIN from Greek *mesos* 'middle'.

mesocarp ■ n. Botany the middle layer of the pericarp of a fruit.

mesocephalic /ˌmɛsə(ʊ)sɪ'falɪk, ˌmɛz-, ˌmiːs-, ˌmiːz-, -kɛ-/ ■ adj. Anatomy having a medium-sized head.

mesoderm ■ n. Embryology the middle layer of cells or tissues of an embryo, or the parts derived from this (e.g. cartilage, muscles, and bone).
- DERIVATIVES **mesodermal** adj.
- ORIGIN C19: from MESO- + Greek *derma* 'skin'.

Mesolithic ■ adj. Archaeology relating to or denoting the middle part of the Stone Age, between the end of the glacial period and the beginnings of agriculture.
- ORIGIN C19: from MESO- + Greek *lithos* 'stone'.

mesomerism /mɪ'sɒmərɪz(ə)m, mɪ'zɒm-/ ■ n. Chemistry old-fashioned term for RESONANCE.
- DERIVATIVES **mesomeric** adj.

mesomorph ■ n. Physiology a person with a compact and muscular body. Compare with ECTOMORPH and ENDOMORPH.
- DERIVATIVES **mesomorphic** adj.
- ORIGIN 1920s: *meso-* from *mesodermal* (being the layer of the embryo giving rise to these physical characteristics) + -MORPH.

meson /'miːzɒn, 'mɛzɒn/ ■ n. Physics a subatomic particle, intermediate in mass between an electron and a proton, that transmits the strong interaction binding nucleons together.
- DERIVATIVES **mesonic** /mɪ'zɒnɪk/ adj.
- ORIGIN 1930s: from MESO- + -ON.

mesopause ■ n. the boundary in the earth's atmosphere between the mesosphere and the thermosphere.

mesopelagic /ˌmɛsə(ʊ)pɪ'ladʒɪk, ˌmɛz-, ˌmiːs-, ˌmiːz-/ ■ adj. Biology inhabiting the intermediate depths of the sea.

mesophyll ■ n. Botany the parenchyma of a leaf, containing many chloroplasts.
- ORIGIN C19: from MESO- + Greek *phullon* 'leaf'.

mesophyte ■ n. Botany a plant needing only a moderate amount of water.
- DERIVATIVES **mesophytic** adj.

Mesopotamian /ˌmɛsəpə'teɪmɪən/ ■ n. a native or inhabitant of Mesopotamia, an ancient region of SW Asia. ■ adj. of or relating to Mesopotamia.

mesosaur ■ n. an extinct small aquatic reptile of the early Permian period, with an elongated body and a long, narrow snout with numerous teeth.
- ORIGIN 1950s: from Greek *mesos* 'middle' + *sauros* 'lizard'.

mesoscale ■ n. an intermediate scale.

mesosphere ■ n. the region of the earth's atmosphere above the stratosphere and below the thermosphere, between about 50 and 80 km in altitude.

mesothelioma /ˌmɛsə(ʊ)ˌθiːlɪ'əʊmə, ˌmɛz-, ˌmiːs-, ˌmiːz-/ ■ n. Medicine cancer of mesothelial tissue, often associated with exposure to asbestos.

mesothelium /ˌmɛsə(ʊ)'θiːlɪəm, ˌmɛz-, ˌmiːs-, ˌmiːz-/ ■ n. (pl. **mesothelia**) Anatomy the epithelium lining the pleurae, peritoneum, and pericardium, derived from the surface layer of the embryonic mesoderm.
- DERIVATIVES **mesothelial** adj.
- ORIGIN C19: from MESO- + a shortened form of EPITHELIUM.

Mesozoic

Mesozoic /ˌmɛsə(ʊ)ˈzəʊɪk, ˌmez-, ˌmiːs-, ˌmiːz-/ ■ adj. Geology relating to or denoting the era between the Palaeozoic and Cenozoic eras (comprising the Triassic, Jurassic, and Cretaceous periods, about 245 to 65 million years ago).
– ORIGIN C19: from MESO- + Greek *zōion* 'animal'.

mesquite /ˈmɛskiːt, mɛˈskiːt/ ■ n. a spiny tree native to the south-western US and Mexico, yielding useful wood, tanbark, medicinal products, and edible pods. [*Prosopis glandulosa* and related species.]
– ORIGIN C18: from Mexican Spanish *mezquite*.

mesquite bean ■ n. an edible pod from the mesquite, used especially to produce flour or as fodder.

mess ■ n. **1** a dirty or untidy state or condition. ▸ euphemistic a domestic animal's excrement. **2** a portion of semi-solid or pulpy food. **3** a confused and problematic situation. ▸ a person whose affairs are in such a situation. **4** a place in which members of the armed forces take their meals. ■ v. **1** make untidy or dirty. ▸ (of a domestic animal) defecate. ▸ make dirty by defecating. **2** take one's meals.
– PHRASAL VERBS **mess about/around** behave in a silly or playful way. ▸ occupy oneself in a pleasantly desultory way. **mess someone about/around** informal cause someone inconvenience or problems. **mess up** informal mishandle a situation. **mess someone up** informal cause someone emotional or psychological problems. **mess with** informal meddle or interfere with.
– ORIGIN Middle English: from Old French *mes* 'portion of food', from late Latin *missum* 'something put on the table', from *mittere* 'send, put'.

message ■ n. **1** a verbal, written, or recorded communication sent by one person to another. **2** a significant point or central theme. ▸ a divinely inspired communication. ■ v. [often as noun **messaging**] send a message to, especially by email.
– PHRASES **get the message** informal understand what is meant.
– ORIGIN Middle English: from Old French, from Latin *missus*, from *mittere* 'send'.

messenger ■ n. a person who carries a message. ■ v. chiefly US send by messenger.
– ORIGIN Middle English: from Old Northern French *messanger*, var. of Old French *messager*, from Latin *missus* (see MESSAGE).

messenger RNA ■ n. the form of RNA in which genetic information transcribed from DNA as a sequence of bases is transferred to a ribosome.

mess hall ■ n. a place where people, especially soldiers, eat together.

messiah /mɪˈsʌɪə/ ■ n. **1** (**the Messiah**) the promised deliverer of the Jewish nation prophesied in the Hebrew Bible. ▸ Jesus regarded by Christians as the Messiah of these prophecies. **2** a leader or saviour.
– DERIVATIVES **messiahship** n.
– ORIGIN Old English: from Hebrew *māšīaḥ* 'anointed'.

messianic /ˌmɛsɪˈanɪk/ ■ adj. **1** of or relating to the Messiah. **2** inspired by hope or belief in a messiah.
– DERIVATIVES **messianism** /mɪˈsʌɪənɪz(ə)m/ n.

Messieurs plural form of MONSIEUR.

mess kit ■ n. **1** military uniform worn on formal occasions in the mess. **2** cooking and eating utensils, especially as used by soldiers.

messmate ■ n. (in the navy) a person with whom one shares accommodation.

Messrs plural form of MR.
– ORIGIN C18: abbrev. of MESSIEURS.

mess tin ■ n. a rectangular metal dish forming part of a mess kit.

messy ■ adj. (-ier, -iest) **1** untidy or dirty. **2** confused and difficult to deal with.
– DERIVATIVES **messily** adv. **messiness** n.

mestizo /mɛˈstiːzəʊ/ ■ n. (fem. **mestiza** /mɛˈstiːzə/), (pl. **-os** (or **-as**)) (in Latin America) a man (or woman) of mixed race, especially the offspring of a Spaniard and an American Indian.
– ORIGIN Spanish, 'mixed', from Latin *mixtus*.

Met ■ abbrev. informal **1** meteorological. **2** metropolitan. **3** (**the Met**) [treated as sing. or pl.] the Metropolitan Police in London.

met past and past participle of MEET¹.

meta- (also **met-** before a vowel or h) ■ comb. form **1** denoting a change of position or condition: *metamorphosis*. **2** denoting position behind, after, or beyond: *metacarpus*. **3** denoting something of a higher or second-order kind: *metalanguage*. **4** Chemistry denoting substitution at two carbon atoms separated by one other in a benzene ring: *metadichlorobenzene*. Compare with ORTHO- and PARA-¹.
– ORIGIN from Greek *meta* 'with, across, or after'.

metabolism /mɪˈtabəlɪz(ə)m/ ■ n. the chemical processes that occur within a living organism to maintain life.
– DERIVATIVES **metabolic** /ˌmɛtəˈbɒlɪk/ adj. **metabolically** adv.
– ORIGIN C19: from Greek *metabolē* 'change'.

metabolite /mɪˈtabəlʌɪt/ ■ n. Biochemistry a substance formed in or necessary for metabolism.

metabolize (also **-ise**) ■ v. process or undergo processing by metabolism.
– DERIVATIVES **metabolizable** (also **-isable**) adj. **metabolizer** (also **-iser**) n.

metacarpus ■ n. (pl. **metacarpi**) the group of five bones of the hand between the wrist (carpus) and the fingers.
– DERIVATIVES **metacarpal** adj. & n.
– ORIGIN Middle English: alteraiton of Greek *metakarpion*.

metafiction ■ n. fiction in which the author self-consciously parodies or departs from novelistic conventions.
– DERIVATIVES **metafictional** adj.

metal ■ n. **1** a solid material which is typically hard, shiny, malleable, fusible, and ductile, with good electrical and thermal conductivity, e.g. iron, copper, and silver. ▸ Heraldry gold and silver. **2** (also **road metal**) broken stone used in road-making. **3** (**metals**) the steel tracks of a railway. **4** molten glass before it is blown or cast. ■ v. (**metalled**, **metalling**; N. Amer. **metaled**, **metaling**) [usu. as adj. **metalled**] **1** make from or coat with metal. **2** make or mend (a road) with road metal.
– DERIVATIVES **metalware** n.
– ORIGIN Middle English: from Old French *metal* or Latin *metallum*, from Greek *metallon* 'mine, quarry, or metal'.

metalanguage ■ n. **1** a form of language or set of terms used for the description or analysis of another language. **2** Logic a system of propositions about propositions.

metaldehyde /mɪˈtaldɪhʌɪd/ ■ n. Chemistry a solid made by polymerizing acetaldehyde, used in slug pellets and as fuel for portable stoves.

metal detector ■ n. an electronic device that gives an audible signal when it is close to metal.

metalinguistics ■ pl. n. [treated as sing.] the branch of linguistics concerned with metalanguages.
– DERIVATIVES **metalinguistic** adj.

metallic ■ adj. of, relating to, or resembling metal. ▸ (of sound) sharp and ringing. ▸ having the sheen or lustre of metal. ■ n. a thing that is made of, contains, or resembles metal.
– DERIVATIVES **metallically** adv. **metallicity** n.

metalliferous ■ adj. containing or producing metal.

metallize (also **-ise**, US also **metalize**) ■ v. **1** coat with metal. **2** make metallic.
– DERIVATIVES **metallization** (also **-isation**) n.

metallography /ˌmɛtəˈlɒɡrəfi/ ■ n. the descriptive science of the structure and properties of metals.
– DERIVATIVES **metallographic** adj. **metallographical** adj. **metallographically** adv.

metalloid ■ n. another term for SEMIMETAL.

metallurgy /mɪˈtalədʒi, ˈmɛt(ə)ˌləːdʒi/ ■ n. the branch of science concerned with the properties, production, and purification of metals.
– DERIVATIVES **metallurgic** /ˌmɛtəˈləːdʒɪk/ adj. **metallurgical** adj. **metallurgically** adv. **metallurgist** n.
– ORIGIN C18: from Greek *metallon* 'metal' + *-ourgia* 'working'.

metalwork ■ n. **1** the art of making things from metal. **2** metal objects collectively.
– DERIVATIVES **metalworker** n. **metalworking** n.

metamere /ˈmɛtəmɪə/ ■ n. Zoology another term for SOMITE.
– DERIVATIVES **metameric** adj. **metamerism** n.
– ORIGIN C19: from META- + Greek *meros* 'part'.

metamorphic ■ adj. **1** Geology (of rock) that has undergone transformation by heat, pressure, or other natural agencies. **2** of or marked by metamorphosis.
– DERIVATIVES **metamorphism** n.
– ORIGIN C19: from META- + Greek *morphē* 'form'.

metamorphose /ˌmɛtəˈmɔːfəʊz/ ■ v. **1** (of an insect or amphibian) undergo metamorphosis. **2** change or cause to change completely. **3** Geology subject (rock) to metamorphism.

metamorphosis /ˌmɛtəˈmɔːfəsɪs, ˌmɛtəmɔːˈfəʊsɪs/ ■ n. (pl. **metamorphoses** /-siːz/) **1** Zoology (in an insect or amphibian) the process of transformation from an immature form to an adult form in two or more distinct stages. **2** a change in form or nature.
– ORIGIN Middle English: from Greek *metamorphōsis*, from *metamorphoun* 'transform, change shape'.

metanoia /ˌmɛtəˈnɔɪə/ ■ n. change in one's way of life resulting from penitence or spiritual conversion.
– ORIGIN C19: from Greek, from *metanoein* 'change one's mind'.

metaphase ■ n. Biology the second stage of cell division, between prophase and anaphase, during which the chromosomes become attached to the spindle fibres.

metaphor ■ n. a figure of speech in which a word or phrase is applied to something to which it is not literally applicable. ▶ a thing regarded as symbolic of something else.
– DERIVATIVES **metaphoric** adj. **metaphorical** adj. **metaphorically** adv.
– ORIGIN C15: from French *métaphore*, from Greek *metaphora*, from *metapherein* 'to transfer'.

metaphrase ■ n. a literal, word-for-word translation. ■ v. alter the phrasing or language of.
– DERIVATIVES **metaphrastic** adj.
– ORIGIN C17: from Greek *metaphrazein* 'word differently'.

metaphysic ■ n. a system of metaphysics.

metaphysical ■ adj. **1** of or relating to metaphysics. ▶ based on abstract reasoning. ▶ transcending physical matter or the laws of nature. **2** denoting certain 17th century English poets known for their subtlety of thought and complex imagery. ■ n. (**the Metaphysicals**) the metaphysical poets.
– DERIVATIVES **metaphysically** adv.

metaphysics ■ pl. n. [usu. treated as sing.] **1** the branch of philosophy concerned with the first principles of things, including abstract concepts such as being and knowing. **2** informal abstract talk; mere theory.
– DERIVATIVES **metaphysician** n.
– ORIGIN C16: from medieval Latin *metaphysica*, from Greek *ta meta ta phusika* 'the things after the Physics', referring to the sequence of Aristotle's works.

metaplasia /ˌmɛtəˈpleɪzɪə/ ■ n. Physiology abnormal change in the nature of a tissue.
– DERIVATIVES **metaplastic** adj.
– ORIGIN C19: from German *Metaplase*, from Greek *metaplassein* 'mould into a new form'.

metapsychology ■ n. the study of mental processes beyond what can be studied experimentally.
– DERIVATIVES **metapsychological** adj.

metasomatism /ˌmɛtəˈsəʊmətɪz(ə)m/ ■ n. Geology change in the chemical composition of a rock.
– DERIVATIVES **metasomatic** adj. **metasomatize** (also **-ise**) v.
– ORIGIN C19: from META- + Greek *sōma*, *somat-* 'body'.

metastable /ˌmɛtəˈsteɪb(ə)l/ ■ adj. Physics **1** (of equilibrium) stable only under small disturbances. **2** (of a substance or particle) theoretically unstable but so long-lived as to be stable for practical purposes.
– DERIVATIVES **metastability** n.

metastasis /mɪˈtastəsɪs/ ■ n. (pl. **metastases** /-siːz/) Medicine the development of secondary tumours at a distance from a primary site of cancer.
– DERIVATIVES **metastasize** (also **-ise**) v. **metastatic** adj.
– ORIGIN C16: from Greek, 'removal or change'.

737 **methamphetamine**

metatarsus ■ n. (pl. **metatarsi**) the bones of the foot, between the ankle and the toes.
– DERIVATIVES **metatarsal** adj. & n.

Metatheria /ˌmɛtəˈθɪərɪə/ ■ pl. n. Zoology a group of mammals which comprises the marsupials. Compare with EUTHERIA.
– DERIVATIVES **metatherian** n. & adj.
– ORIGIN from META- + Greek *thēria*, pl. of *thērion* 'wild animal'.

metathesis /mɪˈtaθɪsɪs/ ■ n. (pl. **metatheses** /-siːz/) **1** Grammar the transposition of sounds or letters in a word. **2** Chemistry another term for DOUBLE DECOMPOSITION.
– ORIGIN C16: from Greek, 'transposition'.

Metazoa /ˌmɛtəˈzəʊə/ ■ pl. n. Zoology a major division of the animal kingdom, comprising all animals other than protozoans and sponges.
– DERIVATIVES **metazoan** n. & adj.
– ORIGIN modern Latin, from META- + *zōia*, pl. of *zōion* 'animal'.

mete[1] /miːt/ ■ v. **1** (**mete something out**) dispense or allot justice, punishment, etc. **2** (in biblical use) measure out.
– ORIGIN Old English *metan* 'measure', of Germanic origin.

mete[2] /miːt/ ■ n. (usu. in phr. **metes and bounds**) a boundary or boundary stone.
– ORIGIN Middle English: from Latin *meta* 'boundary, goal'.

meteor ■ n. a small body of matter from outer space that becomes incandescent as a result of friction with the earth's atmosphere and appears as a streak of light.
– ORIGIN C16: from Greek *meteōron*, from *meteōros* 'lofty'.

meteoric ■ adj. **1** of or relating to meteors or meteorites. **2** (of change or development) very rapid. **3** chiefly Geology relating to or denoting water derived from the atmosphere.
– DERIVATIVES **meteorically** adv.

meteorite ■ n. a piece of rock or metal that has fallen to the earth as a meteor.
– DERIVATIVES **meteoritic** adj.

meteoroid ■ n. Astronomy a small body in the solar system that would become a meteor if it entered the earth's atmosphere.
– DERIVATIVES **meteoroidal** adj.

meteorology /ˌmiːtɪəˈrɒlədʒi/ ■ n. **1** the study of the processes and phenomena of the atmosphere, especially as a means of weather forecasting. **2** the climate and weather of a region.
– DERIVATIVES **meteorological** adj. **meteorologically** adv. **meteorologist** n.
– ORIGIN C16: from Greek *meteōrologia*, from *meteōron* (see METEOR).

meter[1] ■ n. a device that measures and records the quantity, degree, or rate of something. ■ v. [often as adj. **metered**] measure with a meter.
– ORIGIN Middle English: from METE[1].

meter[2] ■ n. US spelling of METRE[1], METRE[2].

-meter ■ comb. form **1** in names of measuring instruments: *thermometer*. **2** Prosody in nouns denoting lines of poetry with a specified number of measures: *hexameter*.
– ORIGIN from Greek *metron* 'measure'.

meth (also **crystal meth**) ■ n. informal the drug methamphetamine.

methadone /ˈmɛθədəʊn/ ■ n. a powerful synthetic analgesic similar to morphine, used as a substitute drug in the treatment of morphine and heroin addiction.
– ORIGIN 1940s: from its chemical name, (6-*di*)*meth*(*yl*)*a*(*mino-4,4-*)*d*(*iphenyl-3-heptan*)*one*.

methaemoglobin /ˌmɛθiːməˈɡləʊbɪn, mɛtˌhiː-/ (US **methemoglobin**) ■ n. Biochemistry a stable oxidized form of haemoglobin which is unable to release oxygen to the tissues.
– DERIVATIVES **methaemoglobinaemia** (US **methemoglobinemia**) n.

methamphetamine /ˌmɛθamˈfɛtəmiːn, -ɪn/ ■ n. a synthetic drug with more rapid and lasting effects than amphetamine, used illegally as a stimulant.

methanal

methanal /ˈmɛθənal/ ■ n. systematic chemical name for FORMALDEHYDE.
– ORIGIN C19: blend of METHANE and ALDEHYDE.

methane /ˈmiːθeɪn, ˈmɛθeɪn/ ■ n. Chemistry a colourless, odourless flammable gas which is the main constituent of natural gas and the simplest member of the alkane series. [CH_4.]
– ORIGIN C19: from METHYL + -ANE².

methanogen /mɛˈθænə(ʊ)dʒ(ə)n, mɛˈθanə(ʊ)-/ ■ n. Biology a methane-producing bacterium.
– DERIVATIVES **methanogenesis** n. **methanogenic** adj.

methanol /ˈmɛθənɒl/ ■ n. Chemistry a toxic flammable liquid alcohol, made chiefly by oxidizing methane. [CH_3OH.]

methedrine /ˈmɛθədrɪn, -driːn/ ■ n. (trademark in the UK) another term for METHAMPHETAMINE.
– ORIGIN 1930s: blend of METHYL and BENZEDRINE.

methemoglobin ■ n. US spelling of METHAEMOGLOBIN.

methi /ˈmeti/ ■ n. another term for FENUGREEK.

methicillin /ˌmɛθɪˈsɪlɪn/ ■ n. Medicine a semi-synthetic form of penicillin.
– ORIGIN 1960s: from *meth(yl)* and *(pen)icillin*.

methinks ■ v. (past **methought**) archaic or humorous it seems to me.
– ORIGIN Old English, from *mē* 'to me' + *thyncth* 'it seems', from *thyncan* 'seem'.

method ■ n. 1 a particular procedure for accomplishing or approaching something. 2 orderliness of thought or behaviour.
– ORIGIN Middle English: from Greek *methodos* 'pursuit of knowledge', from META- + *hodos* 'way'.

method acting ■ n. a technique of acting in which an actor aspires to complete emotional identification with a part.
– DERIVATIVES **method actor** n.

Méthode Cap Classique /mɛˌθɒd kap klaˈsiːk/ ■ n. South African term for MÉTHODE CHAMPENOISE.
– ORIGIN French, 'classic Cape method'.

méthode champenoise /meɪˌtəʊd ʃɒpənˈwɑːz/ ■ n. a method of making sparkling wine by allowing the last stage of fermentation to take place in the bottle.
▶ sparkling wine made in this way.
– ORIGIN French, 'champagne method'.

methodical ■ adj. characterized by method or order.
– DERIVATIVES **methodic** adj. **methodically** adv.

Methodist ■ n. a member of a Christian Protestant denomination originating in the 18th-century evangelistic movement of Charles and John Wesley. ■ adj. of or relating to Methodists or Methodism.
– DERIVATIVES **Methodism** n. **Methodistic** adj.
– ORIGIN prob. from the notion of following a specified 'method' of Bible study.

methodology ■ n. (pl. **-ies**) a system of methods used in a particular field.
– DERIVATIVES **methodological** adj. **methodologically** adv. **methodologist** n.

methotrexate /ˌmɛθəˈtrɛkseɪt, ˌmiːθə-/ ■ n. Medicine a synthetic compound that interferes with cell growth, used to treat leukaemia and other cancers.
– ORIGIN 1950s.

methought past of METHINKS.

meths ■ n. S. African & Brit. informal methylated spirit.

Methuselah ■ n. 1 a very old person. 2 (**methuselah**) a wine bottle of eight times the standard size.
– ORIGIN 1930s: from the name of the biblical patriarch *Methuselah*, said to have lived for 969 years (Genesis 5:27).

methyl /ˈmiːθaɪl, ˈmɛθ-, -θɪl/ ■ n. [as modifier] Chemistry of or denoting the alkyl radical -CH_3, derived from methane.
– ORIGIN C19: back-formation from METHYLENE.

methyl alcohol ■ n. another term for METHANOL.

methylate /ˈmɛθɪleɪt/ ■ v. [often as adj. **methylated**] 1 mix with methanol or methylated spirit. 2 Chemistry introduce a methyl group into.
– DERIVATIVES **methylation** n.

methylated spirit (also **methylated spirits**) ■ n. alcohol for general use, made unfit for drinking by the addition of methanol and pyridine and a violet dye.

methylene /ˈmɛθɪliːn/ ■ n. [as modifier] Chemistry of or denoting the divalent radical -CH_2-.
– ORIGIN C19: from French *méthylène*, from Greek *methu* 'wine' + *hulē* 'wood'.

methylphenidate /ˌmɛθɪlˈfɛnɪdeɪt, ˌmɛθ-, -θɪl-/ ■ n. Medicine a synthetic drug that stimulates the nervous system, used to treat attention deficit disorder.

metical /ˌmɛtɪˈkal/ ■ n. (pl. **meticais** /-ˈkaɪ/) the basic monetary unit of Mozambique.
– ORIGIN Portuguese, from Arabic *miṯkāl*, from *ṯakala* 'to weigh'.

meticulous /mɪˈtɪkjʊləs/ ■ adj. very careful and precise.
– DERIVATIVES **meticulously** adv. **meticulousness** n.
– ORIGIN C16: from Latin *meticulosus*, from *metus* 'fear'.

métier /ˈmɛtjeɪ/ ■ n. 1 a trade, profession, or occupation. 2 an outstanding or advantageous characteristic.
– ORIGIN C18: French, from Latin *ministerium* 'service'.

Metonic cycle /mɪˈtɒnɪk/ ■ n. a period of 19 years (235 lunar months), after which the new and full moons return to the same day of the year.
– ORIGIN named after *Metōn*, an Athenian astronomer of the 5th century BC.

metonym /ˈmɛtənɪm/ ■ n. a word or expression used as a substitute for something with which it is closely associated, e.g. *Washington* for the US government.
– DERIVATIVES **metonymic** adj. **metonymical** adj. **metonymically** adv. **metonymy** /mɪˈtɒnɪmi/ n.
– ORIGIN C19 (*metonymy* C16): from Greek *metōnumia* 'change of name'.

metope /ˈmɛtəʊp, ˈmɛtəpi/ ■ n. Architecture a square space between triglyphs in a Doric frieze.
– ORIGIN C16: from Greek, from *meta* 'between' + *opē* 'hole for a beam end'.

metre¹ (US **meter**) ■ n. the fundamental unit of length in the metric system, equal to 100 centimetres (approximately 39.37 inches).
– DERIVATIVES **metreage** n.
– ORIGIN C18: from French *mètre*, from Greek *metron* 'measure'.

metre² (US **meter**) ■ n. 1 the rhythm of a piece of poetry, determined by the number and length of feet in a line. 2 the basic pulse and rhythm of a piece of music.
– ORIGIN Old English, from Latin *metrum*, from Greek *metron* 'measure'.

metric¹ ■ adj. of or based on the metre; relating to or using the metric system. ■ n. 1 technical a system or standard of measurement. ▶ (**metrics**) (in business) a set of figures or statistics that measure results. 2 informal the metric system.

metric² ■ adj. relating to or composed in a poetic metre. ■ n. the metre of a poem.

-metric ■ comb. form in adjectives corresponding to nouns ending in *-meter* (such as *geometric* corresponding to *geometer* and *geometry*).
– DERIVATIVES **-metrically** comb. form in corresponding adverbs.

metrical ■ adj. 1 of, relating to, or composed in poetic metre. 2 of or involving measurement.
– DERIVATIVES **metrically** adv.

-metrical ■ comb. form equivalent to -METRIC.

metricate ■ v. change or adapt to a metric system of measurement.
– DERIVATIVES **metrication** n.

metric system ■ n. the decimal measuring system based on the metre, litre, and gram as units of length, capacity, and weight or mass.

metric ton (also **metric tonne**) ■ n. a unit of weight equal to 1 000 kilograms (2 205 lb).

metro¹ ■ n. (pl. **-os**) an underground railway system in a city, especially Paris.
– ORIGIN C20: from French *métro*, abbrev. of *métropolitain* (from *Chemin de Fer Métropolitain* 'Metropolitan Railway').

metro² ■ adj. S. African & N. Amer. short for METROPOLITAN. ■ n. S. African short for METROPOLE (in sense 2).

metrology /mɪˈtrɒlədʒi/ ■ n. the scientific study of measurement.
– DERIVATIVES **metrological** adj.
– ORIGIN C19: from Greek *metron* 'measure' + -LOGY.

metronidazole /ˌmɛtrəˈnaɪdəzəʊl/ ■ n. Medicine a synthetic drug used to treat trichomoniasis and similar infections.
– ORIGIN C20: from *me(thyl)* + *(ni)tro-* + *(im)idazole*.

metronome /ˈmɛtrənəʊm/ ■ n. a musicians' device that marks time at a selected rate by giving a regular tick.
– DERIVATIVES **metronomic** adj. **metronomically** adv.
– ORIGIN C19: from Greek *metron* 'measure' + *nomos* 'law'.

metronymic /ˌmɛtrəˈnɪmɪk/ ■ adj. & n. variant spelling of MATRONYMIC.

metropole /ˈmɛtrəpəʊl/ ■ n. **1** the parent state of a colony. **2** S. African a major conurbation. ▸ another term for UNICITY.
– ORIGIN C15: from Old French *metropole*, from Greek *mētēr*, *mētr-* + *polis* (see METROPOLIS).

metropolis /mɪˈtrɒp(ə)lɪs/ ■ n. the capital city of a country. ▸ a large and busy city.
– ORIGIN Middle English: from Greek *mētropolis* 'mother state', from *mētēr*, *mētr-* 'mother' + *polis* 'city'.

metropolitan ■ adj. **1** relating to or denoting a metropolis. **2** S. African relating to a metropole. **3** relating to or denoting the parent state of a colony. **4** Christian Church relating to or denoting a metropolitan or his see. ■ n. **1** Christian Church a bishop having authority over the bishops of a province, in particular (in Orthodox Churches) one ranking above archbishop and below patriarch. **2** an inhabitant of a metropolis.
– ORIGIN Middle English: from late Latin *metropolitanus*, from Greek *mētropolitēs* 'citizen of a mother state', from *mētropolis* (see METROPOLIS).

metrosexual ■ n. informal a heterosexual urban man who enjoys shopping, fashion, and similar interests traditionally associated with women or homosexual men.
– ORIGIN 1990s: blend of METROPOLITAN and HETEROSEXUAL.

-metry ■ comb. form in nouns denoting procedures and systems corresponding to names of instruments ending in *-meter* (such as *calorimetry* corresponding to *calori-meter*).
– ORIGIN from Greek *-metria*, from *-metrēs* 'measurer'.

mettle ■ n. a person's ability to cope with difficulties; spirit and resilience.
– PHRASES **be on one's mettle** be ready or forced to do one's best.
– DERIVATIVES **mettlesome** adj.
– ORIGIN C16: specialized spelling (for figurative senses) of METAL.

meunière /məːnˈjɛː/ ■ adj. [usu. postpos.] cooked or served in lightly browned butter with lemon juice and parsley.
– ORIGIN from French (*à la*) *meunière* '(in the manner of) a miller's wife'.

MeV ■ abbrev. mega-electronvolt(s).

mevrou /məˈfrəʊ/ ■ n. S. African a polite form of address to a woman.
– ORIGIN Afrikaans, from Dutch *mevrouw*.

mew[1] ■ v. (of a cat or gull) make a characteristic high-pitched crying noise. ■ n. a mewing noise.
– ORIGIN Middle English: imitative.

mew[2] Falconry ■ n. a cage or building for trained hawks, especially while they are moulting. ■ v. **1** (of a trained hawk) moult. **2** confine (a moulting trained hawk) to a mew. **3** (often **mew someone up**) confine in a restricting place or situation.
– ORIGIN Middle English: from Old French *mue*, from *muer* 'to moult', from Latin *mutare* 'to change'.

mewl ■ v. [often as adj. **mewling**] **1** cry feebly or querulously. **2** (of a cat or bird) mew.
– ORIGIN Middle English: imitative.

mews ■ n. (pl. same) Brit. **1** a row of houses or flats converted from stables, or built to appear so. **2** a group of stables round a yard or along an alley.
– ORIGIN Middle English: pl. of MEW[2], orig. referring to the royal stables on the site of the hawk mews at Charing Cross, London.

Mexican ■ n. a native or inhabitant of Mexico. ■ adj. of or relating to Mexico.

Mexicano /ˌmɛksɪˈkɑːnəʊ/ ■ n. & adj. informal, chiefly US another term for MEXICAN.
– ORIGIN from Spanish.

Mexican wave ■ n. an effect resembling a moving wave produced by successive sections of a stadium crowd standing up, raising their arms, lowering them, and sitting down again.
– ORIGIN so named because of the repeated practice of this at the 1986 soccer World Cup finals in Mexico City.

meze /ˈmeɪzeɪ/ ■ n. (pl. same or **mezes**) (in Turkish, Greek, and Middle Eastern cookery) a selection of hot and cold hors d'oeuvres.
– ORIGIN from Turkish, 'appetizer'.

mezereon /mɪˈzɪərɪən/ ■ n. a Eurasian shrub with fragrant purplish-red flowers and poisonous red berries. [*Daphne mezereum*.]
– ORIGIN C15: from Arabic *māzaryūn*.

mezuzah /mɛˈzuːzə/ ■ n. (pl. **mezuzahs** or **mezuzoth** /-zəʊt/) a parchment inscribed with religious texts, attached in a case to the doorpost of a Jewish house as a sign of faith.
– ORIGIN C17: from Hebrew *mĕzūzāh* 'doorpost'.

mezzanine /ˈmɛzəniːn, ˈmɛts-/ ■ n. **1** a low storey between two others, typically between the ground and first floors. **2** N. Amer. the lowest balcony of a theatre or the front rows of the balcony.
– ORIGIN C18: from Italian *mezzanino*, diminutive of *mezzano* 'middle', from Latin *medianus* 'median'.

mezzo /ˈmɛtsəʊ/ (also **mezzo-soprano**) ■ n. (pl. **-os**) a female singer with a voice pitched between soprano and contralto.
– ORIGIN C18: from Latin *medius* 'middle'.

mezzo-relievo /ˌmɛtsəʊrɪˈljiːvəʊ/ ■ n. (pl. **-os**) another term for HALF RELIEF.
– ORIGIN C16: from Italian *mezzo-rilievo*.

mezzotint /ˈmɛtsəʊtɪnt, ˈmɛzəʊ-/ ■ n. a print made from an engraved copper or steel plate, the surface of which has been partially roughened, for shading, and partially smoothed, for light areas. ■ v. engrave in mezzotint.
– DERIVATIVES **mezzotinter** n.
– ORIGIN from Italian *mezzotinto*, from *mezzo* 'half' + *tinto* 'tint'.

MF ■ abbrev. medium frequency.

Mfecane /ˌəmfɛˈkɑːni, mfɛˈ|ɑːni/ ■ n. a migration of southern African people, especially that of Zulu and Sotho peoples during the 19th century. ▸ wars associated with the period.
– ORIGIN from isiXhosa *imfecane* 'marauder', rel. to Sesotho DIFAQANE.

Mfengu ■ n. (pl. same) a member of an isiXhosa-speaking people descended from refugee groups who settled in the Eastern Cape after being displaced during the Mfecane.
– ORIGIN C19: from isiXhosa *amamfengu* 'destitute wanderers seeking work', from *fenguza* 'seek work'.

Mg ■ symb. the chemical element magnesium.

mg ■ abbrev. milligram(s).

mgqashiyo /ˌəmkwaˈʃiːjɔ, ˌmǃwaˈʃiːjɔ/ ■ n. S. African a style of popular music with close-harmony singing, typically for three or four female voices.
– ORIGIN from isiZulu *umgqashiyo*, rel. to isiXhosa *umqhashiyo*.

Mgr ■ abbrev. **1** (**mgr**) manager. **2** Monseigneur. **3** Monsignor.

mho /məʊ/ ■ n. (pl. **-os**) the reciprocal of an ohm, a former unit of electrical conductance.
– ORIGIN C19: the word OHM reversed.

MHz ■ abbrev. megahertz.

MI5 ■ abbrev. (in the UK) the governmental agency responsible for internal security and counter-intelligence on British territory (now officially named the Security Service).
– ORIGIN from *Military Intelligence section 5*.

MI6 ■ abbrev. (in the UK) the governmental agency

mi

responsible for matters of internal security and counter-intelligence overseas (now officially named the Secret Intelligence Service).
– ORIGIN from *Military Intelligence section 6*.

mi ▪ n. variant spelling of ME².

MIA ▪ abbrev. chiefly US missing in action.

miaow (also **meow**) ▪ n. the characteristic crying sound of a cat. ▪ v. (of a cat) make a miaow.
– ORIGIN C17: imitative.

miasma /mɪˈazmə, maɪ-/ ▪ n. (pl. **miasmas**) poetic/literary **1** an unpleasant or unhealthy vapour. **2** an oppressive or unpleasant atmosphere.
– DERIVATIVES **miasmal** adj. **miasmatic** adj. **miasmic** adj. **miasmically** adv.
– ORIGIN C17: from Greek, 'defilement', from *miainein* 'pollute'.

mic /mʌɪk/ ▪ n. informal a microphone.

mica /ˈmʌɪkə/ ▪ n. a silicate mineral with a layered structure, found as minute shiny scales in granite and other rocks.
– DERIVATIVES **micaceous** /mɪˈkeɪʃəs/ adj.
– ORIGIN C18: from Latin, 'crumb'.

mica schist ▪ n. a fissile metamorphic rock containing quartz and mica.

mice plural form of MOUSE.

micelle /mɪˈsɛl, maɪˈsɛl/ ▪ n. Chemistry an aggregate of molecules in a colloidal solution.
– DERIVATIVES **micellar** adj.
– ORIGIN C19: coined as a diminutive of Latin *mica* 'crumb'.

Michaelmas /ˈmɪk(ə)lməs/ ▪ n. the feast of St Michael, 29 September.
– ORIGIN Old English *Sanct Michaeles mæsse* 'Saint Michael's Mass', referring to the Archangel.

Michaelmas daisy ▪ n. a North American aster with numerous pinkish-lilac daisy-like flowers which bloom around Michaelmas. [*Aster novi-belgii*.]

Mick ▪ n. informal, offensive **1** an Irishman. **2** a Roman Catholic.
– ORIGIN C19: familiar form of the given name *Michael*.

mickey ▪ n. (in phr. **take the mickey**) informal tease or ridicule someone.
– DERIVATIVES **mickey-taking** n.
– ORIGIN 1950s.

Mickey Finn ▪ n. informal a surreptitiously drugged or doctored drink.
– ORIGIN 1920s: sometimes said to be the name of a notorious Chicago saloon-keeper.

Mickey Mouse ▪ adj. informal ineffective or insignificant.
– ORIGIN the name of a character created by the American cartoonist Walt Disney.

micro ▪ n. (pl. **-os**) **1** a microcomputer. **2** a microprocessor. ▪ adj. extremely small.

micro- ▪ comb. form **1** small: *microbrewery*. ▸ of reduced or restricted size: *microdot*. **2** denoting a factor of one millionth (10⁻⁶): *microgram*.
– ORIGIN from Greek *mikros* 'small'.

microanalysis ▪ n. the quantitative analysis of chemical compounds using a sample of a few milligrams.
– DERIVATIVES **microanalytical** adj.

microbe /ˈmʌɪkrəʊb/ ▪ n. a micro-organism, especially a bacterium causing disease or fermentation.
– DERIVATIVES **microbial** adj. **microbic** adj.
– ORIGIN C19: from Greek *mikros* 'small' + *bios* 'life'.

microbicide /mʌɪˈkrəʊbɪsʌɪd/ ▪ n. a compound that kills microbes or reduces their infectivity, used especially in the prevention of sexually transmitted infections.
– DERIVATIVES **microbicidal** adj.

microbiology ▪ n. the scientific study of micro-organisms.
– DERIVATIVES **microbiological** adj. **microbiologically** adv. **microbiologist** n.

microbrewery ▪ n. (pl. **-ies**) a brewery producing limited quantities of beer.

microcellular ▪ adj. containing or made up of minute cells.

microcephaly /ˌmʌɪkrəʊˈsɛfəli, -ˈkɛfəli/ ▪ n. Medicine abnormal smallness of the head.
– DERIVATIVES **microcephalic** adj. & n. **microcephalous** adj.

microchip ▪ n. a tiny wafer of semi-conducting material used to make an integrated circuit. ▪ v. (**microchipped, microchipping**) implant a microchip under the skin of (a domestic animal) as a means of identification.

microcircuit ▪ n. a minute electric circuit, especially an integrated circuit.

microclimate ▪ n. the climate of a very small or restricted area.
– DERIVATIVES **microclimatic** adj. **microclimatically** adv.

microcode ▪ n. Computing a very low-level instruction set controlling the operation of a computer.

microcomputer ▪ n. a small computer with a microprocessor as its central processor.

microcosm /ˈmʌɪkrə(ʊ)kɒz(ə)m/ ▪ n. **1** a thing regarded as encapsulating in miniature the characteristics of something much larger. **2** humankind regarded as the epitome of the universe.
– DERIVATIVES **microcosmic** /-ˈkɒzmɪk/ adj. **microcosmically** /-ˈkɒzmɪk(ə)li/ adv.
– ORIGIN Middle English: from Old French *microcosme*, from Greek *mikros kosmos* 'little world'.

microcredit ▪ n. the lending of small amounts of money at low interest to small new businesses in the developing world.

microcrystalline ▪ adj. formed of microscopic crystals.

microdot ▪ n. **1** a microphotograph, especially of a printed document, of about 1 mm across. **2** a tiny tablet of LSD.

microeconomics ▪ pl. n. [treated as sing.] the part of economics concerned with single factors and the effects of individual decisions.
– DERIVATIVES **microeconomic** adj.

microelectronics ▪ pl. n. [usu. treated as sing.] the design, manufacture, and use of microchips and microcircuits.
– DERIVATIVES **microelectronic** adj.

microenterprise ▪ n. a very small business, often run by one person.

micro-environment ▪ n. Biology the immediate small-scale environment of an organism.

microevolution ▪ n. Biology evolutionary change within a species or small group of organisms, especially over a short period.

microfauna ▪ n. Ecology microscopic animals living in the soil.

microfibre (US also **microfiber**) ▪ n. a very fine synthetic yarn.

microfiche /ˈmʌɪkrə(ʊ)fiːʃ/ ▪ n. a flat piece of film containing microphotographs of the pages of a newspaper, catalogue, etc.

microfilm ▪ n. a length of film containing microphotographs of a newspaper, catalogue, etc. ▪ v. make a microfilm of.

microflora ▪ n. Biology the micro-organisms of a particular habitat or host organism.

microform ▪ n. microphotographic reproduction on film or paper of a manuscript, map, etc.

microgram (abbrev.: **μg**) ▪ n. one millionth of a gram.

micrograph ▪ n. a photograph taken using a microscope.
– DERIVATIVES **micrographic** adj. **micrographics** pl. n. **micrography** n.

microgravity ▪ n. very weak gravity, as in an orbiting spacecraft.

microhabitat ▪ n. Ecology a habitat of limited extent which differs in character from the surrounding habitat.

microinstruction ▪ n. Computing a single instruction in microcode.

microkernel ▪ n. Computing a small modular part of an operating system kernel which implements its basic features.

microlending ▪ n. the provision of short-term loans of small amounts of cash to low-income earners.
– DERIVATIVES **microlender** n.

VOWELS a cat ɑː arm ɛ bed ɛː hair ə ago əː her ɪ sit i cosy iː see ɒ hot ɔː saw ʌ run

microlight ■ n. a very small, light, one- or two-seater aircraft.

microlitre (US also **microliter**) (abbrev.: μl) ■ n. one millionth of a litre.

micromanage ■ v. N. Amer. control even the smallest part of.
– DERIVATIVES **micromanagement** n. **micromanager** n.

micromesh ■ n. a material consisting of a very fine mesh.

micrometer /mʌɪˈkrɒmɪtə/ ■ n. a gauge which measures small distances or thicknesses.
– DERIVATIVES **micrometry** n.

micrometre /ˈmʌɪkrə(ʊ)ˌmiːtə/ (US **micrometer**) (abbrev.: μm) ■ n. one millionth of a metre.

micron /ˈmʌɪkrɒn/ ■ n. one millionth of a metre.
– ORIGIN C19: from Greek *mikron*, neuter of *mikros* 'small'.

Micronesian ■ n. a native of Micronesia, an island group in the western Pacific. ■ adj. of or relating to Micronesia, its peoples, or their languages.

micronize /ˈmʌɪkrənʌɪz/ (also **-ise**) ■ v. break into very fine particles.

micronutrient ■ n. a chemical element or substance required in trace amounts by living organisms.

micro-organism ■ n. a microscopic organism, especially a bacterium, virus, or fungus.

microphone ■ n. an instrument for converting sound waves into electrical energy variations which may then be amplified, transmitted, or recorded.
– DERIVATIVES **microphonic** adj.

microphotograph ■ n. a photograph reduced to a very small size.
– DERIVATIVES **microphotographic** adj. **microphotography** n.

microphysics ■ pl. n. [treated as sing.] the branch of physics concerned with bodies and phenomena on a microscopic or smaller scale.
– DERIVATIVES **microphysical** adj.

micropore ■ n. a very narrow pore.
– DERIVATIVES **microporous** adj.

microprint ■ n. text reduced by microphotography.

microprobe ■ n. an instrument in which a narrow beam of electrons is focused on to a sample and the resulting fluorescence is analysed to yield chemical information.

microprocessor ■ n. an integrated circuit containing all the functions of a central processing unit of a computer.

micropropagation ■ n. Botany the propagation of plants by growing plantlets in tissue culture and then planting them out.

micropyle /ˈmʌɪkrə(ʊ)pʌɪl/ ■ n. 1 Botany a small opening in the surface of an ovule, which the pollen tube penetrates. 2 Zoology a small opening for spermatozoa in the egg of a fish, insect, etc.
– ORIGIN C19: from MICRO- + Greek *pulē* 'gate'.

microscope ■ n. an optical instrument for viewing very small objects, typically magnifying by several hundred times.
– ORIGIN C17: from MICRO- + -SCOPE.

microscopic ■ adj. 1 so small as to be visible only with a microscope. ▸ informal extremely small. 2 concerned with minute detail. 3 of or relating to a microscope.
– DERIVATIVES **microscopical** adj. **microscopically** adv.

microscopy /mʌɪˈkrɒskəpi/ ■ n. the use of a microscope.
– DERIVATIVES **microscopist** n.

microsecond (abbrev.: μs) ■ n. one millionth of a second.

microsporangium /ˌmʌɪkrə(ʊ)spəˈrandʒɪəm/ ■ n. (pl. **microsporangia** /-dʒɪə/) Botany a sporangium containing microspores, the smaller of two kinds of spore produced by some ferns.

microstructure ■ n. the fine structure (in a metal or other material) which can be made visible and examined with a microscope.
– DERIVATIVES **microstructural** adj.

microsurgery ■ n. intricate surgery performed using miniaturized instruments and a microscope.
– DERIVATIVES **microsurgical** adj.

microswitch ■ n. an electric switch that can be operated rapidly by a small movement.

middle age

microtechnology ■ n. technology that uses micro-electronics.
– DERIVATIVES **microtechnological** adj.

microtome /ˈmʌɪkrə(ʊ)təʊm/ ■ n. chiefly Biology an instrument for cutting extremely thin sections of material for examination under a microscope.

microtone ■ n. Music an interval smaller than a semitone.
– DERIVATIVES **microtonal** adj. **microtonality** n. **microtonally** adv.

microtubule ■ n. Biology a microscopic tubular structure present in numbers in the cytoplasm of cells, sometimes aggregating to form more complex structures.

microvascular ■ adj. of or relating to the smallest blood vessels.

microvillus ■ n. (pl. **microvilli**) Biology each of a large number of minute projections from the surface of some cells.
– DERIVATIVES **microvillar** adj.

microwave ■ n. 1 an electromagnetic wave with a wavelength in the range 0.001–0.3 m, shorter than that of a normal radio wave but longer than those of infrared radiation. 2 short for MICROWAVE OVEN. ■ v. cook (food) in a microwave oven.
– DERIVATIVES **microwaveable** (also **microwavable**) adj.

microwave background ■ n. Astronomy a weak uniform microwave radiation which is detectable in nearly every direction of the sky, believed to be evidence of the big bang.

microwave oven ■ n. an oven that uses microwaves to cook or heat food.

micturate /ˈmɪktjʊreɪt/ ■ v. formal urinate.
– DERIVATIVES **micturition** n.
– ORIGIN C19: back-formation from *micturition* (C18), from Latin *micturire* 'urinate'.

mid[1] ■ adj. 1 of or in the middle part or position of a range. 2 Phonetics (of a vowel) pronounced with the tongue neither high nor low.

mid[2] ■ prep. poetic/literary in the middle of. ▸ in the course of.
– ORIGIN shortening of AMID.

mid- ■ comb. form denoting the middle of: *midsection*. ▸ in the middle; medium; half: *midway*.
– ORIGIN Old English *midd*, of Germanic origin; rel. to Latin *medius* and Greek *mesos*.

Midas touch /ˈmʌɪdəs/ ■ n. (**the Midas touch**) the ability to make a lot of money.
– ORIGIN from *Midas*, king of Phrygia, in Greek mythology given by Dionysus the power to turn everything he touched into gold.

mid-Atlantic ■ adj. 1 situated or occurring in the middle of the Atlantic ocean. 2 having characteristics of both Britain and America. 3 of or relating to states on the middle Atlantic coast of the United States.

midbrain ■ n. Anatomy a small central part of the brainstem, developing from the middle of the primitive or embryonic brain.

midday ■ n. the middle of the day; noon.

middelmannetjie /ˈmɪdlmʌnəki/ (also **middlemannetjie**) ■ n. S. African the ridge or hump between the wheel ruts in an unsurfaced road.
– ORIGIN from Afrikaans, from *middel* 'middle' + *man* 'man' + diminutive suffix.

midden /ˈmɪd(ə)n/ ■ n. a dunghill or refuse heap.
– ORIGIN Middle English *myddyng*, of Scandinavian origin.

middle ■ adj. at an equal distance from the extremities of something; central. ▸ (of a member of a group or series) placed so as to have the same number of members on each side. ▸ intermediate in rank, quality, or ability. ■ n. 1 a middle point or position. 2 informal a person's waist and abdomen. ■ v. (in cricket, tennis, etc.) strike (the ball) with the middle of the bat, racket, or club.
– ORIGIN Old English, of West Germanic origin.

middle age ■ n. the period between youth and old age, about 45 to 60.
– DERIVATIVES **middle-aged** adj.

middle-aged spread

middle-aged spread (also **middle-age spread**) ■ n. the fat that may accumulate in middle age around the waist and abdomen.

Middle Ages ■ pl. n. the period of European history from the fall of the Roman Empire in the West (5th century) to the fall of Constantinople (1453), or, more narrowly, from c.1000 to 1453.

Middle America ■ n. **1** the conservative middle classes of the United States, regarded as characteristically inhabiting the Midwest. **2** Mexico and Central America.
– DERIVATIVES **Middle American** adj. & n.

middlebrow ■ adj. informal, chiefly derogatory demanding or involving only a moderate degree of intellectual application; conventional rather than challenging.

middle C ■ n. Music the C near the middle of the piano keyboard, written on the first leger line below the treble stave or the first leger line above the bass stave.

middle class ■ n. [treated as sing. or pl.] the social group between the upper and working classes; professional and business people. ■ adj. of, relating to, or characteristic of the middle class.

middle distance ■ n. **1** the part of a real or painted landscape between the foreground and the background. **2** [as modifier] (in athletics) denoting or relating to a race distance of between 800 and 5 000 metres.

Middle Dutch ■ n. the Dutch language from c.1100–1500.

middle ear ■ n. the air-filled central cavity of the ear, behind the eardrum.

Middle East ■ n. an area of SW Asia and northern Africa, stretching from the Mediterranean to Pakistan and including the Arabian Peninsula.
– DERIVATIVES **Middle Eastern** adj.

middle eight ■ n. a short section (typically of eight bars) in the middle of a conventionally structured popular song, generally of a different character from the other parts of the song.

Middle England ■ n. the conservative middle classes in England.
– DERIVATIVES **Middle Englander** n.

Middle English ■ n. the English language from c.1150 to c.1470.

middle game ■ n. the phase of a chess game after the opening, when all or most of the pieces still remain on the board.

middle ground ■ n. **1** an area of compromise or possible agreement between two extreme positions. **2** the middle distance of a painting or photograph.

Middle High German ■ n. the language of southern Germany from c.1200–1500.

Middle Low German ■ n. the Low German language (spoken in northern Germany) from c.1200–1500.

middleman ■ n. (pl. **-men**) **1** a person who buys goods from producers and sells them to retailers or consumers. **2** a person who arranges business or political deals between other people.

middle name ■ n. **1** a person's name placed after the first name and before the surname. **2** a quality for which a person is notable: *optimism is my middle name.*

middle-of-the-road ■ adj. **1** moderate. **2** conventional and unadventurous.

middle passage ■ n. historical the sea journey undertaken by slave ships from West Africa to the West Indies.

middle school ■ n. **1** (in the UK) a school for children from about 9 to 13 years old. **2** (in the US and Canada) a junior high school.

middleveld /'mɪdlfelt/ (also **Middleveld**) ■ n. S. African the parts of northern South Africa and central Swaziland lying between 600 and 1 200 metres above sea level.
– ORIGIN partial translation of Afrikaans *middelveld* 'middle land'.

middleware ■ n. Computing software that occupies a position in a hierarchy between the operating system and the applications.

middle watch ■ n. the period from midnight to 4 a.m. on board a ship.

middleweight ■ n. a weight in boxing and other sports intermediate between welterweight and light heavyweight.

middling ■ adj. moderate or average in size, amount, or rank. ▶ neither very good nor very bad. ■ n. (**middlings**) bulk goods of medium grade, especially flour of medium fineness. ■ adv. informal fairly or moderately: *middling rich.*
– DERIVATIVES **middlingly** adv.
– ORIGIN Middle English: prob. from MID- + the adverbial suffix *-ling.*

midfield ■ n. (chiefly in soccer) the central part of the field. ▶ the players in a team who play in a central position between attack and defence.
– DERIVATIVES **midfielder** n.

midge ■ n. **1** a small two-winged fly that forms swarms near water or marshy areas, and of which many kinds feed on blood. [Families Ceratopogonidae (biting midges) and Chironomidae: many species.] ▶ used in names of other small flies whose larvae are pests of plants, e.g. gall midge. **2** informal a small person.
– ORIGIN Old English, of Germanic origin.

midget ■ n. an extremely small person. ▶ [as modifier] extremely small.
– ORIGIN C19: from MIDGE.

midgut ■ n. Zoology the middle part of the alimentary canal, including (in vertebrates) the small intestine.

MIDI ■ n. a standard for interconnecting electronic musical instruments and computers.
– ORIGIN 1980s: acronym from *musical instrument digital interface.*

midi ■ n. (pl. **midis**) a woman's calf-length skirt, dress, or coat.
– ORIGIN 1960s: from MID, on the pattern of *mini.*

midi- ■ comb. form medium-sized; of medium length: *midi-skirt.*

midiron ■ n. Golf an iron with a medium degree of loft, such as a four-, five-, or six-iron.

midi system ■ n. a set of compact stacking hi-fi equipment components.

midland ■ n. the middle part of a country. ▶ (**the Midlands**) the inland counties of central England. ▶ (**the Midlands**) the part of KwaZulu-Natal along the eastern foothills of the Drakensberg. ▶ (**Midland**) a part of the central United States, roughly bounded by Illinois, South Carolina, and Delaware. ■ adj. of or in a midland. ▶ (**Midland**) of or in the English Midlands or the Midland of the United States.
– DERIVATIVES **midlander** n.

midlife ■ n. the central period of a person's life, between around 45 and 60 years old.

midline ■ n. a median line or plane of bilateral symmetry.

midmost ■ adj. & adv. poetic/literary in the most central position.

midnight ■ n. twelve o'clock at night; the middle of the night.

midnight blue ■ n. a very dark blue.

midnight feast ■ n. a secret meal eaten by children late at night.

midnight sun ■ n. the sun when seen at midnight during the summer in either the Arctic or Antarctic Circle.

mid-ocean ridge ■ n. Geology a long, seismically active submarine ridge system situated in the middle of an ocean basin.

mid-off ■ n. Cricket a fielding position on the off side near the bowler.

mid-on ■ n. Cricket a fielding position on the on side near the bowler.

midrib ■ n. a large strengthened vein along the midline of a leaf.

midriff ■ n. the region of the front of the body between the chest and the waist.
– ORIGIN Old English *midhrif*, from MID[1] + *hrif* 'belly'.

midship ■ n. the middle part of a ship or boat.

midshipman ■ n. (pl. **-men**) **1** a rank of officer in the

---

CONSONANTS **b** but **d** dog **f** few **g** get **h** he **j** yes **k** cat **l** leg **m** man **n** no **p** pen **r** red

Royal Navy, above naval cadet and below sub lieutenant. **2** a naval cadet in the US navy.

midships ■ adv. & adj. another term for **AMIDSHIPS**.

midst archaic or poetic/literary ■ prep. in the middle of. ■ n. the middle point or part.
– PHRASES **in our** (or **your, their,** etc.) **midst** among us (or you or them).
– ORIGIN Middle English: from *in middes* 'in the middle'.

midstream ■ n. the middle of a stream or river.
– PHRASES **in midstream 1** in the middle of a stream or river. **2** part-way through an activity, speech, etc.

midsummer ■ n. **1** the middle part of summer. **2** the summer solstice.

Midsummer Day (also **Midsummer's Day**) ■ n. (in the northern hemisphere) 24 June.

midterm ■ n. **1** the middle of a period of office, an academic term, or a pregnancy. **2** N. Amer. an exam in the middle of an academic term.

midtown ■ n. N. Amer. the central part of a city between the downtown and uptown areas.

midway ■ adv. & adj. in or towards the middle of something.

midweek ■ n. the middle of the week. ■ adj. & adv. in the middle of the week.

Midwest ■ n. the region of northern states of the US from Ohio west to the Rocky Mountains.
– DERIVATIVES **Midwestern** adj.

midwicket ■ n. Cricket a fielding position on the leg side, level with the middle of the pitch.

midwife ■ n. (pl. **-wives**) a nurse who is trained to assist women in childbirth.
– DERIVATIVES **midwifery** /-'wɪf(ə)ri/ n.
– ORIGIN Middle English: prob. from the obsolete *mid* 'with' + WIFE (in the archaic sense 'woman').

midwinter ■ n. **1** the middle part of winter. **2** the winter solstice.

mielie ■ n. variant spelling of MEALIE.

mien /miːn/ ■ n. a person's look or manner.
– ORIGIN C16: prob. from French *mine* 'expression', influenced by obsolete *demean* 'bearing, demeanour'.

mifepristone /ˌmɪfɛˈprɪstəʊn/ ■ n. Medicine a synthetic steroid that inhibits the action of progesterone, given orally in early pregnancy to induce abortion.
– ORIGIN 1980s: prob. from Dutch *mifepriston*, from *mife-* (representing *aminophenol*) + *-pr-* (representing *propyl*) + *-ist-* (representing OESTRADIOL) + -ONE.

miff informal ■ v. (usu. **be miffed**) offend or irritate. ■ adj. S. African angry or sulky.
– ORIGIN C17.

miffy ■ adj. informal easily offended or irritated.

miggie /ˈmæxi/ ■ n. variant spelling of MUGGIE.

might¹ ■ modal v. (3rd sing. present **might**) past of MAY¹.
1 used in reported speech to express possibility or permission. ▸ expressing a possibility based on a condition not fulfilled. ▸ expressing annoyance: *you might have told me!* **2** used politely or tentatively in questions and requests. ▸ asking for information, especially condescendingly: *who might you be?* **3** used to express possibility or make a suggestion.

might² ■ n. great power or strength.
– PHRASES **with might and main** with all one's strength or power.
– ORIGIN Old English, of Germanic origin.

mightn't ■ contr. might not.

mighty ■ adj. (**-ier, -iest**) **1** possessing great power or strength. **2** informal very large. ■ adv. informal, chiefly N. Amer. extremely.
– DERIVATIVES **mightily** adv. **mightiness** n.
– ORIGIN Old English, of Germanic origin.

migmatite /ˈmɪgmətʌɪt/ ■ n. Geology a rock composed of two intermingled but distinguishable components, typically a granitic rock within a metamorphic host rock.
– ORIGIN C20: from Greek *migma, migmat-* 'mixture'.

mignonette /ˌmɪnjəˈnɛt/ ■ n. a plant with spikes of small fragrant greenish flowers. [*Reseda odorata* (North Africa) and related species.]

743

– ORIGIN C18: from French *mignonnette*, diminutive of *mignon* 'small and sweet'.

migraine /ˈmiːgreɪn, ˈmʌɪ-/ ■ n. a recurrent throbbing headache, typically affecting one side of the head and often accompanied by nausea and disturbed vision.
– DERIVATIVES **migrainous** adj.
– ORIGIN Middle English: from Greek *hēmikrania*, from *hēmi-* 'half' + *kranion* 'skull'.

migrant ■ n. **1** an animal that migrates. **2** a worker who moves from place to place to do seasonal work. ■ adj. tending to migrate or having migrated.

migrate /mʌɪˈgreɪt, ˈmʌɪgreɪt/ ■ v. **1** (of an animal) move from one habitat to another according to the seasons. **2** (of a person) move to settle in a new area in order to find work. ▸ move from one part of something to another. **3** Computing transfer or cause to transfer from one system to another.
– DERIVATIVES **migration** /-ˈgreɪʃ(ə)n/ n. **migrational** adj. **migrator** n. **migratory** /ˈmʌɪgrət(ə)ri, mʌɪˈgreɪt(ə)ri/ adj.
– ORIGIN C17: from Latin *migrare* 'move, shift'.

mihrab /ˈmiːrɑːb/ ■ n. a niche in the wall of a mosque, at the point nearest to Mecca, towards which the congregation faces to pray.
– ORIGIN from Arabic *miḥrāb* 'place for prayer'.

mikado /mɪˈkɑːdəʊ/ ■ n. historical a title given to the emperor of Japan.
– ORIGIN Japanese, from *mi* 'august' + *kado* 'gate' (a transferred use of 'gate (to the Imperial palace)', an ancient place of audience).

Mike ■ n. a code word representing the letter M, used in radio communication.

mike informal ■ n. a microphone. ■ v. place a microphone close to or in.

mik en druk /mək ən drək/ (also **mik and druk**) S. African informal ■ adj. & n. another term for POINT-AND-SHOOT.
– ORIGIN Afrikaans, 'aim and press'.

mil ■ abbrev. **1** millilitres. **2** millimetres. **3** informal (used in sums of money) millions.

milady /mɪˈleɪdi/ ■ n. (pl. **-ies**) historical or humorous used to address or refer to an English noblewoman.
– ORIGIN C18: from *my lady*.

milage ■ n. variant spelling of MILEAGE.

milch /mɪltʃ/ ■ adj. denoting a domestic mammal giving or kept for milk.
– ORIGIN Middle English: from Old English, from the Germanic base of MILK.

milch cow ■ n. a person or organization that is a source of easy profit.

mild ■ adj. **1** gentle and not easily provoked. **2** of only moderate severity. ▸ not keenly felt: *mild surprise.* ▸ (of a medicine or cosmetic) acting gently. ▸ not sharp or strong in flavour. **3** (of weather) moderately warm; less cold than expected. ■ n. Brit. a kind of dark beer not strongly flavoured with hops.
– DERIVATIVES **mildish** adj. **mildly** adv. **mildness** n.
– ORIGIN Old English, of Germanic origin.

mildew ■ n. a coating of minute fungal hyphae, growing on plants or damp organic material such as paper or leather. ■ v. affect or be affected with mildew.
– DERIVATIVES **mildewy** adj.
– ORIGIN Old English *mildēaw* 'honeydew', of Germanic origin.

mild steel ■ n. steel containing a small percentage of carbon, that is strong and tough but not readily tempered.

mile ■ n. **1** (also **statute mile**) a unit of linear measure equal to 1 760 yards (approximately 1 609 kilometres). **2** historical a Roman measure of 1 000 paces. **3** (**miles**) informal a very long way or a very great amount. ▸ (**miles**) informal by a great amount or a long way: *it is miles better*.
– PHRASES **be miles away** informal be lost in thought. **go the extra mile** be especially assiduous in one's attempt to achieve something. **run a mile** informal run rapidly away; flee. **stand** (or **stick**) **out a mile** informal be very obvious or

mileage

incongruous.
– ORIGIN Old English, from Latin *mil(l)ia*, pl. of *mille* 'thousand'.

mileage (also **milage**) ■ n. **1** a number of miles travelled or covered. **2** informal actual or potential benefit or advantage: *he was getting a lot of mileage out of the mix-up*.

mileometer ■ n. variant spelling of MILOMETER.

milepost ■ n. another term for MILESTONE.

miler ■ n. informal a person or horse trained specially to run a mile.
– DERIVATIVES **miling** n.

milestone ■ n. **1** a stone set up beside a road to mark the distance in miles to a particular place. **2** an event marking a significant new development or stage.

milfoil /ˈmɪlfɔɪl/ ■ n. **1** the common yarrow. **2** (also **water milfoil**) an aquatic plant with finely divided submerged leaves and wind-pollinated flowers. [Genus *Myriophyllum*.]
– ORIGIN Middle English: from Latin *millefolium*, from *mille* 'thousand' + *folium* 'leaf'.

milieu /ˈmiːljəː, miːˈljəː/ ■ n. (pl. **milieux** or **milieus** pronounced same or /-ljəːz/) a person's social environment.
– ORIGIN C19: French, from *mi* 'mid' + *lieu* 'place'.

militant ■ adj. favouring confrontational methods in support of a cause. ■ n. a militant person.
– DERIVATIVES **militancy** n. **militantly** adv.
– ORIGIN Middle English: from Latin *militare* (see MILITATE).

militaria /ˌmɪlɪˈtɛːrɪə/ ■ pl. n. military articles of historical interest.

militarism ■ n. the belief that a country should maintain and readily draw on a strong military capability for the defence or promotion of national interests.
– DERIVATIVES **militarist** n. & adj. **militaristic** adj.

militarize (also **-ise**) ■ v. **1** equip with military resources. **2** give a military character to.
– DERIVATIVES **militarization** (also **-isation**) n. **militarized** (also **-ised**) adj.

military ■ adj. of, relating to, or characteristic of soldiers or armed forces. ■ n. (**the military**) the armed forces of a country.
– DERIVATIVES **militarily** adv.
– ORIGIN Middle English: from French *militaire* or Latin *militaris*, from *miles* 'soldier'.

military attaché ■ n. an army officer serving with an embassy or attached as an observer to a foreign army.

military honours ■ pl. n. ceremonies performed by troops as a mark of respect at the burial of a member of the armed forces.

military-industrial complex ■ n. a country's military establishment and those industries producing arms or other military materials, regarded as a powerful vested interest.

military police ■ n. [treated as pl.] a military corps responsible for policing and disciplinary duties in an army.
– DERIVATIVES **military policeman** n. **military policewoman** n.

militate ■ v. (**militate against**) (of a fact or circumstance) be a powerful or conclusive factor in preventing.
– ORIGIN C16: from Latin *militare* 'serve as a soldier', from *miles* 'soldier'.

USAGE
The verbs **militate** and **mitigate** are often confused. See usage at MITIGATE.

militia /mɪˈlɪʃə/ ■ n. a military force that is raised from the civil population to supplement a regular army in an emergency. ▸ a rebel force acting in opposition to a regular army. ▸ (in the US) all able-bodied civilians eligible by law for military service.
– ORIGIN C16: from Latin, 'military service'.

militiaman ■ n. (pl. **-men**) a member of a militia.

milk ■ n. an opaque white fluid rich in fat and protein, secreted by female mammals for the nourishment of their young. ▸ the milk of cows as a food and drink for humans.
▸ the milk-like juice of certain plants, such as the coconut.
▸ a milk-like liquid with a particular ingredient or use: *cleansing milk*. ■ v. **1** draw milk from (a cow or other animal). ▸ extract sap, venom, or other substances from. **2** exploit or defraud (someone) by taking small amounts of their money over a period of time. ▸ get all possible advantage from (a situation).
– PHRASES **in milk** (of an animal) producing milk. **milk and honey** prosperity and abundance. [with biblical allusion to the prosperity of the Promised Land (Exodus 3:8).]
– ORIGIN Old English *milc*, *milcian*, of Germanic origin.

milk chocolate ■ n. solid chocolate made with the addition of milk.

milker ■ n. **1** a cow or other animal that is kept for milk. **2** a person that milks cows.

milk fever ■ n. **1** an acute illness in female cows or other animals that have just produced young, caused by calcium deficiency. **2** a fever in women caused by infection after childbirth, formerly supposed to be due to the swelling of the breasts with milk.

milkfish ■ n. (pl. same or **-fishes**) a large active silvery fish of the Indo-Pacific region, farmed for food. [*Chanos chanos*.]

milk float ■ n. Brit. an open-sided electrically powered van that is used for delivering milk to houses.

milk glass ■ n. semi-translucent glass, whitened by the addition of various ingredients.

milking stool ■ n. a short three-legged stool, of a kind traditionally used while milking cows.

milk loaf ■ n. a loaf of bread made with milk instead of water.

milkmaid ■ n. chiefly archaic a girl or woman who milks cows or does other work in a dairy.

milkman ■ n. (pl. **-men**) a man who sells and delivers milk.

Milk of Magnesia ■ n. trademark a white suspension of hydrated magnesium carbonate in water, used as an antacid or laxative.

milk pudding ■ n. a baked pudding made of milk and a grain such as rice, sago, or tapioca.

milk round ■ n. Brit. **1** a regular milk delivery along a fixed route. **2** a series of visits to universities and colleges by recruiting staff from large companies.

milk run ■ n. a routine, uneventful journey, especially by aircraft.

milkshake ■ n. a cold drink made from milk whisked with ice cream and fruit or other flavouring.

milksop ■ n. a timid and indecisive person.

milk stout ■ n. a kind of sweet stout made with lactose.

milk tart ■ n. S. African a baked custard tart, flavoured with spice.

milk thistle ■ n. **1** a thistle with a solitary purple flower and glossy marbled leaves, used in herbal medicine. [*Silybum marianum*.] **2** another term for SOWTHISTLE.

milk tooth ■ n. any of a set of early, temporary (deciduous) teeth in children or young mammals.

milk train ■ n. a train that runs very early in the morning to transport milk but also carries passengers.

milkweed ■ n. **1** a herbaceous plant with milky sap. [Genus *Asclepias*.] **2** (also **milkweed butterfly**) another term for MONARCH (in sense 2).

milkwood ■ n. S. African any of several trees that exude a milky sap when injured. [Family Sapotaceae.]

milkwort ■ n. a small plant with blue, pink, or white flowers, formerly supposed to increase a mother's milk production. [*Polygala vulgaris* and related species.]

milky ■ adj. (**-ier**, **-iest**) **1** containing milk. **2** resembling milk; of a soft white colour or clouded appearance.
– DERIVATIVES **milkily** adv. **milkiness** n.

mill ■ n. **1** a building equipped with machinery for grinding grain into flour. ▸ a piece of machinery for grinding grain. **2** a domestic device for grinding a solid substance to powder or pulp: *a pepper mill*. **3** a building fitted with machinery for a manufacturing process: *a steel mill*. ▸ a piece of manufacturing machinery. ■ v. **1** grind in a mill. **2** cut or shape (metal) with a rotating tool. **3** produce regular ribbed markings on the edge of (a coin).

VOWELS   a cat   ɑː arm   ɛ bed   ɛː hair   ə ago   əː her   ɪ sit   i cosy   iː see   ɒ hot   ɔː saw   ʌ run

4 (**mill about/around**) (of people or animals) move around in a confused mass.
– PHRASES **go** (or **put someone**) **through the mill** undergo (or cause someone to undergo) an unpleasant experience.
– DERIVATIVES **millable** adj. **milled** adj.
– ORIGIN Old English, from Latin *mola* 'grindstone, mill', from *molere* 'to grind'.

mill dam ■ n. a dam built across a stream to raise the level of the water so that it will turn the wheel of a watermill.

millefeuille /miːlˈfəːi/ ■ n. a rich cake consisting of thin layers of puff pastry filled with jam and cream.
– ORIGIN French, 'thousand-leaf'.

millefiori /ˌmiːlɪfɪˈɔːri/ ■ n. a kind of ornamental glass in which a number of rods of different colours are fused together and cut into sections which form various patterns, typically embedded in clear glass.
– ORIGIN C19: from Italian *millefiore* 'a thousand flowers'.

millefleurs /ˈmiːlfləː/ ■ n. a pattern of flowers and leaves used especially in tapestry and on porcelain.
– ORIGIN C19: French, 'a thousand flowers'.

millenarian /ˌmɪlɪˈnɛːrɪən/ ■ adj. **1** relating to or believing in Christian millenarianism. **2** denoting a religious or political group seeking rapid and radical change. ■ n. a person who believes in millenarianism.
– ORIGIN C17: from late Latin *millenarius* (see **MILLENARY**).

millenarianism ■ n. the doctrine of or belief in a future (and typically imminent) thousand-year age of blessedness, beginning with or culminating in the Second Coming of Christ (central to the teaching of the Adventists, Mormons, and Jehovah's Witnesses). ▶ belief in a future golden age of peace, justice, and prosperity.
– DERIVATIVES **millenarianist** n. & adj.

millenary /mɪˈlɛnəri, ˈmɪlɪnəri/ ■ n. (pl. **-ies**) **1** a period of a thousand years. **2** a thousandth anniversary. ■ adj. consisting of a thousand.
– ORIGIN C16: from late Latin *millenarius* 'having a thousand'.

millennialism ■ n. another term for **MILLENARIANISM**.
– DERIVATIVES **millennialist** n. & adj.

millennium /mɪˈlɛnɪəm/ ■ n. (pl. **millennia** /-nɪə/ or **millenniums**) **1** a period of a thousand years, especially when calculated from the traditional date of the birth of Christ. ▶ (**the millennium**) Christian Church the prophesied thousand-year reign of Christ at the end of the age (Revelation 20:1–5). ▶ a utopian period of good government, great happiness, and prosperity. **2** an anniversary of a thousand years. **3** (**the millennium**) the point at which one period of a thousand years ends and another begins.
– DERIVATIVES **millennial** adj.
– ORIGIN C17: from Latin *mille* 'thousand', on the pattern of *biennium*.

> USAGE
> The correct spelling is **millennium**, with two **n**s. The spelling with one **n** is a common error, formed by analogy with other similar words correctly spelled with only one **n**, such as **millenarian** and **millenary**.

millennium bug ■ n. an inability in older computing software to deal correctly with dates of 1 January 2000 or later.

miller ■ n. a person who owns or works in a grain mill.

millesimal /mɪˈlɛsɪm(ə)l/ ■ adj. of or relating to division into thousandths; thousandth. ■ n. a thousandth part.
– DERIVATIVES **millesimally** adv.
– ORIGIN C18: from Latin *millesimus*, from *mille* 'thousand'.

millet ■ n. a cereal which bears a large crop of small seeds, used to make flour or alcoholic drinks. [*Panicum miliaceum* and other species.]
– ORIGIN Middle English: from French, diminutive of dialect *mil*, from Latin *milium*.

millhand ■ n. a worker in a mill.

milli- ■ comb. form a thousand, chiefly denoting a factor of one thousandth: *milligram*.
– ORIGIN from Latin *mille* 'thousand'.

milliamp ■ n. short for **MILLIAMPERE**.

milliampere ■ n. one thousandth of an ampere.

milliard /ˈmɪlɪɑːd/ ■ n. Brit. one thousand million.
– ORIGIN C18: French, from *mille* 'thousand'.

millibar ■ n. one thousandth of a bar, the cgs unit of atmospheric pressure equivalent to 100 pascals.

milligram (also **milligramme**) (abbrev.: **mg**) ■ n. one thousandth of a gram.

millilitre (US **milliliter**) (abbrev.: **ml**) ■ n. one thousandth of a litre.

millimetre (US **millimeter**) (abbrev.: **mm**) ■ n. one thousandth of a metre.

milliner ■ n. a person who makes or sells women's hats.
– DERIVATIVES **millinery** n.
– ORIGIN Middle English ('native of Milan', later 'a vendor of fancy goods from Milan'): from the name of the Italian city Milan.

million ■ cardinal number (pl. **millions** or (with numeral or quantifying word) same) **1** (**a/one million**) the number equivalent to the product of a thousand and a thousand; 1 000 000 or 10^6. **2** (also **millions**) informal a very large number or amount.
– DERIVATIVES **millionfold** adj. & adv. **millionth** ordinal number.
– ORIGIN Middle English: prob. from Italian *milione*, from *mille* 'thousand'.

millionaire ■ n. (fem. **millionairess**) a person whose assets are worth one million pounds or dollars or more.
▶ S. African a person with assets of one million rand or more.
– ORIGIN C19: from French *millionnaire*, from *million* (see **MILLION**).

millipede /ˈmɪlɪpiːd/ ■ n. an arthropod with an elongated body composed of many segments, most of which bear two pairs of legs. [Class Diplopoda: many species.]
– ORIGIN C17: from Latin *millepeda* 'woodlouse', from *mille* 'thousand' + *pes*, *ped-* 'foot'.

millisecond ■ n. one thousandth of a second.

millivolt ■ n. one thousandth of a volt.

milliwatt (abbrev.: **mW**) ■ n. one thousandth of a watt.

millpond ■ n. the pool created by a mill dam, providing the head of water that powers a watermill.

mill race ■ n. the channel carrying the swift current of water that drives a mill wheel.

millstone ■ n. **1** each of two circular stones used for grinding grain. **2** a burden of responsibility.

millstream ■ n. the flowing water that drives a mill wheel.

mill wheel ■ n. a wheel used to drive a watermill.

millwright ■ n. a person who designs or builds grain mills or who maintains mill machinery.

milometer /maɪˈlɒmɪtə/ (also **mileometer**) ■ n. Brit. an instrument on a vehicle for recording the number of miles travelled.

milord ■ n. historical or humorous used to address or refer to an English nobleman.
– ORIGIN C17: from *my lord*.

Miltonian /mɪlˈtəʊnɪən/ ■ n. an admirer or follower of the English poet John Milton (1608–74). ■ adj. (also **Miltonic**) of or relating to Milton.

mime ■ n. **1** the expression of action, character, or emotion by gesture and movement and without words, especially as a form of theatrical performance. **2** (in ancient Greece and Rome) a simple farcical drama including mimicry. ■ v. **1** use mime to act out (a play or role). **2** pretend to sing or play an instrument as a recording is being played.
– DERIVATIVES **mimer** n.
– ORIGIN C17: from Latin *mimus*, from Greek *mimos*.

mimesis /mɪˈmiːsɪs, maɪ-/ ■ n. **1** imitative representation of the real world in art and literature. **2** the deliberate imitation of the behaviour of one group of people by another as a factor in social change. **3** Zoology mimicry of another animal or plant.
– DERIVATIVES **mimetic** adj. **mimetically** adv.
– ORIGIN C16: from Greek *mimēsis*, from *mimeisthai* 'to imitate'.

mimic

mimic ■ v. (**mimicked**, **mimicking**) imitate in order to entertain or ridicule. ▶ (of an animal or plant) take on the appearance of (another animal or plant) in order to deter predators or for camouflage. ▶ replicate the effects of. ■ n. 1 a person skilled in mimicking. 2 an animal or plant that mimics.
– DERIVATIVES **mimicker** n. **mimicry** n.
– ORIGIN C16: from Greek *mimikos*, from *mimos* 'mime'.

mimosa /mɪˈməʊzə, -sə/ ■ n. 1 an Australian acacia tree with delicate fern-like leaves and yellow flowers. [*Acacia dealbata*.] 2 a plant of a genus that includes the sensitive plant. [Genus *Mimosa*.]
– ORIGIN from Latin *mimus* 'mime' (because the plant seemingly mimics the sensitivity of an animal).

mimulus /ˈmɪmjʊləs/ ■ n. a plant of a genus which includes the musk plants and the monkey flower. [Genus *Mimulus*.]
– ORIGIN a diminutive of Latin *mimus* 'mime', perhaps with ref. to its mask-like flowers.

min. ■ abbrev. 1 minim (fluid measure). 2 minimum. 3 minute(s).

minaret /ˈmɪnərɛt, ˌmɪnəˈrɛt/ ■ n. a slender tower, especially that of a mosque, with a balcony from which a muezzin calls Muslims to prayer.
– DERIVATIVES **minareted** adj.
– ORIGIN C17: from Spanish *minarete* or Italian *minaretto*, from Arabic *manār(a)* 'lighthouse, minaret', from *nār* 'fire or light'.

minatory /ˈmɪnət(ə)ri/ ■ adj. formal expressing or conveying a threat.
– ORIGIN C16: from late Latin *minatorius*, from *minari* 'threaten'.

mince ■ v. 1 [often as adj. **minced**] cut up or shred (meat) into very small pieces. 2 walk in an affected manner with short, quick steps and swinging hips. ■ n. minced meat.
– PHRASES **mince words** (or **one's words**) [usu. with neg.] voice one's disapproval delicately or gently.
– DERIVATIVES **mincer** n. **mincing** adj. **mincingly** adv.
– ORIGIN Middle English: from Old French *mincier*, from Latin *minutia* 'smallness'.

mincemeat ■ n. a mixture of currants, raisins, apples, candied peel, sugar, spices, and suet.
– PHRASES **make mincemeat of** informal defeat (someone) decisively.

mince pie ■ n. a small pie containing mincemeat, typically eaten at Christmas.

mind ■ n. 1 the faculty of consciousness and thought. 2 the source of a person's thoughts; the intellect. ▶ a person's memory. ▶ a person identified with their intellectual faculties: *he was one of the greatest minds of his time*. 3 a person's attention. ▶ a person's will or determination. ■ v. 1 be distressed or annoyed by; object to. 2 remember or take care to do something: *mind you look after the children*. ▶ give attention to; watch out for: *mind your head!* 3 (also **mind you**) introducing a qualification to a previous statement: *we've got some decorations up—not a lot, mind you.* 4 take care of temporarily. 5 (**be minded**) be inclined to do a particular thing.
– PHRASES **be in** (or **of**) **two minds** be unable to decide between alternatives. **be of one** (or **a different**) **mind** share the same (or hold a different) opinion. **give someone a piece of one's mind** rebuke someone. **have a** (or **a good** or **half a**) **mind to do something** be inclined to do something. **have in mind** intend to do something. **have someone/thing in mind** be thinking of someone or something. **in one's mind's eye** in one's imagination. **mind over matter** the use of will power to overcome physical problems. **mind one's own business** refrain from prying or interfering. **mind one's Ps & Qs** be careful to be polite and avoid giving offence. **mind the shop** informal be in charge of something temporarily. **never mind 1** do not or let us not be concerned or distressed. **2** (also **never you mind**) used in refusing to answer a question: *never mind where I'm going.* **3** let alone: *he found it hard to think, never mind talk.* **out of one's mind** having lost control of one's mental faculties. **put one in mind of** remind one of. **put** (or **set**) **one's mind to** direct all one's attention to. **put someone/thing out of one's mind** stop thinking about someone or something. **to my mind** in my opinion.
– ORIGIN Old English *gemynd* 'memory, thought', of Germanic origin.

mind-bending ■ adj. informal influencing or altering one's state of mind.

mind-blowing ■ adj. informal overwhelmingly impressive.
– DERIVATIVES **mind-blowingly** adv.

mind-boggling ■ adj. informal overwhelming.
– DERIVATIVES **mind-bogglingly** adv.

minded ■ adj. [usu. in combination] inclined to think in a particular way: *liberal-minded scholars*.

minder ■ n. informal a person whose job it is to look after someone or something.

mindful ■ adj. 1 conscious or aware of something. 2 formal inclined or intending to do something.
– DERIVATIVES **mindfully** adv. **mindfulness** n.

mind game ■ n. a series of actions or responses planned for their psychological effect on another.

mindless ■ adj. 1 acting or done without justification and with no concern for the consequences. 2 (**mindless of**) not thinking of or concerned about. 3 (of an activity) simple and repetitive.
– DERIVATIVES **mindlessly** adv. **mindlessness** n.

mind-numbing ■ adj. so extreme or intense as to prevent normal thought.
– DERIVATIVES **mind-numbingly** adv.

mind-reader ■ n. a person who can supposedly discern what another person is thinking.
– DERIVATIVES **mind-reading** n.

mindset ■ n. a habitual way of thinking.

mindshare ■ n. consumer awareness of a product or brand, typically as opposed to market share.

mine[1] ■ possess. pron. referring to a thing or things belonging to or associated with the speaker. ■ possess. det. archaic (used before a vowel) my.
– ORIGIN Old English, of Germanic origin.

mine[2] ■ n. 1 an excavation in the earth for extracting coal or other minerals. 2 an abundant source of something: *a mine of information.* 3 a type of bomb placed on or in the ground or water, which detonates on contact. ■ v. 1 obtain from a mine. ▶ excavate for coal or other minerals. 2 lay a mine or mines on or in. ▶ destroy by means of a mine or mines.
– PHRASES **on the mines** S. African in the employment of a mining company. ▶ in or down a mine.
– DERIVATIVES **mineable** (also **minable**) adj. **mining** n.
– ORIGIN Middle English: from Old French *mine* (n.), *miner* (v.), perhaps of Celtic origin.

mine captain ■ n. S. African the overseer of an area of a mine.

mine dump ■ n. S. African a hill built up from the residue of mining operations.

minefield ■ n. 1 an area planted with explosive mines. 2 a subject or situation presenting unseen hazards.

minehunter ■ n. a warship used for detecting and destroying explosive mines.

miner ■ n. a person who works in a mine. ▶ used in names of burrowing or tunnelling insects and birds, e.g. leaf miner.

mineral ■ n. 1 a solid inorganic substance of natural occurrence. ▶ a substance obtained by mining. ▶ an inorganic substance needed by the human body for good health. 2 (**minerals**) Brit. effervescent soft drinks. ■ adj. of or denoting a mineral.
– ORIGIN Middle English: from medieval Latin *minerale*, neuter of *mineralis*, from *mina* 'ore'.

mineralize (also **-ise**) ■ v. 1 convert (organic matter) wholly or partly into a mineral or inorganic material or structure. 2 impregnate (water or another liquid) with a mineral substance.
– DERIVATIVES **mineralization** (also **-isation**) n.

mineralocorticoid /ˌmɪn(ə)rələ(ʊ)ˈkɔːtɪkɔɪd/ ■ n. Biochemistry a corticosteroid which is involved with maintaining the salt balance in the body, such as aldosterone.

mineralogy ■ n. the scientific study of minerals.

minke

– DERIVATIVES **mineralogical** adj. **mineralogically** adv. **mineralogist** n.

mineral oil ■ n. petroleum, or a distillation product of petroleum.

mineral spirits ■ n. another term for WHITE SPIRIT.

mineral water ■ n. water having some dissolved salts naturally present.

mineral wool ■ n. a substance resembling matted wool and made from inorganic mineral material, used chiefly for packing or insulation.

mineshaft ■ n. a deep, narrow shaft that gives access to a mine.

minestrone /ˌmɪnɪˈstrəʊni/ ■ n. a soup containing vegetables and pasta.
– ORIGIN from Italian.

minesweeper ■ n. a warship equipped for detecting and removing or destroying tethered explosive mines.
– DERIVATIVES **minesweeping** n.

mineworker ■ n. a person who works in a mine; a miner.

Ming ■ n. **1** the dynasty ruling China from 1368 to 1644. **2** [as modifier] denoting Chinese porcelain made during the Ming dynasty, characterized by elaborate designs and vivid colours.
– ORIGIN Chinese, 'clear or bright'.

mingle ■ v. **1** mix or cause to mix together. **2** move around and engage with others at a social function.
– ORIGIN Middle English: from obsolete *meng* 'mix, blend', perhaps influenced by Middle Dutch *mengelen*.

mingy /ˈmɪn(d)ʒi/ ■ adj. (**-ier**, **-iest**) informal mean; ungenerous.
– DERIVATIVES **mingily** adv.
– ORIGIN C20: perhaps a blend of MEAN[2] and STINGY.

mini ■ adj. denoting a miniature version of something. ■ n. (pl. **minis**) a very short skirt or dress.

mini- ■ comb. form very small or minor of its kind; miniature: *minibus*.
– ORIGIN from MINIATURE, reinforced by MINIMUM.

miniature ■ adj. of a much smaller size than normal. ■ n. **1** a thing that is much smaller than normal. ▸ a plant or animal that is a smaller version of an existing variety or breed. ▸ a very small and minutely detailed painting, especially a portrait.
– DERIVATIVES **miniaturist** n. **miniaturization** (also **-isation**) n. **miniaturize** (also **-ise**) v.
– ORIGIN C16: from Italian *miniatura*, from Latin *miniare* 'rubricate, illuminate', from *minium* 'red lead, vermilion' (used to mark particular words in manuscripts).

minibar ■ n. a refrigerator in a hotel room containing a selection of drinks.

minibus ■ n. **1** a small bus for about ten to fifteen passengers. **2** (also **minibus taxi**) S. African another term for TAXI.

minicab ■ n. Brit. a car that is used as a taxi but which must be ordered in advance.

minicam ■ n. a hand-held video camera.

minidisc ■ n. a disc having a format similar to a small CD but able to record sound or data as well as play it back.

minidress ■ n. a very short dress.

minigolf ■ n. an informal version of golf played on a series of short obstacle courses.

minim ■ n. Music a note having the time value of two crotchets or half a semibreve, represented by a ring with a stem.
– ORIGIN Middle English: from Latin *minima*, from *minimus* 'smallest'.

minima plural form of MINIMUM.

minimal ■ adj. **1** of a minimum amount, quantity, or degree. **2** Art characterized by the use of simple or primary forms or structures. ▸ Music characterized by the repetition and gradual alteration of short phrases.
– DERIVATIVES **minimally** adv.
– ORIGIN C17: from Latin *minimus* 'smallest'.

minimalist ■ n. **1** a person who practises or supports the theories of minimal art or music. **2** a person advocating moderate reform in politics. ■ adj. **1** of or relating to minimal art or music. ▸ deliberately simple or basic in design or style. **2** advocating moderate political reform.

– DERIVATIVES **minimalism** n.
– ORIGIN C20: first used with ref. to the Russian Mensheviks; usage in art and music dates from the 1960s.

minimart ■ n. N. Amer. a convenience store.

minimax ■ n. Mathematics the lowest of a set of maximum values.
– ORIGIN 1940s: blend of MINIMUM and MAXIMUM.

mini-me ■ n. informal a person closely resembling a smaller or younger version of another.
– ORIGIN the name of a cloned character in the film *Austin Powers: The Spy Who Shagged Me* (1999).

minimize (also **-ise**) ■ v. **1** reduce to the smallest possible amount or degree. **2** represent or estimate at less than the true value or importance.
– DERIVATIVES **minimization** (also **-isation**) n. **minimizer** (also **-iser**) n.

minimum ■ n. (pl. **minima** or **minimums**) the least or smallest amount, extent, or intensity possible or recorded. ■ adj. smallest or lowest in amount, extent, or intensity.
– ORIGIN C17: from Latin, from *minimus* 'least'.

minimum wage ■ n. the lowest wage permitted by law or by agreement.

mining bee ■ n. a solitary bee that builds long underground tunnels containing nest chambers. [*Andrena* and other genera.]

minion /ˈmɪnjən/ ■ n. a follower or underling of a powerful person, especially a servile or unimportant one.
– ORIGIN C15: from French *mignon*, *mignonne*.

mini-pill ■ n. a contraceptive pill containing a progestogen and not oestrogen.

mini rugby ■ n. a simplified version of rugby with only nine players in a team.

miniseries ■ n. (pl. same) a television drama shown in a small number of episodes.

miniskirt ■ n. a very short skirt.

minister ■ n. **1** a head of a government department. **2** a diplomatic agent, usually ranking below an ambassador, representing a state or sovereign in a foreign country. **3** a member of the clergy. **4** (also **minister general**) the superior of some religious orders. ■ v. **1** (**minister to**) attend to the needs of. **2** act as a minister of religion. **3** administer (a sacrament).
– DERIVATIVES **ministerial** adj. **ministerially** adv. **ministership** n.
– ORIGIN Middle English: from Old French *ministre* (n.), from Latin *minister* 'servant', from *minus* 'less'.

Minister without Portfolio ■ n. a government minister who has cabinet status, but is not in charge of a specific department of state.

ministration ■ n. **1** (usu. **ministrations**) chiefly formal or humorous the provision of assistance or care. **2** the services of a minister of religion or of a religious institution. **3** the action of administering the sacrament.
– DERIVATIVES **ministrant** n.

ministry ■ n. (pl. **-ies**) **1** a government department headed by a minister. **2** chiefly Brit. a period of government under one Prime Minister. **3** the work, vocation, or office of a minister of religion. ▸ spiritual service to others provided by the Christian Church. **4** the action of ministering to someone.

minivan ■ n. a small van fitted with seats for passengers.

mink ■ n. (pl. same or **minks**) a semiaquatic stoat-like carnivore widely farmed for its fur. [*Mustela vison* (N. America) and *M. lutreola* (Eurasia).] ▸ the thick brown fur of the mink.
– PHRASES **mink and manure** S. African informal of or relating to the wealthy suburbs of an urban area or their inhabitants. [with ref. to expensive clothing and horse riding and racing.] ▸ wealthy.
– ORIGIN Middle English: from Swedish.

minke /ˈmɪŋkə, -ki/ ■ n. a small rorqual whale with a dark grey back, white underparts, and pale markings on the fins and behind the head. [*Balaenoptera acutorostrata*.]
– ORIGIN 1930s: prob. from *Meincke*, the name of a Norwegian whaler.

minneola /ˌmɪnɪˈəʊlə/ ■ n. a deep reddish tangelo of a thin-skinned variety.
– ORIGIN C20: named after a town in Florida, US.

minnow ■ n. 1 a small freshwater fish of the carp family, which typically forms large shoals. [*Phoxinus phoxinus*.] ▸ used in names of similar fishes, e.g. mudminnow. ▸ Fishing an artificial lure imitating a minnow. 2 a small or unimportant person or organization.
– ORIGIN Middle English: prob. rel. to Dutch *meun* and German *Münne*, influenced by Anglo-Norman French *menu* 'small, minnow'.

Minoan /mɪˈnəʊən/ ■ adj. relating to or denoting a Bronze Age civilization centred on Crete (*c*.3000–1050 BC). ■ n. an inhabitant of Minoan Crete.
– ORIGIN named after the legendary Cretan king *Minos*.

minor ■ adj. 1 having little importance, seriousness, or significance. 2 Music (of a scale) having intervals of a semitone between the second and third degrees, and (usually) the fifth and sixth, and the seventh and eighth. Contrasted with MAJOR. ▸ (of an interval) characteristic of a minor scale and less by a semitone than the equivalent major interval. ▸ [often postpos.] (of a key or mode) based on a minor scale: *Concerto in A minor*. ■ n. 1 a person under the age of full legal responsibility. 2 Music a minor key, interval, or scale. 3 N. Amer. a student's subsidiary subject or course. 4 a small drab moth which has purplish caterpillars that feed on grass. [Genus *Oligia*.] ■ v. (**minor in**) N. Amer. study or qualify in as a subsidiary subject.
– ORIGIN Middle English: from Latin, 'smaller, less'.

minor axis ■ n. Geometry the shorter axis of an ellipse that is perpendicular to its major axis.

minority ■ n. (pl. **-ies**) 1 the smaller number or part; a number or part representing less than half of the whole. 2 a relatively small group of people, differing from others in race, religion, language, or political persuasion. 3 the state or period of being a minor.
– ORIGIN C15: from French *minorité* or medieval Latin *minoritas*, from Latin *minor* (see MINOR).

minority government ■ n. a government in which the governing party has most seats but still less than half the total.

minor league ■ n. N. Amer. a league below the level of the major league in baseball or American football.
– DERIVATIVES **minor-leaguer** n.

minor orders ■ pl. n. chiefly historical the grades of Catholic or Orthodox clergy below the rank of deacon.

minor planet ■ n. an asteroid.

minor suit ■ n. Bridge diamonds or clubs.

Minotaur /ˈmɪnətɔː, ˈmaɪ-/ ■ n. Greek & Roman Mythology a creature who was half-man and half-bull, kept in a labyrinth by king Minos and killed by Theseus.
– ORIGIN from Greek *Minōtauros* 'bull of Minos'.

minoxidil /mɪˈnɒksɪdɪl/ ■ n. Medicine a synthetic drug which is used as a vasodilator in the treatment of hypertension, and also in lotions to promote hair growth.
– ORIGIN 1970s: from *amino* (see AMINO ACID) + OXIDE + *-dil* (perhaps representing DILATE).

minster ■ n. a large or important church, typically one of cathedral status in the north of England that was built as part of a monastery.
– ORIGIN Old English *mynster*, from Greek *monastērion* (see MONASTERY).

minstrel ■ n. 1 a medieval singer or musician. ▸ a member of a group of entertainers wearing blackface. 2 short for CAPE MINSTREL.
– ORIGIN Middle English: from Old French *menestral* 'entertainer, servant', from Latin *minister* (see MINISTER).

minstrelsy ■ n. the practice of performing as a minstrel.

mint¹ ■ n. 1 an aromatic plant with two-lipped, typically lilac flowers, several kinds of which are used as culinary herbs. [Genus *Mentha*: several species.] ▸ the flavour of mint, especially peppermint. 2 a peppermint sweet.
– DERIVATIVES **minty** adj. (**-ier**, **-iest**)
– ORIGIN Old English *minte*, of West Germanic origin; from Greek *minthē*.

mint² ■ n. 1 a place where money is coined. 2 informal a large sum of money: *it cost a mint*. ■ adj. in pristine condition; as new. ■ v. 1 make (a coin) by stamping metal. 2 [usu. as adj. **minted**] produce for the first time: *newly minted technology*.
– DERIVATIVES **mintage** n. **minter** n.
– ORIGIN Old English *mynet* 'coin', of West Germanic origin; from Latin *moneta* 'money'.

mint julep ■ n. a long drink consisting of bourbon, crushed ice, sugar, and fresh mint.

Minton ■ n. pottery made at Stoke-on-Trent by Thomas Minton (1766–1836) or his factory.

mint sauce ■ n. chopped spearmint in vinegar and sugar, traditionally eaten with lamb.

minuend /ˈmɪnjʊɛnd/ ■ n. Mathematics a quantity or number from which another is to be subtracted.
– ORIGIN C18: from Latin *minuendus*, from *minuere* 'diminish'.

minuet ■ n. 1 a stately ballroom dance in triple time, popular in the 18th century. 2 a piece of music in triple time in the style of such a dance, typically as a movement in a suite, sonata, or symphony.
– ORIGIN C17: from French *menuet*, 'fine, delicate', diminutive of *menu* 'small'.

minus ■ prep. 1 with the subtraction of. 2 (of temperature) falling below zero by: *minus 40 degrees centigrade*. 3 informal lacking: *he was minus a finger*. ■ adj. 1 (before a number) below zero; negative. 2 (after a grade) rather worse than: *C minus*. ■ n. 1 short for MINUS SIGN. 2 informal a disadvantage.
– ORIGIN C15: from Latin, neuter of *minor* 'less'.

minuscule /ˈmɪnəskjuːl/ ■ adj. 1 extremely tiny. 2 of or in lower-case letters, as distinct from capitals or uncials.
– ORIGIN C18: from French, from Latin *minuscula* (*littera*) 'somewhat smaller (letter)'.

USAGE
The correct spelling is **minuscule** rather than **miniscule**.

minus sign ■ n. the symbol –, indicating subtraction or a negative value.

minute¹ /ˈmɪnɪt/ ■ n. 1 a period of time equal to sixty seconds or a sixtieth of an hour. 2 informal a very short time. 3 (also **arc minute** or **minute of arc**) a sixtieth of a degree of angular measurement. (Symbol: ′)
– PHRASES **at the minute** Brit. informal at the present time. **up to the minute** incorporating the very latest information or developments.
– ORIGIN Middle English: from late Latin *minuta* (n.), from *minutus* 'made small'; the senses 'period of sixty seconds' and 'sixtieth of a degree' derive from medieval Latin *pars minuta prima* 'first minute part'.

minute² /maɪˈnjuːt/ ■ adj. (**-est**) 1 extremely small. 2 precise and meticulous: *a minute examination*.
– DERIVATIVES **minutely** adv. **minuteness** n.
– ORIGIN Middle English: from Latin *minutus* 'lessened', from *minuere*.

minute³ /ˈmɪnɪt/ ■ n. 1 (**minutes**) a summarized record of the points discussed at a meeting. 2 an official memorandum. ■ v. 1 record or note (the points discussed at a meeting). 2 send (someone) a minute.
– ORIGIN Middle English: from French *minute*, from the notion of a rough copy in 'small writing' (Latin *scriptura minuta*).

minute gun ■ n. a gun fired at intervals of a minute, especially at a funeral.

minute steak ■ n. a thin slice of steak cooked very quickly.

minutiae /mɪˈnjuːʃiː, maɪ-, -ʃɪaɪ/ (also **minutia** /-ʃə/) ■ pl. n. the small or precise details of something.
– ORIGIN C18: Latin, 'trifles', from *minutus* (see MINUTE²).

minx ■ n. humorous or derogatory an impudent, cunning, or boldly flirtatious girl or young woman.
– ORIGIN C16.

minyan /ˈmɪnjən/ ■ n. (pl. **minyanim** /ˈmɪnjənɪm/) a quorum of ten men over the age of 13 required for traditional Jewish public worship.
– ORIGIN C18: from Hebrew *minyān* 'reckoning'.

Miocene /ˈmaɪə(ʊ)siːn/ ■ adj. Geology relating to or denoting the fourth epoch of the Tertiary period (between the Oligocene and Pliocene epochs, 23.3 to 5.2 million

years ago), a time when the first apes appeared.
– ORIGIN C19: from Greek *meiōn* 'less' + *kainos* 'new'.

miombo ■ n. Ecology a central and southern African vegetation type dominated by deciduous trees of the genera *Brachystegia* and *Julbernardia*, interspersed with grassland.
– ORIGIN from the Kiswahili name for *Brachystegia*.

miosis /mʌɪˈəʊsɪs/ (also **myosis**) ■ n. excessive constriction of the pupil of the eye.
– DERIVATIVES **miotic** adj.
– ORIGIN C19: from Greek *muein* 'shut the eyes'.

mirabelle /ˌmɪrəˈbɛl/ ■ n. **1** a sweet yellow plum-like fruit that is a variety of the greengage. ▸ the tree that bears such fruit. **2** a liqueur distilled from mirabelles.
– ORIGIN C18: from French.

mirabile dictu /mɪˌrɑːbɪleɪ ˈdɪktuː/ ■ adv. wonderful to relate.
– ORIGIN from Latin.

miracidium /ˌmʌɪrəˈsɪdɪəm/ ■ n. (pl. **miracidia**) Zoology a free-swimming ciliated larval stage in which a parasitic fluke passes from the egg to its first host, typically a snail.
– ORIGIN C19: from Greek *meirakidion*, diminutive of *meirakion* 'boy, stripling'.

miracle ■ n. **1** an extraordinary and welcome event that is not explicable by natural or scientific laws, attributed to a divine agency. ▸ a remarkable and very welcome occurrence. **2** an amazing product or achievement, or an outstanding example of something: *a miracle of design*.
– ORIGIN Middle English: from Latin *miraculum* 'object of wonder', from *mirari* 'to wonder', from *mirus* 'wonderful'.

miracle play ■ n. a mystery play.

miraculous ■ adj. having the character of a miracle.
– DERIVATIVES **miraculously** adv. **miraculousness** n.

mirador /ˌmɪrəˈdɔː, ˈmɪrədəː/ ■ n. a turret or tower attached to a building and providing an extensive view.
– ORIGIN C17: from Spanish, from *mirar* 'to look'.

mirage /ˈmɪrɑːʒ, mɪˈrɑːʒ/ ■ n. an optical illusion caused by atmospheric conditions, especially the appearance of a sheet of water in a desert or on a hot road caused by the refraction of light from the sky by heated air.
– ORIGIN C19: from French, from *se mirer* 'be reflected', from Latin *mirare* 'look at'.

mire ■ n. **1** a stretch of swampy or boggy ground. ▸ soft mud or dirt. **2** a state of difficulty from which it is hard to extricate oneself. ■ v. **1** cause to become stuck in mud. ▸ cover or spatter with mud. **2** beset with difficulties.
– ORIGIN Middle English: from Old Norse *mýrr*, of Germanic origin.

mirid /ˈmɪrɪd, ˈmʌɪərɪd/ ■ n. an active plant bug of a large family (Miridae) that includes numerous plant pests.
– ORIGIN 1940s: from *mirus* 'wonderful'.

mirin /ˈmɪrɪn/ ■ n. a rice wine used as a flavouring in Japanese cookery.
– ORIGIN from Japanese.

mirror ■ n. **1** a surface, typically of glass coated with a metal amalgam, which reflects a clear image. **2** something regarded as accurately representing something else. **3** (also **mirror site**) Computing a site on a network which stores the contents copied from another site. ■ v. **1** show a reflection of. **2** correspond to. **3** Computing copy the contents of (a network site) and store at another site. ▸ store copies of data in (two or more hard disks).
– DERIVATIVES **mirrored** adj.
– ORIGIN Middle English: from Old French *mirour*, from Latin *mirare* 'look at'.

mirrorball ■ n. a revolving ball covered with small mirrored facets, used to provide lighting effects at discos or dances.

mirror carp ■ n. a common carp of an ornamental variety that has a row of large shiny plate-like scales along each side.

mirror finish ■ n. a smooth reflective finish.

mirror image ■ n. an identical image, but with the structure reversed, as in a mirror.

mirror writing ■ n. reversed writing resembling ordinary writing reflected in a mirror.

mirth ■ n. amusement; laughter.
– DERIVATIVES **mirthful** adj. **mirthfully** adv.
– ORIGIN Old English, of Germanic origin.

mirthless ■ adj. (of a smile or laugh) lacking real amusement and typically expressing irony.
– DERIVATIVES **mirthlessly** adv. **mirthlessness** n.

miry /ˈmʌɪri/ ■ adj. very muddy or boggy.

MIS ■ abbrev. Computing management information systems.

mis-[1] ■ prefix (added to verbs and their derivatives) wrongly: *misapply*. ▸ badly: *mismanage*. ▸ unsuitably: *misname*.
– ORIGIN Old English, of Germanic origin.

mis-[2] ■ prefix occurring in a few words adopted from French expressing a sense with negative force: *misadventure*.
– ORIGIN from Old French *mes-* (from Latin *minus*), assimilated to **MIS-[1]**.

misadventure ■ n. **1** (also **death by misadventure**) chiefly Brit. & US Law death caused accidentally while performing a legal act without negligence or intent to harm. **2** a mishap.

misaligned ■ adj. incorrectly aligned.
– DERIVATIVES **misalignment** n.

misalliance ■ n. an unsuitable or unhappy alliance or marriage.

misanthrope /ˈmɪz(ə)nθrəʊp, mɪs-/ (also **misanthropist** /mɪˈzanθrəpɪst, mɪˈsan-/) ■ n. a person who dislikes humankind.
– DERIVATIVES **misanthropic** adj. **misanthropical** adj. **misanthropically** adv.
– ORIGIN C16: from Greek *misanthrōpos*, from *misein* 'to hate' + *anthrōpos* 'human being'.

misanthropy /mɪˈzanθrəpi, mɪˈsan-/ ■ n. A dislike of humankind.
– ORIGIN C17: from Greek *misanthrōpia*, from *miso-* 'hating' + *anthrōpos* 'human being'.

misapply ■ v. (**-ies, -ied**) use for the wrong purpose or in the wrong way.
– DERIVATIVES **misapplication** n.

misapprehension ■ n. a mistaken belief.

misappropriate ■ v. dishonestly or unfairly take for one's own use.
– DERIVATIVES **misappropriation** n.

misbegotten ■ adj. **1** badly conceived, designed, or planned. ▸ contemptible. **2** archaic (of a child) illegitimate.

misbehave ■ v. behave badly.
– DERIVATIVES **misbehaviour** n.

misbelief ■ n. a wrong or false belief or opinion.

misc. ■ abbrev. miscellaneous.

miscalculate ■ v. calculate or assess wrongly.
– DERIVATIVES **miscalculation** n.

miscall ■ v. **1** call by a wrong or inappropriate name. **2** archaic or dialect insult verbally.

miscarriage ■ n. the spontaneous or unplanned expulsion of a fetus from the womb before it is able to survive independently.

miscarriage of justice ■ n. a failure of a court or judicial system to attain the ends of justice.

miscarry ■ v. (**-ies, -ied**) **1** have a miscarriage. **2** (of a plan) fail.

miscast ■ v. (past and past part. **miscast**) (usu. **be miscast**) allot an unsuitable role to (an actor).

miscegenation /ˌmɪsɪdʒɪˈneɪʃ(ə)n/ ■ n. the interbreeding of people of different races.
– ORIGIN C19: from Latin *miscere* 'to mix' + *genus* 'race'.

miscellanea /ˌmɪsəˈleɪnɪə/ ■ pl. n. miscellaneous items collected together.
– ORIGIN C16: from Latin, from *miscellaneus* (see **MISCELLANEOUS**).

miscellaneous /ˌmɪsəˈleɪnɪəs/ ■ adj. of various types. ▸ composed of members or elements of different kinds.
– DERIVATIVES **miscellaneously** adv. **miscellaneousness** n.
– ORIGIN C17: from Latin *miscellaneus*, from *miscellus* 'mixed', from *miscere* 'to mix'.

miscellany /mɪˈsɛləni/ ■ n. (pl. **-ies**) a mixture. ▸ a collection of pieces of writing by different authors.
– ORIGIN C16: from French *miscellanées*, from Latin *miscellaneus* (see **MISCELLANEOUS**).

mischance

mischance ■ n. bad luck. ▶ an unlucky occurrence.

mischief ■ n. **1** playful misbehaviour or troublemaking. **2** harm or injury caused by someone or something.
– PHRASES **do someone a mischief** informal injure someone.
– ORIGIN Middle English: from Old French *meschief*, from *meschever* 'come to an unfortunate end'.

mischievous ■ adj. **1** causing or disposed to mischief. **2** intended to cause harm or trouble.
– DERIVATIVES **mischievously** adv. **mischievousness** n.
– ORIGIN Middle English: from Anglo-Norman French *meschevous*, from Old French *meschever* (see **MISCHIEF**).

USAGE
Mischievous is a three-syllable word; do not pronounce it with four syllables, as if it were spelled **mischievious** (mɪsˈtʃiːvɪəs).

miscible /ˈmɪsɪb(ə)l/ ■ adj. (of liquids) forming a homogeneous mixture when added together.
– DERIVATIVES **miscibility** n.
– ORIGIN C16: from medieval Latin *miscibilis*, from Latin *miscere* 'to mix'.

miscommunication ■ n. failure to communicate adequately.

misconceive ■ v. **1** fail to understand correctly. **2** (usu. **be misconceived**) judge or plan badly.

misconception ■ n. a false or mistaken view or opinion.

misconduct ■ n. **1** unacceptable or improper behaviour. **2** mismanagement. ■ v. (**misconduct oneself**) behave in an improper manner.

misconstrue ■ v. (**misconstrues, misconstrued, misconstruing**) interpret wrongly.
– DERIVATIVES **misconstruction** n.

miscount ■ v. count incorrectly. ■ n. an incorrect count.

miscreant /ˈmɪskrɪənt/ ■ n. a person who behaves badly or unlawfully. ■ adj. behaving badly or unlawfully.
– ORIGIN Middle English: from Old French *mescreant*, from *mescreire* 'disbelieve', from *mes-* 'mis-' + *creire* 'believe' (from Latin *credere*).

miscue[1] ■ n. (in billiards and snooker) a failure to cue the ball properly. ▶ (in other sports) a faulty strike, kick, or catch. ■ v. (**miscues, miscued, miscueing** or **miscuing**) perform a miscue.

miscue[2] ■ n. Linguistics a reading error caused by failure to respond correctly to a phonetic or contextual cue.

misdate ■ v. assign an incorrect date to.

misdeed ■ n. a wicked or illegal act.

misdemeanour (US **misdemeanor**) ■ n. a minor wrongdoing. ▶ Law a non-indictable offence, regarded in the US (and formerly the UK) as less serious than a felony.

misdescribe ■ v. describe inaccurately.
– DERIVATIVES **misdescription** n.

misdiagnose ■ v. diagnose incorrectly.
– DERIVATIVES **misdiagnosis** n.

misdial ■ v. (**misdialled, misdialling**; US **misdialed, misdialing**) dial a telephone number incorrectly.

misdirect ■ v. **1** direct wrongly. **2** (of a judge) instruct (a jury) wrongly.
– DERIVATIVES **misdirection** n.

misdoing ■ n. a misdeed.

misdoubt ■ v. chiefly archaic or dialect have doubts about the truth or existence of. ▶ be suspicious about.

mise en scène /ˌmiːz ɒ̃ ˈsɛn/ ■ n. **1** the arrangement of scenery and stage properties in a play. **2** the setting of an event.
– ORIGIN French, 'putting on stage'.

miser ■ n. a person who hoards wealth and spends very little.
– ORIGIN C15: from Latin, 'wretched'.

miserable ■ adj. **1** wretchedly unhappy or uncomfortable. ▶ causing unhappiness or discomfort. ▶ habitually morose. **2** pitiably small or inadequate. ▶ contemptible.
– DERIVATIVES **miserableness** n. **miserably** adv.

– ORIGIN Middle English: from Latin *miserabilis* 'pitiable', from *miserari* 'to pity', from *miser* 'wretched'.

miserere /ˌmɪzəˈrɪəri, -ˈrɛː-/ ■ n. **1** a psalm, prayer, or cry for mercy. **2** another term for **MISERICORD**.
– ORIGIN Middle English: from Latin, 'have mercy!', from *misereri*, from *miser* 'wretched'.

misericord /mɪˈzɛrɪkɔːd/ ■ n. a ledge projecting from the underside of a hinged seat in a choir stall, giving support to someone standing when the seat is folded up.
– ORIGIN Middle English: from Old French *misericorde*, from Latin, from *misericors* 'compassionate', from *misereri* 'to pity' + *cor* 'heart'.

miserly ■ adj. **1** of or characteristic of a miser. **2** (of a quantity) pitiably small.
– DERIVATIVES **miserliness** n.

misery ■ n. (pl. **-ies**) wretched unhappiness or discomfort. ▶ a cause of this. ▶ Brit. informal a person who is constantly miserable.
– PHRASES **put someone/thing out of their misery** kill an animal in pain. ▶ informal release someone from suspense or anxiety.
– ORIGIN Middle English: from Old French *miserie*, from Latin, from *miser* 'wretched'.

misfield ■ v. (in cricket and rugby) field (a ball) badly. ■ n. an instance of misfielding.

misfire ■ v. **1** (of a gun) fail to fire properly. ▶ (of an internal-combustion engine) fail to ignite the fuel correctly or at all. **2** fail to produce the intended result. ■ n. an instance of misfiring.

misfit ■ n. **1** a person whose behaviour or attitude sets them apart from others. **2** something that does not fit or fits badly.

misfortune ■ n. bad luck. ▶ an unfortunate event.

misgive ■ v. (past **misgave**; past part. **misgiven**) poetic/literary (of the mind or heart) fill (someone) with doubt, apprehension, or foreboding.

misgiving ■ n. a feeling of doubt or apprehension about something.

misgovern ■ v. govern unfairly or poorly.
– DERIVATIVES **misgovernment** n.

misguided ■ adj. showing faulty judgement or reasoning.
– DERIVATIVES **misguidedly** adv. **misguidedness** n.

mishandle ■ v. handle wrongly or ineffectively.

mishap ■ n. an unlucky accident.

mishear ■ v. (past and past part. **misheard**) hear incorrectly.

mishit ■ v. (**mishitting**; past and past part. **mishit**) hit or kick (a ball) badly. ■ n. an instance of mishitting.

mishmash ■ n. a confused mixture.
– ORIGIN C15: reduplication of **MASH**.

Mishnah /ˈmɪʃnə/ ■ n. a collection of exegetical material embodying the oral tradition of Jewish law and forming part of the Talmud.
– ORIGIN from Hebrew *mišnāh* '(teaching by) repetition'.

misidentify /ˌmɪsʌɪˈdɛntɪfʌɪ/ ■ v. (**-ies, -ied**) identify incorrectly.
– DERIVATIVES **misidentification** /-fɪˈkeɪʃ(ə)n/ n.

misinform ■ v. give false or inaccurate information to.
– DERIVATIVES **misinformation** n.

misinterpret ■ v. (**misinterpreted, misinterpreting**) interpret wrongly.
– DERIVATIVES **misinterpretation** n.

misjudge ■ v. form an incorrect opinion of. ▶ judge wrongly.
– DERIVATIVES **misjudgement** (also **misjudgment**) n.

miskey ■ v. (**-eys, -eyed**) key (words or data) wrongly.

miskick ■ v. kick (a ball) badly. ■ n. an instance of miskicking.

Miskito /mɪˈskiːtəʊ/ ■ n. (pl. same or **-os**) **1** a member of an American Indian people of the Atlantic coast of Nicaragua and Honduras. **2** the language of this people.
– ORIGIN the name in Miskito.

mislay ■ v. (past and past part. **mislaid**) unintentionally put (an object) where it cannot readily be found.

mislead ■ v. (past and past part. **misled**) cause to have a wrong impression about someone or something.
– DERIVATIVES **misleading** adj. **misleadingly** adv.

mismanage ■ v. manage badly or wrongly.
– DERIVATIVES **mismanagement** n.

mismatch ■ n. 1 a failure to correspond or match. 2 an unequal sporting contest. ■ v. [usu. as adj. **mismatched**] match unsuitably or incorrectly.

mismeasure ■ v. measure or estimate incorrectly.
– DERIVATIVES **mismeasurement** n.

misname ■ v. give a wrong or inappropriate name to.

misnomer ■ n. a wrong or inaccurate name or term. ▸ the wrong use of a name or term.
– ORIGIN Middle English: from Old French *mesnommer*, from *mes-* 'wrongly' + *nommer* 'to name' (from Latin *nomen* 'name').

miso /ˈmiːsəʊ/ ■ n. paste made from fermented soya beans and barley or rice malt, used in Japanese cookery.
– ORIGIN from Japanese.

misogynist /mɪˈsɒdʒ(ə)nɪst, mʌɪ-/ ■ n. a man who hates women.
– DERIVATIVES **misogynistic** adj.

misogyny /mɪˈsɒdʒ(ə)ni, mʌɪ-/ ■ n. hatred of women.
– DERIVATIVES **misogynous** adj.
– ORIGIN C17: from Greek *misos* 'hatred' + *gunē* 'woman'.

misplace ■ v. put in the wrong place.
– DERIVATIVES **misplacement** n.

misplaced ■ adj. incorrectly placed. ▸ unwise or inappropriate.

misplay ■ v. play (a ball or card) wrongly or badly.

misprint ■ n. an error in printed text. ■ v. print incorrectly.

misprision /mɪsˈprɪʒ(ə)n/ (also **misprision of treason** or **felony**) ■ n. Law, chiefly historical the deliberate concealment of one's knowledge of a crime.
– ORIGIN Middle English: from Old French *mesprision* 'error', from *mesprendre*, from *mes-* 'wrongly' + *prendre* 'to take'.

mispronounce ■ v. pronounce wrongly.
– DERIVATIVES **mispronunciation** n.

misquote ■ v. quote inaccurately. ■ n. an inaccurate quote.
– DERIVATIVES **misquotation** n.

misread ■ v. (past and past part. **misread**) read or interpret wrongly.

misreport ■ v. give a false or inaccurate report of.

misrepresent ■ v. give a false or misleading account of.
– DERIVATIVES **misrepresentation** n. **misrepresentative** adj.

misrule ■ n. unfair or inefficient government. ▸ disorder. ■ v. govern badly.

miss[1] ■ v. 1 fail to hit, reach, or come into contact with. ▸ be too late to catch. ▸ fail to notice, hear, or understand. ▸ fail to attend, watch, or participate in. ▸ avoid. 2 (usu. **miss something out**) omit. 3 notice the loss or absence of. ▸ feel regret or sadness at the absence of. 4 (of an engine or vehicle) misfire. ■ n. an instance of missing something.
– PHRASES **give something a miss** informal decide not to do or have something. **miss the boat** (or **bus**) informal be too slow to take advantage of something. **not miss a trick** informal never fail to take advantage of a situation.
– DERIVATIVES **missable** adj.
– ORIGIN Old English, of Germanic origin.

miss[2] ■ n. 1 (**Miss**) a title prefixed to the name of an unmarried woman or girl. ▸ the title of a beauty queen: *Miss World*. ▸ used to address a female shop assistant, teacher, etc. 2 often derogatory or humorous a girl or young woman, especially one regarded as silly.
– DERIVATIVES **missish** adj.
– ORIGIN C17: abbrev. of MISTRESS.

missal /ˈmɪs(ə)l/ ■ n. a book of the texts used in Catholic Mass throughout the year.
– ORIGIN Middle English: from medieval Latin *missale*, from eccles. Latin *missalis* 'relating to the Mass', from *missa* 'Mass'.

misshapen ■ adj. not having the normal or natural shape.

missile ■ n. 1 an object which is forcibly propelled at a target. 2 a weapon that is self-propelled or directed by remote control.
– ORIGIN C17: from Latin *missile* (n.), from *missilis*, from *mittere* 'send'.

missing ■ adj. absent and of unknown whereabouts. ▸ not present when expected or supposed to be. ▸ not yet confirmed as alive, but not known to be dead.

missing link ■ n. a hypothetical fossil form intermediate between two living forms, especially between humans and apes.

mission ■ n. 1 an important assignment, typically involving travel abroad. ▸ [treated as sing. or pl.] a group of people sent on a mission. ▸ an organization or institution involved in a long-term assignment abroad. ▸ a military or scientific expedition. 2 the vocation of a religious organization to spread its faith. ▸ a strongly felt aim or calling. 3 a building or group of buildings used by a Christian mission. 4 informal, chiefly S. African a long and tedious process.
– ORIGIN C16: from Latin *missio(n-)*, from *mittere* 'send'.

missionary ■ n. (pl. **-ies**) a person sent on a religious mission. ■ adj. of or characteristic of a missionary or religious mission.

missionary position ■ n. informal a position for sexual intercourse in which a couple lie face to face with the woman underneath the man.
– ORIGIN said to be so named because early missionaries advocated the position as 'proper' to primitive peoples.

missioner ■ n. 1 a person in charge of a religious mission. 2 a missionary.

mission statement ■ n. a formal summary of the aims and values of an organization.

mission station ■ n. another term for MISSION (in sense 3).

missis /ˈmɪsɪs, -ɪz/ ■ n. variant spelling of MISSUS.

Mississippian ■ adj. 1 of or relating to the US state of Mississippi. 2 Archaeology of or denoting a settled culture of the south-eastern US, dated to AD 800–1300.

missive ■ n. formal or humorous a letter.
– ORIGIN Middle English: from medieval Latin *missivus*, from Latin *mittere* 'send'.

misspell ■ v. (past and past part. **misspelt** or **misspelled**) spell wrongly.

misspend ■ v. (past and past part. **misspent**) [usu. as adj. **misspent**] spend (time or money) foolishly or wastefully.

misstate ■ v. make wrong or inaccurate statements about.
– DERIVATIVES **misstatement** n.

misstep ■ n. 1 a badly judged step. 2 a mistake.

missus /ˈmɪsəz/ (also **missis**) ■ n. informal or humorous a person's wife. ▸ informal a form of address to a woman. ▸ (also **miesies**) S. African dated a title or form of address to a white woman.

missy ■ n. (pl. **-ies**) used as an affectionate or disparaging form of address to a young girl.

mist ■ n. a cloud of tiny water droplets in the atmosphere at or near the earth's surface, limiting visibility to a lesser extent than fog. ▸ a condensed vapour settling on a surface. ▸ a blurring of the sight, especially caused by tears. ■ v. cover or become covered with mist.
– ORIGIN Old English, of Germanic origin.

mistake ■ n. a thing which is not correct. ▸ an error of judgement. ■ v. (past **mistook**; past part. **mistaken**) be wrong about. ▸ (**mistake someone/thing for**) wrongly identify someone or something as.
– DERIVATIVES **mistakable** (also **mistakeable**) adj. **mistakably** (also **mistakeably**) adv.
– ORIGIN Middle English: from Old Norse *mistaka* 'take in error'.

mistaken ■ adj. wrong. ▸ (especially of a belief) based on a misunderstanding or faulty judgement.
– DERIVATIVES **mistakenly** adv. **mistakenness** n.

mist belt ■ n. an area of high humidity and frequent mists, supporting specialized vegetation types. ▸ such an area in the eastern foothills of the Drakensberg.

mister ■ n. full form of MR, often used humorously. ▸ informal a form of address to a man.

mistime ■ v. choose an inappropriate moment to do or say.

mistletoe ■ n. a leathery-leaved parasitic plant which grows on broadleaf trees and bears white berries in winter. [*Viscum album* (Eurasia), *Phoradendron flavescens* (N. America), and other species.]
– ORIGIN Old English *misteltān*, from *mistel* 'mistletoe' (of Germanic origin) + *tān* 'twig'.

mistook past of MISTAKE.

mistral /ˈmɪstr(ə)l, mɪˈstrɑːl/ ■ n. a strong, cold north-westerly wind that blows through the Rhône valley and southern France towards the Mediterranean.
– ORIGIN C17: French, from Latin *magistralis* (*ventus*) 'master wind'.

mistranslate ■ v. translate incorrectly.
– DERIVATIVES **mistranslation** n.

mistreat ■ v. treat badly or unfairly.
– DERIVATIVES **mistreatment** n.

mistress ■ n. 1 a woman in a position of authority or control. ▸ chiefly Brit. a female schoolteacher. ▸ the female owner of a dog, cat, etc. ▸ archaic a female head of a household. 2 a woman skilled in a particular subject or activity: *a mistress of the sound bite*. 3 a woman (other than a wife) having a sexual relationship with a married man. ▸ archaic or poetic/literary a woman loved and courted by a man. 4 (**Mistress**) archaic or dialect Mrs.
– ORIGIN Middle English: from Old French *maistresse*, from *maistre* 'master'.

mistrial ■ n. a trial rendered invalid through an error in proceedings. ▸ US an inconclusive trial.

mistrust ■ v. have no trust in. ■ n. lack of trust.
– DERIVATIVES **mistrustful** adj. **mistrustfully** adv. **mistrustfulness** n.

misty ■ adj. (-ier, -iest) full of, covered with, or accompanied by mist. ▸ indistinct or dim in outline.
– DERIVATIVES **mistily** adv. **mistiness** n.

mistype ■ v. type incorrectly.

misunderstand ■ v. (past and past part. **misunderstood** /-ˈstʊd/) fail to understand correctly.

misunderstanding ■ n. a failure to understand something correctly. ▸ a disagreement.

misuse ■ v. 1 use wrongly. 2 treat badly or unfairly. ■ n. the action of misusing something.

MIT ■ abbrev. Massachusetts Institute of Technology.

mite[1] ■ n. a minute arachnid with four pairs of legs, several kinds of which are parasitic. [Order Acari: many species.]
– ORIGIN Old English, of Germanic origin.

mite[2] ■ n. 1 a small child or animal. 2 a very small amount. ■ adv. (**a mite**) informal a little; slightly.
– ORIGIN Middle English: from Middle Dutch *mīte*.

miter ■ n. & v. US spelling of MITRE.

Mithraism /ˈmɪθreɪɪz(ə)m, ˈmɪθreɪ-/ ■ n. the cult of the ancient Persian god Mithras, a god of light, truth, and honour chiefly worshipped in the first three centuries AD.
– DERIVATIVES **Mithraic** /-ˈθreɪɪk/ adj. **Mithraist** n.

mitigate /ˈmɪtɪɡeɪt/ ■ v. [often as adj. **mitigating**] make less severe, serious, or painful.
– DERIVATIVES **mitigation** n. **mitigator** n. **mitigatory** adj.
– ORIGIN Middle English: from Latin *mitigare* 'soften, alleviate'.

USAGE
The verbs **mitigate** and **militate** are often confused. **Mitigate** means 'make less severe', as in *drainage schemes have helped to mitigate this problem*, while **militate** is used with **against** to mean 'be a powerful factor in preventing', as in *laws that militate against personal freedom*.

mitochondrion /ˌmaɪtə(ʊ)ˈkɒndrɪən/ ■ n. (pl. **mitochondria** /-rɪə/) Biology a structure found in large numbers in most cells, in which respiration and energy production occur.
– DERIVATIVES **mitochondrial** adj.
– ORIGIN C20: from Greek *mitos* 'thread' + *khondrion* (diminutive of *khondros* 'granule').

mitosis /maɪˈtəʊsɪs/ ■ n. (pl. **mitoses**) Biology a type of cell division that results in daughter cells each with the same number and kind of chromosomes as the parent nucleus. Compare with MEIOSIS.
– DERIVATIVES **mitotic** adj.
– ORIGIN C19: from Greek *mitos* 'thread'.

mitral /ˈmaɪtr(ə)l/ ■ adj. Anatomy relating to or denoting the valve between the left atrium and the left ventricle of the heart.
– ORIGIN C17: from Latin *mitra* 'belt or turban' (from the valve's shape).

mitre (US **miter**) ■ n. 1 a tall headdress worn by bishops and senior abbots, tapering to a point at front and back with a deep cleft between. 2 (also **mitre joint**) a joint made between two pieces of wood or other material at an angle of 90°, such that the line of junction bisects this angle. ▸ a diagonal seam of two pieces of fabric that meet at a corner. 3 (also **mitre shell**) a mollusc of warm seas which has a sharply pointed shell with a narrow aperture. [*Mitra* and other genera.] ■ v. join by means of a mitre.
– DERIVATIVES **mitred** adj.
– ORIGIN Middle English: from Greek *mitra* 'belt or turban'.

mitre box ■ n. a guide for a saw when cutting mitre joints.

mitt ■ n. 1 a mitten. ▸ a glove leaving the fingers and thumb-tip exposed. ▸ (also **baseball mitt**) Baseball a large fingerless glove worn by the catcher or first baseman. 2 informal a hand.
– ORIGIN C18: abbrev. of MITTEN.

mitten ■ n. a glove with two sections, one for the thumb and the other for all four fingers.
– DERIVATIVES **mittened** adj.
– ORIGIN Middle English: from Old French *mitaine*, perhaps from *mite* pet name for a cat (because mittens were often made of fur).

mitzvah /ˈmɪtsvə/ ■ n. (pl. **mitzvoth** /-vəʊt/) Judaism 1 a precept or commandment. 2 a good deed done from religious duty.
– ORIGIN C17: from Hebrew *miṣwāh* 'commandment'.

mix ■ v. 1 combine or be able to be combined to form a whole. ▸ make by mixing ingredients. ▸ combine (signals or soundtracks) into one to produce a recording. 2 (**mix something up**) spoil the order or arrangement of something. ▸ (**mix someone/thing up**) confuse someone or something with another. 3 associate with others socially. ■ n. a mixture of two or more different people or things. ▸ the proportion of different people or things constituting a mixture. ▸ a version of a recording mixed in a different way from the original.
– PHRASES **be** (or **get**) **mixed up in** (or **with**) be (or become) involved in or with (dubious or dishonest actions or people). **mix and match** select and combine different but complementary items to form a coordinated set.
– DERIVATIVES **mixable** adj.
– ORIGIN Middle English: back-formation from MIXED.

mixed ■ adj. consisting of different qualities or elements. ▸ involving a mixture of races or social classes. ▸ of or for members of both sexes.
– ORIGIN Middle English: from Old French *mixte*, from Latin *mixtus*, from *miscere* 'to mix'.

mixed bag (also **mixed bunch**) ■ n. a diverse assortment.

mixed blessing ■ n. a thing with advantages and disadvantages.

mixed doubles ■ pl. n. [treated as sing.] (especially in tennis and badminton) a game involving sides each consisting of a man and a woman.

mixed economy ■ n. an economic system combining private and state enterprise.

mixed farming ■ n. farming of both crops and livestock.

mixed grill ■ n. a dish of various grilled meats and vegetables.

mixed marriage ■ n. a marriage between people of different races or religions.

mixed media ■ n. the use of a variety of media in entertainment or art. ■ adj. (**mixed-media**) another term for MULTIMEDIA.

mixed metaphor ■ n. a combination of incompatible metaphors (e.g. *this tower of strength will forge ahead*).

mixed number ■ n. a number consisting of an integer and a proper fraction.

mixed-up ■ adj. informal suffering from psychological or emotional problems.

mixed veld ■ n. S. African land covered with a mixture of grassland and shrubs.

mixer ■ n. 1 a machine or device for mixing things. 2 a person considered in terms of their ability to mix socially: *a good mixer*. 3 a soft drink that can be mixed with alcohol. 4 (in recording and cinematography) a device for merging input signals to produce a combined output. ▸ a person who operates this.

mixer tap ■ n. a tap through which mixed hot and cold water can be drawn by means of separate controls.

mixing desk ■ n. a console where sound signals are mixed.

Mixolydian mode /ˌmɪksəˈlɪdɪən/ ■ n. Music the mode represented by the natural diatonic scale G–G (containing a minor 7th).
– ORIGIN C16: *Mixolydian* from Greek *mixoludios* 'half-Lydian'.

mixture ■ n. a substance made by mixing other substances together. ▸ the process of mixing or being mixed. ▸ (**a mixture of**) a combination of different things in which the components are individually distinct. ▸ the charge of gas or vapour mixed with air admitted to the cylinder of an internal-combustion engine.
– ORIGIN Middle English: from Latin *mixtura*, from *mixtus* (see MIXED).

mix-up ■ n. informal a confusion or misunderstanding.

mizzen /ˈmɪz(ə)n/ (also **mizen**) ■ n. 1 (also **mizzenmast**) the mast aft of a ship's mainmast. 2 (also **mizzensail**) a sail on a mizzenmast.
– ORIGIN Middle English: from Italian, from *mezzano* 'middle', from Latin *medianus* (see MEDIAN) + MAST¹.

mjondolo /(ə)mˈdʒɒnˈdɔlɔ/ (also **jondolo**) ■ n. S. African a shack.
– ORIGIN from isiZulu *umjondolo*.

MK ■ n. short for UMKHONTO WE SIZWE.

Mk ■ abbrev. 1 the German mark. 2 (followed by a numeral) mark (of a vehicle or machine).

mkhukhu /(ə)mˈkuːkuː/ (also **mokhukhu**) ■ n. S. African 1 a shack, especially one built using corrugated iron. 2 another term for MOKHUKHU (in sense 2).
– ORIGIN from isiZulu *umkhukhu*.

ml ■ abbrev. 1 mile(s). 2 millilitre(s).

MLitt ■ abbrev. Master of Letters.
– ORIGIN from Latin *Magister Litterarum*.

Mlle ■ abbrev. (pl. **Mlles**) Mademoiselle.

mm ■ abbrev. millimetre(s).

Mme ■ abbrev. (pl. **Mmes**) Madame.

MMR ■ abbrev. measles, mumps, and rubella (a vaccination given to children).

MMS ■ abbrev. Multimedia Messaging Service, a system that enables cellphones to send and receive colour pictures and sound clips as well as text messages.

MMus ■ abbrev. Master of Music.

Mn ■ symb. the chemical element manganese.

mnemonic /nɪˈmɒnɪk/ ■ n. a device, e.g. a pattern of letters or ideas, which aids the memory. ■ adj. aiding or designed to aid the memory. ▸ of or relating to the power of memory.
– ORIGIN C18: from Greek *mnēmonikos*, from *mnēmōn* 'mindful'.

mnemonics ■ pl. n. [usu. treated as sing.] the study and development of systems for improving and aiding the memory.

MO ■ abbrev. 1 Medical Officer. 2 modus operandi.

Mo ■ symb. the chemical element molybdenum.

mo ■ n. informal a moment.

753

-mo /məʊ/ ■ suffix forming nouns denoting a book size by the number of leaves into which a sheet of paper has been folded: *twelvemo*.
– ORIGIN from the final syllable of Latin ordinal numbers in the ablative singular, such as *duodecimo*.

mo. ■ abbrev. month.

moan ■ n. 1 a long, low sound expressing suffering or sexual pleasure. ▸ a low sound made by the wind. 2 informal a trivial complaint. ■ v. 1 utter or make a moan. ▸ poetic/literary lament. 2 informal complain or grumble.
– DERIVATIVES **moaner** n. **moanful** adj.
– ORIGIN Middle English.

moat ■ n. a deep, wide defensive ditch surrounding a castle or town, typically filled with water. ■ v. [often as adj. **moated**] surround with a moat.
– ORIGIN Middle English: from Old French *mote* 'mound'.

mob ■ n. 1 a disorderly or violent crowd. 2 informal an associated group of people. ▸ (**the Mob**) N. Amer. the Mafia. ▸ (**the mob**) the ordinary people. ■ v. (**mobbed, mobbing**) crowd round in an unruly and excitable way. ▸ N. Amer. crowd into.
– ORIGIN C17: abbrev. of archaic *mobile*, short for Latin *mobile vulgus* 'excitable crowd'.

mob cap ■ n. a large, soft indoor hat covering the hair, worn by women in the 18th and early 19th centuries.
– ORIGIN C18: *mob*, var. of obsolete *mab* 'slut'.

mob-handed ■ adv. Brit. informal in considerable numbers.

mobile /ˈməʊbʌɪl/ ■ adj. able to move or be moved freely or easily. ▸ (of a shop, library, etc.) accommodated in a vehicle so as to travel around. ▸ able or willing to move between occupations, places of residence, or social classes. ■ n. 1 a decorative structure suspended so as to turn freely in the air. 2 short for MOBILE PHONE.
– PHRASES **upwardly** (or **downwardly**) **mobile** moving to a higher (or lower) social class.
– DERIVATIVES **mobility** n.
– ORIGIN C15 (*mobility* Middle English): from Latin *mobilis*, from *movere* 'to move'.

mobile home ■ n. a large caravan used as permanent living accommodation.

mobile phone (also **mobile telephone**) ■ n. another term for CELLPHONE.

mobility allowance ■ n. Brit. a state travel benefit for disabled people.

mobilize (also **-ise**) ■ v. 1 prepare and organize (troops) for active service. ▸ organize (people or resources) for a particular task. 2 make mobile. ▸ make transportable by or as a liquid.
– DERIVATIVES **mobilization** (also **-isation**) n. **mobilizer** (also **-iser**) n.

Möbius strip /ˈməːbɪəs/ ■ n. a surface with one continuous side formed by joining the ends of a rectangle after twisting one end through 180°.
– ORIGIN C20: named after the German mathematician August F. *Möbius*.

mob rule ■ n. political control imposed and enforced by a mob.

mobster ■ n. informal a gangster.

moccasin ■ n. 1 a soft leather slipper or shoe, having the sole turned up and sewn to the upper in a gathered seam, originally worn by North American Indians. 2 a venomous American pit viper. [Genus *Agkistrodon*: three species.]
– ORIGIN C17: from Virginia Algonquian *mockasin*.

mocha /ˈmɒkə/ ■ n. a fine-quality coffee. ▸ a drink or flavouring made with this, typically with chocolate added.
– ORIGIN C18: named after *Mocha*, a port on the Red Sea, from where the coffee was first shipped.

mock ■ v. tease scornfully; ridicule. ▸ mimic scornfully or contemptuously. ■ adj. imitation; pretended. ■ n. (**mocks**) Brit. informal mock examinations.
– DERIVATIVES **mocking** adj. **mockingly** adv.
– ORIGIN Middle English: from Old French *mocquer* 'deride'.

mocker ■ n. a person who mocks.
– PHRASES **put the mockers on** Brit. informal put an end to. ▸ bring bad luck to.

mocker

mockery

mockery ■ n. (pl. **-ies**) ridicule. ▸ an absurd imitation.
– PHRASES **make a mockery of** cause to appear foolish or absurd.

mock-heroic ■ adj. imitating the style of heroic literature to satirise a mundane or prosaic subject.

mockingbird ■ n. a long-tailed American songbird with greyish plumage, noted for mimicking the calls of other birds. [*Mimus polyglottos* and other species.]

mock moon ■ n. Astronomy a paraselene.

mock orange ■ n. a bushy shrub with strongly orange-scented white flowers. [*Philadelphus coronarius* and related species.]

mock sun ■ n. Astronomy a parhelion.

mock-up ■ n. an experimental replica or model of something.

mod ■ adj. informal modern. ■ n. Brit. (especially in the 1960s) a young person of a group characterized by a stylish appearance and the riding of motor scooters.

modal /ˈməʊd(ə)l/ ■ adj. **1** of or relating to mode or form as opposed to substance. **2** Grammar of or denoting the mood of a verb. **3** Logic (of a proposition) in which the predicate is affirmed of the subject with some qualification or condition.
– DERIVATIVES **modally** adv.

modalism ■ n. Theology the doctrine that the persons of the Trinity represent only three modes or aspects of the divine nature.

modality ■ n. (pl. **-ies**) **1** modal quality. **2** a method or procedure. **3** a form of sensory perception.

modal verb ■ n. Grammar an auxiliary verb expressing necessity or possibility, e.g. *must, shall, will*.

mod cons ■ pl. n. informal modern conveniences.

mode ■ n. **1** a way in which something occurs or is done. ▸ Computing a way of operating a system. ▸ Physics any of the kinds or patterns of vibration of an oscillating system. ▸ Logic the character of a modal proposition. ▸ Logic & Grammar another term for MOOD². **2** a style in clothes, art, etc. **3** Statistics the value that occurs most frequently in a given data set. **4** Music a set of musical notes forming a scale and from which melodies and harmonies are constructed.
– ORIGIN Middle English: from Latin *modus* 'measure'.

model ■ n. **1** a three-dimensional representation of a person or thing, typically on a smaller scale. ▸ (in sculpture) a figure in clay or wax, to be reproduced in a more durable material. **2** something used as an example. ▸ a simplified description, especially a mathematical one, of a system or process, to assist calculations and predictions. ▸ a person or thing that is an excellent example of a quality: *she was a model of self-control*. **3** a person employed to display clothes by wearing them. ▸ a person employed to pose for an artist, sculptor, etc. **4** a particular version of a product. ▸ a garment or a copy of a garment by a well-known designer. ■ v. (**modelled**, **modelling**, US **modeled**, **modeling**) **1** fashion or shape (a figure) in clay, wax, etc. ▸ Art cause to appear three-dimensional. **2** (**model something on/after**) use as an example for something. **3** display (clothes) by wearing them. ▸ work as a model.
– DERIVATIVES **modeller** n. **modelling** n.
– ORIGIN C16: from French *modelle*, alteration of Latin *modulus* (see MODULUS).

Model C ■ n. [usu. as modifier] S. African **1** a state school, reserved for white pupils during apartheid but admitting black pupils under a classification scheme effective between 1992 and 1996. ▸ a school formerly falling under this designation. **2** informal, derogatory a characteristic of a black person assumed to have had a more privileged education in such a school: *a model C accent*.

modem /ˈməʊdem/ ■ n. a device for interconverting digital and analogue signals, especially to enable a computer to be connected to a telephone line.
– ORIGIN C20: blend of *modulator* and *demodulator*.

moderate /ˈmɒd(ə)rət/ ■ adj. **1** average in amount, intensity, or degree. **2** not radical or excessively right- or left-wing. ■ n. /ˈmɒd(ə)rət/ a person with moderate views. ■ v. /ˈmɒdəreɪt/ **1** make or become less extreme, intense, or violent. **2** review (examination papers or results) so as to ensure consistency of marking. **3** (in academic and ecclesiastical contexts) preside over (a deliberative body) or act (a debate). **4** monitor (an Internet bulletin board or chat room) for inappropriate or offensive content. **5** Physics retard (neutrons) with a moderator.
– DERIVATIVES **moderately** adv.
– ORIGIN Middle English: from Latin *moderare* 'reduce, control'.

moderation ■ n. **1** the avoidance of excess or extremes, especially in one's behaviour or political opinions. **2** the process of moderating examination papers or results. **3** Physics the retardation of neutrons by a moderator.
– PHRASES **in moderation** within reasonable limits.

moderator ■ n. **1** an arbitrator or mediator. ▸ a presiding officer, especially a chairman of a debate. ▸ a Presbyterian minister presiding over an ecclesiastical body. **2** a person who moderates examination papers. **3** Physics a substance used in a nuclear reactor to retard neutrons. **4** a person who moderates an Internet bulletin board or chat room.
– DERIVATIVES **moderatorship** n.

modern ■ adj. of or relating to the present or recent times. ▸ characterized by or using the most up-to-date techniques, equipment, etc. ▸ denoting a recent style in art, architecture, etc. marked by a departure from traditional styles and values. ■ n. a person who advocates a departure from traditional styles or values.
– DERIVATIVES **modernity** n. **modernness** n.
– ORIGIN Middle English: from late Latin *modernus*, from Latin *modo* 'just now'.

modern English ■ n. English since about 1500.

modern history ■ n. history from the end of the Middle Ages to the present day.

modernism ■ n. modern ideas, methods, or styles. ▸ a movement in the arts or religion that aims to break with traditional forms or ideas.
– DERIVATIVES **modernist** n. & adj. **modernistic** adj.

modernize (also **-ise**) ■ v. adapt to modern needs or habits.
– DERIVATIVES **modernization** (also **-isation**) n. **modernizer** (also **-iser**) n.

modern Latin ■ n. Latin since 1500, used especially in scientific terminology.

modest ■ adj. **1** unassuming in the estimation of one's abilities. **2** relatively moderate, limited, or small. **3** decent; decorous.
– DERIVATIVES **modestly** adv. **modesty** n.
– ORIGIN C16: from French *modeste*, from Latin *modestus* 'keeping due measure', rel. to *modus* 'measure'.

modicum /ˈmɒdɪkəm/ ■ n. a small quantity of something.
– ORIGIN C15: from Latin *modicus* 'moderate', from *modus* 'measure'.

modification ■ n. the action of modifying. ▸ a change made.

modifier ■ n. **1** a person or thing that modifies something. **2** Grammar a word, especially an adjective or noun used attributively, that qualifies the sense of a noun (e.g. *good* and *family* in *a good family house*).

modify ■ v. (**-ies, -ied**) **1** make partial changes to (something) in order to improve it or lessen its severity. **2** Grammar qualify the sense of (a noun).
– DERIVATIVES **modifiable** adj. **modificatory** adj.
– ORIGIN Middle English: from Old French *modifier*, from Latin *modificare*, from *modus* (see MODE).

modillion /məˈdɪljən/ ■ n. Architecture a projecting bracket under the corona of a cornice in the Corinthian and other orders.
– ORIGIN C16: from French *modillon*, from Italian *modiglione*, from Latin *mutulus*.

modish /ˈməʊdɪʃ/ ■ adj. fashionable.
– DERIVATIVES **modishly** adv.

modular ■ adj. employing or involving modules.
– DERIVATIVES **modularity** n.

modulate /ˈmɒdjʊleɪt/ ■ v. **1** exert a modifying influence on; regulate. **2** vary the strength, tone, or pitch of (one's voice). ▸ alter the amplitude or frequency of (an oscillation or signal) in accordance with the variations of a second signal.
– DERIVATIVES **modulation** n. **modulator** n.

– ORIGIN C16 (*modulation* Middle English): from Latin *modulari* 'measure, make melody', from *modulus* (see **MODULUS**).

module ■ n. each of a set of standardized parts or independent units that can be used to construct a more complex structure. ▶ each of a set of independent units of study or training forming part of a course. ▶ an independent self-contained unit of a spacecraft.
– ORIGIN C16: from Latin *modulus* (see **MODULUS**).

modulus /ˈmɒdjʊləs/ ■ n. (pl. **moduli** /-lʌɪ, -liː/) Mathematics **1** another term for **ABSOLUTE VALUE** (in sense 1). ▶ the positive square root of the sum of the squares of the real and imaginary parts of a complex number. **2** a constant factor or ratio, especially one relating a physical effect to the force producing it. **3** a number used as a divisor for considering numbers in sets, numbers being considered congruent when giving the same remainder when divided by it.
– ORIGIN C16: from Latin, 'measure', diminutive of *modus*.

modus operandi /ˌməʊdəs ɒpəˈrandiː, -dʌɪ/ ■ n. (pl. **modi operandi** /ˌməʊdi/) a way of doing something. ▶ the way in which something works.
– ORIGIN Latin, 'way of operating'.

modus vivendi /ˌməʊdəs vɪˈvɛndiː, -dʌɪ/ ■ n. (pl. **modi vivendi** /ˌməʊdi/) **1** an arrangement allowing conflicting parties to coexist peacefully. **2** a way of living.
– ORIGIN Latin, 'way of living'.

moegoe /ˈmʊxʊ/ ■ n. S. African derogatory or humorous a stupid, dull, or gullible person.
– ORIGIN Afrikaans and Tsotsitaal.

moer[1] /muːr, mʊə/ S. African informal ■ v. hit; beat up.
– ORIGIN perhaps from Afrikaans *moor* 'to murder'.

moer[2] /muːr, mʊə/ S. African vulgar slang ■ n. (usu. in phr. **jou moer**) (expressing rage or disgust) stuff you!
– PHRASES **moer and gone** very far away. **the moer in** furiously angry. **moer of a** another term for **MOERSE**.
– ORIGIN Afrikaans, 'mother'.

moerse /ˈmuːrsə/ ■ adj. S. African informal tremendous; mighty.
– ORIGIN Afrikaans, 'mother's, mother of'.

moffie ■ n. S. African informal, derogatory an effeminate man. ▶ a male homosexual or transvestite.
– ORIGIN abbrev. of Afrikaans *moffiedaai* 'hermaphrodite'.

Mogadon /ˈmɒɡədɒn/ ■ n. trademark for **NITRAZEPAM**.

moggie (also **moggy**) ■ n. (pl. **-ies**) informal a cat.
– ORIGIN C17: var. of *Maggie*, familiar form of the given name *Margaret*.

moggy (also **moggie**) ■ adj. (**-ier**, **-iest**) S. African informal highly agitated or upset; crazed.

mogodisano /mɔɡɔdiˈsaːnɔ, mɔɡɔdiˈsaːnəʊ/ ■ n. S. African another term for **STOKVEL**.
– ORIGIN from Sesotho.

Mogul /ˈməʊɡ(ə)l/ (also **Moghul** or **Mughal**) ■ n. **1** a member of the Muslim dynasty of Mongol origin which ruled much of India in the 16th–19th centuries. **2** (**mogul**) informal an important or powerful person.
– ORIGIN from Persian *muġul* 'Mongol'.

mogul /ˈməʊɡ(ə)l/ ■ n. a bump on a ski slope formed by skiers turning.
– ORIGIN 1960s: prob. from southern German dialect *Mugel*, *Mugl*.

mohair ■ n. the hair of the angora goat. ▶ a yarn or fabric made from this.
– ORIGIN C16: from Arabic *muḵayyar* 'cloth made of goat's hair' (literally 'choice, select').

Mohawk ■ n. (pl. same or **Mohawks**) **1** a member of an American Indian people, originally inhabiting parts of what is now upper New York State. **2** the Iroquoian language of this people. **3** chiefly N. Amer. a Mohican haircut.
– ORIGIN from Narragansett (an extinct Algonquian language) *mohowawog* 'maneaters'.

Mohegan /məʊˈhiːɡ(ə)n/ (also **Mohican**) ■ n. **1** a member of an American Indian people formerly inhabiting western parts of Connecticut and Massachusetts. Compare with **MAHICAN**. **2** the extinct Algonquian language of this people. ■ adj. of or relating to the Mohegans or their language.
– ORIGIN from Mohegan, 'people of the tidal waters'.

molar

Mohican[1] /məʊˈhiːk(ə)n, ˈməʊɪk(ə)n/ ■ n. a hairstyle with the head shaved except for a central strip of hair from the forehead to the back of the neck, typically made to stand erect.
– ORIGIN 1960s: erroneously associated with the American Indian people.

Mohican[2] /məʊˈhiːk(ə)n/ ■ adj. & n. old-fashioned variant of **MAHICAN** or **MOHEGAN**.

Moho /ˈməʊhəʊ/ ■ n. Geology the boundary surface between the earth's crust and the mantle.
– ORIGIN 1930s: abbrev. of *Mohorovičić discontinuity*, named after the Yugoslav seismologist Andrija *Mohorovičić*.

Mohs' scale /məʊz/ ■ n. a scale of hardness used in classifying minerals.
– ORIGIN C19: named after the German mineralogist Friedrich *Mohs*.

moiety /ˈmɔɪti/ ■ n. (pl. **-ies**) formal or technical each of two parts into which a thing is or can be divided.
– ORIGIN Middle English: from Old French *moite*, from Latin *medietas* 'middle', from *medius* 'mid, middle'.

moire /mwɑː/ (also **moiré** /ˈmwɑːreɪ/) ■ n. silk fabric subjected to heat and pressure after weaving to give a rippled appearance. ■ adj. (of silk) having a finish of this type. ▶ having a pattern of irregular wavy lines like that of moire.
– ORIGIN C17: from French *moire* 'mohair'; *moiré* is from *moirer* 'give a watered appearance'.

moist ■ adj. **1** slightly wet; damp or humid. ▶ (of a climate) rainy. **2** Medicine marked by a fluid discharge.
– DERIVATIVES **moisten** v. **moistly** adv. **moistness** n.
– ORIGIN Middle English: from Old French *moiste*, from Latin *mucidus* 'mouldy'.

moisture ■ n. water or other liquid diffused in a small quantity as vapour, within a solid, or condensed on a surface.

moisturize (also **-ise**) ■ v. make (something, especially the skin) less dry.

moisturizer ■ n. a cosmetic preparation for moisturizing the skin.

mojo /ˈməʊdʒəʊ/ ■ n. (pl. **-os**) chiefly US a magic charm or spell. ▶ magic.
– ORIGIN C20: prob. of African origin; cf. Gullah *moco* 'witchcraft'.

moke ■ n. Brit. informal a donkey. ▶ Austral./NZ a horse, typically an inferior one.
– ORIGIN C19.

mokhukhu /mɔˈkuːkuː, məʊˈkuːkuː/ ■ n. S. African **1** another term for **MKHUKHU** (in sense 1). **2** an energetic, traditional dance performed by male members of the Zion Christian Church. ▶ the men's group within the Church known for their performance of this dance.

HISTORY
It is believed that the sense 'an energetic traditional dance ...' comes from the time that the Zion Christian Church split into two branches in the middle of the 20th Century. Supporters of one faction are said to have set fire to the *mokhukhus*, or huts, in which members of the other faction lived. A song about the burning huts, accompanied by vigorous dance steps, then came to be associated with a specific group of men within the Zion Christian Church.

mokoro /məˈkɔːrəʊ/ (also **makoro**) ■ n. a dugout canoe propelled with a long pole, used in the Okavango Delta in Botswana. ▶ a similar canoe used for tours of rivers and wetlands in other southern African countries.
– ORIGIN Setswana.

mol /məʊl/ ■ n. Chemistry short for **MOLE**[4].

molal /ˈməʊləl/ ■ adj. Chemistry (of a solution) containing one mole of solute per kilogram of solvent.

molar[1] (also **molar tooth**) ■ n. a grinding tooth at the back of a mammal's mouth.
– ORIGIN Middle English: from Latin *molaris*, from *mola* 'millstone'.

---

s sit   t top   v voice   w we   z zoo   ʃ she   ʒ decision   θ thin   ð this   ŋ ring   x loch   tʃ chip   dʒ jar

molar

molar² ■ adj. acting on or by means of large masses or units.
– ORIGIN C19: from Latin *moles* 'mass'.

molar³ ■ adj. Chemistry of or relating to one mole of a substance. ▸ (of a solution) containing one mole of solute per litre of solvent.
– DERIVATIVES **molarity** n.

molasses ■ n. **1** thick, dark brown juice obtained from raw sugar during the refining process. **2** N. Amer. golden syrup.
– ORIGIN C16: from Portuguese *melaço*, from late Latin *mellacium* 'must', from *mel* 'honey'.

mold ■ n. & v. US spelling of MOULD¹, MOULD², and MOULD³.

molder ■ v.& n. US spelling of MOULDER.

molding ■ n. US spelling of MOULDING.

Moldovan /mɒlˈdəʊv(ə)n/ ■ n. a native or inhabitant of Moldova, a country in SE Europe. ■ adj. of or relating to Moldova.

moldy ■ adj. US spelling of MOULDY.

mole¹ /məʊl/ ■ n. **1** a small burrowing insectivorous mammal with dark velvety fur, a long muzzle, and very small eyes. [Family Talpidae: many species.] **2** a spy who gradually achieves an important position within the security defences of a country. ▸ a betrayer of confidential information.
– ORIGIN Middle English: from the Germanic base of Middle Dutch and Middle Low German *mol*.

mole² /məʊl/ ■ n. a small dark blemish on the skin caused by a high concentration of melanin.
– ORIGIN Old English *māl* 'discoloured spot', of Germanic origin.

mole³ /məʊl/ ■ n. a large solid structure serving as a pier, breakwater, or causeway. ▸ a harbour formed by a mole.
– ORIGIN C16: from French *môle*, from Latin *moles* 'mass'.

mole⁴ /məʊl/ ■ n. Chemistry the SI unit of amount of substance, equal to the quantity containing as many elementary units as there are atoms in 0.012 kg of carbon-12.
– ORIGIN C20: from German *Mol*, from *Molekul* 'molecule'.

mole⁵ /məʊl/ ■ n. Medicine an abnormal mass of tissue in the uterus.
– ORIGIN Middle English: from French *môle*, from Latin *mola* in the sense 'false conception'.

mole cricket ■ n. a large burrowing nocturnal cricket-like insect with broad forelegs. [Family Gryllotalpidae: many species.]

molecular /məˈlɛkjʊlə/ ■ adj. of, relating to, or consisting of molecules.
– DERIVATIVES **molecularly** adv.

molecular biology ■ n. the branch of biology concerned with the macromolecules (e.g. proteins and DNA) essential to life.

molecular weight ■ n. another term for RELATIVE MOLECULAR MASS.

molecule /ˈmɒlɪkjuːl/ ■ n. Chemistry a group of atoms bonded together, representing the smallest fundamental unit of a compound that can take part in a chemical reaction.
– ORIGIN C18: from French *molécule*, from *molecula*, diminutive of Latin *moles* 'mass'.

molehill ■ n. a small mound of earth thrown up by a burrowing mole.
– PHRASES **make a mountain out of a molehill** greatly exaggerate the importance of a minor problem.

mole rat ■ n. a rat-like African rodent that lives underground, with long incisors used in digging. [Many species, mainly in the family Bathyergidae.]

moleskin ■ n. **1** the skin of a mole used as fur. **2** a thick, strong cotton fabric with a shaved pile surface.

mole snake ■ n. a non-venomous African snake feeding on moles and other small mammals. [*Pseudaspis cana*.]

molest ■ v. pester or harass in a hostile way. ▸ assault or abuse sexually.
– DERIVATIVES **molestation** n. **molester** n.
– ORIGIN Middle English: from Latin *molestare* 'annoy', from *molestus* 'troublesome'.

moline /məˈlaɪn/ ■ adj. [postpos.] Heraldry (of a cross) having each extremity broadened, split, and curved back.
– ORIGIN C16: prob. from Anglo-Norman French *moliné*, from *molin* 'mill', because of a resemblance to the iron support of a millstone.

moll ■ n. informal **1** a gangster's female companion. **2** a prostitute.
– ORIGIN C17: familiar form of the given name *Mary*.

mollify /ˈmɒlɪfʌɪ/ ■ v. (-ies, -ied) appease the anger or anxiety of.
– DERIVATIVES **mollification** n.
– ORIGIN Middle English: from French *mollifier* or Latin *mollificare*, from *mollis* 'soft'.

mollisol /ˈmɒlɪsɒl/ ■ n. Soil Science a temperate grassland soil with a dark, humus-rich surface layer containing high concentrations of calcium and magnesium.
– ORIGIN C20: from Latin *mollis* 'soft' + *solum* 'ground, soil'.

mollusc /ˈmɒləsk/ (US **mollusk**) ■ n. Zoology an invertebrate of a large phylum (Mollusca) including snails, slugs, and mussels, with a soft unsegmented body and often an external shell.
– DERIVATIVES **molluscan** /məˈlʌskən/ adj.
– ORIGIN C18: from Latin *molluscus*, from *mollis* 'soft'.

molly (also **mollie**) ■ n. a small live-bearing killifish which has been bred for aquaria in many colours, especially black. [Genus *Poecilia*: several species.]
– ORIGIN 1930s: from *Mollienisia* (former genus name), from the name of Count *Mollien*, French statesman.

mollycoddle ■ v. treat indulgently or overprotectively.
– ORIGIN C19: from *molly* 'girl' (see MOLL) + CODDLE.

Molotov cocktail ■ n. a crude incendiary device, typically a bottle of flammable liquid with a means of ignition.
– ORIGIN named after the Soviet statesman Vyacheslav *Molotov*, who organized their production in the Second World War.

molt ■ v.& n. US spelling of MOULT.

molten /ˈməʊlt(ə)n/ ■ adj. (especially of metal and glass) liquefied by heat.
– ORIGIN Middle English: from MELT.

Moluccan /məˈlʌkən/ ■ n. a native or inhabitant of the Molucca Islands in Indonesia. ■ adj. of or relating to the Molucca Islands.

moly /ˈməʊli/ ■ n. **1** a plant related to the onions, with small yellow flowers. [*Allium moly*.] **2** a mythical herb with white flowers and black roots, having magic properties.
– ORIGIN C16: from Greek *mōlu*.

molybdate /məˈlɪbdeɪt/ ■ n. Chemistry a salt in which the anion contains both molybdenum and oxygen: *ammonium molybdate*.

molybdenite /məˈlɪbdənʌɪt/ ■ n. a blue-grey mineral consisting of molybdenum disulphide.

molybdenum /məˈlɪbdənəm/ ■ n. the chemical element of atomic number 42, a brittle silver-grey metal. (Symbol: **Mo**)
– ORIGIN C19: orig. denoting a salt of lead, from Greek *molubdaina* 'plummet', from *molubdos* 'lead'.

mom ■ n. S. African & N. Amer. informal one's mother.

moment ■ n. **1** a brief period of time. ▸ an exact point in time. **2** formal importance. **3** Physics a turning effect produced by a force on an object, expressed as the product of the force and the distance from its line of action to a given point.
– PHRASES **(at) any moment** very soon. **for the moment** for now. **have one's** (or **its**) **moments** have periods that are better than others. **moment of truth** a time of crisis or test. **of the moment** currently popular, famous, or important.
– ORIGIN Middle English: from Latin *momentum* (see MOMENTUM).

momenta plural form of MOMENTUM.

momentarily ■ adv. **1** for a very short time. **2** N. Amer. very soon.

momentary ■ adj. brief.

moment of inertia ■ n. Physics a quantity expressing a body's tendency to resist angular acceleration.

momentous ■ adj. of great importance or significance.
– DERIVATIVES **momentously** adv. **momentousness** n.

momentum /məˈmɛntəm/ ■ n. (pl. **momenta** /-tə/) **1** Physics the quantity of motion of a moving body, equal to the product of its mass and velocity. **2** impetus gained by movement or progress: *the investigation gathered momentum*.
– ORIGIN C17: from Latin, from *movimentum*, from *movere* 'to move'.

momma ■ n. North American term for **MAMA**.

mommy ■ n. (pl. **-ies**) S. African & N. Amer. informal one's mother.

mommy track ■ n. N. Amer. informal a career path for women who sacrifice some promotions and pay rises in order to devote more time to raising their children.

Mon. ■ abbrev. Monday.

mon- ■ comb. form variant spelling of **MONO-** shortened before a vowel (as in *monamine*).

monad /ˈmɒnad, ˈməʊ-/ ■ n. **1** technical a single unit; the number one. **2** Philosophy (in the philosophy of Leibniz) an indivisible and hence ultimately simple entity, e.g. an atom or a person.
– DERIVATIVES **monadic** adj. **monadism** n. (Philosophy).
– ORIGIN C17: from Greek *monas, monad-* 'unit', from *monos* 'alone'.

monamine ■ n. variant spelling of **MONOAMINE**.

monarch /ˈmɒnək/ ■ n. **1** a sovereign head of state, especially a king, queen, or emperor. **2** a large migratory orange and black butterfly, chiefly North American, whose caterpillars feed on milkweed. [*Danaus plexippus*.] **3** (also **monarch flycatcher**) a flycatcher of Africa, Asia, and Australasia, typically with bold plumage. [Family Monarchidae: many species.]
– DERIVATIVES **monarchial** adj. **monarchic** adj. **monarchical** adj.
– ORIGIN Middle English: from late Latin *monarcha*, from Greek *monarkhēs*, from *monos* 'alone' + *arkhein* 'to rule'.

monarchism ■ n. support for the principle of monarchy.
– DERIVATIVES **monarchist** n. & adj.

monarchy ■ n. (pl. **-ies**) government by a monarch. ▸ a state with a monarch.
– ORIGIN Middle English: from Old French *monarchie*, from Greek *monarkhia* 'the rule of one'.

monastery ■ n. (pl. **-ies**) a community of monks living under religious vows.
– ORIGIN Middle English: from eccles. Greek *monastērion*, from *monazein* 'live alone', from *monos* 'alone'.

monastic ■ adj. of or relating to monks, nuns, etc., or the buildings in which they live. ▸ resembling monks or their way of life. ■ n. a monk or other follower of a monastic rule.
– DERIVATIVES **monastically** adv. **monasticism** n.
– ORIGIN Middle English: from late Latin *monasticus*, from Greek *monastikos*, from *monazein* 'live alone'.

monatomic /ˌmɒnəˈtɒmɪk/ ■ adj. Chemistry consisting of one atom.

Monday ■ n. the day of the week before Tuesday and following Sunday. ■ adv. on Monday. ▸ (**Mondays**) on Mondays; each Monday.
– ORIGIN Old English *Mōnandæg* 'day of the moon', translation of late Latin *lunae dies*.

Monégasque /ˌmɒneɪˈɡask/ ■ n. a native or national of Monaco. ■ adj. of or relating to Monaco or its inhabitants.
– ORIGIN from French.

monetarism ■ n. the theory or practice of controlling the supply of money as the chief method of stabilizing the economy.
– DERIVATIVES **monetarist** n. & adj.

monetary ■ adj. of or relating to money or currency.
– DERIVATIVES **monetarily** adv.

monetize /ˈmʌnɪtaɪz/ (also **monetarize, -ise**) ■ v. **1** convert into or express in the form of currency. **2** [usu. as adj. **monetized** (also **-ised**)] adapt (a society) to the use of money.
– DERIVATIVES **monetization** (also **-isation**) n.

money ■ n. a medium of exchange in the form of coins and banknotes. ▸ (**moneys**) or **monies** formal sums of money. ▸ wealth. ▸ payment or financial gain.
– PHRASES **be in the money** informal have or win a lot of money. **for my money** informal in my opinion or judgement. **money for old rope** (or **money for jam**) informal money or reward earned for little or no effort. **on the money** informal, chiefly N. Amer. accurate; correct. **put one's money where one's mouth is** informal take action to support one's statements or opinions.
– DERIVATIVES **moneyless** adj.
– ORIGIN Middle English: from Old French *moneie*, from Latin *moneta* 'mint, money'.

moneybags ■ pl. n. [treated as sing.] informal a wealthy person.

moneyed (also **monied**) ■ adj. having much money; wealthy.

money-grubbing ■ adj. informal overeager to make money; grasping.
– DERIVATIVES **money-grubber** n.

moneylender ■ n. a person whose business is lending money to others who pay interest.
– DERIVATIVES **moneylending** n. & adj.

money market ■ n. the trade in short-term loans between banks and other financial institutions.

money order ■ n. a printed order for payment of a specified sum, issued by a bank or Post Office.

money spider ■ n. a very small shiny black spider. [Family Linyphiidae.]
– ORIGIN so named because supposed to bring financial luck.

money-spinner ■ n. a thing that brings in a profit.
– DERIVATIVES **money-spinning** adj.

money supply ■ n. the total amount of money in circulation or in existence in a country.

-monger ■ comb. form **1** denoting a dealer or trader in a specified commodity: *fishmonger*. **2** chiefly derogatory denoting a person engaging in a particular activity: *rumour-monger*.
– ORIGIN Old English, from *mangian* 'to traffic', of Germanic origin, from Latin *mango* 'dealer'.

Mongol /ˈmɒŋɡ(ə)l/ ■ n. **1** a native or national of Mongolia; a Mongolian. **2** the Altaic language of this people; Mongolian. **3** (**mongol**) offensive a person with Down's syndrome. ■ adj. of or relating to the people of Mongolia or their language.
– DERIVATIVES **Mongolian** n. & adj. **mongolism** n. (offensive).

Mongoloid ■ adj. **1** of or relating to the broad division of humankind including the indigenous peoples of east Asia, SE Asia, and the Arctic region of North America. **2** (**mongoloid**) offensive affected with Down's syndrome. ■ n. **1** a person of a Mongoloid physical type. **2** offensive a person with Down's syndrome.

> USAGE
> The term **Mongoloid** belongs to a set of terms introduced by 19th-century anthropologists attempting to categorize human races. Such terms are associated with outdated notions of racial types, and so are now potentially offensive and best avoided.

mongoose ■ n. (pl. **mongooses**) a small carnivorous mammal with a long body and tail, native to Africa and Asia. [Family Herpestidae: many species.]
– ORIGIN C17: from Marathi *maṅgūs*.

mongrel ■ n. a dog of no definable type or breed.
– ORIGIN Middle English: of Germanic origin, apparently from a base meaning 'mix'.

monied ■ adj. variant spelling of **MONEYED**.

monies plural form of **MONEY**, as used in financial contexts.

moniker /ˈmɒnɪkə/ (also **monicker**) ■ n. informal a name.
– ORIGIN C19.

moniliform /məˈnɪlɪfɔːm/ ■ adj. Zoology resembling a string of beads.
– ORIGIN C19: from French *moniliforme*, from Latin *monile* 'necklace' + **-IFORM**.

monism

monism /ˈmɒnɪz(ə)m, ˈməʊ-/ ■ n. Philosophy & Theology **1** a theory or doctrine that denies the existence of a distinction or duality, such as that between matter and mind, or God and the world. **2** the doctrine that only one supreme being exists. Compare with **PLURALISM**.
– DERIVATIVES **monist** n. & adj. **monistic** adj.
– ORIGIN C19: from Greek *monos* 'single'.

monitor ■ n. **1** a person or device that monitors something. **2** a school pupil with disciplinary or other special duties. **3** a television receiver used in a studio to view the picture being transmitted from a particular camera. ▸ a screen which displays an image generated by a computer. ▸ a loudspeaker used by performers on stage to hear themselves or in a studio to hear what has been recorded. **4** (also **monitor lizard**) a large tropical Old World lizard with a long neck and a short body, formerly believed to warn of the approach of crocodiles. [Genus *Varanus*: many species.] ■ v. observe and check over a period of time. ▸ maintain regular surveillance over. ▸ listen to and report on (a radio broadcast or telephone conversation).
– DERIVATIVES **monitorial** adj. **monitorship** n.
– ORIGIN C16: from Latin, from *monere* 'warn'.

monk ■ n. a member of a religious community of men typically having a long tail and living in trees in tropical countries.
– DERIVATIVES **monkish** adj. **monkishly** adv. **monkishness** n.
– ORIGIN Old English *munuc*, from Greek *monakhos* 'solitary', from *monos* 'alone'.

monkey ■ n. (pl. **-eys**) **1** a small to medium-sized primate typically having a long tail and living in trees in tropical countries. [Families Cebidae and Callitrichidae (New World), and Cercopithecidae (Old World).] **2** a mischievous person, especially a child. **3** (also **monkey engine**) a piledriving machine consisting of a heavy hammer or ram working vertically in a groove. ■ v. (**-eys**, **-eyed**) (**monkey about/around**) behave in a silly or playful way. ▸ (**monkey with**) tamper with.
– PHRASES **make a monkey of** (or **out of**) make (someone) appear ridiculous. **a monkey on one's back** informal a burdensome problem. ▸ a dependence on drugs. **not give a monkey's** informal not care at all.
– DERIVATIVES **monkeyish** adj.
– ORIGIN C16: perhaps from Low German.

monkey bars ■ pl. n. a piece of playground equipment consisting of a horizontally mounted overhead ladder.

monkey business ■ n. informal mischievous or deceitful behaviour.

monkey flower ■ n. a plant of boggy ground, with yellow or red snapdragon-like flowers. [Genus *Mimulus*.]

monkey gland ■ n. S. African a spicy sauce for meat, made of fruit, onions, tomatoes, peppers, Worcestershire sauce, vinegar, and red wine.

monkey nut ■ n. Brit. a peanut.

monkey orange ■ n. a small southern African evergreen tree bearing hard-shelled fruit with edible pulp but poisonous seeds. [Genus *Strychnos*: several species.]

monkey puzzle ■ n. an evergreen coniferous tree with branches having spirals of tough spiny leaf-like scales, native to Chile. [*Araucaria araucana*.]

monkey rope ■ n. S. African a liana.

monkey suit ■ n. informal a man's evening dress or formal suit.

monkey's wedding ■ n. S. African informal simultaneous rain and sunshine.
– ORIGIN prob. rel to Portuguese *casamento di raposa* 'vixen's wedding', having the same sense.

monkey tricks ■ pl. n. informal, chiefly Brit. mischievous behaviour.

monkey wrench ■ n. an adjustable spanner with large jaws which has its adjusting screw contained in the handle.

monkfish ■ n. (pl. same or **-fishes**) **1** an angel shark. [Genus *Squatina*.] **2** an anglerfish. [Genus *Lophius*.]

Mon-Khmer /ˌmɔːnˈkmɛː/ ■ n. a family of Austro-Asiatic languages of SE Asia, of which the most important are Mon and Khmer.

monk seal ■ n. a seal with a dark back and pale underside, occurring in warm waters of the northern hemisphere. [Genus *Monachus*.]

monkshood ■ n. an aconite with blue or purple flowers. [*Aconitum napellus* (Europe), *A. uncinatum* (N. America), and related species.]

mono ■ adj. **1** monophonic. **2** monochrome. ■ n. (pl. **-os**) **1** monophonic reproduction. **2** monochrome reproduction.

mono- (also **mon-** before a vowel) ■ comb. form **1** one; alone; single: *monocoque*. **2** Chemistry (forming names of compounds) containing one atom or group of a specified kind: *monoamine*.
– ORIGIN from Greek *monos* 'alone'.

monoamine /ˌmɒnəʊˈeɪmiːn/ (also **monamine**) ■ n. Chemistry a compound having a single amine group in its molecule, especially one which is a neurotransmitter (e.g. serotonin, noradrenaline).

monoamine oxidase ■ n. Biochemistry an enzyme (present in most tissues) which catalyses the oxidation and inactivation of monoamine neurotransmitters.

monoamine oxidase inhibitor ■ n. Medicine any of a group of antidepressant drugs which inhibit the action of monoamine oxidase (so allowing accumulation of serotonin and noradrenaline in the brain).

monobasic ■ adj. Chemistry (of an acid) having one replaceable hydrogen atom.

monobloc ■ adj. made as or contained in a single casting.
– ORIGIN C20: from French, from **MONO-** + *bloc* 'block'.

monocarpic /ˌmɒnə(ʊ)ˈkɑːpɪk/ ■ adj. Botany (of a plant) flowering only once and then dying.
– ORIGIN C19: from **MONO-** + Greek *karpos* 'fruit'.

monocausal ■ adj. in terms of a sole cause.

monochromatic ■ adj. **1** containing or using only one colour. **2** Physics (of light or other radiation) of a single wavelength or frequency.

monochromatism ■ n. complete colour blindness in which all colours appear as shades of one colour.

monochromator /ˌmɒnə(ʊ)krəˈmeɪtə, ˌmɒnə(ʊ)ˈkrɒmɪtə/ ■ n. Physics a device used to select radiation of (or very close to) a single wavelength or energy.

monochrome ■ n. representation or reproduction in black and white or in varying tones of only one colour. ■ adj. (of a photograph or picture, or a television screen) consisting of or displaying images in black and white or in varying tones of only one colour.
– ORIGIN C17: from Greek *monokhrōmatos* 'of a single colour'.

monocle /ˈmɒnək(ə)l/ ■ n. a single eyeglass kept in position by the muscles around the eye.
– DERIVATIVES **monocled** adj.
– ORIGIN C19: from late Latin *monoculus* 'one-eyed'.

monocline /ˈmɒnə(ʊ)klaɪn/ ■ n. Geology a bend in rock strata that are otherwise uniformly dipping or horizontal.
– ORIGIN C19: from **MONO-** + Greek *klinein* 'to lean'.

monoclinic ■ adj. denoting a crystal system with three unequal axes of which one is at right angles to the other two.

monoclonal /ˌmɒnə(ʊ)ˈkləʊn(ə)l/ ■ adj. Biology forming a clone which is derived asexually from a single individual or cell.

monoclonal antibody ■ n. an antibody produced by a single clone of cells or cell line and consisting of identical antibody molecules.

monocoque /ˈmɒnə(ʊ)kɒk/ ■ n. an aircraft or vehicle structure in which the chassis is integral with the body.
– ORIGIN C20: from French, from *mono-* 'single' + *coque* 'shell'.

monocot ■ n. Botany short for **MONOCOTYLEDON**.

monocotyledon /ˌmɒnə(ʊ)kɒtɪˈliːd(ə)n/ ■ n. Botany a plant with an embryo bearing a single cotyledon, such plants constituting the smaller (Monocotyledoneae) of the two

classes of flowering species. Compare with **DICOTYLEDON**.
– DERIVATIVES **monocotyledonous** adj.

monocrystalline ■ adj. consisting of a single crystal.

monocular /məˈnɒkjʊlə/ ■ adj. with, for, or in one eye. ■ n. an optical instrument for viewing distant objects with one eye, like one half of a pair of binoculars.
– DERIVATIVES **monocularly** adv.
– ORIGIN C17: from late Latin *monoculus* 'having one eye'.

monoculture ■ n. the cultivation of a single crop in a given area.

monocycle ■ n. a unicycle.

monocyclic /ˌmɒnə(ʊ)ˈsaɪklɪk, -ˈsɪk-/ ■ adj. of or relating to a single cycle of activity.

monocyte /ˈmɒnə(ʊ)saɪt/ ■ n. Physiology a large phagocytic white blood cell with a simple oval nucleus and clear, greyish cytoplasm.

monodactyl /ˌmɒnə(ʊ)ˈdaktɪl/ ■ adj. Zoology having only one finger or toe on each hand or foot.

monodisperse /ˌmɒnə(ʊ)ˈdɪspəːs/ ■ adj. Chemistry (of a colloid) containing particles of uniform size.

monodrama ■ n. a dramatic piece for one performer.

monody /ˈmɒnədi/ ■ n. (pl. **-ies**) **1** an ode sung by a single actor in a Greek tragedy. **2** a poem lamenting a person's death.
– DERIVATIVES **monodic** adj.
– ORIGIN C17: from Greek *monōdia*, from *monōdos* 'singing alone'.

monoecious /məˈniːʃəs/ ■ adj. Biology (of a plant or invertebrate animal) having both the male and female reproductive organs in the same individual; hermaphrodite. Compare with **DIOECIOUS**.
– DERIVATIVES **monoecy** n.
– ORIGIN C18: from Greek *monos* 'single' + *oikos* 'house'.

monofilament (also **monofil**) ■ n. a single strand of man-made fibre. ▶ a type of fishing line using such a strand.

monogamy /məˈnɒɡəmi/ ■ n. **1** the practice of being married to or having a sexual relationship with only one person at a time. **2** Zoology the habit of having only one mate at a time.
– DERIVATIVES **monogamist** n. **monogamous** adj. **monogamously** adv.
– ORIGIN C17: from French *monogamie*, from Greek *monogamia*, from *monos* 'single' + *gamos* 'marriage'.

monogenean /ˌmɒnə(ʊ)dʒɪˈniːən, mɒnəˈdʒɛnɪən/ ■ adj. Zoology relating to or denoting a group of parasitic flukes which only require a single host to complete their life cycle. Compare with **DIGENEAN**.
– ORIGIN 1960s: from modern Latin *Monogenea*, from Greek *monos* 'single' + *genea* 'generation'.

monogenesis /ˌmɒnə(ʊ)ˈdʒɛnɪsɪs/ (also **monogeny** /məˈnɒdʒəni/) ■ n. origination from a single source or place.
– DERIVATIVES **monogenetic** adj.

monoglot /ˈmɒnə(ʊ)ɡlɒt/ ■ adj. using or speaking only one language. ■ n. a monoglot person.
– ORIGIN C19: from Greek *monoglōttos*, from *monos* 'single' + *glōtta* 'tongue'.

monogram ■ n. a motif of two or more interwoven letters, typically a person's initials. ■ v. decorate with a monogram.

monograph ■ n. a detailed written study of a single specialized subject. ■ v. write a monograph on.
– DERIVATIVES **monographer** n. **monographic** adj.

monohull ■ n. a boat with only one hull, as opposed to a catamaran or multihull.

monohybrid ■ n. Genetics a hybrid that is heterozygous with respect to a specified gene.

monohydrate ■ n. Chemistry a hydrate containing one mole of water per mole of the compound.

monokini ■ n. a woman's one-piece beach garment equivalent to the lower half of a bikini. ▶ a cut-out one-piece swimsuit with top and bottom sections linked at the front by fabric mesh, or chain.

monolatry /məˈnɒlətri/ ■ n. the worship of one god without denial of the existence of other gods.

monolayer ■ n. **1** Chemistry a layer one molecule thick. **2** Medicine a cell culture in a layer one cell thick.

monolingual ■ adj. speaking, using, or expressed in only one language.
– DERIVATIVES **monolingualism** n.

monolith ■ n. **1** a large single upright block of stone or concrete, especially a pillar or monument. **2** a very large and indivisible organization or institution.
– ORIGIN C19: from French *monolithe*, from Greek *monolithos*, from *monos* 'single' + *lithos* 'stone'.

monolithic ■ adj. **1** formed of a single large block of stone. **2** very large and uniform or indivisible. **3** Electronics (of a solid-state circuit) composed of active and passive components formed in a single chip.

monologue ■ n. **1** a long speech by one actor in a play or film. **2** a long, tedious speech by one person during a conversation.
– DERIVATIVES **monologic** adj. **monological** adj. **monologist** (also **-loguist**) n. **monologize** (also **-ise**) v.
– ORIGIN C17: from Greek *monologos* 'speaking alone'.

monomania ■ n. obsessive preoccupation with one thing.
– DERIVATIVES **monomaniac** n. & adj. **monomaniacal** adj.

monomer /ˈmɒnəmə/ ■ n. Chemistry a molecule that can be bonded to other identical molecules to form a polymer.
– DERIVATIVES **monomeric** adj.

monometallic ■ adj. consisting of one metal only. ▶ of, involving, or using a standard of currency based on one metal.

monomial /məˈnəʊmɪəl/ Mathematics ■ adj. (of an algebraic expression) consisting of one term. ■ n. a monomial expression.
– ORIGIN C18: from **MONO-**, on the pattern of *binomial*.

monomolecular ■ adj. Chemistry (of a layer) one molecule thick. ▶ consisting of or involving one molecule.

monomorphemic /ˌmɒnə(ʊ)mɔːˈfiːmɪk/ ■ adj. Linguistics consisting of a single morpheme.

monomorphic /ˌmɒnə(ʊ)ˈmɔːfɪk/ ■ adj. Biology (of a species or population) showing little or no variation in morphology or phenotype. ▶ (of an animal species) having sexes that are similar in size and appearance.
– DERIVATIVES **monomorphism** n.
– ORIGIN C19: from **MONO-** + Greek *morphē* 'form'.

mononuclear ■ adj. Biology (of a cell) having one nucleus.

mononucleosis /ˌmɒnə(ʊ)njuːklɪˈəʊsɪs/ ■ n. Medicine an abnormally high proportion of monocytes in the blood, especially associated with glandular fever.

monophonic /ˌmɒnə(ʊ)ˈfɒnɪk/ ■ adj. **1** (of sound reproduction) using only one channel of transmission. Compare with **STEREOPHONIC**. **2** Music having a single melodic line without harmonies or melody in counterpoint.
– DERIVATIVES **monophonically** adv. **monophony** n.

monophthong /ˈmɒnəfθɒŋ/ ■ n. Phonetics a vowel that has a single perceived auditory quality.
– ORIGIN C17: from Greek *monophthongos*, from *monos* 'single' + *phthongos* 'sound'.

monophyletic /ˌmɒnə(ʊ)fʌɪˈlɛtɪk/ ■ adj. Biology (of a group of organisms) descended from a common evolutionary ancestor or ancestral group, especially one not shared with any other group.

Monophysite /məˈnɒfɪsʌɪt/ ■ n. Christian Church a person who holds that there is only one inseparable nature (partly divine, partly and subordinately human) in the person of Christ.
– DERIVATIVES **Monophysitism** n.
– ORIGIN C17: from eccles. Greek *monophusitēs*, from *monos* 'single' + *phusis* 'nature'.

monoplane ■ n. an aircraft with one pair of wings.

monoplegia /ˌmɒnə(ʊ)ˈpliːdʒə/ ■ n. paralysis of one limb or region of the body. Compare with **PARAPLEGIA**.

monopod ■ n. a one-legged support for a camera or fishing rod.
– ORIGIN C19: from Greek *monopodion*, from *monos* 'single' + *pous, pod-* 'foot'.

monopole

monopole ■ n. **1** Physics a single electric charge or magnetic pole, especially a hypothetical isolated magnetic pole. **2** a radio aerial or pylon consisting of a single pole or rod.

monopolist ■ n. a person who has a monopoly.
– DERIVATIVES **monopolistic** adj. **monopolistically** adv.

monopolize (also **-ise**) ■ v. hold or obtain a monopoly on.
– DERIVATIVES **monopolization** (also **-isation**) n. **monopolizer** (also **-iser**) n.

monopoly ■ n. (pl. **-ies**) **1** the exclusive possession or control of the supply of or trade in a commodity or service. ▶ a company or group having a monopoly, or a commodity or service controlled by one. **2** exclusive possession or control of something: *men don't have a monopoly on unrequited love.* **3** (**Monopoly**) trademark a board game in which players engage in simulated property and financial dealings using imitation money.
– ORIGIN C16: from Greek *monopōlion*, from *monos* 'single' + *pōlein* 'sell'.

monopsony /məˈnɒpsəni/ ■ n. (pl. **-ies**) Economics a market situation in which there is only one buyer.
– ORIGIN 1930s: from MONO- + Greek *opsōnein* 'buy provisions'.

monorail ■ n. a railway in which the track consists of a single rail, typically elevated and with the trains suspended from it.

monosaccharide ■ n. Chemistry any of the class of sugars (e.g. glucose) that cannot be hydrolysed to give a simpler sugar.

monoski ■ n. a single broad ski attached to both feet.
– DERIVATIVES **monoskier** n. **monoskiing** n.

monosodium glutamate ■ n. a compound which occurs naturally as a breakdown product of proteins and is used as a flavour enhancer in food.

monospecific ■ adj. Biology **1** relating to or consisting of only one species. **2** (of an antibody) specific to one antigen.

monostable Electronics ■ adj. (of a circuit or device) having only one stable position or state. ■ n. a monostable device or circuit.

monosyllabic ■ adj. **1** consisting of one syllable. **2** using brief words to signify reluctance to engage in conversation.
– DERIVATIVES **monosyllabically** adv. **monosyllable** n.

monotheism /ˈmɒnə(ʊ)ˌθiːɪz(ə)m/ ■ n. the doctrine or belief that there is only one God.
– DERIVATIVES **monotheist** n. & adj. **monotheistic** adj. **monotheistically** adv.
– ORIGIN C17: from MONO- + Greek *theos* 'god'.

monotherapy ■ n. the treatment of a disease with a single drug.

monotone /ˈmɒnətəʊn/ ■ n. a continuing sound that is unchanging in pitch and lacks intonation.
– ORIGIN C17: from late Greek *monotonos*.

monotonic ■ adj. **1** Mathematics (of a function or quantity) varying in such a way that it either never decreases or never increases. **2** speaking or uttered in a monotone.
– DERIVATIVES **monotonically** adv. **monotonicity** n.

monotonous ■ adj. **1** dull, tedious, and repetitious. **2** lacking in variation of tone or pitch.
– DERIVATIVES **monotonously** adv. **monotony** n.

monotreme /ˈmɒnə(ʊ)triːm/ ■ n. Zoology a mammal of a small order (Monotremata) comprising the platypus and the echidnas, distinguished by laying eggs and having a common urogenital and digestive opening.
– ORIGIN C19: from MONO- + Greek *trēma* 'hole'.

monotropy /məˈnɒtrəpi/ ■ n. Chemistry the existence of allotropes of an element, one of which is stable and the others metastable under all known conditions.
– DERIVATIVES **monotrope** n.
– ORIGIN C20: from MONO- + Greek *tropē* 'turning'.

monotype ■ n. a single print taken from a design created in oil paint or printing ink on glass or metal.

monotypic /ˌmɒnə(ʊ)ˈtɪpɪk/ ■ adj. chiefly Biology having only one type or representative, especially (of a genus) containing only one species.

monovalent /ˌmɒnə(ʊ)ˈveɪl(ə)nt/ ■ adj. Chemistry having a valency of one.

monoxide ■ n. Chemistry an oxide containing one atom of oxygen in its molecule or empirical formula.

monozygotic /ˌmɒnə(ʊ)zʌɪˈɡɒtɪk/ ■ adj. (of twins) derived from a single ovum, and so identical.
– ORIGIN C20: from MONO- + ZYGOTE.

monozygous /ˌmɒnə(ʊ)ˈzʌɪɡəs/ ■ adj. another term for MONOZYGOTIC.
– DERIVATIVES **monozygosity** n.

mons /mɒnz/ ■ n. short for MONS PUBIS.

Monsieur /məˈsjə:/ ■ n. (pl. **Messieurs** /mɛˈsjə:/) a title or form of address for a French-speaking man, corresponding to *Mr* or *sir*.
– ORIGIN French, from *mon* 'my' + *sieur* 'lord'.

Monsignor /mɒnˈsiːnjə, ˌmɒnsiːˈnjɔː/ ■ n. (pl. **Monsignori** /-ˈnjɔːri/) the title of various senior Roman Catholic posts, such as a prelate or an officer of the papal court.
– ORIGIN Italian.

monsoon ■ n. **1** a seasonal prevailing wind in the region of the Indian subcontinent and SE Asia, bringing rain when blowing from the south-west. **2** the rainy season accompanying the SW monsoon.
– DERIVATIVES **monsoonal** adj.
– ORIGIN C16: from Portuguese *monção*, from Arabic *mawsim* 'season'.

mons pubis /ˌmɒnz ˈpjuːbɪs/ ■ n. the rounded mass of fatty tissue lying over the joint of the pubic bones.
– ORIGIN C19: Latin, 'mount of the pubes'.

monster ■ n. **1** a large, ugly, and frightening imaginary creature. ▶ an inhumanly cruel or wicked person. ▶ humorous a rude or badly behaved person, typically a child. **2** [as modifier] informal extraordinarily large.
– ORIGIN Middle English: from Old French *monstre*, from Latin *monstrum* 'portent or monster', from *monere* 'warn'.

monstera /mɒnˈstɪərə/ ■ n. a tropical American climbing plant of a genus including the Swiss cheese plant. [Genus *Monstera*.]
– ORIGIN perhaps from Latin *monstrum* 'monster'.

monstrance /ˈmɒnstr(ə)ns/ ■ n. (in the Roman Catholic Church) an open or transparent receptacle in which the consecrated Host is exposed for veneration.
– ORIGIN Middle English: from medieval Latin *monstrantia*, from Latin *monstrare* 'to show'.

monstrosity ■ n. (pl. **-ies**) **1** something very large and unsightly. ▶ a grossly malformed animal, plant, or person. **2** something which is outrageously or offensively wrong.

monstrous ■ adj. **1** very large and ugly or frightening. **2** inhumanly or outrageously evil or wrong.
– DERIVATIVES **monstrously** adv. **monstrousness** n.

mons Veneris /ˌmɒnz ˈvɛnərɪs/ ■ n. (in women) the mons pubis.
– ORIGIN C17: Latin, 'mount of Venus'.

montage /mɒnˈtɑːʒ, ˈmɒntɑːʒ/ ■ n. the technique of producing a picture, film, etc. by piecing together separate sections. ▶ a picture, film, etc. resulting from this.
– ORIGIN C20: French, from *monter* 'to mount'.

montane /ˈmɒnteɪn/ ■ adj. of or inhabiting mountainous country.
– ORIGIN C19: from Latin *montanus*, from *mons* 'mountain'.

montbretia /mɒn(t)ˈbriːʃə/ ■ n. a plant of the iris family with bright orange-yellow trumpet-shaped flowers. [*Crocosmia* × *crocosmiflora*.]
– ORIGIN C19: named after the French botanist A. F. E. Coquebert de *Montbret*.

monte /ˈmɒnti/ ■ n. (usu. **three-card monte**) a game of Mexican origin played with three cards, similar to three-card trick.
– ORIGIN C19: Spanish, 'mountain', also 'heap of cards left after dealing'.

Monte Carlo method ■ n. Statistics a technique in which a large quantity of randomly generated numbers are studied using a probabilistic model to find an approximate solution to a numerical problem.

Montenegrin /ˌmɒntɪˈniːɡrɪn/ ■ n. a native or inhabitant of Montenegro, a republic in the Balkans.

Montessori /ˌmɒntɪˈsɔːri/ ■ n. [usu. as modifier] a system of education for young children that seeks to develop natural interests and activities rather than use formal teaching methods.
– ORIGIN C20: from the name of the Italian educationist Maria *Montessori*.

Montezuma's revenge /ˌmɒntɪˈz(j)uːməz/ ■ n. informal diarrhoea suffered by visitors to Mexico.
– ORIGIN 1960s: from the name of *Montezuma* II, the last Aztec emperor.

month ■ n. each of the twelve named periods into which a year is divided. ▸ a period of time between the same dates in successive calendar months. ▸ a period of 28 days or four weeks.
– PHRASES **a month of Sundays** informal a very long time.
– ORIGIN Old English, of Germanic origin.

monthly ■ adj. done, produced, or occurring once a month. ■ adv. once a month; every month. ■ n. (pl. **-ies**) **1** a magazine that is published once a month. **2** (**monthlies**) informal a menstrual period.

montmorillonite /ˌmɒntməˈrɪlənʌɪt/ ■ n. an aluminium-rich clay mineral which undergoes reversible expansion on absorbing water.
– ORIGIN C19: from *Montmorillon*, the name of a town in France.

monty ■ n. (in phr. **the full monty**) Brit. informal the full amount expected, desired, or possible.
– ORIGIN perhaps from *the full Montague Burton*, 'Sunday-best three-piece suit' (from the name of a tailor), or in ref. to 'the full cooked English breakfast' insisted upon by Field Marshal *Montgomery*.

monument ■ n. **1** a statue, building, or other structure erected to commemorate a notable person or event. **2** a structure or site of historical importance or interest. **3** an enduring and memorable example or reminder: *the house was a monument to untutored taste*.
– ORIGIN Middle English: from Latin *monumentum*, from *monere* 'remind'.

monumental ■ adj. **1** great in importance, extent, or size. **2** of or serving as a monument.
– DERIVATIVES **monumentalism** n. **monumentality** n. **monumentalize** (also **-ise**) v. **monumentally** adv.

-mony ■ suffix forming nouns often denoting an action, state, or quality: *ceremony*.
– ORIGIN from Latin *-monia*, *-monium*.

monzonite /ˈmɒnzənʌɪt/ ■ n. Geology a granular igneous rock containing approximately equal amounts of orthoclase and plagioclase.
– ORIGIN C19: named after Mount *Monzoni* in the Tyrol, Italy.

moo ■ v. (**moos**, **mooed**) make the characteristic deep resonant vocal sound of cattle. ■ n. (pl. **moos**) **1** a sound of this kind. **2** Brit. informal an irritating or disliked woman.
– ORIGIN C16: imitative.

mooch informal ■ v. **1** (usu. **mooch about/around**) Brit. loiter in a bored or listless manner. **2** N. Amer. ask for or obtain (something) without paying for it. ■ n. **1** Brit. an instance of loitering in a bored or listless manner. **2** N. Amer. a beggar or scrounger.
– DERIVATIVES **moocher** n.
– ORIGIN Middle English: prob. from Anglo-Norman French *muscher* 'hide, skulk'.

mood[1] ■ n. **1** a state of mind or feeling. ▸ an angry, irritable, or sullen state of mind. **2** the atmosphere or pervading tone of a work of art. **3** [modifier] inducing or suggestive of a particular mood: *mood music*.
– ORIGIN Old English *mōd*, of Germanic origin.

mood[2] ■ n. **1** Grammar a form or category of a verb expressing fact (indicative mood), command (imperative mood), question (interrogative mood), wish (optative mood), or conditionality (subjunctive mood). **2** Logic any of the valid forms into which each of the figures of a categorical syllogism may occur.
– ORIGIN C16: var. of MODE, influenced by MOOD[1].

moody ■ adj. (**-ier**, **-iest**) **1** given to unpredictable changes of mood, especially sudden bouts of gloominess or sullenness. **2** giving an impression of melancholy or mystery.
– DERIVATIVES **moodily** adv. **moodiness** n.

moolah /ˈmuːlə/ ■ n. informal money.
– ORIGIN 1930s (orig. US).

mooli /ˈmuːli/ ■ n. a radish of a variety with a large slender white root, used especially in Eastern cuisine.
– ORIGIN 1960s: from Hindi *mūlī*, from Sanskrit *mūla* 'root'.

moon ■ n. **1** (also **Moon**) the natural satellite of the earth, visible (chiefly at night) by reflected light from the sun. ▸ a natural satellite of any planet. **2** poetic/literary or humorous a month: *many moons ago*. ■ v. **1** behave or move in a listless or dreamy manner. **2** informal expose one's buttocks to someone in order to insult or amuse them.
– PHRASES **over the moon** informal delighted.
– DERIVATIVES **moonless** adj. **moonlike** adj.
– ORIGIN Old English, of Germanic origin.

moonbag ■ n. S. African a small pouch for valuables, worn on a belt around the hips.

moonbeam ■ n. a ray of moonlight.

moon boot ■ n. a warm, thickly padded boot with an outer shell of fabric or plastic.

mooncalf ■ n. (pl. **mooncalves**) a foolish person.

moon-faced ■ adj. having a round face.

moonfish ■ n. (pl. same or **-fishes**) a deep-bodied, laterally compressed marine fish. [*Mene maculata* (Indo-Pacific) and *Selene setapinnis* (Atlantic).]

moonflower ■ n. a tropical American climbing plant of the convolvulus family, with sweet-smelling trumpet-shaped white flowers which open at dusk and close at midday. [*Ipomoea alba*.]

Moonie ■ n. informal, often derogatory a member of the Unification Church.
– ORIGIN 1970s: from the name of its founder, Sun Myung *Moon*.

moonlight ■ n. the light of the moon. ■ v. (past and past part. **-lighted**) informal do a second job, especially secretly and at night, in addition to one's regular employment.
– DERIVATIVES **moonlighter** n. **moonlit** adj.

moonscape ■ n. a landscape resembling the surface of the moon, especially in being rocky and barren.

moonshine ■ n. **1** foolish talk or ideas. **2** informal, chiefly N. Amer. illicitly distilled or smuggled liquor.

moon shot ■ n. the launching of a spacecraft to the moon.

moonstone ■ n. a pearly white semi-precious stone, especially one consisting of alkali feldspar.

moonstruck ■ adj. unable to think or act normally, especially because of being in love.

moonwalk ■ v. [usu. as noun **moonwalking**] **1** walk on the moon. **2** move or dance in a way reminiscent of the characteristic weightless movement of walking on the moon.
– DERIVATIVES **moonwalker** n.

moony[1] ■ adj. (**-ier**, **-iest**) dreamy and unaware of one's surroundings, especially through being in love.

moony[2] ■ n. S. African a small kite-shaped silvery fish of the Indo-Pacific region. [*Monodactylus falciformis* and *M. argenteus*.]

Moor /mʊə, mɔː/ ■ n. a member of a NW African Muslim people of mixed Berber and Arab descent, that conquered the Iberian peninsula in the 8th century.
– DERIVATIVES **Moorish** adj.
– ORIGIN from Old French *More*, from Greek *Mauros* 'inhabitant of Mauretania' (an ancient region of N. Africa).

moor[1] /mʊə, mɔː/ ■ n. a tract of open uncultivated upland, typically covered with heather.
– DERIVATIVES **moorish** adj. **moory** adj.
– ORIGIN Old English *mōr*, of Germanic origin.

moor[2] /mʊə, mɔː/ ■ v. make fast (a boat) by attaching it by cable or rope to the shore or to an anchor.
– DERIVATIVES **moorage** n.
– ORIGIN C15: prob. from the Germanic base of Dutch *meren*.

moorhen ■ n. an aquatic bird of the rail family with mainly blackish plumage and a red and yellow bill. [*Gallinula chloropus* and other species.]

mooring

mooring (also **moorings**) ■ n. **1** a place where a boat or ship is moored. **2** the ropes, chains, or anchors by which a boat or ship is moored.

Moorish idol ■ n. a disc-shaped fish with bold vertical black-and-white bands and a very tall tapering dorsal fin, of coral reefs in the Indo-Pacific region. [*Zanclus cornutus*.]

moorland (also **moorlands**) ■ n. an extensive area of moor.

moose ■ n. (pl. same) North American term for ELK.
– ORIGIN C17: from Abnaki *mos*.

moot ■ adj. subject to debate, dispute, or uncertainty: *a moot point*. ■ v. raise or suggest (a question or idea). ■ n. **1** Brit. an assembly held for debate, especially in Anglo-Saxon and medieval times. **2** Law a mock trial set up to examine a hypothetical case as an academic exercise.
– ORIGIN Old English *mōt* 'assembly or meeting' and *mōtian* 'to converse', of Germanic origin.

mop ■ n. **1** an implement consisting of a bundle of thick loose strings or a sponge attached to a handle, used for wiping floors. ▶ an act of wiping with a mop. **2** a thick mass of disordered hair. ■ v. (**mopped**, **mopping**) **1** clean or soak up liquid by wiping. **2** (**mop something up**) put an end to or dispose of something.
– DERIVATIVES **moppy** adj.
– ORIGIN C15: perhaps rel. to Latin *mappa* 'napkin'.

mopane /mɒˈpɑːni/ (also **mopani**) ■ n. a southern African tree with a rough, flaking bark, pale green flowers, and butterfly-shaped leaves, which fold together in intense heat. [*Colophospermum mopane*.]
– ORIGIN Setswana.

mopane worm ■ n. a moth caterpillar that feeds on mopane leaves, sometimes used as food. [*Imbrasia belina*.]

mope ■ v. (often **mope around/about**) be listless and apathetic because of unhappiness or boredom. ■ n. informal a depressive or foolish person.
– DERIVATIVES **moper** n. **mopery** n. **mopey** (also **mopy**) adj. **mopily** adv. **mopiness** n. **mopish** adj.
– ORIGIN C16: perhaps of Scandinavian origin; cf. Swedish dialect *mopa* 'to sulk'.

moped /ˈməʊpɛd/ ■ n. a light motor cycle, especially one with an engine capacity of not more than 50 cc.
– ORIGIN 1950s: from Swedish, from (*trampcykel med*) *mo(tor och) ped(aler)* 'pedal cycle with motor and pedals'.

moppet ■ n. informal a small endearingly sweet child.
– ORIGIN C17: from obsolete *moppe* 'baby or rag doll'.

moquette /mɒˈkɛt/ ■ n. a thick pile fabric used for carpets and upholstery.
– ORIGIN 1930s: from French, perhaps from obsolete Italian *mocaiardo* 'mohair'.

mor /mɔː/ ■ n. Soil Science humus formed under acid conditions.
– ORIGIN 1930s: from Danish.

morabaraba /mɒrəˈbɑːrəbə/ (also **marabaraba**) ■ n. a board game in which two players seek to complete rows of three tokens in vertical, horizontal, or diagonal lines.
– ORIGIN Sesotho.

moraine /məˈreɪn/ ■ n. Geology a mass of rocks and sediment carried down and deposited by a glacier.
– DERIVATIVES **morainal** adj. **morainic** adj.
– ORIGIN C18: from Italian dialect *morena*, from French dialect *morre* 'snout'.

moral ■ adj. **1** concerned with the principles of right and wrong behaviour and the goodness or badness of human character. **2** adhering to the code of behaviour that is considered right or acceptable. ■ n. **1** a lesson that can be derived from a story or experience. **2** (**morals**) standards of behaviour, or principles of right and wrong.
– DERIVATIVES **morally** adv.
– ORIGIN Middle English: from Latin *moralis*, from *mos* 'custom', (pl.) *mores* 'morals'.

morale /məˈrɑːl/ ■ n. the confidence, enthusiasm, and discipline of a person or group at a particular time.
– ORIGIN C18: from French *moral*, respelled to preserve the final stress in pronunciation.

moralist ■ n. **1** a person who moralizes, or who teaches or promotes morality. **2** a person who behaves morally.
– DERIVATIVES **moralism** n. **moralistic** adj. **moralistically** adv.

morality ■ n. (pl. **-ies**) **1** principles concerning the distinction between right and wrong or good and bad behaviour. ▶ a system of values and moral principles. **2** the extent to which an action is right or wrong.

morality play ■ n. a kind of drama presenting a moral lesson and having personified abstract qualities as the main characters.

moralize (also **-ise**) ■ v. **1** comment on issues of right and wrong, typically with an unfounded air of superiority. **2** interpret or explain as giving moral lessons. **3** improve the morals of.
– DERIVATIVES **moralization** (also **-isation**) n. **moralizer** (also **-iser**) n. **moralizing** (also **-ising**) adj. **moralizingly** (also **-isingly**) adv.

moral law ■ n. (in some systems of ethics) an absolute principle defining the criteria of right action.

moral majority ■ n. [treated as pl.] a majority of people regarded as favouring strict moral standards. ▶ (**Moral Majority**) a right-wing Christian movement in the US.

moral philosophy ■ n. the branch of philosophy concerned with ethics.

moral sense ■ n. the ability to distinguish between right and wrong.

moral support ■ n. support or help of a psychological rather than physical nature.

moral victory ■ n. a defeat that can be interpreted as a victory in terms of morals or principles.

morass /məˈras/ ■ n. **1** an area of muddy or boggy ground. **2** a complicated or confused situation.
– ORIGIN C15: from Dutch *moeras*, alteration of Middle Dutch *marasch*, from Old French *marais* 'marsh', from medieval Latin *mariscus*.

moratorium /ˌmɒrəˈtɔːrɪəm/ ■ n. (pl. **moratoriums** or **moratoria** /-rɪə/) **1** a temporary prohibition of an activity. **2** Law a legal authorization to debtors to postpone payment.
– ORIGIN C19: from late Latin *moratorius* 'delaying', from Latin *morari* 'delay'.

Moravian ■ n. **1** a native or inhabitant of the region of Moravia in the Czech Republic. **2** a member of a Protestant Church founded by emigrants from Moravia holding views derived from the Hussites and accepting the Bible as the only source of faith. ■ adj. of or relating to Moravia or the Moravian Church.

moray /ˈmɒreɪ, ˈmɒreɪ/ (also **moray eel**) ■ n. an eel-like predatory fish of warm seas which typically hides in crevices. [Family Muraenidae: numerous species.]
– ORIGIN C17: from Portuguese *moréia*, from Greek *muraina*.

morbid ■ adj. **1** characterized by or appealing to an abnormal and unhealthy interest in unpleasant subjects, especially death and disease. **2** Medicine of the nature of or indicative of disease.
– DERIVATIVES **morbidity** n. **morbidly** adv. **morbidness** n.
– ORIGIN C17: from Latin *morbidus*, from *morbus* 'disease'.

morbid anatomy ■ n. the anatomy of diseased organs and tissues.

morceau /mɔːˈsəʊ/ ■ n. (pl. **morceaux**) a short literary or musical composition.
– ORIGIN C18: French, 'morsel, piece'.

mordant /ˈmɔːd(ə)nt/ ■ adj. (especially of humour) sharp or critical; biting. ■ n. a substance that combines with a dye or stain and thereby fixes it in a material. ▶ an adhesive compound for fixing gold leaf. ▶ a corrosive liquid used to etch the lines on a printing plate. ■ v. impregnate or treat (a fabric) with a mordant.
– DERIVATIVES **mordancy** n. **mordantly** adv.
– ORIGIN C15: from French, from *mordre* 'to bite', from Latin *mordere*.

more ■ det. & pron. a greater or additional amount or degree. ■ adv. **1** forming the comparative of adjectives and adverbs, especially those of more than one syllable. **2** to a greater extent. ▶ (**more than**) extremely: *she is more than happy to oblige*. **3** again. **4** moreover.
– PHRASES **more and more** at a continually increasing rate.

more or less speaking imprecisely; to a certain extent. **no more 1** nothing further. **2** no further. **3** (**be no more**) exist no longer. **4** never again. **5** neither.
– ORIGIN Old English *māra*, of Germanic origin.

moreen /məˈriːn/ ■ n. a strong ribbed cotton fabric, used chiefly for curtains.
– ORIGIN C17: perhaps from **MOIRE**.

moreish ■ adj. informal so pleasant to eat that one wants more.

morel /məˈrel/ ■ n. an edible fungus having a brown oval or pointed fruiting body with an irregular honeycombed surface. [*Morchella esculenta* and related species.]
– ORIGIN C17: from French *morille*, from Dutch *morilje*.

morello /mɒˈreləʊ/ ■ n. (pl. **-os**) a dark cherry of a sour kind used in cooking.
– ORIGIN C17: from Italian *morello* 'blackish', from medieval Latin *morellus*, diminutive of Latin *Maurus* 'Moor'.

moreover ■ adv. as a further matter; besides.

mores /ˈmɔːreɪz, -riːz/ ■ pl. n. the customs and conventions of a community.
– ORIGIN C19: from Latin, pl. of *mos* 'custom'.

Moresque /məˈresk, mɔː-/ ■ adj. (of art or architecture) Moorish in style or design.
– ORIGIN Middle English: from Italian *moresco*, from *Moro* 'Moor'.

morganatic /ˌmɔːgəˈnatɪk/ ■ adj. of or denoting a marriage in which neither the spouse of lower rank, nor any children, have any claim to the possessions or title of the spouse of higher rank.
– DERIVATIVES **morganatically** adv.
– ORIGIN C18: from medieval Latin *matrimonium ad morganaticam* 'marriage with a morning gift' (because a gift given by a husband on the morning after the marriage was the wife's sole entitlement).

morgen /ˈmɔːg(ə)n/ ■ n. **1** a South African measure of land equal to about 0.8 hectare or two acres. **2** a Scandinavian and German measure of land equal to about 0.3 hectare or two thirds of an acre.
– ORIGIN C17: from Dutch, or from German *Morgen* 'morning', perhaps from the notion of 'an area of land that can be ploughed in a morning'.

morgue /mɔːg/ ■ n. **1** a mortuary. **2** informal a newspaper's collection of miscellaneous information for use in future obituaries.
– ORIGIN C19: from French, orig. the name of a building in Paris where bodies were kept until identified.

moribund /ˈmɒrɪbʌnd/ ■ adj. **1** at the point of death. **2** in terminal decline; lacking vitality or vigour.
– DERIVATIVES **moribundity** n.
– ORIGIN C18: from Latin *moribundus*, from *mori* 'to die'.

Mormon /ˈmɔːmən/ ■ n. a member of the Church of Jesus Christ of Latter-Day Saints, a religion founded in the US in 1830 by Joseph Smith Jr.
– DERIVATIVES **Mormonism** n.
– ORIGIN the name of a prophet to whom Smith attributed *The Book of Mormon*, a collection of supposed revelations.

morn ■ n. poetic/literary morning.
– ORIGIN Old English, of Germanic origin.

mornay /ˈmɔːneɪ/ ■ adj. denoting or served in a cheese-flavoured white sauce.
– ORIGIN named after *Mornay*, the eldest son of the French cook Joseph Voiron, the inventor of the sauce.

morning ■ n. the period of time between midnight and noon, especially from sunrise to noon. ► sunrise. ■ adv. (**mornings**) informal every morning.
– ORIGIN Middle English: from **MORN**, on the pattern of *evening*.

morning-after pill ■ n. a contraceptive pill that is effective within about seventy-two hours after intercourse.

morning coat ■ n. a man's formal coat with a long back section cut into tails which curves up to join the waist at the front.

morning dress ■ n. a man's formal dress of morning coat and striped trousers.

morning glory ■ n. a climbing plant of the convolvulus family with trumpet-shaped flowers. [*Ipomoea purpureus* and related species.]

morning sickness ■ n. nausea occurring in the first few months of pregnancy.

morning star ■ n. (**the morning star**) a planet, especially Venus, when visible in the east before sunrise.

Moroccan /məˈrɒkən/ ■ n. a native or inhabitant of Morocco. ■ adj. of or relating to Morocco.

morocco ■ n. (pl. **-os**) fine flexible leather made (originally in Morocco) from goatskins tanned with sumac.

morogo /məˈrɒxə/ (also **marog**) ■ n. S. African any of several leafy edible plants that can be cooked and eaten as a vegetable.
– ORIGIN Sesotho and Setswana.

moron ■ n. informal a stupid person.
– DERIVATIVES **moronic** adj. **moronically** adv.
– ORIGIN C20: from Greek, from *mōros* 'foolish'.

morose ■ adj. sullen and ill-tempered.
– DERIVATIVES **morosely** adv. **moroseness** n.
– ORIGIN C16: from Latin *morosus* 'peevish', from *mos* 'manner'.

morph¹ /mɔːf/ ■ n. **1** Biology each of several variant forms of an animal or plant. **2** Linguistics an actual linguistic form.
– ORIGIN 1940s: from Greek *morphē* 'form'.

morph² /mɔːf/ ■ v. change smoothly and gradually from one image to another using computer animation techniques. ■ n. an image processed in this way.
– ORIGIN 1990s: element from **METAMORPHOSIS**.

-morph ■ comb. form denoting something having a specified form or character: *endomorph*.
– ORIGIN from Greek *morphē* 'form'.

morpheme /ˈmɔːfiːm/ ■ n. Linguistics a meaningful morphological unit of a language that cannot be further divided (e.g. *in*, *come*, *-ing*, forming *incoming*).
– DERIVATIVES **morphemic** adj. **morphemically** adv.
– ORIGIN C19: from French *morphème*, from Greek *morphē* 'form'.

morphemics /mɔːˈfiːmɪks/ ■ pl. n. [treated as sing.] Linguistics the study of word structure in terms of morphemes.

morphia /ˈmɔːfɪə/ ■ n. dated morphine.

morphine /ˈmɔːfiːn/ ■ n. an analgesic and narcotic drug obtained from opium and used medicinally to relieve pain.
– ORIGIN C19: from German *Morphin*, from the name of the Roman god of sleep, *Morpheus*.

morphogenesis /ˌmɔːfə(ʊ)ˈdʒɛnɪsɪs/ ■ n. **1** Biology the origin and development of morphological characteristics. **2** Geology the formation of landforms or other structures.
– DERIVATIVES **morphogenetic** adj. **morphogenic** adj.

morphology /mɔːˈfɒlədʒi/ ■ n. (pl. **-ies**) **1** the branch of biology concerned with the forms and structures of living organisms. **2** Linguistics the study of inflections and other forms of words.
– DERIVATIVES **morphologic** adj. **morphological** adj. **morphologically** adv. **morphologist** n.

morphometry /mɔːˈfɒmɪtri/ ■ n. the process of measuring the external shape and dimensions of landforms, living organisms, or other objects.
– DERIVATIVES **morphometric** adj. **morphometrically** adv.

Morris chair ■ n. a type of easy chair with open padded arms and an adjustable back.
– ORIGIN C19: named after the English craftsman William Morris.

morris dance ■ n. a traditional English dance performed outdoors by groups of dancers wearing costumes with small bells attached and carrying handkerchiefs or sticks.
– DERIVATIVES **morris dancer** n. **morris dancing** n.
– ORIGIN Middle English: *morris* from *morys*, var. of *Moorish* (see **MOOR**).

morrow ■ n. (**the morrow**) archaic or poetic/literary the following day.
– ORIGIN Middle English *morwe*, from Old English *morgen*.

Morse (also **Morse code**) ■ n. an alphabet or code in which letters are represented by combinations of long and short light or sound signals.
– ORIGIN C19: named after the American inventor Samuel F. B. Morse.

morsel ■ n. a small piece of food; a mouthful.
– ORIGIN Middle English: from Old French, diminutive of *mors* 'a bite', from Latin *mordere* 'to bite'.

mortadella /ˌmɔːtəˈdɛlə/ ■ n. a type of smooth-textured Italian sausage containing pieces of fat.
– ORIGIN Italian diminutive, from Latin *murtatum* '(sausage) seasoned with myrtle berries'.

mortal ■ adj. 1 (of a living creature) subject to death. 2 causing or liable to cause death; fatal. ▶ (of conflict or an enemy) admitting no reconciliation. ▶ Christian Church denoting a grave sin that is regarded as depriving the soul of divine grace. Often contrasted with **VENIAL**. 3 (of a feeling, especially fear) very intense. ■ n. 1 a mortal being. 2 humorous a person contrasted with those of higher status or ability.
– DERIVATIVES **mortally** adv.
– ORIGIN Middle English: from Latin *mortalis*, from *mors* 'death'.

mortality ■ n. (pl. **-ies**) 1 the state of being mortal. 2 death, especially on a large scale. ▶ (also **mortality rate**) the number of deaths in a given area or period, or from a particular cause.

mortar[1] ■ n. 1 a short smooth-bore gun for firing shells at high angles. 2 a cup-shaped receptacle in which ingredients are crushed or ground in cooking or pharmacy. ■ v. attack or bombard with shells fired from a mortar.
– ORIGIN Old English, from Old French *mortier*, from Latin *mortarium*.

mortar[2] ■ n. a mixture of lime with cement, sand, and water, used in building to bond bricks or stones. ■ v. fix or join using mortar.
– DERIVATIVES **mortarless** adj. **mortary** adj.
– ORIGIN Middle English: from Old French *mortier*, from Latin *mortarium*, prob. a transferred sense denoting a container (see **MORTAR**[1]).

mortar board ■ n. 1 an academic cap with a stiff, flat square top and a tassel. 2 a small square board with a handle on the underside, used by bricklayers for holding mortar.

mortgage /ˈmɔːgɪdʒ/ ■ n. 1 the charging of property by a debtor to a creditor as security for a debt (especially one incurred by the purchase of the property), on the condition that it shall be returned on payment of the debt within a certain period. 2 a loan obtained through the conveyance of property as security. ■ v. convey (a property) to a creditor as security on a loan.
– DERIVATIVES **mortgageable** adj.
– ORIGIN Middle English: from Old French, 'dead pledge', from *mort* 'dead' + *gage* 'pledge'.

mortgage bond ■ n. South African term for **MORTGAGE**.

mortgagee ■ n. the lender in a mortgage, typically a bank or building society.

mortgage rate ■ n. the rate of interest charged by a mortgage lender.

mortgagor /ˌmɔːgɪˈdʒɔː/ ■ n. the borrower in a mortgage, typically a person buying a house.

mortice ■ n. & v. variant spelling of **MORTISE**.

mortician /mɔːˈtɪʃ(ə)n/ ■ n. chiefly N. Amer. an undertaker.
– ORIGIN C19: from Latin *mors, mort-* 'death'.

mortify /ˈmɔːtɪfʌɪ/ ■ v. (**-ies, -ied**) 1 (often **be mortified**) cause to feel embarrassed, ashamed, or humiliated. 2 subdue (physical urges) by self-denial or discipline. 3 (of flesh) be affected by gangrene or necrosis.
– DERIVATIVES **mortification** n. **mortifying** adj. **mortifyingly** adv.
– ORIGIN Middle English: from Old French *mortifier*, from eccles. Latin *mortificare* 'kill, subdue', from Latin *mors* 'death'.

mortise /ˈmɔːtɪs/ (also **mortice**) ■ n. a hole or recess designed to receive a corresponding projection (a tenon) so as to join or lock two parts together. ■ v. join securely by means of a mortise and tenon. ▶ [often as adj. **mortised**] cut a mortise in or through.
– DERIVATIVES **mortiser** n.
– ORIGIN Middle English: from Old French *mortaise*.

mortise lock ■ n. a lock set within the body of a door in a recess or mortise, as opposed to one attached to the door surface.

mortuary /ˈmɔːtjʊəri, -tʃʊ-/ ■ n. (pl. **-ies**) a room or building in which dead bodies are kept until burial or cremation. ■ adj. of or relating to burial or tombs.
– ORIGIN Middle English: from Latin *mortuarius*, from *mortuus* 'dead'.

morula /ˈmɔːr(j)ʊlə/ ■ n. (pl. **morulae** /-liː/) Embryology a solid ball of cells resulting from division of a fertilized ovum, and from which a blastula is formed.
– ORIGIN C19: diminutive of Latin *morum* 'mulberry'.

Mosaic /məʊˈzeɪɪk/ ■ adj. of or associated with Moses.
– ORIGIN C17: from French *mosaïque*.

mosaic /mə(ʊ)ˈzeɪɪk/ ■ n. 1 a picture or pattern produced by arranging together small variously coloured pieces of stone, tile, or glass. ▶ a colourful and variegated pattern. 2 Biology an individual (especially an animal) composed of cells of two genetically different types. 3 (also **mosaic disease**) a virus disease that results in leaf variegation in tobacco, maize, sugar cane, and other plants. ■ v. (**mosaicked, mosaicking**) decorate with a mosaic.
– DERIVATIVES **mosaicist** n.
– ORIGIN Middle English: from French *mosaïque*, from Latin *musi(v)um* 'decoration with small square stones', perhaps from Greek *mousa* 'a muse'.

mosbolletjie /ˈmɒsbɒlǝkɪ/ ■ n. S. African a bun leavened with fermented raisin juice or new wine, flavoured with aniseed, and eaten fresh or as a rusk.
– ORIGIN from S. African Dutch, from *most* 'must' + *bolletje* 'little ball'.

moscato /mɒˈskɑːtəʊ/ ■ n. a sweet Italian dessert wine.
– ORIGIN Italian; rel. to **MUSCAT**.

Moselle /mə(ʊ)ˈzɛl/ (also **Mosel**) ■ n. a light medium-dry white wine produced in the valley of the River Moselle.

Moses basket ■ n. a carrycot or small portable cot made of wickerwork.
– ORIGIN with allusion to the biblical story of Moses being left in a basket among the bulrushes (Exodus 2:3).

mosey informal ■ v. (**-eys, -eyed**) walk or move in a leisurely manner. ■ n. a leisurely walk.
– ORIGIN C19.

MOSFET ■ n. Electronics a field-effect transistor in which there is a thin layer of silicon oxide between the gate and the channel.
– ORIGIN 1960s: acronym from *metal oxide semiconductor field-effect transistor*.

mosh ■ v. dance to rock music in a violent manner involving jumping up and down and deliberately colliding with other dancers.
– ORIGIN 1980s: perhaps from **MASH** or **MUSH**[1].

moskonfyt /ˈmɒskɒnfeɪt/ ■ n. S. African a thick syrup made from grapes, used as a sweetener in cookery and wine production, and as a spread.
– ORIGIN from S. African Dutch *most* 'must' + *konfyt* 'conserve'.

Moslem /ˈmɒzləm/ ■ n. & adj. variant spelling of **MUSLIM**.

Mosotho /məˈsuːtuː/ singular form of **BASOTHO**.

mosque ■ n. a Muslim place of worship.
– ORIGIN Middle English: from French *mosquée*, from Egyptian Arabic *masgid*.

mosquito ■ n. (pl. **-oes**) a slender long-legged fly with aquatic larvae, some kinds of which transmit malaria and other diseases through the bite of the bloodsucking female. [Family Culicidae.]
– ORIGIN C16: from Spanish and Portuguese, diminutive of *mosca*, from Latin *musca* 'fly'.

mosquito net ■ n. a fine net hung across a door or window or around a bed to keep mosquitoes away.

moss ■ n. a small flowerless green plant which grows in low carpets or rounded cushions in damp habitats and reproduces by means of spores. [Class Musci.] ▶ used in names of algae, lichens, and other low-growing plants, e.g. reindeer moss. ■ v. [usu. as adj. **mossed**] cover with moss.
– DERIVATIVES **mossiness** n. **mossy** adj. (**-ier, -iest**).
– ORIGIN Old English *mos* 'bog or moss', of Germanic origin.

moss agate ■ n. agate with moss-like dendritic markings.

moss animal ■ n. a minute sedentary colonial aquatic animal found encrusting rocks or seaweed or forming stalked fronds. [Phylum Bryozoa.]

Mössbauer effect /ˈmɜːsbaʊə/ ■ n. Chemistry an effect in which certain atomic nuclei bound in a crystal emit gamma rays of sharply defined frequency which can be used as a probe of energy levels in other nuclei.
– ORIGIN 1960s: named after the German physicist Rudolf L. *Mössbauer*.

mossie¹ ■ n. S. African informal a sparrow.
– ORIGIN from Dutch *mosje*, diminutive of *mos* 'sparrow'.

mossie² ■ n. (pl. **-ies**) variant spelling of **MOZZIE**.

moss stitch ■ n. alternate plain and purl stitches in knitting.

most ■ det. & pron. **1** greatest in amount or degree. **2** the majority of; nearly all of. ■ adv. **1** to the greatest extent. **2** forming the superlative of adjectives and adverbs, especially those of more than one syllable. **3** extremely; very. **4** N. Amer. informal almost.
– PHRASES **at (the) most** not more than. **be the most** informal be the best of all. **for the most part** in most cases; usually. **make the most of** use or represent to the best advantage.
– ORIGIN Old English, of Germanic origin.

-most ■ suffix forming superlative adjectives and adverbs from prepositions and other words indicating relative position: *innermost*.
– ORIGIN Old English *-mest*, assimilated to **MOST**.

most favoured nation ■ n. a country which has been granted the most favourable trading terms available by another country.

mostly ■ adv. **1** as regards the greater part or number. **2** usually.

most significant bit ■ n. Computing the bit in a binary number which is of the greatest numerical value.

mote ■ n. a speck.
– ORIGIN Old English *mot*, rel. to Dutch *mot* 'dust, sawdust'.

motel ■ n. a roadside hotel designed primarily for motorists, typically having the rooms arranged in low blocks with parking directly outside.
– ORIGIN 1920s: blend of **MOTOR** and **HOTEL**.

motet /məʊˈtet/ ■ n. a short piece of sacred choral music.
– ORIGIN Middle English: from Old French, diminutive of *mot* 'word'.

moth ■ n. a chiefly nocturnal insect having two pairs of broad wings covered in microscopic scales, typically drably coloured and held flat when at rest, and lacking the clubbed antennae of butterflies. [Most superfamilies of the order Lepidoptera.]
– ORIGIN Old English, of Germanic origin.

mothball ■ n. a small pellet of naphthalene or camphor, placed among stored clothes and textiles to deter clothes moths. ■ v. **1** store (clothes) among or in mothballs. **2** put into storage or on hold for an indefinite period.
– PHRASES **in mothballs** in storage or on hold.

moth-eaten ■ adj. **1** damaged by moths. **2** old and disused.

mother /ˈmʌðə/ ■ n. **1** a woman in relation to a child or children to whom she has given birth. ▶ a woman who has care of a child through adoption. ▶ a female animal in relation to its offspring. **2** (**Mother**) (especially as a title or form of address) the head of a female religious community. **3** informal an extreme example or very large specimen: *the mother of all traffic jams*. **4** vulgar slang, chiefly N. Amer. short for **MOTHERFUCKER**. ■ v. **1** bring up (a child) with care and affection. **2** look after kindly and protectively, sometimes excessively so.
– DERIVATIVES **motherhood** n. **mothering** n.
– ORIGIN Old English, of Germanic origin.

motherboard ■ n. Computing a printed circuit board containing the principal components of a microcomputer or other device, with connectors for other circuit boards to be slotted into.

mother country ■ n. a country in relation to its colonies.

motherfucker ■ n. vulgar slang, chiefly N. Amer. a despicable or very unpleasant person or thing.
– DERIVATIVES **motherfucking** adj.

765

mother-in-law ■ n. (pl. **mothers-in-law**) the mother of one's husband or wife.

mother-in-law's tongue ■ n. an African plant of the agave family, which has long slender mottled leaves. [Genus *Sansevieria*.]

motherland ■ n. one's native country.

motherless ■ adj. **1** without a mother. **2** very drunk.

mother lode ■ n. Mining a principal vein of an ore or mineral.

motherly ■ adj. of, resembling, or characteristic of a mother, especially in being caring, protective, and kind.
– DERIVATIVES **motherliness** n.

mother-of-pearl ■ n. a smooth iridescent substance forming the inner layer of the shell of some molluscs, especially oysters and abalones, used as ornamentation.

mother's boy ■ n. a boy or man who is excessively influenced by or attached to his mother.

Mother's Day ■ n. a day of the year on which mothers are particularly honoured by their children.

mother ship ■ n. a large spacecraft or ship from which smaller craft are launched or maintained.

Mother Superior ■ n. the head of a female religious community.

mother-to-be ■ n. (pl. **mothers-to-be**) a woman who is expecting a baby.

mother tongue ■ n. a person's native language.

motif /məʊˈtiːf/ ■ n. **1** a single or recurring image forming a design. **2** a distinctive or dominant theme in a work of art. **3** a decorative device applied to a garment or textile. **4** Biochemistry a distinctive sequence on a protein or DNA, having a three-dimensional structure that allows binding interactions to occur.
– ORIGIN C19: from French.

motile /ˈməʊtaɪl/ ■ adj. Zoology & Botany (of cells, gametes, and single-celled organisms) capable of motion.
– DERIVATIVES **motility** n.
– ORIGIN C19: from Latin *motus* 'motion', on the pattern of *mobile*.

motion ■ n. **1** the action or process of moving or being moved. **2** a movement or gesture. **3** a piece of moving mechanism. **4** a formal proposal put to a legislature or committee. **5** Law an application for a rule or order of court. **6** Brit. an evacuation of the bowels. ▶ a portion of excrement. ■ v. direct (someone) with a gesture.
– PHRASES **go through the motions 1** do something perfunctorily. **2** simulate an action.
– DERIVATIVES **motional** adj. **motionless** adj. **motionlessly** adv.
– ORIGIN Middle English: from Latin *motio(n-)*, from *movere* 'to move'.

motion picture ■ n. chiefly N. Amer. another term for **FILM** (in sense 3).

motivate ■ v. **1** provide with a motive. **2** stimulate the interest of. **3** S. African present facts and arguments in support of a proposal or request.
– DERIVATIVES **motivator** n.

motivation ■ n. **1** a motive. **2** enthusiasm. **3** S. African a presentation of facts and arguments in support of a proposal or request.
– DERIVATIVES **motivational** adj. **motivationally** adv.

motive ■ n. **1** a factor inducing a person to act in a particular way. **2** a motif. ■ adj. **1** producing physical or mechanical motion. **2** acting as a motive.
– DERIVATIVES **motiveless** adj. **motivelessness** n.
– ORIGIN Middle English: from Old French *motif*, from late Latin *motivus*, from *movere* 'to move'.

motive power ■ n. **1** the energy (in the form of steam, electricity, etc.) used to drive machinery. **2** the locomotive engines of a railway system collectively.

mot juste /məʊ ˈʒuːst/ ■ n. (pl. **mots justes** pronunc. same) (**the mot juste**) the exact, appropriate word.

motley

motley /ˈmɒtli/ ■ adj. (**-ier**, **-iest**) varied in appearance or character; disparate. ■ n. **1** a varied mixture. **2** historical the particoloured costume of a jester.
– ORIGIN Middle English.

motocross

motocross ■ n. cross-country racing on motorcycles.
– DERIVATIVES **motocrosser** n.
– ORIGIN C20: abbrev. of MOTOR + CROSS.

motor ■ n. **1** a machine, especially one powered by electricity or internal combustion, that supplies motive power for a vehicle or other device. **2** Brit. informal short for MOTOR CAR. ■ adj. **1** giving, imparting, or producing motion or action. ▶ relating to motor vehicles: *motor insurance*. **2** Physiology relating to muscular movement or the nerves activating it. ■ v. **1** Brit. informal, travel in a car. ▶ informal move or travel quickly.
– DERIVATIVES **motorable** adj.
– ORIGIN Middle English: from Latin, 'mover', from *movere* 'to move'.

Motorail ■ n. a rail service in which cars are transported together with their drivers and passengers.

motorbike ■ n. a motorcycle.

motor boat ■ n. a boat powered by a motor.

motorcade /ˈməʊtəkeɪd/ ■ n. a procession of motor vehicles.
– ORIGIN C20: from MOTOR, on the pattern of *cavalcade*.

motor car ■ n. a car.

motorcycle ■ n. a two-wheeled vehicle that is powered by a motor.
– DERIVATIVES **motorcycling** n. **motorcyclist** n.

motor drive ■ n. a battery-driven motor in a camera, used to wind the film rapidly between exposures.

motorist ■ n. the driver of a car.

motorize (also -ise) ■ v. [usu. as adj. **motorized** (also -ised)] **1** equip (a vehicle or device) with a motor to operate or propel it. **2** equip (troops) with motor transport: *three motorized divisions*.
– DERIVATIVES **motorization** (also -isation) n.

motor lodge (also **motor hotel**) ■ n. a motel.

motormouth ■ n. informal a person who talks quickly and incessantly.
– DERIVATIVES **motormouthed** adj.

motor nerve ■ n. a nerve carrying impulses from the brain or spinal cord to a muscle or gland.

motor neuron ■ n. a nerve cell forming part of a pathway along which impulses pass from the brain or spinal cord to a muscle or gland.

motor neuron disease ■ n. a progressive disease involving degeneration of the motor neurons and wasting of the muscles.

motor racing ■ n. the sport of racing in specially developed fast cars.

motor scooter ■ n. see SCOOTER.

motor sport ■ n. another term for MOTOR RACING.

motor vehicle ■ n. a road vehicle powered by an internal-combustion engine.

motorway ■ n. a road designed for fast traffic, consisting of two or more lanes in each direction and with restricted access and exits.

motor yacht ■ n. a motor-driven boat equipped for cruising.

Motown /ˈməʊtaʊn/ ■ n. trademark soul music released on or reminiscent of the US record label Tamla Motown.
– ORIGIN 1960s: shortening of *Motor Town*, nickname for Detroit, where the record label was founded.

Motswana ■ n. singular form of BATSWANA.

mottle ■ v. mark with patches or spots of a different shade or colour. ■ n. a mottled marking. ▶ a patch or spot forming part of such a marking.
– DERIVATIVES **mottled** adj.
– ORIGIN C18: prob. a back-formation from MOTLEY.

motto ■ n. (pl. **-oes** or **-os**) a short sentence or phrase encapsulating a belief or ideal.
– ORIGIN C16: from Italian, 'word'.

moue /muː/ ■ n. a pout.
– ORIGIN C19: French, earlier 'lip'.

mould[1] (US **mold**) ■ n. **1** a hollow container used to give shape to molten or hot liquid material (such as wax or metal) when it cools and hardens. **2** something made in this way, especially a dish such as a jelly or mousse. **3** a distinctive form, style, or character: *a superb striker in the same mould as Lineker*. **4** a frame or template for producing mouldings. ■ v. **1** form (an object) out of a malleable substance. ▶ give a shape to (a malleable substance). **2** influence the formation or development of. **3** [as adj. **moulded**] (of an ornamental part of a building) shaped to a particular design: *a moulded cornice*.
– PHRASES **break the mould** end a restrictive pattern of events or behaviour by doing things differently.
– DERIVATIVES **mouldable** adj. **moulder** n.
– ORIGIN Middle English: prob. from Old French *modle*, from Latin *modulus* (see MODULUS).

mould[2] (US **mold**) ■ n. a furry growth of minute fungi occurring typically in moist warm conditions on organic matter. ▶ a fungus of this kind.
– ORIGIN Middle English: prob. from obsolete *mould*, from *moul* 'grow mouldy', of Scandinavian origin.

mould[3] (US **mold**) ■ n. soft loose earth, especially when rich in organic matter.
– ORIGIN Old English *molde*, from a Germanic base meaning 'pulverize or grind'.

moulder (US **molder**) ■ v. [often as adj. **mouldering**] slowly decay.
– ORIGIN C16: perhaps from MOULD[3], or rel. to Norwegian dialect *muldra* 'crumble'.

moulding (US **molding**) ■ n. an ornamentally shaped outline as an architectural feature.

mouldy (US **moldy**) ■ adj. (**-ier**, **-iest**) **1** covered with mould. **2** informal, chiefly Brit. dull or depressing.
– DERIVATIVES **mouldiness** n.

moult (US **molt**) ■ v. (of an animal) shed old feathers, hair, or skin, to make way for a new growth. ■ n. a period of moulting.
– ORIGIN Middle English *moute*, from Latin *mutare* 'to change'.

mound ■ n. **1** a raised mass of earth or other compacted material. ▶ Baseball a slight elevation from which the pitcher delivers the ball. **2** a small hill. **3** a heap or pile. **4** a large quantity. ■ v. heap up into a mound.
– ORIGIN C16.

mount[1] ■ v. **1** climb up or on to; ascend. **2** get up on (an animal or bicycle) in order to ride it. ▶ (often **be mounted**) set on horseback; provide with a horse. **3** (of a male animal) get on (a female) for the purpose of copulation. **4** grow larger, more numerous, or more intense: *the costs mount up when you buy a home*. **5** organize and initiate (a campaign or other course of action). **6** set up (a barrier, stall, checkpoint, etc.). **7** fix in position or on a support. **8** (with reference to a picture or photograph) set in or attach to a backing. **9** fix (a specimen) on a microscopic slide. ■ n. **1** a backing on which a picture or photograph is set for display. **2** a support for a piece of equipment. **3** a microscope slide. **4** a stamp hinge. **5** a horse used for riding.
– PHRASES **mount guard** keep watch.
– DERIVATIVES **mountable** adj. **mounted** adj. **mounter** n. **mounting** n.
– ORIGIN Middle English: from Old French *munter*, from Latin *mons*, *mont-* 'mountain'.

mount[2] ■ n. archaic or in place names a mountain or hill: *Mount Everest*.
– ORIGIN Old English *munt*, from Latin *mons*, *mont-* 'mountain'.

mountain ■ n. **1** an elevation of the earth's surface rising abruptly and to a large height from the surrounding level. **2** a large pile or quantity of something. **3** a surplus stock of a commodity.
– PHRASES **move mountains** achieve spectacular and apparently impossible results.
– ORIGIN Middle English: from Old French *montaigne*, from Latin *mons* 'mountain'.

mountain ash ■ n. a small tree with compound leaves, white flowers, and red berries. [*Sorbus aucuparia* and related species.]

mountain bike ■ n. a bicycle with a light sturdy frame, broad deep-treaded tyres, and multiple gears, originally designed for riding on mountainous terrain.
– DERIVATIVES **mountain biker** n. **mountain biking** n.

mountaineering ■ n. the sport or activity of climbing mountains.
– DERIVATIVES **mountaineer** n.

mountain goat ■ n. any goat that lives on mountains, proverbial for its agility.

mountain lion ■ n. North American term for **PUMA**.

mountainous ■ adj. 1 (of a region) having many mountains. 2 huge.

mountain sickness ■ n. altitude sickness.

mountain zebra ■ n. an endangered southern African zebra of mountainous regions. [*Equus zebra* subsp. *zebra* (Cape mountain zebra) and *E. zebra* subsp. *hartmannae* (Hartmann's mountain zebra).]

mountebank /'maʊntɪbaŋk/ ■ n. 1 a swindler. 2 historical a person who sold patent medicines in public places.
– ORIGIN C16: from Italian *montambanco*, from the phr. *monta in banco!* 'climb on the bench!' (with allusion to the raised platform used to attract an audience).

Mountie ■ n. informal a member of the Royal Canadian Mounted Police.

mourn ■ v. feel deep sorrow following the death or loss of. ▸ express this sorrow through conventions such as the wearing of black clothes.
– ORIGIN Old English, of Germanic origin.

mourner ■ n. a person who attends a funeral as a relative or friend of the dead person.

mournful ■ adj. feeling, expressing, or inducing sadness, regret, or grief.
– DERIVATIVES **mournfully** adv. **mournfulness** n.

mourning ■ n. 1 the experience or expression of deep sorrow for someone who has died. 2 black clothes conventionally worn in a period of mourning.

mouse ■ n. (pl. **mice**) 1 a small rodent that typically has a pointed snout, relatively large ears and eyes, and a long tail. [Many species, especially in the family Muridae.] 2 a timid and quiet person. 3 (pl. also **mouses**) a small hand-held device which is dragged across a flat surface to move the cursor on a computer screen, having buttons which are pressed to control computer functions. 4 a dull light brown colour. ■ v. 1 hunt for or catch mice. 2 use a mouse to move a cursor on a computer screen.
– DERIVATIVES **mouser** n.
– ORIGIN Old English, of Germanic origin.

mousebird ■ n. a small gregarious African bird with drab plumage, a crest, and a long tail. [Family Coliidae.]

mouse deer ■ n. another term for **CHEVROTAIN**.

mousetrap ■ n. 1 a trap for catching mice (traditionally baited with cheese). 2 Brit. informal cheese of poor quality.

mousey ■ adj. variant spelling of **MOUSY**.

moussaka /muːˈsɑːkə, ˌmuːsəˈkɑː/ ■ n. a Greek dish consisting of minced lamb, aubergines, and tomatoes, with a cheese sauce on top.
– ORIGIN from Turkish *musakka*.

mousse ■ n. 1 a sweet or savoury dish made as a smooth light mass in which the main ingredient is whipped with cream or egg white, typically served chilled. 2 a soft, light, or aerated preparation for the skin or hair. ■ v. style (hair) using mousse.
– ORIGIN C19: from French, 'moss or froth'.

mousseline /ˈmuːsliːn/ ■ n. 1 a fine, semi-opaque fabric. 2 a soft mousse or whipped sauce.
– ORIGIN C17: from French (see **MUSLIN**).

mousseux /muːˈsəː/ ■ adj. (of wine) sparkling. ■ n. (pl. same) sparkling wine.
– ORIGIN from French, from *mousse* 'froth'.

moustache (US also **mustache**) ■ n. a strip of hair left to grow above the upper lip.
– DERIVATIVES **moustached** adj.
– ORIGIN C16: from Italian *mostaccio*, from Greek *mustax*.

Mousterian /muːˈstɪərɪən/ ■ adj. Archaeology relating to or denoting the main culture of the Middle Palaeolithic period in Europe, between the Acheulian and Aurignacian periods (chiefly 80 000–35 000 years ago).
– ORIGIN C19: from French *moustiérien*, from *Le Moustier*, a cave in SW France where objects from this culture were found.

mousy (also **mousey**) ■ adj. (-ier, -iest) 1 of or like a mouse. 2 (of hair) of a dull, light brown colour. 3 (of a person) timid and ineffectual.
– DERIVATIVES **mousiness** n.

mouth ■ n. (pl. **mouths**) 1 the opening and cavity in the lower part of the human face, surrounded by the lips, through which food and air are taken and vocal sounds are emitted. ▸ the corresponding opening through which an animal takes in food. 2 informal talkativeness; impudence. 3 an opening or entrance to a structure that is hollow, concave, or almost completely enclosed. 4 the opening or entrance to a harbour or bay. ▸ the place where a river enters the sea. ■ v. 1 say (something) in an insincere or pompous way. ▸ (**mouth off**) informal talk in an opinionated or abusive way. 2 move the lips as if to form (words): *she mouthed a silent farewell*. 3 take in or touch with the mouth.
– PHRASES **be all mouth (and no trousers)** informal tend to talk boastfully but not to act on one's words. **keep one's mouth shut** informal say nothing; avoid revealing a secret. **watch one's mouth** informal be careful about what one says.
– DERIVATIVES **-mouthed** adj. **mouther** /ˈmaʊðə/ n. **mouthless** adj.
– ORIGIN Old English, of Germanic origin.

mouth bow ■ n. 1 another term for **JEW'S HARP**. 2 a musical instrument consisting of a curved stick joined at both ends by a taut string, typically played by plucking or striking the string while holding one end of the bow in the mouth, which acts as a resonator.

mouthbrooder ■ n. a freshwater cichlid fish which protects its eggs (and in some cases its young) by carrying them in its mouth. [*Sarotherodon*, *Pseudocrenilabrus* (southern Africa), and other genera.]

mouthful ■ n. (pl. **-fuls**) 1 a quantity of food or drink that fills or can be put in the mouth. 2 a long or complicated word or phrase.
– PHRASES **give someone a mouthful** Brit. informal talk to someone in an angry or abusive way. **say a mouthful** informal say something noteworthy.

mouth organ ■ n. a harmonica.

mouthpart ■ n. any of the appendages surrounding the mouth of an insect or other arthropod and adapted for feeding.

mouthpiece ■ n. 1 a part of a musical instrument, telephone, etc. that is designed to be put in or against the mouth. 2 a person who speaks on behalf of another person or an organization.

mouth-to-mouth ■ adj. denoting a method of artificial respiration in which a person breathes into someone's lungs through their mouth.

mouthwash ■ n. an antiseptic liquid used for rinsing the mouth or gargling.

mouth-watering ■ adj. 1 smelling or looking delicious. 2 highly attractive or tempting.

mouthy ■ adj. (-ier, -iest) informal inclined to talk a lot, especially in an impudent way.

movable (also **moveable**) ■ adj. 1 capable of being moved. 2 denoting a religious feast day that is variable in date from year to year (such as Easter). 3 Law (of property) of the nature of a chattel, as distinct from land or buildings. ■ n. (**movables**) property or possessions not including land or buildings.
– DERIVATIVES **movability** n. **movably** adv.
– ORIGIN Middle English: from Old French, from *moveir* 'to move'.

movable-doh ■ adj. Music denoting a system of solmization (such as tonic sol-fa) in which doh is the keynote of any major scale. Compare with **FIXED-DOH**.

move ■ v. 1 go or cause to go in a specified direction or manner. 2 change or cause to change position. ▸ (**move up**) adjust one's position to be nearer to or make room for someone else. 3 change one's place of residence. ▸ (**move in**) or **out** start (or cease) living or working in a place. 4 take a new job. 5 change or cause to change from one state, opinion, sphere, or activity to another. 6 take or cause to take action. 7 (usu. **be moved**) provoke a strong feeling, especially of sorrow or sympathy, in. 8 make progress: *they are anxious to get things moving.* 9 (**move in/within**) be socially active in (a particular sphere) or among (a particular group). 10 propose for discussion and resolution at a meeting or legislative assembly. 11 (with reference to the bowels) empty or be emptied. ■ n. 1 an

moveable

instance of moving. **2** a change of state or opinion. **3** an action that initiates or advances a process or plan. **4** a manoeuvre in a sport or game. **5** a player's turn during a board game.
– PHRASES **get a move on** informal hurry up. **make a move 1** take action. **2** Brit. set off; leave somewhere.
– ORIGIN Middle English: from Old French *moveir*, from Latin *movere*.

moveable ■ adj. & n. variant spelling of MOVABLE.

movement ■ n. **1** an act of moving. **2** (**movements**) a person's activities during a particular period of time. **3** a group of people working together to advance a shared cause. ▶ a cause of this type. **4** a change or development. **5** Music a principal division of a musical work, that is self-sufficient in terms of key, tempo, and structure. **6** the moving parts of a mechanism, especially a clock or watch.
– ORIGIN Middle English: from medieval Latin *movimentum*, from Latin *movere* 'to move'.

mover ■ n. **1** a person or thing that is moving. **2** a person who instigates or organizes something. **3** chiefly N. Amer. a person who transports furniture to new premises.
– PHRASES **a mover and shaker** a person who initiates events and influences people. [from *movers and shakers*, a phr. from the English poet Arthur O'Shaughnessy's *Music & Moonlight* (1874).]

movie ■ n. **1** a cinema film. **2** (**the movies**) films generally; the film industry.

movie theatre (also **movie house**) ■ n. S. African & N. Amer. a cinema.

moving ■ adj. **1** in motion. **2** arousing strong emotion.
– DERIVATIVES **movingly** adv.

moving-coil ■ adj. (of an electrical device such as a voltmeter or microphone) containing a wire coil suspended in a magnetic field, so that the coil either moves in response to a current or produces a current when it is made to move.

mow ■ v. (past part. **mowed** or **mown**) **1** cut down or trim (grass or a cereal crop) with a machine or scythe. **2** (**mow someone down**) kill someone with a fusillade of bullets or other missiles. ▶ recklessly knock someone down with a car.
– DERIVATIVES **mower** n.
– ORIGIN Old English, of Germanic origin.

mowings ■ pl. n. loose mown grass.

Mozambican /ˌməʊzamˈbiːkən/ ■ n. a native or inhabitant of Mozambique. ■ adj. of or relating to Mozambique or Mozambicans.

Mozartian /məʊtˈsɑːtɪən/ ■ adj. of, relating to, or characteristic of the work of the Austrian composer Wolfgang Amadeus Mozart (1756–91). ■ n. a follower of Mozart.

mozzarella /ˌmɒtsəˈrɛlə/ ■ n. a firm white Italian cheese made from buffalo's or cow's milk.
– ORIGIN Italian, diminutive of *mozza*, denoting a kind of cheese, from *mozzare* 'cut off'.

mozzie (also **mossie**) ■ n. (pl. **-ies**) informal a mosquito.

MP ■ abbrev. **1** Member of Parliament. **2** military police. **3** military policeman.

m.p. ■ abbrev. melting point.

MPC ■ abbrev. multimedia personal computer.

MPEG /ˈɛmpɛɡ/ ■ n. Computing an international standard for encoding and compressing video images.
– ORIGIN C20: from *Motion Pictures Experts Group*.

mpg ■ abbrev. miles per gallon.

mph ■ abbrev. miles per hour.

MPhil ■ abbrev. Master of Philosophy.

mphokoqo /(ə)mpɔˈkɔːkɔ, (ə)mpɔˈkɔːlɔ/ ■ n. variant spelling of UMPHOKOQO.

MPL ■ abbrev. S. African Member of Provincial Legislature.

MPV ■ abbrev. multi-purpose vehicle.

Mr ■ n. **1** a title used before a man's surname or full name (especially when he holds no honorific or professional title). **2** a title used before the name of an office to address a man who holds it: *Mr President*.

– ORIGIN Middle English: orig. an abbrev. of MASTER; cf. MISTER.

MRI ■ abbrev. magnetic resonance imaging.

mridangam /mrɪˈdaŋɡəm/ (also **mridanga**) ■ n. a barrel-shaped double-headed drum with one head larger than the other, used in southern Indian music.
– ORIGIN C19: Tamil alteration of Sanskrit *mrdanga*.

mRNA ■ abbrev. Biology messenger RNA.

Mr Right ■ n. informal a single woman's ideal partner or husband.

Mrs ■ n. a title used before a married woman's surname or full name (especially when she holds no honorific or professional title).
– ORIGIN C17: abbrev. of MISTRESS; cf. MISSUS.

Mrs Grundy ■ n. (pl. **Mrs Grundys**) a person with very conventional standards of propriety.
– ORIGIN C19: a person repeatedly mentioned in T. Morton's comedy *Speed the Plough* (1798).

MS ■ abbrev. **1** manuscript. **2** Master of Science. **3** Master of Surgery. **4** multiple sclerosis.

Ms ■ n. a title used before the surname or full name of a woman regardless of her marital status (a neutral alternative to **Mrs** or **Miss**).
– ORIGIN 1950s: combination of MRS and MISS².

MSB ■ abbrev. most significant bit.

MSc ■ abbrev. Master of Science.

MS-DOS ■ abbrev. Computing, trademark Microsoft disk operating system.

MSG ■ abbrev. monosodium glutamate.

Msgr ■ abbrev. **1** Monseigneur. **2** Monsignor.

MSgt ■ abbrev. Master Sergeant.

MSS /ɛmˈɛsɪz/ ■ abbrev. manuscripts.

MT ■ abbrev. machine translation.

Mt ■ abbrev. [in place names] Mount. ■ symb. the chemical element meitnerium.

MTB ■ abbrev. mountain bike.

MTech ■ abbrev. Master of Technology.

mu /mjuː/ ■ n. **1** the twelfth letter of the Greek alphabet (M, μ), transliterated as 'm'. **2** [as modifier] Physics relating to muons. ■ symb. **1** (μ) micron. **2** (μ) 'micro-' in symbols for units.
– ORIGIN from Greek.

much ■ det. & pron. (**more**, **most**) **1** [often with neg.] a large amount. **2** [with neg.] indicating that someone or something is a poor specimen: *I'm not much of a gardener*. ■ adv. **1** to a great extent; a great deal. **2** [usu. with neg. or in questions] often.
– PHRASES **a bit much** informal somewhat excessive or unreasonable. (**as**) **much as** even though. **how much** used to ask what a particular amount or cost is. **much better** S. African informal very much; like anything. **so much the better** (or **worse**) that is even better (or worse). **too much** too difficult or exhausting to tolerate.
– DERIVATIVES **muchly** adv. (humorous).
– ORIGIN Middle English: shortened from *muchel*, from Old English *micel*.

muchness ■ n. (in phr. (**much**) of a muchness) informal very similar.

mucho /ˈmʊtʃəʊ, ˈmʌtʃəʊ/ informal, humorous ■ det. much or many. ■ adv. very.
– ORIGIN from Spanish.

mucilage /ˈmjuːsɪlɪdʒ/ ■ n. **1** a viscous secretion or bodily fluid. **2** a polysaccharide substance extracted as a viscous or gelatinous solution from plant roots, seeds, etc., used in medicines and adhesives. **3** N. Amer. an adhesive solution; gum or glue.
– DERIVATIVES **mucilaginous** /-ˈladʒɪnəs/ adj.
– ORIGIN Middle English: from late Latin *mucilago* 'musty juice', from Latin *mucus* (see MUCUS).

mucin /ˈmjuːsɪn/ ■ n. Biochemistry a glycoprotein constituent of mucus.
– ORIGIN C19: from MUCUS.

mucinous ■ adj. of, relating to, or covered with mucus.

muck ■ n. **1** dirt or rubbish. **2** manure. ■ v. **1** (**muck something up**) informal spoil something. **2** (**muck something out**) remove manure and other dirt from a

stable, etc. **3** (**muck about/around**) informal, chiefly Brit. behave in a silly or aimless way. ▶ (**muck about/around with something**) spoil something by interfering with it. **4** (**muck someone about/around**) informal, chiefly Brit. treat someone inconsiderately, typically by disrupting their plans. **5** (**muck in**) Brit. informal share tasks or accommodation.
– PHRASES **Lord** (or **Lady**) **Muck** Brit. informal a socially pretentious man (or woman).
– DERIVATIVES **muckiness** n. **mucky** adj. (**-ier, -iest**).
– ORIGIN Middle English *muk*, prob. of Scandinavian origin, from a Germanic base meaning 'soft'.

mucker ■ n. **1** Brit. informal a friend or companion. [1940s: prob. from *muck* in (see MUCK).] **2** US informal, dated a rough or coarse person. [C19: prob. from German *Mucker* 'sulky person'.] **3** a person who removes dirt and waste, especially from mines or stables.

muckraking ■ n. the action of searching out and publicizing scandal about famous people.
– DERIVATIVES **muckrake** v. **muckraker** n.
– ORIGIN coined by US President Theodore Roosevelt in a speech (1906) alluding to Bunyan's *Pilgrim's Progress* and the man with the *muck rake*.

mucosa /mjuːˈkəʊsə/ ■ n. (pl. **mucosae** /-siː/) a mucous membrane.
– DERIVATIVES **mucosal** adj.
– ORIGIN C19: from *mucosus* 'mucous'.

mucous membrane ■ n. a mucus-secreting epithelial tissue lining many body cavities and tubular organs including the gut and respiratory passages.

mucro /ˈmjuːkrəʊ/ ■ n. (pl. **mucrones** /-ˈkrəʊniːz/ or **mucros**) Botany & Zoology a short sharp point at the end of a part or organ.
– DERIVATIVES **mucronate** adj.
– ORIGIN C17: from Latin, 'sharp point'.

mucus /ˈmjuːkəs/ ■ n. **1** a slimy substance secreted by the mucous membranes and glands of animals for lubrication, protection, etc. **2** mucilage from plants.
– DERIVATIVES **mucoid** adj. **mucosity** n. **mucous** adj.
– ORIGIN C17: from Latin.

MUD ■ n. a computer-based text or virtual reality game involving several players.
– ORIGIN C20: from *multi-user dungeon* or *dimension*.

mud ■ n. **1** soft, sticky matter consisting of mixed earth and water. **2** damaging information or allegations.
– PHRASES **drag someone through the mud** slander or denigrate someone publicly. **one's name is mud** informal one is in disgrace or unpopular.
– ORIGIN Middle English: prob. from Middle Low German *mudde*.

mudbank ■ n. a bank of mud on the bed of a river or the bottom of the sea.

mudbath ■ n. **1** a bath in the mud of mineral springs, taken especially to relieve rheumatic complaints. **2** a muddy place.

muddle ■ v. **1** bring into a disordered or confusing state. ▶ (**muddle something up**) confuse two or more things with each other. **2** confuse (a person). **3** busy oneself in a confused and ineffective way. ▶ (**muddle along/through**) cope more or less satisfactorily. ■ n. a muddled state.
– DERIVATIVES **muddled** adj. **muddler** n. **muddling** adj. **muddlingly** adv. **muddly** adj.
– ORIGIN Middle English: perhaps from Middle Dutch *moddelen*, from *modden* 'dabble in mud'.

muddle-headed ■ adj. disorganized or confused.
– DERIVATIVES **muddle-headedness** n.

muddy ■ adj. (**-ier, -iest**) **1** covered in, full of, or reminiscent of mud. **2** clouded; not bright or clear. ■ v. (**-ies, -ied**) **1** cause to become muddy. **2** make unclear: *an attempt to muddy the issue.*
– DERIVATIVES **muddily** adv. **muddiness** n.

mudfish ■ n. (pl. same or **-fishes**) **1** an African freshwater fish with a large mouth and prominent lips that feeds on algae and detritus. [Genus *Labeo*.] **2** an elongated fish that can survive drought by burrowing in the mud. [*Protopterus annectens* (an African lungfish) and genus *Neochanna* (New Zealand).]

mudflap ■ n. a flap that hangs behind the wheel of a vehicle, designed to prevent mud and stones thrown up from the road hitting the bodywork or other vehicles.

769

mug

mudflat ■ n. a stretch of muddy land left uncovered at low tide.

mudguard ■ n. a curved strip or cover over a wheel of a bicycle or motorcycle, designed to protect the vehicle and rider from water and dirt thrown up from the road.

mudminnow ■ n. a small northern-hemisphere stout-bodied freshwater fish that is able to survive low concentrations of oxygen and very low temperatures. [Genus *Umbra*: several species.]

mud pack ■ n. a paste of fuller's earth or a similar substance, applied thickly to the face to improve the condition of the skin.

mudra /ˈmʌdrə/ ■ n. **1** a symbolic hand gesture used in Hindu ceremonies and statuary, and in Indian dance. **2** a movement or pose in yoga.
– ORIGIN from Sanskrit *mudrā* 'sign or token'.

mudskipper (also **mudhopper**) ■ n. a small goby of tropical mangrove swamps which is able to move around out of water. [Genera *Periophthalmus* and *Periophthalmodon*: several species.]

mud-slinging ■ n. informal the casting of insults and accusations.
– DERIVATIVES **mud-sling** v. **mud-slinger** n.

mudstone ■ n. a dark sedimentary rock formed from consolidated mud and lacking the laminations of shale.

muesli /ˈm(j)uːzli/ ■ n. (pl. **mueslis**) a mixture of oats and other cereals, dried fruit, and nuts, typically eaten with milk at breakfast.
– ORIGIN from Swiss German.

muezzin /muːˈɛzɪn/ ■ n. a man who calls Muslims to prayer from the minaret of a mosque.
– ORIGIN C16: var. of Arabic *muʾaḏḏin*, from *aḏḏana* 'proclaim'.

muff[1] ■ n. a short tube made of fur or other warm material into which the hands are placed for warmth.
– ORIGIN C16: from Dutch *mof*, Middle Dutch *muffel*, from medieval Latin *muff(u)la*.

muff[2] informal ■ v. handle clumsily; bungle. ■ n. a mistake or failure, especially a failure to catch a ball cleanly.
– ORIGIN C19.

muffin ■ n. **1** (chiefly N. Amer. **English muffin**) a thick, flattened spongy bread roll made from yeast dough and eaten split, toasted, and buttered. **2** a small domed cake.
– ORIGIN C18.

muffle ■ v. **1** wrap or cover for warmth. **2** wrap or cover (a source of sound) to reduce its loudness. ▶ make (a sound) quieter or less distinct. ■ n. a receptacle in a furnace or kiln in which things can be heated without contact with combustion products.
– ORIGIN Middle English: perhaps from Old French *enmoufler*; the noun (C17) from Old French *moufle* 'thick glove'.

muffler ■ n. **1** a wrap or scarf worn around the neck and face for warmth. **2** a device used to deaden the sound of a drum, bell, piano, or other instrument. **3** chiefly N. Amer. a silencer for a motor vehicle exhaust.

mufti[1] /ˈmʌfti/ ■ n. (pl. **muftis**) a Muslim legal expert who is empowered to give rulings on religious matters.
– ORIGIN C16: from Arabic *muftī*, from *ʾaftā* 'decide a point of law'.

mufti[2] /ˈmʌfti/ ■ n. civilian clothes when worn by military or police staff.
– ORIGIN C19: perhaps humorously from MUFTI[1].

mug[1] ■ n. **1** a large cup, typically cylindrical and with a handle and used without a saucer. **2** informal a person's face. **3** Brit. informal a stupid or gullible person. **4** US informal a hoodlum or thug. ■ v. (**mugged, mugging**) informal **1** attack and rob (someone) in a public place. **2** make faces before an audience or a camera.
– PHRASES **a mug's game** informal an activity likely to be unsuccessful or dangerous.
– DERIVATIVES **mugful** n. (pl. **-fuls**). **mugging** n.
– ORIGIN C16: prob. of Scandinavian origin.

mug[2] ■ v. (**mugged, mugging**) (**mug something up**) Brit. informal learn or study a subject quickly and intensively, especially for an exam.
– ORIGIN C19.

Muganda /mʊˈɡandə/ ■ n. singular form of BAGANDA.

mugger ■ n. a person who attacks and robs another in a public place.

muggie /ˈmʌxi/ (also **miggie**) ■ n. S. African a midge or gnat.
– ORIGIN Afrikaans, 'gnat, midge'.

muggins ■ n. (pl. same or **mugginses**) informal, chiefly Brit. a foolish and gullible person (often used to refer to oneself).
– ORIGIN C19: perhaps a use of the surname *Muggins*, with allusion to MUG[1].

muggy ■ adj. (**-ier**, **-iest**) (of the weather) unpleasantly warm and humid.
– DERIVATIVES **mugginess** n.
– ORIGIN C18: from dialect *mug* 'mist, drizzle', from Old Norse *mugga*.

Mughal /ˈmuːɡɑːl/ ■ n. variant spelling of MOGUL.

mugshot ■ n. informal a photograph of a person's face made for an official purpose, especially police records.

mugwort ■ n. a plant of the daisy family, with aromatic divided leaves that are dark green above and whitish below. [*Artemisia vulgaris* and related species.]
– ORIGIN Old English *mucgwyrt* (see MIDGE, WORT).

Muhammadan /mʊˈhamədən/ (also **Mohammedan**) ■ n. & adj. archaic term for MUSLIM (not favoured by Muslims).
– DERIVATIVES **Muhammadanism** n.
– ORIGIN C17: from the name of the Arab prophet and founder of Islam *Muhammad*.

muishond /ˈmeɪʃɒnt/ ■ n. (pl. same or **muishonde** /-hɒndə/) S. African any of a number of small mammals of the mongoose and weasel family.
– ORIGIN S. African Dutch, from Dutch *muishond* 'weasel'.

mujahedin /ˌmʊdʒɑːhɪˈdiːn/ (also **mujahidin**, **mujaheddin**, or **mujahideen**) ■ pl. n. Islamic guerrilla fighters.
– ORIGIN from Persian and Arabic *mujāhidīn*, colloqial pl. of *mujāhid*, denoting a person who fights a jihad.

mujtahid /mʊdʒˈtɑːhɪd/ ■ n. (pl. **mujtahids** or **mujtahidūn**) a person accepted as an original authority in Islamic law.
– ORIGIN Persian, from Arabic, from *ijtahada* 'strive'.

mulatto /m(j)uːˈlatəʊ/ ■ n. (pl. **-oes** or **-os**) a person with one white and one black parent. ■ adj. relating to or denoting a mulatto or mulattoes.
– ORIGIN C16: from Spanish *mulato* 'young mule or mulatto', from *mulo* 'mule'.

mulberry ■ n. 1 a small tree with dark red or white fruit, native to the Far East and cultivated elsewhere. [*Morus alba* (white mulberry), *M. nigra* (black mulberry), and other species.] ▶ the fruit of this tree. 2 a dark red or purple colour.
– ORIGIN Old English, from Latin *morum* + BERRY.

mulch /mʌl(t)ʃ/ ■ n. a mass of leaves, bark, or compost spread around or over a plant for protection or to enrich the soil. ■ v. apply a mulch. ▶ treat or cover with mulch.
– ORIGIN C17: prob. from dialect *mulch* 'soft', from Old English *melsc*, *mylsc*.

mule[1] ■ n. 1 the offspring of a male donkey and a female horse, typically sterile and used as a beast of burden. Compare with HINNY. 2 a hybrid plant or animal, especially a sterile one. 3 a stupid or obstinate person. 4 (also **spinning mule**) a kind of spinning machine producing yarn on spindles.
– ORIGIN Old English, prob. of Germanic origin, from Latin *mulus*, *mula*.

mule[2] ■ n. a slipper or light shoe without a back.
– ORIGIN C16: from French, 'slipper'.

muleteer /ˌmjuːlɪˈtɪə/ ■ n. a person who drives mules.
– ORIGIN C16: from French *muletier*, from *mulet*, diminutive of Old French *mul* 'mule'.

mulga /ˈmʌlɡə/ ■ n. 1 a small Australian acacia tree or shrub with greyish foliage, which forms dense scrubby growth and is also grown for its wood. [*Acacia aneura*.] 2 an area of scrub or bush dominated by this plant. 3 (**the mulga**) Austral. informal the outback.
– ORIGIN C19: from Yuwaalaraay (an Aboriginal language of New South Wales).

mulgara /mʌlˈɡɑːrə/ ■ n. a rat-sized carnivorous marsupial with a pointed snout, large eyes, and a short crested tail, native to central Australia. [*Dasycercus cristicauda*.]
– ORIGIN 1940s: prob. from Wangganguru (an Aboriginal language) *mardagura*.

mulish /ˈmjuːlɪʃ/ ■ adj. stubborn (like a mule).
– DERIVATIVES **mulishly** adv. **mulishness** n.

mull[1] ■ v. (usu. **mull over**) think about at length.
– ORIGIN C19.

mull[2] ■ v. [usu. as adj. **mulled**] warm (wine or beer) and add sugar and spices to it.
– ORIGIN C17.

mull[3] ■ n. (in Scottish place names) a promontory.
– ORIGIN Middle English: cf. Scottish Gaelic *maol* and Icelandic *múli*.

mull[4] ■ n. humus formed under non-acid conditions.
– ORIGIN 1920s: from Danish *muld* 'soil'.

mull[5] ■ n. a thin muslin, used in bookbinding for joining the spine of a book to its cover.
– ORIGIN C17: abbrev., from Hindi *malmal*.

mullah /ˈmʌlə, ˈmʊlə/ ■ n. a Muslim learned in Islamic theology and sacred law.
– ORIGIN C17: from Persian, Turkish, and Urdu *mullā*, from Arabic *mawlā*.

mullein /ˈmʌlɪn/ ■ n. a plant with woolly leaves and tall spikes of yellow flowers. [*Verbascum thapsus* (great mullein) and related species.]
– ORIGIN Middle English: from Old French *moleine*, of Celtic origin.

Müllerian mimicry /mʊˈlɪərɪən/ ■ n. Zoology a form of mimicry in which two or more noxious animals develop similar appearances as a shared protective device.
– ORIGIN C19: named after the German zoologist Johann F. T. *Müller*.

mullet[1] ■ n. any of various chiefly marine fish that are widely caught for food. [Families Mugilidae (grey mullets) and Mullidae (goatfish).]
– ORIGIN Middle English: from Old French *mulet*, diminutive of Latin *mullus* 'red mullet', from Greek *mullos*.

mullet[2] ■ n. Heraldry a star with five (or more) straight-edged points or rays, as a charge or a mark of cadency for a third son.
– ORIGIN Middle English: from Old French *molette* 'rowel', from Latin *mola* 'grindstone'.

mulligan /ˈmʌlɪɡ(ə)n/ ■ n. informal, chiefly N. Amer. 1 a stew made from odds and ends of food. 2 (in informal golf) an extra stroke allowed after a poor shot, not counted on the scorecard.
– ORIGIN C20: apparently from the surname *Mulligan*.

mulligatawny /ˌmʌlɪɡəˈtɔːni/ ■ n. a spicy meat soup originally made in India.
– ORIGIN from Tamil *miḷaku-taṇṇi* 'pepper-water'.

mullion /ˈmʌljən/ ■ n. a vertical bar between the panes of glass in a window. Compare with TRANSOM (in sense 2).
– DERIVATIVES **mullioned** adj.
– ORIGIN C16: prob. from Old French *moinel* 'middle'.

multi- ■ comb. form more than one; many: *multicultural*.
– ORIGIN from Latin *multus* 'much, many'.

multi-access ■ adj. (of a computer system) allowing the simultaneous connection of a number of terminals.

multiaxial ■ adj. involving or possessing several or many axes.

multicast ■ v. (past and past part. **multicast**) send (data) across a computer network to several users at the same time. ■ n. a set of multicast data.

multicellular ■ adj. (of an organism or part) having or consisting of many cells.
– DERIVATIVES **multicellularity** n.

multicoloured (also **multicolour**; US **-colored**, **-color**) ■ adj. having many colours.

multicultural ■ adj. of, relating to, or constituting several cultural or ethnic groups.
– DERIVATIVES **multiculturalism** n. **multiculturalist** n. & adj. **multiculturally** adv.

multidimensional ■ adj. of or involving several dimensions.
– DERIVATIVES **multidimensionality** n. **multidimensionally** adv.

multidisciplinary ■ adj. involving several academic disciplines or professional specializations.

multi-ethnic ■ adj. of, relating to, or constituting several ethnic groups.

multifaceted ■ adj. having many facets.

multifactorial ■ adj. involving or dependent on a number of factors or causes.

multi-faith ■ adj. involving or characterized by a variety of religions.

multifarious /ˌmʌltɪˈfɛːrɪəs/ ■ adj. having great variety and diversity. ▶ many and various.
– DERIVATIVES **multifariously** adv. **multifariousness** n.
– ORIGIN C16: from Latin *multifarius*.

multifilament ■ adj. denoting a cord or yarn composed of a number of strands or filaments wound together.

multifocal ■ adj. chiefly Medicine & Optics having more than one focus.

multifoil ■ n. Architecture an ornament consisting of more than five foils.

multiform ■ adj. existing in many forms or kinds.
– DERIVATIVES **multiformity** n.

multifunctional (also **multifunction**) ■ adj. having or fulfilling several functions.

multigenerational ■ adj. of or relating to several generations.

multigrade ■ n. 1 an engine oil meeting the requirements of several standard grades. 2 (trademark in the US) a kind of photographic paper made with two emulsions of different sensitivities, from which prints with different levels of contrast can be made.

multigrain ■ adj. (of bread) made from more than one kind of grain.

multigravida /ˌmʌltɪˈɡravɪdə/ ■ n. (pl. **multigravidae** /-diː/) Medicine & Zoology a woman (or female animal) that is or has been pregnant for at least a second time.
– ORIGIN C19: from MULTI-, on the pattern of *primigravida*.

multigym ■ n. an apparatus on which a number of weightlifting and other exercises can be performed.

multihull ■ n. a boat with two or more, especially three, hulls.

multilateral ■ adj. agreed upon or participated in by three or more parties.
– DERIVATIVES **multilateralism** n. **multilateralist** adj. & n. **multilaterally** adv.

multilayer ■ adj. relating to or consisting of several or many layers. ■ n. a multilayer coating or deposit.
– DERIVATIVES **multilayered** adj.

multilingual ■ adj. in or using several languages.
– DERIVATIVES **multilingualism** n. **multilingually** adv.

multimedia ■ adj. using more than one medium of expression or communication. ■ n. Computing an extension of hypertext allowing the provision of audio and video material cross-referenced to a text.

multimeter ■ n. an instrument designed to measure electric current, voltage, and resistance.

multimillion ■ adj. consisting of several million.

multimillionaire ■ n. a person with assets worth several million pounds or dollars.

multinational ■ adj. 1 including or involving several countries or nationalities. 2 operating in several countries. ■ n. a company operating in several countries.
– DERIVATIVES **multinationally** adv.

multinomial /ˌmʌltɪˈnəʊmɪəl/ ■ adj. & n. Mathematics another term for POLYNOMIAL.
– ORIGIN C17: from MULTI-, on the pattern of *binomial*.

multipack ■ n. a package containing a number of similar or identical products sold at a discount compared to the price when bought separately.

multipara /mʌlˈtɪp(ə)rə/ ■ n. (pl. **multiparae** /-riː/) Medicine & Zoology a woman (or female animal) that has had more than one pregnancy resulting in viable offspring.
– DERIVATIVES **multiparous** adj.
– ORIGIN C19: from modern Latin *multiparus* 'multiparous'.

multipartite /ˌmʌltɪˈpɑːtʌɪt/ ■ adj. 1 having several or

multiply

many parts or divisions. 2 Biology (of a virus) existing as two or more separate but incomplete particles. 3 another term for MULTIPARTY.

multiparty ■ adj. of or involving several political parties.

multiphase ■ adj. 1 in, of, or relating to more than one phase. 2 (of an electrical device or circuit) polyphase.

multiplay ■ adj. denoting a compact disc player which can be stacked with a number of discs before needing to be reloaded.

multiplayer ■ n. 1 a compact disc player which can play a number of discs in succession. 2 a multimedia computer and home entertainment system integrating conventional and interactive audio and video functions with those of a personal computer. ■ adj. denoting a computer game for or involving several players.

multiple ■ adj. 1 having or involving several parts or elements. 2 numerous. 3 (of a disease or injury) complex in its nature or effect; affecting several parts of the body. ■ n. a number that may be divided by another a certain number of times without a remainder.
– ORIGIN C17: from late Latin *multiplus*, alteration of Latin *multiplex* (see MULTIPLEX).

multiple-choice ■ adj. (of a question in an examination) accompanied by several possible answers from which the candidate must try to choose the correct one.

multiple fruit ■ n. Botany a fruit formed from carpels derived from several flowers, such as a pineapple.

multiple sclerosis ■ n. see SCLEROSIS.

multiple star ■ n. a group of stars very close together as seen from the earth, especially one whose members are in fact close together and rotate around a common centre.

multiplet ■ n. Physics a group of closely associated things, especially closely spaced spectrum lines or atomic energy levels, or subatomic particles differing only in a single property.
– ORIGIN 1920s: from MULTIPLE, on the pattern of *doublet* and *triplet*.

multiple unit ■ n. a passenger train of two or more carriages powered by integral motors which drive a number of axles.

multiplex ■ adj. 1 consisting of many elements in a complex relationship. 2 involving simultaneous transmission of several messages along a single channel of communication. 3 (of a cinema) having several separate screens within one building. ■ n. 1 a multiplex system or signal. 2 a multiplex cinema. ■ v. incorporate into a multiplex signal or system.
– DERIVATIVES **multiplexer** (also **multiplexor**) n.
– ORIGIN Middle English in the mathematical sense 'multiple': from Latin.

multiplicand /ˌmʌltɪplɪˈkand, ˈmʌltɪplɪˌkand/ ■ n. a quantity which is to be multiplied by another (the multiplier).

multiplication ■ n. 1 the process of multiplying. 2 Mathematics the process of combining matrices, vectors, or other quantities under specific rules to obtain their product.

multiplication sign ■ n. the sign ×, used to indicate that one quantity is to be multiplied by another.

multiplication table ■ n. a list of multiples of a particular number, typically from 1 to 12.

multiplicative /ˈmʌltɪˌplɪkətɪv/ ■ n. subject to or of the nature of multiplication.

multiplicity ■ n. (pl. -ies) a large number or variety.

multiplier ■ n. 1 a quantity by which a given number (the multiplicand) is to be multiplied. 2 Economics a factor by which an increment of income exceeds the resulting increment of saving or investment. 3 a device for increasing by repetition the intensity of an electric current, force, etc. to a measurable level.

multiply[1] /ˈmʌltɪplʌɪ/ ■ v. (-ies, -ied) 1 obtain from (a number) another which contains the first number a specified number of times. 2 increase or cause to increase in number or quantity. 3 increase in number by

multiply

reproducing. **4** propagate (plants).
– DERIVATIVES **multipliable** adj. **multiplicable** adj.
– ORIGIN Middle English: from Old French *multiplier*, from Latin *multiplicare*.

multiply² /ˈmʌltɪpli/ ■ adv. in different ways or respects.

multipolar ■ adj. **1** having many poles or extremities. **2** polarized in several ways or directions.
– DERIVATIVES **multipolarity** n. **multipole** n.

multiprocessing (also **multiprogramming**) ■ n. Computing another term for MULTITASKING.

multiprocessor ■ n. a computer with more than one central processor.

multi-purpose ■ adj. having several purposes.

multiracial ■ adj. consisting of or relating to people of many races.
– DERIVATIVES **multiracialism** n. **multiracialist** adj. & n. **multiracially** adv.

multiskill ■ v. [usu. as noun **multiskilling** or adj. **multiskilled**] acquire, or train to acquire, ability in a variety of disciplines or work skills.

multispectral ■ adj. operating in or involving several regions of the electromagnetic spectrum.

multistage ■ adj. **1** consisting of or relating to several stages or processes. **2** (of a rocket) having at least two sections which contain their own motor and are jettisoned as their fuel runs out. **3** (of a pump, turbine, or similar device) having more than one rotor.

multi-storey (chiefly N. Amer. also **multi-story**) ■ adj. (of a building) having several storeys. ■ n. Brit. informal a multi-storey car park.

multitasking ■ n. Computing **1** the execution of more than one program or task simultaneously by sharing the resources of the computer processor between them. **2** the process of doing several things at the same time.
– DERIVATIVES **multitask** v.

multithreading ■ n. Computing a technique by which a single set of code can be used by several processors at different stages of execution.
– DERIVATIVES **multithreaded** adj.

multi-track ■ adj. relating to or made by the mixing of several separately recorded tracks of sound. ■ n. a multi-track recording. ■ v. record using multi-track recording.
– DERIVATIVES **multi-tracked** adj.

multitude ■ n. **1** a large number of people or things. **2** (**the multitude**) the mass of ordinary people.
– ORIGIN Middle English: from Latin *multitudo*, from *multus* 'many'.

multitudinous /ˌmʌltɪˈtjuːdɪnəs/ ■ adj. **1** very numerous. ▸ consisting of many individuals or elements. **2** poetic/literary (of a body of water) vast.
– DERIVATIVES **multitudinously** adv.
– ORIGIN Latin *multitudo* (see MULTITUDE).

multivalent /ˌmʌltɪˈveɪl(ə)nt/ ■ adj. **1** having many applications, interpretations, or values. **2** Chemistry another term for POLYVALENT.
– DERIVATIVES **multivalence** n. **multivalency** n.

multivalve ■ adj. (of an internal-combustion engine) having more than two valves per cylinder, typically four.

multivariate /ˌmʌltɪˈvɛːrɪət/ ■ adj. Statistics involving two or more variable quantities.

multivendor ■ adj. denoting or relating to computer hardware or software products or network services from more than one supplier.

multiway ■ adj. having several routes, channels, or styles.

mum¹ ■ n. informal, chiefly Brit. another term for MOM.

mum² ■ adj. (in phr. **keep mum**) informal remain silent so as not to reveal a secret.
– PHRASES **mum's the word** do not reveal a secret.
– ORIGIN Middle English: imitative of a sound made with closed lips.

mumble ■ v. **1** say something indistinctly and quietly. **2** bite or chew with toothless gums. ■ n. a quiet and indistinct utterance.
– DERIVATIVES **mumbler** n. **mumbling** adj. **mumblingly** adv.
– ORIGIN Middle English: from MUM².

mumbo-jumbo ■ n. informal language or ritual causing or intended to cause confusion or bewilderment.
– ORIGIN C18 (as *Mumbo Jumbo*, denoting a supposed African idol).

mu-meson ■ n. another term for MUON.

mummer ■ n. an actor in a mummers' play. ▸ archaic or derogatory an actor in the theatre.
– ORIGIN Middle English: from Old French *momeur*, from *momer* 'act in a mime'.

mummers' play (also **mumming play**) ■ n. a traditional English folk play of a type often associated with Christmas and popular in the 18th and early 19th centuries.

mummery ■ n. (pl. **-ies**) **1** a performance by mummers. **2** ridiculous ceremony.

mummify ■ v. (**-ies**, **-ied**) [usu. as adj. **mummified**] **1** (especially in ancient Egypt) preserve (a body) as a mummy. **2** dry up (a body) and so preserve it.
– DERIVATIVES **mummification** n.

mummy¹ ■ n. (pl. **-ies**) informal, chiefly Brit. another term for MOMMY.
– ORIGIN C18: perhaps an alteration of MAMMY.

mummy² ■ n. (pl. **-ies**) (especially in ancient Egypt) a body that has been preserved for burial by embalming and wrapping in bandages.
– ORIGIN Middle English: from French *momie*, from medieval Latin *mumia* and Arabic *mūmiyā* 'embalmed body'.

mumps ■ pl. n. [treated as sing.] a viral disease mainly affecting children, causing swelling of the parotid salivary glands of the face.
– ORIGIN C16: from obsolete *mump* 'grimace'.

mumsy Brit. informal ■ adj. (of a woman) homely and unfashionable. ■ n. chiefly humorous one's mother.
– ORIGIN C19: humorous var. of MUMMY¹.

munch ■ v. eat steadily and audibly.
– DERIVATIVES **muncher** n.
– ORIGIN Middle English: imitative.

Munchausen's syndrome /ˈmʌn(t)ʃˌaʊz(ə)nz/ ■ n. Psychiatry a mental disorder in which a person feigns severe illness so as to obtain medical attention.
– ORIGIN from the name of Baron *Munchausen*, the hero of a book of fantastic tales (1785).

munchies ■ pl. n. informal **1** snacks or small items of food. **2** (**the munchies**) a sudden strong desire for food.

mundane /ˈmʌndeɪn, mʌnˈdeɪn/ ■ adj. **1** lacking interest or excitement. **2** of this earthly world rather than a heavenly or spiritual one.
– DERIVATIVES **mundanely** adv. **mundaneness** n. **mundanity** /-ˈdanɪti/ n. (pl. **-ies**).
– ORIGIN Middle English: from late Latin *mundanus*, from Latin *mundus* 'world'.

mung bean /mʌŋ, muːŋ/ ■ n. **1** a small round green bean grown in the tropics. **2** the plant that produces these beans, chiefly grown as a source of bean sprouts. [*Vigna radiata*.]
– ORIGIN C19: from Hindi *mūng*.

municipal /mjʊˈnɪsɪp(ə)l/ ■ adj. of or relating to a municipality.
– DERIVATIVES **municipalization** (also **-isation**) n. **municipalize** (also **-ise**) v. **municipally** adv.
– ORIGIN C16: from Latin *municipalis*, from *municipium* 'free city' + *capere* 'take'.

municipal bond ■ n. (chiefly in the US) a security issued by or on behalf of a local authority.

municipality ■ n. (pl. **-ies**) a town or district that has local government. ▸ the governing body of such an area.

munificent /mjʊˈnɪfɪs(ə)nt/ ■ adj. very generous.
– DERIVATIVES **munificence** n. **munificently** adv.
– ORIGIN C16: from Latin *munificentior*, from *munificus* 'bountiful'.

munition /mjʊˈnɪʃ(ə)n/ ■ n. (**munitions**) military weapons, ammunition, equipment, and stores. ■ v. supply with munitions.
– ORIGIN Middle English: from Latin *munitio(n-)* 'fortification', from *munire* 'fortify'.

Munro /mʌnˈrəʊ/ ■ n. (pl. **-os**) any of the 277 mountains in Scotland that are at least 3 000 feet high (approximately 914 metres).

– ORIGIN C20: named after Sir Hugh Thomas *Munro*, who published a list of all such mountains in 1891.

muntjac /'mʌntdʒak/ ■ n. a small SE Asian deer with a doglike bark and small tusks. [Genus *Muntiacus*: several species.]
– ORIGIN C18: from Sundanese *minchek*.

muon /'mjuːɒn/ ■ n. Physics an unstable meson with a mass around 200 times that of the electron.
– DERIVATIVES **muonic** adj.
– ORIGIN 1950s: contraction of **MU-MESON**.

mural /'mjʊər(ə)l/ ■ n. a painting executed directly on a wall. ■ adj. of, like, or relating to a wall.
– DERIVATIVES **muralist** n.
– ORIGIN Middle English: from Latin *muralis*, from *murus* 'wall'.

mural crown ■ n. Heraldry a representation of a city wall in the form of a crown, borne above the shield in the arms of distinguished soldiers and of some civic authorities.

murder ■ n. 1 the unlawful premeditated killing of one person by another. 2 informal a very difficult or unpleasant situation or experience. ■ v. 1 kill unlawfully and with premeditation. 2 informal punish severely. 3 informal, chiefly Brit. consume (food or drink) with relish.
– PHRASES **get away with (blue) murder** informal succeed in doing whatever one chooses without being punished. **murder will out** murder cannot remain undetected. **scream (or yell) blue (or N. Amer. bloody) murder** informal make an extravagant and noisy protest.
– DERIVATIVES **murderer** n. **murderess** n.
– ORIGIN Old English, of Germanic origin.

murderous ■ adj. 1 capable of, intending, or involving murder or extreme violence. 2 informal extremely arduous or unpleasant.
– DERIVATIVES **murderously** adv. **murderousness** n.

murine /'mjʊərʌɪn, -rɪn/ ■ adj. Zoology of or relating to mice or related rodents.
– ORIGIN C17: from Latin *murinus*, from *mus* 'mouse'.

murk ■ n. darkness or fog causing poor visibility.
– ORIGIN Old English, of Germanic origin.

murky ■ adj. (-ier, -iest) 1 dark and gloomy. ▸ (of water) dirty or cloudy. 2 deliberately obscure so as to conceal dishonesty or immorality.
– DERIVATIVES **murkily** adv. **murkiness** n.

murmur ■ n. 1 a low continuous background noise. 2 a quietly spoken utterance. ▸ the quiet or subdued expression of a feeling. 3 Medicine a recurring sound heard in the heart through a stethoscope that is usually a sign of disease or damage. ■ v. 1 say something in a murmur. 2 make a low continuous sound.
– PHRASES **without a murmur** without complaining.
– DERIVATIVES **murmurer** n. **murmurous** adj.
– ORIGIN Middle English: from Old French *murmure*, from *murmurer* 'to murmur', from Latin *murmur*.

murmuring ■ n. 1 a low continuous sound. 2 a subdued or private expression of discontent.
– DERIVATIVES **murmuringly** adv.

Murphy's Law ■ n. a supposed law of nature, to the effect that anything that can go wrong will go wrong.

murrain /'mʌrɪn/ ■ n. 1 redwater fever or a similar infectious disease affecting cattle or other animals. 2 archaic a plague or crop blight.
– ORIGIN Middle English: from Old French *morine*, from Latin *mori* 'to die'.

murrey /'mʌri/ ■ n. archaic the deep purple-red colour of a mulberry.
– ORIGIN Middle English: from medieval Latin *moratus*, from *morum* 'mulberry'.

murther /'mɜːðə/ ■ n. & v. archaic spelling of **MURDER**.

MusB (also **Mus Bac**) ■ abbrev. Bachelor of Music.
– ORIGIN from Latin *Musicae Baccalaureus*.

muscadel /ˌmʌskə'dɛl/ ■ n. S. African another term for **MUSCAT** or **MUSCATEL**.

Muscadelle /ˌmʌskə'dɛl/ ■ n. a variety of white grape grown mainly for sweet white wines in Bordeaux and Australia.
– ORIGIN French, from **MUSCAT**.

Muscadet /'mʌskədeɪ, 'mʊsk-/ ■ n. a dry white wine from the Loire region of France.
– ORIGIN French, from *muscade* 'nutmeg'.

muscat /'mʌskat/ ■ n. a variety of white, red, or black grape with a musky scent, grown for wine or eating as fruit or raisins. ▸ a sweet or fortified white wine made from these grapes.
– ORIGIN French, from Provençal, from *musc* 'musk'.

muscatel /ˌmʌskə'tɛl/ ■ n. a muscat grape or a raisin made from such a grape. ▸ a sweet wine made from muscat grapes.
– ORIGIN from Provençal, diminutive of *muscat* (see **MUSCAT**).

muscle ■ n. 1 a band of fibrous tissue in the body that has the ability to contract, producing movement in or maintaining the position of a part of the body. 2 physical power. ▸ political or economic power. ■ v. informal 1 N. Amer. move (an object) by use of physical strength. 2 (**muscle in/into**) force one's way into (another's affairs).
– DERIVATIVES **-muscled** adj. **muscleless** adj. **muscly** adj.
– ORIGIN Middle English: from Latin *musculus*, diminutive of *mus* 'mouse' (some muscles being thought to be mouse-like in form).

muscle-bound ■ adj. having well-developed or over-developed muscles.

muscleman ■ n. (pl. **-men**) a large, strong man, especially one employed to protect someone or intimidate others.

muscovado /ˌmʌskə'vɑːdəʊ/ (also **muscovado sugar**) ■ n. unrefined sugar made from evaporating the juice of sugar cane and draining off the molasses.
– ORIGIN C17: from Portuguese *mascabado (açúcar)* '(sugar) of the lowest quality'.

Muscovite /'mʌskəvʌɪt/ ■ n. a native or citizen of Moscow. ▸ archaic a Russian. ■ adj. of or relating to Moscow. ▸ archaic of or relating to Russia.

muscovite /'mʌskəvʌɪt/ ■ n. a silver-grey form of mica occurring in many igneous and metamorphic rocks.
– ORIGIN C19: from obsolete *Muscovy glass* (in the same sense).

Muscovy duck ■ n. a large tropical American duck with glossy greenish-black plumage. [*Cairina moschata*.]

muscular ■ adj. of or affecting the muscles. ▸ having well-developed muscles.
– DERIVATIVES **muscularity** n. **muscularly** adv.

muscular dystrophy ■ n. a hereditary condition marked by progressive weakening and wasting of the muscles.

muscular rheumatism ■ n. aching pain in the muscles and joints.

musculature /'mʌskjʊlətʃə/ ■ n. the muscular system or arrangement of a body or an organ.
– ORIGIN C19: from Latin *musculus* (see **MUSCLE**).

musculoskeletal /ˌmʌskjʊləʊ'skɛlɪt(ə)l/ ■ adj. relating to or denoting the musculature and skeleton together.

MusD (also **Mus Doc**) ■ abbrev. Doctor of Music.
– ORIGIN from Latin *Musicae Doctor*.

muse[1] ■ n. (**Muse**) Greek & Roman Mythology each of nine goddesses who preside over the arts and sciences. ▸ a woman, or a force personified as a woman, who is the source of inspiration for a creative artist.
– ORIGIN Middle English: from Latin *musa*, from Greek *mousa*.

muse[2] ■ v. (often **muse on**) be absorbed in thought. ▸ say to oneself in a thoughtful manner.
– DERIVATIVES **musing** adj. **musingly** adv.
– ORIGIN Middle English: from Old French *muser* 'meditate, waste time'.

museology /ˌmjuːzɪ'ɒlədʒi/ ■ n. the science or practice of organizing and managing museums.
– DERIVATIVES **museological** adj. **museologist** n.

musette /mjuː'zɛt/ ■ n. 1 a kind of small bagpipe played with bellows, popular in France in the 17th–18th centuries and in later folk music. ▸ a tune or piece of music imitating the sound of this, typically with a drone. 2 a small simple variety of oboe, used chiefly in 19th-century France.
– ORIGIN Middle English: from Old French, diminutive of *muse* 'bagpipe'.

museum ■ n. a building in which objects of historical,

scientific, artistic, or cultural interest are stored and exhibited.
– ORIGIN C17: from Greek *mouseion* 'seat of the Muses'.

museum beetle ■ n. a small beetle whose larvae can cause severe damage to carpets, stored goods, etc. [*Anthrenus museorum* and related species.]

museum piece ■ n. a person or object regarded as old-fashioned or useless.

mush[1] /mʌʃ/ ■ n. 1 a soft, wet, pulpy mass. ▸ N. Amer. thick maize porridge. 2 cloying sentimentality. ■ v. [usu. as adj. **mushed**] reduce to mush.
– DERIVATIVES **mushily** adv. **mushiness** n. **mushy** adj. (**-ier, -iest**).
– ORIGIN C17: prob. a var. of MASH.

mush[2] /mʌʃ/ N. Amer. ■ v. travel across snow with a dog sled. ■ exclam. a command urging on dogs during such a journey.
– DERIVATIVES **musher** n.
– ORIGIN C19: prob. an alteration of French *marchez!* or *marchons!*, from *marcher* 'to advance'.

mushroom ■ n. 1 a spore-producing fungal growth, often edible and typically having a domed cap with gills on the underside. 2 a pale pinkish-brown colour. ■ v. 1 increase or develop rapidly. 2 form a shape resembling that of a mushroom. 3 [usu. as noun **mushrooming**] gather mushrooms.
– DERIVATIVES **mushroomy** adj.
– ORIGIN Middle English: from Old French *mousseron*, from late Latin *mussirio(n-)*.

mushroom cloud ■ n. a mushroom-shaped cloud of dust and debris formed after a nuclear explosion.

mushroom growth ■ n. a sudden development or expansion.

music ■ n. 1 the art or science of combining vocal or instrumental sounds (or both) to produce beauty of form, harmony, and expression of emotion. ▸ The sound so produced. 2 the written or printed signs representing such sound.
– PHRASES **music to one's ears** something that is very pleasant to hear or learn.
– ORIGIN Middle English: from Old French *musique*, from Greek *mousikē* (*tekhnē*) '(art) of the Muses', from *mousa* 'muse'.

musical ■ adj. 1 of, relating to, or accompanied by music. ▸ fond of or skilled in music. 2 pleasant-sounding. ■ n. a play or film in which singing and dancing play an essential part.
– DERIVATIVES **musicality** n. **musicalize** (also **-ise**) v. **musically** adv.

musical box ■ n. Brit. a music box.

musical chairs ■ n. 1 a party game in which players compete for a decreasing number of chairs, the losers in successive rounds being those unable to find a chair to sit on when the accompanying music is stopped. 2 a situation in which people frequently exchange jobs or positions.

musical comedy ■ n. a musical.

musicale /ˌmjuːzɪˈkɑːl/ ■ n. N. Amer. a musical gathering or concert.
– ORIGIN C19: French, from *soirée musicale* 'evening of music'.

musical instrument ■ n. see INSTRUMENT (sense 3).

music box ■ n. a small box which plays a tune when the lid is opened.

music centre ■ n. 1 chiefly Brit. a combined radio, cassette player, and compact disc player. 2 a place where music is played and taught.

music drama ■ n. an opera governed by considerations of dramatic effectiveness, rather than by having a series of formal arias.

music hall ■ n. a form of variety entertainment popular in Britain c.1850–1918, consisting of singing, dancing, comedy, and novelty acts. ▸ a theatre where such entertainment took place.

musician ■ n. a person who plays a musical instrument or is otherwise musically gifted.
– DERIVATIVES **musicianly** adj. **musicianship** n.
– ORIGIN Middle English: from Old French *musicien*, from Latin *musica* (see MUSIC).

musicology ■ n. the study of music as an academic subject.
– DERIVATIVES **musicological** adj. **musicologist** n.
– ORIGIN C20: from French *musicologie*.

music theatre ■ n. a combination of music and drama in modern form distinct from traditional opera, typically for a small group of performers.

musk ■ n. 1 a strong-smelling reddish-brown substance secreted by the male musk deer, used as an ingredient in perfumery. 2 (also **musk plant**) a musk-scented plant related to the monkey flower. [*Mimulus moschatus* and related species.]
– DERIVATIVES **muskiness** n. **musky** adj. (**-ier, -iest**).
– ORIGIN Middle English: from late Latin *muscus*, from Persian *mušk*.

musk deer ■ n. a small East Asian deer without antlers, the male of which produces musk in an abdominal sac. [Genus *Moschus*: several species.]

musket ■ n. historical an infantryman's light gun with a long barrel, typically smooth-bored and fired from the shoulder.
– ORIGIN C16: from French *mousquet*, from Italian *moschetto* 'crossbow bolt'.

musketeer ■ n. historical 1 a soldier armed with a musket. 2 a member of the household troops of the French king in the 17th and 18th centuries.

musketry ■ n. 1 musket fire. 2 musketeers collectively. 3 the art or technique of handling a musket.

musk melon ■ n. a yellow or green melon of a variety which has a raised network of markings on the skin.

Muskogean /ˌmʌskəˈɡiːən, mʌˈskəʊɡɪən/ ■ n. a family of American Indian languages spoken in SE North America, including Creek and Choctaw.

musk ox ■ n. a large heavily built goat-antelope with a thick shaggy coat and a horny boss on the head, native to the tundra of North America and Greenland. [*Ovibos moschatus*.]

muskrat ■ n. a large semiaquatic North American rodent with a musky smell, valued for its fur. [*Ondatra zibethicus*.] ▸ the fur of the muskrat.

Muslim /ˈmʊzlɪm, ˈmʌz-, -s-/ (also **Moslem**) ■ n. a follower of Islam. ■ adj. of or relating to the Muslims or Islam.
– ORIGIN C17: from Arabic, from *'aslama* (see ISLAM).

muslin ■ n. lightweight cotton cloth in a plain weave.
– DERIVATIVES **muslined** adj.
– ORIGIN C17: from French *mousseline*, from Italian *mussolina*, from *Mussolo* 'Mosul' (the place of manufacture in Iraq).

muso /ˈmjuːzəʊ/ ■ n. (pl. **-os**) informal 1 a musician, especially one over-concerned with technique. 2 Brit. a keen music fan.

musquash /ˈmʌskwɒʃ/ ■ n. archaic term for MUSKRAT.
– ORIGIN C17: from Abnaki *mòskwas*.

muss informal, chiefly N. Amer. ■ v. make untidy or messy. ■ n. a mess or muddle.
– DERIVATIVES **mussy** adj. (dated).
– ORIGIN C19: apparently a var. of MESS.

mussel ■ n. 1 a marine bivalve mollusc with a dark brown or purplish-black shell. [*Mytilus edulis* (edible mussel) and other species, family Mytilidae.] 2 a freshwater bivalve mollusc, some kinds of which produce small pearls. [Family Unionidae.]
– ORIGIN Old English, from late Latin *muscula*, from *musculus* (see MUSCLE).

musselcracker ■ n. a large southern African sea bream with powerful molar teeth used for crushing shellfish. [*Sparodon durbanensis* (white musselcracker) and *Cymatoceps nasatus* (black musselcracker), family Sparidae.]

Mussulman /ˈmʌs(ə)lmən/ ■ n. (pl. **Mussulmans** or **Mussulmen**) & adj. archaic term for MUSLIM.
– ORIGIN C16: from Persian *musulmān*, from *muslim* (see MUSLIM).

must[1] ■ modal v. (past **had to** or in reported speech **must**) 1 be obliged to; should. ▸ expressing insistence. 2 expressing

an opinion about something that is very likely. ▪ n. informal something that should not be overlooked or missed.
– ORIGIN Old English *mōste*, from *mōt* 'may', of Germanic origin.

must² ▪ n. grape juice before or during fermentation.
– ORIGIN Old English, from Latin *mustum*, from *mustus* 'new'.

must³ ▪ n. mustiness or mould.
– ORIGIN C17: back-formation from MUSTY.

must⁴ (also **musth**) ▪ n. the frenzied state of a rutting male elephant or camel.
– ORIGIN C19: from Persian *mast* 'intoxicated'.

mustache ▪ n. US spelling of MOUSTACHE.

mustachios /məˈstɑːʃɪəʊz/ ▪ pl. n. a long or elaborate moustache.
– DERIVATIVES **mustachioed** adj.
– ORIGIN C16: from Spanish *mostacho* (sing.), from Italian *mostaccio* (see MOUSTACHE).

mustang /ˈmʌstaŋ/ ▪ n. a small and lightly built feral horse of the south-western US.
– ORIGIN C19: from a blend of Spanish *mestengo* and *mostrenco*, both meaning 'wild or masterless cattle'.

mustard ▪ n. 1 a hot-tasting yellow or brown paste made from the crushed seeds of certain plants, eaten with meat or used as a cooking ingredient. 2 a plant of the cabbage family whose seeds are used to make this paste. [*Brassica nigra* (black mustard), *Sinapis alba* (white mustard, eaten as a seedling with cress), and other species.] 3 a brownish yellow colour.
– DERIVATIVES **mustardy** adj.
– ORIGIN Middle English: from Old French *moustarde*, from Latin *mustum* 'must' (the condiment being orig. prepared with grape must).

mustard gas ▪ n. a colourless oily liquid whose vapour is a powerful irritant and vesicant, used in chemical weapons.

mustard greens ▪ pl. n. chiefly US the leaves of the mustard plant used in salads.

mustard plaster ▪ n. dated a poultice made with mustard.

mustelid /ˈmʌstɪlɪd, mʌˈstɛlɪd/ ▪ n. Zoology a mammal of a family (Mustelidae) including the weasels, martens, skunks, and otters.
– ORIGIN C20: from Latin *mustela* 'weasel'.

muster ▪ v. 1 come or bring (troops) together, especially for inspection or in preparation for battle. ▶ (of a group of people) gather together. 2 summon up (a feeling, attitude, or response). 3 (**muster someone in**) or **out** US enrol someone into (or discharge someone from) military service. ▪ n. an instance of mustering troops.
– PHRASES **pass muster** be accepted as satisfactory.
– ORIGIN Middle English: from Old French *moustrer* (v.), from Latin *monstrare* 'to show'.

muster roll ▪ n. an official list of officers and men in a military unit or ship's company.

musth ▪ n. variant spelling of MUST⁴.

mustn't ▪ contr. must not.

musty ▪ adj. (**-ier**, **-iest**) 1 having a stale or mouldy smell or taste. 2 unoriginal or outdated.
– DERIVATIVES **mustily** adv. **mustiness** n.
– ORIGIN C16: perhaps an alteration of *moisty* 'moist', influenced by MUST².

mutable /ˈmjuːtəb(ə)l/ ▪ adj. liable to change. ▶ poetic/literary inconstant in one's affections.
– DERIVATIVES **mutability** n.
– ORIGIN Middle English: from Latin *mutabilis*, from *mutare* 'to change'.

mutagen /ˈmjuːtədʒ(ə)n/ ▪ n. a substance which causes genetic mutation.
– DERIVATIVES **mutagenesis** n. **mutagenic** adj.
– ORIGIN 1940s: from MUTATION.

mutant ▪ adj. resulting from or showing the effect of mutation. ▪ n. a mutant form.
– ORIGIN C20: from Latin *mutant-*, *mutare* 'to change'.

mutate ▪ v. undergo or cause to undergo mutation.
– DERIVATIVES **mutator** n.
– ORIGIN C19: back-formation from MUTATION.

mutation ▪ n. 1 the action or process of changing. ▶ a change. 2 a change in the structure of a gene resulting in a variant form which may be transmitted to subsequent generations. ▶ a distinct form resulting from such a change. 3 Linguistics (in Celtic languages) change of an initial consonant in a word caused by the preceding word. ▶ (in Germanic languages) umlaut.
– DERIVATIVES **mutational** adj. **mutationally** adv. **mutative** adj.
– ORIGIN Middle English: from Latin *mutatio(n-)*, from *mutare* 'to change'.

mutatis mutandis /muːˌtɑːtɪs muːˈtandɪs, mjuː-, -iːs/ ▪ adv. (used when comparing two or more cases) making necessary alterations while not affecting the main point.
– ORIGIN Latin, 'things being changed that have to be changed'.

mute /mjuːt/ ▪ adj. 1 refraining from speech or temporarily speechless. ▶ dated lacking the faculty of speech. 2 (of a letter) not pronounced. ▪ n. 1 dated a person without the power of speech. ▶ historical (in some Asian countries) a servant who was deprived of the power of speech. 2 a clamp placed over the bridge of a stringed instrument to deaden the resonance without affecting the vibration of the strings. 3 a pad or cone placed in the opening of a brass or other wind instrument. ▪ v. 1 (usu. **be muted**) deaden or muffle the sound of. 2 reduce the strength or intensity of. ▶ [as adj. **muted**] (of colour or lighting) not bright; subdued.
– DERIVATIVES **mutely** adv. **muteness** n.
– ORIGIN Middle English: from Old French *muet*, diminutive of *mu*, from Latin *mutus*.

mute swan ▪ n. the common non-migratory Eurasian swan, with an orange-red bill with a black knob at the base. [*Cygnus olor*.]

muti /ˈmuːti/ ▪ n. S. African 1 traditional medicine, especially that prepared from herbs or parts of animals. ▶ a curative or protective charm. 2 informal any medicine or healing lotion.
– ORIGIN from isiZulu *umuthi* 'plant, tree, medicine'.

mutilate ▪ v. injure or damage severely, typically so as to disfigure.
– DERIVATIVES **mutilation** n. **mutilator** n.
– ORIGIN C16: from Latin *mutilare* 'maim'.

muti murder ▪ n. S. African another term for RITUAL MURDER.

mutineer ▪ n. a person who mutinies.
– ORIGIN C17: from French *mutinier*, from *mutin* 'rebellious'.

mutinous ▪ adj. tending to mutiny; rebellious.
– DERIVATIVES **mutinously** adv.

mutiny ▪ n. (pl. **-ies**) an open rebellion against the proper authorities, especially by soldiers or sailors against their officers. ▪ v. (**-ies**, **-ied**) engage in mutiny; rebel.
– ORIGIN C16: from obsolete *mutine* 'rebellion', from French *mutin* 'mutineer'.

mutism /ˈmjuːtɪz(ə)m/ ▪ n. inability or unwillingness to speak, especially as a result of congenital deafness or brain damage.

mutt ▪ n. informal 1 humorous or derogatory a dog, especially a mongrel. 2 a person regarded as stupid or incompetent.
– ORIGIN C19: shortening of *muttonhead* 'a stupid person'.

mutter ▪ v. say in a barely audible voice. ▶ talk or grumble in secret or in private. ▪ n. a barely audible utterance.
– DERIVATIVES **mutterer** n. **muttering** adj. **mutteringly** adv.
– ORIGIN Middle English: imitative.

mutton ▪ n. the flesh of mature sheep used as food.
– PHRASES **mutton dressed as lamb** informal, derogatory, chiefly Brit. a middle-aged or old woman dressed in a style suitable for a much younger woman.
– DERIVATIVES **muttony** adj.
– ORIGIN Middle English: from Old French *moton*, from medieval Latin *multo(n-)*, prob. of Celtic origin.

mutton chop whiskers ▪ pl. n. the whiskers on a man's cheek when shaped like a meat chop, narrow at the top and broad and rounded at the bottom.

mutual /ˈmjuːtʃʊəl, -tjʊəl/ ▪ adj. 1 experienced or done by

mutual fund

each of two or more parties towards the other or others: *mutual respect*. ▶ (of two or more parties) having the same specified relationship to each other. **2** held in common by two or more parties: *a mutual friend*. **3** denoting a building society or insurance company owned by its members and dividing some or all of its profits between them.
– DERIVATIVES **mutuality** n. **mutually** adv.
– ORIGIN C15: from Old French *mutuel*, from Latin *mutuus* 'mutual, borrowed'.

mutual fund ■ n. a unit trust.

mutual induction ■ n. Physics the production of an electromotive force in a circuit by a change in the current in an adjacent circuit linked to the first by a magnetic field.
– DERIVATIVES **mutual inductance** n.

mutualism ■ n. **1** the doctrine that mutual dependence is necessary to social well-being. **2** Biology symbiosis which is beneficial to both organisms involved.
– DERIVATIVES **mutualist** n. & adj. **mutualistic** adj. **mutualistically** adv.

mutualize (also **-ise**) ■ v. organize (a business) on mutual principles.

muzak /ˈmjuːzak/ ■ n. trademark recorded light background music played through speakers in public places.
– ORIGIN 1930s: alteration of MUSIC.

muzzle ■ n. **1** the projecting part of the face, including the nose and mouth, of an animal such as a dog or horse. ▶ a guard fitted over an animal's muzzle to stop it biting or feeding. **2** the open end of the barrel of a firearm. ■ v. **1** put a muzzle on (an animal). **2** prevent from freedom of expression.
– ORIGIN Middle English: from Old French *musel*, diminutive of medieval Latin *musum*.

muzzy ■ adj. (**-ier**, **-iest**) **1** confused. **2** (of a visual image) blurred. ▶ (of a sound) indistinct.
– DERIVATIVES **muzzily** adv. **muzziness** n.
– ORIGIN C18.

MV ■ abbrev. **1** megavolt(s). **2** motor vessel. **3** muzzle velocity.

MVP ■ abbrev. chiefly N. Amer. most valuable player.

MW ■ abbrev. **1** Malawi (international vehicle registration). **2** medium wave. **3** megawatt(s).

mW ■ abbrev. milliwatt(s).

Mx ■ abbrev. maxwell(s).

MXit ■ n. trademark an application used to send text messages and multimedia between cellphones.

my ■ possess. det. **1** belonging to or associated with the speaker. ▶ used with forms of address in affectionate, sympathetic, humorous, or patronizing contexts. **2** used in various expressions of surprise.
– PHRASES **My Lady** (or **Lord**) a polite form of address to certain titled people.
– ORIGIN Middle English *mi*, from Old English *mīn*.

my- ■ comb. form variant spelling of MYO- shortened before a vowel (as in *myalgia*).

myalgia /maɪˈaldʒə/ ■ n. pain in a muscle or group of muscles.
– DERIVATIVES **myalgic** adj.
– ORIGIN C19: from Greek *mus* 'muscle' + -ALGIA.

myalgic encephalomyelitis (also **myalgic encephalitis**) ■ n. another term for CHRONIC FATIGUE SYNDROME.

mycelium /maɪˈsiːlɪəm/ ■ n. (pl. **mycelia** /-lɪə/) Botany a network of fine white filaments (hyphae) constituting the vegetative part of a fungus.
– DERIVATIVES **mycelial** adj.
– ORIGIN C19: from Greek *mukēs* 'fungus', on the pattern of *epithelium*.

Mycenaean /ˌmaɪsɪˈniːən/ (also **Mycenean**) Archaeology ■ adj. relating to or denoting a late Bronze Age civilization in Greece represented by finds at Mycenae and other ancient cities of the Peloponnese. ■ n. an inhabitant of Mycenae or member of the Mycenaean people.

-mycin ■ comb. form in names of antibiotic compounds derived from fungi: *streptomycin*.
– ORIGIN from MYCO-.

myco- ■ comb. form relating to fungi: *mycotoxin*.
– ORIGIN from Greek *mukēs* 'fungus, mushroom'.

mycobacterium /ˌmaɪkə(ʊ)bakˈtɪərɪəm/ ■ n. (pl. **mycobacteria** /-rɪə/) a bacterium of a group which includes the causative agents of leprosy and tuberculosis.
– DERIVATIVES **mycobacterial** adj.

mycology /maɪˈkɒlədʒi/ ■ n. the scientific study of fungi.
– DERIVATIVES **mycological** adj. **mycologically** adv. **mycologist** n.

mycoplasma /ˌmaɪkə(ʊ)ˈplazmə/ ■ n. (pl. **mycoplasmas** or **mycoplasmata** /-mətə/) a small, typically parasitic bacterium lacking cell walls. [Order Mycoplasmatales.]

mycoprotein ■ n. protein derived from fungi, especially as produced for human consumption.

mycorrhiza /ˌmaɪkə(ʊ)ˈraɪzə/ ■ n. (pl. **mycorrhizae** /-ziː/) Botany a fungus which grows in association with the roots of a plant.
– DERIVATIVES **mycorrhizal** adj.
– ORIGIN C19: from MYCO- + Greek *rhiza* 'root'.

mycosis /maɪˈkəʊsɪs/ ■ n. (pl. **mycoses** /-siːz/) a disease caused by infection with a fungus, such as thrush.
– DERIVATIVES **mycotic** /-ˈkɒtɪk/ adj.

mycotoxin ■ n. any toxic substance produced by a fungus.

myelin /ˈmaɪəlɪn/ ■ n. Anatomy & Physiology a whitish fatty substance forming a sheath around many nerve fibres.
– DERIVATIVES **myelinated** adj. **myelination** n.
– ORIGIN C19: from Greek *muelos* 'marrow'.

myelitis /ˌmaɪəˈlaɪtɪs/ ■ n. Medicine inflammation of the spinal cord.
– ORIGIN C19: from Greek *muelos* 'marrow'.

myeloid /ˈmaɪəlɔɪd/ ■ adj. **1** of or relating to bone marrow. **2** of or relating to the spinal cord.
– ORIGIN C19: from Greek *muelos* 'marrow'.

myeloma /ˌmaɪɪˈləʊmə/ ■ n. (pl. **myelomas** or **myelomata** /-mətə/) Medicine a malignant tumour of the bone marrow.
– ORIGIN C19: from Greek *muelos* 'marrow'.

Mylar /ˈmaɪlɑː/ ■ n. trademark a form of polyester resin made by copolymerizing ethylene glycol and terephthalic acid and used to make heat-resistant plastic films and sheets.
– ORIGIN 1950s: an arbitrary formation.

mylonite /ˈmaɪlənaɪt/ ■ n. Geology a fine-grained metamorphic rock, typically banded, resulting from the grinding or crushing of other rocks.
– ORIGIN C19: from Greek *mulōn* 'mill'.

mynah /ˈmaɪnə/ (also **mynah bird**, **myna**) ■ n. a southern Asian or Australasian starling with a loud call, some kinds of which can mimic human speech. [*Acridotheres tristis* (Indian mynah) and other species.]
– ORIGIN C18: from Hindi *mainā*.

myo- (also **my-** before a vowel) ■ comb. form of muscle; relating to muscles: *myocardium*.
– ORIGIN from Greek *mus*, *mu-* 'mouse or muscle'.

myocardium /ˌmaɪə(ʊ)ˈkɑːdɪəm/ ■ n. Anatomy the muscular tissue of the heart.
– DERIVATIVES **myocardial** adj. **myocarditis** n.
– ORIGIN C19: from MYO- + Greek *kardia* 'heart'.

myoglobin /ˌmaɪə(ʊ)ˈɡləʊbɪn/ ■ n. Biochemistry a red protein containing haem, which carries and stores oxygen in muscle cells.

myology /maɪˈɒlədʒi/ ■ n. the study of the structure, arrangement, and action of muscles.
– DERIVATIVES **myological** adj. **myologist** n.

myopathy /maɪˈɒpəθi/ ■ n. (pl. **-ies**) Medicine a disease of muscle tissue.
– DERIVATIVES **myopathic** adj.

myopia /maɪˈəʊpɪə/ ■ n. **1** short-sightedness. **2** lack of foresight or intellectual insight.
– DERIVATIVES **myopic** /-ˈɒpɪk/ adj. **myopically** /-ˈɒpɪk(ə)li/ adv.
– ORIGIN C18: from late Greek *muōpia*, from Greek *muōps*, from *muein* 'to shut' + *ōps* 'eye'.

myosin /ˈmʌɪə(ʊ)sɪn/ ■ n. Biochemistry a fibrous protein which forms (together with actin) the contractile filaments of muscle cells.

myosis ■ n. variant spelling of MIOSIS.

myositis /ˌmʌɪə(ʊ)ˈsʌɪtɪs/ ■ n. Medicine inflammation and degeneration of muscle tissue.
– ORIGIN C19: from Greek *mus, mu-* 'muscle'.

myosotis /ˌmʌɪə(ʊ)ˈsəʊtɪs/ ■ n. a plant of a genus which includes the forget-me-nots. [Genus *Myosotis*.]
– ORIGIN from Greek *muosōtis*, from *mus, mu-* 'mouse' + *ous, ōt-* 'ear'.

myotonia /ˌmʌɪə(ʊ)ˈtəʊnɪə/ ■ n. inability to relax voluntary muscle after vigorous effort.
– DERIVATIVES **myotonic** adj.
– ORIGIN C19: from MYO- + Greek *tonos* 'tone'.

myriad /ˈmɪrɪəd/ poetic/literary ■ n. 1 an indefinitely great number. 2 (chiefly in classical history) a unit of ten thousand. ■ adj. innumerable. ▶ having innumerable elements: *the myriad political scene.*
– ORIGIN C16: from Greek *murias, muriad-*, from *murioi* '10 000'.

myriapod /ˈmɪrɪəpɒd/ ■ n. Zoology a centipede, millipede, or other arthropod having an elongated body with numerous leg-bearing segments.
– ORIGIN C19: from Greek *murias* (see MYRIAD) + *pous, pod-* 'foot'.

myrmecophile /ˈməːmɪkə(ʊ)fʌɪl, məˈmiːkə(ʊ)-/ ■ n. Biology an invertebrate or plant which has a symbiotic relationship with ants, such as living inside an ants' nest.
– DERIVATIVES **myrmecophilous** adj. **myrmecophily** n.
– ORIGIN C19: from Greek *murmēx, murmēk-* 'ant' + -PHILE.

myrrh /məː/ ■ n. a fragrant gum resin obtained from certain trees and used, especially in the Near East, in perfumery, medicines, and incense.
– ORIGIN Old English, from Greek *murra*, of Semitic origin.

myrtle ■ n. 1 an evergreen shrub with glossy aromatic foliage and white flowers followed by purple-black oval berries. [*Myrtus communis.*] 2 N. Amer. the lesser periwinkle. [*Vinca minor.*]
– ORIGIN Middle English: from medieval Latin *myrtilla*, diminutive of Latin *myrta*, from Greek *murtos*.

myself ■ pron. [first person sing.] 1 [reflexive] used by a speaker to refer to himself or herself as the object of a verb or preposition when he or she is the subject of the clause. 2 [emphatic] I or me personally. 3 poetic/literary term for I[2].
– ORIGIN Old English *me self*, from ME[1] + SELF.

mysid /ˈmʌɪsɪd/ ■ n. Zoology a crustacean of an order (Mysidacea) that comprises the opossum shrimps.
– ORIGIN C20: from *Mysis* (genus name).

mystery ■ n. (pl. **-ies**) 1 something that is difficult or impossible to understand or explain. ▶ secrecy or obscurity. ▶ a person or thing whose identity or nature is puzzling or unknown. 2 a novel, play, or film dealing with a puzzling crime. 3 (**mysteries**) the secret rites of an ancient or tribal religion, to which only initiates are admitted. ▶ archaic the Christian Eucharist. 4 chiefly Christian Church a religious belief based on divine revelation and regarded as beyond human understanding. 5 an incident in the life of Jesus or of a saint as a focus of devotion in the Roman Catholic Church, especially each of those commemorated by one of the decades of the rosary.
– DERIVATIVES **mysterious** adj. **mysteriously** adv. **mysteriousness** n.
– ORIGIN Middle English: from Latin *mysterium*, from Greek *mustērion*.

mystery play ■ n. a popular medieval play based on biblical stories or the lives of the saints.

mystery shopper ■ n. a person employed to visit a shop or restaurant incognito in order to assess the quality of the goods or services.

mystery tour ■ n. a pleasure excursion to an unspecified destination.

mystic ■ n. a person who seeks by contemplation and self-surrender to attain unity with the Deity or the absolute, and so reach truths beyond human understanding. ■ adj. another term for MYSTICAL.
– ORIGIN Middle English: from Greek *mustikos*, from *mustēs* 'initiated person', from *muein* 'close the eyes or lips', also 'initiate'.

mystical ■ adj. 1 of or relating to mystics or mysticism. ▶ having a spiritual symbolic or allegorical significance that transcends human understanding. ▶ of or relating to ancient religious mysteries or other occult rites. 2 inspiring a sense of spiritual mystery, awe, and fascination.
– DERIVATIVES **mystically** adv.

mysticism ■ n. 1 the beliefs or state of mind characteristic of mystics. 2 confused religious belief or thought, especially as associated with a belief in the occult or in mysterious agencies.

mystify ■ v. (**-ies, -ied**) utterly bewilder. ▶ make obscure or mysterious.
– DERIVATIVES **mystification** n. **mystifier** n. **mystifying** adj. **mystifyingly** adv.
– ORIGIN C19: from French *mystifier*, from *mystique* 'mystic' or from *mystère* 'mystery'.

mystique ■ n. a fascinating aura of mystery, awe, and power. ▶ an air of secrecy surrounding an activity or subject, making it impressive or baffling to the layperson.
– ORIGIN C19: from Old French.

myth ■ n. 1 a traditional story concerning the early history of a people or explaining a natural or social phenomenon, and typically involving supernatural beings or events. 2 a widely held but false belief. ▶ a fictitious person or thing. ▶ an exaggerated or idealized conception of a person or thing.
– DERIVATIVES **mythic** adj. **mythical** adj. **mythically** adv.
– ORIGIN C19 (*mythic* C17): from Greek *muthos*.

mythicize (also **-ise**) ■ v. treat as a myth; interpret mythically.
– DERIVATIVES **mythicism** n.

mythography ■ n. 1 the representation of myths, especially in the plastic arts. 2 the creation or collection of myths.
– DERIVATIVES **mythographer** n.

mythology ■ n. (pl. **-ies**) 1 a collection of myths, especially one belonging to a particular religious or cultural tradition. 2 a set of widely held but exaggerated or fictitious stories or beliefs. 3 the study of myths.
– DERIVATIVES **mythologer** n. **mythologic** adj. **mythological** adj. **mythologically** adv. **mythologist** n. **mythologize** (also **-ise**) v. **mythologizer** (also **-iser**) n.
– ORIGIN Middle English: from French *mythologie*, from Greek *muthologia*, from *muthos* 'myth' + *-logia* (see -LOGY).

mythos /ˈmʌɪθɒs, ˈmɪθɒs/ ■ n. (pl. **mythoi** /-θɔɪ/) technical 1 a myth or mythology. 2 an ideology.
– ORIGIN C18: from Greek.

myxo- (also **myx-**) ■ comb. form relating to mucus: *myxo-virus.*
– ORIGIN from Greek *muxa* 'slime, mucus'.

myxoedema /ˌmɪksɪˈdiːmə/ (US **myxedema**) ■ n. Medicine a condition caused by hyperthyroidism, marked by swelling of the skin and underlying tissues.

myxoma /mɪkˈsəʊmə/ ■ n. (pl. **myxomas** or **myxomata** /-mətə/) Medicine a benign tumour of connective tissue containing mucous or gelatinous material.
– DERIVATIVES **myxomatous** adj.

myxomatosis /ˌmɪksəməˈtəʊsɪs/ ■ n. a highly infectious and usually fatal viral disease of rabbits, causing swelling of the mucous membranes and inflammation and discharge around the eyes.

myxovirus /ˈmɪksə(ʊ)ˌvʌɪrəs/ ■ n. any of a group of RNA viruses including the influenza virus.

Mzansi /(ə)mˈzʌntsi, (ə)mˈzɑːnzi/ (also **Mzanzi**) ■ n. S. African 1 informal a nickname for South Africa. 2 [as modifier] denoting a bank account or other personal finance product catering for low-income earners: *an Mzansi account.*
– ORIGIN from isiXhosa and isiZulu *umzansi* 'south' and *uMzansi* 'South Africa'.

Nn

N¹ (also **n**) ■ n. (pl. **Ns** or **N's**) **1** the fourteenth letter of the alphabet. **2** denoting the next after M in a set of items, categories, etc.

N² ■ abbrev. **1** (used in recording moves in chess) knight. [representing the pronunciation of *kn-*, since *k-* represents 'king'.] **2** S. African (in road designations) national road. **3** (chiefly in place names) New. **4** Physics newton(s). **5** Chemistry (with reference to solutions) normal. **6** North or Northern. **7** nuclear. ■ symb. the chemical element nitrogen.

·n ■ abbrev. **1** nano- (10⁻⁹). **2** Grammar neuter. **3** (*n-*) Chemistry normal (denoting straight-chain hydrocarbons). **4** note (used in a book's index to refer to a footnote). **5** Grammar noun. ■ symb. an unspecified or variable number.

'n (also **'n'**) ■ contr. and (used in informal contexts to coordinate two closely connected elements): *rock 'n roll.*

-n¹ ■ suffix variant spelling of -EN².

-n² ■ suffix variant spelling of -EN³.

Na ■ symb. the chemical element sodium.
– ORIGIN from modern Latin *natrium.*

n/a ■ abbrev. **1** not applicable. **2** not available.

NAACP ■ abbrev. National Association for the Advancement of Colored People.

NAAFI /ˈnafi/ ■ abbrev. Navy, Army, and Air Force Institutes. ■ n. (usu. **Naafi**) a canteen or shop run by the NAAFI.

naan ■ n. variant spelling of NAN².

naartjie /ˈnɑːtʃi/ ■ n. S. African a mandarin orange or tangerine.
– ORIGIN from S. African Dutch, prob. from Tamil *nārattai* 'citrus'.

nab ■ v. (**nabbed**, **nabbing**) informal **1** catch (someone) doing something wrong. **2** take or grab suddenly.
– ORIGIN C17 (also *napp*; cf. KIDNAP).

nabob /ˈneɪbɒb/ ■ n. historical **1** a Muslim official or governor under the Mogul empire. **2** a person who returned from India to Europe with a fortune.
– ORIGIN from Portuguese *nababo* or Spanish *nabab,* from Urdu.

naboom /ˈnɑːbʊəm/ ■ n. S. African a tree euphorbia. [*Euphorbia ingens* and other species.]
– ORIGIN from Afrikaans, perhaps from Nama *!na* 'big' + Afrikaans *boom* 'tree'.

nacelle /nəˈsɛl/ ■ n. **1** the outer casing of an aircraft engine. **2** chiefly historical the car of an airship.
– ORIGIN C20: from late Latin *navicella,* diminutive of Latin *navis* 'ship'.

nacho /ˈnatʃəʊ/ ■ n. (pl. **-os**) a small piece of tortilla topped with melted cheese, peppers, etc.
– ORIGIN perhaps from Mexican Spanish *Nacho,* familiar form of *Ignacio* or from Spanish *nacho* 'flat-nosed'.

nacre /ˈneɪkə/ ■ n. mother-of-pearl.
– DERIVATIVES **nacreous** adj.
– ORIGIN C16: from French.

nada /ˈnɑːdə, ˈnadə/ ■ pron. informal, chiefly N. Amer. nothing.
– ORIGIN from Spanish.

nadir /ˈneɪdɪə, ˈnadɪə/ ■ n. **1** Astronomy the point on the celestial sphere directly below an observer. The opposite of ZENITH. **2** the lowest or most unsuccessful point: *his fortunes reached their nadir.*
– ORIGIN Middle English: from Arabic *naẓīr (as-samt)* 'opposite (to the zenith)'.

naevus /ˈniːvəs/ (US **nevus**) ■ n. (pl. **naevi** /-vʌɪ, -viː/) a birthmark or a mole on the skin, especially a birthmark in the form of a raised red patch.
– ORIGIN C19: from Latin.

Nafcoc /ˈnafkɒk/ (also **NAFCOC**) ■ abbrev. (in South Africa) National African Federated Chamber of Commerce and Industry.

naff¹ ■ v. **1** (**naff off**) Brit. informal go away. **2** [as adj. **naffing**] used to emphasize annoyance.
– ORIGIN 1950s: euphemism for FUCK.

naff² ■ adj. S. African & Brit. informal lacking taste or style.
– DERIVATIVES **naffness** n.
– ORIGIN 1960s.

NAFTA (also **Nafta**) ■ abbrev. North American Free Trade Agreement.

nag¹ ■ v. (**nagged**, **nagging**) **1** harass (someone) constantly to do something to which they are averse. **2** [often as adj. **nagging**] be persistently painful or worrying to. ■ n. **1** a person who nags. **2** a persistent feeling of anxiety: *he felt a little nag of doubt.*
– DERIVATIVES **nagger** n. **naggingly** adv. **naggy** adj.
– ORIGIN C19: perhaps of Scandinavian or Low German origin.

nag² ■ n. informal, often derogatory a horse, especially one that is old or in poor health. ▶ archaic a horse suitable for riding rather than as a draught animal.
– ORIGIN Middle English.

naga /ˈnɑːɡə/ ■ n. (in Indian mythology) a member of a semi-divine race, part human, part cobra in form, associated with water and sometimes with mystical initiation.
– ORIGIN from Sanskrit *nāga* 'serpent'.

nagana /nəˈɡɑːnə/ ■ n. trypanosomiasis of cattle, transmitted by tsetse flies.
– ORIGIN C19: from isiZulu *unakane.*

nagmaal /ˈnaxmɑːl/ ■ n. S. African (in the Dutch Reformed Church) holy communion.
– ORIGIN Afrikaans, from Dutch *nachtmaal,* from *nacht* 'night' + *maal* 'meal'.

Nahuatl /ˈnɑːwɑːt(ə)l, nɑːˈwɑːt(ə)l/ ■ n. **1** a member of a group of peoples native to southern Mexico and Central America, including the Aztecs. **2** the language of these peoples.
– ORIGIN via Spanish from Nahuatl.

naiad /ˈnʌɪad/ ■ n. (pl. **naiads** or **naiades** /ˈnʌɪəˌdiːz/) **1** (in classical mythology) a nymph inhabiting a river, spring, or waterfall. **2** the aquatic larva of a dragonfly, mayfly, or stonefly. **3** an aquatic plant with narrow leaves and minute flowers. [Genus *Najas.*]
– ORIGIN from Greek *Naias, Naiad-,* from *naein* 'to flow'.

naiant /ˈneɪənt/ ■ adj. [postpos.] Heraldry (of a fish or marine creature) swimming horizontally.
– ORIGIN C16: from Anglo-Norman French, var. of Old French *noiant, noier* 'to swim'.

naif /nʌɪˈiːf, nɑːˈiːf/ ■ adj. naive. ■ n. a naive person.
– ORIGIN from French *naïf.*

nail ■ n. **1** a small metal spike with a broadened flat head, driven typically into wood to join things together or to serve as a hook. **2** a horny covering on the upper surface of the tip of the finger and toe in humans and other primates. ▶ a hard growth on the upper mandible of some soft-billed birds. ■ v. **1** fasten with a nail or nails. **2** informal detect or catch (someone, especially a suspected criminal). **3** informal (in sport) strike (a ball) forcefully and successfully. ▶ chiefly N. Amer. (of a player) defeat or outwit (an opponent). **4** (**nail someone down**) elicit a firm commitment from someone. **5** (**nail something down**) identify something precisely.
– PHRASES **a nail in the coffin** an action or event likely to have a detrimental or destructive effect. **on the nail** (N. Amer. also **on the barrelhead**) (of payment) without delay.
– DERIVATIVES **-nailed** adj. **nailless** adj.
– ORIGIN Old English, of Germanic origin.

CONSONANTS **b** but **d** dog **f** few **g** get **h** he **j** yes **k** cat **l** leg **m** man **n** no **p** pen **r** red

nail-biting ■ adj. causing great anxiety or tension.
nail enamel ■ n. N. Amer. nail polish.
nailer ■ n. **1** chiefly historical a maker of nails. **2** a power tool for inserting nails.
– DERIVATIVES **nailery** n.
nail file ■ n. a small file or emery board used for smoothing and shaping the fingernails and toenails.
nail head ■ n. an ornament resembling the head of a nail, used chiefly in architecture and on clothing.
nail polish ■ n. varnish applied to the fingernails or toenails to colour them or make them shiny.
nail punch (also **nail set**) ■ n. a tool hit with a hammer to sink the head of a nail below a surface.
nail varnish ■ n. nail polish.
naira /ˈnʌɪrə/ ■ n. the basic monetary unit of Nigeria.
– ORIGIN contraction of *Nigeria*.
naissant /ˈneɪs(ə)nt/ ■ adj. Heraldry (of a charge, especially an animal) issuing from the middle of an ordinary, especially a fess.
– ORIGIN C16: from French, 'being born', from *naître*.
naive /nʌɪˈiːv, nɑːˈiːv/ (also **naïve**) ■ adj. **1** lacking experience, wisdom, or judgement. **2** natural and unaffected. ▸ of or denoting art produced in a style which deliberately rejects sophisticated artistic techniques and has a bold directness resembling a child's work.
– DERIVATIVES **naively** adv. **naiveness** n. **naivety** n.
– ORIGIN C17: from French *naïve*, feminine of *naïf*, from Latin *nativus* 'native, natural'.
naked ■ adj. **1** without clothes. ▸ (of an object) without the usual covering or protection. ▸ (of a tree, plant, or animal) without leaves, hairs, etc. **2** exposed to harm; vulnerable. **3** (of feelings or behaviour) undisguised.
– PHRASES **naked of** devoid of.
– DERIVATIVES **nakedly** adv. **nakedness** n.
– ORIGIN Old English, of Germanic origin.
naked eye ■ n. (**the naked eye**) unassisted vision, without a telescope, microscope, or other device.
naked lady ■ n. another term for BELLADONNA LILY.
naloxone /nəˈlɒksəʊn/ ■ n. Medicine a synthetic drug, similar to morphine, which blocks opiate receptors in the nervous system.
– ORIGIN 1960s: contraction of *N-allylnoroxymorphone*.
Nama /ˈnɑːmə/ ■ n. (pl. same or **Namas**) **1** a member of one of the Khoikhoi peoples of South Africa and SW Namibia. **2** the Khoisan language of this people.
– ORIGIN the name in Nama.

> USAGE
> **Nama** is the standard accepted term in this context. The word **Hottentot**, an older term with a somewhat broader meaning, is obsolete and may now cause offence.

Nama Karoo ■ n. Ecology a vegetation type occurring in the arid western and central part of South Africa, characterized by low-growing shrubs and grasses.
Namaqualand daisy ■ n. a South African daisy with bright yellow, orange, or white flowers, widely grown as an ornamental. [*Dimorphotheca sinuata*.]
– ORIGIN named after the region of *Namaqualand* in the Northern Cape.
namaskar /ˌnʌmʌsˈkɑː/ ■ n. a traditional Indian gesture of greeting, made by bringing the palms together before the face or chest and bowing.
– ORIGIN from Sanskrit *namaskāra*, from *namas* 'bowing' + *kāra* 'action'.
namaste /ˈnʌməsteɪ/ ■ exclam. (in India) a respectful greeting said when giving a namaskar. ■ n. another term for NAMASKAR.
– ORIGIN from Sanskrit *namas* 'bowing' + *te* 'to you'.
namby-pamby derogatory ■ adj. lacking courage or vigour; feeble. ■ n. (pl. **-ies**) a namby-pamby person.
– ORIGIN C18: fanciful formation based on the given name of *Ambrose* Philips, an English writer whose pastorals were ridiculed as insipid.
name ■ n. **1** a word or set of words by which someone or something is known, addressed, or referred to. **2** a famous person. ▸ a reputation, especially a good one. **3** (in the UK) an insurance underwriter belonging to a Lloyd's syndicate. ■ v. **1** give a name to. ▸ identify or mention by name. ▸ (**name someone/thing after**) or N. Amer. also **for** call someone or something by the same name as. **2** specify (a sum, time, or place). ■ adj. (of a person or product) having a well-known name.
– PHRASES **by** (or **of**) **the name of** called. **call someone names** insult someone verbally. **have to one's name** [often with neg.] in one's possession. **in all but name** existing in a particular state but not formally recognized as such. **in someone's name 1** formally registered as belonging to or reserved for someone. **2** on behalf of someone. **in the name of** for the sake of. **make a name for oneself** become famous. **name the day** arrange the date for a specific occasion, especially a wedding. **name names** mention specific names, especially in accusation. **the name of the game** informal the main purpose or most important aspect of a situation.
– DERIVATIVES **nameable** adj.
– ORIGIN Old English, of Germanic origin.
name day ■ n. the feast day of a saint after whom a person is named.
name-dropping ■ n. the practice of casually mentioning the names of famous people one knows in order to impress.
– DERIVATIVES **name-drop** v. **name-dropper** n.
nameless ■ adj. **1** having no name or no known name. **2** difficult to describe. ▸ too horrific to be described. **3** archaic (of a child) illegitimate.
– DERIVATIVES **namelessly** adv. **namelessness** n.
namely ■ adv. that is to say.
nameplate ■ n. a plate attached to something and bearing the name of the owner, occupier, or the thing itself.
namesake ■ n. a person or thing that has the same name as another.
– ORIGIN C17: from the phr. *for the name's sake*.
Namibian /nəˈmɪbɪən/ ■ n. a native or inhabitant of Namibia. ■ adj. of or relating to Namibia.
nan[1] /nan/ ■ n. Brit. informal one's grandmother.
– ORIGIN 1940s: abbrev. of NANNY, or a child's pronunciation of GRAN.
nan[2] /nɑːn/ (also **naan**) ■ n. (in Indian cookery) a type of leavened bread, typically of a flattened teardrop shape.
– ORIGIN from Urdu and Persian *nān*.
nana[1] /ˈnɑːnə/ ■ n. informal a silly person; a fool.
– ORIGIN 1960s: perhaps a shortening of BANANA.
nana[2] /ˈnanə/ (Brit. also **nanna**) ■ n. informal one's grandmother.
– ORIGIN C19: child's pronunciation of NANNY or GRAN.
nancy (also **nance**, **nancy boy**) ■ n. (pl. **-ies**) informal, derogatory an effeminate or homosexual man.
– ORIGIN C20: familiar form of the given name *Ann*.
NAND ■ n. [as modifier] Electronics denoting a gate circuit which produces an output signal unless there are signals on all of its inputs.
– ORIGIN 1950s: from *not and*.
nankeen /nanˈkiːn, nan-/ ■ n. a yellowish cotton cloth. ▸ (**nankeens**) historical trousers made of this cloth.
– ORIGIN C18: from the name of the city of *Nanking* in China, where it was first made.
nanna ■ n. variant spelling of NANA[2].
nanny ■ n. (pl. **-ies**) **1** a person, typically a woman, employed to look after a child in its own home. **2** a person or institution regarded as interfering and overprotective. **3** (also **nanny goat**) a female goat. ■ v. (**-ies**, **-ied**) [usu. as noun **nannying**] be overprotective towards.
– ORIGIN C18: familiar form of the given name *Ann*.
nano- /ˈnanəʊ/ ■ comb. form denoting a factor of 10^{-9}: *nanosecond*. ▸ extremely small; submicroscopic: *nanotube*.
– ORIGIN from Greek *nanos* 'dwarf'.
nanometre /ˈnanə(ʊ)miːtə/ (US **nanometer**) (abbrev.: **nm**) ■ n. one thousand millionth of a metre.
nanosecond (abbrev.: **ns**) ■ n. one thousand millionth of a second.
nanotechnology ■ n. technology on an atomic or

molecular scale, concerned with dimensions of less than 100 nanometres.
– DERIVATIVES **nanotechnological** adj. **nanotechnologist** n.

nanotube ■ n. Chemistry a cylindrical molecule of a fullerene.

nap¹ ■ v. (**napped**, **napping**) sleep lightly or briefly, especially during the day. ▶ n. a short sleep of this type.
– ORIGIN Old English, prob. of Germanic origin.

nap² ■ n. the raised hairs, threads, or similar small projections on the surface of fabric or suede leather.
– DERIVATIVES **napless** adj.
– ORIGIN Middle English *noppe*, from Middle Dutch, Middle Low German *noppe* 'nap'.

nap³ ■ n. **1** a card game resembling whist in which players declare the number of tricks they expect to take, up to five. **2** Brit. the betting of all one's money on one prospective winner. ▶ a tipster's choice for this. ■ v. (**napped**, **napping**) Brit. name (a horse or greyhound) as a probable winner of a race.
– PHRASES **go nap** attempt to take all five tricks in nap. ▶ score or win five times. ▶ risk everything in one attempt.
– ORIGIN C19: abbrev. of *napoleon*, the orig. name of the card game.

napa ■ n. variant spelling of NAPPA.

napalm /ˈneɪpɑːm/ ■ n. a highly flammable sticky jelly consisting of petrol thickened with special soaps, used in incendiary bombs and flame-throwers. ■ v. attack with bombs containing napalm.
– ORIGIN 1940s: from *na(phthenic) and palm(itic acid)*.

nape ■ n. the back of a person's neck.
– ORIGIN Middle English.

napery /ˈneɪp(ə)ri/ ■ n. archaic household linen, especially tablecloths and napkins.
– ORIGIN Middle English: from Old French *naperie*, from *nape* 'tablecloth'.

nap hand ■ n. informal a series of five winning points, victories, etc. in a game or sport.

naphtha /ˈnafθə/ ■ n. Chemistry a flammable oil containing various hydrocarbons, obtained by the dry distillation of organic substances such as coal, shale, or petroleum.
– ORIGIN Middle English, from Latin *naphtha* from Greek, of oriental origin.

naphthalene /ˈnafθəliːn/ ■ n. Chemistry a volatile white crystalline compound produced by the distillation of coal tar, used in mothballs and for chemical manufacture.
– DERIVATIVES **naphthalic** adj.

Napierian logarithm /neɪˈpɪərɪən/ ■ n. another term for NATURAL LOGARITHM.
– ORIGIN C19: named after the Scottish mathematician John Napier (1550–1617).

napkin ■ n. **1** a square piece of cloth or paper used at a meal to wipe the fingers or lips and to protect garments. **2** Brit. dated a baby's nappy. **3** (also **sanitary napkin**) chiefly N. Amer. another term for SANITARY TOWEL.
– ORIGIN Middle English: from Old French *nappe* 'tablecloth', from Latin *mappa* (see MAP).

napoleon ■ n. **1** a gold twenty-franc French coin minted in the reign of Napoleon I. **2** N. Amer. a flaky rectangular pastry with a sweet filling.

Napoleonic /nəpəʊlɪˈɒnɪk/ ■ adj. of, relating to, or characteristic of Napoleon I or his time.

nappa /ˈnapə/ (also **napa**) ■ n. a soft leather made by a special tawing process from the skin of sheep or goats.
– ORIGIN C19: from *Napa*, a valley in California.

nappe /nap/ ■ n. Geology a sheet of rock that has moved sideways over neighbouring strata as a result of an overthrust or folding.
– ORIGIN C19: from French *nappe* 'tablecloth'.

napped¹ ■ adj. (of a textile) having a nap.

napped² ■ adj. (of food) served in a sauce or other liquid.
– ORIGIN 1970s: from French *napper* 'coat with (a sauce)', from *nappe* 'cloth', figuratively 'pool of liquid'.

nappy¹ ■ n. (pl. **-ies**) a piece of absorbent material wrapped round a baby's bottom and between its legs to absorb and retain urine and faeces.
– ORIGIN C20: abbrev. of NAPKIN.

nappy² ■ adj. US informal (of a black person's hair) frizzy.
– ORIGIN C15: from Middle Dutch *noppigh*, Middle Low German *noppich*, from *noppe* (see NAP²).

nappy rash ■ n. inflammation of a baby's skin caused by prolonged contact with a damp nappy.

narc ■ n. informal a member of the narcotics squad in a police force.

narcissism /ˈnɑːsɪsɪz(ə)m, nɑːˈsɪs-/ ■ n. excessive or erotic interest in oneself and one's physical appearance.
– DERIVATIVES **narcissist** n. **narcissistic** adj. **narcissistically** adv.
– ORIGIN C19: from *Narcissus*, the name of a beautiful youth in Greek mythology who fell in love with his own reflection in a pool.

narcissus /nɑːˈsɪsəs/ ■ n. (pl. **narcissi** /-sʌɪ/ or **narcissuses**) a daffodil with a flower that has white or pale outer petals and a shallow orange or yellow centre. [*Narcissus poeticus* and related species.]
– ORIGIN from Greek *narkissos*, perhaps from *narkē* 'numbness', with ref. to its narcotic effects.

narco ■ n. (pl. **-os**) US informal short for NARCOTIC.

narco- ■ comb. form **1** relating to a state of insensibility: *narcolepsy*. **2** relating to narcotic drugs or their use: *narcoterrorism*.
– ORIGIN from Greek *narkē* 'numbness'.

narcolepsy /ˈnɑːkə(ʊ)lɛpsi/ ■ n. Medicine a condition characterized by an extreme tendency to fall asleep whenever in relaxing surroundings.
– DERIVATIVES **narcoleptic** adj. & n.
– ORIGIN C19: from Greek *narkē* 'numbness', on the pattern of *epilepsy*.

narcosis /nɑːˈkəʊsɪs/ ■ n. Medicine a state of stupor, drowsiness, or unconsciousness produced by drugs.
– ORIGIN C17: from Greek *narkōsis*, from *narkoun* 'make numb'.

narcoterrorism ■ n. terrorism associated with the trade in illicit drugs.
– DERIVATIVES **narcoterrorist** n.

narcotic ■ n. a drug or other substance, especially an illegal one, affecting mood or behaviour and used for non-medical purposes. ▶ Medicine a drug which induces drowsiness, stupor, or insensibility, and relieves pain. ■ adj. relating to narcotics.
– DERIVATIVES **narcotically** adv. **narcotism** n. **narcotize** (also **-ise**) v.
– ORIGIN Middle English: from Old French *narcotique*, from Greek *narkōtikos*, from *narkoun* 'make numb'.

nard ■ n. the Himalayan spikenard.
– ORIGIN Old English, from Greek *nardos*; rel. to Sanskrit *nalada*, *narada*.

nares /ˈnɛːriːz/ ■ pl. n. (sing. **naris**) Anatomy & Zoology the nostrils.
– DERIVATIVES **narial** adj.
– ORIGIN C17: pl. of Latin *naris* 'nostril, nose'.

narina trogon ■ n. an African forest bird with iridescent green plumage above and bright red underparts. [*Apaloderma narina*.]

nark informal ■ n. a police informer. ■ v. chiefly Brit. annoy.
– ORIGIN C19: from Romany *nāk* 'nose'.

narky ■ adj. (**-ier**, **-iest**) Brit. informal irritable.

narrate ■ v. give a spoken or written account of. ▶ provide a commentary to accompany (a film, story, etc.).
– DERIVATIVES **narratable** adj. **narration** n. **narrator** n. **narratorial** adj.
– ORIGIN C17 (*narration* Middle English): from Latin *narrare* 'relate'.

narrative ■ n. a spoken or written account of connected events; a story. ▶ the narrated part of a literary work, as distinct from dialogue. ▶ the practice or art of narration. ■ adj. in the form of or concerned with narration.
– DERIVATIVES **narratively** adv. **narrativity** n.

narrow ■ adj. (**-er**, **-est**) **1** of small width in comparison to length. **2** limited in extent, amount, or scope. **3** barely achieved: *a narrow escape*. **4** Phonetics denoting a vowel pronounced with the root of the tongue drawn back so as to narrow the pharynx. ■ v. become or make narrower.

▶ **(narrow something down)** reduce the number of possibilities or options. ■ n. **(narrows)** a narrow channel connecting two larger areas of water.
– DERIVATIVES **narrowish** adj. **narrowly** adv. **narrowness** n.
– ORIGIN Old English, of Germanic origin.

narrowband ■ adj. of or involving signals over a narrow range of frequencies.

narrowboat ■ n. Brit. a canal boat less than 7 ft (2.1 metres) wide with a maximum length of 70 ft (21.3 metres) and steered with a tiller rather than a wheel.

narrowcast ■ v. (past and past part. **narrowcast** or **narrowcasted**) transmit a television programme, especially by cable, to a comparatively small or specialist audience. ■ n. transmission of this type.
– DERIVATIVES **narrowcaster** n.

narrow gauge ■ n. a railway gauge which is narrower than the standard gauge of 4 ft 8½ inches (1.435 m).

narrow-minded ■ adj. not willing to listen to or tolerate other people's views; prejudiced.
– DERIVATIVES **narrow-mindedly** adv. **narrow-mindedness** n.

narrow money ■ n. Economics money in forms that can be used as a medium of exchange, generally notes and coins.

narrow squeak ■ n. informal, chiefly Brit. an escape or victory that is narrowly achieved.

narthex /'nɑːθɛks/ ■ n. an antechamber, porch, or distinct area at the western entrance of some early Christian churches. ▶ an antechamber or large porch in a modern church.
– ORIGIN C17: from Greek *narthēx*.

narwhal /'nɑːw(ə)l/ ■ n. a small Arctic whale, the male of which has a long forward-pointing spirally twisted tusk developed from one of its teeth. [*Monodon monoceros*.]
– ORIGIN C17: from Dutch *narwal*, Danish *narhval*, from Old Norse *nár* 'corpse', with ref. to skin colour.

nary /'nɛːri/ ■ adj. informal or dialect form of NOT.
– ORIGIN C18: from the phr. *ne'er a*.

NASA /'nasə/ ■ abbrev. (in the US) National Aeronautics and Space Administration.

nasal /'neɪz(ə)l/ ■ adj. 1 of or relating to the nose. 2 (of a speech sound) pronounced by the breath resonating in the nose, e.g. *m*, *n*, *ng*, or French *en*, *un*. ▶ (of speech) characterized by resonance in the nose as well as the mouth. ■ n. 1 a nasal speech sound. 2 historical a nosepiece on a helmet.
– DERIVATIVES **nasality** n. **nasally** adv.
– ORIGIN Middle English: from medieval Latin *nasalis*, from Latin *nasus* 'nose'.

nasalize (also **-ise**) ■ v. pronounce or utter (a speech sound) with the breath resonating in the nose.
– DERIVATIVES **nasalization** (also **-isation**) n.

nascent /'nas(ə)nt, 'neɪ-/ ■ adj. 1 just coming into existence and beginning to display signs of future potential. 2 Chemistry (chiefly of hydrogen) freshly generated in a reactive form.
– DERIVATIVES **nascency** /'nas(ə)nsi, 'neɪ-/ n.
– ORIGIN C17: from Latin *nascent-*, *nasci* 'to be born'.

nasogastric ■ adj. reaching or supplying the stomach via the nose.

nasopharynx ■ n. Anatomy the upper part of the pharynx, connecting with the nasal cavity above the soft palate.
– DERIVATIVES **nasopharyngeal** adj.

nasturtium /nə'stəːʃ(ə)m/ ■ n. a South American trailing plant with round leaves and bright orange, yellow, or red flowers, widely grown as an ornamental. [*Tropaeolum majus*.]
– ORIGIN Old English, from Latin, prob. from *naris* 'nose' + *torquere* 'to twist'.

nasty ■ adj. (**-ier**, **-iest**) 1 highly unpleasant or repugnant. 2 unpleasant or spiteful in behaviour. ▶ annoying or unwelcome. 3 physically or mentally damaging or harmful. ■ n. (pl. **-ies**) informal a nasty person or thing.
– DERIVATIVES **nastily** adv. **nastiness** n.
– ORIGIN Middle English.

Nat ■ n. S. African historical a member or supporter of the National Party.

Nat. ■ abbrev. 1 national. 2 nationalist. 3 natural.

National Senior Certificate

natal¹ /'neɪt(ə)l/ ■ adj. of or relating to the place or time of one's birth.
– ORIGIN Middle English: from Latin *natalis*, from *nasci* 'be born'.

natal² /'neɪt(ə)l/ ■ adj. Anatomy relating to the buttocks.
– ORIGIN C19: from Latin *nates*, pl. of *natis* 'buttock, rump'.

natality /nə'talɪti/ ■ n. birth rate.

Natal plum ■ n. S. African another term for NUM-NUM.

natant /'neɪt(ə)nt/ ■ adj. formal, rare swimming or floating.
– DERIVATIVES **natation** /nə'teɪʃ(ə)n/ n.
– ORIGIN C18 (*natation* C16): from Latin *natare* 'swim'.

natch ■ adv. informal naturally.

nation ■ n. a large aggregate of people united by common descent, culture, or language, inhabiting a particular state or territory. ▶ S. African historical (under apartheid) an ethnic group or clan. ▶ a North American Indian people or confederation of peoples.
– DERIVATIVES **nationhood** n.
– ORIGIN Middle English: from Latin *natio(n-)*, from *nasci* 'be born'.

national ■ adj. 1 of, relating to, or characteristic of a nation. 2 owned, controlled, or financially supported by the state. ■ n. 1 a citizen of a particular country. 2 a national newspaper as opposed to a local one.
– DERIVATIVES **nationally** adv.
– ORIGIN C16: from Latin *natio(n-)* (see NATION).

national anthem ■ n. a solemn patriotic song adopted as an expression of national identity.

National Assembly ■ n. an elected legislature in various countries.

national bank ■ n. another term for CENTRAL BANK. ▶ (in the US) a commercial bank which is chartered under the federal government and is a member of the Federal Reserve System.

national curriculum ■ n. a curriculum of study laid down to be taught in state schools.

national debt ■ n. the total amount of money which a country's government has borrowed.

national grid ■ n. 1 S. African & Brit. the network of high-voltage power lines between major power stations. 2 the metric system of geographical coordinates used in maps of the British Isles.

National Guard ■ n. (in the US) the primary reserve military force partly maintained by the states but also available for federal use.

National Health Service ■ n. (in the UK) a government health care system providing cheap or free medical services for all, funded by general taxation.

national income ■ n. the total amount of money earned within a country.

National Insurance ■ n. (in the UK) a system of compulsory payments by employees and employers to provide state assistance for people who are sick, unemployed, or retired.

nationalism ■ n. 1 patriotic feeling, principles, or efforts. ▶ an extreme form of this marked by a feeling of superiority over other countries. 2 advocacy of political independence for a particular country.
– DERIVATIVES **nationalist** n. & adj. **nationalistic** adj. **nationalistically** adv.

nationality ■ n. (pl. **-ies**) 1 the status of belonging to a particular nation. 2 an ethnic group forming a part of one or more political nations.

nationalize (also **-ise**) ■ v. 1 transfer (a major branch of industry or commerce) from private to state ownership or control. 2 make distinctively national. 3 [usu. as adj. **nationalized** (also **-ised**)] naturalize (a foreigner).
– DERIVATIVES **nationalization** (also **-isation**) n. **nationalizer** (also **-iser**) n.

national park ■ n. an area of countryside protected by the state for the enjoyment of the general public or the preservation of wildlife.

national road ■ n. (in South Africa) any of a network of roads between major cities.

National Senior Certificate S. African ■ n. (from 2008

onwards) the school leaving qualification obtained by passing the final year examination in high school.

national service ■ n. a period of compulsory service in the armed forces during peacetime.

National Socialism ■ n. historical the political doctrine of the Nazi Party of Germany.
– DERIVATIVES **National Socialist** n.

nation state ■ n. a sovereign state of which most of the citizens or subjects are united also by factors which define a nation, such as language or common descent.

nationwide ■ adj. & adv. throughout the whole nation.

native ■ n. 1 a person born in a specified place or associated with a place by birth. ▸ a local inhabitant. 2 an animal or plant indigenous to a place. 3 dated, offensive a non-white original inhabitant of a country as regarded by European colonists or travellers. ■ adj. 1 associated with the place or circumstances of a person's birth. ▸ of the indigenous inhabitants of a place. 2 (of a plant or animal) of indigenous origin or growth. 3 innate; in a person's character: *native wit*. 4 (of a metal or other mineral) found in a pure or uncombined state.
– PHRASES **go native** derogatory (of a person living abroad) adopt the way of life of the country one is living in.
– DERIVATIVES **natively** adv. **nativeness** n.
– ORIGIN Middle English: from Latin *nativus*, from *nasci* 'be born'.

Native American ■ n. a member of any of the indigenous peoples of North and South America and the Caribbean Islands. ■ adj. of or relating to these peoples.

USAGE
In the US, **Native American** is now the current accepted term in many contexts. See also **AMERICAN INDIAN**.

native rock ■ n. rock in its original place, i.e. that has not been moved or quarried.

native speaker ■ n. a person who has spoken the language in question from earliest childhood.

nativism /'neɪtɪvɪz(ə)m/ ■ n. 1 the theory or doctrine that concepts and ways of thinking are innate rather than acquired or learned. 2 historical, chiefly US the policy of protecting the interests of native-born or established inhabitants against those of immigrants. 3 a return to or emphasis on traditional or local customs.
– DERIVATIVES **nativist** n. & adj. **nativistic** adj.

nativity ■ n. (pl. **-ies**) 1 the occasion of a person's birth. 2 (usu. **the Nativity**) the birth of Jesus Christ. ▸ the Christian festival of Christ's birth; Christmas.
– ORIGIN Middle English: from Old French *nativité*, from late Latin *nativitas*, from Latin *nativus* (see **NATIVE**).

nativity play ■ n. a play performed at Christmas based on the events surrounding the birth of Jesus Christ.

NATO (also **Nato**) ■ abbrev. North Atlantic Treaty Organization.

natron /'neɪtr(ə)n, 'nat-/ ■ n. a mineral salt found in dried lake beds, consisting of hydrated sodium carbonate.
– ORIGIN C17: from Spanish *natrón*, from Greek *nitron* (see **NITRE**).

natter informal ■ v. chat casually. ■ n. a chat.
– DERIVATIVES **natterer** n.
– ORIGIN C19: imitative.

natterjack toad ■ n. a small European toad with a bright yellow stripe down its back. [*Bufo calamita*.]
– ORIGIN C18: perhaps from **NATTER** (because of its loud croak) + **JACK**.

natty ■ adj. (**-ier**, **-iest**) informal (of a person or their clothing) smart and fashionable.
– DERIVATIVES **nattily** adv. **nattiness** n.
– ORIGIN C18: perhaps rel. to **NEAT**.

Natufian /nɑː'tuːfɪən/ ■ adj. Archaeology relating to or denoting a late Mesolithic culture of the Middle East, dated to about 12 500–10 000 years ago.
– ORIGIN 1930s: from Wadi *an-Natuf*, the type site (a cave north-west of Jerusalem).

natural ■ adj. 1 existing in or derived from nature; not made, caused by, or processed by humankind. ▸ (of fabric) unbleached and undyed; off-white. 2 in accordance with nature; normal. ▸ relaxed and unaffected. ▸ inevitable: *the natural choice*. ▸ (of law or justice) based on innate moral sense. 3 (of a parent or child) related by blood. ▸ chiefly archaic illegitimate. 4 Music (of a note) not sharpened or flattened. ▸ (of a brass instrument) having no valves and able to play only the notes of the harmonic series above a fundamental note. ▸ of or relating to the notes and intervals of the harmonic series. 5 Bridge (of a bid) straightforwardly reflecting one's holding of cards. Often contrasted with **CONVENTIONAL** or **ARTIFICIAL**. ■ n. 1 a person with an innate gift or talent for a particular task or activity. 2 Music a natural note, or a sign (♮) denoting one when a previous sign or the key signature would otherwise demand a sharp or a flat. ▸ any of the longer, lower keys on a keyboard instrument that are normally white. 3 an off-white colour. 4 a hand of cards, throw of dice, or other result which wins immediately.
– DERIVATIVES **naturalness** n.

natural-born ■ adj. having a specified innate characteristic or ability. ▸ archaic having a position by birth.

natural classification ■ n. a scientific classification according to features which are held to be objectively significant, rather than being selected for convenience.

natural frequency ■ n. Physics a frequency at which a system oscillates when not subjected to a continuous or repeated external force.

natural gas ■ n. flammable gas, consisting largely of methane and other hydrocarbons, occurring naturally underground and used as fuel.

natural history ■ n. the scientific study of animals or plants, especially as concerned with observation rather than experiment and presented in popular form.
– DERIVATIVES **natural historian** n.

naturalism ■ n. 1 (in art and literature) a style and theory of representation based on the accurate depiction of detail. 2 a philosophical viewpoint according to which everything arises from natural properties and causes, and supernatural or spiritual explanations are excluded or discounted. ▸ (in moral philosophy) the theory that ethical statements can be derived from non-ethical ones.

naturalist ■ n. 1 an expert in or student of natural history. 2 an exponent or practitioner of naturalism.

naturalistic ■ adj. 1 derived from or imitating real life or nature. 2 based on the theory of naturalism.
– DERIVATIVES **naturalistically** adv.

naturalize (also **-ise**) ■ v. 1 admit (a foreigner) to the citizenship of a country. ▸ alter (an adopted foreign word) so that it conforms more closely to the phonology or orthography of the adopting language. 2 [usu. as adj. **naturalized** (also **-ised**)] establish (a plant or animal) so that it lives wild in a region where it is not indigenous. 3 regard as or cause to appear natural. ▸ explain (a phenomenon) in a naturalistic way.
– DERIVATIVES **naturalization** (also **-isation**) n.

natural language ■ n. a language that has developed naturally in use, as opposed to an artificial language or computer code.

natural law ■ n. 1 a body of unchanging moral principles regarded as a basis for all human conduct. 2 an observable law or laws relating to natural phenomena.

natural life ■ n. the expected span of a person's or animal's life under normal circumstances.

natural logarithm ■ n. Mathematics a logarithm to the base *e* (2.71828 ...).

naturally ■ adv. 1 in a natural manner. 2 of course.

natural magic ■ n. (in the Middle Ages) magic practised for beneficial purposes, involving the making of images, healing, and the use of herbs.

natural numbers ■ pl. n. the positive integers (whole numbers) 1, 2, 3, etc., and sometimes zero as well.

natural philosophy ■ n. archaic natural science, especially physical science.
– DERIVATIVES **natural philosopher** n.

natural religion ■ n. religion based on reason rather than divine revelation, especially deism.

natural resources ■ pl. n. materials or substances occurring in nature which can be exploited for economic gain.

natural science ■ n. a branch of science which deals with the physical world, e.g. physics, chemistry, geology, biology. ▶ the branch of knowledge which deals with the study of the physical world.

natural selection ■ n. Biology the evolutionary process whereby organisms better adapted to their environment tend to survive and produce more offspring.

natural theology ■ n. theology or knowledge of God based on observed facts and experience apart from divine revelation.

natural year ■ n. the tropical or solar year.

nature ■ n. 1 the phenomena of the physical world collectively, including plants, animals, and the landscape, as opposed to humans or human creations. ▶ the physical force regarded as causing and regulating these phenomena. ▶ archaic a living thing's vital functions or needs. 2 the basic or inherent features, qualities, or character of a person or thing. ▶ inborn or hereditary characteristics as an influence on or determinant of personality. Often contrasted with NURTURE.
– PHRASES **someone's better nature** a person's capacity for tolerance, generosity, or sympathy. **in the nature of things** inevitable or inevitably. **in a state of nature 1** in an uncivilized or uncultivated state. **2** totally naked. **3** Christian Church in a morally unregenerate condition, unredeemed by divine grace. **the nature of the beast** informal the inherent or essential character of something.
– DERIVATIVES **-natured** adj.
– ORIGIN Middle English: from Latin *natura* 'birth, nature, quality', from *nasci* 'be born'.

nature cure ■ n. another term for NATUROPATHY.

nature reserve ■ n. a tract of land managed so as to preserve its flora, fauna, and physical features.

nature study ■ n. the practical study of plants, animals, and natural phenomena as a school subject.

nature trail ■ n. a signposted path through the countryside designed to draw attention to natural features.

naturism ■ n. 1 nudism. 2 the worship of nature or natural objects.
– DERIVATIVES **naturist** n. & adj.

naturopathy /ˌneɪtʃəˈrɒpəθi/ ■ n. a system of alternative medicine based on the theory that diseases can be successfully treated or prevented without the use of drugs, by techniques such as control of diet, exercise, and massage.
– DERIVATIVES **naturopath** n. **naturopathic** adj.

Naugahyde /ˈnɔːɡəhaɪd/ ■ n. N. Amer. (trademark in the US) an artificial material designed to resemble leather.
– ORIGIN C20: from *Nauga(tuk)*, the name of a town in Connecticut + *-hyde*, alteration of HIDE².

naught ■ pron. archaic nothing. ■ n. N. Amer. variant spelling of NOUGHT.
– PHRASES **come to naught** be ruined or foiled. **set at naught** disregard; despise.
– ORIGIN Old English *nāwiht*, *-wuht*, from *nā* 'no' + *wiht* 'thing' (see WIGHT).

naughty ■ adj. (-ier, -iest) 1 (especially of a child) disobedient; badly behaved. 2 informal mildly rude or indecent. 3 archaic wicked.
– DERIVATIVES **naughtily** adv. **naughtiness** n.
– ORIGIN Middle English: from NAUGHT.

nauplius /ˈnɔːplɪəs/ ■ n. (pl. **nauplii** /-plɪaɪ, -pliːiː/) Zoology the first larval stage of many crustaceans, having an unsegmented body and a single eye.
– ORIGIN C19: from Latin, denoting a kind of shellfish, or from the Greek name *Nauplios*, the son of the sea god Poseidon in Greek mythology.

nausea /ˈnɔːsɪə, -zɪ-/ ■ n. a feeling of sickness with an inclination to vomit.
– ORIGIN Middle English: from Greek *nausia*, from *naus* 'ship'.

nauseate ■ v. [often as adj. **nauseating**] affect with nausea.
– DERIVATIVES **nauseatingly** adv.

nauseous ■ adj. 1 affected with nausea. 2 causing nausea; offensive to the taste or smell.
– DERIVATIVES **nauseously** adv. **nauseousness** n.
– ORIGIN C17: from Latin *nauseosus*, from *nausea* 'seasickness'.

nautch /nɔːtʃ/ ■ n. (in the Indian subcontinent) a traditional dance performed by professional dancing girls.
– ORIGIN from Hindi *nāc*, from Sanskrit *nṛtya* 'dancing'.

nautical ■ adj. of or concerning sailors or navigation; maritime.
– DERIVATIVES **nautically** adv.
– ORIGIN C16: from Greek *nautikos*, from *nautēs* 'sailor'.

nautical almanac ■ n. a yearbook containing astronomical and tidal information for navigators.

nautical mile ■ n. a unit used in measuring distances at sea, equal to 1 852 metres (2 025 yards) approximately.

nautilus /ˈnɔːtɪləs/ ■ n. (pl. **nautiluses** or **nautili** /-laɪ, -liː/) a cephalopod mollusc with a light external spiral shell and numerous short tentacles around the mouth. [Genus *Nautilus*: several species.]
– DERIVATIVES **nautiloid** n.
– ORIGIN from Greek *nautilos* 'sailor'.

NAV ■ abbrev. net asset value.

Navajo /ˈnavəhəʊ/ (also **Navaho**) ■ n. (pl. same or **-os**) 1 a member of an American Indian people of New Mexico and Arizona. 2 the Athabaskan language of this people.
– ORIGIN from Spanish *Apaches de Navajó* 'apaches from Navajo', from Tewa *navahu* 'fields adjoining an arroyo'.

naval ■ adj. of, in, or relating to a navy or navies.
– ORIGIN Middle English: from Latin *navalis*, from *navis* 'ship'.

naval architecture ■ n. the designing of ships.
– DERIVATIVES **naval architect** n.

naval stores ■ pl. n. materials used in shipping.

Navaratri /ˌnʌvəˈrʌtri/ (also **Navaratra**) ■ n. a Hindu autumn festival extending over the nine nights before Dussehra.
– ORIGIN Sanskrit, 'nine nights'.

navarin /ˈnav(ə)rɪn, -rã/ ■ n. a casserole of lamb or mutton with vegetables.
– ORIGIN from French.

nave¹ ■ n. the central part of a church building, usually separated from the chancel by a step or rail and from adjacent aisles by pillars.
– ORIGIN C17: from Latin *navis* 'ship'.

nave² ■ n. the hub of a wheel.
– ORIGIN Old English *nafu*, of Germanic origin.

navel ■ n. 1 a rounded knotty depression in the centre of a person's belly caused by the detachment of the umbilical cord after birth; the umbilicus. 2 the central point of a place.
– ORIGIN Old English, of Germanic origin.

navel-gazing ■ n. complacent self-absorption or narrow concentration on a single issue.

navel orange ■ n. a large seedless orange of a variety which has a navel-like depression at the top containing a small secondary fruit.

navicular /nəˈvɪkjʊlə/ (also **navicular bone**) ■ n. a boat-shaped bone in the ankle or wrist, especially that in the ankle, between the talus and the cuneiform bones.
– ORIGIN Middle English: from late Latin *navicularis*, from Latin *navicula* 'little ship'.

navigable ■ adj. 1 (of a waterway or sea) able to be sailed on by ships or boats. 2 Computing (of a website) easy to move around in.
– DERIVATIVES **navigability** n.

navigate ■ v. 1 plan and direct the route or course of a ship, aircraft, or other form of transport, especially by using instruments or maps. 2 sail or travel over (a stretch of water or terrain). ▶ guide (a vessel or vehicle) over a specified route or terrain. 3 Computing move around a website, the Internet, etc.
– ORIGIN C16: from Latin *navigare* 'to sail'.

navigation ■ n. 1 the process or activity of navigating. 2 the passage of ships.
– DERIVATIVES **navigational** adj. **navigationally** adv.

navigation lights

navigation lights ▪ pl. n. a set of lights shown by a ship or aircraft at night to indicate its position and orientation.

navigator ▪ n. **1** a person who navigates a ship, aircraft, etc. **2** historical a person who explores by sea. **3** Computing a browser program for accessing data on the World Wide Web or another information system.

navvy ▪ n. (pl. **-ies**) Brit. dated a labourer employed in the excavation and construction of a road, railway, or canal.
– ORIGIN C19: abbrev. of NAVIGATOR.

navy ▪ n. (pl. **-ies**) **1** [treated as sing. or pl.] the branch of a state's armed services which conducts military operations at sea. ▸ poetic/literary a fleet of ships. **2** (also **navy blue**) a dark blue colour.
– ORIGIN Middle English: from Old French *navie* 'ship, fleet', from Latin *navis* 'ship'.

navy yard ▪ n. US a shipyard for the construction, repair, and equipping of naval vessels.

nawab /nʌˈwɑːb/ ▪ n. Indian **1** a native governor during the time of the Mogul empire. **2** a Muslim nobleman or person of high status.
– ORIGIN from Urdu *nawwāb*, var. of Arabic *nuwwāb*, from *nāʾib* 'deputy'.

nay ▪ adv. **1** or rather; and more than that. **2** archaic or dialect no. ▪ n. a negative answer.
– ORIGIN Middle English: from Old Norse *nei*, from *ne* 'not' + *ei* 'ever'.

naysay ▪ v. (past and past part. **-said**) chiefly US say no to; deny or oppose.
– DERIVATIVES **naysayer** n.

Nazarene /ˈnazəriːn, ˌnazəˈriːn/ ▪ n. a native or inhabitant of Nazareth. ▸ **(the Nazarene)** Jesus Christ. ▸ (chiefly in Jewish or Muslim use) a Christian. ▸ a member of an early sect or faction of Jewish Christians. ▪ adj. of or relating to Nazareth or Nazarenes.

Nazareth Baptist Church ▪ n. an indigenous South African church which combines Christianity with Zulu cultural beliefs.

Nazi /ˈnɑːtsi, ˈnɑːzi/ ▪ n. (pl. **Nazis**) historical a member of the National Socialist German Workers' Party. **2** derogatory a person with extreme racist or authoritarian views.
– DERIVATIVES **Nazidom** n. **Nazify** v. (**-ies, -ied**) **Naziism** n. **Nazism** n.
– ORIGIN German, abbrev. representing the pronunciation of *Nati-* in *Nationalsozialist* 'national socialist'.

Nazirite /ˈnazəraɪt/ (also **Nazarite**) ▪ n. an ancient Israelite who had taken certain vows of abstinence.
– ORIGIN from Hebrew *nāzīr* 'consecrated one'.

NB ▪ abbrev. nota bene.

Nb ▪ symb. the chemical element niobium.

NBA ▪ abbrev. (in North America) National Basketball Association.

NBC ▪ abbrev. **1** (in the US) National Broadcasting Com-pany. **2** (of weapons or warfare) nuclear, biological, and chemical.

NC ▪ abbrev. **1** network computer. **2** numerical control.

nca /ʌ, nʌ, nɑː/ S. African informal ▪ adj. good; pleasant; delicious. ▪ exclam. expressing pleasure or enjoyment.
– ORIGIN from isiZulu *mncayi* 'nice'.

NCO ▪ abbrev. non-commissioned officer.

NCOP ▪ abbrev. (in South Africa) National Council of Provinces.

NCS ▪ abbrev. (in South Africa) National Curriculum Statement.

Nd ▪ symb. the chemical element neodymium.

-nd ▪ suffix variant spelling of **-AND, -END**.

n.d. ▪ abbrev. no date.

Ndebele /ˌ(ə)ndəˈbiːli, -ˈbeɪli/ ▪ n. (pl. same or **Ndebeles**) **1** a member of either of two divisions of an Nguni people living in SW Zimbabwe and NE South Africa. **2** another term for ISINDEBELE or SINDEBELE.
– ORIGIN the name in the Nguni languages.

NE ▪ abbrev. north-east or north-eastern.

Ne ▪ symb. the chemical element neon.

né /neɪ/ masc. of NÉE.

Neanderthal /nɪˈandətɑːl/ ▪ n. **1** (also **Neanderthal man**) an extinct human that was widely distributed in ice age Europe between *c.*120 000–35 000 years ago, with a receding forehead and prominent brow ridges. **2** informal an uncivilized or uncouth man.
– ORIGIN C19: from *Neanderthal*, a region in Germany where remains of Neanderthal man were found.

neap /niːp/ ▪ n. (also **neap tide**) a tide just after the first or third quarters of the moon when there is least difference between high and low water. ▪ v. (**be neaped**) (of a boat) be kept aground or in harbour by a neap tide.
– ORIGIN Middle English, from Old English *nēp-* in *nēpflōd* 'neap flood'.

Neapolitan /nɪəˈpɒlɪt(ə)n/ ▪ adj. (of ice cream) made in layers of different colours.

near ▪ adv. **1** at or to a short distance away. **2** a short time away in the future. **3** almost. ▪ prep. (also **near to**) **1** at or to a short distance away from (a place). **2** a short period of time from. **3** almost. **4** similar to. ▪ adj. **1** located a short distance away. **2** only a short time ahead. **3** similar. ▸ close to being (the thing mentioned). ▸ having a close family connection. **4** located on the nearside of a vehicle. Compare with OFF (in sense 3). ▪ v. approach.
– DERIVATIVES **nearish** adj. **nearness** n.
– ORIGIN Middle English: from Old Norse *nær* 'nearer', comparative of *ná*.

nearby ▪ adj. not far away. ▪ adv. (also **near by**) close by.

Nearctic /nɪˈɑːktɪk/ ▪ adj. Zoology relating to or denoting a zoogeographical region comprising North America as far south as northern Mexico, together with Greenland.
– ORIGIN C19: from NEO- + ARCTIC.

near-death experience ▪ n. an unusual experience taking place on the brink of death and recounted by a person on recovery, typically an out-of-body experience or a vision of a tunnel of light.

Near East ▪ n. the countries of SW Asia between the Mediterranean and India (including the Middle East).
– DERIVATIVES **Near Eastern** adj.

nearly ▪ adv. **1** very close to; almost. **2** closely.
– PHRASES **not nearly** nothing like; far from.

near miss ▪ n. **1** a narrowly avoided collision. **2** a bomb or shot that just misses its target.

near money ▪ n. Finance assets which can readily be converted into cash, such as bills of exchange.

nearside ▪ n. (usu. **the nearside**) the side of a vehicle nearest the kerb. Compare with OFFSIDE. ▸ the left side of a horse.

near-sighted ▪ adj. another term for SHORT-SIGHTED.
– DERIVATIVES **near-sightedly** adv. **near-sightedness** n.

neat ▪ adj. **1** in good order; tidy or carefully arranged. **2** done with or demonstrating skill or efficiency. **3** (of a drink of spirits) not diluted or mixed with anything else. **4** informal, chiefly N. Amer. excellent.
– DERIVATIVES **neaten** v. **neatly** adv. **neatness** n.
– ORIGIN C15: from French *net*, from Latin *nitidus* 'shining'.

neath ▪ prep. chiefly poetic/literary beneath.

NEB ▪ abbrev. New English Bible.

Nebuchadnezzar /ˌnɛbjʊkədˈnɛzə/ ▪ n. a very large wine bottle, equivalent in capacity to about twenty regular bottles.
– ORIGIN C20: from *Nebuchadnezzar* II, king of Babylon in the 6th century BC.

nebula /ˈnɛbjʊlə/ ▪ n. (pl. **nebulae** /-liː/ or **nebulas**) **1** Astronomy a cloud of gas or dust in outer space. ▸ old-fashioned term for GALAXY. **2** Medicine a clouded spot on the cornea causing defective vision.
– DERIVATIVES **nebular** adj.
– ORIGIN C17: from Latin, 'mist'.

nebulizer /ˈnɛbjʊlʌɪzə/ (also **-iser**) ▪ n. a device for producing a fine spray of liquid, used e.g. for inhaling a medicinal drug.
– DERIVATIVES **nebulize** (also **-ise**) v.

nebulous /ˈnɛbjʊləs/ ▪ adj. **1** in the form of a cloud or haze; hazy. **2** (of a concept or idea) vague or ill-defined. **3** Astronomy relating to a nebula or nebulae.
– DERIVATIVES **nebulosity** n. **nebulously** adv. **nebulousness** n.

– ORIGIN Middle English: from Latin *nebulosus*, from *nebula* 'mist'.

nebuly /ˈnɛbjʊli/ ■ adj. Heraldry divided or edged with a line formed of deeply interlocking curves.
– ORIGIN C16: from French *nébulé*, from Latin *nebula* 'mist'.

NEC ■ abbrev. National Executive Committee.

necessarily /ˈnɛsəs(ə)rɪli, ˌnɛsəˈsɛrɪli/ ■ adv. as a necessary result; inevitably.

necessary ■ adj. 1 required to be done, achieved, or present; needed. 2 inevitable: *a necessary consequence.* ► Philosophy inevitably resulting from the nature of things, so that the contrary is impossible. ► Philosophy (of an agent) having no independent volition. ■ n. 1 (**necessaries**) the basic requirements of life, such as food and warmth. 2 (**the necessary**) informal the action or item needed.
– ORIGIN Middle English: from Latin *necessarius*, from *necesse* 'be needful'.

necessitarian /nəˌsɛsɪˈtɛːrɪən/ ■ n. Philosophy another term for determinist (see **DETERMINISM**).
– DERIVATIVES **necessitarianism** n.

necessitate ■ v. make necessary as a result or consequence. ► force or compel to do something.

necessitous ■ adj. (of a person) poor; needy.

necessity ■ n. (pl. **-ies**) 1 the state or fact of being necessary. 2 an indispensable thing.
– ORIGIN Middle English: from Old French *necessite*, from Latin *necessitas*, from *necesse* 'needful'.

neck ■ n. 1 the part of a person's or animal's body connecting the head to the rest of the body. 2 a narrow connecting or end part. ► the part of a bottle or other container near the mouth. ► a narrow piece of terrain or sea. 3 the length of a horse's head and neck as a measure of its lead in a race. 4 the part of a violin, guitar, or other instrument that bears the fingerboard. ■ v. 1 informal kiss and caress amorously. 2 become narrow at a particular point when subjected to tension.
– PHRASES **get** (or **catch**) **it in the neck** informal be severely criticized or punished. **neck and neck** level in a race, competition, or comparison. **neck of the woods** informal a particular area or locality. **up to one's neck in** informal heavily, deeply, or busily involved in.
– DERIVATIVES **-necked** adj. **necker** n. **neckless** adj.
– ORIGIN Old English *hnecca* 'back of the neck', of Germanic origin.

neckband ■ n. 1 a strip of material round the neck of a garment. 2 an ornamental band worn round the neck.

neckcloth ■ n. a cravat.

neckerchief ■ n. a square of cloth worn round the neck.

necking ■ n. Architecture a short plain concave section between the capital and the shaft of a classical Doric or Tuscan column.

necklace ■ n. 1 an ornamental chain or string of beads, jewels, or links worn round the neck. 2 (in South Africa) a tyre doused or filled with petrol, placed round a victim's neck and set alight. ■ v. kill with a tyre necklace.

necklet ■ n. a close-fitting, typically rigid ornament worn around the neck.

neckline ■ n. the edge of a woman's garment at or below the neck.

necktie ■ n. N. Amer or dated another term for **TIE** (in sense 2).

necro- ■ comb. form relating to a corpse or death: *necromancy.*
– ORIGIN from Greek *nekros* 'corpse'.

necromancy /ˈnɛkrə(ʊ)ˌmansi/ ■ n. the supposed practice of communicating with the dead, especially in order to predict the future. ► witchcraft, sorcery, or black magic in general.
– DERIVATIVES **necromancer** n. **necromantic** adj.

necrophilia /ˌnɛkrəˈfɪlɪə/ ■ n. sexual intercourse with or attraction towards corpses.
– DERIVATIVES **necrophile** n. **necrophiliac** n. **necrophilic** adj. **necrophilism** n. **necrophilist** n.

necropolis /nɛˈkrɒpəlɪs/ ■ n. a cemetery, especially a large ancient one.
– ORIGIN C19: from Greek, from *nekros* 'dead person' + *polis* 'city'.

necropsy /ˈnɛkrɒpsi, nɛˈkrɒpsi/ ■ n. (pl. **-ies**) another term for **AUTOPSY**.

necrosis /nɛˈkrəʊsɪs/ ■ n. Medicine the death of most or all of the cells in an organ or tissue due to disease, injury, or failure of the blood supply.
– DERIVATIVES **necrotic** adj.
– ORIGIN C17: from Greek *nekrōsis*, from *nekros* 'corpse'.

necrotizing /ˈnɛkrəˌtaɪzɪŋ/ (also **-ising**) ■ adj. causing or accompanied by necrosis.

nectar ■ n. 1 a sugary fluid secreted within flowers to encourage pollination by insects, collected by bees to make into honey. 2 (in Greek and Roman mythology) the drink of the gods. ► a delicious drink. 3 S. African a drink of fruit juice or pulp blended with water.
– DERIVATIVES **nectariferous** adj. **nectarivorous** adj.
– ORIGIN C16: from Greek *nektar*.

nectarine /ˈnɛktərɪn, -iːn/ ■ n. 1 a peach of a variety with smooth, thin, brightly coloured skin and rich firm flesh. 2 the tree bearing this fruit.
– ORIGIN C17: from **NECTAR**.

nectary ■ n. (pl. **-ies**) Botany a nectar-secreting glandular organ in a flower (floral) or on a leaf or stem (extrafloral).

Nedlac /ˈnɛdlak/ (also **NEDLAC**) ■ abbrev. (in South Africa) National Economic Development and Labour Council.

née /neɪ/ ■ adj. (masc. **né**) originally called; born (used in citing a person's former name, especially a married woman's maiden name).
– ORIGIN C18: French, 'born', from *naître*.

need ■ v. 1 require (something) because it is essential or very important rather than just desirable. 2 [usu. with neg. or in questions] expressing necessity or obligation: *need I say more?* 3 archaic be necessary. ■ n. 1 circumstances in which something is necessary; necessity. 2 a thing that is wanted or required. 3 the state of lacking basic necessities such as food, or of requiring help. ■ adv. (**needs**) archaic of necessity.
– PHRASES **needs must** (or **must needs**) it is or was necessary or unavoidable.
– ORIGIN Old English, of Germanic origin.

needful ■ adj. 1 formal necessary; requisite. 2 archaic needy.
– DERIVATIVES **needfully** adv. **needfulness** n.

needle ■ n. 1 a very fine slender piece of metal with a point at one end and a hole or eye for thread at the other, used in sewing. ► a similar, larger instrument used in crochet, knitting, etc. 2 the pointed hollow end of a hypodermic syringe. 3 a stylus used to play records. 4 a thin pointer on a dial, compass, etc. 5 Brit. informal hostility or antagonism provoked by rivalry. 6 the slender, sharp, stiff leaf of a fir or pine tree. 7 a steel pin exploding the cartridge of a breech-loading gun. 8 a beam used as a temporary support during underpinning. ■ v. 1 prick or pierce with a needle. 2 informal provoke or annoy by continual criticism or questioning.
– DERIVATIVES **needler** n.
– ORIGIN Old English, of Germanic origin.

needlecord ■ n. fine-ribbed corduroy fabric.

needlecraft ■ n. needlework.

needlefish ■ n. (pl. same or **-fishes**) another term for **GARFISH**.

needlepoint ■ n. 1 closely stitched embroidery worked over canvas. 2 (also **needlelace**) lace made by hand using a needle rather than bobbins.

needless ■ adj. unnecessary; avoidable.
– PHRASES **needless to say** of course.
– DERIVATIVES **needlessly** adv. **needlessness** n.

needlewoman ■ n. (pl. **-women**) a woman who has particular sewing skills.

needlework ■ n. the art or practice of sewing or embroidery. ► sewn or embroidered items collectively.
– DERIVATIVES **needleworker** n.

needn't ■ contr. need not.

needy ■ adj. (**-ier**, **-iest**) lacking the necessities of life; very poor.
– DERIVATIVES **neediness** n.

neem

neem /niːm/ ■ n. a tropical Old World tree which yields mahogany-like wood, oil, medicinal products, and insecticide. [*Azadirachta indica*.]
– ORIGIN C19: from Sanskrit *nimba*.

ne'er /nɛː/ ■ contr. poetic/literary or dialect never.

ne'er-do-well ■ n. a person who is lazy and irresponsible. ■ adj. lazy and irresponsible.

nefarious /nɪˈfɛːrɪəs/ ■ adj. wicked or criminal.
– DERIVATIVES **nefariously** adv. **nefariousness** n.
– ORIGIN C17: from Latin *nefarius*, from *nefas* 'wrong'.

neg ■ n. informal a photographic negative.

neg. ■ abbrev. negative.

nega- ■ comb. form informal denoting the negative counterpart of a unit of measurement, in particular a unit of energy saved as a result of conservation measures.

negate /nɪˈɡeɪt/ ■ v. **1** nullify; make ineffective. **2** Logic & Grammar make (a clause, sentence, or proposition) negative in meaning. **3** deny the existence of.
– ORIGIN C17 (*negation* Middle English): from Latin *negare* 'deny'.

negation ■ n. **1** the contradiction or denial of something. ▸ Logic a proposition whose assertion specifically denies the truth of another proposition. **2** the absence or opposite of something actual or positive. **3** Mathematics inversion.
– DERIVATIVES **negatory** /nɪˈɡeɪt(ə)ri, ˈnɛɡət(ə)ri/ adj.

negative ■ adj. **1** consisting in or characterized by the absence rather than the presence of distinguishing features. ▸ expressing or implying denial, disagreement, or refusal. ▸ Grammar & Logic stating that something is not the case. Contrasted with **AFFIRMATIVE** and **INTERROGATIVE**. ▸ [as exclam.] (especially in a military context) no. **2** pessimistic, undesirable, or unwelcome. **3** (of a quantity) less than zero. **4** of, containing, producing, or denoting the kind of electric charge carried by electrons. **5** (of a photographic image) showing light and shade or colours reversed from those of the original. ■ n. **1** a word or statement expressing denial, refusal, or negation. ▸ a bad or unwelcome quality or aspect. **2** a negative photographic image from which positive prints may be made. ■ v. **1** reject, veto, or contradict. **2** render ineffective; neutralize.
– DERIVATIVES **negatively** adv. **negativeness** n. **negativism** n. **negativist** n. & adj. **negativistic** adj. **negativity** n.
– ORIGIN Middle English: from late Latin *negativus*, from *negare* (see **NEGATE**).

negative equity ■ n. potential indebtedness arising when the market value of a property falls below the outstanding amount of a mortgage secured on it.

negative feedback ■ n. feedback that tends to reduce the effect by which it is produced.

negative geotropism ■ n. the tendency of plant stems and other parts to grow upwards.

negative pole ■ n. the south-seeking pole of a magnet.

negative sign ■ n. another term for **MINUS SIGN**.

negator /nɪˈɡeɪtə/ ■ n. Grammar a word expressing negation, especially (in English) the word *not*.

neglect ■ v. fail to give proper care or attention to. ▸ fail to do something. ■ n. the state or process of neglecting or being neglected. ▸ failure to do something.
– DERIVATIVES **neglectful** adj. **neglectfully** adv. **neglectfulness** n.
– ORIGIN C16 (*negligence, negligent* Middle English): from Latin *neglegere* 'disregard'.

negligee /ˈnɛɡlɪʒeɪ/ ■ n. a woman's light, filmy dressing gown.
– ORIGIN C18: from French, 'given little thought or attention', from *négliger* 'to neglect'.

negligence ■ n. failure to take proper care over something. ▸ Law breach of a duty of care which results in damage.
– DERIVATIVES **negligent** adj. **negligently** adv.
– ORIGIN Middle English: from Latin *negligentia*, from *negligere*, var. of *neglegere* (see **NEGLECT**).

negligible ■ adj. so small or unimportant as to be not worth considering; insignificant.
– DERIVATIVES **negligibility** /-ˈbɪlɪti/ n. **negligibly** adv.

– ORIGIN C19: from obsolete French, from *négliger* 'to neglect'.

negotiable ■ adj. **1** open to discussion or modification. **2** able to be traversed; passable. **3** able to be transferred or assigned to the legal ownership of another person.
– DERIVATIVES **negotiability** n.

negotiate ■ v. **1** try to reach an agreement or compromise by discussion with others. ▸ obtain or bring about by negotiating. **2** find a way over or through (an obstacle or difficult path). **3** transfer (a cheque, bill, etc.) to the legal ownership of another. ▸ convert (a cheque) into cash or notes.
– DERIVATIVES **negotiant** n. (archaic). **negotiation** n. **negotiator** n.
– ORIGIN C17 (*negotiation* C15): from Latin *negotiari* 'do in the course of business', from *negotium* 'business'.

Negress /ˈniːɡrɪs, -ɡrɛs/ ■ n. a woman or girl of black African origin. See **NEGRO**.

Negritude /ˈnɛɡrɪtjuːd/ ■ n. the quality, fact, or awareness of being of black African origin.

Negro /ˈniːɡrəʊ/ ■ n. (pl. **-oes**) a member of a dark-skinned group of peoples originally native to Africa south of the Sahara.
– ORIGIN from Latin *niger, nigr-* 'black'.

USAGE
Since the 1960s, when the term **black** was favoured as the term to express racial pride, **Negro** (together with related words such as **Negress**) has dropped out of favour, and is now regarded as old-fashioned or offensive.

Negroid ■ adj. of or relating to the division of humankind represented by the indigenous peoples of central and southern Africa.

USAGE
The term **Negroid** belongs to a set of terms introduced by 19th-century anthropologists attempting to categorize human races. Such terms are associated with outdated notions of racial types, and so are now potentially offensive and best avoided.

Negus /ˈniːɡəs/ ■ n. historical a ruler, or the supreme ruler, of Ethiopia.
– ORIGIN from Amharic *n'gus* 'king'.

negus /ˈniːɡəs/ ■ n. historical a hot drink of port, sugar, lemon, and spice.
– ORIGIN C18: named after Colonel Francis *Negus*, who created it.

neigh /neɪ/ ■ n. a characteristic high whinnying sound made by a horse. ■ v. (of a horse) utter a neigh.
– ORIGIN Old English, of imitative origin.

neighbour (US **neighbor**) ■ n. a person living next door to or very near to another. ▸ a person or place in relation to others next to it. ■ v. [usu. as adj. **neighbouring**] be situated next to or very near (another).
– DERIVATIVES **neighbourless** adj. **neighbourliness** n. **neighbourly** adj.
– ORIGIN Old English *nēahgebūr*, from *nēah* 'nigh, near' + *gebūr* 'inhabitant, peasant, farmer'.

neighbourhood (US **neighborhood**) ■ n. a district or community within a town or city. ▸ the area surrounding a particular place, person, or object.
– PHRASES **in the neighbourhood of** approximately; about.

neighbourhood watch ■ n. a scheme of systematic local vigilance by householders to discourage crime, especially burglary.

neither /ˈnaɪðə, ˈniː-/ ■ det. & pron. not the one nor the other of two people or things; not either. ■ adv. **1** used before the first of two (or occasionally more) alternatives (the others being introduced by 'nor') to indicate that they are each untrue or each do not happen. **2** used to introduce a further negative statement.
– ORIGIN Middle English: alteration of Old English *nawther*, from *nāhwæther*, from *nā* 'no' + *hwæther* 'whether'.

nek ■ n. S. African (especially in place names) a low part of a mountain ridge, often forming a pass.
– ORIGIN from S. African Dutch.

nekton /'nɛkt(ə)n, -tɒn/ ■ n. Zoology aquatic animals that are able to swim and move independently of water currents, as distinct from plankton.
– DERIVATIVES **nektonic** adj.
– ORIGIN C19: from Greek *nēktos* 'swimming', from *nēkhein* 'to swim'.

nelly ■ n. (pl. **-ies**) informal **1** a silly person. **2** derogatory an effeminate homosexual man.
– PHRASES **not on your nelly** Brit. certainly not. [orig. as *not on your Nelly Duff*, rhyming slang for 'puff' (i.e. breath of life).]
– ORIGIN C19: from the given name *Nelly*.

nelson ■ n. a wrestling hold in which one arm is passed under the opponent's arm from behind and the hand is applied to the neck (half nelson), or both arms and hands are applied (full nelson).
– ORIGIN C19: apparently from the surname *Nelson*.

nematic /nɪ'matɪk/ ■ adj. relating to or denoting a state of a liquid crystal in which the molecules are oriented in parallel but not arranged in well-defined planes. Compare with SMECTIC.
– ORIGIN C20: from Greek *nēma*, *nēmat-* 'thread'.

nemato- /nɪ'matəʊ, 'nɛmətəʊ/ (also **nemat-** before a vowel) ■ comb. form **1** denoting something thread-like in shape: *nematocyst*. **2** relating to Nematoda.
– ORIGIN from Greek *nēma*, *nēmat-* 'thread'.

nematocyst /nɪ'matə(ʊ)sɪst, 'nɛmət-/ ■ n. Zoology a specialized cell in the tentacles of a jellyfish or other coelenterate, containing a barbed or venomous coiled thread that can be projected in self-defence or to capture prey.

Nematoda /,nɛmə'təʊdə/ ■ pl. n. Zoology a large phylum of worms with slender, unsegmented, cylindrical bodies, including the roundworms, threadworms, and eelworms.
– DERIVATIVES **nematode** /'nɛmətəʊd/ n.

nematology /,nɛmə'tɒlədʒi/ ■ n. the scientific study of nematode worms.
– DERIVATIVES **nematologist** n.

Nembutal /'nɛmbjʊt(ə)l, -taːl/ ■ n. (trademark in the US) the drug sodium pentobarbitone.
– ORIGIN C20: from *N(a)* (*sodium*) + *e*(*thyl*) *m*(*ethyl*) *but*(*yl*), elements of the systematic name.

nem. con. ■ adv. with no one dissenting; unanimously.
– ORIGIN Latin *nemine contradicente*.

Nemertea /,nɛmə'tiːə, nɪ'mɜːtɪə/ ■ pl. n. Zoology a small phylum that comprises the ribbon worms.
– DERIVATIVES **nemertean** adj. & n. **nemertine** /'nɛmətiːn, 'nɛmətʌɪn/ adj. & n.
– ORIGIN from Greek *Nēmertēs*, the name of a sea nymph.

nemesia /nɪ'miːʒə/ ■ n. a plant related to the snapdragon, cultivated for its colourful, funnel-shaped flowers. [Genus *Nemesia*.]
– ORIGIN from Greek *nemesion*, denoting various similar plants.

nemesis /'nɛmɪsɪs/ ■ n. (pl. **nemeses** /-siːz/) the inescapable agent of someone's downfall, especially when deserved. ▸ a downfall caused by such an agent.
– ORIGIN C16: Greek, 'retribution', personified as the goddess of divine punishment.

neo- /'niːəʊ/ ■ comb. form **1** new: *neonate*. **2** a new or revived form of: *neo-Darwinian*.
– ORIGIN from Greek *neos* 'new'.

neoclassicism ■ n. the revival of a classical style or treatment in art, literature, architecture, or music.
– DERIVATIVES **neoclassic** adj. **neoclassical** adj. **neo-classicist** n. & adj.

neocolonialism ■ n. the use of economic, political, or cultural pressures to control or influence other countries, especially former dependencies.
– DERIVATIVES **neocolonial** adj. **neocolonialist** n. & adj.

neocortex ■ n. (pl. **neocortices**) Anatomy a part of the cerebral cortex concerned with sight and hearing in mammals, regarded as the most recently evolved part of the cortex.
– DERIVATIVES **neocortical** adj.

neo-Darwinian ■ adj. Biology of or relating to the modern version of Darwin's theory of evolution by natural selection, incorporating the findings of genetics.
– DERIVATIVES **neo-Darwinism** n. **neo-Darwinist** n.

neodymium /,niːə(ʊ)'dɪmɪəm/ ■ n. the chemical element of atomic number 60, a silvery-white metal of the lanthanide series. (Symbol: **Nd**)
– ORIGIN C19: from NEO- + a shortened form of DIDYMIUM.

Neogene /'niːə(ʊ)dʒiːn/ ■ adj. Geology relating to or denoting the later division of the Tertiary period (comprising the Miocene and Pliocene epochs, from 23.3 to 1.64 million years ago).
– ORIGIN C19: from NEO- + Greek -*genēs* (see -GEN).

neo-Impressionism ■ n. a late 19th-century movement in French painting which sought to improve on Impressionism through a systematic approach to form and colour, particularly using pointillist technique.
– DERIVATIVES **neo-Impressionist** adj. & n.

Neolithic /,niːə(ʊ)'lɪθɪk/ ■ adj. Archaeology relating to or denoting the later part of the Stone Age, when ground or polished stone weapons and implements prevailed.
– ORIGIN C19: from NEO- + Greek *lithos* 'stone'.

neologism /nɪ'ɒlədʒɪz(ə)m/ ■ n. a newly coined word or expression.
– DERIVATIVES **neologist** n. **neologize** (also **-ise**) v.
– ORIGIN C19: from French *néologisme*.

neomycin /,niːə(ʊ)'mʌɪsɪn/ ■ n. Medicine an antibiotic related to streptomycin, active against a wide variety of bacterial infections.

neon ■ n. **1** the chemical element of atomic number 10, an inert gaseous element of the noble gas group. (Symbol: **Ne**) **2** fluorescent lighting and signs using neon or another gas. ▸ [as modifier] very bright or fluorescent in colour.
– ORIGIN C19: from Greek, 'something new', from *neos*.

neonatal /,niːə(ʊ)'neɪt(ə)l/ ■ adj. of or relating to newborn children (or mammals).
– DERIVATIVES **neonatologist** n. **neonatology** n.

neonate /'niːəneɪt/ ■ n. a newborn child or mammal. ▸ Medicine an infant less than four weeks old.
– ORIGIN 1930s: from Greek *neos* 'new' + Latin *nat-*, *nasci* 'be born'.

neon tetra ■ n. see TETRA.

neophyte /'niːə(ʊ)fʌɪt/ ■ n. **1** a person who is new to a subject, skill, or belief. **2** a novice in a religious order, or a newly ordained priest.
– ORIGIN Middle English: from Greek *neophutos* 'newly planted'.

neoplasia /,niːə(ʊ)'pleɪzɪə/ ■ n. Medicine the presence or formation of new, abnormal growth of tissue.
– ORIGIN C19: from NEO- + Greek *plasis* 'formation'.

neoplasm ■ n. a new and abnormal growth of tissue in some part of the body, especially as a characteristic of cancer.

neoplastic¹ ■ adj. Medicine of or relating to a neoplasm or neoplasia.

neoplastic² ■ adj. Art of or relating to neoplasticism.

neoplasticism ■ n. a style of abstract painting characterized by the use of rectangular shapes and primary colours.

Neoplatonism /,niːəʊ'pleɪt(ə)nɪz(ə)m/ ■ n. a philosophical and religious system developed in the 3rd century AD, combining Platonic and other Greek thought with oriental mysticism.
– DERIVATIVES **Neoplatonic** adj. **Neoplatonist** n.

neoprene /'niːə(ʊ)priːn/ ■ n. a synthetic polymer resembling rubber.
– ORIGIN 1930s: from NEO- + *prene*, perhaps from PROPYL.

neoteny /niː'ɒt(ə)ni/ ■ n. Zoology **1** the retention of juvenile features in the adult animal. **2** the sexual maturity of an animal while it is still in a mainly larval state, as in the axolotl.
– DERIVATIVES **neotenic** adj. **neotenous** adj.
– ORIGIN C19: coined in German as *Neotenie*, from Greek *neos* 'new, juvenile' + *teinein* 'extend'.

Neotropical ■ adj. Zoology relating to or denoting a zoogeographical region comprising Central and South America and the Caribbean.
– DERIVATIVES **neotropics** pl. n.

NEPAD ■ abbrev. New Partnership for Africa's Development.

Nepalese /nɛpəˈliːz/ ■ n. a native or inhabitant of Nepal. ■ adj. of or relating to Nepal.

Nepali /nɪˈpɔːli/ ■ n. (pl. same or **Nepalis**) **1** a native or national of Nepal. **2** the Indic official language of Nepal.

nepeta /nɪˈpiːtə/ ■ n. a plant of a genus that includes catmint and several kinds with spikes of blue or violet flowers. [Genus *Nepeta*.]
– ORIGIN from Latin *nepeta* 'calamint' (formerly in this genus).

nepheline /ˈnɛf(ə)lɪn/ ■ n. a colourless, greenish, or brownish aluminosilicate mineral occurring in igneous rocks.
– ORIGIN C19: from French *néphéline*, from Greek *nephelē* 'cloud' (because its fragments become cloudy on immersion in nitric acid).

nephelometer /ˌnɛfəˈlɒmɪtə/ ■ n. an instrument for measuring the size and concentration of suspended particles by means of light scattering.
– ORIGIN C19: from Greek *nephelē* 'cloud' + -METER.

nephew ■ n. a son of one's brother or sister, or of one's brother-in-law or sister-in-law.
– ORIGIN Middle English: from Old French *neveu*, from Latin *nepos* 'grandson, nephew'.

nephr- /nɪfr/ ■ comb. form variant spelling of NEPHRO- shortened before a vowel (as in *nephrectomy*).

nephrectomy /nɪˈfrɛktəmi/ ■ n. (pl. **-ies**) surgical removal of one or both kidneys.

nephridiopore /nɪˈfrɪdɪəpɔː/ ■ n. Zoology the external opening of a nephridium.

nephridium /nɪˈfrɪdɪəm/ ■ n. (pl. **nephridia**) Zoology (in many invertebrates) a minute tube open to the exterior for excretion or osmoregulation.
– DERIVATIVES **nephridial** adj.
– ORIGIN C19: from Greek *nephrion*, diminutive of *nephros* 'kidney', + the diminutive ending *-idium*.

nephrite /ˈnɛfrʌɪt/ ■ n. a pale green or white silicate mineral which is one of the forms of jade.
– ORIGIN C18: from German *Nephrit*, from Greek *nephros* 'kidney' (with ref. to its supposed efficacy in treating kidney disease).

nephritic /nɪˈfrɪtɪk/ ■ adj. renal. ▶ of or relating to nephritis.
– ORIGIN C19: from Greek *nephritikos* (see NEPHRITIS).

nephritis /nɪˈfrʌɪtɪs/ ■ n. Medicine inflammation of the kidneys.
– ORIGIN C16: from Greek, from *nephros* 'kidney'.

nephro- (also **nephr-** before a vowel) ■ comb. form of or relating to the kidneys: *nephrotoxic*.
– ORIGIN from Greek *nephros* 'kidney'.

nephrology /nɛˈfrɒlədʒi/ ■ n. the branch of medicine concerned with the physiology and diseases of the kidneys.
– DERIVATIVES **nephrological** adj. **nephrologist** n.

nephrosis /nɪˈfrəʊsɪs/ ■ n. Medicine kidney disease, especially with oedema and proteinuria.
– DERIVATIVES **nephrotic** adj.

ne plus ultra /ˌneɪ plʌs ˈʊltrɑː/ ■ n. (**the ne plus ultra**) the perfect or most extreme example.
– ORIGIN Latin, 'not further beyond', the supposed inscription on the Pillars of Hercules prohibiting passage by ships.

nepotism /ˈnɛpətɪz(ə)m/ ■ n. the favouring of relatives or friends, especially by giving them jobs.
– DERIVATIVES **nepotist** n. **nepotistic** adj.
– ORIGIN C17: from French *népotisme*, from Italian *nepotismo*, from *nipote* 'nephew' (with ref. to privileges bestowed on the 'nephews' of popes, often really their illegitimate sons).

Neptunian ■ adj. **1** of or relating to the Roman sea god Neptune or to the sea. **2** of or relating to the planet Neptune.

neptunium /nɛpˈtjuːnɪəm/ ■ n. the chemical element of atomic number 93, a radioactive metal of the actinide series. (Symbol: **Np**)
– ORIGIN C19: from the planet *Neptune*, on the pattern of *uranium* (Neptune being the next planet beyond Uranus).

nerd ■ n. informal a person who lacks social skills or is boringly studious.
– DERIVATIVES **nerdish** adj. **nerdishness** n. **nerdy** adj.
– ORIGIN 1950s.

Nereid /ˈnɪərɪɪd/ ■ n. Greek & Roman Mythology any of the sea nymphs, daughters of the old sea god Nereus.

nerine /nɪˈrʌɪni, nəˈriːnə/ ■ n. a bulbous South African plant with narrow strap-shaped petals that are typically crimped and twisted. [Genus *Nerine*.]
– ORIGIN from Greek *Nērēis* 'Nereid'.

neritic /nɪˈrɪtɪk/ ■ adj. Ecology of or denoting the shallow waters overlying the continental shelf.
– ORIGIN C19: from Greek *nēritēs* 'sea mussel', from the name of the sea god Nereus.

neroli /ˈnɪərəli/ (also **neroli oil**) ■ n. an essential oil distilled from the flowers of the Seville orange.
– ORIGIN C17: from Italian *neroli*, said to be the name of an Italian princess.

nerve ■ n. **1** a whitish fibre or bundle of fibres in the body that transmits impulses of sensation between the brain or spinal cord and other parts of the body. **2** (**nerves**) bravery; assurance. ▶ (**one's nerve**) one's steadiness and courage. **3** (**nerves**) nervousness. **4** informal cheek. **5** Botany a prominent unbranched rib in a leaf, especially in the midrib of the leaf of a moss. ■ v. (**nerve oneself**) brace oneself for a demanding situation.
– PHRASES **a bag** (or **bundle**) **of nerves** informal someone who is extremely nervous. **get on someone's nerves** informal irritate someone. **touch** (or **hit**) **a** (**raw**) **nerve** refer to a sensitive topic.
– DERIVATIVES **-nerved** adj.
– ORIGIN Middle English: from Latin *nervus*; rel. to Greek *neuron* 'nerve'.

nerve cell ■ n. a neuron.

nerve centre ■ n. **1** a group of connected nerve cells performing a particular function. **2** the control centre of an organization or operation.

nerve fibre ■ n. the axon of a neuron.

nerve gas ■ n. a poisonous vapour which disrupts the transmission of nerve impulses, causing death or disablement.

nerveless ■ adj. **1** lacking vigour or feeling. **2** confident.
– DERIVATIVES **nervelessly** adv. **nervelessness** n.

nerve-racking (also **nerve-wracking**) ■ adj. stressful; frightening.

nervous ■ adj. **1** easily agitated or alarmed. ▶ apprehensive. ▶ resulting from anxiety or anticipation. **2** relating to or affecting the nerves.
– DERIVATIVES **nervously** adv. **nervousness** n.
– ORIGIN Middle English: from Latin *nervosus* 'sinewy, vigorous', from Latin *nervus* (see NERVE).

nervous breakdown ■ n. a period of mental illness resulting from severe depression or stress.

nervous system ■ n. the network of nerve cells and fibres which transmits nerve impulses between parts of the body.

nervous wreck ■ n. informal a stressed or emotionally exhausted person.

nervy ■ adj. (**-ier**, **-iest**) **1** nervous. ▶ characterized or produced by nervousness. **2** N. Amer. informal bold or impudent.
– DERIVATIVES **nervily** adv. **nerviness** n.

-ness ■ suffix forming nouns chiefly from adjectives: **1** denoting a state or condition: *liveliness*. ▶ an instance of this: *a kindness*. **2** something in a certain state: *wilderness*.
– ORIGIN Old English, of Germanic origin.

nest ■ n. **1** a structure or place made or chosen by a bird for laying eggs and sheltering its young. ▶ a place where an animal or insect breeds or shelters. ▶ a snug or secluded retreat. ▶ a bowl-shaped object likened to a bird's nest. **2** a place filled with undesirable people or things: *a nest of spies*. **3** a set of similar objects of graduated sizes, fitting together for storage. ■ v. **1** use or build a nest. **2** fit (an object or objects) inside a larger one. **3** (especially in computing and linguistics) place in a hierarchical arrangement, typically in a lower position.
– DERIVATIVES **nestful** n. (pl. **-fuls**).
– ORIGIN Old English, of Germanic origin.

nest box (also **nesting box**) ■ n. a box provided for a bird to nest in.

nest egg ■ n. **1** a sum of money saved for the future. **2** a real or artificial egg left in a nest to induce hens to lay there.

nestle ■ v. **1** settle comfortably within or against something. **2** (of a place) lie in a sheltered position.
– ORIGIN Old English, from NEST.

nestling ■ n. a bird that is too young to leave the nest.

Nestorianism /nɛˈstɔːrɪənɪz(ə)m/ ■ n. the Christian doctrine that there were two separate persons in Christ, one human and one divine, maintained by some ancient Churches of the Middle East.
– DERIVATIVES **Nestorian** adj. & n.
– ORIGIN named after *Nestorius*, patriarch of Constantinople (428–31).

net[1] ■ n. **1** a length of open-meshed material of twine, cord, etc., used typically for catching fish. ▸ a net supported by a frame at the end of a handle, used for catching fish or insects. **2** a structure with a net used in various games, e.g. as a goal in football, to divide a tennis court, or to enclose a cricket practice area. **3** a fine fabric with a very open weave. **4** a trap. ▸ a system for selecting or recruiting someone. **5** a communications or broadcasting network. ▸ a network of interconnected computers. ▸ (**the Net**) the Internet. ■ v. (**netted**, **netting**) **1** catch or obtain with or as with a net. **2** (in sport) hit (a ball) into the net; score (a goal). **3** cover with a net.
– DERIVATIVES **netful** n. (pl. **-fuls**).
– ORIGIN Old English, of Germanic origin.

net[2] (also **nett**) ■ adj. **1** (of an amount, value, or price) remaining after a deduction of tax or other contributions. Often contrasted with GROSS. ▸ (of a price) to be paid in full. ▸ (of a weight) excluding that of the packaging. **2** (of an effect or result) overall. ■ v. (**netted**, **netting**) acquire (a sum) as clear profit. ▸ (**net something down/off/out**) exclude a non-net amount when making a calculation, in order to reduce the amount left to a net sum.
– ORIGIN Middle English: from French *net* (see NEAT).

netball ■ n. a seven-a-side game in which goals are scored by throwing an inflated ball through a netted hoop.

nether /ˈnɛðə/ ■ adj. lower in position.
– DERIVATIVES **nethermost** adj.
– ORIGIN Old English, of Germanic origin.

Netherlander ■ n. a native or inhabitant of the Netherlands.
– DERIVATIVES **Netherlandish** adj.

nether regions ■ pl. n. **1** hell; the underworld. **2** euphemistic a person's genitals and bottom.

netherworld ■ n. the underworld; hell.

net national product ■ n. the total value of goods produced and services provided in a country during one year, after depreciation of capital goods has been allowed for.

net profit ■ n. the actual profit after working expenses have been paid.

netsuke /ˈnɛtski, ˈnɛtsʊki/ ■ n. (pl. same or **netsukes**) a carved button-like ornament formerly used in Japan, applied to the end of a cord and tucked into the sash of a kimono, as a means of suspending articles from the sash.
– ORIGIN C19: from Japanese.

nett ■ adj. & v. variant spelling of NET[2].

netting ■ n. netted fabric.

nettle ■ n. a herbaceous plant having jagged leaves covered with stinging hairs. [*Urtica dioica* and other species.] ▸ used in names of plants of a similar appearance, e.g. dead-nettle. ■ v. **1** annoy. **2** sting with nettles.
– PHRASES **grasp the nettle** tackle a difficulty boldly.
– ORIGIN Old English, of Germanic origin.

nettlerash ■ n. another term for URTICARIA.
– ORIGIN from its resemblance to a nettle sting.

nettlesome ■ adj. causing annoyance or difficulty.

network ■ n. **1** an arrangement of intersecting horizontal and vertical lines. **2** a complex system of railways, roads, etc. **3** a group or system of interconnected people or things. ▸ a group of broadcasting stations that connect for the simultaneous broadcast of a programme. ▸ a number of interconnected computers, machines, or operations. ▸ a system of connected electrical conductors. ■ v. **1** connect as or operate with a network. ▸ broadcast on a network. ▸ link (machines) to operate interactively. **2** [often as noun **networking**] interact with others to exchange information and develop useful contacts.
– DERIVATIVES **networkable** adj.

networker ■ n. **1** Computing a person who operates from home or an external office via a computer network. **2** a person who networks with others in a similar field.

neural ■ adj. of or relating to a nerve or the nervous system.
– DERIVATIVES **neurally** adv.
– ORIGIN C19: from Greek *neuron* 'nerve'.

neuralgia /ˌnjʊəˈraldʒə/ ■ n. intense pain along the course of a nerve, especially in the head or face.
– DERIVATIVES **neuralgic** adj.

neural network (also **neural net**) ■ n. a computer system modelled on the human brain and nervous system.

neuritis /ˌnjʊəˈrʌɪtɪs/ ■ n. Medicine inflammation of a peripheral nerve or nerves.
– DERIVATIVES **neuritic** adj.

neuro- ■ comb. form relating to nerves or the nervous system: *neuroanatomy*.
– ORIGIN from Greek *neuron* 'nerve, sinew, tendon'.

neuroanatomy ■ n. the anatomy of the nervous system.
– DERIVATIVES **neuroanatomical** adj. **neuroanatomist** n.

neurobiology ■ n. the biology of the nervous system.
– DERIVATIVES **neurobiological** adj. **neurobiologist** n.

neurofibroma /ˌnjʊərə(ʊ)fʌɪˈbrəʊmə/ ■ n. (pl. **neurofibromas** or **neurofibromata** /-mətə/) Medicine a tumour formed on a nerve cell sheath, frequently symptomless but occasionally malignant.

neurofibromatosis /ˌnjʊərə(ʊ)fʌɪˌbrəʊməˈtəʊsɪs/ ■ n. Medicine a disease in which neurofibromas form throughout the body.

neurogenic /ˌnjʊərə(ʊ)ˈdʒɛnɪk/ ■ adj. Physiology caused by or arising in the nervous system.

neuroleptic /ˌnjʊərə(ʊ)ˈlɛptɪk/ Medicine ■ adj. tending to reduce nervous tension by depressing nerve functions. ■ n. a neuroleptic drug.
– ORIGIN C20: from NEURO- + Greek *lēpsis* 'seizing'.

neurolinguistic programming ■ n. a system of alternative therapy intended to improve self-awareness and change patterns of mental and emotional behaviour.

neurolinguistics ■ pl. n. [treated as sing.] the branch of linguistics concerned with the relationship between language and the brain.
– DERIVATIVES **neurolinguistic** adj.

neurology /ˌnjʊəˈrɒlədʒi/ ■ n. the branch of medicine and biology concerned with the nervous system.
– DERIVATIVES **neurological** adj. **neurologically** adv. **neurologist** n.
– ORIGIN C17: from NEURO- + -LOGY.

neuroma /ˌnjʊəˈrəʊmə/ ■ n. (pl. **neuromas** or **neuromata** /-mətə/) another term for NEUROFIBROMA.

neuromuscular ■ adj. of or relating to nerves and muscles.

neuron /ˈnjʊərɒn/ (also **neurone** /-rəʊn/) ■ n. a specialized cell transmitting nerve impulses.
– DERIVATIVES **neuronal** /-ˈrəʊn(ə)l/ adj. **neuronic** /-ˈrɒnɪk/ adj.
– ORIGIN C19: from Greek *neuron* 'sinew, tendon'; cf. NERVE.

USAGE
In scientific sources the standard spelling is **neuron**. The spelling **neurone** is found only in non-technical sources.

neuropathy /ˌnjʊəˈrɒpəθi/ ■ n. Medicine disease or dysfunction of peripheral nerves.
– DERIVATIVES **neuropathic** adj.

neuropeptide ■ n. Biochemistry any of a group of polypeptide compounds which act as neurotransmitters.

neurophysiology ■ n. the physiology of the nervous system.
– DERIVATIVES **neurophysiological** adj. **neurophysiologist** n.

neuropsychiatry ■ n. psychiatry relating mental disturbance to disordered brain function.
– DERIVATIVES **neuropsychiatric** adj. **neuropsychiatrist** n.

neuropsychology ■ n. the study of the relationship between behaviour and brain function.
– DERIVATIVES **neuropsychological** adj. **neuropsychologist** n.

Neuroptera /ˌnjʊəˈrɒpt(ə)rə/ ■ pl. n. Entomology an order of predatory flying insects, including the lacewings, alderflies, and snake flies, having four finely veined membranous wings.
– DERIVATIVES **neuropteran** n. & adj. **neuropterous** adj.
– ORIGIN from NEURO- in the sense 'veined' + Greek *pteron* 'wing'.

neuroscience ■ n. any or all of the sciences concerned with the nervous system and brain.
– DERIVATIVES **neuroscientist** n.

neurosis /ˌnjʊəˈrəʊsɪs/ ■ n. (pl. **neuroses** /-siːz/) Medicine a relatively mild mental illness not caused by organic disease, involving depression, anxiety, obsessive behaviour, etc. but not a radical loss of touch with reality.
– ORIGIN C18: from NEURO-.

neurosurgery ■ n. surgery performed on the nervous system.
– DERIVATIVES **neurosurgeon** n. **neurosurgical** adj.

neurotic ■ adj. 1 Medicine having, caused by, or relating to neurosis. 2 abnormally sensitive and obsessive. ■ n. a neurotic person.
– DERIVATIVES **neurotically** adv. **neuroticism** n.

neurotoxin /ˌnjʊərəʊˈtɒksɪn/ ■ n. a poison which acts on the nervous system.
– DERIVATIVES **neurotoxic** adj. **neurotoxicity** n.

neurotransmitter ■ n. Physiology a chemical substance released from a nerve fibre and effecting the transfer of an impulse to another nerve, muscle, etc.
– DERIVATIVES **neurotransmission** n.

neurotrophic /ˌnjʊərə(ʊ)ˈtrəʊfɪk, -ˈtrɒfɪk/ ■ adj. Physiology of or relating to the growth of nervous tissue.

neurotropic /ˌnjʊərə(ʊ)ˈtrəʊpɪk, -ˈtrɒpɪk/ ■ adj. Medicine tending to attack or affect the nervous system.
– DERIVATIVES **neurotropism** n.

neuter ■ adj. 1 of or denoting a gender of nouns typically contrasting with masculine and feminine or common. 2 (of an animal) lacking developed sexual organs; castrated or spayed. ▸ (of a plant or flower) having neither functional pistils nor stamens. ■ n. 1 Grammar a neuter word. 2 a non-fertile caste of social insect, especially a worker bee or ant. ▸ a castrated or spayed domestic animal. ■ v. 1 castrate or spay. 2 render ineffective.
– ORIGIN Middle English: from Latin *neuter* 'neither', from *ne-* 'not' + *uter* 'either'.

neutral ■ adj. 1 impartial. ▸ belonging to an impartial state or group. ▸ unbiased. 2 having no strongly marked characteristics. 3 Chemistry neither acid nor alkaline; having a pH of about 7. 4 electrically neither positive nor negative. ■ n. 1 an impartial or unbiased state or person. 2 a neutral colour or shade. 3 a disengaged position of gears. 4 an electrically neutral point, terminal, etc.
– DERIVATIVES **neutrality** n. **neutrally** adv.
– ORIGIN Middle English: from Latin *neutralis* 'of neuter gender', *neuter* (see NEUTER).

neutralism ■ n. a policy of political neutrality.
– DERIVATIVES **neutralist** n.

neutralize (also **-ise**) ■ v. 1 render ineffective by applying an opposite force or effect. 2 make chemically neutral. 3 disarm (a bomb). 4 euphemistic kill; destroy.
– DERIVATIVES **neutralization** (also **-isation**) n. **neutralizer** (also **-iser**) n.

neutrino /njuːˈtriːnəʊ/ ■ n. (pl. **-os**) a neutral subatomic particle with a mass close to zero, rarely interacting with normal matter.
– ORIGIN C20: from Italian, diminutive of *neutro* 'neutral'.

neutron ■ n. a subatomic particle of about the same mass as a proton but without an electric charge, present in all atomic nuclei except those of ordinary hydrogen.
– ORIGIN C20: from NEUTRAL.

neutron bomb ■ n. a nuclear weapon that produces large numbers of neutrons, rather than heat or blast.

neutron star ■ n. Astronomy a celestial object of great density composed predominantly of neutrons, believed to be formed by the gravitational collapse of a star.

neutrophil /ˈnjuːtrə(ʊ)fɪl/ ■ n. Physiology a neutrophilic white blood cell.

neutrophilic ■ adj. Physiology (of a cell or its contents) stained only by neutral dyes.

névé /ˈnɛveɪ/ ■ n. uncompressed granular snow, especially at the head of a glacier.
– ORIGIN C19: from Swiss French, 'glacier'.

never ■ adv. 1 not ever. 2 not at all. ▸ informal definitely or surely not.
– PHRASES **never a one** not one. **well I never!** informal expressing great surprise.
– ORIGIN Old English *næfre*, from *ne* 'not' + *æfre* 'ever'.

nevermore ■ adv. poetic/literary never again.

never-never land ■ n. an imaginary utopian place.
– ORIGIN often with allusion to the ideal country in J. M. Barrie's *Peter Pan*.

nevertheless ■ adv. in spite of that.

nevirapine /nəˈvɪrəpiːn, nəˈvaɪ-/ ■ n. Medicine an antiretroviral drug used in the treatment of HIV, especially to prevent transmission from pregnant women to their babies.

nevus ■ n. (pl. **nevi**) US spelling of NAEVUS.

new ■ adj. 1 not existing before; made, introduced, or discovered recently or now for the first time. ▸ not previously used or owned. 2 (of vegetables) harvested early in the season. 3 seen, experienced, or acquired recently or now for the first time. ▸ (**new to**) unfamiliar or strange to. ▸ (**new to/at**) inexperienced at or unaccustomed to. ▸ (in place names) discovered or founded later than and named after. 4 reinvigorated, restored, or reformed. ▸ superseding and more advanced than others of the same kind: *the new architecture*. ■ adv. newly.
– DERIVATIVES **newish** adj. **newness** n.
– ORIGIN Old English, of Germanic origin.

New Age ■ n. a broad movement characterized by alternative approaches to traditional Western culture, with an interest in spirituality, mysticism, holism, and environmentalism.
– DERIVATIVES **New Ager** n. **New Agey** adj.

New Age music ■ n. a style of chiefly instrumental music characterized by light melodic harmonies and sounds reproduced from the natural world, intended to promote serenity.

newbie ■ n. (pl. **-ies**) informal an inexperienced newcomer.

newborn ■ adj. recently born. ▸ regenerated. ■ n. a newborn child or animal.

Newcastle disease ■ n. an acute infectious viral fever affecting birds, especially poultry.
– ORIGIN 1920s: so named because it was first recorded near Newcastle upon Tyne in NE England in 1927.

newcomer ■ n. 1 a person who has recently arrived. 2 a novice.

newel /ˈnjuːəl/ ■ n. the central supporting pillar of a spiral or winding staircase. ▸ (also **newel post**) the top or bottom supporting post of a stair rail.
– ORIGIN Middle English: from Old French *nouel* 'knob', from medieval Latin *nodellus*, diminutive of Latin *nodus* 'knot'.

New Englander ■ n. a native or inhabitant of New England, an area on the NE coast of the US.

newfangled ■ adj. derogatory newly developed and unfamiliar.
– ORIGIN Middle English: from *newfangle* (now dialect) 'liking what is new', from NEW + element rel. to an Old English word meaning 'to take'.

Newfoundland /ˈnjuːf(ə)n(d)lənd, -land, njuːˈfaʊndlənd/ ■ n. a dog of a very large breed with a thick coarse coat.

newie ■ n. (pl. **-ies**) informal a new person or thing.

new-laid ■ adj. (of an egg) freshly laid.

newly ■ adv. **1** recently. **2** again. ▶ in a new or different manner.

newly-wed ■ n. a recently married person.

new man ■ n. a man who rejects sexist attitudes and the traditional male role.

Newmarket ■ n. a card game in which players put down cards in sequence, hoping to play cards on which bets have been placed.

new maths (N. Amer. **new math**) ■ pl. n. [treated as sing.] a system of teaching mathematics to children, with emphasis on investigation by them and on set theory.

new moon ■ n. **1** the phase of the moon when it first appears as a slender crescent. **2** Astronomy the time at which the moon is in conjunction with the sun and not visible from the earth.

news ■ n. **1** newly received or noteworthy information, especially about recent events. **2** (**the news**) a broadcast or published news report. **3** (**news to**) informal information not previously known to.
– ORIGIN Middle English: pl. of NEW, translating Old French *noveles* or medieval Latin *nova* 'new things'.

news agency ■ n. an organization that collects and distributes news items.

newsagent ■ n. a person or shop selling newspapers, magazines, etc.

newsboy ■ n. another term for NEWSPAPER BOY.

newscast ■ n. a broadcast news report.

newscaster ■ n. a newsreader.

news conference ■ n. a press conference.

newsfeed ■ n. **1** a service by which news is provided on a regular or continuous basis for onward distribution or broadcasting. ▶ an item of information so provided. **2** a system by which data is transferred or exchanged between central computers to provide newsgroup access to networked users.

newsflash ■ n. a single item of important news broadcast separately and often interrupting other programmes.

newsgroup ■ n. a group of Internet users who exchange email on a topic of mutual interest.

news hound ■ n. informal a newspaper reporter.

newsletter ■ n. a bulletin issued periodically to those in a particular group.

newsman (or **newswoman**) ■ n. (pl. **-men** (or **-women**)) a reporter or journalist.

New South Africa ■ n. South Africa in the era following apartheid.

newspaper ■ n. a printed publication, typically issued daily or weekly, consisting of folded unstapled sheets and containing news, articles, and advertisements.

newspaper boy (or **girl**) ■ n. a boy or girl who sells or delivers newspapers.

newspaperman (or **newspaperwoman**) ■ n. (pl. **-men** or **-women**) a male (or female) newspaper journalist.

newspeak ■ n. ambiguous euphemistic language used chiefly in political propaganda.
– ORIGIN 1949: the name of an artificial official language in George Orwell's *Nineteen Eighty-Four*.

newsprint ■ n. cheap, low-quality absorbent printing paper, used chiefly for newspapers.

newsreader ■ n. **1** a person who reads out broadcast news bulletins. **2** Computing a program for reading emails posted to newsgroups.

newsreel ■ n. a short cinema film of news and current affairs.

newsroom ■ n. the area in a newspaper or broadcasting office where news is processed.

news-sheet ■ n. a simple form of newspaper.

news-stand ■ n. a stand for the sale of newspapers.

news ticker ■ n. a coloured strip or band running across the bottom of a computer or television screen, within which the latest news headlines are continuously scrolled.

New Stone Age ■ n. the Neolithic period.

New Style ■ n. the calculation of dates using the Gregorian calendar.

newsvendor ■ n. Brit. a newspaper seller.

news wire ■ n. an up-to-date Internet news service.

newsworthy ■ adj. noteworthy as news.
– DERIVATIVES **newsworthiness** n.

newsy ■ adj. informal (**-ier, -iest**) full of news.

newt ■ n. a small slender-bodied amphibian with a well-developed tail. [*Triturus* and other genera.]
– ORIGIN Middle English: from *an ewt* (ewt from Old English *efeta*), interpreted as *a newt*.

New Testament ■ n. the second part of the Christian Bible, recording the life and teachings of Christ and his earliest followers.

newton (abbrev.: **N**) ■ n. Physics the SI unit of force, equal to the force that would give a mass of one kilogram an acceleration of one metre per second per second.
– ORIGIN C20: named after Sir Isaac *Newton* (1642–1727).

Newtonian ■ adj. **1** Physics relating to or arising from the work of the English scientist Sir Isaac Newton. **2** Astronomy denoting a reflecting telescope with a secondary mirror set at 45° to deflect the light from the main mirror to the eyepiece.

new town ■ n. a planned urban centre created in an undeveloped or rural area.

new wave ■ n. a style of rock music popular in the late 1970s, deriving from punk.

New World ■ n. North and South America regarded collectively, in contrast to Europe, Asia, and Africa.

new year ■ n. the calendar year just begun or about to begin. ▶ the period immediately before and after 31 December.

New Year's Day ■ n. 1 January.

New Year's Eve ■ n. 31 December.

New Zealander ■ n. a native or inhabitant of New Zealand.

New Zealand flax ■ n. another term for FLAX-LILY.

next ■ adj. **1** coming immediately after the time of writing or speaking. ▶ (of a day of the week) nearest (or the nearest but one) after the present. ▶ (of an event) occurring directly after the present one in time. **2** coming immediately after the present one in space, order, or rank. ■ adv. immediately afterwards. ▶ following in the specified order. ■ n. the next person or thing. ■ prep. archaic next to.
– PHRASES **next to 1** beside. **2** following in order or importance. **3** almost. **4** in comparison with. **the next world** (according to some religious beliefs) the place where one goes after death.
– ORIGIN Old English *nēhsta* 'nearest', superlative of *nēah* 'nigh'.

next door ■ adv. & adj. (**next-door**) in or to the next house or room. ■ n. the building, room, or people next door.
– PHRASES **next door to** in the next house or room to.

next of kin ■ n. [treated as sing. or pl.] a person's closest living relative or relatives.

nexus /ˈnɛksəs/ ■ n. (pl. same or **nexuses**) **1** a connection. ▶ a connected group or series. **2** the central and most important point. **3** (**Nexus**) trademark a synthetic drug with euphoric and hallucinogenic effects, often taken illegally.
– ORIGIN C17: from Latin, 'a binding together', from *nectere* 'bind'.

NFL ■ abbrev. National Football League (the top professional league for American football in the US).

NGK /ɛn,xɪəˈkɑː/ (also **NG Kerk**) ■ abbrev. *Nederduits(e) Gereformeerde Kerk*, the Afrikaans name for the DUTCH REFORMED CHURCH.

NGO ■ abbrev. non-governmental organization.

Ngoni /(ə)ŋˈɡəʊni/ ■ n. (pl. same or **Ngonis**) **1** a member of a people living chiefly in Malawi. **2** (**ngoni**) a kind of traditional African drum.
– ORIGIN a local name.

Nguni /(ə)ŋˈɡuːni/ ■ n. (pl. same or **Ngunis**) **1** a member of a group of Bantu-speaking peoples living mainly in southern Africa. **2** the Bantu languages spoken by these peoples, notably isiNdebele, isiXhosa, isiZulu, and siSwati.
– ORIGIN from isiZulu *umnguni, isiNguni*.

Nguni cattle

Nguni cattle ▪ pl. n. animals of an African breed of beef cattle with multicoloured skins.

NHS ▪ abbrev. (in the UK) National Health Service.

Ni ▪ symb. the chemical element nickel.

NIA ▪ abbrev. (in South Africa) National Intelligence Agency.

niacin /ˈnʌɪəsɪn/ ▪ n. another term for NICOTINIC ACID.

nib ▪ n. **1** the pointed end part of a pen, which distributes the ink. ▸ a pointed or projecting part of an object. **2** (**nibs**) shelled and crushed coffee or cocoa beans.
– DERIVATIVES **nibbed** adj.
– ORIGIN C16: prob. from Middle Dutch *nib* or Middle Low German *nibbe*, var. of *nebbe* 'beak'.

nibble ▪ v. **1** take small bites out of. ▸ eat in small amounts. ▸ gently bite at. **2** gradually erode. **3** show cautious interest in a project. ▪ n. **1** an instance of nibbling. **2** a small piece of food bitten off. ▸ (**nibbles**) informal small savoury snacks.
– DERIVATIVES **nibbler** n.
– ORIGIN C15: prob. of Low German or Dutch origin.

niblick /ˈnɪblɪk/ ▪ n. Golf, dated an iron with a heavy, lofted head, used especially for playing out of bunkers.
– ORIGIN C19.

nibs ▪ n. (**his nibs**) informal a mock title used to refer to a self-important man.
– ORIGIN C19.

NiCad /ˈnʌɪkad/ (also US trademark **Nicad**) ▪ n. a battery or cell with a nickel anode, a cadmium cathode, and a potassium hydroxide electrolyte.
– ORIGIN 1950s: blend of NICKEL and CADMIUM.

Nicam /ˈnʌɪkam/ (also **NICAM**) ▪ n. a digital system that provides video signals with high-quality stereo sound.
– ORIGIN 1980s: acronym from *near instantaneously companded* (i.e. compressed and expanded) *audio multiplex*.

Nicaraguan /ˌnɪkəˈragjʊən, -ˈragwən/ ▪ n. a native or inhabitant of Nicaragua. ▪ adj. of or relating to Nicaragua.

nice ▪ adj. **1** pleasant; agreeable; satisfactory. ▸ (of a person) good-natured; kind. **2** fine or subtle. ▸ requiring careful attention. **3** archaic fastidious.
– PHRASES **nice and** —— satisfactory in terms of the quality described. **nice one** informal expressing approval.
– DERIVATIVES **nicely** adv. **niceness** n.
– ORIGIN Middle English (orig. 'stupid', also 'coy, reserved', hence 'fine, subtle'): from Latin *nescius* 'ignorant', from *nescire* 'not know'.

Nicene Creed /ˈnʌɪsiːn, ˈnʌɪ-/ ▪ n. a formal statement of Christian belief, widely used in liturgies and based on that adopted at the first Council of Nicaea in 325.

nicety /ˈnʌɪsɪti/ ▪ n. (pl. **-ies**) (usu. **niceties**) a fine detail or distinction. ▸ accuracy. ▸ a detail of etiquette.
– PHRASES **to a nicety** precisely.
– ORIGIN Middle English: from Old French *nicete*, from Latin *nescius* (see NICE).

niche /niːʃ, nɪtʃ/ ▪ n. **1** a shallow recess, especially one in a wall to display an ornament. **2** (**one's niche**) a comfortable or suitable position in life. **3** a specialized but profitable corner of the market. **4** Ecology a role taken by a type of organism within its community. ▪ v. place or position in a niche.
– ORIGIN C17: from French, 'recess', from *nicher* 'make a nest', from Latin *nidus* 'nest'.

nichrome /ˈnʌɪkrəʊm/ ▪ n. trademark an alloy of nickel and chromium, used chiefly in electrical heating elements.
– ORIGIN C20: blend of NICKEL and CHROME.

nick ▪ n. **1** a small cut or notch. **2** (**the nick**) Brit. informal prison. ▸ a police station. **3** the junction between the floor and side walls in a squash court. ▪ v. **1** make a nick or nicks in. **2** informal steal. ▸ (**nick someone for**) N. Amer. informal cheat someone of. **3** Brit. informal arrest.
– PHRASES **in** —— **nick** Brit. informal in a specified condition. **in the nick of time** only just in time.
– ORIGIN Middle English.

nickel ▪ n. **1** a silvery-white metal resembling iron, the chemical element of atomic number 28. (Symbol: **Ni**) **2** N. Amer. informal a five-cent coin. ▪ v. (**nickelled**, **nickelling**; US **nickeled**, **nickeling**) coat with nickel.
– ORIGIN C18: shortening of German *Kupfernickel*, the copper-coloured ore from which nickel was first obtained, from *Kupfer* 'copper' + *Nickel* 'demon' (with ref. to the ore's failure to yield copper).

nickel brass ▪ n. an alloy of copper, zinc, and nickel.

nickelodeon /ˌnɪkəˈləʊdɪən/ ▪ n. N. Amer. **1** informal, dated a jukebox, originally one operated by the insertion of a nickel. **2** historical a cinema charging one nickel.
– ORIGIN C20: from NICKEL (the coin) + a shortened form of MELODEON.

nickel silver ▪ n. a white alloy of nickel, zinc, and copper.

nickel steel ▪ n. stainless steel containing chromium and nickel.

nicker ▪ v. (of a horse) give a soft breathy whinny. ▪ n. a nickering sound.
– ORIGIN C16: imitative.

nick-nack ▪ n. variant spelling of KNICK-KNACK.

nickname ▪ n. a familiar or humorous name for a person or thing. ▪ v. give a nickname to.
– ORIGIN Middle English: from *an eke-name* (*eke* meaning 'addition'), misinterpreted as *a neke name*.

Niçoise /niːˈswɑːz/ ▪ adj. [postpos.] denoting food garnished with tomatoes, capers, and anchovies: *salade Niçoise*.
– ORIGIN feminine of French *Niçois* 'of Nice', a city in France.

nicotiana /ˌnɪkɒtɪˈɑːnə, -ˈkəʊʃ-/ ▪ n. an ornamental plant related to tobacco, with tubular flowers that are particularly fragrant at night. [*Nicotiana alata* and other species.]
– ORIGIN from modern Latin *nicotiana* (*herba*) 'tobacco (plant)', named after Jaques Nicot, a C16 diplomat who introduced tobacco to France.

nicotinamide /ˌnɪkəˈtɪnəmʌɪd/ ▪ n. Biochemistry the amide of nicotinic acid, found widely in living cells.

nicotine ▪ n. a toxic oily liquid which is the chief active constituent of tobacco.
– ORIGIN C19: from French, from NICOTIANA.

nicotine patch ▪ n. a patch impregnated with nicotine, worn on the skin by a person trying to reduce their craving for cigarettes.

nicotinic acid ▪ n. Biochemistry a vitamin of the B complex which occurs in milk, wheat germ, meat, and other foods and is involved in many metabolic processes.
– DERIVATIVES **nicotinate** n.

nictitating membrane ▪ n. Zoology a whitish membrane forming an inner eyelid in birds, reptiles, and some mammals.
– ORIGIN C18: *nictitating* from medieval Latin *nictitat-* 'blinked', from *nictare*.

nidus /ˈnʌɪdəs/ ▪ n. (pl. **nidi** /-dʌɪ/ or **niduses**) **1** a place in which something is formed or deposited; a site of origin. **2** Medicine a place in which bacteria have multiplied or may multiply; a focus of infection.
– ORIGIN C18: from Latin, 'nest'.

niece ▪ n. a daughter of one's brother or sister, or of one's brother-in-law or sister-in-law.
– ORIGIN Middle English: from Latin *neptis* 'granddaughter', feminine of *nepos* (see NEPHEW).

Nietzschean /ˈniːtʃɪən/ ▪ n. a follower of the German philosopher Friedrich Wilhelm Nietzsche (1844–1900), especially a supporter of his theories of the superman able to rise above the restrictive morality of ordinary men. ▪ adj. of, relating to, or characteristic of Nietzsche or his views.
– DERIVATIVES **Nietzscheanism** n.

niff Brit. informal ▪ n. an unpleasant smell. ▪ v. stink.
– DERIVATIVES **niffy** adj. (**-ier**, **-iest**).
– ORIGIN C20: perhaps from SNIFF.

nifty ▪ adj. (**-ier**, **-iest**) informal particularly good, skilful, or effective. ▸ stylish.
– DERIVATIVES **niftily** adv. **niftiness** n.
– ORIGIN C19.

nigella /nʌɪˈdʒɛlə/ ▪ n. a plant of a genus which includes love-in-a-mist. [Genus *Nigella*.]
– ORIGIN from Latin *nigellus*, diminutive of *niger* 'black'.

Nigerian /nʌɪˈdʒɪərɪən/ ■ n. a native or inhabitant of Nigeria. ■ adj. of or relating to Nigeria.

Niger–Congo ■ adj. denoting or belonging to a large phylum of languages in Africa, named after the Rivers Niger and Congo and comprising the Bantu, Mande, Gur, and Kwa families.

niggard /ˈnɪɡəd/ ■ n. a mean or stingy person. ■ adj. archaic niggardly.
– ORIGIN Middle English: alteration of *nigon*.

niggardly ■ adj. ungenerous. ▸ meagre. ■ adv. archaic in a mean or meagre manner.
– DERIVATIVES **niggardliness** n.

nigger ■ n. offensive a black person.
– ORIGIN C17: from French *nègre*, from Spanish *negro* (see NEGRO).

niggle ■ v. **1** cause slight but persistent annoyance, discomfort, or anxiety. **2** find fault with in a petty way. ■ n. a trifling worry, dispute, or criticism.
– DERIVATIVES **niggling** adj. **nigglingly** adv. **niggly** adj.
– ORIGIN C17: of Scandinavian origin.

nigh ■ adv., prep., & adj. archaic near. ▸ almost.
– ORIGIN Old English, of Germanic origin.

night ■ n. **1** the time from sunset to sunrise. ▸ this as the interval between two days. **2** the darkness of night. ▸ poetic/literary nightfall. **3** an evening. ■ adv. (**nights**) informal at night. ■ exclam. informal short for GOODNIGHT.
– ORIGIN Old English, of Germanic origin.

night adder ■ n. a poisonous nocturnal snake of sub-Saharan Africa. [*Causus rhombeatus* and related species.]

nightbird ■ n. another term for NIGHT OWL.

night blindness ■ n. the inability to see in dim light or at night.

nightcap ■ n. **1** historical a cap worn in bed. **2** a hot or alcoholic drink taken at bedtime.

nightclothes ■ pl. n. clothes worn in bed.

nightclub ■ n. a club that is open at night, typically having a bar and disco or other entertainment.
– DERIVATIVES **nightclubber** n. **nightclubbing** n.

nightdress ■ n. a light, loose garment worn by a woman or girl in bed.

nightfall ■ n. dusk.

nightgown ■ n. **1** a nightdress. **2** archaic a dressing gown.

nighthawk ■ n. North American term for NIGHT OWL.

night heron ■ n. a small short-necked heron that is active mainly at night. [Genus *Nycticorax*: several species.]

nightie ■ n. informal a nightdress.

nightingale ■ n. a small migratory thrush with drab brownish plumage, noted for its rich melodious song which can often be heard at night. [*Luscinia megarhynchos*, family Turdidae.]
– ORIGIN Old English *nihtegala*, of Germanic origin, from NIGHT + a base meaning 'sing'.

nightjar ■ n. a nocturnal insectivorous bird with grey-brown camouflaged plumage, large eyes and gape, and a distinctive call. [Family Caprimulgidae.]

nightlife ■ n. social activities or entertainment available at night.

night light ■ n. a lamp or candle providing a dim light during the night.

nightly ■ adj. **1** happening or done every night. **2** happening, done, or existing in the night. ■ adv. every night.

nightmare ■ n. **1** a frightening or unpleasant dream. **2** a very unpleasant experience or prospect.
– DERIVATIVES **nightmarish** adj. **nightmarishly** adv.
– ORIGIN Middle English: from NIGHT + Old English *mære* 'incubus'.

night owl ■ n. informal a person who is habitually active or wakeful at night.

night safe ■ n. a safe with access from the outer wall of a bank, used for deposits when the bank is closed.

night school ■ n. an institution providing evening classes.

nightshade ■ n. used in the names of a group of poisonous or narcotic plants, e.g. deadly nightshade.
– ORIGIN Old English *nihtscada*, from NIGHT + SHADE, prob. with ref. to dark and poisonous berries.

nightshirt ■ n. a long shirt worn in bed, especially by boys or men.

nightside ■ n. Astronomy the side of a planet or moon facing away from the sun and therefore in darkness.

night soil ■ n. human excrement collected at night from cesspools and privies, sometimes used as manure.

nightspot ■ n. informal a nightclub.

nightstick ■ n. N. Amer. a police officer's truncheon.

night table (also **nightstand**) ■ n. chiefly N. Amer. a small low bedside table.

night-time ■ n. the time between evening and morning.

nightwatchman ■ n. (pl. **-men**) **1** a person who guards a building at night. **2** Cricket an inferior batsman sent in to bat near the end of a day's play.

nightwear ■ n. clothing worn in bed.

nihilism /ˈnʌɪ(h)ɪlɪz(ə)m/ ■ n. **1** the rejection of all religious and moral principles, often in the belief that life is meaningless. **2** Philosophy extreme scepticism, maintaining that nothing has a real existence.
– DERIVATIVES **nihilist** n. **nihilistic** adj.
– ORIGIN C19: from Latin *nihil* 'nothing'.

-nik ■ suffix (forming nouns) denoting a person associated with a specified thing or quality: *beatnik*.
– ORIGIN from Russian and Yiddish.

Nikkei index /ˈnɪkeɪ/ (also **Nikkei average**) ■ n. a figure indicating the relative price of representative shares on the Tokyo Stock Exchange.
– ORIGIN 1970s: *Nikkei*, abbrev. of *Ni(hon) Kei(zai Shimbun)* 'Japanese Economic Journal'.

niks ■ pron. S. African informal nothing.
– ORIGIN from Afrikaans.

nil ■ n. nothing; zero. ■ adj. non-existent.
– ORIGIN C19: from Latin *nihil* 'nothing'.

nil desperandum /ˌdɛspəˈrandəm/ ■ exclam. do not despair; never despair.
– ORIGIN from Latin *nil desperandum Teucro duce* 'no need to despair with Teucer as your leader', from Horace's *Odes* 1.vii.27.

Nile green (or **Nile blue**) ■ n. a pale bluish green.
– ORIGIN C19: suggested by French *eau de Nil* (see EAU DE NIL).

Nile perch ■ n. a large predatory fish found in lakes and rivers in NE and central Africa, widely caught for food. [*Lates niloticus*.]

Nilo-Saharan /ˌnʌɪləʊsəˈhɑːrən/ ■ adj. denoting or belonging to a phylum of languages including the Nilotic family and other languages of northern and eastern Africa.

Nilotic /nʌɪˈlɒtɪk/ ■ adj. **1** of or relating to the River Nile or to the Nile region of Africa. **2** denoting or belonging to a family of languages spoken in Egypt, Sudan, Kenya, and Tanzania.
– ORIGIN via Latin from Greek *Neilōtikos*, from *Neilos* 'Nile'.

nimble ■ adj. (**-er**, **-est**) quick and light in movement or action.
– DERIVATIVES **nimbleness** n. **nimbly** adv.
– ORIGIN Old English *næmel* 'quick to seize or comprehend', rel. to *niman* 'take', of Germanic origin.

nimbostratus /ˌnɪmbə(ʊ)ˈstrɑːtəs, -ˈstreɪtəs/ ■ n. cloud forming a low thick grey layer, from which rain or snow often falls.
– ORIGIN C19: from NIMBUS + STRATUS.

nimbus /ˈnɪmbəs/ ■ n. (pl. **nimbi** /-bʌɪ/ or **nimbuses**) **1** a large grey rain cloud. **2** a luminous cloud or a halo surrounding a supernatural being or saint.
– ORIGIN C17: from Latin, 'cloud, aureole'.

Nimby /ˈnɪmbi/ ■ n. (pl. **Nimbys**) a person who objects to the siting of unpleasant developments in their neighbourhood.
– ORIGIN 1980s: acronym from *not in my back yard*.

nimrod

nimrod /ˈnɪmrɒd/ ▪ n. a skilful hunter.
– ORIGIN C16: from Hebrew *Nimrōḏ*, the name of the great-grandson of Noah, known for his skill as a hunter (see Genesis 10:8-9).

nincompoop /ˈnɪŋkəmpuːp/ ▪ n. a stupid person.
– ORIGIN C17: perhaps from the given name *Nicholas* or from *Nicodemus* (one of the Pharisees).

nine ▪ cardinal number equivalent to the product of three and three; one less than ten; 9. (Roman numeral: **ix** or **IX**.)
– PHRASES **dressed to** (or Brit. **up to**) **the nines** dressed very smartly or fancily.
– DERIVATIVES **ninefold** adj. & adv.
– ORIGIN Old English *nigon*, of Germanic origin.

9/11 (also **9-11**, **nine-eleven**) ▪ n. the day (September 11, 2001) on which hijacked airliners were flown into the World Trade Centre in New York and the Pentagon in Washington. ▸ [as modifier] denoting someone or something associated with or affected by these events.
– ORIGIN from the way the date is written in the US, in which the day is preceded by the year and the month: 2001/9/11.

ninepins ▪ pl. n. [usu. treated as sing.] the traditional form of the game of skittles, using nine pins.
– PHRASES **go down** (or **drop** or **fall**) **like ninepins** succumb in large numbers.

nineteen ▪ cardinal number one more than eighteen; nine more than ten; 19. (Roman numeral: **xix** or **XIX**.)
– DERIVATIVES **nineteenth** ordinal number.
– ORIGIN Old English *nigontȳne*.

nineteenth hole ▪ n. informal, humorous the bar in a golf clubhouse, as reached after a round of eighteen holes.

nine-to-five ▪ adj. of or involving typical office hours. ▪ n. a nine-to-five job.
– DERIVATIVES **nine-to-fiver** n.

ninety ▪ cardinal number (pl. **-ies**) equivalent to the product of nine and ten; ten less than one hundred; 90. (Roman numeral: **xc** or **XC**.)
– DERIVATIVES **ninetieth** ordinal number. **ninetyfold** adj. & adv.
– ORIGIN Old English *nigontig*.

ninja /ˈnɪndʒə/ ▪ n. a person skilled in ninjutsu.
– ORIGIN Japanese, 'spy'.

ninjutsu /nɪnˈdʒʌtsuː/ ▪ n. the traditional Japanese technique of espionage, characterized by stealth and camouflage.
– ORIGIN Japanese, from *nin* 'stealth' + *jutsu* 'art, science'.

ninny ▪ n. (pl. **-ies**) informal a foolish and weak person.
– ORIGIN C16: perhaps from **INNOCENT**.

ninon /ˈniːnɒn/ ▪ n. a lightweight silk dress fabric.
– ORIGIN C20: from French.

ninth ▪ ordinal number **1** constituting number nine in a sequence; 9th. **2** (**a ninth/one ninth**) each of nine equal parts into which something is or may be divided. **3** Music an interval spanning nine consecutive notes in a diatonic scale.
– DERIVATIVES **ninthly** adv.

niobium /nʌɪˈəʊbɪəm/ ▪ n. the chemical element of atomic number 41, a silver-grey metal used in superconducting alloys. (Symbol: **Nb**)
– ORIGIN C19: from *Niobe*, daughter of Tantalus in Greek mythology (because the element was first found in **TANTALITE**).

Nip ▪ n. informal, offensive a Japanese person.
– ORIGIN C20: abbrev. of *Nipponese*, from *Nippon* (the Japanese name for Japan).

nip[1] ▪ v. (**nipped**, **nipping**) **1** pinch, squeeze, or bite sharply. ▸ (**nip something off**) remove something by pinching or squeezing sharply. **2** (of the cold or frost) cause pain or harm to. **3** informal go quickly. **4** US informal steal or snatch. ▪ n. **1** an act of nipping. **2** a feeling of biting cold.
– PHRASES **nip something in the bud** suppress or destroy something at an early stage.
– ORIGIN Middle English: prob. of Low German or Dutch origin.

nip[2] ▪ n. a small quantity or sip of spirits. ▪ v. (**nipped**, **nipping**) take a sip of spirits.
– ORIGIN C18: prob. an abbrev. of the rare term *nipperkin* 'small measure'.

nipa /ˈniːpə, ˈnʌɪpə/ ▪ n. a palm tree with creeping roots, characteristic of mangrove swamps in India and the Pacific islands. [*Nypa fruticans*.]
– ORIGIN C16: from Malay *nīpah*.

nip and tuck ▪ adv. & adj. neck and neck. ▪ n. informal a cosmetic surgical operation.

nipper ▪ n. **1** informal a child. **2** (**nippers**) pliers, pincers, or a similar tool. **3** a creature that nips. ▸ the claw of a crab or lobster.

nipple ▪ n. **1** the small projection in which the mammary ducts of female mammals terminate and from which milk can be secreted. ▸ the corresponding vestigial structure in a male. ▸ N. Amer. the teat of a feeding bottle. **2** a small projection on a machine, especially one from which oil or other fluid is dispensed. ▸ a short section of pipe with a screw thread at each end for coupling. ▪ v. provide with a projection like a nipple.
– ORIGIN C16: perhaps a diminutive of dialect *neb* 'nose, beak'.

nippy ▪ adj. (**-ier**, **-iest**) informal **1** quick; nimble. **2** chilly.
– DERIVATIVES **nippily** adv.

niqab /nɪˈkɑːb/ ▪ n. a veil worn by some Muslim women, covering all of the face and having two holes for the eyes.
– ORIGIN Arabic *niqāb*.

nirvana /nɪəˈvɑːnə/ ▪ n. Buddhism a transcendent state in which there is no suffering or desire, and no sense of self. ▸ a state of perfect happiness.
– ORIGIN from Sanskrit *nirvāṇa*, from *nirvā* 'be extinguished', from *nis* 'out' + *vā-* 'to blow'.

nisei /ˈniːseɪ, niːˈseɪ/ ▪ n. (pl. same or **niseis**) N. Amer. an American or Canadian whose parents immigrated from Japan. Compare with **ISSEI** and **SANSEI**.
– ORIGIN 1940s: from Japanese, 'second generation'.

nisi /ˈnʌɪsʌɪ/ ▪ adj. [postpos.] Law (of a decree, order, or rule) valid or taking effect only after certain conditions are met.
– ORIGIN C19: from Latin, 'unless'.

Nissen hut /ˈnɪs(ə)n/ ▪ n. chiefly Brit. a tunnel-shaped hut of corrugated iron with a cement floor.
– ORIGIN C20: after the British engineer Peter N. *Nissen*.

nit ▪ n. informal **1** the egg or young form of a louse or other parasitic insect, especially the egg of a human head louse. **2** Brit. a stupid person.
– DERIVATIVES **nitty** adj.
– ORIGIN Old English, of West Germanic origin.

niter ▪ n. US spelling of **NITRE**.

nitinol /ˈnɪtɪnɒl/ ▪ n. an alloy of nickel and titanium.
– ORIGIN 1960s: from the chemical symbols **NI** and **TI** + the initial letters of *Naval Ordnance Laboratory* (in Maryland, US).

nit-picking ▪ n. informal fussy or pedantic fault-finding.
– DERIVATIVES **nit-pick** v. **nit-picker** n.

nitrate Chemistry ▪ n. /ˈnʌɪtreɪt/ a salt or ester of nitric acid. ▪ v. /nʌɪˈtreɪt/ treat with nitric acid, especially so as to introduce the group -NO$_2$.
– DERIVATIVES **nitration** n.
– ORIGIN C18: from French (see **NITRE**).

nitrazepam /nʌɪˈtreɪzɪpam, -ˈtrazə-/ ▪ n. Medicine a short-acting drug used to treat insomnia.
– ORIGIN 1960s: from *nitr(o)* + *az(o)-* + *ep(ine)* + *am(ide)*.

nitre /ˈnʌɪtə/ (US **niter**) ▪ n. potassium nitrate; saltpetre.
– ORIGIN Middle English: from Latin *nitrum*, from Greek *nitron*.

nitric acid ▪ n. Chemistry a colourless or pale yellow acid with strong corrosive and oxidizing properties. [HNO$_3$.]

nitric oxide ▪ n. Chemistry a colourless toxic gas made by reduction of nitric acid, reacting immediately with oxygen to form nitrogen dioxide. [NO.]

nitride /ˈnʌɪtrʌɪd/ ▪ n. Chemistry a compound of nitrogen with another element or group.

nitrify /ˈnʌɪtrɪfʌɪ/ ▪ v. (**-ies**, **-ied**) Chemistry convert (ammonia or another nitrogen compound) into nitrites or nitrates.
– DERIVATIVES **nitrification** n.
– ORIGIN C19: from French *nitrifier*.

nitrile /ˈnʌɪtrʌɪl/ ▪ n. Chemistry an organic compound

containing a cyanide group -CN bound to an alkyl group.
– ORIGIN C19: from **NITRE**.

nitrite /'nʌɪtrʌɪt/ ■ n. Chemistry a salt or ester of nitrous acid.

nitro ■ n. short for **NITROGLYCERINE**.

nitro- /'nʌɪtrəʊ/ ■ comb. form **1** of or containing nitric acid, nitrates, or nitrogen: *nitrogenous*. **2** Chemistry containing the group -NO₂: *nitrobenzene*.

nitrobenzene ■ n. Chemistry a yellow oily liquid made by nitrating benzene, used in chemical synthesis.

nitrocellulose ■ n. Chemistry a highly flammable material made by treating cellulose with concentrated nitric acid, used to make explosives and celluloid.

nitrogen /'nʌɪtrədʒ(ə)n/ ■ n. the chemical element of atomic number 7, a colourless, odourless unreactive gas that forms about 78 per cent of the earth's atmosphere. (Symbol: **N**)
– DERIVATIVES **nitrogenous** adj.
– ORIGIN C18: from French *nitrogène* (see **NITRO-**, **-GEN**).

nitrogen cycle ■ n. Ecology the series of processes by which nitrogen and its compounds are interconverted in the environment and in living organisms.

nitrogen dioxide ■ n. Chemistry a reddish-brown poisonous gas formed when many metals dissolve in nitric acid. [NO₂.]

nitrogen fixation ■ n. Biology the chemical processes by which atmospheric nitrogen is assimilated into organic compounds, especially by certain micro-organisms as part of the nitrogen cycle.

nitrogen narcosis ■ n. Medicine a drowsy state induced by breathing air under pressure, e.g. in deep-sea diving.

nitroglycerine (also **nitroglycerin**) ■ n. an explosive yellow liquid made by nitrating glycerol, used in dynamite.

nitrosamine /nʌɪ'trəʊsəmiːn/ ■ n. Chemistry a compound containing the group =NNO attached to two organic groups.
– ORIGIN C19: from *nitroso-* (relating to nitric oxide in combination) + **AMINE**.

nitrous /'nʌɪtrəs/ ■ adj. of or containing nitrogen.
– ORIGIN C17: from Latin *nitrosus* 'nitrous'.

nitrous acid ■ n. Chemistry an unstable, weak acid made by the action of acids on nitrites. [HNO₂.]

nitrous oxide ■ n. Chemistry a colourless gas with a sweetish odour which produces exhilaration or anaesthesia when inhaled and is used as an anaesthetic. [N₂O.]

nitty-gritty ■ n. informal the most important aspects or practical details of a matter.
– ORIGIN 1960s.

nitwit ■ n. informal a silly or foolish person.
– DERIVATIVES **nitwitted** adj. **nitwittedness** n. **nitwittery** n.
– ORIGIN C20: apparently from **NIT** + **WIT**¹.

NIV ■ abbrev. New International Version (of the Bible).

nival /'nʌɪv(ə)l/ ■ adj. of or relating to regions of perpetual snow.
– ORIGIN C17: from Latin *nivalis*, from *nix*, *niv-* 'snow'.

nix informal ■ pron. (S. African also **niks**) nothing. ■ exclam. expressing denial or refusal. ■ v. put an end to; cancel: *he nixed the deal.*
– ORIGIN C18: from German, var. of *nichts* 'nothing'.

Nizari /nɪ'zɑːri/ ■ n. a member of an Ismaili Muslim sect led by the Aga Khan.
– ORIGIN named after the C12 Egyptian Ismaili imam *Nizar*.

Nkosi sikelel' iAfrika /(ə)n'kɔːsi sɪkəl'ɛːli 'ɑːfrɪkʌ/ ■ n. the South African national anthem. ▸ a hymn beginning *Nkosi sikelel' iAfrika* (God bless Africa), adopted as an anthem by the African National Congress and some African countries.
– ORIGIN isiXhosa, 'God bless Africa'.

nm ■ abbrev. **1** nanometre. **2** (also **n.m.**) nautical mile.

NMR ■ abbrev. Physics nuclear magnetic resonance.

NNE ■ abbrev. north-north-east.

NNP ■ abbrev. (in South Africa) New National Party.

NNW ■ abbrev. north-north-west.

No ■ symb. the chemical element nobelium.

No. ■ abbrev. **1** US North. **2** (also **no.**) number. [from Latin *numero*, ablative of *numerus*.]

no ■ det. **1** not any. **2** quite the opposite of: *it was no easy task.* **3** hardly any. ■ exclam. used to give a negative response. ■ adv. **1** [with comparative] not at all: *they were no more able to do it than I was.* **2** Scottish not. ■ n. (pl. **noes**) a negative answer or decision, especially in voting.
– PHRASES **no can do** informal I am unable to do it. **no longer** not now as formerly. **no place** N. Amer. nowhere. **no through road** an indication that passage along a street is blocked or prohibited. **not take no for an answer** persist in spite of refusals. **no two ways about it** no possible doubt about something. **no way** informal under no circumstances; not at all. **no worries** informal, chiefly Austral. all right; fine. **or no** or not.
– ORIGIN Old English *nō*, *nā* (adv.), from *ne* 'not' + *ō*, *ā* 'ever'.

n.o. ■ abbrev. Cricket not out.

no-account ■ adj. informal, chiefly N. Amer. unimportant or worthless.

nob¹ ■ n. Brit. informal a person of wealth or high social position.
– DERIVATIVES **nobby** adj.
– ORIGIN C17 (orig. Scots as *knab*).

nob² ■ n. informal a person's head.
– ORIGIN C17: a var. of **KNOB**.

no-ball Cricket ■ n. an unlawfully delivered ball, counting as an extra run to the batting side if not scored from. ■ v. (of an umpire) declare (a bowler) to have bowled a no-ball.

nobble ■ v. informal, chiefly Brit. **1** try to influence or thwart by underhand or unfair methods. ▸ tamper with (a racehorse) to prevent it from winning a race. **2** accost (someone). **3** obtain dishonestly; steal. ▸ seize.
– ORIGIN C19: prob. a var. of dialect *knobble*, *knubble* 'knock, strike with the knuckles'.

nobbler ■ n. Brit. informal a person who nobbles someone or something.

Nobelist /nəʊ'bɛlɪst/ ■ n. chiefly N. Amer. a winner of a Nobel Prize.

nobelium /nə(ʊ)'biːlɪəm, -'bɛl-/ ■ n. the chemical element of atomic number 102, an artificial radioactive metal of the actinide series. (Symbol: **No**)
– ORIGIN 1950s: from the name of Alfred *Nobel*.

Nobel Prize ■ n. any of six international prizes awarded annually for outstanding work in physics, chemistry, physiology or medicine, literature, economics, and the promotion of peace.
– ORIGIN named after the C19 Swedish chemist and engineer Alfred *Nobel*, who endowed the prizes.

nobility ■ n. (pl. **-ies**) **1** the quality of being noble. **2** the aristocracy.

noble ■ adj. (**-er**, **-est**) **1** belonging by rank, title, or birth to the aristocracy. **2** having fine personal qualities or high moral principles. **3** imposing; magnificent. ■ n.
1 (especially in former times) a person of noble rank or birth. **2** historical a former English gold coin.
– DERIVATIVES **nobleness** n. **nobly** adv.
– ORIGIN Middle English: from Latin (*g*)*nobilis* 'noted, high-born'.

noble gas ■ n. Chemistry any of the gaseous elements helium, neon, argon, krypton, xenon, and radon, which form compounds with difficulty or not at all.

nobleman (or **noblewoman**) ■ n. (pl. **-men** or **-women**) a man (or woman) who belongs to the aristocracy; a peer (or peeress).

noble metal ■ n. Chemistry a metal (e.g. gold, silver, or platinum) that resists attack by acids and other reagents and does not corrode.

noble rot ■ n. a grey mould (*Botrytis cinerea*) cultivated on grapes in order to perfect certain wines.
– ORIGIN 1930s: translation of French *pourriture noble*.

noble savage ■ n. a representative of primitive mankind as idealized in Romantic literature.

noblesse /nəʊ'blɛs/ ■ n. the nobility of a foreign country.
– PHRASES **noblesse oblige** /ɒ'bliːʒ/ privilege entails responsibility.
– ORIGIN French, 'nobility'.

nobody

nobody ■ pron. no person; no one. ■ n. (pl. **-ies**) a person of no importance or authority.
– ORIGIN Middle English: orig. as *no body*.

no-brainer ■ n. informal something that involves little or no mental effort.

nock ■ n. Archery a notch at either end of a bow or at the end of an arrow, for receiving the bowstring. ■ v. fit (an arrow) to the bowstring.
– ORIGIN Middle English: perhaps from Middle Dutch *nocke* 'point, tip'.

no-claim bonus (Brit. **no-claims bonus**) ■ n. a reduction in an insurance premium when no claim has been made during an agreed preceding period.

noctuid /'nɒktjuɪd/ ■ n. Entomology a moth of a large family (Noctuidae), whose members typically have pale or colourful hindwings.
– ORIGIN C19: from Latin *noctua* 'night owl'.

nocturnal ■ adj. done, occurring, or active at night.
– DERIVATIVES **nocturnally** adv.
– ORIGIN C15: from late Latin *nocturnalis*, from Latin *nox, noct-* 'night'.

nocturnal emission ■ n. an involuntary ejaculation of semen during sleep.

nocturne /'nɒktəːn/ ■ n. **1** Music a short composition of a romantic nature. **2** Art a picture of a night scene.
– ORIGIN C19: French, from Latin *nocturnus* 'of the night'.

nocuous /'nɒkjʊəs/ ■ adj. poetic/literary noxious.
– ORIGIN C17: from Latin *nocuus*, from *nocere* 'to hurt'.

nod ■ v. (**nodded, nodding**) **1** lower and raise one's head slightly and briefly, especially in greeting, assent, or understanding, or as a signal. ▸ signify or express in this way: *he nodded his consent*. ▸ move one's head up and down repeatedly. **2** let one's head fall forward when drowsy or asleep. ▸ (**nod off**) informal fall asleep. **3** (**nod something through**) informal approve something by general agreement and without discussion. ■ n. an act of nodding. ▸ a gesture of acknowledgement or concession.
– PHRASES **a nodding acquaintance** a slight acquaintance. **be on nodding terms** know someone slightly. **give someone/thing the nod 1** select or approve someone or something. **2** give someone a signal. **on the nod** Brit. informal by general agreement and without discussion.
– ORIGIN Middle English: perhaps of Low German origin.

noddle ■ n. informal, dated a person's head.
– ORIGIN Middle English.

noddy ■ n. (pl. **-ies**) **1** dated a silly or foolish person. **2** a tropical tern with mainly dark-coloured plumage. [Genera *Anous* and *Procelsterna*.]
– ORIGIN prob. from **NOD**; in sense 2 perhaps with ref. to the birds' nodding during courtship.

node ■ n. technical **1** a point in a network at which lines intersect or branch. ▸ a piece of equipment, such as a computer or peripheral, attached to a network. **2** Botany the part of a plant stem from which one or more leaves emerge. **3** Anatomy a lymph node or other structure consisting of a small mass of differentiated tissue. **4** Physics & Mathematics a point at which the amplitude of vibration in a standing wave system is zero. ▸ a point of zero current or voltage.
– DERIVATIVES **nodal** adj. **nodical** adj.
– ORIGIN Middle English: from Latin *nodus* 'knot'.

node of Ranvier /'rɑːnvɪeɪ/ ■ n. Anatomy a gap in the myelin sheath of a nerve, between adjacent Schwann cells.
– ORIGIN C19: named after the French histologist Louis Antoine *Ranvier*.

nodose /'nəʊdəʊs/ ■ adj. technical characterized by hard or tight lumps; knotty.
– DERIVATIVES **nodosity** n.
– ORIGIN C18: from Latin *nodosus*.

nodule ■ n. **1** a small swelling or aggregation of cells, especially an abnormal one. **2** (usu. **root nodule**) a swelling on a root of a leguminous plant, containing nitrogen-fixing bacteria. **3** a small rounded lump of matter distinct from its surroundings.
– DERIVATIVES **nodular** adj. **nodulated** adj. **nodulation** n. **nodulose** adj. **nodulous** adj.

– ORIGIN Middle English: from Latin *nodulus*, diminutive of *nodus* 'knot'.

Noel (also **Noël**) ■ n. Christmas, especially as a refrain in carols and on Christmas cards.
– ORIGIN C19: French *Noël*, from Latin *natalis* (see **NATAL**[1]).

nogal /'nɒxal/ ■ adv. S. African informal moreover; what is more.
– ORIGIN from Afrikaans, 'fairly, rather'.

noggin ■ n. informal **1** a person's head. **2** a small quantity of alcoholic drink, typically a quarter of a pint.
– ORIGIN C17.

no-go area ■ n. an area to which entry is dangerous, impossible, or forbidden.

Noh /nəʊ/ (also **No**) ■ n. traditional Japanese masked drama with dance and song, evolved from Shinto rites.
– ORIGIN from Japanese.

no-hitter ■ n. Baseball a game in which a pitcher yields no hits to the opposing team.

no-hoper ■ n. informal a person who is not expected to be successful.

nohow ■ adv. informal, chiefly US used to emphasize a negative.

noise ■ n. **1** a sound, especially one that is loud, unpleasant, or disturbing. ▸ continuous or repeated loud, confused sounds. **2** (**noises**) conventional remarks expressing some emotion or purpose: *the government is making the right noises*. **3** technical irregular fluctuations accompanying and tending to obscure an electrical signal or other significant phenomenon. ■ v. **1** (usu. **be noised about**) dated talk about or make known publicly. **2** poetic/literary make much noise.
– PHRASES **make a noise** speak or act in a way designed to attract attention. **noises off 1** sounds made offstage to be heard by the audience of a play. **2** distracting or intrusive background noise.
– DERIVATIVES **noiseless** adj. **noiselessly** adv. **noiselessness** n.
– ORIGIN Middle English: from Latin *nausea* (see **NAUSEA**).

noisette /nwʌ'zɛt/ ■ n. **1** a small round piece of meat, especially lamb. **2** a chocolate made with hazelnuts.
– ORIGIN C19: French, diminutive of *noix* 'nut'.

noisome /'nɔɪs(ə)m/ ■ adj. poetic/literary having an extremely offensive smell. ▸ disagreeable; unpleasant.
– DERIVATIVES **noisomeness** n.
– ORIGIN Middle English: from obsolete *noy* (shortened form of **ANNOY**) + -**SOME**[1].

noisy ■ adj. (**-ier, -iest**) **1** full of or making a lot of noise. **2** technical accompanied by random fluctuations that obscure information.
– DERIVATIVES **noisily** adv. **noisiness** n.

nolle prosequi /ˌnɒlɪ 'prɒsɪkwʌɪ/ ■ n. Law a formal notice of abandonment by a public prosecutor of all or part of a suit, required before a private prosecution can be instituted.
– ORIGIN Latin, 'refuse to pursue'.

Nollywood ■ n. informal the Nigerian film industry.
– ORIGIN on the pattern of *Bollywood*.

nom. ■ abbrev. nominal.

nomad ■ n. a member of a people continually moving to find fresh pasture for its animals and having no permanent home. ▸ a wanderer.
– DERIVATIVES **nomadic** adj. **nomadically** adv. **nomadism** n.
– ORIGIN C16: from French *nomade*, from Greek *nomas*, from *nemein* 'to pasture'.

no-man's-land ■ n. **1** disputed ground between two opposing armies. **2** a piece of unowned land or wasteland.

nom de guerre /ˌnɒm də 'gɛː/ ■ n. (pl. **noms de guerre** pronunc. same) an assumed name under which a person engages in combat.
– ORIGIN French, 'war name'.

nom de plume /ˌnɒm də 'pluːm/ ■ n. (pl. **noms de plume** pronunc. same) a pen name.
– ORIGIN C19: formed from French, on the pattern of *nom de guerre*.

nomenclature /nə(ʊ)'mɛŋklətʃə, 'nəʊmən,kleɪtʃə/ ■ n. the selecting of names for things in a particular field.

▶ a body or system of names. ▶ formal the term or terms applied to someone or something.
– DERIVATIVES **nomenclator** n. **nomenclatural** /-ˈklatʃ(ə)r(ə)l, -kləˈtʃʊər(ə)l/ adj.
– ORIGIN C17: from Latin *nomenclatura*, from *nomen* 'name' + *clatura* 'calling, summoning', from *calare* 'to call'.

nomenklatura /ˌnɒˌmɛnkləˈtjʊərə/ ■ n. often ironic or derogatory governing party appointees to influential public positions, regarded collectively.
– ORIGIN Russian, from Latin *nomenclatura* (see NOMENCLATURE).

nominal ■ adj. 1 existing in name only. ▶ relating to or consisting of names. 2 Grammar headed by or having the function of a noun. 3 (of a sum of money) very small; far below the real value or cost: *a nominal fee.* 4 (of a quantity or dimension) stated but not necessarily corresponding exactly to the real value. 5 informal functioning normally or acceptably.
– DERIVATIVES **nominally** adv.
– ORIGIN C15: from Latin *nominalis*, from *nomen* 'name'.

nominal definition ■ n. Logic a definition that describes something sufficiently to distinguish it from other things, but without describing its essence.

nominalism ■ n. Philosophy the doctrine that universals or general ideas are mere names without any corresponding reality. Often contrasted with REALISM (sense 3).
– DERIVATIVES **nominalist** n. **nominalistic** adj.

nominalize (also -ise) ■ v. Grammar form a noun from (a verb or adjective), e.g. *output, truth,* from *put out, true.*
– DERIVATIVES **nominalization** (also -isation) n.

nominal value ■ n. Economics the value stated on a coin, note, etc.; face value.

nominate ■ v. 1 put forward as a candidate for election or for an honour or award. ▶ appoint to a job or position. 2 specify formally.
– DERIVATIVES **nomination** n. **nominator** n.
– ORIGIN Middle English: from Latin *nominare* 'to name', from *nomen* 'a name'.

nominative /ˈnɒmɪnətɪv/ ■ adj. 1 Grammar denoting a case of nouns, pronouns, and adjectives expressing the subject of a verb. 2 /ˈnɒmɪˌneɪtɪv/ of or appointed by nomination as distinct from election. ■ n. Grammar a word in the nominative case.
– ORIGIN Middle English: from Latin *nominativus*, translating Greek *onomastikē* ⟨*ptōsis*⟩ 'naming (case)'.

nominee ■ n. 1 a person who is nominated. 2 a person or company, not the owner, in whose name a company, stock, etc. is registered.

nomothetic /ˌnɒməˈθɛtɪk, ˌnəʊm-/ ■ adj. of or relating to general scientific laws.
– ORIGIN C17: from obsolete *nomothete* 'legislator', from Greek *nomothetēs*.

-nomy ■ comb. form denoting a specified area of knowledge or its laws: *astronomy.*
– ORIGIN from Greek *-nomia*; rel. to *nomos* 'law' and *nemein* 'distribute'.

non- ■ prefix expressing negation or absence: *non-recognition.* ▶ not of the kind or class described: *non-believer.* ▶ expressing a neutral negative sense where *in-* or *un-* has a special connotation (such as *non-human* compared with *inhuman*).
– ORIGIN from Latin *non* 'not'.

nona- /ˈnɒnə, ˈnəʊnə/ ■ comb. form nine; having nine: *nonagon.*
– ORIGIN from Latin *nonus* 'ninth'.

nonage /ˈnəʊnɪdʒ, ˈnɒn-/ ■ n. formal the period of immaturity or youth.
– ORIGIN Middle English: from Old French *nonage*, from *non-* 'non-' + *age* 'age'.

nonagenarian /ˌnɒnədʒɪˈnɛːrɪən, ˌnəʊn-/ ■ n. a person between 90 and 99 years old.
– ORIGIN C19: from Latin *nonagenarius*, from *nonaginta* 'ninety'.

nonagon /ˈnɒnəg(ə)n/ ■ n. a plane figure with nine straight sides and angles.
– DERIVATIVES **nonagonal** adj.
– ORIGIN C17: from Latin *nonus* 'ninth', on the pattern of *hexagon*.

non-alcoholic ■ adj. (of a drink) not containing alcohol.

non-aligned ■ adj. (chiefly during the cold war) of or denoting countries pursuing a policy of neutrality towards the superpowers.
– DERIVATIVES **non-alignment** n.

non-allergenic ■ adj. not causing an allergic reaction.

non-allergic ■ adj. another term for NON-ALLERGENIC.

non-attributable ■ adj. not able to be attributed to a particular source or cause.
– DERIVATIVES **non-attributably** adv.

non-being ■ n. the state of not being; non-existence.

non-believer ■ n. a person who does not believe in something, especially one who has no religious faith.

non-belligerent ■ adj. not engaged in a war or conflict. ■ n. a non-belligerent nation or person.
– DERIVATIVES **non-belligerence** n.

non-black ■ adj. denoting or relating to a person who is not black or whose origin is not predominantly African. ■ n. a non-black person.

non-capital ■ adj. Law (of an offence) not punishable by death.

nonce[1] /nɒns/ ■ adj. denoting a word or expression coined for one occasion.
– PHRASES **for the nonce** for the present; temporarily.
– ORIGIN Middle English: from *then anes* 'the one (purpose)', from *then,* obsolete oblique form of THE + *ane* 'one' + -s[3].

nonce[2] /nɒns/ ■ n. Brit. informal a sexual deviant, especially a child molester.
– ORIGIN 1970s (orig. prison slang).

nonchalant /ˈnɒnʃ(ə)l(ə)nt/ ■ adj. casually calm and relaxed.
– DERIVATIVES **nonchalance** n. **nonchalantly** adv.
– ORIGIN C18: from French, 'not being concerned', from *nonchaloir*.

non-combatant ■ n. a person who is not engaged in fighting during a war, especially a civilian, army chaplain, or army doctor.

non-commissioned ■ adj. (of an officer in the army, navy, or air force) not holding a rank conferred by a commission.

non-committal ■ adj. not displaying commitment to a definite opinion or policy.
– DERIVATIVES **non-committally** adv.

non-communicant ■ n. Christian Church a person who does not receive Holy Communion.

non compos mentis /ˌnɒn ˌkɒmpɒs ˈmɛntɪs/ ■ adj. not in one's right mind.
– ORIGIN Latin, 'not having control of one's mind'.

non-conductor ■ n. a substance that does not conduct heat or electricity.
– DERIVATIVES **non-conducting** adj.

nonconformist ■ n. a person who does not conform to prevailing ideas or established practice.
▶ (**Non-conformist**) a member of a Protestant Church which dissents from the established Church of England. ■ adj. not conforming to prevailing ideas or established practice.
– DERIVATIVES **nonconformism** n. **nonconformity** n.

non-contributory ■ adj. 1 (of a pension or medical aid) funded by regular payments by the employer, not the employee. 2 (of a state benefit) paid irrespective of taxes or other contributions made by recipients.

non-controversial ■ adj. not controversial (less forceful in meaning than uncontroversial).

non-cooperation ■ n. failure to cooperate, especially as a form of protest.

non-delivery ■ n. chiefly Law failure to provide or deliver goods.

non-denominational ■ adj. open or acceptable to people of any Christian denomination.

nondescript /ˈnɒndɪskrɪpt/ ■ adj. lacking distinctive or

interesting characteristics. ■ n. a nondescript person or thing.
– DERIVATIVES **nondescriptly** adv. **nondescriptness** n.
– ORIGIN C17: from NON- + obsolete *descript* 'described, engraved'.

non-destructive ■ adj. technical (chiefly of methods of testing) not involving damage to the specimen.

non-disjunction ■ n. Genetics failure of a pair of homologous chromosomes to separate normally during nuclear division.

non-drinker ■ n. a person who does not drink alcohol.

non-drip ■ adj. (of paint) formulated so that it does not drip when wet.

none[1] /nʌn/ ■ pron. not any. ▸ no person; no one. ■ adv. (**none the**) [with comparative] by no amount; not at all.
– PHRASES **none other than** used to emphasize the surprising identity of a person or thing. **will have** (or **want**) **none of something** refuse to approve or take part in something.
– ORIGIN Old English *nān*, from *ne* 'not' + *ān* 'one', of Germanic origin.

none[2] /nəʊn/ (also **nones**) ■ n. a service forming part of the Divine Office of the Western Christian Church, traditionally said at the ninth hour of the day (3 p.m.).
– ORIGIN C19: from Latin *nona*, from *nonus* 'ninth'.

nonentity /nɒˈnɛntɪti/ ■ n. (pl. -**ies**) **1** an unimportant person or thing. **2** non-existence.
– ORIGIN C16: from medieval Latin *nonentitas* 'non-existence'.

nones /nəʊnz/ ■ pl. n. **1** (in the ancient Roman calendar) the ninth day before the ides by inclusive reckoning, i.e. the 7th day of March, May, July, October, the 5th of other months. **2** variant spelling of NONE[2].
– ORIGIN from Latin *nonas*, from *nonus* 'ninth'.

non-essential ■ adj. not absolutely necessary. ■ n. a non-essential thing.

nonesuch ■ n. variant spelling of NONSUCH.

nonetheless (also **none the less**) ■ adv. in spite of that; nevertheless.

non-Euclidean ■ adj. denoting systems of geometry that do not obey Euclidean postulates, especially that only one line through a given point can be parallel to a given line.

non-European ■ adj. **1** not in, from, or related to Europe. **2** dated, chiefly S. African relating to a person whose origins are not European or who is not white. ■ n. a person who is not of European origin.

non-event ■ n. an unexpectedly insignificant or uninteresting occasion. ▸ an event that did not happen.

non-existent ■ adj. not existing or not real or present.
– DERIVATIVES **non-existence** n.

non-ferrous ■ adj. relating to or denoting a metal other than iron or steel.

non-fiction ■ n. prose writing that is informative or factual rather than fictional.
– DERIVATIVES **non-fictional** adj.

non-figurative ■ adj. Art abstract.

non-finite ■ adj. **1** not limited in size or extent. **2** Grammar (of a verb form) not limited by tense, person, or number.

non-flammable ■ adj. not catching fire easily.

non-fulfilment ■ n. failure to fulfil or carry out something.

non-functional ■ adj. **1** having no function. **2** not in working order.

non-governmental ■ adj. not belonging to or associated with any government.

non-Hodgkin's lymphoma ■ n. Medicine a form of malignant lymphoma differing from Hodgkin's disease only by the absence of characteristic giant cells.

non-human ■ adj. not human.

non-infectious ■ adj. **1** (of a disease) not liable to be transmitted through the environment. **2** not liable to spread infection.

non-inflammable ■ adj. not catching fire easily.

non-interference ■ n. failure or refusal to intervene without invitation or necessity.

non-intervention ■ n. the policy of not becoming involved in the affairs of others.
– DERIVATIVES **non-interventionism** n. **non-interventionist** adj. & n.

non-invasive ■ adj. **1** (of medical procedures) not involving the introduction of instruments into the body. **2** (chiefly of disease) not tending to spread undesirably.

non-judgemental ■ adj. avoiding moral judgements.

non-linear ■ adj. **1** not linear. **2** Mathematics designating or involving an equation including terms not of the first degree.
– DERIVATIVES **non-linearity** n. **non-linearly** adv.

non-logical ■ adj. not according to the rules of logic (less forceful in meaning than illogical).

non-member ■ n. a person, country, etc. that is not a member of a particular organization.
– DERIVATIVES **non-membership** n.

non-metal ■ n. an element or substance that is not a metal.
– DERIVATIVES **non-metallic** adj.

non-moral ■ adj. not holding or manifesting moral principles.

non-native ■ adj. **1** not native to a particular place. **2** (of a speaker) not having spoken the language in question from earliest childhood.

non-natural ■ adj. not produced by or involving natural processes. ▸ Philosophy existing but not part of the natural world.

non-negative ■ adj. Mathematics either positive or equal to zero.

non-negotiable ■ adj. **1** not open to discussion or modification. **2** not able to be transferred or assigned to the legal ownership of another person.

no-no ■ n. (pl. -**os**) informal a thing that is not possible or acceptable.

non-objective ■ adj. **1** not objective. **2** Art abstract.

non-observance ■ n. failure to observe an obligation, rule, or custom.

no-nonsense ■ adj. simple and straightforward; sensible.

non-operational ■ adj. **1** not involving active duties. **2** not working or in use.

nonpareil /ˌnɒnpəˈreɪl/ ■ adj. unrivalled. ■ n. an unrivalled person or thing.
– ORIGIN Middle English: from French, from *non-* 'not' + *pareil* 'equal'.

non-person ■ n. a person regarded as non-existent or unimportant, or as having no rights.

nonplus /nɒnˈplʌs/ ■ v. (**nonplussed**, **nonplussing**) **1** (usu. **be nonplussed**) surprise and confuse; flummox. **2** [as adj. **nonplussed**] N. Amer. informal unperturbed.
– ORIGIN C16: from Latin *non plus* 'not more'.

non-prescription ■ adj. of or denoting medicines available for sale without a prescription.

non-productive ■ adj. not producing or able to produce (tending to be less forceful in meaning than unproductive).
– DERIVATIVES **non-productively** adv.

non-professional ■ adj. not professional. ■ n. a non-professional person.

non-profit ■ adj. not making or intended to make a profit.

non-proliferation ■ n. the prevention of an increase or spread of something, especially possession of nuclear weapons.

non-proprietary ■ adj. not registered or protected as a trademark or restricted to one manufacturer.

non-resident ■ adj. **1** not living in a particular country or a place of work. ▸ (of a job or course) not requiring residence at the place of work or instruction. **2** Computing (of software) not kept permanently in memory. ■ n. a person not living in a particular place.
– DERIVATIVES **non-residence** n.

non-residential ■ adj. **1** not requiring or providing facilities for people to live on the premises. **2** containing or suitable for commercial premises rather than private houses.

non-resistance ■ n. the policy of not resisting authority.

non-restrictive ■ adj. **1** not involving restrictions or limitations. **2** Grammar (of a clause or phrase) giving additional information about a noun phrase whose particular reference has already been specified.

non-return ■ adj. permitting the flow of air or liquid in one direction only.

non-returnable ■ adj. **1** (especially of a deposit) not repayable in any circumstances. **2** (of bottles) not intended to be returned empty to the suppliers.

non-rigid ■ adj. not rigid. ▸ denoting an airship whose shape is maintained solely by the pressure of the gas inside.

non-scientific ■ adj. not involving or relating to science or scientific methods.
– DERIVATIVES **non-scientist** n.

nonsense ■ n. **1** words that make no sense. **2** foolish or unacceptable behaviour. ▸ an absurd or unthinkable scheme, situation, etc.
– PHRASES **make (a) nonsense of** reduce the value or relevance of (something) to a ridiculous degree.

nonsensical /nɒnˈsɛnsɪk(ə)l/ ■ adj. **1** having no meaning; making no sense. **2** ridiculously impractical or ill-advised.
– DERIVATIVES **nonsensicality** n. **nonsensically** adv.

non sequitur /nɒn ˈsɛkwɪtə/ ■ n. a conclusion or statement that does not logically follow from the previous argument or statement.
– ORIGIN Latin, 'it does not follow'.

non-smoker ■ n. a person who does not smoke tobacco.
– DERIVATIVES **non-smoking** adj.

non-specific ■ adj. not specific. ▸ Medicine not assignable to a particular cause, condition, or category.

non-specific urethritis ■ n. Medicine urethritis due to infection by chlamydiae or other organisms (other than gonococci).

non-standard ■ adj. not average, normal, or usual. ▸ (of language) not of the form that is accepted as standard.

non-starter ■ n. **1** a person or animal that fails to take part in a race. **2** informal something that has no chance of succeeding or being effective.

non-stick ■ adj. (of a pan or surface) covered with a substance that prevents food sticking to it during cooking.

non-stop ■ adj. continuing without stopping or pausing. ▸ (of a passenger vehicle or journey) having no intermediate stops on the way to a destination. ■ adv. without stopping or pausing. ■ n. a non-stop flight or train.

nonsuch /ˈnɒnsʌtʃ/ (also **nonesuch**) ■ n. archaic a person or thing regarded as perfect or excellent.
– ORIGIN C17: coined on the pattern of *nonpareil*.

nonsuit Law ■ v. subject (a plaintiff) to the stoppage of their suit on the grounds of failure to make a legal case or bring sufficient evidence. ■ n. the stoppage of a suit on such grounds.

non-technical ■ adj. not relating to or involving science or technology. ▸ not using technical terms or requiring specialized knowledge.

non-transferable ■ adj. not able to be transferred to the possession of another person.

non-U ■ adj. informal, chiefly Brit. (of language or social behaviour) not characteristic of the upper social classes.

non-uniform ■ adj. not uniform; varying.
– DERIVATIVES **non-uniformity** n. **non-uniformly** adv.

non-union ■ adj. not belonging to or connected with a trade union.

non-use ■ n. the refusal or failure to use something.
– DERIVATIVES **non-usage** n. **non-user** n.

non-venomous ■ adj. of or relating to an animal that does not secrete venom.

non-verbal ■ adj. not involving or using words or speech.
– DERIVATIVES **non-verbally** adv.

non-violent ■ adj. (especially of political or social opposition) not using violence.
– DERIVATIVES **non-violence** n. **non-violently** adv.

non-white ■ adj. denoting or relating to a person who is not white or whose origin is not predominantly European. ■ n. a non-white person.

non-word ■ n. a group of letters or speech sounds that looks or sounds like a word but is not accepted as such by native speakers.

noodle¹ ■ n. (usu. **noodles**) a very thin, long strip of pasta or a similar flour paste.
– ORIGIN C18: from German *Nudel*.

noodle² ■ n. informal **1** a stupid or silly person. **2** a person's head.
– ORIGIN C18.

Nooitgedacht pony /ˈnɔɪtxədɑːxt/ ■ n. S. African a horse of a small sturdy breed that is a cross between the Basotho pony and the Boerperd, known for its hardiness.
– ORIGIN named after the *Nooitgedacht* breeding station near Ermelo, Mpumalanga.

nook ■ n. a corner or recess, especially one offering seclusion or security.
– PHRASES **every nook and cranny** every part of something.
– ORIGIN Middle English.

nooky (also **nookie**) ■ n. informal sexual activity or intercourse.
– ORIGIN C20: perhaps from **NOOK**.

noon ■ n. twelve o'clock in the day; midday.
– ORIGIN Old English *nōn* 'the ninth hour from sunrise, i.e. approximately 3 p.m.', from Latin *nona (hora)* 'ninth (hour)'.

noonday ■ n. the middle of the day.

no one ■ pron. no person; not a single person.

noontide (also **noontime**) ■ n. poetic/literary noon.

noors /nʊərs/ (also **noorsdoring**) ■ S. African a southern African plant of the euphorbia family characterized by milky latex. [Genus *Euphorbia*: numerous species.]
– ORIGIN from Afrikaans, abbrev. of S. African Dutch *noorsedoorn*, from Dutch *norsch* 'gruff, disagreeable' + *doorn* 'thorn'.

noose ■ n. a loop with a running knot which tightens as the rope or wire is pulled, used especially to hang offenders or trap animals. ■ v. apply a noose to; catch with a noose. ▸ form (a rope) into a noose.
– PHRASES **put one's head in a noose** bring about one's own downfall.
– ORIGIN Middle English: prob. via Old French *no(u)s* from Latin *nodus* 'knot'.

nope ■ exclam. informal variant of **NO**.

nor ■ conj. & adv. **1** and not; and not either: *they were neither cheap nor convenient.* ▸ neither: *nor can I.* **2** archaic or dialect than. ■ n. (**NOR**) Electronics **1** a logical operation which gives the value one if and only if all the operands have a value of zero, and otherwise has a value of zero. **2** [as modifier] denoting a gate circuit which produces an output only when there are no signals on any of the input connections.
– ORIGIN Middle English: from Old English *nother* 'neither'.

nor' ■ abbrev. (especially in compounds) north: *nor'west*.

nor- ■ prefix Chemistry denoting an organic compound derived from another by shortening or contraction of a chain or ring by one carbon atom: *noradrenaline*.
– ORIGIN from *nor(mal)*, orig. used to refer to a compound without methyl substituents.

noradrenaline /ˌnɔːrəˈdrɛn(ə)lɪn/ ■ n. Biochemistry an adrenal hormone which functions as a neurotransmitter and is also used as a drug to raise blood pressure.
– ORIGIN 1930s: from **NOR-** + **ADRENALIN**.

Nordic ■ adj. **1** of or relating to Scandinavia, Finland, and Iceland. **2** denoting a physical type of northern European peoples characterized by tall stature, a bony frame, and light colouring. **3** (in skiing) denoting the disciplines of cross-country skiing and ski jumping. ■ n. a native of Scandinavia, Finland, or Iceland.
– ORIGIN from French *nordique*, from *nord* 'north'.

norepinephrine /ˌnɔːrɛpɪˈnɛfrɪn, -riːn/ ■ n. another term for **NORADRENALINE**.

Norfolk jacket ■ n. a loose belted jacket with box pleats, typically made of tweed.

nori /ˈnɔːri/ ■ n. (in Japanese cuisine) seaweed, eaten fresh or dried in sheets.
– ORIGIN from Japanese.

norm ■ n. **1** the usual, typical, or standard thing. ▸ a required or acceptable standard: *the norms of good behaviour*. **2** Mathematics the sum of the squares of the real and imaginary components of a complex number, or the positive square root of this sum.
– ORIGIN C19: from Latin *norma* 'precept, rule, carpenter's square'.

normal ■ adj. **1** conforming to a standard; usual, typical, or expected. **2** technical intersecting a given line or surface at right angles. **3** Medicine containing the same salt concentration as the blood. ▸ Chemistry, dated (of a solution) containing one gram-equivalent of solute per litre. ■ n. **1** the normal state or condition: *her temperature was above normal*. **2** technical a line at right angles to a given line or surface.
– ORIGIN C17: from Latin *normalis*, from *norma* (see NORM).

normal distribution ■ n. Statistics a function that represents the distribution of many random variables as a symmetrical bell-shaped graph.

normality (N. Amer. also **normalcy**) ■ n. the condition of being normal, usual, or typical.

normalize (also **-ise**) ■ v. **1** bring to a normal or standard state. **2** Mathematics multiply by a factor that makes the norm equal to a desired value (usually 1).
– DERIVATIVES **normalization** (also **-isation**) n. **normalizer** (also **-iser**) n.

normally ■ adv. **1** in a normal manner; in the usual way. **2** as a rule. **3** technical at right angles to a given line or surface.

Norman ■ n. **1** a member of a people of mixed Frankish and Scandinavian origin who settled in Normandy in the 10th century; in particular, any of the Normans who conquered England in 1066 or their descendants. ▸ a native or inhabitant of modern Normandy. **2** (also **Norman French**) the northern form of Old French spoken by the Normans. ▸ the French dialect of modern Normandy. ■ adj. of or relating to the Normans or Normandy. ▸ denoting the style of Romanesque architecture used in Britain under the Normans.
– DERIVATIVES **Normanesque** adj. **Normanism** n. **Normanize** (also **-ise**) v.
– ORIGIN Middle English: from Old French *Normans*, pl. of *Normant*, from Old Norse *Northmathr* 'Northman'.

normative ■ adj. formal relating to or deriving from a standard or norm.
– DERIVATIVES **normatively** adv. **normativeness** n.
– ORIGIN C19: from French *normatif, -ive*, from Latin *norma* (see NORM).

Norplant ■ n. trademark a contraceptive implant for women which gradually releases the hormone levonorgestrel.
– ORIGIN 1980s: from (*levo*)*nor*(*gestrel*) (*im*)*plant*.

Norse /nɔːs/ historical ■ n. **1** an ancient or medieval form of Norwegian or a related Scandinavian language. **2** [treated as pl.] Norwegians or Scandinavians. ■ adj. of or relating to Norway or Scandinavia, or their inhabitants or language.
– DERIVATIVES **Norseman** n. (pl. **-men**).
– ORIGIN from Dutch *noor*(*d*)*sch*, from *noord* 'north'.

north ■ n. (usu. **the north**) **1** the direction in which a compass needle normally points, towards the horizon on the left-hand side of a person facing east. **2** the northern part of a country, region, or town. **3** (**the North**) the industrialized capitalist countries, especially those of the northern hemisphere; the First World. ■ adj. **1** lying towards, near, or facing the north. **2** (of a wind) blowing from the north. ■ adv. to or towards the north.
– PHRASES **north by east** (or **west**) between north and north-north-east (or north-north-west).
– DERIVATIVES **northbound** adj. & adv.
– ORIGIN Old English, of Germanic origin.

North American ■ n. a native or inhabitant of North America, especially a citizen of the US or Canada. ■ adj. of or relating to North America.

north-east ■ n. (usu. **the north-east**) **1** the point of the horizon midway between north and east. **2** the north-eastern part of a country, region, or town. ■ adj. **1** lying towards, near, or facing the north-east. **2** (of a wind) from the north-east. ■ adv. to or towards the north-east.
– DERIVATIVES **north-eastern** adj.

northeaster ■ n. a wind blowing from the north-east.

north-easterly ■ adj. & adv. in a north-eastward position or direction. ■ n. another term for NORTHEASTER.

north-eastward ■ adv. (also **north-eastwards**) towards the north-east. ■ adj. situated in, directed towards, or facing the north-east.

northerly ■ adj. & adv. **1** in a northward position or direction. **2** (of a wind) blowing from the north. ■ n. (often **northerlies**) a wind blowing from the north.

northern ■ adj. **1** situated in, directed towards, or facing the north. **2** (usu. **Northern**) living in, coming from, or characteristic of the north.
– DERIVATIVES **northernmost** adj.

Northern blot ■ n. Biology a procedure for identifying specific sequences of messenger RNA.
– ORIGIN suggested by SOUTHERN BLOT.

northerner ■ n. a native or inhabitant of the north of a particular region or country.

Northern Lights ■ pl. n. the aurora borealis (see AURORA).

North Germanic ■ n. a subdivision of the Germanic group of languages, comprising the Scandinavian languages. ■ adj. of or relating to North Germanic.

northing ■ n. **1** distance travelled or measured northward, especially at sea. **2** a figure or line representing northward distance on a map.

North Korean ■ n. a native or inhabitant of North Korea. ■ adj. of or relating to North Korea.

north-north-east ■ n. the compass point or direction midway between north and north-east.

north-north-west ■ n. the compass point or direction midway between north and north-west.

North Star ■ n. the Pole Star.

northward ■ adj. in a northerly direction. ■ adv. (also **northwards**) towards the north. ■ n. (**the northward**) the direction or region to the north.
– DERIVATIVES **northwardly** adj. & adv.

north-west ■ n. (usu. **the north-west**) **1** the point of the horizon midway between north and west. **2** the north-western part of a country, region, or town. ■ adj. **1** lying towards, near, or facing the north-west. **2** (of a wind) blowing from the north-west. ■ adv. to or towards the north-west.
– DERIVATIVES **north-western** adj.

northwester ■ n. a wind blowing from the north-west.

north-westerly ■ adj. & adv. in a north-westward position or direction. ■ n. another term for NORTHWESTER.

north-westward ■ adv. (also **north-westwards**) towards the north-west. ■ adj. situated in, directed towards, or facing the north-west.

Norway lobster ■ n. a small, slender, commercially important European lobster. [*Nephrops norvegicus*.] See also SCAMPI.

Norwegian /nɔːˈwiːdʒ(ə)n/ ■ n. **1** a native or national of Norway, or a person of Norwegian descent. **2** the Scandinavian language spoken in Norway. ■ adj. of or relating to Norway or its people or language.
– ORIGIN from medieval Latin *Norvegia* 'Norway', from Old Norse *Norvegr* 'north way'.

nor'wester ■ n. short for NORTHWESTER.

nos ■ abbrev. numbers.
– ORIGIN pl. of NO.

nose ■ n. **1** the part projecting above the mouth on the face of a person or animal, containing the nostrils and used in breathing and smelling. **2** the sense of smell. ▸ the aroma of a particular substance, especially wine. **3** the front end of an aircraft, car, or other vehicle. ▸ a projecting part. **4** an instinctive talent for detecting something: *he has a nose for a good script*. **5** an act of looking around or prying: *she wanted a good nose round*

the house. ► informal a police informer. ■ v. **1** (of an animal) thrust its nose against or into something. ► smell or sniff (something). **2** look around or pry into something. **3** make one's way slowly ahead, especially in a vehicle.
– PHRASES **by a nose** (of a victory) by a very narrow margin. **cut off one's nose to spite one's face** disadvantage oneself through a wilful attempt to gain an advantage or assert oneself. **get one's nose in front** manage to achieve a winning or leading position. **get up someone's nose** informal irritate or annoy someone. **give someone a bloody nose** inflict a resounding defeat on someone. **keep one's nose clean** informal stay out of trouble. **keep one's nose out of** refrain from interfering in. **nose to tail** (of vehicles) moving or standing close behind one another. **not see further than one's** (or **the end of one's**) **nose** fail to consider different possibilities or to foresee consequences. **on the nose 1** to a person's sense of smell. **2** informal precisely. **put someone's nose out of joint** informal offend someone or hurt their pride. **turn one's nose up at** informal show distaste or contempt for. **under someone's nose** informal directly in front of someone. **with one's nose in the air** haughtily.
– DERIVATIVES **-nosed** adj. **noseless** adj.
– ORIGIN Old English, of West Germanic origin.

nosebag ■ n. a bag containing fodder, hung from a horse's head and into which it can reach to eat.

noseband ■ n. the strap of a bridle that passes over the horse's nose and under its chin.

nosebleed ■ n. an instance of bleeding from the nose.

nose candy ■ n. informal, chiefly N. Amer. cocaine.

nosedive ■ n. **1** a steep downward plunge by an aircraft. **2** a sudden dramatic deterioration. ■ v. make a nosedive.

nose flute ■ n. a flute played by blowing through the nose rather than the mouth.

nosegay ■ n. a small sweet-scented bunch of flowers.
– ORIGIN Middle English: from NOSE + GAY in the obsolete sense 'ornament'.

nose job ■ n. informal an operation involving rhinoplasty or cosmetic surgery on a person's nose.

nose leaf ■ n. a fleshy leaf-shaped structure on the nose of a bat, involved in echolocation.

nosepiece ■ n. **1** the part of a helmet or headdress that protects a person's nose. **2** the part of a microscope to which the objective lenses are attached.

nose tackle (also **nose guard**) ■ n. American Football a defensive lineman positioned opposite the offensive centre.

nosey ■ adj. & v. variant spelling of NOSY.

nosh informal ■ n. food. ■ v. eat enthusiastically or greedily.
– ORIGIN C20: Yiddish.

no-show ■ n. a person who has made a reservation, booking, or appointment but neither keeps nor cancels it.

nosh-up ■ n. informal, chiefly Brit. a large meal.

nosing ■ n. a rounded edge of a step or moulding. ► a metal shield for such an edge.

nosocomial /ˌnɒsə(ʊ)ˈkəʊmɪəl/ ■ adj. Medicine (of a disease) originating in a hospital.
– ORIGIN C19: from Greek *nosokomos* 'person who tends the sick'.

nosode /ˈnɒsəʊd/ ■ n. a preparation of substances secreted in the course of a disease, used in homeopathy.
– ORIGIN C19: from Greek *nosos* 'disease'.

nosology /nɒˈsɒlədʒi/ ■ n. the branch of medical science concerned with the classification of diseases.
– DERIVATIVES **nosological** adj. **nosologist** n.
– ORIGIN C18: from Greek *nosos* 'disease' + -LOGY.

nostalgia ■ n. sentimental longing or wistful affection for a period in the past.
– DERIVATIVES **nostalgic** adj. **nostalgically** adv. **nostalgist** n.
– ORIGIN C18: from Greek *nostos* 'return home' + *algos* 'pain'.

nostril ■ n. either of two external openings of the nasal cavity in vertebrates that admit air to the lungs and smells to the olfactory nerves.
– DERIVATIVES **-nostrilled** adj.
– ORIGIN Old English *nosterl*, *nosthyrl*, from *nosu* 'nose' + *thȳr(e)l* 'hole'.

nostrum /ˈnɒstrəm/ ■ n. **1** a quack medicine. **2** a favourite method for bringing about social or political reform.
– ORIGIN C17: from Latin, used in the sense '(something) of our own making', from *noster* 'our'.

nosy (also **nosey**) ■ adj. (**-ier**, **-iest**) informal showing too much curiosity about other people's affairs.
– DERIVATIVES **nosily** adv. **nosiness** n.

nosy parker ■ n. informal an overly inquisitive person.
– ORIGIN C20: from the picture postcard caption, 'The adventures of Nosey Parker', referring to a peeping Tom in Hyde Park.

not ■ adv. **1** (also **n't** joined to a preceding verb) used chiefly with an auxiliary verb or 'be' to form the negative. **2** used as a short substitute for a negative clause. **3** used to express the negative of other words. ► used with a quantifier to exclude a person or part of a group. ► less than. **4** used in understatements to suggest that the opposite of a following word or phrase is true. ► informal, humorous following and emphatically negating a statement: *that sounds like quality entertainment—not!* ■ n. (**NOT**) Electronics **1** a logical operation which gives the value zero if the operand is one, and vice versa. **2** [as modifier] denoting a gate circuit which produces an output only when there is no input signal. ■ adj. (often **Not**) Art (of paper) not hot-pressed, and having a slightly textured surface.
– ORIGIN Middle English: contraction of NOUGHT.

nota bene /ˌnəʊtə ˈbɛneɪ/ ■ v. formal observe carefully; take special note.
– ORIGIN Latin, 'note well!'

notability ■ n. (pl. **-ies**) a famous or important person.

notable ■ adj. worthy of attention or notice. ■ n. a famous or important person.

notably ■ adv. **1** in particular. **2** in a notable way.

notam /ˈnəʊtəm/ ■ n. a written notification issued to pilots before a flight, advising them of relevant circumstances or precautions.
– ORIGIN 1940s: from *no(tice) t(o) a(ir)m(en)*.

notarize (also **-ise**) ■ v. have (a document) legalized by a notary.

notary /ˈnəʊt(ə)ri/ (in full **notary public**) ■ n. (pl. **-ies**) a person authorized to perform certain legal formalities, especially to draw up or certify contracts, deeds, etc.
– DERIVATIVES **notarial** adj.
– ORIGIN Middle English: from Latin *notarius* 'secretary', from *nota* 'mark'.

notation ■ n. **1** a system of written symbols used to represent numbers, amounts, or elements in a field such as music or mathematics. **2** an annotation.
– DERIVATIVES **notate** v. **notational** adj. **notator** n.
– ORIGIN C16: from Latin *notatio(n-)*, from *notare* (v.), from *nota* 'mark'.

notch ■ n. **1** an indentation or incision on an edge or surface. ► each of a series of holes for the tongue of a buckle. ► a nick made on something to keep a record. **2** a point or degree on a scale. ► S. African a salary increment. **3** N. Amer. a deep, narrow mountain pass. ■ v. **1** make notches in. ► secure or insert by means of notches. **2** score or achieve.
– DERIVATIVES **notcher** n.
– ORIGIN C16: prob. from Anglo-Norman French *noche*, var. of Old French *osche*.

notchback ■ n. a car with a back that extends approximately horizontally from the bottom of the rear window so as to make a distinct angle with it.

notch filter ■ n. Electronics a filter that attenuates signals within a very narrow band of frequencies.

notchy ■ adj. (**-ier**, **-iest**) (of a manual gear-changing mechanism) difficult to use because the lever has to be moved accurately (as if into a narrow notch).

note ■ n. **1** a brief written record of facts, topics, or thoughts, used as an aid to memory. ► an annotation. **2** a short informal written message. ► an official letter sent from the representative of one government to another. ► a short official document of certification. **3** a banknote. ► a written promise or notice of payment of various kinds. **4** a single tone of definite pitch made by a musical instrument

notebook

or the human voice. ▶ a written sign representing the pitch and duration of such a sound. ▶ a key of a piano or similar instrument. **5** a bird's song or call, or a single tone in this. **6** a particular quality or tone expressing a mood or attitude. **7** any of the basic components of a fragrance or flavour. ■ v. **1** pay attention to. **2** record in writing.
– PHRASES **hit** (or **strike**) **the right** (or **wrong**) **note** say or do something in the right (or wrong) way. **of note** important. **strike** (or **sound**) **a note** express (a particular feeling or view). **take note** pay attention.
– ORIGIN Middle English: from Old French *note* (n.), *noter* (v.), from Latin *nota* 'a mark', *notare* 'to mark'.

notebook ■ n. **1** a small book for writing notes in. **2** a portable computer that is smaller than a laptop.

noted ■ adj. well known.

notelet ■ n. a small folded sheet of paper with a decorative design on the front, for an informal letter.

notepad ■ n. **1** a pad of paper for writing notes on. **2** a pocket-sized personal computer in which text is input using a stylus.

notepaper ■ n. paper for writing letters on.

noteworthy ■ adj. interesting or significant.
– DERIVATIVES **noteworthiness** n.

nothing ■ pron. not anything. ▶ something of no importance or concern. ▶ (in calculations) nought. ■ adj. informal of no value or significance. ■ adv. not at all.
– PHRASES **for nothing 1** without payment or charge. **2** to no purpose. **nothing but** only. **nothing doing** informal **1** there is no prospect of success or agreement. **2** nothing is happening. **nothing** (or **nothing else**) **for it** Brit. no alternative. **nothing less than** used to emphasize how extreme something is. **there is nothing to it** there is no difficulty involved. **sweet nothings** words of affection exchanged by lovers. **think nothing of it** do not apologize or feel bound to show gratitude.
– ORIGIN Old English *nān thing* (see NO, THING).

nothingness ■ n. **1** the absence or cessation of existence. **2** worthlessness; insignificance.

notice ■ n. **1** attention; observation. **2** advance notification or warning. ▶ a formal declaration of one's intention to end an agreement, typically one concerning employment or tenancy, at a specified time. **3** a displayed sheet or placard giving news or information. ▶ a small advertisement or announcement in a newspaper or magazine. **4** a short published review of a new film, play, or book. ■ v. **1** become aware of. ▶ archaic remark upon. **2** (**be noticed**) be treated or recognized as noteworthy.
– PHRASES **at short** (or **a moment's**) **notice** with little warning. **put someone on notice** (or **serve notice**) warn someone of something about or likely to occur. **take** (**no**) **notice** (**of**) pay (no) attention (to).
– ORIGIN Middle English: from Latin *notitia* 'being known', from *notus* (see NOTION).

noticeable ■ adj. easily seen or noticed; clear or apparent.
– DERIVATIVES **noticeably** adv.

noticeboard ■ n. a board for displaying notices.

notifiable ■ adj. denoting something, especially a serious infectious disease, that must be reported to the appropriate authorities.

notify ■ v. (**-ies**, **-ied**) inform, typically in a formal or official manner. ▶ report formally or officially.
– DERIVATIVES **notification** n.
– ORIGIN Middle English: from Old French *notifier*, from Latin *notificare* 'make known'.

notion ■ n. **1** a concept or belief. ▶ a vague awareness or understanding. **2** an impulse or desire. **3** (**notions**) chiefly N. Amer. items used in sewing, such as buttons and pins.
– ORIGIN Middle English: from Latin *notio(n-)* 'idea', from *notus* 'known', from *noscere*.

notional ■ adj. **1** hypothetical or imaginary. **2** Linguistics denoting or relating to an approach to grammar which is dependent on the definition of terminology (e.g. 'a verb is a doing word').
– DERIVATIVES **notionally** adv.

notochord /ˈnəʊtə(ʊ)kɔːd/ ■ n. Zoology a cartilaginous skeletal rod supporting the body in all embryonic and some adult chordate animals.
– ORIGIN C19: from Greek *nōton* 'back' + CHORD².

notorious ■ adj. famous for some bad quality or deed.
– DERIVATIVES **notoriety** n. **notoriously** adv.
– ORIGIN C15: from medieval Latin *notorius*, from Latin *notus* 'known'.

no trumps ■ n. Bridge a situation in which no suit is designated as trumps.

notwithstanding ■ prep. in spite of. ■ adv. nevertheless. ■ conj. although.
– ORIGIN Middle English: from NOT + *withstanding*, from WITHSTAND.

nougat /ˈnuːɡɑː, ˈnʌɡət/ ■ n. a sweet made from sugar or honey, nuts, and egg white.
– ORIGIN C19: from French, from Provençal *nogat*, from *noga* 'nut'.

nougatine /ˌnuːɡəˈtiːn/ ■ n. nougat covered with chocolate.
– ORIGIN C19: from NOUGAT.

nought ■ n. the digit o. ■ pron. variant spelling of NAUGHT.

noughts and crosses ■ pl. n. a game in which two players seek to complete a row of either three noughts or three crosses drawn alternately in the spaces of a grid of nine squares.

noun ■ n. Grammar a word (other than a pronoun) used to identify any of a class of people, places, or things (**common noun**), or to name a particular one of these (**proper noun**).
– DERIVATIVES **nounal** adj.
– ORIGIN Middle English: from Latin *nomen* 'name'.

noun phrase ■ n. Grammar a word or group of words that function in a sentence as subject, object, or prepositional object.

nourish ■ v. **1** provide with the food or other substances necessary for growth and health. ▶ enhance the fertility of (soil). **2** keep (a feeling or belief) in one's mind for a long time.
– DERIVATIVES **nourisher** n. **nourishing** adj. **nourishingly** adv.
– ORIGIN Middle English: from Old French *noriss-*, *norir*, from Latin *nutrire* 'feed, cherish'.

nourishment ■ n. the food necessary for growth and health. ▶ the action of nourishing.

nous /naʊs/ ■ n. **1** Brit. informal practical intelligence. **2** Philosophy the mind or intellect.
– ORIGIN C17: from Greek, 'mind, intelligence'.

nouveau /ˈnuːvəʊ/ ■ adj. informal **1** short for NOUVEAU RICHE. **2** up to date.

nouveau riche /ˌnuːvəʊ ˈriːʃ/ ■ n. [treated as pl.] people who have recently acquired wealth, typically those perceived as lacking good taste. ■ adj. of, relating to, or characteristic of such people.
– ORIGIN French, 'new rich'.

nouvelle cuisine /nuːˌvɛl kwɪˈziːn/ ■ n. a modern style of cookery that avoids rich foods and emphasizes the freshness of the ingredients and the presentation of the dishes.
– ORIGIN French, 'new cookery'.

Nov. ■ abbrev. November.

nova /ˈnəʊvə/ ■ n. (pl. **novae** /-viː/ or **novas**) Astronomy a star showing a sudden large increase in brightness and then slowly returning to normal.
– ORIGIN C19: from Latin, from *novus* 'new' (because such stars were thought to be newly formed).

novation /nə(ʊ)ˈveɪʃ(ə)n/ ■ n. Law the substitution of a new contract in place of an old one.
– DERIVATIVES **novate** v.
– ORIGIN C16: from late Latin *novatio(n-)*, from *novare* 'make new'.

novel[1] ■ n. a fictitious prose narrative of book length.
– ORIGIN C16: from Italian *novella* (*storia*) 'new (story)'.

novel[2] ■ adj. interestingly new or unusual.
– ORIGIN Middle English: from Latin *novellus*, from *novus* 'new'.

novelette ■ n. chiefly derogatory a short novel, typically a light romantic one.

novelist ■ n. a writer of novels.

novelistic ■ adj. of or characteristic of novels.

CONSONANTS **b** but **d** dog **f** few **g** get **h** he **j** yes **k** cat **l** leg **m** man **n** no **p** pen **r** red

novelize (also **-ise**) ■ v. convert (a story, typically one in the form of a film) into a novel.
– DERIVATIVES **novelization** (also **-isation**) n.

novella /nəˈvɛlə/ ■ n. a short novel or long short story.
– ORIGIN C20: from Italian, 'novel'.

novelty ■ n. (pl. **-ies**) **1** the quality of being novel. ▸ a new or unfamiliar thing or experience. ▸ [as modifier] denoting something intended to be amusing as a result of its originality or unusualness. **2** a small and inexpensive toy or ornament.

November ■ n. **1** the eleventh month of the year. **2** a code word representing the letter N, used in radio communication.
– ORIGIN Old English, from Latin, from *novem* 'nine' (being orig. the ninth month of the Roman year).

novena /nə(ʊ)ˈviːnə/ ■ n. (in the Roman Catholic Church) a form of worship consisting of special prayers or services on nine successive days.
– ORIGIN C19: from Latin *novem* 'nine'.

novice /ˈnɒvɪs/ ■ n. **1** a person new to and inexperienced in a job or situation. **2** a person who has entered a religious order and is under probation, before taking vows. **3** a racehorse that has not yet won a major prize or reached a level of performance to qualify for important events.
– ORIGIN Middle English: from late Latin *novicius*, from *novus* 'new'.

novitiate /nə(ʊ)ˈvɪʃɪət, -ɪeɪt/ (also **noviciate**) ■ n. **1** the period or state of being a novice. **2** a novice, especially in a religious order. **3** a place housing religious novices.
– ORIGIN C17: from eccles. Latin *noviciatus*, from Latin *novicius* (see **NOVICE**).

novocaine /ˈnəʊvəkeɪn/ ■ n. another term for PROCAINE.
– ORIGIN C20: from Latin *novus* 'new' + *-caine* (from COCAINE).

now ■ adv. **1** at the present time. ▸ at or from this precise moment. ▸ under the present circumstances. **2** used, especially in conversation, to draw attention to something. **3** used in a request, instruction, or question. ■ conj. as a consequence of the fact. ■ adj. informal fashionable.
– PHRASES **now and again** (or **then**) from time to time. **now or never** used to convey urgency. **now you're talking** an expression of enthusiastic agreement or approval.
– DERIVATIVES **nowness** n.
– ORIGIN Old English, of Germanic origin.

nowadays ■ adv. at the present time, in contrast with the past.

noway (also **noways**) ■ adv. dated or N. Amer. not at all.

Nowel (also **Nowell**) ■ n. archaic spelling of NOEL.

nowhere ■ adv. not in or to any place. ■ pron. **1** no place. **2** a place that is remote or uninteresting. ■ adj. informal having no prospect of progress or success.
– PHRASES **be** (or **come**) **nowhere** be badly defeated in a race or competition. **from** (or **out of**) **nowhere** appearing or happening suddenly and unexpectedly. **get** (or **go**) **nowhere** make no progress. **get someone nowhere** be of no benefit to someone. **nowhere near** not nearly.
– ORIGIN Old English *nāhwǣr*.

nowise ■ adv. archaic not at all.

now-now ■ adv. S. African informal **1** at once; immediately. **2** very recently.

nowt /naʊt/ ■ pron. & adv. N. English nothing.

NOx ■ n. oxides of nitrogen, especially as atmospheric pollutants.

noxious /ˈnɒkʃəs/ ■ adj. harmful, poisonous, or very unpleasant.
– DERIVATIVES **noxiously** adv. **noxiousness** n.
– ORIGIN C15: from Latin *noxius*, from *noxa* 'harm'.

nozzle ■ n. a spout at the end of a pipe, hose, or tube used to control a jet of liquid or gas.
– ORIGIN C17: from NOSE.

NP ■ abbrev. **1** S. African historical National Party. **2** notary public.

Np ■ symb. the chemical element neptunium.

n.p. ■ abbrev. **1** new paragraph. **2** (in book classification) no place of publication.

NPA ■ abbrev. (in South Africa) National Prosecuting Authority.

803

npn ■ adj. Electronics denoting a semiconductor device in which two *n*-type regions are separated by a *p*-type region.

NQF ■ abbrev. (in South Africa) National Qualifications Framework.

nr ■ abbrev. near.

NRA ■ abbrev. (in the US) National Rifle Association.

NRF ■ abbrev. (in South Africa) National Research Foundation.

NS ■ abbrev. (in calculating dates) New Style.

ns ■ abbrev. nanosecond.

n/s ■ abbrev. (in personal advertisements) non-smoker; non-smoking.

NSC ■ abbrev. National Senior Certificate.

NT ■ abbrev. **1** New Testament. **2** Bridge no trump(s).

-n't ■ contr. not, used with auxiliary verbs (e.g. *can't*).

Ntate /(ə)nˈtatə/ ■ n. S. African a polite form of address to an older man.
– ORIGIN Sesotho, 'father'.

Nth ■ abbrev. North.

nth /ɛnθ/ ■ adj. **1** Mathematics denoting an unspecified member of a series of numbers or enumerated items. **2** denoting the last or latest item or instance in a long series.
– PHRASES **to the nth degree** to the utmost.

NTP ■ abbrev. Chemistry normal temperature and pressure.

NTSC ■ n. the television broadcasting system used in North America and Japan.
– ORIGIN 1950s: acronym from *National Television Standard Committee*.

n-type ■ adj. Electronics denoting a region in a semiconductor in which electrical conduction is due chiefly to the movement of electrons. Compare with **P-TYPE**.

nu /njuː/ ■ n. the thirteenth letter of the Greek alphabet (N, ν), transliterated as 'n'. ■ symb. (ν) frequency.
– ORIGIN from Greek.

nuance /ˈnjuːɑːns/ ■ n. a subtle difference in or shade of meaning, expression, colour, etc. ■ v. (usu. **be nuanced**) give nuances to.
– ORIGIN C18: from French, 'shade, subtlety'.

nub ■ n. **1** (**the nub**) the crux or central point of a matter. **2** a small lump or protuberance. ▸ a small chunk or nugget of metal or rock.
– ORIGIN C17: apparently a var. of dialect *knub* 'protuberance'.

Nuba /ˈnuːbə/ ■ n. (pl. same or **Nubas**) a member of a Nilotic people inhabiting southern Kordofan in Sudan.
– ORIGIN from Latin *Nubae* 'Nubians'.

nubby (also **nubbly**) ■ adj. chiefly US **1** (of fabric) coarse or knobbly in texture. **2** stubby or lumpy.
– ORIGIN C19: derivative of *nubble* 'small lump'.

Nubian ■ n. **1** a native or inhabitant of an area of southern Egypt and northern Sudan corresponding to the ancient region of Nubia. **2** the Nilo-Saharan language spoken by the Nubians. **3** a goat of a short-haired breed with long pendant ears and long legs, originally from Africa. ■ adj. of or relating to the Nubians or their language, or ancient Nubia.

nubile /ˈnjuːbʌɪl/ ■ adj. (of a girl or woman) youthful but sexually mature and attractive.
– DERIVATIVES **nubility** n.
– ORIGIN C17: from Latin *nubilis* 'marriageable'.

nubuck /ˈnjuːbʌk/ ■ n. cowhide leather which has been rubbed on the flesh side to give a suede-like effect.
– ORIGIN 1970s: perhaps respelling of NEW + BUCK¹.

nucellus /njuːˈsɛləs/ ■ n. (pl. **nucelli**) Botany the central part of an ovule, containing the embryo sac.
– DERIVATIVES **nucellar** adj.
– ORIGIN C19: an irregular diminutive of NUCLEUS.

nucellus

nuclear ■ adj. **1** of or relating to a nucleus. **2** relating to or using energy released in nuclear fission or fusion.
▸ possessing or involving nuclear weapons.

nuclear family ■ n. a couple and their dependent children, regarded as a basic social unit.

nuclear force ■ n. Physics the strong attractive force that holds nucleons together in the atomic nucleus.

nuclear fuel ■ n. a substance that will sustain a fission chain reaction so that it can be used as a source of nuclear energy.

nuclear isomer ■ n. another term for ISOMER (in sense 2).

nuclear magnetic resonance ■ n. the absorption of electromagnetic radiation by certain nuclei (especially protons) in an external magnetic field, used as an analytical and imaging technique.

nuclear medicine ■ n. the branch of medicine concerned with the use of radioactive substances in research, diagnosis, and treatment.

nuclear physics ■ pl. n. [treated as sing.] the physics of atomic nuclei and their interactions, especially in the generation of nuclear energy.

nuclear power ■ n. **1** electric or motive power generated by a nuclear reactor. **2** a country that has nuclear weapons.
–DERIVATIVES **nuclear-powered** adj.

nuclear umbrella ■ n. the supposed protection gained from an alliance with a country possessing nuclear weapons.

nuclear waste ■ n. radioactive waste material, for example from the use or reprocessing of nuclear fuel.

nuclear winter ■ n. a period of abnormal cold and darkness predicted to follow a nuclear war, caused by a layer of smoke and dust in the atmosphere blocking the sun's rays.

nuclease /ˈnjuːkliɛɪz/ ■ n. Biochemistry an enzyme that cleaves nucleic acid chains into smaller units.

nucleate ■ adj. /ˈnjuːklɪət/ chiefly Biology having a nucleus. ■ v. /ˈnjuːklɪeɪt/ [usu. as adj. **nucleated**] **1** form a nucleus. **2** form around a central area.
–DERIVATIVES **nucleation** n.

nuclei plural form of NUCLEUS.

nucleic acid /njuːˈkliːɪk, -ˈkleɪɪk/ ■ n. Biochemistry a complex organic substance, especially DNA or RNA, whose molecules consist of long chains of nucleotides.

nucleo- ■ comb. form representing NUCLEUS, NUCLEAR, or NUCLEIC ACID.

nucleolus /ˌnjuːklɪˈəʊləs/ ■ n. (pl. **nucleoli** /-lʌɪ/) Biology a small dense spherical structure in a cell nucleus during interphase.
–DERIVATIVES **nucleolar** adj.
–ORIGIN C19: from late Latin, diminutive of Latin *nucleus* (see NUCLEUS).

nucleon /ˈnjuːklɒn/ ■ n. Physics a proton or neutron.

nucleonics /ˌnjuːklɪˈɒnɪks/ ■ pl. n. [treated as sing.] the branch of science and technology concerned with atomic nuclei and nuclear power.
–DERIVATIVES **nucleonic** adj.
–ORIGIN 1940s: from NUCLEAR, on the pattern of *electronics*.

nucleophilic /ˌnjuːklɪə(ʊ)ˈfɪlɪk/ ■ adj. Chemistry having a tendency to donate electrons or react with protons. Often contrasted with ELECTROPHILIC.
–DERIVATIVES **nucleophile** n.

nucleoside ■ n. Biochemistry an organic compound consisting of a purine or pyrimidine base linked to a sugar, e.g. adenosine.

nucleosynthesis ■ n. Astronomy the cosmic formation of atoms more complex than the hydrogen atom.
–DERIVATIVES **nucleosynthetic** adj.

nucleotide ■ n. Biochemistry a compound consisting of a nucleoside linked to a phosphate group, forming the basic structural unit of nucleic acids.

nucleus /ˈnjuːklɪəs/ ■ n. (pl. **nuclei** /-lɪʌɪ/) **1** the central and most important part of an object or group. **2** Physics the positively charged central core of an atom, containing nearly all its mass. **3** Biology a structure present in most cells, containing the genetic material. **4** a discrete mass of grey matter in the central nervous system.
–ORIGIN C18: from Latin, 'kernel, inner part', diminutive of *nux, nuc-* 'nut'.

nuclide /ˈnjuːklʌɪd/ ■ n. Physics a distinct kind of atom or nucleus characterized by a specific number of protons and neutrons.
–DERIVATIVES **nuclidic** adj.
–ORIGIN 1940s: from NUCLEUS + *-ide* (from Greek *eidos* 'form').

nude ■ adj. wearing no clothes. ■ n. a naked human figure as a subject in art or photography.
–DERIVATIVES **nudity** n.
–ORIGIN Middle English: from Latin *nudus*.

nudge ■ v. **1** prod gently with one's elbow to attract attention. **2** touch or push gently or gradually. **3** give gentle encouragement to. ■ n. a light touch or push.
–DERIVATIVES **nudger** n.
–ORIGIN C17: perhaps rel. to Norwegian dialect *nugga*, *nyggja* 'to push, rub'.

Nudibranchia /ˌnjuːdɪˈbraŋkɪə/ ■ pl. n. Zoology an order of shell-less marine molluscs comprising the sea slugs.
–DERIVATIVES **nudibranch** /ˈnjuːdɪbraŋk/ n.
–ORIGIN modern Latin, from Latin *nudus* 'nude' + BRANCHIA.

nudist ■ n. a person who goes naked wherever possible.
–DERIVATIVES **nudism** n.

nuée ardente /ˌnjuːeɪ ɑːˈdɒt/ ■ n. Geology an incandescent cloud of gas, ash, and lava fragments ejected from a volcano, typically as part of a pyroclastic flow.
–ORIGIN French, 'burning cloud'.

Nuer /ˈnuːə/ ■ n. (pl. same or **Nuers**) **1** a member of an African people of SE Sudan and Ethiopia. **2** the Nilotic language of this people.
–ORIGIN the name in Dinka.

nuff ■ det., pron., & adv. non-standard spelling of ENOUGH, representing informal speech. ■ det. informal much.

nugatory /ˈnjuːgət(ə)ri, ˈnuː-/ ■ adj. **1** worthless. **2** useless or invalid.
–ORIGIN C17: from Latin *nugatorius*, from *nugari* 'to trifle'.

nugget ■ n. **1** a small lump of gold or other precious metal found ready-formed in the earth. **2** a small but valuable fact.
–DERIVATIVES **nuggety** adj.
–ORIGIN C19: apparently from dialect *nug* 'lump'.

nuisance ■ n. a person or thing causing inconvenience or annoyance. ▸ Law an act which is harmful or offensive to the public or a member of it and for which there is a legal remedy.
–ORIGIN Middle English: from Old French, 'hurt', from Latin *nocere* 'to harm'.

nuke informal ■ n. a nuclear weapon. ■ v. **1** attack or destroy with nuclear weapons. **2** cook or heat up (food) in a microwave oven.

null ■ adj. **1** (usu. in phr. **null and void**) having no legal force; invalid. **2** having or associated with the value zero. ▸ Mathematics (of a set or matrix) having no members, or only zeros as elements. **3** having no positive substance. ■ n. **1** a dummy letter in a cipher. **2** Electronics a condition in which no signal is generated; something generating no signal. ■ v. Electronics cancel out, creating a null.
–ORIGIN Middle English: from French *nul*, from Latin *nullus* 'none', from *ne* 'not' + *ullus* 'any'.

null hypothesis ■ n. (in a statistical test) the hypothesis that any observed differences between two populations are due to sampling or experimental error.

nullify /ˈnʌlɪfʌɪ/ ■ v. (**-ies, -ied**) make null and void.
▸ cancel out.
–DERIVATIVES **nullification** n. **nullifier** n.

nullipara /nʌˈlɪp(ə)rə/ ■ n. (pl. **nulliparae** /nʌˈlɪp(ə)riː/) Medicine & Zoology a woman (or female animal) that has never given birth.
–DERIVATIVES **nulliparous** adj.
–ORIGIN C19: from Latin *nullus* 'none' + *-para*, from *parere* 'bear children'.

nullity ■ n. (pl. **-ies**) **1** Law a thing that is legally void. ▸ the state of being legally void. **2** a thing of no importance or worth. ▸ nothingness.

numb ■ adj. deprived of the power of sensation. ■ v. make numb.
–DERIVATIVES **numbly** adv. **numbness** n.
–ORIGIN Middle English *nome(n)*, from obsolete *nim* 'take'.

number ■ n. **1** an arithmetical value, expressed by a word, symbol, or figure, representing a particular quantity. **2** a quantity or amount. ▸ (**a number of**) several. ▸ (**numbers**) a large quantity or amount; numerical preponderance. **3** a single issue of a magazine. **4** a song, dance, or other musical item. **5** informal an item of clothing of a particular type, regarded with approval: *a little black number*. **6** a grammatical classification of words that consists typically of singular and plural. ■ v. **1** amount to. **2** assign a number to. ▸ count. **3** include as a member of a group.
–PHRASES **by numbers** following simple instructions identified or as if identified by numbers. **someone's** (or **something's**) **days are numbered** someone or something will not survive or remain in power for much longer. **do a number on** N. Amer. informal deceive or disparage. **have someone's number** informal understand a person's real motives or character. **someone's number is up** informal someone is finished or doomed to die. [with ref. to a lottery number or a number by which one may be identified.] **without number** too many to count.
–DERIVATIVES **numberless** adj.
–ORIGIN Middle English: from Old French *nombre* (n.), from Latin *numerus*.

number cruncher ■ n. informal **1** a computer or program capable of performing rapid calculations with large amounts of data. **2** often derogatory a statistician or other person whose job involves dealing with large amounts of numerical data.
–DERIVATIVES **number crunching** n.

numbered account ■ n. a bank account, especially in a Swiss bank, identified only by a number and not bearing the owner's name.

number one informal ■ n. **1** oneself. **2** a person or thing that is foremost in an activity or area. **3** euphemistic urine. ■ adj. most important; foremost.

number plate ■ n. a sign affixed to the front and rear of a vehicle displaying its registration number.

numbers game ■ n. **1** often derogatory the use or manipulation of statistics or figures. **2** (also **numbers racket**) N. Amer. a lottery based on the occurrence of unpredictable numbers in the results of races, a lottery, etc.

number two ■ n. informal **1** a second in command. **2** euphemistic faeces.

numbskull (also **numskull**) ■ n. informal a stupid or foolish person.

numerable ■ adj. able to be counted.
–ORIGIN C16: from Latin *numerabilis*, from *numerare* 'to number'.

numeraire /'njuːmərɛː/ ■ n. Economics an item or commodity acting as a measure of value or as a standard for currency exchange.
–ORIGIN 1960s: from French *numéraire*, from Latin *numerus* 'a number'.

numeral ■ n. a figure, word, or group of figures denoting a number. ■ adj. of or denoting a number.
–ORIGIN Middle English: from late Latin *numeralis*, from Latin *numerus* 'a number'.

numerate /'njuːm(ə)rət/ ■ adj. having a good basic knowledge of arithmetic.
–DERIVATIVES **numeracy** n.
–ORIGIN 1950s: from Latin *numerus* 'a number', on the pattern of *literate*.

numeration ■ n. the action or process of numbering or calculating. ▸ a method or process of numbering or computing.
–ORIGIN Middle English: from Latin *numeratio(n-)* 'payment', from *numerare* 'to number'.

numerator ■ n. the number above the line in a vulgar fraction showing how many of the parts indicated by the denominator are taken, e.g. 2 in ⅔.

numerical ■ adj. of, relating to, or expressed as a number or numbers.
–DERIVATIVES **numerically** adv.
–ORIGIN C17: from medieval Latin *numericus*, from Latin *numerus* 'a number'.

numerical analysis ■ n. the branch of mathematics concerned with the development and use of numerical methods for solving problems.

numerology /ˌnjuːməˈrɒlədʒi/ ■ n. the branch of knowledge concerned with the occult significance of numbers.
–DERIVATIVES **numerological** adj. **numerologist** n.
–ORIGIN C20: from Latin *numerus* 'a number' + -LOGY.

numero uno /ˌnjuːmərəʊ 'uːnəʊ/ ■ n. (pl. **-os**) informal the best or most important person or thing.
–ORIGIN Italian, 'number one'.

numerous ■ adj. many. ▸ consisting of many members.
–DERIVATIVES **numerously** adv. **numerousness** n.
–ORIGIN Middle English: from Latin *numerosus*, from *numerus* 'a number'.

Numidian /njuːˈmɪdɪən/ ■ n. a native or inhabitant of the ancient region of Numidia in North Africa. ■ adj. of or relating to Numidia.

numinous /'njuːmɪnəs/ ■ adj. having a strong religious or spiritual quality.
–ORIGIN C17: from Latin *numen, numin-* 'divine will'.

numismatic /ˌnjuːmɪzˈmatɪk/ ■ adj. of or relating to coins or medals.
–DERIVATIVES **numismatically** adv.
–ORIGIN C18: from French *numismatique*, from Greek *nomisma, nomismat-* 'current coin'.

numismatics ■ pl. n. [usu. treated as sing.] the study or collection of coins, banknotes, and medals.
–DERIVATIVES **numismatist** /njuːˈmɪzmətɪst/ n.

nummulite /'nʌmjʊlʌɪt/ ■ n. Palaeontology the fossilized disc-shaped calcareous shell of a foraminifer.
–ORIGIN C19: from Latin *nummulus*, diminutive of *nummus* 'coin'.

num-num /'nʌmnʌm/ ■ n. S. African a spiny shrub with leathery leaves, white flowers, and fleshy fruits. ▸ the edible fruits of this shrub. [Genus *Carissa*: several species.]
–ORIGIN from Khoikhoi.

numskull ■ n. variant spelling of NUMBSKULL.

nun ■ n. **1** a member of a female religious community, typically one living under vows of poverty, chastity, and obedience. **2** a pigeon of a breed with a crest on its neck.
–DERIVATIVES **nunlike** adj. **nunnish** adj.
–ORIGIN Old English *nonne*, from eccles. Latin *nonna*, feminine of *nonnus* 'monk'.

nunatak /'nʌnətak/ ■ n. an isolated peak of rock projecting above a surface of inland ice or snow.
–ORIGIN C19: from Eskimo *nunataq*.

Nunc Dimittis /ˌnʌŋk dɪˈmɪtɪs/ ■ n. the Song of Simeon (Luke 2:29–32) used as a canticle in Christian liturgy.
–ORIGIN Latin, the opening words of the canticle, '(Lord), now let (your servant) depart'.

nunchaku /nʌnˈtʃakuː/ ■ n. (pl. same or **nunchakus**) a Japanese martial arts weapon consisting of two hardwood sticks joined together by a chain, rope, or thong.
–ORIGIN from Japanese.

nuncio /'nʌnsɪəʊ, 'nʌnʃɪəʊ/ ■ n. (pl. **-os**) (in the Roman Catholic Church) a papal ambassador to a foreign government or court.
–DERIVATIVES **nunciature** n.
–ORIGIN C16: from Italian, from Latin *nuntius* 'messenger'.

nuncupative /'nʌŋkjʊˌpeɪtɪv/ ■ adj. Law (of a will or testament) declared orally, especially by a mortally wounded soldier or sailor.
–ORIGIN C16: from late Latin *nuncupativus*, from Latin *nuncupare* 'declare'.

nunnery ■ n. (pl. **-ies**) a religious house of nuns.

nunu /'nuːnuː/ ■ n. S. African informal an insect, spider, or other small creature; a creepy-crawly.
–ORIGIN from isiZulu *inunu* 'horrible object, monster'.

nuptial /'nʌpʃ(ə)l/ ■ adj. **1** of or relating to marriage or

weddings. **2** Zoology of or denoting characteristic breeding coloration or behaviour. ■ n. (**nuptials**) a wedding.
– ORIGIN C15: from Latin *nuptialis*, from *nuptiae* 'wedding'.

nuptiality ■ n. the frequency or incidence of marriage within a population.

Nurofen /ˈnjʊərəfɛn/ ■ n. trademark for IBUPROFEN.
– ORIGIN invented word on the pattern of *ibuprofen*.

nurse¹ ■ n. a person trained to care for the sick or infirm. ▸ dated a person employed or trained to take charge of young children. ■ v. **1** give medical and other attention to. ▸ work as a nurse. **2** feed or be fed at the breast. **3** treat or hold carefully or protectively. ▸ hold (a cup or glass), drinking from it occasionally. **4** harbour (a belief or feeling) for a long time.
– DERIVATIVES **nursing** n.
– ORIGIN Middle English: contraction of *nourice*, from Latin *nutricius* '(person) that nourishes', from *nutrire* 'nourish'.

nurse² (also **grey nurse**) ■ n. a greyish Australian shark of shallow inshore waters. [*Odontaspis arenarius*.]
– ORIGIN C15: orig. as *nusse*, perhaps derived from *an huss*, denoting a kind of dogfish, from Middle English *husk*.

nurse hound ■ n. a large spotted dogfish of the NE Atlantic, which is caught for food. [*Scyliorhinus stellaris*.]

nurseling ■ n. archaic spelling of NURSLING.

nursemaid ■ n. a woman or girl employed to look after a young child or children. ■ v. look after or be overprotective towards.

nurse practitioner ■ n. a nurse who is qualified to treat certain medical conditions without the direct supervision of a doctor.

nursery ■ n. (pl. **-ies**) **1** a room in a house for the special use of young children. ▸ (also **day nursery**) a nursery school. **2** a place where young plants and trees are grown for sale or for planting elsewhere. **3** a place or natural habitat which breeds or supports animals. **4** [as modifier] denoting a race for two-year-old horses.

nursery class ■ n. a class for the education of children mainly between the ages of three and five.

nurseryman ■ n. (pl. **-men**) a worker in or owner of a plant or tree nursery.

nursery nurse ■ n. Brit. a person trained to look after young children and babies in nurseries, crèches, etc.

nursery rhyme ■ n. a simple traditional song or poem for children.

nursery school ■ n. a school for young children, mainly between the ages of three and five.

nursery slope ■ n. Brit. Skiing a gentle slope suitable for beginners.

nurse shark ■ n. a slow-moving shark with barbels on the snout. [*Ginglymostoma cirratum* (Atlantic) and other species.]

nursing home ■ n. a small private institution for the elderly providing residential accommodation with health care.

nursing officer ■ n. chiefly Brit. a senior nurse with administrative responsibility.

nursling ■ n. dated a baby that is being breastfed.

nurture /ˈnɜːtʃə/ ■ v. **1** rear and encourage the development of (a child). **2** cherish (a hope, belief, or ambition). ■ n. **1** the action or process of nurturing. **2** upbringing, education, and environment as an influence on or determinant of personality. Often contrasted with NATURE.
– DERIVATIVES **nurturance** n. **nurturant** adj. **nurturer** n.
– ORIGIN Middle English: from Old French *noureture* 'nourishment', from Latin *nutrire* 'feed, cherish'.

nut ■ n. **1** a fruit consisting of a hard or tough shell around an edible kernel. ▸ the hard kernel of such a fruit. **2** a small flat piece of metal or other material, typically square or hexagonal, with a threaded hole through it for screwing on to a bolt. ▸ the part at the lower end of a violin bow with a screw for adjusting the tension of the hair. **3** informal a crazy or eccentric person. ▸ an obsessive enthusiast or devotee. **4** informal a person's head. **5** a small lump of coal. **6** (**nuts**) vulgar slang a man's testicles. **7** the fixed ridge on the neck of a stringed instrument over which the strings pass. ■ v. (**nutted**, **nutting**) [usu. as noun **nutting**] archaic gather nuts.
– PHRASES **do one's nut** informal be extremely angry or agitated. **nuts and bolts** informal the basic practical details. **a tough** (or **hard**) **nut to crack** informal a problem or an opponent that is hard to solve or overcome. **use** (or **take**) **a sledgehammer to crack a nut** informal use disproportionately drastic measures to deal with a simple problem.
– ORIGIN Old English, of Germanic origin.

nutation /njuːˈteɪʃ(ə)n/ ■ n. a periodic variation in the inclination of an axis of rotation, especially that causing the earth's precession to follow a wavy rather than a circular path.
– ORIGIN C17: from Latin *nutatio(n-)*, from *nutare* 'to nod'.

nutcase ■ n. informal a mad or foolish person.

nutcracker ■ n. **1** (**nutcrackers**) a device for cracking nuts. **2** a bird of the crow family that feeds on the basic seeds of conifers. [Genus *Nucifraga*: two species.]

nut loaf ■ n. a baked vegetarian dish made from ground or chopped nuts, vegetables, and herbs.

nutmeg ■ n. **1** the hard, aromatic, almost spherical seed of a tropical tree, used as a spice. **2** the evergreen tree that bears these seeds, native to the Moluccas. [*Myristica fragrans*.] ■ v. Soccer (**nutmegged**, **nutmegging**) informal play the ball through the legs of (an opponent).
– ORIGIN Middle English *notemuge*, partial translation of Old French *nois muguede*, from Latin *nux* 'nut' + *muscus* 'musk'.

nutria /ˈnjuːtrɪə/ ■ n. **1** the skin or fur of the coypu. **2** S. African the brown uniform formerly worn by members of the South African Defence Force.
– ORIGIN C19: from Spanish, 'otter'.

nutrient ■ n. a substance that provides nourishment essential for the maintenance of life and for growth.
– ORIGIN C17: from Latin *nutrient-*, *nutrire* 'nourish'.

nutriment ■ n. nourishment; sustenance.
– DERIVATIVES **nutrimental** /-ˈmɛnt(ə)l/ adj.
– ORIGIN Middle English: from Latin *nutrimentum*, from *nutrire* 'nourish'.

nutrition ■ n. **1** the process of ingesting and assimilating nutrients. ▸ food; nourishment. **2** the branch of science concerned with nutrients and their ingestion.
– DERIVATIVES **nutritional** adj. **nutritionally** adv. **nutritionist** (also **nutritionalist**) n.
– ORIGIN Middle English: from late Latin *nutritio(n-)*, from *nutrire* 'nourish'.

nutritious ■ adj. full of nutrients; nourishing.
– DERIVATIVES **nutritiously** adv. **nutritiousness** n.
– ORIGIN C17: from Latin *nutritius* 'that nourishes'.

nutritive ■ adj. **1** of or relating to nutrition. **2** nutritious.
– ORIGIN Middle English: from medieval Latin *nutritivus*, from *nutrire* 'nourish'.

nuts ■ adj. informal mad.

nutshell ■ n. the hard woody covering around the kernel of a nut.
– PHRASES **in a nutshell** in the fewest possible words.

nutter ■ n. informal a mad or eccentric person.

nutty ■ adj. (**-ier**, **-iest**) **1** tasting like nuts. ▸ containing a lot of nuts. **2** informal mad.
– DERIVATIVES **nuttiness** n.

nuzzle ■ v. rub or push against gently with the nose and mouth.
– ORIGIN Middle English: from NOSE, reinforced by Dutch *neuzelen* 'poke with the nose'.

NW ■ abbrev. **1** north-west. **2** north-western.

nyala /ˈnjɑːlə/ ■ n. (pl. same or **nyalas**) **1** a southern African antelope with conspicuous white stripes on the flanks, the male of which has lyre-shaped horns. [*Tragelaphus angasi*.] **2** (**Nyala**) S. African Military an armoured personnel carrier.
– ORIGIN C19: from Xitsonga and Tshivenda.

Nyanja /ˈnjandʒə/ ■ n. (pl. same or **Nyanjas**) **1** a member of a people of Malawi and eastern and central Zambia. **2** the Bantu language of this people.
– ORIGIN a local name, 'lake'.

nylon ■ n. **1** a tough, lightweight, elastic synthetic polymer with a protein-like chemical structure. **2** nylon fabric or yarn. ▸ (**nylons**) stockings or tights made of nylon.
– ORIGIN 1930s: an invented word, on the pattern of *cotton* and *rayon*.

nymph ■ n. **1** a mythological spirit of nature imagined as a beautiful maiden. ▸ poetic/literary a beautiful young woman. **2** an immature form of a dragonfly or other insect that does not undergo complete metamorphosis.
– DERIVATIVES **nymphal** adj. **nymphean** adj.
– ORIGIN Middle English: from Latin *nympha*, from Greek *numphē* 'nymph, bride'.

nymphet /ˈnɪmfɛt, nɪmˈfɛt/ (also **nymphette**) ■ n. an attractive and sexually mature young girl.
– ORIGIN 1950s: from NYMPH.

nympho ■ n. informal a nymphomaniac.

nymphomania ■ n. uncontrollable or excessive sexual desire in a woman.
– DERIVATIVES **nymphomaniac** n. & adj. **nymphomaniacal** adj.
– ORIGIN C18: from Latin *nympha* (see NYMPH) + -MANIA.

NYSE ■ abbrev. New York Stock Exchange.

nystagmus /nɪˈstagməs/ ■ n. rapid involuntary movements of the eyes.
– DERIVATIVES **nystagmic** adj.
– ORIGIN C19: from Greek *nustagmos* 'nodding, drowsiness'.

nystatin /ˈnʌɪstətɪn, ˈnɪs-/ ■ n. an antibiotic used chiefly to treat fungal infections.
– ORIGIN 1950s: from N(ew) Y(ork) Stat(e) (where it was developed).

NZ ■ abbrev. New Zealand.

Oo

O[1] (also **o**) ■ n. (pl. **Os** or **O's**) **1** the fifteenth letter of the alphabet. **2** denoting the next after N in a set of items, categories, etc. **3** a human blood type (in the ABO system) lacking both the A and B antigens. **4** (also **oh**) zero (in a sequence of numerals, especially when spoken).

O[2] ■ abbrev. Cricket (on scorecards) over(s). ■ symb. the chemical element oxygen.

O[3] ■ exclam. **1** archaic spelling of **OH**[1]. **2** used before a name in the vocative.

O' ■ prefix in Irish patronymic names such as *O'Neill*.
–ORIGIN C18: from Irish *ó*, *ua* 'descendant'.

o ■ abbrev. (*o-*) Chemistry ortho-: *o-xylene*.

-o ■ suffix forming chiefly informal or slang variants or derivatives such as *beano*.
–ORIGIN perhaps from **OH**[1], reinforced by abbreviated forms such as *hippo*.

o' ■ prep. short for **OF**, used to represent an informal pronunciation.

oaf ■ n. a stupid, boorish, or clumsy man.
–DERIVATIVES **oafish** adj. **oafishly** adv. **oafishness** n.
–ORIGIN C17: var. of obsolete *auf*, from Old Norse *álfr* 'elf'.

oak ■ n. **1** a large tree which bears acorns and typically has lobed leaves and hard durable wood. [Genus *Quercus*: many species.] ▶ used in names of other trees or plants resembling this, e.g. poison oak. **2** a smoky flavour or nose characteristic of wine aged in oak barrels.
–DERIVATIVES **oaken** adj. (archaic). **oaky** adj.
–ORIGIN Old English *āc*, of Germanic origin.

oaked ■ adj. (of wine) matured in an oak barrel or other container.

oak leaf ■ n. a red or green variety of lettuce which has leaves with serrated edges and a slightly bitter taste.

oakum ■ n. chiefly historical loose fibre obtained by untwisting old rope, used especially in caulking wooden ships.
–ORIGIN Old English *ācumbe* 'off-combings', of Germanic origin.

OAP ■ abbrev. **1** S. African old-age pension. **2** Brit. old-age pensioner.

OAPEC /'əʊpɛk/ ■ abbrev. Organization of Arab Petroleum Exporting Countries.

oar ■ n. a pole with a flat blade, used to row or steer a boat through the water. ▶ a rower.
–PHRASES **put** (or **stick**) **one's oar in** informal give an opinion without being asked.
–DERIVATIVES **oared** adj. **oarless** adj.
–ORIGIN Old English, of Germanic origin.

oarlock ■ n. N. Amer. a rowlock.

oarsman (or **oarswoman**) ■ n. (pl. **-men** or **-women**) a rower.
–DERIVATIVES **oarsmanship** n.

OAS ■ abbrev. Organization of American States.

oasis /əʊ'eɪsɪs/ ■ n. (pl. **oases** /-siːz/) **1** a fertile spot in a desert where the water table rises to ground level. **2** an area or period of calm in the midst of a difficult or hectic place or situation.
–ORIGIN C17: from Greek.

oast house ■ n. a building containing a kiln for drying hops, typically conical in shape with a cowl on top.
–ORIGIN *oast*: Old English, of Germanic origin.

oat ■ n. a cereal plant with a loose branched cluster of florets, cultivated in cool climates. [*Avena sativa* and related species.]
–PHRASES **feel one's oats** N. Amer. informal feel lively and energetic. **get one's oats** Brit. informal have sexual intercourse. **sow one's wild oats** go through a period of wild or promiscuous behaviour while young.
–DERIVATIVES **oaten** adj. (archaic). **oaty** adj.
–ORIGIN Old English.

oatcake ■ n. a thin savoury oatmeal biscuit, traditionally made in Scotland.

oath ■ n. (pl. **oaths**) **1** a solemn promise, often invoking a divine witness, as to the truth of something or as a commitment to future action. **2** a profane or offensive expression of anger or other strong emotions.
–PHRASES **under** (or Brit. **on**) **oath** having sworn to tell the truth, especially in a court of law.
–ORIGIN Old English, of Germanic origin.

oatmeal ■ n. **1** meal made from ground oats and chiefly used in porridge or oatcakes. ▶ porridge made from oatmeal or rolled oats. **2** a greyish-fawn colour flecked with brown.

OAU ■ abbrev. Organization of African Unity.

ob- (also **oc-** before *c*; **of-** before *f*; **op-** before *p*) ■ prefix forming words of mainly Latin origin, meaning: **1** to; towards: *obverse*. **2** against; blocking: *opponent*. ▶ concealment: *occult*. **3** finality or completeness: *obsolete*. **4** technical in a direction or manner contrary to the usual: *obconical*.
–ORIGIN from Latin *ob* 'towards, against, in the way of'.

ob. ■ abbrev. he or she died.
–ORIGIN from Latin *obiit*.

obbligato /ˌɒblɪ'ɡɑːtəʊ/ (US also **obligato**) ■ n. (pl. **obbligatos** or **obbligati**) an instrumental part integral to a piece of music and not to be omitted in performance.
–ORIGIN Italian, 'obligatory'.

obdurate /'ɒbdjʊrət/ ■ adj. stubbornly refusing to change one's opinion or course of action.
–DERIVATIVES **obduracy** n. **obdurately** adv. **obdurateness** n.
–ORIGIN Middle English: from Latin, from *obdurare*, from *ob-* 'in opposition' + *durare* 'harden'.

OBE ■ abbrev. **1** Officer of the Order of the British Empire. **2** outcomes-based education.

obeche /əʊ'biːtʃi/ ■ n. a tropical African tree whose pale wood is used for plywood and veneers. [*Triplochiton scleroxylon*.]
–ORIGIN C20: a term used in Nigeria.

obedience ■ n. **1** compliance with an order or law or submission to another's authority. **2** observance of a monastic rule.
–DERIVATIVES **obedient** adj. **obediently** adv.
–ORIGIN Middle English: from Latin *oboedientia*, from *oboedire* (see **OBEY**).

obeisance /ə(ʊ)'beɪs(ə)ns/ ■ n. deferential respect. ▶ a gesture expressing this, such as a bow.
–DERIVATIVES **obeisant** adj.
–ORIGIN Middle English: from Old French *obeissance*, from *obeir* 'obey'.

obelisk /'ɒb(ə)lɪsk/ ■ n. **1** a tapering stone pillar of square or rectangular cross section, set up as a monument or landmark. **2** another term for **OBELUS**.
–ORIGIN C16: from Greek *obeliskos*, diminutive of *obelos* 'pointed pillar'.

obelus /'ɒb(ə)ləs/ ■ n. (pl. **obeli** /-lʌɪ, -liː/) **1** a symbol (†) used as a reference mark in printed matter, or to indicate that a person is deceased. **2** a mark (− or ÷) used in ancient manuscripts to mark a word or passage as spurious or doubtful.
–ORIGIN Middle English: from Greek *obelos* 'pointed pillar', also 'critical mark'.

obese ■ adj. grossly fat or overweight.
–DERIVATIVES **obesity** n.
–ORIGIN C17: from Latin *obesus* 'having eaten until fat'.

obey ■ v. submit to the authority of. ▶ carry out

VOWELS a cat ɑː arm ɛ bed ɛː hair ə ago əː her ɪ sit i cosy iː see ɒ hot ɔː saw ʌ run

(a command or instruction). ▶ behave in accordance with (a general principle, natural law, etc.).
– ORIGIN Middle English: from Old French *obeir*, from Latin *oboedire*, from *ob-* 'in the direction of' + *audire* 'hear'.

obfuscate /ˈɒbfʌskeɪt/ ■ v. **1** make unclear or unintelligible. **2** bewilder.
– DERIVATIVES **obfuscation** n. **obfuscatory** adj.
– ORIGIN Middle English: from late Latin *obfuscare* 'darken'.

obi /ˈəʊbi/ ■ n. (pl. **obis**) a broad sash worn round the waist of a Japanese kimono.
– ORIGIN Japanese, 'belt'.

obit /ˈɒbɪt, ˈəʊ-/ ■ n. informal an obituary.

obiter /ˈɒbɪtə/ ■ adv. & adj. (chiefly in legal contexts) made or said in passing. ■ n. short for OBITER DICTUM.
– ORIGIN Latin, orig. as the phr. *ob itur* 'by the way'.

obiter dictum /ˈdɪktəm/ ■ n. (pl. **obiter dicta** /ˈdɪktə/) **1** Law a judge's expression of opinion uttered in court or giving judgement, but not essential to the decision and therefore without binding authority. **2** an incidental remark.
– ORIGIN Latin *obiter* 'in passing' + *dictum* 'something that is said'.

obituary /ə(ʊ)ˈbɪtʃʊəri, -tʃəri, -tjʊəri/ ■ n. (pl. **-ies**) a notice of a person's death in a newspaper or periodical, typically including a brief biography.
– DERIVATIVES **obituarist** n.
– ORIGIN C18: from medieval Latin *obituarius*, from Latin *obitus* 'death'.

object ■ n. /ˈɒbdʒɪkt, -dʒɛkt/ **1** a material thing that can be seen and touched. ▶ Philosophy a thing external to the thinking mind or subject. **2** a person or thing to which an action or feeling is directed: *she was the object of attention*. **3** a goal or purpose. **4** Grammar a noun phrase governed by an active transitive verb or by a preposition. **5** Computing a data construct that provides a description of something known to a computer. ■ v. /əbˈdʒɛkt/ express disapproval or opposition.
– PHRASES **no object** not influencing or restricting choices or decisions: *a tycoon for whom money is no object*.
– DERIVATIVES **objectless** adj. **objector** n.
– ORIGIN Middle English: from medieval Latin *objectum* 'thing presented to the mind', from Latin *obicere*, from *ob-* 'in the way of' + *jacere* 'to throw'.

object ball ■ n. Billiards & Snooker the ball at which a player aims the cue ball.

objectify ■ v. (**-ies**, **-ied**) **1** express in a concrete form. **2** degrade to the status of an object: *a sexist attitude that objectifies women*.
– DERIVATIVES **objectification** n.

objection ■ n. the action of challenging or disagreeing with something. ▶ an expression of disapproval or opposition.

objectionable ■ adj. arousing distaste or opposition.
– DERIVATIVES **objectionableness** n. **objectionably** adv.

objective ■ adj. **1** not influenced by personal feelings or opinions in considering and representing facts. **2** not dependent on the mind for existence; actual. **3** Grammar relating to or denoting a case of nouns and pronouns used for the object of a transitive verb or a preposition. ■ n. **1** a goal or aim. **2** the lens in a telescope or microscope nearest to the object observed.
– DERIVATIVES **objectively** adv. **objectiveness** n. **objectivity** n. **objectivization** (also **-isation**) n. **objectivize** (also **-ise**) v.

objectivism ■ n. **1** the tendency to emphasize what is external to or independent of the mind. **2** Philosophy the belief that moral truths exist independently of human knowledge or perception of them.
– DERIVATIVES **objectivist** n. & adj. **objectivistic** adj.

object language ■ n. a language described by means of another language.

object lesson ■ n. a striking practical example of a principle or ideal.

object relations ■ n. Psychoanalysis a psychoanalytical approach which focuses on emotional bonds between one person and another, especially in terms of the capacity to form caring relationships set against interest in and love for the self.

objet d'art /ˌɒbʒeɪ ˈdɑː/ ■ n. (pl. **objets d'art** pronunc. same) a small decorative or artistic object.
– ORIGIN French, 'object of art'.

objet trouvé /ˌɒbʒeɪ ˈtruːveɪ/ ■ n. (pl. **objets trouvés** pronunc. same) an ordinary object found at random and considered as a work of art.
– ORIGIN French, 'found object'.

oblate /ˈɒbleɪt/ ■ n. a person dedicated to a religious life, but typically not having taken full monastic vows.
– ORIGIN C17: from medieval Latin *oblatus*, from Latin *offerre* 'to offer'.

oblation ■ n. a thing presented or offered to God or a god. ▶ Christian Church the presentation of bread and wine to God in the Eucharist.
– ORIGIN Middle English: from late Latin *oblatio(n-)*, from Latin *offerre* 'to offer'.

obligate ■ v. **1** compel legally or morally. **2** US commit (assets) as security. ■ adj. Biology restricted to a particular function or mode of life: *an obligate parasite*.
– DERIVATIVES **obligator** n.
– ORIGIN Middle English: from Latin *obligat-, obligare* (see OBLIGE).

obligation ■ n. **1** an act or course of action to which a person is morally or legally bound. ▶ the condition of being so bound. **2** a debt of gratitude for a service or favour.
– PHRASES **day of obligation** (in the Roman Catholic Church) a day on which all are required to attend Mass.
– DERIVATIVES **obligational** adj.

obligato ■ n. US variant spelling of OBBLIGATO.

obligatory /əˈblɪɡət(ə)ri/ ■ adj. compulsory. ▶ (of a ruling) having binding force.
– DERIVATIVES **obligatorily** adv.

oblige ■ v. **1** (usu. **be obliged to do something**) compel legally or morally. **2** perform a service or favour for. ▶ (**be obliged**) be indebted or grateful.
– ORIGIN Middle English: from Old French *obliger*, from Latin *obligare*, from *ob-* 'towards' + *ligare* 'to bind'.

obliging ■ adj. willing to do a service or kindness; helpful.
– DERIVATIVES **obligingly** adv. **obligingness** n.

oblique /əˈbliːk/ ■ adj. **1** neither parallel nor at right angles; slanting. **2** not explicit or direct. **3** Geometry (of a line, plane figure, or surface) inclined at other than a right angle. ▶ (of an angle) acute or obtuse. ▶ (of a cone, cylinder, etc.) with an axis not perpendicular to the plane of its base. **4** Anatomy (especially of a muscle) neither parallel nor perpendicular to the long axis of a body or limb. ■ n. **1** Brit. another term for SLASH (in sense 3). **2** an oblique muscle.
– DERIVATIVES **obliquely** adv. **obliqueness** n. **obliquity** /əˈblɪkwɪti/ n.
– ORIGIN Middle English: from Latin *obliquus*.

obliterate /əˈblɪtəreɪt/ ■ v. **1** destroy utterly; wipe out. **2** blot out; erase.
– DERIVATIVES **obliteration** n. **obliterative** /-rətɪv/ adj. **obliterator** n.
– ORIGIN C16: from Latin *obliterare* 'strike out, erase', from *littera* 'letter, something written'.

oblivion ■ n. **1** the state of being unaware of what is happening around one. **2** the state of being forgotten. **3** destruction or extinction.
– ORIGIN Middle English: from Latin *oblivio(n-)*, from *oblivisci* 'forget'.

oblivious ■ adj. not aware of what is happening around one.
– DERIVATIVES **obliviously** adv. **obliviousness** n.

oblong ■ adj. having a rectangular shape. ■ n. an oblong object or flat figure.
– ORIGIN Middle English: from Latin *oblongus* 'longish'.

obloquy /ˈɒbləkwi/ ■ n. strong public condemnation.
– ORIGIN Middle English: from late Latin *obloquium* 'contradiction', from Latin *obloqui*, from *ob-* 'against' + *loqui* 'speak'.

obnoxious /əbˈnɒkʃəs/ ■ adj. extremely unpleasant.
– DERIVATIVES **obnoxiously** adv. **obnoxiousness** n.
– ORIGIN C16: from Latin, from *obnoxius* 'exposed to harm', from *ob-* 'towards' + *noxa* 'harm'.

oboe /ˈəʊbəʊ/ ■ n. a woodwind instrument of treble pitch, played with a double reed and having an incisive tone.
– DERIVATIVES **oboist** n.
– ORIGIN C18: from Italian, or from French *hautbois*, from *haut* 'high' + *bois* 'wood'.

oboe d'amore /daˈmɔːreɪ/ ■ n. a type of oboe with a bulbous bell, sounding a minor third lower than the ordinary oboe and used in baroque music.
– ORIGIN C19: from Italian, 'oboe of love'.

obovate /ɒbˈəʊveɪt/ ■ adj. Botany (of a leaf) ovate, with the narrower end at the base.

obscene ■ adj. **1** offensive or disgusting by accepted standards of morality and decency. **2** repugnant.
– DERIVATIVES **obscenely** adv.
– ORIGIN C16: from French *obscène* or Latin *obscaenus* 'ill-omened or abominable'.

obscenity ■ n. (pl. **-ies**) **1** the state or quality of being obscene. **2** an obscene action, image, or expression.

obscurantism /ˌɒbskjʊˈrantɪz(ə)m/ ■ n. the practice of preventing the facts or full details of something from becoming known.
– DERIVATIVES **obscurant** n. & adj. **obscurantist** n. & adj.
– ORIGIN C19: from earlier *obscurant*, denoting a person who obscures something, from Latin *obscurare* 'make dark'.

obscure ■ adj. (**-er**, **-est**) **1** not discovered or known about; uncertain. ▸ not important or well known. **2** not clearly expressed or easily understood. **3** hard to make out; indistinct. ■ v. **1** keep from being seen; conceal. **2** make unclear.
– DERIVATIVES **obscuration** n. **obscurely** adv. **obscurity** n.
– ORIGIN Middle English: from Old French *obscur*, from Latin *obscurus* 'dark'.

obsequies /ˈɒbsɪkwɪz/ ■ pl. n. funeral rites.
– ORIGIN Middle English: from medieval Latin *obsequiae*, from Latin *exsequiae* 'funeral rites', influenced by *obsequium* 'dutiful service'.

obsequious /əbˈsiːkwɪəs/ ■ adj. obedient or attentive to an excessive or servile degree.
– DERIVATIVES **obsequiously** adv. **obsequiousness** n.
– ORIGIN C15: from Latin *obsequiosus*, from *obsequium* 'compliance', from *obsequi* 'follow, comply with'.

observance ■ n. **1** the practice of observing the requirements of law, morality, or ritual. **2** (usu. **observances**) an act performed for religious or ceremonial reasons. ▸ a rule to be followed by a religious order. **3** archaic respect; deference.

observant ■ adj. **1** quick to notice things. **2** observing the rules of a religion.

observation ■ n. **1** the action or process of closely observing or monitoring. **2** the ability to notice significant details. **3** the taking of the sun's or another celestial body's altitude to find a latitude or longitude. **4** a comment based on something one has seen, heard, or noticed.
– DERIVATIVES **observational** adj. **observationally** adv.

observatory ■ n. (pl. **-ies**) a room or building housing an astronomical telescope or other scientific equipment for the study of natural phenomena.

observe ■ v. **1** notice; perceive. ▸ watch attentively. ▸ detect in the course of a scientific study. **2** say; remark: *'It's chilly,' she observed.* **3** fulfil or comply with.
– DERIVATIVES **observable** adj. **observably** adv. **observer** n.
– ORIGIN Middle English: from Old French *observer*, from Latin *observare* 'to watch'.

obsess ■ v. **1** (usu. **be obsessed**) preoccupy continually or to a troubling extent. **2** be preoccupied in this way.
– DERIVATIVES **obsessive** adj. & n. **obsessively** adv. **obsessiveness** n.
– ORIGIN Middle English: from Latin *obsess-*, *obsidere* 'besiege'.

obsession ■ n. **1** the state of being obsessed. **2** an idea or thought that obsesses someone.
– DERIVATIVES **obsessional** adj. **obsessionally** adv.

obsessive-compulsive ■ adj. Psychiatry denoting or relating to a disorder in which a person feels compelled to perform certain actions repeatedly to alleviate persistent fears or intrusive thoughts.

obsidian /əbˈsɪdɪən/ ■ n. a hard, dark, glass-like volcanic rock formed by the rapid solidification of lava without crystallization.
– ORIGIN C17: from Latin *obsidianus*, error for *obsianus*, from *Obsius*, the name (in Pliny) of the discoverer of a similar stone.

obsolescent /ˌɒbsəˈlɛs(ə)nt/ ■ adj. becoming obsolete.
– DERIVATIVES **obsolesce** v. **obsolescence** n.
– ORIGIN C18: from Latin *obsolescere* 'fall into disuse'.

obsolete ■ adj. no longer produced or used; out of date. ■ v. chiefly US cause (a product or idea) to become obsolete by replacing it with something new.
– DERIVATIVES **obsoleteness** n. **obsoletism** n.
– ORIGIN C16: from Latin *obsoletus* 'grown old, worn out', from *obsolescere* 'fall into disuse'.

obstacle ■ n. a thing that blocks one's way or hinders progress.
– ORIGIN Middle English: from Latin *obstaculum*, from *obstare* 'impede'.

obstacle race ■ n. a race in which various obstacles, such as fences and pits, have to be negotiated.

obstetric ■ adj. of or relating to childbirth and the processes associated with it.
– DERIVATIVES **obstetrical** adj. **obstetrically** adv. **obstetrics** pl. n.
– ORIGIN C18: from Latin *obstetricius*, from *obstetrix* 'midwife', from *obstare* 'be present'.

obstetrician /ˌɒbstəˈtrɪʃ(ə)n/ ■ n. a physician or surgeon qualified to practise in obstetrics.

obstinate ■ adj. **1** stubbornly refusing to change one's opinion or chosen course of action. **2** unyielding: *an obstinate problem*.
– DERIVATIVES **obstinacy** n. **obstinately** adv.
– ORIGIN Middle English: from Latin *obstinatus*, *obstinare* 'persist'.

obstreperous /əbˈstrɛp(ə)rəs/ ■ adj. noisy and difficult to control.
– DERIVATIVES **obstreperously** adv. **obstreperousness** n.
– ORIGIN C16: from Latin *obstreperus*, from *obstrepere*, from *ob-* 'against' + *strepere* 'make a noise'.

obstruct ■ v. **1** block; be in the way of. **2** prevent or hinder.
– DERIVATIVES **obstructor** n.
– ORIGIN C16: from Latin *obstruct-*, *obstruere* 'block up'.

obstruction ■ n. **1** the action of obstructing or the state of being obstructed. **2** a thing that obstructs.

obstructionism ■ n. the practice of deliberately impeding or delaying the course of legal, legislative, or other procedures.
– DERIVATIVES **obstructionist** n. & adj.

obstructive ■ adj. **1** causing an obstruction. **2** causing deliberate difficulties and delays: *a culture of obstructive bureaucracy*.
– DERIVATIVES **obstructively** adv. **obstructiveness** n.

obstruent /ˈɒbstrʊənt/ ■ n. Phonetics a fricative or plosive speech sound.
– ORIGIN C17: from Latin *obstruere* 'block up'.

obtain ■ v. **1** acquire or secure. **2** formal be prevalent, customary, or established.
– DERIVATIVES **obtainability** n. **obtainable** adj. **obtainer** n. **obtainment** n. **obtention** n.
– ORIGIN Middle English: from Old French *obtenir*, from Latin *obtinere* 'obtain, gain'.

obtrude ■ v. **1** become obtrusive. **2** impose or force on someone.
– DERIVATIVES **obtruder** n. **obtrusion** n.
– ORIGIN C16: from Latin *obtrudere*, from *ob-* 'towards' + *trudere* 'to push'.

obtrusive ■ adj. noticeable or prominent in an unwelcome or intrusive way.
– DERIVATIVES **obtrusively** adv. **obtrusiveness** n.
– ORIGIN C17: from Latin *obtrus-*, *obtrudere* (see **OBTRUDE**).

obturator /ˈɒbtjʊəreɪtə/ ■ n. Anatomy either of two muscles covering the outer front part of the pelvis on each side and involved in movements of the thigh and hip.
– ORIGIN C18: from medieval Latin, 'obstructor', from *obturare* 'stop up'.

obtuse ■ adj. **1** annoyingly insensitive or slow to understand. **2** (of an angle) more than 90° and less than 180°. **3** not sharp-pointed or sharp-edged; blunt.
– DERIVATIVES **obtusely** adv. **obtuseness** n. **obtusity** n.
– ORIGIN Middle English: from Latin *obtusus*, *obtundere*, from *ob-* 'against' + *tundere* 'to beat'.

obverse ■ n. **1** the side of a coin or medal bearing the head or principal design. **2** the opposite or counterpart of a fact or truth. ■ adj. **1** of or denoting the obverse of a coin or medal. **2** corresponding to something as its opposite or counterpart.
– DERIVATIVES **obversely** adv.
– ORIGIN C17: from Latin *obversus*, *obvertere*, from *ob-* 'towards' + *vertere* 'to turn'.

obviate /ˈɒbvɪeɪt/ ■ v. **1** remove (a need or difficulty). **2** avoid; prevent.
– DERIVATIVES **obviation** n.
– ORIGIN C16: from late Latin *obviare* 'prevent'.

obvious ■ adj. **1** easily perceived or understood; clear. **2** derogatory predictable and lacking in subtlety.
– DERIVATIVES **obviously** adv. **obviousness** n.
– ORIGIN C16: from Latin *obvius*, from the phr. *ob viam* 'in the way'.

OC ■ abbrev. Officer Commanding.

oc- ■ prefix variant spelling of **OB-** assimilated before *c* (as in *occasion*, *occlude*).

ocarina /ˌɒkəˈriːnə/ ■ n. a small wind instrument with holes for the fingers, typically having the shape of a bird.
– ORIGIN C19: from Italian, from *oca* 'goose' (from its shape).

occasion ■ n. **1** a particular event, or the time at which it takes place. ▶ a suitable or opportune time. **2** a special event or celebration. **3** formal reason; cause: *we have occasion to rejoice*. ■ v. formal cause.
– PHRASES **on occasion** from time to time. **rise to the occasion** perform well in response to a special situation. **take occasion** make use of an opportunity to do something.
– ORIGIN Middle English: from Latin *occasio(n-)* 'juncture, reason', from *occidere* 'go down, set'.

occasional ■ adj. **1** occurring infrequently or irregularly. **2** produced on or intended for particular occasions: *occasional verse*.
– DERIVATIVES **occasionality** n. **occasionally** adv.

Occident /ˈɒksɪd(ə)nt/ ■ n. (**the Occident**) formal or poetic/literary the countries of the West, especially Europe and America.
– ORIGIN Middle English: from Latin *occidere* 'go down, set'.

occidental ■ adj. of or relating to the countries of the West. ■ n. (**Occidental**) a native or inhabitant of the West.
– DERIVATIVES **occidentalism** n. **occidentalize** (also **-ise**) v.

occipital bone ■ n. Anatomy the bone which forms the back and base of the skull and encircles the spinal cord.

occipital lobe ■ n. Anatomy the rearmost lobe in each cerebral hemisphere of the brain.

occiput /ˈɒksɪpʌt/ ■ n. Anatomy the back of the head.
– DERIVATIVES **occipital** adj.
– ORIGIN Middle English: from Latin *occiput*, from *ob-* 'against' + *caput* 'head'.

Occitan /ˈɒksɪt(ə)n/ ■ n. the medieval or modern language of Languedoc (southern France), including literary Provençal of the 12th–14th centuries. ■ adj. of or relating to Occitan.
– ORIGIN from French.

occlude /əˈkluːd/ ■ v. **1** stop, close up, or obstruct. **2** Chemistry (of a solid) absorb and retain (a gas or impurity). **3** (of a tooth) come into contact with another in the opposite jaw.
– ORIGIN C16: from Latin *occludere* 'shut up'.

occluded front ■ n. Meteorology a composite front produced by occlusion.

occlusion ■ n. **1** Medicine the blockage or closing of a blood vessel or hollow organ. **2** Meteorology a process by which the cold front of a rotating low-pressure system catches up the warm front, so that the warm air between them is forced upwards. **3** Dentistry the position of the teeth when the jaws are closed.
– DERIVATIVES **occlusive** adj.

occult /ɒˈkʌlt, ˈɒkʌlt/ ■ n. (**the occult**) supernatural beliefs, practices, or phenomena. ■ adj. **1** of, involving, or relating to the occult. **2** esoteric. **3** Medicine (of a disease or process) not accompanied by readily discernible signs or symptoms. ▶ (of blood) abnormally present, but detectable only chemically or microscopically. ■ v. /ɒˈkʌlt/ **1** cut off from view by interposing something. **2** Astronomy (of a celestial body) conceal (an apparently smaller body) from view by passing or being in front of it.
– DERIVATIVES **occultation** n. **occultism** n. **occultist** n. **occultly** adv. **occultness** n.
– ORIGIN C15: from Latin *occultare* 'secrete', from *occult-*, *occulere* 'conceal'.

occupancy ■ n. **1** the action or fact of occupying a place. **2** the proportion of hotel or office accommodation occupied or used.

occupant ■ n. **1** a person who occupies a place at a given time. ▶ Law a person holding property, especially land, in actual possession. **2** the holder of a position or office.

occupation ■ n. **1** the action, state, or period of occupying or being occupied. **2** a job or profession. **3** a way of spending time.
– DERIVATIVES **occupational** adj. **occupationally** adv.

occupational hazard ■ n. a risk accepted as a consequence of a particular occupation.

occupational psychology ■ n. the study of human behaviour at work.
– DERIVATIVES **occupational psychologist** n.

occupational therapy ■ n. the use of particular activities as an aid to recuperation from physical or mental illness.
– DERIVATIVES **occupational therapist** n.

occupy ■ v. (**-ies**, **-ied**) **1** reside or have one's place of business in. ▶ take control of (a place) by military conquest or settlement. ▶ enter and stay in (a building) without authority, especially as a form of protest. **2** fill or take up (a space or time). **3** hold (a position or job). **4** keep (someone) busy, active, or preoccupied.
– DERIVATIVES **occupier** n.
– ORIGIN Middle English: from Old French *occuper*, from Latin *occupare* 'seize'.

occur ■ v. (**occurred**, **occurring**) **1** happen; take place. **2** exist or be found to be present in a place or under a particular set of conditions. **3** (**occur to**) come into the mind of.
– ORIGIN C15: from Latin *occurrere* 'go to meet, present itself', from *ob-* 'against' + *currere* 'to run'.

occurrence /əˈkʌr(ə)ns/ ■ n. **1** the fact or frequency of something occurring. **2** a thing that occurs; an incident or event.

occurrent ■ adj. actually occurring or observable, not potential or hypothetical.

ocean ■ n. a very large expanse of sea; in particular, each of the Atlantic, Pacific, Indian, Arctic, and Antarctic Oceans. ▶ (**the ocean**) chiefly N. Amer. the sea.
– DERIVATIVES **oceanward** adv. & adj. **oceanwards** adv.
– ORIGIN Middle English: from Old French *ocean*, from Greek *ōkeanos* 'great stream encircling the earth's disc'.

oceanarium /ˌəʊʃəˈnɛːrɪəm/ ■ n. (pl. **oceanariums** or **oceanaria** /-rɪə/) a large seawater aquarium.
– ORIGIN 1940s: from OCEAN, on the pattern of *aquarium*.

Oceanian /ˌəʊsɪˈɑːnɪən, -ʃɪ-/ ■ adj. of or relating to Oceania, the islands of the Pacific Ocean and adjacent seas. ■ n. a native or inhabitant of Oceania; a Polynesian.

oceanic /ˌəʊsɪˈanɪk, -ʃɪ-/ ■ adj. **1** of or relating to the ocean. **2** (**Oceanic**) another term for OCEANIAN.

oceanic bonito ■ n. a skipjack tuna.

Oceanid /əʊˈsiːənɪd, ˈəʊʃ(ə)nɪd/ ■ n. (pl. **Oceanids** or **Oceanides** /ˌəʊsɪˈanɪdiːz, ˌəʊʃɪ-/) Greek & Roman Mythology a sea nymph.
– ORIGIN from French *Océanide*, from Greek *ōkeanis*.

oceanography ■ n. the branch of science concerned with the physical and biological properties and phenomena of the sea.
– DERIVATIVES **oceanographer** n. **oceanographic** adj. **oceanographical** adj.

oceanology ■ n. **1** another term for OCEANOGRAPHY. **2** the branch of technology and economics concerned with human use of the sea.
– DERIVATIVES **oceanological** adj. **oceanologist** n.

ocellated /ˈɒsɪleɪtɪd/ ■ adj. (of an animal, or its plumage or body surface) having eye-like markings.

ocellus /əˈsɛləs/ ■ n. (pl. **ocelli** /-lʌɪ, -liː/) Zoology **1** another term for SIMPLE EYE. **2** another term for EYESPOT (in sense 1).
– DERIVATIVES **ocellar** adj.
– ORIGIN C19: from Latin, diminutive of *oculus* 'eye'.

ocelot /ˈɒsɪlɒt, ˈəʊs-/ ■ n. a medium-sized wild cat that has an orange-yellow coat marked with black stripes and spots, native to South and Central America. [*Felis pardalis*.]
– ORIGIN C18: from French, from Nahuatl *tlatlocelotl* 'field tiger'.

och /ɒk, ɒx/ ■ exclam. Scottish & Irish used to express a range of emotions, typically surprise, regret, or disbelief.

oche /ˈɒki/ ■ n. Brit. the line behind which darts players stand when throwing.
– ORIGIN C20: perhaps rel. to Old French *ocher* 'cut a notch in'.

ochre /ˈəʊkə/ (US also **ocher**) ■ n. an earthy pigment containing ferric oxide, varying from light yellow to brown or red.
– DERIVATIVES **ochreish** adj. **ochreous** /ˈəʊkrɪəs/ adj. **ochroid** adj. **ochrous** adj. **ochry** adj.
– ORIGIN Middle English: from Old French *ocre*, from Greek *ōkhra* 'yellow ochre'.

-ock ■ suffix forming nouns originally with diminutive sense: *haddock*. ▸ also occasionally forming words from other sources: *bannock*.
– ORIGIN Old English.

o'clock ■ adv. used to specify the hour when telling the time.
– ORIGIN contraction of *of the clock*.

OCR ■ abbrev. optical character recognition.

-ocracy ■ comb. form see -CRACY.

Oct. ■ abbrev. October.

oct- ■ comb. form variant spelling of OCTA- and OCTO- assimilated before a vowel (as in *octennial*).

oct. ■ abbrev. octavo.

octa- (also **oct-** before a vowel) ■ comb. form eight; having eight: *octahedron*.
– ORIGIN from Greek *oktō* 'eight'.

octad /ˈɒktad/ ■ n. a group or set of eight.
– ORIGIN C19: from Greek *oktas, oktad-*, from *oktō* 'eight'.

octagon ■ n. a plane figure with eight straight sides and eight angles.
– DERIVATIVES **octagonal** adj. **octagonally** adv.
– ORIGIN C16: from Greek *oktagōnos* 'eight-angled'.

octahedron /ˌɒktəˈhiːdrən, -ˈhɛd-/ ■ n. (pl. **octahedra** /-drə/ or **octahedrons**) a three-dimensional shape having eight plane faces, in particular a regular solid figure with eight equal triangular faces.
– DERIVATIVES **octahedral** adj.
– ORIGIN C16: from Greek *oktaedron*, from *oktaedros* 'eight-faced'.

octal /ˈɒkt(ə)l/ ■ adj. relating to or using a system of numerical notation that has 8 rather than 10 as a base. ■ n. the octal system; octal notation.

octamerous /ɒkˈtam(ə)rəs/ ■ adj. Botany & Zoology **1** having parts arranged in groups of eight. **2** consisting of eight joints or parts.

octane ■ n. Chemistry a liquid hydrocarbon of the alkane series, present in petroleum spirit. [C_8H_{18}.]
– ORIGIN C19: from OCTO- 'eight' (denoting eight carbon atoms) + -ANE².

octane number (also **octane rating**) ■ n. a figure indicating the anti-knock properties of a fuel, based on a comparison with a mixture of isooctane and heptane.

octant /ˈɒkt(ə)nt/ ■ n. **1** an arc of a circle equal to one eighth of its circumference, or the area enclosed by such an arc with two radii of the circle. **2** each of eight parts into which a space or solid body is divided by three planes which intersect (especially at right angles) at a single point.
– ORIGIN C17: from Latin *octans, octant-* 'half-quadrant', from *octo* 'eight'.

octavalent /ˌɒktəˈveɪl(ə)nt/ ■ adj. Chemistry having a valency of eight.

octave /ˈɒktɪv/ ■ n. **1** Music a series of eight notes occupying the interval between (and including) two notes, one having twice or half the frequency of vibration of the other. ▸ the interval between these two notes. ▸ each of the two notes at the extremes of this interval. ▸ these two notes sounding together. **2** a group or stanza of eight lines. **3** the seventh day after a Church festival. ▸ a period of eight days beginning with the day of such a festival. **4** Fencing the last of eight parrying positions.
– ORIGIN Middle English: from Latin *octava dies* 'eighth day'.

octavo /ɒkˈtɑːvəʊ, -ˈteɪ-/ (abbrev.: **8vo**) ■ n. (pl. **-os**) a size of book page that results from folding each printed sheet into eight leaves (sixteen pages).
– ORIGIN C16: from Latin *in octavo* 'in an eighth', from *octavus* 'eighth'.

octennial ■ adj. lasting for or recurring every eight years.
– ORIGIN C17: from late Latin *octennium* 'period of eight years'.

octet /ɒkˈtɛt/ ■ n. **1** a group of eight musicians. ▸ a musical composition for eight voices or instruments. **2** a group of eight lines of verse. **3** Chemistry a stable group of eight electrons occupying a single shell in an atom.
– ORIGIN C19: from Italian *ottetto* or German *Oktett*, on the pattern of *duet* and *quartet*.

octo- (also **oct-** before a vowel) ■ comb. form eight; having eight: *octosyllabic*.
– ORIGIN from Latin *octo* or Greek *oktō* 'eight'.

October ■ n. the tenth month of the year.
– ORIGIN Old English, from Latin, from *octo* 'eight' (being orig. the eighth month of the Roman year).

octodecimo /ˌɒktəʊˈdɛsɪməʊ/ ■ n. (pl. **-os**) a size of book page resulting from folding each printed sheet into eighteen leaves (thirty-six pages).
– ORIGIN C19: from Latin *in octodecimo* 'in an eighteenth', from *octodecimus* 'eighteenth'.

octogenarian /ˌɒktə(ʊ)dʒɪˈnɛːrɪən/ ■ n. a person who is between 80 and 89 years old.
– ORIGIN C19: from Latin *octogenarius*, from *octoginta* 'eighty'.

Octopoda /ˌɒktəˈpəʊdə/ ■ pl. n. Zoology an order of cephalopod molluscs that comprises the octopuses.
– DERIVATIVES **octopod** n.
– ORIGIN from Greek *oktōpous, oktōpod-*, from *oktō* 'eight' + *pous* 'foot'.

octopus ■ n. (pl. **octopuses**) a cephalopod mollusc with eight sucker-bearing arms, a soft sac-like body, strong beak-like jaws, and no internal shell. [Order Octopoda: many species.]
– DERIVATIVES **octopoid** adj.
– ORIGIN C18: from Greek *oktōpous* (see OCTOPODA).

> **USAGE**
> The standard plural in English of **octopus** is **octopuses**. However, since the word comes from Greek, the Greek plural form **octopodes** is still occasionally used. The plural form **octopi**, formed according to rules for Latin plurals, is incorrect.

octoroon /ˌɒktəˈruːn/ ■ n. archaic a person whose parents are a quadroon and a white person and who is therefore one-eighth black by descent.
– ORIGIN C19: from OCTO-, on the pattern of *quadroon*.

octuple /ˈɒktjʊp(ə)l, ɒkˈtjuːp(ə)l/ ■ adj. **1** consisting of eight parts or things. **2** eight times as many or as much. ■ v. make or become eight times as numerous or as large.
– ORIGIN C17: from French *octuple* or Latin *octuplus*, from *octo* 'eight' + *-plus*.

octuplet ■ n. each of eight children born at one birth.

ocular /ˈɒkjʊlə/ ■ adj. Medicine of or connected with the eyes or vision. ■ n. another term for EYEPIECE.
– DERIVATIVES **ocularly** adv.

–ORIGIN C16: from late Latin *ocularis*, from Latin *oculus* 'eye'.

ocularist ■ n. a person who makes artificial eyes.

oculist /ˈɒkjʊlɪst/ ■ n. a person who specializes in the medical treatment of diseases or defects of the eye; an ophthalmologist.
–ORIGIN C16: from French *oculiste*, from Latin *oculus* 'eye'.

oculomotor nerves ■ pl. n. Anatomy the pair of cranial nerves supplying muscles around and within the eyeballs.

oculus /ˈɒkjʊləs/ ■ n. (pl. **oculi** /-lʌɪ, -liː/) Architecture **1** a circular window. **2** the central boss of a volute. **3** an opening at the apex of a dome.
–ORIGIN C19: from Latin, 'eye'.

OD informal ■ v. (**OD's**, **OD'd**, **OD'ing**) take an overdose of a drug. ■ n. an overdose.

odalisque /ˈəʊd(ə)lɪsk/ ■ n. historical a female slave or concubine in a harem.
–ORIGIN C17: from French, from Turkish *odalik*, from *oda* 'chamber' + *lik* 'function'.

odd ■ adj. **1** unusual or unexpected; strange. **2** (of whole numbers such as 3 and 5) having one left over as a remainder when divided by two. ▸ denoting a single goal by which one side defeats another in a game where three or more goals are scored. **3** [in combination] in the region of: *fifty-odd years*. **4** occasional: *we have the odd drink together*. ▸ spare; unoccupied: *an odd five minutes*. **5** detached from a pair or set.
–PHRASES **odd one out** a person or thing differing in some way from the other members of a group or set.
–DERIVATIVES **oddish** adj. **oddly** adv. **oddness** n.
–ORIGIN Middle English: from Old Norse *odda-*, as in *odda-mathr* 'third or odd man', from *oddi* 'angle'.

oddball informal ■ n. a strange or eccentric person. ■ adj. strange; bizarre.

oddity ■ n. (pl. **-ies**) **1** the quality of being strange. **2** a strange person or thing.

odd job ■ n. a casual or isolated piece of work, especially one of a routine domestic or manual nature.
–DERIVATIVES **odd-jobber** n. **odd-jobbing** n.

odd-job man ■ n. a man who does odd jobs.

odd lot ■ n. **1** an incomplete set or random mixture of things. **2** US Finance a transaction involving an unusually small number of shares.

oddment ■ n. (usu. **oddments**) an item or piece of something left over from a larger piece or set.

odds ■ pl. n. **1** the ratio between the amounts staked by the parties to a bet, based on the expected probability either way. **2** (**the odds**) the chances of something happening or being the case. **3** (**the odds**) the balance of advantage; superiority in strength, power, or resources: *she clung to the lead against all the odds*.
–PHRASES **at odds** in conflict or at variance. **by all odds** N. Amer. certainly. **it makes no odds** informal, chiefly Brit. it does not matter. [from an earlier use of *odds* in the sense 'difference in advantage or effect'.] **lay odds** be very sure of something. **over the odds** Brit. (especially of a price) above what is generally considered acceptable.
–ORIGIN C16: apparently the pl. of the obsolete noun *odd* 'odd number or odd person'.

odds and ends ■ pl. n. miscellaneous articles or remnants.

odds and sods ■ pl. n. informal miscellaneous people or articles.

odds-on ■ adj. **1** (especially of a horse) rated at evens or less to win. **2** very likely to happen or succeed.

ode ■ n. **1** a lyric poem, typically in the form of an address, written in varied or irregular metre. **2** a classical poem of a kind originally meant to be sung.
–ORIGIN C16: from late Latin *oda*, from Greek *ōidē* 'song', from *aeidein* 'sing'.

-ode¹ ■ comb. form of the nature of a specified thing: *geode*.
–ORIGIN from Greek adjectival ending *-ōdēs*.

-ode² ■ comb. form in names of electrodes, or devices having them: *diode*.
–ORIGIN from Greek *hodos* 'way'.

odiferous /əʊˈdɪf(ə)rəs/ ■ adj. variant spelling of ODORIFEROUS.

odious ■ adj. extremely unpleasant; repulsive.
–DERIVATIVES **odiously** adv. **odiousness** n.
–ORIGIN Middle English: from Old French *odieus*, from Latin *odiosus*, from *odium* 'hatred'.

odium /ˈəʊdɪəm/ ■ n. general or widespread hatred or disgust.
–ORIGIN C17: from Latin, 'hatred', from the verb stem *od-* 'hate'.

odometer /əʊˈdɒmɪtə/ ■ n. an instrument on a wheeled vehicle for measuring the distance it has travelled.
–ORIGIN C18: from French *odomètre*, from Greek *hodos* 'way' + -METER.

Odonata /ˌəʊdəˈnɑːtə/ ■ pl. n. Entomology an order of insects that comprises the dragonflies and damselflies.
–DERIVATIVES **odonate** n. & adj.
–ORIGIN from Greek *odōn* (var. of *odous*) 'tooth', with ref. to the insect's mandibles.

odontoid /ə(ʊ)ˈdɒntɔɪd/ (also **odontoid process**) ■ n. Anatomy a projection from the second cervical vertebra (axis) on which the first (atlas) can pivot.
–ORIGIN C19: from Greek *odontoeidēs*, from *odous* 'tooth' + *eidos* 'form'.

odontology /ˌɒdɒnˈtɒlədʒi, ˌəʊdɒn-/ ■ n. the scientific study of the structure and diseases of teeth.
–DERIVATIVES **odontological** adj. **odontologist** n.

odor ■ n. US spelling of ODOUR.

odorant ■ n. a substance used to give a particular scent or odour to a product.
–ORIGIN Middle English: from Old French, from *odorer*, from Latin *odorare* 'give an odour to'.

odoriferous /ˌəʊdəˈrɪf(ə)rəs/ ■ adj. having an odour.
–DERIVATIVES **odoriferously** adv.
–ORIGIN Middle English: from Latin *odorifer* 'odour-bearing'.

odour (US **odor**) ■ n. a distinctive smell. ▸ a lingering quality or impression.
–PHRASES **be in good** (or **bad**) **odour** informal be in or out of favour.
–DERIVATIVES **odorize** (also **-ise**) v. **odorizer** (also **-iser**) n. **odorous** adj. **odourless** adj.
–ORIGIN Middle English: from Latin *odor* 'smell, scent'.

odyssey /ˈɒdɪsi/ ■ n. (pl. **-eys**) a long and eventful or adventurous journey or process.
–DERIVATIVES **odyssean** /ˌɒdɪˈsiːən/ adj.
–ORIGIN C19: from *Odyssey*, the title of a Greek epic poem attributed to Homer; from Greek *Odusseia*.

Oe ■ abbrev. oersted(s).

OECD ■ abbrev. Organization for Economic Cooperation and Development.

OED ■ abbrev. Oxford English Dictionary.

oedema /ɪˈdiːmə/ (US **edema**) ■ n. a condition characterized by an excess of watery fluid collecting in the cavities or tissues of the body.
–DERIVATIVES **oedematous** adj.
–ORIGIN Middle English: from Greek *oidēma*, from *oidein* 'to swell'.

Oedipus complex ■ n. (in Freudian theory) the complex of emotions aroused in a young child by an unconscious sexual desire for the parent of the opposite sex.
–DERIVATIVES **Oedipal** adj.
–ORIGIN C20: by association with *Oedipus*, who, in Greek mythology, unwittingly killed his father and married his mother.

OEM ■ abbrev. original equipment manufacturer.

oenology /iːˈnɒlədʒi/ (US also **enology**) ■ n. the study of wines.
–DERIVATIVES **oenological** adj. **oenologist** n.
–ORIGIN C19: from Greek *oinos* 'wine' + -LOGY.

oenophile /ˈiːnə(ʊ)fʌɪl/ (US also **enophile**) ■ n. a connoisseur of wines.
–DERIVATIVES **oenophilist** /iːˈnɒfɪlɪst/ n.

o'er ■ adv. & prep. archaic or poetic/literary form of OVER.

oersted (abbrev.: **Oe**) ■ n. Physics a unit of magnetic field strength equivalent to 79.58 amperes per metre.
–ORIGIN C19: named after Danish physicist H. C. *Oersted*.

oesophagitis /ɪˌsɒfəgəˈdʒʌɪtɪs/ (US **esophagitis**) ■ n. Medicine inflammation of the oesophagus.

oesophagus /ɪˈsɒfəgəs/ (US **esophagus**) ■ n. (pl. **oesophagi** /-dʒʌɪ/ or **oesophaguses**) the part of the alimentary canal which connects the throat to the stomach.
– DERIVATIVES **oesophageal** /ɪˌsɒfəˈdʒiːəl, ˌiːsəˈfadʒɪəl/ adj.
– ORIGIN Middle English: from Greek *oisophagos*.

oestradiol /ˌiːstrəˈdʌɪɒl, ˌɛstrə-/ (US **estradiol**) ■ n. Biochemistry a major oestrogen produced in the ovaries.
– ORIGIN 1930s: from OESTRUS.

oestriol /ˈiːstrɪɒl, ˈɛstrɪɒl/ (US also **estriol**) ■ n. Biochemistry an oestrogen which is one of the metabolic products of oestradiol.
– ORIGIN 1930s: from *oestrane* (the parent molecule of most oestrogens).

oestrogen /ˈiːstrədʒ(ə)n, ˈɛstrə-/ (US **estrogen**) ■ n. any of a group of steroid hormones which promote the development and maintenance of female characteristics of the body.
– DERIVATIVES **oestrogenic** adj.
– ORIGIN 1920s: from OESTRUS.

oestrone /ˈiːstrəʊn, ˈɛstrəʊn/ (US **estrone**) ■ n. Biochemistry an oestrogen similar to but less potent than oestradiol.
– ORIGIN 1930s: from *oestrane* (parent molecule of most oestrogens).

oestrus /ˈiːstrəs, ˈɛstrəs/ (US **estrus**) ■ n. a recurring period of sexual receptivity and fertility in many female mammals; heat.
– DERIVATIVES **oestrous** adj.
– ORIGIN C17: from Greek *oistros* 'gadfly or frenzy'.

oeuvre /ˈəːvr(ə)/ ■ n. the body of work of a painter, composer, or author.
– ORIGIN C19: French, 'work'.

of ■ prep. **1** expressing the relationship between a part and a whole. **2** expressing the relationship between a scale or measure and a value. ▸ expressing an age. **3** indicating an association between two entities, typically one of belonging. **4** expressing the relationship between a direction and a point of reference. **5** expressing the relationship between a general category and something which belongs to such a category. **6** expressing the relationship between an abstract concept and a noun denoting the subject or object of the underlying verb. **7** indicating the relationship between a verb and an indirect object. **8** indicating the material constituting something. **9** N. Amer. expressing time in relation to the following hour.
– PHRASES **be of** possess intrinsically or give rise to.
– ORIGIN Old English, of Germanic origin.

of- ■ prefix variant spelling of OB- assimilated before *f* (as in *offend*).

off ■ adv. **1** away from the place in question. **2** so as to be removed or separated. **3** starting a journey or race. **4** so as to bring to an end or be discontinued. **5** (of an electrical appliance or power supply) not functioning or so as to cease to function. **6** having specified material goods or wealth: *how are you off for money?* ■ prep. **1** moving away and often down from. **2** situated or leading in a direction away from. **3** so as to be removed or separated from. **4** informal having a temporary dislike of. ■ adj. **1** unsatisfactory or inadequate. **2** (of food) no longer fresh. **3** located on the side of a vehicle that is normally furthest from the kerb. Compare with NEAR (in sense 4). **4** Brit. informal annoying or unfair. **5** Brit. informal unwell. ■ n. **1** (also **off side**) Cricket the half of the field towards which the batsman's feet are pointed when standing to receive the ball. The opposite of LEG. **2** Brit. informal the start of a race or journey. ■ v. informal **1** leave. **2** N. Amer. kill; murder.
– PHRASES **off and on** intermittently.
– ORIGIN Old English, orig. a var. of OF (which combined the senses of 'of' and 'off').

offal ■ n. **1** the entrails and internal organs of an animal used as food. **2** decaying or waste matter.
– ORIGIN Middle English: prob. suggested by Middle Dutch *afval*, from *af* 'off' + *vallen* 'to fall'.

offbeat ■ adj. **1** Music not coinciding with the beat. **2** informal unconventional; unusual. ■ n. Music any of the normally unaccented beats in a bar.

off-brand N. Amer. ■ adj. denoting or relating to an item of goods of an unknown, unpopular, or inferior brand. ■ n. an unknown, unpopular, or inferior brand.

off break ■ n. Cricket a ball which spins from the off side towards the leg side after pitching.

off-colour ■ adj. **1** slightly unwell. **2** slightly indecent or obscene.

offcut ■ n. a piece of waste material that is left behind after cutting a larger piece.

off-cutter ■ n. Cricket a fast off break.

off drive Cricket ■ n. a drive to the off side.

off-dry ■ adj. (of wine) having an almost dry flavour, with just a trace of sweetness.

offence (US **offense**) ■ n. **1** an act or instance of offending. **2** resentment or hurt. **3** the action of making a military attack. **4** N. Amer. the attacking team in a sport.

offend ■ v. **1** cause to feel hurt or resentful. **2** be displeasing to. **3** commit an illegal act. ▸ break a commonly accepted rule or principle.
– DERIVATIVES **offended** adj. **offendedly** adv. **offender** n.
– ORIGIN Middle English: from Old French *offendre*, from Latin *offendere* 'strike against'.

offensive ■ adj. **1** causing offence. **2** (of a military operation or weapon) involved or used in active attack. **3** chiefly N. Amer. of or relating to the team in possession of the ball or puck in a game. ■ n. **1** a military campaign of attack. **2** a forceful campaign.
– PHRASES **be on the offensive** be ready to act aggressively.
– DERIVATIVES **offensively** adv. **offensiveness** n.

offer ■ v. **1** present or proffer. **2** express readiness to do something for or on behalf of someone. **3** provide (access or opportunity). **4** (often **offer something up**) present (a prayer or sacrifice) to a deity. ■ n. **1** an expression of readiness to do or give something. **2** an amount of money that someone is willing to pay for something. **3** a specially reduced price. **4** a proposal of marriage.
– PHRASES **on offer 1** available. **2** for sale at a reduced price.
– DERIVATIVES **offerer** (or **offeror**) n.
– ORIGIN Old English *offrian* 'sacrifice to a deity', of Germanic origin, from Latin *offerre* 'bestow, present'.

offer document ■ n. a document containing details of a takeover bid which is sent to the shareholders of the target company.

offering ■ n. a thing offered, especially as a gift or contribution. ▸ something offered as a religious sacrifice or token of devotion.

offertory /ˈɒfət(ə)ri/ ■ n. (pl. **-ies**) Christian Church **1** the offering of the bread and wine at the Eucharist. ▸ an anthem accompanying this. **2** a collection of money made at a religious service.
– ORIGIN Middle English: from eccles. Latin *offertorium* 'offering', from late Latin *offert-*, from *offerre* (see OFFER).

off-gas ■ n. a gas which is given off, especially one emitted as the by-product of a chemical process.

offhand ■ adj. ungraciously nonchalant or cool in manner. ■ adv. without previous consideration.
– DERIVATIVES **offhanded** adj. **offhandedly** adv. **offhandedness** n.

office ■ n. **1** a room, set of rooms, or building used as a place of business for non-manual work. **2** a position of authority or service. ▸ tenure of an official position. **3** (usu. **offices**) a service done for others. **4** (also **Divine Office**) Christian Church the services of prayers and psalms said daily by Catholic priests or other clergy.
– ORIGIN Middle English: from Latin *officium* 'performance of a task', from *opus* 'work' + *facere* 'do'.

office boy (or **office girl**) ■ n. a young man (or woman) employed in an office to carry out routine tasks.

officer ■ n. **1** a person holding a position of authority, especially a member of the armed forces who holds a commission or a member of the police force. **2** a holder of a post, especially of a public, civil, or ecclesiastical office. ■ v. provide with an officer or officers.

official ■ adj. **1** of or relating to an authority or public body and its activities and responsibilities. **2** having the approval or authorization of such a body. ■ n. a person holding public office or having official duties.
– DERIVATIVES **officialdom** n. **officialism** n. **officialize** (also **-ise**) v. **officially** adv.

officialese ■ n. the formal and typically verbose style of writing considered to be characteristic of official documents.

official secret ■ n. a piece of information that is important for national security and is officially classified as confidential.

officiant /əˈfɪʃɪənt, -ʃ(ə)nt/ ■ n. a priest or minister who performs a religious service or ceremony.
– ORIGIN C19: from medieval Latin *officiare* 'perform divine service'.

officiate /əˈfɪʃɪeɪt/ ■ v. **1** act as an official. **2** perform a religious service or ceremony.
– DERIVATIVES **officiation** n. **officiator** n.
– ORIGIN C17: from medieval Latin *officiare* 'perform divine service', from *officium* (see OFFICE).

officinal /əˈfɪsɪn(ə)l, ɒfɪˈsiːn(ə)l/ ■ adj. (of a herb or drug) used in medicine.
– DERIVATIVES **officinally** adv.
– ORIGIN C17: from medieval Latin *officinalis* 'storeroom for medicines', from Latin *officina* 'workshop'.

officious ■ adj. asserting authority or interfering in an annoyingly domineering way.
– DERIVATIVES **officiously** adv. **officiousness** n.

offing ■ n. (in phr. **in the offing**) likely to happen or appear soon.
– ORIGIN C17.

offish ■ adj. informal aloof or distant in manner.

off-key ■ adj. & adv. **1** Music not in the correct key or of the correct pitch. **2** inappropriate.

off-kilter ■ adj. & adv. not aligned or balanced. ▸ [as adj.] unconventional or eccentric: *an off-kilter comedy about living in mud.*

off-label ■ adj. relating to the prescription of a drug for a condition other than that for which it has been officially approved.

off-licence ■ n. British term for BOTTLE STORE.

off-limits ■ adj. out of bounds.

off-line Computing ■ adj. not controlled by or directly connected to a computer. ■ adv. while off-line. ▸ with a delay between the production of data and its processing.

offload ■ v. **1** unload (a cargo). **2** rid oneself of. **3** Computing move (data or a task) from one processor to another.

off-peak ■ adj. & adv. at a time when demand is less.

off-piste ■ adj. & adv. Skiing away from prepared ski runs.

off-plan ■ adv. & adj. (of the selling or purchasing of property) before the property is built and with only the plans available for inspection.

offprint ■ n. a printed copy of an article that originally appeared as part of a larger publication.

off-putting ■ adj. unpleasant or disconcerting.
– DERIVATIVES **off-puttingly** adv.

off-ramp ■ n. S. African & N. Amer. an exit road from a freeway.

off-road ■ adv. away from the road; on rough terrain. ■ adj. denoting a vehicle or bicycle for use off-road.
– DERIVATIVES **off-roader** n. **off-roading** n.

off-sales ■ n. a shop that sells mainly alcoholic drink for consumption elsewhere, especially one attached to or owned by a hotel.

off season ■ n. a time of year when a particular activity is not engaged in or a business is quiet.

offset ■ n. **1** a consideration or amount that diminishes or balances the effect of a contrary one. **2** the amount by which something is out of line. **3** Surveying a short distance measured perpendicularly from the main line of measurement. **4** a side shoot from a plant serving for propagation. **5** a spur in a mountain range. **6** Architecture a sloping ledge in a wall or other feature where the thickness of the part above is diminished. **7** a bend in a pipe to carry it past an obstacle. **8** a method of printing in which ink is transferred from a plate or stone to a uniform rubber surface and from that to the paper. ■ v. (**-setting**; past and past part. **-set**) **1** (often **be offset**) counterbalance; compensate for. **2** place out of line. **3** transfer an impression by means of offset printing.

offshoot ■ n. **1** a side shoot on a plant. **2** a thing that develops from something else.

offshore ■ adj. & adv. **1** situated at sea some distance from the shore. **2** (of the wind) blowing towards the sea from the land. **3** of or relating to the business of extracting oil or gas from the seabed. **4** made, situated, or registered abroad. **5** of, relating to, or from a foreign country.

offside ■ adj. & adv. (in games such as football) occupying a position on the field where playing the ball or puck is not allowed, generally through being between the ball and the opponents' goal. ■ n. **1** the fact of being offside. **2** (usu. **the off side**) the side of a vehicle furthest from the kerb. Compare with NEARSIDE. ▸ the right side of a horse.

off spin ■ n. Cricket a type of spin bowling that causes the ball to deviate from the off side towards the leg side after pitching; off breaks.
– DERIVATIVES **off-spinner** n.

offspring ■ n. (pl. same) a person's child or children, or the young of an animal.
– ORIGIN Old English *ofspring* (see OFF, SPRING).

offstage ■ adj. & adv. (in a theatre) not on the stage and so not visible to the audience.

off stump ■ n. Cricket the stump on the off side of a wicket.

off-tackle ■ adj. American Football of, directed towards, or occurring in a part of the offensive line immediately to the outside of either of the tackles.

off-white ■ n. a white colour with a grey or yellowish tinge.

oft ■ adv. archaic or poetic/literary often.
– ORIGIN Old English, of Germanic origin.

often /ˈɒf(ə)n, ˈɒft(ə)n/ ■ adv. (**oftener, oftenest**) **1** frequently. **2** in many instances.
– ORIGIN Middle English: extended form of OFT, prob. influenced by *selden* 'seldom'.

oftentimes ■ adv. archaic or N. Amer. often.
– ORIGIN Middle English: extended form of OFT-TIMES, influenced by OFTEN.

oft-times ■ adv. archaic or poetic/literary often.

ogee /ˈəʊdʒiː, əʊˈdʒiː/ ■ adj. Architecture showing in section an S-shaped curve. ■ n. an S-shaped line or moulding.
– ORIGIN Middle English: from OGIVE.

ogee arch ■ n. Architecture an arch with two ogee curves meeting at the apex.

Ogen /ˈəʊɡən/ ■ n. a small melon with pale orange flesh and an orange skin ribbed with green.
– ORIGIN 1960s: from the name of a kibbutz in Israel.

ogive /ˈəʊdʒaɪv, əʊˈdʒaɪv/ ■ n. Architecture **1** a pointed or Gothic arch. **2** one of the diagonal groins or ribs of a vault.
– DERIVATIVES **ogival** adj.
– ORIGIN Middle English: from French.

ogle ■ v. stare at lecherously. ■ n. a lecherous look.
– DERIVATIVES **ogler** n.
– ORIGIN C17: prob. from Low German or Dutch.

O grade ■ n. short for ORDINARY GRADE.

ogre ■ n. (fem. **ogress**) **1** (in folklore) a man-eating giant. **2** a cruel or terrifying person.
– DERIVATIVES **ogreish** (also **ogrish**) adj.
– ORIGIN C18: from French.

oh¹ ■ exclam. **1** expressing surprise, disappointment, joy, or other emotion. **2** used when responding to something that has just been said.

oh² ■ n. variant spelling of O¹ (in sense 4).

ohm ■ n. the SI unit of electrical resistance, transmitting a current of one ampere when subjected to a potential difference of one volt. (Symbol: Ω)
– DERIVATIVES **ohmic** adj. **ohmically** adv.
– ORIGIN C19: named after the German physicist G. S. *Ohm*.

ohmmeter /ˈəʊmˌmiːtə/ ■ n. an instrument for measuring electrical resistance.

Ohm's law ■ n. Physics a law stating that electric current is proportional to voltage and inversely proportional to resistance.

oho ■ exclam. expressing pleased surprise or recognition.
– ORIGIN Middle English: from O³ + HO.

-oholic ■ suffix variant spelling of -AHOLIC.

OHP ■ abbrev. overhead projector.

OHT ■ abbrev. overhead transparency.

oi (also **oy**) ■ exclam. informal used to attract someone's attention, especially in a rough or angry way.
– ORIGIN 1930s: var. of HOY.

-oid ■ suffix forming adjectives and nouns: **1** Zoology denoting an animal belonging to a higher taxon with a name ending in -oidea: hominoid. **2** denoting form or resemblance: asteroid.
– DERIVATIVES **-oidal** suffix forming corresponding adjectives. **-oidally** suffix forming corresponding adverbs.
– ORIGIN from Greek -oeidēs, rel. to eidos 'form'.

oik (also **oick**) ■ n. Brit. informal an uncouth or obnoxious person.
– ORIGIN 1930s.

oil ■ n. **1** a viscous liquid derived from petroleum, used especially as a fuel or lubricant. ▶ petroleum. **2** any of various viscous liquids which are insoluble in water but soluble in organic solvents and are obtained from animals or plants. **3** Chemistry any of a group of natural esters of glycerol and various fatty acids, which are liquid at room temperature. Compare with FAT. **4** oil paint. ■ v. **1** lubricate, coat, or impregnate with oil. **2** supply with oil as fuel.
– DERIVATIVES **oiled** adj.
– ORIGIN Middle English: from Old French oile, from Latin oleum '(olive) oil'; cf. olea 'olive'.

oil beetle ■ n. a slow-moving flightless beetle that releases a foul-smelling oily secretion when disturbed. [Meloe and other genera.]

oilcake ■ n. a mass of compressed linseed or other plant material left after oil has been extracted, used as fodder or fertilizer.

oilcan ■ n. a can with a long nozzle used for applying oil to machinery.

oilcloth ■ n. cotton fabric treated with oil to make it waterproof.

oil engine ■ n. an internal-combustion engine in which the fuel enters the cylinder as a liquid.

oiler ■ n. **1** an oil tanker. **2** an oilcan or other device used for lubricating machinery. **3** N. Amer. informal an oil well.

oilfield ■ n. an area of land or seabed underlain by strata yielding significant quantities of mineral oil.

oil-fired ■ adj. (especially of a heating system or power station) using oil as fuel.

oil gland ■ n. Botany & Zoology a gland which secretes oil. ▶ Ornithology another term for PREEN GLAND.

oil lamp ■ n. a lamp using oil as fuel.

oilman ■ n. (pl. **-men**) an owner or employee of an oil company.

oil meal ■ n. ground oilcake.

oil paint ■ n. a paste made with ground pigment and a drying oil such as linseed oil, used chiefly by artists.

oil painting ■ n. **1** the art of painting in oils. **2** a picture painted in oils.
– PHRASES **be no oil painting** Brit. informal be rather unattractive.

oil palm ■ n. a tropical West African palm which is the chief source of palm oil. [Elaeis guineensis: several cultivars.]

oil pan ■ n. an engine sump.

oil platform ■ n. a structure designed to stand on the seabed to provide a stable base above water for the drilling and regulation of oil wells.

oil rig ■ n. a structure with equipment for drilling an oil well; an oil platform.

oilseed ■ n. any of a number of seeds from cultivated crops yielding oil, e.g. rape, peanut, or cotton.

oil shale ■ n. fine-grained sedimentary rock from which oil can be extracted.

oilskin ■ n. heavy cotton cloth waterproofed with oil. ▶ (**oilskins**) a set of garments made of oilskin.

oil slick ■ n. a film or layer of oil floating on an expanse of water.

oilstone ■ n. a fine-grained flat stone used with oil for sharpening chisels, planes, or other tools.

oil well ■ n. an artificially made well or shaft in rock from which mineral oil is drawn.

oily ■ adj. (**-ier**, **-iest**) **1** containing, covered with, or soaked in oil. **2** resembling oil. **3** (of a person) unpleasantly smooth and ingratiating.
– DERIVATIVES **oilily** adv. **oiliness** n.

oink ■ n. the characteristic grunting sound of a pig. ■ v. make such a sound.
– ORIGIN 1940s: imitative.

ointment ■ n. a smooth oily substance that is rubbed on the skin for medicinal purposes or as a cosmetic.
– ORIGIN Middle English: alteration of Old French oignement, from Latin unguentum; influenced by Old French oint, from oindre 'anoint'.

Ojibwa /ə(ʊ)ˈdʒɪbweɪ/ ■ n. (pl. same or **Ojibwas**) **1** a member of an American Indian people inhabiting a wide area around Lake Superior. **2** the Algonquian language of this people.
– ORIGIN from Ojibwa ojibwe, said to mean 'puckered', with ref. to their moccasins.

OK (also **okay**) informal ■ exclam. **1** expressing agreement or acquiescence. **2** introducing an utterance. ■ adj. **1** satisfactory, but not especially good. **2** permissible. ■ adv. in a satisfactory manner or to a satisfactory extent. ■ n. an authorization or approval. ■ v. (**OK's**, **OK'd**, **OK'ing**) give approval to.

> HISTORY
> The exclamation **OK** is first recorded in the mid 19th century. It is most probably an abbreviation of orl korrect, a humorous form of all correct, which was popularized as a slogan during US President Martin Van Buren's re-election campaign of 1840. The initials also represented his nickname Old Kinderhook, derived from his birthplace, Kinderhook in New York State.

okapi /ə(ʊ)ˈkɑːpɪ/ ■ n. (pl. same or **okapis**) **1** a large browsing mammal of the giraffe family that lives in the rainforests of the northern Democratic Republic of Congo, having a dark chestnut coat with stripes on the hindquarters and upper legs. [Okapia johnstoni.] **2** S. African trademark a penknife favoured by gangsters.
– ORIGIN C20.

oke (also **okie**) ■ n. S. African informal another term for OU.
– ORIGIN from Afrikaans outjie, from ou + diminutive suffix.

okey-dokey (also **okey-doke**) ■ exclam. variant form of OK.

okra /ˈɒkrə, ˈəʊkrə/ ■ n. a plant of the mallow family with long ridged seed pods, native to the Old World tropics. [Abelmoschus esculentus.] ▶ the immature seed pods of this plant, eaten as a vegetable.
– ORIGIN C18: a W. African word.

-ol ■ suffix Chemistry forming names of organic compounds: **1** denoting alcohols and phenols: retinol. **2** denoting oils and oil-derived compounds: benzol.
– ORIGIN sense 1 from (alcoh)ol; sense 2 from Latin oleum 'oil'.

old ■ adj. (**-er**, **-est**) **1** having lived for a long time; no longer young. ▶ made or built long ago. ▶ possessed or used for a long time. **2** former; previous. **3** dating from far back; long-established or known: old friends. **4** of a specified age: he was fourteen years old. ▶ [as noun] a person or animal of the age specified. **5** informal expressing affection, familiarity, or contempt: good old Mum.
– PHRASES **of old 1** in or belonging to the past. **2** for a long time. **the old days** a period in the past.

– DERIVATIVES **oldish** adj. **oldness** n.
– ORIGIN Old English, of West Germanic origin.

old age ■ n. **1** the later part of normal life. **2** the state of being old.

old-age pension ■ n. a pension paid by the state to retired people above a certain age.
– DERIVATIVES **old-age pensioner** n.

old boy ■ n. **1** a former male pupil of a school. **2** informal an elderly man. ▶ an affectionate form of address for a man or boy.

old boys' club (also **old boys' network**, **old boy network**) ■ n. an informal system through which men are thought to use their positions of influence to help others who went to the same school or university, or who share a similar social background.

old country ■ n. (**the old country**) the native country of a person who has gone to live abroad.

olde /əʊld, ˈəʊldi/ (also **olde worlde**) ■ adj. pseudo-archaic old-fashioned in a way that is intended to be attractively quaint: *Ye Olde Tea Shoppe.*

olden ■ adj. of a former age: *the olden days.*

Old English ■ n. the language of the Anglo-Saxons (up to about 1150), an inflected language with a Germanic vocabulary.

Old English sheepdog ■ n. a large sheepdog of a breed with a shaggy blue-grey and white coat.

old-fashioned ■ adj. according to or favouring styles or views that are no longer current. ■ n. N. Amer. a cocktail consisting chiefly of whisky, bitters, water, and sugar.
– DERIVATIVES **old-fashionedness** n.

Old French ■ n. the French language up to c.1400.

old fruit ■ n. Brit. informal, dated a friendly form of address to a man.

old girl ■ n. **1** a former female pupil of a school, college, or university. **2** informal an elderly woman. ▶ an affectionate term of address to a girl or woman.

Old Glory ■ n. US informal the US national flag.

old gold ■ n. a dull brownish-gold colour.

old-growth ■ adj. (of a tree, forest, etc.) never felled; mature.

old guard ■ n. the original or long-standing members of a group seen as being unwilling to accept change.

old hand ■ n. a person with a lot of experience.

old hat ■ adj. informal tediously familiar or out of date.

Old High German ■ n. the language of southern Germany up to c.1200, from which modern standard German is derived.

Old Icelandic ■ n. Icelandic up to the 16th century, a form of Old Norse in which the medieval sagas were composed.

oldie ■ n. informal an old person or thing, in particular an old song or film that is still well known or popular.

Old Irish ■ n. the Irish Gaelic language up to c.1000, from which modern Irish and Scottish Gaelic are derived.

old lady ■ n. an elderly woman. ▶ (**one's old lady**) informal one's mother, wife, or girlfriend.

old-line ■ adj. N. Amer. **1** holding conservative views. **2** well established.

Old Low German ■ n. the language of northern Germany and the Netherlands up to c.1200, from which modern Dutch and modern Low German are derived.

old maid ■ n. **1** derogatory a single woman regarded as too old for marriage. ▶ a prim and fussy person. **2** a card game in which players collect pairs and try not to be left with an odd penalty card, typically a queen.
– DERIVATIVES **old-maidish** adj.

old man ■ n. an elderly man. ▶ (**one's old man**) informal one's father, husband, or male partner. ▶ Brit. informal an affectionate form of address between men or boys.

old man's beard ■ n. **1** a wild clematis with grey fluffy hairs around the seeds. [*Clematis vitalba* (traveller's joy) and other species.] **2** a lichen forming shaggy greyish growths on trees. [*Usnea barbata* and related species.]

old master ■ n. a great artist of former times, especially of the 13th–17th century in Europe.

old moon ■ n. the moon in its last quarter, before the new moon.

Old Nick ■ n. an informal name for the Devil.

Old Norse ■ n. the North Germanic language of medieval Norway, Iceland, Denmark, and Sweden, from which the modern Scandinavian languages are derived.

Oldowan /ˈɒldə(ʊ)wən/ ■ adj. Archaeology relating to or denoting an early Lower Palaeolithic culture of Africa, dated to about 2.0–1.5 million years ago.
– ORIGIN 1930s: from *Oldoway*, alteration of *Olduvai Gorge* in Tanzania.

Old Pals Act ■ n. informal the tendency of people to use a position of influence to help their friends.

Old Persian ■ n. the Persian language up to the 3rd century BC, written in cuneiform.

Old Saxon ■ n. the dialect of Old Low German spoken in Saxony up to c.1200.

old school ■ n. the traditional form or type: *a gentleman of the old school.*

old stager ■ n. informal a very experienced or long-serving person.

oldster ■ n. informal, chiefly N. Amer. an older person.

Old Stone Age ■ n. the Palaeolithic period.

Old Testament ■ n. the first part of the Christian Bible, comprising thirty-nine books and corresponding approximately to the Hebrew Bible.

old thing ■ n. informal a familiar form of address.

old-time ■ adj. pleasingly traditional or old-fashioned.

old-timer ■ n. informal a very experienced or long-serving person. ▶ N. Amer. an old person.

old wives' tale ■ n. a widely held traditional belief that is now thought to be unscientific or incorrect.

old woman ■ n. **1** an elderly female person. ▶ (**one's old woman**) informal one's mother, wife, or female partner. **2** derogatory a fussy or timid person.
– DERIVATIVES **old-womanish** adj.

Old World ■ n. Europe, Asia, and Africa, regarded collectively as the part of the world known before the discovery of the Americas.

Old Year's Eve ■ n. S. African another term for **NEW YEAR'S EVE**.

ole ■ adj. informal old.

-ole ■ comb. form in names of organic compounds, especially heterocyclic compounds: *thiazole.*
– ORIGIN from Latin *oleum* 'oil'.

olé /əʊˈleɪ/ ■ exclam. bravo!
– ORIGIN from Spanish.

oleaginous /ˌəʊlɪˈadʒɪnəs/ ■ adj. **1** oily or greasy. **2** exaggeratedly complimentary; obsequious.
– ORIGIN Middle English: from French *oléagineux*, from Latin *oleaginus* 'of the olive tree'.

oleander /ˌəʊlɪˈandə/ ■ n. a poisonous evergreen Old World shrub grown in warm countries for its clusters of white, pink, or red flowers. [*Nerium oleander.*]
– ORIGIN C16: from medieval Latin.

oleaster /ˌəʊlɪˈastə/ ■ n. a Eurasian shrub or small tree with fruit resembling an olive. [*Elaeagnus angustifolia* (SE Europe and western Asia) and related species.]
– ORIGIN Middle English: from Latin, from *olea* 'olive tree'.

olecranon /əʊˈlɛkrənɒn, ˌəʊlɪˈkreɪnən/ ■ n. Anatomy a bony prominence at the elbow, on the upper end of the ulna.
– ORIGIN C18: from Greek *ōle(no)kranon*, from *ōlenē* 'elbow' + *kranion* 'head'.

olefin /ˈəʊlɪfɪn/ (also **olefine**) ■ n. Chemistry another term for **ALKENE**.
– DERIVATIVES **olefinic** adj.
– ORIGIN C19: from French *oléfiant* 'oil-forming'.

oleiferous /ˌəʊlɪˈɪf(ə)rəs/ ■ adj. Botany (of seeds, glands, etc.) producing oil.

oleo- /ˈəʊlɪəʊ, ˈɒlɪəʊ/ ■ comb. form relating to or containing oil: *oleomargarine.*
– ORIGIN from Latin *oleum* 'oil'.

oleomargarine

oleomargarine ■ n. a fatty substance extracted from beef fat and widely used in the manufacture of margarine.
▶ N. Amer. dated margarine.

oleoresin ■ n. a natural or artificial mixture of essential oils and a resin, e.g. balsam.

Olestra /ɒˈlɛstrə/ ■ n. trademark a synthetic calorie-free substitute for fat in foods, able to pass through the body without being absorbed.
– ORIGIN 1980s: from (p)ol(y)est(e)r.

oleum /ˈəʊlɪəm/ ■ n. a dense, corrosive liquid consisting of concentrated sulphuric acid containing excess sulphur trioxide in solution.
– ORIGIN C20: from Latin, 'oil'.

O level ■ n. short for ORDINARY LEVEL.

olfaction /ɒlˈfakʃ(ə)n/ ■ n. technical the action or capacity of smelling; the sense of smell.
– ORIGIN C19: from Latin olfactus 'a smell'.

olfactometer /ˌɒlfakˈtɒmɪtə/ ■ n. an instrument for measuring the intensity of an odour or sensitivity to an odour.

olfactory /ɒlˈfakt(ə)ri/ ■ adj. of or relating to the sense of smell.
– ORIGIN C17: from Latin olfactare, from olfacere 'to smell'.

olfactory nerves ■ pl. n. Anatomy the pair of cranial nerves supplying the smell receptors in the nose.

olibanum /ɒˈlɪbənəm/ ■ n. frankincense.
– ORIGIN Middle English: from late Latin libanus, from Greek libanos 'frankincense'.

oligarch /ˈɒlɪɡɑːk/ ■ n. a ruler in an oligarchy.

oligarchy ■ n. (pl. -ies) a small group of people having control of a state. ▶ a state governed by such a group.
– DERIVATIVES **oligarchic** adj. **oligarchical** adj. **oligarchically** adv.
– ORIGIN C15: from Greek oligarkhia, from oligoi 'few' + arkhein 'to rule'.

oligo- ■ comb. form having few; containing a relatively small number of units: oligopoly.
– ORIGIN from Greek oligos 'small', oligoi 'few'.

Oligocene /ˈɒlɪɡə(ʊ)siːn/ ■ adj. Geology relating to or denoting the third epoch of the Tertiary period (between the Eocene and Miocene epochs, 35.4 to 23.3 million years ago), a time when the first primates appeared.
– ORIGIN C19: from OLIGO- + Greek kainos 'new'.

Oligochaeta /ˌɒlɪɡə(ʊ)ˈkiːtə/ ■ pl. n. Zoology a class of annelid worms which includes the earthworms.
– DERIVATIVES **oligochaete** n.
– ORIGIN from OLIGO- + Greek khaitē 'long hair', because they have fewer setae than polychaetes.

oligoclase /ˈɒlɪɡə(ʊ)kleɪz/ ■ n. a feldspar mineral common in siliceous igneous rocks, consisting of a sodium-rich plagioclase.
– ORIGIN C19: from OLIGO- + Greek klasis 'breaking' (because thought to have a less perfect cleavage than albite).

oligodendrocyte /ˌɒlɪɡə(ʊ)ˈdɛndrəsʌɪt/ ■ n. Anatomy a glial cell resembling an astrocyte but with fewer protuberances, concerned with the production of myelin.
– ORIGIN 1930s: from OLIGODENDROGLIA + -CYTE.

oligodendroglia /ˌɒlɪɡə(ʊ)dɛndrəˈɡlʌɪə/ ■ pl. n. Anatomy oligodendrocytes collectively.
– ORIGIN 1920s: from OLIGO- + DENDRO- + GLIA.

oligomer /əˈlɪɡəmə, ˈɒlɪɡ-/ ■ n. Chemistry a polymer whose molecules consist of relatively few repeating units.

oligomerize /əˈlɪɡəmərʌɪz/ (also **-ise**) ■ v. Chemistry join a number of molecules of (a monomer) together to form an oligomer.
– DERIVATIVES **oligomerization** (also **-isation**) n.

oligonucleotide /ˌɒlɪɡə(ʊ)ˈnjuːklɪətʌɪd/ ■ n. Biochemistry a polynucleotide whose molecules contain a relatively small number of nucleotides.

oligopeptide /ˌɒlɪɡə(ʊ)ˈpɛptʌɪd/ ■ n. Biochemistry a peptide whose molecules contain a relatively small number of amino-acid residues.

oligopoly /ˌɒlɪˈɡɒp(ə)li/ ■ n. (pl. -ies) a state of limited competition, in which a market is shared by a small number of producers or sellers.
– DERIVATIVES **oligopolist** n. **oligopolistic** adj.
– ORIGIN C19: from OLIGO-, on the pattern of monopoly.

oligosaccharide /ˌɒlɪɡə(ʊ)ˈsakərʌɪd/ ■ n. Biochemistry a carbohydrate whose molecules are composed of a relatively small number of monosaccharide units.

oligotrophic /ˌɒlɪɡə(ʊ)ˈtrəʊfɪk, -ˈtrɒfɪk/ ■ adj. Ecology (of a body of water) relatively poor in plant nutrients and containing abundant oxygen in the deeper parts.
– DERIVATIVES **oligotrophy** n.

olio /ˈəʊlɪəʊ/ ■ n. (pl. **-os**) 1 a highly spiced stew from Spain and Portugal. 2 a collection or miscellany. 3 a variety act or show.
– ORIGIN C17: from Spanish olla 'stew'.

olivaceous /ˌɒlɪˈveɪʃəs/ ■ adj. technical of a dusky yellowish green colour; olive green.

olive ■ n. 1 a small oval fruit with a hard stone and bitter flesh, green when unripe and bluish black when ripe, used as food and as a source of oil. 2 (also **olive tree**) the small evergreen tree which yields this fruit, native to warm regions of the Old World. [Olea europaea.] 3 (also **olive green**) a greyish-green colour like that of an unripe olive. ▶ [as modifier] (of the complexion) yellowish brown; sallow. 4 a slice of beef or veal made into a roll with stuffing inside and stewed. 5 (also **olive shell**) a marine mollusc with a smooth, roughly cylindrical shell. [Genus Oliva.] 6 Anatomy each of a pair of smooth, oval swellings in the medulla oblongata.
– ORIGIN Middle English: from Latin oliva, from Greek elaia, from elaion 'oil'.

olive branch ■ n. an offer of reconciliation.
– ORIGIN in allusion to the story of Noah in Genesis 8:1, in which a dove returns with an olive branch after the Flood.

olive drab ■ n. a dull olive-green colour, used in some military uniforms.

olive oil ■ n. an oil obtained from olives, used in cookery and salad dressings.

olivine /ˈɒlɪviːn, -ʌɪn/ ■ n. a green or brown silicate mineral occurring in basalt and other igneous rocks.

ollycrock ■ n. S. African another term for ALIKREUKEL.

olm /əʊlm, ɒlm/ ■ n. a pale-skinned blind salamander with external gills which lives in limestone caves in SE Europe. [Proteus anguinus.]
– ORIGIN C19: from German.

Olmec /ˈɒlmɛk/ ■ n. (pl. same or **Olmecs**) 1 a member of a prehistoric people who lived on the Gulf of Mexico. 2 a native people inhabiting this area during the 15th and 16th centuries.
– ORIGIN from Nahuatl Olmecatl, (pl.) Olmeca 'inhabitants of the rubber country'.

-ology ■ comb. form common form of -LOGY.

oloroso /ˌɒləˈrəʊsəʊ/ ■ n. a heavy, dark, medium-sweet sherry.
– ORIGIN Spanish, 'fragrant'.

Olympiad /əˈlɪmpɪad/ ■ n. 1 a celebration of the ancient or modern Olympic Games. ▶ a major national or international contest in a specified activity. 2 a period of four years between Olympic Games, used by the ancient Greeks in dating events.

Olympian ■ adj. 1 associated with Mount Olympus in NE Greece, traditional home of the Greek gods. ▶ resembling or appropriate to a god, especially in superiority and aloofness. 2 relating to the ancient or modern Olympic Games. ■ n. 1 any of the twelve Greek gods regarded as living on Olympus. ▶ a very superior or exalted person. 2 a competitor in the Olympic Games.

Olympic ■ adj. of or relating to ancient Olympia or the Olympic Games. ■ n. (**the Olympics**) the Olympic Games.

Olympic Games ■ pl. n. 1 a sports festival held every four years in different countries, instigated in 1896. 2 an ancient Greek festival with athletic, literary, and musical competitions, held at Olympia every four years.

OM ■ abbrev. Order of Merit.

om /əʊm/ ■ n. Hinduism & Buddhism a mystic syllable, considered the most sacred mantra.
– ORIGIN Sanskrit, sometimes regarded as three sounds, a-u-m, symbolic of the three major Hindu deities.

-oma ■ suffix (forming nouns) denoting tumours and other abnormal growths: *carcinoma*.
– DERIVATIVES **-omatous** suffix forming corresponding adjectives.
– ORIGIN from a Greek suffix denoting the result of verbal action.

Omaha /'əʊməhɑː/ ■ n. (pl. same or **Omahas**) **1** a member of an American Indian people of NE Nebraska. **2** the Siouan language of this people.
– ORIGIN from Omaha *umonhon* 'upstream people'.

Omani /əʊ'mɑːni/ ■ n. a native or inhabitant of Oman. ■ adj. of or relating to Oman.

omasum /əʊ'meɪsəm/ ■ n. (pl. **omasa** /-sə/) Zoology the muscular third stomach of a ruminant animal, between the reticulum and the abomasum.
– ORIGIN C18: from Latin, 'bullock's tripe'.

ombré /'ɒmbreɪ/ ■ adj. (of a fabric) having a design in which the colour is graduated from light to dark.
– ORIGIN French, from *ombrer* 'to shade'.

ombudsman /'ɒmbʊdzmən/ ■ n. (pl. **-men**) an official appointed to investigate individuals' complaints against maladministration, especially that of public authorities.
– ORIGIN 1950s: from Swedish, 'legal representative'.

-ome ■ suffix chiefly Biology forming nouns denoting objects or parts having a specified nature: *rhizome*.
– ORIGIN var. form of **-OMA**.

omega /'əʊmɪɡə/ ■ n. **1** the last letter of the Greek alphabet (Ω, ω), transliterated as 'o' or 'ō'. **2** the last of a series; the final development. ■ symb. (Ω) ohm(s).
– ORIGIN from Greek *ō mega* 'the great O'.

omelette (US also **omelet**) ■ n. a dish of beaten eggs cooked in a frying pan and usually served with a savoury topping or filling.
– ORIGIN French, earlier *amelette*, var. of *alumelle*, from *lemele* 'knife blade'.

omen ■ n. an event regarded as a portent of good or evil.
– ORIGIN C16: from Latin.

omentum /əʊ'mɛntəm/ ■ n. (pl. **omenta** /-tə/) Anatomy a fold of peritoneum connecting the stomach with other abdominal organs.
– DERIVATIVES **omental** adj.
– ORIGIN Middle English: from Latin.

omertà /ˌəʊmɛː'tɑː/ ■ n. a code of silence about criminal activity, practised by the Mafia.
– ORIGIN Italian dialect, var. of *umiltà* 'humility'.

omicron /ə(ʊ)'mʌɪkrɒn/ ■ n. the fifteenth letter of the Greek alphabet (O, o), transliterated as 'o'.
– ORIGIN from Greek *o mikron* 'small o'.

ominous ■ adj. giving the worrying impression that something bad is going to happen.
– DERIVATIVES **ominously** adv. **ominousness** n.
– ORIGIN C16: from Latin *ominosus*, from *omen* 'omen'.

omit ■ v. (**omitted**, **omitting**) leave out or exclude. ▶ fail to do.
– DERIVATIVES **omissible** adj. **omission** n. **omissive** adj.
– ORIGIN Middle English: from Latin *omittere*, from *ob-* 'down' + *mittere* 'let go'.

ommatidium /ˌɒmə'tɪdɪəm/ ■ n. (pl. **ommatidia** /-dɪə/) Entomology each of the optical units that make up the compound eye of an insect.
– ORIGIN C19: from Greek *ommatidion*, diminutive of *omma* 'eye'.

omni- ■ comb. form all; of all things: *omnifarious*. ▶ in all ways or places: *omnipresent*.
– ORIGIN from Latin *omnis* 'all'.

omnibus ■ n. **1** a volume containing several works previously published separately. ▶ chiefly Brit. a single edition of two or more consecutive programmes, especially of soap operas, previously broadcast separately. **2** a bus.
– ORIGIN C19: from Latin, 'for all', dative pl. of *omnis*.

omnicompetent ■ adj. able to deal with all matters or solve all problems. ▶ (of a legislative body) having powers to legislate on all matters.
– DERIVATIVES **omnicompetence** n.

omnidirectional ■ adj. Telecommunications receiving signals from or transmitting in all directions.

omnifarious /ˌɒmnɪ'fɛːrɪəs/ ■ adj. formal comprising or relating to all sorts or varieties.
– ORIGIN C17: from late Latin *omnifarius*.

omnipotent /ɒm'nɪpət(ə)nt/ ■ adj. (especially of a deity) having unlimited or very great power.
– DERIVATIVES **omnipotence** n. **omnipotently** adv.
– ORIGIN Middle English: from Latin *omnipotent-* 'all-powerful'.

omnipresent ■ adj. **1** (of God) present everywhere at the same time. **2** widely or constantly encountered.
– DERIVATIVES **omnipresence** n.
– ORIGIN C17: from medieval Latin *omnipraesent-*.

omniscient /ɒm'nɪsɪənt/ ■ adj. knowing everything.
– DERIVATIVES **omniscience** n. **omnisciently** adv.
– ORIGIN C17: from medieval Latin *omniscient-* 'all-knowing'.

omnisexual ■ adj. involving or characterized by a diverse sexual propensity.

omnium gatherum /ˌɒmnɪəm 'ɡaðərəm/ ■ n. a collection of miscellaneous people or things.
– ORIGIN C16: mock Latin, from Latin *omnium* 'of all' and **GATHER** + the Latin suffix *-um*.

omnivore /'ɒmnɪvɔː/ ■ n. an omnivorous animal.

omnivorous /ɒm'nɪv(ə)rəs/ ■ adj. **1** (of an animal) feeding on a variety of food of both plant and animal origin. **2** indiscriminate in taking in or using whatever is available.
– DERIVATIVES **omnivorously** adv.
– ORIGIN C17: from Latin *omnivorus*.

omophagy /ə(ʊ)'mɒfədʒi/ (also **omophagia**) ■ n. the eating of raw food, especially raw meat.
– ORIGIN C18: from Greek *ōmophagia*, from *ōmos* 'raw' + *-phagia*.

omphalos /'ɒmfəlɒs/ ■ n. (pl. **omphaloi** /-lɔɪ/) **1** (in ancient Greece) a conical stone, especially that at Delphi, representing the navel of the earth. **2** a boss on an ancient Greek shield.
– ORIGIN Greek, 'navel, boss'.

on ■ prep. **1** physically in contact with and supported by (a surface). ▶ located somewhere in the general surface area of (a place). ▶ on to. ▶ in the possession of. **2** forming a distinctive or marked part of the surface of. **3** about; concerning. ▶ having (the thing mentioned) as a basis. **4** as a member of (a committee, jury, etc.) **5** having (the thing mentioned) as a target, aim, or focus. **6** having (the thing mentioned) as a medium for transmitting or storing information. ▶ being broadcast by (a radio or television channel). **7** in the course of (a journey). ▶ while travelling in (a public service vehicle). **8** indicating the day or part of a day during which an event takes place. ▶ at the time of. **9** engaged in. **10** regularly taking (a drug or medicine). **11** paid for by. **12** added to. ■ adv. **1** physically in contact with and supported by a surface. ▶ (of clothing) being worn by a person. **2** indicating continuation of a movement or action. ▶ further forward; in an advanced state. **3** (of an event) taking place or being presented. ▶ due to take place as planned. **4** (of an electrical appliance or power supply) functioning. **5** (of an actor) on stage. ▶ (of an employee) on duty. ■ n. (also **on side**) Cricket the leg side.
– PHRASES **be on about** informal talk about tediously and at length. **be on at** Brit. informal nag or grumble at. **be on to** informal **1** be close to uncovering an illegal or undesirable activity engaged in by (someone). **2** (**be on to something**) have an idea that is likely to lead to an important discovery. **on and on** continually; at tedious length. **on to** moving to a location on the surface of (something) or aboard (a public service vehicle).
– ORIGIN Old English, of Germanic origin.

-on ■ suffix Physics,, Biochemistry,& Chemistry forming nouns: **1** denoting subatomic particles or quanta: *neutron*. **2** denoting molecular units: *codon*. **3** denoting substances: *interferon*.
– ORIGIN sense 1 orig. in *electron*, from **ION**, influenced (as in sense 2) by Greek *on* 'being'; sense 3 is on the pattern of words such as *cotton* or from German *-on*.

onanism /'əʊnənɪz(ə)m/ ■ n. formal **1** masturbation. **2** coitus interruptus.
– DERIVATIVES **onanist** n. **onanistic** adj.
– ORIGIN C18: from French *onanisme* or modern Latin *onanismus*, from the name *Onan* (Genesis 38:9).

on-board ■ adj. **1** situated on board a ship, aircraft, or other vehicle. **2** Computing incorporated into the main circuit board of a computer or computerized device.

once ■ adv. **1** on one occasion or for one time only. ▶ [usu. with neg.] at all; even one occasion. **2** formerly. **3** multiplied by one. ■ conj. as soon as; when.
– PHRASES **all at once 1** suddenly. **2** all at the same time. **at once 1** immediately. **2** simultaneously. **for once** (or **this once**) on this occasion only. **once again** (or **more**) one more time. **once and for all** (or **once for all**) now and for the last time; finally. **once** (or **every once**) **in a while** occasionally. **once or twice** a few times. **once upon a time** at some time in the past.
– ORIGIN Middle English *ones*, genitive of ONE.

once-over ■ n. informal a rapid inspection, search, or piece of work.

onchocerciasis /ˌɒŋkəʊsəːˈsaɪəsɪs, -ˈkaɪəsɪs/ ■ n. technical term for RIVER BLINDNESS.
– ORIGIN C20: from *Onchocerca*, genus name of the filarial parasite causing the disease (from Greek *onkos* 'barb' + *kerkos* 'tail') + -IASIS.

onco- ■ comb. form of or relating to tumours: *oncology*.
– ORIGIN from Greek *onkos* 'mass'.

oncogene /ˈɒŋkə(ʊ)dʒiːn/ ■ n. Medicine a gene which in certain circumstances can transform a cell into a tumour cell.

oncogenic /ˌɒŋkə(ʊ)ˈdʒɛnɪk/ ■ adj. Medicine causing development of a tumour or tumours.
– DERIVATIVES **oncogenesis** n. **oncogenicity** n.

oncology /ɒŋˈkɒlədʒi/ ■ n. Medicine the study and treatment of tumours.
– DERIVATIVES **oncological** adj. **oncologist** n.

oncoming ■ adj. approaching from the front; moving towards one. ■ n. the approach or onset of something.

oncost ■ n. Brit. & Austral. an overhead expense.

ondes martenot /ɒ̃d ˈmɑːt(ə)nəʊ/ ■ n. (pl. same) Music an electronic keyboard producing one note of variable pitch.
– ORIGIN 1950s: from French *ondes musicales* 'musical waves', the orig. name of the instrument) and the name of Maurice *Martenot*, its inventor.

on dit /ɒ̃ ˈdiː/ ■ n. (pl. **on dits** pronunc. same) a piece of gossip; a rumour.
– ORIGIN French, 'they say'.

on drive ■ n. Cricket a drive to the on side.

one ■ cardinal number **1** the lowest cardinal number; half of two; 1. (Roman numeral: **i** or **I**.) **2** single, or a single person or thing. ▶ denoting a particular item of a pair or number of items. ▶ (before a person's name) a certain. ▶ informal, chiefly N. Amer. a noteworthy example of. ▶ identical; the same. **3** informal a joke or story. ■ pron. **1** used to refer to a person or thing previously mentioned or easily identified. **2** a person of a specified kind. **3** [third person sing.] used to refer to the speaker, or any person, as representing people in general.
– PHRASES **at one** in agreement or harmony. **one after another** (or **the other**) following one another in quick succession. **one and all** everyone. **one and only** unique; single. **one another** each other. **one by one** separately and in succession. **one day** at a particular but unspecified time in the past or future. **one or another** (or **the other**) a particular but unspecified one out of a set of items. **one or two** informal a few.
– ORIGIN Old English *ān*, of Germanic origin.

-one ■ suffix Chemistry forming nouns denoting various compounds, especially ketones: *acetone*.
– ORIGIN from Greek patronymic *-ōnē*.

one-armed bandit ■ n. informal a type of slot machine operated by pulling a long handle at the side.

one-dimensional ■ adj. **1** having or relating to a single dimension. **2** lacking depth; superficial.
– DERIVATIVES **one-dimensionality** n.

one-horse race ■ n. a contest in which one competitor is clearly superior to all the others.

one-horse town ■ n. informal a small town with few and poor facilities.

oneiric /ə(ʊ)ˈnʌɪrɪk/ ■ adj. formal of or relating to dreams or dreaming.

oneiromancy /əˈnʌɪrə(ʊ)ˌmansi/ ■ n. the interpretation of dreams in order to foretell the future.
– ORIGIN from Greek *oneiros* 'dream' + -MANCY.

one-liner ■ n. informal a short joke or witty remark.

one-man band ■ n. **1** a street entertainer who plays many instruments at the same time. **2** a person who runs a business alone.

oneness ■ n. **1** the fact or state of being unified, whole, or in harmony. **2** the fact or state of being one in number.

one-night stand (also **one-nighter**) ■ n. **1** informal a sexual relationship lasting only one night. **2** a single performance of a play or show in a particular place.

one-off informal, chiefly Brit. ■ adj. done, made, or happening only once. ■ n. something done, made, or happening only once. ▶ a unique or remarkable person.

oner ■ n. Brit. informal something denoted or characterized by the number one.

onerous /ˈəʊn(ə)rəs, ˈɒn-/ ■ adj. involving an oppressively burdensome amount of effort and difficulty. ▶ Law involving heavy obligations.
– DERIVATIVES **onerousness** n.
– ORIGIN Middle English: from Old French *onereus*, from Latin *onerosus*, from *onus* 'burden'.

oneself ■ pron. [third person sing.] **1** [reflexive] used as the object of a verb or preposition when this is the same as the subject of the clause and the subject is 'one'. **2** [emphatic] used to emphasize that one does something individually or unaided. **3** in one's normal and individual state of body or mind.

one-sided ■ adj. **1** unfairly dealing with or biased towards only one side of a contentious issue. ▶ (of a contest or conflict) grossly unequal. **2** occurring on or having one side only.
– DERIVATIVES **one-sidedly** adv. **one-sidedness** n.

one-step ■ n. a vigorous kind of foxtrot in duple time.

one-time ■ adj. former.

one-track mind ■ n. informal a mind preoccupied with one subject, especially sex.

one-two ■ n. **1** a pair of punches in quick succession, especially with alternate hands. **2** chiefly Soccer a move in which a player plays a short pass to a teammate and moves forward to receive an immediate return pass.

one-up ■ adj. informal having a psychological advantage over someone.

one-upmanship ■ n. informal the technique of gaining an advantage or feeling of superiority over another.

one-way ■ adj. moving or allowing movement in one direction only.

one-world ■ adj. relating to or holding the view that the world's inhabitants are interdependent and should behave accordingly.
– DERIVATIVES **one-worlder** n. **one-worldism** n.

ongoing ■ adj. continuing; still in progress.

onion ■ n. **1** an edible bulb used as a vegetable, having a pungent taste and smell and composed of several concentric layers. **2** the plant that produces this bulb, with spherical heads of greenish-white flowers. [*Allium cepa*.]
– DERIVATIVES **oniony** adj.
– ORIGIN Middle English: from Old French *oignon*, from Latin *unio(n-)*, denoting a kind of onion.

onion dome ■ n. a dome which bulges in the middle and rises to a point, used especially in Russian church architecture.
– DERIVATIVES **onion-domed** adj.

onion-skin paper ■ n. very fine smooth translucent paper.

online ■ adj. & adv. **1** controlled by or connected to a computer. ▶ (of an activity or service) available on or carried out via the Internet: *online banking*. **2** in or into operation or existence.

onlooker ■ n. a non-participating observer; a spectator.
– DERIVATIVES **onlooking** adj.

only ■ adv. **1** and no one or nothing more besides. ▸ no longer ago than. ▸ not until. **2** with the negative or unfortunate result that. ■ adj. alone of its or their kind; single or solitary. ▸ alone deserving consideration. ■ conj. informal except that.
–PHRASES **only just 1** by a very small margin. **2** very recently. **only too** —— to an extreme or regrettable extent.
–ORIGIN Old English *ānlic*.

o.n.o. ■ abbrev. or nearest offer (used in advertisements).

onomastic /ɒnəˈmastɪk/ ■ adj. of or relating to onomastics.
–ORIGIN C16: from Greek *onomastikos*, from *onoma* 'name'.

onomastics ■ pl. n. [usu. treated as sing.] the study of the history and origin of proper names, especially personal names.

onomatopoeia /ˌɒnə(ʊ)matəˈpiːə/ ■ n. the formation of a word from a sound associated with what is named (e.g. *cuckoo*, *sizzle*). ▸ the use of such words for rhetorical effect.
–DERIVATIVES **onomatopoeic** adj. **onomatopoeically** adv.
–ORIGIN C16: from Greek *onomatopoiia* 'word-making', from *onoma* 'name' + *-poios* 'making'.

onrush ■ n. a surging rush forward. ■ v. [usu. as adj. **onrushing**] move forward in a surging rush.

onset ■ n. **1** the beginning of something, especially something unpleasant. **2** archaic a military attack.

onshore ■ adj. & adv. situated or occurring on land. ▸ (of the wind) blowing from the sea towards the land.

onside ■ adj. & adv. **1** (in sport) not offside. **2** informal in or into a position of agreement.

onslaught ■ n. a fierce or destructive attack. ▸ an overwhelmingly large quantity of people or things.
–ORIGIN C17: from Middle Dutch *aenslag*, from *aen* 'on' + *slag* 'blow'.

onstage ■ adj. & adv. (in a theatre) on the stage and so visible to the audience.

on-stream ■ adv. & adj. in or into industrial production or useful operation.

-ont ■ comb. form Biology denoting an individual or cell of a specified type: *schizont*.
–ORIGIN from Greek *ont-* 'being', from *eimi* 'be'.

ontic /ˈɒntɪk/ ■ adj. Philosophy of or relating to entities and the facts about them.
–ORIGIN 1940s: from Greek *ōn*, *ont-* 'being'.

onto ■ prep. variant form of on to (see ON).

ontogenesis /ˌɒntə(ʊ)ˈdʒɛnɪsɪs/ ■ n. Biology the development of an individual organism or anatomical or behavioural feature from the earliest stage to maturity.
–DERIVATIVES **ontogenetic** adj.
–ORIGIN C19: from Greek *ōn*, *ont-* 'being' + *genesis* 'birth'.

ontogeny /ɒnˈtɒdʒəni/ ■ n. the branch of biology concerned with ontogenesis. Compare with PHYLOGENY. ▸ another term for ONTOGENESIS.

ontology /ɒnˈtɒlədʒi/ ■ n. the branch of metaphysics concerned with the nature of being.
–DERIVATIVES **ontological** adj. **ontologically** adv.
–ORIGIN C18: from Greek, from *ōn*, *ont-* 'being' + -LOGY.

onus /ˈəʊnəs/ ■ n. a burden, duty, or responsibility.
–ORIGIN C17: from Latin, 'load or burden'.

onward ■ adv. (also **onwards**) **1** in a continuing forward direction; ahead. ▸ forward in time. **2** so as to make progress or become more successful. ■ adj. (of a journey) moving forward.

Onychophora /ˌɒnɪˈkɒf(ə)rə/ ■ pl. n. Zoology a small phylum of terrestrial invertebrates which comprises the velvet worms.
–DERIVATIVES **onychophoran** adj. & n.
–ORIGIN from Greek *onux*, *onukh-* 'nail, claw' + *-phoros* 'bearing'.

-onym ■ comb. form forming nouns: **1** denoting a type of name: *pseudonym*. **2** denoting a word having a specified relationship to another: *antonym*.
–ORIGIN from Greek, from *-ōnumos*, comb. form of *onoma* 'name'.

onyx /ˈɒnɪks, ˈəʊnɪks/ ■ n. a semi-precious variety of agate with different colours in layers.

821

opal

–ORIGIN Middle English: from Old French *oniche*, *onix*, from Greek *onux* 'fingernail or onyx'.

oo- /ˈəʊə/ ■ comb. form Biology relating to or denoting an egg or ovum: *oogenesis*.
–ORIGIN from Greek *ōion* 'egg'.

oocyte /ˈəʊəsʌɪt/ ■ n. Biology a cell in an ovary which may undergo meiotic division to form an ovum.

oodles ■ pl. n. informal a very great number or amount.
–ORIGIN C19 (orig. US).

oogenesis /ˌəʊəˈdʒɛnɪsɪs/ ■ n. Biology the production or development of an ovum.

oogonium /ˌəʊəˈɡəʊnɪəm/ ■ n. (pl. **oogonia**) **1** Botany the female sex organ of certain algae and fungi. **2** Biology an immature female reproductive cell that gives rise to primary oocytes by mitosis.
–ORIGIN C19: from OO- + Greek *gonos* 'generation'.

ooh ■ exclam. used to express a range of emotions including surprise, delight, or pain. ■ v. (**oohed**, **oohing**) (usu. in phr. **ooh and aah**) utter such an exclamation.

oolite /ˈəʊəlʌɪt/ ■ n. Geology limestone consisting of a mass of rounded grains (**ooliths**) made up of concentric layers.
–DERIVATIVES **oolitic** adj.
–ORIGIN C19: from French *oölithe*, from OO-.

oolith /ˈəʊəlɪθ/ ■ n. Geology any of the rounded grains making up oolite.

oolong /ˈuːlɒŋ/ ■ n. a kind of dark-coloured partly fermented China tea.
–ORIGIN C19: from Chinese *wūlóng* 'black dragon'.

oom /ʊəm/ ■ n. S. African a respectful affectionate title or form of address for an unrelated older man.
–ORIGIN Afrikaans, 'uncle'.

oompah ■ n. informal the rhythmical sound of deep-toned brass instruments in a band.
–ORIGIN C19: imitative.

oomph (also **umph**) ■ n. informal the quality of being exciting, energetic, or sexually attractive.
–ORIGIN 1930s: perhaps imitative.

oophorectomy /ˌəʊəfəˈrɛktəmi/ ■ n. (pl. **-ies**) surgical removal of one or both ovaries.
–ORIGIN C19: from modern Latin *oophoron* 'ovary' + -ECTOMY.

oophoritis /ˌəʊəfəˈrʌɪtɪs/ ■ n. Medicine inflammation of an ovary.

oops ■ exclam. informal used to show recognition of a mistake or minor accident.

oops-a-daisy ■ exclam. variant spelling of UPSY-DAISY.

ooze[1] ■ v. **1** (of a fluid) slowly trickle or seep out. ▸ slowly exude or discharge (a viscous fluid). **2** give a powerful impression of (a quality): *she oozes sex appeal*. ■ n. the sluggish flow of a fluid.
–ORIGIN Old English *wōs* 'juice or sap'.

ooze[2] ■ n. wet mud or slime, especially that found at the bottom of a river, lake, or sea.
–ORIGIN Old English *wāse*; rel. to Old Norse *veisa* 'stagnant pool'.

OP ■ abbrev. **1** observation post. **2** (in the theatre) opposite prompt, the offstage area to the right of an actor. **3** organophosphate(s).

Op. (also **op.**) ■ abbrev. Music (before a number given to each work of a particular composer) opus.

op ■ n. informal **1** a surgical operation. **2** (**ops**) military operations. **3** a radio or telephone operator.

o.p. ■ abbrev. **1** (of a book) out of print. **2** (of alcohol) overproof.

op- ■ suffix variant spelling of OB- assimilated before *p* (as in *oppress*, *oppugn*).

opacity /ə(ʊ)ˈpasɪti/ ■ n. the condition of being opaque.

opal ■ n. a gemstone consisting of a quartz-like form of hydrated silica, typically semi-transparent and showing many small points of shifting colour against a pale or dark ground.
–ORIGIN C16: from French *opale* or Latin *opalus*, prob. from Sanskrit *upala* 'precious stone'.

opalescent

opalescent ■ adj. showing many small points of shifting colour against a pale or dark ground.
– DERIVATIVES **opalescence** n.

opaline /ˈəʊp(ə)lʌɪn, -liːn/ ■ adj. opalescent.

op-amp ■ abbrev. operational amplifier.

opaque /ə(ʊ)ˈpeɪk/ ■ adj. (**-r**, **-st**) **1** not able to be seen through; not transparent. **2** difficult or impossible to understand. ■ n. an opaque thing. ▸ Photography a substance for producing opaque areas on negatives.
– DERIVATIVES **opaquely** adv. **opaqueness** n.
– ORIGIN Middle English *opake*, from Latin *opacus* 'darkened'.

op art ■ n. a form of abstract art that gives the illusion of movement by its use of pattern and colour.
– ORIGIN 1960s: abbrev. of *optical art* on the pattern of *pop art*.

op. cit. ■ adv. in the work already cited.
– ORIGIN from Latin *opere citato*.

ope ■ adj. & v. poetic/literary or archaic form of **OPEN**.

OPEC ■ abbrev. Organization of the Petroleum Exporting Countries.

Op-Ed ■ adj. relating to or denoting a newspaper page opposite the editorial page, devoted to personal comment, feature articles, etc.

open ■ adj. **1** allowing access, passage, or view; not closed, fastened, or restricted. ▸ (of the bowels) not constipated. **2** exposed to the air or to view or attack; not covered or protected. ▸ (**open to**) vulnerable or subject to. ▸ (of land) not covered with buildings or trees. ▸ (of a town or city) officially declared to be undefended, and so immune under international law from bombardment. **3** spread out or unfolded. ▸ (of a book) with the covers parted and able to be read. **4** officially admitting customers or visitors; available for business. ▸ (of an offer or opportunity) still available. **5** frank and communicative. ▸ not concealed; manifest. **6** not finally settled; still admitting of debate. ▸ (often **open to**) accessible to new ideas; receptive. ▸ freely available or accessible. ▸ (**open to**) admitting of; making possible. **7** Music (of a string) allowed to vibrate along its whole length. **8** Phonetics (of a vowel) produced with a relatively wide opening of the mouth and the tongue kept low. ▸ (of a syllable) ending in a vowel. **9** (of an electric circuit) having a break in the conducting path. ■ v. **1** move (a door, window, etc.) so that it is open. ▸ undo or remove the cover or fastening of. ▸ turn on (a tap, valve, etc.) ▸ (**open on to/into**) (of a door, window, etc.) give access to. **2** spread out; unfold or be unfolded. ▸ part the covers of (a book) to read it. ▸ (of a prospect) come into view; spread out. **3** make or become officially ready for customers or visitors. ▸ ceremonially declare (a building, road, etc.) to be completed and ready for use. **4** formally begin or establish. ▸ (**open up**) or **open fire** begin shooting. ▸ (of a counsel in a law court) make a preliminary statement in (a case) before calling witnesses. ▸ Bridge make (the first bid) in the auction. **5** make available or more widely known. ▸ (**open out/up**) become more communicative or confiding. **6** break the conducting path of (an electric circuit). **7** Nautical achieve a clear view of (a place) by sailing past a headland or other obstruction. ■ n. **1** (**the open**) fresh air or open countryside. ▸ (usu. in phr. **bring in/into the open**) a lack of concealment or secrecy. **2** (**Open**) a championship or competition with no restrictions on who may compete.
– PHRASES **the open air** a free or unenclosed space outdoors. **in open court** in a court of law, before the judge and the public. **open-and-shut** (of a case or argument) admitting no doubt or dispute; straightforward.
– DERIVATIVES **openable** adj. **openness** n.
– ORIGIN Old English, of Germanic origin, from the root of the adv. **UP**.

open-air ■ adj. taking place or situated outdoors.

opencast ■ adj. denoting a method of mining in which coal or ore is extracted at or from a level near the earth's surface, rather than from shafts.

open chain ■ n. Chemistry a molecular structure consisting of a chain of atoms with no closed rings.

open cluster ■ n. Astronomy a loose grouping of stars.

open college ■ n. (in the UK) an organization established to provide retraining opportunities, chiefly for the staff of companies.

open day ■ n. a day when members of the public may visit a place or institution to which they do not usually have access.

open-ended ■ adj. having no predetermined limit or boundary.
– DERIVATIVES **open-endedness** n.

opener ■ n. **1** a device for opening something. **2** a person or thing that opens or begins, in particular the first goal in a match or a cricketer who opens the batting.
– PHRASES **for openers** informal to start with; first of all.

open-faced ■ adj. **1** having a frank or ingenuous expression. **2** (of a watch) having no cover other than the glass. **3** (also **open-face**) chiefly N. Amer. (of a sandwich or pie) without an upper layer of bread or pastry.

open-handed ■ adj. **1** (of a blow) delivered with the palm of the hand. **2** generous.
– DERIVATIVES **open-handedly** adv. **open-handedness** n.

open-hearted ■ adj. unrestrainedly warm and kindly.
– DERIVATIVES **open-heartedness** n.

open-heart surgery ■ n. surgery in which the heart is exposed and the blood made to bypass it.

open house ■ n. **1** a place or situation in which all visitors are welcome. **2** N. Amer. an open day.

opening ■ n. **1** an aperture or gap. **2** a beginning; an initial part. ▸ a ceremony at which a building, show, etc. is declared to be open. ▸ a recognized sequence of moves at the beginning of a chess game. **3** an opportunity to achieve something. ▸ an available job or position. ■ adj. coming at the beginning; initial.

open letter ■ n. a letter addressed to a particular person but intended for publication in a newspaper or journal.

openly ■ adv. without concealment, deception, or prevarication; frankly or honestly.
– ORIGIN Old English *openlīce*.

open market ■ n. an unrestricted market with free access by and competition of buyers and sellers.

open marriage ■ n. a marriage in which both partners agree that each may have sexual relations with others.

open mind ■ n. a mind willing to consider new ideas.
– DERIVATIVES **open-minded** adj. **open-mindedly** adv. **open-mindedness** n.

open-necked ■ adj. (of a shirt) worn with the collar unbuttoned and without a tie.

open outcry ■ n. a system of financial trading in which dealers shout their bids and contracts aloud.

open-pit ■ adj. another term for **OPENCAST**.

open-plan ■ adj. (of a room or building) having large rooms with few or no internal dividing walls.

open prison ■ n. Brit. a prison with the minimum of restrictions on prisoners' movements and activities.

open question ■ n. a matter that is not yet decided or is unable to be decided.

open range ■ n. a tract of land without fences or other barriers.

open-reel ■ adj. another term for **REEL-TO-REEL**.

open sandwich ■ n. a sandwich without a top slice of bread.

open season ■ n. the annual period when restrictions on the killing of certain types of wildlife, especially for sport, are lifted.

open secret ■ n. a supposed secret that is in fact known to many people.

open shop ■ n. a place of work where employees do not have to join a trade union.

open side ■ n. Rugby the side of the scrum on which the main line of the opponents' backs is ranged.

open society ■ n. a society characterized by a flexible structure, freedom of belief, and wide dissemination of information.

open-source ■ adj. Computing denoting software for which the original source code is made freely available.

open-toed ■ adj. (of a shoe) not covering the toes.

open-topped (also **open-top**) ▪ adj. (of a vehicle) not having a roof or having a folding or detachable roof.

open verdict ▪ n. Law a verdict of an inquest court affirming the occurrence of a suspicious death but not specifying the cause.

openwork ▪ n. ornamental work in cloth, leather, etc. with regular patterns of openings and holes.

opera[1] ▪ n. a dramatic work in one or more acts that is set to music for singers and instrumentalists. ▸ a building for the performance of opera.
– ORIGIN C17: from Latin, 'labour, work'.

opera[2] plural form of OPUS.

operable ▪ adj. **1** able to be operated. **2** able to be treated by means of a surgical operation.
– DERIVATIVES **operability** n.

opera cloak ▪ n. a cloak of rich material worn over evening clothes, especially by women.

opera glasses ▪ pl. n. small binoculars for use at the opera or theatre.

opera house ▪ n. a theatre for the performance of opera.

operand /ˈɒpərand/ ▪ n. Mathematics the quantity on which an operation is to be done.
– ORIGIN C19: from Latin *operandum*, from *operari* (see OPERATE).

operant /ˈɒp(ə)r(ə)nt/ Psychology ▪ adj. involving the modification of behaviour by the reinforcing or inhibiting effect of its own consequences. ▪ n. an item of behaviour that is not a response to a prior stimulus but something which is initially spontaneous.
– ORIGIN Middle English: from Latin *operari* 'to be at work'.

operate ▪ v. **1** (with reference to a machine, process, etc.) function or control the functioning of. **2** (with reference to an organization) manage or be managed and run. ▸ (of an armed force) conduct military activities. **3** be in effect. **4** perform a surgical operation.
– ORIGIN C17: from Latin *operari*, from *opus* 'work'.

operatic ▪ adj. of, relating to, or characteristic of opera. ▸ extravagantly theatrical.
– DERIVATIVES **operatically** adv.

operating profit ▪ n. a gross profit before deduction of expenses.

operating system ▪ n. the low-level software that supports a computer's basic functions.

operating table ▪ n. a table on which a patient is placed during a surgical operation.

operating theatre (N. Amer. **operating room**) ▪ n. a room in which surgical operations are performed.

operation ▪ n. **1** the action or process of operating. **2** an act of surgery performed on a patient. **3** a concerted action involving a number of people, especially members of the armed forces or the police. **4** a business organization; a company. **5** Mathematics a process in which a number, quantity, expression, etc., is altered or manipulated according to set formal rules.

operational ▪ adj. **1** in or ready for use. **2** relating to the operation of an organization. **3** Philosophy of, relating to, or in accordance with operationalism.
– DERIVATIVES **operationally** adv.

operational amplifier ▪ n. Electronics an amplifier with high gain and high input impedance, used especially in circuits for performing mathematical operations on an input voltage.

operationalism ▪ n. Philosophy a form of positivism which defines scientific concepts in terms of the operations used to determine or prove them.

operationalize (also **-ise**) ▪ v. put into operation or use.

operational research (also **operations research**) ▪ n. a method of mathematically based analysis for providing a quantitive basis for management decisions.

operations room ▪ n. a room from which military or police operations are directed.

operative ▪ adj. **1** functioning; having effect. ▸ (of a word) having the most relevance or significance in a phrase. **2** of or relating to surgery. ▪ n. **1** a worker, especially a skilled one. **2** a private detective or secret agent.
– DERIVATIVES **operatively** adv. **operativeness** n.

operator ▪ n. **1** a person who operates equipment or a machine. ▸ a person who works at the switchboard of a telephone exchange. **2** a person or company that runs a business or enterprise: *a tour operator*. **3** informal a person who acts in a specified, especially manipulative, way: *a smooth operator*. **4** Mathematics a symbol or function denoting an operation (e.g. ×, +).

operculum /ə(ʊ)ˈpɜːkjʊləm/ ▪ n. (pl. **opercula** /-lə/) **1** a flap of skin protecting a fish's gills, typically stiffened by bony plates. **2** a plate that closes the aperture of a gastropod mollusc's shell when the animal is retracted. **3** a lid-like structure of the spore-containing capsule of a moss.
– DERIVATIVES **opercular** adj.
– ORIGIN C18: from Latin, 'lid, covering'.

operetta ▪ n. a short opera, usually on a light or humorous theme and having spoken dialogue.
– ORIGIN C18: from Italian, diminutive of *opera* (see OPERA[1]).

operon /ˈɒpərɒn/ ▪ n. Biology a unit made up of linked genes which is thought to regulate other genes responsible for protein synthesis.
– ORIGIN 1960s: from French *opérer* 'to effect, work'.

Ophidia /ɒˈfɪdɪə/ ▪ pl. n. Zoology a group of reptiles which comprises the snakes.
– DERIVATIVES **ophidian** n. & adj.
– ORIGIN from Greek *ophis*, *ophid-* 'snake'.

ophiolite /ˈɒfɪəlʌɪt/ ▪ n. Geology an igneous rock consisting largely of serpentine.
– DERIVATIVES **ophiolitic** adj.
– ORIGIN C19: from Greek *ophis* 'snake'.

Ophiuroidea /ˌɒfɪ(j)ʊəˈrɔɪdɪə/ ▪ pl. n. Zoology a class of echinoderms that comprises the brittlestars.
– DERIVATIVES **ophiuroid** n. & adj.
– ORIGIN from *Ophiura* (genus name), from Greek *ophis* 'snake' + *oura* 'tail'.

ophthalmia /ɒfˈθalmɪə/ ▪ n. Medicine inflammation of the eye, especially conjunctivitis.
– ORIGIN Middle English: from Greek, from *ophthalmos* 'eye'.

ophthalmic ▪ adj. of or relating to the eye and its diseases.

ophthalmitis /ˌɒfθalˈmʌɪtɪs/ ▪ n. Medicine inflammation of the eye.

ophthalmo- ▪ comb. form Medicine relating to the eyes: *ophthalmoscope*.
– ORIGIN from Greek *ophthalmos* 'eye'.

ophthalmology /ˌɒfθalˈmɒlədʒi/ ▪ n. the branch of medicine concerned with the study and treatment of disorders and diseases of the eye.
– DERIVATIVES **ophthalmological** adj. **ophthalmologist** n.

ophthalmoscope /ɒfˈθalməskəʊp/ ▪ n. an instrument for inspecting the retina and other parts of the eye.
– DERIVATIVES **ophthalmoscopy** n.

-opia ▪ comb. form denoting a visual disorder: *myopia*.
– ORIGIN from Greek *ōps*, *ōp-* 'eye, face'.

opiate ▪ adj. /ˈəʊpɪət/ relating to, resembling, or containing opium. ▪ n. /ˈəʊpɪət/ **1** a drug derived from or related to opium. **2** something inducing a false and unrealistic sense of contentment. ▪ v. /ˈəʊpɪeɪt/ [often as adj. **opiated**] impregnate with opium.

opine ▪ v. formal hold and state as one's opinion.
– ORIGIN Middle English: from Latin *opinari* 'think, believe'.

opinion ▪ n. **1** a view or judgement not necessarily based on fact or knowledge. ▸ the beliefs or views of a large number of people: *the changing climate of opinion*. ▸ an estimation of quality or worth: *he had a high opinion of himself*. **2** Law a formal statement of reasons for a judgement given. ▸ an advocate's advice on the merits of a case.
– PHRASES **be of the opinion that** believe or maintain that. **a matter of opinion** something not capable of being proven either way.
– ORIGIN Middle English: from Latin *opinio(n-)*, from *opinari* 'think, believe'.

opinionated ▪ adj. assertively dogmatic in one's views.

opinion poll

opinion poll ■ n. an assessment of public opinion by questioning of a representative sample, especially to forecast the results of voting.

opioid /'əʊpɪɔɪd/ Biochemistry ■ n. a compound resembling opium in addictive properties or physiological effects. ■ adj. relating to or denoting such compounds.

opisthosoma /ə,pɪsθə'səʊmə/ ■ n. Zoology the abdomen of a spider or other arachnid.

opium ■ n. 1 an addictive drug prepared from the juice of a poppy (*Papaver somniferum*), used illicitly as a narcotic and occasionally in medicine as an analgesic. 2 something inducing a false and unrealistic sense of contentment.
– ORIGIN Middle English: from Greek *opion* 'poppy juice'.

opossum /ə'pɒs(ə)m/ ■ n. 1 an American marsupial which has a naked prehensile tail and hind feet with an opposable thumb. [Family Didelphidae: numerous species.] 2 Austral./NZ a possum.
– ORIGIN C17: from Virginia Algonquian *opassom*, from *op* 'white' + *assom* 'dog'.

opp. ■ abbrev. opposite.

opponent ■ n. a person who opposes.
– ORIGIN C16: from Latin *opponent-, opponere* 'set against'.

opponent muscle ■ n. Anatomy any of several muscles enabling the thumb to be placed front to front against a finger of the same hand.

opportune /'ɒpətjuːn, ˌɒpə'tjuːn/ ■ adj. (of a time) especially convenient or appropriate. ▸ appropriately timed.
– DERIVATIVES **opportunely** adv. **opportuneness** n.

HISTORY
Opportune comes from Latin *opportunus*, denoting a favourable wind blowing towards the harbour (as opposed to one that would blow a ship out to sea), from *ob-* 'in the direction of' and *portus* 'harbour'. From this developed the English sense 'advantageous' and also the noun **opportunity**. The Romans gave the name *Portunus* to the god who protected their harbours: from his name derives the negative word **importunate**, which originally meant 'inconvenient', and the related verb **importune**.

opportunist ■ n. a person who takes advantage of opportunities as and when they arise, regardless of planning or principle. ■ adj. opportunistic.
– DERIVATIVES **opportunism** n.

opportunistic ■ adj. 1 exploiting immediate opportunities, especially in an unplanned or selfish way. 2 Medicine (of an infection) occurring when the immune system is depressed.
– DERIVATIVES **opportunistically** adv.

opportunity ■ n. (pl. -ies) a favourable time or set of circumstances for doing something.
– ORIGIN Middle English: from Latin *opportunitas*, from *opportunus* (see OPPORTUNE).

opportunity cost ■ n. Economics the loss of other alternatives when one alternative is chosen.

opposable ■ adj. (of the thumb of a primate) capable of facing and touching the other digits on the same hand.

oppose ■ v. 1 (also **be opposed to**) disapprove of, resist, or be hostile to. ▸ compete with or fight. 2 [as adj. **opposed**] (of two or more things) contrasting or conflicting. 3 [as adj. **opposing**] opposite.
– DERIVATIVES **opposer** n.
– ORIGIN Middle English: from Old French *opposer*, from Latin *opponere* (see OPPONENT).

opposite ■ adj. 1 situated on the other or further side; facing. ▸ (of angles) between opposite sides of the intersection of two lines. ▸ Botany (of leaves or shoots) arising in pairs at the same level on opposite sides of the stem. 2 completely different. ▸ being the other of a contrasted pair: *the opposite ends of the price range*. ■ n. an opposite person or thing. ■ adv. in an opposite position. ■ prep. 1 in a position opposite to. 2 co-starring beside.
– PHRASES **the opposite sex** women in relation to men or vice versa.
– DERIVATIVES **oppositely** adv.
– ORIGIN Middle English: from Latin *oppositus*, from *opponere* 'set against'.

opposite number ■ n. a person's counterpart in another organization or country.

opposition ■ n. 1 resistance or dissent. ▸ (often **the opposition**) a group of opponents. ▸ (**the Opposition**) the principal parliamentary party opposed to that in office. 2 a contrast or antithesis. 3 Astronomy & Astrology the apparent position of two celestial objects that are directly opposite each other in the sky, especially the position of a planet when opposite the sun.
– DERIVATIVES **oppositional** adj.

oppress ■ v. 1 keep in subjection and hardship. 2 cause to feel distressed or anxious.
– DERIVATIVES **oppression** n. **oppressor** n.
– ORIGIN Middle English: from Old French *oppresser*, from medieval Latin *oppressare*, from Latin *opprimere* 'press against'.

oppressive ■ adj. 1 harsh and authoritarian. 2 weighing heavily on the mind or spirits. 3 (of weather) close and sultry.
– DERIVATIVES **oppressively** adv. **oppressiveness** n.

opprobrious /ə'prəʊbrɪəs/ ■ adj. highly scornful.
– DERIVATIVES **opprobriously** adv.

opprobrium /ə'prəʊbrɪəm/ ■ n. 1 harsh criticism or scorn. 2 public disgrace arising from shameful conduct.
– ORIGIN C17 (*opprobrious* Middle English): from Latin, 'infamy'.

oppugn /ə'pjuːn/ ■ v. archaic dispute the truth or validity of.
– DERIVATIVES **oppugner** n.
– ORIGIN Middle English: from Latin *oppugnare* 'attack, besiege'.

opsonin /'ɒpsənɪn/ ■ n. Biochemistry an antibody or other substance which binds to foreign micro-organisms or cells making them more susceptible to phagocytosis.
– DERIVATIVES **opsonic** adj.
– ORIGIN C20: from Latin *opsonare* 'buy provisions', from Greek *opsōnein*.

opt ■ v. make a choice. ▸ (**opt out**) choose not to participate.
– ORIGIN C19: from French *opter*, from Latin *optare* 'choose, wish'.

optic ■ adj. of or relating to the eye or vision. ■ n. 1 a lens or other optical component in an optical instrument. 2 archaic or humorous the eye. 3 trademark a device fastened to the neck of an inverted bottle for measuring out spirits.
– ORIGIN Middle English: from French *optique* or medieval Latin *opticus*, from Greek *optikos*, from *optos* 'seen'.

optical ■ adj. 1 of or relating to vision, light, or optics. 2 of or using visible light (as opposed to other electromagnetic radiation).
– DERIVATIVES **optically** adv.

optical activity ■ n. Chemistry the property of rotating the plane of polarization of plane-polarized light.
– DERIVATIVES **optically active** adj.

optical character recognition ■ n. the identification of printed characters using photoelectric devices and computer software.

optical density ■ n. Physics the degree to which a refractive medium retards transmitted rays of light.

optical fibre ■ n. a thin glass fibre through which light can be transmitted.

optical glass ■ n. a very pure kind of glass used for lenses.

optical illusion ■ n. a thing that deceives the eye by appearing to be other than it is.

optical isomer ■ n. Chemistry each of two or more isomers with molecules which are mirror images of each other and typically differ in optical activity.

optician ■ n. a person qualified to prescribe and dispense glasses and contact lenses, and to detect eye diseases (optometrist), or to make and supply glasses and contact lenses (dispensing optician).
– ORIGIN C17: from French *opticien*.

optic lobe ■ n. Anatomy a lobe in the midbrain from which the optic nerve partly arises.

optic nerves ▪ pl. n. Anatomy the pair of cranial nerves transmitting retinal impulses to the brain from the eyes.

optics ▪ pl. n. [usu. treated as sing.] the branch of science concerned with vision and the behaviour of light.

optima plural form of **OPTIMUM**.

optimal ▪ adj. best or most favourable.
– DERIVATIVES **optimality** n. **optimally** adv.
– ORIGIN C19: from Latin *optimus* 'best'.

optimism ▪ n. **1** hopefulness and confidence about the future or the success of something. **2** Philosophy the doctrine, especially as set forth by Leibniz, that this world is the best of all possible worlds. ▸ the belief that good must ultimately prevail over evil in the universe.
– DERIVATIVES **optimist** n.
– ORIGIN C18: from French *optimisme*, from Latin *optimum* (see **OPTIMUM**).

optimistic ▪ adj. hopeful and confident about the future. ▸ (especially of an estimate) unrealistically high.
– DERIVATIVES **optimistically** adv.

optimize (also **-ise**) ▪ v. make the best or most effective use of (a situation or resource).
– DERIVATIVES **optimization** (also **-isation**) n. **optimizer** (also **-iser**) n.
– ORIGIN C19: from Latin *optimus* 'best'.

optimum ▪ adj. most conducive to a favourable outcome. ▪ n. (pl. **optima** or **optimums**) the optimum conditions for growth, reproduction, or success.
– ORIGIN C19: from Latin, neuter of *optimus* 'best'.

option ▪ n. **1** a thing that is or may be chosen. ▸ the freedom or right to choose. **2** a right to buy or sell a particular thing at a specified price within a set time. ▪ v. buy or sell an option on.
– PHRASES **keep** (or **leave**) **one's options open** not commit oneself.
– ORIGIN C16: from Latin *optio(n-)*, from *optare* 'choose'.

optional ▪ adj. available to be chosen but not obligatory.
– DERIVATIVES **optionality** n. **optionally** adv.

optocoupler ▪ n. Electronics a device containing light-emitting and light-sensitive components, used to couple isolated circuits.

optoelectronics ▪ pl. n. [treated as sing.] the branch of technology concerned with the combined use of electronics and light.
– DERIVATIVES **optoelectronic** adj.

optometer /ɒpˈtɒmɪtə/ ▪ n. an instrument for testing the refractive power of the eye.
– ORIGIN C18: from Greek *optos* 'seen' + **-METER**.

optometry ▪ n. the occupation of measuring eyesight, prescribing corrective lenses, and detecting eye disease.
– DERIVATIVES **optometric** adj. **optometrist** n.

opulent ▪ adj. ostentatiously rich and luxurious. ▸ wealthy.
– DERIVATIVES **opulence** n. **opulently** adv.
– ORIGIN C16: from Latin *opulent-* 'wealthy, splendid'.

opuntia /ɒˈpʌnʃɪə, ə(ʊ)-/ ▪ n. a cactus of a genus that comprises the prickly pears. [Genus *Opuntia*.]
– ORIGIN C17: from Latin, a name given to a plant growing around *Opus* (stem *Opunt-*), a city in ancient Greece.

opus /ˈəʊpəs, ˈɒp-/ ▪ n. (pl. **opuses** or **opera** /ˈɒp(ə)rə/) **1** Music a separate composition or set of compositions. **2** an artistic work, especially one on a large scale.
– ORIGIN C18: from Latin, 'work'.

opus Dei /ˌəʊpəs ˈdeɪiː, ˈɒpəs/ ▪ n. **1** Christian Church liturgical worship regarded as humankind's primary duty to God. **2** (**Opus Dei**) a Roman Catholic organization of laymen and priests founded in 1928 with the aim of re-establishing Christian ideals in society.
– ORIGIN C19: from medieval Latin, 'work of God'.

OR ▪ abbrev. operational research.

or[1] ▪ conj. **1** used to link alternatives. **2** introducing a synonym or explanation of a preceding word or phrase. **3** otherwise. **4** poetic/literary either. ▪ n. a logical operation which gives the value one if at least one operand has the value one, and otherwise gives a value of zero. ▸ [as modifier] Electronics denoting a gate circuit which produces an output if there is a signal on any of its inputs.
– PHRASES **or so** (after a quantity) approximately.
– ORIGIN Middle English: a reduced form of the obsolete conjunction *other*.

or[2] ▪ n. gold or yellow, as a heraldic tincture.
– ORIGIN C16: from Latin *aurum* 'gold'.

-or[1] ▪ suffix (forming nouns) denoting a person or thing performing the action of a verb, or denoting another agent: *escalator*.
– ORIGIN from Latin, via Anglo-Norman French *-eour* or Old French *-eor*.

-or[2] ▪ suffix forming nouns denoting a state or condition: *terror*.
– ORIGIN from Latin, sometimes via Old French *-or*, *-ur*.

-or[3] ▪ suffix forming adjectives expressing a comparative sense: *junior*.
– ORIGIN via Anglo-Norman French from Latin.

-or[4] ▪ suffix US form of **-OUR**[1].

orache /ˈɒrətʃ/ (also **orach**) ▪ n. a plant with red, yellow, or green leaves sometimes eaten as a vegetable. [*Atriplex hortensis* and related species.]
– ORIGIN Middle English *orage*, from Anglo-Norman French *arasche*, from Latin *atriplex*, from Greek *atraphaxus*.

oracle ▪ n. **1** a priest or priestess acting as a medium for divine advice or prophecy in classical antiquity. **2** an infallible authority. **3** archaic a response or message given by an oracle, especially an ambiguous one.
– ORIGIN Middle English: from Latin *oraculum*, from *orare* 'speak'.

oracular /ɒˈrakjʊlə/ ▪ adj. **1** of or relating to an oracle. **2** hard to interpret. **3** holding or claiming the authority of an oracle.

oracy /ˈɔːrəsi/ ▪ n. the ability to express oneself fluently and grammatically in speech.
– ORIGIN 1960s: from Latin *os*, *or-* 'mouth', on the pattern of *literacy*.

oral ▪ adj. **1** spoken rather than written. **2** of or relating to the mouth. ▸ done or taken by the mouth. ▸ Psychoanalysis relating to or denoting a stage of infantile psychosexual development in which the mouth is the main source of sensuous experience. ▪ n. a spoken examination or test.
– DERIVATIVES **orally** adv.
– ORIGIN C17: from late Latin *oralis*, from Latin *os* 'mouth'.

oral history ▪ n. the collection and study of tape-recorded historical information drawn from the speaker's personal knowledge of past events.

orality ▪ n. the quality of being verbally communicated.

Oral Law ▪ n. Judaism the part of Jewish religious law believed to have been passed down by oral tradition before being collected in the Mishnah.

oral sex ▪ n. sexual activity in which the genitals of one partner are stimulated by the mouth of the other.

oral tradition ▪ n. the transmission of beliefs and customs by oral means, through song, verse, storytelling, etc. ▸ a body of information based on this.

orange ▪ n. **1** a large round citrus fruit with a tough bright reddish-yellow rind. ▸ a drink made from or flavoured with orange juice. **2** the evergreen tree which produces this fruit, native to warm regions of south and SE Asia. [*Citrus sinensis* and related species.] ▸ used in names of other plants with similar fruit or flowers, e.g. Osage orange. **3** a bright reddish-yellow colour. ▪ adj. reddish yellow.
– DERIVATIVES **orangey** (also **orangy**) adj. **orangish** adj.
– ORIGIN Middle English: from Old French *orenge*, from Arabic *nāranj*, from Persian *nārang*.

orangeade ▪ n. Brit. a fizzy soft drink flavoured with orange.

orange flower water ▪ n. a solution of neroli in water, used in perfumery and as a food flavouring.

Orangeman ▪ n. (pl. **-men**) a member of the Orange Order, a Protestant political society in Ireland, especially in Northern Ireland.

orange pekoe ▪ n. a type of black tea made from young leaves.

orange roughy ▪ n. (pl. same or **roughies**) a commercially important edible fish found in deep water off Australia, New Zealand, and Namibia. [*Hoplostethus atlanticus*.]

orangery

orangery ▪ n. (pl. **-ies**) a building like a large conservatory where orange trees are grown.

orange stick ▪ n. a thin stick, pointed at one end and typically made of orange wood, used for manicuring the fingernails.

orang-utan /ɔːˌraŋuːˈtan, əˈraŋuːtan/ (also **-utang** /-uːˈtaŋ/) ▪ n. a large arboreal ape with long red hair, long arms, and hooked hands and feet, native to Borneo and Sumatra. [*Pongo pygmaeus*.]
– ORIGIN C17: from Malay *orang huan* 'forest person'.

oration ▪ n. a formal speech, especially one given on a ceremonial occasion.
– DERIVATIVES **orate** v.
– ORIGIN Middle English: from Latin *oratio(n-)* 'discourse, prayer', from *orare* 'speak, pray'.

orator ▪ n. a proficient public speaker. ▸ (also **public orator**) an official speaking for a university on ceremonial occasions.
– DERIVATIVES **oratorial** adj.
– ORIGIN Middle English: from Anglo-Norman French *oratour*, from Latin *orator* 'speaker, pleader'.

oratorio /ˌɒrəˈtɔːrɪəʊ/ ▪ n. (pl. **-os**) a large-scale semi-dramatic musical work for orchestra and voices on a sacred theme, performed without costume, scenery, or action.
– ORIGIN Italian, from eccles. Latin *oratorium* 'oratory', from the musical services held in the church of the Oratory of St Philip Neri in Rome.

oratory[1] /ˈɒrət(ə)ri/ ▪ n. (pl. **-ies**) a small chapel for private worship.
– ORIGIN Middle English: from Anglo-Norman French *oratorie*, from eccles. Latin *oratorium*, from Latin *orare* 'pray, speak'.

oratory[2] ▪ n. 1 the art or practice of formal public speaking. 2 rhetorical or eloquent language.
– DERIVATIVES **oratorical** /-ˈtɒrɪk(ə)l/ adj.
– ORIGIN C16: from Latin *oratoria*, from *oratorius* 'relating to an orator'.

orb ▪ n. a spherical object or shape. ▸ a golden globe surmounted by a cross, forming part of the regalia of a monarch. ▸ poetic/literary a celestial body. ▸ poetic/literary an eye.
– ORIGIN Middle English: from Latin *orbis* 'ring'.

orbicular /ɔːˈbɪkjʊlə/ ▪ adj. 1 technical having the shape of a flat ring or disc. 2 poetic/literary spherical or rounded. 3 Geology (of a rock) containing spheroidal igneous inclusions.

orbit ▪ n. 1 the regularly repeated elliptical course of a celestial object or spacecraft about a star or planet. 2 a field of activity or influence: *they brought many friends within the orbit of our lives*. 3 the path of an electron round an atomic nucleus. 4 Anatomy the eye socket. ▪ v. (**orbited**, **orbiting**) move in orbit round (a star or planet). ▸ put (a satellite) into orbit.
– PHRASES **into orbit** informal into a state of heightened activity, anger, or excitement.
– ORIGIN C16: from Latin *orbita* 'course, track', from *orbitus* 'circular'.

orbital ▪ adj. 1 of or relating to an orbit or orbits. 2 chiefly Brit. (of a road) passing round the outside of a town. ▪ n. Physics a pattern of electron density representing the possible behaviour of one or more electrons in an atom or molecule.

orbital sander ▪ n. a sander in which the sanding surface has a minute circular motion without rotating relative to the workpiece.

orbiter ▪ n. a spacecraft designed to go into orbit, especially one that does not subsequently land.

orb web ▪ n. a circular vertical spider's web formed of threads radiating from a central point, crossed by radial links that spiral in from the edge.

orc ▪ n. (in fantasy literature and games) a member of an imaginary race of ugly, warlike human-like creatures.
– ORIGIN C16: perhaps from Latin *orcus* 'hell' or Italian *orco* 'monster'; the word was popularized by Tolkien's fantasy adventures.

orca /ˈɔːkə/ ▪ n. another term for **KILLER WHALE**.
– ORIGIN C19: from French *orque* or Latin *orca*, denoting a kind of whale.

Orcadian /ɔːˈkeɪdɪən/ ▪ adj. of or relating to the Orkney Islands or their inhabitants. ▪ n. a native or inhabitant of the Orkney Islands.
– ORIGIN from *Orcades*, the Latin name for the Orkney Islands.

orch. ▪ abbrev. orchestra.

orchard ▪ n. a piece of enclosed land planted with fruit trees.
– DERIVATIVES **orchardist** n.
– ORIGIN Old English *ortgeard*; from Latin *hortus* 'garden' + an element representing **YARD**[2].

orchestra ▪ n. 1 [treated as sing. or pl.] a group of instrumentalists, especially one combining string, woodwind, brass, and percussion sections. 2 (also **orchestra pit**) the part of a theatre where the orchestra plays, typically in front of the stage and on a lower level. 3 N. Amer. the stalls in a theatre.
– DERIVATIVES **orchestral** adj. **orchestrally** adv.
– ORIGIN C17: from Greek *orkhēstra*, from *orkheisthai* 'to dance'.

orchestra stalls ▪ pl. n. chiefly Brit. the front part of the stalls in a theatre.

orchestrate ▪ v. 1 arrange or score (music) for orchestral performance. 2 direct (a situation) to produce a desired effect.
– DERIVATIVES **orchestration** n. **orchestrator** n.

orchid ▪ n. a plant of a large family (Orchidaceae) distinguished by complex showy flowers with a larger central petal at the base and frequently a spur.
– ORIGIN C19: from Greek *orkhis* 'testicle', with ref. to the shape of its tuber.

orchitis /ɔːˈkaɪtɪs/ ▪ n. Medicine inflammation of one or both of the testicles.
– ORIGIN C18: from Greek *orkhis* 'testicle'.

ordain ▪ v. 1 confer holy orders on. 2 order officially. ▸ (of God or fate) decide in advance.
– DERIVATIVES **ordainment** n.
– ORIGIN Middle English: from Anglo-Norman French *ordeiner*, from Latin *ordinare*, from *ordo* (see **ORDER**).

ordeal ▪ n. 1 a prolonged painful or horrific experience. 2 an ancient test of guilt or innocence by subjection of the accused to severe pain, survival of which was taken as divine proof of innocence.
– ORIGIN Old English, of Germanic origin, from a base meaning 'share out'.

order ▪ n. 1 the arrangement or disposition of people or things according to a particular sequence or method. ▸ a state in which everything is in its correct place. ▸ a state in which the laws and rules regulating public behaviour are observed. ▸ the prescribed procedure followed by a meeting, legislative assembly, or court of law. 2 an authoritative command or direction. ▸ a verbal or written request for something to be made, supplied, or served. 3 a social class. ▸ a particular social, political, or economic system. ▸ a rank in the Christian ministry, especially that of bishop, priest, or deacon. ▸ (**orders**) the rank of an ordained minister of the Church. See also **HOLY ORDERS**. ▸ Theology any of the nine grades of angelic beings in the celestial hierarchy. 4 Biology a principal taxonomic category that ranks below class and above family. 5 a society of monks, nuns, or friars living under the same rule. ▸ historical a society of knights constituted in a similar way to a monastic order. ▸ an institution founded by a monarch along the lines of such an order of knights for the purpose of honouring meritorious conduct. ▸ a Masonic or similar fraternity. 6 the quality or nature of something: *poetry of the highest order*. 7 any of the five classical styles of architecture (Doric, Ionic, Corinthian, Tuscan, and Composite) based on proportions of columns and the style of their decoration. 8 Mathematics the degree of complexity of an equation, expression, etc. ▸ the number of elements in a finite group. ▸ the number of rows or columns in a square matrix. ▪ v. 1 give an order. 2 request (something) to be made, supplied, or served. 3 arrange methodically.
– PHRASES **in order 1** in the correct condition for operation or use. **2** appropriate in the circumstances. **in order for** (or **that**) so that. **in order to** with the purpose of doing. **of** (or **on**) **the order of** approximately. **on order** (of

goods) requested but not yet received. **order of battle** the units, formations, and equipment of a military force. **the order of the day 1** the prevailing or required custom or state of affairs. **2** (in a legislature) the business to be considered on a particular day. **out of order 1** (of an electrical or mechanical device) not working properly or at all. **2** Brit. informal unacceptable or wrong.
– ORIGIN Middle English: from Old French *ordre*, from Latin *ordo* 'row, series'.

orderly ■ adj. **1** neatly and methodically arranged. **2** well behaved. ■ n. (pl. **-ies**) **1** an attendant in a hospital responsible for cleaning and other non-medical tasks. **2** a soldier who carries orders or performs minor tasks for an officer.
– DERIVATIVES **orderliness** n.

orderly officer ■ n. Brit. Military the officer in charge of the security and administration of a unit or establishment for a day at a time.

orderly room ■ n. Military the room in a barracks used for regimental or company business.

order of magnitude ■ n. a class in a system of classification determined by size, typically in powers of ten.

Order Paper ■ n. a paper on which the day's business for a legislative assembly is entered.

ordinal ■ n. Christian Church, chiefly historical a service book, especially one with the forms of service used at ordinations. ■ adj. **1** of or relating to order in a series. **2** Biology of or relating to a taxonomic order.
– ORIGIN Middle English: the noun from medieval Latin *ordinale*; the adjective from late Latin *ordinalis* 'relating to order', from *ordo* (see ORDER).

ordinal number ■ n. a number defining a thing's position in a series, such as 'first' or 'second'.

ordinance ■ n. formal **1** an authoritative order. ▶ N. Amer. a by-law. **2** a religious rite.
– ORIGIN Middle English: from Old French *ordenance*, from medieval Latin *ordinantia*, from Latin *ordinare* (see ORDAIN).

ordinand /'ɔːdɪnand/ ■ n. a person who is training to be ordained as a priest or minister.
– ORIGIN C19: from Latin *ordinandus*, from *ordinare* (see ORDAIN).

ordinary ■ adj. **1** with no distinctive features; normal or usual. **2** (of a judge, archbishop, or bishop) exercising authority by virtue of office and not by deputation. ■ n. (pl. **-ies**) **1** a rule or book laying down the order of divine service. **2** Heraldry any of the simplest principal charges used in coats of arms.
– PHRASES **out of the ordinary** unusual.
– DERIVATIVES **ordinarily** adv. **ordinariness** n.
– ORIGIN Middle English: from Latin *ordinarius* 'orderly', from *ordo* 'order'.

ordinary grade ■ n. (in Scotland) the lower of the two main levels of the Scottish Certificate of Education examination. Compare with HIGHER.

ordinary level ■ n. the lower of the two main levels of GCE examination, taken at age 15 or 16. Compare with ADVANCED LEVEL.

ordinary share ■ n. a share entitling its holder to dividends which vary in amount depending on the fortunes of the company. Compare with PREFERENCE SHARE.

ordinate /'ɔːdɪnət/ ■ n. Mathematics a straight line from a point on a graph drawn parallel to the vertical axis and meeting the other; the *y*-coordinate. Compare with ABSCISSA.
– ORIGIN C17: from Latin *linea ordinata applicata* 'line applied parallel'.

ordination ■ n. the action of ordaining someone in holy orders.

ordnance /'ɔːdnəns/ ■ n. **1** mounted guns; cannon. ▶ munitions. **2** a government department dealing especially with military stores and materials.
– ORIGIN Middle English: var. of ORDINANCE.

Ordnance Survey ■ n. (in the UK) an official survey organization preparing large-scale detailed maps of the whole country.

Ordovician /ˌɔːdə'vɪʃɪən/ ■ adj. Geology relating to or denoting the second period of the Palaeozoic era (between the Cambrian and Silurian periods, about 510 to 439 million years ago), a time when the first vertebrates appeared.
– ORIGIN C19: from *Ordovices*, the Latin name of an ancient Brit. tribe.

ordure /'ɔːdjʊə/ ■ n. excrement; dung.
– ORIGIN Middle English: from Old French, from *ord* 'foul', from Latin *horridus* (see HORRID).

ore ■ n. a naturally occurring solid material from which a metal or valuable mineral can be extracted profitably.
– ORIGIN Old English *ōra* 'unwrought metal', of West Germanic origin.

oread /'ɔːrɪad/ ■ n. Greek & Roman Mythology a nymph believed to inhabit mountains.
– ORIGIN from Latin *Oreas, Oread-*, from Greek *Oreias*, from *oros* 'mountain'.

oregano /ˌɒrɪ'gɑːnəʊ, ə'rɛgənəʊ/ ■ n. an aromatic plant related to marjoram, with small purple flowers and leaves used as a culinary herb. [*Origanum vulgare*.]
– ORIGIN C18: from Spanish, var. of ORIGANUM.

Oregon pine ■ n. another term for DOUGLAS FIR.

Oreo /'ɔːrɪəʊ/ ■ n. (pl. **-os**) **1** trademark a chocolate biscuit with a white cream filling. **2** US informal, derogatory an American black person who is seen, especially by other black people, as wishing to be part of the white establishment.

orf ■ n. an infectious disease of sheep and goats characterized by skin lesions and secondary bacterial infection.
– ORIGIN C19: prob. from Old Norse *hrufa*.

organ ■ n. **1** a large musical instrument having rows of pipes supplied with air from bellows and arranged in ranks, each controlled by a stop, and played using a keyboard or by an automatic mechanism. ▶ a smaller instrument without pipes, producing similar sounds electronically. **2** a part of an organism which is typically self-contained and has a specific vital function. ▶ euphemistic a man's penis. **3** a department or organization that performs a specified function. **4** a newspaper or periodical which puts forward the views of a political party or movement.
– DERIVATIVES **organist** n.
– ORIGIN Old English, from Greek *organon* 'tool, sense organ'.

organdie /'ɔːg(ə)ndi, ɔː'gandi/ (US also **organdy**) ■ n. (pl. **-ies**) a fine, translucent, stiff cotton muslin, used chiefly for dresses.
– ORIGIN C19: from French *organdi*.

organelle /ˌɔːgə'nɛl/ ■ n. Biology any of a number of organized or specialized structures within a living cell.
– ORIGIN C20: from modern Latin *organella*, diminutive of Latin *organum* 'organ, tool'.

organ-grinder ■ n. a street musician who plays a barrel organ.

organic ■ adj. **1** relating to or derived from living matter. ▶ Chemistry relating to or denoting compounds containing carbon and chiefly or ultimately of biological origin. Compare with INORGANIC. **2** Physiology of or relating to a bodily organ or organs. ▶ Medicine (of a disease) affecting the structure of an organ. **3** produced or involving production without the use of chemical fertilizers or other artificial chemicals. **4** denoting a harmonious relationship between the elements of a whole. ▶ characterized by natural development.
– DERIVATIVES **organically** adv.

organicism ■ n. the doctrine that everything in nature has an organic basis or is part of an organic whole.

organic law ■ n. a law stating the formal constitution of a nation.

organism ■ n. an individual animal, plant, or single-celled life form. ▶ a whole with interdependent parts, compared to a living being.
– ORIGIN C18: from French *organisme*.

organization (also **-isation**) ■ n. **1** the action of organizing. ▶ systematic arrangement of elements. ▶ a systematic approach to tasks. **2** an organized body of

organization man

people with a particular purpose, such as a business or government department.
- DERIVATIVES **organizational** (also **-isational**) adj. **organizationally** (also **-isationally**) adv.

organization man ■ n. a man who lets his personal life be dominated by the organization he serves.

organize (also **-ise**) ■ v. **1** arrange systematically; order. **2** make arrangements or preparations for. **3** form (people) into a trade union or other political group.
- DERIVATIVES **organizable** (also **-isable**) adj. **organizer** (also **-iser**) n.
- ORIGIN Middle English: from medieval Latin *organizare*, from Latin *organum*, from Greek *organon* 'organ, tool'.

organo- /ˈɔːɡ(ə)nəʊ, ɔːˈɡanəʊ/ ■ comb. form **1** chiefly Biology relating to bodily organs: *organogenesis*. **2** Chemistry (forming names of classes of organic compounds containing a particular element or group) organic: *organophosphate*.
- ORIGIN from Greek *organon* 'organ'; sense 2 from ORGANIC.

organ of Corti ■ n. Anatomy a structure in the cochlea of the inner ear which produces nerve impulses in response to sound vibrations.
- ORIGIN C19: named after the Italian anatomist Alfonso Corti.

organogenesis /ˌɔːɡ(ə)nə(ʊ)ˈdʒɛnɪsɪs, ɔːˌɡan(ə)-/ ■ n. Biology the production and development of the organs of an animal or plant.

organometallic ■ adj. Chemistry (of a compound) containing a metal atom bonded to an organic group or groups.

organophosphate ■ n. any organic compound whose molecule contains one or more phosphate ester groups, especially a pesticide of this kind.

organophosphorus /ˌɔːɡ(ə)nəʊˈfɒsf(ə)rəs/ ■ adj. denoting synthetic organic compounds containing phosphorus.
- DERIVATIVES **organophosphate** n.

organza /ɔːˈɡanzə/ ■ n. a thin, stiff, transparent dress fabric made of silk or a synthetic yarn.
- ORIGIN C19: prob. from *Lorganza*, a US trademark.

orgasm ■ n. the climax of sexual excitement, characterized by intensely pleasurable sensations centred in the genitals. ■ v. have an orgasm.
- ORIGIN C17: from French *orgasme*, from Greek *orgasmos*, from *organ* 'swell, be excited'.

orgasmic ■ adj. **1** of or relating to orgasm. ▶ able to achieve orgasm. **2** informal very enjoyable.
- DERIVATIVES **orgasmically** adv. **orgastic** adj. **orgastically** adv.

orgone /ˈɔːɡəʊn/ ■ n. a supposed excess sexual energy or life force distributed throughout the universe which can be collected and stored for subsequent therapeutic use.
- ORIGIN 1940s: coined by the psychoanalyst Wilhelm Reich, from ORGANISM or ORGANIC.

orgulous /ˈɔːɡjʊləs/ ■ adj. poetic/literary haughty.
- ORIGIN Middle English: from Old French *orguillus*, from *orguill* 'pride'.

orgy ■ n. (pl. **-ies**) **1** a wild party characterized by excessive drinking and indiscriminate sexual activity. **2** excessive indulgence in a specified activity. **3** secret rites used particularly in the worship of Bacchus and Dionysus, celebrated with dancing, drunkenness, and singing.
- DERIVATIVES **orgiastic** adj. **orgiastically** adv.
- ORIGIN C16: from French *orgies*, from Greek *orgia* 'secret rites or revels'.

oribi /ˈɒrɪbi/ ■ n. (pl. same or **oribis**) a small antelope of the African savannah, having a reddish-fawn back and white underparts, the male of which has short vertical horns. [*Ourebia ourebi*.]
- ORIGIN C18: from Afrikaans, from Khoikhoi.

oriel /ˈɔːrɪəl/ ■ n. a large upper-storey bay with a window (oriel window), supported by brackets or on corbels.
- ORIGIN Middle English: from Old French *oriol* 'gallery'.

orient ■ n. /ˈɔːrɪənt, ˈɒr-/ **1** (**the Orient**) poetic/literary the countries of the East, especially east Asia. **2** the special lustre of a pearl of the finest quality (with reference to fine pearls from the East). ■ adj. /ˈɔːrɪənt, ˈɒr-/ poetic/literary oriental. ■ v. /ˈɔːrɪɛnt, ˈɒr-/ **1** align or position relative to the points of a compass or other specified positions.
▶ (**orient oneself**) find one's position in relation to unfamiliar surroundings. **2** tailor to specified circumstances.
- ORIGIN Middle English: from Latin *orient-* 'rising or east', from *oriri* 'to rise'.

oriental (also **Oriental**) ■ adj. **1** of, from, or characteristic of the Far East. ▶ (**Oriental**) Zoology relating to or denoting a zoogeographical region comprising Asia south of the Himalayas and western Indonesia. **2** (of a pearl or other jewel) orient. ■ n. often offensive a person of Far Eastern descent.
- DERIVATIVES **orientalism** n. **orientalist** n. **orientally** adv.

> USAGE
> The term **oriental** is now regarded as old-fashioned and potentially offensive as a term denoting people from the Far East. In US and South African English, **Asian** is the standard accepted term in modern use; in British English, where **Asian** tends to denote people from the Indian subcontinent, specific terms such as **Chinese** or **Japanese** are more likely to be used.

orientalia /ˌɔːrɪənˈteɪlɪə, ˌɒr-/ ■ pl. n. books and other items relating to or characteristic of the Orient.
- ORIGIN C20: from Latin, from *orientalis* 'oriental'.

orientation ■ n. **1** the action of orienting. ▶ a relative position. **2** the direction of someone's interest or attitude, especially political or sexual.
- DERIVATIVES **orientate** v. **orientational** adj.
- ORIGIN C19: apparently from ORIENT.

orientation course ■ n. a course giving information to newcomers to a university or other organization.

orienteering ■ n. a competitive sport in which runners have to find their way across rough country with the aid of a map and compass.
- DERIVATIVES **orienteer** n. & v.
- ORIGIN 1940s: from Swedish *orientering*.

orifice /ˈɒrɪfɪs/ ■ n. an opening, particularly one in the body such as a nostril.
- ORIGIN Middle English: from late Latin *orificium*, from *os, or-* 'mouth' + *facere* 'make'.

oriflamme /ˈɒrɪflam/ ■ n. the sacred scarlet banner of St Denis, given to early French kings on setting out for war.
- ORIGIN Middle English: from Latin *aurum* 'gold' + *flamma* 'flame'.

origami /ˌɒrɪˈɡɑːmi/ ■ n. the Japanese art of folding paper into decorative shapes and figures.
- ORIGIN Japanese, from *oru, -ori* 'fold' + *kami* 'paper'.

origanum /ɒˈrɪɡ(ə)nəm/ ■ n. an aromatic plant of a genus that includes marjoram and oregano. [Genus *Origanum*.]
- ORIGIN Latin, from Greek *origanon*, perhaps from *oros* 'mountain' + *ganos* 'brightness'.

origin ■ n. **1** the point where something begins or arises. ▶ Anatomy the more fixed end or attachment of a muscle. **2** a person's social background or ancestry. **3** Mathematics a fixed point from which coordinates are measured.
- ORIGIN C16: from French *origine*, from Latin *origo*, from *oriri* 'to rise'.

original ■ adj. **1** existing from the beginning; first or earliest. **2** produced first-hand; not a copy. **3** inventive or novel. ■ n. **1** the earliest form of something, from which copies can be made. ▶ (**the original**) the language in which something was first written. **2** an eccentric or unusual person.
- DERIVATIVES **originality** n. **originally** adv.
- ORIGIN Middle English: from Old French, or from Latin *originalis*, from *origo* (see ORIGIN).

original gravity ■ n. (in brewing) the relative density of the wort before it is fermented to produce beer, chiefly dependent on the quantity of fermentable sugars in solution.

original print ■ n. a print made directly from an artist's own woodcut, etching, etc., and printed under the artist's supervision.

original sin ■ n. Christian Church the tendency to evil supposedly innate in all human beings, held to be inherited from Adam in consequence of the Fall.

originate ■ v. have a specified beginning. ► create or initiate.
– DERIVATIVES **origination** n. **originative** adj. **originator** n.

Orimulsion /ˌɒrɪˈmʌlʃ(ə)n/ ■ n. trademark a fuel consisting of an emulsion of bitumen in water.
– ORIGIN 1980s: blend of *Orinoco* (an oil belt in Venezuela where the bitumen was orig. extracted) and **EMULSION**.

O-ring ■ n. a gasket in the form of a ring with a circular cross section.

oriole /ˈɔːrɪəʊl, ˈɔːrɪəl/ ■ n. a brightly coloured arboreal bird with a musical call. [*Oriolus larvatus* (Africa), *O. oriolus*, and related species.]
– ORIGIN C18: from medieval Latin *oriolus*, from Latin *aureolus*, diminutive of *aureus* 'golden'.

Orisha /əˈrɪʃə/ ■ n. (pl. same or **Orishas**) (in southern Nigeria and among certain black religious cults of South America and the Caribbean) any of several minor gods.
– ORIGIN from Yoruba.

orison /ˈɒrɪz(ə)n, -s(ə)n/ ■ n. archaic a prayer.
– ORIGIN Middle English: from Old French *oreison*, from Latin *oratio(n-)* (see **ORATION**).

-orium ■ suffix forming nouns denoting a place for a particular function: *sanatorium*.
– ORIGIN from Latin.

orle /ɔːl/ ■ n. Heraldry a narrow border of charges inset from the edge of a shield.
– ORIGIN C16: from French *ourle*, from *ourler* 'to hem'.

Orlon /ˈɔːlɒn/ ■ n. trademark a synthetic acrylic fibre and fabric used for clothing, knitwear, etc.
– ORIGIN 1950s: invented word, on the pattern of *nylon*.

orlop /ˈɔːlɒp/ (also **orlop deck**) ■ n. the lowest deck of a wooden sailing ship with three or more decks.
– ORIGIN Middle English: from Dutch *overloop* 'covering', from *overlopen* 'run over'.

ormer /ˈɔːmə/ ■ n. an abalone, especially one found chiefly off the Channel Islands. [*Haliotis tuberculata* and other species.]
– ORIGIN C17: Channel Islands French, from French *ormier*, from Latin *auris maris* 'ear of the sea' (because of its ear-like shape).

ormolu /ˈɔːməluː/ ■ n. a gold-coloured alloy of copper, zinc, and tin used in decoration and making ornaments.
– ORIGIN C18: from French *or moulu* 'powdered gold'.

ornament ■ n. /ˈɔːnəm(ə)nt/ an object designed to add beauty to something. ► decorative items collectively; decoration. ► (**ornaments**) Music embellishments made to a melody. ■ v. /ˈɔːnəmɛnt/ beautify.
– DERIVATIVES **ornamentation** n.
– ORIGIN Middle English: from Old French *ournement*, from Latin *ornamentum* 'equipment, ornament', from *ornare* 'adorn'.

ornamental ■ adj. serving or intended as an ornament. ■ n. a plant grown for its attractive appearance.
– DERIVATIVES **ornamentalism** n. **ornamentally** adv.

ornate ■ adj. 1 elaborately or highly decorated. 2 (of literary style) using unusual words and complex constructions.
– DERIVATIVES **ornately** adv. **ornateness** n.
– ORIGIN Middle English: from Latin *ornatus*, *ornare* 'adorn'.

ornery /ˈɔːnəri/ ■ adj. N. Amer. informal bad-tempered.
– ORIGIN C19: var. of **ORDINARY**, representing a dialect pronunciation

ornithine /ˈɔːnɪθiːn/ ■ n. Biochemistry an amino acid which is produced by the body and is important in protein metabolism.
– ORIGIN C19: from **ORNITHO-**, with ref. to a constituent found in bird excrement.

ornithischian /ˌɔːnɪˈθɪskɪən, -ˈθɪʃən/ ■ n. Palaeontology a herbivorous dinosaur of a group with a pelvic structure resembling that of birds. Compare with **SAURISCHIAN**.
– ORIGIN C20: from *Ornithischia* (name of an order), from Greek *ornis* 'bird' + *iskhion* 'hip joint'.

ornitho- ■ comb. form relating to or resembling a bird or birds: *ornithology*.
– ORIGIN from Greek *ornis*, *ornith-* 'bird'.

ornithology /ˌɔːnɪˈθɒlədʒi/ ■ n. the scientific study of birds.
– DERIVATIVES **ornithological** adj. **ornithologically** adv. **ornithologist** n.
– ORIGIN C17: from Greek *ornithologos* 'treating of birds'.

ornithosis /ˌɔːnɪˈθəʊsɪs/ ■ n. another term for **PSITTACOSIS**.

oro- ■ comb. form of or relating to mountains: *orogeny*.
– ORIGIN from Greek *oros* 'mountain'.

orogeny /ɒˈrɒdʒəni/ ■ n. Geology a process in which a section of the earth's crust is folded and deformed by lateral compression to form a mountain range.
– DERIVATIVES **orogenesis** n. **orogenic** adj.

orographic /ˌɒrəˈgrafɪk/ ■ adj. of or relating to mountains, especially as regards their position and form. ► (of clouds or rainfall) resulting from the effects of mountains in forcing moist air to rise.
– DERIVATIVES **orographical** adj.

Oromo /ˈɒrəməʊ/ ■ n. (pl. same or **-os**) 1 a member of an East African people, the largest ethnic group in Ethiopia. 2 the Cushitic language of this people.
– ORIGIN the name in Oromo.

oropharynx /ˌɔːrə(ʊ)ˈfarɪŋks/ ■ n. (pl. **oropharynges** or **oropharynxes**) Anatomy the part of the pharynx that lies between the soft palate and the hyoid bone.
– DERIVATIVES **oropharyngeal** adj.
– ORIGIN C19: from Latin *os*, *-or* 'mouth' + **PHARYNX**.

orotund /ˈɒrə(ʊ)tʌnd, ˈɔː-/ ■ adj. 1 (of the voice) resonant and impressive. 2 (of writing or style) pompous.
– DERIVATIVES **orotundity** n.
– ORIGIN C18: from Latin *ore rotundo* 'with rounded mouth'.

orphan ■ n. 1 a child whose parents are dead. 2 Printing the first line of a paragraph set as the last line of a page or column, considered undesirable. ■ v. (usu. **be orphaned**) make an orphan.
– DERIVATIVES **orphanhood** n.
– ORIGIN Middle English: from Greek *orphanos* 'bereaved'.

orphanage ■ n. a residential institution for the care and education of orphans.

Orphic ■ adj. 1 of or concerning Orpheus, a legendary Greek poet and lyre-player, or the cult of Orphism. 2 of or relating to the artistic movement of Orphism.
– ORIGIN C17: from Greek *Orphikos*, from *Orpheus*.

Orphism /ˈɔːfɪz(ə)m/ ■ n. 1 a mystic religion of ancient Greece, said to have been based on poems by Orpheus, characterized by rites of purification, death, and rebirth. 2 a short-lived art movement (c.1912) within cubism, characterized by a more lyrical use of colour than is found in other cubist works.

orrery /ˈɒrəri/ ■ n. (pl. **-ies**) a clockwork model of the solar system, or of just the sun, earth, and moon.
– ORIGIN C18: named after the fourth Earl of *Orrery*, for whom one was made.

orris /ˈɒrɪs/ (also **orris root**) ■ n. a preparation of the fragrant rootstock of an iris, used in perfumery and formerly in medicine.
– ORIGIN C16: apparently an alteration of **IRIS**.

ortanique /ˌɔːtəˈniːk/ ■ n. a citrus fruit which is a cross between an orange and a tangerine. [*Citrus sinensis* × *reticulata*.]
– ORIGIN blend of **ORANGE**, **TANGERINE**, and **UNIQUE**.

ortho- ■ comb. form 1 straight; rectangular; upright: *orthodontics*. ► correct: *orthoepy*. 2 Chemistry denoting substitution at two adjacent carbon atoms in a benzene ring: *orthodichlorobenzene*. Compare with **META-** and **PARA-**[1]. 3 Chemistry denoting a compound from which a *meta*-compound is formed by dehydration: *orthophosphoric acid*.
– ORIGIN from Greek *orthos* 'straight, right'.

orthochromatic ■ adj. denoting black-and-white photographic film sensitive to all visible light except red.

orthoclase /ˈɔːθəkleɪz/ ■ n. a potassium-rich mineral of the feldspar group, typically white or pink.
– ORIGIN C19: from **ORTHO-** + Greek *klasis* 'breaking' (because of the characteristic two cleavages at right angles).

orthodontics /ˌɔːθəˈdɒntɪks/ (also **orthodontia** /-ˈdɒntɪə/)
■ pl. n. [treated as sing.] the treatment of irregularities in the teeth and jaws.
– DERIVATIVES **orthodontic** adj. **orthodontically** adv. **orthodontist** n.
– ORIGIN C20: from ORTHO- + Greek *odous*, *odont-* 'tooth'.

orthodox ■ adj. **1** conforming with traditional or generally accepted beliefs. **2** conventional; normal. **3** (usu. **Orthodox**) of or relating to Orthodox Judaism or the Orthodox Church.
– DERIVATIVES **orthodoxly** adv.
– ORIGIN Middle English: from Greek *orthodoxos*, from *orthos* 'straight or right' + *doxa* 'opinion'.

Orthodox Church ■ n. a Christian Church or federation of Churches acknowledging the authority of the patriarch of Constantinople and originating in the Greek-speaking Church of the Byzantine Empire.

Orthodox Judaism ■ n. a major branch within Judaism which teaches strict adherence to rabbinical interpretation of Jewish law and its traditional observances.

orthodoxy ■ n. (pl. **-ies**) **1** orthodox theory, doctrine, or practice. ▸ the state of being orthodox. **2** the whole community of Orthodox Jews or Orthodox Christians.

orthoepy /ˈɔːθəʊɛpi, -iːpi, ɔːˈθəʊɪpi/ ■ n. the study of correct or accepted pronunciation.
– DERIVATIVES **orthoepic** /-ˈɛpɪk/ adj. **orthoepist** n.
– ORIGIN C17: from Greek *orthoepeia* 'correct speech'.

orthogenesis /ˌɔːθə(ʊ)ˈdʒɛnɪsɪs/ ■ n. Biology, chiefly historical evolution in which variations follow a particular direction and are not merely sporadic and fortuitous.
– DERIVATIVES **orthogenesist** n. **orthogenetic** adj. **orthogenetically** adv.

orthogonal /ɔːˈθɒɡ(ə)n(ə)l/ ■ adj. **1** of or involving right angles; at right angles to each other. **2** Statistics (of variates) statistically independent.
– DERIVATIVES **orthogonality** n. **orthogonally** adv.
– ORIGIN C16: from Greek *orthogōnios* 'right-angled'.

orthography /ɔːˈθɒɡrəfi/ ■ n. (pl. **-ies**) the conventional spelling system of a language. ▸ the study of spelling and how letters combine to represent sounds and form words.
– DERIVATIVES **orthographer** n. **orthographic** adj. **orthographical** adj. **orthographically** adv.
– ORIGIN Middle English: from Greek *orthographia*, from *orthos* 'correct' + *-graphia* writing.

orthopaedics /ˌɔːθəˈpiːdɪks/ (US **-pedics**) ■ pl. n. [treated as sing.] the branch of medicine concerned with the correction of deformities of bones or muscles.
– DERIVATIVES **orthopaedic** adj. **orthopaedically** adv. **orthopaedist** n.
– ORIGIN C19: from French *orthopédie*, from Greek *orthos* 'right or straight' + *paideia* 'rearing of children'.

orthophosphoric acid /ˌɔːθə(ʊ)fɒsˈfɒrɪk/ ■ n. another term for PHOSPHORIC ACID.
– DERIVATIVES **orthophosphate** n.

Orthoptera /ɔːˈθɒpt(ə)rə/ ■ pl. n. Entomology an order of insects that includes the grasshoppers and crickets.
– DERIVATIVES **orthopteran** n. & adj. **orthopterous** adj.
– ORIGIN from ORTHO- + Greek *pteros* 'wing'.

orthoptics ■ pl. n. [treated as sing.] the study or treatment of irregularities of the eyes, especially those of the eye muscles that prevent normal binocular vision.
– DERIVATIVES **orthoptic** adj. **orthoptist** n.
– ORIGIN C19: from ORTHO- + Greek *optikos* (see OPTIC).

orthorhombic /ˌɔːθə(ʊ)ˈrɒmbɪk/ ■ adj. denoting a crystal system with three unequal axes at right angles.

orthostat /ˈɔːθə(ʊ)stat/ ■ n. Archaeology an upright stone or slab forming part of a structure or set in the ground.
– ORIGIN C20: from Greek *orthostatēs*, from *orthos* 'right or straight' + *statos* 'standing'.

orthostatic ■ adj. **1** Medicine relating to or caused by an upright posture. **2** Archaeology (of a structure) built of orthostats.

orthotic ■ adj. relating to orthotics. ■ n. an artificial support or brace for the limbs or spine.

orthotics /ɔːˈθɒtɪks/ ■ pl. n. [treated as sing.] the branch of medicine concerned with the provision and use of artificial supports or braces.
– DERIVATIVES **orthotist** n.

ortolan /ˈɔːt(ə)lən/ (also **ortolan bunting**) ■ n. a small Eurasian songbird formerly eaten as a delicacy, the male having an olive-green head and yellow throat. [*Emberiza hortulana*.]
– ORIGIN C16: from Provençal, 'gardener'.

Orwellian ■ adj. of or characteristic of the work of the British novelist George Orwell (1903–50), especially with reference to the totalitarian state as depicted in *Nineteen Eighty-four*.

-ory¹ ■ suffix (forming nouns) denoting a place for a particular function: *dormitory*.
– DERIVATIVES **-orial** suffix forming corresponding adjectives.
– ORIGIN from Latin *-oria*, *-orium*.

-ory² ■ suffix forming adjectives (and occasionally nouns) relating to or involving a verbal action: *compulsory*.
– ORIGIN from Latin *-orius*.

oryx /ˈɒrɪks/ ■ n. a large long-horned antelope of arid regions of Africa and Arabia. [Genus *Oryx*: three species.]
– ORIGIN Middle English: from Greek *orux* 'stonemason's pickaxe' (because of its pointed horns).

orzo /ˈɔːtsəʊ/ ■ n. small pieces of pasta, shaped like grains of barley or rice.
– ORIGIN Italian, 'barley'.

OS ■ abbrev. **1** Computing operating system. **2** (in the UK) Ordnance Survey. **3** out of stock.

Os ■ symb. the chemical element osmium.

Oscar ■ n. **1** (trademark in the US) the nickname for a gold statuette given as an Academy award. **2** a code word representing the letter O, used in radio communication.
– ORIGIN one of the several speculative explanations of sense 1 claims that the statuette reminded an executive director of the Academy of Motion Picture Arts and Sciences of her uncle Oscar.

oscar (also **oscar cichlid**) ■ n. a South American cichlid fish with velvety brown young and multicoloured adults, popular in aquaria. [*Astronotus ocellatus*.]

oscillate /ˈɒsɪleɪt/ ■ v. **1** move or swing back and forth at a regular speed. ▸ waver between extremes of opinion or emotion. **2** Physics move or vary with periodic regularity. ▸ cause an electric current or voltage to behave thus.
– DERIVATIVES **oscillation** n. **oscillator** n. **oscillatory** /ɒˈsɪlət(ə)ri, ˈɒsɪlə,t(ə)ri/ adj.
– ORIGIN C18 (*oscillation* C17): from Latin *oscillare* 'swing'.

oscillograph ■ n. a device for recording oscillations, especially those of an electric current.
– DERIVATIVES **oscillogram** n. **oscillographic** adj. **oscillography** n.

oscilloscope ■ n. a device for viewing oscillations by a display on the screen of a cathode ray tube.
– DERIVATIVES **oscilloscopic** adj.

oscine /ˈɒsaɪn, -sɪn/ ■ adj. Ornithology relating to or denoting birds of a large suborder (Oscines) that includes nearly all passerine birds.
– ORIGIN C19: from Latin *oscen*, *oscin-* 'songbird'.

osculum /ˈɒskjʊləm/ ■ n. (pl. **oscula** /-lə/) Zoology a large aperture in a sponge through which water is expelled.
– ORIGIN C17: from Latin, 'little mouth'.

-ose¹ ■ suffix (forming adjectives) having a specified quality: *bellicose*.
– DERIVATIVES **-osely** suffix forming corresponding adverbs. **-oseness** suffix forming corresponding nouns.
– ORIGIN from Latin *-osus*.

-ose² ■ suffix Chemistry forming names of sugars and other carbohydrates: *cellulose*.
– ORIGIN on the pattern of (*gluc*)*ose*.

osier /ˈəʊzɪə/ ■ n. a small Eurasian willow of damp habitats with long flexible shoots used in basketwork. [*Salix viminalis*.] ▸ a willow shoot.
– ORIGIN Middle English: from Old French; cf. medieval Latin *auseria* 'osier bed'.

-osis ■ suffix (pl. **-oses**) denoting a process, condition, or pathological state: *metamorphosis*.
– ORIGIN from Greek *-ōsis*.

-osity ■ suffix forming nouns from adjectives ending in *-ose* (such as *verbosity* from *verbose*) and from adjectives ending in *-ous* (such as *pomposity* from *pompous*).
– ORIGIN from French *-osité* or Latin *-ositas*.

osmic /ˈɒzmɪk/ ■ adj. relating to odours or the sense of smell.
– DERIVATIVES **osmically** adv.
– ORIGIN C20: from Greek *osmē* 'odour'.

osmium /ˈɒzmɪəm/ ■ n. the chemical element of atomic number 76, a hard, dense silvery-white metal. (Symbol: **Os**)
– ORIGIN C19: from Greek *osmē* 'smell' (from the pungent smell of one of its oxides).

osmoregulation ■ n. Biology the maintenance of constant osmotic pressure in the fluids of an organism by the control of water and salt concentrations.
– DERIVATIVES **osmoregulatory** adj.

osmose /ˈɒzməʊs/ ■ v. rare pass by or as if by osmosis.

osmosis /ɒzˈməʊsɪs/ ■ n. **1** Biology & Chemistry a process by which solvent molecules pass through a semipermeable membrane from a less concentrated solution into a more concentrated one. **2** the process of gradual or unconscious assimilation of ideas or knowledge.
– DERIVATIVES **osmotic** adj. **osmotically** adv.
– ORIGIN C19: from Greek *ōsmos* 'a push'.

osmotic pressure /ɒzˈmɒtɪk/ ■ n. Chemistry the pressure that would have to be applied to a pure solvent to prevent it from passing into a given solution by osmosis.

osmunda /ɒzˈmʌndə/ ■ n. a plant of a genus that includes the royal and cinnamon ferns. [Genus *Osmunda*.]
– ORIGIN Anglo-Latin, from Anglo-Norman French *osmunde*.

osnaburg /ˈɒznəbəːɡ/ ■ n. a kind of coarse linen or cotton used chiefly for furnishings and sacks.
– ORIGIN Middle English: alteration of *Osnabrück*, the name of a city in Germany where the cloth was orig. produced.

osprey /ˈɒspri, -preɪ/ ■ n. (pl. **-eys**) a large fish-eating bird of prey with long, narrow wings and a white underside and crown. [*Pandion haliaetus*.]
– ORIGIN Middle English: from Old French *ospres*, apparently from Latin *ossifraga*, from *os* 'bone' + *frangere* 'to break'.

osseous /ˈɒsɪəs/ ■ adj. chiefly Zoology & Medicine consisting of or turned into bone.
– ORIGIN Middle English: from Latin *osseus* 'bony'.

ossicle /ˈɒsɪk(ə)l/ ■ n. **1** Anatomy & Zoology a very small bone, especially one of those in the middle ear. **2** Zoology a small piece of calcified material forming part of the skeleton of an invertebrate animal such as an echinoderm.
– ORIGIN C16: from Latin *ossiculum*, diminutive of *os* 'bone'.

ossify /ˈɒsɪfʌɪ/ ■ v. (**-ies**, **-ied**) **1** turn into bone or bony tissue. **2** (often as adj. **ossified**) cease developing; become inflexible.
– DERIVATIVES **ossification** n.
– ORIGIN C18: from French *ossifier*, from Latin *os*, *oss-* 'bone'.

osso bucco /ˌɒsəʊ ˈbuːkəʊ/ ■ n. an Italian dish made of shin of veal containing marrowbone, stewed in wine with vegetables.
– ORIGIN Italian, 'marrowbone'.

ossuary /ˈɒsjʊəri/ ■ n. (pl. **-ies**) a container or room for the bones of the dead.
– ORIGIN C17: from late Latin *ossuarium*, from Latin *os*, *oss-* 'bone'.

osteitis /ˌɒstɪˈʌɪtɪs/ ■ n. Medicine inflammation of the substance of a bone.
– ORIGIN C19: from Greek *osteon* 'bone'.

ostensible /ɒˈstɛnsɪb(ə)l/ ■ adj. apparently true, but not necessarily so.
– DERIVATIVES **ostensibly** adv.
– ORIGIN C18: from medieval Latin *ostensibilis*, *ostendere* 'stretch out to view'.

ostensive ■ adj. Linguistics denoting a way of defining by direct demonstration, e.g. pointing.
– DERIVATIVES **ostensively** adv. **ostensiveness** n.
– ORIGIN C16: from late Latin *ostensivus*, from *ostens-* (see **OSTENSIBLE**).

ostensory /ɒˈstɛns(ə)ri/ ■ n. (pl. **-ies**) a monstrance.

– ORIGIN C18: from medieval Latin *ostensorium*, from *ostens-* (see **OSTENSIBLE**).

ostentation ■ n. the pretentious display of wealth, skill, or knowledge, designed to impress.
– DERIVATIVES **ostentatious** adj. **ostentatiously** adv. **ostentatiousness** n.
– ORIGIN Middle English: from Latin *ostentatio(n-)*, from *ostentare*, from *ostendere* 'stretch out to view'.

osteo- ■ comb. form of or relating to the bones: *osteoporosis*.
– ORIGIN from Greek *osteon* 'bone'.

osteoarthritis ■ n. Medicine degeneration of joint cartilage and the underlying bone, most common from middle age onward, causing pain and stiffness.
– DERIVATIVES **osteoarthritic** adj.

osteogenesis /ˌɒstɪə(ʊ)ˈdʒɛnɪsɪs/ ■ n. the formation of bone.
– DERIVATIVES **osteogenetic** adj. **osteogenic** adj.

osteogenesis imperfecta /ˌɪmpəˈfɛktə/ ■ n. Medicine an inherited disorder characterized by extreme fragility of the bones.

osteology /ˌɒstɪˈɒlədʒi/ ■ n. the study of the structure and function of the skeleton and bony structures.
– DERIVATIVES **osteological** adj. **osteologically** adv. **osteologist** n.

osteomalacia /ˌɒstɪəʊməˈleɪʃɪə/ ■ n. softening of the bones, typically through a deficiency of vitamin D or calcium.
– ORIGIN C19: from **OSTEO-** + Greek *malakos* 'soft'.

osteomyelitis /ˌɒstɪəʊmʌɪˈlʌɪtɪs/ ■ n. Medicine inflammation of bone or bone marrow.

osteopathy /ˌɒstɪˈɒpəθi/ ■ n. a system of complementary medicine involving the treatment of medical disorders through the manipulation and massage of the skeleton and musculature.
– DERIVATIVES **osteopath** n. **osteopathic** adj. **osteopathically** adv.

osteophyte /ˈɒstɪə(ʊ)fʌɪt/ ■ n. Medicine a bony projection associated with the degeneration of cartilage at joints.

osteoporosis /ˌɒstɪəʊpəˈrəʊsɪs/ ■ n. a medical condition in which the bones become brittle and fragile from loss of tissue, typically as a result of hormonal changes, or deficiency of calcium or vitamin D.
– DERIVATIVES **osteoporotic** adj.
– ORIGIN C19: from **OSTEO-** + Greek *poros* 'passage, pore'.

ostium /ˈɒstɪəm/ ■ n. (pl. **ostia** /ˈɒstɪə/) **1** Anatomy & Zoology an opening into a vessel or cavity of the body. **2** Zoology each of a number of pores in the wall of a sponge, through which water is drawn in.
– ORIGIN C17: from Latin, 'door, opening'.

ostler /ˈɒslə/ (also **hostler**) ■ n. historical a man employed to look after the horses of people staying at an inn.
– ORIGIN Middle English: from Old French *hostelier* 'innkeeper', from *hostel* (see **HOSTEL**).

Ostpolitik /ˈɒstpɒlɪˌtiːk/ ■ n. historical the foreign policy of détente of western European countries with reference to the former communist bloc.
– ORIGIN German, from *Ost* 'east' + *Politik* 'politics'.

ostracize /ˈɒstrəsʌɪz/ (also **-ise**) ■ v. exclude from a society or group. ▶ (in ancient Greece) banish (a citizen) from a city for five or ten years by popular vote.
– DERIVATIVES **ostracism** n.
– ORIGIN C17: from Greek *ostrakizein*, from *ostrakon* 'shell or potsherd' (on which names were written in voting to banish unpopular citizens).

Ostracoda /ˌɒstrəˈkəʊdə/ ■ pl. n. Zoology a class of minute aquatic crustaceans with a hinged shell from which the antennae protrude.
– DERIVATIVES **ostracod** /ˈɒstrəkɒd/ n.
– ORIGIN from Greek *ostrakōdēs* 'testaceous', from *ostrakon* 'shell'.

ostrich ■ n. **1** a large flightless swift-running African bird with a long neck, long legs, and two toes on each foot. [*Struthio camelus*.] **2** a person who refuses to accept facts.
– ORIGIN Middle English: from Old French *ostriche*, from

Latin *avis* 'bird' + late Latin *struthio*, from Greek, from *strouthos* 'sparrow or ostrich'; sense 2 is from the popular belief that ostriches bury their heads in the sand if pursued.

ostrich palace ■ n. another term for **FEATHER PALACE**.

Ostrogoth /ˈɒstrəɡɒθ/ ■ n. a member of the eastern branch of the Goths, who conquered Italy in the 5th–6th centuries AD.
– DERIVATIVES **Ostrogothic** adj.
– ORIGIN from late Latin *Ostrogothi* (pl.), from the Germanic base of **EAST** + late Latin *Gothi* 'Goths'.

OT ■ abbrev. **1** occupational therapist; occupational therapy. **2** Old Testament.

-ot[1] ■ suffix forming nouns which were originally diminutives: *parrot*.
– ORIGIN from French.

-ot[2] ■ suffix (forming nouns) denoting a person of a particular type: *idiot*. ▸ denoting a native of a place: *Cypriot*.
– ORIGIN from Greek *ōtēs*.

OTC ■ abbrev. **1** (in the UK) Officers' Training Corps. **2** over the counter.

other ■ adj. & pron. **1** used to refer to a person or thing that is different from one already mentioned or known. ▸ alternative of two. ▸ those not already mentioned. **2** additional. **3** (**the other**) informal, euphemistic sexual intercourse. **4** (usu. **the Other**) Philosophy & Sociology that which is distinct from, different from, or opposite to something or oneself.
– PHRASES **no other** archaic nothing else. **the other day** (or **night**, **week**, etc.) a few days (or nights, weeks, etc.) ago.
– ORIGIN Old English, of Germanic origin.

other half ■ n. Brit. informal one's wife, husband, or partner.

otherness ■ n. the quality or fact of being different.

other place ■ n. (**the other place**) Brit. humorous **1** hell, as opposed to heaven. **2** the House of Lords as regarded by the House of Commons, and vice versa.

other ranks ■ pl. n. (in the armed forces) all those who are not commissioned officers.

otherwise ■ adv. **1** in different circumstances; or else. **2** in other respects. **3** in a different way. ▸ alternatively. ■ adj. in a different state or situation.
– PHRASES **or** (or **and**) **otherwise** indicating the opposite of something stated.
– ORIGIN Old English *on ōthre wisan*.

other woman ■ n. (**the other woman**) the mistress of a married man.

other world ■ n. the spiritual world or afterlife.

other-worldly ■ adj. **1** of or relating to an imaginary or spiritual world. **2** unworldly.
– DERIVATIVES **other-worldliness** n.

otic /ˈəʊtɪk, ˈɒtɪk/ ■ adj. Anatomy of or relating to the ear.
– ORIGIN C17: from Greek *ōtikos*, from *ous*, *ōt-* 'ear'.

-otic ■ suffix forming adjectives and nouns corresponding to nouns ending in *-osis* (e.g. *neurotic* corresponding to *neurosis*).
– DERIVATIVES **-otically** suffix forming corresponding adverbs.
– ORIGIN from French *-otique*, from Greek *-ōtikos*.

otiose /ˈəʊtɪəʊs, ˈəʊʃɪ-, -z/ ■ adj. serving no practical purpose. ▸ archaic idle.
– DERIVATIVES **otiosely** adv.
– ORIGIN C18: from Latin *otiosus*, from *otium* 'leisure'.

otitis /ə(ʊ)ˈtʌɪtɪs/ ■ n. Medicine inflammation of part of the ear, especially the middle ear (otitis media).
– ORIGIN C18: from Greek *ous*, *ōt-* 'ear'.

oto- /ˈəʊtəʊ/ ■ comb. form of or relating to the ears: *otoscope*.
– ORIGIN from Greek *ous*, *ōt-* 'ear'.

otolaryngology /ˌəʊtə(ʊ)larɪŋˈɡɒlədʒi/ ■ n. the study of diseases of the ear and throat.
– DERIVATIVES **otolaryngological** adj. **otolaryngologist** n.

otolith ■ n. Zoology each of three small oval calcareous bodies in the inner ear of vertebrates, involved in the sensing of gravity and movement.
– DERIVATIVES **otolithic** adj.

otology /əʊˈtɒlədʒi/ ■ n. the study of the anatomy and diseases of the ear.
– DERIVATIVES **otological** adj. **otologist** n.

Otomi /ˌəʊtəˈmiː/ ■ n. (pl. same) a member of an American Indian people inhabiting parts of central Mexico.
– ORIGIN from Nahuatl *otomih* 'unknown'.

otoplasty /ˈəʊtə(ʊ)ˌplasti/ ■ n. (pl. **-ies**) Medicine a surgical operation to enhance the appearance of an ear.

otorhinolaryngology /ˌəʊtə(ʊ)ˌrʌɪnə(ʊ)ˌlarɪŋˈɡɒlədʒi/ ■ n. the study of diseases of the ear, nose, and throat.
– DERIVATIVES **otorhinolaryngological** n.

otoscope ■ n. an instrument for visual examination of the eardrum and passage of the outer ear.
– DERIVATIVES **otoscopic** adj.

OTT ■ abbrev. informal over the top.

ottava rima /ɒˌtɑːvə ˈriːmə/ ■ n. a form of poetry consisting of stanzas of eight lines of ten or eleven syllables, rhyming *abababcc*.
– ORIGIN C18: from Italian, 'eighth rhyme'.

otter ■ n. **1** a semiaquatic fish-eating mammal of the weasel family, with an elongated body, dense fur, and webbed feet. [*Lutra*, *Aonyx*, and other genera.] **2** a piece of board used to carry fishing bait in water.
– ORIGIN Old English, of Germanic origin.

otter board ■ n. either of a pair of boards attached to each side of the mouth of a trawl net, keeping it open as it is pulled through the water.

otto ■ n. another term for **ATTAR**.

Ottoman /ˈɒtəmən/ ■ adj. historical **1** of or relating to the Turkish dynasty of Osman I (Othman I), founded in c.1300. ▸ of or relating to the branch of the Turks to which he belonged. ▸ of or relating to the Ottoman Empire ruled by his successors. **2** Turkish. ■ n. (pl. **Ottomans**) a Turk, especially of the Ottoman period.
– ORIGIN from Arabic *'uṭmānī* (adj.), from *'Uṭmān* 'Othman'.

ottoman ■ n. (pl. **ottomans**) **1** a low upholstered seat without a back or arms, typically serving also as a box, with the seat hinged to form a lid. **2** a heavy ribbed fabric made from silk and either cotton or wool.
– ORIGIN C19: from French *ottomane*, from *ottoman* 'Ottoman'.

OU ■ abbrev. (in the UK) Open University.

ou /əʊ/ ■ n. (pl. **ouens** /ˈəʊənz/ or **ous**) S. African informal a man; a person.
– ORIGIN Afrikaans, prob. from Dutch *ouwe* 'old man'.

oubaas /ˈəʊbɑːs/ ■ n. S. African informal, dated a title or form of address to an older white man who is the owner, manager, or supervisor of an enterprise.
– ORIGIN Afrikaans, from Dutch *oud* 'old' + *baas* 'master'.

oubliette /ˌuːblɪˈɛt/ ■ n. a secret dungeon with access only through a trapdoor in its ceiling.
– ORIGIN C18: from French, from *oublier* 'forget'.

ouboet /ˈəʊbʊt/ ■ n. another term for **BOET** (in sense 2).
– ORIGIN Afrikaans, from *ou* 'old' + *boet* 'brother'.

ouch ■ exclam. used to express pain.
– ORIGIN natural exclamation.

oud /uːd/ ■ n. a form of lute or mandolin played in Arab countries.
– ORIGIN C18: from Arabic *al-ʿūd*.

ouens plural form of **OU**.

ought[1] ■ modal v. (3rd sing. present and past **ought**) **1** used to indicate duty or correctness. ▸ used to indicate a desirable or expected state. ▸ used to give or ask advice. **2** used to indicate something that is probable.
– ORIGIN Old English *āhte*, past tense of *āgan* 'owe'.

ought[2] ■ pron. variant spelling of **AUGHT**.

oughtn't ■ contr. ought not.

Ouija board /ˈwiːdʒə/ ■ n. trademark a board with letters, numbers, and other signs around its edge, to which a planchette or other pointer moves, supposedly in answer to questions from people at a seance.
– ORIGIN C19: *Ouija* from French *oui* 'yes' + German *ja* 'yes'.

ouma /ˈəʊmɑː/ ■ n. S. African informal **1** one's grandmother. **2** a friendly form of address to an elderly woman.
– ORIGIN from Afrikaans.

ounce ■ n. **1** (abbrev.: **oz**) a unit of weight of one sixteenth of a pound avoirdupois (approximately 28 grams). ▸ a unit of one twelfth of a pound troy or apothecaries' measure, equal to 480 grains (approximately 31 grams). **2** a very small amount.
– ORIGIN Middle English: from Old French *unce*, from Latin *uncia* 'twelfth part (of a pound or foot)'; cf. INCH.

oupa /ˈəʊpɑː/ ■ n. S. African informal **1** one's grandfather. **2** a friendly form of address to an elderly man.
– ORIGIN from Afrikaans.

our ■ possess. det. **1** belonging to or associated with the speaker and one or more others previously mentioned or easily identified. ▸ belonging to or associated with people in general. **2** used in formal contexts by a royal person or a writer to refer to something belonging to himself or herself. **3** informal, chiefly N. English used with a name to refer to a relative or friend of the speaker.
– ORIGIN Old English, of Germanic origin.

-our[1] ■ suffix variant spelling of **-OR**[2] surviving in some nouns such as *ardour*, *colour*.

-our[2] ■ suffix variant spelling of **-OR**[1] (as in *saviour*).

Our Father ■ n. Christian Church **1** God. **2** the Lord's Prayer.

Our Lady ■ n. Christian Church Mary, mother of Jesus.

Our Lord ■ n. Christian Church God or Jesus.

ours ■ possess. pron. used to refer to something belonging to or associated with the speaker and one or more others previously mentioned or easily identified.

ourself ■ pron. [first person pl.] used instead of 'ourselves' typically when 'we' refers to people in general.

> USAGE
> The standard reflexive form corresponding to **we** and **us** is **ourselves**, as in *we can only blame ourselves*. The singular form **ourself** is sometimes used, but is not widely accepted in standard English.

ourselves ■ pron. [first person pl.] **1** used as the object of a verb or preposition when this is the same as the subject of the clause and the subject is the speaker and one or more other people considered together. **2** [emphatic] we or us personally.

-ous ■ suffix forming adjectives: **1** characterized by: *mountainous*. **2** Chemistry denoting an element in a lower valency: *sulphurous*. Compare with **-IC**.
– DERIVATIVES **-ously** suffix forming corresponding adverbs. **-ousness** suffix forming corresponding nouns.
– ORIGIN from Anglo-Norman French, or Old French *-eus*, from Latin *-osus*.

oust /aʊst/ ■ v. **1** drive out or expel from a position or place. **2** Law deprive of or exclude from possession of something. ▸ take away (a court's jurisdiction) in a matter.
– ORIGIN Middle English: from Anglo-Norman French *ouster* 'take away', from Latin *obstare* 'oppose, hinder'.

ouster ■ n. **1** Law ejection from a freehold or other possession; deprivation of an inheritance. ▸ removal from the jurisdiction of the courts. ▸ a clause that is or is claimed to be outside the jurisdiction of the courts. **2** chiefly N. Amer. dismissal from a position.

out ■ adv. **1** moving away from a place, especially from one that is enclosed to one that is open. ▸ **outdoors**. ▸ no longer in prison. **2** away from one's usual base or residence. **3** to sea, away from the land. ▸ (of the tide) falling or at its lowest level. **4** so as to be revealed, heard, or known. **5** at or to an end. ▸ so as to no longer exist. **6** at a specified distance away from the goal or a finishing line. ■ prep. non-standard contraction of OUT OF. ■ adj. **1** not at home or one's place of work. **2** revealed. ▸ published. ▸ informal in existence or use. ▸ open about one's homosexuality. **3** no longer existing. ▸ informal no longer in fashion. **4** not possible or worth considering. **5** unconscious. **6** mistaken. **7** (of the ball in tennis, squash, etc.) outside the playing area. **8** Cricket & Baseball no longer batting. **9** (of a flower) open. ■ n. **1** informal a form of escape. **2** Baseball an act of putting a player out. ■ v. **1** informal reveal the homosexuality of. **2** knock out.
– PHRASES **at outs** (N. Amer. **on the outs**) in dispute. **out and about** engaging in normal activity after an illness. **out for** intent on having. **out of 1** from. **2** not having (something). **out of it** informal **1** not included. **2** unaware of what is happening. ▸ Brit. drunk. **out to do something** keenly striving to do something. **out with it** say what you are thinking.
– ORIGIN Old English, of Germanic origin.

out- ■ prefix **1** to the point of surpassing or exceeding: *outperform*. **2** external; separate; from outside: *outbuildings*. **3** away from; outward: *outpost*.

outage /ˈaʊtɪdʒ/ ■ n. a period when a power supply or other service is not available.

out and out ■ adj. absolute. ■ adv. completely.

outback ■ n. (**the outback**) a remote or sparsely populated inland area, especially in Australia.
– DERIVATIVES **outbacker** n.

outbalance ■ v. be more valuable or important than.

outbid ■ v. (**-bidding**; past and past part. **-bid**) bid more for something than.

outboard ■ adj. & adv. on, towards, or near the outside of a ship or aircraft. ▸ (of a motor) portable and attachable to the outside of the stern of a boat. ■ n. an outboard motor. ▸ a boat with such a motor.

outbound ■ adj. & adv. outward bound.

outbrave ■ v. archaic **1** outdo in bravery. **2** face with brave defiance.

outbreak ■ n. a sudden or violent occurrence of war, disease, etc.

outbuilding ■ n. a smaller detached building in the grounds of a main building.

outburst ■ n. a sudden violent occurrence or release of something, especially angry words.

outcast ■ n. a person rejected by their society or social group. ■ adj. rejected or cast out.

outclass ■ v. be far superior to.

outcome ■ n. **1** a consequence. **2** a measurable or quantifiable result. ▸ (**outcomes**) (in education) the skills or knowledge that a learner or student is expected to have acquired on completion of an activity or course.

outcomes-based education ■ n. a system of education that focuses on a set of defined goals and skills that a pupil or student is expected to achieve.

outcrop ■ n. a rock formation that is visible on the surface. ■ v. (**-cropped**, **-cropping**) [often as noun **outcropping**] appear as an outcrop.

outcross ■ v. breed (an animal or plant) with one not closely related. ■ n. an animal or plant resulting from outcrossing.

outcry ■ n. (pl. **-ies**) a strong expression of public disapproval. ▸ an exclamation or shout.

outdated ■ adj. obsolete.
– DERIVATIVES **outdatedness** n.

outdistance ■ v. leave (a competitor or pursuer) far behind.

outdo ■ v. (**-does**, **-doing**; past **-did**; past part. **-done**) be superior to in action or performance.

outdoor ■ adj. done, situated, or used outdoors. ▸ liking the outdoors.

outdoor pursuits ■ pl. n. outdoor sporting or leisure activities.

outdoors ■ adv. in or into the open air. ■ n. any area outside buildings or shelter.
– DERIVATIVES **outdoorsman** n. (pl. **-men**). **outdoorsy** adj. (informal).

outdrive ■ v. (past **-drove**; past part. **-driven**) drive better or faster than. ■ n. an outboard motor.

outer ■ adj. **1** outside; external. ▸ further from the centre or the inside. **2** objective or physical. ■ n. an outer garment or part of one.

outermost ■ adj. furthest from the centre.

outer space ■ n. the physical universe beyond the earth's atmosphere.

outerwear ■ n. clothes worn over other clothes.

outface ■ v. disconcert or defeat by bold confrontation.

outfall ■ n. the place where a river, drain, etc. empties into the sea, a river, or a lake.

outfield ■ n. 1 Cricket the part of the field furthest from the wicket. 2 Baseball the grassy area beyond the infield.
– DERIVATIVES **outfielder** n.

outfight ■ v. (past and past part. **-fought**) beat in a fight.

outfit ■ n. 1 a set of clothes worn together. 2 informal a group of people undertaking a particular activity together. 3 a complete set of equipment needed for a particular purpose. ■ v. (**-fitted, -fitting**) (usu. **be outfitted**) provide with an outfit of clothes or equipment.

outfitter (also **outfitters**) ■ n. 1 dated a shop selling men's clothing. 2 an agent providing equipment, typically for outdoor pursuits.

outflank ■ v. 1 move round the side of (an enemy) so as to outmanoeuvre them. 2 outwit.

outflow ■ n. 1 the action of flowing or moving out. 2 something, such as water, money, etc., that flows or moves out.

outfox ■ v. informal defeat with cunning.

outgas ■ v. (**-gases, -gassing, -gassed**) release or give off as a gas or vapour.

outgoing ■ adj. 1 friendly and confident. 2 leaving an office or position. ▶ going out or away from a place. ■ n. 1 (**outgoings**) one's regular expenditure. 2 an instance of going out.

outgross ■ v. surpass in gross takings or profit.

outgrow ■ v. (past **-grew**; past part. **-grown**) 1 grow too big for. 2 leave behind as one matures. 3 grow faster or taller than.
– PHRASES **outgrow one's strength** Brit. become lanky and weak through too rapid growth.

outgrowth ■ n. 1 something that grows out of something else. 2 a natural development or result. 3 the process of growing out.

outguess ■ v. guess correctly what is intended by.

outgun ■ v. (**-gunned, -gunning**) [often **be outgunned**] have more or better weaponry than. ▶ shoot better than.

outhaul ■ n. Nautical a rope used to haul out the clew of a sail.

outhouse ■ n. a smaller building built on to or in the grounds of a house. ▶ an outside toilet. ■ v. store away from the main storage area.

outie ■ n. S. African informal a down-and-out; a tramp.
– ORIGIN from *out*.

outing ■ n. 1 a short trip taken for pleasure. ▶ a brief journey from home. ▶ informal a public appearance in something. 2 the practice of revealing the homosexuality of a prominent person.

outlandish ■ adj. bizarre or unfamiliar.
– DERIVATIVES **outlandishly** adv. **outlandishness** n.
– ORIGIN Old English *ūtlendisc* 'not native', from *ūtland* 'foreign country'.

outlast ■ v. outlive.

outlaw ■ n. a fugitive from the law. ■ v. ban.
– DERIVATIVES **outlawry** n.
– ORIGIN Old English, from Old Norse *útlagi* (n.) from *útlagr* 'outlawed or banished'.

outlay ■ n. an amount of money spent.

outlet ■ n. 1 a pipe or hole through which water or gas may escape. 2 the mouth of a river. 3 an output socket in an electrical device. 4 a point from which goods are sold or distributed. 5 a means of expressing one's talents, energy, or emotions.

outlier /ˈaʊtlaɪə/ ■ n. 1 a person or thing away or detached from the main body or system. 2 Geology a younger rock formation among older rocks. 3 Statistics a result differing greatly from others in the same sample.

outline ■ n. 1 a line or lines enclosing or indicating the shape of an object in a sketch or diagram. ▶ the contours or bounds of an object. 2 a word in shorthand. 3 a general plan showing essential features but no detail. ▶ the main features of something. ■ v. 1 draw or define the outer edge or shape of. 2 give a summary of.

outliner ■ n. a computer program allowing editing of an outline of the structure of a document.

outlive ■ v. live longer than. ▶ survive or last beyond.

outlook ■ n. 1 a person's point of view or attitude to life. 2 a view. 3 the prospect for the future.

outlying ■ adj. remote.

outmanoeuvre ■ v. evade by moving faster or more skilfully. ▶ use skill and cunning to beat.

outmatch ■ v. be superior to.

outmigration ■ n. migration from one place to another, especially within a country.

outmoded ■ adj. old-fashioned.
– DERIVATIVES **outmodedness** n.

outmost ■ adj. chiefly archaic furthest away.
– ORIGIN Middle English: var. of *utmest* 'utmost'.

outmuscle /aʊtˈmʌs(ə)l/ ■ v. dominate or defeat by superior strength or force.

outnumber ■ v. be more numerous than.

out-of-body experience ■ n. a sensation of being outside one's body, typically of floating and observing oneself from a distance.

out-of-court ■ adj. (of a settlement) made without the intervention of a court.

out of date ■ adj. 1 old-fashioned. 2 no longer valid.

outpace ■ v. go faster than.

outpatient ■ n. a patient attending a hospital for treatment without staying overnight.

outperform ■ v. 1 perform better than. 2 be more profitable than.
– DERIVATIVES **outperformance** n.

outplacement ■ n. the provision of assistance to redundant employees in finding new employment.

outplay ■ v. play better than.

outpoint ■ v. Boxing defeat on points.

outpost ■ n. a small military camp at a distance from the main army. ▶ a remote part of a country or empire. ▶ an isolated or remote branch of something.

outpouring ■ n. 1 something that streams out rapidly. 2 an outburst of strong emotion.

output ■ n. 1 the amount of something produced by a person, machine, or industry. ▶ the process of producing something. ▶ the power, energy, etc. supplied by a device or system. 2 Electronics a place where power or information leaves a system. ■ v. (**-putting**; past and past part. **-put** or **-putted**) (of a computer) produce or supply (data).

outrage ■ n. an extremely strong reaction of anger or indignation. ▶ a cause of outrage. ■ v. 1 arouse outrage in. 2 violate or infringe flagrantly.
– ORIGIN Middle English: from Old French *ou(l)trage*, from Latin *ultra* 'beyond'; influenced by the belief that the word is a compound of OUT and RAGE.

outrageous ■ adj. 1 shockingly bad or excessive. 2 very bold and unusual.
– DERIVATIVES **outrageously** adv. **outrageousness** n.

outran past of OUTRUN.

outrank ■ v. have a higher rank than. ▶ be better or more important than.

outré /ˈuːtreɪ/ ■ adj. unusual and typically rather shocking.
– ORIGIN French, 'exceeded', from *outrer* (see OUTRAGE).

outreach ■ v. /aʊtˈriːtʃ/ reach further than. ▶ poetic/literary reach out. ■ n. /ˈaʊtriːtʃ/ 1 the extent or length of reaching out. 2 an organization's involvement with or influence in the community.

outride ■ v. (past **-rode**; past part. **-ridden**) 1 ride better, faster, or further than. 2 archaic (of a ship) come safely through (a storm).

outrider ■ n. a person in a vehicle or on horseback who escorts or guards another vehicle.
– DERIVATIVES **outriding** n.

outrigger ■ n. a beam, spar, or framework projecting from or over a boat's side. ▶ a stabilizing float or secondary hull fixed parallel to a canoe or small ship. ▶ a boat fitted with such a structure. ▶ a similar projecting

support in another structure.
- DERIVATIVES **outrigged** adj.
- ORIGIN C18: perhaps influenced by the obsolete nautical term *outligger*, in the same sense.

outright ■ adv. **1** altogether. **2** openly. **3** immediately. ▶ not by degrees or instalments. ■ adj. **1** open and direct. **2** complete.

outrode past of OUTRIDE.

outrun ■ v. (-**running**; past -**ran**; past part. -**run**) **1** run or travel faster or further than. ▶ escape from. **2** exceed.

outsell ■ v. (past and past part. -**sold**) be sold in greater quantities than. ▶ sell more of something than.

outset ■ n. the start or beginning.

outshine ■ v. (past and past part. -**shone**) **1** shine more brightly than. **2** be much better than.

outside ■ n. the external side or surface of something. ▶ the part of a path nearer to a road. ▶ the side of a bend or curve where the edge is longer. ▶ the external appearance of someone or something. ■ adj. **1** situated on or near the outside. ▶ (in hockey, soccer, etc.) denoting positions nearer to the sides of the field. **2** not of or belonging to a particular group. ▶ beyond one's immediate personal concerns. ■ prep. & adv. **1** situated or moving beyond the boundaries of. ▶ not being a member of. ▶ (in hockey, soccer, etc.) closer to the side of the field than. **2** beyond the limits or scope of.
- PHRASES **at the outside** at the most. **an outside chance** a remote possibility. **outside of** informal, chiefly N. Amer. beyond the boundaries of. ▶ apart from.

outside broadcast ■ n. a radio or television programme recorded or broadcast live on location.

outside interest ■ n. an interest not connected with one's work or studies.

outsider ■ n. **1** a person who does not belong to a particular group. ▶ a person not accepted by or isolating themselves from society. **2** a competitor thought to have little chance of success.

outsider art ■ n. art produced by untrained artists who work outside the boundaries of the mainstream art world.
- DERIVATIVES **outsider artist** n.

outsize (also **outsized**) ■ adj. exceptionally large.

outskirts ■ pl. n. the outer parts of a town or city.

outsmart ■ v. outwit.

outsold past and past participle of OUTSELL.

outsource ■ v. obtain by contract from an outside supplier. ▶ contract (work) out.

outspan S. African ■ v. (-**spanned**, -**spanning**) unharness (an animal) from a wagon. ■ n. a place for grazing or camping on a wagon journey.
- ORIGIN C19: from Dutch *uitspannen* 'unyoke'.

outspoken ■ adj. frank in stating one's opinions.
- DERIVATIVES **outspokenly** adv. **outspokenness** n.

outspread ■ adj. fully extended or expanded. ■ v. (past and past part. -**spread**) poetic/literary spread out.

outstanding ■ adj. **1** exceptionally good. **2** clearly noticeable. **3** not yet done. ▶ (of a debt) unpaid.
- DERIVATIVES **outstandingly** adv.

outstare ■ v. stare at (someone) for longer than they can stare back.

outstation ■ n. a branch of an organization situated far from its headquarters.

outstay ■ v. **1** stay beyond the limit of (one's expected or permitted time). **2** last longer than (another competitor).

outstretch ■ v. [usu. as adj. **outstretched**] **1** extend or stretch out. **2** go beyond the limit of.

outstrip ■ v. (-**stripped**, -**stripping**) move faster than and overtake. ▶ exceed.

outswinger ■ n. Cricket a ball bowled with a swerve or swing from the leg to the off side.
- DERIVATIVES **outswing** n. **outswinging** adj.

out-take ■ n. a sequence filmed or recorded for a film, programme, etc. but cut from the final version.

out-thrust ■ adj. extended outward. ■ n. a thing which projects outward.

out tray ■ n. a tray on a desk for letters and documents that have been dealt with.

out-turn ■ n. **1** the amount of something produced. **2** a result or consequence.

outvote ■ v. defeat by gaining more votes.

outwait ■ v. wait longer than.

outward ■ adj. **1** of, on, or from the outside. ▶ relating to the external appearance of something rather than its true nature. ▶ archaic outer. **2** going out or away from a place. ■ adv. outwards.
- DERIVATIVES **outwardly** adv. **outwardness** n.

outward bound ■ adj. going away from home. ■ n. (**Outward Bound**) trademark an organization providing naval and adventure training and other outdoor activities for young people.

outwards ■ adv. towards the outside; away from the centre or a place.

outwear ■ v. (past -**wore**; past part. -**worn**) last longer than.

outweigh ■ v. be heavier, greater, or more significant than.

outwit ■ v. (-**witted**, -**witting**) deceive by greater ingenuity.

outwore past of OUTWEAR.

outwork ■ n. **1** an outer section of a fortification or system of defence. **2** work done outside the factory or office which provides it.
- DERIVATIVES **outworker** n.

outworn past participle of OUTWEAR. ■ adj. **1** out of date. **2** worn out.

ouzo /ˈuːzəʊ/ ■ n. a Greek aniseed-flavoured spirit.
- ORIGIN from modern Greek.

ova plural form of OVUM.

oval ■ adj. having a rounded and slightly elongated outline; egg-shaped. ■ n. an oval body, object, or design. ▶ an oval sports field or track.
- DERIVATIVES **ovality** n. **ovalness** n.
- ORIGIN C16: from French, from Latin *ovum* 'egg'.

ovalbumin /əʊˈvalbjʊmɪn/ ■ n. Biochemistry albumin from the white of eggs.
- ORIGIN C19: from Latin *ovi albumen* 'albumen of egg'.

Oval Office ■ n. the office of the US President in the White House.

Ovambo /əʊˈvambəʊ/ (also **Owambo**) ■ n. (pl. same or -**os**) **1** a member of a people of northern Namibia. **2** the Bantu language of this people.
- ORIGIN a local name, from *ova*- (prefix denoting a pl.) + *ambo* 'man of leisure'.

ovarian /əʊˈvɛːrɪən/ ■ adj. of or relating to an ovary or the ovaries.

ovary /ˈəʊv(ə)ri/ ■ n. (pl. -**ies**) **1** a female reproductive organ in which ova or eggs are produced. **2** Botany the base of the carpel of a flower, containing one or more ovules.
- ORIGIN C17: from modern Latin *ovarium*, from Latin *ovum* 'egg'.

ovate /ˈəʊveɪt/ ■ adj. chiefly Biology oval; egg-shaped.
- ORIGIN C18: from Latin *ovatus* 'egg-shaped'.

ovation ■ n. a sustained show of appreciation, especially applause, from an audience.
- ORIGIN C16: from Latin *ovatio(n-)*, from *ovare* 'exult'.

oven ■ n. **1** an enclosed compartment, usually part of a stove, for cooking food. **2** a small furnace or kiln.
- ORIGIN Old English, of Germanic origin.

oven glove ■ n. a padded glove for handling hot dishes from an oven.

ovenproof ■ adj. suitable for use in an oven.

oven-ready ■ adj. (of food) prepared before sale for cooking in an oven.

ovenware ■ n. ovenproof dishes.

over ■ prep. **1** extending upwards from or above. ▶ above so as to cover or protect. **2** beyond. **3** expressing passage or trajectory across. ▶ beyond and falling or hanging from. **4** expressing duration. **5** by means of. **6** at a higher level or layer than. ▶ expressing authority or control. ▶ expressing preference. ▶ expressing majority. **7** higher or more than (a specified number or quantity). **8** on the subject of. ■ adv. **1** expressing passage or trajectory across

an area. ▶ beyond and falling or hanging from a point. **2** in or to the place indicated. **3** used to express action and result. ▶ finished. **4** used to express repetition of a process. ■ n. Cricket a sequence of six balls bowled by a bowler from one end of the pitch.
– PHRASES **be over** be no longer affected by. **over against** adjacent to. ▶ in contrast with. **over and above** in addition to. **over and out** indicating that a message on a two-way radio has finished.
– ORIGIN Old English, of Germanic origin.

over- ■ prefix **1** excessively: *overambitious*. ▶ completely: *overjoyed*. **2** upper; outer; extra: *overcoat*. ▶ over; above: *overcast*.

over-abundant ■ adj. excessive in quantity.
– DERIVATIVES **over-abundance** n. **over-abundantly** adv.

overachieve ■ v. do better than expected, especially at school.
– DERIVATIVES **overachievement** n. **overachiever** n.

overact ■ v. act a role in an exaggerated manner.

overactive ■ adj. excessively active.
– DERIVATIVES **overactivity** n.

overage ■ n. an excess or surplus, especially an amount greater than estimated.

over age ■ adj. over a certain age limit.

overall ■ adj. total. ▶ taking everything into account. ■ adv. taken as a whole. ■ n. (also **overalls**) a loose-fitting garment worn over ordinary clothes for protection.
– DERIVATIVES **overalled** adj.

overambitious ■ adj. excessively ambitious.
– DERIVATIVES **overambition** n. **overambitiously** adv.

overanxious ■ adj. excessively anxious.
– DERIVATIVES **overanxiety** n. **overanxiously** adv.

overarch ■ v. **1** form an arch over. **2** [as adj. **overarching**] all-embracing.

overarm ■ adj. & adv. (of a throw, stroke with a racket, etc.) made with the hand or arm above shoulder-level.

overate past of OVEREAT.

overawe ■ v. (usu. **be overawed**) subdue or inhibit with a sense of awe.

overbalance ■ v. **1** fall or cause to fall due to loss of balance. **2** outweigh.

overbear ■ v. (past **-bore**; past part. **-borne**) overcome by emotional pressure or physical force.

overbearing ■ adj. unpleasantly overpowering.
– DERIVATIVES **overbearingly** adv. **overbearingness** n.

overbid ■ v. (**-bidding**; past and past part. **-bid**) **1** (in an auction) make a higher bid than a previous bid. **2** Bridge bid more than is warranted or manageable. ■ n. a bid higher than another or higher than is justified.
– DERIVATIVES **overbidder** n.

overbite ■ n. Dentistry the overlapping of the lower teeth by the upper.

overblown ■ adj. **1** excessively inflated or pretentious. **2** (of a flower) past its prime.

overboard ■ adv. from a ship into the water.
– PHRASES **go overboard 1** be very enthusiastic. **2** go too far.

overbook ■ v. accept more reservations for (a flight or hotel) than there is room for.

overbore past of OVERBEAR.

overborne past participle of OVERBEAR.

overbought past and past participle of OVERBUY.

overbuild ■ v. (past and past part. **-built**) put up too many buildings in. ▶ build too many of. ▶ build elaborately.

overburden ■ v. burden excessively. ■ n. **1** rock or soil overlying a mineral deposit, archaeological site, etc. **2** an excessive burden.

overbuy ■ v. (past and past part. **-bought**) buy too many or too much of.

overcall Bridge ■ v. bid higher than an opponent. ■ n. an act of overcalling.

overcame past of OVERCOME.

overcapacity ■ n. an excess of productive capacity.

overcapitalize (also **-ise**) ■ v. [usu. as adj. **overcapitalized** (also **-ised**)] provide with an excessive amount of capital. ▶ overestimate the capital value of (a company).

overcareful ■ adj. excessively careful.

overcast ■ adj. **1** (of the sky or weather) cloudy; dull. **2** edged with stitching to prevent fraying. ■ n. cloud covering a large part of the sky. ■ v. (past and past part. **-cast**) **1** cover with clouds or shade. **2** stitch over (a raw edge) to prevent fraying.

overcautious ■ adj. excessively cautious.
– DERIVATIVES **overcaution** n. **overcautiously** adv. **overcautiousness** n.

overcharge ■ v. **1** charge too high a price. **2** put too much electric charge into (a battery).

overclass ■ n. a privileged, wealthy, or powerful section of society.

overcloud ■ v. mar, dim, or obscure.

overcoat ■ n. **1** a long warm coat. **2** a top, final layer of paint or varnish.

overcome ■ v. (past **-came**; past part. **-come**) succeed in dealing with (a problem). ▶ defeat. ▶ (usu. **be overcome**) (of an emotion) overwhelm.

overcommit ■ v. (**-committed**, **-committing**) oblige to do more than is possible. ▶ allocate more (resources) than can be provided.
– DERIVATIVES **overcommitment** n.

overcompensate ■ v. take excessive measures to compensate for something.
– DERIVATIVES **overcompensating** adj. **overcompensation** n. **overcompensatory** adj.

overconfident ■ adj. excessively confident.
– DERIVATIVES **overconfidence** n. **overconfidently** adv.

overcook ■ v. cook too much or for too long.

overcritical ■ adj. inclined to find fault too readily.

overcrop ■ v. (**-cropped**, **-cropping**) [usu. as noun **overcropping**] exhaust (land) by the continuous growing of crops.

overcrowd ■ v. [often as noun **overcrowding**] fill beyond what is usual or comfortable.

overdevelop ■ v. (**-developed**, **-developing**) develop to excess.
– DERIVATIVES **overdevelopment** n.

overdo ■ v. (**-does**; past **-did**; past part. **-done**) exaggerate. ▶ use too much of. ▶ (**overdo it/things**) exhaust oneself. ▶ [often as adj. **overdone**] overcook.
– ORIGIN Old English.

overdose ■ n. an excessive and dangerous dose of a drug. ■ v. take an overdose. ▶ give an overdose to.
– DERIVATIVES **overdosage** /ˌəʊvəˈdəʊsɪdʒ/ n.

overdraft ■ n. a deficit in a bank account caused by drawing more money than the account holds.

overdramatize (also **-ise**) ■ v. react to or portray in an excessively dramatic way.
– DERIVATIVES **overdramatic** adj.

overdraw ■ v. (past **-drew**; past part. **-drawn**) **1** (usu. **be overdrawn**) draw more money from (a bank account) than it holds. ▶ (**be overdrawn**) have taken more money from an account than it holds. **2** exaggerate.

overdress ■ v. (usu. **be overdressed**) dress too elaborately or formally.

overdrive ■ n. **1** a gear in a motor vehicle providing a gear ratio higher than that of the usual top gear. **2** a state of high or excessive activity. **3** a mechanism allowing the exceeding of a normal operating level in equipment.

overdub ■ v. (**-dubbed**, **-dubbing**) record (additional sounds) on an existing recording.

overdue ■ adj. past the time when due. ▶ not having arrived, been born, etc. at the expected time. ▶ (of a library book) retained longer than allowed.

overeager ■ adj. excessively eager.
– DERIVATIVES **overeagerly** adv. **overeagerness** n.

over easy ■ adj. N. Amer. (of an egg) fried on both sides, with the yolk remaining slightly liquid.

overeat ▪ v. (past **-ate**; past part. **-eaten**) [usu. as noun **overeating**] eat too much.
– DERIVATIVES **overeater** n.

over-egg ▪ v. (in phr. **over-egg the pudding**) go too far in doing something; exaggerate.

over-elaborate ▪ adj. excessively elaborate. ▪ v. explain or treat in excessive detail.
– DERIVATIVES **over-elaborately** adv. **over-elaborateness** n. **over-elaboration** n.

overemotional ▪ adj. excessively emotional.
– DERIVATIVES **overemotionally** adv.

overemphasize (also **-ise**) ▪ v. place excessive emphasis on.
– DERIVATIVES **overemphasis** n.

overenthusiasm ▪ n. excessive enthusiasm.
– DERIVATIVES **overenthusiastic** adj. **overenthusiastically** adv.

overestimate ▪ v. form too high an estimate of. ▪ n. an excessively high estimate.
– DERIVATIVES **overestimation** n.

overexcite ▪ v. [usu. as adj. **overexcited**] excite excessively.
– DERIVATIVES **overexcitable** adj. **overexcitement** n.

over-exercise ▪ v. exercise to excess. ▪ n. excessive exercise.

overexert ▪ v. (**overexert oneself**) exert oneself excessively.
– DERIVATIVES **overexertion** n.

overexpose ▪ v. expose too much.
– DERIVATIVES **overexposure** n.

overextend ▪ v. (usu. **be overextended**) **1** make too long. **2** impose an excessive burden on.
– DERIVATIVES **overextension** n.

overfamiliar ▪ adj. **1** too well known. ▸ (**overfamiliar with**) too well acquainted with. **2** inappropriately informal.
– DERIVATIVES **overfamiliarity** n.

overfeed ▪ v. (past and past part. **-fed**) feed too much.

overfill ▪ v. fill to excess.

overfish ▪ v. deplete (a body of water, stock of fish, etc.) by too much fishing.

overflow ▪ v. **1** flow over the brim of a receptacle. ▸ spread over or cover. **2** be excessively full or crowded. **3** (**overflow with**) be very full of (an emotion). ▪ n. **1** the overflowing of a liquid. ▸ the excess not able to be accommodated by a space. **2** (also **overflow pipe**) an outlet for excess water. **3** Computing the generation of a number which is too large for the assigned location.

overfly ▪ v. (**-flies**; past **-flew**; past part. **-flown**) fly over or beyond.
– DERIVATIVES **overflight** n.

overfold ▪ n. Geology a fold in which both the limbs dip in the same direction.

overfond ▪ adj. excessively fond.
– DERIVATIVES **overfondly** adv. **overfondness** n.

overfull ▪ adj. excessively full.

overgarment ▪ n. a garment worn over others.

overgeneralize (also **-ise**) ▪ v. generalize more widely than is justified.
– DERIVATIVES **overgeneralization** (also **-isation**) n.

overgenerous ▪ adj. excessively generous.
– DERIVATIVES **overgenerously** adv.

overglaze ▪ n. decoration or a second glaze applied to glazed ceramic. ▪ adj. (of decoration) applied on a glazed surface.

overgraze ▪ v. graze (grassland) too heavily.

overground ▪ adv. & adj. on or above the ground.

overgrown ▪ adj. **1** grown over with vegetation. **2** grown too large. ▸ chiefly derogatory used in likening an adult to a child.

overgrowth ▪ n. excessive growth.

overhand ▪ adj. & adv. **1** overarm. **2** with the palm downward or inward.

overhand knot ▪ n. a simple knot made by forming a loop and passing a free end through it.

overhang ▪ v. (past and past part. **-hung**) **1** hang over. **2** loom over. ▪ n. **1** an overhanging part. **2** Finance a quantity of securities or commodities large enough to make prices fall if offered for sale.

overhaul ▪ v. **1** examine (machinery or equipment) and repair it if necessary. **2** overtake. ▪ n. an act of overhauling.
– ORIGIN C17: from OVER- + HAUL.

overhead ▪ adv. above one's head; in the sky. ▪ adj. **1** situated overhead. **2** (of a driving mechanism) above the object driven. **3** (of an expense) incurred in the upkeep or running of premises or a business. ▪ n. **1** an overhead cost or expense. **2** a transparency for use with an overhead projector.

overhead projector ▪ n. a device that projects an enlarged image of a transparency by means of an overhead mirror.

overhear ▪ v. (past and past part. **-heard**) hear accidentally or secretly.

overheat ▪ v. **1** make or become too hot. **2** Economics (of an economy) show marked inflation when increased demand results in rising prices.

overindulge ▪ v. **1** indulge to excess. **2** gratify the wishes of to an excessive extent.
– DERIVATIVES **overindulgence** n. **overindulgent** adj.

overinflated ▪ adj. **1** (of a price or value) excessive. ▸ exaggerated. **2** filled with too much air.

overjoyed ▪ adj. extremely happy.

overkill ▪ n. the amount by which destruction or the capacity for destruction exceeds what is necessary. ▸ excessive use, treatment, or action.

overladen ▪ adj. bearing too large a load.

overlaid past and past participle of OVERLAY[1].

overlain past participle of OVERLIE.

overland ▪ adj. & adv. by land. ▪ v. travel a long distance by land. ▸ [usu. as noun **overlanding**] tour in an organized group over a long distance, usually in a truck or similar vehicle.

overlap ▪ v. (**-lapped**, **-lapping**) extend over so as to cover partly. ▸ partly coincide. ▪ n. an overlapping part or amount. ▸ an instance of overlapping.

overlay[1] ▪ v. (past and past part. **-laid**) (often **be overlaid with**) **1** coat the surface of. **2** lie on top of. **3** (of a quality or feeling) become more prominent than (a previous one). ▪ n. a covering. ▸ a transparent sheet over artwork or a map, giving additional detail. ▸ a graphical computer display which can be superimposed on another.

overlay[2] past of OVERLIE.

overleaf ▪ adv. on the other side of the page.

overlie ▪ v. (**-lying**; past **-lay**; past part. **-lain**) lie on top of.

overload ▪ v. **1** load excessively. **2** put too great a demand on (an electrical system). ▪ n. an excessive amount.

overlock ▪ v. prevent fraying of (an edge of cloth) by oversewing it.
– DERIVATIVES **overlocker** n.

overlong ▪ adj. & adv. too long.

overlook ▪ v. **1** fail to notice. ▸ ignore or disregard. ▸ pass over in favour of another. **2** have a view of from above.

overlord ▪ n. a ruler, especially a feudal lord.
– DERIVATIVES **overlordship** n.

overly ▪ adv. excessively.

overlying present participle of OVERLIE.

overman ▪ v. (**-manned**, **-manning**) provide with more people than necessary. ▪ n. (pl. **-men**) Philosophy another term for SUPERMAN. [translation of the German philosopher Friedrich Nietzsche's term *übermensch*.]

overmantel ▪ n. an ornamental structure over a mantelpiece.

overmatch ▪ v. [usu. as adj. **overmatched**] be stronger, better armed, or more skilful than.

overmuch ▪ adv., det., & pron. too much.

overnight ■ adv. **1** for the duration of a night. ▸ during the course of a night. **2** suddenly. ■ adj. **1** for use overnight. ▸ done or happening overnight. **2** sudden. ■ v. stay overnight. ▸ N. Amer. convey (goods) overnight.

overnighter ■ n. **1** chiefly N. Amer. an overnight trip or stay. **2** an overnight bag.

overpaid past and past participle of OVERPAY.

overpaint ■ v. cover with paint. ■ n. paint added as a covering layer.

overpass ■ n. a bridge by which a road or railway line passes over another.

overpay ■ v. (past and past part. **-paid**) pay too much.
– DERIVATIVES **overpayment** n.

overpitch ■ v. [often as adj. **overpitched**] Cricket bowl (a ball) so that it pitches or would pitch too far.

overplay ■ v. overemphasize.
– PHRASES **overplay one's hand** spoil one's chance of success through excessive confidence.

overpopulate ■ v. [usu. as adj. **overpopulated**] populate (an area) in too large numbers.
– DERIVATIVES **overpopulation** n.

overpower ■ v. defeat with superior strength.
▸ overwhelm.
– DERIVATIVES **overpowering** adj. **overpoweringly** adv.

overprice ■ v. [often as adj. **overpriced**] charge too high a price for.

overprint ■ v. **1** print additional matter on. ▸ print with (additional matter). **2** print too many or too much of. **3** Photography make (a print) darker than intended. ■ n. additional matter overprinted. ▸ an overprinted postage stamp.

overproduce ■ v. **1** produce an excess of. **2** record or produce (a song or film) in an excessively elaborate way.
– DERIVATIVES **overproduction** n.

overprotective ■ adj. excessively protective.
– DERIVATIVES **overprotect** v. **overprotection** n. **overprotectiveness** n.

overqualified ■ adj. too highly qualified.

overran past of OVERRUN.

overrate ■ v. [often as adj. **overrated**] rate more highly than is deserved.

overreach ■ v. **1** reach too far. ▸ (**overreach oneself**) try to do more than is possible. **2** (of a horse) bring the hind feet so far forward that they fall alongside or strike the forefeet. ■ n. an injury to a horse's forefoot due to overreaching.

overreact ■ v. react more emotionally or forcibly than is justified.
– DERIVATIVES **overreaction** n.

override ■ v. (past **-rode**; past part. **-ridden**) **1** use one's authority to reject or cancel. **2** interrupt the action of (an automatic function). **3** be more important than. **4** overlap. ■ n. **1** the action or process of overriding. **2** a device on a machine for overriding an automatic function.

overriding ■ adj. **1** more important than any other considerations. **2** extending or moving over.

overripe ■ adj. too ripe.

overrode past of OVERRIDE.

overrule ■ v. reject or disallow by exercising one's superior authority.

overrun ■ v. (**-running**; past **-ran**; past part. **-run**) **1** spread over or occupy (a place) in large numbers. **2** move or extend over or beyond. **3** exceed (an expected or allowed time or cost). **4** rotate faster than (another part of a machine). ■ n. **1** an instance of overrunning. **2** a clear area beyond the end of a runway. **3** the movement of a vehicle at a speed greater than is imparted by the engine.
– ORIGIN Old English (see OVER-, RUN).

oversampling ■ n. Electronics the technique of increasing the apparent sampling frequency of a digital signal by repeating each digit a number of times, in order to facilitate the subsequent filtering of unwanted noise.

oversaw past of OVERSEE.

overseas ■ adv. in or to a foreign country. ■ adj. from, to, or relating to a foreign country. ■ n. foreign countries regarded collectively.

oversee ■ v. (**-sees**; past **-saw**; past part. **-seen**) supervise.
– DERIVATIVES **overseer** n.
– ORIGIN Old English *oferséon* 'look at from above'.

oversell ■ v. (past and past part. **-sold**) **1** sell more of (something) than exists or can be delivered. **2** exaggerate the merits of.

oversensitive ■ adj. excessively sensitive.
– DERIVATIVES **oversensitiveness** n. **oversensitivity** n.

oversew ■ v. (past part. **-sewn** or **-sewed**) sew the edges of two pieces of fabric) with every stitch passing over the join. ▸ join the sections of (a book) in such a way.

oversexed ■ adj. having unusually strong sexual desires.

overshadow ■ v. **1** tower above and cast a shadow over. **2** cast a gloom over. **3** appear more prominent or important than. **4** be more impressive or successful than.
– ORIGIN Old English.

overshoe ■ n. a shoe worn over a normal shoe, typically made either of rubber to protect the normal shoe or of felt to protect a floor surface.

overshoot ■ v. (past and past part. **-shot**) **1** go past (a point) unintentionally. **2** exceed (a financial target or limit). ■ n. an act of overshooting.

overshot past and past participle of OVERSHOOT. ■ adj. denoting an upper jaw which projects beyond the lower jaw.

overside ■ adv. over the side of a ship.

oversight ■ n. **1** an unintentional failure to notice or do something. **2** the action of overseeing.

oversimplify ■ v. (**-ies**, **-ied**) [often as adj. **oversimplified**] simplify (something) so much that a distorted impression of it is given.
– DERIVATIVES **oversimplification** n.

oversized (also **oversize**) ■ adj. bigger than the usual size.

oversleep ■ v. (past and past part. **-slept**) sleep longer or later than one has intended.

oversold past and past participle of OVERSELL.

overspend ■ v. (past and past part. **-spent**) spend too much. ■ n. an act of overspending.

overspill ■ n. **1** an instance of something spilling over. **2** a surplus population moving from an overcrowded area to live elsewhere.

overspread ■ v. (past and past part. **-spread**) cover the surface of; spread over.
– ORIGIN Old English.

overstaff ■ v. provide with more members of staff than are necessary.

overstate ■ v. state too emphatically; exaggerate.
– DERIVATIVES **overstatement** n.

overstay ■ v. stay longer than the duration or limits of.
– DERIVATIVES **overstayer** n.

oversteer ■ v. turn or cause to turn more sharply than is desirable. ■ n. the tendency of a vehicle to oversteer.

overstep ■ v. (**-stepped**, **-stepping**) go beyond (a prescribed or generally accepted limit).
– PHRASES **overstep** (or **overshoot**) **the mark** go beyond what is intended or acceptable.

overstimulate ■ v. stimulate excessively.
– DERIVATIVES **overstimulation** n.

overstitch ■ n. a stitch made over an edge or over another stitch. ■ v. sew with an overstitch.

overstock ■ v. stock with more than is necessary or required. ▸ put more animals in (an area) than it is capable of supporting in terms of food or space. ■ n. chiefly N. Amer. a supply or quantity in excess of demand.

overstorey ■ n. Ecology (pl. **overstoreys**) the uppermost canopy level of a forest, formed by the tallest trees.

overstrain ■ v. subject to an excessive demand on strength, resources, or abilities. ■ n. the action or result of overstraining.

overstress ■ v. **1** subject to too much stress. **2** lay too much emphasis on.

overstretch ■ v. [often as adj. **overstretched**] stretch too much.

overstrike ■ n. the superimposing of one printed character or one coin design on another.

overstrung ■ adj. (of a piano) with strings in sets crossing each other obliquely.

overstuff ■ v. [usu. as adj. **overstuffed**] cover (furniture) completely with a thick layer of stuffing.

oversubscribed ■ adj. 1 (of something for sale) applied for in greater quantities than are available. 2 (of a course or institution) having more applications than available places.

overt /əʊˈvɜːt, ˈəʊvət/ ■ adj. done or shown openly.
–DERIVATIVES **overtly** adv. **overtness** n.
–ORIGIN Middle English: from Old French, from *ovrir* 'to open', from Latin *aperire*.

overtake ■ v. (past **-took**; past part. **-taken**) 1 catch up with and pass while travelling in the same direction. 2 become greater or more successful than. 3 come suddenly or unexpectedly upon.

overtax ■ v. tax excessively.

overthrow ■ v. (past **-threw**; past part. **-thrown**) 1 remove forcibly from power. 2 put an end to through force. 3 throw (a ball) further than the intended distance. ■ n. 1 a removal from power; a defeat or downfall. 2 (in cricket, baseball, etc.) a throw which sends a ball past its intended recipient or target. ▸ a score made because the ball has been overthrown.

overthrust ■ v. (past and past part. **-thrust**) Geology force (a body of rock) over another formation.

overtime ■ n. 1 time worked in addition to one's normal working hours. 2 N. Amer. extra time played at the end of a tie game. ■ adv. in addition to normal working hours.

overtire ■ v. exhaust.
–DERIVATIVES **overtired** adj.

overtone ■ n. 1 a musical tone which is a part of the harmonic series above a fundamental note, and may be heard with it. 2 a subtle or subsidiary quality, implication, or connotation. 3 Physics a component of any oscillation whose frequency is an integral multiple of the fundamental frequency.
–ORIGIN C19: from OVER- + TONE, suggested by German *Oberton*.

overtop ■ v. (**-topped**, **-topping**) 1 exceed in height. 2 (of water) rise over the top of.

overtrain ■ v. train or cause to train too much.

overtrick ■ n. Bridge a trick taken by the declarer in excess of the contract.

overtrousers ■ pl. n. protective or waterproof trousers worn over other trousers.

overture ■ n. 1 an orchestral piece at the beginning of a musical work. ▸ an independent orchestral composition in one movement. 2 an introduction to something more substantial. 3 an approach made with the aim of opening negotiations or establishing a relationship.
–ORIGIN Middle English: from Latin *apertura* 'aperture'.

overturn ■ v. 1 turn over or cause to turn over and come to rest upside down. 2 abolish, invalidate, or reverse (an established fact or system, legal decision, etc.). ■ n. 1 an act of overturning. 2 Ecology the occasional mixing of the water of a thermally stratified lake.

overtype ■ v. type over (another character) on a computer screen. ■ n. a facility allowing overtyping.

overuse ■ v. use too much. ■ n. excessive use.

overvalue ■ v. (**-values**, **-valued**, **-valuing**) 1 overestimate the importance of. 2 fix the value of (something, especially a currency) at too high a level.
–DERIVATIVES **overvaluation** n.

overview ■ n. a general review or summary.

overwater ■ v. apply too much water to.

overweening ■ adj. showing excessive confidence or pride.
–DERIVATIVES **overweeningly** adv.

overweight ■ adj. above a normal, desirable, or permitted weight. ■ n. excessive or extra weight. ■ v. [usu. as adj. **overweighted**] overload.

overwhelm ■ v. 1 bury or drown beneath a huge mass. ▸ give too much of something to: *they were overwhelmed by letters*. 2 defeat completely; overpower. 3 (usu. **be overwhelmed**) have a strong emotional effect on.
–DERIVATIVES **overwhelming** adj. **overwhelmingly** adv.

overwind ■ v. (past and past part. **-wound**) wind (a mechanism) beyond the proper stopping point.

overwinter ■ v. 1 spend the winter in a specified place. 2 (with reference to an insect, plant, etc.) live or maintain through the winter.

overwork ■ v. 1 work or cause to work too hard. 2 [usu. as adj. **overworked**] use (a word or idea) too much and so make it weaker in effect. ■ n. excessive work.

overwound past and past participle of OVERWIND.

overwrite ■ v. (past **-wrote**; past part. **-written**) 1 write on top of (other writing). ▸ another term for OVERTYPE. 2 Computing destroy (data) or the data in (a file) by entering new data in its place. 3 write too elaborately or ornately. 4 (in insurance) accept more risk than the premium income limits allow.
–DERIVATIVES **overwriting** n.

overwrought ■ adj. 1 in a state of nervous excitement or anxiety. 2 (of a piece of writing or a work of art) too elaborate or complicated in design or construction.
–ORIGIN Middle English: archaic past participle of OVERWORK.

overzealous ■ adj. too zealous.
–DERIVATIVES **overzealously** adv. **overzealousness** n.

ovi- ■ comb. form chiefly Zoology of or relating to eggs or ova: *oviparous*.
–ORIGIN from Latin *ovum* 'egg'.

oviduct /ˈəʊvɪdʌkt/ ■ n. the tube through which an ovum or egg passes from an ovary.
–DERIVATIVES **oviductal** adj.

ovine /ˈəʊvaɪn/ ■ adj. of, relating to, affecting, or resembling sheep.
–ORIGIN C19: from late Latin *ovinus*, from Latin *ovis* 'sheep'.

oviparous /əʊˈvɪp(ə)rəs/ ■ adj. Zoology (of an animal) producing young by means of eggs which are hatched after they have been laid by the parent, as in birds. Compare with VIVIPAROUS and OVOVIVIPAROUS.
–DERIVATIVES **oviparity** n.

oviposit /ˌəʊvɪˈpɒzɪt/ ■ v. (**oviposited**, **ovipositing**) Zoology (especially of an insect) lay an egg or eggs.
–DERIVATIVES **oviposition** n.
–ORIGIN C19: from OVI- + Latin *posit-*, *ponere* 'place'.

ovipositor /ˌəʊvɪˈpɒzɪtə/ ■ n. Zoology a tubular organ through which a female insect or fish deposits eggs.

ovoid /ˈəʊvɔɪd/ ■ adj. 1 (of a solid or a three-dimensional surface) more or less egg-shaped. 2 (of a plane figure) oval. ■ n. an ovoid body or surface.
–ORIGIN C19: from French *ovoïde*, from Latin *ovum* 'egg'.

ovoviviparous /ˌəʊvəʊvɪˈvɪp(ə)rəs/ ■ adj. Zoology (of an animal) producing young by means of eggs which are hatched within the body of the parent, as in some snakes. Compare with OVIPAROUS and VIVIPAROUS.
–DERIVATIVES **ovoviviparity** n.

ovulate /ˈɒvjʊleɪt/ ■ v. discharge ova or ovules from the ovary.
–DERIVATIVES **ovulation** n. **ovulatory** adj.
–ORIGIN C19: back-formation from *ovulation*, or from medieval Latin *ovulum* (see OVULE).

ovule /ˈɒvjuːl, ˈəʊ-/ ■ n. Botany the part of the ovary of seed plants that contains the female germ cell and after fertilization becomes the seed.
–DERIVATIVES **ovular** adj.
–ORIGIN C19: from medieval Latin *ovulum*, diminutive of OVUM.

ovum /ˈəʊvəm/ ■ n. (pl. **ova** /ˈəʊvə/) Biology a mature female reproductive cell, which can divide to give rise to an embryo usually only after fertilization by a male cell.
–ORIGIN C18: from Latin, 'egg'.

ow ■ exclam. used to express sudden pain.
–ORIGIN C19: natural exclam.

owe ■ v. 1 have an obligation to pay (money or goods) to

owing

(someone) in return for something received. **2** be under a moral obligation to show (gratitude, respect, etc.) or to offer (an explanation) to (someone). **3** (**owe something to**) have something because of. **4** be indebted to (someone or something) for (something).
– ORIGIN Old English *āgan* 'own, have it as an obligation', of Germanic origin.

owing ■ adj. yet to be paid or supplied.
– PHRASES **owing to** because of or on account of.

owl ■ n. a nocturnal bird of prey with large eyes, a hooked beak, and typically a loud hooting call. [Order Strigiformes: many species.]
– ORIGIN Old English *ūle*, of Germanic origin, from a base imitative of the bird's call.

owlet ■ n. a young or small owl.

owlish ■ adj. **1** like an owl, especially in being wise or solemn. **2** (of glasses or eyes) resembling the large round eyes of an owl.
– DERIVATIVES **owlishly** adv. **owlishness** n.

own ■ adj. & pron. (with a possessive) belonging or relating to the person specified. ▸ done or produced by the person specified. ▸ particular to the person or thing specified; individual. ■ v. **1** possess. **2** formal admit or acknowledge that something is the case. **3** (**own up**) admit to having done something wrong or embarrassing.
– PHRASES **be one's own man** (or **woman**) act independently. **come into its** (or **one's**) **own** become fully effective. **hold one's own** retain a position of strength in a challenging situation.
– DERIVATIVES **-owned** adj. **owner** n. **ownerless** adj.
– ORIGIN Old English *āgen* 'owned, possessed', from *āgan* 'owe'.

own brand ■ n. a product manufactured specially for a retailer and bearing the retailer's name.

owner-occupier ■ n. a person who owns the house, flat, etc. in which they live.
– DERIVATIVES **owner-occupied** adj.

ownership ■ n. the act, state, or right of possessing something.

own goal ■ n. **1** (in soccer) a goal scored when a player inadvertently strikes or deflects the ball into their own team's goal. **2** an act that unintentionally harms one's own interests.

owt /aʊt/ ■ pron. N. English anything.
– ORIGIN C19: var. of AUGHT.

ox ■ n. (pl. **oxen** /ˈɒks(ə)n/) a domesticated bovine animal kept for milk or meat; a cow or bull. See also CATTLE. ▸ used in names of wild animals related to or resembling this, e.g. musk ox. ▸ a castrated bull, especially as a draught animal.
– ORIGIN Old English, of Germanic origin.

ox- ■ comb. form variant spelling of OXY-² reduced before a vowel (as in *oxic*).

oxalic acid /ɒkˈsalɪk/ ■ n. Chemistry a poisonous crystalline organic acid, present in rhubarb leaves, wood sorrel, and other plants.
– DERIVATIVES **oxalate** /ˈɒksəleɪt/ n.
– ORIGIN C18: from French *oxalique*, from Greek *oxalis* 'wood sorrel'.

oxalis /ˈɒksəlɪs, ɒkˈsɑːlɪs/ ■ n. a plant of a genus which includes the wood sorrel, typically having three-lobed leaves and white, yellow, or pink flowers. [Genus *Oxalis*.]
– ORIGIN C17: from Greek, from *oxus* 'sour' (because of its sharp-tasting leaves).

oxbow /ˈɒksbəʊ/ ■ n. **1** a loop formed by a horseshoe bend in a river. **2** the U-shaped piece of an ox-yoke.

oxbow lake ■ n. a curved lake formed from a horseshoe bend in a river where the main stream has cut across the neck and no longer flows around the loop of the bend.

Oxbridge ■ n. Oxford and Cambridge universities regarded together.

oxen plural form of OX.

oxer ■ n. **1** an ox fence. **2** (in showjumping) a jump consisting of a brush fence with a guard rail on one or both sides.

ox-eye daisy ■ n. a Eurasian daisy which has large white flowers with yellow centres. [*Leucanthemum vulgare*.]

ox fence ■ n. a strong fence for confining cattle, consisting of a hedge with a strong guard rail on one side, and usually a ditch on the other.

Oxford ■ n. a type of lace-up shoe with a low heel.
– ORIGIN C19: named after the city of *Oxford* in southern England.

Oxford blue ■ n. Brit. **1** a dark blue, typically with a purple tinge, adopted as the colour of Oxford University. **2** a person who has represented Oxford University in a particular sport.

Oxford comma ■ n. another term for SERIAL COMMA.
– ORIGIN a characteristic of the house style of *Oxford* University Press.

oxhide ■ n. leather made from the hide of an ox.

oxic /ˈɒksɪk/ ■ adj. involving or containing oxygen.

oxidant /ˈɒksɪd(ə)nt/ ■ n. an oxidizing agent.

oxidase /ˈɒksɪdeɪz/ ■ n. Biochemistry an enzyme which promotes the transfer of a hydrogen atom from a particular substrate to an oxygen molecule.

oxidation ■ n. Chemistry the process or result of oxidizing or being oxidized.
– DERIVATIVES **oxidative** adj.
– ORIGIN C18: from French, from *oxider* 'oxidize'.

oxidation number (also **oxidation state**) ■ n. Chemistry a number representing the number of electrons lost or gained by an atom of a particular element when chemically combined.

oxide /ˈɒksaɪd/ ■ n. Chemistry a compound of oxygen with another element or group.
– ORIGIN C18: from French, from *oxygène* 'oxygen'.

oxidize /ˈɒksɪdaɪz/ (also **-ise**) ■ v. combine or cause to combine with oxygen. ▸ Chemistry undergo or cause to undergo a reaction in which electrons are lost to another substance or molecule. The opposite of REDUCE.
– DERIVATIVES **oxidizable** (also **-isable**) adj. **oxidization** (also **-isation**) n. **oxidizer** (also **-iser**) n.

oxidizing agent (also **-ising**) ■ n. Chemistry a substance that tends to bring about oxidation by being reduced and gaining electrons.

oximeter /ɒkˈsɪmɪtə/ ■ n. an instrument for measuring the proportion of oxygenated haemoglobin in the blood.
– DERIVATIVES **oximetry** n.

oxisol /ˈɒksɪsɒl/ ■ n. Soil Science a stable, highly weathered, tropical mineral soil with oxidized subsurface horizons.
– ORIGIN 1960s: from OXIC + -SOL.

Oxon /ˈɒks(ə)n, -sɒn/ ■ abbrev. (in degree titles) of Oxford University.
– ORIGIN from medieval Latin *Oxoniensis*, from *Oxonia* (see OXONIAN).

Oxonian /ɒkˈsəʊnɪən/ ■ adj. of or relating to Oxford or Oxford University. ■ n. a member of Oxford University.
– ORIGIN C16: from *Oxonia*, Latinized name of Oxford, from its old form *Oxenford*.

oxpecker ■ n. a brown African bird related to the starlings, feeding on parasites that infest the skins of large grazing mammals. [Genus *Buphagus*: two species.]

oxtail ■ n. the tail of an ox (used as meat).

ox-tongue ■ n. the tongue of an ox (used as meat).

oxy-¹ ■ comb. form denoting sharpness: *oxytone*.
– ORIGIN from Greek *oxus* 'sharp'.

oxy-² (also **ox-**) ■ comb. form Chemistry representing OXYGEN.

oxyacetylene ■ adj. of or denoting welding or cutting techniques using a very hot flame produced by mixing acetylene and oxygen.

oxyacid ■ n. Chemistry an inorganic acid whose molecules contain oxygen.

oxyanion /ˌɒksɪˈanʌɪən/ ■ n. Chemistry an anion containing one or more oxygen atoms bonded to another element.

oxygen ■ n. the chemical element of atomic number 8, a colourless, odourless reactive gas that forms about 20 per

cent of the earth's atmosphere and is essential to plant and animal life. (Symbol: **O**)
- DERIVATIVES **oxygenous** adj.
- ORIGIN C18: from French (*principe*) *oxygène* 'acidifying constituent' (because at first it was held to be the essential component of acids).

oxygenate /ˈɒksɪdʒəneɪt, ɒkˈsɪdʒ-/ ■ v. supply, treat, charge, or enrich with oxygen.
- DERIVATIVES **oxygenated** adj. **oxygenation** n.

oxygenator ■ n. **1** Medicine an apparatus for oxygenating the blood. **2** an aquatic plant which enriches the surrounding water with oxygen.

oxyhaemoglobin ■ n. Biochemistry a bright red substance formed by the combination of haemoglobin with oxygen, present in oxygenated blood.

oxymoron /ˌɒksɪˈmɔːrɒn/ ■ n. a figure of speech or expressed idea in which apparently contradictory terms appear in conjunction.
- DERIVATIVES **oxymoronic** adj.
- ORIGIN C17: from Greek *oxumōron*, from *oxumōros* 'pointedly foolish', from *oxus* 'sharp' + *mōros* 'foolish'.

oxytocin /ˌɒksɪˈtəʊsɪn/ ■ n. Biochemistry a hormone released by the pituitary gland that causes increased contraction of the womb during labour and stimulates the ejection of milk into the ducts of the breasts.
- ORIGIN 1920s: from Greek *oxutokia* 'sudden delivery', from *oxus* 'sharp' + *tokos* 'childbirth'.

oyster ■ n. **1** a bivalve marine mollusc with a rough, flattened, irregularly oval shell, several kinds of which are farmed for food or pearls. [Ostreidae and other families.] **2** a shade of greyish white.
- PHRASES **the world is one's oyster** one is able to enjoy a broad range of opportunities.
- ORIGIN Middle English: from Old French *oistre*, from Greek *ostreon*.

oystercatcher ■ n. a wading bird with black-and-white or all-black plumage and a strong orange-red bill, feeding chiefly on shellfish. [Genus *Haematopus*.]

oyster mushroom ■ n. an edible fungus with a greyish-brown oyster-shaped cap and a very short or absent stem. [*Pleurotus ostreatus*.]

oyster plant ■ n. another term for SALSIFY.

oyster sauce ■ n. a sauce made with oysters and soy sauce, used especially in oriental cookery.

oy vey /ɔɪ ˈveɪ/ ■ exclam. indicating dismay or grief (used mainly by Yiddish-speakers).
- ORIGIN C19: Yiddish, 'oh woe'.

Oz ■ n. & adj. informal Australia or Australian.
- ORIGIN 1940s: representing a pronunciation of an abbrev. of *Australia*.

oz ■ abbrev. ounce(s).
- ORIGIN from Italian *onza* 'ounce'.

Ozalid /ˈəʊzəlɪd, ˈɒz-/ ■ n. trademark a photocopy made by a process in which a diazonium salt and coupler are present in the paper coating, so that the image develops in the presence of ammonia.
- ORIGIN 1920s: by reversal of DIAZO and insertion of *-l*.

ozone ■ n. **1** an unstable, pungent, toxic form of oxygen with three atoms in its molecule, formed in electrical discharges or by ultraviolet light. **2** informal fresh invigorating air.
- ORIGIN C19: from German *Ozon*, from Greek *ozein* 'to smell'.

ozone-friendly ■ adj. (of manufactured products) not containing chemicals that are destructive to the ozone layer.

ozone hole ■ n. a region of marked thinning of the ozone layer in high latitudes, chiefly in winter, due to CFCs and other atmospheric pollutants.

ozone layer ■ n. a layer in the earth's stratosphere at an altitude of about 10 km (6.2 miles) containing a high concentration of ozone, which absorbs most of the ultraviolet radiation reaching the earth from the sun.

Ozzie ■ n. variant spelling of AUSSIE.

Pp

P¹ (also **p**) ■ n. (pl. **Ps** or **P's**) **1** the sixteenth letter of the alphabet. **2** denoting the next after O in a set of items, categories, etc.

P² ■ abbrev. **1** (in tables of sports results) games played. **2** (on an automatic gear shift) park. **3** (on road signs and street plans) parking. **4** peta- (10^{15}). **5** Physics poise (unit of viscosity). ■ symb. the chemical element phosphorus.

p ■ abbrev. **1** page. **2** (*p*-) Chemistry para-. **3** Brit. penny or pence. **4** pico- (10^{-12}). **5** Chemistry denoting electrons and orbitals possessing one unit of angular momentum. [from *principal*, orig. applied to lines in atomic spectra.] ■ symb. **1** Physics pressure. **2** Statistics probability.

PA ■ abbrev. **1** personal assistant. **2** Press Association. **3** public address.

Pa ■ abbrev. pascal(s). ■ symb. the chemical element protactinium.

pa ■ n. informal father.
– ORIGIN C19: abbrev. of PAPA.

p.a. ■ abbrev. per annum.

paan /pɑːn/ (also **pan**) ■ n. Indian betel leaves prepared and used as a stimulant.
– ORIGIN from Sanskrit *parṇa* 'feather, leaf'.

PABX ■ abbrev. private automatic branch exchange.

PAC ■ abbrev. Pan-Africanist Congress.

pace¹ /peɪs/ ■ n. **1** a single step taken when walking or running. **2** a gait of a horse, especially one of the recognized trained gaits. **3** speed or rate of motion, development, or change. **4** Cricket the state of a wicket as affecting the speed of the ball. ■ v. **1** measure (a distance) by walking it and counting the number of steps taken. **2** walk at a steady speed, especially without a particular destination and as an expression of anxiety. **3** (of a trained horse) move with a distinctive lateral gait in which both legs on the same side are lifted together. **4** lead (another runner in a race) in order to establish a competitive speed. **5** (**pace oneself**) do something at a restrained and steady rate or speed.
– PHRASES **keep pace with** move, develop, or progress at the same speed as. **off the pace** behind the leader or leading group in a race or contest. **put someone through their paces** make someone demonstrate their abilities. **stand** (or **take**) **the pace** be able to keep up with another or others.
– DERIVATIVES **-paced** adj.
– ORIGIN Middle English: from Old French *pas*, from Latin *passus* 'stretch (of the leg)'.

pace² /ˈpɑːtʃeɪ, ˈpeɪsi/ ■ prep. with due respect to.
– ORIGIN Latin, 'in peace', from *pax*.

pace bowler ■ n. Cricket a fast bowler.

pace car ■ n. Motor Racing a car that sets the pace for the warm-up lap before a race but does not take part in it, or one that controls the pace in temporarily hazardous conditions.

pacemaker ■ n. **1** a competitor who sets the pace at the beginning of a race or competition. **2** an artificial device for stimulating and regulating the heart muscle. **3** a part of an organ or of the body which controls rhythmic physiological activity.
– DERIVATIVES **pacemaking** adj. & n.

paceman ■ n. (pl. **-men**) Cricket a fast bowler.

pacer ■ n. **1** a pacemaker. **2** chiefly US a horse bred or trained to pace.

pacesetter ■ n. another term for PACEMAKER (in sense 1).
– DERIVATIVES **pacesetting** adj. & n.

pacey ■ adj. variant spelling of PACY.

pachinko /pəˈtʃɪŋkəʊ/ ■ n. a Japanese form of pinball.
– ORIGIN from Japanese.

pachyderm /ˈpakɪdəːm/ ■ n. a very large mammal with thick skin, especially an elephant, rhinoceros, or hippopotamus.
– DERIVATIVES **pachydermal** adj. **pachydermatous** adj. **pachydermic** adj.
– ORIGIN C19: from French *pachyderme*, from Greek *pakhudermos*, from *pakhus* 'thick' + *derma* 'skin'.

pachytene /ˈpakɪtiːn/ ■ n. Biology the third stage of the prophase of meiosis, during which the paired chromosomes shorten and thicken, the two chromatids of each separate, and exchange of segments between chromatids may occur.
– ORIGIN C20: from Greek *pakhus* 'thick' + *tainia* 'band'.

pacific ■ adj. **1** peaceful in character or intent. **2** (**Pacific**) of or relating to the Pacific Ocean. ■ n. (**the Pacific**) the Pacific Ocean.
– DERIVATIVES **pacifically** adv.
– ORIGIN C16: from Latin *pacificus* 'peacemaking', from *pax* 'peace'.

Pacific Islander ■ n. a native or inhabitant of any of the islands in the South Pacific, especially an aboriginal native of Polynesia.

pacifier ■ n. **1** a person or thing that pacifies. **2** N. Amer. a baby's dummy.

pacifism ■ n. the belief that disputes should be settled by peaceful means and that war and violence are unjustifiable.
– DERIVATIVES **pacifist** n. & adj.
– ORIGIN C20: from French *pacifisme*, from *pacifier* 'pacify'.

pacify ■ v. (**-ies, -ied**) **1** quell the anger or agitation of. **2** bring peace to (a country or warring factions).
– DERIVATIVES **pacification** n.
– ORIGIN C15 (*pacification* Middle English): from Old French *pacefier*, from Latin *pacificare*, from *pax* 'peace'.

pack¹ ■ n. **1** a cardboard or paper container and the items contained within it. **2** a collection of related documents. **3** a set of playing cards. **4** a rucksack. **5** a quantity of foods packed or canned in a particular season. **6** a group of wild animals, especially wolves or wild dogs, living and hunting together. ▶ a group of hounds kept for hunting. **7** (**Pack**) an organized group of Cub Scouts or Brownies. **8** Rugby a team's forwards considered as a group. **9** (**the pack**) the main body of competitors following the leader in a race or competition. **10** chiefly derogatory a group or set of similar things or people: *a pack of lies*. **11** pack ice. **12** a hot or cold pad of absorbent material, used for treating an injury. ■ v. **1** fill (a suitcase or bag) with clothes and other items needed for travel. **2** place in a container for transport or storage. ▶ be capable of being folded up for transport or storage. **3** informal carry (a gun). **4** cram a large number of things into. ▶ [often as adj. **packed**] (of a large number of people) crowd into and fill (a place). **5** cover, surround, or fill.
– PHRASES **pack a punch 1** hit with skill or force. **2** have a powerful effect. **packed out** informal, chiefly Brit. very crowded. **send someone packing** informal dismiss someone peremptorily.
– PHRASAL VERBS **pack something in** informal give up an activity or job. **pack someone off** informal send someone somewhere peremptorily or without much notice. **pack out** S. African unpack. **pack up** informal (of a machine) break down.
– DERIVATIVES **packable** adj. **packer** n.
– ORIGIN Middle English: from Middle Dutch, Middle Low German *pak* (n.), *pakken* (v.).

pack² ■ v. fill (a jury or committee) with people likely to support a particular verdict or decision.

| CONSONANTS | b *but* | d *dog* | f *few* | g *get* | h *he* | j *yes* | k *cat* | l *leg* | m *man* | n *no* | p *pen* | r *red* |

–ORIGIN C16: prob. from the obsolete verb *pact* 'enter into an agreement with', the final *-t* being interpreted as an inflection of the past tense.

package ■ n. **1** an object or group of objects wrapped in paper or packed in a box. ► a packet. **2** (also **package deal**) a set of proposals or terms offered or agreed as a whole. ► (usu. **the package**) S. African informal a payment given to an employee who is made redundant or retires early. **3** informal a package holiday. **4** Computing a collection of programs or subroutines with related functionality. ■ v. **1** put into a box or wrapping. **2** (usu. **be packaged**) present in a particular and advantageous way. **3** combine (various products) for sale as one unit.
–DERIVATIVES **packaged** adj. **packager** n. **packaging** n.
–ORIGIN C16: from PACK[1]; cf. Anglo-Latin *paccagium*.

package holiday (also **package tour**) ■ n. a holiday organized by a travel agent, with arrangements for transport and accommodation made at an inclusive price.

pack animal ■ n. **1** an animal used to carry packs. **2** an animal that lives and hunts in a pack.

pack drill ■ n. a military punishment of marching up and down carrying full equipment.
–PHRASES **no names, no pack drill** punishment will be prevented if names and details are not mentioned.

packed lunch ■ n. a cold lunch carried in a bag or box to work or school or on an excursion.

packet ■ n. **1** a paper or cardboard container. ► S. African a paper or plastic bag. **2** Computing a block of data transmitted across a network. **3** (**a packet**) informal a large sum of money. **4** dated a boat travelling at regular intervals between two ports, originally for the conveyance of mail. ■ v. (**packeted, packeting**) [often as adj. **packeted**] wrap up in a packet.
–ORIGIN C16: diminutive of PACK[1]; cf. Anglo-Latin *paccettum*.

packet radio ■ n. a method of broadcasting that makes use of radio signals carrying packets of data.

packet switching ■ n. Computing & Telecommunications a mode of data transmission in which a message is broken into a number of parts which are sent independently, over whatever route is optimum for each packet, and reassembled at the destination.

Packham (also **Packham's Triumph**) ■ n. a dessert pear of a yellow variety with juicy creamy-white flesh.
–ORIGIN 1900s: named after the Australian grower C. H. Packham.

packhorse ■ n. a horse used to carry loads.

pack ice ■ n. (in polar seas) an expanse of large pieces of floating ice driven together into a mass.

packing ■ n. **1** material used to protect fragile goods in transit. **2** material used to seal a join or assist in lubricating an axle.

packing case ■ n. a large, strong box used for transportation or storage.

packing density ■ n. Computing the density of stored information in terms of bits per unit occupied of its storage medium.

packman ■ n. (pl. **-men**) archaic a pedlar.

pact ■ n. a formal agreement between individuals or parties.
–ORIGIN Middle English: from Latin *pactum* 'something agreed'.

pacy (also **pacey**) ■ adj. (**-ier, -iest**) fast-moving.

pad[1] ■ n. **1** a thick piece of soft or absorbent material. **2** the fleshy underpart of an animal's foot or of a human finger. **3** a protective guard worn over a part of the body by a sports player. **4** a number of sheets of blank paper fastened together at one edge. **5** a flat-topped structure or area used for helicopter take-off and landing or for rocket-launching. **6** Electronics a flat area on a track of a printed circuit or on the edge of an integrated circuit to which wires or component leads can be attached to make an electrical connection. **7** informal a person's home. ■ v. (**padded, padding**) **1** [often as adj. **padded**] fill or cover with a pad. **2** (**pad up**) (in cricket) put on protective pads. ► (of a batsman) deliberately use one's pads to block a ball. **3** (**pad something out**) lengthen a speech or piece of writing with unnecessary material. **4** chiefly N. Amer. defraud by adding false items to (an expenses claim or bill).
–DERIVATIVES **padding** n.
–ORIGIN C16 (in the sense 'bundle of straw to lie on'): the senses may not be of common origin; the meaning 'underpart of an animal's foot' is perhaps rel. to Low German *pad* 'sole of the foot'.

pad[2] ■ v. (**padded, padding**) walk with steady steps making a soft, dull sound. ■ n. the sound of such steps.
–ORIGIN C16: from Low German *padden* 'to tread, go along a path', partly imitative.

padauk /pəˈdaʊk/ (also **padouk**) ■ n. **1** a hard wood from a tropical tree, resembling rosewood. **2** the tree which produces this wood. [*Pterocarpus soyauxii* (W. Africa) and related species.]
–ORIGIN C19: from Burmese.

paddle[1] ■ n. **1** a short pole with a broad blade at one or both ends, used to move a small boat or canoe through the water. **2** a short-handled bat such as that used in table tennis. **3** any of various paddle-shaped instruments used for stirring or mixing. **4** N. Amer. informal a paddle-shaped instrument used for administering corporal punishment. **5** each of the boards fitted round the circumference of a paddle wheel or mill wheel. **6** the fin or flipper of an aquatic mammal or bird. **7** a flat array of solar cells projecting from a spacecraft. **8** Medicine a plastic-covered electrode used in cardiac stimulation. **9** an act of paddling. ■ v. **1** propel (a boat or canoe) with a paddle or paddles. **2** (of a bird or other animal) swim with short fast strokes. **3** informal, chiefly N. Amer. beat with a paddle as a punishment.
–DERIVATIVES **paddler** n.
–ORIGIN Middle English.

paddle[2] ■ v. walk with bare feet in shallow water. ■ n. an act of paddling.
–DERIVATIVES **paddler** n.
–ORIGIN C16.

paddleball ■ n. a game played with a light ball and wooden bat in a four-walled handball court.

paddle steamer (also **paddle boat**) ■ n. a boat powered by steam and propelled by paddle wheels.

paddle wheel ■ n. a large steam-driven wheel with paddles round its circumference, attached to the side or stern of a ship and propelling the ship by its rotation.

paddling pool ■ n. a shallow artificial pool for children to paddle in.

paddock ■ n. **1** a small field or enclosure where horses are kept or exercised. **2** an enclosure adjoining a racecourse or track where horses or cars are gathered and displayed before a race. **3** S. African & Austral./NZ a field or plot of land enclosed by fencing or defined by natural boundaries. ■ v. keep or enclose (a horse) in a paddock.
–ORIGIN C17: apparently a var. of dialect *parrock*.

Paddy ■ n. (pl. **-ies**) informal, chiefly offensive an Irishman.
–ORIGIN C18: familiar form of the Irish given name *Padraig*.

paddy[1] ■ n. (pl. **-ies**) **1** a field where rice is grown. **2** rice still in the husk.
–ORIGIN C17: from Malay *pādī*.

paddy[2] ■ n. Brit. informal a fit of temper.
–ORIGIN C19: from PADDY, associated with obsolete *paddywhack* 'Irishman (given to brawling)'.

paddy wagon ■ n. informal, chiefly N. Amer. a police van.
–ORIGIN 1930s: *paddy* from PADDY.

padkos /ˈpatkɒs/ ■ n. S. African informal food for eating on a journey.
–ORIGIN Afrikaans, from *pad* 'road' + *kos* 'food'.

padlock ■ n. a detachable lock hanging by a pivoted hook on the object fastened. ■ v. [usu. as adj. **padlocked**] secure with a padlock.
–ORIGIN C15: from *pad-* (of unknown origin) + LOCK[1].

padloper /ˈpatˌlʊəpər/ ■ n. a small tortoise with a flattened carapace, native to southern Africa. [Genus *Homopus*: several species.]
–ORIGIN Afrikaans, 'vagabond', from *pad* 'path' + *loper* 'runner'.

padouk /pəˈduːk/ ■ n. variant spelling of PADAUK.

padre /ˈpɑːdreɪ, -dri/ ■ n. informal a chaplain in the armed services.
– ORIGIN C16: from Italian, Spanish, and Portuguese, 'father, priest', from Latin *pater* 'father'.

padrão /pəˈdraʊ/ ■ n. (pl. **padrões**) an inscribed stone pillar erected at places around the southern African coast by early Portuguese explorers to claim the territory for Portugal.
– ORIGIN Portuguese, 'inscribed post, standard'.

padrone /paˈdrəʊneɪ, -ni/ ■ n. a patron or master, especially a Mafia boss.
– ORIGIN from Italian.

padsaw ■ n. a small saw with a narrow blade, for cutting curves.

padstal /ˈpʌtstʌl/ S. African ■ n. a farm stall.
– ORIGIN from Afrikaans *pad* 'road' + *stal* 'stall'.

paean /ˈpiːən/ ■ n. a song of praise or triumph.
– ORIGIN C16: from Greek *paian* 'hymn of thanksgiving to Apollo'.

paederasty ■ n. variant spelling of **PEDERASTY**.

paediatrics /ˌpiːdɪˈatrɪks/ (US **pediatrics**) ■ pl. n. [treated as sing.] the branch of medicine concerned with children and their diseases.
– DERIVATIVES **paediatric** adj. **paediatrician** n.
– ORIGIN C19: from **PAEDO-** + Greek *iatros* 'physician'.

paedo- (US **pedo-**) ■ comb. form of a child; relating to children: *paedophile*.
– ORIGIN from Greek *pais, paid-* 'child, boy'.

paedogenesis /ˌpiːdə(ʊ)ˈdʒɛnɪsɪs/ ■ n. Zoology another term for **NEOTENY** (in sense 2).

paedomorphosis /ˌpiːdə(ʊ)ˈmɔːfəsɪs, -mɔːˈfəʊsɪs/ ■ n. Zoology another term for **NEOTENY** (in sense 1).

paedophile (US **pedophile**) ■ n. a person who is sexually attracted to children.
– DERIVATIVES **paedophilia** n. **paedophiliac** adj. & n.

paella /paɪˈɛlə/ ■ n. a Spanish dish of rice, saffron, chicken, seafood, etc., cooked and served in a large shallow pan.
– ORIGIN Catalan, from Old French *paele*, from Latin *patella* 'pan'.

PAGAD /ˈpagad/ (also **Pagad**) ■ abbrev. (in South Africa) People Against Gangsterism and Drugs.

pagan /ˈpeɪɡ(ə)n/ ■ n. a person holding religious beliefs other than those of the main world religions. ■ adj. of or relating to pagans or their beliefs.
– DERIVATIVES **paganism** n. **paganize** (also **-ise**) v.

HISTORY
The word **pagan** is ultimately from the same root as **peasant**, and entered Middle English via Latin *pagus* 'country district'. Roman soldiers used *paganus* (originally 'rustic, country dweller') to mean 'civilian'; early Christians called themselves *milites* or 'soldiers' enlisted in the 'army' of Christ, and used *paganus* to mean 'heathen' (i.e. not part of that 'army'). The word **heathen** probably developed in a similar way, coming from an adjective meaning 'inhabiting open country, savage'.

---

page¹ ■ n. **1** one side of a leaf of a book, magazine, or newspaper, or the material written or printed on it. **2** both sides of such a leaf considered as a single unit. **3** Computing a section of stored data, especially that which can be displayed on a screen at one time. **4** a particular episode considered as part of a longer history. ■ v. **1** (**page through**) leaf through. ▸ Computing move through and display (text) one page at a time. **2** [usu. as noun **paging**] Computing divide (a piece of software or data) into sections, keeping the most frequently accessed in main memory and storing the rest in virtual memory. **3** paginate (a book).
– DERIVATIVES **-paged** adj.
– ORIGIN C16: from Latin *pagina*, from *pangere* 'fasten'.

page² ■ n. **1** a boy or young man employed in a hotel or club to run errands, open doors, etc. **2** a young boy attending a bride at a wedding. **3** historical a boy in training for knighthood, in the personal service of a knight. **4** historical a man or boy employed as the personal attendant of a person of rank. ■ v. **1** summon over a public address system. **2** contact by means of a pager.
– ORIGIN Middle English: perhaps from Italian *paggio*, from Greek *paidion*, diminutive of *pais* 'boy'.

pageant /ˈpadʒ(ə)nt/ ■ n. **1** an entertainment consisting of a procession of people in elaborate costumes, or an outdoor performance of a historical scene. **2** (also **beauty pageant**) a beauty contest.
– ORIGIN Middle English *pagyn*.

pageantry ■ n. elaborate display or ceremony.

pageboy ■ n. **1** a page in a hotel or attending a bride at a wedding. **2** a woman's hairstyle consisting of a shoulder-length bob with the ends rolled under.

pager ■ n. a small radio device which bleeps or vibrates to inform the wearer that someone wishes to contact them or that it has received a short text message.

Paget's disease /ˈpadʒɪts/ ■ n. **1** a chronic disease of the elderly characterized by alteration of bone tissue, especially in the spine, skull, or pelvis. **2** an inflammation of the nipple associated with breast cancer.
– ORIGIN C19: named after the English surgeon Sir James Paget.

page-turner ■ n. informal an exciting book.
– DERIVATIVES **page-turning** adj. **page-turningly** adv.

paginal /ˈpadʒɪn(ə)l/ ■ adj. of or relating to the pages of a book or periodical.

paginate /ˈpadʒɪneɪt/ ■ v. assign numbers to the pages of a book, journal, etc.
– DERIVATIVES **pagination** n.

pagoda /pəˈɡəʊdə/ ■ n. a Hindu or Buddhist temple or sacred building, typically having a many-tiered tower.
– ORIGIN C16: from Portuguese *pagode*, perhaps from Persian *butkada* 'temple of idols'.

pagoda tree ■ n. a SE Asian leguminous tree with hanging clusters of cream flowers, cultivated as an ornamental. [*Sophora japonica*.]

pah ■ exclam. used to express disgust or contempt.
– ORIGIN C16: natural utterance.

pahoehoe /pəˈhəʊɪhəʊi/ ■ n. Geology basaltic lava forming smooth undulating or ropy masses. Often contrasted with **AA**.
– ORIGIN C19: from Hawaiian.

paid past and past participle of **PAY¹**.
– PHRASES **put paid to** informal stop abruptly; destroy.

paid-up ■ adj. **1** with all subscriptions or charges paid in full. **2** fully committed to a cause, group, etc.: *a fully paid-up postmodernist*.

pail ■ n. a bucket.
– DERIVATIVES **pailful** n. (pl. **-fuls**).
– ORIGIN Middle English: perhaps rel. to Old English *pægel* 'gill, small measure' and Old French *paelle* 'pan, liquid measure, brazier'.

pain ■ n. **1** a strongly unpleasant bodily sensation such as is caused by illness or injury. **2** mental suffering or distress. **3** (also **pain in the neck** or vulgar slang **arse**) informal an annoying or tedious person or thing. **4** (**pains**) careful effort. ■ v. cause mental or physical pain to. ▶ chiefly N. Amer. (of a part of the body) hurt.
– PHRASES **on** (or **under**) **pain of** on penalty of.
– DERIVATIVES **pained** adj.
– ORIGIN Middle English: from Old French *peine*, from Latin *poena* 'penalty', later 'pain'.

painful ■ adj. **1** (of part of the body) affected with pain. **2** causing physical or mental pain.
– DERIVATIVES **painfully** adv. **painfulness** n.

painkiller ■ n. a medicine for relieving pain.
– DERIVATIVES **painkilling** adj.

painless ■ adj. **1** not causing physical pain. **2** involving little effort or stress.
– DERIVATIVES **painlessly** adv. **painlessness** n.

painstaking ■ adj. done with or employing great care and thoroughness.
– DERIVATIVES **painstakingly** adv.

paint ■ n. **1** a substance which is spread over a surface and dries to leave a thin decorative or protective coating. **2** an act of painting. **3** informal cosmetic make-up. **4** Basketball a rectangular area marked near the basket at

each end of a court. **5** Computing the function or capability of producing graphics. ■ v. **1** apply paint to. ▸ apply (a liquid) to a surface with a brush. ▸ (**paint something out**) efface something with paint. **2** depict or produce with paint. ▸ give a description of (something). **3** Computing create (a graphic or screen display) using a paint program. **4** display a mark representing (an aircraft or vehicle) on a radar screen.
- PHRASES **paint the town red** informal go out and enjoy oneself flamboyantly.
- DERIVATIVES **paintable** adj.
- ORIGIN Middle English: from *peint* 'painted', from Old French *peindre*, from Latin *pingere* 'to paint'.

paintball ■ n. **1** a game in which participants simulate military combat, shooting capsules of paint at each other with air guns. **2** such a capsule of paint.

paintbox ■ n. a box holding a palette of dry paints for painting pictures.

paintbrush ■ n. a brush for applying paint.

painted lady ■ n. **1** a migratory butterfly with predominantly orange-brown wings and darker markings. [*Cynthia cardui* and related species.] **2** South African term for some species of GLADIOLUS.

painter[1] ■ n. **1** an artist who paints pictures. **2** a person who paints buildings.
- ORIGIN Middle English: from Anglo-Norman French *peintour*, from Latin *pictor*, from *pingere* 'to paint'.

painter[2] ■ n. a rope attached to the bow of a boat for tying it to a quay.
- ORIGIN Middle English: cf. Old French *pentoir* 'something from which to hang things'.

painterly ■ adj. of or appropriate to a painter; artistic.
- DERIVATIVES **painterliness** n.

painting ■ n. **1** the action or process of painting. **2** a painted picture.

paint shop ■ n. the part of a factory where goods are painted, typically by spraying.

paintwork ■ n. painted surfaces in a building or on a vehicle.

pair ■ n. **1** a set of two things used together or regarded as a unit. **2** an article consisting of two joined or corresponding parts. **3** two people or animals related in some way or considered together. ■ v. join or connect to form a pair. ▸ (**pair off/up**) form a couple.
- DERIVATIVES **paired** adj. **pairing** n. **pairwise** adj. & adv.
- ORIGIN Middle English: from Old French *paire*, from Latin *paria* 'equal things', from *par* 'equal'.

paisley /ˈpeɪzli/ ■ n. a distinctive intricate pattern of curved feather-shaped figures based on an Indian pine cone design.
- ORIGIN C19: named after the town of *Paisley* in Scotland, place of manufacture of a woven woollen cloth orig. incorporating this design.

pajamas ■ pl. n. US spelling of PYJAMAS.

pak choi /pak ˈtʃɔɪ/ (also **bok choy**) ■ n. a Chinese cabbage of a variety with smooth-edged tapering leaves.
- ORIGIN from Chinese (Cantonese dialect) *paâk ts'oi* 'white vegetable'.

Pakeha /ˈpɑːkɪhɑː/ ■ n. NZ a white New Zealander, as opposed to a Maori.
- ORIGIN from Maori.

Paki ■ n. (pl. **Pakis**) Brit. informal, offensive a Pakistani.
- ORIGIN 1960s: abbrev.

Pakistani /ˌpɑːkɪˈstɑːni, ˌpakɪ-, -ˈstani/ ■ n. a native or inhabitant of Pakistan. ■ adj. of or relating to Pakistan or Pakistanis.

pakora /pəˈkɔːrə/ ■ n. (in Indian cookery) a piece of meat or vegetable coated in batter and deep-fried.
- ORIGIN from Hindi *pakoṛā*, denoting a dish of vegetables in gram flour.

pa kua (also **ba gua**) ■ n. **1** a Chinese religious motif incorporating the eight trigrams of the I Ching, arranged around a symbol denoting the balance of yin and yang. **2** a Chinese martial art in which movements are focused on a circle and the defence of eight points around it.
- ORIGIN from Chinese *pa* 'eight' + *kwa* 'symbol, trigram'.

PAL ■ n. the television broadcasting system used in South Africa, Australia, and most of Europe.
- ORIGIN acronym from *Phase Alternate Line* (so named because the colour information in alternate lines is inverted in phase).

pal informal ■ n. a friend. ■ v. (**palled**, **palling**) (**pal up**) form a friendship.
- ORIGIN C17: from Romany, 'brother, mate', from Sanskrit *bhrātṛ* 'brother'.

palace ■ n. a large, impressive building forming the official residence of a sovereign, president, archbishop, etc.
- ORIGIN Middle English: from Old French *paleis*, from Latin *Palatium*, the name of the Palatine hill in ancient Rome, where the house of the emperor was situated.

palace revolution (also **palace coup**) ■ n. the non-violent overthrow of a sovereign or government by senior officials within the ruling group.

paladin /ˈpalədɪn/ ■ n. historical a knight renowned for heroism and chivalry.
- ORIGIN C16: from French *paladin*, from Latin *palatinus* (see PALATINE).

Palaearctic /ˌpalɪˈɑːktɪk, ˌpeɪ-/ (also chiefly US **Palearctic**) ■ adj. Zoology of or denoting a region comprising Eurasia north of the Himalayas, together with North Africa and the temperate part of the Arabian peninsula.

palaeo- /ˈpalɪəʊ, ˈpeɪlɪəʊ/ (US **paleo-**) ■ comb. form older or ancient, especially relating to the geological past: *Palaeolithic.*
- ORIGIN from Greek *palaios* 'ancient'.

palaeoanthropology (US **paleoanthropology**) ■ n. the branch of anthropology concerned with fossil hominids.
- DERIVATIVES **palaeoanthropological** adj. **palaeoanthropologist** n.

palaeobiology (US **paleobiology**) ■ n. the biology of fossil animals and plants.
- DERIVATIVES **palaeobiological** adj. **palaeobiologist** n.

palaeobotany (US **paleobotany**) ■ n. the study of fossil plants.
- DERIVATIVES **palaeobotanical** adj. **palaeobotanist** n.

Palaeocene /ˈpalɪə(ʊ)siːn, ˈpeɪ-/ (US **Paleocene**) ■ adj. Geology relating to or denoting the earliest epoch of the Tertiary period (between the Cretaceous period and the Eocene epoch, about 65 to 56.5 million years ago), a time of rapid development of mammals.
- ORIGIN C19: from PALAEO- + Greek *kainos* 'new'.

palaeoclimate (US **paleoclimate**) ■ n. a climate prevalent at a particular time in the geological past.
- DERIVATIVES **palaeoclimatic** adj. **palaeoclimatologist** n. **palaeoclimatology** n.

palaeoecology (US **paleoecology**) ■ n. the ecology of fossil animals and plants.
- DERIVATIVES **palaeoecological** adj. **palaeoecologist** n.

Palaeogene /ˈpalɪə(ʊ)dʒiːn, ˈpeɪ-/ (US **Paleogene**) ■ adj. Geology relating to or denoting the earlier division of the Tertiary period (comprising the Palaeocene, Eocene, and Oligocene epochs, from about 65 to 23.3 million years ago).
- ORIGIN C19: from PALAEO- + Greek *genēs* (see -GEN).

palaeogeography (US **paleogeography**) ■ n. the study of geographical features at periods in the geological past.
- DERIVATIVES **palaeogeographer** n. **palaeogeographical** adj.

palaeography /ˌpalɪˈɒɡrəfi, peɪ-/ (US **paleography**) ■ n. the study of ancient writing systems and the deciphering and dating of historical manuscripts.
- DERIVATIVES **palaeographer** n. **palaeographic** adj. **palaeographical** /-əˈɡrafɪk(ə)l/ adj. **palaeographically** adv.

Palaeolithic /ˌpalɪə(ʊ)ˈlɪθɪk, ˌpeɪ-/ (US **Paleolithic**) ■ adj. Archaeology relating to or denoting the early phase of the Stone Age, up to the end of the glacial period.
- ORIGIN C19: from PALAEO- + Greek *lithos* 'stone'.

palaeomagnetism (US **paleomagnetism**) ■ n. the branch of geophysics concerned with the magnetism in rocks that was induced by the earth's magnetic field at the time of their formation.
- DERIVATIVES **palaeomagnetic** adj.

palaeontology

palaeontology /ˌpalɪɒnˈtɒlədʒi, ˌpeɪ-/ (US **paleontology**) ■ n. the branch of science concerned with fossil animals and plants.
– DERIVATIVES **palaeontological** adj. **palaeontologist** n.
– ORIGIN C19: from PALAEO- + Greek *onta* 'beings' + -LOGY.

palaeosol /ˈpalɪə(ʊ)sɒl, ˈpeɪ-/ (US **paleosol**) ■ n. Geology a stratum or soil horizon which was formed as a soil in a past geological age.

Palaeotropical (US **Paleotropical**) ■ adj. Botany & Zoology relating to or denoting a region including the tropical parts of the Old World.

Palaeozoic /ˌpalɪə(ʊ)ˈzəʊɪk, ˌpeɪ-/ (US **Paleozoic**) ■ adj. Geology relating to or denoting the era between the Precambrian aeon and the Mesozoic era, about 570 to 245 million years ago.
– ORIGIN C19: from PALAEO- + Greek *zōē* 'life'.

palanquin /ˌpalənˈkiːn/ ■ n. (in India and the East) a covered litter for one passenger, carried on two horizontal poles by four or six bearers.
– ORIGIN C16: from Portuguese *palanquim*, from Sanskrit *palyanka* 'bed, couch'.

palapa /pəˈlapə/ ■ n. a traditional Mexican shelter roofed with palm leaves or branches.
– ORIGIN Mexican Spanish, denoting the palm *Orbignya cohune*.

palatable /ˈpalətəb(ə)l/ ■ adj. 1 pleasant to taste. 2 (of an action or proposal) acceptable.
– DERIVATIVES **palatability** n. **palatably** adv.

palatal /ˈpalət(ə)l/ ■ adj. 1 of or relating to the palate. 2 Phonetics (of a speech sound) made by placing the blade of the tongue against or near the hard palate (e.g. *y* in *yes*). ■ n. Phonetics a palatal sound.
– DERIVATIVES **palatalization** (also **-isation**) n. **palatally** adv.

palate ■ n. 1 the roof of the mouth, separating the cavities of the mouth and nose in vertebrates. 2 a person's ability to distinguish between and appreciate different flavours. 3 the flavour of a wine or beer.
– ORIGIN Middle English: from Latin *palatum*.

palatial ■ adj. resembling a palace, especially in being spacious or grand.
– DERIVATIVES **palatially** adv.
– ORIGIN C18: from Latin *palatium* (see PALACE).

palatinate /pəˈlatɪnət/ ■ n. historical a territory under the jurisdiction of a Count Palatine.

palatine /ˈpalətʌɪn, -tɪn/ ■ adj. chiefly historical (of an official or feudal lord) having local authority that elsewhere belongs only to a sovereign.
– ORIGIN Middle English: from French *palatin(e)*, from Latin *palatinus* 'of the palace'.

palaver /pəˈlɑːvə/ ■ n. 1 informal prolonged and tedious fuss or discussion. 2 dated a parley or improvised conference between two sides.
– ORIGIN C18: from Portuguese *palavra* 'word'.

palazzo /pəˈlatsəʊ/ ■ n. (pl. **palazzos** or **palazzi** /-tsi/) a palatial building, especially in Italy.
– ORIGIN Italian, 'palace'.

palazzo pants ■ pl. n. women's loose wide-legged trousers.

pale[1] ■ adj. 1 containing little colour or pigment; light in colour or shade. ▶ (of a person's face) having little colour, typically as a result of shock, fear, or ill health. 2 unimpressive or inferior: *a pale imitation*. ■ v. 1 become pale in one's face. 2 seem or become less important.
– DERIVATIVES **palely** adv. **paleness** n. **palish** adj.
– ORIGIN Middle English: from Old French *pale*, from Latin *pallidus*.

pale[2] ■ n. 1 a wooden stake used with others to form a fence. 2 a boundary: *within the pale of decency*. 3 Heraldry a broad vertical stripe down the middle of a shield.
– PHRASES **beyond the pale** outside the bounds of acceptable behaviour.

HISTORY

Pale entered Middle English from the Old French word *pal*, from Latin *palus* 'stake'. The idea of a stake forming part of a fence or boundary led to the development of the phrase **beyond the pale**. The term **Pale** was applied to various English-controlled territories, in particular to the area of Ireland under English jurisdiction before the 16th century. The earliest reference (1547) to the **Pale** in Ireland as such draws the contrast between the English Pale and the 'wyld Irysh': the area *beyond the pale* would have been regarded as dangerous and uncivilized by the English.

Palearctic ■ adj. chiefly US variant spelling of PALAEARCTIC.

paleface ■ n. a name supposedly used by North American Indians for a white person.

paleo- ■ comb. form US spelling of PALAEO-.

Palestinian /ˌpalɪˈstɪnɪən/ ■ adj. of or relating to Palestine or its peoples. ■ n. a member of the native Arab population of Palestine.

palette /ˈpalɪt/ ■ n. 1 a thin board or other surface on which an artist lays and mixes colours. 2 the range of colours used by a particular artist or at a particular time. 3 the range or variety of tonal or instrumental colour in a musical piece.
– ORIGIN C18: from French, diminutive of *pale* 'shovel', from Latin *pala* 'spade'.

palette knife ■ n. 1 a thin steel blade with a handle for mixing colours or applying or removing paint. 2 a kitchen knife or spatula with a long, blunt, flexible, round-ended blade.

palfrey /ˈpɔːlfri, ˈpal-/ ■ n. (pl. **-eys**) archaic a docile horse used for ordinary riding, especially by women.
– ORIGIN Middle English: from Old French *palefrei*, from medieval Latin *palefredus*, from Greek *para* 'beside, extra' + Latin *veredus* 'light horse'.

Pali /ˈpɑːliː/ ■ n. an Indic language, closely related to Sanskrit, which developed in northern India in the 5th–2nd centuries BC.
– ORIGIN from Pali *pāli*(-*bhāsā*) 'canonical texts'.

palimony /ˈpalɪməni/ ■ n. informal, chiefly N. Amer. compensation made by one member of an unmarried couple to the other after separation.
– ORIGIN 1970s: from PAL + a shortened form of ALIMONY.

palimpsest /ˈpalɪm(p)sɛst/ ■ n. 1 a parchment or other surface in which later writing has been superimposed on effaced earlier writing. 2 something bearing visible traces of an earlier form.
– ORIGIN C17: from Greek *palimpsēstos*, from *palin* 'again' + *psēstos* 'rubbed smooth'.

palindrome /ˈpalɪndrəʊm/ ■ n. a word or sequence that reads the same backwards as forwards, e.g. *madam*.
– DERIVATIVES **palindromic** /-ˈdrɒmɪk/ adj. **palindromist** n.
– ORIGIN C17: from Greek *palindromos* 'running back again'.

paling /ˈpeɪlɪŋ/ ■ n. a fence made from stakes. ▶ a stake used in such a fence.

palinode /ˈpalɪnəʊd/ ■ n. a poem in which the poet retracts a view or sentiment expressed in a former poem.
– ORIGIN C16: from Greek *palinōidia*, from *palin* 'again' + *ōidē* 'song'.

palisade /ˌpalɪˈseɪd/ ■ n. 1 a fence of stakes or iron railings, forming an enclosure or defence. 2 (**palisades**) US a line of high cliffs. ■ v. [usu. as adj. **palisaded**] enclose or provide with a palisade.
– ORIGIN C17: from French *palissade*, from Provençal, from *palissa* 'paling'.

palisade layer ■ n. Botany a layer of parallel elongated cells below the epidermis of a leaf.

pall[1] /pɔːl/ ■ n. 1 a cloth spread over a coffin, hearse, or tomb. 2 a dark cloud of smoke, dust, etc. 3 an enveloping air of gloom or fear. 4 an ecclesiastical pallium. ▶ Heraldry a Y-shaped charge representing the front of an ecclesiastical pallium.
– ORIGIN Old English *pæll* 'rich (purple) cloth, cloth cover for a chalice', from Latin *pallium* 'covering, cloak'.

pall[2] /pɔːl/ ■ v. become less appealing or interesting through familiarity.
– ORIGIN Middle English: shortening of APPAL.

Palladian /pəˈleɪdɪən/ ■ adj. in or denoting the neoclassical style of the 16th-century Italian architect Andrea Palladio, influential also in the 18th century.
– DERIVATIVES **Palladianism** n.

palladium /pəˈleɪdɪəm/ ■ n. the chemical element of atomic number 46, a rare silvery-white metal resembling platinum. (Symbol: **Pd**)
– ORIGIN C19: from *Pallas*, an asteroid discovered (1803) just before the element.

pall-bearer ■ n. a person helping to carry or officially escorting a coffin at a funeral.

pallet[1] ■ n. **1** a straw mattress. **2** a crude or makeshift bed.
– ORIGIN Middle English: from Anglo-Norman French *paillete*, from *paille* 'straw'.

pallet[2] ■ n. **1** a portable platform on which goods can be moved, stacked, and stored. **2** a flat wooden blade with a handle, used to shape clay or plaster. **3** an artist's palette. **4** a projection on a machine part, serving to change the mode of motion of a wheel.
– DERIVATIVES **palletize** (also **-ise**) v.
– ORIGIN Middle English: from French *palette* 'little blade', from Latin *pala* 'spade'.

pallet[3] ■ n. Heraldry a narrow vertical strip usually borne in groups of two or three.
– ORIGIN C15: diminutive of **PALE**[2].

pallia plural form of **PALLIUM**.

palliasse /ˈpalɪəs/ ■ n. a straw mattress.
– ORIGIN C16: from French *paillasse*.

palliate /ˈpalɪeɪt/ ■ v. **1** make (the symptoms of a disease) less severe without removing the cause. **2** mitigate or disguise (something bad).
– DERIVATIVES **palliation** n.
– ORIGIN Middle English: from late Latin *palliare* 'to cloak', from *pallium* 'cloak'.

palliative /ˈpalɪətɪv/ ■ adj. relieving pain or alleviating a problem without dealing with the cause. ■ n. a palliative remedy or medicine.
– DERIVATIVES **palliatively** adv.

pallid ■ adj. **1** pale, especially because of poor health. **2** feeble or insipid.
– DERIVATIVES **pallidly** adv. **pallidness** n.
– ORIGIN C16: from Latin *pallidus* 'pale'.

pallium /ˈpalɪəm/ ■ n. (pl. **pallia** /-lɪə/ or **palliums**) **1** a woollen vestment conferred by the Pope on an archbishop, consisting of a narrow circular band placed round the shoulders with a short lappet hanging from front and back. **2** a man's large rectangular cloak worn in antiquity.
– ORIGIN Middle English: from Latin, 'covering'.

pall-mall /palˈmal/ ■ n. a 16th- and 17th-century game in which a ball was driven through an iron ring suspended at the end of a long alley.
– ORIGIN from obsolete French *pallemaille*, from Italian *pallamaglio*, from *palla* 'ball' + *maglio* 'mallet'.

pallor ■ n. an unhealthy pale appearance.
– ORIGIN Middle English: from Latin, from *pallere* 'be pale'.

pally ■ adj. (**-ier**, **-iest**) informal having a close, friendly relationship.

palm[1] ■ n. **1** (also **palm tree**) an unbranched evergreen tree with a crown of very long feathered or fan-shaped leaves, growing in tropical and warm regions. [Family Palmae: numerous species.] **2** a leaf of a palm awarded as a prize or viewed as a symbol of victory.
– ORIGIN Old English *palm(a)*, of Germanic origin, from Latin *palma* 'palm (of a hand)', its leaf being likened to a spread hand.

palm[2] ■ n. **1** the inner surface of the hand between the wrist and fingers. **2** the palmate part of a deer's antler. ■ v. **1** conceal (a small object) in the hand, especially as part of a trick. ▶ (**palm something off**) sell or dispose of something by misrepresentation or fraud.
▶ (**palm someone off**) informal persuade someone to accept something by deception. **2** deflect (a ball) with the palm of the hand.
– PHRASES **in the palm of one's hand** under one's control or influence. **read someone's palm** tell someone's fortune by looking at the lines on their palm.
– DERIVATIVES **palmar** /ˈpalmə/ adj. **-palmed** adj. **palmful** n. (pl. **-fuls**)

– ORIGIN Middle English: from Old French *paume*, from Latin *palma*.

palmate /ˈpalmeɪt/ ■ adj. chiefly Botany & Zoology shaped like an open hand with a number of lobes resembling fingers.
– DERIVATIVES **palmated** adj.
– ORIGIN C18: from Latin *palmatus*, from *palma* (see **PALM**[2]).

palmcorder ■ n. a small, hand-held camcorder.

palmer ■ n. **1** historical a pilgrim, especially one who had returned from the Holy Land with a palm branch or leaf as a sign of having undertaken the pilgrimage. **2** a hairy artificial fly used in angling.
– ORIGIN Middle English: from medieval Latin *palmarius* 'pilgrim', from Latin *palma* 'palm'.

palmetto /palˈmɛtəʊ/ ■ n. (pl. **-os**) an American fan palm. [*Sabal palmetto* and other species.]
– ORIGIN C16: from Spanish *palmito* 'small palm'.

palmier /ˈpalmɪeɪ/ ■ n. (pl. pronounced same) a sweet crisp pastry shaped like a palm leaf.
– ORIGIN French, 'palm tree'.

palmiet /ˈpalmɪt/ ■ n. a southern African reed with a woody stem topped by a cluster of long serrated leaves. [*Prionium serratum.*]
– ORIGIN from Dutch, from Portuguese and Spanish *palmito*, diminutive of *palma* 'palm'.

palmistry ■ n. the art or practice of supposedly interpreting a person's character or predicting their future by examining the hand.
– DERIVATIVES **palmist** n.
– ORIGIN Middle English: from **PALM**[2] + *-estry*, later altered to *-istry*.

Palm Sunday ■ n. the Sunday before Easter, on which Christ's entry into Jerusalem is celebrated in many Christian churches by processions in which branches of palms are carried.

palmtop ■ n. a computer small and light enough to be held in one hand.

palm wine ■ n. an alcoholic drink made from fermented palm sap.

palmy ■ adj. (**-ier**, **-iest**) **1** comfortable and prosperous. **2** covered with palms.

palmyra ■ n. an Asian fan palm which yields wood, fibre, and fruit. [*Borassus flabellifer.*]
– ORIGIN C17: from Portuguese *palmeira* 'palm tree', associated with the name of the ancient city of *Palmyra*.

palomino /ˌpaləˈmiːnəʊ/ ■ n. (pl. **-os**) **1** a pale golden or tan-coloured horse with a white mane and tail, originally bred in the south-western US. **2** a variety of white grape used to make sherry and fortified wines.
– ORIGIN C20: from Spanish *palomino* 'young pigeon'.

palooka /pəˈluːkə/ ■ n. informal a lout.
– ORIGIN 1920s.

palp /palp/ ■ n. Zoology each of a pair of elongated segmented appendages near the mouth of an arthropod, usually concerned with the senses of touch and taste.
– ORIGIN C19: from Latin *palpus*, from *palpare* 'to feel'.

palpable /ˈpalpəb(ə)l/ ■ adj. **1** able to be touched or felt. **2** plain to see or comprehend: *a palpable sense of loss*.
– DERIVATIVES **palpability** n. **palpably** adv.
– ORIGIN Middle English: from late Latin *palpabilis*, from Latin *palpare* 'feel, touch gently'.

palpate /ˈpalpeɪt/ ■ v. examine (a part of the body) by touch, especially for medical purposes.
– DERIVATIVES **palpation** n.
– ORIGIN C19 (*palpation* C15): from Latin *palpare* 'touch gently'.

palpitate /ˈpalpɪteɪt/ ■ v. [often as adj. **palpitating**] **1** (of the heart) beat rapidly, strongly, or irregularly. **2** shake; tremble.
– ORIGIN C17 (*palpitation* Middle English): from Latin *palpitare*, from *palpare* 'touch gently'.

palpitation ■ n. (usu. **palpitations**) a noticeably rapid, strong, or irregular heartbeat due to agitation, exertion, or illness.

palsy /ˈpɔːlzi, ˈpɒl-/ ■ n. (pl. **-ies**) dated paralysis, especially

paltry

when accompanied by involuntary tremors. ■ v. (**be palsied**) be affected with palsy.
– ORIGIN Middle English: from Old French *paralisie*, from Latin *paralysis* (see PARALYSIS).

paltry ■ adj. (**-ier, -iest**) **1** (of an amount) very small or meagre. **2** petty; trivial.
– DERIVATIVES **paltriness** n.
– ORIGIN C16: apparently based on dialect *pelt* 'rubbish'.

Paludrine /ˈpaljʊdrɪn, -iːn/ ■ n. trademark for PROGUANIL.

paly /ˈpeɪli/ ■ adj. Heraldry divided into equal vertical stripes.
– ORIGIN Middle English: from Old French *pale* 'divided by stakes', from *pal* 'pale, stake'.

palynology /ˌpalɪˈnɒlədʒi/ ■ n. the study of pollen grains and other spores, especially as found in archaeological or geological deposits.
– DERIVATIVES **palynological** adj. **palynologist** n.
– ORIGIN 1940s: from Greek *palunein* 'sprinkle' + -LOGY.

pampas /ˈpampəs, -z/ ■ n. [treated as sing. or pl.] large treeless plains in South America.
– ORIGIN C18: from Quechua *pampa* 'plain'.

pampas grass ■ n. a tall South American grass with silky flowering plumes. [*Cortaderia selloana*.]

pamper ■ v. indulge (someone) with a great deal of attention and comfort; spoil.
– ORIGIN Middle English: prob. of Low German or Dutch origin.

pamphlet /ˈpamflɪt/ ■ n. a small booklet or leaflet containing information or arguments about a single subject. ■ v. (**pamphleted, pamphleting**) distribute pamphlets to.
– ORIGIN Middle English: from *Pamphilet*, the familiar name of the C12 Latin love poem *Pamphilus, seu de Amore*.

pamphleteer ■ n. a writer of pamphlets, especially controversial political ones.
– DERIVATIVES **pamphleteering** n.

pan[1] /pan/ ■ n. **1** a metal container for cooking food in. **2** a bowl fitted at either end of a pair of scales. **3** a shallow bowl in which gravel and mud is shaken and washed by people seeking gold. **4** Brit. the bowl of a toilet. **5** a hollow in the ground in which water collects or in which a deposit of salt remains after evaporation. **6** a part of the lock that held the priming in old types of gun. **7** a hard stratum of compacted soil. **8** a steel drum. ■ v. (**panned, panning**) **1** informal criticize severely. **2** wash gravel in a pan to separate out (gold). **3** (**pan out**) end up or conclude, especially in a good way.
– PHRASES **go down the pan** informal reach a stage of abject failure or uselessness.
– DERIVATIVES **panful** n. (pl. **-fuls**).
– ORIGIN Old English *panne*, of West Germanic origin, perhaps from Latin *patina* 'dish'.

pan[2] /pan/ ■ v. (**panned, panning**) swing (a video or film camera) in a horizontal or vertical plane to give a panoramic effect or follow a subject. ■ n. a panning movement.
– PHRASES **pan and scan** a technique for narrowing the aspect ratio of a widescreen film to fit a television screen by continuously selecting the most significant portion of the original picture.
– ORIGIN C20: abbrev. of PANORAMA.

pan[3] /pɑːn/ ■ n. variant spelling of PAAN.

pan- ■ comb. form including everything or everyone, especially in relation to the whole of a continent, people, etc.: *pan-African*.
– ORIGIN from Greek *pan*, from *pas* 'all'.

panacea /ˌpanəˈsiːə/ ■ n. a solution or remedy for all difficulties or diseases.
– ORIGIN C16: from Greek *panakeia*, from *panakēs* 'all-healing'.

panache /pəˈnaʃ/ ■ n. flamboyant confidence of style or manner.
– ORIGIN C16: from Italian *pennacchio*, from late Latin *pinnaculum*, diminutive of *pinna* 'feather'.

pan-Africanism ■ n. the principle or advocacy of the political union of all the indigenous inhabitants of Africa.
– DERIVATIVES **pan-African** adj. **pan-Africanist** n. & adj.

panama ■ n. a man's wide-brimmed hat of straw-like material, originally made from the leaves of a tropical palm tree.
– ORIGIN C19: named after the country of *Panama*.

Panamanian /ˌpanəˈmeɪnɪən/ ■ n. a native or inhabitant of Panama. ■ adj. of or relating to Panama.

pan-Americanism ■ n. the principle or advocacy of cooperation among all the countries of North and South America.
– DERIVATIVES **pan-American** adj.

pan-Arabism ■ n. the principle or advocacy of political alliance or union of all the Arab states.
– DERIVATIVES **pan-Arab** adj.

panatella /ˌpanəˈtɛlə/ ■ n. a long thin cigar.
– ORIGIN C19: from Latin American Spanish *panatela*, denoting a long thin biscuit.

pancake ■ n. **1** a thin, flat cake of batter, fried and turned in a pan and typically rolled up with a sweet or savoury filling. **2** theatrical make-up consisting of a flat solid layer of compressed powder. ■ v. informal flatten or become flattened.
– PHRASES (**as**) **flat as a pancake** completely flat.

Pancake Day ■ n. Shrove Tuesday, when pancakes are traditionally eaten.

pancetta /panˈ(t)ʃɛtə/ ■ n. Italian cured belly of pork.
– ORIGIN Italian, diminutive of *pancio* 'belly'.

Panchen Lama /ˌpantʃ(ə)n ˈlɑːmə/ ■ n. a Tibetan lama ranking next after the Dalai Lama.
– ORIGIN Tibetan *panchen*, abbrev. of *pandi-tachen-po* 'great learned one'.

panchromatic ■ adj. denoting black-and-white photographic film sensitive to all visible colours of the spectrum.

pancreas /ˈpaŋkrɪəs/ ■ n. (pl. **pancreases**) a large gland behind the stomach which secretes digestive enzymes into the duodenum.
– DERIVATIVES **pancreatic** adj.
– ORIGIN C16: from Greek *pankreas*, from *pan* 'all' + *kreas* 'flesh'.

pancreatectomy /ˌpaŋkrɪəˈtɛktəmi/ ■ n. (pl. **-ies**) surgical removal of the pancreas.

pancreatin /ˈpaŋkrɪətɪn/ ■ n. a mixture of pancreatic enzymes obtained from animals, given as a medicine to aid digestion.

pancreatitis /ˌpaŋkrɪəˈtʌɪtɪs/ ■ n. Medicine inflammation of the pancreas.

panda /ˈpandə/ ■ n. **1** (also **giant panda**) a large bear-like black-and-white mammal native to bamboo forests in China. [*Ailuropoda melanoleuca*.] **2** (also **red panda**) a Himalayan raccoon-like mammal with thick reddish-brown fur and a bushy tail. [*Ailurus fulgens*.]
– ORIGIN C19: from Nepali.

panda car ■ n. Brit. informal a small police patrol car (originally black and white or blue and white).

pandanus /panˈdeɪnəs, -ˈdan-/ ■ n. a tropical tree or shrub with a twisted stem, long, narrow spiny leaves that yield fibre, and fibrous edible fruit. [Genus *Pandanus*.]
– ORIGIN from Malay *pandan*.

pandemic /panˈdɛmɪk/ ■ adj. (of a disease) prevalent over a whole country or large part of the world. ■ n. an outbreak of such a disease.
– ORIGIN C17: from Greek *pandēmos*, from *pan* 'all' + *dēmos* 'people'.

pandemonium /ˌpandɪˈməʊnɪəm/ ■ n. wild and noisy disorder or confusion; uproar.
– ORIGIN C17 (denoting the place of all demons, in Milton's *Paradise Lost*): from PAN- + Greek *daimōn* 'demon'.

pander ■ v. (**pander to**) gratify or indulge (an immoral or distasteful desire or habit). ■ n. **1** dated a pimp or procurer. **2** archaic a person who panders to the desires of another.
– ORIGIN Middle English: from *Pandare*, the name of a character in Chaucer's *Troilus and Criseyde*.

pandit (also **pundit**) ■ n. a Hindu scholar learned in Sanskrit and Hindu philosophy and religion.

Pandora's box ■ n. a process that once begun generates many complicated problems.
– ORIGIN from *Pandora* in Greek mythology, who was sent to earth with a jar or box of evils and contrary to instructions opened it, letting out all the evils to infect the earth; hope alone remained.

pane ■ n. **1** a single sheet of glass in a window or door. **2** a sheet or page of stamps.
– ORIGIN Middle English: from Old French *pan*, from Latin *pannus* 'piece of cloth'.

panegyric /ˌpanɪˈdʒɪrɪk/ ■ n. a speech or text in praise of someone or something.
– DERIVATIVES **panegyrical** adj.
– ORIGIN C17: from French *panégyrique*, from Greek *panēgurikos* 'of public assembly'.

panegyrize /ˈpanɪdʒɪrʌɪz/ (also **-ise**) ■ v. speak or write in praise of; eulogize.
– DERIVATIVES **panegyrist** n.

panel ■ n. **1** a distinct section, typically rectangular, forming part of or set into a door, vehicle, garment, etc. ▸ a decorated area within a larger design containing a separate subject. **2** a flat board on which instruments or controls are fixed. **3** a small group of people brought together to investigate or decide upon a particular matter. ▸ chiefly N. Amer. a list of available jurors or a jury. ■ v. (**panelled, panelling**; US **paneled, paneling**) [usu. as adj. **panelled**] cover (a wall or other surface) with panels.
– DERIVATIVES **panelling** n.
– ORIGIN Middle English: from Latin *pannus* '(piece of) cloth'.

panel beater ■ n. a person whose job is to beat out the bodywork of motor vehicles.

panel game ■ n. a broadcast quiz played by a panel or team of people.

panellist (US **panelist**) ■ n. a member of a panel, especially in a broadcast game or discussion.

panel pin ■ n. a light, thin nail with a very small head.

panel saw ■ n. a light saw with small teeth, for cutting thin wood.

panel truck ■ n. N. Amer. a small enclosed delivery truck.

panettone /ˌpanɪˈtəʊneɪ, -niː/ ■ n. (pl. **panettoni** /ˌpanɪˈtəʊniː/) a rich Italian bread made with eggs, fruit, and butter, eaten at Christmas.
– ORIGIN Italian, from *panetto* 'cake', diminutive of *pane* 'bread'.

pan-fry ■ v. [often as adj. **pan-fried**] fry in a pan in shallow fat.

pang ■ n. a sudden sharp pain or painful emotion.
– ORIGIN C15: perhaps an alteration of **PRONG**.

panga[1] /ˈpaŋɡə/ ■ n. a bladed African tool like a machete.
– ORIGIN from Kiswahili.

panga[2] ■ n. a sea bream fished commercially off the south-eastern coast of South Africa. [*Pterogymnus laniarius*.]
– ORIGIN prob. from Malay *ikan pangerang*.

pan-Germanism ■ n. the principle or advocacy of a political unification of all Europeans speaking German or a Germanic language.
– DERIVATIVES **pan-German** adj. **pan-Germanic** adj.

Pangloss /ˈpaŋɡlɒs/ ■ n. a person who is optimistic regardless of the circumstances.
– DERIVATIVES **Panglossian** adj.
– ORIGIN C19: from the name of the tutor and philosopher in Voltaire's *Candide* (1759).

pangolin /paŋˈɡəʊlɪn/ ■ n. an insectivorous mammal whose body is covered with horny overlapping scales. [Genus *Manus*.]
– ORIGIN C18: from Malay *peng-guling* 'roller' (from its habit of rolling into a ball).

panhandle ■ n. a narrow strip of territory projecting from the main territory of one state into another. ■ v. N. Amer. informal beg in the street.
– DERIVATIVES **panhandler** n.

Panhellenism /ˌpanˈhɛlənɪzm, -ˈhiːlɪː-/ ■ n. the principle or advocacy of the political union of all Greeks.
– DERIVATIVES **Panhellenic** adj.

panic[1] ■ n. sudden uncontrollable fear or anxiety, often causing wildly unthinking behaviour. ▸ informal frenzied hurry to do something. ■ v. (**panicked, panicking**) be affected by or cause to feel panic. ▸ (**panic someone into**) drive someone through panic into (hasty or rash action).
– PHRASES **panic stations** informal a state of alarm or emergency.
– DERIVATIVES **panicky** adj.
– ORIGIN C17: from French *panique*, from Greek *panikos*, from the name of the Greek god *Pan*, noted for causing terror.

panic[2] (also **panic grass**) ■ n. a cereal or fodder grass of a group including millet. [*Panicum* and other genera.]
– ORIGIN Middle English: from Latin *panicum*, from *panus* 'ear of millet' (literally 'thread wound on a bobbin'), from Greek *pēnion* 'bobbin'.

panic attack ■ n. a sudden overwhelming feeling of acute and disabling anxiety.

panic button ■ n. a button for summoning help in an emergency.

panicle /ˈpanɪk(ə)l/ ■ n. Botany a loose branching cluster of flowers, as in oats.
– ORIGIN C16: from Latin *panicula*, diminutive of *panus* (see **PANIC**[2]).

Panjabi ■ n. (pl. **Panjabis**) & adj. variant spelling of **PUNJABI**.

panjandrum /panˈdʒandrəm/ ■ n. a person who has or claims to have a great deal of authority or influence.
– ORIGIN C19: from *Grand Panjandrum*, an invented phr. in a nonsense verse (1755) by Samuel Foote.

panne /pan/ ■ n. a shining fabric resembling velvet, made of silk or rayon and having a flattened pile.
– ORIGIN C18: from French.

pannier ■ n. **1** a basket, especially one of a pair carried by a beast of burden. ▸ a bag or box fitted on either side of the rear wheel of a bicycle or motorcycle. **2** historical part of a skirt looped up round the hips and supported on a frame.
– ORIGIN Middle English: from Old French *panier*, from Latin *panarium* 'bread basket'.

panoply /ˈpanəpli/ ■ n. **1** a complete or impressive collection or display of something. **2** historical or poetic/literary a complete set of arms or suit of armour.
– DERIVATIVES **panoplied** adj.
– ORIGIN C16: from French *panoplie*, from Greek.

panopticon /panˈɒptɪk(ə)n/ ■ n. historical a circular prison with cells arranged around a central well, from which prisoners could at all times be observed.
– ORIGIN C18: from **PAN-** + Greek *optikon*, from *optikos* 'optic'.

panorama ■ n. **1** an unbroken view of a surrounding region. **2** a complete survey of a subject or sequence of events.
– DERIVATIVES **panoramic** adj. **panoramically** adv.
– ORIGIN C18: from **PAN-** + Greek *horama* 'view'.

pan-pan ■ n. an international radio distress signal, of less urgency than a mayday signal.
– ORIGIN 1920s: *pan* from French *panne* 'breakdown'.

pan pipes ■ pl. n. a musical instrument made from a row of short pipes of varying length fixed together and played by blowing across the top.
– ORIGIN orig. associated with the Greek rural god *Pan*.

PanSALB /ˈpansalb/ ■ abbrev. Pan South African Language Board.

panstick ■ n. a kind of matt cosmetic foundation in stick form, used in theatrical make-up.
– ORIGIN 1940s: from **PANCAKE** + **STICK**[1].

pansy ■ n. **1** a viola with flowers in rich colours, especially of a cultivated variety. [*Viola tricolor* (wild pansy) and related species and hybrids.] **2** informal, derogatory an effeminate or homosexual man. **3** (also **pansy shell**) S. African (the shell-like skeleton of) a small sea urchin with purple markings that resemble a flower; a sand dollar. [*Echinodiscus bisperforatus*.]
– ORIGIN Middle English: from French *pensée* 'thought, pansy', from *penser* 'think'.

pant ■ v. **1** breathe with short, quick breaths, typically from exertion or excitement. ▸ (usu. **pant for**) long for or

pantaloon

to do something. **2** poetic/literary (of the heart or chest) throb violently from strong emotions. ■ n. a short, quick breath.
– DERIVATIVES **panting** adj.
– ORIGIN Middle English: rel. to Old French *pantaisier* 'be agitated, gasp', from Greek *phantasioun* 'cause to imagine', from *phantasia* (see FANTASY).

pantaloon ■ n. (**pantaloons**) women's baggy trousers gathered at the ankles. ▶ historical men's close-fitting breeches fastened below the calf or at the foot. ▶ informal trousers.
– ORIGIN C16: from French *pantalon*, from the Italian name *Pantalone* 'Pantaloon'.

pantechnicon /panˈtɛknɪk(ə)n/ ■ n. a large van for transporting furniture.
– ORIGIN C19: from PAN- + *tekhnikon* 'piece of art', orig. the name of a London bazaar selling artistic work, later converted into a furniture warehouse.

pantheism /ˈpanθiːɪz(ə)m/ ■ n. a doctrine or belief which identifies God with the universe, or regards the universe as a manifestation of God.
– DERIVATIVES **pantheist** n. **pantheistic** adj.
– ORIGIN C18: from PAN- + Greek *theos* 'god'.

pantheon /ˈpanθɪən/ ■ n. **1** all the gods of a people or religion collectively. **2** an ancient temple dedicated to all the gods. **3** a collection of particularly famous or important people.
– ORIGIN Middle English: from Greek *pantheion*, from *pan* 'all' + *theion* 'holy', from *theos* 'god'.

panther ■ n. **1** a leopard, especially a black one. **2** N. Amer. a puma or a jaguar.
– ORIGIN Middle English: from Latin *panthera*, from Greek *panthēr*.

panties ■ pl. n. informal legless underpants worn by women and girls; knickers.

pantihose ■ pl. n. variant spelling of PANTYHOSE.

pantile /ˈpantʌɪl/ ■ n. a roof tile curved to form an S-shaped section, fitted to overlap its neighbour.
– DERIVATIVES **pantiled** adj.
– ORIGIN C17: from PAN¹ + TILE.

panto ■ n. (pl. **-os**) informal a pantomime.

panto- ■ comb. form all; universal: *pantomime*.
– ORIGIN from Greek *pas*, *pant-* 'all'.

Pantocrator /panˈtɒkrətə/ ■ n. a title of Christ represented as the ruler of the universe, especially in Byzantine church decoration.
– ORIGIN C19: from Greek, 'ruler over all'.

pantograph ■ n. **1** an instrument for copying a plan or drawing on a different scale by a system of hinged and jointed rods. **2** a jointed framework conveying a current to an electric train or tram from overhead wires.
– ORIGIN C18: from PANTO- + Greek *-graphos* 'writing'.

pantomime ■ n. **1** a theatrical entertainment involving music, topical jokes, and slapstick comedy, usually produced around Christmas. **2** a dramatic entertainment in which performers express meaning through gestures accompanied by music. **3** informal a ridiculous or confused action or situation. ■ v. express or represent by extravagant and exaggerated mime.
– DERIVATIVES **pantomimic** adj.
– ORIGIN C16: from Latin *pantomimus*, from Greek *pantomimos* (see PANTO-, MIME).

pantry ■ n. (pl. **-ies**) a small room or cupboard in which food, crockery, and cutlery are kept.
– ORIGIN Middle English: from Anglo-Norman French *panterie*, from *paneter* 'baker', from Latin *panis* 'bread'.

pants ■ pl. n. **1** trousers. **2** Brit. underpants or panties.
– PHRASES **catch someone with their pants** (or **trousers**) **down** informal catch someone in an embarrassingly unprepared state. **fly by the seat of one's pants** informal rely on instinct rather than logic or knowledge. **scare** (or **bore** etc.) **the pants off someone** informal make someone extremely scared, bored, etc.
– ORIGIN C19: abbrev. of *pantaloons* (see PANTALOON).

pantsuit (also **pants suit**) ■ n. chiefly N. Amer. a trouser suit.

pantsula /panˈtsuːlə/ (also **mapantsula**) ■ n. (pl. **pantsulas** or **mapantsula**) S. African **1** informal a fashionable young urban black person. **2** a dance style in which each person performs a solo within a circle of dancers doing a repetitive shuffling step. ▶ the music accompanying this dance.
– ORIGIN from Tsotsitaal.

pantyhose (also **pantihose**) ■ pl. n. women's thin nylon tights.

panzer /ˈpanzə/ ■ n. a German armoured unit.
– ORIGIN from German *Panzer* 'coat of mail'.

pap¹ ■ n. **1** bland soft or semi-liquid food such as that suitable for babies or invalids. **2** (in Africa and the Caribbean) maize porridge. **3** worthless or trivial reading matter or entertainment. ■ adj. S. African informal (of a person) lacking strength; feeble. ▶ (of food) soft; limp. ▶ (of an inflatable object) under-inflated.
– PHRASES **pap and** (or **en**) **vleis** S. African a dish of maize porridge and meat.
– ORIGIN Middle English: prob. from Middle Low German, Middle Dutch *pappe*, prob. from Latin *pappare* 'eat'.

pap² ■ n. archaic or dialect a woman's breast or nipple.
– ORIGIN Middle English: prob. of Scandinavian origin, from a base imitative of the sound of sucking.

papa /pəˈpɑː, ˈpɑːpə/ ■ n. **1** N. Amer or dated one's father. **2** a code word representing the letter P, used in radio communication.
– ORIGIN C17: from French, from Greek *papas*.

papacy /ˈpeɪpəsi/ ■ n. (pl. **-ies**) **1** the office or authority of the Pope. **2** the tenure of office of a pope.
– ORIGIN Middle English: from medieval Latin *papatia*, from *papa* 'pope'.

papain /pəˈpeɪɪn, pəˈpʌɪɪn/ ■ n. a protein-digesting enzyme obtained from unripe papaya fruit, used to tenderize meat and as a food supplement to aid digestion.
– ORIGIN C19: from PAPAYA.

papal /ˈpeɪp(ə)l/ ■ adj. of or relating to a pope or the papacy.
– DERIVATIVES **papally** adv.
– ORIGIN Middle English: from medieval Latin *papalis*, from eccles. Latin *papa* 'bishop (of Rome)'.

papalist chiefly historical ■ n. a supporter of the papacy, especially an advocate of papal supremacy. ■ adj. supporting the papacy.

paparazzo /ˌpapəˈratsəʊ/ ■ n. (pl. **paparazzi** /-tsi/) (usu. **paparazzi**) a freelance photographer who pursues celebrities to get photographs of them.
– ORIGIN C20: from Italian, from the name of a character in Fellini's film *La Dolce Vita* (1960).

papaw /pəˈpɔː/ ■ n. variant spelling of PAWPAW.

papaya /pəˈpʌɪə/ ■ n. **1** a fruit shaped like an elongated melon, with edible orange flesh and small black seeds. **2** the fast-growing tree which bears this fruit, native to warm regions of America. [*Carica papaya*.]
– ORIGIN C16: from Spanish and Portuguese (see PAWPAW).

paper ■ n. **1** material manufactured in thin sheets from the pulp of wood or other fibrous substances, used for writing or printing on or as wrapping material. ▶ (**papers**) sheets of paper covered with writing or printing; documents. ▶ [as modifier] officially documented but having no real existence or use: *a paper profit*. **2** a newspaper. **3** a government report or policy document. **4** an essay or dissertation read at a seminar or published in a journal. **5** a set of examination questions to be answered at one session. ▶ the written answers to such questions. **6** theatrical slang free passes of admission to a theatre or other entertainment. ■ v. **1** cover with wallpaper.
▶ (**paper over**) cover (a hole or blemish) with wallpaper.
▶ (**paper over**) disguise (an awkward problem) instead of resolving it. **2** theatrical slang fill (a theatre) by giving out free tickets.
– PHRASES **on paper 1** in writing. **2** in theory rather than in reality.
– DERIVATIVES **paperless** adj. **papery** adj.
– ORIGIN Middle English: from Anglo-Norman French *papir*, from Latin *papyrus* (see PAPYRUS).

paperback ■ n. a book bound in stiff paper or flexible card.

paperbark ■ n. any of several trees with peeling papery bark. [*Acacia sieberiana* and *Albizia tanganyicensis* (Africa), and *Melaleuca* species (Australia).]

CONSONANTS b but d dog f few g get h he j yes k cat l leg m man n no p pen r red

paperboard ■ n. cardboard or pasteboard.

paper boy (or **paper girl**) ■ n. a boy (or girl) who delivers newspapers to people's homes.

paperchase ■ n. 1 Brit. a cross-country race in which the runners follow a trail marked by torn-up paper. 2 informal an excessively bureaucratic procedure.

paper clip ■ n. a piece of bent wire or plastic used for holding several sheets of paper together.

paperhanger ■ n. a person who decorates with wallpaper, especially professionally.

paperknife ■ n. (pl. **paperknives**) a blunt knife used for opening envelopes.

paper money ■ n. money in the form of banknotes.

paper mulberry ■ n. a mulberry tree whose inner bark is used for making paper and tapa cloth. [*Broussonetia papyrifera*.]

paper nautilus ■ n. a small floating octopus, the female of which secretes a thin coiled papery shell in which its eggs are laid. [Genus *Argonauta*.]

paper-pusher ■ n. informal a bureaucrat or menial clerical worker.
– DERIVATIVES **paper-pushing** n. & adj.

paper round (N. Amer. **paper route**) ■ n. a job of regularly delivering newspapers.

paper tape ■ n. paper in the form of a long narrow strip with holes punched in it, used in older computer systems for conveying data or instructions.

paper-thin ■ adj. very thin or insubstantial.

paper tiger ■ n. a person or thing that appears threatening but is ineffectual.

paper trail ■ n. the total amount of written evidence of someone's activities.

paper wasp ■ n. a slender brown wasp which commonly builds papery nests in the overhangs of houses and has a painful sting. [*Polistes fuscatus* and other species.]

paperweight ■ n. a small, heavy object for keeping loose papers in place.

paperwork ■ n. routine work involving written documents such as forms, records, or letters.

papier mâché /ˌpapıeı ˈmaʃeı/ ■ n. a malleable mixture of paper and glue that becomes hard when dry, used to make boxes, ornaments, etc.
– ORIGIN French, 'chewed paper'.

papilla /pəˈpılə/ ■ n. (pl. **papillae** /-liː/) 1 a small rounded protuberance on a part or organ of the body. 2 a small fleshy projection on a plant.
– DERIVATIVES **papillary** adj. **papillate** /ˈpapıleıt, pəˈpılət/ adj. **papillose** /ˈpapıləʊs/ adj.
– ORIGIN C17: from Latin, 'nipple', diminutive of *papula* 'small protuberance'.

papilloma /ˌpapıˈləʊmə/ ■ n. (pl. **papillomas** or **papillomata** /-mətə/) Medicine a small wart-like growth on the skin or on a mucous membrane, derived from the epidermis and usually benign.

papillon /ˈpapılɒn, ˈpapıjõ/ ■ n. a dog of a toy breed with ears suggesting the form of a butterfly.
– ORIGIN C20: from French, 'butterfly', from Latin *papilio(n-)*.

papino ■ n. a variety of small papaya with sweet orange flesh.

papist /ˈpeıpıst/ chiefly derogatory ■ n. 1 a Roman Catholic. 2 another term for **PAPALIST**. ■ adj. Roman Catholic or papalist.
– DERIVATIVES **papism** n. **papistry** n.
– ORIGIN C16: from French *papiste*, from eccles. Latin *papa* 'bishop (of Rome)'.

papoose /pəˈpuːs/ ■ n. chiefly offensive a young North American Indian child.
– ORIGIN C17: from Algonquian *papoos*.

pappardelle /ˌpapɑːˈdɛleı/ ■ pl. n. pasta in the form of broad flat ribbons.
– ORIGIN Italian, from *pappare* 'eat hungrily'.

pappus /ˈpapəs/ ■ n. (pl. **pappi** /-pʌı, -piː/) Botany a tuft of hairs on a seed which assists dispersal by the wind.
– ORIGIN C18: from Greek *pappos*.

pappy¹ ■ n. (pl. **-ies**) a child's word for father.

pappy² ■ adj. of the nature of pap.

paprika /ˈpaprıkə, pəˈpriːkə/ ■ n. a powdered spice with a deep orange-red colour and a mildly pungent flavour, made from certain varieties of sweet pepper.
– ORIGIN C19: from Hungarian.

Pap smear ■ n. 1 a specimen of cellular material taken from the cervix and spread on a microscope slide. 2 (also **Pap test**, **Pap smear test**) a test carried out on a Pap smear to detect cancer of the cervix or womb.
– ORIGIN 1960s: named after the American scientist George N. *Papanicolaou*.

Papuan ■ n. 1 a native or inhabitant of Papua, or of Papua New Guinea. 2 a heterogeneous group of around 750 languages spoken in Papua New Guinea and neighbouring islands. ■ adj. of or relating to Papua or its people or their languages.

papule /ˈpapjuːl/ (also **papula** /-jʊlə/) ■ n. (pl. **papules** or **papulae** /-juliː/) Medicine a small pimple or swelling on the skin, often forming part of a rash.
– DERIVATIVES **papular** adj.
– ORIGIN C18: from Latin *papula*.

papyrus /pəˈpʌırəs/ ■ n. (pl. **papyri** /-rʌı, -riː/ or **papyruses**) 1 a material prepared in ancient Egypt from the pithy stem of a water plant and used in the ancient Mediterranean world for writing or painting on. 2 the tall aquatic sedge from which this material is obtained. [*Cyperus papyrus*.]
– DERIVATIVES **papyrological** adj. **papyrology** n.
– ORIGIN Middle English: from Greek *papuros*.

par ■ n. 1 Golf the number of strokes a first-class player should normally require for a particular hole or course. ▶ a score of this number of strokes at a hole. 2 (usu. in phr. **above**) or **below** or **under par**, or **on a par with**) the usual or expected level or amount. 3 Stock Exchange the face value of a share or other security, as distinct from its market value. ▶ (also **par of exchange**) the recognized value of one country's currency in terms of another's. ■ v. (**parred**, **parring**) Golf play (a hole) in par.
– PHRASES **par for the course** what is normal or expected in any given circumstances.
– ORIGIN C16: from Latin, 'equal', also 'equality'.

par- ■ comb. form variant spelling of **PARA-¹** shortened before a vowel or *h* (as in *paraldehyde*, *parody*, *parhelion*).

par. (also **para.**) ■ abbrev. paragraph.

para /ˈparə/ ■ n. informal a paratrooper.

para-¹ (also **par-**) ■ prefix 1 beside; adjacent to: *parathyroid*. 2 beyond or distinct from, but analogous to: *paramilitary*. 3 Chemistry denoting substitution at diametrically opposite carbon atoms in a benzene ring: *paradichlorobenzene*. Compare with **META-** and **ORTHO-**.
– ORIGIN from Greek *para* 'beside, beyond'.

para-² ■ comb. form denoting something that protects or wards off: *parachute*.
– ORIGIN from the Italian imperative of *parare* 'defend, shield'.

parabat ■ n. S. African a member of the Parachute Battalion of the South African defence forces.

parabiosis /ˌparəbʌıˈəʊsıs/ ■ n. Biology the anatomical joining of two individuals, especially artificially in physiological research.
– DERIVATIVES **parabiotic** adj.
– ORIGIN C20: from **PARA-¹** + Greek *biōsis* 'mode of life'.

parable ■ n. a simple story used to illustrate a moral or spiritual lesson.
– ORIGIN Middle English: from Old French *parabole*, from an eccles. Latin sense 'discourse, allegory' of Latin *parabola* 'comparison', from Greek *parabolē*.

parabola /pəˈrab(ə)lə/ ■ n. (pl. **parabolas** or **parabolae** /-liː/) a symmetrical open plane curve of the kind formed by the intersection of a cone with a plane parallel to its side.
– ORIGIN C16: from Greek *parabolē* 'placing side by side, application', from *ballein* 'to throw'.

parabolic /ˌparəˈbɒlık/ ■ adj. 1 of or like a parabola or part of one. 2 of or expressed in parables.
– DERIVATIVES **parabolical** adj. **parabolically** adv.

paraboloid /pəˈrab(ə)lɔɪd/ ■ n. **1** a solid generated by rotating a parabola about its axis of symmetry. **2** a solid with two or more non-parallel parabolic cross sections.

paracetamol /ˌparəˈsiːtəmɒl, -ˈsɛt-/ ■ n. (pl. same or **paracetamols**) a synthetic compound used to relieve pain and reduce fever.
– ORIGIN 1950s: abbrev. of its chemical name *para-acetylaminophenol*.

parachute ■ n. a cloth canopy which fills with air and allows a person or heavy object attached to it to descend slowly when dropped from a high position, especially in an aircraft. ■ v. drop or cause to drop by parachute.
– DERIVATIVES **parachutist** n.
– ORIGIN C18: from French *para-* 'protection against' + *chute* 'fall'.

Paraclete /ˈparəkliːt/ ■ n. Christian Church the Holy Spirit as advocate or counsellor (John 14:16, 26).
– ORIGIN from Greek *parakletos* 'called in aid'.

parade ■ n. **1** a public procession, especially one celebrating a special day or event. **2** a formal march or gathering of troops for inspection or display. **3** a series or succession: *a parade of celebrities trooped on to his show*. **4** a boastful or ostentatious display. **5** Brit. a public square, promenade, or row of shops. ■ v. **1** walk, march, or display in a parade. **2** display (something) publicly in order to impress or attract attention: *he paraded his knowledge*. **3** (**parade as**) masquerade as.
– DERIVATIVES **parader** n.
– ORIGIN C17: from French, 'a showing', from Latin *parare* 'prepare'.

parade ground ■ n. a place where troops gather for parade.

paradigm /ˈparədʌɪm/ ■ n. **1** technical a typical example, pattern, or model of something. **2** a world view underlying the theories and methodology of a scientific subject. **3** Linguistics a set of items that form mutually exclusive choices in particular syntactic roles. Often contrasted with **SYNTAGM**. **4** Grammar a table of all the inflected forms of a word.
– DERIVATIVES **paradigmatic** /parədɪɡˈmatɪk/ adj. **paradigmatically** adv.
– ORIGIN C15: from Greek *paradeigma*, from *paradeiknunai* 'show side by side'.

paradigm shift ■ n. a fundamental change in approach or underlying assumptions.

paradise /ˈparədʌɪs/ ■ n. **1** (in some religions) heaven. ▶ (**Paradise**) the Garden of Eden. **2** an ideal or idyllic place or state.
– DERIVATIVES **paradisal** adj. **paradisiacal** /-dɪˈsʌɪək(ə)l/ (also **paradisaical** /-dɪˈseɪɪk(ə)l/ or **paradisical** /-ˈdɪsɪk(ə)l/) adj.
– ORIGIN Middle English: from Old French *paradis*, from Greek *paradeisos* 'royal (enclosed) park'.

paradox ■ n. **1** a seemingly absurd or self-contradictory statement or proposition that may in fact be true. ▶ an apparently sound statement or proposition which leads to a logically unacceptable conclusion. **2** a person or thing that combines contradictory features or qualities.
– DERIVATIVES **paradoxical** adj. **paradoxically** adv.
– ORIGIN C16: from Greek *paradoxon* 'contrary (opinion)'.

paraesthesia /ˌparɪsˈθiːzɪə/ (US **paresthesia**) ■ n. (pl. **paraesthesiae** /-ziː/ or **paraesthesias**) Medicine an abnormal sensation, especially 'pins and needles', caused by pressure on or damage to peripheral nerves.
– ORIGIN C19: from **PARA-**[1] + Greek *aisthēsis* 'sensation'.

paraffin ■ n. **1** (also **paraffin wax**) a flammable waxy solid obtained by distilling petroleum or shale and used for sealing and waterproofing and in candles. **2** (also **paraffin oil**) a liquid fuel made similarly, especially kerosene. **3** Chemistry old-fashioned term for **ALKANE**.
– ORIGIN C19: from Latin *parum* 'little' + *affinis* 'related' (from its low reactivity).

paragliding ■ n. a sport in which a person glides through the air by means of a wide parachute after jumping from or being hauled to a height.
– DERIVATIVES **paraglide** v. **paraglider** n.

paragon ■ n. **1** a person or thing regarded as a model of excellence or of a particular quality. **2** a perfect diamond of 100 carats or more.
– ORIGIN C16: from Italian *paragone* 'touchstone', from medieval Greek *parakonē* 'whetstone'.

paragraph ■ n. a distinct section of a piece of writing, indicated by a new line, indentation, or numbering. ■ v. arrange in paragraphs.
– ORIGIN C15: from French *paragraphe*, from Greek *paragraphos* 'short stroke marking a break in sense'.

paragraph mark ■ n. a symbol (usually ¶) used in printed text to mark a new paragraph or as a reference mark.

Paraguayan /ˈparəɡwʌɪən/ ■ n. a native or inhabitant of Paraguay. ■ adj. of or relating to Paraguay.

parakeet /ˈparəkiːt/ (also **parrakeet**) ■ n. a small parrot with predominantly green plumage and a long tail. [*Psittacula, Cyanoramphus*, and other genera.]
– ORIGIN C16: from Old French *paroquet*, Italian *parrocchetto*, and Spanish *periquito*, perhaps from a diminutive meaning 'little wig'.

paralanguage ■ n. the non-lexical component of communication by speech, for example intonation, hesitation noises, gesture, and facial expression.

paralegal chiefly N. Amer. ■ adj. of or relating to auxiliary aspects of the law. ■ n. a person trained in subsidiary legal matters but not fully qualified as a lawyer.

paralinguistic ■ adj. relating to or denoting paralanguage.

paralipsis /ˌparəˈlɪpsɪs/ ■ n. Rhetoric the device of giving emphasis by professing to say little or nothing of a subject, as in *not to mention their unpaid debts*.
– ORIGIN C16: from Greek *paraleipsis* 'passing over', from *paraleipein* 'omit'.

parallax /ˈparəlaks/ ■ n. **1** the apparent difference in the position of an object when viewed from different positions, e.g. through the viewfinder and the lens of a camera. **2** Astronomy the angular difference in the apparent positions of a star observed from opposite sides of the earth's orbit.
– DERIVATIVES **parallactic** adj.
– ORIGIN C16: from Greek *parallaxis* 'a change', from *parallassein* 'to alternate'.

parallel ■ adj. **1** (of lines, planes, or surfaces) side by side and having the same distance continuously between them. **2** occurring or existing at the same time or in a similar way; corresponding. ▶ Computing involving the simultaneous performance of operations. **3** of or denoting electrical components connected in parallel. ■ n. **1** a person or thing that is similar or analogous to another. **2** a similarity or comparison. **3** (also **parallel of latitude**) each of the imaginary parallel circles of constant latitude on the earth's surface. **4** Printing two parallel lines (‖) as a reference mark. ■ v. (**paralleled**, **paralleling**) **1** run or lie parallel to. **2** be similar or corresponding to.
– PHRASES **in parallel 1** taking place at the same time and having no connection. **2** (of electrical components or circuits) connected to common points at each end, so that the current is divided between them.
– DERIVATIVES **parallelism** n. **parallelistic** adj. **parallelization** (also **-isation**) n. (Computing). **parallelize** (also **-ise**) v. (Computing).
– ORIGIN C16: from French *parallèle*, from Greek *parallēlos*, from *para-* 'alongside' + *allēlos* 'one another'.

parallel bars ■ pl. n. a pair of parallel rails on posts, used in gymnastics.

parallel cousin ■ n. the offspring of a parent's sibling; a first cousin.

parallelepiped /ˌparəlɛlɪˈpʌɪpɛd, ˌparəlɛˈlɛpɪpɛd/ ■ n. Geometry a solid body of which each face is a parallelogram.
– ORIGIN C16: from Greek *parallēlepipedon*, from *parallēlos* 'beside another' + *epipedon* 'plane surface'.

parallel imports ■ pl. n. goods imported for sale at less than the manufacturer's official retail price.
– DERIVATIVES **parallel importing** n.

parallel-medium ■ adj. of or relating to an educational system or institution in which two languages of instruction are used, in separate classes. Compare with **DUAL-MEDIUM**.

parallelogram /ˌparəˈlɛləɡram/ ■ n. a four-sided plane rectilinear figure with opposite sides parallel.

- ORIGIN C16: from French *parallélogramme*, from Greek *parallēlogrammon*, from *parallēlos* 'alongside another' + *grammē* 'line'.

parallel processing ■ n. a mode of computer operation in which a process is split into parts, which are executed simultaneously on different processors.

parallel ruler ■ n. an instrument for drawing parallel lines, consisting of two or more rulers connected by jointed crosspieces so as to be always parallel.

paralogism /pəˈralədʒɪz(ə)m/ ■ n. Logic a piece of illogical or fallacious reasoning, especially one which appears superficially logical.
- DERIVATIVES **paralogical** adj. **paralogically** adv. **paralogist** n.
- ORIGIN C16: from French *paralogisme*, from Greek *paralogismos*, from *paralogizesthai* 'reason falsely'.

Paralympics ■ pl. n. [usu. treated as sing.] an international athletic competition for disabled athletes.
- DERIVATIVES **Paralympic** adj.
- ORIGIN 1950s: blend of *paraplegic* and *Olympics*.

paralyse (chiefly US also **paralyze**) ■ v. 1 cause (a person or part of the body) to become partly or wholly incapable of movement. 2 bring to a standstill by causing disruption.
- ORIGIN C19: from French *paralyser*, from *paralysie* 'paralysis'.

paralysis /pəˈralɪsɪs/ ■ n. (pl. **paralyses** /-siːz/) 1 the loss of the ability to move part or most of the body. 2 inability to act or function.
- ORIGIN Old English, from Greek *paralusis*, from *paraluesthai* 'be disabled at the side'.

paralytic ■ adj. 1 of or relating to paralysis. 2 informal, chiefly Brit. extremely drunk. ■ n. a person affected by paralysis.
- DERIVATIVES **paralytically** adv.

paramagnetic ■ adj. (of a substance or body) very weakly attracted by the poles of a magnet, but not retaining any permanent magnetism.
- DERIVATIVES **paramagnetism** n.

paramecium /ˌparəˈmiːsɪəm/ ■ n. Zoology a single-celled freshwater animal which has a characteristic slipper-like shape and is covered with cilia. [Genus *Paramecium*.]
- ORIGIN C18: from Greek *paramēkēs* 'oval'.

paramedic ■ n. a person who is trained to do medical work, especially emergency first aid, but is not a fully qualified doctor.
- DERIVATIVES **paramedical** adj.

parameter /pəˈramɪtə/ ■ n. 1 a measurable or quantifiable characteristic of a system. 2 Mathematics a quantity which is fixed for the case in question but may vary in other cases. 3 a limit or boundary which defines the scope of a particular process or activity.
- DERIVATIVES **parameterization** (also **-isation**) n. **parameterize** (also **-ise**) v. **parametric** adj. **parametrically** adv.
- ORIGIN C17: from Greek *para-* 'beside' + *metron* 'measure'.

parametric equalizer ■ n. an electronic device or computer program which allows any specific part of the frequency range of a signal to be selected and altered in strength.

paramilitary ■ adj. organized on similar lines to a military force. ■ n. (pl. **-ies**) a member of a paramilitary organization.

paramount ■ adj. 1 more important than anything else; supreme. 2 having supreme power.
- DERIVATIVES **paramountcy** n. **paramountly** adv.
- ORIGIN C16: from Anglo-Norman French *paramont*, from Old French *par* 'by' + *amont* 'above'.

paramount chief ■ n. a ruler who has authority over leaders of more than one community, and often has a political role in the national government.

paramour ■ n. archaic or derogatory a lover, especially the illicit partner of a married person.
- ORIGIN Middle English: from Old French *par amour* 'by love'.

paramyxovirus /ˌparəˈmɪksəʊˌvʌɪrəs/ ■ n. Medicine any of a group of RNA viruses including those causing mumps and measles.

parang /ˈpɑːraŋ, ˈpa-/ ■ n. a Malayan machete.
- ORIGIN from Malay.

paranoia /ˌparəˈnɔɪə/ ■ n. 1 a mental condition characterized by delusions of persecution, unwarranted jealousy, or exaggerated self-importance. 2 unjustified suspicion and mistrust of others.
- DERIVATIVES **paranoiac** adj. & n. **paranoiacally** adv. **paranoic** /-ˈnəʊɪk, -ˈnɔɪk/ adj. **paranoically** /-ˈnəʊɪk(ə)li, -ˈnɔɪk(ə)li/ adv.
- ORIGIN C19: from Greek, from *paranoos* 'distracted', from *para* 'irregular' + *noos* 'mind'.

paranoid ■ adj. of, characterized by, or suffering from paranoia. ■ n. a person who is paranoid.

paranormal ■ adj. denoting events or phenomena that are claimed to be beyond the scope of normal scientific understanding.
- DERIVATIVES **paranormally** adv.

paranthropus ■ n. a fossil australopithecine known from remains first found in South Africa. [*Paranthropus robustus*.]
- ORIGIN 1930s: modern Latin, from PARA-[1] + Greek *anthrōpos* 'human being'.

paraparesis /ˌparəpəˈriːsɪs/ ■ n. partial paralysis of the lower limbs.
- DERIVATIVES **paraparetic** adj.

parapente /ˈparəpɒnt/ ■ v. [usu. as noun **parapenting**] take part in the sport of gliding by means of an aerofoil parachute launched from high ground. ■ n. a parachute used for this purpose.
- DERIVATIVES **parapenter** n.
- ORIGIN 1980s: from French, from *para(chute)* + *pente* 'slope'.

parapet /ˈparəpɪt/ ■ n. 1 a low protective wall along the edge of a roof, bridge, or balcony. 2 a protective wall or earth defence along the top of a military trench.
- DERIVATIVES **parapeted** adj.
- ORIGIN C16: from Italian *parapetto* 'chest-high wall', from Latin *pectus* 'chest'.

paraphernalia /ˌparəfəˈneɪlɪə/ ■ n. [treated as sing. or pl.] miscellaneous articles, especially the equipment needed for a particular activity.
- ORIGIN C17: from Greek *parapherna* 'property apart from a dowry'.

paraphrase ■ v. express the meaning of (something) using different words, especially to achieve greater clarity. ■ n. a rewording of a passage.
- DERIVATIVES **paraphrasable** adj. **paraphrastic** adj.
- ORIGIN C16: from Greek *paraphrasis*, from *paraphrazein*, from *para-* (expressing modification) + *phrazein* 'tell'.

paraplegia /ˌparəˈpliːdʒə/ ■ n. paralysis of the legs and lower body, typically caused by spinal injury or disease. Compare with MONOPLEGIA.
- DERIVATIVES **paraplegic** adj. & n.
- ORIGIN C17: from Greek *paraplēgia*, from *paraplēssein* 'strike at the side'.

parapsychic ■ adj. relating to or denoting mental phenomena for which no adequate scientific explanation exists.

parapsychology ■ n. the study of mental phenomena which are excluded from or inexplicable by orthodox scientific psychology (such as hypnosis, telepathy, etc.).
- DERIVATIVES **parapsychological** adj. **parapsychologist** n.

paraquat /ˈparəkwɒt, -kwat/ ■ n. a toxic fast-acting herbicide, which becomes deactivated in the soil.
- ORIGIN 1960s: from PARA-[1] + QUATERNARY.

parasail ■ v. [often as noun **parasailing**] glide through the air wearing an open parachute while being towed by a motor boat. ■ n. a parachute designed for parasailing.

parascending ■ n. Brit. the sport or activity of paragliding or parasailing.
- DERIVATIVES **parascend** v. **parascender** n.

parasitaemia /ˌparəsɪˈtiːmɪə/ (US **parasitemia**) ■ n. Medicine the presence of parasites in the blood.

parasite ■ n. 1 an organism which lives in or on another organism and benefits by deriving nutrients at the other's

parasitic

expense. **2** derogatory a person who habitually relies on or exploits others and gives nothing in return.
– DERIVATIVES **parasiticide** n.
– ORIGIN C16: from Greek *parasitos* '(person) eating at another's table', from *para-* 'alongside' + *sitos* 'food'.

parasitic ■ adj. living as a parasite. ▸ resulting from infestation by a parasite.
– DERIVATIVES **parasitical** adj. **parasitically** adv. **parasitism** n.

parasitize /ˈparəsʌɪtʌɪz, -sɪ-/ (also **-ise**) ■ v. infest or exploit as a parasite.
– DERIVATIVES **parasitization** (also **-isation**) n.

parasitoid /ˈparəsɪtɔɪd/ ■ n. Entomology an insect whose larvae live as parasites which eventually kill their hosts, e.g. an ichneumon wasp.

parasitology ■ n. the study of parasitic organisms.
– DERIVATIVES **parasitological** adj. **parasitologically** adv. **parasitologist** n.

parasol ■ n. **1** a light umbrella used to give shade from the sun. **2** (also **parasol mushroom**) a tall mushroom with a broad scaly greyish-brown cap. [*Lepiota cristata* and related species.]
– ORIGIN C17: from Italian *parasole*, from *para-* 'protecting against' + *sole* 'sun'.

parastatal /ˌparəˈsteɪt(ə)l/ ■ adj. (of an organization or industry) having some political authority and serving the state indirectly. ■ n. a parastatal organization.

parasternal /ˌparəˈstəːn(ə)l/ ■ adj. Anatomy situated beside the sternum.

parasuicide ■ n. Psychiatry apparent attempted suicide without the actual intention of killing oneself.

parasympathetic ■ adj. Physiology relating to or denoting the part of the autonomic nervous system consisting of nerves arising from the brain and the lower end of the spinal cord and supplying the internal organs, blood vessels, and glands.

parasynthesis ■ n. Linguistics a process by which a term is formed by adding a bound morpheme (e.g. *-ed*) to a combination of existing words (e.g. *black-eyed* from *black eye(s)* + *-ed*).
– DERIVATIVES **parasynthetic** adj. **parasynthetically** adv.

paratha /pəˈrɑːtə/ ■ n. (in Indian cookery) a flat, thick piece of unleavened bread fried on a griddle.
– ORIGIN from Hindi *parāṭhā*.

parathion /ˌparəˈθʌɪən/ ■ n. a highly toxic synthetic insecticide containing phosphorus and sulphur.
– ORIGIN 1940s: from PARA-¹ (in sense 2) + THIO- + -ON.

parathyroid ■ n. Anatomy a gland next to the thyroid which secretes a hormone that regulates calcium levels in a person's body.

paratroops ■ pl. n. troops equipped to be dropped by parachute from aircraft.
– DERIVATIVES **paratrooper** n.

paratyphoid ■ n. a fever resembling typhoid, caused by related bacteria.

par avion /pɑː(r) aˈvjɔ̃/ ■ adv. by airmail.
– ORIGIN French, 'by aeroplane'.

parboil ■ v. partly cook by boiling.
– ORIGIN Middle English: from Old French *parbouillir*, from late Latin *perbullire* 'boil thoroughly', from Latin *per-* 'through, thoroughly' (later confused with PART) + *bullire* 'to boil'.

parcel ■ n. **1** an object or collection of objects wrapped in paper in order to be carried or sent by post. **2** a quantity or amount of something, in particular land. **3** (in the diamond trade) a package of rough or cut diamonds. ■ v. (**parcelled**, **parcelling**; US **parceled**, **parceling**) **1** make (something) into a parcel by wrapping it. **2** (**parcel something out**) divide something into portions and then distribute it. **3** Nautical wrap (rope) with strips of tarred canvas to reduce chafing.
– ORIGIN Middle English: from Old French *parcelle*, from Latin *particula* 'small part'.

parcel-gilt ■ adj. (of furniture, silverware, etc.) partly gilded, especially on the inner surface only.

parch ■ v. **1** make or become dry through intense heat. **2** [as adj. **parched**] informal extremely thirsty.
– ORIGIN Middle English.

parchment ■ n. **1** a stiff material made from the prepared skin of a sheep or goat, formerly used as a writing surface. **2** (also **parchment paper**) stiff translucent paper treated to resemble parchment. **3** informal a diploma or other formal document.
– ORIGIN Middle English: from Old French *parchemin*, from a blend of late Latin *pergamina* 'writing material from Pergamum' and *Parthica pellis* 'Parthian skin' (a kind of scarlet leather).

parclose /ˈpɑːkləʊz/ ■ n. a screen or railing in a church enclosing a tomb or altar or separating off a side chapel.
– ORIGIN Middle English: from Old French *parclos(e)*, from *parclore* 'enclose'.

pardon ■ n. **1** the action of forgiving or being forgiven for an error or offence. **2** a remission of the legal consequences of an offence or conviction. **3** Christian Church, historical an indulgence. ■ v. **1** forgive or excuse (a person, error, or offence). **2** release (an offender) from the legal consequences of an offence or conviction. ■ exclam. used to ask a speaker to repeat something because one did not hear or understand it.
– PHRASES **I beg your pardon** (or **pardon me**) used to express polite apology or to indicate that one has not heard or understood something.
– DERIVATIVES **pardonable** adj. **pardonably** adv.
– ORIGIN Middle English: from Old French *pardun* (n.), *pardoner* (v.), from medieval Latin *perdonare* 'concede, remit', from *per-* 'completely' + *donare* 'give'.

pardoner ■ n. historical a person licensed to sell papal pardons or indulgences.

pare ■ v. **1** trim by cutting away the outer edges of. **2** (often **pare something away/down**) reduce or diminish in a number of small successive stages.
– DERIVATIVES **parer** n.
– ORIGIN Middle English: from Old French *parer* 'adorn, prepare', also 'peel, trim', from Latin *parare* 'prepare'.

paregoric /ˌparɪˈɡɒrɪk/ ■ n. a medicine containing opium and camphor, formerly used to treat diarrhoea and coughing in children.
– ORIGIN C17: from Greek *parēgorikos* 'soothing'.

pareiasaurus /pəˌrʌɪəˈsɔːrəs/ ■ n. a large thickset herbivorous reptile of the late Permian period.
– ORIGIN from Greek *pareia* 'cheek' + *sauros* 'lizard'.

paren /pəˈrɛn/ ■ n. Printing a round bracket.
– ORIGIN C20: abbrev. of PARENTHESIS.

parenchyma /pəˈrɛŋkɪmə/ ■ n. **1** Anatomy the functional tissue of an organ as distinguished from the connective and supporting tissue. **2** Botany the cellular tissue found in the softer parts of leaves, pulp of fruits, bark and pith of stems, etc.
– DERIVATIVES **parenchymal** adj. (chiefly Anatomy). **parenchymatous** adj. (chiefly Botany).
– ORIGIN C17: from Greek *parenkhuma* 'something poured in besides', from *para-* 'beside' + *enkhuma* 'infusion'.

parent ■ n. **1** a father or mother. ▸ an animal or plant from which younger ones are derived. **2** an organization or company which owns or controls a number of subsidiaries. **3** archaic a forefather or ancestor. ■ v. [often as noun **parenting**] be or act as a parent to.
– DERIVATIVES **parentage** n. **parental** adj. **parentally** adv. **parentcraft** n. **parenthood** n.
– ORIGIN Middle English: from Latin *parent-*, *parere* 'bring forth'.

parenteral /pəˈrɛnt(ə)r(ə)l/ ■ adj. Medicine (chiefly of nutrition) involving another part of the body than the mouth and alimentary canal. Often contrasted with ENTERAL.
– DERIVATIVES **parenterally** adv.
– ORIGIN C20: from PARA-¹ + Greek *enteron* 'intestine'.

parenthesis /pəˈrɛnθɪsɪs/ ■ n. (pl. **parentheses** /-siːz/) **1** a word or phrase inserted as an explanation or afterthought, in writing usually marked off by brackets, dashes, or commas. **2** (**parentheses**) a pair of round brackets () used to include such a word or phrase.
– DERIVATIVES **parenthesize** (also **-ise**) v. **parenthetic** /ˌpar(ə)nˈθɛtɪk/ adj. **parenthetical** adj. **parenthetically** adv.
– ORIGIN C16: from Greek, from *parentithenai* 'put in beside'.

paresis /pəˈriːsɪs, ˈparɪsɪs/ ■ n. (pl. **pareses** /-siːz/) Medicine **1** muscular weakness or partial paralysis caused by nerve damage or disease. **2** (also **general paresis**) inflammation of the brain in the later stages of syphilis, causing progressive dementia and paralysis.
– DERIVATIVES **paretic** adj.
– ORIGIN C17: from Greek *parienai* 'let go'.

paresthesia ■ n. US spelling of PARAESTHESIA.

pareu /ˈpɑːreɪuː/ (also **pareo**) ■ n. a kind of sarong used as a wrap-around, traditionally worn in Polynesia.
– ORIGIN from Tahitian.

par excellence /pɑːr ˈɛks(ə)l(ə)ns/ ■ adj. [postpos.] better or more than all others of the same kind.
– ORIGIN French, 'by excellence'.

parfait /ˈpɑːfeɪ/ ■ n. **1** a rich cold dessert made with whipped cream, eggs, and fruit. **2** a dessert consisting of layers of ice cream, meringue, and fruit, served in a tall glass.
– ORIGIN from French *parfait* 'perfect'.

parfumerie /pɑːˈfjuːm(ə)ri/ ■ n. (pl. **-ies**) a place where perfume is sold or made.
– ORIGIN from French.

parget /ˈpɑːdʒɪt/ (also **parge** /pɑːdʒ/) ■ v. (**pargeted**, **pargeting**) cover with a patterned or decorative layer of plaster or mortar. ■ n. plaster or mortar applied in this way.
– ORIGIN Middle English: from Old French *parjeter*, from *par-* 'all over' + *jeter* 'to throw'.

parhelion /pɑːˈhiːliən/ ■ n. (pl. **parhelia** /-liə/) a bright spot in the sky on either side of the sun, formed by refraction.
– DERIVATIVES **parhelic** adj.
– ORIGIN C17: from Latin *parelion*, from Greek *para-* 'beside' + *hēlios* 'sun'.

pariah /pəˈrʌɪə/ ■ n. an outcast.
– ORIGIN C17: from Tamil *paṟaiyar* (pl.), '(hereditary) drummers', from *paṟai* 'a drum' (pariahs not being allowed to join in with a religious procession).

pariah dog ■ n. another term for PYE-DOG.

parietal /pəˈrʌɪɪt(ə)l/ ■ adj. **1** Anatomy & Biology of, relating to, or denoting the wall of the body or of a body cavity. **2** Archaeology denoting prehistoric art found on rock walls. ■ n. Anatomy & Zoology a parietal bone or other parietal structure.
– ORIGIN Middle English: from late Latin *parietalis*, from Latin *paries* 'wall'.

parietal bone ■ n. a bone forming the central side and upper back part of each side of the skull.

parietal lobe ■ n. either of the paired lobes of the brain at the top of the head.

parings ■ pl. n. thin strips pared off from something.

pari passu /ˌpɑːriː ˈpasuː, ˌpari/ ■ adv. side by side; equally or equivalently.
– ORIGIN Latin, 'with equal step'.

parish ■ n. **1** (in the Christian Church) a small administrative district with its own church and clergy. **2** Brit. the smallest unit of local government in rural areas.
– ORIGIN Middle English: from Anglo-Norman French *paroche*, from late Latin *parochia*, from Greek *paroikia* 'sojourning', from *para-* 'beside, subsidiary' + *oikos* 'dwelling'.

parish council ■ n. Brit. the administrative body in a local government parish.

parishioner ■ n. a person who lives in a particular Church parish.

parish register ■ n. a book recording christenings, marriages, and burials at a parish church.

Parisian /pəˈrɪziən/ ■ adj. of or relating to Paris. ■ n. a native or inhabitant of Paris.

Parisienne /ˌpaˌrɪziˈɛn/ ■ n. a Parisian girl or woman.

parity[1] /ˈparɪti/ ■ n. **1** equality or equivalence, especially as regards status, pay, or value. **2** Mathematics the fact of being an even or an odd number. **3** Physics the property of a spatial wave equation that either remains the same or changes sign under a given transformation.
– ORIGIN C16: from late Latin *paritas*, from *par* 'equal'.

parity[2] /ˈparɪti/ ■ n. Medicine the fact or condition of having borne a specified number of children.

– ORIGIN C19: from *parous* 'having borne offspring'.

park ■ n. **1** a large public garden in a town, used for recreation. **2** a large enclosed area, typically with woodland and pasture, attached to a country house. **3** an area devoted to a specified purpose: *a wildlife park*. **4** an area in which vehicles may be parked: *a coach park*. ■ v. **1** bring (a vehicle) to a halt and leave it temporarily, typically in a car park or by the side of the road. **2** informal deposit and leave in a convenient place until required: *park your bag by the door*. **3** (**park oneself**) informal sit down.
– ORIGIN Middle English: from Old French *parc*, from medieval Latin *parricus*, of Germanic origin.

parka ■ n. **1** a large windproof hooded jacket for use in cold weather. **2** a hooded jacket made of animal skin, worn by Eskimos.
– ORIGIN C18: via Aleut from Russian.

parkerizing (also **-ising**) ■ n. a rustproofing process involving immersion in a hot acidic solution of a metal phosphate.
– DERIVATIVES **parkerized** (also **-ised**) adj.
– ORIGIN 1920s: from the *Parker* Rust-Proof Company of America.

park home ■ n. a prefabricated building occupied as a permanent home, located with others in a dedicated area of ground.

parking meter ■ n. a coin-operated machine next to a parking space in a street, for receiving a parking fee and indicating the time available.

parking ticket ■ n. a notice informing a driver of a fine imposed for parking illegally.

Parkinson's disease ■ n. a progressive disease of the brain and nervous system marked by tremor, muscular rigidity, and slow, imprecise movement.
– DERIVATIVES **Parkinsonian** adj. **Parkinsonism** n.
– ORIGIN C19: named after the English surgeon James *Parkinson*.

parkland ■ n. (also **parklands**) open land consisting of fields and scattered groups of trees.

Parktown prawn ■ n. S. African a large cricket with long feelers and a prawn-like carapace, a pest in some urban areas. [*Libanasidus vittatus*].

parlance /ˈpɑːl(ə)ns/ ■ n. a particular way of using words, especially one common to those in a subject: *medical parlance*.
– ORIGIN C16: from Old French, from *parler* 'speak', from Latin *parabola* 'comparison' (in late Latin 'speech').

parlay /ˈpɑːleɪ/ ■ v. (**parlay something into**) N. Amer. turn an initial stake or winnings into (a greater amount) by further gambling.
– ORIGIN C19: from French *paroli*, from Latin *par* 'equal'.

parley /ˈpɑːli/ ■ n. (pl. **-eys**) a conference between opposing sides in a dispute, especially regarding an armistice. ■ v. (**-eys**, **-eyed**) hold a parley.
– ORIGIN Middle English: perhaps from Old French *parlee* 'spoken'.

parliament /ˈpɑːləm(ə)nt/ ■ n. the highest legislature of some countries. ▶ the members of this legislature for the period between dissolutions.
– DERIVATIVES **parliamentary** adj.
– ORIGIN Middle English: from Old French *parlement* 'speaking'.

parliamentarian ■ n. a member of a parliament, especially a person well versed in its procedure and debates. ■ adj. of or relating to parliament or parliamentarians.
– DERIVATIVES **parliamentarianism** n.

parlour (US **parlor**) ■ n. **1** dated a sitting room in a private house. **2** a room in a public building for receiving guests or private conversation. **3** a shop or business providing specified goods or services: *a funeral parlour*. **4** a room or building equipped for milking cows.
– ORIGIN Middle English: from Anglo-Norman French *parlur* 'place for speaking', from Latin *parlare* 'speak'.

parlour game ■ n. an indoor game, especially a word game.

parlourmaid

parlourmaid ■ n. historical a maid employed to wait at table.

parlous /ˈpɑːləs/ ■ adj. archaic or humorous full of uncertainty; precarious: *the parlous state of the economy.*
– DERIVATIVES **parlously** adv. **parlousness** n.
– ORIGIN Middle English: contraction of *perilous* (see PERIL).

Parma ham ■ n. a strongly flavoured Italian cured ham, eaten uncooked and thinly sliced.
– ORIGIN named after the city of *Parma* in Italy.

Parma violet ■ n. a scented sweet violet, crystallized and used for food decoration.

Parmesan /pɑːmɪˈzan/ ■ n. a hard, dry Italian cheese used chiefly in grated form.
– ORIGIN C16: from Italian *Parmigiano* 'of *Parma*'.

Parmigiana /ˌpɑːmɪˈdʒɑːnə/ ■ adj. [postpos.] cooked or served with Parmesan cheese.

parochial /pəˈrəʊkɪəl/ ■ adj. 1 of or relating to a Church parish. 2 having a narrow outlook or scope: *parochial attitudes.*
– DERIVATIVES **parochialism** n. **parochiality** n. **parochially** adv.
– ORIGIN Middle English: from eccles. Latin *parochialis*, from *parochia* (see PARISH).

parody ■ n. (pl. -ies) 1 an imitation of the style of a particular writer, artist, or genre with deliberate exaggeration for comic effect. 2 a travesty: *a parody of a smile.* ■ v. (-ies, -ied) produce a parody of.
– DERIVATIVES **parodic** adj. **parodist** n.
– ORIGIN C16: from Greek *parōidia*, from *para-* 'beside' (expressing alteration) + *ōidē* 'ode'.

parol /pəˈrəʊl, ˈpar(ə)l/ ■ adj. Law expressed or agreed orally, or in writing but not under seal.
– PHRASES **by parol** by oral declaration.
– ORIGIN C15: from Old French *parole* (see PAROLE).

parole ■ n. 1 the temporary or permanent release of a prisoner before the expiry of a sentence, on the promise of good behaviour. 2 historical a prisoner of war's word of honour to return or act as a non-belligerent if released. 3 Linguistics the actual language used by people. Contrasted with LANGUE. ■ v. release (a prisoner) on parole.
– DERIVATIVES **parolee** n.
– ORIGIN C15: from Old French, 'word', from eccles. Latin *parabola* 'speech'.

paronym /ˈparənɪm/ ■ n. Linguistics a word which is derived from another word and has a related meaning (e.g. *wishful* from *wish*). ▶ a word which adapts a foreign word with little or no change in form (e.g. *futile* from Latin *futilis*).
– DERIVATIVES **paronymous** adj. **paronymy** n.

parotid /pəˈrɒtɪd/ ■ adj. Anatomy relating to or denoting a pair of large salivary glands situated just in front of each ear.
– ORIGIN C17: from Greek *parōtis*, from *para-* 'beside' + *ous, ōt-* 'ear'.

parotitis /ˌparəˈtʌɪtɪs/ ■ n. Medicine inflammation of the parotid gland, especially (infectious parotitis) mumps.

-parous ■ comb. form Biology bearing offspring of a specified number or in a specified way: *multiparous* | *viviparous.*
– ORIGIN from Latin *-parus* '-bearing', from *parere* 'bring forth, produce'.

Parousia /pəˈruːzɪə/ ■ n. Christian Church the Second Coming.
– ORIGIN Greek, 'being present'.

paroxysm /ˈparəksɪz(ə)m/ ■ n. a sudden attack or violent expression of something: *a paroxysm of weeping.*
– DERIVATIVES **paroxysmal** adj.
– ORIGIN Middle English: from French *paroxysme*, from Greek *paroxusmos*, from *paroxunein* 'exasperate', from *para-* 'beyond' + *oxunein* 'sharpen'.

parp informal ■ n. the honking sound of a car horn. ■ v. make such a sound.
– ORIGIN 1950s: imitative.

parquet /ˈpɑːki, ˈpɑːkeɪ/ ■ n. flooring composed of wooden blocks arranged in a geometric pattern.
– DERIVATIVES **parquetry** n.

– ORIGIN C17 (as v.): from French, 'small park' (i.e. delineated area).

parr ■ n. (pl. same) a young salmon or trout between the stages of fry and smolt.
– ORIGIN C18.

parrakeet ■ n. variant spelling of PARAKEET.

parricide /ˈparɪsʌɪd/ ■ n. 1 the killing of a parent or near relative. 2 a person who commits parricide.
– DERIVATIVES **parricidal** adj.
– ORIGIN C16: from Latin *parricidium*, the first element associated with Latin *pater* 'father' and *parens* 'parent'.

parrot ■ n. a mainly tropical bird, typically brightly coloured, with a strong downcurved hooked bill and a raucous voice, some kinds of which are able to mimic human speech. [Order Psittaciformes: many species.] ■ v. (**parroted**, **parroting**) repeat mechanically.
– ORIGIN C16: prob. from dialect French *perrot*, diminutive of the male given name *Pierre* 'Peter'.

parrot-fashion ■ adv. (of repetition) without thought or understanding.

parrotfish ■ n. (pl. same or **-fishes**) 1 a brightly coloured sea fish with a parrot-like beak. [*Scarus* and other genera.] 2 S. African a marine fish with a parrot-like beak, found off the east coast of southern Africa. [*Oplegnathus conwayi* and other species.]

parry ■ v. (**-ies, -ied**) 1 ward off (a weapon or attack) with a countermove. 2 answer (a question or accusation) evasively. ■ n. (pl. **-ies**) an act of parrying.
– ORIGIN C17: prob. representing French *parez!* 'ward off!', from *parer*.

parse /pɑːz/ ■ v. 1 resolve (a sentence) into its component parts and describe their syntactic roles. 2 Computing analyse (text) into logical syntactic components.
– DERIVATIVES **parser** n.
– ORIGIN C16: perhaps from Middle English *pars* 'parts of speech', from Old French *pars* 'parts'.

parsec /ˈpɑːsɛk/ ■ n. Astronomy a unit of distance equal to about 3.25 light years (3.08×10^{16} metres), corresponding to the distance at which the mean radius of the earth's orbit subtends an angle of one second of arc.
– ORIGIN C20: blend of PARALLAX and SECOND[2].

Parsee /pɑːˈsiː, ˈpɑːsiː/ ■ n. an adherent of Zoroastrianism, especially a descendant of those who fled to India from Persia during the 7th–8th centuries.
– ORIGIN from Persian *pārsī* 'Persian', from *pārs* 'Persia'.

parsimony /ˈpɑːsɪməni/ ■ n. extreme unwillingness to spend money or use resources.
– PHRASES **principle (or law) of parsimony** the scientific principle that things are usually connected in the simplest or most economical way.
– DERIVATIVES **parsimonious** adj. **parsimoniously** adv. **parsimoniousness** n.
– ORIGIN Middle English: from Latin *parsimonia*, from *parcere* 'be sparing'.

parsley ■ n. a plant with white flowers and crinkly or flat leaves used as a culinary herb and garnish. [*Petroselinum crispum.*]
– ORIGIN Old English *petersilie*, from Greek *petroselinon*, from *petra* 'rock' + *selinon* 'parsley', influenced by Old French *peresil*, of the same origin.

parsnip ■ n. 1 a long tapering cream-coloured root with a sweet flavour. 2 the plant of the parsley family which yields this root. [*Pastinaca sativa.*]
– ORIGIN Middle English: from Old French *pasnaie*, from Latin *pastinaca*, rel. to *pastinare* 'dig and trench the ground'.

parson ■ n. a beneficed member of the Anglican clergy; a rector or vicar. ▶ informal any clergyman, especially a Protestant one.
– ORIGIN Middle English: from Old French *persone*, from Latin *persona* 'person'.

parsonage ■ n. a church house provided for a parson.

parson's nose ■ n. informal the fatty extremity of the rump of a cooked fowl.

part ■ n. 1 a piece or segment of something which combined with others makes up the whole. ▶ a component of a machine: *aircraft parts.* 2 a measure allowing comparison between the amounts of different ingredients used in a mixture. ▶ a specified fraction of a whole.

3 some but not all of something. **4 (parts)** informal a region, especially one not clearly specified or delimited. **5** a role played by an actor or actress. ▸ Music a melody or other constituent of harmony assigned to a particular voice or instrument. ▸ the contribution made by someone to an action or situation. **6** N. Amer. a parting in the hair. ■ v. **1** move apart or divide to leave a central space. ▸ leave someone's company. ▸ **(be parted)** leave the company of someone. **2 (part with)** give up possession of; hand over. **3** separate (the hair on either side of a parting) with a comb. ■ adv. partly (often used to contrast different parts of something): *part jazz, part blues.*
– PHRASES **be part and parcel of** be an essential element of. **for my** (or **his, her,** etc.) **part** as far as I am (or he, she, etc.) is concerned. **in part** to some extent though not entirely. **look the part** have an appearance or style of dress appropriate to a particular role or situation. **a man of (many) parts** a man showing great ability in many different areas. **on the part of** (or **on my, their,** etc. **part**) used to ascribe responsibility for something to someone. **part company** cease to be together; go in different directions. **take part** join in or be involved in an activity. **take the part of** give support and encouragement to (someone) in a dispute.
– ORIGIN Old English, from Latin *pars, part-*; verb from Old French *partir*, from Latin *partire* 'divide, share'.

partake ■ v. (past **partook**; past part. **partaken**) **1 (partake in)** formal join in (an activity). **2 (partake of)** be characterized by. **3 (partake of)** eat or drink.
– DERIVATIVES **partaker** n.
– ORIGIN C16: back-formation from *partaker* 'person who takes a part'.

parterre /pɑːˈtɛː/ ■ n. a level space in a garden occupied by an ornamental arrangement of flower beds.
– ORIGIN C17: from French, from *par terre* 'on the ground'.

part exchange ■ n. a method of buying something in which an article that one already owns is given as part of the payment for another, more expensive, article. ■ v. **(part-exchange)** give or take in part exchange.

parthenogenesis /ˌpɑːθɪnə(ʊ)ˈdʒɛnɪsɪs/ ■ n. Biology reproduction from an ovum without fertilization, especially in some invertebrates and lower plants.
– DERIVATIVES **parthenogenetic** adj.
– ORIGIN C19: from Greek *parthenos* 'virgin' + *genesis* 'creation'.

Parthian shot ■ n. another term for PARTING SHOT.
– ORIGIN C19: so named because of the trick used by Parthians of shooting arrows backwards while fleeing.

partial ■ adj. **1** existing only in part; incomplete. **2** favouring one side in a dispute above the other; biased. **3 (partial to)** having a liking for.
– DERIVATIVES **partiality** n. **partially** adv.
– ORIGIN Middle English: from Old French *parcial* (sense 2), French *partiel* (sense 1), from late Latin *partialis*, from *pars* 'part'.

partial derivative ■ n. Mathematics a derivative of a function of two or more variables with respect to one variable, the other(s) being treated as constant.

partial differential equation ■ n. Mathematics an equation containing one or more partial derivatives.

partial eclipse ■ n. an eclipse in which only part of the luminary is obscured or darkened.

partial pressure ■ n. Chemistry the pressure that would be exerted by one of the gases in a mixture if it occupied the same volume on its own.

participate ■ v. take part.
– DERIVATIVES **participant** n. **participation** n. **participative** adj. **participator** n. **participatory** adj.
– ORIGIN C16: from Latin *participare* 'share in', from *pars* 'part' + *capere* 'take'.

participle /ˈpɑːtɪsɪp(ə)l/ ■ n. Grammar a word formed from a verb (e.g. *going, gone, being, been*) and used as an adjective or noun (as in *burnt toast, good breeding*) or used to make compound verb forms (*is going, has been*).
– DERIVATIVES **participial** /-ˈsɪpɪəl/ adj. **participially** /-ˈsɪpɪəli/ adv.
– ORIGIN Middle English: from Old French, by-form of *participe*, from Latin *participium* 'sharing'.

particle ■ n. **1** a minute portion of matter. **2** Physics a subatomic constituent of the physical world, e.g. an electron, proton, neutrino, or photon. **3** Grammar a minor function word that has comparatively little meaning and does not inflect, e.g. *in, up, off,* or *over* used with verbs to make phrasal verbs.
– ORIGIN Middle English: from Latin *particula* 'little part', diminutive of *pars*.

particle board ■ n. another term for CHIPBOARD.

particle physics ■ pl. n. [treated as sing.] the branch of physics concerned with the properties, relationships, and interactions of subatomic particles.

particoloured (US **particolored**) ■ adj. having or consisting of two or more different colours.
– ORIGIN C16: from PARTY² + COLOURED.

particular ■ adj. **1** denoting an individual member of a specified group or class. **2** especially great or intense: *exercise particular care when checking cash.* **3** fastidious about something. **4** Logic denoting a proposition in which something is asserted of some but not all of a class. Contrasted with UNIVERSAL. ■ n. **1** a detail. **2** Philosophy an individual item, as contrasted with a universal quality.
– PHRASES **in particular** used to show that a statement applies to one person or thing more than any other.
– ORIGIN Middle English: from Old French *particuler*, from Latin *particularis*, from *particula* 'small part'.

particularism ■ n. **1** exclusive attachment to one's own group, nation, etc. **2** the principle of leaving each state in an empire or federation free to govern itself and promote its own interests. **3** Theology the doctrine that some but not all people are elected and redeemed.
– DERIVATIVES **particularist** n. & adj. **particularistic** adj.

particularity ■ n. (pl. **-ies**) **1** the quality of being individual. **2** fullness or minuteness of detail. ▸ **(particularities)** small details.

particularize (also **-ise**) ■ v. formal treat individually or in detail.
– DERIVATIVES **particularization** (also **-isation**) n.

particularly ■ adv. **1** to a higher degree than is usual or average. **2** in particular; specifically.

particulate /pɑːˈtɪkjʊlət, -eɪt, pə-/ ■ adj. of, relating to, or in the form of minute particles. ■ n. **(particulates)** matter in such a form.
– ORIGIN C19: from Latin *particula* 'particle'.

parting ■ n. **1** the action of moving away or being separated from someone. **2** the action of dividing something into parts. **3** a line of scalp revealed in a person's hair by combing the hair away in opposite directions on either side.
– PHRASES **a (or the) parting of the ways** a point at which two people must separate or at which a decision must be taken.

parting shot ■ n. a cutting remark made at the moment of departure.

parti pris /ˌpɑːtɪ ˈpriː/ ■ n. (pl. **partis pris** pronunc. same) a preconceived view; a bias. ■ adj. prejudiced; biased.
– ORIGIN French, literally 'side taken'.

partisan /ˈpɑːtɪzan, ˌpɑːtɪˈzan/ ■ n. **1** a strong supporter of a party, cause, or person. **2** a member of an armed group fighting secretly against an occupying force. ■ adj. prejudiced in favour of a particular cause.
– DERIVATIVES **partisanship** n.
– ORIGIN C16: from French, from Italian *partigiano*, from *parte* 'part'.

partita /pɑːˈtiːtə/ ■ n. (pl. **partitas** or **partite** /-teɪ, -ti/) Music a suite, typically for a solo instrument or chamber ensemble.
– ORIGIN C19: from Italian, 'divided off', from *partire*.

-partite /ˈpɑːtaɪt/ ■ suffix (forming adjectives) divided into a specified number of parts: *tripartite.*
– ORIGIN Middle English: from Latin, *partiri* 'divide up'.

partition ■ n. **1** (especially with reference to a country) the action or state of dividing or being divided into parts. **2** a structure dividing a space into two parts, especially a light interior wall. **3** Chemistry the distribution of a solute between two immiscible solvents in contact with one another, in accordance with its differing solubility in each. **4** Computing each of a number of portions into which some operating systems divide memory or storage. ■ v. **1** divide

into parts. **2** divide or separate by erecting a partition.
– DERIVATIVES **partitioner** n. **partitionist** n.
– ORIGIN Middle English: from Latin *partitio(n-)*, from *partiri* 'divide into parts'.

partly ■ adv. to some extent; not completely.

partner ■ n. **1** a person who takes part in an undertaking with another or others, especially in a business or firm with shared risks and profits. **2** either of two people doing something as a couple or pair. **3** either member of a married couple or of an established unmarried couple. ■ v. be the partner of.
– DERIVATIVES **partnerless** adj.
– ORIGIN Middle English: alteration of Anglo-Norman French *parcener* 'partner, joint heir', from Latin *partitio(n-)* 'partition'.

partners' desk (also **partnership desk**) ■ n. a large flat-topped pedestal desk with space for two people to sit opposite each other.

partnership ■ n. **1** the state of being a partner or partners. **2** an association of two or more people as partners. **3** Cricket the number of runs added by a pair of batsmen before one of them is dismissed or the innings ends.

part of speech ■ n. a category to which a word is assigned in accordance with its syntactic functions, e.g. noun, pronoun, adjective, determiner, verb, adverb, preposition, conjunction, and interjection.

partook past of **PARTAKE**.

partridge ■ n. (pl. same or **partridges**) **1** a short-tailed game bird with mainly brown plumage. [*Perdix perdix* and other species.] **2** S. African informal a francolin.
– ORIGIN Middle English *partrich*, from Old French *pertriz*, from Latin *perdix*.

part song ■ n. a secular song with three or more voice parts, typically unaccompanied.

part-time ■ adj. & adv. for only part of the usual working day or week.
– DERIVATIVES **part-timer** n.

parturition /ˌpɑːtjʊˈrɪʃ(ə)n/ ■ n. formal or technical the action of giving birth to young; childbirth.
– ORIGIN C17: from late Latin *parturitio(n-)*, from Latin *parturire* 'be in labour', from *parere* 'bring forth'.

part-way ■ adv. part of the way.

part-work ■ n. a publication appearing in several parts over a period of time.

party[1] ■ n. (pl. **-ies**) **1** a social gathering of invited guests, typically involving eating, drinking, and entertainment. **2** a formally constituted political group that contests elections and attempts to take part in government. **3** a group of people taking part in a particular activity or trip. **4** a person or group forming one side in an agreement or dispute. **5** informal a person, especially one with specified characteristics. ■ v. (**-ies, -ied**) informal enjoy oneself at a party or other lively gathering.
– PHRASES **be party** (or **a party**) to be involved in.
– ORIGIN Middle English: from Old French *partie*, from Latin *partiri* 'divide into parts'.

party[2] ■ adj. Heraldry divided into parts of different tinctures.
– ORIGIN Middle English: from Old French *parti* 'parted'.

party line ■ n. **1** a policy, or the policies collectively, officially adopted by a political party. **2** a telephone line shared by two or more subscribers.

party list ■ n. a proportional representation system in which people vote for a party and seats are filled from lists of candidates according to each party's share of the vote.

party piece ■ n. Brit. a poem, song, or trick regularly performed by someone in order to entertain others.

party politics ■ pl. n. [also treated as sing.] politics that relate to political parties rather than to the public good.
– DERIVATIVES **party political** adj.

party-pooper ■ n. informal a person who throws gloom over social enjoyment.
– DERIVATIVES **party-pooping** n.

party wall ■ n. a wall common to two adjoining buildings or rooms.

parure /pəˈrʊə/ ■ n. a set of jewels intended to be worn together.
– ORIGIN C19: from French, from *parer* 'adorn'.

parvenu /ˈpɑːvənuː, -njuː/ often derogatory ■ n. a person of obscure origin who has gained wealth, influence, or celebrity. ■ adj. relating to or denoting such persons.
– ORIGIN C19: from French, 'arrived', from *parvenir*.

parvovirus /ˈpɑːvəʊˌvʌɪrəs/ ■ n. Medicine any of a class of very small viruses causing contagious disease in dogs and other animals.
– ORIGIN 1960s: from Latin *parvus* 'small' + **VIRUS**.

PAS ■ abbrev. power-assisted steering.

pas /pɑː/ ■ n. (pl. same) a step in dancing, especially in classical ballet.
– ORIGIN from French.

pascal /ˈpask(ə)l/ ■ n. **1** (abbrev.: **Pa**) the SI unit of pressure, equal to one newton per square metre. **2** (**Pascal**) a high-level structured computer programming language.
– ORIGIN 1950s: named after the C17 French scientist Blaise *Pascal*.

Pascal's triangle ■ n. Mathematics a triangular array of numbers in which those at the ends of the rows are 1 and each of the others is the sum of the nearest two numbers in the row above (the apex, 1, being at the top).

paschal /ˈpask(ə)l, ˈpɑːs-/ ■ adj. formal **1** of or relating to Easter. **2** of or relating to the Jewish Passover.
– ORIGIN Middle English: from eccles. Latin *paschalis*, from *pascha* 'feast of Passover', from Hebrew *Pesaḥ*.

pas de chat /ˌpɑː də ˈʃa/ ■ n. (pl. same) Ballet a jump in which each foot in turn is raised to the opposite knee.
– ORIGIN French, 'step of a cat'.

pas de deux /ˌpɑː də ˈdɜː/ ■ n. (pl. same) a dance for a couple.
– ORIGIN French, 'step of two'.

pashmina /paʃˈmiːnə/ ■ n. fine-quality material made from goat's wool.
– ORIGIN Persian, from *pašm* 'wool, down'.

Pashto /ˈpʌʃtəʊ/ ■ n. the language of the Pashtuns, spoken in Afghanistan and northern Pakistan.
– ORIGIN the name in Pashto.

Pashtun /pəʃˈtuːn/ (also **Pakhtun** /pəkˈtuːn/) ■ n. a member of a Pashto-speaking people inhabiting NW Pakistan and SE Afghanistan. Also called **PATHAN**.
– ORIGIN from Pashto *paštūn*.

paso doble /ˌpasə(ʊ) ˈdəʊbleɪ/ ■ n. (pl. **paso dobles**) a fast-paced ballroom dance based on a Latin American marching style. ▸ a piece of music for such a dance.
– ORIGIN 1920s: from Spanish, 'double step'.

paspalum /ˈpasp(ə)ləm/ ■ n. a pasture grass of warm and tropical regions. [Genus *Paspalum*.]
– ORIGIN from Greek *paspalos*, denoting a kind of millet.

pass[1] ■ v. **1** move or cause to move in a specified direction. ▸ change from one state or condition to another. ▸ euphemistic die: *she passed away peacefully*. **2** go past or across; leave behind or on one side in proceeding. ▸ surpass; exceed. ▸ Tennis hit a winning shot past (an opponent). **3** (of time) elapse; go by. ▸ happen; be done or said. ▸ spend or use up (time). ▸ come to an end. **4** transfer (something) to someone, especially by handing or bequeathing it to the next person in a series. ▸ (in ball games) kick, hit, or throw (the ball) to a teammate. **5** be successful in (an examination, test, or course). ▸ judge the performance or standard of (someone or something) to be satisfactory. ▸ (**pass as/for**) be accepted as. **6** approve or put into effect (a proposal or law) by voting on it. **7** pronounce (a judgement or sentence). ▸ utter (remarks, especially criticism). **8** discharge (urine or faeces) from the body. **9** forgo one's turn or an opportunity to do or have something. ▸ [as exclam.] (in response to a question) I do not know. ▸ (of a company) not declare or pay (a dividend). ■ n. **1** an act or instance of moving past or through something. ▸ informal an amorous or sexual advance. ▸ a thrust in fencing. ▸ a juggling trick. ▸ Bridge an act of refraining from bidding during the auction. ▸ Computing a single scan through a set of data or a program. **2** a success in an examination. ▸ Brit. the achievement of a university degree without honours. **3** a card, ticket, or permit giving authorization for the holder

to enter or have access to a place, form of transport, or event. ▶ historical (in South Africa under apartheid) a black person's identity book, used to control travel and residence. **4** (in ball games) an act of passing the ball to a teammate. **5** a state or situation of a specified (usually bad) nature.
– PHRASES **come to a pretty pass** reach a regrettable state of affairs. **pass one's eye over** read cursorily. **pass water** urinate.
– PHRASAL VERBS **pass someone by** happen without being noticed or fully experienced by someone. **pass off** happen or be carried through in a specified (usually satisfactory) way. **pass something off** evade or lightly dismiss an awkward remark. **pass something off as** falsely represent something as. **pass out 1** become unconscious. **2** Brit. complete one's initial training in the armed forces. **pass someone over** ignore the claims of someone to advancement. **pass something over** avoid mentioning or considering something. **pass something up** refrain from taking up an opportunity.
– DERIVATIVES **passer** n.
– ORIGIN Middle English: from Old French *passer*, from Latin *passus* 'pace'.

pass² ■ n. a route over or through mountains.
– PHRASES **sell the pass** Brit. betray a cause.
– ORIGIN Middle English: var. of PACE¹, influenced by PASS¹ and French *pas*.

passable ■ adj. **1** good enough to be acceptable. **2** clear of obstacles and able to be travelled along or on.
– DERIVATIVES **passably** adv.

passage /'pasɪdʒ/ ■ n. **1** the action or process of moving through, under, over, or past something on the way from one place to another. ▶ the action or process of moving forward. ▶ the right to pass through somewhere. ▶ a journey by sea or air. **2** a way through something; a passageway. **3** the process of transition from one state to another. ▶ the passing of a bill into law. **4** a short section or episode from a text, musical composition, game, etc.
– PHRASES **passage of** (or **at**) **arms** a fight or dispute. **work one's passage** work in return for a free place on a voyage.
– ORIGIN Middle English: from Old French, from Latin *passus* 'pace'.

passage grave ■ n. Archaeology a prehistoric megalithic burial chamber inside a mound, with a passage leading to the exterior.

passageway ■ n. a corridor or other narrow passage between buildings or rooms.

passagework ■ n. music affording scope for virtuoso playing.

passant /'pas(ə)nt/ ■ adj. Heraldry (of an animal) represented as walking towards the dexter side, with the right front foot raised.
– ORIGIN Middle English: from Old French, 'proceeding', from *passer*.

passbook ■ n. **1** a book issued by a bank or building society to an account holder, recording transactions. **2** S. African another term for PASS¹ (in sense 3 of the noun).

passé /'paseɪ/ ■ adj. no longer fashionable; out of date.
– ORIGIN French, 'gone by', from *passer*.

passed pawn ■ n. Chess a pawn that no enemy pawn can stop from queening.

passel /'pas(ə)l/ ■ n. informal, chiefly US a large group: *a passel of journalists*.
– ORIGIN C19: representing a pronunciation of PARCEL.

passementerie /'pasm(ə)ntri/ ■ n. decorative textile trimming consisting of gold or silver lace, gimp, or braid.
– ORIGIN C17: from French, from *passement* 'gold lace'.

passenger ■ n. **1** a traveller on a public or private conveyance other than the driver, pilot, or crew. **2** a member of a team who does very little effective work.
– ORIGIN Middle English: from the Old French adj. *passager* 'passing, transitory', from *passage* (see PASSAGE).

passepartout /ˌpaspɑːˈtuː, ˌpɑːs-/ ■ n. a type of card used as a backing in picture framing.
– ORIGIN C17: from French, 'passes everywhere'.

passer-by ■ n. (pl. **passers-by**) a person who happens to be going past something, especially on foot.

passerine /'pasərʌɪn, -riːn/ Ornithology ■ adj. denoting birds of a large order (Passeriformes) distinguished by having feet adapted for perching and including all songbirds. ■ n. a passerine bird.
– ORIGIN C18: from Latin *passer* 'sparrow'.

passible /'pasɪb(ə)l/ ■ adj. Christian Church capable of feeling or suffering.
– DERIVATIVES **passibility** n.
– ORIGIN Middle English: from late Latin *passibilis*, from Latin *pass-*, *pati* 'suffer'.

passim /'pasɪm/ ■ adv. (of references) at various places throughout the text.
– ORIGIN Latin, from *passus*, *pandere* 'scatter'.

passing ■ adj. **1** going past. **2** (of a period of time) going by. **3** carried out quickly and lightly: *a passing glance*. ■ n. **1** the passage of something, especially time. **2** the action of kicking, hitting, or throwing a ball to another team member during a sports match. **3** euphemistic the end of something. ▶ a person's death.
– PHRASES **in passing** briefly and casually.
– DERIVATIVES **passingly** adv.

passing shot ■ n. Tennis a shot aiming the ball beyond and out of reach of one's opponent while they are at or near the net.

passion ■ n. **1** strong and barely controllable emotion. ▶ an outburst of such emotion. **2** intense sexual love. **3** an intense enthusiasm for something. **4** (**the Passion**) Christian Church the suffering and death of Jesus. ▶ a musical setting of this.
– DERIVATIVES **passional** adj. (rare). **passionless** adj.
– ORIGIN Middle English: from late Latin *passio(n-)*, from Latin *pati* 'suffer'.

passionate ■ adj. showing or caused by passion.
– DERIVATIVES **passionately** adv. **passionateness** n.

passion flower ■ n. an evergreen climbing plant of warm regions, with complex white, pink, or red flowers and a pulpy fruit. [Genus *Passiflora*.]

passion fruit ■ n. the edible purple fruit of a passion flower. [*Passiflora edulis*.]

passion play ■ n. a dramatic performance representing Christ's Passion.

Passion Sunday ■ n. the fifth Sunday in Lent.

Passion Week ■ n. the week between Passion Sunday and Palm Sunday.

passivate /'pasɪveɪt/ ■ v. [usu. as adj. **passivated**] make (a metal or other substance) unreactive by coating or otherwise altering its surface.
– DERIVATIVES **passivation** n.

passive ■ adj. **1** accepting or allowing what happens or what others do, without active response or resistance. **2** Grammar denoting a voice of verbs in which the subject undergoes the action of the verb (e.g. *they were killed* as opposed to *he killed them*). The opposite of ACTIVE. **3** denoting a circuit or device containing no source of energy or electromotive force. ▶ (of radar or a satellite) receiving or reflecting radiation rather than generating its own signal. **4** Chemistry unreactive because of a thin inert surface layer of oxide. ■ n. Grammar a passive form of a verb.
– DERIVATIVES **passively** adv. **passiveness** n. **passivity** n.
– ORIGIN Middle English: from Latin *passivus*, from *pass-*, *pati* 'suffer'.

passive immunity ■ n. Physiology short-term immunity resulting from the introduction of antibodies from another person or animal.

passive resistance ■ n. non-violent opposition to authority, especially a refusal to cooperate with legal requirements.

passive smoking ■ n. the involuntary inhaling of smoke from other people's cigarettes, cigars, or pipes.

passivize (also **-ise**) ■ v. Grammar convert into the passive.
– DERIVATIVES **passivizable** (also **-isable**) adj. **passivization** (also **-isation**) n.

pass key ■ n. **1** a key given only to those who are officially allowed access. **2** a master key.

pass laws ■ pl. n. laws formerly in operation in South Africa controlling the rights of black people to residence and travel.

Passover ■ n. the major Jewish spring festival, commemorating the liberation of the Israelites from Egyptian bondage.
– ORIGIN from *pass over*, with ref. to the exemption of the Israelites from the death of their firstborn (Exodus 12).

passport ■ n. an official document issued by a government, certifying the holder's identity and citizenship and entitling them to travel abroad under its protection.
– ORIGIN C15: from French *passeport*, from *passer* 'to pass' + *port* 'seaport'.

password ■ n. a secret word or phrase used to gain admission to something.

past ■ adj. 1 gone by in time and no longer existing. ▸ recently elapsed: *the past twelve months.* 2 Grammar (of a tense) expressing a past action or state. ■ n. 1 (usu. **the past**) a past period or the events in it. ▸ a person's or thing's history or earlier life. 2 Grammar a past tense or form of a verb. ■ prep. 1 to or on the further side of. 2 in front of or from one side to the other of. 3 beyond in time; later than. 4 no longer capable of. 5 beyond the scope of. ■ adv. 1 so as to pass from one side of something to the other. 2 used to indicate the passage of time: *a week went past.*
– PHRASES **not put it past someone** believe someone to be capable of doing something wrong or rash. **past it** informal too old to be any good at anything.
– ORIGIN Middle English: var. of *passed*, from PASS[1].

pasta ■ n. dough extruded or stamped into various shapes (e.g. spaghetti, lasagne) for cooking in boiling water and eating, typically with a savoury sauce.
– ORIGIN C19: from Italian, 'paste'.

paste ■ n. 1 a thick, soft, moist substance, typically produced by mixing dry ingredients with a liquid. 2 an adhesive of this kind. 3 a mixture of kaolin and water of low plasticity, used for making porcelain. 4 a hard vitreous composition used in making imitation gems. ■ v. 1 coat or stick with paste. 2 Computing insert (a section of text) into a document. 3 [often as noun **pasting**] informal beat or defeat severely.
– ORIGIN Middle English: from late Latin *pasta* 'medicinal preparation in the shape of a small square', prob. from Greek, from *pastos* 'sprinkled'.

pasteboard ■ n. thin board made by pasting together sheets of paper.

pastel ■ n. 1 a crayon made of powdered pigments bound with gum or resin. ▸ a work of art created using pastels. 2 a soft and delicate shade of a colour. ■ adj. of or denoting such a shade: *pastel blue curtains.*
– DERIVATIVES **pastellist** (also **pastelist**) n.
– ORIGIN C17: from Italian *pastello*, diminutive of *pasta* 'paste'.

pastern /ˈpast(ə)n/ ■ n. the sloping part of a horse's or other animal's foot between the fetlock and the hoof.
– ORIGIN Middle English: from Old French *pasturon*, from *pasture*, orig. 'strap for hobbling a horse'.

paste-up ■ n. a document prepared by combining and pasting various sections on a backing.

pasteurellosis /ˌpɑːstərɛˈləʊsɪs, ˌpastərɛˈləʊsɪs/ ■ n. a bacterial infection commonly affecting animals and sometimes transferred to humans through bites and scratches.
– ORIGIN C20: from French *pasteurellose*, from *Pasteurella* genus name of the bacterium responsible (named after the C19 French chemist and bacteriologist Louis *Pasteur*).

pasteurize /ˈpɑːstʃəraɪz, -stjə-, ˈpas-/ (also **-ise**) ■ v. [often as adj. **pasteurized** (also **-ised**)] subject (milk, wine, etc.) to a process of partial sterilization, especially by heating.
– DERIVATIVES **pasteurization** (also **-isation**) n. **pasteurizer** (also **-iser**) n.

pastiche /paˈstiːʃ/ ■ n. an artistic work in a style that imitates that of another work, artist, or period. ■ v. create a pastiche of (an artist or work).
– DERIVATIVES **pasticheur** n.
– ORIGIN C19: from Italian *pasticcio*, from late Latin *pasta* 'paste'.

pastille /ˈpast(ə)l, -tɪl/ ■ n. 1 a small sweet or lozenge. 2 a small pellet of aromatic paste burnt as a perfume or deodorizer.
– ORIGIN C17: from Latin *pastillus* 'little loaf, lozenge', from *panis* 'loaf'.

pastime ■ n. an activity that someone does regularly for enjoyment; a hobby.
– ORIGIN C15: from PASS[1] + TIME, translating French *passe-temps*.

pastis /ˈpastɪs, paˈstiːs/ ■ n. (pl. same) an aniseed-flavoured aperitif.
– ORIGIN from French.

past master ■ n. an experienced person particularly skilled at a specified activity.

pastor /ˈpɑːstə/ ■ n. a minister in charge of a Christian church or congregation, especially in some non-episcopal churches. ■ v. be the pastor of.
– DERIVATIVES **pastorate** n. **pastorship** n.
– ORIGIN Middle English: from Anglo-Norman French *pastour*, from Latin *pastor* 'shepherd', from *pascere* 'feed, graze'.

pastoral /ˈpɑːst(ə)r(ə)l/ ■ adj. 1 used for or relating to the farming or grazing of sheep or cattle. 2 portraying country life, especially in an idealized or romanticized form. 3 of or relating to the giving of spiritual guidance. 4 of or denoting a teacher's responsibility for the general well-being of pupils or students. ■ n. a pastoral poem, picture, etc.
– DERIVATIVES **pastoralism** n. **pastorally** adv.

pastoralist ■ n. a member of a nomadic people living chiefly by raising livestock.

past perfect ■ adj. & n. another term for PLUPERFECT.

pastrami /paˈstrɑːmi/ ■ n. highly seasoned smoked beef, typically served in thin slices.
– ORIGIN from Yiddish.

pastry ■ n. (pl. **-ies**) 1 a dough of flour, fat, and water, used as a base and covering in baked dishes such as pies. 2 an item of food consisting of sweet pastry with a cream, jam, or fruit filling.
– ORIGIN Middle English: from PASTE, influenced by Old French *pastaierie*.

pastry cream ■ n. a thick, creamy custard used as a filling for cakes or flans.

pasturage ■ n. 1 land used for pasture. 2 the occupation or process of pasturing animals.

pasture ■ n. 1 land covered mainly with grass, suitable for grazing cattle or sheep. 2 grass and herbage growing on such land. ■ v. put (animals) to graze in a pasture.
– PHRASES **pastures new** somewhere offering new opportunities. [suggested by 'Tomorrow to fresh woods and pastures new' (from the English poet John Milton's *Lycidas*).] **put out to pasture** force to retire.
– ORIGIN Middle English: from late Latin *pastura* 'grazing', from *pascere* 'graze'.

pasty[1] /ˈpasti/ (also **pastie**) ■ n. (pl. **-ies**) chiefly Brit. a folded pastry case filled with seasoned meat and vegetables.
– ORIGIN Middle English: from Old French *paste(e)*, from late Latin *pasta* 'paste'.

pasty[2] /ˈpeɪsti/ ■ adj. (**-ier, -iest**) 1 of or like paste. 2 (of a person's face) unhealthily pale.
– DERIVATIVES **pastiness** n.

Pat. ■ abbrev. Patent.

pat[1] ■ v. (**patted, patting**) 1 touch quickly and gently with the flat of the hand. 2 mould or position with gentle taps. ■ n. 1 a light stroke with the hand. 2 a compact mass of soft material.
– PHRASES **a pat on the back** an expression of congratulation or encouragement.
– ORIGIN Middle English: prob. imitative.

pat[2] ■ adj. simple and somewhat glib or unconvincing: *a pat answer.* ■ adv. conveniently or opportunely.
– PHRASES **have something off** (or **down**) **pat** have something memorized perfectly. **stand pat** chiefly N. Amer. stick stubbornly to one's opinion or decision.
– DERIVATIVES **patly** adv. **patness** n.
– ORIGIN C16: rel. to PAT[1]; orig. 'as if with a pat'.

Patagonian /ˌpatəˈɡəʊniən/ ■ n. a native or inhabitant of the South American region of Patagonia. ■ adj. of or relating to Patagonia.

Patagonian toothfish ■ n. a commercially important

bottom-dwelling fish with powerful jaws and sharp teeth, found in subantarctic waters. [*Dissostichus eleginoides*.]

patas monkey /pəˈtɑː/ ■ n. a central African guenon with reddish-brown fur, a black face, and a white moustache. [*Erythrocebus patas*.]
– ORIGIN C18: *patas* from Wolof *pata*.

patch ■ n. 1 a piece of material used to cover a torn or weak point. ▸ a shield worn over a sightless or injured eye. ▸ a piece of cloth sewn on to clothing as a badge. ▸ an adhesive piece of drug-impregnated material worn on the skin so that the drug may be gradually absorbed. ▸ historical a small black silk disc worn on the face, especially by women in the 17th and 18th centuries. 2 a small area differently coloured or otherwise distinct. 3 a small piece of ground, especially one used for gardening. ▸ informal an area for which someone is responsible or in which they operate. 4 informal a period of time regarded as distinct: *a bad patch*. 5 a temporary electrical or telephone connection. 6 Computing a small piece of code inserted to correct or enhance a program. ■ v. 1 mend, strengthen, or protect by means of a patch. ▸ (usu. **be patched with**) cause to become variegated. ▸ (**patch someone/thing up**) informal treat someone's injuries or repair the damage to something, especially hastily. ▸ (**patch something together**) construct something hastily from unsuitable components. ▸ (**patch up**) informal restore peaceful or friendly relations after (a quarrel or dispute). 2 connect by a temporary electrical, radio, or telephonic connection. 3 Computing improve or correct (a routine or program) by inserting a patch.
– PHRASES **not a patch on** Brit. informal greatly inferior to.
– DERIVATIVES **patcher** n.
– ORIGIN Middle English: perhaps from a var. of Old French *pieche*, var. of *piece* 'piece'.

patchboard ■ n. a board in a switchboard, computer, etc. with a number of sockets that can be connected in various combinations.

patch cord (also **patch lead**) ■ n. an insulated lead with a plug at each end, for use with a patchboard.

patchouli /ˈpatʃʊli, pəˈtʃuːli/ ■ n. an aromatic oil used in perfumery, insecticides, and medicine.
– ORIGIN C19: from Tamil *paccuḷi*.

patch panel ■ n. another term for **PATCHBOARD**.

patch pocket ■ n. a pocket made of a separate piece of cloth sewn on to the outside of a garment.

patch test ■ n. an allergy test in which a range of substances are applied to the skin in light scratches or under a plaster.

patchwork ■ n. 1 needlework in which small pieces of cloth in different designs are sewn together. 2 a thing composed of many different elements so as to appear variegated.

patchy ■ adj. (-ier, -iest) 1 existing or happening in small, isolated areas. 2 not of the same quality throughout; inconsistent.
– DERIVATIVES **patchily** adv. **patchiness** n.

pate /peɪt/ ■ n. archaic or humorous a person's head.
– ORIGIN Middle English.

pâté /ˈpateɪ/ ■ n. a rich savoury paste made from finely minced or mashed meat, fish, or other ingredients.
– ORIGIN French, from Old French *paste* 'pie of seasoned meat'.

pâté de foie gras /ˌpateɪ də fwɑː ˈɡrɑː/ ■ n. a smooth rich paste made from fatted goose liver.
– ORIGIN from French.

patella /pəˈtɛlə/ ■ n. (pl. **patellae** /-liː/) Anatomy the knee-cap.
– DERIVATIVES **patellar** adj. **patellate** /-lət/ adj.
– ORIGIN C16: from Latin, diminutive of *patina* 'shallow dish'.

paten /ˈpat(ə)n/ ■ n. Christian Church a plate for holding the bread during the Eucharist.
– ORIGIN Middle English: from Old French *patene*, from Latin *patina*, from Greek *patanē* 'a plate'.

patent /ˈpat(ə)nt, ˈpeɪt-/ ■ n. a government licence to an individual or body conferring a right or title for a set period, especially the sole right to make, use, or sell an invention. ■ adj. 1 /ˈpeɪt(ə)nt/ easily recognizable; obvious. ▸ Medicine (of a parasitic infection) showing detectable parasites in the tissues or faeces. 2 Medicine (of a duct or aperture) open and unobstructed. 3 made and marketed under a patent. ■ v. obtain a patent for (an invention).
– DERIVATIVES **patency** n. **patentable** adj.
– ORIGIN Middle English: from Old French, from Latin *patent-*, *patere* 'lie open'.

patentee /ˌpeɪt(ə)nˈtiː, ˌpat-/ ■ n. a person or body that obtains or holds a patent for something.

patent leather ■ n. glossy varnished leather, used chiefly for shoes, belts, and handbags.

patently /ˈpeɪt(ə)ntli/ ■ adv. plainly; obviously: *a patently false statement*.

patent medicine ■ n. a medicine made and marketed under a patent and available without prescription.

patent office ■ n. an office from which patents are issued.

pater /ˈpeɪtə/ ■ n. 1 Brit. informal, dated father. 2 Anthropology a person's legal father. Often contrasted with **GENITOR**.
– ORIGIN from Latin.

patera /ˈpat(ə)rə/ ■ n. (pl. **paterae** /-riː/) a broad, shallow bowl-shaped feature on a planet's surface.
– ORIGIN Latin, from *patere* 'be or lie open'.

paterfamilias /ˌpeɪtəfəˈmɪlɪas, ˌpatə-/ ■ n. (pl. **patresfamilias** /ˌpeɪtriːz-, ˌpatriːz-/) the male head of a family or household.
– ORIGIN Latin, 'father of the family'.

paternal ■ adj. 1 of or appropriate to a father. 2 related through the father: *his paternal grandfather*.
– DERIVATIVES **paternally** adv.
– ORIGIN Middle English: from late Latin *paternalis*, from Latin, from *pater* 'father'.

paternalism ■ n. the policy of restricting the freedom and responsibilities of one's subordinates or dependents in their supposed best interest.
– DERIVATIVES **paternalist** n. & adj. **paternalistic** adj. **paternalistically** adv.

paternity ■ n. 1 (especially in legal contexts) the state of being someone's father. 2 paternal origin.

paternity suit ■ n. a court case held to establish the identity of a child's father.

paternity test ■ n. a medical test to determine whether a man could be the father of a particular child.

paternoster /ˌpatəˈnɒstə/ ■ n. 1 (in the Roman Catholic Church) the Lord's Prayer, especially in Latin. 2 a lift consisting of a series of linked doorless compartments moving continuously on an endless belt. 3 a fishing line to which hooks or weights are attached at intervals.
– ORIGIN Old English, from Latin *pater noster* 'our father', the first words of the Lord's Prayer.

path ■ n. (pl. **paths**) 1 a way or track laid down for walking or made by continual treading. 2 the direction in which a person or thing moves. 3 a course of action or conduct.
– DERIVATIVES **pathless** adj.
– ORIGIN Old English *pæth*, of West Germanic origin.

-path ■ comb. form 1 denoting a practitioner of curative treatment: *homeopath*. 2 denoting a person who suffers from a disease: *psychopath*.
– ORIGIN back-formation from **-PATHY**, or from Greek *-pathēs* '-sufferer'.

Pathan /pəˈtɑːn/ ■ n. another term for **PASHTUN**.
– ORIGIN from Hindi *Paṭhān*.

path-breaking ■ adj. pioneering; innovative.
– DERIVATIVES **path-breaker** n.

pathetic ■ adj. 1 arousing pity, especially through vulnerability or sadness. 2 informal miserably inadequate. 3 archaic relating to the emotions.
– DERIVATIVES **pathetically** adv.
– ORIGIN C16: from Greek *pathētikos* 'sensitive', from *pathos* 'suffering'.

pathetic fallacy ■ n. the attribution of human feelings and responses to inanimate things or animals.

pathfinder ■ n. a person who goes ahead and discovers or shows others a path or way.

pathname ■ n. Computing a description of where an item is to be found in a hierarchy of directories.

patho-

patho- ■ comb. form relating to disease: *pathology*.
– ORIGIN from Greek *pathos* 'suffering, disease'.

pathogen /ˈpaθədʒ(ə)n/ ■ n. Medicine a bacterium, virus, or other micro-organism that can cause disease.
– DERIVATIVES **pathogenic** adj. **pathogenicity** n. **pathogenous** /-ˈθɒdʒɪnəs/ adj.

pathogenesis /ˌpaθə(ʊ)ˈdʒɛnɪsɪs/ ■ n. Medicine the manner of development of a disease.
– DERIVATIVES **pathogenetic** adj.

pathognomonic /ˌpaθəɡnə(ʊ)ˈmɒnɪk/ ■ adj. Medicine indicative of a particular disease or condition.
– ORIGIN C17: from Greek *pathognōmonikos* 'skilled in diagnosis', from *pathos* 'suffering' + *gnōmōn* 'judge'.

pathological (US **pathologic**) ■ adj. 1 involving, caused by, or of the nature of a disease. 2 informal compulsive: *a pathological gambler*. 3 of or relating to pathology.
– DERIVATIVES **pathologically** adv.

pathologize (also **-ise**) ■ v. regard or treat as psychologically abnormal.
– DERIVATIVES **pathologization** n.

pathology ■ n. 1 the branch of medicine concerned with the causes and effects of diseases. 2 Medicine the typical behaviour of a specified disease.
– DERIVATIVES **pathologist** n.
– ORIGIN C17: from medieval Latin *pathologia* (see PATHO-, -LOGY).

pathophysiology ■ n. Medicine the disordered physiological processes associated with disease or injury.
– DERIVATIVES **pathophysiologic** adj. **pathophysiological** adj. **pathophysiologically** adv. **pathophysiologist** n.

pathos /ˈpeɪθɒs/ ■ n. a quality that evokes pity or sadness.
– ORIGIN C17: from Greek *pathos* 'suffering'.

pathway ■ n. 1 a path or its course. 2 a sequence of changes or events constituting a progression.

-pathy ■ comb. form 1 denoting feelings: *telepathy*. 2 denoting disorder in a particular part of the body: *neuropathy*. 3 denoting curative treatment of a specified kind: *hydropathy*.
– ORIGIN from Greek *patheia* 'suffering, feeling'.

patience ■ n. 1 the capacity to tolerate delay, trouble, or suffering without becoming angry or upset. 2 a card game for one player, the object of which is to use up all one's cards by forming particular arrangements and sequences.
– PHRASES **lose patience** (or **lose one's patience**) become unable to keep one's temper.
– ORIGIN Middle English: from Latin *patientia*, from *pati* 'suffer'.

patient ■ adj. having or showing patience. ■ n. a person receiving or registered to receive medical treatment.
– DERIVATIVES **patiently** adv.
– ORIGIN Middle English: from Latin *patient-*, *pati* 'suffer'.

patina /ˈpatɪnə/ ■ n. 1 a green or brown film on the surface of old bronze. 2 a sheen on wooden furniture produced by age and polishing. 3 any distinctive surface appearance acquired over time.
– DERIVATIVES **patinated** adj. **patination** n.
– ORIGIN C18: from Latin *patina* 'shallow dish'.

patio ■ n. (pl. **-os**) a paved outdoor area adjoining a house.
– ORIGIN C19: from Spanish.

patio door ■ n. a large glass sliding door leading to a patio, garden, or balcony.

patisserie /pəˈtiːs(ə)ri, -ˈtɪs-/ ■ n. 1 a shop where pastries and cakes are sold. 2 pastries and cakes collectively.
– ORIGIN C16: from French *pâtisserie*, from medieval Latin *pasticium* 'pastry'.

Patna rice ■ n. rice of a variety with long firm grains, originally produced at Patna in India.

patois /ˈpatwɑː/ ■ n. (pl. same /-wɑːz/) the dialect of the common people of a region, differing in various respects from the standard language of the country.
– ORIGIN C17: French, 'rough speech', perhaps from Old French *patoier* 'treat roughly', from *patte* 'paw'.

patresfamilias plural form of PATERFAMILIAS.

patriarch /ˈpeɪtrɪɑːk/ ■ n. 1 the male head of a family or tribe. ▸ an older man who is powerful within a family or organization. ▸ a founder. 2 a biblical figure regarded as a father of the human race. 3 a bishop of one of the most ancient Christian sees (Alexandria, Antioch, Constantinople, Jerusalem, and formerly Rome). ▸ the head of an Eastern Orthodox Church not subject to the external authority of an archbishop. ▸ a Roman Catholic bishop ranking above primates and metropolitans and immediately below the Pope.
– DERIVATIVES **patriarchal** adj. **patriarchally** adv. **patriarchate** n.
– ORIGIN Middle English: from Old French *patriarche*, from Greek *patriarkhēs*, from *patria* 'family' + *arkhēs* 'ruling'.

patriarchy ■ n. (pl. **-ies**) 1 a form of social organization in which the father or eldest male is the head of the family and descent is reckoned through the male line. 2 a system of society or government ruled by men.

patrician /pəˈtrɪʃ(ə)n/ ■ n. 1 an aristocrat or nobleman. 2 a member of the noble class in ancient Rome. 3 N. Amer. a member of a long-established wealthy family. ■ adj. belonging to or characteristic of patricians.
– ORIGIN Middle English: from Old French *patricien*, from Latin *patricius* 'having a noble father', from *pater*, *patr-* 'father'.

patricide /ˈpatrɪsʌɪd/ ■ n. the killing of one's father. ▸ a person who kills their father.
– DERIVATIVES **patricidal** adj.
– ORIGIN C17: from late Latin *patricidium*, alteration of Latin *parricida* (see PARRICIDE).

patrilineal ■ adj. of, relating to, or based on relationship to the father or descent through the male line.
– ORIGIN C20: from Latin *pater*, *patr-* 'father' + LINEAL.

patrimony /ˈpatrɪməni/ ■ n. (pl. **-ies**) 1 property inherited from one's father or male ancestor. 2 heritage. 3 chiefly historical property belonging by ancient endowment or right to a church or other institution.
– DERIVATIVES **patrimonial** /-ˈməʊnɪəl/ adj.
– ORIGIN Middle English: from Latin *patrimonium*, from *pater* 'father'.

patriot /ˈpatrɪət, ˈpeɪt-/ ■ n. a person who vigorously supports their country and is prepared to defend it.
– DERIVATIVES **patriotic** adj. **patriotically** adv. **patriotism** n.
– ORIGIN C16: from French *patriote*, from late Latin *patriota* 'fellow countryman', from Greek, from *patrios* 'of one's fathers', from *patris* 'fatherland'.

patristic /pəˈtrɪstɪk/ ■ adj. of or relating to the early Christian theologians or their writings.
– DERIVATIVES **patristics** pl. n.
– ORIGIN C19: from German *patristisch*, from Latin *pater* 'father'.

patrol ■ n. 1 a person or group sent to keep watch over an area, especially a detachment of guards or police. 2 the action of patrolling an area. 3 an expedition to carry out reconnaissance. 4 a routine operational voyage of a ship or aircraft. ■ v. (**patrolled**, **patrolling**) keep watch over (an area) by regularly walking or travelling around it.
– DERIVATIVES **patroller** n.
– ORIGIN C17: from German *Patrolle*, from French, from *patrouiller* 'paddle in mud', from *patte* 'paw' + dialect (*gad*)*rouille* 'dirty water'.

patrolman ■ n. (pl. **-men**) N. Amer. a patrolling police officer.

patron ■ n. 1 a person who gives financial or other support to a person, organization, cause, etc. 2 a distinguished person who takes an honorary position in a charity. 3 a customer of a restaurant, hotel, etc., especially a regular one.
– DERIVATIVES **patroness** n.
– ORIGIN Middle English: from Latin *patronus* 'protector of clients, defender', from *pater* 'father'.

patronage /ˈpatr(ə)nɪdʒ, ˈpeɪt-/ ■ n. 1 the support given by a patron. 2 the power to control appointments to office or the right to privileges. 3 a patronizing manner. 4 the regular custom attracted by a restaurant, hotel, etc.

patronal /pəˈtrəʊn(ə)l/ ■ adj. of or relating to a patron saint.

patronize (also **-ise**) ■ v. 1 [often as adj. **patronizing** (also **-ising**)] treat with an apparent kindness which betrays a feeling of superiority. 2 frequent (an establishment) as a customer. 3 act as a patron towards (a person, organization, etc.).

- DERIVATIVES **patronization** (also **-isation**) n. **patronizer** (also **-iser**) n. **patronizingly** (also **-isingly**) adv.
patron saint ■ n. the protecting or guiding saint of a person or place.
patronymic /ˌpatrəˈnɪmɪk/ ■ n. a name derived from the name of a father or ancestor, e.g. *Johnson, O'Brien, Ivanovich.*
- ORIGIN C17: from Greek *patrōnumikos*, from *patrōnumos*, from *patēr* 'father' + *onoma* 'name'.
patsy ■ n. (pl. **-ies**) informal, chiefly N. Amer. a person who is taken advantage of, especially by being cheated or blamed for something.
- ORIGIN C20.
patten /ˈpat(ə)n/ ■ n. historical a shoe or clog with a raised sole or set on an iron ring, worn to raise the feet above wet ground.
- ORIGIN Middle English: from Old French *patin*, perhaps from *patte* 'paw'.
patter[1] ■ v. 1 make a repeated light tapping sound. 2 run with quick light steps. ■ n. a repeated light tapping.
- ORIGIN C17: from PAT[1].
patter[2] ■ n. rapid continuous talk, such as that used by a comedian or salesman. ▸ rapid speech included in a comic song. ▸ the jargon of a profession or other group. ■ v. talk trivially at length.
- ORIGIN Middle English: from PATERNOSTER.
pattern ■ n. 1 a repeated decorative design. ▸ an arrangement or sequence regularly found in comparable objects or events. 2 a model or design used as a guide in needlework and other crafts. ▸ a set of instructions to be followed in making a sewn or knitted item. ▸ a model from which a mould is made for a casting. 3 an example for others to follow. 4 a sample of cloth or wallpaper. ■ v. 1 decorate with a pattern. 2 give a regular or intelligible form to. ▸ (**pattern something on/after**) give something a form based on that of (something else).
- DERIVATIVES **patterning** n. **patternless** adj.
- ORIGIN Middle English *patron* 'something serving as a model', from Old French (see PATRON).
patty ■ n. (pl. **-ies**) 1 a small flat cake of minced food, especially meat. 2 a small pie or pasty.
- ORIGIN C17: from French *pâté*, by association with PASTY[1].
pattypan (also **pattypan squash**) ■ n. a small squash of a saucer-shaped variety with a scalloped edge and creamy white flesh.
paua /ˈpɑːwə, ˈpaʊə/ ■ n. a large New Zealand abalone or its shell.
- ORIGIN C19: from Maori.
paucity /ˈpɔːsɪti/ ■ n. the presence of something in only small or insufficient amounts.
- ORIGIN Middle English: from Old French *paucite* or Latin *paucitas*, from *paucus* 'few'.
Pauline /ˈpɔːlʌɪn/ ■ adj. Christian Church relating to or characteristic of St Paul.
Paul Jones ■ n. a ballroom dance in which the dancers change partners after circling in concentric rings.
- ORIGIN 1920s: named after the American admiral John Paul Jones (1747–92).
paunch ■ n. a large or protruding abdomen or stomach. ■ v. disembowel (an animal).
- DERIVATIVES **paunchiness** n. **paunchy** adj.
- ORIGIN Middle English: from Anglo-Norman French *pa(u)nche*, from Latin *pantex* 'intestines'.
pauper ■ n. 1 a very poor person. 2 historical a recipient of poor-law relief.
- DERIVATIVES **pauperdom** n. **pauperism** n. **pauperization** (also **-isation**) n. **pauperize** (also **-ise**) v.
- ORIGIN C15: from Latin, 'poor'.
pause ■ n. 1 a temporary stop in action or speech. 2 a control allowing the temporary interruption of recording, playback, or other process. ■ v. 1 have a pause; stop temporarily. 2 temporarily interrupt (a process or device).
- PHRASES **give pause to someone** (or **give pause for thought**) cause someone to think carefully or hesitate before doing something.
- ORIGIN Middle English: from Latin *pausa*, from Greek *pausis*, from *pausein* 'to stop'.
pavane /pəˈvan, -ˈvɑːn/ (also **pavan** /ˈpav(ə)n/) ■ n. a stately dance, popular in the 16th and 17th centuries and performed in elaborate clothing. ▸ a piece of music for this dance.
- ORIGIN C16: from Italian *pavana*, from *Pavo*, dialect name of the city of *Padua*.
pave ■ v. (often **be paved with**) cover (a piece of ground) with flat stones or bricks.
- PHRASES **pave the way for** create the circumstances to enable (something) to happen or be done.
- DERIVATIVES **paver** n. **paving** n.
- ORIGIN Middle English: from Old French *paver* 'pave'.
pavé /ˈpaveɪ/ ■ n. a setting of precious stones placed so closely together that no metal shows.
- ORIGIN French, 'paved', from *paver*.
pavement ■ n. 1 a raised paved or asphalted path for pedestrians at the side of a road. 2 N. Amer. the hard surface of a road or street. 3 Geology a horizontal expanse of bare rock with cracks or joints: *a limestone pavement.*
- ORIGIN Middle English: from Latin *pavimentum* 'trodden down floor', from *pavire* 'beat, tread down'.
pavement artist ■ n. Brit. an artist who draws with coloured chalks on paving stones to earn money from passers-by.
pavilion ■ n. 1 a building at a cricket ground or other sports ground used for changing and taking refreshments. 2 a summer house or other decorative shelter in a park or large garden. 3 a detached or semi-detached block at a hospital or other building complex. 4 a marquee, especially as used at shows and fairs. 5 a temporary stand or other structure in which items are displayed at a trade exhibition.
- ORIGIN Middle English: from Old French *pavillon*, from Latin *papilio(n-)* 'butterfly or tent'.
paviour /ˈpeɪvjə/ (also **pavior**) ■ n. 1 a paving stone. 2 archaic a person who lays paving stones.
- ORIGIN Middle English: from Old French *paveur*, from *paver* 'pave'.
pavlova ■ n. a dessert consisting of a meringue base and shell filled with whipped cream and fruit.
- ORIGIN 1920s: named after the Russian ballerina Anna *Pavlova*.
Pavlovian /pavˈləʊvɪən/ ■ adj. relating to or denoting classical conditioning as described by the Russian physiologist Ivan P. Pavlov (1849–1936).
paw ■ n. 1 an animal's foot having claws and pads. 2 informal a person's hand. ■ v. 1 feel or scrape with a paw or hoof. 2 informal touch or handle clumsily or lasciviously.
- ORIGIN Middle English: from Old French *poue*, prob. of Germanic origin.
pawky ■ adj. (**-ier, -iest**) chiefly Scottish & N. English drily humorous; sardonic.
- DERIVATIVES **pawkily** adv. **pawkiness** n.
- ORIGIN C17: from Scots and northern English *pawk* 'trick'.
pawl /pɔːl/ ■ n. 1 a pivoted curved bar or lever whose free end engages with the teeth of a cogwheel or ratchet so that the wheel or ratchet can only turn or move one way. 2 each of a set of short stout bars that by engaging with the projections on a capstan, windlass, or winch prevents it from recoiling.
- ORIGIN C17: perhaps from Low German and Dutch *pal* (rel. to *pal* 'fixed').
pawn[1] ■ n. 1 a chess piece of the smallest size and value. 2 a person used by others for their own purposes.
- ORIGIN Middle English: from Anglo-Norman French *poun*, from medieval Latin *pedo* 'foot soldier', from Latin *pes* 'foot'.
pawn[2] ■ v. deposit (an object) with a pawnbroker as security for money lent. ■ n. (usu. **in pawn**) the state of being pawned.
- ORIGIN C15: from Old French *pan* 'pledge, security'.
pawnbroker ■ n. a person who lends money at interest on the security of an article pawned.
- DERIVATIVES **pawnbroking** n.
Pawnee /pɔːˈniː/ ■ n. (pl. same or **Pawnees**) 1 a member of an American Indian confederacy formerly living in

pawnshop

Nebraska, and now mainly in Oklahoma. **2** the language of these people.
– ORIGIN from Canadian French *Pani*, from a N. American Indian language.

pawnshop ■ n. a pawnbroker's shop.

pawpaw /'pɔːpɔː/ (also **papaw**) ■ n. another term for **PAPAYA**.
– ORIGIN C17: from Spanish and Portuguese *papaya*, of Carib origin.

pay¹ ■ v. (past and past part. **paid**) **1** give (someone) money due for work, goods, or a debt incurred. ▶ give (a sum of money) thus owed. ▶ **(pay someone off)** dismiss someone with a final payment. **2** be profitable or advantageous. ▶ **(pay off)** informal yield good results. **3** suffer a loss or misfortune as a consequence of an action. ▶ give what is due or deserved to. ▶ **(pay someone back)** take revenge on someone. **4** give (attention, respect, or a compliment) to. ▶ make (a visit or a call) to. **5** **(pay something out)** let out a rope by slackening it. ■ n. money paid for work.
– PHRASES **in the pay of** employed by. **pay dearly** suffer for a misdemeanour or failure. **pay its** (or **one's**) **way** earn enough to cover its or one's costs. **pay one's last respects** show respect towards a dead person by attending their funeral. **pay one's respects** make a polite visit to someone. **pay through the nose** informal pay much more than a fair price.
– DERIVATIVES **payee** n. **payer** n.
– ORIGIN Middle English: from Old French *paie* (n.), *payer* (v.), from Latin *pacare* 'appease', from *pax* 'peace'.

pay² ■ v. (past and past part. **payed**) Nautical seal (the deck or seams of a wooden ship) with pitch or tar to prevent leakage.
– ORIGIN C17: from Old Northern French *peier*, from Latin *picare*, from *pix* 'pitch'.

payable ■ adj. **1** required to be paid. **2** able to be paid. ■ n. **(payables)** debts owed by a business.

payback ■ n. **1** financial return, especially profit from an investment equal to the initial outlay. **2** informal an act of revenge.

pay channel ■ n. a television channel for which viewers pay a subscription fee additional to that already paid for the basic provision of a cable or satellite service.

pay dirt ■ n. ground containing ore in sufficient quantity to be profitably extracted.
– PHRASES **hit** (or **strike**) **pay dirt** informal find or reach a source of profit.

PAYE ■ abbrev. pay as you earn, the deduction of income tax from an employee's wages by an employer to be paid directly to the government.

paying guest ■ n. a lodger.

payload ■ n. **1** the part of a vehicle's load from which revenue is derived; passengers and cargo. **2** an explosive warhead carried by an aircraft or missile. **3** equipment, personnel, or satellites carried by a spacecraft.

paymaster ■ n. **1** a person who pays another to do something and therefore controls them. **2** an official who pays troops or workers.

payment ■ n. **1** the action of paying or the process of being paid. **2** an amount paid or payable.

pay-off ■ n. informal **1** a payment, especially one made as a bribe or on leaving a job. **2** the return on investment or on a bet. **3** informal a final outcome.

payola /peɪˈəʊlə/ ■ n. chiefly N. Amer. bribery in return for the unofficial promotion of a product in the media.
– ORIGIN 1930s: from PAY¹ + -*ola*.

pay-per-view ■ n. a television service in which viewers are required to pay a fee in order to watch a specific programme.

payphone ■ n. a public telephone that is operated by coins or by a credit or prepaid card.

payroll ■ n. a list of a company's employees and the amount of money they are to be paid.

pay TV ■ n. television broadcasting in which viewers pay by subscription to watch a particular channel.

Pb ■ symb. the chemical element lead.

– ORIGIN from Latin *plumbum*.

PBS ■ abbrev. (in the US) Public Broadcasting System (or Service).

PBX ■ abbrev. private branch exchange, a private telephone switchboard.

PC ■ abbrev. **1** personal computer. **2** police constable. **3** (also **pc**) politically correct; political correctness. **4** Privy Counsellor.

p.c. ■ abbrev. **1** per cent. **2** postcard.

PCB ■ abbrev. **1** Electronics printed circuit board. **2** Chemistry polychlorinated biphenyl.

PCI ■ abbrev. Peripheral Component Interconnect, a standard for connecting computers and their peripherals.

PCM ■ abbrev. pulse code modulation.

PCMCIA ■ abbrev. Personal Computer Memory Card International Association, denoting a standard specification for memory cards and interfaces in personal computers.

PCP ■ abbrev. **1** phencyclidine. **2** Pneumocystis carinii pneumonia.

PCS ■ abbrev. personal communications services, a digital mobile telephony system.

pct. ■ abbrev. N. Amer. per cent.

Pd ■ symb. the chemical element palladium.

pd ■ abbrev. paid.

PDA ■ abbrev. personal digital assistant, a basic palmtop computer.

PDC ■ abbrev. (on a VCR) programme delivery control.

PDF ■ n. Computing a file format for capturing and sending electronic documents in exactly the intended format. ▶ a file in this format.
– ORIGIN 1990s: abbrev. of *Portable Document Format*.

PDQ ■ abbrev. informal pretty damn quick.

PE ■ abbrev. **1** physical education. **2** (in South Africa) Port Elizabeth.

pea ■ n. **1** a spherical green seed eaten as a vegetable. **2** the hardy climbing leguminous plant which yields pods containing peas. [*Pisum sativum*.] **3** used in names of similar or related plants or seeds. e.g. chickpea, sweet pea.
– ORIGIN C17: back-formation from PEASE (interpreted as pl.).

pea-brain ■ n. informal a stupid person.
– DERIVATIVES **pea-brained** adj.

peace ■ n. **1** freedom from disturbance; tranquillity. **2** freedom from or the cessation of war. ▶ a treaty agreeing peace between states at war. **3** (**the peace**) Christian Church an action such as a handshake taking the place of the kiss of peace.
– PHRASES **at peace 1** free from anxiety or distress. **2** euphemistic dead. **hold one's peace** remain silent. **keep the peace** refrain or prevent others from disturbing civil order. **make** (**one's**) **peace** become reconciled.
– ORIGIN Middle English: from Old French *pais*, from Latin *pax* 'peace'.

peaceable ■ adj. **1** inclined to avoid war. **2** free from conflict; peaceful.
– DERIVATIVES **peaceably** adv.
– ORIGIN Middle English: from Old French *peisible*, alteration of *plaisible*, from Latin *placere* 'to please'.

peace dividend ■ n. a sum of public money available for other purposes when spending on defence is reduced.

peaceful ■ adj. **1** free from disturbance; calm. **2** not involving war or violence. **3** inclined to avoid conflict.
– DERIVATIVES **peacefully** adv. **peacefulness** n.

peace-in-the-home ■ n. a creeping Mediterranean plant with masses of tiny leaves, grown as an indoor plant. [*Soleirolia soleirolii*.]

peacekeeping ■ n. the active maintenance of a truce, especially by an international military force.
– DERIVATIVES **peacekeeper** n.

peacenik ■ n. informal, often derogatory a member of a pacifist movement.
– ORIGIN 1960s.

peace offering ■ n. **1** a conciliatory gift. **2** (in biblical use) an offering presented as a thanksgiving to God.

peace officer ■ n. S. African & N. Amer. a civil officer appointed to preserve law and order, such as a traffic policeman.

peace pipe ■ n. a tobacco pipe offered and smoked as a token of peace among North American Indians.

peace sign ■ n. a sign of peace made by holding up the hand with palm out-turned and the first two fingers extended in a V-shape.

peacetime ■ n. a period when a country is not at war.

peach[1] ■ n. 1 a round stone fruit with juicy yellow flesh and downy yellow skin flushed with red. 2 the Chinese tree which bears this fruit. [*Prunus persica*.] 3 a pinkish-orange colour like that of a peach. 4 informal an exceptionally good or attractive person or thing.
– PHRASES **peaches and cream** (of a person's complexion) of a cream colour with downy pink cheeks.
– ORIGIN Middle English: from Old French *pesche*, from Latin *persicum* (*malum*) 'Persian (apple)'.

peach[2] ■ v. (**peach on**) informal inform on.
– ORIGIN Middle English: shortening of archaic *appeach*, from Old French *empechier* (see IMPEACH).

peach bloom ■ n. a matt glaze of reddish pink mottled with green and brown, used on Chinese porcelain.

peach Melba ■ n. a dish of ice cream and peaches with Melba sauce.
– ORIGIN from the name of the Australian operatic soprano Dame Nellie *Melba* (1861–1931).

peachy ■ adj. (-ier, -iest) 1 of the nature or appearance of a peach. 2 (also **peachy keen**) informal attractive or excellent: *everything is just peachy.*
– DERIVATIVES **peachiness** n.

pea coat ■ n. another term for PEA JACKET.

peacock ■ n. a male peafowl, having very long tail feathers with eye-like markings that can be erected and fanned out in display.
– ORIGIN Middle English: from Old English *pēa* (from Latin *pavo*) 'peacock' + COCK.

peacock blue ■ n. a greenish-blue colour like that of a peacock's neck.

peacock butterfly ■ n. a brightly coloured Eurasian butterfly with conspicuous eyespots on its wings. [*Inachis io*.]

peafowl ■ n. a large crested pheasant of which the male is the peacock and the female the peahen. [*Pavo cristatus* (southern Asia) and other species.]

pea green ■ n. a bright green colour.

peahen ■ n. a female peafowl, which has drabber colours and a shorter tail than the male.

pea jacket ■ n. a short double-breasted overcoat of coarse woollen cloth, formerly worn by sailors.
– ORIGIN C18: prob. from Dutch *pijjakker*, from *pij* 'coat of coarse cloth' + *jekker* 'jacket'.

peak ■ n. 1 the pointed top of a mountain. ▶ a mountain with a peak. 2 a stiff brim at the front of a cap. 3 a point in a curve or on a graph, or a value of a physical quantity, which is higher than those around it. ▶ the point of highest activity or achievement. 4 the upper, outer corner of a sail extended by a gaff. ■ v. reach a highest point. ■ adj. maximum. ▶ characterized by maximum activity or demand: *peak hours.*
– DERIVATIVES **peakless** adj.
– ORIGIN C16: prob. a back-formation from *peaked*, var. of dialect *picked* 'pointed'.

peaked[1] ■ adj. (of a cap) having a peak.

peaked[2] ■ adj. gaunt and pale from illness or fatigue.

peak flow meter ■ n. Medicine an instrument used to measure lung capacity in monitoring breathing disorders such as asthma.

peak load ■ n. the maximum of electrical power demand.

peaky ■ adj. (-ier, -iest) pale from illness or fatigue.

peal ■ n. 1 a loud ringing of a bell or bells. ▶ Bell-ringing a series of changes rung on a set of bells. ▶ a set of bells. 2 a loud repeated or reverberating sound of thunder or laughter. ■ v. 1 ring loudly or in a peal. 2 (of laughter or thunder) sound in a peal.
– ORIGIN Middle English: shortening of APPEAL.

peanut ■ n. 1 the oval seed of a South American plant, eaten as a snack or used for making oil or animal feed. 2 the leguminous plant that bears these seeds, which develop in underground pods. [*Arachis hypogaea*.] 3 (**peanuts**) informal a paltry sum of money.

peanut butter ■ n. a spread made from ground roasted peanuts.

peanut gallery ■ n. N. Amer. informal the top gallery in a theatre where the cheaper seats are located.

peanut worm ■ n. a burrowing marine worm with a stout body and a slender retractable part bearing a mouth surrounded by tentacles. [Phylum Sipuncula.]

pear ■ n. 1 a yellowish- or brownish-green edible fruit, narrow at the stalk and wider towards the tip. 2 the tree which bears this fruit. [*Pyrus communis* and related species.]
– ORIGIN Old English, of West Germanic origin, from Latin *pirum*.

pear drop ■ n. a boiled sweet in the shape of a pear, with a pungently sweet flavour.

pearl ■ n. 1 a hard, lustrous spherical mass, typically white or bluish-grey, formed within the shell of an oyster or other bivalve mollusc and highly prized as a gem. ▶ an artificial imitation of this. 2 a thing of great worth: *pearls of wisdom*. 3 a very pale bluish grey or white colour. ■ v. 1 poetic/literary form pearl-like drops. 2 [usu. as noun **pearling**] dive or fish for pearl oysters.
– PHRASES **cast pearls before swine** offer valuable things to people who do not appreciate them.
– DERIVATIVES **pearler** n.
– ORIGIN Middle English: from Old French *perle*, perhaps from Latin *perna* 'leg', extended to denote a leg-of-mutton-shaped bivalve.

pearl barley ■ n. barley reduced to small round grains by grinding.

pearl button ■ n. a button made of real or imitation mother-of-pearl.

pearled ■ adj. 1 adorned with pearls. 2 bluish-grey.

pearlescent ■ adj. having a lustre resembling that of mother-of-pearl.

pearlite ■ n. Metallurgy a finely laminated mixture of ferrite and cementite present in cast iron and steel.
– ORIGIN C19: from PEARL.

pearlized (also **-ised**) ■ adj. made to have a lustre like that of mother-of-pearl.

pearl millet ■ n. a cereal with long cylindrical ears, cultivated in the driest areas of Africa and the Indian subcontinent. [*Pennisetum glaucum*.]

pearl onion ■ n. a very small onion used for pickling.

pearly ■ adj. (-ier, -iest) resembling a pearl in lustre or colour. ■ n. (pl. -ies) (**pearlies**) Brit. 1 a pearly king's or queen's clothes or pearl buttons. 2 (also **pearly whites**) informal a person's teeth.
– DERIVATIVES **pearliness** n.

Pearly Gates ■ pl. n. informal the gates of heaven.

pearly king (or **pearly queen**) ■ n. a London costermonger (or his wife) wearing traditional ceremonial clothes covered with pearl buttons.

pear-shaped ■ adj. having hips that are disproportionately wide in relation to the upper part of the body.
– PHRASES **go pear-shaped** Brit. informal go wrong.

peasant ■ n. 1 a poor smallholder or agricultural labourer of low social status. 2 informal an ignorant, rude, or unsophisticated person.
– DERIVATIVES **peasantry** n. **peasanty** adj.
– ORIGIN Middle English: from Old French *paisent* 'country dweller', from *pais* 'country', from Latin *pagus* 'country district'.

peasant economy ■ n. an agricultural economy in which the family is the basic unit of production.

pease /piːz/ ■ pl. n. archaic peas.
– ORIGIN Old English *pise* 'pea', from Greek *pison*.

pease pudding ■ n. chiefly Brit. a dish of split peas boiled with onion and carrot and mashed to a pulp.

pea-shooter ■ n. a toy weapon consisting of a small tube out of which dried peas are blown.

pea-souper ■ n. Brit. informal a very thick yellowish fog.

peat ■ n. partly decomposed vegetable matter forming a deposit on acidic, boggy ground, dried for use in gardening and as fuel.
– DERIVATIVES **peaty** adj.
– ORIGIN Middle English: from Anglo-Latin *peta*.

peat moss ■ n. **1** a large absorbent moss which grows in dense masses on boggy ground. [Genus *Sphagnum*.] **2** a peat bog.

peau-de-soie /ˌpəʊdəˈswɑː/ ■ n. a smooth, finely ribbed satin fabric of silk or rayon.
– ORIGIN C19: French, 'skin of silk'.

pebble ■ n. a small stone made smooth and round by the action of water or sand. ■ adj. informal (of a spectacle lens) very thick and convex.
– DERIVATIVES **pebbled** adj. **pebbly** adj.
– ORIGIN Old English, as *papel-stān* 'pebble-stone', *pyppelrīpig* 'pebble-stream'.

pebble-dash ■ n. chiefly Brit. mortar with pebbles in it, used as a coating for external walls.
– DERIVATIVES **pebble-dashed** adj.

pebble plant ■ n. another term for STONE PLANT.

pec ■ n. informal a pectoral muscle.

pecan /ˈpiːk(ə)n, pɪˈkan, pɪˈkɑːn/ ■ n. **1** a smooth pinkish-brown nut resembling a walnut. **2** a hickory tree of the southern US, which produces these nuts. [*Carya illinoensis*.]
– ORIGIN C18: from French *pacane*, from Illinois (an American Indian language).

peccadillo /ˌpɛkəˈdɪləʊ/ ■ n. (pl. **-oes** or **-os**) a minor sin or fault.
– ORIGIN C16: from Spanish *pecadillo*, diminutive of *pecado* 'sin'.

peccary /ˈpɛk(ə)ri/ ■ n. (pl. **-ies**) a gregarious piglike mammal found from the south-western US to Paraguay. [Family Tayassuidae: three species.]
– ORIGIN C17: from Carib *pakira*.

peck¹ ■ v. **1** (of a bird) strike or bite with its beak. **2** kiss lightly or perfunctorily. **3** (**peck at**) informal eat (food) listlessly or daintily. **4** type slowly and laboriously. ■ n. **1** an act of pecking. **2** a light or perfunctory kiss.
– ORIGIN Middle English: cf. Middle Low German *pekken* 'peck'.

peck² ■ n. **1** a measure of capacity for dry goods, equal to a quarter of a bushel (approximately 9 litres). **2** archaic a large number or amount of something.
– ORIGIN Middle English: from Anglo-Norman French *pek*.

peck³ ■ v. (of a horse) stumble as a result of striking the ground with the front rather than the flat of the hoof.
– ORIGIN var. of obsolete *pick* 'fix (something pointed) in the ground'.

pecker ■ n. N. Amer. vulgar slang a man's penis.
– PHRASES **keep your pecker up** Brit. informal remain cheerful. [*pecker* prob. in the sense 'beak'.]

pecking order (also **peck order**) ■ n. a hierarchy of status among members of a group, originally as observed among hens.

peckish ■ adj. informal hungry.

pecorino /ˌpɛkəˈriːnəʊ/ ■ n. (pl. **-os**) an Italian cheese made from ewes' milk.
– ORIGIN Italian, from *pecorino* 'of ewes'.

pecten /ˈpɛktɛn/ ■ n. (pl. **pectens** or **pectines** /-tɪniːz/) Zoology a comb-like structure or appendage.
– DERIVATIVES **pectinate** /-nət/ adj. **pectinated** adj.
– ORIGIN Middle English: from Latin *pecten* 'a comb'.

pectin ■ n. a soluble gelatinous polysaccharide present in ripe fruits, used as a setting agent in jams and jellies.
– DERIVATIVES **pectic** adj.
– ORIGIN C19: from Greek *pēktos* 'congealed'.

pectoral /ˈpɛkt(ə)r(ə)l/ ■ adj. of, on, or relating to the breast or chest. ■ n. **1** a pectoral muscle. **2** an ornamental breastplate.
– ORIGIN Middle English: from Latin *pectorale* 'breastplate', from *pectus* 'breast, chest'.

pectoral fin ■ n. Zoology each of a pair of fins situated on either side just behind a fish's head.

pectoral muscle ■ n. each of four large paired muscles which cover the front of the ribcage.

peculation /ˌpɛkjʊˈleɪʃ(ə)n/ ■ n. formal the embezzlement of public funds.
– DERIVATIVES **peculate** v.
– ORIGIN C17: from Latin *peculari* 'peculate'.

peculiar ■ adj. **1** strange or odd. **2** (**peculiar to**) belonging exclusively to. **3** formal particular.
– DERIVATIVES **peculiarly** adv.
– ORIGIN Middle English: from Latin *peculiaris* 'of private property', from *peculium* 'property', from *pecu* 'cattle'.

peculiarity ■ n. (pl. **-ies**) **1** an unusual or distinctive feature or habit. **2** the state of being peculiar.

pecuniary /pɪˈkjuːnɪəri/ ■ adj. formal of, relating to, or consisting of money.
– DERIVATIVES **pecuniarily** adv.
– ORIGIN C16: from Latin *pecuniarius*, from *pecunia* 'money'.

pedagogic /ˌpɛdəˈɡɒɡɪk, -ˈɡɒdʒ-/ ■ adj. of or relating to teaching. ■ n. (**pedagogics**) [treated as sing.] old-fashioned term for PEDAGOGY.
– DERIVATIVES **pedagogical** adj. **pedagogically** adv.

pedagogue /ˈpɛdəɡɒɡ/ ■ n. formal or humorous a teacher, especially a strict or pedantic one.
– ORIGIN Middle English: from Greek *paidagōgos*, denoting a slave who accompanied a child to school (from *pais, paid-* 'boy' + *agōgos* 'guide').

pedagogy /ˈpɛdəɡɒɡi, -ɡɒdʒi/ ■ n. (pl. **-ies**) the profession, science, or theory of teaching.

pedal¹ /ˈpɛd(ə)l/ ■ n. **1** each of a pair of foot-operated levers for powering a bicycle or other vehicle propelled by leg power. **2** a foot-operated throttle, brake, or clutch control in a motor vehicle. **3** each of a set of two or three foot-operated levers on a piano, for sustaining or softening the tone. ▸ a foot-operated lever on other musical instruments, such as a harp or organ. **4** Music short for PEDAL NOTE (in sense 2). ■ v. (**pedalled,** pedalling; US **pedaled, pedaling**) **1** move (a bicycle, pedalo, etc.) by working the pedals. **2** use the pedals of a piano, organ, etc.
– PHRASES **with the pedal to the metal** informal at full speed.
– DERIVATIVES **pedaller** (US **pedaler**) n.
– ORIGIN C17: from French *pédale*, from Latin *pedalis* (see PEDAL²).

pedal² /ˈpɛd(ə)l, ˈpiː-/ ■ adj. chiefly Medicine & Zoology of or relating to the foot or feet.
– ORIGIN C17: from Latin *pedalis*, from *pes* 'foot'.

pedal note (also **pedal point**) ■ n. Music a note sustained in one part (usually the bass) through successive harmonies, some of which are independent of it.

pedalo /ˈpɛdələʊ/ ■ n. (pl. **-os** or **-oes**) a small pedal-operated pleasure boat.
– ORIGIN 1950s: from PEDAL¹ + -O.

pedal pushers ■ n. women's calf-length trousers.

pedal steel guitar ■ n. a musical instrument played like the Hawaiian guitar, but set on a stand with pedals to adjust the tension of the strings.

pedant /ˈpɛd(ə)nt/ ■ n. a person who is excessively concerned with minor detail or with displaying technical knowledge.
– DERIVATIVES **pedantic** adj. **pedantically** adv. **pedantry** n.
– ORIGIN C16: from French *pédant*, from Italian *pedante*.

peddle ■ v. **1** sell (goods, especially small items) by going from place to place. **2** sell (an illegal drug or stolen item). **3** derogatory promote (an idea or view) persistently or widely.
– ORIGIN C16: back-formation from PEDLAR.

peddler ■ n. variant spelling of PEDLAR.

pederasty (also **paederasty**) ■ n. sexual intercourse between a man and a boy.
– DERIVATIVES **pederast** n. **pederastic** adj.
– ORIGIN C17: from Greek *paiderastia*, from *pais, paid-* 'boy' + *erastēs* 'lover'.

pedestal ■ n. **1** the base or support on which a statue, obelisk, or column is mounted. ▶ a position in which one is greatly or uncritically admired: *you shouldn't put him on a pedestal.* **2** each of the two supports of a kneehole desk or table. **3** the supporting column or base of a washbasin or toilet pan.
– ORIGIN C16: from French *piédestal*, from Italian *piedestallo*, from *piè* 'foot' + *di* 'of' + *stallo* 'stall'.

pedestrian ■ n. a person walking rather than travelling in a vehicle. ■ adj. dull; uninspired.
– DERIVATIVES **pedestrianly** adv.
– ORIGIN C18: from Latin *pedester* 'going on foot', also 'written in prose'.

pedestrianize (also **-ise**) ■ v. make (a street or area) accessible only to pedestrians.
– DERIVATIVES **pedestrianization** (also **-isation**) n.

Pedi /ˈpɛdɪ/ ■ n. (pl. same, **Pedis**, or **Bapedi**) **1** a member of the largest group of Sotho people, living in northern South Africa. **2** another term for **SEPEDI**.
– ORIGIN from Sepedi.

pediatrics ■ pl. n. US spelling of **PAEDIATRICS**.

pedicab /ˈpɛdɪkab/ ■ n. a small pedal-operated vehicle serving as a taxi.

pedicel /ˈpɛdɪs(ə)l/ ■ n. **1** Botany a stalk bearing an individual flower in an inflorescence. **2** another term for **PEDICLE**.
– ORIGIN C17: from modern Latin *pedicellus* 'small foot', diminutive of *pes* 'foot'.

pedicle /ˈpɛdɪk(ə)l/ ■ n. **1** Anatomy & Zoology a small stalk-like connecting structure. **2** Medicine part of a skin graft left temporarily attached to its original site.
– ORIGIN C17: from Latin *pediculus* 'small foot', diminutive of *pes*.

pediculosis /pɪˌdɪkjʊˈləʊsɪs/ ■ n. Medicine infestation with lice.
– ORIGIN C19: from Latin *pediculus* 'louse'.

pedicure ■ n. a cosmetic treatment of the feet and toenails. ■ v. [usu. as adj. **pedicured**] give a pedicure to.
– ORIGIN C19: from French *pédicure*, from Latin *pes* 'foot' + *curare* 'attend to'.

pedigree ■ n. **1** the record of descent of an animal, showing it to be pure-bred. **2** a person's lineage or ancestry. ▶ a genealogical table. **3** the history or provenance of a thing.
– DERIVATIVES **pedigreed** adj.
– ORIGIN Middle English: from Anglo-Norman French *pé de grue* 'crane's foot', a mark used to denote succession in pedigrees.

pediment ■ n. **1** Architecture the triangular upper part of the front of a classical building, typically surmounting a portico. **2** Geology a broad expanse of rock debris extending outwards from the foot of a slope.
– DERIVATIVES **pedimental** adj. **pedimented** adj.
– ORIGIN C16.

pedipalp /ˈpɛdɪpalp, ˈpiːdɪpalp/ ■ n. Zoology each of the second pair of appendages attached to the cephalothorax of most arachnids.
– ORIGIN C19: from Latin *pes, ped-* 'foot' + *palpus* 'palp'.

pedlar (also **peddler**) ■ n. **1** an itinerant trader in small goods. **2** a person who sells illegal drugs or stolen goods. **3** a person who peddles an idea or view.
– ORIGIN Middle English: perhaps an alteration of *pedder*, from dialect *ped* 'pannier'.

pedo-[1] ■ comb. form US spelling of **PAEDO-**.

pedo-[2] /ˈpɛdəʊ/ ■ comb. form relating to soil or soil types: *pedogenic.*
– ORIGIN from Greek *pedon* 'ground'.

pedogenic /ˌpɛdə(ʊ)ˈdʒɛnɪk/ ■ adj. relating to or denoting processes occurring in soil or leading to the formation of soil.

pedology /pɪˈdɒlədʒi, pɛ-/ ■ n. another term for **SOIL SCIENCE**.
– DERIVATIVES **pedological** /ˌpɛdəˈlɒdʒɪk(ə)l/ adj. **pedologist** n.

pedometer /pɪˈdɒmɪtə, pɛ-/ ■ n. an instrument for estimating the distance travelled on foot by recording the number of steps taken.
– ORIGIN C18: from French *pédomètre*, from Latin *pes* 'foot'.

peduncle /pɪˈdʌŋk(ə)l/ ■ n. **1** Botany the main stalk of an inflorescence. **2** Zoology a stalk-like connecting structure.
– DERIVATIVES **peduncular** adj. **pedunculate** adj.
– ORIGIN C18: from Latin *pes, ped-* 'foot'.

pee informal ■ v. (**pees**, **peed**, **peeing**) urinate. ■ n. **1** an act of urinating. **2** urine.
– ORIGIN C18: euphemistic use of the initial letter of **PISS**.

peek ■ v. **1** look quickly or furtively. **2** protrude slightly so as to be just visible. ■ n. a quick or furtive look.
– ORIGIN Middle English *pike, pyke*.

peekaboo (also **peek-a-boo**) ■ n. a game played with a young child, which involves hiding and suddenly reappearing, saying 'peekaboo'. ■ adj. **1** (of a garment) made of transparent fabric or having a pattern of small holes. **2** (of a hairstyle) concealing one eye with a fringe or wave.
– ORIGIN C16: from **PEEK** + **BOO**.

peel[1] ■ v. **1** remove the outer covering or skin from (a fruit, vegetable, etc.). **2** (of a surface) lose parts of its outer layer or covering in small strips or pieces. ▶ come off in strips or small pieces. **3** (**peel something away/off**) remove a thin outer covering. ▶ (**peel something off**) or Brit. **peel off** remove an article of clothing. **4** (**peel off**) leave a formation or group by veering away. **5** (**peel out**) N. Amer. informal leave quickly. ■ n. the outer covering or rind of a fruit or vegetable.
– DERIVATIVES **peelings** pl. n.
– ORIGIN Middle English: var. of dialect *pill*, from Latin *pilare* 'to strip hair from', from *pilus* 'hair'.

peel[2] ■ v. Croquet send (another player's ball) through a hoop.
– ORIGIN C19: from the name of Walter H. *Peel*, founder of the All England Croquet Association.

peeler[1] ■ n. a knife or device for peeling fruit and vegetables.

peeler[2] ■ n. Brit. informal, archaic a police officer.
– ORIGIN C19: from the name of the British Prime Minister Sir Robert *Peel* who established the Metropolitan Police.

peen /piːn/ (also **pein**) ■ n. the end of a hammer head opposite the face, typically wedge-shaped or rounded. ■ v. strike with a peen.
– ORIGIN C16: prob. of Scandinavian origin.

peep[1] ■ v. **1** look quickly and furtively. **2** (**peep out**) come slowly or partially into view. ■ n. **1** a quick or furtive look. **2** a momentary or partial view of something.
– ORIGIN C15.

peep[2] ■ n. **1** a weak, high-pitched sound made by a young bird or mammal. ▶ a brief, high-pitched electronic sound. **2** [with neg.] a slight utterance or complaint. ■ v. make a peep.
– ORIGIN Middle English: imitative.

pee-pee ■ n. informal **1** a child's word for an act of urinating. ▶ urine. **2** a penis.

peeper ■ n. **1** a person who peeps, especially in a voyeuristic way. **2** (**peepers**) informal a person's eyes.

peephole ■ n. a small hole in a door through which callers may be identified before the door is opened.

peeping Tom ■ n. a furtive voyeur.
– ORIGIN from the name of the person said to have watched Lady Godiva ride naked through the English city of Coventry.

peep show ■ n. **1** a sequence of pictures viewed through a lens or hole set into a box, formerly offered as a public entertainment. **2** an erotic or pornographic film viewed from a coin-operated booth.

peep sight ■ n. a backsight for rifles with a circular hole through which the foresight is brought into line with the object aimed at.

peep-toe ■ adj. (of a shoe) having the tip cut away to leave the large toe partially exposed.

peepul /ˈpiːpʌl/ (also **pipal**) ■ n. another term for **BO TREE**.
– ORIGIN C18: from Sanskrit *pippala*.

peer[1] ■ v. **1** look with difficulty or concentration. **2** be just visible.
– ORIGIN C16: perhaps a var. of dialect *pire* or from a shortening of **APPEAR**.

peer² ■ n. **1** a member of the nobility in Britain or Ireland, comprising the ranks of duke, marquess, earl, viscount, and baron. **2** a person of the same age, status, or ability as another specified person.
– PHRASES **without peer** unrivalled.
– ORIGIN Middle English: from Old French *peer*, from Latin *par* 'equal'.

peerage ■ n. **1** the title and rank of peer or peeress. **2** (**the peerage**) peers collectively. **3** a book containing a full listing of peers and peeresses.

peeress /ˈpɪərɪs, -rɛs/ ■ n. **1** a woman holding the rank of a peer in her own right. **2** the wife or widow of a peer.

peer group ■ n. a group of people of approximately the same age, status, and interests.

peerless ■ adj. unequalled; unrivalled.
– DERIVATIVES **peerlessly** adv.

peer of the realm ■ n. a member of the class of peers who has the right to sit in the House of Lords.

peer-to-peer ■ adj. Computing denoting a network in which each computer can act as a server for the others.

peeve informal ■ v. annoy; irritate: *he was peeved at being left out.* ■ n. a cause of annoyance.
– ORIGIN C20: back-formation from **PEEVISH**.

peevish ■ adj. irritable.
– DERIVATIVES **peevishly** adv. **peevishness** n.
– ORIGIN Middle English (in the sense 'perverse, coy').

peewit (also **pewit**) ■ n. Brit. the lapwing.
– ORIGIN C16: imitative of the bird's call.

peg ■ n. **1** a short projecting pin or bolt used for hanging things on, securing something in place, or marking a position. ▸ a clip for holding things together or hanging up clothes. **2** chiefly Indian a measure of spirits. **3** a point or limit on a scale, especially of exchange rates. **4** informal a person's leg. **5** a place marked by a peg and allotted to a competitor to fish or shoot from. ■ v. (**pegged**, **pegging**) **1** fix, attach, or mark with a peg or pegs. **2** fix (a price, rate, or amount) at a particular level. **3** N. Amer. informal form a fixed opinion of: *the officer probably has us pegged as anarchists.*
– PHRASES **off the peg** chiefly Brit. (of clothes) ready-made. **a peg to hang a matter on** something used as a pretext or occasion for the treatment of a wider subject. **a square peg in a round hole** a person in a situation unsuited to their abilities or character. **take someone down a peg or two** make someone less arrogant.
– PHRASAL VERBS **peg away** informal work hard over a long period. **peg out 1** informal, chiefly Brit. die. **2** score the winning point at cribbage. **3** Croquet hit the peg with the ball as the final stroke in a game.
– ORIGIN Middle English: prob. of Low German origin.

pegboard ■ n. a board having a regular pattern of small holes for pegs, used chiefly for games or the display of information.

pegbox ■ n. a structure at the head of a stringed instrument where the strings are attached to the tuning pegs.

peg leg ■ n. informal an artificial leg, especially a wooden one.

pegmatite /ˈpɛɡmətʌɪt/ ■ n. Geology a coarsely crystalline granite or other igneous rock with crystals several centimetres in length.
– ORIGIN C19: from Greek *pēgma*, *pēgmat-* 'thing joined together'.

peignoir /ˈpeɪnwɑː/ ■ n. a woman's light dressing gown or negligee.
– ORIGIN French, from *peigner* 'to comb' (because the garment was orig. worn while combing the hair).

pein ■ n. & v. variant spelling of **PEEN**.

pejorative /pɪˈdʒɒrətɪv/ ■ adj. expressing contempt or disapproval.
– DERIVATIVES **pejoratively** adv.
– ORIGIN C19: from French *péjoratif*, *-ive*, from late Latin *pejorare* 'make worse'.

Pekinese /ˌpiːkɪˈniːz/ (also **Pekingese**) ■ n. (pl. same) a lapdog of a short-legged breed with long hair and a snub nose. ■ adj. of or relating to Beijing (Peking), its citizens, or their culture or cuisine.

Peking duck ■ n. a Chinese dish consisting of strips of roast duck served with shredded vegetables and a sweet sauce.

pekoe /ˈpiːkəʊ, ˈpɛ-/ ■ n. a high-quality black tea made from young leaves.
– ORIGIN C18: from Chinese dialect *pekho*, from *pek* 'white' + *ho* 'down' (the leaves being picked when covered with down).

pelage /ˈpɛlɪdʒ/ ■ n. Zoology the fur, hair, or wool of a mammal.
– ORIGIN C19: from Old French *pel* 'hair'.

Pelagian /pɪˈleɪdʒɪən/ ■ adj. of or relating to the theory of an early British monk, Pelagius (c.360–c.420), denying the doctrines of original sin and predestination. ■ n. a follower of Pelagius.
– DERIVATIVES **Pelagianism** n.

pelagic /pɪˈladʒɪk/ ■ adj. **1** of or relating to the open sea. **2** (chiefly of fish) inhabiting the upper layers of the open sea. ▸ (of a bird) inhabiting the open sea and returning to shore only to breed. ■ n. a pelagic fish or bird.
– ORIGIN C17: from Greek *pelagikos*, from *pelagios* 'of the sea'.

pelargonium /ˌpɛləˈɡəʊnɪəm/ ■ n. a shrubby plant native to South Africa, widely cultivated for its red, pink, or white flowers. See also **GERANIUM**. [Genus *Pelargonium*: many species.]
– ORIGIN from Greek *pelargos* 'stork', on the pattern of *geranium*.

pelf ■ n. archaic money, especially when gained dishonestly.
– ORIGIN Middle English: from a var. of Old French *pelfre* 'spoils'.

pelham ■ n. a horse's bit which combines the action of a curb bit and a snaffle.
– ORIGIN C19: from the surname *Pelham*.

pelican ■ n. a large gregarious waterbird with a long bill and an extensible throat pouch for scooping up fish. [Genus *Pelecanus*: several species.]
– ORIGIN Old English *pellicane*, from Greek *pelekan*, prob. based on *pelekus* 'axe' (with ref. to its bill).

pelican crossing ■ n. (in the UK) a pedestrian crossing with traffic lights operated by pedestrians.
– ORIGIN 1960s: *pelican* from *pe(destrian) li(ght) con(trolled)*, altered to conform with the bird's name.

Pelion /ˈpiːlɪən/ ■ n. (in phr. **pile** or **heap Pelion on Ossa**) add an extra difficulty to something which is already onerous.
– ORIGIN the name of a mountain in Greece; the giants of Greek mythology were said to have piled Mounts Olympus and Ossa on its summit in their attempt to reach heaven and destroy the gods.

pelisse /pɪˈliːs/ ■ n. historical **1** a woman's ankle-length cloak with armholes or sleeves. **2** a fur-lined cloak, especially as part of a hussar's uniform.
– ORIGIN C18: medieval Latin *pellicia (vestis)* '(garment) of fur'.

pelite /ˈpiːlʌɪt/ ■ n. Geology a sediment or sedimentary rock composed of very fine clay or mud particles.
– ORIGIN C19: from Greek *pēlos* 'clay, mud'.

pellagra /pɛˈlaɡrə, -ˈleɪɡrə/ ■ n. a disease characterized by dermatitis, diarrhoea, and mental disturbance, caused by a deficiency of nicotinic acid or tryptophan in the diet.
– DERIVATIVES **pellagrous** adj.
– ORIGIN C19: from Italian, from *pelle* 'skin'.

pellet ■ n. **1** a small, rounded, compressed mass of a substance. **2** a piece of small shot or other lightweight bullet. **3** Ornithology a small mass of bones and feathers regurgitated by a bird of prey. ■ v. (**pelleted**, **pelleting**) **1** form into pellets. **2** hit with or as if with pellets.
– DERIVATIVES **pelletize** (also **-ise**) v.
– ORIGIN Middle English: from Old French *pelote* 'metal ball', from a diminutive of Latin *pila* 'ball'.

pellicle /ˈpɛlɪk(ə)l/ ■ n. technical a thin skin, cuticle, membrane, or film.
– ORIGIN Middle English: from French *pellicule*, from Latin *pellicula* 'small piece of skin', diminutive of *pellis*.

pell-mell ■ adj. & adv. in a confused, rushed, or disorderly way. ■ n. a confused mixture; disorder.
– ORIGIN C16: from French *pêle-mêle*, from earlier *pesle mesle, mesle pesle*, reduplication from *mesler* 'to mix'.

pellucid /pɪˈluːsɪd, pɛ-, -ˈljuːsɪd/ ■ adj. **1** translucently clear. **2** easily understood.
– DERIVATIVES **pellucidly** adv.
– ORIGIN C17: from Latin *pellucidus*, from *perlucere* 'shine through'.

Pelmanism /ˈpɛlmənɪz(ə)m/ ■ n. **1** a system of memory training originally devised by the Pelman Institute for the Scientific Development of Mind, Memory, and Personality. **2** a card game in which matching pairs must be selected from memory from cards laid face down.

pelmet ■ n. a narrow border of cloth or wood, fitted across the top of a door or window to conceal the curtain fittings.
– ORIGIN C20: prob. an alteration of French *palmette* 'small palm'.

pelota /pɪˈlɒtə, -ˈləʊtə/ ■ n. **1** a Basque or Spanish ball game played in a walled court with basket-like rackets attached to the hand. **2** the ball used in pelota.
– ORIGIN Spanish, 'ball'.

peloton /ˈpɛlətɒn/ ■ n. the main group of cyclists in a race.
– ORIGIN 1950s: from French, 'small ball' (because of the concentrated grouping of the pack).

pelt[1] ■ v. **1** hurl missiles at. **2** (**pelt down**) (of rain, hail, or snow) fall very heavily. **3** run very quickly. ■ n. archaic an act of pelting.
– PHRASES (**at**) **full pelt** as fast as possible.
– ORIGIN C15.

pelt[2] ■ n. **1** the skin of an animal with the fur, wool, or hair still on it. **2** the raw skin of a sheep or goat, stripped and ready for tanning.
– ORIGIN Middle English: either from obsolete *pellet* 'skin', from Latin *pellis* 'skin', or a back-formation from **PELTRY**.

peltate /ˈpɛlteɪt/ ■ adj. chiefly Botany shield-shaped; more or less circular with a stalk underneath.

peltry ■ n. (also **peltries**) animal pelts collectively.
– ORIGIN Middle English: from Anglo-Norman French *pelterie*, from Old French *pel* 'skin', from Latin *pellis*.

pelvic ■ adj. of or relating to the pelvis.

pelvic fin ■ n. Zoology each of a pair of fins on the underside of a fish's body, attached to the pelvic girdle.

pelvic floor ■ n. the muscular base of the abdomen, attached to the pelvis.

pelvic girdle ■ n. (in vertebrates) the enclosing structure formed by the pelvis.

pelvic inflammatory disease ■ n. inflammation of the female genital tract, accompanied by fever and lower abdominal pain.

pelvis ■ n. (pl. **pelvises** or **pelves** /-viːz/) **1** the large bony frame at the base of the spine to which the lower or hindlimbs are attached. **2** (also **renal pelvis**) the broadened top part of the ureter into which the kidney tubules drain.
– ORIGIN C17: from Latin, 'basin'.

pelycosaur /ˈpɛlɪkəsɔː/ ■ n. a fossil reptile of the late Carboniferous and Permian periods, typically having a spiny sail-like crest on the back.
– ORIGIN C20: from Greek *pelux, peluk-* 'bowl' + *sauros* 'lizard'.

pemmican /ˈpɛmɪk(ə)n/ ■ n. a pressed cake made from pounded dried meat mixed to a paste with melted fat and other ingredients, originally made by North American Indians and later adapted by Arctic explorers.
– ORIGIN from Cree *pimecan*, from *pime* 'fat'.

pemphigus /ˈpɛmfɪɡəs/ ■ n. Medicine a skin disease in which watery blisters form on the skin.
– DERIVATIVES **pemphigoid** adj.
– ORIGIN C18: from Greek *pemphix* 'bubble'.

PEN ■ abbrev. International Association of Poets, Playwrights, Editors, Essayists, and Novelists.

Pen. ■ abbrev. Peninsula.

pen[1] ■ n. an instrument for writing or drawing with ink, typically consisting of a metal nib or ball, or a nylon tip, fitted into a metal or plastic holder. ▶ (**the pen**) writing as an occupation. ▶ an electronic device used in conjunction with a writing surface to enter commands or data into a computer. ■ v. (**penned**, **penning**) write or compose.
– ORIGIN Middle English: from Old French *penne*, from Latin *penna* 'feather'.

pen[2] ■ n. **1** a small enclosure in which sheep, pigs, or other farm animals are kept. **2** a covered dock for a submarine or other warship. ■ v. (**penned**, **penning**) **1** put or keep in a pen. **2** (**pen someone up/in**) confine someone in a restricted space.
– ORIGIN Old English *penn*.

pen[3] ■ n. a female swan.
– ORIGIN C16.

pen[4] ■ n. N. Amer. informal short for **PENITENTIARY**.

penal ■ adj. **1** of, relating to, or prescribing the punishment of offenders under the legal system. ▶ (of an act or offence) punishable by law. **2** (especially of taxation or interest rates) extremely severe.
– DERIVATIVES **penally** adv.
– ORIGIN Middle English: from Old French *penal*, from Latin, from *poena* 'pain, penalty'.

penalize (also **-ise**) ■ v. **1** subject to a penalty or punishment. ▶ put at an unfair disadvantage. **2** Law make or declare (an action) legally punishable.
– DERIVATIVES **penalization** (also **-isation**) n.

penal servitude ■ n. imprisonment with hard labour.

penalty ■ n. (pl. **-ies**) **1** a punishment imposed for breaking a law, rule, or contract. **2** (in sports and games) a handicap imposed on a player or team for infringement of rules, especially a penalty kick. ▶ Bridge points won by the defenders when the declarer fails to make the contract.
– PHRASES **under** (or **on**) **penalty of** under the threat of.
– ORIGIN C16: from medieval Latin *poenalitas*, from *poena* 'pain'.

penalty area ■ n. Soccer the rectangular area marked out in front of each goal, within which a foul by a defender involves the award of a penalty kick.

penalty box ■ n. **1** Soccer another term for **PENALTY AREA**. **2** Ice Hockey an area beside the rink reserved for penalized players and an official who records penalties.

penalty kick ■ n. **1** Soccer a free kick at the goal from the penalty spot, awarded to the attacking team after a foul within the penalty area. **2** Rugby a place kick awarded to a team after an offence by an opponent.

penalty point ■ n. (in the UK) a punishment awarded by the courts for a driving offence and recorded cumulatively on a person's driving licence.

penalty spot ■ n. Soccer the point within the penalty area from which penalty kicks are taken.

penalty try ■ n. Rugby a try awarded to a side when a touchdown is prevented by an offence by the opposition.

penance ■ n. **1** voluntary self-punishment as an open expression of repentance for wrongdoing. **2** a sacrament in which a member of the Church confesses sins to a priest and is given absolution. ▶ a religious observance or other duty imposed as part of this sacrament.
– ORIGIN Middle English: from Latin *paenitentia* 'repentance', from *paenitere* 'be sorry'.

pence plural form of **PENNY** (used for sums of money).

penchant /ˈpɒʃɒ̃/ ■ n. a strong liking or inclination: *she has a penchant for champagne.*
– ORIGIN C17: from French, 'leaning, inclining', from *pencher*.

pencil ■ n. **1** an instrument for writing or drawing, typically consisting of a thin stick of graphite enclosed in a long thin piece of wood or fixed in a thin cylindrical case. **2** Physics a set of light rays, lines, etc. converging to or diverging narrowly from a point. ■ v. (**pencilled**, **pencilling**; US **penciled**, **penciling**) **1** write, draw, or colour with a pencil. **2** (**pencil something in**) arrange or note down something provisionally.
– DERIVATIVES **penciller** n.
– ORIGIN Middle English: from Old French *pincel*, from Latin *peniculus* 'brush', diminutive of *penis* 'tail'.

pencil moustache ■ n. a very thin moustache.

pencil-pusher ■ n. N. Amer. another term for **PEN-PUSHER**.

pencil skirt

pencil skirt ■ n. a very narrow straight skirt.

pendant ■ n. **1** a piece of jewellery that hangs from a necklace chain. **2** a light designed to hang from the ceiling. **3** a short rope hanging from the head of a ship's mast, yardarm, or clew of a sail, used for attaching tackles. **4** Nautical a tapering flag. ■ adj. pendent.
– ORIGIN Middle English: from Old French, 'hanging', from *pendre*, from Latin *pendere*.

pendent ■ adj. **1** hanging down. **2** pending.
– DERIVATIVES **pendency** n.

pendente lite /pɛnˌdɛnteɪ ˈlʌɪti, -ˌdɛnti/ ■ adv. Law during litigation.
– ORIGIN Latin, 'with the lawsuit pending'.

pendentive /pɛnˈdɛntɪv/ ■ n. Architecture a curved triangle of vaulting formed by the intersection of a dome with its supporting arches.
– ORIGIN C18: from the French adjective *pendentif, -ive*, from Latin *pendere* 'hang down'.

pending ■ adj. **1** awaiting decision or settlement. **2** about to happen. ■ prep. until.
– ORIGIN C17: anglicized spelling of French *pendant* 'hanging'.

penduline tit /ˈpɛndjʊlʌɪn/ ■ n. a small titmouse that builds a nest suspended from a branch. [*Anthoscopus minutus* (South Africa), *Remiz pendulinus* (Eurasia), and other species.]
– ORIGIN C19: *penduline* from Latin *pendulus* 'hanging down'.

pendulous /ˈpɛndjʊləs/ ■ adj. hanging down; drooping.
– DERIVATIVES **pendulously** adv.
– ORIGIN C17: from Latin *pendulus* 'hanging down'.

pendulum /ˈpɛndjʊləm/ ■ n. **1** a weight hung from a fixed point so that it can swing freely, especially a rod with a weighted end that regulates the mechanism of a clock. **2** the tendency of a situation to oscillate between extremes: *the pendulum of fashion*.
– DERIVATIVES **pendular** adj.
– ORIGIN C17: from Latin, neuter of *pendulus* 'hanging down'.

peneplain /ˈpiːnɪpleɪn/ ■ n. Geology a level land surface produced by erosion over a long period.
– ORIGIN C19: from Latin *paene* 'almost' + **PLAIN**[1].

penetrant /ˈpɛnɪtr(ə)nt/ ■ n. a substance which can penetrate cracks, pores, and other surface defects. ■ adj. Genetics (of genes) producing characteristic effects in the phenotypes of individuals possessing them.
– DERIVATIVES **penetrance** n. (Genetics).

penetrate ■ v. **1** force a way into or through. ▸ [as adj. **penetrating**] (of a sound) clearly heard through or above other sounds. **2** infiltrate (an enemy organization or a competitor's market). **3** understand or gain insight into (something complex or mysterious). **4** (of a man) insert the penis into the vagina or anus of (a sexual partner).
– DERIVATIVES **penetrability** n. **penetrable** adj. **penetratingly** adv. **penetrator** n.
– ORIGIN C16 (*penetration* Middle English): from Latin *penetrare* 'go into'.

penetration ■ n. **1** the action or process of penetrating. **2** the extent to which a product is recognized and bought by customers in a particular market: *the company achieved remarkable market penetration*. **3** perceptive understanding of complex matters.

penetrative ■ adj. **1** able to penetrate. **2** having or showing deep understanding and insight. **3** (of sexual activity) involving penetration.

penetrometer /ˌpɛnɪˈtrɒmɪtə/ ■ n. an instrument for determining the hardness of a substance by measuring the depth or rate of penetration of a rod or needle driven into it by a known force.

penfriend ■ n. a person with whom one becomes friendly by exchanging letters.

penguin ■ n. a flightless black and white seabird of the southern hemisphere, with wings used as flippers. [Family Spheniscidae: several species.]
– ORIGIN C16 (orig. denoting the great auk).

penicillin ■ n. an antibiotic produced naturally by certain blue moulds, now usually prepared synthetically.
– ORIGIN 1920s: from the genus name *Penicillium*, from Latin *penicillum* 'paintbrush'.

penile /ˈpiːnʌɪl/ ■ adj. of or relating to the penis.
– ORIGIN C19: from Latin *penis* 'tail, penis'.

peninsula /pɪˈnɪnsjʊlə/ ■ n. a long, narrow piece of land projecting out into a sea or lake.
– DERIVATIVES **peninsular** adj.
– ORIGIN C16: from Latin *paeninsula*, from *paene* 'almost' + *insula* 'island'.

> **USAGE**
> Do not confuse the spellings **peninsula** and **peninsular**. **Peninsula** is a noun (*the end of the Cape Peninsula*), whereas **peninsular** is the adjectival form (*the peninsular part of Malaysia*).

penis /ˈpiːnɪs/ ■ n. (pl. **penises** or **penes** /-niːz/) the male copulatory organ, in mammals used also for urination.
– ORIGIN C17: from Latin, 'tail, penis'.

penitent ■ adj. feeling or showing sorrow and regret for having done wrong. ■ n. a person who repents their sins.
– DERIVATIVES **penitence** n. **penitential** adj. **penitently** adv.
– ORIGIN Middle English: from Old French, from Latin *paenitere* 'repent'.

penitentiary /ˌpɛnɪˈtɛnʃ(ə)ri/ ■ n. (pl. **-ies**) N. Amer. a prison for people convicted of serious crimes.
– ORIGIN Middle English: from medieval Latin *paenitentiarius*, from Latin *paenitentia* 'repentance'.

penknife ■ n. (pl. **penknives**) a small knife with a blade which folds into the handle.

penlight ■ n. a small electric torch shaped like a pen.

penman ■ n. (pl. **-men**) **1** dated a person with a specified ability in handwriting. **2** an author.
– DERIVATIVES **penmanship** n.

pen name ■ n. a literary pseudonym.

pennant ■ n. **1** a tapering flag on a ship, especially one flown at the masthead of a vessel in commission. **2** a long triangular or swallow-tailed flag, especially as the military ensign of lancer regiments. **3** N. Amer. a flag denoting a sports championship or identifying a team, club, etc. **4** another term for **PENDANT** (in sense 3).
– ORIGIN C17: blend of **PENDANT** and **PENNON**.

penne /ˈpɛneɪ, ˈpɛni/ ■ pl. n. pasta in the form of short wide tubes.
– ORIGIN Italian, pl. of *penna* 'quill'.

penniless ■ adj. without money; destitute.
– DERIVATIVES **pennilessness** n.

pennon /ˈpɛnən/ ■ n. less common term for **PENNANT**.
– DERIVATIVES **pennoned** adj.
– ORIGIN Middle English: from Old French, from a derivative of Latin *penna* 'feather'.

penn'orth /ˈpɛnəθ/ ■ n. variant spelling of **PENNYWORTH**.

Pennsylvania Dutch (also **Pennsylvania German**) ■ n. a dialect of High German spoken in parts of Pennsylvania.
– ORIGIN Dutch from German *Deutsch* 'German'.

penny ■ n. (pl. **pennies** (for separate coins); **pence** (for a sum of money)) **1** (abbrev.: **p**.) a British bronze coin and monetary unit equal to one hundredth of a pound. **2** (abbrev.: **d**.) a former British coin and monetary unit equal to one twelfth of a shilling and 240th of a pound. **3** N. Amer. informal a one-cent coin. **4** [with neg.] (**a penny**) no money at all.
– PHRASES **be two** (or **ten**) **a penny** chiefly Brit. be plentiful and thus of little value. **in for a penny, in for a pound** expressing an intention to see an undertaking through, however much time, effort, or money this entails. **pennies from heaven** unexpected benefits. **the penny dropped** informal, chiefly Brit. someone has finally realized something. **a penny for your thoughts** a request to someone to say what they are thinking about.
– ORIGIN Old English *penig, penning* of Germanic origin.

penny ante ■ n. chiefly N. Amer. **1** poker played for very small stakes. **2** [as modifier] informal trivial or contemptible.

penny black ■ n. the world's first adhesive postage stamp, issued in Britain in 1840.

penny dreadful ■ n. historical or humorous a cheap, sensational comic or storybook.

penny-farthing ■ n. an early type of bicycle with a very large front wheel and a small rear wheel.

penny loafer ■ n. a casual leather shoe with a decorative slotted leather strip over the upper.

penny-pinching ■ adj. unwilling to spend money; miserly. ■ n. miserliness.
–DERIVATIVES **penny-pincher** n.

penny plain ■ adj. plain and simple.
–ORIGIN C19: with ref. to prints of characters sold for toy theatres, costing one penny for black-and-white ones, and two pennies for coloured ones.

penny post ■ n. historical a system established in the UK in 1840 of carrying letters at a standard charge of one penny each regardless of distance.

pennyroyal ■ n. a small-leaved plant of the mint family, used in herbal medicine. [*Mentha pulegium* (Eurasia) and *Hedeoma pulegioides* (N. America).]
–ORIGIN C16: from Anglo-Norman French *puliol* (from Latin *pulegium* 'thyme') + *real* 'royal'.

penny stock (Brit. **penny share**) ■ n. a low-priced share in a small company.

penny whistle ■ n. a small flute-like instrument made from a thin metal tube, with six finger holes of varying size on top and no thumb holes.

penny wise ■ adj. careful to save small amounts of money.
–PHRASES **penny wise and pound foolish** economical in small matters but extravagant in large ones.

pennyworth (also **penn'orth**) ■ n. **1** an amount of something that may be bought for a penny. **2** (**one's pennyworth**) Brit. one's contribution to a discussion.

penology /piːˈnɒlədʒi, pɪ-/ ■ n. the study of the punishment of crime and of prison management.
–DERIVATIVES **penological** adj. **penologist** n.
–ORIGIN C19: from Latin *poena* 'penalty' + -LOGY.

pen pal ■ n. another term for PENFRIEND.

pen-pusher ■ n. informal a person with a clerical job involving routine paperwork.

pensée /pɒ̃ˈseɪ/ ■ n. a thought or reflection put into literary form; an aphorism.
–ORIGIN from French.

pensile /ˈpɛnsʌɪl/ ■ adj. pendulous.
–ORIGIN C17: from Latin *pensilis*, from *pendere* 'hang'.

pension[1] /ˈpɛnʃ(ə)n/ ■ n. **1** a regular payment made by the state to people at or above the official retirement age and to some widows and disabled people. **2** a regular payment made during a person's retirement from an investment fund to which that person or their employer has contributed during their working life. **3** chiefly historical a regular payment as a reward made to a royal favourite or to enable an artist or scholar to continue their work. ■ v. (**pension someone off**) dismiss someone from employment and pay them a pension.
–DERIVATIVES **pensionability** n. **pensionable** adj. **pensionless** adj.
–ORIGIN Middle English: from Latin *pensio(n-)* 'payment', from *pendere* 'to pay'.

pension[2] /pɒ̃ˈsjɒ̃/ ■ n. a small hotel or boarding house in France and other European countries.
–ORIGIN from French.

pensione /ˌpɛnsɪˈəʊneɪ/ ■ n. (pl. **pensioni** /-ni/) a small hotel or boarding house in Italy.
–ORIGIN from Italian.

pensioner ■ n. a person receiving a pension.

pensive ■ adj. engaged in deep thought.
–DERIVATIVES **pensively** adv. **pensiveness** n.
–ORIGIN Middle English: from Old French *pensif, -ive*, from *penser* 'think', from Latin *pensare* 'ponder'.

penstemon /pɛnˈstiːmən, -ˈstɛmən, ˈpɛnstɪmən/ (also **pentstemon**) ■ n. a North American plant with stems of showy snapdragon-like flowers. [Genus *Penstemon*.]
–ORIGIN from PENTA- + Greek *stēmōn* 'warp', used to mean 'stamen'.

penstock ■ n. **1** a sluice for controlling or directing the flow of water. **2** a channel for conveying water to a hydroelectric station.
–ORIGIN C17: from PEN[2] (meaning 'mill dam') + STOCK.

penta- ■ comb. form five; having five: *pentadactyl*.
–ORIGIN from Greek *pente* 'five'.

pentacle /ˈpɛntək(ə)l/ ■ n. **1** a pentagram, or a symbolic figure inscribed with one. **2** (**pentacles**) one of the suits in some tarot packs, corresponding to coins in others.
–ORIGIN C16: from medieval Latin *pentaculum*, from Greek *penta-* 'five'.

pentad /ˈpɛntad/ ■ n. a group or set of five.
–ORIGIN C17: from Greek *pentas, pentad-*, from *pente* 'five'.

pentadactyl /ˌpɛntəˈdaktɪl/ ■ adj. Zoology having five toes or fingers.

pentagon ■ n. **1** a plane figure with five straight sides and five angles. **2** (**the Pentagon**) the headquarters of the US Department of Defense, near Washington DC.
–DERIVATIVES **pentagonal** adj.
–ORIGIN C16: from Greek, from *pentagōnos* 'five-angled'.

pentagram ■ n. a five-pointed star formed by drawing a continuous line in five straight segments, often used as a mystic and magical symbol.
–ORIGIN C19: from Greek *pentagrammon* (see PENTA-, -GRAM[1]).

pentahedron /ˌpɛntəˈhiːdr(ə)n, -ˈhɛd-/ ■ n. (pl. **pentahedra** /-drə/ or **pentahedrons**) a solid figure with five plane faces.
–DERIVATIVES **pentahedral** adj.
–ORIGIN C18: from PENTA- + -HEDRON.

pentamer /ˈpɛntəmə/ ■ n. Chemistry a polymer comprising five monomer units.
–DERIVATIVES **pentameric** /ˌpɛntəˈmɛrɪk/ adj.

pentamerous /pɛnˈtam(ə)rəs/ ■ adj. Botany & Zoology having parts arranged in groups of five. ▸ consisting of five joints or parts.

pentameter /pɛnˈtamɪtə/ ■ n. Prosody a line of verse consisting of five metrical feet, or (in Greek and Latin verse) of two halves each of two feet and a long syllable.
–ORIGIN C16: from Greek *pentametros* (see PENTA-, -METER).

pentamidine /pɛnˈtamɪdiːn/ ■ n. Medicine a synthetic antibiotic drug used chiefly to treat PCP infection.
–ORIGIN 1940s: from PENTANE + AMIDE.

pentane /ˈpɛnteɪn/ ■ n. Chemistry a volatile liquid hydrocarbon of the alkane series, present in petroleum spirit. [C_5H_{12}.]
–ORIGIN C19: from Greek *pente* 'five' (denoting five carbon atoms) + -ANE[2].

pentangle ■ n. another term for PENTAGRAM.
–ORIGIN Middle English: perhaps from medieval Latin *pentaculum* 'pentacle' (assimilated to Latin *angulus* 'an angle').

pentaprism ■ n. a prism having a five-sided cross section with two silvered surfaces, giving a constant deviation of all rays of light through 90°.

Pentateuch /ˈpɛntətjuːk/ ■ n. the first five books of the Old Testament and Hebrew Scriptures (Genesis, Exodus, Leviticus, Numbers, and Deuteronomy).
–DERIVATIVES **Pentateuchal** adj.
–ORIGIN from eccles. Greek *pentateukhos*, from *penta-* 'five' + *teukhos* 'implement, book'.

pentathlon ■ n. an athletic event comprising five different events for each competitor, in particular (also **modern pentathlon**) a men's event involving fencing, shooting, swimming, riding, and cross-country running.
–DERIVATIVES **pentathlete** n.
–ORIGIN C17: from Greek, from *pente* 'five' + *athlon* 'contest'.

pentatonic /ˌpɛntəˈtɒnɪk/ ■ adj. Music relating to, based on, or denoting a scale of five notes.
–DERIVATIVES **pentatonicism** n.

pentavalent /ˌpɛntəˈveɪl(ə)nt/ ■ adj. Chemistry having a valency of five.

Pentecost /ˈpɛntɪkɒst/ ■ n. **1** the Christian festival celebrating the descent of the Holy Spirit on the disciples of Jesus after his Ascension. **2** the Jewish festival of Shavuoth.
–ORIGIN Old English *pentecosten*, from Greek *pentēkostē*

Pentecostal

(*hēmera*) 'fiftieth (day)' (because the Jewish festival is held on the fiftieth day after the second day of Passover).

Pentecostal ■ adj. **1** of or relating to Pentecost. **2** (in Christian use) emphasizing baptism in the Holy Spirit, evidenced by 'speaking in tongues', prophecy, healing, and exorcism. ■ n. a member of a Pentecostal church.
– DERIVATIVES **Pentecostalism** n. **Pentecostalist** adj. & n.

penthouse ■ n. **1** a flat on the top floor of a tall building, typically luxuriously fitted and offering fine views. **2** archaic an outhouse with a sloping roof, built on the side of a building.
– ORIGIN Middle English *pentis*, shortening of Old French *apentis*, from late Latin *appendicium* 'appendage'; later associated with French *pente* 'slope' and HOUSE.

pentimento /ˌpɛntɪˈmɛntəʊ/ ■ n. (pl. **pentimenti** /-tiː/) a visible trace of earlier painting beneath the paint on a canvas.
– ORIGIN C20: from Italian, 'repentance'.

pentlandite /ˈpɛntləndʌɪt/ ■ n. a bronze-yellow mineral consisting of a sulphide of iron and nickel.
– ORIGIN C19: from the name of the Irish traveller Joseph B. Pentland.

pentobarbitone /ˌpɛntə(ʊ)ˈbɑːbɪtəʊn/ (US **pentobarbital**) ■ n. Medicine a narcotic and sedative barbiturate drug formerly used to relieve insomnia.
– ORIGIN 1930s: from PENTANE + *barbitone*, denoting a sedative barbiturate drug.

Pentothal /ˈpɛntəθal/ ■ n. trademark for THIOPENTONE.

pentstemon ■ n. variant spelling of PENSTEMON.

pent-up ■ adj. closely confined or held back.

penultimate ■ adj. last but one.
– ORIGIN C17: from Latin *paenultimus*, from *paene* 'almost' + *ultimus* 'last', on the pattern of *ultimate*.

penumbra /pɪˈnʌmbrə/ ■ n. (pl. **penumbrae** /-briː/ or **penumbras**) **1** the partially shaded outer region of the shadow cast by an opaque object, especially the area of the earth or moon experiencing a partial eclipse. **2** Astronomy the less dark outer part of a sunspot.
– DERIVATIVES **penumbral** adj.
– ORIGIN C17: from Latin *paene* 'almost' + *umbra* 'shadow'.

penurious /pɪˈnjʊərɪəs/ ■ adj. formal **1** extremely poor. **2** parsimonious.
– DERIVATIVES **penuriously** adv. **penuriousness** n.

penury /ˈpɛnjʊri/ ■ n. extreme poverty.
– ORIGIN Middle English: from Latin *penuria* 'need, scarcity'.

peon /ˈpiːən/ ■ n. **1** /also peɪˈɒn/ a Spanish-American day labourer or unskilled farm worker. ► chiefly N. Amer. a person who does menial work. **2** /also pjuːn/ (in the Indian subcontinent and SE Asia) someone of low rank.
– DERIVATIVES **peonage** n.
– ORIGIN from Portuguese *peão* and Spanish *peón*, from medieval Latin *pedo*, *pedon-* 'walker, foot soldier'.

peony /ˈpiːəni/ ■ n. a herbaceous or shrubby plant of north temperate regions, long cultivated for its showy flowers. [Genus *Paeonia*.]
– ORIGIN Old English *peonie*, from Greek *paiōnia*, from *Paiōn*, the name of the physician of the gods.

people ■ pl. n. **1** human beings in general or considered collectively. ► (**the people**) the mass of citizens in a country; the populace. **2** (**one's people**) one's parents or relatives. **3** (**one's people**) one's employees or supporters. **4** (pl. **peoples**) [treated as sing. or pl.] the members of a particular nation, community, or ethnic group: *the indigenous peoples of Canada*. ■ v. **1** (usu. **be peopled**) (of a particular group of people) inhabit. ► fill or be present in. **2** fill (an area or place) with a particular group of inhabitants.
– DERIVATIVES **peoplehood** n.
– ORIGIN Middle English: from Anglo-Norman French *poeple*, from Latin *populus* 'populace'.

people person ■ n. informal a person who enjoys or is particularly good at interacting with others.

pep informal ■ n. liveliness. ■ v. (**pepped**, **pepping**) (**pep someone/thing up**) make someone or something more lively.
– ORIGIN C20: abbrev. of PEPPER.

peperoni ■ n. variant spelling of PEPPERONI.

peplum /ˈpɛpləm/ ■ n. a short flared, gathered, or pleated strip of fabric attached at the waist of a woman's jacket, dress, or blouse.
– ORIGIN C17: from Greek *peplos* 'outer robe or shawl'.

pepo /ˈpiːpəʊ/ ■ n. (pl. **-os**) any fleshy watery fruit of the melon or cucumber type, with numerous seeds and a firm rind.
– ORIGIN C19: from Latin, 'pumpkin'.

Peppadew (also **pepperdew**) ■ n. trademark a processed small red South African capsicum with a sweet hot taste.

pepper ■ n. **1** a pungent, hot-tasting powder prepared from dried and ground peppercorns, used to flavour food. **2** a climbing vine with berries that are dried as black or white peppercorns. [*Piper nigrum*.] ► used in names of related plants having hot-tasting leaves, or fruits used as a pungent spice, e.g. Jamaica pepper. **3** a capsicum, especially a sweet pepper. ► a reddish and typically hot-tasting spice prepared from various forms of capsicum. **4** Baseball a practice game in which a fielder throws at close range to a batter who hits back to the fielder. ■ v. **1** sprinkle or season with pepper. **2** (usu. **be peppered with**) scatter liberally over or through. **3** hit repeatedly with small missiles or gunshot.
– ORIGIN Old English *piper*, *pipor*, of West Germanic origin; from Greek *peperi*, from Sanskrit *pippalī* 'berry, peppercorn'.

pepper-and-salt ■ adj. flecked or speckled with intermingled dark and light shades.

peppercorn ■ n. the dried berry of a climbing vine, used whole as a spice or crushed or ground to make pepper.

peppercorn rent ■ n. Brit. a very low or nominal rent.
– ORIGIN from the (formerly common) practice of stipulating the payment of a peppercorn as a nominal rent.

pepperdew ■ n. variant spelling of PEPPADEW.

pepper mill ■ n. a device for grinding peppercorns by hand to make pepper.

peppermint ■ n. **1** the aromatic leaves of a plant of the mint family, or an oil obtained from them, used as a flavouring in food. **2** the plant which yields these leaves or oil. [*Mentha × piperita*.] **3** a sweet flavoured with peppermint oil.
– DERIVATIVES **pepperminty** adj.

pepperoni /ˌpɛpəˈrəʊni/ (also **peperoni**) ■ n. beef and pork sausage seasoned with pepper.
– ORIGIN from Italian *peperone* 'chilli'.

pepper pot ■ n. (also **pepper shaker**) a container with a perforated top for sprinkling pepper.

pepper spray ■ n. an aerosol spray containing oils derived from cayenne pepper, irritant to the eyes and respiratory passages and used as a disabling weapon.

pepperwort ■ n. a wild cress with pungent leaves. [Genus *Lepidium*.]

peppery ■ adj. **1** strongly flavoured with pepper or other hot spices. **2** irritable and sharp-tongued.
– DERIVATIVES **pepperiness** n.

pep pill ■ n. informal a pill containing a stimulant drug.

peppy ■ adj. (**-ier**, **-iest**) informal, chiefly N. Amer. lively.
– DERIVATIVES **peppily** adv. **peppiness** n.

pepsin ■ n. Biochemistry the chief digestive enzyme in the stomach, which breaks down proteins into polypeptides.
– ORIGIN C19: from Greek *pepsis* 'digestion'.

pep talk ■ n. informal a talk intended to make someone feel more courageous or enthusiastic.

peptic ■ adj. of or relating to digestion.
– ORIGIN C17: from Greek *peptikos* 'able to digest'.

peptic ulcer ■ n. a lesion in the lining of the digestive tract, typically in the stomach or duodenum, caused by the digestive action of pepsin and stomach acid.

peptide /ˈpɛptʌɪd/ ■ n. Biochemistry a compound consisting of two or more amino acids linked in a chain.
– ORIGIN C20: from German *Peptid*, back-formation from *Polypeptid* 'polypeptide'.

peptone /ˈpɛptəʊn/ ■ n. Biochemistry a soluble protein formed in the early stage of protein digestion.

–ORIGIN C19: from German *Pepton*, from Greek *peptos* 'cooked, digested'.

per ■ prep. **1** for each: *R125 per metre*. **2** by means of. **3** (**as per**) in accordance with. **4** Heraldry divided by a line in the direction of.
–PHRASES **as per usual** as usual.
–ORIGIN Latin, 'through, by means of'.

per- ■ prefix **1** through; all over: *pervade*. ▶ completely; very: *perfect*. ▶ to destruction; to ill effect: *perdition*. **2** Chemistry having the maximum proportion of some element in combination: *peroxide*.
–ORIGIN from Latin (see **PER**).

peradventure archaic or humorous ■ adv. perhaps. ■ n. uncertainty or doubt.
–ORIGIN Middle English: from Old French *per* (or *par*) *auenture* 'by chance'.

perambulate /pəˈrambjʊleɪt/ ■ v. formal walk or travel from place to place.
–DERIVATIVES **perambulation** n. **perambulatory** adj.
–ORIGIN Middle English: from Latin *perambulare* 'walk about'.

perambulator ■ n. formal term for **PRAM**.

per annum ■ adv. for each year.
–ORIGIN C17: Latin.

perborate /pəˈbɔːreɪt/ ■ n. Chemistry a salt which is an oxidized borate containing a peroxide linkage, especially a sodium salt of this kind used as a bleach.

percale /pəˈkeɪl/ ■ n. a closely woven fine cotton fabric.
–ORIGIN C17: from French.

per capita /pəˈkapɪtə/ (also **per caput** /ˈkaput/) ■ adv. & adj. for each person; in relation to people taken individually.
–ORIGIN C17: Latin, 'by heads'.

perceive ■ v. **1** become aware or conscious of. **2** regard as.
–DERIVATIVES **perceivable** adj. **perceiver** n.
–ORIGIN Middle English: from a var. of Old French *perçoivre*, from Latin *percipere* 'seize, understand'.

per cent ■ adv. by a specified amount in or for every hundred. ■ n. one part in every hundred. ▶ the rate, number, or amount in each hundred.
–ORIGIN C16: from **PER** + **CENT**.

percentage ■ n. **1** a rate, number, or amount in each hundred. **2** a proportion of a larger sum of money granted as an allowance or commission. **3** any proportion or share in relation to a whole.

percentile /pəˈsɛntʌɪl/ ■ n. Statistics each of the 100 equal groups into which a population can be divided according to the distribution of values of a particular variable. ▶ each of the 99 intermediate values of a random variable which divide a frequency distribution into 100 such groups.

percept /ˈpəːsɛpt/ ■ n. Philosophy something that is perceived. ▶ a mental concept that is developed as a consequence of the process of perception.
–ORIGIN C19: from Latin *perceptum* 'something perceived', from *percipere* 'seize, understand'.

perceptible ■ adj. (especially of a slight movement or change of state) able to be perceived.
–DERIVATIVES **perceptibility** n. **perceptibly** adv.

perception ■ n. **1** the ability to see, hear, or become aware of something through the senses. ▶ the state of being or process of becoming aware of something in such a way. **2** a way of regarding, understanding, or interpreting something. ▶ intuitive understanding and insight. **3** Psychology the neurophysiological processes, including memory, by which an organism becomes aware of and interprets external stimuli.
–DERIVATIVES **perceptional** adj.
–ORIGIN Middle English: from Latin *perceptio(n-)*, from *percipere* 'seize, understand'.

perceptive ■ adj. having or showing acute insight.
–DERIVATIVES **perceptively** adv. **perceptiveness** n. **perceptivity** /-ˈtɪvɪti/ n.

perceptual ■ adj. of or relating to the ability to interpret or become aware of something through the senses.
–DERIVATIVES **perceptually** adv.

perch[1] ■ n. **1** a thing on which a bird alights or roosts. **2** a high or narrow seat or resting place. ■ v. **1** alight, sit, or rest on a perch. **2** (**be perched**) be situated above or on the edge of something. **3** (**perch someone/thing on**) set or balance someone or something on.
–ORIGIN Middle English: noun from Old French *perche*, from Latin *pertica* 'rod'; verb from Old French *percher*.

perch[2] ■ n. (pl. same or **perches**) a freshwater fish with a high spiny dorsal fin, dark vertical bars on the body, and orange lower fins. [*Perca fluviatilis* (Europe) and other species.] ▶ used in names of similar or related fishes, e.g. Nile perch.
–ORIGIN Middle English: from Old French *perche*, from Greek *perkē*.

perchance ■ adv. archaic or poetic/literary by some chance.
–ORIGIN Middle English: from Old French *par cheance* 'by chance'.

percheron /ˈpəːʃ(ə)rɒn/ ■ n. a powerful draught horse of a grey or black breed, originally from France.
–ORIGIN C19: from French, orig. bred in le *Perche*, a district of northern France.

perchloric acid /pəˈklɒrɪk/ ■ n. Chemistry a fuming toxic liquid with powerful oxidizing properties. [$HClO_4$.]
–DERIVATIVES **perchlorate** n.

perchloroethylene /pəˌklɔːrəʊˈɛθɪliːn/ ■ n. a toxic volatile solvent used as a dry-cleaning fluid. [C_2Cl_4.]

perciform /ˈpəːsɪfɔːm/ ■ adj. Zoology relating to or denoting fish of a very large order (Perciformes) comprising the perches and their relatives.
–ORIGIN C19: from Latin *perca* 'perch' + *forma* 'shape'.

percipient /pəˈsɪpɪənt/ ■ adj. having a perceptive understanding of things. ■ n. (especially in philosophy or with reference to psychic phenomena) a person who is able to perceive things.
–DERIVATIVES **percipience** n. **percipiently** adv.
–ORIGIN C17: from Latin *percipere* 'seize, understand'.

percoid /ˈpəːkɔɪd/ ■ n. Zoology a fish of a large group (superfamily Percoidea) that includes the perches, basses, jacks, snappers, sea breams, etc.
–ORIGIN C19: from Latin *perca* 'perch'.

percolate ■ v. **1** filter through a porous surface or substance. **2** (of information etc.) spread gradually through a group of people. **3** (with reference to coffee) prepare or be prepared in a percolator.
–DERIVATIVES **percolated** adj. **percolation** n.
–ORIGIN C17: from Latin *percolare* 'strain through'.

percolator ■ n. a machine for making coffee, consisting of a pot in which boiling water is circulated through a small chamber that holds the ground beans.

per contra /pəːˈkɒntrə/ ■ adv. on the other hand. ■ n. the opposite side of an account or an assessment.
–ORIGIN C16: from Italian.

percuss /pəˈkʌs/ ■ v. Medicine gently tap (a part of the body) as part of a diagnosis.
–ORIGIN C16: from Latin *percutere* 'strike through'.

percussion ■ n. **1** the action of playing a musical instrument by striking or shaking it. ▶ [as modifier] denoting musical instruments played in this way. ▶ percussion instruments forming a band or section of an orchestra. **2** the striking of one solid object with or against another with some degree of force. **3** Medicine the action of percussing a part of the body.
–DERIVATIVES **percussionist** n. **percussive** adj. **percussively** adv. **percussiveness** n.

percussion cap ■ n. a small amount of explosive powder contained in metal or paper and exploded by striking.

percussion drill ■ n. a hammer drill.

percutaneous /ˌpəːkjuːˈteɪnɪəs/ ■ adj. Medicine made, done, or effected through the skin.
–DERIVATIVES **percutaneously** adv.
–ORIGIN C19: from Latin *per cutem* 'through the skin'.

per diem /pəːˈdiːɛm, ˈdʌɪɛm/ ■ adv. & adj. for each day. ■ n. an allowance or payment made for each day.
–ORIGIN C16: Latin.

perdition /pəˈdɪʃ(ə)n/ ■ n. (in Christian theology) a state of eternal damnation into which a sinful and unpenitent person passes after death.
–ORIGIN Middle English: from Old French *perdiciun*, from Latin *perdere* 'destroy'.

perdurable /pəˈdjʊərəb(ə)l/ ■ adj. formal enduring continuously; permanent.
– DERIVATIVES **perdurably** adv.
– ORIGIN Middle English: from late Latin *perdurabilis*, from Latin *perdurare* 'endure'.

père /pɛː/ ■ n. used after a surname to distinguish a father from a son of the same name.
– ORIGIN French, 'father'.

peregrinate /ˈpɛrɪɡrɪneɪt/ ■ v. archaic or humorous travel or wander from place to place.
– DERIVATIVES **peregrination** n. **peregrinator** n.
– ORIGIN C16 (*peregrination* Middle English): from Latin *peregrinari* 'travel abroad'.

peregrine /ˈpɛrɪɡrɪn/ ■ n. a powerful falcon that breeds chiefly on mountains and coastal cliffs. [*Falco peregrinus*.]
– ORIGIN Middle English: from Latin *peregrinus* 'foreign'; the noun is a translation of the taxonomic name, 'pilgrim falcon', because falconers' birds were caught full-grown on migration, not taken from the nest.

peremptory /pəˈrɛm(p)t(ə)ri, ˈpɛrɪm-/ ■ adj. **1** insisting on immediate attention or obedience; brusque and imperious. **2** Law not open to appeal or challenge; final.
– DERIVATIVES **peremptorily** adv. **peremptoriness** n.
– ORIGIN Middle English: from Latin *peremptorius* 'deadly, decisive', from *perimere* 'destroy, cut off'.

perennial ■ adj. **1** lasting through a year or several years. **2** (of a plant) living for several years. Compare with ANNUAL, BIENNIAL. **3** lasting for a long time; enduring or continually recurring. ▸ continually engaged in a specified activity: *a perennial student*. ■ n. a perennial plant.
– DERIVATIVES **perennially** adv.
– ORIGIN C17: from Latin *perennis* 'lasting the year through'.

perestroika /ˌpɛrɪˈstrɔɪkə/ ■ n. (in the former Soviet Union) the policy or practice of reforming the economic and political system, practised in the 1980s under Mikhail Gorbachev.
– ORIGIN Russian, 'restructuring'.

perfect ■ adj. /ˈpəːfɪkt/ **1** having all the required elements, qualities, or characteristics. **2** free from any flaw; faultless. **3** complete; absolute: *it made perfect sense*. **4** Grammar (of a tense) denoting a completed action or a state or habitual action which began in the past, formed in English with *have* or *has* and the past participle, as in *they have eaten*. **5** Botany (of a flower) having both stamens and carpels present and functional. ■ v. /pəˈfɛkt/ **1** make perfect. **2** bring to completion. ■ n. /ˈpəːfɪkt/ (**the perfect**) Grammar the perfect tense.
– DERIVATIVES **perfecter** n. **perfectibility** n. **perfectible** adj. **perfectly** adv. **perfectness** n.
– ORIGIN Middle English: from Old French *perfet*, from Latin *perfectus*, *perficere* 'complete'.

perfect binding ■ n. a form of bookbinding in which the leaves are bound by gluing, after the back folds have been cut off, rather than sewing.

perfect gas ■ n. another term for IDEAL GAS.

perfection ■ n. **1** the action, process, or condition of perfecting or being perfect. **2** a perfect person or thing.

perfectionism ■ n. refusal to accept any standard short of perfection.
– DERIVATIVES **perfectionist** n. & adj. **perfectionistic** adj.

perfect pitch ■ n. the ability to recognize the pitch of a note or produce any given note.

perfect square ■ n. another term for SQUARE NUMBER.

perfidy /ˈpəːfɪdi/ ■ n. poetic/literary deceitfulness; untrustworthiness.
– DERIVATIVES **perfidious** adj. **perfidiously** adv. **perfidiousness** n.
– ORIGIN C16: from Latin *perfidia*, from *perfidus* 'treacherous'.

perfin /ˈpəːfɪn/ ■ n. Philately a postage stamp perforated with the initials or insignia of an organization.
– ORIGIN 1950s: from *perf*(orated) *in*(itials).

perfoliate /pəˈfəʊlɪət/ ■ adj. Botany (of a stalkless leaf or bract) extended at the base to encircle the node (so that the stem appears to pass through it). ▸ (of a plant) having such leaves.

– ORIGIN C17: from Latin *per-* 'through' + *foliatus* 'leaved'.

perforate /ˈpəːfəreɪt/ ■ v. pierce and make a hole or holes in.
– DERIVATIVES **perforated** adj. **perforator** n.
– ORIGIN Middle English: from Latin *perforare* 'pierce through'.

perforation (/ˌpəːfəˈreɪʃn/) ■ n. a hole made by boring or piercing. ▸ a small hole or row of small holes punched in a sheet of paper. ▸ the action or state of perforating or being perforated.

perforce ■ adv. formal necessarily; inevitably.
– ORIGIN Middle English: from Old French *par force* 'by force'.

perforin /ˈpəːfərɪn/ ■ n. Biochemistry a protein, released by killer cells of the immune system, which destroys targeted cells by creating lesions like pores in their membranes.
– ORIGIN 1980s: from PERFORATE.

perform ■ v. **1** carry out, accomplish, or fulfil (an action, task, or function). **2** work, function, or do something to a specified standard: *the car performs well at low speeds*. **3** (of an investment) yield a profitable return. **4** present (a form of entertainment) to an audience.
– DERIVATIVES **performability** n. **performable** adj. **performer** n.
– ORIGIN Middle English: from Anglo-Norman French *parfourmer*, alteration of Old French *parfournir*, from *par* 'through, to completion' + *fournir* 'furnish, provide'.

performance ■ n. **1** an act of performing a play, concert, or other form of entertainment. **2** a person's rendering of a dramatic role, song, or piece of music. **3** informal a display of exaggerated behaviour; an elaborate fuss. **4** the action or process of performing a task or function. **5** the capabilities of a machine or product. **6** the extent to which an investment is profitable. **7** Linguistics an individual's actual use of a language, including hesitations and errors. Often contrasted with COMPETENCE.

performance art ■ n. an art form that combines visual art with dramatic performance.
– DERIVATIVES **performance artist** n.

performance bond ■ n. a bond issued by a bank or other financial institution, guaranteeing the fulfilment of a particular contract.

performance poetry ■ n. a form of poetry that is performed as a dramatic monologue or exchange and frequently involves extemporization.
– DERIVATIVES **performance poet** n.

performative Linguistics & Philosophy ■ adj. denoting a statement by means of which the speaker performs a particular act (e.g. *I apologize*). ■ n. a performative verb, sentence, or utterance.

performing arts ■ pl. n. forms of creative activity that are performed in front of an audience.

perfume /ˈpəːfjuːm/ ■ n. **1** a fragrant liquid typically made from essential oils, used to impart a pleasant smell to one's body or clothes. **2** a pleasant smell. ■ v. /also pəˈfjuːm/ **1** impart a pleasant smell to. **2** (usu. **be perfumed**) impregnate with perfume or a sweet-smelling ingredient. **3** apply perfume to.
– DERIVATIVES **perfumed** adj. **perfumy** adj.
– ORIGIN C16: from French *parfum* (n.), *parfumer* (v.), from obsolete Italian *parfumare* 'to smoke through'.

perfumery ■ n. (pl. -ies) **1** the process of producing and selling perfumes. **2** a shop that sells perfumes.
– DERIVATIVES **perfumer** n.

perfunctory /pəˈfʌŋ(k)t(ə)ri/ ■ adj. carried out with a minimum of effort or reflection.
– DERIVATIVES **perfunctorily** adv. **perfunctoriness** n.
– ORIGIN C16: from late Latin *perfunctorius* 'careless', from Latin *perfungi* 'have done with, discharge'.

perfuse ■ v. **1** permeate or suffuse with a liquid, colour, quality, etc. **2** Medicine supply (an organ, tissue, or body) with a fluid, typically treated blood or a blood substitute, by circulating it through blood vessels or other natural channels.
– DERIVATIVES **perfusate** n. **perfusion** n. **perfusionist** n.
– ORIGIN Middle English: from Latin *perfundere* 'pour through'.

pergola /ˈpəːɡələ/ ■ n. an arched structure forming a framework for climbing or trailing plants.
– ORIGIN C17: from Latin *pergula* 'projecting roof'.

perhaps ■ adv. **1** expressing uncertainty or possibility. **2** used when making a polite request or suggestion.
– ORIGIN C15: from PER + HAP.

peri- ■ prefix **1** round; about: *pericardium*. **2** Astronomy denoting the point nearest to a specified celestial body: *perihelion*. Compare with APO-.
– ORIGIN from Greek *peri* 'about, around'.

perianth /ˈpɛrɪanθ/ ■ n. Botany the outer part of a flower, consisting of the calyx (sepals) and corolla (petals).
– ORIGIN C18: from French *périanthe*, from Greek *peri* 'around' + *anthos* 'flower'.

pericardium /ˌpɛrɪˈkɑːdɪəm/ ■ n. (pl. **pericardia** /-dɪə/) Anatomy the membrane enclosing the heart.
– DERIVATIVES **pericardial** adj. **pericarditis** n.
– ORIGIN Middle English: from Greek *perikardion*, from *peri* 'around' + *kardia* 'heart'.

pericarp ■ n. Botany the part of a fruit formed from the wall of the ripened ovary.
– ORIGIN C17: from French *péricarpe*, from Greek *perikarpion* 'pod, shell', from *peri-* 'around' + *karpos* 'fruit'.

perichondrium /ˌpɛrɪˈkɒndrɪəm/ ■ n. Anatomy the connective tissue that envelops cartilage where it is not at a joint.
– ORIGIN C18: from PERI- + Greek *khondros* 'cartilage'.

periclase /ˈpɛrɪkleɪz, -s/ ■ n. a colourless mineral consisting of magnesium oxide, occurring chiefly in marble and limestone.
– ORIGIN C19: from Greek *peri* 'utterly' + *klasis* 'breaking' (because it cleaves perfectly).

periderm ■ n. Botany the corky outer layer of a plant stem formed by the cambium or as a response to injury or infection.
– DERIVATIVES **peridermal** adj.
– ORIGIN C19: from PERI- + Greek *derma* 'skin'.

peridot /ˈpɛrɪdɒt/ ■ n. a green semi-precious variety of olivine.
– ORIGIN C18: from Old French *peritot*.

peridotite /ˈpɛrɪdɒtʌɪt/ ■ n. Geology a dense, coarse-grained plutonic rock containing a large amount of olivine, believed to be the main constituent of the earth's mantle.
– DERIVATIVES **peridotitic** adj.

perigee /ˈpɛrɪdʒiː/ ■ n. Astronomy the point in the orbit of the moon or a satellite at which it is nearest to the earth. The opposite of APOGEE.
– ORIGIN C16: from French *périgée*, from Greek *perigeion* 'close round the earth'.

periglacial ■ adj. Geology relating to or denoting an area adjacent to a glacier or ice sheet or otherwise subject to repeated freezing and thawing.

perigynous /pəˈrɪdʒɪnəs/ ■ adj. Botany (of a plant or flower) having the stamens and other floral parts at the same level as the carpels. Compare with EPIGYNOUS and HYPOGYNOUS.
– DERIVATIVES **perigyny** n.

perihelion /ˌpɛrɪˈhiːlɪən/ ■ n. (pl. **perihelia** /-lɪə/) Astronomy the point in the orbit of a planet, asteroid, or comet at which it is closest to the sun. The opposite of APHELION.
– ORIGIN C17: from Greek *peri-* 'around' + *hēlios* 'sun'.

peril ■ n. a situation of serious and immediate danger.
– PHRASES **at one's peril** at one's own risk. **in** (or **at**) **peril of 1** very likely to suffer from. **2** at risk of losing or injuring: *they would be in peril of their life*.
– ORIGIN Middle English: from Latin *peric(u)lum* 'danger', from the base of *experiri* 'to try'.

perilous /ˈpɛrɪləs/ ■ adj. full of or exposed to danger or risk.
– DERIVATIVES **perilously** adv. **perilousness** n.

perilymph ■ n. Anatomy the fluid between the membranous labyrinth of the ear and the bone which encloses it.
– DERIVATIVES **perilymphatic** adj.

perimenopause ■ n. the period of a woman's life shortly before the occurrence of the menopause.
– DERIVATIVES **perimenopausal** adj.

perimeter ■ n. **1** the continuous line forming the boundary of a closed geometrical figure. **2** the outermost parts or boundary of an area or object. **3** an instrument for measuring the extent and characteristics of a person's field of vision.
– DERIVATIVES **perimetric** adj. **perimetry** n.
– ORIGIN Middle English: from Greek *perimetros*, from *peri-* 'around' + *metron* 'measure'.

perinatal ■ adj. Medicine of or relating to the time immediately before and after a birth.
– DERIVATIVES **perinatally** adv. **perinatologist** n. **perinatology** n.

per incuriam /pə(r) ɪnˈkjʊərɪəm/ ■ adv. Law through lack of due regard to the law or to the facts.
– ORIGIN Latin, 'through lack of care'.

perineum /ˌpɛrɪˈniːəm/ ■ n. (pl. **perinea**) Anatomy the area between the anus and the scrotum or vulva.
– DERIVATIVES **perineal** adj.
– ORIGIN Middle English: from Greek *perinaion*.

period ■ n. **1** a length or portion of time. **2** a portion of time characterized by the same prevalent features or conditions. **3** a major division of geological time that is a subdivision of an era and is itself subdivided into epochs. **4** each of the set divisions of the day in a school. **5** (also **menstrual period**) a monthly flow of blood and other material from the lining of the uterus, occurring in women of child-bearing age when not pregnant. **6** chiefly N. Amer. a full stop. **7** Physics the interval of time between successive occurrences of the same state in an oscillatory or cyclic phenomenon. **8** Mathematics the interval between successive equal values of a periodic function. **9** Chemistry a set of elements occupying a horizontal row in the periodic table. **10** Astronomy the time taken by a celestial object to rotate about its axis, or to make one circuit of its orbit. **11** Rhetoric a complex sentence, especially one consisting of several clauses, constructed as part of a formal speech or oration. ■ adj. belonging to or characteristic in style of a past historical time: *period furniture*.
– DERIVATIVES **periodization** (also **-isation**) n. **periodize** (also **-ise**) v.
– ORIGIN Middle English: from Old French *periode*, from Greek *periodos* 'orbit, recurrence, course'.

periodic /ˌpɪərɪˈɒdɪk/ ■ adj. **1** appearing or occurring at intervals. **2** Chemistry relating to the periodic table of the elements or the pattern of chemical properties which underlies it. **3** of or relating to a rhetorical period.
– DERIVATIVES **periodicity** n.

periodic acid /ˌpəːrʌɪˈɒdɪk/ ■ n. Chemistry a hygroscopic solid acid with strong oxidizing properties.
– DERIVATIVES **periodate** /pəˈrʌɪədeɪt/ n.
– ORIGIN C19: from sense 2 of PER- + IODIC ACID.

periodical ■ adj. occurring or appearing at intervals. ▶ (of a magazine or newspaper) published at regular intervals. ■ n. a periodical magazine or newspaper.
– DERIVATIVES **periodically** adv.

periodic function ■ n. Mathematics a function returning to the same value at regular intervals.

periodic table ■ n. Chemistry a table of the chemical elements arranged in order of atomic number, usually in rows, so that elements with similar atomic structure (and hence similar chemical properties) appear in vertical columns.

periodontics /ˌpɛrɪəˈdɒntɪks/ ■ pl. n. [treated as sing.] the branch of dentistry concerned with the structures surrounding and supporting the teeth.
– DERIVATIVES **periodontal** adj. **periodontist** n.
– ORIGIN 1940s: from PERI- + Greek *odous, odont-* 'tooth'.

periodontitis /ˌpɛrɪədɒnˈtʌɪtɪs/ ■ n. Medicine inflammation of the tissue around the teeth.

periodontology /ˌpɛrɪədɒnˈtɒlədʒi/ ■ n. another term for PERIODONTICS.

period piece ■ n. an object or work that is set in or reminiscent of an earlier historical period.

perioperative ■ adj. Medicine (of a process or treatment) occurring or performed at or around the time of an operation.

periosteum /ˌpɛrɪˈɒstɪəm/ ■ n. (pl. **periostea** /-tɪə/) Anatomy a dense layer of vascular connective tissue enveloping the bones except at the surfaces of the joints.
– DERIVATIVES **periosteal** adj. **periostitis** n.

– ORIGIN C16: from Greek *periosteon*, from *peri-* 'around' + *osteon* 'bone'.

peripatetic /ˌpɛrɪpəˈtɛtɪk/ ■ adj. travelling from place to place. ▶ working or based in a succession of places each for a short period.
– DERIVATIVES **peripatetically** adv.
– ORIGIN Middle English: from Old French *peripatetique*, from Greek *peripatētikos* 'walking up and down'.

peri peri (also **piri piri**) ■ n. a hot sauce made with red chilli peppers. ▶ a powdered seasoning made from red chilli peppers. ▶ [as modifier] a dish made with this sauce or seasoning: *peri peri chicken*.
– ORIGIN from African Portuguese *piri piri* 'pepper'.

HISTORY
The word **peri peri** comes from Mozambican Portuguese *piri piri* meaning 'pepper'. Although it came into South African English in the 1950s, it has its roots in the ancient spice trade between the Americas, Africa and Asia. The chilli pepper was brought to Africa's Portuguese colonies from South America in the 16th century and soon became an important part of trade between Africa, Asia and the Middle East. In southern and eastern Africa it is also known as *pilipili* or *pelipeli* and it is likely that the word comes originally from *felfel*, an Arabic word for pepper, which derives ultimately from Sanskrit *pippali*, 'long pepper'.

peripheral ■ adj. **1** of, relating to, or situated on the periphery. **2** marginal. **3** (of a device) able to be attached to and used with a computer, though not an integral part of it. **4** Anatomy near the surface of the body. ■ n. Computing a peripheral device.
– DERIVATIVES **peripherality** n. **peripheralization** (also **-isation**) n. **peripheralize** (also **-ise**) v. **peripherally** adv.

peripheral nervous system ■ n. Anatomy the nervous system outside the brain and spinal cord.

periphery /pəˈrɪf(ə)ri/ ■ n. (pl. **-ies**) **1** the outer limits or edge of an area or object. **2** a marginal or secondary position, part, or aspect.
– ORIGIN C16: from Greek *periphereia* 'circumference'.

periphrasis /pəˈrɪfrəsɪs/ ■ n. (pl. **periphrases** /-siːz/) **1** the use of indirect and circumlocutory speech or writing. **2** Grammar the use of separate words to express a grammatical relationship that is otherwise expressed by inflection, e.g. *did go* as opposed to *went*.
– DERIVATIVES **periphrastic** adj. **periphrastically** adv.
– ORIGIN C16: from Greek, from *periphrazein*, from *peri-* 'around' + *phrazein* 'declare'.

periphyton /pəˈrɪfɪtɒn/ ■ n. Ecology freshwater organisms attached to or clinging to plants and other objects projecting above the bottom sediments.
– DERIVATIVES **periphytic** adj.
– ORIGIN 1960s: from Greek *peri-* 'around' + *phuton* 'plant'.

peripteral /pəˈrɪpt(ə)r(ə)l/ ■ adj. Architecture (of a building) having a single row of pillars on all sides in the style of the temples of ancient Greece.
– ORIGIN C19: from Greek *peripteron*, from *peri-* 'around' + *pteron* 'wing'.

periscope ■ n. an apparatus consisting of a tube attached to a set of mirrors or prisms, by which an observer (typically in a submerged submarine or behind a high obstacle) can see things that are otherwise out of sight.
– DERIVATIVES **periscopic** adj. **periscopically** adv.

perish ■ v. **1** die, especially in large numbers. **2** suffer complete ruin or destruction. **3** rot or decay.
– PHRASES **perish the thought** informal may the thought or idea prove unfounded.
– ORIGIN Middle English: from Old French *periss-*, *perir*, from Latin *perire* 'pass away'.

perishable ■ adj. **1** (of food) likely to rot quickly. **2** having a brief life or significance. ■ n. (**perishables**) things, especially foodstuffs, likely to rot quickly.
– DERIVATIVES **perishability** n.

perishing ■ adj. Brit. informal **1** extremely cold. **2** dated used for emphasis or to express annoyance.
– DERIVATIVES **perishingly** adv.

Perissodactyla /ˌpərɪsə(ʊ)ˈdaktɪlə/ ■ pl. n. Zoology an order of mammals that comprises the horses, rhinoceroses, and tapirs (the odd-toed ungulates).
– DERIVATIVES **perissodactyl** n. & adj.
– ORIGIN from Greek *perissos* 'uneven' + *daktulos* 'finger, toe'.

peristalsis /ˌpɛrɪˈstalsɪs/ ■ n. Physiology the involuntary constriction and relaxation of the muscles of the intestine or another canal, creating wave-like movements which push the contents of the canal forward.
– DERIVATIVES **peristaltic** adj. **peristaltically** adv.
– ORIGIN C19: from Greek *peristallein* 'wrap around'.

peristaltic pump ■ n. a mechanical pump in which pressure is provided by the movement of a constriction along a tube, similar to biological peristalsis.

peristyle ■ n. Architecture a row of columns surrounding a space within a building such as a court or internal garden or edging a veranda or porch.
– ORIGIN C17: from French *péristyle*, from Greek *peristulon*, from *peri-* 'around' + *stulos* 'pillar'.

peritoneum /ˌpɛrɪtəˈniːəm/ ■ n. (pl. **peritoneums** or **peritonea** /-ˈniːə/) Anatomy the serous membrane lining the cavity of the abdomen and covering the abdominal organs.
– DERIVATIVES **peritoneal** adj.
– ORIGIN Middle English: from Greek *peritonaion*, from *peritonos* 'stretched round'.

peritonitis /ˌpɛrɪtəˈnʌɪtɪs/ ■ n. Medicine inflammation of the peritoneum, typically caused by bacterial infection either via the blood or after rupture of an abdominal organ.

periwig ■ n. a highly styled wig worn formerly as a fashionable headdress by both women and men and retained by judges and barristers as part of their professional dress.
– DERIVATIVES **periwigged** adj.
– ORIGIN C16: alteration of archaic *peruke*, from French *peruque*, with *-wi-* representing the French *-u-* sound.

periwinkle[1] ■ n. a plant with flat five-petalled flowers and glossy leaves, some kinds of which contain alkaloids used in medicine. [Genera *Vinca* and *Catharanthus*.]
– ORIGIN Old English *peruince*, from late Latin *pervinca*.

periwinkle[2] ■ n. a small herbivorous shore-dwelling mollusc with a spiral shell. [*Littorina littorea* and other species.]
– ORIGIN C16.

perjure ■ v. (**perjure oneself**) Law commit perjury.
– DERIVATIVES **perjurer** n.
– ORIGIN Middle English: from Old French *parjurer*, from Latin *perjurare* 'swear falsely'.

perjured ■ adj. Law (of evidence) involving wilfully told untruths. ▶ guilty of perjury.

perjury /ˈpəːdʒ(ə)ri/ ■ n. (pl. **-ies**) Law the offence of wilfully telling an untruth in a court after having taken an oath or affirmation.
– DERIVATIVES **perjurious** /-ˈdʒʊərɪəs/ adj.

perk[1] ■ v. (**perk someone upor**) **perk up** make or become more cheerful or lively.
– ORIGIN Middle English: perhaps from an Old French var. of *percher* 'to perch'.

perk[2] ■ n. informal a benefit to which one is entitled as an employee or shareholder of a company. ▶ an advantage or benefit following from a particular situation.
– ORIGIN C19: abbrev. of PERQUISITE.

perky ■ adj. (**-ier**, **-iest**) **1** cheerful and lively. **2** cheeky.
– DERIVATIVES **perkily** adv. **perkiness** n.

Perl ■ n. Computing a high-level programming language used especially for applications running on the World Wide Web.
– ORIGIN 1980s: respelling of PEARL, arbitrarily chosen for its positive connotations.

perlé /ˈpəːleɪ/ ■ n. a semi-sweet, slightly sparkling wine produced in South Africa.
– ORIGIN French, 'beaded', perhaps from an abbrev. of German *Perlwein*, denoting a slightly sparkling wine.

perlemoen /ˈpəːləmʊn/ ■ n. S. African an abalone. [*Haliotis midae*.]
– ORIGIN from obsolete Afrikaans *perlemoer*, from Middle Dutch *perlenmoeder* 'mother-of-pearl', because of the pearlized lining inside the shell.

perlite /'pəːlʌɪt/ ■ n. a form of obsidian consisting of glassy globules, used as insulation or in plant growth media.
– ORIGIN C19: from French, from *perle* 'pearl'.

perlocution ■ n. Philosophy & Linguistics an act of speaking or writing which has an action as its aim but which in itself does not effect or constitute the action, for example persuading or convincing.
– DERIVATIVES **perlocutionary** adj.

perm ■ n. (also **permanent wave**) a method of setting the hair in waves or curls and treating it with chemicals so that the style lasts for several months. ■ v. treat (the hair) in such a way.
– ORIGIN 1920s: abbrev. of PERMANENT.

permaculture ■ n. the development of agricultural ecosystems intended to be sustainable and self-sufficient.
– ORIGIN 1970s: blend of PERMANENT and AGRICULTURE.

permafrost ■ n. a thick subsurface layer of soil that remains below freezing point throughout the year.
– ORIGIN 1940s: from PERMANENT + FROST.

permanent ■ adj. lasting or remaining unchanged indefinitely, or intended to be so; not temporary. ■ n. N. Amer. a perm for the hair.
– DERIVATIVES **permanence** n. **permanency** n. **permanently** adv.
– ORIGIN Middle English: from Latin *permanent-* 'remaining to the end', from *per-* 'through' + *manere* 'remain'.

permanent hardness ■ n. the presence in water of mineral salts (chiefly calcium sulphate) that are not removed by boiling.

permanent magnet ■ n. a magnet that retains its magnetic properties in the absence of an inducing field or current.

permanent tooth ■ n. a tooth in a mammal that replaces a temporary milk tooth and lasts for most of the mammal's life.

permanent wave ■ n. see PERM.

permanent way ■ n. the finished roadbed of a railway together with the track and other permanent equipment.

permanganate /pəˈmaŋɡənət, -eɪt/ ■ n. Chemistry a salt containing the anion MnO_4^-, typically deep purplish-red and with strong oxidizing properties.

permeability ■ n. 1 the state or quality of being permeable. 2 Physics a quantity measuring the influence of a substance on the magnetic flux in the region it occupies.

permeable ■ adj. (of a material or membrane) allowing liquids or gases to pass through it.
– DERIVATIVES **permeabilization** (also **-isation**) n. **permeabilize** (also **-ise**) v.
– ORIGIN Middle English: from Latin *permeabilis*, from *permeare* 'pass through'.

permeance /'pəːmɪəns/ ■ n. Physics the property of allowing the passage of lines of magnetic flux.

permeate ■ v. spread throughout; pervade.
– DERIVATIVES **permeation** n. **permeator** n.
– ORIGIN C17: from Latin *permeare* 'pass through'.

permethrin /pəˈmiːθrɪn/ ■ n. a synthetic insecticide of the pyrethroid class, used chiefly against disease-carrying insects.
– ORIGIN 1970s: from sense 2 of PER- + (*res*)*methrin*, denoting a synthetic pyrethroid.

Permian /'pəːmɪən/ ■ adj. Geology relating to or denoting the last period of the Palaeozoic era (between the Carboniferous and Triassic periods, about 290 to 245 million years ago), a time when reptiles proliferated and many marine animals became extinct.
– ORIGIN C16: from *Perm*, a Russian province with extensive deposits from this period.

per mille /pəː ˈmɪleɪ, ˈmɪli/ (also **per mil** /mɪl/) ■ adv. by a specified amount in or for every thousand.
– ORIGIN C17: from Latin.

permissible ■ adj. allowable; permitted.
– DERIVATIVES **permissibility** n. **permissibly** adv.

permission ■ n. authorization.
– ORIGIN Middle English: from Latin *permissio(n-)*, from *permittere* (see PERMIT).

permissive ■ adj. 1 allowing or characterized by freedom of behaviour. 2 Law allowed but not obligatory; optional.
▸ denoting a path available for public use by the landowner's consent, not as a legal right of way.
– DERIVATIVES **permissively** adv. **permissiveness** n.

permit ■ v. /pəˈmɪt/ (**permitted**, **permitting**) 1 give permission to (someone) or for (something). 2 make possible. 3 (**permit of**) formal allow for; admit of. ■ n. /'pəːmɪt/ an official document giving permission to do something.
– DERIVATIVES **permittee** n. **permitter** n.
– ORIGIN Middle English: from Latin *permittere*, from *per-* 'through' + *mittere* 'send, let go'.

permittivity /ˌpəːmɪˈtɪvɪti/ ■ n. Physics the ability of a substance to store electrical energy in an electric field.

permutate /'pəːmjʊteɪt/ ■ v. change the order or arrangement of.
– ORIGIN C19: a back-formation from PERMUTATION.

permutation ■ n. 1 a way, especially one of several possible variations, in which a set or number of things can be ordered or arranged. 2 Mathematics the action of changing the arrangement of a set of items.
– DERIVATIVES **permutational** adj.
– ORIGIN Middle English: from Latin *permutatio(n-)*, from *permutare* (see PERMUTE).

permute ■ v. submit to a process of alteration, rearrangement, or permutation.
– ORIGIN Middle English: from Latin *permutare* 'change completely'.

pernicious /pəˈnɪʃəs/ ■ adj. having a harmful effect, especially in a gradual or subtle way.
– DERIVATIVES **perniciously** adv. **perniciousness** n.
– ORIGIN Middle English: from Latin *perniciosus* 'destructive', from *pernicies* 'ruin', from *nex* 'death'.

pernicious anaemia ■ n. a deficiency in the production of red blood cells through a lack of vitamin B_{12}.

pernickety ■ adj. informal 1 fussy. 2 requiring a precise or careful approach.
– ORIGIN C19 (orig. Scots).

Pernod /'pəːnəʊ/ ■ n. trademark an aniseed-flavoured aperitif.
– ORIGIN named after the manufacturing firm *Pernod Fils*.

peroneal /ˌpɛrəˈniːəl/ ■ adj. Anatomy relating to or situated in the outer side of the calf of the leg.
– ORIGIN C19: from modern Latin *peronaeus* 'peroneal muscle', from Greek *peronē* 'pin, fibula'.

Peronist /'pɛrənɪst/ ■ adj. of or relating to the activities and social reforms of the Argentinian statesman Juan Domingo Péron (1895–1974). ■ n. a supporter of Péron.

perorate /'pɛrəreɪt/ ■ v. formal 1 speak at length. 2 sum up and conclude a speech.
– ORIGIN C17: from Latin *perorare* 'speak at length'.

peroration ■ n. the concluding part of a speech; the summing up.

perovskite /pəˈrɒfskʌɪt/ ■ n. a yellow, brown, or black mineral consisting largely of calcium titanate.
– ORIGIN C19: from the name of the Russian mineralogist L. A. *Perovsky*.

peroxidase /pəˈrɒksɪdeɪz/ ■ n. Biochemistry an enzyme that catalyses the oxidation of a particular substrate by hydrogen peroxide.

peroxide ■ n. 1 Chemistry a compound containing two oxygen atoms bonded together in its molecule or as the anion O_2^{2-}. 2 hydrogen peroxide, especially as used as a bleach for the hair. ■ v. bleach (hair) with peroxide.
– ORIGIN C19: from sense 2 of PER- + OXIDE.

perp ■ n. N. Amer. informal the perpetrator of a crime.

perpendicular /ˌpəːp(ə)nˈdɪkjʊlə/ ■ adj. 1 at an angle of 90° to a given line, plane, or surface. 2 at an angle of 90° to the ground; vertical. ■ n. a perpendicular line.
– DERIVATIVES **perpendicularity** n. **perpendicularly** adv.
– ORIGIN Middle English: from Latin *perpendicularis*, from *perpendiculum* 'plumb line'.

perpetrate /'pəːpɪtreɪt/ ■ v. carry out or commit (a harmful, illegal, or immoral action).
– DERIVATIVES **perpetration** n. **perpetrator** n.
– ORIGIN C16: from Latin *perpetrare* 'perform'; the English

perpetual

verb was first used in the statutes referring to crime, hence the negative association.

perpetual /pəˈpetʃʊəl, -tjʊəl/ ■ adj. **1** never ending or changing. ▸ denoting or having a position or trophy held for life rather than a limited period. ▸ (of an investment) having no fixed maturity date. **2** occurring repeatedly. **3** (of a plant) blooming or fruiting several times in one season.
- DERIVATIVES **perpetually** adv.
- ORIGIN Middle English: from Latin *perpetualis*, from *perpetuus* 'continuing throughout'.

perpetual calendar ■ n. a calendar in which the day, the month, and the date are adjusted independently to show any combination of the three.

perpetual check ■ n. Chess the situation of play when a draw is obtained by repeated checking of the king.

perpetual motion ■ n. the motion of a hypothetical machine which, once activated, would run forever unless subject to an external force or to wear.

perpetuate /pəˈpetʃʊeɪt, -tjʊ-/ ■ v. cause to continue indefinitely.
- DERIVATIVES **perpetuation** n. **perpetuator** n.
- ORIGIN C16: from Latin *perpetuare* 'make permanent', from *perpetuus* 'continuing throughout'.

perpetuity ■ n. (pl. -ies) **1** the state or quality of lasting forever. **2** a bond or other security with no fixed maturity date. **3** Law a restriction making an estate inalienable perpetually or for a period beyond certain limits fixed by law.

perplex ■ v. cause to feel baffled.
- DERIVATIVES **perplexed** adj. **perplexedly** adv. **perplexing** adj. **perplexingly** adv. **perplexity** n.
- ORIGIN C15: from the obsolete adj. *perplex* 'bewildered', from Latin *perplexus* 'entangled'.

per pro. /pəː ˈprəʊ/ ■ abbrev. per procurationem (used when signing a letter on someone else's behalf); now usually abbreviated to pp.
- ORIGIN from Latin.

perquisite /ˈpəːkwɪzɪt/ ■ n. formal a special right or privilege enjoyed as a result of one's position.
- ORIGIN Middle English: from medieval Latin *perquisitum* 'acquisition', from Latin *perquirere* 'search diligently for'.

per se /pəː ˈseɪ/ ■ adv. by or in itself or themselves.
- ORIGIN from Latin.

persecute ■ v. **1** subject to prolonged hostility and ill-treatment. **2** persistently harass or annoy.
- DERIVATIVES **persecution** n. **persecutor** n. **persecutory** adj.
- ORIGIN Middle English: from Old French *persecuter*, from Latin *persequi* 'follow with hostility'.

persecution complex ■ n. an irrational and obsessive feeling that one is the object of collective hostility or ill-treatment on the part of others.

perseverate /pəˈsɛvəreɪt/ ■ v. Psychology repeat or prolong an action, thought, or utterance after the stimulus that prompted it has ceased.
- DERIVATIVES **perseveration** n.
- ORIGIN C20: from Latin *perseverare* 'abide by strictly' (see PERSEVERE).

persevere ■ v. continue in a course of action in spite of difficulty or with little or no indication of success.
- DERIVATIVES **perseverance** n. **persevering** adj. **perseveringly** adv.
- ORIGIN Middle English: from Old French *perseverer*, from Latin *perseverare* 'abide by strictly', from *perseverus* 'very strict'.

Persian ■ n. **1** a native or national of ancient or modern Persia (or Iran), or a person of Persian descent. **2** the language of modern Iran. ▸ an earlier form of this language spoken in ancient or medieval Persia. **3** a long-haired domestic cat of a breed originating in Persia, having a broad round head and stocky body. **4** another term for BLACKHEAD PERSIAN. ■ adj. of or relating to ancient Persia or modern Iran or its people or language.

Persian carpet ■ n. a carpet or rug woven in Iran in a traditional design incorporating stylized symbolic imagery, or made elsewhere in such a style.

Persian lamb ■ n. the silky, tightly curled fleece of the karakul, used to make clothing.

persiflage /ˈpəːsɪflɑːʒ/ ■ n. formal light mockery or banter.
- ORIGIN C18: from French *persifler* 'to banter'.

persimmon /pəˈsɪmən/ ■ n. **1** an edible fruit resembling a large tomato, with very sweet flesh. **2** the tree which yields this fruit. [*Diospyros virginiana* (America) and *D. kaki* (Japan).]
- ORIGIN C17: alteration of Algonquian *pessemmins*.

persist ■ v. **1** continue firmly or obstinately in an opinion or a course of action in spite of difficulty or opposition. **2** continue to exist.
- ORIGIN C16: from Latin *persistere*, from *per-* 'through, steadfastly' + *sistere* 'to stand'.

persistent ■ adj. **1** persisting or having a tendency to persist. **2** continuing or recurring; prolonged. **3** Botany (of a part of a plant, such as a leaf) remaining attached instead of falling off in the normal manner.
- DERIVATIVES **persistence** n. **persistency** n. **persistently** adv.

persistent vegetative state ■ n. a condition in which a patient is completely unresponsive to stimuli and displays no sign of higher brain function, being kept alive only by medical intervention.

persnickety ■ adj. North American term for PERNICKETY.

person ■ n. (pl. **people** (in most general contexts) or **persons** (chiefly in official and formal contexts)) **1** a human being regarded as an individual. **2** an individual characterized by a preference or liking for a specified thing: *she's not a cat person.* **3** an individual's body: *concealed on his person.* **4** a character in a play or story. **5** Grammar a category used in the classification of pronouns, possessive determiners, and verb forms, according to whether they indicate the speaker (**first person**), the addressee (**second person**), or a third party (**third person**). **6** Christian Church each of the three modes of being of God, namely the Father, the Son, and the Holy Ghost.
- PHRASES **in person** with the personal presence or action of the individual specified.
- ORIGIN Middle English: from Old French *persone*, from Latin *persona* 'actor's mask, character in a play', later 'human being'.

-person ■ comb. form used as a neutral alternative to *-man* in nouns denoting professional status, a position of authority, etc.: *salesperson.*

persona /pəˈsəʊnə, pəː-/ ■ n. (pl. **personas** or **personae** /-niː/) **1** the aspect of a person's character that is presented to or perceived by others. Compare with ANIMA (in sense 2). **2** a role or character adopted by an author or actor.
- ORIGIN C20: Latin, 'mask, character played by an actor'.

personable ■ adj. having a pleasant appearance and manner.
- DERIVATIVES **personableness** n. **personably** adv.

personage ■ n. a person (expressing their importance or elevated status).
- ORIGIN Middle English: from Old French, reinforced by medieval Latin *personagium* 'effigy'.

persona grata /pəˌsəʊnə ˈɡrɑːtə, pəː-/ ■ n. (pl. **personae gratae** /-niː, -tiː/) a person who is acceptable to others.
- ORIGIN Latin, from *persona* + *grata*, feminine of *gratus* 'pleasing'.

personal ■ adj. **1** of, affecting, or belonging to a particular person. **2** involving the presence or action of a particular individual. **3** of or concerning a person's private rather than professional life. **4** making inappropriate or offensive reference to a person's character or appearance: *personal remarks.* **5** of or relating to a person's body: *personal hygiene.* **6** Grammar of or denoting one of the three persons. **7** existing as a self-aware entity, not as an abstraction or an impersonal force: *a personal God.* ■ n. (**personals**) chiefly N. Amer. advertisements or messages in the personal column of a newspaper.
- DERIVATIVES **personally** adv.

personal action ■ n. Law an action brought for compensation or damages for loss of a thing from the person responsible, rather than for recovery of the thing itself.

personal ad ■ n. informal an advertisement or message placed in the personal column of a newspaper.

personal assistant ■ n. a secretary or administrative assistant working for one particular person.

personal column ■ n. a section of a newspaper devoted to private advertisements or messages.

personal computer ■ n. a microcomputer designed for use by one person at a time.

personal identification number (abbrev.: **PIN**) ■ n. a number allocated to an individual and used to validate electronic transactions.

personality ■ n. (pl. **-ies**) **1** the combination of characteristics or qualities that form an individual's distinctive character. **2** the qualities that make someone interesting or popular. **3** a celebrity.

personality disorder ■ n. Psychiatry a deeply ingrained and maladaptive pattern of behaviour, typically causing long-term difficulties in social relationships.

personalize (also **-ise**) ■ v. **1** design or produce (something) to meet someone's individual requirements. **2** make (something) identifiable as belonging to a particular person. **3** cause (an issue or argument) to become concerned with personalities or feelings rather than with general or abstract matters. **4** personify.
– DERIVATIVES **personalization** (also **-isation**) n.

personal organizer (also **-iser**) ■ n. a loose-leaf notebook consisting of separate sections including a diary and address book. ▸ a hand-held microcomputer serving the same purpose.

personal pension ■ n. a pension scheme that is independent of the contributor's employer.

personal pronoun ■ n. each of the pronouns in English (*I*, *you*, *he*, *she*, *it*, *we*, *they*, *me*, *him*, *her*, *us*, and *them*) comprising a set that shows contrasts of person, gender, number, and case.

personal stereo ■ n. a small portable audio cassette or compact disc player, used with lightweight headphones.

personal trainer ■ n. a physical fitness instructor who provides individual exercise training at a gym or a client's home.

personalty /ˈpəːs(ə)n(ə)lti/ ■ n. Law a person's personal property. Compare with **REALTY**.
– ORIGIN C16 (in the legal phr. *in the personalty* 'for damages'): from Anglo-Norman French *personaltie*, from medieval Latin *personalitas*, from Latin, from *persona* (see **PERSON**).

persona non grata ■ n. (pl. **personae non gratae**) an unacceptable or unwelcome person.
– ORIGIN Latin, from *persona* (see **PERSONA**) + *non* 'not' + *grata*, feminine of *gratus* 'pleasing'.

personate ■ v. formal play the part of or pretend to be.
– DERIVATIVES **personation** n.

personify ■ v. (**-ies**, **-ied**) **1** represent (a quality or concept) by a figure in human form. **2** (usu. **be personified**) attribute a personal nature or human characteristics to. **3** represent or embody (a quality or concept) in a physical form.
– DERIVATIVES **personification** n. **personifier** n.

personnel ■ pl. n. people employed in an organization or engaged in an organized undertaking.
– ORIGIN C19: from French.

personnel carrier ■ n. an armoured vehicle for transporting troops.

person of colour ■ n. often offensive a non-white person.

perspective ■ n. **1** the art of representing three-dimensional objects on a two-dimensional surface so as to convey the impression of height, width, depth, and relative distance. **2** a view or prospect. **3** a particular way of regarding something. **4** understanding of the relative importance of things: *we must keep a sense of perspective about what he's done*. **5** an apparent spatial distribution in perceived sound.
– DERIVATIVES **perspectival** adj.
– ORIGIN Middle English: from medieval Latin *perspectiva (ars)* '(science of) optics', from *perspicere* 'look closely'.

perspectivism ■ n. **1** Philosophy the theory that knowledge of a subject is inevitably partial and limited by the individual perspective from which it is viewed. See also **RELATIVISM**. **2** the practice of regarding and analysing a situation or work of art from different points of view.

879

– DERIVATIVES **perspectivist** n.

perspex ■ n. trademark a tough transparent plastic made of an acrylic resin, used as a substitute for glass.
– ORIGIN 1930s: from Latin *perspicere* 'look through'.

perspicacious /ˌpəːspɪˈkeɪʃəs/ ■ adj. having a ready insight into and understanding of things.
– DERIVATIVES **perspicaciously** adv. **perspicacity** n.
– ORIGIN C17: from Latin *perspicax* 'seeing clearly'.

perspicuous /pəˈspɪkjʊəs/ ■ adj. **1** (of an account or representation) clearly expressed and easily understood; lucid. **2** (of a person) expressing things clearly.
– DERIVATIVES **perspicuity** n. **perspicuously** adv.
– ORIGIN C15: from Latin *perspicuus* 'transparent, clear'.

perspire ■ v. give out sweat through the pores of the skin as a result of heat, physical exertion, or stress.
– DERIVATIVES **perspiration** n. **perspiratory** adj.
– ORIGIN C17: from Latin *perspirare*, from *per-* 'through' + *spirare* 'breathe'.

persuade ■ v. **1** cause to do something through reasoning or argument. **2** cause to believe something. **3** (of a situation or event) provide a sound reason for (someone) to do something.
– DERIVATIVES **persuadability** n. **persuadable** adj. **persuader** n. **persuasible** adj.
– ORIGIN C15: from Latin *persuadere*, from *per-* 'through, to completion' + *suadere* 'advise'.

persuasion ■ n. **1** the process of persuading or of being persuaded. **2** a belief or set of beliefs. **3** a group or sect holding a particular belief.

persuasive ■ adj. **1** good at persuading someone to do or believe something. **2** providing sound reasoning or argument.
– DERIVATIVES **persuasively** adv. **persuasiveness** n.

pert ■ adj. **1** attractively lively or cheeky. **2** (of a bodily feature or garment) neat and jaunty.
– DERIVATIVES **pertly** adv. **pertness** n.
– ORIGIN Middle English: from Old French *apert*, from Latin *apertus* 'opened', from *aperire*.

pertain ■ v. **1** be appropriate, related, or applicable. **2** chiefly Law belong to something as a part, appendage, or accessory. **3** be in effect or existence in a specified place or at a specified time: *none of these circumstances pertained during the Jurassic*.
– ORIGIN Middle English: from Old French *partenir*, from Latin *pertinere* 'extend to, have reference to'.

pertinacious /ˌpəːtɪˈneɪʃəs/ ■ adj. formal stubborn; persistent.
– DERIVATIVES **pertinaciously** adv. **pertinaciousness** n. **pertinacity** n.
– ORIGIN C17: from Latin *pertinax* 'holding fast'.

pertinent ■ adj. relevant; appropriate.
– DERIVATIVES **pertinence** n. **pertinency** n. **pertinently** adv.
– ORIGIN Middle English: from Latin *pertinere* (see **PERTAIN**).

perturb ■ v. **1** (usu. **be perturbed**) make anxious or unsettled. **2** alter the normal or regular state or path of (a system, moving object, or process).
– DERIVATIVES **perturbable** adj. **perturbative** /pəˈtəːbətɪv, ˈpəːtəbeɪtɪv/ adj. **perturbing** adj. **perturbingly** adv.
– ORIGIN Middle English: from Latin *perturbare*, from *per-* 'completely' + *turbare* 'disturb'.

perturbation ■ n. **1** anxiety; uneasiness. ▸ a cause of this. **2** the action of perturbing a system, moving object, or process.

pertussis /pəˈtʌsɪs/ ■ n. medical term for **WHOOPING COUGH**.
– ORIGIN C18: from **PER-** + Latin *tussis* 'a cough'.

peruse /pəˈruːz/ ■ v. formal read or examine thoroughly or carefully.
– DERIVATIVES **perusal** n. **peruser** n.
– ORIGIN C15: perhaps from **PER-** + **USE**, or from Anglo-Norman French *peruser* 'examine'.

Peruvian /pəˈruːvɪən/ ■ n. a native or inhabitant of Peru. ■ adj. of or relating to Peru.

Peruvian

perv (also **perve**) informal ▪ n. **1** a sexual pervert. **2** a lecherous look. ▪ v. gaze lecherously.
– DERIVATIVES **pervy** adj. (**-ier**, **-iest**).

pervade ▪ v. spread or be present throughout; suffuse.
– DERIVATIVES **pervasion** n.
– ORIGIN C17: from Latin *pervadere*, from *per-* 'throughout' + *vadere* 'go'.

pervasive ▪ adj. widespread.
– DERIVATIVES **pervasively** adv. **pervasiveness** n.

perverse ▪ adj. **1** showing a deliberate and obstinate desire to behave unacceptably. ▸ sexually perverted. **2** contrary to that which is accepted or expected.
– DERIVATIVES **perversely** adv. **perverseness** n. **perversity** n. (pl. **-ies**).
– ORIGIN Middle English: from Old French *pervers(e)*, from Latin *perversus*, *pervertere* (see **PERVERT**).

perversion ▪ n. the action of perverting. ▸ abnormal or unacceptable sexual behaviour.

pervert ▪ v. **1** alter from its original meaning or state to a corruption of what was first intended. **2** lead away from what is right, natural, or acceptable. ▪ n. a person with abnormal or unacceptable sexual behaviour.
– DERIVATIVES **perverter** n.
– ORIGIN Middle English: from Latin *pervertere*, from *per-* 'thoroughly, to ill effect' + *vertere* 'to turn'.

perverted ▪ adj. characterized by sexually abnormal and unacceptable tendencies.
– DERIVATIVES **pervertedly** adv.

pervious /ˈpəːvɪəs/ ▪ adj. permeable.
– DERIVATIVES **perviousness** n.
– ORIGIN C17: from Latin *pervius* 'having a passage through', from *via* 'way'.

Pesach /ˈpeɪsɑːx/ ▪ n. the Passover festival.
– ORIGIN from Hebrew *Pesaḥ*.

peseta /pəˈseɪtə/ ▪ n. the former monetary unit of Spain.
– ORIGIN Spanish, diminutive of *pesa* 'weight', from Latin *pensa* 'things weighed', from *pendere* 'weigh'.

pesky ▪ adj. (**-ier**, **-iest**) informal annoying.
– DERIVATIVES **peskily** adv. **peskiness** n.
– ORIGIN C18: perhaps rel. to **PEST**.

peso /ˈpeɪsəʊ/ ▪ n. (pl. **-os**) the basic monetary unit of several Latin American countries and of the Philippines.
– ORIGIN Spanish, 'weight', from Latin *pensum* 'something weighed', from *pendere* 'weigh'.

pessary /ˈpɛs(ə)ri/ ▪ n. (pl. **-ies**) **1** a small medicinal or contraceptive soluble block inserted into the vagina. **2** a device inserted into the vagina to support the uterus.
– ORIGIN Middle English: from late Latin *pessarium*, from Greek *pessos* 'oval stone'.

pessimism ▪ n. **1** lack of hope or confidence in the future. **2** Philosophy a belief that this world is as bad as it could be or that evil will ultimately prevail over good.
– DERIVATIVES **pessimist** n. **pessimistic** adj. **pessimistically** adv.
– ORIGIN C18: from Latin *pessimus* 'worst', on the pattern of *optimism*.

pest ▪ n. **1** a destructive insect or other animal that attacks crops, food, or livestock. **2** informal an annoying person or thing. **3** (**the pest**) archaic bubonic plague.
– ORIGIN C15: from French *peste* or Latin *pestis* 'plague'.

pester ▪ v. trouble or annoy with persistent requests or interruptions.
– ORIGIN C16: from French *empestrer* 'encumber', influenced by **PEST**.

pest-house ▪ n. historical a hospital for those with infectious diseases, especially the plague.

pesticide ▪ n. a substance for destroying insects or other pests of plants or animals.
– DERIVATIVES **pesticidal** adj.

pestiferous ▪ adj. **1** poetic/literary harbouring infection and disease. **2** humorous annoying.
– ORIGIN Middle English: from Latin *pestifer* 'bringing pestilence'.

pestilence ▪ n. archaic a fatal epidemic disease, especially bubonic plague.

– ORIGIN Middle English: from Latin *pestilentia*, from *pestis* 'a plague'.

pestilent ▪ adj. **1** deadly. **2** informal, dated annoying.
– DERIVATIVES **pestilently** adv.
– ORIGIN Middle English: from Latin *pestilens* 'unhealthy, destructive', from *pestis* 'plague'.

pestilential ▪ adj. **1** of, relating to, or tending to cause infectious diseases. **2** of the nature of a pest. ▸ informal annoying.

pestle /ˈpɛs(ə)l/ ▪ n. a heavy tool with a rounded end, used for crushing and grinding substances in a mortar. ▸ a mechanical device for grinding, pounding, or stamping. ▪ v. crush or grind with a pestle.
– ORIGIN Middle English: from Old French *pestel*, from Latin *pistillum*, from *pinsere* 'to pound'.

pesto /ˈpɛstəʊ/ ▪ n. a sauce of crushed basil leaves, pine nuts, garlic, Parmesan cheese, and olive oil, typically served with pasta.
– ORIGIN Italian, from *pestare* 'pound, crush'.

PET ▪ abbrev. **1** polyethylene terephthalate. **2** positron emission tomography.

pet[1] ▪ n. **1** a domestic or tamed animal or bird kept for companionship or pleasure. **2** a person treated with special favour. **3** used as an affectionate form of address. ▪ adj. **1** of, relating to, or kept as a pet. **2** favourite or particular: *my pet hate is woodwork*. ▪ v. (**petted**, **petting**) **1** stroke or pat (an animal). **2** caress sexually.
– DERIVATIVES **petter** n.
– ORIGIN C16 (orig. Scots and northern English).

pet[2] ▪ n. a fit of sulking or ill humour.
– ORIGIN C16.

peta- /ˈpɛtə/ ▪ comb. form denoting a factor of 10^{15}: *petabytes*.
– ORIGIN from *pe(n)ta-* (see **PENTA-**), based on the supposed analogy of *tera-* and *tetra-*.

petal ▪ n. each of the segments of the corolla of a flower.
– DERIVATIVES **-petalled** adj. **petal-like** adj. **petaloid** adj.
– ORIGIN C18: from modern Latin *petalum*, from Greek *petalon* 'leaf', from *petalos* 'outspread'.

petard /pɪˈtɑːd/ ▪ n. historical a small bomb made of a metal or wooden box filled with powder. ▸ a kind of firework that explodes with a sharp report.
– PHRASES **hoist with** (or **by**) **one's own petard** having one's schemes against others backfiring on one.
– ORIGIN C16: from French *pétard*, from *péter* 'break wind'.

peter ▪ v. (usu. **peter out**) diminish or come to an end gradually.
– ORIGIN C19.

Peter Pan ▪ n. a person who retains youthful features, or who is immature.
– ORIGIN the hero of J. M. Barrie's play of the same name (1904).

Peter Principle ▪ n. the principle that members of a hierarchy are promoted until they reach the level at which they are no longer competent.
– ORIGIN 1960s: named after the American educationalist Laurence J. *Peter*.

petersham ▪ n. a corded tape used in dressmaking and millinery for stiffening.
– ORIGIN C19: named after the English army officer Lord *Petersham*.

Peter's pence ▪ pl. n. **1** historical an annual tax of one penny from householders with land of a certain value, paid to the papal see. **2** (since 1860) a voluntary payment by Roman Catholics to the papal treasury.
– ORIGIN named after St *Peter*, the first Pope.

Peters projection ▪ n. a world map projection in which areas are shown in correct proportion at the expense of distorted shape.
– ORIGIN named after the German historian Arno *Peters*.

pethidine /ˈpɛθɪdiːn/ ▪ n. Medicine a synthetic compound used as a painkiller, especially for women in labour.
– ORIGIN 1940s: from *p(iper)idine* (from which the drug is derived), with the insertion of *eth(yl)*.

pétillant /ˈpɛtɪjɒ̃/ ▪ adj. (of wine) slightly sparkling.
– ORIGIN from French.

petiole /ˈpɛtɪəʊl/ ▪ n. **1** Botany the stalk that joins a leaf to a stem. **2** Zoology a slender stalk between two structures,

e.g. the abdomen and thorax of an insect.
- DERIVATIVES **petiolar** adj. **petiolate** /-lət/ adj.
- ORIGIN C18: from French *pétiole*, from Latin *petiolus* 'little foot, stalk'.

petit bourgeois ■ adj. of or characteristic of the lower middle class, especially in being conventional and conservative. ■ n. (pl. **petits bourgeois** pronunc. same) a petit bourgeois person.
- ORIGIN French, 'little citizen'.

petite ■ adj. (of a woman) attractively small and dainty.
- ORIGIN C18: French, feminine of *petit* 'small'.

petite bourgeoisie (also **petit bourgeoisie**) ■ n. [treated as sing. or pl.] the lower middle class.
- ORIGIN French, 'little townsfolk'.

petit four /ˌpəti ˈfɔː, ˌpɛti/ ■ n. (pl. **petits fours** /ˈfɔːz/) a very small fancy cake, biscuit, or sweet.
- ORIGIN French, 'little oven'.

petitgrain /ˈpɛtɪɡreɪn/ ■ n. an essential oil with a floral scent, distilled from parts of the orange tree and other citrus plants and used in perfumery.
- ORIGIN from French *petit grain* 'little grain' (from the small green fruits orig. used).

petition ■ n. 1 a formal written request, typically signed by many people, appealing to authority in respect of a cause. ▸ an appeal or request. 2 Law an application to a court for a writ, judicial action in a suit, etc. ■ v. make or present a petition to.
- DERIVATIVES **petitionary** adj. **petitioner** n.
- ORIGIN Middle English: from Latin *petitio(n-)*, from *petere* 'aim at, seek, lay claim to'.

petitio principii /pɪˌtɪʃɪəʊ prɪnˈsɪpɪʌɪ, prɪŋˈkɪp-/ ■ n. Logic a fallacy in which a conclusion is taken for granted in the premises.
- ORIGIN Latin, 'laying claim to a principle'.

petit mal /mal/ ■ n. a mild form of epilepsy characterized by brief spells of unconsciousness without loss of posture. Compare with **GRAND MAL**.
- ORIGIN C19: from French, 'little sickness'.

petit point /pɔɪnt, pwã/ ■ n. embroidery on canvas, using small, diagonal, adjacent stitches.
- ORIGIN C19: from French, 'little stitch'.

petits pois /ˌpəti ˈpwɑː/ ■ pl. n. small, fine peas.
- ORIGIN French, 'small peas'.

pet name ■ n. a name used to express fondness or familiarity.

Petrarchan /pɪˈtrɑːk(ə)n/ ■ adj. denoting a sonnet of the kind used by the Italian poet Petrarch (1304–74), with an octave rhyming *abbaabba*, and a sestet typically rhyming *cdcdcd* or *cdecde*.

petrel /ˈpɛtr(ə)l/ ■ n. a seabird related to the shearwaters, typically flying far from land. [Many species, chiefly in the family Procellariidae.]
- ORIGIN C17: associated with St Peter, from the bird's habit of flying low with legs dangling, and so appearing to walk on the water (see Matthew 14:30).

Petri dish /ˈpetri, ˈpiːtri/ ■ n. a shallow, circular, transparent dish with a flat lid, used for the culture of micro-organisms.
- ORIGIN C19: named after the German bacteriologist Julius R. *Petri*.

petrify ■ v. (**-ies, -ied**) 1 [often as adj. **petrified**] paralyse with fear. 2 change (organic matter) into stone by encrusting or replacing its original substance with a mineral deposit. 3 deprive or become deprived of vitality.
- DERIVATIVES **petrifaction** n. **petrification** n.
- ORIGIN Middle English: from French *pétrifier*, from Latin *petra* 'rock', from Greek.

petro- /ˈpɛtrəʊ/ ■ comb. form 1 of rock; relating to rocks: *petrography*. 2 relating to petroleum: *petrodollar*.
- ORIGIN sense 1 from Greek *petros* 'stone', *petra* 'rock'; sense 2 from **PETROLEUM**.

petrochemical ■ adj. 1 of or relating to the chemical properties and processing of petroleum and natural gas. 2 of or relating to the chemistry of rocks. ■ n. a chemical obtained from petroleum and natural gas.
- DERIVATIVES **petrochemistry** n.

petrodollar ■ n. a notional unit of currency earned from the export of petroleum.

petroglyph /ˈpɛtrə(ʊ)ɡlɪf/ ■ n. a rock carving.
- ORIGIN C19: from **PETRO-** + Greek *glyphē* 'carving'.

petrography /pɛˈtrɒɡrəfi/ ■ n. the study of the composition and properties of rocks.
- DERIVATIVES **petrographer** n. **petrographic** adj. **petrographical** adj.

petrol ■ n. refined petroleum used as fuel in motor vehicles.
- ORIGIN C19: from French *pétrole*, from medieval Latin *petroleum* (see **PETROLEUM**).

petrolatum /ˌpɛtrəˈleɪtəm/ ■ n. another term for **PETROLEUM JELLY**.
- ORIGIN C19: from **PETROL** + Latin suffix *-atum*.

petrol bomb ■ n. a crude bomb consisting of a bottle containing petrol and a cloth wick.

petroleum ■ n. a hydrocarbon oil found in suitable rock strata and extracted and refined to produce fuels including petrol, paraffin, and diesel oil; oil.
- ORIGIN Middle English: from Latin *petra* 'rock' + Latin *oleum* 'oil'.

petroleum ether ■ n. a volatile liquid distilled from petroleum.

petroleum jelly ■ n. a translucent solid mixture of hydrocarbons, used as a lubricant or ointment.

petrology /pɪˈtrɒlədʒi/ ■ n. the study of the origin, structure, and composition of rocks.
- DERIVATIVES **petrologic** adj. **petrological** adj. **petrologist** n.

petrol station ■ n. an establishment selling petrol for motor vehicles.

petticoat ■ n. 1 a woman's light, loose undergarment in the form of a skirt or dress. 2 [as modifier] informal, often derogatory associated with women: *petticoat government*.
- DERIVATIVES **petticoated** adj.
- ORIGIN Middle English: from *petty coat* 'small coat'.

pettifogging ■ adj. petty; trivial.

pettish ■ adj. petulant.
- DERIVATIVES **pettishly** adv. **pettishness** n.

petty ■ adj. (**-ier, -iest**) 1 trivial. 2 mean; small-minded. 3 minor. ▸ Law (of a crime) of lesser importance. Compare with **GRAND** (in sense 2).
- DERIVATIVES **pettily** adv. **pettiness** n.
- ORIGIN Middle English: from a phonetic spelling of the pronunciation of French *petit* 'small'.

petty apartheid ■ n. the principles and policies which dealt with the day-to-day aspects of the apartheid system in South Africa, such as the pass laws, the ban on interracial marriage, and the relegation of black people to separate public facilities, transport, etc.

petty bourgeois ■ n. variant of **PETIT BOURGEOIS**.

petty bourgeoisie ■ n. variant of **PETITE BOURGEOISIE**.

petty cash ■ n. an accessible store of money for expenditure on small items.

petty officer ■ n. a rank of non-commissioned officer in the navy, above leading seaman and below chief petty officer.

petty treason ■ n. see **TREASON**.

petulant /ˈpɛtjʊl(ə)nt/ ■ adj. childishly sulky or bad-tempered.
- DERIVATIVES **petulance** n. **petulantly** adv.
- ORIGIN C16: from French *pétulant*, from Latin *petulant-* 'impudent'.

petunia ■ n. a South American plant of the nightshade family, with white, purple, or red funnel-shaped flowers. [*Petunia × hybrida*.]
- ORIGIN from French *petun*, from Guarani *petý* 'tobacco' (to which these plants are related).

pew ■ n. a long bench with a back, placed in rows in churches for the congregation. ▸ an enclosed seating compartment in some churches for particular worshippers. ▸ Brit. informal a seat.
- ORIGIN Middle English: from Old French *puye* 'balcony', from Latin *podia*, pl. of *podium* 'elevated place'.

pewit ■ n. variant spelling of **PEEWIT**.

pewter ■ n. a grey alloy of tin with copper and antimony (formerly, tin and lead). ▸ utensils made of this.
– DERIVATIVES **pewterer** n.
– ORIGIN Middle English: from Old French *peutre*.

peyote /per'əʊti/ ■ n. **1** a small, soft, blue-green spineless cactus, native to Mexico and the southern US. [*Lophophora williamsii*.] **2** a hallucinogenic drug prepared from this, containing mescaline.
– ORIGIN C19: from Latin American Spanish, from Nahuatl *peyotl*.

Pf. ■ abbrev. pfennig.

pfennig /'(p)fɛnɪg/ ■ n. a former monetary unit of Germany, equal to one hundredth of a mark.
– ORIGIN from German *Pfennig*; rel. to PENNY.

PG ■ abbrev. **1** (in film classification) parental guidance, indicating that some scenes may be considered unsuitable for children. **2** paying guest.

PGA ■ abbrev. Professional Golfers' Association (of America).

PGCE ■ abbrev. Postgraduate Certificate in Education.

PGE ■ abbrev. platinum-group element.

pH ■ n. Chemistry a figure expressing acidity or alkalinity on a logarithmic scale on which 7 is neutral, lower values are more acid and higher values more alkaline.
– ORIGIN C20: from *p* representing German *Potenz* 'power' + *H*, the symbol for hydrogen (the pH being derived from the reciprocal of the hydrogen-ion concentration).

phaeton /'feɪt(ə)n/ ■ n. **1** historical a light, open four-wheeled horse-drawn carriage. **2** US a vintage touring car.
– ORIGIN C18: from French *phaéton*, from *Phaethōn*, son of the sun god Helios in Greek mythology, who was allowed to drive the solar chariot for a day with fatal results.

phage /feɪdʒ, fɑː'ʒ/ ■ n. short for BACTERIOPHAGE.

phagocyte /'fagə(ʊ)saɪt/ ■ n. Physiology a type of body cell which engulfs and absorbs bacteria and other small particles.
– DERIVATIVES **phagocytic** adj.
– ORIGIN C19: from Greek *phago-* 'eating', from *phagein*.

phagocytosis /ˌfagə(ʊ)saɪ'təʊsɪs/ ■ n. Biology the ingestion of bacteria or other particles by phagocytes and amoeboid protozoans.
– DERIVATIVES **phagocytize** (also **-ise**) v. **phagocytose** adj.

-phagous ■ comb. form feeding or subsisting on a specified food: *coprophagous*.
– ORIGIN from Latin *-phagus*, Greek *-phagos*, from *phagein* 'eat'.

-phagy ■ comb. form denoting the practice of eating a specified food: *anthropophagy*.
– ORIGIN from Greek *-phagia*, from *phagein* 'eat'.

phalange /'falan(d)ʒ/ ■ n. Anatomy another term for PHALANX (in sense 3).

phalangeal ■ adj. Anatomy of or relating to a phalanx or the phalanges.

phalanx /'falaŋks/ ■ n. **1** (pl. **phalanxes**) a group of similar people or things. **2** a body of troops or police officers in close formation. ▸ (in ancient Greece) a body of Macedonian infantry with shields touching and spears overlapping. **3** (pl. **phalanges** /fə'lan(d)ʒiːz/) Anatomy a bone of the finger or toe.
– ORIGIN C16: from Greek.

phalarope /'falərəʊp/ ■ n. a small wading or swimming bird with a straight bill and lobed feet. [Genus *Phalaropus*: three species.]
– ORIGIN C18: from Greek *phalaris* 'coot' + *pous*, *pod-* 'foot'.

phallic ■ adj. **1** of, relating to, or resembling a phallus or erect penis. **2** Psychoanalysis of or denoting the genital phase of psychosexual development, especially in males.
– DERIVATIVES **phallically** adv.

phallocentric /ˌfalə(ʊ)'sɛntrɪk/ ■ adj. focused on the phallus as a symbol of male dominance.
– DERIVATIVES **phallocentricity** n. **phallocentrism** n.

phallus /'faləs/ ■ n. (pl. **phalli** /-lʌɪ, -liː/ or **␣phalluses**) a penis, especially when erect. ▸ a representation of this, symbolizing fertility or potency.
– DERIVATIVES **phallicism** n.
– ORIGIN C17: from Greek *phallos*.

Phanerozoic /ˌfan(ə)rə(ʊ)'zəʊɪk/ ■ adj. Geology relating to or denoting the aeon covering the whole of time since the beginning of the Cambrian period about 570 million years ago (comprising the Palaeozoic, Mesozoic, and Cenozoic eras).
– ORIGIN C19: from Greek *phaneros* 'visible, evident' + *zōion* 'animal'.

phantasm /'fantaz(ə)m/ ■ n. poetic/literary an illusion or apparition.
– DERIVATIVES **phantasmal** adj. **phantasmic** adj.
– ORIGIN Middle English: from Old French *fantasme*, from Greek *phantasma*, from *phantazein* 'make visible', from *phainein* 'to show'.

phantasmagoria /ˌfantazmə'ɡɒrɪə, -'ɡɔːrɪə/ ■ n. a sequence of real or imaginary images like that seen in a dream.
– DERIVATIVES **phantasmagoric** adj. **phantasmagorical** adj.
– ORIGIN C19: prob. from French *fantasmagorie*, from *fantasme* 'phantasm'.

phantasy ■ n. chiefly archaic variant spelling of FANTASY.

phantom ■ n. a ghost. ▸ a figment of the imagination. ▸ [as modifier] denoting a person or thing that does not really exist: *phantom withdrawals from ATMs*.
– ORIGIN Middle English: from Old French *fantosme*, from Greek *phantasma* (see PHANTASM).

phantom limb ■ n. a sensation experienced by an amputee that the limb is still there.

phantom pregnancy ■ n. Medicine a condition in which signs of pregnancy are present in a woman who is not pregnant.

pharaoh /'fɛːrəʊ/ ■ n. a ruler in ancient Egypt.
– DERIVATIVES **pharaonic** /ˌfɛː'reɪ'ɒnɪk/ adj.
– ORIGIN Middle English: from Greek *Pharaō*, from Hebrew *par'ōh*, from Egyptian *pr-'o* 'great house'.

pharaoh ant ■ n. a small yellowish ant, native to Africa and a pest of heated buildings worldwide. [*Monomorium pharaonis*.]

Pharisee /'farɪsiː/ ■ n. **1** a member of an ancient Jewish sect, distinguished by strict observance of the traditional and written law, and commonly held to have pretensions to superior sanctity. **2** a self-righteous person.
– DERIVATIVES **Pharisaic** /ˌfarɪ'seɪk/ adj. **Pharisaical** adj. **Pharisaism** /'farɪseɪɪz(ə)m/ n.
– ORIGIN Old English *fariseus*, from Greek *Pharisaios*, from Aramaic *prīšayyā* 'separated ones'.

pharma ■ n. **1** (often in phr. **big pharma**) pharmaceutical companies collectively as a sector of industry. **2** a pharmaceutical company.

pharmaceutical /ˌfɑːmə'sjuːtɪk(ə)l/ ■ adj. of or relating to medicinal drugs, or their preparation, use, or sale. ■ n. a compound manufactured for use as a medicinal drug.
– DERIVATIVES **pharmaceutically** adv. **pharmaceutics** pl. n.
– ORIGIN C17: from Greek *pharmakeutikos*, from *pharmakeutēs* 'druggist', from *pharmakon* 'drug'.

pharmacist ■ n. a person qualified to prepare and dispense medicinal drugs.

pharmacology ■ n. the branch of medicine concerned with the uses, effects, and action of drugs.
– DERIVATIVES **pharmacologic** adj. **pharmacological** adj. **pharmacologically** adv. **pharmacologist** n.
– ORIGIN C18: from modern Latin *pharmacologia*, from Greek *pharmakon* 'drug'.

pharmacopoeia /ˌfɑːməkə'piːə/ (US also **pharmacopeia**) ■ n. **1** a book containing a list of medicinal drugs with their effects and directions for use. **2** a stock of medicinal drugs.
– ORIGIN C17: from Greek *pharmakopoiia* 'art of preparing drugs'.

pharmacy ■ n. (pl. **-ies**) **1** a shop where medicinal drugs are prepared or sold and in which toiletries and other medical goods can be purchased. **2** the science or practice of preparing and dispensing medicinal drugs.
– ORIGIN Middle English: from Old French *farmacie*, from Greek *pharmakeia* 'practice of the druggist', from *pharmakon* 'drug'.

pharyngeal /fəˈrɪn(d)ʒɪəl, ˌfarɪnˈdʒiːəl/ ■ adj. of or relating to the pharynx. ▶ Phonetics (of a speech sound) produced by articulating the root of the tongue with the pharynx.
– ORIGIN C19: from Greek *pharunx, pharung-* 'throat'.

pharyngitis /ˌfarɪŋˈdʒʌɪtɪs/ ■ n. Medicine inflammation of the pharynx.

pharyngo- /fəˈrɪŋɡəʊ/ ■ comb. form of or relating to the pharynx: *pharyngotomy*.
– ORIGIN from Greek *pharunx, pharung-* 'throat'.

pharyngotomy /ˌfarɪŋˈɡɒtəmi/ ■ n. (pl. **-ies**) a surgical incision into the pharynx.

pharynx /ˈfarɪŋks/ ■ n. (pl. **pharynges** /-ˈrɪn(d)ʒiːz/) Anatomy & Zoology the membrane-lined cavity behind the nose and mouth, connecting them to the oesophagus. ▶ (in invertebrates) the part of the alimentary canal immediately behind the mouth.
– ORIGIN C17: from Greek *pharunx, pharung-*.

phase /feɪz/ ■ n. **1** a distinct period or stage in a process of change or development. ▶ each of the aspects of the moon or a planet, according to the amount of its illumination. **2** Zoology a genetic or seasonal variety of an animal's coloration. **3** Chemistry a distinct and homogeneous form of matter separated by its surface from other forms. **4** Physics the relationship in time between the cycles of an oscillating or repeating system and a fixed reference point or a different system. ■ v. (usu. **be phased**) **1** carry out in gradual stages. ▶ (**phase something in/out**) introduce something into (or withdraw something from) use in gradual stages. **2** Physics adjust the phase of (something), especially so as to synchronize it with something else.
– PHRASES **in** (or **out of**) **phase** in (or out of) synchrony or harmony.
– ORIGIN C19: from French *phase*, from Greek *phasis* 'appearance'.

phase angle ■ n. **1** Physics a phase difference expressed as an angle, 360 degrees corresponding to one complete cycle. **2** Astronomy the angle between the lines joining a given planet to the sun and to the earth.

phase-lock ■ v. Electronics fix the frequency of (an oscillator or a laser) relative to a stable lower frequency.

phase shift ■ n. Physics a change in the phase of a waveform.

phase space ■ n. Physics a multidimensional space in which the axes correspond to the coordinates required to specify any state of a system.

phase velocity ■ n. Physics the speed at which a sine wave is propagated, equal to the product of its wavelength and frequency.

phasic /ˈfeɪzɪk/ ■ adj. of or relating to a phase or phases. ▶ chiefly Physiology occurring in phases.

phasing ■ n. **1** division into phases, or the relationship between phases. **2** the modification of a sound signal from an electric guitar or other electronic instrument by combining it with a phase-shifted copy.

phat /fat/ ■ adj. informal excellent.
– ORIGIN 1970s (orig. used to describe a woman, in the sense 'sexy, attractive').

phatic /ˈfatɪk/ ■ adj. (of language) used for general social interaction rather than to convey specific meaning, e.g. *nice morning, isn't it?*
– ORIGIN 1920s: from Greek *phatos* 'spoken' or *phatikos* 'affirming'.

PhD ■ abbrev. Doctor of Philosophy.
– ORIGIN from Latin *philosophiae doctor*.

pheasant ■ n. a large long-tailed game bird native to Asia, the male of which typically has showy plumage. [*Phasianus colchicus* and other species.]
– ORIGIN Middle English: from Old French *fesan*, from Greek *phasianos* '(bird) of *Phasis*', the name of a river in the Caucasus.

pheasantry ■ n. (pl. **-ies**) a place where pheasants are reared or kept.

pheasant's eye ■ n. a plant of the buttercup family which has scarlet flowers with dark centres. [*Adonis autumnalis*.]

phen- ■ comb. form variant spelling of PHENO- shortened before a vowel (as in *phencyclidine*).

phenylketonuria

phencyclidine /fɛnˈsʌɪklɪdiːn/ ■ n. a synthetic compound used as a veterinary anaesthetic and in hallucinogenic drugs such as angel dust.
– ORIGIN 1950s: from PHENO- + CYCLO- + (*piper*)*idine*.

pheno- (also **phen-** before a vowel) ■ comb. form **1** Chemistry derived from benzene: *phenobarbitone*. **2** showing: *phenotype*.
– ORIGIN sense 1 from French *phényle* 'phenyl', from Greek *phaino-* 'shining', from *phainein* 'to show'.

phenobarbital /ˌfiːnə(ʊ)ˈbɑːbɪt(ə)l, ˌfɛn-/ ■ n. another term for PHENOBARBITONE.

phenobarbitone /ˌfiːnə(ʊ)ˈbɑːbɪtəʊn, ˌfɛn-/ ■ n. Medicine a narcotic and sedative barbiturate drug used chiefly to treat epilepsy.

phenocryst /ˈfiːnə(ʊ)krɪst, ˈfɛn-/ ■ n. Geology a large or conspicuous crystal in a porphyritic rock.
– ORIGIN C19: from French *phénocryste*, from Greek *phainein* 'to show' + *krustallos* 'crystal'.

phenol /ˈfiːnɒl/ ■ n. Chemistry a mildly acidic toxic white crystalline solid obtained from coal tar and used in chemical manufacture. See also CARBOLIC ACID. ▶ any compound with a hydroxyl group linked directly to a benzene ring.
– DERIVATIVES **phenolic** adj.
– ORIGIN C19: from French *phénole*, from *phène* 'benzene'.

phenology /fɪˈnɒlədʒi/ ■ n. the study of cyclic and seasonal natural phenomena, especially in relation to climate and plant and animal life.
– DERIVATIVES **phenological** adj.
– ORIGIN C19: from PHENOMENON + -LOGY.

phenomena plural form of PHENOMENON.

phenomenal ■ adj. **1** extraordinary. **2** perceptible by the senses or through immediate experience.
– DERIVATIVES **phenomenalize** (also **-ise**) v. **phenomenally** adv.

phenomenalism ■ n. Philosophy the doctrine that human knowledge is confined to the appearances presented to the senses.
– DERIVATIVES **phenomenalist** n. & adj. **phenomenalistic** adj.

phenomenology /fɪˌnɒmɪˈnɒlədʒi/ ■ n. Philosophy **1** the science of phenomena as distinct from that of the nature of being. **2** an approach that concentrates on the study of consciousness and the objects of direct experience.
– DERIVATIVES **phenomenological** adj. **phenomenologically** adv. **phenomenologist** n.

phenomenon ■ n. (pl. **phenomena**) **1** a fact or situation that is observed to exist or happen, especially one whose cause is in question. **2** Philosophy the object of a person's perception. **3** a remarkable person or thing.
– ORIGIN C16: from Greek *phainomenon* 'thing appearing to view', from *phainein* 'to show'.

USAGE
The word **phenomenon** comes from Greek, and its plural form is **phenomena**. In standard English it is a mistake to treat **phenomena** as if it were a singular form.

phenotype /ˈfiːnə(ʊ)tʌɪp/ ■ n. Biology the observable characteristics of an individual resulting from the interaction of its genotype with the environment.
– DERIVATIVES **phenotypic** adj. **phenotypical** adj. **phenotypically** adv.
– ORIGIN C20: from German *Phaenotypus* (see PHENO-, TYPE).

phenyl /ˈfiːnʌɪl, ˈfɛnɪl/ ■ n. [as modifier] Chemistry of or denoting the radical -C₆H₅, derived from benzene.
– ORIGIN C19: from French *phényle*, from Greek *phaino-* 'shining' (because first used in names of by-products of the manufacture of gas for illumination).

phenylalanine /ˌfiːnʌɪlˈaləniːn, ˌfɛnɪl-/ ■ n. Biochemistry an amino acid widely distributed in plant proteins, an essential nutrient in the diet of vertebrates.

phenylketonuria /ˌfiːnʌɪlˌkiːtə(ʊ)ˈnjʊərɪə, ˌfɛnɪl-/ ■ n. Medicine an inherited inability to metabolize phenylalanine which can result in brain and nerve damage.

phenytoin /ˈfɛnɪtɔɪn/ ■ n. Medicine a synthetic compound used as an anticonvulsant in the treatment of epilepsy.
– ORIGIN 1940s: blend of PHENYL and *hydantoin* a compound found in sugar beet.

pheromone /ˈfɛrəməʊn/ ■ n. Zoology a chemical substance produced and released by an animal, affecting the behaviour or physiology of others of its species.
– DERIVATIVES **pheromonal** adj.
– ORIGIN 1950s: from Greek *pherein* 'convey' + HORMONE.

phew ■ exclam. informal expressing relief.
– ORIGIN C17: imitative of puffing.

phi /fʌɪ/ ■ n. the twenty-first letter of the Greek alphabet (Φ, φ), transliterated as 'ph' or (in modern Greek) 'f'. ■ symb. 1 (φ) a plane angle. 2 (φ) a polar coordinate. Often coupled with θ.
– ORIGIN from Greek.

phial /ˈfʌɪəl/ ■ n. a small cylindrical glass bottle, typically for medical samples or medicines.
– ORIGIN Middle English: from Old French *fiole*, from Greek *phialē*, denoting a broad flat container.

Phi Beta Kappa /ˌfʌɪ ˌbiːtə ˈkapə/ ■ n. (in the US) an honorary society of undergraduates and some graduates, to which members are elected on the basis of high academic achievement. ▸ a member of this society.
– ORIGIN from the initial letters of a Greek motto *philosophia biou kubernētēs* 'philosophy is the guide to life'.

-phil ■ comb. form having a chemical affinity for a substance: *neutrophil*.
– ORIGIN see -PHILE.

phil- ■ comb. form variant spelling of PHILO- shortened before a vowel or *h* (as in *philanthrope*).

philander /fɪˈlandə/ ■ v. (of a man) readily or frequently enter into casual sexual relationships with women.
– DERIVATIVES **philanderer** n.
– ORIGIN C18: from earlier n. *philander* 'man, husband', from Greek *philandros* 'fond of men'.

philanthrope /ˈfɪlənˌθrəʊp/ ■ n. archaic a philanthropist.
– ORIGIN C18: from Greek *philanthrōpos*, from *philein* 'to love' + *anthrōpos* 'human being'.

philanthropist ■ n. a person who seeks to promote the welfare of others, especially by donating money to good causes.
– DERIVATIVES **philanthropic** adj. **philanthropically** adv.

philanthropy /fɪˈlanθrəpi/ ■ n. the desire to promote the welfare of others, especially through the donation of money to good causes.
– DERIVATIVES **philanthropism** n. **philanthropize** (also **-ise**) v.

philately /fɪˈlat(ə)li/ ■ n. the collection and study of postage stamps.
– DERIVATIVES **philatelic** adj. **philatelically** adv. **philatelist** n.
– ORIGIN C19: from French *philatélie*, from *philo-* 'loving' + Greek *ateleia* 'exemption from payment', used to mean a franking mark or postage stamp exempting the recipient from payment.

-phile ■ comb. form denoting a person or thing having a fondness for or tendency towards a specified thing: *bibliophile*.
– ORIGIN from Greek *philos* 'loving'.

philharmonic ■ adj. devoted to music (chiefly used in the names of orchestras).

-philia ■ comb. form denoting fondness, especially an abnormal love for or inclination towards a specified thing: *paedophilia*.
– DERIVATIVES **-philiac** comb. form in corresponding nouns and adjectives. **-philic** comb. form in corresponding adjectives. **-philous** comb. form in corresponding adjectives.
– ORIGIN from Greek *philia* 'fondness'.

philippic /fɪˈlɪpɪk/ ■ n. poetic/literary a bitter verbal attack or denunciation.
– ORIGIN C16: from Greek *philippikos*, the name given to Demosthenes' speeches against Philip II of Macedon, and Cicero's against Mark Antony.

Philippine /ˈfɪlɪpiːn/ ■ adj. of or relating to the Philippines.

Philistine /ˈfɪlɪstʌɪn/ ■ n. 1 a member of a non-Semitic people of ancient Palestine who came into conflict with the Israelites. 2 (**philistine**) a person who is hostile or indifferent to culture and the arts.
– DERIVATIVES **philistinism** /-stɪnɪz(ə)m/ n.

> **HISTORY**
> The connection between uncultured philistines and the Philistines of biblical times, may not seem obvious. The sense 'person hostile or indifferent to culture' arose in the 19th century as a result of a confrontation between townspeople and members of the university of Jena, Germany, in the late 17th century. A sermon on the conflict quoted the phrase 'the Philistines are upon you' (Book of Judges, chapter 16), which led to an association between the townspeople and those hostile to culture.

Phillips ■ adj. trademark denoting a screw with a cross-shaped slot for turning, or a corresponding screwdriver.
– ORIGIN 1930s: from the name of the American manufacturer Henry F. *Phillips*.

Phillips curve ■ n. Economics a supposed inverse relationship between the level of unemployment and the rate of inflation.
– ORIGIN 1960s: named after the NZ economist Alban W. H. *Phillips*.

philo- (also **phil-** before a vowel or *h*) ■ comb. form denoting a liking for a specified thing: *philopatric*.
– ORIGIN from Greek *philein* 'to love' or *philos* 'loving'.

philodendron /ˌfɪləˈdɛndrən/ ■ n. (pl. **philodendrons** or **philodendra** /-drə/) a tropical American climbing plant grown as a greenhouse or indoor plant. [Genus *Philodendron*.]
– ORIGIN C19: from PHILO- + Greek *dendron* 'tree'.

philology ■ n. 1 the study of the structure, historical development, and relationships of a language or languages. 2 chiefly N. Amer. literary or classical scholarship.
– DERIVATIVES **philologian** n. **philological** adj. **philologically** adv. **philologist** n.
– ORIGIN Middle English: from French *philologie*, from Greek *philologia* (see PHILO-, -LOGY).

philosopher ■ n. a person engaged or learned in philosophy.

philosopher's stone ■ n. a mythical substance supposed to change any metal into gold or silver, the discovery of which was the supreme object of alchemy.

philosophical ■ adj. 1 of, relating to, or devoted to the study of philosophy. 2 calm in adverse circumstances.
– DERIVATIVES **philosophic** adj. **philosophically** adv.

philosophize (also **-ise**) ■ v. theorize about fundamental or serious issues, especially tediously. ▸ explain or argue in terms of one's philosophical theories.
– DERIVATIVES **philosophizer** (also **-iser**) n.

philosophy ■ n. (pl. **-ies**) 1 the study of the fundamental nature of knowledge, reality, and existence. ▸ a set of theories of a particular philosopher. 2 the study of the theoretical basis of a branch of knowledge or experience. 3 a theory or attitude that guides one's behaviour.
– ORIGIN Middle English: from Old French *philosophie*, from Greek *philosophia* 'love of wisdom'.

philtre /ˈfɪltə/ (US **philter**) ■ n. a love potion.
– ORIGIN C16: from French *philtre*, from Greek *philtron*, from *philein* 'to love'.

-phily ■ comb. form equivalent to -PHILIA.

phlebitis /flɪˈbʌɪtɪs/ ■ n. Medicine inflammation of the walls of a vein.
– DERIVATIVES **phlebitic** adj.
– ORIGIN C19: from Greek, from *phleps*, *phleb-* 'vein'.

phlebotomy /flɪˈbɒtəmi/ ■ n. (pl. **-ies**) the surgical opening or puncture of a vein to withdraw blood or introduce a fluid.
– DERIVATIVES **phlebotomist** n.
– ORIGIN Middle English: from late Latin *phlebotomia* from Greek, from *phleps*, *phleb-* 'vein' + *-tomia* 'cutting'.

phlegm /flɛm/ ■ n. 1 the thick viscous substance secreted by the mucous membranes of the respiratory passages, especially when produced in excessive quantities during a

cold. **2** (in medieval science and medicine) one of the four bodily humours, believed to be associated with a calm or apathetic temperament. ▸ calmness of temperament.
– DERIVATIVES **phlegmy** adj.
– ORIGIN Middle English, from Old French *fleume*, from late Latin *phlegma* 'clammy moisture (of the body)', from Greek *phlegma* 'inflammation', from *phlegein* 'to burn'.

phlegmatic /flɛgˈmatɪk/ ■ adj. unemotional and stolidly calm.
– DERIVATIVES **phlegmatically** adv.

phloem /ˈfləʊɛm/ ■ n. the vascular tissue in plants which conducts sugars and other metabolic products downwards from the leaves.
– ORIGIN C19: from Greek *phloos* 'bark' + suffix *-ēma*.

phlox /flɒks/ ■ n. a North American plant with dense clusters of colourful scented flowers, grown as an alpine or border plant. [Genus *Phlox*.]
– ORIGIN from Latin, denoting a flame-coloured flower, from Greek, 'flame'.

-phobe ■ comb. form denoting a person having a fear or dislike of a specified thing: *homophobe*.
– ORIGIN from French, from Greek *-phobos* 'fearing', from *phobos* 'fear'.

phobia /ˈfəʊbɪə/ ■ n. an extreme or irrational fear of something.
– DERIVATIVES **phobic** adj. & n.

-phobia ■ comb. form extreme or irrational fear or dislike of a specified thing: *arachnophobia*.
– DERIVATIVES **-phobic** comb. form in corresponding adjectives.
– ORIGIN from Greek.

Phoenician /fəˈnɪʃ(ə)n, -ˈniː-/ ■ n. **1** a member of an ancient Semitic people inhabiting Phoenicia in the eastern Mediterranean. **2** the Semitic language of this people. ■ adj. of or relating to Phoenicia, its people, or its language.

phoenix /ˈfiːnɪks/ ■ n. **1** (in classical mythology) a unique bird of the Arabian desert that burned itself on a funeral pyre every five or six centuries and rose from the ashes with renewed youth. **2** a uniquely remarkable person or thing.
– ORIGIN from Old French *fenix*, from Greek *phoinix* 'Phoenician, reddish purple, or phoenix'.

phon /fɒn/ ■ n. a unit of the perceived loudness of sounds.
– ORIGIN 1930s: from Greek *phōnē* 'sound'.

phonaesthesia /ˌfəʊnəsˈθiːzɪə/ (US also **phonesthesia**) ■ n. attribution of common elements of meaning to certain sound sequences, e.g. initial *sl-*, as in *slow*, *sleep*, *slide*.
– DERIVATIVES **phonaesthetic** adj. **phonaesthetics** pl. n.
– ORIGIN C20: from Greek *phōnē* 'sound' + *aesthesthai* 'perceive'.

phonation /fəˈ(ʊ)neɪʃ(ə)n/ ■ n. Phonetics the production of speech sounds.
– DERIVATIVES **phonate** /fə(ʊ)ˈneɪt/ v. **phonatory** /ˈfəʊnət(ə)ri/ adj.
– ORIGIN C19: from Greek *phōnē* 'sound, voice'.

phone[1] ■ n. **1** a telephone. **2** (**phones**) informal headphones or earphones. ■ v. telephone.

phone[2] ■ n. Phonetics a speech sound.
– ORIGIN C19: from Greek *phōnē* 'sound, voice'.

-phone ■ comb. form **1** denoting an instrument using or connected with sound: *megaphone*. **2** denoting a person who uses a specified language: *francophone*.
– DERIVATIVES **-phonic** comb. form in corresponding adjectives. **-phony** comb. form in corresponding nouns.
– ORIGIN from Greek *phōnē* 'sound, voice'.

phone book ■ n. a telephone directory.

phonecard ■ n. a prepaid card allowing the user to make calls up to a specified number of units on a public telephone.

phone-in ■ n. a radio or television programme during which listeners or viewers telephone the studio and participate.

phoneme /ˈfəʊniːm/ ■ n. Phonetics any of the distinct units of sound that distinguish one word from another, e.g. *p*, *b*, *d*, and *t* in *pad*, *pat*, *bad*, and *bat*.
– DERIVATIVES **phonemic** /-ˈniːmɪk/ adj. **phonemics** pl. n.
– ORIGIN C19: from French *phonème*, from Greek *phōnēma* 'sound, speech', from *phōnein* 'speak'.

phosphine

phonetic /fəˈnɛtɪk/ ■ adj. Phonetics of or relating to speech sounds. ▸ (of a system of writing) having a direct correspondence between symbols and sounds. ▸ of or relating to phonetics.
– DERIVATIVES **phonetically** adv. **phoneticism** n. **phoneticist** n. **phoneticize** (also **-ise**) v.
– ORIGIN C19: from Greek *phōnētikos*, from *phōnein* 'speak'.

phonetics ■ pl. n. [treated as sing.] the study and classification of speech sounds.
– DERIVATIVES **phonetician** n.

phoney (also **phony**) informal ■ adj. (**-ier**, **-iest**) not genuine. ■ n. (pl. **-eys** or **-ies**) a fraudulent person or thing.
– DERIVATIVES **phonily** adv. **phoniness** n.
– ORIGIN C19.

phonic /ˈfəʊnɪk, ˈfɒnɪk/ ■ adj. of or relating to speech sounds. ▸ of or relating to phonics.
– DERIVATIVES **phonically** adv.
– ORIGIN C19: from Greek *phōnē* 'voice'.

phonics ■ pl. n. [treated as sing.] a method of teaching people to read by correlating sounds with alphabetic symbols.

phono ■ adj. denoting a type of plug, and the corresponding socket, used with audio and video equipment, in which one conductor is cylindrical and the other is a central prong that extends beyond it.
– ORIGIN 1940s: abbrev. of **PHONOGRAPH**.

phono- /ˈfəʊnəʊ, ˈfɒn-/ ■ comb. form relating to sound: *phonograph*.
– ORIGIN from Greek *phōnē* 'sound, voice'.

phonocardiogram ■ n. Medicine a record of the sounds made by the heart.

phonograph ■ n. an early form of gramophone able to record and reproduce sound.
– DERIVATIVES **phonographic** adj.

phonolite /ˈfəʊnəlʌɪt/ ■ n. Geology a fine-grained volcanic rock composed of alkali feldspars and nepheline.
– ORIGIN C19: from **PHONO-** 'relating to sound' (because of its resonance when struck).

phonology /fəˈnɒlədʒi/ ■ n. the system of contrastive relationships among the fundamental speech sounds of a language. ▸ the study of these relationships within or between languages.
– DERIVATIVES **phonological** adj. **phonologically** adv. **phonologist** n.

phony ■ adj. & n. variant spelling of **PHONEY**.

phooey informal ■ exclam. used to express disdain or disbelief. ■ n. nonsense.
– ORIGIN 1920s: imitative.

-phore ■ comb. form denoting an agent or bearer of a specified thing: *semaphore*.
– DERIVATIVES **-phorous** comb. form in corresponding adjectives.
– ORIGIN from Greek *-phoros*, *-phoron* 'bearing, bearer', from *pherein* 'to bear'.

phoresy /fəˈriːsi, ˈfɒrəsi/ ■ n. Zoology an association in which one organism travels on the body of another, without being a parasite.
– DERIVATIVES **phoretic** /fəˈrɛtɪk/ adj.
– ORIGIN 1920s: from French *phorésie*, from Greek *phorēsis* 'being carried'.

phosgene /ˈfɒzdʒiːn/ ■ n. Chemistry a poisonous gas formerly used in warfare. [COCl$_2$.]
– ORIGIN C19: from Greek *phōs* 'light' + **-GEN**, with ref. to its original production by the action of sunlight on chlorine and carbon monoxide.

phosphate /ˈfɒsfeɪt/ ■ n. Chemistry a salt or ester of phosphoric acid, typically containing the anion PO$_4^{3-}$ or the group -OPO(OH)$_2$.
– DERIVATIVES **phosphatic** adj.
– ORIGIN C18: from French, from *phosphore* 'phosphorus'.

phosphide /ˈfɒsfʌɪd/ ■ n. Chemistry a binary compound of phosphorus with another element or group.

phosphine /ˈfɒsfiːn/ ■ n. Chemistry a foul-smelling gaseous compound of phosphorus and hydrogen. [PH$_3$.]
– ORIGIN C19: from **PHOSPHO-**.

ʊ put   uː too   ʌɪ my   aʊ how   eɪ day   əʊ no   ɪə near   ɔɪ boy   ʊə poor   ʌɪə fire   aʊə sour

phospho- ■ comb. form representing PHOSPHORUS.

phospholipid /ˌfɒsfə(ʊ)'lɪpɪd/ ■ n. Biochemistry a lipid containing a phosphate group in its molecule.

phosphor /'fɒsfə/ ■ n. **1** a synthetic fluorescent or phosphorescent substance, especially one used to coat the screen of a cathode ray tube. **2** old-fashioned term for PHOSPHORUS.
– ORIGIN C17: from Latin PHOSPHORUS.

phosphorescence ■ n. light emitted by a substance without combustion or perceptible heat. ▸ Physics the emission of radiation in a similar manner to fluorescence but continuing after excitation ceases.
– DERIVATIVES **phosphoresce** v. **phosphorescent** adj.

phosphoric /fɒs'fɒrɪk/ ■ adj. relating to or containing phosphorus. ▸ Chemistry of phosphorus with a valency of five.

phosphoric acid ■ n. Chemistry a crystalline acid obtained by treating phosphates with sulphuric acid, and used in fertilizer and soap manufacture and food processing. [H_3PO_4.]

phosphorite /'fɒsfəraɪt/ ■ n. a sedimentary rock rich in calcium phosphate.
– ORIGIN C18: from PHOSPHORUS.

phosphorous /'fɒsf(ə)rəs/ ■ adj. **1** relating to or containing phosphorus. ▸ Chemistry of phosphorus with a valency of three. **2** phosphorescent.

USAGE
The correct spelling for the noun denoting the chemical element is **phosphorus**, while the correct spelling for the adjective is **phosphorous**.

phosphorus /'fɒsf(ə)rəs/ ■ n. the chemical element of atomic number 15, a poisonous, combustible non-metal which exists as a yellowish waxy solid which ignites spontaneously in air and glows in the dark (white phosphorus), and as a less reactive form used in making matches (red phosphorus). (Symbol: P)
– ORIGIN C17: from Greek *phôsphoros*, from *phôs* 'light' + *-phoros* '-bringing'.

phot /fəʊt/ ■ n. a unit of illumination equal to one lumen per square centimetre.
– ORIGIN C20: from Greek *phôs*, *phôt-* 'light'.

photic ■ adj. **1** technical of or relating to light. **2** Ecology denoting the layers of the ocean reached by sufficient sunlight to allow plant growth.

photo ■ n. (pl. **-os**) a photograph. ■ v. (**-oes**, **-oed**) photograph.

photo- /'fəʊtəʊ/ ■ comb. form **1** relating to light: *photochemical*. **2** relating to photography: *photofit*.
– ORIGIN sense 1 from Greek *phôs*, *phôt-* 'light'.

photobiology ■ n. the study of the effects of light on living organisms.

photocall ■ n. an occasion on which famous people pose for photographers by arrangement.

photo CD ■ n. a compact disc from which still photographs can be displayed on a television screen.

photocell ■ n. short for PHOTOELECTRIC CELL.

photochemical ■ adj. of, relating to, or caused by the chemical action of light. ▸ of or relating to photochemistry.
– DERIVATIVES **photochemically** adv.

photochemistry ■ n. the branch of chemistry concerned with the chemical effects of light.

photochromic ■ adj. undergoing a reversible change in colour when exposed to light of a particular frequency or intensity.
– DERIVATIVES **photochromism** n.
– ORIGIN 1950s: from PHOTO- + Greek *khrōma* 'colour'.

photocomposition ■ n. another term for FILMSETTING.

photoconductivity /ˌfəʊtə(ʊ)kɒndʌk'tɪvɪti/ ■ n. increased electrical conductivity caused by the presence of light.
– DERIVATIVES **photoconductive** adj. **photoconductor** n.

photocopier ■ n. a machine for making photocopies.

photocopy ■ n. (pl. **-ies**) a photographic copy of something produced by a process involving the action of light on a specially prepared surface. ■ v. (**-ies**, **-ied**) make a photocopy of.
– DERIVATIVES **photocopiable** adj.

photodegradable ■ adj. capable of being decomposed by the action of light, especially sunlight.

photodiode ■ n. a semiconductor diode which, when exposed to light, generates a potential difference or changes its electrical resistance.

photodynamic ■ adj. Medicine denoting treatment for cancer involving the injection of a cytotoxic compound which is activated by a laser beam after collecting in the tumour.

photoelectric ■ adj. characterized by or involving the emission of electrons from a surface by the action of light.
– DERIVATIVES **photoelectricity** n.

photoelectric cell ■ n. a device using a photoelectric effect to generate current.

photoelectron ■ n. an electron emitted from an atom by interaction with a photon.

photoemission ■ n. the emission of electrons from a surface caused by the action of light striking it.
– DERIVATIVES **photoemitter** n.

photo finish ■ n. a close finish of a race in which the winner is identifiable only from a photograph of competitors crossing the line.

photofit ■ n. a picture of a person, especially one sought by the police, made from composite photographs of facial features.

photogenic /ˌfəʊtə(ʊ)'dʒɛnɪk, -'dʒiːn-/ ■ adj. **1** looking attractive in photographs. **2** Biology producing or emitting light.
– DERIVATIVES **photogenically** adv.

photogrammetry /ˌfəʊtə(ʊ)'gramɪtri/ ■ n. the use of photography in surveying and mapping to ascertain measurements.
– DERIVATIVES **photogrammetric** adj. **photogrammetrist** n.

photograph ■ n. a picture made with a camera, in which an image is focused on to film and then made visible and permanent by chemical treatment. ■ v. take a photograph of.
– DERIVATIVES **photographable** adj. **photographer** n. **photographic** adj. **photographically** adv.

photographic memory ■ n. an ability to remember information or visual images in great detail.

photography ■ n. the taking and processing of photographs.

photogravure /ˌfəʊtə(ʊ)grə'vjʊə/ ■ n. an image produced from a photographic negative transferred to a metal plate and etched in.
– ORIGIN C19: from French, from *photo-* 'relating to light' + *gravure* 'engraving'.

photojournalism ■ n. the communicating of news by photographs.
– DERIVATIVES **photojournalist** n.

photolysis /fə(ʊ)'tɒlɪsɪs/ ■ n. Chemistry the decomposition or separation of molecules by the action of light.
– DERIVATIVES **photolyse** v. **photolytic** adj.

photometer /fə(ʊ)'tɒmɪtə/ ■ n. an instrument measuring the intensity of light.
– DERIVATIVES **photometric** adj. **photometrically** adv. **photometry** n.

photomicrograph ■ n. another term for MICROGRAPH.
– DERIVATIVES **photomicrography** n.

photomontage /ˌfəʊtəʊmɒn'tɑːʒ/ ■ n. a montage of photographs.

photomosaic ■ n. a large-scale picture or map built up from photographs of small areas.

photomultiplier ■ n. an instrument containing a photoelectric cell and a series of electrodes, used to detect and amplify very faint light.

photon /'fəʊtɒn/ ■ n. Physics a particle representing a quantum of light or other electromagnetic radiation.
– DERIVATIVES **photonic** adj. **photonics** pl. n.
– ORIGIN C20: from Greek *phôs*, *phôt-* 'light', on the pattern of *electron*.

photonegative ■ adj. **1** Biology (of an organism) tending to move away from light. **2** Physics (of a substance) exhibiting a decrease in electrical conductivity under illumination.

photo-offset ■ n. offset printing using plates made photographically.

photo opportunity ■ n. a photocall.

photoperiod ■ n. Botany & Zoology the period of daily illumination received by an organism.
– DERIVATIVES **photoperiodic** adj.

photophobia ■ n. extreme sensitivity to light.
– DERIVATIVES **photophobic** adj.

photopigment ■ n. a pigment whose chemical state depends on its degree of illumination, e.g. those in the retina.

photopositive ■ adj. **1** Biology (of an organism) tending to move towards light. **2** Physics (of a substance) increasing in electrical conductivity under illumination.

photoproduct ■ n. a product of a photochemical reaction.

photorealism ■ n. a style of art and sculpture characterized by the highly detailed depiction of ordinary life with the impersonality of a photograph.
– DERIVATIVES **photorealist** n. & adj. **photorealistic** adj.

photoreceptor ■ n. a structure in an organism that responds to light.

photosensitive ■ adj. responding to light.
– DERIVATIVES **photosensitivity** n.

photo session ■ n. a pre-arranged session in which a photographer takes photographs of someone for publication.

photosetting (also **phototypesetting**) ■ n. another term for FILMSETTING.
– DERIVATIVES **photoset** v. **photosetter** n.

photoshop ■ v. (**photoshops, photoshopping, photoshopped**) alter (a photographic image) digitally using computer software.
– ORIGIN 1990s: from *Adobe Photoshop*, the proprietary name of such a software package.

photosphere ■ n. Astronomy the luminous envelope of a star from which its light and heat radiate.
– DERIVATIVES **photospheric** adj.

photostat /ˈfəʊtə(ʊ)stat/ ■ n. trademark a type of machine for making photocopies on special paper. ▶ a copy made by this means. ■ v. (**photostatted, photostatting**) copy with a photostat.
– DERIVATIVES **photostatic** adj.

photostory ■ n. a strip cartoon with photographs in place of drawings.

photosynthesis ■ n. the process by which green plants use sunlight to synthesize nutrients from carbon dioxide and water.
– DERIVATIVES **photosynthesize** (also **-ise**) v. **photosynthetic** adj. **photosynthetically** adv.

phototaxis /ˌfəʊtəʊˈtaksɪs/ ■ n. (pl. **phototaxes**) Biology the bodily movement of a motile organism in response to light.
– DERIVATIVES **phototactic** adj.

phototransistor ■ n. a transistor that responds to light striking it by generating and amplifying an electric current.

phototropism /ˌfəʊtə(ʊ)ˈtrəʊpɪz(ə)m, fəʊˈtɒtrəˌpɪz(ə)m/ ■ n. Biology the orientation of a plant or other organism in response to light.
– DERIVATIVES **phototropic** adj.

phototypesetting ■ n. variant form of PHOTOSETTING.

photovoltaics ■ pl. n. [treated as sing.] the branch of technology concerned with the production of electric current at the junction of two substances. ▶ [treated as pl.] devices having such a junction.

phrasal verb ■ n. Grammar an idiomatic phrase consisting of a verb and an adverb or preposition, as in *break down* or *see to*.

phrase ■ n. **1** a small group of words standing together as a conceptual unit. ▶ an idiomatic or short pithy expression. **2** Music a group of notes forming a distinct unit within a longer passage. ■ v. **1** put into a particular form of words. **2** [often as noun **phrasing**] divide (music) into phrases in a particular way.
– DERIVATIVES **phrasal** adj. **phrasally** adv.
– ORIGIN C16: from Greek *phrasis*, from *phrazein* 'declare, tell'.

phrase book ■ n. a book for people visiting a foreign country, listing useful expressions and their translations.

phraseology /ˌfreɪzɪˈɒlədʒi/ ■ n. (pl. **-ies**) a particular or characteristic mode of expression.
– DERIVATIVES **phraseological** adj.

phreatic /frɪˈatɪk/ ■ adj. relating to or denoting underground water in the zone below the water table. Compare with VADOSE.
– ORIGIN C19: from Greek *phrear, phreat-* 'a well'.

phrenology /frɪˈnɒlədʒi/ ■ n. chiefly historical the detailed study of the shape and size of the cranium as a supposed indication of character and mental abilities.
– DERIVATIVES **phrenological** adj. **phrenologist** n.
– ORIGIN C19: from Greek *phrēn* 'mind' + -LOGY.

Phrygian /ˈfrɪdʒɪən/ ■ n. **1** a native or inhabitant of Phrygia, an ancient region of west central Asia Minor. **2** the language of the ancient Phrygians, generally classified as Indo-European. ■ adj. of or relating to Phrygia, its people, or their language.

Phrygian mode ■ n. Music the mode represented by the natural diatonic scale E–E (containing a minor 2nd, 3rd, 6th, and 7th).

Phthiraptera /(f)θɪˈraptərə/ ■ pl. n. Entomology an order of insects that comprises the sucking and biting lice.
– ORIGIN from Greek *phtheir* 'louse' + *pteron* 'wing'.

phthisis /ˈ(f)θʌɪsɪs, ˈtʌɪ-/ ■ n. archaic pulmonary tuberculosis or a similar progressive wasting disease.
– ORIGIN C16: from Greek, from *phthinein* 'to decay'.

phut ■ exclam. used to represent a dull abrupt sound as of a slight impact or explosion.
– ORIGIN C19: perhaps from Hindi *phaṭnā* 'to burst'.

phutu /ˈpuːtuː/ ■ n. variant spelling of PUTU.

phycology /fʌɪˈkɒlədʒi/ ■ n. the branch of botany concerned with seaweeds and other algae.
– DERIVATIVES **phycological** adj. **phycologist** n.
– ORIGIN from Greek *phukos* 'seaweed' + -OLOGY.

phyla plural form of PHYLUM.

phylactery /fɪˈlakt(ə)ri/ ■ n. (pl. **-ies**) a small leather box containing Hebrew texts on vellum, worn by Jewish men at morning prayer.
– ORIGIN Middle English: from Greek *phulaktērion* 'amulet', from *phulassein* 'to guard'.

phyletic /fʌɪˈlɛtɪk/ ■ adj. Biology relating to or denoting the evolutionary development of a species or other group.
– ORIGIN C19: from Greek *phuletikos*, from *phuletēs* 'tribesman'.

phyllite /ˈfɪlʌɪt/ ■ n. Geology a fine-grained metamorphic rock with a well-developed laminar structure, intermediate between slate and schist.
– ORIGIN C19: from Greek *phullon* 'leaf'.

phyllo ■ n. variant spelling of FILO.

phyllo- ■ comb. form of a leaf; relating to leaves: *phyllotaxis*.
– ORIGIN from Greek *phullon* 'leaf'.

phyllode /ˈfɪləʊd/ ■ n. Botany a winged leaf stalk which functions as a leaf.
– ORIGIN C19: from Greek *phullōdēs* 'leaf-like'.

phylloquinone /ˌfɪlə(ʊ)ˈkwɪnəʊn/ ■ n. Biochemistry vitamin K₁, a compound found in cabbage, spinach, and other leafy green vegetables, and essential for the blood-clotting process.

phyllotaxis /ˌfɪlə(ʊ)ˈtaksɪs/ (also **phyllotaxy** /-ˈtaksi/) ■ n. Botany the arrangement of leaves on an axis or stem.

phylloxera /ˌfɪlɒkˈsɪərə, fɪˈlɒksərə/ ■ n. a plant louse that is a pest of vines. [*Phylloxera vitifoliae.*]
– ORIGIN C19: from Greek *phullon* 'leaf' + *xēros* 'dry'.

phylogenesis /ˌfʌɪlə(ʊ)ˈdʒɛnɪsɪs/ ■ n. Biology the evolutionary development and diversification of a species

phylogeny

or group of organisms.
- DERIVATIVES **phylogenetic** adj. **phylogenetically** adv.
- ORIGIN C19: from Greek *phulon, phulē* 'race, tribe' + GENESIS.

phylogeny /fʌɪˈlɒdʒ(ə)ni/ ■ n. the branch of biology concerned with phylogenesis. Compare with ONTOGENY. ▶ another term for PHYLOGENESIS.
- DERIVATIVES **phylogenic** adj.

phylum /ˈfʌɪləm/ ■ n. (pl. **phyla** /-lə/) Zoology a principal taxonomic category that ranks above class and below kingdom, equivalent to the division in botany.
- ORIGIN C19: from Greek *phulon* 'race'.

physalis /ˈfʌɪsəlɪs, ˈfɪs-, fʌɪˈseɪlɪs/ ■ n. a plant of a genus that includes the Cape gooseberry and Chinese lantern, which has an inflated lantern-like calyx. [Genus *Physalis*.]
- ORIGIN from Greek *phusallis* 'bladder'.

physic archaic ■ n. medicinal drugs or medical treatment. ■ v. (**physicked**, **physicking**) treat with a medicine.
- ORIGIN Middle English: from Old French *fisique* 'medicine', from Latin *physica*, from Greek *phusikē (epistēmē)* '(knowledge) of nature', from *phusis* 'nature'.

physical ■ adj. **1** of or relating to the body as opposed to the mind. ▶ involving bodily contact or activity: *a physical relationship*. **2** of or relating to things perceived through the senses as opposed to the mind; tangible or concrete. **3** of or relating to physics or the operation of natural forces generally. ■ n. **1** a medical examination to determine a person's bodily fitness. **2** (**physicals**) Stock Exchange stocks held in actual commodities for immediate exchange, as opposed, for example, to futures.
- DERIVATIVES **physicality** /-ˈkalɪti/ n. **physically** adv.

physical anthropology ■ n. the science of human zoology, evolution, and ecology.

physical chemistry ■ n. the branch of chemistry concerned with the application of the techniques and theories of physics to the study of chemical systems.

physical education ■ n. instruction in physical exercise and games, especially in schools.

physical geography ■ n. the branch of geography concerned with natural features.

physicalism ■ n. Philosophy the doctrine that the real world consists simply of the physical world.
- DERIVATIVES **physicalist** n. & adj.

physical sciences ■ pl. n. the sciences concerned with the study of inanimate natural objects, including physics, chemistry, and astronomy.

physical therapy ■ n. US term for PHYSIOTHERAPY.
- DERIVATIVES **physical therapist** n.

physician ■ n. a person qualified to practise medicine, especially one who specializes in diagnosis and medical treatment as distinct from surgery.

physics ■ pl. n. [treated as sing.] the branch of science concerned with the nature and properties of matter and energy. ▶ the physical properties and phenomena of something.
- DERIVATIVES **physicist** n.
- ORIGIN C15: pl. of obsolete *physic* 'physical (thing)', suggested by Latin *physica* (see PHYSIC).

physio ■ n. (pl. **-os**) informal physiotherapy or a physiotherapist.

physio- ■ comb. form **1** relating to nature and natural phenomena: *physiography*. **2** representing PHYSIOLOGY.
- ORIGIN from Greek *phusis* 'nature'.

physiognomy /ˌfɪzɪˈɒ(g)nəmi/ ■ n. (pl. **-ies**) **1** a person's facial features or expression, especially when regarded as indicative of character or ethnic origin. **2** the supposed art of judging character from facial characteristics.
- DERIVATIVES **physiognomic** adj. **physiognomical** adj.
- ORIGIN Middle English: from Old French *phisonomie*, from Greek *phusiognōmonia* 'judging of a man's nature (by his features)', from *gnōmōn* 'judge or interpreter'.

physiology ■ n. the branch of biology concerned with the normal functions of living organisms and their parts. ▶ the way in which a living organism or bodily part functions.
- DERIVATIVES **physiologic** adj. **physiological** adj. **physiologically** adv. **physiologist** n.

physiotherapy (US **physical therapy**) ■ n. the treatment of disease, injury, or deformity by physical methods such as massage and exercise rather than by drugs or surgery.
- DERIVATIVES **physiotherapist** n.

physique /fɪˈziːk/ ■ n. the form, size, and development of a person's body.
- ORIGIN C19: from French, 'physical'.

-phyte ■ comb. form denoting a plant or plant-like organism: *epiphyte*.
- DERIVATIVES **-phytic** comb. form in corresponding adjectives.
- ORIGIN from Greek *phuton* 'a plant'.

phyto- ■ comb. form of a plant; relating to plants: *phytogeography*.

phytochemical ■ n. any of various biologically active compounds found in plants. ■ adj. relating to phytochemistry or phytochemicals.

phytochemistry ■ n. the branch of chemistry concerned with plants and plant products.
- DERIVATIVES **phytochemist** n.

phytochrome ■ n. Biochemistry a blue-green pigment found in many plants, in which it regulates various developmental processes.
- ORIGIN C19: from PHYTO- + Greek *khrōma* 'colour'.

phytogeography ■ n. the branch of botany concerned with the geographical distribution of plants.
- DERIVATIVES **phytogeographic** adj. **phytogeographical** adj.

phytophagous /fʌɪˈtɒfəgəs/ ■ adj. Zoology (especially of an insect or other invertebrate) feeding on plants.

phytoplankton /ˈfʌɪtəʊˌplaŋktən/ ■ n. Biology plankton consisting of microscopic plants.

phytotoxic ■ adj. Botany poisonous to plants.
- DERIVATIVES **phytotoxicity** n.

phytotoxin ■ n. Botany **1** a poisonous substance derived from a plant. **2** a substance, especially one produced by a parasite, that is phytotoxic.

pi /pʌɪ/ ■ n. **1** the sixteenth letter of the Greek alphabet (Π, π), transliterated as 'p'. **2** the numerical value of the ratio of the circumference of a circle to its diameter (approximately 3.14159). **3** [as modifier] Chemistry & Physics (of an electron or orbital) with one unit of angular momentum about an internuclear axis. ■ symb. (Π) mathematical product.
- ORIGIN from Greek: the numerical use comes from the initial letter of Greek *periphereia* 'circumference'.

pia /ˈpʌɪə, ˈpiːə/ (in full **pia mater**) ■ n. Anatomy the delicate innermost membrane enveloping the brain and spinal cord.
- ORIGIN C19: from medieval Latin, in full 'tender mother', translating Arabic *al-'umm ar-raḳīḳa*.

piaffe /pɪˈaf/ Riding ■ n. a movement in which the horse executes a slow elevated trot without moving forward. ■ v. perform such a movement.
- ORIGIN C18: from French *piaffer* 'to strut'.

pianism /ˈpɪənɪz(ə)m/ ■ n. skill or artistry in playing the piano or composing piano music.
- DERIVATIVES **pianistic** adj. **pianistically** adv.

piano[1] /ˈpjɑːnəʊ/ ■ adv. & adj. Music soft or softly.
- ORIGIN Italian, 'soft'.

piano[2] /pɪˈanəʊ/ ■ n. (pl. **-os**) a large keyboard musical instrument with a wooden case enclosing a soundboard and metal strings, which are struck by hammers when the keys are depressed.
- DERIVATIVES **pianist** n.
- ORIGIN C19: from Italian, abbrev. of PIANOFORTE.

piano accordion ■ n. an accordion with the melody played on a small vertical keyboard like that of a piano.

pianoforte /pɪˌanəʊˈfɔːteɪ, -ˈfɔːti/ ■ n. formal term for PIANO.
- ORIGIN C18: from Italian, earlier *piano e forte* 'soft and loud', expressing the gradation in tone.

pianola /ˌpɪəˈnəʊlə/ ■ n. trademark a piano equipped to be played automatically using a piano roll.
- ORIGIN C19: prob. a diminutive of PIANO.

piano organ ■ n. a mechanical piano constructed like a barrel organ.

piano roll ▪ n. a roll of perforated paper which controls the movement of the keys in a pianola.

piastre /pɪˈastə/ (US also **piaster**) ▪ n. a monetary unit of several Middle Eastern countries, equal to one hundredth of a pound.
– ORIGIN from French, from Italian *piastra (d'argento)* 'plate (of silver)'.

piazza /pɪˈatsə/ ▪ n. a public square or marketplace, especially in an Italian town.
– ORIGIN C16: Italian.

pibroch /ˈpiːbrɒk, -brɒx/ ▪ n. a form of music for the Scottish bagpipes involving elaborate variations on a theme, typically of a martial or funerary character.
– ORIGIN C18: from Scottish Gaelic *piobaireachd* 'art of piping', from *piobair* 'piper', from English PIPE.

pic ▪ n. informal a picture, photograph, or film.

pica[1] /ˈpʌɪkə/ ▪ n. Printing 1 a unit of type size and line length equal to 12 points (about ⅙ inch or 4.2 mm). 2 a size of letter in typewriting, with 10 characters to the inch (about 3.9 to the centimetre).
– ORIGIN C16: from Anglo-Latin *pica* 'magpie', commonly identified with a C15 book of rules about Church feasts.

pica[2] /ˈpʌɪkə/ ▪ n. Medicine a tendency or craving to eat substances other than normal food, occurring during childhood or pregnancy or as a symptom of disease.
– ORIGIN C16: from Latin, 'magpie', prob. translating Greek *kissa* 'magpie', also 'false appetite'.

picador /ˈpɪkədɔː/ ▪ n. (in bullfighting) a person on horseback who goads the bull with a lance.
– ORIGIN Spanish, from *picar* 'to prick'.

picante /pɪˈkanteɪ/ ▪ adj. (of food) spicy.
– ORIGIN Spanish, 'pricking, biting'.

picaresque /ˌpɪkəˈrɛsk/ ▪ adj. of or relating to an episodic style of fiction dealing with the adventures of a rough and dishonest but appealing hero.
– ORIGIN C19: from Spanish *picaresco*, from *pícaro* 'rogue'.

picayune /ˌpɪkəˈjuːn/ ▪ adj. N. Amer. informal petty; worthless.
– ORIGIN C19: from French *picaillon*, denoting a Piedmontese copper coin, also used to mean 'cash'.

piccalilli /ˌpɪkəˈlɪli/ ▪ n. (pl. **piccalillies** or **piccalillis**) a pickle of chopped vegetables, mustard, and hot spices.
– ORIGIN C18: prob. from a blend of PICKLE and CHILLI.

piccaninny /ˈpɪkənɪni/ (also **pickaninny** or S. African **piccanin**) ▪ n. (pl. **-ies**) offensive a small black child. ▪ adj. archaic very small.
– ORIGIN C17: from Spanish *pequeño* or Portuguese *pequeno* 'little', *pequenino* 'tiny'.

piccolo ▪ n. (pl. **-os**) a small flute sounding an octave higher than the ordinary one.
– ORIGIN C19: from Italian, 'small (flute)'.

piccy ▪ n. (pl. **-ies**) informal a picture.

pick[1] ▪ v. 1 take hold of and remove (a flower or fruit) from where it is growing. ▸ (often **pick someone/thing up**) take hold of and lift or move. ▸ (**pick up**) Golf take hold of and lift up one's ball, especially when conceding a hole. 2 choose from a number of alternatives. ▸ (**pick one's way**) walk slowly and carefully. 3 (often **pick at**) repeatedly pull at something with one's fingers. ▸ eat in small amounts or without much appetite. ▸ criticize someone in a niggling way. 4 remove unwanted matter from (one's nose or teeth) with a finger or a pointed instrument. 5 pluck the strings of (a guitar or banjo). ▪ n. 1 an act or the right of selecting something. ▸ (**the pick of**) informal the best person or thing in a particular group. 2 Basketball an act of blocking or screening a defensive player from the ball handler.
– PHRASES **pick and choose** select only the best from among a number of alternatives. **pick someone's brains** informal obtain information by questioning someone well informed. **pick a fight** provoke an argument or fight. **pick holes in** find fault with. **pick a lock** open a lock with an instrument other than the proper key. **pick someone's pockets** steal something surreptitiously from another person's pocket.
– PHRASAL VERBS **pick someone/thing off** shoot a member of a group from a distance. **pick on** repeatedly single out for unfair criticism or unkind treatment. **pick someone/thing out** distinguish or select from among a group. ▸ highlight or accentuate by painting or fashioning in a contrasting colour or medium. **pick something over** (or **pick through**) sort through a number of items carefully. **pick up** improve or increase. **pick someone up 1** go somewhere to collect someone. **2** informal casually strike up a relationship with someone as a sexual overture. **3** return to a point or remark made by someone in order to criticize it. **pick something up 1** collect something that has been left elsewhere. **2** obtain, acquire, or learn something. ▸ catch an illness or infection. **3** detect or receive a signal or sound. **4** resume something. **5** (also **pick up on**) refer to or develop a point or topic mentioned earlier. ▸ become aware of or sensitive to something.
– DERIVATIVES **pickable** adj. **picker** n.
– ORIGIN Middle English.

pick[2] ▪ n. 1 a tool headed by a curved bar with a point at one end and a chisel edge or point at the other, used for breaking up hard ground or rock. 2 an instrument for picking. ▸ informal a plectrum.
– ORIGIN Middle English: var. of PIKE[2].

pickaninny ▪ n. variant spelling of PICCANINNY.

pickaxe (US also **pickax**) ▪ n. another term for PICK[2] (in sense 1).
– ORIGIN Middle English *pikoys*, from Old French *picois*, assimilated to AXE.

picket ▪ n. 1 a person or group of people standing outside a workplace trying to persuade others not to enter during a strike. 2 (also **picquet**) a soldier or small body of troops sent out to watch for the enemy. 3 [usu. as modifier] a pointed wooden stake driven into the ground to form a fence or to tether a horse. ▪ v. (**picketed**, **picketing**) act as a picket outside (a workplace).
– DERIVATIVES **picketer** n.
– ORIGIN C17: from French *piquet* 'pointed stake'.

picket fence ▪ n. 1 a wooden fence made of spaced uprights connected by two or more horizontal rails. 2 N. Amer. [often as modifier] a picket fence as a symbol of middle-class domesticity and contentment.

pickings ▪ pl. n. 1 profits or gains, especially those made effortlessly or dishonestly. 2 remaining scraps or left-overs.

pickle ▪ n. 1 a relish consisting of vegetables or fruit preserved in vinegar, brine, or mustard. ▸ N. Amer. a cucumber preserved in this way. ▸ liquid used to preserve food or other perishable items. 2 (**a pickle**) informal a difficult situation. ▪ v. 1 preserve (food) in pickle. 2 immerse (a metal object) in an acid solution for cleaning. 3 [as adj. **pickled**] informal drunk.
– ORIGIN Middle English: from Middle Dutch, Middle Low German *pekel*.

pick-me-up ▪ n. informal a thing that makes one feel more energetic or cheerful.

pickpocket ▪ n. a person who steals from people's pockets.
– DERIVATIVES **pickpocketing** n.

pickup ▪ n. 1 (also **pickup truck**) a small van or truck with low sides. ▸ (**pickup van**) S. African dated a police van. 2 an act of picking up or collecting a person or goods. 3 an improvement, especially in an economy. 4 a device on an electric guitar which converts sound vibrations into electrical signals for amplification. 5 Music a series of introductory notes leading into the opening part of a tune. 6 Fishing a semicircular loop of metal for guiding the line back on to the spool as it is reeled in.

Pickwickian /pɪkˈwɪkɪən/ ▪ adj. of or like Mr Pickwick in Dickens's *Pickwick Papers*, especially in being jovial, plump, or generous.

picky ▪ adj. (**-ier**, **-iest**) informal fastidious, especially excessively so.
– DERIVATIVES **pickiness** n.

picnic ▪ n. a packed meal eaten outdoors, or an occasion when such a meal is eaten. ▪ v. (**picnicked**, **picnicking**) have or take part in a picnic.
– PHRASES **be no picnic** informal be difficult or unpleasant.
– DERIVATIVES **picnicker** n.
– ORIGIN C18: from French *pique-nique*.

pico- /ˈpiːkəʊ, ˈpʌɪkəʊ/ ▪ comb. form denoting a factor of 10^{-12}: *picosecond*. ▸ very small: *picornavirus*.
– ORIGIN from Spanish *pico* 'beak, peak, little bit'.

picornavirus /pɪˈkɔːnəˌvʌɪrəs/ ■ n. any of a group of very small RNA viruses which includes enteroviruses, rhinoviruses, and the virus of foot-and-mouth disease.
– ORIGIN 1960s: from PICO- + RNA + VIRUS.

picquet ■ n. variant spelling of PICKET (in sense 2).

Pict ■ n. a member of an ancient people inhabiting northern Scotland in Roman times.
– DERIVATIVES **Pictish** adj. & n.
– ORIGIN from late Latin *Picti*, perhaps from Latin *pingere* 'to paint or tattoo', or influenced by a local name.

pictograph (also **pictogram**) ■ n. **1** a pictorial symbol for a word or phrase. **2** a pictorial representation of statistics on a chart, graph, or computer screen.
– DERIVATIVES **pictographic** adj. **pictography** n.
– ORIGIN C19: from Latin *pingere* 'to paint' + -GRAPH.

pictorial ■ adj. of or expressed in pictures; illustrated. ■ n. a newspaper or periodical with pictures as a main feature.
– DERIVATIVES **pictorially** adv.
– ORIGIN C17: from late Latin *pictorius*, from Latin *pictor* 'painter', from *pingere* 'to paint'.

picture ■ n. **1** a painting, drawing, or photograph. ▸ a portrait. ▸ an image on a television screen. **2** an impression formed from an account or description: *a full picture of the disaster had not yet emerged*. ▸ (often in phr. **in** (or **out of**) **the picture**) informal a state of being fully informed about or involved in something. **3** a cinema film. ▸ (**the pictures**) the cinema. **4** archaic a person or thing resembling another closely. ■ v. **1** represent in a picture. **2** form a mental image of.
– PHRASES **be** (or **look**) **a picture 1** be beautiful. **2** look amusingly startled. **the big picture** informal the situation as a whole. **a** (or **the**) **picture of** —— the embodiment of a specified state or emotion: *she looked a picture of health*. (**as**) **pretty as a picture** very pretty.
– ORIGIN Middle English: from Latin *pictura*, from *pingere* 'to paint'.

picture book ■ n. a book containing many illustrations, especially one for children.

picture hat ■ n. a woman's highly decorated hat with a wide brim, as worn in 18th-century England.

picture messaging ■ n. a system that enables digital photos and animated graphics to be sent and received by cellphone.

picture palace ■ n. Brit. dated a cinema.

picture-perfect ■ adj. completely lacking in defects or flaws; ideal.

picture postcard ■ n. **1** a postcard with a picture on one side. **2** [as modifier] (of a view) prettily picturesque.

picture rail ■ n. a horizontal strip of wood on a wall from which pictures can be hung.

picturesque ■ adj. visually attractive in a quaint or charming manner. ▸ (of language) unusual and vivid.
– DERIVATIVES **picturesquely** adv. **picturesqueness** n.
– ORIGIN C18: from French *pittoresque*, from Italian *pittore* 'painter', from Latin *pictor*.

picture tube ■ n. Electronics the cathode ray tube of a television set designed for the reproduction of television pictures.

picture window ■ n. a large window consisting of one pane of glass, typically facing an attractive view.

picture-writing ■ n. a mode of recording events by pictorial symbols; pictography.

PID ■ abbrev. pelvic inflammatory disease.

piddle informal ■ v. **1** urinate. **2** (**piddle about/around**) spend time in trifling activities. **3** [as adj. **piddling**] pathetically trivial; trifling. ■ n. an act of urinating. ▸ urine.
– ORIGIN C16: prob. from a blend of PISS and PUDDLE.

piddock /ˈpɪdək/ ■ n. a bivalve mollusc which bores into soft rock or other firm surfaces. [*Pholas* and other genera.]
– ORIGIN C19.

pidgin /ˈpɪdʒɪn/ ■ n. a grammatically simplified form of a language with elements taken from local languages, used for communication between people not sharing a common language.
– ORIGIN C19: Chinese alteration of English *business*.

pi-dog ■ n. variant spelling of PYE-DOG.

pie[1] ■ n. a baked dish of savoury or sweet ingredients encased in or topped with pastry.
– PHRASES (**as**) —— **as pie** informal very ——. **pie in the sky** informal something pleasant to contemplate but very unlikely to be realized.
– ORIGIN Middle English: prob. the same word as PIE[2], the various combinations of ingredients being compared to objects randomly collected by a magpie.

pie[2] ■ n. archaic a magpie. ▸ used in names of similar birds.
– ORIGIN Middle English: from Latin *pica* 'magpie'.

piebald ■ adj. (of a horse) having irregular patches of two colours, typically black and white. ■ n. a piebald horse.
– ORIGIN C16: from PIE[2] (because of the magpie's black-and-white plumage) + BALD (in the obsolete sense 'streaked with white').

piece ■ n. **1** a portion of an object or of material produced by cutting, tearing, or breaking the whole. **2** an item used in constructing something or forming part of a set; a component. ▸ an instance or example: *a crucial piece of evidence*. **3** a musical or written work: *a piece of music*. **4** a figure or token used to make moves in a board game. ▸ Chess a king, queen, bishop, knight, or rook, as opposed to a pawn. **5** a coin of specified value: *a 50c piece*. **6** informal, chiefly N. Amer. a firearm. ■ v. **1** (**piece something together**) assemble something from individual parts. **2** (**piece something out**) archaic extend something.
– PHRASES **go to pieces** become so nervous or upset that one is unable to function normally. **in one piece** unharmed or undamaged. (**all**) **of a piece** entirely consistent. **piece by piece** in slow and small stages. **piece of water** a small lake or pond. **piece of work** informal a person of a specified kind, especially an unpleasant one. **say one's piece** give one's opinion or make a prepared statement. **tear** (or **pull**) **someone/thing to pieces** criticize someone or something harshly.
– DERIVATIVES **piecer** n.
– ORIGIN Middle English: from Old French *piece* (cf. medieval Latin *pecia*, *petium*).

pièce de résistance /ˌpjɛs də reɪˈzɪstɒs/ ■ n. the most important or remarkable feature of a creative work, meal, etc.
– ORIGIN French, 'piece (i.e. means) of resistance'.

piece goods ■ pl. n. fabrics woven in standard lengths for sale.

piece job chiefly S. African ■ n. an occasional short-term job paid for according to the work done.

piecemeal ■ adj. & adv. characterized by unsystematic partial measures taken over a period of time.
– ORIGIN Middle English: from PIECE + *-meal* from Old English *mǣlum*, in the sense 'measure, quantity taken at one time'.

piece of eight ■ n. historical a Spanish dollar, equivalent to eight reals.

piecework ■ n. work paid for according to the quantity, or pieces, produced.
– DERIVATIVES **pieceworker** n.

pie chart (also **pie graph**) ■ n. a type of graph in which a circle is divided into sectors that each represent a proportion of the whole.

piecrust table ■ n. a table with an indented edge like a piecrust.

pied /pʌɪd/ ■ adj. having two or more different colours.
– ORIGIN Middle English: from PIE[2].

pied-à-terre /ˌpjeɪdɑːˈtɛː/ ■ n. (pl. **pieds-à-terre** pronunc. same) a small flat, house, or room kept for occasional use.
– ORIGIN C19: French, 'foot to earth'.

piedmont /ˈpiːdmɒnt/ ■ n. a gentle slope leading from the foot of mountains to a region of flat land.
– ORIGIN C19: from Italian *piemonte* 'mountain foot'.

pied noir /pjɛ ˈnwɑː/ ■ n. (pl. **pieds noirs** pronunc. same) a person of European origin who lived in Algeria during French rule, especially one who returned to Europe after Algerian independence.

– ORIGIN French, 'black foot', so named because of the western-style black leather shoes worn by the first colonists.

Pied Piper ■ n. a person who entices people to follow them, especially to their doom.
– ORIGIN from the legendary German figure, subject of Robert Browning's poem *The Pied Piper of Hamelin* (1842), who rid the town of Hamelin of rats by enticing them away with his music, and when refused the promised payment lured away the town's children.

pie-eyed ■ adj. informal very drunk.

pier ■ n. **1** a structure leading out to sea and used as a landing stage for boats or as a place of entertainment. ▶ a breakwater or mole. **2** Brit. a long narrow structure projecting from an airport terminal and giving access to an aircraft. **3** the pillar of an arch or supporting a bridge. ▶ a wall between windows or other adjacent openings.
– ORIGIN Middle English: from medieval Latin *pera*.

pierce ■ v. **1** make a hole in or through with a sharp pointed object. **2** force or cut a way through: *a shrill voice pierced the air.* **3** [as adj. **piercing**] very sharp, cold, or high-pitched. ▶ very astute or intelligent.
– DERIVATIVES **piercer** n. **piercingly** adv.
– ORIGIN Middle English: from Old French *percer*, from Latin *pertundere* 'bore through'.

pier glass ■ n. a large mirror, used originally to fill wall space between windows.

Pierrot /ˈpɪərəʊ, ˈpjɛrəʊ/ ■ n. a stock male character in French pantomime, with a sad white-painted face, a loose white costume, and a pointed hat.
– ORIGIN French, diminutive of the male given name *Pierre* 'Peter'.

Piesporter /ˈpiːzˌpɔːtə/ ■ n. a white Moselle wine produced in the Piesport region of Germany.

pietà /pjɛrˈtɑː/ ■ n. a picture or sculpture of the Virgin Mary holding the dead body of Christ on her lap or in her arms.
– ORIGIN Italian, from Latin *pietas* 'dutifulness'.

pietas /ˈpʌɪətɑːs, piːˈeɪtɑːs/ ■ n. respect due to an ancestor, country, or institution.
– ORIGIN Latin, 'dutifulness'.

pietism /ˈpʌɪətɪz(ə)m/ ■ n. pious sentiment, especially of an exaggerated or affected nature.
– DERIVATIVES **pietist** n. **pietistic** adj.

piet-my-vrou /ˈpiːtmeɪfrəʊ/ ■ n. S. African the red-chested cuckoo, native to Africa. [*Cuculus solitarius.*]
– ORIGIN S. African Dutch, from the bird's three-note call.

pietra dura /ˌpjɛtrə ˈdʊərə/ ■ n. pictorial mosaic work using semi-precious stones.
– ORIGIN C19: from Italian (pl. *pietre dure*), 'hard stone'.

piety /ˈpʌɪəti/ ■ n. (pl. **-ies**) the quality of being pious or reverent. ▶ a belief accepted with unthinking conventional reverence.
– ORIGIN C16: from Old French *piete*, from Latin *pietas* 'dutifulness', from *pius* (see **PIOUS**).

piezo /pʌɪˈiːzəʊ, ˈpiːzəʊ/ ■ adj. piezoelectric.

piezoelectricity ■ n. electric polarization produced in certain crystals by the application of mechanical stress.
– DERIVATIVES **piezoelectric** adj.
– ORIGIN C19: from Greek *piezein* 'press, squeeze' + **ELECTRICITY**.

piezometer /ˌpʌɪɪˈzɒmɪtə/ ■ n. an instrument for measuring or monitoring pressure in a fluid, especially by determining compressibility.

piffle ■ n. informal nonsense.
– ORIGIN C19: diminutive of imitative *piff-*.

piffling ■ adj. informal trivial; unimportant.

pig ■ n. **1** an omnivorous domesticated hoofed mammal with sparse bristly hair and a flat snout, kept for its meat. [*Sus domesticus.*] ▶ a wild animal related to this; a hog. [Family Suidae.] ▶ N. Amer. a young pig; a piglet. **2** informal a greedy, dirty, or unpleasant person. ▶ Brit. informal an unpleasant or difficult task. **3** informal, derogatory a police officer. **4** an oblong mass of iron or lead from a smelting furnace. ■ v. (**pigged, pigging**) **1** (often **pig out**) informal gorge oneself with food. **2** (often in phr. **pig it**) informal crowd together with others in disorderly or dirty conditions. **3** (of a sow) give birth to piglets; farrow.
– PHRASES **bleed like a (stuck) pig** bleed copiously. **in a**

pig's ear

pig's eye informal, chiefly N. Amer. expressing scornful disbelief. **make a pig of oneself** informal overeat. **make a pig's ear of** Brit. informal handle ineptly. **a pig in a poke** something that is bought or accepted without first being seen or assessed.
– DERIVATIVES **piglet** n. **piglike** adj.
– ORIGIN Middle English: prob. from the first element of Old English *picbrēd* 'acorn, pig bread' (i.e. food for pigs).

pigeon[1] ■ n. a stout seed- or fruit-eating bird with a small head, short legs, and a cooing voice, similar to but generally larger than a dove. [Family Columbidae: many species.]
– ORIGIN Middle English: from Old French *pijon* 'young bird', from late Latin *pipio(n-)* 'young cheeping bird' of imitative origin.

pigeon[2] ■ n. (**one's pigeon**) informal, chiefly Brit. a person's particular responsibility or business.

pigeon-chested (also **pigeon-breasted**) ■ adj. having a narrow, projecting chest.

pigeonhole ■ n. **1** a small recess for a domestic pigeon to nest in. **2** each of a set of small compartments where letters or messages may be left for individuals. **3** a category, especially an overly restrictive one, to which someone or something is assigned. ■ v. **1** assign to a particular category, especially an overly restrictive one. **2** deposit (a document) in a pigeonhole.

pigeon pair ■ n. dialect a boy and girl as twins, or as the only children in a family.

pigeon pea ■ n. **1** a dark red tropical pealike seed. **2** the woody plant which yields these seeds, with pods and foliage that are used as fodder. [*Cajanus cajan.*]

pigeon-toed ■ adj. having the toes or feet turned inwards.

piggery ■ n. (pl. **-ies**) **1** a farm or enclosure where pigs are kept. **2** behaviour regarded as characteristic of pigs, especially greed or unpleasantness.

piggish ■ adj. resembling or likened to a pig, especially in being unpleasant.
– DERIVATIVES **piggishly** adv. **piggishness** n.

piggy ■ n. (pl. **-ies**) **1** a child's word for a pig or piglet. **2** S. African a small grunter, often used by anglers as bait. [*Pomadasys olivaceum.*] ■ adj. resembling or likened to a pig, especially in features or appetite.
– PHRASES **piggy in the middle** chiefly Brit. **1** a game in which two people attempt to throw a ball to each other without a third person in the middle catching it. **2** a person who is placed in an awkward situation between two others.

piggyback ■ n. a ride on someone's back and shoulders. ■ adv. on the back and shoulders of another person. ■ v. **1** carry by or as if by means of a piggyback. **2** mount on or attach to (an existing object or system).

piggy bank ■ n. a money box, especially one shaped like a pig.

pig-headed ■ adj. stupidly obstinate.
– DERIVATIVES **pig-headedly** adv. **pig-headedness** n.

pig-ignorant ■ adj. informal extremely stupid or crude.

pig iron ■ n. crude iron as first obtained from a smelting furnace, in the form of oblong blocks.

pig Latin ■ n. a secret language formed from English by transferring the initial consonant or consonant cluster of each word to the end of the word and adding a vocalic syllable (usually /eɪ/): so *igpay atinlay*.

pigment ■ n. **1** the natural colouring matter of animal or plant tissue. **2** a substance used for colouring or painting, especially a dry powder which constitutes a paint or ink when mixed with oil or water. ■ v. [usu. as adj. **pigmented**] colour with or as if with pigment.
– DERIVATIVES **pigmentary** adj. **pigmentation** n.
– ORIGIN Middle English: from Latin *pigmentum*, from *pingere* 'to paint'.

pigmy ■ n. variant spelling of **PYGMY**.

pigpen ■ n. N. Amer. a pigsty.

pig's ear ■ n. a southern African succulent that has fleshy

pigskin

grey-green leaves margined with red, and orange-red bell-shaped flowers. [*Cotyledon orbiculata*.]

pigskin ■ n. **1** leather made from the hide of a domestic pig. **2** N. Amer. informal a football.

pig-sticking ■ n. the sport of hunting wild boar with a spear, carried out on horseback.
– DERIVATIVES **pig-sticker** n.

pigsty ■ n. (pl. -ies) **1** a pen or enclosure for a pig or pigs. **2** a very dirty or untidy house or room.

pigswill ■ n. kitchen refuse and scraps fed to pigs.

pigtail ■ n. **1** a plaited lock of hair worn singly at the back or on each side of the head. **2** a short length of flexible braided wire connecting a stationary part to a moving part in an electrical device.
– DERIVATIVES **pigtailed** adj.

pigweed ■ n. a North American plant used for fodder, naturalized as a weed in other countries. [Genus *Amaranthus*.]

pike[1] ■ n. (pl. same) a long-bodied predatory freshwater fish with long teeth, native to Eurasia and North America. [*Esox lucius* and related species.] ▸ used in names of similar predatory fish, e.g. garpike.
– ORIGIN Middle English: from PIKE[2] (because of the fish's pointed jaw).

pike[2] ■ n. historical an infantry weapon with a pointed steel or iron head on a long wooden shaft. ■ v. historical thrust through or kill with a pike.
– ORIGIN C16: from French *pique*, back-formation from *piquer* 'pierce', from *pic* 'pick, pike'; sense 2 is prob. of Scandinavian origin.

pike[3] ■ n. short for TURNPIKE.
– PHRASES **come down the pike** N. Amer. appear on the scene; come to notice.

pike[4] ■ n. a jackknife position in diving or gymnastics.
– ORIGIN 1920s.

pikestaff ■ n. historical the wooden shaft of a pike.
– PHRASES **(as) plain as a pikestaff 1** very obvious. **2** ordinary or unattractive in appearance.

pikkie ■ n. S. African informal a small child.
– ORIGIN Afrikaans, 'bantam, little chap', from dialect Dutch, 'chicken'.

pilaf /pɪˈlaf/ (also **pilau**, **pulao**) ■ n. a Middle Eastern or Indian dish of spiced rice or wheat and often meat and vegetables.
– ORIGIN from Turkish *pilâv*.

pilaster /pɪˈlastə/ ■ n. a rectangular column, especially one projecting from a wall.
– DERIVATIVES **pilastered** adj.
– ORIGIN C16: from French *pilastre*, from Italian *pilastro*, from Latin *pila* 'pillar'.

pilchard ■ n. a small marine food fish of the herring family. [*Sardinops* and other genera.]
– ORIGIN C16.

pile[1] ■ n. **1** a heap of things laid or lying one on top of another. ▸ informal a large amount: *the growing pile of work*. **2** a large imposing building: *a Gothic pile*. **3** a series of plates of dissimilar metals laid one on another alternately to produce an electric current. ■ v. **1** place (things) one on top of the other. ▸ **(be piled with)** be stacked or loaded with. ▸ **(pile up)** form a pile or very large quantity. ▸ **(pile something on)** informal intensify or exaggerate something for effect. **2 (pile into/out of)** get into or out of (a vehicle) in a disorganized manner. ▸ **(pile into)** (of a vehicle) crash into.
– PHRASES **make a pile** Brit. informal make a lot of money.
– ORIGIN Middle English: from Latin *pila* 'pillar, pier'.

pile[2] ■ n. **1** a heavy stake or post driven into the ground to support the foundations of a superstructure. **2** Heraldry a triangular charge or ordinary formed by two lines meeting at an acute angle, usually pointing down from the top of the shield. ■ v. strengthen or support with piles.
– ORIGIN Old English *pīl* 'dart, arrow', also 'pointed stake', of Germanic origin.

pile[3] ■ n. the soft projecting surface of a carpet or a fabric such as velvet, consisting of many small threads.
– ORIGIN Middle English: from Latin *pilus* 'hair'.

piledriver ■ n. **1** a machine for driving piles into the ground. **2** Brit. informal a forceful act, blow, or shot.
– DERIVATIVES **piledriving** n. & adj.

pile-up ■ n. informal **1** a crash involving several vehicles. **2** an accumulation of a specified thing.

piles ■ pl. n. haemorrhoids.
– ORIGIN Middle English: prob. from Latin *pila* 'ball' (because of the globular form of external haemorrhoids).

pileus /ˈpaɪlɪəs/ ■ n. (pl. **pilei** /-lɪaɪ/) Botany the cap of a mushroom or toadstool.
– ORIGIN C18: from Latin, 'felt cap'.

pilfer ■ v. steal (things of little value).
– DERIVATIVES **pilferage** n. **pilferer** n.
– ORIGIN Middle English: from Old French *pelfrer* 'to pillage'.

pilgrim ■ n. a person who journeys to a sacred place for religious reasons.
– ORIGIN Middle English: from Provençal *pelegrin*, from Latin *peregrinus* (see PEREGRINE).

pilgrimage ■ n. a pilgrim's journey. ■ v. go on a pilgrimage.

Pilipino /ˌpɪlɪˈpiːnəʊ/ ■ n. & adj. variant of FILIPINO.

pill ■ n. **1** a small round mass of solid medicine for swallowing whole. ▸ **(the Pill)** a contraceptive pill. **2** informal, dated a ball. ■ v. (of knitted fabric) form small balls of fluff on its surface.
– PHRASES **a bitter pill** an unpleasant or painful necessity. **sugar** (or **sweeten**) **the pill** make an unpleasant or painful necessity more palatable.
– ORIGIN Middle English: from Latin *pilula* 'little ball', diminutive of *pila*.

pillage ■ v. rob or steal with violence, especially in wartime. ■ n. the action of pillaging.
– DERIVATIVES **pillager** n.
– ORIGIN Middle English: from Old French, from *piller* 'to plunder'.

pillar ■ n. **1** a tall vertical structure, usually of stone, used as a support for a building or as an ornament or monument. **2** a person or thing providing reliable support: *he was a pillar of his local community*.
– PHRASES **from pillar to post** from one place to another in an unceremonious or fruitless manner.
– DERIVATIVES **pillared** adj.
– ORIGIN Middle English: from Anglo-Norman French *piler*, from Latin *pila* 'pillar'.

pillar box ■ n. a large red cylindrical public postbox.

pillbox ■ n. **1** a small shallow cylindrical box for holding pills. **2** a hat of a similar shape. **3** a small enclosed, partly underground, concrete fort used as an outpost.

pillion ■ n. **1** a seat for a passenger behind a motorcyclist. **2** historical a woman's light saddle. ▸ a cushion attached to the back of a saddle for an additional passenger.
– ORIGIN C15: from Scottish Gaelic *pillean*, Irish *pillín* 'small cushion', diminutive of *pell*, from Latin *pellis* 'skin'.

pillock ■ n. Brit. informal a stupid person.
– ORIGIN C16: var. of archaic *pillicock* 'penis'.

pillory ■ n. (pl. -ies) a wooden framework with holes for the head and hands, in which offenders were formerly imprisoned and exposed to public abuse. ■ v. (-ies, -ied) **1** put in a pillory. **2** attack or ridicule publicly.
– ORIGIN Middle English: from Old French *pilori*, prob. from Provençal *espilori* (perhaps rel. to a Catalan word meaning 'peephole').

pillow ■ n. a rectangular cloth bag stuffed with feathers, wadding, or other soft materials, used to support the head when lying or sleeping. ■ v. rest (one's head) as if on a pillow. ▸ poetic/literary serve as a pillow for.
– DERIVATIVES **pillowy** adj.
– ORIGIN Old English *pyle*, *pylu*, of West Germanic origin, from Latin *pulvinus* 'cushion'.

pillow book ■ n. (in Japanese classical literature) a type of private journal or diary.

pillowcase ■ n. a removable cloth cover for a pillow.

pillow fight ■ n. a mock fight using pillows.

pillow lace ■ n. lace made by hand using a lace pillow.

pillow lava ■ n. lava which has solidified as rounded masses, characteristic of eruption under water.

pillowslip ■ n. a pillowcase.

pillow talk ■ n. intimate conversation in bed.

pill-popper ■ n. informal a person who takes pills freely.
– DERIVATIVES **pill-popping** n.

pilot ■ n. **1** a person who operates the flying controls of an aircraft. **2** a person with expert local knowledge qualified to take charge of a ship entering or leaving a harbour. ▸ a navigational handbook for use at sea. ▸ archaic a guide or leader. **3** [often as modifier] something done or produced as an experiment or test before wider introduction: *a pilot scheme.* ■ v. (**piloted**, **piloting**) **1** act as a pilot of (an aircraft or ship). ▸ guide; steer. **2** test (a scheme, project, etc.) before introducing it more widely.
– DERIVATIVES **pilotage** n. **pilotless** adj.
– ORIGIN C16: from French *pilote*, from medieval Latin *pilotus*, from Greek *pēdon* 'oar', (pl.) 'rudder'.

pilot balloon ■ n. a small meteorological balloon used to track air currents.

pilot chute ■ n. a small parachute used to bring the main one into operation.

pilotfish ■ n. (pl. same or **-fishes**) a fish of warm seas that often swims close to large fish such as sharks. [*Naucrates ductor.*]

pilot house ■ n. another term for **WHEELHOUSE**.

pilot light ■ n. **1** a small gas burner kept alight permanently to light a larger burner when needed, especially on a gas cooker or boiler. **2** an electric indicator light or control light.

pilot officer ■ n. the lowest rank of officer in the RAF.

pilot whale ■ n. a black toothed whale with a square bulbous head. [Genus *Globicephala*: two species.]

Pils /pɪlz, -s/ ■ n. short for **PILSNER**.

Pilsner /ˈpɪlznə, ˈpɪls-/ (also **Pilsener**) ■ n. a lager beer with a strong hop flavour, originally brewed at Pilsen (Plzeň) in the Czech Republic.

pimento /pɪˈmɛntəʊ/ ■ n. (pl. **-os**) **1** variant spelling of PIMIENTO. **2** another term for **ALLSPICE**.

pi-meson ■ n. another term for **PION**.

pimiento /ˌpɪmɪˈɛntəʊ, pɪmˈjɛn-/ (also **pimento**) ■ n. (pl. **-os**) a red sweet pepper.
– ORIGIN C17: from Spanish, from medieval Latin *pigmentum* 'spice'.

pimp ■ n. **1** a man who controls prostitutes and arranges clients for them, taking a percentage of their earnings in return. **2** S. African & Austral. informal a telltale or informer. ■ v. **1** [often as noun **pimping**] act as a pimp. **2** (**pimp on**) S. African & Austral. informal inform on.
– ORIGIN C16.

pimpernel /ˈpɪmpənɛl/ ■ n. a low-growing European plant with bright five-petalled flowers. [*Anagallis arvensis* (scarlet pimpernel) and other species.]
– ORIGIN Middle English: from Old French *pimpernelle*, from Latin *piper* 'pepper'.

pimple ■ n. a small, hard inflamed spot on the skin.
– DERIVATIVES **pimpled** adj. **pimply** adj.
– ORIGIN Middle English: rel. to Old English *piplian* 'break out in pustules'.

PIN (also **PIN number**) ■ abbrev. personal identification number.

pin ■ n. **1** a thin piece of metal with a sharp point at one end and a round head at the other, used for fastening pieces of cloth, paper, etc. ▸ a small brooch or badge. ▸ Medicine a steel rod used to join the ends of fractured bones while they heal. **2** a metal peg that holds down the activating lever of a hand grenade, preventing its explosion. **3** a metal projection from a plug or an integrated circuit which makes an electrical connection with a socket or another part of a circuit. **4** Golf a stick with a flag placed in a hole to mark its position. **5** a skittle in bowling. **6** (**pins**) informal legs. **7** Chess an attack on a piece or pawn which is thereby pinned. ■ v. (**pinned**, **pinning**) **1** attach or fasten with a pin or pins. ▸ (**pin something on**) fix blame or responsibility on. **2** hold someone firmly so they are unable to move. ▸ (**pin someone down**) restrict the actions of an enemy by firing at them. ▸ (**pin someone down**) force someone to be specific about their intentions. **3** Chess hinder or prevent (a piece or pawn) from moving because of the danger to a more valuable piece standing behind it along the line of an attack.

– PHRASES **pin one's hopes** (or **faith**) **on** rely heavily on.
– ORIGIN Old English, of West Germanic origin, from Latin *pinna* 'point, tip, edge'.

pina colada /ˌpiːnə kəˈlɑːdə/ ■ n. a cocktail made with rum, pineapple juice, and coconut.
– ORIGIN from Spanish *piña colada* 'strained pineapple'.

pinafore ■ n. **1** (also **pinafore dress**) a collarless, sleeveless dress worn over a blouse or jumper. **2** Brit. a woman's loose sleeveless garment worn over clothes to keep them clean.
– ORIGIN C18: from PIN + archaic *afore* 'before' (because the term orig. denoted an apron with a bib pinned on the front of a dress).

pinball ■ n. a game in which small metal balls are shot across a sloping board and score points by striking various targets.

pinboard ■ n. a cork-covered board to which messages and pictures may be pinned for display.

pince-nez /ˈpãsneɪ/ ■ n. [treated as sing. or pl.] a pair of eyeglasses with a nose clip instead of earpieces.
– ORIGIN C19: from French, '(that) pinches (the) nose'.

pincer ■ n. **1** (**pincers**) a tool made of two pieces of metal bearing blunt concave jaws arranged like the blades of scissors, used for gripping and pulling things. **2** a front claw of a lobster, crab, or similar crustacean.
– ORIGIN Middle English: from Old French *pincier* 'to pinch'.

pincer movement ■ n. a movement by two separate bodies of troops converging on the enemy.

pinch ■ v. **1** grip (the flesh) tightly and sharply between finger and thumb. ▸ (of a shoe) hurt (a foot) by being too tight. ▸ [often as adj. **pinched**] tighten (the lips or a part of the face), especially with worry or tension. **2** live in a frugal way. **3** informal steal. **4** informal arrest (someone). **5** remove (buds or leaves) to encourage bushy growth. **6** Nautical sail (a boat) so close to the wind that the sails begin to lose power. ■ n. an act of pinching. ▸ an amount of an ingredient that can be held between fingers and thumb.
– PHRASES **at** (or N. Amer. **in**) **a pinch** if absolutely necessary. **feel the pinch** experience hardship, especially financial.
– ORIGIN Middle English: from a var. of Old French *pincier* 'to pinch'.

pinchbeck ■ n. an alloy of copper and zinc resembling gold, used in watchmaking and cheap jewellery. ■ adj. appearing valuable, but actually cheap or tawdry.
– ORIGIN C18: named after the English watchmaker Christopher *Pinchbeck*.

pinch-hit ■ v. Baseball & Cricket bat instead of another, typically at a critical point in the game.
– DERIVATIVES **pinch-hitter** n.

pinchpenny ■ n. (pl. **-ies**) a miserly person.

pinch-run ■ v. Baseball substitute for another as a base runner, typically at a critical point in the game.

pincushion ■ n. **1** a small pad for holding pins. **2** optical distortion in which straight lines along the edge of a screen or lens bulge towards the centre. **3** (also **pincushion protea**) a southern African shrub with rounded flower heads resembling pincushions. [Genus *Leucospermum*.]

pine[1] ■ n. **1** (also **pine tree**) an evergreen coniferous tree having clusters of long needle-shaped leaves, grown for its soft wood or for tar and turpentine. [Genus *Pinus*: many species.] ▸ used in names of coniferous trees of other families, e.g. Chile pine. **2** used in names of unrelated plants that resemble the pines in some way, e.g. screw pine.
– DERIVATIVES **piny** (also **piney**) adj.
– ORIGIN Old English, from Latin *pinus*, reinforced in Middle English by Old French *pin*.

pine[2] ■ v. suffer a mental and physical decline, especially because of a broken heart. ▸ (**pine for**) miss and long for the return of.
– ORIGIN Old English *pīnian* '(cause to) suffer', of Germanic origin, from Latin *poena* 'punishment'.

pineal eye ■ n. Zoology (in some reptiles and lower

vertebrates) an eye-like structure on the top of the head, covered by almost transparent skin and derived from or linked to the pineal gland.

pineal gland /ˈpɪnɪəl, ˈpʌɪ-/ (also **pineal body**) ■ n. a pea-sized conical mass of tissue behind the third ventricle of the brain, secreting a hormone-like substance in some mammals.
– ORIGIN C17: from French *pinéal*, from Latin *pinea* 'pine cone' (with ref. to the shape of the gland).

pineapple ■ n. **1** a large juicy tropical fruit consisting of aromatic edible yellow flesh surrounded by a tough segmented skin and topped with a tuft of stiff leaves. **2** the tropical American plant that bears this fruit, with a spiral of spiny sword-shaped leaves on a thick stem. [*Ananas comosus*.]
– ORIGIN Middle English: from PINE[1] + APPLE.

pineapple flower (also **pineapple lily**) ■ n. a bulbous South African plant with a cluster of flowers surmounted by bracts resembling a pineapple. [Genus *Eucomis*: several species.]

pine cone ■ n. the conical or rounded woody fruit of a pine tree, with scales which open to release the seeds.

pine marten ■ n. an arboreal Eurasian weasel-like mammal with a dark brown coat. [*Martes martes*.]

pine nut ■ n. the edible seed of various pine trees.

pinetum /pʌɪˈniːtəm/ ■ n. (pl. **pineta** /-tə/) a plantation of pine trees or other conifers for scientific or ornamental purposes.
– ORIGIN C19: from Latin, from *pinus* 'pine'.

pin feather ■ n. Ornithology an immature feather, before the veins have expanded and while the shaft is full of fluid.

pinfold ■ n. historical a pound for stray animals.
– ORIGIN Old English *pundfald*, from a base shared by POND and POUND[3] + FOLD[2].

ping ■ n. an abrupt high-pitched ringing sound. ■ v. **1** make or cause to make such a sound. **2** another term for PINK[4].
– DERIVATIVES **pinger** n.
– ORIGIN C19: imitative.

pingo /ˈpɪŋɡəʊ/ ■ n. (pl. **-os**) Geology a dome-shaped mound consisting of a layer of soil over a large core of ice, occurring in permafrost areas.
– ORIGIN 1920S: from Inuit *pinguq* 'nunatak'.

ping-pong ■ n. informal term for TABLE TENNIS.
– ORIGIN C20: imitative of the sound of a bat striking a ball.

pinhead ■ n. **1** the flattened head of a pin. **2** informal a stupid person.

pinhole ■ n. a very small hole.

pinhole camera ■ n. a camera with a pinhole aperture and no lens.

pinion[1] /ˈpɪnjən/ ■ n. the outer part of a bird's wing including the flight feathers. ■ v. **1** tie or hold the arms or legs of. **2** cut off the pinion of (a bird) to prevent flight.
– ORIGIN Middle English: from Old French *pignon*, from Latin *pinna*, *penna* 'feather'.

pinion[2] /ˈpɪnjən/ ■ n. a small cogwheel or spindle engaging with a large cogwheel.
– ORIGIN C17: from French *pignon*, from Latin *pinea* 'pine cone'.

pink[1] ■ adj. **1** of a colour intermediate between red and white, as of coral or salmon. **2** informal, often derogatory left-wing. **3** of or associated with homosexuals: *the pink economy*. ■ n. **1** pink colour, pigment, or material. **2** (**the pink**) informal the best condition or degree. **3** informal, often derogatory a left-wing person.
– DERIVATIVES **pinkish** adj. **pinkly** adv. **pinkness** n. **pinky** adj.
– ORIGIN C17: from PINK[2].

pink[2] ■ n. a plant with sweet-smelling pink or white flowers and slender grey-green leaves. [Genus *Dianthus*.]
– ORIGIN C16: perhaps short for *pink eye* 'small or half-shut eye'.

pink[3] ■ v. cut a scalloped or zigzag edge on.
– ORIGIN C16: cf. Low German *pinken* 'strike, peck'.

pink[4] (also **ping**) ■ v. (of a vehicle engine) make rattling sounds as a result of over-rapid combustion of the fuel–air mixture in the cylinders.
– ORIGIN C20: imitative.

pink[5] ■ n. historical a small square-rigged sailing ship with a narrow, overhanging stern.
– ORIGIN C15: from Middle Dutch *pin(c)ke*.

pink-collar ■ adj. relating to or denoting work traditionally associated with women.

pink elephants ■ pl. n. informal hallucinations supposedly typical of those experienced by a person who is drunk.

pink-eye ■ n. **1** a viral disease of horses, symptoms of which include fever, abortion, and redness of the eyes. **2** conjunctivitis in humans and some livestock.

pink gin ■ n. gin flavoured with angostura bitters.

pinkie ■ n. informal the little finger.
– ORIGIN C19: partly from Dutch *pink* 'the little finger'.

pinking shears ■ pl. n. shears with a serrated blade, used to cut a zigzag edge in fabric to prevent it fraying.

pink noise ■ n. Physics random noise having equal energy per octave, and so having more low-frequency components than white noise.

pinko ■ n. (pl. **-os** or **-oes**) informal, derogatory a person with left-wing or liberal views.

pink slip ■ n. N. Amer. informal a notice of dismissal from employment.

pin money ■ n. a small sum of money for spending on inessentials.
– ORIGIN C17: orig. denoting an allowance to a woman from her husband for dress and other personal expenses.

pinna /ˈpɪnə/ ■ n. (pl. **pinnae** /-niː/) **1** Anatomy & Zoology the external part of the ear in humans and other mammals; the auricle. **2** Botany a primary division of a pinnate leaf, especially of a fern. **3** Zoology any of a number of animal structures resembling fins or wings.
– ORIGIN C18: from a var. of Latin *penna* 'feather, wing, fin'.

pinnace /ˈpɪnɪs/ ■ n. chiefly historical a small boat forming part of the equipment of a warship or other large vessel.
– ORIGIN C16: from French *pinace*, prob. from Latin *pinus* (see PINE[1]).

pinnacle ■ n. **1** a high pointed piece of rock. **2** a small pointed turret built as an ornament on a roof. **3** the most successful point: *the pinnacle of his career*.
– DERIVATIVES **pinnacled** adj.
– ORIGIN Middle English: from late Latin *pinnaculum*, diminutive of *pinna* 'wing, point'.

pinnae plural form of PINNA.

pinnate ■ adj. Botany & Zoology having leaflets or other parts arranged on either side of a stem or axis like the vanes of a feather.
– DERIVATIVES **pinnately** adv. **pinnation** /-ˈneɪʃ(ə)n/ n.
– ORIGIN C18: from Latin *pinnatus* 'feathered', from *pinna*, *penna* (see PINNA).

pinniped /ˈpɪnɪpɛd/ ■ n. Zoology a carnivorous aquatic mammal of an order (Pinnipedia) which comprises the seals, sea lions, and walrus.
– ORIGIN from Latin *pinna* 'wing, fin' + *pes*, *ped-* 'foot'.

pinnule /ˈpɪnjuːl/ ■ n. Botany a secondary division of a pinnate leaf.
– ORIGIN C16: from Latin *pinnula* 'small wing', diminutive of *pinna*.

PIN number ■ n. see PIN.

pinny ■ n. (pl. **-ies**) informal a pinafore.

pinochle /ˈpiːnɒk(ə)l/ ■ n. a North American card game for two or more players using a 48-card pack consisting of two of each card from nine to ace, the object being to score points for various combinations and to win tricks.
▸ the combination of queen of spades and jack of diamonds in this game.
– ORIGIN C19.

pinocytosis /ˌpɪnəʊsʌɪˈtəʊsɪs, ˌpɪnəʊ-, ˌpaɪnəʊ-/ ■ n. Biology the ingestion of liquid into a cell by the budding of small vesicles from the cell membrane.
– ORIGIN C19: from Greek *pino* 'drink' + *-cytosis*.

Pinot /ˈpiːnəʊ/ ■ n. any of several varieties of wine grape, especially Pinot Noir (black) and Pinot Blanc (white).
– ORIGIN French, var. of earlier *Pineau*, diminutive of *pin* 'pine' (because of the shape of the grape cluster).

pinotage /ˈpɪnə(ʊ)tɑːʒ/ ■ n. a variety of red wine grape grown in South Africa, produced by crossing Pinot Noir and other varieties. ▶ a red wine made from this grape.
– ORIGIN blend of *Pinot* (*Noir*) and *Hermitage*, names of types of grape.

pinout ■ n. Electronics a diagram showing the arrangement of pins on an integrated circuit and their functions.

pinpoint ■ n. a tiny dot or point. ■ adj. absolutely precise: *pinpoint accuracy*. ■ v. find or locate exactly.

pinprick ■ n. **1** a prick caused by a pin. **2** a very small dot or amount.

pins and needles ■ pl. n. [treated as sing.] a tingling sensation in a limb recovering from numbness.

pinspot ■ n. a small powerful spotlight.

pinstripe ■ n. a very narrow stripe in cloth, especially of the type used for formal suits.
– DERIVATIVES **pinstriped** adj.

pint ■ n. a unit of liquid or dry capacity equal to one eighth of a gallon, in Britain equal to 0.568 litre and in the US equal to 0.473 litre (for liquid measure) or 0.551 litre (for dry measure). ▶ informal a pint of beer.
– ORIGIN Middle English: from Old French *pinte*.

pintail ■ n. a duck with a long pointed tail. [*Anas acuta* and related species.]

pintle /ˈpɪnt(ə)l/ ■ n. a pin or bolt on which a rudder turns.
– ORIGIN Old English *pintel* 'penis', perhaps a diminutive.

pinto /ˈpɪntəʊ/ ■ n. N. Amer. (pl. **-os**) a piebald horse.
– ORIGIN C19: from Spanish, 'mottled'.

pinto bean ■ n. a medium-sized speckled variety of kidney bean.
– ORIGIN C20: from PINTO, because of the mottled appearance of the bean.

pint-sized ■ adj. informal very small.

pin-tuck ■ n. a very narrow ornamental tuck.

pin-up ■ n. a poster featuring a sexually attractive person, especially a famous one. ▶ a famous person regarded as sexually attractive.

pinwheel ■ n. **1** a small Catherine-wheel firework. **2** something shaped or rotating like a pinwheel. ■ v. spin or rotate like a pinwheel.

pinworm ■ n. a small nematode worm which is an internal parasite of vertebrates. [Family Oxyuridae.]

Pinyin /pɪnˈjɪn/ ■ n. the standard system of romanized spelling for transliterating Chinese.
– ORIGIN 1960s: from Chinese *pīn-yīn* 'spell-sound'.

piolet /pjəʊˈleɪ/ ■ n. Climbing an ice pick.
– ORIGIN C19: from French dialect, 'little pick'.

pion /ˈpaɪɒn/ ■ n. Physics a meson having a mass approximately 270 times that of an electron.
– DERIVATIVES **pionic** adj.
– ORIGIN 1950s: from PI (the letter used as a symbol for the particle) + **-ON**.

pioneer ■ n. **1** a person who is the first to explore or settle a new country or area. ▶ a plant or animal that is among the first to become established in an area. **2** an innovator or developer of new ideas or techniques. **3** a member of an infantry group preparing roads or terrain for the main body of troops. ■ v. **1** be a pioneer of. **2** open up (a road or terrain) as a pioneer.
– DERIVATIVES **pioneering** adj.
– ORIGIN C16: from French *pionnier* 'foot soldier, pioneer'.

pious ■ adj. **1** devoutly religious. **2** making a hypocritical display of virtue. **3** (of a hope) sincere but unlikely to be fulfilled.
– DERIVATIVES **piously** adv. **piousness** n.
– ORIGIN Middle English: from Latin *pius* 'dutiful, pious'.

pip[1] ■ n. a small hard seed in a fruit. ▶ S. African the stone of fruits such as peaches and plums.
– DERIVATIVES **pipless** adj.
– ORIGIN C18: abbrev. of PIPPIN.

pip[2] ■ n. (**the pips**) chiefly Brit. a series of short high-pitched sounds, as used to indicate a time check on the radio or to instruct a caller using a pay telephone to insert more money.
– ORIGIN C20: imitative.

pip[3] ■ n. **1** a star (1–3 according to rank) on the shoulder of an army officer's uniform. **2** any of the spots on a playing card, dice, or domino. **3** an image of an object on a radar screen.
– ORIGIN C16 (orig. *peep*, in the sense 'spot').

pip[4] ■ n. a disease of poultry or other birds causing thick mucus in the throat and white scale on the tongue.
– ORIGIN Middle English: from Middle Dutch *pippe*, prob. from Latin *pituita* 'slime'.

pip[5] ■ v. (**pipped**, **pipping**) informal (usu. **be pipped**) defeat by a small margin or at the last moment.
– PHRASES **pip someone at** (or **to**) **the post** defeat someone at the last moment.
– ORIGIN C19: from PIP[1] or PIP[3].

pipal /ˈpiːp(ə)l/ ■ n. variant spelling of PEEPUL.

pipe ■ n. **1** a tube used to convey water, gas, oil, or other fluids. **2** a device used for smoking tobacco, consisting of a narrow tube with a bowl at one end in which the tobacco is burned, the smoke from which is then drawn into the mouth. **3** a wind instrument consisting of a single tube with holes along its length that are covered by the fingers to produce different notes. ▶ (**pipes**) bagpipes. ▶ (**pipes**) a set of musical pipes joined together, as in pan pipes. ▶ any of the cylindrical tubes by which notes are produced in an organ. ▶ a boatswain's whistle. **4** a high-pitched cry or song, especially of a bird. **5** a cylindrical vein of ore or rock, especially one in which diamonds are found. **6** a large cask for wine, especially as a measure equal to two hogsheads. ■ v. **1** convey through a pipe or pipes. **2** transmit (music, a programme, a signal, etc.) by wire or cable. **3** play (a tune) on a pipe. **4** sing or say in a high, shrill voice. **5** decorate with piping. **6** propagate (a pink or similar plant) by taking a cutting at the joint of a stem.
– PHRASES **put that in one's pipe and smoke it** informal one will have to accept a particular fact, even if it is unwelcome.
– PHRASAL VERBS **pipe someone away** (or **down**) Nautical dismiss someone from duty. **pipe something away** Nautical give a signal for a boat to start. **pipe down** informal stop talking; be less noisy. **pipe up** say something suddenly.
– DERIVATIVES **pipeful** n. (pl. **-fuls**).
– ORIGIN Old English *pipe* 'musical tube', *pīpian* 'play a pipe', of Germanic origin, from Latin *pipare* 'to peep, chirp'.

pipeclay ■ n. a fine white clay, used especially for making tobacco pipes or for whitening leather. ■ v. whiten with pipeclay.

pipe cleaner ■ n. a piece of wire covered with fibre, used to clean a tobacco pipe.

piped music ■ n. pre-recorded background music played through loudspeakers.

pipe dream ■ n. an unattainable or fanciful hope or scheme.
– ORIGIN C19: referring to a dream experienced when smoking an opium pipe.

pipefish ■ n. (pl. same or **-fishes**) a narrow, elongated, marine fish with segmented bony armour beneath the skin and a long tubular snout. [*Syngnathus* and other genera: numerous species.]

pipeline ■ n. **1** a long pipe for conveying oil, gas, etc. over long distances. **2** (in surfing) the hollow formed by the breaking of a large wave. **3** Computing a linear sequence of specialized modules used for pipelining. ■ v. **1** convey by a pipeline. **2** Computing design or execute using the technique of pipelining.
– PHRASES **in the pipeline** in the process of being developed.

pipelining ■ n. **1** the laying of pipelines. ▶ transportation by pipeline. **2** Computing a form of computer organization in which successive steps of an instruction sequence are executed in turn, so that another instruction can be begun before the previous one is finished.

pipe organ ■ n. Music an organ using pipes instead of or as well as reeds.

piper ■ n. a person who plays a pipe or bagpipes.

pipette /pɪˈpɛt/ ■ n. a slender tube with a bulb at one end, filled by sucking liquid into the tube, used for transferring

piping

or measuring out quantities of the liquid. ■ v. pour or draw off using a pipette.
– ORIGIN C19: from French, 'little pipe'.

piping ■ n. 1 lengths of pipe. 2 thin lines of icing or cream, used to decorate cakes and desserts. 3 thin cord covered in fabric, used for decoration and to reinforce seams. 4 the action or art of playing a pipe or pipes.
– PHRASES **piping hot** (of food or water) very hot.

pipistrelle /ˌpɪpɪˈstrɛl, ˈpɪp-/ ■ n. a small insect-eating bat. [Genus *Pipistrellus*.]
– ORIGIN C18: from Italian *pipistrello*, from Latin *vespertilio(n-)* 'bat', from *vesper* 'evening'.

pipit /ˈpɪpɪt/ ■ n. a mainly ground-dwelling songbird of open country, typically having brown streaky plumage. [*Anthus* and other genera.]
– ORIGIN C18: prob. imitative.

pipkin ■ n. a small earthenware pot.
– ORIGIN C16.

pippin ■ n. a red and yellow dessert apple.
– ORIGIN Middle English: from Old French *pepin*.

pipsqueak ■ n. informal an insignificant or contemptible person.

piquant /ˈpiːk(ə)nt, -kɒnt/ ■ adj. 1 having a pleasantly sharp taste or appetizing flavour. 2 pleasantly stimulating or exciting to the mind.
– DERIVATIVES **piquancy** n. **piquantly** adv.
– ORIGIN C16: from French, 'stinging, pricking', from *piquer*.

pique /piːk/ ■ n. a feeling of irritation or resentment resulting from a slight, especially to one's pride: *he left in a fit of pique.* ■ v. (**piques, piqued, piquing**) 1 stimulate (interest or curiosity). 2 (**be piqued**) feel irritated or resentful.
– ORIGIN C16: from French *piquer* 'prick, irritate'.

piqué /ˈpiːkeɪ/ ■ n. firm fabric woven in a ribbed or raised pattern.
– ORIGIN C19: from French, 'backstitched', from *piquer*.

piquet /pɪˈkɛt/ ■ n. a trick-taking card game for two players, using a 32-card pack consisting of the seven to the ace only.
– ORIGIN C17: from French.

PIR ■ abbrev. passive infrared.

piracy ■ n. 1 the practice of attacking and robbing ships at sea. ▶ a similar practice in other contexts, especially hijacking. 2 the unauthorized use or reproduction of another's work: *software piracy*.

piranha /pɪˈrɑːnə, -njə/ ■ n. a deep-bodied South American freshwater fish having very sharp teeth that it uses to tear flesh from prey. [*Serrosalmus* and other genera: several species.]
– ORIGIN C18: from Tupi *piráa* 'fish' + *sainha* 'tooth'.

pirate ■ n. 1 a person who attacks and robs ships at sea. 2 [often as modifier] a person who appropriates or reproduces the work of another for profit without permission: *pirate recordings*. ▶ [often as modifier] a person or organization broadcasting without official authorization: *a pirate radio station.* ■ v. 1 dated rob or plunder (a ship). 2 [often as adj. **pirated**] use or reproduce (another's work) for profit without permission.
– DERIVATIVES **piratic** adj. **piratical** adj. **piratically** adv.
– ORIGIN Middle English: from Latin *pirata*, from Greek *peiratēs*, from *peirein* 'to attempt, attack'.

piri piri /ˈpɪriˌpɪri/ ■ n. variant spelling of **PERI PERI**.

pirogue /pɪˈrəʊg/ ■ n. a long narrow canoe made from a single tree trunk.
– ORIGIN C17: from French, prob. from Carib.

pirouette /ˌpɪruˈɛt/ ■ n. (in ballet) an act of spinning on one foot, typically with the raised foot touching the knee of the supporting leg. ■ v. perform a pirouette.
– ORIGIN C17: from French, 'spinning top'.

piscatorial /ˌpɪskəˈtɔːrɪəl/ (also **piscatory**) ■ adj. of or concerning fishing.
– ORIGIN C19: from Latin, from *piscator* 'fisherman', from *piscis* 'fish'.

Pisces /ˈpaɪsiːz, ˈpɪskiːz/ ■ n. 1 Astronomy a large constellation (the Fish or Fishes), said to represent a pair of fishes tied together by their tails. 2 Astrology the twelfth sign of the zodiac, which the sun enters about 20 February.
– DERIVATIVES **Piscean** /ˈpaɪsɪən/ n. & adj.
– ORIGIN Latin, pl. of *piscis* 'fish'.

pisciculture /ˈpɪsɪˌkʌltʃə/ ■ n. the controlled breeding and rearing of fish.
– DERIVATIVES **piscicultural** adj. **pisciculturist** n.
– ORIGIN C19: from Latin *piscis* 'fish' + **CULTURE**.

piscine /ˈpɪsaɪn/ ■ adj. of or relating to fish.
– ORIGIN C18: from Latin *piscis* 'fish'.

piscivorous /pɪˈsɪv(ə)rəs/ ■ adj. Zoology feeding on fish.
– DERIVATIVES **piscivore** n.
– ORIGIN C17: from Latin *piscis* 'fish' + **-VOROUS**.

piss vulgar slang ■ v. urinate. ■ n. urine. ▶ an act of urinating.
– PHRASES **be** (or **go**) **on the piss** Brit. be engaged in (or go on) a heavy drinking session. **a piece of piss** a very easy thing to do. **piss in the wind** do something that is ineffective. **take the piss** tease or mock someone or something.
– PHRASAL VERBS **piss about/around** Brit. mess around. **piss off** go away. **piss someone off** annoy someone.
– DERIVATIVES **pisser** n.
– ORIGIN Middle English: from Old French *pisser*, prob. of imitative origin.

piss artist ■ n. Brit. vulgar slang 1 a drunkard. 2 an incompetent or useless person.

pissed ■ adj. vulgar slang 1 drunk. 2 (**pissed off**) or N. Amer. **pissed** very annoyed.

piss-up ■ n. vulgar slang a heavy drinking session.

pistachio /pɪˈstɑːʃɪəʊ, pɪˈstatʃəʊ/ ■ n. (pl. **-os**) 1 (also **pistachio nut**) the edible pale green seed of an Asian tree. 2 the evergreen tree which produces this nut, with small brownish-green flowers and oval reddish fruit. [*Pistacia vera*.] 3 a pale green colour.
– ORIGIN Middle English *pistace*, from Old French, later influenced by Italian *pistaccio*, from Greek *pistakion*, from Old Persian.

piste /piːst/ ■ n. a course or run for skiing.
– ORIGIN French, 'racetrack'.

pistil /ˈpɪstɪl/ ■ n. Botany the female organs of a flower, comprising the stigma, style, and ovary.
– ORIGIN C18: from French *pistile* or Latin *pistillum* 'pestle'.

pistillate /ˈpɪstɪlət/ ■ adj. Botany having pistils but no stamens. Compare with **STAMINATE**.

pistol ■ n. a small firearm designed to be held in one hand.
– ORIGIN C16: from obsolete French *pistole*, from German *Pistole*, from Czech *pišt'ala*, orig. in sense 'whistle', hence 'a firearm' by the resemblance in shape.

pistoleer /ˌpɪstəˈlɪə/ ■ n. archaic a soldier armed with a pistol.

pistol grip ■ n. a handle shaped like the butt of a pistol.

pistol-whip ■ v. hit or beat with the butt of a pistol.

piston /ˈpɪst(ə)n/ ■ n. 1 a disc or short cylinder fitting closely within a tube in which it moves up and down against a liquid or gas, used in an internal-combustion engine to derive motion, or in a pump to impart motion. 2 a valve in a brass instrument, depressed to alter the pitch of a note.
– ORIGIN C18: from Italian *pistone*, var. of *pestone* 'large pestle'.

piston ring ■ n. a ring on a piston sealing the gap between the piston and the cylinder wall.

piston rod ■ n. a rod or crankshaft attached to a piston to drive a wheel or to impart motion.

pit¹ ■ n. 1 a large hole in the ground. ▶ a mine or excavation for coal or minerals. 2 an area at the side of a track where racing cars are serviced and refuelled. ▶ a sunken area in a workshop floor allowing access to a car's underside. 3 a hollow or indentation in a surface. 4 short for orchestra pit (see **ORCHESTRA**). 5 a part of the floor of an exchange in which a particular stock or commodity is traded. 6 chiefly historical an enclosure in which animals are made to fight: *a bear pit.* 7 (**the pits**) informal a very bad place or situation: *this really is the pits!* 8 Brit. informal a person's bed. ■ v. (**pitted, pitting**) 1 (**pit someone/thing**

against) set someone or something in conflict or competition with. **2** make a hollow or indentation in the surface of. ▶ sink in or contract so as to form a hollow. **3** drive a racing car into the pit.
—PHRASES **the pit of the stomach** the region of the lower abdomen.
—DERIVATIVES **pitted** adj.
—ORIGIN Old English *pytt*, of West Germanic origin, from Latin *puteus* 'well, shaft'; sense 1 of the verb derives from the former practice of setting animals to fight each other in a pit.

pit² ■ n. the stone of a fruit. ■ v. (**pitted, pitting**) remove the pit from (fruit).
—DERIVATIVES **pitted** adj.
—ORIGIN C19: apparently from Dutch; rel. to PITH.

pita (also **pitta**) ■ n. flat hollow unleavened bread which can be split open to hold a filling.
—ORIGIN modern Greek, 'cake or pie'.

pit-a-pat (also **pitapat**) ■ adv. with a sound like quick light taps. ■ n. a sound of this kind.
—ORIGIN C16: imitative of alternating sounds.

pit bull terrier ■ n. a dog of an American variety of bull terrier, noted for its ferocity.

pitch¹ ■ n. **1** the quality of a sound governed by the rate of vibrations producing it; the degree of highness or lowness of a tone. **2** the steepness of a slope, especially of a roof. ▶ Climbing a section of a climb. **3** a level of intensity, especially a high level: *he brought the machine to a high pitch of development*. **4** an area of ground marked out or used for play in an outdoor team game. ▶ Cricket the strip of ground between the two sets of stumps. **5** Baseball a delivery of the ball by the pitcher. ▶ (also **pitch shot**) Golf a high approach shot on to the green. **6** a form of words used to persuade or influence: *they were impressed by his sales pitch*. **7** Brit. a place where a street vendor or performer stations themselves or sets up a stall. **8** a swaying or oscillation of a ship, aircraft, or vehicle around a horizontal axis perpendicular to the direction of motion. **9** technical the distance between successive corresponding points or lines, for example between the teeth of a cogwheel. ■ v. **1** set at a particular musical pitch. **2** throw or fall heavily or roughly: *she pitched forward into blackness*. **3** Baseball throw (the ball) for the batter. ▶ (**pitch something up**) Cricket bowl a ball so that it bounces near the batsman. ▶ Golf hit (the ball) on to the green with a pitch shot. ▶ Cricket & Golf (of the ball) strike the ground in a particular spot. **4** set or aim at a particular level, target, or audience: *he should pitch his talk at a suitable level*. **5** make a bid to obtain a contract or other business. ▶ try to persuade someone to buy or accept (something). **6** set up and fix in position. **7** (**pitch in**) informal join in enthusiastically with a task or activity. **8** (**pitch up**) informal arrive. **9** (of a moving ship, aircraft, or vehicle) rock or oscillate around a lateral axis, so that the front moves up and down. **10** [often as adj. **pitched**] (chiefly with reference to a roof) slope or cause to slope downwards: *a pitched roof*. **11** pave (a road) with stones.
—PHRASES **make a pitch** make an attempt at or bid for something.
—ORIGIN Middle English: perhaps rel. to Old English *picung* 'stigmata'.

pitch² ■ n. a sticky resinous black or dark brown substance which hardens on cooling, obtained by distilling tar or turpentine and used for waterproofing.
—ORIGIN Old English *pic* (n.), *pician* (v.), of Germanic origin.

pitch and putt ■ n. a form of golf played on a miniature course.

pitch-black (also **pitch-dark**) ■ adj. completely dark.
—DERIVATIVES **pitch-blackness** n.

pitchblende /ˈpɪtʃblɛnd/ ■ n. a form of the mineral uraninite occurring in brown or black pitch-like masses and containing radium.
—ORIGIN C18: from German *Pechblende*, from *Pech* 'pitch' + *Blende*, from *blenden* 'deceive'.

pitched battle ■ n. a battle in which the time and place are determined beforehand, rather than a casual or chance skirmish.

pitcher¹ ■ n. a large jug.
—DERIVATIVES **pitcherful** n. (pl. **-fuls**)
—ORIGIN Middle English: from Old French *pichier* 'pot', from late Latin *picarium*.

897 **pit pony**

pitcher² /ˈpɪtʃə/ ■ n. **1** Baseball the player who pitches the ball. **2** a stone used for paving.

pitcher plant ■ n. a plant with a deep pitcher-shaped fluid-filled pouch in which insects are trapped and absorbed. [Many species, chiefly in the families Sarraceniaceae (New World) and Nepenthaceae (Old World).]

pitchfork ■ n. a farm tool with a long handle and two sharp metal prongs, used for lifting hay. ■ v. **1** lift with a pitchfork. **2** thrust suddenly into an unexpected and difficult situation: *an ordinary intellect pitchforked into power*.
—ORIGIN Middle English: from earlier *pickfork*, influenced by PITCH¹ in the sense 'throw'.

pitchman ■ n. (pl. **-men** /-mɛn/) N. Amer. informal a person delivering a sales pitch.

pitchout ■ n. **1** Baseball a pitch thrown intentionally beyond the reach of the batter to allow the catcher a clear throw at an advancing base runner. **2** American Football a lateral pass.

pitch pine ■ n. a pine tree with hard, heavy, resinous wood.

pitch pipe ■ n. Music a small pipe used to set the correct pitch for the voice or another instrument.

pitchpole ■ v. Nautical (of a boat) overturn so that the stern pitches forward over the bows.
—ORIGIN C17: from PITCH¹ + POLL.

pitchstone ■ n. Geology a dull vitreous rock resembling hardened pitch, formed by weathering of obsidian.

pitchy ■ adj. (**-ier, -iest**) of, like, or as dark as pitch.

piteous ■ adj. deserving or arousing pity.
—DERIVATIVES **piteously** adv. **piteousness** n.
—ORIGIN Middle English: from Old French *piteus*, from Latin *pietas* (see PIETY).

pitfall ■ n. **1** a hidden or unsuspected danger or difficulty. **2** a covered pit for use as a trap.

pith ■ n. **1** spongy white tissue lining the rind of citrus fruits. ▶ Botany the spongy cellular tissue in the stems and branches of many higher plants. **2** the true nature or essence: *the pith and core of socialism*. **3** vigorous and concise expression.
—DERIVATIVES **pithless** adj.
—ORIGIN Old English *pitha*, of West Germanic origin.

pithead ■ n. the top of a mineshaft and the area around it.

pith helmet ■ n. a head covering made from the dried pith of the sola or a similar plant, used for protection from the sun.

pithy ■ adj. (**-ier, -iest**) **1** (of a fruit or plant) containing much pith. **2** (of language or style) terse and vigorously expressive.
—DERIVATIVES **pithily** adv. **pithiness** n.

pitiable ■ adj. **1** deserving or arousing pity. **2** contemptibly poor or small.
—DERIVATIVES **pitiableness** n. **pitiably** adv.

pitiful ■ adj. **1** deserving or arousing pity. ▶ archaic compassionate. **2** very small or poor; inadequate: *a pitiful attempt*.
—DERIVATIVES **pitifully** adv. **pitifulness** n.

pitiless ■ adj. showing no pity; harsh or cruel.
—DERIVATIVES **pitilessly** adv. **pitilessness** n.

pit latrine ■ n. a toilet consisting of a hole in the ground, sometimes with a seat over it.

pitman ■ n. (pl. **-men**) a coal miner.

piton /ˈpiːtɒn/ ■ n. a peg or spike driven into a crack to support a climber or a rope.
—ORIGIN C19: from French, 'eye bolt'.

pitot /ˈpiːtəʊ/ (also **pitot tube**) ■ n. a device for measuring the speed of flow of a fluid, consisting of or containing an open-ended right-angled tube pointing in opposition to the flow.
—ORIGIN C19: named after the C18 French physicist Henri Pitot.

pit pony ■ n. Brit. historical a pony used to haul loads in a coal mine.

pit saw ■ n. historical a large saw with handles at the top and bottom, used in a vertical position by two men, one standing above the timber to be cut, the other in a pit below it.

pit stop ■ n. Motor Racing a brief stop at a pit for servicing and refuelling. ▶ informal a brief rest during a journey.

pitta[1] /ˈpɪtə/ ■ n. variant spelling of PITA.

pitta[2] /ˈpɪtə/ ■ n. a small ground-dwelling thrush-like bird with brightly coloured plumage and a very short tail, found in the Old World tropics. [Genus *Pitta*: many species.]
– ORIGIN C19: from Telugu *piṭṭa* '(young) bird'.

pittance ■ n. a very small or inadequate amount of money.
– ORIGIN Middle English: from Old French *pitance*, from medieval Latin *pitantia*, from Latin *pietas* 'pity'.

pitter-patter ■ n. a sound as of quick light steps or taps. ■ adv. with this sound.
– ORIGIN Middle English: reduplication of PATTER[1].

pit toilet ■ n. another term for PIT LATRINE.

pituitary /pɪˈtjuːɪt(ə)ri/ ■ n. (pl. **-ies**) (in full **pituitary gland** or **pituitary body**) the major endocrine gland, a pea-sized body attached to the base of the brain that is important in controlling growth and the functioning of the other endocrine glands.
– ORIGIN C17: from Latin *pituitarius* 'secreting phlegm'.

pit viper ■ n. a venomous snake of a group found in both America and Asia, distinguished by visible sensory pits on the head which can detect prey by heat. [Numerous genera and species, including the rattlesnakes.]

pity ■ n. (pl. **-ies**) **1** the feeling of sorrow and compassion caused by the sufferings of others. **2** a cause for regret or disappointment: *what a pity*. ■ v. (**-ies**, **-ied**) feel pity for.
– PHRASES **for pity's sake** informal used to express impatience or make an urgent appeal. **more's the pity** informal used to express regret.
– DERIVATIVES **pitying** adj. **pityingly** adv.
– ORIGIN Middle English: from Old French *pite* 'compassion', from Latin *pietas* 'piety'.

pityriasis /ˌpɪtɪˈraɪəsɪs/ ■ n. Medicine a skin disease characterized by the shedding of fine flaky scales.
– ORIGIN C17: from Greek *pituriasis* 'scurf'.

pivot ■ n. **1** the central point, pin, or shaft on which a mechanism turns or oscillates. **2** a person or thing playing a central part in an activity or organization. **3** the person or position from which a body of troops takes its reference point when moving or changing course. ■ v. (**pivoted**, **pivoting**) **1** turn on or as if on a pivot. ▶ provide with or fix on a pivot. **2** (**pivot on**) depend on.
– ORIGIN Middle English: from French, prob. from dialect *pue* 'tooth of a comb' and Spanish *pu(y)a* 'point'.

pivotal ■ adj. **1** fixed on or as if on a pivot. **2** of crucial or central importance.

pixel /ˈpɪks(ə)l, -sɛl/ ■ n. Electronics a minute area of illumination on a display screen, one of many from which an image is composed.
– ORIGIN 1960s: abbrev. of *picture element*.

pixelate /ˈpɪksəleɪt/ (also **pixellate** or **pixilate**) ■ v. divide (an image) into pixels, typically for display or storage in a digital format. ▶ display (a person's image) as a small number of large pixels, typically in order to disguise someone's identity.
– DERIVATIVES **pixelation** n.

pixie (also **pixy**) ■ n. (pl. **-ies**) a supernatural being in folklore, typically portrayed as small and human-like in form, with pointed ears and a pointed hat.
– DERIVATIVES **pixieish** adj.
– ORIGIN C17.

pixilate ■ v. variant spelling of PIXELATE.

pizza /ˈpiːtsə, ˈpɪtsə/ ■ n. a dish of Italian origin, consisting of a flat, round base of dough baked with a topping of tomatoes, cheese, and other ingredients.
– ORIGIN Italian, 'pie'.

pizzazz (also **pizazz** or **pzazz**) ■ n. informal an attractive combination of vitality and style.
– ORIGIN said to have been invented by Diana Vreeland, fashion editor of *Harper's Bazaar* in the 1930s.

pizzeria /ˌpiːtsəˈriːə, ˌpɪtsə-/ ■ n. a place where pizzas are made, sold, or eaten.
– ORIGIN from Italian.

pizzicato /ˌpɪtsɪˈkɑːtəʊ/ Music ■ adv. & adj. plucking the strings of a violin or other stringed instrument with one's finger. ■ n. (pl. **pizzicatos** or **pizzicati** /-ti/) this technique of playing. ▶ a note or passage played in this way.
– ORIGIN Italian, 'pinched, twitched', from *pizzicare*, from *pizza* 'point, edge'.

PJs ■ pl. n. informal pyjamas.

pk ■ abbrev. **1** pack. **2** (also **Pk**) park. **3** peak.

PKU ■ abbrev. phenylketonuria.

P & L ■ abbrev. profit and loss account.

pl. ■ abbrev. **1** (also **Pl.**) place. **2** plate (referring to illustrations in a book). **3** plural.

PLA ■ abbrev. **1** People's Liberation Army. **2** (in the UK) Port of London Authority.

placable /ˈplakəb(ə)l/ ■ adj. archaic easily calmed or placated.

placard /ˈplakɑːd/ ■ n. a sign for public display, either posted on a wall or carried during a demonstration. ■ v. /also plaˈkɑːd/ cover with placards.
– ORIGIN C15: from Old French *placquart*, from *plaquier* 'to plaster, lay flat'.

placate /pləˈkeɪt, ˈplakeɪt, ˈpleɪ-/ ■ v. calm, pacify, or appease.
– DERIVATIVES **placating** adj. **placatingly** adv. **placation** n. **placatory** adj.
– ORIGIN C17: from Latin *placare* 'appease'.

place ■ n. **1** a particular position or point in space; a location. ▶ informal a person's home. ▶ a point in a book reached by a reader at a particular time. **2** a portion of space available or designated for someone. ▶ a vacancy or available position: *a place at university*. ▶ the regular or proper position of something: *lay each slab in place*. **3** a position in a sequence or hierarchy. ▶ a person's rank or status. ▶ a specific role or position: *it's not my place to ask*. ▶ Brit. any of the first three or sometimes four positions in a race. ▶ N. Amer. the second position, especially in a horse race. **4** the position of a figure in a series indicated in decimal notation: *calculate the ratios to one decimal place*. **5** [in place names] a square or short street. ■ v. **1** put in a particular position. **2** find an appropriate place or role for. ▶ arrange for the implementation of (an order, bet, etc.). ▶ order or obtain a connection for (a telephone call). ▶ dispose of (something, especially shares) by selling. ▶ allocate or award a specified position in a sequence or hierarchy. ▶ (**be placed**) Brit. achieve a specified position in a race. ▶ be among the first three or four in a race (or the first three in the US). **4** remember the relevant background of: *she said she couldn't place him*. **5** Rugby & American Football score (a goal) by a place kick.
– PHRASES **give place to** be succeeded or replaced by. **go places** informal **1** travel. **2** be increasingly successful. **in one's place** in one's appropriate (but inferior) position or status. **in place 1** working or ready to work; established. **2** N. Amer. on the spot; not travelling any distance. **in place of** instead of. **out of place** not in the proper position. ▶ in a setting where one is or feels inappropriate or incongruous. **put oneself in another's place** consider a situation from another's point of view. **put someone in his** (or **her**) **place** deflate or humiliate someone regarded as being presumptuous. **take place** occur. **take one's place** take up one's usual or recognized position. **take the place of** replace.
– DERIVATIVES **placeless** adj.
– ORIGIN Middle English: from Old French, from an alteration of Latin *platea* 'open space', from Greek *plateia* (*hodos*) 'broad (way)'.

placebo /pləˈsiːbəʊ/ ■ n. (pl. **-os**) **1** a medicine or regime prescribed for the psychological benefit to the patient rather than for any physiological effect. ▶ a substance that has no therapeutic effect, used as a control in testing new drugs. **2** a measure designed merely to calm or humour another.
– ORIGIN C18: from Latin, 'I shall be acceptable or pleasing', from *placere* 'to please'.

placebo effect ▪ n. a beneficial effect produced by a placebo drug or treatment, due to the patient's belief in that treatment.

place card ▪ n. a card bearing a person's name and used to mark their place at a table.

place kick American Football, Rugby, & Soccer ▪ n. a kick made after the ball is first placed on the ground. ▪ v. (**place-kick**) take a place kick.
– DERIVATIVES **place-kicker** n.

place mat ▪ n. a small protective mat placed underneath a person's dining plate.

placement ▪ n. **1** the action or fact of placing or being placed. **2** the temporary posting of someone in a workplace, especially to gain work experience.

place name ▪ n. the name of a geographical location, such as a town, lake, or mountain.

placenta /pləˈsɛntə/ ▪ n. (pl. **placentae** /-tiː/ or **placentas**) **1** a flattened circular organ in the uterus of pregnant eutherian mammals, nourishing and maintaining the fetus through the umbilical cord. **2** Botany (in flowers) part of the ovary wall to which the ovules are attached.
– ORIGIN C17: from Greek *plakous*, *plakount-* 'flat cake'.

placental ▪ adj. of or relating to a placenta. ▸ Zoology relating to or denoting mammals that possess a placenta; eutherian. ▪ n. Zoology a placental mammal.

placenta praevia /ˈpriːvɪə/ (US **placenta previa**) ▪ n. Medicine a condition in which the placenta partially or wholly blocks the neck of the uterus, so interfering with normal delivery of a baby.
– ORIGIN C19: *praevia* from Latin *praevius* 'going before'.

placentation /ˌplas(ə)nˈteɪʃ(ə)n/ ▪ n. Anatomy, Zoology, & Botany the formation or arrangement of a placenta or placentae.

place of safety ▪ n. **1** (in South Africa) a government facility for the protection of children considered at risk or accused of certain criminal offences. **2** a safe house offering short-term accommodation for abused women and children.

placer[1] ▪ n. [often as modifier] a deposit of sand or gravel in the bed of a river or lake, containing particles of valuable minerals: *placer gold deposits*.
– ORIGIN C19: from Latin American Spanish, 'deposit, shoal'.

placer[2] ▪ n. **1** a person or animal gaining a specified place. **2** a person who places something. **3** Brit. informal a dealer in stolen goods.

placid ▪ adj. not easily upset or excited; calm.
– DERIVATIVES **placidity** n. **placidly** adv.
– ORIGIN C17: from French *placide*, from Latin *placidus*, from *placere* 'to please'.

placing ▪ n. **1** the action or fact of placing or being placed. **2** a ranking given to a competitor in relation to a race or other competition. **3** a post that is found for a job-seeker. **4** a sale or new issue of a large quantity of shares.

placket ▪ n. an opening or slit in a garment, covering fastenings or for access to a pocket, or the flap of fabric under such an opening.
– ORIGIN C17: var. of **PLACARD** in an obsolete sense 'garment worn under an open coat'.

placoderm /ˈplakə(ʊ)dəːm/ ▪ n. a fossil fish of the Devonian period, having the front part of the body encased in broad flat bony plates.
– ORIGIN C19: from Greek *plax*, *plak-* 'flat plate' + *derma* 'skin'.

placoid /ˈplakɔɪd/ ▪ adj. Zoology (of fish scales) tooth-like, being made of dentine with enamel, as in sharks and rays. Compare with **CTENOID** and **GANOID**.
– ORIGIN C19: from Greek *plax*, *plak-* 'flat plate'.

plafond /plaˈfɒ̃(d)/ ▪ n. an ornately decorated ceiling.
– ORIGIN French, from *plat* 'flat' + *fond* 'bottom, base'.

plage /pleɪʒ/ ▪ n. Astronomy an unusually bright region on the sun.
– ORIGIN C19: from French.

plagiarize /ˈpleɪdʒərʌɪz/ (also **-ise**) ▪ v. take (the work or an idea of someone else) and pass it off as one's own.
– DERIVATIVES **plagiarism** n. **plagiarist** n. **plagiaristic** adj. **plagiarizer** (also **-iser**) n.
– ORIGIN C18 (*plagiarism* C17): from Latin *plagiarius* 'kidnapper'.

plagioclase /ˈpleɪdʒɪə(ʊ)kleɪz, ˈplaɡɪəʊ-/ (also **plagioclase feldspar**) ▪ n. a form of feldspar consisting of aluminosilicates of sodium and/or calcium, common in igneous rocks and typically white.
– ORIGIN C19: from Greek *plagios* 'slanting' + *klasis* 'cleavage' (because orig. characterized as having two cleavages at an oblique angle).

plague ▪ n. **1** a contagious bacterial disease characterized by fever and delirium, typically with the formation of buboes (see **BUBONIC PLAGUE**) and sometimes infection of the lungs (pneumonic plague). **2** an unusually large number of insects or animals infesting and causing damage to a place: *a plague of locusts*. ▪ v. (**plagues, plagued, plaguing**) cause continual trouble or distress to. ▸ pester or harass continually.
– ORIGIN Middle English: Latin *plaga* 'stroke, wound', prob. from Greek *plaga*, from a base meaning 'strike'.

plaice ▪ n. (pl. same) a North Atlantic flatfish, brown with orange spots, which is a commercially important food fish. [*Pleuronectes platessa* (Europe) and *Hippoglossoides platessoides* (America).]
– ORIGIN Middle English: from Old French *plaiz*, from late Latin *platessa*, from Greek *platus* 'broad'.

plaid /plad/ ▪ n. chequered or tartan twilled cloth. ▸ a long piece of plaid worn over the shoulder as part of Scottish Highland dress.
– DERIVATIVES **plaided** adj.
– ORIGIN C16: from Scottish Gaelic *plaide* 'blanket'.

plain[1] ▪ adj. **1** not decorated or elaborate; simple or ordinary. ▸ without a pattern; in only one colour. ▸ unmarked; without identification: *a plain envelope*. **2** easy to perceive or understand; clear. ▸ not using concealment or deception; frank: *he recalled her plain speaking*. **3** (of a person) having no pretensions; not remarkable or special. ▸ (of a woman or girl) not marked by any particular beauty; ordinary looking. **4** sheer; simple (used for emphasis). **5** (of a knitting stitch) made by putting the needle through the front of the stitch from left to right. Compare with **PURL**. ▪ adv. informal **1** used for emphasis: *that's just plain stupid*. **2** clearly; unequivocally. ▪ n. a large area of flat land with few trees.
– DERIVATIVES **plainly** adv. **plainness** n.
– ORIGIN Middle English: from Old French *plain*, from Latin *planus*, from a base meaning 'flat'.

plain[2] ▪ v. archaic **1** mourn; lament. **2** complain.
– ORIGIN Middle English: from Old French *plaindre*, from Latin *plangere* 'to lament'.

plainchant ▪ n. another term for **PLAINSONG**.

plain chocolate ▪ n. Brit. dark, slightly bitter, chocolate without added milk.

plain clothes ▪ pl. n. ordinary clothes rather than uniform, especially when worn by police officers.

plain flour ▪ n. another term for **CAKE FLOUR**.

plain sailing ▪ n. smooth and easy progress: *teambuilding was not all plain sailing*.
– ORIGIN C18: prob. a popular use of *plane sailing*, the practice of determining a ship's position on the theory that it is moving on a plane.

Plains Indian ▪ n. a member of any of various North American Indian peoples who formerly inhabited the Great Plains, a vast plains area east of the Rocky Mountains in North America.

plainsman ▪ n. (pl. -men) a person who lives on a plain, especially a frontiersman who lived on the Great Plains of North America.

plainsong ▪ n. unaccompanied church music sung in unison in medieval modes and in free rhythm corresponding to the accentuation of the words, which are taken from the liturgy.
– ORIGIN Middle English: translating Latin *cantus planus*.

plain suit ▪ n. (in bridge and whist) a suit that is not trumps.

plaint ▪ n. chiefly poetic/literary a complaint or lamentation.
– ORIGIN Middle English: from Old French *plainte*, from *plaindre* 'complain'.

plaintiff

plaintiff ■ n. Law a person who brings a case against another in a court of law. Compare with **DEFENDANT**.
– ORIGIN Middle English: from Old French *plaintif* 'plaintive'.

plaintive ■ adj. sounding sad and mournful.
– DERIVATIVES **plaintively** adv. **plaintiveness** n.

plain weave ■ n. a style of weave in which the weft alternates over and under the warp.

plait /plat/ ■ n. a single length of hair, rope, or other material made up of three or more interlaced strands. ■ v. form into a plait or plaits.
– ORIGIN Middle English: from Old French *pleit* 'a fold', from Latin *plicare* 'to fold'.

plan ■ n. 1 a detailed proposal for doing or achieving something. ▸ a scheme for the regular payment of contributions towards a pension, insurance policy, etc.: *a personal pension plan*. 2 an intention or decision about what one is going to do. 3 a map or diagram: *a street plan*. ▸ a scale drawing of a horizontal section showing the layout of a given level of a building. ■ v. (**planned**, **planning**) 1 decide on and arrange in advance. ▸ make preparations for an anticipated event or time. 2 make a plan of.
– DERIVATIVES **planner** n. **planning** n.
– ORIGIN C17: from French, from earlier *plant* 'ground plan, plane surface'.

planar /ˈpleɪnə/ ■ adj. Mathematics of, relating to, or in the form of a plane.

planarian /pləˈnɛːrɪən/ ■ n. Zoology a free-living aquatic flatworm. [Order Tricladida.]
– ORIGIN C19: from Latin *planarius* 'lying flat'.

planchet /ˈplan(t)ʃɪt/ ■ n. a plain metal disc from which a coin is made.
– ORIGIN C17: diminutive of earlier *planch* 'slab of metal', from Old French *planche* 'plank, slab'.

planchette /plɑːnˈʃet/ ■ n. a small board supported on castors, typically heart-shaped and fitted with a vertical pencil, used for automatic writing and in seances.
– ORIGIN C19: from French, 'small plank'.

plane[1] ■ n. 1 a flat surface on which a straight line joining any two points would wholly lie. ▸ an imaginary flat surface through or joining material objects. ▸ a flat surface producing lift by the action of air or water over and under it. 2 a level of existence or thought: *the spiritual plane*. ■ adj. 1 completely level or flat. 2 of or relating to only two-dimensional surfaces or magnitudes: *plane and solid geometry*. ■ v. 1 (of a bird or an airborne object) soar without moving the wings; glide. 2 (of a boat, surfboard, etc.) skim over the surface of water as a result of lift produced hydrodynamically.
– ORIGIN C17: from Latin *planum* 'flat surface', from *planus* 'plain (adj.).

plane[2] ■ n. short for **AEROPLANE**.

plane[3] ■ n. a tool consisting of a block with a projecting steel blade, used to smooth a wooden surface by paring shavings from it. ■ v. smooth with a plane.
– ORIGIN Middle English: from a var. of obsolete French *plaine* 'planing instrument', from Latin *planare* 'make level'.

plane[4] (also **plane tree**) ■ n. a tall spreading tree of the northern hemisphere, with maple-like leaves and bark which peels in uneven patches. [Genus *Platanus*.]
– ORIGIN Middle English: from Latin *platanus*, from Greek *platanos*, from *platus* 'broad'.

plane polarization ■ n. a process restricting the vibrations of electromagnetic radiation, especially light, to one direction.
– DERIVATIVES **plane-polarized** adj.

planer ■ n. another term for **PLANE**[3].

planet ■ n. a celestial body moving in an elliptical orbit round a star. ▸ (**the planet**) the earth. ▸ chiefly Astrology & historical a celestial body distinguished from the fixed stars by having an apparent motion of its own (including the moon and sun).
– PHRASES **what planet are you on?** informal used to indicate that someone is out of touch with reality.
– DERIVATIVES **planetary** adj. **planetologist** n. **planetology** n.
– ORIGIN Middle English: from Old French *planete*, from Greek *planētēs* 'wanderer, planet', from *planan* 'wander'.

plane table ■ n. a surveying instrument used for direct plotting in the field, with a circular drawing board and pivoted alidade.

planetarium /ˌplanɪˈtɛːrɪəm/ ■ n. (pl. **planetariums** or **planetaria** /-rɪə/) 1 a domed building in which images of stars, planets, and constellations are projected for public entertainment or education. 2 another term for **ORRERY**.
– ORIGIN C18: from Latin *planetarius* 'relating to the planets'.

planetary nebula ■ n. Astronomy a ring-shaped nebula formed by an expanding shell of gas round an ageing star.

planetesimal /ˌplanɪˈtɛsɪm(ə)l/ Astronomy ■ n. a minute planet; a body which could come together with many others under gravitation to form a planet. ■ adj. denoting or relating to such bodies.
– ORIGIN C20: from **PLANET**, on the pattern of *infinitesimal*.

planetoid ■ n. another term for **ASTEROID**.

planform ■ n. the shape or outline of an aircraft wing as projected upon a horizontal plane.

plangent /ˈplan(d)ʒ(ə)nt/ ■ adj. chiefly poetic/literary (of a sound) loud and resonant, with a mournful tone.
– DERIVATIVES **plangency** n. **plangently** adv.
– ORIGIN C19: from Latin *plangere* 'to lament'.

planimeter /pləˈnɪmɪtə/ ■ n. an instrument for measuring the area of a plane figure.
– DERIVATIVES **planimetric** adj. **planimetrically** adv. **planimetry** n.

planish /ˈplanɪʃ/ ■ v. flatten (sheet metal) by hammering or rolling.
– DERIVATIVES **planisher** n.
– ORIGIN Middle English: from obsolete French *planiss-*, *planir* 'to smooth'.

planisphere /ˈplanɪsfɪə/ ■ n. a map formed by the projection of a sphere, especially a star map that can be adjusted to show the constellations at a specific time and place.
– DERIVATIVES **planispheric** /-ˈsfɛrɪk/ adj.
– ORIGIN Middle English, from medieval Latin *planisphaerium*, from Latin *planus* 'level' + *sphaera* 'sphere'.

plank ■ n. 1 a long, thin, flat piece of timber, used in building and flooring. 2 a fundamental part of a political or other programme. ■ v. make, provide, or cover with planks.
– PHRASES **walk the plank** (formerly) be forced by pirates to walk blindfold along a plank over the side of a ship to one's death in the sea.
– DERIVATIVES **planking** n.
– ORIGIN Middle English: from late Latin *planca* 'board', from *plancus* 'flat-footed'.

plankton /ˈplaŋ(k)t(ə)n, -tɒn/ ■ n. the small and microscopic organisms drifting or floating in the sea or fresh water, consisting chiefly of diatoms, protozoans, small crustaceans, and the eggs and larval stages of larger animals.
– DERIVATIVES **planktic** adj. **planktonic** adj.
– ORIGIN C19: from Greek *planktos* 'wandering', from *plazein* 'wander'.

planned economy ■ n. an economy in which production, investment, prices, and incomes are determined centrally by the government.

planned obsolescence ■ n. a policy of producing consumer goods that rapidly become obsolete and so require replacing.

planning permission ■ n. formal permission from a local authority for the erection or alteration of buildings or similar development.

plant ■ n. 1 a living organism of the kind exemplified by trees, shrubs, grasses, ferns, and mosses, typically growing in a permanent site, absorbing water and inorganic substances through the roots, and synthesizing nutrients in the leaves by photosynthesis using the green pigment chlorophyll. ▸ a small plant, as distinct from a shrub or tree. 2 a place where an industrial or manufacturing process takes place. ▸ machinery used in an industrial or manufacturing process. 3 a person placed in a group as a

spy or informer. ▶ a thing put among someone's belongings to incriminate or discredit them. **4** Snooker a shot in which the cue ball is made to strike one of two touching or nearly touching balls with the result that the second is potted. ■ v. **1** place (a seed, bulb, or plant) in the ground so that it can grow. ▶ (**plant something out**) place a plant in the ground out of doors. **2** place or fix in a specified position. ▶ secretly place (a bomb). **3** establish (an idea) in someone's mind. **4** found or establish (a colony or community). **5** put or hide (something) among someone's belongings as a plant. ▶ send (someone) to join a group to act as a spy or informer.
−PHRASES **have** (or **keep**) **one's feet firmly planted on the ground** be (or remain) level-headed and sensible.
−DERIVATIVES **plantable** adj. **plantlet** n. **plant-like** adj.
−ORIGIN Old English, from Latin *planta* 'sprout, cutting' and *plantare* 'plant, fix in place'.

Plantagenet /plan'tadʒɪnɪt/ ■ n. a member of the English royal dynasty which held the throne from 1154 until 1485.
−ORIGIN from Latin *planta genista* 'sprig of broom', said to be worn as a crest by and given as a nickname to Geoffrey, count of Anjou, the father of Henry II.

plantain¹ /'plantɪn, -tem/ ■ n. a low-growing plant, typically with a rosette of leaves and a slender green flower spike. [Genus *Plantago*: many species.]
−ORIGIN Middle English: from Latin *plantago*, *plantagin-*, from *planta* 'sole of the foot' (because of its broad prostrate leaves).

plantain² /'plantɪn, -tem/ ■ n. **1** a type of banana containing high levels of starch and little sugar, which is harvested green and widely used as a cooked vegetable in the tropics. **2** the plant which bears this fruit. [*Musa* × *paradisiaca*.]
−ORIGIN C16: from Spanish *plá(n)tano*, prob. by assimilation of a S. American word to the Spanish *plá(n)tano* 'plane tree'.

plantain lily ■ n. another term for HOSTA.

plantar /'plantə/ ■ adj. Anatomy of or relating to the sole of the foot.
−ORIGIN C18: from Latin *plantaris*, from *planta* 'sole'.

plantation ■ n. **1** a large estate on which crops such as coffee, sugar, and tobacco are grown. **2** an area in which trees have been planted, especially for commercial purposes.

planter ■ n. **1** a manager or owner of a plantation. **2** a decorative container in which plants are grown. **3** a machine or person that plants seeds, bulbs, etc.

planter's punch ■ n. a cocktail containing rum, lemon or lime juice, and sugar.
−ORIGIN prob. so called because drunk by plantation owners.

plantigrade /'plantɪgreɪd/ ■ adj. Zoology (of a mammal) walking on the soles of the feet, like a human or a bear. Compare with DIGITIGRADE.
−ORIGIN C19: from Latin *planta* 'sole' + *-gradus* '-walking'.

plant louse ■ n. an aphid or other small bug that infests plants.

plantsman ■ n. (pl. **-men**) an expert in garden plants and gardening.

planula /'planjʊlə/ ■ n. (pl. **planulae** /-liː/) Zoology a free-swimming coelenterate larva with a flattened, ciliated, solid body.
−ORIGIN C19: diminutive of Latin *planus* 'plane, flat'.

plaque /plak, plɑːk/ ■ n. **1** an ornamental tablet fixed to a wall in commemoration of a person or event. **2** a sticky deposit on teeth in which bacteria proliferate. **3** Medicine a small, distinct, typically raised patch on or within the body, caused by local damage or deposition of material. ▶ Microbiology a clear area in a cell culture caused by the inhibition of growth or destruction of cells.
−ORIGIN C19: from Dutch *plak* 'tablet', from *plakken* 'to stick'.

plash poetic/literary ■ n. a splashing sound. ■ v. make or hit with a splash.
−DERIVATIVES **plashy** adj.
−ORIGIN C16: prob. imitative.

plasma /'plazmə/ ■ n. **1** the colourless fluid part of blood, lymph, or milk, in which corpuscles or fat globules are suspended. **2** Physics a gas of positive ions and free electrons with little or no overall electric charge. **3** a bright green translucent ornamental variety of quartz. **4** (also **plasm** /'plaz(ə)m/) cytoplasm or protoplasm.
−DERIVATIVES **plasmatic** adj. **plasmic** adj.
−ORIGIN C18: from Greek *plasma*, from *plassein* 'to shape'.

plasma screen ■ n. a flat display screen which uses an array of cells containing an inert gas which emits ultraviolet radiation when ionized to form a plasma, causing visible light of an appropriate colour to be emitted separately for each cell of the screen.

plasmid /'plazmɪd/ ■ n. Biology a genetic structure in a cell that can replicate independently of the chromosomes, especially a small circular DNA strand in a bacterium or protozoan.
−ORIGIN 1950s: from PLASMA.

plasmin /'plazmɪn/ ■ n. Biochemistry an enzyme formed in the blood which destroys blood clots by attacking fibrin.
−ORIGIN C19: from French *plasmine*, from late Latin *plasma* 'mould, image'.

plasminogen /plaz'mɪnədʒ(ə)n/ ■ n. Biochemistry the inactive precursor of the enzyme plasmin, present in blood.

plasmodium /plaz'məʊdɪəm/ ■ n. (pl. **plasmodia** /-dɪə/) **1** a parasitic protozoan of a genus including that causing malaria. [Genus *Plasmodium*.] **2** Biology a form within the life cycle of some simple organisms such as slime moulds, consisting of a mass of protoplasm containing many nuclei.
−DERIVATIVES **plasmodial** adj.
−ORIGIN C19: from late Latin *plasma* 'mould, formation'.

plaster ■ n. **1** a soft mixture of lime with sand or cement and water for spreading on walls and ceilings to form a smooth hard surface when dried. **2** (also **plaster of Paris**) a hard white substance made by the addition of water to powdered gypsum, used for holding broken bones in place and making sculptures and casts. [so called because the gypsum orig. came from Paris.] **3** (also **sticking plaster**) an adhesive strip of material for covering cuts and wounds. ▶ dated a bandage on which a poultice is spread for application. ■ v. **1** cover with plaster; apply plaster to. **2** coat or cover all over with something, especially to an extent considered excessive: *a face plastered in heavy make-up*. ▶ display widely and conspicuously: *her story was plastered all over the papers*. **3** apply a plaster cast to.
−DERIVATIVES **plasterer** n. **plastery** adj.
−ORIGIN Old English, from medieval Latin *plastrum*, from Greek *emplastron* 'daub, salve'.

plasterboard ■ n. board made of plaster set between two sheets of paper, used especially to line inner walls.

plastered ■ adj. informal very drunk.

plasterwork ■ n. plaster as part of the interior of a building, especially when formed into decorative shapes.

plastic ■ n. **1** a synthetic material made from a wide range of organic polymers such as polyethylene, PVC, nylon, etc., that can be moulded into shape while soft, and then set into a rigid or slightly elastic form. **2** informal credit cards or other plastic cards that can be used as money. ■ adj. **1** made of plastic. **2** easily shaped or moulded. ▶ (in science and technology) of or relating to the permanent deformation of a solid without fracture by the temporary application of force. **3** (in art) of or relating to moulding or modelling in three dimensions, or to produce three-dimensional effects. **4** offering scope for creativity: *words as a plastic medium*. **5** artificial; unnatural: *long-distance flights with their plastic food*.
−DERIVATIVES **plastically** adv. **plasticity** n.
−ORIGIN C17: from French *plastique* or Latin *plasticus*, from Greek *plastikos*, from *plassein* 'to mould'.

plastic arts ■ pl. n. visual art forms that involve modelling or moulding, or the creation of three-dimensional effects.

plastic bullet ■ n. a bullet made of PVC or another plastic, used for riot control.

plastic explosive ■ n. a putty-like explosive capable of being moulded by hand.

plasticine (also **Plasticine**) ■ n. trademark a soft modelling material, used especially by children.

plasticize

plasticize (also **-ise**) ▪ v. [often as adj. **plasticized** (also **-ised**)] 1 make plastic or mouldable, especially by the addition of a plasticizer. 2 treat or make with plastic.

plasticizer (also **-iser**) ▪ n. a substance (typically a solvent) added to a synthetic resin to promote plasticity and to reduce brittleness.

plasticky ▪ adj. 1 resembling plastic. 2 artificial or of inferior quality.

plastic surgery ▪ n. the process of reconstructing or repairing parts of the body by the transfer of tissue, either in the treatment of injury or for cosmetic reasons.
– DERIVATIVES **plastic surgeon** n.

plastid /ˈplastɪd/ ▪ n. Botany any of a class of small organelles in the cytoplasm of plant cells, containing pigment or food.
– ORIGIN C19: from Greek *plastos* 'shaped'.

plastique /plaˈstiːk/ ▪ n. plastic explosive.
– ORIGIN C20: French, 'plastic'.

plastron /ˈplastrən/ ▪ n. Zoology the part of a tortoise's or turtle's shell forming the underside. ▸ a similar ventral plate in some invertebrate animals.
– ORIGIN C16: from Italian *piastrone*, from *piastra* 'breastplate'.

-plasty ▪ comb. form moulding or formation of a specified part, especially a part of the body: *rhinoplasty*.
– ORIGIN from Greek *plastos* 'formed, moulded'.

platanna /pləˈtanə/ ▪ n. an aquatic clawed frog native to sub-Saharan Africa. [*Xenopus laevis* and other species.]
– ORIGIN from S. African Dutch *plathander*, from *plat* 'flat' + *-hander* '-handed one'.

plat du jour /ˌpla dʊˈʒʊə/ ▪ n. (pl. **plats du jour** pronunc. same) a dish specially prepared by a restaurant on a particular day, in addition to the usual menu.
– ORIGIN French, 'dish of the day'.

plate ▪ n. 1 a flat dish, typically circular, from which food is eaten or served. 2 any shallow dish, especially one used for collecting donations in a church. 3 bowls, cups, and other utensils made of gold or silver. ▸ a silver or gold dish or trophy awarded as a prize. 4 a thin, flat sheet or strip of metal or other material, typically one used to join or strengthen or forming part of a machine. ▸ a small, flat piece of metal bearing a name or inscription, designed to be fixed to a wall or door. ▸ short for **NUMBER PLATE**. ▸ Baseball short for **HOME PLATE**. ▸ a horizontal timber laid along the top of a wall to support the ends of joists or rafters. ▸ a light horseshoe for a racehorse. 5 Geology each of the several rigid pieces of the earth's lithosphere which together make up the earth's surface. 6 a sheet of metal or other material bearing an image of type or illustrations from which multiple copies are printed. ▸ a printed photograph or illustration in a book. ▸ a thin sheet of metal or glass coated with a light-sensitive film on which an image is formed, used in larger or older types of camera. 7 a thin piece of metal that acts as an electrode in a capacitor, battery, or cell. ▪ v. 1 cover (a metal object) with a thin coating of a different metal. ▸ cover with plates of metal for decoration or protection. 2 serve or arrange on a plate. 3 Baseball score or cause to score (a run or runs).
– PHRASES **on a plate** informal indicating that something has been achieved with little or no effort. **on one's plate** occupying one's time or energy.
– DERIVATIVES **plateful** n. (pl. **-fuls**) **plater** n. **plating** n.
– ORIGIN Middle English: from medieval Latin *plata* 'plate armour', from Greek *platus* 'flat'; sense 1 represents Old French *plat* 'platter'.

plateau /ˈplatəʊ/ ▪ n. (pl. **plateaux** /-təʊz/ or **plateaus**) 1 an area of fairly level high ground. 2 a state or period of little or no change following a period of activity or progress. ▪ v. (**plateaus**, **plateaued**, **plateauing**) reach a plateau.
– ORIGIN C18: from Old French *platel*, diminutive of *plat* 'level'.

plate glass ▪ n. thick fine-quality glass, used for shop windows and doors and originally cast in plates.

platelet ▪ n. Physiology a small colourless disc-shaped cell fragment without a nucleus, found in large numbers in blood and involved in clotting.

platen /ˈplat(ə)n/ ▪ n. 1 the plate in a small letterpress printing press which presses the paper against the type. 2 the cylindrical roller in a typewriter against which the paper is held.
– ORIGIN C16: from French *platine* 'flat piece' from *plat* 'flat'.

plate tectonics ▪ pl. n. [treated as sing.] a theory explaining the structure of the earth's crust and many associated phenomena as resulting from the interaction of rigid lithospheric plates which move slowly over the underlying mantle.

platform ▪ n. 1 a raised level surface on which people or things can stand. 2 a raised structure along the side of a railway track where passengers get on and off trains. 3 a raised structure standing in the sea from which oil or gas wells can be drilled. 4 Computing a standard for the hardware of a computer system, which determines the kinds of software it can run. 5 the declared policy of a political party or group. ▸ an opportunity to voice one's views: *a platform for discussion*. 6 [usu. as modifier] a very thick sole on a shoe: *platform shoes*.
– ORIGIN C16: from French *plateforme* 'ground plan, flat shape'.

platinize /ˈplatɪnʌɪz/ (also **-ise**) ▪ v. [usu. as adj. **platinized** (also **-ised**)] coat with platinum.
– DERIVATIVES **platinization** (also **-isation**) n.

platinoid /ˈplatɪnɔɪd/ ▪ n. an alloy of copper with zinc, nickel, and sometimes tungsten, used for its high electrical resistance. ▪ adj. (of minerals) resembling or related to platinum.

platinum /ˈplatɪnəm/ ▪ n. 1 a precious silvery-white metal, the chemical element of atomic number 78, used in jewellery, electrical contacts, laboratory equipment, and industrial catalysts. (Symbol: **Pt**) 2 [as modifier] greyish-white or silvery like platinum.
– PHRASES **go platinum** (of a recording) achieve sales meriting a platinum disc.
– ORIGIN C19: alteration of earlier *platina*, from Spanish, diminutive of *plata* 'silver'.

platinum blonde ▪ adj. (of a woman's hair) silvery-blonde. ▪ n. a woman with silvery-blonde hair.

platinum disc ▪ n. a framed platinum disc awarded to a recording artist for sales of a record exceeding a specified high figure.

platinum-group element (also **platinum-group metal**) ▪ n. any of the six metals platinum, palladium, ruthenium, osmium, rhodium, and iridium, which have similar properties and tend to occur together in nature.

platitude /ˈplatɪtjuːd/ ▪ n. a trite, obvious, or insincere remark or statement.
– DERIVATIVES **platitudinize** (also **-ise**) v. **platitudinous** adj.
– ORIGIN C19: from French, from *plat* 'flat'.

Platonic /pləˈtɒnɪk/ ▪ adj. 1 of or associated with the Greek philosopher Plato or his ideas. 2 (**platonic**) (of love or friendship) intimate and affectionate but not sexual.
– DERIVATIVES **platonically** adv.
– ORIGIN C16: from Greek *Platōnikos*, from *Platōn* 'Plato'.

Platonic solid (also **Platonic body**) ▪ n. one of five regular solids (a tetrahedron, cube, octahedron, dodecahedron, or icosahedron).

Platonism /ˈpleɪtənɪz(ə)m/ ▪ n. the philosophy of Plato or his followers, especially that relating to Plato's theory of 'ideas' or 'forms', in which abstract entities ('universals') are contrasted with their objects ('particulars') in the material world. ▸ the theory that numbers or other abstract objects are objective, timeless entities, independent of the physical world and of the symbols used to represent them.
– DERIVATIVES **Platonist** n. & adj.

platoon ▪ n. 1 a subdivision of a company of soldiers, usually commanded by a subaltern or lieutenant and divided into three sections. 2 [as modifier] S. African denoting a system in which a school is used by two different groups of students in the morning and afternoon sessions. ▪ v. S. African use the platoon system in a school.
– DERIVATIVES **platooning** n.
– ORIGIN C17: from French *peloton* 'platoon, small ball', diminutive of *pelote*.

platteland /ˈplatəland/ S. African ■ n. remote country districts. ■ adj. characteristic of country districts; rustic.
– DERIVATIVES **plattelander** n.
– ORIGIN Afrikaans, 'flat land'.

platter ■ n. **1** a large flat serving dish. ▸ a meal or selection of food placed on a platter. **2** Computing a rigid rotating disk on which data is stored in a disk drive; a hard disk.
– PHRASES **on a (silver) platter** informal indicating that something is achieved with little or no effort.
– ORIGIN Middle English: from Anglo-Norman French *plater*, from *plat* (see **PLATE**).

Platyhelminthes /ˌplatɪhɛlˈmɪnθiːz/ ■ pl. n. Zoology a phylum of invertebrates that comprises the flatworms.
– DERIVATIVES **platyhelminth** /ˌplatɪˈhɛlmɪnθ/ n.
– ORIGIN from Greek *platus* 'broad, flat' + *helminth* 'worm'.

platypus /ˈplatɪpəs/ (also **duck-billed platypus**) ■ n. (pl. **platypuses**) a semiaquatic egg-laying Australian mammal with a sensitive pliable bill like that of a duck and webbed feet with venomous spurs. [*Ornithorhynchus anatinus*.]
– ORIGIN C18: from Greek *platupous* 'flat-footed'.

platyrrhine /ˈplatɪraɪn/ ■ adj. Zoology relating to or denoting primates of a group distinguished by having nostrils that are far apart and directed forwards or sideways and typically a prehensile tail, comprising the New World monkeys, marmosets, and tamarins. Compare with **CATARRHINE**.
– ORIGIN C19: from Greek *platus* 'broad, flat' + *rhis, rhin-* 'nose'.

plaudits /ˈplɔːdɪts/ ■ pl. n. praise; enthusiastic approval.
– ORIGIN C17: *plaudit* shortened from Latin *plaudite* 'applaud!' (said by Roman actors at the end of a play), from *plaudere*.

plausible ■ adj. apparently reasonable or probable, without necessarily being so.
– DERIVATIVES **plausibility** n. **plausibly** adv.
– ORIGIN C16: from Latin *plausibilis*, from *plaudere* 'applaud'.

play ■ v. **1** engage in games or other activities for enjoyment rather than for a serious or practical purpose. ▸ amuse oneself by engaging in imaginative pretence. ▸ treat inconsiderately for one's own amusement: *she likes to play with people's emotions*. ▸ tamper with something so as to damage it: *has somebody been playing with these taps?* **2** take part in (a sport or contest). ▸ compete against. ▸ take a specified position in a sports team: *he played in goal*. ▸ strike (a ball) or execute (a stroke). ▸ move (a piece) or display (a playing card) in one's turn in a game. ▸ bet or gamble at or on. **3** be cooperative. **4** represent (a character) in a play or film. ▸ give a performance at (a particular venue). ▸ pretend to be: *the skipper played the innocent*. ▸ (**play someone for**) treat someone as being of (a specified type): *don't imagine you can play me for a fool*. **5** perform on or have the skill to perform on (a musical instrument). ▸ produce (notes) from a musical instrument; perform (a piece of music). ▸ make (a record player, radio, etc.) produce sounds. ▸ accompany (someone) with music in a ceremony or procession. **6** move lightly and quickly; flicker: *a smile played about her lips*. **7** allow (a fish) to exhaust itself on a line before reeling it in. ■ n. **1** games and other activities engaged in for enjoyment, especially by children. ▸ behaviour or speech that is not intended seriously. **2** the progress of a sporting match. ▸ the status of the ball in a game as being available to be played according to the rules: *the ball was put in play*. ▸ a move or manoeuvre in a sport or game. **3** the state of being active, operative, or effective: *luck comes into play*. **4** a dramatic work for the stage or to be broadcast. **5** the ability or freedom of movement in a mechanism. **6** light and constantly changing movement.
– PHRASES **make a play for** informal attempt to attract or attain. **make (great) play of** (or **with**) ostentatiously draw attention to. **make play with** treat frivolously. **play both ends against the middle** keep one's options open by supporting opposing sides. **play something by ear 1** perform music without having to read from a score. **2** (**play it by ear**) informal proceed instinctively according to circumstances rather than according to rules or a plan. **play someone false** prove treacherous or deceitful towards someone. **play fast and loose** behave irresponsibly or immorally. **play for time** use specious excuses or unnecessary manoeuvres to gain time. **play a (or one's) hunch** make an instinctive choice. **play oneself in** become accustomed to the circumstances and conditions of a game or activity. **play into someone's hands** act in such a way as unintentionally to give someone an advantage. **play it cool** informal make an effort to be or appear to be unconcerned. **a play on words** a pun. **play (or play it) safe** avoid taking risks. **play with oneself** informal masturbate. **play with fire** take foolish risks.
– PHRASAL VERBS **play about** (or **around**) behave in a casual or irresponsible way. ▸ informal (of a married person) have an affair. **play along** perform a piece of music at the same time as it is playing on a tape or record. ▸ pretend to cooperate. **play someone along** informal deceive or mislead someone. **play something down** pretend that something is less important than it is. **play someone off** bring other people into conflict for one's own advantage. **play off** (of two competitors) play an extra match to decide a draw or tie. **play on** exploit (someone's weak or vulnerable point). **play up** informal fail to function properly; cause problems. **play something up** emphasize the extent or importance of something. **play up to** humour or flatter.
– DERIVATIVES **playability** n. **playable** adj.
– ORIGIN Old English *pleg(i)an* 'to exercise', *plega* 'brisk movement'.

play-act ■ v. **1** act in a play. **2** engage in histrionic pretence.
– DERIVATIVES **play-acting** n. **play-actor** n.

playback ■ n. the action or process of reproducing previously recorded sound or moving images.

playbill ■ n. **1** a poster announcing a theatrical performance. **2** N. Amer. a theatre programme.

playboy ■ n. a wealthy man who spends his time seeking pleasure, especially sexual pleasure.

player ■ n. **1** a person taking part in a sport or game. **2** a person that is involved and influential in an activity. **3** a person who plays a musical instrument. ▸ a device for playing compact discs, cassettes, etc. **4** an actor.

player-manager ■ n. a person who both plays in a sports team and manages it.

player-piano ■ n. a piano fitted with a pneumatic apparatus enabling it to be played automatically by means of a rotating perforated roll signalling the notes to be played.

playful ■ adj. **1** fond of games and amusement. **2** intended for amusement; light-hearted.
– DERIVATIVES **playfully** adv. **playfulness** n.

playground ■ n. an outdoor area provided for children to play on.

playgroup ■ n. a regular meeting of a group of pre-school children, usually organized by parents.

playhouse ■ n. [usu. in names] a theatre.

playing card ■ n. each of a set of rectangular pieces of card with numbers and symbols on one side (usually 52 cards divided into four suits), used to play various games.

playing field ■ n. a field used for outdoor team games.

playlet ■ n. a short play or dramatic piece.

playlist ■ n. a list of recorded songs or pieces of music chosen to be broadcast on a radio station.

playmaker ■ n. a player in a team game who leads attacks or brings teammates into attacking positions.
– DERIVATIVES **playmaking** n.

playmate ■ n. **1** a friend with whom a child plays. **2** euphemistic a person's lover.

play-off ■ n. an additional match played to decide the outcome of a contest.

playpen ■ n. a small portable enclosure in which a baby or small child can play safely.

play-play S. African ■ n. informal a child's word for make-believe. ■ adj. often ironic fake; pretend.

playroom ■ n. a room in a house that is set aside for children to play in.

playschool ■ n. a playgroup.

PlayStation ■ n. trademark a small console and other equipment used for playing electronic games.

playsuit ■ n. an all-in-one stretchy garment for a baby or very young child, covering the body, arms, and legs. ► a woman's all-in-one garment.

plaything ■ n. **1** a toy. **2** a person treated as amusing but unimportant.

playwright ■ n. a person who writes plays.

plaza ■ n. **1** a public square, marketplace, or similar open space in a built-up area. **2** a shopping centre.
– ORIGIN C17: from Spanish, 'place'.

plc (also **PLC**) ■ abbrev. public limited company.

plea ■ n. **1** a request made in an urgent and emotional manner. **2** Law a formal statement by or on behalf of a defendant or prisoner, stating guilt or innocence in response to a charge, offering an allegation of fact, or claiming that a point of law should apply. ► an excuse or claim of mitigating circumstances.
– PHRASES **plea of tender** Law a plea that the defendant has always been ready to satisfy the plaintiff's claim and now brings the sum into court.
– ORIGIN Middle English: from Old French *plait*, *plaid* 'agreement, discussion', from Latin *placitum* 'a decree', from *placere* 'to please'.

plea-bargaining ■ n. Law an arrangement between prosecution and defendant whereby the defendant pleads guilty to a lesser charge in the expectation of leniency.
– DERIVATIVES **plea-bargain** v. **plea bargain** n.

pleach /pliːtʃ/ ■ v. [usu. as adj. **pleached**] entwine or interlace (tree branches) to form a hedge or provide cover for an outdoor walkway.
– ORIGIN Middle English: from an Old French var. of *plaissier*, from Latin *plectere* 'to plait'.

plead ■ v. (past and past part. **pleaded** or N. Amer. **pled**) **1** make an emotional appeal. **2** present and argue for (a position), especially in court or in another public context. ► Law address a court as an advocate on behalf of a party. ► Law state formally in court whether one is guilty or not guilty of the offence with which one is charged. ► Law invoke (a reason or a point of law) as an accusation or defence: *she pleaded self-defence.* ► offer or present as an excuse for doing or not doing something.
– DERIVATIVES **pleadable** adj. (Law). **pleader** n.
– ORIGIN Middle English: from Old French *plaidier* 'go to law', from *plaid* (see PLEA).

pleading ■ n. **1** the action of making an emotional or earnest appeal. **2** Law a formal statement of the cause of an action or defence. ■ adj. earnestly appealing: *a pleading look.*
– DERIVATIVES **pleadingly** adv.

pleasant ■ adj. (**-er**, **-est**) giving a sense of happy satisfaction or enjoyment. ► (of a person) friendly and considerate; likeable.
– DERIVATIVES **pleasantly** adv. **pleasantness** n.
– ORIGIN Middle English: from Old French *plaisant* 'pleasing', from *plaisir* (see PLEASE).

pleasantry ■ n. (pl. **-ies**) an inconsequential remark made as part of a polite conversation. ► a mild joke.

please ■ v. **1** cause to feel happy and satisfied. **2** (**please oneself**) take only one's own wishes into consideration in deciding how to act or proceed. ► wish or desire to do something: *feel free to wander around as you please.* ► (**it pleases someone to do something**) formal or dated it is someone's choice to do something. ► (**if you please**) used in polite requests or to express indignation. ■ adv. used in polite requests or questions, or to agree to a request or accept an offer. ► used to add urgency and emotion to a request.
– DERIVATIVES **pleasing** adj. **pleasingly** adv.
– ORIGIN Middle English: from Old French *plaisir* 'to please', from Latin *placere*.

pleased ■ adj. feeling or showing pleasure and satisfaction. ► (**pleased to do something**) willing or glad to do something. ► (**pleased with oneself**) excessively proud of one's achievements; self-satisfied.
– DERIVATIVES **pleasedly** adv.

pleasurable ■ adj. pleasing; enjoyable.

– DERIVATIVES **pleasurableness** n. **pleasurably** adv.

pleasure ■ n. **1** a feeling of happy satisfaction and enjoyment. ► enjoyment and entertainment, as opposed to necessity. ► an event or activity from which one derives enjoyment. ► [as modifier] intended for entertainment rather than business: *pleasure boats.* ► sensual gratification. **2** (**one's pleasure**) formal one's wish or desire: *the landlord could terminate the agreement at his pleasure.* ■ v. **1** give sexual enjoyment or satisfaction to. **2** (**pleasure in**) archaic derive enjoyment from.
– ORIGIN Middle English: from Old French *plaisir* 'to please'.

pleasure principle ■ n. Psychoanalysis the instinctive drive to seek pleasure and avoid pain, expressed by the id as a basic motivating force which reduces psychic tension.

pleat ■ n. **1** a double or multiple fold in a garment or other item made of cloth, held by stitching the top or side. **2** a plait. ■ v. [often as adj. **pleated**] fold or form into pleats.
– ORIGIN Middle English: var. of PLAIT.

pleb ■ n. informal, derogatory a member of the lower social classes.
– DERIVATIVES **plebby** adj.

plebeian /plɪˈbiːən/ ■ n. **1** (in ancient Rome) a commoner. **2** a member of the lower social classes. ■ adj. **1** of or relating to the plebeians of ancient Rome. **2** lower-class or lacking in refinement.
– ORIGIN C16: from Latin *plebeius*, from *plebs* 'the common people'.

plebiscite /ˈplɛbɪsʌɪt, -sɪt/ ■ n. the direct vote of all the members of an electorate on an important public question.
– DERIVATIVES **plebiscitary** /-ˈbɪsɪt(ə)ri/ adj.
– ORIGIN C16: from French *plébiscite*, from Latin *plebiscitum*, from *plebs* 'the common people' + *scitum* 'decree'.

plectranthus ■ n. a southern African perennial which bears clusters of mauve, pink, or white flowers, cultivated as an ornamental. [*Plectranthus ecklonii* and related species.]

plectrum /ˈplɛktrəm/ ■ n. (pl. **plectrums** or **plectra** /-trə/) a thin flat piece of plastic or tortoiseshell used to pluck the strings of a guitar or similar musical instrument. ► the corresponding mechanical part which plucks the strings of an instrument such as a harpsichord.
– ORIGIN Middle English: from Greek *plēktron* 'something with which to strike', from *plēssein* 'to strike'.

pled N. Amer. past participle of PLEAD.

pledge ■ n. **1** a solemn promise or undertaking. ► a promise of a donation to charity. ► (**the pledge**) a solemn undertaking to abstain from alcohol. **2** Law a thing that is given as security for the fulfilment of a contract or the payment of a debt and is liable to forfeiture in the event of failure. ► a thing given as a token of love, favour, or loyalty. **3** archaic the drinking of a person's health; a toast. ■ v. **1** solemnly undertake to do or give something. **2** Law give as security for a loan. **3** archaic drink to the health of.
– DERIVATIVES **pledgee** n. (Law). **pledger** n. **pledgor** n. (Law).
– ORIGIN Middle English: from Old French *plege*, from medieval Latin *plebium*, perhaps rel. to the Germanic base of PLIGHT².

-plegia /ˈpliːdʒə/ ■ suffix Medicine forming nouns denoting a kind of paralysis, as *hemiplegia*, *paraplegia*.
– DERIVATIVES **-plegic** suffix forming corresponding adjectives.
– ORIGIN from Greek *plēgē* 'blow, stroke', from *plēssein* 'to strike'.

pleiotropy /plʌɪˈɒtrəpi/ ■ n. Genetics the production by a single gene of two or more apparently unrelated effects.
– DERIVATIVES **pleiotropic** /-ˈtrəʊpɪk, -ˈtrɒpɪk/ adj. **pleiotropism** n.
– ORIGIN 1930s: from Greek *pleiōn* 'more' + *tropē* 'turning'.

Pleistocene /ˈplʌɪstəsiːn/ ■ adj. Geology relating to or denoting the first epoch of the Quaternary period (between the Pliocene and Holocene epochs, from 1.64 million to about 10 000 years ago), a time which included the ice ages and the appearance of humans.
– ORIGIN C19: from Greek *pleistos* 'most' + *kainos* 'new'.

plenary /ˈpliːnəri/ ■ adj. **1** unqualified; absolute. **2** (of a

meeting) to be attended by all participants at a conference or assembly. ■ n. a plenary meeting.
–ORIGIN Middle English: from late Latin *plenarius* 'complete', from *plenus* 'full'.

plenipotentiary /ˌplɛnɪpəˈtɛnʃ(ə)ri/ ■ n. (pl. **-ies**) a person, especially a diplomat, invested with the full power of independent action on behalf of their government. ■ adj. having full power to take independent action. ▶ (of power) absolute.
–ORIGIN C17: from medieval Latin *plenipotentiarius*, from *plenus* 'full' + *potentia* 'power'.

plenitude ■ n. formal an abundance. ▶ the condition of being full or complete.
–ORIGIN Middle English: from late Latin *plenitudo*, from *plenus* 'full'.

plenteous ■ adj. poetic/literary plentiful.
–DERIVATIVES **plenteously** adv. **plenteousness** n.
–ORIGIN Middle English: from Old French *plentivous*, from *plente* 'plenty'.

plentiful ■ adj. existing in or yielding great quantities; abundant.
–DERIVATIVES **plentifully** adv. **plentifulness** n.

plenty /ˈplɛnti/ ■ pron. a large or sufficient amount or quantity; more than enough. ■ n. a situation in which food and other necessities are available in sufficiently large quantities. ■ adv. informal fully; sufficiently.
–ORIGIN Middle English: from Old French *plente*, from Latin *plenitas*, from *plenus* 'full'.

plenum /ˈpliːnəm/ ■ n. 1 an assembly of all the members of a group or committee. 2 Physics a space completely filled with matter, or the whole of space so regarded.
–ORIGIN C17: from Latin, 'full space', from *plenus* 'full'.

pleochroic /ˌpliːə(ʊ)ˈkrəʊɪk/ ■ adj. Crystallography displaying variable colours owing to differential absorption of light according to wavelength, direction, and/or polarization.
–DERIVATIVES **pleochroism** n.
–ORIGIN C19: from Greek *pleōn* 'more' + *khrōs* 'colour'.

plesiosaur /ˈpliːsɪəsɔː, ˈpliːz-/ ■ n. a large fossil marine reptile of the Mesozoic era, with large paddle-like limbs and a long flexible neck.
–ORIGIN C19: from Greek *plēsios* 'near' (because closely related to the lizards) + *sauros* 'lizard'.

plethora /ˈplɛθ(ə)rə/ ■ n. 1 (**a plethora of**) an excess of. 2 Medicine an excess of a bodily fluid, particularly blood.
–DERIVATIVES **plethoric** /ˈplɛθ(ə)rɪk, plɪˈθɒrɪk/ adj. (archaic or Medicine).
–ORIGIN C16: from Greek *plēthōrē*, from *plēthein* 'be full'.

pleura¹ /ˈplʊərə/ ■ n. (pl. **pleurae** /-riː/) each of a pair of serous membranes lining the thorax and enveloping the lungs in humans and other mammals.
–DERIVATIVES **pleural** adj.
–ORIGIN Middle English: from Greek, 'side of the body, rib'.

pleura² plural form of **PLEURON**.

pleurisy /ˈplʊərɪsi/ ■ n. inflammation of the pleurae, causing pain when breathing.
–DERIVATIVES **pleuritic** adj.
–ORIGIN Middle English: from Old French *pleurisie*, from a late Latin alteration of Latin *pleuritis*, from Greek (see **PLEURA¹**).

pleuron /ˈplʊərɒn/ ■ n. (pl. **pleura** /-rə/) Zoology the side wall of each segment of the body of an arthropod.
–ORIGIN C18: from Greek, 'side of the body, rib'.

plexiglas /ˈplɛksɪglɑːs/ ■ n. trademark a tough transparent plastic made of an acrylic resin, used as a substitute for glass.
–ORIGIN 1930s: from Greek *plēxis* 'percussion' + **GLASS**.

plexus ■ n. (pl. same or **plexuses**) 1 Anatomy a network of nerves or vessels in the body. 2 an intricate network or web-like formation.
–DERIVATIVES **plexiform** adj.
–ORIGIN C17: from Latin, 'plaited formation', from *plectere* 'to plait'.

pliable ■ adj. 1 easily bent; flexible. 2 easily influenced or swayed.
–DERIVATIVES **pliability** n. **pliably** adv.
–ORIGIN Middle English: from French, from *plier* (see **PLY¹**).

pliant ■ adj. pliable.
–DERIVATIVES **pliancy** n. **pliantly** adv.

plié /ˈpliːeɪ/ Ballet ■ n. a movement in which a dancer bends the knees and straightens them again, usually with the feet turned right out and heels firmly on the ground. ■ v. perform a plié.
–ORIGIN French, 'bent', from *plier*.

pliers ■ pl. n. pincers with parallel, flat, serrated jaws, used for gripping small objects or bending wire.
–ORIGIN C16: from dialect *ply* 'bend', from French *plier* 'to bend'.

plight¹ ■ n. a dangerous, difficult, or otherwise unfortunate situation.
–ORIGIN Middle English: from Anglo-Norman French *plit* 'fold'.

plight² ■ v. archaic 1 solemnly pledge or promise (faith or loyalty). 2 (**be plighted to**) be engaged to be married to.
–ORIGIN Old English *plihtan* 'endanger', of Germanic origin.

plimsoll (also **plimsole**) ■ n. Brit. a light rubber-soled canvas sports shoe.
–ORIGIN C19: prob. from the resemblance of the side of the sole to a **PLIMSOLL LINE**.

Plimsoll line (also **Plimsoll mark**) ■ n. a marking on a ship's side showing the limit of legal submersion when loaded with cargo under various sea conditions.
–ORIGIN named after the English politician Samuel *Plimsoll*, responsible for the Merchant Shipping Act of 1876.

Plinian /ˈplɪnɪən/ ■ adj. Geology relating to or denoting a type of volcanic eruption in which a narrow stream of gas and ash is violently ejected from a vent to a height of several miles.
–ORIGIN C17: from Italian *pliniano*, with ref. to the eruption of Vesuvius in AD 79, in which Pliny the Elder died.

plinth ■ n. 1 a heavy base supporting a statue or vase. 2 Architecture the lower square slab at the base of a column.
–ORIGIN C16: from Latin *plinthus*, from Greek *plinthos* 'tile, brick, squared stone'.

Pliocene /ˈplaɪə(ʊ)siːn/ ■ adj. Geology relating to or denoting the last epoch of the Tertiary period (between the Miocene and Pleistocene epochs, 5.2 to 1.64 million years ago), a time when the first hominids appeared.
–ORIGIN C19: from Greek *pleiōn* 'more' + *kainos* 'new'.

plissé /ˈpliːseɪ/ ■ adj. (of fabric) treated to give a permanent puckered or crinkled effect. ■ n. material treated in this way.
–ORIGIN C19: French, 'pleated', from *plisser*.

PLO ■ abbrev. Palestine Liberation Organization.

plod ■ v. (**plodded**, **plodding**) walk doggedly and slowly with heavy steps. ▶ work slowly and perseveringly at a dull task. ■ n. 1 a slow, heavy walk. 2 (also **PC Plod**) Brit. informal a police officer.
–DERIVATIVES **plodder** n. **plodding** adj. **ploddingly** adv.
–ORIGIN C16: prob. symbolic of a heavy gait.

-ploid ■ comb. form Biology denoting the number of sets of chromosomes in a cell: *triploid*.
–ORIGIN from (*ha*)*ploid* and (*di*)*ploid*.

ploidy /ˈplɔɪdi/ ■ n. Genetics the number of sets of chromosomes in a cell, or in the cells of an organism.
–ORIGIN 1940s: from (*di*)*ploidy* and (*poly*)*ploidy*.

plonk¹ informal ■ v. 1 set down heavily or carelessly. 2 play unskilfully on a musical instrument. ■ n. a sound as of something being set down heavily.
–ORIGIN C19 (orig. dialect): imitative; cf. **PLUNK**.

plonk² ■ n. informal cheap wine of inferior quality.
–ORIGIN 1930s (orig. Australian): prob. an alteration of *blanc* in French *vin blanc* 'white wine'.

plop ■ n. a short sound as of a small, solid object dropping into water without a splash. ■ v. (**plopped**, **plopping**) fall or drop with such a sound.
–ORIGIN C19: imitative.

plosion /ˈpləʊʒ(ə)n/ ■ n. Phonetics the sudden release of air in the pronunciation of a plosive consonant.

plosive /ˈpləʊsɪv, -z-/ Phonetics ■ adj. denoting a consonant that is produced by stopping the airflow using the lips,

plot

teeth, or palate, followed by a sudden release of air. ■ n. a plosive speech sound.
- ORIGIN C19: shortening of **EXPLOSIVE**.

plot ■ n. **1** a plan made in secret by a group of people to do something illegal or harmful. **2** the main sequence of events in a play, novel, or film. **3** a small piece of ground marked out for building, gardening, etc. **4** a graph showing the relation between two variables. ▶ chiefly US a diagram, chart, or map. ■ v. (**plotted**, **plotting**) **1** secretly make plans to carry out (something illegal or harmful). **2** devise the plot of (a play, novel, or film). **3** mark (a route or position) on a chart. ▶ mark out or allocate (points) on a graph. ▶ make (a curve) by marking out a number of such points. ▶ illustrate by use of a graph.
- DERIVATIVES **plotless** adj. **plotter** n.
- ORIGIN Old English: the sense 'secret plan' is associated with Old French *complot* 'dense crowd, secret project'.

plough (US **plow**) ■ n. **1** a large farming implement with one or more blades fixed in a frame, drawn over soil to turn it over and cut furrows in preparation for the planting of seeds. ▶ land that has been ploughed. **2** (**the Plough**) a prominent formation of seven stars in the constellation Ursa Major (the Great Bear). ■ v. **1** turn up (earth) with a plough. ▶ chiefly N. Amer. clear snow from (a road) using a snowplough. **2** (often **plough into**) (of a vehicle) move in a fast and uncontrolled manner. **3** (of a ship or boat) travel through (an area of water). **4** (often **plough on**) advance or progress laboriously or forcibly. **5** (**plough something in**) invest or reinvest money in a business.
- DERIVATIVES **ploughable** adj. **plougher** n.
- ORIGIN Old English, of Germanic origin.

ploughman's lunch ■ n. a meal of bread and cheese with pickle and salad.

ploughshare ■ n. the main cutting blade of a plough.
- ORIGIN Middle English: from **PLOUGH** + Old English *scær*, *scear* 'ploughshare'.

plover /ˈplʌvə/ ■ n. a short-billed gregarious wading bird, typically found by water but sometimes frequenting grassland, tundra, or mountains. [Family Charadriidae: many species.]
- ORIGIN Middle English: from Anglo-Norman French, from Latin *pluvia* 'rain'.

plow ■ n. & v. US spelling of **PLOUGH**.

ploy ■ n. a cunning plan or action designed to turn a situation to one's own advantage.
- ORIGIN C17 (orig. Scots and northern English in the sense 'pastime').

PLR ■ abbrev. Public Lending Right.

pluck ■ v. **1** take hold of (something) and quickly remove it from its place. ▶ catch hold of and pull quickly. **2** pull the feathers from (a bird's carcass) to prepare it for cooking. ▶ pull some of the hairs from (one's eyebrows) to make them look neater. **3** sound (a stringed musical instrument) with one's finger or a plectrum. **4** (**pluck up**) summon up (enough courage, nerve, etc.) to do something frightening. ■ n. **1** spirited and determined courage. **2** the heart, liver, and lungs of an animal as food.
- DERIVATIVES **-plucker** n.
- ORIGIN Old English, of Germanic origin.

plucky ■ adj. (**-ier**, **-iest**) determined and courageous in the face of difficulties.
- DERIVATIVES **pluckily** adv. **pluckiness** n.

plug ■ n. **1** a piece of solid material fitting tightly into a hole and blocking it up. ▶ a mass of solidified lava filling the neck of a volcano. **2** a device consisting of an insulated casing with metal pins that fit into holes in a socket to make an electrical connection. ▶ informal an electrical socket. **3** informal a piece of publicity promoting a product or event. **4** a piece of tobacco cut from a larger cake for chewing. ▶ (also **plug tobacco**) tobacco in large cakes designed to be cut for chewing. **5** Fishing a lure with one or more hooks attached. ■ v. (**plugged**, **plugging**) **1** block or fill in (a hole or cavity). **2** (**plug something in**) connect an electrical appliance to the mains by means of a socket. ▶ (**plug into**) have or gain access to an information system or area of activity. **3** informal promote (a product or event) by mentioning it publicly. **4** informal shoot or hit. **5** (usu.

plug away) informal proceed steadily and laboriously with a task.
- DERIVATIVES **plugger** n.
- ORIGIN C17: from Middle Dutch and Middle Low German *plugge*.

plughole ■ n. a hole at the lowest point of a bath or sink, down which waste water drains away.
- PHRASES **go down the plughole** informal be unsuccessful, lost, or wasted.

plug-in ■ n. Computing a module or piece of software which can be added to an existing system to give extra features.

plum ■ n. **1** an oval fleshy fruit which is purple, reddish, or yellow when ripe, containing a flattish pointed stone. **2** the tree bearing this fruit. [*Prunus domestica* and related species.] **3** a reddish-purple colour. **4** [usu. as modifier] informal something highly desirable: *a plum job*.
- PHRASES **have a plum in one's mouth** Brit. have an upper-class accent.
- ORIGIN Old English *plūme*, from Latin *prunum* (see **PRUNE¹**).

plumage /ˈpluːmɪdʒ/ ■ n. a bird's feathers collectively.
- DERIVATIVES **-plumaged** adj.
- ORIGIN Middle English: from Old French, from *plume* 'feather'.

plumb¹ ■ v. **1** measure (the depth of a body of water). **2** explore or experience fully or to extremes: *she had plumbed the depths of depravity*. **3** test (an upright surface) to determine the vertical. ■ n. a lead ball or other heavy object attached to a line for finding the depth of water or determining the vertical on an upright surface. ■ adv. **1** informal exactly: *plumb in the centre*. **2** N. Amer. extremely or completely: *they must be plumb crazy*. **3** archaic vertically. ■ adj. **1** vertical. **2** Cricket (of the wicket) level; true.

plumb² ■ v. (**plumb something in**) install a bath, washing machine, etc. and connect it to water and drainage pipes. ▶ install and connect pipes in (a building or room).
- ORIGIN C19: back-formation from **PLUMBER**.

plumbago /plʌmˈbeɪɡəʊ/ ■ n. (pl. **-os**) **1** an evergreen shrub or climber with blue or white flowers. [Genus *Plumbago*.] **2** old-fashioned term for **GRAPHITE**.
- ORIGIN C17: from Latin, from *plumbum* 'lead'.

plumbate /ˈplʌmbeɪt/ ■ n. Chemistry a salt in which the anion contains both lead and oxygen.
- ORIGIN C19: from Latin *plumbum* 'lead'.

plumb bob ■ n. a bob of lead or other heavy material forming the weight of a plumb line.

plumber ■ n. a person who fits and repairs the pipes and fittings of water supply, sanitation, or heating systems.
- ORIGIN Middle English (orig. denoting a person dealing in and working with lead): from Old French *plommier*, from Latin *plumbarius*, from *plumbum* 'lead'.

plumbic /ˈplʌmbɪk/ ■ adj. Chemistry of lead with a valency of four; of lead(IV). Compare with **PLUMBOUS**.
- ORIGIN C18: from Latin *plumbum* 'lead'.

plumbing ■ n. **1** the system of pipes, tanks, and fittings required for the water supply, heating, and sanitation in a building. ▶ the work of installing and maintaining such a system. **2** euphemistic a person's excretory tracts and urinary system.

plumbless /ˈplʌmlɪs/ ■ adj. poetic/literary (of water) extremely deep.

plumb line ■ n. a line with a plumb attached to it.

plumbous /ˈplʌmbəs/ ■ adj. Chemistry of lead with a valency of two; of lead(II). Compare with **PLUMBIC**.
- ORIGIN C17: from Latin *plumbosus* 'full of lead'.

plumb rule ■ n. a plumb line attached to a board, used by builders and surveyors.

plume ■ n. **1** a long, soft feather or arrangement of feathers used by a bird for display or worn on a hat or helmet as decoration. **2** a long spreading cloud of smoke or vapour. **3** Geology a column of magma rising by convection in the earth's mantle.
- DERIVATIVES **plumed** adj. **plumeless** adj. **plumery** n.
- ORIGIN Middle English: from Latin *pluma* 'down'.

plume moth ■ n. a small, slender, long-legged moth with narrow wings divided into feathery plumes. [Family Pterophoridae.]

plummet ■ v. (**plummeted, plummeting**) fall or drop straight down at high speed. ▶ decrease rapidly in value or amount. ■ n. 1 a steep and rapid fall or drop. 2 a plumb or plumb line.
– ORIGIN Middle English: from Old French *plommet* 'small sounding lead', diminutive of *plomb* 'lead'.

plummy ■ adj. (**-ier, -iest**) 1 resembling a plum. 2 Brit. informal (of a person's voice) typical of the English upper classes. 3 Brit. informal choice; highly desirable.

plumose /ˈpluːməʊs, ˈpluːməʊs, -z/ ■ adj. chiefly Biology having many fine filaments or branches which give a feathery appearance.
– ORIGIN C18: from Latin *plumosus* 'full of down or feathers', from *pluma* 'down'.

plump¹ ■ adj. full and rounded in shape. ▶ rather fat. ■ v. (often **plump something up**) make or become full and round.
– DERIVATIVES **plumpish** adj. **plumply** adv. **plumpness** n. **plumpy** adj.
– ORIGIN C15: rel. to Middle Dutch *plomp*, Middle Low German *plump* 'blunt, obtuse'.

plump² ■ v. 1 (often **plump something down**) set or sit down heavily or unceremoniously. 2 (**plump for**) decide definitely in favour of (one of two or more possibilities).
– ORIGIN Middle English: rel. to Middle Low German *plumpen*, Middle Dutch *plompen* 'fall into water'.

plum pudding ■ n. a rich boiled suet pudding containing raisins, currants, and spices.

plum tomato ■ n. a plum-shaped variety of tomato.

plumule /ˈpluːmjuːl/ ■ n. 1 Botany the rudimentary shoot or stem of an embryo plant. 2 Ornithology a bird's down feather, numbers of which form an insulating layer under the contour feathers.
– ORIGIN C18: from French *plumule* or Latin *plumula* 'small feather', diminutive of *pluma* 'down'.

plumy ■ adj. (**-ier, -iest**) resembling or decorated with feathers.

plunder ■ v. forcibly steal goods from, especially in time of war or civil disorder. ■ n. the action of plundering. ▶ property acquired in this way.
– DERIVATIVES **plunderer** n.
– ORIGIN C17: from German *plündern* 'rob of household goods', from Middle High German *plunder* 'household effects'.

plunge ■ v. 1 fall or move suddenly and uncontrollably. ▶ jump or dive quickly and energetically. 2 (often **plunge in**) embark impetuously on a speech or course of action. 3 push or thrust quickly. 4 (**plunge someone/thing into**) suddenly bring someone or something into a specified condition or state. ■ n. an act of plunging.
– PHRASES **take the plunge** informal commit oneself to a bold course of action after consideration.
– ORIGIN Middle English: from Old French *plungier* 'thrust down', from Latin *plumbum* 'lead, plummet'.

plunge pool ■ n. 1 a deep basin at the foot of a waterfall formed by the action of the falling water. 2 a small, deep swimming pool.

plunger ■ n. 1 a part of a device or mechanism that works with a plunging or thrusting movement. 2 a device consisting of a rubber cup on a long handle, used to clear blocked pipes by means of suction.

plunk informal ■ v. 1 play a keyboard or plucked stringed instrument in an unexpressive way. 2 chiefly N. Amer. set down heavily or abruptly. ■ n. 1 a plunking sound. 2 N. Amer. an act of setting something down heavily.
– ORIGIN C19: prob. imitative.

pluperfect Grammar ■ adj. (of a tense) denoting an action completed prior to some past point of time specified or implied, formed in English by *had* and the past participle. ■ n. a verb in the pluperfect tense.
– ORIGIN C15: from Latin (*tempus praeteritum*) *plus quam perfectum* '(past tense) more than perfect'.

plural ■ adj. more than one in number. ▶ Grammar (of a word or form) denoting more than one, or (in languages with dual number) more than two. ■ n. Grammar a plural word or form. ▶ the plural number.
– DERIVATIVES **plurally** adv.
– ORIGIN Middle English: from Old French *plurel* or Latin *pluralis*, from *plus* 'more'.

pluralism ■ n. 1 a condition or system in which two or more states, groups, principles, etc., coexist. ▶ a political theory or system of power-sharing among a number of political parties. 2 Philosophy a theory or system that recognizes more than one ultimate principle. Compare with MONISM.
– DERIVATIVES **pluralist** n. & adj. **pluralistic** adj. **pluralistically** adv.

plurality ■ n. (pl. **-ies**) 1 the fact or state of being plural. 2 a large number of people or things.

pluralize (also **-ise**) ■ v. 1 cause to become more numerous. ▶ cause to be made up of several different elements. 2 give a plural form to (a word).
– DERIVATIVES **pluralization** (also **-isation**) n.

plural society ■ n. a society composed of different ethnic groups or cultural traditions.

plural voting ■ n. the system or practice of casting more than one vote, or of voting in more than one constituency.

pluripotent /ˌplʊərɪˈpəʊt(ə)nt/ ■ adj. Biology (of an immature or stem cell) capable of giving rise to several different cell types.

plus ■ prep. with the addition of. ▶ informal together with. ■ adj. 1 [postpos.] (after a number or amount) at least: *R500 000 plus.* ▶ (after a grade) rather better than: *B plus.* 2 (before a number) above zero; positive. 3 having a positive electric charge. ■ n. 1 short for PLUS SIGN. ▶ a mathematical operation of addition. 2 informal an advantage. ■ conj. informal furthermore; also.
– ORIGIN C16: from Latin, 'more'.

plus ça change /ˌpluː sa ˈʃɒ̃ʒ/ ■ exclam. used to express resigned acknowledgement of the fundamental immutability of things.
– ORIGIN French, from *plus ça change, plus c'est la même chose* 'the more it changes, the more it stays the same'.

plus fours ■ pl. n. baggy knickerbockers reaching below the knee, formerly worn by men for hunting and golf.
– ORIGIN 1920s: so named because the overhang at the knee required an extra four inches of material.

plush ■ n. a rich fabric of silk, cotton, or wool, with a long, soft nap. ■ adj. informal richly luxurious and expensive.
– DERIVATIVES **plushly** adv. **plushness** n. **plushy** adj. (**-ier, -iest**).
– ORIGIN C16: from obsolete French *pluche*, from Old French *peluchier* 'to pluck', from Latin *pilus* 'hair'.

plus-minus (also **plus or minus**) ■ adv. informal approximately; roughly.

plus sign ■ n. the symbol +, indicating addition or a positive value.

plutocracy /pluːˈtɒkrəsi/ ■ n. (pl. **-ies**) government by the wealthy. ▶ a state or society governed in this way. ▶ an elite or ruling class whose power derives from their wealth.
– DERIVATIVES **plutocratic** adj. **plutocratically** adv.
– ORIGIN C17: from Greek *ploutokratia*, from *ploutos* 'wealth' + *kratos* 'strength, authority'.

plutocrat ■ n. often derogatory a person whose power derives from their wealth.

plutonic ■ adj. Geology relating to or denoting igneous rock formed by solidification at considerable depth beneath the earth's surface.
– DERIVATIVES **plutonism** n.

plutonium ■ n. the chemical element of atomic number 94, a dense silvery radioactive metal of the actinide series, used as a fuel in nuclear reactors and as an explosive in nuclear fission weapons. (Symbol: **Pu**)
– ORIGIN 1940s: from the planetary body *Pluto*, on the pattern of *neptunium* (Pluto being the next planetary body beyond Neptune).

pluvial chiefly Geology ■ adj. relating to or characterized by rainfall. ■ n. a period marked by increased rainfall.
– ORIGIN C17: from Latin *pluvialis*, from *pluvia* 'rain'.

ply¹ ■ n. (pl. **-ies**) 1 a thickness or layer of a folded or laminated material. 2 each of a number of multiple layers or strands of which something is made: [in combination] *four-ply*.
– ORIGIN Middle English: from French *plier* 'to fold', from Latin *plicare* 'to fold'.

ply² ▪ v. (-ies, -ied) **1** work steadily with (a tool). ▸ work steadily at (one's business or trade). **2** (of a vessel or vehicle) travel regularly over a route, typically for commercial purposes. **3** (**ply someone with**) provide someone with (food or drink) in a continuous or insistent way. ▸ direct (numerous questions) at someone.
– ORIGIN Middle English: shortening of APPLY.

plywood ▪ n. a type of thin, strong wooden board consisting of two or more layers glued and pressed together.

PM ▪ abbrev. **1** post-mortem. **2** Prime Minister. **3** Provost Marshal.

Pm ▪ symb. the chemical element promethium.

p.m. ▪ abbrev. after noon.
– ORIGIN from Latin *post meridiem*.

PMG ▪ abbrev. **1** Paymaster General. **2** Postmaster General.

PMS ▪ abbrev. premenstrual syndrome.

PMT ▪ abbrev. chiefly Brit. premenstrual tension.

pneumatic ▪ adj. containing or operated by air or gas under pressure.
– DERIVATIVES **pneumatically** adv. **pneumaticity** n.
– ORIGIN C17: from Greek *pneumatikos*, from *pneuma* 'wind'.

pneumatic drill ▪ n. a large, heavy mechanical drill driven by compressed air, used for breaking up a hard surface such as a road.

pneumatics ▪ pl. n. [treated as sing.] the branch of physics or engineering concerned with the mechanical properties of gases.

pneumatic trough ▪ n. Chemistry a shallow liquid-filled container with which gases can be collected by displacing liquid from a jar inverted in the trough.

pneumatophore /ˈnjuːmətəfɔː/ ▪ n. **1** Zoology the gas-filled float of some colonial coelenterates, such as the Portuguese man-of-war. **2** Botany (in mangroves) an aerial root specialized for the exchange of gases.

pneumo- ▪ comb. form **1** of or relating to the lungs: *pneumogastric*. **2** of or relating to the presence of air or gas: *pneumothorax*.
– ORIGIN sense 1 from Greek *pneumōn* 'lung'; sense 2 from Greek *pneuma* 'air'.

pneumococcus /ˌnjuːməˈ(ʊ)kɒkəs/ ▪ n. (pl. **pneumococci** /-ˈkɒk(s)ʌɪ, -ˈkɒk(s)iː/) a bacterium associated with pneumonia and some forms of meningitis. [*Streptococcus pneumoniae*.]
– DERIVATIVES **pneumococcal** adj.

pneumoconiosis /ˌnjuːməˈ(ʊ)kəʊnɪˈəʊsɪs/ ▪ n. Medicine a disease of the lungs due to inhalation of dust, characterized by inflammation, coughing, and fibrosis.
– ORIGIN C19: from PNEUMO- + Greek *konis* 'dust'.

pneumocystis /ˌnjuːməˈ(ʊ)ˈsɪstɪs/ ▪ n. Medicine a parasitic protozoan that can cause fatal pneumonia in people affected with immunodeficiency disease. [*Pneumocystis carinii*.]

pneumonia /njuːˈməʊnɪə/ ▪ n. a lung infection in which the air sacs fill with pus.
– DERIVATIVES **pneumonic** adj.
– ORIGIN C17: from Greek, from *pneumōn* 'lung'.

pneumonitis /ˌnjuːməˈ(ʊ)ˈnʌɪtɪs/ ▪ n. Medicine inflammation of the walls of the alveoli (air sacs) in the lungs, usually caused by a virus.

pneumothorax ▪ n. Medicine the presence of air or gas in the cavity between the lungs and the chest wall, causing collapse of the lung.

p-n junction ▪ n. Electronics a boundary between p-type and n-type material in a semiconductor device, functioning as a rectifier.

PNP ▪ adj. Electronics denoting a semiconductor device in which an *n*-type region is sandwiched between two *p*-type regions.

PO ▪ abbrev. Post Office.

P. & O. ▪ abbrev. Peninsular and Oriental Shipping Company (or Line).

Po ▪ symb. the chemical element polonium.

poach¹ ▪ v. cook by simmering in a small amount of liquid. ▸ cook (an egg) without its shell in or over boiling water.
– DERIVATIVES **poacher** n.
– ORIGIN Middle English: from Old French *pochier* in the sense 'enclose in a bag', from *poche* 'bag, pocket'.

poach² ▪ v. **1** illegally hunt or catch (game or fish) on land that is not one's own or in contravention of official protection. **2** take or acquire in an unfair or clandestine way. **3** (of an animal) trample or cut up (turf) with its hoofs.
– DERIVATIVES **poacher** n.
– ORIGIN C16: rel. to POKE; sense 1 is perhaps partly from French *pocher* (see POACH¹).

PO box ▪ abbrev. post office box.

pochard /ˈpəʊtʃəd, ˈpɒ-/ ▪ n. (pl. same or **pochards**) a diving duck, the male of which typically has a reddish-brown head. [Genera *Netta* and *Aythya*.]
– ORIGIN C16.

pochette /pɒˈʃɛt/ ▪ n. a woman's small handbag shaped like an envelope.
– ORIGIN C19: from French, 'small pocket', diminutive of *poche*.

pock ▪ n. a pockmark.
– DERIVATIVES **pocked** adj.
– ORIGIN Old English *poc* 'pustule', of Germanic origin.

pocket ▪ n. **1** a small bag sewn into or on clothing so as to form part of it, used for carrying small articles. ▸ a pouch-like compartment providing separate storage space. ▸ (**one's pocket**) informal one's financial resources. **2** S. African a narrow sack or mesh bag used for the sale of fruit and vegetables. **3** a small, isolated patch, group, or area. **4** an opening at the corner or on the side of a billiard table into which balls are struck. **5** American Football a protected area behind the line of scrimmage, from which the quarterback throws a pass. ▪ adj. of a suitable size for carrying in a pocket: *a pocket dictionary*. ▪ v. (**pocketed, pocketing**) **1** put into one's pocket. **2** take for oneself, especially dishonestly. **3** Billiards & Snooker drive (a ball) into a pocket.
– PHRASES **in pocket** having enough money or money to spare. ▸ having gained in a transaction. **in someone's pocket 1** dependent on someone financially and therefore under their influence. **2** closely involved with someone. **line one's pocket** make money, especially dishonestly. **out of pocket** having lost money in a transaction. **put one's hand in one's pocket** spend or provide one's own money.
– DERIVATIVES **pocketable** adj. **pocketful** n. (pl. -**fuls**). **pocketless** adj.
– ORIGIN Middle English: from Anglo-Norman French *poket(e)*, diminutive of *poke* 'pouch'.

pocketbook ▪ n. **1** chiefly Brit. a notebook. **2** US a wallet, purse, or handbag.

pocket knife ▪ n. a penknife.

pocket money ▪ n. a small amount of money given to a child by their parents, typically on a regular basis. ▸ a small amount of money suitable for minor expenses.

pocket watch ▪ n. a watch on a chain, intended to be carried in the pocket of a jacket or waistcoat.

pockmark ▪ n. a pitted scar or mark on the skin left by a pustule or spot. ▸ a mark or pitted area disfiguring a surface. ▪ v. cover or disfigure with pockmarks.

pod¹ ▪ n. **1** an elongated seed vessel of a leguminous plant such as the pea, splitting open on both sides when ripe. **2** a self-contained or detachable unit on an aircraft or spacecraft. **3** the egg case of a locust. ▪ v. (**podded, podding**) **1** (of a plant) bear or form pods. **2** remove (peas or beans) from their pods prior to cooking.
– ORIGIN C17: back-formation from dialect *podware*, *podder* 'field crops'.

pod² ▪ n. a small herd or school of marine animals, especially whales.
– ORIGIN C19 (orig. US).

podcast ▪ n. a digital recording of an audio or video broadcast that can be downloaded from the Internet to be played on any of several electronic devices.
– DERIVATIVES **podcaster** n. **podcasting** n.

—ORIGIN early C21: from *iPod*, a proprietary name for a personal audio player.

podger ■ n. a short metal bar used as a lever, especially for tightening a box spanner.

podgy ■ adj. (-ier, -iest) Brit. informal rather fat; chubby.
–DERIVATIVES **podginess** n.

podiatry /pəˈdʌɪətri/ ■ n. another term for CHIROPODY.
–DERIVATIVES **podiatrist** n.
–ORIGIN C20: from Greek *pous, pod-* 'foot' + *iatros* 'physician'.

podium /ˈpəʊdɪəm/ ■ n. (pl. **podiums** or **podia** /-dɪə/) **1** a small platform on which a person may stand to be seen by an audience. ▸ N. Amer. a lectern. **2** a continuous projecting base or pedestal under a building.
–ORIGIN C18: from Greek *podion*, diminutive of *pous* 'foot'.

podzol /ˈpɒdzɒl/ (also **podsol** /-sɒl/) ■ n. Soil Science an infertile acidic soil with a grey subsurface layer, typical of coniferous woodland.
–DERIVATIVES **podzolic** adj. **podzolization** (also **-isation**) n. **podzolize** (also **-ise**) v.
–ORIGIN C20: from Russian, from *pod* 'under' + *zola* 'ashes'.

poem ■ n. a literary composition that is given intensity by particular attention to diction (sometimes involving rhyme), rhythm, and imagery.
–ORIGIN C15: from Greek *poēma*, early var. of *poiēma* 'fiction, poem', from *poiein* 'create'.

poepol /ˈpupəl/ (also **poephol**) ■ n. S. African vulgar slang **1** a person's anus. **2** an idiot or fool.
–ORIGIN from Afrikaans.

poes /pʊs/ ■ n. S. African vulgar slang **1** a woman's genitals. **2** an unpleasant or stupid person.
–ORIGIN Afrikaans.

poesy /ˈpəʊɪzi, -si/ ■ n. archaic or poetic/literary poetry. ▸ the art or composition of poetry.
–ORIGIN Middle English: from Old French *poesie*, from Greek *poēsis*, var. of *poiēsis* 'making, poetry'.

poet ■ n. a person who writes poems. ▸ a person possessing special powers of imagination or expression.
–ORIGIN Middle English: from Old French *poete*, from Greek *poētēs*, var. of *poiētēs* 'maker, poet'.

poetess ■ n. a female poet.

poetic ■ adj. relating to or of the nature of poetry.
–DERIVATIVES **poetical** adj. **poetically** adv. **poeticism** n. **poeticize** (also **-ise**) v.

poetic justice ■ n. fitting or deserved retribution for a person's actions, as encountered in poetry or literature.

poetic licence ■ n. departure from convention or factual accuracy in order to create an artistic effect.

poetics ■ pl. n. [treated as sing.] the art of writing poetry. ▸ the study of linguistic techniques in poetry and literature.

Poet Laureate ■ n. (pl. **Poets Laureate**) an eminent poet appointed by the British royal household to write poems for royal and official occasions.

poetry ■ n. poems collectively or as a genre of literature. ▸ a quality of beauty and intensity of emotion regarded as characteristic of poetry.

po-faced ■ adj. humourless and disapproving.
–ORIGIN 1930s: perhaps from *po* 'chamber pot', influenced by *poker-faced*.

pogo ■ v. (-oes, -oed) informal jump up and down as if on a pogo stick as a form of dancing to rock music, especially punk.

pogo stick ■ n. a toy for jumping about on, consisting of a spring-loaded pole with a handle at the top and rests for the feet near the bottom.
–ORIGIN 1920s.

pogrom /ˈpɒɡrəm, -ɡrɒm, pəˈɡrɒm/ ■ n. an organized massacre of a particular ethnic group, originally that of Jews in Russia or eastern Europe.
–ORIGIN C20: from Russian, 'devastation'.

poignant /ˈpɔɪnjənt/ ■ adj. evoking a keen sense of sadness or regret.
–DERIVATIVES **poignance** n. **poignancy** n. **poignantly** adv.
–ORIGIN Middle English: from Old French, 'pricking', from *poindre*, from Latin *pungere* 'to prick'.

poikilotherm /ˈpɔɪkɪləʊθəːm/ ■ n. Zoology an organism that cannot regulate its body temperature except by behavioural means such as basking or burrowing. Often contrasted with HOMEOTHERM.
–DERIVATIVES **poikilothermal** adj. **poikilothermic** adj. **poikilothermy** n.

poinciana /ˌpɔɪnsɪˈɑːnə/ ■ n. a tropical tree with showy red or red and yellow flowers. [Genera *Caesalpinia* and *Delonix* (formerly *Poinciana*).]
–ORIGIN C18: named after M. de *Poinci*, a C17 governor of the Antilles.

poinsettia /ˌpɔɪnˈsɛtɪə/ ■ n. a shrub with large showy scarlet bracts surrounding the small yellow flowers. [*Euphorbia* (formerly *Poinsettia*) *pulcherrima*.]
–ORIGIN C19: named after the American diplomat and botanist Joel R. *Poinsett*.

point /pɔɪnt/ ■ n. **1** the tapered, sharp end of a tool, weapon, or other object. ▸ Archaeology a pointed flake or blade. ▸ Ballet another term for POINTE. ▸ Boxing the tip of a person's chin as a spot for a blow. ▸ the prong of a deer's antler. **2** a dot or other punctuation mark, in particular a full stop. ▸ a decimal point. ▸ a dot or small stroke used in Semitic languages to indicate vowels or distinguish particular consonants. ▸ a very small dot or mark on a surface. **3** a particular spot, place, or moment. ▸ (**the point of**) the verge or brink of. ▸ (in geometry) something having position but not spatial extent, magnitude, dimension, or direction. **4** a single item or detail in an extended discussion, list, or text. ▸ an argument or idea. ▸ the significant or essential element: *come to the point.* ▸ [usu. with neg. or in questions] advantage or purpose. ▸ (often in phrs **beside/off/to the point**) relevance. ▸ a distinctive feature or characteristic, typically a good one. **5** (in sports and games) a mark or unit of scoring awarded for success or performance. ▸ a unit used in measuring value, achievement, or extent. ▸ (in piquet) the longest suit in a player's hand, containing a specified number of up to eight cards. ▸ a unit of weight (2 mg) for diamonds. **6** each of thirty-two directions marked at equal distances round a compass. ▸ the angular interval between two successive points of a compass, i.e. one eighth of a right angle (11° 15'). **7** a narrow piece of land jutting out into the sea. **8** Brit. a junction of two railway lines, with a pair of linked tapering rails that can be moved laterally to allow a train to pass from one line to the other. **9** Printing a unit of measurement for type sizes and spacing (in the UK and US 0.351 mm, in Europe 0.376 mm). **10** a socket in a wall for connecting a device to an electrical supply or communications network: *a power point.* **11** each of a set of electrical contacts in the distributor of a motor vehicle. **12** Cricket a fielding position on the off side near the batsman. **13** a small leading party of an advanced guard of troops. ▸ chiefly N. Amer. the position at the head of a column or wedge of troops. **14** the extremities of a horse or cat, such as the face, paws, and tail of a Siamese cat. **15** historical a tagged piece of ribbon or cord used for lacing a garment or attaching a hose to a doublet. **16** a short piece of cord at the lower edge of a sail for tying up a reef. ■ v. **1** (often **point at/to**) direct someone's attention in a particular direction by extending one's finger. ▸ (**point something out**) make someone aware of a fact or circumstance. ▸ face in or indicate a particular direction. ▸ (often **point to**) cite or function as evidence. **2** direct or aim (something). **3** (**point something up**) reveal the true nature or importance of something. **4** chiefly Ballet extend (the toes or feet) by tensing the foot and ankle so as to form a point. **5** fill in or repair the joints of (brickwork or tiling) with smoothly finished mortar or cement. ▸ [as noun **pointing**] mortar or cement used in pointing. **6** give a sharp, tapered point to. **7** (of a dog) indicate the presence of (game) by acting as pointer.
–PHRASES **a case in point** an instance or example that illustrates what is being discussed. **make a point of** make a special and noticeable effort to do something. **point the finger** openly accuse someone or apportion blame. **the point of no return** the point in a journey or enterprise at which it becomes essential to continue to its end. **point of sailing** a sailing boat's heading in relation to the wind. **score points** deliberately make oneself appear superior to someone else by making clever remarks. **take someone's point** chiefly Brit. accept the validity of someone's idea or

point-and-shoot

argument. **up to a point** to some extent but not completely.
– ORIGIN Middle English: the noun partly from Old French *point*, from Latin *punctum* 'something that is pricked'; partly from Old French *pointe*, from Latin *puncta* 'pricking'; verb from Old French *pointer*.

point-and-shoot ■ adj. of or relating to a compact camera that adjusts settings such as focus and exposure automatically. ■ n. a camera that is easy to operate.

point-blank ■ adj. & adv. **1** (of a shot or missile) fired from very close to its target. **2** without explanation or qualification: *he refuses point-blank to give interviews.*
– ORIGIN C16: prob. from POINT + BLANK in the sense 'white spot in the centre of a target'.

point break ■ n. (in surfing) a type of wave characteristic of a coast with a headland.

point duty ■ n. Brit. the duties of a police officer or other official stationed at a junction to control traffic.

pointe /pwăt/ ■ n. (pl. pronounced same) Ballet the tips of the toes. ▸ (also **pointe work**) dancing performed on the tips of the toes.
– ORIGIN French, 'tip'.

pointed ■ adj. **1** having a sharpened or tapered tip or end. **2** (of a remark or look) clearly directed and unambiguous in intent.
– DERIVATIVES **pointedly** adv. **pointedness** n.

pointer ■ n. **1** a long, thin piece of metal on a scale or dial which moves to give a reading. ▸ a rod used for pointing to features on a map or chart. ▸ Computing a cursor. ▸ Computing a link. **2** a hint as to what might happen in the future. ▸ a small piece of advice; a tip. **3** a dog of a breed that on scenting game stands rigid looking towards it.

point guard ■ n. Basketball the player who directs the team's offence.

pointillism /'pwantılız(ə)m/ ■ n. a technique of neo-Impressionist painting using tiny dots of various pure colours, which become blended in the viewer's eye.
– DERIVATIVES **pointillist** n. & adj. **pointillistic** adj.
– ORIGIN C20: from French *pointillisme*, from *pointiller* 'mark with dots'.

point lace ■ n. lace made with a needle on a parchment pattern.

pointless ■ adj. **1** having little or no sense or purpose. **2** having scored no points.
– DERIVATIVES **pointlessly** adv. **pointlessness** n.

point man ■ n. **1** the soldier at the head of a patrol. **2** chiefly N. Amer. a person at the forefront of an activity.

point mutation ■ n. Genetics a mutation affecting only one or very few nucleotides in a gene sequence.

point of departure ■ n. the starting point of a line of thought or course of action.

point of honour ■ n. a circumstance that affects one's reputation or conscience.

point of order ■ n. a query in a formal debate or meeting as to whether correct procedure is being followed.

point of view ■ n. **1** a particular attitude or way of considering a matter. **2** the position from which something or someone is observed.

pointsman ■ n. (pl. **-men**) **1** a traffic officer who directs traffic at an intersection. **2** an operator of railway points or junctions.

point source ■ n. Physics a source of energy, such as light or sound, which can be regarded as having negligible dimensions.

point-to-point ■ n. (pl. **point-to-points**) an amateur steeplechase for horses used in hunting, over a set cross-country course.
– DERIVATIVES **point-to-pointer** n. **point-to-pointing** n.

pointy ■ adj. (**-ier**, **-iest**) informal having a pointed tip or end.

pointy-headed ■ adj. N. Amer. informal, chiefly derogatory expert or intellectual.
– DERIVATIVES **pointy head** n.

poise[1] ■ n. **1** graceful and elegant bearing. ▸ composure and dignity of manner. **2** archaic balance; equilibrium. ■ v. **1** be or cause to be balanced or suspended. **2** [as adj. **poised**] composed and elegant or self-assured. **3** (**be poised to do something**) be ready and prepared to do something.
– ORIGIN Middle English: from Old French *pois*, *peis* (n.), *peser* (v.), from Latin *pensum* 'weight'.

poise[2] (abbrev. : **P**) ■ n. Physics a unit of dynamic viscosity, such that a tangential force of one dyne per square centimetre causes a velocity change of one centimetre per second between two parallel planes separated by one centimetre in a liquid.
– ORIGIN C20: from the name of Jean L. M. Poiseuille (1799–1869), French physician.

poison ■ n. **1** a substance that causes death or harm when introduced into or absorbed by a living organism. **2** something that has a destructive or corrupting influence. **3** Chemistry a substance that reduces the activity of a catalyst. **4** Physics an impurity that retards nuclear fission by absorbing neutrons. ■ v. **1** administer poison to or contaminate with poison. **2** corrupt or prove harmful to.
– DERIVATIVES **poisoner** n. **poisoning** n.
– ORIGIN Middle English: from Old French *poison* 'magic potion', from Latin *potio(n-)* 'potion', rel. to *potare* 'to drink'.

poisoned chalice ■ n. an assignment or award which is likely to prove a source of problems for the recipient.

poison ivy ■ n. a North American climbing plant which secretes an irritant oil from its leaves that can cause dermatitis. [*Rhus radicans*.]

poison oak ■ n. a North American climbing shrub related to poison ivy and having similar properties. [*Rhus toxicodendron*.]

poisonous ■ adj. **1** producing or of the nature of poison. **2** extremely unpleasant or malicious.
– DERIVATIVES **poisonously** adv.

poison pen letter ■ n. an anonymous letter that is libellous, abusive, or malicious.

poison pill ■ n. Finance a tactic used by a company threatened with an unwelcome takeover bid to make itself unattractive to the bidder.

Poisson distribution /'pwʌsɒ̃/ ■ n. Statistics a discrete frequency distribution which gives the probability of a number of independent events occurring in a fixed time.
– ORIGIN named after the French mathematical physicist Siméon-Denis *Poisson* (1781–1840).

poke ■ v. **1** jab or prod with a finger or a sharp object. ▸ prod and stir (a fire) with a poker to make it burn more fiercely. **2** (**poke about/around**) look or search around a place. **3** (often **poke out**) thrust out or protrude in a particular direction. ■ n. **1** an act of poking. **2** (also **poke bonnet**) a woman's bonnet with a projecting brim or front, popular in the early 19th century.
– PHRASES **poke fun at** tease or make fun of. **poke one's nose into** informal take an intrusive interest in. **take a poke at someone** informal hit, punch, or criticize someone.
– ORIGIN Middle English.

poker[1] ■ n. a metal rod with a handle, used for prodding and stirring an open fire.

poker[2] ■ n. a card game played by two or more people who bet on the value of the hands dealt to them, sometimes using bluff.
– ORIGIN C19: of US origin; perhaps rel. to German *pochen* 'to brag', *Pochspiel* 'bragging game'.

poker dice ■ pl. n. dice with card designs (from nine to ace) on the faces instead of spots. ▸ [treated as sing.] a dice game in which the thrower aims for combinations of several dice.

poker face ■ n. an impassive expression that hides one's true feelings.
– DERIVATIVES **poker-faced** adj.

pokerwork ■ n. British term for PYROGRAPHY.

pokey ■ n. informal, chiefly N. Amer. prison.
– ORIGIN C20: alteration of *pogey* in the sense 'hostel for the needy', perhaps influenced by POKY.

poky (also **pokey**) ■ adj. (**-ier**, **-iest**) (of a room or building) uncomfortably small and cramped.

– DERIVATIVES **pokily** adv. **pokiness** n.
– ORIGIN C19: from **POKE**, in the sense 'confine'.

pol ■ n. informal, chiefly N. Amer. a politician.

Polack /ˈpəʊlak/ ■ n. derogatory, chiefly N. Amer. a person from Poland or of Polish descent.
– ORIGIN C16: from Polish *Polak*.

polar ■ adj. **1** of or relating to a pole or poles, in particular, of the North or South Pole or their adjacent area. **2** Physics & Chemistry having an electrical or magnetic field. **3** directly opposite in character or tendency. ■ n. Geometry the straight line joining the two points at which tangents from a fixed point touch a conic section.
– ORIGIN C16: from medieval Latin *polaris* 'heavenly', from Latin *polus* (see **POLE**²).

polar bear ■ n. a large white arctic bear which lives mainly on the pack ice. [*Thalarctos maritimus*.]

polar body ■ n. Biology each of the small cells which bud off from an oocyte at the two meiotic divisions and do not develop into ova.

polar cap ■ n. Astronomy a region of ice or other frozen matter surrounding a pole of a planet.

polar coordinates ■ pl. n. Geometry a pair of positional coordinates representing respectively the length of the straight line connecting a given point to the origin and the angle made by this line with a fixed line.

Polari /pəˈlɑːri/ (also **Palari** or **Palare**) ■ n. a form of theatrical slang incorporating Italianate words, rhyming slang, and Romany, used especially by homosexuals.
– ORIGIN C19: from Italian *parlare* 'to speak'.

polarimeter /ˌpəʊləˈrɪmɪtə/ ■ n. an instrument for measuring the polarization of light, especially to determine the optical activity of a substance.
– DERIVATIVES **polarimetric** adj. **polarimetry** n.

polarity ■ n. (pl. **-ies**) **1** the property of having poles or being polar. **2** the direction of a magnetic or electric field.

polarize (also **-ise**) ■ v. **1** Physics restrict the vibrations of (a transverse wave, especially light) wholly or partially to one direction. **2** Physics cause to acquire polarity. **3** [usu. as adj. **polarized** (also **-ised**)] divide into two sharply contrasting groups or sets of beliefs.
– DERIVATIVES **polarization** (also **-isation**) n. **polarizer** (also **-iser**) n.

polarography /ˌpəʊləˈrɒɡrəfi/ ■ n. Chemistry a method of analysis in which a sample is electrolysed using a range of voltages and a plot of current against voltage drawn (showing steps corresponding to particular chemical species).

Polaroid ■ n. **1** trademark a composite material with the property of polarizing light, produced in thin plastic sheets. ▸ (**Polaroids**) sunglasses with lenses of polaroid. **2** a type of camera that produces a finished print rapidly after each exposure. ▸ a photograph taken with such a camera.

polder /ˈpəʊldə/ ■ n. a piece of low-lying land reclaimed from the sea or a river and protected by dykes, especially in the Netherlands.
– ORIGIN C17: from Dutch.

Pole ■ n. a native or national of Poland, or a person of Polish descent.

pole¹ ■ n. **1** a long, slender piece of wood or metal, typically used as a support. ▸ a simple fishing rod. **2** a young tree with a straight slender trunk and no lower branches. ■ v. propel (a boat) with a pole.
– PHRASES **under bare poles** Nautical with no sail set. **up the pole** informal mad.
– ORIGIN Old English *pāl*, of Germanic origin, from Latin *palus* 'stake'.

pole² ■ n. **1** either of the two locations (North Pole or South Pole) on the earth which are the ends of the axis of rotation. ▸ Geometry each of the two points at which the axis of a circle cuts the surface of a sphere. ▸ Geometry a fixed point to which other points or lines are referred, e.g. the origin of polar coordinates. ▸ each of the two opposite points of a magnet at which magnetic forces are strongest. **2** each of two opposed or contradictory principles or ideas.
– PHRASES **be poles apart** have nothing in common.
– DERIVATIVES **poleward** adj. **polewards** adj. & adv.

– ORIGIN Middle English: from Latin *polus*, from Greek *polos* 'pivot, axis, sky'.

poleaxe (US also **poleax**) ■ n. a battleaxe. ▸ a short-handled axe with a spike at the back, formerly used in naval warfare. ▸ a butcher's axe with a hammer head at the back, used to slaughter animals. ■ v. **1** hit, kill, or knock down with or as if with a poleaxe. **2** shock greatly.
– ORIGIN Middle English: rel. to Middle Dutch *pol(l)aex*, Middle Low German *pol(l)exe*.

polecat ■ n. **1** a weasel-like mammal noted for its fetid smell. [Genera *Mustela* (Eurasia) and *Ictonyx* (Africa).] **2** North American term for **SKUNK**.
– ORIGIN Middle English: perhaps from Old French *pole* 'chicken' + **CAT**¹.

pole dancing ■ n. erotic dancing which involves swinging around a fixed pole.
– DERIVATIVES **pole dancer** n.

polemic /pəˈlɛmɪk/ ■ n. a strong verbal or written attack. ▸ (also **polemics**) the art or practice of engaging in controversial debate or dispute. ■ adj. (also **polemical**) of or involving strong or controversial debate.
– DERIVATIVES **polemically** adv. **polemicist** n. **polemicize** (also **-ise**) v.
– ORIGIN C17: from Greek *polemikos*, from *polemos* 'war'.

polenta /pəˈlɛntə/ ■ n. maize flour as used in Italian cookery. ▸ a paste or dough made from this flour, which is boiled and then fried or baked.
– ORIGIN C16: Italian, from Latin, 'pearl barley'.

pole piece ■ n. Physics a mass of iron forming the end of an electromagnet, through which the lines of magnetic force are concentrated and directed.

pole position ■ n. the most favourable position at the start of a motor race.
– ORIGIN 1950s: from a C19 use of *pole* in horse racing, denoting the starting position next to the inside boundary fence.

pole vault ■ n. an athletic event in which competitors attempt to vault over a high bar with the aid of an extremely long flexible pole. ■ v. (**pole-vault**) perform a pole vault.
– DERIVATIVES **pole-vaulter** n.

police ■ n. [treated as pl.] a civil force responsible for the prevention and detection of crime and the maintenance of public order. ▸ members of such a force. ■ v. [often as noun **policing**] control and maintain law and order in (an area), with or as with a police force.
– ORIGIN C15: from medieval Latin *politia* (see **POLICY**¹).

policeman (or **policewoman**) ■ n. (pl. **-men** or **-women**) a member of a police force.

police officer ■ n. a policeman or policewoman.

police record ■ n. a dossier kept by the police on people convicted of crime.

police state ■ n. a totalitarian state controlled by a political police force that secretly supervises the citizens' activities.

police station ■ n. the office or headquarters of a local police force.

policy¹ ■ n. (pl. **-ies**) **1** a course or principle of action adopted or proposed by an organization or individual. **2** archaic prudent or expedient conduct or action.
– ORIGIN Middle English: from Old French *policie* 'civil administration', from Greek *politeia* 'citizenship'.

policy² ■ n. (pl. **-ies**) a contract of insurance.
– ORIGIN C16: from French *police* 'bill of lading, contract of insurance'.

policyholder ■ n. a person or group in whose name an insurance policy is held.

polio ■ n. short for **POLIOMYELITIS**.

poliomyelitis /ˌpəʊlɪəʊmʌɪəˈlʌɪtɪs, ˌpɒlɪəʊ-/ ■ n. Medicine an infectious viral disease that affects the central nervous system and can cause temporary or permanent paralysis.
– ORIGIN C19: from Greek *polios* 'grey' + *muelos* 'marrow'.

poliovirus ■ n. Medicine any of a group of enteroviruses including those that cause poliomyelitis.

polis /ˈpɒlɪs/ ■ n. (pl. **poleis**) a city state in ancient Greece.
– ORIGIN from Greek.

Polish /ˈpəʊlɪʃ/ ■ n. the Western Slavic language of Poland. ■ adj. of or relating to Poland, its inhabitants, or their language.

polish /ˈpɒlɪʃ/ ■ v. **1** make smooth and shiny by rubbing. **2** [often as adj. **polished**] improve, refine, or add the finishing touches to. **3** (**polish something off**) finish or consume something quickly. **4** [as adj. **polished**] (of rice) having had the outer husk removed during milling. ■ n. **1** a substance used to make something smooth and shiny when rubbed in. ▶ an act of polishing. ▶ smoothness or glossiness produced by polishing. **2** refinement or elegance.
– DERIVATIVES **polishable** adj. **polisher** n.
– ORIGIN Middle English: from Old French *poliss-, polir* 'to polish', from Latin *polire*.

Polish notation ■ n. Computing a system of formula notation without brackets or special punctuation, used to represent arithmetical operations.

politburo /ˈpɒlɪtˌbjʊərəʊ/ ■ n. (pl. **-os**) the principal policy-making committee of a communist party, in particular that of the former USSR.
– ORIGIN from Russian *politbyuro*, from *polit(icheskoe) byuro* 'political bureau'.

polite ■ adj. (**-er, -est**) respectful and considerate of other people. ▶ cultured and refined: *polite society*.
– DERIVATIVES **politely** adv. **politeness** n.
– ORIGIN Middle English: from Latin *politus* 'polished, made smooth', from *polire*.

politesse /ˌpɒlɪˈtɛs/ ■ n. formal politeness or etiquette.
– ORIGIN C18: French, from Italian *politezza, pulitezza*, from *pulito* 'polite'.

politic ■ adj. (of an action) seeming sensible and judicious in the circumstances. ▶ (also **politick**) archaic (of a person) prudent and sagacious. ■ v. (**politicked, politicking**) [often as noun **politicking**] often derogatory engage in political activity.
– ORIGIN Middle English: from Old French *politique* 'political', from Greek *politikos*, from *politēs* 'citizen', from *polis* 'city'.

political ■ adj. **1** of or relating to the government or public affairs of a country. ▶ interested in or active in politics. **2** chiefly derogatory done or acting in the interests of status within an organization rather than on principle.
– DERIVATIVES **politically** adv.

political correctness ■ n. the avoidance of forms of expression or action that are perceived to exclude, marginalize, or insult groups of people who are socially disadvantaged or discriminated against.

political economy ■ n. dated economics as a branch of knowledge or academic discipline.
– DERIVATIVES **political economist** n.

politically correct (or **incorrect**) ■ adj. exhibiting (or failing to exhibit) political correctness.

political prisoner ■ n. a person imprisoned for their political beliefs or actions.

political science ■ n. the branch of knowledge concerning political activity and behaviour.
– DERIVATIVES **political scientist** n.

politician ■ n. **1** a person who is professionally involved in politics, especially as a holder of an elected office. **2** a person who acts in a manipulative and devious way, typically to gain advancement.

politicize (also **-ise**) ■ v. [often as adj. **politicized** (also **-ised**)] cause to become politically aware or political in character. ▶ engage in or talk about politics.
– DERIVATIVES **politicization** (also **-isation**) n.

politick ■ adj. archaic spelling of POLITIC.

politico ■ n. (pl. **-os**) informal, chiefly derogatory a politician or person with strong political views.
– ORIGIN Spanish and Italian, 'politic' or 'political person'.

politico- ■ comb. form politically: *politico-ethical*. ▶ political and ...: *politico-economic*.
– ORIGIN from Greek *politikos* 'civic, political'.

politics ■ pl. n. [usu. treated as sing.] **1** the activities associated with the governance of a country or area. ▶ a particular set of political beliefs or principles. **2** activities aimed at improving someone's status within an organization: *office politics*. **3** the principles relating to or inherent in a sphere or activity, especially when concerned with power and status: *the politics of gender*.

polity /ˈpɒlɪti/ ■ n. (pl. **-ies**) a form or process of civil government or constitution. ▶ an organized society; a state as a political entity.
– ORIGIN C16: from obsolete French *politie*, from Greek *politeia* 'citizenship, government'.

polka /ˈpɒlkə, ˈpəʊlkə/ ■ n. a lively dance of Bohemian origin in duple time. ■ v. (**polkas, polkaed** or **polka'd, polkaing**) dance the polka.
– ORIGIN C19: from Czech *půlka* 'half-step'.

polka dot ■ n. each of a number of round dots repeated to form a regular pattern.
– DERIVATIVES **polka-dotted** adj.

poll /pəʊl/ ■ n. **1** the process of voting in an election. ▶ a record of the number of votes cast in an election. ▶ an opinion poll. **2** dialect a person's head or scalp. **3** a hornless animal, especially one of a breed of hornless cattle. ■ v. **1** record the opinion or vote of. ▶ (of a candidate in an election) receive a specified number of votes. **2** cut the horns off (an animal, especially a young cow). ▶ [as adj. **polled**] (of a domestic animal) lacking horns. **3** Telecommunications & Computing check the status of (a device), especially as part of a repeated cycle.
– ORIGIN Middle English: perhaps of Low German origin.

pollack /ˈpɒlək/ (also **pollock**) ■ n. (pl. same or **pollacks**) an edible greenish-brown Atlantic fish of the cod family, with a protruding lower jaw. [*Pollachius pollachius*.]
– ORIGIN Middle English: perhaps of Celtic origin.

pollard /ˈpɒləd/ ■ v. [often as adj. **pollarded**] cut off the top and branches of (a tree) to encourage new growth at the top. ■ n. a tree whose top and branches have been pollarded.
– ORIGIN C17: from POLL + -ARD.

pollen ■ n. a powdery substance discharged from the male part of a flower, each microscopic grain containing a male gamete that can fertilize the female ovule.
– ORIGIN C18: from Latin, 'fine powder'.

pollen basket ■ n. Entomology a flattened area fringed with hairs on the hind leg of a social bee, used for carrying pollen.

pollen count ■ n. an index of the amount of pollen in the air.

pollen tube ■ n. Botany a hollow tube which grows out from a pollen grain into the stigma of a flower on which it is deposited.

pollex /ˈpɒlɛks/ ■ n. (pl. **pollices** /-lɪsiːz/) Zoology the innermost digit of a forelimb, especially the thumb in primates.
– ORIGIN C19: from Latin, 'thumb or big toe'.

pollinate ■ v. deposit pollen in (a flower or plant) and so allow fertilization.
– DERIVATIVES **pollination** n. **pollinator** n.

pollock ■ n. **1** North American term for SAITHE. **2** variant spelling of POLLACK.

pollster /ˈpəʊlstə/ ■ n. a person who conducts or analyses opinion polls.

poll tax ■ n. a tax levied on every adult, without reference to their income or resources.

pollute ■ v. **1** contaminate (water, the air, etc.) with harmful or poisonous substances. **2** corrupt.
– DERIVATIVES **pollutant** adj. & n. **polluter** n. **pollution** n.
– ORIGIN Middle English: from Latin *pollut-, polluere* 'pollute, defile', rel. to *lutum* 'mud'.

Pollyanna ■ n. an excessively cheerful or optimistic person.
– ORIGIN C20: the name of the optimistic heroine created by the American author Eleanor H. Porter (1868–1920).

polo ■ n. a game of Eastern origin with rules similar to hockey, played on horseback with a long-handled mallet.
– ORIGIN C19: from Balti, 'ball'.

polonaise /ˌpɒləˈneɪz/ ■ n. **1** a slow dance of Polish origin in triple time, stately and processional in character. ▶ a piece of music for this dance or in its rhythm. **2** historical a woman's dress with a tight bodice and a skirt open from

the waist downwards, looped up to show a decorative underskirt.
– ORIGIN C18: from French, feminine of *polonais* 'Polish'.

polo neck ■ n. a high, close-fitting, turned-over collar on a sweater.
– DERIVATIVES **polo-necked** adj.

polonium /pə'ləʊnɪəm/ ■ n. the chemical element of atomic number 84, a rare radioactive metal. (Symbol: **Po**)
– ORIGIN C19: from medieval Latin *Polonia* 'Poland' (the native country of Marie Curie, the element's co-discoverer).

polony /pə'ləʊni/ ■ n. (pl. -ies) another term for BOLOGNA.
– ORIGIN C18: an alteration of *Bologna*.

polo shirt ■ n. a casual short-sleeved cotton shirt with a collar and several buttons at the neck.

poltergeist /'pɒltəɡʌɪst/ ■ n. a ghost or other supernatural being supposedly responsible for physical disturbances such as throwing objects about.
– ORIGIN C19: from German *Poltergeist*, from *poltern* 'create a disturbance' + *Geist* 'ghost'.

poltroon /pɒl'truːn/ ■ n. archaic or poetic/literary an utter coward.
– ORIGIN C16: from French *poltron*, from Italian *poltrone*, perhaps from *poltro* 'sluggard'.

poly ■ n. (pl. **polys**) informal **1** polyester. **2** polythene. **3** Brit. a polytechnic.

poly- ■ comb. form many; much: *polychrome*. ▶ Chemistry having many atoms or groups of a particular kind in a molecule (especially a polymer): *polycarbonate*.
– ORIGIN from Greek *polus* 'much', *polloi* 'many'.

polyamide /ˌpɒlɪ'eɪmʌɪd, -'am-/ ■ n. a synthetic polymer, e.g. nylon, made by linking an amino group of one molecule and a carboxylic acid group of another.

polyandry /'pɒliandri/ ■ n. polygamy in which a woman has more than one husband. Compare with POLYGYNY.
– DERIVATIVES **polyandrous** adj.
– ORIGIN C17: from POLY- + Greek *anēr, andr-* 'male'.

polyanthus /ˌpɒlɪ'anθəs/ ■ n. (pl. same) a cultivated hybrid of the wild primrose and primulas. [*Primula × polyantha*.]
– ORIGIN C18: from POLY- + Greek *anthos* 'flower'.

polyatomic ■ adj. consisting of many atoms.

polycarbonate ■ n. a synthetic resin in which the polymer units are linked through carbonate groups.

Polychaeta /ˌpɒlɪ'kiːtə/ ■ pl. n. Zoology a class of marine annelid worms which comprises the bristle worms.
– DERIVATIVES **polychaete** /'pɒlɪkiːt/ n.
– ORIGIN from Greek *polu-* 'many' + *khaitē* 'mane'.

polychlorinated biphenyl ■ n. Chemistry any of a class of toxic chlorinated aromatic compounds, formed as waste in some industrial processes.

polychromatic ■ adj. multicoloured.
– DERIVATIVES **polychromatism** n.

polychrome ■ adj. painted, printed, or decorated in several colours. ■ n. **1** varied colouring. **2** a polychrome work of art.
– DERIVATIVES **polychromed** adj. **polychromy** n.
– ORIGIN C19: from Greek *polukhrōmos*, from *polu-* 'many' + *khrōma* 'colour'.

polyclinic ■ n. a clinic where both general and specialist medical care is available.

polyclonal /ˌpɒlɪ'kləʊn(ə)l/ ■ adj. Biology consisting of or derived from many clones.

polycrystalline ■ adj. consisting of many randomly oriented crystalline parts.

polyculture ■ n. the simultaneous cultivation or exploitation of several crops or kinds of animals.

polycyclic /ˌpɒlɪ'sʌɪklɪk, -'sɪk-/ ■ adj. **1** of, relating to, or resulting from many cycles. **2** Chemistry having several rings of atoms in the molecule.

polydactyl /ˌpɒlɪ'daktɪl/ ■ adj. having more than five fingers or toes on a hand or foot.

polyelectrolyte /ˌpɒlɪ'lɛktrəlʌɪt/ ■ n. Chemistry a polymer with several ionizable groups along the molecule.

polyembryony /ˌpɒlɪ'ɛmbrɪəni/ ■ n. Biology the formation of more than one embryo from a single ovum or seed.

polyester ■ n. a synthetic resin in which the polymer units are linked by ester groups, used chiefly to make textile fibres.

polyethylene /ˌpɒlɪ'ɛθiliːn/ ■ n. another term for POLYTHENE.

polyethylene terephthalate /ˌtɛrəf'θaleɪt/ ■ n. a synthetic resin made from ethylene glycol and terephthalic acid, used to make polyester fibre.

polygamy ■ n. **1** the practice or custom of having more than one wife or husband at the same time. **2** Zoology a pattern of mating in which an animal has more than one mate.
– DERIVATIVES **polygamist** n. **polygamous** adj. **polygamously** adv.
– ORIGIN C16: from French *polygamie*, from Greek *polugamia*, from *polugamos* 'often marrying'.

polygenesis /ˌpɒlɪ'dʒɛnɪsɪs/ ■ n. origination from a number of independent sources or places.
– DERIVATIVES **polygenetic** adj. **polygenism** n.

polygenic /ˌpɒlɪ'dʒɛnɪk/ ■ adj. Genetics relating to or determined by a group of genes which act together to produce observable variation.

polyglot /'pɒlɪɡlɒt/ ■ adj. knowing or using several languages. ■ n. a polyglot person.
– ORIGIN C17: from French *polyglotte*, from Greek, from *polu-* 'many' + *glōtta* 'tongue'.

polygon /'pɒlɪɡ(ə)n/ ■ n. Geometry a plane figure with at least three straight sides and angles, and typically five or more.
– DERIVATIVES **polygonal** adj.
– ORIGIN C16: from Greek *polugōnon*, from *polugōnos* 'many-angled'.

polygraph ■ n. a machine designed to record changes in a person's physiological characteristics, such as pulse and breathing rates, used especially as a lie detector.
– DERIVATIVES **polygraphic** adj.

polygyny /pə'lɪdʒɪni/ ■ n. polygamy in which a man has more than one wife. Compare with POLYANDRY. ▶ Zoology a pattern of mating in which a male animal has more than one mate.
– DERIVATIVES **polygynous** /pə'lɪdʒɪnəs/ adj.
– ORIGIN C18: from POLY- + Greek *gunē* 'woman'.

polyhedron /ˌpɒlɪ'hiːdrən, -'hɛd-/ ■ n. (pl. **polyhedra** /-drə/ or **polyhedrons**) Geometry a solid figure with many plane faces, typically more than six.
– DERIVATIVES **polyhedral** adj. **polyhedric** adj.
– ORIGIN C16: from Greek *poluedron*, from *poluedros* 'many-sided'.

polymath /'pɒlɪmaθ/ ■ n. a person of wide-ranging knowledge or learning.
– DERIVATIVES **polymathic** adj. **polymathy** /pə'lɪməθi/ n.
– ORIGIN C17: from Greek *polumathēs* 'having learned much'.

polymer /'pɒlɪmə/ ■ n. Chemistry a substance with a molecular structure formed from many identical small molecules or other units bonded together.
– DERIVATIVES **polymeric** adj. **polymerization** (also **-isation**) n. **polymerize** (also **-ise**) v.
– ORIGIN C19: from Greek *polumeros* 'having many parts', from *polu-* 'many' + *meros* 'a share'.

polymerous /pə'lɪm(ə)rəs/ ■ adj. Biology having or consisting of many parts.

polymorph ■ n. **1** an organism, object, or material which takes various forms. **2** Physiology a polymorphonuclear leucocyte.
– ORIGIN C19: from Greek *polumorphos*, from *polu-* 'many' + *morphē* 'form'.

polymorphism ■ n. the occurrence of something in several different forms.
– DERIVATIVES **polymorphic** adj. **polymorphous** adj.

polymorphonuclear /ˌpɒlɪˌmɔːfə(ʊ)'njuːklɪə/ ■ adj. Physiology (of a leucocyte) having a nucleus with several lobes and cytoplasm that contains granules.

polymyositis /ˌpɒlɪmʌɪə(ʊ)'sʌɪtɪs/ ■ n. Medicine a condition marked by inflammation and degeneration of skeletal muscle throughout the body.

Polynesian ■ n. **1** a native or inhabitant of Polynesia. **2** a group of Austronesian languages spoken in Polynesia, including Maori, Hawaiian, and Samoan. ■ adj. of or relating to Polynesia, its people, or their languages.

polynomial /ˌpɒlɪˈnəʊmɪəl/ ■ adj. consisting of several terms. ■ n. **1** Mathematics a polynomial expression, especially the sum of several terms containing different powers of the same variable(s). **2** Biology a Latin name with more than two parts.
– ORIGIN C17: from POLY-, on the pattern of *multinomial*.

polynuclear ■ adj. Chemistry another term for POLYCYCLIC.

polynucleotide ■ n. Biochemistry a linear polymer composed of many nucleotide units, constituting a section of a nucleic acid molecule.

polyp /ˈpɒlɪp/ ■ n. **1** Zoology the sedentary form of a coelenterate such as a sea anemone, typically columnar with the mouth uppermost and surrounded by a ring of tentacles. Compare with MEDUSA. **2** Medicine a small growth, usually benign and with a stalk, protruding from a mucous membrane.
– DERIVATIVES **polypoid** adj. & n.
– ORIGIN Middle English: from Old French *polipe*, from Greek *polupous* 'polyp', from *polu-* 'many' + *pous* 'foot'.

polypeptide ■ n. Biochemistry a linear organic polymer consisting of a large number of amino-acid residues, forming all or part of a protein molecule.

polyphagia /ˌpɒlɪˈfeɪdʒə/ ■ n. Zoology the eating of various or all kinds of food.
– DERIVATIVES **polyphagous** adj.

polyphase ■ adj. (of an electrical device) simultaneously using several alternating currents with different phases.

polyphonic ■ adj. **1** having many sounds or voices. **2** Music (especially of vocal music) in two or more parts each having a melody of its own; contrapuntal. ▶ Music (of an instrument) capable of producing more than one note at a time.
– DERIVATIVES **polyphonous** adj. **polyphony** n. (pl. **-ies**).
– ORIGIN C18: from Greek *poluphōnos*, from *polu-* 'many' + *phōnē* 'voice, sound'.

polyphyletic /ˌpɒlɪfʌɪˈlɛtɪk/ ■ adj. Biology (of a group of organisms) derived from more than one common evolutionary ancestor or ancestral group.

polyploid /ˈpɒlɪplɔɪd/ ■ adj. Genetics of or denoting cells or nuclei containing more than two homologous sets of chromosomes.
– DERIVATIVES **polyploidy** n.

polypropylene /ˌpɒlɪˈprəʊpɪliːn/ ■ n. a synthetic resin which is a polymer of propylene.

polyrhythm ■ n. Music the use of two or more different rhythms simultaneously.
– DERIVATIVES **polyrhythmic** adj.

polysaccharide ■ n. Biochemistry a carbohydrate (e.g. starch or cellulose) whose molecules consist of chains of sugar molecules.

polysemy /ˈpɒlɪsiːmi, pəˈlɪsɪmi/ ■ n. Linguistics the coexistence of many possible meanings for a word or phrase.
– DERIVATIVES **polysemic** adj. **polysemous** adj.
– ORIGIN C20: from POLY- + Greek *sēma* 'sign'.

polystyrene /ˌpɒlɪˈstʌɪriːn/ ■ n. a synthetic resin which is a polymer of styrene.

polysulphide (US **polysulfide**) ■ n. Chemistry a compound containing two or more sulphur atoms bonded together as an anion or group.

polysyllabic ■ adj. having more than one syllable. ▶ using words of many syllables.
– DERIVATIVES **polysyllabically** adv. **polysyllable** n.

polytechnic ■ n. an institution of higher education offering courses at degree level or below, especially in vocational subjects.
– ORIGIN C19: from French *polytechnique*, from Greek *polutekhnos*, from *polu-* 'many' + *tekhnē* 'art'.

polytene /ˈpɒlɪtiːn/ ■ adj. Genetics relating to or denoting a giant chromosome composed of many parallel copies of the genetic material.
– ORIGIN 1930S: from POLY- + Greek *tainia* 'band'.

polytetrafluoroethylene /ˌpɒlɪˌtɛtrəˌflʊərəʊˈɛθiliːn, -ˌflɔː-/ ■ n. a tough synthetic resin used to make seals and bearings and to coat non-stick cooking utensils.

polytheism /ˈpɒlɪˌθiːɪz(ə)m/ ■ n. the belief in or worship of more than one god.
– DERIVATIVES **polytheist** n. **polytheistic** adj.
– ORIGIN C17: from French *polythéisme*, from Greek *polutheos* 'of many gods'.

polythene ■ n. a tough, light, flexible synthetic resin made by polymerizing ethylene, chiefly used for packaging.
– ORIGIN 1930S: contraction of POLYETHYLENE.

polythetic /ˌpɒlɪˈθɛtɪk/ ■ adj. of or denoting a classification based on a number of shared characteristics, none of which is essential for membership of the class.
– ORIGIN 1960S: from POLY- + Greek *thetos* 'placed, arranged'.

polytonality ■ n. the simultaneous use of two or more keys in a musical composition.
– DERIVATIVES **polytonal** adj.

polyunsaturated ■ adj. Chemistry (of an organic compound, especially a fat or oil molecule) containing several double or triple bonds between carbon atoms.
– DERIVATIVES **polyunsaturates** pl. n.

polyurethane /ˌpɒlɪˈjʊərɪθeɪn/ ■ n. a synthetic resin in which the polymer units are linked by urethane groups.

polyuria /ˌpɒlɪˈjʊərɪə/ ■ n. Medicine production of abnormally large volumes of dilute urine.

polyvalent /ˌpɒlɪˈveɪl(ə)nt/ ■ adj. **1** Chemistry having a valency of three or more. **2** having many different functions, forms, or facets.

polyvinyl acetate ■ n. a synthetic resin made by polymerizing vinyl acetate, used chiefly in paints and adhesives.

polyvinyl chloride ■ n. a tough chemically resistant synthetic resin made by polymerizing vinyl chloride.

Pom ■ n. **1** short for POMERANIAN. **2** short for POMMY.

pomace /ˈpʌmɪs/ ■ n. (especially in cider-making) the pulpy residue remaining after fruit has been crushed in order to extract its juice. ▶ the pulpy matter remaining after some other substance has been pressed.
– ORIGIN C16: from medieval Latin *pomacium* 'cider'.

pomade /pəˈmeɪd, -ˈmɑːd/ ■ n. a scented preparation for dressing the hair. ■ v. [often as adj. **pomaded**] apply pomade to.
– ORIGIN C16: from French *pommade*, from Latin *pomum* 'apple' (from which it was orig. made).

pomander /pəˈmandə, ˈpɒmənd-/ ■ n. a ball or perforated container of mixed aromatic substances used to perfume a room or cupboard or (formerly) carried as a supposed protection against infection. ▶ an orange studded with cloves and hung in a wardrobe for a similar purpose.
– ORIGIN C15: from Old French *pome d'embre*, from medieval Latin *pomum de ambra* 'apple of ambergris'.

pomatum /pə(ʊ)ˈmeɪtəm/ ■ n. & v. old-fashioned term for POMADE.
– ORIGIN C16: from Latin *pomum* 'apple'.

pome /pəʊm/ ■ n. Botany a fruit consisting of a fleshy enlarged receptacle and a tough central core containing the seeds, e.g. an apple.
– ORIGIN Middle English: from Latin *pomum* 'apple, fruit'.

pomegranate /ˈpɒmɪɡranɪt/ ■ n. **1** a spherical fruit with a tough golden-orange outer skin containing many individual segments of sweet red gelatinous flesh. **2** the tree that bears this fruit, native to North Africa and western Asia. [*Punica granatum*.]
– ORIGIN Middle English: from Old French *pome grenate*, from *pome* 'apple' + *grenate* 'pomegranate' (from Latin (*malum*) *granatum* '(apple) having many seeds').

pomelo /ˈpɒmələʊ, ˈpʌm-/ (also **pummelo**) ■ n. (pl. **-os**) **1** the largest of the citrus fruits, with a thick yellow skin and bitter pulp which resembles grapefruit in flavour. **2** the tree which bears this fruit. [*Citrus maxima*.]
– ORIGIN C19.

Pomeranian ■ n. a small dog of a breed with long silky hair, a pointed muzzle, and pricked ears.
– ORIGIN from *Pomerania*, a region of central Europe.

pomfret /'pɒmfrɪt/ ■ n. an edible deep-bodied sea fish. [*Brama brama* and other species.]
– ORIGIN C18: apparently from Portuguese *pampo*.

pommel /'pʌm(ə)l/ ■ n. **1** the upward curving or projecting part of a saddle in front of the rider. **2** a rounded knob on the end of the handle of a sword, dagger, or old-fashioned gun. ■ v. (**pommelled**, **pommelling**; US **pommeled**, **pommeling**) another term for PUMMEL.
– ORIGIN Middle English: from Old French *pomel*, from a diminutive of Latin *pomum* 'fruit, apple'.

pommel horse ■ n. a vaulting horse fitted with a pair of curved handgrips.

Pommy (also **Pommie**) ■ n. (pl. **-ies**) S. African & Austral./NZ informal, derogatory a British person.
– ORIGIN C20: said by some to be short for *pomegranate*, as a near rhyme to *immigrant*.

pomology /pə(ʊ)'mɒlədʒi/ ■ n. the science of fruit-growing.
– DERIVATIVES **pomological** adj. **pomologist** n.
– ORIGIN C19: from Latin *pomum* 'fruit' + -LOGY.

pomp[1] /pɒmp/ ■ n. **1** ceremony and splendid display. **2** archaic vain and boastful display.
– ORIGIN Middle English: from Old French *pompe*, from Greek *pompē* 'procession, pomp', from *pempein* 'send'.

pomp[2] /pɒmp/ S. African vulgar slang ■ v. (**pomped**, **pomping**) have sexual intercourse with. ■ n. **1** an act of sexual intercourse. **2** a person with whom one has sexual intercourse.
– ORIGIN Afrikaans.

pompadour /'pɒmpədʊə/ ■ n. a woman's hairstyle in which the hair is turned back off the forehead in a roll. ▶ N. Amer. a men's hairstyle in which the hair is combed back from the forehead without a parting. ■ v. [usu. as adj. **pompadoured**] N. Amer. arrange (hair) in a pompadour.
– ORIGIN C19: named after Madame de *Pompadour*, the mistress of Louis XV.

pompano /'pɒmpənəʊ/ ■ n. (pl. **-os**) an edible butterfish of the west coast of North America. [*Peprilus simillimus*.]
– ORIGIN C18: from Spanish *pámpano*, perhaps from *pámpana* 'vine leaf', because of its shape.

pompom (also **pompon**) ■ n. **1** a small woollen ball attached to a garment for decoration. **2** a dahlia, chrysanthemum, or aster with small tightly clustered petals.
– ORIGIN C18: French *pompon*.

pom-pom ■ n. an automatic anti-aircraft cannon, typically mounted on a ship. ▶ S. African historical an automatic machine gun used during the Anglo-Boer War of 1899–1902.
– ORIGIN C19: imitative of the sound of the discharge.

pompom tree ■ n. a small southern African tree with clusters of pink tubular flowers. [*Dais cotinifolia*.]

pompous ■ adj. **1** affectedly grand, solemn, or self-important. **2** archaic characterized by pomp or splendour.
– DERIVATIVES **pomposity** n. **pompously** adv. **pompousness** n.
– ORIGIN Middle English: from Old French *pompeux* 'full of grandeur', from late Latin *pomposus*, from *pompa* 'pomp'.

ponce informal ■ n. **1** a man who lives off a prostitute's earnings. **2** derogatory an effeminate man. ■ v. **1** live off a prostitute's earnings. **2** (**ponce about/around**) behave in an affected or ineffectual way. **3** (**ponce something up**) attempt to improve something by making flashy changes.
– DERIVATIVES **poncey** (also **poncy**) adj.
– ORIGIN C19: perhaps from POUNCE.

poncho ■ n. (pl. **-os**) a garment of a type originally worn in South America, made of a thick piece of woollen cloth with a slit in the middle for the head.
– ORIGIN C18: from Latin American Spanish.

pond ■ n. **1** a fairly small body of still water. **2** (**the pond**) humorous the Atlantic ocean. ■ v. hold back or dam up (flowing water) to form a pond.
– ORIGIN Middle English: alteration of POUND[3].

ponder ■ v. consider carefully.
– ORIGIN Middle English: from Old French *ponderer* 'consider', from Latin *ponderare* 'weigh', from *pondus* 'weight'.

ponderable ■ adj. poetic/literary having appreciable weight or significance.

– ORIGIN C17: from late Latin *ponderabilis*, from *ponderare* (see PONDER).

ponderosa /ˌpɒndə'rəʊzə, -sə/ (also **ponderosa pine**) ■ n. a tall slender North American pine tree, planted for wood and as an ornamental. [*Pinus ponderosa*.]
– ORIGIN C19: from Latin *ponderosus* 'massive'.

ponderous ■ adj. **1** slow and clumsy because of great weight. **2** dull or laborious.
– DERIVATIVES **ponderously** adv. **ponderousness** n.
– ORIGIN Middle English: from Latin *ponderosus*, from *pondus* 'weight'.

Pondo ■ n. (pl. same or **Pondos**) a member of an isiXhosa-speaking people from the eastern part of the Eastern Cape.
– ORIGIN from isiXhosa *amaMpondo* 'the people of Mpondo' (the founding chief).

pondok /'pɒndɒk/ (also **pondokkie** /pɔn'dɒki/) ■ n. S. African a roughly built hut; a shack.
– ORIGIN Afrikaans, from Malay, 'hut, shed'.

pond skater ■ n. a slender predatory bug which moves quickly across the surface film of water. [Family Gerridae.]

pondweed ■ n. a submerged aquatic plant of still or running water. [Families Potamogetonaceae and Aponogetonaceae.]

pong informal ■ n. a strong, unpleasant smell. ■ v. smell strongly and unpleasantly.
– DERIVATIVES **pongy** adj.
– ORIGIN C20.

pongal /'pɒŋg(ə)l/ ■ n. the Tamil New Year festival, celebrated by the cooking of new rice.
– ORIGIN from Tamil *poṅkal* 'swelling' (with ref. to the cooking process of rice).

pongee /pʌn'dʒiː, pɒn-/ ■ n. a soft, unbleached type of Chinese fabric, originally made from threads of raw silk and now also other fibres such as cotton.
– ORIGIN C18: from Chinese (Mandarin) *běnjī* 'own loom' or *běnzhī* 'home-woven'.

pongid /'pɒn(d)ʒɪd/ ■ n. Zoology a primate of a family (Pongidae) which comprises the great apes.
– ORIGIN 1950s: from the genus name *Pongo*, from Congolese *mpongo*.

poniard /'pɒnjəd/ ■ n. historical a small, slim dagger.
– ORIGIN C16: from French *poignard*, from Latin *pugnus* 'fist'.

pons /pɒnz/ ■ n. (pl. **pontes** /'pɒntiːz/) Anatomy the part of the brainstem that links the medulla oblongata and the thalamus.
– ORIGIN C17: from Latin, 'bridge'.

pont /pɒnt/ ■ n. S. African a flat-bottomed ferry worked on cables or ropes.
– ORIGIN from Dutch.

Pontifex Maximus /ˌpɒntɪfɛks 'maksɪməs/ ■ n. (in the Roman Catholic Church) a title of the Pope.
– ORIGIN *Pontifex*, denoting a member of the principal college of priests in ancient Rome, from Latin *pons* 'bridge' + *-fex*, from *facere* 'to make'; *Maximus*, superlative of Latin *magnus* 'great'.

pontiff (also **sovereign** or **supreme pontiff**) ■ n. the Pope.
– ORIGIN C17 (*pontifical* Middle English): from French *pontife*, from Latin *pontifex*.

pontifical /pɒn'tɪfɪk(ə)l/ ■ adj. **1** papal. **2** characterized by a pompous air of infallibility. ■ n. **1** (in the Roman Catholic Church) an office book of the Western Church containing rites to be performed by the Pope or bishops. **2** (**pontificals**) the vestments and insignia of a bishop, cardinal, or abbot.

pontificate ■ v. /pɒn'tɪfɪkeɪt/ **1** (in the Roman Catholic Church) officiate as bishop, especially at Mass. **2** express one's opinions in a pompous and dogmatic way. ■ n. /pɒn'tɪfɪkət/ (also **Pontificate**) (in the Roman Catholic Church) the office or term of office of pope or bishop.
– DERIVATIVES **pontificator** n.
– ORIGIN Middle English: from Latin *pontificatus*, from *pontifex*.

pontine /'pɒntʌɪn/ ■ adj. Anatomy of, relating to, or affecting the pons.
– ORIGIN C19: from Latin *pons, pont-* 'bridge'.

pontoon[1] /pɒn'tu:n/ ■ n. the card game blackjack or vingt-et-un. ▸ a hand of two cards totalling 21 in this game.
– ORIGIN C20: prob. an alteration of *vingt-et-un* 'twenty-one'.

pontoon[2] /pɒn'tu:n/ ■ n. 1 a flat-bottomed boat or hollow metal cylinder used with others to support a temporary bridge or floating landing stage. ▸ a bridge or landing stage supported by pontoons. 2 a large flat-bottomed barge or lighter equipped with cranes and tackle for careening ships and salvage work. 3 either of two floats fitted to an aircraft to enable it to land on water.
– ORIGIN C17: from French *ponton*, from Latin *ponto*, from *pons* 'bridge'.

pony ■ n. (pl. **-ies**) 1 a horse of a small breed, especially one below 15 hands (or 14 hands 2 inches). 2 informal a small glass or measure of liquor. ■ v. (**pony something up**) N. Amer. informal hand over a sum of money, especially to settle an account.
– ORIGIN C17: prob. from French *poulenet* 'small foal'.

ponytail ■ n. a hairstyle in which the hair is drawn back and tied at the back of the head.
– DERIVATIVES **ponytailed** adj.

pony-trekking ■ n. S. African & Brit. the leisure activity of riding across country on a pony or horse.
– DERIVATIVES **pony-trekker** n.

Ponzi scheme /'pɒnzi/ ■ n. a form of fraud in which belief in the success of a non-existent enterprise is fostered by the payment of quick returns to the first investors from money invested by later investors.
– ORIGIN named after Charles *Ponzi*, who carried out such a fraud (1919–20).

poo ■ exclam., n., & v. variant spelling of **POOH**.

pooch ■ n. informal a dog.
– ORIGIN 1920s.

poodle ■ n. 1 a dog of a breed with a curly coat that is usually clipped. 2 a servile or obsequious person. ■ v. Brit. informal move or travel in a leisurely manner.
– ORIGIN C19: from German *Pudel(hund)*, from Low German *pud(d)eln* 'splash in water' (the poodle being a water-dog).

poof[1] /pʊf, pu:f/ (also **pouf**) ■ n. Brit. informal, derogatory an effeminate or homosexual man.
– DERIVATIVES **poofy** adj.
– ORIGIN C19: perhaps from the archaic noun *puff* in the sense 'braggart'.

poof[2] /pʊf/ (also **pouf**) ■ exclam. describing a sudden disappearance or expressing contemptuous dismissal.
– ORIGIN C19: symbolic.

poofter /'pʊftə, 'pu:-/ ■ n. another term for **POOF**[1].
– ORIGIN C20: extended form.

pooh (also **poo**) informal ■ exclam. 1 expressing disgust at an unpleasant smell. 2 expressing impatience or contempt. ■ n. excrement. ▸ an act of defecating. ■ v. defecate.
– ORIGIN C16: natural exclam.

pooh-bah /pu:'bɑ:/ ■ n. a pompous person having much influence or holding many offices simultaneously.
– ORIGIN from the name of a character in W. S. Gilbert's *The Mikado* (1885).

pooh-pooh ■ v. informal dismiss as being foolish or impractical.

pool[1] ■ n. 1 a small area of still water, typically one formed naturally. ▸ a deep place in a river. ▸ (also **swimming pool**) an artificial pool for swimming in. 2 a small, shallow patch of liquid lying on a surface. ■ v. 1 form a pool. 2 (of blood) accumulate in parts of the venous system.
– ORIGIN Old English *pōl*, of West Germanic origin.

pool[2] ■ n. 1 a shared supply of vehicles, people, or resources to be drawn on when needed. ▸ a common fund into which all contributors pay and from which financial backing is provided. ▸ the collective amount of players'
stakes in gambling or sweepstakes. ▸ (**the pools** or **football pools**) a form of gambling on the results of football matches, the winners receiving large sums accumulated from entry money. 2 an arrangement between competing parties to fix prices and share business in order to eliminate competition. 3 a group of contestants who compete against each other in a tournament for the right to advance to the next round. 4 a game played on a billiard table using two sets of seven balls together with one black ball and a white cue ball. ■ v. put (money or other assets) into a common fund. ▸ share for the benefit of all.
– ORIGIN C17: from French *poule* in the sense 'stake, kitty'.

poolroom ■ n. 1 (also **pool hall**) a place for playing pool. 2 N. Amer. a betting shop.

poop[1] ■ n. (also **poop deck**) the aftermost and highest deck of a ship, especially a sailing ship. ■ v. (of a wave) break over the stern of (a ship).
– ORIGIN Middle English: from Old French *pupe*, from a var. of Latin *puppis* 'stern'.

poop[2] ■ v. informal 1 [as adj. **pooped**] exhausted. 2 N. Amer. (**poop out**) stop functioning.
– ORIGIN 1930s.

poop[3] informal ■ n. excrement. ■ v. defecate.
– ORIGIN C18: imitative.

poop[4] ■ n. informal, chiefly N. Amer. up-to-date or inside information.
– ORIGIN 1940s.

pooper scooper (also **poop scoop**) ■ n. an implement for clearing up dog excrement.

poor ■ adj. 1 lacking sufficient money to live at a standard considered comfortable or normal. 2 of a low or inferior standard or quality. ▸ (**poor in**) lacking in. 3 deserving of pity or sympathy.
– PHRASES **the poor man's —** an inferior or cheaper substitute for the thing specified. **poor relation** a person or thing that is considered inferior to others of the same type or group. **take a poor view of** regard with disapproval.
– DERIVATIVES **poorness** n.
– ORIGIN Middle English: from Old French *poure*, from Latin *pauper*.

poor box ■ n. historical a collection box, especially one in a church, for gifts of money to aid the poor.

poorhouse ■ n. Brit. another term for **WORKHOUSE**.

poorly ■ adv. in a poor manner. ■ adj. unwell.

poor-mouth ■ v. N. Amer. & Irish informal talk disparagingly about.

poor relief ■ n. historical financial assistance given to the poor from state or local community funds.

poort /pʊət/ ■ n. S. African a narrow mountain pass.
– ORIGIN S. African Dutch, 'passage'.

poor white ■ n. derogatory a member of an impoverished white underclass.

pooter ■ n. a hollow tubular device used to collect insects or invertebrates by suction.
– ORIGIN 1930s: said to be named after the American entomologist William *Poos* (1891–1987).

pootle ■ v. Brit. informal move or travel in a leisurely manner.
– ORIGIN 1970s: blend of the verbs **POODLE** and **TOOTLE**.

POP (also **PoP**) Computing ■ abbrev. 1 point of presence, denoting equipment that acts as access to the Internet. 2 Post Office Protocol, a standard protocol for accessing email.

pop[1] ■ v. (**popped, popping**) 1 make or cause to make a sudden, sharp, explosive sound. 2 (usu. **pop in/out**) go or come for a short time, often without notice. ▸ (**pop off**) informal die. 3 put or place quickly in a particular position. 4 (of a person's eyes) open wide and appear to bulge, especially with surprise. 5 informal take or inject (a drug). 6 Brit. informal pawn. ■ n. 1 a sudden sharp explosive sound. 2 informal, dated or N. Amer. fizzy soft drink. 3 (also **pop fly** or **pop-up**) Baseball a ball hit high in the air but not far from the home plate.
– PHRASES **— a pop** N. Amer. informal costing a specified amount per item. **have** (or **take**) **a pop at** informal attack.

pop one's clogs informal die. **pop the question** informal propose marriage.
– ORIGIN Middle English: imitative.

pop² ■ n. (also **pop music**) commercial popular music, in particular accessible, tuneful music of a kind popular since the 1950s. ■ adj. **1** of or relating to pop music. **2** often derogatory (especially of a scientific or academic subject) made accessible to the general public.

pop³ ■ n. chiefly US informal term for FATHER.
– ORIGIN C19: abbrev. of POPPA.

pop. ■ abbrev. population.

popadom (also **popadum**) ■ n. variant spelling of POPPADOM.

pop art ■ n. art based on modern popular culture and the mass media, especially as a critical or ironic comment on traditional fine art values.

popcorn ■ n. maize of a variety with hard kernels that swell up and burst open when heated and are then eaten as a snack.

pop culture ■ n. commercial culture based on popular taste.

pope ■ n. **1** (**the Pope**) the Bishop of Rome as head of the Roman Catholic Church. **2** the head of the Coptic Church, the Patriarch of Alexandria.
– PHRASES **is the Pope (a) Catholic?** informal used to indicate that something is blatantly obvious.
– ORIGIN Old English, from eccles. Greek *papas* 'bishop, patriarch', var. of Greek *pappas* 'father'.

Popemobile /ˈpəʊpməbiːl/ ■ n. informal a bulletproof vehicle with a raised viewing area, used by the Pope on official visits.

popery ■ n. derogatory, chiefly archaic Roman Catholicism.

pop-eyed ■ adj. informal having bulging or staring eyes.

pop fly ■ n. Baseball see POP¹.

popgun ■ n. **1** a child's toy gun which shoots a harmless pellet or cork. **2** a small, inefficient, or antiquated gun.

popinjay /ˈpɒpɪndʒeɪ/ ■ n. **1** dated a vain, foppish, or conceited person. **2** archaic a parrot.
– ORIGIN Middle English: from Old French *papingay*, from Arabic *babbaġā*.

popish ■ adj. derogatory Roman Catholic.

poplar ■ n. a tall, fast-growing tree, often grown in shelter belts or for wood and pulp. [Genus *Populus*: many species.]
– ORIGIN Middle English: from Old French *poplier*, from Latin *populus*.

poplin ■ n. a plain-woven fabric, typically a very lightweight cotton, with a corded surface.
– ORIGIN C18: from obsolete French *papeline*, perhaps from Italian *papalina* 'papal', referring to the town of Avignon (residence of popes in exile), where it was first made.

popliteal /pɒˈplɪtɪəl, ˌpɒplɪˈtiːəl/ ■ adj. Anatomy relating to or situated in the hollow at the back of the knee.
– ORIGIN C18: from Latin *poples, poplit-* 'ham'.

pop-out ■ n. Baseball an act of being put out by a caught fly ball. ■ adj. N. Amer. designed to be easily removable.

popover ■ n. N. Amer. a type of very light muffin made from a thin batter, which rises to form a hollow shell when baked.

poppa ■ n. N. Amer. informal term for FATHER.
– ORIGIN C19: alteration of PAPA.

poppadom /ˈpɒpədəm/ (also **poppadum** or **popadom**) ■ n. (in Indian cookery) a large disc of unleavened spiced bread made from ground lentils fried in oil.
– ORIGIN from Tamil *pappaḍam*.

popper ■ n. **1** informal a press stud. **2** informal a small vial of amyl nitrite used for inhalation, which makes a popping sound when opened. **3** a utensil for making popcorn.

poppet ■ n. **1** Brit. informal an endearingly sweet or pretty child. **2** (also **poppet valve**) Engineering a mushroom-shaped valve with a flat end piece that is lifted in and out of an opening by an axial rod.
– ORIGIN Middle English: from Latin *pup(p)a* 'girl, doll'; cf. PUPPET.

poppie ■ n. S. African informal **1** an affectionate form of address for a girl or young woman. **2** derogatory an attractive but superficial young woman.
– ORIGIN Afrikaans, from *pop* 'doll' + the diminutive suffix *-ie*.

popping crease ■ n. Cricket a line across the pitch in front of the stumps, behind which the batsman must keep the bat or one foot grounded to avoid the risk of being stumped or run out.
– ORIGIN C18: from POP¹, perhaps in the obsolete sense 'strike'.

poppy¹ ■ n. a plant having showy flowers, typically red or yellow, and rounded seed capsules. [*Papaver rhoeas* (corn poppy) and other species.]
– ORIGIN Old English, from a medieval Latin alteration of Latin *papaver*.

poppy² ■ adj. (of popular music) tuneful and immediately appealing.

poppycock ■ n. informal nonsense.
– ORIGIN C19: from Dutch dialect *pappekak*, from *pap* 'soft' + *kak* 'dung'.

Poppy Day ■ n. another name for REMEMBRANCE SUNDAY.

pop rivet ■ n. a tubular rivet that is inserted into a hole and clinched by the withdrawing of a central rod. ■ v. (**pop-rivet**) (**-riveted, -riveting**) secure or fasten with pop rivets.

Popsicle ■ n. trademark an ice lolly.
– ORIGIN 1920s: fanciful formation.

popster ■ n. informal a pop musician.

popsy (also **popsie**) ■ n. (pl. **-ies**) informal, chiefly Brit. an attractive young woman.
– ORIGIN C19: alteration of POPPET.

pop-top ■ n. another term for RING PULL.

populace /ˈpɒpjʊləs/ ■ n. [treated as sing. or pl.] the general public.
– ORIGIN C16: from Italian *popolaccio* 'common people'.

popular ■ adj. **1** liked or admired by many or by a particular person or group. **2** intended for or suited to the taste or means of the general public. ▸ (of a belief or attitude) widely held among the general public. **3** (of political activity) of or carried on by the people as a whole.
– DERIVATIVES **popularism** n. **popularity** n. **popularly** adv.
– ORIGIN Middle English: from Latin *popularis*, from *populus* 'people'.

popular front ■ n. a political party or coalition representing left-wing elements.

popularize (also **-ise**) ■ v. make popular. ▸ make (something scientific or academic) accessible or interesting to the general public.
– DERIVATIVES **popularization** (also **-isation**) n. **popularizer** (also **-iser**) n.

popular music ■ n. music appealing to the popular taste, including rock, pop, reggae, dance music, etc.

populate ■ v. **1** form the population of (a place). ▸ cause people to settle in (a place). **2** Computing add data to (a database).
– ORIGIN C16: from medieval Latin *populare* 'supply with people'.

population ■ n. **1** all the inhabitants of a particular place. ▸ a particular group within this. ▸ the action of populating an area. **2** Biology a community of interbreeding organisms. **3** Statistics a finite or infinite collection of items under consideration.

populist ■ n. **1** a member or adherent of a political party seeking to represent the interests of ordinary people. **2** a person who supports or seeks to appeal to the interests of ordinary people. ■ adj. of or relating to a populist.
– DERIVATIVES **populism** n.
– ORIGIN C19: from Latin *populus* 'people'.

populous ■ adj. having a large population.
– ORIGIN Middle English: from late Latin *populosus*, from *populus* 'people'.

pop-up ■ adj. **1** (of a book or greetings card) containing folded pictures that rise up to form a three-dimensional scene or figure when opened. **2** (of an electric toaster) operating so as to push up a piece of toast when it is ready. **3** Computing (of a menu or other utility) able to be

porbeagle

superimposed on the screen being worked on and suppressed rapidly. ■ n. **1** a pop-up menu or other utility. ▸ an unrequested browser window, especially one generated for the purpose of advertising. **2** Baseball see POP¹ (sense 3).

porbeagle /ˈpɔːbiːɡ(ə)l/ ■ n. a large active shark found chiefly in the open seas of the North Atlantic and in the Mediterranean. [*Lamna nasus*.]
– ORIGIN C18: perhaps from Cornish *porth* 'harbour' + *bugel* 'shepherd'.

porcelain /ˈpɔːs(ə)lɪn/ ■ n. a white vitrified translucent ceramic; china. See also HARD-PASTE, SOFT-PASTE. ▸ articles made of this.
– ORIGIN C16: from French *porcelaine*, from Italian *porcellana* 'cowrie shell', hence 'chinaware'.

porcelain clay ■ n. another term for KAOLIN.

porch ■ n. **1** a covered shelter projecting in front of the entrance of a building. **2** N. Amer. a veranda.
– ORIGIN Middle English: from Old French *porche*, from Latin *porticus* 'colonnade', from *porta* 'passage'.

porcine /ˈpɔːsaɪn/ ■ adj. of or resembling a pig or pigs.
– ORIGIN C17: from French *porcin* or Latin *porcinus*, from *porcus* 'pig'.

porcini /pɔːˈtʃiːni/ ■ pl. n. chiefly N. Amer. ceps.
– ORIGIN Italian, 'little pigs'.

porcupine ■ n. a large rodent with defensive spines or quills on the body and tail. [Families Hystricidae (Old World) and Erethizontidae (New World).]
– ORIGIN Middle English: from Old French *porc espin*, from Latin *porcus* 'pig' + *spina* 'thorn'.

porcupine fish ■ n. a spiny tropical marine fish which inflates itself when threatened. [*Diodon hystrix* and other species.]

pore¹ ■ n. a minute opening in the skin or other surface through which gases, liquids, or microscopic particles may pass.
– ORIGIN Middle English: from Greek *poros* 'passage, pore'.

pore² ■ v. **1** (**pore over/through**) be absorbed in the reading or study of. **2** (**pore on/over**) archaic ponder.
– ORIGIN Middle English: perhaps rel. to PEER¹.

porgy /ˈpɔːɡi/ ■ n. (pl. **-ies**) a deep-bodied sea bream of warm coastal waters. [Family Sparidae: many species.]
– ORIGIN C17: alteration of Spanish and Portuguese *pargo*.

Porifera /pəˈrɪf(ə)rə/ ■ pl. n. Zoology a phylum of aquatic invertebrates that comprises the sponges.
– DERIVATIVES **poriferan** adj. & n.
– ORIGIN from Latin *porus* 'pore' + *-fer* 'bearing'.

pork ■ n. **1** the flesh of a pig used as food, especially when uncured. **2** short for PORK BARREL.
– ORIGIN Middle English: from Old French *porc*, from Latin *porcus* 'pig'.

pork barrel ■ n. informal the use of government funds for projects designed to win votes.
– ORIGIN from the use of such a barrel by farmers, to keep a reserve supply of meat.

porker ■ n. **1** a young pig raised and fattened for food. **2** informal, derogatory a fat person.

pork pie ■ n. a raised pie made with minced, cooked pork, eaten cold.

pork-pie hat ■ n. a hat with a flat crown and a brim turned up all round.

pork scratchings ■ pl. n. Brit. crisp pieces of pork fat left after rendering lard, eaten as a snack.

porky ■ adj. (**-ier**, **-iest**) **1** informal fleshy or fat. **2** of or resembling pork. ■ n. (pl. **-ies**) (also **porky-pie**) Brit. rhyming slang a lie.

porn (also **porno**) informal ■ n. pornography. ■ adj. pornographic.

pornography ■ n. printed or visual material intended to stimulate sexual excitement.
– DERIVATIVES **pornographer** n. **pornographic** adj. **pornographically** adv.
– ORIGIN C19: from Greek *pornographos* 'writing about prostitutes'.

porous ■ adj. (of a rock or other material) having minute interstices through which liquid or air may pass.
– DERIVATIVES **porosity** n. **porousness** n.
– ORIGIN Middle English: from Old French *poreux*, from Latin *porus* 'pore'.

porphyria /pɔːˈfɪrɪə/ ■ n. Medicine a rare hereditary disorder of haemoglobin metabolism causing mental disturbance, extreme sensitivity to light, and excretion of dark pigments in the urine.
– ORIGIN 1920s: from Greek *porphura* 'purple'.

porphyritic /ˌpɔːfɪˈrɪtɪk/ ■ adj. Geology relating to or denoting a rock texture containing distinct crystals or crystalline particles embedded in a compact groundmass.

porphyry /ˈpɔːfɪri/ ■ n. (pl. **-ies**) a hard igneous rock containing crystals of feldspar in a fine-grained, typically reddish groundmass.
– ORIGIN Middle English: from Greek *porphurites*, from *porphura* 'purple'.

porpoise /ˈpɔːpəs, -pɔɪs/ ■ n. a small toothed whale with a low triangular dorsal fin and a blunt rounded snout. [*Phocoena phocoena* (harbour porpoise) and other species, family Phocoenidae.]
– ORIGIN Middle English: from Old French *porpois*, from Latin *porcus* 'pig' + *piscis* 'fish'.

porridge ■ n. **1** a dish consisting of oatmeal or another cereal boiled with water or milk. **2** Brit. informal time spent in prison.
– DERIVATIVES **porridgy** adj.
– ORIGIN C16: alteration of POTTAGE.

porringer /ˈpɒrɪn(d)ʒə/ ■ n. historical a small bowl, often with a handle, used for soup or similar dishes.
– ORIGIN Middle English (earlier as *pottinger*): from Old French *potager*, from *potage* 'contents of a pot'.

Porro prism /ˈpɒrəʊ/ ■ n. a prism in which the light is reflected on two 45° surfaces and returned parallel to the incoming beam, especially as used in a conventional pair of binoculars.
– ORIGIN named after the C19 Italian scientist Ignazio Porro.

port¹ ■ n. a town or city with a harbour or access to navigable water where ships load or unload.
– PHRASES **port of call** a place where a ship or person stops on a journey. **port of entry** a harbour or airport where customs officers are stationed to oversee passengers and goods entering or leaving a country.
– ORIGIN Old English, from Latin *portus* 'harbour'.

port² (also **port wine**) ■ n. a sweet dark red (occasionally brown or white) fortified wine, originally from Portugal.
– ORIGIN shortened form of *Oporto*, a port in Portugal from which the wine is shipped.

port³ ■ n. the side of a ship or aircraft that is on the left when one is facing forward. The opposite of STARBOARD. ■ v. turn (a ship or its helm) to port.
– ORIGIN C16: prob. orig. the side turned towards the port.

port⁴ ■ n. **1** an opening in the side of a ship for boarding or loading. ▸ a porthole. **2** an opening for the passage of steam, liquid, or gas. **3** (also **gun port**) an opening in the body of an aircraft or in a wall or armoured vehicle through which a gun may be fired. **4** Electronics a socket in a computer network into which a device can be plugged.
– ORIGIN Old English, from Latin *porta* 'gate'.

port⁵ ■ v. **1** Computing transfer (software) from one system or machine to another. **2** Military carry (a rifle or other weapon) diagonally across and close to the body with the barrel or blade near the left shoulder. ■ n. **1** poetic/literary a person's carriage or bearing. **2** Computing an instance of porting software.
– ORIGIN Middle English: from Old French *port* 'bearing, gait', from Latin *portare* 'carry'.

porta- ■ comb. form denoting something that is movable or portable (often used as part of a proprietary name): *Portakabin*.

portable ■ adj. **1** able to be easily carried or moved. **2** (of a loan or pension) capable of being transferred or adapted in altered circumstances. **3** Computing (of software) able to be ported. ■ n. a portable object.
– DERIVATIVES **portability** n. **portably** adv.

portage /ˈpɔːtɪdʒ/ ■ n. **1** the carrying of a boat or its cargo between two navigable waters. ▸ a place at which this is necessary. **2** archaic the action of carrying or transporting.
– ORIGIN Middle English: from French, from *porter* 'carry'.

Portakabin ■ n. Brit. trademark a portable building used as a temporary office, classroom, etc.
– ORIGIN 1960s: from PORTA- and an alteration of CABIN.

portal¹ ■ n. 1 a doorway, gate, or gateway, especially a large and imposing one. 2 Computing an Internet site providing a directory of links to other sites.
– ORIGIN Middle English: from medieval Latin *portale*, from *portalis* 'like a gate', from Latin *porta* 'door, gate'.

portal² ■ adj. Anatomy of or relating to the transverse fissure of the liver, through which major blood vessels pass.
– ORIGIN C19: from Latin *porta* 'gate'.

portal frame ■ n. Engineering a rigid structural frame consisting essentially of two uprights connected at the top by a third member.

portal vein (in full **hepatic portal vein**) ■ n. Anatomy a vein conveying blood to the liver from the spleen, stomach, pancreas, and intestines.

portcullis ■ n. a strong, heavy grating that can be lowered down grooves on each side of a gateway to block it.
– DERIVATIVES **portcullised** adj.
– ORIGIN Middle English: from Old French *porte coleice* 'sliding door'.

Porte /pɔːt/ (in full **the Sublime** or **Ottoman Porte**) ■ n. the Ottoman court at Constantinople.
– ORIGIN C17: from French *la Sublime Porte* 'the exalted gate', translation of the Turkish title of the central office of the Ottoman government.

portend ■ v. be a sign or warning that (something momentous or calamitous) is likely to happen.
– ORIGIN Middle English: from Latin *portendere*, from *pro-* 'forth' + *tendere* 'stretch'.

portent /ˈpɔːtɛnt, -t(ə)nt/ ■ n. 1 a sign or warning that a momentous or calamitous event is likely to happen. ▶ future significance. 2 archaic an exceptional or wonderful person or thing.
– ORIGIN C16: from Latin *portentum* 'omen, token'.

portentous ■ adj. 1 of or like a portent. 2 overly solemn.
– DERIVATIVES **portentously** adv. **portentousness** n.

porter¹ ■ n. 1 a person employed to carry luggage and other loads. ▶ (also **hospital porter**) a hospital employee who moves equipment or patients. 2 dark brown bitter beer brewed from malt partly charred or browned by drying at a high temperature.
– DERIVATIVES **porterage** n.
– ORIGIN Middle English: from Old French *porteour*, from medieval Latin *portator*, from Latin *portare* 'carry'; sense 2 derives from the beer orig. made for porters.

porter² ■ n. an employee in charge of the entrance of a hotel, block of flats, or other large building.
– ORIGIN Middle English: from Old French *portier*, from late Latin *portarius*, from *porta* 'gate, door'.

porterhouse ■ n. historical, chiefly N. Amer. an establishment at which porter and sometimes steaks were served.

porterhouse steak ■ n. a thick steak cut from the thick end of a sirloin.

portfolio ■ n. (pl. **-os**) 1 a large, thin, flat case for carrying drawings, maps, etc. 2 a set of pieces of creative work intended to demonstrate a person's ability to a potential employer. ▶ a sample of work produced by a pupil or student, collected over a period of time, and used in assessing their progress. 3 a range of investments held by a person or organization. 4 the position and duties of a Minister or Secretary of State.
– ORIGIN C18: from Italian *portafogli*, from *portare* 'carry' + *foglio* 'leaf'.

porthole ■ n. 1 a small window on the outside of a ship or aircraft. 2 historical an opening for firing a cannon through.

portico /ˈpɔːtɪkəʊ/ ■ n. (pl. **-oes** or **-os**) a structure consisting of a roof supported by columns at regular intervals, typically attached as a porch to a building.
– ORIGIN C17: from Latin *porticus* 'porch'.

portière /ˌpɔːtɪˈɛː/ ■ n. a curtain hung over a door or doorway.
– ORIGIN C19: French, from *porte* 'door'.

portion ■ n. 1 a part or a share. ▶ an amount of food suitable for or served to one person. ▶ Law the part or share of an estate given or descending by law to an heir. 2 archaic a person's destiny or lot. 3 (also **marriage portion**) archaic a dowry. ■ v. divide into portions and share out.
– ORIGIN Middle English: from Old French *porcion*, from Latin *portio(n-)*, from the phr. *pro portione* 'in proportion'.

Port Jackson willow ■ n. S. African an Australian acacia that has become naturalized in South Africa. [*Acacia saligna*.]
– ORIGIN from the name of the harbour in Sydney, Australia.

Portland cement ■ n. cement manufactured from chalk and clay.
– ORIGIN so named because it resembles in colour limestone from the Isle of Portland in southern England.

portly ■ adj. (**-ier**, **-iest**) 1 (especially of a man) rather fat. 2 archaic stately or dignified.
– DERIVATIVES **portliness** n.
– ORIGIN C15: from PORT⁵ in the sense 'bearing'.

portmanteau /pɔːtˈmantəʊ/ ■ n. (pl. **portmanteaus** or **portmanteaux** /-əʊz/) 1 a large travelling bag made of stiff leather and opening into two equal parts. 2 [as modifier] consisting of two or more aspects or qualities.
– ORIGIN C16: from French *portemanteau*, from *porter* 'carry' + *manteau* 'mantle'.

portmanteau word ■ n. a word blending the sounds and combining the meanings of two others, e.g. *brunch* from *lunch* and *breakfast*.

portrait ■ n. 1 an artistic representation of a person, especially one depicting only the face or head and shoulders. 2 a description in language or on film or television. 3 [as modifier] denoting a format of printed matter which is higher than it is wide. Compare with LANDSCAPE.
– DERIVATIVES **portraitist** n. **portraiture** n.
– ORIGIN C16: from Old French *portraire* 'portray'.

portray ■ v. 1 depict in a work of art or literature. 2 describe in a particular way. 3 (of an actor) play the part of.
– DERIVATIVES **portrayable** adj. **portrayal** n. **portrayer** n.
– ORIGIN Middle English: from Old French *portraire*, from *traire* 'to draw', from Latin *trahere*.

Port Salut /ˌpɔː saˈluː/ ■ n. a pale, mild type of cheese.
– ORIGIN named after *Port du Salut*, the Trappist monastery in France where it was first produced.

Portuguese /ˌpɔːtjʊˈɡiːz, -tʃʊ-/ ■ n. (pl. same) 1 a native or national of Portugal, or a person of Portuguese descent. 2 the Romance language of Portugal, Brazil, and some African countries. ■ adj. of or relating to Portugal or its people or their language.
– ORIGIN from Portuguese *portuguez*, from medieval Latin *portugalensis*.

Portuguese man-of-war ■ n. a floating jellyfish-like marine coelenterate with a number of polyps, a conspicuous, often blue float, and long stinging tentacles. [*Physalia physalis*.]

port watch ■ n. see WATCH (sense 3).

port wine stain ■ n. a deep red naevus, typically on the face.

POS ■ abbrev. point of sale.

pose ■ v. 1 present or constitute (a problem, danger, question, etc.). 2 assume a particular position in order to be photographed, painted, or drawn. 3 (**pose as**) pretend to be. 4 behave affectedly in order to impress. ■ n. 1 a position assumed in order to be painted, drawn, or photographed. 2 a way of behaving adopted in order to impress or give a false impression.
– ORIGIN Middle English: from Old French *poser* (v.), from late Latin *pausare* 'to pause', which replaced Latin *ponere* 'to place'.

poser¹ ■ n. a person who poses; a poseur.

poser² ■ n. a puzzling question or problem.

poseur /pəʊˈzɜː/ ■ n. a person who behaves affectedly in order to impress.
– ORIGIN French, from *poser* 'to place'.

posey (also **posy**) ■ adj. informal pretentious.

posh informal ■ adj. **1** elegant or stylishly luxurious. **2** chiefly Brit. upper-class.
– DERIVATIVES **poshly** adv. **poshness** n.

posit /'pɒzɪt/ ■ v. (**posited**, **positing**) **1** put forward as fact or as a basis for argument. ▸ (**posit something on**) base something on the truth of (a particular assumption). **2** place. ■ n. Philosophy a statement which is made on the assumption that it will prove to be true.
– ORIGIN C17: from Latin *posit-*, *ponere* 'place'.

position ■ n. **1** a place where someone or something is located or has been put. ▸ the correct place. ▸ a place where part of a military force is posted for strategic purposes. **2** a way in which someone or something is placed or arranged. ▸ the configuration of the pieces and pawns on the board at any point in a game of chess. **3** a situation or set of circumstances. ▸ the state of being advantageously placed in a competitive situation. ▸ a person's place or rank in relation to others. ▸ high rank or social standing. **4** a job. **5** a point of view or attitude. **6** Finance the extent to which an investor, dealer, or speculator has made a commitment in the market by buying or selling securities etc.: *traders were covering short positions*. **7** Logic a proposition laid down or asserted. ■ v. **1** put or arrange in a particular position. **2** promote (a product, service, or business) within a particular sector of a market.
– DERIVATIVES **positional** adj. **positionally** adv.
– ORIGIN Middle English: from Latin *positio(n-)*, from *ponere* 'to place'.

position paper ■ n. (in business and politics) a written report of attitude or intentions regarding a particular matter.

positive ■ adj. **1** consisting in or characterized by the presence rather than the absence of distinguishing features. ▸ expressing or implying affirmation, agreement, or permission. **2** constructive, optimistic, or confident. **3** with no possibility of doubt; certain. **4** (of a quantity) greater than zero. **5** of, containing, producing, or denoting the kind of electric charge opposite to that carried by electrons. **6** (of a photographic image) showing light and shade or colours true to the original. **7** Grammar (of an adjective or adverb) expressing a quality in its basic, primary degree. Contrasted with COMPARATIVE and SUPERLATIVE. **8** chiefly Philosophy dealing only with matters of fact and experience. See also POSITIVISM (sense 1). ■ n. **1** a positive quality or attribute. **2** a positive photographic image, especially one printed from a negative.
– DERIVATIVES **positiveness** n. **positivity** n.
– ORIGIN Middle English: from Old French *positif*, *-ive* or Latin *positivus*, from *ponere* 'place'.

positive discrimination ■ n. British term for AFFIRMATIVE ACTION.

positive feedback ■ n. feedback that tends to enhance the effect by which it is produced.

positive geotropism ■ n. Botany the tendency of roots to grow downwards.

positively ■ adv. **1** in a positive way. **2** used to emphasize that something is the case: *some of the diets may be positively dangerous*.

positive pole ■ n. the north-seeking pole of a magnet.

positive sign ■ n. another term for PLUS SIGN.

positive vetting ■ n. Brit. the investigation of the background and character of a candidate for a Civil Service post that involves access to secret material.

positivism ■ n. Philosophy **1** a philosophical system recognizing only that which can be scientifically verified or which is capable of logical or mathematical proof, and therefore rejecting metaphysics and theism. ▸ another term for LOGICAL POSITIVISM. **2** the theory that laws derive validity from the fact of having been enacted by authority or of deriving logically from existing decisions, rather than from any moral considerations.
– DERIVATIVES **positivist** n. & adj. **positivistic** adj. **positivistically** adv.

positron /'pɒzɪtrɒn/ ■ n. Physics a subatomic particle with the same mass as an electron and a numerically equal but positive charge.
– ORIGIN 1930s: from POSITIVE + -TRON.

posse /'pɒsi/ ■ n. **1** N. Amer. historical a body of men summoned by a sheriff to enforce the law. **2** informal a group of people with a common characteristic, interest, or purpose.
– ORIGIN C17: from medieval Latin, 'power', from Latin *posse* 'be able'.

possess ■ v. **1** have as belonging to one. ▸ Law have possession of as distinct from ownership. **2** have as an ability, quality, or characteristic. ▸ (**possessed of**) in possession of. **3** [usu. as adj. **possessed**] (of a demon or spirit, especially an evil one) have complete power over. **4** (of an emotion, idea, etc.) dominate the mind of. **5** poetic/literary have sexual intercourse with (a woman).
– PHRASES **what possessed you?** used to express surprise at an action regarded as extremely unwise.
– DERIVATIVES **possessor** n. **possessory** adj.
– ORIGIN Middle English: from Old French *possesser*, from Latin *possidere* 'occupy, hold'.

possession ■ n. **1** the state of possessing something. ▸ Law visible power or control, as distinct from lawful ownership. ▸ (in soccer, rugby, and other ball games) temporary control of the ball by a player or team. **2** a thing owned or possessed. ▸ a territory or country controlled or governed by another. **3** the state of being possessed by a demon, emotion, etc.
– DERIVATIVES **possessionless** adj.

possessive ■ adj. **1** demanding someone's total attention and love. **2** showing an unwillingness to share one's possessions. **3** Grammar relating to or denoting the case of nouns and pronouns expressing possession.
– DERIVATIVES **possessively** adv. **possessiveness** n.

possessive determiner ■ n. Grammar a determiner indicating possession, for example *my*.

possessive pronoun ■ n. Grammar a pronoun indicating possession, for example *mine*.

posset /'pɒsɪt/ ■ n. a drink made of hot milk curdled with ale, wine, etc. and typically flavoured with spices, formerly drunk as a delicacy or as a remedy for colds.
– ORIGIN Middle English.

possibility ■ n. (pl. **-ies**) **1** a thing that is possible. **2** the state or fact of being possible. **3** (**possibilities**) unspecified qualities of a promising nature.

possible ■ adj. capable of existing, happening, or being achieved. ▸ that may be so, but that is not certain or probable. ■ n. **1** a possible candidate for a job or member of a team. **2** (**the possible**) that which is likely or achievable.
– ORIGIN Middle English: from Latin *possibilis*, from *posse* 'be able'.

possibly ■ adv. **1** perhaps. **2** in accordance with what is possible.

possie ■ n. variant spelling of POZZIE.

possum ■ n. **1** a tree-dwelling Australasian marsupial, typically with a prehensile tail. [Many species, especially in the family Petauridae.] **2** N. Amer. informal an opossum.
– PHRASES **play possum 1** feign unconsciousness or death (as an opossum does when threatened). **2** feign ignorance.
– ORIGIN C17: shortening of OPOSSUM.

post¹ ■ n. **1** a long, sturdy piece of timber or metal set upright in the ground and used as a support or a marker. ▸ (**the post**) a starting post or winning post. **2** an Internet posting. ■ v. **1** display (a notice) in a public place. **2** announce or publish. ▸ publish the name of (a member of the armed forces) as missing or dead. ▸ send (a message) to an Internet bulletin board or newsgroup, or display (information) online. **3** achieve or record (a particular score or result). **4** (**post up**) Basketball play in a position near the basket, along the side of the key.
– ORIGIN Old English, from Latin *postis* 'doorpost', later 'rod, beam'.

post² ■ n. the official service or system that delivers letters and parcels. ▸ letters and parcels delivered. ▸ a single collection or delivery of post. ■ v. **1** send via the postal system. **2** (in bookkeeping) enter (an item) in a ledger. **3** historical travel with relays of horses. ▸ archaic travel with haste; hurry.
– PHRASES **keep someone posted** keep someone informed of the latest developments or news.

–ORIGIN C16: from French *poste*, from Italian *posta*, from Latin *posita*, from *ponere* 'to place'.

post³ ▪ n. **1** a job. **2** a place where someone is on duty or where an activity is carried out. ▪ v. send to a place to take up an appointment. ▸ station in a particular place.
–ORIGIN C16: from French *poste*, from Italian *posto*, from a contraction of Latin *positum*, from *ponere* 'to place'.

post- ▪ prefix after in time or order: *post-date*.
–ORIGIN from Latin *post* 'after, behind'.

postage ▪ n. the sending of letters and parcels by post. ▸ the amount required to send something by post.

postage stamp ▪ n. an adhesive or printed stamp applied to a letter or parcel to indicate the amount of postage paid.

postal ▪ adj. **1** of or relating to the post. **2** carried out by post: *a postal vote*.
–PHRASES **go postal** US informal go mad, especially from stress. [with ref. to cases in which postal employees have run amok and shot colleagues.]
–DERIVATIVES **postally** adv.

postal code ▪ n. another term for POSTCODE.

postal order ▪ n. an order for payment of a specified sum to a named payee, issued by the Post Office.

post-and-beam ▪ adj. (of a building or a method of construction) having or using a framework of upright and horizontal beams.

postbag ▪ n. British term for MAILBAG.

post-bellum /'bɛləm/ ▪ adj. occurring or existing after a war, in particular the American Civil War.
–ORIGIN C19: from Latin *post* 'after' + *bellum* 'war'.

postbox ▪ n. **1** a large public box having a slot into which letters are posted, for collection by the post office. **2** a box into which mail is delivered, especially one mounted on a post at the entrance to one's property. ▸ S. African short for POST OFFICE BOX.

postcard ▪ n. a card for sending a message by post without an envelope.

post cart ▪ n. S. African historical a horse-drawn vehicle used to transport mail and passengers.

post-chaise /(t)ʃeɪz/ ▪ n. (pl. **post-chaises** pronunc. same) historical a horse-drawn carriage used for long-distance travelling and to carry mail.
–ORIGIN C17: from POST² + CHAISE.

postcode ▪ n. a group of letters and numbers which are added to a postal address to assist the sorting of mail.
–DERIVATIVES **postcoded** adj.

post-coital ▪ adj. occurring or done after sexual intercourse.
–DERIVATIVES **post-coitally** adv.

post-date ▪ v. **1** [usu. as adj. **post-dated**] affix or assign a date later than the actual one to (a document or event). **2** occur or come at a later date than.

postdoc ▪ n. informal a person engaged in postdoctoral research.

postdoctoral ▪ adj. relating to or denoting research undertaken after the completion of a doctorate.

poster ▪ n. a large printed picture or notice used for decoration or advertisement.

poster boy (or **poster girl**) ▪ n. N. Amer. **1** a male (or female) poster child. **2** a male (or female) model who appears in a print advertisement.

poster child ▪ n. N. Amer. a child who appears on a poster in an advertisement for a charitable organization. ▸ a person who epitomizes or represents a specified quality, cause, etc.

poste restante /pəʊst 'rɛst(ə)nt/ ▪ n. a department in a post office that keeps letters for an agreed period until collected by the addressee.
–ORIGIN C18: from French, 'mail remaining'.

posterior ▪ adj. **1** chiefly Anatomy further back in position; of or nearer the rear or hind end. The opposite of ANTERIOR. **2** Medicine relating to or denoting presentation of a fetus in which the rear or caudal end is nearest the cervix and emerges first at birth. **3** formal coming after in time or order; later. ▪ n. humorous a person's buttocks.
–DERIVATIVES **posteriority** n. **posteriorly** adv. (Anatomy).

postmillennialism

–ORIGIN C16: from Latin, comparative of *posterus* 'following', from *post* 'after'.

posterity ▪ n. all future generations.
–ORIGIN Middle English: from Old French *posterite*, from Latin *posteritas*, from *posterus* 'following'.

postern /'pɒst(ə)n, 'pəʊst-/ ▪ n. a back or side entrance.
–ORIGIN Middle English: from Old French *posterne*, from late Latin *posterula*, diminutive of *posterus* 'following'.

poster paint ▪ n. an opaque paint with a water-soluble binder.

post-feminist ▪ adj. coming after the feminism of the 1960s and subsequent decades, in particular moving beyond or rejecting some of the ideas of feminism as out of date. ▪ n. a person holding post-feminist views.
–DERIVATIVES **post-feminism** n.

postglacial ▪ adj. Geology relating to or denoting the period since the last glaciation, about 10 000 years ago.

postgraduate ▪ adj. relating to or denoting a course of study undertaken after completing a first degree. ▪ n. a person engaged in postgraduate study.

post-haste ▪ adv. with great speed or immediacy.
–ORIGIN C16: from the direction 'haste, post, haste', formerly given on letters.

post hoc /hɒk/ ▪ adj. & adv. after the event.
–ORIGIN Latin, 'after this'.

post horn ▪ n. historical a valveless horn used to signal the arrival or departure of a mounted courier or mail coach.

posthumous /'pɒstjʊməs/ ▪ adj. occurring, awarded, or appearing after the death of the originator.
–DERIVATIVES **posthumously** adv.
–ORIGIN C17: from Latin *postumus* 'last' (superlative from *post* 'after'), associated in late Latin with *humus* 'ground', *humare* 'bury'.

postilion /pɒ'stɪlɪən/ (also **postillion**) ▪ n. a person who rides the leading nearside horse of a team or pair drawing a coach or carriage, when there is no coachman.
–ORIGIN C16: from French *postillon*, from Italian *postiglione* 'post-boy', from *posta* (see POST²).

post-Impressionism ▪ n. the work or style of a group of late 19th-century and early 20th-century artists who reacted against the naturalism of the Impressionists, using colour, line, and form to express the emotional response of the artist.
–DERIVATIVES **post-Impressionist** n. & adj. **post-Impressionistic** adj.

post-industrial ▪ adj. of or relating to an economy which no longer relies on heavy industry.
–DERIVATIVES **post-industrialism** n.

posting¹ ▪ n. chiefly Brit. an appointment to a job, especially one abroad or in the armed forces.

posting² ▪ n. a message sent to an Internet bulletin board or newsgroup.

Post-it ▪ n. trademark a piece of paper with an adhesive strip on one side, designed to be stuck prominently to an object or surface and easily removed when necessary.

postlude ▪ n. **1** Music a concluding piece of music. **2** an afterword.
–ORIGIN C19: from POST-, on the pattern of *prelude*.

postman (or **postwoman**) ▪ n. (pl. **-men** or **-women**) a person who is employed to deliver or collect post.

postmark ▪ n. an official mark stamped on a letter or other postal package, giving the place, date, and time of posting, and serving to cancel the postage stamp. ▪ v. stamp with a postmark.

postmaster (or **postmistress**) ▪ n. a person in charge of a post office.

postmaster general ▪ n. the head of a country's postal service.

postmillennial /ˌpəʊs(t)mɪ'lɛnɪəl/ ▪ adj. following the millennium.

postmillennialism ▪ n. (among fundamentalist Christians) the doctrine that the Second Coming of Christ will be the culmination of the prophesied millennium of blessedness.

postmodernism ■ n. a late 20th-century style and concept in the arts and architecture, which represents a departure from modernism and has at its heart a general distrust of theories and ideologies as well as a problematical relationship with the notion of 'art'.
– DERIVATIVES **postmodern** adj. **postmodernist** n. & adj. **postmodernity** n.

post-mortem ■ n. **1** an examination of a dead body to determine the cause of death. **2** an analysis of an event made after it has occurred. ■ adj. **1** of or relating to a post-mortem. **2** happening after death.
– ORIGIN C18: from Latin, 'after death'.

post-natal ■ adj. occurring in or relating to the period after childbirth.
– DERIVATIVES **post-natally** adv.

postnuptial ■ adj. occurring in or relating to the period after marriage.

post office ■ n. the public department or corporation responsible for postal services and (in some countries) telecommunications. ▶ a building where postal business is transacted.

post office box (also **PO box**) ■ n. a private numbered box in a post office or other central location, assigned to a person or organization, to which mail is delivered.

post-op ■ abbrev. post-operative.

post-operative ■ adj. relating to or denoting the period following a surgical operation.

post-partum /ˈpɑːtəm/ ■ adj. Medicine & Veterinary Medicine relating to or characteristic of the period following childbirth or the birth of young.
– ORIGIN C19: from Latin *post partum* 'after childbirth'.

postpone ■ v. arrange for (something) to take place at a time later than that first scheduled.
– DERIVATIVES **postponable** adj. **postponement** n.
– ORIGIN C15: from Latin *postponere*, from *post* 'after' + *ponere* 'to place'.

postposition ■ n. Grammar a word or morpheme placed after the word it governs, for example *-ward* in *homeward*.
– DERIVATIVES **postpositional** adj.
– ORIGIN C19: from PREPOSITION, by substitution of the prefix POST- for *pre-*.

postpositive ■ adj. (of a word) placed after or as a suffix on the word that it relates to. ■ n. a postpositive word.
– DERIVATIVES **postpositively** adv.

postprandial ■ adj. **1** formal or humorous during or relating to the period after a meal. **2** Medicine occurring after a meal.
– ORIGIN C19: from POST- + Latin *prandium* 'a meal'.

postscript ■ n. **1** an additional remark at the end of a letter, following the signature. **2** a sequel.
– ORIGIN C16: from Latin *postscriptum*, from *postscribere* 'write under, add'.

post-structuralism ■ n. an extension and critique of structuralism, especially as used in critical textual analysis, which emphasizes plurality and deferral of meaning and rejects the binary oppositions of structuralism.
– DERIVATIVES **post-structural** adj. **post-structuralist** n. & adj.

post-traumatic stress disorder ■ n. Medicine a condition of persistent mental and emotional stress occurring as a result of injury or severe psychological shock.

postulant /ˈpɒstjʊl(ə)nt/ ■ n. a candidate seeking admission into a religious order.
– ORIGIN C18: from French *postulant* or Latin *postulant-* 'asking', from *postulare* 'ask'.

postulate ■ v. /ˈpɒstjʊleɪt/ suggest or assume the existence, fact, or truth of (something) as a basis for reasoning, discussion, or belief. ■ n. /ˈpɒstjʊlət/ a thing postulated.
– DERIVATIVES **postulation** n. **postulator** n.
– ORIGIN Middle English: from Latin *postulare* 'ask'.

posture ■ n. **1** a particular position of the body. ▶ the way in which a person holds their body. **2** an approach or attitude towards something. ■ v. [often as noun **posturing**] behave in a way that is intended to impress or mislead others.
– DERIVATIVES **postural** adj. **posturer** n.
– ORIGIN C16: from Italian *postura*, from Latin *positura* 'position'.

postviral syndrome (also **postviral fatigue syndrome**) ■ n. myalgic encephalomyelitis following a viral infection.

posy[1] ■ n. (pl. **-ies**) a small bunch of flowers.
– ORIGIN Middle English: contraction of POESY.

posy[2] ■ adj. variant spelling of POSEY.

pot[1] ■ n. **1** a rounded or cylindrical container, especially one of ceramic, used for storage or cooking. **2** a container used for growing plants; a flowerpot. **3** a receptacle used by young children for urinating or defecating into. **4** (**the pot**) the total sum of the bets made on a round in poker, brag, etc. **5** informal a pot belly. **6** informal an engine cylinder. **7** Billiards & Snooker a shot in which a player strikes a ball into a pocket. ■ v. (**potted**, **potting**) **1** plant in a pot. ▶ (**pot on**) transplant from a smaller pot to a larger one. ▶ (**pot up**) transplant from a seed tray to a pot. **2** preserve (food) in a sealed pot or jar. **3** make pottery. **4** Billiards & Snooker strike (a ball) into a pocket. **5** informal hit or kill by shooting. **6** encapsulate (an electrical component or circuit) in a liquid insulating material which sets solid.
– PHRASES **go to pot** informal deteriorate through neglect.
– DERIVATIVES **potful** n. (pl. **-fuls**).
– ORIGIN Old English, prob. reinforced in Middle English by Old French *pot*.

pot[2] ■ n. informal cannabis.
– ORIGIN 1930s: prob. from Mexican Spanish *potiguaya* 'cannabis leaves'.

potable /ˈpəʊtəb(ə)l/ ■ adj. drinkable.
– DERIVATIVES **potability** n.
– ORIGIN Middle English: from French *potable*, from late Latin *potabilis*, from Latin *potare* 'to drink'.

potager /ˈpɒtədʒə/ ■ n. a kitchen garden.
– ORIGIN C17: from French *jardin potager* 'garden providing vegetables for the pot'.

potash ■ n. an alkaline potassium compound, especially potassium carbonate or hydroxide.
– ORIGIN C17: from *pot-ashes*, from obsolete Dutch *potasschen*, orig. obtained by leaching vegetable ashes and evaporating the solution in iron pots.

potassium /pəˈtasɪəm/ ■ n. the chemical element of atomic number 19, a soft silvery-white reactive metal of the alkali-metal group. (Symbol: **K**)
– DERIVATIVES **potassic** adj.
– ORIGIN C19: from POTASH (from French *potasse*).

potassium hydroxide ■ n. a strongly alkaline white deliquescent compound used in many industrial processes, e.g. soap manufacture. [KOH.]

potato ■ n. (pl. **-oes**) **1** a starchy plant tuber which is one of the most important food crops, cooked and eaten as a vegetable. **2** the plant of the nightshade family which produces these tubers on underground runners. [*Solanum tuberosum*.]
– ORIGIN C16 (orig. denoting the sweet potato): from Spanish *patata*, var. of Taino *batata* 'sweet potato'.

pot-au-feu /ˌpɒtəʊˈfəː/ ■ n. a French soup of meat and vegetables cooked in a large pot.
– ORIGIN French, 'pot on the fire'.

pot-bellied stove ■ n. a small bulbous-sided wood-burning stove.

pot belly ■ n. a protruding, rotund stomach.
– DERIVATIVES **pot-bellied** adj.

potboiler ■ n. informal a book, film, etc. produced to make the writer or artist a living by deliberately catering to popular taste.

pot-bound ■ adj. (of a plant) having roots which fill the pot, leaving no room for them to expand.

pot bread ■ n. S. African bread baked in a closed cast-iron pot over an open fire.

Potchefstroom koekoek /ˌpɒtʃəfˌstruəm ˈkʊkʊk/ (also **koekoek**) ■ n. a domestic chicken of a medium-sized South African breed with mottled black and white plumage.

poteen /pɒˈtiːn/ ■ n. chiefly Irish illicitly made whiskey.
– ORIGIN C19: from Irish (*fuisce*) *poitín* 'little pot (of whiskey)', diminutive of *pota* 'pot'.

potent¹ ■ adj. **1** having great power, influence, or effect. **2** (of a male) able to achieve an erection or to reach an orgasm.
– DERIVATIVES **potence** n. **potency** n. **potently** adv.
– ORIGIN Middle English: from Latin *potent-*, *posse* 'be powerful, be able'.

potent² Heraldry ■ adj. [postpos.] **1** formed of crutch-shaped pieces; (especially of a cross) having a straight bar across the end of each extremity. **2** of the fur called potent (as a tincture). ■ n. fur resembling vair, but with the alternating pieces T-shaped.
– ORIGIN Middle English: alteration of Old French *potence* 'crutch', from Latin *potentia* 'power', from *potent-* (see POTENT¹).

potentate ■ n. a monarch or ruler.
– ORIGIN Middle English: from Latin *potentatus* 'dominion', from *potent-* (see POTENT¹).

potential ■ adj. having the capacity to develop into something in the future. ■ n. **1** latent qualities or abilities that may be developed and lead to future success or usefulness. **2** (often **potential for/to do something**) the possibility of something happening or of someone doing something in the future. **3** Physics the quantity determining the energy of mass in a gravitational field or of charge in an electric field.
– DERIVATIVES **potentiality** n. **potentialize** (also **-ise**) v. **potentially** adv.
– ORIGIN Middle English: from late Latin *potentialis*, from *potentia* 'power'.

potential difference ■ n. Physics the difference of electrical potential between two points.

potential energy ■ n. Physics energy possessed by a body by virtue of its position or state. Compare with KINETIC ENERGY.

potentiate /pə(ʊ)ˈtenʃɪeɪt/ ■ v. increase the power or effect of (something such as a drug or physiological reaction).
– ORIGIN C19: from POTENT¹, on the pattern of *substantiate*.

potentiation ■ n. Physiology the increase in strength of nerve impulses along pathways which have been used previously, either short-term or long-term.

potentilla /ˌpəʊt(ə)nˈtɪlə/ ■ n. a plant of a genus that includes the cinquefoils, especially a small shrub with yellow or red flowers. [Genus *Potentilla*: many species.]
– ORIGIN from Latin *potent-* 'being powerful' (with ref. to its herbal qualities) + the diminutive suffix *-illa*.

potentiometer /pə(ʊ)ˌtenʃɪˈɒmɪtə/ ■ n. an instrument for measuring or adjusting an electromotive force by balancing it against a known potential difference.

potentiometry ■ n. Chemistry the measurement of electrical potential as a technique in chemical analysis.
– DERIVATIVES **potentiometric** adj.

pothead ■ n. informal a habitual cannabis smoker.

pothole ■ n. **1** a deep natural underground cave formed by the eroding action of water. ▸ a deep circular hole in a river bed formed by the eroding action of stones in an eddy. **2** a depression or hollow in a road surface caused by wear or subsidence. **3** N. Amer. a lake formed by a natural hollow in the ground in which water has collected. ■ v. Brit. explore underground potholes as a pastime.
– DERIVATIVES **potholed** adj. **potholer** n. **potholing** n.
– ORIGIN C19: from Middle English *pot* 'pit' (perhaps of Scandinavian origin) + HOLE.

potion ■ n. a liquid with healing, magical, or poisonous properties.
– ORIGIN Middle English: from Latin *potio(n-)* 'drink, poisonous draught', rel. to *potare* 'to drink'.

potjie /ˈpɔɪki/ ■ n. S. African a lidded round-bottomed cast-iron pot, often three-legged, used to cook food over an open fire. ▸ short for POTJIEKOS.
– ORIGIN Afrikaans, 'little pot'.

potjiekos /ˈpɔɪkikɒs/ ■ n. S. African a kind of stew cooked in a potjie.
– ORIGIN Afrikaans, from *potjie* 'little pot' + *kos* 'food'.

pot luck ■ n. **1** the chance that whatever is available will prove to be good or acceptable. **2** (**potluck**) [as modifier] denoting a meal in which all the guests bring a different dish to share.

pot-pourri /pəʊˈpʊəri, -ˈriː, pɒtˈpʊəri/ ■ n. (pl. **pot-pourris**)

1 a mixture of dried petals and spices placed in a bowl to perfume a room. **2** a mixture of things; a medley.
– ORIGIN C17 (denoting a stew made of different kinds of meat): from French, 'rotten pot'.

pot roast ■ n. a piece of meat cooked slowly in a covered pot. ■ v. (**pot-roast**) cook (meat) in such a way.

potsherd /ˈpɒtʃəːd/ ■ n. a piece of broken pottery.

potshot ■ n. **1** a shot aimed unexpectedly or at random. ▸ a shot at a game bird or other animal made without regard to hunting rules. **2** a random attack or criticism.
– ORIGIN C19: orig. a *shot* at an animal intended for the *pot*, i.e. for food.

pot still ■ n. a still to which heat is applied directly and not by means of a steam jacket.

pottage ■ n. soup or stew.
– ORIGIN Middle English: from Old French *potage* 'that which is put into a pot'.

potted ■ adj. **1** grown or preserved in a pot. **2** (of a biographical or historical account) put into a short and easily assimilable form. **3** (of an electrical component or circuit) encapsulated in insulating material.

potter¹ (also **putter**) ■ v. **1** occupy oneself in a desultory but pleasant manner. **2** move or go in a casual, unhurried way. ■ n. a spell of pottering.
– DERIVATIVES **potterer** n.
– ORIGIN C16: from dialect *pote* 'to push, kick, or poke'.

potter² ■ n. a person who makes ceramic ware.

potter's wheel ■ n. a horizontal revolving disc on which wet clay is shaped into pots, bowls, etc.

pottery ■ n. (pl. **-ies**) pots, dishes, and other articles made of fired clay. ▸ the craft or profession of making such ware. ▸ a factory or workshop where such ware is made.
– ORIGIN Middle English: from Old French *poterie*, from *potier* 'a potter'.

potting compost ■ n. a mixture of loam, peat, sand, and nutrients, used as a growing medium for plants in containers.

potting shed ■ n. a shed used for potting plants and storing garden tools and supplies.

potto /ˈpɒtəʊ/ (also **potto gibbon**) ■ n. (pl. **-os**) a small nocturnal slow-moving primate with a short tail, living in dense vegetation in the tropical forests of Africa. [*Perodicticus potto*.]
– ORIGIN C18: perhaps from Guinea dialect.

potty¹ ■ adj. (**-ier**, **-iest**) informal, chiefly Brit. **1** foolish; crazy. **2** extremely enthusiastic about someone or something.
– DERIVATIVES **pottiness** n.
– ORIGIN C19.

potty² ■ n. (pl. **-ies**) informal a child's pot for urinating or defecating into.

potty-train ■ v. train (a young child) to use a pot.

pouch ■ n. **1** a small flexible bag. ▸ a lockable bag for mail or dispatches. **2** a pocket-like abdominal receptacle in which marsupials carry their young during lactation. **3** any of a number of similar animal structures, such as those in the cheeks of rodents. ▸ (often **pouches**) a baggy area of skin underneath a person's eyes. ■ v. **1** put into a pouch. **2** make or form into a pouch.
– DERIVATIVES **pouched** adj. **pouchy** adj.
– ORIGIN Middle English: from Old Northern French *pouche*, var. of Old French *poche* 'bag'.

pouf ■ n. variant spelling of POOF¹ or POUFFE. ■ exclam. variant spelling of POOF².

pouffe /puːf/ (also **pouf**) ■ n. a cushioned footstool or low seat with no back.
– ORIGIN C19: from French *pouf*, of imitative origin.

poult /pəʊlt/ ■ n. Farming a young domestic fowl being raised for food.
– ORIGIN Middle English: contraction of PULLET.

poultice /ˈpəʊltɪs/ ■ n. a soft moist mass of material, typically consisting of bran, flour, herbs, etc., applied with a cloth to the body to relieve inflammation. ■ v. apply a poultice to.
– ORIGIN Middle English: from Latin *pultes* (pl.), from *puls* 'pottage, pap'.

poultry /ˈpəʊltri/ ■ n. chickens, turkeys, ducks, and geese; domestic fowl.
– ORIGIN Middle English: from Old French *pouletrie*, from *poulet* 'pullet'.

pounce ■ v. **1** spring or swoop suddenly to catch or as if to catch prey. **2** notice and take swift advantage of a mistake or sign of weakness. ■ n. an act of pouncing.
– DERIVATIVES **pouncer** n.
– ORIGIN Middle English.

pound[1] ■ n. **1** (abbrev.: **lb**) a unit of weight equal to 16 oz avoirdupois (0.4536 kg), or 12 oz troy (0.3732 kg). **2** (also **pound sterling**) (pl. **pounds sterling**) the basic monetary unit of the UK, equal to 100 pence. **3** another term for PUNT[3]. **4** the basic monetary unit of several Middle Eastern countries, Cyprus, and the Sudan.
– PHRASES **one's pound of flesh** something to which one is strictly entitled, but which it is ruthless to demand. [with allusion to Shakespeare's *Merchant of Venice*.] **in the pound seat** (s) in a very favourable position.
– ORIGIN Old English *pund*, of Germanic origin, from Latin (*libra*) *pondo*, denoting a Roman 'pound weight' of 12 ounces.

pound[2] ■ v. **1** strike or hit heavily and repeatedly. ▸ (**pound something out**) produce a document or piece of music with heavy strokes on a keyboard or instrument. ▸ beat or throb with a strong regular rhythm. ▸ walk or run with heavy steps. **2** crush or grind into a powder or paste. **3** informal defeat resoundingly.
– DERIVATIVES **pounding** n.
– ORIGIN Old English *pūnian*.

pound[3] ■ n. a place where stray animals may officially be taken and kept until claimed. ▸ a place where illegally parked motor vehicles removed by the police are kept until the owner pays a fine.
– ORIGIN Middle English.

poundage ■ n. Brit. **1** a commission of a particular amount per pound sterling of the sum involved in a transaction. **2** a percentage of the total earnings of a business, paid as wages. **3** weight.

poundal /ˈpaʊnd(ə)l/ ■ n. Physics a unit of force equal to that required to give a mass of one pound an acceleration of one foot per second per second.
– ORIGIN C19: from POUND[1].

pound cake ■ n. a rich cake originally made with a pound of each chief ingredient.

pounder ■ n. **1** a person or thing that pounds. **2** [in combination] a person or thing weighing or costing a specified number of pounds: *a three-pounder*.

pour ■ v. **1** flow or cause to flow in a steady stream. ▸ (often **pour down**) (of rain) fall heavily. ▸ prepare and serve (a drink). **2** (of people or things) come or go in a steady stream. **3** (**pour something out**) express one's feelings in an unrestrained way.
– PHRASES **pour oil on troubled waters** try to calm a dispute with placatory words.
– DERIVATIVES **pourable** adj. **pourer** n.
– ORIGIN Middle English.

poussin /ˈpuːsã/ ■ n. a chicken killed young for eating.
– ORIGIN from French.

pout ■ v. push one's lips or bottom lip forward as an expression of petulant annoyance or in order to make oneself look sexually attractive. ■ n. a pouting expression.
– DERIVATIVES **pouting** adj. **poutingly** adv. **pouty** adj.
– ORIGIN Middle English: perhaps from Swedish dialect *puta* 'be inflated'.

pouter ■ n. a kind of pigeon that is able to inflate its crop to a considerable extent.

poverty ■ n. **1** the state of being extremely poor. ▸ the renunciation of the right to individual ownership of property as part of a religious vow. **2** the state of being insufficient in amount.
– ORIGIN Middle English: from Old French *poverte*, from Latin *paupertas*, from *pauper* 'poor'.

poverty line (also chiefly S. African **poverty datum line**) ■ n. the estimated minimum level of income needed to secure the necessities of life.

poverty trap ■ n. a situation in which an increase in someone's income is offset by a consequent loss of state benefits.

POW ■ abbrev. prisoner of war.

pow ■ exclam. expressing the sound of a blow or explosion.
– ORIGIN C19 (orig. US): imitative.

powder ■ n. **1** fine dry particles produced by the grinding, crushing, or disintegration of a solid substance. **2** a cosmetic in this form applied to a person's face. **3** dated a medicine in this form. **4** loose, dry, newly fallen snow. **5** short for GUNPOWDER (in sense 1). ■ v. **1** apply powder to; sprinkle or cover with powder. **2** [usu. as adj. **powdered**] reduce to a powder.
– PHRASES **keep one's powder dry** remain cautious and alert. **take a powder** N. Amer. informal depart quickly.
– DERIVATIVES **powdery** adj.
– ORIGIN Middle English: from Old French *poudre*, from Latin *pulvis* 'dust'.

powder blue ■ n. a soft, pale blue.

powder-coat ■ v. cover (an object) with a polyester or epoxy powder, which is then heated to fuse into a protective layer.

powdered sugar ■ n. North American term for ICING SUGAR.

powder keg ■ n. **1** a barrel of gunpowder. **2** a potentially explosive situation.

powder metallurgy ■ n. the production and working of metals as fine powders which can be pressed and sintered to form objects.

powder monkey ■ n. **1** historical a boy employed on a sailing warship to carry powder to the guns. **2** N. Amer. a person who works with explosives.

powder-post beetle ■ n. a small brown beetle whose wood-boring larvae reduce wood to a very fine powder. [Family Lyctidae].

powder puff ■ n. a soft pad for applying powder to the face.

powder room ■ n. euphemistic a women's toilet.

power ■ n. **1** the ability to do something or act in a particular way. **2** the capacity to influence the behaviour of others, the emotions, or the course of events. **3** a right or authority given or delegated to a person or body. ▸ political authority or control. **4** a country viewed in terms of its international influence and military strength: *a world power*. **5** physical strength or force. ▸ capacity or performance of an engine or other device. ▸ the magnifying capacity of a lens. **6** energy that is produced by mechanical, electrical, or other means. ▸ [as modifier] driven by such energy: *a power drill*. **7** Physics the rate of doing work, measured in watts or horse power. **8** Mathematics the product obtained when a number is multiplied by itself a certain number of times. ■ v. **1** supply with power. ▸ (**power something up/down**) switch an electrically powered device on or off. **2** move or cause to move with speed or force: *he powered round a bend*.
– PHRASES **do someone a power of good** informal be very beneficial to someone. **the powers that be** the authorities. [with biblical allusion to Romans 13:1.]
– DERIVATIVES **-powered** adj. **powerless** adj. **powerlessly** adv. **powerlessness** n.
– ORIGIN Middle English: from Anglo-Norman French *poeir*, from Latin *posse* 'be able'.

power-assisted ■ adj. (especially of steering or brakes) using an inanimate source of power to assist manual operation.

powerboat ■ n. a fast motor boat.

power broker ■ n. a person who sets out to affect the distribution of political or economic power by exerting influence or by intrigue.
– DERIVATIVES **power-broking** n. & adj.

power cut ■ n. a temporary withdrawal or failure of an electrical power supply.

power dive ■ n. a steep dive of an aircraft with the engines providing thrust. ■ v. (**power-dive**) perform a power dive.

power factor ■ n. the ratio of the actual power dissipated by a circuit to the product of the rms values of current and voltage.

power forward ■ n. Basketball a large forward who plays in the low post and typically has good shot-blocking and rebounding skills.

powerful ■ adj. having power. ■ adv. chiefly dialect very.
– DERIVATIVES **powerfully** adv. **powerfulness** n.

powerhouse ■ n. a person or thing having great energy or power.

powerlifting ■ n. a form of competitive weightlifting in which contestants attempt three types of lift in a set sequence.
– DERIVATIVES **powerlifter** n.

power of attorney ■ n. Law the written authority to act for another person in specified legal or financial matters.

power pack ■ n. **1** a self-contained and typically transportable unit which stores and supplies electrical power. **2** a transformer for converting an alternating current (from the mains) to a direct current at a different (usually lower) voltage.

power plant ■ n. **1** another term for POWER STATION. **2** an engine or other apparatus which provides power for a machine, building, etc.

power play ■ n. **1** tactics exhibiting or intended to increase a person's power. **2** offensive tactics in a team sport involving the concentration of players in a particular area. **3** Ice Hockey a temporary situation in which one team has a numerical advantage because one or more players is serving a penalty.

power shower ■ n. a shower using an electric pump to produce a high-pressure spray.

power station ■ n. an installation where electrical power is generated.

power steering ■ n. power-assisted steering.

power stroke ■ n. the stage of the cycle of an internal-combustion engine in which the piston is driven outward by the expansion of gases.

power train ■ n. the mechanism that transmits the drive from the engine of a vehicle to its axle.

power-walking ■ n. brisk walking as a form of aerobic exercise.
– DERIVATIVES **power-walk** n. & v. **power-walker** n.

powwow ■ n. **1** a North American Indian ceremony involving feasting and dancing. **2** informal a meeting for discussion among friends or colleagues. ■ v. informal hold a powwow.
– ORIGIN C17: from Narragansett (an extinct Algonquian language) *powah*, *powwaw* 'magician' (literally 'he dreams').

pox ■ n. **1** any of several viral diseases producing a rash of pimples that become pus-filled and leave pockmarks on healing. ▸ (**the pox**) historical smallpox. **2** (**the pox**) informal syphilis.
– PHRASES **a pox on someone** archaic expressing anger with someone.
– ORIGIN Middle English: alteration of *pocks*, pl. of POCK.

poxy ■ adj. (**-ier**, **-iest**) informal, chiefly Brit. of poor quality; worthless.

pozzie ■ n. (also **possie**) S. African & Austral./NZ informal a person's home.
– ORIGIN abbrev. of POSITION (sense 1).

pozzolana /ˌpɒtsəˈlɑːnə/ ■ n. a type of volcanic ash used for mortar or for cement that sets under water.
– ORIGIN C18: from Italian, from *pozz(u)olana* '(earth) of Pozzuoli', a town near Naples.

pp ■ abbrev. **1** (**pp.**) pages. **2** (also **p.p.**) per procurationem (used when signing a letter on someone else's behalf). [Latin 'through the agency of'.]

p. & p. ■ abbrev. postage and packing.

PPE ■ abbrev. philosophy, politics, and economics.

ppi ■ abbrev. Computing pixels per inch.

ppm ■ abbrev. **1** part(s) per million. **2** Computing page(s) per minute.

PPP ■ abbrev. **1** (in computing) point to point protocol. **2** public private partnership. **3** purchasing power parity.

PPS ■ abbrev. post (additional) postscript.

PPV ■ abbrev. pay-per-view.

PR ■ abbrev. **1** proportional representation. **2** public relations.

Pr ■ symb. the chemical element praseodymium.

pr ■ abbrev. **1** pair. **2** archaic per.

practicable ■ adj. **1** able to be done or put into practice successfully. **2** useful.
– DERIVATIVES **practicability** n. **practicably** adv.

practical ■ adj. **1** of or concerned with practice. **2** likely to be effective in real circumstances; feasible. ▸ suitable for a particular purpose. **3** (of a person) realistic in approach. ▸ (of a person) skilled at manual tasks. **4** so nearly the case that it can be regarded as so; virtual. ■ n. an examination or lesson involving the practical application of theories and procedures.
– ORIGIN C16: from archaic *practic* 'practical', from Old French *practique*, from Greek *praktikos* 'concerned with action'.

practicality ■ n. (pl. **-ies**) **1** the quality or state of being practical. **2** (**practicalities**) the aspects of a situation that involve the actual doing or experience of something rather than theories or ideas.

practical joke ■ n. a trick played on someone in order to make them look foolish and to amuse others.
– DERIVATIVES **practical joker** n.

practically ■ adv. **1** in a practical manner. ▸ in practical terms. **2** virtually; almost.

practice ■ n. **1** the actual application or use of a plan or method, as opposed to the theories relating to it. **2** the customary or expected procedure or way of doing something. **3** the practising of a profession. ▸ the business or premises of a doctor or lawyer. **4** the action or process of practising. ■ v. US spelling of PRACTISE.
– PHRASES **in** (or **out of**) **practice** having (or not having) practised an activity or skill on a regular basis.
– ORIGIN Middle English: from PRACTISE, on the pattern of pairs such as *advise*, *advice*.

USAGE
Note that **practice** is the correct spelling for the noun in South African, British, and US English, and is also the spelling of the verb in US English. However, in South African and British English the verb should be spelled **practise**.

practicum /ˈpraktɪkəm/ ■ n. (pl. **practicums**) chiefly N. Amer. a practical section of a course of study.
– ORIGIN C20: from late Latin, from *practicus* 'practical'.

practise (US **practice**) ■ v. **1** perform (an activity) or exercise (a skill) repeatedly or regularly in order to acquire, maintain, or improve proficiency in it. **2** carry out or perform (an activity or custom) habitually or regularly. **3** be engaged in (a particular profession). **4** observe the teaching and rules of (a particular religion). **5** archaic scheme or plot for an evil purpose.
– DERIVATIVES **practised** adj. **practiser** n.
– ORIGIN Middle English: from Old French *practiser*, from Latin *practica* 'practice', from Greek *praktikē*, from *praktikos* (see PRACTICAL).

USAGE
On the difference between **practise** and **practice**, see usage at PRACTICE.

practitioner ■ n. a person actively engaged in an art, discipline, or profession, especially medicine.
– ORIGIN C16: extension of obsolete *practitian*, var. of archaic *practician*.

praesidium ■ n. variant spelling of PRESIDIUM.

praetorian guard ■ n. (in ancient Rome) the bodyguard of the emperor.

pragmatic ■ adj. **1** dealing with things in a way that is based on practical rather than theoretical considerations. **2** relating to philosophical or political pragmatism. **3** Linguistics of or relating to pragmatics.
– DERIVATIVES **pragmatically** adv.
– ORIGIN C16: from Greek *pragmatikos* 'relating to fact'.

pragmatics ■ pl. n. [usu. treated as sing.] the branch of linguistics concerned with language in use and the contexts in which it is used.

pragmatism ■ n. 1 a pragmatic attitude or policy. 2 Philosophy an approach that evaluates theories or beliefs in terms of the success of their practical application.
– DERIVATIVES **pragmatist** n.

prairie ■ n. (in North America) a large open area of grassland.
– ORIGIN C18: from Old French *praerie*, from Latin *pratum* 'meadow'.

prairie dog ■ n. a gregarious ground squirrel that lives in interconnected burrows, native to the grasslands of North America. [Genus *Cynomys*: several species.]

prairie oyster ■ n. a drink made with a raw egg and seasoning, drunk as a cure for a hangover.

praise ■ v. 1 express warm approval of or admiration for. 2 express respect and gratitude towards (a deity). ■ n. 1 the expression of approval or admiration. 2 the expression of respect and gratitude as an act of worship.
– PHRASES **praise be** expressing relief, joy, or gratitude.
– DERIVATIVES **praiseful** adj.
– ORIGIN Middle English: from Old French *preisier* 'to prize, praise', from late Latin *pretiare*, from Latin *pretium* 'price'.

praise singer (also **praise poet**) ■ n. (in some African societies) an orator who proclaims the qualities and accomplishments of a leader on ceremonial occasions.

praiseworthy ■ adj. deserving of praise.
– DERIVATIVES **praiseworthiness** n.

prajna /ˈprajnə/ ■ n. Buddhism direct insight into the truth taught by the Buddha, as a faculty required to attain enlightenment.
– ORIGIN from Sanskrit *prajñā*.

praline /ˈprɑːliːn/ ■ n. a sweet substance made by boiling nuts in sugar and grinding the mixture, used especially as a filling for chocolates.
– ORIGIN C18: from French, named after Marshal de Plessis-*Praslin*, the French soldier whose cook invented it.

pram /pram/ ■ n. a four-wheeled carriage for a baby, pushed by a person on foot.
– ORIGIN C19: contraction of PERAMBULATOR.

prana /ˈprɑːnə/ ■ n. Hinduism breath, considered as a life-giving force.
– ORIGIN from Sanskrit.

pranayama /ˌprɑːnəˈjɑːmə/ ■ n. (in yoga) the regulation of the breath through certain techniques and exercises.
– ORIGIN Sanskrit, from *prāṇa* 'breath' + *āyāma* 'restraint'.

prance ■ v. 1 (of a horse) move with high springy steps. 2 (of a person) walk or move around with ostentatious, exaggerated movements. ■ n. an act of prancing.
– DERIVATIVES **prancer** n.
– ORIGIN Middle English.

prandial /ˈprandɪəl/ ■ adj. during or relating to a meal.
– ORIGIN C19: from Latin *prandium* 'meal'.

prang informal ■ v. crash (a motor vehicle or aircraft). ▸ strike against. ■ n. an act of pranging something; a collision or crash.
– ORIGIN 1940s: imitative.

prank ■ n. a practical joke or mischievous act.
– DERIVATIVES **prankish** adj. **prankishness** n.
– ORIGIN C16.

prankster ■ n. a person fond of playing pranks.

praseodymium /ˌpreɪzɪə(ʊ)ˈdɪmɪəm/ ■ n. the chemical element of atomic number 59, a soft silvery-white metal of the lanthanide series. (Symbol: **Pr**)
– ORIGIN C19: from German *Praseodym*, from Greek *prasios* 'leek-green' (because of its green salts) + German *Didym* 'didymium'.

prat ■ n. Brit. informal an incompetent or stupid person.
– ORIGIN C16.

prate ■ v. talk foolishly or at tedious length.
– ORIGIN Middle English: from Middle Dutch, Middle Low German *praten*, prob. of imitative origin.

pratincole /ˈpratɪŋkəʊl/ ■ n. a long-winged fork-tailed insectivorous bird related to the plovers. [*Glareola pratincola* (Africa and Eurasia) and other species.]
– ORIGIN C18: from Latin *pratum* 'meadow' + *incola* 'inhabitant'.

prattle ■ v. talk at length in a foolish or inconsequential way. ■ n. foolish or inconsequential talk.
– DERIVATIVES **prattler** n.
– ORIGIN C16: from Middle Low German *pratelen*, from *praten* (see PRATE).

prawn ■ n. a marine crustacean which resembles a large shrimp. [*Leander* and other genera.]
– ORIGIN Middle English.

prawn cracker ■ n. (in Chinese cooking) a light prawn-flavoured crisp made from rice or tapioca flour, which puffs up when deep-fried.

praxis /ˈpraksɪs/ ■ n. 1 practice, as distinguished from theory. 2 custom.
– ORIGIN C16: from Greek, 'doing', from *prattein* 'do'.

pray ■ v. 1 address a prayer to God or another deity. 2 wish or hope earnestly for a particular outcome. ■ adv. formal or archaic used in polite requests or questions: *pray continue*.
– ORIGIN Middle English: from Old French *preier*, from Latin *precari* 'entreat'.

prayer /prɛː/ ■ n. 1 a solemn request for help or expression of thanks addressed to God or another deity. 2 (**prayers**) a religious service at which people gather to pray together. 3 an earnest hope or wish.
– PHRASES **not have a prayer** informal have no chance.
– ORIGIN Middle English: from Old French *preiere*, from Latin *precarius* 'obtained by entreaty', from *prex* 'prayer'.

prayerful ■ adj. 1 characterized by the use of prayer. 2 given to praying; devout.
– DERIVATIVES **prayerfully** adv. **prayerfulness** n.

prayer plant ■ n. a Brazilian plant with variegated leaves which are erect at night but lie flat during the day, grown as a house plant. [*Maranta leuconeura*.]

prayer shawl ■ n. Judaism another term for TALLITH.

prayer wheel ■ n. a small revolving cylinder inscribed with or containing prayers, a revolution of which symbolizes the repetition of a prayer, used by Tibetan Buddhists.

praying mantis ■ n. see MANTIS.

pre- ■ prefix before (in time, place, order, degree, or importance): *pre-adolescent*.
– ORIGIN from Latin *prae-*.

preach ■ v. 1 deliver a religious address to an assembled group of people. ▸ publicly proclaim (a religious message). 2 earnestly advocate (a principle): *my parents always preached tolerance*. ▸ (**preach at**) give moral advice to (someone) in a self-righteous way.
– DERIVATIVES **preacher** n. **preachiness** n. **preachy** adj. (**-ier**, **-iest**).
– ORIGIN Middle English: from Old French *prechier*, from Latin *praedicare* 'proclaim', in eccles. Latin 'preach'.

preachify ■ v. (**-ies**, **-ied**) informal preach or moralize tediously.

preamble /priːˈamb(ə)l, ˈpriː-/ ■ n. a preliminary statement; an introduction.
– DERIVATIVES **preambular** adj.
– ORIGIN Middle English: from Old French *preambule*, from late Latin *praeambulus* 'going before'.

preamp ■ n. short for PREAMPLIFIER.

preamplifier ■ n. an electronic device that amplifies a very weak signal and transmits it to a main amplifier.

pre-arrange ■ v. arrange or agree in advance.
– DERIVATIVES **pre-arrangement** n.

prebendary /ˈprɛb(ə)nd(ə)ri/ ■ n. (pl. **-ies**) an honorary canon.

prebiotic ■ adj. existing or occurring before the emergence of life.

Precambrian /priːˈkambrɪən/ ■ adj. Geology relating to or denoting the earliest aeon of the earth's history, preceding the Cambrian period and ending about 570 million years ago (comprising the Archaean and Proterozoic aeons).

precancerous ■ adj. Medicine (of a cell or medical condition) likely to develop into cancer if untreated.

precarious ▪ adj. **1** not securely held or in position; likely to fall. **2** dependent on chance; uncertain.
– DERIVATIVES **precariously** adv. **precariousness** n.
– ORIGIN C17: from Latin *precarius* 'obtained by entreaty', from *prex* 'prayer'.

precast ▪ v. (past and past part. **precast**) [usu. as adj. **precast**] cast (an object or material, typically concrete) in its final shape before positioning.

precaution ▪ n. **1** a measure taken in advance to prevent something undesirable from happening. **2** (**precautions**) informal contraception.
– DERIVATIVES **precautionary** adj.
– ORIGIN C16: from French *précaution*, from Latin *praecavere*, from *prae* 'before' + *cavere* 'take heed, beware of'.

precede ▪ v. come or go before in time, order, or position. ▸ (**precede something with**) preface something with.
– DERIVATIVES **preceding** adj.
– ORIGIN Middle English: from Old French *preceder*, from Latin *praecedere*, from *prae* 'before' + *cedere* 'go'.

precedence /ˈprɛsɪd(ə)ns, ˈpriː-, prɪˈsiːd(ə)ns/ ▪ n. the condition of preceding others in importance, order, or rank. ▸ an acknowledged or legally determined right to such precedence.

precedent ▪ n. /ˈprɛsɪd(ə)nt/ an earlier event or action serving as an example or guide. ▸ Law a previous case or legal decision that may be or (binding precedent) must be followed in subsequent similar cases. ▪ adj. /prɪˈsiːd(ə)nt, ˈprɛsɪ-/ preceding in time, order, or importance.

precentor /prɪˈsɛntə/ ▪ n. **1** a person who leads a congregation in its singing or (in a synagogue) prayers. **2** a minor canon who administers the musical life of a cathedral.
– DERIVATIVES **precent** v. **precentorship** n.
– ORIGIN C17: from French *précenteur* or Latin *praecentor*, from *praecinere* 'sing before'.

precept /ˈpriːsɛpt/ ▪ n. **1** a general rule regulating behaviour or thought. **2** a writ or warrant.
– DERIVATIVES **preceptive** adj.
– ORIGIN Middle English: from Latin *praeceptum*, from *praecipere* 'warn, instruct'.

preceptor /prɪˈsɛptə/ ▪ n. a teacher or instructor.
– DERIVATIVES **preceptorial** /ˌpriːsɛpˈtɔːrɪəl/ adj. **preceptorship** n.

precession ▪ n. **1** Physics the slow movement of the axis of a spinning body around another axis. **2** Astronomy the slow retrograde motion of the equinoctial points along the ecliptic, resulting in the earlier occurrence of equinoxes each year.
– DERIVATIVES **precess** v. **precessional** adj.
– ORIGIN C16: from late Latin *praecessio(n-)*, from *praecedere* (see **PRECEDE**).

precinct /ˈpriːsɪŋ(k)t/ ▪ n. **1** the area within the walls or perceived boundaries of a particular place. ▸ an enclosed or clearly defined area of ground around a cathedral, church, or college. ▸ Brit. an area in a town designated for specific or restricted use, especially one closed to traffic. **2** N. Amer. a district of a city or town as defined for policing or electoral purposes.
– ORIGIN Middle English: from medieval Latin *praecinctum*, from *praecingere* 'encircle'.

preciosity /ˌprɛʃɪˈɒsɪti/ ▪ n. over-refinement in language or art.

precious ▪ adj. **1** having great value. **2** greatly loved or treasured by someone. **3** derogatory affectedly concerned with elegant or refined language or manners. ▪ n. a term of address to a beloved person.
– PHRASES **precious little** (or **few**) informal extremely little (or few).
– DERIVATIVES **preciously** adv. **preciousness** n.
– ORIGIN Middle English: from Old French *precios*, from Latin *pretiosus* 'of great value', from *pretium* 'price'.

precious metals ▪ pl. n. gold, silver, and platinum.

precious stone ▪ n. a highly attractive and valuable piece of mineral, used especially in jewellery.

precipice ▪ n. a tall and very steep rock face or cliff.
– ORIGIN C16: from French *précipice* or Latin *praecipitium*, from *praeceps* 'steep, headlong'.

precipitancy ▪ n. rashness or suddenness of action.

precipitant ▪ n. **1** a cause of a particular action or event. **2** Chemistry a substance that causes precipitation.
– DERIVATIVES **precipitance** n.

precipitate ▪ v. /prɪˈsɪpɪteɪt/ **1** cause (an undesirable event) to happen unexpectedly or prematurely. **2** cause to move suddenly and with force. ▸ (**precipitate someone/thing into**) send someone or something without warning into a particular state or condition. **3** Chemistry cause (a substance) to be deposited in solid form from a solution. ▸ cause (drops of moisture or particles of dust) to be deposited from the atmosphere or from a vapour or suspension. ▪ adj. /prɪˈsɪpɪtət/ done, acting, or occurring suddenly or without careful consideration. ▪ n. /prɪˈsɪpɪtət, -teɪt/ Chemistry a substance precipitated from a solution.
– DERIVATIVES **precipitable** adj. **precipitately** adv. **precipitateness** n.
– ORIGIN C16: from Latin *praecipitat-, praecipitare* 'throw headlong', from *praeceps* 'headlong', from *prae* 'before' + *caput* 'head'.

precipitation ▪ n. **1** Chemistry the action or process of precipitating a substance from a solution. **2** rain, snow, sleet, or hail that falls to or condenses on the ground. **3** archaic the fact or quality of acting precipitately.

precipitator ▪ n. an apparatus for causing precipitation, especially a device for removing dust from a gas.

precipitous /prɪˈsɪpɪtəs/ ▪ adj. **1** dangerously high or steep. **2** (of a change in a condition or situation) sudden and dramatic.
– DERIVATIVES **precipitously** adv. **precipitousness** n.
– ORIGIN C17: from obsolete French *précipiteux*, from Latin *praeceps* (see **PRECIPITATE**).

precis /ˈpreɪsiː/ ▪ n. (pl. same /-siːz/) a summary of a text or speech. ▪ v. (**precises** /-siːz/, **precised** /-siːd/, **precising** /-siːɪŋ/) make a precis of.
– ORIGIN C18: from French *précis* 'precise'.

precise ▪ adj. marked by exactness and accuracy of expression or detail. ▸ (of a person) very attentive to detail; careful in the expression of detail. ▸ exact; particular (used for emphasis).
– DERIVATIVES **precisely** adv. **preciseness** n.
– ORIGIN Middle English: from Old French *prescis*, from Latin *praecidere* 'cut short'.

precision ▪ n. **1** the quality, condition, or fact of being precise. **2** [as modifier] marked by or designed for accuracy and exactness: *a precision instrument*. **3** refinement in a measurement or specification, especially as represented by the number of digits given.

preclinical ▪ adj. Medicine relating to or denoting a stage preceding a clinical stage.

preclude ▪ v. prevent (something) from happening or (someone) from doing something.
– DERIVATIVES **preclusion** n. **preclusive** adj.
– ORIGIN C15: from Latin *praecludere*, from *prae* 'before' + *claudere* 'to shut'.

precocial /prɪˈkəʊʃ(ə)l/ ▪ adj. Zoology relating to or denoting a bird or other animal species whose young are hatched or born in an advanced state and are able to feed themselves almost immediately. Often contrasted with **ALTRICIAL**.
– ORIGIN C19: from *Praecoces*, the name of a former division of birds, from Latin *praecox* 'mature before its time'.

precocious ▪ adj. **1** having developed certain abilities or inclinations at an earlier age than usual. **2** (of a plant) flowering or fruiting earlier than usual.
– DERIVATIVES **precociously** adv. **precociousness** n. **precocity** n.
– ORIGIN C17: from Latin *praecox*, from *praecoquere* 'ripen fully', from *prae* 'before' + *coquere* 'to cook'.

precognition /ˌpriːkɒɡˈnɪʃ(ə)n/ ▪ n. foreknowledge.
– DERIVATIVES **precognitive** adj.

precoital ▪ adj. occurring before sexual intercourse.
– DERIVATIVES **precoitally** adv.

pre-Columbian ▪ adj. of or relating to the history and cultures of the Americas before the arrival of Christopher Columbus in 1492.

preconceived ■ adj. (of an idea or opinion) formed prior to having evidence for its truth or usefulness.
– DERIVATIVES **preconception** n.

precondition ■ n. a condition that must be fulfilled before other things can happen or be done. ■ v. 1 [often as noun **preconditioning**] prepare or condition (someone or something) to behave or react in a certain way under certain conditions. 2 bring into the desired state for use.

preconscious Psychology ■ adj. of or associated with a part of the mind below the level of conscious awareness, from which memories and emotions that have not been repressed can be recalled. ■ n. (**one's/the preconscious**) this part of the mind.
– DERIVATIVES **preconsciousness** n.

precordium /priːˈkɔːdɪəm/ ■ n. Anatomy the region of the thorax immediately in front of or over the heart.
– DERIVATIVES **precordial** adj.
– ORIGIN C19: sing. of Latin *praecordia* 'diaphragm, entrails'.

precursor ■ n. 1 a person or thing that comes before another of the same kind. 2 a substance from which another is formed, especially by metabolic reaction.
– DERIVATIVES **precursory** adj.
– ORIGIN Middle English: from Latin *praecursor*, from *praecurrere*, from *prae* 'beforehand' + *currere* 'to run'.

predacious /prɪˈdeɪʃəs/ ■ adj. (of an animal) predatory.
– DERIVATIVES **predaciousness** n. **predacity** n.
– ORIGIN C18: from Latin *praeda* 'booty'.

pre-date ■ v. exist or occur at a date earlier than.

predation /prɪˈdeɪʃ(ə)n/ ■ n. the preying of one animal on others.
– DERIVATIVES **predate** v.
– ORIGIN C15: from Latin *praedatio(n-)* 'taking of booty', from *praedari* 'seize as plunder', from *praeda* 'booty'.

predator ■ n. 1 an animal that preys on others. 2 a person who exploits others. ▸ a company that tries to take over another.
– DERIVATIVES **predatorily** adv. **predatoriness** n. **predatory** adj.

predatory pricing ■ n. the pricing of goods or services at such a low level that other firms cannot compete and are forced to leave the market.

predecease formal ■ v. die before (another person). ■ n. a death preceding that of another person.

predecessor ■ n. 1 a person who held a job or office before the current holder. 2 a thing that has been followed or replaced by another.
– ORIGIN Middle English: from late Latin *praedecessor*, from Latin *prae* 'beforehand' + *decessor* 'retiring officer'.

pre-democratic ■ adj. denoting a period, society, or political system before the granting of full suffrage. ▸ (of South Africa) denoting or relating to the period before the 1994 elections.

predestination ■ n. (as a doctrine in Christian theology) the divine foreordaining of all that will happen, especially with regard to the salvation of some and not others, as in Calvinism.

predestine ■ v. 1 (of God) destine (someone) for a particular fate or purpose. 2 determine (an outcome) in advance by divine will or fate.
– DERIVATIVES **predestined** adj.

predetermine ■ v. establish or decide in advance. ▸ predestine.
– DERIVATIVES **predeterminable** adj. **predetermination** n. **predetermined** adj.

predeterminer ■ n. Grammar a word or phrase that occurs before a determiner, typically quantifying the noun phrase, for example *both* or *a lot of*.

predicable /ˈprɛdɪkəb(ə)l/ ■ adj. that may be predicated or affirmed. ■ n. a thing that is predicable.
– DERIVATIVES **predicability** n.

predicament ■ n. 1 a difficult situation. 2 Philosophy each of the ten categories in Aristotelian logic.
– ORIGIN Middle English: from late Latin *praedicamentum* 'something predicated' (rendering Greek *katēgoria* 'category'), from Latin *praedicare* (see **PREDICATE**).

predicant /ˈprɛdɪk(ə)nt/ ■ adj. characterized by preaching. ■ n. variant spelling of **PREDIKANT**.
– ORIGIN C16: from Latin *praedicant-* 'declaring', from *praedicare*, in eccles. Latin meaning 'preach'.

predicate ■ n. /ˈprɛdɪkət/ 1 Grammar the part of a sentence or clause containing a verb and stating something about the subject (e.g. *went home* in *John went home*). 2 Logic something which is affirmed or denied concerning an argument of a proposition. ■ v. /ˈprɛdɪkeɪt/ 1 Grammar & Logic state, affirm, or assert (something) about the subject of a sentence or an argument of proposition. 2 (**predicate something on/upon**) found or base something on.
– DERIVATIVES **predication** n.
– ORIGIN Middle English: from Latin *praedicatum* 'something declared', from *praedicare*, from *prae* 'beforehand' + *dicare* 'make known'.

predicate calculus ■ n. the branch of symbolic logic concerned with propositions containing predicates, names, and quantifiers.

predicative /prɪˈdɪkətɪv/ ■ adj. 1 Grammar (of an adjective or other modifier) forming or contained in the predicate, as *old* in *the dog is old* (but not in *the old dog*). Contrasted with **ATTRIBUTIVE**. ▸ denoting a use of the verb *to be* to assert something about the subject. 2 Logic acting as a predicate.
– DERIVATIVES **predicatively** adv.

predict ■ v. state that (a specified event) will happen in the future.
– DERIVATIVES **prediction** n. **predictive** adj. **predictively** adv. **predictor** n.
– ORIGIN C17: from Latin *praedicere* 'make known beforehand, declare', from *prae-* 'beforehand' + *dicere* 'say'.

predictable ■ adj. able to be predicted. ▸ derogatory always behaving or occurring in the way expected.
– DERIVATIVES **predictability** n. **predictably** adv.

predigest ■ v. 1 treat (food) so as to make it more easily digestible when eaten. 2 simplify (information) so that it is easier to absorb.

predikant /ˌprɛdɪˈkant, ˌpriːdə-/ (also **predicant**) ■ n. S. African a minister of the Dutch Reformed Church.
– ORIGIN Dutch, from eccles. Latin *praedicare* 'preach'.

predilection /ˌpriːdɪˈlɛkʃ(ə)n/ ■ n. a preference or special liking for something.
– ORIGIN C18: from French *prédilection*, from Latin *praediligere* 'prefer', from *prae* 'in advance' + *diligere* 'to select'.

predispose ■ v. make liable or inclined to a specified attitude, action, or condition.
– DERIVATIVES **predisposition** n.

prednisolone /prɛdˈnɪsələʊn/ ■ n. Medicine a synthetic steroid resembling prednisone, of which it is a reduced derivative.
– ORIGIN 1950s: from **PREDNISONE**.

prednisone /ˈprɛdnɪzəʊn/ ■ n. Medicine a synthetic drug similar to cortisone, used to relieve rheumatic and allergic conditions and to treat leukaemia.
– ORIGIN 1950s: perhaps from *pre(gnane)* (a synthetic hydrocarbon) + *d(ie)n(e)* + *(cort)isone*.

predominant ■ adj. present as the strongest or main element. ▸ having or exerting the greatest control or power.
– DERIVATIVES **predominance** n. **predominantly** adv.

predominate ■ v. be the strongest or main element. ▸ have or exert control or power.

predominately ■ adv. mainly; for the most part.

pre-echo ■ n. (pl. -oes) 1 a faint copy heard just before an actual sound in a recording, caused by the accidental transfer of signals. 2 a foreshadowing. ■ v. foreshadow.

pre-eclampsia ■ n. a condition in pregnancy characterized by high blood pressure, sometimes with fluid retention and proteinuria.
– DERIVATIVES **pre-eclamptic** adj. & n.

pre-embryo ■ n. a fertilized ovum in the first fourteen days after fertilization, before implantation in the womb.
– DERIVATIVES **pre-embryonic** adj.

preemie /ˈpriːmi/ ■ n. (pl. -ies) S. African & N. Amer. informal a baby born prematurely.

pre-eminent ■ adj. surpassing all others.
– DERIVATIVES **pre-eminence** n. **pre-eminently** adv.

pre-empt ■ v. **1** take action in order to prevent (an attack or other anticipated event) happening; forestall. **2** acquire or appropriate in advance. **3** Bridge make a high opening bid in order to prevent the opponents from bidding effectively.
– DERIVATIVES **pre-emptive** adj. **pre-emptor** n.

pre-emption ■ n. **1** the purchase of goods or shares by one person or party before the opportunity is offered to others. **2** the action of pre-empting or forestalling.
– ORIGIN C17: from medieval Latin *praeemptio(n-)*, from *praeemere* (v.), from *prae* 'in advance' + *emere* 'buy'.

preen ■ v. **1** (of a bird) tidy and clean its feathers with its beak. **2** (of a person) devote effort to making oneself look attractive. **3** (**preen oneself**) congratulate or pride oneself.
– ORIGIN Middle English: apparently a var. of obsolete *prune* (based on Latin *ungere* 'anoint'), in the same sense.

preen gland ■ n. Ornithology a gland at the base of a bird's tail which produces the oil used in preening.

pre-establish ■ v. establish in advance.

pre-exist ■ v. [usu. as adj. **pre-existing**] exist at or from an earlier time. ▸ exist before.
– DERIVATIVES **pre-existence** n. **pre-existent** adj.

pref. ■ abbrev. **1** preface. **2** (with reference to shares) preference or preferred.

prefab ■ n. informal a prefabricated building.

prefabricate ■ v. [usu. as adj. **prefabricated**] manufacture sections of (a building, piece of furniture, etc.) to enable easy assembly on site.
– DERIVATIVES **prefabrication** n.

preface /ˈprɛfəs/ ■ n. an introduction to a book, typically stating its subject, scope, or aims. ■ v. **1** provide with a preface. **2** (**preface something with/by**) introduce or begin a speech or event with or by doing something.
– DERIVATIVES **prefatory** /ˈprɛfət(ə)ri/ adj.
– ORIGIN Middle English: from medieval Latin *praefatia*, from *praefari* (v.), from *prae* 'before' + *fari* 'speak'.

prefect ■ n. **1** a senior pupil authorized to enforce discipline in a school. **2** a chief officer, magistrate, or regional governor in certain countries.
– DERIVATIVES **prefectoral** adj. **prefectorial** adj.
– ORIGIN Middle English: from Latin *praefectus*, *praeficere* 'set in authority over', from *prae* 'before' + *facere* 'make'.

prefecture ■ n. a district under the government of a prefect. ▸ a prefect's office or tenure. ▸ a prefect's official residence.
– DERIVATIVES **prefectural** adj.

prefer ■ v. (**preferred**, **preferring**) **1** like (someone or something) better than another or others; tend to choose. **2** formal submit (a charge or information) for consideration. **3** archaic promote to a prestigious position.
– ORIGIN Middle English: from Old French *preferer*, from Latin *praeferre*, from *prae* 'before' + *ferre* 'to bear, carry'.

preferable ■ adj. more desirable or suitable.
– DERIVATIVES **preferability** n. **preferably** adv.

preference ■ n. **1** a greater liking for one alternative over another or others. ▸ a thing preferred. ▸ favour shown to one person over another or others. **2** Law a prior right, especially in connection with the payment of debts.

preference share (or **stock**) (N. Amer. **preferred share** or **stock**) ■ n. a share which entitles the holder to a fixed dividend whose payment takes priority over that of ordinary share dividends.

preferential ■ adj. **1** of or involving preference or partiality. **2** (of a creditor) having a claim for repayment which will be met before those of other creditors.
– DERIVATIVES **preferentially** adv.

preferment ■ n. promotion or appointment to a position or office.

preferred share ■ n. US term for PREFERENCE SHARE.

prefigure ■ v. be an early indication or version of.
– DERIVATIVES **prefiguration** n. **prefigurative** adj. **prefigurement** n.
– ORIGIN Middle English: from eccles. Latin *praefigurare* 'represent beforehand', from *prae* 'before' + *figurare* 'to form, fashion'.

prefix ■ n. a word, letter, or number placed before another. ▸ an element placed at the beginning of a word to adjust or qualify its meaning (e.g. *ex-*, *non-*, *re-*) or (in some languages) as an inflection. ▸ a title placed before a name (e.g. *Mr*). ■ v. add as a prefix or introduction. ▸ add a prefix or introduction to.
– DERIVATIVES **prefixation** n.
– ORIGIN C16: from Old French *prefixer*, from Latin *praefigere* 'fix in front', from *prae* 'before' + *figere* 'to fix'.

preform ■ v. [usu. as adj. **preformed**] form beforehand.
– DERIVATIVES **preformation** n.

prefrontal ■ adj. Anatomy in or relating to the foremost part of the frontal lobe of the brain.

preglacial ■ adj. before a glacial period.

pregnancy ■ n. (pl. **-ies**) the condition or period of being pregnant.

pregnant ■ adj. **1** (of a woman or female animal) having a child or young developing in the uterus. **2** full of meaning or significance.
– DERIVATIVES **pregnantly** adv.
– ORIGIN Middle English: from Latin *praegnant-*, prob. from *prae* 'before' + the base of *gnasci* 'be born'.

preheat ■ v. heat beforehand.

prehensile /prɪˈhɛnsʌɪl/ ■ adj. (chiefly of an animal's limb or tail) capable of grasping.
– DERIVATIVES **prehensility** n.
– ORIGIN C18: from French *préhensile*, from Latin *prehendere* 'grasp', from *prae* 'before' + *hendere* 'to grasp'.

prehistoric ■ adj. of or relating to prehistory. ▸ informal very old or out of date.
– DERIVATIVES **prehistorically** adv.

prehistory ■ n. **1** the period of time before written records. **2** the events or conditions leading up to a particular phenomenon.
– DERIVATIVES **prehistorian** n.

prehuman ■ adj. relating to or denoting the time before the appearance of human beings. ■ n. a precursor of the human species.

pre-ignition ■ n. premature combustion of the fuel–air mixture in an internal-combustion engine.

pre-industrial ■ adj. before industrialization.

prejudge ■ v. form a judgement on (an issue or person) prematurely and without having adequate information.
– DERIVATIVES **prejudgement** (also **prejudgment**) n.

prejudice ■ n. **1** preconceived opinion that is not based on reason or actual experience. ▸ unjust behaviour formed on such a basis. **2** chiefly Law harm or injury that results or may result from some action or judgement. ■ v. **1** give rise to prejudice in (someone); make biased. **2** chiefly Law cause harm to (a state of affairs).
– PHRASES **without prejudice** Law without detriment to any existing right or claim.
– DERIVATIVES **prejudiced** adj.
– ORIGIN Middle English: from Latin *praejudicium*, from *prae* 'in advance' + *judicium* 'judgement'.

prejudicial ■ adj. harmful to someone or something; detrimental.
– DERIVATIVES **prejudicially** adv.

prelate /ˈprɛlət/ ■ n. formal or historical a bishop or other high ecclesiastical dignitary.
– DERIVATIVES **prelatic** /prɪˈlatɪk/ adj. **prelatical** / prɪˈlatɪk(ə)l/ adj.
– ORIGIN Middle English: from Old French *prelat*, from medieval Latin *praelatus* 'civil dignitary', from Latin *praeferre* 'carry before, place before in esteem'.

prelim /ˈpriːlɪm, prɪˈlɪm/ ■ n. informal **1** a preliminary examination. **2** a preliminary round in a sporting competition. **3** (**prelims**) the pages preceding the main text of a book, including the title, contents, and preface.
– ORIGIN C19: abbrev.

preliminary ■ adj. preceding or done in preparation for something fuller or more important. ■ n. (pl. **-ies**) **1** a preliminary action or event. **2** a preliminary round in a sporting competition. **3** (**preliminaries**) fuller form of prelims (see PRELIM (sense 3)).
– PHRASES **preliminary to** preparatory to; in advance of.

prelinguistic

- DERIVATIVES **preliminarily** adv.
- ORIGIN C17: from French *préliminaire*, from Latin *prae* 'before' + *limen, limin-* 'threshold'.

prelinguistic ■ adj. of or at a stage before the development of language or the acquisition of speech.

preliterate ■ adj. relating to or denoting a society or culture that has not developed the use of writing.

prelude /ˈprɛljuːd/ ■ n. 1 an action or event serving as an introduction to something more important. 2 a piece of music serving as an introduction, e.g. to an act of an opera or to a suite or a fugue. 3 The introductory part of a poem or other literary work. ■ v. serve as a prelude or introduction to.
- DERIVATIVES **preludial** adj.
- ORIGIN C16: from French *prélude*, from Latin *praeludere* 'play beforehand'.

premarital ■ adj. occurring or existing before marriage.
- DERIVATIVES **premaritally** adv.

premature ■ adj. 1 occurring or done before the proper time. 2 (of a baby) born before the end of the full term of gestation.
- DERIVATIVES **prematurely** adv. **prematurity** n.
- ORIGIN Middle English: from Latin *praematurus* 'very early', from *prae* 'before' + *maturus* 'ripe'.

pre-med ■ n. short for PRE-MEDICATION.

pre-medication ■ n. medication given in preparation for an operation or other treatment.

premeditate ■ v. [usu. as adj. **premeditated**] think out or plan (an action, especially a crime) beforehand.
- DERIVATIVES **premeditation** n.
- ORIGIN C16 (*premeditation* Middle English): from Latin *praemeditari*, from *prae* 'before' + *meditari* 'meditate'.

premenopausal /ˌpriːˌmɛnəˈpɔːz(ə)l/ ■ adj. closely preceding the menopause.

premenstrual /priːˈmɛnstruəl/ ■ adj. of, occurring, or experienced before menstruation.
- DERIVATIVES **premenstrually** adv.

premenstrual syndrome ■ n. a complex of symptoms (including emotional tension and fluid retention) experienced by some women prior to menstruation.

premier /ˈprɛmɪə, ˈpriː-/ ■ adj. first in importance, order, or position. ▶ of earliest creation. ■ n. a Prime Minister or other head of government. ▶ (in South Africa, Australia, and Canada) the chief minister of a government of a state or province.
- DERIVATIVES **premiership** n.
- ORIGIN C15: from Old French, 'first', from Latin *primarius* 'principal'.

premier cru /ˌprɛmɪə ˈkruː/ ■ n. (pl. **premiers crus** pronunc. same) (chiefly in France) a wine of a superior grade. Compare with GRAND CRU.
- ORIGIN French, 'first growth'.

premiere /ˈprɛmɪɛː/ ■ n. the first performance of a musical or theatrical work or the first showing of a film. ■ v. give the premiere of.
- ORIGIN C19: French *première*, feminine of *premier* (see PREMIER).

premier grand cru /ˌprɛmɪə grɒ̃ ˈkruː/ ■ n. 1 the highest classification for certain French wines. 2 S. African a dry white wine.
- ORIGIN 1980s: alteration of PREMIER CRU + French *grand* 'great'.

premillennial ■ adj. existing or occurring before a new millennium.

premise ■ n. /ˈprɛmɪs/ (Brit. also **premiss**) Logic a previous statement from which another is inferred. ▶ an underlying assumption. ■ v. /prɪˈmaɪz/ 1 (**premise on/upon**) base (an argument, theory, etc.) on. 2 state or presuppose as a premise.
- ORIGIN Middle English: from Old French *premisse*, from medieval Latin *praemissa (propositio)* '(proposition) set in front', from Latin *praemittere*, from *prae* 'before' + *mittere* 'send'.

premises ■ pl. n. a house or building, together with its land and outbuildings, occupied by a business or considered in an official context.

premium ■ n. (pl. **premiums**) 1 an amount paid for a contract of insurance. 2 a sum added to an ordinary price, charge, or other payment. ▶ [as modifier] (of a commodity) superior and more expensive. 3 something given as a reward or incentive.
- PHRASES **at a premium** 1 scarce and in demand. 2 above the usual price. **put** (or **place**) **a premium on** regard as particularly valuable.
- ORIGIN C17: from Latin *praemium* 'booty, reward', from *prae* 'before' + *emere* 'buy, take'.

premix ■ v. mix in advance. ■ n. a premixed material.

premolar (also **premolar tooth**) ■ n. a tooth situated between the canines and molar teeth.

premonition /ˌprɛməˈnɪʃ(ə)n, ˌpriː-/ ■ n. a strong feeling that something is about to happen.
- DERIVATIVES **premonitory** adj.
- ORIGIN C16: from French *prémonition*, from Latin *praemonere*, from *prae* 'before' + *monere* 'warn'.

prenatal ■ adj. before birth.
- DERIVATIVES **prenatally** adv.

prenominal ■ adj. Grammar preceding a noun.
- DERIVATIVES **prenominally** adv.

prenuptial ■ adj. before marriage.

prenuptial agreement ■ n. an agreement made by a couple before they marry concerning ownership of assets in the event of a divorce.

preoccupation ■ n. the state of being preoccupied. ▶ a matter that preoccupies someone.

preoccupy ■ v. (-ies, -ied) dominate or engross the mind of (someone) to the exclusion of other thoughts.
- ORIGIN C16: from PRE- + OCCUPY, suggested by Latin *praeoccupare* 'seize beforehand'.

pre-op ■ adj. informal short for PREOPERATIVE.

preoperative ■ adj. before a surgical operation.
- DERIVATIVES **preoperatively** adv.

preordain ■ v. (usu. **be preordained**) decide or determine beforehand.

pre-owned ■ adj. (especially of a vehicle) second-hand.

prep¹ ■ n. Brit. informal (especially in a private school) school work done outside lessons. ▶ a period set aside for this.
- ORIGIN C19: abbrev. of PREPARATION or PREPARATORY.

prep² N. Amer. informal ■ v. (**prepped, prepping**) prepare; make ready. ■ n. preparation.
- ORIGIN 1920s: abbrev.

prep. ■ abbrev. preposition.

pre-pack (also **pre-package**) ■ v. [usu. as adj. **pre-packed**] pack or wrap (goods) on the site of production or before sale.

prepaid past and past participle of PREPAY.

preparation ■ n. 1 the action or process of preparing or being prepared. ▶ (usu. **preparations**) something done to get ready for an event or undertaking. 2 a specially made up substance, especially a medicine or food.
- ORIGIN Middle English: from Latin *praeparatio(n-)*, from *praeparare* (see PREPARE).

preparative ■ adj. preparatory. ■ n. a thing which acts as a preparation.
- DERIVATIVES **preparatively** adv.

preparatory ■ adj. serving as or carrying out preparation.
- PHRASES **preparatory to** as a preparation for.
- ORIGIN Middle English: from late Latin *praeparatorius*, *praeparare* (see PREPARE).

preparatory school ■ n. 1 a private school for pupils between the ages of seven and thirteen. 2 N. Amer. a private school that prepares pupils for college or university.

prepare ■ v. 1 make ready for use or consideration. ▶ make (food) ready for cooking or eating. 2 make or get ready to do or deal with something. ▶ (**be prepared to do something**) be willing to do something. 3 make (a substance) by chemical reaction.
- DERIVATIVES **preparer** n.
- ORIGIN Middle English: from French *préparer* or Latin *praeparare*, from *prae* 'before' + *parare* 'make ready'.

preparedness ■ n. a state of readiness, especially for war.

prepay ■ v. (past and past part. **prepaid**) [usu. as adj. **prepaid**] pay for in advance.
– DERIVATIVES **prepayable** adj. **prepayment** n.

pre-plan ■ v. [usu. as adj. **pre-planned**] plan in advance.

preponderant ■ adj. predominant in influence, number, or importance.
– DERIVATIVES **preponderance** n. **preponderantly** adv.
– ORIGIN Middle English: from Latin *preponderant-* 'weighing more', from *praeponderare* (see **PREPONDERATE**).

preponderate ■ v. be preponderant.
– ORIGIN C17: from Latin *praeponderare*, from *prae* 'before' + *ponderare* 'weigh, consider'.

prepose ■ v. Linguistics place (an element or word) in front of another.
– ORIGIN C15: from French *préposer*.

preposition /ˌprɛpəˈzɪʃ(ə)n/ ■ n. Grammar a word governing, and usually preceding, a noun or pronoun and expressing a relation to another word or element, as in 'she arrived *after* dinner' and 'what did you do it *for*?'.
– DERIVATIVES **prepositional** adj. **prepositionally** adv.
– ORIGIN Middle English: from Latin *praepositio(n-)*, from *praeponere* (v.), from *prae* 'before' + *ponere* 'to place'.

prepositional object ■ n. Grammar a noun phrase governed by a preposition.

prepossessing ■ adj. [often with neg.] attractive or appealing in appearance.
– DERIVATIVES **prepossession** n.

preposterous ■ adj. utterly absurd or ridiculous.
– DERIVATIVES **preposterously** adv. **preposterousness** n.
– ORIGIN C16: from Latin *praeposterus* 'reversed, absurd', from *prae* 'before' + *posterus* 'coming after'.

preppy (also **preppie**) N. Amer. informal ■ n. (pl. **-ies**) a pupil of an expensive preparatory school. ■ adj. (**-ier**, **-iest**) of or typical of such a person, especially with reference to their neat style of dress.
– ORIGIN C20: from **PREP SCHOOL**.

preprandial ■ adj. formal or humorous done or taken before dinner.
– ORIGIN C19: from PRE- + Latin *prandium* 'a meal'.

pre-print ■ v. [usu. as adj. **pre-printed**] print in advance. ■ n. a printed document issued before full publication.

pre-process ■ v. subject to preliminary processing.
– DERIVATIVES **pre-processor** n.

pre-production ■ n. work done on a film, broadcast programme, etc. before full-scale production begins.

pre-program ■ v. [usu. as adj. **pre-programmed**] program in advance for ease of use.

prep school ■ n. short for **PREPARATORY SCHOOL**.

pre-pubertal ■ adj. another term for **PRE-PUBESCENT**.
– DERIVATIVES **pre-puberty** n.

pre-pubescent ■ adj. relating to or in the period preceding puberty. ■ n. a pre-pubescent boy or girl.
– DERIVATIVES **pre-pubescence** n.

prepuce /ˈpriːpjuːs/ ■ n. Anatomy 1 technical term for **FORESKIN**. 2 the fold of skin surrounding the clitoris.
– DERIVATIVES **preputial** adj.
– ORIGIN Middle English: from French *prépuce*, from Latin *praeputium*.

pre-qualify ■ v. qualify in advance to take part in a sporting event.

prequel /ˈpriːkw(ə)l/ ■ n. a story or film containing events which precede those of an existing work.
– ORIGIN 1970s: from PRE- + **SEQUEL**.

Pre-Raphaelite /priːˈrafəlʌɪt/ ■ n. a member of a group of English 19th-century artists who sought to emulate the simplicity and sincerity of Italian artists from before the time of Raphael. ■ adj. of or relating to the Pre-Raphaelites. ▸ (especially of women) suggesting Pre-Raphaelite painting in appearance, typically with long, thick, wavy auburn hair and pale skin.
– DERIVATIVES **Pre-Raphaelitism** n.

pre-record ■ v. [often as adj. **pre-recorded**] record (sound or film) in advance.

prerequisite /priːˈrɛkwɪzɪt/ ■ adj. required as a prior condition. ■ n. a prerequisite thing.

prescriptive

prerogative /prɪˈrɒɡətɪv/ ■ n. a right or privilege exclusive to a particular individual or class.
– ORIGIN Middle English: from Latin *praerogativa* '(the verdict of) the political division which was chosen to vote first in the assembly', from *prae* 'before' + *rogare* 'ask'.

Pres. ■ abbrev. President.

presage /ˈprɛsɪdʒ/ ■ v. /also prɪˈseɪdʒ/ be a sign or warning of (an imminent event). ■ n. an omen or portent.
– ORIGIN Middle English: from Latin *praesagium*, from *praesagire* 'forebode', from *prae* 'before' + *sagire* 'perceive keenly'.

presbyopia /ˌprɛzbɪˈəʊpɪə/ ■ n. far-sightedness caused by loss of elasticity of the lens of the eye.
– DERIVATIVES **presbyopic** adj.
– ORIGIN C18: from Greek *presbus* 'old man' + *ōps, ōp-* 'eye'.

presbyter /ˈprɛzbɪtə/ ■ n. historical an elder or minister of the Christian Church. ▸ formal (in Presbyterian Churches) an elder. ▸ formal (in episcopal Churches) a minister of the second order, under the authority of a bishop.
– DERIVATIVES **presbyteral** /-ˈbɪt(ə)r(ə)l/ adj. **presbyterate** n. **presbyterial** adj. **presbyterip** n.
– ORIGIN C16: from Greek *presbuteros* 'elder', comparative of *presbus* 'old (man)'.

Presbyterian /ˌprɛzbɪˈtɪərɪən/ ■ adj. relating to or denoting a Protestant Church or denomination governed by elders all of equal rank. ■ n. a member of a Presbyterian Church.
– DERIVATIVES **Presbyterianism** n.
– ORIGIN C17: from eccles. Latin *presbyterium* (see **PRESBYTERY**).

presbytery /ˈprɛzbɪt(ə)ri/ ■ n. (pl. **-ies**) 1 [treated as sing. or pl.] a body of Church elders, especially (in Presbyterian Churches) an administrative court representing the congregations of a district. ▸ a district represented by such a body. 2 the house of a Roman Catholic parish priest. 3 the eastern part of a church chancel beyond the choir.
– ORIGIN Middle English: from Old French *presbiterie*, from Greek *presbuterion*, from *presbuteros* (see **PRESBYTER**).

pre-school ■ adj. of or relating to the time before a child is old enough to go to school. ■ n. a nursery school.
– DERIVATIVES **pre-schooler** n.

prescient /ˈprɛsɪənt/ ■ adj. having knowledge of events before they take place.
– DERIVATIVES **prescience** n. **presciently** adv.
– ORIGIN C17: from Latin *praescire* 'know beforehand', from *prae* 'before' + *scire* 'know'.

prescind /prɪˈsɪnd/ ■ v. (**prescind from**) formal leave out of consideration. ▸ cut off or separate from something.
– ORIGIN C17: from Latin *praescindere*, from *prae* 'before' + *scindere* 'to cut'.

prescribe ■ v. 1 advise and authorize the use of (a medicine or treatment), especially in writing. 2 recommend as something beneficial. ▸ state authoritatively that (an action or procedure) should be carried out.
– DERIVATIVES **prescriber** n.
– ORIGIN Middle English: from Latin *praescribere* 'direct in writing', from *prae* 'before' + *scribere* 'write'.

prescript /ˈpriːskrɪpt/ ■ n. formal or dated an ordinance, law, or command.
– ORIGIN C16: from Latin *praescriptum* 'something directed in writing', from *praescribere* (see **PRESCRIBE**).

prescription ■ n. 1 an instruction written by a medical practitioner that authorizes a patient to be issued with a medicine or treatment. 2 the action of prescribing. 3 an authoritative recommendation or ruling. 4 (also **positive prescription**) Law the establishment of a claim founded on the basis of long usage or custom. ▸ S. African Law another term for **STATUTE OF LIMITATIONS**.
– ORIGIN Middle English: from Latin *praescriptio(n-)*, from *praescribere* (see **PRESCRIBE**).

prescriptive ■ adj. 1 of or relating to the imposition of a rule or method. 2 (of a right, title, etc.) legally established by long usage or the passage of time.
– DERIVATIVES **prescriptively** adv. **prescriptiveness** n. **prescriptivism** n. **prescriptivist** n. & adj.
– ORIGIN C18: from late Latin *praescriptivus* 'relating to a legal exception', from *praescribere* (see **PRESCRIBE**).

preseason ■ adj. before the start of the season for a particular sport. ■ n. the preseason period.

pre-select ■ v. select in advance.
– DERIVATIVES **pre-selection** n. **pre-selective** adj.

pre-selector ■ n. a device for selecting a mechanical or electrical operation in advance of its execution.

presence ■ n. **1** the state or fact of being present. ▸ a person or thing that is present but not seen. **2** the impressive manner or appearance of a person.
– PHRASES **make one's presence felt** have a strong influence on a situation. **presence of mind** the ability to remain calm and take quick, sensible action in the face of sudden difficulty.
– ORIGIN Middle English: from Latin *praesentia* 'being at hand', from *praeesse* (see PRESENT¹).

presence chamber ■ n. a room in which a monarch or other distinguished person receives visitors.

present¹ /ˈprɛz(ə)nt/ ■ adj. **1** being or occurring in a particular place. **2** existing or occurring now. **3** Grammar (of a tense) expressing an action now going on or habitually performed, or a condition now existing. ■ n. **1** (usu. **the present**) the period of time now occurring. **2** Grammar a present tense or form of a verb.
– PHRASES **at present** now. **for the present** for now; temporarily. **these presents** Law, formal this document.
– ORIGIN Middle English: from Latin *praesent-* 'being at hand', from *praeesse*, from *prae* 'before' + *esse* 'be'.

present² /prɪˈzɛnt/ ■ v. **1** give formally or ceremonially. ▸ (**present someone with**) give (something) to someone in such a way. ▸ offer for acceptance or consideration. **2** formally introduce to someone. ▸ (**present oneself**) appear formally before others. **3** put (a show or exhibition) before the public. ▸ introduce and appear in (a television or radio show). **4** be the cause of (a problem or difficulty). ▸ exhibit (a particular appearance) to others. ▸ represent to others in a particular way. ▸ (**present itself**) (of an opportunity or idea) occur and be available for use or exploitation. ▸ (**present with**) Medicine come forward for medical examination for a particular condition or symptom. ▸ Medicine (of an illness) manifest itself. **5** Medicine (of a part of a fetus) be directed towards the cervix during labour.
– PHRASES **present arms** hold a rifle vertically in front of the body as a salute.
– ORIGIN Middle English: from Old French *presenter*, from Latin *praesentare* 'place before', from *praesent-* (see PRESENT¹).

present³ /ˈprɛz(ə)nt/ ■ n. a thing given to someone as a gift.
– ORIGIN Middle English: from Old French *present*, orig. in the phr. *mettre une chose en present à quelqu'un* 'put a thing into the presence of a person'.

presentable ■ adj. clean, smart, or decent enough to be seen in public.
– DERIVATIVES **presentability** n. **presentably** adv.

presentation ■ n. **1** the action or an instance of presenting or being presented. ▸ the manner or style in which something is presented. ▸ a formal introduction. **2** Medicine the position of a fetus at the time of delivery.
– DERIVATIVES **presentational** adj. **presentationally** adv.
– ORIGIN Middle English: from late Latin *praesentatio(n-)*, from Latin *praesentare* (see PRESENT²).

presenter ■ n. a person who introduces and appears in a television or radio programme.

presentiment /prɪˈzɛntɪm(ə)nt, -ˈsɛn-/ ■ n. an intuitive feeling or foreboding about the future.
– ORIGIN C18: from obsolete French *présentiment*.

presently ■ adv. **1** after a short time; soon. **2** at the present time; now.

preservationist ■ n. a supporter of the preservation of something, especially of historic buildings or artefacts.

preservation order ■ n. chiefly Brit. a legal obligation laid on an owner to preserve a historic building, valuable natural habitat, etc.

preservative ■ n. a substance used to preserve foodstuffs, wood, or other materials against decay. ■ adj. acting to preserve something.

preserve ■ v. **1** maintain in its original or existing state. ▸ keep alive (a memory or quality). **2** keep safe from harm or injury. **3** treat (food) to prevent its decomposition. ▸ prepare (fruit) for long-term storage by boiling it with sugar. ■ n. **1** a foodstuff made with fruit preserved in sugar. **2** something regarded as reserved for a particular person or group. **3** a place where game is protected and kept for private hunting or shooting.
– DERIVATIVES **preservable** adj. **preservation** n. **preserver** n.
– ORIGIN Middle English: from Old French *preserver*, from late Latin *praeservare*, from *prae-* 'before, in advance' + *servare* 'to keep'.

preset ■ v. (**presetting**; past and past part. **preset**) set or adjust (a value that controls the operation of a device) in advance of its use. ■ n. a preset value or control.

pre-shrunk ■ adj. (of a fabric or garment) shrunk during manufacture to prevent further shrinking in use.
– DERIVATIVES **pre-shrink** v.

preside ■ v. be in a position of authority in a meeting, court, etc. ▸ (**preside over**) be in charge of (a situation).
– ORIGIN C17: from French *présider*, from Latin *praesidere*, from *prae* 'before' + *sedere* 'sit'.

presidency ■ n. (pl. **-ies**) the office or status of president. ▸ the period of this.
– ORIGIN C16: from medieval Latin *praesidentia*, from *praesidere* (see PRESIDE).

president ■ n. **1** the elected head of a republican state. ▸ the head of a society, council, college, or other organization. **2** Christian Church the celebrant at a Eucharist.
– DERIVATIVES **presidential** adj. **presidentially** adv. **presidentship** n.
– ORIGIN Middle English: from Latin *praesident-* (see PRESIDE).

presidium /prɪˈsɪdɪəm, -ˈzɪ-/ (also **praesidium**) ■ n. a standing executive committee in a communist country.
– ORIGIN 1920s: from Russian *prezidium*, from Latin *praesidium* (see PRESIDE).

press¹ ■ v. **1** move or cause to move into a position of contact with something by exerting continuous physical force. ▸ exert continuous physical force on, especially in order to operate a device. ▸ squeeze (someone's arm or hand) as a sign of affection. ▸ move in a specified direction by pushing. ▸ (**press on/ahead**) continue in one's action. **2** apply pressure to (something) to flatten, shape, or smooth it, especially by ironing. ▸ extract (juice or oil) by crushing or squeezing fruit, vegetables, etc. ▸ manufacture by moulding under pressure. **3** forcefully put forward (an opinion, claim, etc.). ▸ make strong efforts to persuade or force to do something. ▸ (**press something on/upon**) insist that (someone) accepts an offer or gift. ▸ (of time) be short. ▸ (**be pressed**) have barely enough of something, especially time. ▸ (**be pressed to do something**) have difficulty doing something. ■ n. **1** a device for applying pressure in order to flatten or shape something or to extract juice or oil: *a plant press | an apple press*. **2** a printing press. ▸ a printing or publishing business. **3** (**the press**) [treated as sing. or pl.] newspapers or journalists viewed collectively. ▸ coverage in newspapers and magazines. **4** an act of pressing something. ▸ a closely packed mass of people or things. ▸ dated pressure of business. ▸ Basketball a form of close guarding by the defending team.
– PHRASES **go to press** go to be printed. **press (the) flesh** informal, chiefly N. Amer. greet people by shaking hands.
– ORIGIN Middle English: from Old French *presser* (v.), from Latin *pressare* 'keep pressing', from *premere*.

press² ■ v. **1** (**press into**) put to a specified use, especially as a temporary or makeshift measure. **2** historical force to enlist in the army or navy.
– ORIGIN C16: alteration of obsolete *prest* 'pay given on enlistment, enlistment by such payment', from Old French *prest* 'loan, advance pay', from Latin *praestare* 'provide'.

pressboard ■ n. a smooth, hard, dense board typically made from wood or textile pulp or laminated waste paper.

press conference ■ n. a meeting held with journalists in order to make an announcement or answer questions.

press gang ■ n. historical a body of men employed to enlist men forcibly into service in the army or navy. ■ v. (**press-gang**) force into service.

pressie ■ n. variant spelling of PREZZIE.

pressing ■ adj. requiring quick or immediate action or attention. ▶ expressing something strongly or persistently. ■ n. a gramophone record or other object made by moulding under pressure.
– DERIVATIVES **pressingly** adv.

pressman ■ n. (pl. **-men**) a journalist.

press release ■ n. an official statement issued to journalists on a particular matter.

press stud ■ n. a small fastener engaged by pressing its two halves together.

press-up ■ n. an exercise in which a person lies facing the floor and, keeping their back straight, raises their body by pressing down on their hands.

pressure ■ n. 1 the continuous physical force exerted on or against an object by something in contact with it. ▶ the force per unit area exerted by a fluid against a surface. 2 the use of persuasion, intimidation, etc. to make someone do something. ▶ a feeling of stressful urgency. ■ v. attempt to persuade or coerce into doing something.
– ORIGIN Middle English: from Latin *pressura*, from *premere* 'to squeeze, press'.

pressure cooker ■ n. an airtight pot in which food can be cooked quickly under steam pressure.
– DERIVATIVES **pressure-cook** v.

pressure group ■ n. a group that tries to influence public life in the interest of a particular cause.

pressure hull ■ n. the inner hull of a submarine, in which normal pressure is maintained.

pressure point ■ n. 1 a point on the surface of the body sensitive to pressure. 2 a point where an artery can be pressed against a bone to inhibit bleeding.

pressurize (also **-ise**) ■ v. 1 produce or maintain raised pressure artificially in. 2 attempt to persuade or coerce into doing something.
– DERIVATIVES **pressurization** (also **-isation**) n.

pressurized-water reactor (also **-ised**) ■ n. a nuclear reactor in which the coolant and moderator is water under high pressure.

presswork ■ n. the shaping of metal by pressing or drawing it into a shaped hollow die.

prestidigitation /ˌprɛstɪˌdɪdʒɪˈteɪʃ(ə)n/ ■ n. formal magic tricks performed as entertainment.
– DERIVATIVES **prestidigitator** n.
– ORIGIN C19: from French, from *preste* 'nimble' + Latin *digitus* 'finger'.

prestige ■ n. widespread respect and admiration attracted through a perception of high achievements or quality.
– ORIGIN C17: from French, 'illusion, glamour'.

prestigious ■ adj. inspiring respect and admiration; having high status.
– DERIVATIVES **prestigiously** adv. **prestigiousness** n.

Prestik ■ n. S. African trademark a grey or white putty-like adhesive, typically used to attach paper to walls.

presto (also **hey presto**) ■ exclam. announcing the successful completion of a conjuring trick or other surprising achievement.
– ORIGIN Italian, 'quick, quickly', from Latin *praesto* 'at hand'.

prestressed ■ adj. strengthened by the application of stress during manufacture, especially (of concrete) by means of tensioned rods or wires inserted before setting.
– DERIVATIVES **prestressing** n.

presumably ■ adv. as may reasonably be presumed.

presume ■ v. 1 suppose that something is the case on the basis of probability. ▶ take for granted. 2 be arrogant or impertinent enough to do something. ▶ (**presume on/upon**) unjustifiably regard (something) as entitling one to privileges.
– DERIVATIVES **presumable** adj.
– ORIGIN Middle English: from Old French *presumer*, from Latin *praesumere* 'anticipate', from *prae* 'before' + *sumere* 'take'.

presuming ■ adj. archaic presumptuous.
– DERIVATIVES **presumingly** adv.

presumption ■ n. 1 an act or instance of presuming something to be the case. ▶ an idea that is presumed to be true. ▶ chiefly Law an attitude adopted towards something in the absence of contrary factors. 2 presumptuous behaviour.
– ORIGIN Middle English: from Old French *presumpcion*, from Latin *praesumptio(n)* 'anticipation', from *praesumere* (see PRESUME).

presumptive ■ adj. 1 presumed in the absence of further information. ▶ Law giving grounds for a particular inference or interpretation. 2 another term for PRESUMPTUOUS.
– DERIVATIVES **presumptively** adv.
– ORIGIN Middle English: from French *présomptif, -ive*, from late Latin *praesumptivus*, from *praesumere* (see PRESUME).

presumptuous ■ adj. failing to observe the limits of what is permitted or appropriate.
– DERIVATIVES **presumptuously** adv. **presumptuousness** n.
– ORIGIN Middle English: from Old French *presumptueux*, from late Latin *praesumptuosus*, from *praesumptio* (see PRESUMPTION).

presuppose ■ v. require as a precondition of possibility or coherence. ▶ tacitly assume to be the case.
– DERIVATIVES **presupposition** n.
– ORIGIN Middle English: from Old French *presupposer*, suggested by medieval Latin *praesupponere*, from *prae* 'before' + *supponere* (see SUPPOSE).

prêt-à-porter /ˌprɛtaˈpɔːteɪ/ ■ n. designer clothing sold ready-to-wear.
– ORIGIN French, 'ready to wear'.

pretence (US **pretense**) ■ n. 1 an act of pretending. 2 pretentious behaviour. 3 (**pretence to**) a claim, especially a false or ambitious one.

pretend ■ v. 1 act so as to make it appear that something is the case when in fact it is not. ▶ engage in an imaginative game or fantasy. ▶ simulate (an emotion or quality). 2 (**pretend to**) lay claim to (a quality or title). ■ adj. informal imaginary; make-believe.
– ORIGIN Middle English: from Latin *praetendere* 'stretch forth, claim', from *prae* 'before' + *tendere* 'stretch'.

pretender ■ n. a person who claims or aspires to a title or position.

pretense ■ n. US spelling of PRETENCE.

pretension ■ n. 1 (**pretension to**) a claim or aspiration to something. 2 pretentiousness.
– ORIGIN Middle English: from medieval Latin *praetensio(n-)*, from *praetendere* (see PRETEND).

pre-tension ■ v. apply tension to before manufacture or use.
– DERIVATIVES **pre-tensioner** n.

pretentious ■ adj. attempting to impress by affecting greater importance or merit than is actually possessed.
– DERIVATIVES **pretentiously** adv. **pretentiousness** n.
– ORIGIN C19: from French *prétentieux*, from *prétention* (see PRETENSION).

preterite /ˈprɛt(ə)rɪt/ (US also **preterit**) Grammar ■ adj. expressing a past action or state. ■ n. a simple past tense or form.
– ORIGIN Middle English: from Latin *praeteritus*, from *praeterire* 'pass, go by', from *praeter* 'past, beyond' + *ire* 'go'.

preterm ■ adj. & adv. Medicine born or occurring after a pregnancy significantly shorter than normal.

preternatural /ˌpriːtəˈnatʃ(ə)r(ə)l/ ■ adj. beyond what is normal or natural: *preternatural speed*.
– DERIVATIVES **preternaturally** adv.

pretext ■ n. an ostensible or false reason used to justify an action.
– ORIGIN C16: from Latin *praetextus* 'outward display', from *praetexere* 'to disguise', from *prae* 'before' + *texere* 'weave'.

pretreat ■ v. treat with a chemical before use.
– DERIVATIVES **pretreatment** n.

prettify ■ v. (**-ies, -ied**) make superficially pretty.
– DERIVATIVES **prettification** n. **prettifier** n.

pretty

pretty ■ adj. (**-ier**, **-iest**) **1** attractive in a delicate way without being truly beautiful. **2** informal used ironically to express displeasure: *he led me a pretty dance*. ■ adv. informal to a moderately high degree; fairly. ■ n. (pl. **-ies**) informal a pretty thing; a trinket. ▸ (used condescendingly) an attractive person. ■ v. (**-ies**, **-ied**) make pretty or attractive.
– PHRASES **pretty much** (or **nearly** or **well**) informal very nearly. **a pretty penny** informal a large sum of money. **be sitting pretty** informal be in an advantageous position or situation.
– DERIVATIVES **prettily** adv. **prettiness** n. **prettyish** adj.
– ORIGIN Old English, from a West Germanic base meaning 'trick'.

pretty boy ■ n. informal, often derogatory a foppish or effeminate man.

pretzel /'prets(ə)l/ ■ n. a crisp biscuit baked as a knot or stick and flavoured with salt.
– ORIGIN C19: from German *Pretzel*.

prevail ■ v. **1** prove more powerful; be victorious. ▸ be widespread or current. **2** (**prevail on/upon**) persuade to do something.
– DERIVATIVES **prevailing** adj. **prevailingly** adv.
– ORIGIN Middle English: from Latin *praevalere*, from *prae* 'before' + *valere* 'have power'.

prevailing wind ■ n. a wind from the predominant or most usual direction.

prevalent /'prɛv(ə)l(ə)nt/ ■ adj. widespread in a particular area at a particular time.
– DERIVATIVES **prevalence** n. **prevalently** adv.
– ORIGIN C16: from Latin from *praevalere* (see PREVAIL).

prevaricate /prɪ'varɪkeɪt/ ■ v. speak or act evasively.
– DERIVATIVES **prevarication** n. **prevaricator** n.
– ORIGIN C16 (*prevarication* and *prevaricator* Middle English): from Latin *praevaricari* 'walk crookedly, deviate'.

prevent ■ v. keep from happening or arising. ▸ make unable to do something.
– DERIVATIVES **preventability** n. **preventable** (also **preventible**) adj. **prevention** n.
– ORIGIN Middle English: from Latin *praevenire* 'precede, hinder', from *prae* 'before' + *venire* 'come'.

preventative ■ adj. & n. another term for PREVENTIVE.
– DERIVATIVES **preventatively** adv.

preventer ■ n. **1** a person or thing that prevents something. **2** Nautical an extra line rigged to support a piece of rigging or to prevent the boom from gybing.

preventive ■ adj. designed to prevent something from occurring. ■ n. a preventive medicine or other treatment.
– DERIVATIVES **preventively** adv.

preview ■ n. a viewing or display of something before it is acquired or becomes generally available. ▸ a publicity article, review, or trailer of a forthcoming film, book, etc. ■ v. provide or have a preview of (a product, film, etc.).

previous ■ adj. existing or occurring before in time or order.
– PHRASES **previous to** before.
– DERIVATIVES **previously** adv.
– ORIGIN C17: from Latin *praevius* 'going before', from *prae* 'before' + *via* 'way'.

previously disadvantaged ■ adj. S. African discriminated against under apartheid.

pre-wash ■ n. **1** a preliminary wash, especially in an automatic washing machine. **2** a substance applied as a treatment before washing. ■ v. give a pre-wash to.

prey ■ n. an animal hunted and killed by another for food. ▸ a victim or quarry. ▸ archaic plunder or (in biblical use) a prize. ■ v. (**prey on/upon**) **1** hunt and kill for food. **2** exploit or injure; cause trouble to: *the problem had begun to prey on my mind*.
– ORIGIN Middle English: noun from Old French *preie*, from Latin *praeda* 'booty', verb from Old French *preier*, from Latin *praedari* 'seize as plunder', from *praeda*.

prezzie (also **pressie**) ■ n. informal a present.
– ORIGIN 1930s: abbrev.

priapic /prʌɪ'apɪk/ ■ adj. **1** phallic. **2** Medicine having a persistently (and painfully) erect penis.
– DERIVATIVES **priapism** n.
– ORIGIN C18: from Greek *Priapos*, name of a god of fertility.

Priapulida /ˌprʌɪə'pjuːlɪdə/ ■ pl. n. Zoology a phylum of worm-like marine invertebrates which have a large eversible proboscis.
– DERIVATIVES **priapulid** /prʌɪ'apjulɪd/ n. & adj.
– ORIGIN from *Priapulus* (genus name), from Greek *Priapos* (see PRIAPIC).

price ■ n. the amount of money expected, required, or given in payment for something. ▸ something expended or endured in order to achieve an objective. ▸ the odds in betting. ▸ archaic value; worth. ■ v. decide the price of.
– PHRASES **at any price** no matter what is involved. **at a price** requiring great expense or involving unwelcome consequences. **beyond price** priceless. **a price on someone's head** a reward offered for someone's capture or death. **what price ——? 1** what has or would become of ——? **2** what is the chance of ——?
– ORIGIN Middle English: noun from Old French *pris*, from Latin *pretium* 'value, reward'; verb a var. of earlier *prise* 'estimate the value of' (see PRIZE¹).

priceless ■ adj. **1** so precious that its value cannot be determined. **2** informal very amusing or absurd.
– DERIVATIVES **pricelessly** adv.

price tag ■ n. a label showing the price of an item. ▸ the cost of something.

price-taker ■ n. Economics a company that is obliged to accept the market prices of its products.

pricey (also **pricy**) ■ adj. (**-ier**, **-iest**) informal expensive.

prick ■ v. **1** press briefly or puncture with a sharp point. ▸ (**prick out**) draw or decorate by making small holes in a surface. **2** feel a sensation as though a sharp point were sticking into one. ▸ cause mental or emotional discomfort to. **3** (often **prick up**) (chiefly of a horse or dog) make (the ears) stand erect when on the alert. **4** (**prick out**) plant (seedlings) in small holes made in the earth. ■ n. **1** an act of pricking something. ▸ a small hole or mark made by pricking. **2** a sharp pain caused by being pierced with a fine point. ▸ a sudden feeling of distress, anxiety, etc. **3** vulgar slang a man's penis. ▸ a man regarded as stupid, unpleasant, or contemptible.
– PHRASES **kick against the pricks** hurt oneself by persisting in useless resistance or protest. [with biblical allusion to Acts 9:5.]
– DERIVATIVES **pricker** n.
– ORIGIN Old English, prob. of West Germanic origin.

prickle ■ n. **1** a short spine or pointed outgrowth on the surface of a plant or on the skin of an animal. **2** a tingling or mildly painful sensation on the skin. ■ v. **1** experience or produce a prickle. ▸ cause such a sensation in. **2** react defensively or angrily.
– ORIGIN Old English *pricel* 'instrument for pricking, sensation of being pricked'; from the Germanic base of PRICK.

prickly ■ adj. (**-ier**, **-iest**) **1** covered in or resembling prickles. ▸ having or causing a prickling sensation. **2** ready to take offence. ▸ liable to cause someone to take offence: *a prickly subject*.
– DERIVATIVES **prickliness** n.

prickly heat ■ n. an itchy skin rash experienced in hot moist weather.

prickly pear ■ n. **1** a cactus with flattened, jointed stems which produces prickly, pear-shaped fruits. [*Opuntia ficus-indica* and related species.] **2** the edible orange or red fruit of this plant.

pricy ■ adj. variant spelling of PRICEY.

pride ■ n. **1** a feeling of deep pleasure or satisfaction derived from achievements, qualities, or possessions that do one credit. ▸ something which causes this. **2** consciousness of one's own dignity. ▸ the quality of having an excessively high opinion of oneself. ▸ poetic/ literary the prime of something. **3** a group of lions forming a social unit. ■ v. (**pride oneself on/upon**) be especially proud of (a quality or skill).
– PHRASES **one's pride and joy** a person or thing of which one is very proud. **pride of place** the most prominent or important position.
– DERIVATIVES **prideful** adj. **pridefully** adv.
– ORIGIN Old English *prӯde*, from *prūd* (see PROUD).

Pride-of-de-Kaap (also **Pride of the Cape**) ■ n. S. African an African leguminous shrub or small tree bearing showy red flowers. [*Bauhinia galpinii*.]

Pride of India ■ n. any of several Asian trees cultivated as ornamentals. [*Lagerstroemia indica*, *Koelreuteria paniculata*, and other species.]

prie-dieu /priːˈdjəː/ ■ n. (pl. **prie-dieux** pronunc. same) a narrow desk on which to kneel for prayer.
– ORIGIN C18: French, 'pray God'.

priest ■ n. 1 an ordained minister of the Catholic, Orthodox, or Anglican Church, authorized to perform certain rites and administer certain sacraments. ▸ a person who performs ceremonies in a non-Christian religion. 2 a mallet used to kill fish caught when angling. ■ v. (usu. **be priested**) formal ordain to the priesthood.
– DERIVATIVES **priesthood** n. **priestly** adj.
– ORIGIN Old English, of Germanic origin.

priestess ■ n. a female priest of a non-Christian religion.

priest-in-charge ■ n. (pl. **priests-in-charge**) an Anglican minister who has charge of a parish but has not been formally appointed as its incumbent.

priest's hole ■ n. Brit. historical a hiding place for a Roman Catholic priest during times of religious persecution.

prig ■ n. a self-righteously moralistic person.
– DERIVATIVES **priggery** n. **priggish** adj. **priggishly** adv. **priggishness** n.
– ORIGIN C16 (in sense 'tinker, petty thief', later 'disliked person').

prim ■ adj. (-**mer**, -**mest**) feeling or showing disapproval of anything improper; stiffly correct. ■ v. (**primmed**, **primming**) purse (the mouth or lips) into a prim expression.
– DERIVATIVES **primly** adv. **primness** n.
– ORIGIN C17: prob. from Old French *prin*, Provençal *prim* 'excellent, delicate', from Latin *primus* 'first'.

prima ballerina /ˈpriːmə/ ■ n. the chief female dancer in a ballet or ballet company.
– ORIGIN C19: Italian.

primacy /ˈprʌɪməsi/ ■ n. 1 pre-eminence. 2 Christian Church the office of a primate of the Church.
– ORIGIN Middle English: from Old French *primatie*, from Latin *primas*, *primat-* (see **PRIMATE**[1]).

prima donna ■ n. 1 the chief female singer in an opera or opera company. 2 a very temperamental and self-important person.
– ORIGIN C18: Italian, 'first lady'.

primaeval ■ adj. variant spelling of **PRIMEVAL**.

prima facie /ˌprʌɪmə ˈfeɪʃɪi/ ■ adj. & adv. Law at first sight; accepted as so until proved otherwise.
– ORIGIN Latin, from *primus* 'first' + *facies* 'face'.

primal /ˈprʌɪm(ə)l/ ■ adj. 1 basic; primitive; primeval. 2 Psychology relating to or denoting feelings or behaviour postulated to form the origins of emotional life.
– DERIVATIVES **primally** adv.
– ORIGIN C17: from medieval Latin *primalis*, from Latin *primus* 'first'.

primarily /ˈprʌɪm(ə)rɪli, prʌɪˈmɛr-/ ■ adv. for the most part; mainly.

primary ■ adj. 1 of chief importance; principal. 2 earliest in time or order. ▸ not caused by or based on anything else. 3 relating to or denoting education for children between the ages of about five and eleven. 4 of or denoting the input side of a transformer or other inductive device. 5 Chemistry (of an organic compound) having its functional group on a carbon atom bonded to no more than one other carbon atom. ▸ derived from ammonia by replacement of one hydrogen atom by an organic group. 6 (of a cell or battery) producing current by an irreversible chemical reaction. ■ n. (pl. -**ies**) 1 (in the US) a preliminary election to appoint delegates to a party conference or to select the candidates for a principal, especially presidential, election. 2 Astronomy the body orbited by a smaller body.
– ORIGIN Middle English: from Latin *primarius*, from *primus* 'first'.

primary colour ■ n. any of a group of colours from which all others can be obtained by mixing.

primary feather ■ n. any of the largest flight feathers in a bird's wing.

primary health care ■ n. basic health care available through a community clinic rather than a hospital.

primary industry ■ n. Economics an industry concerned with obtaining or providing raw materials, such as mining or agriculture.

primate[1] /ˈprʌɪmeɪt, -mət/ ■ n. Christian Church the chief bishop or archbishop of a province.
– DERIVATIVES **primatial** /-ˈmeɪʃ(ə)l/ adj.
– ORIGIN Middle English: from Old French *primat*, from Latin *primas* 'of the first rank', from *primus* 'first'.

primate[2] /ˈprʌɪmeɪt/ ■ n. Zoology a mammal of an order (Primates) including the lemurs, bushbabies, tarsiers, marmosets, monkeys, apes, and humans.
– DERIVATIVES **primatological** adj. **primatologist** n. **primatology** n.
– ORIGIN C19: from Latin *primas* (see **PRIMATE**[1]).

primavera /ˌpriːməˈvɛrə/ ■ adj. [postpos.] (of a pasta dish) made with lightly sautéed spring vegetables.
– ORIGIN C19: from Spanish or Italian, denoting the season of spring.

prime[1] ■ adj. 1 of first importance; main; primary. 2 of the best possible quality; excellent. ▸ having all the expected characteristics. ▸ most suitable or likely. 3 (of a number) divisible only by itself and one (e.g. 2, 3, 5, 7, 11). ■ n. 1 a state or time of greatest vigour or success in a person's life. 2 a prime number. 3 Printing a symbol (') written as a distinguishing mark or to denote minutes or feet. 4 Fencing the first of the eight parrying positions. [French.]
– DERIVATIVES **primeness** n.
– ORIGIN Old English *prīm* (n.), from Latin *prima* (*hora*) 'first (hour)', from Latin *primus* 'first'.

prime[2] ■ v. 1 make (something, especially a firearm or bomb) ready for use or action. 2 pour or spray liquid into (a pump or engine) to facilitate its working. 3 prepare (someone) for a situation, especially by giving instructions or information. 4 cover (a surface) with primer.
– ORIGIN C16: prob. from Latin *primus* 'first'.

prime cost ■ n. the direct cost of a commodity in terms of the materials and labour involved.

prime minister ■ n. the head of an elected government; the principal minister of a sovereign or state.

prime mover ■ n. 1 the originator of a plan or project. 2 an initial source of motive power.

primer[1] ■ n. 1 a substance painted on wood, metal, etc. as a preparatory coat. 2 a cap or cylinder containing a compound which ignites the charge in a cartridge or explosive. 3 a small pump for priming an engine.

primer[2] ■ n. a book providing a basic introduction to a subject or used for teaching reading.
– ORIGIN Middle English: from medieval Latin *primarius* (*liber*) 'primary (book)' and *primarium* (*manuale*) 'primary (manual)'.

prime rate ■ n. the lowest rate of interest for commercial borrowing.

prime time ■ n. the time at which a radio or television audience is expected to be greatest.

primeur /priːˈməː/ ■ n. 1 (**primeurs**) fruit or vegetables grown to be available very early in the season. 2 a newly produced wine recently made available.
– ORIGIN French, 'newness'.

primeval /prʌɪˈmiːv(ə)l/ (also **primaeval**) ■ adj. 1 of the earliest time in history. 2 (of behaviour or emotion) instinctive and unreasoning.
– ORIGIN C17: from Latin *primaevus*, from *primus* 'first' + *aevum* 'age'.

primeval soup ■ n. another term for **PRIMORDIAL SOUP**.

primigravida /ˌprɪmɪˈɡravɪdə, ˌprʌɪm-/ ■ n. (pl. **primigravidae** /-diː/) Medicine a woman pregnant for the first time.
– ORIGIN C19: from Latin *primus* 'first' + *gravidus* (see **GRAVID**).

priming ■ n. a substance used for priming something; a primer.

primipara /prʌɪˈmɪp(ə)rə/ ▪ n. (pl. **primiparae** /-riː/) Medicine a woman giving birth for the first time.
– DERIVATIVES **primiparous** adj.
– ORIGIN C19: from *primus* 'first' + *-parus* 'bringing forth' (from *parere*).

primitive ▪ adj. 1 of, relating to, or denoting the earliest times in history or stages in evolution or development. ▸ of or denoting a preliterate, non-industrial society of simple organization. 2 offering an extremely basic level of comfort, convenience, or efficiency. 3 (of behaviour or emotion) instinctive and unreasoning. 4 of or denoting a deliberately simple and direct artistic style. ▪ n. 1 a person belonging to a primitive society. 2 a pre-Renaissance painter, or one employing a primitive style. 3 Computing any of a set of basic geometric shapes generated in computer graphics.
– DERIVATIVES **primitively** adv. **primitiveness** n.
– ORIGIN Middle English: from Old French *primitif, -ive*, from Latin *primitivus* 'first of its kind', from *primus* 'first'.

primitive streak ▪ n. Biology the earliest trace of the embryo in a fertilized ovum.

primitivism ▪ n. adoption of a primitive lifestyle or technique.
– DERIVATIVES **primitivist** n. & adj.

primogenitor /ˌprʌɪmə(ʊ)ˈdʒɛnɪtə/ ▪ n. the earliest ancestor of a people; a progenitor.
– ORIGIN C17: var. of PROGENITOR, on the pattern of *primogeniture*.

primogeniture /ˌprʌɪmə(ʊ)ˈdʒɛnɪtʃə/ ▪ n. the state of being the firstborn child. ▸ a rule or tradition of inheritance by the firstborn child.
– ORIGIN C17: from medieval Latin *primogenitura*, from Latin *primo* 'first' + *genitura* 'geniture'.

primordial /prʌɪˈmɔːdɪəl/ ▪ adj. existing at or from the beginning of time; primitive.
– DERIVATIVES **primordially** adv.
– ORIGIN Middle English: from late Latin *primordialis* 'first of all', from *primordius*, from *primus* 'first' + *ordiri* 'begin'.

primordial soup ▪ n. a solution rich in organic compounds in which life on earth is supposed to have originated.

primp ▪ v. spend time making minor adjustments to.
– ORIGIN C16: rel. to PRIM.

primrose ▪ n. 1 a European woodland and hedgerow plant which produces pale yellow flowers in early spring. [*Primula vulgaris*.] 2 a pale yellow colour.
– PHRASES **primrose path** the pursuit of pleasure, especially when bringing disastrous consequences. [with allusion to Shakespeare's *Hamlet* I. iii. 50.]
– ORIGIN Middle English: cf. Old French *primerose* and medieval Latin *prima rosa* 'first rose'.

primula /ˈprɪmjʊlə/ ▪ n. a plant of a genus that includes primroses, cowslips, and polyanthuses. [Genus *Primula*.]
– ORIGIN from medieval Latin, feminine of *primulus*, diminutive of *primus* 'first'.

Primus /ˈprʌɪməs/ ▪ n. trademark a portable cooking stove that burns vaporized oil.

primus inter pares /ˌpriːməs ɪntə ˈpɑːriːz, ˌprʌɪməs/ ▪ n. a first among equals; the senior or representative member of a group.
– ORIGIN from Latin.

prince ▪ n. 1 a son, grandson, or other close male relative of a monarch. ▸ a male monarch of a small state, actually or nominally subject to a king or emperor. ▸ (in some European countries) a nobleman, usually ranking next below a duke. 2 (**prince of/among**) a man or thing pre-eminent in a particular sphere or group.
– DERIVATIVES **princedom** n.
– ORIGIN Middle English: from Latin *princeps* 'first, chief, sovereign', from *primus* 'first' + *capere* 'take'.

Prince Charming ▪ n. a handsome and honourable young male lover.
– ORIGIN partial translation of French *Roi Charmant* 'King Charming', the title of a C18 fairy-tale romance.

prince consort ▪ n. the husband of a reigning female sovereign who is himself a prince.

princeling ▪ n. chiefly derogatory the ruler of a small principality or domain.

princely ▪ adj. 1 of, relating to, or suitable for a prince. 2 (of a sum of money) generous.

Prince of Darkness ▪ n. the Devil.

Prince of Peace ▪ n. a title of Jesus Christ.

princess ▪ n. 1 a daughter, granddaughter, or other close female relative of a monarch. ▸ the wife or widow of a prince. ▸ a female monarch of a small state, actually or nominally subject to a king or emperor. 2 (**princess of/among**) a woman or thing pre-eminent in a particular sphere or group.
– ORIGIN Middle English: from Old French *princesse*.

principal ▪ adj. 1 first in order of importance; main. 2 denoting an original sum of money invested or lent. ▪ n. 1 the most important or senior person in an organization or group. ▸ the head of a school or college. ▸ (in certain professions) a fully qualified practitioner. 2 a sum of money lent or invested, on which interest is paid. 3 a person for whom another acts as an agent or representative. ▸ Law a person directly responsible for a crime. 4 a main rafter supporting purlins.
– DERIVATIVES **principalship** n.
– ORIGIN Middle English: from Latin *principalis* 'first, original', from *princeps* 'first, chief'.

USAGE
On the confusion of **principal** and **principle**, see usage at PRINCIPLE.

principal boy (or **principal girl**) ▪ n. Brit. a woman who takes the leading male (or female) role in a pantomime.

principality ▪ n. (pl. **-ies**) a state ruled by a prince. ▸ (**the Principality**) Brit. Wales.
– ORIGIN Middle English: from Old French *principalite*, from Latin *principalis* (see PRINCIPAL).

principally ▪ adv. for the most part; chiefly.

principle ▪ n. 1 a fundamental truth or proposition serving as the foundation for belief or action. ▸ a rule or belief governing one's personal behaviour. ▸ morally correct behaviour and attitudes: *a man of principle*. 2 a general scientific theorem or natural law. 3 a fundamental source or basis of something. ▸ a fundamental quality or attribute. 4 Chemistry an active or characteristic constituent of a substance.
– PHRASES **in principle** in theory. **on principle** because of one's adherence to a particular belief.
– ORIGIN Middle English: from Latin *principium* 'source', *principia* (pl.) 'foundations', from *princeps* 'first, chief'.

USAGE
Note that **principle** and **principal** do not have the same meaning. **Principle** is normally used as a noun meaning 'a fundamental basis of a system of thought or belief', as in *this is one of the basic principles of democracy*. **Principal**, on the other hand, is normally an adjective meaning 'main or most important', as in *one of the country's principal cities*. As a noun **principal** refers to the most senior or most important person in an organization: *the College Principal*.

principled ▪ adj. 1 acting in accordance with morality. 2 (of a system or method) based on a given set of rules.

print ▪ v. 1 produce (books, newspapers, etc.) by a mechanical process involving the transfer of text or designs to paper. ▸ produce (text or a picture) in such a way. ▸ publish. ▸ produce a paper copy of (information stored on a computer). 2 produce (a photographic print) from a negative. 3 write clearly without joining the letters. 4 mark with a coloured design or pattern. ▸ make (a mark or indentation) by pressing something on a surface or soft substance. 5 fix firmly or indelibly in someone's mind. ▪ n. 1 the text appearing in a book, newspaper, etc. ▸ the state of being available in published form. ▸ [as modifier] of or relating to the printing industry or the printed media. 2 an indentation or mark left on a surface or soft substance by pressure. ▸ (**prints**) fingerprints. 3 a printed picture or design. ▸ a photograph printed on paper from a negative or transparency. 4 a piece of fabric or clothing with a coloured pattern or design. ▸ a pattern or design of this type.
– PHRASES **appear in print** (of an author) have one's work

published. **in print 1** (of a book) available from the publisher. **2** in published form. **out of print** (of a book) no longer available from the publisher.
– DERIVATIVES **printability** n. **printable** adj.
– ORIGIN Middle English: from Old French *preinte* 'pressed', from *preindre*, from Latin *premere* 'to press'.

printed circuit ■ n. an electronic circuit based on thin strips of a conductor on an insulating board, made by etching.

printer ■ n. **1** a person whose job is commercial printing. **2** a machine for printing text or pictures.

printing ■ n. **1** the production of books, newspapers, etc. **2** a single impression of a book. **3** handwriting in which the letters are written separately.

printing press ■ n. a machine for printing from type or plates.

printing works ■ n. [treated as sing. or pl.] a factory for the printing of newspapers, books, etc.

printmaker ■ n. a person who prints pictures or designs from plates or blocks.
– DERIVATIVES **printmaking** n.

printout ■ n. Computing a page of printed material from a computer's printer.

print run ■ n. the number of copies of a book, magazine, etc. printed at one time.

prion[1] /ˈprʌɪən/ ■ n. a small petrel of southern seas, having a wide bill fringed with comb-like plates for feeding on planktonic crustaceans. [Genus *Pachyptila*: six species.]
– ORIGIN C19: from Greek *priōn* 'a saw' (referring to its bill).

prion[2] /ˈpriːɒn/ ■ n. Microbiology a submicroscopic protein particle believed to be the cause of certain brain diseases such as BSE.
– ORIGIN 1980s: by rearrangement of elements from *pro(teinaceous) in(fectious particle)*.

prior[1] ■ adj. existing or coming before in time, order, or importance. ■ n. N. Amer. informal a previous criminal conviction.
– PHRASES **prior to** before.
– ORIGIN C18: from Latin, 'former, elder', rel. to *prae* 'before'.

prior[2] ■ n. (fem. **prioress**) **1** (in an abbey) the person next in rank below an abbot (or abbess). **2** the head of a house of friars (or nuns).
– ORIGIN Old English, from a medieval Latin noun use of Latin *prior* (see PRIOR[1]).

prioritize (also **-ise**) ■ v. designate or treat as most important. ▶ determine the relative importance of (items or tasks).
– DERIVATIVES **prioritization** (also **-isation**) n.

priority ■ n. (pl. **-ies**) **1** the fact or condition of being regarded as more important. ▶ a thing regarded as more important than others. **2** the right to proceed before other traffic.
– ORIGIN Middle English: from Old French *priorite*, from Latin *prior* (see PRIOR[1]).

priory ■ n. (pl. **-ies**) a monastery or nunnery governed by a prior or prioress.
– ORIGIN Middle English: from medieval Latin *prioria*, from Latin *prior* (see PRIOR[2]).

prise (US **prize**) ■ v. **1** use force in order to open or move apart. **2** (**prise something out of/from**) obtain something from (someone) with effort or difficulty.
– ORIGIN C17: from dialect *prise* 'lever', from Old French *prise* 'grasp, taking hold'.

prism /ˈprɪz(ə)m/ ■ n. **1** Geometry a solid geometric figure whose two ends are similar, equal, and parallel rectilinear figures, and whose sides are parallelograms. **2** Optics a transparent object in this form, especially one with triangular ends used to separate white light into a spectrum of colours.
– ORIGIN C16: from Greek *prisma* 'thing sawn', from *prizein* 'to saw'.

prismatic /prɪzˈmatɪk/ ■ adj. **1** of, relating to, or having the form of a prism. ▶ incorporating a prism or prisms. **2** (of colours) formed, separated, or distributed by as by a prism.

prismoid /ˈprɪzmɔɪd/ ■ n. Geometry a body like a prism, in which the end faces have the same number of sides but are not equal.

prison ■ n. a building for the confinement of criminals or those awaiting trial.
– ORIGIN Old English, from Old French *prisun*, from Latin *prensio(n-)*, *prehensio(n-)* 'laying hold of', from *prehendere*.

prison camp ■ n. a camp where prisoners of war or political prisoners are kept.

prisoner ■ n. a person legally committed to prison. ▶ a person captured and kept confined. ▶ a person trapped by a situation or circumstances.
– PHRASES **take no prisoners** be ruthlessly aggressive or uncompromising in the pursuit of one's objectives.
– ORIGIN Middle English: from Old French *prisonier*, from *prison* (see PRISON).

prisoner of conscience ■ n. a person imprisoned for their political or religious views.

prisoner of state (also **state prisoner**) ■ n. a person confined for political reasons.

prisoner of war ■ n. a person captured and imprisoned by the enemy in war.

prison farm ■ n. a farm on which prisoners are confined and supply the labour.

prissy ■ adj. (**-ier**, **-iest**) fussily respectable; prim.
– DERIVATIVES **prissily** adv. **prissiness** n.
– ORIGIN C19: perhaps a blend of PRIM and SISSY.

pristine /ˈprɪstiːn, -stʌɪn/ ■ adj. in its original condition. ▶ spotless.
– ORIGIN C16: from Latin *pristinus* 'former'.

prithee /ˈprɪði/ ■ exclam. archaic please.
– ORIGIN C16: abbrev. of *I pray thee*.

privacy /ˈprɪvəsi, ˈprʌɪ-/ ■ n. a state in which one is not observed or disturbed by others. ▶ freedom from public attention.

private ■ adj. **1** for or belonging to one particular person or group only. ▶ (of thoughts, feelings, etc.) not to be shared or revealed. ▶ (of a person) not choosing to share their thoughts and feelings. ▶ (of a place) secluded. ▶ alone and undisturbed by others. **2** (of a person) having no official or public position. ▶ not connected with one's work or official position. **3** (of a service or industry) provided or owned by an individual or commercial company rather than the state. ▶ of or relating to a system of education or medical treatment conducted outside the state system and charging fees. **4** relating to or denoting a transaction between individuals. ■ n. **1** the lowest rank in the army, below lance corporal. **2** (**privates**) informal short for PRIVATE PARTS.
– PHRASES **in private** with no one else present.
– DERIVATIVES **privately** adv.
– ORIGIN Middle English: from Latin *privatus* 'withdrawn from public life', from *privare* 'bereave, deprive', from *privus* 'single, individual'.

private bill ■ n. a legislative bill affecting a particular body or individual only.

private company ■ n. a company whose shares may not be offered to the public for sale.

private detective (also **private investigator**) ■ n. a freelance detective carrying out investigations for private clients.

private enterprise ■ n. business or industry managed by independent companies rather than the state.

privateer /ˌprʌɪvəˈtɪə/ ■ n. chiefly historical an armed ship owned by private individuals, holding a government commission and authorized for use in war. ▶ (also **privateersman**) a commander or crew member of a privateer.
– DERIVATIVES **privateering** n.
– ORIGIN C17: from PRIVATE, on the pattern of *volunteer*.

private eye ■ n. informal a private detective.

private income ■ n. income derived from private means.

private law ■ n. a branch of law concerned with the relations between individuals.

private life ■ n. one's personal relationships, interests, etc., as distinct from one's professional or public life.

private means ▪ pl. n. a source of income derived from investments, property, etc., rather than from employment.

private member ▪ n. (in some countries) a member of a parliament who is not a minister or does not hold government office.

private parts ▪ pl. n. euphemistic a person's genitals.

private practice ▪ n. the work of a doctor, lawyer, etc. who is self-employed. ▸ medical practice that is not part of a public health service.

private school ▪ n. **1** a school independent of state control and supported wholly by the payment of fees. **2** N. Amer. a school supported mainly by private individuals.

private secretary ▪ n. **1** a secretary who deals with the personal and confidential concerns of their employer. **2** a civil servant acting as an aide to a senior government official.

private sector ▪ n. the part of the national economy not under direct state control.

private soldier ▪ n. a soldier of the lowest rank.

private view ▪ n. a chance for invited guests to see an art exhibition before it is opened to the public.

private war ▪ n. **1** a feud conducted without regard to the law. **2** hostilities against members of another state without government sanction.

privation /praɪˈveɪʃ(ə)n/ ▪ n. a state in which essentials such as food and warmth are lacking.
– ORIGIN Middle English: from Latin *privatio(n-)*, from *privare* (see PRIVATE).

privative /ˈprɪvətɪv/ ▪ adj. lacking some quality or attribute that is normally present.
– ORIGIN C16: from Latin *privativus* 'denoting privation', from *privat-* (see PRIVATION).

privatize (also **-ise**) ▪ v. transfer (a business, industry, etc.) from public to private ownership.
– DERIVATIVES **privatization** (also **-isation**) n. **privatizer** (also **-iser**) n.

privet /ˈprɪvɪt/ ▪ n. a shrub of the olive family, with small white scented flowers and poisonous black berries. [*Ligustrum ovalifolium* and other species.]
– ORIGIN C16.

privilege ▪ n. **1** a special right, advantage, or immunity for a particular person. ▸ a special benefit or honour. **2** (also **absolute privilege**) (especially in a parliamentary context) the right to say or write something without the risk of punishment. **3** the right of a lawyer or official to refuse to divulge confidential information. ▪ v. formal grant a privilege or privileges to. ▸ (usu. **be privileged from**) exempt from a liability or obligation.
– ORIGIN Middle English: from Latin *privilegium* 'bill or law affecting an individual', from *privus* 'private' + *lex* 'law'.

privileged ▪ adj. **1** having special rights, advantages, or immunities. ▸ having been granted a special honour. **2** (of information) legally protected from being made public.

privity /ˈprɪvɪti/ ▪ n. (pl. **-ies**) Law a relation between two parties that is recognized by law, e.g. that of blood, lease, or service.
– ORIGIN Middle English: from Old French *privete*, from Latin *privus* 'private'.

privy ▪ adj. **1** (**privy to**) sharing in the knowledge of (something secret). **2** archaic hidden; secret. ▪ n. (pl. **-ies**) **1** a toilet in a small shed outside a house. **2** Law a person having a part or interest in any action or matter.
– DERIVATIVES **privily** adv.
– ORIGIN Middle English: from Old French *prive* 'private', from Latin *privatus* (see PRIVATE).

Privy Council ▪ n. a body of advisers appointed by a sovereign or a Governor General (now chiefly on an honorary basis and including government ministers).
– DERIVATIVES **privy counsellor** (also **privy councillor**) n.

privy purse ▪ n. (in the UK) an allowance from the public revenue for the monarch's private expenses.

privy seal ▪ n. (in the UK) a seal affixed to state documents.

prize¹ ▪ n. **1** a thing given as a reward to a winner or in recognition of an outstanding achievement. ▸ something won in a game of chance. ▸ something of great value that is worth struggling to achieve. **2** chiefly historical an enemy ship captured during warfare. ▪ adj. **1** having been or likely to be awarded a prize. **2** outstanding of its kind. ▪ v. value highly.
– ORIGIN Middle English: sense 1 of n. is var. of PRICE, sense 2 is from Old French *prise* 'taking, booty'; v. is from Old French *preisier* (see PRAISE).

prize² ▪ v. US spelling of PRISE.

prizefight ▪ n. a boxing match, typically an unlicensed one, for prize money.
– DERIVATIVES **prizefighter** n. **prizefighting** n.

PRO ▪ abbrev. **1** Public Record Office. **2** public relations officer.

pro¹ informal ▪ n. (pl. **-os**) a professional. ▪ adj. professional.

pro² ▪ n. (pl. **-os**) (usu. in phr. **pros and cons**) an advantage or argument in favour of something. ▪ prep. & adv. in favour of.
– ORIGIN Middle English: from Latin, 'for, on behalf of'.

pro-¹ ▪ prefix **1** favouring; supporting: *pro-choice.* **2** acting as a substitute for: *proconsul.* **3** denoting motion forwards, out, or away: *propel.*
– ORIGIN from Latin *pro* 'in front of, on behalf of, instead of, on account of'.

pro-² ▪ prefix before in time, place, or order: *proactive.*
– ORIGIN from Greek *pro* 'before'.

proactive ▪ adj. creating or controlling a situation rather than just responding to it.
– DERIVATIVES **proactively** adv. **proactivity** n.
– ORIGIN 1930s: from PRO-² (denoting earlier occurrence), on the pattern of *reactive.*

pro-am ▪ adj. involving professionals and amateurs. ▪ n. a pro-am event.

probabilistic ▪ adj. based on or adapted to a theory of probability; involving chance variation.

probability ▪ n. (pl. **-ies**) the extent to which something is probable. ▸ a probable or most probable event.
– PHRASES **in all probability** most probably.

probable ▪ adj. likely to happen or be the case. ▪ n. a person likely to become or do something.
– ORIGIN Middle English: from Latin *probabilis*, from *probare* 'to test, demonstrate'.

probable cause ▪ n. Law, chiefly N. Amer. reasonable grounds.

probably ▪ adv. almost certainly; as far as one knows or can tell.

probate ▪ n. the official proving of a will. ▸ a verified copy of a will with a certificate as handed to the executors.
– ORIGIN Middle English: from Latin *probatum* 'something proved', from *probare* 'to test, prove'.

probation ▪ n. **1** Law the release of an offender from detention, subject to a period of good behaviour under supervision. **2** the process of testing the character or abilities of a person in a certain role.
– DERIVATIVES **probationary** adj.
– ORIGIN Middle English: from Old French *probacion*, from Latin *probatio(n-)*, from *probare* (see PROVE).

probationer ▪ n. **1** a person serving a probationary period in a job or position. **2** an offender on probation.

probation officer ▪ n. a person who supervises offenders on probation.

probative /ˈprəʊbətɪv/ ▪ adj. chiefly Law affording proof or evidence.
– ORIGIN Middle English: from Latin *probativus*, from *probare* (see PROVE).

probe ▪ n. **1** a blunt-ended surgical instrument for exploring a wound or part of the body. **2** a small measuring or testing device, especially an electrode. **3** a projecting device on an aircraft for in-flight refuelling or on a spacecraft for docking with another craft. **4** (also **space probe**) an unmanned exploratory spacecraft. **5** an investigation. ▪ v. physically explore or examine. ▸ enquire into closely.
– DERIVATIVES **probing** adj. **probingly** adv.
– ORIGIN Middle English: from late Latin *proba* 'proof', from Latin *probare* 'to test'.

probiotic /ˌprəʊbaɪˈɒtɪk/ ▪ adj. denoting a substance

which stimulates the growth of microorganisms, especially beneficial ones such as those of the intestinal flora. ■ n. a probiotic substance or preparation.

probit /'prɒbɪt/ ■ n. Statistics a unit of probability based on deviation from the mean of a standard distribution.
– ORIGIN 1930s: from *prob(ability un)it*.

probity /'prəʊbɪti, 'prɒb-/ ■ n. honesty and decency.
– ORIGIN Middle English: from Latin *probitas*, from *probus* 'good'.

problem ■ n. **1** an unwelcome or harmful matter needing to be dealt with and overcome. ▸ a thing that is difficult to achieve. **2** Physics & Mathematics an inquiry starting from given conditions to investigate or demonstrate something.
– ORIGIN Middle English: from Greek *problēma*, from *proballein*, from *pro* 'before' + *ballein* 'to throw'.

problematic ■ adj. constituting or presenting a problem. ■ n. a problematic thing.
– DERIVATIVES **problematical** adj. **problematically** adv.
– ORIGIN C17: from Greek *problēmatikos*, from *problēma* (see PROBLEM).

problematize (also **-ise**) ■ v. make into or regard as a problem.
– DERIVATIVES **problematization** (also **-isation**) n.

pro bono /prəʊ 'bɒnəʊ, 'bəʊnəʊ/ ■ adv. & adj. (also **pro bono publico** /'pʊblɪkəʊ/) denoting legal work undertaken without charge, especially for a client on low income.
– ORIGIN from Latin.

proboscis /prə'bɒsɪs/ ■ n. (pl. **prosbosces** /-siːz/ , **proboscides** /-sɪdiːz/, or **proboscises**) **1** the nose of a mammal, especially when long and mobile like the trunk of an elephant. **2** Zoology an elongated sucking organ or mouth-part.
– ORIGIN C17: from Greek *proboskis* 'means of obtaining food', from *pro* 'before' + *boskein* '(cause to) feed'.

procaine /'prəʊkeɪn/ ■ n. a synthetic compound used as a local anaesthetic.
– ORIGIN C20: from PRO-[1] (denoting substitution) + *-caine* (from COCAINE).

procaryote ■ n. variant spelling of PROKARYOTE.

procedure ■ n. **1** an established or official way of doing something. ▸ a series of actions conducted in a certain order or manner. **2** Computing a subroutine.
– DERIVATIVES **procedural** adj. **procedurally** adv.
– ORIGIN C16: from French *procédure*, from *procéder* (see PROCEED).

proceed ■ v. **1** begin a course of action. ▸ go on to do something. ▸ (of an action) carry on or continue. **2** move forward. **3** Law start a lawsuit against someone. **4** (**proceed from**) originate from.
– ORIGIN Middle English: from Old French *proceder*, from Latin *procedere*, from *pro-* 'forward' + *cedere* 'go'.

proceedings ■ pl. n. **1** an event or a series of activities with a set procedure. **2** Law action taken in a court to settle a dispute. **3** a report of a set of meetings or a conference.

proceeds ■ pl. n. money obtained from an event or activity.
– ORIGIN C17: pl. of the obsolete noun *proceed*, in the same sense, earlier meaning 'procedure'.

process[1] /'prəʊsɛs/ ■ n. **1** a series of actions or steps towards achieving a particular end. ▸ a natural series of changes. **2** [as modifier] Printing relating to or denoting printing using ink in three colours (cyan, magenta, and yellow) and black. **3** Law a summons to appear in court. **4** a natural appendage or outgrowth on or in an organism. ■ v. perform a series of operations to change or preserve. ▸ Computing operate on (data) by means of a program. ▸ deal with, using an established procedure.
– DERIVATIVES **processable** adj.
– ORIGIN Middle English: from Old French *proces*, from Latin *processus* 'progression, course', from *procedere* (see PROCEED).

process[2] /prə'sɛs/ ■ v. walk in procession.
– ORIGIN C19: back-formation from PROCESSION.

procession ■ n. a number of people or vehicles moving forward in an orderly fashion, especially as part of a ceremony. ▸ the action of moving in such a way. ▸ a relentless succession of people or things.
– ORIGIN Old English, from Latin *processio(n-)*, from *procedere* (see PROCEED).

processional ■ adj. of, for, or used in a religious or ceremonial procession.

processor ■ n. a machine that processes something. ▸ Computing a central processing unit.

processual /prə'sɛsjʊəl/ ■ adj. relating to or involving the study of processes.

pro-choice ■ adj. advocating the right of a woman to choose to have an abortion.

proclaim ■ v. announce officially or publicly. ▸ declare (someone) to be. ▸ indicate clearly.
– DERIVATIVES **proclaimer** n. **proclamation** n. **proclamatory** adj.
– ORIGIN Middle English, from Latin *proclamare* 'cry out', from *pro-* 'forth' + *clamare* 'to shout'.

proclivity /prə'klɪvɪti/ ■ n. (pl. **-ies**) an inclination or predisposition.
– ORIGIN C16: from Latin *proclivitas*, from *proclivis* 'inclined', from *pro-* 'forward, down' + *clivus* 'slope'.

proconsul /prəʊ'kɒns(ə)l/ ■ n. **1** a governor of a province in ancient Rome. **2** a governor or deputy consul of a modern colony.
– DERIVATIVES **proconsular** adj.
– ORIGIN from Latin *pro consule* '(one acting) for the consul'.

procrastinate /prə(ʊ)'krastɪneɪt/ ■ v. delay or postpone action.
– DERIVATIVES **procrastination** n. **procrastinator** n.
– ORIGIN C16: from Latin *procrastinare* 'defer till the morning', from *pro-* 'forward' + *crastinus* 'belonging to tomorrow', from *cras* 'tomorrow'.

procreate ■ v. produce young.
– DERIVATIVES **procreation** n. **procreative** adj. **procreator** n.
– ORIGIN Middle English: from Latin *procreare* 'generate, bring forth', from *pro-* 'forth' + *creare* 'create'.

proctitis /prɒk'tʌɪtɪs/ ■ n. Medicine inflammation of the rectum and anus.
– ORIGIN C19: from Greek *prōktos* 'anus'.

proctology /prɒk'tɒlədʒi/ ■ n. the branch of medicine concerned with the anus and rectum.
– DERIVATIVES **proctologist** n.
– ORIGIN C19: from Greek *prōktos* 'anus'.

proctor ■ n. **1** an officer at certain universities having mainly disciplinary functions. **2** N. Amer. an invigilator at an examination.
– DERIVATIVES **proctorial** adj. **proctorship** n.
– ORIGIN Middle English: contraction of PROCURATOR.

procumbent /prə(ʊ)'kʌmb(ə)nt/ ■ adj. Botany (of a plant or stem) growing along the ground without throwing out roots.
– ORIGIN C17: from Latin *procumbent-*, *procumbere* 'fall forwards', from *pro-* 'forwards, down' + a verb rel. to *cubare* 'to lie'.

procurator /'prɒkjʊreɪtə/ ■ n. Law an agent representing others in a court in countries retaining Roman civil law.
– DERIVATIVES **procuratorial** adj. **procuratorship** n.
– ORIGIN Middle English: from Latin *procurator* 'administrator, finance agent', from *procurare* (see PROCURE).

procurator fiscal ■ n. (in Scotland) a local coroner and public prosecutor.

procure ■ v. **1** obtain. ▸ obtain as a prostitute for someone else. **2** Law persuade or cause to do something. ▸ archaic or Law cause to happen.
– DERIVATIVES **procurable** adj. **procurement** n. **procurer** n. **procuress** n.
– ORIGIN Middle English: from Old French *procurer*, from Latin *procurare* 'take care of, manage', from *pro-* 'on behalf of' + *curare* 'see to'.

prod ■ v. (**prodded**, **prodding**) **1** poke with a finger, pointed object, etc. **2** stimulate or persuade to do something. ■ n. **1** a poke. **2** a stimulus or reminder. **3** a pointed implement, typically discharging an electric current and used as a goad.
– DERIVATIVES **prodder** n.
– ORIGIN C16: perhaps a blend of POKE and dialect *brod* 'to goad, prod'.

pro Deo ■ adj. & adv. S. African Law denoting legal assistance granted to a defendant who has committed a serious crime but cannot afford representation. ▶ (of legal and other services) free of charge.
–ORIGIN Latin, 'for God'.

prodigal ■ adj. **1** wastefully extravagant. **2** lavish. ■ n. a prodigal person. ▶ (also **prodigal son** or **daughter**) a person who leaves home to lead a prodigal life but returns repentant.
–DERIVATIVES **prodigality** n. **prodigally** adv.
–ORIGIN Middle English: from late Latin *prodigalis*, from Latin *prodigus* 'lavish'.

prodigal son ■ n. South African term for COBIA.

prodigious /prəˈdɪdʒəs/ ■ adj. **1** remarkably or impressively large. **2** archaic unnatural; abnormal.
–DERIVATIVES **prodigiously** adv. **prodigiousness** n.
–ORIGIN C15: from Latin *prodigiosus*, from *prodigium* (see PRODIGY).

prodigy ■ n. (pl. **-ies**) a person, especially a young one, with exceptional abilities. ▶ an outstanding example of a quality.
–ORIGIN C15: from Latin *prodigium* 'portent'.

prodrug ■ n. a biologically inactive compound which can be metabolized in the body to produce a drug.

produce ■ v. **1** make, manufacture, or create. ▶ create or form as part of a physical, biological, or chemical process. **2** cause to happen or exist. **3** provide for consideration, inspection, or use. **4** administer the financial and managerial aspects of (a film or broadcast) or the staging of (a play). ▶ supervise the making of (a musical recording). ■ n. things that have been produced or grown.
–DERIVATIVES **producer** n. **producible** adj.
–ORIGIN Middle English: from Latin *producere*, from *pro-* 'forward' + *ducere* 'to lead'.

product ■ n. **1** an article or substance manufactured or refined for sale. ▶ a substance produced during a natural, chemical, or manufacturing process. ▶ a result of an action or process. **2** a person whose character has been formed by a particular period or situation. **3** Mathematics a quantity obtained by multiplying quantities together, or from an analogous algebraic operation.
–ORIGIN Middle English: from Latin *productum* 'something produced', from *producere* (see PRODUCE).

production ■ n. **1** the action or process of producing or being produced. ▶ the amount of something produced. ▶ [as modifier] denoting a vehicle manufactured in large numbers, as opposed to a prototype or other special version. **2** a film, record, or play, viewed in terms of its making or staging.
–ORIGIN Middle English: from Latin *productio(n-)*, from *producere* (see PRODUCE).

production line ■ n. another term for ASSEMBLY LINE.

productive ■ adj. **1** producing or able to produce large amounts of goods, crops, etc. ▶ relating to or engaged in the production of goods, crops, etc. **2** achieving or producing a significant amount or result. **3** (**productive of**) producing. **4** Linguistics (of a prefix, suffix, etc.) currently used in forming new words or expressions. **5** Medicine (of a cough) raising mucus from the respiratory tract.
–DERIVATIVES **productively** adv. **productiveness** n.
–ORIGIN C17: from late Latin *productivus*, from *producere* (see PRODUCE).

productivity ■ n. **1** the state or quality of producing something. **2** the effectiveness of productive effort. **3** Ecology the fertility or capacity of a given habitat or area.

product placement ■ n. a practice in which companies pay for their products or services to be featured in films and television programmes.

proem /ˈprəʊɪm/ ■ n. formal a preface or preamble to a book or speech.
–ORIGIN Middle English: from Old French *proeme*, from Greek *prooimion* 'prelude', from *pro* 'before' + *oimē* 'song'.

Prof. ■ abbrev. professor.

prof ■ n. informal a professor.

profane /prəˈfeɪn/ ■ adj. **1** secular rather than religious. ▶ not initiated into religious rites. **2** not respectful of religious practice. ▶ (of language) blasphemous or obscene. ■ v. treat with irreverence.
–DERIVATIVES **profanation** n. **profanely** adv. **profaneness** n. **profaner** n.
–ORIGIN Middle English: from Latin *profanus* 'outside the temple, not sacred', from *pro* 'before' + *fanum* 'temple'.

profanity /prəˈfanɪti/ ■ n. (pl. **-ies**) profane language or behaviour. ▶ a swear word.

profess ■ v. **1** claim that one has (a quality or feeling). **2** affirm one's faith in or allegiance to (a religion). ▶ (**be professed**) be received into a religious order under vows. **3** dated or humorous teach (a subject) as a professor.
–ORIGIN Middle English: from Latin *profess-*, *profiteri* 'declare publicly', from *pro-* 'before' + *fateri* 'confess'.

professed ■ adj. **1** (of a quality, feeling, etc.) claimed openly but typically falsely. **2** self-acknowledged: *a professed commitment to human rights*. **3** having taken the vows of a religious order.

professedly ■ adv. ostensibly.

profession ■ n. **1** a paid occupation, especially one involving training and a formal qualification. ▶ [treated as sing. or pl.] a body of people engaged in a profession. **2** an open but typically false claim: *a profession of allegiance*. **3** a declaration of belief in a religion. ▶ the vows made on entering a religious order.
–PHRASES **the oldest profession** humorous prostitution.
–ORIGIN Middle English: from Latin *professio(n-)*, from *profiteri* (see PROFESS).

professional ■ adj. **1** of, relating to, or belonging to a profession. ▶ worthy of or appropriate to a professional person. **2** engaged in an activity as a paid occupation rather than as an amateur. **3** informal, derogatory habitually engaged in a particular activity: *a professional timewaster*. ■ n. a professional person. ▶ a person having impressive competence in a particular activity.
–DERIVATIVES **professionalization** (also **-isation**) n. **professionalize** (also **-ise**) v. **professionally** adv.

professional foul ■ n. (especially in soccer) a deliberate foul to prevent an opponent from scoring.

professionalism ■ n. **1** the competence or skill expected of a professional. **2** the practising of an activity by professionals rather than amateurs.

professor ■ n. **1** a university academic of the highest rank; the holder of a university chair. ▶ N. Amer. a university teacher. **2** a person who affirms a faith in or allegiance to something.
–DERIVATIVES **professorial** adj. **professoriate** n. **professorship** n.
–ORIGIN Middle English: from Latin *professor*, from *profiteri* (see PROFESS).

proffer ■ v. offer.
–ORIGIN Middle English: from Anglo-Norman French *proffrir*, from Latin *pro-* 'before' + *offerre* 'to offer'.

proficient ■ adj. competent; skilled.
–DERIVATIVES **proficiency** n. **proficiently** adv.
–ORIGIN C16: from Latin *proficient-*, *proficere* 'to advance', from *pro-* 'on behalf of' + *facere* 'do, make'.

profile ■ n. **1** an outline of something, especially a face, as seen from one side. **2** a vertical cross section of something. **3** a graphical or other representation of information recorded in quantified form. **4** a short descriptive article about someone. **5** the extent to which a person or organization attracts public notice. ■ v. **1** describe in a short article. **2** (**be profiled**) appear in outline.
–PHRASES **in profile** as seen from one side. **keep a low profile** remain inconspicuous.
–DERIVATIVES **profiler** n.
–ORIGIN C17: from obsolete Italian *profilo*, from *pro-* 'forth' + *filare* 'to spin', formerly 'draw a line', from Latin, from *filum* 'thread'.

profiling ■ n. the analysis of a person's psychological and behavioural characteristics, so as to assess or predict their capabilities or to identify a subgroup of people.

profit ■ n. **1** a financial gain, especially the difference between an initial outlay and the subsequent amount earned. **2** advantage; benefit. ■ v. (**profited, profiting**) benefit, especially financially. ▶ be beneficial to.
–DERIVATIVES **profitability** n. **profitable** adj. **profitably** adv. **profitless** adj.

– ORIGIN Middle English: from Latin *profectus* 'progress, profit', from *proficere* 'to advance', from *pro-* 'on behalf of' + *facere* 'do'.

profit and loss account ■ n. an account to which incomes and gains are credited and expenses and losses debited, so as to show the net profit or loss over a period.

profiteer ■ v. [often as noun **profiteering**] make an excessive or unfair profit. ■ n. a person who profiteers.

profiterole ■ n. a small ball of soft, sweet choux pastry filled with cream and covered with chocolate sauce.
– ORIGIN French, diminutive of *profit* 'profit'.

profit margin ■ n. the amount by which revenue from sales exceeds costs in a business.

profit-sharing ■ n. a system in which the people who work for a company receive a direct share of the profits.

profit-taking ■ n. the sale of securities that have risen in price.

profligate /ˈprɒflɪɡət/ ■ adj. recklessly extravagant or wasteful. ▸ licentious; dissolute. ■ n. a profligate person.
– DERIVATIVES **profligacy** n. **profligately** adv.
– ORIGIN C16: from Latin *profligatus* 'dissolute', from *profligare* 'overthrow, ruin', from *pro-* 'forward, down' + *fligere* 'strike down'.

pro forma /prəʊ ˈfɔːmə/ ■ adv. as a matter of form or politeness. ■ adj. 1 done or produced as a matter of form. ▸ denoting a standard document or form. 2 (of a financial statement) showing potential or expected income, costs, assets, or liabilities. ■ n. a standard document or form.
– ORIGIN C16: from Latin.

profound ■ adj. (**-er**, **-est**) 1 very great or intense: *profound social changes*. ▸ (of a disease or disability) severe. 2 showing great knowledge or insight. ▸ demanding deep study or thought. 3 archaic very deep.
– DERIVATIVES **profoundly** adv. **profoundness** n.
– ORIGIN Middle English: from Latin *profundus* 'deep', from *pro* 'before' + *fundus* 'bottom'.

profundity ■ n. (pl. **-ies**) 1 great depth of insight or knowledge. 2 great depth or intensity of a state, quality, or emotion.

profuse ■ adj. plentiful; abundant.
– DERIVATIVES **profusely** adv. **profuseness** n. **profusion** n.
– ORIGIN Middle English: from Latin *profusus* 'lavish, spread out', from *profundere*, from *pro-* 'forth' + *fundere* 'pour'.

prog informal ■ n. a television or radio programme. ■ adj. (of rock music) progressive.

progenitor /prə(ʊ)ˈdʒɛnɪtə/ ■ n. 1 an ancestor or parent. 2 the originator of an artistic, political, or intellectual movement.
– ORIGIN Middle English: from Latin *progenitor*, from *progignere*, from *pro-* 'forward' + *gignere* 'beget'.

progeny /ˈprɒdʒ(ə)ni/ ■ n. [treated as sing. or pl.] offspring.
– ORIGIN Middle English: from Old French *progenie*, from Latin *progenies*, from *progignere* (see **PROGENITOR**).

progesterone /prəˈdʒɛstərəʊn/ ■ n. Biochemistry a steroid hormone released by the corpus luteum that stimulates the uterus to prepare for pregnancy.
– ORIGIN 1930s: blend of **PROGESTIN** and the German synonym *Luteosteron* (from **CORPUS LUTEUM** + **STEROL**).

progestin /prə(ʊ)ˈdʒɛstɪn/ ■ n. Biochemistry another term for **PROGESTOGEN**.
– ORIGIN 1930s: from **PRO-**[1] + **GESTATION**.

progestogen /prə(ʊ)ˈdʒɛstədʒ(ə)n/ ■ n. Biochemistry a steroid hormone that maintains pregnancy and prevents further ovulation.

prognathous /ˈprɒɡˌneɪθəs, prɒɡˈnæθəs/ ■ adj. having a projecting lower jaw or chin. ▸ (of a jaw or chin) projecting.
– DERIVATIVES **prognathic** /prɒɡˈnæθɪk/ adj. **prognathism** n.
– ORIGIN C19: from **PRO-**[2] + Greek *gnathos* 'jaw'.

prognosis /prɒɡˈnəʊsɪs/ ■ n. (pl. **prognoses** /-siːz/) a forecast, especially of the likely course of a disease or ailment.
– ORIGIN C17: from Greek *prognōsis*, from *pro-* 'before' + *gignōskein* 'know'.

prognostic /prɒɡˈnɒstɪk/ ■ adj. predicting the likely course of a disease or ailment.

– ORIGIN Middle English: from Greek *prognōstikos*, from *prognōsis* (see **PROGNOSIS**).

prognosticate ■ v. foretell; prophesy.
– DERIVATIVES **prognostication** n. **prognosticator** n.

prograde /ˈprəʊɡreɪd/ ■ adj. 1 Astronomy proceeding from west to east; direct. The opposite of **RETROGRADE**. 2 Geology (of metamorphism) resulting from an increase in temperature or pressure. ■ v. Geology (of a coastline) advance towards the sea as a result of accumulation of sediment.
– ORIGIN C20: from **PRO-**[1] + **RETROGRADE**.

programmatic ■ adj. 1 of the nature of or according to a programme, schedule, or method. 2 of the nature of programme music.
– DERIVATIVES **programmatically** adv.

programme (US **program**) ■ n. 1 a planned series of events. ▸ a set of related measures or activities with a long-term aim. 2 a sheet or booklet detailing items or performers at an event. 3 a radio or television broadcast. 4 (**program**) a series of coded software instructions to control the operation of a computer or other machine. ■ v. (**programmed**, **programming**; US **programed**, **programing**) 1 (**program**) provide (a computer or other machine) with a program. ▸ input (instructions) into a computer or other machine. 2 cause to behave in a predetermined way. 3 arrange according to a plan or schedule. ▸ plan; schedule.
– DERIVATIVES **programmability** n. **programmable** adj. **programming** n.
– ORIGIN C17: from Greek *programma*, from *prographein* 'write publicly', from *pro* 'before' + *graphein* 'write'.

programme music ■ n. music intended to evoke images or tell a story. Compare with **ABSOLUTE MUSIC**.

programmer ■ n. 1 a person who writes computer programs. 2 a device controlling the operation of something according to a prescribed programme.

progress ■ n. 1 forward or onward movement towards a destination. 2 development towards a better, more complete, or more modern condition. ■ v. 1 move or develop towards a destination or an improved or advanced condition. 2 [usu. as adj. **progressed**] Astrology calculate the position of (a planet) or of all the planets and coordinates of (a chart).
– ORIGIN Middle English: from Latin *progressus* 'an advance', from *progredi*, from *pro-* 'forward' + *gradi* 'to walk'.

progression ■ n. 1 a gradual movement or development towards a destination or a more advanced state. ▸ a succession. ▸ Music a passage or movement from one note or chord to another. 2 a sequence of numbers following a mathematical rule. 3 Astrology a predictive technique in which the daily movement of the planets represents a year in the subject's life.

progressive ■ adj. 1 proceeding gradually or in stages: *a progressive decline in popularity*. ▸ (of a disease or ailment) increasing in severity. ▸ (of tax) increasing as a proportion of the sum taxed as that sum increases. 2 (of a card game or dance) involving a series of sections for which participants successively change place. 3 favouring social reform. ▸ favouring change or innovation. 4 Grammar denoting an aspect or tense of a verb expressing an action in progress, e.g. *am writing*. ■ n. a person advocating social reform.
– DERIVATIVES **progressively** adv. **progressiveness** n. **progressivism** n. **progressivist** n. & adj.

proguanil /prəʊˈɡwɑːnɪl/ ■ n. Medicine a bitter-tasting synthetic compound used in the prevention and treatment of malaria.
– ORIGIN 1940s: from *pro(pyl)* + *(bi)guan(ide)*.

prohibit ■ v. (**prohibited**, **prohibiting**) 1 formally forbid by law, rule, etc. 2 prevent.
– DERIVATIVES **prohibitory** adj.
– ORIGIN Middle English: from Latin *prohibit-*, *prohibere* 'keep in check', from *pro-* 'in front' + *habere* 'to hold'.

prohibited degrees ■ pl. n. another term for the forbidden degrees (see **FORBID**).

prohibition /ˌprəʊhɪˈbɪʃ(ə)n, prəʊɪ-/ ■ n. 1 the action of prohibiting. 2 English Law a writ from a superior court

prohibitive

forbidding an inferior court from proceeding in a suit deemed to be beyond its cognizance. **3 (Prohibition)** the prevention by law of the manufacture and sale of alcohol, especially in the US from 1920–1933.
– DERIVATIVES **prohibitionary** adj. **Prohibitionist** n.
– ORIGIN Middle English: from Latin *prohibitio(n-)*, from *prohibere* (see PROHIBIT).

prohibitive ■ adj. **1** serving to forbid, restrict, or prevent. **2** (of a price or charge) excessively high.
– DERIVATIVES **prohibitively** adv.
– ORIGIN Middle English: from French *prohibitif, -ive* or Latin *prohibitivus*, from *prohibere* (see PROHIBIT).

project ■ n. **1** an enterprise carefully planned to achieve a particular aim. ▶ a proposed or planned undertaking. **2** a piece of research work by a schoolchild or student. **3** (also **housing project**) a government-subsidized estate or block of homes. ■ v. **1** estimate or forecast on the basis of present trends. ▶ [often as adj. **projected**] plan. **2** protrude. **3** throw or cause to move forward or outward. ▶ cause (light, shadow, or an image) to fall on a surface. ▶ cause (a sound) to be heard at a distance. **4** present or promote. ▶ display (an emotion or quality) in one's behaviour. **5** (**project something on to**) attribute an emotion to (another person), especially unconsciously. **6** Geometry draw straight lines through (a given figure) to produce a corresponding figure on a surface or line. **7** represent (the earth's surface, the heavens, etc.) on a plane surface.
– ORIGIN Middle English: from Latin *projectum* 'something prominent', from *proicere*, from *pro-* 'forth' + *jacere* 'to throw'.

projectile ■ n. a missile fired or thrown at a target. ■ adj. **1** of or relating to a projectile. **2** propelled with great force.
– ORIGIN C17: from *project-*, from *proicere* (see PROJECT).

projection ■ n. **1** an estimate or forecast based on present trends. **2** the projecting of an image, sound, etc. **3** the presentation or promotion of someone or something in a particular way. ▶ a mental image viewed as reality. **4** the unconscious transfer of one's own desires or emotions to another person. **5** a protruding thing. **6** a map or diagram made by projecting a given figure, area, etc.
– DERIVATIVES **projectionist** n.

projective ■ adj. **1** Geometry relating to or derived by projection. ▶ (of a property) unchanged by projection. **2** Psychology relating to the projection of desires or emotions.
– DERIVATIVES **projectively** adv.

projective geometry ■ n. the study of the projective properties of geometric figures.

projector ■ n. a device used to project rays of light, especially an apparatus for projecting slides or film on to a screen.

prokaryote /prəʊˈkarɪəʊt, -ɒt/ (also **procaryote**) ■ n. Biology a single-celled organism with neither a distinct nucleus with a membrane nor other specialized structures (i.e. a bacterium or archaean). Compare with EUKARYOTE.
– DERIVATIVES **prokaryotic** adj.
– ORIGIN 1960s: from PRO-² + Greek *karuon* 'nut, kernel' + *-ote* as in ZYGOTE.

prolactin /prəʊˈlaktɪn/ ■ n. Biochemistry a hormone from the anterior pituitary gland stimulating milk production after childbirth.
– ORIGIN 1930s: from PRO-² + LACTATION.

prolapse ■ n. /ˈprəʊlaps, prəˈlaps/ a slipping forward or down of a part or organ of the body. ▶ a prolapsed part or organ. ■ v. /prəʊˈlaps/ [usu. as adj. **prolapsed**] (of a part or organ of the body) slip forward or down.
– ORIGIN C18: from Latin *prolaps-, prolabi*, from *pro-* 'forward, down' + *labi* 'to slip'.

prolapsed disc (also **prolapsed intervertebral disc**) ■ n. another term for SLIPPED DISC.

prolate /ˈprəʊleɪt/ ■ adj. Geometry (of a spheroid) lengthened in the direction of a polar diameter.
– ORIGIN C17: from Latin *prolatus* 'carried forward', from *proferre* 'prolong', from *pro-* 'forward' + *ferre* 'carry'.

prole informal, derogatory ■ n. a member of the working class. ■ adj. working class.

– ORIGIN C19: abbrev. of PROLETARIAT.

proleg ■ n. Entomology a fleshy abdominal limb of a caterpillar or similar insect larva.

proletarian /ˌprəʊlɪˈtɛːrɪən/ ■ adj. of or relating to the proletariat. ■ n. a member of the proletariat.
– DERIVATIVES **proletarianism** n. **proletarianization** (also **-isation**) n. **proletarianize** (also **-ise**) v.
– ORIGIN C17: from Latin *proletarius*, from *proles* 'offspring', denoting a person without wealth, serving the state only by producing offspring.

proletariat ■ n. [treated as sing. or pl.] **1** workers or working-class people (often used with reference to Marxism). **2** the lowest class of citizens in ancient Rome.
– ORIGIN C19: from French *prolétariat*, from Latin *proletarius* (see PROLETARIAN).

pro-life ■ adj. seeking to ban abortion and euthanasia.
– DERIVATIVES **pro-lifer** n.

proliferate /prəˈlɪfəreɪt/ ■ v. reproduce rapidly; increase rapidly in number.
– DERIVATIVES **proliferative** adj. **proliferator** n.
– ORIGIN C19: back-formation from PROLIFERATION.

proliferation ■ n. rapid reproduction or increase in numbers. ▶ a large number of something.
– ORIGIN C19: from French *prolifération*, from *prolifère* 'proliferous'.

prolific ■ adj. **1** producing much fruit or foliage or many offspring. **2** (of an artist, author, etc.) producing many works. **3** plentiful.
– DERIVATIVES **prolificacy** n. **prolifically** adv. **prolificness** n.
– ORIGIN C17: from medieval Latin *prolificus*, from Latin *proles* 'offspring'.

proline /ˈprəʊliːn/ ■ n. Biochemistry an amino acid which is a constituent of most proteins, especially collagen.
– ORIGIN C20: contraction of the chemical name *p(yr)rol(id)ine-2-carboxylic acid*.

prolix /ˈprəʊlɪks, prəˈlɪks/ ■ adj. (of speech or writing) tediously lengthy.
– DERIVATIVES **prolixity** n. **prolixly** adv.
– ORIGIN Middle English: from Latin *prolixus* 'poured forth, extended', from *pro-* 'outward' + *liquere* 'be liquid'.

prologue (US **prolog**) ■ n. **1** a separate introductory section of a literary or musical work. ▶ an introductory scene in a play. **2** an event or action leading to another.
– ORIGIN Middle English: from Greek *prologos*, from *pro-* 'before' + *logos* 'saying'.

prolong ■ v. **1** extend the duration of. **2** technical extend in spatial length.
– DERIVATIVES **prolongation** n.
– ORIGIN Middle English: from Old French *prolonguer*, from late Latin *prolongare*, from *pro-* 'forward, onward' + *longus* 'long'.

prolonged ■ adj. lengthy.
– DERIVATIVES **prolongedly** adv.

prom ■ n. informal **1** Brit. short for PROMENADE (in sense 1). **2** (also **Prom**) Brit. a promenade concert. **3** N. Amer. a formal dance, especially one at a high school or college.

promenade /ˌprɒməˈnɑːd, -ˈneɪd, ˈprɒm-/ ■ n. **1** a paved public walk, especially one along a seafront. **2** a leisurely walk, ride, or drive, typically in a public place so as to meet or be seen by others. **3** (in country dancing) a movement resembling a march made by couples in formation. ■ v. take a promenade. ▶ dated escort (someone) about a place, especially for display.
– ORIGIN C16: from French, from *se promener* 'to walk', from *promener* 'take for a walk'.

promenade concert ■ n. Brit. a concert of classical music at which part of the audience stands in an area without seating, for which tickets are sold at a reduced price.

promenade deck ■ n. an upper, open-air deck on a passenger ship.

promenader ■ n. **1** a person who takes a promenade. **2** Brit. a person standing at a promenade concert.

Promethean /prəˈmiːθɪən/ ■ adj. daring or skilful like Prometheus, a demigod in Greek mythology who stole fire from the gods and gave it to the human race.

promethium /prəˈmiːθɪəm/ ■ n. the chemical element of

atomic number 61, an unstable radioactive metal of the lanthanide series. (Symbol: **Pm**)
– ORIGIN 1940s: from the name of *Prometheus* (see **PROMETHEAN**).

prominence ■ n. **1** the state of being prominent. **2** a thing that projects from something. ▸ Astronomy a stream of incandescent gas projecting above the sun's chromosphere.

prominent ■ adj. **1** important; famous. **2** protuberant. **3** particularly noticeable. ■ n. (also **prominent moth**) a drab-coloured moth with tufts on the forewings which stick up while it is at rest. [Family Notodontidae: many species.]
– DERIVATIVES **prominency** n. **prominently** adv.
– ORIGIN Middle English: from Latin *prominent-*, *prominere* 'jut out'.

promiscuous /prə'mɪskjʊəs/ ■ adj. **1** having or characterized by many transient sexual relationships. **2** indiscriminate or casual. ▸ wide-ranging; unselective.
– DERIVATIVES **promiscuity** n. **promiscuously** adv. **promiscuousness** n.
– ORIGIN C17: from Latin *promiscuus* 'indiscriminate', from *miscere* 'to mix'.

promise ■ n. **1** an assurance that one will do something or that something will happen. ▸ an indication that something is likely to occur: *the promise of spring*. **2** potential excellence. ■ v. **1** make a promise. ▸ (**be promised**) archaic be pledged to marry. **2** give good grounds for expecting. **3** (**promise oneself**) firmly intend.
– PHRASES **on a promise** informal confidently assured of something.
– DERIVATIVES **promiser** n.
– ORIGIN Middle English: from Latin *promissum* 'something promised', from *promittere* 'put forth, promise', from *pro-* 'forward' + *mittere* 'send'.

promised land ■ n. **1** (**the Promised Land**) (in the Bible) the land of Canaan, promised to Abraham and his descendants (Genesis 12:7). **2** a place or situation where great happiness is expected.

promisee ■ n. Law a person to whom a promise is made.

promising ■ adj. showing great potential.
– DERIVATIVES **promisingly** adv.

promisor ■ n. Law a person who makes a promise.

promissory /'prɒmɪs(ə)ri/ ■ adj. chiefly Law conveying or implying a promise.
– ORIGIN Middle English: from medieval Latin *promissorius*, from *promittere* (see **PROMISE**).

promissory note ■ n. a signed document containing a written promise to pay a stated sum to a specified person or the bearer at a specified date or on demand.

promo /'prəʊməʊ/ ■ n. (pl. **-os**) informal a promotional film, video, etc.

promontory /'prɒm(ə)nt(ə)ri/ ■ n. (pl. **-ies**) **1** a point of high land jutting out into the sea or a lake. **2** Anatomy a protuberance on an organ or other bodily structure.
– ORIGIN C16: from Latin *promontorium*, var. (influenced by *mons* 'mountain') of *promunturium*.

promote ■ v. **1** further the progress of; support or encourage. ▸ publicize. **2** raise to a higher position or rank. **3** Chemistry (of an additive) increase the activity of (a catalyst). **4** Chess exchange (a pawn) for a more powerful piece when it reaches the opponent's end of the board.
– DERIVATIVES **promotability** n. **promotable** adj. **promoter** n. **promotive** adj.
– ORIGIN Middle English: from Latin *promovere* 'move forward', from *pro-* 'forward, onward' + *movere* 'to move'.

promotion ■ n. **1** activity that supports or encourages. **2** the publicizing of a product or venture so as to increase sales or public awareness; a publicity campaign. ▸ (**promotions**) the activity or business of organizing such publicity. **3** the action of raising someone to a higher position or rank or the fact of being so raised. ▸ the transfer of a sports team to a higher division of a league.
– DERIVATIVES **promotional** adj.

prompt ■ v. **1** cause or bring about. ▸ (**prompt someone to/to do something**) cause someone to take a course of action. **2** assist or encourage (a hesitating speaker). ▸ supply a forgotten word or line to (an actor). ■ n. **1** an act of prompting a hesitating speaker. ▸ a word or phrase used in prompting an actor. ▸ a prompter. **2** Computing a word or symbol on a VDU screen to show that input is required. ■ adj. done or acting without delay. ▸ arriving precisely at a pre-arranged time. ▸ (of goods) for immediate delivery and payment. ■ adv. Brit. exactly (with reference to a specified time).
– DERIVATIVES **prompting** n. **promptitude** n. **promptly** adv. **promptness** n.
– ORIGIN Middle English: from Old French *prompt* or Latin *promptus* 'brought to light', also 'prepared, ready', from *promere* 'to produce', from *pro-* 'out, forth' + *emere* 'take'.

prompt book ■ n. an annotated copy of a play used by a prompter.

prompter ■ n. a person who prompts the actors during the performance of a play.

promulgate /'prɒm(ə)lɡeɪt/ ■ v. promote or make widely known. ▸ put (a law or decree) into effect by official proclamation.
– DERIVATIVES **promulgation** n. **promulgator** n.
– ORIGIN C16 (*promulgation* C15): from Latin *promulgare*, from *pro-* 'out, publicly' + *mulgere* 'cause to come forth' (literally 'to milk').

prone ■ adj. **1** (**prone to**) likely or liable to suffer from, do, or experience (something unfortunate). **2** lying flat, especially face downwards. ▸ with the palm of the hand facing downwards.
– DERIVATIVES **proneness** n.
– ORIGIN Middle English: from Latin *pronus* 'leaning forward', from *pro* 'forwards'.

prong ■ n. **1** each of two or more projecting pointed parts on a fork or other device. **2** each of the separate parts of an attack or operation. ■ v. pierce or stab with a fork.
– DERIVATIVES **-pronged** adj.
– ORIGIN C15: perhaps rel. to Middle Low German *prange* 'pinching instrument'.

pronk ■ v. (of an antelope, especially a springbok) leap in the air with an arched back and stiff legs. ■ n. an instance of pronking.
– ORIGIN C19: from Afrikaans, 'show off', from Dutch *pronken* 'to strut'.

pronominal /prəʊ'nɒmɪn(ə)l/ ■ adj. of, relating to, or serving as a pronoun.
– DERIVATIVES **pronominalization** (also **-isation**) n. **pronominalize** (also **-ise**) v. **pronominally** adv.
– ORIGIN C17: from late Latin *pronominalis* 'belonging to a pronoun', from Latin *pronomen* (see **PRONOUN**).

pronoun ■ n. a word used instead of a noun to indicate someone or something already mentioned or known, e.g. *I, she, this*.
– ORIGIN Middle English: from **PRO-**[1] + **NOUN**, suggested by Latin *pronomen*, from *pro-* 'for, in place of' + *nomen* 'name'.

pronounce /prə'naʊns/ ■ v. **1** make the sound of (a word or part of a word). **2** declare or announce. ▸ (**pronounce on**) pass judgement or make a decision on.
– DERIVATIVES **pronounceability** n. **pronounceable** adj. **pronouncer** n.
– ORIGIN Middle English: from Old French *pronuncier*, from Latin *pronuntiare*, from *pro-* 'out, forth' + *nuntiare* 'announce', from *nuntius* 'messenger'.

pronounced ■ adj. very noticeable.
– DERIVATIVES **pronouncedly** adv.

pronouncement ■ n. a formal or authoritative announcement or declaration.

pronto ■ adv. informal promptly.
– ORIGIN C20: from Spanish.

pronunciation /prənʌnsɪ'eɪʃ(ə)n/ ■ n. the way in which a word is pronounced.

> USAGE
>
> The word **pronunciation** is often pronounced, by analogy with **pronounce**, as if the second syllable rhymed with **bounce**. This is not correct in standard English: the standard pronunciation has the second syllable rhyming with **dunce**.

pro-nuncio /prəʊ'nʌnsɪəʊ, -ʃɪəʊ/ ■ n. (pl. **-os**) a papal ambassador to a country that does not accord the Pope's

proof

ambassador automatic precedence.
– ORIGIN 1960s: from Italian *pro-nunzio*, from *pro-* 'before' + *nunzio* 'nuncio'.

proof ■ n. **1** evidence establishing a fact or the truth of a statement. ▶ Law the evidence in a trial. ▶ the proving of the truth of a statement. **2** a series of stages in the resolution of a mathematical or philosophical problem. **3** Printing a trial impression of a page used for making corrections before final printing. ▶ a trial photographic print. ▶ each of a limited number of impressions from an engraved plate, especially before the ordinary issue is printed. ▶ a specially struck specimen coin with a polished or frosted finish. **4** the strength of distilled alcoholic liquor, relative to proof spirit taken as a standard of 100. ■ adj. [often in combination] resistant: *bulletproof*. ■ v. **1** make waterproof. **2** make a proof of (a printed work, engraving, etc.). ▶ proof-read (a text). **3** N. Amer. activate (yeast). ▶ knead (dough) until light and smooth. ▶ (of dough) prove.
– ORIGIN Middle English *preve*, from Old French *proeve*, from late Latin *proba*, from Latin *probare* 'to test, prove'.

proof positive ■ n. final or absolute proof of something.

proof-read ■ v. read (printer's proofs or other material) and mark any errors.
– DERIVATIVES **proof-reader** n.

proof sheet ■ n. Printing a proof.

proof spirit ■ n. a mixture of alcohol and water containing 57.1 per cent alcohol by volume, used as a standard of strength of distilled alcoholic liquor.

prop[1] ■ n. **1** a pole or beam used as a temporary support. **2** a major source of support or assistance. **3** (also **prop forward**) Rugby a forward at either end of the front row of a scrum. ■ v. (**propped**, **propping**) **1** support with or as with a prop. ▶ lean against something else. **2** (**prop someone/thing up**) support or assist someone or something that would otherwise fail or decline.
– ORIGIN Middle English: prob. from Middle Dutch *proppe* 'support (for vines)'.

prop[2] ■ n. a portable object used on the set of a play or film.
– ORIGIN C19: abbrev. of PROPERTY.

prop[3] ■ n. informal an aircraft propeller.

prop. ■ abbrev. **1** proposition. **2** proprietor.

propaganda ■ n. information, especially of a biased or misleading nature, used to promote a political cause or point of view. ▶ the dissemination of such information.
– ORIGIN Italian, from modern Latin *congregatio de propaganda fide* 'congregation for propagation of the faith'.

propagandist chiefly derogatory ■ n. a person who disseminates propaganda. ■ adj. consisting of or spreading propaganda.
– DERIVATIVES **propagandism** n. **propagandistic** adj. **propagandistically** adv. **propagandize** (also **-ise**) v.

propagate ■ v. **1** breed by natural processes from the parent stock. ▶ cause to increase in number or amount. **2** promote (an idea, knowledge, etc.) widely. **3** transmit or be transmitted in a particular direction.
– DERIVATIVES **propagation** n. **propagative** adj.
– ORIGIN Middle English: from Latin *propagare* 'multiply from layers or shoots'; rel. to *propago* 'young shoot'.

propagator ■ n. **1** a covered, heated container of earth or compost, used for germinating seedlings. **2** a person who propagates an idea, knowledge, etc.

propagule /'prɒpəgjuːl/ ■ n. Botany a detachable structure that can give rise to a new plant, e.g. a bud, sucker, or spore.
– ORIGIN C19: diminutive of Latin *propago* 'shoot, runner'.

propane /'prəʊpeɪn/ ■ n. Chemistry a flammable hydrocarbon gas of the alkane series, present in natural gas and used as bottled fuel. [C_3H_8].
– ORIGIN C19: from *propionic acid*, a fatty acid + -ANE[2].

propel ■ v. (**propelled**, **propelling**) drive or push forwards. ▶ drive into a particular situation.
– ORIGIN Middle English: from Latin *propellere*, from *pro-* 'forward' + *pellere* 'to drive'.

propellant ■ n. **1** an inert fluid, liquefied under pressure, in which the active contents of an aerosol are dispersed. **2** an explosive that fires bullets from a firearm. **3** a substance used as a reagent in a rocket engine to provide thrust. ■ adj. variant of PROPELLENT.
– ORIGIN C17: orig. from Latin *propellere* 'drive ahead (of oneself)'.

propellent ■ adj. capable of propelling something.

propeller ■ n. a revolving shaft with two or more broad, angled blades, for propelling a ship or aircraft.

propeller shaft ■ n. a shaft transmitting power from an engine to a propeller or to the wheels of a vehicle.

propeller turbine ■ n. a turboprop.

propensity ■ n. (pl. **-ies**) an inclination or tendency.
– ORIGIN C16: from archaic *propense*, from Latin *propendere*, from *pro-* 'forward, down' + *pendere* 'hang'.

proper ■ adj. **1** truly what something is said or regarded to be; genuine: *she's never had a proper job.* ▶ [postpos.] strictly so called: *the World Cup proper.* **2** suitable or appropriate; correct. ▶ respectable. **3** (**proper to**) belonging or relating exclusively to. ▶ (of a psalm, prayer, etc.) appointed for a particular day or occasion. ▶ archaic belonging to oneself. **4** [usu. postpos.] Heraldry in the natural colours. **5** archaic or dialect good-looking. ■ adv. Brit. informal or dialect correctly. ▶ thoroughly.
– DERIVATIVES **properness** n.
– ORIGIN Middle English: from Old French *propre*, from Latin *proprius* 'one's own, special'.

proper fraction ■ n. a fraction that is less than one, with the numerator less than the denominator.

properly ■ adv. **1** correctly. ▶ suitably; respectably. **2** in the strict sense. **3** informal, chiefly Brit. completely.

proper noun (also **proper name**) ■ n. a name for an individual person, place, or organization, having an initial capital letter. Often contrasted with COMMON NOUN.

propertied ■ adj. owning property and land.

property ■ n. (pl. **-ies**) **1** a thing or things belonging to someone. **2** a building and the land belonging to it. ▶ (**properties**) shares or investments in property. **3** Law ownership. **4** a characteristic of something. **5** old-fashioned term for PROP[2].
– ORIGIN Middle English: from a var. of Old French *propriete*, from Latin *proprietas*, from *proprius* (see PROPER).

property qualification ■ n. chiefly historical a qualification for office or for the exercise of a right, based on the ownership of property.

prop forward ■ n. see PROP[1] (sense 3).

prophase ■ n. Biology the first stage of cell division, before metaphase, during which the chromosomes become visible as paired chromatids.
– ORIGIN C19: from PRO-[2] + PHASE.

prophecy /'prɒfɪsi/ ■ n. (pl. **-ies**) a prediction. ▶ the faculty or practice of prophesying.
– ORIGIN Middle English: from Old French *profecie*, from Greek *prophēteia*, from *prophētēs* (see PROPHET).

prophesy /'prɒfɪsʌɪ/ ■ v. (**-ies**, **-ied**) **1** predict. **2** speak or write by divine inspiration.
– DERIVATIVES **prophesier** n.
– ORIGIN Middle English: from Old French *profecier*, from *profecie* (see PROPHECY); the different spellings of *prophesy* and *prophecy* were established after 1700.

prophet ■ n. (fem. **prophetess**) **1** an inspired teacher or proclaimer of the will of God. ▶ (**the Prophet**) (among Muslims) Muhammad. ▶ (**the Prophet**) (among Mormons) Joseph Smith or one of his successors. **2** a person who predicts the future. ▶ a person who advocates a new belief or theory. **3** (**the Prophets**) (in Christian use) the prophetic writings of the Old Testament. ▶ (in Jewish use) one of the three canonical divisions of the Hebrew Bible.
– DERIVATIVES **prophethood** n.
– ORIGIN Middle English: from Old French *prophete*, from Greek *prophētēs* 'spokesman', from *pro* 'before' + *phētēs* 'speaker', from *phēnai* 'speak'.

prophetic /prə'fɛtɪk/ ■ adj. **1** accurately predicting the future. **2** of, relating to, or characteristic of a prophet or prophecy.
– DERIVATIVES **prophetical** adj. **prophetically** adv.

prophylactic /ˌprɒfɪ'laktɪk/ ■ adj. intended to prevent

disease. ■ n. **1** a preventative medicine or course of action. **2** chiefly N. Amer. a condom.
– DERIVATIVES **prophylactically** adv.
– ORIGIN C16: from Greek *prophulaktikos*, from *pro* 'before' + *phulassein* 'to guard'.

prophylaxis /ˌprɒfɪˈlaksɪs/ ■ n. action taken to prevent disease.
– ORIGIN C19: from **PRO-²** + Greek *phulaxis* 'act of guarding'.

propinquity /prəˈpɪŋkwɪti/ ■ n. proximity.
– ORIGIN Middle English: from Old French *propinquité*, from Latin *propinquitas*, from *propinquus* 'near'.

propitiate /prəˈpɪʃɪeɪt/ ■ v. appease.
– DERIVATIVES **propitiator** n. **propitiatory** adj.
– ORIGIN C16: from Latin *propitiat-*, *propitiare* 'make favourable', from *propitius* (see **PROPITIOUS**).

propitiation ■ n. **1** appeasement. **2** Christian Church atonement, especially that of Christ.
– ORIGIN Middle English: from late Latin *propitiatio(n-)*, from *propitiare* (see **PROPITIATE**).

propitious /prəˈpɪʃəs/ ■ adj. favourable.
– DERIVATIVES **propitiously** adv. **propitiousness** n.
– ORIGIN Middle English: from Old French *propicieus* or Latin *propitius* 'favourable, gracious'.

prop jet ■ n. a turboprop aircraft or engine.

propolis /ˈprɒp(ə)lɪs/ ■ n. a red or brown resinous substance collected by honeybees from tree buds for constructing and varnishing honeycombs.
– ORIGIN C17: from Greek *propolis* 'suburb', also 'bee glue', from *pro* 'before' + *polis* 'city'.

proponent /prəˈpəʊnənt/ ■ n. a person who advocates a theory, proposal, or project.
– ORIGIN C16: from Latin *proponere* (see **PROPOUND**).

proportion ■ n. **1** a part, share, or number considered in relation to a whole. ▸ the ratio of one thing to another. ▸ the correct or pleasing relation of things or between the parts of a whole. **2** (**proportions**) dimensions; size.
■ v. formal adjust so as to have a particular or suitable relationship to something else.
– PHRASES **in** (or **out of**) **proportion** according (or not according) to a particular relationship in size, amount, or degree. ▸ regarded without (or with) exaggeration. **sense of proportion** the ability to judge the relative importance of things.
– DERIVATIVES **proportioned** adj. **proportionless** adj.
– ORIGIN Middle English: from Latin *proportio(n-)*, from *pro portione* 'in respect of (its or a person's) share'.

proportional ■ adj. **1** corresponding in size or amount to something else. **2** Mathematics (of a variable quantity) having a constant ratio to another quantity.
– DERIVATIVES **proportionality** n. **proportionally** adv.

proportional representation ■ n. an electoral system in which parties gain seats in proportion to the number of votes cast for them.

proportionate ■ adj. another term for **PROPORTIONAL**.
– DERIVATIVES **proportionately** adv.

proposal ■ n. **1** a plan or suggestion. ▸ the action of proposing something. **2** an offer of marriage.

propose ■ v. **1** put forward (an idea or plan) for consideration by others. ▸ nominate for an office or position. ▸ put forward (a motion) to a legislature or committee. **2** make an offer of marriage to someone.
– DERIVATIVES **proposer** n.
– ORIGIN Middle English: from Old French *proposer*, from Latin *proponere* (see **PROPOUND**).

proposition ■ n. **1** a statement expressing a judgement or opinion. ▸ Logic a statement expressing a concept that can be true or false. ▸ Mathematics a formal statement of a theorem or problem. **2** a proposed scheme or plan. **3** informal an offer of sexual intercourse. **4** a matter or person to be dealt with, with reference to the likelihood of a successful outcome. ■ v. informal make an offer, especially of sexual intercourse, to.
– DERIVATIVES **propositional** adj.
– ORIGIN Middle English: from Latin *propositio(n-)*, from *proponere* (see **PROPOUND**).

propound /prəˈpaʊnd/ ■ v. put forward (an idea, theory, etc.) for consideration.
– DERIVATIVES **propounder** n.
– ORIGIN C16: from Latin *proponere* 'set forth', from *pro-* 'forward' + *ponere* 'put'.

propranolol /prəʊˈpranəlɒl/ ■ n. Medicine a synthetic beta blocker used mainly to treat cardiac arrhythmia.
– ORIGIN 1960s: from *pro(pyl)* + *pr(op)anol*, with the reduplication of *-ol*.

proprietary ■ adj. **1** of, relating to, or characteristic of an owner or ownership. **2** (of a product) marketed under a registered trade name.
– ORIGIN Middle English: from late Latin *proprietarius* 'proprietor', from *proprietas* (see **PROPERTY**).

proprietary name (also **proprietary term**) ■ n. a name of a product or service registered as a trademark.

proprietor ■ n. (fem. **proprietress**) **1** the owner of a business. **2** a holder of property.
– DERIVATIVES **proprietorship** n.

proprietorial /prəˌprʌɪəˈtɔːrɪəl/ ■ adj. behaving as if one owned someone or something; possessive.
– DERIVATIVES **proprietorially** adv.

propriety ■ n. (pl. **-ies**) correctness concerning standards of behaviour or morals. ▸ (**proprieties**) the details or rules of conventionally accepted behaviour. ▸ appropriateness; rightness.
– ORIGIN Middle English: from Old French *propriete*, from Latin *proprietas* (see **PROPERTY**).

proprioceptive /ˌprəʊprɪə(ʊ)ˈsɛptɪv/ ■ adj. Physiology of or denoting stimuli produced and perceived within an organism, especially those relating to position and movement of the body.
– DERIVATIVES **proprioception** n. **proprioceptor** n.
– ORIGIN C20: from Latin *proprius* 'own' + **RECEPTIVE**.

propshaft ■ n. a propeller shaft.

propulsion ■ n. the action of driving or pushing forward.
– DERIVATIVES **propulsive** adj.
– ORIGIN C17: from medieval Latin *propulsio(n-)*, from Latin *propellere* 'drive before (oneself)'.

propulsor ■ n. a ducted propeller swivelled to give forward, upward, or downward flight to an airship.

propyl /ˈprəʊpʌɪl, -pɪl/ ■ n. [as modifier] Chemistry of or denoting the alkyl radical -C_3H_7, derived from propane: *propyl alcohol*.

propylene /ˈprəʊpɪliːn/ ■ n. Chemistry a gaseous hydrocarbon of the alkene series, made by cracking alkanes. [C_3H_6.]

pro rata /prəʊ ˈrɑːtə, ˈreɪtə/ ■ adj. proportional. ■ adv. proportionally.
– ORIGIN C16: Latin, 'according to the rate'.

prorogue /prəˈrəʊg/ ■ v. (**prorogues**, **prorogued**, **proroguing**) discontinue a session of (a parliament or assembly) without dissolving it.
– DERIVATIVES **prorogation** /-rəˈgeɪʃ(ə)n/ n.
– ORIGIN Middle English: from Latin *prorogare* 'prolong, extend', from *pro-* 'in front of, publicly' + *rogare* 'ask'.

prosaic /prə(ʊ)ˈzeɪɪk/ ■ adj. **1** having the style or diction of prose. **2** commonplace; unromantic.
– DERIVATIVES **prosaically** adv. **prosaicness** n.
– ORIGIN C16: from late Latin *prosaicus*, from Latin *prosa* (see **PROSE**).

prosaist /ˈprəʊzeɪɪst/ ■ n. **1** a person who writes in prose. **2** a prosaic person.
– DERIVATIVES **prosaism** n.
– ORIGIN C19: from French *prosaïste*, from Latin *prosa* (see **PROSE**).

proscenium /prə(ʊ)ˈsiːnɪəm/ ■ n. (pl. **prosceniums** or **proscenia** /-nɪə/) the part of a stage in front of the curtain. ▸ (also **proscenium arch**) an arch framing the opening between the stage and the auditorium. ▸ the stage of an ancient theatre.
– ORIGIN C17: from Greek *proskēnion*, from *pro* 'before' + *skēnē* 'stage'.

prosciutto /prəˈʃuːtəʊ/ ■ n. raw cured Italian ham.
– ORIGIN from Italian.

proscribe ■ v. forbid, especially by law. ▸ denounce or condemn. ▸ historical outlaw (someone).
– DERIVATIVES **proscription** n. **proscriptive** adj.
– ORIGIN Middle English: from Latin *proscribere*, from *pro-* 'in front of' + *scribere* 'write'.

prose

prose ■ n. **1** ordinary written or spoken language, without metrical structure. **2** another term for SEQUENCE (in sense 4). ■ v. talk tediously.
– DERIVATIVES **proser** n.
– ORIGIN Middle English: from Latin *prosa (oratio)* 'straightforward (discourse)', feminine of *prosus*, earlier *prorsus* 'direct'.

Prosecco ■ n. a variety of wine grape grown in the Veneto region of NE Italy. ▸ a sparkling wine made from this grape.
– ORIGIN Italian, prob. from *Prosecco*, a town near Trieste.

prosecute ■ v. **1** institute legal proceedings against. ▸ institute legal proceedings in respect of (a claim or offence). ▸ conduct the case against the party being accused or sued in a lawsuit. **2** continue with a view to completion.
– DERIVATIVES **prosecutable** adj.
– ORIGIN Middle English: from Latin *prosecut-*, *prosequi* 'pursue, accompany', from *pro-* 'onward' + *sequi* 'follow'.

prosecution ■ n. **1** the prosecuting of someone in respect of a criminal charge. ▸ (**the prosecution**) [treated as sing. or pl.] the party prosecuting someone in a lawsuit. **2** the continuation of a course of action with a view to its completion.

prosecutor ■ n. a person, especially a public official, who prosecutes someone. ▸ an advocate or other lawyer who conducts the case against a defendant.
– DERIVATIVES **prosecutorial** adj.

proselyte /ˈprɒsɪlʌɪt/ ■ n. a convert from one opinion, religion, or party to another. ▸ a Gentile who has converted to Judaism.
– DERIVATIVES **proselytism** /-lɪtɪz(ə)m/ n.
– ORIGIN Middle English: from Greek *prosēluthos* 'stranger, convert', from *prosēluth-*, *proserkhesthai* 'approach'.

proselytize /ˈprɒsɪlɪtʌɪz/ (also **-ise**) ■ v. convert from one religion, belief, or opinion to another.
– DERIVATIVES **proselytizer** (also **-iser**) n.

prosimian /prəʊˈsɪmɪən/ ■ n. Zoology a primate of a sub-order (Prosimii) that includes the lemurs, lorises, bushbabies, and tarsiers.
– ORIGIN C19: from PRO-² + SIMIAN.

prosody /ˈprɒsədi/ ■ n. **1** the patterns of rhythm and sound used in poetry. ▸ the study of these patterns. **2** the patterns of stress and intonation in a language.
– DERIVATIVES **prosodic** adj. **prosodist** n.
– ORIGIN C15: from Latin *prosodia* 'accent of a syllable', from Greek *prosōidia* 'song sung to music, tone of a syllable', from *pros* 'towards' + *ōidē* 'song'.

prosopopoeia /ˌprɒsəpəˈpiːə/ ■ n. a figure of speech in which an abstract thing is personified or an imagined or absent person is represented as speaking.
– ORIGIN C16: from Greek *prosōpopoiia*, from *prosōpon* 'person' + *poiein* 'to make'.

prospect ■ n. **1** the possibility or likelihood of some future event occurring. ▸ a mental picture of a future or anticipated event. ▸ (**prospects**) chances or opportunities for success. **2** a person regarded as a potential customer or as likely to be successful. **3** an extensive view of landscape. **4** a place likely to yield mineral deposits. ■ v. search for mineral deposits, especially by means of drilling and excavation.
– DERIVATIVES **prospectless** adj. **prospector** n.
– ORIGIN Middle English: from Latin *prospectus* 'view', from *prospicere* 'look forward'.

prospective ■ adj. expected or likely to happen or be in the future.
– DERIVATIVES **prospectively** adv. **prospectiveness** n.

prospectus ■ n. (pl. **prospectuses**) a printed booklet advertising a school or university or giving details of a share offer.
– ORIGIN C18: from Latin, 'view, prospect', from *prospicere* 'look forward'.

prosper ■ v. succeed or flourish, especially financially; thrive. ▸ poetic/literary make successful.
– ORIGIN Middle English: from Old French *prosperer*, from Latin *prosperare*, from *prosperus* 'doing well'.

prosperous ■ adj. successful or flourishing, especially financially.
– DERIVATIVES **prosperity** n. **prosperously** adv. **prosperousness** n.

prostaglandin /ˌprɒstəˈɡlandɪn/ ■ n. Biochemistry any of a group of compounds with varying hormone-like effects, notably the promotion of uterine contractions.
– ORIGIN 1930s: from PROSTATE + GLAND¹.

prostate ■ n. a gland surrounding the neck of the bladder in male mammals and releasing a fluid component of semen.
– DERIVATIVES **prostatic** adj.
– ORIGIN C17: from Greek *prostatēs* 'one that stands before'.

prosthesis /prɒsˈθiːsɪs, ˈprɒsθɪˌsɪs/ ■ n. (pl. **prostheses** /-siːz/) an artificial body part.
– DERIVATIVES **prosthetic** /-ˈθɛtɪk/ adj. **prosthetically** adv.
– ORIGIN C16: from Greek *prosthesis*, from *prostithenai* 'add'.

prosthetic group ■ n. Biochemistry a non-protein group forming part of or combined with a protein.

prosthetics /prɒsˈθɛtɪks/ ■ pl. n. **1** artificial body parts; prostheses. ▸ pieces of flexible material applied to actors' faces to transform their appearance. **2** [treated as sing.] the branch of surgery concerned with the making and fitting of artificial body parts.
– DERIVATIVES **prosthetist** /ˈprɒsθɪtɪst/ n.

prostitute ■ n. a person, typically a woman, who engages in sexual activity for payment. ■ v. (often **prostitute oneself**) **1** offer (someone) as a prostitute. **2** put to an unworthy or corrupt use for the sake of gain.
– DERIVATIVES **prostitution** n. **prostitutor** n.
– ORIGIN C16: from Latin *prostituere* 'expose publicly, offer for sale'.

prostrate ■ adj. /ˈprɒstreɪt/ **1** lying stretched out on the ground with one's face downwards. **2** completely overcome with distress or exhaustion. **3** Botany growing along the ground. ■ v. /prɒˈstreɪt/ **1** (**prostrate oneself**) throw oneself flat on the ground in reverence or submission. **2** (of distress, exhaustion, or illness) completely overcome (someone).
– DERIVATIVES **prostration** n.
– ORIGIN Middle English: from Latin *prostrat-*, *prosternere* 'throw down'.

prosy /ˈprəʊzi/ ■ adj. (**-ier**, **-iest**) (of speech or writing) showing no imagination; commonplace or dull.
– DERIVATIVES **prosily** adv. **prosiness** n.

prot- ■ comb. form variant spelling of PROTO- before a vowel (as in *protanopia*).

protactinium /ˌprəʊtakˈtɪnɪəm/ ■ n. the chemical element of atomic number 91, a radioactive metal of the actinide series, occurring in small amounts as a product of the natural decay of uranium. (Symbol: **Pa**)
– ORIGIN C20: from PROTO- + ACTINIUM, so named because one of its isotopes decays to form actinium.

protagonist ■ n. **1** the leading character or one of the major characters in a drama, film, or novel. ▸ a prominent figure in a real situation. **2** an advocate or champion of a particular cause or idea.
– ORIGIN C17: from Greek *prōtagōnistēs*, from *prōtos* 'first in importance' + *agōnistēs* 'actor'.

protandrous /prəʊˈtandrəs/ ■ adj. Botany & Zoology (of a hermaphrodite flower or animal) having the male reproductive organs come to maturity before the female. The opposite of PROTOGYNOUS.
– DERIVATIVES **protandry** n.

protanopia /ˌprəʊtəˈnəʊpɪə/ ■ n. colour blindness resulting from insensitivity to red light, causing confusion of greens, reds, and yellows. Compare with DEUTERANOPIA, TRITANOPIA.
– ORIGIN C20: from PROTO- 'original' (red being regarded as the first component of colour vision) + AN-¹ + -OPIA.

protea /ˈprəʊtɪə/ ■ n. a chiefly South African evergreen shrub with large cone-like flower heads surrounded by brightly coloured bracts. [Genus *Protea*: many species.]
– ORIGIN from *Proteus* (see PROTEAN), with ref. to the many species of the genus.

protean /ˈprəʊtiən, prəʊˈtiːən/ ▪ adj. tending or able to change or adapt; variable or versatile.
– ORIGIN C16: from the minor Greek sea god *Proteus* (who was able to change shape at will).

protease /ˈprəʊtieɪz/ ▪ n. Biochemistry an enzyme which breaks down proteins and peptides.
– ORIGIN C20: from PROTEIN.

protect ▪ v. **1** keep safe from harm or injury. ▸ [often as adj. **protected**] aim to preserve (a threatened plant or animal species) by legislating against collecting or hunting. **2** Economics shield (a domestic industry) from competition by imposing import duties on foreign goods. **3** provide funds to meet (a bill of exchange or commercial draft).
– DERIVATIVES **protectable** adj.
– ORIGIN Middle English: from Latin *protect-*, *protegere* 'cover in front'.

protectant ▪ n. a substance that provides protection, e.g. against disease or ultraviolet radiation.

protection ▪ n. **1** the action or state of protecting or being protected. ▸ a person or thing that protects. ▸ a condom. ▸ a document guaranteeing immunity from harm to the person specified in it. **2** the payment of money to criminals to prevent them from attacking oneself or one's property.

protectionism ▪ n. Economics the theory or practice of shielding a country's domestic industries from foreign competition by taxing imports.
– DERIVATIVES **protectionist** n. & adj.

protective ▪ adj. **1** serving, intended, or wishing to protect. **2** Economics of or relating to the protection of domestic industries from foreign competition. ▪ n. Brit. a thing that protects. ▸ dated a condom.
– DERIVATIVES **protectively** adv. **protectiveness** n.

protective custody ▪ n. the detention of a person for their own protection.

protector ▪ n. **1** a person or thing that protects. **2** (**Protector**) historical a regent in charge of a kingdom during the minority, absence, or incapacity of the sovereign.
– DERIVATIVES **protectoral** adj. **protectorship** n. **protectress** n.

protectorate ▪ n. **1** a state that is controlled and protected by another. ▸ the relationship between a state of this kind and the one that controls it. **2** (**Protectorate**) historical the position or office of a Protector.

protégé /ˈprɒtɪʒeɪ, -teʒeɪ, ˈprəʊ-/ ▪ n. (fem. **protégée**) a person who is guided and supported by an older and more experienced or influential person.
– ORIGIN C18: French, 'protected', from *protéger*.

protein ▪ n. any of a class of nitrogenous organic compounds forming structural components of body tissues and constituting an important part of the diet.
– DERIVATIVES **proteinaceous** adj.
– ORIGIN C19: from French *protéine*, German *Protein*, from Greek *prōteios* 'primary'.

proteinuria /ˌprəʊtiːˈnjʊərɪə/ ▪ n. Medicine the presence of abnormal quantities of protein in the urine, possibly indicating damage to the kidneys.

pro tem /prəʊ ˈtɛm/ ▪ adv. & adj. for the time being.
– ORIGIN abbrev. of Latin *pro tempore*.

proteolysis /ˌprəʊtiˈɒlɪsɪs/ ▪ n. Biochemistry the breakdown of proteins or peptides into amino acids by the action of enzymes.
– DERIVATIVES **proteolytic** adj. **proteolytically** adv.

Proterozoic /ˌprəʊt(ə)rəˈzəʊɪk/ ▪ adj. Geology relating to or denoting the later part of the Precambrian aeon (between the Archaean aeon and the Cambrian period, about 2 500 to 570 million years ago), in which the earliest forms of life evolved.
– ORIGIN C20: from Greek *proteros* 'former' + *zōē* 'life', *zōos* 'living'.

protest ▪ n. **1** a statement or action expressing disapproval of or objection to something. ▸ an organized public demonstration objecting to an official policy or course of action. **2** Law a written declaration, typically by a notary public, that a bill has been presented and payment or acceptance refused. ▪ v. **1** express an objection to what someone has said or done. ▸ engage in public protest. **2** make an emphatic declaration or denial in response to an accusation or criticism. **3** Law write or obtain a protest in regard to (a bill).
– DERIVATIVES **protester** n. **protesting** adj. **protestingly** adv. **protestor** n.
– ORIGIN Middle English: from Old French *protester*, from Latin *protestari* 'assert formally', from *testis* 'a witness'.

Protestant /ˈprɒtɪst(ə)nt/ ▪ n. a member or follower of any of the Western Christian Churches that are separate from the Roman Catholic Church in accordance with the principles of the Reformation. ▪ adj. of, relating to, or belonging to any of the Protestant Churches.
– DERIVATIVES **Protestantism** n.
– ORIGIN C16: from Latin *protestant-* 'protesting', from Latin *protestari* (see PROTEST).

Protestant ethic (also **Protestant work ethic**) ▪ n. the view that a person's duty and responsibility is to achieve success through hard work and thrift.

protestation /ˌprɒtɪˈsteɪʃ(ə)n/ ▪ n. an emphatic declaration that something is or is not the case. ▸ an objection or protest.

proteus /ˈprəʊtiəs/ ▪ n. **1** a bacterium found in the intestines of animals and in the soil. [Genus *Proteus*.] **2** another term for OLM.
– ORIGIN C19: from *Proteus* (see PROTEAN).

prothallus /prəʊˈθaləs/ ▪ n. (pl. **prothalli** /-lʌɪ, -liː/) Botany the gametophyte of ferns and related plants.
– DERIVATIVES **prothallial** adj.
– ORIGIN C19: from PRO-² + Greek *thallos* 'green shoot'.

prothrombin /prəʊˈθrɒmbɪn/ ▪ n. Biochemistry a protein present in blood plasma which is converted into active thrombin during coagulation.

Protista /prəʊˈtɪstə/ ▪ pl. n. Biology a kingdom or large grouping of typically single-celled organisms including the protozoans, slime moulds, and simple algae and fungi.
– DERIVATIVES **protist** /ˈprəʊtɪst/ n. **protistan** adj. & n. **protistology** n.
– ORIGIN from Greek *prōtista*, from *prōtistos* 'very first'.

protium /ˈprəʊtiəm/ ▪ n. Chemistry the common, stable isotope of hydrogen, as distinct from deuterium and tritium.
– ORIGIN 1930s: from Greek *prōtos* 'first'.

Proto ▪ n. S. African trademark a type of breathing apparatus that filters out toxic gases and supplies oxygen to the wearer. ▸ [as modifier] denoting a person or team equipped to carry out underground rescue operations.

proto- (usu. **prot-** before a vowel) ▪ comb. form original; primitive: *prototype*. ▸ first; anterior; relating to a precursor: *protozoon*.
– ORIGIN from Greek *prōtos* 'first'.

protoceratops /ˌprəʊtə(ʊ)ˈsɛrətɒps/ ▪ n. a small quadrupedal dinosaur of the late Cretaceous period, having a bony frill above the neck and probably ancestral to triceratops.

protocol ▪ n. **1** the official procedure or system of rules governing affairs of state or diplomatic occasions. ▸ the accepted code of procedure or behaviour in a particular situation. **2** the original draft of a diplomatic document, especially of the terms of a treaty agreed to in conference and signed by the parties. ▸ an amendment to a treaty or convention. **3** a formal record of scientific experimental observations. ▸ a procedure for carrying out a scientific experiment or a course of medical treatment. **4** Computing a set of rules governing the exchange or transmission of data between devices.
– ORIGIN Middle English: from Old French *prothocole*, from Greek *prōtokollon* 'first page, flyleaf'.

protogynous /prəʊˈtɒdʒɪnəs/ ▪ adj. Botany & Zoology (of a hermaphrodite flower or animal) having the female reproductive organs come to maturity before the male. The opposite of PROTANDROUS.
– DERIVATIVES **protogyny** n.

Proto-Indo-European ▪ n. the lost language from which all Indo-European languages derive.

proton /ˈprəʊtɒn/ ▪ n. Physics a stable subatomic particle occurring in all atomic nuclei, with a positive electric charge equal in magnitude to that of an electron.
– DERIVATIVES **protonic** adj.
– ORIGIN 1920s: from Greek, from *prōtos* 'first'.

protonate /ˈprəʊtəneɪt/ ■ v. Chemistry transfer a proton to (a molecule, group, or atom) which forms a coordinate bond to the proton.
– DERIVATIVES **protonation** n.

protoplasm /ˈprəʊtə(ʊ)ˌplaz(ə)m/ ■ n. Biology the colourless material comprising the living part of a cell, including the cytoplasm, nucleus, and other organelles.
– DERIVATIVES **protoplasmic** adj.
– ORIGIN C19: from Greek *prōtoplasma* (see PROTO-, PLASMA).

protoplast /ˈprəʊtə(ʊ)plast, -plɑːst/ ■ n. chiefly Botany the protoplasm of a living plant or bacterial cell whose cell wall has been removed.
– ORIGIN C19: from Greek *prōtoplastos* 'first formed'.

prototype ■ n. 1 a first or preliminary form from which other forms are developed or copied. 2 a typical example of something. ■ v. make a prototype of.
– DERIVATIVES **prototypal** adj. **prototypic** adj. **prototypical** adj. **prototypically** adv.
– ORIGIN C16: from Greek *prōtotupos* (see PROTO-, TYPE).

Protozoa /ˌprəʊtəˈzəʊə/ ■ pl. n. Zoology a phylum or group of phyla comprising the single-celled microscopic animals such as amoebas, flagellates, ciliates, and sporo-zoans.
– DERIVATIVES **protozoal** adj. **protozoan** n. & adj. **protozoic** adj. **protozoon** n.
– ORIGIN from PROTO- + Greek *zōion* 'animal'.

protract ■ v. prolong; draw out.
– DERIVATIVES **protracted** adj. **protractedly** adv. **protractedness** n.
– ORIGIN C16: from Latin *protract-*, *protrahere* 'prolong', from *pro-* 'out' + *trahere* 'to draw'.

protraction ■ n. 1 the action or state of prolonging or being prolonged. 2 the action of extending a part of the body.

protractor ■ n. 1 an instrument for measuring angles, typically in the form of a flat semicircle marked with degrees along the curved edge. 2 chiefly Zoology a muscle serving to extend a part of the body.

protrude ■ v. extend beyond or above a surface. ▸ (of an animal) cause (a body part) to do this.
– DERIVATIVES **protrusible** adj. **protrusion** n. **protrusive** adj.
– ORIGIN C17: from Latin *protrudere*, from *pro-* 'forward, out' + *trudere* 'to thrust'.

protuberance /prəˈtjuːb(ə)r(ə)ns/ ■ n. a thing that protrudes. ▸ the fact or state of protruding.

protuberant ■ adj. protruding; bulging.
– ORIGIN C17: from late Latin *protuberare* 'swell out'.

proud ■ adj. 1 feeling pride or satisfaction in one's own or another's achievements. ▸ poetic/literary imposing; splendid. 2 having or showing a high opinion of oneself. ▸ conscious of one's own dignity. 3 slightly projecting from a surface. ▸ (of flesh) overgrown round a healing wound.
– PHRASES **do someone proud** informal act in a way that gives someone cause to feel pleased or satisfied. ▸ treat or entertain someone very well.
– DERIVATIVES **proudly** adv. **proudness** n.
– ORIGIN Old English *prūt*, *prūd*, from Old French *prud* 'valiant', from Latin *prodesse* 'be of value'.

prove /pruːv/ ■ v. (past part. **proved** or **proven** /ˈpruːv(ə)n, ˈprəʊ-/) 1 demonstrate by evidence or argument the truth or existence of. ▸ Law establish the genuineness and validity of (a will). 2 be seen or found to be: *the scheme has proved a great success*. ▸ demonstrate to be. ▸ (**prove oneself**) demonstrate one's abilities or courage. 3 subject (a gun) to a testing process. 4 (of bread dough) become aerated by the action of yeast; rise.
– PHRASES **not proven** Scots Law a verdict that there is insufficient evidence to establish guilt or innocence.
– DERIVATIVES **provability** n. **provable** adj. **provably** adv.
– ORIGIN Middle English: from Old French *prover*, from Latin *probare* 'test, approve, demonstrate'.

provenance /ˈprɒv(ə)nəns/ ■ n. 1 the place of origin or earliest known history of something. 2 a record of ownership of a work of art or an antique.
– ORIGIN C18: from French, from *provenir* 'come or stem from'.

Provençal /ˌprɒvɒ̃ˈsɑːl/ ■ n. 1 a native or inhabitant of Provence. 2 the language of Provence. ■ adj. relating to or denoting Provence or its people or language.

provençale /ˌprɒvɒ̃ˈsɑːl/ ■ adj. [postpos.] denoting a dish cooked in a sauce made with tomatoes, garlic, and olive oil, as characteristic of Provençal cuisine.
– ORIGIN from French *à la provençale* 'in the Provençal style'.

provender /ˈprɒvɪndə/ ■ n. 1 animal fodder. 2 often humorous food.
– ORIGIN Middle English: from Old French *provendre*, from Latin *praebenda* 'things to be supplied'.

proverb ■ n. a short pithy saying in general use, stating a general truth or piece of advice.
– ORIGIN Middle English: from Old French *proverbe*, from Latin *proverbium*, from *pro-* '(put) forth' + *verbum* 'word'.

proverbial ■ adj. 1 referred to in a proverb or idiom. 2 well known, especially so as to be stereotypical.
– DERIVATIVES **proverbiality** n. **proverbially** adv.

pro-vice-chancellor ■ n. an assistant or deputy vice-chancellor of a university.

provide ■ v. 1 make available for use; supply. ▸ (**provide someone with**) equip or supply someone with. 2 (**provide for**) make adequate preparation or arrangements for. ▸ (of a law) enable or allow (something to be done). 3 stipulate in a will or other legal document.
– DERIVATIVES **provider** n.
– ORIGIN Middle English: from Latin *providere* 'foresee, attend to'.

provided ■ conj. on the condition or understanding that.

providence ■ n. 1 the protective care of God or of nature as a spiritual power. ▸ (**Providence**) God or nature as providing such care. 2 timely preparation for future eventualities.

provident ■ adj. making or indicative of timely preparation for the future.
– DERIVATIVES **providently** adv.

provident fund ■ n. an investment fund contributed to by employees, employers, and (sometimes) the state, out of which a lump sum is provided to each employee on retirement.

providential ■ adj. 1 occurring at a favourable time; opportune. 2 involving divine foresight or interference.
– DERIVATIVES **providentially** adv.

providing ■ conj. on the condition or understanding that.

province ■ n. 1 a principal administrative division of a country or empire. ▸ (**the Province**) Brit. Northern Ireland. ▸ Christian Church a district under an archbishop or a metropolitan. 2 (**one's province**) an area in which one has special knowledge, interest, or responsibility. 3 (**the provinces**) the whole of a country outside the capital, especially when regarded as lacking in sophistication or culture.
– ORIGIN Middle English: from Latin *provincia* 'charge, province'.

provincial ■ adj. 1 of or concerning a province of a country or empire. 2 of or concerning the regions outside the capital city of a country, especially when regarded as unsophisticated or narrow-minded. ■ n. 1 an inhabitant of a province of a country or empire. 2 an inhabitant of the regions outside the capital city of a country.
– DERIVATIVES **provinciality** n. **provincialization** (also **-isation**) n. **provincially** adv.

provincialism ■ n. 1 the way of life or mode of thought characteristic of the regions outside the capital city of a country, especially when regarded as unsophisticated or narrow-minded. ▸ narrow-mindedness, insularity, or lack of sophistication. 2 concern for one's own area or region at the expense of national or supranational unity. 3 a word or phrase peculiar to a local area. 4 the degree to which plant or animal communities are restricted to particular areas.
– DERIVATIVES **provincialist** n. & adj.

proving ground ■ n. an area or situation in which a person or thing is tested or proved.

provirus /ˈprəʊvʌɪrəs/ ■ n. Microbiology the genetic material of a virus as incorporated into, and able to replicate with, the genome of a host cell.
– DERIVATIVES **proviral** adj.

provision ■ n. **1** the action of providing or supplying. ▸ something supplied or provided. ▸ (**provision for/against**) arrangements for future eventualities or requirements. **2** (**provisions**) supplies of food, drink, or equipment, especially for a journey. **3** a condition or requirement in a legal document. **4** an amount set aside out of profits in the accounts of an organization for a known liability. ■ v. **1** supply with provisions. **2** set aside a provision for a known liability.
– DERIVATIVES **provisioner** n.

provisional ■ adj. **1** arranged or existing for the present, possibly to be changed later. **2** (**Provisional**) denoting or relating to the unofficial wings of the IRA and Sinn Fein. ■ n. (**Provisional**) a member of the Provisional wings of the IRA or Sinn Fein.
– DERIVATIVES **provisionality** n. **provisionally** adv.

proviso /prəˈvaɪzəʊ/ ■ n. (pl. **-os**) a condition attached to an agreement.
– ORIGIN Middle English: from the medieval Latin phr. *proviso* (*quod*) 'it being provided (that)'.

provisory ■ adj. **1** subject to a proviso; conditional. **2** provisional.

provitamin ■ n. Biochemistry a substance which is converted into a vitamin within an organism.

provocation ■ n. the action of provoking. ▸ action or speech that provokes. ▸ Law action or speech held to be likely to prompt physical retaliation.

provocative ■ adj. **1** causing annoyance, anger, or another strong reaction, especially deliberately. **2** arousing sexual desire or interest, especially deliberately.
– DERIVATIVES **provocatively** adv. **provocativeness** n.

provoke ■ v. **1** stimulate (a reaction or emotion, typically a strong or unwelcome one) in someone. **2** deliberately annoy or anger. ▸ incite to do or feel something, especially by arousing anger.
– DERIVATIVES **provokable** adj. **provoker** n. **provoking** adj. **provokingly** adv.
– ORIGIN Middle English: from Old French *provoquer*, from Latin *provocare* 'challenge', from *pro-* 'forth' + *vocare* 'to call'.

provolone /ˌprɒvəˈləʊneɪ, -ˈləʊni/ ■ n. an Italian soft smoked cheese made from cow's milk.
– ORIGIN Italian, from *provola* 'buffalo's milk cheese'.

provost /ˈprɒvəst/ ■ n. **1** Brit. the position of head in certain university colleges and public schools. ▸ N. Amer. a senior administrative officer in certain universities. **2** the head of a chapter in a cathedral. **3** short for PROVOST MARSHAL.
– DERIVATIVES **provostship** n.
– ORIGIN Old English *profost* 'head of a chapter, prior', from medieval Latin *propositus*, Latin *praepositus* 'head, chief'.

provost marshal ■ n. the head of military police in camp or on active service.

prow /praʊ/ ■ n. the pointed front part of a ship; the bow.
– ORIGIN C16: from Old French *proue*, from Provençal *proa*, from Greek *prōira*.

prowess ■ n. **1** skill or expertise in a particular activity or field. **2** bravery in battle.
– ORIGIN Middle English: from Old French *proesce*, from *prou* 'valiant'.

prowl ■ v. move about stealthily or restlessly in search of or as if in search of prey. ■ n. an act of prowling.
– DERIVATIVES **prowler** n.
– ORIGIN Middle English.

proxemics /prɒkˈsiːmɪks/ ■ pl. n. [treated as sing.] the branch of study concerned with the amount of space that people set between themselves and others.
– ORIGIN 1960s: from PROXIMITY.

proximal ■ adj. chiefly Anatomy situated nearer to the centre of the body or an area or the point of attachment. The opposite of DISTAL.
– DERIVATIVES **proximally** adv.

proximate ■ adj. **1** closest in space, time, or relationship: *the proximate cause of the symptoms*. **2** nearly accurate; approximate.
– DERIVATIVES **proximately** adv. **proximation** n.
– ORIGIN C16: from Latin *proximare* 'draw near', from *proximus* 'nearest'.

proximity ■ n. nearness in space, time, or relationship.

– ORIGIN C15: from French *proximité*, from Latin *proximitas*, from *proximus* 'nearest'.

proximo /ˈprɒksɪməʊ/ ■ adj. [postpos.] dated of next month.
– ORIGIN from Latin *proximo mense* 'in the next month'.

proxy ■ n. (pl. **-ies**) **1** the authority to represent someone else, especially in voting. ▸ a person authorized to act on behalf of another. **2** a figure used to represent the value of something in a calculation.
– ORIGIN Middle English: contraction of *procuracy*, from Latin *procurare* 'take care of, manage', from *pro-* 'on behalf of' + *curare* 'manage, see to'.

Prozac /ˈprəʊzak/ ■ n. trademark for FLUOXETINE.
– ORIGIN 1980s: an invented name.

prude ■ n. a person who is easily shocked by matters relating to sex or nudity.
– DERIVATIVES **prudery** n. **prudish** adj. **prudishly** adv. **prudishness** n.
– ORIGIN C18: from French, back-formation from *prudefemme*, feminine of *prud'homme* 'good man and true'.

prudent ■ adj. acting with or showing care and thought for the future.
– DERIVATIVES **prudence** n. **prudently** adv.
– ORIGIN Middle English: from Latin *prudent-*, contraction of *provident-* (see PROVIDENT).

prudential ■ adj. involving or showing care and forethought, typically in business.
– DERIVATIVES **prudentially** adv.
– ORIGIN Middle English: from PRUDENT.

prune¹ ■ n. **1** a plum preserved by drying and having a black, wrinkled appearance. **2** informal a disagreeable person.
– ORIGIN Middle English: from Greek *prou(m)non* 'plum'.

prune² ■ v. **1** trim (a tree, shrub, or bush) by cutting away dead or overgrown branches or stems. **2** remove superfluous or unwanted parts from. ■ n. an instance of pruning.
– DERIVATIVES **pruner** n.
– ORIGIN C15: from Old French *pro(o)ignier*, possibly based on Latin *rotundus* 'round'.

prunus /ˈpruːnəs/ ■ n. a tree or shrub of a large genus that includes cherry, almond, plum, peach, and apricot trees. [Genus *Prunus*.]
– ORIGIN from Latin, 'plum tree'.

prurient /ˈprʊərɪənt/ ■ adj. having or encouraging an excessive interest in sexual matters.
– DERIVATIVES **prurience** n. **pruriency** n. **pruriently** adv.
– ORIGIN C16: from Latin *prurient-*, *prurire* 'itch, long, be wanton'.

prurigo /prʊəˈraɪɡəʊ/ ■ n. Medicine a chronic skin disease causing severe itching.
– DERIVATIVES **pruriginous** /prʊəˈrɪdʒɪnəs/ adj.
– ORIGIN C17: from Latin, from *prurire* 'to itch'.

pruritus /prʊˈraɪtəs/ ■ n. Medicine severe itching of the skin, as a symptom of various ailments.
– DERIVATIVES **pruritic** adj.
– ORIGIN C17: from Latin, 'itching'.

prusik /ˈprʌsɪk/ ■ adj. Climbing relating to or denoting a method of ascending or descending a rope by means of two movable loops attached by a special knot which tightens under pressure.
– DERIVATIVES **prusiking** n.
– ORIGIN 1930s: from the name of Austrian mountaineer Karl *Prusik*.

Prussian ■ n. a native or inhabitant of the former German kingdom of Prussia. ■ adj. of or relating to Prussia.

Prussian blue ■ n. a deep blue pigment used in painting and dyeing, made from or in imitation of ferric ferrocyanide.

prussic acid /ˈprʌsɪk/ ■ n. old-fashioned term for HYDROCYANIC ACID.
– DERIVATIVES **prussiate** n.
– ORIGIN C18: *prussic* from French *prussique* 'relating to Prussian blue'.

pry¹ ▪ v. (-ies, -ied) enquire too intrusively into a person's private affairs.
– DERIVATIVES **prying** adj. **pryingly** adv.
– ORIGIN Middle English.

pry² ▪ v. (-ies, -ied) chiefly N. Amer. another term for PRISE.
– ORIGIN C19: from PRISE.

PS ▪ abbrev. **1** postscript. **2** (in the theatre) prompt side.

Ps. ▪ abbrev. (pl. **Pss.**) Psalm or Psalms.

psalm /sɑːm/ ▪ n. a sacred song or hymn, in particular any of those contained in the biblical Book of Psalms. ▸ (**the Psalms** or **the Book of Psalms**) a book of the Bible comprising a collection of religious verses, sung or recited in both Jewish and Christian worship.
– DERIVATIVES **psalmic** adj. **psalmist** n.
– ORIGIN Old English (p)sealm, from Greek psalmos 'song sung to harp music'.

psalmody /'sɑːmədi, 'sɑːlm-/ ▪ n. the singing of psalms or similar sacred canticles. ▸ psalms arranged for singing.
– DERIVATIVES **psalmodic** adj. **psalmodist** n.
– ORIGIN Middle English: from Greek psalmōidia 'singing to a harp'.

psalter /'sɔːltə, 'sɒl-/ ▪ n. a copy of the biblical Psalms, especially for liturgical use. ▸ (**the psalter**) the Book of Psalms.
– ORIGIN Old English (p)saltere, from Greek psaltērion 'stringed instrument'.

psaltery /'sɔːlt(ə)ri, 'sɒl-/ ▪ n. (pl. -ies) an ancient and medieval musical instrument like a dulcimer but played by plucking the strings with the fingers or a plectrum.
– ORIGIN Middle English, from Old French sauterie, from Latin psalterium (see PSALTER).

PSBR ▪ abbrev. public-sector borrowing requirement.

psephology /sɛ'fɒlədʒi, sɪ-/ ▪ n. the statistical study of elections and trends in voting.
– DERIVATIVES **psephological** adj. **psephologist** n.
– ORIGIN 1950s: from Greek psēphos 'pebble, vote'.

pseud /sjuːd/ ▪ n. informal a pretentious person; a poseur.

pseud- ▪ comb. form variant spelling of PSEUDO- reduced before a vowel.

pseudo /'sjuːdəʊ/ ▪ adj. not genuine; fake, pretentious, or insincere. ▪ n. (pl. -os) a pretentious or insincere person.

pseudo- (also **pseud-** before a vowel) ▪ comb. form **1** false; not genuine: pseudonym. **2** resembling or imitating: pseudo-hallucination.
– ORIGIN from Greek pseudēs 'false', pseudos 'falsehood'.

pseudomonas /ˌsjuːdə(ʊ)'məʊnəs, sjuː'dɒmənəs/ ▪ n. Microbiology a bacterium of a genus occurring typically in soil and detritus. [Genus Pseudomonas.]
– ORIGIN from PSEUDO- + monas 'monad'.

pseudomorph /'sjuːdə(ʊ)mɔːf/ ▪ n. Crystallography a crystal consisting of one mineral but having the form of another.
– DERIVATIVES **pseudomorphic** adj. **pseudomorphism** n. **pseudomorphous** adj.
– ORIGIN C19: from PSEUDO- + Greek morphē 'form'.

pseudonym /'sjuːdənɪm/ ▪ n. a fictitious name, especially one used by an author.
– ORIGIN C19: from French pseudonyme, from Greek pseudōnymos, from pseudēs 'false' + onoma 'name'.

pseudonymous /sjuː'dɒnɪməs/ ▪ adj. writing or written under a false name.
– DERIVATIVES **pseudonymity** /-'nɪmɪti/ n. **pseudonymously** adv.

pseudopodium /ˌsjuːdə(ʊ)'pəʊdɪəm/ ▪ n. (pl. **pseudopodia** /-dɪə/) Biology a temporary protrusion of the surface of an amoeboid cell for movement and feeding.

pseudopregnancy ▪ n. (pl. -ies) another term for PHANTOM PREGNANCY.

pseudoscience ▪ n. a collection of beliefs or practices mistakenly regarded as being based on scientific method.
– DERIVATIVES **pseudoscientific** adj. **pseudoscientist** n.

pshaw /pʃɔː, ʃɔː/ ▪ exclam. dated or humorous an expression of contempt or impatience.

psi /psʌɪ, sʌɪ/ ▪ n. **1** the twenty-third letter of the Greek alphabet (Ψ, ψ), transliterated as 'ps'. **2** supposed parapsychological or psychic faculties or phenomena.
– ORIGIN from Greek.

p.s.i. ▪ abbrev. pounds per square inch.

psittacine /'sɪtəkʌɪn, -sʌɪn/ Ornithology ▪ adj. of, relating to, or denoting birds of the parrot family. ▪ n. a bird of the parrot family.
– ORIGIN C19: from Latin psittacinus 'of a parrot', from psittacus, from Greek psittakos 'parrot'.

psittacosis /ˌsɪtə'kəʊsɪs/ ▪ n. a contagious disease of birds, caused by chlamydiae and transmissible (especially from parrots) to human beings as a form of pneumonia.
– ORIGIN C19: from Latin psittacus 'parrot'.

psoas /'səʊas/ ▪ n. Anatomy each of a pair of large muscles used in flexing the hip.
– ORIGIN C16: from Greek, from psoa.

psoriasis /sɒ'rʌɪəsɪs/ ▪ n. Medicine a skin disease marked by red, itchy, scaly patches.
– DERIVATIVES **psoriatic** /ˌsɔːrɪ'atɪk/ adj.
– ORIGIN C17: from Greek psōriasis, from psōrian 'to itch'.

psst ▪ exclam. used to attract someone's attention surreptitiously.

PST ▪ abbrev. Pacific Standard Time.

psych /sʌɪk/ (also **psyche**) ▪ v. **1** (often **psych someone up**) informal mentally prepare (someone) for a testing task or occasion. ▸ (**psych someone out**) intimidate an opponent or rival by appearing very confident or aggressive. **2** informal subject (someone) to psychological investigation or psychotherapy. **3** (usu. **psyche**) Bridge make a psychic bid. ▪ n. **1** informal a psychiatrist or psychologist. ▸ psychiatry or psychology. **2** (usu. **psyche**) Bridge a psychic bid.

psyche /'sʌɪki/ ▪ n. the human soul, mind, or spirit.
– ORIGIN C17: from Greek psukhē 'breath, life, soul'.

psychedelia /ˌsʌɪkə'diːlɪə/ ▪ n. music, culture, or art based on the experiences produced by psychedelic drugs.

psychedelic /ˌsʌɪkə'dɛlɪk, -'diːlɪk/ ▪ adj. **1** relating to or denoting drugs (especially LSD) that produce hallucinations and apparent expansion of consciousness. **2** relating to or denoting a style of rock music characterized by musical experimentation and drug-related lyrics. **3** having an intense, vivid colour or a swirling abstract pattern. ▪ n. a psychedelic drug.
– DERIVATIVES **psychedelically** adv.
– ORIGIN 1950s: from PSYCHE + Greek dēlos 'clear, manifest'.

psychiatrist ▪ n. a medical practitioner specializing in the diagnosis and treatment of mental illness.

psychiatry /sʌɪ'kʌɪətri/ ▪ n. the branch of medicine concerned with the study and treatment of mental illness, emotional disturbance, and abnormal behaviour.
– DERIVATIVES **psychiatric** /ˌsʌɪkɪ'atrɪk/ adj. **psychiatrically** adv.
– ORIGIN C19: from Greek psukhē 'soul, mind' + iatreia 'healing', from iatros 'healer'.

psychic /'sʌɪkɪk/ ▪ adj. **1** relating to or denoting faculties or phenomena that are apparently inexplicable by natural laws, especially involving telepathy or clairvoyance. ▸ (of a person) appearing or considered to be telepathic or clairvoyant. **2** of or relating to the soul or mind. **3** Bridge denoting a bid that deliberately misrepresents the bidder's hand, in order to mislead the opponents. ▪ n. **1** a person considered or claiming to have psychic powers; a medium. **2** (**psychics**) [treated as sing. or pl.] the study of psychic phenomena.
– DERIVATIVES **psychical** adj. **psychically** adv. **psychism** n.

psycho ▪ n. (pl. -os) informal a psychopath.

psycho- ▪ comb. form relating to the mind or psychology: psychometrics.
– ORIGIN from Greek psukhē 'breath, soul, mind'.

psychoactive ▪ adj. (chiefly of a drug) affecting the mind.

psychoanalysis ▪ n. a system of psychological theory and therapy which aims to treat mental disorders by investigating the interaction of conscious and unconscious elements in the mind and bringing repressed fears and conflicts into the conscious mind.
– DERIVATIVES **psychoanalyse** (US **psychoanalyze**) v. **psychoanalyst** n. **psychoanalytic** adj. **psychoanalytical** adj. **psychoanalytically** adv.

psychobabble ▪ n. informal, derogatory jargon used in popular psychology.

psychobiology ■ n. the branch of science concerned with the biological basis of behaviour and mental phenomena.
– DERIVATIVES **psychobiological** adj. **psychobiologist** n.

psychodrama ■ n. **1** a form of psychotherapy in which patients act out events from their past. **2** a play, film, or novel in which psychological elements are the main interest.

psychodynamics ■ pl. n. [treated as sing.] the interrelation of the unconscious and conscious mental and emotional forces that determine personality and motivation. ▸ the branch of psychology concerned with this.
– DERIVATIVES **psychodynamic** adj. **psychodynamically** adv.

psychogenesis /ˌsʌɪkə(ʊ)ˈdʒɛnɪsɪs/ ■ n. the psychological cause to which a mental illness or behavioural disturbance may be attributed.

psychogenic /ˌsʌɪkə(ʊ)ˈdʒɛnɪk/ ■ adj. having a psychological origin or cause rather than a physical one.

psychographics ■ pl. n. [treated as sing.] the study and classification of people according to their attitudes, aspirations, etc., especially in market research.
– DERIVATIVES **psychographic** adj.

psychokinesis /ˌsʌɪkəʊkɪˈniːsɪs, -kʌɪ-/ ■ n. the supposed ability to move objects by mental effort alone.
– DERIVATIVES **psychokinetic** adj.

psycholinguistics ■ pl. n. [treated as sing.] the study of the relationships between linguistic behaviour and psychological processes, including the process of language acquisition.
– DERIVATIVES **psycholinguist** n. **psycholinguistic** adj.

psychological ■ adj. **1** of, affecting, or arising in the mind; related to the mental and emotional state of a person. **2** of or relating to psychology.
– DERIVATIVES **psychologically** adv.

psychological warfare ■ n. actions intended to reduce an opponent's morale.

psychologism ■ n. Philosophy a tendency to interpret events or arguments in subjective terms, or to exaggerate the relevance of psychological factors.

psychology ■ n. **1** the scientific study of the human mind and its functions, especially those affecting behaviour in a given context. **2** the mental characteristics or attitude of a person. ▸ the mental factors governing a situation or activity.
– DERIVATIVES **psychologist** n. **psychologize** (also **-ise**) v.

psychometrics ■ pl. n. [treated as sing.] the science of measuring mental capacities and processes.

psychometry /sʌɪˈkɒmɪtri/ ■ n. **1** the supposed ability to discover facts about an event or person by touching inanimate objects associated with them. **2** another term for **PSYCHOMETRICS**.
– DERIVATIVES **psychometric** /ˌsʌɪkə(ʊ)ˈmɛtrɪk/ adj. **psychometrically** adv. **psychometrist** n.

psychomotor ■ adj. of or relating to the origination of movement in conscious mental activity.

psychoneurosis ■ n. another term for **NEUROSIS**.

psychopath ■ n. a person suffering from chronic mental disorder with abnormal or violent social behaviour.
– DERIVATIVES **psychopathic** adj. **psychopathically** adv.

psychopathology ■ n. the scientific study of mental disorders. ▸ features of people's mental health considered collectively. ▸ mental or behavioural disorder.
– DERIVATIVES **psychopathological** adj. **psychopathologist** n.

psychopathy /sʌɪˈkɒpəθi/ ■ n. mental illness or disorder.

psychopharmacology ■ n. the branch of psychiatry concerned with the effects of drugs on the mind and behaviour.
– DERIVATIVES **psychopharmacological** adj. **psychopharmacologist** n.

psychophysics ■ pl. n. [treated as sing.] the branch of psychology concerned with the relations between physical stimuli and mental phenomena.
– DERIVATIVES **psychophysical** adj.

psychophysiology ■ n. Psychology the study of the relationship between physiological and psychological phenomena.
– DERIVATIVES **psychophysiological** adj. **psychophysiologist** n.

psychosexual ■ adj. of or involving the psychological aspects of the sexual impulse.
– DERIVATIVES **psychosexually** adv.

psychosis /sʌɪˈkəʊsɪs/ ■ n. (pl. **psychoses** /-siːz/) a severe mental disorder in which thought and emotions are so impaired that contact is lost with external reality.

psychosocial ■ adj. of or relating to the interrelation of social factors and individual thought and behaviour.
– DERIVATIVES **psychosocially** adv.

psychosomatic /ˌsʌɪkə(ʊ)səˈmatɪk/ ■ adj. **1** (of a physical illness) caused or aggravated by a mental factor such as internal conflict or stress. **2** of or relating to the interaction of mind and body.
– DERIVATIVES **psychosomatically** adv.

psychosurgery ■ n. brain surgery, such as leucotomy, used to treat mental disorder.
– DERIVATIVES **psychosurgical** adj.

psychosynthesis ■ n. the integration of separated elements of the psyche or personality.

psychotherapy ■ n. the treatment of mental disorder by psychological rather than medical means.
– DERIVATIVES **psychotherapeutic** adj. **psychotherapist** n.

psychotic /sʌɪˈkɒtɪk/ ■ adj. of, denoting, or suffering from a psychosis. ■ n. a psychotic person.
– DERIVATIVES **psychotically** adv.

psychotronic /ˌsʌɪkə(ʊ)ˈtrɒnɪk/ ■ adj. **1** denoting or relating to a genre of low-budget films with a science fiction, horror, or fantasy theme. **2** of or relating to psychotronics.

psychotronics ■ pl. n. [treated as sing.] a particular branch of parapsychology which supposes an energy or force to emanate from living organisms and affect matter.
– ORIGIN 1970s.

psychotropic /ˌsʌɪkə(ʊ)ˈtrəʊpɪk, ˌsʌɪkə(ʊ)ˈtrɒpɪk/ ■ adj. relating to or denoting drugs that affect a person's mental state.

psychrometer /sʌɪˈkrɒmɪtə/ ■ n. a hygrometer consisting of wet and dry-bulb thermometers, the difference in the two thermometer readings being used to determine atmospheric humidity.
– ORIGIN C18: from Greek *psukhros* 'cold' + **-METER**.

psyllid /ˈsɪlɪd/ ■ n. Entomology a minute insect of a family (Psyllidae) that comprises the jumping plant lice.
– ORIGIN C19: from Greek *psulla* 'flea'.

psyllium /ˈsɪlɪəm/ ■ n. a leafy-stemmed plantain, the seeds of which are used as a laxative and as a bulking agent in the treatment of obesity. [*Plantago psafra*.]
– ORIGIN C16: from Greek *psullion*, from *psulla* 'flea' (because the seeds resemble fleas).

PT ■ abbrev. physical training.

Pt ■ abbrev. **1** Part. **2** (**pt**) pint. **3** (in scoring) point. **4** Printing point (as a unit of measurement). **5** (**Pt.**) Point (on maps). **6** (**pt**) port (a side of a ship or aircraft). ■ symb. the chemical element platinum.

PTA ■ abbrev. parent–teacher association.

ptarmigan /ˈtɑːmɪɡ(ə)n/ ■ n. a grouse of northern mountains and the Arctic, changing to white plumage in winter. [*Lagopus mutus*.]
– ORIGIN C16: from Scottish Gaelic *tàrmachan*; spelling influenced by Greek words starting with *pt*-.

Pte ■ abbrev. Private (in the army).

pteranodon /tɛˈranədɒn/ ■ n. a large tailless pterosaur of the Cretaceous period, with a long toothless beak and a long bony crest.
– ORIGIN from Greek *pteron* 'wing' + *an-* 'without' + *odous* 'tooth'.

pteridology /ˌtɛrɪˈdɒlədʒi/ ■ n. the study of ferns and related plants.
– DERIVATIVES **pteridological** adj. **pteridologist** n.
– ORIGIN C19: from Greek *pteris*, *pterid-* 'fern'.

Pteridophyta /ˌtɛrɪdə(ʊ)ˈfʌɪtə/ ■ pl. n. Botany a division of flowerless plants which comprises the ferns, horsetails,

ptero-

and clubmosses.
- DERIVATIVES **pteridophyte** /ˈtɛrɪdə(ʊ)faɪt/ n.
- ORIGIN from Greek *pteris, pterid-* 'fern' + *phuton* 'plant'.

ptero- /ˈtɛrəʊ/ ■ comb. form relating to wings; having wings: *pterosaur.*
- ORIGIN from Greek *pteron* 'feather, wing'.

pterobranch /ˈtɛrə(ʊ)braŋk/ ■ n. Zoology a minute tube-dwelling colonial acorn worm of a class (Pterobranchia) found chiefly in deep water.

pterodactyl /ˌtɛrəˈdaktɪl/ ■ n. a pterosaur of the late Jurassic period, with a long slender head and neck and a very short tail. ▸ (in general use) any pterosaur.
- ORIGIN C19: from Greek *pteron* 'wing' + *daktulos* 'finger'.

pteropod /ˈtɛrəpɒd/ ■ n. Zoology a sea butterfly.
- ORIGIN C19: from Greek *pteron* 'wing' + *pous, pod-* 'foot'.

pterosaur /ˈtɛrəsɔː/ ■ n. a fossil warm-blooded flying reptile of the Jurassic and Cretaceous periods, with membranous wings supported by a greatly lengthened fourth finger.
- ORIGIN C19: from Greek *pteron* 'wing' + *sauros* 'lizard'.

Pterygota /ˌtɛrɪˈɡəʊtə/ ■ pl. n. Entomology a large group of insects that comprises those that have wings or winged ancestors, including the majority of modern species.
- DERIVATIVES **pterygote** n.
- ORIGIN modern Latin, from Greek *pterugōtos* 'winged', from *pteron* 'wing'.

PTFE ■ abbrev. polytetrafluoroethylene.

PTO ■ abbrev. **1** please turn over. **2** (also **pto**) power take-off.

Ptolemaic /ˌtɒləˈmeɪɪk/ ■ adj. **1** of or relating to the 2nd-century Greek astronomer Ptolemy. **2** of or relating to the Ptolemies, rulers of Egypt 304–30 BC.

Ptolemaic system (also **Ptolemaic theory**) ■ n. Astronomy, historical the theory that the earth is the stationary centre of the universe, with the planets moving in epicyclic orbits within surrounding concentric spheres. Compare with COPERNICAN SYSTEM.

ptomaine /ˈtəʊmeɪn/ ■ n. Chemistry, dated any of a group of amine compounds of unpleasant taste and odour formed in putrefying animal and vegetable matter and formerly thought to cause food poisoning.
- ORIGIN C19: from French *ptomaïne*, from Italian *ptomaina*, from Greek *ptōma* 'corpse'.

ptosis /ˈtəʊsɪs/ ■ n. Medicine drooping of the upper eyelid due to paralysis or disease, or as a congenital condition.
- DERIVATIVES **ptotic** /ˈtəʊtɪk/ adj.
- ORIGIN C18: from Greek *ptōsis*, from *piptein* 'to fall'.

PTSD ■ abbrev. post-traumatic stress disorder.

Pty ■ abbrev. S. African & Austral./NZ proprietary.

ptyalin /ˈtʌɪəlɪn/ ■ n. Biochemistry a form of amylase found in the saliva of humans and some other animals.
- ORIGIN C19: from Greek *ptualon* 'spittle'.

p-type ■ adj. Electronics denoting a region in a semiconductor in which electrical conduction is due chiefly to the movement of positive holes. Compare with N-TYPE.

Pu ■ symb. the chemical element plutonium.

pub chiefly Brit. ■ n. an establishment for the sale and consumption of beer and other drinks, often also serving food. ■ v. [usu. as noun **pubbing**] informal frequent pubs.
- ORIGIN C19: abbrev. of PUBLIC HOUSE.

pub. ■ abbrev. **1** publication(s). **2** published. **3** publisher.

pub crawl informal chiefly Brit. ■ n. a tour taking in several pubs, with one or more drinks at each. ■ v. (**pub-crawl**) go on a pub crawl.

puberty ■ n. the period during which adolescents reach sexual maturity and become capable of reproduction.
- DERIVATIVES **pubertal** adj.
- ORIGIN Middle English: from Latin *pubertas*, from *puber* 'adult'.

pubes ■ n. **1** /ˈpjuːbiːz/ (pl. same) the lower part of the abdomen at the front of the pelvis, covered with hair from puberty. **2** /ˈpjuːbiːz/ plural form of PUBIS. **3** /pjuːbz/ informal pubic hairs.
- ORIGIN C16: from Latin, 'pubic hair, groin, genitals'.

pubescence /pjuːˈbɛs(ə)ns/ ■ n. **1** the time when puberty begins. **2** Botany & Zoology soft down on the leaves and stems of plants or on various parts of animals, especially insects.
- DERIVATIVES **pubescent** adj. & n.
- ORIGIN Middle English: from Latin *pubescent-, pubescere* 'reach puberty'.

pubic ■ adj. of or relating to the pubes or pubis.

pubis /ˈpjuːbɪs/ ■ n. (pl. **pubes** /-biːz/) either of a pair of bones forming the two sides of the pelvis.
- ORIGIN C16: from Latin *os pubis* 'bone of the pubes'.

public ■ adj. **1** of, concerning, or open to the people as a whole. ▸ involved in the affairs of the community, especially in government or entertainment: *a public figure.* **2** done, perceived, or existing in open view. **3** of or provided by the state rather than an independent, commercial company. ■ n. (**the public**) [treated as sing. or pl.] ordinary people in general; the community.
- PHRASES **go public 1** become a public company. **2** reveal details about a previously private concern. **in public** in view of other people; when others are present.
- DERIVATIVES **publicly** adv.
- ORIGIN Middle English: from Latin *publicus*, blend of *poplicus* 'of the people' and *pubes* 'adult'.

public address system ■ n. a system of microphones, amplifiers, and loudspeakers used to amplify speech or music.

publican ■ n. **1** Brit. a person who owns or manages a pub. **2** (in ancient Roman and biblical times) a collector or farmer of taxes.
- ORIGIN Middle English: from Old French *publicain*, from Latin *publicanus*, from *publicum* 'public revenue'.

publication ■ n. **1** the action or process of publishing something. **2** a book or journal that is published.

public bar ■ n. Brit. the more plainly furnished bar in a pub.

public bill ■ n. a bill of legislation affecting the public as a whole.

public company ■ n. a company whose shares are traded freely on a stock exchange.

public defender ■ n. US Law a lawyer employed by the state in a criminal trial to represent a defendant who is unable to afford legal assistance.

public enemy ■ n. a notorious wanted criminal.

public house ■ n. formal term for PUB.

public housing ■ n. another term for SOCIAL HOUSING.

publicist ■ n. a person responsible for publicizing a product, person, or company.
- DERIVATIVES **publicistic** adj.

publicity ■ n. notice or attention given to someone or something by the media. ▸ the giving out of information for advertising or promotional purposes. ▸ material or information used for such a purpose.

publicize (also **-ise**) ■ v. **1** make widely known. **2** give out publicity about; advertise or promote.

public key encryption ■ n. a cryptographic system which needs two keys in special relation, a public one used for encryption, and a private one used for decryption.

public law ■ n. the law of relations between individuals and the state.

public lending right ■ n. the right of authors to receive payment when their books are lent out by public libraries.

public limited company ■ n. a company with statutory minimum capital requirements and shares offered to the public subject to conditions of limited liability.

public nuisance ■ n. Brit. **1** an act that is illegal because it interferes with the rights of the public generally. **2** informal an obnoxious or dangerous person or group.

public prosecutor ■ n. a law officer who conducts criminal proceedings on behalf of the state or in the public interest.

Public Protector ■ n. (in South Africa) a national or provincial ombudsman.

public purse ■ n. the funds raised by a government by taxation or other means.

Public Record Office ▪ n. (in the UK) an institution where official archives are kept for public inspection.

public relations ▪ pl. n. the professional maintenance of a favourable public image by an organization or famous person. ▸ the relationship between an organization or famous person and the public.

public school ▪ n. **1** (in the UK) a private fee-paying secondary school. **2** (chiefly in North America) a school supported by public funds.

public sector ▪ n. the part of an economy that is controlled by the state.

public servant ▪ n. a person who works for the state or for local government.

public service ▪ n. another term for CIVIL SERVICE.

public spirit ▪ n. willingness to do things that help the public.
– DERIVATIVES **public-spirited** adj. **public-spiritedly** adv. **public-spiritedness** n.

public transport (N. Amer. **public transportation**) ▪ n. buses, trains, and other forms of transport that are available to the public, charge set fares, and run on fixed routes.

public utility ▪ n. an organization supplying the community with electricity, gas, water, or sewerage.

public works ▪ pl. n. the work of building roads, schools, hospitals, etc., carried out by the state for the community.

publish ▪ v. **1** prepare and issue (a book, journal, or piece of music) for public sale. ▸ print in a book or journal so as to make generally known. **2** formally announce or read (an edict or marriage banns). **3** Law communicate (a libel) to a third party.
– DERIVATIVES **publishable** adj. **publishing** n.
– ORIGIN Middle English: from Latin *publicare* 'make public', from *publicus* (see PUBLIC).

publisher ▪ n. **1** a company or person that prepares and issues books, journals, or music for sale. **2** chiefly N. Amer. a newspaper proprietor.

puce /pjuːs/ ▪ n. a dark red or purple-brown colour.
– ORIGIN C18: from French *puce*, 'flea(-colour)'.

puck ▪ n. a black disc made of hard rubber, used in ice hockey.
– ORIGIN C19.

pucker ▪ v. tightly gather or contract into wrinkles or small folds. ▪ n. a wrinkle or small fold.
– ORIGIN C16: prob. from Anglo-Norman French *poke* 'pouch', rel. to POCKET (suggesting the formation of small purse-like gatherings).

puckish ▪ adj. playful, especially in a mischievous way.
– DERIVATIVES **puckishly** adv.

pud ▪ n. informal short for PUDDING.

pudding ▪ n. **1** a cooked sweet dish served after the main course of a meal. ▸ the dessert course of a meal. ▸ N. Amer. a dessert with a soft or creamy consistency. **2** a sweet or savoury steamed dish made with suet and flour. **3** informal a fat, dumpy, or stupid person.
– DERIVATIVES **puddingy** adj.
– ORIGIN Middle English: apparently from Old French *boudin* 'black pudding', from Latin *botellus* 'sausage, small intestine'.

pudding basin ▪ n. **1** a deep round bowl used for cooking steamed puddings. **2** [as modifier] denoting a hairstyle produced or seemingly produced by inverting a pudding basin on a person's head and cutting away all the hair that sticks out under it.

pudding face ▪ n. informal a large fat face.
– DERIVATIVES **pudding-faced** adj.

puddle ▪ n. **1** a small pool of liquid, especially of rainwater on the ground. **2** clay and sand mixed with water and used as a watertight covering for embankments. ▪ v. **1** cover with or form puddles. **2** line (a hole) with puddle. ▸ knead (clay and sand) into puddle. ▸ work (mixed water and clay) to separate gold or opal. **3** [usu. as noun **puddling**] chiefly historical stir (molten iron) with iron oxide in a furnace, to produce wrought iron by oxidizing carbon.
– DERIVATIVES **puddler** n. **puddly** adj.
– ORIGIN Middle English: diminutive of Old English *pudd* 'ditch, furrow'.

puddle jumper ▪ n. informal, chiefly N. Amer. a small light aircraft used for short trips.

pudendum /pjuːˈdɛndəm/ ▪ n. (pl. **pudenda** /-də/) a person's external genitals, especially a woman's.
– DERIVATIVES **pudendal** adj. **pudic** /ˈpjuːdɪk/ adj.
– ORIGIN C17: from Latin *pudenda (membra)* '(parts) to be ashamed of', from *pudere* 'be ashamed'.

pudgy ▪ adj. (-ier, -iest) informal rather fat.
– DERIVATIVES **pudgily** adv. **pudginess** n.

pueblo /ˈpwɛbləʊ/ ▪ n. (pl. -os) **1** a town or village in Spain, Latin America, or the south-western US, especially an American Indian settlement. **2** (**Pueblo**) (pl. same or -os) a member of any of various American Indian peoples, including the Hopi, occupying pueblo settlements chiefly in New Mexico and Arizona.
– ORIGIN Spanish, 'people'.

puerile /ˈpjʊərʌɪl/ ▪ adj. childishly silly and trivial.
– DERIVATIVES **puerilely** adv. **puerility** /pjʊəˈrɪlɪti/ n. (pl. -ies).
– ORIGIN C16: from French *puéril* or Latin *puerilis*, from *puer* 'boy'.

puerperal fever ▪ n. fever caused by uterine infection following childbirth.

puerperium /ˌpjuːəˈpɛrɪəm, ˌpjuːəˈpɪərɪəm/ ▪ n. Medicine the period of about six weeks after childbirth during which the mother's reproductive organs return to their original non-pregnant condition.
– DERIVATIVES **puerperal** adj.
– ORIGIN C17: from Latin, from *puerperus* 'parturient', from *puer* 'child' + *-parus* 'bearing'.

Puerto Rican /ˌpwɛːtəʊ ˈriːkən/ ▪ n. a native or inhabitant of Puerto Rico. ▪ adj. of or relating to Puerto Rico.

puff ▪ n. **1** a short burst of breath or wind. ▸ a small quantity of vapour or smoke emitted in one blast. ▸ an act of drawing quickly on a pipe, cigarette, or cigar. ▸ informal breath. **2** a light pastry case containing a sweet or savoury filling. **3** informal a complimentary review of a book, play, etc. ▪ v. **1** breathe in repeated short gasps. ▸ move with short, noisy breaths or bursts of air or steam. ▸ blow (dust, smoke, etc.) with quick breaths or blasts. ▸ smoke a pipe, cigarette, or cigar. ▸ (**be puffed/puffed out**) be out of breath. **2** (**puff out/up**) or **puff something out/up** become swollen or cause something to swell. ▸ cause to become conceited.
– PHRASES **puff and blow** breathe in gasps during or after exertion.
– DERIVATIVES **puffer** n.
– ORIGIN Middle English: imitative of the sound of a breath, perhaps from Old English *pyf* (n.), *pyffan* (v.).

puff adder ▪ n. a large, sluggish African viper which inflates the upper part of its body and hisses loudly when under threat. [*Bitis arietans*.]

puffa jacket ▪ n. Brit. a type of thick padded jacket.

puffball ▪ n. **1** a fungus that produces a large round fruiting body which ruptures when ripe to release a cloud of spores. [*Lycoperdon* and other genera.] **2** a short full skirt gathered around the hemline to produce a soft puffy shape.

pufferfish ▪ n. (pl. same or -fishes) a stout-bodied fish which inflates itself like a balloon when threatened. [Family Tetraodontidae.]

puffery ▪ n. exaggerated or false praise.

puffin ▪ n. a hole-nesting northern auk with a large head and a massive brightly coloured triangular bill. [*Fratercula arctica* and other species.]
– ORIGIN Middle English: perhaps from PUFF.

puff pastry ▪ n. light flaky pastry.

puff sleeve (also **puffed sleeve**) ▪ n. a short sleeve gathered at the top and cuff and full in the middle.

puffy ▪ adj. (-ier, -iest) **1** softly inflated. **2** (of a part of the body) swollen and soft.
– DERIVATIVES **puffily** adv. **puffiness** n.

pug[1] ▪ n. a dog of a dwarf breed like a bulldog with a broad flat nose and deeply wrinkled face.
– ORIGIN C18: perhaps of Low German origin.

pug[2] ▪ n. loam or clay mixed and worked into a soft,

pug

plastic condition without air pockets for making bricks or pottery. ■ v. (**pugged**, **pugging**) 1 [usu. as adj. **pugged**] prepare (clay) in this way. 2 [usu. as noun **pugging**] pack (a space) with pug, sawdust, or other material in order to deaden sound.
– ORIGIN C19.

pug[3] ■ n. the footprint of an animal. ■ v. (**pugged**, **pugging**) track (an animal) by its footprints.
– ORIGIN C19: from Hindi *pag* 'footprint'.

pugilist /ˈpjuːdʒɪlɪst/ ■ n. dated or humorous a boxer.
– DERIVATIVES **pugilism** n. **pugilistic** adj.
– ORIGIN C18: from Latin *pugil* 'boxer'.

pugnacious /pʌɡˈneɪʃəs/ ■ adj. eager or quick to argue, quarrel, or fight.
– DERIVATIVES **pugnaciously** adv. **pugnacity** n.
– ORIGIN C17: from Latin *pugnax, pugnac-*, from *pugnare* 'to fight'.

pug nose ■ n. a short nose with an upturned tip.
– DERIVATIVES **pug-nosed** adj.

puisne /ˈpjuːni/ ■ adj. Law (in South Africa, the UK, and some other countries) denoting a judge of a superior court inferior in rank to chief justices or judges president.
– ORIGIN C16: from Old French, from *puis* 'afterwards' + *ne* 'born'.

puissance /ˈpjuːɪs(ə)ns, ˈpwiː-, ˈpwɪ-/ ■ n. 1 /also ˈpwiːsɒs/ a competitive test of a horse's ability to jump large obstacles in showjumping. 2 archaic or poetic/literary great power, influence, or prowess.

puissant /ˈpjuːɪs(ə)nt, ˈpwiː-, ˈpwɪ-/ ■ adj. archaic or poetic/literary having great power or influence.
– DERIVATIVES **puissantly** adv.
– ORIGIN Middle English: from Old French *posse* 'be able'.

puja /ˈpuːdʒɑː/ ■ n. a Hindu ceremonial offering.
– ORIGIN from Sanskrit *pūjā* 'worship'.

pujari /pʊˈdʒɑːri/ ■ n. (pl. **pujaris**) a Hindu priest.
– ORIGIN from Sanskrit *pūjā* 'worship'.

puke ■ v.& n. informal vomit.
– DERIVATIVES **pukey** adj.
– ORIGIN C16: prob. imitative.

pukka /ˈpʌkə/ (also **pukkah**) ■ adj. informal 1 proper or genuine. ▶ of or appropriate to high or respectable society. 2 excellent.
– ORIGIN C17: from Hindi *pakkā* 'cooked, ripe, substantial'.

puku /ˈpuːkuː/ ■ n. (pl. **pukus**) a southern African antelope with a shaggy golden-yellow coat and short thick horns. [*Kobus vardonii*].
– ORIGIN C19: from isiZulu *mpuku*.

pula /ˈpuːlə/ ■ n. (pl. same) the basic monetary unit of Botswana, equal to 100 thebe.
– ORIGIN Setswana, 'rain'.

pulao /pəˈlaʊ/ ■ n. variant spelling of PILAF.

pulchritude /ˈpʌlkrɪtjuːd/ ■ n. poetic/literary beauty.
– DERIVATIVES **pulchritudinous** adj.
– ORIGIN Middle English: from Latin *pulchritudo*, from *pulcher* 'beautiful'.

pule /pjuːl/ ■ v. [often as adj. **puling**] poetic/literary cry querulously or weakly.
– ORIGIN Middle English: prob. imitative.

Pulitzer Prize ■ n. an award for an achievement in American journalism, literature, or music.
– ORIGIN named after the C19 Hungarian-born American newspaper proprietor Joseph *Pulitzer*.

pull ■ v. 1 exert force on so as to cause movement towards oneself or the origin of the force. ▶ be attached to the front and be the source of forward movement of (a vehicle). ▶ remove by pulling. ▶ informal bring out (a weapon) for use. ▶ Brit. draw (beer) from a barrel to serve. ▶ (**pull at/on**) inhale deeply while drawing on (a cigarette). ▶ damage (a muscle, ligament, etc.) by abnormal strain. 2 move steadily: *the bus pulled away*. ▶ move one's body against resistance. 3 attract as a customer; cause to show interest. ▶ informal succeed in attracting sexually. 4 informal cancel or withdraw (an entertainment or advertisement). ▶ arrest. ▶ check the speed of (a horse), especially so as to make it lose a race. 5 Cricket play (the ball) round to the leg side from the off. ▶ Golf & Baseball strike (the ball) so that it travels to the left (or, with a left-handed player, the right). 6 print (a proof). ■ n. 1 an act of pulling something. ▶ a handle to hold while pulling. ▶ a deep draught of a drink. ▶ an injury to a muscle or ligament caused by abnormal strain. 2 a force, influence, or compulsion. 3 a printer's proof.
– PHRASES **pull someone's leg** deceive someone playfully; tease someone. **pull the plug** informal prevent something from happening or continuing. **pull (one's) punches** [usu. with neg.] be less forceful, severe, or violent than one could be. **pull strings** make use of one's influence and contacts to gain an advantage. **pull the strings** be in control of events or of other people's actions. **pull together** cooperate in a task or undertaking. **pull oneself together** recover control of one's emotions. **pull one's weight** do one's fair share of work.
– PHRASAL VERBS **pull back** (or **pull someone/thing back**) 1 withdraw from an undertaking. 2 improve or restore a team's position in a sporting contest. **pull something down** 1 demolish a building. 2 informal earn a sum of money. **pull someone in** informal arrest someone. **pull something in 1** succeed in securing or obtaining something. ▶ informal earn a sum of money. 2 use reins to check a horse. **pull something off** informal succeed in achieving or winning something difficult. **pull out** withdraw from an undertaking. ▶ retreat from an area. **pull round** chiefly Brit. recover from an illness. **pull through** get through an illness or other dangerous or difficult situation. **pull up** (of a vehicle) come to a halt. **pull someone up** cause someone to stop or pause; check someone. ▶ reprimand someone.
– DERIVATIVES **puller** n.
– ORIGIN Old English *pullian* 'pluck, snatch'.

pullet ■ n. a young hen, especially one less than one year old.
– ORIGIN Middle English: from Old French *poulet*, diminutive of *poule*, from Latin *pullus* 'chicken, young animal'.

pulley ■ n. (pl. **-eys**) a wheel with a grooved rim around which a cord passes, used to raise heavy weights. ▶ a wheel or drum fixed on a shaft and turned by a belt, used to increase speed or power. ■ v. (**-eys**, **-eyed**) hoist with a pulley.
– ORIGIN Middle English: from Old French *polie*, prob. from a medieval Greek diminutive of *polos* 'pivot, axis'.

Pullman ■ n. (pl. **Pullmans**) a railway carriage or train affording special comfort.
– ORIGIN C19: named after its American designer George M. *Pullman*.

pull-out ■ n. a section of a magazine or newspaper that is designed to be detached and kept for rereading. ■ adj. designed to be pulled out or detached.

pullover ■ n. a knitted garment put on over the head and covering the top half of the body.

pullulate /ˈpʌljʊleɪt/ ■ v. [often as adj. **pullulating**] breed or spread so as to become extremely common. ▶ be very crowded; be full of life and activity.
– DERIVATIVES **pullulation** n.
– ORIGIN C17: from Latin *pullulare* 'sprout', from *pullulus*, diminutive of *pullus* 'young animal'.

pull-up ■ n. an exercise involving raising oneself with one's arms by pulling up against a horizontal bar fixed above one's head.

pulmonaria /ˌpʌlməˈnɛːrɪə/ ■ n. a Eurasian plant of a genus that includes lungwort. [Genus *Pulmonaria*.]
– ORIGIN from medieval Latin *pulmonaria* (*herba*), from Latin *pulmonarius* 'relating to the lungs' (from the belief in its efficacy in curing lung diseases).

pulmonary /ˈpʌlmən(ə)ri/ ■ adj. of or relating to the lungs.
– ORIGIN C17: from Latin *pulmonarius*, from *pulmo, pulmon-* 'lung'.

pulmonary artery ■ n. the artery carrying blood from the right ventricle of the heart to the lungs for oxygenation.

pulmonary vein ■ n. a vein carrying oxygenated blood from the lungs to the left atrium of the heart.

Pulmonata /ˌpʌlməˈneɪtə/ ■ pl. n. Zoology a group of molluscs which includes the land snails and slugs and many freshwater snails.
– DERIVATIVES **pulmonate** n. & adj.

– ORIGIN from Latin *pulmo, pulmon-* 'lung'.

pulmonic /pʌlˈmɒnɪk/ ■ adj. another term for **PULMONARY**.

pulp ■ n. **1** a soft, wet, shapeless mass of material. ▸ the soft fleshy part of a fruit. ▸ a soft wet mass of fibres derived from rags or wood, used in papermaking. **2** vascular tissue filling the interior cavity and root canals of a tooth. **3** Mining pulverized ore mixed with water. **4** [as modifier] denoting popular or sensational writing, generally regarded as being of poor quality. ■ v. **1** crush into a pulp. **2** withdraw (a publication) from the market and recycle the paper.
– DERIVATIVES **pulper** n. **pulpiness** n. **pulpy** adj.
– ORIGIN Middle English: from Latin *pulpa*; sense 4 is from the printing of such material on cheap paper.

pulpit ■ n. **1** a raised enclosed platform in a church or chapel from which the preacher delivers a sermon. **2** a guard rail enclosing a small area at the bow of a yacht.
– ORIGIN Middle English: from Latin *pulpitum* 'scaffold, platform'.

pulsar /ˈpʌlsɑː/ ■ n. Astronomy a celestial object, thought to be a rapidly rotating neutron star, that emits regular rapid pulses of radio waves.
– ORIGIN 1960s: from *puls(ating st)ar*, on the pattern of *quasar*.

pulsate /pʌlˈseɪt, ˈpʌlseɪt/ ■ v. **1** expand and contract with strong regular movements. **2** (often as adj. **pulsating**) produce a regular throbbing sensation or sound.
– DERIVATIVES **pulsation** n. **pulsator** n. **pulsatory** /ˈpʌlsət(ə)ri/ adj.
– ORIGIN C17 (*pulsation* Middle English): from Latin *pulsare* 'throb, pulse'.

pulsatile /ˈpʌlsətaɪl/ ■ adj. chiefly Physiology pulsating; relating to pulsation.
– ORIGIN Middle English: from medieval Latin *pulsatilis* (in *vena pulsatilis* 'artery'), from *pulsare* (see **PULSATE**).

pulse¹ ■ n. **1** the rhythmical throbbing of the arteries as blood is propelled through them. ▸ each successive throb of the arteries or heart. **2** a single vibration or short burst of sound, electric current, light, or other wave. **3** a musical beat or other regular rhythm. **4** the centre of activity in an area or field: *those close to the financial and economic pulse*. **5** Biochemistry a measured amount of an isotopic label given to a culture of cells. ■ v. **1** pulsate. **2** modulate (a wave or beam) so that it becomes a series of pulses. **3** apply a pulsed signal to (a device).
– PHRASES **feel** (or **take**) **the pulse of** ascertain the mood or opinion of.
– DERIVATIVES **pulseless** adj.
– ORIGIN Middle English: from Latin *pulsus* 'beating', from *pellere* 'to drive, beat'.

pulse² ■ n. the edible seeds of various leguminous plants, e.g. lentils. ▸ the plant or plants producing such seeds.
– ORIGIN Middle English: from Old French *pols*, from Latin *puls* 'porridge of meal or pulse'.

pulse code modulation ■ n. Electronics a technique of modulating the amplitude of an analogue signal to represent digital information as a series of pulses.

pulverize (also **-ise**) ■ v. **1** reduce to fine particles. **2** informal defeat utterly.
– DERIVATIVES **pulverizable** (also **-isable**) adj. **pulverization** (also **-isation**) n. **pulverizer** (also **-iser**) n.
– ORIGIN Middle English: from late Latin *pulverizare*, from *pulvis* 'dust'.

puma ■ n. a large American wild cat with a plain tawny to greyish coat. [*Felis concolor*.]
– ORIGIN C18: from Quechua.

pumice /ˈpʌmɪs/ ■ n. a light and porous form of solidified lava.
– DERIVATIVES **pumiceous** /pjuːˈmɪʃəs/ adj.
– ORIGIN Middle English: from Old French *pomis*, from a Latin var. of *pumex, pumic-*.

pummel ■ v. (**pummelled**, **pummelling**; US **pummeled**, **pummeling**) strike repeatedly, especially with the fists.
– ORIGIN C16: var. of **POMMEL**.

pummelo ■ n. variant spelling of **POMELO**.

pump¹ ■ n. **1** a mechanical device using suction or pressure to raise or move liquids, compress gases, or force air into inflatable objects. **2** Physiology a mechanism in living cells by which specific ions are moved against a cell membrane against a concentration gradient. ■ v. **1** force (liquid, gas, etc.) to move by or as if by means of a pump. ▸ move in spurts as though driven by a pump. **2** (often **pump something up**) fill (something) with (liquid, gas, etc.). ▸ (**pump something up**) informal turn up the volume of music. ▸ [as adj. **pumped up**] informal very enthusiastic or excited. **3** move or cause to move vigorously up and down. **4** informal try to elicit information from (someone) by persistent questioning.
– PHRASES **pump iron** informal exercise with weights.
– ORIGIN Middle English: rel. to Dutch *pomp* 'ship's pump'.

pump² ■ n. **1** a light shoe for dancing. **2** N. Amer. a court shoe.
– ORIGIN C16.

pump-action ■ adj. **1** denoting a repeating firearm in which a new round is brought into the breech by a slide action in line with the barrel. **2** denoting an unpressurized spray dispenser for a liquid that is worked by finger action.

pumped (also **pumped up**) ■ adj. informal, chiefly N. Amer. filled with enthusiasm or excitement.

pumpernickel /ˈpʊmpəˌnɪk(ə)l, ˈpʌm-/ ■ n. dark, dense German bread made from coarsely ground wholemeal rye.
– ORIGIN C18: transferred use of German *Pumpernickel* 'lout, bumpkin'.

pumpkin ■ n. **1** a large rounded orange-yellow fruit with a thick rind and edible flesh. **2** a plant of the gourd family bearing this fruit, native to warm regions of America. [*Cucurbita pepo* and related species.]
– ORIGIN C17: alteration of *pumpion*, from obsolete French *pompon*, from Greek *pepōn* (see **PEPO**).

pump-priming ■ n. **1** the introduction of fluid into a pump to prepare it for working. **2** the stimulation of economic activity by investment.
– DERIVATIVES **pump-prime** v. **pump-primer** n.

pun ■ n. a joke exploiting the different meanings of a word or the fact that there are words of the same sound and different meanings. ■ v. (**punned**, **punning**) [often as adj. **punning**] make a pun.
– DERIVATIVES **punningly** adv. **punster** n.
– ORIGIN C17: perhaps an abbrev. of obsolete *pundigrion*.

punch¹ ■ v. **1** strike with the fist. **2** press (a button or key on a machine). ▸ (**punch in**) or **out** N. Amer. (of an employee) clock in (or out). ■ n. **1** a blow with the fist. **2** informal effectiveness; impact.
– PHRASES **punch above one's weight** informal engage in an activity perceived as beyond one's abilities. **punch the clock** N. Amer. (of an employee) clock in or out.
– DERIVATIVES **puncher** n.
– ORIGIN Middle English: var. of **POUNCE**.

punch² ■ n. **1** a device or machine for making holes in materials such as paper and metal. **2** a tool or machine for impressing a design or stamping a die on a material. ■ v. pierce a hole in (a material) with or as if with a punch. ▸ pierce (a hole) with or as if with a punch.
– ORIGIN C16: perhaps an abbrev. of *puncheon* 'short post', or from **PUNCH¹**.

punch³ ■ n. a drink made from wine or spirits mixed with water, fruit juices, spices, etc.
– ORIGIN C17: apparently from Sanskrit *pañca* 'five, five kinds of' (because the drink had five ingredients).

punch⁴ ■ n. (**Punch**) a grotesque, hook-nosed humpbacked buffoon, the chief male character of the Punch and Judy puppet show.
– PHRASES **as pleased** (or **proud**) **as Punch** feeling great delight or pride.
– ORIGIN C17: abbrev. of **PUNCHINELLO**.

punchbag ■ n. a suspended stuffed cylindrical bag, used for punching as exercise or training, especially by boxers.

punchball ■ n. a suspended or mounted stuffed or inflated ball, used for punching as exercise or training, especially by boxers.

punchbowl ■ n. a deep bowl for mixing and serving punch.

punch-drunk ■ adj. stupefied by or as if by a series of heavy blows.

punched card (also **punchcard**) ■ n. a card perforated according to a code, for controlling the operation of a machine, formerly used to program computers.

punched tape ■ n. a paper tape perforated according to a code, formerly used for conveying instructions or data to a data processor.

puncheon /ˈpʌn(t)ʃ(ə)n/ ■ n. historical a large cask for liquids or other commodities.
– ORIGIN Middle English: from Old French *poinchon*.

Punchinello /ˌpʌn(t)ʃɪˈnɛləʊ/ ■ n. (pl. -os) another name for PUNCH⁴.
– ORIGIN C17: alteration of Neapolitan dialect *Polecenella*, perhaps a diminutive of *pollecena* 'young turkey cock with a hooked beak'.

punchline ■ n. the culmination of a joke or story, providing the humour or climax.

punch-up ■ n. informal a brawl.

punchy ■ adj. (-ier, -iest) effective; forceful.
– DERIVATIVES **punchily** adv. **punchiness** n.

punctate /ˈpʌŋ(k)teɪt/ ■ adj. Biology studded with or denoting dots or tiny holes.
– DERIVATIVES **punctation** n.
– ORIGIN C18: from Latin *punctum* 'point'.

punctilious /pʌŋ(k)ˈtɪlɪəs/ ■ adj. showing great attention to detail or correct behaviour.
– DERIVATIVES **punctiliously** adv. **punctiliousness** n.
– ORIGIN C17: from French *pointilleux*, from *pointille*, from Italian *puntiglio*, diminutive of *punto* 'point'.

punctual /ˈpʌŋ(k)tʃʊəl, -tjʊəl/ ■ adj. happening or doing something at the appointed time.
– DERIVATIVES **punctuality** n. **punctually** adv.
– ORIGIN C17: from medieval Latin *punctualis*, from Latin *punctum* 'a point'.

punctuate /ˈpʌŋ(k)tʃʊeɪt, -tjʊ-/ ■ v. 1 occur at intervals throughout. ▸ (**punctuate something with**) interrupt an activity with. 2 insert punctuation marks in.
– ORIGIN C17: from medieval Latin *punctuare* 'bring to a point'.

punctuated equilibrium ■ n. Biology the hypothesis that evolutionary development is marked by isolated episodes of rapid speciation between long periods of little or no change.

punctuation ■ n. the marks, such as full stop, comma, and brackets, used in writing to separate sentences and their elements and to clarify meaning. ▸ the use of such marks.
– DERIVATIVES **punctuational** adj.

puncture ■ n. a small hole caused by a sharp object, especially one in a tyre. ■ v. 1 make a puncture in. 2 cause a sudden collapse of (a mood, feeling, etc.).
– ORIGIN Middle English: from Latin *punctura*, from *pungere* 'prick'.

pundit /ˈpʌndɪt/ ■ n. 1 an expert who frequently expresses opinion in public. 2 variant spelling of PANDIT.
– DERIVATIVES **punditry** n.
– ORIGIN from Sanskrit *paṇḍita* 'learned'.

pungent ■ adj. 1 having a sharply strong taste or smell. 2 (of remarks or humour) sharp and caustic.
– DERIVATIVES **pungency** n. **pungently** adv.
– ORIGIN C16: from Latin *pungere* 'prick'.

Punic /ˈpjuːnɪk/ ■ adj. Carthaginian. ■ n. the language of ancient Carthage, related to Phoenician.
– ORIGIN from Latin *Punicus* (earlier *Poenicus*), from *Poenus*, from Greek *Phoinix* 'Phoenician'.

punish ■ v. 1 inflict a penalty on as retribution for an offence. ▸ inflict a penalty on someone for (an offence). 2 treat harshly.
– DERIVATIVES **punishable** adj. **punisher** n. **punishing** adj. **punishingly** adv.
– ORIGIN Middle English: from Old French *puniss-*, *punir* 'punish', from Latin *punire*, from *poena* 'penalty'.

punishment ■ n. 1 the action of punishing or the state of being punished. ▸ the penalty inflicted. 2 informal rough treatment.

punitive /ˈpjuːnɪtɪv/ ■ adj. inflicting or intended as punishment.
– DERIVATIVES **punitively** adv. **punitiveness** n.
– ORIGIN C17: from medieval Latin *punitivus*, from Latin *punire* (see PUNISH).

punitive damages ■ pl. n. Law damages exceeding simple compensation and awarded to punish the defendant.

Punjabi /pʌnˈdʒɑːbi, pʊn-/ (also **Panjabi**) ■ n. (pl. **Punjabis**) 1 a native or inhabitant of Punjab. 2 the Indic language of Punjab. ■ adj. of or relating to Punjab or its people or language.

punk ■ n. 1 (also **punk rock**) a loud, fast-moving, and aggressive form of rock music, popular in the late 1970s. ▸ (also **punk rocker**) an admirer or player of such music. 2 informal, chiefly N. Amer. a worthless person; a thug or criminal. ■ adj. of or relating to punk rock and its associated subculture.
– DERIVATIVES **punkish** adj. **punky** adj.
– ORIGIN C17: perhaps rel. to archaic *punk* 'prostitute', also to SPUNK.

punkah /ˈpʌŋkə, -kɑː/ ■ n. chiefly historical (in India) a large cloth fan on a frame suspended from the ceiling, worked by a cord.
– ORIGIN from Sanskrit *pakṣaka*, from *pakṣa* 'wing'.

punnet ■ n. a small light basket or other container for fruit or vegetables.
– ORIGIN C19: perhaps a diminutive of dialect *pun* 'a pound'.

punt¹ /pʌnt/ ■ n. a long, narrow, flat-bottomed boat, square at both ends and propelled with a long pole. ■ v. travel or convey in a punt.
– ORIGIN Old English, from Latin *ponto*, denoting a flat-bottomed ferry boat.

punt² /pʌnt/ ■ v. 1 American Football & Rugby kick the ball after it has dropped from the hands and before it reaches the ground. 2 Soccer kick (the ball) a long distance upfield. ■ n. a kick of this kind.
– ORIGIN C19: prob. from dialect *punt* 'push forcibly'.

punt³ /pʌnt/ informal, chiefly Brit. ■ v. bet or speculate. ■ n. a bet.
– ORIGIN C18: from French *ponte* 'player against the bank'.

punt⁴ /pʊnt/ ■ n. the former monetary unit of the Republic of Ireland.
– ORIGIN Irish, 'pound'.

punter ■ n. 1 informal a person who gambles, places a bet, or makes a risky investment. 2 Brit. informal a customer or client.

puny /ˈpjuːni/ ■ adj. (-ier, -iest) 1 small and weak. 2 meagre.
– DERIVATIVES **punily** adv. **puniness** n.
– ORIGIN C16: phonetic spelling of PUISNE.

pup ■ n. 1 a young dog. 2 a young wolf, seal, rat, or other mammal. 3 dated, chiefly Brit. a cheeky or arrogant boy or young man. ■ v. (**pupped**, **pupping**) give birth to a pup or pups.
– PHRASES **sell someone a pup** Brit. informal swindle someone, especially by selling something worthless.
– ORIGIN C16: back-formation from PUPPY, interpreted as a diminutive.

pupa /ˈpjuːpə/ ■ n. (pl. **pupae** /-piː/) an insect in its inactive immature form between larva and adult, e.g. a chrysalis.
– DERIVATIVES **pupal** adj.
– ORIGIN C18: from Latin *pupa* 'girl, doll'.

pupate ■ v. become a pupa.
– DERIVATIVES **pupation** n.

pupil¹ ■ n. 1 a person who is taught by another, especially a schoolchild. 2 a trainee advocate or barrister.

HISTORY
The two English words **pupil** are related to each other, and to **poppet**, **puppet**, and **pupa**, through their Latin root, *pupa* 'girl, doll'. **Pupil** entered English via Old French from the Latin forms *pupillus* (diminutive of *pupus* 'boy') and *pupilla* (diminutive of *pupa* 'girl'); it originally meant 'orphan or ward', and did not take on its modern meaning until the 16th century. **Pupil** meaning 'the centre of the eye' is from the feminine form *pupilla* (literally 'little doll' or 'young girl'): it acquired its English meaning from the phenomenon whereby one can see a tiny reflected image of oneself in another person's eyes.

pupil² ■ n. the dark circular opening in the centre of the

iris of the eye, which varies in size to regulate the amount of light reaching the retina.
- DERIVATIVES **pupillary** adj.
- ORIGIN Middle English: from Old French *pupille* or Latin *pupilla*, diminutive of *pupa* 'doll' (from the tiny reflected images visible in the eye).

pupillage ■ n. **1** the state of being a pupil. **2** Law apprenticeship to a member of the Bar, which qualifies an advocate or barrister to practise independently.

pupiparous /pjuːˈpɪp(ə)rəs/ ■ adj. Entomology (of certain flies, e.g. the tsetse) producing young which are already ready to pupate.
- ORIGIN C19: from modern Latin *pupipara* from *pupiparus* 'bringing forth young'.

puppet ■ n. **1** a movable model of a person or animal, typically moved either by strings or by a hand inside it, used to entertain. **2** a person under the control of another.
- DERIVATIVES **puppeteer** n. **puppeteering** n. **puppetry** n.
- ORIGIN C16: later form of POPPET.

puppy ■ n. (pl. **-ies**) **1** a young dog. **2** informal, dated a conceited or arrogant young man.
- DERIVATIVES **puppyhood** n. **puppyish** adj.
- ORIGIN C15: perhaps from Old French *poupee* 'doll, toy'.

puppy fat ■ n. fat on the body of a child which disappears around adolescence.

puppy love ■ n. intense but relatively short-lived love, typically associated with adolescents.

pup tent ■ n. N. Amer. a small triangular tent, especially one for two people and without side walls.

purblind /ˈpɜːblaɪnd/ ■ adj. **1** having impaired or defective vision. **2** dim-witted.
- DERIVATIVES **purblindness** n.
- ORIGIN Middle English: from PURE 'utterly' + BLIND.

purchase ■ v. **1** buy. **2** Nautical haul up (a rope, cable, or anchor) by means of a pulley or lever. ■ n. **1** the action of buying. ▸ a thing bought. ▸ Law the acquisition of property by one's personal action and not by inheritance. **2** firm contact or grip. **3** a pulley or similar device for moving heavy objects.
- DERIVATIVES **purchasable** adj. **purchaser** n.
- ORIGIN Middle English: from Old French *pourchacier* 'seek to obtain or bring about'.

purchase tax ■ n. a tax added to the price of goods sold to consumers.

purdah /ˈpɜːdə/ ■ n. the practice in certain Muslim and Hindu societies of screening women from men or strangers by means of a curtain or all-enveloping clothes.
- ORIGIN C19: from Urdu and Persian *parda* 'veil, curtain'.

pure ■ adj. **1** not mixed or adulterated with any other substance or material. ▸ (of an animal or plant) of unmixed origin or descent. **2** innocent or morally good. **3** (of a sound) perfectly in tune and with a clear tone. **4** (of a subject) theoretical rather than practical. Compare with APPLIED. **5** complete; nothing but. **6** Phonetics (of a vowel) not joined with another to form a diphthong.
- DERIVATIVES **purely** adv. **pureness** n.
- ORIGIN Middle English: from Old French *pur* 'pure', from Latin *purus*.

pure-bred ■ adj. (of an animal) bred from parents of the same breed or variety.

purée /ˈpjʊəreɪ/ ■ n. a smooth pulp of liquidized or crushed fruit or vegetables. ■ v. (**purées, puréed, puréeing**) make a purée of.
- ORIGIN C18: French, 'purified', from *purer*.

pure mathematics ■ pl. n. see MATHEMATICS.

pure play ■ n. [usu. as modifier] a company that focuses exclusively on a particular product or service in order to obtain a large market share. ▸ a company that operates only on the Internet.

purgation /pəˈgeɪʃ(ə)n/ ■ n. **1** cleansing or purification. **2** evacuation of the bowels brought about by laxatives.
- ORIGIN Middle English: from Old French *purgacion*, from Latin, from *purgare* (see PURGE).

purgative /ˈpɜːgətɪv/ ■ adj. strongly laxative in effect. ■ n. a laxative.

purgatory /ˈpɜːgət(ə)ri/ ■ n. (pl. **-ies**) **1** (in Catholic doctrine) a place or state of suffering inhabited by the souls of sinners who are expiating their sins before going to heaven. **2** mental anguish.
- DERIVATIVES **purgatorial** adj.
- ORIGIN Middle English: from Anglo-Norman French *purgatorie* or medieval Latin *purgatorium*, from *purgare* (see PURGE).

purge ■ v. **1** rid of an unwanted feeling or condition. **2** remove (a group of people considered undesirable) from an organization or place. **3** remove by a cleansing process. **4** [often as noun **purging**] evacuate one's bowels, especially as a result of taking a laxative. **5** Law atone for or wipe out (contempt of court). ■ n. an act of purging people from an organization or place.
- DERIVATIVES **purger** n.
- ORIGIN Middle English: from Old French *purgier*, from Latin *purgare* 'purify', from *purus* 'pure'.

puri /ˈpʊːri/ ■ n. (pl. **puris**) (in Indian cookery) a small, round, flat piece of unleavened bread, deep-fried and served with meat or vegetables.
- ORIGIN from Sanskrit *pūrikā*.

purify ■ v. (**-ies, -ied**) remove contaminants from; make pure.
- DERIVATIVES **purification** n. **purificatory** adj. **purifier** n.
- ORIGIN Middle English: from Old French *purifier*, from Latin *purificare*, from *purus* 'pure'.

purine /ˈpjʊəriːn/ ■ n. Chemistry a colourless crystalline bicyclic compound with basic properties. ▸ (also **purine base**) a substituted derivative of this, especially adenine or guanine present in DNA.
- ORIGIN C19: from German *Purin*, from Latin *purus* 'pure' + *uricum* 'uric acid' (which it forms on oxidation).

purism ■ n. **1** scrupulous observance of traditional rules or structures, especially in language or style. **2** (**Purism**) an early 20th-century artistic style and movement rejecting cubism and emphasizing purity of geometric form and the representation of recognizable objects.
- DERIVATIVES **purist** n. **puristic** adj.

puritan ■ n. **1** (**Puritan**) a member of a group of English Protestants who regarded the Reformation of the Church under Elizabeth I as incomplete and sought to simplify and regulate forms of worship. **2** a person with censorious moral beliefs, especially about self-indulgence and sex. ■ adj. **1** (**Puritan**) of or relating to the Puritans. **2** characteristic of a puritan.
- DERIVATIVES **puritanical** adj. **puritanically** adv. **puritanism** (also **Puritanism**) n.
- ORIGIN C16: from late Latin *puritas* 'purity'.

purity ■ n. the state of being pure.

purl ■ adj. (of a knitting stitch) made by putting the needle through the front of the stitch from right to left. Compare with PLAIN[1] (in sense 5). ■ v. knit with a purl stitch.
- ORIGIN C17.

purlieu /ˈpɜːljuː/ ■ n. (**purlieus**) the area near or surrounding a place.
- ORIGIN C15: prob. an alteration (suggested by French *lieu* 'place') of Anglo-Norman French *puralee* 'a going round to settle the boundaries'.

purlin /ˈpɜːlɪn/ ■ n. a horizontal beam along the length of a roof, resting on principals and supporting the common rafters or boards.
- ORIGIN Middle English: perhaps of French origin.

purloin /pəˈlɔɪn/ ■ v. formal or humorous steal.
- DERIVATIVES **purloiner** n.
- ORIGIN Middle English: from Anglo-Norman French *purloigner* 'put away'.

purple ■ n. **1** a colour intermediate between red and blue. **2** (also **Tyrian purple**) a crimson dye obtained from some molluscs, formerly used for fabric worn by an emperor or senior magistrate in ancient Rome or Byzantium. ▸ (**the purple**) (in ancient Rome) a position of rank, authority, or privilege. **3** the scarlet official dress of a cardinal. ■ adj. of a colour intermediate between red and blue. ■ v. become or make purple in colour.
- PHRASES **born in** (or **to**) **the purple** born into a reigning family or privileged class.
- DERIVATIVES **purpleness** n. **purplish** adj. **purply** adj.
- ORIGIN Old English, from Latin *purpura* 'purple', from Greek *porphura*, denoting molluscs that yielded a crimson dye, also cloth dyed with this.

purple heart ■ n. **1** (**Purple Heart**) (in the US) a

purple passage

decoration for those wounded or killed in action. **2** the hard, dark purplish-brown wood of a large American rainforest tree (genus *Peltogyne*).

purple passage ■ n. an excessively ornate passage in a literary composition.

purple patch ■ n. **1** informal a run of success or good luck. **2** another term for PURPLE PASSAGE.

purple prose ■ n. prose that is too ornate.

purport ■ v. /pəˈpɔːt/ appear to be or do, especially falsely. ■ n. /ˈpəːpɔːt/ **1** the meaning or substance of a document or speech. **2** the purpose of a person or thing.
– DERIVATIVES **purported** adj. **purportedly** adv.
– ORIGIN Middle English: from Old French *purporter*, from medieval Latin *proportare*, from Latin *pro-* 'forth' + *portare* 'carry, bear'.

purpose ■ n. **1** the reason for which something is done or for which something exists. **2** resolve or determination. ■ v. formal have as one's objective.
– PHRASES **on purpose** intentionally. **to the purpose** relevant or useful.
– DERIVATIVES **purposeless** adj. **purposelessly** adv. **purposelessness** n.
– ORIGIN Middle English: from Old French *porpos*, from *porposer*, var. of *proposer* (see PROPOSE).

purposeful ■ adj. **1** resolute. **2** having a purpose.
– DERIVATIVES **purposefully** adv. **purposefulness** n.

USAGE
The adverbs **purposefully**, **purposely**, and **purposively** have different meanings. **Purposely** means 'on purpose, deliberately', while **purposefully** means 'resolutely' or 'with a strong purpose', as in *he strode purposefully through the courtyard*. The uncommon word **purposively** means 'with a particular purpose'.

purposely ■ adv. deliberately; on purpose.

purposive ■ adj. having or done with a purpose.
– DERIVATIVES **purposively** adv. **purposiveness** n.

purpura /ˈpəːpjʊrə/ ■ n. Medicine a rash of purple spots on the skin caused by internal bleeding from small blood vessels.
– DERIVATIVES **purpuric** /-ˈpjʊərɪk/ adj.
– ORIGIN C18: from Greek *porphura* 'purple'.

purr ■ v. **1** (of a cat) make a low continuous vibratory sound expressing contentment. **2** (of a vehicle or engine) move or run smoothly while making a similar sound. ■ n. a purring sound.
– ORIGIN C17: imitative.

purse ■ n. **1** a small pouch of leather or plastic used for carrying money. **2** N. Amer. a handbag. **3** an amount of money available; funds. ▸ a sum of money given as a prize in a sporting contest. ■ v. (with reference to the lips) pucker or contract.
– PHRASES **hold the purse strings** have control of expenditure.
– ORIGIN Old English, alteration of late Latin *bursa*, from Greek *bursa* 'hide, leather'.

purser ■ n. an officer on a ship who keeps the accounts, especially the head steward on a passenger vessel.

purse seine /seɪn/ ■ n. a seine net which may be drawn into the shape of a bag, used for catching shoal fish.
– DERIVATIVES **purse-seiner** n.

purslane /ˈpəːslɪn/ ■ n. a small fleshy-leaved plant of damp or marshy habitats, some kinds of which are edible. [*Portulaca oleracea* and other species.]
– ORIGIN Middle English: from Old French *porcelaine*, prob. from Latin *porcil(l)aca*, var. of *portulaca*.

pursuance ■ n. formal the carrying out or pursuing of something.

pursuant /pəˈsjuːənt/ ■ adv. (**pursuant to**) formal in accordance with (a law, resolution, etc.).
– DERIVATIVES **pursuantly** adv.
– ORIGIN Middle English *poursuiant*: from Old French, 'pursuing', from *poursuir*; later influenced in spelling by PURSUE.

pursue ■ v. (**pursues, pursued, pursuing**) **1** follow in order to catch or attack. **2** seek to attain (a goal).

3 proceed along (a path or route). **4** follow or continue with (a course of action). ▸ continue to investigate or discuss.
– DERIVATIVES **pursuable** adj. **pursuer** n.
– ORIGIN Middle English: from Anglo-Norman French *pursuer*, from Latin *prosequi* 'prosecute'.

pursuit ■ n. **1** the action of pursuing. **2** a recreational or sporting activity. **3** a cycling race in which competitors set off from different parts of a track and attempt to overtake one another.
– ORIGIN Middle English: from Anglo-Norman French *purseute* 'following after', from *pursuer* (see PURSUE).

purulent /ˈpjʊərʊl(ə)nt/ ■ adj. Medicine consisting of, containing, or discharging pus.
– ORIGIN Middle English: from Latin *purulentus*, from *pus, pur-* 'pus'.

purvey ■ v. provide or supply (food, drink, or other goods) as one's business.
– DERIVATIVES **purveyor** n.
– ORIGIN Middle English: from Anglo-Norman French *purveier*, from Latin *providere* (see PROVIDE).

purveyance ■ n. the action of purveying.

purview ■ n. **1** the scope of the influence or concerns of something. **2** a range of experience or thought.
– ORIGIN Middle English: from Anglo-Norman French *purveu, purveier* (see PURVEY).

pus ■ n. a thick yellowish or greenish opaque liquid produced in infected tissue, consisting of dead white blood cells and bacteria with tissue debris and serum.
– ORIGIN Middle English: from Latin.

push ■ v. **1** exert force on (someone or something) in order to move them away from oneself. ▸ hold and exert force on (something) so as to cause it to move in front of one. ▸ move one's body or a part of it forcefully into a specified position. ▸ (**push off**) exert pressure with an oar so as to move a boat out from a bank. ▸ move forward by using force. ▸ (**push in**) go in front of people who are already queuing. ▸ (**push ahead**) proceed with or continue a course of action. ▸ (**push along/off**) informal go away; depart. **3** urge (someone) to greater effort. ▸ (**push for**) demand persistently. **4** informal promote the use, sale, or acceptance of. ▸ sell (a narcotic drug) illegally. **5** (**be pushed**) informal have very little of something, especially time. **6** (**be pushing**) informal be nearly (a particular age). ■ n. **1** an act of pushing. **2** a vigorous effort. ▸ forcefulness and enterprise. **3** (**a push**) informal something that is hard to achieve.
– PHRASES **at a push** informal only if necessary or with a certain degree of difficulty. **get** (or **give someone**) **the push** (or **shove**) Brit. informal **1** be dismissed (or dismiss someone) from a job. **2** be rejected in (or end) a relationship. **push one's luck** informal take a risk on the assumption that one will continue to be successful or in favour. **when push comes to shove** informal when one must commit oneself to an action or decision.
– DERIVATIVES **pusher** n.
– ORIGIN Middle English: from Old French *pousser*, from Latin *pulsare* (see PULSE¹).

pushbike ■ n. Brit. informal a bicycle.

pushcart ■ n. a small handcart or barrow.

pushchair ■ n. a folding chair on wheels, in which a baby or young child can be pushed along.

pushover ■ n. **1** informal a person who is easy to overcome or influence. ▸ a thing that is very easily done. **2** Rugby a try in which one side in a scrum pushes the ball over the opponents' goal line.

pushpin ■ n. chiefly N. Amer. a drawing pin with a spherical or cylindrical plastic head.

pushpit ■ n. a raised safety rail in the stern of a yacht.
– ORIGIN 1960s: humorous formation, suggested by PULPIT.

push poll ■ n. an ostensible opinion poll in which the true objective is to sway voters using loaded questions.
– DERIVATIVES **push-polling** n.

push-pull ■ adj. **1** operated by pushing and pulling. **2** Electronics denoting an arrangement of two matched transistors or valves conducting alternately.

pushrod ■ n. a rod operated by cams that opens and closes the valves in an internal-combustion engine.

push-start ■ v. start (a motor vehicle) by pushing it in order to make the engine turn. ■ n. an act of push-starting.

push technology ■ n. Computing a service in which the user downloads software from a provider which then continually supplies information from the Internet in categories selected by the user.

push-up ■ n. another term for PRESS-UP.

pushy ■ adj. (**-ier**, **-iest**) excessively self-assertive or ambitious.
– DERIVATIVES **pushily** adv. **pushiness** n.

pusillanimous /ˌpjuːsɪˈlanɪməs/ ■ adj. timid.
– DERIVATIVES **pusillanimity** /-ləˈnɪmɪti/ n. **pusillanimously** adv.
– ORIGIN Middle English: from eccles. Latin *pusillanimis*, from *pusillus* 'very small' + *animus* 'mind'.

puss ■ n. informal **1** a cat (especially as a form of address). **2** a coquettish girl or young woman: *a glamour puss*.
– ORIGIN C16: prob. from Middle Low German *pūs* or Dutch *poes*.

pussy ■ n. (pl. **-ies**) **1** (also **pussy cat**) informal a cat. **2** vulgar slang a woman's genitals. ▶ women collectively, considered sexually.

pussyfoot ■ v. **1** act in an excessively cautious or non-committal way. **2** move stealthily.
– DERIVATIVES **pussyfooter** n.

pussy willow ■ n. a willow with soft fluffy catkins that appear before the leaves, e.g. a sallow.

pustule /ˈpʌstjuːl/ ■ n. a small blister or pimple containing pus.
– DERIVATIVES **pustular** adj.
– ORIGIN Middle English: from Latin *pustula*.

put ■ v. (**putting**; past and past part. **put**) **1** move to or place in a particular position. ▶ (of a ship) proceed in a particular direction: *the boat put out to sea*. **2** bring into a particular state or condition: *they tried to put me at ease*. ▶ express in a particular way: *to put it bluntly, he was not really divorced*. **3** (**put something on/on to**) cause to carry or be subject to something: *commentators put the blame on Congress*. ▶ assign a particular value, figure, or limit to. **4** throw (a shot or weight) as an athletic sport. ■ n. a throw of the shot or weight.
– PHRASES **put someone's eyes out** blind someone, especially in a violent way. **put foot** S. African informal go fast or accelerate, especially in a car. **put one's hands together** applaud. **put one's hands up** raise one's hands in surrender. **put it to** make a statement or allegation to (someone) and challenge them to deny it. **put one over on** informal deceive (someone) into accepting something false. **put up or shut up** informal justify oneself or remain silent.
– PHRASAL VERBS **put about** Nautical (of a ship) turn on the opposite tack. **put something about** spread information or rumours. **put something aside** (or **by**) save money for future use. **put someone away** informal confine someone in a prison or psychiatric hospital. **put something away 1** save money for future use. **2** informal consume food or drink in large quantities. **put someone down** informal lower someone's self-esteem by publicly criticizing them. **put something down 1** suppress a rebellion, coup, or riot by force. **2** kill an animal because it is sick, injured, or old. **3** pay a specified sum as a deposit. **4** preserve or store food or wine for future use. **put something down to** attribute something to. **put someone off 1** cancel or postpone an appointment with someone. **2** cause someone to feel dislike or lose enthusiasm. **3** distract someone. **put something off** postpone something. **put something on 1** present or provide a play, service, etc. **2** become heavier by a specified amount. **3** assume a particular expression, accent, etc. **put someone on to** draw someone's attention to. **put out for** informal, chiefly N. Amer. agree to have sexual intercourse with. **put someone out** inconvenience, upset, or annoy someone. **put something out 1** dislocate a joint. **2** (of an engine or motor) produce a particular amount of power. **put someone through 1** subject someone to a gruelling or unpleasant experience. **2** connect someone by telephone to another person or place. **3** pay for one's child to attend school or college. **put something to 1** submit something to (someone) for consideration. **2** couple an animal with (another of the opposite sex) for breeding. **put up** offer or show (a particular degree of resistance or skill) in a fight,

959

putty

contest, etc. **put someone up 1** accommodate someone temporarily. **2** propose someone for election or adoption. **put something up 1** present something for discussion or consideration. **2** publish banns. **3** provide money as backing for an enterprise. **4** offer something for sale or auction. **5** cause game to rise from cover. **6** archaic return a sword to its sheath. **put upon** [often as adj. **put-upon**] informal take advantage of (someone) by exploiting their good nature. **put someone up to** informal encourage someone to do (something wrong or unwise). **put up with** tolerate; endure.
– ORIGIN Old English; of unknown origin; cf. dialect *pote* 'to push, thrust' (an early sense of *put*).

putative /ˈpjuːtətɪv/ ■ adj. generally considered or reputed to be.
– DERIVATIVES **putatively** adv.
– ORIGIN Middle English: from Old French *putatif*, *-ive* or late Latin *putativus*, from Latin *putare* 'think'.

put-down ■ n. informal a remark intended to humiliate or criticize someone.

put-in ■ n. Rugby another term for THROW-IN (in sense 2).

putonghua /puːˈtʊŋhwɑː/ ■ n. the standard spoken form of modern Chinese, based on the dialect of Beijing.
– ORIGIN Chinese, 'common spoken language'.

put option ■ n. Stock Exchange an option to sell assets at an agreed price on or before a particular date.

put-put /ˈpʌtpʌt/ ■ n. & v. another term for PUTTER[2].

putrefy /ˈpjuːtrɪfʌɪ/ ■ v. (**-ies**, **-ied**) decay or rot and produce a fetid smell.
– DERIVATIVES **putrefaction** n. **putrefactive** adj.
– ORIGIN Middle English: from Latin *putrefacere*, from *puter*, *putr-* 'rotten'.

putrescent /pjuːˈtrɛs(ə)nt/ ■ adj. undergoing the process of decay; rotting.
– DERIVATIVES **putrescence** n.
– ORIGIN C18: from Latin *putrescent-*, from *putrere* (see PUTRID).

putrescible ■ adj. liable to decay.

putrid ■ adj. **1** decaying or rotting and emitting a fetid smell. **2** informal very unpleasant.
– DERIVATIVES **putridity** n. **putridly** adv. **putridness** n.
– ORIGIN Middle English: from Latin *putridus*, from *putrere* 'to rot', from *puter*, *putr-* 'rotten'.

putsch /pʊtʃ/ ■ n. a violent attempt to overthrow a government.
– ORIGIN 1920s: from Swiss German, 'thrust, blow'.

putt /pʌt/ ■ v. (**putted**, **putting**) strike a golf ball gently so that it rolls into or near a hole. ■ n. a stroke of this kind.
– ORIGIN C17 (orig. Scots).

puttee /ˈpʌti/ ■ n. a long strip of cloth wound spirally round the leg from ankle to knee for protection and support.
– ORIGIN C19: from Hindi *paṭṭī* 'band, bandage'.

putter[1] /ˈpʌtə/ ■ n. a golf club designed for putting, typically with a flat-faced mallet-like head.

putter[2] /ˈpʌtə/ ■ n. the rapid intermittent sound of a small petrol engine. ■ v. move with or make such a sound.
– ORIGIN 1940s: imitative.

putter[3] /ˈpʌtə/ ■ v. another term for POTTER[1].
– ORIGIN C19.

putting green ■ n. (in golf) a smooth area of short grass surrounding a hole.

putto /ˈpʊtəʊ/ ■ n. (pl. **putti** /-tiː/) a representation of a naked child, especially a cherub or a cupid in Renaissance art.
– ORIGIN Italian, 'boy'.

Putt-Putt ■ n. trademark a type of minigolf.

putty ■ n. **1** a malleable paste, made from whiting and raw linseed oil, that gradually hardens and is used chiefly for sealing glass in window frames. ▶ a malleable substance used as a filler, modelling material, etc. **2** a polishing powder, usually made from tin oxide, used in jewellery

---

s sit　t top　v voice　w we　z zoo　ʃ she　ʒ decision　θ thin　ð this　ŋ ring　x loch　tʃ chip　dʒ jar

putu

work. ■ v. (-ies, -ied) seal or cover with putty.
– PHRASES **be (like) putty in someone's hands** be easily manipulated by someone.
– ORIGIN C17: from French *potée* 'potful'.

putu /ˈpuːtuː/ (also **phutu**) ■ n. S. African thick maize porridge.
– ORIGIN from isiZulu *uphuthu*, prob. from *putu* 'crumbling to pieces'.

put-up job ■ n. informal something devised so as to deceive.

puzzle ■ v. **1** confuse because difficult to understand. **2** think hard about something difficult to understand. ■ n. **1** a game, toy, or problem designed to test ingenuity or knowledge. **2** a puzzling person or thing.
– DERIVATIVES **puzzlement** n. **puzzler** n. **puzzling** adj. **puzzlingly** adv.
– ORIGIN C16.

puzzle bush ■ n. a shrub or small tree with fragrant white, lilac, or purple flowers, native to southern Africa. [*Ehretia rigida*.]

PVA ■ abbrev. polyvinyl acetate.

PVC ■ abbrev. polyvinyl chloride.

PVS ■ abbrev. Medicine **1** persistent vegetative state. **2** postviral syndrome.

p.w. ■ abbrev. per week.

PWA ■ abbrev. person with Aids.

PWR ■ abbrev. pressurized-water reactor.

pye-dog /ˈpaɪdɒɡ/ (also **pi-dog**) ■ n. (in Asia) a half-wild stray mongrel.
– ORIGIN C19: from Anglo-Indian *pye*, Hindi *pāhī* 'outsider' + DOG.

pyelitis /ˌpaɪəˈlaɪtɪs/ ■ n. Medicine inflammation of the renal pelvis.
– ORIGIN C19: from Greek *puelos* 'trough, basin'.

pygidium /paɪˈdʒɪdɪəm, -ˈɡɪdɪəm/ ■ n. (pl. **pygidia** /-ɪə/) Zoology the terminal part or hind segment of the body in certain invertebrates.
– ORIGIN C19: from Greek *pugē* 'rump'.

pygmy (also **pigmy**) ■ n. (pl. **-ies**) **1** a member of certain peoples of very short stature in equatorial Africa or parts of SE Asia. **2** a person who is deficient in a particular respect: *he regarded them as intellectual pygmies*. ■ adj. very small; dwarf.
– ORIGIN Middle English: from Greek *pugmaios* 'dwarf', from *pugmē* 'the length measured from elbow to knuckles'.

pygmy chimpanzee ■ n. another term for BONOBO.

pyjamas (US **pajamas**) ■ pl. n. a suit of loose trousers and jacket for sleeping in.
– ORIGIN C19: from Urdu and Persian, from *pāy* 'leg' + *jāma* 'clothing'.

pylon ■ n. **1** (also **electricity pylon**) a tall tower-like structure for carrying electricity cables. **2** a pillar-like structure on the wing of an aircraft used for carrying an engine or other load. **3** a tower or post marking a path for light aircraft, cars, or other vehicles, especially in racing.
– ORIGIN C19: from Greek *pulōn*, from *pulē* 'gate'.

pylorus /paɪˈlɔːrəs/ ■ n. (pl. **pylori** /-rʌɪ/) Anatomy the opening from the stomach into the duodenum.
– DERIVATIVES **pyloric** adj.
– ORIGIN C17: from Greek *pulouros* 'gatekeeper'.

pyoderma /ˌpaɪə(ʊ)ˈdəːmə/ ■ n. Medicine a skin infection with formation of pus.
– ORIGIN 1930s: from Greek *puo-* (from *puon* 'pus') + *derma* 'skin'.

pyogenic /ˌpaɪə(ʊ)ˈdʒɛnɪk/ ■ adj. Medicine involving or relating to the production of pus.
– ORIGIN C19: from Greek *puo-* (from *puon* 'pus') + -GENIC.

pyracantha /ˌpaɪrəˈkanθə/ ■ n. a thorny evergreen Eurasian shrub with white flowers and bright red or yellow berries. [Genus *Pyracantha*.]
– ORIGIN from Greek *purakantha*, the name of an unidentified plant, from *pur* 'fire' + *akantha* 'thorn'.

pyramid /ˈpɪrəmɪd/ ■ n. **1** a monumental stone structure with a square or triangular base and sloping sides that meet in a point at the top, especially one built as a royal tomb in ancient Egypt. **2** Geometry a polyhedron of which one face is a polygon and the other faces are triangles with a common vertex. **3** Anatomy a pyramid-shaped structure, especially in the brain. **4** a system of financial growth achieved by a small initial investment.
– DERIVATIVES **pyramidical** /-ˈmɪdɪk(ə)l/ adj. **pyramidically** adv.
– ORIGIN Middle English: from Greek *puramis, puramid-*.

pyramidal /pɪˈramɪd(ə)l/ ■ adj. **1** resembling a pyramid in shape. **2** Anatomy & Medicine relating to or denoting a tract of motor nerves within the pyramid of the medulla oblongata.
– DERIVATIVES **pyramidally** adv.

pyramid selling ■ n. a system of selling goods in which agency rights are sold to an increasing number of distributors at successively lower levels.

pyre ■ n. a heap of combustible material, especially one for burning a corpse as part of a funeral ceremony.
– ORIGIN C17: from Greek *pura*, from *pur* 'fire'.

Pyrenean /ˌpɪrəˈniːən/ ■ adj. of or relating to the Pyrenees.

pyrethrin /paɪˈriːθrɪn/ ■ n. Chemistry any of a group of insecticidal compounds present in pyrethrum flowers.
– DERIVATIVES **pyrethroid** n.

pyrethrum /paɪˈriːθrəm/ ■ n. **1** an aromatic plant of the daisy family, typically with feathery foliage and brightly coloured flowers. [Genus *Tanacetum* (formerly *Pyrethrum*): several species.] **2** an insecticide made from the dried flowers of these plants.
– ORIGIN Middle English: from Greek *purethron* 'feverfew'.

pyretic /paɪˈrɛtɪk, pɪ-/ ■ adj. feverish or inducing fever.
– ORIGIN C18: from Greek *puretos* 'fever'.

Pyrex ■ n. trademark a hard heat-resistant type of glass.
– ORIGIN C20: an invented word.

pyrexia /paɪˈrɛksɪə, pɪ-/ ■ n. Medicine fever.
– DERIVATIVES **pyrexial** adj. **pyrexic** adj.
– ORIGIN C18: from Greek *purexis*, from *puressein* 'be feverish'.

pyridine /ˈpɪrɪdiːn/ ■ n. Chemistry a colourless volatile heterocyclic liquid with an unpleasant odour, present in coal tar and used as a solvent.
– ORIGIN C19: from Greek *pur* 'fire'.

pyridoxine /ˌpɪrɪˈdɒksɪn, -iːn/ ■ n. Biochemistry vitamin B_6, a compound present chiefly in cereals, liver oils, and yeast, and important in the metabolism of fats.
– ORIGIN 1930s: from *pyrid(ine)*.

pyriform /ˈpɪrɪfɔːm/ ■ adj. Biology pear-shaped.
– ORIGIN C18: from *pyrum*, misspelling of Latin *pirum* 'pear', + -IFORM.

pyrimidine /pɪˈrɪmɪdiːn/ ■ n. Chemistry a colourless crystalline heterocyclic compound with basic properties. ▶ (also **pyrimidine base**) a substituted derivative of this, especially thymine or cytosine present in DNA.
– ORIGIN C19: from German *Pyrimidin*, from PYRIDINE, with the insertion of *-im-* from IMIDE.

pyrites /paɪˈrʌɪtiːz/ (also **iron pyrites**, **pyrite**) ■ n. a shiny yellow mineral consisting of iron disulphide, occurring as intersecting cubic crystals. See also COPPER PYRITES.
– DERIVATIVES **pyritic** adj. **pyritization** (also **-isation**) n. **pyritize** (also **-ise**) v.
– ORIGIN Middle English: from Greek *puritēs* 'of fire', from *pur* 'fire'.

pyro- ■ comb. form **1** of or relating to fire: *pyromania*. **2** Chemistry & Mineralogy formed or affected by heat: *pyroxene*.
– ORIGIN from Greek *pur* 'fire'.

pyroclastic /ˌpaɪrə(ʊ)ˈklastɪk/ Geology ■ adj. of or denoting rock fragments or ash erupted by a volcano, especially as a hot, dense, destructive flow. ■ n. (**pyroclastics**) pyroclastic material.
– DERIVATIVES **pyroclast** n.

pyrogenic ■ adj. **1** Medicine inducing fever. **2** resulting from combustion or heating.
– DERIVATIVES **pyrogenicity** n.

pyrography /paɪˈrɒɡrəfi/ ■ n. the art or technique of decorating wood or leather by burning a design on the surface with a heated metallic point.

pyrolysis /pʌɪˈrɒlɪsɪs/ ■ n. Chemistry decomposition brought about by high temperatures.
– DERIVATIVES **pyrolyse** (US **pyrolyze**) v. **pyrolytic** adj.

pyromania ■ n. an obsessive desire to set fire to things.
– DERIVATIVES **pyromaniac** n. **pyromaniacal** adj. **pyromanic** adj.

pyrometer /pʌɪˈrɒmɪtə/ ■ n. an instrument for measuring high temperatures, especially in furnaces and kilns.
– DERIVATIVES **pyrometric** adj. **pyrometrically** adv. **pyrometry** n.

pyrope /ˈpʌɪrəʊp/ ■ n. a deep red variety of garnet.
– ORIGIN C19: from German *Pyrop*, from Greek *purōpos* 'gold-bronze', literally 'fiery-eyed'.

pyrophoric /ˌpʌɪrə(ʊ)ˈfɒrɪk/ ■ adj. **1** liable to ignite spontaneously in air. **2** (of an alloy) emitting sparks when scratched or struck.
– ORIGIN C19: from Greek *purophoros* 'fire-bearing'.

pyrotechnic /ˌpʌɪrə(ʊ)ˈtɛknɪk/ ■ adj. **1** of or relating to fireworks. **2** brilliant or spectacular.
– DERIVATIVES **pyrotechnical** adj. **pyrotechnist** n.
– ORIGIN C19: from PYRO- + Greek *tekhnē* 'art'.

pyrotechnics ■ pl. n. **1** a firework display. ▶ [treated as sing.] the art of making fireworks or staging firework displays. **2** a spectacular performance or display: *vocal pyrotechnics*.

pyroxene /pʌɪˈrɒksiːn/ ■ n. any of a large class of rock-forming silicate minerals typically occurring as prismatic crystals.
– ORIGIN C19: from PYRO- + Greek *xenos* 'stranger' (because supposedly alien to igneous rocks).

pyrrhic /ˈpɪrɪk/ ■ adj. (of a victory) won at too great a cost to have been worthwhile for the victor.
– ORIGIN C19: from the name of *Pyrrhus*, a king of Epirus who defeated the Romans at Asculum in 279 BC but sustained heavy losses.

pyruvic acid /pʌɪˈruːvɪk/ ■ n. Biochemistry a yellowish organic acid which is an intermediate in many metabolic processes.
– DERIVATIVES **pyruvate** n.
– ORIGIN C19: from modern Latin *acidum pyruvicum*, from *acidum* 'acid' + *pyruvicum* from PYRO- (denoting an acid) + Latin *uva* 'grape'.

Pythagoras' theorem ■ n. the theorem that the square on the hypotenuse of a right-angled triangle is equal in area to the sum of the squares on the other two sides.

Pythagorean /pʌɪˌθagəˈriːən/ ■ adj. of or relating to the Greek philosopher and mathematician Pythagoras (*c.*580–500 BC) or his philosophy. ■ n. a follower of Pythagoras.

python ■ n. a large non-venomous snake which kills prey by constriction. [*Python* (tropical Asia and Africa) and other genera in Australasia: many species.]
– DERIVATIVES **pythonic** adj.
– ORIGIN C16: from Greek *Puthōn*, the name of a huge serpent killed by Apollo.

python dance ■ n. another term for DOMBA (in sense 2).

Pythonesque /pʌɪθəˈnɛsk/ ■ adj. resembling the absurdist or surrealist humour of *Monty Python's Flying Circus*, a British television comedy series (1969–74).

pyuria /pʌɪˈjʊərɪə/ ■ n. Medicine the presence of pus in the urine, typically from bacterial infection.
– ORIGIN C19: from Greek *puon* 'pus' + -URIA.

pzazz ■ n. variant spelling of PIZZAZZ.

Qq

Q¹ (also **q**) ■ n. (pl. **Qs** or **Q's**) **1** the seventeenth letter of the alphabet. **2** denoting the next after P in a set of items, categories, etc.

Q² ■ abbrev. **1** quarter (used to refer to a specified quarter of the financial year): *Q4*. **2** queen (used especially in card games and chess). **3** question.

q ■ symb. Physics electric charge.
– ORIGIN C19: initial letter of *quantity*.

QA ■ abbrev. quality assurance.

Qabalah ■ n. variant spelling of **KABBALAH**.

Qatari /kaˈtɑːri/ ■ n. a native or inhabitant of Qatar, a country in the Persian Gulf. ■ adj. of or relating to Qatar.

qawwali /kəˈvɑːli/ ■ n. a style of Muslim devotional music associated particularly with Sufis in Pakistan.
– ORIGIN from Arabic *qawwāli*, from *Qawwāl* 'loquacious', also 'singer'.

QC ■ abbrev. **1** quality control. **2** Law Queen's Counsel.

QCD ■ abbrev. quantum chromodynamics.

QED ■ abbrev. **1** quantum electrodynamics. **2** quod erat demonstrandum.

Q fever ■ n. an infectious fever caused by rickettsiae.
– ORIGIN 1930s: from *Q* for *query* + **FEVER**.

qi /kiː/ ■ n. variant spelling of **CHI²**.

qibla ■ n. variant spelling of **KIBLAH**.

qigong /tʃiːˈɡɒŋ/ ■ n. a Chinese system of physical exercises and breathing control related to tai chi.
– ORIGIN from Chinese.

QM ■ abbrev. Quartermaster.

QMG ■ abbrev. Quartermaster General.

QMS ■ abbrev. Quartermaster Sergeant.

qr ■ abbrev. quarter(s).

Q-ship ■ n. a merchant ship with concealed weapons, used in an attempt to destroy submarines.
– ORIGIN FIRST WORLD WAR: from *Q* as a non-explicit symbol of the type of vessel + **SHIP**.

QSO ■ abbrev. quasi-stellar object, a quasar.

qt ■ abbrev. quart(s).

q.t. ■ n. (in phr. **on the q.t.**) informal secretly.
– ORIGIN C19: abbrev. of *quiet*.

qua /kweɪ, kwɑː/ ■ conj. formal in the capacity of.
– ORIGIN Latin, from *qui* 'who'.

quack¹ ■ n. the characteristic harsh sound made by a duck. ■ v. make this sound.
– ORIGIN C16: imitative.

quack² ■ n. **1** an unqualified person who dishonestly claims to have medical knowledge. **2** informal a doctor.
– DERIVATIVES **quackery** n. **quackish** adj.
– ORIGIN C17: abbrev. of *quacksalver*, from Dutch, prob. from obsolete *quacken* 'prattle' + *salf*, *zalf* (see **SALVE**).

quad ■ n. **1** a quadrangle. **2** a quadruplet. **3** quadraphonic. **4** (in telephony) a group of four insulated conductors twisted together.

quad bike ■ n. a motorcycle with four large tyres, for off-road use.

quadrangle ■ n. **1** a four-sided geometrical figure, especially a square or rectangle. **2** a square or rectangular courtyard enclosed by buildings.
– ORIGIN Middle English: from late Latin *quadrangulum* 'square', from *quadrangulus*, from Latin *quadri-* 'four' + *angulus* 'corner, angle'.

quadrangular ■ adj. **1** having four sides. **2** involving four teams competing against each other.

quadrant ■ n. technical **1** each of four parts of a circle, plane, body, etc. divided by two lines or planes at right angles. **2** historical an instrument for taking angular measurements, consisting of a graduated quarter circle and a sighting mechanism. **3** a frame, typically in the form of a quarter circle, enclosing a steering mechanism or control lever.
– DERIVATIVES **quadrantal** adj.
– ORIGIN Middle English: from Latin *quadrans*, *quadrant-* 'quarter', from *quattuor* 'four'.

quadraphonic (also **quadrophonic**) ■ adj. (of sound reproduction) transmitted through four channels.
– DERIVATIVES **quadraphonically** adv. **quadraphonics** pl. n. **quadraphony** /-ˈdrɒf(ə)ni/ n.
– ORIGIN 1960s: from **QUADRI-** + a shortened form of **STEREOPHONIC**.

quadrat /ˈkwɒdrət/ ■ n. Ecology a randomly selected small area used in assessing the local distribution of plants or animals.
– ORIGIN C20: var. of **QUADRATE**.

quadrate /ˈkwɒdrət/ ■ n. (also **quadrate bone**) Zoology a squarish bone in the skull of a bird or reptile, with which the jaw articulates. ■ adj. roughly square or rectangular.
– ORIGIN Middle English: from Latin *quadrare* 'make square', from *quattuor* 'four'.

quadratic /kwɒˈdratɪk/ ■ adj. Mathematics involving the second and no higher power of an unknown quantity or variable.
– ORIGIN C17: from French *quadratique* or modern Latin *quadraticus*, from *quadrare* (see **QUADRATE**).

quadrature /ˈkwɒdrətʃə/ ■ n. **1** Astronomy the position of the moon or a planet when 90° from the sun in the sky. **2** Electronics a phase difference of 90° between two waves of the same frequency.
– ORIGIN C16: from Latin *quadratura* 'a square', from *quadrare* (see **QUADRATE**).

quadrennial /kwɒˈdrɛnɪəl/ ■ adj. lasting for or recurring every four years.
– DERIVATIVES **quadrennially** adv.
– ORIGIN C17: from Latin *quadrennium*, from *quadri-* 'four' + *annus* 'year'.

quadri- ■ comb. form four; having four: *quadriplegia*.
– ORIGIN from Latin, from *quattuor* 'four'.

quadric /ˈkwɒdrɪk/ ■ adj. Geometry denoting a surface or curve described by an equation of the second degree.
– ORIGIN C19: from Latin *quadra* 'square'.

quadriceps /ˈkwɒdrɪsɛps/ ■ n. (pl. same) a large muscle at the front of the thigh which acts to extend the leg.
– ORIGIN C16: from Latin, 'four-headed', from *quadri-* 'four' + *-ceps* (from *caput* 'head').

quadrilateral ■ n. a four-sided figure. ■ adj. having four straight sides.
– ORIGIN C17: from late Latin *quadrilaterus*.

quadrille¹ /kwɒˈdrɪl/ ■ n. a square dance performed typically by four couples and containing five figures, each of which is a complete dance in itself. ▸ a piece of music for such a dance.
– ORIGIN C18: from Spanish *cuadrilla* or Italian *quadriglia* 'troop, company'.

quadrille² /kwɒˈdrɪl/ ■ n. a trick-taking card game for four players using a pack lacking eights, nines, and tens, fashionable in the 18th century.
– ORIGIN C18: from French, perhaps from Spanish *cuartillo*, from *cuarto* 'fourth'.

quadrille³ /kwɒˈdrɪl/ ■ n. paper printed with a ruled grid of small squares.
– ORIGIN C19: from French *quadrillé*, from *quadrille* 'small square'.

| CONSONANTS | b but | d dog | f few | g get | h he | j yes | k cat | l leg | m man | n no | p pen | r red |

quadrillion /kwɒˈdrɪljən/ ■ cardinal number (pl. **quadrillions** or (with numeral) same) a thousand raised to the power of five (10¹⁵).
– DERIVATIVES **quadrillionth** ordinal number.
– ORIGIN C17: from French, from *million*, by substitution of QUADRI- for the initial letters.

quadripartite /ˌkwɒdrɪˈpɑːtʌɪt/ ■ adj. **1** consisting of four parts. **2** shared by or involving four parties.

quadriplegia /ˌkwɒdrɪˈpliːdʒə/ ■ n. Medicine paralysis of all four limbs.
– DERIVATIVES **quadriplegic** adj. & n.

quadrivalent /ˌkwɒdrɪˈveɪl(ə)nt/ ■ adj. Chemistry another term for TETRAVALENT.

quadroon /kwɒˈdruːn/ ■ n. a person whose parents are a mulatto and a white person and who is therefore one-quarter black by descent.
– ORIGIN C18: from Spanish *cuarterón*, from *cuarto* 'quarter'; later assimilated to words beginning with QUADRI-.

quadrophonic ■ adj. variant spelling of QUADRAPHONIC.

quadruped /ˈkwɒdrʊpɛd/ ■ n. an animal which has four feet, especially an ungulate mammal.
– DERIVATIVES **quadrupedal** /-ˈpiːd(ə)l, -ˈruːpɪd(ə)l/ adj. **quadrupedalism** n.
– ORIGIN C17: from French *quadrupède* or Latin *quadrupes*, from *quadru-* 'four' + *pes* 'foot'.

quadruple /ˈkwɒdrʊp(ə)l, kwɒˈdruːp(ə)l/ ■ adj. **1** consisting of four parts or elements. **2** consisting of four times as much or as many. **3** (of time in music) having four beats in a bar. ■ v. increase or be increased fourfold. ■ n. a quadruple thing, number, or amount.
– DERIVATIVES **quadruply** adv.
– ORIGIN Middle English: from Latin *quadruplus*, from *quadru-* 'four' + *-plus* as in *duplus* (see DUPLE).

quadruplet /ˈkwɒdrʊplɪt, kwɒˈdruːplɪt/ ■ n. each of four children born at one birth.
– ORIGIN C18: from QUADRUPLE, on the pattern of *triplet*.

quadruplicate ■ adj. /kwɒˈdruːplɪkət/ **1** consisting of four parts or elements. **2** of which four copies are made. ■ v. /kwɒˈdruːplɪkeɪt/ **1** multiply by four. **2** [usu. as adj. **quadruplicated**] make or provide four copies of.
– DERIVATIVES **quadruplication** n. **quadruplicity** n.
– ORIGIN C17: from Latin *quadruplicare* 'quadruple'.

quadrupole /ˈkwɒdrʊpəʊl/ ■ n. Physics a unit or arrangement of four equal monopoles or two equal dipoles with alternating polarity.

quaff /kwɒf/ ■ v. drink (something) heartily.
– DERIVATIVES **quaffable** adj. **quaffer** n.
– ORIGIN C16: prob. imitative of the sound of drinking.

quagga /ˈkwaxə/ ■ n. an extinct South African zebra with a yellowish-brown coat with darker stripes. [*Equus quagga*.]
– ORIGIN S. African Dutch, prob. from Khoikhoi, imitative of its braying.

quagmire /ˈkwagmʌɪə, ˈkwɒg-/ ■ n. **1** a soft boggy area of land that gives way underfoot. **2** a complex or difficult situation.

quaich /kweɪx, -x/ (also **quaigh**) ■ n. Scottish a shallow drinking cup, typically with two handles.
– ORIGIN C16: from Scottish Gaelic *cuach* 'cup'.

quail¹ ■ n. (pl. same or **quails**) a small short-tailed game bird. [*Coturnix coturnix* and other species.]
– ORIGIN Middle English: from Old French *quaille*, from medieval Latin *coacula* (prob. imitative of its call).

quail² ■ v. feel or show fear or apprehension.
– ORIGIN Middle English.

quaint ■ adj. attractively unusual or old-fashioned.
– DERIVATIVES **quaintly** adv. **quaintness** n.
– ORIGIN Middle English: from Old French *cointe*, from Latin *cognoscere* 'ascertain'.

quake ■ v. **1** (especially of the earth) shake or tremble. **2** shudder with fear. ■ n. informal an earthquake.
– DERIVATIVES **quaky** adj. (-ier, -iest).
– ORIGIN Old English *cwacian*.

Quaker ■ n. a member of the Religious Society of Friends, a Christian movement devoted to peaceful principles and rejecting both formal ministry and all set forms of worship.
– DERIVATIVES **Quakerish** adj. **Quakerism** n.

– ORIGIN from QUAKE, perhaps alluding to the founder's direction to his followers to 'tremble at the name of the Lord'.

quaking grass ■ n. a grass with oval or heart-shaped flower heads which tremble in the wind. [Genus *Briza*.]

quale /ˈkweɪli/ ■ n. (pl. **qualia** /ˈkweɪlɪə/) Philosophy a quality or property as perceived or experienced by a person.
– ORIGIN C17: from Latin, from *qualis* 'of what kind'.

qualification ■ n. **1** the action of qualifying or the fact of becoming qualified. **2** a pass of an examination or an official completion of a course. **3** a quality that qualifies someone for a job or activity. **4** a condition that must be fulfilled before a right can be acquired. **5** a statement or assertion that qualifies another.
– DERIVATIVES **qualificatory** adj.

qualify ■ v. (-ies, -ied) **1** (often **qualify for**) be entitled to a benefit or privilege by fulfilling a necessary condition. ▸ fulfill the necessary conditions to be eligible for a competition. ▸ be or make properly entitled to be classed in a particular way. **2** become officially recognized as a practitioner of a profession or activity, typically by undertaking a course and passing examinations. ▸ make competent or knowledgeable enough to do something. **3** make (a statement or assertion) less absolute. ▸ archaic make less severe or extreme. **4** Grammar (of a word or phrase) attribute a quality to (another word, especially a preceding noun).
– DERIVATIVES **qualifiable** adj. **qualifier** n.
– ORIGIN Middle English: from French *qualifier*, from medieval Latin *qualificare*, from Latin *qualis* (see QUALITY).

qualitative /ˈkwɒlɪtətɪv/ ■ adj. **1** of, concerned with, or measured by quality. Often contrasted with QUANTITATIVE. **2** Grammar (of an adjective) describing the quality of something in size, appearance, etc.
– DERIVATIVES **qualitatively** adv.
– ORIGIN Middle English: from late Latin *qualitativus*, from Latin *qualitas* (see QUALITY).

qualitative analysis ■ n. Chemistry identification of the constituents present in a substance.

quality ■ n. (pl. -ies) **1** the standard of something as measured against other things of a similar kind. ▸ general excellence. ▸ archaic high social standing. **2** a distinctive attribute or characteristic. ▸ Phonetics the distinguishing characteristic or characteristics of a speech sound.
– ORIGIN Middle English: from Old French *qualite*, from Latin *qualitas*, from *qualis* 'of what kind, of such a kind'.

quality control ■ n. a system of maintaining standards in manufactured products by testing a sample of the output against the specification.
– DERIVATIVES **quality controller** n.

quality time ■ n. time devoted exclusively to another person in order to strengthen a relationship.

qualm /kwɑːm, kwɔːm/ ■ n. **1** a feeling of doubt or unease, especially about one's conduct. **2** archaic a momentary faint or sick feeling.
– DERIVATIVES **qualmish** adj.
– ORIGIN C16: perhaps rel. to Old English *cw(e)alm* 'pain', of Germanic origin.

quandary /ˈkwɒnd(ə)ri/ ■ n. (pl. -ies) a state of uncertainty over what to do in a difficult situation: *Kate was in a quandary*.
– ORIGIN C16: perhaps partly from Latin *quando* 'when'.

quango /ˈkwaŋɡəʊ/ ■ n. (pl. -os) Brit., chiefly derogatory a semi-public administrative body with financial support from and senior appointments made by the government.
– ORIGIN 1970s (orig. US): acronym from *quasi* (or *quasi-autonomous*) *non-government(al) organization*.

quanta plural form of QUANTUM.

quantal /ˈkwɒnt(ə)l/ ■ adj. technical composed of discrete units or quanta; varying in steps rather than continuously.
– DERIVATIVES **quantally** adv.

quantifier ■ n. **1** Logic an expression (e.g. *some*) that indicates the scope of a term to which it is attached. **2** Grammar a determiner or pronoun indicative of quantity (e.g. *all*).

quantify ▪ v. (-ies, -ied) 1 express or measure the quantity of. 2 Logic define the application of (a term or proposition) by the use of a quantifier.
– DERIVATIVES **quantifiability** n. **quantifiable** adj. **quantification** n.
– ORIGIN C16: from medieval Latin *quantificare*, from Latin *quantus* 'how much'.

quantitate /ˈkwɒntɪteɪt/ ▪ v. Medicine & Biology determine the quantity or extent of.
– DERIVATIVES **quantitation** n.
– ORIGIN 1960s: from QUANTITY.

quantitative /ˈkwɒntɪˌteɪtɪv, -ˌtətɪv/ ▪ adj. 1 of, concerned with, or measured by quantity. Often contrasted with QUALITATIVE. 2 denoting or relating to verse whose metre is based on the length of syllables, as in Latin, as opposed to the stress, as in English.
– DERIVATIVES **quantitatively** adv.
– ORIGIN C16: from medieval Latin *quantitativus*, from Latin *quantitas* (see QUANTITY).

quantitative analysis ▪ n. Chemistry measurement of the quantities of particular constituents present in a substance.

quantitive ▪ adj. another term for QUANTITATIVE.
– DERIVATIVES **quantitively** adv.

quantity ▪ n. (pl. -ies) 1 a certain amount or number. ▸ a considerable number or amount. 2 the property of something that is measurable: *wages depended on quantity of output, regardless of quality*.
– ORIGIN Middle English: from Old French *quantite*, from Latin *quantitas*, from *quantus* 'how great, how much'.

quantity surveyor ▪ n. a person who calculates the amount and cost of materials needed for building work.

quantize (also **-ise**) ▪ v. 1 Physics form into quanta; make subject to quantum theory. 2 Electronics approximate (a continuously varying signal) by one whose amplitude is restricted to prescribed values.
– DERIVATIVES **quantization** (also **-isation**) n. **quantizer** (also **-iser**) n.

quantum /ˈkwɒntəm/ ▪ n. (pl. **quanta** /-tə/) 1 Physics a discrete quantity of energy proportional in magnitude to a particular frequency of radiation and corresponding e.g. to a single photon or to a transition of an atom between energy states. ▸ an analogous unit amount of something. 2 a total amount, especially a large amount of money legally payable in damages. ▸ a share.
– ORIGIN C16: from Latin, from *quantus* (see QUANTITY).

quantum chromodynamics ▪ pl. n. [treated as sing.] Physics a theory in which the strong interaction is described in terms of an interaction between quarks transmitted by gluons.
– ORIGIN *chromodynamics* from CHROMO-[2] 'colour' (property of quarks) + DYNAMICS.

quantum computer ▪ n. a computer which makes use of the quantum states of subatomic particles to store information.
– DERIVATIVES **quantum computing** n.

quantum electrodynamics ▪ pl. n. [treated as sing.] a theory concerned with the electromagnetic field and its interaction with electrically charged particles.

quantum jump ▪ n. 1 Physics an abrupt transition of an electron, atom, etc. from one state to another, with the absorption or emission of a quantum. 2 (also **quantum leap**) a sudden large increase or advance.

quantum mechanics ▪ pl. n. [treated as sing.] the mathematical description of the motion and interaction of subatomic particles in terms of quanta, incorporating the idea that particles can also be regarded as waves.
– DERIVATIVES **quantum-mechanical** adj.

quantum number ▪ n. Physics a number expressing the value of some property of a particle which occurs in quanta.

quantum theory ▪ n. Physics a theory of matter and energy based on the concept of quanta.

quarantine ▪ n. a state, period, or place of isolation for people or animals that have arrived from elsewhere or been exposed to contagious disease. ▪ v. put in quarantine.

HISTORY
Quarantine entered English in the 16th century, coming from Italian *quarantina*, meaning 'forty days', from *quaranta* 'forty'. It denoted a period of forty days during which a newly widowed woman was entitled to remain in her late husband's house. The current sense is first recorded in 1663, in Samuel Pepys's *Diary*. From then on the emphasis of the word was on the state of isolation rather than the number of days (which depended on the incubation period of the disease in question).

quark[1] /kwɑːk, kwɔːk/ ▪ n. Physics any of a group of subatomic particles carrying a fractional electric charge, postulated as building blocks of the hadrons.
– ORIGIN 1960s: invented by the American physicist Murray Gell-Mann and associated with the line 'Three quarks for Muster Mark' in Joyce's *Finnegans Wake* (1939).

quark[2] /kwɑːk/ ▪ n. a type of low-fat curd cheese.
– ORIGIN 1930s: from German *Quark* 'curd, curds'.

quarrel[1] ▪ n. 1 an angry argument or disagreement. 2 a reason for disagreement. ▪ v. (**quarrelled**, **quarrelling**; US **quarreled**, **quarreling**) have a quarrel. ▸ (**quarrel with**) disagree with.
– DERIVATIVES **quarreller** n.
– ORIGIN Middle English: from Old French *querele*, from Latin *querel(l)a* 'complaint', from *queri* 'complain'.

quarrel[2] ▪ n. historical a short heavy square-headed arrow or bolt for a crossbow.
– ORIGIN Middle English: from late Latin *quadrus* 'square'.

quarrelsome ▪ adj. given to or characterized by quarrelling.
– DERIVATIVES **quarrelsomely** adv. **quarrelsomeness** n.

quarry[1] ▪ n. (pl. -ies) a place, typically a large pit, from which stone or other materials may be extracted. ▪ v. (-ies, -ied) extract from a quarry. ▸ cut into (rock or ground) to obtain stone or other materials.
– DERIVATIVES **quarrier** n. **quarryman** n. (pl. **-men**).
– ORIGIN Middle English: from Old French *quarriere*, from Latin *quadrum* 'a square'.

quarry[2] ▪ n. (pl. -ies) an animal being hunted. ▸ a person or thing being chased or sought.
– ORIGIN Middle English: from Old French *cuiree*, from Latin *cor* 'heart'.

quarry[3] ▪ n. (pl. -ies) 1 a diamond-shaped pane in a lattice window. 2 (also **quarry tile**) an unglazed floor tile.
– ORIGIN C16: alteration of QUARREL[2], which in Middle English denoted a lattice windowpane.

quart ▪ n. 1 a unit of liquid capacity equal to a quarter of a gallon or two pints, equivalent in Britain to approximately 1.13 litres and in US to approximately 0.94 litre. ▸ N. Amer. a unit of dry capacity equivalent to approximately 1.10 litres. 2 /kɑːt/ (also **quarte** or **carte**) Fencing the fourth of eight parrying positions. 3 (in piquet) a sequence of four cards of the same suit.
– ORIGIN Middle English: from Old French *quarte*, from Latin *quarta (pars)* 'fourth (part)', from *quartus* 'fourth'.

quartan /ˈkwɔːt(ə)n/ ▪ adj. Medicine denoting a mild form of malaria causing a fever that recurs every third day.
– ORIGIN Middle English: from Latin (*febris*) *quartana*, from Latin *quartus* 'fourth' (because, by inclusive reckoning, the fever recurs every fourth day).

quarter ▪ n. 1 each of four equal or corresponding parts into which something is or can be divided. 2 a period of three months, used especially in reference to financial transactions. ▸ chiefly US each of four terms into which a school or university year may be divided. 3 a quarter-hour. 4 (**quarters**) the haunches or hindquarters of a horse. 5 a US or Canadian coin worth 25 cents. 6 a part of a town or city with a specific character or use. 7 the direction of one of the points of the compass. 8 either side of a ship aft of the beam. 9 a person, group, area, etc. regarded as the source of something: *help from an unexpected quarter*. 10 (**quarters**) rooms or lodgings. 11 (in combat) pity or mercy. 12 Heraldry each of four or more roughly equal divisions of a shield. ▸ a square charge covering the top left quarter of the field. ▪ v. 1 divide into quarters. ▸ historical cut the body of (an executed person) into four parts. 2 (**be quartered**) be stationed or lodged.

3 range over (an area) in all directions. **4** Heraldry display (different coats of arms) in quarters of a shield.
– ORIGIN Middle English: from Old French *quartier*, from Latin, from *quartus* 'fourth', from *quattuor* 'four'.

quarterback American Football ■ n. a player stationed behind the centre who directs a team's offensive play. ■ v. play as a quarterback for.

quarter binding ■ n. a type of bookbinding in which the spine is bound in one material and the rest of the cover in another.
– DERIVATIVES **quarter-bound** adj.

quarter day ■ n. Brit. each of four days on which some tenancies begin and end and quarterly payments fall due.

quarterdeck ■ n. **1** the part of a ship's upper deck near the stern, traditionally reserved for officers or for ceremonial use. **2** the officers of a ship or the navy.

quarter-final ■ n. a match of a knockout competition preceding the semi-final.

Quarter Horse ■ n. a horse of a small stocky agile breed, reputed to be the fastest breed over a quarter of a mile.

quarter-hour ■ n. **1** (also **quarter of an hour**) a period of fifteen minutes. **2** a point of time fifteen minutes before or after a full hour of the clock.

quartering ■ n. **1** (**quarterings**) Heraldry the coats of arms on a shield denoting the marriages held in a family of the heiresses of others. **2** the provision of lodgings, especially for troops. **3** division into quarters.

quarter-light ■ n. a window in the side of a motor vehicle other than a main door window.

quarterly ■ adj. **1** produced or occurring once every quarter of a year. **2** Heraldry divided into quarters. ■ adv. **1** once every quarter of a year. **2** Heraldry in the four, or in two diagonally opposite, quarters of a shield. ■ n. (pl. **-ies**) a publication produced four times a year.

quartermaster ■ n. **1** a regimental officer in charge of quartering and supplies. **2** a naval petty officer responsible for steering and signals.

Quartermaster General ■ n. the head of the army department in charge of the quartering and equipment of troops.

quarter note Music ■ n. **1** a crotchet. **2** (in tonic sol-fa) a semiquaver.

quarter plate ■ n. **1** Brit. a photographic plate measuring 3¼ × 4¼ inches (*c*.8.3 × 10.8 cm). **2** a photograph reproduced from this.

quarter-pounder ■ n. a hamburger weighing a quarter of a pound.

quarter sessions ■ pl. n. historical (in England, Wales, and Northern Ireland) a court of limited criminal and civil jurisdiction and of appeal, usually held quarterly.

quarterstaff ■ n. a stout pole 6–8 feet long, formerly used as a weapon.

quarter tone ■ n. Music half a semitone.

quartet (also **quartette**) ■ n. **1** a group of four people playing music or singing together. ▶ a composition for such a group. **2** a set of four people or things.
– ORIGIN C17: from French *quartette*, from Italian, from *quarto* 'fourth', from Latin *quartus*.

quartic /ˈkwɔːtɪk/ ■ adj. Mathematics denoting an equation, curve, etc. involving the fourth and no higher power of an unknown quantity or variable.
– ORIGIN C19: from Latin *quartus* 'fourth'.

quartile /ˈkwɔːtʌɪl/ ■ n. Statistics each of four equal groups into which a population can be divided according to the distribution of values of a particular variable.
– ORIGIN C19: from medieval Latin *quartilis*, from Latin *quartus* 'fourth'.

quarto /ˈkwɔːtəʊ/ (abbrev.: **4to**) ■ n. (pl. **-os**) a page or paper size resulting from folding a sheet into four leaves, typically 10 inches × 8 inches (254 × 203 mm). ▶ a book of this size.
– ORIGIN C16: from Latin (*in*) *quarto* '(in) the fourth (of a sheet)', from *quartus* 'fourth'.

quartz ■ n. a hard mineral consisting of silica, typically occurring as colourless or white hexagonal prisms.
– ORIGIN C18: from German *Quarz*, from Polish dialect *kwardy* 'hard'.

quartz clock (or **watch**) ■ n. a clock (or watch) regulated by vibrations of an electrically driven quartz crystal.

quartzite ■ n. Geology compact, hard, granular rock consisting essentially of quartz.

quasar /ˈkweɪzɑː, -sɑː/ ■ n. Astronomy a massive and extremely remote celestial object which emits large amounts of energy and typically shows a starlike image.
– ORIGIN 1960s: contraction of *quasi-stellar*.

quash ■ v. **1** reject as invalid, especially by legal procedure. **2** suppress: *rumours of job losses were quashed*.
– ORIGIN Middle English: from Old French *quasser* 'annul', from late Latin *cassare*, from *cassus* 'null, void'.

quasi- /ˈkweɪzaɪ, -saɪ, ˈkwɑːzi/ ■ comb. form **1** seemingly: *quasiscientific*. **2** being partly or almost: *quasicrystalline*.
– ORIGIN from Latin *quasi* 'as if, almost'.

quatercentenary /ˌkwatəsɛnˈtiːn(ə)ri, -ˈtɛn-, ˌkweɪtə-/ ■ n. (pl. **-ies**) a four-hundredth anniversary.
– ORIGIN C19: from Latin *quater* 'four times' + CENTENARY.

quaternary /kwəˈtəːn(ə)ri/ ■ adj. **1** fourth in order or rank. **2** (**Quaternary**) Geology relating to or denoting the most recent period in the Cenozoic era, following the Tertiary period (comprising the Pleistocene and Holocene epochs and beginning 1.64 million years ago). **3** Chemistry denoting an ammonium compound containing a cation of the form NR_4^+, where R represents organic groups.
– ORIGIN Middle English: from Latin *quaternarius*, from *quaterni* 'four at once', from *quater* 'four times', from *quattuor* 'four'.

quatrain /ˈkwɒtreɪn/ ■ n. a stanza of four lines, typically with alternate rhymes.
– ORIGIN C16: from French, from *quatre* 'four'.

quatrefoil /ˈkatrəfɔɪl/ ■ n. an ornamental design of four lobes or leaves, resembling a flower or clover leaf.
– ORIGIN C15: from Old French *quatre* 'four' + *foil* 'leaf'.

quattrocento /ˌkwatrə(ʊ)ˈtʃɛntəʊ/ ■ n. the 15th century as a period of Italian art or architecture.
– ORIGIN Italian, '400' (shortened from *milquattrocento* '1400').

quaver ■ v. (of a voice) tremble. ■ n. **1** a tremble in a voice. **2** Music a note having the value of an eighth of a semibreve or half a crotchet, represented by a large dot with a hooked stem.
– DERIVATIVES **quavering** adj. **quaveringly** adv. **quavery** adj.
– ORIGIN Middle English: from dialect *quave* 'quake, tremble', prob. from an Old English word rel. to QUAKE.

quay ■ n. a platform lying alongside or projecting into water for loading and unloading ships.
– DERIVATIVES **quayage** n.
– ORIGIN Middle English *key*, from Old French *kay*, of Celtic origin.

quayside ■ n. a quay and the area around it.

quean /kwiːn/ ■ n. archaic **1** an impudent girl or woman. **2** a prostitute.
– ORIGIN Old English *cwene* 'woman', of Germanic origin.

queasy ■ adj. (**-ier**, **-iest**) **1** nauseous. ▶ inducing nausea. **2** slightly nervous or worried.
– DERIVATIVES **queasily** adv. **queasiness** n.
– ORIGIN Middle English *queisy*, *coisy*, perhaps rel. to Old French *coisier* 'to hurt'.

Quebec /kwɪˈbɛk/ ■ n. a code word representing the letter Q, used in radio communication.

Quechua /ˈkɛtʃwə/ (also **Quecha** /ˈkɛtʃə/, **Quichua**) ■ n. (pl. same or **Quechuas**) **1** a member of an American Indian people of Peru and neighbouring countries. **2** the language or group of languages of this people.
– DERIVATIVES **Quechuan** adj. & n.
– ORIGIN Spanish, from Quechua *ghechwa* 'temperate valleys'.

queen ■ n. **1** the female ruler of an independent state, especially one who inherits the position by right of birth. ▶ (also **queen consort**) a king's wife. ▶ a woman or girl holding the most important position in a festival or event. **2** a woman or thing regarded as the finest or most important in its sphere or group. **3** the most powerful

Queen Anne

chess piece, able to move in any direction. **4** a playing card bearing a representation of a queen, ranking next below a king. **5** Entomology a reproductive female in a colony of ants, bees, wasps, or termites. **6** an adult female cat that has not been spayed. **7** informal a flamboyantly effeminate male homosexual. ■ v. **1** (**queen it**) (of a woman) act in an unpleasantly superior way. **2** Chess convert (a pawn) into a queen when it reaches the opponent's end of the board.
– DERIVATIVES **queendom** n. **queen-like** adj. **queenliness** n. **queenly** adj. (**-ier**, **-iest**). **queenship** n.
– ORIGIN Old English *cwēn*, of Germanic origin.

Queen Anne ■ adj. denoting a style of English furniture or architecture characteristic of the early 18th century.
– ORIGIN named after *Queen Anne*, who reigned in Britain 1702–1714.

Queen Anne's lace ■ n. cow parsley.

queen bee ■ n. **1** the single reproductive female in a colony of honeybees. **2** informal a woman with a dominant or controlling position.

queen dowager ■ n. the widow of a king.

queenfish ■ n. (pl. same or **-fishes**) a blue-grey marine fish with blotches along the sides of its body, living near reefs and popular as a game fish. [Family Carangidae.]

queen mother ■ n. the widow of a king and mother of the sovereign.

queen of puddings ■ n. a pudding made with bread, jam, and meringue.

Queen of the May ■ n. a May queen.

queen post ■ n. either of two upright timbers between the tie beam and principal rafters of a roof truss.

Queen's Bench ■ n. (in the UK) a division of the High Court of Justice.

Queensberry Rules /ˈkwiːnzbər(ə)ri/ ■ pl. n. the standard rules of boxing.
– ORIGIN C19: named after the 8th Marquess of *Queensberry*, who supervised the preparation of the rules in 1867.

queen's bishop ■ n. Chess each player's bishop on the queenside at the start of a game.

Queen's colour ■ n. (in the UK) a union flag carried by a regiment along with its regimental colour.

Queen's Counsel ■ n. Brit. a senior barrister appointed on the recommendation of the Lord Chancellor.

Queen's English ■ n. the English language as correctly written and spoken in Britain.

Queen's highway ■ n. Brit. the public road network.

queenside ■ n. Chess the half of the board on which each queen stands at the start of a game (the left-hand side for White, right for Black).

queen-sized (also **queen-size**) ■ adj. of a larger size than the standard but smaller than king-sized.

queen's knight ■ n. Chess each player's knight on the queenside at the start of a game.

Queen's Messenger ■ n. (in the UK) a courier in the diplomatic service.

queen's pawn ■ n. Chess the pawn immediately in front of each player's queen at the start of a game.

queen's rook ■ n. Chess each player's rook on the queenside at the start of a game.

Queen's Speech ■ n. (in the UK) a statement read by the sovereign at the opening of parliament, detailing the government's proposed legislative programme.

queensware ■ n. fine, cream-coloured Wedgwood pottery.
– ORIGIN C18 (as *Queen's ware*): named in honour of Queen Charlotte (wife of the British king George III).

queer ■ adj. **1** strange; odd. ▶ Brit. informal, dated slightly ill. **2** informal, derogatory (of a man) homosexual. ■ n. informal, derogatory a homosexual man. ■ v. informal spoil or ruin.
– PHRASES **in Queer Street** Brit. informal, dated in difficulty or debt. **queer someone's pitch** Brit. spoil someone's plans or chances of doing something.
– DERIVATIVES **queerish** adj. **queerly** adv. **queerness** n.
– ORIGIN C16: considered to be from German *quer* 'oblique, perverse', but the origin is doubtful.

> **USAGE**
> The word **queer** was first used to mean 'homosexual' in the early 20th century: it was originally, and usually still is, a deliberately derogatory term when used by heterosexual people. In recent years, however, gay people have taken the word **queer** and deliberately used it in place of **gay** or **homosexual**, in an attempt, by using the word positively, to deprive it of its negative power.

quelea /ˈkwiːlɪə/ ■ n. a brownish African weaver bird. [Genus *Quelea*: three species.]
– ORIGIN perhaps from medieval Latin *qualea* 'quail'.

quell ■ v. **1** put an end to, typically by force. **2** subdue or suppress.
– DERIVATIVES **queller** n.
– ORIGIN Old English *cwellan* 'kill', of Germanic origin.

Quena /ˈkwɛnə/ ■ n. another term for **KHOIKHOI**.

quench ■ v. **1** satisfy (thirst) by drinking. **2** satisfy (a desire). **3** extinguish (a fire). ▶ rapidly cool (hot metal). **4** stifle (a feeling). ▶ dated reduce to silence. **5** Physics suppress or damp (luminescence, an oscillation, etc.). ■ n. an act of quenching something very hot.
– DERIVATIVES **quenchable** adj. **quencher** n. **quenchless** adj. (poetic/literary).
– ORIGIN Old English *-cwencan* (in *acwencan* 'put out, extinguish'), of Germanic origin.

quenelle /kəˈnɛl/ ■ n. a small seasoned ball of fish or meat.
– ORIGIN French, prob. from Alsatian German *knödel*.

quern /kwəːn/ ■ n. a simple hand mill for grinding grain, typically consisting of two circular stones (quernstones).
– ORIGIN Old English, of Germanic origin.

querulous /ˈkwɛrʊləs, ˈkwɛrjʊləs/ ■ adj. complaining in a petulant or whining manner.
– DERIVATIVES **querulously** adv. **querulousness** n.
– ORIGIN C15: from late Latin *querulosus*, from Latin *querulus*, from *queri* 'complain'.

query ■ n. (pl. **-ies**) **1** a question, especially one expressing doubt. **2** chiefly Printing a question mark. ■ v. (**-ies**, **-ied**) ask a query about something.
– ORIGIN C17: anglicized form of Latin *quaere!*, from Latin *quaerere* 'ask, seek'.

quest ■ n. **1** a long or arduous search. **2** (in medieval romance) an expedition by a knight to accomplish a prescribed task. ■ v. search for something.
– DERIVATIVES **quester** (also **questor**) n. **questing** adj. **questingly** adv.
– ORIGIN Middle English: from Old French *queste* (n.), *quester* (v.), from Latin *quaerere* 'ask, seek'.

question ■ n. **1** a sentence worded or expressed so as to elicit information. **2** a doubt. ▶ the raising of a doubt or objection. **3** a problem requiring resolution. **4** a matter or concern depending on conditions: *a question of age*. ■ v. **1** ask questions of. **2** express doubt about; object to.
– PHRASES **come** (or **bring**) **into question** become (or raise) an issue for further consideration or discussion. **in question 1** being considered or discussed. **2** in doubt. **no question of** no possibility of. **out of the question** not possible. **put the question** require supporters and opponents of a debated proposal to record their votes.
– DERIVATIVES **questioner** n. **questioning** adj. **questioningly** adv.
– ORIGIN Middle English: from Old French *question* (n.), *questionner* (v.), from Latin *quaestio(n-)*, from *quaerere* 'ask, seek'.

questionable ■ adj. **1** open to doubt. **2** of suspect morality, honesty, value, etc.
– DERIVATIVES **questionability** n. **questionableness** n. **questionably** adv.

questionary ■ n. (pl. **-ies**) chiefly Medicine a questionnaire.

question mark ■ n. a punctuation mark (?) indicating a question.

question master ■ n. Brit. the questioner in a quiz or panel game.

questionnaire /ˌkwɛstʃəˈnɛː, ˌkɛstjə-/ ■ n. a set of printed

questions, usually with a choice of answers, devised for a survey or statistical study.
– ORIGIN C19: from French, from *questionner* 'to question'.

question time ■ n. a period during proceedings in some parliaments when MPs may question ministers.

queue ■ n. 1 a line or sequence of people or vehicles awaiting their turn to be attended to or to proceed. ▸ Computing a list of data items, commands, etc., stored so as to be retrievable in a definite order. 2 archaic a plait of hair worn at the back. ■ v. (**queues, queued, queuing** or **queueing**) wait in a queue. ▸ Computing arrange in a queue.
– ORIGIN C16: from French, based on Latin *cauda* 'tail'.

queue-jump ■ v. Brit. move forward out of turn in a queue.
– DERIVATIVES **queue-jumper** n.

quibble ■ n. a slight objection or criticism. ■ v. argue about a trivial matter.
– DERIVATIVES **quibbler** n. **quibbling** adj. **quibblingly** adv.
– ORIGIN C17: diminutive of obsolete *quib* 'a petty objection', prob. from Latin *quibus*, from *qui, quae, quod* 'who, what, which', freq. used in legal documents.

quiche /kiːʃ/ ■ n. a baked flan with a savoury filling thickened with eggs.
– ORIGIN French, from Alsatian dialect *Küchen*.

Quichua /ˈkɪtʃwə/ ■ n. variant of **QUECHUA**.

quick ■ adj. 1 moving fast or doing something in a short time. ▸ lasting a short time. ▸ prompt. 2 intelligent. ▸ (of one's eye or ear) alert. 3 (of a person's temper) easily roused. ■ n. 1 (**the quick**) the tender flesh below the growing part of a fingernail or toenail. ▸ the central or most sensitive part of someone or something. 2 [as pl. n. **the quick**] archaic those who are living.
– PHRASES **cut someone to the quick** cause someone deep distress. **a quick one** informal a rapidly consumed alcoholic drink.
– DERIVATIVES **quickly** adv. **quickness** n.
– ORIGIN Old English *cwic, cwicu* 'alive, animated, alert', of Germanic origin.

quicken ■ v. 1 make or become quicker. 2 stimulate or be stimulated. ▸ give or restore life to. 3 archaic (of a woman) reach a stage in pregnancy when the fetus can be felt to move. ▸ (of a fetus) begin to show signs of life.

quick-fire ■ adj. 1 unhesitating and rapid. 2 (of a gun) firing shots in rapid succession.

quick fix ■ n. a speedy but inadequate solution.

quickie informal ■ n. 1 a rapidly consumed alcoholic drink. 2 a brief act of sexual intercourse. ■ adj. done or made quickly.

quicklime ■ n. a white caustic alkaline substance consisting of calcium oxide, obtained by heating limestone.

quick march ■ n. a brisk military march.

quicksand ■ n. (also **quicksands**) loose wet sand that sucks in anything resting on it.

quicksilver ■ n. 1 liquid mercury. 2 [as modifier] moving or changing rapidly.

quickstep ■ n. a fast foxtrot in 4/4 time. ■ v. (**-stepped, -stepping**) dance the quickstep.

quick-tempered ■ adj. easily angered.

quick time ■ n. Military marching at about 120 paces per minute.

quick trick ■ n. Bridge a card such as an ace that can normally be relied on to win a trick.

quick-witted ■ adj. showing an ability to think or respond quickly.
– DERIVATIVES **quick-wittedness** n.

quid[1] ■ n. (pl. same) Brit. informal one pound sterling.
– PHRASES **quids in** Brit. informal profiting or likely to profit from something.
– ORIGIN C17.

quid[2] ■ n. a lump of chewing tobacco.
– ORIGIN C18: var. of **CUD**.

quiddity /ˈkwɪdɪti/ ■ n. (pl. **-ies**) chiefly Philosophy the inherent nature or essence of a person or thing.
– ORIGIN Middle English: from medieval Latin *quidditas*, from Latin *quid* 'what'.

quid pro quo /ˌkwɪd prəʊ ˈkwəʊ/ ■ n. (pl. **-os**) a favour or advantage given in return for something.
– ORIGIN Latin, 'something for something'.

quiescent /kwɪˈes(ə)nt, kwʌɪ-/ ■ adj. in a state or period of inactivity.
– DERIVATIVES **quiescence** n. **quiescently** adv.
– ORIGIN C17: from Latin *quiescent-, quiescere* 'be still', from *quies* 'quiet'.

quiet ■ adj. (**-er, -est**) 1 making little or no noise. ▸ free from activity, disturbance, or excitement. ▸ undisturbed; uninterrupted. 2 discreet, moderate, or restrained. ▸ (of a person) tranquil and reserved. ▸ (of a colour or garment) unobtrusive. ■ n. silence; calm. ■ v. chiefly N. Amer. make or become quiet.
– PHRASES **keep quiet** refrain from speaking or revealing a secret. **keep something quiet** keep something secret. **on the quiet** informal secretly or unobtrusively.
– DERIVATIVES **quieten** v. **quietly** adv. **quietness** n.
– ORIGIN Middle English: from Latin *quies, quiet-* 'repose, quiet'.

quietism ■ n. 1 (in the Christian faith) devotional contemplation and abandonment of the will as a form of religious mysticism. 2 calm acceptance of things, without resistance.
– DERIVATIVES **quietist** n. & adj. **quietistic** adj.
– ORIGIN C17: from Italian *quietismo*, from Latin *quies, quiet-* 'quiet'.

quietude ■ n. a state of calmness and quiet.
– ORIGIN C16: from French *quiétude* or medieval Latin *quietudo*, from Latin *quietus* 'quiet'.

quietus /kwʌɪˈiːtəs/ ■ n. (pl. **quietuses**) 1 death or a cause of death, regarded as a release from life. 2 archaic something calming or soothing.
– ORIGIN Middle English: abbrev. of medieval Latin *quietus est*, orig. used as a form of receipt on payment of a debt.

quiff ■ n. chiefly Brit. a man's tuft of hair, brushed upwards and backwards from the forehead.
– ORIGIN C19.

quill ■ n. 1 a main wing or tail feather of a bird. ▸ the hollow shaft of a feather, especially the lower part that lacks barbs. 2 a pen made from a quill. 3 a hollow sharp spine of a porcupine, hedgehog, etc.
– ORIGIN Middle English: prob. from Middle Low German *quiele*.

quilling ■ n. a type of ornamental craftwork involving the shaping of paper, fabric, or glass into delicate pleats or folds.

quilt ■ n. a warm bed covering made of padding enclosed between layers of fabric and kept in place by lines of decorative stitching. ▸ a bedspread of similar design. ■ v. [often as adj. **quilted**] join (layers of fabric or padding) with stitching to form a bed covering, a warm garment, or for decorative effect.
– DERIVATIVES **quilter** n. **quilting** n.
– ORIGIN Middle English: from Old French *cuilte*, from Latin *culcita* 'mattress, cushion'.

quin ■ n. informal, chiefly Brit. a quintuplet.

quinary /ˈkwʌɪnəri/ ■ adj. of or relating to the number five; fifth.
– ORIGIN C17: from Latin *quinarius*, from *quini* 'five at once, a set of five', from *quinque* 'five'.

quince ■ n. 1 a hard, acid, pear-shaped fruit used in preserves or as flavouring. 2 the Asian shrub or small tree which bears this fruit. [*Cydonia oblonga*.] 3 (**Japanese quince**) another term for **JAPONICA**.
– ORIGIN Middle English: from Old French *cooin*, from Latin (*malum*) *cotoneum*, var. of (*malum*) *cydonium* 'apple of *Cydonia* (= Chania, in Crete)'.

quincentenary /ˌkwɪnsenˈtiːn(ə)ri, -ˈten-/ ■ n. (pl. **-ies**) a five-hundredth anniversary.
– DERIVATIVES **quincentennial** n. & adj.
– ORIGIN C19: from Latin *quinque* 'five' + **CENTENARY**.

quincunx /ˈkwɪŋkʌŋks/ ■ n. (pl. **quincunxes**) an arrangement of five objects with four at the corners of a square or rectangle and the fifth at its centre.
– DERIVATIVES **quincuncial** adj.
– ORIGIN C17: from Latin, 'five twelfths', from *quinque* 'five' + *uncia* 'twelfth'.

quinella /kwɪˈnɛlə/ ■ n. a bet predicting the first two places in a race, but not necessarily in the correct order.
– ORIGIN 1940s (orig. US): from Latin American Spanish *quiniela*.

quinine /ˈkwɪniːn, kwɪˈniːn/ ■ n. a bitter crystalline compound present in cinchona bark, used as a tonic and as an antimalarial drug.
– ORIGIN C19: from Spanish *quina* 'cinchona bark', from Quechua *kina* 'bark'.

quinoa /ˈkiːnəʊə, kwɪˈnəʊə/ ■ n. 1 a goosefoot found in the Andes, cultivated for its edible starchy seeds. [*Chenopodium quinoa*.] 2 the seeds of this plant, used as food and to make alcoholic drinks.
– ORIGIN C17: Spanish spelling of Quechua *kinua, kinoa*.

quinoline /ˈkwɪnəliːn/ ■ n. Chemistry a pungent oily liquid present in coal tar and bone oil.
– ORIGIN C19: from Spanish *quina* (see QUININE).

quinquennial /kwɪŋˈkwɛnɪəl/ ■ adj. lasting for or recurring every five years.
– DERIVATIVES **quinquennially** adv.
– ORIGIN C15: from Latin *quinquennis*, from *quinque* 'five' + *annus* 'year'.

quinsy /ˈkwɪnzi/ ■ n. inflammation of the throat, especially an abscess near the tonsils.
– ORIGIN Middle English: from medieval Latin *quinancia*, from Greek *kunankhē* 'canine quinsy', from *kun-* 'dog' + *ankhein* 'throttle'.

quinta /ˈkwɪntə, ˈkɪntə/ ■ n. (in Spain, Portugal, and Latin America) a large country house. ▸ a wine-growing estate, especially in Portugal.
– ORIGIN Spanish and Portuguese, from *quinta parte* 'fifth part' (with ref. to the amount of a farm's produce paid in rent).

quintal /ˈkwɪnt(ə)l/ ■ n. 1 a unit of weight equal to a hundredweight (112 lb) or, formerly, 100 lb. 2 a unit of weight equal to 100 kg.
– ORIGIN Middle English: from medieval Latin *quintale*, from Arabic *ḳinṭār*, from Latin *centenarius* 'containing a hundred'.

quinte /kãt/ ■ n. Fencing the fifth of eight parrying positions.
– ORIGIN C18: French, from Latin *quintus* 'fifth', from *quinque* 'five'.

quintessence /kwɪnˈtɛs(ə)ns/ ■ n. 1 the most perfect or typical example. ▸ a central intrinsic aspect of something. 2 a refined essence or extract of a substance.

HISTORY
The word **quintessence** comes from the medieval Latin term *quinta essentia*, meaning 'fifth essence', and denoted a fifth substance believed to exist in addition to the four elements air, earth, fire, and water. Medieval philosophers believed that this 'fifth essence' was the substance of which the celestial bodies were composed, and that it was present in all things.

quintessential /ˌkwɪntɪˈsɛnʃ(ə)l/ ■ adj. representing the most perfect or typical example.
– DERIVATIVES **quintessentially** adv.

quintet ■ n. 1 a group of five people playing music or singing together. ▸ a composition for such a group. 2 a set of five people or things.
– ORIGIN C18: from French *quintette* or Italian *quintetto*, from *quinto* 'fifth', from Latin *quintus*.

quintile /ˈkwɪntɪl, -ʌɪl/ ■ n. Statistics each of five equal groups into which a population can be divided according to the distribution of values of a variable.
– ORIGIN C17: from Latin *quintilis*, from *quintus* 'fifth'.

quintillion /kwɪnˈtɪljən/ ■ cardinal number (pl. **quintillions** or (with numeral) same) a thousand raised to the power of six (10^{18}).
– DERIVATIVES **quintillionth** ordinal number.
– ORIGIN C17: from French, from *million*, by substitution of the prefix *quinti-* 'five' for the initial letters.

quintuple /ˈkwɪntjʊp(ə)l, kwɪnˈtjuːp(ə)l/ ■ adj. 1 consisting of five parts or elements. 2 five times as much or as many. 3 (of time in music) having five beats in a bar. ■ v. increase or be increased fivefold. ■ n. a quintuple thing, number, or amount.
– DERIVATIVES **quintuply** adv.
– ORIGIN C16: from medieval Latin *quintuplus*, from Latin *quintus* 'fifth' + *-plus* as in *duplus* (see DUPLE).

quintuplet /ˈkwɪntjʊˌplɪt, kwɪnˈtjuːplɪt/ ■ n. each of five children born at one birth.
– ORIGIN C19: from QUINTUPLE, on the pattern of *triplet*.

quintuplicate ■ adj. 1 fivefold. 2 of which five copies are made. ■ v. multiply by five.

quip ■ n. a witty remark. ■ v. (**quipped, quipping**) make a quip.
– DERIVATIVES **quipster** n.
– ORIGIN C16: perhaps from Latin *quippe* 'indeed, forsooth'.

quire /kwʌɪə/ ■ n. 1 four sheets of paper or parchment folded to form eight leaves, as in medieval manuscripts. 2 any collection of leaves one within another in a manuscript or book. 3 25 (formerly 24) sheets of paper; one twentieth of a ream.
– ORIGIN Middle English: from Old French *quaier*, from Latin *quaterni* 'set of four'.

quirk ■ n. 1 a peculiar behavioural habit. 2 a strange chance occurrence. 3 a sudden twist, turn, or curve. 4 Architecture an acute hollow between convex or other mouldings. ■ v. move or be moved suddenly or jerkily.
– DERIVATIVES **quirkish** adj.
– ORIGIN C16.

quirky ■ adj. (**-ier, -iest**) having or characterized by peculiar or unexpected traits or aspects.
– DERIVATIVES **quirkily** adv. **quirkiness** n.

quirt /kwəːt/ ■ n. a short-handled riding whip with a braided leather lash. ■ v. hit with a quirt.
– ORIGIN C19 (orig. US): from Spanish *cuerda* 'cord' (from Latin *chorda* 'cord') or from Mexican Spanish *cuarta* 'whip'.

quisling /ˈkwɪzlɪŋ/ ■ n. a traitor collaborating with an occupying enemy force.
– ORIGIN SECOND WORLD WAR: from the name of Major Vidkun *Quisling*, who ruled Norway on behalf of the German occupying forces.

quit ■ v. (**quitting**; past and past part. **quitted** or **quit**) 1 leave, especially permanently. 2 informal resign from (a job). 3 informal, chiefly N. Amer. stop or discontinue. 4 (**quit oneself**) archaic behave in a specified way. ■ adj. (**quit of**) rid of.
– ORIGIN Middle English: from Old French *quiter* (v.), *quite* (adj.), from Latin *quietus*, from *quiescere* 'be still', from *quies* 'quiet'.

quite ■ adv. 1 absolutely; completely. 2 fairly; moderately. ■ exclam. (also **quite so**) expressing agreement.
– PHRASES **quite a ——** a remarkable or impressive (person or thing). **quite a lot** (or **a bit**) a considerable number or amount. **quite some** a considerable amount of.
– ORIGIN Middle English: from the obsolete adj. *quite*, var. of QUIT.

quit rent ■ n. S. African historical an annual rent paid to secure long-term or permanent tenancy of a piece of land.

quits ■ adj. on equal terms by retaliation or repayment.
– PHRASES **call it quits** 1 agree that terms are now equal. 2 decide to abandon an activity.
– ORIGIN C15: perhaps an abbrev. of medieval Latin *quittus*, from Latin *quietus*, used as a receipt (see QUIETUS).

quittance ■ n. archaic or poetic/literary a release from a debt or obligation. ▸ a document certifying this; a receipt.
– ORIGIN Middle English: from Old French *quitance*, from *quiter* (see QUIT).

quitter ■ n. informal a person who gives up easily.

quiver[1] ■ v. shake or tremble with a slight rapid motion. ▸ cause to make a slight rapid motion. ■ n. a slight trembling movement or sound.
– DERIVATIVES **quivering** adj. **quiveringly** adv. **quivery** adj.
– ORIGIN Middle English: from Old English *cwifer* 'nimble, quick'.

quiver[2] ■ n. an archer's portable case for arrows.
– PHRASES **an arrow in the quiver** one of a number of resources that can be drawn on.
– ORIGIN Middle English: from Anglo-Norman French *quiveir*, of West Germanic origin.

quiver tree ■ n. a large tree-like southern African aloe, whose branches were used by the San people to make quivers. [*Aloe dichotoma*.]

qui vive /kiː ˈviːv/ ■ n. (in phr. **on the qui vive**) on the alert or lookout.
– ORIGIN C16: from French, '(long) live who?', i.e. 'on whose side are you?', used as a sentry's challenge.

quixotic /kwɪkˈsɒtɪk/ ■ adj. impractically idealistic or fanciful.
– DERIVATIVES **quixotically** adv. **quixotism** /ˈkwɪksətɪz(ə)m/ n. **quixotry** /ˈkwɪksətri/ n.
– ORIGIN C18: from the name of Don *Quixote*, hero of Cervantes' romance.

quiz[1] ■ n. (pl. **quizzes**) 1 a test of knowledge, especially as a competition for entertainment. 2 N. Amer. an informal written test. ■ v. (**quizzes**, **quizzed**, **quizzing**) 1 question (someone). 2 N. Amer. give an informal written test to.
– ORIGIN C19 (as v.; orig. US): possibly from QUIZ[2].

quiz[2] ■ v. archaic (**quizzes**, **quizzed**, **quizzing**) 1 look intently at through or as if through an eyeglass. 2 make fun of.
– ORIGIN C18: possibly a deliberately coined nonsense word.

quizmaster ■ n. a question master.

quizzical ■ adj. indicating mild or amused puzzlement.
– DERIVATIVES **quizzicality** n. **quizzically** adv. **quizzicalness** n.

quod erat demonstrandum /kwɒd ˌerat demənˈstrandʊm/ ■ used, especially at the conclusion of a formal proof, to convey that something demonstrates the truth of one's claim.
– ORIGIN Latin, 'which was to be demonstrated'.

quoin /kɔɪn, kwɔɪn/ ■ n. 1 an external angle of a wall or building. 2 a wedge for raising the level of a gun barrel or to keep it from rolling. ■ v. provide with quoins.
– DERIVATIVES **quoining** n.
– ORIGIN Middle English: var. of COIN, used earlier in the sense 'cornerstone, wedge'.

quoit /kɔɪt, kwɔɪt/ ■ n. 1 a ring of iron, rope, or rubber thrown in a game to encircle or land as near as possible to an upright peg. ▸ (**quoits**) [treated as sing.] a game of aiming and throwing quoits. 2 the flat covering stone of a dolmen. ▸ a dolmen.
– ORIGIN Middle English: prob. of French origin.

quondam /ˈkwɒndəm, -dam/ ■ adj. formal former.
– ORIGIN C16: from Latin, 'formerly'.

Quonset /ˈkwɒnsɪt/ (also **Quonset hut**) ■ n. N. Amer. trademark a prefabricated building with a semicylindrical corrugated roof.
– ORIGIN SECOND WORLD WAR: named after *Quonset* Point, Rhode Island, where such huts were first made.

quorate /ˈkwɔːrət, -reɪt/ ■ adj. (of a meeting) attended by a quorum.

Quorn /kwɔːn/ ■ n. Brit. trademark a form of mycoprotein used as a meat substitute.
– ORIGIN 1980s: the name of a former company in the Leicestershire village of Quorndon.

quorum /ˈkwɔːrəm/ ■ n. (pl. **quorums**) the minimum number of members of an assembly or society that must be present at a meeting to make the proceedings valid.
– ORIGIN Middle English: used in commissions for committee members designated by the Latin *quorum vos ... unum* (*duos*, etc.) *esse volumus* 'of whom we wish that you ... be one (two, etc.)'.

quota ■ n. 1 a limited quantity of a product which may be produced, exported, or imported. 2 a share of something that one is entitled to receive or bound to contribute. 3 a fixed number of a group allowed or required to do something, e.g. immigrants entering a country. ▸ (in a system of proportional representation) the minimum number of votes required to elect a candidate. 4 a minimum number or proportion (e.g. of women or a racial group) required to achieve representivity in a specified activity or enterprise. ▸ [as modifier] denoting someone or something associated with the achievement of such representivity: *a quota system* | *quota players*.
– ORIGIN C17: from medieval Latin *quota* (*pars*) 'how great (a part)', from *quotus*, from *quot* 'how many'.

quotable ■ adj. suitable for or worth quoting.
– DERIVATIVES **quotability** n.

quotation ■ n. 1 a group of words from a text or speech repeated by someone other than the originator. ▸ a short musical passage or visual image taken from one piece of music or work of art and used in another. ▸ the action of quoting from a text, work of art, etc. 2 a formal statement of the estimated cost of a job or service. ▸ Stock Exchange a price offered by a market-maker for the sale or purchase of a stock. 3 Stock Exchange a registration granted to a company enabling their shares to be officially listed and traded.
– ORIGIN C16: from medieval Latin *quotatio(n-)*, from *quotare* (see QUOTE).

quotation mark ■ n. each of a set of punctuation marks, single (' ') or double (" "), used either to mark the beginning and end of a title or quotation, or to indicate slang or jargon words.

quote ■ v. 1 repeat or copy out (a passage from a text or speech by another). ▸ repeat a passage or statement from. 2 (**quote someone/thing as**) put forward or describe someone or something as being. 3 give someone (an estimated price). ▸ (**quote someone/thing at/as**) name someone or something at (specified odds). 4 Stock Exchange give (a company) a listing on a stock exchange. ■ n. 1 a quotation. 2 (**quotes**) quotation marks.
– PHRASES **quote —— unquote** informal used parenthetically to indicate the beginning and end of a quotation.
– ORIGIN Middle English (orig. 'mark a book with numbers or marginal references'): from medieval Latin *quotare*, from *quot* 'how many', or from medieval Latin *quota* (see QUOTA).

quoth /kwəʊθ/ ■ v. archaic or humorous said (used only in first and third person singular before the subject).
– ORIGIN Middle English: from obsolete *quethe* 'say, declare', of Germanic origin.

quotidian /kwɒˈtɪdɪən, kwəʊ-/ ■ adj. 1 daily. 2 ordinary or everyday. 3 Medicine denoting the malignant form of malaria.
– ORIGIN Middle English: from Latin *quotidianus*, earlier *cotidianus*, from *cotidie* 'daily'.

quotient /ˈkwəʊʃ(ə)nt/ ■ n. 1 Mathematics a result obtained by dividing one quantity by another. 2 a degree or amount of a specified quality.
– ORIGIN Middle English: from Latin *quotiens* 'how many times', from *quot* 'how many'.

Qur'an /kəˈrɑːn/ (also **Quran**) ■ n. Arabic spelling of KORAN.

q.v. ■ abbrev. used to direct a reader to another part of a text for further information.
– ORIGIN from Latin *quod vide* 'which see'.

qwerty /ˈkwəːti/ ■ adj. denoting the standard layout on English-language typewriters and keyboards, having *q*, *w*, *e*, *r*, *t*, and *y* as the first keys on the top row of letters.

Rr

R¹ (also **r**) ■ n. (pl. **Rs** or **R's**) **1** the eighteenth letter of the alphabet. **2** denoting the next after Q in a set of items, categories, etc.
– PHRASES **the three Rs** reading, writing, and arithmetic, regarded as the fundamentals of learning.

R² ■ abbrev. **1** rand. **2** Regina or Rex. **3** (®) registered as a trademark. **4** (in the US) Republican. **5** N. Amer. (in film classification) restricted (to viewers over a certain age). **6** (on a gear shift) reverse. **7** (**R.**) River. **8** roentgen(s). **9** rook (in chess). **10** Cricket (on scorecards) run(s). ■ symb. **1** Chemistry an unspecified organic radical. **2** electrical resistance.

r ■ abbrev. **1** recto. **2** right. **3** Law rule. ■ symb. radius.

RA ■ abbrev. (in the UK) Royal Academician or Royal Academy.

Ra ■ symb. the chemical element radium.

rabbi /ˈrabʌɪ/ ■ n. (pl. **rabbis**) **1** a Jewish scholar or teacher, especially of Jewish law. **2** a Jewish religious leader.
– DERIVATIVES **rabbinate** /ˈrabɪnət/ n.
– ORIGIN Old English, from Hebrew *rabbī* 'my master', from *raḥ* 'master'.

rabbinic /rəˈbɪnɪk/ ■ adj. of or relating to rabbis or to Jewish law or teachings.
– DERIVATIVES **rabbinical** adj. **rabbinically** adv.

rabbit ■ n. a burrowing gregarious plant-eating mammal, with long ears, long hind legs, and a short tail. [*Oryctolagus cuniculus* and other species.] ▶ the fur of the rabbit. ▶ N. Amer. a hare. ■ v. (**rabbited**, **rabbiting**) **1** [usu. as noun **rabbiting**] hunt rabbits. **2** informal chatter.
– DERIVATIVES **rabbity** adj.
– ORIGIN Middle English: apparently from Old French (cf. French dialect *rabotte* 'young rabbit'), perhaps of Dutch origin.

rabbitfish ■ n. (pl. same or **-fishes**) a blunt-nosed fish with rabbit-like teeth or jaws. [*Chimaera monstrosa* (Atlantic), *Siganus oramin* (Indo-Pacific), and other species.]

rabbit punch ■ n. a sharp chop with the edge of the hand to the back of the neck.

rabble ■ n. **1** a disorderly crowd. **2** (**the rabble**) ordinary people regarded as socially inferior or uncouth.
– ORIGIN Middle English: perhaps rel. to dialect *rabble* 'to gabble'.

rabble-rouser ■ n. a person who stirs up a crowd, especially for political reasons.
– DERIVATIVES **rabble-rousing** adj. & n.

Rabelaisian /ˌrabəˈleɪziən/ ■ n. an admirer of the French satirist François Rabelais (c.1494–1553). ■ adj. of or like Rabelais or his writings; marked by exuberant imagination and earthy humour.

rabid /ˈrabɪd, ˈreɪ-/ ■ adj. **1** extreme; fanatical. **2** of, relating to, or affected with rabies.
– DERIVATIVES **rabidity** /rəˈbɪdɪti/ n. **rabidly** adv. **rabidness** n.
– ORIGIN C17: from Latin *rabidus*, from *rabere* 'to rave'.

rabies /ˈreɪbiːz, -ɪz/ ■ n. a dangerous viral disease of dogs and other mammals, transmissible through the saliva to humans and causing madness and convulsions.
– ORIGIN C16: from Latin, from *rabere* 'rave'.

RAC ■ abbrev. (in the UK) Royal Automobile Club.

raccoon /rəˈkuːn/ (also **racoon**) ■ n. a greyish-brown omnivorous American mammal with a black facial mask and a ringed tail. [Genus *Procyon*: two species.]
– ORIGIN C17: from Virginia Algonquian *arougchun*.

race¹ ■ n. **1** a competition between runners, horses, vehicles, etc. to see which is fastest over a set course. ▶ (**the races**) a series of races for horses or dogs, held at a fixed time on a set course. ▶ a situation in which people compete to be first to achieve something. **2** a strong or rapid current flowing through a narrow channel. **3** a water channel, especially one in a mill or mine. **4** a smooth ring-shaped groove or guide for a ball bearing or roller bearing. **5** a fenced passageway in a stockyard through which animals pass singly for branding, loading, etc. **6** (in weaving) the channel along which the shuttle moves. ■ v. **1** compete in a race. ▶ compete regularly in races as a sport. ▶ prepare and enter (an animal or vehicle) for races. **2** move or progress swiftly. ▶ operate or cause to operate at excessive speed.
– ORIGIN Old English, from Old Norse *rás* 'current'.

race² ■ n. **1** each of the major divisions of humankind, having distinct physical characteristics. ▶ racial origin or distinction. ▶ an ethnic group. ▶ a group descended from a common ancestor. **2** a group of people or things with a common feature. **3** Biology a distinct population within a species; a subspecies.
– ORIGIN C16: from Italian *razza*.

> **USAGE**
> In recent years, the associations of **race** with the ideologies and theories that grew out of the work of 19th-century anthropologists and physiologists has led to the use of the word **race** itself becoming problematic. Although still used in general contexts, it is now often replaced by other words which are less emotionally charged, such as **people**(**s**) or **community**.

racecard ■ n. a programme giving information about the races at a race meeting.

racecourse ■ n. a ground or track for horse or dog racing.

racehorse ■ n. a horse bred and trained for racing.

racemate /ˈrasɪmeɪt/ ■ n. Chemistry a racemic mixture.

raceme /ˈrasiːm, rəˈsiːm/ ■ n. Botany a flower cluster with the separate flowers attached by short stalks along a central stem, the flowers at the base developing first. Compare with **CYME**.
– ORIGIN C18: from Latin *racemus* 'bunch of grapes'.

race meeting ■ n. a sporting event consisting of a series of horse races held at one course.

race memory ■ n. a supposedly inherited subconscious memory of events in human history or prehistory.

racemic /rəˈsiːmɪk, rəˈsɛmɪk/ ■ adj. Chemistry composed of dextrorotatory and laevorotatory forms in equal proportion.
– DERIVATIVES **racemize** /ˈrasɪmʌɪz/ (also **-ise**) v.
– ORIGIN C19: from French *racémique* 'derived from grape juice' (orig. referring to tartaric acid).

racemose /ˈrasɪməʊs, -z/ ■ adj. Botany of the form of a raceme.
– ORIGIN C17: from Latin *racemosus*, from *racemus* (see **RACEME**).

racer ■ n. **1** an animal or vehicle used for racing. ▶ a person who competes in races. **2** a harmless fast-moving slender snake. [*Coluber constrictor* (N. America) and other species.] **3** a circular horizontal rail along which the carriage or traversing platform of a heavy gun moves.

race relations ■ pl. n. relations between members of different races within a country.

racetrack ■ n. **1** a racecourse. **2** a track for motor racing.

raceway ■ n. chiefly N. Amer. **1** a water channel, especially an artificial one for rearing fish. **2** a groove or race for bearings. **3** a pipe or tubing enclosing electric wires. **4** a track for trotting, pacing, or harness racing. ▶ a race-track.

rachis /ˈreɪkɪs/ ■ n. (pl. **rachides** /-kɪdiːz/) **1** Botany a stem of a grass or other plant bearing flower stalks at short

---

CONSONANTS   **b** but   **d** dog   **f** few   **g** get   **h** he   **j** yes   **k** cat   **l** leg   **m** man   **n** no   **p** pen   **r** red

intervals. ▶ the midrib of a compound leaf or frond. **2** Ornithology the shaft of a feather.
–ORIGIN C18: from Greek *rhakhis* 'spine'.

Rachmanism /ˈrakmənɪz(ə)m/ ■ n. Brit. the exploitation and intimidation of tenants by unscrupulous landlords.
–ORIGIN 1960s: named after the notorious London landlord Peter *Rachman*.

racial ■ adj. **1** of or relating to a race. **2** relating to relations or differences between races.
–DERIVATIVES **racially** adv.

racialism ■ n. racism.
–DERIVATIVES **racialist** n. & adj. **racialize** (also **-ise**) v.

racing ■ n. a sport involving races. ■ adj. **1** moving swiftly. **2** (of a person) following horse racing.

racing car ■ n. a car built for racing.

racing driver ■ n. a driver of racing cars.

racism ■ n. **1** the belief that there are characteristics, abilities, or qualities specific to each race. **2** discrimination against or antagonism towards other races.
–DERIVATIVES **racist** n. & adj.

rack[1] ■ n. **1** a framework for holding or storing things. ▶ a vertically barred holder for animal fodder. **2** a cogged or toothed bar or rail engaging with a wheel or pinion, or using pegs to adjust the position of something. **3** (**the rack**) historical an instrument of torture consisting of a frame on which the victim was tied by the wrists and ankles and stretched. **4** a triangular frame for positioning pool balls. **5** a digital effects unit for a guitar or other instrument. ■ v. **1** (also **wrack**) cause extreme physical or mental pain to. **2** place in or on a rack. **3** (**rack something up**) accumulate or achieve something.
–PHRASES **rack** (or **wrack**) **one's brains** make a great mental effort.
–ORIGIN Middle English: from Middle Dutch *rec*, Middle Low German *rek* 'horizontal bar or shelf', prob. from *recken* 'to stretch, reach'.

rack[2] ■ n. a horse's gait between a trot and a canter. ■ v. move with such a gait.
–ORIGIN C16.

rack[3] ■ n. a joint of meat, especially lamb, including the front ribs.
–ORIGIN C16.

rack[4] (also **wrack**) ■ n. (in phr. **go to rack and ruin**) gradually deteriorate due to neglect.
–ORIGIN Old English *wræc* 'vengeance, destruction', rel. to WREAK.

rack[5] ■ v. draw off (wine, beer, etc.) from the sediment in the barrel.
–ORIGIN C15: from Provençal *arracar*, from *raca* 'stems and husks of grapes, dregs'.

rack[6] ■ n. variant spelling of WRACK[3].

rack-and-pinion ■ adj. denoting a mechanism using a fixed cogged or toothed bar or rail engaging with a smaller cog.

racket[1] (also **racquet**) ■ n. a bat with a round or oval frame strung with catgut, nylon, etc., used especially in tennis, badminton, and squash.
–ORIGIN C16: from French *raquette* (see RACKETS).

racket[2] ■ n. **1** a loud unpleasant noise. **2** informal a fraudulent scheme for obtaining money. ▶ a person's line of business. ■ v. (**racketed**, **racketing**) (**racket about/around**) enjoy oneself socially.
–DERIVATIVES **rackety** adj.
–ORIGIN C16: perhaps imitative of clattering.

racketeer ■ n. a person engaging in fraudulent business dealings.
–DERIVATIVES **racketeering** n.

rackets ■ pl. n. [treated as sing.] a ball game for two or four people played with rackets in a four-walled court, using a harder ball than squash.
–ORIGIN Middle English: from French *raquette*, from Arabic *rāha*, *rāhat-* 'palm of the hand'.

rack railway ■ n. a railway for steep slopes, having a toothed rack between the bearing rails which engages with a cogwheel under the locomotive.

rack rent ■ n. a very high rent.

–ORIGIN C16: from RACK[1] (in the sense 'cause stress') + RENT[1].

raclette /raˈklɛt/ ■ n. a Swiss dish of melted cheese, typically with potatoes.
–ORIGIN French, 'small scraper', referring to the practice of scraping the cheese on to a plate as it melts.

raconteur /ˌrakɒnˈtəː/ ■ n. (fem. **raconteuse** /ˌrakɒnˈtəːz/) a skilful teller of anecdotes.
–ORIGIN C19: French, from *raconter* 'relate, recount'.

racoon ■ n. variant spelling of RACCOON.

racquet ■ n. variant spelling of RACKET[1].

racy ■ adj. (**-ier**, **-iest**) **1** suggestive; risqué. ▶ showing vigour or spirit. **2** (of a wine, flavour, etc.) having a characteristic quality in a high degree. **3** (of a vehicle or animal) suitable for racing.
–DERIVATIVES **racily** adv. **raciness** n.

rad[1] ■ abbrev. radian(s).

rad[2] ■ n. Physics a unit of absorbed dose of ionizing radiation, corresponding to the absorption of 0.01 joule per kilogram of absorbing material.
–ORIGIN C20: acronym from *radiation absorbed dose*.

rad[3] ■ adj. informal excellent.
–ORIGIN 1980s: prob. an abbrev. of RADICAL.

RADA /ˈrɑːdə/ ■ abbrev. (in the UK) Royal Academy of Dramatic Art.

radar ■ n. a system for detecting the presence, direction, and speed of aircraft, ships, etc., by sending out pulses of radio waves which are reflected off the object back to the source. ▶ used to indicate that someone or something has or has not come to the attention of a person or group: *he's off the radar in South Africa but in his country of birth he's a well-known figure.*
–ORIGIN 1940s: from *ra(dio) d(etection) a(nd) r(anging)*.

radar gun ■ n. a hand-held radar device used by traffic police to estimate a vehicle's speed.

radar trap ■ n. an area of road in which radar is used by the police to detect speeding vehicles.

raddled ■ adj. (of a person) showing signs of age or fatigue.

radial ■ adj. **1** of or arranged like rays or the radii of a circle; diverging in lines from a common centre. ▶ (of a road) running from a town centre to an outlying district. **2** (also **radial-ply**) denoting a tyre in which the layers of fabric have their cords running at right angles to the circumference of the tyre. **3** denoting an internal-combustion engine with its cylinders fixed like the spokes of a wheel around a rotating crankshaft. **4** Anatomy & Zoology of or relating to the radius. ■ n. a radial tyre.
–DERIVATIVES **radially** adv.
–ORIGIN C16: from medieval Latin *radialis*, from Latin *radius* (see RADIUS).

radial symmetry ■ n. chiefly Biology symmetry about a central axis, as in a starfish.

radial velocity ■ n. chiefly Astronomy the velocity of a star or other body along the line of sight of an observer.

radian /ˈreɪdɪən/ ■ n. a unit of measurement of angles equal to about 57.3°, equivalent to the angle subtended at the centre of a circle by an arc equal in length to the radius.

radiant ■ adj. **1** shining or glowing brightly. ▶ emanating great joy, love, or health. ▶ (of an emotion or quality) emanating powerfully. **2** transmitted by electromagnetic radiation, rather than conduction or convection. ▶ (of an appliance) emitting radiant energy for cooking or heating. ■ n. **1** a point or object from which light or heat radiates. **2** Astronomy the apparent focal point of a meteor shower.
–DERIVATIVES **radiance** n. **radiantly** adv.
–ORIGIN Middle English: from Latin *radiant-*, *radiare* (see RADIATE).

radiate ■ v. **1** emit (light, heat, or other energy) in the form of rays or waves. ▶ be emitted in such a way. ▶ emanate (a strong feeling or quality). **2** diverge from or as if from a central point. **3** Biology (of an animal or plant

radiation

group) evolve into a variety of forms.
– DERIVATIVES **radiative** adj.
– ORIGIN C17: from Latin *radiare* 'emit in rays', from *radius* 'ray, spoke'.

radiation ■ n. **1** the action or process of radiating. **2** Physics energy emitted as electromagnetic waves or subatomic particles.

radiation sickness ■ n. illness caused by exposure to X-rays, gamma rays, or other radiation.

radiation therapy (also **radiation treatment**) ■ n. radiotherapy.

radiator ■ n. **1** a thing that emits light, heat, or sound. **2** a heating device consisting of a metal case through which hot water is pumped by a central heating system. ▸ a portable oil or electric heater resembling this. **3** a cooling device in a vehicle or aircraft engine consisting of a bank of thin tubes in which circulating water is cooled by the surrounding air.

radical ■ adj. **1** of, relating to, or affecting the fundamental nature of something. ▸ innovative or progressive. **2** (of surgery) thorough and intended to be completely curative. **3** advocating thorough political or social reform; politically extreme. **4** Mathematics of the root of a number or quantity. **5** denoting or relating to the roots of a word. **6** Botany of or coming from the root or stem base of a plant. **7** informal excellent. ■ n. **1** an advocate of radical political or social reform. **2** Chemistry a group of atoms behaving as a unit in a number of compounds. See also **FREE RADICAL**. **3** the root or base form of a word. ▸ any of the basic set of Chinese characters constituting semantically or functionally significant elements in the composition of other characters. **4** Mathematics a quantity forming or expressed as the root of another.
– DERIVATIVES **radicalism** n. **radicalization** (also **-isation**) n. **radicalize** (also **-ise**) v. **radically** adv. **radicalness** n.
– ORIGIN Middle English: from late Latin *radicalis*, from Latin *radix* 'root'.

radical chic ■ n. the fashionable affectation of radical left-wing views. ▸ the dress, lifestyle, etc. associated with this.
– ORIGIN 1970: coined by the American writer Tom Wolfe.

radicchio /raˈdiːkɪəʊ/ ■ n. (pl. **-os**) chicory of a variety with dark red leaves.
– ORIGIN from Italian.

radices plural form of **RADIX**.

radicle /ˈrædɪk(ə)l/ ■ n. **1** Botany the part of a plant embryo that develops into the primary root. **2** Anatomy a root-like subdivision of a nerve or vein.
– ORIGIN C17: from Latin *radicula*, diminutive of *radix* 'root'.

radii plural form of **RADIUS**.

radio ■ n. (pl. **-os**) **1** the transmission and reception of radio waves, especially those carrying audio messages. **2** broadcasting sound. ▸ a broadcasting station or channel. **3** an apparatus for receiving radio programmes. ▸ an apparatus capable of receiving and transmitting radio messages. ■ v. (**-oes, -oed**) send a message by radio. ▸ communicate with by radio.
– ORIGIN C20: abbrev. of **RADIOTELEPHONE**.

radio- ■ comb. form **1** denoting radio waves or broad-casting: *radiogram*. **2** Physics connected with rays, radiation, or radioactivity: *radiograph*. ▸ denoting artificially prepared radioisotopes: *radio-cobalt*. **3** Anatomy relating to the radius: *radio-carpal*.

radioactive ■ adj. emitting or relating to the emission of ionizing radiation or particles.
– DERIVATIVES **radioactively** adv.

radioactivity ■ n. the emission of ionizing radiation or particles caused by the spontaneous disintegration of atomic nuclei. ▸ radioactive particles.

radio astronomy ■ n. the branch of astronomy concerned with radio emissions from celestial objects.

radiobiology ■ n. the branch of biology concerned with the effects of ionizing radiation and the use of radiological techniques.
– DERIVATIVES **radiobiological** adj. **radiobiologist** n.

radio car ■ n. a car with a two-way radio.

radiocarbon ■ n. a radioactive isotope of carbon, especially carbon-14 used in carbon dating.

radiochemistry ■ n. the branch of chemistry concerned with radioactive substances.
– DERIVATIVES **radiochemical** adj.

radio-controlled ■ adj. controllable from a distance by radio.

radio frequency ■ n. a frequency or band of frequencies in the range 10^4 to 10^{11} or 10^{12} hertz, suitable for use in telecommunications.

radiogenic /ˌreɪdɪə(ʊ)ˈdʒɛnɪk, -ˈdʒiːn-/ ■ adj. **1** produced by radioactivity. **2** suitable for broadcasting by radio.

radiogram ■ n. **1** Brit. a combined radio and record player. [from **RADIO-** + **GRAMOPHONE**.] **2** a radiograph. **3** dated a telegram sent by radio.

radiograph ■ n. an image produced on a sensitive plate or film by X-rays or other radiation. ■ v. produce a radiograph of.
– DERIVATIVES **radiographic** adj. **radiographically** adv.

radiography ■ n. the process or occupation of taking radiographs to assist in medical examinations.
– DERIVATIVES **radiographer** n.

radioimmunoassay ■ n. Medicine a technique for measuring antibody levels using radioactively labelled antigens.

radioisotope ■ n. Chemistry a radioactive isotope.
– DERIVATIVES **radioisotopic** adj.

radiolaria /ˌreɪdɪə(ʊ)ˈlɛːrɪə/ ■ pl. n. Zoology single-celled aquatic animals having a spherical amoebalike body with a spiny skeleton of silica. [Phylum Actinopoda.]
– DERIVATIVES **radiolarian** n. & adj.
– ORIGIN C19: from late Latin *radiolus* 'faint ray', diminutive of *radius* 'ray'.

radiology ■ n. the science of X-rays and other high-energy radiation, especially as used in medicine.
– DERIVATIVES **radiologic** adj. **radiological** adj. **radiologically** adv. **radiologist** n.

radiometer /ˌreɪdɪˈɒmɪtə/ ■ n. an instrument for detecting or measuring radiation.
– DERIVATIVES **radiometry** n.

radiometric ■ adj. Physics of or relating to the measurement of radioactivity.
– DERIVATIVES **radiometrically** adv.

radionics /ˌreɪdɪˈɒnɪks/ ■ pl. n. [treated as sing.] a system of alternative medicine based on the study of radiation supposedly emitted by living matter.
– ORIGIN 1940s: from **RADIO-**, on the pattern of *electronics*.

radionuclide ■ n. a radioactive nuclide.

radiopaque /ˌreɪdɪəʊˈpeɪk/ (also **radio-opaque**) ■ adj. opaque to X-rays.

radiophonic ■ adj. relating to or denoting sound produced electronically.

radioscopy /ˌreɪdɪˈɒskəpi/ ■ n. Physics the examination by X-rays of objects opaque to light.
– DERIVATIVES **radioscopic** adj.

radiotelephone ■ n. a telephone using radio transmission.
– DERIVATIVES **radiotelephonic** adj. **radiotelephony** n.

radio telescope ■ n. Astronomy an instrument used to detect radio emissions from the sky.

radiotherapy ■ n. the treatment of cancer or other disease using X-rays or similar radiation.
– DERIVATIVES **radiotherapeutic** adj. **radiotherapist** n.

radio wave ■ n. an electromagnetic wave of radio frequency.

radish ■ n. **1** a pungent-tasting edible root, typically small, spherical, and red, and eaten raw. **2** the plant of the cabbage family which yields this root. [*Raphanus sativus*.]
– ORIGIN Old English *rædic*, from Latin *radix* 'root'.

radium /ˈreɪdɪəm/ ■ n. the chemical element of atomic number 88, a radioactive metal of the alkaline earth series. (Symbol: **Ra**)
– ORIGIN C19: from Latin *radius* 'ray'.

radius /ˈreɪdɪəs/ ■ n. (pl. **radii** /-dɪaɪ/ or **radiuses**) **1** a straight line from the centre to the circumference of a circle or sphere. ▸ a radial line from the focus to any point

of a curve. **2** a specified distance from a centre in all directions. **3** Anatomy & Zoology a bone of the forearm or forelimb, in humans the thicker and shorter of two. **4** Zoology a radially symmetric feature in an echinoderm or coelenterate, e.g. an arm of a starfish. ■ v. (**radiused**, **radiusing**) [often as adj. **radiused**] make (a corner or edge) rounded.
– ORIGIN C16: from Latin, 'staff, spoke, ray'.

radix /'radɪks, 'reɪ-/ ■ n. (pl. **radices** /-dɪsiːz/) Mathematics the base of a system of numeration.
– ORIGIN C17: from Latin, 'root'.

radome /'reɪdəʊm/ ■ n. a dome or other structure protecting radar equipment and made from material transparent to radio waves.
– ORIGIN 1940s: blend of RADAR and DOME.

radon /'reɪdɒn/ ■ n. the chemical element of atomic number 86, a rare radioactive noble gas. (Symbol: **Rn**)
– ORIGIN C20: from RADIUM (from which it is formed by radioactive decay), on the pattern of *argon*.

radula /'radjʊlə/ ■ n. (pl. **radulae** /-liː/) Zoology (in a mollusc) a rasp-like structure for scraping off food particles and drawing them into the mouth.
– ORIGIN C19: from Latin, 'scraper', from *radere* 'to scrape'.

RAF ■ abbrev. **1** (in South Africa) Road Accident Fund. **2** (in the UK) Royal Air Force.

raffia ■ n. **1** a palm tree of tropical Africa and Madagascar, with a short trunk and extremely long leaves. [*Raphia ruffia*.] **2** the fibre from these leaves, used for making hats, baskets, etc.
– ORIGIN C18: from Malagasy.

raffinate /'rafɪneɪt/ ■ n. Chemistry a liquid which has been purified by extraction with a solvent.
– ORIGIN 1920s: from French *raffiner* or German *raffinieren* 'refine'.

raffish ■ adj. slightly disreputable, especially in an attractive manner.
– DERIVATIVES **raffishly** adv. **raffishness** n.
– ORIGIN C19: from RIFF-RAFF.

raffle ■ n. a lottery with goods as prizes. ■ v. offer as a prize in a raffle.
– ORIGIN Middle English (denoting a dice game): from French.

rafflesia /rəˈfliːzɪə, -'zɪə/ ■ n. a Malaysian and Indonesian parasitic plant with a single very large flower which smells of carrion. [Genus *Rafflesia*.]
– ORIGIN named after the British colonial administrator Sir T. Stamford *Raffles*.

raft[1] ■ n. **1** a flat buoyant structure of timber or other materials fastened together, used as a boat or floating platform. ▸ a small inflatable boat. **2** a floating mass of fallen trees, ice, etc. **3** a foundation of reinforced concrete for a building. ■ v. **1** travel or transport on or as if on a raft. **2** make into or transport as a raft.
– DERIVATIVES **rafter** n. **rafting** n.
– ORIGIN Middle English: from Old Norse *raptr* 'rafter'.

raft[2] ■ n. a large amount of something.
– ORIGIN C19: alteration of dialect *raff* 'abundance' (perhaps of Scandinavian origin), by association with RAFT[1] in sense 2.

rafter ■ n. a beam forming part of the internal framework of a roof.
– DERIVATIVES **raftered** adj.
– ORIGIN Old English *ræfter*, of Germanic origin; rel. to RAFT[1].

rag[1] /rag/ ■ n. **1** a piece of old cloth, especially one torn from a larger piece. ▸ (**rags**) old or tattered clothes. **2** (**rags**) the remnants of something. **3** informal a low-quality newspaper. ■ v. give a decorative effect to by applying paint with a rag.
– PHRASES **on the rag** informal, chiefly N. Amer. menstruating. **lose one's rag** informal lose one's temper.
– ORIGIN Middle English: prob. a back-formation from RAGGED or RAGGY.

rag[2] /rag/ ■ n. **1** a programme of entertainments organized by students to raise money for charity. **2** informal, dated a prank. ■ v. (**ragged**, **ragging**) **1** make fun of loudly and boisterously. **2** rebuke severely.
– ORIGIN C18.

rag[3] /rag/ ■ n. **1** a large coarse roofing slate. **2** (also **ragstone**) Brit. a hard coarse sedimentary rock that can be broken into thick slabs.
– ORIGIN Middle English: later associated with RAG[1].

rag[4] /rag/ ■ n. a ragtime composition or tune.
– ORIGIN C19: perhaps from RAGGED.

raga /'rɑːgə, 'rɑːgɑː/ ■ n. (in Indian music) a characteristic pattern of notes used as a basis for improvisation.
– ORIGIN C18: from Sanskrit, 'colour, musical tone'.

ragamuffin (also **raggamuffin**) ■ n. **1** a person in ragged, dirty clothes. **2** an exponent or follower of ragga, typically wearing ragged clothes. ▸ another term for RAGGA.
– ORIGIN Middle English: prob. from RAG[1], with a fanciful suffix.

rag-and-bone man ■ n. chiefly Brit. an itinerant dealer in old clothes and other second-hand items.

ragbag ■ n. **1** a bag for storing rags and old clothes. **2** a miscellaneous collection. **3** informal an untidily dressed woman.

rag doll ■ n. a doll made from cloth.

rage ■ n. **1** violent uncontrollable anger. ▸ [in combination] violent anger associated with conflict arising from a particular context: *road rage*. ▸ the violent action of a natural agency. **2** a vehement desire or passion. ▸ poetic/literary prophetic, poetic, or martial enthusiasm or ardour. ■ v. feel or express rage. ▸ continue violently or with great force.
– PHRASES **all the rage** temporarily very popular or fashionable.
– DERIVATIVES **raging** adj.
– ORIGIN Middle English: from Old French *rage* (n.), *rager* (v.), from a var. of Latin *rabies* (see RABIES).

ragga /'ragə/ ■ n. a style of dance music in which a DJ improvises lyrics over a backing track.
– ORIGIN 1990s: from RAGAMUFFIN, because of the clothing worn by its followers.

raggamuffin ■ n. variant spelling of RAGAMUFFIN.

ragged /'ragɪd/ ■ adj. **1** (of cloth or clothes) old and torn. ▸ wearing such clothes. **2** rough or irregular. ▸ (of an animal) having a rough, shaggy coat. ▸ lacking finish, smoothness, or uniformity. ▸ Printing (especially of a right margin) uneven. **3** suffering from exhaustion or stress.
– PHRASES **run someone ragged** exhaust someone.
– DERIVATIVES **raggedly** adv. **raggedness** n. **raggedy** adj.
– ORIGIN Middle English: of Scandinavian origin.

ragged robin ■ n. a pink-flowered European campion with divided petals that give it a tattered appearance. [*Lychnis flos-cuculi*.]

ragged-tooth shark ■ n. a large shark with a brown or grey back and paler underparts that occurs in tropical and temperate oceans. [*Carcharias taurus* and *Odontaspis ferox*.]

raggie (also **raggy**) ■ n. S. African informal another term for RAGGED-TOOTH SHARK.

raggle-taggle ■ adj. untidy and scruffy.
– ORIGIN C20: a fanciful var. of RAGTAG.

raggy informal ■ adj. (**-ier**, **-iest**) ragged. **2** variant spelling of RAGGIE.
– ORIGIN Old English, of Scandinavian origin.

raglan ■ adj. having or denoting sleeves continuing in one piece up to the neck of a garment. ■ n. an overcoat with raglan sleeves.
– ORIGIN C19: named after Lord *Raglan*, a British commander in the Crimean War.

ragout /ra'guː/ ■ n. a highly seasoned dish of chopped meat stewed with vegetables.
– ORIGIN from French *ragoût*, from *ragoûter* 'revive the taste of'.

rag paper ■ n. paper made from cotton.

rag-roll ■ v. create a striped or marbled effect on (a surface) by painting it with a rag crumpled up into a roll.
– DERIVATIVES **rag-rolled** adj. **rag-rolling** n.

rag rug ■ n. a rug made from small strips of fabric hooked into or pushed through a material such as hessian.

ragstone ■ n. see RAG[3] (sense 2).

ragtag

ragtag ■ adj. untidy, disorganized, or incongruously varied in character.
– ORIGIN C19: superseding earlier *tag-rag* and *tag and rag* (see RAG¹, TAG¹).

ragtime ■ n. music characterized by a syncopated melodic line and regularly accented accompaniment, evolved by black American musicians in the 1890s and played especially on the piano.

rag trade ■ n. informal the clothing or fashion industry.

raguly /ˈragjuli/ ■ adj. Heraldry having an edge with oblique notches like a row of sawn-off branches.
– ORIGIN C17: perhaps from RAGGED.

ragworm ■ n. a predatory marine bristle worm, often used as bait by fishermen. [Family Nereidae.]

ragwort ■ n. a yellow-flowered ragged-leaved European plant of the daisy family, toxic to livestock. [*Senecio jacobaea* and related species.]

rah-rah ■ adj. informal marked by great or uncritical enthusiasm or excitement.

rai /raɪ/ ■ n. a style of music fusing Arabic and Algerian folk elements with Western rock.
– ORIGIN 1980s: perhaps from Arabic *ha er-ray* 'that's the thinking, here is the view', a phr. found in the songs.

RAID ■ abbrev. Computing redundant array of independent (or inexpensive) disks, a system for providing greater capacity, security, etc. by using several disk drives.

raid ■ n. 1 a rapid surprise attack on people or premises. 2 a surprise visit by police to arrest suspects or seize illicit goods. 3 Stock Exchange a hostile attempt to buy a controlling interest in the shares of a company. ■ v. 1 conduct a raid on. 2 quickly and illicitly take something from (a place).
– DERIVATIVES **raider** n.
– ORIGIN Middle English: Scots var. of ROAD in the early senses 'journey on horseback, foray'.

rail¹ /reɪl/ ■ n. 1 a bar or series of bars fixed on upright supports or attached to a wall or ceiling, serving as part of a fence or barrier or used to hang things on. 2 a steel bar or continuous line of bars laid on the ground as one of a pair forming a railway track. 3 railways as a means of transport. 4 a horizontal piece in the frame of a panelled door or sash window. Compare with STILE². 5 the edge of a surfboard or sailboard. 6 Electronics a conductor which is maintained at a fixed potential and to which other parts of a circuit are connected. ■ v. 1 provide or enclose with a rail or rails. 2 convey (goods) by rail.
– PHRASES **go off the rails** informal begin behaving in an uncontrolled way. **on the rails** informal functioning in a normal or regulated way.
– DERIVATIVES **railage** n.
– ORIGIN Middle English: from Old French *reille* 'iron rod', from Latin *regula* 'straight stick, rule'.

rail² ■ v. (**rail against/at**) complain or protest strongly about or to.
– ORIGIN Middle English: from French *railler*, from an alteration of Latin *rugire* 'to bellow'.

rail³ ■ n. a secretive waterside bird with typically drab grey and brown plumage. [*Rallus* and other genera, family Rallidae.]
– ORIGIN Middle English: from Old Northern French *raille*, perhaps of imitative origin.

railcar ■ n. a powered railway passenger vehicle designed to operate singly or as part of a multiple unit. ▸ (**rail car**) N. Amer. any railway carriage or wagon.

railcard ■ n. Brit. a pass entitling the holder to reduced rail fares.

railhead ■ n. 1 a point on a railway from which roads and other transport routes begin. 2 the furthest point reached in constructing a railway.

railing ■ n. (usu. **railings**) a fence or barrier made of rails.

raillery /ˈreɪləri/ ■ n. good-humoured teasing.
– ORIGIN C17: from French *raillerie*, from *railler* (see RAIL²).

railman ■ n. (pl. **-men**) another term for RAILWAYMAN.

railroad ■ n. North American term for RAILWAY. ■ v. informal 1 rush or coerce (someone) into doing something.
▸ cause (a measure) to be passed or approved quickly by applying pressure. 2 N. Amer. send (someone) to prison unjustly.

railway ■ n. 1 a track made of rails along which trains run. 2 a system of such tracks with the trains, organization, and personnel required for its working.

railwayman ■ n. (pl. **-men**) a man who works on a railway.

raiment /ˈreɪm(ə)nt/ ■ n. archaic or poetic/literary clothing.
– ORIGIN Middle English: shortening of obsolete *arrayment* 'dress, outfit'.

rain ■ n. 1 the condensed moisture of the atmosphere falling visibly in separate drops. ▸ (**rains**) falls of rain. 2 a large quantity of things falling or descending: *a rain of blows*. ■ v. 1 (**it rains**), **it is raining**, etc. rain falls. ▸ poetic/literary send down rain. 2 (**be rained off**) (of an event) be terminated or cancelled because of rain. 3 fall or cause to fall in large quantities: *it was just raining glass*.
– PHRASES **be as right as rain** be perfectly fit and well. **rain cats and dogs** rain heavily.
– DERIVATIVES **rainless** adj.
– ORIGIN Old English *regn* (n.), *regnian* (v.), of Germanic origin.

rainbird ■ n. a bird that is said to foretell rain by its call, especially (in South Africa) Burchell's coucal. [*Centropus superciliosus*.]

rainbow ■ n. 1 an arch of colours visible in the sky, caused by the refraction and dispersion of the sun's light by water droplets in the atmosphere. 2 a wide range of things of different colours or kinds. ▸ [as modifier] S. African denoting or relating to the multiracial and/or multicultural characteristics of South Africa.
– ORIGIN Old English *regnboga* (see RAIN, BOW¹).

rainbow coalition ■ n. a political alliance of differing groups, especially one comprising minorities and other disadvantaged groups.

rainbow nation ■ n. post-apartheid South Africa seen in terms of its cultural diversity and inclusiveness.

rainbow runner ■ n. a colourfully striped fish of the jack family, of warm seas worldwide. [*Elagatis bipinnulata*.]

rainbow trout ■ n. a large trout with reddish sides, native to western North America and introduced widely elsewhere for food or sport. [*Oncorhynchus mykiss*.]

rain check ■ n. N. Amer. a ticket given for later use when an outdoor event is interrupted or postponed by rain.
– PHRASES **take a rain check** politely refuse an offer, with the implication that one may take it up at a later date.

raincoat ■ n. a long coat made from waterproofed or water-resistant fabric.

raindrop ■ n. a single drop of rain.

rainfall ■ n. 1 the fall of rain. 2 the quantity of rain falling within a given area in a given time.

rainforest ■ n. a luxuriant, dense forest found in tropical areas with consistently heavy rainfall.

rain frog ■ n. a stout-bodied African burrowing frog. [Genus *Breviceps*: several species.]

rainmaker ■ n. 1 a person who attempts to cause rain to fall. 2 N. Amer. informal a person who is highly successful, especially in business.
– DERIVATIVES **rainmaking** n.

rain shadow ■ n. a relatively dry region sheltered from prevailing rain-bearing winds by a range of hills.

rainstorm ■ n. a storm with heavy rain.

rainswept ■ adj. frequently or recently exposed to rain and wind.

rainwater ■ n. water that has fallen as rain.

rainy ■ adj. (**-ier**, **-iest**) having or characterized by considerable rainfall.
– PHRASES **a rainy day** a time in the future when money may be needed.

raise ■ v. 1 lift or move to a higher position or level. ▸ set upright. 2 construct or build (a structure). 3 increase the amount, level, or strength of. ▸ promote to a higher rank. 4 (**raise something to**) Mathematics multiply a quantity to (a specified power). 5 (in poker or brag) bet (a specified amount) more than (another player). ▸ Bridge make a higher bid in the same suit as that bid by (one's partner).

6 cause to be heard, felt, or considered: *doubts have been raised.* **7** generate (an invoice or other document). **8** collect or levy (money or resources). **9** bring up (a child). **10** breed or grow (animals or plants). **11** wake from sleep or bring back from death. **12** abandon or force to abandon (a blockade, embargo, etc.). **13** drive (an animal) from its lair. **14** (of someone at sea) come in sight of (land or another ship). ▶ informal establish contact with (someone), especially by telephone or radio. **15** Physiology stimulate production of (an antiserum, antibody, etc.) against the appropriate target cell or substance. ■ n. **1** an increase in salary. **2** an act of raising a stake or bid. **3** Weightlifting an act of lifting or raising a part of the body while holding a weight.
–PHRASES **raise hell** informal make a noisy disturbance. ▶ complain vociferously. **raise the roof** make or cause people to make a great deal of noise, especially cheering. **raise one's voice** speak more loudly.
–DERIVATIVES **raiser** n.
–ORIGIN Middle English: from Old Norse *reisa*; rel. to the verb REAR².

raised beach ■ n. Geology a former beach now above water level owing to changes since its formation.

raisin ■ n. a partially dried grape.
–DERIVATIVES **raisiny** adj.
–ORIGIN Middle English: from Old French, 'grape', from Latin *racemus* 'grape bunch'.

raison d'être /ˌreɪzɒ̃ ˈdɛtr/ ■ n. (pl. **raisons d'être** pronunc. same) the most important reason or purpose for someone or something's existence.
–ORIGIN French, 'reason for being'.

raita /ˈrʌɪtə/ ■ n. an Indian side dish of yogurt containing chopped cucumber or other vegetables, and spices.
–ORIGIN from Hindi *rāytā*.

Raj /rɑːdʒ/ ■ n. (**the Raj**) historical British sovereignty in India.
–ORIGIN from Hindi *rāj* 'reign'.

raja /ˈrɑːdʒɑː/ (also **rajah**) ■ n. historical an Indian king or prince.
–ORIGIN from Hindi *rājā*, Sanskrit *rājan* 'king'.

raja yoga ■ n. a form of yoga intended to achieve control over the mind and emotions.
–ORIGIN from Sanskrit, from *rājan* 'king' + YOGA.

rake¹ ■ n. **1** an implement consisting of a pole having at its end a toothed crossbar or fine tines, used for drawing together leaves, cut grass, etc. or smoothing loose soil or gravel. **2** an act of raking. ■ v. **1** draw together with a rake. **2** make smooth with a rake. **3** scratch or scrape with a long sweeping movement. **4** draw or drag (something) through something with a long sweeping movement. **5** sweep with gunfire, a look, or a beam of light. **6** (**rake through**) search or rummage through.
–PHRASES **rake over** (**old**) **coals** (or **rake over the ashes**) chiefly Brit. revive the memory of a past event.
–PHRASAL VERBS **rake it in** informal make a lot of money. **rake something up/over** revive the memory of an incident or period of time that is best forgotten.
–DERIVATIVES **raker** n.
–ORIGIN Old English, of Germanic origin, from a base meaning 'heap up'; the verb is partly from Old Norse *raka* 'to scrape, shave'.

rake² ■ n. a fashionable or wealthy man of dissolute habits.
–ORIGIN C17: abbrev. of archaic *rakehell* in the same sense.

rake³ ■ v. **1** set at a sloping angle. **2** (of a ship's mast or funnel) incline from the perpendicular towards the stern. **3** (of a ship's bow or stern) project at its upper part beyond the keel. ■ n. the angle at which a thing slopes.
–ORIGIN C17: prob. rel. to German *ragen* 'to project'.

rake-off ■ n. informal a commission or share of the profits from a deal, especially one that is disreputable.

raki /rəˈkiː, ˈrɑːki/ ■ n. a strong alcoholic spirit made in eastern Europe or the Middle East.
–ORIGIN from Turkish *rak*.

rakish ■ adj. having a dashing, jaunty, or slightly disreputable quality or appearance.
–DERIVATIVES **rakishly** adv. **rakishness** n.
–ORIGIN C18: from RAKE².

raku /ˈrɑːkuː/ ■ n. a kind of lead-glazed Japanese earthenware, used especially for the tea ceremony.
–ORIGIN Japanese, 'enjoyment'.

rale /rɑːl/ ■ n. (usu. **rales**) Medicine an abnormal rattling sound heard when examining unhealthy lungs with a stethoscope.
–ORIGIN C19: from French *râle*, from *râler* 'to rattle'.

rally ■ v. (**-ies, -ied**) **1** (with reference to troops) bring or come together again in order to continue fighting. **2** bring or come together for concerted action. **3** assemble in a mass meeting. **4** recover or cause to recover in health, spirits, or poise. **5** (of share, currency, or commodity prices) increase after a fall. **6** drive in a rally. ■ n. (pl. **-ies**) **1** a mass meeting held as a protest or in support of a cause. **2** an open-air event for people who own a particular kind of vehicle. **3** a competition for motor vehicles in which they are driven a long distance over public roads or rough terrain. **4** a quick or marked recovery. **5** (in tennis and other racket sports) an extended exchange of strokes between players.
–DERIVATIVES **rallyist** n.
–ORIGIN C17: from French *rallier*, from *re-* 'again' + *allier* 'to ally'.

rallycross ■ n. a form of motor racing in which cars are driven in heats over a course including rough terrain and tarmac roads, but not public roads.

rallying ■ n. **1** the action or process of bringing or coming together. ▶ [as modifier] having the effect of calling people to action: *a rallying cry*. **2** the action or sport of participating in a motor rally.

RAM ■ abbrev. Computing random-access memory.

ram ■ n. **1** an uncastrated male sheep. ▶ the male of certain other animals, e.g. a bushbuck. **2** short for BATTERING RAM. **3** the falling weight of a piledriving machine. **4** a hydraulic water-raising or lifting machine. **5** historical a projecting part of the bow of a warship, for piercing the sides of other ships. ■ v. (**rammed, ramming**) **1** roughly force (something) into place. **2** (of a vehicle or vessel) be driven violently into. **3** (**ram into**) crash violently against. **4** [often as adj. **rammed**] beat (earth or the ground) with a heavy implement to make it hard and firm.
–DERIVATIVES **rammer** n.
–ORIGIN Old English *ram(m)*, of Germanic origin.

Ramadan /ˈraməˌdan, ˌraməˈdan/ (also **Ramadhan** /-zan/) ■ n. the ninth month of the Muslim year, during which strict fasting is observed from sunrise to sunset.
–ORIGIN from Arabic *ramaḍān*, from *ramaḍa* 'be hot'; supposedly because the fasting period was orig. in one of the hot months.

ram air ■ n. air which is forced to enter a moving aperture, such as the air intake of an aircraft.

Ramapithecus /ˌrɑːməˈpɪθɪkəs/ ■ n. a genus of fossil anthropoid apes known from remains found in Miocene deposits in SW Asia and East Africa.
–ORIGIN from the name of the Hindu god *Rama* + Greek *pithēkos* 'ape'.

ramble ■ v. **1** walk for pleasure in the countryside. **2** (of a plant) grow over walls, fences, etc. **3** (often **ramble on**) talk or write at length in a confused or inconsequential way. ■ n. a walk taken for pleasure in the countryside.
–DERIVATIVES **rambler** n. **rambling** adj. & n.
–ORIGIN Middle English: prob. rel. to Middle Dutch *rammelen* (used of animals in the sense 'wander about on heat').

Rambo /ˈrambəʊ/ ■ n. an extremely tough and aggressive man.
–ORIGIN the name of the hero of David Morrell's novel *First Blood* (1972), popularized in the films *First Blood* (1982) and *Rambo: First Blood Part II* (1985).

rambunctious /ramˈbʌŋ(k)ʃəs/ ■ adj. informal, chiefly N. Amer. uncontrollably exuberant.
–DERIVATIVES **rambunctiously** adv. **rambunctiousness** n.
–ORIGIN C19.

rambutan /ramˈb(j)uːt(ə)n/ ■ n. **1** a red, plum-sized tropical fruit with soft spines and a slightly acidic taste. **2** the Malaysian tree that bears this fruit. [*Nephelium lappaceum*.]
–ORIGIN C18: from Malay *rambūtan*, from *rambut* 'hair', with allusion to the fruit's spines.

ramekin

ramekin /ˈramɪkɪn, ˈramkɪn/ ■ n. a small dish for baking and serving an individual portion of food.
– ORIGIN C17: from French *ramequin*, of Low German or Dutch origin.

ramen /ˈrɑːmɛn/ ■ pl. n. (in oriental cuisine) quick-cooking noodles.
– ORIGIN Japanese, from Chinese *lā* 'to pull' + *miàn* 'noodles'.

ramie /ˈrami/ ■ n. 1 a vegetable fibre noted for its length and toughness, used in the manufacture of textiles. 2 the plant of the nettle family which yields this fibre, native to tropical Asia. [*Boehmeria nivea*.]
– ORIGIN C19: from Malay *rami*.

ramification ■ n. 1 the action or state of ramifying or being ramified. 2 (usu. **ramifications**) a complex consequence of an action or event. 3 a subdivision of a complex structure or process.

ramify /ˈramɪfʌɪ/ ■ v. (**-ies, -ied**) form or cause to form branches; spread or cause to spread and branch out.
– DERIVATIVES **ramified** adj.
– ORIGIN Middle English: from Old French *ramifier*, from medieval Latin *ramificare*, from Latin *ramus* 'branch'.

ramjet ■ n. a type of jet engine in which the air drawn in for combustion is compressed solely by the forward motion of the aircraft.

ramp ■ n. 1 a sloping surface joining two different levels. 2 a movable set of steps for entering or leaving an aircraft. 3 S. African & N. Amer. an inclined slip road leading to or from a main road or freeway. 4 Brit. a speed bump. 5 an upward bend in a stair rail. 6 an electrical waveform in which the voltage increases or decreases linearly with time. 7 informal a swindle involving a fraudulent increase of the price of a share. ■ v. 1 provide with a ramp. 2 (of an electrical waveform) increase or decrease in voltage linearly with time. 3 [usu. as noun **ramping**] purchase shares or other securities in order to raise their price fraudulently. 4 (**ramp up** or **ramp something up**) (especially in reference to the production of goods) increase or cause something to increase in amount. 5 archaic (of an animal) rear up on its hind legs, as if climbing.
– ORIGIN Middle English: from Old French *ramper* 'creep, crawl'.

rampage ■ v. /ramˈpeɪdʒ/ rush around in a violent and uncontrollable manner. ■ n. /ramˈpeɪdʒ, ˈrampeɪdʒ/ an instance of rampaging.
– DERIVATIVES **rampager** n.
– ORIGIN C17: perhaps from RAMP and RAGE.

rampant ■ adj. 1 flourishing or spreading unchecked. 2 unrestrained in action or performance. 3 (of a plant) lush in growth. 4 [usu. postpos.] Heraldry (of an animal) represented standing on its left hind foot with its forefoot in the air.
– DERIVATIVES **rampancy** n. **rampantly** adv.

HISTORY

Rampant entered Middle English from Old French, in which it meant 'crawling' (from *ramper* 'to crawl'). As in French, early use in English had the adjective following the noun, especially in heraldry, as in 'lion rampant', in which the lion is depicted in profile, standing on its left hind foot, with forefeet and tail raised. By extension to other wild animals rearing up in a threatening manner, **rampant** acquired the sense 'fierce', from which developed the current meaning 'unrestrained'.

---

rampart ■ n. a defensive wall of a castle or walled city, having a broad top with a walkway.
– ORIGIN C16: from French *rempart*, from *remparer* 'fortify, take possession of again', based on Latin *ante* 'before' + *parare* 'prepare'.

ram raid ■ n. a robbery in which a shop window is rammed with a vehicle and looted.
– DERIVATIVES **ram-raider** n. **ram-raiding** n.

ramrod ■ n. a rod for ramming down the charge of a muzzle-loading firearm. ■ v. (**ramrodded, ramrodding**) (**ramrod something through**) chiefly N. Amer. force a proposed measure to be accepted or completed quickly.

ramshackle ■ adj. in a state of severe disrepair.
– ORIGIN C19: alteration of earlier *ramshackled*, from obsolete *ransackled* 'ransacked'.

ramus /ˈreɪməs/ ■ n. (pl. **rami** /ˈreɪmʌɪ, ˈreɪmiː/) 1 Anatomy & Zoology a projecting structure, especially a branch of a bone or nerve. 2 Ornithology a barb of a feather.
– ORIGIN C17: from Latin, 'branch'.

ran past of RUN.

ranch ■ n. 1 a large farm, especially in the western US and Canada, where cattle or other animals are bred. 2 (also **ranch house**) N. Amer. a single-storey house. 3 (also **ranch dressing**) N. Amer. a type of thick white salad dressing made with sour cream. ■ v. run a ranch. ▸ breed (animals) on a ranch.
– DERIVATIVES **rancher** n. **ranching** n.
– ORIGIN C19: from Spanish *rancho* 'group of persons eating together'.

rancid ■ adj. (of foods containing fat or oil) smelling or tasting unpleasant as a result of being stale.
– DERIVATIVES **rancidity** n.
– ORIGIN C17: from Latin *rancidus* 'stinking'.

rancour (US **rancor**) ■ n. bitterness; resentment.
– DERIVATIVES **rancorous** adj.
– ORIGIN Middle English: from late Latin *rancor* 'rankness', rel. to Latin *rancidus* 'stinking'.

rand /rand, rant/ ■ n. 1 (usu. **Rand**) the basic monetary unit of South Africa, equal to 100 cents. 2 (**the Rand**) the chief industrial and gold-mining region of South Africa, centred around Johannesburg. 3 S. African a long rocky hillock.
– ORIGIN from Dutch *rand* 'edge, border'; sense 2 a shortening of WITWATERSRAND.

R & B ■ abbrev. rhythm and blues.

R & D ■ abbrev. research and development.

Randlord ■ n. S. African, often derogatory a wealthy or powerful person, especially from one of the Johannesburg mining houses.

random ■ adj. 1 made, done, or happening without method or conscious decision. 2 Statistics governed by or involving equal chances for each item. 3 (of masonry or something similarly constructed) with stones or components of irregular size and shape.
– DERIVATIVES **randomization** (also **-isation**) n. **randomize** (also **-ise**) v. **randomly** adv. **randomness** n.
– ORIGIN Middle English: from Old French *randon* 'great speed', from *randir* 'gallop', from a Germanic root.

random access ■ n. Computing the process of transferring information to or from memory in which every memory location can be accessed directly rather than being accessed in a fixed sequence.

random error ■ n. Statistics an error in measurement caused by factors which vary from one measurement to another.

random walk ■ n. Physics a series of movements of an object or changes in a variable that follow no discernible pattern or trend.

R & R ■ abbrev. 1 Medicine rescue and resuscitation. 2 informal rest and recreation. 3 (also **R'n'R**) rock and roll.

randy ■ adj. (**-ier, -iest**) informal sexually aroused or excited.
– DERIVATIVES **randily** adv. **randiness** n.
– ORIGIN C17: perhaps from obsolete *rand* 'rant, rave', from obsolete Dutch *randen* 'to rant'.

rang past of RING².

range ■ n. 1 the area of variation between limits on a particular scale. 2 a set of different things of the same general type. 3 the scope or extent of a person's or thing's abilities or capacity. 4 the distance within which a sense, detector, transmitter, etc. is effective. ▸ the distance that can be covered by a vehicle or aircraft without refuelling. ▸ the distance attained or attainable by a gun, projectile, etc. ▸ the distance between a camera and the subject to be photographed. 5 a line or series of mountains or hills. 6 a large area of open land for grazing or hunting. 7 an area used as a testing ground for military equipment. ▸ (also **shooting range**) an area with targets for shooting practice. 8 the area over which a plant or animal is distributed. ■ v. 1 vary or extend between specified limits. 2 run or extend in a line in a particular direction. 3 place or arrange in a row or rows or in a specified order or manner. 4 (**range someone against** or **be ranged against**) place oneself or

---

VOWELS a cat ɑː arm ɛ bed ɛː hair ə ago əː her ɪ sit i cosy iː see ɒ hot ɔː saw ʌ run

be placed in opposition to. **5** Brit. Printing (with reference to type) align or be aligned at the ends of successive lines. **6** travel or wander over a wide area. **7** embrace a wide number of different topics.
– ORIGIN Middle English: from Old French *range* 'row, rank', from *rangier* 'put in order', from *rang* 'rank'.

rangefinder ■ n. an instrument for estimating the distance of an object, especially for use with a camera or gun.

ranger ■ n. **1** a keeper of a park, forest, or area of countryside. **2** a member of a body of armed men. **3** (**Ranger** or **Ranger Guide**) a member of the senior branch of the Guides.

ranging pole (also **ranging rod**) ■ n. Surveying a pole or rod used for setting a straight line.

rangy /ˈreɪn(d)ʒi/ ■ adj. (**-ier, -iest**) (of a person) tall and slim; long-limbed.
– DERIVATIVES **ranginess** n.

ranitidine /rəˈnɪtɪdiːn, -ˈnaɪt-/ ■ n. Medicine a synthetic compound with antihistamine properties, used to treat ulcers and related conditions.
– ORIGIN 1970s.

rank[1] ■ n. **1** a position within a fixed hierarchy, especially that of the armed forces. **2** high social standing. **3** a single line of soldiers or police officers drawn up abreast. ▸ a regular row or line of things or people. **4** (**the ranks**) (in the armed forces) those who are not commissioned officers. **5** (**ranks**) the people belonging to or constituting a group or class: *the ranks of the unemployed.* **6** Chess each of the eight rows of eight squares running from side to side across a chessboard. Compare with **FILE**[1] (in sense 3). **7** short for **TAXI RANK**. ■ v. **1** give (someone or something) a rank within a grading system. **2** hold a specified rank. **3** US take precedence over (someone) in respect to rank.
– PHRASES **break rank** (or **ranks**) **1** (of soldiers or police officers) fail to remain in line. **2** fail to maintain solidarity. **close ranks 1** (of soldiers or police officers) come closer together in a line. **2** unite in action to defend common interests. **keep rank** (of soldiers or police officers) remain in line. **pull rank** take unfair advantage of one's seniority.
– ORIGIN Middle English: from Old French *ranc*, of Germanic origin.

rank[2] ■ adj. **1** (of vegetation) growing too thickly. **2** having a foul smell. **3** conspicuously undesirable; flagrant.
– DERIVATIVES **rankly** adv. **rankness** n.
– ORIGIN Old English *ranc* 'proud, rebellious, sturdy', also 'fully grown', of Germanic origin.

rank and file ■ n. [treated as pl.] the ordinary members of an organization as opposed to its leaders.
– ORIGIN referring to the 'ranks' and 'files' into which privates and non-commissioned officers form on parade.

rank correlation ■ n. Statistics an assessment of the degree of correlation between two ways of ranking the members of a set.

ranker ■ n. **1** chiefly Brit. a soldier in the ranks; a private. ▸ a commissioned officer who has been in the ranks. **2** [in combination] a person or animal of a specified rank: *a top-ranker.*

ranking ■ n. **1** a position in a hierarchy or scale. **2** the action of giving a rank or status to someone or something. ■ adj. [in combination] having a specified rank: *high-ranking officers.* ▸ N. Amer. having a high rank.

rankle ■ v. **1** (of a comment or fact) cause annoyance or resentment. ▸ chiefly N. Amer. annoy or irritate (someone). **2** archaic (of a wound or sore) continue to be painful; fester.
– ORIGIN Middle English: from Old French *rancler*, from *rancle, draoncle* 'festering sore', from medieval Latin *dracunculus*, diminutive of *draco* 'serpent'.

ransack ■ v. **1** go hurriedly through (a place) stealing things and causing damage. **2** thoroughly search.
– DERIVATIVES **ransacker** n.
– ORIGIN Middle English: from Old Norse *rannsaka*, from *rann* 'house' + an element rel. to *sækja* 'seek'.

ransom ■ n. a sum of money demanded or paid for the release of a captive. ■ v. obtain the release of (someone) by paying a ransom. ▸ detain (someone) and demand a ransom for their release.
– PHRASES **hold someone to ransom 1** hold someone captive and demand payment for their release. **2** demand concessions from a person or organization by threatening damaging action. **a king's ransom** a huge amount of money.
– ORIGIN Middle English: from Old French *ransoun* (n.), *ransouner* (v.), from Latin *redemptio(n-)* (see **REDEMPTION**).

rant ■ v. speak or shout at length in a wild, impassioned way. ■ n. a spell of ranting.
– DERIVATIVES **ranter** n.
– ORIGIN C16: from Dutch *ranten* 'talk nonsense, rave'.

ranunculus /rəˈnʌŋkjʊləs/ ■ n. (pl. **ranunculuses** or **ranunculi** /-laɪ, -liː/) a plant of a genus that includes the buttercups and water crowfoots, typically having yellow or white bowl-shaped flowers and lobed or toothed leaves. [Genus *Ranunculus*: many species.]
– ORIGIN from Latin, 'little frog', diminutive of *rana*.

rap[1] ■ v. (**rapped, rapping**) **1** strike (a hard surface) with a series of rapid audible blows. ▸ strike (something) against a hard surface in such a way. ▸ strike (someone or something) sharply. **2** (usu. **rap something out**) say something sharply or suddenly. **3** informal, chiefly N. Amer. talk or chat in an easy and familiar manner. **4** perform rap music. ■ n. **1** a quick, sharp knock or blow. **2** informal a rebuke or criticism. **3** a type of popular music of US origin in which words are recited rhythmically over an instrumental backing. **4** informal, chiefly N. Amer. an impromptu talk or discussion. **5** informal, chiefly N. Amer. a criminal charge: *a murder rap.*
– PHRASES **beat the rap** N. Amer. informal escape punishment for or be acquitted of a crime. **take the rap** informal be punished or blamed for something.
– DERIVATIVES **rapper** n.
– ORIGIN Middle English: prob. imitative and of Scandinavian origin.

rap[2] ■ n. the smallest amount: *he doesn't care a rap.*
– ORIGIN C19: from Irish *ropaire* 'robber'; used as the name of a counterfeit coin in C18 Ireland.

rapacious /rəˈpeɪʃəs/ ■ adj. aggressively greedy.
– DERIVATIVES **rapaciously** adv. **rapaciousness** n. **rapacity** n.
– ORIGIN C17: from Latin *rapac-, rapax* (from *rapere* 'to snatch').

rape[1] ■ v. **1** (of a man) force (another person) to have sexual intercourse with him against their will. **2** spoil or destroy (a place). ■ n. **1** an act or the crime of raping someone. **2** the act of raping a place or area.
– DERIVATIVES **raper** n. (chiefly US).
– ORIGIN Middle English: from Anglo-Norman French *rap* (n.), *raper* (v.), from Latin *rapere* 'seize'.

rape[2] ■ n. a plant of the cabbage family with bright yellow flowers, especially a variety (oilseed rape) grown for its oil-rich seed and as stockfeed. [*Brassica napus*.]
– ORIGIN Middle English: from Latin *rapum, rapa* 'turnip'.

rapeseed ■ n. seeds of the rape plant, used for oil.

raphe /ˈreɪfi/ ■ n. (pl. **raphae** /ˈreɪfiː/) Biology a groove, ridge, or seam in an organ or tissue, typically marking the line where two halves fused in the embryo.
– ORIGIN C18: from Greek *rhaphē* 'seam'.

rapid ■ adj. happening in a short time or at great speed. ■ n. (usu. **rapids**) a fast-flowing and turbulent part of the course of a river.
– DERIVATIVES **rapidity** n. **rapidly** adv. **rapidness** n.
– ORIGIN C17: from Latin *rapidus*, from *rapere* 'take by force'.

rapid eye movement ■ n. the jerky movement of a person's eyes that occurs in REM sleep.

rapier ■ n. a thin, light sharp-pointed sword used for thrusting.
– ORIGIN C16: from French *rapière*, from *râpe* 'rasp, grater' (because the perforated hilt resembles a rasp).

rapine /ˈrapaɪn, -pɪn/ ■ n. poetic/literary the violent seizure of property.
– ORIGIN Middle English: from Old French, or from Latin *rapina*, from *rapere* 'seize'.

rapist ■ n. a man who commits rape.

rappel /raˈpɛl/ ■ n. & v. (**rappelled, rappelling**) another term for **ABSEIL**.
– ORIGIN 1930s: from French, 'a recalling', from *rappeler* in

rapport

the sense 'bring back to oneself' (with ref. to the rope manoeuvre).

rapport /ra'pɔː/ ■ n. a close and harmonious relationship in which there is common understanding.
– ORIGIN C17: French, from *rapporter* 'bring back'.

rapporteur /ˌrapɔːˈtɜː/ ■ n. a person appointed by an organization to report on its meetings.
– ORIGIN C18: French, from *rapporter* 'bring back'.

rapprochement /raˈprɒʃmɒ̃/ ■ n. the establishment or resumption of harmonious relations.
– ORIGIN French, from *rapprocher*, from *re-* (expressing intensive force) + *approcher* 'to approach'.

rapscallion /rapˈskaliən/ ■ n. archaic or humorous a mischievous person.
– ORIGIN C17: alteration of earlier *rascallion*, perhaps from RASCAL.

rapt ■ adj. 1 fully absorbed and intent; fascinated. 2 enraptured.
– DERIVATIVES **raptly** adv.
– ORIGIN Middle English: from Latin *raptus* 'seized', from *rapere*.

raptor ■ n. 1 a bird of prey. 2 informal a dromaeosaurid dinosaur, such as a velociraptor.
– ORIGIN Middle English: from Latin, 'plunderer', from *rapere* 'seize'.

raptorial ■ adj. chiefly Zoology 1 predatory. 2 adapted for seizing prey.

rapture ■ n. 1 a feeling of intense pleasure or joy. 2 (**raptures**) the expression of intense pleasure or enthusiasm.
– DERIVATIVES **rapturous** adj. **rapturously** adv.
– ORIGIN C16: from medieval Latin *raptura* 'seizing', partly influenced by RAPT.

rara avis /ˌrɑːrə ˈeɪvɪs, ˌrɑːrə ˈɑːvɪs/ ■ n. (pl. **rarae aves** /-riː, -viːz/) another term for RARE BIRD.
– ORIGIN from Latin.

rare¹ ■ adj. (**rarer**, **rarest**) 1 occurring very infrequently. 2 remarkable: *a player of rare skill*.
– DERIVATIVES **rareness** n.
– ORIGIN Middle English: from Latin *rarus*.

rare² ■ adj. (**rarer**, **rarest**) (of red meat) lightly cooked, so that the inside is still red.
– ORIGIN C18: var. of obsolete *rear* 'half-cooked'.

rare bird ■ n. an exceptional person or thing.
– ORIGIN translating Latin *rara avis* (Juvenal's *Satires*, vi.165).

rarebit (also **Welsh rarebit** or **Welsh rabbit**) ■ n. a dish of melted and seasoned cheese on toast.
– ORIGIN C18.

rare earth (also **rare-earth element** or **metal**) ■ n. Chemistry any of a group of chemically similar metallic elements comprising the lanthanide series and (usually) scandium and yttrium.

raree show /ˈrɛːriː/ ■ n. archaic a form of street entertainment, especially one carried in a box, such as a peep show.
– ORIGIN C17: representing *rare show*, as pronounced by Savoyard showmen.

rarefaction /ˌrɛːrɪˈfakʃ(ə)n/ ■ n. reduction of the density of something, especially air or a gas.
– ORIGIN C17: from medieval Latin *rarefactio(n-)*, from *rarefacere* 'grow thin, become rare'.

rarefied /ˈrɛːrɪfaɪd/ ■ adj. 1 (of air) of lower pressure than usual; thin. 2 very esoteric or refined.

rare gas ■ n. another term for NOBLE GAS.

rarely ■ adv. 1 not often; seldom. 2 archaic remarkably well. ▶ to an unusual degree.

raring ■ adj. informal very eager to do something: *she was raring to go*.
– ORIGIN 1920s: from *rare*, dialect var. of ROAR or REAR².

rarity ■ n. (pl. **-ies**) 1 the state or quality of being rare. 2 a rare thing.

rascal ■ n. a mischievous or cheeky person, especially a child.
– DERIVATIVES **rascality** n. **rascally** adj.
– ORIGIN Middle English: from Old French *rascaille* 'rabble'.

rash¹ ■ adj. acting or done impetuously, without careful consideration.
– DERIVATIVES **rashly** adv. **rashness** n.
– ORIGIN Middle English: of Germanic origin.

rash² ■ n. 1 an area of reddening of a person's skin, sometimes with raised spots. 2 an unwelcome series of things happening within a short space of time: *a rash of strikes*.
– ORIGIN C18: prob. rel. to Old French *rasche* 'eruptive sores, scurf'.

rasher ■ n. a thin slice of bacon.
– ORIGIN C16.

rasp ■ n. 1 a coarse file for use on metal, wood, or other hard material. 2 a harsh, grating noise. ■ v. 1 file with a rasp. 2 (of a rough surface or object) scrape in a painful or unpleasant way. 3 make a harsh, grating noise.
– DERIVATIVES **rasping** adj. **raspingly** adv. **raspy** adj.
– ORIGIN Middle English (as v.): from Old French *rasper*, perhaps of Germanic origin.

raspberry ■ n. 1 an edible soft fruit related to the blackberry, consisting of a cluster of reddish-pink aggregate drupes. 2 the prickly shrub which yields this fruit. [*Rubus idaeus*.] 3 informal a sound made with the tongue and lips, expressing derision or contempt. [from **raspberry tart**, rhyming slang for 'fart'.]
– ORIGIN C17: from dialect *rasp*, abbrev. of obsolete *raspis* 'raspberry', + BERRY.

Rasta /ˈrastə/ ■ n. & adj. informal short for RASTAFARIAN.

Rastafarian /ˌrastəˈfɑːriən, -ˈfɛːriən/ ■ adj. of or relating to a religious movement of Jamaican origin holding that Emperor Haile Selassie of Ethiopia was the Messiah and that black people are the chosen people. ■ n. a member of this movement.
– DERIVATIVES **Rastafarianism** n.
– ORIGIN from *Ras Tafari*, the name by which Haile Selassie was known (1916–30).

Rastaman /ˈrastəman/ ■ n. (pl. **-men**) informal a male Rastafarian.

raster /ˈrastə/ ■ n. a rectangular pattern of parallel scanning lines followed by the electron beam on a television screen or computer monitor.
– ORIGIN C20: from German *Raster* 'screen', from Latin *rastrum* 'rake'.

rasterize (also **-ise**) ■ v. Computing convert (an image stored as an outline) into pixels that can be displayed on a screen or printed.
– DERIVATIVES **rasterization** (also **-isation**) n. **rasterizer** (also **-iser**) n.

rat ■ n. 1 a rodent resembling a large, long-tailed mouse, typically considered a serious pest. [*Rattus norvegicus* (brown rat), *R. rattus* (black or ship rat), and many other species.] 2 informal a despicable person. 3 informal an informer. ■ exclam. (**rats**) informal expressing mild annoyance. ■ v. (**ratted**, **ratting**) 1 hunt or kill rats. 2 informal desert one's party, side, or cause. 3 (**rat on someone** or US also **rat someone out**) informal inform on someone. 4 (**rat on**) informal break (an agreement or promise).
– DERIVATIVES **ratting** n.
– ORIGIN Old English *ræt*, prob. of Romance origin; reinforced in Middle English by Old French *rat*.

ratable ■ adj. variant spelling of RATEABLE.

ratafia /ˌratəˈfiːə/ ■ n. 1 a liqueur flavoured with almonds or the kernels of peaches, apricots, or cherries. 2 an almond-flavoured biscuit like a small macaroon.
– ORIGIN C17: from French.

rat-arsed ■ adj. vulgar slang, chiefly Brit. very drunk.

ratatouille /ˌratəˈtuːi, -ˈtwiː/ ■ n. a vegetable dish consisting of onions, courgettes, tomatoes, aubergines, and peppers, stewed in oil.
– ORIGIN a French dialect word.

ratbag ■ n. informal, chiefly Brit. an unpleasant or disliked person.

ratchet ■ n. a device consisting of a bar or wheel with a set of angled teeth in which a pawl, cog, or tooth engages, allowing motion in one direction only. ■ v. (**ratcheted**,

---

CONSONANTS b but d dog f few g get h he j yes k cat l leg m man n no p pen r red

ratcheting) **1** operate by means of a ratchet. **2** (**ratchet something up/down**) cause something to rise (or fall) as a step in an irreversible process.
– ORIGIN C17: from French *rochet*, orig. denoting a blunt lance head, later in the sense 'bobbin, ratchet'.

rate[1] ■ *n.* **1** a measure, quantity, or frequency. **2** the speed with which something moves, happens, or changes. **3** a fixed price paid or charged for something. **4** the amount of a charge or payment expressed as a percentage of some other amount, or as a basis of calculation. **5** (**rates**) a tax on commercial and private land and buildings paid to a local authority. ■ *v.* **1** assign a standard or value to (something) according to a particular scale. **2** consider to be of a certain quality or standard. ▸ informal have a high opinion of. ▸ be worthy of; merit. **3** assess the value of (a property) for the purpose of levying rates.
– PHRASES **at any rate** whatever happens or may have happened. **at this** (or **that**) **rate** if things continue in this or that way; should a certain assumption be true.
– ORIGIN Middle English: from medieval Latin *rata* (from Latin *pro rata parte* 'according to the proportional share'), from *ratus* 'reckoned', from *reri*.

rate[2] ■ *v.* archaic scold angrily.
– ORIGIN Middle English.

rateable (also **ratable**) ■ *adj.* able to be rated or estimated.
– DERIVATIVES **rateably** *adv.*

rateable value ■ *n.* a value ascribed to a commercial property based on its size, location, etc., used to determine the rates payable by its owner.

ratel /ˈreɪt(ə)l, ˈrɑː-/ ■ *n.* **1** another term for HONEY BADGER. **2** (**Ratel**) S. African Military a six-wheeled armoured personnel carrier and infantry combat vehicle.
– ORIGIN C18: from Afrikaans.

rate of exchange ■ *n.* another term for EXCHANGE RATE.

ratepayer ■ *n.* a person liable to pay rates.

rather ■ *adv.* **1** (**would rather**) indicating one's preference in a particular matter. **2** to a certain or significant extent or degree. **3** on the contrary. **4** more precisely. **5** instead of; as opposed to. ■ *exclam.* Brit. dated expressing emphatic affirmation, agreement, or acceptance.
– PHRASES **had rather** poetic/literary or archaic would rather.
– ORIGIN Old English *hrathor* 'earlier, sooner', from *hræth* 'prompt'.

ratify ■ *v.* (**-ies**, **-ied**) give formal consent to; make officially valid.
– DERIVATIVES **ratifiable** *adj.* **ratification** *n.*
– ORIGIN Middle English: from Old French *ratifier*, from medieval Latin *ratificare*, from Latin *ratus* (see RATE[1]).

rating ■ *n.* **1** a classification or ranking based on quality, standard, or performance. **2** the value of a property or condition which is claimed to be standard, optimal, or limiting for a material, device, etc. **3** (**ratings**) the estimated audience size of a particular television or radio programme. **4** any of the classes into which racing yachts are assigned according to dimensions. **5** Brit. a non-commissioned sailor in the navy.

ratio ■ *n.* (pl. **-os**) the quantitative relation between two amounts showing the number of times one value contains or is contained within the other.
– ORIGIN C17: from Latin, 'reckoning', from *reri* 'reckon'.

ratiocinate /ˌratɪˈɒsɪneɪt, ˌraʃɪ-/ ■ *v.* formal form judgements by a process of logic; reason.
– DERIVATIVES **ratiocination** *n.*
– ORIGIN C17: from Latin *ratiocinari* 'deliberate, calculate', from *ratio* (see RATIO).

ration ■ *n.* **1** a fixed amount of a commodity officially allowed to each person during a time of shortage, as in wartime. **2** (**rations**) an amount of food supplied on a regular basis to members of the armed forces during a war. **3** (**rations**) food; provisions. ■ *v.* **1** limit the supply of (a commodity) to fixed rations. **2** limit the amount of a commodity available to (someone).
– ORIGIN C18: from Latin *ratio(n-)* 'reckoning, ratio'.

rational ■ *adj.* **1** based on or in accordance with reason or logic. **2** (of a person) able to think sensibly or logically. **3** endowed with the capacity to reason. **4** Mathematics (of a number, quantity, or expression) expressible or, or containing quantities which are expressible, as a ratio of whole numbers.
– DERIVATIVES **rationality** *n.* **rationally** *adv.*

– ORIGIN Middle English: from Latin *rationalis*, from *ratio(n-)* (see RATIO).

rationale /ˌraʃəˈnɑːl/ ■ *n.* a set of reasons or a logical basis for a course of action or a particular belief.
– ORIGIN C17: from Latin *rationalis* (see RATIONAL).

rationalism ■ *n.* **1** the practice or principle of basing opinions and actions on reason and knowledge rather than on religious belief or emotional response. **2** Philosophy the theory that reason rather than experience is the foundation of certainty in knowledge.
– DERIVATIVES **rationalist** *n.* **rationalistic** *adj.* **rationalistically** *adv.*

rationalize (also **-ise**) ■ *v.* **1** attempt to justify (an action or attitude) with logical reasoning. **2** reorganize (a process or system) in such a way as to make it more logical and consistent. **3** make (a company or industry) more efficient by dispensing with superfluous personnel or equipment. **4** Mathematics convert to a rational form.
– DERIVATIVES **rationalization** (also **-isation**) *n.*

ratite /ˈratʌɪt/ Ornithology ■ *adj.* denoting a bird having a flat breastbone without a keel and so unable to fly, such as an ostrich, emu, etc. ■ *n.* a ratite bird.
– ORIGIN C19: from Latin *ratis* 'raft'.

rat-kangaroo ■ *n.* a small rat-like Australian marsupial with long hindlimbs used for hopping. [Family Potoroidae: several species.]

ratlines /ˈratlɪnz/ ■ *pl. n.* a series of small rope lines fastened across a sailing ship's shrouds like the rungs of a ladder, used for climbing the rigging.
– ORIGIN Middle English.

ratoon /rəˈtuːn/ ■ *n.* a new shoot springing from the base of a crop plant, especially sugar cane, after cropping.
– ORIGIN C17: from Spanish *retoño* 'a sprout'.

rat pack[1] ■ *n.* informal a group of journalists and photographers perceived as aggressive or relentless in their pursuit of stories.

rat pack[2] ■ *n.* S. African military slang a food pack.

rat race ■ *n.* informal a way of life in which people are caught up in a fiercely competitive struggle for wealth or power.

rat run ■ *n.* Brit. informal a minor street used by drivers during peak periods to avoid congestion on main routes.

rat snake ■ *n.* a harmless constricting snake that feeds on rats and other small mammals. [*Elaphe obsoleta* (N. America), *Ptyas mucosus* (Asia), and other species.]

rat-tail ■ *n.* **1** (also **rat's tail**) a narrow hairless tail like that of a rat, or something that resembles one. **2** (**rat's tails**) Brit. informal hair hanging in lank, damp, or greasy strands. **3** another term for GRENADIER (in sense 2).

rattan /rəˈtan/ ■ *n.* **1** the thin, jointed stems of a palm, used to make furniture. **2** a length of such a stem used as a walking stick. **3** the tropical climbing palm which yields these stems. [Genus *Calamus*.]
– ORIGIN C17: from Malay *rotan*, prob. from *raut* 'pare, trim'.

rat-tat (also **rat-tat-tat**) ■ *n.* a rapping sound.
– ORIGIN C17: imitative.

ratted ■ *adj.* Brit. informal very drunk.

ratter ■ *n.* a dog or other animal used for hunting rats.

rattle ■ *v.* **1** make or cause to make a rapid succession of short, sharp knocking or clinking sounds. **2** move or travel somewhere while making such sounds: *trains rattled past.* **3** (**rattle about/around in**) be in or occupy (an unnecessarily or undesirably large space). **4** informal cause to feel nervous, worried, or irritated. **5** (**rattle something off**) say, perform, or produce something quickly and effortlessly. **6** (**rattle on/away**) talk rapidly and at length. ■ *n.* **1** a rattling sound. **2** a thing that makes a rattling sound, in particular a baby's toy consisting of a container filled with small pellets. **3** a gurgling sound in the throat. **4** the set of horny rings at the end of a rattlesnake's tail.
– PHRASES **rattle sabres** threaten to take aggressive action.
– DERIVATIVES **rattly** *adj.*
– ORIGIN Middle English: rel. to Middle Dutch and Low German *ratelen*, of imitative origin.

rattler ■ n. 1 a thing that rattles, especially an old or rickety vehicle. 2 N. Amer. informal a rattlesnake.

rattlesnake ■ n. a heavy-bodied American pit viper with a series of horny rings on the tail that produce a characteristic rattling sound when vibrated as a warning. [Genera *Crotalus* and *Sistrurus*: several species.]

rattletrap ■ n. informal an old or rickety vehicle.

rattling ■ adj. 1 making a rattle. 2 informal, dated very good of its kind: *a rattling good story*.

ratty ■ adj. (-ier, -iest) 1 resembling or characteristic of a rat. 2 infested with rats. 3 informal shabby, untidy, or in bad condition. 4 informal bad-tempered and irritable.
–DERIVATIVES **rattily** adv. **rattiness** n.

raucous /'rɔːkəs/ ■ adj. making or constituting a harsh, loud noise.
–DERIVATIVES **raucously** adv. **raucousness** n.
–ORIGIN C18: from Latin *raucus* 'hoarse'.

raunch ■ n. informal energetic earthiness or vulgarity.
–ORIGIN 1960s: back-formation from RAUNCHY.

raunchy ■ adj. (-ier, -iest) informal 1 energetically earthy and sexually explicit. 2 chiefly US slovenly or grubby.
–DERIVATIVES **raunchily** adv. **raunchiness** n.
–ORIGIN 1930s.

ravage ■ v. cause extensive damage to; devastate. ■ n. (**ravages**) the destructive effects of something.
–DERIVATIVES **ravager** n.
–ORIGIN C17: from French *ravager*, from earlier *ravage*, alteration of *ravine* 'rush of water'.

rave ■ v. 1 talk wildly or incoherently. 2 speak or write about someone or something with great enthusiasm or admiration. 3 informal attend or take part in a rave party. ■ n. 1 informal an extremely enthusiastic appraisal of someone or something. 2 a person or thing that inspires intense and widely shared enthusiasm. 3 informal a lively party involving dancing and drinking. 4 informal a very large party or event with dancing to loud, fast electronic music. ▸ electronic dance music of the kind played at a rave.
–ORIGIN Middle English: prob. from Old Northern French *raver*.

ravel ■ v. (**ravelled, ravelling**; US **raveled, raveling**) 1 (**ravel something out**) untangle something. 2 unravel; fray. 3 confuse or complicate (a question or situation).
–ORIGIN Middle English: prob. from Dutch *ravelen* 'fray out, tangle'.

raven /'reɪv(ə)n/ ■ n. a large heavily built black crow. [*Corvus corax* and related species.] ■ adj. (especially of hair) of a glossy black colour.
–ORIGIN Old English, of Germanic origin.

ravening ■ adj. voracious; rapacious.

ravenous ■ adj. voraciously hungry.
–DERIVATIVES **ravenously** adv. **ravenousness** n.
–ORIGIN Middle English: from Old French *ravineus*, from *raviner* 'to ravage', from Latin *rapina* 'pillage'.

raver ■ n. 1 informal a person who has an exciting and uninhibited social life. 2 informal a person who regularly goes to raves. 3 a person who talks wildly or incoherently.

ravine /rə'viːn/ ■ n. a deep, narrow gorge with steep sides.
–DERIVATIVES **ravined** adj.
–ORIGIN C18: from French, 'violent rush'.

raving ■ n. (usu. **ravings**) wild or incoherent talk. ■ adj. & adv. informal extremely or conspicuously: *raving mad*.

ravioli /ˌravɪ'əʊli/ ■ pl. n. small pasta envelopes containing minced meat, cheese, or vegetables.
–ORIGIN from Italian.

ravish ■ v. archaic or poetic/literary 1 fill with intense delight; enrapture. 2 seize and carry off by force. 3 rape.
–DERIVATIVES **ravisher** n. **ravishment** n.
–ORIGIN Middle English: from Old French *raviss-, ravir*, from Latin *rapere* 'seize'.

ravishing ■ adj. causing intense delight; entrancing.
–DERIVATIVES **ravishingly** adv.

raw ■ adj. 1 (of food) uncooked. 2 (of a material or substance) in its natural state; not processed. 3 (of data) not organized, analysed, or evaluated. 4 (of the edge of a piece of cloth) not having a hem or selvedge. 5 new and lacking in experience in an activity or job. 6 (of the skin) red and painful, especially as the result of abrasion. ▸ (of the nerves) very sensitive. 7 (of an emotion or quality) strong and undisguised. 8 (of the weather) bleak, cold, and damp.
–PHRASES **in the raw** 1 in its true state. 2 informal naked. **touch someone on the raw** upset someone by referring to a subject about which they are very sensitive.
–DERIVATIVES **rawish** adj. **rawly** adv. **rawness** n.
–ORIGIN Old English, of Germanic origin.

raw-boned ■ adj. having a bony or gaunt physique.

rawhide ■ n. stiff untanned leather.

Rawlplug /'rɔːlplʌɡ/ ■ n. trademark a thin plastic or fibre sheath that is inserted into a hole in masonry in order to hold a screw.
–ORIGIN C20: from *Rawlings* (the name of the engineers who introduced it) + PLUG.

raw material ■ n. a basic material from which a product is made.

ray[1] ■ n. 1 each of the lines in which light seems to stream from the sun or any luminous body, or pass through a small opening. 2 the straight line in which light or other electromagnetic radiation travels to a given point. 3 (**rays**) a specified form of non-luminous radiation: *ultra-violet rays*. 4 Mathematics any of a set of straight lines passing through one point. 5 an initial or slight indication of a positive or welcome quality: *a ray of hope*. 6 Botany any of the individual strap-shaped florets around the edge of the flower of a daisy or related plant. ■ v. spread from or as if from a central point.
–PHRASES **catch some rays** informal sunbathe. **ray of sunshine** informal a person who brings happiness into the lives of others.
–DERIVATIVES **-rayed** adj. **rayless** adj.
–ORIGIN Middle English: from Old French *rai*, from Latin *radius* 'spoke, ray'.

ray[2] ■ n. a broad flat cartilaginous fish with wing-like pectoral fins and a long slender tail. [Order Batiformes: many species.]
–ORIGIN Middle English: from Old French *raie*, from Latin *raia*.

ray[3] (also **re**) ■ n. Music (in tonic sol-fa) the second note of a major scale. ▸ the note D in the fixed-doh system.
–ORIGIN Middle English *re*, representing (as an arbitrary name for the note) the first syllable of *resonare*, taken from a Latin hymn.

Raynaud's disease /'reɪnəʊ/ (also **Raynaud's syndrome**) ■ n. a disease characterized by whiteness, numbness, or pain in the fingers, typically brought on by constant cold or vibration.
–ORIGIN C19: named after the French physician Maurice *Raynaud*.

rayon ■ n. a textile fibre or fabric made from regenerated cellulose (viscose).
–ORIGIN 1920s: an arbitrary formation.

raze ■ v. tear down and destroy (a building, town, etc.).
–ORIGIN Middle English: from Old French *raser* 'shave closely', from Latin *radere* 'scrape'.

razor ■ n. an instrument with a sharp blade, used to shave unwanted hair from the face or body.
–ORIGIN Middle English: from Old French *rasor*, from *raser* (see RAZE).

razor blade ■ n. a blade used in a razor, typically a thin flat piece of metal with a sharp edge or edges used in a safety razor.

razor shell ■ n. a burrowing bivalve mollusc with a long straight shell. [Family Solenidae.]

razor wire ■ n. a metal wire or ribbon with sharp edges or studded with small sharp blades, used as a defensive barrier.

razzle-dazzle ■ n. another term for RAZZMATAZZ.
–ORIGIN C19: reduplication of DAZZLE.

razzmatazz (also **razzamatazz**) ■ n. informal noisy, showy, and exciting activity and display.
–ORIGIN C19: prob. an alteration of RAZZLE-DAZZLE.

RB ■ abbrev. Botswana (international vehicle registration).
–ORIGIN from *Republic of Botswana*.

Rb ■ symb. the chemical element rubidium.
RBI ■ abbrev. Baseball run(s) batted in.
RC ■ abbrev. **1** reinforced concrete. **2** Electronics resistance/capacitance (or resistor/capacitor). **3** Roman Catholic.
RCA ■ abbrev. (in the UK) Royal College of Art.
RCM ■ abbrev. (in the UK) Royal College of Music.
RCMP ■ abbrev. Royal Canadian Mounted Police.
RCN ■ abbrev. (in the UK) Royal College of Nursing.
Rd ■ abbrev. Road (used in street names).
RDA ■ abbrev. recommended daily (or dietary) allowance.
RDBMS ■ abbrev. Computing relational database management system.
RDI ■ abbrev. recommended (or reference) daily intake.
RDP ■ abbrev. Reconstruction and Development Programme. ■ n. (in South Africa) a strategy advanced between 1994 and 1996 by the first democratic government to redress the socio-economic and political inequalities created by apartheid. ▸ [as modifier] denoting policies, projects, or resources associated with or resulting from this strategy: *RDP houses*.
RDX ■ n. a type of high explosive.
– ORIGIN 1940S: from R(*esearch*) D(*epartment*) (*E*)x(*plosive*).
Re ■ symb. the chemical element rhenium.
re¹ /riː, reɪ/ ■ prep. **1** in the matter of (used in headings or to introduce a reference). **2** about; concerning.
– ORIGIN Latin, ablative of *res* 'thing'.
re² ■ n. variant spelling of RAY³.
re- ■ prefix **1** once more; afresh; anew: *reactivate*. ▸ return to a previous state: *restore*. **2** (also **red-**) in return; mutually: *resemble*. ▸ in opposition: *repel*. **3** behind or after: *relic*. ▸ in a withdrawn state: *reticent*. ▸ back and away; down: *recede*. **4** with frequentative or intensive force: *resound*. **5** with negative force: *recant*.
– ORIGIN from Latin *re-*, *red-* 'again, back'.

> **USAGE**
> Words formed with **re-** tend to be unhyphenated: *restore*, *reacquaint*. An exception to this occurs when the word to which **re-** attaches begins with **e**, in which case a hyphen is often inserted for clarity: **re-examine**, **re-enter**. A hyphen is sometimes also used where the word formed with the prefix would be identical to an already existing word: **re-cover** (meaning 'cover again') not **recover** (meaning 'get better in health').

reach ■ v. **1** stretch out an arm in a specified direction in order to touch or grasp something. ▸ (**reach something out**) stretch out one's hand or arm. ▸ (**reach something down**) stretch upwards to pick something up and bring it down to a lower level. ▸ hand (something) to. **2** be able to touch (something) with an outstretched arm or leg. **3** arrive at or attain; extend to. **4** succeed in achieving. **5** make contact with. **6** (of a broadcast or other communication) be received by. **7** succeed in influencing or having an effect on. **8** Nautical sail with the wind blowing from the side. ■ n. **1** an act of reaching. **2** the distance to which someone can stretch out their hand (used especially of a boxer). **3** the extent or range of something's application, effect, or influence. **4** (often **reaches**) a continuous extent of land or water, especially a stretch of river between two bends. **5** Nautical a distance traversed in reaching.
– DERIVATIVES **reachable** adj.
– ORIGIN Old English, of West Germanic origin.

react ■ v. **1** respond to something in a particular way or with particular behaviour. **2** (**react against**) respond with hostility or a contrary course of action to. **3** suffer from adverse physiological effects after ingesting, breathing, or touching a substance. **4** Chemistry & Physics interact and undergo a chemical or physical change. **5** Stock Exchange (of share prices) fall after rising.
– ORIGIN C17: from RE- (expressing intensive force or reversal) + ACT, orig. suggested by medieval Latin *reagere* 'do again'.

reactance ■ n. Physics the non-resistive component of impedance in an AC circuit, arising from inductance and/or capacitance.

reactant ■ n. Chemistry a substance that takes part in and undergoes change during a reaction.

readily

reaction ■ n. **1** an instance of reacting to or against something. **2** (**reactions**) a person's ability to respond physically and mentally to external stimuli. **3** opposition to political or social progress or reform. **4** a process in which substances interact causing chemical or physical change. **5** Physics a force exerted in opposition to an applied force.
– DERIVATIVES **reactionist** n. & adj.

reactionary ■ adj. opposing political or social progress or reform. ■ n. (pl. **-ies**) a person holding reactionary views.

reaction formation ■ n. Psychoanalysis the tendency of a repressed wish or feeling to be expressed at a conscious level in a contrasting form.

reactivate ■ v. restore to a state of activity.
– DERIVATIVES **reactivation** n.

reactive ■ adj. **1** showing a response to a stimulus. **2** acting in response to a situation rather than creating or controlling it. **3** having a tendency to react chemically. **4** Physiology showing an immune response to a specific antigen. **5** (of an illness) caused by a reaction to something. **6** Physics of or relating to reactance.
– DERIVATIVES **reactivity** n.

reactor ■ n. **1** (also **nuclear reactor**) an apparatus or structure in which fissile material can be made to undergo a controlled, self-sustaining nuclear reaction releasing energy. **2** a container or apparatus in which substances are made to react chemically. **3** Medicine a person who reacts to a drug, antigen, etc. **4** Physics a coil or other component which provides reactance in a circuit.

read ■ v. (past and past part. **read**) **1** look at and comprehend the meaning of (written or printed matter) by interpreting the characters or symbols of which it is composed. ▸ speak (written or printed words) aloud. ▸ (of a passage, text, or sign) contain or consist of specified words; have a certain wording. **2** habitually read (a particular newspaper or journal). **3** discover (information) by reading it in a written or printed source. ▸ [as adj. **read**] having a specified level of knowledge as a result of reading: *she was well read*. **4** understand or interpret the nature or significance of. ▸ (of a piece of writing) convey a specified impression to the reader: *it read like a cry for help*. **5** proof-read. **6** present (a bill or other measure) before a legislative assembly. **7** inspect and record the figure indicated on (a measuring instrument). ▸ indicate a specified measurement or figure. **8** chiefly Brit. study (an academic subject) at a university. **9** (of a computer) copy or transfer (data). ▸ enter or extract (data) in an electronic storage device. **10** hear and understand the words of (someone speaking on a radio transmitter). ■ n. **1** chiefly Brit. a period or act of reading. **2** informal a book considered in terms of its readability.
– PHRASES **read between the lines** look for or discover a meaning that is hidden or implied rather than explicitly stated. **read someone's mind** (or **thoughts**) discern what someone is thinking. **read my lips** N. Amer. informal listen carefully. **take something as read** assume something without the need for further discussion.
– PHRASAL VERBS **read something into** attribute a meaning or significance to (something) that it may not in fact possess. **read up on something** (or **read something up**) acquire information about a particular subject by reading.
– ORIGIN Old English, of Germanic origin.

readable ■ adj. **1** able to be read or deciphered; legible. **2** easy or enjoyable to read.
– DERIVATIVES **readability** n. **readably** adv.

reader ■ n. **1** a person who reads. **2** a person who reports to a publisher on the merits of manuscripts submitted for publication. **3** (**Reader**) a university lecturer of the highest grade below professor. **4** short for LAY READER. **5** a book containing extracts of a text or texts for teaching purposes. **6** a device that produces on a screen a readable image from a microfiche or microfilm.
– DERIVATIVES **readerly** adj.

readership ■ n. [treated as sing. or pl.] the readers of a newspaper or magazine regarded collectively.

readily ■ adv. **1** without hesitation; willingly. **2** without difficulty; easily.

readiness ■ n. the state or quality of being ready.

reading ■ n. **1** the action or skill of reading. **2** an instance of something being read to an audience. **3** an interpretation of a text. **4** a figure recorded on a measuring instrument. **5** a stage of debate in parliament through which a bill must pass before it can become law.

reading age ■ n. a child's reading ability expressed with reference to an average age at which a comparable ability is found.

readjust ■ v. set or adjust again. ▶ adjust or adapt to a changed situation or environment.
– DERIVATIVES **readjustment** n.

read-only memory ■ n. Computing memory read at high speed but not capable of being changed by program instructions.

read-write ■ adj. Computing capable of reading existing data and accepting alterations or further input.

ready ■ adj. (**-ier**, **-iest**) **1** in a suitable state for an activity or situation; fully prepared. **2** made suitable and available for immediate use. **3** easily available or obtained; within reach. **4** willing to do something. **5** immediate, quick, or prompt. **6** in such a condition as to be likely to do something. ■ v. (**-ies**, **-ied**) make (something) ready.
– PHRASES **at the ready** prepared or available for immediate use. **make ready** prepare.
– ORIGIN Middle English: from Old English, from a Germanic base meaning 'arrange, prepare'.

ready-made ■ adj. **1** made to a standard size or specification rather than to order. **2** readily available: *ready-made answers*. **3** (of food) sold ready or almost ready to be served. ■ n. a ready-made article.

ready-mixed ■ adj. (of concrete, paint, food, etc.) having some or all of the constituents already mixed together.
– DERIVATIVES **ready-mix** n.

ready money (also **ready cash**) ■ n. money in the form of cash that is immediately available.

ready-to-wear ■ adj. (of clothes) sold through shops rather than made to order for an individual customer.

reafforest ■ v. another term for REFOREST.
– DERIVATIVES **reafforestation** n.

reagent /rɪˈeɪdʒ(ə)nt/ ■ n. a substance or mixture for use in chemical analysis or other reactions.

real /riːl/ ■ adj. **1** actually existing or occurring in fact; not imagined or supposed. **2** significant; serious: *a real danger*. **3** Philosophy relating to something as it is, not merely as it may be described or distinguished. **4** not artificial or made in imitation of something; genuine. **5** rightly so called; proper: *he's my idea of a real man*. **6** adjusted for changes in the value of money; assessed by purchasing power. **7** Mathematics (of a number or quantity) having no imaginary part. **8** Optics (of an image) such that the light that forms it actually passes through it; not virtual. ■ adv. informal, chiefly N. Amer. really; very.
– PHRASES **for real** informal as a serious or actual concern.
– DERIVATIVES **realness** n.
– ORIGIN Middle English: from late Latin *realis*, from Latin *res* 'thing'.

real account ■ n. Finance an account dealing with the material assets of a business, such as its property.

real ale ■ n. chiefly Brit. cask-conditioned beer that is served traditionally, without additional gas pressure.

real estate ■ n. real property; land.

realia /reɪˈɑːlɪə, rɪˈeɪlɪə/ ■ n. objects and material from everyday life used as teaching aids.
– ORIGIN 1950s: from late Latin, from *realis* (see REAL).

realign ■ v. **1** change or restore to a different or former position or state. **2** (**realign oneself with**) change one's position or attitude with regard to.
– DERIVATIVES **realignment** n.

realism ■ n. **1** the practice of accepting a situation as it is and dealing with it accordingly. **2** (in art or literature) the representation of things in a way that is accurate and true to life. **3** Philosophy the doctrine that universals or abstract concepts have an objective or absolute existence. Often contrasted with NOMINALISM.
– DERIVATIVES **realist** n.

realistic ■ adj. **1** having a sensible and practical idea of what can be achieved or expected. **2** representing things in a way that is accurate and true to life.
– DERIVATIVES **realistically** adv.

reality ■ n. (pl. **-ies**) **1** the state of things as they actually exist, as opposed to an idealistic or notional idea of them. ▶ [as modifier] denoting television programmes based on real people or situations, intended to be entertaining rather than informative: *reality TV*. **2** a thing that is actually experienced or seen. **3** the quality of being lifelike. **4** the state or quality of having existence or substance. **5** Philosophy existence that is absolute, self-sufficient, or objective, and not subject to human decisions or conventions.

reality principle ■ n. Psychoanalysis (in Freudian theory) the control by the ego of the pleasure-seeking activity of the id in order to meet the demands of the external world.

reality testing ■ n. Psychology the objective evaluation of an emotion or thought against real life, as a faculty present in normal individuals but defective in psychotics.

reality TV ■ n. television featuring ordinary people in unscripted situations, typically in a group cut off from civilization.

realize (also **-ise**) ■ v. **1** become fully aware of as a fact; understand clearly. **2** cause to happen. **3** achieve (something desired or anticipated); fulfil. **4** give actual or physical form to (a concept or work). **5** sell for or make a profit of. **6** convert (an asset) into cash.
– DERIVATIVES **realizability** (also **-isability**) n. **realizable** (also **-isable**) adj. **realization** (also **-isation**) n. **realizer** (also **-iser**) n.
– ORIGIN C17: from REAL, on the pattern of French *réaliser*.

really ■ adv. **1** in reality; in actual fact. **2** very; thoroughly: *he writes really well*. ■ exclam. expressing interest, surprise, doubt, or protest.

realm ■ n. **1** archaic or poetic/literary a kingdom. **2** a field or domain of activity or interest.
– ORIGIN Middle English *rewme*, from Old French *reaume*, from Latin *regimen* (see REGIMEN); the spelling with *-l-* was influenced by Old French *reiel* 'royal'.

realpolitik /reɪˈɑːlpɒlɪˌtiːk/ ■ n. politics based on practical rather than moral or ideological considerations.
– ORIGIN C20: from German *Realpolitik* 'practical politics'.

real property ■ n. Law property consisting of land or buildings.

real tennis ■ n. the original form of tennis, played with a solid ball on an enclosed court.

real time ■ n. **1** the actual time during which something occurs. **2** [as modifier] Computing relating to or denoting a system in which input data is available virtually immediately as feedback to the process from which it is coming, e.g. in a missile guidance system.

realtor /ˈrɪəltə/ ■ n. N. Amer. an estate agent.
– ORIGIN C20: from REALTY.

realty /ˈrɪəltɪ/ ■ n. Law a person's real property. Compare with PERSONALTY.

ream[1] ■ n. **1** 500 (formerly 480) sheets of paper. **2** a large quantity of something, especially paper.
– ORIGIN Middle English: from Old French *raime*, from Arabic *rizma* 'bundle'.

ream[2] ■ v. widen (a bore or hole) with a special tool.
– ORIGIN C19.

reamer ■ n. a tool for widening or shaping holes.

reanalyse ■ v. conduct a further analysis of something.
– DERIVATIVES **reanalysis** n.

reanimate ■ v. revive.
– DERIVATIVES **reanimation** n.

reap ■ v. **1** cut or harvest a crop from (land). **2** receive as a consequence of one's own or others' actions.
– ORIGIN Old English.

reaper ■ n. **1** a person or machine that harvests a crop. **2** (**the Reaper** or **the Grim Reaper**) a personification of death as a cloaked skeleton wielding a large scythe.

reappear ■ v. appear again.
– DERIVATIVES **reappearance** n.

reappoint ■ v. appoint again to a position previously held.
– DERIVATIVES **reappointment** n.

reappraise ■ v. appraise again or differently.
– DERIVATIVES **reappraisal** n.

rear¹ ■ n. **1** the back or hindmost part of something. **2** (also **rear end**) informal a person's buttocks. ■ adj. at the back.
– PHRASES **bring up the rear 1** be at the very end of a queue. **2** come last in a race.
– ORIGIN Middle English from Old French *rere*, from Latin *retro* 'back'.

rear² ■ v. **1** bring up (a child). ▸ (of an animal) care for (young) until fully grown. ▸ breed and raise (animals). ▸ grow or cultivate (plants). **2** (of an animal) raise itself upright on its hind legs. ▸ set or lift upright. **3** (of a building, mountain, etc.) extend or appear to extend to a great height.
– DERIVATIVES **rearer** n.
– ORIGIN Old English *rǣran* 'set upright, construct, elevate', of Germanic origin.

rear admiral ■ n. a rank of naval officer below vice admiral.

rearguard ■ n. **1** the soldiers at the rear of a body of troops, especially those protecting a retreating army. **2** a reactionary or conservative faction.
– ORIGIN Middle English: from Old French *rereguarde*.

rearguard action ■ n. a defensive action carried out by a retreating army.

rear light ■ n. a tail light.

rearm ■ v. provide with or acquire a new supply of weapons.
– DERIVATIVES **rearmament** n.

rearmost ■ adj. furthest back.

rearrange ■ v. arrange again in a different way.
– DERIVATIVES **rearrangement** n.

rearrest ■ v. arrest again. ■ n. an act of rearresting someone.

rear-view mirror ■ n. a mirror fixed inside the windscreen of a motor vehicle enabling the driver to see the vehicle or road behind.

rearward ■ adj. directed towards the back. ■ adv. (also **rearwards**) towards the back.

rear-wheel drive ■ n. a transmission system that provides power to the rear wheels of a motor vehicle.

reason ■ n. **1** a cause, explanation, or justification. ▸ good or obvious cause to do something. ▸ Logic a premise of an argument in support of a belief, especially a minor premise given after the conclusion. **2** the power of the mind to think, understand, and form judgements logically. ▸ (**one's reason**) one's sanity. **3** what is right, practical, or possible. ■ v. **1** think, understand, and form judgements logically. ▸ (**reason something out**) find a solution to a problem by considering possible options. **2** (**reason with**) persuade with rational argument.
– PHRASES **by reason of** formal because of. **listen to reason** be persuaded to act sensibly. **it stands to reason** it is obvious or logical.
– DERIVATIVES **reasoned** adj. **reasoner** n. **reasonless** adj. (archaic).
– ORIGIN Middle English: from Old French *reisun* (n.), *raisoner* (v.), from a var. of Latin *ratio(n-)*, from *reri* 'consider'.

reasonable ■ adj. **1** fair and sensible. **2** as much as is appropriate or fair; moderate. ▸ fairly good. ▸ relatively inexpensive.
– DERIVATIVES **reasonableness** n. **reasonably** adv.
– ORIGIN Middle English: from Old French *raisonable*, suggested by Latin *rationabilis* 'rational', from *ratio* (see REASON).

reassemble ■ v. assemble again; put back together.
– DERIVATIVES **reassembly** n.

reassert ■ v. assert again.
– DERIVATIVES **reassertion** n.

reassess ■ v. assess again, especially differently.
– DERIVATIVES **reassessment** n.

reassign ■ v. assign again or differently.
– DERIVATIVES **reassignment** n.

reassure ■ v. allay the doubts and fears of.
– DERIVATIVES **reassurance** n. **reassuring** adj. **reassuringly** adv.

reattach ■ v. attach again.
– DERIVATIVES **reattachment** n.

reattempt ■ v. attempt again.

reave /riːv/ ■ v. (past and past part. **reft** /rɛft/) archaic (often **be reft of**) rob of something by force. ▸ steal.
– ORIGIN Old English, of Germanic origin.

reawaken ■ v. awaken again.

rebadge ■ v. relaunch (a product) under a new name or logo.

rebarbative /rɪˈbɑːbətɪv/ ■ adj. formal unattractive and objectionable.
– ORIGIN C19: from French *rébarbatif*, *-ive*, from Old French *se rebarber* 'face each other "beard to beard" aggressively', from *barbe* 'beard'.

rebase ■ v. establish a new base level for (a tax level, price index, etc.).

rebate¹ /ˈriːbeɪt/ ■ n. **1** a partial refund to someone who has paid too much for tax, rent, or a utility. **2** a deduction or discount on a sum due. ■ v. pay back as a rebate.
– DERIVATIVES **rebatable** adj.
– ORIGIN Middle English: from Anglo-Norman French *rebatre* 'beat back', also 'deduct'.

rebate² /ˈriːbeɪt/ ■ n. a step-shaped recess cut in a piece of wood, typically forming a match to the edge or tongue of another piece. ■ v. (**rebated**, **rebating**) **1** make a rebate in. **2** join or fix with a rebate.
– ORIGIN C17: from Old French *rabbat* 'abatement, recess'.

rebbe /ˈrɛbə/ ■ n. Judaism a rabbi, especially a Hasidic religious leader.
– ORIGIN Yiddish, from Hebrew *rabbī* 'rabbi'.

rebbetzin /ˈrɛbɪtsɪn/ (also **rebbitzin**) ■ n. Judaism **1** the wife of a rabbi. **2** a female religious teacher.
– ORIGIN Yiddish, feminine of *rebbe* (see REBBE).

rebel ■ n. /ˈrɛb(ə)l/ a person who rebels. ■ v. /rɪˈbɛl/ (**rebelled**, **rebelling**) rise in opposition or armed resistance to an established government or ruler. ▸ resist authority, control, or convention. ▸ show or feel repugnance.
– ORIGIN Middle English: from Old French *rebelle* (n.), *rebeller* (v.), from Latin *rebellis*, from *bellum* 'war'.

rebellion ■ n. **1** armed resistance to an established government or ruler. **2** defiance of authority or control.
– ORIGIN Middle English: from Latin *rebellio(n-)*, from *rebellis* (see REBEL).

rebellious ■ adj. **1** showing a desire to rebel. ▸ engaged in rebellion. **2** unmanageable.
– DERIVATIVES **rebelliously** adv. **rebelliousness** n.

rebid ■ v. (**rebidding**; past and past part. **rebid**) bid again. ■ n. a further bid.

rebind ■ v. (past and past part. **rebound**) give a new binding to (a book).

rebirth ■ n. **1** reincarnation. **2** a revival.

rebirthing ■ n. a form of therapy involving controlled breathing intended to simulate the trauma of being born.
– DERIVATIVES **rebirther** n.

reboot ■ v. boot (a computer system) again. ■ n. an act or instance of rebooting.

rebore ■ v. make a new or wider boring in (the cylinders of an internal-combustion engine). ■ n. an act of reboring. ▸ an engine with rebored cylinders.

reborn ■ adj. **1** brought back to life or activity. **2** born-again.

rebound¹ ■ v. /rɪˈbaʊnd/ **1** bounce back after hitting a hard surface. **2** recover in value, amount, or strength. **3** (**rebound on/upon**) have an unexpected adverse consequence for. **4** Basketball gain possession of a missed shot after it bounces off the backboard or basket rim. ■ n. /ˈriːbaʊnd/ **1** a ball or shot that rebounds. ▸ Basketball a recovery of possession of a missed shot. **2** an instance of recovering in value, amount, or strength. **3** [usu. as modifier] Medicine recurrence of a condition after withdrawal of treatment: *rebound hypertension*.
– PHRASES **on the rebound** while still distressed after the ending of a romantic relationship.
– ORIGIN Middle English: from Old French *rebondir*, from *re-* 'back' + *bondir* 'bounce up'.

rebound² past and past participle of **REBIND**.

rebrand ■ v. [usu. as noun **rebranding**] change the corporate image of.

rebreather ■ n. an aqualung in which the diver's exhaled breath is partially purified of carbon dioxide, mixed with more oxygen, and then breathed again.

rebroadcast ■ v. (past **rebroadcast** or **rebroadcasted**; past part. **rebroadcast**) broadcast again. ■ n. a repeated broadcast.

rebuff ■ v. reject in an abrupt or ungracious manner. ■ n. an abrupt rejection.
– ORIGIN C16: from obsolete French *rebuffe* (n.), from Italian *ri-* (expressing opposition) + *buffo* 'a gust, puff', of imitative origin.

rebuild ■ v. (past and past part. **rebuilt**) build again. ■ n. 1 an instance of rebuilding. 2 a thing that has been rebuilt.
– DERIVATIVES **rebuilder** n.

rebuke ■ v. criticize or reprimand sharply. ■ n. a sharp criticism.
– DERIVATIVES **rebuker** n.
– ORIGIN Middle English: from Old Northern French *rebuker*, from *re-* 'back, down' + *bukier* 'to beat'.

rebut /rɪˈbʌt/ ■ v. (**rebutted**, **rebutting**) claim or prove to be false.
– DERIVATIVES **rebuttable** adj.
– ORIGIN Middle English: from Anglo-Norman French *rebuter*, from Old French *re-* (expressing opposition) + *boter* 'to butt'.

rebuttal ■ n. a refutation or contradiction.

recalcitrant /rɪˈkalsɪtr(ə)nt/ ■ adj. obstinately uncooperative. ■ n. a recalcitrant person.
– DERIVATIVES **recalcitrance** n. **recalcitrantly** adv.
– ORIGIN C19: from Latin *recalcitrare* 'kick out with the heels', from *calx* 'heel'.

recalculate ■ v. calculate again.
– DERIVATIVES **recalculation** n.

recall /rɪˈkɔːl/ ■ v. 1 remember. ► cause one to remember or think of. ► (**recall someone/thing to**) bring back the memory of someone or something to. 2 call up (stored computer data). 3 officially order to return. ► (of a manufacturer) request the return of (faulty products). 4 reselect (a sports player) as a member of a team. 5 bring out of a state of inattention. ■ n. /also ˈriːkɔːl/ 1 the action or faculty of remembering. 2 an act of officially recalling someone or something.
– PHRASES **beyond recall** in such a way that restoration is impossible.
– DERIVATIVES **recallable** adj.
– ORIGIN C16: from RE- + CALL, suggested by Latin *revocare* or French *rappeler* 'call back'.

recant /rɪˈkant/ ■ v. renounce a former opinion or belief, especially one considered heretical.
– DERIVATIVES **recantation** /ˌriːkanˈteɪʃ(ə)n/ n.
– ORIGIN C16: from Latin *recantare* 'revoke', from *re-* (expressing reversal) + *cantare* 'sing, chant'.

recap informal ■ v. (**recapped**, **recapping**) recapitulate. ■ n. a recapitulation.

recapitalize (also **-ise**) ■ v. provide (a business) with more capital.
– DERIVATIVES **recapitalization** (also **-isation**) n.

recapitulate /ˌriːkəˈpɪtjʊleɪt/ ■ v. summarize and state again the main points of.
– DERIVATIVES **recapitulatory** adj.
– ORIGIN C16: from late Latin *recapitulat-* 'gone through heading by heading', from *re-* 'again' + *capitulum* 'chapter' (diminutive of *caput* 'head').

recapitulation /ˌriːkəpɪtjʊˈleɪʃ(ə)n/ ■ n. 1 an act or instance of recapitulating something. 2 Music a part of a movement (especially one in sonata form) in which themes from the exposition are restated.

recapture ■ v. 1 capture (an escapee). 2 recover (something taken or lost). 3 recreate (a past time, event, or feeling). ■ n. an act of recapturing.

recast ■ v. (past and past part. **recast**) 1 cast (metal) again or differently. 2 present in a different form or style. 3 allocate roles in (a play or film) to different actors.

recce /ˈrɛki/ informal ■ n. 1 reconnaissance. 2 (also **Recce**) S. African historical a soldier belonging to the reconnaissance unit of the SADF. ■ v. (**recced**, **recceing**) reconnoitre.

recd ■ abbrev. received.

recede ■ v. 1 move back or further away. 2 gradually diminish. 3 (of a man's hair) cease to grow at the temples and above the forehead. 4 [usu. as adj. **receding**] (of a facial feature) slope backwards.
– ORIGIN C15: from Latin *recedere*, from *re-* 'back' + *cedere* 'go'.

receipt ■ n. 1 the action of receiving something or the fact of its being received. ► a written acknowledgement of this. ► (**receipts**) an amount of money received over a period by an organization. 2 archaic a recipe. ■ v. [usu. as adj. **receipted**] mark (a bill) as paid.
– ORIGIN Middle English: from Anglo-Norman French *receite*, from medieval Latin *recepta* 'received', from Latin *recipere*.

receivable ■ adj. able to be received. ■ n. (**receivables**) amounts owed to a business, regarded as assets.

receive ■ v. 1 be given, presented with, or paid. ► take delivery of. ► buy or accept (goods known to be stolen). 2 detect or pick up (broadcast signals). 3 form (an idea or impression) from an experience. 4 (in tennis and similar games) be the player to whom the server serves (the ball). 5 consent to hear (an oath or confession). 6 serve as a receptacle for. 7 suffer, experience, or be subject to. ► respond to in a specified way. ► meet with (a specified reaction). 8 [as adj. **received**] widely accepted as authoritative or true. 8 greet or welcome formally. ► be visited by. ► admit as a member. 9 accommodate.
– PHRASES **be at** (or **on**) **the receiving end** informal be subjected to something unpleasant.
– ORIGIN Middle English: from Anglo-Norman French *receivre*, from Latin *recipere*, from *re-* 'back' + *capere* 'take'.

received pronunciation (also **received standard**) ■ n. the standard form of British English pronunciation, based on educated speech in southern England.

receiver ■ n. 1 a person or thing that receives something. 2 a piece of radio or television apparatus converting broadcast signals into sound or images. ► a telephone handset. 3 (Brit. also **official receiver**) a person appointed to manage the financial affairs of a bankrupt business. 4 American Football a player who specializes in catching passes.

Receiver of Revenue ■ n. an official of the South African Revenue Service responsible for collecting taxes. ► (also **the Receiver**) informal the inland revenue service.

receivership ■ n. the state of being managed by an official receiver.

recent ■ adj. 1 having happened or been done lately; belonging to a period of time not long ago. 2 (**Recent**) Geology another term for HOLOCENE.
– DERIVATIVES **recency** n. **recently** adv. **recentness** n.
– ORIGIN Middle English: from Latin *recens*, *recent-* or French *récent*.

receptacle /rɪˈsɛptək(ə)l/ ■ n. 1 an object or space used to contain something. 2 chiefly Zoology an organ or structure which receives a secretion, eggs, etc. 3 Botany the base of a flower, flower head, or other sexual organ.
– ORIGIN Middle English: from Latin *receptaculum*, from *recipere* (see RECEIVE).

reception ■ n. 1 the action or process of receiving someone or something. ► the way in which something is received. 2 a formal social occasion held to welcome someone or celebrate an event. 3 the area in a hotel, office, etc. where visitors are greeted. 4 the first class in an infant or primary school. 5 the quality with which broadcast signals are received.
– ORIGIN Middle English: from Latin *receptio(n-)*, from *recipere* (see RECEIVE).

receptionist ■ n. a person who greets and deals with clients and visitors to a surgery, office, hotel, etc.

reception order ■ n. an order authorizing the detention of a patient in a psychiatric hospital.

reception room ■ n. a function room in a hotel or other building. ▶ a room in a private house suitable for entertaining visitors.

receptive ■ adj. **1** able or willing to receive something. ▶ willing to consider new suggestions and ideas. **2** (of a female animal) ready to mate.
– DERIVATIVES **receptively** adv. **receptiveness** n. **receptivity** n.

receptor /rɪˈsɛptə/ ■ n. Physiology **1** an organ or cell that responds to external stimuli and transmits signals to a sensory nerve. **2** a tissue or substance which responds to a particular neurotransmitter, hormone, etc.
– ORIGIN C20: coined in German from Latin *receptor*, from *recipere* (see RECEIVE).

recess /rɪˈsɛs, ˈriːsɛs/ ■ n. **1** a small space set back in a wall. ▶ a hollow in something. ▶ (**recesses**) remote, secluded, or secret places. **2** a period when the proceedings of a parliament, law court, etc. are temporarily suspended. ▶ chiefly N. Amer. a break between school classes. ■ v. **1** [usu. as adj. **recessed**] set (a fitment) back into a wall or surface. **2** chiefly N. Amer. (of proceedings) be temporarily suspended. ▶ (of an official body) suspend its proceedings temporarily.
– ORIGIN C16: from Latin *recessus*, from *recedere* (see RECEDE).

recession ■ n. **1** a temporary economic decline during which trade and industrial activity are reduced. **2** chiefly Astronomy the action of receding.
– DERIVATIVES **recessionary** adj.
– ORIGIN C17: from Latin *recessio(n-)*, from *recedere* (see RECEDE).

recessional ■ adj. of or relating to recession. ■ n. a hymn sung while the clergy and choir withdraw after a service.

recessive ■ adj. **1** Genetics relating to or denoting heritable characteristics controlled by genes which are expressed in offspring only when inherited from both parents. Often contrasted with DOMINANT. **2** undergoing an economic recession. **3** Phonetics (of stress) tending to fall on the first syllable. ■ n. Genetics a recessive trait or gene.
– DERIVATIVES **recessively** adv. **recessiveness** n. **recessivity** n.
– ORIGIN C17: from RECESS, on the pattern of *excessive*.

recharge ■ v. **1** charge or be charged again. **2** return to a normal state of mind or strength after exertion. ■ n. the replenishment of an aquifer with water.
– DERIVATIVES **rechargeable** adj. **recharger** n.

recheck ■ v. check again. ■ n. an act of rechecking.

rechristen ■ v. give a new name to.

recidivist /rɪˈsɪdɪvɪst/ ■ n. a convicted criminal who reoffends.
– DERIVATIVES **recidivism** n. **recidivistic** adj.
– ORIGIN C19: from French *récidiviste*, from *récidiver* 'fall back', from Latin *recidivus*, *recidere*, from *re-* 'back' + *cadere* 'to fall'.

recipe /ˈrɛsɪpi/ ■ n. **1** a set of instructions for preparing a dish. **2** something likely to lead to a particular outcome: *a recipe for disaster*.
– ORIGIN Middle English: from Latin, 'receive!', from *recipere*.

recipient ■ n. a receiver of something.
– ORIGIN C16: from Latin *recipient-*, *recipere* 'receive'.

reciprocal /rɪˈsɪprək(ə)l/ ■ adj. **1** given, felt, or done in return. **2** (of an agreement or arrangement) bearing on or binding two parties equally. **3** Grammar (of a pronoun or verb) expressing mutual action or relationship. **4** (of a course or bearing) opposite in direction. ■ n. **1** Mathematics the quantity obtained by dividing the number one by a given quantity. **2** Grammar a reciprocal pronoun or verb.
– DERIVATIVES **reciprocality** n. **reciprocally** adv.
– ORIGIN C16: from Latin *reciprocus*, from *re-* 'back' + *pro-* 'forward'.

reciprocate /rɪˈsɪprəkeɪt/ ■ v. **1** respond to (a gesture or action) with a corresponding one. ▶ return (love, affection, etc.) to someone who gives it. **2** [usu. as adj. **reciprocating**] (of a machine part) move backwards and forwards in a straight line.
– DERIVATIVES **reciprocation** n. **reciprocator** n.
– ORIGIN C16: from Latin *reciprocare*, from *reciprocus* (see RECIPROCAL).

reciprocating engine ■ n. a piston engine.

reciprocity /ˌrɛsɪˈprɒsɪti/ ■ n. the practice of exchanging things with others for mutual benefit.
– ORIGIN C18: from French *réciprocité*, from *réciproque*, from Latin *reciprocus* (see RECIPROCATE).

recirculate ■ v. circulate again.
– DERIVATIVES **recirculation** n.

recital ■ n. **1** the performance of a programme of music by a soloist or small group. **2** the enumeration of connected names, facts, or elements. **3** Law the part of a legal document giving factual information.
– DERIVATIVES **recitalist** n.

recitative /ˌrɛsɪtəˈtiːv/ ■ n. musical declamation of the kind usual in the narrative and dialogue parts of opera and oratorio.

recite ■ v. **1** repeat aloud or declaim from memory before an audience. **2** state (names, facts, etc.) in order.
– DERIVATIVES **recitation** n. **reciter** n.
– ORIGIN Middle English: from Latin *recitare* 'read out', from *re-* (expressing intensive force) + *citare* 'cite'.

reckless ■ adj. without thought or care for the consequences of an action.
– DERIVATIVES **recklessly** adv. **recklessness** n.
– ORIGIN Old English, from a Germanic base meaning 'care'.

reckon ■ v. **1** calculate. **2** informal be of the opinion. **3** regard in a specified way. ▶ (**reckon someone/thing among**) include someone or something in (a group). ▶ (**reckon on/to**) informal have a specified view or opinion of. **4** (**reckon on**) rely on or be sure of. ▶ informal expect. **5** (**reckon with** (or **without**)) take (or fail to take) into account.
– PHRASES **a —— to be reckoned with** (or **to reckon with**) a thing or person not to be ignored or underestimated.
– ORIGIN Old English *(ge)recenian* 'recount, relate', of West Germanic origin.

reckoner (also **ready reckoner**) ■ n. a book, table, etc. listing standard numerical calculations or other kinds of information.

reckoning ■ n. **1** the action of calculating or estimating something. **2** an opinion or judgement. **3** archaic a bill or account, or its settlement. **4** the working out of consequences or retribution for one's actions: *a terrible reckoning*.
– PHRASES **into** (or **out of**) **the reckoning** into or out of contention for selection, victory, etc.

reclaim ■ v. **1** retrieve or recover. **2** redeem from a state of vice. **3** bring (waste land or land formerly under water) under cultivation. ▶ recycle. ■ n. the action of reclaiming or being reclaimed.
– DERIVATIVES **reclaimable** adj. **reclaimer** n. **reclamation** n.
– ORIGIN Middle English: from Old French *reclamer*, from Latin *reclamare* 'cry out against', from *re-* 'back' + *clamare* 'to shout'.

reclassify ■ v. (**-ies**, **-ied**) classify differently.
– DERIVATIVES **reclassification** n.

recline ■ v. **1** lean or lie back in a relaxed position. **2** (of a seat) have a back able to move into a sloping position.
– DERIVATIVES **reclinable** adj.
– ORIGIN Middle English: from Old French *recliner* or Latin *reclinare* 'bend back, recline', from *re-* 'back' + *clinare* 'to bend'.

recliner ■ n. **1** a person who reclines. **2** an armchair with a reclining back.

reclothe ■ v. clothe again or differently.

recluse /rɪˈkluːs/ ■ n. a person who avoids others and lives a solitary life.
– DERIVATIVES **reclusion** n. **reclusive** adj. **reclusiveness** n.
– ORIGIN Middle English: from Old French *reclus*, from Latin *recludere* 'enclose', from *re-* 'again' + *claudere* 'to shut'.

recode ■ v. code differently.

recognition ■ n. the action or process of recognizing or being recognized.
– ORIGIN C15: from Latin *recognitio(n-)*, from *recognoscere* (see RECOGNIZE).

recognizance /rɪˈkɒ(g)nɪz(ə)ns/ (also **recognisance**) ▪ n. Law a bond by which a person undertakes before a court or magistrate to observe some condition, e.g. to appear when summoned.
– ORIGIN Middle English: from Old French *reconnissance*, from *reconnaistre* 'recognize'.

recognize (also **-ise**) ▪ v. **1** identify as already known; know again. ▸ (of a computer or other device) identify and respond correctly to (a sound, character, etc.). **2** acknowledge the existence, validity, or legality of. ▸ formally acknowledge that (a country or government) is eligible to be dealt with as a member of the international community. **3** reward formally. **4** (of a person chairing a meeting or debate) call on (someone) to speak.
– DERIVATIVES **recognizability** (also **-isability**) n. **recognizable** (also **-isable**) adj. **recognizably** (also **-isably**) adv. **recognizer** (also **-iser**) n.
– ORIGIN Middle English: from Old French *reconniss-*, *reconnaistre*, from Latin *recognoscere* 'know again, recall to mind', from *re-* 'again' + *cognoscere* 'learn'.

recoil ▪ v. **1** suddenly spring back or flinch in fear, horror, or disgust. ▸ feel such emotions at the thought of something. **2** (of a gun) move abruptly backwards as a reaction on firing. ▸ spring back through force of impact or elasticity. **3** (**recoil on/upon**) (of an action) have an adverse consequence for (the originator). ▪ n. the action of recoiling.
– DERIVATIVES **recoilless** adj.
– ORIGIN Middle English: from Old French *reculer* 'move back', from Latin *culus* 'buttocks'.

recollect[1] /ˌrɛkəˈlɛkt/ ▪ v. remember.
– ORIGIN C16: from Latin *recollect-*, *recolligere* 'gather back', from *re-* 'back' + *colligere* 'collect'.

recollect[2] /ˌriːkəˈlɛkt/ ▪ v. (**recollect oneself**) compose oneself.
– ORIGIN C17: from RE- + COLLECT[1].

recollection /ˌrɛkəˈlɛkʃ(ə)n/ ▪ n. **1** the action or faculty of remembering. **2** a memory.
– DERIVATIVES **recollective** adj.

recombinant /rɪˈkɒmbɪnənt/ Genetics ▪ adj. relating to or denoting genetic material, cells, etc. formed by recombination. ▪ n. a recombinant gene, cell, etc.

recombination ▪ n. **1** the process of recombining things. **2** Genetics the rearrangement of genetic material, especially by crossing over in chromosomes or by the artificial joining of DNA segments.

recombine ▪ v. combine or cause to combine again or differently.

recommence ▪ v. begin or cause to begin again.
– DERIVATIVES **recommencement** n.

recommend ▪ v. **1** put forward with approval as being suitable for a purpose or role. ▸ advise as a course of action. ▸ advise to do something. **2** make appealing or desirable. **3** (**recommend someone/thing to**) archaic commend or entrust someone or something to.
– DERIVATIVES **recommendable** adj. **recommendatory** adj. **recommender** n.
– ORIGIN Middle English: from medieval Latin *recommendare*, from Latin *re-* (expressing intensive force) + *commendare* 'commit to the care of'.

recommendation /ˌrɛkəmɛnˈdeɪʃ(ə)n/ ▪ n. a suggestion or proposal as to the best course of action. ▸ the action of recommending.

recommission ▪ v. commission again.

recompense /ˈrɛkəmpɛns/ ▪ v. compensate. ▸ pay or reward for effort or work. ▸ make amends to or reward someone for (loss, harm, or effort). ▪ n. compensation or reward.
– ORIGIN Middle English: from late Latin *recompensare*, from Latin *re-* 'again' (also expressing intensive force) + *compensare* 'weigh one thing against another'.

recompose ▪ v. compose again or differently.
– DERIVATIVES **recomposition** n.

reconcile /ˈrɛkənsʌɪl/ ▪ v. **1** restore friendly relations between. ▸ settle (a quarrel). **2** make or show to be compatible. **3** (**reconcile someone to**) make someone accept (a disagreeable thing).
– DERIVATIVES **reconcilability** n. **reconcilable** adj. **reconcilement** n. **reconciler** n. **reconciliatory** adj.
– ORIGIN Middle English: from Latin *reconciliare*, from Latin *re-* 'back' (also expressing intensive force) + *conciliare* 'bring together'.

reconciliation /ˌrɛk(ə)nsɪlɪˈeɪʃ(ə)n/ ▪ n. the action of reconciling. ▸ an instance or occasion of friendly relations being restored.

recondite /ˈrɛk(ə)ndʌɪt, rɪˈkɒn-/ ▪ adj. (of a subject or knowledge) obscure.
– ORIGIN C17: from Latin *reconditus* 'hidden, put away', from *recondere*, from *re-* 'back' + *condere* 'put together, secrete'.

recondition ▪ v. **1** condition again. **2** overhaul or renovate.

reconfigure ▪ v. configure differently.
– DERIVATIVES **reconfiguration** n.

reconnaissance /rɪˈkɒnɪs(ə)ns/ ▪ n. military observation of a region to locate an enemy or ascertain strategic features. ▸ preliminary surveying or research.
– ORIGIN C19: from French, from *reconnaître* (see RECONNOITRE).

reconnect ▪ v. connect again.
– DERIVATIVES **reconnection** n.

reconnoitre /ˌrɛkəˈnɔɪtə/ (US **reconnoiter**) ▪ v. make a military observation of (a region). ▪ n. informal an act of reconnoitring.
– ORIGIN C18: from obsolete French *reconnoître*, from Latin *recognoscere* (see RECOGNIZE).

reconsecrate ▪ v. consecrate again.
– DERIVATIVES **reconsecration** n.

reconsider ▪ v. consider again.
– DERIVATIVES **reconsideration** n.

reconsolidate ▪ v. consolidate again or anew.
– DERIVATIVES **reconsolidation** n.

reconstitute ▪ v. **1** reconstruct. ▸ change the form and organization of (an institution). **2** restore (something dried) to its original state by adding water.
– DERIVATIVES **reconstitution** n.

reconstruct ▪ v. **1** construct again. **2** form an impression, model, or re-enactment of (something) from evidence.
– DERIVATIVES **reconstructable** (also **reconstructible**) adj. **reconstruction** n. **reconstructive** adj. **reconstructor** n.

Reconstruction and Development Programme ▪ n. full form of RDP.

reconvene ▪ v. convene or cause to convene again.

reconvert ▪ v. convert back to a former state.
– DERIVATIVES **reconversion** n.

record ▪ n. **1** a piece of evidence about the past, especially a written or other permanent account of something. ▸ Law an official report of the proceedings and judgement in a court. **2** a person or thing's previous conduct or performance. ▸ a criminal record. **3** the best performance or most remarkable event of its kind on record. **4** a thin plastic disc carrying recorded sound in grooves on each surface, for reproduction by a record player. ▸ a piece or collection of music reproduced on such a disc or on another medium. **5** Computing a number of related items of information handled as a unit. ▪ v. **1** make a record of. ▸ state or express officially. **2** convert (sound, a broadcast, etc.) into permanent form for later reproduction. ▸ produce (music or a programme) by such means.
– PHRASES **for the record** so that the true facts are recorded or known. **on record** officially measured and noted. **on** (or **off**) **the record** made (or not made) as an official or attributable statement. **put** (or **set**) **the record straight** correct a misapprehension.
– DERIVATIVES **recordable** adj. **recording** n.
– ORIGIN Middle English: from Old French *record* 'remembrance', from *recorder* 'bring to remembrance', from Latin *recordari* 'remember', from *cor*, *cord-* 'heart'.

record-breaking ▪ adj. surpassing a record.
– DERIVATIVES **record-breaker** n.

recorded delivery ▪ n. a service in which the post office or other mail carrier obtains a signature from the recipient as a record that an item has been delivered.

recorder ▪ n. **1** an apparatus for recording sound, pictures, or data. **2** a person who keeps records.

3 a simple woodwind instrument without keys, played by blowing air through a shaped mouthpiece.
– ORIGIN Middle English: from Anglo-Norman French *recordour*, from Old French *recorder* 'bring to remembrance'; partly reinforced by the verb RECORD.

record player ■ n. an apparatus for reproducing sound from gramophone records.

recount¹ /rɪˈkaʊnt/ ■ v. give an account of something.
– ORIGIN Middle English: from Old Northern French *reconter* 'tell again', from Old French *counter* (see COUNT¹).

recount² ■ v. /riːˈkaʊnt/ count again. ■ n. /ˈriːkaʊnt/ an act of counting something again.

recoup ■ v. **1** regain (something lost). ▸ reimburse or compensate for money spent or lost. ▸ regain (lost physical or mental resources); recover. **2** Law deduct or keep back (part of a sum due).
– DERIVATIVES **recoupable** adj. **recoupment** n.
– ORIGIN C17: from French *recouper* 'retrench, cut back', from *re-* 'back' + *couper* 'to cut'.

recourse ■ n. **1** a source of help in a difficult situation. ▸ (**recourse to**) use of as a recourse. **2** the legal right to demand compensation or payment.
– PHRASES **without recourse** Finance a formula used to disclaim responsibility for future non-payment.
– ORIGIN Middle English: from Old French *recours*, from Latin *recursus*, from *re-* 'back, again' + *cursus* 'course, running'.

recover ■ v. **1** return to a normal state of health, mind, or strength. **2** find or regain possession of. ▸ regain control of (oneself or a physical or mental state). ▸ regain or secure (compensation). **3** remove or extract (an energy source, chemical, etc.) for use, reuse, or waste treatment.
– DERIVATIVES **recoverability** n. **recoverable** adj. **recoverer** n.
– ORIGIN Middle English: from Anglo-Norman French *recoverer*, from Latin *recuperare* 'get again'.

re-cover ■ v. put a new cover or covering on.

recovery ■ n. (pl. **-ies**) **1** an act or the process of recovering. ▸ the action of taking a vehicle that has broken down or crashed for repair. **2** (also **recovery shot**) Golf a stroke bringing the ball out of the rough or a bunker. **3** (in rowing, swimming, etc.) the action of returning the paddle, leg, or arm to its initial position for a new stroke.

recovery position ■ n. a position used to prevent an unconscious person from choking, the body being placed face downwards and slightly to the side, supported by bent limbs.

recreate ■ v. create again. ▸ reproduce.

recreation¹ /ˌrɛkrɪˈeɪʃ(ə)n/ ■ n. enjoyable leisure activity.
– ORIGIN Middle English: from Latin *recreatio(n-)*, from *recreare* 'create again, renew'.

recreation² /ˌriːkrɪˈeɪʃ(ə)n/ ■ n. the action of recreating something.

recreational ■ adj. of or relating to recreation. ▸ relating to or denoting drugs taken occasionally for enjoyment.
– DERIVATIVES **recreationally** v.

recreation ground ■ n. a piece of public land used for sports and games.

recreative /ˈrɛkrɪˌeɪtɪv, ˌriːkrɪˈeɪtɪv/ ■ adj. recreational.

recriminate /rɪˈkrɪmɪneɪt/ ■ v. make recriminations.
– DERIVATIVES **recriminatory** adj.
– ORIGIN C17: from medieval Latin *recriminari* 'accuse in return', from *re-* (expressing opposition) + *criminare* 'accuse'.

recrimination ■ n. (usu. **recriminations**) an accusation in response to one from someone else.

recross ■ v. cross again.

recrudesce /ˌriːkruːˈdɛs, ˌrɛk-/ ■ v. formal break out again; recur.
– DERIVATIVES **recrudescence** n. **recrudescent** adj.
– ORIGIN C19 (*recrudescence* C18): from Latin *recrudescere* 'become raw again', from *re-* 'again' + *crudus* 'raw'.

recruit ■ v. enlist (someone) in the armed forces. ▸ enrol (someone) as a member or worker in an organization. ▸ informal persuade to do or help with something. ■ n. a newly recruited person.

– ORIGIN C17: from obsolete French dialect *recrute*, from Latin *recrescere* 'grow again'.

recruitment ■ n. **1** the action of recruiting people. **2** Ecology the increase in a natural population as progeny grow and immigrants arrive.

recta plural form of RECTUM.

rectal ■ adj. of, relating to, or affecting the rectum.
– DERIVATIVES **rectally** adv.

rectangle ■ n. a plane figure with four straight sides and four right angles, especially one with unequal adjacent sides.
– ORIGIN C16: from medieval Latin *rectangulum*, from Latin *rectus* 'straight' + *angulus* 'an angle'.

rectangular ■ adj. **1** denoting or shaped like a rectangle. ▸ (of a solid) having a rectangular base, section, or side. **2** placed or having parts placed at right angles.
– DERIVATIVES **rectangularity** n. **rectangularly** adv.

rectified spirit ■ n. a mixture of ethanol (95.6 per cent) and water produced as an azeotrope by distillation.

rectifier ■ n. an electrical device converting an alternating current into a direct one by allowing it to flow in one direction only.

rectify ■ v. (**-ies**, **-ied**) **1** put right; correct. **2** convert (alternating current) to direct current. **3** find a straight line equal in length to (a curve).
– DERIVATIVES **rectifiable** adj. **rectification** n.
– ORIGIN Middle English: from Old French *rectifier*, from medieval Latin *rectificare*, from Latin *rectus* 'right'.

rectilinear /ˌrɛktɪˈlɪnɪə/ (also **rectilineal** /-nɪəl/) ■ adj. contained by, consisting of, or moving in a straight line or lines.
– DERIVATIVES **rectilinearity** n. **rectilinearly** adv.
– ORIGIN C17: from late Latin *rectilineus*, from Latin *rectus* 'straight' + *linea* 'line'.

rectitude ■ n. formal morally correct behaviour.
– ORIGIN Middle English: from late Latin *rectitudo*, from Latin *rectus* 'right, straight'.

recto ■ n. (pl. **-os**) a right-hand page of an open book, or the front of a loose document. Contrasted with VERSO.
– ORIGIN C19: from Latin *recto* (*folio*) 'on the right (leaf)'.

rector ■ n. **1** (in some Anglican Churches) a member of the clergy in charge of a parish. ▸ (in the Roman Catholic Church) a priest in charge of a church or a religious institution. **2** the head of certain universities, colleges, and schools.
– DERIVATIVES **rectorate** n. **rectorial** adj. **rectorship** n.
– ORIGIN Middle English: from Latin *rector* 'ruler', from *regere* 'rule'.

rectory ■ n. (pl. **-ies**) a rector's house.

rectrices /ˈrɛktrɪsiːz/ ■ pl. n. (sing. **rectrix** /-trɪks/) Ornithology the larger feathers in a bird's tail, used for steering in flight.
– ORIGIN C18: from Latin, from *rector* (see RECTOR).

rectum ■ n. (pl. **rectums** or **recta** /-tə/) the final section of the large intestine, terminating at the anus.
– ORIGIN C16: from Latin *rectum* (*intestinum*) 'straight (intestine)'.

recumbent /rɪˈkʌmb(ə)nt/ ■ adj. **1** lying down. **2** (of a plant) growing close to the ground.
– DERIVATIVES **recumbency** n. **recumbently** adv.
– ORIGIN C17: from Latin *recumbent-*, *recumbere* 'recline', from *re-* 'back' + a verb rel. to *cubare* 'to lie'.

recuperate /rɪˈkuːpəreɪt/ ■ v. **1** recover from illness or exertion. **2** regain (something lost).
– DERIVATIVES **recuperable** adj. **recuperation** n. **recuperative** adj.
– ORIGIN C16 (*recuperation* C15): from Latin *recuperare* 'regain', from *re-* 'back' + *capere* 'take'.

recur ■ v. (**recurred**, **recurring**) occur again. ▸ (of a thought, image, etc.) come back to one's mind. ▸ (**recur to**) go back to in thought or speech.
– DERIVATIVES **recurrence** n. **recurring** adj.
– ORIGIN Middle English: from Latin *recurrere*, from *re-* 'again, back' + *currere* 'run'.

recurrent ■ adj. occurring often or repeatedly.
– DERIVATIVES **recurrently** adv.

recurring decimal ■ n. a decimal fraction in which a figure or group of figures is repeated indefinitely, as in 0.666...

recursion /rɪˈkɜːʃ(ə)n/ ■ n. chiefly Mathematics & Linguistics the repeated application of a procedure or rule to successive results of the process. ▸ a recursive procedure or formula.

recursive ■ adj. 1 chiefly Mathematics & Linguistics relating to or characterized by recursion. 2 Computing relating to or denoting a program or routine a part of which requires the application of the whole.
– DERIVATIVES **recursively** adv.

recurve ■ v. chiefly Biology bend backwards.
– DERIVATIVES **recurvature** n.

recuse /rɪˈkjuːz/ ■ v. (**recuse oneself**) chiefly S. African & N. Amer. (especially of a judge) excuse oneself because of a possible lack of impartiality.
– DERIVATIVES **recusal** n.
– ORIGIN Middle English: from Latin *recusare* 'to refuse', from *re-* (expressing opposition) + *causa* 'a cause'.

recycle ■ v. 1 convert (waste) into reusable material. ▸ use again. 2 return (material) to a previous stage in a cyclic process.
– DERIVATIVES **recyclability** n. **recyclable** adj. **recycler** n.

red ■ adj. (**redder**, **reddest**) 1 of a colour at the end of the spectrum next to orange and opposite violet, as of blood, fire, or rubies. ▸ (of hair or fur) of a reddish-brown colour. ▸ (of a person's face) red due to embarrassment, anger, or heat. 2 (of wine) made from dark grapes and coloured by their skins. 3 denoting a red light or flag used as a signal to stop. ▸ denoting something forbidden, dangerous, or urgent. 4 (of a ski run) of the second-highest level of difficulty. 5 informal, chiefly derogatory communist or socialist. 6 S. African denoting the red ochre traditionally used by Xhosa peoples to smear the body and clothing. ▸ often derogatory conservative; resistant to change. ■ n. 1 red colour or pigment. 2 informal, chiefly derogatory a communist or socialist. 3 (**the red**) the situation of having spent more than is in one's bank account.
– PHRASES **the red planet** Mars. **see red** informal become very angry suddenly.
– DERIVATIVES **reddish** adj. **reddy** adj. **redly** adv. **redness** n.
– ORIGIN Old English, of Germanic origin.

red- ■ prefix variant of RE- before a vowel (as in *redolent*).

red admiral ■ n. a migratory butterfly of the northern hemisphere, having dark wings with red bands and white spots. [*Vanessa atalanta*.]

red algae ■ pl. n. a large group of algae that includes many red seaweeds. [Division Rhodophyta.]

red ant ■ n. 1 any of several species of reddish army ant. [*Dorylus helvolus* and other species.] ▸ another term for FIRE ANT. 2 S. African (**Red Ant**) a member of a private security firm empowered by a local authority to execute eviction orders [so named because they wear red overalls].

red-bait ■ n. S. African a large sea squirt used as fishing bait. [*Pyura stolonifera*.]

red blood cell ■ n. less technical term for ERYTHROCYTE.

red-blooded ■ adj. (of a man) vigorous or virile.
– DERIVATIVES **red-bloodedness** n.

red-brick ■ adj. 1 built with red bricks. 2 (of a British university) founded in the late 19th or early 20th century.

red card ■ n. (especially in soccer) a red card shown by the referee to a player being sent off the field. ■ v. (**red-card**) (of a referee) show a red card to.

red carpet ■ n. a long, narrow red carpet for a distinguished visitor to walk along.

red cell ■ n. less technical term for ERYTHROCYTE.

red cent ■ n. N. Amer. 1 a one-cent coin, formerly made of copper. 2 [usu. with neg.] the smallest amount of money.

redcoat ■ n. historical a British soldier.

red coral ■ n. a branching pinkish-red horny coral used in jewellery. [Genus *Corallium*.]

Red Crescent ■ n. a national branch in Muslim countries of the International Movement of the Red Cross and the Red Crescent.

Red Cross ■ n. the International Movement of the Red Cross and the Red Crescent, an organization bringing relief to victims of war or natural disaster.

redcurrant ■ n. 1 a small edible red berry. 2 the shrub which produces this fruit, related to the blackcurrant. [*Ribes rubrum*.]

red data list (or **red data book**) ■ n. a list (or book) which categorizes plant and animal species according to their risk of extinction after an assessment of their conservation status.

red deer ■ n. a deer of the northern hemisphere with a rich red-brown summer coat that turns brownish-grey in winter, the male having large antlers. [*Cervus elaphus*.]

redden ■ v. 1 make or become red. 2 blush.
– DERIVATIVES **reddening** n.

red dwarf ■ n. Astronomy a small, old, relatively cool star.

redecorate ■ v. decorate again or differently.
– DERIVATIVES **redecoration** n.

rededicate ■ v. dedicate again.
– DERIVATIVES **rededication** n.

redeem ■ v. 1 compensate for the faults or bad aspects of. ▸ (**redeem oneself**) make up for one's poor past performance or behaviour. ▸ save from sin, error, or evil. 2 gain or regain possession of in exchange for payment. ▸ Finance repay (a stock, bond, etc.) at the maturity date. ▸ exchange (a coupon) for goods or money. ▸ clear (a debt). 3 fulfil (a pledge or promise).
– DERIVATIVES **redeemable** adj. **redeeming** adj.
– ORIGIN Middle English: from Latin *redimere*, from *re-* 'back' + *emere* 'buy'.

redeemer ■ n. 1 a person who redeems someone or something. 2 (**the Redeemer**) Christ.

redefine ■ v. define again or differently.
– DERIVATIVES **redefinition** n.

redemption ■ n. 1 the action of redeeming someone or something, or of being redeemed. 2 a thing that saves someone from error or evil.
– DERIVATIVES **redemptive** adj.
– ORIGIN Middle English: from Latin *redemptio(n-)*, from *redimere* (see REDEEM).

red ensign ■ n. a red flag with the Union Jack in the top corner next to the flagstaff, flown by British-registered ships.

redeploy ■ v. deploy again or differently.
– DERIVATIVES **redeployment** n.

redesign ■ v. design again or differently. ■ n. the action or process of redesigning something.

redetermine ■ v. determine again or differently.
– DERIVATIVES **redetermination** n.

redevelop ■ v. develop again or differently.
– DERIVATIVES **redeveloper** n. **redevelopment** n.

red-eye ■ n. 1 the effect in photography of people appearing to have red eyes, caused by a reflection from the retina when the flashgun is too near the camera lens. 2 (also **red-eye flight**) informal, chiefly N. Amer. a flight on which one cannot expect much sleep. 3 (**red eye**) S. African another term for ROOIKRANS.

red-faced ■ adj. embarrassed; ashamed.

red flag ■ n. 1 a warning of danger. 2 the symbol of socialist revolution.

red giant ■ n. Astronomy a very large luminous star of low surface temperature.

red gold ■ n. an alloy of gold and copper.

red grouse ■ n. a British moorland grouse with reddish-brown plumage. [*Lagopus lagopus scoticus*.]

red gum ■ n. an Australian gum tree with smooth bark and hard dark red wood. [*Eucalyptus camaldulensis* and other species.] ▸ astringent reddish kino gum from such a tree.

red-handed ■ adj. in or just after the act of doing something wrong.

redhead ■ n. a person, especially a woman, with red hair.

red herring ■ n. 1 a dried smoked herring. 2 a misleading clue or distraction. [so named from the practice of using the scent of red herring in training hounds.]

red-hot ■ adj. 1 so hot as to glow red. 2 extremely exciting or popular. 3 very passionate.

VOWELS a cat ɑː arm ɛ bed ɛː hair ə ago əː her ɪ sit i cosy iː see ɒ hot ɔː saw ʌ run

red-hot poker ■ n. a South African plant with tall erect spikes of tubular flowers, the upper ones of which are red and the lower ones yellow. [*Kniphofia uvaria*.]

redial ■ v. (**redialled, redialling**; US **redialed, redialing**) dial (a telephone number) again. ■ n. the facility on a telephone by which the number just dialled may be redialled by pressing a single button.

redid past of REDO.

rediffusion ■ n. the relaying of broadcast programmes, especially by cable from a central receiver.

Red Indian ■ n. old-fashioned term for AMERICAN INDIAN.

redingote /ˈrɛdɪŋɡəʊt/ ■ n. a woman's long coat with a cutaway or contrasting front.
– ORIGIN C18: French, from English *riding coat*.

redirect ■ v. direct differently.
– DERIVATIVES **redirection** n.

rediscount Finance ■ v. (of a central bank) discount (a bill of exchange) that has already been discounted by a commercial bank. ■ n. the action of rediscounting.

rediscover ■ v. discover again.
– DERIVATIVES **rediscovery** n. (pl. **-ies**).

redistribute ■ v. distribute again or differently.
– DERIVATIVES **redistribution** n. **redistributive** adj.

redistributionist ■ n. a person who advocates the redistribution of wealth.

redivide ■ v. divide again or differently.
– DERIVATIVES **redivision** n.

red lead ■ n. red lead oxide used as a pigment.

Red Leicester ■ n. see LEICESTER (sense 1).

red-letter day ■ n. a noteworthy or memorable day.
– ORIGIN C18: from the practice of highlighting a festival in red on a calendar.

red light ■ n. a red light instructing moving vehicles to stop.

red-light district ■ n. an area with many brothels, strip clubs, etc.
– ORIGIN from the use of a red light as the sign of a brothel.

redline informal ■ v. 1 drive with (the car engine) at its maximum rpm. 2 refuse (a loan or insurance) to someone due to their area of residence. ■ n. the maximum number of revolutions per minute for a car engine.
– DERIVATIVES **redlining** n.
– ORIGIN from the use of *red* as a limit marker, in sense 2 a ring marking part of a map.

red list ■ n. another term for RED DATA LIST.

red man ■ n. offensive an American Indian.

red meat ■ n. meat that is red when raw, e.g. beef or lamb.

red mullet ■ n. an elongated food fish with long barbels on the chin, living in warmer seas. [*Muletus surmuletus* and other species.]

redneck ■ n. N. Amer. informal, derogatory a working-class white person from the southern US, especially a politically conservative one.
– DERIVATIVES **rednecked** adj.

redo ■ v. (**redoes**; past **redid**; past part. **redone**) do again or differently. ▶ informal redecorate.

redolent /ˈrɛd(ə)l(ə)nt/ ■ adj. (**redolent of/with**) strongly reminiscent or suggestive of. ▶ poetic/literary strongly smelling of.
– DERIVATIVES **redolence** n. **redolently** adv.
– ORIGIN Middle English: from Latin *redolent-* 'giving out a strong smell', from *re(d)-* 'back, again' + *olere* 'to smell'.

redouble ■ v. 1 make or become much greater, more intense, or more numerous. 2 Bridge double a bid already doubled by an opponent. ■ n. Bridge a call that redoubles a bid.
– ORIGIN Middle English: from French *redoubler*, from *re-* 'again' + *doubler* 'to double'.

redoubt ■ n. Military a temporary or supplementary fortification, typically square or polygonal and without flanking defences.
– ORIGIN C17: from French *redoute*, from medieval Latin *reductus* 'refuge', from Latin *reducere* 'withdraw'; the *-b-* was added by association with DOUBT.

redoubtable ■ adj. often humorous (of a person) formidable, especially as an opponent.
– DERIVATIVES **redoubtably** adv.
– ORIGIN Middle English: from Old French *redoutable*, from *redouter* 'to fear', from *re-* (expressing intensive force) + *douter* 'to doubt'.

redound /rɪˈdaʊnd/ ■ v. 1 (**redound to**) formal contribute greatly to (a person's credit or honour). 2 (**redound upon**) archaic rebound on.
– ORIGIN Middle English: from Old French *redonder*, from Latin *redundare* 'surge', from *re(d)-* 'again' + *unda* 'a wave'.

redox /ˈriːdɒks, ˈrɛdɒks/ ■ n. [usu. as modifier] Chemistry oxidation and reduction considered together: *redox reactions*.
– ORIGIN 1920s: blend.

red pepper ■ n. the ripe red fruit of a sweet pepper.

redpoll /ˈrɛdpəʊl/ ■ n. 1 a mainly brown finch with a red forehead, related to the linnet. [*Acanthis flammea*.] 2 (**red poll**) an animal of a breed of red-haired polled cattle.

Red Queen hypothesis ■ n. Biology the hypothesis that organisms are constantly struggling to keep up in an evolutionary race between predator and prey species.
– ORIGIN C20: named from a passage in Lewis Carroll's *Through the Looking Glass*, in which the Red Queen tells Alice that 'it takes all the running you can do to stay in the same place'.

redraft ■ v. draft differently. ■ n. a redrafted document or text.

redraw ■ v. (past **redrew**; past part. **redrawn**) draw or draw up again or differently.

redress ■ v. remedy or set right. ■ n. remedy or compensation for a wrong or grievance.
– PHRASES **redress the balance** restore equality in a situation.
– DERIVATIVES **redressable** adj. **redressal** n.
– ORIGIN Middle English: the verb from Old French *redresser*; the noun via Anglo-Norman French *redresse*.

re-dress ■ v. dress again or differently.

red roan ■ adj. (of an animal's coat) bay or chestnut mixed with white or grey. ■ n. a red roan animal.

red rock rabbit ■ n. a nocturnal southern African rabbit that lives in rocky terrain. [Genus *Pronolagus*: three species.]

red rose ■ n. Brit. the emblem of Lancashire. ▶ historical the emblem of the Lancastrians.

red salmon ■ n. the sockeye salmon.

red setter ■ n. less formal term for IRISH SETTER.

redshank ■ n. a large sandpiper with long red legs. [*Tringa totanus* and *T. erythropus*.]

red shift ■ n. Astronomy the displacement of the spectrum to longer wavelengths in the light from distant celestial objects moving away from the observer. Compare with BLUE SHIFT.

redskin ■ n. dated or offensive an American Indian.

red snapper ■ n. an edible reddish marine fish. [*Sebastes ruberrimus* (N. Pacific) and genus *Lutjanus* (tropics).]

red squirrel ■ n. a small squirrel with a reddish coat. [*Sciurus vulgaris* (Eurasia) and *Tamiasciurus hudsonicus* (N. America).]

redstart ■ n. a small Eurasian and North African songbird of the thrush family with a reddish tail. [*Phoenicurus phoenicurus* and other species.]

red tape ■ n. excessive bureaucracy or adherence to rules, especially in public business.
– ORIGIN C18: so named because of the red or pink tape used to bind official documents.

red tide ■ n. a discoloration of seawater caused by a bloom of toxic red dinoflagellates.

reduce ■ v. 1 make or become smaller or less in amount, degree, or size. ▶ boil (a sauce or other liquid) so that it becomes thicker and more concentrated. ▶ chiefly N. Amer. (of a person) lose weight. 2 (**reduce someone/thing to**) bring someone or something by force or necessity to (an undesirable state or action). 3 (**reduce something to**)

reducing agent

change something to (a simpler or more basic form). ▸ convert a fraction to (the form with the lowest terms). **4** Chemistry cause to combine chemically with hydrogen. ▸ undergo or cause to undergo a reaction in which electrons are gained from another substance or molecule. The opposite of **OXIDIZE**. **5** restore (a dislocated body part) to its proper position.
-PHRASES **reduced circumstances** poverty after relative prosperity. **reduce someone to the ranks** demote a non-commissioned officer to an ordinary soldier.
-DERIVATIVES **reducer** n. **reducibility** n. **reducible** adj.
-ORIGIN Middle English: from Latin *reducere*, from *re-* 'back, again' + *ducere* 'bring, lead'.

reducing agent ■ n. Chemistry a substance that tends to bring about reduction by being oxidized and losing electrons.

reductant ■ n. Chemistry a reducing agent.

reductase /rɪˈdʌkteɪz/ ■ n. Biochemistry an enzyme which promotes chemical reduction.

reductio ad absurdum /rɪˌdʌktɪəʊ ad abˈsəːdəm/ ■ n. Philosophy a method of proving the falsity of a premise by showing that its logical consequence is absurd or contradictory.
-ORIGIN Latin, 'reduction to the absurd'.

reduction ■ n. **1** the action or fact of reducing something. ▸ the amount by which something is reduced. **2** an arrangement of an orchestral score for piano or a smaller group of performers. **3** a smaller copy of a picture or photograph. **4** a thick and concentrated liquid or sauce.

reduction gear ■ n. a system of gearwheels in which the driven shaft rotates more slowly than the driving shaft.

reductionism ■ n. often derogatory the practice of analysing and describing a complex phenomenon in terms of its simple or fundamental constituents, especially when this is said to provide a sufficient explanation.
-DERIVATIVES **reductionist** n. & adj. **reductionistic** adj.

reductive ■ adj. **1** tending to present a subject or problem in a simplified form, especially one viewed as crude. ▸ (with reference to art) minimal. **2** of or relating to chemical reduction.
-DERIVATIVES **reductively** adv. **reductiveness** n.

reductivism ■ n. **1** minimalism. **2** reductionism.

redundant ■ adj. **1** no longer needed or useful; superfluous. ▸ (of words) able to be omitted without loss of meaning or function. ▸ Engineering (of a component) not strictly necessary but included in case another component fails. **2** unemployed.
-DERIVATIVES **redundancy** n. (pl. **-ies**). **redundantly** adv.
-ORIGIN C16: from Latin *redundant-, redundare* (see **REDOUND**).

reduplicate ■ v. **1** repeat or copy so as to form another of the same kind. **2** repeat (a linguistic element) exactly or with a slight change (e.g. *hurly-burly*).
-DERIVATIVES **reduplication** n. **reduplicative** adj.
-ORIGIN C16 (*reduplication* Middle English): from late Latin *reduplicare* 'double again', from *re-* 'again' + *duplicare* (see **DUPLICATE**).

redux /ˈriːdʌks/ ■ adj. [postpos.] revived; restored.
-ORIGIN C19: from Latin, from *reducere* 'bring back'.

redwater (also **redwater fever**) ■ n. babesiosis in cattle.

redwing ■ n. **1** a small migratory thrush of northern Europe, with red underwings. [*Turdus iliacus*.] **2** any of various other red-winged birds.

redwood ■ n. a giant coniferous tree with reddish wood, native to California and Oregon. [*Sequoia sempervirens* (California redwood) and *Sequoiadendron giganteum* (giant redwood).] ▸ used in names of other trees with reddish wood.

redworm ■ n. **1** a red earthworm used to make compost and as fishing bait. [*Lumbricus rubellus*.] **2** a parasitic nematode worm affecting horses. [Genus *Strongylus*.]

red zone ■ n. a dangerous or forbidden region, or one in which an activity is prohibited.

re-echo ■ v. (**-oes, -oed**) echo again or repeatedly.

reed ■ n. **1** a tall, slender-leaved plant of the grass family, growing in water or on marshy ground. [Genera *Phragmites* and *Arundo*: several species.] ▸ used in names of similar plants growing in wet habitats, e.g. **bur-reed**. **2** a tall, thin, straight stalk of a reed, used especially for thatching. ▸ Brit. straw for thatching. **3** poetic/literary a rustic musical pipe made from reeds or straw. **4** a piece of thin cane or metal which vibrates in a current of air to produce the sound of various musical instruments, as in the mouthpiece of a clarinet or at the base of some organ pipes. ▸ a wind instrument played with a reed. **5** (also **broken reed**) a weak or impressionable person. **6** a weaver's comb-like implement for separating the warp and positioning the weft. **7** an electrical contact in a magnetically operated switch or relay.
-DERIVATIVES **reeded** adj.
-ORIGIN Old English, of West Germanic origin.

reed bed ■ n. an area of water or marshland dominated by reeds.

reedbuck ■ n. an African antelope with a distinctive whistling call, the male of which has stout forward-curved horns. [Genus *Redunca*: three species.]

reed bunting ■ n. a Eurasian bunting that frequents reed beds and hedgerows, the male having a black head and white collar. [*Emberiza schoeniclus*.]

reed dance ■ n. a dance ceremony performed by several peoples of southern Africa, especially an annual celebration by unmarried girls in Swaziland and KwaZulu-Natal.

reeding ■ n. a small semi-cylindrical moulding.

re-edit ■ v. (**re-edited, re-editing**) edit again.
-DERIVATIVES **re-edition** n.

reed mace ■ n. a tall reed-like water plant with a dark brown velvety cylindrical flower head. [*Typha latifolia* and related species.]

reed pipe ■ n. a simple wind instrument having or made from a reed. ▸ an organ pipe with a reed.

re-educate ■ v. educate or train to behave or think differently.
-DERIVATIVES **re-education** n.

reed warbler ■ n. a Eurasian and African songbird with plain plumage, frequenting reed beds. [Genus *Acrocephalus*: several species.]

reedy ■ adj. (**-ier, -iest**) **1** (of a sound or voice) high and thin in tone. **2** full of or edged with reeds. **3** (of a person) tall and thin.
-DERIVATIVES **reediness** n.

reef[1] ■ n. **1** a ridge of jagged rock, coral, or sand just above or below the surface of the sea. **2** a vein of gold or other ore. **3** (**the Reef**) another term for **RAND** (in sense 2).
-ORIGIN C16: from Middle Low German and Middle Dutch *rif, ref*, from Old Norse *rif* 'rib'.

reef[2] Nautical ■ n. each of several strips across a sail which can be taken in or rolled up to reduce the area exposed to the wind. ■ v. take in one or more reefs of (a sail).
-ORIGIN Middle English: from Middle Dutch *reef, rif*, from Old Norse *rif* 'rib'.

reefer[1] ■ n. informal a cannabis cigarette. ▸ cannabis.
-ORIGIN 1930S: perhaps rel. to Mexican Spanish *grifo* '(smoker of) cannabis'.

reefer[2] ■ n. informal a refrigerated truck, railway wagon, or ship.
-ORIGIN C20: abbrev.

reefer jacket ■ n. a thick close-fitting double-breasted jacket.

reef knot ■ n. a double knot made symmetrically to hold securely and cast off easily.

reefpoint ■ n. Nautical each of several short pieces of rope attached to a sail to secure it when reefed.

reek ■ v. **1** have a foul smell. ▸ archaic give off smoke, steam, or fumes. **2** (**reek of**) be suggestive of (something unpleasant). ■ n. a foul smell.
-ORIGIN Old English *rēocan* 'give out smoke or vapour', *rēc* (n.) 'smoke', of Germanic origin.

reel ■ n. **1** a cylinder on which film, wire, thread, etc. can be wound. ▸ a length of something wound on a reel. **2** a part of a film. **3** a lively Scottish or Irish folk dance. ▸ a piece of music for a reel, typically in simple or duple time. ■ v. **1** (**reel something in**) wind a line on to a reel by turning the reel. ▸ bring something attached to a line,

especially a fish, towards one by turning a reel. **2** (**reel something off**) say or recite something rapidly and effortlessly. **3** stagger or lurch violently. ▸ feel giddy or bewildered.
– DERIVATIVES **reeler** n.
– ORIGIN Old English.

re-elect ■ v. (usu. **be re-elected**) elect again.
– DERIVATIVES **re-election** n.

re-eligible ■ adj. eligible for re-election.

reel-to-reel ■ adj. denoting a tape recorder in which the tape passes between two reels mounted separately rather than within a cassette.

re-emerge ■ v. emerge again.
– DERIVATIVES **re-emergence** n. **re-emergent** adj.

re-emphasize (also **-ise**) ■ v. emphasize again.
– DERIVATIVES **re-emphasis** n.

re-enact ■ v. **1** act out (a past event). **2** enact (a repealed law) once more.
– DERIVATIVES **re-enactment** n.

re-engineer ■ v. **1** redesign (a machine). **2** [often as noun **re-engineering**] restructure (a company or its operations).

re-enter ■ v. enter again.
– DERIVATIVES **re-entrance** n.

re-entrant ■ adj. (of an angle) pointing inwards. The opposite of SALIENT.

re-entry ■ n. (pl. **-ies**) **1** the action or process of re-entering something. ▸ the return of a spacecraft or missile into the earth's atmosphere. **2** a visible duplication of part of the design for a postage stamp.

reeve[1] ■ n. historical a local official, in particular the chief magistrate of a town or district in Anglo-Saxon England.
– ORIGIN Old English.

reeve[2] ■ v. (past and past part. **rove** or **reeved**) Nautical thread (a rope or rod) through a ring or other aperture.
– ORIGIN C17: prob. from Dutch *reven*.

reeve[3] ■ n. a female ruff (bird).
– ORIGIN C17: var. of dialect *ree*.

re-examine ■ v. examine again or further. ▸ Law examine (a witness) again, after cross-examination by the opposing counsel.
– DERIVATIVES **re-examination** n.

re-export ■ v. /ˌriːɪkˈspɔːt, -ɛk-/ export (imported goods), typically after further processing or manufacture. ■ n. /riːˈɛkspɔːt/ the action of re-exporting. ▸ a thing that has or will be re-exported.
– DERIVATIVES **re-exportation** n. **re-exporter** n.

ref ■ n. informal (in sports) a referee.

ref. ■ abbrev. **1** reference. **2** refer to.

reface ■ v. put a new facing on (a building).

refection ■ n. poetic/literary refreshment by food or drink. ▸ a meal or snack.
– ORIGIN Middle English: from Latin *refectio(n-)*, from *reficere* (see REFECTORY).

refectory ■ n. (pl. **-ies**) a room used for communal meals, especially in an educational or religious institution.
– ORIGIN Middle English: from late Latin *refectorium*, from Latin *reficere* 'refresh, renew'.

refectory table ■ n. a long, narrow table.

refer /rɪˈfəː/ ■ v. (**referred**, **referring**) **1** (**refer to**) mention or allude to. ▸ (**refer someone to**) direct the attention of someone to. ▸ (**refer to**) (of a word or phrase) describe or denote. **2** (**refer something to**) pass a matter to (a higher body) for a decision. ▸ send to a medical specialist. ▸ (**refer to**) consult (a source of information). **3** fail (a candidate in an examination).
– PHRASES **refer to drawer** a phrase used by banks when suspending payment of a cheque.
– DERIVATIVES **referable** /rɪˈfəːrəb(ə)l, ˈrɛf(ə)r-/ adj. **referrer** n.
– ORIGIN Middle English: from Old French *referer* or Latin *referre* 'carry back'.

referee ■ n. **1** an official who watches a game or match closely to ensure that the rules are adhered to. **2** a person willing to testify in writing about the character or ability of a job applicant. **3** a person appointed to examine and assess an academic work for publication. ■ v. (**referees**, **refereed**, **refereeing**) officiate as referee at or over.

991

reflection

reference ■ n. **1** the action of mentioning something. ▸ a mention or citation of a source of information in a book or article. **2** the action of referring to a source of information or higher authority. **3** a letter from a previous employer testifying to someone's ability or reliability. ■ v. provide (a book or article) with references.
– PHRASES **terms of reference** the scope and limitations of an activity or area of knowledge. **with** (or **in**) **reference to** in relation to; as regards.

reference group ■ n. a social group which a person takes as a standard in forming attitudes and behaviour.

reference library ■ n. a library in which the books are for consultation rather than for loan.

reference point ■ n. a basis or standard for evaluation or comparison.

referendum /ˌrɛfəˈrɛndəm/ ■ n. (pl. **referendums** or **referenda** /-də/) a general vote by the electorate on a single political question which has been referred to them for a direct decision.
– ORIGIN C19: from Latin, 'referring' or 'something to be referred', from *referre* (see REFER).

referent ■ n. Linguistics the thing in the world that a word or phrase denotes or stands for.

referential ■ adj. **1** containing or of the nature of a reference or references. **2** Linguistics of or relating to a referent, in particular having the external world rather than a text or language as a referent.
– DERIVATIVES **referentiality** n. **referentially** adv.

referral ■ n. the action of referring someone or something for consultation or review, especially the directing of a patient by a GP to a specialist.

referred pain ■ n. Medicine pain felt in a part of the body other than its actual source.

refill ■ v. /riːˈfɪl/ fill or become full again. ■ n. /ˈriːfɪl/ an act of refilling or a glass that is refilled.
– DERIVATIVES **refillable** adj.

refinance ■ v. finance again, typically with new loans at a lower rate of interest.

refine ■ v. **1** remove impurities or unwanted elements from. **2** make minor changes so as to improve (a theory or method). **3** [as adj. **refined**] elegant and cultured.
– DERIVATIVES **refiner** n.
– ORIGIN C16: from RE- + the verb FINE[1], influenced by French *raffiner*.

refinement ■ n. **1** the action or process of refining. ▸ an improvement. **2** elegance, sophistication, and good taste.

refinery ■ n. (pl. **-ies**) an industrial installation where a substance is refined.

refinish ■ v. apply a new finish to (a surface or object). ■ n. an act of refinishing a surface or object.

refit ■ v. (**refitted**, **refitting**) replace or repair machinery, equipment, and fittings in (a ship, building, etc.). ■ n. an act of refitting.

reflag ■ v. (**reflagged**, **reflagging**) change the national registration of (a ship).

reflate ■ v. (of a government) expand the level of output of (an economy) by either fiscal or monetary policy.
– DERIVATIVES **reflation** n. **reflationary** adj.
– ORIGIN 1930s: from RE-, on the pattern of *inflate*, *deflate*.

reflect ■ v. **1** (of a surface or body) throw back (heat, light, or sound) without absorbing it. ▸ (of a mirror or shiny surface) show an image of. **2** embody or represent in a faithful or appropriate way: *the letters reflect all aspects of his life*. ▸ (**reflect well/badly on**) bring about a good or bad impression of. **3** (**reflect on/upon**) think deeply or carefully about.
– ORIGIN Middle English: from Latin *reflectere*, from *re-* 'back' + *flectere* 'to bend'.

reflectance ■ n. Physics a property of a surface equal to the proportion of incident light which it reflects or scatters.

reflecting telescope ■ n. a telescope in which a mirror is used to collect and focus light.

reflection ■ n. **1** the fact or phenomenon of light, heat, sound, etc. being reflected. ▸ something reflected or an

reflective

image so formed. **2** a thing bringing discredit. **3** serious thought or consideration. ▸ a considered idea, expressed in writing or speech. **4** Mathematics the symmetry operation of inverting something with respect to a plane.

reflective ■ adj. **1** providing or capable of providing a reflection. ▸ produced by reflection. **2** thoughtful.
– DERIVATIVES **reflectively** adv. **reflectiveness** n. **reflectivity** n.

reflector ■ n. **1** a piece of reflective material, e.g. a red one on the back of a motor vehicle or bicycle. **2** an object or device which reflects radio waves, seismic vibrations, sound, or other waves.

reflex ■ n. **1** an action performed without conscious thought as a response to a stimulus. ▸ (in reflexology) a response in a part of the body to stimulation of a corresponding point on the feet, hands, or head. **2** a thing that reproduces the essential features or qualities of something else. **3** a word formed by development from an earlier stage of a language. **4** archaic a reflected source of light. ■ adj. **1** (of an action) performed as a reflex. **2** (of an angle) exceeding 180°.
– DERIVATIVES **reflexly** adv.
– ORIGIN C16: from Latin *reflexus* 'a bending back', from *reflectere* (see REFLECT).

reflex arc ■ n. Physiology the nerve pathway involved in a reflex action.

reflex camera ■ n. a camera with a ground-glass focusing screen on which the image is formed by a combination of lens and mirror, enabling a scene to be correctly composed and focused.

reflexion ■ n. archaic spelling of REFLECTION.

reflexive ■ adj. **1** Grammar denoting a pronoun that refers back to the subject of the clause in which it is used, e.g. *myself*. ▸ (of a verb or clause) having a reflexive pronoun as its object (e.g. *wash oneself*). **2** Logic (of a relation) always holding between a term and itself. **3** (of a method or theory in the social sciences) taking account of itself or of the effect of the researcher on what is being investigated. **4** (of an action) performed without conscious thought.
– DERIVATIVES **reflexively** adv. **reflexiveness** n. **reflexivity** n.

reflexology ■ n. a system of massage used to relieve tension and treat illness, based on the theory that there are reflex points on the feet, hands, and head linked to every part of the body.
– DERIVATIVES **reflexologist** n.

refloat ■ v. set afloat again.

reflux /'ri:flʌks/ ■ n. **1** Chemistry the process of boiling a liquid so that any vapour is liquefied and returned to the stock. **2** technical the flowing back of a bodily fluid. ■ v. Chemistry **1** boil or cause to boil under reflux. **2** technical (of a bodily fluid) flow back.

refocus ■ v. (**refocused**, **refocusing** or **refocussed**, **refocussing**) **1** adjust the focus of (a lens or one's eyes). **2** focus (attention or resources) on something new or different.

reforest ■ v. replant with trees; cover again with forest.
– DERIVATIVES **reforestation** n.

reform ■ v. **1** make changes in (something, especially an institution or practice) in order to improve it. ▸ cause (someone) to relinquish an immoral or criminal lifestyle. **2** Chemistry subject (hydrocarbons) to a catalytic process in which straight-chain molecules are converted to branched forms. ■ n. the action or process of reforming.
– DERIVATIVES **reformative** adj. **reformed** adj. **reformer** n.
– ORIGIN Middle English: from Latin *reformare*, from *re-* 'back' + *formare* 'to form'.

re-form ■ v. form or cause to form again.
– DERIVATIVES **re-formation** n.

reformat ■ v. (**reformatted**, **reformatting**) chiefly Computing give a new format to.

reformation ■ n. **1** the action or process of reforming. **2** (**the Reformation**) a 16th-century movement for the reform of abuses in the Roman Church, ending in the establishment of the Reformed and Protestant Churches.
– DERIVATIVES **reformational** adj.

reformatory /rɪ'fɔːmət(ə)ri/ ■ n. (pl. **-ies**) S. African or dated an institution to which young offenders are sent as an alternative to prison. ■ adj. tending or intended to produce reform.

Reformed Church ■ n. a Church that has accepted the principles of the Reformation, especially a Calvinist Church (as distinct from Lutheran).

reformist ■ adj. supporting or advocating gradual reform rather than abolition or revolution. ■ n. a supporter or advocate of such a policy.
– DERIVATIVES **reformism** n.

Reform Judaism ■ n. a form of Judaism which has reformed or abandoned aspects of Orthodox Jewish worship and ritual in an attempt to adapt to modern life.
– DERIVATIVES **Reform Jew** n.

reform school ■ n. another term for REFORMATORY.

reformulate ■ v. formulate again or differently.
– DERIVATIVES **reformulation** n.

refract ■ v. (of water, air, or glass) make (a ray of light) change direction when it enters at an angle. ▸ change the direction of propagation of (radio, sound, or other waves) by causing them to travel at different speeds at different points along the wave front.
– ORIGIN C17: from Latin *refract-*, *refringere* 'break up'.

refracting telescope ■ n. a telescope which uses a converging lens to collect the light.

refraction ■ n. the fact or phenomenon of light, radio waves, etc., being refracted.
– DERIVATIVES **refractive** adj.

refractive index ■ n. Physics the ratio of the velocity of light in a vacuum to its velocity in a specified medium.

refractometer /,ri:frak'tɒmɪtə/ ■ n. an instrument for measuring a refractive index.
– DERIVATIVES **refractometry** n.

refractor ■ n. **1** a lens or other object which causes refraction. **2** a refracting telescope.

refractory ■ adj. formal **1** stubborn or unmanageable. **2** resistant to a process or stimulus. ▸ Medicine not yielding to treatment. ▸ technical heat-resistant; hard to melt or fuse.
– DERIVATIVES **refractoriness** n.
– ORIGIN C17: from Latin *refractarius* 'stubborn' (see also REFRACT).

refrain¹ ■ v. (usu. **refrain from**) stop oneself from doing something.
– ORIGIN Middle English: from Old French *refrener*, from Latin *refrenare*, from *re-* (expressing intensive force) + *frenum* 'bridle'.

refrain² ■ n. a repeated line or number of lines in a poem or song, typically at the end of each verse. ▸ the musical accompaniment for a refrain.
– ORIGIN Middle English: from Old French *refraindre* 'break', from Latin *refringere* 'break up' (because the refrain 'broke' the sequence).

refresh ■ v. give new strength or energy to. ▸ jog (someone's memory) by going over previous information. ▸ revise or update (skills, knowledge, etc.).
– ORIGIN Middle English: from Old French *refreschier*, from *re-* 'back' + *fres(che)* 'fresh'.

refresher ■ n. an activity that refreshes one's skills or knowledge.

refreshing ■ adj. **1** serving to refresh. **2** welcome or stimulating because new or different.
– DERIVATIVES **refreshingly** adv.

refreshment ■ n. **1** a light snack or drink. **2** the giving of fresh strength or energy.

refried beans ■ pl. n. (in Mexican cooking) pinto beans boiled and fried in advance and reheated when required.

refrigerant ■ n. a substance used for refrigeration. ■ adj. causing cooling or refrigeration.

refrigerate ■ v. subject (food or drink) to cold in order to chill or preserve it.
– DERIVATIVES **refrigeration** n.
– ORIGIN Middle English: from Latin *refrigerare* 'make cool', from *re-* 'back' + *frigus* 'cold'.

refrigerator ■ n. an appliance or compartment which is artificially kept cool and used to store food and drink.

reft past and past participle of REAVE.

refuel ■ v. (**refuelled**, **refuelling**; US **refueled**, **refueling**) (with reference to a vehicle) supply or be supplied with more fuel.

refuge ■ n. a place or state of safety from danger or trouble.
– ORIGIN Middle English: from Old French, from Latin *refugium*, from Latin *re-* 'back' + *fugere* 'flee'.

refugee ■ n. a person who has been forced to leave their country in order to escape war, persecution, or natural disaster.
– ORIGIN C17: from French *réfugié* 'gone in search of refuge', from *refuge* (see **REFUGE**).

refugium /rɪˈfjuːdʒɪəm/ ■ n. (pl. **refugia** /-dʒɪə/) Biology an area in which a population of organisms can survive a period of unfavourable conditions, especially glaciation.
– ORIGIN 1950s: from Latin, 'place of refuge'.

refulgent /rɪˈfʌldʒ(ə)nt/ ■ adj. poetic/literary shining very brightly.
– DERIVATIVES **refulgence** n. **refulgently** adv.
– ORIGIN C15: from Latin *refulgent-*, *refulgere* 'shine out'.

refund ■ v. /rɪˈfʌnd/ pay back (money). ▶ pay back money to. ■ n. /ˈriːfʌnd/ a refunded sum of money.
– DERIVATIVES **refundable** adj.
– ORIGIN Middle English: from Latin *refundere*, from *re-* 'back' + *fundere* 'pour'.

refurbish ■ v. renovate and redecorate.
– DERIVATIVES **refurbishment** n.

refuse[1] /rɪˈfjuːz/ ■ v. indicate unwillingness. ▶ indicate unwillingness to accept or grant (something offered or requested). ▶ (of a horse) decline to jump (a fence or other obstacle).
– DERIVATIVES **refusal** n. **refuser** n.
– ORIGIN Middle English: from Old French *refuser*, prob. an alteration of Latin *recusare* 'to refuse', influenced by *refutare* 'refute'.

refuse[2] /ˈrefjuːs/ ■ n. matter thrown away as worthless.
– ORIGIN Middle English: perhaps from Old French *refusé* 'refused', from *refuser* (see **REFUSE**[1]).

refusenik /rɪˈfjuːznɪk/ ■ n. 1 a Jew in the former Soviet Union who was refused permission to emigrate to Israel. 2 a person who refuses to comply with orders or the law, especially as a protest.
– ORIGIN 1970s: from **REFUSE**[1].

refute /rɪˈfjuːt/ ■ v. 1 prove (a statement or the person advancing it) to be wrong. 2 deny (a statement or accusation).
– DERIVATIVES **refutable** adj. **refutation** n.
– ORIGIN C16: from Latin *refutare* 'repel, rebut'.

regain ■ v. 1 obtain possession or use of (something) again after losing it. 2 get back to.

regal ■ adj. of, resembling, or fit for a monarch, especially in being magnificent or dignified.
– DERIVATIVES **regally** adv.
– ORIGIN Middle English: from Latin *regalis*, from *rex, reg-* 'king'.

regale ■ v. 1 entertain with conversation. 2 lavishly supply with food or drink.
– ORIGIN C17: from French *régaler*, from *re-* (expressing intensive force) + Old French *gale* 'pleasure'.

regalia /rɪˈɡeɪlɪə/ ■ pl. n. [treated as sing. or pl.] 1 the insignia of royalty, especially the crown and other ornaments used at a coronation. 2 the distinctive clothing and trappings of high office, worn at formal occasions.
– ORIGIN C16: from medieval Latin, 'royal privileges', from *regalis* 'regal'.

regality ■ n. (pl. **-ies**) the state of being a monarch.

regard ■ v. 1 consider in a particular way. 2 gaze at in a specified fashion. ■ n. 1 heed or concern: *she rescued him without regard for herself*. 2 high opinion; esteem. ▶ (**regards**) best wishes (used especially at the end of letters). 3 a steady look.
– PHRASES **as regards** concerning. **in this** (or **that**) **regard** in connection with the point previously mentioned. **with** (or **in** or **having**) **regard to** as concerns.
– ORIGIN Middle English: from Old French *regarder* 'to watch', from *re-* (expressing intensive force) + *garder* (see **GUARD**).

regardant /rɪˈɡɑːd(ə)nt/ ■ adj. Heraldry looking backwards.
– ORIGIN Middle English: from Anglo-Norman French and Old French, from *regarder* 'look (again)'.

regarding ■ prep. about; concerning.

regardless ■ adv. despite the prevailing circumstances.
– PHRASES **regardless of** without regard for.
– DERIVATIVES **regardlessly** adv.

regatta ■ n. a sporting event consisting of a series of boat or yacht races.
– ORIGIN C17: from Italian (Venetian dialect), 'a fight or contest'.

regd ■ abbrev. registered.

regency /ˈriːdʒ(ə)nsi/ ■ n. (pl. **-ies**) the office or period of government by a regent. ▶ a commission acting as regent. ■ adj. (**Regency**) relating to or denoting a broadly neoclassical style of British architecture, clothing, and furniture of the late 18th and early 19th centuries.
– ORIGIN Middle English: from medieval Latin *regentia*, from Latin *regent-* (see **REGENT**).

regenerate ■ v. /rɪˈdʒenəreɪt/ 1 (of a living organism) regrow (new tissue). ▶ (of an organ or tissue) regrow. 2 bring new and more vigorous life to (an area or institution). 3 (especially in Christian use) give a new and higher spiritual nature to. 4 [usu. as adj. **regenerated**] Chemistry precipitate (cellulose) as fibres following chemical processing. ■ adj. /rɪˈdʒen(ə)rət/ reborn, especially in a spiritual or moral sense.
– DERIVATIVES **regeneration** n. **regenerative** adj. **regeneratively** adv. **regenerator** n.
– ORIGIN Middle English: from Latin *regeneratus*, *regenerare* 'create again'.

regenerative braking ■ n. a method of braking in which energy is extracted from the parts braked, to be stored and reused.

regent ■ n. 1 a person appointed to administer a state because the monarch is a minor or is absent or incapacitated. 2 N. Amer. a member of the governing body of a university or other academic institution. ■ adj. [postpos.] acting as regent: *Prince Regent*.
– ORIGIN Middle English: from Latin *regent-*, *regere* 'to rule'.

reggae /ˈreɡeɪ/ ■ n. a style of popular music with a strongly accented subsidiary beat, originating in Jamaica.
– ORIGIN perhaps rel. to Jamaican English *rege-rege* 'quarrel, row'.

regicide /ˈredʒɪsaɪd/ ■ n. the killing of a king. ▶ a person who does this.
– DERIVATIVES **regicidal** adj.
– ORIGIN C16: from Latin *rex, reg-* 'king' + **-CIDE**.

regime /reɪˈʒiːm/ ■ n. 1 a government, especially an authoritarian one. 2 a systematic or ordered way of doing something.
– ORIGIN C15: French *régime*, from Latin *regimen* (see **REGIMEN**).

regimen /ˈredʒɪmən/ ■ n. a therapeutic course of medical treatment, often including recommendations as to diet and exercise.
– ORIGIN Middle English: from Latin, from *regere* 'to rule'.

regiment ■ n. /ˈredʒɪm(ə)nt/ 1 a permanent unit of an army, typically divided into several smaller units and often into two battalions. 2 a large number of people or things. ■ v. /ˈredʒɪment/ (usu. **be regimented**) organize according to a strict system.
– DERIVATIVES **regimental** adj. **regimentally** adv. **regimentation** n.
– ORIGIN Middle English: from late Latin *regimentum* 'rule', from *regere* 'to rule'.

regimental colour ■ n. a regimental standard in the form of a silk flag carried by a particular regiment.

Regina /rɪˈdʒaɪnə/ ■ n. the reigning British queen (used following a name or in the titles of lawsuits in British courts, e.g. *Regina v. Jones*: the Crown versus Jones).
– ORIGIN Latin, 'queen'.

region ■ n. 1 an area of a country or the world having definable characteristics but not always fixed boundaries. ▶ an administrative district of a city or country. 2 a part of the body, especially around or near an organ.
– PHRASES **in the region of** approximately.
– DERIVATIVES **regional** adj. & n. **regionalization** (also

regionalism

-isation) n. **regionalize** (also **-ise**) v. **regionally** adv.
– ORIGIN Middle English: from Latin *regio(n-)* 'direction, district', from *regere* 'to rule, direct'.

regionalism ■ n. **1** the theory or practice of regional rather than central systems of administration or economic, cultural, or political affiliation. **2** a linguistic feature peculiar to a particular region.
– DERIVATIVES **regionalist** n. & adj.

register ■ n. **1** an official list or record. ▶ a record of attendance, for example of pupils in a class. **2** a particular part of the range of a voice or instrument. **3** Linguistics a variety of a language determined by degree of formality and choice of vocabulary, pronunciation, and syntax. **4** Printing & Photography the exact correspondence of the position of colour components in a printed positive. ▶ Printing the exact correspondence of the position of printed matter on the two sides of a leaf. **5** (in electronic devices) a location in a store of data, used for a specific purpose and with quick access time. **6** a sliding device controlling a set of organ pipes which share a tonal quality. ▶ a set of organ pipes so controlled. ■ v. **1** enter in or place on a register. ▶ put one's name on a register, especially as an eligible voter or as a guest in a hotel. **2** express (an opinion or emotion). ▶ (of an emotion) show in a person's face or gestures. ▶ [usu. with neg.] become aware of. **3** (of an instrument) detect and show (a reading) automatically. ▶ (of an event) give rise to a specified reading on an instrument. **4** entrust (a letter or parcel) to a post office for transmission by registered post. **5** Printing & Photography correspond or cause to correspond exactly in position.
– DERIVATIVES **registrable** adj.
– ORIGIN Middle English: from medieval Latin *regestrum*, from late Latin *regesta* 'things recorded', from *regerere* 'enter, record'.

registered post ■ n. a postal procedure with special precautions for safety and for compensation in case of loss.

register office ■ n. a local government building where civil marriages are conducted and births, marriages, and deaths are recorded with the issue of certificates.

registrant ■ n. a person who registers.

registrar /ˈrɛdʒɪstrɑː, ˌrɛdʒɪˈstrɑː/ ■ n. **1** an official responsible for keeping a register or official records. **2** the chief administrative officer in a university. **3** the judicial and administrative officer of the High Court. **4** a middle-ranking hospital doctor undergoing training as a specialist.
– DERIVATIVES **registrarship** n.
– ORIGIN C17: from medieval Latin *registrarius*, from *registrum* (see REGISTER).

registration ■ n. **1** the action or process of registering or of being registered. **2** (also **registration mark** or **registration number**) the series of letters and figures identifying a motor vehicle, displayed on a number plate.

registration document (also **vehicle registration document**) ■ n. a document giving registered information about a vehicle, such as the owner's name and the date of its manufacture.

registration plate ■ n. another term for NUMBER PLATE.

registry ■ n. (pl. **-ies**) **1** a place where registers are kept. **2** registration.

registry office ■ n. another term for REGISTER OFFICE (in informal and non-official use).

Regius professor /ˈriːdʒɪəs/ ■ n. (in the UK) the holder of a university chair founded by a sovereign or filled by Crown appointment.
– ORIGIN Latin *regius* 'royal', from *rex* 'king'.

regmaker /ˈrɛxmɑːkə/ ■ n. S. African informal a medicine or (alcoholic) drink taken to cure a hangover.
– ORIGIN Afrikaans, from *reg* 'right' + *maker* 'maker'.

regnal /ˈrɛɡn(ə)l/ ■ adj. of a reign or monarch.
– ORIGIN C17: from Anglo-Latin *regnalis*, from Latin *regnum* 'kingdom'.

regolith /ˈrɛɡ(ə)lɪθ/ ■ n. Geology the layer of unconsolidated solid material covering the bedrock of a planet.
– ORIGIN C19: from Greek *rhēgos* 'rug, blanket' + -LITH.

regrade ■ v. grade again or differently.

regress ■ v. /rɪˈɡrɛs/ **1** return to a former state. ▶ return mentally to a former stage of life or a supposed previous life. **2** Astronomy move in a retrograde direction. ■ n. /ˈriːɡrɛs/ **1** the action of regressing. **2** Philosophy a series of statements in which a logical procedure is continually reapplied to its own result without approaching a useful conclusion.
– ORIGIN Middle English: from Latin *regressus*, from *regredi* 'go back, return'.

regression ■ n. **1** a return to a former state. ▶ a return to an earlier stage of life or a supposed previous life. **2** Statistics a measure of the relation between the mean value of one variable and corresponding values of other variables.

regressive ■ adj. **1** tending to regress or characterized by regression. **2** (of a tax) taking a proportionally greater amount from those on lower incomes.
– DERIVATIVES **regressively** adv. **regressiveness** n.

regret ■ v. (**regretted**, **regretting**) feel or express sorrow, repentance, or disappointment over. ■ n. a feeling of sorrow, repentance, or disappointment. ▶ used in polite formulas to express apology or sadness.
– DERIVATIVES **regretful** adj. **regretfulness** n.
– ORIGIN Middle English: from Old French *regreter* 'bewail (the dead)'.

regretfully ■ adv. **1** in a regretful manner. **2** it is regrettable that.

regrettable ■ adj. giving rise to regret; undesirable.
– DERIVATIVES **regrettably** adv.

regroup ■ v. reassemble into organized groups, typically after being attacked or defeated.

regrow ■ v. (past **regrew**; past part. **regrown**) grow or cause to grow again.
– DERIVATIVES **regrowth** n.

Regt ■ abbrev. Regiment.

regular ■ adj. **1** arranged in a constant or definite pattern, especially with the same space between individual instances. ▶ recurring at short uniform intervals. **2** doing the same thing often or at uniform intervals: *regular worshippers*. ▶ done or happening frequently. **3** conforming to or governed by an accepted standard of procedure or convention. ▶ of or belonging to the permanent professional armed forces of a country. ▶ properly trained or qualified and pursuing a full-time occupation. **4** usual or customary. ▶ chiefly N. Amer. of an ordinary kind. ▶ N. Amer. not pretentious or arrogant; ordinary and friendly: *a regular guy*. ▶ (chiefly in commercial use) denoting merchandise of average size. **5** Grammar (of a word) following the normal pattern of inflection. **6** Geometry (of a figure) having all sides and all angles equal. ▶ (of a solid) bounded by a number of equal figures. **7** Botany (of a flower) having radial symmetry. ■ n. a regular customer, member of a team, etc. ▶ a regular member of the armed forces.
– DERIVATIVES **regularity** n. (pl. **-ies**). **regularization** (also **-isation**) n. **regularize** (also **-ise**) v. **regularly** adv.
– ORIGIN Middle English: from Latin *regularis*, from *regula* 'rule'.

regular expression ■ n. Computing a sequence of symbols and characters which uses syntax rules to express a string or pattern to be searched for within a list, piece of text, etc.

regulate ■ v. **1** control or maintain the rate or speed of (a machine or process). **2** control or supervise by means of rules and regulations.
– DERIVATIVES **regulative** adj. **regulator** n. **regulatory** adj.
– ORIGIN Middle English: from late Latin *regulare* 'direct, regulate', from Latin *regula* 'rule'.

regulation ■ n. **1** a rule or directive made and maintained by an authority. ▶ [as modifier] in accordance with regulations. **2** the action or process of regulating or being regulated.

regurgitate /rɪˈɡɜːdʒɪteɪt/ ■ v. **1** bring (swallowed food) up again to the mouth. **2** repeat (information) without analysing or comprehending it.
– DERIVATIVES **regurgitation** n.
– ORIGIN C16: from medieval Latin *regurgitare*, from *re-* 'again' + *gurges, gurgit-* 'whirlpool'.

rehab /'riːhab/ informal ■ n. rehabilitation.

rehabilitate ■ v. **1** restore to health or normal life by training and therapy after imprisonment, addiction, or illness. **2** restore the standing or reputation of. **3** restore to a former condition.
– DERIVATIVES **rehabilitation** n. **rehabilitative** adj.
– ORIGIN C16 (*rehabilitation* C15): from medieval Latin *rehabilitare*, from Latin *re-* 'again' + *habilitare* 'make able', from *habilis* 'able'.

rehash ■ v. reuse (old ideas or material) without significant change or improvement. ■ n. an instance of rehashing.

rehearsal ■ n. a trial performance of a play or other work for later public performance. ▸ the action or process of rehearsing.

rehearse ■ v. **1** practise (a play, piece of music, or other work) for later public performance. **2** state (a list of points that have been made many times before).
– DERIVATIVES **rehearser** n.
– ORIGIN Middle English: from Old French *rehercier*, perhaps from *re-* 'again' + *hercer* 'to harrow', from *herse* (see HEARSE).

reheat ■ v. heat again.

rehouse ■ v. provide with new housing.

rehydrate ■ v. absorb or cause to absorb moisture after dehydration.
– DERIVATIVES **rehydration** n.

Reich /rʌɪk, -x/ ■ n. the former German state, most often used to refer to the Third Reich (the Nazi regime, 1933–45).
– ORIGIN German, 'empire'.

Reichstag /'rʌɪxsˌtɑːɡ, 'rʌɪks-/ ■ n. the main legislature of the German state under the Second and Third Reichs.
– ORIGIN German, from *Reichs* 'of the empire' + *Tag* 'assembly'.

reify /'riːɪfʌɪ, 'reɪɪ-/ ■ v. (**-ies**, **-ied**) formal make (something abstract) more concrete or real.
– DERIVATIVES **reification** n.
– ORIGIN C19: from Latin *res*, *re-* 'thing'.

reign ■ v. **1** rule as monarch. **2** [as adj. **reigning**] (of a sports player or team) currently holding a particular title. **3** prevail: *confusion reigned.* ■ n. **1** the period of rule of a monarch. **2** the period during which someone or something is predominant or pre-eminent.
– ORIGIN Middle English: from Old French *reignier* 'to reign', *reigne* 'kingdom', from Latin *regnum*.

USAGE
The correct phrase is **a free rein**, not **a free reign**.

reign of terror ■ n. a period of remorseless repression or bloodshed.

reiki /'reɪki/ ■ n. a healing technique based on the principle that the therapist can channel energy into the patient by means of touch, to activate the natural healing processes of the patient's body.
– ORIGIN Japanese, 'universal life energy'.

reimburse /ˌriːɪmˈbəːs/ ■ v. repay (a person who has spent or lost money). ▸ repay (a sum of money that has been spent or lost).
– DERIVATIVES **reimbursable** adj. **reimbursement** n.
– ORIGIN C17: from RE- + obsolete *imburse* 'put in a purse', from medieval Latin *imbursare*, from late Latin *bursa* 'purse'.

reimport ■ v. import (goods processed or made from exported materials). ■ n. the action of reimporting.
– DERIVATIVES **reimportation** n.

rein ■ n. **1** a long, narrow strap attached at one end to a horse's bit, typically used in pairs to guide or check a horse in riding or driving. ▸ a similar device used to restrain a young child. **2** (**reins**) the power to direct and control: *a new chairperson will soon take over the reins.* ■ v. **1** check or guide (a horse) by pulling on its reins. **2** (often **rein someone/thing in/back**) restrain.
– PHRASES **draw rein** Brit. stop one's horse. (a) **free rein** freedom of action or expression. **keep a tight rein on** exercise strict control over.
– ORIGIN Middle English: from Old French *rene*, from Latin *retinere* 'retain'.

USAGE
The phrase **a free rein**, which derives from the literal meaning of allowing a horse to move freely without being controlled by reins, is sometimes misinterpreted and wrongly written as **a free reign**.

reincarnate ■ v. /ˌriːɪnˈkɑːneɪt/ cause (someone) to undergo rebirth in another body. ■ adj. /ˌriːɪnˈkɑːnət/ [usu. postpos.] reborn in another body.

reincarnation ■ n. the rebirth of a soul in a new body. ▸ a person or animal in whom a soul is believed to have been reborn.

reindeer ■ n. (pl. same or **reindeers**) a deer with large branching antlers, native to the northern tundra and subarctic and domesticated in parts of Eurasia. [*Rangifer tarandus*.]
– ORIGIN Middle English: from Old Norse *hreindýri*, from *hreinn* 'reindeer' + *dýr* 'deer'.

reindeer moss ■ n. a bluish-grey arctic lichen, eaten by reindeer in winter. [*Cladonia rangiferina*.]

reinfect ■ v. cause to become infected again.
– DERIVATIVES **reinfection** n.

reinforce ■ v. **1** strengthen (a military force) with additional personnel or material. **2** give added strength to.
– DERIVATIVES **reinforcement** n. **reinforcer** n.
– ORIGIN Middle English: from French *renforcer*, influenced by *inforce*, an obsolete spelling of ENFORCE.

reinforced concrete ■ n. concrete in which metal bars or wire are embedded to increase its tensile strength.

reinstall ■ v. **1** place or fix in position again. ▸ install (computer software) again. **2** reinstate in a position of authority.
– DERIVATIVES **reinstallation** n.

reinstate ■ v. restore to a former position or state.
– DERIVATIVES **reinstatement** n.

reinsure ■ v. (of an insurer) transfer (all or part of a risk) to another insurer to provide protection against the risk of the first insurance.
– DERIVATIVES **reinsurance** n. **reinsurer** n.

reintegrate ■ v. **1** restore (elements regarded as disparate) to unity. **2** integrate back into society.
– DERIVATIVES **reintegration** n.

reinterpret ■ v. (**reinterpreted**, **reinterpreting**) interpret in a new or different light.
– DERIVATIVES **reinterpretation** n.

reintroduce ■ v. **1** bring (something, especially a law or system) into effect again. **2** put (a species of animal or plant) back into a former habitat.
– DERIVATIVES **reintroduction** n.

reinvent ■ v. change so much so as to appear entirely new.
– PHRASES **reinvent the wheel** waste a great deal of time or effort in creating something that already exists.
– DERIVATIVES **reinvention** n.

reinvest ■ v. put (the profit on a previous investment) back into the same scheme.
– DERIVATIVES **reinvestment** n.

reinvigorate ■ v. give new energy or strength to.
– DERIVATIVES **reinvigoration** n.

reissue ■ v. (**reissues**, **reissued**, **reissuing**) make a new supply or different form of (a book, record, or other product) available for sale. ■ n. a new issue of such a product.

reiterate ■ v. say something again or repeatedly.
– DERIVATIVES **reiteration** n. **reiterative** adj.
– ORIGIN Middle English: from Latin *reiterare* 'go over again'.

reject ■ v. /rɪˈdʒɛkt/ **1** dismiss as inadequate or faulty. ▸ refuse to consider or agree to. **2** fail to show due affection or concern for. **3** Medicine show a damaging immune response to (a transplanted organ or tissue). ■ n. /ˈriːdʒɛkt/ a rejected person or thing.
– DERIVATIVES **rejection** n.
– ORIGIN Middle English: from Latin *reicere* 'throw back'.

rejig

rejig ■ v. (**rejigged**, **rejigging**) rearrange.

rejoice ■ v. feel or show great joy.
– DERIVATIVES **rejoicing** n. & adj. **rejoicingly** adv.
– ORIGIN Middle English: from Old French *rejoiss-, rejoir*, from *re-* (expressing intensive force) + *joir* 'experience joy'.

rejoin¹ ■ v. **1** join together again. **2** return to.

rejoin² ■ v. say in reply; retort.
– ORIGIN Middle English: from Old French *rejoindre*, from *re-* 'again' + *joindre* 'to join'.

rejoinder ■ n. a sharp or witty reply.
– ORIGIN Middle English: from Anglo-Norman French *rejoindre* (see REJOIN²).

rejuvenate /rɪ'dʒuːvəneɪt/ ■ v. **1** make or cause to appear younger or more vital. **2** [often as adj. **rejuvenated**] restore (a river or stream) to a condition characteristic of a younger landscape.
– DERIVATIVES **rejuvenation** n. **rejuvenator** n.
– ORIGIN C19: from RE- + Latin *juvenis* 'young'.

rejuvenescence /rɪˌdʒuːvə'nɛsəns/ ■ n. the renewal of youth or vitality.
– ORIGIN C17: from late Latin *rejuvenescere*, from Latin *re-* 'again' + *juvenis* 'young'.

rekey ■ v. chiefly Computing key (text or other data) again.

rekindle ■ v. **1** relight (a fire). **2** revive (something lapsed or lost).

-rel ■ suffix forming nouns with diminutive or derogatory force such as *cockerel*.
– ORIGIN from Old French *-erel(le)*.

relaid past and past participle of RELAY².

relapse /rɪ'laps/ ■ v. **1** (of a sick or injured person) deteriorate after a period of improvement. **2** (**relapse into**) return to (a worse or less active state). ■ n. /also 'riː-/ a deterioration in health after a temporary improvement.
– ORIGIN Middle English: from Latin *relaps-, relabi* 'slip back'.

relapsing fever ■ n. an infectious bacterial disease marked by recurrent fever.

relate ■ v. **1** give an account of. **2** (**be related**) be connected by blood or marriage. **3** establish a causal connection between. ▸ (**relate to**) concern. **4** (**relate to**) feel sympathy with.
– DERIVATIVES **relatable** adj. **related** adj. **relatedness** n. **relater** (also **relator**) n.
– ORIGIN C16 (*relation* Middle English): from Latin *relat-, referre* 'bring back' (see REFER).

relation ■ n. **1** the way in which two or more people or things are connected or related. ▸ (**relations**) the way in which two or more people or groups feel about and behave towards each other. **2** a relative. **3** the action of telling a story. **4** (**relations**) formal sexual intercourse.
– PHRASES **in relation to** in connection with.
– DERIVATIVES **relational** adj. **relationally** adv.

relational database ■ n. Computing a database structured to recognize relations between stored items.

relationship ■ n. **1** the way in which two or more people or things are connected, or the state of being connected. ▸ the way in which two or more people or groups regard and behave towards each other. **2** an emotional and sexual association between two people.

relative /'rɛlətɪv/ ■ adj. **1** considered in relation or in proportion to something else. ▸ existing or possessing a characteristic only in comparison to something else. **2** Grammar denoting a pronoun, determiner, or adverb that refers to an expressed or implied antecedent and attaches a subordinate clause to it, e.g. *which*. ▸ (of a clause) attached to an antecedent by a relative word. ■ n. **1** a person connected by blood or marriage. ▸ a species related to another by common origin. **2** Philosophy a term or concept which is dependent on something else.
– PHRASES **relative to 1** compared with or in relation to. **2** concerning.
– DERIVATIVES **relatival** /-'taɪv(ə)l/ adj. **relatively** adv.

relative atomic mass ■ n. Chemistry the ratio of the average mass of one atom of an element to one twelfth of the mass of an atom of carbon-12.

relative density ■ n. Chemistry the ratio of the density of a substance to a standard density, usually that of water or air.

relative humidity ■ n. the amount of water vapour present in air, expressed as a percentage of the amount needed for saturation at the same temperature.

relative molecular mass ■ n. Chemistry the ratio of the average mass of one molecule of an element or compound to one twelfth of the mass of an atom of carbon-12.

relativism /'rɛlətɪvɪz(ə)m/ ■ n. the doctrine that knowledge, truth, and morality exist in relation to culture, society, or historical context, and are not absolute.
– DERIVATIVES **relativist** n.

relativistic ■ adj. Physics accurately described only by the theory of relativity.
– DERIVATIVES **relativistically** adv.

relativity ■ n. **1** the absence of standards of absolute and universal application. **2** Physics a description of matter, energy, space, and time according to Einstein's theories based on the importance of relative motion and the principle that the speed of light is constant for all observers.

relativize (also **-ise**) ■ v. chiefly Linguistics & Philosophy make or treat as relative.
– DERIVATIVES **relativization** (also **-isation**) n.

relaunch ■ v. launch again or in a different form. ■ n. an instance of relaunching.

relax ■ v. **1** make or become less tense or anxious. ▸ cause (a limb or muscle) to become less rigid. **2** rest from work or engage in a recreational activity. **3** make (a rule or restriction) less strict.
– DERIVATIVES **relaxed** adj. **relaxedly** adv. **relaxer** n.
– ORIGIN Middle English: from Latin *relaxare*, from *re-* (expressing intensive force) + *laxus* 'lax, loose'.

relaxant ■ n. a drug used to promote relaxation or reduce tension. ▸ a thing having a relaxing effect. ■ adj. causing relaxation.

relaxation ■ n. **1** the action of relaxing or the state of being relaxed. **2** Physics the return of a system to equilibrium following disturbance.

relay¹ /'riːleɪ/ ■ n. **1** a group of people or animals engaged in a task for a period of time and then replaced by a similar group. ▸ a race between teams of runners, each team member in turn covering part of the total distance. **2** an electrical device which is activated by a current in one circuit to open or close another circuit. **3** a device to receive, reinforce, and retransmit a signal. ▸ a message, programme, etc. transmitted by such a device. ■ v. /also rɪ'leɪ/ **1** receive and pass on (information or a message). **2** broadcast by means of a relay.
– ORIGIN Middle English: from Old French *relai* (n.), *relayer* (v.), from Latin *laxare* 'slacken'.

relay² /riː'leɪ/ ■ v. (past and past part. **relaid**) lay again or differently.

release ■ v. **1** set free. **2** allow (information) to be generally available. ▸ make (a film or recording) available to the public. **3** allow to move or flow freely. ▸ remove (part of a machine or appliance) from a fixed position, allowing something else to move or function. **4** Law remit or discharge (a debt). ▸ surrender (a right). ▸ make over (property or money) to another. ■ n. **1** the action or process of releasing or being released. ▸ a film or other product released to the public. **2** a handle or catch that releases part of a mechanism. **3** Law the action of releasing property, money, or a right to another. ▸ a document effecting this.
– DERIVATIVES **releasable** adj. **releasee** n. (Law). **releaser** n. **releasor** n. (Law).
– ORIGIN Middle English: from Old French *reles* (n.), *relesser* (v.), from Latin *relaxare* (see RELAX).

relegate ■ v. **1** assign an inferior rank or position to. **2** (usu. **be relegated**) transfer (a sports team) to a lower division of a league.
– DERIVATIVES **relegation** n.
– ORIGIN Middle English: from Latin *relegare* 'send away'.

relent ■ v. **1** abandon or mitigate a harsh intention or cruel treatment. **2** become less intense.

−ORIGIN Middle English: from Latin *re-* 'back' + *lentare* 'to bend'.

relentless ■ adj. **1** oppressively constant. **2** harsh or inflexible.
−DERIVATIVES **relentlessly** adv. **relentlessness** n.

relevant ■ adj. closely connected or appropriate to the matter in hand.
−DERIVATIVES **relevance** n. **relevancy** n. **relevantly** adv.
−ORIGIN C16: from medieval Latin *relevant-* 'raising up', from Latin *relevare*.

relevé /ˌrələˈveɪ/ ■ n. **1** Ballet a movement in which the dancer rises on the tips of the toes. **2** Ecology each of a number of small plots of vegetation, analysed as a sample of a wider area.
−ORIGIN French, 'raised up'.

reliable ■ adj. able to be relied on.
−DERIVATIVES **reliability** n. **reliably** adv.

reliance ■ n. dependence on or trust in someone or something.
−DERIVATIVES **reliant** adj.

relic ■ n. **1** an object of interest surviving from an earlier time. ▸ a surviving but outdated object, custom, or belief. **2** a part of a deceased holy person's body or belongings kept as an object of reverence.
−ORIGIN Middle English: from Old French *relique*, from Latin *reliquiae*, from *reliquus* 'remaining'.

relict /ˈrɛlɪkt/ ■ n. an organism or other thing which has survived from an earlier period. ▸ Ecology a population, formerly more widespread, that survives in only a few localities.
−ORIGIN Middle English: from Latin *relictus*, *relinquere* 'leave behind'.

relief ■ n. **1** the alleviation or removal of pain, anxiety, or distress. ▸ a feeling or cause of relief. ▸ (usu. **light relief**) a temporary break in a generally tense or tedious situation. **2** financial or practical assistance given to those in special need or difficulty. **3** a person or group of people replacing others who have been on duty. **4** the raising of a siege on a town. **5** distinctness due to being accentuated. **6** a method of moulding, carving, or stamping in which the design stands out from the surface, to a greater (high relief) or lesser (low relief) extent. ▸ a representation of relief given by an arrangement of line, colour, etc.
−PHRASES **in relief** Baseball acting as a substitute pitcher. **on relief** chiefly N. Amer. receiving state assistance because of need.
−ORIGIN Middle English: from Old French, from *relever* 'raise up, relieve', from Latin *relevare* 'raise again, alleviate'; sense 6 via French from Italian *rilievo*, from *rilevare* 'raise'.

relief map ■ n. **1** a map indicating hills and valleys by shading rather than by contour lines alone. **2** a map model with elevations and depressions representing hills and valleys, typically on an exaggerated relative scale.

relief printing ■ n. printing from raised images, as in letterpress and flexography.

relief road ■ n. chiefly Brit. a road taking traffic around, rather than through, a congested urban area.

relieve ■ v. **1** alleviate or remove (pain, distress, or difficulty). ▸ (usu. **be relieved**) cause (someone) to stop feeling distressed or anxious. **2** release (someone) from duty by taking their place. **3** (**relieve someone of**) take (a burden or responsibility) from someone. **4** bring military support for (a besieged place). **5** make less tedious or monotonous. **6** (**relieve oneself**) formal or euphemistic urinate or defecate.
−DERIVATIVES **relievable** adj. **relieved** adj. **relievedly** adv. **reliever** n.
−ORIGIN Middle English: from Old French *relever*, from Latin *relevare*, from *re-* (expressing intensive force) + *levare* 'raise'.

relight ■ v. (past and past part. **relighted** or **relit**) light again.

religio- /rɪˈlɪdʒɪəʊ/ ■ comb. form religious and ...: *religio-political*.

religion ■ n. **1** the belief in and worship of a superhuman controlling power, especially a personal God or gods. ▸ a particular system of faith and worship. **2** a pursuit or interest followed with devotion.

remake

−ORIGIN Middle English (orig. in the sense 'life under monastic vows'): from Latin *religio(n-)* 'obligation, reverence'.

religionism ■ n. excessive religious zeal.
−DERIVATIVES **religionist** n.

religiose /rɪˈlɪdʒɪəʊs/ ■ adj. excessively religious.
−DERIVATIVES **religiosity** n.

religious ■ adj. **1** of, concerned with, or believing in a religion. ▸ belonging or relating to a monastic order or other group united by their practice of religion. **2** treated or regarded with a devotion and scrupulousness appropriate to worship. ■ n. (pl. same) a person bound by monastic vows.
−DERIVATIVES **religiously** adv. **religiousness** n.

relinquish ■ v. voluntarily cease to keep or claim; give up.
−DERIVATIVES **relinquishment** n.
−ORIGIN Middle English: from Old French *relinquiss-*, *relinquir*, from Latin *relinquere*, from *re-* (expressing intensive force) + *linquere* 'to leave'.

reliquary /ˈrɛlɪkwəri/ ■ n. (pl. **-ies**) a container for holy relics.
−ORIGIN C16: from French *reliquaire*, from Old French *relique* (see RELIC).

relish ■ n. **1** great enjoyment. ▸ pleasurable anticipation. **2** a piquant sauce or pickle eaten with plain food to add flavour. ■ v. enjoy greatly. ▸ anticipate with pleasure.
−DERIVATIVES **relishable** adj.
−ORIGIN Middle English: from Old French *reles* 'remainder', from *relaisser* 'to release'.

relive ■ v. live through (an experience or feeling) again in one's imagination.

reload ■ v. load (something, especially a gun) again.

relocate ■ v. move to a new place and establish one's home or business there.
−DERIVATIVES **relocation** n.

reluctance ■ n. **1** unwillingness. **2** Physics the property of a magnetic circuit of opposing the passage of magnetic flux lines, equal to the ratio of the magnetomotive force to the magnetic flux.

reluctant ■ adj. unwilling and hesitant.
−DERIVATIVES **reluctantly** adv.
−ORIGIN C17: from Latin *reluctant-*, *reluctari* 'struggle against'.

rely ■ v. (-**ies**, -**ied**) (**rely on/upon**) **1** depend on with full trust. **2** be dependent on.
−ORIGIN Middle English: from Old French *relier* 'bind together', from Latin *religare*, from *re-* (expressing intensive force) + *ligare* 'bind'.

REM ■ abbrev. rapid eye movement.

rem ■ n. (pl. same) a unit of effective absorbed dose of ionizing radiation in human tissue, loosely equivalent to one roentgen of X-rays.
−ORIGIN 1940s: acronym from *roentgen equivalent man*.

remade past and past participle of REMAKE.

remain ■ v. **1** be in the same place or condition during further time. ▸ continue to be: *he remained alert*. **2** be left over after others or other parts have been completed, used, or dealt with.
−ORIGIN Middle English: from Old French *remain-*, *remanoir*, from Latin *remanere*, from *re-* (expressing intensive force) + *manere* 'to stay'.

remainder ■ n. **1** a part, number, or quantity that is left over. ▸ the number which is left over in a division in which one quantity does not exactly divide another. **2** a part that is still to come. **3** a copy of a book left unsold when demand has fallen. **4** Law an interest in an estate that becomes effective in possession only when a prior interest (devised at the same time) ends. ■ v. (often **be remaindered**) dispose of (a book left unsold) at a reduced price.
−ORIGIN Middle English: from Latin *remanere* (see REMAIN).

remains ■ pl. n. **1** things remaining. **2** historical or archaeological relics. **3** a person's body after death.

remake ■ v. (past and past part. **remade**) make again or

remand

differently. ■ n. a film or piece of music that has been filmed or recorded again and re-released.

remand Law ■ v. place (an accused person) on bail or in custody, especially when a trial is adjourned. ■ n. a committal to custody.
– PHRASES **on remand** in custody pending trial.
– ORIGIN Middle English: from late Latin *remandare*, from *re-* 'back' + *mandare* 'commit'.

remanent /ˈrɛmənənt/ ■ adj. (of magnetism) remaining after the magnetizing field has been removed.
– DERIVATIVES **remanence** n.
– ORIGIN Middle English: from Latin *remanent-*, *remanere* 'remain'.

remark ■ v. 1 say as a comment; mention. 2 regard with attention; notice. ■ n. a comment. ▸ notice or comment.
– ORIGIN C16: from French *remarquer* 'note again'.

re-mark ■ v. mark (an examination paper or piece of academic work) again.

remarkable ■ adj. extraordinary or striking.
– DERIVATIVES **remarkableness** n. **remarkably** adv.

remarry ■ v. (-ies, -ied) marry again.
– DERIVATIVES **remarriage** n.

remaster ■ v. make a new master of (a recording), typically in order to improve the sound quality.

rematch ■ n. a second match or game between two sports teams or players.

remedial ■ adj. 1 giving or intended as a remedy. 2 provided or intended for children with learning difficulties.
– DERIVATIVES **remedially** adv.

remediation /rɪˌmiːdɪˈeɪʃ(ə)n/ ■ n. 1 the action of remedying something, in particular environmental damage. 2 the giving of remedial teaching or therapy.
– DERIVATIVES **remediate** v.
– ORIGIN C19: from Latin *remediatio(n-)*, from *remediare* (see REMEDY).

remedy ■ n. (pl. -ies) 1 a medicine or treatment for a disease or injury. 2 a means of counteracting or eliminating something undesirable. 3 a means of legal reparation. ■ v. (-ies, -ied) rectify (an undesirable situation).
– DERIVATIVES **remediable** adj.
– ORIGIN Middle English: from Anglo-Norman French *remedie*, from Latin *remedium*, from *re-* 'back' + *mederi* 'heal'.

remember ■ v. 1 have in or be able to bring to one's mind (someone or something from the past). ▸ bear (someone) in mind by making them a gift, making provision for them, or mentioning them in prayer.
▸ (**remember oneself**) recover one's manners after a lapse. 2 keep (something necessary or advisable) in mind. 3 (**remember someone to**) convey greetings from one person to (another).
– ORIGIN Middle English: from Old French *remembrer*, from late Latin *rememorari* 'call to mind'.

remembrance ■ n. the action of remembering. ▸ a memory. ▸ a thing kept or given as a reminder or in commemoration of someone.

Remembrance Day ■ n. another term for REMEMBRANCE SUNDAY.

Remembrance Sunday ■ n. the Sunday nearest 11 November, when those who were killed in the First and Second World Wars and later conflicts are commemorated.

remiges /ˈrɛmɪdʒiːz/ ■ pl. n. (sing. **remex** /ˈriːmɛks/) Ornithology flight feathers.
– ORIGIN C18: from Latin, 'rowers'.

remind ■ v. cause (someone) to remember something or to do something. ▸ (**remind someone of**) cause someone to think of (something) because of a resemblance.
– ORIGIN C17: from RE- + the verb MIND.

reminder ■ n. a thing that causes someone to remember something. ▸ a letter sent to remind someone to pay a bill.

remineralize (also **-ise**) ■ v. restore the depleted mineral content of (teeth or other body tissue).
– DERIVATIVES **remineralization** (also **-isation**) n.

reminisce /ˌrɛmɪˈnɪs/ ■ v. indulge in reminiscence.

reminiscence ■ n. a story told about a past event remembered by the narrator. ▸ the enjoyable recollection of past events.
– ORIGIN C16: from late Latin *reminiscentia*, from Latin *reminisci* 'remember'.

reminiscent ■ adj. 1 (usu. **reminiscent of**) tending to remind one of something. 2 absorbed in memories.
– DERIVATIVES **reminiscently** adv.

remise /rɪˈmiːz/ ■ v. Fencing make a second thrust after the first has failed.
– ORIGIN French, from *remettre* 'put back'.

remiss /rɪˈmɪs/ ■ adj. lacking care or attention to duty.
– DERIVATIVES **remissly** adv. **remissness** n.
– ORIGIN Middle English: from Latin *remissus*, *remittere* 'slacken'.

remission ■ n. 1 the cancellation of a debt, charge, or penalty. ▸ the reduction of a prison sentence, especially as a reward for good behaviour. 2 a temporary diminution of the severity of disease or pain. 3 formal forgiveness of sins.
– ORIGIN Middle English: from Latin *remissio(n-)*, from *remittere* (see REMIT).

remit ■ v. /rɪˈmɪt/ (**remitted**, **remitting**) 1 refrain from exacting or inflicting (a debt or punishment). 2 send (money) in payment, especially by post. 3 refer (a matter for decision) to an authority. ▸ Law send back (a case) to a lower court. ▸ Law send (someone) from one tribunal to another for a trial or hearing. ■ n. /ˈriːmɪt, rɪˈmɪt/ the task or area of activity officially assigned to an individual or organization.
– DERIVATIVES **remittable** adj. **remittal** n. **remitter** n.
– ORIGIN Middle English: from Latin *remiss-*, *remittere* 'send back, restore'.

remittance ■ n. a sum of money remitted. ▸ the action of remitting money.

remittent ■ adj. (of a fever) characterized by fluctuating body temperatures.

remix ■ v. mix again. ▸ produce a different version of (a musical recording) by altering the balance of the separate tracks. ■ n. a remixed musical recording.
– DERIVATIVES **remixer** n.

remnant ■ n. 1 a small remaining quantity. ▸ a piece of cloth left when the greater part has been used or sold. 2 a surviving trace. ■ adj. remaining.
– ORIGIN Middle English: from Old French *remenant*, from *remenoir*, *remanoir* 'remain'.

remodel ■ v. (**remodelled**, **remodelling**; US **remodeled**, **remodeling**) 1 change the structure or form of. 2 shape (a figure or object) again or differently.

remold ■ v. US spelling of REMOULD.

remonstrance /rɪˈmɒnstr(ə)ns/ ■ n. a forcefully reproachful protest.

remonstrate /ˈrɛmənstreɪt/ ■ v. make a forcefully reproachful protest.
– DERIVATIVES **remonstration** n. **remonstrative** adj.
– ORIGIN C16: from medieval Latin *remonstrare* 'demonstrate', from Latin *re-* (expressing intensive force) + *monstrare* 'to show'.

remora /ˈrɛmərə/ ■ n. a slender sea fish which attaches itself to large fish by means of a sucker on top of the head. [*Remora remora* and other species, family Echeneidae.]
– ORIGIN C16: from Latin, 'hindrance' (because of the former belief that the fish slowed down ships).

remorse ■ n. deep regret or guilt for a wrong committed.
– DERIVATIVES **remorseful** adj. **remorsefully** adv.
– ORIGIN Middle English: from medieval Latin *remorsus*, from Latin *remordere* 'vex', from *re-* (expressing intensive force) + *mordere* 'to bite'.

remorseless ■ adj. 1 without remorse. 2 (of something unpleasant) relentless.
– DERIVATIVES **remorselessly** adv. **remorselessness** n.

remortgage ■ v. take out another or a different mortgage on. ■ n. a different or additional mortgage.

remote ■ adj. (-er, -est) 1 far away in space or time.
▸ situated far from the main centres of population.
2 distantly related. ▸ having very little connection with.
3 (of a chance or possibility) unlikely to occur. 4 aloof and unfriendly in manner. 5 Computing denoting a device which

can only be accessed by means of a network. Compare with LOCAL. ■ n. a remote control device.
–DERIVATIVES **remotely** adv. **remoteness** n.
–ORIGIN Middle English: from Latin *remotus, removere* (see REMOVE).

remote control ■ n. control of a machine or apparatus from a distance by means of signals transmitted from a radio or electronic device. ▸ (also **remote controller**) a device that controls an apparatus in this way.
–DERIVATIVES **remote-controlled** adj.

remote sensing ■ n. the scanning of the earth by satellite or high-flying aircraft in order to obtain information about it.

remould (US **remold**) ■ v. /riːˈməʊld/ **1** mould again or differently. **2** Brit. put a new tread on (a worn tyre). ■ n. /ˈriːməʊld/ a remoulded tyre.

remount ■ v. /riːˈmaʊnt/ **1** get on (a horse or vehicle) again. **2** attach to a new frame or setting. **3** mount (a course of action) again. ■ n. /ˈriːmaʊnt/ a fresh horse for a rider.

removal ■ n. **1** the action of removing. **2** the transfer of furniture and other contents when moving house. **3** short for FORCED REMOVAL.

remove ■ v. **1** take off or away from the position occupied. ▸ abolish or get rid of. ▸ dismiss from a post. ▸ (**remove to**) dated relocate to (another place). **2** (**be removed**) be very different from. **3** [as adj. **removed**] separated by a particular number of steps of descent: *his second cousin once removed*. ■ n. a degree of remoteness or separation.
–DERIVATIVES **removability** n. **removable** adj. **remover** n.
–ORIGIN Middle English: from Latin *removere*, from *re-* 'back' + *movere* 'to move'.

REM sleep ■ n. a kind of sleep that occurs at intervals during the night and is characterized by rapid eye movement, more dreaming and bodily movement, and faster pulse and breathing.

remuage /ˌrɛmjuˈɑːʒ/ ■ n. the periodic turning or shaking of bottled wine, especially champagne, to move sediment towards the cork.
–ORIGIN French, 'moving about'.

remunerate /rɪˈmjuːnəreɪt/ ■ v. pay for services rendered or work done.
–DERIVATIVES **remuneration** n. **remunerative** adj.
–ORIGIN C16 (*remuneration* Middle English): from Latin *remunerari* 'reward, recompense'.

Renaissance /rɪˈneɪs(ə)ns, -ɒs/ ■ n. **1** the revival of art and literature under the influence of classical models in the 14th–16th centuries. **2** (**renaissance**) a revival of or renewed interest in something.
–ORIGIN from French *renaissance*, from *re-* 'back, again' + *naissance* 'birth'.

Renaissance man ■ n. a person with many talents or interests, especially in the humanities.

renal /ˈriːn(ə)l/ ■ adj. technical of or relating to the kidneys.
–ORIGIN C17: from French *rénal*, from late Latin *renalis*, from Latin *renes* 'kidneys'.

renal calculus ■ n. another term for KIDNEY STONE.

renal pelvis ■ n. see PELVIS (sense 2).

rename ■ v. give a new name to.

renascence /rɪˈnas(ə)ns, -ˈneɪ-/ ■ n. the revival or renewal of something.

renascent ■ adj. becoming active again.
–ORIGIN C18: from Latin *renascent-, renasci* 'to be born again'.

rend ■ v. (past and past part. **rent**) poetic/literary **1** tear to pieces. **2** cause great emotional pain to.
–PHRASES **rend the air** sound piercingly. **rend one's garments** (or **hair**) tear one's clothes (or pull one's hair out) as a sign of extreme grief of distress.
–ORIGIN Old English, rel. to Middle Low German *rende*.

render ■ v. **1** provide or give (a service, help, etc.). ▸ submit for inspection, consideration, or payment. ▸ poetic/literary hand over; surrender. **2** cause to be or become. **3** represent or depict artistically. ▸ perform (a piece of music). ▸ translate. **4** melt down (fat). **5** cover (stone or brick) with a coat of plaster. **6** Computing process (an image) in order to make it appear solid and three-dimensional. ■ n. a first coat of plaster applied to a brick or stone surface.
–DERIVATIVES **renderer** n.
–ORIGIN Middle English: from Old French *rendre*, from an alteration of Latin *reddere* 'give back'.

rendering ■ n. **1** a performance of a piece of music or drama. ▸ an artistic depiction. **2** a translation. **3** the action of rendering a wall. ▸ the plaster so applied. **4** the action of giving or surrendering something.

rendezvous /ˈrɒndɪvuː, -deɪvuː/ ■ n. (pl. same /-vuːz/) a meeting at an agreed time and place. ▸ a meeting place. ■ v. (**rendezvouses** /-vuːz/, **rendezvoused** /-vuːd/, **rendezvousing** /-vuːɪŋ/) meet at an agreed time and place.
–ORIGIN C16: from French *rendez-vous!* 'present yourselves!', from *se rendre*.

rendition ■ n. **1** a rendering of a dramatic, musical, or artistic work. **2** a translation. **3** (also **extraordinary rendition**) (especially in the US) the practice of having a foreign criminal or terrorist suspect covertly to be interrogated in a country with less rigorous regulations for the humane treatment of prisoners.
–ORIGIN C17: from obsolete French, from *rendre* 'give back, render'.

rendzina /rɛn(d)ˈziːnə/ ■ n. Soil Science a fertile lime-rich soil with dark humus above a pale soft calcareous layer, typical of grassland.
–ORIGIN 1920s: from Polish *rędzina*.

renegade /ˈrɛnɪɡeɪd/ ■ n. a person who deserts and betrays an organization, country, or set of principles. ■ adj. having treacherously changed allegiance.
–ORIGIN C15: from Spanish *renegado*, from medieval Latin *renegatus, renegare* 'renounce'.

renege /rɪˈneɪɡ, rɪˈniːɡ/ ■ v. **1** go back on a promise, undertaking, or contract. **2** another term for REVOKE (in sense 2).
–DERIVATIVES **reneger** n.
–ORIGIN C16: from medieval Latin *renegare*, from Latin *re-* (expressing intensive force) + *negare* 'deny'.

renegotiate ■ v. negotiate again in order to change the original agreed terms.
–DERIVATIVES **renegotiable** adj. **renegotiation** n.

renew ■ v. **1** resume or re-establish after an interruption. **2** give fresh life or strength to. **3** extend the period of validity of (a licence, subscription, or contract). **4** replace or restore (something broken or worn out).
–DERIVATIVES **renewal** n. **renewer** n.

renewable ■ adj. **1** capable of being renewed. **2** (of energy or its source) not depleted when used.
–DERIVATIVES **renewability** n.

reniform /ˈriːnɪfɔːm/ ■ adj. chiefly Mineralogy & Botany kidney-shaped.
–ORIGIN C18: from Latin *ren* 'kidney' + -IFORM.

renin /ˈriːnɪn/ ■ n. Biochemistry an enzyme secreted by and stored in the kidneys which promotes the production of the protein angiotensin.
–ORIGIN C19: from Latin *ren* 'kidney'.

renminbi ■ n. (pl. same) the system of currency of China. ▸ another term for YUAN.
–ORIGIN from Chinese *rénmínbì*, from *rénmín* 'people' + *bì* 'currency'.

rennet /ˈrɛnɪt/ ■ n. a preparation containing rennin, used in curdling milk for cheese.
–ORIGIN C15: prob. rel. to RUN.

rennin /ˈrɛnɪn/ ■ n. Biochemistry an enzyme secreted into the stomach of unweaned mammals causing the curdling of milk.
–ORIGIN C19: from RENNET.

renosterbos /rəˈnɔːstəˌbɒs, rəˈnɒstəˌbɒs/ (also **rhenosterbos**) ■ n. a South African shrub with small greyish leaves and inconspicuous flowers. [*Elytropappus rhinocerotis*.]
–ORIGIN Afrikaans, from *renoster* 'rhinoceros' + *bos* 'bush'.

renosterveld /rəˈnɔːstəˌfɛlt, rəˈnɒstəˌfɛlt/ (also **renosterbosveld**) ■ n. Ecology a vegetation type that forms part of the Cape Floral Kingdom, characterized by grassland and plants of the daisy family.
–ORIGIN Afrikaans, from *renoster* 'rhinoceros' + VELD.

renounce

renounce ■ v. **1** formally declare one's abandonment of (a claim, right, or possession). ▶ Law refuse or resign a right or position, especially one as an heir or trustee. **2** refuse to recognize any longer. **3** abandon (a cause, bad habit, or way of life).
– DERIVATIVES **renounceable** adj. **renouncement** n. **renouncer** n.
– ORIGIN Middle English: from Old French *renoncer*, from Latin *renuntiare* 'protest against'.

renovate /ˈrɛnəveɪt/ ■ v. restore (something old) to a good state of repair.
– DERIVATIVES **renovation** n. **renovator** n.
– ORIGIN C16 (*renovation* Middle English): from Latin *renovare* 'make new again'.

renown ■ n. the state of being famous.
– DERIVATIVES **renowned** adj.
– ORIGIN Middle English: from Anglo-Norman French *renoun*, from Old French *renomer* 'make famous', from *re-* (expressing intensive force) + *nomer* 'to name'.

rent¹ ■ n. **1** a tenant's regular payment to a landlord for the use of property or land. **2** a sum paid for the hire of equipment. ■ v. pay someone for the use of. ▶ let someone use (something) in return for payment.
– DERIVATIVES **rentability** n. **rentable** adj. **renter** n.
– ORIGIN Middle English: from Old French *rente*, from a root shared by RENDER.

rent² ■ n. a large tear in a piece of fabric.
– ORIGIN C16: from obsolete *rent* 'pull to pieces', var. of REND.

rent³ past and past participle of REND.

rent-a- ■ comb. form often humorous denoting availability for hire of a specified thing: *rent-a-crowd*.

rental ■ n. an amount paid or received as rent. ▶ the action of renting. ■ adj. of, relating to, or available for rent.

rent boy ■ n. informal a young male prostitute.

rent roll ■ n. a register of a landlord's lands and buildings with the rents due from them. ▶ a landlord's total income from rent.

renumber ■ v. change the number or numbers assigned to.

renunciation ■ n. **1** the action of renouncing. **2** Law a document expressing renunciation.
– DERIVATIVES **renunciant** n. & adj.
– ORIGIN Middle English: from late Latin *renuntiatio(n-)*, from Latin *renuntiare* (see RENOUNCE).

renvoi /ˈrɒvwʌ/ ■ n. Law the action or process of referring a case or dispute to the jurisdiction of another country.
– ORIGIN C19: French, from *renvoyer* 'send back'.

reoccupy ■ v. (-ies, -ied) occupy again.
– DERIVATIVES **reoccupation** n.

reoccur ■ v. (**reoccurred**, **reoccurring**) occur again or repeatedly.
– DERIVATIVES **reoccurrence** n.

reoffend ■ v. commit a further offence.
– DERIVATIVES **reoffender** n.

reopen ■ v. open again.

reorder ■ v. **1** order again. **2** arrange again. ■ n. a renewed or repeated order for goods.

reorganize (also **-ise**) ■ v. change the way in which (something) is organized.
– DERIVATIVES **reorganization** (also **-isation**) n. **reorganizer** (also **-iser**) n.

reorient /riːˈɔːrɪɛnt, -ˈɒr-/ ■ v. **1** change the focus or direction of. **2** (**reorient oneself**) find one's bearings again.
– DERIVATIVES **reorientate** v. **reorientation** n.

Rep. ■ abbrev. **1** (in the US Congress) Representative. **2** Republic. **3** US a Republican.

rep¹ informal ■ n. a representative. ■ v. (**repped**, **repping**) act as a sales representative.

rep² ■ n. informal repertory. ▶ a repertory theatre or company.

rep³ (also **repp**) ■ n. a fabric with a ribbed surface, used in curtains and upholstery.

– ORIGIN C19: from French *reps*.

rep⁴ ■ n. (in bodybuilding) a repetition of a set of exercises. ■ v. (as an instruction in knitting patterns) repeat.

repack ■ v. pack (a suitcase or bag) again.

repackage ■ v. package again or differently.

repaginate ■ v. renumber the pages of.
– DERIVATIVES **repagination** n.

repaid past and past participle of REPAY.

repaint ■ v. cover with a new coat of paint. ■ n. an act of repainting.

repair¹ ■ v. **1** restore (something damaged, worn, or faulty) to a good condition. **2** set right (a rift in relations). ■ n. **1** the action of repairing. ▶ a result of this. **2** the relative physical condition of an object.
– DERIVATIVES **repairable** adj. **repairer** n.
– ORIGIN Middle English: from Old French *reparer*, from Latin *reparare*, from *re-* 'back' + *parare* 'make ready'.

repair² ■ v. (**repair to**) formal or humorous go to (a place).
– ORIGIN Middle English: from Old French *repairer*, from late Latin *repatriare* (see REPATRIATE).

reparable /ˈrɛp(ə)rəb(ə)l/ ■ adj. able to be repaired or rectified.
– ORIGIN C16: from Latin *reparabilis*, from *reparare* (see REPAIR¹).

reparation /ˌrɛpəˈreɪʃ(ə)n/ ■ n. **1** the making of amends for a wrong. ▶ (**reparations**) the compensation for war damage paid by a defeated state. **2** the action of repairing something.
– DERIVATIVES **reparative** /ˈrɛp(ə)rətɪv, rɪˈparətɪv/ adj.
– ORIGIN Middle English: from late Latin *reparatio(n-)*, from *reparare* (see REPAIR¹).

repartee /ˌrɛpɑːˈtiː/ ■ n. conversation or speech characterized by quick, witty comments or replies.
– ORIGIN C17: from French *repartie* 'replied promptly', from *repartir*, from *re-* 'again' + *partir* 'set off'.

repast /rɪˈpɑːst/ ■ n. formal a meal.
– ORIGIN Middle English: from Old French, from late Latin *repascere*, from *re-* (expressing intensive force) + *pascere* 'to feed'.

repatriate /riːˈpatrɪeɪt, -ˈpeɪ-/ ■ v. send (someone) back to their own country. ■ n. a person who has been repatriated.
– DERIVATIVES **repatriation** n.
– ORIGIN C17 (*repatriation* C16): from late Latin *repatriare* 'return to one's country'.

repay ■ v. (past and past part. **repaid**) **1** pay back (a loan). ▶ pay back money owed to (someone). **2** do or give something as recompense for (a favour or kindness received). **3** be worth subjecting to (a specified action).
– DERIVATIVES **repayable** adj. **repayment** n.

repayment mortgage ■ n. a mortgage in which the borrower repays the capital and interest together in fixed instalments over a fixed period.

repeal ■ v. revoke or annul (a law or act of parliament). ■ n. the action of repealing.
– DERIVATIVES **repealable** adj.
– ORIGIN Middle English: from Anglo-Norman French *repeler*, from Old French *re-* (expressing reversal) + *apeler* 'to call, appeal'.

repeat ■ v. **1** say or do again. ▶ (**repeat oneself**) say or do the same thing again. **2** (of food) be tasted after being swallowed, as a result of indigestion. ■ n. **1** an instance of repeating or being repeated. ▶ [as modifier] occurring, done, or used more than once: *a repeat prescription*. **2** a repeated broadcast of a television or radio programme. **3** a decorative pattern which is repeated uniformly over a surface.
– DERIVATIVES **repeatability** n. **repeatable** adj. **repeated** adj. **repeatedly** adv. **repeater** n. **repeating** adj.
– ORIGIN Middle English: from Latin *repetere*, from *re-* 'back' + *petere* 'seek'.

repêchage /ˈrɛpəʃɑːʒ/ ■ n. (in rowing and other sports) a contest in which the runners-up in the eliminating heats compete for a place in the final.
– ORIGIN C20: French, from *repêcher* 'fish out, rescue'.

repel ■ v. (**repelled**, **repelling**) **1** drive or force back or away. **2** be repulsive or distasteful to. **3** (of a magnetic pole or electric field) force (something similarly

magnetized or charged) away. **4** (of a substance) resist mixing with or be impervious to.
– DERIVATIVES **repeller** n.
– ORIGIN Middle English: from Latin *repellere*, from *re-* 'back' + *pellere* 'to drive'.

repellent (also **repellant**) ■ adj. **1** able to repel a particular thing; impervious to: *water-repellent nylon*. **2** causing disgust or distaste. ■ n. **1** a substance that dissuades insects or other pests from approaching or settling. **2** a substance used to treat something to make it impervious to water or dirt.
– DERIVATIVES **repellence** n. **repellency** n. **repellently** adv.

repent ■ v. feel or express sincere regret or remorse.
– DERIVATIVES **repentance** n. **repentant** adj. **repenter** n.
– ORIGIN Middle English: from Old French *repentir*, from Latin *paenitere* 'cause to repent'.

repercussion ■ n. (usu. **repercussions**) a consequence of an event or action.
– DERIVATIVES **repercussive** adj.
– ORIGIN Middle English: from Latin *repercussio(n-)*, from *repercutere* 'cause to rebound, push back'.

repertoire /ˈrɛpətwɑː/ ■ n. the body of pieces known or regularly performed by a performer or company.
– ORIGIN C19: from French *répertoire*, from late Latin *repertorium* (see REPERTORY).

repertory /ˈrɛpət(ə)ri/ ■ n. (pl. **-ies**) **1** the performance by a company of the plays, operas, or ballets in its repertoire at regular short intervals. **2** another term for REPERTOIRE. **3** a repository or collection.
– ORIGIN C16: from late Latin *repertorium*, from Latin *reperire* 'find, discover'.

repertory company ■ n. a theatrical company that performs plays from its repertoire for regular short periods of time.

répétiteur /rɛˌpɛtɪˈtəː/ ■ n. a tutor or coach of ballet dancers or musicians, especially opera singers.
– ORIGIN from French.

repetition ■ n. the act or an instance of repeating or being repeated. ▸ a thing that repeats another.
– DERIVATIVES **repetitional** adj. **repetitious** adj. **repetitiously** adv. **repetitiousness** n.
– ORIGIN Middle English: from Latin *repetitio(n-)*, from *repetere* (see REPEAT).

repetitive ■ adj. containing or characterized by repetition.
– DERIVATIVES **repetitively** adv. **repetitiveness** n.

repetitive strain injury ■ n. a condition in which the prolonged performance of repetitive actions, typically with the hands, causes pain or impairment of function in the tendons and muscles involved.

rephrase ■ v. express in an alternative way.

repine ■ v. poetic/literary be discontented; fret.
– ORIGIN C16: from RE- + PINE², on the pattern of *repent*.

replace ■ v. **1** take the place of. **2** provide a substitute for. **3** put back in a previous place or position.
– DERIVATIVES **replaceable** adj. **replacement** n. **replacer** n.

replan ■ v. (**replanned**, **replanning**) plan (something) differently or again.

replant ■ v. plant again, especially in a new pot or site. ▸ provide (an area) with new plants or trees.

replay ■ v. **1** play back (a recording). **2** play (a match) again. ■ n. the act or an instance of replaying.

replenish ■ v. **1** fill up again. **2** restore to a former level or condition.
– DERIVATIVES **replenisher** n. **replenishment** n.
– ORIGIN Middle English: from Old French *repleniss-*, *replenir*, from *re-* 'again' + *plenir* 'fill'.

replete /rɪˈpliːt/ ■ adj. **1** filled or well-supplied with something. **2** very full with food; sated.
– DERIVATIVES **repletion** n.
– ORIGIN Middle English: from Old French *replet(e)* or Latin *repletus* 'filled up', from *replere*, from *re-* 'back, again' + *plere* 'fill'.

replica ■ n. an exact copy or model of something, especially one on a smaller scale.
– ORIGIN C18: from Italian, from *replicare* 'to reply'.

replicase /ˈrɛplɪkeɪz/ ■ n. Biochemistry an enzyme which catalyses the synthesis of a complementary RNA molecule using an RNA template.
– ORIGIN 1960s: from REPLICATE.

replicate ■ v. /ˈrɛplɪkeɪt/ make an exact copy of; reproduce. ▸ (**replicate itself**) (of genetic material or a living organism) reproduce or give rise to a copy of itself. ▸ repeat (a scientific experiment or trial) to obtain a consistent result. ■ adj. /ˈrɛplɪkət/ of the nature of a copy. ▸ of or relating to a replicated experiment or trial. ■ n. /ˈrɛplɪkət/ a close or exact copy; a replica. ▸ a replicated experiment or trial.
– DERIVATIVES **replicability** /ˌrɛplɪkəˈbɪlɪti/ n. **replicable** /ˈrɛplɪkəb(ə)l/ adj. **replication** n. **replicative** adj.
– ORIGIN Middle English: from Latin *replicare*, from *re-* 'back, again' + *plicare* 'to fold'.

replicator ■ n. **1** a thing which replicates another. **2** Biology a structural gene at which replication of a specific replicon is believed to be initiated.

replicon /ˈrɛplɪkɒn/ ■ n. Biology a nucleic acid molecule, or part of one, which replicates as a unit, beginning at a specific site within it.
– ORIGIN 1960s: from *replication* (see REPLICATE).

reply ■ v. (**-ies, -ied**) say or write something in response to something said or written. ■ n. (pl. **-ies**) **1** the action of replying. **2** a spoken or written response. ▸ Law a plaintiff's response to the defendant's plea.
– DERIVATIVES **replier** n.
– ORIGIN Middle English: from Old French *replier*, from Latin *replicare* 'repeat', later 'make a reply' (see REPLICATE).

repopulate ■ v. introduce a population into (a previously occupied area or country).
– DERIVATIVES **repopulation** n.

repo rate ■ n. the interest rate set by a central bank for lending to other banks, used as the benchmark for interest rates generally.
– ORIGIN 1960s: shortening of REPURCHASE.

report ■ v. **1** give a spoken or written account of something. ▸ convey information about an event or situation. **2** make a formal complaint about. **3** present oneself as having arrived at a particular place or as ready to do something. **4** (**report to**) be responsible to (a supervisor or manager). ■ n. **1** an account given of a matter after investigation or consideration. **2** a piece of information about an event or situation. ▸ talk; rumour. **3** a teacher's written assessment of a pupil's work and progress. **4** Law a detailed formal account of a case heard in a court. **5** a sudden loud noise of or like an explosion or gunfire.
– DERIVATIVES **reportable** adj. **reported** adj. **reportedly** adv.
– ORIGIN Middle English: from Old French *reporter* (v.), *report* (n.), from Latin *reportare* 'bring back'.

reportage /ˌrɛpɔːˈtɑːʒ, rɪˈpɔːtɪdʒ/ ■ n. the reporting of news by the press and the broadcasting media. ▸ factual, journalistic presentation in a book or other text.
– ORIGIN C17: French, from Old French *reporter* (see REPORT).

report back ■ n. an account of something a person or group has been asked to do or investigate. ■ v. give a report back.

report card ■ n. **1** a teacher's written assessment of a pupil's work and progress. **2** an evaluation of performance.

reported speech ■ n. a speaker's words reported in subordinate clauses governed by a verb conveying the action of speaking, with the required changes of person and tense (e.g. *he said that he would go*, based on *I will go*). Contrasted with DIRECT SPEECH.

reporter ■ n. a person who reports news for a newspaper or broadcasting company.

repose¹ /rɪˈpəʊz/ ■ n. **1** a state of restfulness or tranquillity. **2** composure. ■ v. rest. ▸ be situated or kept in a particular place.
– DERIVATIVES **reposeful** adj.
– ORIGIN Middle English: from Old French *repos* (n.), *reposer* (v.), from late Latin *repausare*, from *re-* (expressing intensive force) + *pausare* 'to pause'.

repose

repose² /rɪˈpəʊz/ ■ v. (**repose something in**) place something, especially one's confidence or trust, in.
– ORIGIN Middle English: from RE- + POSE, suggested by Latin *reponere* 'replace'.

reposition ■ v. place in a different position; adjust or alter the position of. ▸ change the image of (a company, product, etc.) to target a different market.

repository /rɪˈpɒzɪt(ə)ri/ ■ n. (pl. **-ies**) 1 a place where or receptacle in which things are stored. 2 a place where something is found in significant quantities.
– ORIGIN C15: from Old French *repositoire* or Latin *repositorium*, from *reponere* (see REPOSE²).

repossess ■ v. retake possession of (something) when a buyer defaults on payments.
– DERIVATIVES **repossession** n. **repossessor** n.

repot ■ v. (**repotted**, **repotting**) put (a plant) in another pot.

repp ■ n. variant spelling of REP³.

repr. ■ abbrev. reprint or reprinted.

reprehend /ˌreprɪˈhend/ ■ v. reprimand.
– DERIVATIVES **reprehension** n.
– ORIGIN Middle English: from Latin *reprehendere* 'seize, check, rebuke'.

reprehensible ■ adj. deserving censure or condemnation.
– DERIVATIVES **reprehensibility** n. **reprehensibly** adv.
– ORIGIN Middle English: from late Latin *reprehensibilis*, from *reprehendere* (see REPREHEND).

represent ■ v. 1 be entitled or appointed to act or speak for. ▸ be an elected Member of Parliament or member of a legislature for. ▸ act as a substitute for. 2 constitute; amount to. ▸ be a specimen or example of; typify. ▸ (**be represented**) be present to a particular degree. 3 depict in a work of art. ▸ portray in a particular way. ▸ signify, symbolize, or embody. 4 formal state or point out.
– DERIVATIVES **representability** n. **representable** adj.
– ORIGIN Middle English: from Old French *representer* or Latin *repraesentare*, from *re-* (expressing intensive force) + *praesentare* 'to present'.

re-present ■ v. present again.
– DERIVATIVES **re-presentation** n.

representation ■ n. 1 the action or an instance of representing or being represented. 2 an image, model, or other depiction of something. 3 (**representations**) statements made to an authority to communicate an opinion or register a protest.

representational ■ adj. 1 of, relating to, or characterized by representation. 2 relating to or denoting art which depicts the physical appearance of things.

representationalism /ˌreprɪzenˈteɪʃ(ə)n(ə)lɪz(ə)m/ (also **representationism**) ■ n. 1 the practice or advocacy of representational art. 2 Philosophy the doctrine that thought is the manipulation of mental representations which correspond to external states or objects.
– DERIVATIVES **representationalist** (also **representationist**) adj. & n.

representative ■ adj. 1 typical of a class or group. ▸ containing typical examples of many or all types. 2 (of a legislative or deliberative assembly) consisting of people chosen to act and speak on behalf of a wider group. ▸ (of a government or political system) based on such representation of the people. 3 serving as a portrayal of something. ■ n. 1 a person chosen or appointed to act or speak for another or others. 2 an agent of a firm who travels to potential clients to sell its products. 3 an example of a class or group.
– DERIVATIVES **representatively** adv. **representativeness** n.

representivity (also **representativity**) ■ n. the inclusion of a representative proportion (from a specified group). ▸ chiefly S. African the inclusion of a population group that has been under-represented in the past, especially previously disadvantaged people.

repress ■ v. 1 subdue by force. 2 restrain, prevent, or inhibit. ▸ suppress (a thought, feeling, or desire) in oneself so that it becomes or remains unconscious. 3 Biology prevent the transcription of (a gene).

– DERIVATIVES **represser** n. **repressible** adj. **repression** n.
– ORIGIN Middle English: from Latin *repress-*, *reprimere* 'press back, check'.

repressed ■ adj. 1 oppressed. 2 (of a thought, feeling, or desire) kept suppressed and unconscious in one's mind. ▸ suppressing one's feelings and desires.

repressive ■ adj. inhibiting or restraining personal freedom; oppressive.
– DERIVATIVES **repressively** adv. **repressiveness** n.

reprieve ■ v. cancel or postpone the punishment or demise of. ■ n. such a cancellation or postponement.
– ORIGIN C15: from Anglo-Norman French *repris*, from *reprendre*, from Latin *re-* 'back' + *prehendere* 'seize'.

reprimand /ˈreprɪmɑːnd/ ■ n. a formal expression of disapproval. ■ v. address a reprimand to.
– ORIGIN C17: from French *réprimande*, from Latin *reprimenda* 'things to be held in check', from *reprimere* (see REPRESS).

reprint ■ v. print again or in a different form. ■ n. 1 an act of reprinting. 2 a copy of a book or other material that has been reprinted. ▸ an offprint.

reprisal ■ n. an act of retaliation.
– ORIGIN Middle English: from Anglo-Norman French *reprisaille*, from medieval Latin *reprisalia*, from Latin *repraehendere* (see REPREHEND).

reprise /rɪˈpriːz/ ■ n. 1 a repeated passage in music. 2 a further performance of something. ■ v. repeat (a piece of music or a performance).
– ORIGIN C18: French, 'taken up again', from *reprendre* (see REPRIEVE).

repro ■ n. (pl. **-os**) informal a reproduction or copy. ▸ the reproduction or copying of a document or image.

reproach ■ v. 1 express to (someone) one's disapproval of or disappointment in their actions. 2 (**reproach someone with**) accuse someone of. ■ n. an expression of disapproval or disappointment.
– PHRASES **above** (or **beyond**) **reproach** such that no criticism can be made; perfect.
– DERIVATIVES **reproachable** adj. **reproacher** n. **reproaching** adj. **reproachingly** adv.
– ORIGIN Middle English: from Old French *reprochier* (v.), from a base meaning 'bring back close', from Latin *prope* 'near'.

reproachful ■ adj. expressing disapproval or disappointment.
– DERIVATIVES **reproachfully** adv. **reproachfulness** n.

reprobate /ˈreprəbeɪt/ ■ n. an unprincipled person. ■ adj. unprincipled.
– DERIVATIVES **reprobation** n.
– ORIGIN Middle English: from Latin *reprobare* 'disapprove'.

reprocess ■ v. process (something, especially spent nuclear fuel) again or differently, in order to reuse it.

reproduce ■ v. 1 produce a copy or representation of. ▸ create something in a different medium or context that is very similar to. 2 (of an organism) produce offspring.
– DERIVATIVES **reproducer** n. **reproducibility** n. **reproducible** adj. **reproducibly** adv.

reproduction ■ n. 1 the action or process of reproducing. ▸ the quality of reproduced sound. 2 a copy of a work of art, especially a print made of a painting. ▸ [as modifier] made to imitate the style of an earlier period or particular craftsman.

reproductive ■ adj. relating to or effecting reproduction: *the female reproductive system.*
– DERIVATIVES **reproductively** adv. **reproductiveness** n. **reproductivity** n.

reprogram (also **reprogramme**) ■ v. (**reprogrammed**, **reprogramming**; US also **reprogramed**, **reprograming**) program (a computer) again.
– DERIVATIVES **reprogrammable** adj.

reprographics ■ pl. n. [treated as sing.] reprography.

reprography /rɪˈprɒɡrəfi/ ■ n. the science and practice of reproducing documents and graphic material.
– DERIVATIVES **reprographer** n. **reprographic** adj.
– ORIGIN 1960s: from REPRODUCE + -GRAPHY.

reproof¹ ■ n. a rebuke or reprimand.
– ORIGIN Middle English: from Old French *reprove*, from *reprover* 'reprove'.

reprove ■ v. rebuke or reprimand.
– DERIVATIVES **reprovable** adj. **reprover** n. **reproving** adj. **reprovingly** adv.
– ORIGIN Middle English: from Old French *reprover*, from late Latin *reprobare* (see REPROBATE).

reptile ■ n. **1** a cold-blooded vertebrate animal of a class (Reptilia) that includes snakes, lizards, crocodiles, turtles, and tortoises, typically having a dry scaly skin and laying soft-shelled eggs on land. **2** informal a person regarded with loathing and contempt.
– DERIVATIVES **reptilian** adj. & n.
– ORIGIN Middle English: from late Latin *reptilis*, from Latin *repere* 'crawl'.

republic ■ n. a state in which supreme power is held by the people and their elected representatives, and which has an elected or nominated president rather than a monarch.
– ORIGIN C16: from French *république*, from Latin *respublica*, from *res* 'concern' + *publicus* 'of the people, public'.

republican ■ adj. **1** belonging to or characteristic of a republic. **2** advocating republican government. **3** (**Republican**) (in the US) supporting the Republican Party. ■ n. **1** a person advocating republican government. **2** (**Republican**) (in the US) a member or supporter of the Republican Party. **3** (**Republican**) an advocate of a united Ireland.
– DERIVATIVES **republicanism** n.

repudiate /rɪˈpjuːdɪeɪt/ ■ v. **1** refuse to accept or be associated with. **2** deny the truth or validity of. **3** chiefly Law refuse to fulfil or discharge (an agreement, obligation, or debt). **4** archaic disown or divorce (one's wife).
– DERIVATIVES **repudiation** n. **repudiator** n. **repudiatory** /rɪˈpjuːdɪətˌ(ə)ri/ adj. (Law).
– ORIGIN Middle English: from Latin *repudiatus* 'divorced, cast off', from *repudium* 'divorce'.

repugnance /rɪˈpʌɡnəns/ ■ n. intense disgust.
– DERIVATIVES **repugnancy** n.
– ORIGIN Middle English: from Old French *repugnance* or Latin *repugnantia*, from *repugnare* 'oppose'.

repugnant ■ adj. **1** extremely distasteful; unacceptable. **2** (**repugnant to**) in conflict with; incompatible with.
– DERIVATIVES **repugnantly** adv.

repulse ■ v. **1** drive back (an attacking enemy) by force. ▸ rebuff or refuse to accept. **2** cause to feel intense distaste or disgust. ■ n. the action or an instant of repulsing or being repulsed.
– ORIGIN Middle English: from Latin *repuls-*, *repellere* (see REPEL).

repulsion ■ n. **1** a feeling of intense distaste or disgust. **2** Physics a force under the influence of which objects tend to move away from each other, e.g. through having the same magnetic polarity or electric charge.

repulsive ■ adj. **1** arousing intense distaste or disgust. **2** of or relating to repulsion between physical objects.
– DERIVATIVES **repulsively** adv. **repulsiveness** n.

repurchase ■ v. buy (something) back. ■ n. the action of buying something back.

reputable ■ adj. having a good reputation.
– DERIVATIVES **reputably** adv.
– ORIGIN C17: from medieval Latin *reputabilis*, from *reputare* (see REPUTE).

reputation ■ n. the beliefs or opinions that are generally held about someone or something. ▸ a widespread belief that someone or something has a particular characteristic.
– ORIGIN Middle English: from Latin *reputatio(n-)*, from *reputare* (see REPUTE).

repute ■ n. **1** the opinion generally held of someone or something. **2** the state of being highly regarded. ■ v. (**be reputed**) be generally regarded as having done something or as having particular characteristics. ▸ [as adj. **reputed**] being generally believed to exist.
– DERIVATIVES **reputedly** adv.
– ORIGIN Middle English: from Old French *reputer* or Latin *reputare* 'think over'.

request ■ n. an act of asking politely or formally for something. ▸ a thing that is asked for in such a way. ■ v. politely or formally ask for. ▸ politely or formally ask (someone) to do something.
– DERIVATIVES **requester** n.

– ORIGIN Middle English: from Old French *requeste* (n.), from Latin *requirere* (see REQUIRE).

requiem /ˈrɛkwɪəm, -ɪɛm/ ■ n. **1** a Mass for the repose of the souls of the dead. **2** a musical composition setting parts of such a Mass. **3** an act or token of remembrance.
– ORIGIN Middle English: from Latin (first word of the Mass), from *requies* 'rest'.

require ■ v. **1** need or depend on. ▸ wish to have. **2** instruct or expect (someone) to do something. ▸ (**require something of**) regard an action or quality as due from. ▸ specify as compulsory: *required by law*.
– DERIVATIVES **requirer** n.
– ORIGIN Middle English: from Latin *requirere*, from *re-* (expressing intensive force) + *quaerere* 'seek'.

requirement ■ n. **1** a thing that is needed or wanted. **2** a thing that is compulsory; a necessary condition.

requisite /ˈrɛkwɪzɪt/ ■ adj. made necessary by particular circumstances or regulations. ■ n. a thing that is necessary for the achievement of a specified end.
– ORIGIN Middle English: from Latin *requisitus* 'searched for, deemed necessary', from *requirere* (see REQUIRE).

requisition /ˌrɛkwɪˈzɪʃ(ə)n/ ■ n. **1** an official order laying claim to the use of property or materials. **2** the appropriation of goods for military or public use. **3** a formal written demand that something should be performed or put into operation. ■ v. demand the use, supply, or performance of through the issue of a requisition.
– DERIVATIVES **requisitioner** n.
– ORIGIN Middle English: from Latin *requisitio(n-)*, from *requirere* (see REQUIRE).

requite /rɪˈkwaɪt/ ■ v. formal **1** make appropriate return for (a favour or demonstration of affection, or a wrong-doing). **2** return a favour to (someone).
– DERIVATIVES **requital** n.
– ORIGIN C16: from RE- + obsolete *quite*, var. of QUIT.

reran past of RERUN.

reread ■ v. (past and past part. **reread**) read (a text) again. ■ n. an act of rereading.

reredos /ˈrɪədɒs/ ■ n. (pl. same) an ornamental screen at the back of an altar in a church.
– ORIGIN Middle English: from Old French *areredos*, from *arere* 'behind' + *dos* 'back'.

re-release ■ v. release (a recording or film) again. ■ n. a re-released recording or film.

re-route ■ v. send by or along a different route.

rerun ■ v. (**rerunning**; past **reran**; past part. **rerun**) show, stage, or perform again. ■ n. a rerun event, competition, or programme.

resale ■ n. the sale of a thing previously bought.
– DERIVATIVES **resaleable** (also **resalable**) adj.

resat past and past participle of RESIT.

reschedule ■ v. **1** change the time of (a planned event). **2** arrange a new scheme of repayments of (a debt).

rescind /rɪˈsɪnd/ ■ v. revoke, cancel, or repeal (a law, order, or agreement).
– DERIVATIVES **rescindable** adj.
– ORIGIN C16: from Latin *rescindere*, from *re-* (expressing intensive force) + *scindere* 'to divide, split'.

rescission /rɪˈsɪʒ(ə)n/ ■ n. formal the rescinding of a law, order, or agreement.
– ORIGIN C17: from late Latin *rescissio(n-)*, from *rescindere* (see RESCIND).

rescue ■ v. (**rescues**, **rescued**, **rescuing**) save from a dangerous or distressing situation. ■ n. an act of rescuing or being rescued.
– DERIVATIVES **rescuable** adj. **rescuer** n.
– ORIGIN Middle English: from Old French *rescoure* from Latin *re-* (expressing intensive force) + *excutere* 'shake out, discard'.

reseal ■ v. seal (something) again.
– DERIVATIVES **resealable** adj.

research /rɪˈsəːtʃ, ˈriːsəːtʃ/ ■ n. the systematic investigation into and study of materials and sources in

research and development

order to establish facts or verify information. ■ v. carry out research into.
– DERIVATIVES **researchable** adj. **researcher** n.
– ORIGIN C16: from obsolete French *recerche* (n.), *recercher* (v.), from Old French *re-* (expressing intensive force) + *cerchier* 'to search'.

research and development ■ n. (in industry) work directed towards innovation in and improvement of products and processes.

reseat ■ v. 1 seat again. 2 realign or repair (something) to fit it into its correct position. 3 equip with new seats.

resect /rɪˈsɛkt/ ■ v. [often as adj. **resected**] Surgery cut out (tissue or part of an organ).
– DERIVATIVES **resectable** adj. **resection** n. **resectional** adj.
– ORIGIN C17: from Latin *resecare* 'to cut off', from *re-* 'back' + *secare* 'to cut'.

reselect ■ v. select again or differently.
– DERIVATIVES **reselection** n.

resell ■ v. (past and past part. **resold**) sell (something one has bought) to someone else.
– DERIVATIVES **reseller** n.

resemblance ■ n. the state of resembling. ▸ a way in which two or more things resemble each other.
– DERIVATIVES **resemblant** adj.

resemble ■ v. have a similar appearance to or features in common with.
– ORIGIN Middle English: from Old French *resembler*, from Latin *similare*, from *similis* 'like'.

resent ■ v. feel bitterness or indignation at.
– ORIGIN C16: from obsolete French *resentir*, from *re-* (expressing intensive force) + *sentir* 'feel', from Latin *sentire*.

resentful ■ adj. feeling or expressing bitterness or indignation.
– DERIVATIVES **resentfully** adv. **resentfulness** n.

resentment ■ n. bitterness; indignation.

reserpine /rɪˈsɜːpiːn/ ■ n. Medicine a compound of the alkaloid class obtained from a snakeroot plant, used in the treatment of hypertension.
– ORIGIN 1950s: from the species name *R(auwolfia) serp(entina)*, named after the German botanist Leonhard Rauwolf.

reservation ■ n. 1 the action of reserving. ▸ an arrangement whereby something has been reserved. 2 an area of land set aside for occupation by indigenous peoples. 3 Law a right or interest retained in an estate being conveyed. 4 a qualification or expression of doubt attached to a statement or claim.

reserve ■ v. 1 retain for future use. 2 arrange for (a seat, ticket, etc.) to be kept for the use of a particular person. 3 retain or hold (a right or entitlement). 4 refrain from delivering (a judgement or decision) without due consideration or evidence. ■ n. 1 (often **reserves**) a reserved supply of a commodity. ▸ funds kept available by a bank, company, or government. ▸ a part of a company's profits added to capital rather than paid as a dividend. 2 a force or body of troops used to reinforce or protect others, or additional to the regular forces and available in an emergency. 3 an extra player in a team, serving as a possible substitute. ▸ (**the reserves**) the second-choice team. 4 another term for RESERVATION (in sense 2). 5 a protected area for wildlife. 6 a lack of warmth or openness. 7 qualification or doubt attached to a statement or claim.
– DERIVATIVES **reservable** adj. **reserver** n.
– ORIGIN Middle English: from Old French *reserver*, from Latin *reservare* 'keep back'.

reserve bank ■ n. 1 S. African & Austral./NZ a central bank. 2 (in the US) a regional bank operating under and implementing the policies of the Federal Reserve.

reserve currency ■ n. a strong currency widely used in international trade that a central bank is prepared to hold as part of its foreign exchange reserves.

reserved ■ adj. slow to reveal emotion or opinions.
– DERIVATIVES **reservedly** adv. **reservedness** n.

reserved word ■ n. Computing a word in a programming language which has a fixed meaning and cannot be redefined by the programmer.

reserve price ■ n. the price stipulated as the lowest acceptable by the seller for an item sold at auction.

reservist ■ n. a member of a military reserve force.

reservoir ■ n. 1 a large natural or artificial lake used as a source of water supply. ▸ S. African a large storage tank used as a water supply. ▸ a supply or source of something. 2 a place where fluid collects, especially in rock strata or in the body. 3 a receptacle or part of a machine designed to hold fluid.
– ORIGIN C17: from French *réservoir*, from *réserver* 'to reserve, keep'.

reset ■ v. (**resetting**; past and past part. **reset**) 1 set again or differently. 2 Electronics cause (a binary device) to enter the state representing the numeral 0.
– DERIVATIVES **resettability** n. **resettable** adj.

resettle ■ v. settle or cause to settle in a different place.
– DERIVATIVES **resettlement** n.

res gestae /reɪz ˈɡɛstaɪ, riːz ˈdʒɛstiː/ ■ pl. n. Law the events, circumstances, or remarks which relate to a particular case, especially as constituting admissible evidence in a court of law.
– ORIGIN Latin, 'things done'.

reshape ■ v. shape or form (something) differently or again.

reshuffle ■ v. 1 interchange the positions of (members of a team, especially government ministers). 2 rearrange. ■ n. an act of reshuffling.

reside ■ v. 1 have one's permanent home in a particular place. 2 (of a right or legal power) belong to a person or body. 3 (of a quality) be present or inherent in something.
– ORIGIN Middle English: prob. a back-formation from RESIDENT, influenced by French *résider* or Latin *residere* 'remain'.

residence ■ n. 1 the fact of residing somewhere. 2 the place where a person resides; a person's home. 3 the official house of a government minister or other official figure. 4 short for hall of residence (see HALL sense 3).
– PHRASES **artist** (or **writer**) **in residence** an artist or writer who is based for a set period within a college or other institution and is available for teaching purposes.

residence time ■ n. technical the average length of time during which a substance, object, etc. is in a given location or condition.

residency ■ n. (pl. **-ies**) 1 the fact of living in a place. 2 a residential post held by an artist or writer. 3 N. Amer. a period of specialized medical training in a hospital; the position of a resident.

resident ■ n. 1 a person who lives somewhere on a long-term basis. ▸ a bird, butterfly, or other animal of a species that does not migrate. 2 N. Amer. a medical graduate engaged in specialized practice under supervision in a hospital. ■ adj. 1 living somewhere on a long-term basis. ▸ having quarters on the premises of one's work. ▸ attached to and working regularly for a particular institution. ▸ (of a bird, butterfly, or other animal) non-migratory. 2 (of a computer program, file, etc.) immediately available in computer memory, rather than having to be loaded from elsewhere.
– ORIGIN Middle English: from Latin *residere* 'remain'.

residential ■ adj. 1 designed for people to live in. ▸ providing accommodation in addition to other services. ▸ occupied by private houses. 2 concerning or relating to residence.
– DERIVATIVES **residentially** adv.

residentiary ■ adj. 1 relating to or involving residence. 2 (of a canon) required to live officially in a cathedral or collegiate church.

residua plural form of RESIDUUM.

residual ■ adj. 1 remaining after the greater part or quantity has gone or been subtracted. ▸ (of a physical state or property) remaining after the removal of or present in the absence of a causative agent. 2 (of an experimental or arithmetical error) not accounted for or eliminated. 3 (of a soil or other deposit) formed in situ by weathering. ■ n. 1 a residual quantity. 2 a difference between a value

measured in a scientific experiment and the theoretical or true value.
— DERIVATIVES **residually** adv.

residual current device ∎ n. a current-activated circuit-breaker used as a safety device for mains-operated electrical tools and appliances.

residuary ∎ adj. **1** technical residual. **2** Law of or relating to the residue of an estate.

residue /ˈrɛzɪdjuː/ ∎ n. **1** a small amount of something that remains after the main part has gone or been taken or used. ▸ a substance that remains after a process such as combustion or evaporation. **2** Law the part of an estate that is left after the payment of charges, debts, and bequests.
— ORIGIN Middle English: from Old French *residu*, from Latin *residuum* (see RESIDUUM).

residuum /rɪˈzɪdjuəm/ ∎ n. (pl. **residua** /-djuə/) chiefly technical a residue.
— ORIGIN C17: from Latin, from *residuus*, *residere* 'to remain'.

resign ∎ v. **1** voluntarily leave a job or position of office. **2** (**be resigned**) accept that something undesirable cannot be avoided. **3** archaic surrender oneself to another's guidance.
— DERIVATIVES **resigned** adj. **resignedly** adv. **resignedness** n.
— ORIGIN Middle English: from Old French *resigner*, from Latin *resignare* 'unseal, cancel'.

re-sign ∎ v. sign (a document or contract) again.

resignation ∎ n. **1** an act of resigning. ▸ a document conveying an intention to resign. **2** acceptance of something undesirable but inevitable.

resilient ∎ adj. **1** (of a substance or object) able to recoil or spring back into shape after bending, stretching, or being compressed. **2** (of a person or animal) able to withstand or recover quickly from difficult conditions.
— DERIVATIVES **resilience** n. **resiliency** n. **resiliently** adv.
— ORIGIN C17: from Latin *resilient-* 'leaping back', from *resilire* 'to recoil'.

resin /ˈrɛzɪn/ ∎ n. **1** a sticky flammable organic substance exuded by some trees and other plants. **2** a solid or liquid synthetic organic polymer used as the basis of plastics, adhesives, varnishes, etc. ∎ v. (**resined**, **resining**) rub or treat with resin.
— DERIVATIVES **resined** adj. **resinous** adj.
— ORIGIN Middle English: from Latin *resina*; rel. to Greek *rhētinē* 'pine resin'.

res ipsa loquitur /ˌreɪz ˌɪpsə ˈlɒkwɪtə/ ∎ n. Law the principle that the occurrence of an accident implies negligence.
— ORIGIN Latin, 'the matter speaks for itself'.

resist ∎ v. **1** withstand the action or effect of. **2** try to prevent by action or argument. **3** refrain from (something tempting). **4** struggle against. ∎ n. a resistant substance applied as a coating to protect a surface during some process, for example to prevent dye or glaze adhering.
— DERIVATIVES **resister** n. **resistibility** n. **resistible** adj.
— ORIGIN Middle English: from Old French *resister* or Latin *resistere*, from *re-* (expressing opposition) + *sistere* 'stop'.

resistance ∎ n. **1** the action of resisting. **2** armed or violent opposition. **3** (also **resistance movement**) a secret organization resisting political authority. ▸ (**the Resistance**) the underground movement formed in France during the Second World War to fight the German occupying forces and the Vichy government. **4** the impeding effect exerted by one material thing on another. **5** the ability not to be affected by something. ▸ Medicine & Biology lack of sensitivity to a drug, insecticide, etc., especially as a result of continued exposure or genetic change. **6** the degree to which a material or device opposes the passage of an electric current, causing energy dissipation. ▸ a resistor.
— PHRASES **the line** (or **path**) **of least resistance** the easiest course of action.
— DERIVATIVES **resistant** adj.

resistive /rɪˈzɪstɪv/ ∎ adj. **1** technical able to resist something. **2** Physics of or concerning electrical resistance.

resistivity /ˌriːzɪˈstɪvɪti/ ∎ n. Physics a measure of the resisting power of a specified material to the flow of an electric current.

resistor ∎ n. Physics a device having resistance to the passage of an electric current.

resit ∎ v. (**resitting**; past and past part. **resat**) take (an examination) again after failing. ∎ n. an examination held for this purpose.

resite ∎ v. place or situate in a different place.

resize ∎ v. alter the size of (something, especially a computer window or image).

res judicata /reɪz ˌdʒuːdɪˈkɑːtə/ ∎ n. (pl. **res judicatae** /ˌdʒuːdɪˈkɑːtaɪ, ˌdʒuːdɪˈkɑːtiː/) Law a matter that has been adjudicated by a competent court and may not be pursued further by the same parties.
— ORIGIN Latin, 'judged matter'.

reskill ∎ v. teach (a person, especially one who is unemployed) new skills.

resold past and past participle of RESELL.

resolute /ˈrɛzəluːt/ ∎ adj. determined; unwavering.
— DERIVATIVES **resolutely** adv. **resoluteness** n.
— ORIGIN Middle English: from Latin *resolutus* 'loosened, released, paid', from *resolvere* (see RESOLVE).

resolution ∎ n. **1** the quality of being resolute. **2** a firm decision. ▸ a formal expression of opinion or intention agreed on by a legislative body. **3** the action of solving a problem or dispute. **4** Medicine the disappearance of a symptom or condition. **5** the process of reducing or separating something into components. **6** the smallest interval measurable by a telescope or other scientific instrument. **7** the degree of detail visible in a photographic or television image.

resolve ∎ v. **1** settle or find a solution to. ▸ Medicine cause (a symptom or condition) to heal or disappear. **2** decide firmly on a course of action. ▸ (of a legislative body) take a decision by a formal vote. **3** (**resolve something into**) reduce a subject or statement into (separate elements or a more elementary form). **4** (of something seen at a distance) turn into a different form when seen more clearly. ▸ (of optical or photographic equipment) separate or distinguish between (closely adjacent objects). **5** Physics analyse (a force or velocity) into components acting in particular directions. ∎ n. **1** firm determination. **2** US a formal resolution by a legislative body or public meeting.
— DERIVATIVES **resolvable** adj. **resolved** adj. **resolvedly** adv. **resolver** n.
— ORIGIN Middle English: from Latin *resolvere*, from *re-* (expressing intensive force) + *solvere* 'loosen'.

resolving power ∎ n. the ability of an optical instrument or type of film to separate or distinguish small or closely adjacent images.

resonance ∎ n. **1** the quality of being resonant. **2** Physics the reinforcement or prolongation of sound by reflection or synchronous vibration. **3** Mechanics enhanced vibration of an object subjected to an oscillating force close to a natural frequency of the object. **4** the condition in which an electric circuit produces the largest possible response to an applied oscillating signal. **5** Physics a short-lived subatomic particle that is an excited state of a more stable particle. **6** Astronomy the occurrence of a simple ratio between the periods of revolution of two orbiting bodies. **7** Chemistry the state of having a molecular structure which cannot adequately be represented by a single structural formula but is a composite of two or more structures of higher energy.

resonant ∎ adj. **1** (of sound) deep, clear, and continuing to sound or ring. ▸ (of a room, musical instrument, or hollow body) tending to reinforce or prolong sounds, especially by synchronous vibration. ▸ (**resonant with**) filled or resounding with (a sound). **2** having the ability to evoke or suggest enduring images, memories, or emotions. **3** (of a colour) enhancing another or others by contrast. **4** technical relating to or bringing about resonance in a circuit, atom, or other object.
— DERIVATIVES **resonantly** adv.
— ORIGIN C16 (*resonance* Middle English): from Latin *resonant-*, *resonare*, from *re-* (expressing intensive force) + *sonare* 'to sound'.

resonate ∎ v. **1** be resonant. **2** chiefly US (of an idea or action) meet with someone's agreement. **3** technical

resonator

produce electrical or mechanical resonance.
– ORIGIN C19: from Latin *resonare* (see RESOUND).

resonator ■ n. **1** anything that resonates. **2** a body or device that increases the resonance of a sound, especially a hollow part of a musical instrument. **3** an apparatus used for the detection of radio waves.

resorb /rɪˈsɔːb/ ■ v. **1** absorb again. **2** Physiology remove (cells, tissue, etc.) by gradual breakdown into component materials and dispersal in the circulation.
– ORIGIN C17: from Latin *resorbere*, from *re-* (expressing intensive force) + *sorbere* 'absorb'.

resorption /rɪˈzɔːpʃ(ə)n, -ˈsɔːp-/ ■ n. the process or action of resorbing or being resorbed.
– DERIVATIVES **resorptive** adj.

resort ■ v. (**resort to**) turn to and adopt (a strategy or course of action) so as to resolve a difficult situation. ■ n. **1** a place frequented for holidays or recreation or for a particular purpose. **2** the action of resorting to something. ▸ a strategy or course of action resorted to.
– PHRASES **as a first** (or **last** or **final**) **resort** before anything else is attempted (or when all else has failed).
– DERIVATIVES **resorter** n.
– ORIGIN Middle English: from Old French *resortir*, from *re-* 'again' + *sortir* 'come or go out'.

resound /rɪˈzaʊnd/ ■ v. **1** fill or be filled with a ringing, booming, or echoing sound. **2** (of fame, success, etc.) be much talked of. ▸ [as adj. **resounding**] emphatic; unmistakable: *a resounding success*.
– DERIVATIVES **resoundingly** adv.
– ORIGIN Middle English: from RE- + SOUND¹, suggested by Old French *resoner* or Latin *resonare* 'sound again'.

resource /rɪˈsɔːs, rɪˈzɔːs/ ■ n. **1** (usu. **resources**) a stock or supply of materials or assets. **2** an action or strategy adopted in adverse circumstances. ▸ (**resources**) personal attributes and capabilities that sustain one in adverse circumstances. ▸ a teaching aid. ■ v. provide with resources.
– DERIVATIVES **resourceless** adj.
– ORIGIN C17: from obsolete French *ressourse*, from Old French dialect *resourdre* 'rise again, recover', from Latin *surgere* 'to rise'.

resourceful ■ adj. having the ability to find quick and clever ways to overcome difficulties.
– DERIVATIVES **resourcefully** adv. **resourcefulness** n.

respect ■ n. **1** a feeling of deep admiration for someone elicited by their qualities or achievements. ▸ (**respects**) polite greetings. **2** due regard for the feelings or rights of others. **3** a particular aspect, point, or detail. ■ v. **1** feel or have respect for. **2** avoid harming or interfering with. ▸ agree to recognize and abide by.
– PHRASES **in respect of** (or **with respect to**) as regards; with reference to.
– DERIVATIVES **respecter** n. **respectful** adj. **respectfully** adv. **respectfulness** n.
– ORIGIN Middle English: from Latin *respectus*, from *respicere* 'look back at, regard'.

respectable ■ adj. **1** regarded by society as being proper, correct, and good. **2** of some merit or importance. ▸ adequate or acceptable in number, size, or amount.
– DERIVATIVES **respectability** n. **respectably** adv.

respecting ■ prep. with reference or regard to.

respective ■ adj. belonging or relating separately to each of two or more people or things.

respectively ■ adv. separately or individually and in the order already mentioned.

respiration ■ n. **1** the action of breathing. ▸ a single breath. **2** Biology a process in living organisms involving the production of energy, typically with the intake of oxygen and the release of carbon dioxide.
– ORIGIN Middle English: from Latin *respiratio(n-)*, from *respirare* (see RESPIRE).

respirator ■ n. **1** an apparatus worn over the mouth and nose or the entire face to prevent the inhalation of dust, smoke, or other noxious substances. **2** an apparatus used to induce artificial respiration.

respiratory /rɪˈspɪrət(ə)ri, ˈrɛsp(ə)rət(ə)ri, rɪˈspʌɪ-/ ■ adj. of, relating to, or affecting respiration or the organs of respiration.

respiratory tract ■ n. the passage formed by the mouth, nose, throat, and lungs, through which air passes during breathing.

respire ■ v. breathe. ▸ (of a plant) carry out respiration.
– DERIVATIVES **respirable** adj.
– ORIGIN Middle English: from Old French *respirer* or Latin *respirare* 'breathe out'.

respite /ˈrɛspaɪt, -spɪt/ ■ n. a short period of rest or relief from something difficult or unpleasant.
– ORIGIN Middle English: from Old French *respit*, from Latin *respectus* 'refuge, consideration'.

respite care ■ n. temporary care of a sick, elderly, or disabled person, providing relief for their usual carer.

resplendent /rɪˈsplɛnd(ə)nt/ ■ adj. attractive and impressive through being richly colourful or sumptuous.
– DERIVATIVES **resplendence** n. **resplendency** n. **resplendently** adv.
– ORIGIN Middle English: from Latin *resplendent-*, *resplendere* 'shine out'.

respond ■ v. say or do something in reply or as a reaction. ■ n. Architecture a half-pillar or half-pier attached to a wall to support an arch.
– DERIVATIVES **responder** n.
– ORIGIN Middle English: from Old French, from *respondre* 'to answer', from Latin *respondere*, from *re-* 'again' + *spondere* 'to pledge'.

respondent ■ n. **1** a defendant in a lawsuit, especially one in an appeal or divorce case. **2** a person who responds to a questionnaire or an advertisement. ■ adj. **1** in the position of defendant in a lawsuit. **2** responding to something.

response ■ n. **1** an instance of responding; an answer or reaction. **2** Physiology an excitation of a nerve impulse.
– ORIGIN Middle English: from Old French *respons* or Latin *responsum*, from *respondere* (see RESPOND).

responsibility ■ n. (pl. -**ies**) **1** the state or fact of being responsible. **2** the opportunity or ability to act independently and take decisions without authorization. ▸ (often **responsibilities**) a thing which one is required to do as part of a job, role, or legal obligation.

responsible ■ adj. **1** having an obligation to do something, or having control over or care for someone. **2** being the primary cause of something and so able to be blamed or credited for it. ▸ (**responsible to**) reporting to; answerable to. ▸ morally accountable for one's behaviour. **3** (of a job or position) involving important duties or decisions or control over others. **4** capable of being trusted.
– DERIVATIVES **responsibleness** n. **responsibly** adv.
– ORIGIN C16: from obsolete French *responsible*, from Latin *respondere* (see RESPOND).

responsive ■ adj. **1** responding readily and positively. **2** in response; answering.
– DERIVATIVES **responsively** adv. **responsiveness** n.

respray ■ v. /riːˈspreɪ/ spray with a new coat of paint. ■ n. /ˈriːspreɪ/ an instance of respraying.

rest¹ ■ v. **1** cease work or movement in order to relax or recover strength. ▸ allow to be inactive in order to regain or save strength or energy. ▸ lie buried. ▸ (of a problem or subject) be left without further investigation or discussion. **2** place or be placed so as to stay in a specified position. ▸ (**rest on**) (of a look) alight or be steadily directed on. ▸ (**rest on**) be based on or grounded in; depend on. ▸ (**rest something in/on**) place hope, trust, or confidence on or in. ▸ (often **rest with**) (of power, responsibility, etc.) belong to a specified person or group. **3** N. Amer. conclude the case for the prosecution or defence in a court of law. ■ n. **1** the action or a period of resting. ▸ a motionless state. **2** an object that is used to hold or support something.
– PHRASES **rest one's case** conclude one's presentation of evidence and arguments in a lawsuit.
– ORIGIN Old English, of Germanic origin, from a root meaning 'league' or 'mile' (referring to a distance after which one rests).

rest² ■ n. the remaining part of something. ▸ [treated as pl.] the remaining people or things; the others. ■ v. remain or be left in a specified condition.

– ORIGIN Middle English: from Old French *reste* (n.), *rester* (v.), from Latin *restare* 'remain'.

restart ■ v. start again.

restaurant /ˈrest(ə)rɒnt, -r(ə)nt, -rō/ ■ n. a place where people pay to sit and eat meals that are cooked and served on the premises.
– ORIGIN C19: from French, from *restaurer* 'provide food for' (literally 'restore to a former state').

restaurateur /ˌrest(ə)rəˈtɔː, ˌrestɒr-/ ■ n. a person who owns and manages a restaurant.
– ORIGIN C18: French, from *restaurer* (see RESTAURANT).

rest camp ■ n. a fenced enclosure in a nature reserve providing accommodation for tourists.

restful ■ adj. having a quiet and soothing quality.
– DERIVATIVES **restfully** adv. **restfulness** n.

rest home ■ n. a residential institution where old or frail people are cared for.

restio ■ n. a plant of the reed family which in South Africa forms an important component of the fynbos biome. [Family Restionaceae: numerous species.]

restitutio in integrum /ˌrestɪˌtjuːtɪəʊ ɪn ɪnˈtɛɡrəm/ ■ n. Law restoration of an injured party to the situation which would have prevailed had no injury been sustained.
– ORIGIN Latin, 'restoration to the whole (i.e. uninjured) state'.

restitution ■ n. **1** the restoration of something lost or stolen to its proper owner. **2** recompense for injury or loss. **3** the restoration of something to its original state. ▸ Physics the resumption of an object's original shape or position through elastic recoil.
– DERIVATIVES **restitutive** adj.
– ORIGIN Middle English: from Latin *restitutio(n-)*, from *restituere* 'restore'.

restive ■ adj. unable to keep still or silent; restless.
– DERIVATIVES **restively** adv. **restiveness** n.
– ORIGIN C16: from Old French *restif, -ive*, from Latin *restare* 'remain'.

restless ■ adj. unable to rest as a result of anxiety or boredom. ▸ offering no physical or emotional rest; involving constant activity.
– DERIVATIVES **restlessly** adv. **restlessness** n.

restock ■ v. replenish with fresh stock or supplies.

restoration ■ n. **1** the action or process of restoring. **2** the return of a monarch to a throne, a head of state to government, or a regime to power. ▸ (**the Restoration**) the re-establishment of Charles II as King of England in 1660, or the period following this.

restorative ■ adj. **1** having the ability to restore health, strength, or a feeling of well-being. **2** Surgery & Dentistry relating to or concerned with the restoration of a damaged tooth or other part of the body. ■ n. something, especially a medicine or drink, that restores health, strength, or well-being.
– DERIVATIVES **restoratively** adv.

restore ■ v. **1** bring back (a previous right, practice, or situation); reinstate. ▸ return (someone or something) to a former condition or position. **2** repair or renovate. **3** give (something stolen or removed) back to the original owner.
– DERIVATIVES **restorable** adj. **restorer** n.
– ORIGIN Middle English: from Old French *restorer*, from Latin *restaurare* 'rebuild, restore'.

restrain ■ v. **1** prevent from doing something; keep under control or within limits. ▸ deprive of freedom of movement or personal liberty. **2** repress (a strong emotion).
– DERIVATIVES **restrainable** adj. **restrainer** n. **restraining** adj.
– ORIGIN Middle English: from Old French *restreign-, restreindre*, from Latin *restringere*, from *re-* 'back' + *stringere* 'to tie'.

restrained ■ adj. **1** reserved, unemotional, or dispassionate. **2** understated and subtle; not ornate.
– DERIVATIVES **restrainedly** adv.

restraining order ■ n. a temporary court order issued to prohibit an individual from carrying out a particular action, especially approaching or contacting a specified person.

restraint ■ n. **1** the action of restraining. ▸ a measure or condition that restrains. ▸ a device which limits or prevents freedom of movement. **2** dispassionate or moderate behaviour; self-control. ▸ understatement, especially of artistic expression.
– ORIGIN Middle English: from Old French *restreinte*, from *restreindre* (see RESTRAIN).

restraint of trade ■ n. Law **1** action that interferes with free competition in a market. **2** a clause in a contract that restricts a person's right to carry on their trade or profession.

restrict ■ v. **1** put a limit on; keep under control. **2** deprive of freedom of movement or action.
– ORIGIN C16 (*restriction* Middle English): from Latin *restrict-, restringere* (see RESTRAIN).

restricted ■ adj. **1** limited in extent, number, or scope. **2** not to be revealed or open to the public for reasons of national security.
– DERIVATIVES **restrictedly** adv. **restrictedness** n.

restriction ■ n. **1** a limiting condition or measure. **2** the action or state of restricting or being restricted.
– DERIVATIVES **restrictionism** n. **restrictionist** adj. & n.

restriction enzyme (also **restriction endonuclease**) ■ n. Biochemistry an enzyme with the property of cleaving DNA molecules at or near a specific sequence of bases.

restriction fragment ■ n. Biochemistry a fragment of a DNA molecule that has been cleaved by a restriction enzyme.

restrictive ■ adj. **1** imposing restrictions. **2** Grammar (of a relative clause or descriptive phrase) serving to specify the particular instance or instances being mentioned.
– DERIVATIVES **restrictively** adv. **restrictiveness** n.

restrictive covenant ■ n. Law a covenant imposing a restriction on the use of land so that the value and enjoyment of adjoining land will be preserved.

restrictive practice ■ n. an arrangement in industry or trade that restricts or controls competition between firms.

restring ■ v. (past and past part. **restrung**) **1** fit new strings to. **2** string (beads) again.

restroom ■ n. chiefly N. Amer. a toilet in a public building.

restructure ■ v. **1** organize differently. **2** Finance convert (a debt) into debt that is repayable at a later time.

restyle ■ v. **1** rearrange or remake in a new shape or layout. **2** give a new designation to. ■ n. an instance of restyling.

result ■ n. **1** a consequence, effect, or outcome. ▸ (also **results**) a satisfactory outcome: *persistence guarantees results*. **2** an item of information or a quantity or formula obtained by experiment or calculation. **3** a final score, mark, or placing in a sporting event or examination. **4** (usu. **results**) the outcome of a business's trading over a given period, expressed as a statement of profit or loss. ■ v. occur or follow as a result. ▸ (**result in**) have a specified end or outcome).
– ORIGIN Middle English: from medieval Latin *resultare* 'to result', earlier 'spring back', from *re-* (expressing intensive force) + *saltare*, from *salire* 'to jump'.

resultant ■ adj. occurring or produced as a result. ■ n. technical a force or other vector quantity which is equivalent to two or more component vectors acting at the same point.

resume ■ v. begin again or continue after a pause or interruption. ▸ take or put on again; return to the use of.
– DERIVATIVES **resumable** adj. **resumption** n.
– ORIGIN Middle English: from Old French *resumer* or Latin *resumere*, from *re-* 'back' + *sumere* 'take'.

résumé /ˈrɛzjʊmeɪ/ ■ n. **1** a summary. **2** a curriculum vitae.
– ORIGIN C19: French, 'resumed', from *résumer*.

resurface ■ v. **1** put a new coating on or re-form (a surface). **2** come back up to the surface of deep water. **3** arise or become evident again.

resurgent ■ adj. increasing or reviving after a period of little activity, popularity, or occurrence.
– DERIVATIVES **resurgence** n.
– ORIGIN C18: from Latin *resurgent-, resurgere* 'rise again'.

resurrect ■ v. 1 restore to life. 2 revive the practice, use, or memory of.
– ORIGIN C18: back-formation from RESURRECTION.

resurrection ■ n. the action or fact of resurrecting or being resurrected. ▸ **(the Resurrection)** (in Christian belief) Christ's rising from the dead. ▸ **(the Resurrection)** (in Christian belief) the rising of the dead at the Last Judgement.
– ORIGIN Middle English: from Old French, from late Latin *resurrectio(n-)*, from *resurgere* (see RESURGENT).

resuscitate /rɪˈsʌsɪteɪt/ ■ v. 1 revive from unconsciousness. 2 make active or vigorous again.
– DERIVATIVES **resuscitation** n. **resuscitative** adj. **resuscitator** n.
– ORIGIN C16 (*resuscitation* C15): from Latin *resuscitare* 'raise again'.

ret. ■ abbrev. retired.

retail /ˈriːteɪl/ ■ n. the sale of goods to the public for use or consumption rather than for resale. ■ adv. being sold in such a way. ■ v. /also rɪˈteɪl/ 1 sell (goods) in such a way. ▸ **(retail at/for)** be sold in this way for (a specified price). 2 recount or relate details of.
– DERIVATIVES **retailer** n.
– ORIGIN Middle English: from Old French *retaille* 'a piece cut off', from *retaillier*, from *re-* (expressing intensive force) + *tailler* 'to cut'.

retail price index ■ n. (in the UK) an index of the variation in the prices of retail goods and other items.

retain ■ v. 1 continue to have; keep possession of. ▸ not abolish, discard, or alter. ▸ keep in one's memory. 2 absorb and continue to hold (a substance). 3 keep in place; hold fixed. 4 keep engaged in one's service. ▸ secure the services of (a professional) with a preliminary payment.
– DERIVATIVES **retainability** n. **retainable** adj. **retaining** adj. **retainment** n.
– ORIGIN Middle English: from Old French *retenir*, from Latin *retinere*, from *re-* 'back' + *tenere* 'hold'.

retainer ■ n. 1 a thing that holds something in place. 2 a fee paid in advance to some professionals, in order to secure their services for use when required. 3 a servant who has worked for a person or family for a long time.

retaining wall ■ n. a wall that holds back earth or water on one side of it.

retake ■ v. (past **retook**; past part. **retaken**) 1 take (a test or examination) again. 2 regain possession of. ■ n. an instance of filming a scene or recording a piece of music again.

retaliate /rɪˈtalɪeɪt/ ■ v. make an attack or assault in return for a similar attack.
– DERIVATIVES **retaliation** n. **retaliative** adj. **retaliator** n. **retaliatory** adj.
– ORIGIN C17 (*retaliation* C16): from Latin *retaliare* 'return in kind'.

retard ■ v. /rɪˈtɑːd/ delay or hold back in terms of development or progress.
– DERIVATIVES **retardation** n. **retarder** n.
– ORIGIN C15 (*retardation* Middle English): from French *retarder*, from Latin *retardare*, from *re-* 'back' + *tardus* 'slow'.

retardant ■ adj. [in combination] preventing or inhibiting: *fire-retardant polymers*.
– DERIVATIVES **retardancy** n.

retarded ■ adj. less advanced in mental, physical, or social development than is usual for one's age.

retch ■ v. make the sound and movement of vomiting. ■ n. an instance of retching.
– ORIGIN C19: var. of dialect *reach*, from a Germanic base meaning 'spittle'.

retd ■ abbrev. retired.

retell ■ v. (past and past part. **retold**) tell (a story) again or differently.

retention ■ n. 1 the act of retaining or state of being retained. 2 failure to eliminate a substance from the body.
– ORIGIN Middle English: from Latin *retentio(n-)*, from *retinere* (see RETAIN).

retentive ■ adj. 1 (of a person's memory) effective in retaining facts and impressions. 2 able to retain or hold in place.
– DERIVATIVES **retentively** adv. **retentiveness** n.

retentivity ■ n. (pl. **-ies**) Physics the ability of a substance to retain or resist magnetization.

rethink ■ v. (past and past part. **rethought**) assess or consider (a policy or course of action) again. ■ n. an instance of rethinking.

reticent /ˈrɛtɪs(ə)nt/ ■ adj. not revealing one's thoughts or feelings readily.
– DERIVATIVES **reticence** n. **reticently** adv.
– ORIGIN C19 (*reticence* C17): from Latin *reticere* 'remain silent'.

reticula plural form of RETICULUM.

reticular formation (also **reticular activating system**) ■ n. Anatomy a diffuse network of nerve pathways in the brainstem connecting the spinal cord, cerebrum, and cerebellum.

reticulate ■ v. /rɪˈtɪkjʊleɪt/ divide or mark in such a way as to resemble a net or network. ■ adj. /rɪˈtɪkjʊlət/ chiefly Botany & Zoology reticulated.
– DERIVATIVES **reticulation** n.
– ORIGIN C17: from Latin *reticulatus* 'reticulated', from *reticulum* (see RETICULUM).

reticulated ■ adj. 1 constructed, arranged, or marked like a net or network. 2 Architecture relating to or denoting a style of decorated tracery characterized by circular shapes drawn at top and bottom into ogees, resulting in a net-like framework.

reticulated python ■ n. a very large Asian python patterned with dark patches outlined in black. [*Python reticulatus*.]

reticule /ˈrɛtɪkjuːl/ ■ n. chiefly historical a woman's small handbag, typically having a drawstring and decorated with embroidery or beading.
– ORIGIN C18: from French *réticule*, from Latin *reticulum* (see RETICULUM).

reticulocyte /rɪˈtɪkjʊlə(ʊ)sʌɪt/ ■ n. Physiology an immature red blood cell without a nucleus, having a granular or reticulated appearance when suitably stained.

reticuloendothelial /rɪˌtɪkjʊləʊɛndə(ʊ)ˈθiːlɪəl/ ■ adj. Physiology relating to or denoting a system of fixed and circulating phagocytic cells involved in the immune response.
– ORIGIN 1920s: from RETICULUM + *endothelial* (see ENDOTHELIUM).

reticulum /rɪˈtɪkjʊləm/ ■ n. (pl. **reticula** /-lə/) 1 a fine network or net-like structure. 2 Zoology the second stomach of a ruminant, having a honeycomb-like structure, receiving food from the rumen and passing it to the omasum.
– DERIVATIVES **reticular** adj.
– ORIGIN C17 (*reticular* C16): from Latin, diminutive of *rete* 'net'.

retina /ˈrɛtɪnə/ ■ n. (pl. **retinas** or **retinae** /-niː/) a layer at the back of the eyeball that contains cells sensitive to light, which trigger nerve impulses that pass via the optic nerve to the brain, where a visual image is formed.
– DERIVATIVES **retinal** adj. **retinitis** n.
– ORIGIN Middle English: from Latin *rete* 'net'.

retinitis pigmentosa /ˌpɪgmɛnˈtəʊsə/ ■ n. Medicine a hereditary eye disease characterized by black pigmentation and gradual degeneration of the retina.
– ORIGIN C19: *pigmentosa*, from Latin *pigmentosus*, from *pigmentum* 'pigment'.

retinoid /ˈrɛtɪnɔɪd/ ■ n. Biochemistry any of a group of compounds having effects like those of vitamin A.

retinol /ˈrɛtɪnɒl/ ■ n. Biochemistry vitamin A, a yellow compound which is essential for growth and vision in dim light and is found in vegetables, egg yolk, and fish-liver oil.

retinopathy /ˌrɛtɪˈnɒpəθi/ ■ n. Medicine disease of the retina which results in impairment or loss of vision.

retinue /ˈrɛtɪnjuː/ ■ n. a group of advisers or assistants accompanying an important person.
– ORIGIN Middle English: from Old French *retenue*, from *retenir* 'keep back, retain'.

retire ■ v. 1 leave one's job and cease to work, especially because one has reached a particular age. ▸ (of a sports player) cease to play competitively. 2 withdraw from a

race or match because of accident or injury. ▶ Baseball put out (a batter); cause (a side) to end a turn at bat. **3** withdraw to or from a particular place. ▶ (of a jury) leave the courtroom to decide the verdict of a trial. **4** go to bed. **5** Finance pay off or cancel (a debt).
–DERIVATIVES **retired** adj.
–ORIGIN C16: from French *retirer*, from *re-* 'back' + *tirer* 'draw'.

retirement ■ n. **1** the action or fact of retiring. **2** the period of one's life after retiring from work. **3** seclusion.

retirement pension ■ n. another term for OLD-AGE PENSION.

retiring ■ adj. tending to avoid company; shy.

retold past and past participle of RETELL.

retook past of RETAKE.

retool ■ v. **1** equip (a factory) with new or adapted tools. **2** chiefly N. Amer. adapt, alter, or prepare for a new purpose or challenge.

retort[1] ■ v. say something sharp, angry, or witty in answer to a remark or accusation. ■ n. a sharp, angry, or witty reply.
–ORIGIN C15: from Latin *retort-*, *retorquere* 'twist back'.

retort[2] ■ n. **1** a container or furnace for carrying out a chemical process on a large or industrial scale. **2** historical a glass container with a long neck, used in distilling liquids and other chemical operations. ■ v. heat in a retort.
–ORIGIN C17: from French *retorte*, from medieval Latin *retorta*, from *retorquere* 'twist back' (with ref. to the long recurved neck of the laboratory container).

retouch ■ v. improve or repair (a painting, photograph, etc.) by making slight additions or alterations.
–DERIVATIVES **retoucher** n.

retrace ■ v. **1** go back over (the same route that one has just taken). ▶ discover and follow (a route or course taken by someone else). **2** trace (something) back to its source or beginning.

retract ■ v. **1** draw or be drawn back or back in. **2** withdraw (a statement or accusation) as untrue or unjustified. ▶ withdraw or go back on (an undertaking or promise).
–DERIVATIVES **retractable** adj. **retraction** n. **retractor** n.
–ORIGIN Middle English: from Latin *retract-*, *retrahere* 'draw back'; the senses 'withdraw (a statement)' and 'go back on' from *retractare* 'reconsider'.

retractile /rɪˈtraktʌɪl/ ■ adj. Zoology capable of being retracted.

retrain ■ v. teach or learn new skills, especially for a different job.

retread ■ v. **1** (past **retrod**; past part. **retrodden**) go back over (a path or one's steps). **2** (past and past part. **retreaded**) put a new tread on (a worn tyre). ■ n. **1** a tyre that has been given a new tread. **2** informal an altered or rearranged version of something.

retreat ■ v. (of an army) withdraw from confrontation with enemy forces. ▶ move back from a difficult or uncomfortable situation. ▶ withdraw to a quiet or secluded place. ■ n. **1** an act of retreating. ▶ a signal for a military force to withdraw. **2** a quiet or secluded place. ▶ a period or place of seclusion for the purposes of prayer and meditation.
–ORIGIN Middle English: from Old French *retret* (n.), *retraiter* (v.), from Latin *retrahere* (see RETRACT).

retrench ■ v. reduce costs or spending in response to economic difficulty. ▶ chiefly S. African & Austral. make (an employee) redundant in order to reduce costs.
–DERIVATIVES **retrenchment** n.
–ORIGIN C16: from obsolete French *retrencher*, var. of *retrancher*, from *re-* (expressing reversal) + *trancher* 'to cut, slice'.

retrial ■ n. Law a second or further trial.

retribution ■ n. punishment inflicted in the spirit of moral outrage or personal vengeance.
–DERIVATIVES **retributive** /rɪˈtrɪbjʊtɪv/ adj. **retributory** /rɪˈtrɪbjʊt(ə)ri/ adj.
–ORIGIN Middle English: from late Latin *retributio(n-)*, from *retribuere* 'assign again'.

retrieve ■ v. **1** get or bring back. **2** (of a dog) find and bring back (game that has been shot). **3** find or extract (information stored in a computer). **4** rescue from a state of difficulty or collapse.
–DERIVATIVES **retrievable** adj. **retrieval** n.
–ORIGIN Middle English: from Old French *retroeve-*, *retrover* 'find again'.

retriever ■ n. a dog of a breed used for retrieving game.

retro ■ adj. imitative of a style from the recent past. ■ n. retro clothes, music, or style.
–ORIGIN 1960s: from French *rétro*, abbrev. of *rétrograde* 'retrograde'.

retro- ■ comb. form **1** denoting action that is directed backwards or is reciprocal: *retrospect*. **2** denoting location behind: *retrochoir*.
–ORIGIN from Latin *retro* 'backwards'.

retroactive ■ adj. (especially of legislation) taking effect from a date in the past.
–DERIVATIVES **retroactively** adv. **retroactivity** n.

retrocede /ˌrɛtrə(ʊ)ˈsiːd/ ■ v. cede (territory) back again.
–DERIVATIVES **retrocession** n.

retrod past of RETREAD (in sense 1).

retrodden past participle of RETREAD (in sense 1).

retrofit /ˈrɛtrəʊfɪt/ ■ v. (**retrofitted**, **retrofitting**) fit with a component or accessory not fitted during manufacture. ■ n. an act of retrofitting.
–ORIGIN 1950s: blend of RETROACTIVE and REFIT.

retroflex /ˈrɛtrə(ʊ)flɛks/ (also **retroflexed**) ■ adj. **1** Anatomy turned backwards. **2** Phonetics pronounced with the tip of the tongue curled up towards the hard palate.
–DERIVATIVES **retroflexion** n.
–ORIGIN C18: from Latin *retroflex-*, *retroflectere* 'bend backwards'.

retrograde ■ adj. **1** directed or moving backwards. ▶ (of the order of something) reversed; inverse. **2** reverting to an earlier and inferior condition. **3** Geology (of a metamorphic change) resulting from a decrease in temperature or pressure. **4** Astronomy & Astrology (of the apparent motion of a planet) in a reverse direction from normal (so from east to west), resulting from the relative orbital progress of the earth and the planet. The opposite of PROGRADE. **5** Astronomy (of the orbit or rotation of a planet or planetary satellite) in a reverse direction from that normal in the solar system. ■ v. go back in position or time.
–DERIVATIVES **retrogradation** n.
–ORIGIN Middle English: from Latin *retrogradus*, from *retro* 'backwards' + *gradus* 'step'.

retrogress /ˌrɛtrə(ʊ)ˈɡrɛs/ ■ v. go back to an earlier and typically inferior state; engage in retrogression.

retrogression ■ n. **1** the process of retrogressing. **2** Astronomy retrogradation.
–DERIVATIVES **retrogressive** adj.
–ORIGIN C17: from RETRO-, on the pattern of *progression*.

retrospect ■ n. a survey or review of a past course of events or period of time.
–PHRASES **in retrospect** when looking back on a past event or situation; with hindsight.
–DERIVATIVES **retrospection** n.
–ORIGIN C17: from RETRO-, on the pattern of *prospect*.

retrospective ■ adj. **1** looking back on or dealing with past events or situations. ▶ (of an exhibition or compilation) showing the development of an artist's work over a period of time. **2** (of a statute or legal decision) taking effect from a date in the past. ■ n. a retrospective exhibition or compilation.
–DERIVATIVES **retrospectively** adv.

retrotransposon /ˌrɛtrəʊtransˈpəʊzɒn, -trɑːns-, -tranz-/ ■ n. Genetics a transposon whose sequence shows homology with that of a retrovirus.

retroussé /rəˈtruːseɪ/ ■ adj. (of a person's nose) turned up at the tip.
–ORIGIN C19: French, 'tucked up', from *retrousser*.

retroverted /ˈrɛtrəvɜːt/ ■ adj. Anatomy (of the uterus) tilted abnormally backwards.
–DERIVATIVES **retroversion** n.
–ORIGIN C18: from Latin *retrovertere* 'turn backwards'.

retroviral ■ adj. of the nature of, caused by, or relating to a retrovirus.

retrovirus /ˈretrəʊˌvʌɪrəs/ ■ n. Biology any of a group of RNA viruses which insert a DNA copy of their genome into the host cell in order to replicate, e.g. HIV.
– ORIGIN 1970s: from the initial letters of *reverse transcriptase* + VIRUS.

retry ■ v. (-ies, -ied) Law try (a defendant or case) again.

retsina /retˈsiːnə/ ■ n. a Greek white wine flavoured with resin.
– ORIGIN from modern Greek.

retune ■ v. tune again or differently.

return ■ v. 1 come or go back to a place. ▸ (**return to**) go back to (a particular state or activity). ▸ (of a sensation) come back after a period of absence. ▸ give or send back or put back in place. 2 feel, say, or do (the same feeling, action, etc.) in response. ▸ (in tennis and other sports) hit or send (the ball) back to an opponent. 3 (of a judge or jury) state or present (a verdict). 4 yield or make (a profit). 5 (of an electorate) elect (someone) to office. 6 Bridge lead (a card) after taking a trick. 7 Architecture continue (a wall) in a changed direction, especially at right angles. ■ n. 1 an act of returning. 2 a thing which has been returned, especially an unwanted ticket for an event. 3 (also **return ticket**) a ticket allowing travel to a place and back again. 4 an electrical conductor bringing a current back to its source. 5 (also **return match** or **game**) a second contest between the same opponents. 6 (also **returns**) a profit from an investment. 7 an official report or statement submitted in response to a formal demand. ▸ Law an endorsement or report by a court officer or sheriff on a writ. 8 (also **carriage return**) a mechanism or key on a typewriter that returns the carriage to a fixed position at the start of a new line. ▸ (also **return key**) a key pressed on a computer keyboard to simulate a carriage return. 9 Architecture a part receding from the line of the front, for example the side of a house or of a window opening.
– PHRASES **by return (of post)** in the next available mail delivery to the sender. **many happy returns (of the day)** a greeting to someone on their birthday.
– DERIVATIVES **returnable** adj. **returner** n.
– ORIGIN Middle English: from Old French *returner*, from Latin *re-* 'back' + *tornare* 'to turn'.

return crease ■ n. Cricket each of two lines on either side of the wicket between which the bowler must deliver the ball.

returnee ■ n. 1 a refugee returning from abroad. 2 a person returning to work after an extended absence.

returning officer ■ n. the official in each constituency or electorate who conducts an election and announces the result.

retype ■ v. type (text) again.

reunify ■ v. (-ies, -ied) restore political unity to.
– DERIVATIVES **reunification** n.

reunion ■ n. 1 the process or an instance of reuniting. 2 a social gathering attended by members of a group of people who have not seen each other for some time.

reunite ■ v. come together or cause to come together again after a period of separation or disunity.

reuse ■ v. /riːˈjuːz/ use again or more than once. ■ n. /riːˈjuːs/ the action of using something again.
– DERIVATIVES **reusable** adj.

Reuters /ˈrɔɪtəz/ ■ n. an international news and financial information organization, established in London in 1851.
– ORIGIN C19: named after the founder P. J. *Reuter*.

Rev. ■ abbrev. Reverend.

rev informal ■ n. (**revs**) the number of revolutions of an engine per minute. ■ v. (**revved, revving**) increase the running speed of (an engine) by pressing the accelerator, especially while the clutch is disengaged.

revalue ■ v. (**revalues, revalued, revaluing**) value again.
– DERIVATIVES **revaluation** n.

revamp ■ v. give new and improved form, structure, or appearance to. ■ n. a new and improved version.

revanchism /rɪˈvan(t)ʃɪz(ə)m/ ■ n. a policy of seeking to retaliate, especially to recover lost territory.
– DERIVATIVES **revanchist** adj. & n.
– ORIGIN C20: from French *revanche* 'revenge'.

rev counter ■ n. an instrument that measures the rate of revolutions of an engine.

Revd ■ abbrev. Reverend.

reveal[1] ■ v. 1 disclose (previously unknown or secret information). ▸ make known to humans by divine or supernatural means. 2 cause or allow to be seen.
– DERIVATIVES **revealer** n.
– ORIGIN Middle English: from Latin *revelare*, from *re-* 'again' (expressing reversal) + *velum* 'veil'.

reveal[2] ■ n. either side surface of an aperture in a wall for a door or window.
– ORIGIN C17: from obsolete *revale* 'to lower', from Old French *revaler*, from *re-* 'back' + *avaler* 'go down, sink'.

revealing ■ adj. 1 divulging interesting or significant information. 2 (of a garment) allowing much of the wearer's body to be seen.
– DERIVATIVES **revealingly** adv.

revegetate ■ v. produce new vegetation on (disturbed or barren ground).
– DERIVATIVES **revegetation** n.

reveille /rɪˈvali/ ■ n. a military waking signal sounded especially on a bugle or drum.
– ORIGIN C17: from French *réveillez!* 'wake up!', from *réveiller*, based on Latin *vigilare* 'keep watch'.

revel ■ v. (**revelled, revelling**; US **reveled, reveling**) 1 engage in lively and noisy festivities. 2 (**revel in**) gain great pleasure from. ■ n. (**revels**) lively and noisy festivities.
– DERIVATIVES **reveller** n. **revelry** n. (pl. -ies).
– ORIGIN Middle English: from Old French *reveler* 'rise up in rebellion', from Latin *rebellare* 'to rebel'.

revelation ■ n. 1 a surprising disclosure. ▸ the revealing of something previously unknown. ▸ a surprising or remarkable thing. 2 a divine or supernatural disclosure to humans. ▸ (**Revelation** or informal **Revelations**) (in full **the Revelation of St John the Divine**) the last book of the New Testament, recounting a divine revelation of the future to St John.
– DERIVATIVES **revelational** adj.
– ORIGIN Middle English: from late Latin *revelatio(n-)*, from *revelare* (see REVEAL[1]).

revelatory /ˌrevəˈleɪt(ə)ri, ˈrev(ə)lət(ə)ri/ ■ adj. revealing.

revenant /ˈrev(ə)nənt/ ■ n. a person who has returned, especially supposedly from the dead.
– ORIGIN C19: French, 'coming back', from *revenir*.

revenge ■ n. retaliation for an injury or wrong. ▸ the desire to inflict this. ■ v. (**revenge oneself or be revenged**) chiefly poetic/literary inflict revenge for an injury or wrong done to oneself. ▸ inflict revenge on behalf of (someone else).
– DERIVATIVES **revenger** n. (poetic/literary).
– ORIGIN Middle English: from Old French *revencher*, from late Latin *revindicare*, from *re-* (expressing intensive force) + *vindicare* 'claim, avenge'.

revengeful ■ adj. eager for revenge.
– DERIVATIVES **revengefully** adv. **revengefulness** n.

revenue ■ n. income, especially when of a company and of a substantial nature. ▸ a state's annual income from which public expenses are met. ▸ (**revenues**) items or amounts constituting revenue. ▸ (**the revenue**) the department of the civil service collecting revenue.
– ORIGIN Middle English: from Old French *revenu(e)* 'returned', from *revenir*, from Latin *revenire* 'return'.

reverb /ˈriːvəːb, rɪˈvəːb/ ■ n. an effect whereby the sound from an amplifier or amplified musical instrument is made to reverberate. ▸ a device producing this effect.

reverberate ■ v. 1 (of a loud noise) be repeated as an echo. 2 have continuing serious effects.
– DERIVATIVES **reverberant** adj. **reverberantly** adv. **reverberation** n. **reverberative** adj. **reverberator** n. **reverberatory** adj.
– ORIGIN C15 (*reverberation* Middle English): from Latin *reverberare* 'strike again', from *re-* 'back' + *verberare* 'to lash'.

reverberatory furnace ■ n. a furnace in which the roof and walls are heated by flames and radiate heat on to material in the centre.

revere /rɪ'vɪə/ ■ v. respect or admire deeply.
– ORIGIN C17: from French *révérer* or Latin *revereri*, from *re-* (expressing intensive force) + *vereri* 'to fear'.

reverence ■ n. **1** deep respect. **2** archaic a bow or curtsy. **3** (**His/Your** etc. **Reverence**) a title given to a member of the clergy. ■ v. regard or treat with reverence.
– ORIGIN Middle English: from Latin *reverentia*, from *revereri* (see REVERE).

reverend ■ adj. a title or form of address to members of the clergy. ■ n. informal a clergyman.
– ORIGIN Middle English: from Latin *reverendus* 'person to be revered', from *revereri* (see REVERE).

Reverend Mother ■ n. the title of the Mother Superior of a convent.

reverent ■ adj. showing reverence.
– DERIVATIVES **reverential** adj. **reverentially** adv. **reverently** adv.

reverie /'rɛv(ə)ri/ ■ n. a daydream.
– ORIGIN C17: from Old French *reverie* 'rejoicing, revelry', from *rever* 'be delirious'.

revers /rɪ'vɪə/ ■ n. (pl. same /-'vɪəz/) the turned-back edge of a garment revealing the underside, especially at the lapel.
– ORIGIN C19: from French, 'reverse'.

reversal ■ n. **1** a change to an opposite direction, position, or course of action. ▸ Law an annulment of a judgement made by a lower court or authority. ▸ an adverse change of fortune. **2** Photography direct production of a positive image from an exposed film or plate.

reverse /rɪ'vəːs/ ■ v. **1** move or cause to move backwards. **2** turn the other way round or up or inside out. **3** make the opposite of what it was. ▸ swap (positions or functions). **4** Law revoke or annul (a judgement by a lower court or authority). ■ adj. **1** going in or turned towards the opposite direction. ▸ operating or behaving in a way contrary to that which is usual or expected. **2** Geology denoting a fault in which a relative downward movement occurred in the strata on the underside of the fault plane. ■ n. **1** a complete change of direction or action. **2** reverse gear. **3** (**the reverse**) the opposite or contrary. **4** a setback or defeat. **5** American Football a play in which the direction of attack is reversed. **6** the opposite side or face to the observer. ▸ a left-hand page of an open book, or the back of a loose document. ▸ the side of a coin or medal bearing the value or secondary design.
– PHRASES **reverse arms** hold a rifle with the butt upwards. **reverse the charges** make the recipient of a telephone call responsible for payment.
– DERIVATIVES **reversely** adv. **reverser** n.
– ORIGIN Middle English: from Old French *revers*, from Latin *revers-, revertere* 'turn back'.

reverse engineering ■ n. the reproduction of another manufacturer's product after detailed examination of its construction or composition.

reverse gear ■ n. a gear making a vehicle or piece of machinery move or work backwards.

reverse light (also **reversing light**) ■ n. a white light at the rear of a vehicle that shines when the vehicle is reversing.

reverse takeover ■ n. a takeover of a public company by a smaller company.

reversible ■ adj. **1** able to be turned the other way round. ▸ (of a garment or fabric) faced on both sides so as to be worn or used with either outside. **2** (of the effects of a process or condition) capable of being reversed so that the previous state is restored.
– DERIVATIVES **reversibility** n. **reversibly** adv.

reversion /rɪ'vəːʃ(ə)n/ ■ n. **1** a return to a previous state, practice, or belief. **2** a sum payable on a person's death, especially by way of life insurance.
– DERIVATIVES **reversionary** adj.

revert ■ v. (**revert to**) return to (a previous state, condition, etc.).
– ORIGIN Middle English: from Old French *revertir* or Latin *revertere* 'turn back'.

revet /rɪ'vɛt/ ■ v. (**revetted, revetting**) [usu. as adj. **revetted**] face (a rampart, wall, etc.) with masonry, especially in fortification.
– ORIGIN C19: from French *revêtir*, from late Latin *revestire*, from *re-* 'again' + *vestire* 'clothe'.

revetment /rɪ'vɛtm(ə)nt/ ■ n. a retaining wall or facing of masonry, supporting or protecting a rampart, wall, etc.
– ORIGIN C18: from French *revêtement*, from *revêtir* (see REVET).

review ■ n. **1** a formal assessment of something with the intention of instituting change if necessary. ▸ Law a reconsideration of a judgement or sentence by a higher court or authority. **2** a critical appraisal of a book, play, or other work. ▸ a periodical with critical articles on current events and the arts. ▸ a retrospective survey or report. **3** a ceremonial display and formal inspection of military or naval forces. **4** a facility for playing a tape recording during a fast wind. ■ v. **1** carry out or write a review of. **2** view or inspect again.
– DERIVATIVES **reviewable** adj. **reviewal** n. **reviewer** n.
– ORIGIN Middle English: from obsolete French *reveue*, from *revoir* 'see again'.

revile ■ v. (usu. **be reviled**) criticize abusively.
– DERIVATIVES **revilement** n.
– ORIGIN Middle English: from Old French *reviler*, from *vil* 'vile'.

revise ■ v. **1** examine and improve or amend (something, especially written matter). ▸ reconsider and alter (an opinion or judgement). **2** reread work done previously to improve one's knowledge, typically for an examination. ■ n. Printing a proof including corrections made in an earlier proof.
– DERIVATIVES **revisable** adj. **revisal** n. **reviser** n. **revisory** adj.
– ORIGIN C16: from French *réviser* 'look at', or Latin *revisere* 'look at again'.

revision ■ n. the action of revising. ▸ a revised edition or form.
– DERIVATIVES **revisionary** adj.

revisionism ■ n. often derogatory **1** a policy of revision or modification, especially of Marxism on evolutionary socialist or pluralist principles. **2** the theory or practice of revising one's attitude to something.
– DERIVATIVES **revisionist** n. & adj.

revisit ■ v. (**revisits, revisiting, revisited**) come back to or visit again. ▸ consider (a situation or problem) again or from a different perspective.

revitalize (also **-ise**) ■ v. imbue with new life and vitality.
– DERIVATIVES **revitalization** (also **-isation**) n.

revival ■ n. **1** an improvement in the condition or strength of something. **2** an instance of something becoming popular, active, or important again. ▸ a reawakening of religious fervour, especially by means of evangelistic meetings. **3** a new production of an old play.

revivalism ■ n. **1** belief in or the promotion of a revival of religious fervour. **2** a tendency or desire to revive a former custom or practice.
– DERIVATIVES **revivalist** n. & adj.

revive ■ v. restore to or regain life, consciousness, or strength. ▸ restore interest in or the popularity of. ▸ restore or improve the position or condition of.
– DERIVATIVES **revivable** adj. **reviver** n.
– ORIGIN Middle English: from Old French *revivre* or late Latin *revivere*, from Latin *re-* 'back' + *vivere* 'live'.

revivify /rɪ'vɪvɪfʌɪ/ ■ v. (**-ies, -ied**) give new life or vigour to.
– DERIVATIVES **revivification** n.

revoke ■ v. **1** end the validity or operation of (a decree, decision, or promise). **2** (in card games) fail to follow suit despite being able to do so.
– DERIVATIVES **revocability** n. **revocable** adj. **revocation** n. **revocatory** adj. **revoker** n.
– ORIGIN Middle English: from Old French *revoquer* or Latin *revocare*, from *re-* 'back' + *vocare* 'to call'.

revolt ■ v. **1** rise in rebellion. ▸ refuse to acknowledge someone or something as having authority. **2** (often **be revolted**) cause to feel disgust. ■ n. an attempt to end the authority of a person or body by rebelling. ▸ a refusal to obey or conform.
– DERIVATIVES **revolting** adj. **revoltingly** adv.
– ORIGIN C16: from French *révolte* (n.), *révolter* (v.), based on Latin *revolvere* (see REVOLVE).

revolute /ˈrɛvəl(j)uːt/ ▪ adj. Botany (especially of the edge of a leaf) curved or curled back.
– ORIGIN C18: from Latin *revolutus* 'unrolled', from *revolvere* (see REVOLVE).

revolution ▪ n. 1 a forcible overthrow of a government or social order, in favour of a new system. ▸ (in Marxism) the class struggle expected to lead to political change and the triumph of communism. 2 a dramatic and wide-reaching change. 3 an instance of revolving. ▸ motion in orbit or in a circular course or round an axis or centre. ▸ the single completion of an orbit or rotation.
– DERIVATIVES **revolutionism** n. **revolutionist** n.
– ORIGIN Middle English: from late Latin *revolutio(n-)*, from *revolvere* (see REVOLVE).

revolutionary ▪ adj. 1 involving or causing dramatic change or innovation. 2 engaged in, promoting, or relating to political revolution. ▪ n. (pl. **-ies**) a person who revolts or advocates revolution.

revolutionize (also **-ise**) ▪ v. change radically or fundamentally.

revolve ▪ v. 1 move in a circle on a central axis. ▸ (**revolve about/around**) move in a circular orbit around. 2 (**revolve around**) treat as the most important point or element.
– ORIGIN Middle English: from Latin *revolvere*, from *re-* 'back' (also expressing intensive force) + *volvere* 'roll'.

revolver ▪ n. a pistol with revolving chambers enabling several shots to be fired without reloading.

revolving credit ▪ n. credit that is automatically renewed as debts are paid off.

revolving door ▪ n. 1 an entrance to a large building in which four partitions turn about a central axis. 2 a situation or place in which the same events or problems recur in a continuous cycle.

revue /rɪˈvjuː/ ▪ n. a light theatrical entertainment of short sketches, songs, and dances, typically dealing satirically with topical issues.
– ORIGIN French, 'review'.

revulsion ▪ n. a sense of disgust and loathing.
– ORIGIN C16: from Latin *revulsio(n-)*, from *revellere* 'tear out'.

reward ▪ n. a thing given in recognition of service, effort, or achievement. ▸ a fair return for good or bad behaviour. ▸ a sum offered for the detection of a criminal, the restoration of lost property, etc. ▪ v. give a reward to. ▸ show one's appreciation of (an action or quality) by making a gift. ▸ (**be rewarded**) receive what one deserves.
– PHRASES **go to one's reward** euphemistic die.
– DERIVATIVES **rewardless** adj.
– ORIGIN Middle English: from Anglo-Norman French, var. of Old French *reguard* 'regard, heed'.

rewarding ▪ adj. providing satisfaction.
– DERIVATIVES **rewardingly** adv.

rewind ▪ v. (past and past part. **rewound**) wind (a film or tape) back to the beginning. ▪ n. a mechanism for rewinding a film or tape.
– DERIVATIVES **rewinder** n.

rewire ▪ v. provide with new electric wiring.

reword ▪ v. put into different words.

rework ▪ v. alter, revise, or reshape.

rewound past and past participle of REWIND.

rewritable ▪ adj. Computing (of a storage device) supporting overwriting of previously recorded data.

rewrite ▪ v. (past **rewrote**; past part. **rewritten**) write again in an altered or improved form. ▪ n. an instance of rewriting something. ▸ a text that has been rewritten.

Rex ▪ n. the reigning king (following a name or in the titles of lawsuits, e.g. *Rex v. Jones*: the Crown versus Jones).
– ORIGIN Latin, 'king'.

Rexine /ˈrɛksiːn/ ▪ n. trademark an artificial leather, used in upholstery and bookbinding.
– ORIGIN C20.

Reye's syndrome /ˈreɪz, ˈraɪz/ ▪ n. a life-threatening metabolic disorder in young children, of uncertain cause.
– ORIGIN 1960s: named after the Australian paediatrician Ralph D. K. Reye.

Reynard /ˈrɛnɑːd, ˈreɪ-/ ▪ n. poetic/literary a fox.
– ORIGIN from Old French *renart*; influenced by Middle Dutch *Reynaerd*.

Rf ▪ symb. the chemical element rutherfordium.

r.f. ▪ abbrev. radio frequency.

RFC ▪ abbrev. 1 Computing request for comment. 2 historical Royal Flying Corps. 3 Rugby Football Club.

RFID ▪ abbrev. radio frequency identification, a method for tracking goods by means of tags which transmit a radio signal.

Rg ▪ symb. the chemical element roentgenium.

Rh ▪ abbrev. rhesus (factor). ▪ symb. the chemical element rhodium.

r.h. ▪ abbrev. right hand.

Rhaeto-Romance /ˌriːtə(ʊ)rəʊˈmans/ (also **Rhaeto-Romanic** /-ˈmanɪk/) ▪ adj. relating to or denoting the Romance dialects spoken in parts of SE Switzerland, NE Italy, and Tyrol. ▪ n. any of these dialects.
– ORIGIN from Latin *Rhaetus* 'of Rhaetia' (a Roman province in the Alps) + ROMANCE.

rhapsodist ▪ n. 1 a person who rhapsodizes. 2 a reciter of epic poems, especially in ancient Greece.

rhapsodize (also **-ise**) ▪ v. enthuse about someone or something.

rhapsody ▪ n. (pl. **-ies**) 1 an enthusiastic or ecstatic expression of feeling. 2 Music a piece of music in one extended movement, typically emotional in character.
– DERIVATIVES **rhapsodic** adj.
– ORIGIN C16: from Greek *rhapsōidia*, from *rhaptein* 'to stitch' + *ōidē* 'song, ode'.

RHD ▪ abbrev. right-hand drive.

rhea /ˈriːə/ ▪ n. a large flightless bird of South American grasslands, resembling a small ostrich with greyish-brown plumage. [*Rhea americana* and *Pterocnemia pennata*.]
– ORIGIN C19: from the name of *Rhea*, a Titan in Greek mythology.

rhebok /ˈriːbɒk/ (also **rhebuck**) ▪ n. a small South African antelope with a woolly brownish-grey coat, a long slender neck, and short straight horns. [*Pelea capreolus*.]
– ORIGIN C18: from Dutch *reebok* 'roebuck'.

rheme /riːm/ ▪ n. Linguistics the part of a clause giving information about the theme.
– ORIGIN C19: from Greek *rhēma* 'that which is said'.

Rhenish /ˈrɛnɪʃ/ ▪ adj. of the Rhine and adjacent regions.
– ORIGIN Middle English: from Anglo-Norman French *reneis*, from Latin *Rhenanus*, from *Rhenus* 'Rhine'.

rhenium /ˈriːnɪəm/ ▪ n. the chemical element of atomic number 75, a rare silvery-white metal. (Symbol: **Re**)
– ORIGIN 1920s: from *Rhenus* (see RHENISH).

rheology /rɪˈɒlədʒi/ ▪ n. the branch of physics concerned with the deformation and flow of matter.
– DERIVATIVES **rheological** adj.
– ORIGIN 1920s: from Greek *rheos* 'stream' + -LOGY.

rheostat /ˈriːəstat/ ▪ n. an electrical instrument used to control a current by varying the resistance.
– DERIVATIVES **rheostatic** adj.
– ORIGIN C19: from Greek *rheos* 'stream' + -STAT.

rhesus baby /ˈriːsəs/ ▪ n. a baby suffering from haemolytic disease of the newborn.
– ORIGIN 1960s: see RHESUS FACTOR.

rhesus factor ▪ n. an antigen occurring on red blood cells which is a cause of haemolytic disease of the newborn and of incompatibility in blood transfusions.
– ORIGIN 1940s: from RHESUS MONKEY, in which the antigen was first observed.

rhesus monkey ▪ n. a small brown macaque with red skin on the face and rump, native to southern Asia. [*Macaca mulatta*.]
– ORIGIN C19: *rhesus*: arbitrary use of Latin *Rhesus*, from Greek *Rhēsos*, a mythical king of Thrace.

rhesus negative ▪ adj. lacking the rhesus factor.

rhesus positive ▪ adj. having the rhesus factor.

rhetoric /ˈrɛtərɪk/ ▪ n. the art of effective or persuasive speaking or writing. ▸ language with a persuasive or

impressive effect, but often lacking sincerity or meaningful content.
– ORIGIN Middle English: from Old French *rethorique*, from Greek *rhētorikē (tekhnē)* '(art) of rhetoric', from *rhētōr* 'orator'.

rhetorical /rɪˈtɒrɪk(ə)l/ ■ adj. **1** of, relating to, or concerned with rhetoric. ▸ expressed in terms intended to persuade or impress. **2** (of a question) asked for effect or to make a statement rather than to elicit information.
– DERIVATIVES **rhetorically** adv.

rhetorician ■ n. **1** an expert in formal rhetoric. **2** a speaker whose words are intended to impress or persuade.

rheum /ruːm/ ■ n. chiefly poetic/literary a watery fluid that collects in or drips from the nose or eyes.
– DERIVATIVES **rheumy** adj.
– ORIGIN Middle English: from Old French *reume*, from Greek *rheuma* 'stream', from *rhein* 'to flow'.

rheumatic /ˈruːmətɪk/ ■ adj. of, relating to, caused by, or suffering from rheumatism. ■ n. a rheumatic person.
– DERIVATIVES **rheumatically** adv. **rheumaticky** adj. (informal).
– ORIGIN Middle English: from Old French *reumatique*, from Greek *rheumatikos*, from *rheuma* (see RHEUM).

rheumatic fever ■ n. an acute fever marked by inflammation and pain in the joints, caused by a streptococcal infection.

rheumatics ■ pl. n. [usu. treated as sing.] informal rheumatism.

rheumatism ■ n. any disease marked by inflammation and pain in the joints, muscles, or fibrous tissue, especially rheumatoid arthritis.
– ORIGIN C17: from French *rhumatisme*, from Greek *rheumatismos*, from *rheumatizein* 'to snuffle', from *rheuma* 'stream' (because it was believed to be caused by the internal flow of 'watery' humours).

rheumatoid /ˈruːmətɔɪd/ ■ adj. Medicine relating to, affected by, or resembling rheumatism.

rheumatoid arthritis ■ n. a chronic progressive disease causing inflammation in the joints and resulting in painful deformity and immobility.

rheumatology /ˌruːməˈtɒlədʒi/ ■ n. Medicine the study of rheumatism, arthritis, and other disorders of the joints, muscles, and ligaments.
– DERIVATIVES **rheumatological** adj. **rheumatologist** n.

rhinestone ■ n. an imitation diamond.
– ORIGIN C19: translating French *caillou du Rhin* 'pebble of the Rhine'.

rhinitis /rʌɪˈnʌɪtɪs, rɪ-/ ■ n. Medicine inflammation of the mucous membrane of the nose, caused by a viral infection or an allergic reaction.

rhino ■ n. (pl. same or **-os**) informal a rhinoceros.

rhino- ■ comb. form of or relating to the nose: *rhinoplasty*.
– ORIGIN from Greek *rhis, rhin-* 'nose'.

rhinoceros /rʌɪˈnɒs(ə)rəs/ ■ n. (pl. same or **rhinoceroses**) a large, heavily built plant-eating mammal with one or two horns on the nose and thick folded skin, native to Africa and South Asia. [Family Rhinocerotidae: five species.]
– ORIGIN Middle English: from Greek *rhinokerōs*, from *rhis, rhin-* 'nose' + *keras* 'horn'.

rhinoceros beetle ■ n. a very large mainly tropical beetle, the male of which has a curved horn on the head and typically another on the thorax. [*Oryctes rhinoceros* and other species.]

rhinoplasty /ˈrʌɪnə(ʊ)ˌplasti/ ■ n. (pl. **-ies**) Medicine plastic surgery performed on the nose.
– DERIVATIVES **rhinoplastic** adj.

rhinovirus /ˈrʌɪnəʊˌvʌɪrəs/ ■ n. Medicine any of a group of viruses including those which cause some forms of the common cold.

rhizo- ■ comb. form Botany relating to a root or roots: *rhizobium*.
– ORIGIN from Greek *rhiza* 'root'.

rhizobium /rʌɪˈzəʊbɪəm/ ■ n. a nitrogen-fixing bacterium that is common in the soil, especially in the root nodules of leguminous plants.
– ORIGIN 1920s: from RHIZO- + Greek *bios* 'life'.

rhizoid /ˈrʌɪzɔɪd/ ■ n. Botany a filamentous root-like outgrowth on the underside of the thallus in mosses and other lower plants.
– DERIVATIVES **rhizoidal** adj.

rhizome /ˈrʌɪzəʊm/ ■ n. Botany a continuously growing horizontal underground stem with lateral shoots and adventitious roots at intervals.
– ORIGIN C19: from Greek *rhizōma*, from *rhizousthai* 'take root', from *rhiza* 'root'.

Rhizopoda /ˌrʌɪzəˈpəʊdə, rʌɪˈzɒpədə/ ■ pl. n. Zoology a phylum of single-celled animals including the amoebas.
– DERIVATIVES **rhizopod** n.
– ORIGIN from RHIZO- + Greek *pous, pod-* 'foot'.

rhizosphere /ˈrʌɪzə(ʊ)ˌsfiːə/ ■ n. Ecology the region of soil in the vicinity of plant roots.

rho /rəʊ/ ■ n. the seventeenth letter of the Greek alphabet (Ρ, ρ), transliterated as 'r' or 'rh'. ■ symb. (ρ) density.
– ORIGIN from Greek.

Rhode Island Red ■ n. a bird of a breed of reddish-black domestic chicken, originally from Rhode Island.

Rhodes grass ■ n. a tufted perennial grass native to southern Africa, cultivated for pasturage and hay. [*Chloris gayana*.]

Rhodesian /rəʊˈdiːʃ(ə)n, -ˈdiːʒ(ə)n/ ■ n. a native or inhabitant of Rhodesia (now Zimbabwe). ■ adj. of or relating to Rhodesia.

Rhodesian ridgeback ■ n. a large dog of a breed having a short coat and a ridge of hair growing along the back in the opposite direction to the rest of the coat.

Rhodes Scholarship ■ n. any of several scholarships awarded annually and tenable at Oxford University by students from certain Commonwealth countries, the US, and Germany.
– DERIVATIVES **Rhodes Scholar** n.
– ORIGIN named after the South African statesman Cecil *Rhodes*, who founded the scholarships in 1902.

rhodium /ˈrəʊdɪəm/ ■ n. the chemical element of atomic number 45, a hard, dense silvery-white metal. (Symbol: **Rh**)
– ORIGIN C19: from Greek *rhodon* 'rose' (from the colour of its salts).

rhodochrosite /ˌrəʊdə(ʊ)ˈkrəʊsʌɪt/ ■ n. a mineral consisting of manganese carbonate, typically pink, brown, or grey.
– ORIGIN C19: from Greek *rhodokhrōs* 'rose-coloured'.

rhododendron /ˌrəʊdəˈdɛndr(ə)n/ ■ n. a shrub or small tree of the heather family, with large clusters of bell-shaped flowers and typically with large evergreen leaves. [Genus *Rhododendron*.]
– ORIGIN from Greek *rhodon* 'rose' + *dendron* 'tree'.

Rhodophyta /ˌrəʊdə(ʊ)ˈfʌɪtə/ ■ pl. n. Botany a division of lower plants comprising the red algae.
– DERIVATIVES **rhodophyte** n.
– ORIGIN from Greek *rhodon* 'rose' + *phuta* 'plants'.

rhodopsin /rə(ʊ)ˈdɒpsɪn/ ■ n. another term for VISUAL PURPLE.
– ORIGIN C19: from Greek *rhodon* 'rose' + *opsis* 'sight'.

rhomb /rɒm(b)/ ■ n. a rhombus.
– DERIVATIVES **rhombic** adj.

rhombi plural form of RHOMBUS.

rhombohedron /ˌrɒmbə(ʊ)ˈhiːdr(ə)n, -ˈhɛd-/ ■ n. (pl. **rhombohedra** /-drə/ or **rhombohedrons**) a solid figure whose faces are six equal rhombuses.
– DERIVATIVES **rhombohedral** adj.
– ORIGIN C19: from RHOMBUS + -HEDRON.

rhomboid /ˈrɒmbɔɪd/ ■ adj. having or resembling the shape of a rhombus. ■ n. a quadrilateral of which only the opposite sides and angles are equal.
– DERIVATIVES **rhomboidal** adj.

rhomboideus /rɒmˈbɔɪdɪəs/ ■ n. (pl. **rhomboidei** /-dɪʌɪ/) Anatomy a muscle connecting the shoulder blade to the vertebrae.
– ORIGIN C19: modern Latin, from *rhomboideus (musculus)* (see RHOMBOID).

rhombus /ˈrɒmbəs/ ■ n. (pl. **rhombuses** or **rhombi** /-bʌɪ/)

Geometry a parallelogram with oblique angles and equal sides.
– ORIGIN C16: from Greek *rhombos*.

rhotic /ˈrəʊtɪk/ ■ adj. Phonetics relating to or denoting a variety of English (e.g. in America and SW England) in which *r* is pronounced before a consonant (as in *hard*) and at the ends of words (as in *far*).
– ORIGIN 1960s: from Greek *rhot-*, stem of *rho* (see RHO).

rhubarb ■ n. 1 a large-leaved plant of the dock family which produces thick reddish or green leaf stalks. [*Rheum rhaponticum* and related species.] ▸ the cooked leaf stalks of this plant, eaten as a dessert. 2 informal noise made by a group of actors to give the impression of indistinct background conversation. ▸ nonsense.
– ORIGIN Middle English: from Old French *reubarbe*, from medieval Latin *rheubarbarum*, alteration of *rhabarbarum* 'foreign rhubarb', from Greek *rha* 'rhubarb' + *barbaros* 'foreign'.

rhumb /rʌm/ (also **rhumb line**) ■ n. Nautical an imaginary line on the earth's surface cutting all meridians at the same angle, used to plot a ship's course on a chart.
– ORIGIN C16: from French *rumb* (earlier *ryn (de vent)* 'point of the compass'); associated with Latin *rhombus* (see RHOMBUS).

rhumba ■ n. variant spelling of RUMBA.

rhyme ■ n. 1 correspondence of sound between words or the endings of words, especially when used in poetry. ▸ a word with the same sound as another. 2 a short poem with rhyming lines. ▸ rhyming poetry or verse. ■ v. 1 (of a word, syllable, or line) have or end with a sound that corresponds to another. ▸ (**rhyme something with**) treat a word as rhyming with (another). ▸ (of a poem or song) be composed in rhyme. 2 poetic/literary compose verse or poetry.
– PHRASES **rhyme or reason** [with neg.] logical explanation.
– DERIVATIVES **rhymer** n.
– ORIGIN Middle English *rime*, from medieval Latin *rithmus*, from Greek *rhuthmos* (see RHYTHM).

rhyme scheme ■ n. the pattern of rhymes in a poem or verse.

rhyming slang ■ n. a type of slang that replaces words with rhyming words or phrases, typically with the rhyming element omitted (e.g. *butcher's*, short for *butcher's hook*, meaning 'look').

rhyolite /ˈrʌɪəlʌɪt/ ■ n. Geology a pale fine-grained volcanic rock of granitic composition.
– ORIGIN C19: from German *Rhyolit*, from Greek *rhuax* 'lava stream' + *lithos* 'stone'.

rhythm /ˈrɪð(ə)m/ ■ n. 1 a strong, regular repeated pattern of movement or sound. ▸ the systematic arrangement of musical sounds, according to duration and periodical stress. ▸ a type of pattern formed by this. 2 a person's natural feeling for rhythm. 3 the measured flow of words and phrases in verse or prose as determined by the length of and stress on syllables. 4 a regularly recurring sequence of events or actions.
– DERIVATIVES **rhythmless** adj.
– ORIGIN C16: from French *rhythme*, from Greek *rhuthmos*, rel. to *rhein* 'to flow'.

rhythm and blues ■ n. popular music of US origin, arising from a combination of blues with jazz rhythms.

rhythmic ■ adj. 1 having or relating to rhythm. 2 occurring regularly.
– DERIVATIVES **rhythmical** adj. **rhythmically** adv.

rhythmic gymnastics ■ pl. n. [usu. treated as sing.] a form of gymnastics with dance-like routines, typically involving the use of ribbons or hoops.

rhythmicity ■ n. rhythmical quality or character.

rhythm method ■ n. a method of birth control involving the avoidance of sexual intercourse when ovulation is likely to occur.

rhythm section ■ n. the part of a pop or jazz group supplying the rhythm, in particular the bass and drums.

ria /ˈriːə/ ■ n. Geography a long narrow inlet formed by the partial submergence of a river valley.
– ORIGIN C19: from Spanish *ría* 'estuary'.

rial /riˈɑːl/ (also **riyal**) ■ n. 1 the basic monetary unit of Iran and Oman. 2 (usu. **riyal**) the basic monetary unit of Saudi Arabia, Qatar, and Yemen.
– ORIGIN from Arabic *riyāl*, from Spanish *real* 'royal'.

rib ■ n. 1 each of a series of slender curved bones articulated in pairs to the spine, protecting the thoracic cavity and its organs. ▸ an animal rib with meat adhering to it used as food. 2 Architecture a curved member supporting a vault or defining its form. 3 a curved transverse strut of metal or timber in a ship, forming part of the framework of the hull. 4 each of the curved pieces of wood forming the body of a lute or violin. 5 each of the hinged rods supporting the fabric of an umbrella. 6 Aeronautics a structural member in an aerofoil. 7 a vein of a leaf or an insect's wing. 8 Knitting alternate plain and purl stitches producing a ridged, slightly elastic fabric. ■ v. (**ribbed**, **ribbing**) 1 (usu. **be ribbed**) mark with or form into raised bands or ridges. 2 informal tease good-naturedly.
– DERIVATIVES **ribber** n.
– ORIGIN Old English, of Germanic origin.

RIBA ■ abbrev. Royal Institute of British Architects.

ribald /ˈrɪb(ə)ld, ˈrʌɪbɔːld/ ■ adj. coarsely or irreverently humorous.
– ORIGIN Middle English: from Old French *ribauld*, from *riber* 'indulge in licentious pleasures', from a Germanic base meaning 'prostitute'.

ribaldry ■ n. ribald talk or behaviour.

riband /ˈrɪb(ə)nd/ ■ n. archaic a ribbon.
– ORIGIN Middle English: from Old French *riban*, prob. from a Germanic compound of BAND[1].

ribbed ■ adj. having a pattern of raised bands. ▸ Architecture strengthened with ribs.

ribbing ■ n. 1 a rib-like structure or pattern. 2 informal good-natured teasing.

ribbon ■ n. 1 a long, narrow strip of fabric, used for tying something or for decoration. ▸ a ribbon of a special colour or design awarded as a prize or worn to indicate the holding of an honour. 2 a long, narrow strip of something. 3 a narrow band of impregnated material wound on a spool and forming the inking agent in some typewriters and computer printers. ■ v. extend or move in a long narrow strip.
– PHRASES **cut** (or **tear**) **something to ribbons** cut (or tear) something into ragged strips. ▸ damage something severely.
– DERIVATIVES **ribboned** adj.
– ORIGIN C16: var. of RIBAND.

ribbon development ■ n. the building of houses along a main road.

ribcage ■ n. the bony frame formed by the ribs.

rib-eye ■ n. a cut of beef from the outer side of the ribs.

riboflavin /ˌrʌɪbə(ʊ)ˈfleɪvɪn/ ■ n. Biochemistry vitamin B_2, a yellow compound essential for energy production and present especially in milk, liver, and green vegetables.
– ORIGIN 1930s: from RIBOSE + Latin *flavus* 'yellow'.

ribonucleic acid /ˌrʌɪbə(ʊ)njuːˈkleɪɪk, -ˈkliːɪk/ ■ n. see RNA.
– ORIGIN 1930s: *ribonucleic* from RIBOSE + NUCLEIC ACID.

ribose /ˈrʌɪbəʊz, -s/ ■ n. Biochemistry a sugar which is a constituent of nucleosides and several vitamins and enzymes.
– ORIGIN C19: alteration of *arabinose*, a related sugar.

ribosome /ˈrʌɪbə(ʊ)səʊm/ ■ n. Biochemistry a minute particle of RNA and protein found in cells, involved in the synthesis of polypeptides and proteins.
– DERIVATIVES **ribosomal** adj.
– ORIGIN 1950s: from RIBONUCLEIC ACID + -SOME[3].

ribozyme /ˈrʌɪbə(ʊ)zʌɪm/ ■ n. Biochemistry an RNA molecule capable of acting as an enzyme.
– ORIGIN 1980s: blend of RIBONUCLEIC ACID and ENZYME.

rib-tickler ■ n. informal a very amusing joke or story.
– DERIVATIVES **rib-tickling** adj. **rib-ticklingly** adv.

rice ■ n. a swamp grass which is cultivated as a source of food, especially in Asia. [*Oryza sativa* and other species.] ▸ the grains of this cereal used as food.
– ORIGIN Middle English: from Old French *ris*, from Italian *riso*, from Greek *oruza*.

rice bowl ■ n. an area in which rice is grown in abundance.

ricepaper ■ n. thin translucent edible paper made from the flattened and dried pith of a shrub, used in oriental painting and in baking biscuits and cakes.

ricer ■ n. N. Amer. a utensil with small holes through which soft food is pushed to form particles resembling rice grains.

rich ■ adj. **1** having a great deal of money or assets. ▸ (of a country or region) having valuable natural resources or a successful economy. ▸ of expensive materials or workmanship. **2** plentiful; abundant. ▸ (**rich in**) having (something) in large amounts. ▸ (of food) containing much fat, spice, etc. ▸ (of the mixture in an internal-combustion engine) containing a high proportion of fuel. **3** (of a colour, sound, or smell) pleasantly deep and strong. **4** full of interesting diversity or complexity. **5** producing or yielding a large quantity of something. ▸ (of soil or land) fertile. **6** informal (of a remark) causing ironic amusement or indignation.
– DERIVATIVES **richen** v. **richness** n.
– ORIGIN Old English *rīce* 'powerful, wealthy', of Germanic origin; from Celtic; reinforced in Middle English by Old French *riche* 'rich, powerful'.

-rich ■ comb. form containing a large amount of something specified: *protein-rich*.

riches ■ pl. n. material wealth. ▸ valuable natural resources.
– ORIGIN Middle English: var. of archaic *richesse*, from Old French *richeise*, from *riche* 'rich'.

richly ■ adv. **1** in an elaborate, generous, or plentiful way. **2** fully: *a richly deserved holiday*.

Richter scale /ˈrɪktə/ ■ n. Geology a logarithmic scale for expressing the magnitude of an earthquake on the basis of seismograph oscillations.
– ORIGIN 1930s: named after the American geologist Charles F. *Richter*.

ricin /ˈraɪsɪn, ˈrɪsɪn/ ■ n. a highly toxic protein obtained from the pressed seeds of the castor oil plant.
– ORIGIN C19: from *Ricinus communis* (denoting the castor oil plant).

rick[1] ■ n. **1** a stack of hay, corn, or straw, especially one built into a regular shape and thatched. **2** N. Amer. a pile of firewood smaller than a cord.
– ORIGIN Old English, of Germanic origin.

rick[2] ■ n. a slight sprain or strain, especially in the neck or back. ■ v. strain (one's neck or back) slightly.
– ORIGIN C18.

rickets /ˈrɪkɪts/ ■ n. [treated as sing. or pl.] Medicine a disease of children caused by vitamin D deficiency, characterized by softening and distortion of the bones typically resulting in bow legs.
– ORIGIN C17: perhaps an alteration of Greek *rhakhitis*, from *rhakhis* 'spine'.

rickettsia /rɪˈkɛtsɪə/ ■ n. (pl. **rickettsiae** /-iː/ or **rickettsias**) any of a group of very small bacteria that cause typhus and other febrile diseases. [Genus *Rickettsia*.]
– DERIVATIVES **rickettsial** adj.
– ORIGIN named after the American pathologist Howard Taylor *Ricketts*.

rickety ■ adj. **1** poorly made and likely to collapse. **2** suffering from rickets.
– DERIVATIVES **ricketiness** n.
– ORIGIN C17: from **RICKETS**.

rickrack ■ n. braided trimming in a zigzag pattern, used on clothes.
– ORIGIN C19: of unknown origin.

rickshaw ■ n. a light two-wheeled hooded vehicle drawn by one or more people, chiefly used in Asian countries.
– ORIGIN C19: abbrev. of Japanese *jinriksha*, from *jin* 'man' + *riki* 'strength' + *sha* 'vehicle'.

ricochet /ˈrɪkəʃeɪ, -ʃɛt/ ■ v. (**ricocheted** /-ʃeɪd/, **ricocheting** /-ʃeɪɪŋ/ or **ricochetted** /-ʃɛtɪd/, **ricochetting** /-ʃɛtɪŋ/) (of a bullet or other projectile) rebound off a surface. ▸ move or appear to move in such a way. ■ n. a shot or hit that ricochets. ▸ the ricocheting action of a bullet or other projectile.
– ORIGIN C18: from French.

ricotta /rɪˈkɒtə/ ■ n. a soft white unsalted Italian cheese.
– ORIGIN Italian, 'recooked, cooked twice'.

RICS ■ abbrev. (in the UK) Royal Institution of Chartered Surveyors.

rictus /ˈrɪktəs/ ■ n. a fixed grimace or grin.
– DERIVATIVES **rictal** adj.
– ORIGIN C19: from Latin, 'open mouth', from *rict-*, *ringi* 'to gape'.

rid ■ v. (**ridding**; past and past part. **rid**) (**rid someone/thing of**) make someone or something free of (an unwanted person or thing). ▸ (**be** (or **get**) **rid of**) be freed or relieved of.
– ORIGIN Middle English: from Old Norse *rythja*.

riddance ■ n. the action of getting rid of someone or something.
– PHRASES **good riddance** expressing relief at being rid of someone or something.

ridden past participle of **RIDE**.

riddle[1] ■ n. a question or statement phrased so as to require ingenuity in ascertaining its answer or meaning. ▸ a person or thing that is difficult to understand. ■ v. archaic speak in or pose riddles. ▸ explain (a riddle) to.
– DERIVATIVES **riddler** n.
– ORIGIN Old English *rǣdels*, *rǣdelse* 'opinion, conjecture, riddle'.

riddle[2] ■ v. **1** (usu. **be riddled**) make many holes in, especially with gunshot. ▸ fill or permeate with something undesirable. **2** pass through a riddle. ■ n. a large coarse sieve, especially one for separating ashes from cinders or sand from gravel.
– ORIGIN Old English, of Germanic origin.

riddling ■ adj. expressed in riddles; enigmatic.

ride ■ v. (past **rode**; past part. **ridden**) **1** sit on and control the movement of (a horse, bicycle, or motorcycle). ▸ (usu. **ride in/on**) travel in or on (a vehicle or horse). ▸ S. African transport (goods). ▸ compete in (a race) on a horse, bicycle, or motorcycle. ▸ N. Amer. travel in (a lift or vehicle). **2** be carried or supported by (something with great momentum). ▸ (of a vessel) sail or float. ▸ (**ride something out**) come safely through something. ▸ yield to (a blow) so as to reduce its impact. **3** project or overlap. ▸ (**ride up**) (of a garment) gradually move upwards out of its proper position. **4** (**ride on**) depend on. **5** [often in combination] (**be ridden**) be full of or dominated by: *crime-ridden streets*. **6** vulgar slang have sexual intercourse with. ■ n. **1** an act of riding. **2** N. Amer. a person giving a lift in a vehicle. **3** US informal a motor vehicle. **4** a path for horse riding. **5** a roller coaster, roundabout, etc. ridden at a fair or amusement park. **6** (also **ride cymbal**) a cymbal keeping up a continuous rhythm. **7** vulgar slang an act of sexual intercourse.
– PHRASES **be riding for a fall** informal be acting in a reckless way that invites failure. **let something ride** take no immediate action over something. **ride high** be successful. **ride shotgun** chiefly N. Amer. travel as a guard next to the driver of a vehicle. **ride to hounds** chiefly Brit. go fox-hunting on horseback. **a rough** (or **easy**) **ride** a difficult (or easy) time. **take someone for a ride** informal deceive someone.
– DERIVATIVES **rideable** (also **ridable**) adj.
– ORIGIN Old English, of Germanic origin.

rider ■ n. **1** a person who rides a horse, bicycle, motorcycle, etc. **2** an added condition or proviso. ▸ an addition or amendment to a bill. ▸ a recommendation or comment added by the jury to a judicial verdict.
– DERIVATIVES **riderless** adj.

ridership ■ n. the number of passengers using a particular form of public transport.

ridge ■ n. **1** a long narrow hilltop, mountain range, or watershed. **2** the edge formed where the two sloping sides of a roof meet at the top. **3** Meteorology an elongated region of high barometric pressure. **4** a narrow raised band on a surface. **5** a raised strip of arable land, especially one of a set separated by furrows. ■ v. [often as adj. **ridged**] mark with or form into ridges.
– ORIGIN Old English *hrycg* 'spine, crest', of Germanic origin.

ridgeback ■ n. short for **RHODESIAN RIDGEBACK**.

ridge piece

ridge piece (also **ridge tree**) ■ n. a horizontal beam along the ridge of a roof, into which the rafters are fixed.

ridge pole ■ n. **1** the horizontal pole of a long tent. **2** a ridge pole.

ridge tent ■ n. a tent with a central ridge supported by a pole or frame at each end.

ridge tile ■ n. a curved tile used in making a roof ridge.

ridgeway ■ n. a road or track along a ridge.

ridicule ■ n. mockery or derision. ■ v. subject to ridicule.
– ORIGIN C17: from Latin *ridiculum*, from *ridiculus* 'laughable', from *ridere* 'to laugh'.

ridiculous ■ adj. inviting ridicule; absurd.
– DERIVATIVES **ridiculously** adv. **ridiculousness** n.
– ORIGIN C16: from Latin *ridiculosus*, from *ridiculus* (see RIDICULE).

riding ■ n. the sport or activity of riding horses.

riding crop ■ n. a short flexible whip with a loop for the hand, used when riding horses.

riding habit ■ n. a woman's riding dress, consisting of a skirt and a double-breasted jacket.

riding light ■ n. a light shown by a ship at anchor.

ridley ■ n. (pl. **-eys**) a small turtle of tropical seas. [*Lepidochelys kempi* and *Latin olivacea*.]
– ORIGIN 1940s.

riel /ˈriːəl/ ■ n. the basic monetary unit of Cambodia.
– ORIGIN from Khmer.

riempie /ˈrɪmpɪ/ ■ n. S. African a strip of worked leather, used especially in making seats for chairs and benches. ▸ [as modifier] denoting a piece of furniture with a seat made of these strips.
– ORIGIN Afrikaans, from *riem* 'leather, thong'.

Riesling /ˈriːzlɪŋ, ˈriːs-/ ■ n. a variety of wine grape grown especially in Germany and Austria. ▸ a dry white wine made from this grape.
– ORIGIN from German.

rietbok /ˈriːtbɒk/ ■ n. S. African another term for REEDBUCK.
– ORIGIN C18: from S. African Dutch *riet* 'reed' + *bok* 'antelope, goat'.

rifampicin /rɪˈfæmpɪsɪn/ (also **rifampin**) ■ n. Medicine a bacterial antibiotic used chiefly to treat tuberculosis and leprosy.
– ORIGIN 1960s: from *rifamycin* (a related antibiotic) + *pi-* from *piperazine* (a synthetic compound used as an anthelmintic).

rife ■ adj. (especially of something undesirable) widespread. ▸ (**rife with**) full of.
– DERIVATIVES **rifeness** n.
– ORIGIN Old English, prob. from Old Norse *rífr* 'acceptable'.

riff ■ n. a short repeated phrase in popular music or jazz. ■ v. [usu. as noun **riffing**] play riffs.
– ORIGIN 1930s: abbrev. of RIFFLE.

riffle ■ v. **1** turn over something, especially pages, quickly and casually. ▸ (**riffle through**) search quickly through. ▸ ruffle. **2** shuffle (playing cards) by flicking up and releasing the corners of two piles of cards so that they intermingle. ■ n. **1** an act of riffling. **2** chiefly N. Amer. a shallow part of a stream or river. ▸ a patch of waves or ripples.
– ORIGIN C18: perhaps from a var. of RUFFLE, influenced by RIPPLE.

riff-raff ■ n. disreputable or undesirable people.
– ORIGIN C15: from Old French *rif et raf* 'one and all, every bit', of Germanic origin.

rifle[1] ■ n. **1** a gun, especially one fired from shoulder level, having a long spirally grooved barrel to make a bullet spin and thereby increase accuracy over a long distance. **2** (**rifles**) troops armed with rifles. ■ v. **1** [usu. as adj. **rifled**] make spiral grooves in (a gun or its barrel or bore). **2** hit or kick (a ball) hard and straight.
– ORIGIN C17: from French *rifler* 'graze, scratch', of Germanic origin.

rifle[2] ■ v. search through something hurriedly in order to find or steal something. ▸ steal.
– ORIGIN Middle English: from Old French *rifler* 'graze, plunder', of Germanic origin.

rifleman ■ n. (pl. **-men**) a soldier armed with a rifle.

rifle range ■ n. a place for practising rifle shooting.

rifling ■ n. spiral grooves on the inside of a rifle barrel.

rift ■ n. **1** a crack, split, or break in something. **2** a serious break in friendly relations. **3** Geology a rift valley. ■ v. [often as adj. **rifted**] chiefly Geology move or force to move apart.
– ORIGIN Middle English: of Scandinavian origin.

rift valley ■ n. a steep-sided valley formed by subsidence of the earth's surface between nearly parallel faults.

rig[1] ■ v. (**rigged**, **rigging**) **1** provide (a boat) with sails and rigging. ▸ assemble and adjust (the equipment of a sailing boat, aircraft, etc.) in readiness for operation. ▸ (often **rig something up**) set up (a device or structure), typically in a makeshift way. **2** (often **rig someone up**) provide with clothes of a particular type. ■ n. **1** the arrangement of a boat's sails and rigging. ▸ the sail, mast, and boom of a windsurfer. **2** an apparatus or device for a particular purpose. ▸ an oil rig or drilling rig. ▸ (in CB and short-wave radio) a transmitter and receiver. ▸ a type of construction for fishing tackle that bears the bait and hook. **3** a person's costume or outfit. **4** chiefly N. Amer. & Austral./NZ a truck.
– DERIVATIVES **-rigged** adj.
– ORIGIN C15: perhaps of Scandinavian origin.

rig[2] ■ v. (**rigged**, **rigging**) manage or conduct fraudulently so as to gain an advantage.
– ORIGIN C18.

rigatoni /ˌrɪɡəˈtəʊni/ ■ pl. n. pasta in the form of short hollow fluted tubes.
– ORIGIN from Italian.

rigger ■ n. **1** [in combination] a ship rigged in a particular way. **2** a person who attends to the rigging of a sailing ship, aircraft, or parachute. **3** a person who erects and maintains scaffolding, cranes, etc. **4** a person who works on an oil rig.

rigging ■ n. **1** the system of ropes or chains supporting a ship's masts and controlling or setting the yards and sails. **2** the ropes and wires supporting the structure of an airship, biplane, hang-glider, or parachute. ▸ the cables and fittings controlling the flight surfaces and engines of an aircraft.

right ■ adj. **1** morally good, justified, or acceptable. **2** factually correct. ▸ most appropriate. ▸ socially fashionable or important. **3** in a satisfactory, sound, or normal state or condition. **4** on, towards, or relating to the side of a human body or of a thing which is to the east when the person or thing is facing north. **5** informal, chiefly Brit. complete; absolute: *I felt a right idiot*. **6** of or relating to a right-wing person or group. ■ adv. **1** to the furthest or most complete extent or degree. ▸ exactly; directly. ▸ informal immediately. ▸ dialect or archaic very. **2** correctly. ▸ satisfactorily. **3** on or to the right side. ■ n. **1** that which is morally right. **2** a moral or legal entitlement to have or do something. ▸ (**rights**) the authority to perform, publish, or film a particular work or event. **3** (**the right**) the right-hand part, side, or direction. ▸ a right turn. ▸ a person's right fist, or a blow given with it. **4** (often **the Right**) [treated as sing. or pl.] a group or political party favouring conservative views. ■ v. **1** restore to a normal or upright position. ▸ restore to a normal or correct condition. **2** rectify. ■ exclam. informal indicating agreement or acknowledging a statement or order.
– PHRASES **bang** (or N. Amer. **dead**) **to rights** informal (of a criminal) with positive proof of guilt. **be in the right** be justified in one's views or actions. **by rights** if things were fair or correct. **do right by** treat fairly. **in one's own right** as a result of one's own claims, qualifications, or efforts. (**as**) **of right** (or **by right**) due to a moral or legal claim or entitlement. **put** (or **set**) **someone right** tell someone the true facts of a situation. **put** (or **set**) **something to rights** restore something to its correct or normal state. (**as**) **right as rain** informal completely well or healthy. **right** (or **straight**) **away** (or informal **off**) immediately. **right on** informal expressing support, approval, or encouragement. **a right one** Brit. informal a silly or foolish person.
– DERIVATIVES **righter** n. **rightmost** adj. **rightness** n. **rightward** adj. & adv. **rightwards** adv.
– ORIGIN Old English, of Germanic origin; rel. to Latin *rectus* 'ruled'.

VOWELS a cat ɑː arm ɛ bed eː hair ə ago əː her ɪ sit i cosy iː see ɒ hot ɔː saw ʌ run

right about (also **right about-face**) ▪ n. Military a right turn through 180° so as to face in the opposite direction.

right angle ▪ n. an angle of 90°, as in a corner of a square.
– PHRASES **at right angles to** forming an angle of 90° with.
– DERIVATIVES **right-angled** adj.

right ascension ▪ n. Astronomy position measured along the celestial equator, expressed in hours, minutes, and seconds.

right back ▪ n. a defender in soccer or field hockey who plays primarily on the right of the field.

right bank ▪ n. the bank of a river on the right as one faces downstream.

right brain ▪ n. the right-hand side of the human brain, believed to be associated with creative thought and the emotions.

righteous /ˈraɪtʃəs/ ▪ adj. morally right or justifiable.
– DERIVATIVES **righteously** adv. **righteousness** n.
– ORIGIN Old English *rihtwīs*, from *riht* 'right' + *wīs* 'manner, state, condition'; the change in the ending was by association with words such as *bounteous*.

right field ▪ n. Baseball the part of the outfield to the right of the batter when facing the pitcher.
– DERIVATIVES **right fielder** n.

rightful ▪ adj. having a legitimate right to something. ▸ legitimately claimed; fitting.
– DERIVATIVES **rightfully** adv. **rightfulness** n.

right hand ▪ n. 1 the hand of a person's right side. ▸ the region or direction on the right side. 2 the most important position next to someone. ▸ an indispensable assistant. ▪ adj. on or towards the right side. ▸ done with or using the right hand.

right-hand drive ▪ n. a motor-vehicle steering system with the steering wheel and other controls fitted on the right side, for use in countries where vehicles drive on the left side of the road.

right-handed ▪ adj. 1 using or done with the right hand. 2 going towards or turning to the right. ▸ (of a screw) advanced by turning clockwise.
– DERIVATIVES **right-handedly** adv. **right-handedness** n.

right-hander ▪ n. 1 a right-handed person. 2 a blow struck with the right hand.

right-hand man ▪ n. an indispensable helper or chief assistant.

Right Honourable ▪ adj. a title given to certain high officials such as government ministers.

rightism ▪ n. the political views or policies of the right.
– DERIVATIVES **rightist** n. & adj.

rightly ▪ adv. correctly. ▸ with good reason. ▸ in accordance with justice or what is morally right.

right-minded ▪ adj. having sound views and principles.

righto (also chiefly Brit. **righty-ho**) ▪ exclam. informal expressing agreement or assent.

right of abode ▪ n. a person's right to live in a country.

right of way ▪ n. 1 the legal right to pass along a specific route through property belonging to another. ▸ a thoroughfare subject to such a right. 2 the right of a pedestrian, vehicle, or ship to proceed with precedence over others in a situation or place.

right-on ▪ adj. informal, often derogatory in keeping with fashionable liberal or left-wing opinions and values.

Right Reverend ▪ adj. a title given to a bishop.

right side ▪ n. the side of something intended to be uppermost or foremost.
– PHRASES **on the right side of** on the safe, appropriate, or desirable side of. **right side out** not inside out.

rights issue ▪ n. an issue of shares offered at a special price by a company to its existing shareholders.

rightsize ▪ v. convert to an appropriate or optimum size, in particular shed staff from (an organization).

right-thinking ▪ adj. right-minded.

right-to-life ▪ adj. another term for **PRO-LIFE**.
– DERIVATIVES **right-to-lifer** n.

right triangle ▪ n. N. Amer. a right-angled triangle.

right whale ▪ n. a baleen whale with a large head and a deeply curved jaw, of Arctic and temperate waters.

1017

[*Balaena glacialis* and other species.]
– ORIGIN C18: so named because it was regarded as the 'right' whale to hunt.

right wing ▪ n. 1 the conservative or reactionary section of a political party or system. [see **LEFT WING**.] 2 the right side of a sports team on the field or of an army.
– DERIVATIVES **right-winger** n.

righty-ho ▪ exclam. variant of **RIGHTO**.

rigid ▪ adj. 1 unable to bend or be forced out of shape. ▸ (of a person) stiff and unmoving. 2 not able to be changed or adapted. ▪ n. a truck which is not articulated.
– DERIVATIVES **rigidify** v. **rigidity** n. **rigidly** adv. **rigidness** n.
– ORIGIN Middle English: from Latin *rigidus*, from *rigere* 'be stiff'.

rigmarole /ˈrɪɡmərəʊl/ ▪ n. a lengthy and complicated procedure. ▸ a long, rambling story.
– ORIGIN C18: an alteration of *ragman roll*, orig. denoting a legal document recording a list of offences.

rigor[1] /ˈrɪɡɔː, ˈraɪɡɔː, -ɡə/ ▪ n. 1 Medicine a sudden feeling of cold accompanied by shivering and a rise in temperature, especially at the onset or height of a fever. 2 short for **RIGOR MORTIS**.
– ORIGIN Middle English: from Latin, 'stiffness', from *rigere* 'be stiff'.

rigor[2] ▪ n. US spelling of **RIGOUR**.

rigorism ▪ n. extreme strictness in interpreting a law or principle.
– DERIVATIVES **rigorist** n. & adj.

rigor mortis /ˈmɔːtɪs/ ▪ n. Medicine stiffening of the joints and muscles a few hours after death, lasting from one to four days.
– ORIGIN C19: from Latin, 'stiffness of death'.

rigorous ▪ adj. 1 extremely thorough, exhaustive, or accurate. 2 (of a rule, system, etc.) strictly applied or adhered to. ▸ adhering strictly to a belief, opinion, or system. 3 (of weather) harsh.
– DERIVATIVES **rigorously** adv. **rigorousness** n.
– ORIGIN Middle English: from Old French *rigorous* or late Latin *rigorosus*, from *rigor* (see **RIGOR**[1]).

rigour (US **rigor**) ▪ n. 1 the quality of being rigorous. 2 (**rigours**) demanding, difficult, or extreme conditions.
– ORIGIN Middle English: from Old French *rigour* from Latin *rigor* 'stiffness'.

Rig Veda /rɪɡ ˈveɪdə, ˈviːdə/ ▪ n. the oldest and principal of the Vedas.
– ORIGIN from Sanskrit *ṛgveda*, from *ṛc* '(sacred) stanza' + **VEDA**.

rile ▪ v. informal annoy or irritate.
– ORIGIN C19: var. of **ROIL**.

Riley ▪ n. (in phr. **the life of Riley**) informal a luxurious or carefree existence.
– ORIGIN C20.

rill /rɪl/ ▪ n. 1 a small stream. 2 a shallow channel cut in soil or rocks by running water. ▸ variant spelling of **RILLE**.
– ORIGIN C16: prob. of Low German origin.

rille /rɪl/ (also **rill**) ▪ n. Astronomy a fissure or narrow channel on the moon's surface.
– ORIGIN C19: from German (see **RILL**).

rim[1] ▪ n. 1 the upper or outer edge of something, typically something circular. ▸ (also **wheel rim**) the outer edge of a wheel, on which the tyre is fitted. ▸ the part of a spectacle frame surrounding the lenses. 2 the limit or boundary of something. ▸ an encircling stain or deposit. ▪ v. (**rimmed**, **rimming**) (usu. **be rimmed**) provide with a rim.
– DERIVATIVES **rimless** adj. **-rimmed** adj.
– ORIGIN Old English *rima* 'a border, coast', rel. to Old Norse *rimi* 'ridge, strip of land'.

rim[2] ▪ v. (**rimmed**, **rimming**) vulgar slang lick or suck the anus of (a partner) for sexual stimulation.
– ORIGIN C20: perhaps var. of **REAM**[2].

rime[1] /raɪm/ ▪ n. (also **rime ice**) frost formed on cold objects by the rapid freezing of water vapour in cloud or fog. ▸ poetic/literary hoar frost. ▪ v. poetic/literary cover with hoar frost.
– DERIVATIVES **rimy** adj. (**-ier**, **-iest**).
– ORIGIN Old English, of Germanic origin.

rime

rime² ■ n. & v. archaic spelling of RHYME.

rimfire ■ adj. (of a cartridge) having the primer around the edge of the base. ▸ (of a rifle) adapted for such cartridges.

rind ■ n. a tough outer layer or covering, especially of fruit, cheese, or bacon.
– DERIVATIVES **-rinded** adj. **rindless** adj.
– ORIGIN Old English *rind(e)*.

rinderpest /'rɪndəpɛst/ ■ n. an infectious viral disease of ruminants, especially cattle, characterized by fever and dysentery.
– ORIGIN C19: from German, from *Rinder* 'cattle' + *Pest* 'plague'.

ring¹ ■ n. **1** a small circular band, typically of precious metal, worn on a finger as an ornament or as a token of marriage or engagement. **2** a circular band, article, or mark. ▸ a thin band of rock and ice particles round a planet. ▸ a flat circular heating device forming part of a gas or electric hob. ▸ Archaeology a circular prehistoric earthwork, typically consisting of a bank and ditch. **3** an enclosed space in which a sport, performance, or show takes place. **4** a circle of people or things. ▸ a group of people with a shared interest or goal, especially one involving illegal activity. **5** Chemistry a number of atoms bonded together to form a closed loop in a molecule. ■ v. **1** surround. ▸ draw a circle round. **2** Ornithology put an identifying strip around the leg of (a bird). **3** put a circular band through the nose of (a bull, pig, etc.) to lead or control it.
– PHRASES **hold the ring** monitor a dispute or conflict without becoming involved. **run** (or **make**) **rings round** (or **around**) informal outclass or outwit (someone) easily.
– DERIVATIVES **ringed** adj. **ringless** adj.
– ORIGIN Old English *hring*, of Germanic origin.

ring² ■ v. (past **rang**; past part. **rung**) **1** make or cause to make a clear resonant or vibrating sound. ▸ (of a telephone) ring repeatedly to signal an incoming call. ▸ call for attention by sounding a bell. ▸ (often **ring with**) reverberate with a sound. ▸ (of the ears) be filled with a buzzing or humming sound due to a blow or loud noise. ▸ (**ring something up**) record an amount on a cash register. **2** call by telephone. ▸ (**ring off**) chiefly Brit. end a telephone call by replacing the receiver. **3** sound (the hour, a peal, etc.) on a bell or bells. ▸ (**ring someone/thing in**) or **out** usher someone or something in (or out) by or as if by ringing a bell. **4** convey a specified impression or quality: *her story rings true*. ▸ (**ring with**) be filled with (a quality). ■ n. **1** an act or instance of ringing. ▸ a loud clear sound or tone. **2** informal a telephone call. **3** a quality conveyed by something heard: *the tale had a ring of truth*. **4** a set of bells, especially church bells.
– PHRASES **ring down** (or **up**) **the curtain 1** lower (or raise) a theatre curtain. **2** mark the end (or beginning) of something.
– ORIGIN Old English *hringan*, of Germanic origin, perhaps imitative.

ring-a-ring o' roses ■ n. a children's singing game in which players hold hands and dance in a circle, falling down at the end of the song.
– ORIGIN said to refer to the inflamed ('rose-coloured') ring of buboes, symptomatic of the plague.

ringbark ■ v. remove a ring of bark from (a tree) to kill it or to check rapid growth and improve fruit production.

ring binder ■ n. a loose-leaf binder with ring-shaped clasps that can be opened to pass through holes in the paper.
– DERIVATIVES **ring-bound** adj.

ringbolt ■ n. a bolt with a ring attached for fitting a rope to.

ringer ■ n. **1** informal a person's or thing's double. ▸ an athlete or horse fraudulently substituted for another in a competition. **2** a person or device that rings something.

Ringer's solution ■ n. Biology a physiological saline solution containing sodium chloride and salts of potassium and calcium.
– ORIGIN C19: named after the English physician Sydney Ringer.

ring fence ■ n. a fence completely enclosing a piece of land. **2** an effective barrier. ■ v. (**ring-fence**) **1** enclose with a ring fence. **2** guarantee that (funds for a particular purpose) will not be spent on anything else.

ring finger ■ n. the finger next to the little finger, especially of the left hand, on which the wedding ring is worn.

ringgit /'rɪŋgɪt/ ■ n. (pl. same or **ringgits**) the basic monetary unit of Malaysia.
– ORIGIN from Malay.

ringing ■ adj. **1** having a clear resonant sound. **2** (of a statement) forceful and unequivocal.
– DERIVATIVES **ringingly** adv.

ringleader ■ n. a person who leads an illicit activity.

ringlet ■ n. **1** a corkscrew-shaped curl of hair. **2** a brown butterfly with wings bearing eyespots. [*Ypthima asterope* (Africa), *Aphantopus hyperantus* (Europe), and other species.]
– DERIVATIVES **ringletted** (also **ringleted**) adj. **ringlety** adj.

ring main ■ n. **1** an electrical supply serving a series of consumers and returning to the original source. **2** an electric circuit serving a number of power points, with one fuse in the supply.

ringmaster ■ n. the person directing a circus performance.

ringneck ■ n. a bird with a ring of colour round the neck.
– DERIVATIVES **ring-necked** adj.

ring pull ■ n. a ring on a can that is pulled to open it.

ring road ■ n. a bypass encircling a town.

ringside ■ n. the area beside a boxing ring or circus ring.
– DERIVATIVES **ringsider** n.

ringside seat ■ n. an advantageous position from which to observe something.

ring spanner ■ n. a spanner in which the jaws form a ring which fits completely around a nut.

ringtail ■ n. a mammal or bird having a tail marked with a ring or rings.
– DERIVATIVES **ring-tailed** adj.

ring-tailed lemur ■ n. a grey lemur with black rings around the eyes and a distinctive black-and-white banded tail. [*Lemur catta*].

ringtone ■ n. a sound made by a cellphone when an incoming call is received.

ringworm ■ n. a contagious itching skin disease occurring in small circular patches, caused by any of a number of fungi and affecting chiefly the scalp or feet.

rink ■ n. **1** (also **ice rink**) an enclosed area of ice for skating, ice hockey, or curling. ▸ (also **roller rink**) a smooth enclosed floor for roller skating. ▸ (also **bowling rink**) the strip of a bowling green used for a match. **2** a team in curling or bowls.
– ORIGIN Middle English: perhaps orig. from Old French *renc* 'rank'.

rinkhals /'rɪŋkhals/ ■ n. a large spitting cobra of southern Africa, with one or two white rings across the throat. [*Hemachatus haemachatus*.]
– ORIGIN C18: from Afrikaans *rinkhals*, from *ring* 'ring' + *hals* 'neck'.

rinky-dink ■ adj. informal, chiefly N. Amer. old-fashioned, amateurish, or shoddy.
– ORIGIN C19.

Rinpoche /'rɪmpɒtʃeɪ/ ■ n. a religious teacher held in high regard among Tibetan Buddhists.
– ORIGIN Tibetan, 'precious jewel'.

rinse ■ v. wash with clean water to remove soap or dirt. ▸ **rinse something off/out**) remove (soap or dirt) by rinsing. ■ n. **1** an act of rinsing. **2** an antiseptic solution for cleansing the mouth. **3** a preparation for conditioning or tinting the hair.
– DERIVATIVES **rinser** n.
– ORIGIN Middle English: from Old French *rincer*.

Rioja /rɪ'ɒhə, rɪ'ɒkə/ ■ n. a wine produced in La Rioja, Spain.

riot ■ n. **1** a violent disturbance of the peace by a crowd. **2** a confused or lavish combination or display: *a riot of colour*. **3** (**a riot**) informal a highly amusing or entertaining person or thing. ■ v. **1** take part in a riot. **2** behave in an unrestrained way.

– PHRASES **read the Riot Act** give a severe warning or reprimand. **run riot 1** behave or be displayed in a violent and unrestrained way. **2** proliferate or spread uncontrollably.
– DERIVATIVES **rioter** n.
– ORIGIN Middle English: from Old French *riote* 'debate', from *rioter* 'to quarrel'.

riot girl (also **riot grrrl**) ■ n. a member of a movement of young feminists favouring aggressive punk-style rock music.

riotous ■ adj. **1** marked by or involving public disorder. ▸ involving wild and uncontrolled behaviour. **2** having a vivid, varied appearance.
– DERIVATIVES **riotously** adv. **riotousness** n.

RIP ■ abbrev. rest in peace (used on graves).
– ORIGIN from Latin *requiescat* (or (pl.) *requiescant*) *in pace*.

rip¹ ■ v. (**ripped**, **ripping**) **1** tear or pull forcibly away from something or someone. ▸ tear. ▸ (**rip something up**) tear something into small pieces. **2** move forcefully and rapidly. **3** (**rip into**) informal make a vehement verbal attack on. **4** (**rip someone off**) informal cheat someone, especially financially. ▸ (**rip something off**) informal steal or plagiarize something. ■ n. a long tear or cut.
– PHRASES **let rip** informal proceed vigorously or without restraint. ▸ express oneself vehemently.
– ORIGIN Middle English.

rip² ■ n. a stretch of fast-flowing and rough water caused by the meeting of currents.
– ORIGIN C18: perhaps rel. to RIP¹.

riparian /rʌɪˈpɛːrɪən/ ■ adj. of, relating to, or situated on the banks of a river.
– ORIGIN C19: from Latin *riparius*, from *ripa* 'bank'.

ripcord ■ n. a cord that is pulled to open a parachute.

rip current ■ n. an intermittent strong surface current flowing seaward from the shore.

ripe ■ adj. **1** (of fruit or grain) ready for harvesting and eating. ▸ (of a cheese or wine) fully matured. **2** (**ripe for**) arrived at a fitting time for. **3** (of a person's age) advanced. **4** (**ripe with**) full of. **5** (of a female fish or insect) ready to lay eggs or spawn.
– DERIVATIVES **ripely** adv. **ripeness** n.
– ORIGIN Old English, of West Germanic origin.

ripen ■ v. become or make ripe.

rip-off ■ n. informal **1** an article that is greatly overpriced. **2** an inferior imitation.

riposte /rɪˈpɒst/ ■ n. **1** a quick clever reply. **2** a quick return thrust in fencing. ■ v. make a riposte.
– ORIGIN C18: from French *risposte* (n.), from Italian *risposta* 'response'.

ripper ■ n. a person or thing that rips.

ripping ■ adj. Brit. informal, dated excellent.
– DERIVATIVES **rippingly** adv.

ripple ■ n. **1** a small wave or series of waves. ▸ Physics a small wave in which the dominant force is surface tension rather than gravity. **2** a gentle rising and falling sound that spreads through a group of people. ▸ a feeling that spreads through someone or something. **3** a small periodic voltage variation superposed on a direct voltage or low-frequency alternating voltage. **4** a type of ice cream with wavy lines of coloured flavoured syrup running through it. ■ v. **1** form or cause to form ripples. **2** (of a sound or feeling) spread through a person or place.
– DERIVATIVES **ripplet** n. **ripply** adj.
– ORIGIN C17.

ripple marks ■ pl. n. a system of parallel wavy ridges and furrows left on sand, mud, or rock by the action of water or wind.

rip-roaring ■ adj. full of energy and vigour.
– DERIVATIVES **rip-roaringly** adv.

ripsaw ■ n. a coarse saw for cutting wood along the grain.

ripsnorting ■ adj. informal showing great vigour or intensity.

ripstop ■ n. nylon fabric that is woven so that a tear will not spread.

rip tide ■ n. another term for RIP².

RISC ■ n. [usu. as modifier] computers or computing based on a form of microprocessor designed to perform a limited set of operations extremely quickly.
– ORIGIN 1980s: acronym from *reduced instruction set computer* (or *computing*).

rise ■ v. (past **rose**; past part. **risen**) **1** come or go up. ▸ reach a higher social or professional position. ▸ (**rise above**) succeed in not being constrained by. **2** get up from lying, sitting, or kneeling. ▸ (of a meeting or a session of a court) adjourn. **3** (of land) incline upwards. ▸ (of a structure or natural feature) be much taller than the surrounding landscape. **4** (of the sun, moon, or stars) appear above the horizon. **5** increase in number, size, intensity, or quality. **6** (**rise to**) respond adequately to (a challenging situation). **7** (often **rise up**) cease to be submissive or peaceful. **8** (of a river) have its source: *the Euphrates rises in Turkey*. **9** be restored to life. ■ n. **1** an act or instance of rising. **2** an upward slope or hill. **3** an increase in salary or wages. **4** the source of a river. **5** the vertical height of a step, arch, or incline. ▸ another term for RISER (in sense 2).
– PHRASES **get** (or **take**) **a rise out of** informal provoke an angry or irritated response from. **on the rise 1** increasing. **2** becoming more successful. **rise and shine** informal wake up and get out of bed promptly.
– ORIGIN Old English *rīsan* 'make an attack, get out of bed', of Germanic origin.

riser ■ n. **1** a person who habitually gets out of bed at a particular time of the morning: *an early riser*. **2** a vertical section between the treads of a staircase. **3** a vertical pipe for the upward flow of liquid or gas. **4** a low platform on a stage or in an auditorium. **5** a strip of webbing joining the harness and the rigging lines of a parachute or paraglider.

rishi /ˈrɪʃi/ ■ n. (pl. **rishis**) a Hindu sage or saint.
– ORIGIN from Sanskrit *ṛṣi*.

risible /ˈrɪzɪb(ə)l/ ■ adj. such as to provoke laughter.
– DERIVATIVES **risibility** n. **risibly** adv.
– ORIGIN C16: from late Latin *risibilis*, from Latin *ridere* 'to laugh'.

rising ■ adj. **1** approaching a specified age. **2** [postpos.] Heraldry (of a bird) depicted with the wings open but not fully displayed, as if preparing for flight. ■ n. a revolt.

rising damp ■ n. moisture absorbed from the ground into a wall.

risk ■ n. **1** a situation involving exposure to danger. ▸ the possibility that something unpleasant will happen. **2** a person or thing causing a risk or regarded in relation to risk: *a fire risk*. ■ v. expose to danger or loss. ▸ act in such a way as to incur the risk of. ▸ incur risk by engaging in (an action).
– PHRASES **at one's** (**own**) **risk** taking responsibility for one's own safety or possessions. **run** (or **take**) **a risk** (or **risks**) act in such a way as to expose oneself to danger.
– ORIGIN C17: from French *risque* (n.), *risquer* (v.), from Italian *risco* 'danger' and *rischiare* 'run into danger'.

risk capital ■ n. another term for VENTURE CAPITAL.

risky ■ adj. (**-ier**, **-iest**) **1** involving risk. **2** risqué.
– DERIVATIVES **riskily** adv. **riskiness** n.

risotto /rɪˈzɒtəʊ/ ■ n. (pl. **-os**) an Italian dish of rice cooked in stock with ingredients such as meat or sea-food.
– ORIGIN Italian, from *riso* 'rice'.

risqué /ˈriːskeɪ, ˈrɪskeɪ, riːˈskeɪ/ ■ adj. slightly indecent and liable to shock.
– ORIGIN C19: French, from *risquer* 'to risk'.

rissole ■ n. a compressed mixture of meat and spices, coated in breadcrumbs and fried.
– ORIGIN C18: from Old French dialect *ruissole*, from late Latin *russeolus* 'reddish'.

Ritalin /ˈrɪtəlɪn/ ■ n. trademark for METHYLPHENIDATE.
– ORIGIN 1940s: invented word.

rite ■ n. **1** a religious or other solemn ceremony or act. **2** a body of customary observances characteristic of a Church or a part of it.
– PHRASES **rite of passage** a ceremony or event, e.g. marriage, marking an important stage in someone's life.
– ORIGIN Middle English: from Latin *ritus* '(religious) usage'.

ritual ■ n. **1** a religious or solemn ceremony involving a series of actions performed according to a prescribed order. ▸ a prescribed order of performing such a ceremony. **2** a series of actions habitually and invariably

ritualism

followed by someone. ■ adj. of, relating to, or done as a ritual.
– DERIVATIVES **ritually** adv.
– ORIGIN C16: from Latin *ritualis*, from *ritus* (see RITE).

ritualism ■ n. the regular observance or practice of ritual, especially when excessive or without regard to its function.
– DERIVATIVES **ritualist** n. **ritualistic** adj. **ritualistically** adv.

ritualize (also **-ise**) ■ v. [usu. as adj. **ritualized** (also **-ised**)] 1 make into a ritual by following a pattern of actions or behaviour. 2 Zoology retain (a behaviour pattern) as a form of display or interaction, without its original function.
– DERIVATIVES **ritualization** (also **-isation**) n.

ritual murder ■ n. S. African murder committed to obtain human body parts for use as charms or potions or in religious rites.

ritzy ■ adj. (**-ier**, **-iest**) informal expensively stylish.
– DERIVATIVES **ritzily** adv. **ritziness** n.

rival ■ n. a person or thing competing with another for superiority or the same objective. ▶ [with neg.] a person or thing equal to another in quality. ■ v. (**rivalled**, **rivalling**; US **rivaled**, **rivaling**) be comparable to.
– DERIVATIVES **rivalrous** adj. **rivalry** n. (pl. **-ies**).
– ORIGIN C16: from Latin *rivalis*, orig. in the sense 'person using the same stream as another', from *rivus* 'stream'.

rive /raɪv/ ■ v. (past **rived**; past part. **riven** /ˈrɪv(ə)n/) (usu. **be riven**) tear apart. ▶ archaic (with reference to wood or stone) split.
– ORIGIN Middle English: from Old Norse *rífa*.

river ■ n. 1 a large natural flow of water travelling along a channel to the sea, a lake, or another river. 2 a large quantity of a flowing substance.
– PHRASES **sell someone down the river** informal betray someone. [orig. with ref. to the sale of a troublesome slave to a plantation owner on the lower Mississippi, in the southern US, where conditions were relatively harsher.]
– DERIVATIVES **rivered** adj. **riverless** adj.
– ORIGIN Middle English: from Anglo-Norman French, from Latin *riparius*, from *ripa* 'bank of a river'.

river blindness ■ n. a tropical skin disease, sometimes also causing blindness, caused by a parasitic filarial worm and transmitted by blackflies which breed in rivers.

river capture ■ n. Geology the natural diversion of the headwaters of one stream into the channel of another, due to erosion.

riverine /ˈrɪvəraɪn/ ■ adj. technical or poetic/literary of, relating to, or situated on a river or riverbank.

river lily (also **scarlet river lily**) ■ n. a South African plant with strap-like leaves and scarlet star-shaped flowers. [*Hesperantha* (formerly *Schizostylis*) *coccinea*.]

rivet /ˈrɪvɪt/ ■ n. a short metal pin or bolt for holding together two metal plates, its headless end being beaten out or pressed down when in place. ■ v. (**riveted**, **riveting**) 1 join or fasten with a rivet or rivets. 2 (usu. **be riveted**) completely engross. ▶ direct (one's eyes or attention) intently.
– DERIVATIVES **riveter** n. **riveting** adj. **rivetingly** adv.
– ORIGIN Middle English: from Old French, from *river* 'fix, clinch'.

riviera /ˌrɪviˈɛːrə/ ■ n. a coastal region with a subtropical climate and vegetation. ▶ (**the Riviera**) part of the Mediterranean coastal region of southern France and northern Italy.
– ORIGIN C18: from Italian, 'seashore'.

rivulet /ˈrɪvjʊlɪt/ ■ n. a very small stream.
– ORIGIN C16: alteration of obsolete *riveret* (from French, 'small river').

rix-dollar /ˈrɪksdɒlə/ ■ n. historical a unit of currency introduced by the Dutch into certain former colonies, including the Cape.
– ORIGIN from Dutch *rijksdaalder*, from *rijks* 'imperial' + *daalder* 'dollar'.

riyal ■ n. variant spelling of RIAL.

rm ■ abbrev. room.

rms ■ abbrev. root mean square.

RN ■ abbrev. 1 (in the UK) Royal Navy. 2 (chiefly in North America) Registered Nurse.

Rn ■ symb. the chemical element radon.

RNA ■ n. Biochemistry ribonucleic acid, a substance in living cells which carries instructions from DNA for controlling the synthesis of proteins and in some viruses carries genetic information instead of DNA.

RNase ■ n. Biochemistry an enzyme which breaks down RNA into smaller molecules.
– ORIGIN 1950s: from **RNA**.

RNA virus ■ n. a virus in which the genetic information is stored in the form of RNA (as opposed to DNA).

roach[1] ■ n. (pl. same) a common European freshwater fish of the carp family. [*Rutilus rutilus*.]
– ORIGIN Middle English: from Old French *roche*.

roach[2] ■ n. informal 1 chiefly N. Amer. a cockroach. 2 a roll of card or paper that forms the butt of a cannabis cigarette.

roach[3] ■ n. Nautical a curved part of a fore-and-aft sail extending beyond a straight line between its corners, especially on the leech side.
– ORIGIN C18.

road ■ n. 1 a wide way between places, especially one surfaced for use by vehicles. 2 a way to achieving a particular outcome. 3 a partly sheltered stretch of water near the shore in which ships can ride at anchor: *Boston Roads*. 4 an underground passage or gallery in a mine.
– PHRASES **down the road** informal in the future. **in** (or **out of**) **the** (or **one's**) **road** informal in (or out of) someone's way. **one for the road** informal a final alcoholic drink before leaving. **on the road** 1 on a long journey or series of journeys. ▶ without a permanent home and moving from place to place. 2 (of a car) able to be driven.
– DERIVATIVES **roadless** adj.
– ORIGIN Old English *rād* 'journey on horseback, foray', of Germanic origin; rel. to RIDE.

Road Accident Fund ■ n. S. African a government fund providing compensation for a person injured in a motor accident for which they were not to blame.

roadbed ■ n. 1 the material laid down to form a road. 2 another term for TRACKBED.

roadblock ■ n. a barrier put across a road by the police or army to stop and examine traffic.

road hog ■ n. informal a motorist who drives recklessly or inconsiderately.

roadholding ■ n. the ability of a vehicle to remain stable when moving, especially when cornering at high speeds.

roadhouse ■ n. a pub, club, or restaurant on a country road.

road hump ■ n. another term for SPEED BUMP.

roadie ■ n. informal a person employed by a touring band of musicians to set up and maintain equipment.

road kill ■ n. a killing of an animal on the road by a vehicle. ▶ animals so killed.

road manager ■ n. the organizer and supervisor of a musicians' tour.

road map ■ n. 1 a map showing the roads of a country or area. 2 a document setting out the procedure for achieving a goal: *a road map for peace*.

road movie ■ n. a film of a genre in which the main character spends most of the time travelling.

road pricing ■ n. the practice of charging motorists to use busy roads at certain times, especially to relieve congestion in urban areas.

road rage ■ n. violent anger arising from conflict with the driver of another motor vehicle.

roadroller ■ n. a motor vehicle with a heavy roller, used in road-making.

roadrunner ■ n. a fast-running long-tailed bird of the cuckoo family, found chiefly in arid country from the southern US to Central America. [Genus *Geococcyx*: two species.]

roadshow ■ n. each of a series of radio or television programmes broadcast on location from different venues. ▶ a touring political or promotional campaign. ▶ a touring show of pop musicians.

roadside ■ n. [often as modifier] the strip of land beside a road.

roadstead ■ n. another term for ROAD (in sense 3).
– ORIGIN C16: from ROAD + STEAD in the sense 'a place'.

roadster ■ n. **1** an open-top motor car with two seats. **2** a motorcycle designed to be used on the road, rather than for racing.

road tax ■ n. a tax payable on motor vehicles using public roads.

road test ■ n. **1** a test of the performance of a vehicle or engine on the road. **2** a test of equipment carried out in working conditions. ■ v. (**road-test**) subject to a road test.

roadway ■ n. a road. ▶ the part of a road intended for vehicles, in contrast to the pavement or verge.

roadwork ■ n. **1** (**roadworks**) repairs to roads or to utilities under roads. **2** athletic exercise or training involving running on roads.

roadworthy ■ adj. (of a vehicle) fit to be used on the road.
– DERIVATIVES **roadworthiness** n.

roam ■ v. wander over, through, or about (a place). ▶ (of a person's eyes or hands) pass lightly over. ■ n. an aimless walk.
– DERIVATIVES **roamer** n.
– ORIGIN Middle English.

roaming ■ n. a term in wireless telecommunications referring to the extending of connectivity to a location other than the home location. ▶ a service that allows cellphone users to make or receive calls in countries outside their local GSM network.

roan ■ adj. denoting an animal, especially a horse or cow, having a coat of a main colour thickly interspersed with hairs of another colour, typically bay, chestnut, or black mixed with white. ■ n. a roan animal.
– ORIGIN C16: from Old French.

roan antelope ■ n. a large grey-brown African antelope with backward-curving horns and distinctive black and white facial markings. [*Hippotragus equinus*.]

roar ■ n. a full, deep, prolonged sound as made by a lion, natural force, or engine. ▶ a loud, deep sound uttered by a person, especially as an expression of pain, anger, or great amusement. ■ v. **1** make or utter a roar. ▶ express in a roar. ▶ laugh loudly. ▶ (of a horse) make a loud noise in breathing as a symptom of disease of the larynx. **2** (especially of a vehicle) move at high speed making a roar. ▶ act or happen fast and decisively.
– DERIVATIVES **roarer** n.
– ORIGIN Old English, imitative of a deep prolonged cry, of West Germanic origin.

roaring ■ adj. informal unmistakable; emphatic: *a roaring success*.
– PHRASES **do a roaring trade** (or **business**) informal do very good business. **the roaring forties** stormy ocean tracts between latitudes 40° and 50° south. **the roaring twenties** the prosperous years of the 1920s.
– DERIVATIVES **roaringly** adv.

roast ■ v. **1** (with reference to food, especially meat) cook or be cooked by prolonged exposure to heat in an oven or over a fire. ▶ process (a foodstuff, metal ore, etc.) by subjecting it to intense heat. **2** make or become very warm. **3** criticize or reprimand severely. ■ adj. (of food) having been roasted. ■ n. **1** a joint of meat that has been roasted or that is intended for roasting. **2** the process of roasting something, especially coffee. ▶ a particular type of roasted coffee. **3** an outdoor party at which meat is roasted.
– DERIVATIVES **roaster** n.
– ORIGIN Middle English: from Old French *rostir*, of West Germanic origin.

roasting informal ■ adj. very hot and dry. ■ n. a severe criticism or reprimand.

rob ■ v. (**robbed**, **robbing**) **1** take property unlawfully from (a person or place) by force or threat of force. ▶ informal steal. ▶ informal overcharge. **2** deprive of something needed, deserved, or significant.
– PHRASES **rob Peter to pay Paul** deprive one person of something in order to pay another. [prob. with ref. to the saints and apostles *Peter* and *Paul*; the allusion is uncertain.]
– DERIVATIVES **robber** n.
– ORIGIN Middle English: from Old French *rober*, of Germanic origin.

robber baron ■ n. a ruthless plutocrat.

robber fly ■ n. a large powerful predatory fly which darts out and grabs insect prey on the wing. [Family Asilidae.]

robbery ■ n. (pl. **-ies**) the action of robbing a person or place. ▶ informal unashamed swindling or overcharging.

robe ■ n. a long, loose outer garment reaching to the ankles. ▶ such a garment worn, especially on formal or ceremonial occasions, as an indication of the wearer's rank, office, or profession. ■ v. [usu. as adj. **robed**] clothe in or put on a robe or robes.
– ORIGIN Middle English: from Old French, from the Germanic base (in the sense 'booty') of ROB (because clothing was an important component of booty).

robin ■ n. **1** a small European songbird of the thrush family with a red breast and brown back and wings. [*Erithacus rubecula*.] **2** (also **American robin**) a large North American thrush with an orange-red breast. [*Turdus migratorius*.] **3** used in names of numerous similar or related birds, e.g. Cape robin.
– ORIGIN C16: from Old French, familiar form of the given name *Robert*.

robinia /rə'bɪnɪə/ ■ n. a North American tree or shrub of a genus that includes the false acacia. [Genus *Robinia*.]
– ORIGIN named after Jean and Vespasien *Robin*, C17 French gardeners.

robin's-egg blue ■ n. N. Amer. a greenish-blue colour.

robot /'rəʊbɒt/ ■ n. **1** a machine capable of carrying out a complex series of actions automatically, especially one programmable by a computer. **2** S. African a set of automatic traffic lights.
– DERIVATIVES **robotization** (also **-isation**) n. **robotize** (also **-ise**) v.
– ORIGIN from Czech, from *robota* 'forced labour'; the term was coined in K. Čapek's play *R.U.R.* 'Rossum's Universal Robots' (1920).

robotic /rə(ʊ)'bɒtɪk/ ■ adj. **1** of or relating to robots. **2** mechanical, stiff, or unemotional.
– DERIVATIVES **robotically** adv.

robotics ■ pl. n. [treated as sing.] the branch of technology concerned with the design, construction, operation, and application of robots.

robust ■ adj. (**-er**, **-est**) **1** sturdy or resilient. ▶ strong and healthy. **2** not perturbed by or attending to subtleties. **3** (of wine or food) strong and rich in flavour or smell.
– DERIVATIVES **robustly** adv. **robustness** n.
– ORIGIN C16: from Latin *robustus* 'firm and hard'.

robusta ■ n. coffee beans from a West African species of coffee plant (*Coffea canephora*, formerly *robusta*).
– ORIGIN C20: from Latin *robustus* 'robust'.

roc ■ n. a gigantic mythological bird described in the Arabian Nights.
– ORIGIN C16: from Persian *ruk*.

ROCE ■ abbrev. Finance return on capital employed.

roche moutonnée /ˌrɒʃ muːˈtɒneɪ/ ■ n. (pl. **roches moutonnées** pronunc. same) Geology a small bare outcrop of rock shaped by glacial erosion, with one side smooth and gently sloping and the other steep, rough, and irregular.
– ORIGIN C19: French, 'fleecy rock'.

rock[1] ■ n. **1** the hard mineral material of the earth's crust, exposed on the surface or underlying the soil. ▶ a mass of this projecting out of the ground or water. ▶ a boulder. ▶ a stone of any size. **2** Geology any natural material with a distinctive mineral composition. **3** Brit. a kind of hard confectionery in the form of cylindrical peppermint-flavoured sticks. **4** informal a diamond or other precious stone. **5** informal a small piece of crack cocaine. **6** (**rocks**) vulgar slang a man's testicles.
– PHRASES **between a rock and a hard place** informal faced with two equally difficult alternatives. **get one's rocks off** vulgar slang have an orgasm. **on the rocks** informal **1** experiencing difficulties and likely to fail. **2** (of a drink) served undiluted and with ice cubes.
– DERIVATIVES **rockless** adj. **rock-like** adj.
– ORIGIN Middle English: from Old French *rocque*, from medieval Latin *rocca*.

rock[2] ■ v. **1** move gently to and fro or from side to side. ▶ shake, especially because of an earthquake or explosion. **2** cause great shock or distress to. **3** informal dance to or

rockabilly

play rock music. **4** informal have an atmosphere of excitement or much social activity. ■ n. **1** (also **rock music**) a form of popular music derived from rock and roll and pop music. ▸ rock and roll. **2** a rocking movement.
– PHRASAL VERBS **rock up** arrive; turn up.
– ORIGIN Old English, prob. from a Germanic base meaning 'remove, move'.

rockabilly ■ n. a type of popular music, originating in the south-eastern US, combining elements of rock and roll and country music.
– ORIGIN 1950s: blend of ROCK AND ROLL and HILLBILLY.

rock and roll (also **rock 'n' roll**) ■ n. a type of popular dance music originating in the 1950s from an amalgamation of rhythm and blues and country music.
– DERIVATIVES **rock and roller** n.

rock art ■ n. a design produced on a rock face or cave wall, usually by painting or carving.

rock-bottom ■ adj. at the lowest possible level. ■ n. (**rock bottom**) the lowest possible level.

rock-bound ■ adj. (of a coast or shore) rocky and inaccessible.

rockburst ■ n. a sudden, violent rupture or collapse of highly stressed rock in a mine.

rock climbing ■ n. the sport or pastime of climbing rock faces, especially with the aid of ropes and special equipment.
– DERIVATIVES **rock climb** n. **rock climber** n.

rock cod ■ n. any of several marine fishes that live in rocky habitats, especially in southern African and Australian waters. [Many species, mainly in the family Serranidae.]

rock crystal ■ n. transparent quartz, typically in the form of colourless hexagonal crystals.

rock dove ■ n. a mainly blue-grey Old World pigeon, the ancestor of most domestic and feral pigeons. [*Columba livia*.]

rocker ■ n. **1** a person who performs, dances to, or enjoys rock music. ▸ a rock song. ▸ Brit. a young person, especially in the 1960s, belonging to a subculture characterized by leather clothing, riding motorcycles, and a liking for rock music. **2** a rocking chair. **3** a curved bar or similar support on which something such as a chair can rock. ▸ a rocking device forming part of a mechanism. **4** the amount of curvature in the longitudinal contour of a boat or surfboard.
– PHRASES **off one's rocker** informal mad.

rocker switch ■ n. an electrical on/off switch incorporating a spring-loaded rocker.

rockery ■ n. (pl. **-ies**) a heaped arrangement of rocks with soil between them, planted with rock plants.

rocket[1] ■ n. **1** a cylindrical projectile that can be propelled by the combustion of its contents. ▸ a missile or spacecraft propelled by an engine providing thrust on the same principle. **2** Brit. informal a severe reprimand. ■ v. (**rocketed**, **rocketing**) **1** (of an amount, price, etc.) increase very rapidly and suddenly. **2** move or progress very rapidly. **3** attack with rocket-propelled missiles.
– ORIGIN C17: from French *roquette*, from Italian *rocchetto*, diminutive of *rocca* 'distaff (for spinning)', with ref. to its cylindrical shape.

rocket[2] ■ n. an edible Mediterranean plant of the cabbage family, eaten in salads. [*Eruca vesicaria* subsp. *sativa*.]
– ORIGIN C15: from French *roquette*, from Italian *ruchetta*, diminutive of *ruca*, from Latin *eruca* 'downy-stemmed plant'.

rocketeer ■ n. a person who designs or operates space rockets.

rocketry ■ n. the branch of science and technology concerned with rockets.

rocket scientist ■ n. [usu. with neg.] informal a very intelligent person.

rock face ■ n. a bare vertical surface of natural rock.

rockfall ■ n. a descent of loose rocks. ▸ a mass of fallen rock.

rock garden ■ n. a garden in which rocks or rockeries are the main feature.

rockhopper ■ n. a small penguin with a yellowish crest, breeding on subantarctic coastal cliffs. [*Eudyptes chrysocome*.]

rockhound ■ n. informal, chiefly N. Amer. a geologist or amateur collector of mineral specimens.
– DERIVATIVES **rockhounding** n.

rock hyrax ■ n. a rabbit-sized mammal, with greyish brown fur, short ears, and short legs. [*Procavia capensis*.]

rocking chair ■ n. a chair mounted on rockers or springs.

rocking horse ■ n. a model of a horse mounted on rockers or springs for a child to ride on.

rock lobster ■ n. another term for SPINY LOBSTER.

rock 'n' roll ■ n. variant spelling of ROCK AND ROLL.

rock painting ■ n. a painting on rock done with charcoal or ochre pigments mixed with animal fat or blood, gum, water, etc.

rock pigeon ■ n. **1** another term for ROCK DOVE. **2** a reddish-brown African pigeon with white-spotted upper parts and a red mask. [*Columba guinea*.]

rock plant ■ n. a plant that grows on or among rocks.

rock pool ■ n. a pool of water among rocks, typically along a shoreline.

rock rabbit ■ n. **1** another term for HYRAX. **2** short for RED ROCK RABBIT.

rock rose ■ n. a herbaceous or shrubby plant with rose-like flowers, native to temperate and warm regions. [Genera *Cistus* and *Helianthemum*.]

rock salmon ■ n. a tropical snapper found both in the sea and in rivers, valued for food and sport. [*Lutjanus argentimaculatus*.]

rock salt ■ n. common salt occurring naturally as a mineral.

rockslide ■ n. a rockfall.

rock solid ■ adj. completely firm or stable.

rocksteady ■ n. an early form of reggae music originating in Jamaica in the 1960s, characterized by a slow tempo.

rockumentary ■ n. informal a documentary about rock music and musicians.
– ORIGIN 1970s: from ROCK[2] + DOCUMENTARY.

rock wool ■ n. inorganic material made into matted fibre, used especially for insulation or soundproofing.

rocky[1] ■ adj. (**-ier**, **-iest**) consisting of or formed of rock. ▸ full of rocks.
– DERIVATIVES **rockiness** n.

rocky[2] ■ adj. (**-ier**, **-iest**) unsteady or unstable.
– DERIVATIVES **rockily** adv. **rockiness** n.

Rocky Mountain spotted fever ■ n. see SPOTTED FEVER.

rococo /rəˈkəʊkəʊ/ ■ adj. **1** relating to or denoting an elaborately ornate late baroque style of European furniture or architecture of the 18th century, characterized by asymmetrical patterns involving motifs and scrollwork. **2** (of music or literature) highly ornamented and florid. ■ n. the rococo style.
– ORIGIN C19: from French, alteration of *rocaille* denoting an elaborate style of ornamentation using pebbles, from *roc* 'rock'.

rod ■ n. **1** a thin straight bar, especially of wood or metal. **2** a fishing rod. **3** a slender straight stick. ▸ (**the rod**) the use of a stick for caning or flogging. **4** Anatomy one of two types of light-sensitive cell present in the retina of the eye, responsible mainly for monochrome vision in poor light. Compare with CONE (in sense 3).
– PHRASES **make a rod for one's own back** do something likely to cause difficulties for oneself later. **rule someone/thing with a rod of iron** control or govern someone or something very harshly.
– DERIVATIVES **rodless** adj. **rod-like** adj.
– ORIGIN Old English, prob. rel. to Old Norse *rudda* 'club'.

rode past of RIDE.

rodent ■ n. a mammal of an order (Rodentia) that includes rats, mice, squirrels, and porcupines,

distinguished by strong constantly growing incisors and no canine teeth.
– ORIGIN C19: from Latin *rodent-, rodere* 'gnaw'.

rodenticide /rəˈdɛntɪsaɪd/ ■ n. a poison used to kill rodents.

rodent ulcer ■ n. Medicine a slow-growing malignant tumour of the face (basal cell carcinoma).

rodeo /ˈrəʊdɪəʊ, rəˈdeɪəʊ/ ■ n. (pl. **-os**) an exhibition or contest in which cowboys show their skill at riding broncos, roping calves, etc. ▸ a similar exhibition or contest demonstrating other skills, such as motorcycle riding.
– ORIGIN C19: from Spanish, from *rodear* 'go round'.

rodomontade /ˌrɒdə(ʊ)mɒnˈteɪd/ ■ n. boastful or inflated talk or behaviour.
– ORIGIN C17: from obsolete Italian *rodomontada*, from *rodomonte*, from the name of a boastful character in the medieval *Orlando* epics.

ROE ■ abbrev. Finance return on equity.

roe[1] ■ n. 1 (also **hard roe**) the mass of eggs contained in the ovaries of a female fish or shellfish, especially when ripe and used as food. 2 (**soft roe**) the ripe testes of a male fish, especially when used as food.
– ORIGIN Middle English: rel. to Middle Low German, Middle Dutch *roge*.

roe[2] (also **roe deer**) ■ n. (pl. same or **roes**) a small Eurasian deer with a reddish summer coat that turns greyish in winter. [*Capriolus capriolus.*]
– ORIGIN Old English, of Germanic origin.

roentgen /ˈrʌntjən, ˈrɜːnt-, ˈrɒnt-/ (also **röntgen**) (abbrev.: **R**) ■ n. a unit of ionizing radiation, the amount producing one electrostatic unit of positive or negative ionic charge in one cubic centimetre of air under standard conditions.
– ORIGIN 1920s: named after the German physicist and discoverer of X-rays Wilhelm Conrad *Röntgen*.

roentgenium /ˈrʌntjənɪəm/ ■ n. the chemical element of atomic number 111, a radioactive element produced artificially. (Symbol: **Rg**)
– ORIGIN C21: named after Wilhelm Conrad *Röntgen* (see ROENTGEN).

roentgenology /ˌrʌntjəˈnɒlədʒi, ˌrɜːnt-, ˌrɒnt-/ (also **röntgenology**) ■ n. chiefly Medicine another term for RADIOLOGY.

rogan josh /ˌrəʊɡ(ə)n ˈdʒɒʃ/ ■ n. an Indian dish of curried meat, typically lamb, in a rich tomato-based sauce.
– ORIGIN from Urdu *roġan joś*.

Rogation Days ■ pl. n. (in the Western Christian Church) the three days before Ascension Day, traditionally marked by fasting and prayer.

roger ■ exclam. your message has been received and understood (used in radio communication). ■ v. Brit. vulgar slang (of a man) have sexual intercourse with.
– ORIGIN C16: from the given name *Roger*; verb from an obsolete sense ('penis') of the noun.

rogue ■ n. 1 a dishonest or unprincipled man. ▸ a mischievous but likeable person. 2 [usu. as modifier] an elephant or other large wild animal with destructive tendencies driven away or living apart from the herd. ▸ a person or thing that is defective, aberrant, or unpredictable. ▸ a seedling or plant deviating from the standard variety. ■ v. remove rogue plants or seedlings from (a crop).
– DERIVATIVES **roguery** n. (pl. **-ies**).
– ORIGIN C16: prob. from Latin *rogare* 'beg, ask', and rel. to obsolete slang *roger* 'vagrant beggar'.

rogues' gallery ■ n. informal a collection of photographs of known criminals, used by police to identify suspects.

roguish ■ adj. 1 characteristic of a rogue. 2 playfully mischievous: *a roguish smile.*
– DERIVATIVES **roguishly** adv. **roguishness** n.

Rohypnol /rəʊˈhɪpnɒl/ ■ n. trademark a powerful sedative drug of the benzodiazepine class.
– ORIGIN 1980s: invented name.

ROI ■ abbrev. Finance return on investment.

roil /rɔɪl/ ■ v. make (a liquid) turbid by disturbing the sediment. ▸ (of a liquid) move in a turbulent manner.
– ORIGIN C16: perhaps from Old French *ruiler* 'mix mortar'.

roister /ˈrɔɪstə/ ■ v. enjoy oneself or celebrate in a noisy or boisterous way.
– DERIVATIVES **roisterer** n. **roisterous** adj.
– ORIGIN C16: from obsolete *roister* 'roisterer', from French *rustre* 'ruffian'.

role ■ n. 1 an actor's part in a play, film, etc. 2 a person's or thing's function in a particular situation.
– ORIGIN C17: from obsolete French *roule* 'roll', referring orig. to the roll of paper on which the actor's part was written.

role model ■ n. a person looked to by others as an example to be imitated.

role playing (also **role play**) ■ n. 1 the acting out of a particular role, either consciously (as a technique in psychotherapy or training) or unconsciously (in accordance with the perceived expectations of society). 2 participation in a role-playing game.
– DERIVATIVES **role-play** v. **role player** n.

role-playing game ■ n. a game in which players take on the roles of imaginary characters who engage in adventures, typically in a fantasy setting.

Rolfing ■ n. a deep massage technique aimed at releasing muscular tension at skeletal level.
– DERIVATIVES **Rolf** v.
– ORIGIN 1970s: from the name of the American physiotherapist Ida P. *Rolf.*

roll ■ v. 1 move by turning over and over on an axis. ▸ turn over to face a different direction. ▸ (of a moving ship, aircraft, or vehicle) sway on an axis parallel to the direction of motion. ▸ S. African & N. Amer. informal overturn (a vehicle). ▸ throw (a die or dice). 2 (with reference to a vehicle or other wheeled object) move or cause to move along. ▸ (of waves, smoke, cloud, or fog) move or flow forward with an undulating motion. ▸ (of a drop of liquid) flow. ▸ (of time) elapse steadily: *the years rolled by.* ▸ [as adj. **rolling**] steady and continuous: *a rolling programme of reforms.* ▸ [usu. as adj. **rolling**] (of land) extend in gentle undulations. ▸ (of credits for a film or television programme) be displayed as if moving on a roller up the screen. ▸ (with reference to a machine, device, or system) begin or cause to begin operating. 3 (often **roll something up**) turn (something flexible) over and over on itself to form a cylindrical or spherical shape. ▸ curl up tightly. 4 flatten (something) by passing a roller over it or by passing it between rollers. 5 (of a loud, deep sound such as that of thunder) reverberate. ▸ pronounce (a consonant, typically an *r*) with a trill. ▸ (of words) flow mellifluously: *the names rolled off his lips.* 6 informal rob (a drunk or sleeping person). ■ n. 1 a cylinder formed by rolling flexible material. ▸ a cylindrical mass or a number of items arranged in a cylindrical shape. ▸ an item of food made by wrapping a flat sheet of pastry, cake, meat, or fish round a filling. 2 a rolling movement. ▸ a gymnastic exercise in which the body is rolled into a tucked position and turned in a forward or backward circle. 3 a prolonged, deep, reverberating sound. ▸ Music drumming consisting of a sustained, rapid alternation of single or double strokes by each stick. 4 a very small loaf of bread. 5 a roller used to shape metal in a rolling mill. 6 an official list or register of names. ▸ the total numbers on such a list. ▸ a document, typically an official record, in scroll form.
– PHRASES **a roll in the hay** (or **the sack**) informal an act of sexual intercourse. **be rolling in it** (or **money**) informal be very rich. **on a roll** informal experiencing a prolonged spell of success or good luck. **roll of honour** a list of people whose deeds are honoured, especially a list of those who have died in battle. **roll up one's sleeves** prepare to fight or work. **roll with the punches** 1 (of a boxer) move one's body away from an opponent's blows so as to lessen the impact. 2 adapt oneself to adverse circumstances. **strike someone off the roll** debar someone from practising their profession as a penalty for misconduct.
– PHRASAL VERBS **roll something back** reverse the progress or reduce the importance of something. **roll in** informal 1 be received in large amounts. 2 arrive in a casual way in spite of being late. **roll on —** informal used to indicate that one wants a particular time or event to come quickly. **roll something out** officially launch a new product. **roll something over** Finance contrive or extend a

particular financial arrangement. **roll up** informal arrive.
– DERIVATIVES **rollable** adj.
– ORIGIN Middle English: from Old French *rolle* (n.), *roller* (v.), from Latin *rotulus* 'a roll, little wheel', diminutive of *rota*.

rollback ■ n. **1** chiefly N. Amer. a reduction. **2** Computing the process of restoring a database or program to a previous defined state.

roll bar ■ n. a metal bar running up the sides and across the top of a car, strengthening its frame and protecting the occupants if the vehicle overturns.

roll cage ■ n. a framework of reinforcements protecting a car's passenger cabin in the event that it should roll on to its roof.

roll-call ■ n. the process of calling out a list of names to establish who is present.

rolled gold ■ n. gold in the form of a thin coating applied to a baser metal by rolling.

rolled oats ■ pl. n. oats that have been husked and crushed.

roller ■ n. **1** a cylinder that rotates about a central axis and is used in various machines and devices to move, flatten, or spread something. **2** a small cylinder on which hair is rolled in order to produce curls. **3** (also **roller bandage**) a long surgical bandage rolled up for convenient application. **4** a long swelling wave that appears to roll steadily towards the shore. **5** a brightly coloured crow-sized bird, predominantly blue and having a characteristic tumbling display flight. [*Coracias garrulus* and other species.]

rollerball ■ n. **1** a ballpoint pen using relatively thin ink. **2** Computing an input device containing a ball which is moved with the fingers to control the cursor.

roller bearing ■ n. a bearing similar to a ball bearing but using small cylindrical rollers instead of balls. ▶ a roller used in such a bearing.

Rollerblade ■ n. trademark an in-line skate. ■ v. skate using Rollerblades.
– DERIVATIVES **rollerblader** n.

roller blind ■ n. a window blind fitted on a roller.

roller coaster ■ n. a fairground attraction consisting of a light railway track with many tight turns and steep slopes, on which people ride in small fast open carriages. ■ v. (**roller-coaster** or **roller-coast**) move or occur in the dramatically changeable manner of a roller coaster.

roller skate ■ n. each of a pair of boots or metal frames fitted to shoes with four or more small wheels, for gliding across a hard surface.
– DERIVATIVES **roller skater** n. **roller skating** n.

roller towel ■ n. a long towel with the ends joined and hung on a roller.

roll film ■ n. photographic film with a protective lightproof backing paper wound on to a spool.

rollicking[1] ■ adj. exuberantly lively and amusing.
– DERIVATIVES **rollick** v.
– ORIGIN C19: prob. dialect, perhaps a blend of ROMP and FROLIC.

rollicking[2] (also **rollocking**) ■ n. Brit. informal a severe reprimand.
– ORIGIN C20: euphemistic alteration of BOLLOCKING.

rolling mill ■ n. a factory or machine for rolling steel or other metal into sheets.

rolling pin ■ n. a cylinder for rolling out dough.

rolling stock ■ n. locomotives, carriages, or other vehicles used on a railway.

rolling stone ■ n. a person who is unwilling to settle for long in one place.
– ORIGIN from the proverb 'a rolling stone gathers no moss'.

rolling strike ■ n. a strike consisting of a coordinated series of consecutive limited strikes by small groups of workers.

rollmop ■ n. a rolled uncooked pickled herring fillet.
– ORIGIN C20: from German *Rollmops*.

roll neck ■ n. a high loosely turned-over collar.
– DERIVATIVES **roll-necked** adj.

rollocking ■ n. variant spelling of ROLLICKING[2].

roll-on ■ adj. (of a deodorant or cosmetic) applied by means of a rotating ball in the neck of the container. ■ n. **1** a roll-on deodorant or cosmetic. **2** Brit. a light elastic corset.

roll-on roll-off ■ adj. denoting a ferry or other vessel in which vehicles are driven directly on at the start of the voyage and driven off at the end of it.

roll-out ■ n. **1** the unveiling or launch of a new aircraft, spacecraft, or product. **2** American Football a play in which a quarterback moves out toward the sideline before attempting to pass.

rollover ■ n. **1** Finance the extension or transfer of a debt or other financial arrangement. **2** (in a lottery) the accumulative carry-over of prize money to the following draw.

roll-top desk ■ n. a writing desk with a semicircular flexible cover sliding in curved grooves.

roll-up ■ n. (chiefly N. Amer. also **roll-your-own**) Brit. informal a hand-rolled cigarette. ■ adj. Finance denoting an investment fund in which returns are reinvested and tax liabilities can be reduced.

Rolodex /ˈrəʊlə(ʊ)dɛks/ ■ n. trademark a type of desktop card index.

roly-poly ■ n. (also **roly-poly pudding**) Brit. a pudding made of a sheet of suet pastry covered with jam or fruit, formed into a roll, and steamed or baked. ■ adj. informal round and plump.
– ORIGIN C17: fanciful formation from ROLL.

ROM ■ abbrev. Computing read-only memory.

romaine /rəʊˈmeɪn/ ■ n. a cos lettuce.
– ORIGIN C20: from French, feminine of *romain* 'Roman'.

Roman ■ adj. **1** of or relating to ancient or modern Rome. **2** denoting the alphabet used for writing Latin, English, and most European languages, developed in ancient Rome. **3** (**roman**) (of type) of a plain upright kind used in ordinary print, especially as distinguished from italic and Gothic. ■ n. **1** an inhabitant of ancient or modern Rome. **2** (**roman**) roman type.

roman (also **red roman**) ■ n. a reddish sea bream of southern African coastal waters. [*Chrysoblephus laticeps*.]
– ORIGIN C19: from Afrikaans *rooiman*, from *rooi* 'red' + *man* 'man', from S. African Dutch *roodeman*.

roman-à-clef /ˌrəʊmɒ̃ːˈkleɪ/ ■ n. (pl. **romans-à-clef** pronunc. same) a novel in which real people or events appear with invented names.
– ORIGIN French, 'novel with a key'.

Roman blind ■ n. a window blind made of fabric that draws up into pleats.

Roman candle ■ n. a firework giving off a series of flaming coloured balls and sparks.

Roman Catholic ■ adj. of or relating to the Roman Catholic Church. ■ n. a member of this Church.
– DERIVATIVES **Roman Catholicism** n.
– ORIGIN C16: translation of Latin (*Ecclesia*) *Romana Catholica* (*et Apostolica*) 'Roman Catholic (and Apostolic Church)', first used as a conciliatory term in place of *Roman*, *Romanist*, or *Romish*, considered derogatory.

Roman Catholic Church ■ n. the part of the Christian Church which acknowledges the Pope as its head, especially as it has developed since the Reformation.

Romance /rə(ʊ)ˈmans, ˈrəʊmans/ ■ n. the group of Indo-European languages descended from Latin, principally French, Spanish, Portuguese, Italian, Catalan, Occitan, and Romanian. ■ adj. relating to or denoting this group of languages.
– ORIGIN Middle English (orig. denoting the vernacular language of France as opposed to Latin): from Old French *romanz*, from Latin *Romanicus* 'Roman'.

romance /rə(ʊ)ˈmans, ˈrəʊmans/ ■ n. **1** a pleasurable feeling of excitement and wonder associated with love. ▶ a love affair, especially a relatively brief and lighthearted one. ▶ a book or film dealing with love in a sentimental or idealized way. **2** a quality or feeling of mystery, excitement, and remoteness from everyday life. **3** a medieval tale dealing with a hero of chivalry, of the kind

common in the Romance languages. ■ v. 1 dated be involved in an amorous relationship with (someone). ▸ informal seek the attention or custom of, especially by use of flattery. 2 romanticize.
– ORIGIN Middle English (orig. denoting a composition in the vernacular as opposed to works in Latin): from ROMANCE.

Roman-Dutch law ■ n. the law code that forms the basis of South African law, combining elements of Roman and Dutch law.

Roman Empire ■ n. the empire under Roman rule established in 27 BC and divided in AD 395 into the Western or Latin and Eastern or Greek Empire.

Romanesque /ˌrəʊməˈnɛsk/ ■ adj. of or relating to a style of architecture which prevailed in Europe c.900–1200, with massive vaulting and round arches. ■ n. Romanesque architecture.
– ORIGIN French, from *roman* 'romance'.

roman-fleuve /ˌrɒmɒ̃ˈfləːv/ ■ n. (pl. **romans-fleuves** pronunc. same) a novel or sequence of novels dealing with the lives of a family or other group of people over a prolonged period of time.
– ORIGIN French, 'river novel'.

Roman holiday ■ n. an occasion on which enjoyment or profit is derived from others' suffering.
– ORIGIN C19: from Byron's *Childe Harold*, orig. with ref. to a holiday given for a gladiatorial combat.

Romanian (also **Rumanian**) ■ n. 1 a native or national of Romania, or a person of Romanian descent. 2 the Romance language of Romania. ■ adj. of or relating to Romania or its people or language.

romanize /ˈrəʊmənaɪz/ (also **-ise**) ■ v. 1 historical bring under Roman influence or authority. 2 make Roman Catholic in character. 3 put (text) into the Roman alphabet or into roman type.
– DERIVATIVES **romanization** (also **-isation**) n.

Roman law ■ n. the law code of the ancient Romans forming the basis of civil law in many countries today.

Roman nose ■ n. a nose with a high bridge.

Roman numeral ■ n. any of the letters representing numbers in the Roman numerical system: I = 1, V = 5, X = 10, L = 50, C = 100, D = 500, M = 1 000.

Romansh /rə(ʊ)ˈmanʃ, -ˈmɑːnʃ/ (also **Rumansh**) ■ n. the Rhaeto-Romance language spoken in the Swiss canton of Grisons, an official language of Switzerland.
– ORIGIN from Romansh *Roman(t)sch*, from medieval Latin *romanice* 'in the Romance manner'.

romantic ■ adj. 1 inclined towards or suggestive of romance. ▸ relating to love, especially in a sentimental or idealized way. 2 of, characterized by, or suggestive of an idealized view of reality. 3 (**Romantic**) denoting or relating to romanticism. ■ n. 1 a person with romantic beliefs or attitudes. 2 (**Romantic**) a writer or artist of the Romantic movement.
– DERIVATIVES **romantically** adv.
– ORIGIN C17: from archaic *romaunt* 'tale of chivalry', from an Old French var. of *romanz* (see ROMANCE).

romanticism ■ n. a movement in the arts and literature which originated in the late 18th century, emphasizing inspiration, subjectivity, and the primacy of the individual.
– DERIVATIVES **romanticist** n.

romanticize (also **-ise**) ■ v. deal with or describe in an idealized or unrealistic fashion.
– DERIVATIVES **romanticization** (also **-isation**) n.

Romany /ˈrɒməni, ˈrəʊ-/ ■ n. (pl. **-ies**) 1 the Indo-European language of the gypsies. 2 a gypsy.
– ORIGIN C19: from Romany *Romani*, sing. *Romano*.

Romeo /ˈrəʊmiəʊ/ ■ n. 1 (pl. **-os**) an attractive, passionate male seducer or lover. 2 a code word representing the letter R, used in radio communication.
– ORIGIN from the name of the hero of Shakespeare's romantic tragedy *Romeo and Juliet*.

romer /ˈrəʊmə/ (also **romer scale**) ■ n. a small piece of plastic or card used to determine the precise reference of a point within the grid printed on a map.
– ORIGIN 1930s: named after its British inventor Carrol *Romer*.

Romish /ˈrəʊmɪʃ/ ■ adj. chiefly derogative Roman Catholic.

romp ■ v. 1 play about roughly and energetically.

2 informal achieve something easily. ▸ (**romp home/in**) finish as the easy winner of a race or other contest. ■ n. 1 a spell of romping. 2 a light-hearted film or other work. 3 informal an easy victory.
– ORIGIN C18: perhaps an alteration of RAMP.

rompers (also **romper suit**) ■ pl. n. 1 a young child's one-piece outer garment. 2 a similar garment for adults, worn as overalls or sportswear.

rondavel /rɒnˈdɑːv(ə)l/ ■ n. S. African a circular dwelling with a conical roof.
– ORIGIN from Afrikaans *rondawel*.

rondeau /ˈrɒndəʊ/ ■ n. (pl. **rondeaux** pronunc. same or /-əʊz/) a poem of ten or thirteen lines with only two rhymes throughout and with the opening words used twice as a refrain.
– ORIGIN C16: French, later form of *rondel*, from *rond* 'round'.

rondo /ˈrɒndəʊ/ ■ n. (pl. **-os**) a musical form with a recurring leading theme, often found in the final movement of a sonata or concerto.
– ORIGIN C18: Italian, from French *rondeau* (see RONDEAU).

rongo-rongo /ˌrɒŋɡəʊˈrɒŋɡəʊ/ ■ n. Archaeology an ancient script of hieroglyphic signs found on wooden tablets on Easter Island.
– ORIGIN C20: a local word.

röntgen ■ n. variant spelling of ROENTGEN.

roo ■ n. Austral. informal a kangaroo.

rood /ruːd/ ■ n. a crucifix, especially one positioned above the rood screen of a church or on a beam over the entrance to the chancel.
– ORIGIN Old English.

rood screen ■ n. a screen of wood or stone separating the nave from the chancel of a church.

roof ■ n. (pl. **roofs**) 1 the structure forming the upper covering of a building or vehicle. ▸ the top inner surface of a covered area or space. 2 the upper limit or level of prices or wages. ■ v. (usu. **be roofed**) cover with a roof.
▸ function as the roof of.
– PHRASES **go through the roof** informal (of prices or figures) reach extreme levels. **hit** (or **go through**) **the roof** informal suddenly become very angry.
– DERIVATIVES **roofer** n. **roofing** n. **roofless** adj.
– ORIGIN Old English, of Germanic origin.

roofing sheet ■ n. a sheet of corrugated iron, asbestos, or other material used in the construction of roofs.

roof light ■ n. 1 a window panel built into a roof. 2 a small interior light on the ceiling of a motor vehicle. 3 a flashing warning light on the top of a police car or other emergency vehicle.

roof of the mouth ■ n. the palate.

roof prism ■ n. a reflecting prism in which the reflecting surface is in two parts that are angled like the two sides of a pitched roof.

roof rack ■ n. a framework for carrying luggage on the roof of a vehicle.

roof-tree ■ n. a horizontal beam along the ridge of a roof.

roof wetting ■ n. a ceremony or party to mark the completion of a new building.

rooibos /ˈrɔɪbɒs/ ■ n. S. African an evergreen shrub whose leaves can be used to make tea. [Genus *Aspalathus*.]
– ORIGIN C20: from Afrikaans, 'red bush'.

rooigras /ˈrɔɪxrɑs/ ■ n. S. African a reddish-coloured African grass, used as pasture. [*Themeda triandra*.]
– ORIGIN Afrikaans, 'red grass'.

rooikat /ˈrɔɪkʌt/ S. African ■ (pl. **rooikats** or **rooikatte**/-tə/) another term for CARACAL.
– ORIGIN Afrikaans *rooi* 'red' + *kat* 'cat'.

rooikrans /ˈrɔɪkrɑːns/ ■ n. S. African a yellow-flowered Australian wattle that has become invasive in South Africa. [*Acacia cyclops*.]
– ORIGIN Afrikaans, 'red garland' (because of its red seed stalk).

rooinek /ˈrɔɪnɛk/ ■ n. S. African informal, derogatory an English person or an English-speaking South African.
– ORIGIN Afrikaans, 'red-neck'.

rook[1] ■ n. a gregarious Eurasian crow with black plumage and a bare face, nesting in colonies in treetops. [*Corvus frugilegus*.] ■ v. informal defraud, swindle, or overcharge.
– ORIGIN Old English *hrōc*, prob. imitative and of Germanic origin.

rook[2] ■ n. a chess piece, typically with its top in the shape of a battlement, that can move in any direction along a rank or file on which it stands.
– ORIGIN Middle English: from Old French *rock*, from Arabic *rukk*.

rookery ■ n. (pl. **-ies**) 1 a breeding colony of rooks, typically seen as a collection of nests high in a clump of trees. 2 a breeding colony of seabirds (especially penguins), seals, or turtles.

rookie ■ n. informal a new recruit, especially in the army or police. ▶ an inexperienced member of a sports team; a novice.
– ORIGIN C19: perhaps an alteration of **RECRUIT**, influenced by **ROOK**[1].

room /ruːm, rʊm/ ■ n. 1 space viewed in terms of its capacity to accommodate contents or allow action: *she was trapped without room to move.* 2 a part of a building enclosed by walls, floor, and ceiling. ▶ (**rooms**) a set of rooms rented out to lodgers. 3 opportunity or scope: *room for improvement*. ■ v. chiefly N. Amer. share lodgings, especially at a college or similar institution.
– PHRASES **no** (or **not**) **room to swing a cat** humorous a very confined space. [*cat* in the sense 'cat-o'-nine-tails'.]
– DERIVATIVES **-roomed** adj. **roomful** n. (pl. **-fuls**).
– ORIGIN Old English, of Germanic origin.

roomie ■ n. N. Amer. informal a room-mate.

rooming house ■ n. chiefly N. Amer. a lodging house.

room-mate ■ n. a person occupying the same room as another. ▶ N. Amer. a person occupying the same room, flat, or house as another.

room service ■ n. provision of food and drink to hotel guests in their rooms.

room temperature ■ n. a comfortable ambient temperature, generally taken as about 20°C.

roomy ■ adj. (**-ier**, **-iest**) having plenty of room; spacious.
– DERIVATIVES **roomily** adv. **roominess** n.

roost ■ n. a place where birds regularly settle to rest at night, or where bats congregate to rest in the day. ■ v. (of a bird or bat) settle or congregate for rest.

rooster ■ n. a male domestic fowl.

roosterbrood /ˈrʊəstəˌbrʊət/ (also **roosterkoek** /ˈrʊəstəˌkʊk/) ■ n. S. African a type of bread roll cooked on a griddle or in the ashes of a fire.
– ORIGIN Afrikaans, from *rooster* 'gridiron' + *koek* 'cake'.

root[1] ■ n. 1 a part of a plant normally below ground, which acts as a support and collects water and nourishment. ▶ a turnip, carrot, or other vegetable which grows as such a part of a plant. 2 the embedded part of a bodily organ or structure such as a hair. 3 the basic cause, source, or origin: *we need to get to the root of the problem*. ▶ (**roots**) family, ethnic, or cultural origins as the reasons for one's emotional attachment to a place or community. ▶ [as modifier] (**roots**) denoting something, especially music, from a non-Western ethnic or cultural origin: *roots music*. 4 Linguistics a morpheme, not necessarily surviving as a word in itself, from which words have been made by the addition of prefixes or suffixes or by other modification. 5 (also **root note**) Music the fundamental note of a chord. 6 (in biblical use) a descendant. 7 Mathematics a number or quantity that when multiplied by itself one or more times gives a specified number or quantity. ▶ a value of an unknown quantity satisfying a given equation. ■ v. 1 (with reference to a plant or cutting) establish or cause to establish roots. 2 (usu. **be rooted**) establish deeply and firmly. ▶ (**be rooted in**) have as a source or origin. 3 [often as adj. **rooted**] cause to stand immobile through fear or amazement. 4 (**root someone/thing out/up**) find and get rid of someone or something.
– PHRASES **at root** fundamentally. **put down roots** begin to have a settled life in a place. **root and branch** (of a process or operation) thorough or radical. **take root** become fixed or established.
– DERIVATIVES **rootedness** n. **rootless** adj. **rootlessness** n. **rootlet** n. **root-like** adj. **rooty** adj.
– ORIGIN Old English *rōt*, from Old Norse *rót*.

root[2] ■ v. 1 (of an animal) turn up the ground with its snout in search of food. ▶ rummage. 2 (**root for**) informal support enthusiastically. ■ n. an act of rooting.
– ORIGIN Old English *wrōtan*, of Germanic origin; rel. to Old English *wrōt* 'snout'.

root beer ■ n. N. Amer. an effervescent drink made from an extract of the roots and bark of certain plants.

root canal ■ n. 1 the pulp-filled cavity in the root of a tooth. 2 a procedure to replace infected pulp in a root canal with an inert material.

rootin'-tootin' ■ adj. N. Amer. informal boisterous, noisy, or lively.
– ORIGIN C19: reduplication of *rooting* in the sense 'inquisitive'.

rootle ■ v. Brit. informal term for **ROOT**[2].
– ORIGIN C19: frequentative of **ROOT**[2].

root mean square ■ n. Mathematics the square root of the arithmetic mean of the squares of a set of values.

root nodule ■ n. see **NODULE** (sense 2).

rootstock ■ n. 1 a rhizome. 2 a plant on to which another variety is grafted. 3 a primary form or source from which offshoots have arisen.

rootsy ■ adj. informal (of music) unpolished and emphasizing its traditional or ethnic origins.

root vegetable ■ n. the fleshy enlarged root of a plant used as a vegetable, e.g. a carrot.

rope ■ n. 1 a length of stout cord made by twisting together strands of hemp, sisal, nylon, etc. ▶ (**the ropes**) the ropes enclosing a boxing or wrestling ring. ▶ (**the rope**) execution by hanging. 2 a quantity of roughly spherical objects strung together. 3 (**the ropes**) informal the established procedures in an organization or area of activity: *I showed her the ropes*. ■ v. 1 catch, fasten, or secure with rope. ▶ Climbing (of a party of climbers) connect each other together with a rope. 2 (**rope someone in/into**) persuade someone, despite reluctance, to take part in.
– PHRASES **on the rope** Climbing roped together. **on the ropes** 1 Boxing forced against the ropes by the opponent's attack. 2 in state of near collapse.
– DERIVATIVES **roping** n.
– ORIGIN Old English, of Germanic origin.

rope ladder ■ n. two long ropes connected by short crosspieces, used as a ladder.

ropesight ■ n. Bell-ringing skill in judging when to pull on a bell rope in change-ringing.

ropeway ■ n. a transport system, used especially in mines or mountainous areas, in which carriers are suspended from moving cables powered by a motor.

ropy (also **ropey**) ■ adj. (**-ier**, **-iest**) 1 resembling a rope. 2 Brit. informal poor in quality or health.
– DERIVATIVES **ropily** adv. **ropiness** n.

Roquefort /ˈrɒkfɔː/ ■ n. trademark a soft blue cheese made from ewes' milk.
– ORIGIN from the name of a village in southern France.

roquette /rɒˈket/ ■ n. another term for **ROCKET**[2].
– ORIGIN from French.

ro-ro ■ abbrev. roll-on roll-off.

rorqual /ˈrɔːkw(ə)l/ ■ n. a baleen whale of a small group with pleated skin on the underside, e.g. the blue, fin, and humpback whales. [Family Balaenopteridae.]
– ORIGIN C19: from Norwegian *røyrkval* 'fin whale', from Old Norse *reythr*, the specific name, + *hvalr* 'whale'.

Rorschach test /ˈrɔːʃɑːk/ ■ n. Psychology a test used in psychoanalysis, in which a standard set of symmetrical ink blots of different shapes and colours is presented one by one to the subject, who is asked to describe what they suggest or resemble.
– ORIGIN 1920s: named after the Swiss psychiatrist Hermann *Rorschach*.

rosace /ˈrəʊzeɪs/ ■ n. an ornamentation resembling a rose, in particular a rose window.
– ORIGIN C19: from Latin *rosaceus*, from *rosa* 'rose'.

rosacea /rəʊˈzeɪʃɪə/ (also **acne rosacea**) ■ n. Medicine a

condition in which certain facial blood vessels enlarge, giving the cheeks and nose a flushed appearance.
– ORIGIN C19: from Latin, from *rosaceus* in the sense 'rose-coloured'.

rosary /ˈrəʊz(ə)ri/ ■ n. (pl. **-ies**) **1** (in the Roman Catholic Church) a form of devotion in which five (or fifteen) decades of Hail Marys are repeated, each decade preceded by an Our Father and followed by a Glory Be. **2** a string of beads for keeping count in such a devotion or in the devotions of some other religions.
– ORIGIN Middle English: from Latin *rosarium* 'rose garden', from *rosa* 'rose'.

rose[1] ■ n. **1** a prickly bush or shrub that typically bears red, pink, yellow, or white fragrant flowers, native to north temperate regions and widely grown as an ornamental. [Genus *Rosa*: many species and varieties.] ▸ used in names of other plants with similar flowers, e.g. Christmas rose. ▸ a stylized representation of a rose in heraldry or decoration. **2** a perforated cap attached to a shower, the spout of a watering can, or the end of a hose to produce a spray. **3** a warm pink or light crimson colour. ▸ (**roses**) a rosy complexion. **4** (**roses**) favourable circumstances or ease of success: *everything was coming up roses*. ■ v. poetic/literary make rosy.
– PHRASES **come up** (or **out**) **smelling of roses** emerge from a difficult situation with reputation intact.
– DERIVATIVES **rose-like** adj.
– ORIGIN Old English, of Germanic origin, from Latin *rosa*.

rose[2] past of RISE.

rosé /ˈrəʊzeɪ/ ■ n. any light pink wine, coloured by only brief contact with red grape skins.
– ORIGIN French, 'pink'.

roseapple ■ n. a tropical evergreen tree cultivated for its foliage and fragrant fruit. [*Syzygium jambos* (SE Asia) and related species.]

roseate /ˈrəʊziət/ ■ adj. rose-coloured.

rosebay ■ n. **1** (also **rosebay willowherb**) a tall willowherb with pink flowers, native to north temperate regions. [*Epilobium angustifolium*.] **2** N. Amer. an azalea. [Genus *Rhododendron*.] **3** another term for OLEANDER.

rosebud ■ n. the bud of a rose.

rose-coloured ■ adj. **1** of a warm pink colour. **2** referring to a naively optimistic or unfoundedly favourable viewpoint: *you are still seeing the profession through rose-coloured spectacles*.

rose-cut ■ adj. (of a gem) cut in tiny triangular facets.

rose hip ■ n. see HIP[2].

rose madder ■ n. a pale shade of pink.

rose mallow ■ n. an ornamental hibiscus. [Genus *Hibiscus*, in particular *H. rosa-sinensis*.]

rosemary ■ n. an evergreen aromatic shrub of the mint family, native to southern Europe, the leaves of which are used as a culinary herb, in perfumery, and formerly as an emblem of remembrance. [*Rosmarinus officinalis*.]
– ORIGIN Middle English *rosmarine*, from Latin *ros marinus*, from *ros* 'dew' + *marinus* 'of the sea'; also influenced by ROSE[1] and Mary, mother of Jesus.

rose of Jericho ■ n. a desert plant whose dead branches fold inwards to form a ball, native to North Africa and the Middle East. [*Anastatica hierochuntica*.]

rose of Sharon ■ n. **1** an ornamental hibiscus. [*Hibiscus syriacus*.] **2** a low shrub with dense foliage and large golden-yellow flowers, native to SE Europe and Asia Minor. [*Hypericum calycinum*.] **3** (in biblical use) a flowering plant whose identity is unknown.
– ORIGIN from *Sharon*, a region of fertile coastal plain in present-day Israel.

roseola /rə(ʊ)ˈziːələ/ ■ n. Medicine a rose-coloured rash occurring in measles, typhoid fever, syphilis, and some other diseases.
– ORIGIN C19: var. of RUBEOLA, from Latin *roseus* 'rose-coloured'.

rose quartz ■ n. a translucent pink variety of quartz.

rose-tinted ■ adj. another term for ROSE-COLOURED.

rosette ■ n. **1** a rose-shaped decoration, typically made of ribbon, worn by supporters of a team or political party or awarded as a prize. **2** a design or growth resembling a rose. ▸ Architecture a carved or moulded ornament resembling or representing a rose. **3** a radiating arrangement of horizontally spreading leaves at the base of a low-growing plant.
– DERIVATIVES **rosetted** adj.
– ORIGIN C18: from French, diminutive of *rose* (see ROSE[1]).

rose water ■ n. scented water made with rose petals.

rose window ■ n. a circular window with mullions or tracery radiating in a form suggestive of a rose.

rosewood ■ n. **1** a close-grained tropical timber with a distinctive fragrance, used for making furniture and musical instruments. **2** the tree which produces this wood. [Genus *Dalbergia*: several species, in particular *D. nigra* of Brazil.] ▸ used in names of other trees which yield similar wood, e.g. African rosewood.

Rosh Hashana /ˌrɒʃ həˈʃɑːnə/ (also **Rosh Hashanah**) ■ n. the Jewish New Year festival, held on the first (sometimes the second) day of Tishri (in September).
– ORIGIN Hebrew, 'head of the year'.

Roshi /ˈrəʊʃi/ ■ n. (pl. **Roshis**) the spiritual leader of a community of Zen Buddhist monks.
– ORIGIN from Japanese.

Rosicrucian /ˌrəʊzɪˈkruːʃ(ə)n/ ■ n. a member of a secretive society devoted to the study of metaphysical, mystical, and alchemical lore. ■ adj. of or relating to the Rosicrucians.
– DERIVATIVES **Rosicrucianism** n.
– ORIGIN from *rosa crucis* (or *crux*), Latinization of the name of Christian *Rosenkreuz*, legendary C15 founder of the movement.

rosin /ˈrɒzɪn/ ■ n. resin, especially the solid amber residue obtained after the distillation of crude turpentine oleoresin, used in adhesives, varnishes, and inks and for treating the bows of stringed instruments. ■ v. (**rosined**, **rosining**) rub or treat with rosin.
– DERIVATIVES **rosiny** adj.
– ORIGIN Middle English: from medieval Latin *rosina*, from Latin *resina* (see RESIN).

roster /ˈrɒstə, ˈrəʊst-/ ■ n. a list or plan showing turns of duty or leave for individuals or groups in an organization. ▸ a list of names, in particular of sports players available for team selection. ■ v. (usu. **be rostered**) assign according to a duty roster.
– ORIGIN C18: from Dutch *rooster* 'list', earlier 'gridiron', with ref. to its parallel lines.

rostral /ˈrɒstr(ə)l/ ■ adj. **1** Anatomy at or near the front end of the body: *the rostral portion of the brain*. **2** Zoology of or on the rostrum.

rostrum /ˈrɒstrəm/ ■ n. (pl. **rostra** /-trə/ or **rostrums**) **1** a raised platform on which a person stands to make a public speech, play music, or conduct an orchestra. ▸ a similar platform for supporting a film or television camera. **2** chiefly Zoology a beak-like projection.
– DERIVATIVES **rostrate** /-strət/ adj. (chiefly Zoology).
– ORIGIN C16: from Latin, 'beak'; orig. used to denote an orator's platform in Rome, which was decorated with the beaks of captured galleys.

rosy ■ adj. (**-ier**, **-iest**) **1** (especially of a person's skin) rose-red or pink, typically as an indication of health or youthfulness: *rosy cheeks*. **2** promising or suggesting good fortune; hopeful.
– DERIVATIVES **rosily** adv. **rosiness** n.

rot ■ v. (**rotted**, **rotting**) **1** decompose by the action of bacteria and fungi; decay or cause to decay. **2** gradually deteriorate or decline. ■ n. **1** the process of decaying. ▸ rotten or decayed matter. **2** (**the rot**) a process of deterioration; a decline in standards: *there is enough talent to stop the rot*. **3** any of a number of fungal or bacterial diseases that cause tissue deterioration, especially in plants. ▸ liver rot in sheep. **4** informal nonsense; rubbish.
– ORIGIN Old English, of Germanic origin.

rota ■ n. chiefly Brit. a list showing times and names for people to take their turn to undertake certain duties.
– ORIGIN C17: from Latin, 'wheel'.

Rotarian ■ n. a member of Rotary, a worldwide charitable society of business and professional people organized into local Rotary clubs. ■ adj. of or relating to Rotary.

rotary 1028

rotary ■ adj. revolving around a centre or axis; rotational. ▶ acting by means of rotation; having a rotating part or parts: *a rotary mower.* ■ n. (pl. **-ies**) a rotary machine or device.
– ORIGIN C18: from medieval Latin *rotarius*, from *rota* 'wheel'.

rotary press ■ n. a printing press that prints from a rotating cylindrical surface on to paper forced against it by another cylinder.

rotary wing ■ n. an aerofoil that rotates in an approximately horizontal plane, providing all or most of the lift in a helicopter or autogiro.

rotate /rə(ʊ)'teɪt/ ■ v. **1** move or cause to move in a circle round an axis. **2** pass to each member of a group in a regularly recurring order. **3** grow (different crops) in succession on a particular piece of land.
– DERIVATIVES **rotatable** adj. **rotating** adj. **rotative** /'rəʊtətɪv/ adj. **rotatory** /'rəʊtət(ə)ri, -'teɪt(ə)ri/ adj.
– ORIGIN C17 (*rotation* C16): from Latin *rotare* 'turn in a circle', from *rota* 'wheel'.

rotation ■ n. the action or process of rotating.
– DERIVATIVES **rotational** adj. **rotationally** adv.

rotator ■ n. **1** a thing which rotates or which causes something to rotate. **2** Anatomy a muscle whose contraction causes or assists in the rotation of a part of the body.

rotavator /'rəʊtəveɪtə/ (also **rotovator**) ■ n. trademark a machine with rotating blades for breaking up or tilling the soil.
– DERIVATIVES **rotavate** v.
– ORIGIN 1930s: blend of **ROTARY** + **CULTIVATOR**.

rotavirus /'rəʊtə,vʌɪrəs/ ■ n. Medicine any of a group of wheel-shaped RNA viruses, some of which cause acute enteritis in humans.
– ORIGIN 1970s: from Latin *rota* 'wheel' + **VIRUS**.

rote ■ n. mechanical or habitual repetition: *a poem learnt by rote.*
– ORIGIN Middle English.

rotgut ■ n. informal poor-quality and potentially harmful alcoholic liquor.

roti /'rəʊti/ ■ n. (pl. **rotis**) (in Indian cooking) bread, especially a flat round bread cooked on a griddle.
– ORIGIN from Hindi *roṭī*.

Rotifera /rəʊ'tɪf(ə)rə/ ■ pl. n. Zoology a small phylum of minute multicellular aquatic animals which have a characteristic wheel-like ciliated organ used in swimming and feeding.
– DERIVATIVES **rotifer** /'rəʊtɪfə/ n.
– ORIGIN from Latin *rota* 'wheel' + *ferre* 'to bear'.

rotisserie /rəʊ(ʊ)'tɪs(ə)ri/ ■ n. **1** a restaurant specializing in roasted or barbecued meat. **2** a rotating spit for roasting and barbecuing meat.
– ORIGIN C19: from French *rôtisserie*, from *rôtir* 'to roast'.

rotogravure /ˌrəʊtə(ʊ)grə'vjʊə/ ■ n. a printing system using a rotary press with intaglio cylinders. ▶ chiefly N. Amer. a sheet or magazine printed with this system.
– ORIGIN C20: from German *Rotogravur*, part of the name of a printing company.

rotor ■ n. **1** the rotating part of a turbine, electric motor, or other device. **2** a hub with a number of radiating blades that is rotated to provide the lift for a helicopter.
– ORIGIN C20: from **ROTATOR**.

rotorcraft ■ n. (pl. same) a rotary wing aircraft, such as a helicopter or autogiro.

rotoscope ■ n. a device which projects and enlarges individual frames of filmed live action to permit them to be used to create composite film sequences. ■ v. transfer into another film sequence using a rotoscope.
– ORIGIN 1950s.

rotovator ■ n. variant spelling of **ROTAVATOR**.

rotten ■ adj. (**-er**, **-est**) **1** suffering from decay. **2** corrupt. **3** informal very bad or unpleasant. ■ adv. informal very much: *your mother spoiled you rotten.*
– DERIVATIVES **rottenly** adv. **rottenness** n.
– ORIGIN Middle English: from Old Norse *rotinn*.

rotter ■ n. informal, dated a cruel, mean, or unkind person.

Rottweiler /'rɒtvʌɪlə, -wʌɪlə/ ■ n. a large powerful dog of a tall black-and-tan breed.
– ORIGIN C20: German, from *Rottweil*, the name of a town in SW Germany.

rotund /rə(ʊ)'tʌnd/ ■ adj. large and plump. ▶ round; spherical.
– DERIVATIVES **rotundity** n. **rotundly** adv.
– ORIGIN C15: from Latin *rotundus*, from *rotare* 'rotate'.

rotunda ■ n. a round building or room, especially one with a dome.
– ORIGIN C17: alteration of Italian *rotonda* (*camera*) 'round (chamber)', from *rotondo*.

rouble /'ruːb(ə)l/ (also **ruble**) ■ n. the basic monetary unit of Russia and some other former republics of the USSR, equal to 100 kopeks.
– ORIGIN from Russian *rubl'*.

roué /'ruːeɪ/ ■ n. a debauched man, especially an elderly one.
– ORIGIN C19: French, 'broken on a wheel', referring to the instrument of torture thought to be deserved by such a person.

rouge /ruːʒ/ ■ n. a red powder or cream used as a cosmetic for colouring the cheeks or lips. ■ v. colour with rouge.
– ORIGIN Middle English: from French, 'red', from Latin *rubeus*.

rough ■ adj. **1** having an uneven or irregular surface; not smooth or level. ▶ (of terrain) having many obstacles; difficult to cross. **2** (of a voice) harsh and rasping. ▶ (of wine or another alcoholic drink) sharp or harsh in taste. **3** not gentle; violent or boisterous: *rough treatment.* ▶ (of weather or the sea) wild and stormy. **4** informal difficult and unpleasant. **5** not finished tidily; plain and basic. ▶ not worked out or correct in every detail; approximate: *a rough draft | a rough guess.* ▶ lacking sophistication or refinement. ▶ n. **1** chiefly Brit. a disreputable and violent person. **2** (on a golf course) the area of longer grass around the fairway and the green. **3** a preliminary sketch. **4** an uncut precious stone. ■ v. **1** work or shape in a rough, preliminary fashion. **2** make uneven. **3** (**rough it**) informal live in discomfort with only basic necessities. **4** (**rough someone up**) informal beat someone up.
– PHRASES **bit of rough** informal a male sexual partner whose toughness or lack of sophistication is a source of attraction. **in the rough 1** in a natural state; without decoration or other treatment. **2** in difficulties. **rough and ready** crude but effective. ▶ unsophisticated or unrefined. **the rough edge** (or **side**) **of one's tongue** a scolding. **rough edges** small imperfections in something that is otherwise satisfactory. **rough justice** treatment that is not scrupulously fair or in accordance with the law. **sleep rough** sleep in uncomfortable conditions, typically out of doors. **take the rough with the smooth** accept the difficult or unpleasant aspects of life as well as the good.
– DERIVATIVES **roughish** adj. **roughness** n.
– ORIGIN Old English, of West Germanic origin.

roughage ■ n. fibrous indigestible material in vegetable foodstuffs which aids the passage of food and waste products through the gut. ▶ Farming coarse, fibrous fodder.

rough and tumble ■ n. a situation without rules or organization.
– ORIGIN C19: orig. boxing slang.

roughcast ■ n. plaster of lime, cement, and gravel, used on outside walls. ■ adj. **1** coated with roughcast. **2** (of a person) lacking refinement. ■ v. coat with roughcast.

rough cut ■ n. the first version of a film after preliminary editing. ■ v. (**rough-cut**) make a rough cut or rough copy of.

rough diamond ■ n. **1** an uncut diamond. **2** a person who is of good character but lacks manners or education.

roughen ■ v. make or become rough.

rough-hew ■ v. **1** shape (wood or stone) roughly or without smoothing off. **2** [as adj. **rough-hewn**] (of a person) uncultivated or uncouth.

rough house informal, chiefly N. Amer. ■ n. a violent disturbance. ■ v. (**rough-house**) act or treat in a rough, violent manner.

roughly ■ adv. **1** in a rough or harsh manner. **2** approximately.

VOWELS a cat ɑː arm ɛ bed ɛː hair ə ago əː her ɪ sit i cosy iː see ɒ hot ɔː saw ʌ run

roughneck ■ n. 1 informal a rough, uncouth person. 2 an oil rig worker. ■ v. work on an oil rig.
– DERIVATIVES **roughnecking** n.

roughshod ■ adj. archaic (of a horse) having shoes with nail heads projecting to prevent slipping.
– PHRASES **ride roughshod over** arrogantly or inconsiderately disregard.

rough trade ■ n. informal male homosexual prostitution, especially when involving brutality or sadism. ▸ homosexuals of this kind.

rouille /'ruːi/ ■ n. a Provençal sauce made from pounded red chillies, garlic, breadcrumbs, and stock.
– ORIGIN French, 'rust', with ref. to the colour.

roulade /ruːˈlɑːd/ ■ n. 1 a piece of meat, sponge, or other food, spread with a filling and rolled up. 2 a florid passage of runs in classical music for a solo virtuoso.
– ORIGIN French, from *rouler* 'to roll'.

roulette ■ n. 1 a gambling game in which a ball is dropped on to a revolving wheel with numbered compartments, the players betting on the number at which the ball comes to rest. 2 a tool or machine with a revolving toothed wheel, used in engraving or for making perforations between postage stamps. ■ v. use a roulette to make perforations in.
– ORIGIN C18: from French, diminutive of *rouelle* 'wheel'.

Roumanian /ruːˈmeɪniən/ ■ adj. & n. old-fashioned variant of **ROMANIAN**.

round ■ adj. 1 shaped like a circle or cylinder. 2 shaped like a sphere. ▸ having a curved surface with no sharp projections. 3 (of a person's shoulders) bent forward. 4 (of a voice) rich and mellow. 5 (of a number) expressed in convenient units rather than exactly, for example to the nearest whole number. ▸ used to show that a figure has been completely and exactly reached: *the batsman made a round 100*. 6 frank and truthful: *she berated him in good round terms*. ■ n. 1 a circular piece or section. 2 an act of visiting a number of people or places in turn, especially in a fixed order as part of one's duties: *a newspaper round*. ▸ a regularly recurring sequence of activities. 3 each of a sequence of sessions in a process, especially in a sports contest. ▸ a single division of a game or contest, especially in a boxing or wrestling match. ▸ an act of playing all the holes in a golf course once. 4 Music a song for three or more unaccompanied voices or parts, each singing the same theme but starting one after another. 5 a set of drinks bought for all the members of a group, typically as part of a sequence in which each member in turn buys such a set. 6 Brit. a slice of bread. ▸ the quantity of sandwiches made from two slices of bread. 7 the amount of ammunition needed to fire one shot. ▸ Archery a fixed number of arrows shot from a fixed distance. ■ adv. chiefly Brit. 1 so as to rotate or cause rotation. ▸ so as to cover the whole area surrounding a particular centre. 2 so as to rotate and face in the opposite direction. ▸ used in describing the relative position of something: *it's the wrong way round*. 3 so as to surround. ▸ so as to give support. 4 so as to reach a new place or position. 5 used to suggest idle and purposeless motion or activity. ■ prep. chiefly Brit. 1 on every side of (a focal point). 2 so as to encircle. 3 from or on the other side of. 4 so as to cover the whole of. ■ v. 1 pass and go round. 2 make (a figure) less exact but more convenient for calculations: *we'll round the weight up to the nearest kilo*. 3 become or cause to become round in shape. 4 Phonetics pronounce (a vowel) with the lips narrowed and protruded.
– PHRASES **go the round** (or **rounds**) be passed on from person to person. **in the round** 1 (of sculpture) standing free, rather than carved in relief. 2 (of theatre) with the audience placed on at least three sides of the stage. 3 fully and thoroughly; with all aspects shown.
– PHRASAL VERBS **round something off** 1 make the edges of something smooth. 2 complete something in a satisfying or suitable way. **round on** make a sudden attack on. **round someone/thing up** drive or collect a number of people or animals together.
– DERIVATIVES **roundish** adj. **roundness** n.
– ORIGIN Middle English: from the Old French stem *round-*, from a var. of Latin *rotundus* 'rotund'.

roundabout ■ n. 1 another term for **TRAFFIC CIRCLE**. 2 a large revolving device in a playground, for children to ride on. ▸ a merry-go-round. ■ adj. 1 not following a short direct route; circuitous. 2 not clear and direct; circumlocutory.

roundball ■ n. US informal term for **BASKETBALL**.
– DERIVATIVES **roundballer** n.

round dance ■ n. 1 a folk dance in which the dancers form one large circle. 2 a ballroom dance such as a waltz or polka in which couples move in circles round the ballroom.

rounded ■ adj. 1 round or curved. 2 well developed in all aspects; complete and balanced: *a rounded human being*.

roundel /'raʊnd(ə)l/ ■ n. 1 a small disc, especially a decorative medallion. ▸ a circular identifying mark painted on military aircraft. 2 a variation of the rondeau, consisting of three stanzas of three lines each, rhyming alternately, with the opening words repeated as a refrain after the first and third stanzas.
– ORIGIN Middle English: from Old French *rondel*, from *ro(u)nd-* (see **ROUND**).

roundelay /'raʊndəleɪ/ ■ n. poetic/literary 1 a short simple song with a refrain. 2 a circle dance.
– ORIGIN Middle English: from Old French *rondelet*, from *rondel*, from *rond* 'round'.

rounders ■ pl. n. [treated as sing.] a ball game similar to baseball, in which players run round a circuit of bases after hitting the ball with a cylindrical wooden bat, scoring a rounder if all four bases are reached before the ball is fielded.

Roundhead ■ n. historical a member or supporter of the Parliamentary party in the English Civil War.
– ORIGIN with ref. to their short-cropped hair.

roundhouse ■ n. informal a blow given with a wide sweep of the arm.

roundly ■ adv. 1 in a vehement or emphatic manner. ▸ thoroughly. 2 in a circular or roughly circular shape.

round robin ■ n. 1 a tournament in which each competitor plays in turn against every other. 2 a petition, especially one with signatures written in a circle to conceal the order of writing.

round table ■ n. [usu. as modifier] an assembly where parties meet on equal terms for discussion: *round-table talks*.

round trip ■ n. a journey to a place and back again.

round turn ■ n. a complete turn of a rope around another rope or an anchoring point.

round-up ■ n. 1 a systematic gathering together of people or things. 2 a summary of facts or events.

roundwood ■ n. timber which is left as small logs, typically taken from near the tops of trees and used for furniture.

roundworm ■ n. a nematode worm, especially a parasitic one found in the intestines of mammals. [Many species, including the large *Ascaris lumbricoides* in humans.]

roup /ruːp/ ■ n. an infectious disease of poultry affecting the respiratory tract.
– DERIVATIVES **roupy** adj.
– ORIGIN C16.

rouse /raʊz/ ■ v. 1 bring out of sleep; awaken. ▸ cease to sleep; wake up. 2 bring out of inactivity. 3 excite; provoke: *his evasiveness roused my curiosity*. 4 stir (a liquid, especially beer while brewing).
– DERIVATIVES **rousable** adj. **rouser** n.
– ORIGIN Middle English: prob. from Anglo-Norman French.

rousing ■ adj. stirring: *a rousing speech*.
– DERIVATIVES **rousingly** adv.

roust /raʊst/ ■ v. 1 cause to get up or start moving; rouse. 2 N. Amer. informal treat roughly; harass.
– ORIGIN C17: perhaps an alteration of **ROUSE**.

roustabout /'raʊstəbaʊt/ ■ n. an unskilled or casual labourer, especially a labourer on an oil rig.
– ORIGIN C19: from **ROUST**.

rout[1] /raʊt/ ■ n. 1 a disorderly retreat of defeated troops. ▸ a decisive defeat. 2 archaic a disorderly or tumultuous crowd of people. ■ v. defeat utterly and force to retreat.
– PHRASES **put to rout** put to flight; defeat utterly.
– ORIGIN Middle English: from Latin *rupt-*, *rumpere* 'break', via obsolete French *route*.

rout² /raʊt/ ■ v. **1** cut a groove in (a surface). **2** another term for ROOT². ▸ force to leave a place.
– ORIGIN C16: alteration of the verb ROOT².

route /ruːt/ ■ n. **1** a way or course taken in getting from a starting point to a destination. ▸ the line of a road, path, railway, etc. **2** N. Amer. a round travelled in delivering, selling, or collecting goods. ■ v. (**routeing** or **routing**) send or direct along a specified course.
– ORIGIN Middle English: from Old French *rute* 'road', from Latin *rupta* (*via*) 'broken (way)', from *rumpere*.

router¹ /ˈraʊtə/ ■ n. a power tool with a shaped cutter, used in carpentry.

router² /ˈruːtə/ ■ n. Computing a device which forwards data packets to the appropriate parts of a network.

routine ■ n. **1** a sequence of actions regularly followed; a fixed unvarying programme. **2** a set sequence in a theatrical or comic performance. ■ adj. **1** performed as part of a regular procedure: *a routine inspection*. **2** characteristic of routine; without variety.
– DERIVATIVES **routinely** adv. **routinization** (also **-isation**) n. **routinize** (also **ise**) v.
– ORIGIN C17: from French, from *route* (see ROUTE).

roux /ruː/ ■ n. (pl. same) Cookery a mixture of fat (especially butter) and flour used in making sauces.
– ORIGIN from French (*beurre*) *roux* 'browned (butter)'.

ROV ■ abbrev. remotely operated vehicle.

rove¹ ■ v. **1** travel constantly without a fixed destination; wander. ▸ [usu. as adj. **roving**] travel for one's work, having no fixed base: *a roving reporter*. **2** (of eyes) look around in all directions.
– ORIGIN C15: perhaps from dialect *rave* 'to stray', prob. of Scandinavian origin.

rove² past of REEVE².

rove³ ■ n. a small metal plate or ring for a rivet to pass through, especially in boatbuilding.
– ORIGIN Middle English: from Old Norse *ró*, with the addition of *-v-*.

rove beetle ■ n. a long-bodied beetle with very short wing cases, typically found among decaying matter.

rover¹ ■ n. **1** a person who spends their time wandering. **2** (in various sports) a player not restricted to a particular position on the field. **3** (**Rovers**) a senior branch of the Scout Association, for men and women above the age of 18. **4** a vehicle for driving over rough terrain. **5** Archery a mark for long-distance shooting. ▸ a mark chosen at random and not at a determined range.

rover² ■ n. archaic a pirate.
– ORIGIN Middle English: from Middle Low German, Middle Dutch *röver*, from *röven* 'rob'.

row¹ /rəʊ/ ■ n. a number of people or things in a more or less straight line.
– PHRASES **a hard** (or **tough**) **row to hoe** a difficult task. **in a row 1** forming a line. **2** informal in succession.
– ORIGIN Old English *rāw*, of Germanic origin.

row² /rəʊ/ ■ v. **1** propel (a boat) with oars. ▸ travel by propelling a boat in this way. **2** engage in the sport of rowing. ▸ (**row someone down**) overtake a team in a rowing race. ▸ (**row over**) complete the course of a boat race with little effort. ■ n. a spell of rowing.
– DERIVATIVES **rower** n. **rowing** n.
– ORIGIN Old English *rōwan*, of Germanic origin.

row³ /raʊ/ informal ■ n. **1** an acrimonious quarrel. **2** a loud noise or uproar. **3** Brit. a severe reprimand. ■ v. **1** have a row. **2** Brit. rebuke severely.
– ORIGIN C18.

rowan /ˈrəʊən, ˈraʊən/ ■ n. another term for MOUNTAIN ASH.
– ORIGIN C15: of Scandinavian origin.

rowdy ■ adj. (**-ier**, **-iest**) noisy and disorderly. ■ n. (pl. **-ies**) a rowdy person.
– DERIVATIVES **rowdily** adv. **rowdiness** n. **rowdyism** n.
– ORIGIN C19 (orig. US in the sense 'lawless backwoodsman').

rowel /ˈraʊ(ə)l/ ■ n. a spiked revolving disc at the end of a spur. ■ v. (**rowelled**, **rowelling**; US **roweled**, **roweling**) use a rowel to urge on (a horse).

– ORIGIN Middle English: from Old French *roel(e)*, from late Latin *rotella*, diminutive of Latin *rota* 'wheel'.

row house ■ n. N. Amer. a terrace house.

rowing machine ■ n. an exercise machine with oars and a sliding seat.

rowlock /ˈrɒlək, ˈrʌlək/ ■ n. a fitting on the gunwale of a boat which serves as a fulcrum for an oar and keeps it in place.
– ORIGIN C18: alteration of OARLOCK, influenced by ROW².

royal ■ adj. **1** of, relating to, or having the status of a king or queen or a member of their family. **2** of a quality or size suitable for a king or queen; splendid. ■ n. informal a member of a royal family.
– DERIVATIVES **royally** adv.
– ORIGIN Middle English: from Old French *roial*, from Latin *regalis* 'regal'.

royal antelope ■ n. a West African antelope with an arched back, short neck, and a red and brown coat with white underparts. [*Neotragus pygmaeus*, family Bovidae.]

royal assent ■ n. (in the UK) assent of the sovereign to a bill which has been passed by Parliament, and which thus becomes an Act of Parliament.

royal blue ■ n. a deep, vivid blue.

Royal Commission ■ n. a commission of inquiry appointed by the Crown on the recommendation of the government.

royal flush ■ n. (in poker) the highest straight flush, including ace, king, queen, jack, and ten all in the same suit.

Royal Gala ■ n. a New Zealand dessert apple of a variety with red and yellow skin.
– ORIGIN 1960s: orig. *Gala*, but renamed following a royal visit.

royal icing ■ n. hard white icing, typically used to decorate fruit cakes.

royalist ■ n. **1** a person who supports the principle of monarchy. **2** a supporter of the King against Parliament in the English Civil War. ■ adj. giving support to the monarchy.
– DERIVATIVES **royalism** n.

royal jelly ■ n. a substance secreted by honeybee workers and fed by them to larvae which are being raised as potential queen bees.

royal palm ■ n. a New World palm which is widely cultivated as an avenue tree. [Genus *Roystonea*: several species, in particular *R. regia*.]

royal stag ■ n. Brit. a red deer stag with a head of twelve or more points.

royal standard ■ n. a banner bearing the royal coat of arms, flown in the presence of royalty.

royalty ■ n. (pl. **-ies**) **1** people of royal blood or status. ▸ an individual member of a royal family. ▸ the status or power of a king or queen. **2** a sum paid for the use of a patent or to an author or composer for each copy of a book sold or for each public performance of a work. **3** a royal right (now especially over minerals) granted by a sovereign. ▸ a payment made by a producer of minerals, oil, or natural gas to the owner of the site or of the mineral rights.

royal warrant ■ n. a warrant issued by the sovereign, in particular one authorizing a company to display the royal arms, indicating that goods or services are supplied to the royal family.

RP ■ abbrev. received pronunciation.

RPG ■ abbrev. **1** report program generator (a high-level commercial programming language). **2** rocket-propelled grenade. **3** role-playing game.

RPI ■ abbrev. Brit. retail price index.

rpm ■ abbrev. revolutions per minute.

rpt ■ abbrev. report.

RPV ■ abbrev. remotely piloted vehicle.

RRP ■ abbrev. recommended retail price.

RSA ■ abbrev. **1** Republic of South Africa. **2** Royal Society of Arts.

RSC ■ abbrev. Royal Shakespeare Company.

RSI ■ abbrev. repetitive strain injury.

RSJ ■ abbrev. rolled steel joist.

RSM ■ abbrev. (in the British army) Regimental Sergeant Major.

RSV ■ abbrev. Revised Standard Version (of the Bible).

RSVP ■ abbrev. répondez s'il vous plaît; please reply (used at the end of invitations).
– ORIGIN from French.

rt ■ abbrev. right.

rte ■ abbrev. route.

RTF ■ abbrev. Computing rich text format.

Rt Hon. ■ abbrev. Right Honourable.

Rt Revd (also **Rt Rev.**) ■ abbrev. Right Reverend.

RU486 ■ n. trademark for MIFEPRISTONE.

Ru ■ symb. the chemical element ruthenium.

rub ■ v. (**rubbed**, **rubbing**) **1** apply firm pressure against the surface of, using a repeated back and forth motion. ▸ move to and fro against a surface. ▸ apply with a rubbing action: *she rubbed some cream on her nose.* ▸ (**rub something in/into/through**) blend or mix ingredients together using a rubbing action: *rub in the fat.* ▸ (**rub something down**) dry, smooth, or clean something by rubbing. ▸ (**rub something out**) erase pencil marks with a rubber. ▸ (**rub off**) be transferred by contact or association. **2** (**rub along**) informal, chiefly Brit. cope or get along without undue difficulty. **3** reproduce the design of (a sepulchral brass or a stone) by rubbing paper laid on it with pencil or chalk. **4** Bowls (of a bowl) be slowed or diverted by the unevenness of the ground. ■ n. **1** an act of rubbing. **2** an ointment designed to be rubbed on the skin. **3** (usu. **the rub**) the central or most important difficulty. [from Shakespeare's *Hamlet* (III. i. 65).] **4** Bowls an inequality of the ground impeding or diverting a bowl; the diversion or hindering of a bowl by this.
– PHRASES **the rub of the green 1** Golf an accidental or unpredictable influence on the course or position of the ball. **2** good fortune. **rub one's hands** rub one's hands together to show keen satisfaction. **rub it in** (or **rub someone's nose in something**) informal emphatically draw someone's attention to an embarrassing or painful fact. **rub noses** rub one's nose against someone else's in greeting (especially as traditional among Maoris and some other peoples). **rub shoulders** (or N. Amer. **elbows**) associate or come into contact. **rub someone** (or **rub someone up**) **the wrong way** anger or irritate someone.
– ORIGIN Middle English: perhaps from Low German *rubben*.

rubato /rʊˈbɑːtəʊ/ (also **tempo rubato**) ■ n. (pl. **rubatos** or **rubati** /-tiː/) Music the temporary disregard for strict tempo to allow an expressive quickening or slackening.
– ORIGIN Italian, 'robbed'.

rubber[1] ■ n. **1** a contest consisting of a series of matches between the same sides in cricket, tennis, and other games. **2** Bridge a unit of play in which one side scores bonus points for winning the best of three games.
– ORIGIN C16.

rubber[2] ■ n. **1** a tough elastic polymeric substance made from the latex of a tropical plant or synthetically. **2** a piece of such material used for erasing pencil marks. **3** N. Amer. informal a condom. **4** (**rubbers**) N. Amer. rubber boots; galoshes.
– DERIVATIVES **rubberiness** n. **rubberize** (also **-ise**) v. **rubbery** adj.
– ORIGIN C16: from RUB.

rubber band ■ n. a loop of rubber for holding things together.

rubber bullet ■ n. a bullet made of rubber, used especially in riot control.

rubber cement ■ n. a cement or adhesive containing rubber in a solvent.

rubber duck ■ n. an inflatable flat-bottomed rubber dinghy, often motorized.

rubberneck informal ■ n. a person who turns their head to stare at something in a foolish manner. ■ v. stare in such a way.
– DERIVATIVES **rubbernecker** n.

rubber plant ■ n. an evergreen tree of the fig family, which has large dark green shiny leaves and was formerly grown as a source of rubber. [*Ficus elastica*.]

rubber stamp ■ n. **1** a hand-held device for imprinting dates, addresses, etc. **2** a person acting to give automatic authorization, without having the authority or ability to question or reject. ■ v. (**rubber-stamp**) **1** apply a rubber stamp to. **2** approve automatically without proper consideration.

rubber tree ■ n. a tree that produces the latex from which rubber is manufactured, native to the Amazonian rainforest. [*Hevea brasiliensis*.]

rubbing ■ n. **1** the action of rubbing. **2** an impression of a design on brass or stone, made by rubbing.

rubbing alcohol ■ n. denatured alcohol used as an antiseptic or in massage.

rubbish ■ n. **1** waste material; refuse or litter. **2** material that is considered unimportant or valueless. ▸ nonsense; worthless talk or ideas. ▸ informal a worthless person. ■ v. informal criticize and reject as worthless. ■ adj. Brit. informal very bad.
– DERIVATIVES **rubbishy** adj.
– ORIGIN Middle English: from Anglo-Norman French *rubbous*; perhaps rel. to Old French *robe* 'spoils'.

rubble ■ n. waste or rough fragments of stone, brick, concrete, etc., especially as the debris from the demolition of buildings.
– DERIVATIVES **rubbled** adj. **rubbly** adj.
– ORIGIN Middle English: perhaps from an Anglo-Norman French alteration of Old French *robe* 'spoils'.

rubella /ruːˈbɛlə/ ■ n. a contagious viral disease, with symptoms like mild measles; German measles.
– ORIGIN C19: from Latin *rubellus* 'reddish'.

rubeola /ruːˈbiːələ/ ■ n. medical term for MEASLES.
– ORIGIN C17: from medieval Latin, diminutive of Latin *rubeus* 'red'.

rubescent /ruːˈbɛs(ə)nt/ ■ adj. chiefly poetic/literary reddening; blushing.
– ORIGIN C18: from Latin *rubescent-*, *rubescere* 'redden', from *ruber* 'red'.

Rubicon /ˈruːbɪk(ə)n, -kɒn/ ■ n. a point of no return.
– ORIGIN the name of a stream in NE Italy marking the ancient boundary between Italy and Cisalpine Gaul, which Julius Caesar crossed in 49 BC, breaking the law and so committing himself to war.

rubicund /ˈruːbɪk(ə)nd/ ■ adj. having a ruddy complexion.
– DERIVATIVES **rubicundity** /-ˈkʌndɪti/ n.
– ORIGIN Middle English: from Latin *rubicundus*, from *rubere* 'be red'.

rubidium /ruːˈbɪdɪəm/ ■ n. the chemical element of atomic number 37, a rare soft silvery reactive metal of the alkali metal group. (Symbol: **Rb**)
– ORIGIN C19: from Latin *rubidus* 'red' (with ref. to lines in its spectrum).

Rubik's cube /ˈruːbɪks/ ■ n. a puzzle in the form of a plastic cube covered with multicoloured squares, which the player attempts to turn so that all the squares on each face are of the same colour.
– ORIGIN 1980s: named after its Hungarian inventor Erno Rubik.

ruble ■ n. variant spelling of ROUBLE.

rubric /ˈruːbrɪk/ ■ n. **1** a heading on a document. **2** a set of instructions or rules. ▸ a direction in a liturgical book as to how a church service should be conducted.
– DERIVATIVES **rubrical** adj.
– ORIGIN Middle English *rubrish*, from Old French *rubriche*, from Latin *rubrica* (*terra*) 'red (earth or ochre as writing material)'.

ruby ■ n. (pl. **-ies**) **1** a precious stone consisting of corundum in colour varieties varying from deep crimson or purple to pale rose. **2** an intense deep red colour.
– ORIGIN Middle English: from Old French *rubi*, from medieval Latin *rubinus*, from Latin *rubeus* 'red'.

ruby wedding ■ n. the fortieth anniversary of a wedding.

ruche /ruːʃ/ ■ n. a frill or pleat of fabric.
– DERIVATIVES **ruched** adj. **ruching** n.
– ORIGIN C19: from medieval Latin *rusca* 'tree bark', of Celtic origin.

ruck¹ ■ n. **1** Rugby a loose scrum formed around a player with the ball on the ground. Compare with MAUL. ▶ Australian Rules a group of three players who follow the play without fixed positions. **2** a tightly packed crowd of people. ■ v. Rugby & Australian Rules take part in a ruck.
– ORIGIN Middle English: of Scandinavian origin.

ruck² ■ v. make or form wrinkles, creases, or folds. ■ n. a crease or wrinkle.
– ORIGIN C18: from Old Norse *hrukka*.

rucksack /'rʌksak, 'ruk-/ ■ n. a bag with two shoulder straps which allow it to be carried on the back, used by hikers.
– ORIGIN C19: from German, from *rucken* (var. of *Rücken* 'back') + *Sack* 'bag, sack'.

ruckus /'rʌkəs/ ■ n. a row or commotion.
– ORIGIN C19: perhaps rel. to RUCTION and RUMPUS.

ruction ■ n. informal a disturbance or quarrel. ▶ (**ructions**) trouble.
– ORIGIN C19: perhaps associated with INSURRECTION.

rudaceous /ru'deɪʃəs/ ■ adj. Geology (of rock) composed of fragments of relatively large size (larger than sand grains).
– ORIGIN C20: from Latin *rudus* 'rubble'.

rudbeckia /rʌd'bɛkɪə, rʌd-/ ■ n. a North American plant of the daisy family, with yellow or orange flowers and a dark cone-like centre. [Genus *Rudbeckia*.]
– ORIGIN named after the Swedish botanist Olaf *Rudbeck* (1660–1740).

rudder ■ n. a flat piece hinged vertically near the stern of a boat for steering. ▶ a vertical aerofoil pivoted from the tailplane of an aircraft, for controlling movement about the vertical axis. ▶ application of the rudder in steering a boat or aircraft.
– ORIGIN Old English *rōther* 'paddle, oar', of West Germanic origin.

rudderless ■ adj. **1** lacking a rudder. **2** lacking direction.

ruddy ■ adj. (**-ier**, **-iest**) **1** (especially of a person's face) having a healthy red colour. **2** Brit. informal, dated used as a euphemism for 'bloody'. ■ v. (**-ies**, **-ied**) make ruddy in colour.
– DERIVATIVES **ruddily** adv. (rare). **ruddiness** n.
– ORIGIN Old English *rudig*, from archaic *rud* 'red colour'.

rude ■ adj. **1** offensively impolite or ill-mannered. ▶ referring to sex in a way considered improper and offensive. **2** very abrupt: *a rude awakening*. **3** chiefly Brit. vigorous or hearty. **4** dated roughly made or done; lacking sophistication. ▶ archaic ignorant and uneducated.
– DERIVATIVES **rudely** adv. **rudeness** n. **rudery** n.
– ORIGIN Middle English: from Latin *rudis* 'unwrought', 'uncultivated'; rel. to *rudus* 'broken stone'.

ruderal /'ruːd(ə)r(ə)l/ Botany ■ adj. (of a plant) growing on waste ground or among rubbish. ■ n. a ruderal plant.
– ORIGIN C19: from Latin *rudera*, pl. of *rudus* 'rubble'.

rudiment /'ruːdɪm(ə)nt/ ■ n. **1** (**rudiments**) the first principles of a subject. ▶ an elementary or primitive form of something. **2** Music a basic pattern used by drummers, such as the roll.
– ORIGIN C16: from Latin *rudimentum*, from *rudis* 'unwrought'.

rudimentary /ˌruːdɪ'ment(ə)ri/ ■ adj. **1** involving or limited to basic principles. **2** of or relating to an immature, undeveloped, or basic form.
– DERIVATIVES **rudimentarily** adv.

rue¹ ■ v. (**rues**, **rued**, **rueing** or **ruing**) bitterly regret (a past event or action) and wish it undone. ■ n. archaic **1** repentance; regret. **2** compassion; pity.
– ORIGIN Old English *hrēow* 'repentance', *hrēowan* 'affect with contrition', of Germanic origin.

rue² ■ n. a perennial evergreen shrub with bitter strong-scented lobed leaves which are used in herbal medicine. [*Ruta graveolens*.]
– ORIGIN Middle English: from Greek *rhutē*.

rueful ■ adj. expressing regret, especially in a wry or humorous way.
– DERIVATIVES **ruefully** adv. **ruefulness** n.

ruff¹ ■ n. **1** a projecting starched frill worn round the neck, characteristic of Elizabethan and Jacobean costume. **2** a projecting or conspicuously coloured ring of feathers or hair round the neck of a bird or mammal. **3** a pigeon of a domestic breed with a ruff of feathers. **4** (pl. same or **ruffs**) a North Eurasian wading bird, the male of which has a large ruff and ear tufts in the breeding season. [*Philomachus pugnax*; the female is called a reeve.]
– ORIGIN C16: prob. from a var. of ROUGH.

ruff² ■ v. (in bridge and whist) play a trump in a trick which was led in a different suit. ▶ play a trump on (a card). ■ n. an act of ruffing or opportunity to ruff.
– ORIGIN C16: from Old French *rouffle* (perhaps an alteration of Italian *trionfo* 'a trump').

ruffian ■ n. a violent or lawless person.
– DERIVATIVES **ruffianism** n. **ruffianly** adj.
– ORIGIN C15: from Old French *ruffian*, from Italian *ruffiano*, perhaps from dialect *rofia* 'scab, scurf', of Germanic origin.

ruffle ■ v. **1** make or become disarranged; disrupt the smooth surface of. ▶ (of a bird) erect (its feathers) in anger or display. **2** disconcert or upset the composure of. **3** [usu. as adj. **ruffled**] ornament with or gather into a frill. ■ n. **1** an ornamental gathered frill on a garment. **2** a low continuous drum beat.
– ORIGIN Middle English.

rufous /'ruːfəs/ ■ adj. reddish brown in colour. ■ n. a reddish-brown colour.
– ORIGIN C18: from Latin *rufus* 'red, reddish'.

rug ■ n. **1** a small carpet. ▶ chiefly Brit. a thick woollen blanket. **2** informal, chiefly N. Amer. a toupee or wig.
– PHRASES **pull the rug out from under** abruptly expose or withdraw support from.
– ORIGIN C16: prob. of Scandinavian origin.

rugby (also **rugby football**) ■ n. a team game played with an oval ball that may be kicked, carried, and passed by hand, in which points are won by scoring a try or by kicking the ball over the crossbar of the opponents' goal.
– ORIGIN C19: named after *Rugby* School in central England, where the game was first played.

rugby league ■ n. a form of rugby played in teams of thirteen, in which professionalism has always been allowed.

rugby union ■ n. a form of rugby played in teams of fifteen, traditionally strictly amateur but opened to professionalism in 1995.

rugged /'rʌɡɪd/ ■ adj. **1** having a rocky and uneven surface. **2** having or requiring toughness and determination. ▶ (of a man) having attractively masculine, rough-hewn features.
– DERIVATIVES **ruggedly** adv. **ruggedness** n.
– ORIGIN Middle English: prob. of Scandinavian origin.

ruggedized (also **-ised**) ■ adj. chiefly N. Amer. designed or improved to be hard-wearing: *ruggedized computers*.
– DERIVATIVES **ruggedization** (also **-isation**) n.

rugger ■ n. Brit. informal rugby.

rugger-bugger ■ n. an aggressively masculine young man who is enthusiastic about sport.

rugosa /ruː'ɡəʊzə/ ■ n. a SE Asian rose with dark green wrinkled leaves and deep pink flowers. [*Rosa rugosa*.]
– ORIGIN C19: from Latin *rugosus* (see RUGOSE).

rugose /'ruːɡəʊs, ruː'ɡəʊs/ ■ adj. chiefly Biology wrinkled; corrugated.
– DERIVATIVES **rugosity** n.
– ORIGIN Middle English: from Latin *rugosus*, from *ruga* 'wrinkle'.

rug rat ■ n. N. Amer. informal a small child.

ruin ■ n. **1** physical destruction or collapse. **2** a building (or the remains of a building) that has suffered much damage. **3** a dramatic decline; a downfall. ■ v. **1** damage irreparably; reduce to a state of ruin. ▶ reduce to poverty or bankruptcy. **2** poetic/literary fall headlong.
– PHRASES **in ruins** in a state of complete collapse.
– ORIGIN Middle English: from Old French *ruine*, from Latin *ruina*, from *ruere* 'to fall'.

ruination ■ n. the action or fact of ruining or the state of being ruined.

ruinous ■ adj. **1** disastrous or destructive. **2** in ruins; dilapidated.
– DERIVATIVES **ruinously** adv. **ruinousness** n.

rule ■ n. **1** a regulation or principle governing conduct or procedure within a particular sphere. **2** control or government: *an end to Soviet rule.* **3** a code of practice and discipline for a religious community: *the Rule of St Benedict.* **4** (**the rule**) the normal or customary state of things. **5** a straight strip of rigid material used for measuring; a ruler. **6** a thin printed line or dash. ■ v. **1** exercise ultimate power over (a people or nation). ▸ exert a powerful and restricting influence on. ▸ be prevalent; be the norm. **2** pronounce authoritatively and legally to be the case. **3** [often as adj. **ruled**] make parallel lines on (paper). ▸ make (a straight line) with a ruler. **4** (**rule something out/in**) exclude (or include) something as a possibility.
– PHRASES **as a rule** usually, but not always. **rule of law** the restriction of power by well-defined and established laws. **rule of thumb** a broadly accurate guide or principle, based on practice rather than theory. **rule the roost** be in complete control.
– DERIVATIVES **ruleless** adj.
– ORIGIN Middle English: from Old French *reule* (n.), *reuler* (v.), from Latin *regula* 'straight stick'.

rule nisi ■ n. (pl. **rules nisi**) Law a court order valid for a fixed period, at the end of which arguments may be presented against its being made final.
– ORIGIN Latin *nisi* 'unless'.

rule of the road ■ n. a custom or law regulating the direction in which two cars, ships, etc. should move to pass one another to avoid collision.

ruler ■ n. **1** a person or agent exercising government or dominion. **2** a straight-edged strip of rigid material, marked at regular intervals and used to draw straight lines or measure distances.
– DERIVATIVES **rulership** n.

ruling ■ n. an authoritative decision or pronouncement. ■ adj. exercising rule.

rum¹ ■ n. an alcoholic spirit distilled from sugar-cane residues or molasses.
– ORIGIN C17: perhaps an abbrev. of obsolete *rumbullion*, in the same sense.

rum² ■ adj. (**rummer**, **rummest**) Brit. informal, dated odd; peculiar.
– DERIVATIVES **rumly** adv. **rumness** n.
– ORIGIN C18.

Rumanian /ruːˈmeɪnɪən/ ■ adj. & n. variant spelling of **ROMANIAN**.

rumba /ˈrʌmbə/ (also **rhumba**) ■ n. a rhythmic dance with Spanish and African elements, originating in Cuba. ▸ a ballroom dance based on this. ■ v. (**rumbas**, **rumbaed** /-bəd/ or **rumba'd**, **rumbaing** /-bə(r)ɪŋ/) dance the rumba.
– ORIGIN 1920s: from Latin American Spanish.

rum baba ■ n. see BABA¹.

rumble ■ v. **1** make a continuous deep, resonant sound. ▸ move with such a sound. **2** (**rumble on**) (of a dispute) continue in a persistent but low-key way. **3** Brit. informal discover (an illicit activity or its perpetrator): *it wouldn't need a genius to rumble his little game.* **4** US informal take part in a street fight. ■ n. a continuous deep, resonant sound like distant thunder.
– DERIVATIVES **rumbler** n. **rumbling** adj.
– ORIGIN Middle English: prob. from Middle Dutch *rommelen*, *rummelen*, of imitative origin.

rumble strip ■ n. a series of raised strips set in a road, changing the noise a vehicle's tyres make on the surface and so warning drivers of speed restrictions or an approaching hazard.

rumbustious /rʌmˈbʌstʃəs, -tɪəs/ ■ adj. informal; chiefly Brit. boisterous or unruly.
– DERIVATIVES **rumbustiously** adv. **rumbustiousness** n.
– ORIGIN C18: prob. an alteration of archaic *robustious* 'boisterous, robust'.

rum butter ■ n. a rich, sweet, rum-flavoured sauce made with butter and sugar.

rumen /ˈruːmɛn/ ■ n. (pl. **rumens** or **rumina** /-mɪnə/) Zoology the first stomach of a ruminant, which receives food or cud, partly digests it, and passes it to the reticulum.
– ORIGIN C18: from Latin, 'throat'.

run

ruminant ■ n. **1** an even-toed ungulate mammal of a type that chews the cud, comprising cattle, sheep, antelopes, deer, giraffes, and their relatives. **2** a person given to meditation. ■ adj. of or relating to ruminants.
– ORIGIN C17: from Latin *ruminari* 'chew over again', from *rumen* (see RUMEN).

ruminate /ˈruːmɪneɪt/ ■ v. **1** think deeply about something. **2** (of a ruminant) chew the cud.
– DERIVATIVES **rumination** n. **ruminative** adj. **ruminatively** adv. **ruminator** n.
– ORIGIN C16: from Latin *ruminari* 'chew over'.

rummage ■ v. search unsystematically and untidily for something. ▸ make a thorough search of (a vessel). ■ n. an act of rummaging.
– DERIVATIVES **rummager** n.

HISTORY
Rummage came into English in the late 15th century, from the Old French word *arrumage*, which was based on *arrumer* 'stow in a hold'. In early use it meant 'arrange items in the hold of a ship', which gave rise to the sense 'make a search of a vessel' (which is still used in the context of customs officers going about their duties) and then to the main modern meaning. **Rummage** is connected to **room**, through the shared Middle Dutch root *ruim* 'room'.

rummage sale ■ n. chiefly N. Amer. a jumble sale.

rummer ■ n. a large stemmed drinking glass.
– ORIGIN C17: of Low Dutch origin; rel. to Dutch *roemer*.

rummy¹ ■ n. a card game in which the players try to form sets and sequences of cards.
– ORIGIN C20.

rummy² ■ adj. (**-ier**, **-iest**) another term for RUM².

rumour (US **rumor**) ■ n. a currently circulating story or report of unverified or doubtful truth. ■ v. (**be rumoured**) be circulated as a rumour.
– ORIGIN Middle English: from Old French *rumur*, from Latin *rumor* 'noise'.

rump ■ n. **1** the hind part of the body of a mammal or the lower back of a bird. ▸ chiefly humorous a person's buttocks. **2** a small or unimportant remnant.
– DERIVATIVES **rumpless** adj.
– ORIGIN Middle English: prob. of Scandinavian origin; cf. Danish and Norwegian *rumpe* 'backside'.

rumple ■ v. [usu. as adj. **rumpled**] give a ruffled or dishevelled appearance to. ■ n. an untidy state.
– DERIVATIVES **rumply** adj.
– ORIGIN C16: from Middle Dutch *rompel*.

rumpus ■ n. (pl. **rumpuses**) a noisy disturbance.
– ORIGIN C18: prob. fanciful.

rumpus room ■ n. N. Amer. & Austral./NZ a room for playing games or other noisy activities.

run ■ v. (**running**; past **ran** /ran/; past part. **run**) **1** move at a speed faster than a walk, never having both or all feet on the ground at the same time. ▸ enter or be entered in a race. ▸ (of hounds) chase or hunt their quarry. ▸ (of a boat) sail straight and fast directly before the wind. ▸ (of a migratory fish) go upriver from the sea in order to spawn. **2** move about in a hurried and hectic way. **3** pass or cause to pass: *Helen ran her fingers through her hair.* ▸ move or cause to move forcefully: *the tanker ran aground.* ▸ informal fail to stop at (a red traffic light). ▸ navigate (rapids or a waterfall) in a boat. **4** flow or cause to flow. ▸ cause water to flow over. ▸ emit or exude a liquid: *her nose was running.* ▸ (of dye or colour) dissolve and spread when wet. **5** (of a bus, train, etc.) make a regular journey on a particular route. ▸ transport in a car: *I'll run you home.* **6** be in charge of; manage or organize. ▸ continue, operate, or proceed: *everything's running according to plan.* ▸ own, maintain, and use (a vehicle). **7** be in or cause to be in operation; function or cause to function. **8** (**run in**) (of a quality or trait) be common or inherent in. **9** stand as a candidate. **10** pass into or reach a specified state or level. **11** (of a stocking or pair of tights) develop a ladder. **12** publish or be published in a newspaper or magazine. **13** smuggle (goods). ■ n. **1** an act or spell of

runabout

running. ▶ a running pace. **2** a journey or route. ▶ a short excursion made in a car. **3** Cricket a unit of scoring achieved by hitting the ball so that both batsmen are able to run between the wickets. ▶ Baseball a point scored by the batter returning to the home plate after touching the bases. **4** a spell of producing, proceeding, or operating: *a run of bad luck*. ▶ a continuous stretch or length of something. ▶ a rapid series of musical notes. ▶ a sequence of cards of the same suit. **5** a widespread and sudden demand: *a big run on nostalgia toys*. **6** a course or track made or regularly used: *a ski run*. **7** (**the run**) the average or usual type: *he stood out from the general run of soldiers*. **8** an enclosed area in which animals or birds may run freely in the open. ▶ (**the run of**) free and unrestricted use of or access to somewhere. **9** a ladder in stockings or tights. **10** a downward trickle of liquid. **11** a small stream or brook. **12** (**the runs**) informal diarrhoea. **13** Nautical the after part of a ship's bottom where it rises and narrows towards the stern. **14** an annual mass migration of fish up or down a river.
– PHRASES **be run off one's feet** be extremely busy. **a (good) run for one's money 1** challenging competition or opposition. **2** reward or enjoyment in return for one's efforts. **on the run 1** escaping from arrest. **2** while running or moving. **run before one can walk** attempt something difficult before one has grasped the basic skills. **run dry 1** (of a well or river) cease to flow or have any water. **2** (of a supply) be completely used up. (**make a**) **run for it** attempt to escape by running away. **run foul** (or chiefly N. Amer. **afoul**) **of 1** Nautical collide or become entangled with. **2** come into conflict with. **run low** (or **short**) (of a supply) become depleted. **run off at the mouth** N. Amer. informal talk excessively or indiscreetly. **run a temperature** be suffering from a high temperature. **run someone/thing to earth** (or **ground**) chase a quarry to its lair. **run to ruin** archaic fall into disrepair.
– PHRASAL VERBS **run across** meet or find by chance. **run after** informal pursue persistently. **run along** informal go away. **run away 1** take flight; escape. **2** try to avoid facing up to danger or difficulty. **run away with 1** escape the control of: *Susan's imagination was running away with her*. **2** win (a competition or prize) easily. **run something by** (or **past**) tell (someone) about something, in order to ascertain an opinion or reaction. **run someone/thing down 1** (of a vehicle) hit and knock over a person or animal. **2** criticize someone or something unfairly or unkindly. **3** discover someone or something after a search. **4** (also **run down**) reduce or become reduced in size or resources. **5** lose or cause to lose power; stop or cause to stop functioning. **6** gradually deteriorate or cause to deteriorate. **run someone in** informal arrest someone. **run something in** use something new in such a way as not to make maximum demands upon it. **run into 1** collide with. ▶ meet by chance. **2** experience (a problem or difficult situation). **run off** informal escape; abscond. **run something off 1** produce a copy on a machine. **2** write or recite something quickly and with little effort. **3** drain liquid from a container. **run on** continue without stopping; go on longer than is expected. **run out 1** use up or be used up. **2** become no longer valid. **3** (of rope) be paid out. **4** extend; project. **run someone out** Cricket dismiss a batsman by dislodging the bails with the ball while the batsman is still running. **run over 1** overflow. **2** exceed (a limit). **run someone/thing over** knock down a person or animal in a vehicle. **run someone/thing through** stab a person or animal so as to kill them. **run through** (or **over**) go over quickly or briefly as a rehearsal or reminder. **run to 1** extend to or reach. **2** show a tendency towards. **run something up 1** allow a bill, score, etc. to accumulate. **2** make something quickly or hurriedly. **3** raise a flag. **run up against** experience or meet (a difficulty or problem). **run with** proceed with; accept.
– DERIVATIVES **runnable** adj.
– ORIGIN Old English *rinnan, irnan* (v.), of Germanic origin; the current form with *-u-* is first recorded in C16.

runabout ■ n. a small car or light aircraft, especially one used for short journeys.

runaround ■ n. informal **1** (**the runaround**) deceitful or evasive treatment. **2** a runabout.

runaway ■ n. **1** a person who has run away from their home or an institution. **2** [as modifier] (of an animal or vehicle) running out of control. ▶ happening or done quickly or uncontrollably: *runaway success*.

rundown ■ n. a brief analysis or summary. ■ adj. (**run-down**) **1** in a poor or neglected state. **2** tired and rather unwell, especially through overwork.

rune /ruːn/ ■ n. **1** a letter of an ancient Germanic alphabet, related to the Roman alphabet, used especially in Scandinavia. ▶ a mysterious symbol, especially in a spell or incantation. **2** an ancient Scandinavian poem or part of one.
– DERIVATIVES **runic** adj.
– ORIGIN Old English *rūn* 'a secret, mystery'; reintroduced in the late C17 under the influence of Old Norse *rúnir, rúnar* 'magic signs, hidden lore'.

rung[1] ■ n. **1** a horizontal support on a ladder for a person's foot. ▶ a strengthening crosspiece in the structure of a chair. **2** a level in a hierarchical structure.
– DERIVATIVES **runged** adj. **rungless** adj.
– ORIGIN Old English *hrung*.

rung[2] past participle of RING[2].

run-in ■ n. **1** the approach to an action or event. **2** informal a disagreement or fight.

runnel ■ n. **1** a gutter. **2** a brook or stream.
– ORIGIN C16: var. of dialect *rindle*.

runner ■ n. **1** a person or animal that runs. ▶ a horse that runs in a particular race. ▶ a messenger, collector, or agent for a bank, bookmaker, or similar. ▶ an orderly in the army. **2** a vehicle or machine that runs in a satisfactory or specified way. **3** Brit. informal an idea that has a chance of being accepted. **4** a rod, groove, or blade on which something slides. ▶ a roller for moving a heavy article. ▶ a ring capable of sliding or being drawn along a strap or rod. ▶ Nautical a rope in a single block with one end round a tackle block and the other having a hook. **5** a shoot which grows along the ground and can take root at points along its length. ▶ a climbing plant, or one that spreads by means of runners. **6** a long, narrow rug or strip of carpet. **7** used in names of fast-swimming fish of the jack family, e.g. rainbow runner.
– PHRASES **do a runner** Brit. informal leave hastily, in order to escape or avoid something.

runner bean ■ n. chiefly Brit. a Central American climbing bean plant with scarlet flowers, widely cultivated for its long green edible pods. [*Phaseolus coccineus*].

runner-up ■ n. (pl. **runners-up**) a competitor or team taking second place in a contest.

running ■ n. **1** the activity or movement of a runner. **2** the action or business of managing or operating. ■ adj. **1** (of water) flowing naturally or supplied through pipes and taps. ▶ exuding liquid or pus: *a running sore*. **2** continuous or recurring: *a running joke*. **3** done while running. **4** [postpos.] consecutive; in succession: *he failed to turn up for the third week running*.
– PHRASES **in** (or **out of**) **the running** (or **no longer in**) contention. **make the running** set the pace. **take up the running** take over as pacesetter.

running back ■ n. American Football an offensive player who specializes in carrying the ball.

running battle ■ n. a military engagement which does not occur at a fixed location.

running belay ■ n. Climbing a device attached to a rock face through which a climbing rope runs freely, acting as a pulley if the climber falls.

running board ■ n. a footboard extending along the side of a vehicle.

running commentary ■ n. a verbal description of events, given as they occur.

running head ■ n. a heading printed at the top of each page of a book or chapter.

running knot ■ n. a knot that slips along the rope and changes the size of a noose.

running lights ■ pl. n. **1** another term for NAVIGATION LIGHTS. **2** small lights on a motor vehicle that remain illuminated while the vehicle is running.

running mate ■ n. chiefly US an election candidate for the lesser of two closely associated political offices.

running repairs ▪ pl. n. minor or temporary repairs carried out on machinery while it is in use.

running stitch ▪ n. a simple needlework stitch consisting of a line of small even stitches which run back and forth through the cloth.

runny ▪ adj. (-ier, -iest) 1 more liquid in consistency than is usual or expected. 2 (of a person's nose) producing or discharging mucus.

run-off ▪ n. 1 a further contest after a tie or inconclusive result. 2 the draining away of rainfall or other liquid from the surface of an area. ▸ the liquid that drains in this way.

run-of-the-mill ▪ adj. lacking unusual or special aspects; ordinary.

run-out ▪ n. 1 Cricket the dismissal of a batsman by being run out. 2 informal a short session of play or practice in a sport. 3 a length of time or space over which something gradually lessens or ceases.

runt ▪ n. 1 a small pig or other animal, especially the smallest in a litter. 2 a pigeon of a large domestic breed.
– DERIVATIVES **runty** adj.
– ORIGIN C16 (in the sense 'old or decayed tree stump').

run-through ▪ n. 1 a rehearsal. 2 a brief outline or summary.

run-time ▪ n. Computing 1 the length of time a program takes to run. ▸ the time at which a program is run. 2 a cut-down version of a program that can be run but not changed.

run-up ▪ n. 1 the preparatory period before a notable event. 2 an act of running briefly to gain momentum before bowling, performing a jump, etc. 3 Golf a low approach shot that bounces and runs forward.

runway ▪ n. 1 a strip of hard ground along which aircraft take off and land. 2 a raised gangway extending into an auditorium, especially as used for fashion shows. 3 an animal run.

rupee /ruːˈpiː, ˈruːpiː/ ▪ n. the basic monetary unit of India, Pakistan, Sri Lanka, Nepal, Mauritius, and the Seychelles.
– ORIGIN from Sanskrit *rūpya* 'wrought silver'.

rupiah /ruːˈpiːə/ ▪ n. the basic monetary unit of Indonesia.
– ORIGIN Indonesian, from Hindi *rūpyah* (see RUPEE).

rupture ▪ v. 1 break or burst suddenly. ▸ cause to break or burst suddenly. ▸ (**be ruptured**) or **rupture oneself** suffer an abdominal hernia. 2 breach or disturb (a harmonious situation). ▪ n. 1 an instance of rupturing. 2 an abdominal hernia.
– ORIGIN Middle English: from Old French *rupture* or Latin *ruptura*, from *rumpere* 'to break'.

rural ▪ adj. in, relating to, or characteristic of the countryside rather than the town.
– DERIVATIVES **ruralism** n. **ruralist** n. **rurality** n. **ruralization** (also **-isation**) n. **ruralize** (also **-ise**) v. **rurally** adv.
– ORIGIN Middle English: from late Latin *ruralis*, from *rus*, *rur-* 'country'.

Ruritanian /ˌrʊərɪˈteɪnɪən/ ▪ adj. relating to or characteristic of romantic adventure or its setting.
– ORIGIN C19: from *Ruritania*, an imaginary kingdom in SE Europe used as the setting for the novels of courtly intrigue and romance written by the English novelist Anthony Hope.

ruse /ruːz/ ▪ n. a stratagem or trick.
– ORIGIN Middle English: from Old French, from *ruser* 'use trickery', earlier 'drive back', perhaps from Latin *rursus* 'backwards'.

rush¹ ▪ v. 1 move or act or cause to move or act with urgent haste. ▸ take somewhere with urgent haste. ▸ (**rush something out**) produce and distribute something very quickly. ▸ deal with (something) hurriedly. 2 (of air or a liquid) flow strongly. 3 dash towards (someone or something) in an attempt to attack or capture them or it. ▸ American Football advance towards (an opposing player, especially the quarterback). ▸ American Football gain a specified amount of ground by running forward with the ball. 4 informal overcharge (a customer). ▪ n. 1 the action or an instance of rushing. 2 a flurry of hasty activity. 3 a sudden strong demand for a commodity. 4 a sudden intensity of feeling. 5 a sudden thrill experienced after taking certain drugs. 6 (**rushes**) the first prints made of a film after a period of shooting.

– PHRASES **rush one's fences** Brit. act with undue haste. **a rush of blood (to the head)** a sudden attack of wild irrationality.
– DERIVATIVES **rusher** n. **rushing** adj.
– ORIGIN Middle English: from an Anglo-Norman French var. of Old French *ruser* 'drive back'.

rush² ▪ n. 1 a marsh or waterside plant with slender stem-like pith-filled leaves, some kinds of which are used for matting, baskets, etc. [Genus *Juncus*.] 2 used in names of similar plants, e.g. flowering rush.
– DERIVATIVES **rushy** adj.
– ORIGIN Old English, of Germanic origin.

rush hour ▪ n. a time at the start and end of the working day when traffic is at its heaviest.

rushlight ▪ n. historical a candle made by dipping the pith of a rush in tallow.

rusk ▪ n. a dry biscuit or piece of rebaked bread.
– ORIGIN C16: from Spanish or Portuguese *rosca* 'twist, coil, roll of bread'.

russet ▪ adj. reddish brown. ▪ n. 1 a reddish-brown colour. 2 a dessert apple of a variety with a slightly rough greenish-brown skin.
– DERIVATIVES **russety** adj.
– ORIGIN Middle English: from an Anglo-Norman French var. of Old French *rousset*, diminutive of *rous* 'red', from Latin *russus* 'red'.

Russian ▪ n. 1 a native or national of Russia, or a person of Russian descent. 2 the language of Russia, an Eastern Slavic language written in the Cyrillic alphabet. ▪ adj. of or relating to Russia, its people, or their language.
– DERIVATIVES **Russianization** (also **-isation**) n. **Russianize** (also **-ise**) v. **Russianness** n.

Russian doll ▪ n. each of a set of brightly painted hollow wooden dolls of varying sizes, designed to fit inside each other.

Russian Orthodox Church ▪ n. the national Church of Russia.

Russian roulette ▪ n. a dangerous game of chance in which a single bullet is loaded into the chamber of a revolver, the cylinder is spun, and people take it in turns to hold the gun to their own head and fire it.

Russian tea ▪ n. tea laced with rum and typically served with lemon.

Russian vine ▪ n. a fast-growing Asian climbing plant of the dock family, with long clusters of white or pink flowers. [*Fallopia baldschuanica*.]

Russify /ˈrʌsɪfaɪ/ ▪ v. (**-ies**, **-ied**) make Russian in character.
– DERIVATIVES **Russification** n.

Russki /ˈrʌski/ (also **Russky**) ▪ n. (pl. **Russkis** or **Russkies**) informal, often offensive a Russian.
– ORIGIN C19: from Russian *russkiĭ* 'Russian', or from RUSSIAN, on the pattern of Russian surnames ending in *-skiĭ*.

Russo- ▪ comb. form Russian; Russian and ...: *Russo-Japanese*. ▸ relating to Russia.

Russophile /ˈrʌsə(ʊ)faɪl/ ▪ n. a person who admires or is fond of Russia and things Russian.
– DERIVATIVES **Russophilia** n.

Russophobe /ˈrʌsə(ʊ)fəʊb/ ▪ n. a person who dislikes Russia and things Russian.
– DERIVATIVES **Russophobia** n.

russula /ˈrʌsələ/ ▪ n. a woodland toadstool that typically has a brightly coloured flattened cap and a white stem and gills. [Genus *Russula*: numerous species.]
– ORIGIN from Latin *russus* 'red' (because many have a red cap).

rust ▪ n. 1 a reddish- or yellowish-brown flaking coating of iron oxide that is formed on iron or steel by oxidation, especially in the presence of moisture. 2 a fungal disease of plants which results in reddish or brownish patches. 3 a reddish-brown colour. ▪ v. be affected with rust.
– DERIVATIVES **rustless** adj.
– ORIGIN Old English *rūst*, of Germanic origin.

rust belt ■ n. informal a region characterized by declining industry and a falling population, especially in the American Midwest and NE states.

rust bucket ■ n. informal, often humorous a vehicle or ship which is old and badly rusted.

rustic ■ adj. **1** of or characteristic of life in the country. ▸ having a simplicity and charm that is considered typical of the countryside. **2** made of rough branches or timber. **3** (of masonry) having a rough-hewn or roughened surface or sunken joints. ■ n. often derogatory an unsophisticated country person.
– DERIVATIVES **rustically** adv. **rusticity** n.
– ORIGIN Middle English: from Latin *rusticus*, from *rus* 'the country'.

rusticate /ˈrʌstɪkeɪt/ ■ v. **1** S. African & Brit. suspend (a student) from a university as a punishment. **2** fashion (masonry) in large blocks with sunken joints and a roughened surface.
– DERIVATIVES **rustication** n.
– ORIGIN C15: from Latin *rusticari* 'live in the country', from *rusticus* (see RUSTIC).

rustle ■ v. **1** make a soft, muffled crackling sound like that caused by the movement of dry leaves or paper. ▸ move with such a sound. **2** round up and steal (cattle, horses, or sheep). **3** (**rustle something up**) informal produce something quickly. ■ n. a rustling sound.
– DERIVATIVES **rustler** n.
– ORIGIN Middle English: imitative.

rustproof ■ adj. not susceptible to corrosion by rust. ■ v. make rustproof.

rusty ■ adj. (**-ier**, **-iest**) **1** affected by rust. **2** rust-coloured. **3** (of knowledge or a skill) impaired by lack of recent practice.
– DERIVATIVES **rustily** adv. **rustiness** n.

rut[1] ■ n. **1** a long deep track made by the repeated passage of the wheels of vehicles. **2** a routine or pattern of behaviour that has become dull and unproductive but is hard to change.
– DERIVATIVES **rutted** adj. **rutty** adj.
– ORIGIN C16: prob. from Old French *rute* (see ROUTE).

rut[2] ■ n. an annual period of sexual activity in deer and some other mammals, during which the males fight each other for access to the females. ■ v. (**rutted**, **rutting**) engage in such activity.
– ORIGIN Middle English: from Latin *rugitus*, from *rugire* 'to roar'.

rutabaga /ˌruːtəˈbeɪɡə/ ■ n. chiefly N. Amer. a swede.
– ORIGIN C18: from Swedish dialect *rotabagge*.

ruth ■ n. archaic a feeling of pity, distress, or grief.
– ORIGIN Middle English: from RUE[1], prob. influenced by Old Norse *hrygth*.

Ruthenian /ruːˈθiːnɪən/ ■ n. a native or inhabitant of Ruthenia, a region of central Europe. ■ adj. of or relating to Ruthenia.

ruthenium /rʊˈθiːnɪəm/ ■ n. the chemical element of atomic number 44, a hard silvery-white metal. (Symbol: **Ru**)
– ORIGIN C19: from *Ruthenia* (see RUTHENIAN), because it was discovered in ores from the Urals.

rutherfordium /ˌrʌðəˈfɔːdɪəm/ ■ n. the chemical element of atomic number 104, a very unstable element made by high-energy atomic collisions. (Symbol: **Rf**)
– ORIGIN 1960s: named after the New Zealand physicist Ernest *Rutherford*.

ruthless ■ adj. having or showing no compassion.
– DERIVATIVES **ruthlessly** adv. **ruthlessness** n.
– ORIGIN Middle English: from RUTH.

rutile /ˈruːtɪl, ˈruːtaɪl/ ■ n. a black or reddish-brown mineral consisting of titanium dioxide, typically occurring as needle-like crystals.
– ORIGIN C19: from German *Rutil*, from Latin *rutilus* 'reddish'.

RV ■ abbrev. **1** N. Amer. recreational vehicle (especially a motorized caravan). **2** a rendezvous point. **3** Revised Version (of the Bible).

Rwandan /ruːˈandən/ (also **Rwandese** /ruːˈandiːz/) ■ n. a native or inhabitant of Rwanda, a country in central Africa. ■ adj. of or relating to Rwanda or Rwandans.

-ry suffix a shortened form of -ERY (as in *devilry*).

rye ■ n. **1** a wheat-like cereal plant which tolerates poor soils and low temperatures. [*Secale cereale*.] **2** (also **rye whisky**) whisky in which a significant amount of the grain used in distillation is fermented rye. **3** short for RYE BREAD.
– ORIGIN Old English, of Germanic origin.

rye bread ■ n. a dense, chewy bread made with rye flour.

ryegrass ■ n. a grass used for fodder and lawns. [Genus *Lolium*: several species, in particular *L. perenne*.]
– ORIGIN C18: alteration of obsolete *ray-grass*.

ryu /rɪˈuː/ ■ n. (pl. same or **ryus**) a school or style in Japanese arts, especially in the martial arts.
– ORIGIN from Japanese.

Ss

S¹ (also **s**) ■ n. (pl. **Ss** or **S's**) **1** the nineteenth letter of the alphabet. **2** denoting the next after R in a set of items, categories, etc.

S² ■ abbrev. **1** (chiefly in Catholic use) Saint. **2** siemens. **3** small (as a clothes size). **4** South or Southern. ■ symb. **1** the chemical element sulphur. **2** Chemistry entropy.

s ■ abbrev. **1** second(s). **2** Law section (of an act). **3** shilling(s). **4** Chemistry solid. **5** (in genealogies) son(s). **6** Chemistry denoting electrons and orbitals possessing zero angular momentum and total symmetry. [s from *sharp*, orig. applied to lines in atomic spectra.] ■ symb. (in mathematical formulae) distance.

's /s, z after a vowel sound or voiced consonant/ ■ contr. informal **1** is. **2** has. **3** us. **4** does.

-s¹ /s, z after a vowel sound or voiced consonant/ ■ suffix denoting the plurals of nouns (as in *wagons*). Compare with **-ES¹**.
– ORIGIN Old English pl. ending *-as*.

-s² /s, z after a vowel sound or voiced consonant/ ■ suffix forming the third person singular of the present of verbs (as in *sews*). Compare with **-ES²**.
– ORIGIN Old English dialect.

-s³ /s, z after a vowel sound or voiced consonant/ ■ suffix **1** forming adverbs such as *besides*. **2** forming possessive pronouns such as *hers*.
– ORIGIN Old English *-es*.

-s⁴ /s, z after a vowel sound or voiced consonant/ ■ suffix forming nicknames or pet names: *ducks*.
– ORIGIN suggested by **-s¹**.

-'s¹ /s, z after a vowel sound or voiced consonant, ɪz after a sibilant/ ■ suffix denoting possession in singular nouns, also in plural nouns not having a final *-s*: *John's book*.
– ORIGIN Old English, genitive sing. ending.

-'s² /s, z after a vowel sound or voiced consonant, ɪz after a sibilant/ ■ suffix denoting the plural of a letter or symbol: *9's*.

SA ■ abbrev. **1** Salvation Army. **2** South Africa.

sa ■ exclam. S. African used to incite a dog to attack.
– ORIGIN prob. from Dutch, 'at him, come on!'

SAA ■ abbrev. South African Airways.

SAAF ■ abbrev. South African Air Force.

Saanen /ˈsɑːnən/ ■ n. a dairy goat of a white hornless breed, first developed in the region of Saanen in Switzerland.

sabbatarian /ˌsabəˈtɛːrɪən/ ■ n. a strict observer of the sabbath. ■ adj. relating to or upholding the observance of the sabbath.
– DERIVATIVES **sabbatarianism** n.
– ORIGIN C17: from late Latin *sabbatarius*, from Latin *sabbatum* 'sabbath'.

sabbath ■ n. **1** (often **the Sabbath**) a day of religious observance and abstinence from work, kept by Jews from Friday evening to Saturday evening, and by most Christians on Sunday. **2** (also **witches' sabbath**) a supposed annual midnight meeting of witches with the Devil.
– ORIGIN Old English, from Latin *sabbatum*, from Hebrew *šabbāt*, from *šābat* 'to rest'.

sabbatical /səˈbatɪk(ə)l/ ■ n. a period of paid leave granted to a university teacher for study or travel (traditionally one year for every seven years worked). ■ adj. of or relating to a sabbatical.
– ORIGIN C16: from Greek *sabbatikos* 'of the sabbath'.

SABC ■ abbrev. South African Broadcasting Corporation.

saber ■ n. & v. US spelling of **SABRE**.

sabkha /ˈsabkə, -xə/ ■ n. Geography an area of coastal flats subject to periodic flooding and evaporation which result in the accumulation of aeolian clays, evaporites, and salts, typically found in North Africa and Arabia.
– ORIGIN C19: from Arabic *sabka* 'salt flat'.

sable¹ /ˈseɪb(ə)l/ ■ n. a marten with a short tail and dark brown fur, native to Japan and Siberia. [*Martes zibellina*.] ▸ the fur of the sable.
– ORIGIN Middle English: from Old French, in the sense 'sable fur', from medieval Latin *sabelum*, of Slavic origin.

sable² /ˈseɪb(ə)l/ ■ adj. poetic/literary or Heraldry black. ■ n. **1** poetic/literary or Heraldry black. ▸ (**sables**) archaic mourning garments. **2** (also **sable antelope**) a large African antelope with long curved horns, the male of which has a black coat and the female a russet coat. [*Hippotragus niger*.]
– ORIGIN Middle English: from Old French (as a heraldic term), generally taken to be identical with **SABLE¹**, although sable fur is dark brown.

sablefish ■ n. (pl. same or **-fishes**) a large commercially important fish with a slaty-blue to black back, occurring throughout the North Pacific. [*Anoplopoma fimbria*.]

sabot /ˈsabəʊ/ ■ n. **1** a kind of simple shoe, shaped and hollowed out from a single block of wood. **2** a device which ensures the correct positioning of a bullet or shell in the barrel of a gun.
– ORIGIN C17: French, blend of *savate* 'shoe' and *botte* 'boot'.

sabotage /ˈsabətɑːʒ/ ■ v. deliberately destroy or obstruct, especially for political or military advantage. ■ n. the action of sabotaging.
– ORIGIN C20: from French, from *saboter* 'kick with sabots, wilfully destroy'.

saboteur /ˌsabəˈtəː/ ■ n. a person who engages in sabotage.
– ORIGIN C20: from French.

sabra /ˈsabrə/ ■ n. a Jew born in Israel (or before 1948 in Palestine).
– ORIGIN from modern Hebrew *ṣabbār* 'opuntia fruit' (opuntias being common in coastal regions of Israel).

sabre /ˈseɪbə/ (US **saber**) ■ n. **1** a heavy cavalry sword with a curved blade and a single cutting edge. ▸ historical a cavalry soldier and horse. **2** a light fencing sword with a tapering, typically curved blade.
– ORIGIN C17: from French, alteration of obsolete *sable*, from German *Sabel*, from Hungarian *szablya*.

sabre-rattling ■ n. the display or threat of military force.

sabre saw ■ n. a portable electric jigsaw.

sabretache /ˈsabətaʃ/ ■ n. historical a flat satchel on long straps worn by some cavalry officers from the left of the waist belt.
– ORIGIN C19: from German *Säbeltasche*, from *Säbel* 'sabre' + *Tasche* 'pocket'.

sabretooth ■ n. a large extinct carnivore of the cat family with massive curved upper canine teeth. [*Smilodon* (Pleistocene) and other genera.]
– DERIVATIVES **sabre-toothed** adj.

sabreur /saˈbrəː/ ■ n. a cavalryman or fencer using a sabre.
– ORIGIN French, from *sabrer* 'strike with a sabre'.

SABS ■ abbrev. South African Bureau of Standards.

sac /sak/ ■ n. a hollow, flexible structure resembling a bag or pouch. ▸ a cavity enclosed by a membrane within a living organism. ▸ the distended membrane surrounding a hernia, cyst, or tumour.
– ORIGIN C18: from French *sac* or Latin *saccus* 'sack, bag'.

saccade /saˈkɑːd/ ■ n. (usu. **saccades**) a rapid movement of the eye between fixation points.
– DERIVATIVES **saccadic** /saˈkadɪk/ adj.
– ORIGIN C18: from French, 'violent pull'.

saccharide /ˈsakərʌɪd/ ■ n. Biochemistry another term for **SUGAR** (in sense 2).
– ORIGIN C19: from modern Latin *saccharum* 'sugar'.

saccharin

saccharin /ˈsakərɪn/ ■ n. a sweet-tasting synthetic compound used as a substitute for sugar.
– ORIGIN C19: from modern Latin *saccharum* 'sugar'.

saccharine /ˈsakərʌɪn, -ɪn, -iːn/ ■ adj. **1** excessively sweet or sentimental. **2** relating to or containing sugar. ■ n. another term for **SACCHARIN**.
– ORIGIN C17: from modern Latin *saccharum*.

SACCI ■ abbrev. South African Chamber of Commerce and Industry.

saccule /ˈsakjuːl/ (also **sacculus** /ˈsakjʊləs/) ■ n. Biology & Anatomy **1** a small sac, pouch, or cyst. **2** the smaller of the two fluid-filled sacs forming part of the labyrinth of the inner ear. Compare with **UTRICLE**.
– DERIVATIVES **saccular** adj. **sacculated** adj. **sacculation** n.
– ORIGIN C18: from Latin, diminutive of *saccus* 'sack'.

sacerdotal /ˌsasəˈdəʊt(ə)l, ˌsakə-/ ■ adj. **1** relating to priests or the priesthood. **2** Theology relating to or denoting a doctrine which ascribes sacrificial functions and spiritual or supernatural powers to ordained priests.
– ORIGIN Middle English: from Latin *sacerdotalis*, from *sacerdos* 'priest'.

Sachertorte /ˈzaxəˌtɔːtə/ ■ n. (pl. **Sachertorten** /-ˌtɔːt(ə)n/) a chocolate gateau with apricot jam filling.
– ORIGIN German, from the name of the pastry chef Franz Sacher + *Torte* 'tart, pastry'.

sachet /ˈsaʃeɪ/ ■ n. a small sealed bag or packet containing a small quantity of something.
– ORIGIN C19: from French, 'little bag', diminutive of *sac*, from Latin *saccus* 'sack, bag'.

sack¹ ■ n. **1** a large bag made of a material such as hessian or thick paper, used for storing and carrying goods. **2** (**the sack**) informal dismissal from employment. **3** (**the sack**) informal bed. **4** Baseball, informal a base. **5** American Football a tackle of a quarterback behind the line of scrimmage. ■ v. **1** informal dismiss from employment. **2** (**sack out**) informal, chiefly N. Amer. go to sleep or bed. **3** American Football tackle with a sack. **4** put into a sack or sacks.
– PHRASES **hit the sack** informal go to bed.
– DERIVATIVES **sackable** adj. **sackful** n. (pl. **-fuls**).
– ORIGIN Old English *sacc*, from Latin *saccus* 'sack, sackcloth', from Greek *sakkos*, of Semitic origin.

sack² ■ v. plunder and destroy (used chiefly in historical contexts). ■ n. an instance of sacking.
– ORIGIN C16: from French *sac*, in the phr. *mettre à sac* 'put to sack', on the model of Italian *fare il sacco*, *mettere a sacco*, which perhaps orig. referred to filling a sack with plunder.

sack³ ■ n. historical a dry white wine formerly imported into Britain from Spain and the Canaries.
– ORIGIN C16: from the phr. *wyne seck*, from French *vin sec* 'dry wine'.

sackbut /ˈsakbʌt/ ■ n. an early form of trombone used in Renaissance music.
– ORIGIN C15: from French *saquebute*, from obsolete *saqueboute* 'hook for pulling a man off a horse'.

sackcloth ■ n. a coarse fabric woven from flax or hemp.
– PHRASES **sackcloth and ashes** used with allusion to the wearing of sackcloth and having ashes sprinkled on the head as a sign of penitence or mourning.

sacking ■ n. **1** an act of sacking someone or something. **2** coarse material for making sacks; sackcloth.

sack race ■ n. a children's race in which each competitor is confined within a sack and moves forward by jumping.

sack suit ■ n. chiefly N. Amer. a suit with a straight loose-fitting jacket.

SACOB /ˈsakɒb/ (also **Sacob**) ■ abbrev. South African Chamber of Business.

SACP ■ abbrev. South African Communist Party.

sacra plural form of **SACRUM**.

sacral /ˈseɪkr(ə)l, ˈsak-/ ■ adj. **1** Anatomy of or relating to the sacrum. **2** of, for, or relating to sacred rites or symbols.
– DERIVATIVES **sacrality** n.

sacralize /ˈseɪkrəlʌɪz/ (also **-ise**) ■ v. imbue with or treat as having a sacred character or quality.
– DERIVATIVES **sacralization** (also **-isation**) n.

sacrament /ˈsakrəm(ə)nt/ ■ n. **1** (in the Christian Church) a religious ceremony or ritual regarded as imparting divine grace, such as baptism, the Eucharist, and (in the Catholic and many Orthodox Churches) penance and the anointing of the sick. **2** (also **the Blessed Sacrament** or **the Holy Sacrament**) (in Catholic use) the consecrated elements of the Eucharist, especially the bread or Host. **3** a thing of mysterious or sacred significance; a religious symbol.
– ORIGIN Middle English: from Old French *sacrement*, from Latin *sacramentum* 'solemn oath', used in Christian Latin as a translation of Greek *mustērion* 'mystery'.

sacramental ■ adj. relating to or constituting a sacrament or the sacraments. ■ n. an observance analogous to but not reckoned among the sacraments, such as the use of holy water or the sign of the cross.
– DERIVATIVES **sacramentalism** n. **sacramentally** adv.

sacred /ˈseɪkrɪd/ ■ adj. **1** connected with a deity and so deserving veneration; holy. ▸ (of writing or text) embodying the doctrines of a religion. ▸ sacrosanct. **2** religious rather than secular.
– DERIVATIVES **sacredly** adv. **sacredness** n.
– ORIGIN Middle English: from archaic *sacre* 'consecrate', from Old French *sacrer*, from Latin *sacrare*, from *sacer* 'holy'.

sacred cow ■ n. an idea, custom, or institution held, especially unreasonably, to be above criticism (with reference to the respect of Hindus for the cow as a sacred animal).

sacred ibis ■ n. a mainly white ibis with a bare black head and neck, native to Africa and the Middle East and venerated by the ancient Egyptians. [*Threskiornis aethiopicus*.]

sacrifice ■ n. **1** the practice or an act of killing an animal or person or surrendering a possession as an offering to a deity. ▸ an animal, person, or object offered in this way. **2** an act of giving up something of value for the sake of something that is of greater value or importance. **3** (also **sacrifice bunt** or **sacrifice fly**) Baseball a bunted or fly ball which puts the batter out but allows a base-runner to advance. ■ v. offer or give up as a sacrifice.
– DERIVATIVES **sacrificial** adj. **sacrificially** adv.
– ORIGIN Middle English: from Latin *sacrificium*; rel. to *sacrificus* 'sacrificial', from *sacer* 'holy'.

sacrilege /ˈsakrɪlɪdʒ/ ■ n. violation or misuse of something regarded as sacred or as having great value.
– DERIVATIVES **sacrilegious** adj. **sacrilegiously** adv.
– ORIGIN Middle English: from Latin *sacrilegium*, from *sacrilegus* 'stealer of sacred things', from *sacer* 'sacred' + *legere* 'take possession of'.

sacrist /ˈsakrɪst, ˈseɪ-/ ■ n. another term for **SACRISTAN**.

sacristan /ˈsakrɪstən/ ■ n. **1** a person in charge of a sacristy. **2** archaic the sexton of a parish church.
– ORIGIN Middle English: from medieval Latin *sacristanus*, from Latin *sacer* 'sacred'.

sacristy /ˈsakrɪsti/ ■ n. (pl. **-ies**) a room in a church where a priest prepares for a service, and where vestments and other things used in worship are kept.
– ORIGIN Middle English: from French *sacristie*, from medieval Latin *sacristia*, from Latin *sacer* 'sacred'.

sacro- /ˈseɪkrəʊ, ˈsakrəʊ-/ ■ comb. form of or relating to the sacrum: *sacroiliac*.
– ORIGIN from Latin (*os*) *sacrum* 'sacrum'.

sacroiliac /ˌseɪkrəʊˈɪlɪak, ˌsak-/ ■ adj. Anatomy relating to the sacrum and the ilium. ▸ denoting the rigid joint at the back of the pelvis between the sacrum and the ilium.

sacrosanct /ˈsakrə(ʊ)saŋ(k)t, ˈseɪk-/ ■ adj. regarded as too important or valuable to be interfered with.
– DERIVATIVES **sacrosanctity** n.
– ORIGIN C15: from Latin *sacrosanctus*, from *sacro* 'by a sacred rite' + *sanctus* 'holy'.

sacrum /ˈseɪkrəm, ˈsak-/ ■ n. (pl. **sacra** /-krə/ or **sacrums**) Anatomy a triangular bone in the lower back formed from fused vertebrae and situated between the two hip bones of the pelvis.
– ORIGIN C18: from Latin *os sacrum*, translation of Greek *hieron osteon* 'sacred bone' (from the belief that the soul resides in it).

SAD ■ abbrev. seasonal affective disorder.

sad ■ adj. (**sadder**, **saddest**) **1** feeling sorrow; unhappy. ▸ causing or characterized by sorrow or regret. **2** informal pathetically inadequate or unfashionable.
– DERIVATIVES **sadness** n.
– ORIGIN Old English *sæd* 'sated, weary', also 'weighty, dense', of Germanic origin.

SADC ■ abbrev. Southern African Development Community.

sadden ■ v. (often **be saddened**) cause to feel sad.

saddle ■ n. **1** a seat with a raised ridge at the front and back, fastened on the back of a horse for riding. **2** a seat on a bicycle or motorcycle. **3** a low part of a ridge between two higher points or peaks. **4** a shaped support for a cable, pipe, or other object. **5** the lower part of the back in a mammal or fowl, especially when distinct in shape or marking. **6** a joint of meat consisting of the two loins. ■ v. **1** put a saddle on (a horse). **2** (usu. **be saddled with**) burden with an onerous responsibility or task. **3** (of a trainer) enter (a horse) for a race.
– PHRASES **in the saddle 1** on horseback. **2** in a position of control or responsibility.
– ORIGIN Old English, of Germanic origin.

saddleback ■ n. **1** Architecture a tower roof which has two opposite gables connected by a pitched section. **2** a hill with a ridge along the top that dips in the middle. **3** a pig of a black breed with a white stripe across the back.
– DERIVATIVES **saddlebacked** adj.

saddlebag ■ n. a bag attached to a saddle.

saddle-bow ■ n. chiefly archaic the pommel of a saddle, or a similar curved part behind the rider.

saddlecloth ■ n. a cloth laid on a horse's back under the saddle.

saddle horse ■ n. **1** a wooden frame or stand on which saddles are cleaned or stored. **2** chiefly N. Amer. a horse kept for riding only.

saddler ■ n. someone who makes, repairs, or deals in saddlery.

saddlery ■ n. (pl. **-ies**) saddles, bridles, and other equipment for horses. ▸ the making or repairing of such equipment. ▸ a saddler's business or premises.

saddle soap ■ n. soft soap used for cleaning leather.

saddle-sore ■ n. a bruise or sore on a horse's back, caused by an ill-fitting saddle. ■ adj. chafed by a saddle.

saddle stitch ■ n. a stitch of thread or a wire staple passed through the fold of a magazine or booklet. ■ v. (**saddle-stitch**) sew with such a stitch.

saddle tank ■ n. a small steam locomotive with a water tank that fits over the top and sides of the boiler like a saddle.

Sadducee /ˈsadjʊsiː/ ■ n. a member of an ancient Jewish sect that denied the resurrection of the dead, the existence of spirits, and the obligation of oral tradition, emphasizing acceptance of the written Law alone.
– DERIVATIVES **Sadducean** /-ˈsiːən/ adj.
– ORIGIN Old English *sadducēas* (pl.), from Greek *Saddoukaios*, from Hebrew *ṣĕḏōqī* in the sense 'descendant of Zadok' (2 Samuel 8:17).

SADF ■ abbrev. historical South African Defence Force.

sadhu /ˈsɑːduː/ ■ n. Indian a holy man, sage, or ascetic.
– ORIGIN from Sanskrit.

sadism ■ n. the tendency to derive sexual gratification or general pleasure from inflicting pain, suffering, or humiliation on others.
– DERIVATIVES **sadist** n. **sadistic** adj. **sadistically** adv.
– ORIGIN C19: from French *sadisme*, from the name of the C18 French writer the Marquis de *Sade*.

sadly ■ adv. **1** in a sad manner. **2** it is sad or regrettable that; regrettably.

sadomasochism /ˌseɪdəʊˈmasəkɪz(ə)m/ ■ n. the psychological tendency or sexual practice characterized by a combination of sadism and masochism.
– DERIVATIVES **sadomasochist** n. **sadomasochistic** adj.

sad sack ■ n. informal, chiefly US an inept blundering person.

sadza ■ n. (especially in Zimbabwe) stiff porridge made of ground maize or millet.
– ORIGIN from Shona.

sae ■ abbrev. stamped addressed envelope.

SAFA /ˈsɑːfə/ (also **Safa**) ■ abbrev. South African Football Association.

safari ■ n. (pl. **safaris**) an expedition to observe or hunt animals in their natural habitat.
– ORIGIN C19: from Kiswahili, from Arabic *safara* 'to travel'.

safari jacket ■ n. a belted lightweight jacket, typically having short sleeves and four patch pockets.

safari park ■ n. an area of parkland where wild animals are kept in the open and may be observed by visitors driving through.

safari suit ■ n. a lightweight suit consisting of a safari jacket with matching trousers, shorts, or skirt.

safe ■ adj. **1** protected from or not exposed to danger or risk; not likely to be harmed or lost. ▸ not causing or leading to harm or injury. ▸ (of a place) affording security or protection. **2** often derogatory cautious and unenterprising. **3** (of an assertion, verdict, etc.) based on good reasons or evidence and not likely to be proved wrong. **4** uninjured; with no harm done. **5** informal excellent. ■ n. **1** a strong fireproof cabinet with a complex lock, used for the storage of valuables. **2** N. Amer. informal a condom.
– PHRASES **to be on the safe side** in order to have a margin of security against risks.
– DERIVATIVES **safely** adv. **safeness** n.
– ORIGIN Middle English: from Old French *sauf*, from Latin *salvus* 'uninjured'.

safe bet ■ n. **1** a bet that is certain to succeed. **2** something that can be confidently predicted.

safe-breaker (also **safe-blower** or **safe-cracker**) ■ n. a person who breaks open and robs safes.

safe conduct ■ n. immunity from arrest or harm when passing through an area.

safe deposit (also **safety deposit**) ■ n. a strongroom or safe within a bank or hotel.

safeguard ■ n. a measure taken to protect or prevent something. ■ v. protect with a safeguard.
– ORIGIN Middle English: from Old French *sauve garde*, from *sauve* 'safe' + *garde* 'guard'.

safe house ■ n. **1** a house in a secret location, used by spies or criminals in hiding. ▸ a house in a secret location used by law enforcement agencies to protect key witnesses in criminal investigations. **2** a house used as a refuge for women and children under threat from domestic violence.

safe keeping ■ n. preservation in a safe place.

safelight ■ n. a light with a coloured filter that can be used in a darkroom without affecting photosensitive film or paper.

safe period ■ n. the time during and near a woman's menstrual period when conception is least likely.

safe seat ■ n. a parliamentary seat that is likely to be retained with a large majority in an election.

safe sex ■ n. sexual activity in which people take precautions to protect themselves against sexually transmitted diseases such as Aids.

safety ■ n. (pl. **-ies**) **1** the condition of being safe. ▸ [as modifier] denoting something designed to prevent injury or damage: *a safety barrier*. **2** American Football a defensive back who plays in a deep position. **3** American Football a play in which the ball is downed by the offence in their own end zone, scoring two points to the defence.

safety belt ■ n. a belt or strap securing a person to their seat in a vehicle or aircraft.

safety cage ■ n. a framework of reinforced struts protecting a car's passenger cabin against crash damage.

safety catch ■ n. a device that prevents a gun being fired or a machine being operated accidentally.

safety curtain ■ n. a fireproof curtain that can be lowered between the stage and the main part of a theatre to prevent the spread of fire.

safety deposit ■ n. another term for **SAFE DEPOSIT**.

safety factor ■ n. **1** a margin of security against risks. **2** the ratio of a material's strength to an expected strain.

safety fuse

safety fuse ■ n. **1** a protective electric fuse. **2** a fuse that burns at a constant slow rate, used for the controlled firing of a detonator.

safety glass ■ n. glass that has been toughened or laminated so that it is less likely to splinter when broken.

safety lamp ■ n. historical a miner's portable lamp with a flame protected by wire gauze to reduce the risk of explosion from ignited methane (firedamp).

safety match ■ n. a match that ignites only when struck on a specially prepared surface, especially the side of a matchbox.

safety net ■ n. **1** a net placed to catch an acrobat in case of a fall. **2** a safeguard against adversity.

safety pin ■ n. a pin with a point that is bent back to the head and is held in a guard when closed.

safety razor ■ n. a razor with a guard to reduce the risk of cutting the skin.

safety valve ■ n. **1** a valve that opens automatically to relieve excessive pressure. **2** a means of giving harmless vent to feelings of tension or stress.

Saffer (also **Saffie**) informal ■ n. a South African, especially an expatriate. ■ adj. South African.

safflower ■ n. an orange-flowered thistle-like plant with seeds that yield an edible oil and petals that were formerly used to produce a red or yellow dye. [*Carthamus tinctorius*.]
– ORIGIN Middle English: from Dutch *saffloer* or German *Saflor*, from Arabic *aṣfar* 'yellow'.

saffron ■ n. **1** an orange-yellow spice used for flavouring and colouring food, made from the dried stigmas of a crocus. **2** (also **saffron crocus**) an autumn-flowering crocus with reddish-purple flowers that yields this spice. [*Crocus sativus*.]
– ORIGIN Middle English: from Old French *safran*, from Arabic *zaʿfarān*.

sag ■ v. (**sagged**, **sagging**) sink, subside, or bulge downwards gradually under weight or pressure or through lack of strength. ▸ hang down loosely or unevenly. ■ n. an instance of sagging.
– DERIVATIVES **saggy** adj.
– ORIGIN Middle English: prob. rel. to Middle Low German *sacken*, Dutch *zakken* 'subside'.

saga /ˈsɑːɡə/ ■ n. **1** a long story of heroic achievement, especially a medieval prose narrative in Old Norse or Old Icelandic. **2** a long, involved account or series of incidents.
– ORIGIN C18: from Old Norse, 'narrative'.

sagacious /səˈɡeɪʃəs/ ■ adj. having or showing good judgement.
– DERIVATIVES **sagaciously** adv. **sagacity** n.
– ORIGIN C17 (*sagacity* C15): from Latin *sagax, sagac-* 'wise'.

sage[1] ■ n. an aromatic plant with greyish-green leaves used as a culinary herb, native to southern Europe and the Mediterranean. [*Salvia officinalis*.] ▸ used in names of similar aromatic plants, e.g. wood sage.
– ORIGIN Middle English: from Old French *sauge*, from Latin *salvia* 'healing plant', from *salvus* 'safe'.

sage[2] ■ n. (especially in ancient history or legend) a man recognized for his wisdom. ■ adj. wise; judicious.
– DERIVATIVES **sagely** adv. **sageness** n.
– ORIGIN Middle English: from Latin *sapere* 'be wise'.

sagebrush ■ n. a shrubby aromatic North American plant of the daisy family. [*Artemisia tridentata* and related species.] ▸ semi-arid country dominated by this plant.

sage green ■ n. a greyish-green colour like that of sage leaves.

sage grouse ■ n. a large grouse of western North America with long pointed tail feathers, noted for the male's courtship display in which air sacs are inflated to make a popping sound. [*Centrocercus urophasianus*.]

sagewood ■ n. a shrub or small tree of southern Africa, with clusters of lilac flowers and hairy leaves resembling sage. [*Buddleja salviifolia*.]

sagittal /ˈsadʒɪt(ə)l, səˈdʒɪt-/ ■ adj. Anatomy **1** relating to or denoting the suture on top of the skull which runs between the parietal bones in a front to back direction. **2** of or in a plane parallel to this suture, especially that dividing the body into left and right halves.
– ORIGIN Middle English: from medieval Latin *sagittalis*, from Latin *sagitta* 'arrow'.

sagittal crest ■ n. Zoology (in many mammals) a bony ridge on the top of the skull to which the jaw muscles are attached.

Sagittarius /ˌsadʒɪˈtɛːrɪəs/ ■ n. **1** Astronomy a large constellation (the Archer), said to represent a centaur carrying a bow and arrow. **2** Astrology the ninth sign of the zodiac, which the sun enters about 22 November.
– DERIVATIVES **Sagittarian** n. & adj.
– ORIGIN from Latin.

sagittate /ˈsadʒɪteɪt/ ■ adj. Botany shaped like an arrowhead.
– ORIGIN C18: from Latin *sagitta* 'arrow'.

sago /ˈseɪɡəʊ/ ■ n. (pl. **-os**) **1** edible starch obtained from a palm, dried to produce a flour or processed into a granular form. **2** a sweet dish made from sago and milk. **3** (**sago palm**) the palm from which most sago is obtained, growing in freshwater swamps in SE Asia. [*Metroxylon sagu*.] ▸ any of a number of other palms or cycads which yield a similar starch.
– ORIGIN C16: from Malay *sagu*.

saguaro /səˈɡwɑːrəʊ, -ˈwɑː-/ (also **saguaro cactus**) ■ n. (pl. **-os**) a giant cactus whose branches are shaped like candelabra, native to the SW United States and Mexico. [*Carnegiea gigantea*.]
– ORIGIN C19: from Mexican Spanish.

Saharan /səˈhɑːrən/ ■ adj. of or relating to the Sahara Desert.

Sahelian /səˈhiːlɪən/ ■ adj. of or relating to the Sahel, a semi-arid region of North Africa.

sahib /ˈsɑː(h)ɪb, sɑːb/ ■ n. Indian a polite title or form of address for a man.
– ORIGIN Urdu, from Arabic *ṣāḥib* 'friend, lord'.

said past and past participle of SAY. ■ adj. denoting someone or something already mentioned or named: *the said agreement*.

sail ■ n. **1** a piece of material extended on a mast to catch the wind and propel a boat or ship. ▸ a wind-catching apparatus attached to the arm of a windmill. ▸ S. African a canvas sheet or tarpaulin. ▸ a structure by which an animal is propelled across the surface of water by the wind, e.g. the float of a Portuguese man-of-war. **2** a voyage or excursion in a sailing boat or ship. ■ v. **1** travel in a sailing boat as a sport or for recreation. ▸ travel in a ship or boat using sails or engine power. ▸ begin a voyage; leave a harbour. ▸ travel by ship on or across (a sea) or on (a route). ▸ navigate or control (a boat or ship). **2** move smoothly and rapidly or in a stately or confident manner. ▸ (**sail through**) informal succeed easily at (something, especially a test or examination). ▸ (**sail into**) informal attack physically or verbally with force.
– PHRASES **in** (or **under**) **full sail** with all the sails in position or fully spread. **sail close to** (or **near**) **the wind 1** sail as nearly against the wind as possible. **2** behave or operate in a risky way. **under sail** with the sails hoisted.
– DERIVATIVES **sailed** adj. **sailing** n.
– ORIGIN Old English, of Germanic origin.

sailboard ■ n. a board with a mast and a sail, used in windsurfing.
– DERIVATIVES **sailboarder** n. **sailboarding** n.

sailboat ■ n. North American term for SAILING BOAT.

sailcloth ■ n. a canvas or other strong fabric used for making sails. ▸ a similar fabric used for making durable clothes.

sailer ■ n. a sailing boat or ship of specified power or manner of sailing.

sailfish ■ n. (pl. same or **-fishes**) an edible migratory billfish with a high sail-like dorsal fin. [*Istiophorus platypterus* and related species.]

sailing boat ■ n. a boat propelled by sails.

sailing ship ■ n. a ship propelled by sails.

sailor ■ n. a person who works as a member of the crew of a commercial or naval ship or boat, especially one who is below the rank of officer. ▸ a person who sails as a sport or recreation. ▸ (**a good/bad sailor**) a person who rarely (or often) becomes sick at sea in rough weather.

– DERIVATIVES **sailorly** adj.
– ORIGIN C17: var. of obsolete *sailer*.

sailor collar ■ n. a collar cut deep and square at the back, tapering to a V-neck at the front.

sailor hat ■ n. another term for BOATER (in sense 1).

sailor suit ■ n. a suit of blue and white material resembling the dress uniform of an ordinary seaman, especially as fashionable dress for young boys during the 19th century.

sailplane ■ n. a glider designed for sustained flight.

sainfoin /'seɪnfɔɪn, 'san-/ ■ n. a pink-flowered leguminous plant native to Asia, grown widely for fodder. [*Onobrychis viciifolia*.]
– ORIGIN C17: from obsolete French *saintfoin*, from modern Latin *sanum foenum* 'wholesome hay' (with ref. to its medicinal properties).

saint /seɪnt, before a name usually s(ə)nt/ ■ n. **1** a person who is acknowledged as holy or virtuous and regarded in Christian faith as being in heaven after death. ▶ a person of exalted virtue who is canonized by the Church after death and who may be the object of veneration and prayers for intercession. ▶ informal a very virtuous person. **2** (**Saint**) a member of the Church of Jesus Christ of Latter-Day Saints; a Mormon. ■ v. **1** formally recognize as a saint; canonize. **2** [as adj. **sainted**] worthy of being a saint; very virtuous: *his sainted sister*.
– DERIVATIVES **saintdom** n. **sainthood** n. **saintliness** n. **saintly** adj. **saintship** n.
– ORIGIN Middle English, from Old French *seint*, from Latin *sanctus* 'holy', from *sancire* 'consecrate'.

saintpaulia /s(ə)nt'pɔːlɪə/ ■ n. an African violet. [Genus *Saintpaulia*.]
– ORIGIN from the name of the German explorer Baron W. von *Saint Paul* (1860–1910).

saint's day ■ n. (in the Christian Church) a day on which a saint is particularly commemorated.

saith /sɛθ/ archaic third person singular present of SAY.

saithe /seɪθ/ ■ n. a North Atlantic food fish of the cod family. [*Pollachius virens*.]
– ORIGIN C16: from Old Norse *seithr*.

sake[1] /seɪk/ ■ n. **1** (**for the sake of something**) for the purpose of or in the interest of something; in order to achieve or preserve something. ▶ (**for its own sake**) or **something for something's sake** or **for the sake of it** indicating something that is done as an end in itself rather than to achieve some other purpose. ▶ (**for old times' sake**) in memory of former times; in acknowledgement of a shared past. **2** (**for the sake of someone**) out of consideration for or in order to help someone. **3** (**for God's**) or **goodness etc. sake** expressing impatience, annoyance, urgency, or desperation.
– ORIGIN Old English *sacu* 'contention, crime', of Germanic origin, from a base meaning 'affair, legal action'.

sake[2] /'sɑːki, 'sakeɪ/ ■ n. a Japanese alcoholic drink made from fermented rice.
– ORIGIN from Japanese.

saker /'seɪkə/ ■ n. a large falcon with a brown back and whitish head, used in falconry. [*Falco cherrug*.]
– ORIGIN Middle English: from Old French *sacre*, from Arabic *ṣaḳr* 'falcon'.

saki /'sɑːki/ ■ n. (pl. **sakis**) a tropical American monkey with coarse fur and a long bushy non-prehensile tail. [Genera *Pithecia* and *Chiropotes*: several species.]
– ORIGIN C18: from Tupi *saui*.

sakkie-sakkie /'sakɪsakɪ/ ■ n. S. African a style of boeremusiek. ▶ a lively dance performed to this music.
– ORIGIN Afrikaans, prob. echoic.

Sakti ■ n. variant spelling of SHAKTI.

salaam /sə'lɑːm/ ■ n. a gesture of greeting or respect in Arabic-speaking and Muslim countries, consisting of a low bow of the head and body with the hand or fingers touching the forehead. ■ v. make a salaam.
– ORIGIN C17: from Arabic (*al-*)*salām* ('*alaikum*) 'peace (be upon you)'.

salable ■ adj. variant spelling of SALEABLE.

salacious /sə'leɪʃəs/ ■ adj. having or conveying undue or indecent interest in sexual matters.
– DERIVATIVES **salaciously** adv. **salaciousness** n.
– ORIGIN C17: from Latin *salax, salac-*, from *salire* 'to leap'.

1041 **salesman**

salad ■ n. a dish consisting of a mixture of raw vegetables or other cold ingredients, typically served with a dressing.
– ORIGIN Middle English: from Old French *salade*, from Latin *sal* 'salt'.

salad cream ■ n. a creamy salad dressing resembling mayonnaise.

salad days ■ pl. n. (**one's salad days**) **1** the period when one is young and inexperienced. **2** the peak or heyday of something.
– ORIGIN from Shakespeare's *Antony and Cleopatra* (I. v. 72).

salamander /'salə,mandə/ ■ n. **1** a long-tailed amphibian resembling a newt and typically with bright markings. [Order Urodela: many species.] **2** a mythical lizard-like creature said to live in fire or to be able to withstand its effects. **3** a metal plate heated and placed over food to brown it.
– DERIVATIVES **salamandrine** /-'mandrɪn/ adj.
– ORIGIN Middle English: from Old French *salamandre*, from Greek *salamandra*.

salami /sə'lɑːmi/ ■ n. (pl. same or **salamis**) a type of highly seasoned preserved sausage, originally from Italy.
– ORIGIN Italian, pl. of *salame*, from a late Latin word meaning 'to salt'.

sal ammoniac /ˌsal ə'məʊnɪak/ ■ n. dated ammonium chloride, a white crystalline salt.
– ORIGIN Middle English: from Latin *sal ammoniacus* 'salt of Ammon', from Greek *ammōniakos* 'of Ammon', used as a name for the salt and gum obtained near the temple of Jupiter *Ammon* at Siwa in Egypt.

salariat /sə'lɛːrɪat/ ■ n. (**the salariat**) salaried white-collar workers.
– ORIGIN C20: from French, from *salaire* 'salary'.

salary ■ n. (pl. **-ies**) a fixed regular payment made usually on a monthly basis by an employer to an employee, especially a professional or white-collar worker. ■ v. (**-ies, -ied**) pay a salary to.
– DERIVATIVES **salaried** adj.
– ORIGIN Middle English: from Anglo-Norman French *salarie*, from Latin *salarium*, orig. denoting a Roman soldier's allowance to buy salt, from *sal* 'salt'.

salaryman ■ n. (pl. **-men**) (in Japan) a white-collar worker.

salat /sa'lɑːt/ ■ n. the ritual prayer of Muslims, performed five times daily in a set form.
– ORIGIN Arabic, pl. of *salāh* 'prayer, worship'.

salbutamol /sal'bjuːtəmɒl/ ■ n. Medicine a synthetic compound related to aspirin, used as a bronchodilator in the treatment of asthma and other conditions involving constriction of the airways.
– ORIGIN 1960s: from *sal*(*icylic acid*) + *but*(*yl*) + *am*(*ine*).

salchow /'salkəʊ/ ■ n. a jump in figure skating from the backward inside edge of one skate to the backward outside edge of the other, with one or more full turns in the air.
– ORIGIN 1920s: named after the Swedish skater Ulrich *Salchow*.

sale ■ n. **1** the exchange of a commodity for money; the process of selling something. ▶ (**sales**) a quantity or amount sold. **2** (**sales**) the activity or profession of selling. **3** a period in which goods are disposed of at reduced prices. **4** a public or charitable event at which goods are sold. ▶ a public auction.
– PHRASES **for** (or **on**) **sale** offered for purchase. **sale or return** an arrangement by which a purchaser takes a quantity of goods with the right to return any surplus without payment.
– ORIGIN Old English *sala*, from Old Norse *sala*, of Germanic origin.

saleable (also **salable**) ■ adj. fit or able to be sold.
– DERIVATIVES **saleability** (also **salability**) n.

saleroom (also **salesroom**) ■ n. chiefly Brit. a room in which auctions are held.

sales clerk ■ n. a shop assistant.

Salesian /sə'liːzɪən, -ʒ(ə)n/ ■ adj. of or relating to a Roman Catholic educational religious order named after St Francis de Sales. ■ n. a member of this order.

salesman (or **saleswoman**) ■ n. (pl. **-men** or **-women**) a

salesperson

person whose job involves selling or promoting commercial products.
– DERIVATIVES **salesmanship** n.

salesperson ■ n. (pl. **-persons** or **-people**) a salesman or saleswoman.

Salian /ˈseɪlɪən/ ■ adj. of or relating to the Salii, a 4th-century Frankish people. ■ n. a member of this people.

Salic /ˈsalɪk, ˈseɪ-/ ■ adj. another term for SALIAN.

Salic law ■ n. historical a law excluding females from dynastic succession, especially as the alleged fundamental law of the French monarchy.

salicylic acid /ˌsalɪˈsɪlɪk/ ■ n. Chemistry a bitter compound present in certain plants, used as a fungicide and in the manufacture of aspirin and dyestuffs.
– DERIVATIVES **salicylate** /səˈlɪsɪleɪt/ n.
– ORIGIN C19: from French *salicyle*, the radical of the acid, from Latin *salix, salic-* 'willow'.

salient /ˈseɪlɪənt/ ■ adj. 1 most noticeable or important. 2 (of an angle) pointing outwards. The opposite of RE-ENTRANT. 3 [postpos.] Heraldry (of an animal) standing on its hind legs with the front legs and paws raised, as if leaping. ■ n. 1 a piece of land or section of fortification that juts out to form an angle. 2 an outward bulge in a military line.
– DERIVATIVES **salience** n. **saliency** n. **saliently** adv.
– ORIGIN C16: from Latin *salient-, salire* 'to leap'.

Salientia /ˌseɪlɪˈɛnʃɪə, -ˈɛnt-/ ■ pl. n. Zoology another term for ANURA.
– DERIVATIVES **salientian** n. & adj.
– ORIGIN from Latin *salire* 'to leap'.

saline /ˈseɪlʌɪn/ ■ adj. 1 containing or impregnated with salt. 2 chiefly Medicine (of a solution) containing sodium chloride and/or a salt or salts of magnesium or another alkali metal. ■ n. a saline solution.
– DERIVATIVES **salinity** n. **salinization** (also **-isation**) n.
– ORIGIN C15: from Latin *sal* 'salt'.

salinometer /ˌsalɪˈnɒmɪtə/ ■ n. an instrument for measuring the salinity of water.

Salish /ˈseɪlɪʃ/ ■ n. (pl. same) 1 a member of a group of American Indian peoples inhabiting areas of the north-western US and the west coast of Canada. 2 the group of related languages spoken by the Salish.
– ORIGIN a local name, literally 'Flatheads'.

saliva /səˈlʌɪvə/ ■ n. a watery liquid secreted into the mouth by glands, providing lubrication for chewing and swallowing, and aiding digestion.
– DERIVATIVES **salivary** /səˈlʌɪ-, ˈsalɪ-/ adj.
– ORIGIN Middle English: from Latin.

salivate /ˈsalɪveɪt/ ■ v. 1 secrete saliva, especially in anticipation of food. ▸ cause to produce a copious secretion of saliva. 2 display great relish at the sight or prospect of something.
– DERIVATIVES **salivation** n.
– ORIGIN C17: from Latin *salivare* 'produce saliva', from *saliva* (see SALIVA).

sallow[1] ■ adj. (**-er**, **-est**) (of a person's face or complexion) of a yellowish or pale brown colour.
– DERIVATIVES **sallowness** n.
– ORIGIN Old English *salo* 'dusky', of Germanic origin.

sallow[2] ■ n. chiefly Brit. a willow tree of a typically low-growing or shrubby kind. [*Salix cinerea* and related species.]
– ORIGIN Old English, of Germanic origin; rel. to Latin *salix* 'willow'.

sally[1] ■ n. (pl. **-ies**) 1 a sortie. 2 a witty or lively retort. ■ v. (**-ies**, **-ied**) make a sortie; set forth.
– ORIGIN Middle English: from French *saillie*, from *saillir* 'come or jut out', from Old French *salir* 'to leap', from Latin *salire*.

sally[2] ■ n. (pl. **-ies**) the part of a bell rope that has coloured wool woven into it to provide a grip for the bell-ringer's hands.
– ORIGIN C17: perhaps from SALLY[1] in the sense 'leaping motion'.

sally port ■ n. a small exit point in a fortification for the passage of troops when making a sortie.

salmanazar /ˌsalməˈneɪzə/ ■ n. a wine bottle of approximately twelve times the standard size.
– ORIGIN 1930s: named after *Shalmaneser*, an ancient king of Assyria.

salmon /ˈsamən/ ■ n. (pl. same or (especially of types) **salmons**) 1 a large edible fish that matures in the sea and migrates to freshwater streams to spawn. [*Salmo salar* (Atlantic) and genus *Oncorhynchus* (Pacific).] ▸ any of various unrelated marine fish resembling this, e.g. Cape salmon. ▸ the flesh of such a fish as food. 2 a pale pink colour like that of the flesh of a salmon.
– DERIVATIVES **salmony** adj.
– ORIGIN Middle English, from Anglo-Norman French *saumoun*, from Latin *salmo*.

salmonella /ˌsalməˈnɛlə/ ■ n. (pl. **salmonellae** /-liː/) a bacterium that occurs mainly in the gut and can cause food poisoning. [Genus *Salmonella*.] ▸ food poisoning caused by this.
– DERIVATIVES **salmonellosis** /-ˈləʊsɪs/ n.
– ORIGIN named after the American veterinary surgeon Daniel E. *Salmon*.

salmonid /ˈsalmənɪd, salˈmɒnɪd/ ■ n. Zoology a fish of a family (Salmonidae) including salmon, trout, charr, and whitefish.

salmon ladder (also **salmon leap**) ■ n. a series of natural steps in a cascade or steeply sloping river bed, or a similar arrangement incorporated into a dam, allowing salmon to pass upstream.

salmon trout ■ n. a large trout or trout-like fish, especially a sea trout.

salomie /səˈluəmi/ (also **salomi**) ■ n. S. African a roti rolled around a curry filling.

salon ■ n. 1 an establishment where a hairdresser, beautician, or couturier conducts their trade. 2 a reception room in a large house. 3 chiefly historical a regular gathering of writers, artists, etc., held in a fashionable household. 4 (**Salon**) an annual exhibition of the work of living artists held by the Royal Academy of Painting and Sculpture in Paris (originally in the Salon d'Apollon in the Louvre).
– ORIGIN C17: from French (see SALOON).

saloon ■ n. 1 a public room or building used for a specified purpose. ▸ (also **saloon bar**) another term for LOUNGE BAR. ▸ a large public room for use as a lounge on a ship. 2 N. Amer. historical or humorous a place where alcoholic drinks may be bought and drunk. 3 (also **saloon car**) a car having a closed body and separate boot. 4 (also **saloon car**) a luxurious railway carriage used as a lounge or restaurant or as private accommodation.
– ORIGIN C18: from French *salon*, from Italian *salone* 'large hall', from *sala* 'hall'.

saloon deck ■ n. a deck on the same level as a ship's saloon, for the use of passengers.

salpiglossis /ˌsalpɪˈglɒsɪs/ ■ n. a South American plant of the nightshade family, with brightly patterned funnel-shaped flowers. [Genus *Salpiglossis*.]
– ORIGIN from Greek *salpinx* 'trumpet' + *glōssa* 'tongue'.

salpingectomy /ˌsalpɪŋˈdʒɛktəmi/ ■ n. (pl. **-ies**) surgical removal of the Fallopian tubes.
– ORIGIN from SALPINGO- + -ECTOMY.

salpingitis /ˌsalpɪŋˈdʒʌɪtɪs/ ■ n. Medicine inflammation of the Fallopian tubes.

salpingo- /salˈpɪŋɡəʊ/ (also **salping-** before a vowel) ■ comb. form relating to the Fallopian tubes.
– ORIGIN from Greek *salpinx, salping-* 'trumpet'.

salsa /ˈsalsə/ ■ n. 1 a type of Latin American dance music incorporating elements of jazz and rock. ▸ a dance performed to this music. 2 (especially in Latin American cookery) a spicy tomato sauce.
– ORIGIN Spanish, 'sauce', extended in American Spanish to denote the dance.

salsa verde /ˌsalsə ˈvəːdeɪ, ˈvəːdi/ ■ n. 1 an Italian sauce made with olive oil, garlic, capers, anchovies, vinegar or lemon juice, and parsley. 2 a Mexican sauce of chopped onion, garlic, coriander, parsley, and hot peppers.
– ORIGIN Spanish, 'green sauce'.

salsify /ˈsalsɪfi/ ■ n. 1 an edible plant of the daisy family,

with a long root like that of a parsnip. [*Tragopogon porrifolius*.] **2** the root of this plant used as a vegetable.
– ORIGIN C17: from French *salsifis*, from obsolete Italian *salsefica*.

SALT /sɔːlt, sɒlt/ ■ abbrev. Strategic Arms Limitation Talks.

salt /sɔːlt, sɒlt/ ■ n. **1** (also **common salt**) sodium chloride, a white crystalline substance which gives seawater its characteristic taste and is used for seasoning or preserving food. ▸ poetic/literary something which adds freshness or piquancy. **2** Chemistry any chemical compound formed by the reaction of an acid with a base, with the hydrogen of the acid replaced by a metal or other cation. **3** (usu. **old salt**) informal an experienced sailor. ■ adj. impregnated with salt. ■ v. **1** [often as adj. **salted**] season or preserve with salt. ▸ make piquant or more interesting. ▸ sprinkle (a road or path) with salt in order to melt snow or ice. **2** informal fraudulently make (a mine) appear to be a paying one by placing rich ore into it. **3** (**salt something away**) informal secretly store or put by something, especially money. **4** [as adj. **salted**] (of a horse) having developed a resistance to disease by surviving it. **5** (**salt something out**) cause soap to separate from lye by adding salt. ▸ Chemistry cause an organic compound to separate from an aqueous solution by adding an electrolyte.
– PHRASES **rub salt into the wound** make a painful experience even more painful. **the salt of the earth** a person of great goodness and strength of character. [with biblical allusion to Matthew 5:13.] **sit below the salt** be of lower social standing. [from the former custom of placing a salt cellar in the middle of a dining table with the host at one end.] **take something with a pinch** (or **grain**) **of salt** regard something as exaggerated; believe only part of something. **worth one's salt** good or competent at one's job or allotted task.
– DERIVATIVES **saltish** adj. **saltless** adj. **saltness** n.
– ORIGIN Old English *sealt* (n.), of Germanic origin.

salt-and-pepper ■ adj. another way of saying PEPPER-AND-SALT.

saltation /salˈteɪʃ(ə)n, sɔː-, sɒ-/ ■ n. **1** Biology abrupt evolutionary change; sudden large-scale mutation. **2** Geology the transport of hard particles over an uneven surface in a turbulent flow of air or water.
– DERIVATIVES **saltatory** /ˈsaltət(ə)ri, sɔː-, ˈsɒ-/ adj.
– ORIGIN C17: from Latin *saltatio(n-)*, from *saltare* 'to dance', from *salire* 'to leap'.

saltbox ■ n. N. Amer. a frame house having up to three storeys at the front and one fewer at the back with a steeply pitched roof.

salt bridge ■ n. Chemistry **1** a tube containing an electrolyte (typically in the form of a gel), providing electrical contact between two solutions. **2** a link between electrically charged acidic and basic groups, especially on different parts of a large molecule such as a protein.

saltbush ■ n. a salt-tolerant orache plant, sometimes planted on saline soils. [Genus *Atriplex*: several species including *A. vestita*.]

salt cellar ■ n. a dish or container for storing salt, typically a closed container with perforations in the lid for sprinkling.
– ORIGIN Middle English: from SALT + obsolete *saler*, from Old French *salier* 'salt-box', from Latin *salarium* (see SALARY); the change in spelling was due to association with CELLAR.

salt fish ■ n. fish, especially cod, that has been preserved in salt.

salt flats ■ pl. n. areas of flat land covered with a layer of salt.

salt glaze ■ n. a hard glaze with a pitted surface, produced on stoneware by adding salt to the kiln during firing.
– DERIVATIVES **salt-glazed** adj. **salt glazing** n.

saltimbocca /ˌsaltɪmˈbɒkə/ ■ n. a dish consisting of rolled pieces of veal or poultry cooked with herbs, bacon, and other flavourings.
– ORIGIN Italian, 'leap into the mouth'.

saltine /sɔːlˈtiːn, sɒ-/ ■ n. N. Amer. a thin crisp savoury biscuit baked with salt sprinkled on its surface.
– ORIGIN from SALT.

salting ■ n. (usu. **saltings**) Brit. an area of coastal land that is regularly covered by the tide.

1043 **salvage**

saltire /ˈsaltʌɪə, ˈsɔː-/ ■ n. Heraldry a diagonal cross as a heraldic ordinary.
– ORIGIN Middle English: from Old French *saultoir* 'stirrup cord, saltire', from Latin *saltare* 'to dance'.

salt lick ■ n. a place where animals go to lick salt from the ground. ▸ a block of salt provided for animals to lick.

salt marsh ■ n. an area of coastal grassland that is regularly flooded by seawater.

salt pan ■ n. a shallow container or depression in the ground in which salt water evaporates to leave a deposit of salt.

saltpetre /sɔːltˈpiːtə, sɒ-/ (US **saltpeter**) ■ n. potassium nitrate or (Chile saltpetre) sodium nitrate.
– ORIGIN Middle English: from Old French *salpetre*, from medieval Latin *salpetra*, prob. representing *sal petrae* 'salt of rock' (i.e. found as an encrustation).

salt spoon ■ n. a tiny spoon with a roundish deep bowl, used for serving oneself with salt.

saltwater ■ adj. of or found in salt water; living in the sea.

saltwort ■ n. a plant of the goosefoot family, typically growing in salt marshes, which is rich in alkali. [Genus *Salsola*.]

salty ■ adj. (**-ier**, **-iest**) **1** tasting of, containing, or preserved with salt. **2** (of language or humour) down-to-earth; coarse.
– DERIVATIVES **saltily** adv. **saltiness** n.

salubrious /səˈluːbrɪəs/ ■ adj. **1** health-giving; healthy. **2** (of a place) pleasant; not run-down.
– DERIVATIVES **salubriously** adv. **salubriousness** n. **salubrity** n.
– ORIGIN C16: from Latin *salubris*, from *salus* 'health'.

saluki /səˈluːki/ ■ n. (pl. **salukis**) a tall, swift, slender dog of a silky-coated breed with large drooping ears and fringed feet.
– ORIGIN C19: from Arabic *salūkī*.

salut /saˈluː/ ■ exclam. used as a toast.
– ORIGIN from French.

salutary /ˈsaljʊt(ə)ri/ ■ adj. **1** (of something disadvantageous) beneficial in providing an opportunity for learning from experience. **2** archaic health-giving.
– ORIGIN Middle English: from French *salutaire* or Latin *salutaris*, from *salus* 'health'.

salutation ■ n. a greeting.
– DERIVATIVES **salutational** adj.
– ORIGIN Middle English: from Latin *salutatio(n-)*, from *salutare* (see SALUTE).

salutatory /səˈljuːtət(ə)ri/ ■ adj. relating to or of the nature of a salutation. ■ n. (pl. **-ies**) N. Amer. an address of welcome, especially one given as an oration by the student ranking second highest in a graduating class at a university or college.

salute ■ n. **1** a gesture of respect and recognition. **2** a prescribed or specified movement, typically a raising of a hand to the head, made as a salute by a member of a military or similar force. **3** the discharge of a gun or guns as a formal or ceremonial sign of respect or celebration. **4** Fencing the formal performance of certain guards or other movements by fencers before engaging. ■ v. **1** make a formal salute to. **2** greet. **3** show or express admiration and respect for.
– DERIVATIVES **saluter** n.
– ORIGIN Middle English: from Latin *salutare* 'greet, pay one's respects to', from *salus* 'health, greeting'; the noun partly from Old French *salut*.

Salvadorean /ˌsalvəˈdɔːrɪən/ ■ n. a native or inhabitant of El Salvador. ■ adj. of or relating to El Salvador.

salvage ■ v. **1** rescue (a ship or its cargo) from loss at sea. **2** retrieve or preserve from loss or destruction. ■ n. **1** the process or an instance of salvaging. **2** the cargo saved from a wrecked or sunken ship. ▸ Law payment made or due to a person who has saved a ship or its cargo.
– DERIVATIVES **salvageable** adj. **salvager** n.
– ORIGIN C17: from medieval Latin *salvagium*, from Latin *salvare* 'to save'.

salvage yard ▪ n. a place where disused machinery, vehicles, etc. are broken up and parts salvaged.

salvation ▪ n. **1** Theology deliverance from sin and its consequences, believed by Christians to be brought about by faith in Christ. **2** preservation or deliverance from harm, ruin, or loss. ▸ (**one's salvation**) a source or means of being saved in this way.
– ORIGIN Middle English: from Old French *salvacion*, from eccles. Latin *salvation-* (from *salvare* 'to save'), translating Greek *sōtēria*.

salvationist ▪ n. (**Salvationist**) a member of the Salvation Army, a Christian evangelical organization. ▪ adj. **1** of or relating to salvation. **2** (**Salvationist**) of or relating to the Salvation Army.
– DERIVATIVES **salvationism** n.

salve ▪ n. **1** an ointment used to soothe or promote healing of the skin. **2** something that soothes wounded feelings or an uneasy conscience. ▪ v. apply a salve to; soothe.
– ORIGIN Old English, of Germanic origin.

salver ▪ n. a tray, typically one made of silver and used in formal circumstances.
– ORIGIN C17: from French *salve* 'tray for presenting food to the king', from Spanish *salva* 'sampling of food', from *salvar* 'make safe'.

salvia ▪ n. a plant of a genus including sage, especially one cultivated for its spikes of bright flowers. [Genus *Salvia*.]
– ORIGIN from Latin *salvia* 'sage'.

salvo ▪ n. (pl. **-os** or **-oes**) **1** a simultaneous discharge of artillery or other guns in a battle. **2** a sudden vigorous series of aggressive statements or acts.
– ORIGIN C16: from French *salve*, Italian *salva* 'salutation'.

sal volatile /ˌsal vəˈlatɪli/ ▪ n. a scented solution of ammonium carbonate in alcohol, used as smelling salts.
– ORIGIN C17: modern Latin, 'volatile salt'.

salvor /ˈsalvə, ˈsalvɔː/ ▪ n. a person engaged in salvage of a ship or items lost at sea.

salwar /sʌlˈwɑː/ (also **shalwar**) ▪ n. a pair of light, loose, pleated trousers tapering to a tight fit around the ankles, worn by women from the Indian subcontinent, typically with a long tunic (kameez).
– ORIGIN from Persian and Urdu *šalwār*.

SAM ▪ abbrev. surface-to-air missile.

samadhi /sʌˈmɑːdi/ ▪ n. (pl. **samadhis**) Hinduism & Buddhism a state of intense concentration achieved through meditation.
– ORIGIN from Sanskrit *samādhi* 'contemplation'.

samango monkey ▪ n. a southern African guenon with blue-grey fur and black markings on its legs and shoulders. [*Cercopithecus mitis*.]
– ORIGIN C19: from isiZulu *insimango*, prob. rel. to *isimanga* 'something surprising or wondrous'.

Samaritan ▪ n. **1** (usu. **good Samaritan**) a charitable or helpful person (with reference to Luke 10:33). **2** a member of a people inhabiting Samaria in biblical times, or of the modern community claiming descent from them. **3** the dialect of Aramaic formerly spoken in Samaria. **4** (**the Samaritans**) (in the UK) an organization which counsels those in distress, mainly through a telephone service. ▪ adj. of or relating to Samaria or the Samaritans.
– DERIVATIVES **Samaritanism** n.
– ORIGIN from late Latin *Samaritanus*, from Greek *Samareitēs*, from *Samareia* 'Samaria'.

samarium /səˈmɛːrɪəm/ ▪ n. the chemical element of atomic number 62, a hard silvery-white metal of the lanthanide series. (Symbol: **Sm**)
– ORIGIN C19: from *samar(skite)*, a mineral in which its spectrum was first observed (named after *Samarsky*, a C19 Russian official).

Sama Veda /ˈsɑːmə/ ▪ n. one of the four Vedas, a collection of liturgical chants.
– ORIGIN from Sanskrit *sāmaveda*, from *sāman* 'chant' and VEDA.

samba /ˈsambə/ ▪ n. a Brazilian dance of African origin. ▸ a ballroom dance based on this. ▪ v. (**sambas, sambaed** /-bəd/ or **samba'd, sambaing** /-bə(r)ɪŋ/) dance the samba.
– ORIGIN C19: from Portuguese, of African origin.

sambal /ˈsambal/ ▪ n. (in oriental cookery) relish made with vegetables or fruit and spices.
– ORIGIN from Malay.

sambar /ˈsambə/ ▪ n. a dark brown southern Asian woodland deer with branched antlers. [*Cervus unicolor*.]
– ORIGIN C17: from Hindi *sābar*, from Sanskrit *śambara*.

Sambo ▪ n. (pl. **-os** or **-oes**) offensive a black person.
– ORIGIN C18: perhaps from Fula *sambo* 'uncle'.

Sam Browne ▪ n. a leather belt with a supporting strap that passes over the right shoulder, worn by army and police officers.
– ORIGIN C20: named after the British military commander Sir *Sam*uel J. *Brown*(*e*).

sambuca /samˈbuːkə/ ▪ n. an Italian aniseed-flavoured liqueur.
– ORIGIN Italian, from Latin *sambucus* 'elder tree'.

Samburu /samˈbuːruː/ ▪ n. (pl. same) **1** a member of a mainly pastoral people of northern Kenya. **2** the Nilotic language of this people.
– ORIGIN a local name.

same ▪ adj. (**the same**) **1** identical; unchanged. **2** (**this/that same**) referring to a person or thing just mentioned. ▪ pron. **1** (**the same**) the same thing as previously mentioned. ▸ identical people or things. **2** the person or thing just mentioned. ▪ adv. in the same way.
– PHRASES **all** (or **just**) **the same** nevertheless. ▸ anyway. **at the same time 1** simultaneously. **2** on the other hand. **same difference** informal no difference. **same here** informal the same applies to me. (**the**) **same to you!** may you do or have the same thing.
– DERIVATIVES **sameness** n.
– ORIGIN Middle English: from Old Norse *sami*.

samey ▪ adj. (**-ier, -iest**) Brit. informal monotonous.
– DERIVATIVES **sameyness** n.

Samhain /saʊn, ˈsaʊɪn, ˈsawɪn, Irish ˈsəʊnʲ/ ▪ n. **1** November, celebrated by the ancient Celts as a festival marking the beginning of winter and their new year.
– ORIGIN Irish, from Old Irish *samain*.

Sami /ˈsɑːmi, sɑːm/ ▪ pl. n. the Lapps of northern Scandinavia.
– ORIGIN Lappish.

USAGE
Sami is the term by which the Lapps themselves prefer to be known. See **LAPP**.

Samian /ˈseɪmɪən/ ▪ n. a native or inhabitant of Samos, a Greek island in the Aegean. ▪ adj. of or relating to Samos.

Samian ware ▪ n. a type of fine, glossy, reddish-brown pottery widely made in the Roman Empire.

samisen /ˈsamɪsɛn/ (also **shamisen** /ˈʃamɪsɛn/) ▪ n. a Japanese three-stringed lute with a square body, played with a large plectrum.
– ORIGIN C17: Japanese, from Chinese *san-hsien*, from *san* 'three' + *hsien* 'string'.

samite /ˈsamʌɪt, ˈseɪ-/ ▪ n. a rich silk fabric interwoven with gold and silver threads, made in the Middle Ages.
– ORIGIN Middle English: from Old French *samit*, from medieval Greek *hexamiton*, from Greek *hexa-* 'six' + *mitos* 'thread'.

samizdat /ˈsamɪzdat, ˌsamɪzˈdat/ ▪ n. the clandestine copying and distribution of literature banned by the state, especially formerly in the communist countries of eastern Europe.
– ORIGIN 1960s: Russian, 'self-publishing house'.

Samoan ▪ n. **1** a native or inhabitant of Samoa. **2** the Polynesian language of Samoa. ▪ adj. of or relating to Samoa, its people, or their language.

samoosa /səˈmuːsə/ (also **samosa** /səˈməʊsə/) ▪ n. a triangular fried pastry containing spiced vegetables or meat.
– ORIGIN from Persian and Urdu.

samovar /ˈsaməvɑː, ˌsaməˈvɑː/ ▪ n. a highly decorated Russian tea urn.
– ORIGIN Russian, 'self-boiler'.

Samoyed /ˈsaməjɛd, ˈsamɔɪjɛd/ ▪ n. a dog of a white Arctic breed.
– ORIGIN from Russian *samoed*.

samp ■ n. S. African & US coarsely ground maize, or porridge made from this.
– ORIGIN C17: from Algonquian *nasamp* 'softened by water'.

sampan /ˈsampan/ ■ n. a small boat used in the Far East, typically with an oar or oars at the stern.
– ORIGIN C17: from Chinese *san-ban*, from *san* 'three' + *ban* 'board'.

samphire /ˈsamfʌɪə/ ■ n. a fleshy-leaved European plant which grows near the sea. [*Crithmum maritimum* (rock samphire) and other species.]
– ORIGIN C16: from French (*herbe de*) *Saint Pierre* 'St Peter('s herb)'.

sample ■ n. 1 a small part or quantity intended to show what the whole is like. ▶ Statistics a portion of a population, serving as a basis for estimates of the attributes of the whole population. 2 a specimen taken for scientific testing or analysis. 3 a sound created by sampling. ■ v. 1 take a sample or samples of. 2 get a representative experience of. 3 Electronics ascertain the momentary value of (an analogue signal) many times a second so as to convert the signal to digital form.
– ORIGIN Middle English: from an Anglo-Norman French var. of Old French *essample* 'example'.

sampler ■ n. 1 a piece of embroidery worked in various stitches as a specimen of skill. 2 a representative collection or example of something. 3 a person or device that takes samples. ▶ a device for sampling music and sound.
– ORIGIN Middle English: from Old French *essamplaire* 'exemplar'.

sampling ■ n. 1 the taking of a sample or samples. ▶ Statistics a sample. 2 the technique of digitally encoding music or sound and reusing it as part of a composition or recording.

sampling frame ■ n. Statistics a list of the items or people forming a population from which a sample is taken.

samsara /sʌmˈsɑːrə/ ■ n. Hinduism & Buddhism the cycle of death and rebirth to which life in the material world is bound.
– ORIGIN from Sanskrit *saṃsāra*.

samskara /sʌmˈskɑːrə/ ■ n. Hinduism a purificatory ceremony or rite marking a major event in one's life.
– ORIGIN from Sanskrit *saṃskāra* 'a making perfect, preparation'.

samurai /ˈsam(j)ʊrʌɪ/ ■ n. (pl. same) historical a member of a powerful military caste in feudal Japan.
– ORIGIN from Japanese.

San /sɑːn/ ■ n. (pl. same) 1 a member of the Bushmen of southern Africa. See BUSHMAN. 2 the group of Khoisan languages spoken by these peoples.
– ORIGIN from Nama *sān* 'aboriginals, settlers'.

san ■ n. informal a sanatorium.

sanatorium /ˌsanəˈtɔːrɪəm/ ■ n. (pl. **sanatoriums** or **sanatoria** /-rɪə/) an establishment for the treatment of people who are convalescing or have a chronic illness. ▶ a place in a boarding school for children who are unwell.
– ORIGIN C19: from Latin *sanare* 'heal'.

Sancerre /sɒ̃ˈsɛː/ ■ n. a light white wine produced in the part of France around Sancerre.

sanctify /ˈsaŋ(k)tɪfʌɪ/ ■ v. (**-ies, -ied**) 1 consecrate. 2 make legitimate or binding by religious sanction. 3 free from sin. 4 give the appearance of being right or good.
– DERIVATIVES **sanctification** n. **sanctifier** n.
– ORIGIN Middle English: from Old French *saintifier*, from eccles. Latin *sanctificare*, from Latin *sanctus* 'holy'.

sanctimonious /ˌsaŋ(k)tɪˈməʊnɪəs/ ■ adj. derogatory making a show of being morally superior.
– DERIVATIVES **sanctimoniously** adv. **sanctimoniousness** n. **sanctimony** /ˈsaŋ(k)tɪməni/ n.
– ORIGIN C17: from Latin *sanctimonia* 'sanctity', from *sanctus* 'holy'.

sanction ■ n. 1 a threatened penalty for disobeying a law or rule. ▶ (**sanctions**) measures taken by a state to coerce another to conform to an international agreement or norms of conduct. 2 official permission or approval for an action. ▶ official confirmation or ratification of a law. ▶ Law, historical a law or decree, especially an ecclesiastical one. ■ v. 1 give official sanction for. 2 impose a sanction or penalty on.
– DERIVATIVES **sanctionable** adj.
– ORIGIN Middle English: from Latin *sanctio(n-)*, from *sancire* 'ratify'.

sanctitude ■ n. formal holiness; saintliness.
– ORIGIN Middle English: from Latin *sanctitudo*, from *sanctus* 'holy'.

sanctity ■ n. (pl. **-ies**) 1 holiness; saintliness. 2 ultimate importance and inviolability.
– ORIGIN Middle English: from Old French *sainctite*, reinforced by Latin *sanctitas*, from *sanctus* 'holy'.

sanctuary ■ n. (pl. **-ies**) 1 a place of refuge or safety. ▶ immunity from arrest. 2 a nature reserve. ▶ a place where injured or unwanted animals are cared for. 3 a holy place. ▶ the innermost recess or holiest part of a temple. ▶ the part of the chancel of a church containing the high altar.
– ORIGIN Middle English: from Old French *sanctuaire*, from Latin *sanctuarium*, from *sanctus* 'holy'.

sanctum /ˈsaŋ(k)təm/ ■ n. (pl. **sanctums**) 1 a sacred place, especially a shrine in a temple or church. 2 a private place.
– ORIGIN C16: from Latin, from *sanctus* 'holy', from *sancire* 'consecrate'.

sanctum sanctorum /saŋ(k)ˈtɔːrəm/ ■ n. (pl. **sancta sanctorum** or **sanctum sanctorums**) the holy of holies in the Jewish temple.
– ORIGIN Middle English: Latin *sanctum* (see SANCTUM) + *sanctorum* 'of holy places', translating Hebrew *qōdeš haqqŏdāšîm* 'holy of holies'.

Sanctus /ˈsaŋ(k)təs/ ■ n. Christian Church a hymn beginning *Sanctus, sanctus, sanctus* (Holy, holy, holy) forming a set part of the Mass.
– ORIGIN Middle English: from Latin, 'holy'.

sand ■ n. 1 a loose granular substance, typically pale yellowish brown, resulting from the erosion of siliceous and other rocks and forming a major constituent of beaches, river beds, the seabed, and deserts. ▶ (**sands**) an expanse of sand. ▶ technical sediment whose particles are larger than silt. 2 a pale yellow-brown colour. ■ v. 1 smooth with sandpaper or a sander. 2 sprinkle or overlay with sand.
– PHRASES **the sands (of time) are running out** the allotted time is nearly at an end. [with ref. to the sand of an hourglass.]
– ORIGIN Old English, of Germanic origin.

sandal[1] ■ n. a light shoe with an openwork upper or straps attaching the sole to the foot.
– DERIVATIVES **sandalled** (US **sandaled**) adj.
– ORIGIN Middle English: from Greek *sandalion*, diminutive of *sandalon* 'wooden shoe', prob. of Asiatic origin.

sandal[2] ■ n. short for SANDALWOOD.

sandalwood ■ n. 1 the fragrant wood of an Indian or SE Asian tree. ▶ perfume or incense derived from this wood. 2 the tree yielding this wood. [*Santalum album* (white sandalwood) and other species.]
– ORIGIN C16: *sandal* from medieval Latin *sandalum* (from Sanskrit *candana*) + WOOD.

sandarac /ˈsandərak/ ■ n. a gum resin obtained from a cypress (genus *Tetraclinis*), used in making varnish.
– ORIGIN Middle English: from Latin *sandaraca*, from Greek *sandarakē*, of Asiatic origin.

sandbag ■ n. a bag of sand, used for defensive purposes or as ballast in a boat. ■ v. (**-bagged, -bagging**) 1 [usu. as adj. **sandbagged**] barricade with sandbags. 2 hit or fell with or as if with a blow from a sandbag. 3 N. Amer. bully. 4 deliberately underperform in a contest to gain an unfair advantage.
– DERIVATIVES **sandbagger** n.

sandbank ■ n. a deposit of sand forming a shallow area in the sea or a river.

sandbar ■ n. a long, narrow sandbank.

sandblast ■ v. roughen or clean with a jet of sand driven by compressed air or steam. ■ n. such a jet of sand.
– DERIVATIVES **sandblaster** n.

sandboard ■ n. a long, narrow board, often a modified snowboard, used for sliding down sand dunes.
– DERIVATIVES **sandboarder** n. **sandboarding** n.

sandbox

sandbox ■ n. N. Amer. a sandpit.

sandboy ■ n. (in phr. (**as**) **happy as a sandboy**) extremely happy or carefree.
– ORIGIN prob. orig. denoting a boy hawking sand.

sandcastle ■ n. a model of a castle built out of sand.

sand dollar ■ n. a flattened sea urchin which lives partly buried in sand, feeding on detritus. [Order Clypeasteroida: many species.]

sand eel ■ n. a small elongated marine fish living in shallow waters of the northern hemisphere, often found burrowing in the sand. [*Ammodytes tobianus* (Europe) and other species.]

sander ■ n. a power tool used for smoothing a surface with sandpaper or other abrasive material.

sanderling /ˈsandəlɪŋ/ ■ n. a small migratory sandpiper, typically seen running after receding waves on the beach. [*Calidris alba*.]
– ORIGIN C17.

SANDF ■ abbrev. South African National Defence Force.

sand flea ■ n. **1** another term for CHIGGER. **2** another term for SANDHOPPER.

sandfly ■ n. (pl. **-flies**) a small hairy biting fly of tropical and subtropical regions, which transmits a number of diseases. [*Phlebotomus* and other genera.]

sandgrouse ■ n. (pl. same) a seed-eating ground-dwelling bird with brownish plumage, found in arid regions. [Genera *Pterocles* and *Syrrhaptes*: several species.]

sandhopper ■ n. a small seashore crustacean which typically lives among seaweed and leaps when disturbed. [*Orchestia* and other genera.]

Sandinista /ˌsandɪˈniːstə/ ■ n. a member of a left-wing Nicaraguan political organization, in power from 1979 until 1990.
– ORIGIN named after a similar organization founded by the nationalist leader Augusto César *Sandino*.

sand iron ■ n. Golf a sand wedge.

sandlot ■ n. N. Amer. a piece of unoccupied land used by children for games.

sandman ■ n. (**the sandman**) a fictional man supposed to make children sleep by sprinkling sand in their eyes.

sand martin ■ n. a small gregarious swallow with dark brown and white plumage, excavating nest holes in sandy banks near water. [*Riparia riparia* and other species.]

sandpaper ■ n. paper with sand or another abrasive stuck to it, used for smoothing wooden or other surfaces. ■ v. smooth with sandpaper.
– DERIVATIVES **sandpapery** adj.

sandpiper ■ n. a wading bird, typically long-billed and long-legged and frequenting coastal areas. [*Calidris*, *Tringa*, and other genera; family Scolopacidae: numerous species.]

sandpit ■ n. **1** a shallow box or hollow, partly filled with sand for children to play in. **2** a quarry from which sand is excavated.

sand shark ■ n. **1** a voracious brown-spotted tropical Atlantic shark. [*Odontaspis taurus*.] **2** a ray, dogfish, or small shark of shallow coastal waters.

sandstone ■ n. sedimentary rock consisting of sand or quartz grains cemented together, typically red, yellow, or brown in colour.

sandstorm ■ n. a strong wind in a desert carrying clouds of sand.

sandveld /ˈsandfelt/ ■ n. S. African land characterized by having dry, sandy soil.
– ORIGIN C19: from Afrikaans *sandveld*, from S. African Dutch *zandveld* 'sandy region'.

sand wedge ■ n. Golf a heavy, lofted iron used for hitting the ball out of sand.

sandwich /ˈsan(d)wɪdʒ, -wɪtʃ/ ■ n. **1** an item of food consisting of two pieces of bread with a filling between them. **2** Brit. a sponge cake of two or more layers with jam or cream between them. ■ v. (**sandwich something between**) insert something between (two people or things). ▸ (**sandwich things together**) squeeze two things together.
– ORIGIN C18: named after the 4th Earl of *Sandwich*, an English nobleman said to have eaten food in this form.

sandwich board ■ n. a pair of advertisement boards connected by straps by which they are hung over a person's shoulders.

sandwich course ■ n. a training course with alternate periods of formal instruction and practical experience.

sandwich tern ■ n. a large crested tern. [*Sterna sandvicensis*.]
– ORIGIN C18: named after *Sandwich*, a town in southern England.

sandwort ■ n. a low-growing plant of the pink family, typically having small white flowers and growing in dry sandy ground. [*Arenaria* and other genera.]

sandy ■ adj. (**-ier**, **-iest**) **1** covered in or consisting of sand. **2** (especially of hair) light yellowish brown.
– DERIVATIVES **sandiness** n. **sandyish** adj.
– ORIGIN Old English *sandig* (see SAND).

sand yacht ■ n. a wind-driven three-wheeled vehicle with a sail, used for racing on beaches.

sane ■ adj. **1** of sound mind; not mad. **2** reasonable; sensible.
– DERIVATIVES **sanely** adv. **saneness** n.
– ORIGIN C17: from Latin *sanus* 'healthy'.

sang past of SING.

sangar /ˈsaŋɡə/ ■ n. a small protected structure built up from the ground, used for observing or firing from.
– ORIGIN C19: from Pashto, prob. from Persian *sang* 'stone'.

sangfroid /sɒ̃ˈfrwɑː/ ■ n. composure or coolness under trying circumstances.
– ORIGIN C18: from French *sang-froid* 'cold blood'.

sangha /ˈsaŋɡə/ ■ n. the Buddhist monastic order.
– ORIGIN from Sanskrit *saṃgha* 'community'.

Sangiovese /ˌsandʒɪə(ʊ)ˈveɪzɪ/ ■ n. a variety of black wine grape used to make Chianti and other Italian red wines.
– ORIGIN from Italian.

sangoma /saŋˈɡɔːmə/ ■ n. (in southern Africa) a traditional healer or diviner.
– ORIGIN from isiZulu *isangoma*.

sangrail /saŋˈɡreɪl/ (also **sangreal**) ■ n. another term for GRAIL.
– ORIGIN Middle English: from Old French *saint graal* 'Holy Grail'.

sangria /saŋˈɡriːə/ ■ n. a Spanish drink of red wine, lemonade, fruit, and spices.
– ORIGIN Spanish, 'bleeding'.

sanguinary /ˈsaŋɡwɪn(ə)ri/ ■ adj. chiefly archaic involving or causing much bloodshed.
– ORIGIN Middle English: from Latin *sanguinarius*, from *sanguis* 'blood'.

sanguine /ˈsaŋɡwɪn/ ■ adj. **1** cheerfully optimistic. **2** (in medieval medicine) having a predominance of blood among the bodily humours, supposedly marked by a ruddy complexion and an optimistic disposition. ▸ archaic (of the complexion) ruddy. **3** poetic/literary blood-red. ■ n. a blood-red colour.
– DERIVATIVES **sanguinely** adv. **sanguineness** n.
– ORIGIN Middle English: from Old French *sanguin(e)* 'blood red', from Latin *sanguineus* 'of blood', from *sanguis* 'blood'.

Sanhedrin /ˈsanɪdrɪn, sanˈhiːdrɪn, sanˈhɛdrɪn/ (also **Sanhedrim** /-rɪm/) ■ n. the highest court of justice and the supreme council in ancient Jerusalem.
– ORIGIN from late Hebrew *sanhedrīn*, from Greek *sunedrion* 'council', from *sun-* 'with' + *hedra* 'seat'.

sanidine /ˈsanɪdiːn/ ■ n. a high-temperature mineral of the alkali feldspar group.
– ORIGIN C19: from Greek *sanis*, *sanid-* 'board'.

sanitarian ■ n. chiefly archaic a person responsible for public health or in favour of public health reform.
– ORIGIN C19: from SANITARY.

sanitarium /ˌsanɪˈtɛːrɪəm/ ■ n. (pl. **sanitariums** or **sanitaria** /-rɪə/) North American term for SANATORIUM.
– ORIGIN C19: from Latin *sanitas* 'health'.

sanitary ■ adj. **1** of or relating to conditions affecting hygiene and health. **2** hygienic.
– DERIVATIVES **sanitarily** adv. **sanitariness** n.

–ORIGIN C19: from French *sanitaire*, from Latin *sanitas* 'health', from *sanus* 'healthy'.

sanitary protection ▪ n. sanitary towels and tampons collectively.

sanitary towel (N. Amer. **sanitary napkin**) ▪ n. an absorbent pad worn by women to absorb menstrual blood.

sanitaryware ▪ n. toilet bowls, cisterns, and other fittings.

sanitation ▪ n. conditions relating to public health.
–ORIGIN C19: from SANITARY.

sanitize (also **-ise**) ▪ v. **1** make hygienic. **2** derogatory make more acceptable.
–DERIVATIVES **sanitization** (also **-isation**) n. **sanitizer** (also **-iser**) n.

sanity ▪ n. the condition of being sane. ▸ reasonable and rational behaviour.
–ORIGIN Middle English: from Latin *sanitas* 'health', from *sanus* 'healthy'.

sank past of SINK[1].

sannyasi /sənˈjɑːsi/ (also **sanyasi** or **sannyasin**) ▪ n. (pl. same) a Hindu religious mendicant.
–ORIGIN from Sanskrit *saṃnyāsin* 'laying aside, ascetic', from *saṃ* 'together' + *ni* 'down' + *as* 'throw'.

sans /sanz/ ▪ prep. poetic/literary or humorous without.
–ORIGIN Middle English: from Old French *sanz*, from a var. of Latin *sine* 'without'.

sansei /ˈsanseɪ/ ▪ n. (pl. same) N. Amer. an American or Canadian whose grandparents immigrated from Japan. Compare with NISEI and ISSEI.
–ORIGIN 1940s: Japanese, from *san* 'third' + *sei* 'generation'.

Sanskrit /ˈsanskrɪt/ ▪ n. an ancient Indo-European language of India, still used as a language of religion and scholarship and from which many Indic languages are derived.
–ORIGIN from Sanskrit *saṃskṛta* 'composed, elaborated', from *saṃ* 'together' + *kṛ* 'make' + the participial ending *-ta*.

sans serif /san ˈsɛrɪf/ (also **sanserif**) Printing ▪ n. a style of type without serifs. ▪ adj. without serifs.
–ORIGIN C19: from French *sans* 'without' + SERIF.

Santa (also **SANTA**) ▪ abbrev. South African National Tuberculosis Association.

Santa Claus (also informal **Santa**) ▪ n. Father Christmas.
–ORIGIN orig. US, an alteration of Dutch dialect *Sante Klaas* 'St Nicholas'.

santeria /ˌsantɛˈriːə/ ▪ n. a pantheistic Afro-Cuban religious cult developed from the beliefs of the Yoruba people and having some elements of Catholicism.
–ORIGIN Spanish, 'holiness'.

santolina /ˌsantəˈliːnə/ ▪ n. a plant of a genus including cotton lavender. [Genus *Santolina*.]
–ORIGIN perhaps an alteration of *Santonica* (*herba*) '(plant) of the Santoni', a tribe from Aquitaine, France.

sanyasi ▪ n. variant spelling of SANNYASI.

SAP ▪ abbrev. historical South African Police.

sap[1] ▪ n. **1** the fluid, chiefly water with dissolved sugars and mineral salts, circulating in the vascular system of a plant. **2** vigour or energy. ▪ v. (**sapped**, **sapping**) gradually weaken (a person's strength or power). ▸ (**sap someone of**) drain someone of (strength or power).
–DERIVATIVES **sapless** adj.
–ORIGIN Old English, prob. of Germanic origin; the verb is derived from SAP[2], in the sense 'undermine'.

sap[2] ▪ n. historical a tunnel or trench to conceal an assailant's approach to a fortified place. ▪ v. (**sapped**, **sapping**) **1** historical dig a sap. **2** archaic make insecure by removing the foundations.
–ORIGIN C16: from French *saper*, from Italian *zappare*, from *zappa* 'spade, spadework', prob. from Arabic *sarab* 'underground passage'.

sap[3] ▪ n. informal, chiefly N. Amer. a foolish and gullible person.
–ORIGIN C19: abbrev. of dialect *sapskull* 'person with a head like sapwood'.

Sapa /ˈsɑːpə/ (also **SAPA**) ▪ abbrev. South African Press Association.

sapele /səˈpiːli/ ▪ n. a large tropical African hardwood tree, with reddish-brown wood resembling mahogany. [Genus *Entandrophragma*.]
–ORIGIN C20: from the name of a port on the Benin River, Nigeria.

sap green ▪ n. a vivid yellowish-green pigment made from buckthorn berries.

saphenous /səˈfiːnəs/ ▪ adj. Anatomy relating to or denoting either of the two large superficial veins in the leg.
–ORIGIN C19: from medieval Latin *saphena* 'vein'.

sapid /ˈsapɪd/ ▪ adj. chiefly N. Amer. **1** flavoursome. **2** pleasant or interesting.
–ORIGIN C17: from Latin *sapidus*, from *sapere* 'to taste'.

sapient /ˈseɪpɪənt/ ▪ adj. **1** formal wise, or attempting to appear wise. **2** of or relating to the human species (*Homo sapiens*).
–DERIVATIVES **sapience** n. **sapiently** adv.
–ORIGIN Middle English: from Latin *sapient-*, *sapere* 'to be wise'.

sapiential ▪ adj. poetic/literary of or relating to wisdom.
–ORIGIN C15: from eccles. Latin *sapientialis*, from Latin *sapientia* 'wisdom'.

sapling ▪ n. **1** a young, slender tree. **2** poetic/literary a young and slender or inexperienced person.
–ORIGIN Middle English: from SAP[1].

sapodilla /ˌsapəˈdɪlə/ ▪ n. **1** a large evergreen tropical American tree which has hard durable wood and yields chicle. [*Manilkara zapota*.] **2** (also **sapodilla plum**) the sweet brownish bristly fruit of this tree.
–ORIGIN C17: from Spanish *zapotillo*, diminutive of *zapote*, from Nahuatl *tzápotl*.

saponify /səˈpɒnɪfʌɪ/ ▪ v. (**-ies**, **-ied**) Chemistry turn (fat or oil) into soap by reaction with an alkali. ▸ convert (any ester) into an alcohol and a salt by alkaline hydrolysis.
–DERIVATIVES **saponification** n.
–ORIGIN C19: from French *saponifier*, from Latin *sapo*, *sapon-* 'soap'.

sapper ▪ n. **1** a military engineer who lays or detects and disarms mines. **2** Brit. a soldier in the Corps of Royal Engineers.
–ORIGIN C17: from SAP[2].

sapphic /ˈsafɪk/ ▪ adj. **1** (**Sapphic**) of or relating to the Greek lyric poet Sappho, or her poetry expressing love and affection for women. **2** formal or humorous of or relating to lesbians or lesbianism.
–ORIGIN C16: from French *saphique*, from Greek *Sapphikos*, from *Sapphō*.

sapphire /ˈsafʌɪə/ ▪ n. **1** a transparent precious stone, typically blue, which is a form of corundum. **2** a bright blue colour.
–DERIVATIVES **sapphirine** /ˈsafɪrʌɪn/ adj.
–ORIGIN Middle English: from Old French *safir*, from Greek *sappheiros*, prob. denoting lapis lazuli.

sapphism /ˈsafɪz(ə)m/ ▪ n. formal or humorous lesbianism.

sappy (**-ier**, **-iest**) **1** informal, chiefly N. Amer. over-sentimental. **2** (of a plant) containing a lot of sap.
–DERIVATIVES **sappily** adv. **sappiness** n.

sapro- ▪ comb. form Biology relating to putrefaction or decay: *saprogenic*.
–ORIGIN from Greek *sapros* 'putrid'.

saprogenic /ˌsaprə(ʊ)ˈdʒɛnɪk/ ▪ adj. Biology causing or produced by putrefaction or decay.

saprophagous /səˈprɒfəɡəs/ ▪ adj. Biology feeding on decaying matter.

saprophyte /ˈsaprə(ʊ)fʌɪt/ ▪ n. Biology a plant, fungus, or micro-organism that lives on decaying matter.
–DERIVATIVES **saprophytic** adj.

saprotrophic ▪ adj. Biology feeding on decaying organic matter.

SAPS ▪ abbrev. South African Police Service.

sapsucker ▪ n. an American woodpecker that pecks rows of small holes in trees and visits them for sap and insects. [*Sphyrapicus*: four species.]

sapwood ▪ n. the soft outer layers of new wood between the heartwood and the bark.

SAQA

SAQA /ˈsakwə/ ■ abbrev. South African Qualifications Authority.

SAR ■ abbrev. search and rescue (an emergency service).

saraband /ˈsarəband/ (also **sarabande**) ■ n. a slow, stately Spanish dance in triple time. ▸ a piece of music for this.
– ORIGIN C17: from French *sarabande*, from Spanish and Italian *zarabanda*.

Saracen /ˈsarəs(ə)n/ ■ n. **1** an Arab or Muslim, especially at the time of the Crusades. **2** a nomad of the Syrian and Arabian desert at the time of the Roman Empire.
– DERIVATIVES **Saracenic** adj.
– ORIGIN Middle English, from Old French *sarrazin*, from late Greek *Sarakēnos*, perhaps from Arabic *šarḳī* 'eastern'.

Saracen's head ■ n. a conventionalized depiction of the head of a Saracen as a heraldic charge or inn sign.

Saran /səˈran/ (also **Saran Wrap**) ■ n. N. Amer. trademark cling film.
– ORIGIN 1940s.

sarangi /səˈrangi, saːˈrʌngi/ ■ n. (pl. **sarangis**) an Indian stringed instrument played with a bow.
– ORIGIN from Hindi *sāraṅgī*.

sarape /səˈrɑːpeɪ/ ■ n. variant of SERAPE.

sarcasm ■ n. the use of irony to mock or convey contempt.
– DERIVATIVES **sarcastic** adj. **sarcastically** adv.
– ORIGIN C16: from French *sarcasme*, from late Greek *sarkasmos*, from Greek *sarkazein* 'tear flesh', later 'gnash the teeth, speak bitterly', from *sarx* 'flesh'.

sarcolemma /ˌsɑːkə(ʊ)ˈlɛmə/ ■ n. Physiology the fine transparent tubular sheath enveloping the fibres of skeletal muscles.
– DERIVATIVES **sarcolemmal** adj.
– ORIGIN C19: from Greek *sarx*, *sark-* 'flesh' + *lemma* 'husk'.

sarcoma /sɑːˈkəʊmə/ ■ n. (pl. **sarcomas** or **sarcomata** /-mətə/) Medicine a malignant tumour of connective or other non-epithelial tissue.
– DERIVATIVES **sarcomatosis** n. **sarcomatous** adj.
– ORIGIN C19: from Greek *sarkōma*, from *sarkoun* 'become fleshy', from *sarx* 'flesh'.

sarcophagus /sɑːˈkɒfəɡəs/ ■ n. (pl. **sarcophagi** /-gʌɪ, -dʒʌɪ/) a stone coffin, typically associated with ancient Egypt, Rome, and Greece.
– ORIGIN Middle English: from Greek *sarkophagos* 'flesh-consuming', from *sarx* 'flesh' + *-phagos* '-eating'.

sarcoplasm /ˈsɑːkə(ʊ)plaz(ə)m/ ■ n. Physiology the cytoplasm of striated muscle cells.
– DERIVATIVES **sarcoplasmic** adj.
– ORIGIN C19: from Greek *sarx*, *sark-* 'flesh' + PLASMA.

sarcoptic mange /sɑːˈkɒptɪk/ ■ n. a form of mange chiefly affecting the abdomen and hindquarters.
– ORIGIN C19: from *Sarcoptes*, genus name of the itch mite, from Greek *sarx*, *sark-* 'flesh'.

sard /sɑːd/ ■ n. a yellow or brownish-red variety of chalcedony.
– ORIGIN Middle English: from French *sarde* or Latin *sarda*, from Greek *sardios*, prob. from *Sardō* 'Sardinia'.

sardar /ˈsɑːdɑː/ (also **sirdar**) ■ n. chiefly Indian a leader.
– ORIGIN from Persian and Urdu *sar-dār*.

sardine /sɑːˈdiːn/ ■ n. a young pilchard or other young or small herring-like fish. ■ v. informal pack closely together.
– PHRASES **packed like sardines** crowded close together, as sardines in tins.
– ORIGIN Middle English: from Latin *sardina*, from *sarda*, prob. from *Sardō* 'Sardinia'.

Sardinian ■ adj. of or relating to Sardinia, its people, or their language. ■ n. **1** a native or inhabitant of Sardinia. **2** the Romance language of Sardinia, which has several distinct dialects.

sardonic /sɑːˈdɒnɪk/ ■ adj. grimly mocking or cynical.
– DERIVATIVES **sardonically** adv. **sardonicism** n.
– ORIGIN C17: from French *sardonique*, earlier *sardonien*, from Greek *sardonios* 'of Sardinia', alteration of *sardanios*, used to describe bitter or scornful laughter.

sardonyx /ˈsɑːdənɪks/ ■ n. onyx in which white layers alternate with sard.
– ORIGIN Middle English: from Greek *sardonux*, prob. from *sardios* 'sardius' + *onux* 'onyx'.

saree ■ n. variant spelling of SARI.

Sarfu /ˈsɑːfuː/ (also **SARFU**) ■ abbrev. South African Rugby Football Union.

sargassum /sɑːˈɡasəm/ (also **sargasso**) ■ n. a brown seaweed with berry-like air bladders, typically floating in large masses. [Genus *Sargassum*.]
– ORIGIN C16: from Portuguese *sargaço*.

sarge ■ n. informal sergeant.

sari /ˈsɑːri/ (also **saree**) ■ n. (pl. **saris** or **sarees**) a garment consisting of a length of cotton or silk elaborately draped around the body, traditionally worn by women from the Indian subcontinent.
– ORIGIN C18: from Hindi *sāṛī*.

sarin /ˈsɑːrɪn/ ■ n. an organophosphorus nerve gas, developed during the Second World War.
– ORIGIN from German *Sarin*.

sarky ■ adj. (**-ier**, **-iest**) informal, chiefly Brit. sarcastic.
– DERIVATIVES **sarkily** adv. **sarkiness** n.

sarmie ■ n. S. African informal a sandwich.

sarnie ■ n. Brit. informal a sandwich.

sarod /səˈrəʊd/ ■ n. a lute used in classical North Indian music.
– ORIGIN Urdu, from Persian *surod* 'song, melody'.

sarong /səˈrɒŋ/ ■ n. a garment consisting of a long piece of cloth wrapped round the body and tucked at the waist or under the armpits, traditionally worn in SE Asia and now also by Western women.
– ORIGIN C19: Malay, 'sheath'.

SARS ■ abbrev. **1** South African Revenue Service. **2** (also **Sars**) severe acute respiratory syndrome.

sarsaparilla /ˌsɑːs(ə)pəˈrɪlə/ ■ n. **1** a preparation of the dried rhizomes of various plants, especially smilax, used to flavour some drinks and medicines and formerly as a tonic. ▸ a sweet drink flavoured with this. **2** the tropical American climbing plant from which these rhizomes are obtained. [*Smilax regelii* and other species.]
– ORIGIN C16: from Spanish *zarzaparilla*, from *zarza* 'bramble' + a diminutive of *parra* 'vine'.

sarsen /ˈsɑːs(ə)n/ ■ n. a silicified sandstone boulder of a kind used at Stonehenge and in other prehistoric monuments in southern England.
– ORIGIN C17: prob. a var. of SARACEN.

sarsenet /ˈsɑːsnɪt/ (also **sarcenet**) ■ n. a fine soft silk fabric.
– ORIGIN Middle English: from Anglo-Norman French *sarzinett*, perhaps a diminutive of *sarzin* 'Saracen', suggested by Old French *drap sarrasinois* 'Saracen cloth'.

sartorial /sɑːˈtɔːrɪəl/ ■ adj. of or relating to tailoring, clothes, or style of dress.
– DERIVATIVES **sartorially** adv.
– ORIGIN C19: from Latin *sartor* 'tailor', from *sarcire* 'to patch'.

sartorius /sɑːˈtɔːrɪəs/ ■ n. Anatomy a long, narrow muscle running obliquely across the front of each thigh.
– ORIGIN C18: from Latin *sartor* 'tailor' (because the muscle is used when sitting cross-legged, a position associated with tailors).

SAS ■ abbrev. **1** South African Ship. **2** Special Air Service.

SASE ■ abbrev. self-addressed stamped envelope.

sash[1] ■ n. a long strip or loop of cloth worn over one shoulder or round the waist.
– DERIVATIVES **sashed** adj.
– ORIGIN C16: from Arabic *šāš* 'muslin, turban'.

sash[2] ■ n. a frame holding the glass in a window, typically one of two sliding frames in a sash window.
– DERIVATIVES **sashed** adj.
– ORIGIN C17: alteration of CHASSIS.

sashay /saˈʃeɪ/ ■ v. informal, chiefly N. Amer. **1** walk ostentatiously, with exaggerated hip and shoulder movements. **2** perform the sashay. ■ n. (in American square dancing) a figure in which partners circle each other by taking sideways steps.
– ORIGIN C19: alteration of CHASSÉ.

sash cord ■ n. a strong cord attaching either of the weights of a sash window to a sash.

sashimi /ˈsaʃɪmi/ ■ n. a Japanese dish of bite-sized pieces

of raw fish eaten with soy sauce and horseradish paste.
– ORIGIN from Japanese.

sash window ■ n. a window with one or two sashes which can be slid vertically to open it.

Sasquatch /ˈsaskwatʃ, -wɒtʃ/ ■ n. another name for **BIGFOOT**.
– ORIGIN C20: Salish.

sass N. Amer. informal ■ n. cheek. ■ v. be cheeky to.
– ORIGIN C19: var. of **SAUCE**.

sassafras /ˈsasəfras/ ■ n. 1 a deciduous North American tree with aromatic leaves and bark. [*Sassafras albidum*.] 2 an extract of the leaves or bark of this tree, used medicinally or in perfumery.
– ORIGIN C16: from Spanish *sasafrs*, from Latin *saxifraga* 'saxifrage'.

Sassenach /ˈsasənax, -nak/ derogatory Scottish & Irish ■ n. an English person. ■ adj. English.
– ORIGIN C18: from Scottish Gaelic *Sasunnoch*, Irish *Sasanach*, from Latin *Saxones* 'Saxons'.

sassy ■ adj. (**-ier, -iest**) informal, chiefly N. Amer. bold and spirited; cheeky.
– DERIVATIVES **sassily** adv. **sassiness** n.
– ORIGIN C19: var. of **SAUCY**.

SAT ■ abbrev. 1 trademark (in the US) Scholastic Aptitude Test. 2 standard assessment task.

Sat. ■ abbrev. Saturday.

sat past and past participle of **SIT**.

Satan ■ n. the Devil; Lucifer.
– ORIGIN Old English, from Hebrew *śāṭān* 'adversary', from *śāṭan* 'plot against'.

satanic ■ adj. 1 of or characteristic of Satan. 2 connected with satanism.
– DERIVATIVES **satanically** adv.

satanism ■ n. the worship of Satan, typically involving a travesty of Christian symbols and practices.
– DERIVATIVES **satanist** n. & adj.

satay /ˈsateɪ/ (also **saté**) ■ n. an Indonesian and Malaysian dish consisting of small pieces of meat grilled on a skewer and served with spiced sauce.
– ORIGIN from Malay *satai*, Indonesian *sate*.

SATB ■ abbrev. soprano, alto, tenor, and bass (as a combination of singing voices required for a piece of music).

satchel ■ n. a shoulder bag with a long strap, used especially for school books.
– ORIGIN Middle English: from Old French *sachel*, from Latin *saccellus* 'small bag'.

satcom (also **SATCOM**) ■ n. satellite communications.

sate[1] ■ v. 1 satisfy fully. 2 supply with as much as or more than is desired or can be managed.
– ORIGIN C17: prob. an alteration of dialect *sade*, from Old English *sadian* 'become sated or weary'.

sate[2] ■ v. archaic spelling of **SAT**.

saté ■ n. variant spelling of **SATAY**.

sateen /saˈtiːn/ ■ n. a cotton fabric woven like satin with a glossy surface.
– ORIGIN C19: alteration of **SATIN**, on the pattern of *velveteen*.

satellite ■ n. 1 an artificial body placed in orbit round the earth or another planet to collect information or for communication. ▸ [as modifier] using or relating to satellite technology. ▸ satellite television. 2 Astronomy a celestial body orbiting a planet. 3 a thing separate from something else but dependent on or controlled by it. ▸ a small town, country, etc. dependent on another.
– ORIGIN C16: from French *satellite* or Latin *satelles*, *satellit-* 'attendant'.

satellite dish ■ n. a bowl-shaped aerial with which signals are transmitted to or received from a communications satellite.

satellite television ■ n. television in which the signals are broadcast via satellite.

satiate /ˈseɪʃɪeɪt/ ■ v. another term for **SATE**[1]. ■ adj. archaic fully satisfied.
– DERIVATIVES **satiable** adj. (archaic). **satiation** n.
– ORIGIN Middle English: from Latin *satiatus*, from *satiare*, from *satis* 'enough'.

satiety /səˈtʌɪɪti/ ■ n. the feeling or state of being sated.
– ORIGIN C16: from Old French *saciete*, from Latin *satietas*, from *satis* 'enough'.

satin ■ n. 1 a smooth, glossy fabric, usually of silk, produced by a weave in which the threads of the warp are caught and looped by the weft only at certain intervals. 2 [as modifier] denoting or having a smooth, glossy surface or finish. ■ v. (**satined, satining**) give a satin surface to.
– DERIVATIVES **satiny** adj.
– ORIGIN Middle English: from Arabic *zaytūnī* 'of Tsinkiang', a town in China.

satin stitch ■ n. a long straight embroidery stitch, giving the appearance of satin.

satinwood ■ n. 1 glossy yellowish wood valued for cabinetwork. 2 the tropical tree that produces this wood. [*Chloroxylon swietenia* (India and Sri Lanka), *Zanthoxylum flava* (Caribbean region), and other species.]

satire /ˈsatʌɪə/ ■ n. 1 the use of humour, irony, exaggeration, or ridicule to expose and criticize people's stupidity or vices. 2 a play, novel, etc. using satire. ▸ (in Latin literature) a literary miscellany, especially a poem ridiculing prevalent vices or follies.
– DERIVATIVES **satirist** n.
– ORIGIN C16: from Latin *satira*, later form of *satura* 'poetic medley'.

satiric /səˈtɪrɪk/ ■ adj. another term for **SATIRICAL**.

satirical ■ adj. containing or using satire. ▸ sarcastic; humorously critical.
– DERIVATIVES **satirically** adv.
– ORIGIN C16: from late Latin *satiricus*, from *satira* (see **SATIRE**).

satirize /ˈsatɪrʌɪz/ (also **-ise**) ■ v. deride and criticize by means of satire.
– DERIVATIVES **satirization** (also **-isation**) n.

satisfaction ■ n. 1 the state of being satisfied. 2 Law the payment of a debt or fulfilment of an obligation or claim. 3 [with neg.] what is felt to be owed or due to one. 4 Christian Church Christ's atonement for sin. 5 historical the chance to defend one's honour in a duel.
– ORIGIN Middle English: from Latin *satisfactio(n-)*, from *satisfacere* (see **SATISFY**).

satisfactory ■ adj. fulfilling expectations or needs; acceptable.
– DERIVATIVES **satisfactorily** adv. **satisfactoriness** n.
– ORIGIN Middle English: from Old French *satisfactoire* or medieval Latin *satisfactorius*, from Latin *satisfacere* (see **SATISFY**).

satisfice /ˈsatɪsfʌɪs/ ■ v. formal satisfy only the minimum requirements necessary to achieve a particular goal.
– ORIGIN C16: alteration of **SATISFY**, influenced by Latin *satisfacere*.

satisfy ■ v. (**-ies, -ied**) 1 meet the expectations, needs, or desires of. ▸ fulfil (a desire or need). 2 provide with adequate information about or proof of something. 3 comply with (a condition, obligation, or demand). 4 Mathematics (of a quantity) make (an equation) true.
– DERIVATIVES **satisfiability** n. **satisfiable** adj. **satisfied** adj. **satisfying** adj. **satisfyingly** adv.
– ORIGIN Middle English: from Old French *satisfier*, from Latin *satisfacere* 'to content', from *satis* 'enough' + *facere* 'make'.

satnav /ˈsatnav/ ■ n. navigation using information from satellites.

satori /saˈtɔːri/ ■ n. Buddhism sudden enlightenment.
– ORIGIN Japanese, 'awakening'.

Satour /ˈsatɔː/ ■ abbrev. South African Tourism.

satphone ■ n. a telephone that transmits its signal via a geostationary communications satellite.

satrap /ˈsatrap/ ■ n. 1 a provincial governor in the ancient Persian empire. 2 a subordinate or local ruler.
– ORIGIN Middle English: from Old French *satrape* or Latin *satrapa*, from Old Persian *kšathra-pāvan* 'country-protector'.

satrapy /ˈsatrəpi/ ■ n. (pl. **-ies**) a province governed by a satrap.

satsuma /satˈsuːmə/ ■ n. 1 a tangerine of a hardy

saturate

loose-skinned variety, originally grown in Japan. **2** /also 'satsumə, -sjʊ-/ (**Satsuma** or **Satsuma ware**) Japanese pottery, often elaborately painted, with a crackled cream-coloured glaze.
– ORIGIN C19: named after the former Japanese province of *Satsuma*.

saturate ■ v. /'satʃəreɪt/ **1** soak thoroughly with water or other liquid. **2** cause to combine with, dissolve, or hold the greatest possible quantity of another substance. ▸ (usu. **be saturated with**) fill until no more can be held or absorbed. **3** magnetize or charge (a substance or device) fully. **4** supply (a market) beyond the point at which the demand for a product is satisfied. ■ n. /'satʃərət/ a saturated fat. ■ adj. /'satʃərət/ poetic/literary saturated with moisture.
– DERIVATIVES **saturable** adj.
– ORIGIN Middle English: from Latin *saturare* 'fill, glut', from *satur* 'full'.

saturated ■ adj. **1** Chemistry (of a solution) containing the largest possible amount of solute. **2** Chemistry (of an organic molecule) containing the greatest possible number of hydrogen atoms, without double or triple bonds. **3** (of colour) bright, rich, and free from an admixture of white.

saturation ■ n. **1** the action of saturating or state of being saturated. **2** [as modifier] to the fullest extent.

saturation diving ■ n. diving in which the diver's bloodstream is saturated with helium or other gas at the pressure of the surrounding water, so that decompression time is independent of the duration of the dive.

saturation point ■ n. the stage beyond which no more can be absorbed or accepted.

Saturday ■ n. the day of the week before Sunday and following Friday. ■ adv. on Saturday. ▸ (**Saturdays**) on Saturdays; each Saturday.
– ORIGIN Old English *Sætern(es)dæg*, translation of Latin *Saturni dies* 'day of Saturn'.

Saturday night special ■ n. informal, chiefly N. Amer. a cheap low-calibre pistol or revolver.

Saturnalia /ˌsatə'neɪlɪə/ ■ n. [treated as sing. or pl.] the ancient Roman festival of Saturn in December, a period of unrestrained merrymaking. ▸ (**saturnalia**) an occasion of wild revelry.
– DERIVATIVES **saturnalian** adj.
– ORIGIN Latin, 'matters relating to Saturn', from *Saturnalis*.

Saturnian ■ adj. of or relating to the planet Saturn.

saturniid /sə'tə:nɪɪd/ ■ n. Entomology a moth of a family (Saturniidae) which includes the emperor moths and the giant Indian silk moths.
– ORIGIN C19: from the genus name *Saturnia*.

saturnine /'satənʌɪn/ ■ adj. gloomy. ▸ (of looks, etc.) dark and brooding.
– DERIVATIVES **saturninely** adv.
– ORIGIN Middle English: from Old French *saturnin*, from medieval Latin *Saturninus* 'of Saturn' (associated with slowness and gloom by astrologers).

satyagraha /sʌ'tjɑːɡrəhɑː/ ■ n. passive political resistance, especially as advocated by Mahatma Gandhi against British rule in India.
– ORIGIN Sanskrit, from *satya* 'truth' + *āgraha* 'obstinacy'.

satyr /'satə/ ■ n. **1** Greek & Roman Mythology one of a class of lustful, drunken woodland gods, represented as a man with a horse's ears and tail or (in Roman representations) with a goat's ears, tail, legs, and horns. **2** a man with strong sexual desires.
– DERIVATIVES **satyric** adj.
– ORIGIN Middle English: from Old French *satyre*, or from Greek *saturos*.

sauce ■ n. **1** thick liquid served with food to add moistness and flavour. **2** N. Amer. stewed fruit, especially apples. **3** (**the sauce**) informal, chiefly N. Amer. alcoholic drink. **4** informal, chiefly Brit. impertinence. ■ v. **1** (usu. **be sauced**) season with a sauce. **2** make more interesting and exciting. **3** informal be impudent to.
– DERIVATIVES **sauceless** adj.
– ORIGIN Middle English: from Latin *salsus* 'salted', from *salere* 'to salt', from *sal* 'salt'.

sauce boat ■ n. a long, narrow jug for serving sauce.

sauced ■ adj. informal, chiefly N. Amer. drunk.

saucepan ■ n. a deep cooking pan, typically round, made of metal, and with one long handle and a lid.
– DERIVATIVES **saucepanful** n. (pl. **-fuls**).

saucer ■ n. a shallow dish, typically with a central circular indentation, on which a cup is placed.
– DERIVATIVES **saucerful** n. (pl. **-fuls**). **saucerless** adj.
– ORIGIN Middle English: from Old French *saussier(e)* 'sauce boat', prob. suggested by late Latin *salsarium*.

saucier /'səʊsɪeɪ/ ■ n. a chef who prepares sauces.
– ORIGIN from French.

saucy ■ adj. (**-ier**, **-iest**) informal **1** sexually suggestive, typically in a humorous way. **2** chiefly N. Amer. bold, lively, and spirited. **3** covered with sauce.
– DERIVATIVES **saucily** adv. **sauciness** n.

Saudi /'saʊdi, 'sɔːdi/ ■ n. (pl. **Saudis**) a citizen of Saudi Arabia, or a member of its ruling dynasty. ■ adj. of or relating to Saudi Arabia or its ruling dynasty.
– ORIGIN from the name of Abdul-Aziz ibn *Saud*, first king of Saudi Arabia.

Saudi Arabian ■ n. a native or inhabitant of Saudi Arabia. ■ adj. of or relating to Saudi Arabia.

sauerkraut /'saʊəkraʊt/ ■ n. a German dish of chopped pickled cabbage.
– ORIGIN from German, from *sauer* 'sour' + *Kraut* 'vegetable'.

sauna /'sɔːnə/ ■ n. **1** a small room used as a hot-air or steam bath for cleaning and refreshing the body. **2** a session in a sauna.
– ORIGIN C19: from Finnish.

saunter ■ v. walk in a slow, relaxed manner. ■ n. a leisurely stroll.
– DERIVATIVES **saunterer** n.
– ORIGIN Middle English.

-saur ■ comb. form forming names of reptiles, especially extinct ones: *ichthyosaur*.
– ORIGIN from Greek *sauros* 'lizard'; cf. **-SAURUS**.

saurian /'sɔːrɪən/ ■ adj. of or like a lizard. ■ n. a large reptile, especially a dinosaur.
– ORIGIN C19: from Greek *sauros* 'lizard'.

saurischian /sɔː'rɪskɪən, -'rɪʃɪən/ ■ n. Palaeontology a dinosaur of a group with a pelvic structure resembling that of lizards. Compare with **ORNITHISCHIAN**.
– ORIGIN C19: from Greek *sauros* 'lizard' + *iskhion* 'hip joint'.

sauropod /'sɔːrəpɒd, 'saʊr-/ ■ n. an apatosaurus, brachiosaurus, or similar huge herbivorous dinosaur with a long neck and tail and massive limbs.
– ORIGIN C19: from Greek *sauros* 'lizard' + *pous, pod-* 'foot'.

-saurus ■ comb. form forming genus names of reptiles, especially extinct ones: *stegosaurus*.
– ORIGIN cf. **-SAUR**.

saury /'sɔːri/ ■ n. (pl. **-ies**) a long slender-bodied edible marine fish with an elongated snout. [*Scomberesox saurus* (Atlantic), *Cololabis saira* (Pacific), and other species.]
– ORIGIN C18: from Greek *sauros* 'horse mackerel'.

sausage ■ n. **1** a short cylindrical tube of minced pork, beef, etc. encased in a skin, typically sold raw and grilled or fried before eating. ▸ a cylindrical tube of minced meat seasoned and cooked or preserved, sold mainly to be eaten cold in slices. **2** a sausage-shaped object.
– PHRASES **not a sausage** Brit. informal nothing at all.
– ORIGIN Middle English: from Old Northern French *saussiche*, from medieval Latin *salsicia*, from Latin *salsus* (see **SAUCE**).

sausage dog ■ n. informal term for **DACHSHUND**.

sausage meat ■ n. minced meat with spices and a binder such as cereal, used in sausages or as a stuffing.

sausage roll ■ n. a piece of sausage meat baked in a roll of pastry.

sausage tree ■ n. a tropical African tree with red bell-shaped flowers and pendulous sausage-shaped fruits. [*Kigelia africana*.]

sauté /'səʊteɪ/ ■ adj. fried quickly in a little hot fat. ■ n. **1** a dish cooked in such a way. **2** Ballet a jump off both feet, landing in the same position. ■ v. (**sautés**, **sautéed** or **sautéd**, **sautéing**) cook in such a way.

– ORIGIN C19: French, 'jumped', from *sauter*.

Sauternes /sə(ʊ)ˈtɜːn/ ■ n. a sweet white wine from Sauternes in the Bordeaux region of France.

Sauvignon /ˈsəʊvɪnjɒ̃/ (also **Sauvignon Blanc**) ■ n. a variety of white wine grape. ▸ a white wine made from this grape.
– ORIGIN from French.

savage ■ adj. 1 fierce, violent, and uncontrolled. ▸ cruel and vicious. 2 primitive; uncivilized. 3 (of a place) wild; uncultivated. ■ n. 1 a member of a people regarded as primitive and uncivilized. 2 a brutal or vicious person. ■ v. 1 (especially of a dog) attack ferociously. 2 criticize brutally.
– DERIVATIVES **savagely** adv. **savageness** n. **savagery** n.
– ORIGIN Middle English: from Old French *sauvage* 'wild', from Latin *silvaticus* 'of the woods', from *silva* 'a wood'.

savannah (also **savanna**) ■ n. a grassy plain in tropical and subtropical regions, with few trees.
– ORIGIN C16: from Spanish *sabana*, from Taino *zavana*.

savant /ˈsav(ə)nt/ ■ n. a learned person.
– ORIGIN C18: French, 'knowing (person)', from *savoir*.

savarin /ˈsavərɪn/ ■ n. a light ring-shaped cake made with yeast and soaked in liqueur-flavoured syrup.
– ORIGIN named after the French gastronome Anthelme Brillat-Savarin.

savate /səˈvɑːt/ ■ n. a French method of boxing using feet and fists.
– ORIGIN French, orig. denoting an ill-fitting shoe.

save[1] ■ v. 1 keep safe or rescue from harm or danger. ▸ prevent from dying. ▸ (in Christian use) preserve (a soul) from damnation. 2 store up for future use. ▸ preserve. 3 Computing keep (data) by moving a copy to a storage location. 4 (**save it**) N. Amer. informal be quiet. 5 avoid the need to use up or spend. ▸ avoid, lessen, or guard against. 6 prevent an opponent from scoring (a goal or point) or from winning (the game). ▸ Baseball (of a relief pitcher) preserve (a winning position) gained by another pitcher. ■ n. chiefly Soccer an act of preventing an opponent's scoring. ▸ Baseball an instance of saving a winning position.
– PHRASES **save one's breath** not bother to say something pointless. **save the day** (or **situation**) provide a solution to a problem. **save someone's skin** (or **neck** or **bacon**) rescue someone from difficulty.
– DERIVATIVES **savable** (also **saveable**) adj.
– ORIGIN Middle English: from Old French *sauver*, from late Latin *salvare*, from Latin *salvus* 'safe'.

save[2] ■ prep. & conj. formal or poetic/literary except; other than.
– ORIGIN Middle English: from Old French *sauf*, *sauve*, from Latin *salvus* 'safe', used in phrs such as *salvo jure*, *salva innocentia* 'with no violation of right or innocence'.

save as you earn ■ n. a method of saving money that carries tax privileges.

saveloy /ˈsavəlɔɪ/ ■ n. Brit. a seasoned red pork sausage, dried and smoked and sold ready to eat.
– ORIGIN C19: alteration of obsolete French *cervelat*; from Italian *cervellata*; cf. **CERVELAT**.

saver ■ n. 1 a person who regularly saves money through a bank or recognized scheme. 2 [in combination] something that prevents a particular resource from being used up. 3 a reduced travel fare.

saving ■ n. 1 an economy of or reduction in money, time, etc. 2 (**savings**) money saved, especially through a bank or official scheme. 3 Law a reservation; an exception. ■ adj. [in combination] preventing waste of a particular resource. ■ prep. except.
– ORIGIN Middle English: from **SAVE**[1]; the preposition prob. from **SAVE**[2].

saving grace ■ n. 1 the redeeming grace of God. 2 a redeeming quality or characteristic.

savings account ■ n. an interest-earning account with a bank or savings institution to which certain conditions may apply, such as a specified minimum balance.

savings and loan (also **savings and loan association**) ■ n. (in the US) an institution which accepts savings at interest and lends money to savers.

savings bank ■ n. a non-profit-making financial institution receiving small deposits at interest.

savings certificate ■ n. a document issued to savers guaranteeing fixed interest on a deposit.

saviour (US **savior**) ■ n. 1 a person who saves someone or something from danger or harm. 2 (**the/our Saviour**) (in Christianity) God or Jesus Christ.
– ORIGIN Middle English: from Old French *sauveour*, from eccles. Latin *salvator* (translating Greek *sōtēr*), from late Latin *salvare* 'to save'.

savoir faire /ˌsavwɑː ˈfɛː/ ■ n. the ability to act appropriately in social situations.
– ORIGIN C19: French, 'know how to do'.

savor ■ v.& n. US spelling of **SAVOUR**.

savory[1] ■ n. an aromatic plant of the mint family, used as a culinary herb. [*Satureja hortensis* (summer savory) and *S. montana* (winter savory).]
– ORIGIN Middle English: perhaps from Old English *sætherie* or from Latin *satureia*.

savory[2] ■ adj. & n. US spelling of **SAVOURY**.

savour (US **savor**) ■ v. 1 appreciate and enjoy the taste of (good food or drink). ▸ enjoy or appreciate to the full. 2 (**savour of**) have a suggestion or trace of. ■ n. 1 a characteristic taste, flavour, or smell. 2 a suggestion or trace.
– DERIVATIVES **savourless** adj.
– ORIGIN Middle English: from Latin *sapor*, from *sapere* 'to taste'.

savoury (US **savory**) ■ adj. 1 (of food) salty or spicy rather than sweet. 2 [usu. with neg.] morally wholesome or acceptable. ■ n. (pl. **-ies**) a savoury snack.
– DERIVATIVES **savouriness** n.
– ORIGIN Middle English: from Old French *savoure* 'tasty, fragrant', from Latin *sapor* 'taste'.

savoy ■ n. a cabbage of a hardy variety with densely wrinkled leaves.
– ORIGIN C16: from Savoy, an area of SE France.

savvy informal ■ n. shrewdness. ■ adj. (**-ier**, **-iest**) shrewd and knowledgeable.
– ORIGIN C18: orig. pidgin English imitating Spanish *sabe usted* 'you know'.

saw[1] ■ n. a hand tool for cutting wood, etc., typically with a long, thin serrated blade and operated using a backwards and forwards movement. ▸ a mechanical power-driven cutting tool with a toothed rotating disc or moving band. ■ v. (past part. **sawn** or **sawed**) cut, make, or form with a saw. ▸ cut as if with a saw, especially roughly. ▸ make rapid sawlike motions.
– ORIGIN Old English *saga*, of Germanic origin.

saw[2] past of **SEE**[1].

saw[3] ■ n. a proverb or maxim.
– ORIGIN Old English *sagu* 'a saying, speech', of Germanic origin.

sawbench ■ n. a circular saw mounted under a bench so that the blade projects up through a slot.

sawbones ■ n. (pl. same) informal, dated a doctor or surgeon.

saw doctor ■ n. a person or device that sharpens saws.

sawdust ■ n. powdery particles of wood produced by sawing.

sawed-off ■ adj. & n. another term for **SAWN-OFF**.

sawfish ■ n. (pl. same or **-fishes**) a large fish related to the rays, with a long flattened snout bearing large blunt teeth along each side. [Family Pristidae: several species.]

sawfly ■ n. (pl. **-flies**) an insect related to the wasps, with a saw-like tube used in laying eggs in plant tissues. [Suborder Symphyta: many species.]

sawgrass ■ n. chiefly N. Amer. a sedge with spiny-edged leaves. [Genus *Cladium*.]

sawhorse ■ n. N. Amer. a rack supporting wood for sawing.

sawmill ■ n. a factory in which logs are sawn by machine.

sawn past participle of **SAW**[1].

sawn-off (also **sawed-off**) ■ adj. 1 (of a gun) having a shortened barrel for ease of handling and a wider field of fire. 2 informal (of a garment) having been cut short.

sawtooth (also **sawtoothed**) ■ adj. **1** shaped like the teeth of a saw. **2** (of a waveform) showing a slow linear rise and rapid linear fall or vice versa.

sawyer ■ n. **1** a person who saws timber. **2** a large insect whose larvae bore tunnels in wood. [Genus *Monochamus* (a longhorn beetle) and other species.]
– ORIGIN Middle English: from SAW¹.

sax ■ n. informal **1** a saxophone. **2** a saxophone player.

saxe ■ n. a light blue colour with a greyish tinge.
– ORIGIN C19: from French, 'Saxony', the source of a dye of this colour.

saxhorn ■ n. a brass instrument with valves and a funnel-shaped mouthpiece, used mainly in military and brass bands.
– ORIGIN from the name of the Belgian instrument-makers Charles J. *Sax* and his son Antoine-Joseph 'Adolphe' *Sax* + HORN.

saxifrage /ˈsaksɪfreɪdʒ/ ■ n. a low-growing plant of poor soils, bearing small white, yellow, or red flowers and forming rosettes of succulent leaves or hummocks of mossy leaves. [Genus *Saxifraga*.]
– ORIGIN Middle English: from Old French *saxifrage* or late Latin *saxifraga* (*herba*), from Latin *saxum* 'rock' + *frangere* 'break'.

Saxon ■ n. **1** a member of a Germanic people that conquered and settled in much of southern England in the 5th–6th centuries. **2** a native of modern Saxony in Germany. **3** (**Old Saxon**) the West Germanic language of the ancient Saxons. **4** another term for OLD ENGLISH. **5** the Low German dialect of modern Saxony. ■ adj. **1** of or relating to the Anglo-Saxons, their language, or their period of dominance in England (5th–11th centuries). **2** of or relating to Saxony or the continental Saxons.
– ORIGIN Middle English: from Old French, from late Latin and Greek *Saxones* (pl.), of West Germanic origin.

saxony /ˈsaks(ə)ni/ ■ n. a fine kind of wool. ▸ a fine-quality cloth made from this wool.
– ORIGIN C19: from *Saxony*, a large region of Germany.

saxophone /ˈsaksəfəʊn/ ■ n. a member of a family of metal wind instruments with a reed like a clarinet, used especially in jazz and dance music.
– DERIVATIVES **saxophonic** /-ˈfɒnɪk/ adj. **saxophonist** /ˈsaksəfəʊnɪst/ n.
– ORIGIN from the name of Adolphe *Sax* (see SAXHORN) + -PHONE.

say ■ v. (**says**; past and past part. **said**) **1** utter words so as to convey information, an opinion, an instruction, etc. ▸ (of a text or symbol) convey information or instructions. ▸ (of a clock or watch) indicate (a time). ▸ (**be said**) be asserted or reported. ▸ recite (a speech or formula). **2** (**say something for**) present a consideration in favour of or excusing. **3** assume as a hypothesis. ■ exclam. N. Amer. informal used to express surprise or to draw attention to a remark or question. ■ n. an opportunity to state one's opinion or feelings. ▸ an opportunity to influence events.
– PHRASES **go without saying** be obvious. **I say!** Brit. dated used to express surprise or to draw attention to a remark. **say the word** give permission or instructions. **there is no saying** it is impossible to know. **they say** it is rumoured. **when all is said and done** when everything is taken into account.
– DERIVATIVES **sayable** adj. **-sayer** n.
– ORIGIN Old English, of Germanic origin.

SAYE ■ abbrev. save as you earn.

saying ■ n. a short, commonly known expression containing advice or wisdom; an adage or maxim.
– PHRASES **as** (or **so**) **the saying goes** (or **is**) used to introduce a proverb, cliché, etc.

say-so ■ n. informal **1** the power or action of deciding or allowing something. **2** mere assertion.

Sb ■ symb. the chemical element antimony.
– ORIGIN from Latin *stibium*.

SBS ■ abbrev. **1** sick building syndrome. **2** Special Boat Service.

SC ■ abbrev. Law senior counsel.

Sc ■ symb. the chemical element scandium.

S.C. ■ abbrev. small capitals.

sc. ■ abbrev. scilicet.

scab ■ n. **1** a dry, rough protective crust that forms over a cut or wound during healing. **2** mange or a similar skin disease in animals. ▸ any of a number of fungal diseases of plants in which rough patches develop, especially on apples and potatoes. **3** informal a person or thing regarded with contempt. ▸ a person who refuses to strike or who takes the place of a striking worker. ■ v. (**scabbed**, **scabbing**) **1** [usu. as adj. **scabbed**] become encrusted with a scab or scabs. **2** act or work as a scab.
– DERIVATIVES **scabbiness** n. **scabby** adj.
– ORIGIN Middle English: from Old Norse *skabb*.

scabbard /ˈskabəd/ ■ n. a sheath for the blade of a sword or dagger. ▸ a sheath for a gun or other weapon or tool.
– ORIGIN Middle English: from Anglo-Norman French *escalberc*, from a Germanic compound of words meaning 'cut' and 'protect'.

scabies /ˈskeɪbiːz/ ■ n. a contagious skin disease marked by itching and small raised red spots, caused by the itch mite.
– ORIGIN Middle English: from Latin, from *scabere* 'to scratch'.

scabious /ˈskeɪbiəs/ ■ n. a plant of the teasel family, with blue, pink, or white pincushion-shaped flowers. [*Scabiosa*, *Knautia*, and other genera.] ■ adj. affected with mange; scabby.
– ORIGIN Middle English: from Latin *scabiosus* 'rough, scabby' and medieval Latin *scabiosa* (*herba*) 'rough, scabby (plant)', formerly regarded as a cure for skin disease.

scabrous /ˈskeɪbrəs, ˈskabrəs/ ■ adj. **1** rough and covered with, or as if with, scabs. **2** salacious or sordid.
– DERIVATIVES **scabrously** adv. **scabrousness** n.
– ORIGIN C16: from French *scabreux* or late Latin *scabrosus*, from Latin *scaber* 'rough'.

scad ■ n. another term for JACK (in sense 10) or MAASBANKER.
– ORIGIN C17.

scads ■ pl. n. informal, chiefly N. Amer. a large number or quantity.
– ORIGIN C19.

scaffold /ˈskafəʊld, -f(ə)ld/ ■ n. **1** a raised wooden platform used formerly for public executions. **2** a structure made using scaffolding. ■ v. attach scaffolding to.
– DERIVATIVES **scaffolder** n.
– ORIGIN Middle English: from Old French (*e*)*schaffaut*, from the base of CATAFALQUE.

scaffolding ■ n. a temporary structure on the outside of a building, made of wooden planks and metal poles, used while building, repairing, or cleaning. ▸ the materials used in such a structure.

scag ■ n. variant spelling of SKAG.

scagliola /skalˈjəʊlə/ ■ n. imitation marble or other stone, made of plaster mixed with glue and dyes which is then painted or polished.
– ORIGIN C18: from Italian *scagliuola*, diminutive of *scaglia* 'a scale'.

scalable ■ adj. **1** able to be scaled or climbed. **2** able to be changed in size or scale. **3** technical able to be graded according to a scale.
– DERIVATIVES **scalability** n.

scalar /ˈskeɪlə/ Mathematics & Physics ■ adj. (of a quantity) having only magnitude, not direction. ■ n. a scalar quantity.
– ORIGIN C17: from Latin *scalaris*, from *scala* (see SCALE³).

scalar product ■ n. Mathematics a quantity (written as **a.b** or **ab**) equal to the product of the magnitudes of two vectors and the cosine of the angle between them.

scalawag ■ n. variant spelling of SCALLYWAG.

scald ■ v. **1** injure with very hot liquid or steam. **2** heat (milk or other liquid) to near boiling point. ▸ immerse briefly in boiling water. ▸ archaic clean by rinsing with boiling water. **3** cause to feel a searing sensation like that of boiling water on skin. ■ n. **1** a burn or other injury caused by hot liquid or steam. **2** any of a number of plant diseases which produce a similar effect to that of scalding, especially a disease of fruit marked by browning and

caused by excessive sunlight, bad storage conditions, or atmospheric pollution.
– PHRASES **like a scalded cat** at a very fast speed.
– DERIVATIVES **scalding** adj.
– ORIGIN Middle English: from Anglo-Norman French *escalder*, from late Latin *excaldare*, from Latin *ex-* 'thoroughly' + *calidus* 'hot'.

scale¹ ■ n. **1** each of the small overlapping horny or bony plates protecting the skin of fish and reptiles. ▸ each of numerous microscopic tile-like structures covering the wings of butterflies and moths. ▸ a rudimentary leaf, feather, or bract. **2** a thick dry flake of skin. **3** a flaky deposit, in particular: ▸ a white deposit formed in a kettle, boiler, etc. by the evaporation of water containing lime. ▸ tartar formed on teeth. ▸ a coating of oxide formed on heated metal. ■ v. **1** remove scale or scales from. **2** [often as noun **scaling**] (especially of the skin) form scales. ▸ come off in scales; flake off.
– PHRASES **the scales fall from someone's eyes** someone is no longer deceived. [with biblical ref. to Acts 9:18.]
– DERIVATIVES **-scaled** adj. **scaleless** adj. **scaler** n.
– ORIGIN Middle English: shortening of Old French *escale*, from the Germanic base of SCALE².

scale² ■ n. (usu. **scales**) an instrument for weighing, originally a simple balance but now usually a device with an electronic or other internal weighing mechanism. ▸ either of the dishes on a simple balance. ■ v. have a weight of.
– PHRASES **throw something on** (or **into**) **the scale** contribute something to one side of an argument or debate. **tip** (or **turn**) **the scales** (or **balance**) be the deciding factor; make the critical difference.
– ORIGIN Middle English: from Old Norse *skál* 'bowl', of Germanic origin.

scale³ ■ n. **1** a graduated range of values forming a standard system for measuring or grading something. ▸ a measuring instrument based on such a system. **2** the relative size or extent of something: *no one foresaw the scale of the disaster.* ▸ a ratio of size in a map, model, drawing, or plan. **3** Music an arrangement of the notes in any system of music in ascending or descending order of pitch. ■ v. **1** climb up or over (something high and steep). **2** represent or draw according to a common scale. ▸ (of a quantity or property) be variable according to a particular scale. **3** (**scale something back/down**) or **up** reduce (or increase) something in size, number, or extent.
– PHRASES **to scale** with a uniform reduction or enlargement: *not drawn to scale.* **in scale** in proportion to the surroundings.
– DERIVATIVES **scaler** n.
– ORIGIN Middle English: from Latin *scala* 'ladder', from the base of *scandere* 'to climb'.

scale armour ■ n. historical armour consisting of small overlapping plates of metal, leather, or horn.

scale board ■ n. very thin wood used (especially formerly) in bookbinding, making hatboxes, and backing pictures.

scale insect ■ n. a small bug which secretes a protective shield-like scale and spends its life attached to a single plant. [Family Coccidae: many species.]

scale leaf ■ n. Botany a small modified leaf, as on a rhizome or forming part of a bulb.

scalene /ˈskeɪliːn/ ■ adj. (of a triangle) having sides unequal in length.
– ORIGIN C17: from Greek *skalēnos* 'unequal'.

scalenus /skəˈliːnəs/ ■ n. (pl. **scaleni** /-naɪ/) any of several muscles extending from the neck to the first and second ribs.
– ORIGIN C18: from late Latin *scalenus* (*musculus*) (see SCALENE).

scallion /ˈskalɪən/ ■ n. a long-necked onion with a small bulb, in particular a shallot or spring onion.
– ORIGIN Middle English: from Anglo-Norman French *scaloun*, from Latin *Ascalonia* (*caepa*) '(onion) of *Ascalon*', a port in ancient Palestine.

scallop /ˈskɒləp, ˈskaləp/ ■ n. **1** an edible bivalve mollusc with a ribbed fan-shaped shell, which swims by rapidly opening and closing the shell valves. [*Chlamys*, *Pecten*, and other genera.] ▸ a scallop shell or similarly shaped dish used for baking or serving food. **2** each of a series of convex rounded projections forming an ornamental edging in material, knitting, etc. **3** another term for ESCALOPE. ■ v. (**scalloped**, **scalloping**) **1** [usu. as adj. **scalloped**] ornament with scallops. ▸ shape in the form of a scallop shell. **2** [usu. as noun **scalloping**] N. Amer. gather or dredge for scallops. **3** bake with milk or a sauce.
– ORIGIN Middle English: shortening of Old French *escalope*, prob. of Germanic origin.

scallywag (US also **scalawag**) ■ n. informal a mischievous person; a rascal.
– ORIGIN C19: perhaps orig. in the sense 'undersized cattle'.

scalp ■ n. **1** the skin covering the top and back of the head. **2** historical the scalp with the hair cut away from an enemy's head as a battle trophy, a former practice among American Indians. ■ v. **1** take the scalp of (an enemy). ▸ informal punish severely. **2** informal, chiefly N. Amer. resell (shares or tickets) at a large or quick profit.
– DERIVATIVES **scalper** n.
– ORIGIN Middle English: prob. of Scandinavian origin.

scalpel ■ n. a knife with a small sharp blade, as used by a surgeon.
– ORIGIN C18: from Latin *scalpellum*, diminutive of *scalprum* 'chisel', from *scalpere* 'to scratch'.

scaly ■ adj. (**-ier**, **-iest**) **1** covered in scales. **2** (of skin) dry and flaking.
– DERIVATIVES **scaliness** n.

scaly anteater ■ n. another term for PANGOLIN.

scam ■ n. informal a dishonest scheme; a fraud. ■ v. (**scammed**, **scamming**) swindle.
– DERIVATIVES **scammer** n.
– ORIGIN 1960s.

scamp ■ n. informal a mischievous person, especially a child.
– DERIVATIVES **scampish** adj.
– ORIGIN C18: from obsolete *scamp* 'rob on the highway', prob. from Middle Dutch *schampen* 'slip away'.

scamper ■ v. run with quick light steps, especially through fear or excitement. ■ n. an act of scampering.
– ORIGIN C17.

scampi ■ n. [treated as sing. or pl.] Norway lobsters when prepared or cooked, typically fried in breadcrumbs.
– ORIGIN from Italian.

Scamto (also **Scamtho**) ■ n. variant spelling of ISICAMTHO.

scan ■ v. (**scanned**, **scanning**) **1** look at quickly in order to identify relevant features or information. **2** traverse with a detector or an electromagnetic beam, especially to obtain an image. ▸ cause (a beam) to traverse across a surface or object. ▸ resolve (a picture) into its elements of light and shade in a pre-arranged pattern for the purposes of television transmission. ▸ convert (a document or picture) into digital form for storage or processing on a computer. **3** analyse the metre of (a line of verse) by reading with appropriate intonation or by examining the pattern of feet or syllables. ▸ (of verse) conform to metrical principles. ■ n. **1** an act of scanning. **2** a medical examination using a scanner. ▸ an image obtained by scanning or with a scanner.
– DERIVATIVES **scannable** adj.
– ORIGIN Middle English: from Latin *scandere* 'climb' (in late Latin 'scan (verses)'), by analogy with the raising and lowering of one's foot when marking rhythm.

scandal ■ n. an action or event regarded as morally or legally wrong and causing general public outrage. ▸ outrage, rumour, or gossip arising from this.
– DERIVATIVES **scandalous** adj. **scandalously** adv. **scandalousness** n.
– ORIGIN Middle English: from Old French *scandale*, from eccles. Latin *scandalum* 'cause of offence', from Greek *skandalon* 'snare, stumbling block'.

scandalize (also **-ise**) ■ v. shock or horrify by a violation of propriety or morality.

scandent /ˈskandənt/ ■ adj. having a climbing habit.
– ORIGIN C17: from Latin *scandent-*, *scandere* 'climb'.

Scandinavian ■ adj. of or relating to Scandinavia, its people, or their languages. ■ n. **1** a native or inhabitant of Scandinavia, or a person of Scandinavian descent. **2** the northern branch of the Germanic languages, comprising

scandium

Danish, Norwegian, Swedish, Icelandic, and Faroese (the language of the Faroe Islands), all descended from Old Norse.

scandium /ˈskandɪəm/ ■ n. the chemical element of atomic number 21, a soft silvery-white metal resembling the rare-earth elements. (Symbol: **Sc**)
– ORIGIN C19: from *Scandia*, contraction of *Scandinavia* (where minerals are found containing this element).

scanner ■ n. **1** Medicine a machine that examines the body through the use of radiation, ultrasound, or magnetic resonance imaging, as a diagnostic aid. **2** a device that scans documents and converts them into digital data.

scanning electron microscope ■ n. an electron microscope in which the surface of a specimen is scanned by a beam of electrons that are reflected to form an image.

scanning tunnelling microscope ■ n. a high-resolution microscope using neither light nor an electron beam, but with an ultra-fine tip able to reveal atomic and molecular details of surfaces.

scansion /ˈskanʃ(ə)n/ ■ n. the action of scanning a line of verse to determine its rhythm. ▸ the rhythm of a line of verse.
– ORIGIN C17: from Latin *scansio(n-)*, from *scandere* 'to climb'.

scant ■ adj. barely sufficient or adequate. ▸ barely amounting to the amount specified: *a scant two pounds.*
– DERIVATIVES **scantly** adv. **scantness** n.
– ORIGIN Middle English: from Old Norse *skamt*, from *skammr* 'short'.

scantling ■ n. **1** a timber beam of small cross section. ▸ the size to which a piece of timber or stone is measured and cut. **2** (often **scantlings**) a set of standard dimensions for parts of a structure, especially in shipbuilding.
– ORIGIN C16: from Old French *escantillon* 'sample'.

scanty ■ adj. (**-ier**, **-iest**) small or insufficient in quantity or amount. ▸ (of clothing) revealing; skimpy.
– DERIVATIVES **scantily** adv. **scantiness** n.

-scape ■ comb. form denoting a specified type of scene: *moonscape.*
– ORIGIN on the pattern of (*land*)*scape*.

scapegoat ■ n. a person who is blamed for the wrongdoings or mistakes of others. ■ v. make a scapegoat of.
– ORIGIN C16: from archaic *scape* 'escape' + GOAT.

scapegrace ■ n. archaic a mischievous person; a rascal.
– ORIGIN C19: from archaic *scape* 'escape' + GRACE, i.e. a person who lacks the grace of God.

scaphoid /ˈskafɔɪd/ ■ n. Anatomy a large carpal bone articulating with the radius below the thumb.
– ORIGIN C18: from Greek *skaphoeidēs*, from *skaphos* 'boat'.

scapula /ˈskapjʊlə/ ■ n. (pl. **scapulae** /-liː/ or **scapulas**) Anatomy technical term for SHOULDER BLADE.
– ORIGIN C16: sing. of Latin *scapulae* 'shoulder blades'.

scapular ■ adj. Anatomy & Zoology of or relating to the shoulder or shoulder blade. ▸ Ornithology denoting a feather covering the shoulder, growing above the region where the wing joins the body. ■ n. **1** a short monastic cloak covering the shoulders. **2** Medicine a bandage passing over and around the shoulders.
– ORIGIN C15: from late Latin *scapulare*, from *scapula* 'shoulder'.

scar ■ n. **1** a mark left on the skin or within body tissue after the healing of a wound or burn. ▸ a mark left at the point of separation of a leaf, frond, or other part from a plant. **2** a lasting effect left following an unpleasant experience. **3** a steep high cliff or rock outcrop. ■ v. (**scarred**, **scarring**) mark or be marked with a scar or scars.
– DERIVATIVES **scarless** adj.
– ORIGIN Middle English: from Old French *escharre*, from Greek *eskhara* 'scab'; sense 3 is from Old Norse *sker* 'low reef'.

scarab /ˈskarəb/ ■ n. **1** a large dung beetle, regarded as sacred in ancient Egypt. [*Scarabaeus sacer.*] ▸ any scarabaeid. **2** an ancient Egyptian gem in the form of a scarab beetle, engraved with hieroglyphs on the flat underside.
– ORIGIN C16: from Latin *scarabaeus*, from Greek *skarabeios*.

scarabaeid /ˌskarəˈbiːɪd/ ■ n. Entomology a beetle of a family (Scarabaeidae) including the scarab, chafers, and many dung beetles.

scarce ■ adj. (of a resource) insufficient for the demand. ▸ rare. ■ adv. archaic scarcely.
– PHRASES **make oneself scarce** informal leave a place, especially so as to avoid a difficult situation.
– DERIVATIVES **scarcely** adv. **scarceness** n. **scarcity** n.
– ORIGIN Middle English: from Anglo-Norman French *escars*, from a Romance word meaning 'selected'.

scare /skɛː/ ■ v. **1** cause great fear or nervousness in; frighten. ▸ (**scare someone away/off**) drive or keep someone away by fear. ▸ become scared. **2** (**scare something up**) informal, chiefly N. Amer. find or obtain something. ■ n. a sudden attack of fright. ▸ a period of general anxiety or alarm about something: *a bomb scare.*
– DERIVATIVES **scared** adj. **scarer** n.
– ORIGIN Middle English: from Old Norse *skirra* 'frighten', from *skjarr* 'timid'.

scarecrow ■ n. an object made to resemble a human figure, set up to scare birds away from a field where crops are growing.

scaredy-cat ■ n. informal a timid person.

scarf[1] ■ n. (pl. **scarves** or **scarfs**) a length or square of fabric worn around the neck or head.
– DERIVATIVES **scarfed** (also **scarved**) adj.
– ORIGIN C16: prob. from Old Northern French *escarpe*, prob. identical with Old French *escharpe* 'pilgrim's scrip'.

scarf[2] ■ v. join the ends of (two pieces of timber or metal) by bevelling or notching them so that they fit together. ■ n. an instance of scarfing; a joint made by scarfing.
– ORIGIN Middle English: prob. from Old Norse.

scarf[3] ■ v. N. Amer. informal eat or drink hungrily or enthusiastically.
– ORIGIN 1960s: var. of SCOFF[2].

scarify[1] /ˈskarɪfʌɪ, ˈskɛːrɪ-/ ■ v. (**-ies**, **-ied**) **1** cut and remove debris from (a lawn). **2** break up the surface of (soil or a road or pavement). **3** make shallow incisions in (the skin), as a medical procedure or traditional cosmetic practice. **4** criticize severely and hurtfully.
– DERIVATIVES **scarification** n. **scarifier** n.
– ORIGIN Middle English: from Old French *scarifier*, from Greek *skariphasthai* 'scratch an outline', from *skariphos* 'stylus'.

scarify[2] /ˈskɛːrɪfʌɪ/ ■ v. (**-ies**, **-ied**) [usu. as adj. **scarifying**] informal frighten.
– ORIGIN C18: from SCARE.

scarlatina /ˌskɑːləˈtiːnə/ (also **scarletina**) ■ n. another term for SCARLET FEVER.
– ORIGIN C19: from Italian *scarlattina*, from *scarlatto* 'scarlet'.

scarlet ■ n. a brilliant red colour.
– ORIGIN Middle English: shortening of Old French *escarlate*, from medieval Latin *scarlata*, from late Latin *sigillatus* 'decorated with small images', from *sigillum* 'small image'.

scarlet fever ■ n. an infectious bacterial disease affecting especially children, and causing fever and a scarlet rash.

scarletina ■ n. variant spelling of SCARLATINA.

scarlet river lily ■ n. another term for RIVER LILY.

scarlet runner ■ n. another term for RUNNER BEAN.

scarlet woman ■ n. a notoriously promiscuous or immoral woman.
– ORIGIN C19: orig. applied as a derogatory ref. to the Roman Catholic Church.

scarp ■ n. a very steep bank or slope; an escarpment. ■ v. cut or erode so as to form a scarp.
– ORIGIN C16: from Italian *scarpa*.

scarper ■ v. Brit. informal run away.
– ORIGIN C19: prob. from Italian *scappare* 'to escape', influenced by rhyming slang *Scapa Flow* 'go'.

scarp slope ■ n. Geology the steeper slope of a cuesta, cutting across the underlying strata. Often contrasted with DIP SLOPE.

Scart (also **SCART**) ■ n. a 21-pin socket used to connect video equipment.
– ORIGIN 1980s: acronym from French *Syndicat des Constructeurs des Appareils Radiorécepteurs et Téléviseurs*, the committee which designed the connector.

scarves plural form of SCARF¹.

scary ■ adj. (**-ier**, **-iest**) informal frightening; causing fear.
– DERIVATIVES **scarily** adv. **scariness** n.

scat¹ ■ v. (**scatted**, **scatting**) informal go away; leave.
– ORIGIN C19: perhaps an abbrev. of SCATTER, or from the sound of a hiss + *-cat*.

scat² ■ n. improvised jazz singing in which the voice is used in imitation of an instrument. ■ v. (**scatted**, **scatting**) sing in such a way.
– ORIGIN 1920s: prob. imitative.

scat³ ■ n. droppings, especially those of carnivorous mammals.
– ORIGIN 1950s: from Greek *skōr*, *skat-* 'dung'.

scathe /skeɪð/ archaic ■ v. harm; injure. ■ n. harm; injury.
– ORIGIN Middle English: from Old Norse *skathi* (n.), *skatha* (v.).

scathing ■ adj. witheringly scornful; severely critical.
– DERIVATIVES **scathingly** adv.

scatology /skəˈtɒlədʒi/ ■ n. a preoccupation with excrement and excretion.
– DERIVATIVES **scatological** adj.
– ORIGIN C19: from Greek *skōr*, *skat-* 'dung' + -LOGY.

scatter ■ v. throw in various random directions. ▸ separate or cause to separate and move off in different directions. ▸ (**be scattered**) occur or be found at various places rather than all together. ▸ Physics deflect or diffuse (electromagnetic radiation or particles). ■ n. a small, dispersed amount of something.
– DERIVATIVES **scatterer** n. **scattering** n.
– ORIGIN Middle English: prob. a var. of SHATTER.

scatterbrain ■ n. a person who tends to be disorganized and lacking in concentration.
– DERIVATIVES **scatterbrained** adj.

scatter cushion ■ n. a small cushion placed randomly so as to create a casual effect.

scatter diagram (also **scatter plot** or **scattergram**) ■ n. Statistics a graph in which the values of two variables are plotted along two axes, the pattern of the resulting points revealing any correlation present.

scattergun ■ n. 1 chiefly N. Amer. a shotgun. 2 (also **scattershot**) [as modifier] covering a broad range in a random and unsystematic way: *the scattergun approach*.

scatter rug ■ n. a small decorative rug designed to be placed with a casual effect.

scatty ■ adj. (**-ier**, **-iest**) informal absent-minded and disorganized.
– DERIVATIVES **scattily** adv. **scattiness** n.
– ORIGIN C20: abbrev. of *scatterbrained*.

scavenge /ˈskavɪn(d)ʒ/ ■ v. 1 search for and collect (anything usable) from discarded waste. ▸ search for (carrion) as food. 2 remove (combustion products) from an internal-combustion engine cylinder on the return stroke of the piston. 3 Chemistry combine with and remove (molecules, radicals, etc.) from a particular medium.
– ORIGIN C17: back-formation from SCAVENGER.

scavenger ■ n. 1 a person or animal that scavenges. 2 Chemistry a substance that reacts with and removes particular molecules, radicals, etc.
– ORIGIN C16: from Anglo-Norman French *scawager*, from Old Northern French *escauwer* 'inspect'; the term orig. denoted an officer who collected *scavage*, a toll on foreign merchants' goods.

ScD ■ abbrev. Doctor of Science.
– ORIGIN from Latin *scientiae doctor*.

scenario /sɪˈnɑːrɪəʊ/ ■ n. (pl. **-os**) 1 a written outline of a film, novel, or stage work giving details of the plot and individual scenes. ▸ a setting, in particular for a work of art or literature. 2 a postulated sequence or development of events.
– ORIGIN C19: from Italian, from Latin *scena* 'scene'.

scene ■ n. 1 the place where an incident in real life or fiction occurs or occurred. ▸ a landscape. ▸ a representation of an incident, or the incident itself: *scenes of 1930s America.* 2 a sequence of continuous action in a play, film, opera, etc. ▸ a subdivision of an act in a play, in which the time is continuous and the setting fixed. ▸ the pieces of scenery used in a play or opera. 3 a public display of emotion or anger. 4 a specified area of activity or interest.
– PHRASES **behind the scenes** out of public view. **change of scene** a move to different surroundings. **come** (or **appear** or **arrive**) **on the scene** arrive; appear. **hit** (or **make**) **the scene** US arrive; appear. **not one's scene** informal not something one enjoys or is interested in.
– ORIGIN C16: from Latin *scena*, from Greek *skēnē* 'tent, stage'.

scenery ■ n. 1 the natural features of a landscape considered in terms of their appearance, especially when picturesque. 2 the painted background used to represent the fictional surroundings on a stage or film set.
– ORIGIN C18: from Italian *scenario* (see SCENARIO).

scenic ■ adj. 1 of or relating to impressive or beautiful natural scenery: *the scenic route*. 2 of or relating to theatrical scenery. 3 (of a picture) representing an incident.
– DERIVATIVES **scenically** adv.

scenic railway ■ n. an attraction at a fair consisting of a miniature railway that goes past natural features and artificial scenery.

scenography ■ n. 1 the design and painting of theatrical scenery. 2 (in painting and drawing) the representation of objects in perspective.
– DERIVATIVES **scenographic** adj.

scent ■ n. 1 a distinctive smell, especially one that is pleasant. 2 pleasant-smelling liquid worn on the skin; perfume. 3 a trail indicated by the characteristic smell of an animal. ▸ a trail of evidence assisting someone in a search or investigation. ■ v. 1 impart a pleasant scent to. 2 discern by the sense of smell. ▸ sense the presence or imminence of: *the Premier scented victory last night*.
– DERIVATIVES **scented** adj. **scentless** adj.
– ORIGIN Middle English: from Old French *sentir* 'perceive, smell', from Latin *sentire*.

scent gland ■ n. an animal gland that secretes an odorous pheromone or defensive substance.

scent mark ■ n. (also **scent marking**) an odoriferous substance containing a pheromone that is deposited by a mammal from a scent gland or in the urine or faeces. ■ v. (**scent-mark**) (of a mammal) deposit a scent mark.

scepter ■ n. US spelling of SCEPTRE.

sceptic (US **skeptic**) ■ n. 1 a person inclined to question or doubt accepted opinions. ▸ a person who doubts the truth of Christianity and other religions; an atheist. 2 Philosophy a philosopher who denies the possibility of knowledge, or even rational belief, in certain spheres.
– DERIVATIVES **sceptical** adj. **scepticism** n.
– ORIGIN C16: from French *sceptique*, or from Greek *skeptikos*, from *skepsis* 'inquiry, doubt'.

sceptre (US **scepter**) ■ n. a staff carried by rulers on ceremonial occasions as a symbol of sovereignty.
– DERIVATIVES **sceptred** adj.
– ORIGIN Middle English: from Old French *ceptre*, from Greek *skēptron*, from *skēptein* 'lean on'.

Schadenfreude /ˈʃɑːd(ə)nˌfrɔɪdə/ ■ n. pleasure derived from another's misfortune.
– ORIGIN German, from *Schaden* 'harm' + *Freude* 'joy'.

schanz /skans, skɑːns/ (also **schans**) ■ n. S. African historical a defensive fortification of stones or earth.
– ORIGIN from Dutch, 'defensive works'.

schedule /ˈʃɛdjuːl, ˈskɛd-/ ■ n. 1 a plan for carrying out a process or procedure, giving lists of intended events and times. ▸ a timetable. 2 chiefly Law an appendix to a formal document or statute, especially as a list, table, or inventory. ■ v. 1 arrange or plan to take place at a particular time. 2 include in a schedule.
– PHRASES **to** (or **on** or **according to**) **schedule** on time; as planned.
– DERIVATIVES **schedular** adj. **scheduler** n.
– ORIGIN Middle English: from Old French *cedule*, from late Latin *schedula* 'slip of paper', diminutive of *scheda*, from Greek *skhedē* 'papyrus leaf'.

scheduled ■ adj. forming part of a schedule. ▶ (of an airline or flight) forming part of a regular service rather than specially chartered.

scheduled caste ■ n. the official name given in India to the untouchable caste, who are given special concessions in recognition of their disadvantaged status.

scheduled tribe ■ n. (in India) a category of people officially regarded as socially disadvantaged, who are granted special concessions in recognition of this.

scheelite /ˈʃiːlʌɪt/ ■ n. a fluorescent mineral, white when pure, which consists of calcium tungstate and is an important ore of tungsten.
– ORIGIN C19: from the name of the C18 Swedish chemist Karl W. *Scheele*.

schema /ˈskiːmə/ ■ n. (pl. **schemata** /-mətə/ or **schemas**) **1** technical a representation of a plan or theory in the form of an outline or model. **2** Logic a syllogistic figure. **3** (in Kantian philosophy) a conception of what is common to all members of a class; a general or essential type.
– ORIGIN C18: from Greek *skhēma* 'form, figure'.

schematic ■ adj. **1** (of a diagram or representation) symbolic and simplified. **2** (of thought, ideas, etc.) simplistic or formulaic in character: *a highly schematic reading of the play.* ■ n. technical a schematic diagram, in particular of an electric or electronic circuit.
– DERIVATIVES **schematically** adv.

schematism ■ n. arrangement or presentation according to a scheme or schema.

schematize (also **-ise**) ■ v. arrange or represent in a schematic form.
– DERIVATIVES **schematization** (also **-isation**) n.

scheme ■ n. **1** a systematic plan or arrangement for attaining some particular object or putting a particular idea into effect. ▶ a particular ordered system or arrangement: *a classical rhyme scheme.* **2** a secret or underhand plan; a plot. ■ v. **1** make a scheme, especially a devious one or with intent to do something wrong. **2** arrange according to a colour scheme.
– DERIVATIVES **schemer** n. **scheming** adj. & n. **schemingly** adv.
– ORIGIN C16: from Latin *schema* (see SCHEMA).

schemozzle ■ n. variant spelling of SHEMOZZLE.

scherzo /ˈskɛːtsəʊ/ ■ n. (pl. **scherzos** or **scherzi** /-tsi/) Music a vigorous, light, or playful composition, typically comprising a movement in a symphony or sonata.
– ORIGIN Italian, 'jest'.

Schiff base ■ n. Chemistry an organic compound having the structure R¹R²C=NR³ (where R¹,²,³ are alkyl groups and R¹ may be hydrogen).
– ORIGIN C19: named after the German chemist Hugo *Schiff*.

schilling /ˈʃɪlɪŋ/ ■ n. the former monetary unit of Austria.

schipperke /ˈskɪpəki, ˈʃɪp-, -kə/ ■ n. a small black tailless dog of a breed with a ruff of fur round its neck.
– ORIGIN from Dutch dialect, 'little boatman', with ref. to its use as a watchdog on barges.

schism /ˈsɪz(ə)m, ˈskɪz(ə)m/ ■ n. **1** a division between strongly opposed parties, caused by differences in opinion or belief. **2** the formal separation of a Church into two Churches or the secession of a group owing to doctrinal and other differences.
– ORIGIN Middle English: from Old French *scisme*, from Greek *skhisma* 'cleft', from *skhizein* 'to split'.

schismatic ■ adj. of, characterized by, or favouring schism. ■ n. chiefly historical (especially in the Christian Church) a person who promotes schism.
– DERIVATIVES **schismatically** adv.

schist /ʃɪst/ ■ n. Geology a coarse-grained metamorphic rock which consists of layers of different minerals and can be split into thin irregular plates.
– ORIGIN C18: from French *schiste*, from Greek *skhistos* 'split', from the base of *skhizein* 'cleave'.

schistose /ˈʃɪstəʊs/ ■ adj. Geology having a laminar structure like that of schist.
– DERIVATIVES **schistosity** n.

schistosome /ˈʃɪstə(ʊ)səʊm/ ■ n. Zoology & Medicine a parasitic flatworm which causes bilharzia in humans, infesting freshwater snails when immature and the blood vessels of birds and mammals when adult. [Genus *Schistosoma*.]
– ORIGIN C20: from Greek *skhistos* 'divided' + *sōma* 'body'.

schistosomiasis /ˌʃɪstə(ʊ)səˈmʌɪəsɪs/ ■ n. another term for BILHARZIA.

schizanthus /skɪtˈsanθəs/ ■ n. a South American plant of the nightshade family, with irregularly lobed showy flowers marked with contrasting colours. [Genus *Schizanthus*.]
– ORIGIN from Greek *skhizein* 'to split' + *anthos* 'flower'.

schizo ■ adj. & n. (pl. **-os**) informal schizophrenic.

schizo- ■ comb. form **1** divided; split: *schizocarp.* **2** relating to schizophrenia: *schizotype.*
– ORIGIN from Greek *skhizein* 'to split'.

schizocarp /ˈskʌɪzə(ʊ)kɑːp, ˈskɪts-/ ■ n. Botany a dry fruit that splits into single-seeded parts when ripe.
– ORIGIN C19: from SCHIZO- + Greek *karpos* 'fruit'.

schizogony /ʃʌɪˈzɒɡəni, skɪts-/ ■ n. Biology asexual reproduction by multiple fission, found in some protozoans.
– DERIVATIVES **schizogonous** adj.
– ORIGIN C19: from SCHIZO- + Greek *-gonia* 'production'.

schizoid /ˈskɪtsɔɪd, ˈskɪdz-/ ■ adj. denoting a personality type characterized by emotional aloofness and solitary habits. ▶ informal resembling schizophrenia in having contradictory elements; mad or crazy.

schizont /ˈʃʌɪzɒnt, ˈskɪ-/ ■ n. Biology (in certain sporozoan protozoans) a cell that divides by schizogony to form daughter cells.
– ORIGIN C20: from SCHIZO- + -ONT.

schizophrenia /ˌskɪtsə(ʊ)ˈfriːnɪə/ ■ n. a long-term mental disorder of a type involving a breakdown in the relation between thought, emotion, and behaviour, leading to faulty perception, inappropriate actions and feelings, and withdrawal from reality into fantasy and delusion.
– ORIGIN C20: from Greek *skhizein* 'to split' + *phrēn* 'mind'.

schizophrenic /ˌskɪtsə(ʊ)ˈfrɛnɪk/ ■ adj. **1** characterized by or suffering from schizophrenia. **2** characterized by mutually contradictory or inconsistent elements. ■ n. a person suffering from schizophrenia.
– DERIVATIVES **schizophrenically** adv.

schlemiel /ʃləˈmiːl/ ■ n. N. Amer. informal a stupid, awkward, or unlucky person.
– ORIGIN C19: from Yiddish *shlemiel*.

schlep /ʃlɛp/ (also **schlepp**) informal, chiefly S. African & N. Amer. ■ v. (**schlepped**, **schlepping**) **1** haul or carry with difficulty. **2** go or move reluctantly or with effort. ■ n. a tedious or difficult journey.
– ORIGIN C20: from Yiddish *shlepn* 'drag', from Middle High German *sleppen*.

schlieren /ˈʃliərən/ ■ pl. n. **1** technical discernible layers in a transparent material that differ from the surrounding material in density or composition. **2** Geology irregular streaks or masses in igneous rock.
– ORIGIN C19: from German *Schlieren*, pl. of *Schliere* 'streak'.

schlock /ʃlɒk/ ■ n. informal, chiefly N. Amer. cheap or inferior goods; trash.
– DERIVATIVES **schlocky** adj.
– ORIGIN C20: from Yiddish *shlak* 'an apoplectic stroke', *shlog* 'wretch, untidy person'.

schmaltz /ʃmɔːlts, ʃmalts/ ■ n. informal excessive sentimentality.
– DERIVATIVES **schmaltzy** adj. (**-ier**, **-iest**).
– ORIGIN 1930s: from Yiddish *shmaltz*, from German *Schmalz* 'dripping, lard'.

schmooze /ʃmuːz/ chiefly N. Amer. ■ v. chat; gossip. ▶ chat to (someone) in order to gain an advantage. ■ n. an intimate conversation.
– DERIVATIVES **schmoozer** n. **schmoozy** adj.
– ORIGIN C19: from Yiddish *shmuesn* 'converse, chat'.

schmuck /ʃmʌk/ ■ n. N. Amer. informal a foolish or contemptible person.
– ORIGIN C19: from Yiddish *shmok* 'penis'.

schnapps /ʃnaps/ ■ n. a strong alcoholic drink resembling gin.

– ORIGIN from German *Schnaps*, 'dram of liquor', from Low German and Dutch *snaps* 'mouthful'.

schnauzer /'ʃnauzə/ ■ n. a dog of a German breed with a close wiry coat and heavy whiskers round the muzzle.
– ORIGIN C20: from German, from *Schnauze* 'muzzle, snout'.

schnitzel /'ʃnɪtz(ə)l/ ■ n. a thin slice of veal or other pale meat, coated in breadcrumbs and fried.
– ORIGIN from German *Schnitzel*, 'slice'.

schnozz /ʃnɒz/ (also **schnozzle** or **schnozzola**) ■ n. N. Amer. informal a person's nose.
– ORIGIN 1940s: from Yiddish *shnoytz*, from German *Schnauze* 'snout'.

scholar ■ n. 1 a specialist in a particular branch of study, especially the humanities; a distinguished academic. ▶ chiefly archaic a person who is highly educated or has an aptitude for study. 2 a university student holding a scholarship. 3 archaic or dialect a student or pupil.
– ORIGIN Old English *scol(i)ere* 'student', from late Latin *scholaris*, from Greek *skholē* (see **SCHOOL**[1]).

scholarly ■ adj. involving academic study or dedicated to academic pursuits.
– DERIVATIVES **scholarliness** n.

scholarship ■ n. 1 academic achievement; learning of a high level. 2 a grant made to support a student's education, awarded on the basis of academic or other achievement.

scholastic ■ adj. 1 of or concerning schools and education. 2 Philosophy & Theology of or relating to medieval scholasticism. ▶ typical of scholasticism in being pedantic or overly subtle. ■ n. Philosophy & Theology, historical an adherent of scholasticism; a schoolman.
– DERIVATIVES **scholastically** adv.
– ORIGIN C16: from Greek *skholastikos* 'studious', from *skholazein*, from *skholē* (see **SCHOOL**[1]).

scholasticism /skə'lastɪˌsɪz(ə)m/ ■ n. 1 the system of theology and philosophy taught in medieval European universities, based on Aristotelian logic and the writings of the early Christian Fathers and having a strong emphasis on tradition and dogma. 2 narrow-minded insistence on traditional doctrine.

scholiast /'skəʊlɪast/ ■ n. historical a commentator on ancient or classical literature.
– DERIVATIVES **scholiastic** adj.

scholium /'skəʊlɪəm/ ■ n. (pl. **scholia** /-lɪə/) historical a marginal note made by a scholiast.
– ORIGIN C16: from Greek *skholion*, from *skholē* 'learned discussion'.

school[1] ■ n. 1 an institution for educating children. ▶ a day's work at school; lessons. 2 any institution at which instruction is given in a particular discipline: *a dancing school.* ▶ N. Amer. informal a university. ▶ a department or faculty of a university: *the School of Dental Medicine.* 3 a group of people sharing similar ideas, methods, or style. ▶ a specified style, approach, or method. ■ v. 1 S. African & N. Amer. send to school; educate. 2 train in a particular skill or activity. ▶ Riding train (a horse).
– PHRASES **school of thought** a particular way of thinking.
– ORIGIN Old English *scōl, scolu*, from Greek *skholē* 'leisure, philosophy, lecture-place', reinforced in Middle English by Old French *escole*.

school[2] ■ n. a large group of fish or sea mammals. ■ v. (of fish or sea mammals) form a school.
– ORIGIN Middle English: from Middle Low German, Middle Dutch *schōle*, of West Germanic origin.

schoolboy (or **schoolgirl**) ■ n. a boy (or girl) attending school.

schoolchild ■ n. (pl. -**children**) a child attending school.

schooler ■ n. [in combination] a pupil or student of a particular level or status: *a pre-schooler*.

schoolhouse ■ n. 1 a building used as a school, especially in a rural community. 2 Brit., chiefly historical a house adjoining a school, lived in by the schoolteacher.

schooling ■ n. 1 education received at school. 2 Riding the training of a horse on the flat or over fences.

schoolmarm ■ n. a schoolmistress, especially one regarded as prim and strict.
– DERIVATIVES **schoolmarmish** adj.

schoolmaster ■ n. a male teacher in a school.

Scientology

– DERIVATIVES **schoolmastering** n. **schoolmasterly** adj.

schoolmate ■ n. informal a fellow pupil.

schoolmistress ■ n. a female teacher in a school.

schoolteacher ■ n. a person who teaches in a school.
– DERIVATIVES **schoolteaching** n.

schooner /'skuːnə/ ■ n. 1 a sailing ship with two or more masts, typically with the foremast smaller than the mainmast. 2 Brit. a large glass for sherry.
– ORIGIN C18: perhaps from dialect *scun* 'skim along', influenced by Dutch words beginning with *sch-*.

schottische /ʃɒ'tiːʃ, 'ʃɒtɪʃ/ ■ n. a dance resembling a slow polka.
– ORIGIN C19: from German *der schottische Tanz* 'the Scottish dance'.

schuss /ʃʊs/ ■ n. a straight downhill run on skis. ■ v. perform a schuss.
– ORIGIN 1930s: from German *Schuss* 'shot'.

schwa /ʃwɑː/ ■ n. Phonetics the unstressed central vowel (as in *a* moment *a*go), represented by the symbol /ə/ in the International Phonetic Alphabet.
– ORIGIN C19: from Hebrew *šĕwā*.

schwarma /'ʃwɑːmə/ (also **shwarma**) ■ n. a type of sandwich of Middle Eastern origin, consisting of spiced meat cooked on a spit and served in pita bread.
– ORIGIN colloquial Arabic *šāwirma*, from Turkish *çivirme* 'sliced meat roasted on a spit' from *çevirmek* 'turn, rotate'.

sciagraphy /sʌɪ'agrəfi/ (also **skiagraphy**) ■ n. the use of shading to show perspective in architectural or technical drawing.
– DERIVATIVES **sciagram** n. **sciagraph** n. & v. **sciagraphic** adj.
– ORIGIN C16: from French *sciagraphie*, from Greek *skiagraphia*, from *skia* 'shadow'.

sciatic /sʌɪ'atɪk/ ■ adj. 1 of or relating to the hip. 2 of or affecting the sciatic nerve. ▶ suffering from or liable to sciatica.
– DERIVATIVES **sciatically** adv.
– ORIGIN C16: from French *sciatique*, from Greek *iskhiadikos* 'relating to the hips', from *iskhion* 'hip joint'.

sciatica ■ n. pain affecting the back, hip, and outer side of the leg, caused by compression of a spinal nerve root in the lower back.
– ORIGIN Middle English: from late Latin *sciatica* (*passio*) '(affliction) of sciatica' (see **SCIATIC**).

sciatic nerve ■ n. Anatomy a major nerve extending from the lower end of the spinal cord down the back of the thigh.

science ■ n. 1 the intellectual and practical activity encompassing the systematic study of the structure and behaviour of the physical and natural world through observation and experiment. 2 a systematically organized body of knowledge on any subject.
– ORIGIN Middle English: from Latin *scientia*, from *scire* 'know'.

science fiction ■ n. fiction based on imagined future worlds portraying scientific or technological changes.

science park ■ n. an area devoted to scientific research or the development of science-based industries.

scienter /sʌɪ'entə/ ■ n. Law the fact of an act having been done knowingly, especially as grounds for civil damages.
– ORIGIN Latin, from *scire* 'know'.

scientific ■ adj. 1 of, relating to, or based on science. 2 systematic; methodical.
– DERIVATIVES **scientifically** adv. **scientificity** n.
– ORIGIN C16: from French *scientifique* or late Latin *scientificus* 'producing knowledge', from *scientia* (see **SCIENCE**).

scientism ■ n. thought or expression regarded as characteristic of scientists. ▶ excessive belief in the power of scientific knowledge and techniques.
– DERIVATIVES **scientistic** adj.

scientist ■ n. a person who is studying or has expert knowledge of one or more of the natural or physical sciences.

Scientology ■ n. trademark a religious system based on the

sci-fi

seeking of self-knowledge and spiritual fulfilment through graded courses of study and training.
- DERIVATIVES **Scientologist** n.
- ORIGIN from Latin *scientia* 'knowledge' + -LOGY.

sci-fi ■ n. informal short for SCIENCE FICTION.

scilicet /'saɪlɪsɛt, 'skiːlɪkɛt/ ■ adv. that is to say; namely (introducing a missing word or an explanation).
- ORIGIN Latin, from *scire licet* 'one is permitted to know'.

scilla /'sɪlə/ ■ n. a plant of the lily family which typically bears small blue star- or bell-shaped flowers and glossy strap-like leaves. [Genus *Scilla*.]
- ORIGIN from Latin *scilla* 'sea onion', from Greek *skilla*.

scimitar /'sɪmɪtə/ ■ n. a short sword with a curved blade that broadens towards the point, used originally in Eastern countries.
- ORIGIN C16: from French *cimeterre* or Italian *scimitarra*.

scintigraphy /sɪn'tɪgrəfi/ ■ n. Medicine a technique in which a scintillation counter or similar detector is used with a radioactive tracer to obtain an image of a bodily organ.
- DERIVATIVES **scintigraphic** adj.
- ORIGIN 1950s: from SCINTILLATION + -GRAPHY.

scintilla /sɪn'tɪlə/ ■ n. a tiny trace or amount: *not a scintilla of doubt*.
- ORIGIN C17: Latin, 'spark'.

scintillate /'sɪntɪleɪt/ ■ v. emit flashes of light; sparkle.
▶ Physics fluoresce momentarily when struck by a charged particle or photon.
- DERIVATIVES **scintillant** adj. & n.
- ORIGIN C17: from Latin *scintillare* 'to sparkle', from *scintilla* 'spark'.

scintillating ■ adj. 1 sparkling or shining brightly. 2 brilliant and exciting: *his scintillating wit*.
- DERIVATIVES **scintillatingly** adv.

scintillation ■ n. 1 a flash of light. ▶ the process or state of emitting flashes. 2 Physics a small flash of visible or ultraviolet light emitted by fluorescence in a phosphor when struck by a charged particle or high-energy photon. 3 Astronomy the twinkling of the stars, caused by the earth's atmosphere diffracting starlight unevenly.

scintillator ■ n. Physics 1 a material that scintillates. 2 a detector for charged particles and gamma rays in which scintillations are amplified by a photomultiplier, giving an electrical output signal.

scion /'saɪən/ ■ n. 1 (US also **cion**) a young shoot or twig of a plant, especially one cut for grafting or rooting. 2 a descendant of a notable family or one with a long lineage.
- ORIGIN Middle English: from Old French *ciun* 'shoot, twig'.

scirocco ■ n. variant spelling of SIROCCO.

scission /'sɪʃ(ə)n/ ■ n. 1 a division or split; a schism. 2 chiefly Biochemistry breakage of a chemical bond.
- ORIGIN Middle English: from late Latin *scissio(n-)*, from *scindere* 'cut, cleave'.

scissor ■ v. 1 cut with scissors. 2 move or cause to move in a way resembling the action of scissors.

scissor hold (also **scissors hold**) ■ n. Wrestling a hold in which the opponent's body or head is gripped between the legs which are then locked at the feet to apply pressure.

scissors ■ pl. n. 1 (also **a pair of scissors**) an instrument used for cutting cloth and paper, consisting of two crossing blades pivoted in the middle and operated by thumb and fingers inserted in rings at each end. 2 (also **scissor**) [as modifier] denoting an action in which two things cross each other or open and close like a pair of scissors: *a scissor kick*.
- ORIGIN Middle English: from Old French *cisoires*, from late Latin *cisorium* 'cutting instrument'; the *sc-* spelling arose by association with the Latin stem *sciss-* 'cut'.

sclera /'sklɪərə/ ■ n. Anatomy the white outer layer of the eyeball.
- DERIVATIVES **scleral** adj.
- ORIGIN C19: from Greek *sklēros* 'hard'.

Scleractinia /ˌsklɛrak'tɪnɪə/ ■ pl. n. Zoology an order of coelenterates that comprises the stony corals.
- DERIVATIVES **scleractinian** n. & adj.

- ORIGIN from Greek *sklēros* 'hard' + *aktis, aktin-* 'ray'.

sclerenchyma /sklɪə'rɛŋkɪmə, sklɛ-/ ■ n. Botany strengthening tissue in a plant, formed from cells with thickened walls.
- DERIVATIVES **sclerenchymatous** adj.
- ORIGIN C19: from Greek *sklēros* 'hard' + *enkhuma* 'infusion'.

sclerite /'sklɪərʌɪt, 'sklɛ-/ ■ n. Zoology a component section of an exoskeleton, especially each of the plates forming the skeleton of an arthropod.
- ORIGIN C19: from Greek *sklēros* 'hard'.

scleritis /sklɪə'rʌɪtɪs, sklɛ-/ ■ n. Medicine inflammation of the sclera of the eye.

sclero- /'sklɪərəʊ/ ■ comb. form hard; hardened; hardening: *sclerotherapy*.
- ORIGIN from Greek *sklēros* 'hard'.

scleroderma /ˌsklɪərə'dəːmə/ ■ n. Medicine a chronic hardening and contraction of the skin and connective tissue, either locally or throughout the body.

sclerophyll /'sklɪərəfɪl, 'sklɛ-/ ■ n. Botany a woody plant with evergreen leaves that are tough and thick in order to reduce water loss.
- DERIVATIVES **sclerophyllous** /-'rɒfɪləs/ adj.
- ORIGIN C20: from Greek *sklēros* 'hard' + *phullon* 'leaf'.

scleroprotein /ˌsklɪərə(ʊ)'prəʊtiːn, ˌsklɛ-/ ■ n. Biochemistry an insoluble structural protein such as keratin, collagen, or elastin.

sclerose /sklɪə'rəʊs, sklə-, 'sklɪə-/ ■ v. Medicine [usu. as adj. **sclerosed** or **sclerosing**] affect with sclerosis.

sclerosis /sklɪə'rəʊsɪs, sklə-/ ■ n. Medicine 1 abnormal hardening of body tissue. 2 (in full **multiple sclerosis**) a chronic, typically progressive disease involving damage to the sheaths of nerve cells in the brain and spinal cord, whose symptoms may include numbness, impairment of speech and muscular coordination, blurred vision, and severe fatigue.
- ORIGIN Middle English: from Greek *sklērōsis*, from *sklēroun* 'harden'.

sclerotherapy /ˌsklɪərə(ʊ)'θɛrəpi, ˌsklɛ-/ ■ n. Medicine the treatment of varicose blood vessels by the injection of an irritant which causes inflammation, coagulation of blood, and narrowing of the blood vessel wall.

sclerotic /sklɪə'rɒtɪk, sklə-/ ■ adj. 1 Medicine of or having sclerosis. 2 Anatomy of or relating to the sclera. 3 rigid; unable to adapt: *sclerotic management*. ■ n. another term for SCLERA.

sclerotin /'sklɪərətɪn, 'sklɛ-/ ■ n. Biochemistry a structural protein which forms the cuticles of insects and is hardened and darkened by a natural tanning process.
- ORIGIN 1940s: from SCLERO-, on the pattern of *keratin*.

sclerotized /'sklɪərətʌɪzd, 'sklɛ-/ (also **-ised**) ■ adj. Entomology hardened by conversion into sclerotin.
- DERIVATIVES **sclerotization** (also **-isation**) n.

scoff[1] ■ v. speak about something in a scornfully derisive way. ■ n. an expression of scornful derision.
- DERIVATIVES **scoffer** n. **scoffing** adj. **scoffingly** adv.
- ORIGIN Middle English: perhaps of Scandinavian origin.

scoff[2] informal ■ v. eat quickly and greedily. ■ n. food.
- ORIGIN C18: the verb a var. of Scots and dialect *scaff*; the noun from Afrikaans *schoff*, representing Dutch *schoft* 'quarter of a day, meal'.

scold ■ v. angrily remonstrate with or rebuke. ■ n. archaic a woman who nags or grumbles constantly.
- DERIVATIVES **scolder** n.
- ORIGIN Middle English: prob. from Old Norse *skáld* 'skald'.

scoliosis /ˌskɒlɪ'əʊsɪs, ˌskəʊ-/ ■ n. Medicine abnormal lateral curvature of the spine.
- DERIVATIVES **scoliotic** adj.
- ORIGIN C18: from Greek, from *skolios* 'bent'.

scollop ■ n. & v. archaic spelling of SCALLOP.

sconce ■ n. a candle holder attached to a wall with an ornamental bracket.
- ORIGIN Middle English: from Old French *esconse* 'lantern' or medieval Latin *sconsa* from Latin *absconsa* (*laterna*) 'dark (lantern)', from *abscondere* 'to hide'.

scone /skɒn, skəʊn/ ■ n. a small unsweetened or lightly sweetened cake made from flour, fat, and milk.

–ORIGIN C16: perhaps from Middle Dutch *schoon(broot)* 'fine (bread)'.

scoop ■ n. **1** a utensil resembling a spoon, having a short handle and a deep bowl, used for extracting liquids or substances from a container. ▶ the bowl-shaped part of a digging machine or dredger. ▶ a long-handled spoon-like surgical instrument. **2** informal a piece of news published or broadcast in advance of being released by other newspapers or broadcast stations. ▶ **(the scoop)** N. Amer. the latest news. ■ v. **1** pick up with a scoop. ▶ create (a hollow) with or as if with a scoop. ▶ pick or gather up in a swift, fluid movement: *he laughed and scooped her up in his arms.* **2** informal publish a scoop. **3** win.
–DERIVATIVES **scooper** n. **scoopful** n. (pl. **-fuls**).
–ORIGIN Middle English: from Middle Dutch, Middle Low German *schōpe* 'waterwheel bucket.'

scoop neck ■ n. a deeply curved wide neckline on a woman's garment.
–DERIVATIVES **scoop-necked** adj.

scoot ■ v. informal go or leave somewhere quickly. ▶ move or cause to move with a rapid, darting motion.
–ORIGIN C18.

scooter ■ n. **1** (also **motor scooter**) a light two-wheeled motorcycle. **2** any small light vehicle able to travel quickly across water or snow. **3** a child's toy consisting of a footboard mounted on two wheels and a long steering handle, propelled by pushing one foot against the ground. ■ v. travel or ride on a scooter.
–DERIVATIVES **scooterist** n.

scope[1] ■ n. **1** the extent of the area or subject matter that something deals with or to which it is relevant: *these complex matters are beyond the scope of this book.* **2** the opportunity or possibility for doing something. **3** Nautical the length of cable extended when a ship rides at anchor.
–ORIGIN C16: from Italian *scopo* 'aim', from Greek *skopos* 'target'.

scope[2] ■ n. informal a telescope, microscope, or other device having a name ending in *-scope.* ■ v. N. Amer. informal look at carefully; scan. ▶ assess; weigh up.

-scope ■ comb. form denoting an instrument for observing or examining: *telescope.*
–DERIVATIVES **-scopic** comb. form in corresponding adjectives.
–ORIGIN from Greek *skopein* 'look at'.

scops owl /skɒps/ ■ n. a small owl with ear tufts. [*Otus senegalensis* (Africa) and related species.]
–ORIGIN C18: from *Scops* (former genus name), from Greek *skōps.*

-scopy ■ comb. form indicating observation or examination: *microscopy.*
–ORIGIN from Greek *skopia* 'observation', from *skopein* 'examine, look at'.

scorch ■ v. **1** become burnt or cause to become burnt on the surface or edges. ▶ [often as adj. **scorched**] cause to become dried out and withered as a result of extreme heat. **2** informal move very fast. ■ n. the burning or charring of the surface of something.
–DERIVATIVES **scorching** adj. **scorchingly** adv.
–ORIGIN Middle English: perhaps rel. to Old Norse *skorpna* 'be shrivelled'.

scorched earth policy ■ n. a military strategy of burning or destroying all crops and resources that might be of use to an enemy force.

scorcher ■ n. informal **1** a day or period of very hot weather. **2** Brit. a remarkable or powerful example of something: *a scorcher of a story.*

score ■ n. **1** the number of points, goals, runs, etc. achieved in a game by an individual. ▶ a mark or grade. **2** (**the score**) informal the state of affairs; the real facts. **3** (pl. same) a group or set of twenty. ▶ a large amount or number: *he sent scores of letters to friends.* **4** a written representation of a musical composition showing all the vocal and instrumental parts. **5** a notch or line cut or scratched into a surface. **6** informal an act of buying illegal drugs. ▶ informal the proceeds of a crime. ■ v. **1** gain (a point, goal, run, etc.) in a competitive game. ▶ be worth (a number of points). ▶ record the score during a game.
▶ Baseball cause (a teammate) to score. **2** orchestrate or arrange (a piece of music). ▶ compose the music for (a film or play). **3** cut or scratch a mark or notch on (a surface).
▶ (**score something out/through**) delete text by drawing a line through it. **4** informal secure (a success or an advantage). ▶ be successful. ▶ succeed in obtaining (illegal drugs). ▶ succeed in attracting a sexual partner. **5** (**score off**) or **score points off** informal outdo or humiliate, especially in an argument.
–PHRASES **know the score** informal be aware of the essential facts. **on the score of** Brit. because of. **on that** (or **this**) **score** so far as that (or this) is concerned. **settle** (or **pay**) **a** (or **the**) **score** take revenge on someone.
–DERIVATIVES **scoreless** adj. **scorer** n.
–ORIGIN Old English *scoru* 'set of twenty', from Old Norse *skor* 'notch, twenty', of Germanic origin; verb from Old Norse *skora* 'make an incision'.

scorecard ■ n. **1** (also **scoresheet** or **scorebook**) a card, sheet, or book in which scores are entered. **2** a card listing the names, positions, etc. of players in a team.

scoreline ■ n. the number of points or goals scored in a match.

scoria /ˈskɔːrɪə/ ■ n. (pl. **scoriae** /-riː/) **1** basaltic lava ejected as fragments from a volcano, typically with a frothy texture. **2** slag separated from molten metal during smelting.
–DERIVATIVES **scoriaceous** /-ˈeɪʃəs/ adj.
–ORIGIN Middle English: from Greek *skōria* 'refuse', from *skōr* 'dung'.

scorn ■ n. contempt or disdain expressed openly. ■ v. **1** express scorn for. **2** reject in a contemptuous way.
–DERIVATIVES **scorner** n. **scornful** adj. **scornfully** adv. **scornfulness** n.
–ORIGIN Middle English: shortening of Old French *escarn* (n.), *escharnir* (v.), of Germanic origin.

Scorpio ■ n. Astrology the eighth sign of the zodiac (the Scorpion), which the sun enters about 23 October.
–DERIVATIVES **Scorpian** n. & adj.
–ORIGIN from Latin.

scorpion ■ n. **1** an arachnid with lobster-like pincers and a poisonous sting at the end of its tail. [Order Scorpiones.]
▶ used in names of similar arachnids and insects, e.g. false scorpion. **2** (**the Scorpions**) (in South Africa) the popular name for the Directorate of Special Operations, a special investigating unit focusing on organized crime and dissolved in 2009. ▶ used in names of governmental investigative units specializing in crime affecting specific sectors, e.g. the environment or water affairs: *Green Scorpions, Blue Scorpions.*
–ORIGIN Middle English: from Latin *scorpio(n-),* based on Greek *skorpios* 'scorpion'.

scorpionfish ■ n. (pl. same or **-fishes**) a marine fish, typically red, with spines on the head that are sometimes venomous. [Family Scorpaenidae: many species.]

scorpion fly ■ n. a slender predatory insect with membranous wings, the males of which have a swollen abdomen curved up like a scorpion's sting. [Family Panorpidae.]

scorzonera /ˌskɔːzə(ʊ)ˈnɪərə/ ■ n. a plant of the daisy family with tapering purple-brown edible roots, which can be eaten as a vegetable. [*Scorzonera hispanica.*]
–ORIGIN C17: from Italian, from *scorzone,* from an alteration of medieval Latin *curtio(n-)* 'venomous snake' (against whose venom the plant may have been regarded as an antidote).

Scot ■ n. a native of Scotland or a person of Scottish descent.
–ORIGIN Old English *Scottas* (pl.), from late Latin *Scottus.*

Scotch ■ adj. old-fashioned term for **SCOTTISH**. ■ n. **1** short for **SCOTCH WHISKY**. **2** [as pl. n. **the Scotch**] dated the people of Scotland.
–ORIGIN C16: contraction of **SCOTTISH**.

scotch ■ v. decisively put an end to.
–ORIGIN C17.

Scotch broth ■ n. a traditional Scottish soup made from meat stock with pearl barley and vegetables.

Scotch call (also **Scotch ring**) ■ n. S. African informal a pre-arranged telephone call that is left unanswered and ended after a few rings, which acts as a message or signal to the recipient.

scotch cart ■ n. S. African a small horse- or ox-drawn

tip-up cart, used for carrying rubble, refuse, etc.
– ORIGIN adaptation of S. African Dutch *skotskar*, from German *Schuttkarren* 'dustcart'.

Scotch egg ■ n. a hard-boiled egg enclosed in sausage meat, rolled in breadcrumbs, and fried.

Scotchgard ■ n. trademark a preparation for giving a waterproof stain-resistant finish to textiles and other materials.

Scotchlite ■ n. trademark a light-reflecting material containing a layer of minute glass lenses.

Scotch mist ■ n. a thick drizzly mist of a kind common in the Scottish Highlands.

Scotch ring ■ n. S. African informal another term for SCOTCH CALL.

Scotch tape ■ n. trademark, chiefly N. Amer. transparent adhesive tape.

Scotch whisky ■ n. whisky distilled in Scotland.

scot-free ■ adv. without suffering any punishment or injury.
– ORIGIN from archaic *scot* denoting a tax, from Old Norse *skot* 'a shot'.

scotia /ˈskəʊʃə/ ■ n. Architecture a concave moulding, especially at the base of a column.
– ORIGIN C16: from Greek *skotia*, from *skotos* 'darkness', with ref. to the shadow produced.

Scoticism ■ n. variant spelling of SCOTTICISM.

scotoma /skɒˈtəʊmə, skə(ʊ)-/ ■ n. (pl. **scotomas** or **scotomata** /-mətə/) Medicine a partial loss of vision or blind spot in an otherwise normal visual field.
– ORIGIN C16: from Greek *skotōma*, from *skotoun* 'darken', from *skotos* 'darkness'.

Scots ■ adj. another term for SCOTTISH. ■ n. the form of English used in Scotland.

Scotsman[1] (or **Scotswoman**) ■ n. (pl. **-men** or **-women**) a native or national of Scotland or a person of Scottish descent.

Scotsman[2] ■ n. an edible sea bream of the east coast of southern Africa. [*Polysteganus praeorbitalis*.]

Scots pine ■ n. a pine tree, now widely planted for commercial use, forming the dominant tree of the old Caledonian pine forest of the Scottish Highlands. [*Pinus sylvestris*.]

Scotticism /ˈskɒtɪsɪz(ə)m/ (also **Scoticism**) ■ n. a characteristically Scottish phrase, word, or idiom.

Scottie ■ n. informal 1 (also **Scottie dog**) a Scottish terrier. 2 a nickname for a Scotsman.

Scottish ■ adj. of or relating to Scotland or its people. ■ n. [as pl. n. **the Scottish**] the people of Scotland.
– DERIVATIVES **Scottishness** n.

Scottish Blackface ■ n. a long-coated sheep of a hardy breed developed in upland areas of northern Britain.

Scottish Nationalist ■ n. a member or supporter of Scottish nationalism or of the Scottish National Party.

Scottish terrier ■ n. a small terrier of a rough-haired short-legged breed.

scoundrel ■ n. a dishonest or unscrupulous person; a rogue.
– DERIVATIVES **scoundrelism** n. **scoundrelly** adj.
– ORIGIN C16.

scour[1] ■ v. 1 clean or brighten by vigorous rubbing, typically with an abrasive or detergent. ▸ remove (dirt or unwanted matter) by rubbing in such a way. 2 (of running water) erode (a channel or pool). 3 (of livestock) suffer from diarrhoea. ■ n. 1 the action of scouring or the state of being scoured. 2 (also **scours**) diarrhoea in livestock, especially cattle and pigs.
– DERIVATIVES **scourer** n.
– ORIGIN Middle English: from Middle Dutch, Middle Low German *schüren*, from Old French *escurer*, from late Latin *excurare* 'clean (off)'.

scour[2] ■ v. 1 subject to a thorough search. 2 move rapidly.
– ORIGIN Middle English: rel. to obsolete *scour* 'moving hastily'.

scourge ■ n. 1 historical a whip used as an instrument of punishment. 2 a person or thing causing great trouble or suffering. ■ v. 1 historical whip with a scourge. 2 cause great suffering to.
– DERIVATIVES **scourger** n. (historical).
– ORIGIN Middle English: shortening of Old French *escorge* (n.), *escorgier* (v.), from Latin *ex-* 'thoroughly' + *corrigia* 'thong, whip'.

Scouse /skaʊs/ Brit. informal ■ n. 1 the dialect or accent of people from Liverpool. 2 (also **Scouser**) a person from Liverpool. ■ adj. of or relating to Liverpool.
– ORIGIN C19: abbrev. of *lobscouse* denoting a stew formerly eaten by sailors.

scout ■ n. 1 a soldier or other person sent out ahead of a main force so as to gather information about the enemy's position, strength, or movements. ▸ a ship or aircraft employed for reconnaissance. 2 (also **Scout**) a member of the Scout Association. 3 a talent scout. 4 (also **scout bee**) a honeybee that searches for a new site for a swarm to settle or for a new food source. 5 an instance of scouting. 6 a domestic worker at a college at Oxford University. ■ v. 1 make a detailed search of a place. ▸ explore or examine so as to gather information: *they are keen to scout out business opportunities*. 2 act as a scout.
– DERIVATIVES **scouter** n. **scouting** n.
– ORIGIN Middle English: from Old French *escouter*, *ascolter* 'listen', from Latin *auscultare*.

scout car ■ n. a fast armoured vehicle used for military reconnaissance and liaison.

scow /skaʊ/ ■ n. 1 a wide-beamed sailing dinghy. 2 chiefly N. Amer. a flat-bottomed boat used for transporting cargo to and from ships in harbour.
– ORIGIN C17: from Dutch *schouw* 'ferry boat'.

scowl ■ n. an angry or bad-tempered expression. ■ v. frown in an angry or bad-tempered way.
– DERIVATIVES **scowler** n.
– ORIGIN Middle English: prob. of Scandinavian origin.

SCR ■ abbrev. Senior Common Room.

scrabble ■ v. 1 scratch or grope around with one's fingers to find, collect, or hold on to something. 2 move quickly and in a disorderly manner; scramble. ■ n. 1 an act of scrabbling. 2 a disorderly struggle or fight. 3 (**Scrabble**) trademark a board game in which players build up words from small lettered squares or tiles.
– ORIGIN C16: from Middle Dutch *schrabbelen*, from *schrabben* 'to scrape'.

scrag ■ v. (**scragged**, **scragging**) informal, chiefly Brit. handle roughly; beat up. ■ n. an unattractively thin person or animal.
– ORIGIN C16: perhaps an alteration of Scots and northern English *crag* 'neck'; verb from the early use 'hang, strangle'.

scrag-end ■ n. Brit. the inferior end of a neck of mutton.

scraggy ■ adj. (**-ier**, **-iest**) 1 scrawny. 2 (also chiefly N. Amer. **scraggly**) ragged or untidy in form or appearance.
– DERIVATIVES **scraggily** adv. **scragginess** n.

scram ■ v. (**scrammed**, **scramming**) informal go away or leave quickly.
– ORIGIN C20: prob. from SCRAMBLE.

scramble ■ v. 1 move or make one's way quickly and awkwardly, typically by using one's hands as well as one's feet. ▸ informal act in a hurried, disorderly, or undignified manner: *firms scrambled to win public-sector contracts*. 2 (with reference to fighter aircraft) take off or cause to take off immediately in an emergency or for action. 3 make or become jumbled or muddled. ▸ cook (beaten eggs with a little liquid) in a pan. 4 make (a broadcast transmission or telephone conversation) unintelligible unless received by an appropriate decoding device. 5 American Football (of a quarterback) run with the ball behind the line of scrimmage, avoiding tackles. ■ n. 1 an act of scrambling. 2 a walk up steep terrain involving the use of one's hands. 3 a motorcycle race over rough and hilly ground. 4 a disordered mixture.
– DERIVATIVES **scrambling** n.
– ORIGIN C16: imitative; cf. dialect *scamble* 'stumble' and *cramble* 'crawl'.

scrambled egg ■ n. 1 (also **scrambled eggs**) a dish of eggs prepared by beating with a little liquid and then cooking and stirring gently. 2 informal gold braid on a military officer's cap.

scrambler ■ n. **1** a device for scrambling. **2** a person who walks over steep, mountainous terrain as a pastime. ▸ a motorcycle for racing over rough ground. **3** a plant with long slender stems supported by other plants.

scrap¹ ■ n. **1** a small piece or amount of something, especially one that is left over after the greater part has been used. ▸ (**scraps**) bits of uneaten food left after a meal. **2** material, especially metal, discarded for reprocessing. ■ v. (**scrapped**, **scrapping**) **1** remove (an old or redundant vehicle, vessel, or machine) from use or service, especially so as to convert it to scrap metal. **2** abolish or cancel (a plan, policy, or law).
–ORIGIN Middle English: from Old Norse *skrap* 'scraps'; rel. to *skrapa* 'to scrape'.

scrap² informal ■ n. a fight or quarrel, especially a minor or spontaneous one. ■ v. (**scrapped**, **scrapping**) engage in such a fight or quarrel. ▸ compete fiercely.
–DERIVATIVES **scrapper** n.
–ORIGIN C17: perhaps from **SCRAPE**.

scrapbook ■ n. a book of blank pages for sticking cuttings, drawings, or pictures in. ■ v. [often as noun **scrapbooking**] compile or create a scrapbook, especially as a hobby.
–DERIVATIVES **scrapbooker** n.

scrape ■ v. **1** drag or pull a hard or sharp implement across (a surface or object). ▸ use a sharp or hard implement to remove (dirt or unwanted matter). **2** rub or cause to rub against a rough or hard surface. ▸ humorous play a violin tunelessly. **3** just manage to achieve, succeed, or pass. ▸ (**scrape something together/up**) collect or accumulate something with difficulty. ▸ try to save as much money as possible; economize. ▸ (**scrape by/along**) manage to live with difficulty. ■ n. **1** an act or sound of scraping. ▸ an injury or mark caused by scraping. ▸ Brit. a thinly applied layer of butter or margarine on bread. **2** informal an embarrassing or difficult predicament. **3** archaic an obsequious bow in which one foot is drawn backwards along the ground.
–PHRASES **scrape acquaintance with** dated contrive to get to know. **scrape the barrel** (or **the bottom of the barrel**) informal be reduced to using the last and poorest resources.
–DERIVATIVES **scraper** n. **scraping** adj. & n.
–ORIGIN Old English *scrapian* 'scratch with the fingernails', of Germanic origin, reinforced by Old Norse *skrapa* or Middle Dutch *schrapen* 'to scratch'.

scraperboard ■ n. cardboard or board with a blackened surface which can be scraped off for making white line drawings.

scrap heap ■ n. a pile of discarded materials or articles.

scrapie ■ n. a disease of sheep involving the central nervous system, characterized by a lack of coordination causing affected animals to rub against objects for support.
–ORIGIN C20: from **SCRAPE**.

scrapple ■ n. US scraps of pork or other meat stewed with maize meal and shaped into large cakes.

scrappy ■ adj. (**-ier**, **-iest**) **1** consisting of disorganized, untidy, or incomplete parts. **2** N. Amer. informal determined, argumentative, or pugnacious.
–DERIVATIVES **scrappily** adv. **scrappiness** n.

scrapyard ■ n. a place where scrap is collected before being discarded, reused, or recycled.

scratch ■ v. **1** score or mark with a sharp or pointed object. ▸ make a long, narrow superficial wound in the skin of. ▸ rub (a part of one's body) with one's fingernails to relieve itching. ▸ (of a bird or mammal) rake the ground with the beak or claws in search of food. ▸ (often **scratch around/along**) make a living or find resources with difficulty. **2** cancel or strike out (writing) with a pen or pencil. ▸ withdraw from a competition. ▸ cancel or abandon (an undertaking or project). **3** play a record using the scratch technique. ■ n. **1** a mark or wound made by scratching. ▸ informal a slight or insignificant wound or injury. ▸ an act or spell of scratching. **2** the starting point in a handicap for a competitor receiving no odds. ▸ Golf a handicap of zero, indicating that a player is good enough to achieve par on a course. **3** a technique, used especially in rap music, of stopping a record by hand and moving it back and forwards to give a rhythmic scratching effect. **4** informal money. ■ adj. **1** assembled or made from whatever is available. **2** (of a sports competitor or event) with no handicap given.
–PHRASES **from scratch** from the very beginning, especially without making use of any previous work. **scratch one's head** informal think hard in order to find a solution. **scratch the surface** deal with or investigate a matter only in the most superficial way. **up to scratch** up to the required standard; satisfactory.
–DERIVATIVES **scratcher** n. **scratching** n.
–ORIGIN Middle English: prob. a blend of the synonymous dialect words *scrat* and *cratch*.

scratchboard ■ n. another term for **SCRAPERBOARD**.

scratch card ■ n. a card with a section or sections coated in an opaque waxy substance which may be scraped away to reveal a symbol indicating whether a prize has been won.

scratch pad ■ n. chiefly N. Amer. a notepad.

scratchplate ■ n. a plate attached to the front of a guitar to protect it from being scratched by the plectrum.

scratchy ■ adj. (**-ier**, **-iest**) causing or characterized by scratching. ▸ (of a voice or sound) rough; grating. ▸ (of a record) making a crackling sound because of scratches on the surface.
–DERIVATIVES **scratchily** adv. **scratchiness** n.

scrawl ■ v. write in a hurried, careless way. ■ n. an example of hurried, careless writing.
–DERIVATIVES **scrawly** adj.
–ORIGIN C17: an alteration of **CRAWL**, perhaps influenced by obsolete *scrawl* 'sprawl'.

scrawny ■ adj. (**-ier**, **-iest**) unattractively thin and bony.
–DERIVATIVES **scrawniness** n.
–ORIGIN C19: var. of dialect *scranny*; cf. archaic *scrannel* 'weak, feeble'.

scream ■ v. **1** make a long, loud, piercing cry or sound, especially expressing extreme emotion or pain. **2** move very rapidly with or as if with such a sound. ■ n. **1** a screaming cry or sound. **2** (**a scream**) informal an irresistibly funny person or thing.
–ORIGIN Middle English: perhaps from Middle Dutch.

screamer ■ n. **1** a person or thing that makes a screaming sound. **2** informal a thing remarkable for speed or impact.

screamingly ■ adv. to a very great extent; extremely: *it was screamingly obvious*.

scree ■ n. a mass of small loose stones that form or cover a slope on a mountain.
–ORIGIN C18: prob. from Old Norse *skritha* 'landslip'.

screech ■ n. a loud, harsh, piercing cry or sound. ■ v. **1** make a screech. **2** move rapidly with a screech.
–DERIVATIVES **screecher** n. **screechy** adj. (**-ier**, **-iest**).
–ORIGIN C16: alteration of archaic *scritch*, of imitative origin.

screech owl ■ n. **1** Brit. another term for **BARN OWL**. **2** a small American owl with a screeching call. [*Otus asio* and related species.]

screed ■ n. **1** a long speech or piece of writing, typically a tedious one. **2** a levelled layer of material (e.g. cement) applied to a floor or other surface.
–DERIVATIVES **screeding** n.
–ORIGIN Middle English: prob. a var. of **SHRED**.

screen ■ n. **1** an upright partition used to divide a room, give shelter, or provide concealment. ▸ a windscreen of a motor vehicle. ▸ a frame with fine wire netting used to keep out flying insects. **2** the surface of a cathode ray tube or similar electronic device, especially that of a television, VDU, or monitor, on which images and data are displayed. ▸ a blank surface on which a photographic image is projected. ▸ (**the screen**) films or television. ▸ Photography a flat piece of ground glass on which the image formed by a camera lens is focused. **3** Printing a transparent finely ruled plate or film used in half-tone reproduction. **4** a system or act of screening for the presence or absence of something. **5** a large sieve or riddle. **6** Military a detachment of troops or ships detailed to cover the movements of the main body. **7** a part of an electrical or other instrument which protects it from or prevents it causing electromagnetic interference. ▸ (also **screen grid**) Electronics a grid placed between the control grid and the anode of a valve to

screenplay

reduce the capacitance between these electrodes. ■ v. **1** conceal, protect, or shelter with a screen. ▸ protect from something dangerous or unpleasant. **2** show (a film or video) or broadcast (a television programme). **3** test for the presence or absence of a disease. ▸ investigate (someone), typically to ascertain suitability for a job. **4** pass (a substance such as grain or coal) through a large sieve or screen, especially so as to sort it into different sizes. **5** Printing project (a photograph or other image) through a screen so as to reproduce it as a half-tone.
– DERIVATIVES **screenable** adj. **screener** n. **screenful** n. (pl. **-fuls**). **screening** n.
– ORIGIN Middle English: shortening of Old Northern French *escren*, of Germanic origin.

screenplay ■ n. the script of a film, including acting instructions and scene directions.

screen-print ■ v. [often as adj. **screen-printed**] force ink on to (a surface) through a prepared screen of fine material so as to create a picture or pattern. ■ n. (**screen print**) a picture or design produced by screen-printing.

screen saver ■ n. Computing a program which, after a set time, replaces an unchanging screen display with a moving image to prevent damage to the phosphor.

screen test ■ n. a filmed test to ascertain whether an actor is suitable for a film role. ■ v. (**screen-test**) give such a test to.

screenwriter ■ n. a person who writes a screenplay.
– DERIVATIVES **screenwriting** n.

screw ■ n. **1** a short, slender, sharp-pointed metal pin with a raised helical thread running around it and a slotted head, used to join things together by being rotated in under pressure. ▸ a cylinder with a helical ridge or thread running round the outside that can be turned to seal an opening, apply pressure, adjust position, etc. ▸ (**the screws**) historical an instrument of torture acting in this way. **2** an act of turning a screw. ▸ Brit. a small twisted-up piece of paper containing a substance such as salt or tobacco. **3** (also **screw propeller**) a ship's or aircraft's propeller. **4** informal, derogatory a prison warder. **5** vulgar slang an act of sexual intercourse. ■ v. **1** fasten or tighten with a screw or screws. ▸ rotate (something) so as to attach or remove it by means of a spiral thread. ▸ impart spin or curl to (a ball or shot). ▸ (**screw something around/round**) turn one's head or body round sharply. **2** informal cheat or swindle. ▸ informal ruin or render ineffective. **3** vulgar slang have sexual intercourse with. ▸ informal used to express anger or contempt.
– PHRASES **have one's head screwed on (the right way)** informal have common sense. **have a screw loose** informal be slightly eccentric or mentally disturbed. **put** (or **turn** or **tighten**) **the screw** (or **screws**) **on** informal exert strong psychological pressure on.
– PHRASAL VERBS **screw around 1** vulgar slang have many different sexual partners. **2** informal fool about. **screw someone over** informal, chiefly US treat someone unfairly; cheat or swindle someone. **screw up** informal completely mismanage or mishandle a situation. **screw someone up** informal cause someone to be emotionally or mentally disturbed. **screw something up 1** crush a piece of paper or fabric into a tight mass. **2** tense the muscles of one's face or around one's eyes. **2** informal cause something to fail or go wrong. **3** summon up one's courage.
– DERIVATIVES **screwable** adj. **screwer** n.
– ORIGIN Middle English: from Old French *escroue* 'female screw, nut', from Latin *scrofa* 'sow', later 'screw'.

screwball chiefly N. Amer. ■ n. **1** Baseball a ball pitched with reverse spin as compared to a curve ball. **2** informal a crazy or eccentric person. ■ adj. informal crazy; absurd. ▸ relating to or denoting a style of fast-moving comedy film involving eccentric characters or ridiculous situations.
– DERIVATIVES **screwballer** n.

screw cap ■ n. a round cap or lid that can be screwed on to a bottle or jar.
– DERIVATIVES **screw-capped** adj.

screw coupling ■ n. a female screw with threads at both ends for joining lengths of pipes or rods.

screwdriver ■ n. **1** a tool with a shaped tip that fits into the head of a screw to turn it. **2** a cocktail made from vodka and orange juice.

screw eye ■ n. a screw with a loop for passing a cord through, instead of a slotted head.

screw gear ■ n. a gear consisting of an endless screw with a cogwheel or pinion.

screw hook ■ n. a hook with a point and thread for fastening it to woodwork.

screw jack ■ n. a vehicle jack worked by a screw device.

screw pine ■ n. another term for PANDANUS.

screw plate ■ n. a steel plate with threaded holes for making male screws.

screw tap ■ n. a tool for making female screws.

screw top ■ n. a round cap or lid that can be screwed on to a bottle or jar.
– DERIVATIVES **screw-topped** adj.

screw valve ■ n. a stopcock opened and shut by a screw.

screwy ■ adj. (**-ier**, **-iest**) informal, chiefly N. Amer. rather odd or eccentric.
– DERIVATIVES **screwiness** n.

scribble ■ v. **1** write or draw carelessly or hurriedly. **2** informal write for a living or as a hobby. ■ n. a piece of writing or a picture produced carelessly or hurriedly.
– DERIVATIVES **scribbler** n. **scribbly** adj.
– ORIGIN Middle English: from medieval Latin *scribillare*, diminutive of Latin *scribere* 'write'.

scribe ■ n. **1** historical a person who copied out documents. ▸ informal, often humorous a writer, especially a journalist. **2** Judaism an ancient Jewish record-keeper or, later, a professional theologian and jurist. **3** (also **scriber** or **scribe awl**) a pointed instrument used for making marks to guide a saw or in signwriting. ■ v. **1** chiefly poetic/literary write. **2** mark with a pointed instrument.
– DERIVATIVES **scribal** adj.
– ORIGIN Middle English: from Latin *scriba*, from *scribere* 'write'; the verb is perhaps a shortening of DESCRIBE.

scrim ■ n. **1** strong, coarse fabric used for heavy-duty lining or upholstery. **2** Theatre a piece of gauze cloth that appears opaque until lit from behind, used as a screen or backcloth. **3** something that conceals or obscures.
– ORIGIN C18.

scrimmage ■ n. **1** a confused struggle or fight. **2** American Football a sequence of play beginning with the placing of the ball on the ground with its longest axis at right angles to the goal line. ■ v. American Football engage in a scrimmage. ▸ put (the ball) into a scrimmage.
– DERIVATIVES **scrimmager** n.
– ORIGIN Middle English: alteration of dialect *scrimish*, var. of SKIRMISH.

scrimp ■ v. be thrifty or parsimonious; economize.
– ORIGIN C18: from Scots *scrimp* 'meagre'; perhaps rel. to SHRIMP.

scrimshaw ■ v. adorn (shells, ivory, or other materials) with carved designs. ■ n. work done in such a way.
– ORIGIN C19: perhaps influenced by the surname *Scrimshaw*.

scrip[1] ■ n. a provisional certificate of money subscribed to a bank or company, entitling the holder to a formal certificate and dividends. ▸ certificates of this type collectively. ▸ Finance an issue of additional shares to shareholders in proportion to the shares already held.
– ORIGIN C18: abbrev. of *subscription receipt*.

scrip[2] ■ n. historical a small bag or pouch, as carried by a pilgrim, shepherd, or beggar.
– ORIGIN Middle English: prob. a shortening of Old French *escrepe* 'purse'.

scrip[3] ■ n. another term for SCRIPT[2].

script[1] ■ n. **1** handwriting as distinct from print; written characters. ▸ writing using a particular alphabet: *Russian script*. **2** the written text of a play, film, or broadcast. **3** a candidate's written answers in an examination. ■ v. write a script for.
– ORIGIN Middle English: shortening of Old French *escript*, from Latin *scriptum*, from *scribere* 'write'.

script[2] ■ n. informal a doctor's prescription.

scriptorium /skrɪpˈtɔːrɪəm/ ■ n. (pl. **scriptoria** /-rɪə/ or **scriptoriums**) chiefly historical a room set apart for writing,

especially one in a monastery where manuscripts were copied.
– ORIGIN C18: from Latin *script-*, *scribere* 'write'.

scriptural ■ adj. of, from, or relating to the Bible.
– DERIVATIVES **scripturally** adv.

scripture /'skrɪptʃə/ (also **scriptures**) ■ n. the sacred writings of Christianity contained in the Bible. ▸ the sacred writings of another religion.
– ORIGIN Middle English: from Latin *scriptura* 'writings', from *script-*, *scribere* 'write'.

scriptwriter ■ n. a person who writes a script for a play, film, or broadcast.
– DERIVATIVES **scriptwriting** n.

scrivener /'skrɪv(ə)nə/ ■ n. historical a clerk, scribe, or notary.
– ORIGIN Middle English: shortening of Old French *escrivein*, from Latin *scriba* (see SCRIBE).

scrofula /'skrɒfjʊlə/ ■ n. chiefly historical a disease with glandular swellings, probably a form of tuberculosis.
– DERIVATIVES **scrofulous** adj.
– ORIGIN Middle English: from medieval Latin, diminutive of Latin *scrofa* 'breeding sow' (said to be subject to the disease).

scroll ■ n. 1 a roll of parchment or paper for writing or painting on. ▸ an ancient book or document on such a roll. 2 an ornamental design or carving resembling a partly unrolled scroll of parchment. ■ v. 1 move displayed text or graphics on a computer screen in order to view different parts of them. 2 cause to move like paper rolling or unrolling.
– DERIVATIVES **scrollable** adj. **scroller** n. **scrolling** n.
– ORIGIN Middle English: alteration of obsolete *scrow* 'roll', shortening of ESCROW.

scroll bar ■ n. a long thin section at the edge of a computer display by which material can be scrolled using a mouse.

scrolled ■ adj. having an ornamental design or carving resembling a scroll of parchment.

scroll saw ■ n. a narrow-bladed saw for cutting decorative spiral lines or patterns.

scrollwork ■ n. decoration consisting of spiral lines or patterns.

Scrooge ■ n. a person who is mean with money.
– ORIGIN from the name of Ebenezer *Scrooge*, a miserly curmudgeon in Charles Dickens's novel *A Christmas Carol*.

scrotum /'skrəʊtəm/ ■ n. (pl. **scrota** /-tə/ or **scrotums**) a pouch of skin containing the testicles.
– DERIVATIVES **scrotal** adj.
– ORIGIN C16: from Latin.

scrounge informal ■ v. seek to obtain (something) at the expense of others or by stealth. ▸ (often **scrounge something up**) search for or obtain by searching. ■ n. an act or the action of scrounging.
– DERIVATIVES **scrounger** n.
– ORIGIN C20: var. of dialect *scrunge* 'steal'.

scrub¹ ■ v. (**scrubbed**, **scrubbing**) 1 rub hard so as to clean. ▸ (**scrub up**) thoroughly clean one's hands and arms before performing surgery. 2 informal cancel or abandon. 3 use water to remove impurities from (gas or vapour). ■ n. 1 an act of scrubbing. 2 a semi-abrasive cosmetic lotion applied to the face or body in order to cleanse the skin. 3 (**scrubs**) special hygienic clothing worn by surgeons during operations.
– ORIGIN C16: prob. from Middle Low German, Middle Dutch *schrobben*, *schrubben*.

scrub² ■ n. 1 vegetation consisting mainly of brushwood or stunted forest growth. ▸ (also **scrubs**) land covered with such vegetation. 2 [as modifier] denoting a shrubby or small form of a plant.
– DERIVATIVES **scrubby** adj.
– ORIGIN Middle English: var. of SHRUB.

scrubber ■ n. 1 a person or thing that scrubs. ▸ an apparatus using water or a solution for purifying gases or vapours. 2 derogatory, chiefly Brit. a sexually promiscuous woman.

scrub hare ■ n. a chiefly nocturnal African hare with a greyish coat and white underparts. [*Lepus saxatilis*.]

scruff¹ ■ n. the back of a person's or animal's neck.

1063 **scud**

– ORIGIN C18: alteration of dialect *scuff*.

scruff² ■ n. Brit. informal a scruffy person.
– ORIGIN C16: var. of SCURF.

scruffy ■ adj. (**-ier**, **-iest**) shabby and untidy or dirty.
– DERIVATIVES **scruffily** adv. **scruffiness** n.

scrum ■ n. 1 Rugby an ordered formation of players in which the forwards of each team push against each other with arms interlocked and heads down and the ball is thrown in to restart play. 2 Brit. informal a disorderly crowd. ■ v. (**scrummed**, **scrumming**) 1 Rugby form or take part in a scrum. 2 informal jostle; crowd.
– ORIGIN C19: abbrev. of SCRUMMAGE.

scrum half ■ n. Rugby a halfback who puts the ball into the scrum and stands ready to receive it again.

scrummage ■ n. & v. fuller form of SCRUM.
– DERIVATIVES **scrummager** n.
– ORIGIN C19: var. of SCRIMMAGE.

scrummy ■ adj. (**-ier**, **-iest**) informal delicious.
– ORIGIN C20: from SCRUMPTIOUS.

scrump ■ v. Brit. informal steal (fruit) from an orchard or garden.
– ORIGIN C19: from dialect *scrump* 'withered apple'.

scrumple ■ v. Brit. crumple (paper or cloth).
– ORIGIN C16: alteration of CRUMPLE.

scrumptious ■ adj. informal (of food) extremely appetizing or delicious. ▸ (of a person) very attractive.
– DERIVATIVES **scrumptiously** adv. **scrumptiousness** n.
– ORIGIN C19.

scrumpy ■ n. Brit. rough strong cider, especially as made in the West Country of England.

scrunch ■ v. 1 make a loud crunching noise. 2 crush or squeeze into a compact mass. ▸ style (hair) by squeezing in the hands to give a tousled look. ■ n. a loud crunching noise.
– ORIGIN C18: prob. imitative; cf. CRUNCH.

scrunchy ■ adj. making a loud crunching noise when crushed or compressed. ■ n. (also **scrunchie**) (pl. **-ies**) a circular band of fabric-covered elastic used for fastening the hair.

scruple ■ n. a feeling of doubt or hesitation with regard to the morality or propriety of an action. ■ v. hesitate or be reluctant to do something that one thinks may be wrong.
– ORIGIN Middle English: from French *scrupule* or Latin *scrupulus*, from *scrupus* 'rough pebble', (figuratively) 'anxiety'.

scrupulous ■ adj. 1 diligent, thorough, and attentive to details. 2 very concerned to avoid doing wrong.
– DERIVATIVES **scrupulosity** n. **scrupulously** adv. **scrupulousness** n.
– ORIGIN Middle English: from French *scrupuleux* or Latin *scrupulosus*, from *scrupulus* (see SCRUPLE).

scrutineer ■ n. a person who examines or inspects something closely and thoroughly. ▸ a person who supervises the conduct of an election or competition.

scrutinize (also **-ise**) ■ v. examine or inspect closely and thoroughly.
– DERIVATIVES **scrutinization** (also **-isation**) n. **scrutinizer** (also **-iser**) n.

scrutiny ■ n. (pl. **-ies**) critical observation or examination.
– ORIGIN Middle English: from Latin *scrutinium*, from *scrutari* 'to search' (orig. 'sort rubbish', from *scruta* 'rubbish').

scry /skraɪ/ ■ v. (**-ies**, **-ied**) foretell the future, especially using a crystal ball.
– DERIVATIVES **scryer** n.
– ORIGIN C16: shortening of DESCRY.

SCSI ■ abbrev. Computing small computer system interface.

scuba /'sku:bə, 'skju:bə/ ■ n. an aqualung.
– ORIGIN 1950s: acronym from *self-contained underwater breathing apparatus*.

scuba-diving ■ n. the sport or pastime of swimming underwater using a scuba.
– DERIVATIVES **scuba-dive** v. **scuba-diver** n.

scud ■ v. (**scudded**, **scudding**) move fast in a straight line because as or if driven by the wind. ■ n. 1 chiefly poetic/

scuff

literary vapoury clouds or spray driven fast by the wind. ▶ a driving shower of rain. **2** the action of scudding.
– ORIGIN C16: perhaps an alteration of **SCUT**, reflecting the sense 'race like a hare'.

scuff ■ v. scrape (a shoe or other object) against something. ▶ [often as adj. **scuffed**] mark by scuffing. ▶ drag (one's feet) when walking. ■ n. a mark made by scuffing.
– ORIGIN C18: perhaps of imitative origin.

scuffle ■ n. **1** a short, confused fight or struggle at close quarters. **2** an act or sound of moving in a scuffling manner. ■ v. **1** engage in a scuffle. **2** move in a hurried, confused, or shuffling way.
– ORIGIN C16: prob. of Scandinavian origin; cf. Swedish *skuffa* 'to push'.

scull ■ n. each of a pair of small oars used by a single rower. ▶ an oar placed over the stern of a boat to propel it with a side to side motion. ▶ a light, narrow boat propelled with a scull or a pair of sculls. ▶ (**sculls**) a race between boats in which each participant uses a pair of oars. ■ v. propel a boat with sculls.
– DERIVATIVES **sculler** n.
– ORIGIN Middle English.

scullery /ˈskʌl(ə)ri/ ■ n. (pl. **-ies**) a small kitchen or room at the back of a house used for washing dishes and other dirty household work.
– ORIGIN Middle English: from Old French *escuelerie*, from *escuele* 'dish', from Latin *scutella* 'salver'.

scullion ■ n. archaic a servant assigned the most menial kitchen tasks.
– ORIGIN C15: perhaps influenced by **SCULLERY**.

sculpt (also **sculp**) ■ v. create or represent by sculpture.

sculptor ■ n. (fem. **sculptress**) an artist who makes sculptures.

sculpture ■ n. **1** the art of making three-dimensional representative or abstract forms, especially by carving stone or wood or by casting metal or plaster. ▶ a work of such a kind. **2** raised or sunken patterns on a shell, pollen grain, etc. ■ v. make or represent by sculpture. ▶ [usu. as adj. **sculptured**] form or shape as if by sculpture, especially with strong, smooth curves.
– DERIVATIVES **sculptural** adj. **sculpturally** adv. **sculpturesque** adj. **sculpturing** n.
– ORIGIN Middle English: from Latin *sculptura*, from *sculpere* 'carve'.

scum ■ n. **1** a layer of dirt or froth on the surface of a liquid. **2** informal a worthless or contemptible person or group of people. ■ v. (**scummed**, **scumming**) cover or become covered with a layer of scum.
– DERIVATIVES **scummy** adj. (**-ier**, **-iest**).
– ORIGIN Middle English: from Middle Low German, Middle Dutch *schūm*, of Germanic origin.

scumbag ■ n. informal a contemptible person.

scumble /ˈskʌmb(ə)l/ Art ■ v. give a softer or duller effect to (a picture or colour) by applying a very thin coat of opaque paint or a layer of light pencil or charcoal shading. ■ n. a coat of paint or layer of shading applied in this way, or the effect thus produced.
– ORIGIN C17: perhaps from **SCUM**.

scupper[1] ■ n. a hole in a ship's side to allow water to run away from the deck.
– ORIGIN Middle English: perhaps from Old French *escopir* 'to spit'.

scupper[2] ■ v. **1** sink (a ship) deliberately. **2** informal prevent from working or succeeding; thwart.
– ORIGIN C19.

scurf ■ n. flakes on the surface of the skin that form as fresh skin develops below, occurring especially as dandruff. ▶ a similar flaky deposit on a plant resulting from a fungal infection.
– DERIVATIVES **scurfy** adj.
– ORIGIN Old English *sceorf*, from the base of *sceorfan* 'gnaw', *sceorfian* 'cut to shreds'.

scurrilous /ˈskʌrɪləs/ ■ adj. making scandalous claims about someone with the intention of damaging their reputation. ▶ humorously insulting.
– DERIVATIVES **scurrility** n. (pl. **-ies**). **scurrilously** adv. **scurrilousness** n.

– ORIGIN C16: from French *scurrile* or Latin *scurrilus*, from *scurra* 'buffoon'.

scurry ■ v. (**-ies**, **-ied**) move hurriedly with short quick steps. ■ n. **1** a situation of hurried and confused movement. **2** a flurry of rain or snow.
– ORIGIN C19: abbrev. of *hurry-scurry*, reduplication of **HURRY**.

scurvy ■ n. a disease caused by a deficiency of vitamin C, characterized by swollen bleeding gums and the opening of previously healed wounds. ■ adj. (**-ier**, **-iest**) archaic worthless or contemptible.
– DERIVATIVES **scurvily** adv.
– ORIGIN Middle English: from **SCURF**.

scut ■ n. the short tail of a hare, rabbit, or deer.
– ORIGIN Middle English: cf. obsolete *scut* 'short', also 'shorten'.

scuta plural form of **SCUTUM**.

scute /skjuːt/ ■ n. Zoology a thickened horny or bony plate on a turtle's shell or on the back of a crocodile, stegosaurus, etc.
– ORIGIN Middle English: from Latin **SCUTUM**.

scutellum /skjuːˈtɛləm/ ■ n. (pl. **scutella** /-lə/) **1** Botany a modified cotyledon in the embryo of a grass seed. **2** Entomology one of the dorsal sclerites of an insect's thorax.
– DERIVATIVES **scutellar** adj.
– ORIGIN C18: diminutive of Latin *scutum* 'shield'.

scutter chiefly Brit. ■ v. move hurriedly with short steps. ■ n. an act or sound of scuttering.
– ORIGIN C18: perhaps an alteration of **SCUTTLE**[2].

scuttle[1] ■ n. **1** a metal container with a sloping hinged lid and a handle, used to fetch and store coal for a domestic fire. **2** the part of a car's bodywork between the windscreen and the bonnet.
– ORIGIN Old English *scutel* 'dish, platter', from Old Norse *skutill*, from Latin *scutella* 'dish'.

scuttle[2] ■ v. run hurriedly or furtively with short quick steps. ■ n. an act or sound of scuttling.
– ORIGIN C15: cf. dialect *scuddle*, from **SCUD**.

scuttle[3] ■ v. **1** sink (one's own ship) deliberately. **2** deliberately cause (a scheme) to fail. ■ n. an opening with a lid in a ship's deck or side.
– ORIGIN C15: perhaps from Old French *escoutille*, from the Spanish diminutive *escotilla* 'hatchway'.

scuttlebutt ■ n. informal, chiefly N. Amer. rumour; gossip.
– ORIGIN C19.

scutum /ˈskjuːtəm/ ■ n. (pl: **scuta** /-tə/) **1** Zoology another term for **SCUTE**. **2** Entomology the second dorsal sclerite in each thoracic segment of an insect.
– ORIGIN C18: from Latin, 'oblong shield'.

scuzz ■ n. informal, chiefly N. Amer. something disgusting or disreputable. ▶ a disreputable or unpleasant person.
– DERIVATIVES **scuzzy** adj.
– ORIGIN 1960s: prob. an informal abbrev. of *disgusting*.

Scyphozoa /ˌsaɪfəˈzəʊə, ˌskaɪf-, ˌskɪf-/ ■ pl. n. Zoology a class of marine coelenterates which comprises the jelly-fishes.
– DERIVATIVES **scyphozoan** n. & adj.
– ORIGIN from Greek *skuphos* 'drinking cup' + *zōion* 'animal'.

scythe ■ n. a tool used for cutting crops such as grass or corn, with a long curved blade at the end of a long pole attached to one or two short handles. ■ v. **1** cut with a scythe. **2** move through or penetrate rapidly and forcefully.
– ORIGIN Old English, of Germanic origin.

SD ■ abbrev. Swaziland (international vehicle registration).

SDI ■ abbrev. **1** S. African Spatial Development Initiative. **2** Strategic Defense Initiative.

SDR ■ abbrev. special drawing right (from the International Monetary Fund).

SE ■ abbrev. **1** south-east. **2** south-eastern.

Se ■ symb. the chemical element selenium.

se- ■ prefix in words adopted from Latin originally meaning 'apart' (as in *separate*) or meaning 'without' (as in *secure*).
– ORIGIN from Latin *se-*.

sea ■ n. **1** the expanse of salt water that covers most of the

earth's surface and surrounds its land masses. ▶ a roughly definable area of this: *the Black Sea.* ▶ (also **seas**) waves as opposed to calm sea. **2** a vast expanse or quantity: *a sea of faces.*
–PHRASES **at sea 1** sailing on the sea. **2** (also **all at sea**) confused; uncertain. **put** (**out**) **to sea** leave land on a voyage. **one's sea legs** one's ability to keep one's balance and not feel seasick when on board a moving ship.
–DERIVATIVES **seaward** adj. & adv. **seawards** adv.
–ORIGIN Old English, of Germanic origin.

sea anchor ■ n. an object dragged in the water behind a boat in order to keep its bows pointing into the waves or to lessen leeway.

sea anemone ■ n. a sedentary marine coelenterate with a columnar body which bears a ring of stinging tentacles around the mouth. [Order Actiniaria.]

sea bamboo ■ n. a large kelp found along the west coast of South Africa. [*Ecklonia maxima*.]

sea bass ■ n. a marine fish with a spiny dorsal fin, resembling the freshwater perch. [Many species, mainly in the family Serranidae.]

seabed ■ n. the ground under the sea; the ocean floor.

seabird ■ n. a bird that frequents the sea or coast.

seaboard ■ n. a region bordering the sea; the coastline.

seaborgium /siˈbɔːgɪəm/ ■ n. the chemical element of atomic number 106, a very unstable element made by high-energy atomic collisions. (Symbol: **Sg**)
–ORIGIN 1990s: named after the American nuclear chemist Glenn *Seaborg*.

sea bream ■ n. a deep-bodied marine fish that resembles the freshwater bream. [Several species, mainly in the family Sparidae.]

sea breeze ■ n. a breeze blowing towards the land from the sea.

SeaCat ■ n. trademark a large, high-speed catamaran used as a passenger and car ferry on short sea crossings.

sea change ■ n. a profound or notable transformation.
–ORIGIN from Shakespeare's *Tempest* (I. ii. 403).

sea chest ■ n. a sailor's storage chest.

sea cow ■ n. **1** a sirenian, especially a manatee. **2** archaic a hippopotamus.

sea cucumber ■ n. an echinoderm having a thick worm-like body with tentacles around the mouth. [Class Holothuroidea.]

sea dog ■ n. informal an old or experienced sailor.

sea eagle ■ n. a large fish-eating eagle that frequents coasts and wetlands. [*Haliaeetus albicilla* and related species.]

sea elephant ■ n. another term for ELEPHANT SEAL.

sea fan ■ n. a horny coral with a vertical tree- or fan-like skeleton. [Order Gorgonacea.]

seafaring ■ adj. travelling by sea. ■ n. travel by sea.
–DERIVATIVES **seafarer** n.

seafood ■ n. shellfish and sea fish served as food.

seafront ■ n. another term for BEACHFRONT.

sea-girt ■ adj. poetic/literary surrounded by sea.

seagoing ■ adj. **1** (of a ship) suitable for voyages on the sea. **2** characterized by or relating to travelling by sea.

sea gooseberry ■ n. a common comb jelly with a spherical body bearing two long retractile branching tentacles. [*Pleurobrachia pileus*.]

sea grape ■ n. a salt-resistant tree of the dock family, bearing grape-like bunches of edible purple fruit. [*Coccoloba uvifera*.]

seagrass ■ n. eelgrass or a similar grass-like plant that grows near the sea.

sea green ■ n. a pale bluish green colour.

seagull ■ n. a gull.

sea hare ■ n. a large sea slug which has a minute internal shell and lateral extensions to the foot. [*Aplysia* and other genera.]

sea holly ■ n. a spiny-leaved European plant of the parsley family, with metallic blue teasel-like flowers, growing in sandy places by the sea. [*Eryngium maritimum*.]

sea horse ■ n. a small marine fish with an upright posture and a head and neck suggestive of a horse. [Genus *Hippocampus*: many species.]

sea-island cotton ■ n. a fine-quality long-stapled cotton grown on islands off the southern US.

seakale ■ n. a maritime plant of the cabbage family cultivated for its edible young shoots. [*Crambe maritima*.]

seakeeping ■ n. the ability of a vessel to withstand rough conditions at sea.

seal[1] ■ n. **1** a device or substance used to join two things together or render something impervious. ▶ the state or fact of being joined or rendered impervious with a seal. **2** a piece of wax, lead, etc. with an individual design stamped into it, attached to a document as a guarantee of authenticity. ▶ a design embossed in paper for this purpose. ▶ an engraved device used for stamping a seal. ▶ a decorative adhesive stamp. **3** a confirmation or guarantee: *a seal of approval.* **4** (**the seal**) or **the seal of the confessional** the obligation on a priest not to divulge anything said during confession. **5** the water standing in the trap of a drain to prevent foul air from rising. ■ v. **1** fasten or close securely. ▶ (**seal something off**) isolate an area by preventing or monitoring entrance to and exit from it. **2** apply a non-porous coating to (a surface) to make it impervious. **3** conclude, establish, or secure definitively: *victory was sealed.* **4** authenticate (a document) with a seal.
–PHRASES **my lips are sealed** I will not discuss or reveal a particular secret. **put** (or **set**) **the seal on** finally confirm or conclude. **set** (or **put**) **one's seal to** (or **on**) mark with one's distinctive character.
–DERIVATIVES **sealable** adj.
–ORIGIN Middle English: from Old French *seel* (n.), *seeler* (v.), from Latin *sigillum* 'small picture', diminutive of *signum* 'a sign'.

seal[2] ■ n. a fish-eating aquatic mammal with a streamlined body and feet developed as flippers. [Families Phocidae and Otariidae (eared seals): many species.] ■ v. [usu. as noun **sealing**] hunt for seals.
–ORIGIN Old English *seolh*, of Germanic origin.

sealant ■ n. material used for sealing something so as to make it airtight or watertight.

sea lavender ■ n. a chiefly maritime plant with small pink or lilac funnel-shaped flowers. [Genus *Limonium*.]

sea lawyer ■ n. informal an eloquently and obstinately argumentative person.

sealed-beam ■ adj. denoting a vehicle headlamp with a sealed unit consisting of the light source, reflector, and lens.

sealed orders ■ pl. n. Military orders which are not to be opened before a specified time.

sealer[1] ■ n. a device or substance used to seal something.

sealer[2] ■ n. a ship or person engaged in hunting seals.

sea lettuce ■ n. an edible seaweed with green fronds that resemble lettuce leaves. [*Ulva lactuca*.]

sea level ■ n. the level of the sea's surface, used in reckoning the height of geographical features and as a barometric standard.

sea lily ■ n. a sedentary marine echinoderm which has a small body on a jointed stalk, with feather-like arms to trap food. [Class Crinoidea.]

sealing wax ■ n. a mixture of shellac and rosin with turpentine and pigment, softened by heating and used to make seals.

sea lion ■ n. an eared seal occurring mainly on Pacific coasts, the large male of which has a mane on the neck and shoulders. [Five genera and species in the family Otariidae.]

sealpoint ■ n. a dark brown marking on the fur of the head, tail, and paws of a Siamese cat. ▶ a cat with such markings.

sealskin ■ n. the skin or prepared fur of a seal, especially when made into a garment.

seam ■ n. **1** a line where two pieces of fabric are sewn together in a garment or other article. ▶ a line where the

seaman

edges of two pieces of wood or other material touch each other. **2** an underground layer of a mineral such as coal or gold. **3** a long thin indentation or scar. ■ v. **1** join with a seam. **2** [usu. as adj. **seamed**] make a long narrow indentation in.
– PHRASES **bursting** (or **bulging**) **at the seams** informal full to overflowing. **come** (or **fall**) **apart at the seams** informal be in a very poor condition and near to collapse.
– ORIGIN Old English, of Germanic origin.

seaman ■ n. (pl. **-men**) a sailor, especially one below the rank of officer.
– DERIVATIVES **seamanlike** adj. **seamanship** n.

seam bowler ■ n. Cricket a bowler who makes the ball deviate by causing it to bounce on its seam.
– DERIVATIVES **seam bowling** n.

seamer ■ n. **1** Cricket another term for SEAM BOWLER. ▶ a ball which deviates by bouncing on its seam. **2** a person who seams garments.

sea mile ■ n. a unit of distance equal to a minute of arc of a great circle, varying between approximately 2 014 yards (1 842 metres) at the equator and 2 035 yards (1 861 metres) at the pole.

seamless ■ adj. smooth and without seams or obvious joins.
– DERIVATIVES **seamlessly** adv.

seamount ■ n. a submarine mountain.

seamstress ■ n. a woman who sews, especially as a job.
– ORIGIN C16: from archaic *seamster*, *sempster* 'tailor, seamstress'.

seamy ■ adj. (**-ier**, **-iest**) sordid and disreputable.
– DERIVATIVES **seaminess** n.

seance /ˈseɪəns, -ɒs, -ɑːns/ ■ n. a meeting at which people attempt to make contact with the dead.
– ORIGIN C18: French *séance*, from Old French *seoir*, from Latin *sedere* 'sit'.

sea pen ■ n. a marine coelenterate related to the corals, forming a feather-shaped colony with a horny or calcareous skeleton. [Order Pennatulacea.]

sea pink ■ n. another term for THRIFT (in sense 3).

seaplane ■ n. an aircraft with floats or skis instead of wheels, designed to land on and take off from water.

seaport ■ n. a town or city with a harbour for seagoing ships.

SEAQ ■ abbrev. (in the UK) Stock Exchange Automated Quotations.

sear ■ v. **1** burn or scorch with a sudden intense heat. ▶ brown (food) quickly at a high temperature. **2** [usu. as adj. **searing**] (of pain) be experienced as a sudden burning sensation. ■ adj. (also **sere**) poetic/literary withered.
– DERIVATIVES **searingly** adv.
– ORIGIN Old English, of Germanic origin.

search ■ v. **1** try to find something by looking or otherwise seeking carefully and thoroughly. ▶ examine thoroughly in order to find something. ▶ look for information in (a computer network or database) by using a search engine. **2** [as adj. **searching**] scrutinizing thoroughly, especially in a disconcerting way. ■ n. (often in phr. **in search of**) an act of searching. ▶ Law an investigation of public records to find if a property is subject to any liabilities or encumbrances.
– PHRASES **search me!** informal I do not know.
– DERIVATIVES **searchable** adj. **searcher** n. **searchingly** adv.
– ORIGIN Middle English: from Old French *cerchier* (v.), from late Latin *circare* 'go round', from Latin *circus* 'circle'.

search engine ■ n. Computing a program for the retrieval of data, files, or documents from a database or network, especially the Internet.

searchlight ■ n. a powerful outdoor electric light with a concentrated beam that can be turned in the required direction.

search party ■ n. a group of people organized to look for someone or something that is lost.

search warrant ■ n. a legal document authorizing a police officer or other official to enter and search premises.

sea robin ■ n. a gurnard (fish), especially one of warm seas, with brightly coloured wing-like pectoral fins.

sea room ■ n. clear space at sea for a ship to turn or manoeuvre in.

sea salt ■ n. salt produced by the evaporation of seawater.

seascape ■ n. a view or picture of an expanse of sea.

sea serpent ■ n. a legendary serpent-like sea monster.

seashell ■ n. the shell of a marine mollusc.

seashore ■ n. an area of sandy, stony, or rocky land bordering and level with the sea. ▶ Law the land between high- and low-water marks.

seasick ■ adj. suffering from nausea caused by the motion of a ship at sea.
– DERIVATIVES **seasickness** n.

seaside ■ n. a place by the sea, especially a beach area or holiday resort.

sea slug ■ n. a shell-less marine mollusc with external gills and a number of appendages on the upper surface. [Order Nudibranchia.]

sea snail ■ n. a marine mollusc, especially one with a spiral shell. [Subclass Prosobranchia.]

sea snake ■ n. a venomous marine snake found in warm coastal waters of the Indian and Pacific oceans. [Subfamily Hydrophiinae: several species.]

season ■ n. **1** each of the four divisions of the year (spring, summer, autumn, and winter) marked by particular weather patterns and daylight hours. ▶ a period of the year characterized by particular climatic conditions: *the dry season*. ▶ the time of year when a particular fruit, vegetable, etc., is plentiful and in good condition. **2** a period of the year characterized by an activity or event, especially a particular sport. ▶ (**the season**) chiefly Brit. the time of year traditionally marked by fashionable upper-class social events. **3** (usu. in phr. **in season**) a period when a female mammal is ready to mate. **4** archaic a proper or suitable time: *to everything there is a season*. ■ v. **1** add salt, herbs, or spices to (food). **2** add an enlivening quality or feature to. **3** keep (wood) so as to dry it for use as timber. **4** [as adj. **seasoned**] accustomed to particular conditions; experienced.
– ORIGIN Middle English: from Old French *seson*, from Latin *satio(n-)* 'sowing', later 'time of sowing'.

seasonable ■ adj. usual for or appropriate to a particular season of the year.
– DERIVATIVES **seasonability** n. **seasonableness** n. **seasonably** adv.

seasonal ■ adj. relating to or characteristic of a particular season of the year. ▶ fluctuating according to the season.
– DERIVATIVES **seasonality** n. **seasonally** adv.

seasonal affective disorder ■ n. depression associated with late autumn and winter and thought to be caused by a lack of light.

seasoning ■ n. salt, herbs, or spices added to food to enhance the flavour.

season ticket ■ n. a ticket allowing travel within a particular period or admission to a series of events.

sea squirt ■ n. a marine tunicate which has a bag-like body with orifices through which water flows into and out of a central pharynx. [Class Ascidiacea.]

sea state ■ n. the degree of turbulence at sea, generally measured on a scale of 0 to 9 according to average wave height.

seat ■ n. **1** a thing made or used for sitting on, such as a chair or stool. ▶ the roughly horizontal part of a chair. ▶ a sitting place for a passenger in a vehicle or for a member of an audience. **2** a person's buttocks. **3** a place in an elected parliament or council. ▶ chiefly Brit. a parliamentary constituency. **4** a site or location. ▶ a large country house and estate belonging to an aristocratic family: *a country seat*. **5** a part of a machine that supports or guides another part. ■ v. arrange for (someone) to sit somewhere. ▶ (**seat oneself**) or **be seated** sit down. ▶ (of a place) have sufficient seats for. ▶ fit in position.
– DERIVATIVES **seating** n. **seatless** adj.

CONSONANTS   **b** but   **d** dog   **f** few   **g** get   **h** he   **j** yes   **k** cat   **l** leg   **m** man   **n** no   **p** pen   **r** red

– ORIGIN Middle English: from Old Norse *sæti*, from the Germanic base of **SIT**.

seat belt ■ n. a belt used to secure someone in the seat of a motor vehicle or aircraft.

-seater ■ comb. form denoting a vehicle, sofa, or building with a specified number of seats: *a six-seater*.

SEATO ■ abbrev. South-East Asia Treaty Organization.

sea trout ■ n. 1 Brit. a brown trout of a salmon-like migratory race. [*Salmo trutta trutta*.] 2 N. Amer. a trout-like marine fish of the drum family occurring in the western Atlantic. [Genus *Cynoscion*: several species.]

sea urchin ■ n. a marine echinoderm which has a spherical or flattened shell covered in mobile spines, with a mouth on the underside and calcareous jaws. [Class Echinoidea.]

sea wall ■ n. a wall or embankment erected to prevent the sea encroaching on an area of land.

seaway ■ n. a waterway or channel used by or capable of accommodating ships.

seaweed ■ n. large algae growing in the sea or on rocks below the high-water mark.

seaworthy ■ adj. (of a boat) in a good enough condition to sail on the sea.
– DERIVATIVES **seaworthiness** n.

sebaceous /sɪˈbeɪʃəs/ ■ adj. technical of or relating to oil or fat. ▸ of or relating to a sebaceous gland or its secretion.
– ORIGIN C18: from Latin *sebaceus*, from *sebum* 'tallow'.

sebaceous cyst ■ n. a swelling in the skin arising in a sebaceous gland, typically filled with yellowish sebum.

sebaceous gland ■ n. a small gland in the skin which secretes a lubricating oily matter (sebum) into the hair follicles to lubricate the skin and hair.

seborrhoea /ˌsɛbəˈriːə/ (US **seborrhea**) ■ n. Medicine excessive discharge of sebum from the sebaceous glands.
– DERIVATIVES **seborrhoeic** adj.

sebum /ˈsiːbəm/ ■ n. an oily secretion of the sebaceous glands.
– ORIGIN C19: from Latin *sebum* 'grease'.

Sec. ■ abbrev. secretary.

sec[1] ■ abbrev. secant.

sec[2] ■ n. informal a second or a very short space of time.

sec[3] ■ adj. (of wine) dry.
– ORIGIN French, from Latin *siccus*.

sec. ■ abbrev. second(s).

secant /ˈsiːk(ə)nt, ˈsɛk-/ ■ n. 1 Mathematics the ratio of the hypotenuse (in a right-angled triangle) to the shorter side adjacent to an acute angle. 2 Geometry a straight line that cuts a curve in two or more parts.
– ORIGIN C16; from French *sécante*, from Latin *secare* 'to cut'.

secateurs /ˌsɛkəˈtɜːz, ˈsɛkətəːz/ ■ pl. n. a pair of pruning clippers for use with one hand.
– ORIGIN C19: pl. of French *sécateur* 'cutter', from Latin *secare* 'to cut'.

secco /ˈsɛkəʊ/ ■ n. the technique of painting on dry plaster with pigments mixed in water.
– ORIGIN C19: from Italian, 'dry', from Latin *siccus*.

secede /sɪˈsiːd/ ■ v. withdraw formally from membership of a federal union or a political or religious organization.
– ORIGIN C18: from Latin *secedere*, from *se-* 'apart' + *cedere* 'go'.

secession /sɪˈsɛʃ(ə)n/ ■ n. the action of seceding from a federation or organization. ▸ (**the Secession**) historical the withdrawal of eleven Southern states from the US Union in 1860, leading to the Civil War.
– DERIVATIVES **secessional** adj. **secessionism** n. **secessionist** n.

seclude ■ v. keep (someone) away from other people.
– ORIGIN Middle English: from Latin *secludere*, from *se-* 'apart' + *claudere* 'to shut'.

secluded ■ adj. (of a place) not seen or visited by many people; sheltered and private.

seclusion ■ n. the state of being private and away from other people.
– DERIVATIVES **seclusive** adj.

Seconal /ˈsɛkənal, -(ə)l/ ■ n. trademark a barbiturate drug

1067   **second-degree**

used as a sedative and hypnotic.
– ORIGIN 1930s: blend of **SECONDARY** and **ALLYL**.

second[1] /ˈsɛk(ə)nd/ ■ ordinal number 1 constituting number two in a sequence; coming after the first in time or order; 2nd. ▸ **secondly**. ▸ (**seconds**) informal a second course or second helping of food at a meal. ▸ denoting someone or something reminiscent of a better-known predecessor: *the conflict could turn into a second Vietnam*. 2 subordinate or inferior in position, rank, or importance. ▸ denoting the second highest division in the results of the examinations for a university degree.
▸ (**seconds**) goods of an inferior quality. 3 Music an interval spanning two consecutive notes in a diatonic scale. ▸ the note which is higher by this interval than the tonic of a diatonic scale or root of a chord. 4 an attendant assisting a combatant in a duel or boxing match. ■ v. formally support or endorse (a nomination or resolution) before adoption or further discussion. ▸ express agreement with.
– PHRASES **second to none** the best, worst, fastest, etc.
– DERIVATIVES **seconder** n. **secondly** adv.
– ORIGIN Middle English: from Latin *secundus* 'following, second', from *sequi* 'follow'.

second[2] /ˈsɛk(ə)nd/ ■ n. 1 (abbrev: **s** or ″) a sixtieth of a minute of time, which as the SI unit of time is defined in terms of the natural periodicity of the radiation of a caesium-133 atom. ▸ informal a very short time. 2 (also **arc second** or **second of arc**) a sixtieth of a minute of angular distance. (Symbol: ″)
– ORIGIN Middle English: from medieval Latin *secunda* (*minuta*) 'second (minute)', from *secundus*, referring to the 'second' operation of dividing an hour by sixty.

second[3] /sɪˈkɒnd/ ■ v. temporarily transfer (a worker) to another position.
– DERIVATIVES **secondee** /-ˈdiː/ n. **secondment** n.
– ORIGIN C19: from French *en second* 'in the second rank (of officers)'.

secondary ■ adj. 1 coming after, less important than, or resulting from something primary. 2 of or relating to education for children from the age of eleven to sixteen or eighteen. 3 of or denoting the output side of a transformer or other inductive device. 4 Chemistry (of an organic compound) having its functional group on a carbon atom bonded to two other carbon atoms. ▸ derived from ammonia by replacement of two hydrogen atoms by organic groups.
– DERIVATIVES **secondarily** adv. **secondariness** n.

secondary colour ■ n. a colour resulting from the mixing of two primary colours.

secondary feather ■ n. any of the flight feathers growing from the second joint of a bird's wing.

secondary industry ■ n. Economics industry that converts raw materials into commodities and products; manufacturing industry.

secondary modern school ■ n. chiefly historical (in the UK) a secondary school for children not selected for grammar or technical schools.

secondary picketing ■ n. picketing of a firm not directly involved in a particular dispute.

secondary sexual characteristics ■ pl. n. physical characteristics developed at puberty which distinguish between the sexes but are not involved in reproduction.

second ballot ■ n. a further ballot held to confirm the selection of a candidate where a previous ballot did not yield an absolute majority.

second best ■ adj. next after the best. ■ n. a less adequate or less desirable alternative.

second chamber ■ n. the upper house of a parliament with two chambers.

second class ■ n. 1 a set of people or things grouped together as the second best. 2 the second-best accommodation in an aircraft, train, or ship. 3 Brit. the second-highest division in the results of the examinations for a university degree. ■ adj. & adv. of the second-best quality or in the second class.

Second Coming ■ n. Christian Church the prophesied return of Christ to Earth at the Last Judgement.

second-degree ■ adj. 1 Medicine denoting burns that

cause blistering but not permanent scars. **2** Law, chiefly N. Amer. denoting a category of a crime, especially murder, that is less serious than a first-degree crime.

seconde /səˈkōd/ ■ n. Fencing the second of eight parrying positions.
– ORIGIN C18: from French, from *second* 'second'.

second economy ■ n. another term for INFORMAL ECONOMY.

second-generation ■ adj. **1** denoting the offspring of parents who have immigrated to a particular country. **2** of a more advanced stage of technology than previous models or systems.

second-guess ■ v. **1** anticipate or predict (someone's actions or thoughts) by guesswork. **2** judge or criticize (someone) with hindsight.

second hand ■ n. an extra hand in some watches and clocks which moves round to indicate the seconds.

second-hand ■ adj. & adv. **1** (of goods) having had a previous owner; not new. **2** accepted on another's authority and not from original investigation.
– PHRASES **at second hand** by hearsay rather than direct observation or experience.

second in command ■ n. the officer next in authority to the commanding or chief officer.

second lieutenant ■ n. the lowest commissioned rank in the army and air force, below lieutenant.

second line ■ n. **1** a battle line behind the front line to support it and make good its losses. **2** [as modifier] ranking second in strength, effectiveness, or ability.

second mate ■ n. another term for SECOND OFFICER.

second name ■ n. Brit. a surname.

second nature ■ n. a tendency or habit that has become instinctive.

second officer ■ n. an assistant mate on a merchant ship.

second person ■ n. see PERSON (sense 5).

second position ■ n. **1** Ballet a posture in which the feet form a straight line, being turned out to either side with the heels separated by the distance of a small step. **2** Music a position of the left hand on the fingerboard of a stringed instrument nearer to the bridge than the first position.

second-rate ■ adj. of mediocre or inferior quality.
– DERIVATIVES **second-rater** n.

second reading ■ n. a second presentation of a bill to a legislative assembly.

second sight ■ n. the supposed ability to perceive future or distant events; clairvoyance.
– DERIVATIVES **second-sighted** adj.

second string ■ n. an alternative resource or course of action in case another one fails.

second thoughts (US also **second thought**) ■ pl. n. a change of opinion or resolve reached after reconsidering something.

second wind ■ n. regained ability to breathe freely during exercise, after having been out of breath.

Second World ■ n. the former communist block consisting of the Soviet Union and some countries in eastern Europe.

secret ■ adj. not known or seen or not meant to be known or seen by others. ▸ fond of having or keeping secrets; secretive. ■ n. **1** something kept or meant to be kept secret. ▸ something not properly understood; a mystery: *the secrets of the universe*. **2** a valid but not commonly known method of achieving something: *the secret of a happy marriage is compromise*.
– DERIVATIVES **secrecy** n. **secretly** adv.
– ORIGIN Middle English: from Latin *secretus* 'separate, set apart', from *secernere*, from *se-* 'apart' + *cernere* 'sift'.

secret agent ■ n. a spy acting for a country.

secretaire /ˌsekrɪˈteː/ ■ n. a small writing desk; an escritoire.
– ORIGIN C18: from French *secrétaire* 'secretary'.

secretariat /ˌsekrɪˈteːrɪət/ ■ n. a governmental administrative office or department.

– ORIGIN C19: from French *secrétariat*, from medieval Latin *secretariatus*, from *secretarius* (see SECRETARY).

secretary ■ n. (pl. **-ies**) **1** a person employed to assist with correspondence, keep records, etc. **2** an official of a society or other organization who conducts its correspondence and keeps its records. **3** the principal assistant of a government minister or ambassador.
– DERIVATIVES **secretarial** adj. **secretaryship** n.
– ORIGIN Middle English: from late Latin *secretarius* 'confidential officer', from Latin *secretum* 'a secret' (see SECRET).

secretary bird ■ n. a slender long-legged African bird of prey that feeds on snakes, having a crest like a quill pen behind the ear. [*Sagittarius serpentarius*.]

Secretary General ■ n. (pl. **Secretaries General**) the title of the principal administrator of some organizations.

Secretary of State ■ n. **1** (in the UK) the head of a major government department. **2** (in the US) the head of the State Department, responsible for foreign affairs.

secrete¹ /sɪˈkriːt/ ■ v. (of a cell, gland, or organ) produce by secretion.
– DERIVATIVES **secretory** adj.

secrete² /sɪˈkriːt/ ■ v. conceal; hide.
– ORIGIN C18: alteration of the obsolete verb *secret* 'keep secret'.

secretion ■ n. a process by which substances are produced and discharged from a cell, gland, or organ for a particular function in the organism or for excretion. ▸ a substance discharged in such a way.
– ORIGIN C17: from French *sécrétion* or Latin *secretio(n-)* 'separation', from *secernere* 'move apart'.

secretive ■ adj. inclined to conceal feelings and intentions or not to disclose information.
– DERIVATIVES **secretively** adv. **secretiveness** n.
– ORIGIN C19: back-formation from *secretiveness*, suggested by French *secrétivité*, from *secret* 'secret'.

secret police ■ n. [treated as pl.] a police force working in secret against a government's political opponents.

secret service ■ n. **1** a government department concerned with espionage. **2** (**Secret Service**) (in the US) a branch of the Treasury Department dealing with counterfeiting and providing protection for the President.

secret society ■ n. an organization whose members are sworn to secrecy about its activities.

sect ■ n. **1** a religious group or faction regarded as heretical or as deviating from orthodox tradition. **2** a group with extreme or dangerous philosophical or political ideas.
– ORIGIN Middle English: from Old French *secte* or Latin *secta* 'following', hence 'faction, party', from *sequi* 'follow'.

sect. ■ abbrev. section.

sectarian ■ adj. denoting, concerning, or deriving from a sect or sects. ▸ carried out on the grounds of membership of a sect, denomination, or other group: *sectarian killings*. ■ n. a member or follower of a sect.
– DERIVATIVES **sectarianism** n.

section ■ n. **1** any of the more or less distinct parts into which something is or may be divided or from which it is made up. ▸ chiefly N. Amer. a particular district of a town. **2** a distinct group within a larger body of people or things. ▸ a subdivision of an army platoon. **3** the cutting of a solid by or along a plane. ▸ the shape resulting from cutting a solid along a plane. ▸ a representation of the internal structure of something as if it has been cut through. **4** Surgery a separation by cutting. ■ v. **1** divide into sections. **2** Surgery divide by cutting.
– DERIVATIVES **sectional** adj. **sectionally** adv. **sectioned** adj.
– ORIGIN Middle English: from French *section* or Latin *sectio(n-)*, from *secare* 'to cut'.

sectionalism ■ n. restriction of interest to parochial concerns.
– DERIVATIVES **sectionalist** n. & adj.

sectional title ■ n. S. African Law a right to the individual ownership of one or more sections of a divided property, for example an apartment block or housing complex, with joint ownership in common property and amenities.

Section 21 company ■ n. S. African a non-profit

company with charitable, cultural, educational, or similar aims, that is incorporated under Section 21 of the Companies Act of 1973.

section mark ■ n. a sign (§) used as a reference mark or to indicate a section of a book.

sector ■ n. **1** an area or portion that is distinct from others. ▸ a distinct part of an economy, society, or sphere of activity. ▸ a subdivision of an area for military operations. **2** the plane figure enclosed by two radii of a circle or ellipse and the arc between them. **3** a mathematical instrument consisting of two arms hinged at one end and marked with sines, tangents, etc. for making diagrams.
– DERIVATIVES **sectoral** adj.
– ORIGIN C16: a technical use of Latin *sector* 'cutter'.

secular /ˈsɛkjʊlə/ ■ adj. **1** not religious, sacred, or spiritual. **2** Christian Church not subject to or bound by religious rule. **3** Astronomy of or denoting slow changes in the motion of the sun or planets.
– DERIVATIVES **secularism** n. **secularist** n. **secularity** n. **secularization** (also **-isation**) n. **secularize** (also **-ise**) v. **secularly** adv.
– ORIGIN Middle English: senses 1 and 2 from Old French *seculer*, from Latin *saecularis*, from *saeculum* 'generation', used in Christian Latin to mean 'the world'; sense 3 from Latin *saecularis* 'relating to an age or period'.

secure ■ adj. **1** fixed or fastened so as not to give way, become loose, or be lost. **2** certain to remain safe and unthreatened. ▸ protected against attack or other criminal activity. **3** feeling free from fear or anxiety. ▸ (**secure of**) dated feeling no doubts about attaining. **4** (of a place of detention) having provisions against the escape of inmates. ■ v. **1** make secure; fix or fasten securely. **2** protect against threats. **3** succeed in obtaining. ▸ seek to guarantee repayment of (a loan) by having a right to take possession of an asset in the event of non-payment. **4** Surgery compress (a blood vessel) to prevent bleeding.
– PHRASES **secure arms** Military hold a rifle with the muzzle downward and the lock in the armpit to guard it from rain.
– DERIVATIVES **securable** adj. **securely** adv. **securement** n. **secureness** n.
– ORIGIN C16 (*security* Middle English): from Latin *securus*, from *se-* 'without' + *cura* 'care'.

securitize (also **-ise**) ■ v. [often as adj. **securitized,** (also **-ised**)] convert (an asset, especially a loan) into marketable securities, typically for the purpose of raising cash.
– DERIVATIVES **securitization** (also **-isation**) n.

security ■ n. (pl. **-ies**) **1** the state of being or feeling secure. **2** the safety of people or property against criminal activity. ▸ the safety of a state or organization against activities such as terrorism. ▸ measures taken to ensure safety. **3** a thing deposited or pledged as a guarantee of the fulfilment of an undertaking or the repayment of a loan, to be forfeited in case of default. **4** a certificate attesting credit, the ownership of stocks or bonds, or the right to ownership connected with tradable derivatives.

security blanket ■ n. **1** a blanket or other familiar object which is a comfort to a child. **2** an official sanction imposed on information in order to maintain complete secrecy.

security complex (also **security estate** or **security village**) ■ n. an enclosed residential development with controlled access.

security gate ■ n. a steel gate, often put in front of a door, protecting a building or area against forced entry.

securocrat /səˈkjʊərə(ʊ)krat/ ■ n. a military or police officer who holds an influential position in government. ▸ an advocate of close military or police involvement in government.
– ORIGIN blend of **SECURITY** and **BUREAUCRAT**.

sedan /sɪˈdan/ ■ n. **1** (also **sedan chair**) an enclosed chair for conveying one person, carried between horizontal poles by two porters, common in the 17th and 18th centuries. **2** a motor car for four or more people.
– ORIGIN perhaps an alteration of an Italian dialect word, from Latin *sella* 'saddle'.

sedate[1] ■ adj. **1** calm and unhurried. **2** staid and rather dull.
– DERIVATIVES **sedately** adv. **sedateness** n.
– ORIGIN Middle English: from Latin *sedare* 'settle', from *sedere* 'sit'.

sedate[2] ■ v. put under sedation.
– ORIGIN 1960s: back-formation from **SEDATION**.

sedation ■ n. the administering of a sedative drug to produce a state of calm or sleep.
– ORIGIN C16: from Latin *sedatio(n-)*, from *sedare* (see **SEDATE**[1]).

sedative ■ adj. promoting calm or inducing sleep. ■ n. a sedative drug.
– ORIGIN Middle English: from Old French *sedatif* or medieval Latin *sedativus*, from Latin *sedare* (see **SEDATE**[1]).

sedentary /ˈsɛd(ə)nt(ə)ri/ ■ adj. **1** tending to spend much time seated. ▸ (of work or a way of life) characterized by much sitting and little physical exercise. ▸ sitting. **2** Anthropology inhabiting the same locality throughout life.
– DERIVATIVES **sedentariness** n.
– ORIGIN C16: from Latin *sedentarius*, from *sedere* 'sit'.

Seder /ˈseɪdə/ ■ n. a Jewish ritual service and ceremonial dinner for the first night or first two nights of Passover.
– ORIGIN from Hebrew *sēḏer* 'order, procedure'.

sedge ■ n. a grass-like plant with triangular stems and inconspicuous flowers, growing typically in wet ground. [*Carex* and other genera.]
– DERIVATIVES **sedgy** adj.
– ORIGIN Old English, of Germanic origin.

sedge warbler ■ n. a common migratory songbird with streaky brown plumage, frequenting marshes and reed beds. [*Acrocephalus schoenobaenus*.]

sediment ■ n. **1** matter that settles to the bottom of a liquid. **2** Geology particulate matter carried by water or wind and deposited on the land surface or seabed. ■ v. settle or deposit as sediment.
– DERIVATIVES **sedimentation** n.
– ORIGIN C16: from French *sédiment* or Latin *sedimentum* 'settling'.

sedimentary ■ adj. of or relating to sediment. ▸ Geology (of rock) that has formed from sediment deposited by water or wind.

sedition ■ n. conduct or speech inciting rebellion against the authority of a state or monarch.
– DERIVATIVES **seditious** adj. **seditiously** adv.
– ORIGIN Middle English: from Latin *seditio(n-)*, from *sed-* 'apart' + *itio(n-)* 'going'.

seduce ■ v. **1** persuade to do something inadvisable. **2** entice into sexual activity.
– DERIVATIVES **seducer** n. **seduction** n. **seductress** n.
– ORIGIN C15 (*seduction* Middle English): from Latin *seducere*, from *se-* 'away' + *ducere* 'to lead'.

seductive ■ adj. tempting and attractive.
– DERIVATIVES **seductively** adv. **seductiveness** n.

sedulous /ˈsɛdjʊləs/ ■ adj. showing dedication and diligence.
– DERIVATIVES **sedulity** /sɪˈdjuːlɪti/ n. **sedulously** adv. **sedulousness** n.
– ORIGIN C16: from Latin *sedulus* 'zealous'.

sedum /ˈsiːdəm/ ■ n. a fleshy-leaved plant of a large genus including the stonecrops, with small star-shaped flowers. [Genus *Sedum*.]
– ORIGIN from modern Latin, denoting a houseleek.

see[1] ■ v. (**sees, seeing**; past **saw**; past part. **seen**) **1** perceive with the eyes. ▸ watch (a game, film, or other entertainment). ▸ experience or witness (an event or situation). **2** deduce after reflection or from information. ▸ ascertain after inquiry or consultation. **3** regard in a specified way. ▸ envisage. **4** meet (someone one knows) socially or by chance. ▸ meet regularly as a boyfriend or girlfriend. ▸ consult (a specialist or professional). ▸ give an interview or consultation to. **5** escort to a specified place. **6** (**see to**) attend to. **7** ensure. **8** (in poker or brag) equal the bet of (an opponent) and require them to reveal their cards to determine who has won the hand.
– PHRASES **let me see** said as an appeal for time to think before speaking. **see here!** said for emphasis or to express a protest. **see one's way clear to do** (or **doing**) **something** find that it is possible or convenient to do something. **see someone coming** recognize a person who can be fooled.

see

see someone right Brit. informal make sure that a person is appropriately rewarded or looked after. **see the back of** informal be rid of.
- PHRASAL VERBS **see about** attend to. **see something of** spend a specified amount of time with (someone) socially. **see someone off 1** accompany a person who is leaving to their point of departure. **2** repel an intruder or counter someone posing a threat. **see something out** chiefly Brit. come to the end of a period of time or undertaking. **see through** detect the true nature of. **see someone through** support a person for the duration of a difficult time. **see something through** persist with an undertaking until it is completed.
- ORIGIN Old English, of Germanic origin.

see² ■ n. the place in which a cathedral church stands, identified as the seat of authority of a bishop or archbishop.
- ORIGIN Middle English: from Anglo-Norman French *sed*, from Latin *sedere* 'sit'.

seed ■ n. **1** a flowering plant's unit of reproduction, capable of developing into another such plant. ▸ a quantity of these. **2** the beginning of a feeling, process, or condition. **3** archaic a man's semen. **4** archaic (chiefly in biblical use) offspring or descendants. **5** a small crystal introduced into a liquid to act as a nucleus for crystallization. **6** any of a number of stronger competitors in a sports tournament who have been assigned a position in an ordered list to ensure they do not play each other in the early rounds. ■ v. **1** sow (land) with seeds. ▸ sow (seed). **2** produce or drop seeds. **3** remove the seeds from. **4** initiate the development or growth of. **5** place a crystalline substance in (a cloud or solution) in order to cause condensation or crystallization. **6** give (a competitor) the status of seed in a tournament.
- PHRASES **go** (or **run**) **to seed 1** cease flowering as the seeds develop. **2** deteriorate in condition or strength.
- DERIVATIVES **seeded** adj. **seedless** adj.
- ORIGIN Old English, of Germanic origin.

seedbed ■ n. a bed of fine soil in which seedlings are germinated.

seed cake ■ n. cake containing caraway seeds.

seed capital ■ n. another term for SEED MONEY.

seedcorn ■ n. **1** good-quality corn kept for seed. **2** Brit. assets set aside for the generation of future profit.

seeder ■ n. a machine for sowing seed.

seed head ■ n. a flower head in seed.

seed leaf ■ n. Botany a cotyledon.

seedling ■ n. a young plant, especially one raised from seed and not from a cutting.

seed money ■ n. money allocated to initiate a project.

seed pearl ■ n. a very small pearl.

seed potato ■ n. a potato intended for replanting to produce a new plant.

seedsman ■ n. (pl. **-men**) a person who deals in seeds as a profession.

seedy ■ adj. (**-ier**, **-iest**) **1** sordid or squalid. **2** dated unwell.
- DERIVATIVES **seedily** adv. **seediness** n.

seeing ■ conj. because; since. ■ n. Astronomy the quality of observed images as determined by atmospheric conditions.

Seeing Eye dog ■ n. trademark, chiefly N. Amer. a guide dog for the blind.

seek ■ v. (past and past part. **sought**) **1** attempt to find. ▸ (**seek someone/thing out**) search for and find someone or something. **2** attempt to obtain or do. **3** ask for.
- DERIVATIVES **seeker** n.
- ORIGIN Old English, of Germanic origin.

seem ■ v. **1** give the impression of being. **2** (**cannot seem to do something**) be unable to do something, despite having tried.
- ORIGIN Middle English: from Old Norse *sœma* 'to honour', from *sœmr* 'fitting'.

seeming ■ adj. apparent. ▸ [in combination] giving the impression of having a specified quality: *an angry-seeming man.* ■ n. poetic/literary outward appearance, especially when deceptive or different from reality.
- DERIVATIVES **seemingly** adv.

seemly ■ adj. conforming to propriety or good taste.
- DERIVATIVES **seemliness** n.
- ORIGIN Middle English: from Old Norse *sœmiligr*, from *sœmr* 'fitting'.

seen past participle of SEE¹.

See of Rome ■ n. another term for HOLY SEE.

seep ■ v. (of a liquid) flow or leak slowly through porous material or small holes. ■ n. N. Amer. a place where petroleum or water seeps out of the ground.
- DERIVATIVES **seepage** n.
- ORIGIN C18: perhaps a dialect form of Old English *sīpian* 'to soak'.

seer /'siːə, sɪə/ ■ n. **1** a person of supposed supernatural insight who sees visions of the future. **2** chiefly archaic a person who sees something specified.

seersucker ■ n. a fabric with a surface consisting of puckered and flat sections.
- ORIGIN C18: from Persian *šir o šakar* 'milk and sugar', (by transference) 'striped cotton garment'.

see-saw ■ n. **1** a long plank balanced on a fixed support, on each end of which children sit and move up and down by pushing the ground alternately with their feet. **2** a situation characterized by rapid, repeated changes from one state or position to another. ■ v. change rapidly and repeatedly from one state or position to another and back again.
- ORIGIN C17: reduplication of the verb SAW¹.

seethe ■ v. **1** (of a liquid) boil or be turbulent as if boiling. **2** be filled with intense but unexpressed anger. **3** be crowded with people or things moving about in a rapid or hectic way.
- ORIGIN Old English *sēothan* 'make or keep boiling'.

see-through ■ adj. (especially of clothing) translucent.

Sefer /'sɛfə/ ■ n. (pl. **Sifrei**) Judaism a book of Hebrew religious literature.
- ORIGIN from Hebrew *sēp̱er tōrāh* 'book of (the) Law'.

segment /'sɛgm(ə)nt/ ■ n. **1** each of the parts into which something is or may be divided. **2** Geometry a part of a circle cut off by a chord, or a part of a sphere cut off by a plane not passing through the centre. **3** Phonetics the smallest distinct part of a spoken utterance, especially with regard to vowel and consonant sounds. **4** Zoology each of a series of similar anatomical units of which the body and appendages of some animals are composed. ■ v. /usu. sɛɡˈmɛnt/ divide into segments.
- DERIVATIVES **segmentary** adj. **segmentation** n.
- ORIGIN C16: from Latin *segmentum*, from *secare* 'to cut'.

segmental ■ adj. **1** composed of segments. ▸ Phonetics denoting or relating to the division of speech into segments. **2** Architecture denoting an arch in which the curve forms a shallow arc of a circle, less than a semicircle.
- DERIVATIVES **segmentalization** (also **-isation**) n. **segmentalize** (also **-ise**) v. **segmentally** adv.

segregate¹ /'sɛɡrɪɡeɪt/ ■ v. **1** set apart from the rest or from each other. **2** separate along racial, sexual, or religious lines. **3** Genetics (of pairs of alleles) be separated at meiosis and transmitted independently via separate gametes.
- DERIVATIVES **segregable** adj. **segregative** adj.
- ORIGIN C16: from Latin *segregare* 'separate from the flock'.

segregate² /'sɛɡrɪɡət/ ■ n. Genetics an allele that has undergone segregation.
- ORIGIN C19: from Latin *segregatus* 'separate', from *segregare* (see SEGREGATE¹).

segregation ■ n. the action of segregating or the state of being segregated.
- DERIVATIVES **segregational** adj. **segregationist** n. & adj.

segue /'sɛɡweɪ/ ■ v. (**segues**, **segued**, **seguing**) (in music and film) move without interruption from one song, melody, or scene to another. ■ n. an instance of this.
- ORIGIN Italian, 'follows'.

seicento /seɪ'tʃɛntəʊ/ ■ n. the style of Italian art and literature of the 17th century.
- DERIVATIVES **seicentist** n.
- ORIGIN Italian, '600', shortened from *mille seicento* '1600', used with ref. to the years 1600–99.

seiche /seɪʃ/ ■ n. a temporary disturbance or oscillation in the water level of a lake or partially enclosed body of water, especially one caused by changes in atmospheric pressure.
– ORIGIN C19: from Swiss French, perhaps from German *Seiche* 'sinking (of water)'.

seif /siːf, seɪf/ ■ n. a sand dune in the form of a long narrow ridge.
– ORIGIN C20: from Arabic *sayf* 'sword' (because of the shape).

seigneur /seɪˈnjəː/ (also **seignior** /ˈseɪnjə/) ■ n. a feudal lord; the lord of a manor.
– DERIVATIVES **seigneurial** adj.
– ORIGIN C16: from Latin *senior* 'older, elder'.

seigniorage /ˈseɪnjərɪdʒ/ (also **seignorage**) ■ n. profit made by a government by issuing currency, especially the difference between the face value of coins and their production costs.
– ORIGIN Middle English: from Old French *seignorage*, from *seigneur* (see SEIGNEUR).

seigniory /ˈseɪnjəri/ (also **seignory**) ■ n. (pl. **-ies**) the position, authority, or domain of a feudal lord.
– ORIGIN Middle English: from Old French *seignorie*, from *seigneur* (see SEIGNEUR).

seine /seɪn/ ■ n. a fishing net which hangs vertically in the water with floats at the top and weights at the bottom edge, the ends being drawn together to encircle the fish. ■ v. fish or catch with a seine.
– DERIVATIVES **seiner** n.
– ORIGIN Old English *segne*, of West Germanic origin, from Greek *sagēnē*; reinforced in Middle English by Old French *saine*.

seise ■ v. see SEIZE (sense 5).

seismic /ˈsaɪzmɪk/ ■ adj. 1 of or relating to earthquakes or other vibrations of the earth and its crust. ▸ relating to or denoting geological surveying methods involving vibrations produced artificially by explosions. 2 of enormous proportions or effect.
– DERIVATIVES **seismical** adj. **seismically** adv.
– ORIGIN C19: from Greek *seismos* 'earthquake'.

seismicity /saɪzˈmɪsɪti/ ■ n. Geology the occurrence or frequency of earthquakes in a region.

seismo- ■ comb. form of an earthquake; relating to earthquakes: *seismograph*.
– ORIGIN from Greek *seismos* 'earthquake'.

seismogram /ˈsaɪzmə(ʊ)ɡram/ ■ n. a record produced by a seismograph.

seismograph /ˈsaɪzmə(ʊ)ɡrɑːf/ ■ n. an instrument that measures and records details of earthquakes, such as force and duration.
– DERIVATIVES **seismographic** adj. **seismographical** adj.

seismology /saɪzˈmɒlədʒi/ ■ n. the branch of science concerned with earthquakes and related phenomena.
– DERIVATIVES **seismological** adj. **seismologically** adv. **seismologist** n.

seismometer /saɪzˈmɒmɪtə/ ■ n. another term for SEISMOGRAPH.

sei whale /seɪ/ ■ n. a small rorqual with dark steely-grey skin and white grooves on the belly. [*Balaenoptera borealis*.]
– ORIGIN C20: from Norwegian *sejhval*.

seize ■ v. 1 take hold of suddenly and forcibly. ▸ take forcible possession of. ▸ (of the police or another authority) take possession of by warrant or legal right. 2 take (an opportunity) eagerly and decisively. ▸ (**seize on/upon**) take eager advantage of. 3 affect suddenly or acutely. 4 (of a machine with moving parts or a moving part in a machine) become jammed. 5 (also **seise**) (**be seized of**) English Law be in legal possession of.
– DERIVATIVES **seizable** adj.
– ORIGIN Middle English: from Old French *seizir*, from the medieval Latin phr. *ad proprium sacire* 'claim as one's own', from a Germanic base meaning 'procedure'.

seizure ■ n. 1 the action of seizing. 2 a sudden attack of illness, especially a stroke or an epileptic fit.

sejant /ˈsiːdʒ(ə)nt/ ■ adj. [postpos.] Heraldry (of an animal) sitting upright.
– ORIGIN C15: alteration of an Old French var. of *seant* 'sitting'.

Sekt /zɛkt/ ■ n. a German sparkling white wine.
– ORIGIN from German.

selachian /sɪˈleɪkɪən/ ■ n. Zoology a cartilaginous fish of a group that comprises the sharks and dogfishes.
– ORIGIN C19: from Greek *selakhos* 'shark'.

seldom ■ adv. not often.
– ORIGIN Old English *seldan*, of Germanic origin, from a base meaning 'strange, wonderful'.

select ■ v. carefully choose as being the best or most suitable. ■ adj. 1 carefully chosen from a larger number as being the best. 2 used by or consisting of a wealthy or sophisticated elite.
– DERIVATIVES **selectable** adj.
– ORIGIN C16: from Latin *select-*, *seligere* 'choose'.

select committee ■ n. a small parliamentary committee appointed for a special purpose.

selection ■ n. the action or fact of selecting. ▸ a number of selected things. ▸ a range of things from which a choice may be made. ▸ a horse or horses tipped as worth bets in a race or meeting.

selectional ■ adj. Linguistics denoting or relating to the process by which only certain words or structures can occur naturally, normally, or correctly in the context of other words.
– DERIVATIVES **selectionally** adv.

selective ■ adj. 1 relating to or involving selection. ▸ tending to choose carefully. 2 (of a process or agent) affecting some things and not others.
– DERIVATIVES **selectively** adv. **selectiveness** n. **selectivity** n.

selector ■ n. 1 a person appointed to select a team in a sport. 2 a device for selecting a particular gear or other setting of a machine or device.

selenite /ˈsɛlɪnʌɪt/ ■ n. a form of gypsum occurring as transparent crystals or thin plates.
– ORIGIN C17: from Greek *selēnitēs lithos* 'moonstone'.

selenium /sɪˈliːnɪəm/ ■ n. the chemical element of atomic number 34, a grey crystalline non-metal with semi-conducting properties. (Symbol: **Se**)
– DERIVATIVES **selenide** n.
– ORIGIN C19: from Greek *selēnē* 'moon'.

selenography /ˌsɛlɪˈnɒɡrəfi, ˌsiː-/ ■ n. the scientific mapping of the moon.
– DERIVATIVES **selenographic** adj.

Seleucid /sɪˈluːsɪd/ ■ n. a member of a dynasty ruling over Syria and a great part of western Asia from 311 to 65 BC.
– ORIGIN from *Seleucus* Nicator (the name of the founder, one of Alexander the Great's generals).

self ■ n. (pl. **selves**) a person's essential being that distinguishes them from others, especially considered as the object of introspection or reflexive action. ▸ a person's particular nature or personality. ▸ one's own interests or pleasure. ■ pron. (pl. **selves**) 1 (**one's self**) used ironically to refer in specified favourable terms to oneself or someone else: *a picture of my good self*. 2 used on counterfoils, cheques, and other papers to refer to the holder or person who has signed. ■ adj. (of a trimming, woven design, etc.) of the same material or colour as the rest. ■ v. chiefly Botany self-pollinate; self-fertilize.
– ORIGIN Old English, of Germanic origin.

self- /sɛlf/ ■ comb. form 1 of or directed towards oneself or itself: *self-hatred*. 2 by one's own efforts; by its own action: *self-adjusting*. 3 on, in, for, or relating to oneself or itself: *self-adhesive*.

self-abandonment (also **self-abandon**) ■ n. the action of completely surrendering oneself to a desire or impulse.
– DERIVATIVES **self-abandoned** adj.

self-absorption ■ n. 1 preoccupation with one's own emotions, interests, or situation. 2 Physics the absorption by a body of radiation which it has itself emitted.
– DERIVATIVES **self-absorbed** adj.

self-abuse ■ n. 1 behaviour which causes damage or harm to oneself. 2 euphemistic masturbation.

self-addressed ■ adj. (especially of an envelope) bearing one's own address.

self-adhesive ■ adj. adhering without requiring moistening.

self-adjusting ■ adj. (chiefly of machinery) adjusting itself to meet varying requirements.

self-advertisement ■ n. the active publicizing of oneself.
–DERIVATIVES **self-advertiser** n. **self-advertising** adj.

self-affirmation ■ n. the recognition and assertion of the existence and value of one's individual self.

self-alienation ■ n. the distancing of oneself from one's feelings or activities, such as may occur in mental illness.

self-appointed ■ adj. having assumed a position or role without the endorsement of others.

self-assembly ■ n. **1** the construction of a piece of furniture from materials sold in kit form. **2** Biology the spontaneous formation of a ribosome, virus, etc. in a medium containing the appropriate components.
–DERIVATIVES **self-assemble** v.

self-assertion ■ n. the confident and forceful expression or promotion of oneself or one's views.
–DERIVATIVES **self-assertive** adj. **self-assertiveness** n.

self-assessment ■ n. **1** assessment of oneself or one's performance in relation to an objective standard. **2** calculation of one's own taxable liability.

self-assurance ■ n. confidence in one's own abilities or character.
–DERIVATIVES **self-assured** adj. **self-assuredly** adv.

self-awareness ■ n. conscious knowledge of one's own character, feelings, motives, and desires.
–DERIVATIVES **self-aware** adj.

self-build ■ n. the building of homes by their owners.

self-cancelling ■ adj. **1** having elements which contradict or negate one another. **2** (of a mechanical device) designed to stop working automatically when no longer required.

self-catering ■ adj. (of a holiday or accommodation) offering facilities for people to cook their own meals. ■ n. the action of catering for oneself.

self-censorship ■ n. the exercising of control over what one says and does, especially to avoid reprisal.

self-centred ■ adj. preoccupied with oneself and one's affairs.
–DERIVATIVES **self-centredly** adv. **self-centredness** n.

self-certification ■ n. the practice of attesting something about oneself in a formal statement, rather than asking a disinterested party to do so. ▶ the practice, for the purpose of claiming sick pay, by which an employee rather than a doctor declares in writing that an absence was due to illness.

self-certify ■ v. attest (one's financial standing) in a formal statement. ▶ [as adj. **self-certified**] (of a loan or mortgage) obtained as a result of such self-certification.

self-colour ■ n. **1** a single uniform colour. **2** the natural colour of something.
–DERIVATIVES **self-coloured** adj.

self-conceit ■ n. another term for SELF-CONGRATULATION.
–DERIVATIVES **self-conceited** adj.

self-confessed ■ adj. having openly admitted to being a person with certain characteristics.
–DERIVATIVES **self-confessedly** adv. **self-confession** n. **self-confessional** adj.

self-confidence ■ n. a feeling of trust in one's abilities, qualities, and judgement.
–DERIVATIVES **self-confident** adj. **self-confidently** adv.

self-congratulation ■ n. undue pride regarding one's achievements or qualities.
–DERIVATIVES **self-congratulatory** adj.

self-conscious ■ adj. **1** nervous or awkward because unduly aware of oneself or one's actions. **2** (especially of an action) deliberate and with full awareness. **3** Philosophy & Psychology having knowledge of one's own existence, especially the knowledge of oneself as a conscious being.
–DERIVATIVES **self-consciously** adv. **self-consciousness** n.

self-contained ■ adj. **1** complete, or having all that is needed, in itself. ▶ (of accommodation) having its own kitchen and bathroom, and typically its own private entrance. **2** not depending on or influenced by others.
–DERIVATIVES **self-containment** n.

self-contradiction ■ n. inconsistency between aspects or parts of a whole.
–DERIVATIVES **self-contradicting** adj. **self-contradictory** adj.

self-control ■ n. the ability to control one's emotions or behaviour, especially in difficult situations.
–DERIVATIVES **self-controlled** adj.

self-deception ■ n. the action or practice of deceiving oneself into believing that a false or unvalidated feeling, idea, or situation is true.
–DERIVATIVES **self-deceit** n. **self-deceiver** n. **self-deceiving** adj. **self-deceptive** adj.

self-defeating ■ adj. (of an action or policy) unable to achieve the end it is designed to bring about.

self-defence ■ n. the defence of one's person or interests, especially through the use of physical force, which is permitted in certain cases as an answer to a charge of violent crime.

self-denial ■ n. the denial of one's own interests and needs.
–DERIVATIVES **self-denying** adj.

self-deprecating ■ adj. modest about or critical of oneself, especially humorously so.
–DERIVATIVES **self-deprecatingly** adv. **self-deprecation** n. **self-deprecatory** adj.

self-depreciatory ■ adj. another term for SELF-DEPRECATING.
–DERIVATIVES **self-depreciation** n.

self-destruct ■ v. explode or disintegrate automatically, having been preset to do so.

self-destructive ■ adj. destroying or causing harm to oneself.
–DERIVATIVES **self-destruction** n. **self-destructively** adv.

self-determination ■ n. **1** the process by which a country determines its own statehood and forms its own allegiances and government. **2** the process by which a person controls their own life.

self-directed ■ adj. **1** (of an emotion, statement, or activity) directed at one's self. **2** (of an activity) under one's own control.
–DERIVATIVES **self-direction** n.

self-discipline ■ n. the ability to control one's feelings and overcome one's weaknesses.
–DERIVATIVES **self-disciplined** adj.

self-doubt ■ n. lack of confidence in oneself and one's abilities.

self-drive ■ adj. **1** (of a hired vehicle) driven by the hirer. **2** (of a holiday) involving use of one's own car rather than transport arranged by the operator.

self-educated ■ adj. educated largely through one's own efforts, rather than by formal instruction.
–DERIVATIVES **self-education** n.

self-effacing ■ adj. not claiming attention for oneself.
–DERIVATIVES **self-effacement** n. **self-effacingly** adv.

self-employed ■ adj. working for oneself as a freelance or the owner of a business rather than for an employer.
–DERIVATIVES **self-employment** n.

self-enclosed ■ adj. (of a person, community, or system) not choosing or able to communicate with others or with external systems.

self-esteem ■ n. confidence in one's own worth or abilities.

self-evaluation ■ n. another term for SELF-ASSESSMENT.

self-evident ■ adj. not needing to be demonstrated or explained.
–DERIVATIVES **self-evidence** n. **self-evidently** adv.

self-examination ■ n. **1** the study of one's behaviour and motivations. **2** the examination of one's body for signs of illness.

self-explanatory ■ adj. not needing explanation.

self-expression ■ n. the expression of one's feelings, thoughts, or ideas, especially in writing, art, music, or dance.

– DERIVATIVES **self-expressive** adj.

self-feeder ■ n. **1** a furnace or machine that renews its own fuel or material automatically. **2** a device for supplying food to farm animals automatically.
– DERIVATIVES **self-feeding** adj.

self-fertile ■ adj. Botany (of a plant) capable of self-fertilization.

self-fertilization (also **-isation**) ■ n. Biology the fertilization of plants and some invertebrate animals by their own pollen or sperm.
– DERIVATIVES **self-fertilize** (also **-ise**) v.

self-financing ■ adj. (of an organization or enterprise) having or generating enough income to finance itself.
– DERIVATIVES **self-financed** adj.

self-flagellation ■ n. **1** the action of flogging oneself, especially as a form of religious discipline. **2** excessive self-criticism.

self-fulfilling ■ adj. (of an opinion or prediction) bound to be proved correct or to come true as a result of behaviour caused by its being expressed.

self-governing ■ adj. (of a former colony or dependency) administering its own affairs.

self-government ■ n. **1** government of a country by its own people, especially after having been a colony. **2** another term for SELF-CONTROL.
– DERIVATIVES **self-governed** adj.

self-harm ■ n. deliberate injury to oneself, typically as a manifestation of a psychological or psychiatric disorder. ■ v. commit self-harm.
– DERIVATIVES **self-harmer** n.

self-heal ■ n. a purple-flowered Eurasian plant of the mint family, formerly used for healing wounds. [*Prunella vulgaris*.]

self-help ■ n. the use of one's own efforts and resources to achieve things without relying on others.

selfhood ■ n. the quality that constitutes one's individuality.

self-identification ■ n. the attribution of certain characteristics or qualities to oneself.

self-image ■ n. the idea one has of one's abilities, appearance, and personality.

self-immolation ■ n. the offering of oneself as a sacrifice, especially by burning.

self-importance ■ n. an exaggerated sense of one's own value or importance.
– DERIVATIVES **self-important** adj. **self-importantly** adv.

self-improvement ■ n. the improvement of one's knowledge, status, or character by one's own efforts.

self-induced ■ adj. **1** brought about by oneself. **2** produced by electrical self-induction.

self-induction ■ n. Physics the induction of an electromotive force in a circuit when the current in that circuit is varied.

self-indulgent ■ adj. indulging or tending to indulge one's desires.
– DERIVATIVES **self-indulgence** n. **self-indulgently** adv.

self-inflicted ■ adj. (of a wound or other harm) inflicted on oneself.

self-insurance ■ n. insurance of oneself or one's interests by maintaining a fund to cover possible losses rather than by purchasing an insurance policy.

self-interest ■ n. one's personal interest or advantage, especially when pursued without regard for others.
– DERIVATIVES **self-interested** adj.

self-involved ■ adj. wrapped up in oneself or one's own thoughts.
– DERIVATIVES **self-involvement** n.

selfish ■ adj. concerned chiefly with one's own personal profit or pleasure at the expense of consideration for others.
– DERIVATIVES **selfishly** adv. **selfishness** n.

selfless ■ adj. concerned more with the needs and wishes of others than with one's own.
– DERIVATIVES **selflessly** adv. **selflessness** n.

self-limiting ■ adj. Medicine (of a condition) ultimately resolving itself without treatment.

1073

self-reliance

self-liquidating ■ adj. denoting an asset, project, etc. that earns sufficiently over a certain period to pay for its cost.

self-loading ■ adj. (especially of a gun) loading automatically.
– DERIVATIVES **self-loader** n.

self-love ■ n. regard for one's own well-being and happiness.

self-made ■ adj. **1** having become successful or rich by one's own efforts. **2** made by oneself.

self-management ■ n. **1** management of or by oneself. **2** the distribution of political control to individual regions of a state, especially as a form of socialism.
– DERIVATIVES **self-managing** adj.

self-medicate ■ v. administer medication to oneself without medical supervision.
– DERIVATIVES **self-medication** n.

self-motivated ■ adj. motivated to do something because of one's own enthusiasm or interest, without needing pressure from others.
– DERIVATIVES **self-motivating** adj. **self-motivation** n.

self-mutilation ■ n. deliberate injury to one's own body.

self-opinionated ■ adj. having an arrogantly high regard for oneself or one's own opinions.
– DERIVATIVES **self-opinion** n.

self-parody ■ n. the intentional or inadvertent parodying of one's own behaviour, style, etc.
– DERIVATIVES **self-parodic** adj. **self-parodying** adj.

self-perpetuating ■ adj. perpetuating itself or oneself without external agency or intervention.
– DERIVATIVES **self-perpetuation** n.

self-pity ■ n. excessive unhappiness over one's own troubles.
– DERIVATIVES **self-pitying** adj. **self-pityingly** adv.

self-policing ■ n. the process of keeping order or maintaining control within a community without accountability or reference to an external authority.

self-pollination ■ n. Botany the pollination of a flower by pollen from the same plant.
– DERIVATIVES **self-pollinate** v. **self-pollinator** n.

self-portrait ■ n. a portrait by an artist of himself or herself.
– DERIVATIVES **self-portraiture** n.

self-possessed ■ adj. calm, confident, and in control of one's feelings.
– DERIVATIVES **self-possession** n.

self-preservation ■ n. the protection of oneself from harm or death, especially regarded as a basic instinct in human beings and animals.

self-proclaimed ■ adj. proclaimed to be such by oneself, without endorsement by others.

self-promotion ■ n. the action of promoting or publicizing oneself or one's abilities, especially in a forceful way.
– DERIVATIVES **self-promoter** n. **self-promoting** adj.

self-propelled ■ adj. moving or able to move without external propulsion or agency.
– DERIVATIVES **self-propelling** adj.

self-raising flour ■ n. flour that has a raising agent already added.

self-realization (also **-isation**) ■ n. fulfilment of one's own potential.

self-referential ■ adj. (especially of a literary or other creative work) making reference to itself, its creator, or their other work.
– DERIVATIVES **self-referentiality** n. **self-referentially** adv.

self-regard ■ n. **1** consideration for oneself. **2** vanity.
– DERIVATIVES **self-regarding** adj.

self-regulating ■ adj. regulating itself without intervention from external bodies.
– DERIVATIVES **self-regulation** n. **self-regulatory** adj.

self-reliance ■ n. reliance on one's own powers and resources rather than those of others.
– DERIVATIVES **self-reliant** adj. **self-reliantly** adv.

self-replicating ■ adj. capable of reproducing or giving rise to a copy of itself.

self-respect ■ n. pride and confidence in oneself.
– DERIVATIVES **self-respecting** adj.

self-restraint ■ n. self-control.
– DERIVATIVES **self-restrained** adj.

self-revealing ■ adj. revealing one's character or motives, especially inadvertently.
– DERIVATIVES **self-revelation** n. **self-revelatory** adj.

self-righteous ■ adj. certain that one is totally correct or morally superior.
– DERIVATIVES **self-righteously** adv. **self-righteousness** n.

self-righting ■ adj. (of a boat) designed to right itself when capsized.

self-rule ■ n. another term for SELF-GOVERNMENT (in sense 1).

self-sacrifice ■ n. the giving up of one's own interests or wishes in order to help others or advance a cause.
– DERIVATIVES **self-sacrificial** adj. **self-sacrificing** adj.

selfsame ■ adj. exactly the same.

self-satisfied ■ adj. smugly complacent.
– DERIVATIVES **self-satisfaction** n.

self-sealing ■ adj. **1** (of a tyre, fuel tank, etc.) able to seal small punctures automatically. **2** (of an envelope) self-adhesive.

self-seed ■ v. (of a plant) propagate itself by seed.
– DERIVATIVES **self-seeder** n.

self-seeking ■ adj. pursuing one's own welfare and interests before those of others.
– DERIVATIVES **self-seeker** n.

self-selection ■ n. **1** the action of putting oneself forward for something. **2** the action of selecting something for oneself.
– DERIVATIVES **self-selecting** adj.

self-service ■ adj. denoting a shop, restaurant, or other outlet where customers select goods for themselves and pay at a checkout. ■ n. a self-service system or outlet.

self-serving ■ adj. another term for SELF-SEEKING.

self-sow ■ v. (of a plant) propagate itself by seed.

self-starter ■ n. **1** a self-motivated and ambitious person who acts on their own initiative. **2** dated the starter of a motor-vehicle engine.
– DERIVATIVES **self-starting** adj.

self-sterile ■ adj. Biology incapable of self-fertilization.
– DERIVATIVES **self-sterility** n.

self-styled ■ adj. using a description or title that one has given oneself.

self-sufficient ■ adj. **1** able to satisfy one's basic needs without outside help, especially with regard to the production of food. **2** emotionally and intellectually independent.
– DERIVATIVES **self-sufficiency** n. **self-sufficiently** adv.

self-supporting ■ adj. **1** having the resources to be able to survive without outside assistance. **2** staying up or upright without being supported by something else.
– DERIVATIVES **self-support** n.

self-surrender ■ n. the surrender of oneself or one's will to an external influence, an emotion, etc.

self-sustaining ■ adj. able to continue in a healthy state without outside assistance.
– DERIVATIVES **self-sustained** adj.

self-tailing ■ adj. (of a winch) designed to maintain constant tension in the rope so that it does not slip.

self-tapping ■ adj. (of a screw) able to cut a thread in the material into which it is inserted.

self-taught ■ adj. having acquired knowledge or skill on one's own initiative rather than through formal instruction or training.

self-timer ■ n. a mechanism in a camera that introduces a delay between the operation of the shutter release and the opening of the shutter, enabling the photographer to be included in the photograph.

self-willed ■ adj. obstinately pursuing one's own wishes.
– DERIVATIVES **self-will** n.

self-winding ■ adj. (chiefly of a watch) wound by automatic means rather than by hand.

self-worth ■ n. another term for SELF-ESTEEM.

Seljuk /'sɛldʒuːk/ ■ n. a member of any of the Turkish dynasties which ruled Asia Minor in the 11th to 13th centuries.
– ORIGIN from Turkish *seljūq*, the name of the reputed ancestor of the dynasty.

selkie (also **selky** or **silkie**) ■ n. (pl. **-ies**) Scottish a mythical creature that resembles a seal in the water but assumes human form on land.
– ORIGIN from *selch*, var. of SEAL.

sell ■ v. (past and past part. **sold**) **1** hand over in exchange for money. ▸ deal in. ▸ be subject to a specified demand on the market: *the book didn't sell well.* ▸ (**sell out**) sell all of one's stock of something. ▸ (**sell oneself**) have sex in exchange for money. **2** persuade someone of the merits of. ▸ make enthusiastic about. **3** (**sell someone out**) betray someone for one's own financial or material benefit. ▸ (**sell out**) abandon one's principles for reasons of expedience. ■ n. informal an act of selling or attempting to sell.
– PHRASES **sell someone/thing short** fail to recognize or state the true value of someone or something. **sell one's soul** (**to the devil**) be willing to do anything, no matter how wrong it is, in order to achieve one's objective.
– DERIVATIVES **sellable** adj.
– ORIGIN Old English, of Germanic origin.

sell-by date ■ n. **1** a date marked on a perishable product indicating the recommended time by which it should be sold. **2** informal a time after which something or someone is no longer considered desirable or effective.

seller ■ n. **1** a person who sells. **2** a product that sells in a specified way.
– PHRASES **seller's** (or **sellers'**) **market** an economic situation in which goods or shares are scarce and sellers can keep prices high.

selling point ■ n. a feature of a product for sale that makes it attractive to customers.

sell-off ■ n. a sale of assets, typically at a low price, carried out in order to dispose of them rather than as normal trade. ▸ a sale of shares, bonds, or commodities, especially one that causes a fall in price.

Sellotape ■ n. trademark transparent adhesive tape. ■ v. fasten or stick with Sellotape.
– ORIGIN 1940s: from an alteration of CELLULOSE + TAPE.

sell-out ■ n. **1** the selling of an entire stock of something. ▸ an event for which all tickets are sold. **2** a sale of a business or company. **3** a betrayal. ▸ a collaborator or informer.

sell-through ■ n. **1** the ratio of the quantity of goods sold by a retail outlet to the quantity distributed to it wholesale. **2** the retail sale of something, especially a pre-recorded video cassette, as opposed to its rental.

seltzer /'sɛltzə/ ■ n. dated soda water.
– ORIGIN C18: alteration of German *Selterser*.

selvedge /'sɛlvɪdʒ/ (also **selvage**) ■ n. **1** an edge produced on woven fabric during manufacture that prevents it from unravelling. **2** Geology a zone of altered rock at the edge of a rock mass.
– ORIGIN Middle English: from an alteration of SELF + EDGE.

selves plural form of SELF.

SEM ■ abbrev. scanning electron microscope.

semantic /sɪ'mantɪk/ ■ adj. relating to meaning in language or logic.
– DERIVATIVES **semantically** adv. **semanticity** n.
– ORIGIN C17: from French *sémantique*, from Greek *sēmantikos* 'significant'.

semantic field ■ n. Linguistics a lexical set of semantically related items, for example verbs of perception.

semantics ■ pl. n. [usu. treated as sing.] **1** the branch of linguistics and logic concerned with meaning. **2** the meaning of a word, phrase, sentence, or text.
– DERIVATIVES **semantician** n. **semanticist** n.

semaphore ■ n. **1** a system of sending messages by holding the arms or two flags or poles in certain positions according to an alphabetic code. **2** an apparatus for

signalling in this way, consisting of an upright with movable parts. ■ v. send by semaphore or by signals resembling semaphore.
– DERIVATIVES **semaphoric** adj. **semaphorically** adv.
– ORIGIN C19: from French *sémaphore*, from Greek *sēma* 'sign' + *-phoros*.

semasiology /sɪˌmeɪzɪˈɒlədʒi/ ■ n. the branch of knowledge concerned with concepts and the terms that represent them.
– DERIVATIVES **semasiological** adj.
– ORIGIN C19: from German *Semasiologie*, from Greek *sēmasia* 'meaning'.

semblance ■ n. 1 the outward appearance or apparent form of something. 2 archaic resemblance.
– ORIGIN Middle English: from Old French, from *sembler* 'seem', from Latin *similare* 'simulate'.

semen /ˈsiːmən/ ■ n. the male reproductive fluid, containing spermatozoa in suspension.
– ORIGIN Middle English: from Latin, 'seed', from *serere* 'to sow'.

semester /sɪˈmɛstə/ ■ n. a half-year term in a school or university.
– ORIGIN C19: from German *Semester*, from Latin *semestris* 'six-monthly'.

semi ■ n. (pl. **semis**) informal 1 Brit. a semi-detached house. 2 a semi-final.

semi- ■ prefix 1 half: *semicircular*. ► occurring or appearing twice in a specified period: *semi-annual*. 2 partly: *semi-conscious*. ► almost: *semi-darkness*.
– ORIGIN from Latin; rel. to Greek *hemi-*.

semi-acoustic ■ adj. (of a guitar) having both one or more pickups and a hollow body, typically with f-holes.

semi-annual ■ adj. occurring twice a year.
– DERIVATIVES **semi-annually** adv.

semiaquatic ■ adj. 1 (of an animal) living partly on land and partly in water. 2 (of a plant) growing in very wet or waterlogged ground.

semi-automatic ■ adj. partially automatic. ► (of a firearm) having a mechanism for self-loading but not for continuous firing.

semi-autonomous ■ adj. 1 having a degree of self-government. 2 acting independently to some degree.

semibold ■ adj. Printing printed in a typeface with thick strokes but not as thick as bold.

semibreve /ˈsɛmɪbriːv/ ■ n. Music a note having the time value of two minims or four crotchets, represented by a ring with no stem.

semicircle ■ n. a half of a circle or of its circumference.
– DERIVATIVES **semicircular** adj.

semicircular canals ■ pl. n. a system of three fluid-filled bony channels in the inner ear, involved in sensing and maintaining balance.

semicolon /ˌsɛmɪˈkəʊlən, -ˈkəʊlɒn/ ■ n. a punctuation mark (;) indicating a more pronounced pause than that indicated by a comma.

semiconductor ■ n. a solid, e.g. silicon, whose conductivity is between that of an insulator and a conductive metal and increases with temperature.
– DERIVATIVES **semi-conducting** adj.

semi-conscious ■ adj. partially conscious.

semi-cylinder ■ n. Geometry half of a cylinder cut longitudinally.
– DERIVATIVES **semi-cylindrical** adj.

semi-detached ■ adj. (of a house) joined to another house on one side only by a common wall.

semi-documentary ■ adj. (of a film) having a factual background and a fictitious story.

semi-dome ■ n. Architecture a half-dome formed by vertical section.

semi-double ■ adj. (of a flower) intermediate between single and double in having only the outer stamens converted to petals.

semi-final ■ n. a match or round immediately preceding the final.
– DERIVATIVES **semi-finalist** n.

semi-finished ■ adj. prepared for the final stage of manufacture.

semi-fluid ■ adj. having a thick consistency between solid and liquid.

semi-independent ■ adj. 1 having some degree of independence or autonomy. 2 (of an institution) not wholly supported by public funds.

semi-infinite ■ adj. Mathematics (of a line or solid) limited in one direction and stretching to infinity in the other.

semi-invalid ■ n. a partially disabled or somewhat infirm person.

semi-liquid ■ adj. another term for SEMI-FLUID.

semi-literate ■ adj. 1 unable to read or write with ease or fluency. 2 (of a text) poorly written. ■ n. a semi-literate person.
– DERIVATIVES **semi-literacy** n.

Sémillon /ˈsɛmɪjɔ̃/ ■ n. a variety of white wine grape grown in France and elsewhere. ► a white wine made from this grape.
– ORIGIN French dialect, from Latin *semen* 'seed'.

semilunar ■ adj. chiefly Anatomy shaped like a half-moon or crescent.

semilunar valve ■ n. Anatomy each of a pair of valves in the heart at the bases of the aorta and the pulmonary artery.

semimetal ■ n. Chemistry an element (e.g. arsenic or tin) whose properties are intermediate between those of metals and solid non-metals or semiconductors.
– DERIVATIVES **semimetallic** adj.

semi-modal ■ n. a verb that functions to some extent like a modal verb, typically in the way it forms negative and interrogative constructions (e.g. *need* and *dare* in English).

semi-monocoque ■ adj. relating to or denoting aircraft or vehicle structures combining a load-bearing shell with integral frames.

semi-monthly ■ adj. occurring or published twice a month.

seminal ■ adj. 1 (of a work, event, or person) strongly influencing later developments. 2 relating to or denoting semen. 3 Botany of, relating to, or derived from the seed of a plant.
– DERIVATIVES **seminally** adv.
– ORIGIN Middle English: from Old French *seminal* or Latin *seminalis*, from *semen* 'seed'.

seminar /ˈsɛmɪnɑː/ ■ n. 1 a conference or other meeting for discussion or training. 2 a small group of students at university, meeting to discuss topics with a teacher.
– ORIGIN C19: from German *Seminar*, from Latin *seminarium* (see SEMINARY).

seminary /ˈsɛmɪn(ə)ri/ ■ n. (pl. **-ies**) a training college for priests or rabbis.
– DERIVATIVES **seminarian** /-ˈnɛːrɪən/ n. **seminarist** n.
– ORIGIN Middle English: from Latin *seminarium*, from *seminarius* 'of seed', from *semen* 'seed'.

seminiferous /ˌsɛmɪˈnɪf(ə)rəs/ ■ adj. producing or conveying semen.
– ORIGIN C17: from Latin *semen, semin-* 'seed' + -FEROUS.

semi-official ■ adj. having some, but not full, official authority or recognition.
– DERIVATIVES **semi-officially** adv.

semiology /ˌsiːmɪˈɒlədʒi, ˌsɛmɪ-/ ■ n. another term for SEMIOTICS.
– DERIVATIVES **semiological** adj. **semiologist** n.
– ORIGIN C20: from Greek *sēmeion* 'sign' + -LOGY.

semiosis /ˌsiːmɪˈəʊsɪs, ˌsɛmɪ-/ ■ n. Linguistics the process of signification in language or literature.
– ORIGIN C20: from Greek *sēmeiosis* '(inference from) a sign'.

semiotics /ˌsiːmɪˈɒtɪks, ˌsɛmɪ-/ ■ pl. n. [treated as sing.] the study of signs and symbols and their use or interpretation.
– DERIVATIVES **semiotic** adj. **semiotically** adv. **semiotician** /-əˈtɪʃ(ə)n/ n.
– ORIGIN C19: from Greek *sēmeiotikos* 'of signs'.

semipermeable ■ adj. permeable only to certain substances, especially allowing the passage of a solvent but not of the solute.

semi-precious ■ adj. denoting minerals which can be used as gems but are considered to be less valuable than precious stones.

semi-professional ■ adj. receiving payment for an activity but not relying on it for a living. ■ n. a semi-professional person.

semi-prone position ■ n. another term for RECOVERY POSITION.

semiquaver /ˈsɛmɪˌkweɪvə/ ■ n. Music a note having the time value of a sixteenth of a semibreve or half a quaver, represented by a large dot with a two-hooked stem.

semi-retired ■ adj. having retired from employment or an occupation but continuing to work part-time or occasionally.
– DERIVATIVES **semi-retirement** n.

semi-rigid ■ adj. (of an inflatable boat) having a rigid hull and inflatable sponsons.

semi-skilled ■ adj. (of work or a worker) having or needing some, but not extensive, training.

semi-skimmed ■ adj. Brit. (of milk) having had some of the cream removed.

semi-solid ■ adj. highly viscous; slightly thicker than semi-fluid.

semi-submersible ■ adj. denoting an oil or gas drilling platform or barge with submerged hollow pontoons able to be flooded with water when the vessel is anchored on site in order to provide stability.

semi-sweet ■ adj. 1 (of food) slightly sweetened, but less so than normal. 2 (of wine) slightly sweeter than medium dry.

semi-synthetic ■ adj. Chemistry made by synthesis from a naturally occurring material.

Semite /ˈsiːmaɪt, ˈsɛm-/ ■ n. a member of a people speaking a Semitic language, in particular the Jews and Arabs.
– ORIGIN from Greek *Sēm* 'Shem', son of Noah in the Bible, from whom these people are traditionally descended.

Semitic /sɪˈmɪtɪk/ ■ n. an Afro-Asiatic subfamily of languages that includes Hebrew, Arabic, and Aramaic and certain ancient languages such as Phoenician. ■ adj. of or relating to these languages or their speakers.

semitone ■ n. Music the smallest interval used in classical Western music, equal to a twelfth of an octave or half a tone.

semi-trailer ■ n. a trailer having wheels at the back but supported at the front by a towing vehicle. ▶ an articulated truck.

semi-tropics ■ pl. n. another term for SUBTROPICS.
– DERIVATIVES **semi-tropical** adj.

semivowel ■ n. a speech sound intermediate between a vowel and a consonant, e.g. *w* or *y*.

semolina ■ n. the hard grains left after the milling of flour, used in puddings and in pasta.
– ORIGIN C18: from Italian *semolino*, diminutive of *semola* 'bran'.

sempiternal /ˌsɛmpɪˈtɜːn(ə)l/ ■ adj. eternal and unchanging; everlasting.
– DERIVATIVES **sempiternally** adv. **sempiternity** n.
– ORIGIN Middle English: from Latin *sempiternus*, from *semper* 'always' + *aeternus* 'eternal'.

sempstress /ˈsɛm(p)strɪs/ ■ n. another term for SEAMSTRESS.

Semtex ■ n. a very pliable, odourless plastic explosive.
– ORIGIN 1980s: prob. a blend of *Semtin* (the name of a village in the Czech Republic near the place of production) and EXPLOSIVE.

Sen. ■ abbrev. 1 N. Amer. Senate. 2 N. Amer. Senator. 3 Senior.

senate ■ n. 1 the smaller upper assembly in the US, US states, France, and other countries. ▶ the governing body of a university or college. 2 the state council of the ancient Roman republic and empire.
– ORIGIN Middle English: from Old French *senat*, from Latin *senatus*, from *senex* 'old man'.

senator ■ n. a member of a senate.
– DERIVATIVES **senatorial** adj. **senatorship** n.

send ■ v. (past and past part. **sent**) 1 cause to go or be taken or delivered to a particular destination. ▶ (**send someone to**) arrange for someone to attend (an institution). 2 cause to move sharply or quickly; propel. 3 cause to be in a specified state: *it nearly sent me crazy*. 4 informal cause to feel ecstasy or elation.
– PHRASES **send someone to Coventry** chiefly Brit. refuse to associate with or speak to someone. **send word** send a message.
– PHRASAL VERBS **send someone down** Brit. 1 expel a student from a university. 2 informal sentence someone to imprisonment. **send for** 1 order or instruct (someone) to come to one; summon. 2 order by post. **send someone off** (of a soccer or rugby referee) order a player to leave the field and take no further part in the game. **send someone/thing up** informal ridicule someone or something by exaggerated imitation.
– DERIVATIVES **sendable** adj. **sender** n.
– ORIGIN Old English, of Germanic origin.

sendal /ˈsɛnd(ə)l/ ■ n. historical a fine silk material used to make ceremonial robes and banners.
– ORIGIN Middle English: from Old French *cendal*, from Greek *sindōn*.

send-off ■ n. a celebratory demonstration of goodwill at a person's departure.

send-up ■ n. informal a parody or exaggerated imitation of someone or something.

senecio /səˈniːsɪəʊ, -ʃɪəʊ/ ■ n. (pl. -os) a plant of a genus that includes ragwort and groundsel. [Genus *Senecio*.]
– ORIGIN from Latin, 'old man, groundsel', with ref. to the hairy white fruits.

Senegalese /ˌsɛnɪɡəˈliːz/ ■ n. a native or inhabitant of Senegal. ■ adj. of or relating to Senegal.

senesce /sɪˈnɛs/ ■ v. Biology (of a living organism) deteriorate with age.
– DERIVATIVES **senescence** n. **senescent** adj.
– ORIGIN C17: from Latin *senescere*, from *senex* 'old'.

seneschal /ˈsɛnɪʃ(ə)l/ ■ n. 1 historical the steward or majordomo of a medieval great house. 2 chiefly historical a governor or other administrative or judicial officer.
– ORIGIN Middle English: from medieval Latin *seniscalus*, from a Germanic compound meaning 'old' and 'servant'.

senhor /sɛnˈjɔː/ ■ n. (in Portuguese-speaking countries) a form of address for a man, corresponding to *Mr* or *sir*.
– ORIGIN Portuguese, from Latin *senior* (see SENIOR).

senhora /sɛnˈjɔːrə/ ■ n. (in Portuguese-speaking countries) a form of address for a woman, corresponding to *Mrs* or *madam*.

senhorita /ˌsɛnjəˈriːtə/ ■ n. (in Portuguese-speaking countries) a form of address for a young woman, corresponding to *Miss*.

senile ■ adj. having the weaknesses or diseases of old age, especially a loss of mental faculties. ▶ characteristic of or caused by old age.
– DERIVATIVES **senility** n.
– ORIGIN C17: from Latin *senilis*, from *senex* 'old man'.

senile dementia ■ n. severe mental deterioration in old age, characterized by loss of memory and lack of control of bodily functions.

senior /ˈsiːnɪə, ˈsiːnjə/ ■ adj. 1 of a more advanced age. ▶ of, for, or denoting schoolchildren above a certain age, typically in (the UK) eleven or (in South Africa) twelve. ▶ US of the final year at a university or high school. ▶ [postpos.] denoting the elder of two with the same name in a family. 2 high or higher in rank or status. ■ n. 1 a person who is a specified number of years older than someone else: *she was two years his senior*. 2 a student in one of the higher forms of a senior school. 3 (in sport) a competitor of above a certain age or of the highest status. 4 an elderly person, especially an old-age pensioner.
– DERIVATIVES **seniority** n.
– ORIGIN Middle English: from Latin, 'older, older man', comparative of *senex* 'old man, old'.

senior citizen ■ n. an elderly person, especially an old-age pensioner.

senior common room ■ n. a room used for social purposes by fellows, lecturers, and other senior members of a college or university.

senior counsel ■ n. S. African Law a senior advocate appointed by the President.

senior high school ■ n. N. Amer. a secondary school typically comprising the three highest grades.

senior nursing officer ■ n. Brit. the person in charge of nursing services in a hospital.

senior phase ■ n. S. African the period of school education comprising grades 7–9.

senior registrar ■ n. a hospital doctor undergoing specialist training, one grade below that of consultant.

senior school ■ n. a secondary school, typically for children between the ages of eleven or twelve and eighteen.

Senior Service ■ n. Brit. the Royal Navy.

senna ■ n. **1** the cassia tree. **2** a laxative prepared from the dried pods of this tree.
– ORIGIN C16: from medieval Latin *sena*, from Arabic *sanā*.

sennet /ˈsɛnɪt/ ■ n. (in the stage directions of Elizabethan plays) a call on a trumpet or cornet to signal the ceremonial entrance or exit of an actor.
– ORIGIN C16: perhaps a var. of **SIGNET**.

sennight /ˈsɛnaɪt/ ■ n. archaic a week.
– ORIGIN Old English *seofon nihta* 'seven nights'.

sennit ■ n. plaited straw, hemp, or similar material used to make hats.

Senr ■ abbrev. Senior (in names).

sensate /ˈsɛnseɪt, -sət/ ■ adj. perceiving or perceived with the senses.

sensation ■ n. **1** a physical feeling or perception resulting from something that happens to or comes into contact with the body. ▸ the capacity to have such feelings or perceptions. **2** an inexplicable awareness or impression. **3** a widespread reaction of interest and excitement. ▸ a person or thing that arouses such interest and excitement.
– ORIGIN C17: from medieval Latin *sensatio(n-)*, from Latin *sensus* (see **SENSE**).

sensational ■ adj. **1** causing or seeking to cause great public interest and excitement. **2** informal very impressive or attractive.
– DERIVATIVES **sensationalize** (also **-ise**) v. **sensationally** adv.

sensationalism ■ n. **1** the deliberate use of sensational stories or language in the media. **2** Philosophy another term for **PHENOMENALISM**.
– DERIVATIVES **sensationalist** n. & adj. **sensationalistic** adj.

sense ■ n. **1** a faculty by which the body perceives an external stimulus; one of the faculties of sight, smell, hearing, taste, and touch. ▸ (**one's senses**) one's sanity. **2** an awareness of something or feeling that something is the case. **3** a sane and realistic attitude to situations and problems. ▸ a reasonable or comprehensible rationale. **4** a way in which an expression or situation can be interpreted; a meaning. **5** chiefly Mathematics & Physics the property distinguishing two opposite but otherwise identical things, e.g. motion in opposite directions. ■ v. **1** perceive by a sense or senses. ▸ be vaguely or indefinably aware of. **2** (of a machine or similar device) detect.
– PHRASES **make sense** be intelligible, justifiable, or practicable. **make sense of** find meaning or coherence in.
– ORIGIN Middle English: from Latin *sensus* 'faculty of feeling, thought, meaning', from *sentire* 'feel'.

sense datum ■ n. Philosophy an immediate object of perception which is not a material object.

sensei /ˈsɛnseɪ/ ■ n. (pl. same) (in martial arts) a teacher.
– ORIGIN Japanese, from *sen* 'previous' + *sei* 'birth'.

senseless ■ adj. **1** unconscious or incapable of sensation. **2** without discernible meaning or purpose. ▸ lacking common sense; wildly foolish.
– DERIVATIVES **senselessly** adv. **senselessness** n.

sense organ ■ n. an organ of the body which responds to external stimuli by conveying impulses to the sensory nervous system.

sensibility ■ n. (pl. **-ies**) (also **sensibilities**) the ability to appreciate and respond to complex emotional or aesthetic influences; sensitivity. ▸ (**sensibilities**) a person's tendency to be offended or shocked.

sensible ■ adj. **1** wise and prudent; having or showing common sense. ▸ practical and functional rather than decorative. **2** archaic readily perceived; appreciable. ▸ (**sensible of/to**) able to notice or appreciate.
– DERIVATIVES **sensibleness** n. **sensibly** adv.
– ORIGIN Middle English: from Latin *sensibilis*, from *sensus* (see **SENSE**).

sensillum /sɛnˈsɪləm/ ■ n. (pl. **sensilla** /sɛnˈsɪlə/) Zoology (in some invertebrates) a simple sensory receptor consisting of a modified cell or cells of the cuticle or epidermis.
– ORIGIN C20: diminutive of Latin *sensus* 'sense'.

sensitive ■ adj. **1** quick to detect, respond to, or be affected by slight changes, signals, or influences. ▸ (of photographic materials) responding rapidly to the action of light. **2** quickly and delicately appreciating the feelings of others. **3** easily offended or upset. **4** kept secret or with restrictions on disclosure. ■ n. a person supposedly able to respond to paranormal influences.
– DERIVATIVES **sensitively** adv. **sensitiveness** n.
– ORIGIN Middle English: from Old French *sensitif* or medieval Latin *sensitivus*, from Latin *sentire* 'feel'.

sensitive plant ■ n. a tropical American plant of the pea family, whose leaflets fold together and leaves bend down when touched. [*Mimosa pudica*.]

sensitivity ■ n. (pl. **-ies**) **1** the quality or condition of being sensitive. **2** (**sensitivities**) a person's feelings which might be easily offended or hurt.

sensitize (also **-ise**) ■ v. cause to respond to certain stimuli; make sensitive.
– DERIVATIVES **sensitization** (also **-isation**) n. **sensitizer** (also **-iser**) n.

sensor ■ n. a device which detects or measures a physical property.

sensorimotor /ˌsɛns(ə)rɪˈməʊtə/ ■ adj. Physiology (of nerves or their actions) having or involving both sensory and motor functions or pathways.

sensorium /sɛnˈsɔːrɪəm/ ■ n. (pl. **sensoria** /-rɪə/ or **sensoriums**) the sensory apparatus or faculties considered as a whole.
– DERIVATIVES **sensorial** adj. **sensorially** adv.
– ORIGIN C17: from Latin *sens-*, *sentire* 'perceive'.

sensory ■ adj. of or relating to sensation or the senses.
– DERIVATIVES **sensorily** adv.

sensual /ˈsɛnsjʊəl, -ʃʊəl/ ■ adj. **1** of or relating to the physical senses, especially as a source of pleasure. **2** arousing sexual or other physical gratification.
– DERIVATIVES **sensualism** n. **sensualist** n. **sensuality** n. **sensualize** (also **-ise**) v. **sensually** adv.
– ORIGIN Middle English: from late Latin *sensualis*, from *sensus* (see **SENSE**).

USAGE
The words **sensual** and **sensuous** are frequently used interchangeably to mean 'gratifying the senses', especially in a sexual sense. This goes against a traditional distinction, by which **sensuous** is the more neutral term, meaning 'relating to the senses rather than the intellect'. Evidence suggests that the 'neutral' use of **sensuous** is rare in modern English; if a neutral use is intended it is advisable to use alternative wording.

sensu lato /ˌsɛnsuː ˈlɑːtəʊ/ ■ adv. formal in the broad sense.
– ORIGIN Latin.

sensum /ˈsɛnsəm/ ■ n. (pl. **sensa** /-sə/) Philosophy a sense datum.
– ORIGIN C19: Latin, 'something sensed', from *sentire* 'feel'.

sensuous /ˈsɛnsjʊəs, ˈsɛnʃʊəs/ ■ adj. **1** relating to or affecting the senses rather than the intellect. **2** attractive or gratifying physically, especially sexually.
– DERIVATIVES **sensuously** adv. **sensuousness** n.
– ORIGIN C17: from Latin *sensus* 'sense'.

sensu stricto /ˌsɛnsuː ˈstrɪktəʊ/ ■ adv. formal strictly speaking; in the narrow sense.
– ORIGIN Latin, 'in the restricted sense'.

sent past and past participle of **SEND**.

sente /ˈsɛntɪ/ ■ n. (pl. **lisente** /lɪˈsɛntɪ/) a monetary unit of Lesotho, equal to one hundredth of a loti.
– ORIGIN from Sesotho.

sentence

sentence ■ n. **1** a set of words that is complete in itself, conveying a statement, question, exclamation, or command and typically containing a subject and predicate. ► Logic a series of signs or symbols expressing a proposition in an artificial or logical language. **2** the punishment assigned to a defendant found guilty by a court. ■ v. declare the punishment decided for (an offender).
– ORIGIN Middle English: from Latin *sententia* 'opinion'.

sentential /sɛnˈtɛnʃ(ə)l/ ■ adj. Grammar & Logic of or relating to a sentence.

sententious /sɛnˈtɛnʃəs/ ■ adj. given to moralizing in a pompous or affected manner.
– DERIVATIVES **sententiously** adv. **sententiousness** n.
– ORIGIN Middle English: from Latin *sententiosus*, from *sententia* (see SENTENCE).

sentient /ˈsɛnʃ(ə)nt/ ■ adj. able to perceive or feel things.
– DERIVATIVES **sentience** n. **sentiently** adv.
– ORIGIN C17: from Latin *sentient-*, *sentire* 'to feel'.

sentiment ■ n. **1** a view, opinion, or feeling. ► general feeling or opinion. **2** exaggerated and self-indulgent feelings of tenderness, sadness, or nostalgia.
– ORIGIN Middle English: from Old French *sentement*, from medieval Latin *sentimentum*, from Latin *sentire* 'feel'.

sentimental ■ adj. deriving from feelings of tenderness, sadness, or nostalgia. ► having or arousing such feelings in an exaggerated and self-indulgent way.
– PHRASES **sentimental value** value of an object deriving from personal or emotional associations rather than material worth.
– DERIVATIVES **sentimentalism** n. **sentimentalist** n. **sentimentality** n. **sentimentalization** (also **-isation**) n. **sentimentalize** (also **-ise**) v. **sentimentally** adv.

sentinel /ˈsɛntɪn(ə)l/ ■ n. **1** a soldier or guard whose job is to stand and keep watch. **2** Medicine a thing that acts as an indicator of the presence of disease. ■ v. (**sentinelled**, **sentinelling**; US **sentineled**, **sentineling**) keep watch over.
– ORIGIN C16: from French *sentinelle*, from Italian *sentinella*.

sentry ■ n. (pl. **-ies**) a soldier stationed to keep guard or to control access to a place.
– ORIGIN C17: perhaps from obsolete *centrinel*, var. of SENTINEL.

sentry box ■ n. a structure providing shelter for a standing sentry.

señor /sɛˈnjɔː/ ■ n. (pl. **señores** /-reɪz/) (in Spanish-speaking countries) a form of address for a man, corresponding to *Mr* or *sir*.
– ORIGIN Spanish, from Latin *senior* (see SENIOR).

señora /sɛˈnjɔːrə/ ■ n. (in Spanish-speaking countries) a form of address for a woman, corresponding to *Mrs* or *madam*.

señorita /ˌsɛnjəˈriːtə/ ■ n. (in Spanish-speaking countries) a form of address for an unmarried woman, corresponding to *Miss*.

sepal /ˈsɛp(ə)l, ˈsiːp(ə)l/ ■ n. Botany each of the parts of the calyx of a flower, enclosing the petals and typically green and leaf-like.
– ORIGIN C19: from French *sépale*, modern Latin *sepalum*, from Greek *skepē* 'covering', influenced by French *pétale* 'petal'.

separable ■ adj. able to be separated or treated separately.
– DERIVATIVES **separability** n. **separableness** n. **separably** adv.

separate ■ adj. /ˈsɛp(ə)rət/ forming or viewed as a unit apart or by itself; not joined or united with others. ► different; distinct. ■ v. /ˈsɛpəreɪt/ **1** move or come apart; make or become detached or disconnected. ► stop living together as a couple. **2** divide into constituent or distinct elements. ► extract or remove for use or rejection. ► distinguish between or from another; consider individually. **3** form a distinction or boundary between. ■ n. /ˈsɛp(ə)rət/ (**separates**) things forming units by themselves, in particular individual items of clothing suitable for wearing in different combinations.

– DERIVATIVES **separately** adv. **separateness** n. **separator** n.
– ORIGIN Middle English: from Latin *separare* 'disjoin, divide', from *se-* 'apart' + *parare* 'prepare'.

separate development ■ n. S. African historical (under apartheid) the policy of creating a homeland for each of the officially designated black communities in South Africa.

separation ■ n. **1** the action or state of separating or being separated. ► the state in which a husband and wife remain married but live apart. **2** distinction between the signals carried by the two channels of a stereophonic system. **3** Physics & Aeronautics the generation of a turbulent boundary layer between a surface and a moving fluid.
– PHRASES **separation of powers** the vesting of the legislative, executive, and judiciary powers of government in separate bodies.

separatism ■ n. the advocacy or practice of separation of a group of people from a larger body on the basis of ethnicity, religion, or gender.
– DERIVATIVES **separatist** n. & adj.

Sepedi /sɛˈpɛːdi/ ■ n. the language of the Bapedi people, the core dialect of Sesotho sa Leboa. ► another term for SESOTHO SA LEBOA.
– ORIGIN the name in Sepedi.

Sephardi /sɪˈfɑːdi/ ■ n. (pl. **Sephardim** /-dɪm/) a Jew of Spanish or Portuguese descent. ► any Jew of the Middle East or North Africa.
– DERIVATIVES **Sephardic** adj.
– ORIGIN modern Hebrew, from *sĕp̄āraḏ*, a country mentioned in Obadiah 20 and taken to be Spain.

sepia /ˈsiːpɪə/ ■ n. **1** a reddish-brown colour associated particularly with early monochrome photographs. **2** a brown pigment prepared from cuttlefish ink, used in monochrome drawing and in watercolours.
– ORIGIN Middle English: from Greek *sēpia*.

sepoy /ˈsiːpɔɪ, sɪˈpɔɪ/ ■ n. historical an Indian soldier serving under British or other European rulers.
– ORIGIN from Urdu and Persian *sipāhī* 'soldier'.

seppuku /sɛˈpuːkuː/ ■ n. another term for HARA-KIRI.
– ORIGIN Japanese, from *setsu* 'to cut' + *fuku* 'abdomen'.

sepsis /ˈsɛpsɪs/ ■ n. Medicine the presence in tissues of harmful bacteria and their toxins, typically through infection of a wound.
– ORIGIN C19: from Greek *sēpsis*, from *sēpein* 'make rotten'.

Sept. ■ abbrev. September.

septa plural form of SEPTUM.

septal ■ adj. **1** Anatomy & Biology relating to a septum or septa. **2** Archaeology (of a stone or slab) separating compartments in a burial chamber.

septate ■ adj. Anatomy & Biology having or partitioned by a septum or septa.
– DERIVATIVES **septation** n.

septcentenary /ˌsɛp(t)sɛnˈtiːn(ə)ri, -ˈtɛn-/ ■ n. (pl. **-ies**) the seven-hundredth anniversary of a significant event.

September ■ n. the ninth month of the year.
– ORIGIN Old English, from Latin *septem* 'seven' (being orig. the seventh month of the Roman year).

septenary /ˈsɛptɪn(ə)ri, -ˈtiːn(ə)ri/ ■ adj. of, relating to, or divided into seven. ■ n. (pl. **-ies**) a group or set of seven, in particular a period of seven years.
– ORIGIN Middle English: from Latin *septenarius*, from *septeni* 'in sevens'.

septennial ■ adj. lasting for or recurring every seven years.
– ORIGIN C17: from late Latin *septennis*, from Latin *septem* 'seven' + *annus* 'year'.

septet /sɛpˈtɛt/ (also **septette**) ■ n. a group of seven people playing music or singing together. ► a composition for such a group.
– ORIGIN C19: from German *Septett*, from Latin *septem* 'seven'.

septic /ˈsɛptɪk/ ■ adj. **1** (of a wound or a part of the body) infected with bacteria. **2** denoting a drainage system incorporating a septic tank.
– DERIVATIVES **septically** adv. **septicity** /-ˈtɪsɪti/ n.
– ORIGIN C17: from Greek *sēptikos*, from *sēpein* 'make rotten'.

septicaemia /ˌsɛptɪˈsiːmɪə/ (US **septicemia**) ■ n. blood poisoning, especially that caused by bacteria or their toxins.
– DERIVATIVES **septicaemic** adj.

septic tank ■ n. a tank, typically underground, in which sewage is allowed to decompose through bacterial activity before draining by means of a soakaway.

septimal /ˈsɛptɪm(ə)l/ ■ adj. of or relating to the number seven.
– ORIGIN C19: from Latin *septimus* 'seventh'.

septime /ˈsɛptɪm, -tiːm/ ■ n. Fencing the seventh of the eight parrying positions.
– ORIGIN C19: from Latin *septimus* 'seventh'.

septivalent /ˌsɛptɪˈveɪl(ə)nt/ ■ adj. Chemistry another term for **HEPTAVALENT**.

septoria /sɛpˈtɔːrɪə/ ■ n. a fungus of a genus that includes many kinds that cause diseases in plants. [Genus *Septoria*.]
– ORIGIN from Latin *septum* (see **SEPTUM**).

septuagenarian /ˌsɛptjʊədʒɪˈnɛːrɪən/ ■ n. a person who is between 70 and 79 years old.
– ORIGIN C18: from Latin *septuagenarius*, from *septuaginta* 'seventy'.

septum /ˈsɛptəm/ ■ n. (pl. **septa** /-tə/) chiefly Anatomy & Biology a partition separating two chambers, such as that between the nostrils or the chambers of the heart.
– ORIGIN C17: from Latin *septum*, from *sepire* 'enclose'.

septuple /ˈsɛptjʊp(ə)l, sɛpˈtjuːp(ə)l/ ■ adj. 1 consisting of seven parts or elements. ▶ (of time in music) having seven beats in a bar. 2 consisting of seven times as much or as many as usual. ■ v. multiply by seven; increase sevenfold.
– ORIGIN C17: from late Latin *septuplus*, from Latin *septem* 'seven'.

septuplet /ˈsɛptjʊplɪt, sɛpˈtjuːplɪt/ ■ n. each of seven children born at one birth.
– ORIGIN C19: from **SEPTUPLE**, on the pattern of *triplet*.

sepulchral /sɪˈpʌlkr(ə)l/ ■ adj. 1 of or relating to a tomb or interment. 2 gloomy; dismal.
– DERIVATIVES **sepulchrally** adv.

sepulchre /ˈsɛp(ə)lkə/ (US **sepulcher**) ■ n. a small room or monument, cut in rock or built of stone, in which a dead person is laid or buried. ■ v. chiefly poetic/literary lay or bury in or as if in a sepulchre.
– ORIGIN Middle English: from Latin *sepulcrum* 'burial place', from *sepelire* 'bury'.

seq. (also **seqq.**) ■ adv. short for **ET SEQ**.

sequel ■ n. 1 a published, broadcast, or recorded work that continues the story or develops the theme of an earlier one. 2 something that takes place after or as a result of an earlier event.
– ORIGIN Middle English: from Old French *sequelle* or Latin *sequella*, from *sequi* 'follow'.

sequela /sɪˈkwiːlə/ ■ n. (pl. **sequelae** /-liː/) Medicine a condition which is the consequence of a previous disease or injury.
– ORIGIN C18: from Latin, from *sequi* 'follow'.

sequence ■ n. 1 a particular order in which related events, movements, etc., follow each other. ▶ Music a repetition of a phrase or melody at a higher or lower pitch. 2 a set of related events, movements, etc., that follow each other in a particular order. ▶ a set of three or more playing cards of the same suit next to each other in value. 3 a part of a film dealing with one particular event or topic. ■ v. 1 arrange in a sequence. 2 play or record (music) with a sequencer.
– ORIGIN Middle English: from late Latin *sequentia*, from Latin *sequi* 'to follow'.

sequence dancing ■ n. a type of ballroom dancing in which the couples all perform the same steps and movements simultaneously.

sequence of tenses ■ n. Grammar the dependence of the tense of a subordinate verb on the tense of the verb in the main clause (e.g. *I think that you* are *wrong*; *I thought that you* were *wrong*).

sequencer ■ n. 1 a programmable electronic device for storing sequences of musical notes, chords, or rhythms and transmitting them to an electronic musical instrument. 2 Biochemistry an apparatus for ascertaining the sequence of amino acids or other monomers in a biological polymer.

sequential ■ adj. forming or following in a logical order or sequence.
– DERIVATIVES **sequentiality** n. **sequentially** adv.

sequester /sɪˈkwɛstə/ ■ v. 1 [often as adj. **sequestered**] isolate or hide away. 2 another term for **SEQUESTRATE**. 3 Chemistry form a chelate or other stable compound with (an ion, molecule, etc.) so that it cannot react.
– ORIGIN Middle English: from Old French *sequestrer* or late Latin *sequestrare* 'commit for safe keeping', from Latin *sequester* 'trustee'.

sequestrate /sɪˈkwɛstreɪt, ˈsiːkwɪs-/ ■ v. 1 take legal possession of (assets) until a debt has been paid or other claims have been met. ▶ legally place (the property of a bankrupt) in the hands of a trustee for division among the creditors. ▶ declare bankrupt. 2 take forcible possession of; confiscate.
– DERIVATIVES **sequestrable** adj. **sequestrator** /ˈsiːkwɪˌstreɪtə/ n.

sequestration /ˌsiːkwɪˈstreɪʃ(ə)n/ ■ n. the action of sequestrating or sequestering.

sequestrum /sɪˈkwɛstrəm/ ■ n. (pl. **sequestra** /-trə/) Medicine a piece of dead bone tissue formed within a diseased or injured bone, typically in chronic osteomyelitis.
– ORIGIN C19: from Latin *sequester* 'standing apart'.

sequin ■ n. a small, shiny disc sewn on to clothing for decoration.
– DERIVATIVES **sequinned** (also **sequined**) adj.
– ORIGIN C16: from Italian *zecchino*, from *zecca* 'a mint', from Arabic *sikka* 'a die for coining'.

sequoia /sɪˈkwɔɪə/ ■ n. a redwood tree, especially the California redwood.
– ORIGIN from *Sequoya*, the name of the Cherokee Indian who invented the Cherokee syllabary.

sera plural form of **SERUM**.

serac /ˈsɛrak, sɛˈrak/ ■ n. a pinnacle or ridge of ice on the surface of a glacier.
– ORIGIN C19: from Swiss French *sérac*, orig. the name of a compact white cheese.

seraglio /sɛˈrɑːlɪəʊ, sɪ-/ ■ n. (pl. **-os**) 1 the women's apartments in a Muslim palace. ▶ a harem. 2 historical a Turkish palace, especially the Sultan's court and government offices at Constantinople.
– ORIGIN C16: from Italian *serraglio*, from Persian *sarāy* 'palace'.

serape /sɛˈrɑːpeɪ/ (also **sarape**) ■ n. a shawl or blanket worn as a cloak by people from Latin America.
– ORIGIN from Mexican Spanish.

seraph /ˈsɛrəf/ ■ n. (pl. **seraphim** /-fɪm/ or **seraphs**) an angelic being associated with light, ardour, and purity.
– DERIVATIVES **seraphic** adj. **seraphically** adv.
– ORIGIN Old English, back-formation from *seraphim* (pl.), from Hebrew *śĕrāpîm*.

Serb ■ n. a native or national of Serbia, or a person of Serbian descent.

Serbian ■ n. 1 the Southern Slavic language of the Serbs, almost identical to Croatian but written in the Cyrillic alphabet. 2 a Serb. ■ adj. of or relating to Serbia, the Serbs, or their language.

Serbo-Croat /ˌsəːbəʊˈkrəʊat/ (also **Serbo-Croatian** /-krəʊˈeɪʃ(ə)n/) ■ n. the Southern Slavic language spoken in Serbia, Croatia, and elsewhere in the former Yugoslavia.

sere ■ adj. variant spelling of **SEAR**.

serenade ■ n. 1 a piece of music sung or played in the open air, especially by a man at night under the window of his beloved. 2 another term for **SERENATA**. ■ v. entertain with a serenade.
– DERIVATIVES **serenader** n.
– ORIGIN C17: from French *sérénade*, from Italian *serenata*, from *sereno* 'serene'.

serenata /ˌsɛrəˈnɑːtə/ ■ n. Music 1 a cantata with a pastoral subject. 2 a simple form of suite for orchestra or wind band.
– ORIGIN Italian (see **SERENADE**).

serendipity /ˌsɛr(ə)nˈdɪpɪti/ ■ n. the occurrence and

serene

development of events by chance in a happy or beneficial way.
– DERIVATIVES **serendipitous** adj. **serendipitously** adv.
– ORIGIN 1754: coined by Horace Walpole, suggested by *The Three Princes of Serendip*, the title of a fairy tale in which the heroes were always making fortunate discoveries.

serene ■ adj. calm, peaceful, and untroubled; tranquil.
– DERIVATIVES **serenely** adv. **serenity** n.
– ORIGIN Middle English: from Latin *serenus*.

serf ■ n. (in the feudal system) an agricultural labourer who was tied to working on a particular estate.
– DERIVATIVES **serfage** n. **serfdom** n.
– ORIGIN C15: from Latin *servus* 'slave'.

serge /sɑːdʒ/ ■ n. a durable twilled woollen or worsted fabric.
– ORIGIN Middle English: from Old French *sarge*, from a var. of Latin *serica* (*lana*) 'silken (wool)', from *sericus* (see SILK).

sergeant /ˈsɑːdʒ(ə)nt/ ■ n. 1 a rank of non-commissioned officer in the army or air force, above corporal and below staff sergeant or flight sergeant. 2 S. African & Brit. a police officer ranking below an inspector. 3 US a police officer ranking below a lieutenant.
– ORIGIN Middle English: from Old French *sergent*, from Latin *servire* 'serve'.

sergeant-at-arms ■ n. variant spelling of SERJEANT-AT-ARMS.

sergeant major ■ n. 1 a non-commissioned officer of the highest rank. 2 a warrant officer.

Sergt ■ abbrev. Sergeant.

serial ■ adj. 1 consisting of, forming part of, or taking place in a series. 2 repeatedly committing the same offence or following a characteristic behaviour pattern: *a serial killer*. 3 Computing (of a device) involving the transfer of data as a single sequence of bits. ■ n. 1 a published or broadcast story or play appearing in regular instalments. 2 (in a library) a periodical.
– DERIVATIVES **seriality** n. **serially** adv.
– ORIGIN C19: from SERIES, perhaps suggested by French *sérial*.

serial comma (also **Oxford comma**) ■ n. a comma used after the penultimate item in a list of three or more items, before 'and' or 'or' (e.g. *an Italian painter, sculptor, and architect*).

serialism ■ n. Music a compositional technique using a fixed series of notes which is subject to change only in specific ways.
– DERIVATIVES **serialist** adj. & n.

serialize (also **-ise**) ■ v. 1 publish or broadcast (a story or play) in regular instalments. 2 arrange in a series.
– DERIVATIVES **serialization** (also **-isation**) n.

serial number ■ n. an identification number showing the position of a manufactured or printed item in a series.

seriate technical ■ adj. /ˈsɪərɪət/ arranged or occurring in one or more series. ■ v. /ˈsɪərɪeɪt/ arrange in a sequence according to prescribed criteria.
– DERIVATIVES **seriation** n.

seriatim /ˌsɪərɪˈeɪtɪm, ˌsɛrɪ-/ ■ adv. formal taking one subject after another in regular order; point by point.
– ORIGIN C15: from Latin *series*, on the pattern of Latin *gradatim*.

sericulture /ˈsɛrɪˌkʌltʃə/ ■ n. the production of silk and the rearing of silkworms for this purpose.
– DERIVATIVES **sericultural** adj. **sericulturist** n.
– ORIGIN C19: abbrev. of French *sériciculture*, from late Latin *sericum* 'silk' + French *culture* 'cultivation'.

series ■ n. (pl. same) 1 a number of similar or related things coming one after another. ▶ a set of books, periodicals, etc., published in a common format. ▶ a set of stamps, banknotes, or coins issued at a particular time. 2 a sequence of related television or radio programmes. 3 [as modifier] having or denoting electrical components connected in series. 4 Geology a range of strata corresponding to an epoch in time, being a subdivision of a system and itself subdivided into stages.
– PHRASES **in series** (of electrical components or circuits) arranged so that the current passes through each successively.
– ORIGIN C17: from Latin, 'row, chain', from *serere* 'join, connect'.

serif /ˈsɛrɪf/ ■ n. a slight projection finishing off a stroke of a letter, as in T contrasted with T.
– DERIVATIVES **seriffed** adj.
– ORIGIN C19: perhaps from Dutch *schreef* 'dash, line'.

serigraph /ˈsɛrɪɡrɑːf/ ■ n. chiefly N. Amer. a printed design produced by means of a silk screen.
– DERIVATIVES **serigrapher** n. **serigraphy** n.
– ORIGIN C19: from Latin *sericum* 'silk' + -GRAPH.

seringa ■ n. variant spelling of SYRINGA.

serio-comic /ˈsɪərɪəʊ-/ ■ adj. combining the serious and the comic.
– DERIVATIVES **serio-comically** adv.

serious ■ adj. 1 demanding or characterized by careful consideration or application. ▶ solemn or thoughtful. 2 sincere and in earnest, rather than joking or half-hearted. 3 significant or worrying in terms of danger or risk: *serious injury*. 4 informal substantial in terms of size, number, or quality: *serious money*.
– DERIVATIVES **seriousness** n.
– ORIGIN Middle English: from Old French *serieux* or late Latin *seriosus*, from *serius* 'earnest, serious'.

seriously ■ adv. in a serious manner or to a serious extent.
– PHRASES **take someone/thing seriously** regard someone or something as important and worthy of attention.

serjeant-at-arms (also **sergeant-at-arms**) ■ n. (pl. **serjeants-at-arms**) 1 an official of a legislative assembly whose duties include maintaining order and security. 2 historical a knight or armed officer in the service of the monarch or a lord.

sermon ■ n. 1 a talk on a religious or moral subject, especially one given during a church service. 2 informal a long or tedious piece of admonition or reproof.
– DERIVATIVES **sermonic** adj. **sermonize** (also **-ise**) v. **sermonizer** (also **-iser**) n.
– ORIGIN Middle English: from Latin *sermo(n-)* 'discourse, talk'.

sero- ■ comb. form relating to serum: *serotype*.

seroconvert /ˌsɪərəʊkənˈvɜːt/ ■ v. Medicine undergo a change from a seronegative to a seropositive condition.
– DERIVATIVES **seroconversion** n.

serology /sɪəˈrɒlədʒi/ ■ n. the scientific study or diagnostic examination of blood serum.
– DERIVATIVES **serologic** adj. **serological** adj. **serologically** adv. **serologist** n.

seropositive (or **seronegative**) ■ adj. Medicine giving a positive (or negative) result in a test of blood serum, especially for the presence of a virus.
– DERIVATIVES **seronegativity** n. **seropositivity** n.

serosa /sɪˈrəʊsə/ ■ n. Physiology the tissue of a serous membrane.
– DERIVATIVES **serosal** adj. **serositis** n.
– ORIGIN from medieval Latin *serosus* 'serous'.

serotine /ˈsɛrətiːn/ ■ n. a medium-sized insectivorous bat. [*Eptesicus capensis* (Africa) and other species.]
– ORIGIN C18: from French *sérotine*, from Latin *serotinus* 'of the evening, late'.

serotonin /ˌsɛrəˈtəʊnɪn/ ■ n. Biochemistry a compound present in blood platelets and serum, which constricts the blood vessels and acts as a neurotransmitter.
– ORIGIN 1940s: from SERUM + TONIC.

serotype /ˈsɪərə(ʊ)taɪp/ Microbiology ■ n. a serologically distinguishable strain of a micro-organism. ■ v. assign to a particular serotype.
– DERIVATIVES **serotypic** /ˌsɪərə(ʊ)ˈtɪpɪk/ adj.

serous /ˈsɪərəs/ ■ adj. Physiology of, resembling, or producing serum.
– ORIGIN Middle English: from French *séreux* or medieval Latin *serosus*, from *serum* (see SERUM).

serous membrane ■ n. a smooth transparent two-layered membrane lining certain internal cavities of the body and lubricated by a fluid derived from serum.

serpent ■ n. 1 chiefly poetic/literary a large snake. ▶ a dragon or other mythical snake-like reptile. ▶ (**the Serpent**) a biblical name for Satan (see Genesis 3, Revelation 20). ▶ a sly or treacherous person. 2 historical a bass wind

instrument made of leather-covered wood in three U-shaped turns, with a cup-shaped mouthpiece and few keys.
– ORIGIN Middle English: from Latin *serpent-*, *serpere* 'to creep'.

serpentine /'sə:p(ə)ntʌɪn/ ■ adj. of or like a serpent or snake. ▶ winding and twisting. ▶ complex, cunning, or treacherous. ■ n. a dark green mineral consisting of hydrated magnesium silicate, sometimes mottled or spotted like a snake's skin.

serpentinite /'sə:p(ə)ntɪ,nʌɪt/ ■ n. Geology a metamorphic rock consisting largely of serpentine.

serrate /'sɛreɪt/ ■ adj. chiefly Botany serrated.

serrated ■ adj. having or denoting a jagged edge; saw-like.
– ORIGIN Middle English: from late Latin *serratus*, from Latin *serra* 'saw'.

serration ■ n. a tooth or point of a serrated edge or surface.

serried ■ adj. (of rows of people or things) standing close together.
– ORIGIN C17: from *serry* 'press close', prob. from French *serré* 'close together'.

serum /'sɪərəm/ ■ n. (pl. **sera** /-rə/ or **serums**) 1 an amber-coloured, protein-rich liquid which separates out when blood coagulates. 2 the blood serum of an animal, used to provide immunity to a pathogen or toxin by inoculation or as a diagnostic agent.
– ORIGIN C17: from Latin, 'whey'.

serval /'sə:v(ə)l/ ■ n. a slender African wild cat with long legs, large ears, and a black-spotted orange-brown coat. [*Felis serval*.]
– ORIGIN C18: from Portuguese *cerval* 'deer-like', from *cervo* 'deer'.

servant ■ n. a person employed to perform duties for others, especially in a house on domestic duties or as a personal attendant. ▶ a person employed in the service of a government. ▶ a devoted and helpful follower or supporter.
– ORIGIN Middle English: from Old French, '(person) serving', from *servir* 'to serve'.

serve ■ v. 1 perform duties or services for. ▶ be employed as a member of the armed forces. ▶ spend (a period) in office, in an apprenticeship, or in prison. 2 present food or drink to (someone). ▶ (of food or drink) be enough for. ▶ attend to (a customer in a shop). ▶ Christian Church act as a server at the celebration of the Eucharist. 3 Law formally deliver (a summons or writ) to the person to whom it is addressed. 4 be of use in achieving something or fulfilling a purpose. ▶ treat in a specified way. ▶ (of a male breeding animal) copulate with (a female). 5 (in tennis and other racket sports) hit the ball or shuttlecock to begin play for each point of a game. 6 Nautical bind (a rope) with thin cord to protect or strengthen it. ■ n. an act of serving in tennis, badminton, etc.
– PHRASES **serve someone right** be someone's deserved punishment or misfortune. **serve one's** (or **its**) **turn** be useful. ▶ (**serve someone's turn**) be useful to someone.
– ORIGIN Middle English: from Old French *servir*, from Latin *servire*, from *servus* 'slave'.

server ■ n. 1 a person or thing that serves. 2 a computer or computer program which manages access to a centralized resource or service in a network.

servery ■ n. (pl. **-ies**) a counter, hatch, or room from which meals are served.

service ■ n. 1 the action or process of serving. ▶ an act of assistance. ▶ a period of employment with a company or organization: *he retired after 40 years' service*. ▶ (often in phrs **in**) or **out of service**) use for a particular purpose. ▶ (often in phr. **in service**) employment as a servant. 2 a system supplying a public need such as transport, or utilities such as electricity and water. ▶ a public department or organization run by the state: *the probation service*. ▶ (**the services**) the armed forces. 3 a ceremony of religious worship according to a prescribed form. 4 a set of matching crockery used for serving a particular meal. 5 (in tennis, badminton, etc.) a serve. 6 a periodic routine inspection and maintenance of a vehicle or other machine. ■ v. 1 perform routine maintenance or repair work on (a vehicle or machine). ▶ provide a service or services for. 2 pay interest on (a debt). 3 (of a male animal) mate with (a female animal).

– PHRASES **be at someone's service** be ready to assist someone whenever required. **be of service** be available to assist someone.
– ORIGIN Old English, from Old French *servise* or Latin *servitium* 'slavery', from *servus* 'slave'.

serviceable ■ adj. 1 fulfilling its function adequately; usable or in working order. 2 functional and durable rather than attractive.
– DERIVATIVES **serviceability** n. **serviceably** adv.

service area ■ n. chiefly Brit. a roadside area where services are available to motorists.

service book ■ n. a book of authorized forms of worship used in a church.

service charge ■ n. an extra charge made for serving customers in a restaurant. ▶ a charge made for maintenance on a rented property.

service dress ■ n. chiefly Brit. military uniform worn on formal but not ceremonial occasions.

serviced site ■ n. a plot of land intended for residential or commercial development supplied with electricity, sanitation, and water points.

service flat ■ n. Brit. a rented flat in which domestic service and sometimes meals are provided by the management.

service industry ■ n. a business that does work for a customer, and sometimes provides goods, but is not involved in manufacturing.

service line ■ n. (in tennis and other racket sports) a line on a court marking the limit of the area into which the ball must be served.

serviceman (or **servicewoman**) ■ n. (pl. **-men** or **-women**) 1 a person serving in the armed forces. 2 a person providing maintenance for machinery.

service provider ■ n. Computing a company which gives its subscribers access to the Internet.

service road ■ n. a subsidiary road running parallel to a main road and giving access to houses, shops, or businesses.

service station ■ n. a roadside establishment selling petrol and oil and sometimes offering vehicle maintenance.

serviette ■ n. a table napkin.
– ORIGIN C15: from Old French, from *servir* 'to serve'.

servile ■ adj. 1 excessively willing to serve or please others. 2 of or characteristic of a slave or slaves.
– DERIVATIVES **servilely** adv. **servility** n.
– ORIGIN Middle English: from Latin *servilis*, from *servus* 'slave'.

serving ■ n. a quantity of food suitable for or served to one person.

servingman (or **servingwoman**) ■ n. (pl. **-men** or **-women**) archaic a domestic servant or attendant.

servitor /'sə:vɪtə/ ■ n. archaic a person who serves or attends on a social superior.
– DERIVATIVES **servitorship** n.
– ORIGIN Middle English: from late Latin, from *servit-*, *servire* (see **SERVE**).

servitude /'sə:vɪtjuːd/ ■ n. 1 the state of being a slave or completely subject to someone more powerful. 2 Law the subjection of property to certain rights that allow one person to cross or use another's land for a specific purpose.
– ORIGIN Middle English: from Latin *servitudo*, from *servus* 'slave'.

servo ■ n. (pl. **-os**) short for **SERVOMECHANISM** or **SERVOMOTOR**.
– ORIGIN C19: from Latin *servus* 'slave'.

servomechanism ■ n. a powered mechanism producing motion or forces at a higher level of energy than the input level, e.g. in the brakes and steering of large motor vehicles.

servomotor ■ n. the motive element in a servomechanism.

sesame /'sɛsəmi/ ■ n. a tall annual herbaceous plant of tropical and subtropical areas of the Old World, cultivated

sesamoid

for its oil-rich seeds. [*Sesamum indicum*.]
– PHRASES **open sesame** a free or unrestricted means of admission or access. [from the magic formula in the tale of Ali Baba and the Forty Thieves.]
– ORIGIN Middle English: from Greek *sēsamon*, *sēsamē*; cf. Arabic *simsim*.

sesamoid /ˈsɛsəmɔɪd/ (also **sesamoid bone**) ■ n. a small bony nodule developed in a tendon passing over an angular structure, especially in the hands and feet.
– ORIGIN C17: from SESAME, with ref. to the similarity in shape of a sesame seed.

Sesotho /sɛˈsuːtuː/ ■ n. the Southern Sotho language of the Basotho people.
– ORIGIN the name in Sesotho.

Sesotho sa Leboa ■ n. the Northern Sotho language spoken by the Basotho people of Limpopo province.
– ORIGIN the name in Sesotho sa Leboa, 'Northern Sotho'.

sesqui- ■ comb. form denoting one and a half: *sesquicentenary*. ▸ Chemistry (of a compound) in which a particular element or group is present in a ratio of 3:2 compared with another.
– ORIGIN from Latin *semi-* (see SEMI-) + *que* 'and'.

sesquicentenary /ˌsɛskwɪsɛnˈtiːn(ə)ri, -ˈtɛn-/ ■ n. (pl. **-ies**) the one-hundred-and-fiftieth anniversary of a significant event.
– DERIVATIVES **sesquicentennial** adj. & n.

sessile /ˈsɛsʌɪl, ˈsɛsɪl/ ■ adj. Biology 1 (of an organism) fixed in one place; immobile. 2 (of a structure) attached directly by its base without a stalk or peduncle.
– ORIGIN C18: from Latin *sessilis*, from *sedere* 'sit'.

session ■ n. 1 a period devoted to a particular activity: *a training session*. ▸ a period of recording music in a studio. 2 (often in phr. **in session**) a meeting of a deliberative or judicial body to conduct its business. ▸ a period during which such meetings are regularly held. 3 an academic year. ▸ the period during which a school has classes. 4 the governing body of a Presbyterian Church.
– DERIVATIVES **sessional** adj.
– ORIGIN Middle English: from Latin *sessio(n-)*, from *sess-* (see SESSILE).

session clerk ■ n. a chief lay official in the session of a Presbyterian Church.

session musician ■ n. a freelance musician hired to play on recording sessions.

sesterce /ˈsɛstəːs/ (also **sestertius** /sɛˈstəːʃəs/) ■ n. (pl. **sesterces** /-siːz/ or **sestertii** /-ˈstəːʃiː/) an ancient Roman coin and monetary unit equal to one quarter of a denarius.
– ORIGIN from Latin *sestertius*.

sestet /sɛsˈtɛt/ ■ n. Prosody the last six lines of a sonnet.
– ORIGIN C19: from Italian *sestetto*, from *sesto*, from Latin *sextus* 'a sixth'.

sestina /sɛˈstiːnə/ ■ n. Prosody a poem with six stanzas of six lines and a final triplet, all stanzas having the same six words at the line-ends in six different sequences.
– ORIGIN C19: from Italian, from *sesto* (see SESTET).

set¹ ■ v. (**setting**; past and past part. **set**) 1 put, lay, or stand (something) in a specified place or position. ▸ (**be set**) be situated in a specified place or position. ▸ represent (a story) as happening at a specified time or in a specified place. ▸ mount a precious stone in (a piece of jewellery). ▸ Printing arrange (type or text) as required. ▸ prepare (a table) for a meal by placing cutlery, crockery, etc., on it. ▸ (**set something to**) add (music) to a written work. ▸ Nautical put (a sail) up in position to catch the wind. 2 put, bring, or place into a specified state: *the hostages were set free*. ▸ instruct (someone) to do something. ▸ give someone (a task): *the problem we have been set*. ▸ establish as (an example or record). ▸ decide on or fix (a time, value, or limit). 3 adjust (a device) as required. 4 harden into a solid, semi-solid, or fixed state. ▸ arrange (damp hair) into the required style. ▸ put (a broken or dislocated bone or limb) into the correct position for healing. ▸ (of a hunting dog) adopt a rigid attitude indicating the presence of game. 5 (of the sun, moon, etc.) appear to move towards and below the earth's horizon as the earth rotates. 6 (of a tide or current) take or have a specified direction or course. 7 chiefly N. Amer. start (a fire). 8 (of blossom or a tree) form into or produce (fruit). 9 informal or dialect sit. 10 (of a dancer) acknowledge one's partner using the steps prescribed. 11 give the teeth of (a saw) an alternate outward inclination.
– PHRASES **set one's heart** (or **hopes**) **on** have a strong desire for or to do. **set out one's stall** display or show off one's abilities or attributes. **set sail** hoist the sails of a boat. ▸ begin a voyage. **set one's teeth** clench one's teeth together. ▸ become resolute. **set the wheels in motion** begin a process or put a plan into action.
– PHRASAL VERBS **set about 1** start doing something with vigour or determination. **2** Brit. informal attack (someone). **set someone against** cause someone to be in opposition or conflict with. **set something (off) against** offset something against. **set someone apart** give someone an air of unusual superiority. **set something apart** separate something and keep it for a special purpose. **set something aside 1** save or keep something for a particular purpose. ▸ remove land from agricultural production. **2** annul a legal decision or process. **set someone/thing back 1** delay or impede the progress of someone or something. **2** informal cost someone a particular amount of money. **set something by** archaic or US save something for future use. **set someone down** stop and allow someone to alight from a vehicle. **set something down** record something in writing or as an authoritative rule or principle. **set forth** begin a journey or trip. **set something forth** state or describe something in writing or speech. **set forward** archaic start on a journey. **set in** (of something unwelcome) begin and seem likely to continue. **set something in** insert something, especially a sleeve, into a garment. **set off** begin a journey. **set something off 1** cause a bomb or alarm to go off. **2** serve as decorative embellishment to. **set on** (or **upon**) attack (someone) violently. **set someone/thing on** (or **upon**) cause or urge a person or animal to attack. **set out 1** begin a journey. **2** aim or intend to do something. **set something out** arrange or display something in a particular order or position. **set to** begin doing something vigorously. **set someone up 1** establish someone in a particular capacity or role. **2** informal restore or enhance the health of someone. **3** informal make an innocent person appear guilty of something. **set something up 1** place or erect something in position. **2** establish a business, institution, etc. **3** begin making a loud sound.
– ORIGIN Old English *settan*, of Germanic origin.

set² ■ n. 1 a group or collection of things belonging or used together or resembling one another. ▸ a group of people with common interests or occupations: *the literary set*. ▸ a group of pupils or students who are taught together. ▸ (in tennis, darts, and other games) a group of games counting as a unit towards a match. ▸ (in jazz or popular music) a sequence of songs or pieces constituting or forming part of a live show or recording. ▸ a group of people making up the required number for a country dance. ▸ Mathematics & Logic a collection of distinct entities regarded as a unit, being either individually specified or (more usually) satisfying specified conditions. **2** the way in which something is set, disposed, or positioned. ▸ (also **dead set**) a setter's pointing in the presence of game. ▸ a warp or bend in wood, metal, etc., caused by continued strain or pressure. **3** a radio or television receiver. **4** a collection of scenery, stage furniture, etc., used for a scene in a play or film. **5** a cutting, young plant, or bulb used in the propagation of new plants. ▸ a young fruit that has just formed. **6** the last coat of plaster on a wall. **7** variant spelling of SETT. **8** Snooker another term for PLANT (in sense 4).
– PHRASES **make a dead set at** Brit. make a determined attempt to win the affections of. [by association with hunting (see *dead set* above).]
– ORIGIN Middle English: partly from Old French *sette*, from Latin *secta* 'sect', partly from SET¹.

set³ ■ adj. 1 fixed or arranged in advance. ▸ (of a restaurant menu) offered at a fixed price with a limited choice of dishes. ▸ (of a book) prescribed for study. ▸ having a conventional or predetermined wording; formulaic. 2 firmly fixed and unchanging. 3 ready, prepared, or likely to do something: *we're all set for tonight!* ▸ (**set against**) firmly opposed to. ▸ (**set on**) determined to do.
– ORIGIN Old English, from SET¹.

SETA /ˈsiːtə/ ■ abbrev. (in South Africa) Sector Education and Training Authority.

seta /ˈsiːtə/ ■ n. (pl. setae /-tiː/) chiefly Zoology a stiff hair-like or bristle-like structure.
– DERIVATIVES **setaceous** /-ˈteɪʃəs/ adj. **setal** adj.
– ORIGIN C18: from Latin, 'bristle'.

set-aside ■ n. the policy of taking land out of production to reduce crop surpluses. ▶ land taken out of production in this way.

setback ■ n. **1** a reversal or check in progress. **2** Architecture a plain, flat offset in a wall. **3** the distance by which a building is set back from the property line.

se-tenant /siːˈtɛnənt/ ■ adj. Philately (of stamps of different designs) joined together side by side as when printed.
– ORIGIN C20: from French, 'holding together'.

SETI ■ abbrev. search for extraterrestrial intelligence.

set-off ■ n. **1** an item or amount set off against another. ▶ Law a counterbalancing debt pleaded by the defendant in an action to recover money due. **2** Printing the unwanted transference of ink from one printed sheet or page to another.

setose /ˈsiːtəʊs, -z/ ■ adj. chiefly Zoology bearing bristles or setae; bristly.
– ORIGIN C17: from Latin *seta* 'bristle'.

set phrase ■ n. an unvarying phrase having a specific meaning or being the only context in which a word appears.

set piece ■ n. **1** a passage or section of a novel, film, etc., arranged for maximum effect. ▶ a formal and carefully structured speech. **2** a carefully organized and practised move in a team game. **3** an arrangement of fireworks forming a picture or design.

set point ■ n. (in tennis and other sports) a point which if won by one of the players will also win them a set.

set screw ■ n. a screw for adjusting or clamping parts of a machine.

set shot ■ n. Basketball a shot at the basket made without jumping.

set square ■ n. a right-angled triangular plate for drawing lines, especially at 90°, 45°, 60°, or 30°.

Setswana /sɛˈtswɑːnə/ ■ n. the Bantu language of the Tswana people.
– ORIGIN the name in Setswana.

sett (also **set**) ■ n. **1** the earth or burrow of a badger. **2** a granite paving block.
– ORIGIN Middle English: var. of SET².

settee ■ n. a long upholstered seat for more than one person, typically with a back and arms.
– ORIGIN C18: perhaps a var. of SETTLE².

setter ■ n. **1** a dog of a large long-haired breed trained to stand rigid when scenting game. **2** a person or thing that sets something.

set theory ■ n. the branch of mathematics concerned with the formal properties and applications of sets.

setting /ˈsɛtɪŋ/ ■ n. **1** the surroundings of a place or the location where an event happens. ▶ the place and time at which a story is represented as happening. **2** a piece of metal in which a precious stone or gem is fixed to form a piece of jewellery. **3** a piece of vocal or choral music composed for particular words. **4** (also **place setting**) a complete set of crockery and cutlery for one person at a meal. **5** a level at which a machine or device can be adjusted to operate.

settle¹ ■ v. **1** reach an agreement or decision about (an argument or problem); resolve. ▶ (**settle for**) accept or agree to (something less than satisfactory). **2** pay (a debt or account). ▶ (**settle something on**) give money or property to (someone) through a deed of settlement or a will. **3** (often **settle down**) adopt a more steady or secure style of life, especially through establishing a permanent home. ▶ make one's permanent home somewhere. ▶ establish a colony in a place. ▶ begin to feel comfortable or established in a new situation. ▶ (**settle down to**) apply oneself to. ▶ become or make calmer or quieter. **4** sit or come to rest in a comfortable position. **5** fall or come down on to a surface. ▶ (of suspended particles) sink slowly in a liquid to form sediment. ▶ (of an object) gradually sink down under its own weight. ▶ (of a ship) begin to sink. **6** dated silence (a troublesome person) by some means.
– DERIVATIVES **settleable** adj.
– ORIGIN Old English *setlan* 'to seat, place', from SETTLE².

settle² ■ n. a wooden bench with a high back and arms, typically incorporating a box under the seat.
– ORIGIN Old English *setl* 'a place to sit', of Germanic origin; rel. to Latin *sella* 'seat'.

settlement ■ n. **1** the action or process of settling. **2** an official agreement intended to resolve a dispute or conflict. **3** a place where people establish a community. **4** Law an arrangement whereby property passes to a person or succession of people as dictated by the settlor.

settler ■ n. a person who settles in an area, especially one with no or few previous inhabitants. ▶ S. African historical a British colonist, especially one of a group who settled on the eastern frontier of the Cape Colony in 1820. ▶ informal, often derogatory any white South African.

settlor /ˈsɛtlə/ ■ n. Law a person who makes a settlement, especially of a property.

set-to ■ n. (pl. **-os**) informal a fight or argument.

set-top box ■ n. a device for viewing cable or satellite television or giving television access to the Internet. ▶ a device which converts a digital television signal to analogue for viewing on a conventional set.

set-up ■ n. informal **1** the way in which something is organized or arranged. ▶ an organization or arrangement. ▶ a set of equipment for a particular activity. **2** a scheme or trick intended to incriminate or deceive someone. ▶ chiefly N. Amer. a contest with a pre-arranged outcome.

seven ■ cardinal number **1** equivalent to the sum of three and four; one more than six, or three less than ten; 7. (Roman numeral: **vii** or **VII**.) **2** (**sevens**) seven-a-side rugby.
– PHRASES **the seven deadly sins** (in Christian tradition) the sins of pride, covetousness, lust, anger, gluttony, envy, and sloth. **the seven seas** all the oceans of the world. **the Seven Wonders of the World** the seven most spectacular man-made structures of the ancient world. **the seven year itch** a supposed tendency to infidelity after seven years of marriage.
– DERIVATIVES **sevenfold** adj. & adv.
– ORIGIN Old English *seofon*, of Germanic origin.

seventeen ■ cardinal number one more than sixteen, or seven more than ten; 17. (Roman numeral: **xvii** or **XVII**.)
– DERIVATIVES **seventeenth** adj. & n.
– ORIGIN Old English *seofontiene*, from the Germanic base of SEVEN.

seventh ■ ordinal number **1** constituting number seven in a sequence; 7th. **2** (**a seventh/one seventh**) each of seven equal parts into which something is or may be divided. **3** Music an interval spanning seven consecutive notes in a diatonic scale. ▶ the note which is higher by this interval than the tonic of a diatonic scale or root of a chord. ▶ a chord in which the seventh note of the scale forms an important component.
– DERIVATIVES **seventhly** adv.

Seventh-Day Adventist ■ n. a member of a strict Protestant sect which preaches the imminent return of Christ to Earth and observes Saturday as the sabbath.

seventy ■ cardinal number (pl. **-ies**) the number equivalent to the product of seven and ten; ten less than eighty; 70. (Roman numeral: **lxx** or **LXX**.)
– DERIVATIVES **seventieth** ordinal number . **seventyfold** adj. & adv.
– ORIGIN Old English *hundseofontig*, from *hund-* (of uncertain origin) + *seofon* 'seven'.

seventy-four ■ n. a southern African sea bream with longitudinal dotted blue stripes along its flanks. [*Polystegnus undulosus*.]
– ORIGIN C19: named after C18 battleships called *seventy-fours* from the number of gun ports along the sides.

sever ■ v. **1** divide by cutting or slicing. **2** put an end to (a connection or relationship).
– DERIVATIVES **severable** adj.
– ORIGIN Middle English: from Anglo-Norman French *severer*, from Latin *separare* 'disjoin, divide'.

several ■ det. & pron. more than two but not many. ■ adj. **1** separate or respective. **2** Law applied or regarded separately.
– DERIVATIVES **severally** adv.
– ORIGIN Middle English: from medieval Latin *separalis*, from Latin *separ* 'separate, different'.

severance ■ n. **1** the action of ending a connection or relationship. **2** the state of being separated or cut off. **3** dismissal or discharge from employment.

severance pay ■ n. money paid to an employee on the early termination of a contract.

severe ■ adj. **1** (of something bad, undesirable, or difficult) very great; intense. **2** strict or harsh. **3** very plain in style or appearance.
– DERIVATIVES **severely** adv. **severity** n.
– ORIGIN C16: from French *sévère* or Latin *severus*.

seviche /sɛˈviːtʃeɪ/ ■ n. variant spelling of CEVICHE.

Seville orange /ˈsɛvɪl/ ■ n. a bitter orange used for marmalade.
– ORIGIN from *Seville* in Spain.

Sèvres /ˈsɛvr(ə)/ ■ n. a type of fine porcelain characterized by elaborate decoration on backgrounds of intense colour.
– ORIGIN from *Sèvres* in the suburbs of Paris, the place of manufacture.

sevruga /sɛvˈruːɡə/ ■ n. a migratory sturgeon found only in the basins of the Caspian and Black Seas, fished for its caviar. [*Acipenser stellatus*.]
– ORIGIN C16: from Russian *sevryuga*.

sew ■ v. (past part. **sewn** or **sewed**) **1** join, fasten, or repair by making stitches with a needle and thread or a sewing machine. **2** (**sew something up**) informal bring something to a favourable state or conclusion.
– ORIGIN Old English *siwan*, of Germanic origin.

sewage /ˈsuːɪdʒ/ ■ n. waste water and excrement conveyed in sewers.
– ORIGIN C19: from SEWER[1].

sewage works (also **sewage farm**) ■ n. a place where sewage is treated to produce safe effluent or residues.

sewer[1] /ˈsuːə, ˈsjuːə/ ■ n. an underground conduit for carrying off drainage water and waste matter.
– ORIGIN Middle English: from Old Northern French *seuwiere* 'channel to drain the overflow from a fish pond', from Latin *ex-* 'out of' + *aqua* 'water'.

sewer[2] /ˈsəʊə/ ■ n. a person that sews.

sewerage ■ n. **1** the provision of drainage by sewers. **2** US term for SEWAGE.

sewing machine ■ n. a machine with a mechanically driven needle for sewing or stitching cloth.

sewn past participle of SEW.

sex ■ n. **1** either of the two main categories (male and female) into which humans and most other living things are divided on the basis of their reproductive functions. ▸ the fact of belonging to one of these categories. ▸ the group of all members of either sex. **2** sexual activity, specifically sexual intercourse. ▸ euphemistic a person's genitals. ■ v. determine the sex of.
– DERIVATIVES **sexer** n.
– ORIGIN Middle English: from Old French *sexe* or Latin *sexus*.

sexagenarian /ˌsɛksədʒɪˈnɛːrɪən/ ■ n. a person who is between 60 and 69 years old.
– ORIGIN C18: from Latin *sexagenarius*, from *sexaginta* 'sixty'.

sex appeal ■ n. the quality of being attractive in a sexual way.

sex bomb ■ n. informal a woman who is very sexually attractive.

sexcentenary /ˌsɛk(s)sɛnˈtiːn(ə)ri, -ˈtɛn-/ ■ n. (pl. **-ies**) the six-hundredth anniversary of a significant event.

sex chromosome ■ n. a chromosome concerned in determining the sex of an organism (in mammals the X and Y chromosomes).

sex drive ■ n. the urge to seek satisfaction of sexual needs.

sexed ■ adj. **1** having specified sexual appetites: *highly sexed*. **2** having sexual characteristics.

sexennial /sɛkˈsɛnɪəl/ ■ adj. lasting for or recurring every six years.
– ORIGIN C17: from Latin *sexennium* 'period of six years', from *sex* 'six' + *annus* 'year'.

sex hormone ■ n. a hormone affecting sexual development or reproduction, such as oestrogen or testosterone.

sexism ■ n. prejudice, stereotyping, or discrimination, typically against women, on the basis of sex.
– DERIVATIVES **sexist** adj. & n.

sexivalent /ˌsɛksɪˈveɪl(ə)nt/ ■ adj. Chemistry another term for HEXAVALENT.

sex kitten ■ n. informal a young woman who asserts or exploits her sexual attractiveness.

sexless ■ adj. **1** lacking in sexual desire, activity, or attractiveness. **2** neither male nor female.
– DERIVATIVES **sexlessly** adv. **sexlessness** n.

sex life ■ n. a person's sexual activity and relationships considered as a whole.

sex object ■ n. a person regarded chiefly in terms of their sexual attractiveness or availability.

sexology ■ n. the study of human sexual life or relationships.
– DERIVATIVES **sexological** adj. **sexologist** n.

sexploitation ■ n. informal the commercial exploitation of sex or sexually explicit material.

sexpot ■ n. informal a sexy person.

sex symbol ■ n. a person widely noted for their sexual attractiveness.

sextant /ˈsɛkst(ə)nt/ ■ n. an instrument with a graduated arc of 60° and a sighting mechanism, used for measuring the angular distances between objects and especially for taking altitudes in navigation and surveying.
– ORIGIN C16: from Latin *sextans* 'sixth part', from *sextus* 'sixth'.

sextet (also **sextette**) ■ n. **1** a group of six people playing music or singing together. ▸ a composition for such a group. **2** a set of six people or things.
– ORIGIN C19: alteration of SESTET, suggested by Latin *sex* 'six'.

sextillion /sɛksˈtɪljən/ ■ cardinal number (pl. **sextillions** or (with numeral) same) a thousand raised to the seventh power (10^{21}).
– DERIVATIVES **sextillionth** ordinal number.
– ORIGIN C17: from French *million*, by substitution of the prefix *sexti-* 'six' (from Latin *sextus* 'sixth').

sexton ■ n. a person who looks after a church and churchyard, typically acting as bell-ringer and grave-digger.
– ORIGIN Middle English: from Anglo-Norman French *segrestein*, from medieval Latin *sacristanus* (see SACRISTAN).

sex tourism ■ n. travel abroad with the aim of taking advantage of the lack of restrictions on sexual activity and prostitution in some countries.
– DERIVATIVES **sex tourist** n.

sextuple /ˈsɛkstjʊp(ə)l, sɛksˈtjuːp(ə)l/ ■ adj. **1** consisting of six parts or elements. **2** six times as much or as many. ■ v. increase or be increased sixfold. ■ n. a sixfold number or amount.
– ORIGIN C17: from medieval Latin *sextuplus*, from Latin *sex* 'six'.

sextuplet /ˈsɛkstjʊplɪt, sɛksˈtjuːplɪt/ ■ n. each of six children born at one birth.
– ORIGIN C19: from SEXTUPLE, on the pattern of *triplet*.

sexual ■ adj. **1** relating to the instincts, physiological processes, and activities connected with physical attraction or intimate physical contact between individuals. **2** of or relating to the two sexes or to gender. **3** (of reproduction) involving the fusion of gametes.
– DERIVATIVES **sexualization** (also **-isation**) n. **sexualize** (also **-ise**) v. **sexually** adv.

sexual harassment ■ n. the repeated making of unwanted sexual advances or obscene remarks to a person, especially in a workplace.

sexual intercourse ■ n. sexual contact between individuals involving penetration, especially the insertion of a man's erect penis into a woman's vagina culminating in orgasm and the ejaculation of semen.

sexuality ■ n. (pl. **-ies**) capacity for sexual feelings. ▶ a person's sexual orientation or preference. ▶ sexual activity.

sexual orientation ■ n. a person's sexual identity in relation to the gender to which they are attracted; the fact of being heterosexual, homosexual, or bisexual.

sexual politics ■ pl. n. [treated as sing.] relations between the sexes regarded in terms of power.

sexual selection ■ n. Biology natural selection arising through preference by one sex for certain characteristics in individuals of the other sex.

sex worker ■ n. euphemistic a prostitute.

sexy ■ adj. (**-ier, -iest**) **1** sexually attractive or exciting. ▶ sexually aroused. **2** informal very exciting or appealing.
– DERIVATIVES **sexily** adv. **sexiness** n.

Seychellois /seɪʃelˈwɑː/ ■ n. a native or inhabitant of the Seychelles. ■ adj. of or relating to the Seychelles.

sfumato /sfuːˈmɑːtəʊ/ ■ n. Art the technique of allowing tones and colours to shade gradually into one another.
– ORIGIN C19: Italian, 'shaded off', from *sfumare*.

SFX ■ abbrev. **1** sound effects. **2** special effects.
– ORIGIN *FX* representing a pronunciation of *effects*.

SG ■ abbrev. Physics specific gravity.

Sg ■ symb. the chemical element seaborgium.

SGB ■ abbrev. **1** School Governing Body. **2** S. African Standards Generating Body.

SGML ■ abbrev. Computing Standard Generalized Mark-up Language, a system for encoding electronic texts so that they can be displayed in any desired format.

sgraffito /sɡrɑːˈfiːtəʊ/ ■ n. (pl. **sgraffiti** /-tiː/) a form of decoration made by scratching through a surface to reveal a lower layer of a contrasting colour.
– ORIGIN C18: Italian, 'scratched away', from *sgraffiare*.

Sgt ■ abbrev. Sergeant.

shabby ■ adj. (**-ier, -iest**) **1** worn out or dilapidated. ▶ dressed in old or worn clothes. **2** mean and unfair.
– DERIVATIVES **shabbily** adv. **shabbiness** n.
– ORIGIN C17: from dialect *shab* 'scab', from a Germanic base meaning 'itch'.

shack ■ n. a roughly built hut or cabin; a small makeshift dwelling. ■ v. (**shack up**) informal live with someone as a lover.
– ORIGIN C19: perhaps from Mexican *jacal*, Nahuatl *xacatli* 'wooden hut'.

shack farming ■ n. S. African the renting out of undeveloped land for the construction of informal dwellings. ▶ the construction and renting out of a backyard shack.
– DERIVATIVES **shack farm** n. & v. **shack farmer** n.

shackland ■ n. S. African informal another term for INFORMAL SETTLEMENT.

shackle ■ n. **1** (**shackles**) a pair of fetters connected by a chain, used to fasten a prisoner's wrists or ankles together. ▶ restraints or impediments. **2** a metal link, typically U-shaped, closed by a bolt and used to secure a chain or rope to something. ■ v. **1** chain with shackles. **2** restrain; limit.
– ORIGIN Old English *sc(e)acul* 'fetter', of Germanic origin.

shad ■ n. (pl. same or **shads**) **1** an edible herring-like marine fish that enters rivers to spawn. [Genera *Alosa* and *Caspialosa*: several species.] **2** S. African (in KwaZulu-Natal) another term for BLUEFISH.
– ORIGIN Old English.

shaddock /ˈʃadək/ ■ n. another term for POMELO.
– ORIGIN C17: named after Captain *Shaddock*, who introduced it to the West Indies.

shade ■ n. **1** comparative darkness and coolness caused by shelter from direct sunlight. **2** a position of relative inferiority or obscurity. **3** a colour, especially with regard to how light or dark it is. ▶ a slight degree of difference between colours. **4** a slightly differing variety: *all shades of opinion*. **5** a slight amount. **6** a lampshade. **7** N. Amer. a screen or blind on a window. **8** (**shades**) informal sunglasses. **9** poetic/literary a ghost. ■ v. **1** screen from direct light. ▶ cover, moderate, or exclude the light of. **2** darken or colour with parallel pencil lines or a block of colour. **3** informal narrowly win. **4** reduce or decline in amount, rate, or price.
– PHRASES **shades of** —— suggestive or reminiscent of someone or something.
– DERIVATIVES **shadeless** adj. **shader** n.
– ORIGIN Old English, of Germanic origin.

shading ■ n. **1** the representation of light and shade on a drawing or map. **2** a very slight variation. **3** something providing shade.

shadoof /ʃəˈduːf/ ■ n. a pole with a bucket and counterpoise used especially in Egypt for raising water.
– ORIGIN C19: from Egyptian Arabic *šādūf*.

shadow ■ n. **1** a dark area or shape produced by a body coming between light rays and a surface. ▶ partial or complete darkness. ▶ a dark patch or area. **2** an air or expression of sadness and gloom. **3** a position of relative inferiority or obscurity. **4** [with neg.] the slightest trace. **5** a weak or inferior remnant or version of something. **6** an inseparable attendant or companion. ▶ a person secretly following and observing another. **7** [as modifier] denoting the opposition counterpart of a government minister. ■ v. **1** envelop in shadow; cast a shadow over. **2** follow and observe secretly. ▶ accompany (a worker) in their daily activities for experience of or insight into a job.
– DERIVATIVES **shadower** n. **shadowiness** n. **shadowless** adj. **shadowy** adj. (**-ier, -iest**).
– ORIGIN Old English, of Germanic origin.

shadow-box ■ v. spar with an imaginary opponent as a form of training.

shadow economy ■ n. Economics illicit economic activity existing alongside a country's official economy, e.g. black market transactions and undeclared work.

shadowgraph ■ n. **1** an image formed by the shadow of an object on a surface. **2** an image formed when light shone through a fluid is refracted differently by regions of different density. **3** a radiograph.

shadowland ■ n. poetic/literary an indeterminate borderland between places or states.

shadow price ■ n. Economics the estimated price of something for which no market price exists.

shadow theatre ■ n. a display in which the shadows of flat jointed puppets are cast on a screen which is viewed by the audience from the other side.

shady ■ adj. (**-ier, -iest**) **1** situated in or full of shade. **2** giving shade. **3** informal of doubtful honesty or legality.
– DERIVATIVES **shadily** adv. **shadiness** n.

shaft ■ n. **1** a long, narrow part or section forming the handle of a tool or club, the body of a spear or arrow, or similar. ▶ an arrow or spear. ▶ a column, especially the part between the base and capital. ▶ a long cylindrical rotating rod for the transmission of motive power in a machine. ▶ each of the pair of poles between which a horse is harnessed to a vehicle. **2** a ray of light or bolt of lightning. **3** a sudden flash of a quality or feeling. ▶ a witty, wounding, or provoking remark. **4** vulgar slang a man's penis. **5** a long, narrow, typically vertical hole giving access to a mine, accommodating a lift, etc. ■ v. **1** (of light) shine in beams. **2** vulgar slang (of a man) have sexual intercourse with. **3** informal treat harshly or unfairly.
– DERIVATIVES **shafted** adj.
– ORIGIN Old English *scæft, sceaft* 'handle, pole', of Germanic origin.

shafting ■ n. a system of shafts for transmitting motive power in a machine.

shag[1] ■ n. **1** a carpet or rug with a long, rough pile. ▶ [as modifier] (of pile) long and rough. **2** a thick, tangled hairstyle. **3** coarse cut tobacco.
– ORIGIN Old English *sceacga* 'rough matted hair', of Germanic origin.

shag[2] ■ n. a cormorant.
– ORIGIN C16: perhaps a use of SHAG[1], with ref. to the bird's 'shaggy' crest.

shag[3] vulgar slang ■ v. (**shagged, shagging**) have sexual intercourse with. ■ n. an act of sexual intercourse.
– DERIVATIVES **shagger** n.
– ORIGIN C18.

shag[4] ■ v. Baseball chase or catch (fly balls) for practice.
– ORIGIN C20.

shaggy ■ adj. (**-ier, -iest**) (of hair or fur) long, thick, and

shagreen

unkempt. ▸ having shaggy hair or fur. ▸ of or having a covering resembling shaggy hair.
- PHRASES **shaggy-dog story** a long, rambling story or joke, amusing only because it is absurdly inconsequential. [orig. an anecdote of this type, about a shaggy-haired dog (1945).]
- DERIVATIVES **shaggily** adv. **shagginess** n.

shagreen /ʃəˈɡriːn/ ■ n. **1** sharkskin used for decoration or as an abrasive. **2** untanned leather with a rough granulated surface.
- ORIGIN C17: var. of CHAGRIN, literally 'rough skin'.

shah /ʃɑː/ ■ n. historical a title of the former monarch of Iran.
- DERIVATIVES **shahdom** n.
- ORIGIN C16: from Persian *šāh*, from Old Persian *kšāyaṭiya* 'king'.

Shaitan /ʃeɪˈtɑːn/ ■ n. (in Muslim countries) Satan or an evil spirit.
- ORIGIN from Arabic *šayṭān*.

shake ■ v. (past **shook**; past part. **shaken**) **1** tremble or vibrate or cause to do so. ▸ tremble uncontrollably with strong emotion. **2** move forcefully or quickly up and down or to and fro. ▸ remove from something by shaking. ▸ brandish in anger or as a warning. **3** (often **shake someone/thing off**) informal get rid of or put an end to (someone or something unwanted). **4** shock or astonish. ▸ cause a change of mood by shocking or disturbing. ▸ weaken or impair (confidence, a belief, etc.). ■ n. **1** an act of shaking. **2** an amount sprinkled from a container. **2** informal a milkshake. **3** (**the shakes**) informal a fit of trembling or shivering.
- PHRASES **get** (or **give someone**) **a fair shake** informal get (or give someone) fair treatment. **in two shakes** (**of a lamb's tail**) informal very quickly. **no great shakes** informal not very good or significant. **shake the dust off one's feet** leave indignantly or disdainfully. **shake a leg** informal make a start; rouse oneself.
- PHRASAL VERBS **shake someone down** N. Amer. informal extort money from someone. **shake on** informal confirm (an agreement) by shaking hands. **shake someone up** rouse someone from lethargy or apathy. **shake something up** make radical changes to the structure of an institution or system.
- ORIGIN Old English, of Germanic origin.

shakedown ■ n. informal **1** a radical change or restructuring. **2** a thorough search. **3** a test of a new product or model.

shaken past participle of SHAKE.

shaken baby syndrome ■ n. a condition characterized by cranial injury, retinal haemorrhage, etc. observed in infants who have been violently jolted.

shaker ■ n. **1** a container used for mixing ingredients by shaking. ▸ a container with a pierced top from which a powder is poured by shaking. **2** (**Shaker**) a member of an American Christian sect dedicated to a simple lifestyle. ▸ [as modifier] denoting a style of elegantly functional furniture traditionally produced by Shakers.
- DERIVATIVES **Shakeress** n. **Shakerism** n.

Shakespearean /ʃeɪkˈspɪəriən/ (also **Shakespearian**) ■ adj. of, relating to, or in the style of William Shakespeare or his works. ■ n. an expert in or student of Shakespeare's works.

shake-up (also **shake-out**) ■ n. informal a radical reorganization.

shako /ˈʃeɪkəʊ, ˈʃakəʊ/ ■ n. (pl. **-os**) a cylindrical or conical military hat with a peak and a plume or pompom.
- ORIGIN C19: from Hungarian, from *csák* 'peak', from German *Zacken* 'spike'.

Shakti /ˈʃʌkti/ (also **Sakti**) ■ n. Hinduism the female principle of divine energy.
- ORIGIN from Sanskrit *śakti* 'power, divine energy'.

shaky ■ adj. (**-ier**, **-iest**) **1** shaking or trembling. **2** unstable. ▸ not safe or reliable.
- DERIVATIVES **shakily** adv. **shakiness** n.

shale ■ n. soft finely stratified sedimentary rock formed from consolidated mud or clay.
- DERIVATIVES **shaly** (also **shaley**) adj.
- ORIGIN C18: prob. from German *Schale*; rel. to English dialect *shale* 'dish'.

shale oil ■ n. mineral oil distilled from bituminous shale.

shall ■ modal v. (3rd sing. present **shall**) **1** (in the first person) expressing the future tense. **2** expressing a strong assertion or intention. **3** expressing an instruction or command. **4** used in questions indicating offers or suggestions.
- ORIGIN Old English, of Germanic origin, from a base meaning 'owe'.

> **USAGE**
> There are traditional rules as to when to use **shall** and **will**. In practice, however, these rules are not followed so strictly and the contracted forms (**I'll**, **she'll**, etc.) are frequently used instead, especially in spoken and informal contexts. See "*shall* and *will*" in *Guide to Good English* p. SP 14.

shallot /ʃəˈlɒt/ ■ n. **1** a small onion-like bulb, used in cookery and pickling. **2** the plant which produces these bulbs. [*Allium ascalonicum*.]
- ORIGIN C17: shortening of *eschalot*, from French *eschalotte*, alteration of Old French *eschaloigne*.

shallow ■ adj. **1** of little depth. **2** not showing, requiring, or capable of serious thought. ■ n. (**shallows**) a shallow area of water. ■ v. become shallow.
- DERIVATIVES **shallowly** adv. **shallowness** n.
- ORIGIN Middle English.

shalom /ʃəˈlɒm/ ■ exclam. used as salutation by Jews at meeting or parting.
- ORIGIN from Hebrew *šālōm* 'peace'.

shalt archaic second person singular of SHALL.

shalwar /ʃʌlˈwɑː/ ■ n. variant spelling of SALWAR.

sham ■ n. **1** a person or thing that is not what they are purported to be. **2** pretence. ■ adj. bogus; false. ■ v. (**shammed**, **shamming**) **1** falsely present something as the truth. **2** pretend to be or to be experiencing.
- DERIVATIVES **shammer** n.
- ORIGIN C17: perhaps a northern English var. of SHAME.

shaman /ˈʃamən, ˈʃeɪm-/ ■ n. (pl. **shamans**) (in some traditional societies) a person believed to work with good and evil spirits in healing, divining, etc.
- DERIVATIVES **shamanic** /ʃəˈmanɪk/ adj. **shamanism** n. **shamanist** n. & adj. **shamanistic** adj.
- ORIGIN C17: from German *Schamane* and Russian *shaman*, from Tungus (a Siberian language) *šaman*.

shamateur ■ n. derogatory a sports player who makes money from sporting activities though classified as amateur.
- DERIVATIVES **shamateurism** n.
- ORIGIN C19: blend of SHAM and AMATEUR.

shamba /ˈʃambə/ ■ n. (in East Africa) a cultivated plot of ground.
- ORIGIN from Kiswahili.

shamble ■ v. move with a slow, shuffling, awkward gait. ■ n. a shambling gait.
- ORIGIN C16: prob. from dialect *shamble* 'ungainly', perhaps from the phr. *shamble legs*, with ref. to the legs of shamble tables.

shambles ■ n. **1** informal a chaotic state. **2** a scene of carnage.
- ORIGIN Middle English: pl. of earlier *shamble* 'stool, stall', of West Germanic origin, from Latin *scamellum*, diminutive of *scamnum* 'bench'.

shambolic ■ adj. informal chaotic, disorganized, or mismanaged.
- ORIGIN 1970S: from SHAMBLES.

shame ■ n. **1** a feeling of humiliation or distress caused by the consciousness of wrong or foolish behaviour. **2** dishonour. ▸ a person or thing bringing dishonour. **3** a regrettable or unfortunate thing. ■ v. cause to feel ashamed. ■ exclam. informal **1** used to express sympathy or pity. **2** S. African used to express pleasure, especially at something charmingly small or endearing.
- PHRASES **put someone to shame** shame someone by outdoing or surpassing them. **shame on you!** you should be ashamed.
- ORIGIN Old English, of Germanic origin.

shamefaced ■ adj. showing shame.

–DERIVATIVES **shamefacedly** adv. **shamefacedness** n.
–ORIGIN C16: alteration of archaic *shamefast*, by association with FACE.

shameful ■ adj. worthy of or causing shame.
–DERIVATIVES **shamefully** adv. **shamefulness** n.

shameless ■ adj. showing a lack of shame.
–DERIVATIVES **shamelessly** adv. **shamelessness** n.

shammy (also **shammy leather**) ■ n. (pl. **-ies**) informal term for CHAMOIS (in sense 2).
–ORIGIN C18: a phonetic spelling.

shampoo ■ n. **1** a liquid preparation for washing the hair. ▸ a similar substance for cleaning a carpet, car, etc. **2** an act of washing with shampoo. ■ v. (**shampoos, shampooed**) wash or clean with shampoo.
–ORIGIN C18: from Hindi *cāmpo!* 'press!', from *cāmpnā*.

shamrock ■ n. a low-growing clover-like plant with three-lobed leaves, the national emblem of Ireland. [*Trifolium minus* and other species.]
–ORIGIN C16: from Irish *seamróg* 'trefoil', diminutive of *seamar* 'clover'.

Shan /ʃɑːn/ ■ n. (pl. same or **Shans**) a member of a people living mainly in northern Burma (Myanmar) and adjacent parts of China.
–ORIGIN from Burmese.

shandy ■ n. (pl. **-ies**) beer mixed with lemonade or ginger beer.
–ORIGIN C19: abbrev. of *shandygaff*, in the same sense.

Shangaan /ˈʃaŋɡɑːn/ ■ n. (pl. same or **Shangaans**) **1** a member of the Tsonga people of southern Africa. **2** the Bantu language of this people.
–ORIGIN prob. named after the founding chief *Soshangane*.

shanghai /ʃaŋˈhʌɪ/ ■ v. (**shanghais, shanghaied, shanghaiing**) **1** historical force to join a ship's crew by underhand means. **2** informal coerce or trick into a place or action.
–ORIGIN C19: from *Shanghai*, a major Chinese seaport.

Shangri-La /ˌʃaŋɡrɪˈlɑː/ ■ n. an imaginary earthly paradise.
–ORIGIN the name of a Tibetan utopia in James Hilton's *Lost Horizon* (1933), from *Shangri* (an invented name) + Tibetan *la* 'mountain pass'.

shank ■ n. **1** a person's leg, especially the lower part. ▸ the lower part of an animal's foreleg, especially as a cut of meat. **2** a long narrow part of a tool connecting the handle to the operational end. ▸ the stem of a key, spoon, anchor, etc. ▸ the straight part of a nail or fish hook. **3** a part by which something is attached to something else. **4** the band of a ring. **5** the narrow middle of the sole of a shoe. ■ v. Golf strike (a ball) with the heel of the club.
–DERIVATIVES **-shanked** adj.
–ORIGIN Old English, of West Germanic origin.

Shanks's pony (also **Shanks's mare**) ■ n. one's own legs as a means of conveyance.
–ORIGIN C18: first recorded as *shanks-nag* in R. Fergusson's *Poems* (1785).

shan't ■ contr. shall not.

shantung /ʃanˈtʌŋ/ ■ n. a soft dress fabric spun from tussore silk.
–ORIGIN C19: from *Shantung* in China, where it was orig. made.

shanty[1] ■ n. (pl. **-ies**) a small, crudely built shack.
–ORIGIN C19: perhaps from Canadian French *chantier* 'lumberjack's cabin, logging camp'.

shanty[2] (also **sea shanty**) ■ n. (pl. **-ies**) a song with alternating solo and chorus, originally sung by sailors working together.
–ORIGIN C19: prob. from French *chantez!* 'sing!', from *chanter*.

shanty town ■ n. a deprived area consisting of large numbers of shanty dwellings.

shape ■ n. **1** the external form or outline of someone or something. ▸ a specific form or guise assumed by someone or something. ▸ a piece of material, paper, etc., made or cut in a particular form. **2** the condition or state of someone or something. ▸ the distinctive nature or qualities of something. **3** definite or orderly arrangement. ■ v. **1** give a particular shape or form to. ▸ make (something) fit the form of something else. **2** determine the nature of. **3** (often **shape up**) develop in a particular way. **4** (**shape up**) become physically fit. ▸ (**shape something up**) informal improve something. **5** form or produce (a sound or words).
–PHRASES **in (good) shape** in good physical condition. **in the shape of** by way of. **lick (or knock or whip) someone/something into shape** act forcefully to bring someone or something into a better state. **out of shape 1** not having its usual or original shape. **2** in poor physical condition. **take shape** assume a distinct form.
–DERIVATIVES **shapable** (also **shapeable**) adj. **shaped** adj. **shaper** n.
–ORIGIN Old English *gesceap* 'external form, creation', *sceppan* 'create', of Germanic origin.

shapeless ■ adj. lacking definite or attractive shape.
–DERIVATIVES **shapelessly** adv. **shapelessness** n.

shapely ■ adj. (**-ier, -iest**) having an attractive or well-proportioned shape.
–DERIVATIVES **shapeliness** n.

shard ■ n. a sharp piece of broken ceramic, metal, glass, etc.
–ORIGIN Old English *sceard* 'gap, notch, potsherd', of Germanic origin.

share ■ n. **1** a part or portion of a larger amount which is divided among or contributed by a number of people. ▸ any of the equal parts into which a company's capital is divided. ▸ part-ownership of property. **2** the allotted or due amount of something expected to be had or done. ▸ a contribution to something. ■ v. **1** have a share of with another or others. ▸ (often **share something out**) give a share of (something) to another or others. ▸ possess in common with others. ▸ (**share in**) have a part in (an activity). **2** tell someone about.
–PHRASES **share and share alike** have or receive an equal share.
–DERIVATIVES **shareable** (also **sharable**) adj. **sharer** n.
–ORIGIN Old English, of Germanic origin.

sharecropper ■ n. a tenant farmer who gives a part of each crop as rent.
–DERIVATIVES **sharecrop** v. (**-cropped, -cropping**).

shareholder ■ n. an owner of shares in a company.
–DERIVATIVES **shareholding** n.

share option ■ n. an option for an employee to buy shares in their company at a discount or at a stated fixed price.

shareware ■ n. Computing software that is available free of charge and often distributed informally for evaluation.

sharia /ʃəˈriːə/ (also **shariah** or **shariat** /ʃəˈriːət/) ■ n. Islamic canonical law based on the teachings of the Koran and the traditions of the Prophet.
–ORIGIN from Arabic *šarīʿa*; the var. *shariat* from Urdu and Persian.

shark[1] ■ n. **1** a long-bodied cartilaginous marine fish, typically predatory and voracious, with a prominent dorsal fin. [Many species in the subclass Elasmobranchii.] **2** a small black SE Asian freshwater fish, popular in aquaria. [*Labeo bicolor* and *Morulius chrysophekadion*.]
–ORIGIN Middle English.

shark[2] ■ n. informal a person who exploits or swindles others.
–ORIGIN C16: perhaps from German *Schurke* 'worthless rogue', influenced by SHARK[1].

shark net ■ n. an underwater net that prevents sharks from entering a bathing area, protecting swimmers from attack.

sharkskin ■ n. a stiff, slightly lustrous synthetic fabric.

sharon fruit /ˈʃɛːr(ə)n, ˈʃar(ə)n/ ■ n. a persimmon, especially of an orange variety grown in Israel.
–ORIGIN from *Sharon*, a fertile coastal plain in Israel.

sharp ■ adj. **1** having an edge or point able to cut or pierce something. ▸ tapering to a point or edge. ▸ (of sand or gravel) composed of angular grains. **2** producing a sudden, piercing sensation or effect. **3** (of a food, taste, or smell) acidic and intense. **4** (of a sound) sudden and penetrating. **5** (of words or a speaker) critical or hurtful. ▸ (of an emotion or experience) painful. **6** clearly defined. **7** informal smart and stylish. **8** sudden and marked. ▸ making a sudden change of direction: *a sharp bend*.

9 showing speed of perception, comprehension, or response. ▶ quick to take advantage, especially in a dishonest way. **10** (of musical sound) above true or normal pitch. ▶ [postpos.] (of a note) a semitone higher than a specified note. ▶ [postpos.] (of a key) having a sharp or sharps in the signature. ■ adv. **1** punctually: *at 7.30 sharp*. **2** suddenly or abruptly. **3** above the true or normal pitch of musical sound. ■ n. **1** a musical note raised a semitone above natural pitch. ▶ the sign (♯) indicating this. **2** a long, sharply pointed needle used for general sewing. ▶ a thing with a sharp edge or point. ■ exclam. S. African informal another term for **SHARP SHARP**.
– DERIVATIVES **sharply** adv. **sharpness** n.
– ORIGIN Old English *sc(e)arp*, of Germanic origin.

Shar Pei /ʃɑː 'peɪ/ ■ n. (pl. **Shar Peis**) a compact squarely built dog of a Chinese breed, with a wrinkly skin and short bristly coat.
– ORIGIN 1970s: from Chinese *shā pí* 'sand skin'.

sharpen ■ v. make or become sharp.
– DERIVATIVES **sharpener** n.

sharp-featured ■ adj. having well-defined facial features.

sharpish informal ■ adj. fairly sharp. ■ adv. chiefly Brit. quickly; soon.

sharp practice ■ n. dishonest or barely honest dealings.

sharp sharp (also **sharp**) ■ exclam. S. African informal **1** expressing approval, acceptance or agreement. **2** used as a greeting at meeting or parting.

sharpshooter ■ n. a person skilled in shooting.
– DERIVATIVES **sharpshooting** n. & adj.

sharp-tongued ■ adj. given to using harsh or critical language.

sharp-witted ■ adj. perceptive or intelligent.
– DERIVATIVES **sharp-wittedly** adv. **sharp-wittedness** n.

shashlik /ˈʃaʃlɪk/ ■ n. (pl. same or **shashliks**) (in Asia and eastern Europe) a mutton kebab.
– ORIGIN from Russian *shashlyk*, from Turkish *şiş* 'spit, skewer'.

Shasta daisy /ˈʃastə/ ■ n. a tall Pyrenean plant bearing a single large white daisy-like flower. [*Leucanthemum maximum*.]
– ORIGIN C19: named after Mount *Shasta* in California.

shat past and past participle of **SHIT**.

shatter ■ v. **1** break or cause to break suddenly and violently into pieces. ▶ damage or destroy. **2** upset greatly. **3** [usu. as adj. **shattered**] informal exhaust.
– DERIVATIVES **shatterer** n. **shattering** adj. **shatteringly** adv. **shatterproof** adj.
– ORIGIN Middle English: perhaps imitative.

shave ■ v. **1** cut the hair off one's face with a razor. ▶ cut the hair off (a person or part of the body) with a razor. **2** cut (a thin slice or slices) off something. **3** reduce by a small amount. **4** pass or send something very close to. ■ n. **1** an act of shaving. **2** a tool for shaving very thin slices or layers from wood.
– ORIGIN Old English, of Germanic origin.

shaven ■ adj. shaved.

shaver ■ n. **1** an electric razor. **2** informal, dated a young lad.

Shavian /ˈʃeɪvɪən/ ■ adj. of, relating to, or in the manner of the Irish dramatist George Bernard Shaw (1856–1950) or his works or ideas. ■ n. an admirer of Shaw or his work.
– ORIGIN from *Shavius*, Latinized form of *Shaw*.

shaving ■ n. **1** a thin strip cut off a surface. **2** [as modifier] used when shaving.

Shavuoth /ʃəˈvuːəs, ʃɑːvʊˈɒt/ (also **Shavuot**) ■ n. a major Jewish festival held fifty days after the second day of Passover, originally a harvest festival but now also commemorating the giving of the Torah.
– ORIGIN from Hebrew *šābūʿōt* 'weeks', with ref. to the weeks between Passover and Pentecost.

shawl ■ n. a piece of fabric worn by women over the shoulders or head or wrapped round a baby.
– DERIVATIVES **shawled** adj.
– ORIGIN from Urdu and Persian *šāl*, prob. from *Shāliāt*, the name of a town in India.

shawl collar ■ n. a rounded collar without lapel notches that extends down the front of a garment.

shawm /ʃɔːm/ ■ n. a medieval and Renaissance wind instrument, forerunner of the oboe.
– ORIGIN Middle English: from Old French *chalemel*, from Greek *kalamos* 'reed'.

Shawnee /ʃɔːˈniː/ ■ n. (pl. same or **Shawnees**) **1** a member of an American Indian people formerly living in the eastern US. **2** the Algonquian language of this people.
– ORIGIN the name in Delaware.

shayile /ˈʃaɪˌiːle/ (also **tjaila**) S. African informal ■ v. knock off; stop work. ■ n. (also **shayile time** or **tjaila time**) knocking off time; the end of the working day.
– ORIGIN from isiXhosa *-tshayile*, isiZulu *-shayile*, or Setswana *-chaile* 'finished'.

shaykh ■ n. variant spelling of **SHEIKH**.

shazam /ʃəˈzam/ ■ exclam. used to introduce something extraordinary.
– ORIGIN 1940s: an invented word, used by conjurors.

she ■ pron. [third person sing.] **1** used to refer to a woman, girl, or female animal previously mentioned or easily identified. **2** used to refer to a ship, country, or other inanimate thing regarded as female. **3** any female person (in modern use, now largely replaced by 'anyone' or 'the person'). ■ n. a female; a woman.
– ORIGIN Middle English: prob. a phonetic development of the Old English *hēo*, *hīe*.

shea butter ■ n. a fatty substance from the nuts of the shea, a small tropical African tree (*Vitellaria paradoxa* or *Butyrospermum parkii*), used in cosmetic skin preparations, food, etc.

sheaf ■ n. (pl. **sheaves**) **1** a bundle of grain stalks laid lengthways and tied together after reaping. **2** a bundle of objects, especially papers. ■ v. bundle into sheaves.
– ORIGIN Old English, of Germanic origin.

shear ■ v. (past part. **shorn** or **sheared**) **1** cut the wool off (a sheep or other animal). ▶ cut off with scissors or shears. ▶ (**be shorn of**) have something cut off. **2** break off or cause to break off, owing to a structural strain. ■ n. a strain produced by pressure in the structure of a substance, when its layers are laterally shifted in relation to each other.
– DERIVATIVES **shearer** n.
– ORIGIN Old English, of Germanic origin, from a base meaning 'divide, shear, shave'.

shearling ■ n. a sheep that has been shorn once. ▶ wool or fleece from such a sheep. ▶ chiefly US a coat made from such wool.

shears (also **a pair of shears**) ■ pl. n. a cutting instrument in which two blades move past each other, like very large scissors.
– ORIGIN Old English *scēara* (pl.) 'scissors, cutting instrument', of Germanic origin.

shearwater ■ n. **1** a long-winged seabird related to the petrels, often flying low over the water far from land. [*Puffinus* and other genera: many species.] **2** North American term for **SKIMMER** (in sense 2).

sheath ■ n. (pl. **sheaths** /ʃiːðz, ʃiːθs/) **1** a cover for the blade of a knife or sword. **2** a structure in living tissue which closely envelops another. **3** a protective covering around an electric cable. **4** a condom. **5** (also **sheath dress**) a close-fitting dress.
– DERIVATIVES **sheathless** adj.
– ORIGIN Old English, of Germanic origin.

sheathe /ʃiːð/ ■ v. **1** put (a knife or sword) into a sheath. **2** (often **be sheathed in**) encase in a close-fitting or protective covering.
– ORIGIN Middle English: from **SHEATH**.

sheathing /ˈʃiːðɪŋ/ ■ n. protective casing or covering.

sheath knife ■ n. a short knife similar to a dagger, carried in a sheath.

sheave[1] ■ v. another term for **SHEAF**.
– ORIGIN C16: from **SHEAVES**.

sheave[2] ■ n. a wheel with a groove for a rope to run on, as in a pulley block.
– ORIGIN Middle English: from a Germanic base meaning 'wheel, pulley'.

sheaves plural form of **SHEAF**.

shebang /ʃɪˈbaŋ/ ■ n. informal a matter, operation, or set of circumstances: *the whole shebang.*
– ORIGIN C19.

shebeen /ʃɪˈbiːn/ ■ n. (especially in Ireland, Scotland, and South Africa) an unlicensed establishment or private house selling alcoholic liquor.
– DERIVATIVES **shebeener** n.
– ORIGIN C18: from Anglo-Irish *síbín*, from *séibe* 'mugful'.

shed[1] ■ n. a simple roofed structure, typically of wood and used for storage or to shelter animals. ▶ a larger structure, typically with one or more sides open, for storing vehicles or machinery. ■ v. (**shedded**, **shedding**) park (a vehicle) in a depot.
– ORIGIN C15: apparently a var. of **SHADE**.

shed[2] ■ v. (**shedding**; past and past part. **shed**) 1 (of a plant) allow (leaves or fruit) to fall to the ground. ▶ (of a reptile, insect, etc.) allow (its skin, shell, etc.) to come off, to be replaced by another growing underneath. ▶ lose (hair) as a result of moulting, disease, or age. 2 take off (clothes). 3 discard. 4 cast or give off (light). 5 resist the absorption of. 6 accidentally drop or spill.
– PHRASES **shed tears** cry.
– ORIGIN Old English *sc(e)ādan* 'separate out (one selected group), divide', also 'scatter', of Germanic origin.

she'd ■ contr. 1 she had. 2 she would.

she-devil ■ n. a malicious or spiteful woman.

shedload ■ n. Brit. informal a large amount or number.
– ORIGIN 1990s: from **SHED**[1] + **LOAD**; perhaps euphemistic after **SHITLOAD**.

sheen ■ n. a soft lustre on a surface. ■ v. poetic/literary shine or cause to shine softly.
– ORIGIN C17: from obsolete *sheen* 'beautiful, resplendent'.

sheeny ■ adj. lustrous.

sheep ■ n. (pl. same) 1 a domesticated ruminant mammal with a thick woolly coat, kept in flocks for its wool or meat. [*Ovis aries*.] ▶ a wild mammal related to this. 2 a person who is too easily influenced or led. 3 a member of a minister's congregation.
– PHRASES **make sheep's eyes at** look at (someone) in a foolishly amorous way.
– DERIVATIVES **sheeplike** adj.
– ORIGIN Old English, of West Germanic origin; sense 3 with biblical allusion to Luke 15:6.

sheep dip ■ n. 1 a liquid preparation for cleansing sheep of parasites or preserving their wool. 2 a place where sheep are dipped in this.

sheepdog ■ n. 1 a dog trained to guard and herd sheep. 2 a dog of a breed suitable for this.

sheepdog trials ■ pl. n. a public competitive display of the skills of sheepdogs.

sheepish ■ adj. showing embarrassment from shame or shyness.
– DERIVATIVES **sheepishly** adv. **sheepishness** n.

sheepshank ■ n. a knot used to shorten a rope, made by taking two loops of rope and securing them to the standing rope with two half hitches.

sheepskin ■ n. a sheep's skin with the wool on, especially when made into a garment or rug. ▶ leather from a sheep's skin used in bookbinding.

sheer[1] ■ adj. 1 nothing other than; unmitigated: *sheer hard work.* 2 (of a cliff, wall, etc.) perpendicular or nearly so. 3 (of a fabric) very thin. ■ adv. perpendicularly.
– DERIVATIVES **sheerly** adv. **sheerness** n.
– ORIGIN Middle English: prob. an alteration of dialect *shire* 'pure, clear', from the Germanic base of **SHINE**.

sheer[2] ■ v. 1 (especially of a boat) swerve or change course quickly. 2 avoid or move away from an unpleasant topic. ■ n. a sudden deviation from a course.
– ORIGIN C17: perhaps from Middle Low German *scheren* 'to shear'.

sheer[3] ■ n. the upward slope of a ship's lines towards the bow and stern.
– ORIGIN C17: prob. from **SHEAR**.

sheer legs ■ pl. n. [treated as sing.] a hoisting apparatus made from poles joined at or near the top and separated at the bottom, used for masting ships and lifting heavy objects.

sheet[1] ■ n. 1 a large rectangular piece of cotton or other fabric, used on a bed to cover the mattress or as a layer beneath blankets. 2 a broad flat piece of metal or glass. 3 a rectangular piece of paper. ▶ a quantity of text or data on a sheet of paper. ▶ Printing a flat piece of paper as opposed to a reel of continuous paper, the pages of a book, or a folded map. ▶ a set of unseparated postage stamps. 4 an extensive unbroken surface area of something. ▶ a broad moving mass of flames or water. ■ v. 1 cover with or wrap in a sheet of cloth. 2 (of rain) fall heavily.
– ORIGIN Old English, of Germanic origin.

sheet[2] Nautical ■ n. 1 a rope attached to the lower corner of a sail. 2 (**sheets**) the space at the bow or stern of an open boat. ■ v. (**sheet something in/out**) make a sail more or less taut. ▶ (**sheet something home**) set a sail as flat as possible.
– PHRASES **two** (or **three**) **sheets to the wind** informal drunk.
– ORIGIN Old English *scēata* 'lower corner of a sail', of Germanic origin.

sheet anchor ■ n. 1 an additional anchor for use in emergencies. 2 a dependable person or thing relied upon in the last resort.
– ORIGIN C15: perhaps rel. to obsolete *shot*, denoting two cables spliced together.

sheet bend ■ n. a method of temporarily fastening one rope through the loop of another.

sheeting ■ n. material formed into or used as a sheet.

sheet lightning ■ n. lightning with its brightness diffused by reflection within clouds.

sheet metal ■ n. metal formed into thin sheets.

sheet music ■ n. 1 printed music, as opposed to performed or recorded music. 2 music published in single or interleaved sheets.

Sheetrock ■ n. US trademark plasterboard made of gypsum layered between sheets of heavy paper.

Sheffield plate ■ n. copper plated with silver, especially as produced in Sheffield from 1760 to 1840.

sheikh /ʃeɪk, ʃiːk/ (also **shaykh** or **sheik**) ■ n. 1 an Arab leader, especially the chief or head of a tribe, family, or village. 2 a leader in a Muslim community or organization.
– DERIVATIVES **sheikhdom** n.
– ORIGIN C16: from Arabic *šayk* 'old man, sheikh', from *šāka* 'be or grow old'.

sheila ■ n. Austral./NZ informal a girl or woman.
– ORIGIN C19: orig. as *shaler*, later assimilated to the given name *Sheila*.

shekel /ˈʃɛk(ə)l/ ■ n. 1 the basic monetary unit of modern Israel. 2 historical a silver coin and unit of weight used in ancient Israel and the Middle East. 3 (**shekels**) informal money; wealth.
– ORIGIN from Hebrew *šeqel*, from *šāqal* 'weigh'.

Shekinah /ʃɪˈkʌɪnə/ (also **Shekhinah**) ■ n. Judaism the glory of the divine presence, represented as light or interpreted (in Kabbalism) as a divine feminine aspect.
– ORIGIN C17: from late Hebrew, from *šākan* 'dwell, rest'.

shelduck /ˈʃɛldʌk/ ■ n. (pl. same or **shelducks**) a large goose-like duck with boldly marked plumage. [*Tadorna* and other genera.]
– ORIGIN C18: prob. from dialect *sheld* 'pied' (rel. to Middle Dutch *schillede* 'variegated') + **DUCK**[1]; *sheldrake* (sometimes used for the male) dates from Middle English.

shelf ■ n. (pl. **shelves**) 1 a flat length of wood or rigid material attached to a wall or forming part of a piece of furniture, providing a surface for the storage or display of objects. 2 a ledge of rock or protruding strip of land. ▶ a submarine bank, or a part of the continental shelf.
– PHRASES **off the shelf** not designed or made to order. **on the shelf 1** no longer useful or desirable. **2** past an age when one might expect to be married.
– DERIVATIVES **shelf-ful** n. (pl. **-fuls**). **shelf-like** adj.
– ORIGIN Middle English: from Middle Low German *schelf*; rel. to Old English *scylfe* 'partition', *scylf* 'crag'.

shelf life ■ n. the length of time for which an item remains usable, edible, or saleable.

shelf mark ■ n. a notation on a book showing its place in a library.

shell

shell ■ n. **1** the hard protective outer case of a mollusc or crustacean. ▶ the thin outer covering of a bird's or reptile's egg. ▶ the outer case of a nut kernel or seed. ▶ the carapace of a tortoise, turtle, or terrapin. ▶ the wing cases of a beetle. ▶ the integument of an insect pupa or chrysalis. **2** an explosive artillery projectile or bomb. ▶ a hollow metal or paper case used as a container for fireworks, explosives, or cartridges. ▶ chiefly N. Amer. a cartridge. **3** something resembling or likened to a shell, especially a hollow case. **4** an outer form without substance. **5** the walls of an unfinished or gutted building. **6** a light racing boat. **7** the metal framework of a vehicle body. **8** an inner or roughly made coffin. **9** the handguard of a sword. **10** Physics each of a set of orbitals in an atom, occupied by electrons of similar energies. ■ v. **1** bombard with shells. **2** remove the shell or pod from. **3** (**shell out**) informal pay a specified amount of money, especially an amount regarded as excessive.
– PHRASES **come out of one's shell** cease to be shy.
– DERIVATIVES **-shelled** adj. **shell-less** adj. **shell-like** adj. **shelly** adj.
– ORIGIN Old English, of Germanic origin.

she'll /ʃəl/ contr. she shall; she will.

shellac /ʃəˈlak/ ■ n. lac resin melted into thin flakes, used for making varnish. ■ v. (**shellacked**, **shellacking**) **1** [often as adj. **shellacked**] varnish with shellac. **2** N. Amer. informal defeat decisively.
– ORIGIN C17: from SHELL + LAC, translating French *laque en écailles* 'lac in thin plates'.

shell bit ■ n. a gouge-shaped boring bit.

shell company ■ n. a non-trading company used as a vehicle for various financial manoeuvres.

shell egg ■ n. an egg sold in its natural state in the shell.

shellfire ■ n. bombardment by shells.

shellfish ■ n. (pl. same) an aquatic shelled mollusc or crustacean, especially an edible one.

shell game ■ n. a deceptive and evasive action or ploy.

shell heap (also **shell mound**) ■ n. Archaeology a kitchen midden consisting mainly of shells.

shell lime ■ n. fine-quality lime produced by roasting seashells.

shell pink ■ n. a delicate pale pink.

shell program ■ n. Computing a program providing an interface between the user and the operating system.

shell shock ■ n. psychological disturbance caused by prolonged exposure to active warfare.
– DERIVATIVES **shell-shocked** adj.

shell suit ■ n. a casual outfit consisting of a loose jacket and trousers with a soft lining and a shiny polyester outer shell.

shell top ■ n. a short sleeveless top, typically having a simple shape with a high neckline.

shell-work ■ n. ornamentation consisting of shells cemented on to a surface.

shelter ■ n. **1** a place giving protection from bad weather or danger. **2** a place providing food and accommodation for the homeless. **3** an animal sanctuary. **4** a shielded condition; protection. ■ v. **1** provide with shelter. ▶ find refuge or take cover. **2** [often as adj. **sheltered**] prevent from having to do or face something difficult. **3** protect (income) from taxation.
– DERIVATIVES **shelterer** n. **shelterless** adj.
– ORIGIN C16: perhaps from obsolete *sheltron* 'phalanx', from Old English *scieldtruma*, 'shield troop'.

shelter belt ■ n. a line of trees or shrubs planted to protect an area from fierce weather.

sheltered housing (also **sheltered accommodation**) ■ n. Brit. accommodation for the elderly or handicapped consisting of private independent units with some shared facilities and a warden.

shelterwood ■ n. mature trees left standing to shelter saplings.

sheltie (also **shelty**) ■ n. (pl. **-ies**) a Shetland pony or sheepdog.
– ORIGIN C17: prob. representing an Orkney pronunciation of Old Norse *Hjalti* 'Shetlander'.

shelve[1] ■ v. **1** place on a shelf. **2** abandon or defer (a plan or project). **3** fit with shelves.
– ORIGIN C16: from *shelves*, pl. of SHELF.

shelve[2] ■ v. (of ground) slope downwards.
– ORIGIN Middle English: perhaps from SHELF.

shelves plural form of SHELF.

shelving ■ n. shelves collectively.

Shembe Church /ˈʃɛmbɛ/ (also **Shembe**) ■ n. another term for NAZARETH BAPTIST CHURCH.
– ORIGIN C20: from the name of its founder, Isaiah *Shembe*.

shemozzle /ʃɪˈmɒz(ə)l/ (also **schemozzle**) ■ n. informal a muddle.
– ORIGIN C19: Yiddish, suggested by late Hebrew *šel-lō-mazzāl* 'of no luck'.

shenanigans /ʃɪˈnanɪɡ(ə)nz/ ■ pl. n. informal **1** secret or dishonest activity. **2** mischief.
– ORIGIN C19.

Sheol /ˈʃiːəʊl, ˈʃiːɒl/ ■ n. the Hebrew underworld, abode of the dead.
– ORIGIN from Hebrew.

shepherd ■ n. **1** a person who tends sheep. **2** a member of the clergy providing spiritual care and guidance for a congregation. ■ v. **1** [usu. as noun **shepherding**] tend (sheep). **2** guide or direct somewhere. **3** give spiritual or other guidance to.
– DERIVATIVES **shepherdess** n.
– ORIGIN Old English *scēaphierde*, from SHEEP + obsolete *herd* 'herdsman'.

shepherd dog ■ n. a sheepdog.

shepherd's crook ■ n. a shepherd's staff with a hook at one end.

shepherd's pie ■ n. a dish of minced meat under a layer of mashed potato.

shepherd's plaid ■ n. a small black-and-white check pattern. ▶ woollen cloth with this pattern.

shepherd's purse ■ n. a white-flowered weed of the cabbage family, with triangular or heart-shaped seed pods. [*Capsella bursa-pastoris*.]

shepherd's tree ■ n. a southern African shrub or small tree with pale grey or white bark and a small umbrella-shaped crown. [*Boscia albitrunca* and related species.]

sherardize /ˈʃɛrədʌɪz/ (also **-ise**) ■ v. coat (iron or steel) with zinc by heating it in contact with zinc dust.
– ORIGIN C20: from the name of the English inventor *Sherard* Cowper-Coles.

Sheraton /ˈʃɛrət(ə)n/ ■ adj. (of furniture) designed by or in the simple, graceful style of the English furniture-maker Thomas Sheraton (1751–1806).

sherbet ■ n. **1** a flavoured sweet effervescent powder eaten alone or made into a drink. **2** (especially in Arab countries) a drink of sweet diluted fruit juices. **3** N. Amer. water ice; sorbet. **4** Austral. humorous beer.
– ORIGIN C17: from Turkish *şerbet*, from Arabic *šarba* 'drink', from *šariba* 'to drink'.

sherd /ʃəːd/ ■ n. another term for POTSHERD.

sheriff ■ n. **1** (also **sheriff of the court**) S. African an officer who carries out orders of the court, such as executing summonses. **2** (also **high sheriff**) (in England and Wales) the chief executive officer of the Crown in a county, having administrative and judicial functions. **3** (in Scotland) a judge. **4** US an elected officer in a county, responsible for keeping the peace.
– DERIVATIVES **sheriffdom** n. **sheriffhood** n. **sheriffship** n.
– ORIGIN Old English *scīrgerēfa* (see SHIRE, REEVE[1]).

Sherpa /ˈʃəːpə/ ■ n. (pl. same or **Sherpas**) a member of a Himalayan people living on the borders of Nepal and Tibet.
– ORIGIN from Tibetan *sharpa* 'inhabitant of an Eastern country'.

sherry ■ n. (pl. **-ies**) a fortified wine originally and mainly from southern Spain.
– ORIGIN C16: alteration of archaic *sherris*, from Spanish (*vino de*) *Xeres* 'Xeres (wine)' (Xeres being the former name of the city of Jerez de la Frontera).

she's ■ contr. **1** she is. **2** she has.

CONSONANTS **b** but **d** dog **f** few **g** get **h** he **j** yes **k** cat **l** leg **m** man **n** no **p** pen **r** red

Shetlander /ˈʃɛtləndə/ ■ n. a native or inhabitant of the Shetland Islands.

Shetland pony ■ n. a pony of a small, hardy rough-coated breed.

Shetland sheepdog ■ n. a small dog of a collie-like breed.

shew ■ v. old-fashioned variant of **SHOW**.

shh (also **sh**) ■ exclam. used to call for silence.
– ORIGIN C19: var. of **HUSH**.

Shia /ˈʃiːə/ (also **Shi'a**) ■ n. (pl. same or **Shias**) one of the two main branches of Islam, regarding Ali, the fourth caliph, as Muhammad's first true successor. Compare with **SUNNI**.
▸ a Muslim who adheres to this branch of Islam.
– ORIGIN from Arabic šīʿa 'party (of Ali)'.

shiatsu /ʃiˈatsuː/ ■ n. a Japanese therapy based on the same principles as acupuncture, in which pressure is applied with the hands to points on the body.
– ORIGIN 1960s: Japanese, 'finger pressure'.

shibboleth /ˈʃɪbəlɛθ/ ■ n. a custom, principle, or belief distinguishing a particular class or group of people.
– ORIGIN C17: from Hebrew šibbōleṯ 'ear of corn', used as a test of nationality by its difficult pronunciation (Judges 12:6).

shibobo /ʃɪˈbɔːbɔː/ informal Soccer S. African ■ n. a kick or dribble executed through an opponent's legs. ■ v. (**shiboboed**, **shiboboing**) kick or dribble a ball through an opponent's legs.

shied past and past participle of **SHY²**.

shield ■ n. 1 a broad piece of armour held by straps or a handle on one side, used for protection against blows or missiles. 2 a sporting trophy consisting of an engraved metal plate mounted on a piece of wood. 3 a US police officer's badge. 4 a person or thing providing protection. ▸ a protective plate, screen, or other structure. ■ v. 1 protect from a danger, risk, etc. ▸ enclose or screen (machinery) to protect the user. 2 prevent from being seen. 3 prevent or reduce the escape of sound, light, or other radiation from.
– DERIVATIVES **shieldless** adj.
– ORIGIN Old English, of Germanic origin, from a base meaning 'divide, separate'.

shield bug ■ n. a heteropterous bug with a flattened, shield-shaped body. [Many species in Pentatomidae and other families.]

shield-nose snake (also **shield-nosed snake**) ■ n. a short, thickset southern African snake with a shield-like rostrum which it uses for burrowing. [*Aspidelaps scutatus*.]

shield volcano ■ n. Geology a very broad volcano with gently sloping sides.

shift /ʃɪft/ ■ v. 1 move or change or cause to move or change from one position to another. ▸ move one's body slightly due to discomfort. 2 Brit. informal move quickly. ▸ (**shift oneself**) Brit. informal move or rouse oneself. 3 informal sell (merchandise) quickly or in large quantities. 4 change gear. ■ n. 1 a slight change in position, direction, or tendency. 2 a key used to switch between two sets of characters or functions on a keyboard. 3 a gear lever or gear-changing mechanism. 4 Building the positioning of successive rows of bricks so that their ends do not coincide. 5 each of two or more periods in which different groups of workers do the same jobs in relay. ▸ a group of people who work in this way. 6 a straight unwaisted dress. ▸ historical a long, loose undergarment.
– PHRASES **make shift** dated manage or contrive to do something. **shift for oneself** manage alone as best one can. **shift one's ground** change one's position in an argument.
– DERIVATIVES **shiftable** adj. **shifter** n.
– ORIGIN Old English *sciftan* 'arrange, apportion' (also Middle English, 'change, replace'), of Germanic origin.

shifting spanner ■ n. an adjustable multi-purpose spanner.

shiftless ■ adj. lazy, indolent, and lacking ambition.
– DERIVATIVES **shiftlessly** adv. **shiftlessness** n.

shifty ■ adj. (-**ier**, -**iest**) informal 1 deceitful or evasive. 2 constantly changing.
– DERIVATIVES **shiftily** adv. **shiftiness** n.

shigella /ʃɪˈɡɛlə/ ■ n. (pl. same or **shigellae** /-liː/) a bacterium of a genus including some kinds responsible for dysentery. [Genus *Shigella*.]
– ORIGIN from the name of the Japanese bacteriologist Kiyoshi *Shiga*.

shih-tzu /ʃiːˈtsuː/ ■ n. a dog of a breed with long silky erect hair and short legs.
– ORIGIN 1920s: from Chinese *shizi* 'lion'.

shiitake /ʃiːˈtɑːkeɪ, ʃɪ-/ ■ n. an edible mushroom cultivated in Japan and China. [*Lentinus edodes*.]
– ORIGIN C19: from Japanese, from *shii*, denoting a kind of oak + *take* 'mushroom'.

Shiite /ˈʃiːʌɪt/ (also **Shi'ite**) ■ n. an adherent of the Shia branch of Islam. ■ adj. of or relating to Shia.
– DERIVATIVES **Shiism** /ˈʃiːɪz(ə)m/ (also **Shi'ism**) n.

shiksa /ˈʃɪksə/ ■ n. derogatory (used especially by Jews) a gentile girl or woman.
– ORIGIN C19: from Yiddish *shikse*, from Hebrew *šiqṣāh*, from *šeqeṣ* 'detested thing'.

shillelagh /ʃɪˈleɪlə, -li/ ■ n. (in Ireland) a cudgel of blackthorn or oak.
– ORIGIN C18: from the name of the town *Shillelagh*, in Co. Wicklow, Ireland.

shilling ■ n. 1 a former British coin and monetary unit equal to one twentieth of a pound or twelve pence. 2 the basic monetary unit of Kenya, Tanzania, and Uganda, equal to 100 cents.
– PHRASES **not the full shilling** Brit. informal not very clever. **take the King's** (or **Queen's**) **shilling** Brit. enlist as a soldier. [with ref. to the former practice of paying a shilling to a new recruit.]
– ORIGIN Old English, of Germanic origin.

shilly-shally ■ v. (-**ies**, -**ied**) be indecisive. ■ n. indecisive behaviour.
– DERIVATIVES **shilly-shallyer** (also -**shallier**) n.
– ORIGIN C18: orig. as *shill I, shall I*, reduplication of *shall I*?

shim ■ n. a washer or thin strip of material used to align parts, make them fit, or reduce wear. ■ v. (**shimmed**, **shimming**) wedge or fill up with a shim.
– ORIGIN C18.

shimmer ■ v. shine with a soft tremulous light. ■ n. a light with such qualities.
– DERIVATIVES **shimmering** adj. **shimmeringly** adv. **shimmery** adj.
– ORIGIN Old English *scymrian*, of Germanic origin.

shimmy ■ n. (pl. -**ies**) 1 a kind of ragtime dance in which the whole body shakes or sways. 2 shaking, especially abnormal vibration of the wheels of a motor vehicle. ■ v. (-**ies**, -**ied**) 1 dance the shimmy. 2 shake or vibrate abnormally. 3 move swiftly and effortlessly.
– ORIGIN C20.

shin ■ n. the front of the leg below the knee. ▸ a cut of beef from the lower part of a cow's leg. ■ v. (**shinned**, **shinning**) (**shin up/down**) climb quickly up or down by gripping with one's arms and legs.
– ORIGIN Old English, prob. from a Germanic base meaning 'narrow or thin piece'.

shin bone ■ n. the tibia.

shindig ■ n. informal 1 a large, lively party. 2 a noisy disturbance or quarrel.
– ORIGIN C19: prob. from **SHIN** and **DIG**, influenced later by **SHINDY**.

shindy ■ n. (pl. -**ies**) informal 1 a noisy disturbance or quarrel. 2 a large, lively party.
– ORIGIN C19: perhaps an alteration of **SHINTY**.

shine ■ v. (past and past part. **shone** or **shined**) 1 give out a bright light; glow with reflected light. ▸ direct (a torch or other light) somewhere. ▸ (of a person's eyes) be bright with the expression of emotion. 2 [often as adj. **shining**] excel at something. 3 (**shine through**) (of a quality or skill) be clearly evident. 4 (past and past part. **shined**) polish. ■ n. 1 a quality of brightness, especially through reflecting light. 2 an act of polishing.
– PHRASES **take the shine off** spoil the brilliance or excitement of. **take a shine to** informal develop a liking for.
– DERIVATIVES **shiningly** adv.
– ORIGIN Old English, of Germanic origin.

shiner ■ n. 1 a thing that shines. 2 a person or thing that polishes something. 3 informal a black eye.

shingle

shingle¹ ■ n. a mass of small rounded pebbles, especially on a seashore.
– DERIVATIVES **shingly** adj.
– ORIGIN Middle English.

shingle² ■ n. **1** a rectangular wooden tile used on walls or roofs. **2** dated a woman's short haircut, tapering from the back of the head to the nape of the neck. **3** N. Amer. a small signboard, especially one outside an office. ■ v. **1** roof or clad with shingles. **2** dated cut (hair) in a shingle.
– PHRASES **hang out one's shingle** N. Amer. begin to practise a profession.
– ORIGIN Middle English: apparently from Latin *scindula*, earlier *scandula* 'a split piece of wood'.

shingles ■ pl. n. [treated as sing.] an acute painful inflammation of nerve endings, with a skin eruption often forming a girdle around the body, caused by the herpes zoster virus.
– ORIGIN Middle English: representing medieval Latin *cingulus*, var. of Latin *cingulum* 'girdle'.

Shinkansen /ˈʃɪnkɑːnˌsɛn/ ■ n. (pl. same) (in Japan) a railway system carrying high-speed passenger trains. ▶ a train operating on such a system.
– ORIGIN Japanese, from *shin* 'new' + *kansen* 'main line'.

shin pad ■ n. a protective pad worn on the shins when playing soccer and other sports.

shin splints ■ pl. n. [treated as sing. or pl.] acute pain in the shin and lower leg caused by prolonged running on hard surfaces.

Shinto /ˈʃɪntəʊ/ ■ n. a Japanese religion incorporating the worship of ancestors and nature spirits.
– DERIVATIVES **Shintoism** n. **Shintoist** n.
– ORIGIN Japanese, from Chinese *shen dao* 'way of the gods'.

shinty ■ n. (pl. **-ies**) a Scottish twelve-a-side game resembling hockey, played with curved sticks and taller goalposts and derived from hurling.
– ORIGIN C18: prob. from the cry *shin ye, shin you, shin t' ye*, used in the game.

shiny ■ adj. (**-ier, -iest**) reflecting light because very smooth, clean, or polished.
– DERIVATIVES **shinily** adv. **shininess** n.

ship ■ n. **1** a large seagoing boat. ▶ a sailing vessel with a bowsprit and three or more square-cut masts. **2** a spaceship. **3** N. Amer. an aircraft. ■ v. (**shipped, shipping**) **1** transport on a ship. ▶ transport by other means. ▶ (of a sailor) take service on a ship. **2** Electronics make (a product) available for purchase. **3** (of a boat) take in (water) over the side. **4** take (oars) from the rowlocks and lay them inside a boat. ▶ fix (a rudder, mast, etc.) in place on a ship.
– PHRASES **a sinking ship** a failing organization or endeavour. **take ship** set off on a voyage by ship. **when one's ship comes in** (or **home**) when one's fortune is made.
– DERIVATIVES **shipless** adj. **shipload** n. **shippable** adj. **shipper** n.
– ORIGIN Old English *scip* (n.), later *scipian* (v.), of Germanic origin.

-ship ■ suffix forming nouns: **1** denoting a quality or condition: *companionship*. **2** denoting status, office, or honour: *citizenship*. ▶ denoting a tenure of office: *chairmanship*. **3** denoting a skill in a certain capacity: *workmanship*. **4** denoting the collective individuals of a group: *membership*.
– ORIGIN Old English *-scipe, scype*, of Germanic origin.

shipboard ■ n. [as modifier] used or occurring on board a ship.
– PHRASES **on shipboard** on board a ship.

ship-breaker ■ n. a contractor who breaks up old ships for scrap.

shipbroker ■ n. a broker who arranges charters, cargo space, and passenger bookings on ships.

shipbuilder ■ n. a person or company that designs and builds ships.
– DERIVATIVES **shipbuilding** n.

ship burial ■ n. Archaeology a burial in a wooden ship under a mound, carried out in Britain in Anglo-Saxon and Viking times.

ship canal ■ n. a canal large enough for use by ships.

shiplap ■ v. fit (boards) together by halving so that each overlaps the one below. ■ n. shiplapped boards, typically used for cladding. ▶ a joint between boards made by halving.

shipmaster ■ n. a ship's captain.

shipmate ■ n. a fellow member of a ship's crew.

shipment ■ n. **1** the action of shipping goods. **2** a consignment of goods shipped.

ship of the desert ■ n. poetic/literary a camel.

ship of the line ■ n. historical a warship of the largest size, used in the line of battle.

shipowner ■ n. a person owning a ship or shares in a ship.

shipping ■ n. **1** ships collectively. **2** the transport of goods by sea or other means.

shipping agent ■ n. an agent in a port who transacts a ship's business for the owner.

ship's biscuit ■ n. a hard, coarse kind of biscuit formerly taken on sea voyages.

ship's company ■ n. the crew of a ship.

shipshape ■ adj. orderly and neat.

ship-to-shore ■ adj. from a ship to land. ■ n. a radiotelephone for such use.

shipway ■ n. a slope on which a ship is built and down which it slides to be launched.

shipworm ■ n. another term for TEREDO.

shipwreck ■ n. the destruction of a ship at sea by sinking or breaking up. ▶ a ship so destroyed. ■ v. (**be shipwrecked**) suffer a shipwreck.

shipwright ■ n. a shipbuilder.

shipyard ■ n. a place where ships are built and repaired.

Shiraz /ˈʃɪəraz, ʃɪˈraz/ ■ n. a variety of black wine grape. ▶ a red wine made from this grape.
– ORIGIN from *Shiraz* in Iran, an alteration of French *syrah*, from the belief that the vine was brought from Iran by the Crusades.

shire /ˈʃʌɪə/ ■ n. Brit. a county, especially in England. ▶ (**the Shires**) the parts of England regarded as strongholds of traditional rural culture, especially the rural Midlands.
– ORIGIN Old English *scīr* 'care, official charge, county', of Germanic origin.

-shire /ʃɪə, ʃə/ ■ comb. form forming the names of counties: *Oxfordshire*.

shire horse ■ n. a heavy powerful horse of a draught breed, originally from the English Midlands.

shirk ■ v. avoid or neglect (a duty or responsibility).
– DERIVATIVES **shirker** n.
– ORIGIN C17: from obsolete *shirk* 'sponger', perhaps from German *Schurke* 'scoundrel'.

shirr /ʃəː/ ■ v. [often as adj. **shirred**] gather (fabric) by means of drawn or elasticized threads in parallel rows.
– ORIGIN C19.

shirt ■ n. **1** a garment for the upper body, with a collar and sleeves and buttons down the front. ▶ a similar garment of stretchable material without full fastenings, worn for sports. **2** Brit. a place on a particular sports team.
– PHRASES **keep your shirt on** informal stay calm. **lose one's shirt** informal lose all one's possessions. **put one's shirt on** Brit. informal bet all one has on. **the shirt off one's back** informal one's last remaining possessions.
– DERIVATIVES **shirted** adj. **shirtless** adj.
– ORIGIN Old English *scyrte*, of Germanic origin; prob. from a base meaning 'short garment'.

shirt dress ■ n. a dress with a collar and button fastening in the style of a shirt, without a seam at the waist.

shirting ■ n. fabric for making shirts.

shirtsleeve ■ n. the sleeve of a shirt.
– PHRASES **in (one's) shirtsleeves** wearing a shirt with nothing over it.
– DERIVATIVES **shirtsleeved** adj.

shirt tail ■ n. the curved part of a shirt which comes below the waist.

shirtwaister ■ n. a shirt dress with a seam at the waist.

shirty ■ adj. (**-ier, -iest**) informal ill-tempered or annoyed.

—DERIVATIVES **shirtily** adv. **shirtiness** n.

shisha /ˈʃiːʃə/ ▪ n. (in Egypt and other Arabic-speaking countries) a hookah. ▸ tobacco for smoking in a hookah.
—ORIGIN Egyptian Arabic *shiisha*, from Turkish.

shish kebab /ˌʃɪʃ kɪˈbab/ ▪ n. a dish of pieces of marinated meat and vegetables cooked and served on skewers.
—ORIGIN from Turkish *şiş kebap*, from *şiş* 'skewer' + *kebap* 'roast meat'.

shit vulgar slang ▪ v. (**shitting**; past and past part. **shitted** or **shit** or **shat**) **1** defecate. **2** (**shit oneself**) be very frightened. ▪ n. **1** faeces. ▸ an act of defecating. **2** a contemptible person. ▸ something worthless; rubbish. **3** an intoxicating drug, especially cannabis. ▪ exclam. expressing disgust or annoyance.
—PHRASES **be shitting bricks** be extremely nervous or frightened. **in the shit** in trouble. **not give a shit** not care at all. **be up shit creek (without a paddle)** be in an awkward predicament. **when the shit hits the fan** when the disastrous consequences of something become known.
—ORIGIN Old English *scitte* 'diarrhoea', of Germanic origin.

shite ▪ n. & exclam. vulgar slang another term for **SHIT**.

shit-faced ▪ adj. vulgar slang drunk or stoned.

shit-hot ▪ adj. vulgar slang excellent.

shitless ▪ adj. (in phr. **be scared shitless**) vulgar slang be extremely frightened.

shitlist ▪ n. vulgar slang a list of those whom one dislikes or plans to harm.

shitload ▪ n. vulgar slang a large amount or number.

shit-scared ▪ adj. vulgar slang terrified.

shit-stirrer ▪ n. vulgar slang a person who takes pleasure in causing trouble or discord.
—DERIVATIVES **shit-stirring** n.

shitty ▪ adj. (-ier, -iest) vulgar slang **1** contemptible. ▸ awful. **2** covered with excrement.

shiva /ˈʃɪvə/ (also **shivah**) ▪ n. Judaism a period of seven days' formal mourning for the dead, beginning immediately after the funeral.
—ORIGIN from Hebrew *šib'āh* 'seven'.

shiver[1] ▪ v. shake slightly and uncontrollably as a result of being cold, frightened, or excited. ▪ n. a momentary trembling movement. ▸ (**the shivers**) a spell or attack of shivering.
—DERIVATIVES **shiverer** n. **shivering** adj. **shiveringly** adv. **shivery** adj.
—ORIGIN Middle English *chivere*, perhaps an alteration of *chavele* 'to chatter', from Old English *ceafl* 'jaw'.

shiver[2] ▪ n. a splinter. ▪ v. break into shivers.
—PHRASES **shiver my timbers** a mock oath attributed to sailors.
—ORIGIN Middle English: from a Germanic base meaning 'to split'.

Shoah /ˈʃəʊə/ ▪ n. (in Jewish use) the Holocaust.
—ORIGIN modern Hebrew, 'catastrophe'.

shoal[1] ▪ n. a large number of fish swimming together. ▪ v. (of fish) form shoals.
—ORIGIN C16: prob. from Middle Dutch *schōle* 'troop'.

shoal[2] ▪ n. **1** an area of shallow water. **2** a submerged sandbank visible at low water. ▪ v. (of water) become shallower.
—DERIVATIVES **shoaly** adj.
—ORIGIN Old English *sceald*, of Germanic origin.

shock[1] ▪ n. **1** a sudden upsetting or surprising event or experience, or the resulting feeling. ▸ short for **ELECTRIC SHOCK**. **2** an acute medical condition associated with a fall in blood pressure, caused by loss of blood, severe burns, sudden emotional stress, etc. **3** a violent shaking movement caused by an impact, explosion, or tremor. **4** short for **SHOCK ABSORBER**. ▪ v. **1** cause (someone) to feel surprised and upset. ▸ offend the moral feelings of; outrage. **2** affect with physiological shock, or with an electric shock.
—DERIVATIVES **shockability** n. **shockable** adj. **shockproof** adj.
—ORIGIN C16: from French *choc* (n.), *choquer* (v.).

shock[2] ▪ n. a group of twelve sheaves of grain placed upright and supporting each other to allow the grain to dry and ripen. ▪ v. arrange in shocks.

—ORIGIN Middle English: perhaps from Middle Dutch, Middle Low German *schok*.

shock[3] ▪ n. an unkempt or thick mass of hair.
—ORIGIN C17 (denoting a dog with long shaggy hair).

shock absorber ▪ n. a device for absorbing jolts and vibrations, especially on a vehicle.

shock cord ▪ n. heavy elasticated cord; bungee cord.

shocker ▪ n. informal a person or thing that shocks, especially through being unacceptable or sensational.

shock-headed ▪ adj. having thick, shaggy, and unkempt hair.

shocking ▪ adj. **1** causing shock or disgust. **2** informal very bad.
—DERIVATIVES **shockingly** adv. **shockingness** n.

shocking pink ▪ n. a vibrant shade of pink.

shock jock ▪ n. informal a radio disc jockey who expresses opinions in a deliberately offensive or provocative way.

shock tactics ▪ pl. n. the use of sudden violent or extreme action to shock someone into doing something.

shock therapy (also **shock treatment**) ▪ n. treatment of chronic mental conditions by electroconvulsive therapy or by inducing physiological shock.

shock troops ▪ pl. n. troops trained for carrying out sudden assaults.

shock wave ▪ n. an intense travelling pressure wave caused by explosion or by a body moving faster than sound.

shod past and past participle of **SHOE**.

shoddy ▪ adj. (-ier, -iest) **1** badly made or done. **2** lacking moral principle; sordid. ▪ n. an inferior yarn or fabric made from shredded woollen waste.
—DERIVATIVES **shoddily** adv. **shoddiness** n.
—ORIGIN C19.

shoe ▪ n. **1** a covering for the foot having a sturdy sole and not reaching above the ankle. ▸ a horseshoe. **2** a drag for a wheel. **3** a socket on a camera for fitting a flash unit. **4** a metal rim or ferrule, especially on the runner of a sledge. ▪ v. (**shoes, shoeing**; past and past part. **shod**) **1** fit (a horse) with a shoe or shoes. **2** (**be shod**) be wearing shoes of a specified kind. **3** protect with a metal shoe.
—PHRASES **be (or put oneself) in another person's shoes** imagine oneself in another's situation or predicament. **dead men's shoes** property or a position coveted by a prospective successor but available only on a person's death. **wait for the other shoe to drop** informal, chiefly N. Amer. be prepared for a further or consequential event to occur.
—DERIVATIVES **shoeless** adj.
—ORIGIN Old English, of Germanic origin.

shoebill ▪ n. an African stork with grey plumage and a very large bill shaped like a clog. [*Balaeniceps rex*.]

shoebox ▪ n. **1** a box in which a pair of shoes is delivered or sold. **2** informal a very cramped room or space.

shoehorn ▪ n. a curved instrument used for easing one's heel into a shoe. ▪ v. force into an inadequate space.

shoelace ▪ n. a cord or leather strip passed through eyelets or hooks on opposite sides of a shoe and pulled tight and fastened.

shoemaker ▪ n. a person who makes shoes and other footwear as a profession.
—DERIVATIVES **shoemaking** n.

shoeshine ▪ n. chiefly N. Amer. an act of polishing someone's shoes.
—DERIVATIVES **shoeshiner** n.

shoestring ▪ n. **1** N. Amer. a shoelace. **2** informal a small or inadequate budget: *living on a shoestring*.

shoe tree ▪ n. a shaped block inserted into a shoe when it is not being worn to keep it in shape.

shofar /ˈʃəʊfɑː/ ▪ n. (pl. **shofars** or **shofroth** /ˈʃəʊfrəʊt/) a ram's-horn trumpet used by Jews in religious ceremonies and as an ancient battle signal.
—ORIGIN from Hebrew *šōpār*, (pl.) *šōpārōt*.

shogun /ˈʃəʊɡʊn/ ■ n. (in feudal Japan) a hereditary commander-in-chief.
– DERIVATIVES **shogunate** /-nət/ n.
– ORIGIN Japanese, from Chinese *jiāng jūn* 'general'.

shoji /ˈʃəʊdʒi/ ■ n. (pl. same or **shojis**) (in Japan) a sliding door made of a latticed screen covered with white paper.
– ORIGIN from Japanese *shōji*.

Shona /ˈʃəʊnə/ ■ n. (pl. same or **Shonas**) **1** a member of a group of peoples inhabiting parts of southern Africa, particularly Zimbabwe. **2** any of the closely related Bantu languages spoken by these peoples.
– ORIGIN the name in Shona.

shone past and past participle of SHINE.

shongololo ■ n. variant spelling of SONGOLOLO.

shoo ■ exclam. used to frighten or drive away a person or animal. ■ v. (**shoos**, **shooed**) cause to go away by waving one's arms and saying 'shoo'.

shoo-in ■ n. a person or thing that is certain to succeed or win.

shook past of SHAKE.

shoot ■ v. (past and past part. **shot**) **1** kill or wound (a person or animal) with a bullet or arrow. ▸ cause (a gun) to fire. ▸ hunt game with a gun. ▸ (**shoot someone/thing down**) bring down an aircraft or person by shooting. **2** move suddenly and rapidly. ▸ [as adj. **shooting**] (of a pain) sudden and piercing. ▸ direct (a glance, question, or remark) at someone. **3** (in soccer, basketball, etc.) kick, hit, or throw the ball or puck in an attempt to score a goal. ▸ informal make (a specified score) for a round of golf. ▸ N. Amer. informal play a game of (pool, dice, or cards). **4** film or photograph (a scene, film, etc.). **5** send out buds or shoots; germinate. **6** (**shoot up**) informal inject oneself with a narcotic drug. **7** plane (the edge of a board) accurately. **8** (of a boat) sweep swiftly down or under (rapids, a waterfall, or a bridge). ▸ informal drive past (a traffic light at red). ▸ move (a door bolt) to fasten or unfasten a door. ■ n. **1** a young branch or sucker springing from the main stock of a tree or other plant. **2** an occasion when a group of people hunt and shoot game for sport. ▸ Brit. land used for shooting game. **3** an occasion of taking photographs professionally or making a film or video: *a fashion shoot*. **4** variant spelling of CHUTE¹. **5** a rapid in a stream. ■ exclam. N. Amer. informal used as a euphemism for 'shit'.
– PHRASES **shoot the breeze** (or **the bull**) N. Amer. informal have a casual conversation. **shoot one's cuffs** pull one's shirt cuffs out to project beyond the cuffs of one's jacket or coat. **shoot from the hip** informal react suddenly or without careful consideration. **shoot oneself in the foot** informal inadvertently make a situation worse for oneself. **shoot a line** Brit. informal describe something in an exaggerated, untruthful, or boastful way. **shoot one's mouth off** informal talk boastfully or indiscreetly. **the whole shooting match** informal everything.
– PHRASAL VERBS **shoot something out** (usu. **be shot out**) kill all of a species of game in an area.
– DERIVATIVES **shootable** adj.
– ORIGIN Old English, of Germanic origin.

shooter ■ n. **1** a person who uses a gun. ▸ informal a gun. **2** (in netball, basketball, etc.) a player whose role is to attempt to score goals. ▸ a person who throws a dice. **3** Cricket a bowled ball that moves rapidly along the ground after pitching. **4** informal a small drink of spirits.

shooting gallery ■ n. **1** a room or fairground booth for recreational shooting at targets. **2** N. Amer. informal a place used for injecting drugs.

shooting star ■ n. a small, rapidly moving meteor burning up on entering the earth's atmosphere.

shooting stick ■ n. a walking stick with a handle that unfolds to form a seat and a sharpened end which can be stuck firmly in the ground.

shootist ■ n. N. Amer. informal a person who shoots, especially a marksman.

shoot-out ■ n. **1** informal a decisive gun battle. **2** (usu. **penalty shoot-out**) Soccer a tiebreaker decided by each side taking a specified number of penalty kicks.

shop ■ n. **1** a building or part of a building where goods or services are sold. ▸ informal an act of going shopping. **2** a place where things are manufactured or repaired; a workshop. **3** (often in phr. **talk shop**) matters concerning one's work, especially when discussed at an inappropriate time. ■ v. (**shopped**, **shopping**) **1** go to a shop or shops to buy goods. ▸ (**shop around**) look for the best available price or rate for something. **2** informal, chiefly Brit. inform on (someone).
– ORIGIN Middle English: shortening of Old French *eschoppe* 'lean-to booth', of West Germanic origin.

shopaholic ■ n. informal a compulsive shopper.

shop assistant ■ n. a person who serves customers in a shop.

shopfitter ■ n. a person whose job it is to fit the counters, shelves, etc. with which a shop is equipped.
– DERIVATIVES **shopfitting** n.

shop floor ■ n. the part of a workshop or factory where production as distinct from administrative work is carried out.

shopfront ■ n. the facade of a shop.

shopkeeper ■ n. the owner and manager of a shop.
– DERIVATIVES **shopkeeping** n.

shoplifting ■ n. the theft of goods from a shop by someone pretending to be a customer.
– DERIVATIVES **shoplift** v. **shoplifter** n.

shopper ■ n. **1** a person who is shopping. **2** Brit. a bag for holding shopping, attached to wheels and pushed or pulled along.

shopping ■ n. **1** the purchasing of goods from shops. **2** goods bought from shops, especially food and household goods.

shopping centre ■ n. an area or complex of shops.

shopping list ■ n. a list of purchases to be made. ▸ a list of items to be considered or acted on.

shop-soiled ■ adj. (of an article) made dirty or imperfect by being displayed or handled in a shop.

shop steward ■ n. a person elected by workers in a factory to represent them in dealings with management.

shop window ■ n. **1** a display window of a shop. **2** a position that allows a person or organization to demonstrate their strengths.

shopworn ■ adj. chiefly N. Amer. another term for SHOP-SOILED.

shore¹ ■ n. **1** the land along the edge of a sea, lake, etc. **2** (also **shores**) poetic/literary a country or other geographic area bounded by a coast: *distant shores*.
– PHRASES **in shore** on the water near land or nearer to land. **on shore** ashore; on land.
– DERIVATIVES **shoreless** adj. **shoreward** adj. & adv. **shorewards** adv.
– ORIGIN Middle English: from Middle Dutch, Middle Low German *schōre*.

shore² ■ n. a prop or beam set obliquely against something weak or unstable as a support. ■ v. (often **shore something up**) support or hold up with shores.
– DERIVATIVES **shoring** n.
– ORIGIN Middle English: from Middle Dutch, Middle Low German *schore* 'prop'.

shore leave ■ n. leisure time spent ashore by a sailor.

shoreline ■ n. the line along which a large body of water meets the land.

shorn past participle of SHEAR.

short ■ adj. **1** of a small length or duration. ▸ (of a ball in sport) travelling only a small distance before bouncing. **2** relatively small in extent. **3** (of a person) small in height. **4** (**short of/on**) not having enough of (something); lacking or deficient in. ▸ in insufficient supply. **5** (of a person) terse; uncivil. **6** Phonetics (of a vowel) categorized as short with regard to quality and length (e.g. in standard British English the vowel /ʊ/ in *good*). ▸ Prosody (of a vowel or syllable) having the lesser of the two recognized durations. **7** (of odds or a chance) reflecting or representing a high level of probability. **8** Finance (of shares or other assets) sold in advance of being acquired. ▸ (of a security) maturing at a relatively early date. **9** (of pastry) containing a high proportion of fat to flour and therefore crumbly. ▸ (of clay) having poor plasticity. ■ adv. (in sport) at, to, or over a short distance. ▸ not as far as the point aimed

at. ■ n. 1 Brit. informal a strong alcoholic drink, especially spirits, served in small measures. 2 a short film as opposed to a feature film. ▶ a short sound, vowel, or syllable. ▶ a short circuit. 3 Finance a person who sells short. ▶ (**shorts**) short-dated stocks. 4 (**shorts**) a mixture of bran and coarse flour. ■ v. short-circuit.
– PHRASES **be caught** (or Brit. **taken**) **short 1** be put at a disadvantage. **2** Brit. informal urgently need to urinate or defecate. **a brick short of a load** (or **two sandwiches short of a picnic**, etc.) informal (of a person) stupid or crazy. **bring** (or **pull**) **someone up short** cause someone to stop or pause abruptly. **for short** as an abbreviation or nickname. **get** (or **have**) **someone by the short and curlies** informal have complete control of a person. **go short** not have enough of something, especially food. **in short** to sum up; briefly. **in short order** chiefly N. Amer. immediately; rapidly. **in the short run** (or **term**) in the near future. **in short supply** (of a commodity) scarce. **make short work of** accomplish, consume, or destroy quickly. **short and sweet** brief and pleasant. **short for** an abbreviation or nickname for. **short of 1** less than. **2** not reaching as far as. **3** without going so far as (some extreme action). **short of breath** panting; short-winded. **stop short** stop suddenly or abruptly.
– DERIVATIVES **shortish** adj. **shortness** n.
– ORIGIN Old English *sceort*, of Germanic origin.

short-acting ■ adj. (chiefly of a drug) having effects that only last for a short time.

shortage ■ n. a state or situation in which something needed cannot be obtained in sufficient amounts.

short-arm ■ adj. denoting a blow or throw executed with the arm not fully extended or with motion from the elbow only.

short back and sides ■ n. a haircut in which the hair is cut short at the back and the sides.

shortbread ■ n. a crisp, rich, crumbly type of biscuit made with butter, flour, and sugar.

shortcake ■ n. 1 another term for SHORTBREAD. 2 N. Amer. a rich dessert made from short pastry and topped with fruit and whipped cream.

short change ■ n. insufficient money given as change. ■ v. (**short-change**) 1 cheat by giving short change. 2 treat unfairly by withholding something of value.

short circuit ■ n. an electrical circuit of lower than usual resistance, especially one formed unintentionally. ■ v. (**short-circuit**) 1 suffer or cause to suffer a short circuit. 2 shorten (a process or activity) by using a more direct but irregular method.

shortcoming ■ n. a failure to meet a certain standard; a fault or defect.

shortcrust pastry ■ n. crumbly pastry made with flour, fat, and a little water.

short cut ■ n. 1 an alternative route that is shorter than the one usually taken. 2 an accelerated but somewhat irregular way of doing something.

short-dated ■ adj. (of a stock or bond) due for early payment or redemption.

short division ■ n. arithmetical division in which the quotient is written directly without a succession of intermediate workings.

shorten ■ v. 1 make or become shorter. 2 Nautical reduce the amount of (sail spread).

shortening ■ n. fat used for making pastry.

shortfall ■ n. a deficit of something required or expected.

short fuse ■ n. informal a quick temper.
– DERIVATIVES **short-fused** adj.

shorthair ■ n. a cat of a short-haired breed.

shorthand ■ n. 1 a method of rapid writing by means of abbreviations and symbols, used especially for taking dictation. 2 a short and simple way of expressing or referring to something.

short-handed ■ adj. not having enough or the usual number of staff or crew. ▶ Ice Hockey (of a goal) scored by a team playing with fewer players on the ice than their opponent. ▶ Ice Hockey (of a situation) occurring while or because a team has fewer than six players on the ice. ■ adv. with fewer staff, crew, or players than usual.

shorthand typist ■ n. a typist qualified to take and transcribe shorthand.

short haul ■ n. a relatively short distance in terms of travel or the transport of goods.

short head ■ n. Horse Racing a distance less than the length of a horse's head.

shorthorn ■ n. an animal of a breed of cattle with short horns.

shortie ■ n. variant spelling of SHORTY.

shortlist ■ n. a list of selected candidates from which a final choice is made. ■ v. put on a shortlist.

short-lived ■ adj. lasting only a short time.

shortly ■ adv. 1 in a short time; soon. 2 in a few words; briefly. ▶ abruptly, sharply, or curtly.

short measure ■ n. an amount less than that which is declared or paid for.

short-order ■ adj. N. Amer. of or denoting food dishes which can be quickly prepared and served: *a short-order cook.*

short-pitched ■ adj. Cricket (of a delivery) bowled so that the ball bounces relatively near the bowler.

short-range ■ adj. 1 able to be used or be effective only over short distances. 2 of or over a short period of future time.

short rib ■ n. 1 Brit. another term for FLOATING RIB. 2 (**short ribs**) chiefly N. Amer. a narrow cut of beef containing the ends of the ribs near to the breastbone.

shorts ■ pl. n. 1 short trousers that reach only to the knees or thighs. 2 N. Amer. men's underpants.

short shrift ■ n. rapid and unsympathetic dismissal; curt treatment.

short sight ■ n. the inability to see things clearly unless they are relatively close to the eyes; myopia.

short-sighted ■ adj. 1 having short sight. 2 lacking imagination or foresight.
– DERIVATIVES **short-sightedly** adv. **short-sightedness** n.

short-staffed ■ adj. not having enough or the usual number of staff.

shortstop /'ʃɔːtstɒp/ ■ n. Baseball a fielder positioned between second and third base.

short story ■ n. a story with a fully developed theme but significantly shorter and less elaborate than a novel.

short temper ■ n. a tendency to lose one's temper quickly.
– DERIVATIVES **short-tempered** adj.

short-termism ■ n. concentration on immediate profit or advantage at the expense of long-term security.

short time ■ n. the condition of working fewer than the regular hours per day or days per week.

short title ■ n. an abbreviated form of a title of a book or document.

short waist ■ n. a high waist on a woman's dress or a person's body.
– DERIVATIVES **short-waisted** adj.

short wave ■ n. a radio wave of a wavelength between about 10 and 100 m (and a frequency of about 3 to 30 MHz). ▶ broadcasting using radio waves of this wavelength.

short weight ■ n. weight that is less than that declared.

short-winded ■ adj. out of breath, or tending to run out of breath quickly.

shorty (also **shortie**) ■ n. (pl. **-ies**) informal 1 a short person. 2 chiefly Brit. a short dress, nightdress, or raincoat.

shot[1] ■ n. 1 the firing of a gun or cannon. ▶ a person with a specified level of ability in shooting: *he was an excellent shot.* ▶ a critical or aggressive remark. 2 a hit, stroke, or kick of the ball in sports, in particular an attempt to score. ▶ informal an attempt to do something. 3 (pl. same) a ball of stone or metal fired from a large gun or cannon. ▶ (also **lead shot**) tiny lead pellets used in a single charge or cartridge in a shotgun. ▶ a heavy ball thrown by a shot-putter. 4 a photograph. ▶ a film sequence photographed continuously by one camera. ▶ the range of

shot

a camera's view: *standing just out of shot.* **5** informal a small drink of spirits. ▸ an injection of a drug or vaccine. **6** the launch of a rocket: *a moon shot.*
– PHRASES **give it one's best shot** informal do the best that one can. **like a shot** informal without hesitation; willingly. **a shot in the arm** informal an encouraging stimulus.
– ORIGIN Old English, of Germanic origin; from the base of SHOOT.

shot² past and past participle of SHOOT. ■ adj. **1** (of coloured cloth) woven with a warp and weft of different colours, giving a contrasting effect when looked at from different angles. ▸ interspersed with a different colour. **2** informal ruined or worn out.
– PHRASES **get** (or **be**) **shot of** Brit. informal get (or be) rid of. **shot through with** suffused with. **shot to pieces** (or **to hell**) informal ruined.

shot-blast ■ v. clean or strip (a surface) by directing a high-speed stream of steel particles at it.

shot glass ■ n. a small glass used for serving spirits.

shotgun ■ n. a smooth-bore gun for firing small shot at short range.

shotgun marriage (also **shotgun wedding**) ■ n. informal an enforced or hurried wedding, especially because the bride is pregnant.

shot hole ■ n. **1** a hole made by the passage of a shot. **2** a hole bored in rock for the insertion of a blasting charge. **3** a small round hole made in a leaf by a fungus or bacterium, or in wood by a boring beetle.

shot-peen ■ v. shape (sheet metal) by bombarding it with a stream of metal shot.

shot put ■ n. an athletic contest in which a very heavy round ball is thrown as far as possible.
– DERIVATIVES **shot-putter** n. **shot-putting** n.

shottist ■ n. a person who takes part in shooting as a competitive sport.

should ■ modal v. (3rd sing. **should**) **1** used to indicate obligation, duty, or correctness. ▸ used to give or ask advice or suggestions. **2** used to indicate what is probable. **3** formal expressing the conditional mood. ▸ (in the first person) indicating the consequence of an imagined event. ▸ referring to a possible event or situation. **4** used in a clause with 'that' after a main clause describing feelings. **5** used in a clause with 'that' expressing purpose. **6** (in the first person) expressing a polite request or acceptance. **7** (in the first person) expressing a conjecture or hope.
– ORIGIN Old English *sceolde*: past of SHALL.

> **USAGE**
> There are traditional rules about the use of **should** and **would**, but these are no longer strictly followed. See "*should* and *would*" in *Guide to Good English* p. SP 14.

shoulder ■ n. **1** the joint between the upper arm or forelimb and the main part of the body. ▸ the part of a bird or insect at which the wing is attached. **2** a part of something resembling a shoulder, in particular a point at which a steep slope descends from a plateau or highland area. **3** short for HARD SHOULDER. ■ v. **1** put (something heavy) over one's shoulder or shoulders to carry. **2** take on (a burden or responsibility). **3** push out of one's way with one's shoulder.
– PHRASES **be looking over one's shoulder** be anxious or insecure about a possible danger. **put one's shoulder to the wheel** set to work vigorously. **shoulder arms** hold a rifle against the right side of the body, barrel upwards. **shoulder to shoulder** side by side or acting together.
– DERIVATIVES **-shouldered** adj.
– ORIGIN Old English, of West Germanic origin.

shoulder bag ■ n. a bag with a long strap that is hung over the shoulder.

shoulder belt ■ n. a bandolier or other strap passing over one shoulder and under the opposite arm.

shoulder blade ■ n. either of the large, flat, triangular bones which lie against the ribs in the upper back; the scapula.

shoulder pad ■ n. a pad sewn into the shoulder of a garment to provide shape or give protection.

shoulder season ■ n. a travel period between peak and off-peak seasons.

shoulder strap ■ n. **1** a narrow strip of material going over the shoulder from front to back of a garment. **2** a long strap attached to a bag for carrying it over the shoulder. **3** a strip of cloth from shoulder to collar on a military uniform, coat, etc.

shouldn't ■ contr. should not.

shout ■ v. speak or call out very loudly. ▸ (**shout at**) reprimand loudly. ▸ (**shout someone down**) prevent someone from speaking or being heard by shouting. ■ n. **1** a loud cry or call. **2** (**one's shout**) Brit. & Austral./NZ informal one's turn to buy a round of drinks.
– PHRASES **all over bar the shouting** informal (of a contest) almost finished and therefore virtually decided. **give someone a shout** informal call on or get in touch with someone. **in with a shout** informal having a good chance. **shout the odds** talk loudly and in an opinionated way.
– DERIVATIVES **shouter** n. **shouty** adj. (informal).
– ORIGIN Middle English: perhaps rel. to SHOOT; cf. Old Norse *skúta* 'a taunt'.

shouting match ■ n. informal a loud quarrel.

shove ■ v. **1** push roughly. **2** informal put (something) somewhere carelessly or roughly. ▸ (**shove it**) used to express angry dismissal. ■ n. a strong push.
– PHRASAL VERBS **shove off 1** informal go away. **2** push away from the shore in a boat. **shove up** informal move oneself to make room for someone.
– ORIGIN Old English, of Germanic origin; rel. to SHUFFLE.

shovel ■ n. a tool resembling a spade with a broad blade and upturned sides, used for moving coal, earth, snow, etc. ■ v. (**shovelled**, **shovelling**; US **shoveled**, **shoveling**) **1** move with a shovel. **2** (**shovel something down/in**) informal eat food quickly and in large quantities.
– DERIVATIVES **shovelful** n. (pl. **-fuls**).
– ORIGIN Old English *scofl*, of Germanic origin.

shoveller (US **shoveler**) ■ n. **1** a person or thing that shovels something. **2** (usu. **shoveler**) a dabbling duck with a long broad bill. [Genus *Anas*: four species.]

show ■ v. (past part. **shown** or **showed**) **1** be, allow, or cause to be visible. ▸ exhibit or produce for inspection. ▸ present (a film or television programme) on a screen for viewing. ▸ represent or depict in art. ▸ (**show oneself** or **one's face**) allow oneself to be seen; appear in public. ▸ (also **show up**) informal arrive for an appointment or at a gathering. **2** display or allow to be perceived (a quality, emotion, or characteristic). ▸ accord or treat someone with (a specified quality). **3** demonstrate or prove. ▸ explain or demonstrate something to. ▸ conduct or lead: *show them in, please.* **4** N. Amer. finish third or in the first three in a race. **5** informal (of a woman) be visibly pregnant. ■ n. **1** a spectacle or display. **2** a play or other stage performance, especially a musical. ▸ a light entertainment programme on television or radio. ▸ an event or competition involving the public display of animals, plants, or products. ▸ informal an undertaking, project, or organization: *I run the show.* **3** an outward appearance or display of a quality or feeling. ▸ (often in phr. **for show**) an outward display intended to give a false impression. **4** Medicine a discharge of blood and mucus from the vagina at the onset of labour or menstruation.
– PHRASES **all over the show** another way of saying all over the place (see ALL). **get the show on the road** informal begin an undertaking or enterprise. **good** (or **bad** or **poor**) **show!** informal, dated used to express approval (or disapproval or dissatisfaction). **have something** (or **nothing**) **to show for** have a (or no) visible result of (one's work or experience). **on show** be being exhibited. **show cause** Law produce satisfactory grounds for application of (or exemption from) a procedure or penalty. **show (someone) a clean pair of heels** informal run away from (someone) extremely fast. **show someone the door** dismiss or eject someone. **show one's hand** (or **cards**) disclose one's plans. **show of force** a demonstration of the forces at one's command or of one's readiness to use them. **show of hands** a vote by the raising of hands. **show one's teeth** Brit. use one's power or authority in an aggressive or intimidating way. **show willing** display a willingness to help.
– PHRASAL VERBS **show off** informal boastfully display one's abilities or accomplishments. **show something off** display something that is a source of pride. **show out** Bridge reveal

that one has no cards of a particular suit. **show someone round** (or chiefly N. Amer. **around**) point out interesting features in a place or building to someone. **show someone/thing up 1** expose someone or something as being bad or faulty. **2** (**show someone up**) informal embarrass or humiliate someone.
– ORIGIN Old English *scēawian* 'look at, inspect', from a West Germanic base meaning 'look'.

show-and-tell ■ n. chiefly N. Amer. a teaching method in which pupils bring items to class and describe them to their classmates.

showband ■ n. **1** a band which plays cover versions of popular songs. **2** a jazz band which performs with theatrical extravagance.

showbiz ■ n. informal term for SHOW BUSINESS.
– DERIVATIVES **showbizzy** adj.

showboat ■ n. **1** (in the US) a river steamer on which theatrical performances are given. **2** informal, chiefly N. Amer. a show-off; an exhibitionist. ■ v. informal, chiefly N. Amer. show off.
– DERIVATIVES **showboater** n.

show business ■ n. the theatre, films, television, and pop music as a profession or industry.

showcard ■ n. a large card bearing a conspicuous design, used in advertising, teaching, etc.

showcase ■ n. **1** a glass case used for displaying articles in a shop or museum. **2** a place or occasion for presenting something to general attention. ■ v. exhibit; display.

showdown ■ n. **1** a final test or confrontation intended to settle a dispute. **2** (in poker or brag) the requirement at the end of a round that the players who remain in should show their cards to determine which is the strongest hand.

shower /'ʃaʊə/ ■ n. **1** a brief and usually light fall of rain or snow. **2** a mass of small things falling or moving at once. ▶ a large number of things happening or given at the same time: *a shower of awards*. ▶ a group of particles produced by a cosmic-ray particle in the earth's atmosphere. **3** a cubicle or bath in which a person stands under a spray of water to wash. ▶ an act of washing oneself in a shower. **4** a party at which presents are given to a woman who is about to get married or have a baby. **5** Brit. informal an incompetent or worthless group of people. ■ v. **1** fall, throw, or be thrown in a shower: *broken glass showered down.* **2** (**shower something on/upon**) or **shower someone with** give a great number of things to someone. **3** wash oneself in a shower.
– ORIGIN Old English *scūr* 'light fall of rain', of Germanic origin.

showerproof ■ adj. (of a garment) resistant to light rain. ■ v. make showerproof.

showery ■ adj. characterized by frequent showers of rain.

showgirl ■ n. an actress who sings and dances in musicals, variety acts, etc.

showground ■ n. an area of land on which a show takes place.

show house (also **show home**) ■ n. **1** a house offered for sale and open to public viewing to increase the likelihood of a purchase. **2** a house or flat in a newly built complex which is furnished and decorated to be shown to prospective buyers.

showing ■ n. **1** a presentation of a cinema film or television programme. **2** a performance of a specified quality: *poor opinion poll showings*.

showjumping ■ n. the competitive sport of riding horses over a course of fences and other obstacles in an arena, with penalty points for errors.
– DERIVATIVES **showjump** v. **showjumper** n.

showman ■ n. (pl. **-men**) **1** the manager or presenter of a circus, fair, or other variety show. **2** a person skilled at entertaining, theatrical presentation, or performance.
– DERIVATIVES **showmanship** n.

shown past participle of SHOW.

show-off ■ n. informal a person who boastfully displays their abilities or accomplishments.

showpiece ■ n. **1** something which attracts admiration as an outstanding example of its type. **2** an item of work presented for exhibition or display.

showplace ■ n. a place of beauty or interest attracting many visitors.

showreel ■ n. a short videotape containing examples of an actor's or director's work for showing to potential employers.

showroom ■ n. a room used to display cars, furniture, or other goods for sale.

show-stopper ■ n. informal a performance or item receiving prolonged applause.
– DERIVATIVES **show-stopping** adj.

show trial ■ n. a judicial trial held in public with the intention of influencing or satisfying public opinion, rather than of ensuring justice.

showy ■ adj. (**-ier**, **-iest**) strikingly bright, colourful, or ostentatious.
– DERIVATIVES **showily** adv. **showiness** n.

shoyu /'ʃəʊjuː/ ■ n. a type of Japanese soy sauce.
– ORIGIN from Japanese *shōyu*.

shrank past of SHRINK.

shrapnel /'ʃrapn(ə)l/ ■ n. small metal fragments thrown out by the explosion of a shell, bomb, etc. ▶ shells designed to burst short of the target and shower it with such fragments.
– ORIGIN C19: named after the British soldier General Henry *Shrapnel*, inventor of shrapnel shells.

shred ■ n. **1** a strip of material that has been torn, cut, or scraped from something larger. **2** a very small amount. ■ v. (**shredded**, **shredding**) tear or cut into shreds.
– ORIGIN Old English *scrēad* 'piece cut off', *scrēadian* 'trim, prune', of West Germanic.

shredder ■ n. a device for shredding something, especially documents.

shrew ■ n. **1** a small mouse-like insectivorous mammal with a long pointed snout and tiny eyes. [Family Soricidae: many species.] **2** a bad-tempered or aggressively assertive woman.
– DERIVATIVES **shrewish** adj. **shrewishly** adv. **shrewishness** n.
– ORIGIN Old English *scrēawa*, *scrēwa*, of Germanic origin.

shrewd ■ adj. having or showing sharp powers of judgement; astute.
– DERIVATIVES **shrewdly** adv. **shrewdness** n.
– ORIGIN Middle English: from SHREW in the sense 'evil person or thing', or from obsolete *shrew* 'to curse'.

shriek ■ v. utter a high-pitched piercing sound, cry, or words. ■ n. **1** a high-pitched piercing cry or sound. **2** informal an exclamation mark.
– DERIVATIVES **shrieker** n. **shrieking** adj. **shriekingly** adv.
– ORIGIN C15: imitative.

shrift ■ n. archaic confession, especially to a priest. ▶ absolution by a priest. See also SHORT SHRIFT.
– ORIGIN Old English *scrift* 'penance imposed after confession', from SHRIVE.

shrike ■ n. a predatory songbird with a hooked bill, often impaling its prey on thorns. [Family Laniidae: many species.] ▶ used in names of birds of other families, e.g. bush-shrike.
– ORIGIN C16: perhaps rel. to Old English *scrīc* 'thrush' and Middle Low German *schrīk*, 'corncrake', of imitative origin.

shrill ■ adj. (of a voice or sound) high-pitched and piercing. ▶ derogatory (of a complaint or demand) loud and forceful. ■ v. make a shrill noise.
– DERIVATIVES **shrillness** n. **shrilly** adv.
– ORIGIN Middle English, of Germanic origin.

shrimp ■ n. (pl. same or **shrimps**) a small free-swimming edible crustacean with ten legs, mainly marine. [*Pandalus, Crangon*, and other genera.] **2** informal, derogatory a small, physically weak person. ■ v. fish for shrimps.
– DERIVATIVES **shrimper** n.
– ORIGIN Middle English: prob. rel. to Middle Low German *schrempen* 'to wrinkle', Middle High German *schrimpfen* 'to contract'.

shrimp plant ■ n. a Mexican shrub with clusters of small flowers in pinkish-brown bracts, said to resemble shrimps. [*Justicia brandegeana*.]

shrine

shrine ■ n. **1** a place regarded as holy because of its associations with a divinity or a sacred person. **2** a casket containing sacred relics; a reliquary. ▸ a niche or enclosure containing a religious statue or other object. ■ v. poetic/literary enshrine.
– ORIGIN Old English *scrīn* 'cabinet, chest, reliquary', of Germanic origin.

shrink ■ v. (past **shrank**; past part. **shrunk** or (especially as adj.) **shrunken**) **1** become or make smaller in size or amount; contract. ▸ (of clothes or material) become smaller as a result of being immersed in water. **2** move back or away in fear or disgust. ▸ (**shrink from**) be averse to or unwilling to do (something). ■ n. informal a psychiatrist.
– DERIVATIVES **shrinkable** adj. **shrinker** n.
– ORIGIN Old English, of Germanic origin; noun from *headshrinker*.

shrinkage ■ n. **1** the process, fact, or amount of shrinking. **2** an allowance made for reduction in the takings of a business due to wastage or theft.

shrinking violet ■ n. informal an exaggeratedly shy person.

shrink wrap ■ n. clinging transparent plastic film used to enclose an article as packaging. ■ v. (**shrink-wrap**) enclose in shrink wrap.

shrive /ʃrʌɪv/ ■ v. (past **shrove**; past part. **shriven**) archaic (of a priest) hear the confession of, assign penance to, and absolve. ▸ (**shrive oneself**) present oneself to a priest for confession, penance, and absolution.
– ORIGIN Old English *scrīfan* 'impose as a penance', of Germanic origin, from Latin *scribere* 'write'.

shrivel ■ v. (**shrivelled**, **shrivelling**; US **shriveled**, **shriveling**) wrinkle and contract, or cause to wrinkle and contract, through loss of moisture.
– ORIGIN C16: perhaps of Scandinavian origin.

shroom ■ n. informal short for MAGIC MUSHROOM or MUSHROOM.

shroud ■ n. **1** a length of cloth or an enveloping garment in which a dead person is wrapped for burial. **2** a thing that envelops or obscures: *a shroud of mist*. **3** technical a protective casing or cover. **4** (**shrouds**) a set of ropes forming part of the standing rigging of a sailing boat and supporting the mast or topmast. ▸ (also **shroud line**) each of the lines joining the canopy of a parachute to the harness. ■ v. **1** wrap or dress in a shroud. **2** cover or envelop so as to conceal from view.
– ORIGIN Old English *scrūd* 'garment, clothing', of Germanic origin, from a base meaning 'cut'.

shrove past of SHRIVE.

Shrovetide ■ n. Shrove Tuesday and the two days preceding it, when it was formerly customary to attend confession.

Shrove Tuesday ■ n. (in the Western Christian Church) the day before Ash Wednesday, traditionally marked by feasting before the Lenten fast.

shrub ■ n. a woody plant which is smaller than a tree and has several main stems arising at or near the ground.
– DERIVATIVES **shrubby** adj.
– ORIGIN Old English *scrubb*, *scrybb* 'shrubbery'.

shrubbery ■ n. (pl. **-ies**) **1** an area in a garden planted with shrubs. **2** a clump of shrubs collectively.

shrug ■ v. (**shrugged**, **shrugging**) raise (one's shoulders) slightly and momentarily to express doubt, ignorance, or indifference. ▸ (**shrug something off**) dismiss something as unimportant. ■ n. an act or instance of shrugging one's shoulders.
– ORIGIN Middle English.

shrunk (also **shrunken**) past participle of SHRINK.

shtook /ʃtʊk/ (also **schtuck**) ■ n. informal trouble.
– ORIGIN 1930s.

shtum /ʃtʊm/ (also **schtum**) ■ adj. informal silent; non-communicative.
– ORIGIN 1950s: Yiddish, from German *stumm*.

shuck /ʃʌk/ chiefly N. Amer. ■ n. an outer covering such as a husk or pod, especially the husk of an ear of maize. ▸ the shell of an oyster or clam. ■ v. **1** remove the shucks from. **2** informal abandon; get rid of. ▸ take off (a garment).
– ORIGIN C17.

shucks ■ exclam. informal, chiefly N. Amer. used to express surprise, regret, etc.

shudder ■ v. tremble or shake convulsively, especially as a result of fear or repugnance. ■ n. an act of shuddering.
– DERIVATIVES **shuddering** adj. **shudderingly** adv. **shuddery** adj.
– ORIGIN Middle English: from Middle Dutch *schūderen*, from a Germanic base meaning 'shake'.

shuffle /ʃʌf(ə)l/ ■ v. **1** walk by dragging one's feet along or without lifting them fully from the ground. ▸ restlessly shift one's position. ▸ (**shuffle something off/shuffle out of something**) get out of or avoid a responsibility or obligation. **2** rearrange (a pack of cards) by sliding them over each other quickly. ▸ (**shuffle through**) sort or look through (a number of things) hurriedly. **3** move (people or things) around into different positions or a different order. ■ n. **1** a shuffling movement, walk, or sound. ▸ a quick dragging or scraping movement of the feet in dancing. ▸ a dance performed with such steps. **2** an act of shuffling a pack of cards. **3** a change of order or relative positions; a reshuffle. **4** a facility on a CD player for playing tracks in an arbitrary order.
– DERIVATIVES **shuffler** n.
– ORIGIN C16: perhaps from Low German *schuffeln* 'walk clumsily', also 'deal dishonestly, shuffle (cards)', of Germanic origin.

shufti /ʃʊfti/ ■ n. (pl. **shuftis**) Brit. informal a quick look or reconnoitre.
– ORIGIN 1940s: from Arabic *šāfa* 'try to see'.

shul /ʃuːl/ ■ n. a synagogue.
– ORIGIN C19: Yiddish, from German *Schule* 'school'.

shun ■ v. (**shunned**, **shunning**) persistently avoid, ignore, or reject.
– ORIGIN Old English *scunian* 'abhor, shrink back with fear'.

shunt ■ v. **1** slowly push or pull (a railway vehicle or vehicles) so as to make up or remove from a train. ▸ push or shove. ▸ direct or divert to a less important place or position. **2** provide (an electrical circuit) with a shunt, through which some of the current may be diverted. ■ n. **1** an act of shunting. **2** Brit. informal a motor accident, especially a collision of vehicles travelling one close behind the other. **3** an electrical conductor joining two points of a circuit. **4** Surgery an alternative path created for the passage of blood or other fluid.
– ORIGIN Middle English (in the sense 'move suddenly aside'): perhaps from SHUN.

shunter ■ n. **1** a small locomotive used for shunting. **2** a railway worker engaged in such work.

shuriken /ʃʊərɪkɛn/ ■ n. a weapon in the form of a star with projecting blades or points, used as a missile in some martial arts.
– ORIGIN Japanese, 'dagger in the hand'.

shush /ʃʊʃ, ʃʌʃ/ ■ exclam. be quiet. ■ n. **1** an utterance of 'shush'. **2** a soft swishing or rustling sound. ■ v. **1** tell or signal to be silent. ▸ become or remain silent. **2** move with or make a soft swishing or rustling sound.

shut ■ v. (**shutting**; past and past part. **shut**) **1** move or cause to move into position to block an opening. ▸ (usu. **shut someone/thing in/out**) confine or exclude by closing something such as a door. ▸ (**shut someone out**) prevent an opponent from scoring in a game. ▸ (**shut up**) or **shut someone up** informal stop or cause someone to stop talking. **2** fold or bring together the sides or parts of. **3** chiefly Brit. make or become unavailable for business or service. ▸ (**shut down**) or **shut something down** cease or cause something to cease business or operation. **4** (**shut off**) or **shut something off** stop or cause something to stop flowing or working.
– PHRASES **be** (or **get**) **shut of** informal be (or get) rid of. **shut up shop** cease trading, either temporarily or permanently.
– ORIGIN Old English *scyttan* 'put (a bolt) in position to hold fast', of West Germanic origin.

shutdown ■ n. a closure of a factory or instance of turning off a machine or computer.

shut-eye ■ n. informal sleep.

shut-out bid ■ n. Bridge a high bid intended to end the auction; a pre-emptive bid.

shutter ■ n. **1** each of a pair of hinged panels fixed inside

or outside a window that can be closed for security or privacy or to keep out the light. **2** Photography a device that opens and closes to expose the film in a camera. ■ v. close the shutters of (a window or building).
– DERIVATIVES **shuttering** n. **shutterless** adj.

shutterbug ■ n. informal, an enthusiastic photographer.

shuttle ■ n. **1** a form of transport that travels regularly between two places. **2** a bobbin with two pointed ends used for carrying the weft thread across between the warp threads in weaving. ▸ a bobbin carrying the lower thread in a sewing machine. **3** short for SHUTTLECOCK. ■ v. travel regularly between two or more places. ▸ transport in a shuttle.
– ORIGIN Old English *scytel* 'dart, missile', of Germanic origin.

shuttlecock ■ n. a light cone-shaped object struck with rackets in the games of badminton and battledore, traditionally of cork with feathers attached.

shuttle diplomacy ■ n. negotiations conducted by a mediator who travels between two or more parties that are reluctant to hold direct discussions.

shwarma /ˈʃwɑːmə/ ■ n. variant spelling of SCHWARMA.

shweshwe /ˈʃwɛʃwɛː/ ■ n. S. African an inexpensive cotton cloth, typically with white floral or geometric designs on a dark blue or dark brown background.
– ORIGIN from Sesotho *-shweshwe* (or *-shoeshoe*), 'of the people of Moshesh (Moshoeshoe)'.

shy[1] ■ adj. (**shyer**, **shyest**) **1** nervous or timid in the company of other people. ▸ (**shy of/about**) slow or reluctant to do. ▸ [in combination] having a specified dislike or aversion: *camera-shy*. ▸ (of a wild animal) reluctant to remain in sight of humans. **2** (**shy of**) informal less than; short of or before. **3** (of a plant) not bearing flowers or fruit well or prolifically. ■ v. (**-ies**, **-ied**) (especially of a horse) start suddenly aside in fright. ▸ (**shy from**) avoid through nervousness or lack of confidence. ■ n. a sudden startled movement, especially of a frightened horse.
– DERIVATIVES **shyly** adv. **shyness** n.
– ORIGIN Old English *scēoh* '(of a horse) easily frightened', of Germanic origin;.

shy[2] ■ v. (**-ies**, **-ied**) fling or throw at a target. ■ n. (pl. **-ies**) (often in phr. **have a shy at**) an act of shying.
– ORIGIN C18.

shyster ■ n. informal a person, especially a lawyer, who uses unscrupulous methods.
– ORIGIN C19: said to be from *Scheuster*, the name of a lawyer, perhaps reinforced by German *Scheisser* 'worthless person'.

SI ■ abbrev. Système International, the international system of units of measurement based on the metre, kilogram, second, ampere, kelvin, candela, and mole, together with prefixes indicating multiplication or division by powers of ten.

Si ■ symb. the chemical element silicon.

si /siː/ ■ n. Music another term for TE.
– ORIGIN C18: from the initial letters of *Sancte Iohannes*, the closing words of a Latin hymn.

sialic acid /sʌɪˈalɪk/ ■ n. Biochemistry a substance present in saliva, consisting of a sugar with amino and ester groups.
– ORIGIN 1950s: from Greek *sialon* 'saliva'.

Siamese ■ n. (pl. same) **1** dated a native of Siam (now Thailand) in SE Asia. **2** (also **Siamese cat**) a cat of a lightly built short-haired breed characterized by slanting blue eyes and pale fur with darker points. ■ adj. dated of or relating to Siam, its people, or their language.

Siamese twins ■ pl. n. twins that are physically joined at birth, in some cases sharing organs.
– ORIGIN with ref. to the *Siamese* men Chang and Eng (1811–74), who were joined at the waist.

SIB ■ abbrev. Securities and Investment Board.

sib ■ n. chiefly Zoology a sibling.
– ORIGIN Old English, 'relative' and 'related by birth'.

Siberian /sʌɪˈbɪərɪən/ ■ n. a native or inhabitant of Siberia. ■ adj. of or relating to Siberia.

sibilant ■ adj. **1** making or characterized by a hissing sound. **2** Phonetics (of a speech sound) sounded with a hissing effect, for example *s*, *sh*. ■ n. Phonetics a sibilant speech sound.
– DERIVATIVES **sibilance** n.

1099

sickly

– ORIGIN C17: from Latin *sibilare* 'hiss'.

siblicide /ˈsɪblɪsʌɪd/ ■ n. Zoology the killing of a sibling or siblings.

sibling ■ n. each of two or more children or offspring having one or both parents in common; a brother or sister.
– ORIGIN Old English, in the sense 'relative' (see SIB, -LING).

sibship ■ n. chiefly Zoology a group of offspring having the same two parents.

sibyl ■ n. (in ancient times) a woman supposedly able to utter the oracles and prophecies of a god. ▸ poetic/literary a woman able to foretell the future.
– DERIVATIVES **sibylline** adj.
– ORIGIN from Old French *Sibile* or medieval Latin *Sibilla*, from Greek *Sibulla*.

sic /sɪk/ ■ adv. (after a copied or quoted word) written exactly as it stands in the original.
– ORIGIN Latin, 'so, thus'.

Sicilian ■ n. a native or inhabitant of Sicily. ■ adj. of or relating to Sicily.

siciliano /sɪˌtʃɪlɪˈɑːnəʊ, -ˌsɪlɪ-/ (also **siciliana**) ■ n. (pl. **-os**) a dance, song, or instrumental piece in 6/8 or 12/8 time, typically in a minor key and evoking a pastoral mood.
– ORIGIN Italian, 'Sicilian'.

sick[1] ■ adj. **1** affected by physical or mental illness. **2** feeling nauseous and wanting to vomit. **3** informal disappointed, mortified, or miserable. **4** (**sick of**) bored by or annoyed with through excessive exposure; weary of. **5** informal (of humour) dealing offensively with unpleasant or upsetting subjects. ▸ having abnormal or unnatural tendencies; perverted. **6** archaic pining or longing. ■ n. Brit. informal vomit. ■ v. (**sick something up**) Brit. informal bring something up by vomiting.
– PHRASES **be sick 1** be ill. **2** Brit. vomit. **get sick 1** be ill. **2** N. Amer. vomit. **sick to one's stomach 1** nauseous. **2** disgusted.
– DERIVATIVES **sickish** adj.
– ORIGIN Old English *sēoc*, of Germanic origin.

sick[2] ■ v. **1** (**sick something on**) set a dog on. **2** (**sick someone on**) informal set someone to pursue, keep watch on, or accompany.
– ORIGIN C19: dialect var. of SEEK.

sickbay ■ n. a room or building set aside for sick people, especially on a ship.

sickbed ■ n. an invalid's bed.

sick building syndrome ■ n. a condition marked by headaches, respiratory problems, etc. affecting office workers, attributed to factors such as poor ventilation in the working environment.

sicken ■ v. **1** become disgusted or appalled. ▸ [as adj. **sickening**] informal very irritating or annoying. ▸ archaic feel disgust or horror. **2** become ill. ▸ (**sicken for**) begin to show symptoms of (a particular illness).
– DERIVATIVES **sickeningly** adv.

sickener ■ n. informal something which causes disgust or severe disappointment.

sick headache ■ n. a headache accompanied by nausea, particularly a migraine.

sickie ■ n. informal, chiefly Brit. a period of sick leave taken when one is not actually ill.

sickle ■ n. a short-handled farming tool with a semicircular blade, used for cutting corn, lopping, or trimming.
– ORIGIN Old English *sicol*, of Germanic origin, from Latin *secula*, from *secare* 'to cut'.

sick leave ■ n. leave of absence granted because of illness.

sickle-cell anaemia (also **sickle-cell disease**) ■ n. a severe hereditary form of anaemia in which a mutated form of haemoglobin distorts the red blood cells into a crescent shape at low oxygen levels.

sickly ■ adj. (**-ier**, **-iest**) **1** often ill; in poor health. ▸ causing, characterized by, or indicative of poor health. **2** inducing discomfort or nausea: *a sickly green*. ▸ excessively sentimental or mawkish.
– DERIVATIVES **sickliness** n.

sick-making ■ adj. informal nauseatingly unpleasant, shocking, or sentimental.

sickness ■ n. 1 the state of being ill. ▸ a particular type of illness or disease. 2 nausea or vomiting.

sickness benefit ■ n. (in the UK) benefit paid weekly by the state to an individual for sickness which interrupts paid employment.

sicko ■ n. (pl. -os) informal a mentally ill or perverted person, especially a dangerous one.

sickroom ■ n. a room occupied by or set apart for people who are unwell.

siddha /ˈsɪdə/ ■ n. Hinduism an ascetic who has achieved enlightenment.
– ORIGIN from Sanskrit.

siddhi /ˈsɪdi/ ■ n. (pl. **siddhis**) Hinduism 1 complete understanding; enlightenment. 2 a paranormal power possessed by a siddha.
– ORIGIN from Sanskrit.

side ■ n. 1 a position to the left or right of an object, place, or central point. 2 either of the two halves of something regarded as divided by an imaginary central line. 3 an upright or sloping surface of a structure or object that is not the top or bottom and generally not the front or back. ▸ each of the flat surfaces of a solid object. ▸ each of the lines forming the boundary of a plane rectilinear figure. ▸ each of the two surfaces of something flat and thin, e.g. paper. ▸ each of the two faces of a record or of the two separate tracks on a cassette tape. 4 a part or region near the edge and away from the middle of something. ▸ [as modifier] subsidiary or less important: *a side dish.* 5 a person or group opposing another or others in a dispute or contest. ▸ the cause, interests, or attitude of one person or group. ▸ a particular aspect: *he had a disagreeable side.* ▸ a person's kinship or line of descent as traced through either their father or mother: *Richard was of French descent on his mother's side.* 6 a sports team. 7 (also **side spin**) horizontal spinning motion given to a ball, especially by hitting it on one side. ■ v. (**side with/against**) support or oppose in a conflict or dispute.
– PHRASES **from side to side 1** alternately left and right from a central point. **2** across the entire width; right across. **on the side 1** in addition to one's regular job. **2** secretly, especially as an illicit sexual relationship. **3** N. Amer. served separately from the main dish. **side by side** close together and facing the same way. **take sides** support one person or cause against another or others.
– DERIVATIVES **-sided** adj. **-sidedly** adv. **-sidedness** n. **sideward** adj. & adv. **sidewards** adv.
– ORIGIN Old English *side* 'left or right part of the body', of Germanic origin.

sidearm ■ n. a weapon worn at a person's side, such as a pistol.

sideband ■ n. Telecommunications each of two frequency bands either side of the carrier wave, which contain the modulated signal.

sidebar ■ n. chiefly N. Amer. 1 a short note or supplement placed alongside a main article of text. ▸ a side issue. 2 (in a court of law) a discussion between the lawyers and the judge held out of earshot of the jury. 3 (**the Side Bar**) (in South Africa) attorneys collectively. See also BAR (sense 6).

sideboard ■ n. 1 a flat-topped piece of furniture with cupboards and drawers, used for storing crockery, glasses, etc. 2 Brit. a sideburn.

sideburn ■ n. a strip of hair grown by a man down each side of the face in front of his ears.
– ORIGIN C19: orig. *burnside*, from the name of General *Burnside*, who affected this style.

sidecar ■ n. a small, low vehicle attached to the side of a motorcycle for carrying passengers.

side chain ■ n. Chemistry a group of atoms attached to the main part of a molecule with a ring or chain structure.

side chair ■ n. an upright wooden chair without arms.

side drum ■ n. a small drum in the form of a short cylinder with a membrane at each end, the upper one being struck with hard sticks and the lower one often fitted with rattling cords or wires (snares).

side effect ■ n. a secondary, typically undesirable effect of a drug or medical treatment.

side-foot ■ v. kick (a ball) with the inside of the foot.

side glance ■ n. a sideways or brief glance.

side issue ■ n. a subsidiary point or topic connected to or raised by some other issue.

sidekick ■ n. informal a person's assistant or junior associate.

sidelight ■ n. 1 Brit. a small supplementary light on either side of a motor vehicle's headlights. ▸ (**sidelights**) a ship's navigation lights. 2 a narrow pane of glass set alongside a door or larger window. 3 a piece of incidental information that helps to clarify or enliven a subject.

sideline ■ n. 1 an activity done in addition to one's main job. 2 either of the two lines bounding the longer sides of a football field, basketball court, or similar. 3 (**the sidelines**) a position of observing a situation rather than being directly involved in it. ■ v. remove or bar from a team, game, or active position.

sidelong ■ adj. & adv. directed to or from one side; sideways.
– ORIGIN Middle English: alteration of *sideling*, from SIDE + the adverbial suffix *-ling*.

sideman ■ n. (pl. -men) a supporting musician in a jazz band or rock group.

side-on ■ adj. & adv. on, from, or towards a side.

sidereal /saɪˈdɪərɪəl/ ■ adj. relating to the distant stars, especially with reference to their apparent positions and diurnal motion.
– ORIGIN C17: from Latin *sidereus*, from *sidus* 'star'.

sidereal day ■ n. Astronomy the time between consecutive meridional transits of the First Point of Aries, almost four minutes shorter than the solar day.

sidereal period ■ n. Astronomy the period of revolution of one body about another, measured with respect to the distant stars.

sidereal time ■ n. Astronomy time reckoned from the motion of the earth (or a planet) relative to the distant stars (rather than with respect to the sun).

sidereal year ■ n. Astronomy the sidereal period of the earth about the sun, about twenty minutes longer than the solar year.

siderite /ˈsaɪdəraɪt, ˈsɪd-/ ■ n. a brown mineral consisting of ferrous carbonate.
– DERIVATIVES **sideritic** adj.
– ORIGIN C16 (denoting lodestone): from Greek *sidēros* 'iron'.

side road ■ n. a minor or subsidiary road, especially one joining or diverging from a main road.

siderophore /ˈsɪdərə(ʊ)fɔː, ˈsaɪ-/ ■ n. Biochemistry a molecule which binds and transports iron in micro-organisms.
– ORIGIN from Greek *sidēros* 'iron' + -PHORE.

side saddle ■ n. a saddle in which the rider has both feet on the same side of the horse, used by women riders wearing skirts. ■ adv. (**side-saddle**) sitting in this position on a horse.

side salad ■ n. a salad served as a side dish.

sideshow ■ n. 1 a small show or stall at an exhibition, fair, or circus. 2 a minor but diverting incident or issue.

side-slip ■ n. 1 a sideways skid or slip. 2 Aeronautics a sideways movement of an aircraft, especially downwards towards the inside of a turn. ■ v. perform a side-slip.

sidesman ■ n. (pl. -men) Brit. a churchwarden's assistant.

side-splitting ■ adj. informal extremely amusing.
– DERIVATIVES **side-splittingly** adv.

sidestep ■ v. (-stepped, -stepping) 1 avoid by stepping sideways. 2 avoid dealing with or discussing. ■ n. an instance of sidestepping.

side street ■ n. a minor or subsidiary street.

sidestroke ■ n. a swimming stroke similar to the breaststroke in which the swimmer lies on their side.

sideswipe ■ n. 1 a passing critical remark. 2 a glancing blow from or on the side, especially of a motor vehicle. ■ v. strike with a glancing blow.

sidetrack ■ v. distract from an immediate or important issue.

sidewalk ■ n. N. Amer. a pavement.

sidewall ■ n. the side of a tyre.

sideways ■ adv. & adj. **1** to, towards, or from the side. ▸ so as to occupy a job or position at the same level as one previously held. **2** unconventional or unorthodox: *a sideways look at daily life.*

side whiskers ■ pl. n. whiskers or sideburns on a man's cheeks.

side wind ■ n. a wind blowing predominantly from one side.

sidewinder /ˈsaɪdˌwaɪndə/ ■ n. a nocturnal burrowing rattlesnake that moves sideways over sand by throwing its body into S-shaped curves. [*Crotalus cerastes*.]

sidewise ■ adv. & adj. another term for SIDEWAYS.

siding ■ n. **1** a short track at the side of and opening on to a railway line, for shunting or stabling trains. ▸ S. African a scheduled stop for goods and passenger trains, often in open country. **2** N. Amer. cladding material for the outside of a building.

sidle ■ v. walk in a furtive or stealthy manner, especially sideways or obliquely. ■ n. an instance of sidling.
– ORIGIN C17: back-formation from *sideling* (see SIDELONG).

SIDS ■ abbrev. sudden infant death syndrome.

siege ■ n. **1** a military operation in which enemy forces surround a town or building, cutting off essential supplies, with the aim of compelling the surrender of those inside. **2** a similar operation by a police team to compel the surrender of an armed person.
– PHRASES **lay siege to** conduct a siege of. **under siege** undergoing a siege.
– ORIGIN Middle English: from Old French *sege*, from *asegier* 'besiege'.

siege mentality ■ n. a defensive or paranoid attitude based on the belief that others are hostile towards one.

siemens /ˈsiːmənz/ (abbrev.: **S**) ■ n. Physics the SI unit of conductance, equal to one reciprocal ohm.
– ORIGIN 1930s: named after the German-born British engineer Sir Charles William *Siemens*.

sienna ■ n. a kind of ferruginous earth used as a pigment in painting, normally yellowish-brown in colour (**raw sienna**) or deep reddish-brown when roasted (**burnt sienna**).
– ORIGIN C18: from Italian (*terra di*) *Sienna* '(earth of) Siena'.

sierra /sɪˈɛrə, sɪˈɛːrə/ ■ n. **1** (especially in Spanish-speaking countries or the western US) a long jagged mountain chain. **2** a code word representing the letter S, used in radio communication.
– ORIGIN C16: Spanish, from Latin *serra* 'saw'.

Sierra Leonean /lɪˈəʊnɪən/ ■ n. a native or inhabitant of Sierra Leone, a country in West Africa. ■ adj. of or relating to Sierra Leone.

siesta /sɪˈɛstə/ ■ n. an afternoon rest or nap, especially one taken during the hottest hours of the day in a hot climate.
– ORIGIN C17: Spanish, from Latin *sexta* (*hora*) 'sixth hour'.

sieve /sɪv/ ■ n. a utensil consisting of a wire or plastic mesh held in a frame, used for straining solids from liquids, for separating coarser from finer particles, or for reducing soft solids to a pulp. ■ v. **1** put through a sieve. **2** (**sieve through**) examine in detail.
– ORIGIN Old English, of West Germanic origin.

sievert /ˈsiːvət/ (abbrev.: **Sv**) ■ n. Physics the SI unit of dose equivalent, defined as a dose which delivers a joule of energy per kilogram of recipient mass.
– ORIGIN 1940s: named after the Swedish physicist Rolf M. *Sievert*.

sift ■ v. **1** put (a dry substance) through a sieve so as to remove lumps or large particles. **2** cause to flow or pass as through a sieve. **3** (**sift down**) (of snow, ash, light, etc.) descend lightly or sparsely as if having passed through a sieve. **4** examine thoroughly so as to isolate that which is important or useful.
– DERIVATIVES **sifted** adj. **sifter** n. **sifting** n.
– ORIGIN Old English, of West Germanic origin.

SIG ■ abbrev. Computing special interest group.

sig ■ n. Computing, informal a short personalized message at the end of an email message.
– ORIGIN 1990s: abbrev. of SIGNATURE.

Sigatoka /ˌsɪɡəˈtəʊkə/ ■ n. a fungal disease of banana plants.
– ORIGIN 1920s: named after a district in Fiji.

sigh ■ n. **1** a long, deep, audible exhalation expressing sadness, tiredness, relief, etc. **2** a sound resembling this. ■ v. **1** emit a sigh. **2** (**sigh for**) poetic/literary yearn for.
– ORIGIN Middle English: prob. a back-formation from *sighte*, from Old English *sīcan*.

sight ■ n. **1** the faculty or power of seeing. **2** the action or fact of seeing someone or something. **3** the area or distance within which someone can see or something can be seen. **4** a thing that one sees or that can be seen. **5** (**sights**) places of interest to tourists and other visitors. **6** (**a sight**) informal a person or thing having a ridiculous or unattractive appearance. **7** (usu. **sights**) a device on a gun or optical instrument used for assisting in precise aim or observation. ■ v. **1** manage to see or briefly observe. **2** take aim by looking through the sights of a gun. **3** take a detailed visual measurement with or as with a sight. **4** adjust the sight of (a gun or optical instrument).
– PHRASES **at first sight** at the first glimpse; on the first impression. **catch sight of** glimpse for a moment. **in sight 1** visible. **2** near at hand; close to being achieved or realized. **in** (or **within**) **sight of 1** so as to see or be seen from. **2** within reach of; close to attaining. **in** (or **within**) **one's sights 1** visible, especially through the sights of one's gun. **2** within the scope of one's ambitions or expectations. **lose sight of 1** be no longer able to see. **2** fail to consider, be aware of, or remember. **on** (or **at**) **sight** as soon as someone or something has been seen. **out of sight 1** not visible. **2** (also **outasight**) informal extremely good; excellent. **raise** (or **lower**) **one's sights** become more (or less) ambitious; increase (or lower) one's expectations. **set one's sights on** hope strongly to achieve or reach. **a sight ——** informal indicating considerable extent: *she is a sight cleverer than Sarah.* **a sight for sore eyes** informal a person or thing that one is extremely pleased or relieved to see. **a sight to behold** a person or thing that is particularly impressive or worth seeing.
– DERIVATIVES **sighted** adj. **sighting** n.
– ORIGIN Old English (*ge*)*sihth* 'something seen', of West Germanic origin.

sight glass ■ n. a transparent tube or window through which the level of liquid in a reservoir or supply line can be checked visually.

sighting shot ■ n. an experimental shot to guide shooters in adjusting their sights.

sightless ■ adj. **1** unable to see; blind. **2** poetic/literary invisible.
– DERIVATIVES **sightlessly** adv. **sightlessness** n.

sight line ■ n. a hypothetical line from someone's eye to what is seen.

sightly ■ adj. pleasing to the eye.

sight-read ■ v. read and perform (music) at sight, without preparation.
– DERIVATIVES **sight-reader** n.

sight screen ■ n. Cricket a large white or black screen placed near the boundary in line with the wicket to help the batsman see the ball.

sightseeing ■ n. the activity of visiting places of interest in a particular location.
– DERIVATIVES **sightsee** v. **sightseer** n.

sight-sing ■ v. sing (music) at sight, without preparation.

sight unseen ■ adv. without the opportunity to look at the object in question beforehand.

sigil /ˈsɪdʒɪl/ ■ n. a sign or symbol.
– ORIGIN Middle English: from late Latin *sigillum* 'sign'.

SIGINT /ˈsɪɡɪnt/ ■ abbrev. signals intelligence.

siglum /ˈsɪɡləm/ ■ n. (pl. **sigla** /-lə/) a letter or symbol which stands for a word or name, especially to denote a particular manuscript or edition of a text.
– ORIGIN C18: from late Latin *sigla* (pl.), perhaps from *singulus* 'single'.

sigma /ˈsɪɡmə/ ■ n. **1** the eighteenth letter of the Greek

sigmoid

alphabet (Σ, σ, or at the end of a word ς), transliterated as 's'. **2** [as modifier] Chemistry & Physics (of an electron or orbital) with zero angular momentum about an internuclear axis. ■ symb. **1** (Σ) mathematical sum. **2** (σ) standard deviation.
– ORIGIN from Greek.

sigmoid /ˈsɪɡmɔɪd/ ■ adj. **1** curved like the uncial sigma; crescent-shaped. **2** S-shaped. **3** Anatomy of or denoting the curved part of the colon leading into the rectum.
– DERIVATIVES **sigmoidal** adj.
– ORIGIN C17: from Greek *sigmoeidēs*, from *sigma* (see SIGMA).

sigmoidoscopy /ˌsɪɡmɔɪˈdɒskəpi/ ■ n. examination of the sigmoid colon by means of a flexible tube inserted through the anus.
– DERIVATIVES **sigmoidoscope** n. **sigmoidoscopic** adj.

sign ■ n. **1** an object, quality, or event whose presence or occurrence indicates the probable presence, occurrence, or advent of something else. **2** Medicine an indication of a disease detectable by a medical practitioner even if not apparent to the patient. Compare with SYMPTOM. **3** N. Amer. the trail of a wild animal. **4** a signal conveying information or an instruction. **5** a public notice giving information or instructions in a written or symbolic form. **6** a gesture used in sign language. **7** a symbol or word used to represent an operation, instruction, concept, or object in algebra, music, or other subjects. **8** Astrology each of the twelve equal sections into which the zodiac is divided, named from the constellations formerly situated in each, and associated with successive periods of the year according to the position of the sun on the ecliptic. **9** Mathematics the positiveness or negativeness of a quantity. ■ v. **1** write one's name on (something) for the purposes of identification or authorization. ▶ write (one's name) for such a purpose. **2** (with reference to a sports player, musician, etc.) engage for or commit oneself to work by signing a contract. **3** use gestures to convey information or instructions. **4** communicate in sign language. **5** (usu. **be signed**) indicate with signposts or other markers.
– PHRASAL VERBS **sign in** sign a register on arrival in a hotel or workplace. **sign someone in** record someone's arrival in a register. **sign off 1** complete a letter, broadcast, or other message. **2** sign to record that one is leaving work for the day. **sign someone off** record that someone is entitled to miss work. **sign on 1** commit oneself to employment, membership of a society, etc. **2** Brit. register as unemployed. **sign someone on** take someone into one's employment. **sign out** sign a register to record one's departure from a hotel or workplace. **sign someone out** authorize someone's release or record their departure by signing a register. **sign something out** sign to indicate that one has borrowed or hired something. **sign up 1** commit oneself to a period of employment, education, etc. **2** (also **sign something up**) conclude a business deal. **sign someone up** formally engage someone in employment.
– DERIVATIVES **signed** adj. **signer** n.
– ORIGIN Middle English: from Old French *signe* (n.), *signer* (v.), from Latin *signum* 'mark, token'.

signage ■ n. signs collectively, especially commercial or public display signs.

signal¹ ■ n. **1** a gesture, action, or sound conveying information or an instruction. **2** an indication of a state of affairs. **3** an event or statement that provides the impulse or occasion for something to happen. **4** a light or semaphore on a railway, giving indications to train drivers of whether or not to proceed. **5** Bridge a pre-arranged convention of bidding or play intended to convey information to one's partner. **6** an electrical impulse or radio wave transmitted or received. ■ v. (**signalled**, **signalling**; US **signaled**, **signaling**) **1** transmit a signal. **2** instruct or indicate by means of a signal.
– DERIVATIVES **signaller** n.
– ORIGIN Middle English: from medieval Latin *signale*, from Latin *signum* (see SIGN).

signal² ■ adj. striking; outstanding.
– DERIVATIVES **signally** adv.
– ORIGIN C17: from French *signalé*, from Italian *segnalato* 'distinguished', from *segnale* 'a signal'.

signal box ■ n. a building beside a railway track from which signals, points, and other equipment are controlled.

signalize (also **-ise**) ■ v. **1** mark or indicate. **2** provide (an intersection) with traffic signals.

signalman ■ n. (pl. **-men**) **1** a railway worker responsible for operating signals and points. **2** a person responsible for sending and receiving naval or military signals.

signal-to-noise ratio ■ n. the ratio of the strength of an electrical or other signal carrying information to that of unwanted interference, generally expressed in decibels.

signatory /ˈsɪɡnət(ə)ri/ ■ n. (pl. **-ies**) a party that has signed an agreement.
– ORIGIN C19: from Latin *signatorius* 'of sealing', from *signare* (see SIGNATURE).

signature ■ n. **1** a person's name written in a distinctive way as a form of identification or authorization. **2** the action of applying one's signature. **3** a distinctive product or characteristic by which someone or something can be identified. **4** Music short for KEY SIGNATURE or TIME SIGNATURE. **5** Printing a letter or figure printed at the foot of one or more pages of each sheet of a book as a guide in binding. **6** a printed sheet after being folded to form a group of pages.
– ORIGIN C16: from medieval Latin *signatura* 'sign manual', from Latin *signare* 'to sign, mark'.

signature on delivery ■ n. South African term for RECORDED DELIVERY.

signature tune ■ n. a distinctive piece of music associated with a particular programme or performer on television or radio.

signboard ■ n. **1** a board displaying the name or logo of a business or product. **2** a board displaying a sign to direct traffic or travellers.

signee ■ n. a person who has signed a contract or other official document.

signet ■ n. historical a small seal, especially one set in a ring, used instead of or with a signature to give authentication to an official document.
– ORIGIN Middle English: from Old French, or from medieval Latin *signetum*, diminutive of *signum* 'token, seal'.

signet ring ■ n. a ring with a seal set into it.

significance ■ n. **1** the quality of being significant; importance. **2** the unstated meaning to be found in words or events. **3** (also **statistical significance**) the extent to which a result deviates from that expected to arise simply from random variation or errors in sampling.
– ORIGIN Middle English: from Old French, or from Latin *significantia*, from *significare* 'indicate, portend'.

significant ■ adj. **1** having an unstated meaning; indicative of something. **2** extensive or important enough to merit attention. **3** Statistics of, relating to, or having significance.
– DERIVATIVES **significantly** adv.

significant figure ■ n. Mathematics each of the digits of a number that are used to express it to the required degree of accuracy, starting from the first non-zero digit.

signified ■ n. Linguistics the meaning or idea expressed by a sign, as distinct from the physical form in which it is expressed.

signifier ■ n. Linguistics a sign's physical form (such as a sound, printed word, or image) as distinct from its meaning.

signify ■ v. (**-ies**, **-ied**) **1** be an indication of. **2** be a symbol of; have as meaning. **3** (of a person) indicate or declare (a feeling or intention). **4** [with neg.] be of importance.
– DERIVATIVES **signification** n.
– ORIGIN Middle English: from Old French *signifier*, from Latin *significare* 'indicate, portend', from *signum* 'token'.

signing ■ n. **1** a person who has recently been signed to join a sports team, record company, etc. **2** an event at which an author signs copies of their book to gain publicity and sales. **3** sign language. **4** the provision of signs in a street.

sign language ■ n. a system of communication used among and with deaf people, consisting of facial and manual gestures and signs.

signor /ˈsiːnjɔː, siːˈnjɔː/ (also **signore**) ■ n. (pl. **signori**

/-'njɔːriː/) a title or form of address used of or to an Italian-speaking man, corresponding to *Mr* or *sir*.
– ORIGIN Italian, from Latin *senior* (see SENIOR).

signora /siːˈnjɔːrə/ ■ n. a title or form of address used of or to an Italian-speaking married woman, corresponding to *Mrs* or *madam*.
– ORIGIN Italian, feminine of *signor* (see SIGNOR).

signorina /ˌsiːnjəˈriːnə/ ■ n. a title or form of address used of or to an Italian-speaking unmarried woman, corresponding to *Miss*.
– ORIGIN Italian, diminutive of *signora* (see SIGNORA).

signpost ■ n. a sign on a post, giving information such as the direction and distance to a nearby town. ■ v. 1 provide (an area) with a signpost or signposts. 2 indicate (a place or feature) with a signpost.

signwriter ■ n. a person who paints commercial signs and advertisements.
– DERIVATIVES **signwriting** n.

sika /ˈsiːkə/ (also **sika deer**) ■ n. a forest-dwelling deer with a greyish winter coat that turns yellowish-brown with white spots in summer, native to eastern Asia and naturalized in parts of Europe. [*Cervus nippon*.]
– ORIGIN C19: from Japanese *shika*.

Sikh /siːk/ ■ n. an adherent of Sikhism. ■ adj. of or relating to Sikhs or Sikhism.
– ORIGIN from Punjabi 'disciple', from Sanskrit *śiṣya*.

Sikhism /ˈsiːkɪz(ə)m, ˈsɪk-/ ■ n. a monotheistic religion founded in Punjab in the 15th century by Guru Nanak.

silage /ˈsaɪlɪdʒ/ ■ n. grass or other green fodder that is compacted and stored in airtight conditions, without first being dried, and used as animal feed in the winter.
– ORIGIN C19: alteration of *ensilage*, influenced by SILO.

silane /ˈsaɪleɪn/ ■ n. Chemistry a spontaneously flammable gaseous compound of silicon and hydrogen. [SiH$_4$.] ▶ any of the series of silicon hydrides analogous to the alkanes.
– ORIGIN C20: from SILICON.

silence ■ n. 1 complete absence of sound. 2 the fact or state of abstaining from speech. 3 the avoidance of mentioning or discussing something. ■ v. 1 make silent. 2 fit with a silencer.
– DERIVATIVES **silenced** adj.
– ORIGIN Middle English: from Latin *silentium*, from *silere* 'be silent'.

silencer ■ n. a device for reducing the noise emitted by a mechanism, especially a gun or exhaust system.

silent ■ adj. 1 not making or accompanied by any sound. ▶ (of a film) without an accompanying soundtrack. 2 not speaking or not spoken aloud. ▶ not prone to speak much. 3 (of a letter) written but not pronounced, e.g. *b* in *doubt*. 4 saying or recording nothing on a particular subject.
– DERIVATIVES **silently** adv.

silent partner ■ n. another term for SLEEPING PARTNER.

Silesian /saɪˈliːziən, -ˈliːʒən/ ■ n. a native or inhabitant of Silesia, a region of central Europe. ■ adj. of or relating to Silesia.

silex /ˈsaɪlɛks/ ■ n. silica, especially quartz or flint.
– ORIGIN C16: from Latin, 'flint'.

silhouette /ˌsɪluˈɛt/ ■ n. 1 the dark shape and outline of someone or something visible in restricted light against a brighter background. 2 a representation of someone or something showing the shape and outline only, typically coloured in solid black. ■ v. cast or show as a silhouette.
– ORIGIN C18: named after the French author and politician Étienne de *Silhouette*.

silica /ˈsɪlɪkə/ ■ n. silicon dioxide, a hard, unreactive, colourless compound which occurs as quartz and as the principal constituent of sandstone and other rocks. [SiO$_2$.]
– DERIVATIVES **siliceous** /sɪˈlɪʃəs/ (also **silicious**) adj.
– ORIGIN C19: from Latin *silex, silic-* 'flint'.

silica gel ■ n. hydrated silica in a hard granular hygroscopic form used as a desiccant.

silicate /ˈsɪlɪkeɪt, -kət/ ■ n. 1 Chemistry a salt in which the anion contains both silicon and oxygen. 2 a mineral consisting of silica combined with metal oxides, as a common constituent of rocks.

silicic /sɪˈlɪsɪk/ ■ adj. Geology (of rocks) rich in silica.

silicic acid ■ n. Chemistry a hydrated form of silica made by acidifying solutions of silicates.

silicide /ˈsɪlɪsaɪd/ ■ n. Chemistry a compound of silicon with a metal or other element.

silicify /sɪˈlɪsɪfaɪ/ ■ v. (**-ies, -ied**) convert into or impregnate with silica.
– DERIVATIVES **silicification** n. **silicified** adj.

silicon /ˈsɪlɪk(ə)n/ ■ n. the chemical element of atomic number 14, a shiny grey crystalline non-metal used in semi-conducting properties, used in making electronic circuits. (Symbol: **Si**)
– ORIGIN C19: alteration of earlier *silicium*, from Latin *silex, silic-* 'flint'.

silicon carbide ■ n. a hard refractory compound of silicon and carbon; carborundum. [SiC.]

silicon chip ■ n. a microchip.

silicone /ˈsɪlɪkəʊn/ ■ n. a durable synthetic resin with a structure based on chains of silicon and oxygen atoms with organic side chains. ■ v. treat with a silicone.
– DERIVATIVES **siliconize** (also **-ise**) v. **siliconized** (also **-ised**) adj.

silicosis /ˌsɪlɪˈkəʊsɪs/ ■ n. Medicine lung fibrosis caused by the inhalation of dust containing silica.
– DERIVATIVES **silicotic** adj.

silk ■ n. 1 a fine, strong, soft lustrous fibre produced by silkworms in making cocoons. 2 thread or fabric made from this fibre. 3 (**silks**) garments made from silk, especially as worn by a jockey in the colours of a particular horse owner. 4 (**silks**) the silky styles of the female maize flower.
– PHRASES **take silk** (in South Africa) become a senior counsel or (in the UK) become a Queen's (or King's) Counsel.
– DERIVATIVES **silken** adj.
– ORIGIN Old English *sioloc, seolec*, from Latin *sericus*, from Greek *Sēres*, the name given to the inhabitants of the Far Eastern countries from which silk first came overland to Europe.

silk-cotton tree ■ n. a tree which produces kapok. [*Bombax ceiba* (India) and *Ceiba pentandra* (the ceiba, tropical America).]

silk hat ■ n. a man's tall, cylindrical hat covered with black silk plush.

silkie ■ n. (pl. **-ies**) 1 a small chicken of a breed characterized by long soft plumage. 2 variant spelling of SELKIE.

silk moth ■ n. a large moth with a caterpillar that produces silk. [*Bombyx mori* (Asia) and other species.]

silk screen ■ n. a screen of fine mesh used in screen printing. ■ v. (**silk-screen**) print, decorate, or reproduce using a silk screen.

silkworm ■ n. a caterpillar of a domesticated silk moth, which spins a silk cocoon that is processed to yield silk fibre.

silky ■ adj. (**-ier, -iest**) 1 of or resembling silk. 2 suave and smooth: *a silky, seductive voice*.
– DERIVATIVES **silkily** adv. **silkiness** n.

sill ■ n. 1 (also **cill**) Building a shelf or slab of stone, wood, or metal at the foot of a window or doorway. 2 a strong horizontal member at the base of any structure, e.g. in the frame of a motor or rail vehicle. 3 Geology a tabular sheet of igneous rock intruded between and parallel with the existing strata. Compare with DYKE^1. 4 an underwater ridge or rock ledge extending across the bed of a body of water.
– ORIGIN Old English *syll, sylle* 'horizontal beam forming a foundation', of Germanic origin.

sillimanite /ˈsɪlɪmənaɪt/ ■ n. an aluminosilicate mineral typically occurring as fibrous masses, commonly in schist or gneiss.
– ORIGIN C19: from the name of the American chemist Benjamin *Silliman*.

silly ■ adj. (**-ier, -iest**) 1 lacking in common sense or judgement; foolish. 2 trivial or frivolous. 3 archaic weak-minded. 4 archaic helpless; defenceless. 5 Cricket denoting fielding positions very close to the batsman: *silly mid-on*. ■ n. (pl. **-ies**) informal a silly person.
– PHRASES **the silly season** high summer, regarded as a

silly billy

time of frivolous behaviour and the season when newspapers often publish trivial material because of a lack of important news.
– DERIVATIVES **sillily** adv. **silliness** n.

HISTORY
Silly entered English (spelled *seely*) in the 13th century from a Germanic source, in the senses 'happy, blissful' and 'lucky, auspicious'. From this the senses 'spiritually blessed' and 'pious and holy' arose. A subtle development in meaning from 'innocent, harmless' (often referring to animals) to 'deserving of pity' led to 'feeble' and then, from the early 16th century, 'foolish, simple'. The spelling **silly** is recorded from the 15th century.

silly billy ■ n. informal a foolish person.
silo /'saɪləʊ/ ■ n. (pl. **-os**) **1** a tall tower or pit on a farm, used to store grain. **2** a pit or other airtight structure in which green crops are compressed and stored as silage. **3** an underground chamber in which a guided missile is kept ready for firing.
– ORIGIN C19: from Spanish, from Greek *siros* 'corn pit'.

silt ■ n. **1** fine sand, clay, or other material carried by running water and deposited as a sediment. **2** technical sediment whose particles are between clay and sand in size (typically 0.002–0.06 mm). ■ v. fill or block or become filled or blocked with silt.
– DERIVATIVES **siltation** n. **silting** n. **silty** adj.
– ORIGIN Middle English: prob. orig. denoting a salty deposit and of Scandinavian origin.

siltstone ■ n. fine-grained sedimentary rock consisting of consolidated silt.

Silurian /sʌɪ'ljʊərɪən, sɪ-/ ■ adj. Geology relating to or denoting the third period of the Palaeozoic era (between the Ordovician and Devonian periods, about 439 to 409 million years ago), a time when land plants and the first true fish appeared.
– ORIGIN C18: from *Silures*, the Latin name of a people of ancient SE Wales.

silvan ■ adj. variant spelling of SYLVAN.

silver ■ n. **1** a precious shiny greyish-white metal, the chemical element of atomic number 47. (Symbol: **Ag**) **2** a shiny grey-white colour or appearance like that of silver. **3** silver dishes, containers, or cutlery. ▶ household cutlery of any material. **4** coins made from silver or from a metal that resembles silver. ■ v. **1** coat or plate with silver. **2** provide (mirror glass) with a backing of a silver-coloured material in order to make it reflective. **3** poetic/literary (especially of the moon) give a silvery appearance to. **4** (with reference to hair) turn or cause to turn grey or white.
– PHRASES **be born with a silver spoon in one's mouth** be born into a wealthy family of high social standing. **the silver screen** the cinema industry.
– DERIVATIVES **silvered** adj. **silveriness** n. **silvering** n. **silverware** n. **silvery** adj.
– ORIGIN Old English *seolfor*, of Germanic origin.

silver age ■ n. a period regarded as notable but inferior to a golden age.

silverback ■ n. a mature male mountain gorilla, which is distinguished by an area of white or silvery hair across the back and is the dominant member of its social group.

silver birch ■ n. a Eurasian birch with silver-grey bark. [*Betula pendula*.]

silver bullet ■ n. a simple and seemingly magical solution to a complex problem.
– ORIGIN from the belief that a silver bullet was the only weapon that could kill a werewolf.

silverfish ■ n. (pl. same or **-fishes**) a silvery bristletail that lives in buildings, chiefly nocturnal and feeding on starchy materials. [*Ctenolepisma longicaudata* and *Lepisma saccharina*.]

silver fox ■ n. a red fox of a North American variety which has black fur with white tips.

silver gilt ■ n. gilded silver.

silver jubilee ■ n. the twenty-fifth anniversary of a significant event.

silver medal ■ n. a medal made of or coloured silver, customarily awarded for second place in a race or competition.

silver plate ■ n. **1** a thin layer of silver electroplated or otherwise applied as a coating to another metal. **2** plates, dishes, etc. made of or plated with silver. ■ v. (**silver-plate**) cover with a thin layer of silver.

silver service ■ n. a style of serving food at formal meals in which the server uses a silver spoon and fork in one hand to place food on the diner's plate.

silverside ■ n. **1** the upper side of a round of beef from the outside of the leg. **2** (also **silversides**) a small, slender, chiefly marine fish with a bright silver line along its sides. [Family Atherinidae: numerous species.]

silversmith ■ n. a person who makes silver articles.
– DERIVATIVES **silversmithing** n.

silver tongue ■ n. a tendency to be eloquent and persuasive in speaking.
– DERIVATIVES **silver-tongued** adj.

silver tree ■ n. a South African tree which has light silvery-green leaves covered with fine down. [*Leucadendron argenteum*.]

silver wedding ■ n. the twenty-fifth anniversary of a wedding.

silviculture /'sɪlvɪˌkʌltʃə/ ■ n. the growing and cultivation of trees.
– DERIVATIVES **silvicultural** adj. **silviculturist** n.
– ORIGIN C19: from French *sylviculture*, from Latin *silva* 'wood' + French *culture* 'cultivation'.

sim ■ n. informal a video game that simulates an activity such as flying an aircraft or playing a sport.
– ORIGIN C20: abbrev. of *simulation* (see SIMULATE).

simazine /'sɪməziːn, 'sʌɪ-/ ■ n. a synthetic herbicide derived from triazine.
– ORIGIN 1950s: blend of SYMMETRICAL and TRIAZINE.

simian /'sɪmɪən/ ■ adj. of, relating to, or resembling apes or monkeys. ■ n. an ape or monkey.
– ORIGIN C17: from Latin *simia* 'ape', perhaps from Greek *simos* 'flat-nosed'.

similar ■ adj. **1** of the same kind in appearance, character, or quantity, without being identical. **2** Geometry (of geometrical figures) having the same angles and proportions, though of different sizes. ■ n. **1** chiefly archaic a person or thing similar to another. **2** a substance that produces effects resembling the symptoms of a disease (the basis of homeopathic treatment).
– DERIVATIVES **similarity** n. **similarly** adv.
– ORIGIN C16: from French *similaire* or medieval Latin *similaris*, from Latin *similis* 'like'.

simile /'sɪmɪli/ ■ n. a figure of speech involving the comparison of one thing with another thing of a different kind (e.g. *as solid as a rock*).
– ORIGIN Middle English: from Latin, from *similis* 'like'.

similitude /sɪ'mɪlɪtjuːd/ ■ n. the quality or state of being similar.
– ORIGIN Middle English: from Latin *similitudo*, from *similis* 'like'.

SIMM ■ abbrev. Computing single in-line memory module.

Simmental /'sɪm(ə)ntɑːl/ ■ n. an animal of a red and white breed of cattle farmed for both meat and milk.
– ORIGIN 1950s: named after a valley in central Switzerland.

simmer ■ v. **1** stay or cause to stay just below boiling point while bubbling gently. **2** be in a state of suppressed anger or excitement. ▶ (**simmer down**) become calmer and quieter. ■ n. a state or temperature just below boiling point.
– ORIGIN C17: alteration of dialect *simper* (in the same sense).

simnel cake /'sɪmn(ə)l/ ■ n. chiefly Brit. a rich fruit cake covered with marzipan, eaten especially at Easter or during Lent.
– ORIGIN C17: *simnel* from Old French *simenel*, from Latin *simila* or Greek *semidalis* 'fine flour'.

simony /'sʌɪməni, 'sɪm-/ ■ n. chiefly historical the buying or selling of pardons, benefices, and other ecclesiastical privileges.
– DERIVATIVES **simoniac** /-'məʊnɪak/ adj. & n. **simoniacal** /-'nʌɪək(ə)l/ adj.

sinfonietta

simpatico /sɪmˈpatɪkəʊ/ ■ adj. **1** likeable and easy to get on with. **2** similar in attributes or interests; compatible.
– ORIGIN from Italian and Spanish.

simper ■ v. smile in an affectedly coquettish, coy, or ingratiating manner. ■ n. such a smile.
– DERIVATIVES **simpering** adj. **simperingly** adv.
– ORIGIN C16: cf. German *zimpfer* 'elegant, delicate'.

simple ■ adj. (-er, -est) **1** easily understood or done. **2** plain and uncomplicated in form, nature, or design. ▸ humble and unpretentious. **3** composed of a single element; not compound. ▸ Botany (of a leaf or stem) not divided or branched. ▸ (of a lens, microscope, etc.) consisting of a single lens or component. **4** of very low intelligence. **5** (in English grammar) denoting a tense formed without an auxiliary. **6** (of interest) payable on the sum loaned only. Compare with COMPOUND[1]. ■ n. chiefly historical a medicinal herb, or a medicine made from one.
– DERIVATIVES **simpleness** n.
– ORIGIN Middle English: from Latin *simplus*.

simple eye ■ n. a small eye of an insect or other arthropod which has only one lens, typically present in one or more pairs. Contrasted with COMPOUND EYE.

simple fracture ■ n. a fracture of the bone only, without damage to the surrounding tissues or breaking of the skin.

simple harmonic motion ■ n. Physics oscillatory motion under a retarding force proportional to the amount of displacement from an equilibrium position.

simple-minded ■ adj. having or showing very little intelligence or judgement.
– DERIVATIVES **simple-mindedly** adv. **simple-mindedness** n.

simple sentence ■ n. a sentence consisting of only one clause, with a single subject and predicate.

Simple Simon ■ n. a foolish or gullible person.
– ORIGIN prob. from the name of a character in various nursery rhymes.

simple time ■ n. Music musical rhythm or metre in which each beat in a bar may be subdivided simply into halves or quarters. Compare with COMPOUND TIME.

simpleton ■ n. a foolish or gullible person.
– ORIGIN C17: from SIMPLE, on the pattern of surnames derived from place names ending in *-ton*.

simplex ■ adj. technical **1** composed of or characterized by a single part or structure. **2** (of a communication system, computer circuit, etc.) only allowing transmission of signals in one direction at a time. ■ n. **1** a simple or uncompounded word. **2** S. African a single-storey unit in a housing complex.
– ORIGIN C16: from Latin, 'single', var. of *simplus* 'simple'.

simpliciter /sɪmˈplɪsɪtə/ ■ adv. chiefly Law simply; unconditionally.
– ORIGIN Latin, 'simply'.

simplicity ■ n. **1** the quality or condition of being simple. **2** a thing that is simple.
– ORIGIN Middle English: from Old French *simplicite* or Latin *simplicitas*, from *simplex* (see SIMPLEX).

simplify ■ v. (-ies, -ied) make more simple.
– DERIVATIVES **simplification** n.

simplistic ■ adj. treating complex issues and problems as simpler they really are.
– DERIVATIVES **simplistically** adv.

simply ■ adv. **1** in a simple manner. **2** merely; just. **3** absolutely; completely (used for emphasis).

simulacrum /ˌsɪmjʊˈleɪkrəm/ ■ n. (pl. **simulacra** /-krə/ or **simulacrums**) **1** an image or representation of someone or something. **2** an unsatisfactory imitation or substitute.
– ORIGIN C16: from Latin, from *simulare* (see SIMULATE).

simulate /ˈsɪmjʊleɪt/ ■ v. imitate or reproduce the appearance, character, or conditions of.
– DERIVATIVES **simulant** n. **simulation** n. **simulative** adj.
– ORIGIN C17 (*simulation* Middle English): from Latin *simulare* 'copy, represent'.

simulator ■ n. a machine that simulates the controls and conditions of a real vehicle, process, etc., used for training or testing.

simulcast /ˈsɪm(ə)lkɑːst/ ■ n. **1** a simultaneous transmission of the same programme on radio and television, or on two or more channels. **2** N. Amer. a live transmission of a public celebration or sports event. ■ v. broadcast (such a transmission).
– ORIGIN 1940s: blend of SIMULTANEOUS and BROADCAST.

simultaneous /ˌsɪm(ə)lˈteɪnɪəs/ ■ adj. occurring, operating, or done at the same time.
– DERIVATIVES **simultaneity** /-təˈnɪːɪti, -təˈneɪɪti/ n. **simultaneously** adv. **simultaneousness** n.
– ORIGIN C17: from Latin *simul* 'at the same time', prob. influenced by late Latin *momentaneus*.

simultaneous equations ■ pl. n. equations involving two or more unknowns that are to have the same values in each equation.

sin[1] /sɪn/ ■ n. **1** an immoral act considered to be a transgression against divine law. **2** an act regarded as a serious offence. ■ v. (**sinned**, **sinning**) commit a sin. ▸ (**sin against**) cause offence or harm to.
– PHRASES **for one's sins** humorous, chiefly Brit. as a punishment. **live in sin** often humorous (of an unmarried couple) live together.
– DERIVATIVES **sinful** adj. **sinfully** adv. **sinfulness** n. **sinless** adj. **sinlessly** adv. **sinlessness** n.
– ORIGIN Old English *synn* (n.), *syngian* (v.); prob. rel. to Latin *sons* 'guilty'.

sin[2] /sɪn/ ■ abbrev. sine.

sin bin informal ■ n. (in sport, especially ice hockey) a box or bench to which offending players can be sent as a penalty during a game. ■ v. (**sin-bin**) send (a player) to a sin bin.

since ■ prep. in the intervening period between (the time mentioned) and the time under consideration. ■ conj. **1** during or in the time after. **2** for the reason that; because. ■ adv. **1** from the time mentioned until the present or the time under consideration. **2** ago.
– ORIGIN Middle English: contraction of obsolete *sithence*, or from dialect *sin*, both from *sithen* 'thereupon, afterwards, ever since'.

sincere ■ adj. (-er, -est) proceeding from or characterized by genuine feelings; free from pretence or deceit.
– DERIVATIVES **sincerely** adv. **sincereness** n. **sincerity** n.
– ORIGIN C16: from Latin *sincerus* 'clean, pure'.

Sindebele /sɪnˈdeɪbəli, ˌsɪndəˈbeɪli/ ■ n. (especially in Zimbabwe) another term for ISINDEBELE.

sine /saɪn/ ■ n. Mathematics the trigonometric function that is equal to the ratio of the side opposite a given angle in a right-angled triangle) to the hypotenuse.
– ORIGIN C16: from Latin *sinus* 'curve', used in medieval Latin as a translation of Arabic *jayb* 'pocket, sine'.

sinecure /ˈsaɪnɪkjʊə, ˈsɪn-/ ■ n. a position requiring little or no work but giving the holder status or financial benefit.
– DERIVATIVES **sinecurism** n. **sinecurist** n.
– ORIGIN C17: from Latin *sine cura* 'without care'.

sine curve (also **sine wave**) ■ n. a curve representing periodic oscillations of constant amplitude as given by a sine function.

sine die /ˌsiːneɪ ˈdiːeɪ, ˌsaɪnɪ ˈdʌɪiː/ ■ adv. (with reference to an adjournment) with no appointed date for resumption.
– ORIGIN Latin, 'without a day'.

sine qua non /ˌkweɪ ˈnɒn, ˌkwɑː ˈnəʊn/ ■ n. a thing that is absolutely essential.
– ORIGIN Latin, '(cause) without which not'.

sinew ■ n. **1** a piece of tough fibrous tissue uniting muscle to bone; a tendon or ligament. **2** (**sinews**) the parts of a structure or system that give it strength or bind it together.
– DERIVATIVES **sinewed** adj. **sinewy** adj.
– ORIGIN Old English *sin(e)we* 'tendon', of Germanic origin.

sinfonia /sɪnˈfəʊnɪə, ˌsɪnfəˈniːə/ ■ n. Music **1** a symphony. ▸ (in baroque music) an orchestral piece used as an introduction to an opera, cantata, or suite. **2** a small symphony orchestra.
– ORIGIN from Italian.

sinfonietta /ˌsɪnfəʊnɪˈɛtə/ ■ n. Music **1** a short or simple symphony. **2** a small symphony orchestra.
– ORIGIN Italian, diminutive of *sinfonia* (see SINFONIA).

sing

sing ▪ v. (past **sang**; past part. **sung**) **1** make musical sounds with the voice, especially words with a set tune. ▸ perform (a song) in this way. ▸ (**sing along**) sing in accompaniment to a song or piece of music. **2** (of a bird) make characteristic melodious whistling and twittering sounds. **3** make a high-pitched sound. **4** informal act as an informer to the police. **5** recount or celebrate, especially in poetry: *sing someone's praises*. ▪ n. informal an act or spell of singing.
– DERIVATIVES **singable** adj. **singer** n. **singing** n. & adj.
– ORIGIN Old English *singan* (v.), of Germanic origin.

sing. ▪ abbrev. singular.

singalong ▪ n. an informal occasion when people sing together in a group.

Singaporean /ˌsɪŋəˈpɔːrɪən/ ▪ n. a native or inhabitant of Singapore. ▪ adj. of or relating to Singapore.

singe ▪ v. (**singeing**) **1** burn or be burnt lightly or superficially. **2** burn the bristles or down off (the carcass of a pig or fowl) to prepare it for cooking. ▪ n. a light or superficial burn.
– ORIGIN Old English, of West Germanic origin.

Singhalese /ˌsɪŋɡəˈliːz/ ▪ n. & adj. variant spelling of SINHALESE.

single ▪ adj. **1** only one; not one of several. ▸ regarded as distinct from others in a group. ▸ [with neg.] even one (used for emphasis): *they didn't receive a single reply*. ▸ designed or suitable for one person. **2** not involved in a stable romantic or sexual relationship. **3** consisting of one part. ▸ (of a flower) having only one whorl of petals. **4** (of a ticket) valid for an outward journey only. **5** archaic free from duplicity or deceit: *a pure and single heart*. ▪ n. **1** a single person or thing. **2** a short record with one song on each side. **3** Cricket a hit for one run. ▸ Baseball a hit which allows the batter to proceed safely to first base. **4** (**singles**) (especially in tennis and badminton) a game or competition for individual players. ▪ v. **1** (**single someone/thing out**) choose someone or something from a group for special treatment. **2** thin out (seedlings or saplings). **3** reduce (a railway track) to a single line. **4** Baseball hit a single. ▸ cause (a run) to be scored by hitting a single. ▸ advance (a runner) by hitting a single.
– DERIVATIVES **singleness** n. **singly** adv.
– ORIGIN Middle English: from Latin *singulus*, rel. to *simplus* 'simple'.

single-action ▪ adj. (of a gun) needing to be cocked by hand before it can be fired.

single-blind ▪ adj. denoting a test or experiment in which information that may bias the results is concealed from either tester or subject.

single bond ▪ n. a chemical bond in which one pair of electrons is shared between two atoms.

single-breasted ▪ adj. (of a jacket or coat) fastened by one row of buttons at the centre of the front.

single-cell protein ▪ n. protein derived from a culture of single-celled organisms, used especially as a food supplement.

single combat ▪ n. fighting between two people.

single cream ▪ n. thin cream with a relatively low fat content.

single-decker ▪ n. chiefly Brit. a bus having only one floor or level.

single-ended ▪ adj. (of an electronic device) designed for use with unbalanced signals and therefore having one input and one output terminal connected to earth.

single file ▪ n. a line of people or things arranged one behind another. ▪ adv. one behind another.

single-handed ▪ adv. & adj. **1** done without help from others. **2** done or designed to be used with one hand.
– DERIVATIVES **single-handedly** adv. **single-hander** n.

single-lens reflex ▪ adj. denoting a reflex camera in which the lens that forms the image on the film also provides the image in the viewfinder.

single malt ▪ n. whisky that has not been blended with any other malt.

single market ▪ n. an association of countries trading with each other without restrictions or tariffs.

single-minded ▪ adj. concentrating purposefully on one particular thing.
– DERIVATIVES **single-mindedly** adv. **single-mindedness** n.

single parent ▪ n. a person bringing up a child or children without a partner.

single-source ▪ v. give a franchise to a single supplier for (a particular product).

singlet ▪ n. **1** chiefly Brit. a vest or similar sleeveless garment. **2** Physics a single line in a spectrum, not part of a multiplet. **3** Physics a state or energy level with zero spin, giving a single value for a particular quantum number.
– ORIGIN C18 (orig. denoting a man's short jacket): from SINGLE (because the garment was unlined), on the pattern of *doublet*.

singleton ▪ n. **1** a single person or thing of the kind under consideration. ▸ a child or animal born singly, rather than one of a multiple birth. ▸ (in card games, especially bridge) a card that is the only one of its suit in a hand. **2** informal a person who is not in a long-term relationship. **3** Mathematics a set which contains exactly one element.
– ORIGIN C19: from SINGLE, on the pattern of *simpleton*.

single transferable vote ▪ n. an electoral system of proportional representation in which a person's vote can be transferred to a second or further choice of candidate.

single-vision ▪ adj. denoting glasses of which each lens is a single optical element; not bifocal.

sing-song ▪ adj. (of a person's voice) having a repeated rising and falling rhythm. ▪ n. informal an informal gathering for singing.

singular ▪ adj. **1** exceptionally good or great; remarkable. ▸ strange or eccentric in some respect. **2** single; unique. ▸ Grammar (of a word or form) denoting or referring to just one person or thing. **3** Physics relating to or of the nature of a singularity. ▪ n. Grammar the singular form of a word.
– DERIVATIVES **singularly** adv.
– ORIGIN Middle English: from Latin *singularis*, from *singulus* (see SINGLE).

singularity ▪ n. (pl. **-ies**) **1** the state, fact, or quality of being singular. **2** Physics & Mathematics a point at which a function takes an infinite value, especially a point of infinite density at the centre of a black hole.

singularize (also **-ise**) ▪ v. **1** make distinct or conspicuous. **2** give a singular form to (a word).
– DERIVATIVES **singularization** (also **-isation**) n.

Sinhalese /ˌsɪnhəˈliːz, ˌsɪnə-/ (also **Singhalese**, **Sinhala** /sɪnˈhɑːlə/) ▪ n. (pl. same) **1** a member of an Indian people now forming the majority of the population of Sri Lanka. **2** an Indic language spoken by this people, descended from Sanskrit. ▪ adj. of or relating to the Sinhalese or their language.
– ORIGIN from Sanskrit *Siṅhala* 'Sri Lanka'.

sinister ▪ adj. **1** suggestive of evil or harm. **2** archaic & Heraldry on or towards the left-hand side (in a coat of arms, from the bearer's point of view, i.e. the right as it is depicted). The opposite of DEXTER1.
– DERIVATIVES **sinisterly** adv. **sinisterness** n.
– ORIGIN Middle English: from Old French *sinistre* or Latin *sinister* 'left'.

sinistral /ˈsɪnɪstr(ə)l/ ▪ adj. **1** of or on the left side or the left hand. The opposite of DEXTRAL. ▸ left-handed. **2** Geology relating to or denoting a strike-slip fault in which the motion of the block on the further side of the fault is towards the left.
– DERIVATIVES **sinistrality** n. **sinistrally** adv.

Sinitic /sɪˈnɪtɪk/ ▪ adj. relating to or denoting the division of the Sino-Tibetan language family that includes the many forms of Chinese.
– ORIGIN from Greek *Sinai* 'the Chinese', from Arabic *ṣīn*, denoting the Chinese empire.

sink[1] ▪ v. (past **sank**; past part. **sunk**) **1** go down below the surface of liquid; become submerged. ▸ (with reference to a ship) go or cause to go to the bottom of the sea. **2** disappear and not be seen or heard of again. ▸ conceal or ignore: *they agreed to sink their differences*. ▸ cause to fail. **3** drop downwards. ▸ lower oneself or drop down gently. ▸ pocket (a ball) in snooker or billiards. ▸ Golf hit the ball into the hole with (a putt or other shot). **4** (**sink in**)

CONSONANTS **b** but **d** dog **f** few **g** get **h** he **j** yes **k** cat **l** leg **m** man **n** no **p** pen **r** red

(of words or facts) become fully understood. **5** insert beneath a surface. ▸ (**sink something into**) cause something sharp to penetrate (a surface). ▸ excavate (a well) or bore (a shaft) vertically downwards. **6** gradually decrease or decline in amount or intensity. **7** lapse or fall into a particular state or condition. **8** (**sink something in/into**) put money or energy into.
– PHRASES **a** (or **that**) **sinking feeling** an unpleasant bodily sensation caused by apprehension or dismay. **sink or swim** fail or succeed by one's own efforts.
– DERIVATIVES **sinkable** adj. **sinkage** n.
– ORIGIN Old English *sincan*, of Germanic origin.

sink² ■ n. **1** a fixed basin with a water supply and outflow pipe. **2** short for SINKHOLE. **3** a pool or marsh in which a river's water disappears by evaporation or percolation. **4** technical a body or process which absorbs or removes energy or a particular component from a system. The opposite of SOURCE.
– ORIGIN Middle English: from SINK¹.

sinker ■ n. **1** a weight used to sink a fishing line or sounding line. **2** (also **sinker ball**) Baseball a pitch which drops markedly as it nears home plate.

sinkhole ■ n. **1** a cavity in the ground, especially in a limestone formation, caused by water erosion and providing a route for surface water to disappear underground. **2** a deep cavity in the ground, caused by subsidence resulting from underground mining.

sinking fund ■ n. a fund formed by periodically setting aside money for the gradual repayment of a debt or replacement of a wasting asset.

sinner ■ n. a person who sins.

sinnet /'sɪnɪt/ ■ n. Nautical braided cords and ropes in flat, round, or square form.
– ORIGIN C17.

Sino- /'saɪnəʊ/ ■ comb. form Chinese; Chinese and ...: *Sino-American*. ▸ relating to China.
– ORIGIN from Greek *Sinai* (see SINITIC).

sino-atrial node /ˌsaɪnəʊˈeɪtrɪəl/ ■ n. Anatomy a small body of specialized muscle tissue in the wall of the heart that acts as a pacemaker.
– ORIGIN C20: from SINUS + *atrial* (see ATRIUM).

sinology /saɪˈnɒlədʒi, sɪ-/ ■ n. the study of Chinese language, history, and culture.
– DERIVATIVES **sinological** adj. **sinologist** n.

Sino-Tibetan ■ adj. relating to or denoting a large language family of eastern Asia which includes Chinese, Burmese, Tibetan, and (in some classifications) Thai. ■ n. this language family.

sinter /'sɪntə/ ■ n. **1** Geology a hard siliceous or calcareous deposit precipitated from mineral springs. **2** solid material which has been sintered. ■ v. coalesce or cause to coalesce from powder into solid by heating (and usually also by compression).
– ORIGIN C18: from German *Sinter*.

sinuous /'sɪnjʊəs/ ■ adj. **1** having many curves and turns. **2** lithe and supple.
– DERIVATIVES **sinuosity** n. **sinuously** adv. **sinuousness** n.
– ORIGIN C16: from French *sinueux* or Latin *sinuosus*, from *sinus* 'a bend'.

sinus /'saɪnəs/ ■ n. **1** Anatomy & Zoology a cavity within a bone or other tissue, especially one in the bones of the face or skull connecting with the nasal cavities. **2** Anatomy & Zoology an irregular venous or lymphatic cavity, reservoir, or dilated vessel. **3** Medicine an infected tract leading from a deep-seated infection and discharging pus to the surface. **4** [as modifier] Physiology relating to the sino-atrial node of the heart: *sinus rhythm*.
– DERIVATIVES **sinusitis** n.
– ORIGIN Middle English: from Latin, 'a recess, bend'.

sinusoid /'saɪnəsɔɪd/ ■ n. **1** another term for SINE CURVE. **2** Anatomy a small irregularly shaped blood vessel found in certain organs, especially the liver.
– DERIVATIVES **sinusoidal** adj. **sinusoidally** adv.

Sion /'saɪən/ ■ n. variant spelling of ZION.

Siouan /'suːən/ ■ n. a family of North American Indian languages spoken by the Sioux and related people, including Dakota and Crow. ■ adj. relating to or denoting this language family.

Sioux /suː/ ■ n. (pl. same) another term for the Dakota people of North America or their language.
– ORIGIN N. American French, from *Nadouessioux* from Ojibwa *nātowēssiwak*.

sip ■ v. (**sipped**, **sipping**) drink (something) by taking small mouthfuls. ■ n. a small mouthful of liquid.
– DERIVATIVES **sipper** n.
– ORIGIN Middle English.

siphon /'saɪf(ə)n/ (also **syphon**) ■ n. **1** a tube used to convey liquid upwards from a container and then down to a lower level, the flow being forced initially by suction and maintained by atmospheric pressure and gravity. **2** Zoology a tubular organ in an aquatic animal through which water is drawn in or expelled. ■ v. **1** draw off or convey (liquid) by means of a siphon. **2** draw off (small amounts of money) over a period of time, especially illicitly: *he's been siphoning money off the firm*.
– DERIVATIVES **siphonage** n.
– ORIGIN Middle English: from Greek *siphōn* 'pipe'.

Siphonaptera /ˌsaɪfəˈnapt(ə)rə/ ■ pl. n. Entomology an order of insects that comprises the fleas.
– ORIGIN from Greek *siphōn* 'tube' + *apteros* 'wingless'.

Siphonophora /ˌsaɪfəˈnɒf(ə)rə/ ■ pl. n. Zoology an order of colonial marine coelenterates that includes the Portuguese man-of-war, having a float or swimming bell for drifting or swimming on the open sea.
– DERIVATIVES **siphonophore** /saɪˈfɒnəfɔː/ n.
– ORIGIN from Greek *siphōn* 'tube' + *pherein* 'to bear'.

sir (also **Sir**) ■ n. **1** a polite or respectful form of address to a man. **2** used to address a man at the beginning of a formal or business letter. **3** used as a title before the forename of a knight or baronet.
– ORIGIN Middle English: reduced form of SIRE.

sirdar ■ n. variant spelling of SARDAR.

sire /saɪə/ ■ n. **1** the male parent of an animal, especially a stallion or bull kept for breeding. **2** a father or other male forebear. **3** archaic a respectful form of address to someone of high social status, especially a king. ■ v. be the sire of.
– ORIGIN Middle English: from Old French, from an alteration of Latin *senior* (see SENIOR).

siree /sɪˈriː/ (also **sirree**) ■ exclam. N. Amer. informal sir (used for emphasis, especially after *yes* and *no*).
– ORIGIN C19: from SIR + the emphatic suffix *-ee*.

siren ■ n. **1** a device that makes a loud prolonged signal or warning sound. **2** Greek & Roman Mythology each of a number of women or winged creatures whose singing lured unwary sailors on to rocks. **3** a woman who is considered to be alluring but also dangerous in some way.
– PHRASES **siren song** (or **call**) the appeal of something that is alluring but also potentially dangerous.
– ORIGIN Middle English: from Old French *sirene*, from Latin *Siren*, from Greek *Seirēn*.

Sirenia /saɪˈriːnɪə/ ■ pl. n. Zoology an order of large aquatic plant-eating mammals which includes the manatees and dugong.
– DERIVATIVES **sirenian** n. & adj.
– ORIGIN modern Latin (see SIREN).

Sir Galahad ■ n. see GALAHAD.

sirloin ■ n. the choicer part of a loin of beef.
– ORIGIN Middle English: from Old French (see SUR-¹, LOIN).

sirocco /sɪˈrɒkəʊ/ (also **scirocco**) ■ n. (pl. **-os**) a hot wind blowing from North Africa across the Mediterranean to southern Europe.
– ORIGIN C17: from Italian *scirocco*, from Spanish Arabic *šalūk* 'east wind'.

sirrah /'sɪrə/ ■ n. archaic a term of address to a man or boy, especially one younger or of lower status than the speaker.
– ORIGIN C16: prob. from SIRE, when still two syllables in Middle English.

sirup ■ n. US spelling of SYRUP.

SIS ■ abbrev. (in the UK) Secret Intelligence Service.

sis¹ /sɪs/ ■ n. informal sister.

sis² /sɪs, səs/ ■ exclam. S. African informal used to express disgust, contempt, or disappointment.
– ORIGIN from Afrikaans *sies*, perhaps from Khoikhoi (t)*si*.

sisal /'saɪs(ə)l/ ■ n. **1** a Mexican agave with large fleshy leaves, cultivated for the fibre it yields. [*Agave sisalana*.]

2 the fibre made from this plant, used especially for ropes or matting.
– ORIGIN C19: from *Sisal*, the name of a port in Yucatán, Mexico.

sisi /ˈsɪsi/ ■ n. S. African a friendly form of address to a woman or girl.
– ORIGIN from isiXhosa *usisi*.

siskin ■ n. a small songbird with yellow or brown plumage and streaks of a darker colour. [Genera *Carduelis* and *Serinus*: several species.]
– ORIGIN C16: from Middle Dutch *siseken*, of Slavic origin.

sissy (also **cissy**) informal ■ n. (pl. **-ies**) a person regarded as feeble or effeminate. ■ adj. (**-ier**, **-iest**) feeble or effeminate.
– DERIVATIVES **sissified** adj. **sissyish** adj.
– ORIGIN C19: from **SIS**[1].

sister ■ n. **1** a woman or girl in relation to other daughters and sons of her parents. **2** a female friend or associate. ▸ N. Amer. a fellow black woman. **3** [as modifier] denoting an organization or a place which bears a relationship to another of common origin or allegiance. **4** (often **Sister**) a member of a religious order of women. **5** (often **Sister**) a senior female nurse.
– DERIVATIVES **sisterliness** n. **sisterly** adj.
– ORIGIN Old English, of Germanic origin.

sisterhood ■ n. **1** the relationship between sisters. **2** a feeling of kinship with and closeness to a group of women or all women. **3** (often **Sisterhood**) an association or community of women linked by a common interest, religion, or trade.

sister-in-law ■ n. (pl. **sisters-in-law**) **1** the sister of one's wife or husband. **2** the wife of one's brother or brother-in-law.

Sistine /ˈsɪstiːn, -tʌɪn/ ■ adj. of or relating to any of the popes called Sixtus, especially Sixtus IV.
– ORIGIN from Italian *Sistino*, from *Sisto* 'Sixtus'.

siSwati /sɪˈswɑːti/ ■ n. the Nguni language of the Swazi people.

Sisyphean /ˌsɪsɪˈfiːən/ ■ adj. (of a task) such that it can never be completed.
– ORIGIN C16: from *Sisyphus* in Greek mythology, who was condemned to the eternal task of rolling a large stone to the top of a hill, from which it always rolled down again.

sit ■ v. (**sitting**; past and past part. **sat** /sat/) **1** be or cause to be in a position in which one's weight is supported by one's buttocks rather than one's feet and one's back is upright. ▸ (of an animal) rest with the hind legs bent and the body close to the ground. ▸ (of a bird) remain on its nest to incubate its egg. ▸ (**sit for**) pose for (an artist or photographer). **2** be or remain in a particular position or state. ▸ (**sit with**) be harmonious with. **3** (of a parliament, committee, court of law, etc.) be engaged in its business. ▸ serve as a member of a council, jury, or other official body. ▸ chiefly Brit. take (an examination). **4** (of a table or room) have enough seats for. **5** [usu. in combination] look after children, pets, or a house while the parents or owners are away: *they want me to house-sit for them*. ■ n. a period of sitting.
– PHRASES **sit tight** informal **1** remain firmly in one's place. **2** refrain from taking action or changing one's mind.
– PHRASAL VERBS **sit in 1** (of demonstrators) occupy a place as a form of protest. **2** attend a meeting without taking an active part. **sit in for** temporarily carry out the duties of. **sit on** informal **1** fail to deal with. **2** subdue or suppress. **sit something out** not take part in an event or activity. ▸ wait without taking action until an unwelcome situation or process is over. **sit up 1** move from a lying or slouching to a sitting position. **2** refrain from going to bed until later than usual.
– ORIGIN Old English *sittan*, of Germanic origin.

sitar /ˈsɪtɑː, sɪˈtɑː/ ■ n. a large, long-necked Indian lute with movable frets, played with a wire pick.
– DERIVATIVES **sitarist** /sɪˈtɑːrɪst/ n.
– ORIGIN from Persian *sitār*, from *sih* 'three' + *tār* 'string'.

sitatunga /ˌsɪtəˈtʌŋɡə/ ■ n. a brown or greyish antelope with splayed hoofs and, in the male, spiral horns, inhabiting swampy areas in central and East Africa. [*Tragelaphus spekii*.]
– ORIGIN C19: from Kiswahili.

sitcom ■ n. informal a situation comedy.
– ORIGIN 1960s: abbrev.

sit-down ■ adj. **1** denoting a meal eaten sitting at a table. **2** denoting a protest in which demonstrators occupy their workplace or sit down on the ground in a public place, refusing to leave until their demands are met. ■ n. **1** a period of sitting down. **2** a sit-down protest.

SITE ■ abbrev. (in South Africa) standard income tax on employees.

site ■ n. **1** an area of ground on which something is located. **2** a place where a particular event or activity is occurring or has occurred. **3** short for **WEBSITE**. ■ v. fix or build in a particular place.
– ORIGIN Middle English: from Anglo-Norman French, or from Latin *situs* 'local position'.

sitrep ■ n. informal a report on the current military situation in a particular area.
– ORIGIN 1940s: from *sit*(*uation*) *rep*(*ort*).

sits vac ■ pl. n. Brit. informal situations vacant. See **SITUATION**.

sitter ■ n. **1** a person who sits, especially for a portrait or examination. **2** a sitting hen. **3** [usu. in combination] a person who looks after children, pets, or a house while the parents or owners are away: *a house-sitter*. **4** a person who provides care and companionship for people who are ill. **5** informal (in sport) an easy catch or shot.

sitting ■ n. **1** a period or spell of sitting. **2** a period of time when a group of people are served a meal. ■ adj. **1** in a seated position. **2** currently present or in office.

sitting duck (also **sitting target**) ■ n. informal a person or thing with no protection against attack.

sitting room ■ n. a room that is furnished for sitting and relaxing in.

sitting tenant ■ n. a tenant already in occupation of premises, especially when there is a change of owner.

situate ■ v. /ˈsɪtʃueɪt, -tjʊ-/ **1** (usu. **be situated**) place in a particular location or context. **2** (**be situated**) be in a specified financial or marital position.
– ORIGIN Middle English: from medieval Latin *situare* 'place', from Latin *situs* 'site'.

situation ■ n. **1** a set of circumstances in which one finds oneself. **2** the location and surroundings of a place. **3** a job.
– PHRASES **situations vacant** (or **wanted**) jobs currently available (or sought).
– DERIVATIVES **situational** adj. **situationally** adv.

situation comedy ■ n. a television or radio series in which the same set of characters are involved in various amusing situations.

situationism ■ n. **1** the theory that human behaviour is determined by surrounding circumstances rather than by personal qualities. **2** a revolutionary political theory which regards modern industrial society as being inevitably oppressive and exploitative.
– DERIVATIVES **situationist** n. & adj.

sit-up ■ n. a physical exercise designed to strengthen the abdominal muscles, in which a person sits up from a supine position without using the arms for leverage.

sitz bath /sɪts/ ■ n. a bath in which only the buttocks and hips are immersed in water.
– ORIGIN C19: partial translation of German *Sitzbad*, from *sitzen* 'sit' + *Bad* 'bath'.

six ■ cardinal number **1** equivalent to the product of two and three; one more than five, or four less than ten; 6. (Roman numeral: **vi** or **VI**.) **2** Cricket a hit that reaches the boundary without first striking the ground, scoring six runs. **3** a group of six Brownies or Cubs.
– PHRASES **at sixes and sevens** in a state of confusion or disarray. **knock** (or **hit**) **someone for six** informal utterly surprise or overcome someone. **six feet under** informal dead and buried. **six of one and half a dozen of the other** a situation in which there is little difference between two alternatives.
– DERIVATIVES **sixfold** adj. & adv.
– ORIGIN Old English *siex*, *six*, *syx*, of Germanic origin.

sixer ■ n. the leader of a group of six Brownies or Cubs.

six-gun ■ n. another term for **SIX-SHOOTER**.

six-pack ■ n. **1** a pack of six cans of beer. **2** informal a set of well-developed abdominal muscles.

sixpence ■ n. Brit. **1** a small coin worth six old pence (2½ p), withdrawn in 1980. **2** the sum of six pence, especially before decimalization (1971).

sixpenny ■ adj. Brit. costing or worth six pence, especially before decimalization (1971).

six-shooter ■ n. a revolver with six chambers.

sixte /sɪkst/ ■ n. Fencing the sixth of the eight parrying positions.
– ORIGIN C19: French, from Latin *sextus* 'sixth'.

sixteen ■ cardinal number equivalent to the product of four and four; one more than fifteen, or six more than ten; 16. (Roman numeral: **xvi** or **XVI**.)
– DERIVATIVES **sixteenth** ordinal number.
– ORIGIN Old English *siextīene*.

sixth ■ ordinal number **1** constituting number six in a sequence; 6th. **2** (**a sixth/one sixth**) each of six equal parts into which something is or may be divided. **3** the sixth form of a school. **4** Music an interval spanning six consecutive notes in a diatonic major or minor scale, e.g. C to A (major sixth) or A to F (minor sixth).
– DERIVATIVES **sixthly** adv.

sixth sense ■ n. a supposed intuitive faculty giving awareness not explicable in terms of normal perception.

sixty ■ cardinal number (pl. **-ies**) the number equivalent to the product of six and ten; ten more than fifty; 60. (Roman numeral: **lx** or **LX**.)
– DERIVATIVES **sixtieth** ordinal number. **sixtyfold** adj. & adv.
– ORIGIN Old English *siextig*.

sixty-four thousand dollar question ■ n. informal something that is not known and on which a great deal depends.
– ORIGIN 1940s: orig. *sixty-four dollar question*, from a question posed for the top prize in a broadcast quiz show.

sixty-nine ■ n. another term for **SOIXANTE-NEUF**.

sizable ■ adj. variant spelling of **SIZEABLE**.

size¹ ■ n. **1** a thing's overall dimensions or magnitude. **2** each of the classes into which garments or other articles are divided according to how large they are. ■ v. **1** alter or sort in terms of size or according to size. **2** (**size something up**) estimate or measure something's dimensions. **3** (**size someone/thing up**) informal form an estimate or rough judgement of someone or something.
– PHRASES **of a size** (of two or more people or things) having the same dimensions. **that's the size of it** informal that is the truth about a situation, however unpalatable. **to size** to the dimensions wanted.
– DERIVATIVES **-sized** (also **-size**) adj. **sizer** n.
– ORIGIN Middle English: from Old French *sise*, from *assise* 'ordinance', or a shortening of **ASSIZE**.

size² ■ n. a gelatinous solution used in glazing paper, stiffening textiles, and preparing plastered walls for decoration. ■ v. treat with size.
– ORIGIN Middle English: perhaps the same word as **SIZE**¹.

sizeable (also **sizable**) ■ adj. fairly large.
– DERIVATIVES **sizeably** adv.

sizeism (also **sizism**) ■ n. prejudice or discrimination on the grounds of a person's size.
– DERIVATIVES **sizeist** adj.

sizzle ■ v. **1** (of food) make a hissing sound when frying or roasting. **2** informal be very hot. **3** informal be very exciting or passionate, especially sexually. ■ n. an instance or the sound of sizzling.
– DERIVATIVES **sizzler** n. **sizzling** adj.
– ORIGIN C17: imitative.

sjambok /ˈʃambɒk/ ■ n. (in South Africa) a long, stiff whip, originally made of rhinoceros hide. ■ v. flog with a sjambok.
– DERIVATIVES **sjambokking** n.
– ORIGIN from S. African Dutch *tjambok*, from Urdu *chābuk*.

ska /skɑː/ ■ n. a style of fast popular music having a strong offbeat and originating in Jamaica in the 1960s, a forerunner of reggae.
– ORIGIN 1960s.

skaapsteker /ˈskɑːpˌstɪəkə/ ■ n. a greyish or olive-brown southern African snake, common in grassland. [*Psammophylax rhombeatus* and *P. tritaeniatus*.]

1109 **skeleton**

– ORIGIN C19: Afrikaans, from S. African Dutch *schaapsteker*, from *schaap* 'sheep' + *steker* 'piercer'.

skag (also **scag**) ■ n. informal, chiefly N. Amer. heroin.
– ORIGIN C20.

skank /skaŋk/ ■ n. a dance performed to reggae music, characterized by rhythmically bending forward, raising the knees, and extending the hands palms-downwards. ▸ reggae music suitable for such dancing. ■ v. play reggae music or dance in this style.
– DERIVATIVES **skanking** adj.
– ORIGIN 1970s.

skanky ■ adj. informal, chiefly N. Amer. very unpleasant.

skarn /skɑːn/ ■ n. Geology lime-bearing siliceous rock produced by the metamorphic alteration of limestone or dolomite.
– ORIGIN C20: from Swedish, 'dung, filth'.

skate¹ ■ n. **1** an ice skate or roller skate. **2** a wheeled device used to move a heavy or unwieldy object. ■ v. **1** move on ice skates or roller skates in a gliding fashion. ▸ ride on a skateboard. **2** (**skate over/round/around**) pass over or refer only fleetingly to (a subject or problem). ▸ (**skate through**) make quick and easy progress through.
– PHRASES **get one's skates on** Brit. informal hurry up.
– DERIVATIVES **skater** n. **skating** n.
– ORIGIN C17: from Dutch *schaats* (sing. but interpreted as pl.), from Old French *eschasse* 'stilt'.

skate² ■ n. (pl. same or **skates**) an edible marine fish of the ray family with a diamond-shaped body. [Family Rajidae: numerous species.]
– ORIGIN Middle English: from Old Norse *skata*.

skate³ ■ n. informal, dated or S. African a disreputable or contemptible person, especially a man.
– ORIGIN C19: perhaps influenced by Afrikaans *skuit*.

skateboard ■ n. a short narrow board with two small wheels fixed to the bottom of either end, on which a person can ride in a standing or crouching position. ■ v. [often as noun **skateboarding**] ride on a skateboard.
– DERIVATIVES **skateboarder** n.

skatepark ■ n. an area designated and equipped for skateboarding.

skedaddle /skɪˈdad(ə)l/ ■ v. informal depart quickly or hurriedly.
– ORIGIN C19.

skedonk /skəˈdɒŋk/ ■ n. S. African informal an old, battered car.
– ORIGIN 1970s: perhaps imitative.

skeet (also **skeet shooting**) ■ n. a shooting sport in which a clay target is thrown from a trap to simulate the flight of a bird.
– ORIGIN 1920s: perhaps a pseudo-archaic alteration of the verb **SHOOT**.

skeg ■ n. a tapering or projecting after section of a vessel's keel. ▸ a fin underneath the rear of a surfboard.
– ORIGIN C17: from Old Norse *skegg* 'beard', perhaps from Dutch *scheg*.

skein /skeɪn/ ■ n. **1** a length of thread or yarn, loosely coiled and knotted. **2** a flock of wild geese or swans in flight, typically in a V-shaped formation.
– ORIGIN Middle English: shortening of Old French *escaigne*.

skeletal /ˈskɛlɪt(ə)l, skəˈliːt(ə)l/ ■ adj. **1** relating to or functioning as a skeleton. ▸ very thin; emaciated. **2** existing only in outline or as a framework.
– DERIVATIVES **skeletally** adv.

skeletal muscle ■ n. another term for **STRIATED MUSCLE**.

skeleton ■ n. **1** an internal or external framework of bone, cartilage, or other rigid material supporting or containing the body of an animal or plant. ▸ a very thin or emaciated person or animal. **2** a supporting framework, basic structure, or essential part. ▸ [as modifier] denoting an essential or minimum number of people or things: *a skeleton staff*.
– PHRASES **skeleton in the cupboard** (or **closet**) a discreditable or embarrassing fact that someone wishes to keep secret.
– DERIVATIVES **skeletonize** (also **-ise**) v.
– ORIGIN C16: from Greek, from *skeletos* 'dried up'.

skeleton key

skeleton key ■ n. a key designed to fit many locks by having the interior of the bit hollowed.

skelm /ˈskɛl(ə)m/ S. African informal ■ n. a scoundrel. ■ adj. (of a person) sly; corrupt.
– ORIGIN Afrikaans, from Dutch *schelm*.

skep (also **skip**) ■ n. **1** a straw or wicker beehive. **2** archaic a wooden or wicker basket.
– ORIGIN Old English *sceppe* 'basket', from Old Norse *skeppa* 'basket, bushel'.

skeptic ■ n. US spelling of SCEPTIC.

skerry /ˈskɛri/ ■ n. (pl. **-ies**) Scottish a reef or rocky island.
– ORIGIN C17: Orkney dialect, from Old Norse *sker*.

sketch ■ n. **1** a rough or unfinished drawing or painting. ▸ a brief written or spoken account or description. **2** a short humorous play, scene, or performance. ■ v. make a sketch of. ▸ give a brief account or general outline of.
– DERIVATIVES **sketcher** n.
– ORIGIN C17: from Dutch *schets* or German *Skizze*, from Italian *schizzo*, based on Greek *skhedios* 'done extempore'.

sketchbook (also **sketch pad**) ■ n. a pad of drawing paper for sketching on.

sketch map ■ n. a roughly drawn map that shows only basic details.

sketchy ■ adj. (**-ier**, **-iest**) not thorough or detailed.
– DERIVATIVES **sketchily** adv. **sketchiness** n.

skew ■ adj. **1** neither parallel nor at right angles to a specified or implied line; askew. **2** Statistics (of a statistical distribution) not symmetrical. **3** Mathematics (of a pair of lines) neither parallel nor intersecting. ▸ (of a curve) not lying in a plane. ■ n. **1** an oblique angle; a slant. **2** a bias towards one particular group or subject. **3** Statistics the state of not being symmetrical. ■ v. **1** suddenly change direction or move at an angle. **2** make biased or distorted. **3** Statistics cause (a distribution) to be asymmetrical.
– DERIVATIVES **skewness** n.
– ORIGIN Middle English: shortening of Old Northern French *eskiuwer*, var. of Old French *eschiver* 'eschew'.

skewbald ■ adj. (of a horse) with irregular patches of white and another colour (properly not black). ■ n. a skewbald horse.
– ORIGIN C17: from obsolete *skewed* 'skewbald', on the pattern of *piebald*.

skewer ■ n. a long piece of wood or metal used for holding pieces of food together during cooking. ■ v. fasten together or pierce with a pin or skewer.
– ORIGIN Middle English.

skew-whiff ■ adv. & adj. informal, chiefly Brit. not straight; askew.

ski ■ n. (pl. **skis**) each of a pair of long, narrow pieces of hard flexible material fastened under the feet for travelling over snow. ▸ a similar device attached beneath a vehicle or aircraft. ■ v. (**skis**, **skied**, **skiing** or **ski-ing**) travel over snow on skis.
– DERIVATIVES **skiable** adj. **skiing** n.
– ORIGIN C18: from Norwegian, from Old Norse *skíth* 'billet, snowshoe'.

ski-bob ■ n. a device resembling a bicycle with skis instead of wheels, used for sliding down snow-covered slopes. ■ v. ride a ski-bob.

skid ■ v. (**skidded**, **skidding**) **1** (of a vehicle) slide, typically sideways, on slippery ground or as a result of stopping or turning too quickly. ▸ slip; slide. **2** fasten a skid to (a wheel) as a brake. ■ n. **1** an act of skidding. **2** a runner attached to the underside of an aircraft for use when landing on snow or grass. ▸ N. Amer. each of a set of wooden rollers for moving a log or other heavy object. **3** a braking device consisting of a wooden or metal shoe that prevents a wheel from revolving. **4** a beam or plank of wood used to support a ship under construction or repair.
– PHRASES **hit the skids** informal begin a rapid decline. **on the skids** informal in a bad state; failing. **put the skids under** informal hasten the decline or failure of.
– ORIGIN C17: perhaps rel. to Old Norse *skíth* (see SKI).

skidoo /skɪˈduː/ trademark, chiefly N. Amer. ■ n. a motorized toboggan. ■ v. (**skidoos**, **skidooed**) ride on a skidoo.
– ORIGIN C20: an arbitrary formation from SKI.

skidpan (N. Amer. **skidpad**) ■ n. a slippery road surface prepared for drivers to practise control of skidding.

skid row ■ n. informal, chiefly N. Amer. a run-down part of a town frequented by vagrants and alcoholics.
– ORIGIN 1930s: alteration of *skid road* denoting a road formed of *skids* over which logs were hauled, thence a part of town frequented by loggers.

skier ■ n. a person who skis.

skiff ■ n. a light rowing boat or sculling boat, typically for one person.
– ORIGIN C15: from French *esquif*, from Italian *schifo*, of Germanic origin.

skiffle ■ n. **1** Brit. a kind of folk music popular in the 1950s, often incorporating improvised instruments such as washboards. **2** US a style of 1920s and 1930s jazz using both improvised and conventional instruments.
– ORIGIN 1920s: perhaps imitative.

skijoring /ˈskiːdʒɔːrɪŋ, -ˈdʒɔː-/ ■ n. the sport or recreation of being pulled over snow or ice on skis by a horse or dog.
– ORIGIN 1920s: from Norwegian *skikjøring*, from *ski* 'ski' + *kjøre* 'drive'.

ski jump ■ n. a steep slope levelling off before a sharp drop to allow a skier to leap through the air. ▸ a leap made from such a slope.
– DERIVATIVES **ski jumper** n. **ski jumping** n.

skilful (also chiefly N. Amer. **skillful**) ■ adj. having or showing skill.
– DERIVATIVES **skilfully** adv. **skilfulness** n.

ski lift ■ n. a system used to transport skiers up a slope to the top of a run, typically consisting of moving seats attached to an overhead cable.

skill ■ n. the ability to do something well; expertise or dexterity. ■ v. [usu. as noun **skilling**] train (a worker) to do a particular task.
– DERIVATIVES **skilless** adj. (archaic).
– ORIGIN Old English *scele* 'knowledge', from Old Norse *skil* 'discernment, knowledge'.

skilled ■ adj. having or showing skill. ▸ (of work) requiring special abilities or training.

skillet ■ n. **1** a frying pan. **2** Brit. historical a small metal cooking pot with a long handle, typically with legs.
– ORIGIN Middle English: perhaps from Old French *escuelete*, diminutive of *escuele* 'platter', from late Latin *scutella*.

skilly ■ n. Brit., chiefly historical thin broth, typically made from oatmeal and water and flavoured with meat.
– ORIGIN C19: abbrev. of archaic *skilligalee*.

skim ■ v. (**skimmed**, **skimming**) **1** remove (a substance) from the surface of a liquid. **2** move quickly and lightly over or on a surface or through the air. ▸ throw (a flat stone) so that it bounces several times on the surface of water. **3** read (something) quickly, noting only the important points. ▸ (**skim over**) deal with or treat briefly or superficially. **4** informal steal or embezzle (money) in small amounts over a period of time. ■ n. **1** a thin layer of a substance on the surface of a liquid. **2** an act of reading something quickly or superficially.
– ORIGIN Middle English: back-formation from SKIMMER, or from Old French *escumer*, from *escume* 'scum, foam'.

ski mask ■ n. a protective covering for the head and face, with holes for the eyes, nose, and mouth.

skimmed milk (also **skim milk**) ■ n. milk from which the cream has been removed.

skimmer ■ n. **1** a person or thing that skims. **2** a long-winged seabird which feeds by skimming over the water surface with its knife-like lower mandible immersed. [Genus *Rynchops*: three species.] **3** chiefly N. Amer. a flat, broad-brimmed straw hat. ▸ informal a close-fitting dress.
– ORIGIN Middle English: from Old French *escumoir*, from *escumer* 'skim', from *escume* 'scum'.

skimobile /ˈskiːməbiːl/ ■ n. N. Amer. a motor vehicle for travelling over snow, with caterpillar tracks at the back and steerable skis in front.

skimp ■ v. (often **skimp on**) expend fewer resources on something than are necessary in an attempt to economize.
– ORIGIN C18.

CONSONANTS   **b** but   **d** dog   **f** few   **g** get   **h** he   **j** yes   **k** cat   **l** leg   **m** man   **n** no   **p** pen   **r** red

skimpy ■ adj. (-ier, -iest) providing or consisting of less than is necessary; meagre. ▶ (of clothes) short and revealing.
—DERIVATIVES **skimpily** adv. **skimpiness** n.

skin ■ n. 1 the thin layer of tissue forming the natural outer covering of the body of a person or animal. ▶ the skin of a dead animal used as material for clothing or other items. ▶ a container made from the skin of an animal such as a goat, used for holding liquids. 2 the peel or outer layer of a fruit or vegetable. ▶ the outermost layer of a structure such as an aircraft. ▶ the thin outer covering of a sausage. ▶ a thin layer forming on the surface of a hot liquid as it cools. 3 Brit. informal a skinhead. 4 informal a drum or drumhead. 5 [as modifier] informal relating to or denoting pornography: *the skin trade.* 6 informal a cigarette paper. ■ v. (**skinned, skinning**) 1 remove the skin from. ▶ graze (a part of one's body). 2 archaic cover with or form skin. 3 informal take money from or swindle. 4 Soccer, informal take the ball past (a defender) with ease.
—PHRASES **be skin and bone** be very thin. **by the skin of one's teeth** by a very narrow margin. **get under someone's skin** informal 1 annoy or irritate someone intensely. 2 fill someone's mind in a compelling and persistent way. 3 reach or display a deep understanding of someone. **give someone (some) skin** US informal shake or slap hands together as a gesture of friendship or solidarity. **have a thick (or thin) skin** be insensitive (or oversensitive) to criticism or insults. **it's no skin off my nose** (or US **off my back**) informal one is not offended or adversely affected. **under the skin** in reality, as opposed to superficial appearances.
—DERIVATIVES **skinless** adj. **skinned** adj. **skinner** n.
—ORIGIN Old English *scinn*, from Old Norse *skinn*.

skin-deep ■ adj. not deep or lasting; superficial.

skinder /ˈskɪnə/ (also **skinner**) S. African informal ■ n. gossip. ■ v. engage in gossip.
—ORIGIN Afrikaans, 'to gossip, slander'.

skin diving ■ n. the action or sport of swimming under water without a diving suit, typically using an aqualung and flippers.
—DERIVATIVES **skin-dive** v. **skin-diver** n.

skinflint ■ n. informal a person who spends as little money as possible; a miser.

skinful ■ n. Brit. informal enough alcoholic drink to make one drunk.

skinhead ■ n. a young person of a subculture characterized by close-cropped hair and heavy boots, often perceived as aggressive, violent, and racist.

skink ■ n. a smooth-bodied lizard with short or absent limbs. [Family Scincidae: numerous species.]
—ORIGIN C16: from French *scinc* or Latin *scincus*, from Greek *skinkos*.

skinny ■ adj. (-ier, -iest) 1 (of a person) unattractively thin. 2 (of an article of clothing) tight-fitting. 3 informal (of coffee) made with skimmed or semi-skimmed milk. ■ n. (**the (inside) skinny**) N. Amer. informal confidential information or gossip.
—DERIVATIVES **skinniness** n.

skinny-dip informal ■ v. swim naked. ■ n. a naked swim.
—DERIVATIVES **skinny-dipper** n.

skinny-rib ■ n. a tightly fitting sweater or cardigan.

skint ■ adj. Brit. informal having little or no money available.
—ORIGIN 1920s: var. of colloquial *skinned*, in the same sense, from SKIN.

skin test ■ n. a test to determine whether an immune reaction is elicited when a substance is applied to or injected into the skin.

skintight ■ adj. (of a garment) very close-fitting.

skip¹ ■ v. (**skipped, skipping**) 1 move along lightly, stepping from one foot to the other with a hop or bounce. ▶ throw (a stone) so that it skims the surface of water. 2 jump repeatedly over a rope which is held at both ends and turned over the head and under the feet. 3 jump lightly over. ▶ omit or move quickly and unmethodically over (a stage or point). ▶ fail to attend or deal with; miss. ▶ informal leave quickly and secretly. ■ n. a skipping movement.
—ORIGIN Middle English: prob. of Scandinavian origin.

skip² ■ n. 1 a large transportable open-topped container for bulky refuse. 2 a cage or bucket in which workers or materials are lowered and raised in mines and quarries. 3 variant spelling of SKEP.

skip³ ■ n. the captain or director of a side at bowls or curling. ■ v. (**skipped, skipping**) act as skip of (a side).
—ORIGIN C19: abbrev. of SKIPPER¹.

ski pants ■ pl. n. women's trousers made of stretchy fabric with tapering legs and an elastic stirrup under each foot.

skipjack ■ n. 1 (also **skipjack tuna**) a small tuna with dark horizontal stripes. [*Katsuwonus pelamis*.] 2 another term for CLICK BEETLE. 3 a sloop-rigged sailing boat of a kind used off the east coast of the US.
—ORIGIN C18: from SKIP¹ + JACK¹ (with ref. to the fish's habit of jumping out of the water).

ski-plane ■ n. an aircraft having its undercarriage fitted with skis for landing on snow or ice.

skipper¹ informal ■ n. the captain of a ship, boat, or aircraft. ▶ the captain of a side in a game or sport. ■ v. act as captain of.
—ORIGIN Middle English: from Middle Dutch, Middle Low German *schipper*, from *schip* 'ship'.

skipper² ■ n. South African term for T-SHIRT.

skipper³ ■ n. 1 a person or thing that skips. 2 a small brownish moth-like butterfly with rapid darting flight. [Family Hesperiidae: many species.]

skirl /skɜːl/ ■ n. a shrill sound, especially that of bagpipes. ■ v. (of bagpipes) make such a sound.
—ORIGIN Middle English: prob. of Scandinavian origin.

skirmish ■ n. an episode of irregular or unpremeditated fighting, especially between small or outlying parts of armies. ■ v. [often as noun **skirmishing**] engage in a skirmish.
—DERIVATIVES **skirmisher** n.
—ORIGIN Middle English: from Old French *eskirmiss-, eskirmir*, from a Germanic verb meaning 'defend'.

skirt ■ n. 1 a woman's outer garment fastened around the waist and hanging down around the legs. ▶ the part of a coat or dress that hangs below the waist. ▶ informal women regarded as objects of sexual desire. 2 a surface that conceals or protects the wheels or underside of a vehicle or aircraft. 3 an animal's diaphragm and other membranes as food. ▶ Brit. a cut of meat from the lower flank. 4 a small flap on a saddle covering the bar from which the stirrup hangs. 5 archaic an edge, border, or extreme part. ■ v. (also **skirt along/around**) go round or past the edge of. ▶ avoid dealing with.
—DERIVATIVES **-skirted** adj.
—ORIGIN Middle English: from Old Norse *skyrta* 'shirt'.

skirting (also **skirting board**) ■ n. a wooden board running along the base of an interior wall.

skit ■ n. a short comedy sketch or piece of humorous writing, especially a parody.
—ORIGIN C18: rel. to the rare verb *skit* 'move lightly and rapidly', perhaps from Old Norse (cf. *skjóta* 'shoot').

skitter ■ v. 1 move lightly and quickly or hurriedly. 2 draw (bait) jerkily across the surface of the water as a technique in fishing.
—ORIGIN C19: perhaps of Old Norse origin.

skittery ■ adj. restless; skittish.

skittish ■ adj. (of a horse) nervous; inclined to shy. ▶ lively and unpredictable; playful.
—DERIVATIVES **skittishly** adv. **skittishness** n.
—ORIGIN Middle English: perhaps from the rare verb *skit* (see SKIT).

skittle ■ n. 1 (**skittles**) [treated as sing.] a game played with wooden pins, typically nine in number, set up at the end of an alley to be bowled down with a wooden ball or disc. ▶ (also **table skittles**) a game played with similar pins set up on a board to be knocked down by swinging a suspended ball. 2 a pin used in the game of skittles. 3 (**skittles**) [treated as sing.] Brit. informal chess that is not played seriously. ■ v. knock over as if in a game of skittles. ▶ Cricket get (batsmen) out in rapid succession.
—ORIGIN C17.

skive¹ /skaɪv/ informal ■ v. avoid work or a duty; shirk. ■ n.

skive an instance of shirking. ► an easy option.
– DERIVATIVES **skiver** n.
– ORIGIN C20: perhaps from French *esquiver* 'slink away'.

skive[2] /skʌɪv/ ■ v. technical pare (the edge of a piece of leather or other material) to reduce its thickness.
– ORIGIN C19: from Old Norse *skífa*.

skivvy ■ n. (pl. **-ies**) **1** Brit. informal a low-ranking female domestic servant. ► a person doing menial work. **2** US a lightweight high-necked long-sleeved garment. ► a T-shirt or short-sleeved vest. ► (**skivvies**) N. Amer. trademark underwear of vest and underpants. ■ v. (**-ies**, **-ied**) informal do menial household tasks.
– ORIGIN C20.

skokiaan /'skɒkɪɑːn/ ■ n. S. African home-brewed liquor made primarily of yeast, sugar, and water.
– ORIGIN perhaps from isiZulu *isikokeyana* 'small enclosure' (from the practice of hiding illicit liquor in holes in the ground), or from isiXhosa *koka* 'make drunk'.

skol /skɒl, skəʊl/ (also **skoal**) ■ exclam. used as a toast before drinking.
– ORIGIN C17: from Danish and Norwegian *skaal*, Swedish *skål*, from Old Norse *skál* 'bowl'.

skollie /'skɒli/ (also **skolly**) ■ n. (pl. **-ies**) S. African informal a gang member; a petty criminal.
– ORIGIN from Afrikaans, prob. from Dutch *schoelje* 'rogue'.

skop, skiet en donder /'skɒp 'skiːt ən 'dɒnə/ (also **skop, skiet and donder** or **donner**) S. African informal ■ n. action entertainment provided by a film, book, computer game, etc. that is characterized by violence. ■ adj. of, relating to, or resembling such entertainment.
– ORIGIN 1970s: Afrikaans, 'kick, shoot, and beat up'.

skottel /'skɒtl/ (also **skottel braai**) ■ n. S. African a large bowl-shaped metal pan that is attached to a gas cylinder and used for outdoor cooking.
– ORIGIN Afrikaans, 'dish', from Dutch *schotel*.

skua /'skjuːə/ ■ n. a large predatory seabird, chiefly brown, which pursues other birds to make them disgorge fish. [*Catharacta skua* (great skua), *Stercorarius parasiticus* (Arctic skua), and related species.]
– ORIGIN C17: from Faroese (the language of the Faroe Islands) *skúvur*, from Old Norse *skufr* (prob. imitative).

skulduggery /skʌl'dʌg(ə)ri/ (also **skullduggery**) ■ n. underhand or unscrupulous behaviour; trickery.
– ORIGIN C19: alteration of Scots *sculduddery*.

skulk ■ v. hide or move around secretly, typically with a sinister or cowardly motive. ■ n. a group of foxes.
– DERIVATIVES **skulker** n.
– ORIGIN Middle English: of Scandinavian origin.

skull ■ n. a bone framework enclosing the brain of a vertebrate. ► informal a person's head or brain. ■ v. informal hit on the head.
– PHRASES **out of one's skull** informal **1** out of one's mind; crazy. **2** very drunk. **skull and crossbones** a representation of a skull with two thigh bones crossed below it as an emblem of piracy or death.
– DERIVATIVES **-skulled** adj.
– ORIGIN Middle English *scolle*.

skullcap ■ n. **1** a small close-fitting peakless cap or protective helmet. **2** the top part of the skull. **3** a plant of the mint family, whose tubular flowers have a helmet-shaped cup at the base. [Genus *Scutellaria*.]

skunk ■ n. **1** a black-and-white striped American mammal of the weasel family, able to spray foul-smelling irritant liquid from its anal glands at attackers. [*Mephitis mephitis* and other species.] **2** informal a contemptible person. ■ v. N. Amer. informal defeat (an opponent) overwhelmingly, especially by preventing them from scoring at all.
– ORIGIN C17: from Abnaki *segankw*.

skunk cabbage ■ n. a North American arum, the flower of which has a distinctive unpleasant smell. [*Lysichiton americanum* and *Symplocarpus foetidus*.]

skunkworks ■ pl. n. [usu. treated as sing.] US informal a small experimental laboratory or department of a company or institution.
– ORIGIN 1970s: allegedly from an association with the *Skonk Works*, an illegal still in the Li'l Abner comic strip.

sky ■ n. (pl. **-ies**) **1** the region of the atmosphere and outer space seen from the earth. **2** poetic/literary heaven; heavenly power. ■ v. (**-ies**, **-ied**) informal hit (a ball) high into the air.
– PHRASES **the sky is the limit** there is practically no limit. **to the skies** very highly; enthusiastically. **under the open sky** out of doors.
– DERIVATIVES **skyless** adj. **skyward** adj. & adv. **skywards** adv.
– ORIGIN Middle English, from Old Norse *ský* 'cloud'.

sky blue ■ n. a bright clear blue.

skybox ■ n. N. Amer. a luxurious enclosed seating area high up in a sports arena.

sky burial ■ n. a Tibetan funeral ritual involving the exposure of a dismembered corpse to sacred vultures.

skycap ■ n. N. Amer. a porter at an airport.

skydiving ■ n. the sport of jumping from an aircraft and performing acrobatic manoeuvres in the air under free fall before landing by parachute.
– DERIVATIVES **skydive** v. **skydiver** n.

Skye terrier ■ n. a small long-haired terrier of a slate-coloured or fawn-coloured Scottish breed.

skyglow ■ n. brightness of the night sky in a built-up area as a result of light pollution.

sky-high ■ adv. & adj. **1** as if reaching the sky; very high. **2** at or to a very high level; very great.

skyhook ■ n. Climbing a small flattened hook, with an eye for attaching a rope, fixed temporarily into a rock face.

skyjack ■ v. hijack (an aircraft). ■ n. an act of skyjacking.
– DERIVATIVES **skyjacker** n.

skylark ■ n. a common Eurasian and North African lark of open country, noted for its prolonged song given in hovering flight. [*Alauda arvensis*.] ■ v. play practical jokes or indulge in horseplay.

skylight ■ n. a window set in a roof or ceiling at the same angle.

skyline ■ n. an outline of land and buildings defined against the sky.

skylit (also **skylighted**) ■ adj. fitted with or lit by a skylight or skylights.

skyrocket ■ n. a rocket designed to explode high in the air as a signal or firework. ■ v. (**-rocketed**, **-rocketing**) informal (of a price or amount) increase very rapidly.

skyscape ■ n. a view or picture of an expanse of sky.

skyscraper ■ n. a very tall building of many storeys.

sky surfing ■ n. the sport of jumping from an aircraft and surfing through the air on a board before landing by parachute.

skywatch ■ v. informal observe or monitor the sky, especially for heavenly bodies or aircraft.
– DERIVATIVES **skywatcher** n.

sky wave ■ n. a radio wave reflected from the ionosphere.

skyway ■ n. chiefly N. Amer. **1** a recognized route followed by aircraft. **2** (also **skywalk**) a covered overhead walkway between buildings.

skywriting ■ n. words in the form of smoke trails made by an aircraft, especially for advertising.
– DERIVATIVES **skywriter** n.

S & L ■ abbrev. savings and loan.

slab ■ n. **1** a large, thick, flat piece of solid material, in particular stone, concrete, or heavy food. **2** a flat, heavy table top or counter used for food preparation. ► a table used for laying a body on in a mortuary. **3** an outer piece of timber sawn from a log. **4** Climbing a large, smooth body of rock lying at a sharp angle to the horizontal. ■ v. (**slabbed**, **slabbing**) remove slabs from (a log or tree) to prepare it for sawing into planks.
– DERIVATIVES **slabbed** adj. **slabby** adj.
– ORIGIN Middle English.

slack[1] ■ adj. **1** not taut or held tightly in position; loose. **2** (of business or trade) not busy; quiet. **3** careless, lazy, or negligent. **4** (of a tide) neither ebbing nor flowing. ■ n. **1** the part of a rope or line which is not held taut. **2** (**slacks**) casual trousers. **3** informal a spell of inactivity or laziness. ■ v. **1** loosen or reduce the intensity or speed of; slacken. ► (**slack off/up**) decrease in intensity or speed. **2** informal work slowly or lazily. **3** slake (lime).
– PHRASES **cut someone some slack** N. Amer. informal allow

someone some leeway in their conduct. **take** (or **pick**) **up the slack 1** improve the use of resources to avoid an undesirable lull in business. **2** pull on the loose part of a rope to make it taut.
– DERIVATIVES **slacken** v. **slackly** adv. **slackness** n.
– ORIGIN Old English *slæc* 'inclined to be lazy, unhurried', of Germanic origin.

slack[2] ■ n. coal dust or small pieces of coal.
– ORIGIN Middle English: prob. from Low German or Dutch.

slacker ■ n. informal **1** a person who avoids work or effort. **2** chiefly N. Amer. a young person of a subculture characterized by apathy and aimlessness.

slack water ■ n. the state of the tide when it is turning, especially at low tide.

slag ■ n. **1** stony waste matter separated from metals during the smelting or refining of ore. ▶ similar material produced by a volcano; scoria. **2** informal, derogatory a promiscuous woman. ▶ a contemptible or insignificant person. ■ v. (**slagged**, **slagging**) **1** [usu. as noun **slagging**] produce deposits of slag. **2** (often **slag someone off**) informal criticize abusively.
– DERIVATIVES **slaggy** adj. (**-ier**, **-iest**).
– ORIGIN C16: from Middle Low German *slagge*, perhaps from *slagen* 'strike', with ref. to fragments formed by hammering.

slag heap ■ n. a hill or area of refuse from a mine or industrial site.

slag wool ■ n. mineral wool made from blast-furnace slag.

slain past participle of **SLAY**.

slainte /ˈslɑːntʃə/ ■ exclam. used as a toast before drinking.
– ORIGIN from Scottish Gaelic *slàinte* 'health'.

slake ■ v. **1** quench (one's thirst). ▶ satisfy (a desire). **2** combine (quicklime) with water to produce calcium hydroxide.
– ORIGIN Old English *slacian* 'become less eager', also 'slacken', from *slæc* (see **SLACK**[1]).

slaked lime ■ n. calcium hydroxide, made by adding water to quicklime.

slalom /ˈslɑːləm/ ■ n. a ski race down a winding course marked out by poles. ▶ a canoeing or sailing race over a similar course. ■ v. move or race in a winding path, avoiding obstacles.
– ORIGIN 1920s: from Norwegian, 'sloping track'.

slam[1] ■ v. (**slammed**, **slamming**) **1** shut or be shut forcefully and loudly. ▶ push or put somewhere with great force. ▶ (often **slam into**) crash or strike heavily into. ▶ put into action suddenly or forcefully: *I slammed on the brakes*. ▶ short for **SLAM-DANCE**. **2** informal criticize severely. **3** informal, chiefly N. Amer. easily score points against or defeat. ■ n. **1** a loud bang caused by the forceful shutting of something. **2** chiefly US a poetry contest in which competitors recite their entries and are judged by members of the audience.
– ORIGIN C17: prob. of Scandinavian origin.

slam[2] ■ n. Bridge a grand slam (all thirteen tricks) or small slam (twelve tricks), for which bonus points are scored if bid and made.
– ORIGIN C17: perhaps from obsolete *slampant* 'trickery'.

slam-bang ■ adj. informal, chiefly N. Amer. exciting and energetic. ▶ direct and forceful.

slam-dance ■ n. chiefly N. Amer. a form of dancing to rock music in which the dancers deliberately collide with one another. ■ v. perform a slam-dance.
– DERIVATIVES **slam-dancer** n. **slam dancing** n.

slam dunk ■ n. **1** Basketball a shot thrust down through the basket. **2** N. Amer. informal a foregone conclusion or certainty. ■ v. (**slam-dunk**) **1** Basketball thrust (the ball) down through the basket. **2** N. Amer. informal defeat or dismiss decisively.

slammer ■ n. **1** informal prison. **2** (also **tequila slammer**) a cocktail made with tequila and champagne or another fizzy drink, which is covered, slammed on the table, and then drunk in one.

slander ■ n. defamation. ▶ UK Law spoken defamation. Compare with **LIBEL**. ▶ a false and malicious spoken statement. ■ v. make such statements about.

1113

– DERIVATIVES **slanderer** n. **slanderous** adj. **slanderously** adv.
– ORIGIN Middle English: from Old French *esclandre*, *escandle*, from late Latin *scandalum* (see **SCANDAL**).

slang ■ n. informal language that is more common in speech than in writing and is typically restricted to a particular context or group. ■ v. informal attack (someone) using abusive language.
– DERIVATIVES **slangily** adv. **slanginess** n. **slangy** adj. (**-ier**, **-iest**).
– ORIGIN C18.

slanging match ■ n. a prolonged exchange of insults.

slant ■ v. **1** diverge from the vertical or horizontal; slope or lean. **2** [often as adj. **slanted**] present or view (information) from a particular angle, especially in a biased or unfair way. ■ n. **1** a sloping position. **2** a point of view. ■ adj. sloping.
– DERIVATIVES **slantwise** adv. & adv.
– ORIGIN Middle English: var. of dialect *slent*, of Scandinavian origin, prob. influenced by **ASLANT**.

slap ■ v. (**slapped**, **slapping**) **1** hit or strike with the palm of one's hand or a flat object. ▶ hit against with the sound of such an action. ▶ (**slap someone down**) informal reprimand someone forcefully. **2** (**slap something on**) apply something quickly, carelessly, or forcefully. ▶ informal impose a fine or other penalty on. ■ n. an act or sound of slapping. ■ adv. (also **slap bang**) informal suddenly and directly, especially with great force. ▶ exactly; right.
– PHRASES **slap in the face** an unexpected rejection or affront. **slap on the back** a congratulation or commendation. **slap on the wrist** a mild reprimand or punishment.
– ORIGIN Middle English: prob. imitative.

slap and tickle ■ n. informal physical amorous play.

slap bass ■ n. a style of playing double bass or bass guitar by pulling and releasing the strings sharply against the fingerboard.

slap chips ■ pl. n. S. African informal deep-fried potato chips, as distinct from potato crisps.
– ORIGIN *slap* prob. from Afrikaans, 'soft'.

slapdash ■ adj. & adv. done too hurriedly and carelessly.

slap-happy ■ adj. informal **1** cheerfully casual or flippant. **2** dazed or stupefied from happiness or relief.

slap shot ■ n. Ice Hockey a hard shot struck with a sharp slapping motion.

slapstick ■ n. comedy based on deliberately clumsy actions and humorously embarrassing events.

slap-up ■ adj. informal (of a meal) large and sumptuous.

slash ■ v. **1** cut with a violent sweeping movement. **2** informal reduce (a price, quantity, etc.) greatly. ▶ [as adj. **slashing**] vigorously incisive or effective. ■ n. **1** a cut made with a wide, sweeping stroke. **2** a bright patch or flash of colour or light. **3** an oblique stroke (/) used between alternatives, in fractions and ratios, or between separate elements of a text. **4** informal an act of urinating. **5** debris resulting from the felling or destruction of trees.
– ORIGIN Middle English: perhaps imitative, or from Old French *esclachier* 'break in pieces'.

slash-and-burn ■ adj. relating to or denoting a method of agriculture in which vegetation is cut down and burned off before new seeds are sown.

slasher ■ n. **1** a person or thing that slashes. **2** (also **slasher film**) informal a horror film, especially one in which victims are slashed with knives.

slasto /ˈslɑːstəʊ/ ■ n. S. African trademark flooring and tiling material consisting of slate-like shale.
– ORIGIN blend of *slate* and *stone*.

slat ■ n. a thin, narrow piece of wood or other material, especially one of a series which overlap or fit into each other.
– DERIVATIVES **slatted** adj.
– ORIGIN Middle English: shortening of Old French *esclat* 'splinter'.

slate ■ n. **1** a fine-grained grey, green, or bluish-purple metamorphic rock easily split into smooth, flat plates. ▶ a flat plate of such rock used as roofing material. **2** a plate of

slate

slater

slate formerly used in schools for writing on. **3** a bluish-grey colour. **4** a list of candidates for election to a post or office. ▸ Brit. a record of a person's debt or credit: *put it on the slate.* ■ v. **1** cover (a roof) with slates. **2** informal criticize severely. **3** schedule; plan.
– DERIVATIVES **slaty** adj.
– ORIGIN Middle English *sclate, sklate*, shortening of Old French *esclate*, synonymous with *esclat* (see SLAT).

slater ■ n. **1** a person who slates roofs for a living. **2** a woodlouse or similar isopod crustacean.

slather /ˈslaðə/ ■ v. informal spread or smear thickly or liberally.
– ORIGIN C19.

slattern /ˈslat(ə)n/ ■ n. dated a dirty, untidy woman.
– DERIVATIVES **slatternliness** n. **slatternly** adj.
– ORIGIN C17: rel. to *slattering* 'slovenly', from dialect *slatter* 'to spill, slop'.

slaughter /ˈslɔːtə/ ■ n. **1** the killing of farm animals for food. **2** the killing of a large number of people in a cruel or violent way. **3** informal a thorough defeat. ■ v. **1** kill (animals) for food. **2** kill (people) in a cruel or violent way. **3** informal defeat (an opponent) thoroughly.
– DERIVATIVES **slaughterer** n. **slaughterous** adj.
– ORIGIN Middle English: from Old Norse *slátr* 'butcher's meat'; rel. to SLAY.

slaughterhouse ■ n. a place where animals are slaughtered for food.

Slav /slɑːv/ ■ n. a member of a group of peoples in central and eastern Europe speaking Slavic languages.
– ORIGIN from medieval Latin *Sclavus*, late Greek *Sklabos*.

slave ■ n. **1** historical a person who is the legal property of another and is forced to obey them. ▸ a person who is excessively dependent upon or controlled by something: *a slave to fashion.* **2** a device, or part of one, directly controlled by another. Compare with MASTER. ■ v. **1** work excessively hard. **2** [as noun **slaving**] historical the action or process of enslaving people. **3** subject (a device) to control by another.
– ORIGIN Middle English: shortening of Old French *esclave*, equivalent of medieval Latin *sclava* (feminine) 'Slavonic (captive)'.

slave bangle (also **slave bracelet**) ■ n. a bangle or bracelet worn above the elbow.

slave bell ■ n. (in South Africa) a large bell formerly used on farms in the Cape Colony to summon slaves to work.

slave-driver ■ n. informal a person who works others very hard.
– DERIVATIVES **slave-drive** v.

slave labour ■ n. labour which is coerced and inadequately rewarded.

slaver[1] /ˈsleɪvə/ ■ n. historical a person dealing in or owning slaves. ▸ a ship used for transporting slaves.

slaver[2] /ˈslavə, ˈsleɪvə/ ■ n. saliva running from the mouth. ■ v. **1** let saliva run from the mouth. **2** (usu. **slaver over**) show excessive desire.
– ORIGIN Middle English: prob. from Low German.

slavery ■ n. the state of being a slave. ▸ the practice or system of owning slaves.

slave trade ■ n. chiefly historical the procuring, transporting, and selling of human beings as slaves.
– DERIVATIVES **slave trader** n.

Slavic /ˈslɑːvɪk, ˈslavɪk/ ■ n. the branch of the Indo-European language family that includes Russian, Polish, Czech, Bulgarian, and Serbo-Croat. ■ adj. relating to or denoting this branch of languages or their speakers.

slavish ■ adj. **1** showing no attempt at originality. **2** servile or submissive.
– DERIVATIVES **slavishly** adv. **slavishness** n.

Slavonic /sləˈvɒnɪk/ ■ n. & adj. another term for SLAVIC.

slaw ■ n. N. Amer. coleslaw.
– ORIGIN C18: from Dutch *sla*, shortened from *salade* 'salad'.

slay ■ v. (past **slew**; past part. **slain**) **1** archaic or poetic/literary kill in a violent way. ▸ N. Amer. murder (someone). **2** informal greatly impress or amuse.

– DERIVATIVES **slayer** n.
– ORIGIN Old English *slēan* 'strike, kill', of Germanic origin.

SLBM ■ abbrev. submarine-launched ballistic missile.

sleaze informal ■ n. immoral, sordid, and corrupt behaviour or material. ▸ (also **sleazebag** or **sleazeball**) informal, chiefly N. Amer. a sordid, corrupt, or immoral person. ■ v. behave in an immoral, corrupt, or sordid way.
– ORIGIN 1960s: back-formation from SLEAZY.

sleazy ■ adj. (-ier, -iest) sordid, corrupt, or immoral. ▸ (of a place) squalid and seedy.
– DERIVATIVES **sleazily** adv. **sleaziness** n.
– ORIGIN C17.

sled ■ n. & v. (**sledded**, **sledding**) North American term for SLEDGE[1].
– ORIGIN Middle English: from Middle Low German *sledde*.

sledge[1] ■ n. a vehicle on runners for travelling over snow or ice, either pushed, pulled, or allowed to slide downhill. ■ v. ride or carry on a sledge.
– DERIVATIVES **sledging** n.
– ORIGIN C16: from Middle Dutch *sleedse*.

sledge[2] ■ n. a sledgehammer. ■ v. [usu. as noun **sledging**] Cricket (of a fielder) make offensive remarks to (an opposing batsman).
– ORIGIN Old English *slecg* (n.), from a Germanic base meaning 'to strike'.

sledgehammer ■ n. **1** a large, heavy hammer used for breaking rocks, driving in posts, etc. **2** [as modifier] very powerful, forceful, or unsubtle: *sledgehammer blows.*

sleek ■ adj. **1** (especially of hair or fur) smooth, glossy, and healthy-looking. **2** wealthy and well-groomed in appearance. ▸ elegant and streamlined. ■ v. make (the hair) sleek by applying pressure or moisture.
– DERIVATIVES **sleekly** adv. **sleekness** n. **sleeky** adj.
– ORIGIN Middle English: a later var. of SLICK.

sleep ■ n. **1** a regularly recurring condition of body and mind in which the nervous system is inactive, the eyes closed, the postural muscles relaxed, and consciousness practically suspended. **2** a gummy secretion found in the corners of the eyes after sleep. ■ v. (past and past part. **slept** /slɛpt/) **1** rest in such a condition. ▸ (**sleep something off**) recover from something by going to sleep. ▸ (**sleep in**) remain asleep or in bed later than usual in the morning. **2** provide (a specified number of people) with beds or bedrooms. **3** (**sleep together/with**) have sexual intercourse or be involved in a sexual relationship. ▸ (**sleep around**) have many casual sexual partners.
– PHRASES **put someone to sleep** make someone unconscious with drugs or anaesthetic. **put something to sleep** kill an animal painlessly. **sleep like a log** (or **top**) sleep very soundly.
– DERIVATIVES **sleepless** adj. **sleeplessly** adv. **sleeplessness** n.
– ORIGIN Old English, of Germanic origin.

sleeper ■ n. **1** a person or animal that is asleep. ▸ a person who sleeps in a specified manner: *a light sleeper.* **2** a sleeping car or a train carrying sleeping cars. **3** a film, book, play, etc. that suddenly achieves success after initially attracting little attention. **4** a secret agent who remains inactive for a long period while establishing a secure position. **5** a ring or bar worn in a pierced ear to keep the hole from closing. **6** a wooden or concrete beam laid transversely under railway track to support it.

sleeper couch ■ n. a couch or sofa that can be converted into a bed.

sleeping bag ■ n. a warm lined padded bag to sleep in, especially when camping.

sleeping car (Brit. also **sleeping carriage**) ■ n. a railway carriage provided with beds or berths.

sleeping draught ■ n. Brit. dated a drink or drug intended to induce sleep.

sleeping partner ■ n. a partner not sharing in the actual work of a firm.

sleeping pill ■ n. a tablet of a sleep-inducing drug.

sleeping policeman ■ n. a speed bump.

sleeping sickness ■ n. a tropical disease caused by a parasitic protozoan (trypanosome) transmitted by the bite of the tsetse fly, marked by extreme lethargy.

sleepover ■ n. an occasion of spending the night away from home.

sleepsuit ■ n. a young child's one-piece garment, typically worn as nightwear.

sleepwalk ■ v. walk around and sometimes perform other actions while asleep.
– DERIVATIVES **sleepwalker** n.

sleepy ■ adj. (**-ier**, **-iest**) 1 needing or ready for sleep. 2 (of a place) without much activity. ▸ not dynamic or able to respond to change.
– DERIVATIVES **sleepily** adv. **sleepiness** n.

sleepyhead ■ n. informal a sleepy or inattentive person.

sleet ■ n. rain containing some ice, or snow melting as it falls. ■ v. (**it sleets,**) it is sleeting, etc. sleet falls.
– DERIVATIVES **sleety** adj.
– ORIGIN Middle English: of Germanic origin.

sleeve ■ n. 1 the part of a garment that wholly or partly covers a person's arm. 2 a protective paper or cardboard cover for a record. ▸ a protective or connecting tube fitting over a rod, spindle, or smaller tube.
– PHRASES **up one's sleeve** kept secret and in reserve for use when needed.
– DERIVATIVES **sleeved** adj. **sleeveless** adj.
– ORIGIN Old English *slēfe, sliefe*), *slȳf*.

sleeve note ■ n. an article printed on a CD or record cover giving information about the music or musician.

sleeve nut ■ n. a long nut with right-hand and left-hand screw threads for drawing together conversely threaded pipes or shafts.

sleeving ■ n. Brit. tubular covering for electrical or other cables.

sleigh ■ n. a sledge drawn by horses or reindeer. ■ v. ride on a sleigh.
– ORIGIN C17: from Dutch *slee*.

sleigh bell ■ n. a tinkling bell attached to the harness of a sleigh horse.

sleight /slaɪt/ ■ n. poetic/literary the use of dexterity or cunning, especially so as to deceive.
– PHRASES **sleight of hand** manual dexterity, typically in performing conjuring tricks. ▸ skilful deception.
– ORIGIN Middle English *sleghth* 'cunning, skill', from Old Norse *slœgth*, from *slœgr* 'sly'.

slender ■ adj. (**-er**, **-est**) 1 gracefully thin. 2 barely sufficient: *people of slender means.*
– DERIVATIVES **slenderly** adv. **slenderness** n.
– ORIGIN Middle English.

slept past and past participle of SLEEP.

sleuth /sluːθ/ informal ■ n. a detective. ■ v. [often as noun **sleuthing**] carry out a search or investigation in the manner of a detective.
– ORIGIN Middle English: from Old Norse *slóth*.

slew[1] (also **slue**) ■ v. 1 turn or slide violently or uncontrollably. 2 [usu. as noun **slewing**] (of an electronic device) give a maximum response to a sudden large increase in input. ■ n. a slewing movement.
– ORIGIN C18 (orig. in nautical use).

slew[2] past of SLAY.

slew[3] ■ n. informal, chiefly N. Amer. a large number or quantity.
– ORIGIN C19: from Irish *sluagh*.

slice ■ n. 1 a thin, broad piece of food cut from a larger portion. ▸ a portion or share. 2 a utensil with a broad, flat blade for lifting foods such as cake and fish. 3 (in sports) a sliced stroke or shot. ■ v. 1 cut into slices. ▸ (often **slice something off/from**) cut with or as if with a sharp implement. 2 move easily and quickly. 3 Golf strike (the ball) so that it curves away to the right (for a left-handed player, the left). ▸ (in other sports) propel (the ball) with a glancing contact so that it travels forward spinning.
– PHRASES **slice and dice** divide a quantity of information up into smaller parts, especially in order to analyse it more closely or in different ways.
– DERIVATIVES **sliceable** adj. **slicer** n.
– ORIGIN Middle English: shortening of Old French *esclice* 'splinter', from the verb *esclicier*, of Germanic origin.

slick ■ adj. 1 done or operating in an impressively smooth and efficient way. ▸ glibly assured. 2 (of skin or hair) smooth and glossy. ▸ (of a surface) smooth, wet, and slippery. ■ n. 1 an oil slick. 2 a racing-car or bicycle tyre without a tread, for use in dry weather conditions. ■ v. make (hair) flat and slick with water, oil, or cream. ▸ cover with a film of liquid.
– DERIVATIVES **slickly** adv. **slickness** n.
– ORIGIN Middle English: prob. from Old English and rel. to Old Norse *slíkr* 'smooth'.

slickenside ■ n. Geology a polished and striated rock surface that results from friction along a fault or bedding plane.
– ORIGIN C18: from a dialect var. of SLICK + SIDE.

slicker ■ n. chiefly N. Amer. 1 short for CITY SLICKER. 2 a raincoat made of smooth material.

slide ■ v. (past and past part. **slid**) 1 move along a smooth surface, especially downwards, while maintaining continuous contact with it. 2 change gradually to a worse condition or lower level. ■ n. 1 a structure with a smooth sloping surface for children to slide down. 2 an act of sliding. ▸ a part of a machine or instrument that slides. 3 a rectangular piece of glass on which an object is mounted or placed for examination under a microscope. 4 a mounted transparency, especially one placed in a projector for viewing on a screen. 5 Brit. a hairslide.
– DERIVATIVES **slidable** adj. **slidably** adv.
– ORIGIN Old English.

slide guitar ■ n. a style of guitar playing in which a glissando effect is produced by moving a bottleneck or similar device over the strings.

slider ■ n. 1 a knob or lever which is moved horizontally or vertically to control a variable. 2 Baseball a pitch that moves laterally as it nears home plate.

slide rule ■ n. a ruler with a sliding central strip, marked with logarithmic scales and used for making rapid calculations.

slide valve ■ n. a piece that opens and closes an aperture by sliding across it.

sliding scale ■ n. a scale of fees, wages, etc., that varies in accordance with variation of some standard.

slight ■ adj. 1 small in degree; inconsiderable. ▸ not profound or substantial. 2 not sturdy and strongly built. ■ v. insult (someone) by treating them without proper respect or attention. ■ n. an insult caused by a failure to show someone proper respect or attention.
– DERIVATIVES **slighting** adj. **slightingly** adv. **slightness** n.
– ORIGIN Middle English: from Old Norse *sléttr* (adj.) 'smooth', *slétta* (v.), of Germanic origin.

slightly ■ adv. 1 to a small degree; inconsiderably: *he lowered his voice slightly.* 2 (with reference to a person's build) in a slender way: *a slightly built girl.*

slily ■ adv. variant spelling of slyly (see SLY).

slim ■ adj. (**-er**, **-est**) 1 gracefully thin; slenderly built. ▸ small in width and long and narrow in shape. 2 very small: *a slim chance.* 3 S. African crafty or unscrupulous. ■ v. (**slimmed**, **slimming**) make or become thinner, especially by dieting and sometimes exercising. ▸ reduce (an organization) to a smaller size to make it more efficient. ■ n. 1 a course or period of slimming. 2 (also **slim disease**) another term for AIDS.
– DERIVATIVES **slimly** adv. **slimmer** n. **slimness** n.
– ORIGIN C17: from Low German or Dutch, from a base meaning 'slanting, cross, bad'.

slime ■ n. an unpleasantly moist, soft, and slippery substance. ■ v. cover with slime.
– ORIGIN Old English, of Germanic origin.

slimeball ■ n. informal a repulsive or despicable person.

slime mould ■ n. a simple organism that consists of creeping jelly-like protoplasm containing nuclei, or a mass of amoeboid cells. [Division Myxomycota or (regarded as a protist) phylum Gymnomyxa.]

slimes dam ■ n. Mining, chiefly S. African a disposal pond for ore tailings.

slimline ■ adj. 1 slender in design or build. 2 (of food or drink) low in calories.

slimy ■ adj. (**-ier**, **-iest**) 1 covered by or having the feel or consistency of slime. 2 informal repulsively obsequious.
– DERIVATIVES **slimily** adv. **sliminess** n.

sling ■ n. 1 a flexible strap or belt used in the form of a loop to support or raise a hanging weight. ▸ a bandage or soft strap looped round the neck to support an injured

slingback

arm. ▶ a pouch or frame for carrying a baby, supported by a strap round the neck or shoulders. **2** a simple weapon in the form of a strap or loop, used to hurl stones or other small missiles. ■ v. (past and past part. **slung**) **1** suspend or carry loosely with or as with a sling or strap. **2** informal throw; fling. **3** hurl from a sling or similar weapon.
– PHRASES **put someone's** (or **have one's**) **ass in a sling** N. Amer. vulgar slang cause someone to be (or be) in trouble.
– DERIVATIVES **slinger** n.
– ORIGIN Middle English: prob. from Low German.

slingback ■ n. a shoe held in place by a strap around the ankle above the heel.

slingshot ■ n. a hand-held catapult. ▶ a shot from a slingshot. ■ v. (**-shotting**; past and past part. **-shot** or **-shotted**) forcefully accelerate.

slink ■ v. (past and past part. **slunk**) move quietly with gliding steps, in a stealthy or sensuous manner. ▶ come or go unobtrusively or furtively. ■ n. an act of slinking.
– ORIGIN Old English *slincan* 'crawl, creep'.

slinky ■ adj. (**-ier**, **-iest**) informal graceful and sinuous in movement or form.
– DERIVATIVES **slinkily** adv. **slinkiness** n.

slip¹ ■ v. (**slipped**, **slipping**) **1** lose one's balance or footing and slide unintentionally for a short distance. ▶ accidentally slide or move out of position or from someone's grasp. ▶ fail to grip or make proper contact with a surface. **2** pass gradually to a worse condition. ▶ (usu. **slip up**) make a careless error. **3** move or place quietly, quickly, or stealthily. **4** escape or get loose from (a means of restraint). ▶ fail to be remembered by (one's mind or memory). ▶ release (a hunting dog) from restraint. ▶ release (the clutch of a motor vehicle) slightly or for a moment. **5** Knitting move (a stitch) to the other needle without knitting it. ■ n. **1** an act of slipping. ▶ a sideways movement of an aircraft in flight. **2** a minor or careless mistake. **3** a loose-fitting garment, especially a short petticoat. **4** Cricket a fielding position close behind the batsman on the off side. **5** short for **SLIPWAY**.
– PHRASES **give someone the slip** informal evade or escape from someone. **let something slip** reveal something inadvertently in conversation. **slip of the pen** (or **the tongue**) a minor mistake in writing (or speech).
– DERIVATIVES **slippage** n.
– ORIGIN Middle English: prob. from Middle Low German *slippen* (v.).

slip² ■ n. **1** a small piece of paper for writing on or that gives printed information. **2** a long, thin, narrow strip of wood or other material. **3** (**a slip of a ——**) a small, slim young person: *a slip of a girl*. **4** a cutting taken from a plant for grafting or planting; a scion.
– ORIGIN Middle English: prob. from Middle Dutch, Middle Low German *slippe* 'cut, strip'.

slip³ ■ n. a creamy mixture of clay, water, and typically a pigment of some kind, used for decorating earthenware.
– ORIGIN C17: cf. Norwegian *slip(a)* 'slime'.

slip case ■ n. a close-fitting case open at one side or end for an object such as a book.

slip casting ■ n. the manufacture of ceramic ware by allowing slip to solidify in a mould.
– DERIVATIVES **slip-cast** adj.

slip cover ■ n. **1** a detachable cover for a chair or sofa. **2** a jacket or slip case for a book.

slip knot ■ n. **1** a knot that can be undone by a pull. **2** a running knot.

slip-on ■ adj. (of shoes or clothes) having no fastenings and therefore able to be put on and taken off quickly. ■ n. a slip-on shoe or garment.

slipped ■ adj. Heraldry (of a flower or leaf) depicted with a stalk.

slipped disc ■ n. a displaced or protruding spinal disc which presses on nearby nerves, causing back pain or sciatica.

slipper ■ n. a comfortable slip-on shoe that is worn indoors. ▶ a light slip-on shoe, especially one used for dancing.
– DERIVATIVES **slippered** adj.

slipper bath ■ n. chiefly historical a bath with one high end to lean against and the other end covered in.

slippery ■ adj. **1** difficult to hold firmly or stand on through being smooth, wet, or slimy. **2** (of a person) evasive and unpredictable. ▶ (of a word or concept) changing in meaning according to context or point of view.
– PHRASES **slippery slope** a course of action likely to lead to something bad.
– DERIVATIVES **slipperily** adv. **slipperiness** n.
– ORIGIN C15: from dialect *slipper* 'slippery', prob. suggested by Luther's *schlipfferig*.

slippery elm ■ n. a North American elm with slimy inner bark, used medicinally. [*Ulmus fulva*.]

slippy ■ adj. (**-ier**, **-iest**) informal slippery.
– DERIVATIVES **slippiness** n.

slip ring ■ n. a ring for sliding electrical contact in a dynamo or electric motor.

slip road ■ n. a road entering or leaving a highway or dual carriageway.

slipshod ■ adj. **1** lacking in care, thought, or organization. **2** archaic (of shoes) worn down at the heel.
– ORIGIN C16: from **SLIP¹** + **SHOD**.

slip-slop ■ n. S. African another term for **FLIP-FLOP** (in sense 1).

slip stitch ■ n. **1** (in sewing) a loose stitch joining layers of fabric and not visible externally. **2** Knitting a type of stitch in which the stitches are moved from one needle to the other without being knitted. ■ v. (**slip-stitch**) sew or knit with slip stitches.

slipstream ■ n. **1** a current of air or water driven back by a revolving propeller or jet engine. ▶ the partial vacuum created in the wake of a moving vehicle. **2** an assisting force regarded as drawing something along in its wake. ■ v. follow in the slipstream of a vehicle, especially when awaiting an opportunity to overtake in motor racing.

slip-up ■ n. informal a mistake or blunder.

slipware ■ n. pottery decorated with slip (see **SLIP³**).

slipway ■ n. a slope leading into water, used for launching and landing boats and ships or for building and repairing them.

slit ■ n. a long, narrow cut or opening. ■ v. (**slitting**; past and past part. **slit**) **1** make a slit in. ▶ cut into strips. **2** (past and past part. **slitted**) form (one's eyes) into slits.
– DERIVATIVES **slitter** n.
– ORIGIN Old English *slite* (n.); rel. to *slītan* 'split, rend', of Germanic origin.

slither ■ v. move smoothly over a surface with a twisting or oscillating motion. ▶ slide or slip unsteadily on a loose or slippery surface. ■ n. **1** a slithering movement. **2** a sliver.
– DERIVATIVES **slithery** adj.
– ORIGIN Middle English: alteration of dialect *slidder*, from the base of **SLIDE**.

slit trench ■ n. a narrow trench for a soldier or a small group of soldiers and their equipment.

slitty ■ adj. (**-ier**, **-iest**) chiefly derogatory (of the eyes) long and narrow.

sliver /ˈslɪvə, ˈslaɪ-/ ■ n. a small, narrow, sharp piece cut or split off a larger piece. ■ v. cut or break into slivers.
– ORIGIN Middle English: from dialect *slive* 'cleave'.

slivovitz /ˈslɪvəvɪts/ ■ n. a type of plum brandy made chiefly in the former Yugoslavia and in Romania.
– ORIGIN from Serbo-Croat *šljivovica*, from *šljiva* 'plum'.

slob informal ■ n. a lazy and slovenly person. ■ v. behave in a lazy and slovenly manner.
– DERIVATIVES **slobbish** adj. **slobbishness** n. **slobby** adj.
– ORIGIN C18: from Irish *slab* 'mud', from Anglo-Irish *slab* 'ooze, sludge', prob. of Scandinavian origin.

slobber ■ v. **1** have saliva dripping copiously from the mouth. **2** (**slobber over**) show excessive enthusiasm for. ■ n. saliva dripping copiously from the mouth.
– DERIVATIVES **slobbery** adj.
– ORIGIN Middle English: prob. from Middle Dutch *slobberen* 'walk through mud', also 'feed noisily', of imitative origin.

sloe ■ n. the small bluish-black fruit of the European

blackthorn, with a sharp sour taste.
–ORIGIN Old English, of Germanic origin.

sloe-eyed ■ adj. having attractive dark almond-shaped eyes.

sloe gin ■ n. a liqueur made by steeping sloes in gin.

slog ■ v. (**slogged**, **slogging**) 1 work hard over a period of time. ▶ walk or move with difficulty or effort. 2 hit or strike forcefully. ▶ (**slog it out**) fight or compete fiercely. ■ n. 1 a spell of difficult, tiring work or travelling. 2 a forceful hit or strike.
–DERIVATIVES **slogger** n.
–ORIGIN C19.

slogan ■ n. a short, memorable phrase used in advertising or associated with a political party or group.
–ORIGIN C16: from Scottish Gaelic *sluagh-ghairm*, from *sluagh* 'army' + *gairm* 'shout'.

sloganeer chiefly N. Amer. ■ v. [usu. as noun **sloganeering**] employ or invent slogans, especially in a political context. ■ n. a person who does this.

slo-mo ■ n. short for SLOW MOTION.

sloop ■ n. 1 a one-masted sailing boat with a mainsail and jib rigged fore and aft. 2 (also **sloop of war**) historical a small square-rigged sailing warship with two or three masts. 3 a small anti-submarine warship used for convoy escort in the Second World War.
–ORIGIN C17: from Dutch *sloep(e)*.

sloot /sluːt/ (also **sluit**) ■ n. S. African a deep gully eroded by rainfall. ▶ historical a narrow water channel constructed for irrigation.
–ORIGIN Afrikaans, from Dutch *sloot* 'ditch'.

slop ■ v. (**slopped**, **slopping**) 1 (of a liquid) spill or flow over the edge of a container. ▶ apply casually or carelessly. ▶ (**slop out**) (especially in prison) empty the contents of a chamber pot. 2 (**slop through**) wade through (a wet or muddy area). 3 (**slop about/around**) chiefly Brit. dress in an untidy or casual manner. ■ n. 1 (**slops**) waste water or liquid that has to be emptied by hand. ▶ semi-liquid kitchen refuse. ▶ unappetizing weak, semi-liquid food. 2 Nautical a choppy sea.
–ORIGIN C16: prob. rel. to SLIP[3].

slope ■ n. a surface of which one end or side is at a higher level than another. ▶ a difference in level or sideways position between two ends or sides. ▶ a part of the side of a hill or mountain, especially as a place for skiing. ■ v. 1 be inclined from a horizontal or vertical line; slant up or down. 2 informal move in an idle or aimless manner.
▶ (**slope off**) leave unobtrusively, typically in order to evade work or duty.
–PHRASES **slope arms** Military hold a rifle with the barrel on the left shoulder and the butt in the left hand.
–ORIGIN C16: from the obsolete adverb *slope*, a shortening of archaic *aslope* 'in a sloping position'.

sloppy ■ adj. (**-ier**, **-iest**) 1 (of semi-fluid matter) containing too much liquid; watery. 2 careless and unsystematic; excessively casual. 3 (of a garment) casual and loose-fitting. 4 weakly or foolishly sentimental.
–DERIVATIVES **sloppily** adv. **sloppiness** n.

sloppy joe ■ n. informal 1 a long, loose-fitting sweater. 2 N. Amer. a hamburger in which the minced-beef filling is made into a kind of meat sauce.

slosh ■ v. (of liquid in a container) move irregularly with a splashing sound. ▶ move through liquid with a splashing sound. ▶ pour (liquid) clumsily. ■ n. an act or sound of splashing. ▶ a quantity of liquid that is poured out.
–ORIGIN C19: var. of SLUSH.

sloshed ■ adj. informal drunk.

sloshy ■ adj. (**-ier**, **-iest**) 1 wet and sticky; slushy. 2 excessively sentimental; sloppy.

slot[1] ■ n. 1 a long, narrow aperture or slit into which something may be fitted or inserted. 2 an allotted place in an arrangement or scheme such as a broadcasting schedule. ■ v. (**slotted**, **slotting**) place or be placed into a slot. ▶ (**slot in/into**) fit easily into (a new role or situation).
–DERIVATIVES **slotted** adj.
–ORIGIN Middle English: from Old French *esclot*.

slot[2] ■ n. the track of a deer, visible as slotted footprints in soft ground.
–ORIGIN C16: from Old French *esclot* 'hoofprint of a horse', prob. from Old Norse *slóth* 'trail'.

slotback ■ n. American Football a back between the tackle and the split end.

sloth /sləʊθ/ ■ n. 1 reluctance to work or make an effort; laziness. 2 a slow-moving tropical American mammal that hangs upside down from branches using its long limbs and hooked claws. [Genus *Bradypus* (three-toed sloths) and *Choloepus* (two-toed sloths).]
–DERIVATIVES **slothful** adj. **slothfully** adv. **slothfulness** n.
–ORIGIN Old English: from SLOW + -TH[2].

slot machine ■ n. 1 a coin-operated gambling machine that generates random combinations of symbols, certain combinations winning money for the player. 2 a vending machine.

slouch ■ v. stand, move, or sit in a lazy, drooping way. ■ n. 1 a lazy, drooping posture or movement. 2 [usu. with neg.] informal an incompetent person: *he was no slouch at making a buck.*
–DERIVATIVES **slouchy** adj.
–ORIGIN C16.

slouch hat ■ n. a hat with a wide flexible brim.

slough[1] /slaʊ/ ■ n. 1 a swamp. 2 a situation characterized by lack of progress or activity.
–DERIVATIVES **sloughy** adj.
–ORIGIN Old English.

slough[2] /slʌf/ ■ v. 1 (of an animal, especially a snake) cast off or shed (an old skin). 2 (**slough away/down**) (of soil or rock) collapse or slide into a hole or depression. ■ n. the dropping off of dead tissue from living flesh.
–DERIVATIVES **sloughy** adj.
–ORIGIN Middle English: perhaps rel. to Low German *slu(we)* 'husk, peel'.

Slovak /ˈsləʊvak/ ■ n. 1 a native or national of Slovakia, or a person of Slovak descent. 2 the language of Slovakia.
–ORIGIN the name in Slovak, from a Slavic root shared with SLOVENE and perhaps rel. to *slovo* 'word'.

Slovakian /sləˈvakɪən, -ˈvɑːkɪən/ ■ n. a native or inhabitant of Slovakia. ■ adj. of or relating to Slovakia.

sloven /ˈslʌv(ə)n/ ■ n. dated a person who is habitually untidy or careless.
–ORIGIN C15: perhaps from Flemish *sloef* 'dirty' or Dutch *slof* 'careless, negligent'.

Slovene /ˈsləʊviːn, sləʊˈviːn/ ■ n. a native or national of Slovenia, or a person of Slovene descent.
–DERIVATIVES **Slovenian** n. & adj.

slovenly ■ adj. 1 untidy and dirty. 2 careless; excessively casual.
–DERIVATIVES **slovenliness** n.

slow ■ adj. 1 moving or capable of moving only at a low speed. ▶ lasting or taking a long time. 2 (of a clock or watch) showing a time earlier than the correct time. 3 not prompt to understand, think, or learn. 4 uneventful and rather dull. ▶ (of business) with little activity; slack. 5 Photography (of a film) needing long exposure. 6 (of a fire or oven) burning or giving off heat gently. ■ v. (often **slow down/up**) reduce one's speed or the speed of a vehicle or process. ▶ live or work less actively or intensely.
–PHRASES **slow but** (or **and**) **sure** not quick but achieving the required result eventually.
–DERIVATIVES **slowish** adj. **slowly** adv. **slowness** n.
–ORIGIN Old English *slāw* 'slow-witted, sluggish', of Germanic origin.

slowcoach ■ n. informal a person who acts or moves slowly.

slow cooker ■ n. a large electric pot used for cooking food very slowly.

slow handclap ■ n. a slow, rhythmic clapping by an audience as a sign of displeasure or impatience.

slow march ■ n. a military marching pace approximately half the speed of the quick march.

slow match ■ n. historical a slow-burning wick or cord for lighting explosives.

slow motion ■ n. the action of showing film or video more slowly than it was made or recorded, so that the action appears much slower than in real life.

slowpoke ■ n. informal North American term for SLOWCOACH.

slow puncture ■ n. a puncture causing only gradual deflation of a tyre.

slow virus ■ n. a virus or virus-like organism that multiplies slowly in the host organism and has a long incubation period.

slow-worm ■ n. a small snake-like legless European lizard that gives birth to live young. [*Anguis fragilis.*]
– ORIGIN Old English *slāwyrm*, from *slā-* (of uncertain origin) + *wyrm* 'snake'.

SLR ■ abbrev. **1** self-loading rifle. **2** single-lens reflex.

slub ■ n. a lump or thick place in yarn or thread. ▶ fabric woven from yarn with such a texture. ■ adj. (of fabric) having an irregular appearance caused by uneven thickness of the warp.
– DERIVATIVES **slubbed** adj.
– ORIGIN C18.

sludge ■ n. **1** thick, soft, wet mud or a similar viscous mixture. ▶ dirty oil or industrial waste. **2** an unattractive muddy shade of brown or green.
– DERIVATIVES **sludgy** adj.
– ORIGIN C17.

slue ■ v.& n. variant spelling of SLEW¹.

slug¹ ■ n. **1** a tough-skinned terrestrial mollusc which lacks a shell and secretes a film of mucus for protection. [Order Stylommatophora.] **2** an amount of an alcoholic drink that is gulped or poured. **3** a bullet. ■ v. (**slugged**, **slugging**) gulp (something, typically alcohol).
– ORIGIN Middle English: prob. of Scandinavian origin.

slug² informal ■ v. (**slugged**, **slugging**) strike with a hard blow. ▶ (**slug it out**) settle a dispute or contest by fighting or competing fiercely. ■ n. a hard blow.
– DERIVATIVES **slugger** n.
– ORIGIN C19.

sluggard ■ n. a lazy, sluggish person.
– DERIVATIVES **sluggardliness** n. **sluggardly** adj.
– ORIGIN Middle English: from the rare verb *slug* 'be lazy or slow'.

sluggish ■ adj. slow-moving or inactive. ▶ lacking energy or alertness.
– DERIVATIVES **sluggishly** adv. **sluggishness** n.
– ORIGIN Middle English: from the noun SLUG¹ or the verb *slug* (see SLUGGARD).

slug pellet ■ n. a pellet containing a substance poisonous to slugs, placed among growing plants to prevent them being damaged.

sluice /sluːs/ ■ n. **1** (also **sluice gate**) a sliding gate or other device for controlling the flow of water. **2** (also **sluiceway**) an artificial water channel for carrying off overflow or surplus water. **3** an act of rinsing or showering with water. ■ v. wash or rinse freely with a stream or shower of water.
– ORIGIN Middle English: from Old French *escluse* 'sluice gate', from Latin *excludere* 'exclude'.

sluit /sluːt, ˈsluːɪt/ ■ n. variant spelling of SLOOT.

slum ■ n. a squalid and overcrowded urban area inhabited by very poor people. ▶ a house in such a place. ■ v. (**slummed**, **slumming**) (often **slum it**) informal voluntarily spend time in uncomfortable conditions or at a lower social level than one's own.
– DERIVATIVES **slummer** n. **slumminess** n. **slummy** adj.
– ORIGIN C19 (orig. slang, in the sense 'room').

slumber poetic/literary ■ v. sleep. ■ n. a sleep.
– DERIVATIVES **slumberer** n. **slumberous** (also **slumbrous**) adj.
– ORIGIN Middle English: alteration of Scots and northern English *sloom*, in the same sense. The *-b-* was added for ease of pronunciation.

slumlord ■ n. informal a landlord of slum property, especially one who profiteers.

slump ■ v. **1** sit, lean, or fall heavily and limply. **2** fail or decline substantially or over a prolonged period. ■ n. **1** an instance of slumping. **2** a prolonged period of abnormally low economic activity.
– DERIVATIVES **slumped** adj. **slumpy** adj.
– ORIGIN C17: prob. imitative and rel. to Norwegian *slumpe* 'to fall'.

slung past and past participle of SLING.

slunk past and past participle of SLINK.

slur ■ v. (**slurred**, **slurring**) **1** (with reference to speech) articulate or be articulated indistinctly. **2** pass over (a fact or aspect) so as to conceal or minimize it. **3** Music perform (a group of two or more notes) in a smooth, flowing manner. ▶ mark (notes) with a slur. ■ n. **1** an insinuation or allegation. **2** an indistinct utterance. **3** Music a curved line indicating that notes are to be slurred.
– DERIVATIVES **slurred** adj.
– ORIGIN Middle English ('thin mud', later as verb meaning 'smear' and 'disparage').

slurp ■ v. eat or drink with a loud sucking sound. ■ n. an act or sound of slurping.
– DERIVATIVES **slurpy** adj.
– ORIGIN C17: from Dutch *slurpen*.

slurry ■ n. (pl. **-ies**) a semi-liquid mixture, especially of fine particles of manure, cement, or coal and water.
– ORIGIN Middle English: rel. to dialect *slur* 'thin mud'.

slush ■ n. **1** partially melted snow or ice. **2** watery mud. **3** informal excessive sentiment. ■ v. make a soft splashing sound.
– DERIVATIVES **slushiness** n. **slushy** adj.
– ORIGIN C17: prob. imitative.

slush fund ■ n. a reserve of money used for illicit purposes, especially political bribery.
– ORIGIN C19: orig. nautical slang denoting money collected to buy luxuries, from the sale of watery food known as *slush*.

slut ■ n. a slovenly or promiscuous woman.
– DERIVATIVES **sluttish** adj. **sluttishness** n.
– ORIGIN Middle English.

sly ■ adj. (**slyer**, **slyest**) **1** having a cunning and deceitful nature. **2** (of a remark, glance, or expression) insinuating. **3** (of an action) surreptitious.
– PHRASES **on the sly** in a surreptitious fashion.
– DERIVATIVES **slyly** (also **slily**) adv. **slyness** n.
– ORIGIN Middle English: from Old Norse *slœgr* 'cunning'.

Sm ■ symb. the chemical element samarium.

smack¹ ■ n. **1** a sharp blow or slap, especially one given with the palm of the hand. **2** a loud, sharp sound made by or as by such a blow. **3** a loud kiss. ■ v. **1** hit with a smack. **2** smash, drive, or put forcefully into or on to something. **3** part (one's lips) noisily. ■ adv. (also **smack bang**) informal **1** in a sudden and violent way. **2** (N. Amer. also **smack dab**) exactly; precisely.
– PHRASES **a smack in the face** (or **eye**) informal a strong rebuff.
– ORIGIN C16: from Middle Dutch *smacken*, of imitative origin.

smack² ■ v. (**smack of**) **1** have a flavour or smell of. **2** suggest the presence or effects of. ■ n. (**a smack of**) a flavour, smell, or suggestion of.
– ORIGIN Old English *smæc* 'flavour, smell', of Germanic origin.

smack³ ■ n. a single-masted sailing boat used for coasting or fishing.
– ORIGIN C17: from Dutch *smak*.

smack⁴ ■ n. informal heroin.
– ORIGIN 1940s: prob. an alteration of Yiddish *shmek* 'a sniff'.

smacker (also **smackeroo**) ■ n. informal **1** a loud kiss. **2** (in South Africa) a rand, (in the UK) a pound sterling, or (in the US) a dollar.

small ■ adj. **1** of a size that is less than normal or usual. **2** not great in amount, number, strength, or power. **3** not fully grown or developed; young. **4** insignificant; unimportant. **5** (of a business or its owner) operating on a modest scale. ■ n. (**smalls**) informal underwear. ■ adv. **1** into small pieces. **2** in a small manner or size.
– PHRASES **feel** (or **look**) **small** feel (or look) contemptibly weak or insignificant. **the small of the back** the part of a person's back where the spine curves in at the level of the waist. **the small screen** television as a medium.
– DERIVATIVES **smallish** adj. **smallness** n.
– ORIGIN Old English, of Germanic origin.

small arms ■ pl. n. portable firearms.

small beer ■ n. a thing that is considered unimportant.

small-bore ■ adj. denoting a firearm with a narrow bore, in international and Olympic shooting generally .22 inch calibre (5.6 millimetre bore).

small-cap ■ adj. Finance denoting or relating to the stock of a company with a small capitalization.

small capital ■ n. a capital letter which is of the same height as a lower-case x in the same typeface, as THIS.

small change ■ n. 1 money in the form of coins of low value. 2 a thing that is considered trivial.

small claims court ■ n. a local court in which claims for small sums of money can be heard and decided quickly and cheaply, without legal representation.

small forward ■ n. Basketball a versatile forward who is effective outside the key as well as near the net.

small fry ■ pl. n. 1 young or small fish. 2 young or insignificant people or things.

smallholding ■ n. an agricultural holding that is smaller than a farm.
– DERIVATIVES **smallholder** n.

small hours ■ pl. n. (**the small hours**) the early hours of the morning after midnight.

small intestine ■ n. the part of the intestine that runs between the stomach and the large intestine, consisting of the duodenum, the jejunum, and the ileum.

small letter ■ n. a lower-case letter, as distinct from a capital letter.

small-minded ■ adj. having a narrow outlook; petty.
– DERIVATIVES **small-mindedly** adv. **small-mindedness** n.

smallpox ■ n. an acute contagious viral disease, with fever and pustules usually leaving permanent scars.

small print ■ n. 1 printed matter in small type. 2 inconspicuous but binding details or conditions printed in an agreement or contract.

small-scale ■ adj. of limited size or extent.

small slam ■ n. Bridge the bidding and winning of twelve of the thirteen tricks.

small talk ■ n. polite conversation about uncontroversial matters.

small-time ■ adj. informal unimportant; minor.
– DERIVATIVES **small-timer** n.

small-town ■ adj. relating to or characteristic of a small town, especially in being unsophisticated or petty.

smarm informal ■ v. 1 behave in an ingratiating way. 2 smooth down (one's hair), especially with oil or gel. ■ n. ingratiating behaviour.
– ORIGIN C19: orig. dialect 'smear, bedaub'.

smarmy ■ adj. (**-ier, -iest**) informal excessively flattering or ingratiating.
– DERIVATIVES **smarmily** adv. **smarminess** n.

smart ■ adj. 1 clean, tidy, and stylish. 2 bright and fresh in appearance. 3 (of a place) fashionable and upmarket. 4 informal having a quick intelligence. ▶ (of a device) capable of independent and seemingly intelligent action. ▶ chiefly N. Amer. impertinently clever or sarcastic. 5 quick; brisk. ■ v. 1 present a sharp, stinging pain. 2 feel upset and annoyed. ■ n. 1 (**smarts**) N. Amer. informal intelligence; acumen. 2 a smarting pain. ■ adv. archaic in a quick or brisk manner.
– PHRASES **look smart** chiefly Brit. be quick.
– DERIVATIVES **smarting** adj. **smartingly** adv. **smartly** adv. **smartness** n.
– ORIGIN Old English, of West Germanic origin.

smart alec (also **smart aleck**) ■ n. informal a person considered irritating in always having a clever answer to a question.
– DERIVATIVES **smart-alecky** adj.
– ORIGIN C19: from SMART + *Alec*, diminutive of the given name *Alexander*.

smart-arse (US **smart-ass**) ■ n. informal another term for SMART ALEC.

smart card ■ n. a plastic card with a built-in microprocessor, used for electronic processes such as financial transactions and personal identification.

smarten ■ v. (often **smarten up**) make or become smarter.

smartish ■ adv. informal, chiefly Brit. quickly; briskly.

smart mouth N. Amer. informal ■ n. a tendency to make impudent remarks. ■ v. (**smart-mouth**) make impudent remarks.
– DERIVATIVES **smart-mouthed** adj.

smartphone ■ n. a cellphone which incorporates a palmtop computer or PDA.

smash ■ v. 1 break or cause to break violently into pieces. ▶ (**smash down**) violently knock down. 2 crash and severely damage (a vehicle). ▶ (**smash into**) hit or collide with forcefully. 3 (in sport) strike (the ball) or score (a goal, run, etc.) with great force. ▶ (in tennis, badminton, and similar sports) strike (the ball or shuttlecock) downwards with a hard overarm stroke. 4 completely defeat, destroy, or foil. ■ n. 1 an act, instance, or sound of smashing. 2 (also **smash hit**) informal a very successful song, film, or show. ■ adv. with a sudden smash.
– ORIGIN C18: prob. imitative, representing a blend of words such as *smack*, *smite* with *bash*, *mash*, etc.

smash-and-grab ■ adj. denoting a robbery in which the thief smashes a shop window and seizes goods.

smashed ■ adj. informal very drunk.

smasher ■ n. 1 a person or device that smashes something. 2 Brit. informal a very attractive or impressive person or thing.

smashing ■ adj. informal, chiefly Brit. excellent; wonderful.
– DERIVATIVES **smashingly** adv.

smash-up ■ n. informal a violent collision between vehicles.

smattering (also **smatter**) ■ n. 1 a small amount. 2 a slight knowledge of a language or subject.
– ORIGIN C16: from *smatter* 'talk ignorantly, prate'.

smear ■ v. 1 coat or mark with a greasy or sticky substance. 2 spread (a greasy or sticky substance) over a surface. 3 blur or smudge. 4 damage the reputation of (someone) by false or unwarranted accusations. ■ n. 1 a greasy or sticky mark. 2 a false or unwarranted accusation. 3 a sample thinly spread on a microscopic slide. ▶ short for SMEAR TEST or PAP SMEAR. 4 Climbing an insecure foothold.
– DERIVATIVES **smearer** n. **smeary** adj.
– ORIGIN Old English *smierwan* (v.), *smeoru* 'ointment, grease', of Germanic origin.

smear test ■ n. a Pap smear.

smectic /'smɛktɪk/ ■ adj. denoting or involving a state of a liquid crystal in which the molecules are oriented in parallel and arranged in well-defined planes. Compare with NEMATIC.
– ORIGIN C17: from Greek *smēktikos* 'cleansing' (because of the soap-like consistency).

smegma /'smɛgmə/ ■ n. a sebaceous secretion in the folds of the skin, especially under a man's foreskin.
– ORIGIN C19: from Greek *smēgma* 'soap'.

smell ■ n. 1 the faculty of perceiving odours by means of the organs in the nose. 2 a quality in something that is perceived by this faculty; an odour. ▶ an unpleasant odour. 3 an act of inhaling in order to ascertain an odour. ■ v. (past and past part. **smelt** or **smelled**) 1 perceive or detect the odour of. ▶ sniff at (something) in order to ascertain its odour. 2 (**smell something out**) detect or discover something by the faculty of smell. 3 detect or suspect by means of instinct or intuition. ▶ (also **smell someone out**) S. African (of a traditional healer or diviner) identify a witch or evil-doer. 4 emit an odour of a specified kind. ▶ have a strong or unpleasant odour. 5 be suggestive of something.
– PHRASES **smell a rat** informal suspect trickery.
– DERIVATIVES **smellable** adj. **smeller** n. **smelliness** n. **-smelling** adj. **smelly** adj.
– ORIGIN Middle English.

smelling-out ■ n. S. African an act or instance of identifying a witch or evil-doer.

smelling salts ■ pl. n. chiefly historical a pungent substance typically consisting of ammonium carbonate mixed with perfume, sniffed as a restorative.

smelt[1] ■ v. extract (metal) from its ore by a process involving heating and melting.
– DERIVATIVES **smelter** n. **smelting** n.
– ORIGIN C16: from Middle Dutch, Middle Low German *smelten*.

smelt

smelt² past and past participle of SMELL.

smidge ■ n. informal another term for SMIDGEN.

smidgen (also **smidgeon** or **smidgin**) ■ n. informal a tiny amount.
– ORIGIN C19: perhaps from Scots *smitch* in the same sense.

smilax /'smaɪlaks/ ■ n. **1** a climbing shrub with hooks and tendrils, several South American species of which yield sarsaparilla from their roots. [Genus *Smilax*.] **2** a climbing asparagus with decorative foliage, native to southern Africa. [*Asparagus asparagoides*.]
– ORIGIN C16: from Greek, 'bindweed'.

smile ■ v. **1** form one's features into a pleased, friendly, or amused expression, with the corners of the mouth turned up. **2** (**smile at/on/upon**) regard favourably or indulgently. ■ n. an act of smiling; a smiling expression.
– DERIVATIVES **smiler** n. **smiling** adj. **smilingly** adv.
– ORIGIN Middle English: perhaps of Scandinavian origin.

smiley (also **smilie**) ■ adj. informal smiling; cheerful. ■ n. (pl. **-eys** or **-ies**) **1** a symbol representing a smiling face, formed by the characters :-) and used in electronic communications. **2** S. African informal a cooked sheep's head.

smirch /smɜːtʃ/ ■ v. **1** make dirty. **2** discredit; taint. ■ n. **1** a dirty mark or stain. **2** a flaw.
– ORIGIN C15: prob. symbolic.

smirk ■ v. smile in an irritatingly smug or silly way. ■ n. a smug or silly smile.
– DERIVATIVES **smirker** n. **smirking** adj. **smirkingly** adv. **smirky** adj.
– ORIGIN Old English *sme(a)rcian*, from a base shared by SMILE.

smite ■ v. (past **smote**; past part. **smitten**) **1** archaic or poetic/literary strike with a firm blow. **2** archaic or poetic/literary defeat or conquer. **3** (usu. **be smitten**) (especially of a disease) attack or affect severely. **4** (**be smitten**) be strongly attracted to someone or something. ■ n. archaic or poetic/literary a firm blow.
– DERIVATIVES **smiter** n.
– ORIGIN Old English *smītan* 'to smear, blemish', of Germanic origin.

smith ■ n. a worker in metal. ▶ short for BLACKSMITH. ■ v. treat (metal) by heating, hammering, and forging it.
– ORIGIN Old English, of Germanic origin.

-smith ■ comb. form denoting a person skilled in creating something with a specified material: *goldsmith*.

smithereens /ˌsmɪðə'riːnz/ (also **smithers** /'smɪðəz/) ■ pl. n. informal small pieces.
– ORIGIN C19: prob. from Irish *smidirín*.

smithery ■ n. the work of or goods made by a smith.

smithy /'smɪði/ ■ n. (pl. **-ies**) a blacksmith's workshop; a forge.
– ORIGIN Middle English, from Old Norse *smithja*.

smitten past participle of SMITE.

SMME ■ abbrev. chiefly S. African small, medium, and/or microenterprises.

smock ■ n. **1** a loose dress or blouse having the upper part closely gathered in smocking. **2** a loose overall worn to protect one's clothes. ■ v. decorate with smocking.
– DERIVATIVES **smocked** adj.
– ORIGIN Old English *smoc* 'woman's loose-fitting undergarment'.

smocking ■ n. decoration on a garment created by gathering a section of the material into tight pleats and holding them together with parallel stitches in an ornamental pattern.

smog ■ n. fog or haze intensified by smoke or other atmospheric pollutants.
– DERIVATIVES **smoggy** adj.
– ORIGIN C20: blend of SMOKE and FOG.

smoke ■ n. **1** a visible suspension of carbon or other particles in the air, typically one emitted from a burning substance. **2** an act of smoking tobacco. **3** informal a cigarette or cigar. ■ v. **1** emit smoke. **2** inhale and exhale the smoke of tobacco or a drug. **3** cure or preserve (meat or fish) by exposure to smoke. **4** treat (glass) so as to darken it. **5** fumigate, cleanse, or purify by exposure to smoke. ▶ subdue (bees in a hive) by exposing them to smoke. **6** (**smoke someone/thing out**) drive someone or something out of a place by using smoke.
– PHRASES **go up in smoke** informal **1** be destroyed by fire. **2** (of a plan) come to nothing. **no smoke without fire** rumours usually have some basis in fact. **smoke and mirrors** the use of misleading or irrelevant information to obscure or embellish the truth. **smoke like a chimney** smoke tobacco incessantly.
– DERIVATIVES **smokable** (also **smokeable**) adj. **smoked** adj. **smokeless** adj. **smoking** adj. & n.
– ORIGIN Old English, from the Germanic base of *smēocan* 'emit smoke'.

smoke alarm ■ n. a device that detects and gives a warning of the presence of smoke.

smoke bomb ■ n. a bomb that emits dense smoke as it explodes.

smokebox ■ n. **1** a smoke-producing oven for smoking food. **2** the chamber in a steam engine or boiler between the flues and the funnel or chimney stack. **3** another term for SMOKER (in sense 3).

smoke bush ■ n. another term for SMOKE TREE.

smokehouse ■ n. a shed or room for smoking fish or meat.

smokeless zone ■ n. a district in which it is illegal to create smoke and where only smokeless fuel may be used.

smoker ■ n. **1** a person who smokes tobacco regularly. **2** a person or device that smokes fish or meat. **3** a device which emits smoke for subduing bees in a hive.

smokescreen ■ n. **1** a cloud of smoke created to conceal military operations. **2** irrelevant activity designed to disguise someone's real intentions or activities.

smoke signal ■ n. a column of smoke used to convey a message to a distant person.

smokestack ■ n. a chimney or funnel for discharging smoke from a locomotive, ship, factory, etc.

smoke tree ■ n. a shrub or small tree which bears feathery plumes of purple or reddish flowers and fruit, giving it a smoky appearance. [*Cotinus coggygria* (formerly *Rhus cotinus*).]

smoking gun ■ n. a piece of incontrovertible incriminating evidence.

smoking jacket ■ n. a man's comfortable jacket, typically made of velvet, formerly worn while smoking after dinner.

smoky ■ adj. (**-ier**, **-iest**) **1** producing, filled with, smelling of, or resembling smoke. **2** having the taste or aroma of smoked food.
– DERIVATIVES **smokily** adv. **smokiness** n.

smoky quartz ■ n. a semi-precious variety of quartz ranging in colour from light greyish-brown to nearly black.

smolder ■ v. US spelling of SMOULDER.

smolt /sməʊlt/ ■ n. a young salmon or trout after the parr stage, when it becomes silvery and migrates to the sea for the first time.
– ORIGIN Middle English (orig. Scots and northern English).

smooch informal ■ v. kiss and cuddle amorously. ■ n. a spell of smooching.
– DERIVATIVES **smoocher** n. **smoochy** adj. (**-ier**, **-iest**).
– ORIGIN 1930s: from dialect *smouch*, of imitative origin.

smoorsnoek /'smʊə(r)snʊk/ (also **smoorvis** /'smʊə(r)fɪs/) ■ n. S. African a Cape Malay dish of smoked fish, typically snoek, braised with vegetables and rice.
– ORIGIN Afrikaans, from *smoor* 'to stew' + *snoek*.

smooth ■ adj. **1** having an even and regular surface; free from projections or indentations. ▶ (of a liquid) having an even consistency; without lumps. **2** (of movement) without jerks. **3** without problems or difficulties. **4** (of a flavour) without harshness or bitterness. **5** suavely or unctuously charming. ■ v. (also **smoothe**) make smooth.
– DERIVATIVES **smoother** n. **smoothish** adj. **smoothly** adv. **smoothness** n.
– ORIGIN Old English, prob. of Germanic origin.

smooth-bore ■ n. a gun with an unrifled barrel.

smooth-faced ■ adj. clean-shaven.

VOWELS a cat ɑː arm ɛ bed ɛː hair ə ago əː her ɪ sit i cosy iː see ɒ hot ɔː saw ʌ run

smooth hound ■ n. a small shark which typically lives close to the seabed in shallow waters. [Genus *Mustelus*: two species.]

smoothie ■ n. **1** informal a man with a smooth, suave manner. **2** a thick, smooth drink of fresh fruit puréed with milk, yogurt, or ice cream.

smoothing plane ■ n. a small plane for finishing the surface of wood.

smooth muscle ■ n. Physiology muscle tissue in which the contractile fibrils are not highly ordered, occurring in the gut and other internal organs and not under voluntary control. Often contrasted with **STRIATED MUSCLE**.

smooth talk ■ n. persuasively charming or flattering language. ■ v. (**smooth-talk**) informal address or persuade with smooth talk.
–DERIVATIVES **smooth-talker** n. **smooth-talking** adj.

smooth tongue ■ n. the tendency to use smooth talk.
–DERIVATIVES **smooth-tongued** adj.

smorgasbord /ˈsmɔːɡəsbɔːd/ ■ n. a range of open sandwiches and savoury delicacies served as hors d'oeuvres or a buffet.
–ORIGIN Swedish, from *smörgås* '(slice of) bread and butter' + *bord* 'table'.

smote past of **SMITE**.

smother ■ v. **1** suffocate by covering the nose and mouth. **2** extinguish (a fire) by covering it. **3** (**smother someone/thing in/with**) cover someone or something entirely with. **4** cause to feel trapped and oppressed. **5** suppress (a feeling or action). ■ n. a mass of something that stifles or obscures.
–ORIGIN Middle English: from the base of Old English *smorian* 'suffocate'.

smothered mate ■ n. Chess checkmate in which the king has no vacant square to move to and is checkmated by a knight.

smoulder (US also **smolder**) ■ v. **1** burn slowly with smoke but no flame. **2** (with reference to an intense feeling) express or be expressed in a barely suppressed state. ■ n. an instance of smouldering.
–DERIVATIVES **smouldering** adj. **smoulderingly** adv.
–ORIGIN Middle English: rel. to Dutch *smeulen*.

smous /sməʊs/ ■ n. (pl. **smouse** or **smouses**) S. African historical an itinerant Jewish pedlar.
–ORIGIN from S. African Dutch 'hawker, pedlar', transferred use of Dutch 'Jew, usurer'.

SMS ■ abbrev. short message service, a system that enables cellphone users to send and receive text messages. ■ n. a text message that is sent or received using SMS. ■ v. (**SMSs** or **SMSes**, **SMSing**, **SMSed**) send someone a text message using SMS.

SMTP ■ abbrev. Simple Mail Transfer (or Transport) Protocol, a standard for the transmission of electronic mail on a computer network.

smudge ■ v. make or become blurred or smeared. ■ n. a smudged mark or image.
–DERIVATIVES **smudgily** adv. **smudginess** n. **smudgy** adj. (**-ier**, **-iest**).
–ORIGIN Middle English.

smug ■ adj. (**smugger**, **smuggest**) irritatingly pleased with oneself; self-satisfied.
–DERIVATIVES **smugly** adv. **smugness** n.
–ORIGIN C16: from Low German *smuk* 'pretty'.

smuggle ■ v. **1** move (goods) illegally into or out of a country. **2** convey secretly and illicitly.
–DERIVATIVES **smuggler** n. **smuggling** n.
–ORIGIN C17: from Low German *smuggelen*.

smut ■ n. **1** a small flake of soot or dirt. **2** a fungal disease of cereals in which parts of the ear change to black powder. **3** indecent or obscene talk, writing, or pictures. ■ v. (**smutted**, **smutting**) **1** mark with smuts. **2** infect with smut.
–DERIVATIVES **smuttily** adv. **smuttiness** n. **smutty** adj. (**-ier**, **-iest**).
–ORIGIN Middle English.

Sn ■ symb. the chemical element tin.
–ORIGIN from late Latin *stannum* 'tin'.

snack ■ n. a small quantity of food or a light meal, eaten between meals or in place of a meal. ■ v. eat a snack.
–ORIGIN Middle English: from Middle Dutch *snac(k)*, from *snacken* 'to bite', var. of *snappen*.

snaffle ■ n. a simple bit on a bridle, used with a single set of reins. ■ v. informal illicitly take for oneself.
–ORIGIN C16: prob. from Low German or Dutch; the verb (C19) is perhaps of a different origin.

snafu /snaˈfuː, ˈsnafuː/ informal, chiefly N. Amer. ■ n. a confused or chaotic state; a mess. ■ v. throw into confusion or chaos.
–ORIGIN 1940s: acronym from *situation normal: all fouled (or fucked) up*.

snag ■ n. **1** an unexpected or hidden obstacle or drawback. **2** a sharp, angular, or jagged projection. **3** a small rent or tear. **4** (in forestry) a dead tree. ■ v. (**snagged**, **snagging**) **1** catch or tear or become caught or torn on a snag. **2** N. Amer. informal catch; obtain.
–DERIVATIVES **snaggy** adj.
–ORIGIN C16: prob. of Scandinavian origin.

snaggle ■ n. a tangled or knotted mass. ■ v. become knotted or tangled.
–ORIGIN C20: from **SNAG**.

snaggle-toothed ■ adj. having irregular or projecting teeth.

snail ■ n. a slow-moving mollusc with a spiral shell into which the whole body can be withdrawn. [Many species in the class Gastropoda.]
–ORIGIN Old English, of Germanic origin.

snail mail ■ n. informal the ordinary post as opposed to email.

snake ■ n. **1** a predatory reptile with a long slender limbless supple body, many kinds of which have a venomous bite. [Suborder Ophidia: many species.] **2** (also **snake in the grass**) a treacherous or deceitful person. **3** (in full **plumber's snake**) a long flexible wire for clearing obstacles in piping. ■ v. move or extend with the twisting motion of a snake.
–ORIGIN Old English, of Germanic origin.

snakebird ■ n. another term for **DARTER** (in sense 1).

snakeboard ■ n. trademark a type of skateboard consisting of two footplates joined by a bar, allowing for greater speed and manoeuvrability than with a standard skateboard.
–DERIVATIVES **snakeboarder** n. **snakeboarding** n.

snake charmer ■ n. an entertainer who appears to make snakes move by playing music.

snake eyes ■ pl. n. [treated as sing.] a throw of two ones with a pair of dice.

snake mackerel ■ n. another term for **ESCOLAR**.

snake oil ■ n. informal, chiefly N. Amer. a substance with no real medicinal value sold as a cure-all.

snakes and ladders ■ pl. n. [treated as sing.] a children's board game in which players proceed up ladders or fall back down snakes depicted on the board.

snaky ■ adj. (**-ier**, **-iest**) **1** long and sinuous like a snake. **2** cold and cunning.
–DERIVATIVES **snakily** adv. **snakiness** n.

snap ■ v. (**snapped**, **snapping**) **1** break or cause to break with a sharp cracking sound. **2** (of an animal) make a sudden audible bite. ▶ (**snap something up**) quickly secure something that is in short supply. **3** open or close with a brisk movement or sharp sound. **4** suddenly lose one's self-control. ▶ say something quickly and irritably. **5** (**snap out of**) informal get out of (a bad mood) by a sudden effort. **6** take a snapshot of. **7** American Football put (the ball) into play by a quick backward movement. ■ n. **1** an act of snapping; a sudden snapping sound or movement. **2** a brief spell of cold or otherwise distinctive weather. **3** vigour; liveliness. **4** a snapshot. **5** a card game in which players compete to call 'snap' as soon as two cards of the same type are exposed. **6** a crisp, brittle biscuit. ■ adj. done or taken on the spur of the moment: *a snap decision*.
–DERIVATIVES **snapping** adj. **snappingly** adv.
–ORIGIN C15: prob. from Middle Dutch or Middle Low German *snappen* 'seize'; partly imitative.

snap-brim

snap-brim ■ adj. denoting a hat with a brim that can be turned up and down at opposite sides.

snapdragon ■ n. a plant bearing spikes of brightly coloured two-lobed flowers which gape like a mouth when a bee lands on the curved lip. [*Antirrhinum majus*.]

snap fastener ■ n. another term for PRESS STUD.

snap hook (also **snap link**) ■ n. a hook with a spring allowing the entrance but preventing the escape of a cord, link, etc.

snap-lock ■ adj. denoting a device or component which is fastened automatically when pushed into position.

snap pea ■ n. another term for SUGAR SNAP.

snapper ■ n. **1** a marine fish noted for snapping its toothed jaws. [Many species, chiefly in the family Lutjanidae.] **2** a snapping turtle.

snapping turtle ■ n. a large American freshwater turtle with strong hooked jaws. [*Chelydra serpentina* and *Macroclemys temminckii* (the alligator snapper).]

snappish ■ adj. **1** (of a dog) irritable and inclined to bite. **2** (of a person) irritable; curt.
– DERIVATIVES **snappishly** adv. **snappishness** n.

snappy ■ adj. (**-ier, -iest**) informal **1** irritable; curt. **2** cleverly concise: *a snappy catchphrase*. **3** neat and stylish: *a snappy dresser*.
– PHRASES **make it snappy** do it quickly.
– DERIVATIVES **snappily** adv. **snappiness** n.

snap roll ■ n. a manoeuvre in which an aircraft makes a single quick revolution about its longitudinal axis while flying horizontally.

snapshot ■ n. **1** an informal photograph, taken quickly. **2** (**snap shot**) a shot in soccer or hockey taken quickly with little backlift.

snare ■ n. **1** a trap for catching small animals, consisting of a loop of wire or cord that pulls tight. ▸ Surgery a wire loop for severing polyps or other growths. **2** a length of wire, gut, or hide stretched across a drumhead to produce a rattling sound. ▸ (also **snare drum**) another term for SIDE DRUM. ■ v. catch in a snare.
– DERIVATIVES **snarer** n.
– ORIGIN Old English, from Old Norse *snara*; sense 2 is prob. from Middle Low German, Middle Dutch *snare* 'harp string'.

snarky ■ adj. (**-ier, -iest**) informal sharply critical.
– ORIGIN C20: from dialect verb *snark* 'snore, snort', 'find fault'.

snarl[1] ■ v. **1** growl with bared teeth. **2** say something aggressively. ■ n. an act or sound of snarling.
– DERIVATIVES **snarler** n. **snarling** adj. **snarlingly** adv. **snarly** adj.
– ORIGIN C16: extension of obsolete *snar*, of Germanic origin.

snarl[2] ■ v. (**snarl up**) entangle or become entangled. ■ n. a knot or tangle.
– ORIGIN Middle English: from SNARE.

snarl-up ■ n. informal **1** a traffic jam. **2** a muddle.

snatch ■ v. seize quickly and deftly. ▸ informal steal or kidnap by seizing suddenly. ▸ quickly secure or obtain. ■ n. **1** an act of snatching. **2** a fragment of music or talk. **3** Weightlifting the rapid raising of a weight from the floor to above the head in one movement.
– DERIVATIVES **snatcher** n. **snatchy** adj.
– ORIGIN Middle English *sna(c)che* (v.) 'suddenly snap at', (n.) 'a snare'.

snazzy ■ adj. (**-ier, -iest**) informal smart; stylish.
– DERIVATIVES **snazzily** adv. **snazziness** n.
– ORIGIN 1960s.

sneak ■ v. (past and past part. **sneaked** or informal **snuck**) **1** move, go, or convey in a furtive or stealthy manner. ▸ stealthily acquire or obtain: *she sneaked a glance at her watch*. **2** Brit. informal inform someone in authority of a person's misdeeds. ■ n. informal **1** a furtive person. **2** Brit. a telltale. ■ adj. acting or done surreptitiously: *a sneak preview*.
– DERIVATIVES **sneakily** adv. **sneakiness** n. **sneaky** adj. (**-ier, -iest**).
– ORIGIN C16: perhaps rel. to obsolete *snike* 'to creep'.

sneaker ■ n. chiefly N. Amer. a soft shoe worn for sports or casual occasions.

sneaking ■ adj. (of a feeling) persistent in one's mind but reluctantly held; nagging.
– DERIVATIVES **sneakingly** adv.

sneer ■ n. a contemptuous or mocking smile, remark, or tone. ■ v. smile or speak in a contemptuous or mocking manner.
– DERIVATIVES **sneerer** n. **sneering** adj. **sneeringly** adv.
– ORIGIN Middle English: prob. of imitative origin.

sneeze ■ v. make a sudden involuntary expulsion of air from the nose and mouth due to irritation of one's nostrils. ■ n. an act or the sound of sneezing.
– PHRASES **not to be sneezed at** informal not to be rejected without careful consideration.
– DERIVATIVES **sneezer** n. **sneezy** adj.
– ORIGIN Middle English: apparently an alteration of Middle English *fnese* due to misreading or misprinting (after initial *fn-* had become unfamiliar).

sneezewood ■ n. a southern African tree, the saw-dust of which causes violent sneezing. [*Ptaeroxylon obliquum*.] ▸ the hard wood of this tree, used for fencing and making furniture.

snick ■ v. **1** cut a small notch or incision in. **2** Cricket deflect (the ball) slightly with the edge of the bat; deflect a ball delivered by (a bowler) in this way. **3** make or cause to make a sharp click. ■ n. **1** a small notch or cut. **2** Cricket a slight deflection of the ball by the bat. **3** a sharp click.
– ORIGIN C17: prob. from obsolete *snick or snee* 'fight with knives'.

snicker ■ v. **1** snigger. **2** (of a horse) whinny. ■ n. a snigger or whinny.
– DERIVATIVES **snickering** adj. **snickeringly** adv.
– ORIGIN C17: imitative.

snide ■ adj. **1** derogatory or mocking in an indirect way. **2** chiefly N. Amer. (of a person) devious and underhand. ■ n. a snide person or remark.
– DERIVATIVES **snidely** adv. **snideness** n. **snidey** adj.
– ORIGIN C19.

sniff ■ v. **1** draw air audibly through the nose. **2** (**sniff at**) show contempt or dislike for: *the price is not to be sniffed at*. **3** (**sniff around/round**) informal investigate something covertly. ▸ (**sniff something out**) informal discover something by covert investigation. ■ n. **1** an act or sound of sniffing. **2** informal a hint or sign.
– DERIVATIVES **sniffer** n.
– ORIGIN Middle English: imitative.

sniffer dog ■ n. informal a dog trained to find drugs or explosives by smell.

sniffle ■ v. sniff slightly or repeatedly, typically because of a cold or fit of crying. ■ n. **1** an act of sniffling. **2** a slight head cold.
– DERIVATIVES **sniffler** n. **sniffly** adj.
– ORIGIN C17: imitative.

sniffy ■ adj. (**-ier, -iest**) informal scornful; contemptuous.
– DERIVATIVES **sniffily** adv. **sniffiness** n.

snifter ■ n. informal **1** a small quantity of an alcoholic drink. **2** chiefly N. Amer. a balloon glass for brandy.
– ORIGIN C19: imitative; cf. dialect *snift* 'to snort'.

snigger ■ n. a smothered or half-suppressed laugh. ■ v. give such a laugh.
– DERIVATIVES **sniggerer** n. **sniggering** adj. **sniggeringly** adv. **sniggery** adj.
– ORIGIN C18: later var. of SNICKER.

snip ■ v. (**snipped, snipping**) cut with scissors or shears, with small, quick strokes. ■ n. **1** an act of snipping. **2** a small piece that has been cut off. **3** Brit. informal a bargain. **4** informal a thing that is easily achieved. **5** (**snips**) hand shears for cutting metal.
– ORIGIN C16: from Low German *snip* 'small piece'.

snipe /snʌɪp/ ■ n. (pl. same or **snipes**) a wading bird with brown camouflaged plumage and a long straight bill. [*Gallinago* and other genera.] ■ v. **1** shoot at someone from a hiding place at long range. **2** make a sly or petty verbal attack.
– DERIVATIVES **sniper** n. **sniping** adj. & n.
– ORIGIN Middle English: prob. of Scandinavian origin.

snippet ■ n. a small piece or brief extract.
– DERIVATIVES **snippety** adj.

snippy ■ adj. (-ier, -iest) informal curt or sharp.
– DERIVATIVES **snippily** adv. **snippiness** n.

snit ■ n. N. Amer. informal a fit of irritation or pique.
– ORIGIN 1930s.

snitch informal ■ v. **1** steal. **2** inform on someone. ■ n. an informer.
– ORIGIN C17.

snivel ■ v. (**snivelled, snivelling**; US **sniveled, sniveling**) **1** cry and sniffle. **2** complain in a whining or tearful way. ■ n. a spell of snivelling.
– DERIVATIVES **sniveller** n. **snivelling** adj. **snivellingly** adv.
– ORIGIN Old English *snyflung* 'mucus', from *snofl*, in the same sense.

snob ■ n. a person who has an exaggerated respect for high social position or wealth and who looks down on those regarded as socially inferior. ▸ a person with a similar respect for tastes considered superior in a particular area: *a wine snob*.
– DERIVATIVES **snobbery** n. (pl. **-ies**) **snobbish** adj. **snobbishly** adv. **snobbishness** n. **snobbism** n. **snobby** adj. (-ier, -iest).

HISTORY
When it first appeared, as a dialect word in the late 18th century, **snob** meant 'cobbler'. It next surfaced as a Cambridge University slang term for a non-member of the university, and then came to refer to any ordinary person lacking high rank or status. The main modern sense, of a person who looks down on those regarded as socially inferior, is first recorded in 1848, in *The Book of Snobs* by William Makepeace Thackeray. Folk etymology connects **snob** with the Latin phrase *sine nobilitate* 'without nobility', but there is no convincing evidence for this.

snoek /snuk/ ■ n. S. African a long, slender fish of southern seas, highly valued as food. [*Thyrsites atun* and other species.]
– ORIGIN Afrikaans, from Dutch, 'pike'.

snog informal ■ v. (**snogged, snogging**) kiss and caress amorously. ■ n. an act or spell of snogging.
– DERIVATIVES **snogger** n.
– ORIGIN 1940s: of unknown origin.

snood /snuːd/ ■ n. **1** an ornamental hairnet or pouch worn over the hair at the back of a woman's head. **2** a wide ring of knitted material worn as a hood or scarf. **3** a short line attaching a hook to a main line in sea fishing.
– ORIGIN Old English *snōd*.

snook[1] /snuːk/ ■ n. (in phr. **cock a snook**) informal, chiefly Brit. place one's hand so that the thumb touches one's nose and the fingers are spread out, in order to express contempt. ▸ openly show contempt or a lack of respect for someone or something.
– ORIGIN C18.

snook[2] /snuːk/ ■ n. a large edible game fish of the Caribbean. [*Centropomus undecimalis*.]
– ORIGIN C17: from Dutch *snoek*.

snooker ■ n. **1** a game played with cues on a billiard table in which the players use a white cue ball to pocket the other balls in a set order. **2** a position in a game of snooker or pool in which a player cannot make a direct shot at any permitted ball. ■ v. subject to a snooker. ▸ (**be snookered**) informal be ruined or placed in an impossible position.
– ORIGIN C19.

snoop informal ■ v. investigate or look around furtively in an attempt to find out something. ■ n. **1** an act of snooping. **2** a person who snoops.
– DERIVATIVES **snooper** n. **snoopy** adj.
– ORIGIN C19: from Dutch *snæpen* 'eat on the sly'.

snoot ■ n. **1** informal a person's nose. **2** informal a snob. **3** an attachment used to produce a narrow beam from a spotlight.
– ORIGIN C19: var. of **SNOUT**.

snooty ■ adj. (-ier, -iest) informal showing disapproval of or contempt towards others, especially those considered to be socially inferior.
– DERIVATIVES **snootily** adv. **snootiness** n.
– ORIGIN C20: from **SNOOT**.

snooze informal ■ n. a short, light sleep. ■ v. have a snooze.
– DERIVATIVES **snoozer** n. **snoozy** adj. (-ier, -iest).
– ORIGIN C18.

snooze button ■ n. a control on a clock which sets an alarm to repeat after a short interval.

snore ■ n. a snorting or grunting sound in a person's breathing while they are asleep. ■ v. make such a sound while asleep.
– DERIVATIVES **snorer** n.
– ORIGIN Middle English: prob. imitative.

snorkel /ˈsnɔːk(ə)l/ ■ n. a tube for a swimmer to breathe through while under water. ■ v. (**snorkelled, snorkelling**; US **snorkeled, snorkeling**) swim using a snorkel.
– DERIVATIVES **snorkeller** n. **snorkelling** n.
– ORIGIN 1940s: from German *Schnorchel*.

snort ■ n. **1** an explosive sound made by the sudden forcing of breath through the nose. **2** informal an inhaled dose of cocaine. **3** informal a measure of an alcoholic drink. ■ v. **1** make a snort. ▸ express indignation or derision by making a snort. **2** informal inhale (cocaine).
– DERIVATIVES **snorter** n.
– ORIGIN Middle English: prob. imitative.

snot ■ n. informal **1** nasal mucus. **2** a contemptible person.
– ORIGIN Middle English: prob. from Middle Dutch, Middle Low German.

snot-nosed ■ adj. informal **1** childish and inexperienced. **2** considering oneself superior; snobbish.

snotty ■ adj. (-ier, -iest) informal **1** full of or covered with nasal mucus. **2** having a superior or conceited attitude.
– DERIVATIVES **snottily** adv. **snottiness** n.

snout ■ n. **1** the projecting nose and mouth of an animal, especially a mammal. ▸ the projecting front or end of something such as a pistol. **2** Brit. informal a cigarette. ▸ tobacco. **3** Brit. informal a police informer.
– DERIVATIVES **snouted** adj. **snouty** adj.
– ORIGIN Middle English: from Middle Dutch, Middle Low German *snūt*.

snow ■ n. **1** atmospheric water vapour frozen into ice crystals and falling in light white flakes or lying on the ground as a white layer. ▸ (**snows**) falls of snow. **2** a mass of flickering white spots on a television or radar screen, caused by interference or a poor signal. **3** informal cocaine. ■ v. **1** (**it snows**), it is snowing, etc. snow falls. ▸ (**be snowed in/up**) be confined or blocked by a large quantity of snow. **2** arrive in overwhelming quantities: *in the last week it had snowed letters.* ▸ (**be snowed under**) be overwhelmed with a large quantity of something, especially work. **3** informal, chiefly N. Amer. mislead or charm (someone) with elaborate and insincere words.
– DERIVATIVES **snowily** adv. **snowiness** n. **snowless** adj. **snowy** adj. (-ier, -iest).
– ORIGIN Old English, of Germanic origin.

snowball ■ n. **1** a ball of packed snow. **2** a thing that grows rapidly in size, intensity, or importance. **3** a cocktail containing advocaat and lemonade. ■ v. **1** throw snowballs at. **2** increase rapidly in size, intensity, or importance.

snowberry ■ n. a North American shrub of the honeysuckle family, bearing white berries and often cultivated as an ornamental or for hedging. [*Symphoricarpos albus*.]

snow-blind ■ adj. temporarily blinded by the glare of light reflected by a large expanse of snow.
– DERIVATIVES **snow blindness** n.

snowboard ■ n. a board resembling a short, broad ski, used for sliding downhill on snow. ■ v. slide downhill on a snowboard.
– DERIVATIVES **snowboarder** n. **snowboarding** n.

snow boot ■ n. a warm padded waterproof boot worn in the snow.

snowbound ■ adj. prevented from travelling or going out by snow or snowy weather. ▸ cut off or inaccessible because of snow.

snowcap ■ n. a covering of snow on the top of a mountain.
– DERIVATIVES **snow-capped** adj.

snowcat (also US trademark **Sno-Cat**) ■ n. a tracked vehicle

snowdrift

for travelling over snow.
– ORIGIN 1940s: from SNOW + CATERPILLAR.

snowdrift ■ n. a bank of deep snow heaped up by the wind.

snowdrop ■ n. a bulbous plant which bears drooping white flowers during the late winter. [*Galanthus nivalis*.]

snowfall ■ n. 1 a fall of snow. 2 the quantity of snow falling within a given area in a given time.

snowfield ■ n. a permanent wide expanse of snow in mountainous or polar regions.

snowflake ■ n. each of the many feathery ice crystals, typically displaying delicate sixfold symmetry, that fall as snow.

snow goose ■ n. a gregarious goose that breeds in Arctic Canada and Greenland, typically having white plumage with black wing tips. [*Anser caerulescens*.]

snow job ■ n. informal a deception or concealment of one's real motive in an attempt to flatter or persuade.

snow leopard ■ n. a rare large cat which has pale grey fur patterned with dark blotches and rings, living in the Altai mountains, Hindu Kush, and Himalayas. [*Panthera uncia*.]

snowline ■ n. the altitude in a particular place above which some snow remains on the ground throughout the year.

snowman ■ n. (pl. **-men**) a representation of a human figure created with compressed snow.

snowmobile /'snəʊməbiːl/ ■ n. a motor vehicle, especially one with runners or caterpillar tracks, for travelling over snow.

snowpack ■ n. a mass of lying snow that is compressed and hardened by its own weight.

snow pea ■ n. chiefly N. Amer. another term for MANGETOUT.

snowplough (US **snowplow**) ■ n. 1 an implement or vehicle for clearing roads of snow. 2 Skiing an act of turning the points of one's skis inwards in order to slow down or turn.

snowscape ■ n. a landscape covered in snow. ▸ a picture of such a landscape.

snowshoe ■ n. a flat device resembling a racket, which is attached to the sole of a boot and used for walking on snow. ■ v. proceed wearing snowshoes.
– DERIVATIVES **snowshoer** n.

snowstorm ■ n. a heavy fall of snow accompanied by a high wind.

snowy owl ■ n. a large northern owl that breeds mainly in the Arctic tundra, the male being entirely white and the female having darker markings. [*Nyctea scandiaca*.]

Snr ■ abbrev. Senior.

snub ■ v. (**snubbed**, **snubbing**) 1 ignore or spurn disdainfully. 2 restrict the movement of (a horse or boat) by means of a rope wound round a post. ■ n. an act of snubbing. ■ adj. (of a person's nose) short and turned up at the end.
– ORIGIN Middle English: from Old Norse *snubba* 'chide, check the growth of'.

snubber ■ n. 1 a simple fluid shock absorber. 2 an electric circuit intended to suppress voltage spikes.

snuck informal, chiefly N. Amer. past and past participle of SNEAK.

snuff[1] ■ v. 1 extinguish (a candle). 2 (**snuff out**) abruptly put an end to. ▸ (**snuff it**) informal die. 3 trim the charred wick from (a candle). ■ n. the charred part of a candle wick.
– ORIGIN Middle English.

snuff[2] ■ n. powdered tobacco that is sniffed up the nostril. ■ v. inhale or sniff at.
– PHRASES **up to snuff** informal up to the required standard. ▸ in good health.
– ORIGIN Middle English: from Middle Dutch *snuffen* 'to snuffle'.

snuffer ■ n. a small hollow metal cone on the end of a handle, used to extinguish a candle by smothering the flame.

snuffle ■ v. 1 breathe noisily through the nose due to a cold or crying. 2 (of an animal) make repeated sniffing sounds. ■ n. 1 a snuffling sound. 2 (**the snuffles**) informal a cold.
– DERIVATIVES **snuffler** n. **snuffly** adj.
– ORIGIN C16: prob. from Low German and Dutch *snuffelen*.

snuff movie ■ n. informal a pornographic film or video recording of an actual murder.

snug ■ adj. (**snugger**, **snuggest**) 1 warm and cosy. 2 very tight or close-fitting. ■ n. Brit. a small, cosy public room in a pub or small hotel.
– DERIVATIVES **snugly** adv. **snugness** n.
– ORIGIN C16: prob. of Low German or Dutch origin.

snuggle ■ v. settle into a warm, comfortable position.
– ORIGIN C17: from SNUG.

So. ■ abbrev. South.

so[1] ■ adv. 1 to such a great extent. ▸ extremely; very much. 2 [with neg.] to the same extent: *he isn't so bad*. 3 referring back to something previously mentioned: *I believe so*. ▸ similarly: *so have I*. 4 in the way described or demonstrated; thus. ■ conj. 1 and for this reason; therefore. 2 (**so that**) with the result or aim that. 3 and then. 4 introducing a question or concluding statement. 5 in the same way; correspondingly.
– PHRASES **and so on** (or **forth**) and similar things; et cetera. **only so much** only a limited amount. **so be it** an expression of acceptance or resignation. **so long** S. African informal for the time being; meanwhile. **so long!** informal goodbye. **so much as** [with neg.] even: *without so much as a word*. **so to speak** (or **say**) indicating that one is relating or describing something in an unusual or metaphorical way.
– ORIGIN Old English, of Germanic origin.

so[2] ■ n. variant spelling of SOH.

-so ■ comb. form equivalent to -SOEVER.

soak ■ v. 1 make or become thoroughly wet by immersion in liquid. 2 make extremely wet: *the rain soaked their hair*. 3 (**soak something up**) absorb a liquid. ▸ expose oneself to something beneficial or enjoyable. 4 (**soak oneself in**) immerse oneself in (a particular experience). 5 informal impose heavy charges or taxation on. 6 archaic, informal drink heavily. ■ n. 1 an act or spell of soaking. 2 informal a heavy drinker.
– DERIVATIVES **soakage** n. **soaked** adj.
– ORIGIN Old English *socian*; rel. to *sūcan* 'to suck'.

soakaway (S. African also **soak pit**) ■ n. a pit through which waste water drains slowly out into the surrounding soil.

soaking (also **soaking wet**) ■ adj. extremely wet. ■ n. an act of soaking something.

so-and-so ■ n. (pl. -os) 1 a person or thing whose name the speaker does not know, remember, or need to specify. 2 informal a person who is disliked or considered to have a particular unfavourable characteristic: *a nosy so-and-so*.

soap ■ n. 1 a substance used with water for washing and cleaning, made of a compound of natural oils or fats with sodium hydroxide or another strong alkali, and typically perfumed. 2 informal a soap opera. ■ v. wash with soap.
– DERIVATIVES **soapily** adv. **soapiness** n. **soapless** adj. **soapy** adj. (-ier, -iest).
– ORIGIN Old English, of West Germanic origin.

soapberry ■ n. 1 a tree or shrub with berries that produce a soapy froth when crushed. [Several species, mainly of the genus *Sapindus*.] 2 the berry of such a plant.

soapbox ■ n. a box or crate used as a makeshift stand for public speaking.

soap opera (also informal **soap**, **soapie**) ■ n. a television or radio drama serial dealing with daily events in the lives of the same group of characters.
– ORIGIN 1930s: so named because such serials were orig. sponsored in the US by soap manufacturers.

soapstone ■ n. a soft rock consisting largely of steatite (talc).

soapwort ■ n. a European plant of the pink family, with fragrant pink or white flowers and leaves that were formerly used to make soap. [*Saponaria officinalis*.]

soar ■ v. **1** fly or rise high into the air. ▶ glide high in the air. **2** increase rapidly above the usual level.
– DERIVATIVES **soarer** n. **soaring** adj.
– ORIGIN Middle English: shortening of Old French *essorer*, from Latin *ex-* 'out of' + *aura* 'breeze'.

Soave /'swɑːveɪ, səʊ'ɑːveɪ/ ■ n. a dry white wine produced in the region of northern Italy around Soave.

sob ■ v. (**sobbed**, **sobbing**) cry making loud, convulsive gasps. ▶ say while sobbing. ■ n. an act or sound of sobbing.
– DERIVATIVES **sobbing** adj. **sobbingly** adv.
– ORIGIN Middle English: perhaps of Dutch or Low German origin.

s.o.b. ■ abbrev. N. Amer. informal son of a bitch.

soba /'səʊbə/ ■ n. Japanese noodles made from buckwheat flour.
– ORIGIN from Japanese.

sober ■ adj. (**-er**, **-est**) **1** not affected by alcohol; not drunk. **2** serious; thoughtful. **3** muted in colour. ■ v. **1** (usu. **sober up**) make or become sober after drinking alcohol. **2** make or become serious.
– DERIVATIVES **sobering** adj. **soberingly** adv. **soberly** adv.
– ORIGIN Middle English: from Old French *sobre*, from Latin *sobrius*.

sobersides ■ n. informal, chiefly N. Amer. a sedate and serious person.
– DERIVATIVES **sobersided** adj.

sobriety /sə'brʌɪəti/ ■ n. the state or quality of being sober.
– ORIGIN Middle English: from Old French *sobriete* or Latin *sobrietas*, from *sobrius* (see **SOBER**).

sobriquet /'səʊbrɪkeɪ/ (also **soubriquet**) ■ n. a person's nickname.
– ORIGIN C17: French, orig. in the sense 'tap under the chin'.

sob story ■ n. informal a story or account intended to arouse sympathy.

Soc. ■ abbrev. **1** Socialist. **2** Society.

soca /'səʊkə/ ■ n. calypso music with elements of soul, originally from Trinidad.
– ORIGIN 1970s: blend of **SOUL** and **CALYPSO**.

so-called ■ adj. commonly designated by the name or term specified. ▶ expressing one's view that such a name or term is inappropriate: *her so-called friends*.

soccer ■ n. a form of football played by two teams of eleven players with a round ball which may not be handled during play except by the goalkeepers, the object of the game being to score goals by kicking or heading the ball into the opponents' goal.
– ORIGIN C19: shortening of **ASSOC.** (from **ASSOCIATION FOOTBALL**) + **-ER³**.

sociable ■ adj. engaging readily with other people. ▶ marked by friendliness.
– DERIVATIVES **sociability** n. **sociableness** n. **sociably** adv.
– ORIGIN C16: from Latin *sociabilis*, from *sociare* 'unite', from *socius* 'companion'.

social ■ adj. **1** of or relating to society or its organization. ▶ of or relating to rank and status in society: *a woman of high social standing*. **2** needing companionship; suited to living in communities. **3** relating to or designed for activities in which people meet each other for pleasure. **4** (of birds, insects, or mammals) breeding or living in colonies or organized communities. ■ n. an informal social gathering organized by the members of a particular club or group.
– DERIVATIVES **sociality** n. **socially** adv.
– ORIGIN Middle English: from Latin *socialis* 'allied', from *socius* 'friend'.

social anthropology (also **cultural anthropology**) ■ n. the comparative study of human societies and cultures and their development.

social capital ■ n. the networks of relationships among people who live and work in a particular society, enabling that society to function effectively.

social climber ■ n. derogatory a person who is anxious to gain a higher social status.
– DERIVATIVES **social climbing** n.

social contract (also **social compact**) ■ n. an implicit agreement among the members of a society to cooperate for mutual social benefit, for example by sacrificing some individual freedom for state protection (originally promoted by theorists such as Thomas Hobbes, John Locke, and Jean-Jacques Rousseau).

social credit ■ n. the economic theory that consumer purchasing power should be increased either by subsidizing producers so that they can lower prices or by distributing the profits of industry to consumers.

social Darwinism ■ n. the theory that individuals, groups, and peoples are subject to the same Darwinian laws of natural selection as plants and animals (now largely discredited).

social democracy ■ n. a socialist system of government achieved by democratic means.
– DERIVATIVES **social democrat** n.

social fund ■ n. (in the UK) a social security fund from which loans or grants are made to people in need.

social geography ■ n. the study of people and their environment with particular emphasis on social factors.

social gospel ■ n. Christian faith practised as a call not just to personal conversion but to social reform.

social housing ■ n. housing provided for people on low incomes, subsidized by public funds.

social insurance ■ n. a system of compulsory contribution to provide state assistance in sickness, unemployment, etc.

socialism ■ n. a political and economic theory of social organization which advocates that the means of production, distribution, and exchange should be owned or regulated by the community as a whole. ▶ (in Marxist theory) a transitional social state between the overthrow of capitalism and the realization of Communism.
– DERIVATIVES **socialist** n. & adj. **socialistic** adj. **socialistically** adv.

socialist realism ■ n. the theory that art, literature, and music should reflect and promote the ideals of a socialist society (especially in the Soviet Union under Stalin).

socialite ■ n. a person who is well known in fashionable society and is fond of social activities.

socialize (also **-ise**) ■ v. **1** mix socially with others. **2** make (someone) behave in a way that is acceptable to society. **3** organize according to the principles of socialism.
– DERIVATIVES **socialization** (also **-isation**) n. **socialized** (also **-ised**) adj. **socializing** (also **-ising**) adj.

socialized medicine (also **socialised medicine**) ■ n. chiefly US the provision of medical and hospital care for all by means of public funds.

social market economy (also **social market**) ■ n. an economic system based on a free market operated in conjunction with state provision for those unable to sell their labour, such as the elderly or unemployed.

social media ■ n. websites or similar online services designed to facilitate the publication of text, images, audio and video material, etc., typically for the purposes of social networking. ▶ material published online using such services.

social networking ■ n. the activity of interacting with other people in digital environments, e.g. by using or creating websites accessible to other users connected to the World Wide Web.

social partner ■ n. an individual or organization, such as an employer, trade union, or employee, participating in a cooperative relationship for the mutual benefit of all concerned.

social psychology ■ n. the branch of psychology concerned with social interactions.
– DERIVATIVES **social psychologist** n.

social realism ■ n. the realistic depiction in art of contemporary life, as a means of social or political comment.

social science ■ n. the scientific study of human society and social relationships. ▶ a subject within this field, such as economics or politics.
– DERIVATIVES **social scientist** n.

social secretary

social secretary ■ n. a person who arranges the social activities of a person or organization.

social security ■ n. **1** monetary assistance from the state for people with an inadequate or no income. **2** (**Social Security**) (in the US) a federal insurance scheme providing benefits for pensioners, the unemployed, and the disabled.

social service ■ n. **1** (**social services**) government services provided for the benefit of the community, such as education, medical care, and housing. **2** activity aiming to promote the welfare of others.

social studies ■ pl. n. [treated as sing.] the study of human society.

social wage ■ n. the cost per person of the amenities provided within a society from public funds.

social work ■ n. work carried out by trained personnel with the aim of alleviating the conditions of those people in a community suffering from social deprivation.
– DERIVATIVES **social worker** n.

society ■ n. (pl. -**ies**) **1** the aggregate of people living together in a more or less ordered community. ▸ a particular community of people. ▸ (also **high society**) people who are fashionable, wealthy, and influential, regarded as forming a distinct group. **2** a plant or animal community. **3** an organization or club formed for a particular purpose or activity. **4** the situation of being in the company of other people: *she shunned the society of others.*
– DERIVATIVES **societal** adj. **societally** adv.
– ORIGIN C16: from French *société*, from Latin *societas*, from *socius* 'companion'.

socio- /ˈsəʊsɪəʊ, ˈsəʊʃɪəʊ/ ■ comb. form **1** relating to society; society and …: *socio-economic*. **2** relating to sociology; sociology and …: *sociolinguistics*.
– ORIGIN from Latin *socius* 'companion'.

sociobiology ■ n. the scientific study of the biological (especially ecological and evolutionary) aspects of social behaviour in animals and humans.
– DERIVATIVES **sociobiological** adj. **sociobiologically** adv. **sociobiologist** n.

socioecology ■ n. the branch of science concerned with the interactions among the members of a species, and between them and the environment.
– DERIVATIVES **socioecological** adj. **socioecologist** n.

socio-economic ■ adj. relating to or concerned with the interaction of social and economic factors.
– DERIVATIVES **socio-economically** adv.

sociolect /ˈsəʊsɪə(ʊ)lɛkt, ˈsəʊʃɪə(ʊ)-/ ■ n. the dialect of a particular social class.
– ORIGIN 1970s: from SOCIO- + -*lect* as in DIALECT.

sociolinguistics ■ pl. n. [treated as sing.] the study of language in relation to social factors.
– DERIVATIVES **sociolinguist** n. **sociolinguistic** adj. **sociolinguistically** adv.

sociology ■ n. the study of the development, structure, and functioning of human society. ▸ the study of social problems.
– DERIVATIVES **sociological** adj. **sociologically** adv. **sociologist** n.

sociopath /ˈsəʊsɪə(ʊ)paθ, ˈsəʊʃɪə(ʊ)-/ ■ n. a person with a personality disorder manifesting itself in extreme antisocial attitudes and behaviour.
– DERIVATIVES **sociopathic** adj. **sociopathy** n.

sock ■ n. **1** a knitted garment for the foot and lower part of the leg. **2** an insole. **3** a white marking on the lower part of a horse's leg. **4** informal a hard blow. ■ v. informal **1** hit forcefully. **2** (**sock something away**) N. Amer. save up money. **3** (usu. **be socked in**) N. Amer. envelop or make impassable by inhospitable weather conditions.
– PHRASES **knock** (or **blow**) **someone's socks off** informal amaze or impress someone. **knock the socks off** informal surpass or beat. **pull one's socks up** informal make an effort to improve. **put a sock in it** informal stop talking. **sock it to someone** informal attack or make a forceful impression on someone.
– ORIGIN Old English *socc* 'light shoe', of Germanic origin, from Latin *soccus* 'comic actor's shoe, slipper', from Greek *sukkhos*.

socket ■ n. **1** a hollow in which something fits or revolves. **2** an electrical device receiving a plug or light bulb to make a connection. ■ v. (**socketed**, **socketing**) place in or fit with a socket.
– ORIGIN Middle English: from an Anglo-Norman French diminutive of Old French *soc* 'ploughshare', prob. of Celtic origin.

socket wrench ■ n. a ratchet tool with detachable sockets for tightening and untightening nuts of different sizes.

sockeye ■ n. a commercially valuable salmon of the North Pacific region. [*Oncorhynchus nerka*.]
– ORIGIN C19: from Salish *sukai* 'fish of fishes'.

Socratic /səˈkratɪk/ ■ adj. of or relating to the Athenian philosopher Socrates (469–399 BC) or his philosophy or methods. ■ n. a follower of Socrates.
– DERIVATIVES **Socratically** adv.

Socratic irony ■ n. a pose of ignorance assumed in order to entice others into making statements that can then be challenged.

sod[1] ■ n. turf. ▸ a piece of turf.
– PHRASES **under the sod** dead and buried.
– ORIGIN Middle English: from Middle Dutch, Middle Low German *sode*.

sod[2] vulgar slang, chiefly Brit. ■ n. **1** an unpleasant person. ▸ a person of a specified kind. **2** a difficult or problematic thing. ■ v. (**sodded**, **sodding**) used to express anger or annoyance. ▸ (**sod off**) go away. ▸ [as adj. **sodding**] used as a general term of contempt.
– PHRASES **sod all** absolutely nothing.
– ORIGIN C19: abbrev. of SODOMITE.

soda ■ n. **1** (also **soda water**) carbonated water (originally made with sodium bicarbonate). ▸ chiefly N. Amer. a sweet carbonated drink. **2** sodium carbonate. ▸ sodium in chemical combination: *nitrate of soda*.
– ORIGIN Middle English: from Arabic *suwwad* 'saltwort'.

soda ash ■ n. commercially manufactured anhydrous sodium carbonate.

soda bread ■ n. bread leavened with baking soda.

soda fountain ■ n. chiefly N. Amer. a device dispensing soda water or soft drinks. ▸ a shop or counter selling drinks from such a device.

soda lime ■ n. a mixture of calcium oxide and sodium hydroxide.

sodalite /ˈsəʊdəlʌɪt/ ■ n. a blue mineral consisting of an aluminosilicate and chloride of sodium.
– ORIGIN C19: from SODA + -LITE.

sodality /səʊˈdalɪti/ ■ n. (pl. -**ies**) a confraternity or association, especially a Roman Catholic religious guild or brotherhood.
– ORIGIN C17: from French *sodalité* or Latin *sodalitas*, from *sodalis* 'comrade'.

soda pop ■ n. US informal a sweet carbonated drink.

soda siphon ■ n. a bottle from which carbonated water is dispensed by allowing the gas pressure to force it out.

soda water ■ n. see SODA (sense 1).

sodden ■ adj. **1** soaked through. **2** [in combination] having drunk an excessive amount of a particular alcoholic drink: *whisky-sodden*.
– ORIGIN Middle English: archaic past participle of SEETHE.

sodium ■ n. the chemical element of atomic number 11, a soft silver-white reactive metal of the alkali-metal group. (Symbol: **Na**)
– DERIVATIVES **sodic** adj. (Mineralogy).
– ORIGIN C19: from SODA.

sodium bicarbonate ■ n. a soluble white powder used in fire extinguishers and effervescent drinks and as a raising agent in baking. [$NaHCO_3$.]

sodium carbonate ■ n. a white alkaline compound used in making soap and glass. [Na_2CO_3.]

sodium chloride ■ n. the chemical name for common salt. [$NaCl$.]

sodium hydroxide ■ n. a strongly alkaline white deliquescent compound used in many industrial processes. [$NaOH$.]

sodium thiosulphate ■ n. a white soluble compound used in photography as a fixer. [$Na_2S_2O_3$.]

sodium-vapour lamp (also **sodium lamp**) ■ n. a lamp in which an electrical discharge in sodium vapour gives a yellow light.

Sodom /'sɒdəm/ ■ n. a wicked or depraved place.
– ORIGIN from *Sodom*, a town in ancient Palestine destroyed for its wickedness (Genesis 19:24).

sodomite /'sɒdəmʌɪt/ ■ n. a person who engages in sodomy.
– ORIGIN Middle English: from late Latin *Sodomita*, from Greek *Sodomitēs* 'inhabitant of Sodom'.

sodomy ■ n. anal intercourse.
– DERIVATIVES **sodomize** (also **-ise**) v.
– ORIGIN Middle English: from medieval Latin *sodomia*, from late Latin *peccatum Sodomiticum* 'sin of Sodom' (after Genesis 19:5, which implies that the men of Sodom practised homosexual rape).

Sod's Law ■ n. another name for MURPHY'S LAW.

soetkoekie ■ n. S. African a traditional spiced biscuit.
– ORIGIN Afrikaans, from S. African Dutch *soet* 'sweet' + *koek* 'cake'.

soever ■ adv. archaic or poetic/literary of any kind; to any extent.

-soever ■ comb. form of any kind; to any extent: *whosoever*.
– ORIGIN Middle English: orig. as the phr. *so ever*.

sofa ■ n. a long upholstered seat with a back and arms, for two or more people.
– ORIGIN C17: from French, from Arabic *ṣuffa*.

sofa bed ■ n. another term for SLEEPER COUCH.

soffit /'sɒfɪt/ ■ n. the underside of an arch, a balcony, overhanging eaves, etc.
– ORIGIN C17: from French *soffite* or Italian *soffitto*, from Latin *suffixus* 'fastened below'.

soft ■ adj. **1** easy to mould, cut, compress, or fold. **2** not rough or coarse. **3** quiet and gentle. ▸ (of a consonant) pronounced as a fricative (as *c* in *ice*). **4** (of light or shadow) pleasingly subtle. **5** sympathetic or lenient, especially excessively so. ▸ denoting a faction within a political party that is willing to compromise. ▸ informal (of a job or way of life) requiring little effort. **6** informal foolish. ▸ (**soft on**) infatuated with. **7** (of a market, currency, or commodity) falling or likely to fall in value. **8** (of a drink) not alcoholic. ▸ (of a drug) not likely to cause addiction. **9** (of water) free from mineral salts. **10** (of radiation) having little penetrating power. **11** (also **soft-core**) (of pornography) suggestive but not explicit. ■ adv. softly.
– PHRASES **have a soft spot for** be fond of. **soft touch** (also **easy touch**) informal a person who is easily persuaded or imposed upon.
– DERIVATIVES **softish** adj. **softly** adv. **softness** n.
– ORIGIN Old English *sōfte* 'agreeable, calm, gentle', of West Germanic origin.

softback ■ adj. & n. another term for PAPERBACK.

softball ■ n. a modified form of baseball played on a smaller field with a larger, softer ball.

soft-boiled ■ adj. (of an egg) lightly boiled, leaving the yolk soft or liquid.

soft-centred ■ adj. **1** (of a sweet) having a soft filling. **2** (of a person) compassionate or sentimental.

soft coal ■ n. bituminous coal.

soft copy ■ n. Computing a legible version of a piece of information, stored or displayed on a computer.

soft-core ■ adj. another term for SOFT (in sense 11).

soften ■ v. **1** make or become soft or softer. **2** (often **soften someone/thing up**) undermine the resistance of.

softener ■ n. a substance or device that softens something, especially a fabric conditioner.

soft focus ■ n. deliberate slight blurring or lack of definition in a photograph or film.

soft fruit ■ n. a small stoneless fruit, e.g. a strawberry.

soft furnishings ■ pl. n. curtains, chair coverings, and other cloth items used to decorate a room.

soft goods ■ pl. n. textiles.

soft-headed ■ adj. not intelligent.
– DERIVATIVES **soft-headedness** n.

soft-hearted ■ adj. kind and compassionate.
– DERIVATIVES **soft-heartedness** n.

soil mechanics

softie (also **softy**) ■ n. (pl. **-ies**) informal a weak or soft-hearted person.

soft iron ■ n. easily magnetizable iron with a low carbon content, used to make the cores of solenoids.

soft loan ■ n. a loan made on terms very favourable to the borrower.

softly-softly ■ adj. cautious and patient.

soft-nosed ■ adj. (of a bullet) expanding on impact.

soft palate ■ n. the fleshy, flexible part towards the back of the roof of the mouth.

soft-paste ■ adj. denoting artificial porcelain, typically containing ground glass and fired at a comparatively low temperature.

soft pedal ■ n. a pedal on a piano that can be pressed to soften the tone. ■ v. (**soft-pedal**) **1** Music play with the soft pedal down. **2** play down the unpleasant aspects of.

soft power ■ n. a persuasive approach to international relations, typically involving the use of economic or cultural influence. Compare with HARD POWER.

soft roe ■ n. see ROE[1].

soft sell ■ n. subtly persuasive selling. ■ v. (**soft-sell**) sell by such a method.

soft-shoe ■ n. a tap dance performed in soft-soled shoes. ■ v. perform such a dance.

soft shoulder ■ n. chiefly N. Amer. an unmetalled strip of land at the side of a road.

soft soap ■ n. **1** a semi-fluid soap, especially one made with potassium rather than sodium salts. **2** informal persuasive flattery. ■ v. (**soft-soap**) informal use flattery to persuade or cajole.

soft target ■ n. a relatively vulnerable person or thing.

soft-top ■ n. a motor vehicle with a roof that can be folded back.

software ■ n. programs and other operating information used by a computer. Compare with HARDWARE.

softwood ■ n. **1** the wood from a conifer as distinguished from that of broadleaved trees. **2** (in gardening) young pliable growth on shrubs or bushes from which cuttings can be taken.

softy ■ n. variant spelling of SOFTIE.

soggy ■ adj. (**-ier**, **-iest**) very wet and soft.
– DERIVATIVES **soggily** adv. **sogginess** n.
– ORIGIN C18: from dialect *sog* 'a swamp'.

soh /səʊ/ (also **so** or **sol**) ■ n. Music (in tonic sol-fa) the fifth note of a major scale. ▸ the note G in the fixed-doh system.
– ORIGIN Middle English *sol*: representing (as an arbitrary name for the note) the first syllable of *solve*, taken from a Latin hymn.

SOHO ■ abbrev. (with reference to marketing electronic products) small office, home office.

soi-disant /ˌswɑːdiːˈzɒ̃/ ■ adj. self-styled: *a soi-disant novelist*.
– ORIGIN French, from *soi* 'oneself' + *disant* 'saying'.

soigné /ˈswʌnjeɪ/ ■ adj. (fem. **soignée** pronunc. same) elegant and well groomed.
– ORIGIN from French *soigner* 'take care of'.

soil[1] ■ n. **1** the upper layer of earth in which plants grow, a black or dark brown material typically consisting of organic remains, clay, and rock particles. **2** the territory of a particular nation.
– DERIVATIVES **soil-less** adj.
– ORIGIN Middle English: from Anglo-Norman French, perhaps representing Latin *solium* 'seat', associated with *solum* 'ground'.

soil[2] ■ v. **1** make dirty. ▸ make dirty by defecating in or on. **2** bring discredit to. ■ n. **1** waste matter, especially sewage. **2** archaic a stain.
– ORIGIN Middle English: from Old French *soiller*, from Latin *sucula*, diminutive of *sus* 'pig'.

soil mechanics ■ pl. n. [usu. treated as sing.] the study of the properties and behaviour of soil as they affect civil engineering.

soil pipe ■ n. a sewage or waste water pipe.

soil science ■ n. the branch of science concerned with the formation, nature, ecology, and classification of soil.

soil stack ■ n. a pipe which takes the waste water from the upstairs plumbing system of a building.

soirée /ˈswɑːreɪ/ ■ n. an evening party or gathering, typically in a private house, for conversation or music.
– ORIGIN French, from *soir* 'evening'.

soixante-neuf /ˌswasɒntˈnɜːf/ ■ n. informal sexual activity between two people involving mutual oral stimulation of the genitals.
– ORIGIN French, 'sixty-nine', from the position of the couple.

sojourn /ˈsɒdʒ(ə)n, -dʒɜːn/ formal ■ n. a temporary stay. ■ v. stay temporarily.
– DERIVATIVES **sojourner** n.
– ORIGIN Middle English: from Old French *sojourner*, from Latin *sub-* 'under' + late Latin *diurnum* 'day'.

sol[1] /sɒl/ ■ n. variant of **SOH**.

sol[2] /sɒl/ ■ n. Chemistry a fluid suspension of a colloidal solid in a liquid.
– ORIGIN C19: abbrev. of **SOLUTION**.

-sol ■ comb. form in nouns denoting different kinds and states of soil: *histosol*.
– ORIGIN from Latin *solum* 'soil'.

sola /ˈsəʊlə/ ■ n. an Indian swamp plant of the pea family, with stems that yield the pith used to make sola topis. [*Aeschynomene indica*.]
– ORIGIN C19: from Bengali *solā*, Hindi *śolā*.

solace /ˈsɒlɪs/ ■ n. comfort or consolation in time of distress. ■ v. give solace to.
– ORIGIN Middle English: from Old French *solas, solacier*, from Latin *solari* 'to console'.

solar[1] /ˈsəʊlə/ ■ adj. of, relating to, or determined by the sun or its rays.
– ORIGIN Middle English: from Latin *solaris*, from *sol* 'sun'.

solar[2] /ˈsɒlə, ˈsəʊlə/ ■ n. Brit. an upper chamber in a medieval house.
– ORIGIN Middle English: from Anglo-Norman French *soler*, from Latin *solarium* 'gallery, terrace'.

solar battery (also **solar cell**) ■ n. a device converting solar radiation into electricity.

solar day ■ n. the time between successive meridian transits of the sun at a particular place.

solar eclipse ■ n. an eclipse in which the sun is obscured by the moon.

solar energy ■ n. radiant energy emitted by the sun.
▸ solar power.

solar flare ■ n. Astronomy a brief eruption of intense high-energy radiation from the sun's surface.

solarium /səˈlɛːrɪəm/ ■ n. (pl. **solariums** or **solaria** /-rɪə/) 1 a room equipped with sunlamps or sunbeds. 2 a room with extensive areas of glass to admit sunlight.
– ORIGIN C19: from Latin, 'sundial, place for sunning oneself', from Latin *sol* 'sun'.

solar panel ■ n. a panel designed to absorb the sun's rays as a source of energy for generating electricity or heating.

solar plexus ■ n. a complex of ganglia and radiating nerves of the sympathetic system at the pit of the stomach.

solar power ■ n. power obtained by harnessing the energy of the sun's rays.

solar system ■ n. the sun together with the planets, asteroids, comets, etc. in orbit around it.

solar wind ■ n. the continuous flow of charged particles from the sun which permeates the solar system.

solar year ■ n. the time between successive spring or autumn equinoxes, or winter or summer solstices (365 days, 5 hours, 48 minutes, and 46 seconds).

SOLAS /ˈsəʊləs/ ■ n. the provisions made during a series of international conventions governing maritime safety.
– ORIGIN 1960s: acronym from *safety of life at sea*.

solatium /səˈleɪʃɪəm/ ■ n. (pl. **solatia** /-ʃɪə/) formal a thing given as compensation or consolation.
– ORIGIN C19: from Latin, 'solace'.

sola topi ■ n. an Indian sun hat made from the pith of the sola plant.

sold past and past participle of **SELL**.

solder /ˈsəʊldə, ˈsɒldə/ ■ n. a low-melting alloy, especially one based on lead and tin, used for joining less fusible metals. ■ v. join with solder.
– DERIVATIVES **solderable** adj. **solderer** n.
– ORIGIN Middle English: from Old French *soudure, souder*, from Latin *solidare* 'fasten together', from *solidus* 'solid'.

soldering iron ■ n. an electrical tool for melting and applying solder.

soldier ■ n. 1 a person who serves in an army. ▸ (also **common soldier** or **private soldier**) a private in an army. 2 Entomology a wingless caste of ant or termite with a large modified head and jaws, involved chiefly in defence. 3 Brit. informal a strip of bread or toast, dipped into a soft-boiled egg. 4 an upright brick, timber, or other building element. ■ v. 1 serve as a soldier. 2 (**soldier on**) informal persevere.
– DERIVATIVES **soldierly** adj.
– ORIGIN Middle English: from Old French *soldier*, from *soulde* '(soldier's) pay', from Latin *solidus* (see **SOLIDUS**).

soldier of fortune ■ n. a mercenary.

soldiery ■ n. (pl. **-ies**) 1 soldiers collectively. 2 military training or knowledge.

sole[1] ■ n. 1 the underside of a person's foot. ▸ the section forming the underside of a piece of footwear. 2 the underside of a tool or implement, e.g. a plane or the head of a golf club. ■ v. (usu. **be soled**) put a new sole on (a shoe).
– DERIVATIVES **-soled** adj.
– ORIGIN Middle English: from Latin *solea* 'sandal, sill', from *solum* 'bottom, pavement, sole'.

sole[2] ■ n. an edible marine flatfish. [Several species in the families Soleidae, Pleuronectidae, and Bothidae.]
– ORIGIN Middle English: from Provençal *sola*, from Latin *solea* (see **SOLE[1]**), named from its shape.

sole[3] ■ adj. 1 one and only. ▸ belonging or restricted to one person or group. 2 archaic (especially of a woman) unmarried. ▸ alone.
– ORIGIN Middle English: from Old French *soule*, from Latin *solus* 'alone'.

solecism /ˈsɒlɪsɪz(ə)m/ ■ n. a grammatical mistake. ▸ a piece of bad manners or incorrect behaviour.
– DERIVATIVES **solecistic** /-ˈsɪstɪk/ adj.
– ORIGIN C16: from French *solécisme*, or from Greek *soloikismos*, from *soloikos* 'speaking incorrectly'.

solely ■ adv. not involving anyone or anything else; only.

solemn ■ adj. 1 formal and dignified: *a solemn procession*. 2 not cheerful; serious. ▸ deeply sincere.
– DERIVATIVES **solemnly** adv. **solemnness** n.
– ORIGIN Middle English: from Old French *solemne*, from Latin *sollemnis* 'customary, celebrated at a fixed date', from *sollus* 'entire'.

solemnity /səˈlɛmnɪti/ ■ n. (pl. **-ies**) 1 the state or quality of being solemn. 2 a solemn rite or ceremony.

solemnize /ˈsɒləmnaɪz/ (also **-ise**) ■ v. duly perform (a ceremony, especially that of marriage). ▸ mark with a formal ceremony.
– DERIVATIVES **solemnization** (also **-isation**) n.

Solemn Mass ■ n. another term for **HIGH MASS**.

solenoid /ˈsəʊlənɔɪd, ˈsɒl-/ ■ n. a cylindrical coil of wire acting as a magnet when carrying electric current.
– DERIVATIVES **solenoidal** adj.
– ORIGIN C19: from French *solénoïde*, from Greek *sōlēn* 'channel, pipe'.

soleplate ■ n. a metal plate forming the base of an electric iron, machine saw, or other machine.

sole proprietor (also **sole trader**) ■ n. an exclusive owner of a business, where the owner and the business are not separate legal entities.
– DERIVATIVES **sole proprietorship** n.

sol-fa /ˈsɒlfɑː/ ■ n. short for **TONIC SOL-FA**. ■ v. (**sol-fas, sol-faed, sol-faing**) sing using the sol-fa syllables.

soli plural form of **SOLO**.

solicit ■ v. (**solicited, soliciting**) 1 ask for or try to obtain (something) from someone. ▸ ask for something from.

2 accost someone and offer one's or someone else's services as a prostitute.
– DERIVATIVES **solicitation** n.
– ORIGIN Middle English: from Old French *solliciter*, from Latin *sollicitare* 'agitate', from *sollicitus* 'anxious', from *sollus* 'entire' + *citus* (from *ciere* 'set in motion').

solicitor ■ n. **1** Brit. & Austral. an attorney. Compare with BARRISTER. ▶ N. Amer. the chief law officer of a city, town, or government department. **2** N. Amer. a canvasser.

Solicitor General ■ n. (pl. **Solicitors General**) (in the UK) the Crown law officer below the Attorney General or (in Scotland) below the Lord Advocate. ▶ (in the US) the law officer below the Attorney General.

solicitous ■ adj. showing interest or concern.
– DERIVATIVES **solicitously** adv. **solicitousness** n.
– ORIGIN C16: from Latin *sollicitus* (see SOLICIT).

solicitude ■ n. care or concern.
– ORIGIN Middle English: from Old French *sollicitude*, from Latin *sollicitudo*, from *sollicitus* (see SOLICIT).

solid ■ adj. (**-er**, **-est**) **1** firm and stable in shape: *solid fuel*. ▶ strongly built or made. **2** Geometry three-dimensional. ▶ relating to three-dimensional objects. **3** not hollow or having spaces or gaps. ▶ consisting of the same substance throughout. **4** dependable; reliable. ▶ sound but without special qualities. ■ n. **1** a solid substance or object. ▶ (**solids**) food that is not liquid. **2** Geometry a three-dimensional body or geometric figure.
– DERIVATIVES **solidity** n. **solidly** adv. **solidness** n.
– ORIGIN Middle English: from Latin *solidus*; rel. to *salvus* 'safe' and *sollus* 'entire'.

solid angle ■ n. a three-dimensional angle, such as that formed by the apex of a cone.

solidarity ■ n. unity or agreement of feeling or action, especially among individuals with a common interest.
– ORIGIN C19: from French *solidarité*, from *solidaire* 'solidary'.

solidary ■ adj. characterized by solidarity.
– ORIGIN C19: from French *solidaire*, from *solide* 'solid'.

solidi plural form of SOLIDUS.

solidify ■ v. (**-ies**, **-ied**) make or become hard or solid.
– DERIVATIVES **solidification** n. **solidifier** n.

solid solution ■ n. Chemistry a solid mixture containing a minor component uniformly distributed within the crystal lattice of the major component.

solid state ■ n. the state of matter in which materials are not fluid but retain their boundaries without support. ■ adj. (**solid-state**) making use of the electronic properties of solid semiconductors (as opposed to valves).

solidus /'sɒlɪdəs/ ■ n. (pl. **solidi** /-dʌɪ/) **1** another term for SLASH (in sense 3). **2** Chemistry a curve in a graph of the temperature and composition of a mixture, below which the substance is entirely solid. **3** historical a gold coin of the later Roman Empire.
– ORIGIN Latin, 'solid'; sense 3 is from Latin *solidus* (*nummus*).

solifluction /ˌsɒlɪˈflʌkʃ(ə)n, ˌsəʊlɪ-/ ■ n. Geology the gradual movement of wet soil down a slope.
– ORIGIN C20: from Latin *solum* 'soil' + *fluctio(n-)* 'flowing', from *fluere* 'to flow'.

soliloquy /səˈlɪləkwi/ ■ n. (pl. **-ies**) an act of speaking one's thoughts aloud when alone or regardless of hearers, especially by a character in a play.
– DERIVATIVES **soliloquist** n. **soliloquize** (also **-ise**) v.
– ORIGIN Middle English: from late Latin *soliloquium*, from Latin *solus* 'alone' + *loqui* 'speak'.

solipsism /'sɒlɪpsɪz(ə)m/ ■ n. the view that the self is all that can be known to exist.
– DERIVATIVES **solipsist** n. **solipsistic** adj. **solipsistically** adv.
– ORIGIN C19: from Latin *solus* 'alone' + *ipse* 'self'.

solitaire /ˈsɒlɪtɛː, ˌsɒlɪˈtɛː/ ■ n. **1** a game for one player played by removing pegs from a board one at a time by jumping others over them from adjacent holes, the object being to be left with only one peg. **2** the card game patience. **3** a single diamond or other gem in a piece of jewellery. ▶ a ring with a single gem.
– ORIGIN C18: from French, from Latin *solitarius* (see SOLITARY).

solitary ■ adj. **1** done or existing alone. ▶ (of a bee, wasp, etc.) not social or colonial. **2** secluded or isolated. **3** [often with neg.] single; only. **4** (of a flower or other part) borne singly. ■ n. (pl. **-ies**) **1** a recluse or hermit. **2** informal solitary confinement.
– DERIVATIVES **solitarily** adv. **solitariness** n.
– ORIGIN Middle English: from Latin *solitarius*, from *solus* 'alone'.

solitary confinement ■ n. the isolation of a prisoner in a separate cell as a punishment.

solitude ■ n. the state of being alone. ▶ a lonely or uninhabited place.
– ORIGIN Middle English: from Latin *solitudo*, from *solus* 'alone'.

solmization /ˌsɒlmɪˈzeɪʃ(ə)n/ (also **-isation**) ■ n. Music a system of associating each note of a scale with a particular syllable (typically the sequence doh, ray, me, fah, so, la, te), especially to teach singing.
– DERIVATIVES **solmizate** (also **-isate**) v.
– ORIGIN C17: from French *solmisation*, from *sol* 'soh' + *mi* (see ME²).

solo ■ n. (pl. **-os**) **1** (pl. **solos** or **soli**) a piece of music, song, or dance for one performer. **2** an unaccompanied flight by a pilot. **3** (also **solo whist**) a card game resembling whist in which the players make bids and the highest bidder plays against the others. ▶ a bid by which a player undertakes to win five tricks in this game. ■ adj. & adv. for or done by one person. ■ v. (**-oes**, **-oed**) **1** perform a solo. **2** fly an aircraft unaccompanied.
– ORIGIN C17: from Italian, from Latin *solus* 'alone'.

soloist ■ n. a performer of a solo.

Solomon /'sɒləmən/ ■ n. a very wise person.
– DERIVATIVES **Solomonic** /sɒləˈmɒnɪk/ adj.
– ORIGIN the name of a king of ancient Israel *c.*970–*c.*930 BC, famed for his wisdom.

solstice /'sɒlstɪs/ ■ n. each of the two times in the year, respectively at midsummer and midwinter, when the sun reaches its highest or lowest point in the sky at noon, marked by the longest and shortest days.
– DERIVATIVES **solstitial** adj.
– ORIGIN Middle English: from Latin *solstitium*, from *sol* 'sun' + *stit-*, *sistere* 'stop, be stationary'.

solubilize /'sɒljʊbɪlʌɪz/ (also **-ise**) ■ v. technical make soluble or more soluble.
– DERIVATIVES **solubilization** (also **-isation**) n.

soluble ■ adj. **1** (of a substance) able to be dissolved, especially in water. **2** able to be solved.
– DERIVATIVES **solubility** n.
– ORIGIN Middle English: from late Latin *solubilis*, from *solvere* (see SOLVE).

solute /'sɒljuːt, sɒˈljuːt/ ■ n. the minor component in a solution, dissolved in the solvent.
– ORIGIN C19: from Latin *solutus* 'loosened', from *solvere*.

solution ■ n. **1** a means of solving a problem. ▶ the correct answer to a puzzle. **2** a liquid mixture in which the minor component (the solute) is uniformly distributed within the major component (the solvent). ▶ the process or state of being dissolved.
– ORIGIN Middle English: from Latin *solutio(n-)*, from *solvere* (see SOLVE).

Solutrean /səˈluːtrɪən/ ■ adj. Archaeology relating to or denoting an Upper Palaeolithic culture of central and SW France and parts of Iberia, dated to about 21 000–18 000 years ago.
– ORIGIN C19: from *Solutré* in eastern France, where objects from this culture were found.

solvate Chemistry ■ v. /sɒlˈveɪt/ (of a solvent) enter into reversible chemical combination with (a solute). ■ n. /'sɒlveɪt/ a complex formed by solvation.
– DERIVATIVES **solvation** n.
– ORIGIN C20: from SOLVE + -ATE¹.

solve ■ v. find an answer to, explanation for, or way of dealing with (a problem or mystery).
– DERIVATIVES **solvable** adj. **solver** n.
– ORIGIN Middle English: from Latin *solvere* 'loosen, unfasten'.

solvent ■ adj. **1** having assets in excess of liabilities. **2** able to dissolve other substances. ■ n. **1** the liquid in which a solute is dissolved to form a solution. ▶ a liquid

solvent abuse

used for dissolving other substances. **2** something that weakens or dispels a particular attitude or situation.
– DERIVATIVES **solvency** n.
– ORIGIN C17: from Latin *solvere* 'loose, unfasten'.

solvent abuse ■ n. the use of certain volatile organic solvents as intoxicants by inhalation, e.g. glue-sniffing.

soma /ˈsəʊmə/ ■ n. **1** Biology the parts of an organism other than the reproductive cells. **2** the body as distinct from the soul, mind, or psyche.
– ORIGIN C19: from Greek *sōma* 'body'.

Somali /səˈmɑːli/ ■ n. (pl. same or **Somalis**) **1** a member of a mainly Muslim people of Somalia. **2** the Cushitic language of this people, also spoken in Djibouti and parts of Kenya and Ethiopia. **3** a native or national of Somalia. ■ adj. of or relating to Somalia, the Somalis, or their language.
– DERIVATIVES **Somalian** adj. & n.
– ORIGIN the name in Somali.

somatic /səˈmatɪk/ ■ adj. of or relating to the body, especially as distinct from the mind.
– DERIVATIVES **somatically** adv.
– ORIGIN C18: from Greek *sōmatikos*, from *sōma* 'body'.

somatic cell ■ n. Biology any cell of an organism other than the reproductive cells.

somatization /ˌsəʊmətʌɪˈzeɪʃ(ə)n/ (also **-isation**) ■ n. Psychiatry the production of recurrent and multiple medical symptoms with no discernible organic cause.

somato- ■ comb. form of or relating to the human or animal body: *somatotype*.
– ORIGIN from Greek *sōma*, *sōmat-* 'body'.

somatostatin /ˌsəʊmətə(ʊ)ˈstatɪn/ ■ n. Biochemistry a hormone which inhibits gastric secretion and somatotrophin release.

somatotrophin /ˌsəʊmətə(ʊ)ˈtrəʊfɪn/ ■ n. Biochemistry a growth hormone secreted by the anterior pituitary gland.

somatotype ■ n. a category to which people are assigned according to their bodily physique (usually endomorphic, mesomorphic, or ectomorphic).
– DERIVATIVES **somatotyping** n.
– ORIGIN 1940S: coined by W. H. Sheldon in *Varieties of Human Physique*.

sombre (US also **somber**) ■ adj. **1** dark or dull. **2** oppressively solemn or sober.
– DERIVATIVES **sombrely** adv. **sombreness** n.
– ORIGIN C18: from French, from Latin *sub* 'under' + *umbra* 'shade'.

sombrero /sɒmˈbrɛːrəʊ/ ■ n. (pl. **-os**) a broad-brimmed felt or straw hat, typically worn in Mexico and the south-western US.
– ORIGIN from Spanish.

some[1] ■ det. **1** an unspecified amount or number of. **2** denoting an unknown or unspecified person or thing. **3** (used with a number) approximately. **4** a considerable amount or number of. **5** at least a small amount or number of. **6** expressing admiration: *that was some goal*. ▸ used ironically to express disapproval or disbelief. ■ pron. **1** an unspecified number or amount of people or things. **2** at least a small number or amount of people or things. ■ adv. informal, chiefly N. Amer. to some extent.
– PHRASES **and then some** informal and plenty more than that.
– ORIGIN Old English *sum*, of Germanic origin.

-some[1] ■ suffix forming adjectives meaning: **1** productive of: *loathsome*. **2** characterized by being: *wholesome*. ▸ apt to: *tiresome*.
– ORIGIN Old English *-sum*.

-some[2] ■ suffix (forming nouns) denoting a group of a specified number: *foursome*.
– ORIGIN Old English *sum* 'some'.

-some[3] ■ comb. form denoting a portion of a body, especially a particle of a cell: *chromosome*.
– ORIGIN from Greek *sōma* 'body'.

somebody ■ pron. someone.

some day (also **someday**) ■ adv. at some time in the future.

somehow ■ adv. in some way. ▸ for an unknown or unspecified reason.

someone ■ pron. **1** an unknown or unspecified person. **2** a person of importance or authority.

someplace ■ adv. & pron. informal, chiefly N. Amer. somewhere.

somersault /ˈsʌməsɒlt, -sɔːlt/ ■ n. **1** an acrobatic movement in which a person turns head over heels in the air or on the ground and finishes on their feet. **2** a dramatic upset or reversal of policy or opinion. ■ v. perform a somersault.
– ORIGIN C16: from Old French *sombresault*, from Provençal *sobresaut*, from *sobre* 'above' + *saut* 'leap'.

something ■ pron. **1** an unspecified or unknown thing. **2** an unspecified or unknown amount or degree. ■ adv. **1** informal used for emphasis with a following adjective: *my back hurts something terrible*. **2** archaic or dialect somewhat.
– PHRASES **quite** (or **really**) **something** informal something impressive or notable. **something else** informal an exceptional person or thing. **something of** to some degree. **thirty-something** (**forty-something**, etc.) informal an unspecified age between thirty and forty (forty and fifty, etc.).

sometime ■ adv. at some unspecified or unknown time. ■ adj. **1** former. **2** N. Amer. occasional.

sometimes ■ adv. occasionally.

someway (also **someways**) ■ adv. informal, chiefly N. Amer. by some means.

somewhat ■ adv. to some extent.
– PHRASES **somewhat of** something of.

somewhen ■ adv. informal at some time.

somewhere ■ adv. **1** in or to some place. **2** used to indicate an approximate amount. ■ pron. some unspecified place.
– PHRASES **get somewhere** informal make progress; achieve success.

somite /ˈsəʊmʌɪt/ ■ n. Zoology each of a number of body segments containing the same internal structures, e.g. in an earthworm.
– ORIGIN C19: from Greek *sōma* 'body'.

sommelier /ˈsɒm(ə)ljeɪ, sɒˈmɛljeɪ/ ■ n. a waiter who serves wine.
– ORIGIN C19: French, 'butler'.

sommer /ˈsɒmə/ ■ adv. S. African informal just; simply.
– ORIGIN from Afrikaans.

somnambulism /sɒmˈnambjʊlɪz(ə)m/ ■ n. sleepwalking.
– DERIVATIVES **somnambulant** adj. **somnambulantly** adv. **somnambulist** n. **somnambulistic** adj. **somnambulistically** adv.
– ORIGIN C18: from French *somnambulisme*, from Latin *somnus* 'sleep' + *ambulare* 'to walk'.

somnolent /ˈsɒmnəl(ə)nt/ ■ adj. sleepy; drowsy. ▸ inducing drowsiness.
– DERIVATIVES **somnolence** n. **somnolency** n. **somnolently** adv.
– ORIGIN Middle English: from Latin *somnolentus*, from *somnus* 'sleep'.

son ■ n. **1** a boy or man in relation to his parents. ▸ a male descendant. ▸ a man regarded as the product of a particular influence or environment. **2** (**the Son**) (in Christian belief) the second person of the Trinity; Christ. **3** (also **my son**) used as a form of address for a boy or younger man.
– PHRASES **son of a bitch** (pl. **sons of bitches**) informal used as a general term of abuse. **son of a gun** (pl. **sons of guns**) informal a jocular way of addressing or referring to someone.
– DERIVATIVES **sonship** n.
– ORIGIN Old English, of Germanic origin.

sonar /ˈsəʊnɑː/ ■ n. **1** a system for the detection of objects under water based on the emission and measured reflection of sound pulses. ▸ an apparatus used for this. **2** the method of echolocation used in water or air by animals such as whales and bats.
– ORIGIN 1940S: from *so*(*und*) *na*(*vigation and*) *r*(*anging*), on the pattern of *radar*.

sonata /səˈnɑːtə/ ■ n. a classical composition for an instrumental soloist, often with a piano accompaniment.

—ORIGIN C17: Italian, 'sounded' (orig. as distinct from 'sung'), from *sonare*.

sonata form ■ n. a type of composition in three sections (exposition, development, and recapitulation) in which two themes or subjects are explored according to set key relationships.

sonatina /ˌsɒnəˈtiːnə/ ■ n. a simple or short sonata.
—ORIGIN C18: Italian, diminutive of **SONATA**.

sonde /sɒnd/ ■ n. a probe that transmits information about its surroundings underground or under water.
—ORIGIN C20: from French, 'sounding (line)'.

sone /səʊn/ ■ n. a unit of subjective loudness, equal to 40 phons.
—ORIGIN 1930s: from Latin *sonus* 'a sound'.

son et lumière /ˌsɒn eɪ ˈluːmjɛː/ ■ n. an entertainment held by night at a historic monument or building, telling its history by the use of lighting effects and recorded sound.
—ORIGIN French, 'sound and light'.

song ■ n. 1 a short poem or other set of words set to music. ▶ singing or vocal music. ▶ a musical composition suggestive of a song. 2 the musical phrases uttered by some birds, whales, and insects, used chiefly for territorial defence or for attracting mates. 3 a poem, especially one in rhymed stanzas. ▶ archaic poetry.
—PHRASES **for a song** informal very cheaply. **on song** Brit. informal performing well. **a song and dance** informal a fuss. ▶ N. Amer. a long and pointless or evasive explanation.
—ORIGIN Old English, of Germanic origin.

songbird ■ n. a bird with a musical song. ▶ Ornithology any oscine bird.

songbook ■ n. a collection of songs with music.

song cycle ■ n. a set of related songs forming a single musical entity.

Songhai /sɒŋˈɡʌɪ/ ■ n. (pl. same or **Songhais**) 1 a member of a people of West Africa living mainly in Niger and Mali. 2 the Nilo-Saharan language of this people.
—ORIGIN the name in Songhai.

songololo /ˌsɒŋɡəˈlɔlɔ/ (also **shongololo** /ˌʃɒŋɡəˈlɔlɔ/) ■ n. S. African a millipede.
—ORIGIN from isiXhosa and isiZulu, from *ukus(h)onga* 'roll up'.

songsmith ■ n. informal a writer of popular songs.

songster ■ n. (fem. **songstress**) 1 a person who sings. 2 a writer of songs or verse. 3 a songbird.

song thrush ■ n. a thrush with a buff spotted breast and a song in which phrases are repeated two or three times. [*Turdus philomelos*.]

songwriter ■ n. a writer of songs or the music for them.
—DERIVATIVES **songwriting** n.

sonic ■ adj. 1 relating to or using sound waves. 2 denoting or having a speed equal to that of sound.
—DERIVATIVES **sonically** adv.
—ORIGIN 1920s: from Latin *sonus* 'sound'.

sonic boom ■ n. an explosive noise caused by the shock wave from an aircraft or other object travelling faster than the speed of sound.

sonics ■ pl. n. musical sounds artificially produced or reproduced.

son-in-law ■ n. (pl. **sons-in-law**) the husband of one's daughter.

sonnet ■ n. a poem of fourteen lines using any of a number of formal rhyme schemes, in English typically having ten syllables per line.
—ORIGIN C16: from French, or from Italian *sonetto*, diminutive of *suono* 'a sound'.

sonneteer /ˌsɒnɪˈtɪə/ ■ n. a writer of sonnets.

sonny ■ n. informal a familiar form of address to a young boy. ▶ (also **Sonny Jim**) a humorous or patronizing way of addressing a man.

sono- /ˈsəʊnəʊ, ˈsɒnəʊ/ ■ comb. form of or relating to sound: *sonogram*.
—ORIGIN from Latin *sonus* 'sound'.

sonobuoy ■ n. a buoy detecting underwater sounds and transmitting them by radio.

Son of Man ■ n. Jesus Christ.

sonogram ■ n. 1 a graph showing the distribution of energy at different frequencies in a sound. 2 a visual image produced from an ultrasound examination.
—DERIVATIVES **sonograph** n. **sonographic** adj. **sonography** n.

sonoluminescence ■ n. Physics luminescence associated with the passage of sound waves.
—DERIVATIVES **sonoluminescent** adj.

sonorant /ˈsɒn(ə)r(ə)nt, səˈnɔːr(ə)nt/ ■ n. Phonetics a sound produced with the vocal cord so positioned that spontaneous voicing is possible.
—ORIGIN 1930s: from **SONOROUS**.

sonorous /ˈsɒn(ə)rəs, səˈnɔːrəs/ ■ adj. 1 (of a sound) deep and full. 2 capable of producing a deep or ringing sound. 3 using imposing language.
—DERIVATIVES **sonority** n. **sonorously** adv. **sonorousness** n.
—ORIGIN C17: from Latin *sonorus*, from *sonor* 'sound'.

soon ■ adv. 1 in or after a short time. ▶ early. 2 readily (used to indicate a preference).
—PHRASES **no sooner than** as soon as; at the very moment that. **sooner or later** eventually.
—DERIVATIVES **soonish** adv.
—ORIGIN Old English *sōna* 'immediately', of West Germanic origin.

soot ■ n. a black powdery or flaky substance consisting largely of amorphous carbon, produced by the incomplete burning of organic matter. ■ v. cover or clog with soot.
—ORIGIN Old English, of Germanic origin.

sooth /suːθ/ ■ n. archaic truth.
—PHRASES **in sooth** truly.
—ORIGIN Old English *sōth* (orig. as adj. 'genuine, true'), of Germanic origin.

soothe ■ v. gently calm. ▶ reduce pain or discomfort in. ▶ relieve (pain).
—DERIVATIVES **soother** n. **soothing** adj. **soothingly** adv.
—ORIGIN Old English *sōthian* 'verify, show to be true', from *sōth* 'true'.

soothsayer ■ n. a person supposed to be able to foresee the future.
—DERIVATIVES **soothsaying** n.
—ORIGIN Middle English (in the sense 'person who speaks the truth'): see **SOOTH**.

sooty ■ adj. (**-ier, -iest**) covered with or coloured like soot.
—DERIVATIVES **sootily** adv. **sootiness** n.

sop ■ n. 1 a thing given or done to appease or bribe someone. 2 a piece of bread dipped in gravy, soup, or sauce. ■ v. (**sopped, sopping**) (**sop something up**) soak up liquid.
—ORIGIN Old English *soppian* 'dip (bread) in liquid', prob. from Old English *sūpan* 'sup'.

sophism /ˈsɒfɪz(ə)m/ ■ n. a fallacious argument, especially one used to deceive.
—ORIGIN Middle English: from Old French *sophime*, from Greek *sophisma* 'clever device', from *sophizesthai* (see **SOPHIST**).

sophist /ˈsɒfɪst/ ■ n. 1 a paid teacher of philosophy and rhetoric in ancient Greece, associated in popular thought with moral scepticism and specious reasoning. 2 a person who uses clever but fallacious arguments.
—DERIVATIVES **sophistic** /səˈfɪstɪk/ adj. **sophistical** /səˈfɪstɪk(ə)l/ adj. **sophistically** adv.
—ORIGIN C16: from Greek *sophistēs*, from *sophizesthai* 'devise, become wise', from *sophos* 'wise'.

sophisticate ■ v. 1 cause to become discerning and aware of complex issues through education or experience. ▶ develop into a more complex form. 2 archaic talk or reason in a complex and educated manner. ▶ mislead or corrupt by sophistry. ■ n. a sophisticated person.
—DERIVATIVES **sophistication** n.
—ORIGIN Middle English: from medieval Latin *sophisticatus* 'tampered with', from *sophisticare*, from *sophisticus* 'sophistic'.

sophisticated ■ adj. 1 (of a machine, system, or technique) highly complex. ▶ (of a person) aware of and able to interpret complex issues. 2 showing worldly experience and knowledge of fashion and culture.

sophistry

▸ appealing to sophisticated people.
– DERIVATIVES **sophisticatedly** adv.

HISTORY
Sophisticate and **sophisticated** entered English in the Middle Ages, the verb meaning 'mix with a foreign substance' and the adjective 'adulterated'. The root is the medieval Latin verb *sophisticare* 'tamper with', which goes back to Greek *sophistēs* 'deviser, sophist' and ultimately to *sophos* 'wise'. Until the late 19th century, when it acquired the sense 'worldly and experienced', **sophisticated** meant 'adulterated' or 'deprived of natural simplicity'; it did not take on the meaning 'highly developed and complex' until 1945.

sophistry /ˈsɒfɪstri/ ■ n. (pl. **-ies**) the use of fallacious arguments, especially to deceive. ▸ a fallacious argument.

sophomore /ˈsɒfəmɔː/ ■ n. N. Amer. a second-year university or high-school student.
– DERIVATIVES **sophomoric** adj.
– ORIGIN C17: perhaps from earlier *sophumer*, from *sophum, sophom* (obsolete vars of SOPHISM).

soporific /ˌsɒpəˈrɪfɪk/ ■ adj. inducing drowsiness or sleep. ▸ sleepy. ■ n. a soporific drug or other agent.
– DERIVATIVES **soporifically** adv.
– ORIGIN C17: from Latin *sopor* 'sleep'.

sopping ■ adj. wet through.
– ORIGIN C19: from SOP.

soppy ■ adj. (**-ier, -iest**) informal **1** self-indulgently sentimental. **2** feeble.
– DERIVATIVES **soppily** adv. **soppiness** n.
– ORIGIN C19: from SOP.

soprano /səˈprɑːnəʊ/ ■ n. (pl. **-os**) **1** the highest singing voice. ▸ a singer with such a voice. **2** an instrument of a high or the highest pitch in its family.
– ORIGIN C18: Italian, from *sopra* 'above', from Latin *supra*.

soprano recorder ■ n. a descant recorder.

sorbent /ˈsɔːb(ə)nt/ ■ n. Chemistry a substance which collects molecules of another substance by sorption.

sorbet /ˈsɔːbeɪ, -bɪt/ ■ n. **1** a water ice. **2** archaic an Arabian sherbet.
– ORIGIN C16: from French, from Italian *sorbetto*, from Turkish *şerbet*, from Arabic *šariba* 'to drink'.

sorcerer ■ n. (fem. **sorceress**) a person believed to have magic powers.
– DERIVATIVES **sorcerous** adj. **sorcery** n.
– ORIGIN Middle English: from Old French *sorcier*, from Latin *sors* 'lot'.

sordid ■ adj. **1** involving ignoble actions and motives. **2** dirty or squalid.
– DERIVATIVES **sordidly** adv. **sordidness** n.
– ORIGIN Middle English: from French *sordide* or Latin *sordidus*, from *sordere* 'be dirty'.

sore ■ adj. **1** painful or aching. ▸ suffering pain. **2** informal, chiefly N. Amer. upset and angry. **3** severe; urgent. ■ n. **1** a raw or painful place on the body. **2** a source of distress or annoyance. ■ adv. archaic extremely; severely.
– PHRASES **sore point** an issue about which someone feels distressed or annoyed. **stand** (or **stick**) **out like a sore thumb** be quite obviously different.
– DERIVATIVES **soreness** n.
– ORIGIN Old English, of Germanic origin.

sorehead ■ n. N. Amer. informal a person who is angry or easily irritated.

sorely ■ adv. extremely; badly.

sorghum /ˈsɔːɡəm/ ■ n. a cereal which is a major source of grain and stockfeed, native to warm regions of the Old World. [*Sorghum bicolor* and related species.]
– ORIGIN C16: from Italian *sorgo*, perhaps from a var. of Latin *syricum* 'Syrian'.

sorghum beer ■ n. S. African an alcoholic drink made from fermented sorghum millet.

sori plural form of SORUS.

Soroptimist ■ n. a member of Soroptimist International, a worldwide service organization for business and professional women.

– ORIGIN 1920s: from Latin *soror* 'sister' + 'optimist' (see OPTIMISM).

sorority /səˈrɒrɪti/ ■ n. (pl. **-ies**) N. Amer. a society for female students in a university or college.
– ORIGIN C16: from medieval Latin *sororitas*, or from Latin *soror* 'sister'.

sorption /ˈsɔːpʃ(ə)n/ ■ n. Chemistry absorption and adsorption considered as a single process.
– ORIGIN C20: back-formation from *absorption* and *adsorption*.

sorrel¹ /ˈsɒr(ə)l/ ■ n. an edible plant of the dock family with arrow-shaped leaves and an acidic flavour. [*Rumex acetosa* and other species.] ▸ used in names of other plants with acid leaves, e.g. wood sorrel.
– ORIGIN Middle English: from Old French *sorele*, of Germanic origin.

sorrel² /ˈsɒr(ə)l/ ■ n. a horse with a light reddish-brown coat. ▸ a light reddish-brown colour.
– ORIGIN Middle English: from Old French *sorel*, from *sor* 'yellowish', from a Germanic adj. meaning 'dry'.

sorrow ■ n. a feeling of deep distress caused by loss or disappointment. ▸ a cause of sorrow. ▸ the outward expression of grief. ■ v. feel sorrow.
– DERIVATIVES **sorrowful** adj. **sorrowfully** adv. **sorrowfulness** n.
– ORIGIN Old English, of Germanic origin.

sorry ■ adj. (**-ier, -iest**) **1** feeling distress, especially through sympathy with someone else's misfortune. ▸ (**sorry for**) filled with compassion for. **2** feeling regret or penitence. ▸ used to express apology. **3** in a poor or pitiful state. ▸ unpleasant and regrettable.
– DERIVATIVES **sorrily** adv. **sorriness** n.
– ORIGIN Old English *sārig* 'pained, distressed', of West Germanic origin.

sort ■ n. **1** a category of people or things with a common feature. ▸ informal a person with a specified nature. **2** archaic a manner or way. **3** Computing the arrangement of data in a prescribed sequence. ■ v. **1** arrange systematically in groups. ▸ separate from a mixed group. ▸ (**sort through**) look at in succession for classification or to make a selection. **2** (**sort someone/thing out**) resolve a problem or difficulty. ▸ (**sort someone out**) informal deal with a troublesome person.
– PHRASES **of a sort** (or **of sorts**) of a somewhat unusual or inferior kind. **out of sorts** slightly unwell or unhappy. **sort of** informal to some extent.
– DERIVATIVES **sortable** adj. **sorter** n.
– ORIGIN Middle English: from Old French *sorte*, from Latin *sors* 'lot, condition'.

sorted ■ adj. informal, chiefly Brit. **1** organized; arranged. **2** having obtained illegal drugs. **3** emotionally well balanced.

sortie ■ n. **1** an attack by troops coming out from a position of defence. ▸ an operational flight by a single military aircraft. **2** a short trip. ■ v. (**sorties, sortied, sortieing**) make a sortie.
– ORIGIN C18: from French, from *sortir* 'go out'.

sorting office ■ n. a place in which mail is sorted according to its destination.

sorus /ˈsɔːrəs/ ■ n. (pl. **sori** /-raɪ/) Botany a cluster of spore-producing receptacles on the underside of a fern frond.
– ORIGIN C19: from Greek *sōros* 'heap'.

SOS ■ n. an international coded signal of extreme distress, used especially by ships at sea. ▸ an urgent appeal for help. ▸ a message broadcast to an untraceable person in an emergency.
– ORIGIN C20: letters chosen as being easily transmitted and recognized in Morse code; by folk etymology an abbrev. of *save our souls*.

sosatie /səˈsɑːti/ ■ n. S. African a dish of cubes of curried or spiced meat or vegetables grilled on a skewer; a kebab.
– ORIGIN C19: from S. African Dutch *sasaatje*, from Javanese *sesate* 'skewered meat'.

sosatie stick ■ n. S. African a wooden skewer used in cooking.

so-so ■ adj. neither very good nor very bad.

sot ■ n. a habitual drunkard.
– DERIVATIVES **sottish** adj.

– ORIGIN Old English *sott* 'foolish person', from medieval Latin *sottus*, reinforced by Old French *sot* 'foolish'.

soteriology /sə(ʊ)ˌtɪərɪˈɒlədʒi, sɒ-/ ■ n. Theology the doctrine of salvation.
– DERIVATIVES **soteriological** adj.
– ORIGIN C19: from Greek *sōtēria* 'salvation' + -LOGY.

Sotho /ˈsuːtuː/ ■ n. (pl. same or **-os**) **1** a member of a group of peoples living chiefly in Botswana, Lesotho, and South Africa. **2** the Bantu languages spoken by these peoples.
– ORIGIN the stem of BASOTHO and SESOTHO.

Sotho-Tswana ■ n. a collective term for the Sotho and Tswana peoples of southern Africa or their languages.

sotto voce /ˌsɒtəʊ ˈvəʊtʃeɪ/ ■ adv. & adj. in a quiet voice.
– ORIGIN from Italian *sotto* 'under' + *voce* 'voice'.

sou /suː/ ■ n. historical a former French coin of low value. ▸ [usu. with neg.] informal a very small amount of money.
– ORIGIN French, from Old French *sout* from Latin *solidus* (see SOLIDUS).

soubrette /suːˈbrɛt/ ■ n. a pert maidservant or similar female role in a comedy.
– ORIGIN C18: French, from Provençal *soubreto*, from *soubret* 'coy', from Latin *superare* 'be above'.

soubriquet /ˈsuːbrɪkeɪ/ ■ n. variant spelling of SOBRIQUET.

soufflé ■ n. a light, spongy baked dish made typically by adding flavoured egg yolks to stiffly beaten egg whites.
– ORIGIN French, 'blown', from *souffler*, from Latin *sufflare* 'to blow'.

sough /saʊ, sʌf/ ■ v. (of the wind, sea, etc.) make a moaning, whistling, or rushing sound. ■ n. a sound of this type.
– ORIGIN Old English, of Germanic origin.

sought past and past participle of SEEK.

sought after ■ adj. much in demand.

souk /suːk/ (also **suk**, **sukh**, or **suq**) ■ n. an Arab bazaar.
– ORIGIN from Arabic *sūk*.

soukous /ˈsuːkuːs/ ■ n. a style of African popular music with syncopated rhythms and intricate contrasting guitar melodies.
– ORIGIN perhaps from French *secouer* 'to shake'.

soul ■ n. **1** the spiritual or immaterial part of a human, regarded as immortal. ▸ one's moral or emotional nature or sense of identity. ▸ emotional or intellectual energy or intensity. **2** short for SOUL MUSIC. **3** a person regarded as the embodiment of some quality: *he was the soul of discretion*. ▸ an individual. ▸ a person regarded with affection or pity.
– PHRASES **lost soul** a soul that is damned. ▸ chiefly humorous a person who seems unable to cope with everyday life. **upon my soul** dated an exclamation of surprise.
– DERIVATIVES **-souled** adj.
– ORIGIN Old English, of Germanic origin.

soul-destroying ■ adj. unbearably monotonous.

soul food ■ n. food traditionally associated with black people of the southern US.

soulful ■ adj. expressing deep and typically sorrowful feeling.
– DERIVATIVES **soulfully** adv. **soulfulness** n.

soulless ■ adj. **1** lacking character and individuality. ▸ (of an activity) tedious and uninspiring. **2** lacking or suggesting a lack of human feelings.
– DERIVATIVES **soullessly** adv. **soullessness** n.

soulmate ■ n. a person ideally suited to another.

soul music ■ n. a kind of music incorporating elements of rhythm and blues and gospel music, popularized by African Americans.

soul-searching ■ n. close examination of one's emotions and motives. ■ adj. characterized by such examination.

soulster ■ n. informal a singer of soul music.

sound¹ ■ n. **1** vibrations which travel through the air or another medium and are sensed by the ear. ▸ a thing that can be heard. **2** (also **musical sound**) sound produced by continuous and regular vibrations, as opposed to noise. **3** music, speech, and sound effects accompanying a film or broadcast. ▸ radio broadcasting as distinct from television. **4** an idea or impression conveyed by words. ■ v. **1** emit or cause to emit sound. ▸ utter. **2** convey a specified impression when heard. **3** (**sound off**) express one's opinions loudly or forcefully. **4** test (the lungs or another body cavity) by noting the sound they produce.
– DERIVATIVES **soundless** adj. **soundlessly** adv. **soundlessness** n.
– ORIGIN Middle English *soun*, from Anglo-Norman French *soun* (n.), *suner* (v.), from Latin *sonus*.

sound² ■ adj. **1** in good condition. ▸ based on reason or judgement. ▸ competent or reliable. ▸ financially secure. **2** (of sleep) deep and unbroken. **3** severe: *a sound thrashing*. ■ adv. soundly.
– DERIVATIVES **soundly** adv. **soundness** n.
– ORIGIN Middle English: from Old English *gesund*, of West Germanic origin.

sound³ ■ v. **1** ascertain (the depth of water) by means of a line or pole or using sound echoes. **2** Medicine examine (the bladder or other internal cavity) with a long surgical probe. **3** (**sound someone out**) question someone discreetly or cautiously. **4** (especially of a whale) dive steeply to a great depth. ■ n. a long surgical probe, typically with a curved, blunt end.
– DERIVATIVES **sounder** n.
– ORIGIN Middle English: from Old French *sonder*, from Latin *sub-* 'below' + *unda* 'wave'.

sound⁴ ■ n. a narrow stretch of water forming an inlet or connecting two larger bodies of water.
– ORIGIN Middle English: from Old Norse *sund* 'swimming, strait'.

soundalike ■ n. a person or thing sounding very like another.

sound barrier ■ n. the speed of sound, regarded as presenting problems of drag, controllability, etc. for aircraft.

sound bite ■ n. a short extract from a recorded interview, chosen for its pungency or aptness.

soundboard (also **sounding board**) ■ n. a thin board under the strings of a piano or similar instrument to increase the sound produced.

soundbox ■ n. the hollow chamber forming the body of a stringed instrument and providing resonance.

sound card ■ n. a device which can be slotted into a computer to allow the use of audio components for multimedia applications.

soundcheck ■ n. a test of sound equipment before a musical performance or recording.

sound effect ■ n. a sound other than speech or music made artificially for use in a play, film, etc.

sound engineer ■ n. a technician dealing with acoustics for a broadcast or musical performance.

soundhole ■ n. a hole in the belly of a stringed instrument.

sounding¹ ■ n. **1** the action of sounding the depth of water. ▸ a measurement taken by sounding. ▸ the determination of any physical property at a depth in the sea or at a height in the atmosphere. **2** (**soundings**) information or evidence ascertained before taking action.

sounding² ■ adj. archaic giving forth sound. ▸ having an imposing sound but little substance.

sounding board ■ n. **1** a board over or behind a pulpit or stage to reflect a speaker's voice forward. **2** a soundboard. **3** a person whose reactions to ideas are used as a test of their validity or likely success. ▸ a channel through which ideas are disseminated.

sounding line ■ n. a weighted line used to measure the depth of water under a boat.

soundproof ■ adj. preventing the passage of sound. ■ v. make soundproof.

soundscape ■ n. a piece of music considered in terms of its component sounds.

sound shift ■ n. Linguistics a change in the pronunciation of a set of speech sounds as a language evolves.

sound system ■ n. a set of equipment for the reproduction and amplification of sound.

soundtrack ■ n. **1** the sound accompaniment to a film.

sound wave

2 a strip on the edge of a film on which sound is recorded. ■ v. provide (a film) with a soundtrack.

sound wave ■ n. Physics a wave of compression and rarefaction, by which sound is propagated in an elastic medium such as air.

soup ■ n. 1 a savoury liquid dish made by boiling meat, fish, or vegetables in stock or water. 2 US informal nitroglycerine or gelignite, especially as used for safe-breaking. ■ v. (**soup something up**) [often as adj. **souped-up**] informal increase the power and efficiency of an engine. ▶ make something more elaborate or impressive.
– PHRASES **in the soup** informal in trouble.
– ORIGIN Middle English: from Old French *soupe* 'sop, broth', from late Latin *suppa*, of Germanic origin.

soupçon /'suːpsɒn, -sɒ̃/ ■ n. a very small quantity.
– ORIGIN C18: French, from Old French *souspeçon*, from medieval Latin *suspectio* (see SUSPICION).

soup kitchen ■ n. a place where free food is served to the homeless or destitute.

soup plate ■ n. a deep, wide-rimmed plate in which soup is served.

soup spoon ■ n. a large spoon with a round bowl, used for eating soup.

soupy ■ adj. (-ier, -iest) 1 having the appearance or consistency of soup. 2 informal mawkishly sentimental.
– DERIVATIVES **soupily** adv. **soupiness** n.

sour ■ adj. 1 having an acid taste like lemon or vinegar. 2 (of food, especially milk) having gone bad because of fermentation. ▶ having a rancid smell. 3 showing resentment, disappointment, or anger. 4 (of soil) deficient in lime. 5 (of petroleum or natural gas) containing a high proportion of sulphur. ■ n. a cocktail made by mixing a spirit with lemon or lime juice. ■ v. make or become sour.
– PHRASES **go** (or **turn**) **sour** become less pleasant; turn out badly. **sour grapes** an attitude in which someone affects to despise something because they cannot have it themselves.
– DERIVATIVES **sourish** adj. **sourly** adv. **sourness** n.
– ORIGIN Old English, of Germanic origin.

source ■ n. 1 a place, person, or thing from which something originates. ▶ a spring or fountain head from which a river or stream issues. 2 a person who provides information. ▶ a book or document providing evidence for research. 3 technical a body or process by which energy or a component enters a system. The opposite of SINK[2]. ■ v. obtain from a particular source. ▶ find out where to obtain.
– PHRASES **at source** at the point of origin or issue.
– ORIGIN Middle English: from Old French *sours(e)*, from *sourdre* 'to rise', from Latin *surgere*.

sourcebook ■ n. a collection of writings for the study of a particular subject.

source code ■ n. Computing a text listing of commands to be compiled into an executable computer program.

source criticism ■ n. the analysis and study of sources used by biblical authors.

sour cream ■ n. cream deliberately fermented by adding certain bacteria.

sourdough ■ n. leaven for making bread, consisting of fermenting dough, originally that left over from a previous baking. ▶ bread made using such leaven.

sour fig ■ n. a creeping succulent plant with fleshy leaves and brightly coloured flowers, native to South Africa. [Genus *Carpobrotus*: several species.] ▶ the edible fruit of this plant.

sour grass ■ n. grass which is coarse, unpalatable, or of low nutritional value.

sourpuss ■ n. informal a bad-tempered or habitually sullen person.
– ORIGIN 1930s: from SOUR + dialect *puss* 'face', from Irish *pus* 'mouth'.

soursop ■ n. 1 a large acidic custard apple with white fibrous flesh. 2 the evergreen tropical American tree which bears this fruit. [*Annona muricata*.]

sourveld /'saʊəfelt/ ■ n. S. African uncultivated land covered with grasses lacking nutritional value.
– ORIGIN C18: partial translation of S. African Dutch *zuurveld*, from *zuur* 'sour, unpalatable' + *veld* 'land, countryside'.

sous- /suː(z)/ ■ prefix (in words adopted from French) subordinate: *sous-chef*.
– ORIGIN from French *sous* 'under'.

sousaphone /'suːzəfəʊn/ ■ n. an American form of tuba with a wide bell pointing forward above the player's head.
– DERIVATIVES **sousaphonist** /-'zɒf(ə)nɪst/ n.
– ORIGIN 1920s: named after the American composer J. P. Sousa, on the pattern of *saxophone*.

souse /saʊs/ ■ v. 1 soak in or drench with liquid. 2 [often as adj. **soused**] put (gherkins, fish, etc.) in pickle or a marinade: *soused herring*. 3 [as adj. **soused**] informal drunk. ■ n. 1 liquid used for pickling. 2 informal a drunkard.
– ORIGIN Middle English: from Old French *sous* 'pickle', of Germanic origin.

souslik /'suːslɪk/ ■ n. a short-tailed Eurasian and Arctic ground squirrel. [*Spermophilus citellus* and related species.]
– ORIGIN C18: from Russian.

sou sou ■ n. another term for CHAYOTE.

sous vide /suː 'viːd/ ■ n. a method of treating food by partial cooking followed by vacuum-sealing and chilling. ■ adj. & adv. involving such preparation.
– ORIGIN French, 'under vacuum'.

soutane /suː'tɑːn/ ■ n. a type of cassock worn by Roman Catholic priests.
– ORIGIN C19: from French, from Italian *sottana*, from *sotto* 'under', from Latin *subtus*.

souterrain /'suːtəreɪn/ ■ n. chiefly Archaeology an underground chamber or passage.
– ORIGIN C18: from French, from *sous* 'under' + *terre* 'earth'.

south ■ n. (usu. **the south**) 1 the direction towards the point of the horizon 90° clockwise from east. 2 the southern part of a country, region, or town. ▶ (**the South**) the Southern states of the United States. 3 (**the South**) another term for THIRD WORLD. ■ adj. 1 lying towards, near, or facing the south. 2 (of a wind) blowing from the south. ■ adv. to or towards the south. ■ v. move towards the south.
– PHRASES **south by east** (or **west**) between south and south-south-east (or south-south-west).
– DERIVATIVES **southbound** adj. & adv.
– ORIGIN Old English, of Germanic origin.

South African ■ n. a native or inhabitant of South Africa. ■ adj. of or relating to South Africa.

South African Dutch ■ n. the Afrikaans language from the 17th to the 19th centuries, during its development from Dutch. ■ adj. dated of or relating to Afrikaans-speaking South Africans.

South Africanism ■ n. 1 a word or phrase peculiar to or originating in South Africa. 2 the qualities typical of South Africa and South Africans.

South African War ■ n. another term for the 1899–1902 ANGLO-BOER WAR.

South American ■ n. a native or inhabitant of South America. ■ adj. of or relating to South America.

south-east ■ n. (usu. **the south-east**) 1 the direction towards the point of the horizon midway between south and east. 2 the south-eastern part of a country, region, or town. ■ adj. 1 lying towards, near, or facing the south-east. 2 (of a wind) blowing from the south-east. ■ adv. to or towards the south-east.
– DERIVATIVES **south-eastern** adj.

southeaster ■ n. a wind blowing from the south-east.

south-easterly ■ adj. & adv. in a south-eastward position or direction. ■ n. another term for SOUTHEASTER.

south-eastward ■ adv. (also **south-eastwards**) towards the south-east. ■ adj. situated in, directed towards, or facing the south-east.

southerly ■ adj. & adv. 1 in a southward position or direction. 2 (of a wind) blowing from the south. ■ n. (often **southerlies**) a wind blowing from the south.

southern ■ adj. 1 situated, directed towards, or facing the

south. **2** (usu. **Southern**) living in, coming from, or characteristic of the south.
– DERIVATIVES **southernmost** adj.

Southern Baptist ■ n. a member of a large convention of Baptist churches in the US, typically having a fundamentalist and evangelistic approach to Christianity.

Southern blot ■ n. Biology a procedure for identifying specific sequences of DNA.
– ORIGIN C20: named after the British biochemist Edwin M. Southern.

Southern Comfort ■ n. trademark a whisky-based liqueur of US origin.

southerner ■ n. a native or inhabitant of the south of a particular region or country.

southern-fried ■ adj. chiefly N. Amer. (of food, especially chicken) coated in flour, egg, and breadcrumbs and then deep-fried.

Southern Lights ■ pl. n. the aurora australis (see AURORA).

southernwood ■ n. a bushy artemisia of southern Europe. [*Artemisia abrotanum*.]

South Korean ■ n. a native or inhabitant of South Korea. ■ adj. of or relating to South Korea.

southpaw ■ n. a left-handed boxer who leads with the right hand. ▸ informal, chiefly N. Amer. a left-hander in any sphere.
– ORIGIN C19: from PAW.

south-south-east ■ n. the compass point or direction midway between south and south-east.

south-south-west ■ n. the compass point or direction midway between south and south-west.

southward /'saʊθwəd Nautical/, /'sʌðəd/ ■ adj. in a southerly direction. ■ adv. (also **southwards**) towards the south. ■ n. (**the southward**) the direction or region to the south.
– DERIVATIVES **southwardly** adj. & adv.

south-west ■ n. **1** (usu. **the south-west**) the direction towards the point of the horizon midway between south and west. **2** the south-western part of a country, region, or town. ■ adj. **1** lying towards, near, or facing the south-west. **2** (of a wind) blowing from the south-west. ■ adv. to or towards the south-west.
– DERIVATIVES **south-western** adj.

southwester ■ n. a wind blowing from the south-west.

south-westerly ■ adj. & adv. in a south-westward position or direction. ■ n. another term for SOUTHWESTER.

south-westward ■ adv. (also **south-westwards**) towards the south-west. ■ adj. situated in, directed toward, or facing the south-west.

soutie /'saʊti/ (also vulgar slang **soutpiel** /'saʊtpi:l/) ■ n. S. African informal, derogatory an English-speaking South African or a person of English descent, especially a man.
– ORIGIN 1940s: Afrikaans, shortening of *soutpiel*, from *sout* 'salt' + *piel* 'penis' (from the idea of a man straddling Britain and South Africa with his penis in the Mediterranean Sea).

souvenir /ˌsuːvə'nɪə/ ■ n. a thing that is kept as a reminder of a person, place, or event.
– ORIGIN C18: from French, from *souvenir* 'remember', from Latin *subvenire* 'occur to the mind'.

souvlaki /suː'vlɑːki/ ■ n. (pl. **souvlakia** /-kɪə/ or **souvlakis**) a Greek dish of pieces of meat grilled on a skewer.
– ORIGIN from modern Greek.

sou'wester /saʊ'wɛstə/ ■ n. a waterproof hat with a broad flap covering the neck.

sovereign ■ n. **1** a supreme ruler, especially a monarch. **2** a former British gold coin worth one pound sterling, now only minted for commemorative purposes. ■ adj. **1** possessing supreme or ultimate power. ▸ archaic or poetic/literary possessing royal power and status. **2** (of a nation or its affairs) acting or done independently and without outside interference.
– DERIVATIVES **sovereignly** adv.
– ORIGIN Middle English: from Old French *soverain*, from Latin *super* 'above'.

sovereignty ■ n. (pl. **-ies**) **1** supreme power or authority. ▸ the authority of a state to govern itself or another state. **2** a self-governing state.

soviet /'səʊvɪət, 'sɒv-/ ■ n. **1** an elected local, district, or national council in the former USSR. ▸ a revolutionary council of workers or peasants in Russia before 1917. **2** (**Soviet**) a citizen of the former USSR. ■ adj. (**Soviet**) of or concerning the former Soviet Union.
– DERIVATIVES **Sovietism** n. **Sovietization** (also **-isation**) n. **Sovietize** (also **-ise**) v.
– ORIGIN C20: from Russian *sovet* 'council'.

Sovietologist /ˌsəʊvɪə'tɒlədʒɪst, ˌsɒ-/ ■ n. a student of or expert on the former Soviet Union.
– DERIVATIVES **Sovietological** adj. **Sovietology** n.

sovkhoz /'sɒvkɒz, sʌv'kɔːz/ ■ n. (pl. same, **sovkhozes** /'sɒvkɒzɪz, sʌv'kɔːzɪz/, or **sovkhozy** /'sɒvkɒzi, sʌv'kɔːzi/) a state-owned farm in the former USSR.
– ORIGIN Russian, from *sov*(*etskoe*) *khoz*(*yaĭstvo*) 'Soviet farm'.

sow[1] /səʊ/ ■ v. (past **sowed** /səʊd/; past part. **sown** /səʊn/ or **sowed**) **1** plant (seed) by scattering it on or in the earth. ▸ plant (an area) with seed. **2** disseminate or introduce (something unwelcome): *the new policy has sown confusion and doubt.*
– DERIVATIVES **sower** n.
– ORIGIN Old English *sāwan*, of Germanic origin.

sow[2] /saʊ/ ■ n. **1** an adult female pig, especially one which has farrowed. ▸ the female of certain other mammals, e.g. the guinea pig. **2** a large block of metal (larger than a 'pig') made by smelting.
– ORIGIN Old English *sugu*.

sow bug /'saʊ/ ■ n. chiefly N. Amer. another term for WOODLOUSE.

Sowetan /sə'wɛtən, -'weɪtən/ ■ n. a native or inhabitant of Soweto. ■ adj. of or relating to Soweto.

Soweto Day ■ n. less formal term for YOUTH DAY.

sown past participle of SOW[1].

sowthistle /'saʊθɪs(ə)l/ ■ n. a plant with yellow flowers, thistle-like leaves, and milky sap. [Genus *Sonchus*.]

soy ■ n. **1** (also **soy sauce**) a sauce made with fermented soya beans, used in Chinese and Japanese cooking. **2** another term for SOYA.
– ORIGIN from Japanese *shō-yu*, from Chinese *shi-yu*, from *shi* 'salted beans' + *yu* 'oil'.

soya ■ n. **1** protein derived from the beans of an Asian plant, used as a replacement for animal protein in certain foods. ▸ chiefly Brit. soy sauce. **2** the widely cultivated plant of the pea family which produces these beans. [*Glycine max*.]
– ORIGIN C17: from Dutch *soja*, from Malay *soi* (see SOY).

soya milk ■ n. the liquid obtained by suspending soya bean flour in water, used as a fat-free substitute for milk, particularly by vegans.

sozzled ■ adj. informal very drunk.
– ORIGIN C19: from *sozzle* 'mix sloppily', prob. of imitative origin.

sp. ■ abbrev. species (usually singular).

spa ■ n. a mineral spring considered to have health-giving properties. ▸ a place or resort with such a spring. ▸ a commercial establishment offering health and beauty treatment.
– ORIGIN C17: from *Spa*, a small town in eastern Belgium noted for its mineral springs.

space ■ n. **1** a continuous area or expanse which is free or unoccupied. ▸ a gap between printed or written words or characters. ▸ pages in a newspaper, or time between broadcast programmes, available for advertising. ▸ the freedom and scope to live and develop as one wishes. ▸ Telecommunications one of two possible states of a signal in certain systems. The opposite of MARK[1]. **2** an interval of time (often used to emphasize that the time is short): *both cars were stolen in the space of a few hours.* **3** the dimensions of height, depth, and width within which all things exist and move. ▸ (also **outer space**) the physical universe beyond the earth's atmosphere. ▸ the near-vacuum extending between the planets and stars. **4** Mathematics a mathematical concept generally regarded as a set of points having some specified structure. ■ v. **1** position (two or more items) at a distance from one another. ▸ (in printing or writing) insert spaces between.

space age

2 (be spaced out or chiefly N. Amer. **space out)** informal be or become euphoric or disorientated, especially from taking drugs.
- DERIVATIVES **spacer** n. **spacing** n.
- ORIGIN Middle English: shortening of Old French *espace*, from Latin *spatium*.

space age ■ n. **(the space age)** the era starting when the exploration of space became possible. ■ adj. **(space-age)** very modern; technologically advanced.

space bar ■ n. a long key on a typewriter or computer keyboard for making a space between words.

space blanket ■ n. a light metal-coated sheet designed to retain heat, originally developed for use during space travel.

space cadet ■ n. **1** a trainee astronaut. **2** informal a person perceived as out of touch with reality.

space capsule ■ n. a small spacecraft or the part of a larger one that contains the instruments or crew, designed to be returned to earth.

spacecraft ■ n. (pl. same or **spacecrafts**) a vehicle used for travelling in space.

spacefaring ■ n. the action or activity of travelling in space.
- DERIVATIVES **spacefarer** n.

space frame ■ n. a three-dimensional structural framework designed to withstand loads applied at any point.

space heater ■ n. a heater used to warm an enclosed space within a building.
- DERIVATIVES **space-heated** adj. **space heating** n.

spaceman ■ n. (pl. **-men**) a male astronaut.

space–time ■ n. Physics the concepts of time and three-dimensional space regarded as fused in a four-dimensional continuum.

space opera ■ n. informal a novel or drama set in outer space.

spaceplane ■ n. an aircraft that takes off and lands conventionally but is capable of entry into orbit or travel through space.

spaceport ■ n. a base from which spacecraft are launched.

space probe ■ n. see **PROBE**.

spaceship ■ n. a manned spacecraft.

space shuttle ■ n. a rocket-launched spacecraft able to land like an unpowered aircraft, used to make journeys between earth and earth orbit.

space station ■ n. a large artificial satellite used as a long-term base for manned operations in space.

spacesuit ■ n. a sealed and pressurized suit designed to allow an astronaut to survive in space.

space walk ■ n. an excursion by an astronaut outside a spacecraft.

spacey (also **spacy**) ■ adj. (**-ier**, **-iest**) informal out of touch with reality. ▶ (of popular music) drifting and ethereal.

spacial ■ adj. variant spelling of **SPATIAL**.

spacious ■ adj. (of a room or building) having plenty of space.
- DERIVATIVES **spaciously** adv. **spaciousness** n.
- ORIGIN Middle English: from Old French *spacios* or Latin *spatiosus*, from *spatium* (see **SPACE**).

spade¹ ■ n. **1** a tool with a sharp-edged, rectangular metal blade and a long handle, used for digging. **2** [as modifier] shaped like a spade: *a spade bit*. ■ v. dig over with a spade. ▶ move or lift with a spade.
- PHRASES **call a spade a spade** speak plainly and frankly.
- DERIVATIVES **spadeful** n. (pl. **-fuls**).
- ORIGIN Old English *spadu*, *spada*, of Germanic origin.

spade² ■ n. **1** (**spades**) one of the four suits in a conventional pack of playing cards, denoted by a black inverted heart-shaped figure with a small stalk. ▶ (**a spade**) a card of this suit. **2** informal, offensive a black person.
- PHRASES **in spades** informal in large amounts or to a high degree.
- ORIGIN C16: from Italian *spade*, pl. of *spada* 'sword', from Greek *spathē*.

spadefish ■ n. (pl. same or **-fishes**) a fish with an almost disc-shaped body, found in tropical inshore waters. [*Chaetodipterus* and other genera.]

spadework ■ n. hard or routine preparatory work.

spaetzle /ˈʃpetslə, ˈʃpets(ə)l/ (also **spätzle**) ■ pl. n. small dough dumplings of a type made in southern Germany and Alsace.
- ORIGIN from German dialect *Spätzle* 'little sparrows'.

spaghetti /spəˈɡeti/ ■ pl. n. pasta made in solid strings, between macaroni and vermicelli in thickness.
- ORIGIN Italian, pl. of the diminutive of *spago* 'string'.

spaghetti Bolognese /ˌbɒləˈneɪz/ ■ n. a dish of spaghetti with a sauce of minced beef, tomato, onion, and herbs.
- ORIGIN Italian, 'spaghetti of Bologna'.

spaghettini /ˌspaɡɛˈtiːni/ ■ pl. n. pasta in the form of strings of thin spaghetti.
- ORIGIN Italian, diminutive of *spaghetti*.

spaghetti strap ■ n. a thin rounded shoulder strap on an item of women's clothing.

spaghetti western ■ n. informal a western film made cheaply in Europe by an Italian director.

spake archaic or poetic/literary past of **SPEAK**.

spall /spɔːl/ ■ n. a splinter or chip of rock. ■ v. break or cause to break into spalls.
- ORIGIN Middle English.

spallation /spɔːˈleɪʃ(ə)n/ ■ n. Geology separation of fragments from the surface of a rock.

spalted /ˈspɔːltəd/ ■ adj. (of wood) containing blackish irregular lines as a result of fungal decay.
- ORIGIN 1970s: from dialect *spalt* 'to splinter'.

spam ■ n. **1** trademark a tinned meat product made mainly from ham. **2** irrelevant or inappropriate messages sent on the Internet to a large number of newsgroups or users. ■ v. send the same message indiscriminately (to large numbers of users) on the Internet.
- DERIVATIVES **spammer** n. **spamming** n.
- ORIGIN 1930s: apparently from *sp(iced h)am*; the Internet sense apparently derives from a sketch by the British 'Monty Python' comedy group, set in a café in which every item on the menu includes spam.

span¹ ■ n. **1** the full extent of something from end to end; the amount of space covered. ▶ a part of a bridge between piers or supports. **2** the length of time for which something lasts. **3** the maximum distance between the tips of the thumb and little finger, taken as the basis of a measurement equal to 9 inches. ■ v. (**spanned**, **spanning**) extend across or over.
- ORIGIN Old English, 'distance between thumb and little finger', of Germanic origin.

span² ■ n. **1** Nautical a rope with its ends fastened at different points in order to provide a purchase. **2** a team of people or animals, especially a matched pair of horses or oxen.
- ORIGIN C16: from Dutch or Low German *spannen*.

span³ ■ adj. see **SPICK AND SPAN**.

span⁴ chiefly archaic past of **SPIN**.

spandex ■ n. trademark a type of stretchy polyurethane fabric.
- ORIGIN 1950s: an arbitrary formation from **EXPAND**.

spandrel /ˈspandrɪl/ ■ n. Architecture the almost triangular space between one side of the outer curve of an arch, a wall, and the ceiling or framework. ▶ the space between the shoulders of adjoining arches and the ceiling or moulding above.
- ORIGIN Middle English: perhaps from Anglo-Norman French *spaund(e)re*, or from *espaundre* 'expand'.

spangle ■ n. **1** a small thin piece of glittering material, used to ornament a garment; a sequin. **2** a spot of bright colour or light. ■ v. cover with spangles or sparkling objects.
- DERIVATIVES **spangly** adj.
- ORIGIN Middle English: diminutive from obsolete *spang* 'glittering ornament', from Middle Dutch *spange* 'buckle'.

Spanglish /ˈspaŋɡlɪʃ/ ■ n. hybrid language combining words and idioms from both Spanish and English.

Spaniard /'spanjəd/ ■ n. a native or national of Spain, or a person of Spanish descent.
– ORIGIN Middle English: shortening of Old French *Espaignart*.

spaniel ■ n. a dog of a breed with a long silky coat and drooping ears.
– ORIGIN Middle English: from Old French *espaigneul* 'Spanish (dog)', from Latin *Hispaniolus* 'Spanish'.

Spanish ■ n. the main language of Spain and of much of Central and South America. ■ adj. of or relating to Spain, its people, or their language.
– DERIVATIVES **Spanishness** n.

Spanish-American ■ n. a native or inhabitant of the Spanish-speaking countries of Central and South America. ■ adj. of or relating to the Spanish-speaking countries or peoples of Central and South America.

Spanish flu ■ n. influenza caused by an influenza virus of type A, in particular that of the pandemic which began in 1918.

Spanish fly ■ n. a toxic preparation of the dried bodies of a bright green blister beetle (*Lytta vesicatoria*), formerly used in medicine as a counterirritant and sometimes taken as an aphrodisiac.

Spanish guitar ■ n. the standard six-stringed acoustic guitar, used especially for classical and folk music.

Spanish moss ■ n. a tropical American plant which grows as silvery-green festoons on trees, obtaining water and nutrients directly through its surface. [*Tillandsia usneoides*.]

Spanish omelette ■ n. an omelette containing chopped vegetables, especially potatoes.

Spanish onion ■ n. a large onion with a mild flavour.

Spanish rice ■ n. a dish of rice cooked with onions, peppers, tomatoes, and spices.

spank ■ v. slap with one's open hand or a flat object, especially on the buttocks as a punishment. ■ n. a slap or series of slaps of this type.
– ORIGIN C18: perhaps imitative.

spanking ■ adj. 1 lively; brisk. 2 informal very good; impressive or pleasing: *it's in spanking condition*. ■ n. a series of spanks.

spanner ■ n. a tool with a shaped opening or jaws for gripping and turning a nut or bolt.
– PHRASES **spanner in the works** a person or thing that prevents the successful implementation of a plan.
– ORIGIN C18: from German *spannen* 'draw tight'.

spanspek /'spanspɛk/ ■ n. South African term for MUSK MELON or CANTALOUPE.
– ORIGIN from Afrikaans.

spar[1] ■ n. a thick, strong pole such as is used for a mast or yard on a ship. ▶ the main longitudinal beam of an aircraft wing.
– ORIGIN Middle English: shortening of Old French *esparre*, or from Old Norse *sperra*.

spar[2] ■ v. (**sparred**, **sparring**) 1 make the motions of boxing without landing heavy blows, as a form of training. 2 engage in argument without marked hostility. ■ n. a period or bout of sparring.
– ORIGIN Old English *sperran*, *spyrran* 'strike out'.

spar[3] ■ n. a crystalline, easily cleavable, translucent or transparent mineral.
– DERIVATIVES **sparry** adj.
– ORIGIN C16: from Middle Low German.

sparaxis /spə'raksɪs/ ■ n. a South African plant with slender sword-shaped leaves and showy multicoloured flowers. [Genus *Sparaxis*.]
– ORIGIN from Greek, 'laceration', from *sparassein* 'to tear'.

spare ■ adj. 1 additional to what is required for ordinary use. ▶ not currently in use or occupied. 2 with no excess fat; thin. 3 elegantly simple. ■ n. 1 an item kept in case another item of the same type is lost, broken, or worn out. 2 (in tenpin bowling) an act of knocking down all the pins with two balls. ■ v. 1 give (something of which one has enough) to. ▶ make free or available. 2 refrain from killing or harming. ▶ refrain from inflicting (harm) on: *they were been spared the violence*.
– PHRASES **go spare** Brit. informal become extremely angry or distraught. **spare no expense** (or **no expense spared**) be prepared to pay any amount. **to spare** left over.
– DERIVATIVES **sparely** adv. **spareness** n.
– ORIGIN Old English *spær* 'not plentiful, meagre', *sparian* 'refrain from injuring or using', of Germanic origin.

spare rib ■ n. (usu. **spare ribs**) a trimmed rib of pork.
– ORIGIN C16: prob. a transposition of Middle Low German *ribbesper*; also associated with SPARE.

spare tyre ■ n. 1 an extra tyre carried in a motor vehicle for use in case of puncture. 2 informal a roll of fat round a person's waist.

sparid /'sparɪd, 'spɛɪrɪd/ ■ n. Zoology a fish of the sea bream family (Sparidae), whose members have deep bodies with long spiny dorsal fins.
– ORIGIN 1960s: from Greek *sparos* 'sea bream'.

sparing ■ adj. moderate; economical.
– DERIVATIVES **sparingly** adv. **sparingness** n.

spark[1] ■ n. 1 a small fiery particle thrown off from a fire, alight in ashes, or produced by striking together two surfaces. 2 a light produced by a sudden disruptive electrical discharge through the air. ▶ a discharge such as this serving to ignite the explosive mixture in an internal-combustion engine. 3 a small bright object or point. 4 a small but concentrated amount or trace: *a tiny spark of anger*. ▶ a sense of liveliness and excitement. ■ v. 1 emit sparks. ▶ produce sparks at the point where an electric circuit is interrupted. 2 ignite. 3 (usu. **spark something off**) provide the stimulus for.
– DERIVATIVES **sparkless** adj. **sparky** adj.
– ORIGIN Old English.

spark[2] ■ n. (in phr. **bright spark**) a lively person.
– ORIGIN C16: prob. from SPARK[1].

spark chamber ■ n. Physics an apparatus designed to show ionizing particles.

spark gap ■ n. a space between electrical terminals across which a transient discharge passes.

sparkle ■ v. 1 shine brightly with flashes of light. 2 be vivacious and witty. 3 [as adj. **sparkling**] (of drink) effervescent. ■ n. 1 a glittering flash of light. 2 vivacity and wit.
– DERIVATIVES **sparklingly** adv. **sparkly** adj.
– ORIGIN Middle English: from SPARK[1].

sparkler ■ n. a hand-held firework that emits sparks.

spark plug (also **sparking plug**) ■ n. a device for firing the explosive mixture in an internal-combustion engine.

sparrow ■ n. a small, typically brown and grey finch-like bird related to the weaver birds. [*Passer domesticus* (house sparrow) and other species.] ▶ used in names of many other birds which resemble this, e.g. Java sparrow.
– ORIGIN Old English, of Germanic origin.

sparrowhawk ■ n. a small Old World hawk that preys on small birds. [*Accipiter nisus* and related species.] ▶ N. Amer. the American kestrel (*Falco sparverius*).

sparse ■ adj. thinly dispersed.
– DERIVATIVES **sparsely** adv. **sparseness** n. **sparsity** n.
– ORIGIN C18: from Latin *sparsus*, from *spargere* 'scatter'.

Spartan ■ adj. 1 of or relating to Sparta, a city state in ancient Greece. 2 (usu. **spartan**) frugal; indifferent to comfort or luxury. ■ n. a citizen of Sparta.

spasm ■ n. 1 a sudden involuntary muscular contraction or convulsive movement. 2 a sudden brief spell of activity or sensation.
– ORIGIN Middle English: from Old French *spasme*, or from Greek *spasmos*, from *span* 'pull'.

spasmodic ■ adj. 1 occurring or done in brief, irregular bursts. 2 of or caused by a spasm or spasms.
– DERIVATIVES **spasmodically** adv.
– ORIGIN C17: from Greek *spasmōdēs*, from *spasma* (see SPASM).

spastic ■ adj. 1 relating to or affected by muscle spasm. ▶ of or having a form of muscular weakness (spastic paralysis) typical of cerebral palsy, involving reflex resistance to passive movement of the limbs and difficulty in initiating and controlling muscular movement. 2 informal, offensive incompetent or uncoordinated. ■ n. 1 a person with cerebral palsy. 2 informal, offensive an incompetent or uncoordinated person. – DERIVATIVES **spastically** adv. **spasticity** n. – ORIGIN C18: from Greek *spastikos* 'pulling', from *span* 'pull'.

> **USAGE**
> In modern use the term **spastic** is likely to cause offence. It is preferable to use phrasing such as *people with cerebral palsy* instead.

spat[1] past and past participle of SPIT[1].

spat[2] ■ n. **1** a short cloth gaiter covering the instep and ankle. **2** a cover for the upper part of an aircraft wheel. – ORIGIN C19: abbrev. of SPATTERDASH.

spat[3] informal ■ n. a petty quarrel. ■ v. (**spatted**, **spatting**) quarrel pettily. – ORIGIN C19: prob. imitative.

spat[4] ■ n. the spawn or larvae of shellfish, especially oysters. – ORIGIN C17: from Anglo-Norman French.

spatchcock ■ n. a chicken or game bird split open and grilled. ■ v. **1** prepare (a poultry or game bird) in this way. **2** informal, chiefly Brit. add (a phrase, sentence, etc.) in a context where it is inappropriate. – ORIGIN C18 (orig. Irish usage): perhaps rel. to DISPATCH + COCK.

spate ■ n. **1** a large number of similar things or events coming in quick succession. **2** chiefly Brit. a sudden flood in a river. – PHRASES **in** (**full**) **spate** (of a river) overflowing. – ORIGIN Middle English.

spathulate /ˈspatjʊlət/ ■ adj. variant spelling of SPATULATE.

spatial /ˈspeɪʃ(ə)l/ (also **spacial**) ■ adj. of or relating to space. – DERIVATIVES **spatiality** n. **spatialization** (also **-isation**) n. **spatialize** (also **-ise**) v. **spatially** adv. – ORIGIN C19: from Latin *spatium* 'space'.

spatio-temporal /ˌspeɪʃɪəʊˈtɛmp(ə)r(ə)l/ ■ adj. Physics & Philosophy belonging to both space and time or to space–time. – DERIVATIVES **spatio-temporally** adv.

Spätlese /ˈʃpɛtˌleɪzə/ ■ n. (pl. **Spätleses** or **Spätlesen** /-ˌleɪz(ə)n/) a white wine of German origin or style made from grapes harvested late in the season. – ORIGIN from German, from *spät* 'late' + *Lese* 'picking, vintage'.

spatter ■ v. cover with drops or spots. ▸ splash or be splashed over a surface. ■ n. a spray or splash. – ORIGIN C16: from a base shared by Dutch, Low German *spatten* 'burst, spout'.

spatterdash ■ n. historical a long gaiter or legging, worn especially when riding.

spatula ■ n. an implement with a broad, flat, blunt blade, used especially for mixing or spreading. – ORIGIN C16: from Latin, var. of *spathula*, diminutive of *spatha* 'spathe'.

spatulate /ˈspatjʊlət/ ■ adj. having a broad, rounded end. ▸ (also **spathulate**) Botany & Zoology broad at the apex and tapered to the base.

spätzle ■ pl. n. variant spelling of SPAETZLE.

spavin /ˈspavɪn/ ■ n. a disorder of a horse's hock. – DERIVATIVES **spavined** adj. – ORIGIN Middle English: shortening of Old French *espavin*, var. of *esparvain*, of Germanic origin.

spawn ■ v. **1** (of a fish, frog, mollusc, etc.) release or deposit eggs. ▸ chiefly derogatory (of a person) produce (off-spring). **2** produce or generate; give rise to. ■ n. **1** the eggs of fish, frogs, etc. **2** chiefly derogatory offspring. **3** the mycelium of a fungus, especially a cultivated mushroom. – DERIVATIVES **spawner** n. – ORIGIN Middle English: shortening of Anglo-Norman French *espaundre* 'to shed roe', var. of Old French *espandre* 'pour out'.

spay ■ v. sterilize (a female animal) by removing the ovaries.

– ORIGIN Middle English: shortening of Old French *espeer* 'cut with a sword', from *espee* 'sword', from Latin *spatha* 'spathe'.

spaza /ˈspɑːzə/ (also **spaza shop**) ■ n. S. African a small shop of a kind originally operating informally in townships, often based in a private house. – ORIGIN from township slang *spaza* 'camouflaged'.

SPCA ■ abbrev. Society for the Prevention of Cruelty to Animals.

speak ■ v. (past **spoke**; past part. **spoken**) **1** say something. ▸ make a speech. ▸ communicate in or be able to communicate in (a specified language). ▸ (**speak for**) express the views or position of. ▸ (**speak out/up**) express one's opinions frankly and publicly. ▸ (**speak up**) speak more loudly. **2** (**speak to**) talk to in order to advise, pass on information, etc. ▸ appeal or relate to. **3** (of behaviour, an event, etc.) serve as evidence for something. **4** make a sound. – PHRASES **speak in tongues** speak in an unknown language during Christian worship, regarded as one of the gifts of the Holy Spirit (Acts 2). **speak one's mind** express one's opinions frankly. **speak volumes** convey a great deal without using words: *a look that spoke volumes*. **speak well** (or **ill**) **of** praise (or criticize). **to speak of** of a substantial or important nature: *I've no capital—well, none to speak of*. – DERIVATIVES **speakable** adj. – ORIGIN Old English, of West Germanic origin.

-speak ■ comb. form forming nouns denoting a manner of speaking, characteristic of a specified group: *technospeak*. – ORIGIN on the pattern of (*New*)*speak*.

speakeasy ■ n. (pl. **-ies**) informal (in the US during Prohibition) an illicit liquor shop or drinking club.

speaker ■ n. **1** a person who speaks, especially at a formal occasion. **2** (**Speaker**) the presiding officer in a legislative assembly. **3** short for LOUDSPEAKER. – DERIVATIVES **speakership** n.

speakerphone ■ n. a telephone with a loudspeaker and microphone, which does not need to be held in the hand.

speaking ■ n. the action of expressing oneself in speech or giving speeches. ■ adj. **1** used for or engaged in speech. ▸ able to communicate in a specified language. **2** conveying meaning as though in words. – PHRASES **on speaking terms** slightly acquainted; moderately friendly.

speaking trumpet ■ n. historical an instrument for making the voice carry, especially at sea.

speaking tube ■ n. a pipe for conveying a person's voice from one room or building to another.

spear ■ n. **1** a metal weapon with a pointed tip and a long shaft, used for thrusting or throwing. **2** a plant shoot, especially a pointed stem of asparagus or broccoli. **3** [as modifier] denoting the male side or members of a family. Compare with DISTAFF. ■ v. pierce or strike with a spear or other pointed object. – ORIGIN Old English, of Germanic origin.

spearfish ■ n. (pl. same or **-fishes**) a billfish that resembles the marlin. [Genus *Tetrapturus*: several species.]

speargrass ■ n. any of a number of grasses with hard pointed seed heads. [*Heteropogon*, *Stipa*, and other genera.]

speargun ■ n. a gun used to propel a spear in underwater fishing.

spearhead ■ n. **1** the point of a spear. **2** an individual or group leading an attack or movement. ■ v. lead (an attack or movement).

spearmint ■ n. the common garden mint, which is used as a culinary herb and in flavouring. [*Mentha spicata*.]

spec[1] ■ n. (in phr. **on spec**) informal in the hope of success but without any specific preparation or plan. – ORIGIN C18: abbrev. of *speculation*.

spec[2] ■ n. informal short for SPECIFICATION.

special ■ adj. **1** better, greater, or otherwise different from what is usual. **2** designed for or belonging to a particular person, place, or event. ▸ (of a subject) studied in particular depth. **3** used to denote education for children with particular needs. ■ n. **1** something designed or organized for a particular occasion or purpose. ▸ a dish not on the regular menu but served on a particular day.

2 a person assigned to a special duty.
– DERIVATIVES **specialness** n.
– ORIGIN Middle English: shortening of Old French *especial* 'especial', or from Latin *specialis*, from *species* (see SPECIES).

Special Branch ■ n. (in some countries) the police department dealing with political security.

special case ■ n. Law a written statement of fact presented by litigants to a court.

special constable ■ n. a person who is trained to act as a police officer on particular occasions, especially in times of emergency.

special delivery ■ n. a service offering delivery of an item of mail within a short time period or outside normal hours.

special drawing rights ■ pl. n. a form of international money created by the International Monetary Fund, defined as a weighted average of various convertible currencies.

special effects ■ pl. n. illusions created for films and television by props, camerawork, computer graphics, etc.

special forces ■ pl. n. the units of a country's armed forces that undertake counterterrorist and other specialized operations.

specialist ■ n. a person who concentrates on a particular subject or activity; a person highly skilled in a specific field. ■ adj. of, relating to, or involving detailed knowledge or a specific focus within a field.
– DERIVATIVES **specialism** n.

speciality /ˌspeʃɪˈalɪti/ (chiefly N. Amer. & Medicine also **specialty**) ■ n. (pl. **-ies**) **1** a pursuit, area of study, or skill to which someone has devoted themselves and in which they are expert. ▶ a product for which a person or region is famous. **2** (usu. **specialty**) a branch of medicine or surgery.
– ORIGIN Middle English: from Old French *especialite* or late Latin *specialitas*, from Latin *specialis* (see SPECIAL).

specialize (also **-ise**) ■ v. concentrate on and become expert in a particular skill or area. ▶ make a habit of engaging in. ▶ (usu. **be specialized** also **-ised**) Biology adapt or set apart (an organ or part) to serve a special function.
– DERIVATIVES **specialization** (also **-isation**) n. **specialized** (also **-ised**) adj.

specially ■ adv. for a special purpose.

special needs (also **special educational needs**) ■ pl. n. particular educational requirements resulting from learning difficulties, physical disability, or emotional and behavioural difficulties.

special pleading ■ n. argument in which the speaker deliberately ignores aspects that are unfavourable to their point of view.

special school ■ n. a school catering for children with special needs.

special sort ■ n. Printing a character, such as an accented letter or a symbol, not normally included in a font.

special team ■ n. American Football a squad that is used for kick-offs, punts, and other special plays.

specialty /ˈspeʃ(ə)lti/ ■ n. (pl. **-ies**) chiefly N. Amer. & Medicine another term for SPECIALITY.
– ORIGIN Middle English: shortening of Old French *especialte*, from *especial* (see SPECIAL).

speciation /ˌspiːʃɪˈeɪʃ(ə)n, ˌspiːs-/ ■ n. Biology the formation of new and distinct species in the course of evolution.
– DERIVATIVES **speciate** v.

specie /ˈspiːʃiː, ˈspiːʃi/ ■ n. money in the form of coins rather than notes.
– PHRASES **in specie 1** in coin. **2** Law in the real, precise, or actual form specified.
– ORIGIN C16: from Latin, from *species* 'form, kind'.

species /ˈspiːʃiːz, -ʃɪz, ˈspiːs-/ ■ n. (pl. same) **1** Biology a group of living organisms consisting of similar individuals capable of exchanging genes or interbreeding, considered as the basic unit of taxonomy and denoted by a Latin binomial, e.g. *Homo sapiens*. **2** [as modifier] denoting a plant belonging to a distinct species rather than to one of the many varieties produced by hybridization: *a species rose*. **3** a kind or sort. **4** Christian Church the visible form of each of the elements of consecrated bread and wine in the Eucharist.

– ORIGIN Middle English: from Latin, 'appearance, form, beauty', from *specere* 'to look'.

speciesism /ˈspiːʃiːˌzɪz(ə)m, ˈspiːs-/ ■ n. the assumption of human superiority over other creatures, leading to the exploitation of animals.
– DERIVATIVES **speciesist** adj. & n.

specific /spəˈsɪfɪk/ ■ adj. **1** clearly defined or identified. ▶ precise and clear: *when ordering goods be specific*. ▶ of or relating uniquely to a particular subject. **2** Biology of, relating to, or connected with species or a species. **3** (of a duty or a tax) levied at a fixed rate per physical unit of the thing taxed, regardless of its price. **4** Physics of or denoting a physical quantity expressed in terms of a unit mass, volume, or other measure, or calculated as a ratio to the corresponding value for a substance used as a reference. ■ n. **1** chiefly dated a medicine or remedy effective in treating a particular disease or part of the body. **2** (usu. **specifics**) a precise detail.
– DERIVATIVES **specifically** adv. **specificity** /ˌspɛsɪˈfɪsɪti/ n. **specificness** n.
– ORIGIN C17: from late Latin *specificus*, from Latin *species* (see SPECIES).

specification /ˌspɛsɪfɪˈkeɪʃ(ə)n/ ■ n. **1** the action of specifying. ▶ (usu. **specifications**) a detailed description of the design and materials used to make something. ▶ a description of an invention accompanying an application for a patent. **2** a standard of workmanship, materials, etc. required to be met in a piece of work.

specific charge ■ n. Physics the ratio of the charge of an ion or subatomic particle to its mass.

specific epithet ■ n. chiefly Botany the second element in the Latin binomial name of a species, which distinguishes the species from others in the same genus.

specific gravity ■ n. another term for RELATIVE DENSITY.

specific heat capacity ■ n. Physics the heat required to raise the temperature of the unit mass of a given substance by a given amount (usually one degree).

specific performance ■ n. Law the performance of a contractual duty, as ordered in cases where damages would not be adequate remedy.

specify ■ v. (**-ies**, **-ied**) **1** identify clearly and definitely. **2** include in an architect's or engineer's specifications.
– DERIVATIVES **specifiable** adj. **specifier** n.

specimen /ˈspɛsɪmɪn/ ■ n. **1** an individual animal, plant, object, etc. used as an example of its species or type for scientific study or display. ▶ an example of something regarded as typical of its class or group: [as modifier] *a specimen signature*. ▶ informal used to refer humorously to a person or animal. **2** a sample for medical testing, especially of urine.
– ORIGIN C17: from Latin, from *specere* 'to look'.

specious /ˈspiːʃəs/ ■ adj. superficially plausible, but actually wrong. ▶ misleadingly attractive in appearance.
– DERIVATIVES **speciously** adv. **speciousness** n.
– ORIGIN Middle English: from Latin *speciosus* 'fair, plausible, specious', from *species* (see SPECIES).

speck ■ n. a tiny spot. ▶ a small particle. ■ v. mark with small spots.
– DERIVATIVES **speckless** adj.
– ORIGIN Old English *specca*.

speckle ■ n. a small spot or patch of colour. ■ v. mark with speckles.
– DERIVATIVES **speckled** adj.
– ORIGIN Middle English: from Middle Dutch *spekkel*.

specs ■ pl. n. informal a pair of spectacles.

spectacle ■ n. a visually striking performance or display.
– PHRASES **make a spectacle of oneself** draw attention to oneself by behaving in a ridiculous way in public.
– ORIGIN Middle English: from Latin *spectaculum* 'public show', from *spectare*, from *specere* 'to look'.

spectacled ■ adj. **1** wearing spectacles. **2** used in names of animals with markings around the eyes that resemble spectacles.

spectacles ■ pl. n. a pair of glasses.

spectacular ■ adj. **1** very impressive, striking, or

spectate

dramatic. **2** strikingly large; marked. ■ n. a performance or event produced on a large scale and with striking effects.
– DERIVATIVES **spectacularly** adv.

spectate ■ v. be a spectator.
– ORIGIN C18: back-formation from SPECTATOR.

spectator ■ n. a person who watches at a show, game, or other event.
– ORIGIN C16: from French *spectateur* or Latin *spectator*, from *spectare* (see SPECTACLE).

specter ■ n. US spelling of SPECTRE.

spectra plural form of SPECTRUM.

spectral ■ adj. **1** of or like a spectre. **2** of or concerning spectra or the spectrum.
– DERIVATIVES **spectrally** adv.

spectre (US **specter**) ■ n. **1** a ghost. **2** something unpleasant or dangerous imagined or expected: *the spectre of nuclear holocaust.*
– ORIGIN C17: from French *spectre* or Latin *spectrum* (see SPECTRUM).

spectro- ■ comb. form representing SPECTRUM.

spectrogram ■ n. a visual or electronic record of a spectrum.

spectrograph ■ n. an apparatus for photographing or otherwise recording spectra.
– DERIVATIVES **spectrographic** adj. **spectrographically** adv. **spectrography** n.

spectrometer /spɛkˈtrɒmɪtə/ ■ n. an apparatus used for recording and measuring spectra, especially as a method of analysis.
– DERIVATIVES **spectrometric** adj. **spectrometry** n.

spectrophotometer /ˌspɛktrə(ʊ)fəʊˈtɒmɪtə/ ■ n. an apparatus for measuring the intensity of light in a part of the spectrum, especially as transmitted or emitted by particular substances.
– DERIVATIVES **spectrophotometric** /-təˈmɛtrɪk/ adj. **spectrophotometry** n.

spectroscope ■ n. an apparatus for producing and recording spectra for examination.

spectroscopy ■ n. the branch of science concerned with the investigation and measurement of spectra produced when matter interacts with or emits electromagnetic radiation.
– DERIVATIVES **spectroscopic** adj. **spectroscopically** adv. **spectroscopist** n.

spectrum ■ n. (pl. **spectra** /-trə/) **1** a band of colours produced by separation of the components of light by their different degrees of refraction according to wavelength, e.g. in a rainbow. ▸ the entire range of wavelengths of electromagnetic radiation. ▸ a characteristic series of frequencies of electromagnetic radiation emitted or absorbed by a substance. ▸ the components of a sound or other phenomenon arranged according to frequency, energy, etc. **2** a scale extending between two points; a range: *the political spectrum.*
– ORIGIN C17: from Latin, 'image, apparition', from *specere* 'to look'.

specula plural form of SPECULUM.

specular /ˈspɛkjʊlə/ ■ adj. of, relating to, or having the properties of a mirror.
– ORIGIN C16: from Latin *specularis*, from *speculum* (see SPECULUM).

speculate /ˈspɛkjʊleɪt/ ■ v. **1** form a theory or conjecture without firm evidence. **2** invest in stocks, property, or other ventures in the hope of gain but with the risk of loss.
– DERIVATIVES **speculation** n. **speculator** n.
– ORIGIN C16: from Latin *speculari* 'observe', from *specula* 'watchtower', from *specere* 'to look'.

speculative ■ adj. **1** engaged in, expressing, or based on conjecture rather than knowledge. **2** (of an investment) involving a high risk of loss.
– DERIVATIVES **speculatively** adv. **speculativeness** n.

speculum /ˈspɛkjʊləm/ ■ n. (pl. **specula** /-lə/) **1** Medicine a metal instrument that is used to dilate an orifice or canal in the body to allow inspection. **2** Ornithology a bright patch of plumage on the wings of certain birds, especially ducks.

3 a mirror or reflector, especially (formerly) a metallic mirror in a reflecting telescope.
– ORIGIN Middle English: from Latin, 'mirror', from *specere* 'to look'.

sped past and past participle of SPEED.

speech ■ n. **1** the expression of or the ability to express thoughts and feelings by articulate sounds. **2** a formal address delivered to an audience. ▸ a sequence of lines written for one character in a play.
– ORIGIN Old English, of West Germanic origin.

speech act ■ n. Linguistics & Philosophy an utterance considered as an action, particularly with regard to its intention, purpose, or effect.

speech day ■ n. an annual event held at some schools at which speeches are made and prizes are presented.

speechify ■ v. (**-ies**, **-ied**) deliver a speech, especially in a tedious or pompous way.

speechless ■ adj. unable to speak, especially as the temporary result of shock or strong emotion.
– DERIVATIVES **speechlessly** adv. **speechlessness** n.

speech-reading ■ n. lip-reading.

speech recognition ■ n. the process of enabling a computer to identify and respond to the sounds produced in human speech.

speech therapy ■ n. treatment to help people with speech and language problems.
– DERIVATIVES **speech therapist** n.

speed ■ n. **1** the rate at which someone or something moves or operates or is able to move or operate. ▸ rapidity of movement or action. **2** each of the possible gear ratios of a bicycle. **3** the light-gathering power or f-number of a camera lens. ▸ the duration of a photographic exposure. ▸ the sensitivity of photographic film to light. **4** informal an amphetamine drug, especially methamphetamine. **5** archaic success; prosperity. ■ v. (past and past part. **speeded** or **sped**) **1** move quickly. ▸ (**speed up**) move or work more quickly. **2** (of a motorist) travel at a speed greater than the legal limit. **3** informal take or be under the influence of an amphetamine drug. **4** archaic make prosperous or successful: *may God speed you.*
– PHRASES **at speed** quickly. **up to speed 1** operating at full speed or capacity. **2** fully informed or up to date.
– DERIVATIVES **speeder** n.
– ORIGIN Old English, from the Germanic base of Old English *spōwan* 'prosper, succeed'.

speedball ■ n. **1** informal a mixture of cocaine with heroin. **2** US a ball game resembling soccer but in which the ball may be handled.

speedboat ■ n. a motor boat designed for high speed.

speed bump (also **speed hump**) ■ n. a ridge set in a road to control the speed of vehicles.

speed camera ■ n. a roadside camera designed to catch speeding vehicles by taking video footage or a photograph.

speed dial ■ n. a function on some telephones which allows numbers to be entered into a memory and dialled with the push of a single button. ■ v. (**speed-dial**) (**speed-dials**, **speed-dialling**, **speed-dialled**) dial (a telephone number) by using a speed dial function.

speed limit ■ n. the maximum speed at which a vehicle may legally travel on a particular stretch of road.

speedo ■ n. (pl. **-os**) informal short for SPEEDOMETER.

speedometer /spiːˈdɒmɪtə/ ■ n. an instrument on a vehicle's dashboard indicating its speed.

speedster ■ n. informal a person or thing that operates well at high speed.

speedway ■ n. a form of motorcycle racing in which the riders race laps around an oval dirt track. ▸ a stadium or track used for this sport.

speedwell ■ n. a small creeping plant with blue or pink flowers. [Genus *Veronica*: several species.]

speedy ■ adj. (**-ier**, **-iest**) **1** done or occurring quickly. **2** moving quickly.
– DERIVATIVES **speedily** adv. **speediness** n.

spekboom /ˈspɛkbʊəm/ ■ n. S. African a southern African shrub with round fleshy leaves and pink flowers, sometimes used as fodder. [*Portulacaria afra*.]
– ORIGIN C19: from Afrikaans, from *spek* 'bacon' + *boom* 'tree'.

speleology /ˌspiːlɪˈɒlədʒi, ˌspɛl-/ ■ n. the study or exploration of caves.
– DERIVATIVES **speleological** adj. **speleologist** n.
– ORIGIN C19: from French *spéléologie*, from Greek *spēlaion* 'cave'.

speleothem /ˈspiːlɪə(ʊ)θɛm/ ■ n. Geology a structure formed in a cave by the deposition of minerals from water, e.g. a stalactite or stalagmite.
– ORIGIN 1950s: from Greek *spēlaion* 'cave' + *thema* 'deposit'.

spell[1] ■ v. (past and past part. **spelled** or **spelt**) 1 write or name the letters that form (a word) in correct sequence. ▸ (of letters) make up or form (a word). 2 be a sign of; lead to: *the plans would spell disaster for the economy.* 3 (**spell something out**) explain something simply and in detail.
– DERIVATIVES **spelling** n.
– ORIGIN Middle English: shortening of Old French *espeller*, from the Germanic base of SPELL[2].

spell[2] ■ n. 1 a form of words used as a magical charm or incantation. 2 a state of enchantment or influence induced by or as if by a spell.
– ORIGIN Old English *spel(l)* 'narration', of Germanic origin.

spell[3] ■ n. 1 a short period of time. ▸ Austral./NZ a period of rest from work. 2 Cricket a series of overs in which a particular bowler bowls. ■ v. chiefly N. Amer. take someone's place in order to allow them to rest briefly. ▸ Austral./NZ take a brief rest.
– ORIGIN C16: var. of dialect *spele* 'take the place of'.

spellbind ■ v. (past and past part. **spellbound**) hold the complete attention of, as if by a spell.
– DERIVATIVES **spellbinder** n. **spellbinding** adj. **spell-bindingly** adv.

spellchecker (also **spelling checker**) ■ n. a computer program which checks the spelling of words in files of text, usually by comparing them with a stored list of words.
– DERIVATIVES **spellcheck** v. & n.

speller ■ n. 1 a person of a specified spelling ability. 2 chiefly N. Amer. a book for teaching spelling. ▸ short for SPELLCHECKER.

spelling bee ■ n. a spelling competition.

spelt[1] past and past participle of SPELL[1].

spelt[2] ■ n. an old kind of wheat with bearded ears and spikelets that each contain two narrow grains, favoured as a health food. [*Triticum spelta*.]
– ORIGIN Old English, from Old Saxon *spelta*.

spelter /ˈspɛltə/ ■ n. commercial crude smelted zinc. ▸ a solder or other alloy in which zinc is the main constituent.
– ORIGIN C17: cf. Old French *espeautre*, Middle Dutch *speauter*; rel. to PEWTER.

spelunking /spɪˈlʌŋkɪŋ/ ■ n. chiefly N. Amer. the exploration of caves, especially as a hobby.
– DERIVATIVES **spelunker** n.
– ORIGIN 1940s: from obsolete *spelunk* 'cave', from Latin *spelunca*.

spencer ■ n. 1 a short, close-fitting jacket, worn by women and children in the early 19th century. 2 a thin woollen vest.
– ORIGIN prob. named after the second Earl *Spencer* (1758–1834), English politician.

spend ■ v. (past and past part. **spent**) 1 pay out (money) in buying or hiring goods or services. 2 use or use up (energy or resources); exhaust. ▸ pass (time) in a specified way. ■ n. informal an amount of money paid out.
– PHRASES **spend a penny** Brit. informal, euphemistic urinate.
– DERIVATIVES **spendable** adj. **spender** n.
– ORIGIN Old English, from Latin *expendere* 'pay out'; also a shortening of obsolete *dispend*, from Latin *dispendere* 'pay out'.

spending money ■ n. an allowance for entertainment and day-to-day expenditure.

spendthrift ■ n. a person who spends money in an extravagant, irresponsible way.

Spenserian /spɛnˈsɪərɪən/ ■ adj. of, relating to, or in the style of the English poet Edmund Spenser (c.1552–99) or his works.

spent past and past participle of SPEND. ■ adj. used up; exhausted.

spermine

sperm ■ n. (pl. same or **sperms**) 1 semen. ▸ a spermatozoon. 2 short for SPERM WHALE.
– ORIGIN Middle English: from Greek *sperma* 'seed', from *speirein* 'to sow'.

spermaceti /ˌspɜːməˈsiːti, -ˈsɛti/ ■ n. a white waxy substance obtained from an organ in the head of the sperm whale, which focuses acoustic signals and aids in the control of buoyancy, and was formerly used in candles and ointments.
– ORIGIN C15: from late Latin *sperma* 'sperm' + *ceti* 'of a whale', from Greek *kētos* 'whale', from the belief that it was whale spawn.

spermatheca /ˌspɜːməˈθiːkə/ ■ n. (pl. **spermathecae** /-ˈθiːkiː/) Zoology a receptacle in many female or hermaphrodite invertebrates in which sperm is stored after mating.
– ORIGIN C19: from late Latin *sperma* 'sperm' + THECA.

spermatic cord ■ n. (in mammals) a bundle of nerves, ducts, and blood vessels connecting the testicles to the abdominal cavity.

spermatid /ˈspɜːmətɪd/ ■ n. Biology an immature male sex cell formed from a spermatocyte, which may develop into a spermatozoon without further division.
– DERIVATIVES **spermatidal** /ˌspɜːməˈtʌɪd(ə)l/ adj.

spermato- ■ comb. form Biology relating to sperm or seeds: *spermatozoid*.
– ORIGIN from Greek *sperma, spermat-* 'sperm'.

spermatocyte /ˈspɜːmətə(ʊ)sʌɪt, spəˈmat-/ ■ n. Biology a cell produced at the second stage in the formation of spermatozoa, formed from a spermatogonium and dividing by meiosis into spermatids.

spermatogenesis /ˌspɜːmətə(ʊ)ˈdʒɛnɪsɪs, spəˌmat-/ ■ n. Biology the production or development of mature spermatozoa.

spermatogonium /ˌspɜːmətə(ʊ)ˈɡəʊnɪəm, spəˌmat-/ ■ n. (pl. **spermatogonia** /-nɪə/) Biology a cell produced at an early stage in the formation of spermatozoa, giving rise by mitosis to spermatocytes.
– DERIVATIVES **spermatogonial** adj.
– ORIGIN C19: from SPERM + modern Latin *gonium*, from Greek *gonos* 'offspring, seed'.

spermatophore /ˈspɜːmətə(ʊ)fɔː, spəˈmat-/ ■ n. Zoology a protein capsule containing a mass of spermatozoa, transferred during mating in various insects, arthropods, cephalopod molluscs, etc.

spermatophyte /ˈspɜːmətə(ʊ)fʌɪt, spəˈmat-/ ■ n. Botany a plant of a large division that comprises those that bear seeds, including the gymnosperms and angiosperms.

spermatozoid /ˌspɜːmətə(ʊ)ˈzəʊɪd, spəˌmat-/ ■ n. Botany a motile male gamete produced by a lower plant or a gymnosperm.

spermatozoon /ˌspɜːmətə(ʊ)ˈzəʊɒn, spəˌmat-/ ■ n. (pl. **spermatozoa** /-ˈzəʊə/) Biology the mature motile male sex cell of an animal, by which the ovum is fertilized, typically having a compact head and one or more long flagella for swimming.
– DERIVATIVES **spermatozoal** adj. **spermatozoan** adj.
– ORIGIN C19: from Greek *sperma, spermat-* 'seed' + *zōion* 'animal'.

sperm bank ■ n. a place where semen is kept in cold storage for use in artificial insemination.

sperm count ■ n. a measure of the number of spermatozoa per measured amount of semen, used as an indication of a man's fertility.

spermicide ■ n. a substance that kills spermatozoa, used as a contraceptive.
– DERIVATIVES **spermicidal** adj.

spermidine /ˈspɜːmɪdiːn/ ■ n. Biochemistry a colourless compound with a similar distribution and effect to spermine.
– ORIGIN 1920s: from SPERM.

spermine /ˈspɜːmiːn/ ■ n. Biochemistry a deliquescent compound which acts to stabilize various components of living cells and is widely distributed in living and decaying tissues.

sperm oil

sperm oil ■ n. an oil found with spermaceti in the head of the sperm whale, used formerly as a lubricant.

sperm whale ■ n. a toothed whale with a massive head, feeding at great depths largely on squid. [*Physeter macrocephalus* and other species.]
– ORIGIN C19: abbrev. of SPERMACETI.

spessartine /ˈspɛsətiːn/ ■ n. a form of garnet containing manganese and aluminium, occurring as orange-red to dark brown crystals.
– ORIGIN C19: from French, from *Spessart*, the name of a district in NW Bavaria.

spew ■ v. **1** expel or be expelled in large quantities rapidly and forcibly. **2** informal vomit. ■ n. informal vomit.
– ORIGIN Old English, of Germanic origin.

SPF ■ abbrev. sun protection factor.

sphagnum /ˈsfagnəm/ ■ n. a plant of a genus that comprises the peat mosses. [Genus *Sphagnum*.]
– ORIGIN C18: from Greek *sphagnos*, denoting a kind of moss.

sphalerite /ˈsfalərʌɪt/ ■ n. a shiny mineral, yellow to dark brown or black in colour, consisting of zinc sulphide.
– ORIGIN C19: from Greek *sphaleros* 'deceptive'.

sphene /sfiːn/ ■ n. a greenish-yellow or brown mineral consisting of a silicate of calcium and titanium, occurring in granitic and metamorphic rocks in wedge-shaped crystals.
– ORIGIN C19: from French *sphène*, from Greek *sphēn* 'wedge'.

sphenoid /ˈsfiːnɔɪd/ ■ n. Anatomy a large compound bone which forms the base of the cranium.
– DERIVATIVES **sphenoidal** adj.
– ORIGIN C18: from Greek *sphēnoeidēs*, from *sphēn* 'wedge'.

sphere ■ n. **1** a round solid figure, with every point on its surface equidistant from its centre. **2** each of a series of revolving concentrically arranged spherical shells in which celestial bodies were formerly thought to be set in a fixed relationship. ▸ chiefly poetic/literary a celestial body. **3** an area of activity, interest, or expertise; a group or section distinguished and unified by a particular characteristic. ■ v. archaic enclose in or form into a sphere.
– PHRASES **music (or harmony) of the spheres** the natural harmonic tones supposedly produced by the movement of the celestial spheres or the bodies fixed in them.
– ORIGIN Middle English: from Old French *espere*, from late Latin *sphera*, from Greek *sphaira* 'ball'.

-sphere ■ comb. form denoting a structure or region of spherical form, especially a region round the earth: *ionosphere*.

spheric /ˈsfɛrɪk/ ■ adj. spherical.
– DERIVATIVES **sphericity** n.

spherical ■ adj. shaped like a sphere. ▸ of or relating to the properties of spheres.
– DERIVATIVES **spherically** adv.
– ORIGIN C15: from Greek *sphairikos*, from *sphaira* (see SPHERE).

spherical aberration ■ n. a loss of definition in the image arising from the surface geometry of a spherical mirror or lens.

spherical coordinates ■ pl. n. coordinates that locate a point in three dimensions in terms of its distance from the origin and two angles defined with reference to vertical and horizontal planes.

spherical triangle ■ n. a triangle formed by three arcs of great circles on a sphere.

spheroid /ˈsfɪərɔɪd/ ■ n. a sphere-like but not perfectly spherical body.
– DERIVATIVES **spheroidal** adj. **spheroidicity** n.

spherule /ˈsfɛrjuːl/ ■ n. a small sphere.
– ORIGIN C17: from late Latin *sphaerula*, diminutive of Latin *sphaera* (see SPHERE).

spherulite /ˈsfɛrjʊlʌɪt/ ■ n. chiefly Geology a small spheroidal mass of crystals grouped radially around a point.
– DERIVATIVES **spherulitic** adj.
– ORIGIN C19: from SPHERULE.

sphincter /ˈsfɪŋktə/ ■ n. Anatomy a ring of muscle surrounding and serving to guard or close an opening.
– DERIVATIVES **sphincteral** adj. **sphincteric** adj.
– ORIGIN C16: from Greek *sphinktēr*, from *sphingein* 'bind tight'.

sphingosine /ˈsfɪŋɡə(ʊ)sʌɪn/ ■ n. Biochemistry a basic compound which is a constituent of a number of substances important in the metabolism of nerve cells.
– ORIGIN C19: from Greek *Sphing-*, *Sphinx* 'sphinx', with ref. to the enigmatic nature of the compound.

sphinx ■ n. **1** an ancient Egyptian stone figure having a lion's body and a human or animal head. **2** an enigmatic or inscrutable person.
– ORIGIN Middle English: from Greek *Sphinx* (from *sphingein* 'draw tight'), the name of a winged monster in Greek mythology, having a woman's head and a lion's body, who propounded a riddle and killed those who failed to solve it.

sphygmo- /ˈsfɪɡməʊ/ ■ comb. form Physiology of or relating to the pulse or pulsation.
– ORIGIN from Greek *sphugmos* 'pulse'.

sphygmomanometer /ˌsfɪɡməʊməˈnɒmɪtə/ ■ n. an instrument for measuring blood pressure, typically consisting of an inflatable rubber cuff which is applied to the arm and connected to a column of mercury next to a graduated scale.
– DERIVATIVES **sphygmomanometry** n.

Sphynx /sfɪŋks/ ■ n. a cat of a hairless breed, originally from North America.

spic ■ n. US informal, offensive a Spanish-speaking person from Central or South America or the Caribbean, especially a Mexican.
– ORIGIN C20: abbrev. of US slang *spiggoty*, in the same sense: perhaps an alteration of *speak the* in 'no speak the English.'

spic and span ■ adj. variant spelling of SPICK AND SPAN.

spice ■ n. **1** an aromatic or pungent vegetable substance used to flavour food, e.g. pepper. **2** an element providing interest and excitement. ■ v. **1** (often as adj. **spiced**) flavour with spice. **2** (often **spice something up**) make more exciting or interesting.
– ORIGIN Middle English: shortening of Old French *espice*, from Latin *species* 'sort, kind'.

spick and span (also **spic and span**) ■ adj. neat, clean, and well looked after.
– ORIGIN C16: from *spick and span new*, emphatic extension of dialect *span new*, from Old Norse *spán-nýr*, from *spánn* 'chip' + *nýr* 'new'; *spick* influenced by Dutch *spiksplinternieuw* 'splinter new'.

spicule /ˈspɪkjuːl/ ■ n. **1** chiefly Zoology a small needle-like structure, in particular any of those making up the skeleton of a sponge. **2** Astronomy a short-lived jet of gas in the sun's corona.
– DERIVATIVES **spicular** adj. **spiculate** /-lət/ adj. **spiculation** n.
– ORIGIN C18: from modern Latin *spicula*, *spiculum*, diminutive of *spica* 'ear of grain'.

spicy (also **spicey**) ■ adj. (-ier, -iest) **1** flavoured with spice. **2** mildly indecent.
– DERIVATIVES **spicily** adv. **spiciness** n.

spider ■ n. **1** an eight-legged predatory arachnid with an unsegmented body consisting of a fused head and thorax and a rounded abdomen, most kinds of which spin webs in which to capture insects. [Order Araneae.] ▸ used in names of other arachnids, e.g. sea spider. **2** a long-legged rest for a billiard cue that can be placed over a ball without touching it. **3** Brit. a set of radiating elastic ties used to hold a load in place on a vehicle. **4** another term for CRAWLER (in sense 2). ■ v. **1** move in a scuttling manner suggestive of a spider. **2** form a pattern suggestive of a spider or its web.
– ORIGIN Old English *spīthra*, from *spinnan* (see SPIN).

spider crab ■ n. a crab with long thin legs and a compact pear-shaped body. [*Macropodia* and other genera.]

spider mite ■ n. an active plant-feeding mite resembling a minute spider. [*Tetranychus urticae* (red spider mite) and other species.]

spider monkey ■ n. a South American monkey with very long limbs and a long prehensile tail. [Genus *Brachyteles*: four species.]

spider plant ■ n. another term for HEN AND CHICKENS.

spidery ▪ adj. resembling a spider, especially having long, thin, angular lines like a spider's legs.

spiel /ʃpiːl, spiːl/ informal ▪ n. an elaborate and glib speech or story, typically one used by a salesperson. ▪ v. speak or utter at length or glibly.
– ORIGIN C19: from German *Spiel* 'a game'.

spiff ▪ v. (**spiff someone/thing up**) informal make someone or something smart or stylish.
– ORIGIN C19: perhaps from dialect *spiff* 'well dressed'.

spiffing ▪ adj. informal, dated excellent; splendid.
– ORIGIN C19.

spiffy ▪ adj. (**-ier, -iest**) informal smart or stylish.
– ORIGIN C19.

spigot /ˈspɪɡət/ ▪ n. **1** a small peg or plug, especially for insertion into the vent of a cask. **2** US a tap. ▸ a device for controlling the flow of liquid in a tap. **3** the plain end of a section of a pipe fitting into the socket of the next one.
– ORIGIN Middle English: perhaps an alteration of Provençal *espigou(n)*, from Latin *spiculum*, diminutive of *spicum*, var. of *spica* 'spike'.

spike¹ ▪ n. **1** a thin, pointed piece of metal or another rigid material. ▸ a large stout nail. ▸ each of several metal points set into the sole of a sports shoe to prevent slipping. ▸ (**spikes**) a pair of sports shoes with spikes. ▸ a pointed metal rod standing on a base and used for filing bills or journalistic material rejected for publication. **2** a sharp increase in magnitude or intensity. ▸ Electronics a pulse of very short duration. ▪ v. **1** impale on or pierce with a spike. ▸ historical render (a gun) useless by plugging up the vent with a spike. **2** form into or cover with sharp points. **3** (of a newspaper editor) reject (a story) by or as if by filing it on a spike. ▸ thwart. **4** informal lace (drink or food) with alcohol or a drug surreptitiously. ▸ Physics & Chemistry enrich with a particular isotope. **5** increase and then decrease sharply. **6** (in volleyball) hit (the ball) forcefully from a position near the net so that it moves downward into the opposite court. ▸ American Football fling (the ball) forcefully to the ground, typically in celebration of a touchdown or victory.
– PHRASES **spike someone's guns** thwart someone's plans.
– ORIGIN Middle English: perhaps from Middle Low German, Middle Dutch *spiker*.

spike² ▪ n. Botany a flower cluster formed of many flower heads attached directly to a long stem.
– ORIGIN Middle English: from Latin *spica* 'spike, ear of corn'.

spikelet ▪ n. Botany the basic unit of a grass flower, consisting of two glumes or outer bracts at the base and one or more florets above.

spikenard /ˈspʌɪknɑːd/ ▪ n. **1** a costly perfumed ointment much valued in ancient times. **2** the Himalayan plant of the valerian family that produces the rhizome from which this ointment was prepared. [*Nardostachys grandiflora*.]
– ORIGIN Middle English: from medieval Latin *spica nardi* (see SPIKE², NARD), translating Greek *nardostakhus*.

spiky ▪ adj. (**-ier, -iest**) **1** like a spike or spikes or having many spikes. **2** informal easily offended or annoyed.
– DERIVATIVES **spikily** adv. **spikiness** n.

spile /spʌɪl/ ▪ n. a small wooden peg or spigot.
– ORIGIN C16: from Middle Dutch, Middle Low German, 'wooden peg'.

spill¹ ▪ v. (past and past part. **spilt** or **spilled**) **1** (with reference to liquid) flow or cause to flow over the edge of its container. **2** (with reference to contents or occupants) be discharged or cause to be discharged from a container or place. **3** informal reveal (confidential information). **4** Nautical let (wind) out of a sail, typically by slackening the sheets. ▪ n. **1** a quantity of liquid that has spilled or been spilt. ▸ an instance of a liquid spilling or being spilt. **2** a fall from a horse or bicycle.
– PHRASES **spill the beans** informal reveal secret information unintentionally or indiscreetly. **spill (someone's) blood** kill or wound people. **spill one's guts** informal reveal much information in an uninhibited way.
– DERIVATIVES **spillage** n. **spiller** n.
– ORIGIN Old English *spillan* 'kill, waste, shed (blood)'.

spill² ▪ n. a thin strip of paper or wood used for lighting a fire, pipe, etc.
– ORIGIN Middle English (in the sense 'sharp fragment of wood').

spillikins /ˈspɪlɪkɪnz/ ▪ pl. n. [treated as sing.] a game played with a heap of small rods of wood, bone, or plastic, in which players try to remove one at a time without disturbing the others.
– ORIGIN C18: from SPILL².

spillover ▪ n. **1** an instance of spilling over into another area. ▸ a thing that spills or has spilt over. **2** an unexpected consequence or by-product.

spillway ▪ n. a passage for surplus water from a dam.

spilt past and past participle of SPILL¹.

spin ▪ v. (**spinning**; past and past part. **spun**) **1** turn or cause to turn round quickly. ▸ (of a person's head) give a sensation of dizziness. ▸ chiefly Cricket (with reference to a ball) move or cause to move through the air with a revolving motion. **2** draw out (wool, cotton, or other material) and convert it into threads. ▸ make (threads) in this way. ▸ (of a spider or a silkworm or other insect) produce (gossamer or silk) or construct (a web or cocoon) by extruding a fine viscous thread from a special gland. **3** (**spin something out**) make something last as long as possible. **4** (**spin out**) (of a driver or car) lose control in a skid. **5** (**spin something off**) (of a parent company) turn a subsidiary into a new and separate company. **6** informal give information a particular emphasis or bias, especially a favourable one. **7** fish with a spinner. ▪ n. **1** a spinning motion. ▸ a fast revolving motion of an aircraft as it descends rapidly. ▸ Physics the intrinsic angular momentum of a subatomic particle. **2** informal a brief trip in a vehicle for pleasure. **3** a favourable bias or slant given to information.
– PHRASES **flat spin 1** a spin in which an aircraft descends in tight circles while remaining horizontal. **2** informal a state of agitation. **spin a yarn** tell a long, far-fetched story.
– ORIGIN Old English *spinnan* 'draw out and twist (fibre)'.

spina bifida /ˌspʌɪnə ˈbɪfɪdə/ ▪ n. a congenital defect in which part of the spinal cord is exposed through a gap in the backbone, and which can cause paralysis and mental handicap.
– ORIGIN C18: modern Latin (see SPINE, BIFID).

spinach /ˈspɪnɪdʒ, -ɪtʃ/ ▪ n. an Asian plant of the goosefoot family, with large dark green leaves which are eaten as a vegetable. [*Spinacia oleracea*.]
– DERIVATIVES **spinachy** adj.
– ORIGIN Middle English: prob. from Old French *espinache*, from Persian *aspānāk*.

spinach beet ▪ n. beet of a variety cultivated for its spinach-like leaves.

spinal ▪ adj. of or relating to the spine.
– DERIVATIVES **spinally** adv.

spinal canal ▪ n. a cavity which runs successively through each of the vertebrae and encloses the spinal cord.

spinal column ▪ n. the spine.

spinal cord ▪ n. the cylindrical bundle of nerve fibres which is enclosed in the spine and connected to the brain, with which it forms the central nervous system.

spinal tap ▪ n. another term for LUMBAR PUNCTURE.

spindle ▪ n. **1** a slender rounded rod with tapered ends used in hand spinning to twist and wind thread from a mass of wool or flax held on a distaff. ▸ a pin bearing the bobbin of a spinning machine. **2** a rod or pin serving as an axis that revolves or on which something revolves. **3** a turned piece of wood used as a banister or chair leg. **4** Biology a slender mass of microtubules formed when a cell divides. **5** a measure of length for yarn, equal to 15 120 yards (13 826 metres) for cotton or 14 400 yards (13 167 metres) for linen.
– ORIGIN Old English *spinel*, from the base of SPIN.

spindle-shanks ▪ pl. n. informal, dated **1** long thin legs. **2** [treated as sing.] a person with such legs.
– DERIVATIVES **spindle-shanked** adj.

spindle-shaped ▪ adj. having a circular cross section and tapering towards each end.

spindly ▪ adj. long or tall and thin.

spin doctor ▪ n. informal a spokesperson for a political

spindrift

party or politician employed to give a favourable interpretation of events to the media.

spindrift ■ n. **1** spray blown from the crests of waves by the wind. **2** driving snow.
– ORIGIN C17: var. of *spoondrift*, from archaic *spoon* 'run before wind or sea' + DRIFT.

spin dryer ■ n. a machine for extracting water from wet clothes by spinning them in a revolving perforated drum.
– DERIVATIVES **spin-dry** v.

spine ■ n. **1** a series of vertebrae extending from the skull to the small of the back, enclosing the spinal cord and providing support for the thorax and abdomen; the backbone. **2** a central feature or main source of strength. **3** the part of a book's jacket or cover that encloses the inner edges of the pages. **4** chiefly Zoology & Botany a prickle or other hard pointed projection or structure.
– DERIVATIVES **-spined** adj.
– ORIGIN Middle English: shortening of Old French *espine*, or from Latin *spina* 'thorn, backbone'.

spine-chiller ■ n. a story or film that inspires terror and excitement.
– DERIVATIVES **spine-chilling** adj.

spinel /spɪˈnɛl, ˈspɪn(ə)l/ ■ n. a hard glassy mineral consisting chiefly of magnesium and aluminium oxides. ▶ Chemistry any of a class of similar crystalline oxides.
– ORIGIN C16: from French *spinelle*, from Italian *spinella*, diminutive of *spina* 'thorn'.

spineless ■ adj. **1** having no spine; invertebrate. **2** (of an animal or plant) lacking spines. **3** weak and purposeless.
– DERIVATIVES **spinelessly** adv. **spinelessness** n.

spinet /spɪˈnɛt, ˈspɪnɪt/ ■ n. a small harpsichord with the strings set obliquely to the keyboard, popular in the 18th century.
– ORIGIN C17: shortening of obsolete French *espinette*, from Italian *spinetta* 'virginal, spinet', diminutive of *spina* (see SPINE), the strings being plucked by quills.

spine-tingling ■ adj. informal thrilling or pleasurably frightening.

spinnaker /ˈspɪnəkə/ ■ n. a large three-cornered sail set forward of the mainsail of a racing yacht when running before the wind.
– ORIGIN C19: apparently from *Sphinx*, the name of the yacht first using it.

spinner ■ n. **1** a person occupied in spinning thread. **2** Cricket a bowler who is expert in spinning the ball. **3** (also **spinnerbait**) Fishing a lure designed to revolve when pulled through the water. ▶ a type of fishing fly, used chiefly for trout.

spinneret /ˈspɪnərɛt/ ■ n. **1** Zoology any of a number of different organs through which the silk, gossamer, or thread of spiders, silkworms, and certain other insects is produced. **2** (in the production of man-made fibres) a cap or plate with a number of small holes through which a fibre-forming solution is forced.

spinney ■ n. (pl. **-eys**) Brit. a small area of trees and bushes.
– ORIGIN C16: shortening of Old French *espinei*, from Latin *spinetum* 'thicket'.

spinning ■ n. trademark an intense form of aerobic exercise performed on stationary exercise bikes and led by an instructor who sets the constantly varying pace.

spinning jenny ■ n. historical a machine for spinning with more than one spindle at a time.

spinning mule ■ n. see MULE[1] (sense 4).

spinning top ■ n. see TOP[2].

spinning wheel ■ n. an apparatus for spinning yarn or thread with a spindle driven by a wheel attached to a crank or treadle.

spin-off ■ n. **1** a product or incidental benefit produced during or after the primary activity. **2** a subsidiary of a parent company that has been sold off, creating a new company.

spinose /ˈspʌɪnəʊs, spʌɪˈnəʊs/ (also **spinous** /ˈspʌɪnəs/) ■ adj. chiefly Botany & Zoology having spines; spiny.

spin-out ■ n. N. Amer. informal **1** another term for SPIN-OFF. **2** a skidding spin by a vehicle out of control.

spinster ■ n. chiefly derogatory an unmarried woman, typically an older woman beyond the usual age for marriage.
– DERIVATIVES **spinsterhood** n. **spinsterish** adj.
– ORIGIN Middle English (in the sense 'woman who spins'): from SPIN.

spinthariscope /spɪnˈθarɪskəʊp/ ■ n. Physics an instrument that shows the incidence of alpha particles by flashes on a fluorescent screen.
– ORIGIN C20: from Greek *spintharis* 'spark' + -SCOPE.

spinto /ˈspɪntəʊ/ ■ n. (pl. **-os**) a lyric soprano or tenor voice of powerful dramatic quality.
– ORIGIN 1950s: Italian, 'pushed', from *spingere* 'push'.

spiny ■ adj. (**-ier**, **-iest**) full of or covered with prickles.
– DERIVATIVES **spininess** n.

spiny anteater ■ n. another term for ECHIDNA.

spiny lobster ■ n. a large edible crustacean with a spiny shell and long heavy antennae, but without large claws. [Family Palinuridae: several species.]

spiracle /ˈspʌɪrək(ə)l/ ■ n. Zoology an external respiratory opening in insects, cartilaginous fish, and other animals.
– DERIVATIVES **spiracular** adj.
– ORIGIN C18: from Latin *spiraculum*, from *spirare* 'breathe'.

spiraea /spʌɪˈriːə/ (chiefly US also **spirea**) ■ n. a shrub of the rose family with clusters of small white or pink flowers, cultivated as an ornamental. [Genus *Spiraea*.]
– ORIGIN from Greek *speiraia*, from *speira* 'a coil'.

spiral ■ adj. winding in a continuous and gradually widening (or tightening) curve around a central point or axis. ▶ winding in a continuous curve of constant diameter about a central axis, as though along a cylinder; helical. ▶ Astronomy denoting galaxies in which the stars and gas clouds are concentrated mainly in spiral arms. ■ n. **1** a spiral curve, shape, or pattern. **2** a progressive rise or fall of prices, wages, etc., each responding to an upward or downward stimulus provided by a previous one. ▶ a process of progressive deterioration. ■ v. (**spiralled**, **spiralling**; US **spiraled**, **spiraling**) **1** take or cause to follow a spiral course. **2** show a continuous and dramatic increase. ▶ (**spiral down/downward**) decrease continuously.
– DERIVATIVES **spirally** adv.
– ORIGIN C16: from medieval Latin *spiralis*, from Latin *spira*, from Greek *speira* 'a coil'.

spiral-bound ■ adj. (of a book or notepad) bound with a wire or plastic spiral threaded through a row of holes along one edge.

spire ■ n. a tapering conical or pyramidal structure on the top of a building, typically a church tower.
– DERIVATIVES **spired** adj. **spiry** adj.
– ORIGIN Old English *spir* 'tall slender stem of a plant'.

spirea ■ n. US variant spelling of SPIRAEA.

spirillum /spʌɪˈrɪləm/ ■ n. (pl. **spirilla** /-lə/) a bacterium with a rigid spiral structure, found in stagnant water and sometimes causing disease.
– ORIGIN diminutive of Latin *spira* 'a coil'.

spirit ■ n. **1** the non-physical part of a person which is the seat of emotions and character. ▶ this regarded as surviving after the death of the body, often manifested as a ghost. ▶ a supernatural being. **2** the prevailing or typical quality or mood: *the nation's egalitarian spirit.* ▶ a person identified with their role or most prominent quality: *he was a leading spirit in the conference.* ▶ (**spirits**) a person's mood. **3** courage, energy, and determination. **4** the real meaning or intention of something as opposed to its strict verbal interpretation. **5** strong distilled liquor such as rum. ▶ [with modifier] a volatile liquid, especially a fuel, prepared by distillation: *aviation spirit.* ■ v. (**spirited**, **spiriting**) (usu. **spirit something away**) convey rapidly and secretly.
– PHRASES **in** (or **in the**) **spirit** in thought or intention though not physically. **when the spirit moves someone** when someone feels inclined to do something.
– ORIGIN Middle English: from Latin *spiritus* 'breath, spirit', from *spirare* 'breathe'.

spirited ■ adj. **1** full of energy, enthusiasm, and determination. **2** [in combination] having a specified character or mood: *a generous-spirited man.*
– DERIVATIVES **spiritedly** adv. **spiritedness** n.

spirit gum ▪ n. a quick-drying solution of gum, chiefly used by actors to attach false hair to their faces.

spiritism ▪ n. another term for SPIRITUALISM (in sense 1).
– DERIVATIVES **spiritist** adj. & n. **spiritistic** adj.

spirit lamp ▪ n. a lamp burning methylated or other volatile spirits instead of oil.

spiritless ▪ adj. lacking courage, energy, or determination.
– DERIVATIVES **spiritlessly** adv. **spiritlessness** n.

spirit level ▪ n. a device consisting of a sealed glass tube partially filled with alcohol or other liquid, containing an air bubble whose position reveals whether a surface is perfectly level.

spiritous ▪ adj. another term for SPIRITUOUS.

spiritual /ˈspɪrɪtʃʊəl, -tjʊəl/ ▪ adj. **1** of, relating to, or affecting the human spirit as opposed to material or physical things. **2** of or relating to religion or religious belief. ▪ n. (also **negro spiritual**) a religious song of a kind associated with black Christians of the southern US.
– DERIVATIVES **spirituality** n. **spiritualization** (also **-isation**) n. **spiritualize** (also **-ise**) v. **spiritually** adv.

spiritualism ▪ n. **1** a system of belief or religious practice based on supposed communication with the spirits of the dead, especially through mediums. **2** Philosophy the doctrine that the spirit exists as distinct from matter, or that spirit is the only reality.
– DERIVATIVES **spiritualist** n. **spiritualistic** adj.

spirituous /ˈspɪrɪtjʊəs/ ▪ adj. formal or archaic containing much alcohol.
– ORIGIN C16: from Latin *spiritus* 'spirit', or from French *spiritueux*.

spiro-¹ ▪ comb. form **1** spiral; in a spiral: *spirochaete*. **2** Chemistry denoting a molecule with two rings with one atom common to both.
– ORIGIN from Latin *spira*, Greek *speira* 'a coil'.

spiro-² ▪ comb. form relating to breathing: *spirometer*.
– ORIGIN from Latin *spirare* 'breathe'.

spirochaete /ˈspaɪrə(ʊ)kiːt/ (US **spirochete**) ▪ n. a flexible spirally twisted bacterium of an order (Spirochaetales) including that responsible for syphilis.
– ORIGIN C19: from SPIRO-¹ + Greek *khaitē* 'long hair'.

spirogyra /ˌspaɪrə(ʊ)ˈdʒaɪrə/ ▪ n. Botany a filamentous green alga of a genus that includes blanket weed. [Genus *Spirogyra*.]
– ORIGIN from SPIRO-¹ + Greek *guros*, *gura* 'round'.

spirometer /spaɪˈrɒmɪtə/ ▪ n. an instrument for measuring the air capacity of the lungs.
– DERIVATIVES **spirometry** n.

spirt ▪ v. & n. old-fashioned spelling of SPURT.

spirulina /ˌspɪrʊˈlaɪnə, ˌspaɪrʊ-/ ▪ n. a filamentous cyanobacterium of a genus typically forming tangled masses in warm alkaline lakes. [Genus *Spirulina*.]
– ORIGIN from *spirula* 'small spiral (shell)'.

spit¹ ▪ v. (**spitting**; past and past part. **spat** or **spit**) **1** eject saliva forcibly from one's mouth. ▸ forcibly eject (food or liquid) from one's mouth. **2** utter in a hostile way. **3** (of a fire or something being cooked) emit small bursts of sparks or hot fat with a series of explosive noises. **4** (**it spits**), **it is spitting**, etc. light rain falls. ▪ n. **1** saliva. **2** an act of spitting.
– PHRASES **be the spit** (or **the dead spit**) **of** informal look exactly like. [see SPITTING IMAGE.] **spit blood** feel or express vehement anger. **spit in the eye** (or **face**) **of** show contempt or scorn for. **spit it out** [in imper.] informal say something unhesitatingly.
– ORIGIN Old English *spittan*, of imitative origin.

spit² ▪ n. **1** a long, thin metal rod pushed through meat in order to hold and turn it while it is roasted over an open fire. **2** a narrow point of land projecting into the sea. ▪ v. (**spitted**, **spitting**) put a spit through (meat).
– DERIVATIVES **spitty** adj.
– ORIGIN Old English *spitu*, of West Germanic origin.

spit³ ▪ n. (pl. same or **spits**) a layer of earth whose depth is equal to the length of the blade of a spade.
– ORIGIN C16: from Middle Dutch and Middle Low German; prob. rel. to SPIT².

spit and polish ▪ n. thorough cleaning and polishing, especially by a soldier.

spitball N. Amer. ▪ n. **1** a ball of chewed paper used as a missile. **2** Baseball an illegal swerving pitch made with a ball moistened with saliva or sweat.
– DERIVATIVES **spitballer** n.

spite ▪ n. a desire to hurt, annoy, or offend. ▪ v. deliberately hurt, annoy, or offend.
– PHRASES **in spite of** without being affected by the particular factor mentioned. **in spite of oneself** although one did not want or expect to do so.
– DERIVATIVES **spiteful** adj. **spitefully** adv. **spitefulness** n.
– ORIGIN Middle English: shortening of Old French *despit* 'contempt', *despiter* 'show contempt for'.

spitfire ▪ n. a person with a fierce temper.

spit-roast ▪ v. [usu. as adj. **spit-roasted**] cook (a piece of meat) on a spit.

spitting cobra ▪ n. an African cobra that defends itself by spitting venom from the fangs. [*Naja nigricollis* and other species.]

spitting image ▪ n. (**the spitting image of**) informal the exact double of.
– ORIGIN C19: orig. as *the spit of* or *the spit and image of*; perhaps from the idea of a person being formed from the spit of another, so great is the similarity between them.

spittle ▪ n. saliva, especially as ejected from the mouth.
– DERIVATIVES **spittly** adj.
– ORIGIN C15: alteration of dialect *spattle*, by association with SPIT¹.

spittlebug ▪ n. another term for FROGHOPPER.

spittoon /spɪˈtuːn/ ▪ n. a container for spitting into.

spitz ▪ n. a dog of a small breed with a pointed muzzle, especially a Pomeranian.
– ORIGIN C19: from German *Spitz(hund)*, from *spitz* 'pointed' + *Hund* 'dog'.

spiv ▪ n. Brit. informal a man, typically a flashy dresser, who makes a living by disreputable dealings.
– DERIVATIVES **spivvish** adj. **spivvy** adj.
– ORIGIN 1930s: perhaps rel. to SPIFFY.

splanchnic /ˈsplaŋknɪk/ ▪ adj. of or relating to the viscera or internal organs, especially those of the abdomen.
– ORIGIN C17: from Greek *splankhnikos*, from *splankhna* 'entrails'.

splash ▪ v. **1** make (liquid) strike or fall on something in drops. ▸ (of a liquid) fall or be scattered in drops. ▸ strike or move around in water, causing it to fly about. ▸ (**splash down**) (of a spacecraft) land on water. **2** display (a story or photograph) in a prominent place in a newspaper or magazine. **3** (**splash out**) or **splash money out** informal spend money freely. **4** (**be splashed with**) be decorated with scattered patches of. ▪ n. **1** an instance of splashing or the sound made by this. ▸ a small quantity of liquid that has splashed on to a surface. ▸ a small quantity of liquid added to a drink. **2** a bright patch of colour. **3** informal a prominent news feature or story.
– PHRASES **make a splash** informal attract a great deal of attention.
– DERIVATIVES **splashy** adj. (**-ier**, **-iest**).
– ORIGIN C18: alteration of PLASH.

splashback ▪ n. a panel behind a sink or stove that protects the wall from splashes.

splat¹ ▪ n. a piece of thin wood in the centre of a chair back.
– ORIGIN C19: from obsolete *splat* 'split up'; rel. to SPLIT.

splat² informal ▪ n. a sound of something soft and wet or heavy striking a surface. ▪ adv. with a splat. ▪ v. (**splatted**, **splatting**) hit or land with a splat.
– ORIGIN C19: abbrev. of SPLATTER.

splatter ▪ v. splash with a sticky or viscous liquid. ▸ (of such a liquid) splash. ▪ n. **1** a splash of a sticky or viscous liquid. **2** [as modifier] informal denoting or referring to films featuring many violent and gruesome deaths.
– ORIGIN C18: imitative.

splay ▪ v. **1** spread or be spread out or further apart. **2** [usu. as adj. **splayed**] construct (a window, doorway, or other aperture) so that it is wider at one side of the wall than the other. ▪ n. **1** a tapered widening of a road at an intersection to increase visibility. **2** a surface making an

splay-footed

oblique angle with another, especially a splayed window or other aperture. ■ adj. [usu. in combination] turned outward or widened: *the girl sat splay-legged.*
– ORIGIN Middle English: shortening of DISPLAY.

splay-footed ■ n. having a broad flat foot turned outward.
– DERIVATIVES **splay-foot** n.

spleen ■ n. 1 Anatomy an abdominal organ involved in the production and removal of blood cells and forming part of the immune system. 2 bad temper; spite.
– DERIVATIVES **spleenful** adj.
– ORIGIN Middle English: shortening of Old French *esplen*, from Greek *splēn*; sense 2 derives from the former belief that the spleen was the seat of bad temper.

splen- ■ comb. form Anatomy of or relating to the spleen: *splenectomy.*
– ORIGIN from Greek *splēn* 'spleen'.

splendid ■ adj. 1 magnificent; very impressive. 2 informal excellent.
– DERIVATIVES **splendidly** adv. **splendidness** n.
– ORIGIN C17: from French *splendide* or Latin *splendidus*, from *splendere* 'shine'.

splendiferous /splɛnˈdɪf(ə)rəs/ ■ adj. informal, humorous splendid.
– DERIVATIVES **splendiferously** adv. **splendiferousness** n.
– ORIGIN C19: from SPLENDOUR.

splendour (US **splendor**) ■ n. splendid appearance.
– ORIGIN Middle English: from Anglo-Norman French *splendur* or Latin *splendor*, from *splendere* 'shine'.

splenectomy /splɪˈnɛktəmi/ ■ n. (pl. **-ies**) a surgical operation involving removal of the spleen.

splenetic /splɪˈnɛtɪk/ ■ adj. bad-tempered or spiteful.
– DERIVATIVES **splenetically** adv.
– ORIGIN Middle English: from late Latin *spleneticus*, from Greek *splēn* (see SPLEEN).

splenic /ˈsplɛnɪk, ˈspliːnɪk/ ■ adj. of or relating to the spleen.

splenitis /splɪˈnʌɪtɪs/ ■ n. Medicine inflammation of the spleen.

splenomegaly /ˌspliːnə(ʊ)ˈmɛg(ə)li/ ■ n. abnormal enlargement of the spleen.
– ORIGIN C20: from SPLEN- + Greek *megas, megal-* 'great'.

splice ■ v. join (a rope or ropes) by interweaving the strands at the ends. ▸ join (pieces of timber, film, or tape) at the ends. ▸ Genetics join or insert (a gene or gene fragment). ■ n. a spliced join. ▸ the wedge-shaped tang of a cricket-bat handle, forming a joint with the blade.
– PHRASES **get** (or **be**) **spliced** informal get married. **splice the main brace** Brit. historical (in the navy) serve out an extra tot of rum.
– DERIVATIVES **splicer** n.
– ORIGIN C16: prob. from Middle Dutch *splissen*.

spliff ■ n. informal a cannabis cigarette.
– ORIGIN 1930s.

spline /splʌɪn/ ■ n. 1 a rectangular key fitting into grooves in the hub and shaft of a wheel, especially one formed integrally with the shaft which allows movement of the wheel on the shaft. ▸ a corresponding groove in a hub along which the key may slide. 2 a slat. 3 a flexible wood or rubber strip used especially in drawing large curves. ■ v. secure by means of a spline. ▸ [usu. as adj. **splined**] fit with a spline.
– ORIGIN C18: perhaps rel. to SPLINTER.

splint ■ n. 1 a strip of rigid material for supporting a broken bone when it has been set. 2 a long, thin strip of wood used in basketwork or to light a fire. 3 a bony enlargement on the inside of a horse's leg. ■ v. secure with a splint or splints.
– ORIGIN Middle English: from Middle Dutch, Middle Low German *splinte* 'metal plate or pin'.

splint bone ■ n. either of two small bones in the foreleg of a horse or other large quadruped, lying behind and close to the cannon bone.

splinter ■ n. a small, thin, sharp piece of wood, glass, etc. broken off from a larger piece. ■ v. break or cause to break into splinters.

– DERIVATIVES **splintery** adj.
– ORIGIN Middle English: from Middle Dutch *splinter, splenter*.

splinter group (also **splinter party**) ■ n. a small organization that has broken away from a larger one.

splinter-proof ■ adj. 1 capable of withstanding splinters from bursting shells or bombs. 2 not producing splinters when broken.

split ■ v. (**splitting**; past and past part. **split**) 1 break or cause to break forcibly into parts. ▸ cause the fission of (an atom). 2 divide or cause to divide into parts or groups. ▸ (often **split up**) end a marriage or other relationship. 3 informal (of one's head) suffer great pain from a headache. 4 (usu. **split on**) informal betray the secrets of or inform on someone. 5 informal leave, especially suddenly. ■ n. 1 a tear, crack, or fissure. 2 an instance of splitting or being split. 3 (**the splits**) (in gymnastics and dance) an act of leaping in the air or sitting down with the legs straight and at right angles to the body, one in front and the other behind, or one at each side. 4 half a bottle or glass of champagne or other liquor. 5 the time taken to complete a recognized part of a race, or the point in the race where such a time is measured.
– PHRASES **split the difference** take the average of two proposed amounts. **split one's sides** informal be convulsed with laughter. **split the vote** (of a candidate or minority party) attract votes from another candidate or party with the result that both are defeated by a third.
– DERIVATIVES **splitter** n.
– ORIGIN C16: from Middle Dutch *splitten*.

split end ■ n. a tip of a person's hair which has split from dryness or ill-treatment.

split infinitive ■ n. a construction consisting of an infinitive with an adverb or other word inserted between *to* and the verb, e.g. *she seems to really like it.*

> **USAGE**
> It is still widely held that splitting infinitives is wrong, a view based on an analogy with Latin. In Latin, infinitives cannot be split as they consist of only one word (e.g. *amare* 'to love'). It is therefore said that they should not be split in English either. But English is not the same as Latin, and the avoidance of a split infinitive can change the emphasis of a sentence or sound awkward (as in *she seems really to like it*). For this reason, the rule about avoiding split infinitives is not followed so strictly today, although it is best not to split them in formal writing.

split-level ■ adj. 1 (of a room or building) having the floor level of one part about half a storey above or below the floor level of an adjacent part. 2 (of a stove) having the oven and hob in separately installed units.

split pea ■ n. a pea dried and split in half for cooking.

split pin ■ n. a metal cotter pin with two arms passed through a hole, held in place by the springing apart of the arms.

split ring ■ n. a small steel ring with two spiral turns, such as a key ring.

split screen ■ n. a cinema, television, or computer screen on which two or more separate images are displayed.

split second ■ n. a very brief moment of time. ■ adj. (**split-second**) very rapid or accurate.

split shift ■ n. a working shift comprising two or more separate periods of duty in a day.

split shot ■ n. 1 small pellets used to weight a fishing line. 2 Croquet a stroke driving two touching balls in different directions.

splittism ■ n. (among communists, or in communist countries) the pursuance of factional interests in opposition to official Communist Party policy.
– DERIVATIVES **splittist** n.

splodge ■ n. & v. chiefly Brit. another term for SPLOTCH.
– DERIVATIVES **splodgy** adj.

splosh informal ■ v. move with a soft splashing sound. ■ n. a splash or splashing sound.
– ORIGIN C19: imitative.

splotch informal ■ n. a spot, splash, or smear. ■ v. make a splotch on.
– DERIVATIVES **splotchy** adj.

– ORIGIN C17: perhaps a blend of **spot** and obsolete *plotch* 'blotch'.

splurge informal ■ n. **1** a sudden burst of extravagance. **2** a large or excessive amount. ■ v. spend extravagantly.
– ORIGIN C19 (orig. US): prob. imitative.

splurt informal ■ n. a sudden gush of liquid. ■ v. push out with force.
– ORIGIN C18: imitative.

splutter ■ v. **1** make a series of short explosive spitting or choking sounds. **2** say in a rapid indistinct way. ■ n. a spluttering sound.
– DERIVATIVES **splutterer** n. **spluttering** adj. & n.
– ORIGIN C17: imitative.

Spode /spəʊd/ ■ n. trademark fine ornately decorated pottery or porcelain made at the factories of the English potter Josiah Spode (1755–1827) or his successors.

spodumene /ˈspɒdjʊmiːn/ ■ n. a translucent, typically greyish-white aluminosilicate mineral which is an important source of lithium.
– ORIGIN C19: from French *spodumène*, from Greek *spodousthai* 'burn to ashes'.

spoil ■ v. (past and past part. **spoilt** or **spoiled**) **1** diminish or destroy the value or quality of. ▸ (of food) become unfit for eating. ▸ mark (a ballot paper) incorrectly so as to invalidate one's vote. **2** harm the character of (a child) by being too indulgent. ▸ treat with great or excessive kindness or generosity. **3** (**be spoiling for**) be extremely or aggressively eager for. ■ n. **1** (**spoils**) stolen goods. **2** waste material brought up during the course of an excavation or a dredging or mining operation.
– PHRASES **be spoilt for choice** have so many options that it is difficult to make a choice.
– DERIVATIVES **spoilage** n.
– ORIGIN Middle English: shortening of Old French *espoille* (n.), *espoillier* (v.), from Latin *spoliare*, from *spolium* 'plunder, skin stripped from an animal'.

spoiler ■ n. **1** a person or thing that spoils. **2** a flap on an aircraft wing which can be projected to create drag and so reduce speed. ▸ a similar device on a motor vehicle intended to improve road-holding at high speeds.

spoilsport ■ n. a person who spoils others' pleasure.

spoils system ■ n. chiefly US the practice of a successful political party of giving public office to its supporters.

spoilt past and past participle of **SPOIL**.

spoke[1] ■ n. **1** each of the bars or wire rods connecting the centre of a wheel to its rim. **2** each of a set of radial handles projecting from a ship's wheel. **3** each of the metal rods in an umbrella to which the material is attached.
– PHRASES **put a spoke in someone's wheel** prevent someone from carrying out a plan.
– DERIVATIVES **-spoked** adj.
– ORIGIN Old English, of West Germanic origin, from the base of **SPIKE**[1].

spoke[2] past of **SPEAK**.

spoken past participle of **SPEAK**. ■ adj. [in combination] speaking in a specified way: *a soft-spoken man.*
– PHRASES **be spoken for 1** be already claimed or reserved. **2** already have a romantic commitment.

spokeshave /ˈspəʊkʃeɪv/ ■ n. a small plane with a handle on each side of its blade, used for shaping curved surfaces (originally wheel spokes).

spokesman (or **spokeswoman**) ■ n. (pl. **-men** or **-women**) a person who makes statements on behalf of a group.
– ORIGIN C16: from **SPOKE**[2], on the pattern of *craftsman*.

spokesperson ■ n. (pl. **-persons** or **-people**) a spokesman or spokeswoman (used as a neutral alternative).

spoliation /ˌspəʊlɪˈeɪʃ(ə)n/ ■ n. **1** the action of spoiling. **2** the action of plundering.
– DERIVATIVES **spoliator** n.
– ORIGIN Middle English: from Latin *spoliatio(n-)*, from *spoliare* (see **SPOIL**).

spondaic /spɒnˈdeɪɪk/ ■ adj. Prosody of or concerning spondees. ▸ (of a hexameter) having a spondee as its fifth foot.

spondee /ˈspɒndiː/ ■ n. Prosody a foot consisting of two long (or stressed) syllables.
– ORIGIN Middle English: from Greek *spondeios (pous)* '(foot) of a libation', from *spondē* 'libation' (being characteristic of music accompanying libations).

spondulicks /spɒnˈdjuːlɪks/ ■ pl. n. Brit. informal money.
– ORIGIN C19.

spondylitis /ˌspɒndɪˈlʌɪtɪs/ ■ n. Medicine inflammation of the joints of the backbone. See also **ANKYLOSING SPONDYLITIS**.
– ORIGIN C19: from Latin *spondylus* 'vertebra'.

sponge ■ n. **1** a sedentary aquatic invertebrate with a soft porous body supported by a framework of fibres or spicules. [Phylum Porifera.] **2** a piece of a soft, light, porous, absorbent substance originally consisting of the fibrous skeleton of a sponge but now usually made of synthetic material, used for washing, as padding, etc. ▸ a piece of sponge impregnated with spermicide and inserted into a woman's vagina as a form of barrier contraceptive. **3** a very light cake made with eggs, sugar, and flour but little or no fat. **4** informal a person who lives at someone else's expense. **5** informal a heavy drinker. **6** metal in a porous form. ■ v. (**sponging** or **spongeing**) **1** wipe or clean with a wet sponge or cloth. **2** (often **sponge off**) informal obtain money or food from others without giving anything in return. **3** give a decorative effect to (a wall or surface) by applying paint with a sponge. ▸ decorate (pottery) using a sponge.
– DERIVATIVES **spongeable** adj. **sponge-like** adj.
– ORIGIN Old English, from Greek *spongia*, later form of *spongos*, reinforced in Middle English by Old French *esponge*.

sponge bag ■ n. Brit. a toilet bag.

sponge cloth ■ n. soft, lightly woven cloth with a slightly wrinkled surface.

sponge pudding ■ n. Brit. a steamed or baked pudding of fat, flour, and eggs.

sponger ■ n. informal a person who lives at others' expense.

sponge rubber ■ n. rubber latex processed into a sponge-like substance.

spongiform /ˈspʌndʒɪfɔːm/ ■ adj. chiefly Veterinary Medicine having, relating to, or denoting a porous structure or consistency resembling that of a sponge.

spongy /ˈspʌn(d)ʒi/ ■ adj. (**-ier**, **-iest**) **1** like a sponge, especially in being porous, compressible, or absorbent. **2** (of metal) having an open, porous structure. **3** (of a motor vehicle's braking system) lacking firmness.
– DERIVATIVES **spongily** adv. **sponginess** n.

sponson /ˈspɒns(ə)n/ ■ n. **1** a gun platform standing out from a warship's side. **2** a short subsidiary wing that serves to stabilize a seaplane. **3** a buoyancy chamber in a canoe.
– ORIGIN C19.

sponsor ■ n. **1** a person or organization that pays all or some of the costs of a television programme, event, etc. in return for advertising. **2** a person who pledges money to a charity after another person has participated in a fund-raising event. **3** a person who introduces and supports a proposal for legislation. **4** a person taking official responsibility for the actions of another. ▸ Christian Church a godparent at a child's baptism. ▸ a person presenting a candidate for confirmation. ■ v. be a sponsor for.
– DERIVATIVES **sponsorship** n.
– ORIGIN C17: from Latin, from *spondere* 'promise solemnly'.

spontaneous /spɒnˈteɪnɪəs/ ■ adj. **1** performed or occurring as a result of an unpremeditated inner impulse and without external stimulus. ▸ (of a process or event) occurring without apparent external cause. **2** open, natural, and uninhibited.
– DERIVATIVES **spontaneity** n. **spontaneously** adv.
– ORIGIN C17: from late Latin *spontaneus*, from *(sua) sponte* 'of (one's) own accord'.

spontaneous combustion ■ n. the ignition of organic matter without apparent cause, especially through heat generated internally by rapid oxidation.

spoof informal ■ n. **1** a parody, typically of a film or a genre of film. **2** a hoax. ■ v. **1** parody. **2** hoax. **3** interfere with

spook

(radio or radar signals) so as to make them useless.
- DERIVATIVES **spoofer** n. **spoofery** n.
- ORIGIN C19: coined by the English comedian Arthur Roberts.

spook informal ■ n. **1** a ghost. **2** a spy. ■ v. frighten or become frightened.
- ORIGIN C19: from Dutch.

spooky ■ adj. (**-ier**, **-iest**) informal sinister or ghostly.
- DERIVATIVES **spookily** adv. **spookiness** n.

spool ■ n. a cylindrical device on which thread, film, magnetic tape, fishing line, etc. can be wound. ■ v. **1** wind or be wound on to a spool. **2** Computing send (data for printing or peripheral processing) to an intermediate store. **3** (**spool up**) increase the speed of rotation of a device to the working speed.
- ORIGIN Middle English: shortening of Old French *espole* or from Middle Low German *spôle*, of West Germanic origin; sense 2 of the verb is an acronym from *simultaneous peripheral operation online*.

spoon ■ n. **1** an implement consisting of a small, shallow oval or round bowl on a long handle, used for eating, stirring, and serving food. ▸ (**spoons**) a pair of spoons held in the hand and beaten together rhythmically as a percussion instrument. **2** (also **spoon bait**) a fishing lure designed to wobble when pulled through the water. **3** an oar with a broad curved blade. ■ v. **1** transfer with a spoon. **2** informal, dated (of a couple) behave in an amorous way. **3** hit (a ball) up into the air with a soft or weak stroke.
- DERIVATIVES **spooner** n. **spoonful** n. (pl. **-fuls**).
- ORIGIN Old English *spōn* 'chip of wood', of Germanic origin.

spoonbill ■ n. a tall mainly white or pinkish wading bird related to ibises, having a long bill with a very broad flat tip. [Genera *Platalea* and *Ajaia*: several species.]

spoonerism ■ n. an error in speech in which the initial sounds or letters of two or more words are accidentally transposed, often to humorous effect, as in *you have hissed the mystery lectures*.
- ORIGIN C20: named after the English scholar Revd W. A. Spooner, who reputedly made such errors in speaking.

spoon-feed ■ v. **1** feed (a baby or infirm adult) using a spoon. **2** provide (someone) with so much help or information that they do not need to think for themselves.

spoor /spʊə, spɔː/ ■ n. the track or scent of an animal. ■ v. follow the spoor of.
- DERIVATIVES **spoorer** n.
- ORIGIN C19: from Afrikaans, from Middle Dutch *spor*.

sporadic /spəˈradɪk/ ■ adj. occurring at irregular intervals or only in a few places.
- DERIVATIVES **sporadically** adv.
- ORIGIN C17: from Greek *sporadikos*, from *sporas* 'scattered'; rel. to *speirein* 'to sow'.

sporangium /spəˈran(d)ʒɪəm/ ■ n. (pl. **sporangia** /-dʒɪə/) Botany (in ferns and lower plants) a receptacle in which asexual spores are formed.
- DERIVATIVES **sporangial** adj.
- ORIGIN C19: from Greek *spora* 'spore' + *angeion* 'vessel'.

spore ■ n. **1** Biology a minute, typically single-celled, reproductive unit characteristic of lower plants, fungi, and protozoans, capable of giving rise to a new individual without sexual fusion. **2** Microbiology (in bacteria) a rounded resistant form adopted by a bacterial cell in adverse conditions.
- ORIGIN C19: from Greek *spora* 'sowing, seed'.

sporo- ■ comb. form Biology of or relating to spores: *sporo-genesis*.
- ORIGIN from Greek *spora* 'spore'.

sporocyst ■ n. Zoology **1** a larva of a parasitic fluke in a sac-like form after infection of the host's tissues. **2** (in parasitic sporozoans) an encysted zygote in an invertebrate host.

sporogenesis /ˌspɔːrə(ʊ)ˈdʒɛnɪsɪs, ˌspɒrə(ʊ)-/ ■ n. chiefly Botany the process of spore formation.

sporogony /spəˈrɒɡəni/ ■ n. Zoology the asexual process of spore formation in parasitic sporozoans.

sporophore /ˈspɒrəfɔː, ˈspɔː-/ ■ n. Botany the spore-bearing structure of a fungus.

sporophyte /ˈspɒrəfʌɪt, ˈspɔː-/ ■ n. Botany (in the life cycle of plants with alternating generations, e.g. ferns) the asexual phase (typically diploid), which produces spores from which the gametophyte arises.
- DERIVATIVES **sporophytic** adj.

Sporozoa /ˌspɒrəˈzəʊə/ ■ pl. n. Zoology a phylum of mainly parasitic protozoans with complex life cycles, including the organisms responsible for malaria, toxoplasmosis, etc.
- DERIVATIVES **sporozoan** n. & adj.
- ORIGIN from **SPORO-** + Greek *zōia* 'animals'.

sporozoite /ˌspɒrə(ʊ)ˈzəʊʌɪt, ˌspɔː-/ ■ n. Zoology & Medicine a motile spore-like stage in the life cycle of some sporozoans.
- ORIGIN C19: from **SPORO-** + Greek *zoion* 'animal'.

sporran /ˈspɒr(ə)n/ ■ n. a small pouch worn at the front of the kilt as part of men's Scottish Highland dress.
- ORIGIN C18: from Scottish Gaelic *sporan*.

sport ■ n. **1** an activity involving physical exertion and skill in which an individual or team competes against another or others for entertainment. **2** informal a person who behaves in a good or specified way in response to teasing, defeat, etc. **3** chiefly Austral./NZ a friendly form of address, especially between unacquainted men. **4** a spontaneously mutated animal or plant showing abnormal or striking variation from the parent type. **5** dated entertainment; fun. ■ v. **1** wear or display (a distinctive or noticeable item). **2** amuse oneself or play in a lively, energetic way.
- PHRASES **the sport of kings** horse racing.
- DERIVATIVES **sporter** n.
- ORIGIN Middle English: shortening of **DISPORT**.

sporting ■ adj. **1** connected with or interested in sport. **2** fair and generous in one's behaviour or dealing with others.
- DERIVATIVES **sportingly** adv.

sporting chance ■ n. a reasonable chance of winning or succeeding.

sporting code ■ n. **1** the rules and regulations governing a particular sport. **2** (also **sports code**) a particular sport, e.g. tennis or cricket.

sportive ■ adj. playful; light-hearted.
- DERIVATIVES **sportively** adv. **sportiveness** n.

sports bar ■ n. a bar where televised sport is shown continuously.

sports car ■ n. a low-built, often convertible, car designed for performance at high speeds.

sportscast ■ n. chiefly N. Amer. a broadcast of sports news or a sports event.
- DERIVATIVES **sportscaster** n.

sports drink ■ n. a flavoured soft drink containing a balance of carbohydrates and electrolytes, designed to prevent dehydration resulting from strenuous exercise.

sports jacket (US also **sport jacket** or **sports coat**) ■ n. a man's jacket resembling a suit jacket, for informal wear.

sportsman (or **sportswoman**) ■ n. (pl. **-men** or **-women**) **1** a person who takes part in a sport, especially as a professional. **2** a person who behaves sportingly.
- DERIVATIVES **sportsmanlike** adj. **sportsmanship** n.

sportsperson ■ n. (pl. **-persons** or **-people**) a sportsman or sportswoman (used as a neutral alternative).

sportster ■ n. a sports car.

sportswear ■ n. clothes worn for sport or for casual outdoor use.

sport utility ■ n. a high-performance four-wheel-drive vehicle.

sporty ■ adj. (**-ier**, **-iest**) informal **1** fond of or good at sport. **2** (of clothing) suitable for wearing for sport or for casual use. **3** (of a car) compact and with fast acceleration.
- DERIVATIVES **sportily** adv. **sportiness** n.

sporulate /ˈspɒrjʊleɪt/ ■ v. Biology produce or form a spore or spores.
- DERIVATIVES **sporulation** n.

spot ■ n. **1** a small round or roundish mark, differing in colour or texture from the surface around it. **2** a pimple. **3** a particular place, point, or position. ▸ a small feature or part with a particular quality: *his bald spot*. ▸ a place for an individual item within a show. **4** informal, chiefly Brit. a small amount of something: *a spot of lunch*. **5** [as modifier]

denoting a system of trading in which commodities or currencies are delivered and paid for immediately after a sale. ■ v. (**spotted**, **spotting**) **1** see, notice, or recognize (someone or something) that is difficult to detect or sought-after. ▸ Military locate an enemy's position, typically from the air. **2** mark or become marked with spots. **3** (**it spots**), **it is spotting, etc.** rain slightly. **4** place (a ball) on its designated starting point on a billiard table.
– PHRASES **hit the spot** informal be exactly what is required. **in a spot** informal in a difficult situation. **on the spot 1** immediately. **2** at the scene of an action or event. **3** chiefly Brit. (of an action) performed without moving from one's original position. **put someone on the spot** informal force someone into a situation in which they must respond or act.
– DERIVATIVES **spotted** adj.
– ORIGIN Middle English: perhaps from Middle Dutch *spotte*.

spot ball ■ n. Billiards one of two white cue balls, distinguished from the other by two black spots.

spot check ■ n. a test made without warning on a randomly selected subject. ■ v. (**spot-check**) subject to a spot check.

spot height ■ n. the altitude of a point, especially as shown on a map.

spot kick ■ n. another term for PENALTY KICK.

spotlamp ■ n. another term for SPOTLIGHT.

spotless ■ adj. absolutely clean or pure.
– DERIVATIVES **spotlessly** adv. **spotlessness** n.

spotlight ■ n. **1** a lamp projecting a narrow, intense beam of light directly on to a place or person. **2** (**the spotlight**) intense public attention. ■ v. (past and past part. **-lighted** or **-lit**) **1** illuminate with a spotlight. **2** direct attention to.

spot on ■ adj. & adv. informal completely accurate or accurately.

spotted dick ■ n. Brit. a suet pudding containing currants.

spotted fever ■ n. a disease characterized by fever and skin spots, especially (also Rocky Mountain spotted fever) a rickettsial disease transmitted by ticks.

spotted hyena ■ n. an African hyena that has a yellowish-brown coat with irregular dark spots, noted for its loud laughing call. [*Crocuta crocuta*.]

spotter ■ n. **1** [usu. in combination] a person who observes or looks for a particular thing as a hobby or job: *bus-spotters*. **2** an aviator or aircraft employed in spotting enemy positions.

spotty ■ adj. (**-ier**, **-iest**) **1** marked with or having spots. **2** chiefly N. Amer. of uneven quality.
– DERIVATIVES **spottily** adv. **spottiness** n.

spot-weld ■ v. join by welding at a number of separate points. ■ n. (**spot weld**) a weld so made.
– DERIVATIVES **spot-welder** n.

spousal /'spauz(ə)l/ ■ adj. of or relating to marriage or to a husband or wife.

spouse /spauz, -s/ ■ n. a husband or wife.
– ORIGIN Middle English: from Old French *spous(e)*, var. of *espous(e)*, from Latin *sponsus* (masculine), *sponsa* (feminine), from *spondere* 'betroth'.

spout ■ n. **1** a projecting tube or lip through or over which liquid can be poured from a container. **2** a stream of liquid issuing with great force. **3** a pipe, trough, or chute for conveying liquid, grain, etc. ■ v. **1** send out or issue forcibly in a stream. **2** express (one's views) in a lengthy or declamatory way.
– PHRASES **up the spout** Brit. informal **1** useless, ruined, or wasted. **2** (of a woman) pregnant. **3** (of a bullet or cartridge) in the barrel of a gun and ready to be fired.
– DERIVATIVES **spouted** adj. **spouter** n. **spoutless** adj.
– ORIGIN Middle English: from Middle Dutch *spouten*, from an imitative base shared by Old Norse *spýta* 'to spit'.

spp. ■ abbrev. species (plural).

spraddle ■ v. [usu. as adj. **spraddled**] chiefly N. Amer. spread (one's legs) far apart.
– ORIGIN C17: prob. from *sprad*, dialect past participle of SPREAD.

sprain ■ v. wrench the ligaments of (an ankle, wrist, or other joint) violently so as to cause pain and swelling but not dislocation. ■ n. the result of such a wrench.
– ORIGIN C17.

sprang past of SPRING.

sprat ■ n. a small marine fish of the herring family, caught for food and fish products. [*Sprattus sprattus* (Europe) and other species.] ▸ informal any small sea fish. ■ v. (**spratted**, **spratting**) fish for sprats.
– PHRASES **a sprat to catch a mackerel** Brit. a small outlay or risk ventured in the hope of a significant return.
– ORIGIN C16: var. of Old English *sprot*.

sprawl ■ v. **1** sit, lie, or fall with one's limbs spread out in an ungainly way. **2** spread out irregularly over a large area. ■ n. **1** a sprawling position or movement. **2** a sprawling group or mass. ▸ the disorganized expansion of an urban or industrial area into the adjoining countryside.
– DERIVATIVES **sprawling** n. & adj. **sprawlingly** adv.
– ORIGIN Old English *spreawlian* 'move the limbs convulsively'.

spray[1] ■ n. liquid sent through the air in tiny drops. ▸ a liquid preparation which can be forced out of an aerosol or other container in a spray. ■ v. **1** apply (liquid) in a spray. ▸ cover or treat with a spray. ▸ (of liquid) be sent through the air in a spray. ▸ (of a male cat) direct a stream of urine over (an object or area) to mark a territory. **2** scatter over an area with force.
– DERIVATIVES **sprayable** adj. **sprayer** n.
– ORIGIN C17: rel. to Middle Dutch *spra(e)yen* 'sprinkle'.

spray[2] ■ n. **1** a stem or small branch of a tree or plant, bearing flowers and foliage. **2** a bunch of cut flowers arranged in an attractive way.
– ORIGIN Middle English: representing Old English (*e*)*sprei*, recorded in personal and place names.

spraydeck ■ n. a flexible cover fitted to the opening in the top of a kayak to form a waterproof seal around the canoeist's body.

spray-dry ■ v. dry (a foodstuff or a ceramic material) by spraying particles of it into a current of hot air.
– DERIVATIVES **spray-dryer** n.

spray gun ■ n. a device resembling a gun which is used to spray a liquid such as paint under pressure.

sprayskirt ■ n. another term for SPRAYDECK.

spread ■ v. (past and past part. **spread**) **1** open out so as to increase in surface area, width, or length. ▸ stretch out (limbs, hands, fingers, or wings) so that they are far apart. **2** extend or distribute over a wide area or a specified period of time. ▸ (**spread out**) (of a group of people) move apart so as to cover a wider area. ▸ gradually reach or cause to reach a wider area or more people. **3** apply (a substance) in an even layer. ▸ cover (a surface) with a substance in such a way. ▸ be able to be applied in such a way. ■ n. **1** the fact or action of spreading. **2** the extent, width, or area covered by something. ▸ an expanse. **3** the range of something. ▸ the difference between two rates or prices. **4** a soft paste that can be spread on bread. **5** an article or advertisement covering several columns or pages of a newspaper or magazine. **6** N. Amer. a large farm or ranch. **7** informal a large and elaborate meal.
– PHRASES **spread oneself too thin** be involved in so many different activities that one's time and energy are not used to good effect.
– DERIVATIVES **spreadable** adj.
– ORIGIN Old English, of West Germanic origin.

spread betting ■ n. a form of betting in which the bettor wins or loses money according to the margin by which the value of a particular outcome varies from the spread of expected values quoted by the bookmaker.

spreadeagle ■ v. **1** (usu. **be spreadeagled**) stretch (someone) out with their arms and legs extended. **2** informal utterly defeat (an opponent in a sporting contest).

spreader ■ n. **1** a device for spreading. ▸ a bar attached to a yacht's mast so as to spread the angle of the upper shrouds. **2** a person who disseminates something.

spreadsheet ■ n. a computer program used chiefly for accounting, in which figures arranged in a grid can be manipulated and used in calculations.

spree ■ n. a spell of unrestrained activity of a particular kind.
– ORIGIN C18.

sprig[1] ■ n. 1 a small stem bearing leaves or flowers, taken from a bush or plant. 2 a descendant or younger member of a family or social class. ■ v. apply moulded decorations to (a piece of pottery). ▸ [as adj. **sprigged**] (of fabric or wallpaper) decorated with a design of sprigs.
– DERIVATIVES **spriggy** adj.
– ORIGIN Middle English: rel. to Low German *sprick*.

sprig[2] ■ n. a small tapering tack with no head, used chiefly to hold glass in a window frame until the putty dries.
– ORIGIN Middle English.

sprightly (also **spritely**) ■ adj. (-ier, -iest) (especially of an old person) lively; energetic.
– DERIVATIVES **sprightliness** n.
– ORIGIN late C16: from *spright*, rare var. of **SPRITE**.

spring ■ v. (past **sprang** or chiefly N. Amer. **sprung**; past part. **sprung**) 1 move suddenly or rapidly upwards or forwards. ▸ cause (a game bird) to rise from cover. 2 move suddenly by or as if by the action of a spring. 3 operate or cause to operate by means of a spring mechanism. 4 (**spring from**) originate or appear from. ▸ (**spring up**) suddenly develop or appear. ▸ (**spring something on**) present something suddenly or unexpectedly to. 5 informal bring about the escape or release of (a prisoner). 6 [usu. as adj. **sprung**] provide (a vehicle or item of furniture) with springs. 7 (of wood) become warped or split. 8 (**spring for**) N. Amer. & Austral. informal pay for. ■ n. 1 the season after winter and before summer, in which vegetation begins to appear. ▸ Astronomy the period from the vernal equinox to the summer solstice. 2 an elastic device, typically a helical metal coil, that can be pressed or pulled but returns to its former shape when released. ▸ elastic quality. 3 a sudden jump upwards or forwards. 4 a place where water wells up from an underground source. 5 an upward curvature of a ship's deck planking from the horizontal. ▸ a split in a wooden plank or spar under strain. 6 Nautical a hawser laid out from a ship's bow or stern and secured to a fixed point in order to prevent movement or assist manoeuvring.
– PHRASES **spring a leak** (of a boat or container) develop a leak. [orig. in nautical use, referring to timbers springing out of position.]
– DERIVATIVES **springless** adj. **springlet** n. (poetic/literary). **springlike** adj.
– ORIGIN Old English, of Germanic origin.

spring balance ■ n. a balance that measures weight by the tension of a spring.

springboard ■ n. 1 a strong, flexible board from which a diver or gymnast may jump in order to gain added impetus. 2 a thing providing impetus to an action or enterprise.

springbok /ˈsprɪŋbɒk/ ■ n. (also **springbuck**) a southern African gazelle with a characteristic habit of leaping when disturbed. [*Antidorcas marsupialis*.]
– ORIGIN C18: from Afrikaans, from Dutch *springen* 'to spring' + *bok* 'antelope'.

spring chicken ■ n. [usu. with neg.] informal a young person.

spring clean ■ n. a thorough cleaning of a house or room, typically undertaken in spring. ■ v. (**spring-clean**) clean thoroughly.

springe /sprɪn(d)ʒ/ ■ n. a noose or snare for catching small game.
– ORIGIN Middle English: from the base of **SPRING**.

springer ■ n. 1 (also **springer spaniel**) a small spaniel of a breed originally used to spring game. 2 Architecture the lowest stone in an arch, where the curve begins. 3 S. African another term for **LADYFISH**. 4 a cow near to calving.

spring fever ■ n. a feeling of restlessness and excitement felt at the beginning of spring.

spring greens ■ pl. n. the leaves of young cabbage plants of a variety that does not develop a heart.

springhare (also **springhaas**) ■ n. a nocturnal African rodent with powerful hind legs and feet, long ears, and a long bushy tail. [*Pedetes capensis*.]
– ORIGIN from S. African Dutch *springhaas*, from Dutch *spring* 'jumping' + *haas* 'hare'.

spring-loaded ■ adj. containing a compressed or stretched spring pressing one part against another.

spring lock ■ n. a type of lock with a spring-loaded bolt which requires a key only to open it, as distinct from a deadlock.

spring onion ■ n. an onion taken from the ground before the bulb has formed, typically eaten raw in salad.

spring roll ■ n. a Chinese snack consisting of a pancake filled with vegetables and sometimes meat, rolled into a cylinder and fried.

springtail ■ n. a minute wingless insect which has a spring-like organ under the abdomen that enables it to leap when disturbed. [Order Collembola.]

springtide ■ n. poetic/literary springtime.

spring tide ■ n. a tide just after a new or full moon, when there is the greatest difference between high and low water.

springy ■ adj. (-ier, -iest) 1 springing back quickly when squeezed or stretched. 2 (of movements) light and confident.
– DERIVATIVES **springily** adv. **springiness** n.

sprinkle ■ v. 1 scatter or pour small drops or particles over. ▸ scatter or pour (small drops or particles) over an object or surface. 2 distribute something randomly throughout. ■ n. 1 a small quantity or amount that is sprinkled. 2 (**sprinkles**) tiny sugar strands and balls used for decorating cakes and desserts.
– ORIGIN Middle English: perhaps from Middle Dutch *sprenkelen*.

sprinkler ■ n. 1 a device for watering lawns. 2 an automatic fire extinguisher installed in a ceiling.

sprinkling ■ n. a small, thinly distributed amount.

sprint ■ v. run at full speed over a short distance. ■ n. an act or spell of sprinting. ▸ a short, fast race.
– DERIVATIVES **sprinter** n. **sprinting** n.
– ORIGIN C18: rel. to Swedish *spritta*.

sprit ■ n. Nautical a small spar reaching diagonally from a mast to the upper outer corner of a sail.
– ORIGIN Old English *spréot* '(punting) pole'.

sprite ■ n. 1 an elf or fairy. 2 Computing a graphical figure which can be moved and manipulated as a single entity.
– ORIGIN Middle English: from *sprit*, a contraction of **SPIRIT**.

spritely ■ adj. variant spelling of **SPRIGHTLY**.

spritz ■ v. squirt or spray in quick short bursts at or on to. ■ n. an act or instance of spritzing.
– ORIGIN C20: from German *spritzen* 'to squirt'.

spritzer ■ n. a mixture of wine and soda water.
– ORIGIN 1960s: from German *Spritzer* 'a splash'.

sprocket ■ n. 1 each of several projections on the rim of a wheel that engage with the links of a chain or with holes in film, tape, or paper. 2 (also **sprocket wheel**) a wheel with projections of this kind.
– ORIGIN C16 (denoting a triangular piece of timber used in a roof).

sprog informal, chiefly derogatory Brit. ■ n. 1 a child. 2 military slang a recruit or trainee. ■ v. (**sprogged, sprogging**) have a baby.
– ORIGIN 1940s: perhaps from obsolete *sprag* 'lively young man'.

sprout ■ v. produce shoots. ▸ grow (plant shoots or hair). ▸ start to grow or develop. ■ n. 1 a shoot of a plant. 2 short for **BRUSSELS SPROUT**.
– ORIGIN Middle English: of West Germanic origin.

spruce[1] ■ adj. neat and smart. ■ v. (**spruce someone/thing up**) make a person or place smarter.
– DERIVATIVES **sprucely** adv. **spruceness** n.
– ORIGIN C16: perhaps from **SPRUCE**[2] in the obsolete sense 'Prussian'.

spruce[2] ■ n. a widespread coniferous tree which has a distinctive conical shape and hanging cones, grown for wood, pulp, and Christmas trees. [Genus *Picea*: many species.]
– ORIGIN Middle English: alteration of obsolete *Pruce* 'Prussia'.

sprue[1] /spruː/ ■ n. 1 a channel through which metal or

plastic is poured into a mould. **2** a piece of metal or plastic which has solidified in a sprue.
– ORIGIN C19.

sprue² /spruː/ ■ n. a disease characterized by ulceration of the mouth and chronic enteritis, suffered by visitors to tropical regions.
– ORIGIN C19: from Dutch *spruw* 'thrush'.

spruit /spreɪt/ ■ n. S. African a small watercourse, typically dry except during the rainy season.
– ORIGIN Afrikaans, from Dutch 'offshoot'.

sprung past participle and (especially in North America) past of SPRING.

spry ■ adj. (-er, -est) (especially of an old person) lively.
– DERIVATIVES **spryly** adv. **spryness** n.
– ORIGIN C18.

spud ■ n. **1** informal a potato. **2** a small, narrow spade. ■ v. (**spudded, spudding**) make the initial drilling for (an oil well).
– ORIGIN Middle English.

spud wrench ■ n. a long bar with a socket on the end for tightening bolts.

spumante /spuːˈmanteɪ, -ˈmanti/ ■ n. an Italian sparkling white wine.
– ORIGIN Italian, 'sparkling'.

spume /spjuːm/ poetic/literary ■ n. froth or foam, especially that found on waves. ■ v. froth or foam.
– DERIVATIVES **spumous** adj. **spumy** adj.
– ORIGIN Middle English: from Old French (*e*)*spume* or Latin *spuma*.

spun past and past participle of SPIN.

spunk ■ n. **1** informal courage and determination. **2** Brit. vulgar slang semen.
– DERIVATIVES **spunkily** adv. **spunky** adj. (-ier, -iest).
– ORIGIN C16: perhaps a blend of SPARK¹ and obsolete *funk* 'spark'.

spun sugar ■ n. stiff sugar syrup drawn out into long filaments and used to make candyfloss or as a decoration for sweet dishes.

spur ■ n. **1** a device with a small spike or a spiked wheel, worn on a rider's heel for urging a horse forward. **2** an incentive. **3** a projection from a mountain or mountain range. ▸ Botany a slender tubular projection from the base of a flower, e.g. an orchid, typically containing nectar. ▸ a short fruit-bearing side shoot. ▸ a horny spike on the back of the leg of a cock or male game bird. **4** a short branch road or railway line. **5** a small support for ceramic ware in a kiln. ■ v. (**spurred, spurring**) **1** urge (a horse) forward with spurs. **2** (often **spur someone on**) encourage; give an incentive to. **3** prune in (a side shoot) so as to form a spur close to the stem.
– PHRASES **on the spur of the moment** on a momentary impulse.
– DERIVATIVES **spurless** adj. **spurred** adj.
– ORIGIN Old English, of Germanic origin.

spurge /spɜːdʒ/ ■ n. a plant or shrub with milky latex and small, typically greenish flowers. [Genus *Euphorbia*: numerous species.]
– ORIGIN Middle English: shortening of Old French *espurge*, from *espurgier*, from Latin *expurgare* 'cleanse' (because of the purgative properties of the milky latex).

spur gear ■ n. another term for SPUR WHEEL.

spurious /ˈspjʊərɪəs/ ■ adj. **1** false or fake. **2** (of a line of reasoning) apparently but not actually valid.
– DERIVATIVES **spuriously** adv. **spuriousness** n.
– ORIGIN C16: from Latin *spurius* 'false'.

spurn ■ v. reject with disdain or contempt.
– DERIVATIVES **spurner** n.
– ORIGIN Old English, rel. to Latin *spernere* 'to scorn'.

spurrey /ˈspʌri/ (also **spurry**) ■ n. (pl. -eys or -ies) a small plant of the pink family with pink or white flowers. [Genera *Spergula* and *Spergularia*: several species.]
– ORIGIN C16: from Dutch *spurrie*; prob. rel. to medieval Latin *spergula*.

spurt ■ v. **1** gush or cause to gush out in a sudden stream. **2** move with a sudden burst of speed. ■ n. **1** a sudden gushing stream. **2** a sudden burst of activity or speed.
– ORIGIN C16.

spur wheel ■ n. a gearwheel with teeth projecting parallel to the wheel's axis.

sputnik /ˈspʊtnɪk, ˈspʌt-/ ■ n. each of a series of Soviet satellites, the first of which (launched in October 1957) was the first artificial satellite to be placed in orbit.
– ORIGIN Russian, 'fellow-traveller'.

sputter ■ v. **1** make a series of soft explosive sounds. **2** speak in a series of incoherent bursts. **3** Physics deposit (metal) on a surface by using fast ions to eject particles of it from a target. ■ n. a sputtering sound.
– DERIVATIVES **sputterer** n.
– ORIGIN C16: from Dutch *sputteren*, of imitative origin.

sputum /ˈspjuːtəm/ ■ n. a mixture of saliva and mucus coughed up from the respiratory tract, typically as a result of infection or other disease.
– ORIGIN C17: from Latin, from *spuere* 'to spit'.

spy ■ n. (pl. **-ies**) **1** a person employed by a government or other organization to collect and report secret information on an enemy or competitor. **2** a person who observes others secretly. ■ v. (-ies, -ied) **1** be a spy. ▸ (**spy on**) observe furtively. **2** observe or notice.
– PHRASES **spy out the land** collect information about a situation before deciding how to act.
– ORIGIN Middle English: shortening of Old French *espie* 'espying', *espier* 'espy', of Germanic origin.

spyglass ■ n. a small telescope.

spyhole ■ n. Brit. a peephole.

spyware ■ n. Computing software that enables a user to obtain covert information about someone's computer activities by transmitting data covertly from their hard drive.

SQ (also **sq**) ■ abbrev. according to quantity (ordered), typically used of a price on a restaurant menu.
– ORIGIN from French *selon quantité*.

sq ■ abbrev. square.

SQL ■ abbrev. Computing Structured Query Language, an international standard for database manipulation.

Sqn Ldr ■ abbrev. Squadron Leader.

squab /skwɒb/ ■ n. **1** a young unfledged pigeon. **2** Brit. the padded back or side of a vehicle seat. ▸ a thick cushion, especially one covering the seat of a chair or sofa.
– ORIGIN C17: cf. obsolete *quab* 'shapeless thing' and Swedish dialect *skvabba* 'fat woman'.

squabble ■ n. a trivial noisy quarrel. ■ v. engage in a squabble.
– DERIVATIVES **squabbler** n.
– ORIGIN C17: prob. imitative; cf. Swedish dialect *skvabbel* 'a dispute'.

squab pie ■ n. Brit. pigeon pie.

squacco heron /ˈskwakəʊ/ ■ n. a small crested buff and white heron found in southern Europe, the Middle East, and Africa. [*Ardeola ralloides*.]
– ORIGIN C18: *squacco* from Italian dialect *sguacco*.

squad ■ n. [treated as sing. or pl.] **1** a small number of soldiers assembled for drill or assigned to a particular task. **2** a group of sports players from which a team is chosen. **3** a division of a police force dealing with a particular type of crime.
– ORIGIN C17: shortening of French *escouade*, var. of *escadre*, from Italian *squadra* 'square'.

squad car ■ n. a police patrol car.

squaddie (also **squaddy**) ■ n. (pl. -ies) Brit. informal a private soldier.

squadron ■ n. **1** an operational unit in an air force consisting of two or more flights of aircraft. **2** a principal division of an armoured regiment, consisting of two or more troops. **3** a group of warships detached on a particular duty or under the command of a flag officer.
– ORIGIN C16: from Italian *squadrone*, from *squadra* 'square'.

squadron leader ■ n. a rank of officer in the RAF, above flight lieutenant and below wing commander.

squalid ■ adj. **1** extremely dirty and unpleasant. **2** showing a contemptible lack of moral standards.
– DERIVATIVES **squalidly** adv. **squalidness** n.
– ORIGIN C16: from Latin *squalidus*, from *squalere* 'be rough or dirty'.

squall

squall /skwɔːl/ ■ n. **1** a sudden violent gust of wind or localized storm, especially one bringing rain, snow, or sleet. **2** a loud cry. ■ v. (of a baby or small child) cry noisily and continuously.
– DERIVATIVES **squally** adj.
– ORIGIN C17: prob. an alteration of SQUEAL, influenced by BAWL.

squall line ■ n. Meteorology a narrow band of high winds and storms associated with a cold front.

squalor /ˈskwɒlə/ ■ n. the state of being squalid.
– ORIGIN C17: from Latin, from *squalere* 'be dirty'.

Squamata /skwəˈmɑːtə/ ■ pl. n. Zoology a large order of reptiles comprising the snakes, lizards, and worm lizards.
– DERIVATIVES **squamate** adj. & n.
– ORIGIN from Latin *squama* 'scale'.

squamous /ˈskweɪməs/ ■ adj. **1** covered with or characterized by scales. **2** Anatomy of or denoting a layer of epithelium consisting of very thin flattened cells. **3** Anatomy denoting the flat portion of the temporal bone which forms part of the side of the skull.
– ORIGIN Middle English: from Latin *squamosus*, from *squama* 'scale'.

squander ■ v. waste in a reckless or foolish manner.
– DERIVATIVES **squanderer** n.
– ORIGIN C16.

square ■ n. **1** a plane figure with four equal straight sides and four right angles. **2** an open, typically four-sided, area surrounded by buildings. **3** an area within a military barracks or camp used for drill. **4** Cricket a closer-cut area at the centre of a ground, any strip of which may be prepared as a wicket. **5** the product of a number multiplied by itself. **6** an L-shaped or T-shaped instrument used for obtaining or testing right angles. **7** informal a person considered to be old-fashioned or boringly conventional. ■ adj. **1** having the shape or approximate shape of a square. ▸ having or forming a right angle, exactly or approximately. **2** denoting a unit of measurement equal to the area of a square whose side is of the unit specified. ▸ [postpos.] denoting the length of each side of a square shape or object. **3** at right angles. ▸ Cricket & Soccer in a direction transversely across the field or pitch. **4** broad and solid in shape. **5** level or parallel. ▸ properly arranged. ▸ on even terms. **6** fair and honest. **7** informal old-fashioned or boringly conventional. **8** (of rhythm) simple and straightforward. ■ adv. **1** directly; straight. **2** Cricket & Soccer in a direction transversely across the field or pitch. ■ v. **1** make square or rectangular. ▸ [usu. as adj. **squared**] mark out in squares. **2** multiply (a number) by itself. **3** make or be compatible. **4** balance (an account) or settle (a bill or debt). ▸ make the score of (a match or game) even. **5** informal secure the help or acquiescence of (someone), especially by offering an inducement. **6** bring (one's shoulders) into a position in which they appear square and broad. **7** Nautical set (a yard or other part of a ship) at right angles to the keel or other point of reference.
– PHRASES **back to** (or **at**) **square one** informal back to where one started, with no progress having been made. **on the square 1** informal honest; straightforward. **2** having membership of the Freemasons. **out of square** not at right angles. **square the circle 1** construct a square equal in area to a given circle (a problem incapable of a purely geometrical solution). **2** do something considered to be impossible. **a square deal** see DEAL[1]. **a square peg in a round hole** see PEG.
– PHRASAL VERBS **square something away** N. Amer. deal with something in a satisfactory way. **square off** N. Amer. another way of saying square up. **square up 1** assume the attitude of a person about to fight. **2** (**square up to**) face and tackle (a difficulty or problem) resolutely.
– DERIVATIVES **squareness** n. **squarer** n. **squarish** adj.
– ORIGIN Middle English: shortening of Old French *esquare* (n.), *esquarrer* (v.), from Latin *quadra* 'square'.

square-bashing ■ n. Brit. informal military drill performed repeatedly on a barrack square.

square dance ■ n. a country dance that starts with four couples facing one another in a square, with the steps and movements shouted out by a caller.
– DERIVATIVES **square dancer** n.

square eyes ■ pl. n. humorous eyes supposedly affected by excessive television viewing.
– DERIVATIVES **square-eyed** adj.

square knot ■ n. another term for REEF KNOT.

square leg ■ n. Cricket a fielding position level with the batsman approximately halfway towards the boundary on the leg side.

squarely ■ adv. without deviation or equivocation; directly.

square meal ■ n. a substantial and balanced meal.
– ORIGIN said to derive from nautical use, with ref. to the square platters on which meals were served.

square measure ■ n. a unit of measurement relating to area.

square number ■ n. the product of a number multiplied by itself, e.g. 1, 4, 9, 16, with respect to 1, 2, 3, 4.

square-rigged ■ adj. (of a sailing ship) having the principal sails at right angles to the length of the ship, supported by horizontal yards attached to the mast or masts.

square-rigger ■ n. a square-rigged sailing ship.

square root ■ n. a number which produces a specified quantity when multiplied by itself.

square-toed ■ adj. (of shoes) having broad, square toes.

square wave ■ n. Electronics a periodic wave that varies abruptly in amplitude between two fixed values.

squash[1] ■ v. **1** crush or squeeze (something) so that it becomes flat, soft, or out of shape. ▸ squeeze or force into a restricted space. **2** suppress or subdue. ▸ firmly reject (an idea or suggestion). ▸ silence (someone), typically with a humiliating remark. ■ n. **1** a state of being squashed. **2** a concentrated liquid made from fruit juice and sugar, diluted to make a drink. **3** (also **squash rackets**) a game in which two players use rackets to hit a small, soft rubber ball against the walls of a closed court.
– DERIVATIVES **squashily** adv. **squashiness** n. **squashy** adj. (**-ier**, **-iest**).
– ORIGIN C16: alteration of QUASH.

squash[2] ■ n. (pl. same or **squashes**) **1** a gourd with flesh that can be cooked and eaten as a vegetable. **2** the plant which produces such gourds. [Several species and varieties of the genus *Cucurbita*.]
– ORIGIN C17: abbrev. of Narragansett (an extinct Algonquian language) *asquutasquash*.

squat ■ v. (**squatted**, **squatting**) **1** crouch or sit with the knees bent and the heels close to or touching the buttocks or thighs. **2** unlawfully occupy an uninhabited building or area of land. ■ adj. (**squatter**, **squattest**) short or low, and disproportionately broad or wide. ■ n. **1** a squatting position or movement. ▸ Weightlifting an exercise in which a person squats down and rises again with a barbell behind their neck. **2** a building occupied by squatters. ▸ an act of squatting in an uninhabited building. **3** informal, chiefly N. Amer. short for DIDDLY-SQUAT.
– DERIVATIVES **squatly** adv. **squatness** n.
– ORIGIN Middle English: from Old French *esquatir* 'flatten', from Latin *coactus*, from *cogere* 'compel'.

squatter ■ n. a person who squats in a building or on unused land.

squatter camp ■ n. another term for INFORMAL SETTLEMENT.

squat thrust ■ n. an exercise in which the legs are thrust backwards to their full extent from a squatting position with the hands on the floor.

squaw /skwɔː/ ■ n. offensive an American Indian woman or wife.
– ORIGIN C17: from Narragansett (an extinct Algonquian language) *squaws* 'woman'.

squawk ■ v. **1** (of a bird) make a loud, harsh noise. **2** say something in a loud, discordant tone. ▸ complain about something. ■ n. an act of squawking.
– DERIVATIVES **squawker** n.
– ORIGIN C19: imitative.

squeak ■ n. a short, high-pitched sound or cry. ▸ [with neg.] a single remark or communication. ■ v. **1** make a squeak. ▸ say something in a high-pitched tone. **2** informal inform on someone. **3** informal achieve something by a narrow margin.

squeaker ■ n. 1 a person or thing that squeaks. 2 a young pigeon.
– DERIVATIVES **squeakily** adv. **squeakiness** n. **squeaky** adj. (**-ier**, **-iest**).
– ORIGIN Middle English: imitative.

squeaky clean ■ adj. informal 1 completely clean. 2 beyond reproach.

squeal ■ n. a long, high-pitched cry or noise. ■ v. 1 make a squeal. ▶ say something in a high-pitched, excited tone. 2 complain. 3 informal inform on someone.
– DERIVATIVES **squealer** n.
– ORIGIN Middle English: imitative.

squeamish ■ adj. 1 easily nauseated or disgusted. 2 having fastidious moral views.
– DERIVATIVES **squeamishly** adv. **squeamishness** n.
– ORIGIN Middle English: alteration of dialect *squeamous*, from Anglo-Norman French *escoymos*.

squeegee /'skwiːdʒiː/ ■ n. a scraping implement with a rubber-edged blade, typically used for cleaning windows. ▶ a similar small instrument or roller used especially in developing photographs. ■ v. (**squeegees**, **squeegeed**, **squeegeeing**) clean or scrape with a squeegee.
– ORIGIN C19: from archaic *squeege* 'to press', form of SQUEEZE.

squeeze ■ v. 1 firmly press from opposite or all sides, typically with the fingers. ▶ extract (liquid or a soft substance) from something by squeezing. 2 (usu. **squeeze something out of/from**) obtain from someone with difficulty. ▶ informal put pressure on (someone) to supply information, authorization, etc. ▶ have a damaging or restricting effect on: *the economy is being squeezed by foreign debt repayments*. ▶ Bridge force (an opponent) to discard a guarding or potentially winning card. 3 (**squeeze something off**) informal shoot a round or shot from a gun. ▶ take a photograph. 4 (**squeeze in/into/through**) manage to get into or through (a restricted space). ▶ (**squeeze up**) move closer to and press tightly against someone or something. ▶ (**squeeze someone/thing in**) manage to find time for someone or something. ▶ (**squeeze someone/thing out**) force someone or something out of a domain or activity. ■ n. 1 an act of squeezing or state of being squeezed. 2 a hug. 3 a small amount of liquid extracted by squeezing. 4 dated a crowded social gathering. 5 a strong financial demand or pressure. ▶ informal money illegally extorted or exacted from someone. 6 a moulding or cast of an object, or a copy of a design, obtained by pressing a pliable substance round or over it. 7 Bridge a tactic that forces an opponent to discard an important card. 8 (also **squeeze play**) Baseball an act of hitting a ball short to the infield to enable a runner on third base to start for home as soon as the ball is pitched. 9 (often **main squeeze**) N. Amer. informal a person's girlfriend or boyfriend.
– PHRASES **put the squeeze on** informal coerce or pressurize.
– DERIVATIVES **squeezable** adj. **squeezer** n.
– ORIGIN C16: from earlier *squise*, from obsolete *queise*.

squeeze box ■ n. informal an accordion or concertina.

squeezy ■ adj. (especially of a container) flexible and able to be squeezed to force out the contents.

squelch ■ v. 1 make a soft sucking sound as that of treading in thick mud. 2 informal forcefully silence or suppress. ■ n. 1 a squelching sound. 2 Electronics a circuit that suppresses the output of a radio receiver if the signal strength falls below a certain level.
– DERIVATIVES **squelcher** n. **squelchy** adj.
– ORIGIN C17: imitative.

squib ■ n. 1 a small firework that hisses before exploding. 2 a short piece of satirical writing. 3 informal a small or weak person.
– ORIGIN C16: perhaps imitative of a small explosion.

SQUID ■ abbrev. Physics superconducting quantum interference device (used in very sensitive magnetometers).

squid ■ n. (pl. same or **squids**) an elongated, fast-swimming cephalopod mollusc with eight arms and two long tentacles. [*Loligo* and other genera: many species.] ▶ the flesh of this animal as food. ▶ an artificial fishing bait resembling a squid.
– ORIGIN C16.

squidge ■ v. informal squash or crush. ▶ squelch.

– ORIGIN C19: perhaps imitative.

squidgy ■ adj. (**-ier**, **-iest**) informal, chiefly Brit. soft and moist.

squiffy ■ adj. (**-ier**, **-iest**) informal 1 chiefly Brit. slightly drunk. 2 askew; awry.
– ORIGIN C19.

squiggle ■ n. a short line that curls and loops irregularly. ■ v. chiefly N. Amer. wriggle; squirm.
– DERIVATIVES **squiggly** adj.
– ORIGIN C19: perhaps a blend of SQUIRM and WIGGLE or WRIGGLE.

squill ■ n. a small plant resembling a hyacinth, with clusters of violet-blue or blue-striped flowers. [Genera *Scilla* and *Puschkinia*.]
– ORIGIN Middle English: from Greek *skilla*.

squillion /'skwɪljən/ ■ cardinal number (pl. **squillions** or (with numeral) same) informal an indefinite very large number.
– ORIGIN 1940s: fanciful formation on the pattern of *billion* and *trillion*.

squinch[1] ■ n. a straight or arched structure across an interior angle of a square tower, bearing a superstructure such as a dome.
– ORIGIN C15: alteration of obsolete *scunch*.

squinch[2] ■ v. chiefly N. Amer. tense up the muscles of (one's eyes or face).
– ORIGIN C19: perhaps a blend of SQUEEZE and PINCH.

squint ■ v. 1 look at someone or something with partly closed eyes. ▶ partly close (one's eyes). 2 have a squint affecting one eye. ■ n. 1 a permanent deviation in the direction of the gaze of one eye. 2 informal a quick or casual look.
– DERIVATIVES **squinter** n. **squinty** adj.
– ORIGIN C16: shortening of obsolete *asquint* 'with a glance to one side', perhaps from A-[2] + a Low German or Dutch word rel. to modern Dutch *schuinte* 'slant'.

squint-eyed ■ adj. derogatory having a squint.

squire ■ n. 1 chiefly Brit. a country gentleman, especially the chief landowner in an area. 2 Brit. informal used as a friendly form of address by one man to another. 3 historical a young nobleman acting as an attendant to a knight before becoming a knight himself. ■ v. (of a man) accompany or escort (a woman). ▶ dated (of a man) have a romantic relationship with (a woman).
– DERIVATIVES **squiredom** n. **squireship** n.
– ORIGIN Middle English: shortening of Old French *esquier* 'esquire'.

squirearchy /'skwʌɪəˌrɑːki/ ■ n. (pl. **-ies**) landowners collectively.
– DERIVATIVES **squirearch** n. **squirearchical** adj.
– ORIGIN C18: from SQUIRE, on the pattern of *hierarchy*.

squirm ■ v. wriggle or twist the body from side to side, especially due to nervousness or discomfort. ▶ be embarrassed or ashamed. ■ n. a wriggling movement.
– DERIVATIVES **squirmer** n. **squirmy** adj.
– ORIGIN C17: symbolic of writhing movement; prob. associated with WORM.

squirrel ■ n. an agile tree-dwelling rodent with a bushy tail, typically feeding on nuts and seeds. [*Sciurus* and other genera: numerous species.] ▶ used in names of other rodents of the same family (Sciuridae), e.g. ground squirrel. ■ v. (**squirrelled**, **squirrelling**; US also **squirreled**, **squirreling**) 1 (**squirrel something away**) hide money or valuables in a safe place. 2 move about inquisitively or busily.
– ORIGIN Middle English: shortening of Old French *esquireul*, from a diminutive of Latin *sciurus*, from Greek *skiouros*, from *skia* 'shade' + *oura* 'tail'.

squirrel cage ■ n. 1 a rotating cylindrical cage in which a small captive animal can exercise as on a treadmill. 2 a monotonous or repetitive activity. 3 a form of rotor in small electric motors, resembling a squirrel cage.

squirrelfish ■ n. (pl. same or **-fishes**) a large-eyed marine fish, typically brightly coloured, that lives around reefs in warm seas. [Family Holocentridae: several species.]

squirrelly ■ adj. 1 relating to or resembling a squirrel. 2 informal, chiefly N. Amer. restless or nervous. ▶ eccentric.

squirt ■ v. 1 (with reference to a liquid) be or cause to be

squirt gun

ejected in a thin jet from a small opening. ▸ wet with a jet of liquid. **2** transmit (information) in highly compressed or speeded-up form. ■ *n*. **1** a thin jet of liquid. ▸ a device from which liquid may be squirted. **2** *informal* a puny or insignificant person. **3** a compressed radio signal transmitted at high speed.
– DERIVATIVES **squirter** *n*.
– ORIGIN Middle English: imitative.

squirt gun ■ *n*. N. Amer. a water pistol.

squish ■ *v*. make a soft squelching sound. ▸ *informal* squash. ▸ (**squish in/into**) *informal* squeeze oneself into. ■ *n*. a soft squelching sound.
– DERIVATIVES **squishy** *adj*. (**-ier**, **-iest**).
– ORIGIN C17: imitative.

squitters (also **the squits**) ■ *pl. n. informal* diarrhoea.
– ORIGIN C17: perhaps from dialect *squit* 'to squirt'.

squiz ■ *n*. S. African & Austral./NZ *informal* a look or glance.
– ORIGIN C20: prob. a blend of QUIZ[2] and SQUINT.

Sr ■ *abbrev*. **1** senior (in names). **2** Señor. **3** Signor. **4** Sister (in a religious order). ■ *symb*. the chemical element strontium.

sr ■ *abbrev*. steradian(s).

SRAM ■ *abbrev. Electronics* static random-access memory.

SRC ■ *abbrev*. Student Representative Council.

Sri Lankan /srɪ ˈlaŋkən, ʃrɪ/ ■ *n*. a native or inhabitant of Sri Lanka. ■ *adj*. of or relating to Sri Lanka.

SRN ■ *abbrev*. (in the UK) State Registered Nurse.

SS[1] ■ *abbrev*. **1** Saints. **2** steamship.

SS[2] ■ *n*. the Nazi special police force.
– ORIGIN *abbrev*. of German *Schutzstaffel* 'defence squadron'.

SSC ■ *abbrev. Physics* superconducting super collider.

SSE ■ *abbrev*. south-south-east.

SSL ■ *abbrev. Computing* Secure Sockets Layer, a protocol which uses public key encryption for the secure transmission of data over the Internet.

ssp. ■ *abbrev*. subspecies.

SSRI ■ *abbrev. Medicine* selective serotonin reuptake inhibitor, any of a group of antidepressant drugs (including Prozac) which inhibit the uptake of serotonin in the brain.

SSW ■ *abbrev*. south-south-west.

St ■ *abbrev*. **1** Saint. **2** Street.

st ■ *abbrev*. **1** stone (in weight). **2** *Cricket* (on scorecards) stumped by.

-st ■ *suffix* variant of -EST[2].

Sta. ■ *abbrev*. railway station.

stab ■ *v*. (**stabbed**, **stabbing**) **1** thrust a knife or other pointed weapon into. **2** thrust a pointed object at. **3** (usu. **stab at**) (of a pain or painful thing) cause a sudden sharp sensation. ■ *n*. **1** an act of stabbing. ▸ a wound made by stabbing. **2** a sudden sharp feeling or pain. **3** (**a stab at**) *informal* an attempt to do.
– PHRASES **stab someone in the back** betray someone.
– DERIVATIVES **stabber** *n*. **stabbing** *n*. & *adj*.
– ORIGIN Middle English.

Stabat Mater /ˌstɑːbat ˈmɑːtə, ˈmeɪtə/ ■ *n*. a medieval Latin hymn on the suffering of the Virgin Mary at the Crucifixion.
– ORIGIN from the opening words *Stabat mater dolorosa* 'Stood the mother, full of grief'.

stability ■ *n*. the state of being stable.

stabilize (also **-ise**) ■ *v*. make or become stable.
– DERIVATIVES **stabilization** (also **-isation**) *n*.

stabilizer (also **-iser**) ■ *n*. **1** the horizontal tailplane of an aircraft. **2** a gyroscopic device used to reduce the rolling of a ship. **3** (**stabilizers**) a pair of small supporting wheels fitted on a child's bicycle. **4** a substance preventing the breakdown of emulsions, especially in food or paint.

stable[1] ■ *adj*. (**-er**, **-est**) **1** not likely to give way or overturn; firmly fixed. **2** not deteriorating in health after an injury or operation. **3** emotionally well-balanced. **4** not likely to change or fail. **5** not liable to undergo chemical decomposition or radioactive decay.
– DERIVATIVES **stably** *adv*.
– ORIGIN Middle English: from Latin *stabilis*, from the base of *stare* 'to stand'.

stable[2] ■ *n*. **1** a building for housing horses. **2** an establishment where racehorses are kept and trained. **3** an establishment producing particular types of people or things. ■ *v*. put or keep (a horse) in a stable.
– DERIVATIVES **stableful** *n*. (pl. **-fuls**).
– ORIGIN Middle English: shortening of Old French *estable* 'stable, pigsty', from Latin *stabulum*, from the base of *stare* 'to stand'.

stable boy (or **stable girl**, also Brit. **stable lad**) ■ *n*. a boy or man (or girl or woman) employed in a stable.

stable companion ■ *n*. a stablemate.

stable door ■ *n*. a door of a kind found in a stable, divided into two parts horizontally so that one half may be shut and the other left open.

Stableford /ˈsteɪb(ə)lfəd/ ■ *n*. a form of strokeplay golf in which points are awarded according to the number of strokes taken to complete each hole.
– ORIGIN named after its American inventor Frank B. Stableford.

stablemate ■ *n*. **1** a horse, especially a racehorse, from the same stable as another. **2** a person or product from the same organization or background as another.

stabling ■ *n*. accommodation for horses.

staccato /stəˈkɑːtəʊ/ ■ *adv*. & *adj*. with each sound or note sharply detached or separated from the others. ■ *n*. (pl. **-os**) a series of short, detached sounds or words.
– ORIGIN Italian, 'detached'.

stack ■ *n*. **1** a pile, especially a neat one. **2** a rectangular or cylindrical pile of hay, straw, etc. **3** *informal* a large quantity of something. **4** a vertical arrangement of hi-fi or guitar amplification equipment. **5** a number of aircraft flying in circles at different altitudes around the same point while waiting to land at an airport. **6** a pyramidal group of rifles. **7** (**the stacks**) compact units of shelving in part of a library normally closed to the public. **8** *Computing* a set of storage locations from which the most recently stored item is the first to be retrieved. **9** a chimney or vertical exhaust pipe. ■ *v*. **1** arrange in a stack. ▸ fill or cover with stacks of things. **2** cause (aircraft) to fly in stacks. **3** shuffle or arrange (a pack of cards) dishonestly. **4** (**be stacked against/in favour of**) (of a situation) be overwhelmingly likely to produce an unfavourable or favourable outcome for. **5** (**stack up**) N. Amer. *informal* measure up; compare. **6** (in snowboarding) fall over.
– DERIVATIVES **stackable** *adj*. **stacker** *n*.
– ORIGIN Middle English: from Old Norse *stakkr* 'haystack', of Germanic origin.

stacked ■ *adj*. **1** arranged in a stack or stacks. **2** filled or covered with goods. **3** (of a heel) made from thin layers of wood or leather glued one on top of the other. **4** (of a pack of cards) shuffled or arranged dishonestly. **5** *informal* (of a woman) having large breasts.

stadium ■ *n*. (pl. **stadiums** or **stadia** /ˈsteɪdɪə/) an athletic or sports ground with tiers of seats for spectators.
– ORIGIN Middle English: from Greek *stadion*.

stadtholder /ˈstadˌhəʊldə, ˈstat-/ (also **stadholder**) ■ *n*. *historical* the chief magistrate of the United Provinces of the Netherlands.
– DERIVATIVES **stadtholdership** *n*.
– ORIGIN C16: from Dutch *stadhouder* 'deputy', from *stad* 'place' + *houder* 'holder'.

staff ■ *n*. **1** [treated as sing. or pl.] the employees of a particular organization. **2** [treated as sing. or pl.] a group of officers assisting an officer in command of an army formation or administration headquarters. ▸ (usu. **Staff**) short for STAFF SERGEANT. **3** a long stick used as a support or weapon. ▸ a rod or sceptre held as a sign of office or authority. ▸ *Surveying* a rod for measuring distances or heights. **4** *Music* another term for STAVE (in sense 2). ■ *v*. (usu. **be staffed**) provide with staff.
– PHRASES **the staff of life** bread or another staple food.
– ORIGIN Old English, of Germanic origin.

staffage /stəˈfɑːʒ/ ■ *n*. accessory items in a painting, especially figures in a landscape.
– ORIGIN C19: from German, from *staffieren* 'decorate', perhaps from Old French *estoffer*, from *estoffe* 'stuff'.

staff college ■ n. a college at which military officers are trained for staff duties.

staffer ■ n. a member of a staff.

staff notation ■ n. Music notation by means of a stave, especially as distinct from the tonic sol-fa.

staff nurse ■ n. an experienced nurse less senior than a sister or charge nurse.

staff officer ■ n. a military officer serving on the staff of a headquarters or government department.

Staffordshire bull terrier ■ n. a terrier of a small, stocky breed, with a short, broad head and dropped ears.

staffroom ■ n. a common room for teachers in a school or college.

staff sergeant ■ n. a rank of non-commissioned officer in the army, above sergeant and below warrant officer.

stag ■ n. 1 a fully adult male deer. 2 [as modifier] denoting a social gathering attended by men only. 3 Stock Exchange a person who applies for shares in a new issue with a view to selling at once for a profit. ■ v. (**stagged, stagging**) Stock Exchange buy (shares in a new issue) and sell them at once for a profit.
– ORIGIN Middle English: rel. to Old Norse *steggr* 'male bird'.

stag beetle ■ n. a large dark beetle, the male of which has large branched jaws resembling antlers. [*Lucanus cervus* and other species.]

stage ■ n. 1 a point, period, or step in a process or development. ▸ a section of a journey or race. 2 each of two or more sections of a rocket or spacecraft that are jettisoned in turn when their propellant is exhausted. 3 Electronics a part of a circuit containing a single amplifying transistor or valve. 4 a raised floor or platform on which actors, entertainers, or speakers perform. ▸ (**the stage**) the acting or theatrical profession. 5 a scene of action or forum of debate. 6 (on a microscope) a raised plate on which a slide or specimen is placed for examination. 7 Geology a range of strata corresponding to an age in time, forming a subdivision of a series. 8 archaic term for STAGECOACH. ■ v. present a performance of (a play or other show). ▸ organize and participate in (a public event). ▸ cause (something dramatic or unexpected) to happen.
– PHRASES **hold the stage** dominate a scene of action or forum of debate. **set the stage for** prepare the conditions for. **stage left** (or **right**) on the left (or right) side of a stage from the point of view of a performer facing the audience.
– DERIVATIVES **stageability** n. **stageable** adj.
– ORIGIN Middle English: shortening of Old French *estage* 'dwelling', from Latin *stare* 'to stand'.

stagecoach ■ n. a large closed horse-drawn vehicle formerly used to carry passengers and often mail along a regular route.

stagecraft ■ n. skill in writing or staging plays.

stage direction ■ n. an instruction in a play script indicating the position or tone of an actor, or specifying sound effects, lighting, etc.

stage door ■ n. a staff entrance from the street to the backstage area of a theatre.

stage fright ■ n. nervousness before or during a performance.

stagehand ■ n. a person dealing with scenery or props during a play.

stage-manage ■ v. 1 be the stage manager of. 2 arrange carefully to create a certain effect.
– DERIVATIVES **stage management** n.

stage manager ■ n. the person responsible for lighting and other technical arrangements for a stage play.

stage name ■ n. a name assumed for professional purposes by an actor.

stage-struck ■ adj. having a passionate love of the theatre and wishing to become an actor.

stage whisper ■ n. a loud whisper by an actor on stage, intended to be heard by the audience.

stagey ■ adj. variant spelling of STAGY.

stagflation ■ n. Economics persistent high inflation combined with high unemployment and stagnant demand in a country's economy.
– ORIGIN 1960s: blend of *stagnation* and INFLATION.

stagger ■ v. 1 walk or move unsteadily, as if about to fall. 2 astonish. 3 spread over a period of time. 4 arrange (objects or parts) so that they are not in line. ■ n. 1 an act of staggering. 2 (**the stagger**) the staggered arrangement of the runners on a track at the start of a race.
– DERIVATIVES **staggering** n. & adj. **staggeringly** adv.
– ORIGIN Middle English: from Old Norse *stakra*, from *staka* 'push, stagger'.

staggers ■ pl. n. [usu. treated as sing.] 1 a diseased condition of farm animals manifested by staggering or loss of balance. 2 (**the staggers**) the inability to stand or walk steadily.

staghorn fern (also **stag's-horn fern**) ■ n. a fern with fronds that resemble antlers, occurring in tropical rainforests and typically epiphytic. [Genus *Platycerium*.]

staging ■ n. 1 an instance or method of staging something. 2 a stage or set of stages or platforms for performers or between levels of scaffolding. ▸ Brit. shelving for plants in a greenhouse.

staging area ■ n. a stopping place or assembly point en route to a destination.

staging post ■ n. a place at which people or vehicles regularly stop during a journey.

stagnant /'stagnənt/ ■ adj. (of water or air) motionless and often having an unpleasant smell as a consequence. ▸ showing little activity.
– DERIVATIVES **stagnancy** n. **stagnantly** adv.
– ORIGIN C17: from Latin *stagnare* 'form a pool of standing water', from *stagnum* 'pool'.

stagnate /stag'neɪt, 'stagneɪt/ ■ v. become stagnant.
– DERIVATIVES **stagnation** n.
– ORIGIN C17: from Latin *stagnare* 'settle as a still pool', from *stagnum* 'pool'.

stag night (also **stag party**) ■ n. an all-male celebration, especially one held for a man about to be married.

stagy /'steɪdʒi/ (also **stagey**) ■ adj. (**-ier, -iest**) excessively theatrical or exaggerated.
– DERIVATIVES **stagily** adv. **staginess** n.

staid ■ adj. respectable and unadventurous.
– DERIVATIVES **staidly** adv. **staidness** n.
– ORIGIN C16: archaic past participle of STAY[1].

stain ■ v. 1 mark or discolour with something that is not easily removed. 2 damage (someone's or something's reputation). 3 colour with a penetrative dye or chemical. ■ n. 1 a stubborn discoloured patch or dirty mark. 2 a thing that damages a reputation. 3 a dye or chemical used to colour materials. ▸ Biology a dye used to colour organic tissue for laboratory study.
– DERIVATIVES **stainable** adj. **stainer** n.
– ORIGIN Middle English: shortening of archaic *distain*, from Old French *desteindre* 'tinge with a different colour'.

stained glass ■ n. coloured glass used to form decorative or pictorial designs, typically set in a lead framework and used for church windows.

stainless ■ adj. unmarked by or resistant to stains.

stainless steel ■ n. a form of steel containing chromium, resistant to tarnishing and rust.

stair ■ n. each of a set of fixed steps. ▸ (**stairs**) a set of such steps leading from one floor of a building to another.
– ORIGIN Old English, of Germanic origin, from a base meaning 'climb'.

staircase ■ n. a set of stairs and its surrounding structure. ▸ Brit. a part of a large building containing a staircase.

stairhead ■ n. chiefly Brit. a landing at the top of a set of stairs.

stairlift ■ n. a lift in the form of a chair that can be raised or lowered at the edge of a domestic staircase.

stair rod ■ n. a rod securing a carpet in the angle between two steps.

stairway ■ n. a staircase.

stairwell ■ n. a shaft in which a staircase is built.

stake[1] ■ n. 1 a strong post with a point at one end, driven into the ground to support a tree, form part of a fence, etc. 2 historical a wooden post to which a person was tied before being burned alive as a punishment. 3 a territorial

division of the Mormon Church. ■ v. 1 support (a plant) with a stake. 2 (**stake something out**) mark an area with stakes so as to claim ownership. 3 (**stake someone/thing out**) informal keep a place or person under surveillance.
– PHRASES **pull up stakes** N. Amer. move or go to live elsewhere. **stake a claim** assert one's right to something.
– ORIGIN Old English *staca*, of West Germanic origin.

stake² ■ n. 1 a sum of money gambled on a risky game or venture. 2 a share or interest in a business or situation. 3 (**stakes**) prize money. ▶ [in names] a horse race in which the owners of the horses running contribute to the prize money. 4 (**stakes**) a competitive situation: *one step ahead in the fashion stakes.* ■ v. 1 **gamble** (money or something of value). 2 N. Amer. informal give financial or other support to.
– PHRASES **at stake** 1 at risk. 2 at issue or in question.
– ORIGIN Middle English: perhaps a specialized usage of STAKE¹.

stake boat ■ n. an anchored boat used to mark the course for a boat race.

stakebuilding ■ n. Finance the building up of a holding of shares in a company.

stakeholder ■ n. 1 an independent party with whom money or counters wagered are deposited. 2 a person with an interest or concern in something.

stake net ■ n. a fishing net hung on stakes.

stake-out ■ n. informal a period of secret surveillance.

staker ■ n. a person who stakes money on something.

Stakhanovite /stəˈkɑːnəvʌɪt, -ˈkæn-/ ■ n. a worker who is exceptionally productive or zealous.
– DERIVATIVES **Stakhanovism** n. **Stakhanovist** n. & adj.
– ORIGIN 1930s: from the name of the Russian coal miner Aleksei Grigorevich *Stakhanov*.

stalactite /ˈstaləktʌɪt/ ■ n. a tapering structure hanging from the roof of a cave, formed of calcium salts deposited by dripping water.
– DERIVATIVES **stalactitic** adj.
– ORIGIN C17: from Greek *stalaktos* 'dripping', from *stalassein* 'to drip'.

Stalag /ˈstalag, ˈʃtalag/ ■ n. (in the Second World War) a German prison camp.
– ORIGIN German, contraction of *Stammlager*, from *Stamm* 'base, main stock' + *Lager* 'camp'.

stalagmite /ˈstaləgmʌɪt/ ■ n. a mound or tapering column rising from the floor of a cave, formed of calcium salts deposited by dripping water.
– DERIVATIVES **stalagmitic** adj.
– ORIGIN C17: from Greek *stalagma* 'a drop', from *stalassein* (see STALACTITE).

stale ■ adj. (**staler**, **stalest**) 1 (of food) no longer fresh or pleasant to eat. 2 no longer new and interesting. 3 (of a person) no longer performing well because of having done something for too long. 4 (of a cheque or legal claim) invalid because out of date. ■ v. make or become stale.
– DERIVATIVES **stalely** adv. **staleness** n.
– ORIGIN Middle English: prob. from Anglo-Norman French and Old French, from *estaler* 'to halt'.

stalemate ■ n. 1 Chess a position counting as a draw, in which a player is not in check but can only move into check. 2 a situation in which further progress by opposing parties seems impossible. ■ v. bring to or cause to reach stalemate.
– ORIGIN C18: from Anglo-Norman French *estale* 'position', from *estaler* 'be placed' + MATE².

Stalinism ■ n. the ideology and policies adopted by the Soviet Communist Party leader and head of state Joseph Stalin (1879–1953), based on centralization, totalitarianism, and the pursuit of communism.
– DERIVATIVES **Stalinist** n. & adj.

stalk¹ ■ n. 1 the main stem of a herbaceous plant. ▶ the attachment or support of a leaf, flower, or fruit. 2 a similar support for a sessile animal, or for an organ in an animal. 3 a slender support or stem.
– DERIVATIVES **-stalked** adj. **stalkless** adj. **stalk-like** adj. **stalky** adj.
– ORIGIN Middle English: prob. a diminutive of dialect *stale* 'rung of a ladder, long handle'.

stalk² ■ v. 1 pursue or approach stealthily. ▶ harass or persecute with unwanted and obsessive attention. ▶ chiefly poetic/literary move silently or threateningly through. 2 stride in a proud, stiff, or angry manner. ■ n. 1 a stealthy pursuit. 2 a stiff, striding gait.
– DERIVATIVES **stalker** n.
– ORIGIN Old English (*bistealcian* 'walk cautiously or stealthily'), of Germanic origin.

stalking horse ■ n. 1 a false pretext concealing someone's real intentions. 2 a candidate for the leadership of a political party who stands only in order to provoke the election and thus allow a stronger candidate to come forward.
– ORIGIN C16: from the former practice of using a horse trained to allow a fowler to hide behind it.

stall ■ n. 1 a stand, booth, or compartment for the sale of goods in a market. 2 an individual compartment for an animal in a stable or cowshed, enclosed on three sides. ▶ a stable or cowshed. ▶ (also **starting stall**) a cage-like compartment in which a horse is held prior to the start of a race. 3 a compartment for one person in a set of toilets, shower cubicles, etc. 4 a seat in the choir or chancel of a church, enclosed at the back and sides and often canopied, typically reserved for a member of the clergy. 5 (**stalls**) the ground-floor seats in a theatre. 6 an instance of an engine or vehicle stalling. ■ v. 1 (with reference to a motor vehicle or its engine) stop or cause to stop running. ▶ (of an aircraft) be moving at a speed too low to allow effective operation of the controls. ▶ Nautical (of a sailing boat) have insufficient wind power to give controlled motion. 2 stop or cause to stop making progress. 3 prevaricate. ▶ delay or divert by prevarication. 4 keep (an animal) in a stall.
– ORIGIN Old English *steall* 'stable or cattle shed', of Germanic origin.

stall-feed ■ v. feed and keep (an animal) in a stall, especially in order to fatten it.

stallholder ■ n. a person in charge of a market stall.

stallion ■ n. an uncastrated adult male horse.
– ORIGIN Middle English: from an Anglo-Norman French var. of Old French *estalon*, from a derivative of a Germanic base shared by STALL.

stalwart /ˈstɔːlwət, ˈstal-/ ■ adj. 1 loyal, reliable, and hard-working. 2 dated sturdy. ■ n. a stalwart supporter or participant in an organization.
– DERIVATIVES **stalwartly** adv. **stalwartness** n.
– ORIGIN Middle English: Scots var. of obsolete *stalworth*, from Old English *stǽl* 'place' + *weorth* 'worth'.

stamen /ˈsteɪmən/ ■ n. Botany a male fertilizing organ of a flower, typically consisting of a pollen-containing anther and a filament.
– ORIGIN C17: from Latin, 'warp in an upright loom, thread'.

stamina ■ n. the ability to sustain prolonged physical or mental effort.
– ORIGIN C17: from Latin, pl. of STAMEN in the sense 'threads spun by the Fates'.

staminate /ˈstamɪnət/ ■ adj. Botany having stamens but no pistils. Compare with PISTILLATE.

staminode /ˈstamɪnəʊd/ ■ n. Botany a sterile or abortive stamen.

stammer ■ v. speak with sudden involuntary pauses and a tendency to repeat the initial letters of words. ▶ utter (words) in such a way. ■ n. a tendency to stammer.
– DERIVATIVES **stammerer** n. **stammering** n. & adj. **stammeringly** adv.
– ORIGIN Old English, of West Germanic origin.

stamp ■ v. 1 bring down (one's foot) heavily on the ground or an object. ▶ crush, flatten, or remove with a heavy blow from one's foot. 2 walk with heavy, forceful steps. 3 (**stamp something out**) suppress or put an end to something. 4 impress a pattern or mark on with a stamp. ▶ impress (a pattern or mark). ▶ cut out using a die or mould. 5 fix a postage stamp to. ■ n. 1 an instrument for stamping a pattern or mark, especially an engraved or inked block or die. ▶ a mark or pattern made by a stamp. 2 a characteristic or distinctive impression or quality. ▶ a particular type of person or thing. 3 a small adhesive piece of paper recording payment of postage. 4 an act or sound of stamping the foot.
– DERIVATIVES **stamper** n.
– ORIGIN Middle English: of Germanic origin; reinforced by Old French *estamper* 'to stamp'.

stamp duty ■ n. a duty levied on the legal recognition of certain documents.

stampede ■ n. a sudden panicked rush of a number of horses, cattle, etc. ▸ a sudden rapid movement or reaction of a mass of people due to interest or panic. ■ v. take part or cause to take part in a stampede.
– DERIVATIVES **stampeder** n.
– ORIGIN C19: Mexican Spanish use of Spanish *estampida* 'crash, uproar', of Germanic origin.

stamp hinge ■ n. a small piece of gummed transparent paper for fixing postage stamps in an album.

stamping ground (also **stomping ground**) ■ n. a place one regularly frequents.

stamp mealies (also **stamped mealies**) ■ n. S. African another term for SAMP.

stamp office ■ n. an office issuing government stamps and receiving stamp duty.

stance /stɑːns, stans/ ■ n. 1 the way in which someone stands, especially when deliberately adopted. 2 a standpoint. 3 Climbing a ledge or foothold.
– ORIGIN Middle English: from French, from Italian *stanza*.

stanch /stɔːn(t)ʃ, stɑːn(t)ʃ/ ■ v. chiefly US variant spelling of STAUNCH².

stanchion /ˈstɑːnʃ(ə)n/ ■ n. an upright bar, post, or frame forming a support or barrier.
– DERIVATIVES **stanchioned** adj.
– ORIGIN Middle English: from Anglo-Norman French *stanchon*, from Old French *estanchon*, from *estance* 'a support', prob. from Latin *stare* 'stand'.

stand ■ v. (past and past part. **stood**) 1 be in or rise to an upright position, supported by one's feet. ▸ move in this position to a specified place. 2 place or be situated in a particular position. ▸ (especially of a vehicle) remain stationary. ▸ (of a ship) remain on a specified course. 3 (of food, liquid, etc.) rest without disturbance. 4 be in a specified state or condition. ▸ (of a building) remain upright and entire. ▸ remain valid or unaltered. ▸ be of a specified height. 5 adopt a particular attitude towards an issue. 6 be likely to do something: *investors stood to lose heavily.* 7 act in a specified capacity: *he stood security for the government's borrowings.* 8 (also **stand at stud**) (of a stallion) be available for breeding. 9 [usu. with neg.] tolerate or like. ▸ withstand without being damaged. 10 be a candidate in an election. 11 umpire a cricket match. 12 provide (food or drink) for (someone) at one's expense. ■ n. 1 an attitude towards a particular issue. ▸ a determined effort to hold one's ground or resist something. ▸ Cricket a partnership. 2 a large raised tiered structure for spectators. ▸ a raised platform for a band, orchestra, or speaker. ▸ a rack, base, or item of furniture for holding or displaying something. ▸ a small temporary stall or booth from which promotional goods are sold or displayed. ▸ (**the stand**) a witness box. 3 the place where someone usually stands or sits. ▸ a place where vehicles wait for passengers. 4 a cessation from motion or progress. 5 a group of trees or other plants. 6 S. African a plot of land.
– PHRASES **stand and deliver!** a highwayman's order to hand over money and valuables. **stand on one's own (two) feet** be or become self-reliant or independent. **stand trial** be tried in a court of law. **stand up and be counted** state publicly one's support for someone or something.
– PHRASAL VERBS **stand alone** be unequalled. **stand by 1** look on without intervening. **2** support or remain loyal to. ▸ adhere to. **3** be ready to take action if required. **stand down 1** (also **stand aside**) resign from a position or office. **2** (**stand down**) or **stand someone down** relax or cause someone to relax after a state of readiness. **3** (of a witness) leave the witness box after giving evidence. **stand for 1** be an abbreviation of or symbol for. **2** [with neg.] endure or tolerate. **stand in 1** deputize. **2** Nautical sail closer to the shore. **stand off** move or keep away. ▸ Nautical sail further away from the shore. **stand on 1** be scrupulous in the observance of. **2** Nautical continue on the same course. **stand out 1** project. ▸ be easily noticeable. ▸ be clearly better. **2** persist in opposition to or support of something. **stand over** (or **stand something over**) be postponed or cause something to be postponed. **stand to** Military stand ready for an attack. **stand someone up** informal fail to keep a date. **stand up for** speak or act in support of. **stand up to 1** make a spirited defence against. **2** be resistant to the harmful effects of.
– ORIGIN Old English, of Germanic origin.

standard ■ n. 1 a level of quality or attainment. ▸ a required or agreed level of quality or attainment. ▸ S. African former term for GRADE (in sense 3). 2 something used as a measure, norm, or model in comparative evaluations. ▸ (**standards**) principles of honourable, decent behaviour. ▸ a system by which the value of a currency is defined in terms of gold or silver. 3 a military or ceremonial flag. 4 a tree that grows on an erect stem of full height. ▸ a shrub grafted on an erect stem and trained in tree form. 5 an upright water or gas pipe. ■ adj. used or accepted as normal or average. ▸ (of a size, measure, etc.) such as is regularly used or produced. ▸ (of a work, writer, etc.) viewed as authoritative and so widely read.
– PHRASES **raise one's** (or **the**) **standard** take up arms.
– DERIVATIVES **standardly** adv.
– ORIGIN Middle English: shortening of Old French *estendart*, from *estendre* 'extend'.

standard assessment task ■ n. (in the UK) a standard test given to schoolchildren to assess their progress in a core subject of the national curriculum.

standard-bearer ■ n. 1 a soldier carrying the standard of a unit, regiment, or army. 2 a leading figure in a cause or movement.

Standardbred ■ n. a horse of a breed able to attain a specified speed, developed especially for trotting.

standard deviation ■ n. Statistics a quantity calculated to indicate the extent of deviation for a group as a whole.

Standard Grade ■ n. 1 (in South Africa) the lower of the two levels at which subjects could be studied for matriculation. Compare with HIGHER GRADE. 2 (in Scotland) an examination equivalent to the GCSE.

standardize (also **-ise**) ■ v. cause to conform to a standard. ▸ (**standardize on**) adopt as one's standard. ▸ determine the properties of by comparison with a standard.
– DERIVATIVES **standardizable** (also **-isable**) adj. **standardization** (also **-isation**) n.

standard lamp ■ n. chiefly Brit. a lamp with a tall stem whose base stands on the floor.

standard of living ■ n. the degree of material comfort available to a person or community.

standard time ■ n. a uniform time for places in approximately the same longitude.

standby ■ n. (pl. **standbys**) 1 readiness for duty or immediate deployment. ▸ a person or thing ready to be deployed in an emergency. 2 the state of waiting to secure an unreserved place for a journey or performance.

standee /stanˈdiː/ ■ n. chiefly N. Amer. a person who is standing.

stand-in ■ n. a substitute.

standing ■ n. 1 position, status, or reputation. 2 duration: *a squabble of long standing.* ■ adj. 1 (of a jump or start of a race) performed from rest or an upright position. 2 long-term or regularly repeated: *a standing invitation.* 3 (of water) stagnant or still. 4 (of corn) not yet reaped.
– PHRASES **all standing** Nautical without time to lower the sails. **in good standing** on good terms. **leave someone/thing standing** informal be much better or faster than someone or something else.

standing committee ■ n. a permanent committee meeting regularly.

standing joke ■ n. something regularly causing amusement or provoking ridicule.

standing order ■ n. 1 British term for STOP ORDER. 2 an order placed on a regular basis with a retailer. 3 (**standing orders**) rulings governing the procedures of a parliament, council, etc.

standing ovation ■ n. a period of prolonged applause during which the audience rise to their feet.

standing stone ■ n. another term for MENHIR.

standing wave ■ n. Physics a vibration of a system in

stand-off

which some particular points remain fixed while others between them vibrate with the maximum amplitude.

stand-off ■ n. **1** a deadlock between two equally matched opponents. **2** Rugby another term for **FLY HALF**.

stand-offish ■ adj. informal distant and cold in manner.
– DERIVATIVES **stand-offishly** adv. **stand-offishness** n.

standout ■ n. informal an outstanding person or thing.

standpipe ■ n. a vertical pipe extending from a water supply, especially one connecting a temporary tap to the mains.

standpoint ■ n. **1** an attitude towards a particular issue. **2** the position from which a scene or an object is viewed.

St Andrew's cross ■ n. a diagonal or X-shaped cross, especially white on a blue background (as a national emblem of Scotland).

standstill /'stan(d)stɪl/ ■ n. a situation or condition without movement or activity.

stand-up ■ adj. **1** involving or used by people standing up. **2** (of a comedian) performing by standing in front of an audience and telling jokes. ▸ (of comedy) performed in such a way. **3** (of a fight or argument) involving direct confrontation; loud or violent. **4** designed to stay upright or erect. ■ n. a stand-up comedian. ▸ stand-up comedy.

stank past of **STINK**.

Stanley knife ■ n. trademark a utility knife with a short, strong replaceable blade.

stannic /'stanɪk/ ■ adj. Chemistry of tin with a valency of four; of tin(IV).
– ORIGIN C18: from late Latin *stannum* 'tin'.

stannous /'stanəs/ ■ adj. Chemistry of tin with a valency of two; of tin(II).
– ORIGIN C19: from late Latin *stannum* 'tin'.

stanza /'stanzə/ ■ n. a group of lines forming the basic recurring metrical unit in a poem.
– DERIVATIVES **stanza'd** (also **stanzaed**) adj. **stanzaic** /-'zeɪɪk/ adj.
– ORIGIN C16: from Italian, 'standing place', also 'stanza'.

stapelia /stə'piːlɪə/ ■ n. a plant of a genus of southern African succulents, often with flowers that emit an odour like that of rotting flesh, attracting flies that act as pollinators. [Genus *Stapelia*.]

stapeliad ■ n. any of several closely related leafless succulent plants that occur in warm, dry climates. [*Stapelia* and other genera in the subfamily Asclepiadoideae.]

stapes /'steɪpiːz/ ■ n. (pl. same) Anatomy a small stirrup-shaped bone in the middle ear, transmitting vibrations from the incus to the inner ear.
– ORIGIN C17: from modern Latin, 'stirrup'.

staph /staf/ ■ n. informal short for **STAPHYLOCOCCUS**.

staphylococcus /ˌstafɪlə(ʊ)'kɒkəs/ ■ n. (pl. **staphylococci** /-'kɒk(s)ʌɪ, -'kɒk(s)iː/) a bacterium of a genus including many pathogenic kinds that cause pus formation. [Genus *Staphylococcus*.]
– DERIVATIVES **staphylococcal** adj.
– ORIGIN from Greek *staphulē* 'bunch of grapes' + *kokkos* 'berry'.

staple¹ ■ n. **1** a small flattened U-shaped piece of wire used to fasten papers together. **2** a small U-shaped metal bar with pointed ends for driving into wood to hold electric wires, battens, etc. in place. ■ v. secure with a staple or staples.
– ORIGIN Old English *stapol*, of Germanic origin.

staple² ■ n. **1** a main or important element of something. **2** the fibre of cotton or wool considered with regard to its length and fineness. **3** historical a centre of trade in a specified commodity. ■ adj. main or important.
– ORIGIN Middle English: from Old French *estaple* 'market', from Middle Low German, Middle Dutch *stapel* 'pillar, emporium'.

staple gun ■ n. a hand-held mechanical tool for driving staples into a hard surface.

stapler ■ n. a device for fastening papers together with staples.

star ■ n. **1** a fixed luminous point in the night sky which is a large, remote incandescent body like the sun. **2** a stylized representation of a star, typically with five or more points. ▸ a star-shaped symbol indicating a category of excellence. ▸ used in names of starfishes and similar echinoderms, e.g. cushion star. **3** a famous or talented entertainer or sports player. ▸ an outstanding person or thing. **4** Astrology a planet, constellation, or configuration regarded as influencing one's fortunes or personality.
▸ (**stars**) a horoscope. **5** a white patch on the forehead of a horse or other animal. ■ v. (**starred, starring**) **1** (of a film, play, etc.) have (someone) as a principal performer. ▸ (of a performer) have a principal role in a film, play, etc.
2 decorate or cover with star-shaped marks or objects.
▸ mark for special notice or recommendation with a star.
– PHRASES **see stars** seem to see flashes of light, especially as a result of a blow on the head.
– DERIVATIVES **stardom** n. **starless** adj. **starlike** adj.
– ORIGIN Old English, of Germanic origin.

star anise ■ n. a small star-shaped fruit of a Chinese tree (*Illicium verum*), having an aniseed flavour and used in Asian cookery.

starboard /'stɑːbɔːd, -bəd/ ■ n. the side of a ship or aircraft on the right when one is facing forward. The opposite of **PORT³**. ■ v. turn (a ship or its helm) to starboard.
– ORIGIN Old English *stēorbord* 'rudder side' (see **STEER¹**, **BOARD**), because early Teutonic sailing vessels were steered with a paddle on the right side.

starboard watch ■ n. see **WATCH** (sense 3).

starburst ■ n. a pattern of lines or rays radiating from a central point. ▸ an explosion producing such an effect. ▸ a camera lens attachment that produces such a pattern.

starch ■ n. **1** an odourless, tasteless carbohydrate which is obtained chiefly from cereals and potatoes and is an important constituent of the human diet. **2** powder or spray made from this substance, used to stiffen fabric. **3** stiffness of manner. ■ v. stiffen with starch.
– DERIVATIVES **starchily** adv. **starchiness** n. **starchy** adj. (**-ier, -iest**).
– ORIGIN Old English, of Germanic origin.

star-crossed ■ adj. poetic/literary ill-fated.

stare ■ v. **1** look fixedly at someone or something with the eyes wide open. ▸ (**stare someone out/down**) look fixedly at someone until they feel forced to look away. **2** be unpleasantly prominent or striking. ■ n. an act of staring.
– PHRASES **be staring someone in the face** be glaringly obvious.
– DERIVATIVES **starer** n.
– ORIGIN Old English, of Germanic origin, from a base meaning 'be rigid'.

stare decisis /ˌstɛːrɪ dɪ'sʌɪsɪs, ˌstɑːreɪ dɪ'siːsɪs/ ■ n. Law the legal principle of determining points in litigation according to precedent.
– ORIGIN Latin, 'stand by things decided'.

starfish ■ n. (pl. same or **-fishes**) a marine echinoderm with five or more radiating arms bearing tube feet underneath. [Class Asteroidea: many species.]

starfruit ■ n. another term for **CARAMBOLA**.

stargazer ■ n. **1** informal an astronomer or astrologer. **2** a fish with electric organs that normally stays buried in the sand with only its eyes protruding. [Families Uranoscopidae and Dactyloscopidae.]
– DERIVATIVES **stargaze** v.

stark ■ adj. **1** severe or bare in appearance. **2** unpleasantly or sharply clear. **3** complete; sheer: *stark terror*.
– PHRASES **stark naked** completely naked. **stark raving** (or **staring**) **mad** informal completely mad.
– DERIVATIVES **starkly** adv. **starkness** n.
– ORIGIN Old English *stearc* 'unyielding, severe', of Germanic origin.

starkers ■ adj. informal completely naked.

Starking (also **Star King**) ■ n. a dessert apple of a soft-fleshed variety with a red and yellow skin.

starlet ■ n. informal a promising young actress or sportswoman.

starlight ■ n. light coming from the stars.

starling ■ n. a gregarious songbird typically with dark lustrous or iridescent plumage. [Family Sturnidae: several species.]

– ORIGIN Old English, from *stær* 'starling', of Germanic origin.

starlit ■ adj. lit by stars.

star network ■ n. a data or communication network in which all nodes are independently connected to one central unit.

Star of David ■ n. a six-pointed figure consisting of two interlaced equilateral triangles, used as a Jewish and Israeli symbol.

starry ■ adj. (**-ier**, **-iest**) **1** full of or lit by stars. ▶ resembling a star. **2** informal of or relating to stars in entertainment.
– DERIVATIVES **starrily** adv. **starriness** n.

starry-eyed ■ adj. naively enthusiastic or idealistic.

Stars and Stripes ■ pl. n. [treated as sing.] the national flag of the US.

star sapphire ■ n. a cabochon sapphire that reflects a starlike image resulting from its regular internal structure.

star shell ■ n. an explosive projectile which bursts in the air to light up an enemy's position.

starship ■ n. (in science fiction) a large manned spaceship for interstellar travel.

star sign ■ n. a sign of the zodiac.

star-spangled ■ adj. **1** poetic/literary covered or decorated with stars. **2** informal glitteringly successful.

star-struck ■ adj. fascinated and greatly impressed by famous people.

star-studded ■ adj. **1** (of the sky) filled with stars. **2** informal featuring a number of famous people.

start ■ v. **1** come or bring into being. ▶ begin to do. ▶ begin to attend (a school, college, etc.) or engage in (an occupation). **2** cause to happen. ▶ begin to operate. ▶ cause or enable to begin doing something. ▶ signal (competitors) to begin a race. **3** (**start at**) cost at least (a specified amount). **4** begin to move or travel. **5** give a small jump or jerking movement from surprise. ▶ poetic/literary move or appear suddenly. ▶ rouse (game) from its lair. ▶ (of eyes) bulge. ■ n. **1** the beginning. ▶ an act of beginning. **2** an advantage given at the beginning of a race. **3** a sudden movement of surprise.
– PHRASES **for a start** in the first place. **start something** informal cause trouble. **to start with** as the first thing to be taken into account.
– PHRASAL VERBS **start in** informal begin doing something. ▶ (**start in on**) N. Amer. begin to do or deal with. ▶ (**start in on**) N. Amer. attack verbally. **start off** (or **start someone/thing off**) begin (or cause someone or something to begin) working, operating, etc. **start on 1** begin to work on or deal with. **2** informal begin to talk in a critical or hostile way to. **start over** N. Amer. make a new beginning. **start out** (or **up**) embark on a venture or undertaking.
– ORIGIN Old English *styrtan* 'to caper, leap', of Germanic origin.

starter ■ n. **1** the first course of a meal. **2** an automatic device for starting a machine. **3** a person who signals the start of a race. **4** a competitor taking part in a race or game at the start. ▶ Baseball the pitcher who starts the game. **5** a person or thing starting in a specified way: *a slow starter*. **6** a topic or question with which to start a discussion or course of study. **7** a preparation used to initiate souring, fermentation, etc.
– PHRASES **for starters** informal first of all. **under starter's orders** (of horses, runners, etc.) waiting for the signal to start a race.

starter home ■ n. a small house or flat designed for people buying their first home.

starting block ■ n. a shaped rigid block for bracing the feet of a runner at the start of a race.

starting gate ■ n. a barrier raised at the start of a race, especially in horse racing, to ensure a simultaneous start.

starting pistol ■ n. a pistol used to signal the start of a race.

starting post ■ n. a marker indicating the starting place for a race.

starting price ■ n. the final odds at the start of a horse race.

startle ■ v. cause to feel sudden shock or alarm.
– DERIVATIVES **startler** n.

– ORIGIN Old English *steartlian* 'kick, struggle', from the base of **START**.

startling ■ adj. **1** alarming. **2** very surprising or remarkable.
– DERIVATIVES **startlingly** adv.

star turn ■ n. the act giving the most heralded or impressive performance in a programme.

starve ■ v. suffer or die or cause to suffer or die from hunger. ▶ (**starve someone out**) or **into** force someone out of (a place) or into (a specified state) by starving them. ▶ (usu. **be starved of**) or US **for** deprive of. ▶ (**be starving**) or **starved** informal feel very hungry.
– DERIVATIVES **starvation** n.
– ORIGIN Old English *steorfan* 'to die', of Germanic origin, prob. from a base meaning 'be rigid'.

starveling /ˈstɑːvlɪŋ/ archaic ■ adj. starving or emaciated. ■ n. a starveling person or animal.

stash informal ■ v. store safely in a secret place. ■ n. a secret store of something.
– ORIGIN C18.

stasis /ˈsteɪsɪs, ˈstɑ-/ ■ n. **1** formal or technical a period or state of inactivity or equilibrium. **2** Medicine a stoppage of flow of a body fluid.
– ORIGIN C18: from Greek, 'standing, stoppage', from *sta-*, base of *histanai* 'to stand'.

-stasis ■ comb. form (pl. **-stases**) Physiology slowing down; stopping: *haemostasis*.
– DERIVATIVES **-static** comb. form in corresponding adjectives.
– ORIGIN from Greek *stasis* 'standing, stoppage'.

stat¹ /stat/ ■ abbrev. informal **1** photostat. **2** statistic(s). **3** thermostat.

stat² /stat/ ■ adv. (in a medical direction or prescription) immediately.
– ORIGIN C19: abbrev. of Latin *statim*.

-stat ■ comb. form denoting instruments, substances, etc. maintaining a controlled state: *thermostat*.
– ORIGIN partly from (*helio*)*stat*, partly a back-formation from **STATIC**.

statant /ˈsteɪtənt/ ■ adj. Heraldry (of an animal) standing with all four paws on the ground.
– ORIGIN C15: from Latin *stat-* 'fixed, stationary', from *stare* 'to stand'.

state ■ n. **1** the condition of someone or something. ▶ a physical condition as regards internal or molecular form or structure. ▶ (**a state**) informal an agitated, disorderly, or dirty condition. **2** a nation or territory considered as an organized political community under one government. ▶ an organized political community or area forming part of a federal republic. ▶ (**the States**) the US. **3** the civil government of a country. **4** pomp and ceremony associated with monarchy or government. ■ v. express definitely or clearly in speech or writing. ▶ chiefly Law specify the facts of (a case) for consideration.
– PHRASES **state of affairs** (or **things**) a situation. **state-of-the-art** incorporating the newest ideas and most up-to-date features. **state of emergency** a situation of national danger or disaster in which a government suspends normal constitutional procedures. **state of grace** a state of being free from sin. **the state of play** Brit. the score at a particular time in a cricket or football match. ▶ the current situation.
– DERIVATIVES **statable** (also **stateable**) adj. **statehood** n.
– ORIGIN Middle English: partly a shortening of **ESTATE**, partly from Latin *status* (see **STATUS**).

state attorney ■ n. **1** S. African a lawyer representing the government in court. **2** (also **state's attorney**) US a lawyer representing a state in court.

state capitalism ■ n. a political system in which the state has control of production and the use of capital.

statecraft ■ n. the skilful management of state affairs.

State Department ■ n. (in the US) the department of foreign affairs.

stateless ■ adj. not recognized as a citizen of any country.
– DERIVATIVES **statelessness** n.

stately

stately ■ adj. (**-ier**, **-iest**) dignified, imposing, or grand.
– DERIVATIVES **stateliness** n.

stately home ■ n. Brit. a large and fine house occupied or formerly occupied by an aristocratic family.

statement ■ n. **1** a definite or clear expression of something in speech or writing. ▶ a formal account of facts or events, especially one given to the police or in court. **2** a document setting out items of debit and credit between a bank or other organization and a customer.

state prisoner ■ n. another term for PRISONER OF STATE.

state prosecutor ■ n. another term for PUBLIC PROSECUTOR.

stateroom /'steɪtruːm, -rʊm/ ■ n. **1** a large room in a palace or public building, for use on formal occasions. **2** a captain's or superior officer's room on a ship. ▶ a private compartment on a ship.

state school ■ n. a school funded and controlled by the state.

state's evidence ■ n. S. African & US Law evidence for the prosecution given by a participant in or accomplice to the crime being tried.

States General (also **Estates General**) ■ n. the legislative body in the Netherlands from the 15th to the 18th century, and in France until 1789.

statesman /'steɪtsmən/ (or **stateswoman**) ■ n. (pl. **-men** or **-women**) a skilled, experienced, and respected political leader or figure.
– DERIVATIVES **statesmanlike** adj. **statesmanship** n.
– ORIGIN C16: from *state's man*, translating French *homme d'état*.

state socialism ■ n. a political system in which the state has control of industries and services.

state trial ■ n. prosecution by the state.

statewide ■ adj. & adv. extending throughout a state in the US.

static /'statɪk/ ■ adj. **1** lacking movement, action, or change. **2** Physics concerned with bodies at rest or forces in equilibrium. Often contrasted with DYNAMIC. **3** relating to or denoting electric charges acquired by objects that cannot conduct a current. ■ n. **1** static electricity. **2** crackling or hissing on a telephone, radio, etc.
– DERIVATIVES **statically** adv.
– ORIGIN C16: from Greek *statikē* (*tekhnē*) 'science of weighing'; the adjective from Greek *statikos* 'causing to stand', from the verb *histanai*.

statice /'statɪsi/ ■ n. another term for SEA LAVENDER.
– ORIGIN C18: from *Statice* (former genus name), from Greek *statikos* 'causing to stand still' (because the plant was used to staunch blood).

static line ■ n. a cord used instead of a rip cord for opening a parachute, attached at one end to the aircraft and temporarily snapped to the parachute at the other.

statics ■ pl. n. **1** [usu. treated as sing.] the branch of mechanics concerned with bodies at rest and forces in equilibrium. Compare with DYNAMICS. **2** another term for STATIC (in sense 2).

statin /'statɪn/ ■ n. Medicine any of a group of drugs which act to reduce levels of cholesterol in the blood.

station ■ n. **1** a place where passenger trains stop on a railway line, typically with platforms and buildings. **2** a place where a specified activity or service is based: *a radar station*. **3** a broadcasting company of a specified kind. **4** the place where someone or something stands or is placed for a particular purpose or duty. ▶ dated one's social rank or position. **5** Austral./NZ a large sheep or cattle farm. ■ v. assign to a station.
– ORIGIN Middle English: from Latin *statio(n-)*, from *stare* 'to stand'.

stationary ■ adj. **1** not moving. **2** not changing in quantity or condition.
– ORIGIN Middle English: from Latin *stationarius*, from *statio(n-)* (see STATION).

USAGE
The words **stationary** and **stationery** are often confused. **Stationary** is an adjective which means 'not moving or changing', as in *a car collided with a stationary vehicle*, whereas **stationery** is a noun which means 'writing materials', as in *I wrote to Ann on the hotel stationery*.

stationary bicycle ■ n. an exercise bike.

stationary point ■ n. Mathematics a point on a curve where the gradient is zero.

stationary wave ■ n. Physics another term for STANDING WAVE.

stationer ■ n. a seller of stationery.
– ORIGIN Middle English: from medieval Latin *stationarius* 'tradesman (at a fixed location)'.

stationery ■ n. paper and other materials needed for writing.

USAGE
On the confusion of **stationery** and **stationary**, see usage at STATIONARY.

station house ■ n. chiefly N. Amer. a police or fire station.

stationmaster ■ n. an official in charge of a railway station.

Station of the Cross ■ n. each of a series of fourteen pictures representing incidents during Jesus' progress from Pilate's house to his crucifixion at Calvary.

station wagon ■ n. an estate car.

statism /'steɪtɪz(ə)m/ ■ n. a political system in which the state has substantial central control over social and economic affairs.
– DERIVATIVES **statist** n. & adj.

statistic ■ n. a fact or piece of data obtained from a study of a large quantity of numerical data. ■ adj. statistical.
– ORIGIN C18: from German *statistisch* (adj.), *Statistik* (n.).

statistical ■ adj. of or relating to statistics.
– DERIVATIVES **statistically** adv.

statistical mechanics ■ pl. n. [treated as sing.] the description of physical phenomena in terms of a statistical treatment of the behaviour of large numbers of atoms or molecules, especially as regards the distribution of energy among them.

statistical significance ■ n. see SIGNIFICANCE.

statistics ■ pl. n. [treated as sing.] the practice or science of collecting and analysing numerical data in large quantities, especially for the purpose of inferring proportions in a whole from those in a representative sample.
– DERIVATIVES **statistician** n.

statocyst ■ n. Zoology an organ of balance and orientation in some aquatic invertebrates.

statolith ■ n. Zoology a calcareous particle in a statocyst, which stimulates sensory receptors in response to gravity.

stator /'steɪtə/ ■ n. the stationary part of an electric generator or motor.
– ORIGIN C19: from STATIONARY, on the pattern of *rotor*.

stats ■ pl. n. informal statistics.

statuary /'statjʊəri, -tʃʊə-/ ■ n. statues collectively.
– ORIGIN C16: from Latin *statuarius*, from *statua* (see STATUE).

statue /'statjuː, -tʃuː/ ■ n. a carved or cast figure of a person or animal, especially one that is life-size or larger.
– DERIVATIVES **statued** adj.
– ORIGIN Middle English: from Latin *statua*, from *stare* 'to stand'.

statuesque /ˌstatjʊ'ɛsk, -tʃʊ-/ ■ adj. attractively tall, graceful, and dignified.
– DERIVATIVES **statuesquely** adv. **statuesqueness** n.
– ORIGIN C18: from STATUE, on the pattern of *picturesque*.

statuette ■ n. a small statue.
– ORIGIN C19: from French, diminutive of *statue*.

stature ■ n. **1** a person's natural height when standing. **2** importance or reputation gained by ability or achievement.
– ORIGIN Middle English: from Latin *statura*, from *stare* 'to stand'.

status ▪ n. **1** relative social or professional standing. ▸ high rank or social standing. ▸ the official classification given to a person, country, etc., determining their rights or responsibilities. **2** the position of affairs at a particular time.
– ORIGIN C18: from Latin, 'standing', from *stare* 'to stand'.

status epilepticus /ˌɛpɪˈlɛptɪkəs/ ▪ n. Medicine a condition in which epileptic fits follow one another without recovery of consciousness between them.

status quo /ˈkwəʊ/ ▪ n. the existing state of affairs.
– ORIGIN Latin, 'the state in which'.

status quo ante /kwəʊ ˈanti/ ▪ n. the previous state of affairs.
– ORIGIN Latin, 'the state in which before'.

status symbol ▪ n. a possession taken to indicate a person's wealth or high status.

statute /ˈstatjuːt, -tʃuːt/ ▪ n. a written law passed by a legislative body. ▸ a rule of an organization or institution.
– ORIGIN Middle English: from Old French *statut*, from late Latin *statutum*, from Latin *statuere* 'set up' from *status* (see STATUS).

statute-barred ▪ adj. English Law (especially of a debt claim) no longer legally enforceable due to the lapse of time.

statute book ▪ n. a book in which laws are written. ▸ **(the statute book)** a nation's laws collectively.

statute law ▪ n. the body of principles and rules of law laid down in statutes.

statute of limitations ▪ n. Law a statute limiting the period for the bringing of certain kinds of actions.

statutory /ˈstatjʊt(ə)ri, -tʃʊ-/ ▪ adj. **1** required, permitted, or enacted by statute. **2** having come to be required or expected due to being done regularly.
– DERIVATIVES **statutorily** adv.

statutory instrument ▪ n. Law a government or executive order of subordinate legislation.

statutory rape ▪ n. US Law the offence of having sexual intercourse with a minor.

statutory tenant ▪ n. Law a person who is legally entitled to remain in a property although their original tenancy has expired.

staunch[1] /stɔːn(t)ʃ/ ▪ adj. very loyal and committed.
– DERIVATIVES **staunchly** adv. **staunchness** n.
– ORIGIN Middle English: from Old French *estanche, estanc*, from a base meaning 'dried up, weary'.

staunch[2] /stɔːn(t)ʃ, stɑːn(t)ʃ/ (US also **stanch**) ▪ v. stop or restrict (a flow of blood from a wound); stop from bleeding.
– ORIGIN Middle English: from Old French *estanchier*, from the base of STAUNCH[1].

staurolite /ˈstɔːrəlʌɪt/ ▪ n. a brown glassy mineral consisting of a silicate of aluminium and iron.
– ORIGIN C19: from Greek *stauros* 'cross' (the mineral is often twinned in the shape of a cross).

stave ▪ n. **1** a vertical wooden post or plank in a building or other structure. ▸ any of the lengths of wood fixed side by side to make a barrel, bucket, etc. ▸ a strong wooden stick or iron pole used as a weapon. **2** (also **staff**) Music a set of five parallel lines on or between any of which a note is written to indicate its pitch. **3** a verse or stanza of a poem. ▪ v. **1** (past and past part. **staved** or **stove**) **(stave something in)** break something by forcing it inwards or piercing it roughly with a hole. **2** (past and past part. **staved**) **(stave something off)** avert or delay something bad or dangerous.
– ORIGIN Middle English: back-formation from *staves*, var. pl. form of STAFF.

stay[1] ▪ v. **1** remain in the same place. ▸ **(stay on)** continue to study, work, or be somewhere after others have left. ▸ **(stay over)** stay for the night at someone's home or a hotel. ▸ **(stay up)** not go to bed. **2** remain in a specified state or position. ▸ continue, persevere, or keep up with (an activity or person). **3** live somewhere temporarily as a visitor or guest. ▸ S. African & Scottish live permanently. **4** stop, delay, or prevent, in particular suspend or postpone (judicial proceedings) or refrain from pressing (charges). ▸ assuage (hunger) for a short time. **5** poetic/literary support or prop up. ▪ n. **1** a period of staying somewhere. **2** a curb or check, especially a suspension or postponement of judicial proceedings. **3** a device used as a brace or support. **4** (**stays**) historical a corset made of two pieces laced together and stiffened by strips of whalebone.
– PHRASES **stay the course** (or **distance**) keep going to the end of a race or contest. ▸ pursue a difficult task or activity to the end. **a stay of execution** a delay in carrying out a court order. **stay put** remain somewhere without moving. **stay well** S. African expressing good wishes on parting, said to the person staying behind.
– DERIVATIVES **stayer** n.
– ORIGIN Middle English: from Anglo-Norman French *estai-*, stem of Old French *ester*, from Latin *stare* 'to stand'; in the sense 'support', partly from Old French *estaye* (n.), *estayer* (v.), of Germanic origin.

stay[2] ▪ n. **1** a large rope, wire, or rod used to support a ship's mast. **2** a guy or rope supporting a flagstaff or other upright pole. **3** a supporting wire or cable on an aircraft. ▪ v. secure or steady by means of a stay.
– ORIGIN Old English *stæg*, of Germanic origin, from a base meaning 'be firm'.

staying power ▪ n. informal endurance or stamina.

staysail /ˈsteɪseɪl, -s(ə)l/ ▪ n. a triangular fore-and-aft sail extended on a stay.

stay stitching ▪ n. stitching placed along a bias or curved seam to prevent the fabric of a garment from stretching while the garment is being made.

St Bernard ▪ n. a very large dog of a breed originally kept to rescue travellers by the monks of the hospice on the Great St Bernard, a pass across the Alps.

STD ▪ abbrev. sexually transmitted disease.

stead ▪ n. the place or role that someone or something should have or fill: *appointed in his stead*.
– PHRASES **stand someone in good stead** be advantageous to someone over time or in the future.
– ORIGIN Old English *stede* 'place', of Germanic origin.

steadfast /ˈstɛdfɑːst, -fəst/ ▪ adj. resolutely or dutifully firm and unwavering.
– DERIVATIVES **steadfastly** adv. **steadfastness** n.
– ORIGIN Old English *stedefæst* 'standing firm' (see STEAD, FAST[1]).

Steadicam ▪ n. trademark a lightweight mounting for a film camera which keeps it steady for filming when hand-held or moving.

steady ▪ adj. (-**ier**, -**iest**) **1** firmly fixed, supported, or balanced. **2** not faltering or wavering; controlled. **3** sensible and reliable. **4** regular, even, and continuous in development, frequency, or intensity. ▪ v. (-**ies**, -**ied**) make or become steady. ▪ exclam. a warning to keep calm or take care. ▪ n. (pl. -**ies**) informal a person's regular boyfriend or girlfriend.
– PHRASES **go steady** informal have a regular romantic or sexual relationship with someone. **steady on!** Brit. calm down; be more reasonable.
– DERIVATIVES **steadier** n. **steadily** adv. **steadiness** n. **steadying** adj. & n.
– ORIGIN Middle English: from STEAD.

steady-going ▪ adj. moderate and sensible.

steady-state theory ▪ n. a cosmological theory which holds that the universe is eternal and maintained by constant creation of matter.

steak ▪ n. **1** high-quality beef taken from the hindquarters of the animal, typically cut into thick slices for grilling or frying. ▸ a thick slice of other meat or fish. **2** poorer-quality beef that is cubed or minced and cooked by braising or stewing.
– ORIGIN Middle English: from Old Norse *steik*; rel. to *steikja* 'roast on a spit' and *stikna* 'be roasted'.

steak tartare ▪ n. a dish consisting of raw minced steak mixed with raw egg.

steal ▪ v. (past **stole**; past part. **stolen**) **1** take (something) without permission or legal right and without intending to return it. ▸ dishonestly pass off (another person's ideas) as one's own. **2** take (something) surreptitiously: *I stole a glance at my watch*. **3** move somewhere quietly or surreptitiously. **4** (in various sports) gain (an advantage, a run, or possession of the ball) unexpectedly or by exploiting the temporary distraction of an opponent.

stealth

▶ Baseball run to (a base) while the pitcher is in the act of delivery. ■ n. **1** informal a bargain. **2** Baseball an act of stealing a base.
– PHRASES **steal a march on** gain an advantage over by taking early action. **steal someone's heart** win someone's love. **steal the show** attract the most attention and praise. **steal someone's thunder** win praise or attention for oneself by pre-empting someone else's attempt to impress.
– DERIVATIVES **stealer** n.
– ORIGIN Old English, of Germanic origin.

stealth ■ n. **1** cautious and surreptitious action or movement. **2** [as modifier] (chiefly of aircraft) designed in accordance with technology which makes detection by radar or sonar difficult: *a stealth bomber*.
– ORIGIN Middle English: prob. representing an Old English word rel. to STEAL.

stealth tax ■ n. a form of taxation levied in a covert or indirect manner.

stealthy ■ adj. (**-ier**, **-iest**) characterized by stealth.
– DERIVATIVES **stealthily** adv. **stealthiness** n.

steam ■ n. **1** the hot vapour into which water is converted when heated, which condenses in the air into a mist of minute water droplets. **2** the expansive force of this vapour used as a source of power for machines. **3** momentum; impetus: *the dispute gathered steam*. ■ v. **1** give off or produce steam. ▶ (**steam up**) or **steam something up** become or cause something to become misted over with steam. **2** cook (food) by heating it in steam from boiling water. **3** clean or otherwise treat with steam. ▶ apply steam to (something fixed with adhesive) so as to open or loosen it. **4** (of a ship or train) travel somewhere under steam power. **5** (**be/get steamed up**) be or become extremely agitated or angry. **6** informal come, go, or move somewhere rapidly or in a forceful way.
– PHRASES **get up** (or **pick up**) **steam 1** generate enough pressure to drive a steam engine. **2** (of an activity, project, etc.) gradually gain impetus. **have steam coming out of one's ears** informal be extremely angry. **let** (or **blow**) **off steam** informal get rid of pent-up energy or strong emotion. **run out of** (or **lose**) **steam** informal lose impetus or enthusiasm. **under one's own steam** without assistance from others.
– ORIGIN Old English *stēam* 'vapour', *stēman* 'emit a scent, be exhaled', of Germanic origin.

steam bath ■ n. a room that is filled with hot steam for the purpose of cleaning and refreshing the body and for relaxation. ▶ a session in such a bath.

steamboat ■ n. a boat that is propelled by a steam engine, especially (in the US) a paddle-wheel craft of a type used widely on rivers in the 19th century.

steam distillation ■ n. Chemistry distillation of a liquid in a current of steam.

steamed ■ adj. (of food) cooked by steaming.

steam engine ■ n. an engine that uses the expansion or rapid condensation of steam to generate power. ▶ a steam locomotive.

steamer ■ n. **1** a ship or boat powered by steam. **2** a type of saucepan in which food can be steamed. **3** a device used to direct a jet of hot steam on to a garment in order to remove creases. **4** informal a wetsuit.

steamer trunk ■ n. a sturdy trunk designed or intended for use on board a steamboat.

steaming ■ adj. **1** giving off steam. **2** Brit. informal extremely drunk. **3** Brit. informal very angry.

steam iron ■ n. an electric iron that emits steam from holes in its flat surface.

steam jacket ■ n. a steam-filled casing that is fitted around a cylinder in order to heat its contents.

steamroller ■ n. a heavy, slow-moving vehicle with a roller, used to flatten the surfaces of roads during construction. ■ v. (also **steamroll**) (of a government or other authority) forcibly pass (a measure) by restricting debate or otherwise overriding opposition. ▶ force (someone) into doing or accepting something.

steam turbine ■ n. a turbine in which a high-velocity jet of steam rotates a bladed disc or drum.

steamy ■ adj. (**-ier**, **-iest**) **1** producing, filled with, or clouded with steam. **2** hot and humid. **3** informal of or involving erotic sexual activity.
– DERIVATIVES **steamily** adv. **steaminess** n.

stearic acid /'stɪərɪk, stɪ'arɪk/ ■ n. Chemistry a solid saturated fatty acid obtained from animal or vegetable fats.
– DERIVATIVES **stearate** /'stɪəreɪt/ n.
– ORIGIN C19: *stearic* from French *stéarique*, from Greek *stear* 'tallow'.

stearin /'stɪərɪn/ ■ n. a white crystalline substance which is the main constituent of tallow and suet.
– ORIGIN C19: from French *stéarine*, from Greek *stear* 'tallow'.

steatite /'stɪətʌɪt/ ■ n. the mineral talc occurring in consolidated form, especially as soapstone.
– DERIVATIVES **steatitic** adj.
– ORIGIN C18: from Greek *steatitēs*, from *stear* 'tallow'.

steatosis /,stɪə'təʊsɪs/ ■ n. Medicine infiltration of liver cells with fat, associated with disturbance of the metabolism.

steed ■ n. archaic or poetic/literary a horse.
– ORIGIN Old English *stēda* 'stallion'.

steel ■ n. **1** a hard, strong grey or bluish-grey alloy of iron with carbon and usually other elements, used extensively as a structural and fabricating material. **2** a rod of roughened steel on which knives are sharpened. **3** strength and determination: *nerves of steel*. ■ v. mentally prepare (oneself) to do or face something difficult.
– ORIGIN Old English *stȳle*, *stēli*, of Germanic origin.

steel band ■ n. a band that plays music on steel drums.

steel drum (also **steel pan**) ■ n. a percussion instrument originating in Trinidad, made out of an oil drum with one end beaten down and divided by grooves into sections to give different notes.

steel engraving ■ n. the process or action of engraving a design into a steel plate. ▶ a print made using this process.

steelhead ■ n. a large, migratory form of rainbow trout found in the sea.

steel wool ■ n. fine strands of steel matted together into a mass, used as an abrasive.

steelworks ■ pl. n. [usu. treated as sing.] a factory where steel is manufactured.
– DERIVATIVES **steelworker** n.

steely ■ adj. (**-ier**, **-iest**) **1** resembling steel in colour, brightness, or strength. **2** coldly determined; severe.
– DERIVATIVES **steeliness** n.

steen /stiːn, stɪən/ ■ n. S. African former term for CHENIN BLANC.
– ORIGIN from S. African Dutch, shortening of *steendruiven*, from *steen* 'stone' + *druiven* 'grapes'.

steenbok /'stɪənbɒk/ (also **steinbok** or **steenbuck**) ■ n. a small African antelope with large ears and a small tail, the male of which has smooth upright horns. [*Raphicerus campestris*.]
– ORIGIN C18: from Dutch, from *steen* 'stone' + *bok* 'buck'.

steenbras /'stɪənbrɑːs/ ■ n. (pl. **same**) a sea bream of South African coastal waters, popular with anglers. [*Petrus rupestris* (**red steenbras**), *Lithognathus lithognathus* (**white steenbras**), and other species.]
– ORIGIN from Dutch, from *steen* stone + *brasem* 'bream'.

steep[1] ■ adj. **1** rising or falling sharply; almost perpendicular. **2** (of a rise or fall in an amount) very large or rapid. **3** informal (of a price or demand) not reasonable; excessive. ▶ (of a claim or account) exaggerated.
– DERIVATIVES **steepish** adj. **steeply** adv. **steepness** n.
– ORIGIN Old English *stēap* 'extending to a great height', of West Germanic origin.

steep[2] ■ v. **1** soak or be soaked in water or other liquid. **2** (usu. **be steeped in**) fill or imbue with a particular quality or influence.
– ORIGIN Middle English: of Germanic origin.

steepen ■ v. become or cause to become steeper.

steeple ■ n. a church tower and spire.
– DERIVATIVES **steepled** adj.
– ORIGIN Old English, of Germanic origin.

steeplechase ■ n. a horse race run on a racecourse having ditches and hedges as jumps. ▶ a running race in

which runners must clear hurdles and water jumps.
– DERIVATIVES **steeplechaser** n. **steeplechasing** n.
– ORIGIN C18: from STEEPLE (because orig. a steeple marked the finishing point across country) + CHASE[1].

steeplejack ■ n. a person who climbs tall structures such as chimneys and steeples in order to carry out repairs.

steer[1] ■ v. **1** guide or control the movement of (a vehicle, ship, etc.). ▸ follow (a course) in a specified direction. **2** direct or guide in a particular direction. ■ n. **1** the type of steering of a vehicle. **2** informal a piece of advice or information.
– PHRASES **steer clear of** take care to avoid.
– DERIVATIVES **steerable** adj. **steerer** n. **steering** n.
– ORIGIN Old English *stīeran*, of Germanic origin.

steer[2] ■ n. another term for BULLOCK.
– ORIGIN Old English *stēor*, of Germanic origin.

steerage ■ n. **1** historical the part of a ship providing accommodation for passengers with the cheapest tickets. **2** archaic or poetic/literary the action of steering a boat.

steer-by-wire ■ n. a semi-automatic and typically computer-regulated system for controlling various functions of a motor vehicle.

steering column ■ n. a shaft that connects the steering wheel of a vehicle to the rest of the steering mechanism.

steering committee (also **steering group**) ■ n. a committee that decides on the priorities or order of business of an organization.

steering wheel ■ n. a wheel that a driver rotates in order to steer a vehicle.

steersman ■ n. (pl. **-men**) a person who steers a boat or ship.

stegosaur /ˈstɛɡəsɔː/ (also **stegosaurus** /ˌstɛɡəˈsɔːrəs/) ■ n. a quadrupedal herbivorous dinosaur with a double row of large bony plates along the back.
– ORIGIN from Greek *stegē* 'covering' + *sauros* 'lizard'.

stein[1] /stʌɪn/ ■ n. a large earthenware beer mug.
– ORIGIN C19: from German *Stein* 'stone'.

stein[2] /stʌɪn/ ■ n. S. African a semi-sweet white wine.
– ORIGIN perhaps an alteration of STEEN, or from German *Steinwein*, a dry white wine produced in Germany.

steinbok /ˈstʌɪnbɒk/ ■ n. variant spelling of STEENBOK.

stele /stiːl, ˈstiːli/ ■ n. Botany the central core of the stem and root of a vascular plant, consisting of the vascular tissue (xylem and phloem) and associated supporting tissue.
– DERIVATIVES **stelar** adj.
– ORIGIN C19: from Greek *stēlē* 'standing block'.

stellar /ˈstɛlə/ ■ adj. **1** of or relating to a star or stars. **2** informal of or having the quality of a star performer; excellent.
– DERIVATIVES **stelliform** adj.
– ORIGIN C17: from late Latin *stellaris*, from Latin *stella* 'star'.

stellar wind ■ n. Astronomy a continuous flow of charged particles from a star.

stellate /ˈstɛleɪt, -lət/ ■ adj. arranged in a radiating pattern like that of a star.
– DERIVATIVES **stellated** adj.
– ORIGIN C17: from Latin *stellatus*, from *stella* 'star'.

St Elmo's fire /ˈɛlməʊz/ ■ n. a phenomenon in which a luminous electrical discharge appears on a ship or aircraft during a storm.
– ORIGIN regarded as a sign of protection given by *St Elmo*, the patron saint of sailors.

stem[1] ■ n. **1** the main body or stalk of a plant or shrub. ▸ the stalk supporting a fruit, flower, or leaf, and attaching it to a larger branch, twig, or stalk. **2** a long, thin supportive or main section of something, such as that of a wine glass or tobacco pipe. **3** a rod or cylinder in a mechanism. **4** a vertical stroke in a letter or musical note. **5** Grammar the root or main part of a word, to which inflections or formative elements are added. **6** the main upright timber or metal piece at the bow of a ship. ■ v. (**stemmed**, **stemming**) **1** (**stem from**) originate in or be caused by. **2** remove the stems from (fruit or tobacco leaves).
– PHRASES **from stem to stern** from one end to the other, especially of a ship.
– DERIVATIVES **stemmed** adj. **stemless** adj.
– ORIGIN Old English *stemn*, *stefn*, of Germanic origin.

stem[2] ■ v. (**stemmed**, **stemming**) **1** stop or restrict (the flow of something). **2** Skiing slide the tail of one ski or both skis outwards in order to turn or slow down.
– ORIGIN Middle English: from Old Norse *stemma*, of Germanic origin; the skiing term (early C20) is from the German verb *stemmen*.

stem cell ■ n. Biology an undifferentiated cell of a multicellular organism which is capable of giving rise to indefinitely more cells of the same type, and from which certain other kinds of cell arise by differentiation.

stem ginger ■ n. pieces of crystallized or preserved ginger.

stem stitch ■ n. an embroidery stitch forming a continuous line of long, overlapped stitches.

stem turn ■ n. Skiing a turn made by stemming with the upper ski and lifting the lower one parallel to it towards the end.

stemware ■ n. goblets and stemmed glasses regarded collectively.

stench ■ n. a strong and very unpleasant smell.
– ORIGIN Old English *stenc* 'smell', of Germanic origin.

stencil ■ n. a thin sheet of card, plastic, or metal with a pattern or letters cut out of it, used to produce the cut design on the surface below by the application of ink or paint through the holes. ■ v. (**stencilled**, **stencilling**; US **stenciled**, **stenciling**) decorate using a stencil. ▸ produce (a design) with a stencil.
– DERIVATIVES **stencilled** adj. **stencilling** n.
– ORIGIN C18: from earlier *stansel* 'ornament with various colours', from Latin *scintilla* 'spark'.

Sten gun ■ n. a type of lightweight British sub-machine gun.
– ORIGIN 1940s: from the initials of the inventors' surnames, Shepherd and Turpin, suggested by BREN GUN.

stenography /stɪˈnɒɡrəfi/ ■ n. N. Amer. the action or process of writing in shorthand and transcribing the shorthand on a typewriter.
– DERIVATIVES **stenographer** n. **stenographic** adj.
– ORIGIN C17: from Greek *stenos* 'narrow' + -GRAPHY.

stenohaline /ˌstɛnəʊˈheɪlʌɪn, -liːn/ ■ adj. Ecology able to tolerate only a narrow range of salinity. Often contrasted with EURYHALINE.
– ORIGIN 1930s: from Greek *stenos* 'narrow' + *halinos* 'of salt'.

stenosis /stɪˈnəʊsɪs/ ■ n. (pl. **stenoses**) Medicine the abnormal narrowing of a passage in the body.
– DERIVATIVES **stenosed** adj. **stenosing** adj. **stenotic** adj.
– ORIGIN C19: from Greek *stenōsis* 'narrowing', from *stenoun* 'make narrow'.

stenothermal /ˌstɛnə(ʊ)ˈθəːm(ə)l/ ■ adj. Ecology able to tolerate only a small range of temperature. Often contrasted with EURYTHERMAL.
– ORIGIN C19: from Greek *stenos* 'narrow' + THERMAL.

stent ■ n. Medicine **1** a splint placed inside a duct, canal, or blood vessel to aid healing or relieve an obstruction. **2** an impression or cast of a part or body cavity, used to maintain pressure so as to promote healing, especially of a skin graft.
– ORIGIN C19: from the name of the English dentist Charles T. *Stent*.

stenter ■ n. another term for TENTER.
– ORIGIN from Scots *stent* 'set up (a tent)', perhaps a shortening of EXTEND.

stentorian /stɛnˈtɔːrɪən/ ■ adj. (of a person's voice) loud and powerful.

step ■ n. **1** an act or movement of putting one leg in front of the other in walking or running. ▸ the distance covered by such a movement. ▸ a short and easily walked distance. **2** one of the sequences of movement of the feet which make up a dance. **3** a flat surface, especially one in a series, on which to place one's foot when moving from one level to another. ▸ a doorstep. ▸ a rung of a ladder. ▸ Climbing a foothold cut in a slope of ice. **4** a block fixed to a boat's keel in order to take the base of a mast or other fitting. **5** Physics an abrupt change in the value of a

quantity, especially voltage. **6** a position or grade in a scale or hierarchy. **7** a measure or action, especially one of a series taken in order to deal with or achieve a particular thing. **8** step aerobics. ▪ v. (**stepped**, **stepping**) **1** lift and set down one's foot or one foot after the other in order to walk somewhere or move to a new position. **2** Nautical set up (a mast) in its step.
– PHRASES **follow** (or **tread**) **in someone's steps** do as someone else did, especially in making a journey or following a career. **in** (or **out of**) **step 1** walking, marching, or dancing in the same (or a different) rhythm and pace as others. **2** conforming (or not conforming) to what others are doing or thinking. **3** Physics (of two or more oscillations or other cyclic phenomena) having (or not having) the same frequency and always in the same phase. **mind** (or **watch**) **one's step** walk or act carefully. **step into someone's shoes** take control of a task or job from another person. **step on it** informal go faster. **step out of line** behave inappropriately or disobediently. **step up to the plate** N. Amer. take action in response to an opportunity or crisis. **step up to the plate** N. Amer. take action in response to an opportunity or crisis.
– PHRASAL VERBS **step aside** another way of saying step down. **step back** mentally withdraw from a situation in order to consider it objectively. **step down** withdraw or resign from a position or office. **step something down** decrease voltage by using a transformer. **step forward** offer one's help or services. **step in 1** become involved in a difficult situation, especially in order to help. **2** act as a substitute for someone. **step out 1** leave a room or building, typically for a short time. **2** walk with long or vigorous steps. **step something up** increase the amount, speed, or intensity of something. ▸ increase voltage using a transformer.
– DERIVATIVES **stepped** adj. **stepwise** adj.
– ORIGIN Old English *stæpe* (n.), *stæppan* (v.), of Germanic origin.

step- ▪ comb. form denoting a relationship resulting from a remarriage: *stepmother*.
– ORIGIN Old English *stēop-*, from a Germanic base meaning 'bereaved, orphaned'.

step aerobics ▪ pl. n. [treated as sing. or pl.] a type of aerobics that involves stepping up on to and down from a portable block.

stepbrother ▪ n. a son of one's stepparent, by a marriage other than one's own father or mother.

step change ▪ n. (in business or politics) a significant change in policy or attitude, especially one that results in an improvement or increase.

stepchild ▪ n. (pl. **-children**) a child of one's husband or wife by a previous marriage.

stepdaughter ▪ n. a daughter of one's husband or wife by a previous marriage.

stepfather ▪ n. a man who is married to one's mother after the divorce of one's parents or the death of one's father.

stephanotis /ˌstɛfəˈnəʊtɪs/ ▪ n. a Madagascan climbing plant cultivated for its fragrant waxy white flowers. [Genus *Stephanotis*.]
– ORIGIN from Greek, 'fit for a wreath', from *stephanos* 'wreath'.

stepladder ▪ n. a short folding ladder with flat steps and a small platform.

stepmother ▪ n. a woman who is married to one's father after the divorce of one's parents or the death of one's mother.

steppe /stɛp/ ▪ n. a large area of flat unforested grassland in SE Europe or Siberia.
– ORIGIN C17: from Russian *step'*.

stepper ▪ n. **1** an electric motor or other device which moves or rotates in a series of small discrete steps. **2** a portable block used in step aerobics.

stepping stone ▪ n. **1** a raised stone on which to step when crossing a stream or muddy area. **2** an action that helps one to make progress towards a specified goal.

stepsister ▪ n. a daughter of one's stepparent by a marriage other than with one's own father or mother.

stepson ▪ n. a son of one's husband or wife by a previous marriage.

-ster ▪ suffix **1** denoting a person engaged in or associated with a particular activity or thing: *songster*. **2** denoting a person having a particular quality: *youngster*.
– ORIGIN Old English, of Germanic origin.

steradian /stəˈreɪdɪən/ (abbrev.: **sr**) ▪ n. the SI unit of solid angle, equal to the angle at the centre of a sphere subtended by a part of the surface equal in area to the square of the radius.
– ORIGIN C19: from Greek *stereos* 'solid' + RADIAN.

stereo /ˈstɛrɪəʊ, ˈstɪərɪəʊ/ ▪ n. (pl. **-os**) **1** stereophonic sound. **2** a stereophonic CD player, record player, etc. ▪ adj. **1** stereophonic. **2** stereoscopic.

stereo- ▪ comb. form having or relating to three dimensions: *stereography* | *stereophonic*.
– ORIGIN from Greek *stereos* 'solid'.

stereochemistry ▪ n. the branch of chemistry concerned with the three-dimensional arrangement of atoms in molecules and the effect of this on reactions.
– DERIVATIVES **stereochemical** adj. **stereochemically** adv.

stereogram ▪ n. a diagram or computer-generated image giving a three-dimensional representation of a solid object or surface.

stereography ▪ n. the representation of three-dimensional things on a two-dimensional surface, as in cartography.
– DERIVATIVES **stereograph** n. **stereographic** adj.

stereoisomer /ˌstɛrɪəʊˈaɪsəmə, ˌstɪə-/ ▪ n. Chemistry each of two or more molecules differing only in the spatial arrangement of their atoms.
– DERIVATIVES **stereoisomeric** adj. **stereoisomerism** n.

stereolithography ▪ n. the creation layer by layer of a three-dimensional object from a computer-generated design, using a liquid polymer which hardens on contact with a moving laser beam.

stereophonic /ˌstɛrɪə(ʊ)ˈfɒnɪk, ˌstɪərɪə(ʊ)-/ ▪ adj. of or denoting sound recording and reproduction using two or more channels. Compare with MONOPHONIC.
– DERIVATIVES **stereophonically** adv. **stereophony** /-ˈɒf(ə)ni/ n.

stereopsis /ˌstɛrɪˈɒpsɪs, ˌstɪərɪ-/ ▪ n. the perception of depth produced by the reception in the brain of visual stimuli from both eyes in combination; binocular vision.
– DERIVATIVES **stereoptic** adj.
– ORIGIN C20: from STEREO- + Greek *opsis* 'sight'.

stereoscope /ˈstɛrɪə(ʊ)skəʊp, ˈstɪə-/ ▪ n. a device by which two photographs of the same object taken at slightly different angles are viewed together, creating an impression of depth and solidity.
– DERIVATIVES **stereoscopic** adj. **stereoscopically** adv. **stereoscopy** n.

stereoselective /ˌstɛrɪəʊsɪˈlɛktɪv, ˌstɪə-/ ▪ adj. Chemistry (of a reaction) preferentially producing a particular stereoisomeric form of the product.
– DERIVATIVES **stereoselectivity** n.

stereospecific ▪ adj. Chemistry another term for STEREOSELECTIVE.
– DERIVATIVES **stereospecifically** adv. **stereospecificity** n.

stereotactic /ˌstɛrɪə(ʊ)ˈtaktɪk, ˌstɪərɪə(ʊ)-/ (also **stereotaxic** /-ˈtaksɪk/) ▪ adj. relating to or denoting techniques for surgical treatment or scientific investigation that permit the accurate positioning of probes inside the brain or other parts of the body.
– DERIVATIVES **stereotactically** adv. **stereotaxis** n.

stereotype ▪ n. an image or idea of a particular type of person or thing that has become fixed through being widely held. ▪ v. view or represent as a stereotype.
– DERIVATIVES **stereotypic** adj. **stereotypical** adj. **stereotypically** adv. **stereotypy** n.
– ORIGIN C18: from French *stéréotype* (adj.).

steric /ˈstɛrɪk, ˈstɪərɪk/ ▪ adj. Chemistry of or relating to the spatial arrangement of atoms in a molecule, especially as it affects reactions.
– DERIVATIVES **sterically** adv.
– ORIGIN C19: from Greek *stereos* 'solid'.

sterilant /ˈstɛrɪl(ə)nt/ ▪ n. an agent used to destroy micro-organisms, or pests and diseases in soil.

sterile ▪ adj. **1** not able to produce children or young.

▶ (of a plant) not able to produce fruit or seeds. ▶ (of land or soil) too poor in quality to produce crops. **2** lacking in imagination, creativity, or excitement. **3** free from bacteria or other living micro-organisms.
– DERIVATIVES **sterilely** adv. **sterility** n.
– ORIGIN Middle English: from Old French, or from Latin *sterilis*; rel. to Greek *steira* 'barren cow'.

sterilize (also **-ise**) ■ v. **1** make sterile. **2** deprive of the ability to produce offspring by removing or blocking the sex organs.
– DERIVATIVES **sterilizable** (also **-isable**) adj. **sterilization** (also **-isation**) n. **sterilized** (also **-ised**) adj. **sterilizer** (also **-iser**) n.

sterling ■ n. British money. ■ adj. (of a person or their work) excellent; of great value.
– ORIGIN Middle English: prob. from *steorra* 'star' (because some early Norman pennies bore a small star).

sterling silver ■ n. silver of at least 92¼ per cent purity.

stern[1] ■ adj. **1** grimly serious or strict, especially in the exercise of discipline. **2** severe; demanding.
– DERIVATIVES **sternly** adv. **sternness** n.
– ORIGIN Old English *styrne*, prob. from the West Germanic base of STARE.

stern[2] ■ n. the rearmost part of a ship or boat.
– DERIVATIVES **sterned** adj. **sternmost** adj. **sternwards** adv.
– ORIGIN Middle English: prob. from Old Norse *stjórn* 'steering', from *stýra* 'to steer'.

sternal ■ adj. of or relating to the sternum.

sternal rib ■ n. another term for TRUE RIB.

sternocleidomastoid /ˌstɜːnə(ʊ)ˌklʌɪdəʊˈmastɔɪd/ ■ n. Anatomy each of a pair of long muscles which connect the sternum, clavicle, and mastoid process and serve to turn and nod the neck.

sternpost ■ n. the central upright support at the stern of a boat, traditionally bearing the rudder.

sternum /ˈstɜːnəm/ ■ n. (pl. **sternums** or **sterna** /-nə/) **1** the breastbone. **2** Zoology a thickened ventral plate on each segment of the body of an arthropod.
– ORIGIN C17: from Greek *sternon* 'chest'.

steroid /ˈstɪərɔɪd, ˈstɛrɔɪd/ ■ n. Biochemistry any of a large class of organic compounds (including many hormones, alkaloids, and vitamins) with a molecule containing four rings of carbon atoms.
– DERIVATIVES **steroidal** adj.
– ORIGIN 1930s: from STEROL.

sterol /ˈstɪərɒl, ˈstɛrɒl/ ■ n. Biochemistry any of a group of naturally occurring unsaturated steroid alcohols, typically waxy solids.
– ORIGIN C20: independent usage of the ending of words such as CHOLESTEROL.

stertorous /ˈstɜːt(ə)rəs/ ■ adj. (of breathing) noisy and laboured.
– DERIVATIVES **stertorously** adv.
– ORIGIN C19: from modern Latin *stertor* 'snoring sound', from Latin *stertere* 'to snore'.

stet ■ v. (**stetted**, **stetting**) let it stand (used as an instruction on a printed proof to ignore a correction). ▶ write such an instruction against.
– ORIGIN Latin, 'let it stand', from *stare* 'to stand'.

stethoscope /ˈstɛθəskəʊp/ ■ n. a medical instrument for listening to the action of someone's heart or breathing, having a small disc-shaped resonator that is placed against the chest and two tubes connected to earpieces.
– DERIVATIVES **stethoscopic** adj.
– ORIGIN C19: from French *stéthoscope*, from Greek *stēthos* 'breast' + *skopein* 'look at'.

Stetson /ˈstɛts(ə)n/ ■ n. (trademark in the US) a hat with a high crown and a very wide brim, traditionally worn by cowboys and ranchers in the US.
– ORIGIN C19: named after the American hat manufacturer John B. Stetson.

stevedore /ˈstiːvədɔː/ ■ n. a person employed at a dock to load and unload ships.
– ORIGIN C18: from Spanish *estivador*, from *estivar* 'stow a cargo', from Latin *stipare* 'pack tight'.

stew[1] ■ n. **1** a dish of meat and vegetables cooked slowly in liquid in a closed dish or pan. **2** informal a state of anxiety or agitation. **3** archaic a brothel. ■ v. **1** cook or be cooked slowly in liquid in a closed dish or pan. ▶ chiefly Brit.

stick

(of tea) become strong and bitter with prolonged brewing. **2** informal remain in a heated or stifling atmosphere. **3** informal remain in an anxious or agitated state.
– PHRASES **stew in one's own juice** informal be left to suffer the consequences of one's own actions.
– ORIGIN Middle English: from Old French *estuve*, *estuver* 'heat in steam', prob. from Greek *tuphos* 'smoke, steam'.

stew[2] ■ n. Brit. a pond or large tank for keeping fish for eating.
– ORIGIN Middle English: from Old French *estui*, from *estoier* 'confine'.

steward ■ n. **1** a person who looks after the passengers on a ship or aircraft. **2** a person responsible for supplies of food to a college, club, etc. **3** an official appointed to supervise arrangements at a large public event. **4** short for SHOP STEWARD. **5** a person employed to manage another's property, especially a large house or estate. ▶ chiefly historical an officer of the British royal household, especially an administrator of Crown estates. ■ v. act as a steward of.
– DERIVATIVES **stewardship** n.
– ORIGIN Old English *stiweard*, from *stig*, prob. in the sense 'house, hall' + *weard* 'ward'.

stewardess /ˈstjuːədɪs, ˌstjuːəˈdɛs/ ■ n. a woman who looks after the passengers on a ship or aircraft.

stewed ■ adj. informal drunk.

stewpot ■ n. a large pot in which stews are cooked.

stg ■ abbrev. sterling.

St George's cross ■ n. a +-shaped cross, red on a white background (especially as a national emblem of England).

Sth ■ abbrev. south.

St Helenian /hɛˈliːnɪən/ ■ n. a native or inhabitant of the South Atlantic island of St Helena. ■ adj. of or relating to St Helena.

STI ■ abbrev. sexually transmitted infection.

stibnite /ˈstɪbnʌɪt/ ■ n. a lead-grey mineral consisting of antimony sulphide.
– ORIGIN C19: from Latin *stibium* 'black antimony'.

stick[1] ■ n. **1** a thin piece of wood that has fallen or been cut off a tree. ▶ a stick used for support in walking or as a weapon. **2** (in hockey, polo, etc.) a long, thin implement with a curved head or angled blade, used to hit or direct the ball or puck. ▶ (**sticks**) (in field hockey) the foul play of raising the stick above the shoulder. **3** a long, thin object or piece of something: *a stick of dynamite*. **4** a conductor's baton. **5** a gear or control lever. **6** a group of bombs or paratroopers dropped from an aircraft. **7** a small group of soldiers assigned to a particular duty. **8** the threat of punishment as a means of persuasion as contrasted with the 'carrot' or enticement). ▶ Brit. informal severe criticism or treatment. **9** (**the sticks**) informal, derogatory rural areas. **10** Stock Exchange a large quantity of unsold stock, especially the proportion of shares which must be taken up by underwriters after an unsuccessful issue.
– PHRASES **up sticks** Brit. informal go to live elsewhere. [from nautical slang *to up sticks* 'set up a boat's mast' (ready for departure).]
– ORIGIN Old English *sticca* 'peg, stick, spoon', of West Germanic origin.

stick[2] ■ v. (past and past part. **stuck**) **1** insert, thrust, or push (an object or its point) into or through something. ▶ (**stick in/into/through**) be or remain fixed with its point embedded in. ▶ stab or pierce with a sharp object. **2** put somewhere in a quick or careless way. ▶ informal used to express angry dismissal of a particular thing: *they can stick the job*. **3** protrude or extend in a certain direction. **4** adhere or cause to adhere. **5** (**be stuck**) be fixed in a particular position or unable to move or be moved. ▶ be unable to progress with a task or find the answer or solution. ▶ (**be stuck for**) be at a loss for or in need of. ▶ (**be stuck with**) informal be unable to get rid of or escape from: *they were stuck with each other*. ▶ (**be stuck on**) informal be infatuated with. **6** informal accept; tolerate; endure: *I can't stick Geoffrey*. ▶ (**stick at**) informal persevere with (a task or endeavour). ▶ (**stick it out**) informal put up with or persevere with something difficult or disagreeable.
– PHRASES **get stuck in** (or **into**) informal start doing something with determination. **stick in one's throat** (or

sticker

craw) be difficult or impossible to accept. **stick it to** informal, chiefly N. Amer. treat harshly. **stick one's neck out** informal risk incurring criticism or anger by acting or speaking boldly.
– PHRASAL VERBS **stick around** informal remain in or near a place. **stick by** continue to support or be loyal to. **stick something on** informal place the blame for a mistake or wrongdoing on. **stick out** be extremely noticeable. **stick out for** refuse to accept less than. **stick to** continue or confine oneself to doing, using, or practising. **stick together** informal remain united or mutually loyal. **stick someone/thing up** informal, chiefly N. Amer. rob someone or something at gunpoint. **stick up for** support or defend. **stick with** informal persevere or continue with.
– DERIVATIVES **stickability** n.
– ORIGIN Old English *stician*, of Germanic origin.

sticker ■ n. an adhesive label or notice.

stick fighting ■ n. a form of martial art that uses a stick or staff as a weapon. ▶ S. African a contest among rural Xhosa and Zulu youths in which two opponents each fight with a pair of sticks, one used for attack the other for defence.
– DERIVATIVES **stick fight** n. & v. **stick fighter** n.

stick insect ■ n. a long, slender, slow-moving insect that resembles a twig. [Family Phasmatidae: many species.]

stick-in-the-mud ■ n. informal a person who resists change.

stickleback ■ n. a small freshwater or coastal fish with sharp spines along its back, widely distributed in the northern hemisphere. [*Gasterosteus aculeatus* and other species.]
– ORIGIN Middle English: from Old English *sticel* 'thorn, sting' + *bæc* 'back'.

stickler ■ n. a person who insists on a certain quality or type of behaviour.
– ORIGIN C16: from obsolete *stickle* 'be umpire', alteration of obsolete *stightle* 'to control', from Old English *stiht(i)an* 'set in order'.

stick shift ■ n. N. Amer. a gear lever or manual transmission.

stick-up ■ n. informal, chiefly US an armed robbery in which a gun is used to threaten people.

sticky ■ adj. (-ier, -iest) 1 tending or designed to stick; adhesive. ▶ glutinous; viscous. 2 (of the weather) hot and humid; muggy. 3 damp with sweat. 4 informal difficult; awkward. 5 (of wine) sweet; fortified. ■ n. (pl. -ies) a fortified, late harvest, or dessert wine.
– PHRASES **come to a sticky end** be led by one's own actions to ruin or an unpleasant death. **sticky fingers** informal a propensity to steal.
– DERIVATIVES **stickily** adv. **stickiness** n.

stickybeak informal Austral./NZ ■ n. an inquisitive person. ■ v. pry.

sticky-fingered ■ adj. informal given to stealing.

stiff ■ adj. 1 not easily bent; rigid. ▶ not moving freely; difficult to turn or operate. ▶ unable to move easily and without pain. 2 not relaxed or friendly; constrained. 3 severe or strong: *they face stiff fines*. ▶ (of a wind) blowing strongly. ▶ (of an alcoholic drink) strong. 4 (**stiff with**) informal full of. 5 (—— **stiff**) informal having a specified unpleasant feeling to an extreme extent: *scared stiff*. ■ n. informal 1 a dead body. 2 chiefly N. Amer. a boring, conventional person. ■ v. informal 1 N. Amer. cheat (someone). 2 kill.
– PHRASES **a stiff upper lip** a quality of uncomplaining stoicism.
– DERIVATIVES **stiffish** adj. **stiffly** adv. **stiffness** n.
– ORIGIN Old English, of Germanic origin.

stiff-arm ■ v. tackle or fend off by extending an arm rigidly.

stiffen ■ v. 1 make or become stiff. 2 make or become stronger or more steadfast.
– DERIVATIVES **stiffener** n. **stiffening** n.

stiff-necked ■ adj. haughty and stubborn.

stiffy[1] ■ n. (pl. -ies) vulgar slang an erection of a man's penis.

stiffy[2] ■ n. (pl. -ies) Computing, chiefly S. African a 3½-inch diskette contained in a rigid casing.

stifle[1] ■ v. 1 prevent from breathing freely; suffocate. 2 smother or suppress: *she stifled a giggle*. ▶ prevent or constrain (an activity or idea).
– DERIVATIVES **stifling** adj. **stiflingly** adv.
– ORIGIN Middle English: perhaps from Old French *estouffer* 'smother, stifle'.

stifle[2] ■ n. a joint in the legs of horses, dogs, and other animals, equivalent to the knee in humans.
– ORIGIN Middle English.

stigma /ˈstɪgmə/ ■ n. (pl. **stigmas** or especially in sense 2 **stigmata** /-mətə, -ˈmɑːtə/) 1 a mark of disgrace associated with a particular circumstance, quality, or person. 2 (**stigmata**) (in Christian tradition) marks corresponding to those left on Christ's body by the Crucifixion. 3 Medicine a visible sign or characteristic of a disease. ▶ a mark or spot on the skin. 4 Botany the part of a pistil that receives the pollen during pollination.
– ORIGIN C16: from Greek *stigma* 'a mark made by a pointed instrument, a dot'.

stigmatic ■ adj. 1 of or relating to a stigma or stigmas. 2 another term for ANASTIGMATIC.
– DERIVATIVES **stigmatically** adv.
– ORIGIN C16: from Latin *stigma*, *stigmat-*.

stigmatize (also **-ise**) ■ v. 1 (usu. **be stigmatized**) (also **-ised**) regard as worthy of disgrace. 2 mark with stigmata.
– DERIVATIVES **stigmatization** (also **-isation**) n.

stilboestrol /stɪlˈbiːstrɒl/ (US **stilbestrol**) ■ n. Biochemistry a powerful synthetic oestrogen used in hormone therapy, as a post-coital contraceptive, and as a growth-promoting agent for livestock.
– ORIGIN 1930s: from *stilbene*, a synthetic hydrocarbon, + OESTRUS.

stile[1] ■ n. an arrangement of steps set into a fence or wall that allows people to climb over.
– ORIGIN Old English *stigel*, from a Germanic root meaning 'to climb'.

stile[2] ■ n. a vertical piece in the frame of a panelled door or sash window. Compare with RAIL[1].
– ORIGIN C17: prob. from Dutch *stijl* 'pillar, doorpost'.

stiletto ■ n. (pl. **-os**) 1 a thin, high tapering heel on a woman's shoe. 2 a short dagger with a tapering blade.
– ORIGIN C17: from Italian, diminutive of *stilo* 'dagger'.

still[1] ■ adj. 1 not moving. 2 (of air or water) undisturbed by wind, sound, or current. 3 (of a drink) not effervescent. ■ n. 1 a state of deep and quiet calm: *the still of the night*. 2 a photograph or a single shot from a cinema film. ■ adv. 1 even now or at a particular time: *it was still raining*. 2 nevertheless. 3 even (used with comparatives for emphasis): *better still*. ■ v. make or become still.
– DERIVATIVES **stillness** n.
– ORIGIN Old English, of West Germanic origin, from a base meaning 'be fixed, stand'.

still[2] ■ n. an apparatus for distilling alcoholic drinks such as whisky.
– ORIGIN C16: from the rare verb *still* 'extract by distillation', shortening of DISTIL.

stillbirth ■ n. the birth of an infant that has died in the womb.
– DERIVATIVES **stillborn** adj.

still life ■ n. (pl. **still lifes**) a painting or drawing of a static arrangement of objects, typically flowers and/or fruit.

still room ■ n. Brit. historical a room in a large house used to store preserves and to prepare tea and coffee.
– ORIGIN C18: orig. denoting a room with a still.

stilly poetic/literary ■ adv. /ˈstɪlli/ quietly and with little movement. ■ adj. /ˈstɪli/ still and quiet.

stilt ■ n. 1 either of a pair of upright poles with supports for the feet enabling the user to walk raised above the ground. 2 each of a set of posts or piles supporting a building. 3 a long-billed wading bird, predominantly black and white, with very long slender legs. [Genera *Himantopus* and *Cladorhynchus*: several species.]
– ORIGIN Middle English: of Germanic origin.

stilted ■ adj. 1 (of speech or writing) stiff and self-conscious or unnatural. 2 standing on stilts. 3 Architecture (of an arch) with pieces of upright masonry

between the imposts and the springers.
– DERIVATIVES **stiltedly** adv. **stiltedness** n.

Stilton ■ n. trademark a kind of strong, rich blue cheese, originally made in Leicestershire in central England.
– ORIGIN so named because it was formerly sold at a coaching inn in *Stilton*, Cambridgeshire.

stimulant ■ n. 1 a substance that acts to increase physiological or nervous activity in the body. 2 something that promotes activity, interest, or enthusiasm. ■ adj. acting as a stimulant.

stimulate ■ v. 1 apply or act as a stimulus to. 2 animate or excite.
– DERIVATIVES **stimulating** adj. **stimulatingly** adv. **stimulation** n. **stimulative** adj. **stimulator** n. **stimulatory** adj.
– ORIGIN C16: from Latin *stimulare* 'urge, goad'.

stimulus /ˈstɪmjʊləs/ ■ n. (pl. **stimuli** /-lʌɪ, -liː/) 1 a thing that evokes a specific functional reaction in an organ or tissue. 2 something that promotes activity, interest, or enthusiasm.
– ORIGIN C17: from Latin, 'goad, spur, incentive'.

sting ■ n. 1 a small sharp-pointed organ of an insect, plant, etc. capable of inflicting a painful wound by injecting poison. 2 a wound from such an organ. 3 a sharp tingling sensation or hurtful effect. 4 informal a carefully planned undercover operation. ■ v. (past and past part. **stung**) 1 wound with a sting. 2 produce a stinging sensation. ▸ hurt; upset. ▸ (**sting someone into**) goad someone into. 3 informal swindle or exorbitantly overcharge.
– PHRASES **sting in the tail** an unexpected and unpleasant end to something.
– DERIVATIVES **stinger** n. **stinging** adj. **stingingly** adv. **stingless** adj.
– ORIGIN Old English, of Germanic origin.

stinging nettle ■ n. a nettle covered in stinging hairs. [*Urtica dioica* and related species.]

stingray ■ n. a marine ray with a long poisonous serrated spine at the base of the tail. [Families Dasyatidae and Urolophidae: several species.]

stingy /ˈstɪn(d)ʒi/ ■ adj. (**-ier**, **-iest**) informal mean; ungenerous.
– DERIVATIVES **stingily** adv. **stinginess** n.
– ORIGIN C17: perhaps a dialect var. of STING.

stink ■ v. (past **stank** or **stunk**; past part. **stunk**) 1 have a strong unpleasant smell. ▸ (**stink a place out**) fill a place with such a smell. 2 informal be contemptible or scandalous. ▸ (**stink of**) be highly suggestive of (something disapproved of). ■ n. 1 a strong, unpleasant smell. 2 informal a row or fuss.
– PHRASES **like stink** informal extremely hard or intensely.
– DERIVATIVES **stinky** adj. (informal).
– ORIGIN Old English *stincan*, of West Germanic origin.

stink bomb ■ n. a small container holding a sulphurous compound that is released when the container is broken, emitting a very unpleasant smell.

stink bug ■ n. a shield bug which emits a foul smell when handled or molested.

stinker ■ n. informal 1 a person or thing that stinks. 2 a contemptible or very unpleasant person or thing. 3 a difficult task.

stinkhorn ■ n. a fungus with a rounded greenish-brown gelatinous head that turns into a foul-smelling slime containing the spores. [Family Phallaceae: many species.]

stinking ■ adj. 1 foul-smelling. 2 informal contemptible or very unpleasant. ■ adv. informal extremely: *stinking rich*.
– DERIVATIVES **stinkingly** adv.

stinkwood ■ n. any of several trees, some of which yield wood with an unpleasant odour. [*Ocotea bullata* (black stinkwood) and *Celtis africana* (white stinkwood) (South Africa), and other species elsewhere.]

stint[1] ■ v. [often with neg.] be restrictive or ungenerous towards or in the supply of. ▸ (**stint on**) be restrictive or frugal in acquiring or providing: *he doesn't stint on wining and dining*. ■ n. 1 an allotted period of work. 2 limitation of supply or effort.
– ORIGIN Old English *styntan* 'make blunt', of Germanic origin.

stint[2] ■ n. a very small short-legged northern sandpiper.

[*Calidris minuta* (little stint) and related species.]
– ORIGIN Middle English.

stipe /stʌɪp/ ■ n. Botany a stalk or stem, especially of a seaweed, fungus, or fern frond.
– ORIGIN C18: from French, from Latin *stipes* (see STIPES).

stipend /ˈstʌɪpɛnd/ ■ n. a fixed regular sum paid as a salary or as expenses to a clergyman, teacher, or public official.
– ORIGIN Middle English: from Old French *stipendie* or Latin *stipendium*, from *stips* 'wages' + *pendere* 'to pay'.

stipendiary /stʌɪˈpɛndɪəri, stɪ-/ ■ adj. 1 receiving a stipend; working for pay rather than voluntarily. 2 of, relating to, or of the nature of a stipend. ■ n. (pl. **-ies**) a person receiving a stipend.

stipes /ˈstʌɪpiːz/ ■ n. (pl. **stipites** /ˈstɪpɪtiːz/) 1 Zoology a part or organ resembling a stalk, especially the second joint of the maxilla of an insect. 2 Botany more technical term for STIPE.
– DERIVATIVES **stipitate** adj. (Botany).
– ORIGIN C18: from Latin, 'log, tree trunk'.

stipple ■ v. 1 (in drawing, painting, or engraving) mark (a surface) with numerous small dots or specks. 2 produce a decorative effect on (paint or other material) by roughening its surface when wet. ■ n. the process, technique, or effect of stippling.
– DERIVATIVES **stippler** n. **stippling** n.
– ORIGIN C17: from Dutch *stippelen*, from *stippen* 'to prick', from *stip* 'a point'.

stipulate[1] /ˈstɪpjʊleɪt/ ■ v. demand or specify as part of a bargain or agreement.
– DERIVATIVES **stipulation** n. **stipulator** n.
– ORIGIN C17: from Latin *stipulari* 'demand as a formal promise'.

stipulate[2] /ˈstɪpjʊlət/ ■ adj. Botany having stipules.
– ORIGIN C18: from Latin *stipula* (see STIPULE).

stipule /ˈstɪpjuːl/ ■ n. Botany a small leaf-like appendage to a leaf, typically borne in pairs at the base of the leaf stalk.
– DERIVATIVES **stipular** adj.
– ORIGIN C18: from French *stipule* or Latin *stipula* 'straw'.

stir[1] ■ v. (**stirred**, **stirring**) 1 move an implement round and round in (a liquid or other substance) in order to mix it thoroughly. 2 move or cause to move slightly. ▸ wake or rise from sleep. ▸ begin or cause to begin to be active. 3 arouse strong feeling in. ▸ arouse or prompt (a feeling or memory). 4 informal deliberately cause trouble. ■ n. 1 an act or an instance of stirring or being stirred. 2 a disturbance or commotion.
– DERIVATIVES **stirrer** n. **stirring** adj. & n. **stirringly** adv.
– ORIGIN Old English *styrian*, of Germanic origin.

stir[2] ■ n. informal prison.
– ORIGIN C19: perhaps from Romany *sturbin* 'jail'.

stir-crazy ■ adj. informal, chiefly N. Amer. psychologically disturbed as a result of being confined or imprisoned.

stir-fry ■ v. fry rapidly over a high heat while stirring briskly. ■ n. a stir-fried dish.
– DERIVATIVES **stir-fried** adj.

Stirling engine ■ n. a machine used to provide power or refrigeration which operates on a closed cycle in which a working fluid is cyclically compressed and expanded at different temperatures.
– ORIGIN named after the C19 Scottish engineer Robert *Stirling*.

stirrup ■ n. 1 each of a pair of devices attached at either side of a horse's saddle, in the form of a loop with a flat base to support the rider's foot. 2 (**lithotomy stirrups**) a pair of metal supports for the ankles used during gynaecological examinations and childbirth (originally used in lithotomy). 3 another term for STAPES.
– ORIGIN Old English *stigrāp*, from the Germanic base of obsolete *sty* 'climb' + ROPE.

stirrup cup ■ n. an alcoholic drink offered to a person on horseback who is about to depart.

stirrup pants ■ pl. n. a pair of stretch trousers having a band of elastic at the bottom of each leg which passes under the arch of the foot.

stirrup pump ■ n. chiefly historical a portable

hand-operated water pump with a footrest resembling a stirrup, used to extinguish small fires.

stishovite /ˈstɪʃəvaɪt/ ■ n. a dense form of silica produced by very high pressures, e.g. in meteorite craters.
– ORIGIN 1960s: from the name of the Russian chemist Sergei M. *Stishov*.

stitch ■ n. **1** a loop of thread or yarn resulting from a single pass or movement of the needle in sewing, knitting, or crocheting. ▶ a method of sewing, knitting, or crocheting producing a particular pattern: *an embroidery stitch*. **2** [usu. with neg.] informal the smallest item of clothing: *swimming around with not a stitch on*. **3** a sudden sharp pain in the side of the body, caused by strenuous exercise. ■ v. **1** make or mend with stitches; apply a stitch or stitches to. **2** (**stitch someone up**) Brit. informal manipulate a situation to someone's disadvantage. ▶ (**stitch something up**) manipulate a situation or secure a deal to one's own advantage.
– PHRASES **in stitches** informal laughing uncontrollably.
– DERIVATIVES **stitcher** n. **stitchery** n. **stitching** n.
– ORIGIN Old English, of Germanic origin.

St John's wort ■ n. a herbaceous plant or shrub with distinctive yellow five-petalled flowers and paired oval leaves. [Genus *Hypericum*: many species.]
– ORIGIN so named because some species come into flower near the feast day of St John the Baptist (24 June).

St Louis encephalitis ■ n. a form of viral encephalitis which can be fatal and is transmitted by mosquitoes.
– ORIGIN from the name of *St Louis* in Missouri, US.

St Lucian /ˈluːʃ(ə)n/ ■ n. a native or inhabitant of the Caribbean island of St Lucia. ■ adj. of or relating to St Lucia.

STM ■ abbrev. scanning tunnelling microscope.

stoat ■ n. a small carnivorous mammal of the weasel family with chestnut fur (which in northern areas turns white in winter), white underparts, and a black-tipped tail. [*Mustela erminea*.]
– ORIGIN Middle English.

stochastic /stəˈkastɪk/ ■ adj. having a random probability distribution or pattern that may be analysed statistically but not predicted precisely.
– DERIVATIVES **stochastically** adv.
– ORIGIN C17: from Greek *stokhastikos*, from *stokhazesthai* 'aim at, guess', from *stokhos* 'aim'.

stock ■ n. **1** a supply of goods or materials available for sale or use. **2** farm animals bred and kept for their meat or milk; livestock. **3** the capital raised by a company through the issue and subscription of shares. ▶ (usu. **stocks**) a portion of this as held by an individual or group as an investment. ▶ securities issued by the government in fixed units with a fixed rate of interest. **4** water in which bones, meat, fish, or vegetables have been slowly simmered. ▶ the raw material from which a specified commodity can be manufactured. **5** a person's ancestry or line of descent. ▶ a breed, variety, or population of an animal or plant. **6** the trunk or woody stem of a tree or shrub, especially one into which a graft (scion) is inserted. ▶ the perennial part of a herbaceous plant, especially a rhizome. **7** a plant cultivated for its fragrant flowers, typically lilac, pink, or white. [Genus *Matthiola*: several species.] **8** (**the stocks**) [treated as sing. or pl.] historical an instrument of punishment consisting of a wooden structure with holes for securing a person's feet and hands, in which criminals were locked and exposed to public ridicule or assault. **9** the part of a rifle or other firearm to which the barrel and firing mechanism are attached. ▶ the crossbar of an anchor. ▶ the handle of a whip, fishing rod, etc. **10** a band of white material tied like a cravat and worn as a part of formal horse-riding dress. ▶ a piece of black material worn under a clerical collar. **11** (**stocks**) a frame used to support a ship or boat when out of water. ■ adj. **1** usually kept in stock and thus regularly available for sale. **2** constantly recurring; common or conventional: *the stock characters in every cowboy film*. ■ v. have or keep a stock of.
▶ provide or fill with a stock of something. ▶ (**stock up**) amass stocks of something.
– PHRASES **in** (or **out of**) **stock** available (or unavailable) for immediate sale or use. **put stock in** have a specified amount of belief or faith in. **take stock** make an overall assessment of a particular situation.
– DERIVATIVES **stockless** adj.
– ORIGIN Old English *stoc*(*c*) 'trunk, block of wood, post', of Germanic origin.

stockade ■ n. **1** a barrier or enclosure formed from upright wooden posts or stakes. **2** chiefly N. Amer. a military prison. ■ v. enclose with a stockade.
– DERIVATIVES **stockaded** adj.
– ORIGIN C17: shortening of obsolete French *estocade*, from Spanish *estacada*, from the Germanic base of STAKE[1].

stockbreeder ■ n. a farmer who breeds livestock.
– DERIVATIVES **stockbreeding** n.

stockbroker ■ n. a broker who buys and sells securities on a stock exchange on behalf of clients.
– DERIVATIVES **stockbrokerage** n. **stockbroking** n.

stockbroker belt ■ n. Brit. an affluent residential area outside a large city.

stock car ■ n. **1** an ordinary car that has been strengthened for use in a type of race in which competing cars collide with each other. **2** N. Amer. a railway wagon for transporting livestock.

stock cube ■ n. a cube of concentrated dehydrated meat, vegetable, or fish stock for use in cooking.

stocker ■ n. a person who stocks the shelves of a shop or supermarket.

stock exchange ■ n. a market in which securities are bought and sold.

stockfish ■ n. (pl. same or **-fishes**) **1** S. African the hake, a commercially important food fish. [*Merluccius capensis* and *M. paradoxus*.] **2** cod or a similar fish split and dried in the open air without salt.
– ORIGIN Middle English: from Middle Low German, Middle Dutch *stokvisch*.

stockholder ■ n. **1** chiefly N. Amer. a shareholder. **2** a holder of supplies for manufacturers.
– DERIVATIVES **stockholding** n.

stockinet (also **stockinette**) ■ n. a soft, loosely knitted stretch fabric used for cleaning, wrapping, or bandaging.
– ORIGIN C18: prob. an alteration of *stocking-net*.

stocking ■ n. **1** a woman's garment that fits closely over the foot and leg, typically made of fine knitted nylon yarn, held up by suspenders or an elasticated strip at the upper thigh. ▶ a cylindrical bandage or other medical covering for the leg resembling a stocking. **2** US or archaic a long sock worn by men. **3** a real or ornamental stocking hung up by children on Christmas Eve for Father Christmas to fill with presents. **4** a white marking of the lower part of a horse's leg, extending as far as, or just beyond, the knee or hock.
– DERIVATIVES **stockinged** adj. **stockingless** adj.
– ORIGIN C16: from STOCK in the dialect sense 'stocking'.

stocking cap ■ n. a knitted conical hat with a long tapered end that hangs down.

stocking filler (N. Amer. **stocking stuffer**) ■ n. a small present suitable for putting in a Christmas stocking.

stocking mask ■ n. a nylon stocking pulled over the face to disguise the features, used by criminals.

stocking stitch ■ n. a knitting stitch consisting of alternate rows of plain and purl stitch.

stock-in-trade ■ n. **1** the typical subject or commodity a person, company, or profession uses or deals in. **2** the type of stock kept regularly by a shop.

stockist ■ n. a retailer that stocks goods of a particular type for sale.

stockman ■ n. (pl. **-men**) **1** a person who looks after livestock. **2** US an owner of livestock.

stock market ■ n. a stock exchange.

stock option ■ n. another term for SHARE OPTION.

stockpile ■ n. a large accumulated stock of goods or materials. ■ v. accumulate a large stock of.
– DERIVATIVES **stockpiler** n.

stockpot ■ n. a pot in which stock is prepared by long, slow cooking.

stock split ■ n. an issue of new shares in a company to existing shareholders in proportion to their current holdings.

stock-still ■ adv. without any movement; completely still.

stocktaking ■ n. the action or process of recording the

amount of stock held by a business.
- DERIVATIVES **stocktake** n. **stocktaker** n.

stocky ■ adj. (-ier, -iest) (especially of a person) short and sturdy.
- DERIVATIVES **stockily** adv. **stockiness** n.

stodge ■ n. informal, chiefly Brit. **1** food that is heavy, filling, and high in carbohydrates. **2** dull and uninspired material or work.
- DERIVATIVES **stodgily** adv. **stodginess** n. **stodgy** adj.
- ORIGIN C17: suggested by STUFF and dialect *podge* 'excess weight, fat'.

stoep /stuːp/ ■ n. S. African a veranda in front of a house.
- ORIGIN Afrikaans, from Dutch.

stoic /ˈstəʊɪk/ ■ n. a stoical person. ■ adj. stoical.
- ORIGIN Middle English: from Greek *stōikos* (with ref. to the teaching of the ancient Greek philosopher Zeno, in the *Stoa Poikilē* or 'Painted Porch', at Athens).

stoical /ˈstəʊɪk(ə)l/ ■ adj. enduring pain and hardship without showing one's feelings or complaining.
- DERIVATIVES **stoically** adv.

stoichiometry /ˌstɔɪkɪˈɒmɪtri/ ■ n. Chemistry the relationship between the relative quantities of substances taking part in a reaction or forming a compound, typically a ratio of whole integers.
- DERIVATIVES **stoichiometric** adj. **stoichiometrically** adv.
- ORIGIN C19: from Greek *stoikheion* 'element' + -METRY.

stoicism /ˈstəʊɪsɪz(ə)m/ ■ n. stoical behaviour.

stoke ■ v. **1** add coal to (a fire, furnace, etc.). **2** encourage or incite (a strong emotion). **3** (**stoke up**) informal consume a large quantity of food to give one energy.
- ORIGIN C17: back-formation from STOKER.

stoker ■ n. **1** a person who tends the furnace on a steamship or steam train. **2** a mechanical device for supplying fuel to a furnace.
- ORIGIN C17: from Dutch, from *stoken* 'stoke (a furnace)', from Middle Dutch *stoken* 'push, poke'.

stokvel /ˈstɒkfɛl/ ■ n. S. African an informal group savings scheme that provides small-scale rotating loans.
- ORIGIN adaptation of *stock-fair* resulting from a pronunciation mistakenly suggesting that the word is from Afrikaans; so named from the rotating cattle auctions held by English settlers in the 19th century.

STOL ■ abbrev. Aeronautics short take-off and landing.

stole[1] ■ n. **1** a woman's long scarf or shawl, worn loosely over the shoulders. **2** a priest's vestment worn over the shoulders and hanging down to the knee or below.
- ORIGIN Old English, from Greek *stolē* 'clothing', from *stellein* 'array'.

stole[2] past of STEAL.

stolen past participle of STEAL.

stolid ■ adj. calm, dependable, and showing little emotion or animation.
- DERIVATIVES **stolidity** n. **stolidly** adv. **stolidness** n.
- ORIGIN C16: from obsolete French *stolide* or Latin *stolidus*, perhaps rel. to *stultus* 'foolish'.

stollen /ˈstɒlən, ˈʃtɒ-/ ■ n. a rich German fruit and nut loaf.
- ORIGIN from German *Stollen*.

stolon /ˈstəʊlɒn/ ■ n. **1** Botany a creeping horizontal stem or runner that takes root at several points to form new plants. **2** Zoology a branched stem-like structure attaching a colony of hydroids to the substrate.
- DERIVATIVES **stolonate** adj. **stoloniferous** adj.
- ORIGIN C17: from Latin *stolo, stolon-* 'shoot, scion'.

stoma /ˈstəʊmə/ ■ n. (pl. **stomas** or **stomata** /-mətə/) **1** Botany any of the minute pores in the epidermis of the leaf or stem of a plant, allowing movement of gases in and out of the intercellular spaces. **2** Zoology a small mouth-like opening in some lower animals. **3** Medicine an artificial opening made into a hollow organ, especially one on the surface of the body leading to the gut or trachea.
- DERIVATIVES **stomal** adj.
- ORIGIN C17: from Greek *stoma* 'mouth'.

stomach ■ n. **1** an internal organ in which the first part of digestion occurs, being (in humans and many mammals) a pear-shaped enlargement of the alimentary canal linking the oesophagus to the small intestine. ► each of four such organs in a ruminant. **2** the abdominal area of the body; the belly. **3** [usu. with neg.] an appetite or desire for something. ■ v. **1** [usu. with neg.] consume (food or drink) without feeling or being sick: *he cannot stomach milk*. **2** endure or accept: *what I won't stomach is thieving*.
- PHRASES **a strong stomach** an ability to see or do unpleasant things without feeling sick or squeamish.
- DERIVATIVES **stomachful** n. (pl. **-fuls**).
- ORIGIN Middle English: from Old French *estomac, stomaque*, from Greek *stomakhos* 'gullet'.

stomacher ■ n. historical a V-shaped ornamental panel worn over the chest and stomach by men and women in the 16th century, later only by women.
- ORIGIN Middle English: prob. a shortening of Old French *estomachier*, from *estomac* (see STOMACH).

stomata plural form of STOMA.

stomate /ˈstəʊmeɪt/ ■ n. Botany another term for STOMA.
- DERIVATIVES **stomatal** adj.
- ORIGIN C19: apparently an English sing. of STOMATA.

stomatitis /ˌstəʊməˈtʌɪtɪs, ˌstɒ-/ ■ n. Medicine inflammation of the mucous membrane of the mouth.
- ORIGIN C19: from *stoma, stomat-* 'mouth'.

stomp ■ v. **1** tread heavily and noisily, typically in order to show anger. **2** dance with heavy stamping steps. ■ n. a tune or dance with a fast tempo and a heavy beat.
- DERIVATIVES **stomper** n. **stomping** adj. **stompy** adj.
- ORIGIN C19 (orig. US dialect): var. of STAMP.

stompie /ˈstɒmpi/ ■ n. S. African a cigarette end.
- PHRASES **pick up stompies** overhear and interrupt a conversation.
- ORIGIN from Afrikaans *stomp* 'stump'.

stomping ground ■ n. another term for STAMPING GROUND.

stone ■ n. **1** hard, solid non-metallic mineral matter of which rock is made. ► a small piece of stone found on the ground. ► a piece of stone shaped for a purpose, especially one of commemoration or demarcation. ► Astronomy a meteorite made of rock, as opposed to metal. **2** a gem. **3** Medicine a gallstone or kidney stone; a calculus. **4** a hard seed in a cherry, plum, peach, etc. **5** (pl. same) Brit. a unit of weight equal to 14 lb (6.35 kg). **6** a whitish or brownish-grey colour. ■ v. **1** throw stones at in order to injure or kill. **2** remove the stone from (a fruit). **3** build, face, or pave with stone. ■ adv. extremely or totally: *stone cold*.
- PHRASES **leave no stone unturned** try every possible course of action in order to achieve something. **a stone's throw** a short distance. **stone me!** (or **stone the crows!**) Brit. informal an exclamation of surprise or shock.
- DERIVATIVES **stoneless** adj.
- ORIGIN Old English, of Germanic origin.

Stone Age ■ n. a prehistoric period when weapons and tools were made of stone, preceding the Bronze Age.

stonechat ■ n. a small bird of the thrush family, with a call like two stones being knocked together. [*Saxicola torquata* and related species.]

stone circle ■ n. a megalithic monument consisting of stones or menhirs arranged more or less in a circle.

stonecrop ■ n. a small fleshy-leaved plant which typically has star-shaped yellow or white flowers and grows among rocks or on walls. [Genus *Sedum*: many species.]

stoned ■ adj. informal under the influence of drugs, especially cannabis, or alcohol.

stonefish ■ n. (pl. same or **-fishes**) a tropical Indo-Pacific fish of bizarre appearance which rests motionless in the sand with its venomous dorsal spines projecting. [*Synanceia verrucosa* and other species.]

stonefly ■ n. (pl. **-flies**) a slender insect with transparent membranous wings, the larvae of which live in clean running water. [Order Plecoptera: many families.]

stone fruit ■ n. a fruit with flesh or pulp enclosing a stone, such as a peach, plum, or cherry.

stoneground ■ adj. (of flour) ground with millstones.

stonemason ■ n. a person who cuts, prepares, and builds with stone.
- DERIVATIVES **stonemasonry** n.

stone pine ■ n. an umbrella-shaped southern European pine tree with seeds that are eaten as pine nuts. [*Pinus pinea*.]

stone plant ■ n. a succulent plant of a large family native to southern Africa. [Family Mesembryanthemaceae (Aizoaceae): several genera, including *Lithops*.]

stonewall ■ v. **1** delay or block by refusing to answer questions or by giving evasive replies, especially in politics. **2** Cricket bat extremely defensively.
– DERIVATIVES **stonewaller** n.

stoneware ■ n. a type of pottery which is impermeable and partly vitrified but opaque.

stonewashed (also **stonewash**) ■ adj. (of a garment or fabric, especially denim) washed with abrasives to produce a worn or faded appearance.

stonework ■ n. **1** the parts of a building that are made of stone. **2** the work of a mason.
– DERIVATIVES **stoneworker** n.

stonker ■ n. Brit. informal something very large or impressive of its kind.
– DERIVATIVES **stonking** adj.

stony ■ adj. (-ier, -iest) **1** full of stones. **2** of or resembling stone. **3** cold and unfeeling.
– PHRASES **fall on stony ground** (of words or a suggestion) be ignored or badly received. [with biblical ref. to the parable of the sower (Matthew 13:5).]
– DERIVATIVES **stonily** adv. **stoniness** n.

stony broke ■ adj. informal entirely without money.

stood past and past participle of **STAND**.

stooge ■ n. **1** derogatory a subordinate used by another to do routine or unpleasant work. **2** a performer whose act involves being the butt of a comedian's jokes. ■ v. informal move about aimlessly.
– ORIGIN C20.

stook /stʊk, stuːk/ Brit. ■ n. a group of sheaves of grain stood on end in a field. ■ v. arrange in stooks.
– ORIGIN Middle English: from or rel. to Middle Low German *stūke*.

stool ■ n. **1** a seat without a back or arms, typically resting on three or four legs or on a single pedestal. **2** chiefly Medicine a piece of faeces. **3** a root or stump of a tree or plant from which shoots spring. ■ v. throw up shoots from the root. ▸ cut back (a plant) to or near ground level in order to induce new growth.
– PHRASES **fall between two stools** fail to be or take either of two satisfactory alternatives.
– ORIGIN Old English, of Germanic origin.

stool pigeon ■ n. **1** a police informer. **2** a person acting as a decoy.
– ORIGIN C19: so named from the original use of a pigeon fixed to a stool as a decoy.

stoop¹ ■ v. **1** bend one's head or body forwards and downwards. ▸ have the head and shoulders habitually bent forwards. **2** lower one's moral standards so far as to do something reprehensible. **3** (of a bird of prey) swoop down on a quarry. ■ n. **1** a stooping posture. **2** the downward swoop of a bird of prey.
– ORIGIN Old English *stūpian* (v.), of Germanic origin.

stoop² ■ n. N. Amer. a porch with steps in front of a house or other building.
– ORIGIN C18: from Dutch *stoep* (see **STOEP**).

stop ■ v. (**stopped**, **stopping**) **1** come or cause to come to an end. ▸ discontinue an action, practice, or habit. **2** prevent from happening or from doing something. ▸ instruct a bank to withhold payment on (a cheque). ▸ refuse to supply as usual. ▸ Boxing defeat (an opponent) by a knockout. **3** cease or cause to cease moving or operating. ▸ (of a bus or train) call at a designated place to pick up or set down passengers. ▸ Brit. informal stay somewhere for a short time. **4** block or close up (a hole or leak). **5** obtain the required pitch from (the string of a violin or similar instrument) by pressing at the appropriate point with the finger. ■ n. **1** an act of stopping. ▸ a place designated for a bus or train to stop. **2** an object or part of a mechanism which prevents movement. ▸ Bridge a high card that prevents the opponents from establishing a particular suit. ▸ Nautical a stopper. **3** Phonetics a consonant produced with complete closure of the vocal tract. **4** a set of organ pipes of a particular tone and range of pitch. ▸ (also **stop knob**) a knob, lever, etc. in an organ or harpsichord which brings into play a set of pipes or strings of a particular tone and range of pitch. **5** Photography the effective diameter of a lens. ▸ a device for reducing this. ▸ a unit of change of relative aperture or exposure (with a reduction of one stop equivalent to halving it).
– PHRASES **pull out all the stops** make a very great effort to achieve something. **put a stop to** cause (an activity) to end. **stop dead** (or **short**) suddenly cease moving, speaking, or acting. **stop payment** instruct a bank to withhold payment on a cheque.
– PHRASAL VERBS **stop by** (or **in**) call briefly and informally as a visitor. **stop something down** Photography reduce the aperture of a lens with a diaphragm. **stop off** (or **over**) pay a short visit en route to one's ultimate destination. **stop up** Brit. informal refrain from going to bed.
– DERIVATIVES **stoppable** adj.
– ORIGIN Old English (*for*)*stoppian* 'block up (an aperture)', of West Germanic origin, from late Latin *stuppare* 'to stuff'.

stopcock ■ n. an externally operated valve regulating the flow of a liquid or gas through a pipe.

stope /stəʊp/ ■ n. a step-like working in a mine. ■ v. [usu. as noun **stoping**] cut a series of stopes in.
– ORIGIN C18: apparently rel. to **STEP**.

stopgap ■ n. a temporary solution or substitute.

stop-go ■ n. the alternate restriction and stimulation of economic demand by a government.

stop knob ■ n. see **STOP** sense 4.

stop light ■ n. a red traffic signal.

stop list ■ n. **1** a list of people with whom members of an association are forbidden to do business. **2** a list of words automatically omitted from a computer-generated concordance or index.

stop-motion ■ n. a technique of cinematographic animation whereby the camera is repeatedly stopped and started to give the impression of movement.

stop order ■ n. S. African an instruction to a bank by an account holder to make regular fixed payments to another account.

stoppage ■ n. **1** an instance of stopping or being stopped. ▸ an instance of industrial action. **2** a blockage.

stoppage time ■ n. another term for **INJURY TIME**.

stopper ■ n. **1** a plug for sealing a hole, especially in the neck of a bottle. **2** (in soccer or American football) a player whose function is to block attacks on goal from the middle of the field. **3** Baseball a pitcher who prevents opponents from scoring highly. **4** (in sailing or climbing) a rope or clamp for preventing a rope or cable from being run out. ■ v. [usu. as adj. **stoppered**] seal with a stopper.
– PHRASES **put a** (or **the**) **stopper on** informal prevent.

stop press ■ n. late news inserted in a newspaper or periodical either just before printing or after printing has begun.

stop street ■ n. an intersection at which drivers must come to a complete stop before continuing.

stop volley ■ n. Tennis a checked volley played close to the net, dropping the ball dead on the other side.

stopwatch ■ n. a special watch with buttons that start, stop, and then zero the display, used to time races.

storage ■ n. **1** the action of storing. **2** space available for storing. **3** a charge for warehouse storage.

storage battery (also **storage cell**) ■ n. a battery (or cell) used for storing electrical energy.

storage heater ■ n. Brit. an electric heater that accumulates heat during the night (when electricity is cheaper) and releases it during the day.

store ■ n. **1** a quantity or supply kept for use as needed. ▸ (**stores**) supplies kept for use by members of the military or other institutions. **2** a place where things are kept for future use or sale. ▸ a shop. **3** Brit. a computer memory. **4** a sheep, steer, cow, or pig acquired or kept for fattening. ■ v. **1** keep or accumulate for future use. **2** retain or enter (information) for future electronic retrieval. **3** (**be stored with**) have a useful supply of.

strafe

—PHRASES **in store** about to happen. **set** (or **lay** or **put**) **store by** (or **on**) consider to be of a particular degree of importance: *she set much store by privacy.*
—DERIVATIVES **storable** adj. **storer** n.
—ORIGIN Middle English: shortening of Old French *estore* (n.), *estorer* (v.), from Latin *instaurare* 'renew'.

store card ■ n. a credit card that can be used only in one store or chain of stores.

storefront ■ n. another term for SHOPFRONT.

storehouse ■ n. **1** a building used for storing goods. **2** a repository.

storekeeper ■ n. a shopkeeper.

storeman ■ n. (pl. **-men**) a man responsible for stored goods.

storeroom ■ n. a room in which items are stored.

storey (N. Amer. also **story**) ■ n. (pl. **-eys** or **-ies**) a part of a building comprising all the rooms that are on the same level.
—DERIVATIVES **-storeyed** (N. Amer. also **-storied**) adj.
—ORIGIN Middle English: shortening of Latin *historia* 'history', a special use in Anglo-Latin, perhaps orig. denoting a tier of painted windows or sculptures representing a historical subject.

stork ■ n. a very tall long-legged bird with a long heavy bill and typically white and black plumage. [Family Coconiidae: several species.]
—ORIGIN Old English *storc*, of Germanic origin.

storm ■ n. **1** a violent disturbance of the atmosphere with strong winds and usually rain, thunder, lightning, or snow. **2** a sudden violent display of strong feeling. **3** a direct assault by troops. ■ v. **1** move angrily or forcefully in a specified direction. **2** (of troops) suddenly attack and capture (a place). **3** shout angrily.
—PHRASES **go down a storm** be enthusiastically received. **a storm in a teacup** Brit. great anger or excitement about a trivial matter. **take something by storm 1** capture a place by a sudden and violent attack. **2** have great and rapid success. —— **up a storm** chiefly N. Amer. perform the specified action with great enthusiasm and energy.
—DERIVATIVES **stormproof** adj.
—ORIGIN Old English, of Germanic origin.

stormbound ■ adj. prevented by storms from starting or continuing a journey.

storm cloud ■ n. **1** a heavy, dark rain cloud. **2** (**storm clouds**) an ominous state of affairs.

storm drain (chiefly S. African & Austral./NZ **stormwater drain**) ■ n. a drain built to carry away excess water in times of heavy rain.

stormer ■ n. informal a thing which is particularly impressive of its kind.
—DERIVATIVES **storming** adj.

storm flap ■ n. a flap intended to protect an opening or fastening on a tent or coat from the effects of rain.

storm lantern ■ n. a hurricane lamp.

storm petrel ■ n. a small petrel with blackish plumage, formerly believed to be a harbinger of bad weather. [*Hydrobates pelagicus* (NE Atlantic and Mediterranean) and other species.]

storm sail ■ n. a sail of smaller size and stronger material than the corresponding one used ordinarily.

storm troops ■ pl. n. another term for SHOCK TROOPS.
—DERIVATIVES **storm trooper** n.

stormwater drain ■ n. another term for STORM DRAIN.
—DERIVATIVES **stormwater drainage** n.

stormy ■ adj. (**-ier**, **-iest**) **1** affected or disturbed by a storm. **2** full of angry or violent outbursts of feeling.
—DERIVATIVES **stormily** adv. **storminess** n.

stormy petrel ■ n. **1** dated term for STORM PETREL. **2** a person who delights in conflict or attracts controversy.

story[1] ■ n. (pl. **-ies**) **1** an account of imaginary or real people and events told for entertainment. ▸ a storyline. **2** an account of past events, experiences, etc. ▸ an item of news. **3** informal a lie.
—PHRASES **the same old story** a bad situation that is tediously familiar. **the story goes** it is said. **the story of one's life** informal a misfortune that has happened too often in one's experience. **to cut** (N. Amer. **make**) **a long story short** used to end an account of events quickly.
—ORIGIN Middle English: shortening of Anglo-Norman French *estorie*, from Latin *historia* (see HISTORY).

story[2] ■ n. N. Amer. variant spelling of STOREY.

storyboard ■ n. a sequence of drawings representing the shots planned for a film or television production.

storybook ■ n. **1** a book containing a story or stories for children. **2** [as modifier] idyllically perfect.

story editor ■ n. an editor who advises on the content and form of film or television scripts.

storyline ■ n. the plot of a novel, play, film, or other narrative form.

storyteller ■ n. a person who tells stories.
—DERIVATIVES **storytelling** n. & adj.

stoup /stu:p/ ■ n. **1** a basin for holy water in a church. **2** archaic a flagon or beaker.
—ORIGIN Middle English: from Old Norse *staup*, of Germanic origin.

stout ■ adj. **1** rather fat or heavily built. **2** (of an object) sturdy and thick. **3** brave and determined. ■ n. a kind of strong, dark beer brewed with roasted malt or barley.
—DERIVATIVES **stoutish** adj. **stoutly** adv. **stoutness** n.
—ORIGIN Middle English: from Anglo-Norman French and Old French dialect, of West Germanic origin.

stout-hearted ■ adj. courageous or determined.
—DERIVATIVES **stout-heartedly** adv. **stout-heartedness** n.

stove[1] ■ n. an apparatus for cooking or heating that operates by burning fuel or using electricity. ■ v. heat (an object) in a stove so as to apply a desired coating.
—ORIGIN Middle English: from Middle Dutch or Middle Low German *stove*; perhaps rel. to STEW[1].

stove[2] past and past participle of STAVE.

stove enamel ■ n. Brit. a heatproof enamel produced by heat treatment in a stove.

stovepipe ■ n. a pipe taking the smoke and gases from a stove up through a roof or to a chimney.

stovepipe hat ■ n. a type of tall top hat.

stow ■ v. **1** pack or store (an object) tidily in an appropriate place. **2** (**stow away**) conceal oneself on a ship, aircraft, etc. so as to travel without paying or surreptitiously.
—PHRASES **stow it!** Brit. informal be quiet!
—DERIVATIVES **stowage** n.
—ORIGIN Middle English: shortening of BESTOW.

stowaway ■ n. a person who stows away.

STP ■ abbrev. **1** Physiology short-term potentiation. **2** Chemistry standard temperature and pressure.

St Peter's fish ■ n. a tilapia with a dark mark near each pectoral fin, native to North Africa and the Middle East. [*Sarotherodon galileus*.]
—ORIGIN with biblical allusion to Matthew 17:27.

str. ■ abbrev. strait.

strabismus /strə'bɪzməs/ ■ n. the condition of having a squint.
—DERIVATIVES **strabismic** adj.
—ORIGIN C17: from Greek *strabismos*, from *strabizein* 'to squint'.

Strad ■ n. informal a Stradivarius.

straddle ■ v. **1** sit or stand with one leg on either side of. **2** extend across both sides of. **3** N. Amer. maintain an equivocal position regarding (a political issue). ■ n. **1** an act of straddling. **2** Stock Exchange a simultaneous purchase of options to buy and to sell a security or commodity at a fixed price.
—DERIVATIVES **straddler** n.
—ORIGIN C16: alteration of dialect *striddle*, back-formation from *striddling* 'astride'.

Stradivarius /ˌstrædɪˈvɛːrɪəs/ ■ n. a violin or other stringed instrument made by the Italian violin-maker Antonio Stradivari (c.1644–1737) or his followers.
—ORIGIN C19: Latinized form of *Stradivari*.

strafe /strɑːf, streɪf/ ■ v. attack with machine-gun fire or

straggle

bombs from low-flying aircraft. ■ n. an act of strafing.
– ORIGIN C20: humorous adaptation of the German First World War catchphrase *Gott strafe England* 'may God punish England'.

straggle ■ v. 1 move along slowly so as to trail behind the person or people in front. 2 grow or spread out in an irregular, untidy way. ■ n. an irregular and untidy group.
– DERIVATIVES **straggler** n. **straggly** adj.
– ORIGIN Middle English: perhaps from dialect *strake* 'go'.

straight ■ adj. 1 extending uniformly in one direction only; without a curve or bend. 2 properly positioned so as to be level, upright, or symmetrical. ▸ in proper order or condition. 3 not evasive; honest. ▸ (of a choice) simple. ▸ (of thinking) clear and logical. 4 in continuous succession. 5 (of an alcoholic drink) undiluted. 6 (of drama) serious as opposed to comic or musical. 7 informal conventional or respectable. 8 informal heterosexual. ■ adv. 1 in a straight line or in a straight manner. 2 archaic at once. ■ n. 1 the straight part of something, especially the concluding stretch of a racecourse. 2 (in poker) a continuous sequence of five cards. 3 informal a conventional person.
– PHRASES **go straight** live an honest life after being a criminal. **a straight face** a blank or serious facial expression, especially when trying not to laugh. **the straight and narrow** the honest and morally acceptable way of living. **straight away** immediately. **a straight fight** a contest between just two opponents. **straight from the shoulder** (of words) frank or direct. **straight off** (or **out**) informal without hesitation or deliberation.
– DERIVATIVES **straightish** adj. **straightly** adv. **straightness** n.
– ORIGIN Middle English: archaic past participle of **STRETCH**.

straight angle ■ n. Mathematics an angle of 180°.

straight-arm ■ v. informal push away (an opponent or obstacle) with the arm outstretched.

straightaway ■ adv. variant spelling of straight away at STRAIGHT. ■ adj. N. Amer. extending or moving in a straight line.

straight chain ■ n. Chemistry a chain of atoms in a molecule that is neither branched nor formed into a ring.

straight edge ■ n. a bar with one edge accurately straight, used for testing straightness.

straight-eight (or **straight-six**) ■ n. an internal-combustion engine with eight (or six) cylinders in line.

straighten ■ v. 1 make or become straight. ▸ stand or sit erect after bending. 2 (**straighten up**) (of a vehicle, ship, or aircraft) stop turning and move in a straight line.
– DERIVATIVES **straightener** n.

straight flush ■ n. (in poker or brag) a hand of cards all of one suit and in a continuous sequence.

straightforward ■ adj. 1 easy to do or understand. 2 honest and open.
– DERIVATIVES **straightforwardly** adv. **straightforwardness** n.

straightjacket ■ n. & v. variant spelling of STRAITJACKET.

straight-laced ■ adj. variant spelling of STRAIT-LACED.

straight-line ■ adj. Finance (of depreciation) allocating a given percentage of the cost of an asset each year for a fixed period.

straight man ■ n. a comedian's stooge.

straight razor ■ n. another term for CUT-THROAT RAZOR.

straight shooter ■ n. informal an honest and forthright person.
– DERIVATIVES **straight-shooting** adj.

straight-up ■ adj. N. Amer. informal honest; trustworthy.

straightway ■ adv. archaic form of straight away (see STRAIGHT).

strain¹ ■ v. 1 force (a part of one's body or oneself) to make an unusually great effort. ▸ injure (a limb, muscle, or organ) by overexertion. ▸ make a strenuous and continuous effort. 2 make severe or excessive demands on. 3 pull or push forcibly at something. 4 pour (a mainly liquid substance) through a sieve or similar device to separate out any solid matter. ▸ drain off (liquid) in this way. ■ n. 1 a force tending to strain something to an extreme degree. ▸ Physics the magnitude of a deformation, equal to the change in the dimension of a deformed object divided by its original dimension. 2 an injury caused by straining a muscle, limb, etc. 3 a severe demand on strength or resources. ▸ a state of tension or exhaustion resulting from this. 4 the sound of a piece of music as it is played or performed.
– DERIVATIVES **strainable** adj.
– ORIGIN Middle English: from Old French *estreindre*, from Latin *stringere* 'draw tight'.

strain² ■ n. 1 a distinct breed, stock, or variety of an animal, plant, or other organism. 2 a tendency in a person's character.
– ORIGIN Old English *strīon* 'acquisition, gain', of Germanic origin.

strained ■ adj. 1 not relaxed or comfortable; showing signs of strain. 2 produced by deliberate effort; artificial or laboured.

strainer ■ n. a device for straining liquids, having holes punched in it or made of crossed wire.

strait ■ n. 1 (also **straits**) a narrow passage of water connecting two seas or other large areas of water. 2 (**straits**) a situation characterized by a specified degree of trouble or difficulty: *in dire straits.* ■ adj. archaic 1 narrow or cramped. 2 strict or rigorous.
– DERIVATIVES **straitly** adv. **straitness** n.
– ORIGIN Middle English: shortening of Old French *estreit* 'tight, narrow', from Latin *strictus* (see STRICT).

straiten ■ v. 1 [as adj. **straitened**] restricted in range. ▸ restricted because of poverty: *they lived in straitened circumstances.* 2 archaic make or become narrow.

straitjacket (also **straightjacket**) ■ n. 1 a strong garment with long sleeves which can be tied together to confine the arms of a violent prisoner or mental patient. 2 a severe restriction. ■ v. (-**jacketed**, -**jacketing**) restrain with or as if with a straitjacket.

strait-laced (also **straight-laced**) ■ adj. having or showing very strict moral attitudes.

strake ■ n. 1 a continuous line of planking or plates from the stem to the stern of a ship or boat. 2 a protruding ridge fitted to an aircraft or other structure to improve aerodynamic stability.
– ORIGIN Middle English: from Anglo-Latin *stracus*; prob. from the Germanic base of STRETCH.

strand¹ ■ v. [often as adj. **stranded**] 1 drive or leave aground on a shore. 2 leave without the means to move from a place. ■ n. poetic/literary the shore of a sea, lake, or large river.
– DERIVATIVES **stranding** n.
– ORIGIN Old English.

strand² ■ n. 1 a single thin length of thread, wire, etc., especially as twisted together with others. 2 an element that forms part of a complex whole.
– DERIVATIVES **stranded** adj.
– ORIGIN C15.

Strandloper /ˈstrantloəpə/ ■ n. S. African historical a member of a Khoisan people living on the west coast of South Africa when the first white settlers arrived.
– ORIGIN from Dutch *strandlooper*, from *strand* 'beach' + *looper* 'walker'.

strandveld /ˈstrantfɛlt/ ■ n. S. African uncultivated coastal land characterized by loose, sandy soil and semi-succulent vegetation.
– ORIGIN C19: from Afrikaans, from *strand* 'beach' + *veld* 'land, countryside'.

strandwolf /ˈstrantvɔlf, ˈstrandwʊlf/ ■ n. S. African the brown hyena.
– ORIGIN from S. African Dutch, from *strand* 'beach' + *wolf* 'wolf', or from English *strand* + *wolf* (because of its habit of scavenging along the shore).

strange ■ adj. 1 unusual or surprising. 2 not previously visited, seen, or encountered. ▸ (**strange to/at/in**) archaic unaccustomed to or unfamiliar with. 3 Physics having a non-zero value for strangeness.
– PHRASES **feel strange** 1 feel indefinably unwell. 2 be uncomfortable in a situation. **strange to say** (or poetic/literary **tell**) it is surprising or unusual that.
– DERIVATIVES **strangely** adv.

–ORIGIN Middle English: shortening of Old French *estrange*, from Latin *extraneus* 'external, strange'.

strangeness ■ n. **1** the state or fact of being strange. **2** Physics one of the six flavours of quark.

stranger ■ n. **1** a person whom one does not know. **2** a person who does not know, or is not known in, a particular place. **3** (**stranger to**) a person entirely unaccustomed to (a feeling, experience, or situation).
–ORIGIN Middle English: shortening of Old French *estrangier*, from Latin *extraneus* (see STRANGE).

strangle ■ v. **1** squeeze or constrict the neck of, especially so as to cause death. **2** suppress or hinder (an impulse, action, or sound).
–DERIVATIVES **strangler** n.
–ORIGIN Middle English: shortening of Old French *estrangler*, from Latin *strangulare*, from Greek, from *strangalē* 'halter'.

stranglehold ■ n. **1** a grip around the neck of a person that can kill by asphyxiation if held for long enough. **2** complete or overwhelming control.

strangles ■ pl. n. [usu. treated as sing.] bacterial infection of the upper respiratory tract of horses, causing enlarged lymph nodes in the throat.

strangulate /ˈstraŋɡjʊleɪt/ ■ v. [often as adj. **strangulated**] **1** Medicine prevent blood circulation through (a part, especially a hernia) by constriction. **2** informal strangle. ▸ [as adj. **strangulated**] sounding as though the speaker's throat is constricted.
–DERIVATIVES **strangulation** n.
–ORIGIN C17: from Latin *strangulare* 'choke' (see STRANGLE).

strap ■ n. **1** a strip of leather, cloth, or other flexible material, used for fastening, securing, carrying, or holding on to. **2** a strip of metal, often hinged, used for fastening or securing. **3** (**the strap**) punishment by beating with a leather strap. ■ v. (**strapped**, **strapping**) **1** fasten or secure with a strap. **2** bind (an injured part of the body) with adhesive plaster. **3** beat with a leather strap. **4** [as adj. **strapped**] informal short of money: *I'm constantly strapped for cash*.
–DERIVATIVES **strapless** adj. **strappy** adj.
–ORIGIN C16: dialect form of STROP[1].

strap hinge ■ n. a hinge with long leaves or flaps for screwing on to the surface of a door or gate.

strapline ■ n. a subsidiary heading or caption in a newspaper or magazine.

strapping[1] ■ adj. (especially of a young person) big and strong.

strapping[2] ■ n. **1** adhesive plaster for strapping injuries. **2** leather or metal straps.

strapwork ■ n. ornamentation imitating pierced and interlaced straps.

strata plural form of STRATUM.

stratagem /ˈstratədʒəm/ ■ n. a plan or scheme intended to outwit an opponent.
–ORIGIN C15: from French *stratagème*, from Greek *stratēgēma*, from *stratēgein* 'be a general'.

stratal ■ adj. of or relating to strata or a stratum.

strategic /strəˈtiːdʒɪk/ ■ adj. **1** forming part of a long-term plan or aim to achieve a specific purpose. **2** relating to the gaining of overall or long-term military advantage. ▸ (of bombing or weapons) done or for use against an enemy's territory or infrastructure. Often contrasted with TACTICAL.
–DERIVATIVES **strategical** adj. **strategically** adv.

strategy /ˈstratɪdʒi/ ■ n. (pl. **-ies**) **1** a plan designed to achieve a particular long-term aim. **2** the art of planning and directing military activity in a war or battle. Often contrasted with tactics (see TACTIC (sense 2)). ▸ a plan so devised.
–DERIVATIVES **strategist** n. **strategize** (also **-ise**) v.
–ORIGIN C19: from French *stratégie*, from Greek *stratēgia* 'generalship', from *stratēgos* 'general'.

strath /straθ/ ■ n. Scottish a broad river valley.
–ORIGIN C16: from Scottish Gaelic *srath*.

stratify /ˈstratɪfʌɪ/ ■ v. (**-ies**, **-ied**) **1** [usu. as adj. **stratified**] form or arrange into strata. **2** arrange or classify. **3** place (seeds) close together in layers in moist sand or peat to preserve them or to help them germinate.

1173 **streak**

–DERIVATIVES **stratification** n. **stratiform** adj.

stratigraphy /strəˈtɪɡrəfi/ ■ n. **1** the branch of geology concerned with the order and relative dating of strata. **2** the analysis of the order and position of layers of archaeological remains. **3** the structure of a particular set of strata.
–DERIVATIVES **stratigraphic** adj. **stratigraphical** adj.
–ORIGIN C19: from STRATUM + -GRAPHY.

stratocumulus /ˌstratə(ʊ)ˈkjuːmjʊləs, ˌstreɪ-, ˌstrɑː-/ ■ n. cloud forming a low layer of clumped or broken grey masses.

stratosphere /ˈstratəˌsfɪə/ ■ n. **1** the layer of the earth's atmosphere above the troposphere, extending to about 50 km above the earth's surface (the lower boundary of the mesosphere). **2** informal the very highest levels of something: *the fashion stratosphere*.
–DERIVATIVES **stratospheric** /-ˈsfɛrɪk/ adj. **stratospherically** adv.

stratum /ˈstrɑːtəm, ˈstreɪtəm/ ■ n. (pl. **strata** /-tə/) **1** a layer or a series of layers of rock. **2** a thin layer within any structure. **3** a level or class of society.
–ORIGIN C16: from Latin, 'something spread or laid down', from *sternere* 'strew'.

stratum corneum /ˌstrɑːtəm ˈkɔːnɪəm/ ■ n. Anatomy the relatively tough outer layer of the skin.
–ORIGIN Latin, 'horny layer'.

stratus /ˈstrɑːtəs, ˈstreɪtəs/ ■ n. cloud forming a continuous horizontal grey sheet, often with rain or snow.
–ORIGIN C19: from Latin, 'strewn', from *sternere*.

straw ■ n. **1** dried stalks of grain, used especially as fodder or for thatching, packing, or weaving. **2** a single dried stalk of grain. **3** a thin hollow tube of paper or plastic for sucking drink from a glass or bottle. **4** a pale yellow colour like that of straw.
–PHRASES **clutch** (or **grasp** or **catch**) **at straws** resort in desperation to unlikely or inadequate means of salvation. **draw the short straw** be chosen to perform an unpleasant task. **the last** (or **final**) **straw** a further minor difficulty that comes after a series of difficulties and makes a situation unbearable. [from the proverb *the last straw breaks the (laden) camel's back*.] **a straw in the wind** a slight hint of future developments.
–DERIVATIVES **strawy** adj.
–ORIGIN Old English *strēaw*, of Germanic origin.

strawberry ■ n. **1** a sweet soft red fruit with a seed-studded surface. **2** the low-growing plant which produces this fruit, with white flowers, lobed leaves, and runners. [Genus *Fragaria*.] **3** a deep pinkish-red colour.
–ORIGIN Old English *strēa(w)berige*, *strēowberige* (see STRAW, BERRY).

strawberry blonde ■ adj. denoting hair that is a light reddish-blonde colour. ■ n. a woman with such hair.

strawberry mark ■ n. a soft red birthmark.

strawberry roan ■ adj. denoting an animal's coat which is chestnut mixed with white or grey.

strawberry tree ■ n. a small European tree bearing clusters of whitish flowers and strawberry-like fruit. [*Arbutus unedo*.]

straw man ■ n. **1** a person who is a sham. **2** a sham argument.

straw poll (also **straw vote**) ■ n. an unofficial ballot conducted as a test of opinion.

stray ■ v. **1** move away aimlessly from a group or from the right course or place. ▸ (of the eyes or a hand) move idly in a specified direction. **2** be unfaithful to a spouse or partner. ■ adj. **1** not in the right place; separated from a group. **2** (of a domestic animal) having no home or having wandered away from home. **3** Physics arising naturally but unwanted and usually detrimental: *stray voltages*. ■ n. **1** a stray person or thing, especially a domestic animal. **2** (**strays**) electrical phenomena interfering with radio reception.
–DERIVATIVES **strayer** n.
–ORIGIN Middle English: shortening of Anglo-Norman French *estrayer* (v.), *strey* (n.), partly from ASTRAY.

streak ■ n. **1** a long, thin mark of a different substance or colour from its surroundings. **2** an element of a specified

streaky

kind in someone's character: *a ruthless streak*. **3** a spell of specified success or luck. ▪ **v. 1** mark with streaks. **2** move very fast in a specified direction. **3** informal run naked in a public place so as to shock or amuse.
- PHRASES **like a streak** informal very fast. **streak of lightning** a flash of lightning.
- DERIVATIVES **streaker** n. **streaking** n.
- ORIGIN Old English, of Germanic origin.

streaky ▪ adj. (**-ier**, **-iest**) **1** having streaks. ▸ (of bacon) from the belly, thus having alternate strips of fat and lean. **2** informal, chiefly N. Amer. unpredictable; variable.
- DERIVATIVES **streakily** adv. **streakiness** n.

stream ▪ n. **1** a small, narrow river. **2** a continuous flow of liquid, air, gas, people, or things. **3** Brit. a group in which schoolchildren of the same age and ability are taught. ▪ v. **1** (of liquid) run in a continuous flow. ▸ (of a mass of people or things) move in a continuous flow. **2** (usu. **be streaming**) run with tears, sweat, or other liquid. **3** float at full extent in the wind. **4** Brit. put (schoolchildren) in streams.
- PHRASES **against** (or **with**) **the stream** against (or with) the prevailing view or tendency. **on stream** in or into operation or existence.
- DERIVATIVES **streamlet** n.
- ORIGIN Old English *strēam* (n.), of Germanic origin.

streamer ▪ n. **1** a long, narrow strip of material used as a decoration or flag. **2** a banner headline in a newspaper. **3** Fishing a fly with feathers attached. **4** Astronomy an elongated mass of luminous matter, e.g. in an aurora. **5** (also **tape streamer**) Computing a device for writing data very quickly on to magnetic tape.

streaming ▪ adj. (of a cold) accompanied by copious running of the nose and eyes.

streamline ▪ v. **1** [usu. as adj. **streamlined**] design or provide with a form that presents very little resistance to a flow of air or water. **2** make (an organization or system) more efficient by employing faster or simpler working methods. ▪ n. a line along which the flow of a moving fluid is least turbulent. ▪ adj. (of fluid flow) free from turbulence.

stream of consciousness ▪ n. a literary style in which the continuous flow of a person's thoughts and reactions to events is recorded without interruption by objective description or conventional dialogue.

street ▪ n. **1** a public road in a city, town, or village, typically with buildings on one or both sides. **2** [as modifier] of or relating to the subculture of fashionable urban youth. **3** [as modifier] homeless: *street children*.
- PHRASES **on the streets 1** homeless. **2** working as a prostitute. **streets ahead** informal greatly superior. **up** (or **right up**) **one's street** (or **alley**) informal well suited to one's tastes, interests, or abilities.
- ORIGIN Old English, of West Germanic origin, from late Latin *strāta* (via) 'paved (way)', from *sternere* 'lay down'.

street Arab ▪ n. archaic a street child.

streetcar ▪ n. N. Amer. a tram.

street child (also informal **street kid**) ▪ n. an indigent child who lives or works on the streets.

street credibility (also informal **street cred**) ▪ n. acceptability among young fashionable urban people.

street door ▪ n. the main door of a house opening on the street.

street furniture ▪ n. objects placed or fixed in the street for public use, such as postboxes or road signs.

street-legal ▪ adj. (of a vehicle) meeting all legal requirements for use on ordinary roads.

street light (also **street lamp**) ▪ n. a light illuminating a road, typically mounted on a tall post.
- DERIVATIVES **street lighting** n.

street name ▪ n. the name of a stockbroking firm, bank, or dealer in which stock is held on behalf of a purchaser.

street-smart ▪ adj. another term for STREETWISE.

street value ▪ n. the price a commodity, especially an amount of drugs, would fetch if sold illicitly.

streetwalker ▪ n. a prostitute who seeks clients in the street.
- DERIVATIVES **streetwalking** n. & adj.

streetwise ▪ adj. informal having the skills and knowledge necessary for dealing with modern urban life.

strelitzia /strəˈlɪtsɪə/ ▪ n. a southern African plant of a genus including the bird of paradise flower. [Genus *Strelitzia*.]
- ORIGIN named after Charlotte of Mecklenburg-*Strelitz* (1744–1818), queen of the British king George III.

strength /strɛŋθ, strɛŋkθ/ ▪ n. **1** the quality or state of being strong. **2** a good or beneficial quality or attribute. ▸ poetic/literary a source of mental or emotional support. **3** the number of people comprising a group. ▸ a full complement of people: *below strength*.
- PHRASES **from strength** from a secure or advantageous position. **go from strength to strength** progress with increasing success. **in strength** in large numbers. **on the strength of** on the basis or with the justification of. **tower** (or **pillar**) **of strength** a person who can be relied upon to support and comfort others.
- ORIGIN Old English, from the Germanic base of STRONG.

strengthen /ˈstrɛŋθ(ə)n, -ŋkθ(ə)n/ ▪ v. make or become stronger.
- PHRASES **strengthen someone's hand** (or **hands**) enable a person to act more effectively.
- DERIVATIVES **strengthener** n.

strenuous /ˈstrɛnjʊəs/ ▪ adj. requiring or using great exertion.
- DERIVATIVES **strenuously** adv. **strenuousness** n.
- ORIGIN C17: from Latin *strenuus* 'brisk'.

strep ▪ n. Medicine, informal short for STREPTOCOCCUS.

strep throat ▪ n. a sore throat with fever caused by streptococcal infection.

strepto- ▪ comb. form twisted; in the form of a twisted chain: *streptomycete*. ▸ associated with streptococci or streptomycetes.
- ORIGIN from Greek *streptos* 'twisted'.

streptocarpus /ˌstrɛptə(ʊ)ˈkɑːpəs/ ▪ n. an African plant with funnel-shaped pink, white, or violet flowers, cultivated as indoor or greenhouse plants. [Genus *Streptocarpus*.]
- ORIGIN from STREPTO- + Greek *karpos* 'fruit'.

streptococcus /ˌstrɛptə(ʊ)ˈkɒkəs/ ▪ n. (pl. **streptococci** /-ˈkɒk(s)aɪ, -ˈkɒk(s)iː/) a bacterium of a genus including the agents of souring of milk and dental decay and the pathogens causing scarlet fever and pneumonia. [Genus *Streptococcus*.]
- DERIVATIVES **streptococcal** adj.

streptomycete /ˌstrɛptə(ʊ)ˈmaɪsiːt/ ▪ n. (pl. **streptomycetes** /-ˈmaɪsiːts, -maɪˈsiːtiːz/) a bacterium which occurs chiefly in soil and of which some kinds yield antibiotics. [*Streptomyces* and related genera.]
- ORIGIN 1950s: from *Streptomyces*, from STREPTO- + Greek *mukēs, mukēt-* 'fungus'.

streptomycin /ˌstrɛptə(ʊ)ˈmaɪsɪn/ ▪ n. Medicine a bacterial antibiotic used against tuberculosis.

stress ▪ n. **1** pressure or tension exerted on a material object. ▸ Physics the magnitude of this measured in units of force per unit area. **2** a state of mental, emotional, or other strain. **3** particular emphasis. ▸ emphasis given to a syllable or word in speech. ▪ v. **1** emphasize. ▸ give emphasis to (a syllable or word) when pronouncing it. **2** subject to stress.
- DERIVATIVES **stressless** adj. **stressor** n.
- ORIGIN Middle English: shortening of DISTRESS, or partly from Old French *estresse* 'narrowness, oppression', from Latin *strictus* (see STRICT).

stressful ▪ adj. causing mental or emotional stress.
- DERIVATIVES **stressfully** adv. **stressfulness** n.

stretch ▪ v. **1** (of something soft or elastic) be made or be able to be made longer or wider without tearing or breaking. ▸ pull (something) tightly from one point to another or across a space. **2** straighten or extend one's body or a part of one's body to its full length. **3** last or cause to last longer than expected. ▸ (of finances or resources) be sufficient for a particular purpose. **4** extend over an area or period of time. **5** make demands on. ▪ n. **1** an act of stretching. ▸ the fact or condition of being stretched. ▸ the capacity to stretch or be stretched; elasticity. **2** a continuous expanse or period. ▸ informal a period of time spent in prison. ▸ chiefly N. Amer. a straight

part of a racetrack, typically the home straight. ▸ Nautical the distance covered on one tack. **3** [usu. as modifier] informal a motor vehicle or aircraft modified so as to have extended seating or storage capacity. **4** a difficult or demanding task.
- PHRASES **at full stretch** using the maximum amount of one's resources or energy. **at a stretch 1** in one continuous period. **2** just possible but with difficulty. **stretch one's legs** go for a short walk, typically after sitting for some time. **stretch a point** allow or do something not usually acceptable.
- DERIVATIVES **stretchability** n. **stretchable** adj. **stretchiness** n. **stretchy** adj. (**-ier, -iest**).
- ORIGIN Old English, of West Germanic origin.

stretcher ▪ n. **1** a framework of two poles with a long piece of canvas slung between them, used for carrying sick, injured, or dead people. ▸ S. African & Austral./NZ a camp bed. **2** a wooden frame over which a canvas is stretched ready for painting. **3** a rod or bar joining and supporting chair legs. **4** a board in a boat against which a rower presses their feet for support. **5** a brick or stone laid with its long side along the face of a wall. Compare with HEADER (in sense 3). ▪ v. carry on a stretcher.

stretch marks ▪ pl. n. marks on the skin, especially on the abdomen, caused by distention of the skin from obesity or during pregnancy.

streusel /ˈstrɔɪz(ə)l, ˈstruːz(ə)l/ ▪ n. a crumbly topping or filling for a cake or pastry, made from fat, flour, sugar, and often cinnamon.
- ORIGIN from German *Streusel*, from *streuen* 'sprinkle'.

strew ▪ v. (past part. **strewn** or **strewed**) (usu. **be strewn**) scatter untidily over a surface or area. ▸ (usu. **be strewn with**) cover (a surface or area) with untidily scattered things.
- ORIGIN Old English, of Germanic origin.

strewth (also **struth**) ▪ exclam. informal used to express surprise or dismay.
- ORIGIN C19: contraction of *God's truth*.

stria /ˈstraɪə/ ▪ n. (pl. **striae** /-iː/) technical a linear mark, ridge, or groove, especially one of a number of similar parallel features.
- ORIGIN C17: from Latin, 'furrow'.

striate technical ▪ adj. /ˈstraɪət, ˈstraɪeɪt/ marked with striae. ▪ v. /ˈstraɪeɪt/ [usu. as adj. **striated**] mark with striae.
- DERIVATIVES **striation** n.

striated muscle ▪ n. Physiology muscle tissue in which the contractile fibrils are aligned in parallel bundles, occurring in the muscles attached to bones and under voluntary control. Often contrasted with SMOOTH MUSCLE.

striatum /straɪˈeɪtəm/ ▪ n. (pl. **striata** /straɪˈeɪtə/) Anatomy short for CORPUS STRIATUM.

stricken North American or archaic past participle of STRIKE. ▪ adj. seriously affected by an undesirable condition or unpleasant feeling. ▸ (of a face or look) showing great distress.

strict ▪ adj. **1** demanding that rules concerning behaviour are obeyed. ▸ (of a rule) demanding total compliance; rigidly enforced. **2** following rules or beliefs exactly. **3** not allowing deviation or relaxation.
- DERIVATIVES **strictly** adv. **strictness** n.
- ORIGIN Middle English: from Latin *strictus*, *stringere* 'tighten'.

strict construction ▪ n. Law a literal interpretation of a statute or document by a court.

strict liability ▪ n. Law liability which does not depend on actual negligence or intent to harm.

stricture /ˈstrɪktʃə/ ▪ n. **1** a rule restricting behaviour or action. **2** a sternly critical remark. **3** Medicine abnormal narrowing of a canal or duct in the body.
- DERIVATIVES **strictured** adj.
- ORIGIN Middle English: from Latin *strictura*, from *stringere* (see STRICT).

stride ▪ v. (past **strode**; past part. **stridden**) **1** walk with long, decisive steps. **2** (**stride across/over**) cross (an obstacle) with one long step. ▪ n. **1** a long, decisive step. ▸ the length of a step or manner of taking steps. **2** a step in progress towards an aim. ▸ (**one's stride**) a good or regular rate of progress, especially after a slow start. **3** (**strides**) Brit. informal trousers.
- PHRASES **take something in one's stride** deal with

1175 **strike-breaker**

something difficult in a calm way.
- DERIVATIVES **strider** n.
- ORIGIN Old English *stride* (n.) 'single long step', *stridan* (v.) 'stand or walk with the legs wide apart', prob. from a Germanic base meaning 'strive, quarrel'.

strident ▪ adj. **1** loud and harsh. **2** presenting a point of view in an excessively forceful way. **3** Phonetics sibilant.
- DERIVATIVES **stridency** n. **stridently** adv.

stridor /ˈstraɪdə/ ▪ n. a strident sound. ▸ Medicine a harsh vibrating noise when breathing, caused by obstruction of the windpipe or larynx.
- ORIGIN C17: from Latin, from *stridere* 'to creak'.

stridulate /ˈstrɪdjʊleɪt/ ▪ v. (of an insect, especially a male cricket or grasshopper) make a shrill sound by rubbing the legs, wings, or other parts of the body together.
- DERIVATIVES **stridulant** adj. **stridulation** n. **stridulatory** adj.
- ORIGIN C19: from French *striduler*, from Latin *stridulus* 'creaking'.

strife ▪ n. angry or bitter disagreement; conflict.
- ORIGIN Middle English: shortening of Old French *estrif*.

strike ▪ v. (past and past part. **struck** /strʌk/) **1** deliver a blow to. ▸ accidentally hit (a part of one's body) against something. ▸ come into forcible contact with. ▸ (in sporting contexts) hit or kick (a ball) so as to score a run, point, or goal. ▸ ignite (a match) by rubbing it briskly against an abrasive surface. ▸ bring (an electric arc) into being. **2** (of a disaster, disease, etc.) occur suddenly and have harmful effects on. ▸ attack suddenly. ▸ (**strike something into**) cause a strong emotion in. ▸ cause to become suddenly: *he was struck dumb*. **3** suddenly come into the mind of. ▸ cause to have a particular impression. ▸ (**be struck by/with**) find particularly interesting or impressive. ▸ (**be struck on**) informal be deeply fond of. **4** (of employees) refuse to work as a form of organized protest. ▸ undertake such action against (an employer). **5** cancel or remove by or as if by crossing out with a pen. ▸ (**strike someone off**) officially remove someone from membership of a professional group. **6** move or proceed vigorously or purposefully. ▸ (**strike out**) start out on a new or independent course. **7** reach (an agreement, balance, or compromise). ▸ (in financial contexts) reach (a figure) by balancing an account. **8** (of a clock) indicate the time by sounding a chime or stroke. **9** make (a coin or medal) by stamping metal. **10** discover (gold, minerals, or oil) by drilling or mining. ▸ (**strike on/upon**) discover or think of, especially unexpectedly. **11** take down or dismantle (a tent, camp, or theatrical scenery). ▸ lower or take down (a flag or sail). **12** insert (a cutting of a plant) in soil to take root. ▸ develop roots. **13** Fishing secure a hook in the mouth of a fish by jerking or tightening the line after it has taken the bait or fly. ▪ n. **1** an act of striking by employees. ▸ a refusal to do something as an organized protest: *a rent strike*. **2** a sudden attack, typically a military one. **3** (in sporting contexts) an act of striking a ball. ▸ (in tenpin bowling) an act of knocking down all the pins with one's first ball. ▸ Baseball a batter's unsuccessful attempt to hit a pitched ball. ▸ Baseball a pitch that passes through the strike zone. **4** an act of striking gold, minerals, or oil. **5** the horizontal or compass direction of a stratum, fault, or other geological feature.
- PHRASES **strike an attitude** (or **pose**) hold one's body in a particular position to create an impression. **strike a blow for** (or **at** or **against**) do something to help (or hinder) a cause, belief, or principle. **strike while the iron is hot** make use of an opportunity immediately.
- PHRASAL VERBS **strike back 1** retaliate. **2** (of a gas burner) burn from an internal point before the gas has become mixed with air. **strike someone out** (or **strike out**) **1** Baseball dismiss someone (or be dismissed) by means of three strikes. **2** (**strike out**) N. Amer. informal be unsuccessful. **strike up** (or **strike something up**) **1** begin to play a piece of music. **2** (**strike something up**) begin a friendship or conversation with someone.
- ORIGIN Old English *strīcan* 'go, flow' and 'rub lightly', of West Germanic origin.

strike-breaker ▪ n. a person who works or is employed in place of others who are on strike.
- DERIVATIVES **strike-break** v.

strike force ▪ n. [treated as sing. or pl.] a military force equipped and organized for sudden attack.

strikeout ▪ n. Baseball an out called when a batter has made three strikes.

strike pay ▪ n. money paid to strikers by their trade union.

strike price ▪ n. Finance **1** the price fixed by the seller of a security after receiving bids in a tender offer. **2** the price at which a put or call option can be exercised.

striker ▪ n. **1** an employee on strike. **2** the player who is to strike the ball in a game; a player considered in terms of ability to strike the ball. ▸ (chiefly in soccer) a forward or attacker.

strike rate ▪ n. the success rate of a sports team, typically in scoring goals or runs.

strike-slip fault ▪ n. Geology a fault in which rock strata are displaced mainly in a horizontal direction, parallel to the line of the fault.

strike zone ▪ n. Baseball an imaginary area over home plate extending from the armpits to the knees of a batter in the batting position.

striking ▪ adj. **1** noticeable. **2** dramatically good-looking or beautiful.
–DERIVATIVES **strikingly** adv.

striking circle ▪ n. an elongated semicircle on a hockey field in front of the goal, from within which the ball must be hit in order to score.

striking price ▪ n. another term for **STRIKE PRICE**.

strimmer ▪ n. trademark British term for **WEED EATER**.
–ORIGIN 1970s: prob. a blend of **STRING** and **TRIMMER**.

Strine /strʌɪn/ ▪ n. informal Australian English or the Australian accent.
–ORIGIN 1960s: representing *Australian* in Strine.

string ▪ n. **1** material consisting of threads of cotton, hemp, etc. twisted together to form a thin length. ▸ a piece of such material. **2** a length of catgut or wire on a musical instrument, producing a note by vibration. ▸ (**strings**) the stringed instruments in an orchestra. **3** a piece of catgut, nylon, etc., interwoven with others to form the head of a sports racket. **4** a set of things tied or threaded together on a thin cord. **5** a sequence of similar items or events. ▸ Computing a linear sequence of characters, words, or other data. ▸ a group of racehorses trained at one stable. ▸ a reserve team or player holding a specified position in an order of preference. ▸ a player assigned a specified rank in a team in an individual sport. **6** a tough piece of fibre in vegetables, meat, or other food. **7** Physics a hypothetical one-dimensional sub-atomic particle having the dynamical properties of a flexible loop. ▸ (also **cosmic string**) a hypothetical thread-like concentration of energy within the structure of space–time. ▪ v. (past and past part. **strung**) **1** arrange on or as on a string. ▸ (**be strung**) or **be strung out** be arranged in a long line. **2** fit a string or strings to (a musical instrument, a racket, or a bow). **3** remove the strings from (a bean). **4** informal, chiefly N. Amer. hoax. **5** work as a stringer in journalism. **6** Billiards determine the order of play by striking the cue ball from baulk to rebound as far as possible from the top cushion.
–PHRASES **no strings attached** informal there are no special conditions or restrictions. **on a string** under one's control or influence.
–PHRASAL VERBS **string along** informal stay with a person or group as long as it is convenient. **string someone along** informal mislead someone deliberately over a length of time. **string something out 1** prolong something. **2** (**be strung out**) be nervous or tense. **3** (**be strung out**) N. Amer. be under the influence of alcohol or drugs. **string someone up 1** kill someone by hanging. **2** (**be strung up**) Brit. be tense or nervous.
–DERIVATIVES **stringed** adj. **stringless** adj. **string-like** adj.
–ORIGIN Old English, of Germanic origin.

string bass ▪ n. (especially among jazz musicians) a double bass.

string bean ▪ n. any of various beans eaten in their fibrous pods, especially runner beans or French beans.

stringent /ˈstrɪn(d)ʒ(ə)nt/ ▪ adj. (of regulations or requirements) strict, precise, and exacting.
–DERIVATIVES **stringency** n. **stringently** adv.
–ORIGIN C17: from Latin *stringere* 'draw tight'.

stringer ▪ n. **1** a longitudinal structural piece in a framework, especially that of a ship or aircraft. **2** informal a journalist who is not on the regular staff of a newspaper, but who is retained on a part-time basis to report on a particular place.

string quartet ▪ n. a chamber music ensemble consisting of first and second violins, viola, and cello. ▸ a piece of music for such an ensemble.

string tie ▪ n. a very narrow necktie.

string vest ▪ n. a man's undergarment made of a meshed fabric.

stringy ▪ adj. (**-ier**, **-iest**) **1** resembling string in being long and thin. **2** tall, wiry, and thin. **3** (of food) tough and fibrous. **4** (of a liquid) viscous; forming strings.
–DERIVATIVES **stringily** adv. **stringiness** n.

strip[1] ▪ v. (**stripped**, **stripping**) **1** remove all coverings or clothes from. ▸ take off one's clothes. **2** leave bare of accessories or fittings. ▸ remove the accessory fittings of or take apart (a machine, motor vehicle, etc.) for inspection or adjustment. **3** remove (paint) from a surface with solvent. **4** (**strip someone of**) deprive someone of (rank, power, or property). **5** sell off (the assets of a company) for profit. **6** tear the thread or teeth from (a screw, gearwheel, etc.). ▪ n. **1** an act of undressing, especially in a striptease. ▸ [as modifier] used for or involving the performance of stripteases. **2** the identifying outfit worn by the members of a sports team while playing.
–ORIGIN Middle English: of Germanic origin; sense 2 of the noun is perhaps from the notion of clothing to which a player 'strips' down.

strip[2] ▪ n. **1** a long, narrow piece of cloth, paper, etc. ▸ steel or other metal in the form of narrow flat bars. **2** a long, narrow area of land. ▸ chiefly N. Amer. a main road lined with shops and other facilities.
–ORIGIN Middle English: rel. to Middle Low German *strippe* 'strap, thong', prob. also to **STRIPE**.

stripe ▪ n. **1** a long narrow band or strip of a different colour or texture from the surface on either side of it. **2** a chevron sewn on to a uniform to denote military rank. **3** chiefly N. Amer. a type or category. ▪ v. (usu. **be striped**) mark with stripes.
–DERIVATIVES **striped** adj. **stripy** (also **stripey**) adj.
–ORIGIN Middle English: perhaps a back-formation from *striped*, of Dutch or Low German origin.

strip light ▪ n. a tubular fluorescent lamp.

stripling ▪ n. archaic or humorous a young man.
–ORIGIN Middle English: prob. from **STRIP**[2] (from the notion of 'narrowness', i.e. slimness).

strip mill ▪ n. a mill in which steel slabs are rolled into strips.

strip-mine ▪ v. obtain (ore or coal) by opencast mining. ▪ n. (**strip mine**) an opencast mine.

stripper ▪ n. **1** a device or substance for stripping. **2** a striptease performer.

strippergram ▪ n. a novelty greetings message delivered by a man or woman who accompanies it with a striptease act.

strip poker ▪ n. a form of poker in which a player with a losing hand takes off an item of clothing as a forfeit.

strip-search ▪ v. search (someone) for concealed drugs, weapons, or other items, by stripping off their clothes. ▪ n. an act of strip-searching.

striptease ▪ n. a form of entertainment in which a performer gradually undresses to music in a sexually exciting way.
–DERIVATIVES **stripteaser** n.

strive ▪ v. (past **strove** or **strived**; past part. **striven** or **strived**) make great efforts. ▸ (**strive against**) fight vigorously against.
–DERIVATIVES **striver** n.
–ORIGIN Middle English: shortening of Old French *estriver*; rel. to *estrif* 'strife'.

strobe informal ▪ n. **1** a stroboscope. ▸ a stroboscopic lamp. **2** N. Amer. an electronic flash for a camera. ▪ v. **1** flash intermittently. **2** exhibit or give rise to strobing.

strobilus /ˈstrəʊbɪləs/ ■ n. (pl. **strobili** /-lʌɪ, -liː/) Botany **1** the cone of a pine, fir, or other conifer. **2** a cone-like structure.
– ORIGIN C18: from Greek *strobilos*, from *strephein* 'to twist'.

strobing /ˈstrəʊbɪŋ/ ■ n. **1** irregular movement and loss of continuity of lines and stripes in a television picture. **2** jerkiness in what should be a smooth movement of a cinematographic image.

stroboscope /ˈstrəʊbəskəʊp/ ■ n. Physics an instrument which shines a bright light at rapid intervals so that a moving or rotating object appears stationary.
– DERIVATIVES **stroboscopic** adj. **stroboscopically** adv.
– ORIGIN C19: from Greek *strobos* 'whirling' + -SCOPE.

strode past of STRIDE.

stroganoff /ˈstrɒɡənɒf/ ■ n. a dish in which the central ingredient, typically strips of beef, is cooked in a sauce containing sour cream.
– ORIGIN named after the Russian diplomat Count Pavel Stroganov (1772–1817).

stroke ■ n. **1** an act of hitting: *he received three strokes of the cane.* ▸ Golf an act of hitting the ball with a club, as a unit of scoring. ▸ a sound made by a striking clock. **2** a mark made by drawing a pen, pencil, or paintbrush once across paper or canvas. ▸ a line forming part of a written or printed character. ▸ a short diagonal line separating characters or figures. **3** an act of stroking. **4** one of a series of repeated movements. ▸ the whole motion of a piston in either direction. ▸ a style of moving the arms and legs in swimming. ▸ the mode or action of moving the oar in rowing. ▸ (also **stroke oar**) the oarsman nearest the stern, setting the timing for the other rowers. **5** a sudden disabling attack or loss of consciousness caused by an interruption in the flow of blood to the brain. ■ v. move one's hand with gentle pressure over (a surface).
– PHRASES **at a** (or **one**) **stroke** by a single action having immediate effect. **not** (or **never**) **do a stroke of work** do no work at all. **on the stroke of —** precisely at the specified time. **put someone off their stroke** disconcert someone so that they make a mistake or hesitate. **stroke of genius** an outstandingly original idea. **stroke of luck** (or **good luck**) a fortunate unexpected occurrence.
– ORIGIN Old English *strācian* 'caress lightly', of Germanic origin.

stroke play ■ n. play in golf in which the score is reckoned by counting the number of strokes taken overall. Compare with MATCH PLAY.
– DERIVATIVES **stroke player** n.

stroll ■ v. **1** walk in a leisurely way. **2** achieve a sporting victory easily. ■ n. **1** a short leisurely walk. **2** a victory easily achieved.
– ORIGIN C17: prob. from German *strollen*, *strolchen*, from *Strolch* 'vagabond'.

stroller ■ n. **1** a pushchair. **2** S. African a street child, especially one in Cape Town.

stroma /ˈstrəʊmə/ ■ n. (pl. **stromata** /-mətə/) Biology **1** the supportive tissue or matrix of an organ, tumour, cell, etc. **2** a cushion-like mass of fungal tissue containing spore-bearing structures.
– DERIVATIVES **stromal** adj. (chiefly Anatomy).
– ORIGIN C19: from Greek *strōma* 'coverlet'.

stromatolite /strə(ʊ)ˈmatəlʌɪt/ ■ n. Biology a calcareous mound built up of layers of blue-green algae and trapped sediment, especially as fossilized in Precambrian rocks.
– ORIGIN 1930s: from modern Latin *stroma*, *stromat*- 'layer, covering', from Greek.

strong ■ adj. (**-er**, **-est**) **1** physically powerful. **2** done with or exerting great force. ▸ (of language or actions) forceful and extreme. **3** able to withstand great force or pressure. ▸ secure, stable, or firmly established. ▸ (of a market) having steadily high or rising prices. **4** great in intensity or degree: *strong competition for land.* ▸ (of something seen or heard) not soft or muted. ▸ pungent and full-flavoured. ▸ (of a solution or drink) containing a large proportion of a substance. **5** great in power, influence, or ability. **6** used after a number to indicate the size of a group. **7** Grammar denoting a class of verbs in Germanic languages that form the past tense and past participle by a change of vowel within the stem rather than by addition of a suffix (e.g. *swim*, *swam*, *swum*).
– PHRASES **come on strong** informal behave aggressively or assertively. **going strong** informal continuing to be healthy, vigorous, or successful. **strong on 1** good at. **2** possessing large quantities of.
– DERIVATIVES **strongish** adj. **strongly** adv.
– ORIGIN Old English, of Germanic origin.

strong-arm ■ adj. using or characterized by force or violence.

strongbox ■ n. a small lockable metal box in which valuables may be kept.

strong drink ■ n. alcohol, especially spirits.

stronghold ■ n. **1** a place that has been fortified against attack. **2** a place of strong support for a cause or political party.

strongman ■ n. (pl. **-men**) **1** a man of great physical strength, especially one who performs feats of strength for entertainment. **2** a leader who rules by the exercise of threats, force, or violence.

strongpoint ■ n. a specially fortified defensive position.

strongroom ■ n. a room, typically one in a bank, designed to protect valuable items against fire and theft.

strong suit ■ n. **1** (in bridge or whist) a holding of a number of high cards of one suit in a hand. **2** a thing at which a person excels.

strongyle /ˈstrɒndʒɪl/ ■ n. a nematode worm of a group that includes several common disease-causing parasites of mammals and birds. [Genus *Strongylus*. See also REDWORM (sense 2).]
– ORIGIN C19: from Greek *strongulos* 'round'.

strontium /ˈstrɒntɪəm, ˈstrɒnʃ(ɪ)əm/ ■ n. the chemical element of atomic number 38, a soft silver-white metal of the alkaline earth series. (Symbol: **Sr**)
– ORIGIN C19: from *strontian* denoting native strontium carbonate from *Strontian*, a parish in Scotland where it was discovered.

strop[1] ■ n. **1** a device, typically a strip of leather, for sharpening razors. **2** Nautical a collar of leather, spliced rope, or iron, used for handling cargo. ■ v. (**stropped**, **stropping**) sharpen on or with a strop.
– ORIGIN Middle English: prob. a West Germanic adoption of Latin *stroppus* 'thong'.

strop[2] ■ n. informal, chiefly Brit. a temper.
– ORIGIN C20: prob. a back-formation from STROPPY.

strophe /ˈstrəʊfi/ ■ n. **1** the first section of an ancient Greek choral ode or of one division of it. **2** a group of lines forming a section of a lyric poem.
– DERIVATIVES **strophic** adj.
– ORIGIN C17: from Greek *strophē* 'turning'.

stroppy ■ adj. (**-ier**, **-iest**) informal bad-tempered; argumentative.
– DERIVATIVES **stroppily** adv. **stroppiness** n.
– ORIGIN 1950s: perhaps an abbrev. of OBSTREPEROUS.

strove past of STRIVE.

struck past and past participle of STRIKE.

structural ■ adj. of, relating to, or forming part of a structure.
– DERIVATIVES **structurally** adv.

structural engineering ■ n. the branch of civil engineering concerned with large modern buildings and similar structures.
– DERIVATIVES **structural engineer** n.

structural formula ■ n. Chemistry a formula which shows the arrangement of atoms in a molecule.

structuralism ■ n. a method of interpretation and analysis of human cognition, behaviour, culture, and experience, which focuses on relationships of contrast between elements in a conceptual system.
– DERIVATIVES **structuralist** n. & adj.

structural linguistics ■ pl. n. [treated as sing.] the branch of linguistics concerned with language as a system of interrelated structures.

structural steel ■ n. strong mild steel in shapes suited to construction work.

structural unemployment ■ n. unemployment

structuration

resulting from industrial reorganization due to technological change, rather than fluctuations in supply or demand.

structuration ■ n. the state or process of organization in a structured form.

structure ■ n. **1** the arrangement of and relations between the parts of something complex. **2** a building or other object constructed from several parts. **3** the quality of being well organized. ■ v. give structure to.
– DERIVATIVES **structureless** adj.
– ORIGIN Middle English: from Latin *structura*, from *struere* 'to build'.

structure plan ■ n. a plan drawn up by a local planning authority for the use of a prescribed area of land.

strudel /ˈstruːd(ə)l, ˈʃtruː-/ ■ n. a confection of thin pastry rolled up round a fruit filling and baked.
– ORIGIN from German *Strudel* 'whirlpool'.

struggle ■ v. **1** make forceful efforts to get free. **2** strive under difficult circumstances to do something. ▶ have difficulty in gaining recognition or a living. **3** contend or compete. **4** make one's way with difficulty. ■ n. **1** an act of struggling. **2** a very difficult task. **3** (**the struggle**) (in South Africa) organized resistance to apartheid and its institutions.
– DERIVATIVES **struggler** n.
– ORIGIN Middle English: perhaps of imitative origin.

strum ■ v. (**strummed, strumming**) play (a guitar or similar instrument) by sweeping the thumb or a plectrum up or down the strings. ▶ play casually or unskilfully on a stringed instrument. ■ n. an instance or the sound of strumming.
– DERIVATIVES **strummer** n.
– ORIGIN C18: imitative.

strumpet ■ n. archaic or humorous a female prostitute or a promiscuous woman.
– ORIGIN Middle English.

strung past and past participle of STRING.

strut ■ n. **1** a bar forming part of a framework and designed to resist compression. **2** a strutting gait. ■ v. (**strutted, strutting**) walk with a stiff, erect, and conceited gait.
– PHRASES **strut one's stuff** informal dance or behave in a confident and expressive way.
– DERIVATIVES **strutter** n. **strutting** adj. **struttingly** adv.
– ORIGIN Old English *strūtian* 'protrude stiffly', of Germanic origin.

struth ■ exclam. variant spelling of STREWTH.

strychnine /ˈstrɪkniːn, -ɪn/ ■ n. a bitter and highly poisonous alkaloid obtained from the southern Asian nux vomica tree (*Strychnos nux-vomica*) and related plants.
– ORIGIN C19: from Greek *strukhnos*, denoting a kind of nightshade.

Sts ■ abbrev. Saints.

St Swithin's day ■ n. 15 July, a Church festival commemorating St Swithin and popularly believed to be a day on which, if it rains, it will continue raining for the next forty days.

Stuart (also **Stewart**) ■ adj. of or relating to the royal family ruling Scotland 1371–1714 and Britain 1603–1714. ■ n. a member of this family.

stub ■ n. **1** the truncated remnant of a pencil, cigarette, or similar-shaped object after use. **2** a truncated or unusually short thing: *he wagged his little stub of tail*. **3** the counterfoil of a cheque, ticket, or other document. **4** [as modifier] denoting a projection or hole that goes only part of the way through a surface. ■ v. (**stubbed, stubbing**) **1** accidentally strike (one's toe) against something. **2** extinguish (a cigarette) by pressing the lighted end against something.
– DERIVATIVES **stubbily** adv. **stubbiness** n.
– ORIGIN Old English *stub(b)* 'stump of a tree', of Germanic origin.

stub axle ■ n. an axle supporting only one wheel of a pair on opposite sides of a vehicle.

stubble ■ n. **1** the cut stalks of cereal plants left in the ground after harvesting. **2** short, stiff hairs growing on a man's face when he has not shaved for a while.
– DERIVATIVES **stubbled** adj. **stubbly** adj.
– ORIGIN Middle English: from Anglo-Norman French *stuble*, from Latin *stupla, stupula*, vars of *stipula* 'straw'.

stubborn ■ adj. **1** determined not to change one's attitude or position. **2** difficult to move, remove, or cure.
– DERIVATIVES **stubbornly** adv. **stubbornness** n.
– ORIGIN Middle English.

stubby ■ adj. (**-ier, -iest**) short and thick.

stucco ■ n. fine plaster used for coating wall surfaces or moulding into architectural decorations. ■ v. (**-oes, -oed**) [usu. as adj. **stuccoed**] coat or decorate with stucco.
– ORIGIN C16: from Italian.

stuck past participle of STICK².

stuck-up ■ adj. informal snobbishly aloof.

stud¹ ■ n. **1** a large-headed piece of metal that pierces and projects from a surface, especially for decoration. ▶ a small projection fixed to the base of a shoe or boot to provide better grip. ▶ a small object projecting slightly from a road surface as a marker. **2** a small piece of jewellery which is pushed through a pierced ear or nostril. **3** a fastener consisting of two buttons joined with a bar, used in formal wear to fasten a shirt front or to fasten a collar to a shirt. **4** an upright timber in a wall to which laths and plasterboard are nailed. ▶ US the height of a room as indicated by the length of this. ■ v. (**studded, studding**) (usu. **be studded**) **1** decorate with studs or similar small objects. **2** strew or scatter: *the sky was studded with stars*.
– DERIVATIVES **studding** n.
– ORIGIN Old English *studu, stuthu* 'post, upright prop'.

stud² ■ n. **1** an establishment where horses or other domesticated animals are kept for breeding. **2** (also **stud horse**) a stallion. **3** informal a sexually active or virile young man. **4** (also **stud poker**) a form of poker in which the first card of a player's hand is dealt face down and the others face up, with betting after each round of the deal.
– ORIGIN Old English *stōd*, of Germanic origin.

stud book ■ n. a book containing the pedigrees of pure-bred animals, particularly horses.

student ■ n. **1** a person studying at a university or other place of higher education. ▶ chiefly N. Amer. a school pupil. ▶ [as modifier] denoting someone who is studying to enter a particular profession: *a student nurse*. **2** a person who takes a particular interest in a subject.
– DERIVATIVES **studentship** n. **studenty** adj. (informal).
– ORIGIN Middle English: from Latin *studere* 'apply oneself to', rel. to *studium* 'painstaking application'.

Student's t-test ■ n. a test for statistical significance based on a fraction (*t*) whose numerator is drawn from a normal distribution with a mean of zero, and whose denominator is the root mean square of a number of terms drawn from the same normal distribution.
– ORIGIN C20: *Student*, the pseudonym of William Sealy Gosset, English brewery employee.

stud horse ■ n. see STUD² (sense 2).

studio ■ n. (pl. **-os**) **1** a room where an artist works or where dancers practise. **2** a room from which television or radio programmes are broadcast, or in which they are recorded. **3** a place where films or musical or sound recordings are made. **4** a film production company. **5** a studio flat.
– ORIGIN C19: from Italian, from Latin *studium* (see STUDY).

studio couch ■ n. chiefly N. Amer. a sofa bed.

studio flat ■ n. a flat containing one main room.

studio theatre ■ n. a small theatre where experimental and innovative productions are staged.

studious ■ adj. **1** spending a lot of time studying or reading. **2** done deliberately or with great care.
– DERIVATIVES **studiously** adv. **studiousness** n.
– ORIGIN Middle English: from Latin *studiosus*, from *studium* 'painstaking application'.

stud poker ■ n. see STUD² (sense 4).

study ■ n. (pl. **-ies**) **1** the devotion of time and attention to acquiring knowledge, especially from books. **2** a detailed investigation and analysis of a subject or situation. **3** a room for reading, writing, or academic work. **4** a piece of work, especially a drawing, done for practice or as an experiment. ▶ a musical composition designed to develop a player's technical skill. **5** (**a study in**) a good example of

(a quality or emotion): *he perched on the bed, a study in misery.* **6** theatrical slang a person who memorizes a role at a specified speed. ■ v. (-ies, -ied) **1** acquire knowledge on. ▶ make a study of. ▶ apply oneself to study. ▶ (**study up**) US learn intensively about something, especially in preparation for a test. ▶ (of an actor) try to learn (the words of one's role). **2** look at closely in order to observe or read. **3** [as adj. **studied**] done with deliberate and careful effort.
- PHRASES **in a brown study** absorbed in one's thoughts. [apparently orig. from *brown* in the sense 'gloomy'.]
- DERIVATIVES **studiedly** adv. **studiedness** n.
- ORIGIN Middle English: shortening of Old French *estudie* (n.), *estudier* (v.), both from Latin *studium* 'painstaking application'.

study hall ■ n. N. Amer. the period of time in a school curriculum designated for study and the preparation of homework.

stuff ■ n. **1** matter, material, articles, or activities of a specified or indeterminate kind. ▶ informal drink or drugs. ▶ (**the stuff**) informal money. ▶ (**one's stuff**) one's area of expertise. **2** basic characteristics; substance: *Healey was made of sterner stuff.* **3** Brit. dated woollen fabric, especially as distinct from silk, cotton, and linen. **4** N. Amer. (in sport) spin given to a ball. **5** informal, dated nonsense; rubbish. ■ v. **1** fill tightly with something. ▶ force tightly into a receptacle or space. ▶ fill out the skin of (a dead animal or bird) with material to restore the original shape and appearance. ▶ push hastily into a space. ▶ (**be stuffed up**) have one's nose blocked up with catarrh. ▶ informal eat greedily. ▶ (**be stuffed**) S. African informal be damaged or broken. **2** [usu. in imper.] informal used to express indifference or rejection. **3** informal defeat heavily in sport. **4** vulgar slang (of a man) have sexual intercourse with. **5** place bogus votes in (a ballot box).
- PHRASES **get stuffed** [usu. in imper.] informal said to express dismissal or contempt. **that's the stuff** informal that is good or what is needed.
- PHRASAL VERBS **stuff around** S. African & Austral./NZ informal engage in trivial or foolish activity. **stuff someone around** S. African & Austral./NZ informal waste someone's time. **stuff off** S. African & Austral./NZ informal go away. **stuff something up** (also **stuff up**) S. African & Austral./NZ informal **1** damage or ruin something. **2** do something badly or act incompetently.
- DERIVATIVES **-stuffer** n.
- ORIGIN Middle English: shortening of Old French *estoffe* 'material, furniture', *estoffer* 'equip, furnish', from Greek *stuphein* 'draw together'.

stuffed shirt ■ n. informal a conservative, pompous person.

stuffing ■ n. **1** a mixture used to stuff poultry or meat before cooking. **2** padding used to stuff cushions, furniture, or soft toys.
- PHRASES **knock** (or **take**) **the stuffing out of** informal severely impair the confidence or strength of.

stuffing box ■ n. a casing in which material such as greased wool is compressed around a shaft or axle to form a seal against gas or liquid.

stuffy ■ adj. (-ier, -iest) **1** lacking fresh air or ventilation. **2** conventional and narrow-minded. **3** (of a person's nose) blocked up.
- DERIVATIVES **stuffily** adv. **stuffiness** n.

stultify /ˈstʌltɪfʌɪ/ ■ v. (-ies, -ied) **1** [usu. as adj. **stultifying**] cause to feel bored or enervated. **2** cause to appear foolish or absurd.
- DERIVATIVES **stultification** n.
- ORIGIN C18: from late Latin *stultificare*, from Latin *stultus* 'foolish'.

stumble ■ v. **1** trip or momentarily lose one's balance. ▶ walk unsteadily. **2** make a mistake or repeated mistakes in speaking. **3** (**stumble across/on/upon**) find by chance. ■ n. an act of stumbling.
- DERIVATIVES **stumbler** n. **stumbling** adj. **stumblingly** adv.
- ORIGIN Middle English: from Old Norse, from the Germanic base of STAMMER.

stumbling block ■ n. an obstacle.

stump ■ n. **1** the part of a tree trunk left projecting from the ground after the rest has fallen or been felled. **2** a projecting remnant of something worn away or cut or broken off. **3** Cricket each of the three upright pieces of wood which form a wicket. ▶ (**stumps**) informal close of play. **4** a cylinder with conical ends made of rolled paper or other soft material, used in art for softening or blending pencil or crayon marks. **5** [as modifier] engaged in or involving political campaigning. ■ v. **1** (usu. **be stumped**) baffle. **2** Cricket (of a wicketkeeper) dismiss (a batsman) by dislodging the bails with the ball while the batsman is out of the crease but not running. **3** walk stiffly and noisily. **4** (**stump something up**) informal pay a sum of money. **5** chiefly N. Amer. travel around (a district) making political speeches. **6** use a stump on (a drawing, line, etc.).
- PHRASES **on the stump** informal engaged in political campaigning.
- ORIGIN Middle English: from Middle Low German *stump(e)* or Middle Dutch *stomp*; sense 5 of the noun refers to the use of a tree stump as a platform for a speaker.

stumper ■ n. informal a puzzling question.

stumpnose ■ n. (pl. same) S. African a southern African sea bream, popular with anglers. [*Rhabdosargus* and other genera, family Sparidae.]
- ORIGIN translation of S. African Dutch *stompneus*, from Dutch *stomp* 'blunt' + *neus* 'nose, snout'.

stumpy ■ adj. (-ier, -iest) short and thick; squat.
- DERIVATIVES **stumpily** adv. **stumpiness** n.

stun ■ v. (**stunned, stunning**) **1** knock unconscious or into a dazed or semi-conscious state. **2** astonish or shock (someone) so that they are temporarily unable to react.
- ORIGIN Middle English: shortening of Old French *estoner* 'astonish'.

stung past and past participle of STING.

stun gun ■ n. a device used to immobilize an attacker without causing serious injury.

stunk past and past participle of STINK.

stunner ■ n. informal a strikingly beautiful or impressive person or thing. ▶ an amazing turn of events.

stunning ■ adj. extremely impressive or attractive.
- DERIVATIVES **stunningly** adv.

stunt[1] ■ v. [often as adj. **stunted**] retard the growth or development of. ▶ frustrate and spoil.
- DERIVATIVES **stuntedness** n.
- ORIGIN C16: from dialect *stunt* 'foolish, stubborn', of Germanic origin.

stunt[2] ■ n. an action displaying spectacular skill and daring. ▶ something unusual done to attract attention. ■ v. perform stunts, especially aerobatics.
- ORIGIN C19 (orig. US college slang).

stuntman (or **stuntwoman**) ■ n. (pl. -men or -women) a person taking an actor's place in performing dangerous stunts.

stupa /ˈstuːpə/ ■ n. a dome-shaped building erected as a Buddhist shrine.
- ORIGIN from Sanskrit *stūpa*.

stupefy /ˈstjuːpɪfʌɪ/ ■ v. (-ies, -ied) **1** make (someone) unable to think or feel properly. **2** astonish and shock.
- DERIVATIVES **stupefaction** n. **stupefying** adj. **stupefyingly** adv.
- ORIGIN Middle English: from French *stupéfier*, from Latin *stupefacere*, from *stupere* 'be struck senseless'.

stupendous /stjuːˈpɛndəs/ ■ adj. extremely impressive.
- DERIVATIVES **stupendously** adv. **stupendousness** n.
- ORIGIN C16: from Latin *stupendus* 'to be wondered at', from *stupere*.

stupid ■ adj. (-er, -est) **1** lacking intelligence or common sense. ▶ informal used to express exasperation or boredom: *stop messing about with your stupid paintings!* **2** dazed and unable to think clearly.
- DERIVATIVES **stupidity** n. **stupidly** adv. **stupidness** n.
- ORIGIN C16: from French *stupide* or Latin *stupidus*, from *stupere* 'be amazed or stunned'.

stupor /ˈstjuːpə/ ■ n. a state of near-unconsciousness or insensibility.
- ORIGIN Middle English: from Latin, from *stupere* 'be amazed or stunned'.

sturdy ■ adj. (-ier, -iest) strongly and solidly built or made. ▶ confident and determined: *a sturdy independence.*
- DERIVATIVES **sturdily** adv. **sturdiness** n.
- ORIGIN Middle English: shortening of Old French *esturdi*

'stunned, dazed'; perhaps from Latin *turdus* 'a thrush' (cf. the French phr. *soûl comme une grive* 'drunk as a thrush').

sturgeon /ˈstəːdʒ(ə)n/ ■ n. a very large primitive fish with bony plates on the body, commercially important for its caviar and flesh. [Family Acipenseridae: several species.]
– ORIGIN Middle English: from Anglo-Norman French, of Germanic origin.

Sturm und Drang /ˌʃtʊəm ʊnt ˈdraŋ/ ■ n. an 18th-century German literary and artistic movement characterized by the expression of emotional unrest and a rejection of neoclassical literary norms.
– ORIGIN German, 'storm and stress'.

stutter ■ v. talk with continued involuntary repetition of sounds, especially initial consonants. ▶ (of a machine or gun) produce a series of short, sharp sounds. ■ n. a tendency to stutter while speaking.
– DERIVATIVES **stutterer** n. **stuttering** adj.
– ORIGIN C16: from dialect *stut*, of Germanic origin.

St Vitus's dance /ˈvʌɪtəsɪz/ ■ n. old-fashioned term for **SYDENHAM'S CHOREA**.
– ORIGIN so named because a visit to St Vitus's shrine was believed to alleviate the disease.

sty[1] ■ n. (pl. **-ies**) a pigsty.
– ORIGIN Old English *sti*- (in *stifearh* 'sty pig'), prob. identical with *stig* 'hall' (see **STEWARD**), of Germanic origin.

sty[2] (also **stye**) ■ n. (pl. **sties** or **styes**) an inflamed swelling on the edge of an eyelid.
– ORIGIN C17: from dialect *styany*, from *styan*, from Old English *stīgend* 'riser' + **EYE**.

Stygian /ˈstɪdʒɪən/ ■ adj. poetic/literary very dark.
– ORIGIN from the River *Styx*, an underworld river in Greek mythology.

style ■ n. 1 a manner of doing something. ▶ a way of painting, writing, etc., characteristic of a particular period, person, etc. 2 a distinctive appearance, design, or arrangement. 3 elegance and sophistication. 4 an official or legal title. 5 Botany a narrow, typically elongated extension of the ovary, bearing the stigma. ■ v. 1 design, make, or arrange in a particular form. 2 designate with a particular name, description, or title.
– DERIVATIVES **styleless** adj. **styler** n.
– ORIGIN Middle English: from Old French *stile*, from Latin *stilus*.

-style ■ suffix (forming adjectives and adverbs) in a manner characteristic of: *family-style*.

stylet /ˈstʌɪlɪt/ ■ n. Medicine a slender probe. ▶ a wire or piece of plastic run through a catheter or cannula to stiffen or clear it.
– ORIGIN C17: from French *stilet*, from Italian *stiletto* (see **STILETTO**).

styli plural form of **STYLUS**.

stylish ■ adj. having or displaying a good sense of style. ▶ fashionably elegant.
– DERIVATIVES **stylishly** adv. **stylishness** n.

stylist ■ n. 1 a person who designs fashionable clothes or cuts hair. 2 a writer noted for their literary style. ▶ (in sport or music) a person who performs with style.

stylistic ■ adj. of or concerning style, especially literary style.
– DERIVATIVES **stylistically** adv.

stylistics ■ pl. n. [treated as sing.] the study of the literary styles of particular genres or writers.

stylize (also **-ise**) ■ v. [usu. as adj. **stylized** (also **-ised**)] depict or treat in a mannered and non-realistic style.
– DERIVATIVES **stylization** (also **-isation**) n.

stylograph ■ n. a kind of fountain pen having a fine perforated tube instead of a split nib.
– ORIGIN C19: from **STYLUS** + **-GRAPH**.

styloid ■ adj. technical resembling a stylus or pen. ▶ Anatomy denoting a slender projection of bone, such as those at the lower ends of the ulna and radius.

stylus /ˈstʌɪləs/ ■ n. (pl. **styli** /-lʌɪ, -liː/ or **styluses**) 1 a hard point, typically of diamond or sapphire, following a groove in a gramophone record and transmitting the recorded sound for reproduction. 2 an ancient writing implement for scratching letters on wax-covered tablets. ▶ a similar implement for engraving and tracing.
– ORIGIN C18: erroneous spelling of Latin *stilus*.

stymie /ˈstʌɪmi/ ■ v. (**stymies**, **stymied**, **stymying** or **stymieing**) informal prevent or hinder the progress of.
– ORIGIN C19 (orig. a golfing term, denoting a situation on the green where a ball obstructs the shot of another player).

styrene /ˈstʌɪriːn/ ■ n. Chemistry an unsaturated liquid hydrocarbon obtained as a petroleum by-product and used to make plastics and resins.
– ORIGIN C19: from *styrax*, denoting a fragrant gum resin, from Greek *sturax*.

styrofoam ■ n. (trademark in the US) a kind of expanded polystyrene, used especially for making food containers.
– ORIGIN 1950s: from **POLYSTYRENE** + **FOAM**.

stywe pap /ˈsteɪvə pap/ ■ n. S. African firm maize meal porridge.
– ORIGIN Afrikaans, from *styf* 'stiff' + *pap* 'porridge'.

suasion /ˈsweɪʒ(ə)n/ ■ n. formal persuasion as opposed to force or compulsion.
– ORIGIN Middle English: from Old French, or from Latin *suasio(n-)*, from *suadere* 'to urge'.

suave /swɑːv/ ■ adj. (**suaver**, **suavest**) (of a man) charming, confident, and elegant.
– DERIVATIVES **suavely** adv. **suaveness** n. **suavity** /-vɪti/ n. (pl. **-ies**).
– ORIGIN Middle English: from Old French, or from Latin *suavis* 'agreeable'.

sub informal ■ n. 1 a submarine. 2 a subscription. 3 a substitute, especially in a sporting team. 4 a subeditor. 5 Brit. an advance or loan against expected income. ■ v. (**subbed**, **subbing**) 1 act as a substitute. 2 Brit. lend or advance a sum to. 3 subedit.

sub- (also **suc-** before *c*; **suf-** before *f*; **sug-** before *g*; **sup-** before *p*; **sur-** before *r*; **sus-** before *c, p, t*) ■ prefix 1 at, to, or from a lower level or position: *subalpine*. ▶ lower in rank or importance: *subdeacon*. 2 somewhat; nearly; more or less: *subantarctic*. 3 denoting subsequent or secondary action of the same kind: *subdivision*. 4 denoting support: *subvention*. 5 Chemistry in names of compounds containing a relatively small proportion of a component: *suboxide*.
– ORIGIN from Latin *sub* 'under, close to'.

subacute ■ adj. 1 Medicine (of a condition) between acute and chronic. 2 moderately acute in shape or angle.

subaerial ■ adj. Geology existing, occurring, or formed in the open air or on the earth's surface, not under water or underground.

subalpine ■ adj. of or situated on the higher slopes of mountains just below the treeline.

subaltern /ˈsʌb(ə)lt(ə)n/ ■ n. an officer in the British army below the rank of captain, especially a second lieutenant. ■ adj. of lower status.
– ORIGIN C16: from late Latin *subalternus*, from Latin *sub-* 'next below' + *alternus* 'every other'.

subantarctic ■ adj. of or relating to the region immediately north of the Antarctic Circle.

sub-aqua ■ adj. of or relating to swimming or exploring under water, especially with an aqualung.

sub-aquatic ■ adj. underwater.

subaqueous ■ adj. existing, formed, or taking place under water.

subarctic ■ adj. of or relating to the region immediately south of the Arctic Circle.

sub-assembly ■ n. (pl. **-ies**) a unit assembled separately but designed to be incorporated with other units into a larger manufactured product.

subatomic ■ adj. smaller than or occurring within an atom.

Sub-Boreal /ˈbɔːrɪəl/ ■ adj. Geology relating to or denoting the fourth climatic stage of the postglacial period in northern Europe (about 5 000 to 2 800 years ago).

subcategory ■ n. (pl. **-ies**) a secondary or subordinate category.
– DERIVATIVES **subcategorization** (also **-isation**) n. **subcategorize** (also **-ise**) v.

subclass ■ n. a secondary or subordinate class. ▶ Biology a taxonomic category that ranks below class and above order.

sub-clause ■ n. **1** chiefly Law a subsidiary section of a clause of a bill, contract, or treaty. **2** Grammar a subordinate clause.

subclavian /sʌbˈkleɪvɪən/ ■ adj. Anatomy relating to or denoting an artery or vein which serves the neck and arm on the left or right side of the body.
– ORIGIN C17: from *sub* 'under' + *clavis* (see **CLAVICLE**).

subclinical ■ adj. Medicine relating to or denoting a disease which is not severe enough to present readily observable symptoms.

subconscious ■ adj. of or concerning the part of the mind of which one is not fully aware but which influences one's actions and feelings. ■ n. (**one's/the subconscious**) this part of the mind.
– DERIVATIVES **subconsciously** adv. **subconsciousness** n.

subcontinent ■ n. a large distinguishable part of a continent, such as North America or southern Africa.
– DERIVATIVES **subcontinental** adj.

subcontract ■ v. /sʌbkənˈtrakt/ employ a firm or person outside one's company to do (work). ▸ carry out work for a company as part of a larger project. ■ n. /sʌbˈkɒntrakt/ a contract to do work for another company as part of a larger project.

subcontractor ■ n. a firm or person that carries out work for a company as part of a larger project.

subcortical ■ adj. Anatomy below the cortex.

subcostal ■ adj. Anatomy beneath a rib; below the ribs.

subcritical ■ adj. Physics **1** (in nuclear physics) containing or involving less than the critical mass. **2** (of a flow of fluid) slower than the speed at which waves travel in the fluid.

subculture ■ n. a cultural group within a larger culture, often having beliefs or interests at variance with those of the larger culture.
– DERIVATIVES **subcultural** adj.

subcutaneous ■ adj. Anatomy & Medicine situated or applied under the skin.
– DERIVATIVES **subcutaneously** adv.

subdeacon ■ n. (in some Christian Churches) a minister of an order ranking below deacon.

subdivide ■ v. divide (something that has already been divided or that is a separate unit).

subdivision ■ n. **1** the action of subdividing or being subdivided. ▸ a secondary or subordinate division. **2** N. Amer. & Austral./NZ an area of land divided into plots for sale.

subdominant ■ n. Music the fourth note of the diatonic scale of any key.

subduction /səbˈdʌkʃ(ə)n/ ■ n. Geology the sideways and downward movement of the edge of a plate of the earth's crust into the mantle beneath another plate.
– DERIVATIVES **subduct** v.
– ORIGIN 1970s: from Latin *subductio(n-)*, from *subducere* 'draw from below'.

subdue ■ v. (**subdues**, **subdued**, **subduing**) overcome, quieten, or bring under control. ▸ bring (a country) under control by force.
– ORIGIN Middle English: from Anglo-Norman French *suduire*, from Latin *subducere* 'draw from below'.

subdued ■ adj. **1** (of a person) quiet and rather reflective or depressed. **2** (of colour or lighting) soft; muted.

subdural /sʌbˈdjʊər(ə)l/ ■ adj. Anatomy situated or occurring between the dura mater and the arachnoid membrane of the brain and spinal cord.

subedit ■ v. (**subedited**, **subediting**) check and correct (newspaper or magazine text) before printing, typically also writing headlines and captions.
– DERIVATIVES **subeditor** n.

subfamily ■ n. (pl. **-ies**) a subdivision of a group. ▸ Biology a taxonomic category that ranks below family and above tribe or genus.

subfloor ■ n. the foundation for a floor in a building.

subframe ■ n. a supporting frame.

subgenus ■ n. (pl. **subgenera**) Biology a taxonomic category that ranks below genus and above species.
– DERIVATIVES **subgeneric** adj.

subglacial ■ adj. Geology situated or occurring underneath a glacier or ice sheet.

subgroup ■ n. a subdivision of a group.

sub-heading (also **sub-head**) ■ n. a heading given to a subsection of a piece of writing.

subhuman ■ adj. **1** of a lower order of being than the human. **2** derogatory not worthy of a human being; debased or depraved. ■ n. a subhuman creature or person.

subjacent /səbˈdʒeɪs(ə)nt/ ■ adj. technical situated below something else.
– ORIGIN C16: from Latin *subjacent-* 'lying underneath', from *sub-* 'under' + *jacere* 'to lie'.

subject ■ n. /ˈsʌbdʒɪkt/ **1** a person or thing that is being discussed or dealt with or that gives rise to something. ▸ Logic the part of a proposition about which a statement is made. ▸ a person who is the focus of scientific or medical attention or experiment. **2** a branch of knowledge studied or taught in a school, college, or university. **3** Grammar a noun phrase about which the rest of the clause is predicated. **4** a member of a state owing allegiance to its monarch or supreme ruler. **5** Philosophy a thinking or feeling entity; the conscious mind or ego. ▸ the central substance or core of a thing as opposed to its attributes. ■ adj. /ˈsʌbdʒɪkt/ (**subject to**) **1** likely or prone to be affected by (something bad). **2** dependent or conditional upon. **3** under the control or authority of. ■ adv. /ˈsʌbdʒɪkt/ (**subject to**) conditionally upon. ■ v. /səbˈdʒɛkt/ (usu. **subject someone/thing to**) cause or force to undergo.
– DERIVATIVES **subjection** n. **subjectless** adj.
– ORIGIN Middle English: from Old French *suget*, from Latin *subject-*, *subicere* 'bring under'.

subjective ■ adj. **1** based on or influenced by personal feelings, tastes, or opinions. **2** dependent on the mind for existence. **3** Grammar relating to or denoting a case of nouns and pronouns used for the subject of a sentence.
– DERIVATIVES **subjectively** adv. **subjectiveness** n. **subjectivity** n.

subjectivism ■ n. Philosophy the doctrine that knowledge is merely subjective and that there is no external or objective truth.
– DERIVATIVES **subjectivist** n. & adj.

subject matter ■ n. the topic dealt with or the subject represented in a debate, exposition, or work of art.

subjoin ■ v. formal add (comments or supplementary information) at the end of a speech or text.
– ORIGIN C16: from obsolete French *subjoindre*, from Latin *subjungere*, from *sub-* 'in addition' + *jungere* 'to join'.

sub judice /sʌb ˈdʒuːdɪsi, sʊb ˈjuːdɪkeɪ/ ■ adj. Law under judicial consideration and therefore prohibited from public discussion elsewhere.
– ORIGIN Latin, 'under a judge'.

subjugate /ˈsʌbdʒʊɡeɪt/ ■ v. (often **subjugate someone/thing to**) bring under domination or control, especially by conquest.
– DERIVATIVES **subjugation** n. **subjugator** n.
– ORIGIN Middle English: from late Latin *subjugare* 'bring under a yoke', from *jugum* 'yoke'.

subjunctive /səbˈdʒʌŋ(k)tɪv/ Grammar ■ adj. denoting a mood of verbs expressing what is imagined or wished or possible. Compare with **INDICATIVE**. ■ n. a verb in the subjunctive mood.
– DERIVATIVES **subjunctively** adv.
– ORIGIN C16: from French *subjonctif*, *-ive* or late Latin *subjunctivus*, from *subjungere* (see **SUBJOIN**), rendering Greek *hupotaktikos* 'subjoined'.

USAGE
See **Subjunctive** in *Guide to Good English* p. SP 14.

sublease ■ n. & v. another term for **SUBLET**.

sub-lessee ■ n. a person who holds a sublease.

sub-lessor ■ n. a person who grants a sublease.

sublet ■ v. /sʌbˈlɛt/ (**subletting**; past and past part. **sublet**) lease (a property) to a subtenant. ■ n. /ˈsʌblɛt/ a lease of a property by a tenant to a subtenant.

sub lieutenant ■ n. a rank of officer in the navy, above ensign and below lieutenant.

sublimate /ˈsʌblɪmeɪt/ ■ v. **1** (in psychoanalytic theory)

sublime

divert or modify (an instinctual impulse) into a culturally higher or socially more acceptable activity. **2** transform into a purer or idealized form. **3** Chemistry another term for SUBLIME. ■ n. /also ˈsʌblɪmət/ Chemistry a solid deposit of a substance which has sublimed.
– DERIVATIVES **sublimation** n.
– ORIGIN Middle English: from Latin *sublimare* 'raise up'.

sublime ■ adj. (-er, -est) **1** of such excellence, grandeur, or beauty as to inspire great admiration or awe. **2** extreme or unparalleled: *the sublime confidence of youth.* ■ v. **1** Chemistry (with reference to a solid substance) change directly into vapour when heated, typically forming a solid deposit again on cooling. **2** archaic elevate to a high degree of purity or excellence.
– DERIVATIVES **sublimely** adv. **sublimity** n.
– ORIGIN C16: from Latin *sublimis*, from *sub-* 'up to' + a second element perhaps rel. to *limen* 'threshold', *limus* 'oblique'.

subliminal /səˈblɪmɪn(ə)l/ ■ adj. Psychology (of a stimulus or mental process) perceived by or affecting someone's mind without their being aware of it.
– DERIVATIVES **subliminally** adv.
– ORIGIN C19: from SUB- + Latin *limen*, *limin-* 'threshold'.

subliminal advertising ■ n. advertising that uses images and sounds to influence consumers subliminally.

sublingual ■ adj. Anatomy & Medicine situated or applied under the tongue. ▸ denoting a pair of small salivary glands beneath the tongue.
– DERIVATIVES **sublingually** adv.

sublittoral /sʌbˈlɪt(ə)r(ə)l/ ■ adj. chiefly Ecology living, growing, or situated near to or just behind the shore.

subluxation /ˌsʌblʌkˈseɪʃ(ə)n/ ■ n. Medicine a partial dislocation.

sub-machine gun ■ n. a hand-held lightweight machine gun.

submandibular /ˌsʌbmanˈdɪbjʊlə/ ■ adj. Anatomy situated beneath the jaw or mandible.

submandibular gland (also **submaxillary gland**) ■ n. Anatomy either of a pair of salivary glands situated below the parotid glands.

submarine ■ n. **1** a streamlined warship designed to operate completely submerged in the sea for long periods. **2** (also **submarine sandwich**) N. Amer. a sandwich made of a long roll filled with meat, cheese, and salad. ■ adj. existing, occurring, done, or used under the surface of the sea.
– DERIVATIVES **submariner** n.

submediant ■ n. Music the sixth note of the diatonic scale of any key.

submerge ■ v. **1** cause to be under water. ▸ descend below the surface of water. **2** completely cover or obscure.
– DERIVATIVES **submergence** n. **submergible** adj.
– ORIGIN C17: from Latin *submergere*, from *sub-* 'under' + *mergere* 'to dip'.

submerse /səbˈməːs/ ■ v. technical submerge.
– ORIGIN Middle English: from Latin *submers-* 'plunged below', from *submergere* (see SUBMERGE).

submersible ■ adj. designed to operate while submerged. ■ n. a small boat or craft that is submersible.

submersion ■ n. the action or state of submerging or being submerged.

submicroscopic ■ adj. too small to be seen by an ordinary light microscope.

submission ■ n. **1** the action or fact of submitting. ▸ Wrestling an act of surrendering to a hold by one's opponent. **2** a proposal or application submitted for consideration. ▸ Law a proposition or argument presented by counsel to a judge or jury.

submissive ■ adj. meekly obedient or passive.
– DERIVATIVES **submissively** adv. **submissiveness** n.

submit ■ v. (**submitted**, **submitting**) **1** accept or yield to a superior force or stronger person. **2** (usu. **submit something to**) subject to a particular process, treatment, or condition. ▸ (**submit oneself to**) consent to undergo. ▸ agree to refer a matter to a third party for decision or adjudication. **3** present (a proposal or application) for consideration or judgement. ▸ (especially in judicial contexts) suggest; argue.
– DERIVATIVES **submitter** n.
– ORIGIN Middle English: from Latin *submittere*, from *sub-* 'under' + *mittere* 'send, put'.

submodifier ■ n. Grammar an adverb used in front of an adjective or another adverb to modify its meaning, e.g. *very* in *very cold.*

submucosa /ˌsʌbmjuːˈkəʊsə/ ■ n. (pl. **submucosae**) Physiology the layer of areolar connective tissue lying beneath a mucous membrane.
– DERIVATIVES **submucosal** adj.
– ORIGIN C19: from modern Latin *submucosa* (*membrana*), from *submucosus* 'submucous'.

submultiple ■ n. a number that can be divided exactly into a specified number.

subnormal ■ adj. not reaching a level regarded as usual, especially with respect to intelligence or development.
– DERIVATIVES **subnormality** n.

sub-nuclear ■ adj. Physics occurring in or smaller than an atomic nucleus.

suboptimal ■ adj. technical of less than the highest standard or quality.

suborder ■ n. Biology a taxonomic category that ranks below order and above family.

subordinary ■ n. (pl. **-ies**) Heraldry a simple device or bearing that is less common than the ordinaries.

subordinate ■ adj. /səˈbɔːdɪnət/ lower in rank or position. ▸ of less or secondary importance. ■ n. /səˈbɔːdɪnət/ a person under the authority or control of another. ■ v. /səˈbɔːdɪnet/ treat or regard as subordinate. ▸ make subservient or dependent.
– DERIVATIVES **subordinately** adv. **subordination** n. **subordinative** adj.
– ORIGIN Middle English: from medieval Latin *subordinatus* 'placed in an inferior rank', from Latin *sub-* 'below' + *ordinare* 'ordain'.

subordinate clause ■ n. a clause that forms part of and is dependent on a main clause (e.g. 'when it rang' in 'she answered the phone when it rang').

subordinate legislation ■ n. Law law which is enacted under delegated powers.

subordinating conjunction ■ n. a conjunction that introduces a subordinating clause, e.g. *although*, *because*. Contrasted with COORDINATING CONJUNCTION.

suborn /səˈbɔːn/ ■ v. bribe or otherwise induce (someone) to commit an unlawful act such as perjury.
– DERIVATIVES **subornation** n. **suborner** n.
– ORIGIN C16: from Latin *subornare* 'incite secretly', from *sub-* 'secretly' + *ornare* 'equip'.

suboxide ■ n. Chemistry an oxide containing the lowest or an unusually small proportion of oxygen.

subphylum ■ n. (pl. **subphyla**) Zoology a taxonomic category that ranks below phylum and above class.

sub-plot ■ n. a subordinate plot in a play, novel, etc.

subpoena /səˈpiːnə/ Law ■ n. a writ ordering a person to attend a court. ■ v. (**subpoenas**, **subpoenaed** or **subpoena'd**, **subpoenaing**) summon with a subpoena. ▸ require (a document or other evidence) to be submitted to a court.
– ORIGIN Middle English: from Latin *sub poena* 'under penalty' (the first words of the writ).

sub-post office ■ n. (in the UK) a small local post office offering fewer services than a main post office.

subprogram ■ n. Computing a subroutine.

subrogation /ˌsʌbrəˈɡeɪʃ(ə)n/ ■ n. Law the substitution of one person or group by another in respect of a debt or insurance claim, accompanied by the transfer of any associated rights and duties.
– DERIVATIVES **subrogate** /ˈsʌbrəɡeɪt/ v.
– ORIGIN Middle English: from late Latin *subrogatio(n-)*, from *subrogare* 'choose as substitute'.

sub rosa /sʌb ˈrəʊzə/ ■ adj. & adv. formal happening or done in secret.
– ORIGIN Latin, 'under the rose', as an emblem of secrecy.

subroutine ■ n. Computing a set of instructions designed to perform a frequently used operation within a program.

sub-Saharan ■ adj. from or forming part of the African regions south of the Sahara desert.

subsample ■ n. a sample drawn from a larger sample. ■ v. take a subsample from.

subscribe ■ v. 1 (usu. **subscribe to**) arrange to receive something, especially a periodical, regularly by paying in advance. ▸ contribute or undertake to contribute a sum of money to a project or cause. ▸ apply to participate in. ▸ apply for an issue of shares. ▸ (of a bookseller) agree before publication to take a certain number of copies of a book. 2 formal sign (a will, contract, etc.). 3 (**subscribe to**) feel agreement with (an idea or proposal).
– DERIVATIVES **subscriber** n.
– ORIGIN Middle English: from Latin *subscript-*, *subscribere*, from *sub-* 'under' + *scribere* 'write'.

subscriber trunk dialling ■ n. the automatic connection of trunk calls by dialling without the assistance of an operator.

subscript ■ adj. (of a letter, figure, or symbol) written or printed below the line. ■ n. a subscript letter, figure, or symbol.

subscription ■ n. 1 the action or fact of subscribing. ▸ a payment to subscribe to something. 2 formal a signature or short piece of writing at the end of a document.

subscription concert ■ n. one of a series of concerts for which tickets are sold mainly in advance.

subsection ■ n. a division of a section.

subsense ■ n. a subsidiary sense of a word defined in a dictionary.

subsequence¹ /'sʌbsɪkw(ə)ns/ ■ n. formal the state of following or being a consequence of something.

subsequence² /'sʌb,siːkw(ə)ns/ ■ n. a sequence contained in or derived from another sequence.

subsequent ■ adj. coming after something in time.
– DERIVATIVES **subsequently** adv.
– ORIGIN Middle English: from Old French, or from Latin *subsequent-*, *subsequi* 'follow after'.

subserve ■ v. formal help to further or promote.
– ORIGIN C17: from Latin *subservient-*, *subservire* (see **SUB-**, **SERVE**).

subservient ■ adj. (often **subservient to**) 1 prepared to obey others unquestioningly; obsequious. 2 less important; subordinate.
– DERIVATIVES **subservience** n. **subserviency** n. **subserviently** adv.

subset ■ n. a part of a larger group of related things. ▸ Mathematics a set of which all the elements are contained in another set.

subshrub ■ n. Botany a dwarf shrub, especially one that is woody only at the base.

subside ■ v. 1 become less intense, violent, or severe. ▸ (**subside into**) give way to (an overwhelming feeling). 2 (of water) go down to a lower or the normal level. ▸ (of a swelling) reduce until gone. 3 (of a building) sink lower into the ground. ▸ (of the ground) cave in; sink. ▸ informal sink into a sitting, kneeling, or lying position.
– ORIGIN C17: from Latin *subsidere*, from *sub-* 'below' + *sidere* 'settle'.

subsidence /səb'sʌɪd(ə)ns, 'sʌbsɪd(ə)ns/ ■ n. the gradual caving in or sinking of an area of land.

subsidiarity /səb,sɪdɪ'arɪti/ ■ n. (in politics) the principle that a central authority should have a subsidiary function, performing only those tasks which cannot be performed at a more local level.

subsidiary ■ adj. less important than but related or supplementary to. ▸ (of a company) controlled by a holding or parent company. ■ n. (pl. **-ies**) a subsidiary company.
– ORIGIN C16: from Latin *subsidiarius*, from *subsidium* (see **SUBSIDY**).

subsidize (also **-ise**) ■ v. support (an organization or activity) financially. ▸ pay part of the cost of producing (something) to reduce its price.
– DERIVATIVES **subsidization** (also **-isation**) n. **subsidizer** (also **-iser**) n.

subsidy ■ n. (pl. **-ies**) 1 a sum of money granted from public funds to help an industry or business keep the price of a commodity or service low. ▸ a sum of money granted to support an undertaking held to be in the public interest. ▸ a grant or contribution of money. 2 historical a parliamentary grant to the sovereign for state needs. ▸ a tax levied on a particular occasion.
– ORIGIN Middle English: from Anglo-Norman French *subsidie*, from Latin *subsidium* 'assistance'.

subsist ■ v. 1 maintain or support oneself, especially at a minimal level. 2 chiefly Law remain in being, force, or effect. ▸ (**subsist in**) be attributable to.
– DERIVATIVES **subsistent** adj.
– ORIGIN C16: from Latin *subsistere* 'stand firm'.

subsistence ■ n. 1 the action or fact of subsisting. ▸ the means of doing this. ▸ [as modifier] denoting or relating to production at a level sufficient only for one's own use or consumption, without any surplus for trade: *subsistence agriculture*. 2 chiefly Law the state of remaining in force or effect.

subsistence allowance (also **subsistence money**) ■ n. an allowance or advance on wages, especially when granted as travelling expenses.

subsistence level (also **subsistence wage**) ■ n. a standard of living (or wage) that provides only the bare necessities of life.

subsoil ■ n. the soil lying immediately under the surface soil. ■ v. [usu. as noun **subsoiling**] plough (land) so as to cut into the subsoil.
– DERIVATIVES **subsoiler** n.

subsonic ■ adj. relating to or flying at a speed or speeds less than that of sound.
– DERIVATIVES **subsonically** adv.

subspecies ■ n. (pl. same) Biology a taxonomic category that ranks below species, typically a fairly permanent geographically isolated race.
– DERIVATIVES **subspecific** adj.

substance ■ n. 1 a particular kind of matter with uniform properties. ▸ an intoxicating or narcotic drug. 2 the real physical matter of which a person or thing consists. ▸ solid basis in reality or fact: *the claim has no substance*. ▸ dependability or stability. 3 the quality of being important, valid, or significant. ▸ the most important or essential part or meaning. ▸ the subject matter of a text or work of art, especially as contrasted with its form or style. ▸ wealth and possessions: *a woman of substance*. 4 Philosophy the essential nature underlying phenomena, which is subject to changes and accidents.
– PHRASES **in substance** essentially.
– ORIGIN Middle English: from Latin *substantia* 'being, essence', from *substare* 'stand firm'.

substance abuse ■ n. inappropriate use of or addiction to alcohol, drugs, or intoxicating chemical substances.

sub-standard ■ adj. 1 below the usual or required standard. 2 another term for **NON-STANDARD**.

substantial ■ adj. 1 of considerable importance, size, or worth. ▸ strongly built or made. ▸ important in material or social terms; wealthy. 2 concerning the essentials of something. 3 real and tangible rather than imaginary.
– DERIVATIVES **substantiality** n.

substantialism ■ n. Philosophy the doctrine that behind phenomena there are substantial realities.

substantially ■ adv. 1 to a great or significant extent. 2 for the most part; essentially.

substantiate /səb'stanʃɪeɪt/ ■ v. provide evidence to support or prove the truth of.
– DERIVATIVES **substantiation** n.
– ORIGIN C17: from medieval Latin *substantiare* 'give substance'.

substantive /'sʌbst(ə)ntɪv/ ■ adj. /also səb'stantɪv/ 1 having a firm basis in reality and so important or meaningful. 2 having a separate and independent existence. ▸ (of a rank or appointment) permanent. ▸ (of a dye) not needing a mordant. ▸ (of an enactment, motion, or resolution) made in due form as such; not amended. 3 (of law) defining rights and duties as opposed to giving the rules by which such rights are established. ■ n. Grammar, dated a noun.
– DERIVATIVES **substantival** /-'tʌɪv(ə)l/ adj. **substantively** adv.

substation ■ n. **1** a set of equipment reducing the high voltage of electrical power transmission to that suitable for supply to consumers. **2** a subordinate police station or fire station.

substituent /səb'stɪtjʊənt/ ■ n. Chemistry an atom or group of atoms taking the place of another or occupying a specified position in a molecule.

substitute ■ n. **1** a person or thing acting or serving in place of another. **2** a sports player nominated as eligible to replace another after a match has begun. **3** Scots Law a deputy. ■ v. **1** (usu. **substitute something for**) use, add, or serve in place of. ▸ (usu. **substitute something with**) replace with another. ▸ Chemistry replace (an atom or group in a molecule) with another. **2** replace (a sports player) with a substitute during a match.
– DERIVATIVES **substitutability** n. **substitutable** adj. **substitution** n. **substitutional** adj. **substitutionary** adj. **substitutive** adj.
– ORIGIN Middle English: from Latin *substitut-*, *substituere* 'put in place of'.

substrate /'sʌbstreɪt/ ■ n. **1** the surface or material on which an organism lives, grows, or feeds. **2** the substance on which an enzyme acts. **3** a surface on which something is deposited or inscribed.
– ORIGIN C19: anglicized form of SUBSTRATUM.

substratum /sʌb'strɑːtəm, -'streɪtəm/ ■ n. (pl. **substrata**) **1** an underlying layer or substance, in particular a layer of rock or soil beneath the surface of the ground. **2** a foundation or basis.

substructure ■ n. an underlying or supporting structure.
– DERIVATIVES **substructural** adj.

subsume /səb'sjuːm/ ■ v. include or absorb in something else.
– DERIVATIVES **subsumable** adj. **subsumption** n.
– ORIGIN C16: from medieval Latin *subsumere*, from *sub-* 'from below' + *sumere* 'take'.

subtenant ■ n. a person who leases property from a tenant.
– DERIVATIVES **subtenancy** n.

subtend /sʌb'tɛnd/ ■ v. (of a line, arc, etc.) form (an angle) at a particular point when straight lines from its extremities meet. ▸ (of an angle or chord) have bounding lines or points that meet or coincide with those of (a line or arc).
– ORIGIN C16: from Latin *subtendere*, from *sub-* 'under' + *tendere* 'stretch'.

subterfuge /'sʌbtəfjuːdʒ/ ■ n. a trick or deception used in order to achieve one's goal.
– ORIGIN C16: from late Latin *subterfugium*, from Latin *subterfugere* 'escape secretly', from *subter-* 'beneath' + *fugere* 'flee'.

subterranean /ˌsʌbtə'reɪniən/ ■ adj. **1** existing, occurring, or done under the earth's surface. **2** secret.
– DERIVATIVES **subterraneously** adv.
– ORIGIN C17: from Latin *subterraneus*, from *sub-* 'below' + *terra* 'earth'.

subtext ■ n. an underlying theme in a piece of writing or speech.

subtitle ■ n. **1** (**subtitles**) captions displayed at the bottom of a cinema or television screen that translate or transcribe the dialogue or narrative. **2** a subordinate title of a published work or article. ■ v. provide with a subtitle or subtitles.

subtle ■ adj. (**-er**, **-est**) **1** so delicate or precise as to be difficult to analyse or describe: *a subtle distinction*. ▸ capable of making fine distinctions. ▸ delicately complex and understated: *subtle lighting*. **2** making use of clever and indirect methods to achieve something. **3** archaic crafty; cunning.
– DERIVATIVES **subtleness** n. **subtlety** n. **subtly** adv.
– ORIGIN Middle English: from Old French *sotil*, from Latin *subtilis*.

subtotal ■ n. the total of one set of a larger group of figures to be added. ■ v. (**subtotalled**, **subtotalling**; US **subtotaled**, **subtotaling**) add (numbers) so as to obtain a subtotal. ■ adj. Medicine (of an injury or a surgical operation) partial; not total.

subtract ■ v. take away (a number or amount) from another to calculate the difference. ▸ remove (a part of something).
– DERIVATIVES **subtraction** n. **subtractive** adj.
– ORIGIN C16 (*subtraction* Middle English): from Latin *subtract-*, *subtrahere* 'draw away'.

subtrahend /'sʌbtrə,hɛnd/ ■ n. Mathematics a quantity or number to be subtracted from another.
– ORIGIN C17: from Latin *subtrahendus* 'to be taken away', from *subtrahere* (see SUBTRACT).

subtropics ■ pl. n. the regions adjacent to or bordering on the tropics.
– DERIVATIVES **subtropical** adj.

subtype ■ n. a secondary or subordinate type.

subunit ■ n. a distinct component of something.

suburb ■ n. an outlying district of a city, especially a residential one.
– DERIVATIVES **suburban** adj. **suburbanite** n. **suburbanization** (also **-isation**) n. **suburbanize** (also **-ise**) v.
– ORIGIN Middle English: from Old French *suburbe* or Latin *suburbium*, from *sub-* 'near to' + *urbs* 'city'.

suburbia ■ n. the suburbs viewed collectively.

subvent ■ v. formal support or assist by the payment of a subvention.

subvention ■ n. a grant of money, especially from a government.
– ORIGIN Middle English: from late Latin *subventio(n-)*, from Latin *subvenire* 'assist'.

subversive ■ adj. seeking or intended to subvert an established system or institution. ■ n. a subversive person.
– DERIVATIVES **subversively** adv. **subversiveness** n.

subvert ■ v. undermine the power and authority of (an established system or institution).
– DERIVATIVES **subversion** n. **subverter** n.
– ORIGIN Middle English: from Old French *subvertir* or Latin *subvers-*, *subvertere*, from *sub-* 'from below' + *vertere* 'to turn'.

subway ■ n. **1** chiefly Brit. a tunnel under a road for use by pedestrians. **2** chiefly N. Amer. an underground railway.

subwoofer ■ n. a loudspeaker component designed to reproduce very low bass frequencies.

sub-zero ■ adj. (of temperature) lower than zero; below freezing.

suc- ■ prefix variant spelling of SUB- assimilated before *c* (as in *succeed*, *succussion*).

succeed ■ v. **1** achieve an aim or purpose. ▸ attain fame, wealth, or social status. **2** take over an office, title, etc., from (someone). ▸ (often **succeed to**) become the new rightful holder of an office, title, etc. **3** come after and take the place of: *her embarrassment was succeeded by fear*.
– ORIGIN Middle English: from Old French *succeder* or Latin *success-*, *succedere* 'come close after'.

succès de scandale /suk,seɪ də skɒn'dɑːl/ ■ n. a success due to notoriety or a thing's scandalous nature.
– ORIGIN French, 'success of scandal'.

succès d'estime /suk,seɪ dɛ'stiːm/ ■ n. (pl. same) a success in terms of critical appreciation as opposed to popularity or commercial gain.
– ORIGIN French, 'success of opinion'.

success ■ n. the accomplishment of an aim or purpose. ▸ the attainment of fame, wealth, or social status. ▸ a person or thing that achieves success.
– ORIGIN C16: from Latin *successus*, from *succedere* (see SUCCEED).

successful ■ adj. accomplishing an aim or purpose. ▸ having achieved fame, wealth, or social status.
– DERIVATIVES **successfully** adv. **successfulness** n.

succession ■ n. **1** a number of people or things following one after the other. **2** the action, process, or right of inheriting an office, title, etc. **3** Ecology the process by which a plant or animal community successively gives way to another until a stable climax is reached.
– PHRASES **in quick** (or **rapid**) **succession** following one another at short intervals. **in succession** following one after the other without interruption. **in succession to** inheriting or elected to the place of.
– DERIVATIVES **successional** adj.

successive ■ adj. following one another or following others.
– DERIVATIVES **successively** adv. **successiveness** n.

successor ■ n. a person or thing that succeeds another.

success story ■ n. informal a successful person or thing.

succinct /səkˈsɪŋ(k)t/ ■ adj. briefly and clearly expressed.
– DERIVATIVES **succinctly** adv. **succinctness** n.
– ORIGIN Middle English: from Latin *succinct-, succingere* 'tuck up', from *sub-* 'from below' + *cingere* 'gird'.

succour /ˈsʌkə/ (US **succor**) ■ n. assistance and support in times of hardship and distress. ■ v. give assistance or aid to.
– ORIGIN Middle English: from medieval Latin *succursus*, from Latin *succurrere* 'run to the help of'.

succubus /ˈsʌkjʊbəs/ ■ n. (pl. **succubi** /-bʌɪ/) a female demon believed to have sexual intercourse with sleeping men.
– ORIGIN Middle English: from medieval Latin *succubus* 'prostitute', from *succubare*, from *sub-* 'under' + *cubare* 'to lie'.

succulent ■ adj. 1 (of food) tender, juicy, and tasty. 2 Botany (of a plant, especially a xerophyte) having thick fleshy leaves or stems adapted to storing water. ■ n. Botany a succulent plant.
– DERIVATIVES **succulence** n. **succulently** adv.
– ORIGIN C17: from Latin *succulentus*, from *succus* 'juice'.

succulent Karoo ■ n. Ecology a vegetation type occurring in the arid western part of South Africa, characterized by succulents and plants of the daisy family.

succumb ■ v. 1 (often **succumb to**) fail to resist (pressure, temptation, etc.). 2 die from the effect of a disease or injury.
– ORIGIN C15: from Old French *succomber* or Latin *succumbere*, from *sub-* 'under' + a verb rel. to *cubare* 'to lie'.

succuss /səˈkʌs/ ■ v. (in preparing homeopathic remedies) shake (a solution) vigorously.
– DERIVATIVES **succussion** n.
– ORIGIN C19: from Latin *succuss-, succutere* 'shake'.

such ■ det., predet., & pron. 1 of the type previously mentioned. 2 (**such ―― as/that**) of the type about to be mentioned. 3 to so high a degree; so great.
– PHRASES **and such** and similar things. **as such** in the exact sense of the word. **such-and-such** an unspecified person or thing. **such as** 1 for example. 2 of a kind that; like. 3 archaic those who. **such as it is** what little there is; for what it's worth. **such a one** such a person or thing. **such that** to the extent that.
– ORIGIN Old English *swilc, swylc*, from the Germanic bases of SO[1] and ALIKE.

suchlike ■ pron. things of the type mentioned. ■ det. of the type mentioned.

suck ■ v. 1 draw into the mouth by contracting the muscles of the lip and mouth to make a partial vacuum. ▸ hold (something) in the mouth and draw at it by contracting the lip and cheek muscles. ▸ draw in a specified direction by creating a vacuum. ▸ (of a pump) make a gurgling sound as a result of sucking air instead of water. 2 (usu. **suck someone in/into**) involve (someone) in something without their choosing. 3 (**suck up**) informal attempt to gain advantage by behaving obsequiously. 4 informal, chiefly N. Amer. be very bad or disagreeable: *the weather here sucks*. ■ n. an act or sound of sucking. ■ exclam. (**sucks**) Brit. informal used to express derision and defiance.
– PHRASES **give suck** archaic suckle. **suck someone dry** exhaust someone's physical, material, or emotional resources. **suck something out of** (or **from**) **one's thumb** S. African informal fabricate a statement; base something on guesswork.
– ORIGIN Old English *sūcan* (v.), from an Indo-European imitative root.

sucker ■ n. 1 a rubber cup that adheres to a surface by suction. ▸ a flat or concave organ enabling an animal to cling to a surface by suction. 2 the piston of a suction pump. ▸ a pipe through which liquid is drawn by suction. 3 informal a gullible or easily deceived person. ▸ (**a sucker for**) a person especially susceptible to or fond of (a specified thing). 4 informal, chiefly N. Amer. an unspecified person or thing. 5 Botany a shoot springing from the base of a tree or other plant, especially one arising from the root at some distance from the trunk. ▸ a side shoot from an axillary bud. 6 informal a lollipop. ■ v. 1 Botany (of a plant) produce suckers. 2 informal, chiefly N. Amer. fool or trick (someone).

sucker punch ■ n. an unexpected punch or blow.

sucking ■ adj. (of a child or animal) not yet weaned.

suckle ■ v. (with reference to a baby or young animal) feed from the breast or teat.
– DERIVATIVES **suckler** n.
– ORIGIN Middle English: prob. a back-formation from SUCKLING.

suckling ■ n. an unweaned child or animal.
– ORIGIN Middle English: from SUCK.

sucrase /ˈs(j)uːkreɪz/ ■ n. another term for INVERTASE.

sucrose /ˈs(j)uːkrəʊz, -əʊs/ ■ n. Chemistry a compound which is the chief component of cane or beet sugar.
– ORIGIN C19: from French *sucre* 'sugar'.

suction ■ n. the production of a partial vacuum by the removal of air in order to force fluid into a vacant space or procure adhesion. ■ v. remove using suction.
– ORIGIN C17: from late Latin *suctio(n-)*. from Latin *sugere* 'suck'.

suction pump ■ n. a pump for drawing liquid through a pipe into a chamber emptied by a piston.

Sudanese /suːdəˈniːz/ ■ n. a native or inhabitant of the Sudan. ■ adj. of or relating to the Sudan.

sudd /sʌd/ ■ n. an area of floating vegetation in a stretch of the White Nile, thick enough to impede navigation.
– ORIGIN Arabic, 'obstruction'.

sudden ■ adj. occurring or done quickly and unexpectedly.
– PHRASES (**all**) **of a sudden** (or archaic **on a sudden**) suddenly.
– DERIVATIVES **suddenness** n.
– ORIGIN Middle English: from Anglo-Norman French *sudein*, from an alteration of Latin *subitaneus*, from *subitus* 'sudden'.

sudden death ■ n. a means of deciding the winner in a tied match, in which play continues and the winner is the first side or player to score.

sudden infant death syndrome ■ n. technical term for COT DEATH.

suddenly ■ adv. quickly and unexpectedly.

sudoku /suːˈdɒkuː, suːˈdəʊkuː/ ■ n. a number puzzle in which players insert numbers into a grid consisting of nine squares subdivided into a further nine squares.
– ORIGIN early C21: from Japanese *su doku*.

suds ■ pl. n. 1 froth made from soap and water. 2 N. Amer. informal beer. ■ v. chiefly N. Amer. cover or wash in soapy water. ▸ form suds.
– DERIVATIVES **sudsy** adj.
– ORIGIN C19: perhaps orig. denoting the flood water of fens; cf. Middle Low German *sudde*, Middle Dutch *sudse* 'marsh, bog'.

sue ■ v. (**sues, sued, suing**) 1 institute legal proceedings against (a person or institution), typically for redress. 2 formal appeal formally to a person for something.
– DERIVATIVES **suer** n.
– ORIGIN Middle English: from Anglo-Norman French *suer*, from Latin *sequi* 'follow'.

suede ■ n. leather, especially the skin of a young goat, with the flesh side rubbed to make a velvety nap.
– ORIGIN C17: from French (*gants de*) *Suède* '(gloves of) Sweden'.

suet /ˈs(j)uːɪt/ ■ n. the hard white fat on the kidneys and loins of cattle, sheep, and other animals, used in making foods.
– DERIVATIVES **suety** adj.
– ORIGIN Middle English: from Anglo-Norman French, from the synonymous word *su*, from Latin *sebum* 'tallow'.

suet pudding ■ n. a boiled or steamed pudding of suet and flour.

suf- ■ prefix variant spelling of SUB- assimilated before *f* (as in *suffocate, suffuse*).

suffer ■ v. 1 experience or be subjected to (something bad

sufferance

or unpleasant). ▸ (**suffer from**) be affected by or subject to (an illness or ailment). ▸ become or appear worse in quality. **2** archaic tolerate. ▸ allow (someone) to do something.
– DERIVATIVES **sufferable** adj. **sufferer** n.
– ORIGIN Middle English: from Anglo-Norman French *suffrir*, from Latin *sufferre*, from *sub-* 'from below' + *ferre* 'to bear'.

sufferance ■ n. **1** absence of objection rather than genuine approval; toleration. **2** archaic patient endurance.

suffice /sə'fʌɪs/ ■ v. be enough or adequate. ▸ meet the needs of.
– PHRASES **suffice (it) to say** used to indicate that one is withholding something for reasons of discretion or brevity.
– ORIGIN Middle English: from Old French *suffis-*, *suffire*, from Latin *sufficient-*, *sufficere* 'put under, meet the need of'.

sufficiency ■ n. (pl. **-ies**) **1** the condition or quality of being sufficient. ▸ an adequate amount, especially of something essential. **2** archaic self-sufficiency or independence of character.

sufficient ■ adj. & det. enough; adequate.
– DERIVATIVES **sufficiently** adv.
– ORIGIN Middle English: from Old French, or from Latin *sufficient-* (see **SUFFICE**).

suffix /'sʌfɪks/ ■ n. **1** a morpheme added at the end of a word to form a derivative (e.g. *-ation*). **2** Mathematics another term for **SUBSCRIPT**. ■ v. /also sə'fɪks/ append, especially as a suffix.
– DERIVATIVES **suffixation** n.
– ORIGIN C18: from modern Latin *suffixum*, from Latin *suffigere*, from *sub-* 'subordinately' + *figere* 'fasten'.

suffocate ■ v. die or cause to die from lack of air or inability to breathe. ▸ have or cause to have difficulty in breathing.
– DERIVATIVES **suffocating** adj. **suffocatingly** adv. **suffocation** n.
– ORIGIN C15: from Latin *suffocare* 'stifle', from *sub-* 'below' + *fauces* 'throat'.

suffragan /'sʌfrəg(ə)n/ (also **suffragan bishop** or **bishop suffragan**) ■ n. a bishop appointed to help a diocesan bishop. ▸ a bishop in relation to his archbishop or metropolitan.
– ORIGIN Middle English: from Anglo-Norman French and Old French, representing medieval Latin *suffraganeus* 'assistant (bishop)', from Latin *suffragium* 'suffrage'.

suffrage /'sʌfrɪdʒ/ ■ n. **1** the right to vote in political elections. ▸ archaic a vote given for a person or in assent to a proposal. **2** (**suffrages**) (in the Book of Common Prayer) the intercessory petitions pronounced by a priest in the Litany. ▸ a series of petitions pronounced by the priest with the responses of the congregation.
– DERIVATIVES **suffragism** n.
– ORIGIN Middle English: from Latin *suffragium*, reinforced by French *suffrage*.

suffragette /ˌsʌfrə'dʒɛt/ ■ n. historical a woman seeking the right to vote through organized protest.

suffragist ■ n. chiefly historical a person advocating the extension of suffrage, especially to women.

suffuse /sə'fjuːz/ ■ v. (often **be suffused with**) gradually spread through or over.
– DERIVATIVES **suffusion** n.
– ORIGIN C16: from Latin *suffus-*, *suffundere* 'pour into'.

Sufi /'suːfi/ ■ n. (pl. **Sufis**) a Muslim ascetic and mystic.
– DERIVATIVES **Sufic** adj. **Sufism** n.
– ORIGIN C17: from Arabic *ṣūfī*, perhaps from *ṣūf* 'wool' (referring to the woollen garment worn).

sug- ■ prefix variant spelling of **SUB-** assimilated before *g* (as in *suggest*).

sugar ■ n. **1** a sweet crystalline substance obtained especially from sugar cane and sugar beet, consisting essentially of sucrose and used as a sweetener in food and drink. **2** any of the class of soluble, crystalline, typically sweet-tasting carbohydrates found in living tissues and exemplified by glucose and sucrose. **3** informal, chiefly N. Amer. used as a term of endearment. ■ v. **1** sweeten, sprinkle, or coat with sugar. ▸ make more agreeable or palatable. **2** [as noun **sugaring**] N. Amer. the boiling down of maple sap until it thickens into syrup or crystallizes into sugar.
– DERIVATIVES **sugarless** adj.
– ORIGIN Middle English: from Old French *sukere*, from Italian *zucchero*, prob. from Arabic *sukkar*.

sugar bean ■ n. a reddish-brown speckled variety of the common bean (*Phaseolus vulgaris*).

sugar beet ■ n. beet of a variety from which sugar is extracted.

sugarbird ■ n. a southern African songbird with a long slender bill and very long tail. [*Promerops cafer* (Cape sugarbird) and *P. gurneyi* (Gurney's sugarbird).]

sugarbush ■ n. a South African protea with nectar-rich red flowers, widely cultivated as an ornamental. [*Protea repens*.] ▸ S. African any protea.

sugar candy ■ n. fuller form of **CANDY**.

sugar cane ■ n. a perennial tropical grass with tall stout jointed stems from which sugar is extracted. [*Saccharum officinarum*.]

sugar-coated ■ adj. superficially attractive or excessively sentimental.
– DERIVATIVES **sugar-coat** v.

sugarcraft ■ n. the art of creating confectionery or cake decorations from sugar paste.

sugar daddy ■ n. informal a rich older man who lavishes gifts on a young woman in return for her company or sexual favours.

sugar gum ■ n. an Australian eucalyptus with sweet foliage. [*Eucalyptus cladocalyx* and other species.]

sugarloaf ■ n. a conical moulded mass of sugar.

sugar lump ■ n. a small cube of compacted sugar used for sweetening hot drinks.

sugar maple ■ n. a North American maple, the sap of which is used to make maple sugar and maple syrup. [*Acer saccharum*.]

sugarplum ■ n. archaic a small round boiled sweet.

sugar snap (also **sugar snap pea**, **sugar pea**) ■ n. mangetout, especially of a variety with thicker and more rounded pods.

sugar soap ■ n. an alkaline preparation containing washing soda and soap, used for cleaning or removing paint.

sugary ■ adj. **1** resembling, or containing much, sugar. **2** excessively sentimental.
– DERIVATIVES **sugariness** n.

suggest ■ v. **1** put forward for consideration. ▸ (**suggest itself**) (of an idea) come into one's mind. **2** cause one to think that (something) exists or is the case; evoke. ▸ state or express indirectly.
– DERIVATIVES **suggester** n.
– ORIGIN C16 (**suggestion** Middle English): from Latin *suggest-*, *suggerere* 'suggest, prompt', from *sub-* 'from below' + *gerere* 'bring'.

suggestible ■ adj. open to suggestion; easily swayed.
– DERIVATIVES **suggestibility** n.

suggestion ■ n. **1** an idea or plan put forward for consideration. ▸ the action of suggesting. **2** something that implies or indicates a certain fact or situation. **3** a slight trace or indication: *a suggestion of a smile*. **4** Psychology the influencing of a person to accept a belief or impulse uncritically.

suggestive ■ adj. **1** (often **suggestive of**) tending to suggest or evoke something. **2** hinting at or bringing to mind sexual matters; mildly indecent.
– DERIVATIVES **suggestively** adv. **suggestiveness** n.

suicide /'s(j)uːɪsʌɪd/ ■ n. **1** the action of killing oneself intentionally. ▸ a person who does this. ▸ [as modifier] relating to or denoting a military operation carried out by people who do not expect to survive it: *a suicide bomber*. **2** a course of action which is disastrously damaging to one's own interests. ■ v. intentionally kill oneself.
– DERIVATIVES **suicidal** adj. **suicidally** adv.
– ORIGIN C17: from modern Latin *suicida* 'act of suicide', *suicidium* 'person who commits suicide', from Latin *sui* 'of oneself' + *caedere* 'kill'.

suicide pact ■ n. an agreement between two or more people to commit suicide together.

sui generis /ˌsuːʌɪ ˈdʒɛn(ə)rɪs, suːiː, sjuː-, ˈgɛn-/ ■ adj. unique.
– ORIGIN Latin, 'of its own kind'.

sui juris /ˈdʒʊərɪs, ˈjʊə-/ ■ adj. Law of age; independent.
– ORIGIN Latin, 'of one's own right'.

suint /swɪnt/ ■ n. the natural grease in sheep's wool, from which lanolin is obtained.
– ORIGIN C18: from French, from *suer* 'sweat'.

suit ■ n. 1 a set of outer clothes made of the same fabric and designed to be worn together, typically consisting of a jacket and trousers or a jacket and skirt. ▶ a set of clothes for a particular activity: *a jogging suit*. ▶ informal a high-ranking business executive. 2 any of the sets into which a pack of playing cards is divided (in conventional packs spades, hearts, diamonds, and clubs). 3 short for LAWSUIT. 4 the process of trying to win a woman's affection with a view to marriage. ▶ poetic/literary a petition or entreaty made to a person in authority. ■ v. 1 be convenient for or acceptable to. ▶ (**suit oneself**) act entirely according to one's own wishes. ▶ [as adj. **suited**] appropriate or fitting. 2 go well with or enhance the features, figure, or character of (someone). 3 N. Amer. put on clothes.
– PHRASES **suit the action to the word** carry out one's stated intentions. **suit someone's book** Brit. informal be convenient or acceptable to someone. **suit someone down to the ground** be extremely convenient or appropriate for someone.
– DERIVATIVES **suited** adj. **suiting** n.
– ORIGIN Middle English: from Anglo-Norman French *siwte*, from Romance verb based on Latin *sequi* 'follow'.

suitable ■ adj. right or appropriate for a particular person, purpose, or situation.
– DERIVATIVES **suitability** n. **suitableness** n. **suitably** adv.

suitcase ■ n. a case with a handle and a hinged lid, used for carrying clothes and other personal possessions.

suite /swiːt/ ■ n. 1 a set of rooms for one person's or family's use or for a particular purpose. 2 a set of furniture of the same design. 3 Music a set of instrumental compositions to be played in succession. ▶ a set of pieces from an opera or musical arranged as one instrumental work. 4 a group of people in attendance on a monarch or other person of high rank.
– ORIGIN C17: from Anglo-Norman French *siwte* (see SUIT).

suitor /ˈs(j)uːtə/ ■ n. a man who pursues a relationship with a woman with a view to marriage. ▶ a prospective buyer of a business or corporation.
– ORIGIN Middle English: from Anglo-Norman French *seutor*, from Latin *secutor*, from *sequi* 'follow'.

suk (also **sukh**) ■ n. variant spelling of SOUK.

sukiyaki /ˌsʊkɪˈjaki, -ˈjɑːki/ ■ n. a Japanese dish of sliced meat, especially beef, fried rapidly with vegetables and sauce.
– ORIGIN from Japanese.

sulcus /ˈsʌlkəs/ ■ n. (pl. **sulci** /-sʌɪ/) Anatomy a groove or furrow, especially one on the surface of the brain.
– ORIGIN C17: from Latin, 'furrow, wrinkle'.

sulfur etc. ■ n. US spelling of SULPHUR etc.

sulk ■ v. be silent, morose, and bad-tempered through annoyance or disappointment. ■ n. a period of sulking.
– DERIVATIVES **sulker** n.
– ORIGIN C18: perhaps a back-formation from SULKY.

sulky ■ adj. (-ier, -iest) morose, bad-tempered, and resentful. ■ n. (pl. -ies) a light two-wheeled horse-drawn vehicle for one person, used chiefly in trotting races.
– DERIVATIVES **sulkily** adv. **sulkiness** n.
– ORIGIN C18: perhaps from obsolete *sulke* 'hard to dispose of'.

sullage /ˈsʌlɪdʒ/ ■ n. waste from household sinks, showers, and baths, but not toilets.
– ORIGIN C16: perhaps from Anglo-Norman French *suillage*, from *suiller* 'to soil'.

sullen ■ adj. bad-tempered and sulky.
– DERIVATIVES **sullenly** adv. **sullenness** n.
– ORIGIN Middle English (in the sense 'solitary, averse to company'): from Anglo-Norman French *sulein*, from *sol* 'sole'.

1187

sum

sully /ˈsʌli/ ■ v. (-ies, -ied) poetic/literary or ironic damage the purity or integrity of; defile.
– ORIGIN C16: perhaps from French *souiller* 'to soil'.

sulpha /ˈsʌlfə/ (US **sulfa**) ■ n. [usu. as modifier] short for SULPHONAMIDE: *sulpha drugs*.

sulphamic acid /sʌlˈfamɪk/ (US **sulfamic acid**) ■ n. Chemistry a crystalline acid used in cleaning agents.
– DERIVATIVES **sulphamate** /ˈsʌlfəmeɪt/ n.
– ORIGIN C19: from SULPHUR + AMIDE.

sulphanilamide /ˌsʌlfəˈnɪləmʌɪd/ (US **sulfanilamide**) ■ n. Medicine a synthetic antibacterial compound which is the basis of the sulphonamide drugs.
– ORIGIN 1930s: from *sulphanilic* (from SULPHUR + ANILINE) + AMIDE.

sulphate /ˈsʌlfeɪt/ (US **sulfate**) ■ n. Chemistry a salt or ester of sulphuric acid.

sulphide /ˈsʌlfʌɪd/ (US **sulfide**) ■ n. Chemistry a compound of sulphur with another element or group.

sulphite /ˈsʌlfʌɪt/ (US **sulfite**) ■ n. Chemistry a salt of sulphurous acid.

sulphonamide /sʌlˈfɒnəmʌɪd/ (US **sulfonamide**) ■ n. Medicine any of a class of drugs, derived from sulphanilamide, which are able to prevent the multiplication of some pathogenic bacteria.
– ORIGIN C19: from SULPHONE + AMIDE.

sulphonate /ˈsʌlfəneɪt/ (US **sulfonate**) Chemistry ■ n. a salt or ester of a sulphonic acid. ■ v. convert into a sulphonate.
– DERIVATIVES **sulphonation** n.

sulphone /ˈsʌlfəʊn/ (US **sulfone**) ■ n. Chemistry an organic compound containing the group -SO$_2$- linking two organic groups.

sulphonic acid (US **sulfonic**) ■ n. Chemistry an organic acid containing the group -SO$_2$OH.

sulphur (US & Chemistry **sulfur**) ■ n. 1 the chemical element of atomic number 16, a combustible non-metal which typically occurs as yellow crystals. ▶ the material of which hellfire and lightning were formerly believed to consist. (Symbol: **S**) 2 a pale greenish-yellow colour.
– DERIVATIVES **sulphureous** adj. **sulphury** adj.
– ORIGIN Middle English: from Anglo-Norman French *sulfre*, from Latin *sulfur, sulphur*.

sulphur dioxide ■ n. Chemistry a colourless pungent toxic gas formed by burning sulphur. [SO$_2$.]

sulphuretted hydrogen /ˌsʌlfjʊˈrɛtɪd/ (US **sulfureted**) ■ n. Chemistry archaic term for HYDROGEN SULPHIDE.

sulphuric /sʌlˈfjʊərɪk/ (US **sulfuric**) ■ adj. containing sulphur or sulphuric acid.

sulphuric acid ■ n. a strong acid made by oxidizing solutions of sulphur dioxide. [H$_2$SO$_4$.]

sulphurous /ˈsʌlf(ə)rəs/ (US **sulfurous**) ■ adj. 1 containing or derived from sulphur. 2 pale yellow. 3 marked by anger or profanity.

sulphurous acid ■ n. Chemistry an unstable weak acid formed when sulphur dioxide dissolves in water. [H$_2$SO$_3$.]

sulphur spring ■ n. a spring impregnated with sulphur or its compounds.

sultan ■ n. a Muslim sovereign.
– DERIVATIVES **sultanate** n.
– ORIGIN C16: from French, or from medieval Latin *sultanus*, from Arabic *sulṭān* 'power, ruler'.

sultana ■ n. 1 a small light brown seedless raisin. 2 a wife or concubine of a sultan. ▶ any other woman in a sultan's family.
– ORIGIN C16: from Italian, from *sultano* (see SULTAN).

sultry /ˈsʌltri/ ■ adj. (-ier, -iest) 1 (of the weather) hot and humid. 2 displaying or suggesting passion; provocative.
– DERIVATIVES **sultrily** adv. **sultriness** n.
– ORIGIN C16: from obsolete *sulter* 'swelter'.

sum ■ n. 1 a particular amount of money. 2 (**the sum of**) the total amount resulting from the addition of two or more numbers or amounts. ▶ the total amount of something that exists. 3 an arithmetical problem, especially at an elementary level. ■ v. (**summed**,

---

s sit   t top   v voice   w we   z zoo   ʃ she   ʒ decision   θ thin   ð this   ŋ ring   x loch   tʃ chip   dʒ jar

summing) 1 (sum someone/thing up) concisely describe the nature or character of someone or something. ▶ **(sum up)** summarize briefly. **2** technical find the sum of (two or more amounts).
– PHRASES **in sum** to sum up.
– ORIGIN Middle English: from Latin *summa* 'main part, sum total', from *summus* 'highest'.

sumac /'s(j)uːmak, 'ʃuː-/ (also **sumach**) ■ n. a shrub or small tree with compound leaves, conical clusters of fruits, and bright autumn colours. [Genera *Rhus* and *Cotinus*: several species.]
– ORIGIN Middle English: from Old French *sumac* or medieval Latin *sumac(h)*, from Arabic *summāḳ*.

Sumatran /sʊˈmɑːtrən/ ■ n. a native or inhabitant of the Indonesian island of Sumatra. ■ adj. of or relating to Sumatra.

Sumerian /sʊˈmɪərɪən, sjuː-/ ■ n. **1** a member of an indigenous non-Semitic people of ancient Sumer in Babylonia. **2** the language of this people, the oldest known written language. ■ adj. of or relating to Sumer or the Sumerians or their language.

summa /'sʊmə, 'sʌmə/ ■ n. (pl. **summae** /-miː/) poetic/literary a summary of what is known of a subject.
– ORIGIN C18: from Latin, 'sum total'.

summa cum laude /ˌsʌmə kʌm 'lɔːdiː, ˌsʊmə kʊm 'laʊdeɪ/ ■ adv. & adj. (of a degree, diploma, etc.) with the highest distinction.
– ORIGIN Latin, 'with highest praise'.

summary ■ n. (pl. **-ies**) a brief statement of the main points of something. ■ adj. **1** dispensing with needless details or formalities. **2** Law (of a judicial process) conducted without the customary legal formalities. ▶ (of a conviction) made by a judge or magistrate without a jury.
– DERIVATIVES **summarily** adv. **summariness** n. **summarization** (also **-isation**) n. **summarize** (also **-ise**) v. **summarizer** (also **-iser**) n.
– ORIGIN Middle English: from Latin *summarius*, from *summa* (see SUM).

summary jurisdiction ■ n. Law the authority of a court to use summary proceedings and arrive at a judgement.

summary offence ■ n. Law an offence within the scope of a summary court.

summation /sʌˈmeɪʃ(ə)n/ ■ n. **1** the process of adding things together. ▶ a sum total. **2** the action of summing up. ▶ a summary.
– DERIVATIVES **summational** adj. **summative** adj.

summer ■ n. **1** the season after spring and before autumn, when the weather is warmest. ▶ Astronomy the period from the summer solstice to the autumnal equinox. **2 (summers)** poetic/literary years, especially of a person's age. ■ v. spend the summer in a particular place. ▶ pasture (cattle) for the summer.
– DERIVATIVES **summery** adj.
– ORIGIN Old English *sumor*, of Germanic origin.

summer camp ■ n. see CAMP[1] (sense 2).

summer house ■ n. a small building in a garden, used for relaxation during fine weather.

summer lightning ■ n. distant sheet lightning without audible thunder, typically occurring on a summer night.

summer pudding ■ n. Brit. a pudding of soft summer fruit encased in bread or sponge.

summersault ■ n. & v. archaic spelling of SOMERSAULT.

summer school ■ n. a course of lectures held during school and university summer vacations.

summer season ■ n. the summer period when most people take holidays.

summer squash ■ n. a squash of a variety eaten before the seeds and rind have hardened, unsuitable for storage.

summer stock ■ n. N. Amer. theatrical productions by a repertory company organized for the summer season, especially at holiday resorts.

summertime ■ n. the season or period of summer.

summer time ■ n. chiefly Brit. another term for DAYLIGHT SAVING TIME.

summer-weight ■ adj. (of clothes) light and cool.

summing-up ■ n. a summary. ▶ Law a judge's review of evidence at the end of a case, with a direction to the jury regarding points of law.

summit ■ n. **1** the highest point of a hill or mountain. **2** the highest attainable level of achievement. **3** a meeting between heads of government.
– ORIGIN Middle English: from Old French *somete*, from *som* 'top', from Latin *summus* 'highest'.

summon ■ v. **1** authoritatively call on (someone) to be present, especially to appear in a law court. **2** call people to attend (a meeting). **3** (usu. **summon something up**) cause (a quality or reaction) to emerge from within oneself: *she managed to summon up a smile*.
– DERIVATIVES **summonable** adj. **summoner** n.
– ORIGIN Middle English: from Old French *somondre*, from Latin *summonere* 'give a hint', later 'call, summon', from *sub-* 'secretly' + *monere* 'warn'.

summons ■ n. (pl. **summonses**) **1** an order to appear in a law court. **2** an act of summoning. ■ v. chiefly Law serve with a summons.
– ORIGIN Middle English: from Old French *sumunse*, from Latin *summonita*, from *summonere* (see SUMMON).

summum bonum /ˌsʊməm 'bɒnʊm, ˌsʌməm 'bəʊnəm/ ■ n. the highest good, especially as the ultimate goal according to which values and priorities are established in an ethical system.
– ORIGIN from Latin.

sumo /'suːməʊ/ ■ n. (pl. **-os**) a Japanese form of heavyweight wrestling, in which a wrestler wins a bout by forcing his opponent outside a marked circle or by making him touch the ground with any part of his body except the soles of his feet.
– ORIGIN from Japanese *sūmo*.

sump ■ n. **1** the base of an internal-combustion engine, which serves as a reservoir of oil for the lubrication system. **2** a depression in the floor of a mine or cave in which water collects. **3** a cesspool.
– ORIGIN Middle English: from Middle Dutch or Low German *sump*, or (in the mining sense) from German *Sumpf*.

sumptuary /'sʌm(p)tjʊəri/ ■ adj. chiefly historical relating to or denoting laws that limit private expenditure on food and personal items.
– ORIGIN C17: from Latin *sumptuarius*, from *sumptus* 'cost'.

sumptuous ■ adj. splendid and expensive-looking.
– DERIVATIVES **sumptuosity** n. **sumptuously** adv. **sumptuousness** n.
– ORIGIN Middle English: from Old French *somptueux*, from Latin *sumptuosus*, from *sumptus* (see SUMPTUARY).

sum total ■ n. another term for SUM (in sense 2).

Sun. ■ abbrev. Sunday.

sun ■ n. **1** (also **Sun**) the star round which the earth orbits. ▶ any similar star, with or without planets. **2** the light or warmth received from the sun. ■ v. (**sunned**, **sunning**) (**sun oneself**) sit or lie in the sun. ▶ expose to the sun.
– PHRASES **against the sun** Nautical against the direction of the sun's apparent movement (in the northern hemisphere); anticlockwise. **shoot the sun** Nautical ascertain the altitude of the sun with a sextant in order to determine one's latitude. **under the sun** in existence. **with the sun** Nautical in the direction of the sun's apparent movement (in the northern hemisphere); clockwise.
– DERIVATIVES **sunless** adj. **sunlessness** n. **sunlike** adj. **sunward** adj. & adv. **sunwards** adv.
– ORIGIN Old English *sunne*, of Germanic origin.

sun-baked ■ adj. exposed to the heat of the sun.

sunbath ■ n. a period of sunbathing.

sunbathe ■ v. sit or lie in the sun to get a suntan.
– DERIVATIVES **sunbather** n.

sunbeam ■ n. a ray of sunlight.

sun bear (also **Malayan sun bear**) ■ n. a small mainly nocturnal bear which has a brownish-black coat with a light-coloured mark on the chest, native to SE Asia. [*Helarctos malayanus*.]

sunbed ■ n. **1** a lounger used for sunbathing. **2** an apparatus for acquiring a tan, consisting of two banks of sunlamps between which one lies or stands.

sunbelt ▪ n. a strip of territory receiving a high amount of sunshine, especially the southern US from California to Florida.

sunbird ▪ n. a small, brightly coloured bird of warmer parts of the Old World, resembling a hummingbird but not able to hover. [Family Nectariniidae: numerous species.]

sunblind ▪ n. a window blind used to exclude the sun.

sunblock ▪ n. a cream or lotion for protecting the skin from sunburn.

sun bonnet ▪ n. a child's close-fitting peaked cotton hat that protects the head and neck from the sun.

sunburn ▪ n. inflammation of the skin caused by overexposure to the ultraviolet rays of the sun. ▪ v. (past and past part. **sunburned** or **sunburnt**) (**be sunburned**) suffer from sunburn.

sunburst ▪ n. 1 a sudden brief appearance of the full sun from behind clouds. 2 a design or ornament representing the sun and its rays.

suncream ▪ n. a creamy preparation for protecting the skin from sunburn and typically to promote a suntan.

sundae ▪ n. a dish of ice cream with added ingredients such as fruit, nuts, and syrup.
– ORIGIN C19 (orig. US): perhaps an alteration of SUNDAY, either because the dish was made with ice cream left over from Sunday, or because it was sold only on Sundays.

Sundanese /ˌsʌndəˈniːz/ ▪ n. (pl. same) 1 a member of a mainly Muslim people of western Java. 2 the Indonesian language of this people. ▪ adj. of or relating to the Sundanese or their language.
– ORIGIN from Sundanese *Sunda*, the western part of Java.

Sunday ▪ n. the day of the week before Monday and following Saturday, observed by Christians as a day of rest and religious worship. ▪ adv. on Sunday. ▸ (**Sundays**) on Sundays; each Sunday.
– ORIGIN Old English *Sunnandæg* 'day of the sun', translation of Latin *dies solis*.

Sunday best ▪ n. a person's best clothes.

Sunday driver ▪ n. a person who drives over-cautiously or unskilfully.

Sunday painter ▪ n. an amateur painter.

Sunday school ▪ n. a class held on Sundays to teach children about Christianity.

sun deck ▪ n. 1 the deck of a yacht or cruise ship that is open to the sky. 2 N. Amer. a terrace or balcony positioned to catch the sun.

sunder ▪ v. poetic/literary split apart.
– PHRASES **in sunder** apart or into pieces.
– ORIGIN Old English.

sundew ▪ n. a small carnivorous plant of boggy places, with leaves bearing sticky hairs for trapping insects. [Genus *Drosera*: several species.]

sundial ▪ n. an instrument showing the time by the shadow of a pointer cast by the sun on to a plate marked in hours.

sun dog ▪ n. another term for PARHELION.

sundown ▪ n. sunset.

sundowner ▪ n. informal an alcoholic drink taken at sunset.

sundress ▪ n. a light, loose sleeveless dress, typically having a wide neckline and thin shoulder straps.

sundry ▪ adj. of various kinds. ▪ n. (pl. -**ies**) (**sundries**) various items not important enough to be mentioned individually.
– ORIGIN Old English *syndrig* 'distinct, separate'.

sun-dry ▪ v. [usu. as adj. **sun-dried**] dry in the sun, as opposed to using artificial heat.

sun filter ▪ n. another term for SUNSCREEN.

sunfish ▪ n. (pl. same or -**fishes**) 1 a large, short-tailed sea fish with tall dorsal and anal fins near the rear of the body. [*Mola mola* and other species.] 2 a nest-building North American freshwater fish. [Several species in the family Centrarchidae.]

sunflower ▪ n. a tall North American plant with very large golden-rayed flowers, grown for its edible seeds which yield oil. [*Helianthus annus*.]

sung past participle of SING.

sunglasses ▪ pl. n. glasses tinted to protect the eyes from sunlight or glare.

sun helmet ▪ n. chiefly historical a rigid hat made of cork or a similar material, worn in tropical climates.

sunk past and past participle of SINK[1].

sunken past participle of SINK[1]. ▪ adj. 1 having sunk. 2 at a lower level than the surrounding area. ▸ (of a person's eyes or cheeks) deeply recessed.

sun-kissed ▪ adj. made warm or brown by the sun.

sunlamp ▪ n. 1 a lamp emitting ultraviolet rays, used chiefly to produce an artificial suntan or in therapy. 2 a large lamp with a parabolic reflector used in film-making.

sunlight ▪ n. light from the sun.
– DERIVATIVES **sunlit** adj.

Sunna /ˈsʊnə, ˈsʌnə/ ▪ n. the traditional portion of Muslim law based on Muhammad's words or acts, accepted (together with the Koran) as authoritative by Muslims.
– ORIGIN Arabic, 'form, way, rule'.

Sunni /ˈsʊni, ˈsʌni/ ▪ n. (pl. same or **Sunnis**) one of the two main branches of Islam, differing from Shia in its understanding of the Sunna and in its acceptance of the first three caliphs. Compare with SHIA. ▸ a Muslim who adheres to this branch of Islam.
– DERIVATIVES **Sunnite** adj. & n.
– ORIGIN Arabic, 'custom, normative rule'.

sunny ▪ adj. (-**ier**, **sunniest**) 1 bright with or receiving much sunlight. 2 cheerful.
– PHRASES **sunny side up** N. Amer. (of an egg) fried on one side only.
– DERIVATIVES **sunnily** adv. **sunniness** n.

sunray ▪ n. a radiating line or broadening stripe resembling a ray of the sun.

sunrise ▪ n. the time in the morning when the sun rises. ▸ the colours and light visible in the sky at sunrise.

sunrise industry ▪ n. a new and growing industry.

sunroof ▪ n. a panel in the roof of a car that can be opened for extra ventilation.

sunscreen ▪ n. a cream or lotion rubbed on to the skin to protect it from the sun.

sunset ▪ n. 1 the time in the evening when the sun sets. ▸ the colours and light visible in the sky at sunset. 2 the final declining phase of something. 3 [as modifier] denoting a clause or provision under which an agency or programme is to be disbanded or terminated at the end of a fixed period unless it is formally renewed.

sunset industry ▪ n. an old and declining industry.

sunshade ▪ n. a parasol, awning, or other device giving protection from the sun.

sunshine ▪ n. 1 sunlight unbroken by cloud. 2 cheerfulness or happiness. 3 informal, chiefly Brit. used as a familiar form of address.
– DERIVATIVES **sunshiny** adj.

sun sign ▪ n. Astrology another term for BIRTH SIGN.

sun spider ▪ n. a fast-moving predatory arachnid with a pair of massive vertical pincers. [Order Solifugae.]

sunspot ▪ n. Astronomy a temporary, relatively darker and cooler patch on the sun's surface, associated with the sun's magnetic field.

sunstone ▪ n. a chatoyant gem consisting of feldspar, with a red or gold lustre.

sunstroke ▪ n. heatstroke brought about by excessive exposure to the sun.

sunsuit ▪ n. a child's suit of clothes, typically consisting of shorts and top, worn in hot weather.

suntan ▪ n. a golden-brown colouring of the skin caused by exposure to the sun. ▪ v. [usu. as adj. **suntanned**] expose to the sun to achieve a suntan.

suntrap ▪ n. Brit. a place sheltered from the wind and positioned to receive much sunshine.

sunup ▪ n. sunrise.

sun visor ■ n. a small hinged screen above a vehicle's windscreen that can be lowered to protect the occupants' eyes from bright sunlight.

sup ■ v. (**supped, supping**) dated eat supper.
– ORIGIN Middle English: from Old French *super*, of Germanic origin.

sup- ■ prefix variant spelling of **SUB-** assimilated before *p* (as in *suppurate*).

super ■ adj. **1** informal excellent. **2** (of a manufactured product) of extra fine quality. ▸ a grade of petrol having a high octane rating. **3** Building short for **SUPERFICIAL**. ■ adv. informal especially. ■ n. informal a superintendent.

super- ■ comb. form **1** above; over; beyond: *superstructure*. **2** to a great or extreme degree: *superabundant*. **3** extra large of its kind: *supercontinent*. ▸ having greater influence, capacity, etc. than another of its kind: *superpower*. **4** of a higher kind (especially in names of classificatory divisions): *superfamily*.
– ORIGIN Latin, from *super* 'above, beyond'.

superabundant ■ adj. formal or literary term for **OVER-ABUNDANT**.
– DERIVATIVES **superabundance** n. **superabundantly** adv.

superadd ■ v. add to what has already been added.
– DERIVATIVES **superaddition** n.

superannuate /ˌs(j)uːpərˈanjueɪt/ ■ v. **1** retire with a pension. ▸ [as adj. **superannuated**] belonging to a superannuation scheme. **2** [as adj. **superannuated**] too old or outdated to be effective or useful.
– DERIVATIVES **superannuable** adj.
– ORIGIN C17: from medieval Latin *superannuatus*, from Latin *super-* 'over' + *annus* 'year'.

superannuation ■ n. regular payment made into a fund by an employee towards a future pension. ▸ a pension of this type.

superb ■ adj. **1** excellent. **2** magnificent or splendid.
– DERIVATIVES **superbly** adv. **superbness** n.
– ORIGIN C16: from Latin *superbus* 'proud, magnificent'.

superbike ■ n. a high-performance motorcycle.

superbug ■ n. informal a bacterium, insect, etc. regarded as having enhanced qualities, especially of resistance to antibiotics or pesticides.

supercar ■ n. a high-performance sports car.

supercargo ■ n. (pl. **-oes** or **-os**) a representative of the ship's owner on board a merchant ship, responsible for the supervision and sale of the cargo.
– ORIGIN C17: alteration of *supracargo*, from Spanish *sobrecargo*, from *sobre* 'over' + *cargo* 'cargo'.

supercede ■ v. variant spelling of **SUPERSEDE**.

USAGE
The spelling **supercede** is widely regarded as an error: see **SUPERSEDE**.

supercharge ■ v. **1** provide with a supercharger. **2** [as adj. **supercharged**] having powerful emotional associations.

supercharger ■ n. a device that increases the pressure of the fuel-air mixture in an internal-combustion engine, thereby giving greater efficiency.

superciliary /ˌs(j)uːpəˈsɪliəri/ ■ adj. of or relating to the eyebrow or the region over the eye.
– ORIGIN C18: from Latin *supercilium* 'eyebrow'.

supercilious ■ adj. having an air of contemptuous superiority.
– DERIVATIVES **superciliously** adv. **superciliousness** n.
– ORIGIN C16: from Latin *superciliosus* 'haughty', from *supercilium* 'eyebrow'.

superclass ■ n. Biology a taxonomic category that ranks above class and below phylum.

supercomputer ■ n. a particularly powerful mainframe computer.
– DERIVATIVES **supercomputing** n.

superconductivity ■ n. Physics the property of zero electrical resistance in some substances at very low temperatures.
– DERIVATIVES **superconduct** v. **superconducting** adj. **superconductive** adj. **superconductor** n.

superconscious ■ adj. transcending human or normal consciousness.
– DERIVATIVES **superconsciousness** n.

supercontinent ■ n. a large land mass believed to have divided in the geological past to form some of the present continents.

supercool ■ v. Chemistry cool (a liquid) below its freezing point without solidification or crystallization.

supercritical ■ adj. Physics greater than or above a critical threshold such as critical mass or temperature.

super-duper ■ adj. informal, humorous excellent; super.

superego ■ n. (pl. **-os**) Psychoanalysis the part of the mind that acts as a self-critical conscience, reflecting social standards learned from parents and teachers. Compare with **EGO** and **ID**.

supererogation /ˌs(j)uːpərɛrəˈɡeɪʃ(ə)n/ ■ n. the performance of more work than duty requires.
– DERIVATIVES **supererogatory** /-ɪˈrɒɡət(ə)ri/ adj.
– ORIGIN C16: from late Latin *supererogatio(n-)*, from *supererogare* 'pay in addition'.

superette ■ n. chiefly US a small supermarket.
– ORIGIN 1930s: from **SUPERMARKET** + **-ETTE**.

superfamily ■ n. (pl. **-ies**) Biology a taxonomic category that ranks above family and below order.

superficial ■ adj. **1** existing or occurring at or on the surface. **2** apparent rather than actual. **3** not thorough or deep; cursory. ▸ lacking depth of character or understanding. **4** Building denoting a quantity of a material expressed in terms of area covered.
– DERIVATIVES **superficiality** /-ʃɪˈalɪti/ n. (pl. **-ies**). **superficially** adv. **superficialness** n.
– ORIGIN Middle English: from late Latin *superficialis*, from Latin *superficies*, from *super-* 'above' + *facies* 'face'.

superfine ■ adj. **1** of especially high quality. **2** very fine: *superfine face powder*.

superfluidity ■ n. Physics the property of flowing without friction or viscosity, as shown by liquid helium below about 2.18 kelvin.
– DERIVATIVES **superfluid** n. & adj.

superfluous ■ adj. unnecessary, especially through being more than enough.
– DERIVATIVES **superfluity** n. (pl. **-ies**). **superfluously** adv. **superfluousness** n.
– ORIGIN Middle English: from Latin *superfluus*, from *super-* 'over' + *fluere* 'to flow'.

superfood ■ n. a nutrient-rich food considered to be especially beneficial for health and well-being.

supergiant ■ n. Astronomy a star that is greater and more luminous than a giant.

superglue ■ n. a very strong quick-setting adhesive, typically based on cyanoacrylates.

supergrass ■ n. informal a police informer who implicates a large number of people.

supergroup ■ n. a rock group formed by musicians already famous from playing in other groups.

superheat ■ v. Physics **1** heat (a liquid) under pressure above its boiling point without vaporization. **2** heat (steam or other vapour) above the temperature of the liquid from which it was formed.
– DERIVATIVES **superheater** n.

superheavyweight ■ n. a weight above heavyweight in boxing and other sports.

superhero ■ n. (pl. **-oes**) a benevolent fictional character with superhuman powers.

superheterodyne /ˌs(j)uːpəˈhɛt(ə)rə(ʊ)dʌɪn/ ■ adj. relating to or denoting a system of radio and television reception in which the receiver produces a tunable signal which is combined with the incoming signal to produce a predetermined intermediate frequency, on which most of the amplification is formed.
– ORIGIN 1920s: from **SUPERSONIC** + rare *heterodyne*, denoting the production of a lower frequency by combining two almost equal high frequencies.

superhuman ■ adj. having or showing ability or powers above those of a normal human being.
– DERIVATIVES **superhumanly** adv.

superimpose ■ v. place or lay (one thing) over another, typically so that both are evident.

—DERIVATIVES **superimposable** adj. **superimposition** n.

superintend ■ v. act as superintendent of.
—DERIVATIVES **superintendence** n. **superintendency** n.
—ORIGIN C17 (*superintendent* C16): from eccles. Latin *superintendere*, translating Greek *episkopein*.

superintendent ■ n. **1** a person who supervises or is in charge of an organization, department, etc. **2** a police officer ranking above captain (in South Africa) or chief inspector (in the UK). **3** (in the US) the chief of a police department. **4** N. Amer. the caretaker of a building.

superior ■ adj. **1** higher in rank, status, or quality. ▶ of high standard or quality. ▶ greater in size or power. **2** chiefly Anatomy further above or out; higher in position. ▶ Botany (of the ovary of a flower) situated above the sepals and petals. **3** (of a letter, figure, or symbol) written or printed above the line. **4** (**superior to**) above yielding to or being influenced by. **5** conceited. ■ n. **1** a person of superior rank. ▶ the head of a monastery or other religious institution. **2** Printing a superior letter, figure, or symbol.
—DERIVATIVES **superiority** n. **superiorly** adv.
—ORIGIN Middle English: from Latin *superior*, comparative of *superus* 'that is above', from *super* 'above'.

superior court ■ n. Law **1** a higher court whose decisions have weight as precedents and which is not subject to control by any other court except by way of appeal. **2** (in some US states) a court of appeals or a court of general jurisdiction.

superiority complex ■ n. an attitude of superiority which conceals actual feelings of inferiority and failure.

superior planet ■ n. Astronomy any of the planets Mars, Jupiter, Saturn, Uranus, and Neptune, and formerly including Pluto, whose orbits are further from the sun than the earth's.

superjacent /ˌs(j)uːpəˈdʒeɪs(ə)nt/ ■ adj. technical overlying.
—ORIGIN C16: from Latin *superjacent-*, from *super-* 'over' + *jacere* 'to lie'.

superlative /sɪuːˈpɜːlətɪv/ ■ adj. **1** of the highest quality or degree. **2** Grammar (of an adjective or adverb) expressing the highest or a very high degree of a quality (e.g. *bravest, most fiercely*). Contrasted with POSITIVE and COMPARATIVE. ■ n. a hyperbolical expression of praise.
—DERIVATIVES **superlatively** adv. **superlativeness** n.
—ORIGIN Middle English: from Old French *superlatif, -ive*, from late Latin *superlativus*, from Latin *superlatus*, from *superferre* 'carry beyond'.

superluminal /ˌs(j)uːˈpəˈluːmɪn(ə)l/ ■ adj. Physics denoting or having a speed greater than that of light.
—ORIGIN 1950s: from SUPER- + Latin *lumen, lumin-* 'a light'.

superman ■ n. (pl. **-men**) **1** another term for ÜBERMENSCH. **2** informal a man with exceptional physical or mental ability.
—ORIGIN C20: from SUPER- + MAN, coined by G. B. Shaw in imitation of German *Übermensch* (used by Nietzsche).

supermarket ■ n. a large self-service shop selling foods and household goods.

supermini ■ n. (pl. **superminis**) a type of small car with a relatively powerful engine.

supermodel ■ n. a highly successful fashion model enjoying celebrity status.

supernal /s(j)uːˈpɜːn(ə)l/ ■ adj. chiefly poetic/literary **1** of or relating to the sky or the heavens. **2** supremely excellent.
—DERIVATIVES **supernally** adv.
—ORIGIN Middle English: from medieval Latin *supernalis*, from Latin *supernus*, from *super* 'above'.

supernatant /ˌs(j)uːpəˈneɪt(ə)nt/ ■ adj. technical denoting the liquid lying above a solid residue after crystallization, centrifugation, or other process.

supernatural ■ adj. **1** (of a manifestation or event) attributed to some force beyond scientific understanding or the laws of nature. **2** exceptionally or extraordinarily great. ■ n. (**the supernatural**) supernatural manifestations or events.
—DERIVATIVES **supernaturalism** n. **supernaturalist** n. **supernaturally** adv.

supernormal ■ adj. beyond what is normal.

supernova /ˌs(j)uːpəˈnəʊvə/ ■ n. (pl. **supernovae** /-viː/ or **supernovas**) Astronomy a star that undergoes a catastrophic explosion, becoming suddenly very much brighter.

superstructure

supernumerary /ˌs(j)uːpəˈnjuːm(ə)r(ə)ri/ ■ adj. **1** present in excess of the normal or requisite number. **2** not belonging to a regular staff but engaged for extra work. ■ n. (pl. **-ies**) a supernumerary person or thing.
—ORIGIN C17: from late Latin *supernumerarius* '(soldier) added to a legion after it is complete'.

superorder ■ n. Biology a taxonomic category that ranks above order and below class.

superordinate /ˌs(j)uːpərˈɔːdɪnət/ ■ n. **1** a thing that represents a superior order or category within a system of classification. ▶ Linguistics a word whose meaning includes the meaning of one or more other words. **2** a person of superior rank or status. ■ adj. superior in status.
—ORIGIN C17: from SUPER-, on the pattern of *subordinate*.

superovulation ■ n. stimulation of the ovaries by the use of fertility drugs.

superoxide ■ n. Chemistry an oxide containing the anion O_2^-.

superphosphate ■ n. a fertilizer made by treating phosphate rock with sulphuric or phosphoric acid.

superpose ■ v. place (something) on or above something else, especially so that they coincide.
—DERIVATIVES **superposed** adj. **superposition** n.
—ORIGIN C19: from French *superposer*.

superpower ■ n. any of the top few most powerful and influential nations of the world.

supersaturate ■ v. Chemistry increase the concentration of (a solution) beyond saturation point.
—DERIVATIVES **supersaturation** n.

superscribe ■ v. **1** write or print (an inscription) at the top of or on the outside of a document. **2** write or print (a character, word, or line) above an existing one.
—DERIVATIVES **superscription** n.
—ORIGIN C15: from Latin *superscribere*, from *super-* 'over' + *scribere* 'write'.

superscript ■ adj. (of a letter, figure, or symbol) written or printed above the line.
—ORIGIN C19: from Latin *superscriptus, superscribere* 'write above'.

supersede /ˌs(j)uːpəˈsiːd/ ■ v. take the place of; supplant.
—DERIVATIVES **supersession** n.
—ORIGIN C15: from Old French *superseder*, from Latin *supersedere* 'be superior to'.

USAGE
The standard spelling is **supersede** rather than **supercede**. Although the **c** spelling is still often regarded as incorrect, it is now being entered without comment in some modern dictionaries.

supersonic ■ adj. involving or denoting a speed greater than that of sound.
—DERIVATIVES **supersonically** adv.

supersonics ■ pl. n. [treated as sing.] another term for ULTRASONICS.

superstar ■ n. an extremely famous and successful performer or sports player.
—DERIVATIVES **superstardom** n.

superstate ■ n. a large and powerful state formed from a federation or union of nations.

superstation ■ n. N. Amer. a television station using satellite technology to broadcast over a very large area, especially an entire continent.

superstition ■ n. excessively credulous belief in and reverence for the supernatural. ▶ a widely held but irrational belief in supernatural influences, especially as bringing good or bad luck.
—DERIVATIVES **superstitious** adj. **superstitiously** adv. **superstitiousness** n.
—ORIGIN Middle English: from Latin *superstitio(n-)*, from *super-* 'over' + *stare* 'to stand'.

superstore ■ n. a very large out-of-town supermarket.

superstructure ■ n. **1** a structure built on top of something else. ▶ the part of a building above its foundations. **2** a concept or idea based on others. **3** (in Marxist theory) the institutions and culture considered to

supersymmetry

result from or reflect the economic system underlying a society.
– DERIVATIVES **superstructural** adj.

supersymmetry ■ n. Physics a very general type of mathematical symmetry which relates fermions and bosons.
– DERIVATIVES **supersymmetric** adj.

supertanker ■ n. a very large oil tanker.

supertax ■ n. an additional tax on something already taxed.

supertonic ■ n. Music the second note of the diatonic scale of any key; the note above the tonic.

supervene /ˌs(j)uːpəˈviːn/ ■ v. **1** occur as an interruption or change to an existing situation. **2** Philosophy (of a fact or property) be entailed by or consequent on the existence or establishment of another.
– DERIVATIVES **supervenient** adj. **supervention** n.
– ORIGIN C17: from Latin *supervenire*, from *super-* 'in addition' + *venire* 'come'.

supervise ■ v. observe and direct the execution of (a task or activity) or the work of (a person).
– DERIVATIVES **supervision** n. **supervisor** n. **supervisory** adj.
– ORIGIN C15: from medieval Latin *supervis-*, *supervidere* 'survey, supervise'.

supervision order ■ n. English Law a court order placing a child or young person under the supervision of a local authority or a probation officer in a case of delinquency or where care proceedings are appropriate.

superwoman ■ n. (pl. -**women**) informal a woman with exceptional physical or mental ability.

supine /ˈs(j)uːpʌɪn/ ■ adj. **1** lying face upwards. ▸ with the palm of the hand upwards. **2** failing to act as a result of moral weakness or indolence. ■ n. a Latin verbal noun used only in the accusative and ablative cases, especially to denote purpose (e.g. *mirabile dictu* 'wonderful to relate').
– DERIVATIVES **supinely** adv. **supineness** n.
– ORIGIN Middle English: from Latin *supinus* 'bent backwards'.

supp ■ n. informal, chiefly S. African & Austral. a supplementary examination.

supper ■ n. a light or informal evening meal.
– PHRASES **sing for one's supper** provide a service in return for a benefit.
– DERIVATIVES **supperless** adj.
– ORIGIN Middle English: from Old French *super* 'to sup' (see SUP).

supplant ■ v. supersede and replace.
– DERIVATIVES **supplanter** n.
– ORIGIN Middle English: from Old French *supplanter* or Latin *supplantare* 'trip up', from *sub-* 'from below' + *planta* 'sole'.

supple ■ adj. (-**er**, -**est**) flexible or pliant. ■ v. make more flexible.
– DERIVATIVES **supplely** (also **supply**) adv. **suppleness** n.
– ORIGIN Middle English: from Old French *souple*, from Latin *supplex*, *supplic-* 'submissive', from *sub-* 'under' + *placere* 'propitiate'.

supplement ■ n. **1** a thing added to something else to enhance or complete it. **2** a separate section, especially a colour magazine, added to a newspaper or periodical. **3** an additional charge payable for an extra service or facility. **4** Geometry the amount by which a given angle is less than 180°. ■ v. provide a supplement for.
– DERIVATIVES **supplemental** adj. **supplementally** adv. **supplementation** n.
– ORIGIN Middle English: from Latin *supplementum*, from *supplere* (see SUPPLY[1]).

supplementary ■ adj. completing or enhancing something. ■ n. (pl. -**ies**) a supplementary person or thing. ▸ a question asked in parliament following the answer to a tabled one.
– DERIVATIVES **supplementarily** adv.

supplementary angle ■ n. Mathematics either of two angles whose sum is 180°.

supplementary examination (also **supplementary exam**) ■ n. (in universities) an additional examination granted to students who narrowly fail in their first attempt.

Supplex /ˈsʌplɛks/ ■ n. trademark a synthetic stretchable fabric which is permeable to air and water vapour, used in sports and outdoor clothing.

suppliant /ˈsʌplɪənt/ ■ n. a person who supplicates. ■ adj. making or expressing a humble or earnest plea.
– DERIVATIVES **suppliantly** adv.

supplicate /ˈsʌplɪkeɪt/ ■ v. ask or beg for something earnestly or humbly.
– DERIVATIVES **supplicant** adj. & n. **supplication** n. **supplicatory** adj.
– ORIGIN Middle English: from Latin *supplicare* 'implore', from *sub-* 'from below' + *placere* 'propitiate'.

supply[1] /səˈplʌɪ/ ■ v. (-**ies**, -**ied**) make (something needed) available to someone. ▸ provide with something needed. ▸ be adequate to satisfy (a requirement or demand). ■ n. (pl. -**ies**) **1** a stock or amount of something supplied or available. ▸ the action of supplying. **2** [usu. as modifier] a person, especially a schoolteacher, acting as a temporary substitute for another.
– PHRASES **supply and demand** the amount of a good or service available and the desire of buyers for it, considered as factors regulating its price.
– DERIVATIVES **supplier** n.
– ORIGIN Middle English: from Old French *soupleer*, from Latin *supplere* 'fill up'.

supply[2] /ˈsʌpli/ ■ adv. variant spelling of **supplely** (see SUPPLE).

supply-side ■ adj. Economics denoting a policy designed to increase output and employment by reducing taxation and other forms of restriction.
– DERIVATIVES **supply-sider** n.

support ■ v. **1** bear all or part of the weight of. **2** give assistance, encouragement, or approval to. ▸ be actively interested in (a sports team). ▸ [as adj. **supporting**] (of an actor or a role) of secondary importance to the leading roles in a play or film. ▸ (of a pop or rock group or performer) function as a secondary act to (another) at a concert. **3** provide with a home and the necessities of life. ▸ be capable of sustaining. **4** corroborate. **5** endure; tolerate. ■ n. **1** a person or thing that supports. ▸ the action of supporting or the state of being so supported. **2** assistance, encouragement, or approval.
– DERIVATIVES **supportability** n. **supportable** adj.
– ORIGIN Middle English: from Old French *supporter*, from Latin *supportare*, from *sub-* 'from below' + *portare* 'carry'.

supporter ■ n. **1** a person who supports a sports team, policy, etc. **2** Heraldry a representation of an animal or other figure, typically one of a pair, holding up or standing beside an escutcheon.

supportive ■ adj. providing encouragement or emotional help.
– DERIVATIVES **supportively** adv. **supportiveness** n.

support price ■ n. a minimum price guaranteed to a farmer for agricultural produce and maintained by subsidy or the buying in of surplus stock.

suppose ■ v. **1** think or assume that something is true or probable, but without proof. ▸ (of a theory or argument) assume or require that something is the case as a precondition. ▸ [in imper.] used to introduce a suggestion. **2** (**be supposed to do something**) be required or expected to do something.
– DERIVATIVES **supposable** adj.
– ORIGIN Middle English: from Old French *supposer*, from Latin *supponere*, from *sub-* 'from below' + *ponere* 'to place'.

supposedly ■ adv. according to what is generally believed or supposed.

supposition ■ n. an assumption or hypothesis.
– DERIVATIVES **suppositional** adj.

suppositious ■ adj. based on assumption rather than fact.

suppository ■ n. (pl. -**ies**) a solid medical preparation in a roughly conical or cylindrical shape, designed to dissolve after insertion into the rectum or vagina.
– ORIGIN Middle English: from medieval Latin *suppositorium*, from late Latin *suppositorius* 'placed underneath'.

VOWELS a cat ɑː arm ɛ bed ɛː hair ə ago əː her ɪ sit i cosy iː see ɒ hot ɔː saw ʌ run

suppress ■ v. **1** forcibly put an end to. **2** prevent from being expressed or published. ▸ Psychoanalysis consciously avoid thinking of (an unpleasant idea or memory). **3** prevent or inhibit (a process or phenomenon).
– DERIVATIVES **suppressible** adj. **suppression** n. **suppressive** adj. **suppressor** n.
– ORIGIN Middle English: from Latin *suppress-, supprimere* 'press down'.

suppressant ■ n. a drug or other substance which acts to suppress something.

suppurate /ˈsʌpjʊreɪt/ ■ v. form or discharge pus.
– DERIVATIVES **suppuration** n. **suppurative** /-rətɪv/ adj.
– ORIGIN Middle English: from Latin *sub-* 'below' + *pus, pur-* 'pus'.

supra /ˈs(j)uːprə/ ■ adv. formal (in academic or legal texts) someone or something mentioned earlier.
– ORIGIN from Latin.

supra- /ˈs(j)uːprə/ ■ prefix **1** above: *suprarenal.* **2** beyond; transcending: *supranational.*
– ORIGIN from Latin *supra* 'above, beyond, before in time'.

supranational ■ adj. having power or influence that transcends national boundaries or governments.
– DERIVATIVES **supranationalism** n. **supranationality** n.

suprarenal ■ adj. Anatomy another term for ADRENAL.

suprasegmental ■ adj. Linguistics denoting a feature of an utterance other than the consonantal and vocalic components, for example (in English) stress and intonation.

supremacist ■ n. an advocate of the supremacy of a particular group, especially one determined by race or sex. ■ adj. relating to or advocating such supremacy.
– DERIVATIVES **supremacism** n.

supreme ■ adj. **1** highest in authority or rank. **2** very great or greatest; most important. ▸ (of a penalty or sacrifice) involving death. ■ n. (also **suprême**) a rich cream sauce or a dish served in this.
– PHRASES **the Supreme Being** a name for God.
– DERIVATIVES **supremacy** n. **supremely** adv.
– ORIGIN C15: from Latin *supremus,* superlative of *superus* 'that is above'; noun from French *suprême.*

supreme court ■ n. the highest judicial court in a country or state.

supreme pontiff ■ n. see PONTIFF.

Supreme Soviet ■ n. the governing council of the former USSR or one of its constituent republics.

supremo /s(j)uːˈpriːməʊ, -ˈpreɪməʊ/ ■ n. (pl. -os) informal **1** a person in overall charge. **2** a person with great authority or skill in a certain area.
– ORIGIN Spanish, 'supreme'.

Supt ■ abbrev. Superintendent.

suq ■ n. variant spelling of SOUK.

sur-¹ ■ prefix equivalent to SUPER-.
– ORIGIN from French.

sur-² ■ prefix variant spelling of SUB- assimilated before *r* (as in *surrogate*).

sura /ˈsʊərə/ (also **surah**) ■ n. a chapter or section of the Koran.
– ORIGIN from Arabic *sūra.*

surcease ■ n. archaic or N. Amer. **1** cessation. **2** relief.
– ORIGIN Middle English: from Old French *sursis, surseoir* 'refrain, delay', from Latin *supersedere* (see SUPERSEDE); the change in the ending was due to association with CEASE.

surcharge ■ n. an additional charge or payment. ▸ an amount in an official account not passed by the auditor and having to be refunded by the person responsible. ▸ the showing of an omission in an account for which credit should have been given. ■ v. exact a surcharge from.

surcingle /ˈsəːsɪŋɡ(ə)l/ ■ n. a wide strap which runs over the back and under the belly of a horse, used to keep a rug or other equipment in place.
– ORIGIN Middle English: from Old French *surcengle,* from *cengle* 'girth', from Latin *cingula,* from *cingere* 'gird'.

surcoat /ˈsəːkəʊt/ ■ n. historical an outer coat or garment of rich material, typically worn over armour.
– ORIGIN Middle English: from Old French *surcot,* from *sur* 'over' + *cot* 'coat'.

surd /səːd/ ■ n. Mathematics an irrational number.
– ORIGIN C16: from Latin *surdus* 'deaf, mute'; as a mathematical term, translating Greek *alogos* 'irrational, speechless'.

sure /ʃʊə, ʃɔː/ ■ adj. **1** completely confident that one is right. **2** (**sure of/to do something**) certain to receive, get, or do something. **3** undoubtedly true; completely reliable. ■ adv. [often as exclam.] informal certainly.
– PHRASES **be sure** [usu. in imper.] do not fail. **for sure** informal without doubt. **make sure** confirm or ensure. **sure enough** informal used to introduce a statement that confirms something previously predicted. **sure thing** informal a certainty. ▸ [as exclam.] chiefly N. Amer. certainly. **to be sure** certainly; it must be admitted.
– DERIVATIVES **sureness** n.
– ORIGIN Middle English: from Old French *sur,* from Latin *securus* 'free from care'.

sure-fire ■ adj. informal certain to succeed.

sure-footed ■ adj. **1** unlikely to stumble or slip. **2** confident and competent.
– DERIVATIVES **sure-footedly** adv. **sure-footedness** n.

surely ■ adv. **1** it must be true that (used for emphasis). ▸ certainly. ▸ [as exclam.] informal, chiefly N. Amer. of course. **2** with assurance.

surety /ˈʃʊərɪti, ˈʃʊəti/ ■ n. (pl. **-ies**) **1** a person who takes responsibility for another's undertaking, e.g. the payment of a debt. **2** money given as a guarantee that someone will do something. **3** the state of being sure.
– PHRASES **of** (or **for**) **a surety** archaic for certain. **stand surety** become a surety.
– DERIVATIVES **suretyship** n.
– ORIGIN Middle English: from Old French *surte,* from Latin *securitas* (see SECURITY).

surf ■ n. the mass or line of foam formed by waves breaking on a seashore or reef. ■ v. **1** stand or lie on a surfboard and ride on the crest of a wave towards the shore. **2** occupy oneself by moving from site to site on (the Internet).
– DERIVATIVES **surfer** n. **surfing** n. **surfy** adj.
– ORIGIN C17: from obsolete *suff,* perhaps influenced by the spelling of *surge.*

surface ■ n. **1** the outside part or uppermost layer of something. ▸ (also **surface area**) the area of this. **2** the upper limit of a body of liquid. **3** outward appearance as distinct from less obvious aspects. **4** Geometry a set of points that has length and breadth but no thickness. ■ adj. of, relating to, or occurring on the surface. ▸ carried by or denoting transportation by sea or overland as contrasted with by air. ■ v. **1** rise or come up to the surface. **2** become apparent. **3** provide (something, especially a road) with a particular surface. **4** informal appear after having been asleep.
– DERIVATIVES **surfaced** adj. **surfacer** n.
– ORIGIN C17: from French (see SUR-¹, FACE), suggested by Latin *superficies.*

surface-active ■ adj. (of a substance) tending to reduce the surface tension of a liquid in which it is dissolved.

surface structure ■ n. (in transformational grammar) the structure of a phrase or sentence in a language, as opposed to its underlying logical form. Contrasted with DEEP STRUCTURE.

surface tension ■ n. the tension of the surface film of a liquid, which tends to minimize surface area.

surface-to-air ■ adj. (of a missile) designed to be fired from the ground or a vessel at an aircraft.

surface-to-surface ■ adj. (of a missile) designed to be fired from one point on the ground or a vessel at another such point or vessel.

surfactant /səːˈfakt(ə)nt/ ■ n. a surface-active substance.
– ORIGIN 1950s: from *surf(ace)-act(ive).*

surfboard ■ n. a long, narrow board used in surfing.

surfcasting ■ n. fishing by casting a line into the sea from the shore.

surfeit ■ n. **1** an excess. **2** archaic an illness caused or regarded as being caused by excessive eating or drinking. ■ v. (**surfeited, surfeiting**) cause to be wearied

surficial

of something through excess.
– ORIGIN Middle English: from Old French *surfeit*, from Latin *super-* 'above, in excess' + *facere* 'do'.

surficial /ˈsəːfɪʃ(ə)l/ ■ adj. Geology of or relating to the earth's surface.
– DERIVATIVES **surficially** adv.
– ORIGIN C19: from SURFACE, on the pattern of *superficial*.

surf 'n' turf (also **surf and turf**) ■ n. a dish containing both seafood and meat, typically shellfish and steak.

surge ■ n. **1** a sudden powerful forward or upward movement: *tidal surges.* **2** a sudden large temporary increase. **3** a powerful rush of an emotion or feeling. ■ v. **1** move in a surge. **2** increase suddenly and powerfully. **3** Nautical (of a rope, chain, or windlass) slip back with a jerk.
– ORIGIN C15: the noun from Old French *sourgeon*; the verb partly from the Old French stem *sourge-*, from Latin *surgere* 'to rise'.

surgeon ■ n. **1** a medical practitioner qualified to practise surgery. **2** a doctor in the navy.
– ORIGIN Middle English: from Anglo-Norman French *surgien*, contraction of Old French *serurgien*, from Latin *chirurgia*, from Greek *kheirourgia* 'handiwork, surgery'.

surgeonfish ■ n. (pl. same or **-fishes**) a tropical marine fish with a scalpel-like spine on each side of the tail. [Family Acanthuridae: many species.]

surgeon general ■ n. (pl. **surgeons general**) the head of a public health service or of the medical service of the armed forces.

surgery ■ n. (pl. **-ies**) **1** the branch of medicine concerned with treatment of bodily injuries or disorders by incision or manipulation, especially with instruments. **2** a place where a medical practitioner treats or advises patients. **3** Brit. an occasion on which an MP, lawyer, or other professional person gives advice.
– ORIGIN Middle English: from Old French *surgerie*, contraction of *serurgerie*, from *serurgien* (see SURGEON).

surge tank ■ n. a tank designed to neutralize sudden changes of pressure in a flow of liquid.

surgical ■ adj. **1** of, relating to, or used in surgery. **2** (of a special garment or appliance) worn to correct or relieve an injury, illness, or deformity. **3** denoting something done with great precision, especially a military attack from the air.
– DERIVATIVES **surgically** adv.

surgical spirit ■ n. methylated spirit (often with oil of wintergreen) used especially for cleansing the skin before injections or surgery.

suricate /ˈs(j)ʊərɪkeɪt/ ■ n. a gregarious burrowing meerkat with dark bands on the back and a black-tipped tail, native to southern Africa. [*Suricata suricatta.*]
– ORIGIN C18: from a local African word.

Surinamer /ˌsʊərɪˈnɑːmə, -ˈnɑːmə/ ■ n. a native or inhabitant of Surinam, a country on the NE coast of South America.
– DERIVATIVES **Surinamese** /-nəˈmiːz/ adj. & n.

surly ■ adj. (**-ier, -iest**) bad-tempered and unfriendly.
– DERIVATIVES **surlily** adv. **surliness** n.
– ORIGIN C16: alteration of obsolete *sirly* (see SIR).

surmise /səˈmaɪz/ ■ v. suppose without having evidence. ■ n. a supposition or guess.
– ORIGIN Middle English: from Anglo-Norman French and Old French *surmise*, from *surmettre* 'accuse', from late Latin *supermittere* 'put in afterwards'.

surmount ■ v. **1** overcome (a difficulty or obstacle). **2** stand or be placed on top of.
– DERIVATIVES **surmountable** adj.
– ORIGIN Middle English: from Old French *surmonter* (see SUR-¹, MOUNT¹).

surname ■ n. **1** a hereditary name common to all members of a family, as distinct from a forename. **2** archaic a descriptive or allusive name, title, or epithet added to a person's name. ■ v. give a surname to.
– ORIGIN Middle English: partial translation of Anglo-Norman French *surnoun*, suggested by medieval Latin *supernomen*.

surpass ■ v. be greater or better than. ▶ [as adj. **surpassing**] archaic or poetic/literary incomparable or outstanding.
– DERIVATIVES **surpassable** adj. **surpassingly** adv.
– ORIGIN C16: from French *surpasser*, from *sur-* 'above' + *passer* 'to pass'.

surplice /ˈsəːplɪs/ ■ n. a loose white linen vestment worn over a cassock by clergy and choristers at Christian church services.
– DERIVATIVES **surpliced** adj.
– ORIGIN Middle English: from Old French *sourpelis*, from medieval Latin *superpellicium*, from *super-* 'above' + *pellicia* 'fur garment'.

surplus ■ n. an amount left over when requirements have been met. ▶ an excess of income or assets over expenditure or liabilities in a given period. ▶ the excess value of a company's assets over the face value of its stock. ■ adj. excess; extra.
– ORIGIN Middle English: from Old French *sourplus*, from medieval Latin *superplus*, from *super-* 'in addition' + *plus* 'more'.

surplus value ■ n. Economics (in Marxist theory) the excess of value produced by the labour of workers over the wages they are paid.

surprise ■ n. **1** a feeling of mild astonishment or shock caused by something unexpected. **2** an unexpected or astonishing thing. ■ v. **1** cause to feel surprise. **2** capture, attack, or discover suddenly and unexpectedly.
– PHRASES **take someone/thing by surprise** attack or capture someone or something unexpectedly. ▶ (**take someone by surprise**) happen unexpectedly to someone.
– DERIVATIVES **surprised** adj. **surprisedly** adv. **surprising** adj. **surprisingly** adv. **surprisingness** n.
– ORIGIN Middle English: from Old French, from *surprendre*, from medieval Latin *superprehendere* 'seize'.

surreal ■ adj. having the qualities of surrealism; bizarre.
– DERIVATIVES **surreality** n. **surreally** adv.

surrealism ■ n. a 20th-century avant-garde movement in art and literature which sought to release the creative potential of the unconscious mind, for example by the irrational juxtaposition of images.
– DERIVATIVES **surrealist** n. & adj. **surrealistic** adj. **surrealistically** adv.
– ORIGIN C20: from French *surréalisme* (see SUR-¹, REALISM).

surrender ■ v. **1** cease resistance to an opponent and submit to their authority. **2** give up (a person, right, or possession) on compulsion or demand. ▶ give up (a lease) before its expiry. **3** (**surrender to**) abandon oneself entirely to (a powerful emotion or influence). **4** (of a person assured) cancel (a life insurance policy) and receive back a proportion of the premiums paid. ■ n. the action of surrendering.
– PHRASES **surrender to bail** Law duly appear in court after release on bail.
– ORIGIN Middle English: from Anglo-Norman French (see SUR-¹, RENDER).

surrender value ■ n. the amount payable to a person who surrenders a life insurance policy.

surreptitious /ˌsʌrəpˈtɪʃəs/ ■ adj. covert or clandestine.
– DERIVATIVES **surreptitiously** adv. **surreptitiousness** n.
– ORIGIN Middle English: from Latin *surreptitius*, from *surripere*, from *sub-* 'secretly' + *rapere* 'seize'.

surrogate /ˈsʌrəgət/ ■ n. a substitute, especially a person deputizing for another in a specific role or office. ▶ (in the Christian Church) a bishop's deputy who grants marriage licences.
– DERIVATIVES **surrogacy** n.
– ORIGIN C17: from Latin *surrogare* 'elect as a substitute'.

surrogate mother ■ n. a woman who bears a child on behalf of another woman, either from her own egg or from the implantation in her womb of a fertilized egg from the other woman.

surround ■ v. **1** be all round; encircle. **2** be associated with: *the killings were surrounded by controversy.* ■ n. **1** a border or edging. **2** (**surrounds**) surroundings.
– ORIGIN Middle English: from Old French *souronder*, from late Latin *superundare*, from *super-* 'over' + *undare* 'to flow'; later associated with ROUND.

surroundings ■ pl. n. the conditions or area around a person or thing.

surtax ■ n. an additional tax on something already taxed, especially a higher rate of tax on incomes above a certain level.

surtitle ■ n. a caption projected on a screen above the stage in an opera, translating the text being sung. ■ v. provide with surtitles.

surtout /ˈsɜːtuː, səˈtuː(t)/ ■ n. historical a man's greatcoat of a similar style to a frock coat.
– ORIGIN C17: from French, from *sur* 'over' + *tout* 'everything'.

surveillance /səˈveɪl(ə)ns, -ˈveɪəns/ ■ n. close observation, especially of a suspected spy or criminal.
– ORIGIN C19: from French, from *sur-* 'over' + *veiller* 'watch'.

survey ■ v. /səˈveɪ/ **1** look carefully and thoroughly at. **2** examine and record the area and features of (an area of land) so as to construct a map, plan, or description. **3** examine and report on the condition of (a building), especially for a prospective buyer. **4** conduct a survey among (a group of people). ■ n. /ˈsɜːveɪ/ **1** a general view, examination, or description. ▸ an investigation of the opinions or experience of a group of people, based on a series of questions. **2** an act of surveying. **3** a map, plan, or report obtained by surveying.
– ORIGIN Middle English: from Anglo-Norman French *surveier*, from medieval Latin *supervidere*, from *super-* 'over' + *videre* 'to see'.

surveyor ■ n. **1** a person who surveys land, buildings, etc. as a profession. **2** an official inspector, especially for measurement and valuation purposes.

survival ■ n. **1** the state or fact of surviving. **2** an object or practice that has survived from an earlier time.
– PHRASES **survival of the fittest** the continued existence of the organisms best adapted to their environment; natural selection.

survivalism ■ n. **1** the policy of trying to ensure one's own survival or that of one's social or national group. **2** the practising of outdoor survival skills as a sport or hobby.
– DERIVATIVES **survivalist** n. & adj.

survival kit ■ n. a pack of emergency equipment, including food, medical supplies, and tools, especially as carried by members of the armed forces.

survive ■ v. continue to live or exist. ▸ continue to live or exist in spite of (an accident or ordeal). ▸ remain alive after the death of.
– DERIVATIVES **survivable** adj.
– ORIGIN Middle English: from Old French *sourvivre*, from Latin *supervivere*, from *super-* 'in addition' + *vivere* 'live'.

survivor ■ n. **1** a person who has survived. **2** Law the remaining party under a joint will.
– DERIVATIVES **survivorship** n.

sus /sʌs/ ■ n. Brit. informal suspicion of having committed a crime. ▸ [as modifier] historical relating to or denoting a law under which a person could be arrested on suspicion of having committed an offence. ■ v. variant spelling of SUSS.

sus- ■ prefix variant spelling of SUB- before *c*, *p*, *t* (as in *susceptible*, *suspend*).

susceptibility ■ n. (pl. **-ies**) **1** the state or fact of being susceptible. **2** (**susceptibilities**) a person's feelings, regarded as being easily hurt. **3** Physics the ratio of the magnetization produced in a material to the magnetizing force.

susceptible /səˈsɛptɪb(ə)l/ ■ adj. **1** (often **susceptible to**) likely to be influenced or harmed by a particular thing. ▸ easily influenced by feelings or emotions. **2** (**susceptible of**) capable or admitting of.
– DERIVATIVES **susceptibly** adv.
– ORIGIN C17: from late Latin *susceptibilis*, from Latin *suscipere* 'take up, sustain'.

sushi /ˈsuːʃi, ˈsʊʃi/ ■ n. a Japanese dish consisting of small balls or rolls of vinegar-flavoured cold rice served with a garnish of vegetables, egg, or raw seafood.
– ORIGIN from Japanese.

suspect ■ v. /səˈspɛkt/ **1** believe (something) to be probable or possible. ▸ believe (someone) to be guilty of a crime or offence, without certain proof. **2** doubt the genuineness or truth of. ■ n. /ˈsʌspɛkt/ a person suspected of a crime or offence. ■ adj. /ˈsʌspɛkt/ possibly dangerous or false.

– ORIGIN Middle English: from Latin *suspectus*, *suspicere* 'mistrust', from *sub-* 'from below' + *specere* 'to look'.

suspend ■ v. **1** halt temporarily. **2** debar temporarily from a post, duties, etc. as a punishment. **3** defer or delay (an action, event, or judgement). ▸ Law (of a judge or court) cause (an imposed sentence) to be unenforced as long as no further offence is committed within a specified period. **4** hang from somewhere. **5** (**be suspended**) be dispersed in a suspension.
– PHRASES **suspend payment** (of a company) cease to meet its financial obligations as a result of insolvency or insufficient funds.
– ORIGIN Middle English: from Old French *suspendre* or Latin *suspendere*, from *sub-* 'from below' + *pendere* 'hang'.

suspended animation ■ n. temporary cessation of most vital functions, without death.

suspended ceiling ■ n. a ceiling with a space between it and the floor above from which it hangs.

suspender ■ n. **1** an elastic strap attached to a belt or garter, fastened to the top of a stocking to hold it up. **2** (**suspenders**) N. Amer. a pair of braces for holding up trousers.

suspender belt ■ n. a woman's undergarment consisting of a decorative belt and suspenders.

suspense ■ n. **1** a state or feeling of excited or anxious uncertainty about what may happen. **2** chiefly Law the temporary cessation or suspension of something.
– DERIVATIVES **suspenseful** adj.
– ORIGIN Middle English: from Old French *suspens* 'abeyance', from Latin *suspensus*, *suspendere* (see SUSPEND).

suspense account ■ n. an account in which items are entered temporarily before allocation to the correct or final account.

suspension ■ n. **1** the action of suspending or the condition of being suspended. **2** the system of springs and shock absorbers by which a vehicle is supported on its wheels. **3** a mixture in which particles are dispersed throughout the bulk of a fluid.

suspension bridge ■ n. a bridge in which the deck is suspended from cables running between towers.

suspensive ■ adj. of or relating to the suspension of an event, action, or legal obligation.

suspensory ■ adj. **1** holding and supporting an organ or part. **2** of or relating to the suspension of an event, action, or legal obligation.

suspicion ■ n. **1** a feeling that something is possible or probable or that someone is guilty of a crime or offence. **2** cautious distrust. **3** a very slight trace: *a suspicion of a smile*.
– PHRASES **above suspicion** too good or honest to be thought capable of wrongdoing. **under suspicion** suspected of wrongdoing.
– ORIGIN Middle English: from Anglo-Norman French *suspeciun*, from medieval Latin *suspectio(n-)*, from *suspicere* 'mistrust'.

suspicious ■ adj. having or showing cautious distrust. ▸ causing one to believe that someone or something is questionable, dishonest, or dangerous. ▸ believing that someone is involved in illegal or dishonest activity.
– DERIVATIVES **suspiciously** adv. **suspiciousness** n.

suss (also **sus**) informal ■ v. (**sussed**, **sussing**) **1** realize. ▸ understand the true character or nature of. **2** [as adj. **sussed**] clever and well informed. ■ n. knowledge or awareness of a specified kind: *business suss*.
– ORIGIN 1930s: abbrev. of SUSPECT, SUSPICION.

sustain ■ v. **1** strengthen or support physically or mentally. ▸ bear (the weight of an object). **2** keep (something) going over time or continuously. **3** suffer (something unpleasant). **4** uphold or confirm the justice or validity of.
– DERIVATIVES **sustained** adj. **sustainedly** adv. **sustainer** n. **sustainment** n.
– ORIGIN Middle English: from Old French *soustenir*, from Latin *sustinere*, from *sub-* 'from below' + *tenere* 'hold'.

sustainable

sustainable ■ adj. able to be sustained.
– DERIVATIVES **sustainability** n. **sustainably** adv.

sustained yield ■ n. a level of exploitation or crop production which is maintained by restricting the quantity harvested to avoid long-term depletion.

sustenance ■ n. 1 food and drink regarded as sustaining life. 2 the sustaining of someone or something in life or existence.
– ORIGIN Middle English: from Old French *soustenance*, from *soustenir* (see SUSTAIN).

susurration /ˌs(j)uːsʌˈreɪʃ(ə)n/ (also **susurrus** /s(j)uːˈsʌrəs/) ■ n. poetic/literary whispering or rustling.
– ORIGIN Middle English: from late Latin *susurratio(n-)*, from Latin *susurrare* 'to murmur, hum'.

sutherlandia ■ n. a plant of a genus that comprises the cancer bushes. [Genus *Sutherlandia*.]

sutler /ˈsʌtlə/ ■ n. historical a person who followed an army and sold provisions to the soldiers.
– ORIGIN C16: from obsolete Dutch *soeteler*, from *soetelen* 'perform mean duties'.

sutra /ˈsuːtrə/ ■ n. 1 a rule or aphorism in Sanskrit literature, or a set of these on grammar or Hindu law or philosophy. See also KAMA SUTRA. 2 a Buddhist or Jainist scripture.
– ORIGIN from Sanskrit *sūtra* 'thread, rule', from *siv* 'sew'.

suttee /sʌˈtiː, ˈsʌti/ ■ n. (pl. **suttees**) the former Hindu practice of a widow immolating herself on her husband's funeral pyre.
– ORIGIN Hindi, from Sanskrit *sati* 'faithful wife', from *sat* 'good'.

suture /ˈsuːtʃə/ ■ n. 1 a stitch or row of stitches holding together the edges of a wound or surgical incision. ▸ a thread or wire used for this. 2 the action of suturing. 3 chiefly Anatomy a seam-like immovable junction between two parts, especially between bones of the skull. ■ v. stitch up with a suture.
– DERIVATIVES **sutural** adj.
– ORIGIN Middle English: from Latin *sutura*, from *suere* 'sew'.

SUV ■ abbrev. sport utility vehicle.

suzerain /ˈsuːzəreɪn/ ■ n. 1 a sovereign or state having some control over another state that is internally autonomous. 2 a feudal overlord.
– DERIVATIVES **suzerainty** n.
– ORIGIN C19: from French, apparently from *sus* 'above', suggested by *souverain* 'sovereign'.

Sv ■ abbrev. sievert(s).

s.v. ■ abbrev. (in textual references) under the word or heading given.
– ORIGIN from Latin *sub voce* or *sub verbo* 'under the voice/word'.

svelte ■ adj. slender and elegant.
– ORIGIN C19: from French, from Italian *svelto*.

Svengali /svenˈɡɑːli/ ■ n. a person who exercises a controlling influence on another, especially for a sinister purpose.
– ORIGIN *Svengali*, a musician in George du Maurier's novel *Trilby* (1894) who controls Trilby's stage singing hypnotically.

SVGA ■ abbrev. super video graphics array, a high-resolution standard for monitors and screens.

S-VHS ■ abbrev. super video home system, an improved version of VHS.

SW ■ abbrev. 1 south-west. 2 south-western.

swab ■ n. 1 an absorbent pad used in surgery and medicine for cleaning wounds or applying medication. ▸ a specimen of a secretion taken with a swab. 2 a mop or other absorbent device for cleaning or mopping up. 3 archaic a contemptible person. ■ v. (**swabbed**, **swabbing**) clean or absorb with a swab.
– ORIGIN C17: back-formation from *swabber* 'sailor detailed to swab decks', from early modern Dutch *zwabber*.

swaddle ■ v. wrap in garments or cloth.
– ORIGIN Middle English: from SWATHE[2].

swaddling clothes ■ pl. n. historical cloth bands wrapped round a newborn child to calm it.

swag ■ n. 1 an ornamental festoon of flowers, fruit, and greenery. ▸ a curtain or drape fastened to hang in a drooping curve. 2 informal money or goods taken by a thief or burglar. 3 Austral./NZ a traveller's or miner's bundle of personal belongings. ■ v. (**swagged**, **swagging**) 1 arrange in or decorate with swags. 2 chiefly poetic/literary hang or sway heavily.
– ORIGIN Middle English: prob. of Scandinavian origin.

swage /sweɪdʒ/ ■ n. 1 a tool or die for shaping metal by hammering or pressure. 2 a groove, ridge, or other moulding on an object. ■ v. shape or compress using a swage.
– ORIGIN Middle English: from Old French *souage* 'decorative groove'.

swagger ■ v. walk or behave arrogantly or self-importantly. ■ n. an arrogant or self-important gait or manner.
– DERIVATIVES **swaggerer** n. **swaggering** adj. **swaggeringly** adv.
– ORIGIN C16: apparently from SWAG.

swagger stick ■ n. a short cane carried by a military officer.

swagman ■ n. (pl. -men) Austral./NZ a man carrying a swag; an itinerant worker.

Swahili /swəˈhiːli, swɑː-/ ■ n. (pl. same) 1 a Bantu language widely used as a lingua franca in East Africa. 2 a member of a people of Zanzibar and nearby coastal regions.
– ORIGIN from Arabic *sawāḥil*, pl. of *sāḥil* 'coast'.

swain ■ n. 1 archaic a country youth. 2 poetic/literary a young lover or suitor.
– ORIGIN Old English, from Old Norse *sveinn* 'lad'.

swale ■ n. a low or hollow place, especially a marshy depression between ridges. ▸ a ditch or furrow dug along a contour line to channel and conserve rainwater and assist in soil infiltration.
– ORIGIN C16.

swallow[1] ■ v. 1 cause or allow (food, drink, etc.) to pass down the throat. ▸ make a similar movement of the throat, especially through fear or nervousness. 2 take in and cause to disappear; engulf. 3 put up with or meekly accept. ▸ resist expressing: *he swallowed his pride*. 4 believe (an untrue or unlikely statement) unquestioningly. ■ n. an act of swallowing something.
– DERIVATIVES **swallowable** adj. **swallower** n.
– ORIGIN Old English *swelgan*, of Germanic origin.

swallow[2] ■ n. a migratory swift-flying insectivorous songbird with a forked tail. [Family Hirundinidae: several genera, in particular *Hirundo*.]
– ORIGIN Old English *swealwe*, of Germanic origin.

swallow dive ■ n. a dive performed with one's arms outspread until close to the water.

swallow hole ■ n. another term for SINKHOLE (in sense 1).

swallowtail ■ n. 1 a deeply forked tail. 2 a large brightly coloured butterfly with tail-like projections on the hindwings. [Genus *Papilio*.]
– DERIVATIVES **swallow-tailed** adj.

swam past of SWIM.

swami /ˈswɑːmi/ ■ n. (pl. **swamis**) a male Hindu religious teacher.
– ORIGIN from Hindi *swāmī* 'master, prince', from Sanskrit *svāmin*.

swamp ■ n. an area of waterlogged ground; a bog or marsh. ■ v. 1 overwhelm or flood with water. 2 overwhelm with too much of something; inundate.
– DERIVATIVES **swampish** adj. **swampy** adj.
– ORIGIN C17: prob. from a Germanic base meaning 'sponge' or 'fungus'.

swamp fever ■ n. a contagious and usually fatal viral disease of horses.

swan ■ n. a large waterbird, typically all white, with a long flexible neck, short legs, and webbed feet. [Several species, chiefly in the genus *Cygnus*.] ■ v. (**swanned**, **swanning**) informal move or go in a casual, irresponsible, or ostentatious way.
– DERIVATIVES **swanlike** adj.
– ORIGIN Old English, of Germanic origin.

swan dive ■ n. chiefly N. Amer. a swallow dive.

swank informal ▪ v. display one's wealth, knowledge, or achievements so as to impress others. ▪ n. behaviour, talk, or display intended to impress others. ▪ adj. another term for SWANKY.
– ORIGIN C19.

swanky ▪ adj. (**-ier**, **-iest**) informal **1** stylishly luxurious and expensive. **2** inclined to show off.
– DERIVATIVES **swankily** adv. **swankiness** n.

swan neck ▪ n. a curved structure shaped like a swan's neck.
– DERIVATIVES **swan-necked** adj.

swannery ▪ n. (pl. **-ies**) a place where swans are kept or bred.

swansdown ▪ n. **1** the fine down of a swan, used for trimmings and powder puffs. **2** a thick cotton fabric with a soft nap on one side. ▸ a soft, thick woollen fabric containing a little silk or cotton.

swansong ▪ n. the final performance or activity of a person's career.
– ORIGIN C19: suggested by German *Schwanengesang*, denoting a song fabled to be sung by a dying swan.

swap (also **swop**) ▪ v. (**swapped**, **swapping**) exchange or substitute. ▪ n. an act of exchanging one thing for another.
– DERIVATIVES **swappable** adj. **swapper** n.
– ORIGIN Middle English (in the sense 'throw forcibly'): prob. imitative of a resounding blow.

swapfile ▪ n. Computing a file on a hard disk used for programs transferred from the processor's memory.

SWAPO /ˈswɑːpəʊ/ ▪ abbrev. South West Africa People's Organization.

sward /swɔːd/ ▪ n. an expanse of short grass. ▸ the upper layer of soil, especially when covered with grass.
– DERIVATIVES **swarded** adj.
– ORIGIN Old English *sweard* 'skin'.

sware archaic past of SWEAR.

swarf /swɑːf/ ▪ n. fine chips or filings produced by machining.
– ORIGIN C16: either from Old English *geswearf* 'filings' or from Old Norse *svarf* 'file dust'.

swarm ▪ n. a large or dense group of flying insects, people, or things. ▪ v. **1** move in or form a swarm. **2** somewhere in large numbers. ▸ (**swarm with**) be crowded or overrun with.
– PHRASAL VERBS **swarm up** climb rapidly by gripping with one's hands and feet.
– DERIVATIVES **swarmer** n.
– ORIGIN Old English, of Germanic origin.

swart /swɔːt/ ▪ adj. archaic or poetic/literary swarthy.
– ORIGIN Old English, of Germanic origin.

swart gevaar /ˌswɑːt xəˈfɑː/ ▪ n. S. African historical (under apartheid) the supposed threat which the black majority posed to the white population.
– ORIGIN Afrikaans, 'black peril'.

swarthy ▪ adj. (**-ier**, **-iest**) dark-complexioned.
– DERIVATIVES **swarthily** adv. **swarthiness** n.
– ORIGIN C16: alteration of obsolete *swarty* (from SWART).

swash¹ ▪ v. **1** (of water) move with a splashing sound. **2** archaic flamboyantly swagger about or wield a sword. ▪ n. the rush of seawater up the beach after the breaking of a wave. ▸ archaic the motion or sound of water washing against something.
– ORIGIN C16: imitative.

swash² ▪ adj. Printing denoting an ornamental written or printed character, typically a capital letter.
– ORIGIN C17.

swashbuckler ▪ n. a person who takes a flamboyant part in daring adventures. ▸ a film or book portraying such a person.
– DERIVATIVES **swashbuckling** adj.
– ORIGIN C16: from SWASH¹ + BUCKLER.

swastika /ˈswɒstɪkə/ ▪ n. an ancient symbol in the form of an equal-armed cross with each arm continued at a right angle, used (in clockwise form) as the emblem of the German Nazi party.
– ORIGIN C19: from Sanskrit *svastika*, from *svasti* 'well-being', from *su* 'good' + *asti* 'being'.

swat ▪ v. (**swatted**, **swatting**) hit or crush with a sharp blow from a flat object. ▪ n. such a sharp blow.

– ORIGIN C17: northern English dialect and US var. of SQUAT.

swatch ▪ n. a piece of fabric used as a sample. ▸ a number of these bound together.
– ORIGIN C16: orig. Scots and northern English.

swathe¹ /sweɪð, swɒð/ (chiefly N. Amer. also **swath** /sweɪð/)
▪ n. (pl. **swathes** or **swaths** /swɔːðs, swɔːðs, swɒðs/) **1** a row or line of grass, corn, etc. as it falls when mown or reaped. **2** a broad strip or area: *vast swathes of countryside.*
– PHRASES **cut a swathe through** pass through (an area) causing destruction or upheaval.
– ORIGIN Old English *swæth*, *swathu* 'track, trace', of West Germanic origin.

swathe² /sweɪð/ ▪ v. wrap in several layers of fabric. ▪ n. a strip of material in which something is wrapped.
– ORIGIN Old English *swath-* (n.), *swathian* (v.).

SWAT team /swɒt/ ▪ n. (in the US) a group of elite police marksmen who specialize in high-risk tasks such as hostage rescue.
– ORIGIN 1980s: acronym from *Special Weapons and Tactics*.

sway ▪ v. **1** move slowly or rhythmically backwards and forwards or from side to side. **2** cause to change in opinion, action, etc.; influence. **3** poetic/literary rule; govern. ▪ n. **1** a rhythmical movement from side to side. **2** influence; rule.
– PHRASES **hold sway** have great power or influence.
– ORIGIN Middle English: rel. to Low German *swājen* 'be blown to and fro' and Dutch *zwaaien* 'swing, walk totteringly'.

swayback ▪ n. an abnormally hollowed back, especially in a horse.
– DERIVATIVES **sway-backed** adj.

Swazi /ˈswɑːzi/ ▪ n. (pl. same or **Swazis**) **1** a member of a people inhabiting Swaziland and parts of north-eastern South Africa. ▸ a native or national of Swaziland. **2** another term for SISWATI. ▪ adj. of or relating to Swaziland, its people, or their language.
– ORIGIN from the name of *Mswati*, a C19 king of the Swazis.

swear ▪ v. (past **swore**; past part. **sworn**) **1** state or promise solemnly or on oath. ▸ (**swear someone in**) admit someone to a position or office by directing them to take a formal oath. ▸ compel to observe a certain course of action: *I am sworn to secrecy.* ▸ (**swear to**) give an assurance that something is the case. ▸ (**swear off**) informal promise to abstain from. ▸ (**swear by**) informal have or express great confidence in. ▸ (**swear something out**) US Law obtain the issue of a warrant for arrest by making a charge on oath. **2** use offensive language, especially to express anger.
– PHRASES **swear blind** (or N. Amer. **swear up and down**) informal affirm something emphatically.
– DERIVATIVES **swearer** n.
– ORIGIN Old English, of Germanic origin.

swear word ▪ n. an offensive or obscene word.

sweat ▪ n. **1** moisture exuded through the pores of the skin, especially as a reaction to heat, physical exertion, or anxiety. **2** informal a state of anxiety or distress. ▸ informal hard work; a laborious undertaking. **3** (**sweats**) informal, chiefly N. Amer. a sweatsuit; sweatpants. ▪ v. (past and past part. **sweated** or N. Amer. **sweat**) **1** exude sweat. ▸ (**sweat something out/off**) get rid of something by exuding sweat. ▸ cause to exude sweat by exercise or exertion. ▸ exert a great deal of strenuous effort. ▸ be or remain in a state of extreme anxiety. ▸ N. Amer. informal worry about. **2** (of a substance) exude moisture. **3** cook (chopped vegetables) slowly in a pan with a small amount of fat. **4** subject (metal) to surface melting, especially to fasten or join by solder without a soldering iron.
– PHRASES **break (a) sweat** informal exert oneself physically. **by the sweat of one's brow** by one's own hard labour. **no sweat** informal used to convey that one perceives no difficulty or problem with something. **sweat blood** informal make an extraordinarily strenuous effort. ▸ be extremely anxious. **sweat it out** informal endure prolonged heat, exertion, or anxiety.
– ORIGIN Old English, of Germanic origin.

sweatband

sweatband ■ n. a band of absorbent material worn to soak up sweat.

sweated ■ adj. of or denoting manual workers employed for long hours and under poor conditions: *sweated labour*.

sweat equity ■ n. informal an interest in a property earned by a tenant in return for labour towards upkeep or restoration.

sweater ■ n. a pullover with long sleeves. ▸ a sweatshirt.

sweat gland ■ n. a coiled tubular gland in the skin, secreting sweat.

sweat lodge ■ n. a hut used by North American Indians for ritual steam baths.

sweatpants ■ pl. n. loose trousers with an elasticated or drawstring waist, worn for exercise or leisure.

sweatshirt ■ n. a loose sweater, typically of knitted cotton, worn for exercise or leisure.

sweatshop ■ n. a factory or workshop employing sweated labour.

sweatsuit ■ n. a suit consisting of a sweatshirt and sweatpants.

sweaty ■ adj. (-ier, -iest) exuding, soaked in, or inducing sweat.
– DERIVATIVES **sweatily** adv. **sweatiness** n.

Swede ■ n. a native or national of Sweden, or a person of Swedish descent.
– ORIGIN from Middle Low German and Middle Dutch *Swēde*, prob. from Old Norse, from *Svíar* 'Swedes' + *thjóth* 'people'.

swede ■ n. a large, round yellow-fleshed root vegetable, originally from Sweden. ▸ the variety of rape which produces this root.

Swedish ■ n. the Scandinavian language of Sweden. ■ adj. of or relating to Sweden, its people, or their language.

sweep ■ v. (past and past part. **swept**) 1 clean (an area) by brushing away dirt or litter. ▸ move or remove by brushing. ▸ move or push with great force in a particular direction. ▸ (**sweep something away/aside**) remove something swiftly and suddenly. 2 search or survey (an area) for something. 3 pass or traverse swiftly and smoothly in a particular direction. ▸ affect (an area or place) swiftly and widely: *violence swept the country*. ▸ extend continuously, especially in an arc or curve. ▸ Cricket hit to the leg side by bringing the bat across the body from a half-kneeling position. ■ n. 1 an act of sweeping. ▸ short for CHIMNEY SWEEP. 2 a long, swift, curving movement. ▸ Electronics the movement of a beam across the screen of a cathode ray tube. 3 a long, typically curved stretch of road, river, etc. 4 the range or scope of something. 5 informal a sweepstake. 6 N. Amer. an instance of winning every event, award, or place in a contest. 7 a long heavy oar. 8 a sail of a windmill.
– PHRASES **sweep the board** win every event or prize in a contest.
– ORIGIN Old English, of Germanic origin.

sweeper ■ n. 1 a person or device that cleans by sweeping. 2 Soccer a player stationed behind the other defenders, free to defend at any point across the field.

sweeping ■ adj. 1 extending or performed in a long, continuous curve. 2 wide in range or effect. ▸ (of a statement) taking no account of particular cases or exceptions; too general. ■ n. (**sweepings**) dirt or refuse collected by sweeping.
– DERIVATIVES **sweepingly** adv. **sweepingness** n.

sweepstake ■ n. (also **sweepstakes**) a form of gambling, especially on sporting events, in which all the stakes are divided among the winners.

sweet ■ adj. 1 having the pleasant taste characteristic of sugar or honey; not salt, sour, or bitter. 2 (of air, water, etc.) fresh, pure, and untainted. ▸ fragrant. 3 pleasing in general; delightful. ▸ melodious or harmonious. ▸ chiefly US denoting music, especially jazz, played at a steady tempo without improvisation. 4 (of a person or action) pleasant and kind or thoughtful. ▸ charming and endearing. ▸ (**sweet on**) informal, dated infatuated with or in love with. ▸ dear; beloved. ■ n. 1 a small shaped piece of confectionery made with sugar. 2 a sweet dish forming a course of a meal; a pudding or dessert. 3 used as a very affectionate form of address.
– PHRASES **keep someone sweet** informal keep someone well disposed towards oneself, especially by favours or bribery.
– DERIVATIVES **sweetish** adj. **sweetly** adv.
– ORIGIN Old English, of Germanic origin.

sweet-and-sour ■ adj. cooked with both sugar and a sour substance, as vinegar or lemon.

sweetbread ■ n. the thymus gland (or, rarely, the pancreas) of an animal, used for food.

sweetbriar ■ n. a wild rose with fragrant leaves and flowers. [*Rosa eglanteria*.]

sweet butter ■ n. unsalted butter made from fresh pasteurized cream.

sweet cicely ■ n. see CICELY.

sweetcorn ■ n. maize of a variety with kernels that have a high sugar content, eaten as a vegetable.

sweeten ■ v. 1 make or become sweet or sweeter. 2 make more agreeable or acceptable.

sweetener ■ n. 1 a substance used to sweeten food or drink, especially one other than sugar. 2 informal an inducement, especially in the form of money or a concession.

sweet Fanny Adams ■ n. see FANNY ADAMS.

sweet flag ■ n. a waterside plant of the arum family with leaves like an iris and roots used medicinally and as a flavouring. [*Acorus calamus*.]

sweetgrass ■ n. any of a number of grasses which are fragrant or attractive to livestock. [*Glyceria*, *Hierochloe*, and other genera.]

sweet gum ■ n. a North American liquidambar tree which yields a balsam and decorative heartwood. [*Liquidambar styraciflua*.]

sweetheart ■ n. 1 a person that one is in love with. ▸ used as a term of endearment or affectionate form of address. 2 [as modifier] informal denoting an arrangement reached privately by two sides in their own interests: *a sweetheart deal*.

sweetheart neckline ■ n. a low neckline shaped like the top of a heart.

sweetie ■ n. informal 1 a sweet. 2 (also **sweetie-pie**) used as a term of endearment.

sweetlips ■ n. (pl. same) a fish of Indo-Pacific seas that changes its colour and markings with age. [*Plectorhynchus* and other genera: several species.]

sweetmeat ■ n. archaic an item of confectionery or sweet food.

sweet milk ■ n. fresh whole milk, as opposed to buttermilk.

sweetness ■ n. the quality of being sweet.
– PHRASES **sweetness and light** good-natured benevolence or harmony.

sweet pea ■ n. a climbing plant of the pea family, cultivated for its colourful fragrant flowers. [*Lathyrus odoratus* and related species.]

sweet pepper ■ n. a large green, yellow, orange, or red variety of capsicum with a mild or sweet flavour.

sweet potato ■ n. 1 an edible tuber with pinkish-orange slightly sweet flesh. 2 the Central American climbing plant which yields this tuber, widely cultivated in warm countries. [*Ipomoea batatas*.]

sweet-talk ■ v. informal persuade to do something by insincere flattery or kind words.

sweet thorn (also **Karoo thorn**) ■ n. a southern African acacia with long straight paired thorns and yellow flowers. [*Acacia karroo*.]

sweet tooth ■ n. (pl. **sweet tooths**) a great liking for sweet-tasting foods.
– DERIVATIVES **sweet-toothed** adj.

sweetveld /ˈswiːtfɛlt/ ■ n. S. African uncultivated land covered with nutritious grazing.
– ORIGIN C18: partial translation of Dutch *zoeteveld*, from *zoet* 'sweet, good' + *veld* 'land, countryside'.

sweet violet ■ n. a sweet-scented violet with heart-shaped leaves, used in perfumery and as a flavouring. [*Viola odorata*.]

sweet william ■ n. a fragrant garden pink with flattened clusters of vivid red, pink, or white flowers. [*Dianthus barbatus*.]

swell ■ v. (past part. **swollen** or **swelled**) **1** become larger or rounder in size, especially as a result of an accumulation of fluid. **2** become or make greater in intensity, amount, or volume. ■ n. **1** a full or gently rounded form. **2** a gradual increase in sound, amount, or intensity. ▸ a welling up of a feeling. **3** a slow, regular movement of the sea in rolling waves that do not break. **4** informal, dated a fashionable or stylish person of wealth or high social position. ■ adj. N. Amer. informal, dated excellent; very good. ■ adv. N. Amer. informal, dated excellently; very well.
– ORIGIN Old English, of Germanic origin.

swelling ■ n. an abnormal enlargement of a part of the body as a result of an accumulation of fluid. ▸ a natural rounded protuberance.

swelter ■ v. be uncomfortably hot. ■ n. an uncomfortably hot atmosphere.
– DERIVATIVES **sweltering** adj. **swelteringly** adv.
– ORIGIN Middle English: from dialect *swelt* 'perish', of Germanic origin.

swept past and past participle of **SWEEP**.

swept-wing ■ adj. (of an aircraft) having wings directed backwards from the fuselage.

swerve ■ v. abruptly diverge or cause to diverge from a straight course. ■ n. such a change of course. ▸ a tendency to swerve imparted to a ball.
– ORIGIN Old English *sweorfan* 'depart, leave, turn aside', of Germanic origin.

SWG ■ abbrev. standard wire gauge.

swidden /ˈswɪd(ə)n/ ■ n. the practice of clearing land for cultivation by slashing and burning vegetation. ▸ an area of land cleared in this way.
– ORIGIN C18: from dialect *swithen* 'to burn'.

swift ■ adj. **1** happening quickly or promptly. **2** moving or capable of moving at high speed. ■ adv. poetic/literary (except in combination) swiftly: *a swift-acting poison*. ■ n. **1** a fast-flying insectivorous bird with long, slender wings, spending most of its life on the wing. [*Apus* and other genera, family Apodidae.] **2** a moth, typically yellow-brown, with fast darting flight. [Family Hepialidae.]
– DERIVATIVES **swiftly** adv. **swiftness** n.
– ORIGIN Old English, from the Germanic base of Old English *swifan* 'move in a course, sweep'.

swig ■ v. (**swigged**, **swigging**) drink in large draughts. ■ n. a large draught of drink.
– ORIGIN C16.

swill ■ v. **1** Brit. wash or rinse out (an area or container) by pouring large amounts of water over or into it. ▸ cause to swirl round in a container or cavity. **2** informal drink greedily or in large quantities. ■ n. **1** kitchen refuse and waste food mixed with water for feeding to pigs. **2** informal a large mouthful of a drink.
– ORIGIN Old English.

swim ■ v. (**swimming**; past **swam**; past part. **swum**) **1** propel oneself through water by bodily movement. ▸ cross (a stretch of water) in this way. ▸ float. **2** be immersed in or covered with liquid. **3** appear to whirl before one's eyes. ▸ experience a dizzily confusing sensation. ■ n. an act or period of swimming.
– PHRASES **in the swim** involved in or aware of current affairs or events.
– DERIVATIVES **swimmable** adj. **swimmer** n. **swimming** n.
– ORIGIN Old English, of Germanic origin.

swim bladder ■ n. a gas-filled sac in a fish's body, used to maintain buoyancy.

swimfeeder ■ n. Fishing a small perforated container for bait, used to attract fish.

swimming costume ■ n. a garment worn for swimming, especially a woman's one-piece swimsuit.

swimmingly ■ adv. informal smoothly and satisfactorily.

swimming trunks (also **swim trunks**) ■ pl. n. shorts worn by men for swimming.

swimsuit ■ n. a woman's one-piece swimming costume.
– DERIVATIVES **swimsuited** adj.

1199

swipe

swimwear ■ n. clothing worn for swimming.

swindle ■ v. use deception to deprive of money or possessions. ▸ obtain fraudulently. ■ n. a fraudulent scheme or action.
– DERIVATIVES **swindler** n.
– ORIGIN C18: back-formation from *swindler*, from German *Schwindler*, from *schwindeln* 'be giddy', also 'tell lies'.

swine ■ n. **1** (pl. same) formal or N. Amer. a pig. **2** (pl. same or **swines**) informal a contemptible or disgusting person.
– DERIVATIVES **swinish** adj. **swinishness** n.
– ORIGIN Old English, of Germanic origin.

swine fever ■ n. an intestinal viral disease of pigs.

swine flu ■ n. influenza caused by a strain of influenza virus of type H1N1, thought to have been transmitted from pigs to humans in 2009 resulting in a pandemic.

swineherd ■ n. chiefly historical a person who tends pigs.

swine vesicular disease ■ n. an infectious viral disease of pigs causing blisters around the mouth and feet.

swing ■ v. (past and past part. **swung**) **1** move or cause to move back and forth or from side to side while or as if suspended. ▸ informal be executed by hanging. **2** move by grasping a support and leaping. ▸ move quickly round to the opposite direction. **3** move or cause to move in a smooth, curving line. ▸ (**swing at**) attempt to hit or punch, especially with a wide curving movement. ▸ throw (a punch) with such a movement. **4** shift or cause to shift from one opinion, mood, or state of affairs to another. ▸ have a decisive influence on (a vote, judgement, etc.). ▸ informal succeed in bringing about. **5** play music with an easy flowing but vigorous rhythm. **6** informal be lively, exciting, or fashionable. **7** informal be promiscuous, especially by swapping sexual partners. ■ n. **1** a seat suspended by ropes or chains, on which someone can sit and swing back and forth. **2** an act of swinging. ▸ the manner in which a golf club or a bat is swung. ▸ the motion of swinging. ▸ Cricket sideways deviation of the ball. **3** a discernible change in public opinion, especially in an election. **4** a style of jazz or dance music with an easy flowing but vigorous rhythm.
– PHRASES **get** (**back**) **into the swing of things** informal become accustomed to (or return to) an activity or routine. **go with a swing** informal (of a party or other event) be lively and enjoyable. **in full swing** at the height of activity. **swings and roundabouts** a situation in which different actions result in no eventual gain or loss.
– DERIVATIVES **swinger** n. **swingy** adj.
– ORIGIN Old English *swingan* 'to beat, whip', *geswing* 'a stroke with a weapon', of Germanic origin.

swingbin ■ n. a rubbish bin with a lid that swings shut.

swing bridge ■ n. a bridge that can be swung to one side to allow ships to pass.

swing coat ■ n. a coat cut so as to swing when the wearer moves.

swing door ■ n. a door that can be opened in either direction and swings back when released.

swingeing ■ adj. chiefly Brit. severe or otherwise extreme.
– DERIVATIVES **swingeingly** adv.

swinging ■ adj. informal lively, exciting, and fashionable. ▸ sexually liberated or promiscuous.
– DERIVATIVES **swingingly** adv.

swingman ■ n. (pl. -**men**) Basketball a player who can play both guard and forward.

swingometer /swɪŋˈɒmɪtə/ ■ n. informal a device or computerized display used to demonstrate the effect of a political swing in an election.

swing shift ■ n. N. Amer. a work shift from afternoon to late evening.

swing-wing ■ n. an aircraft wing that can move from a right-angled to a swept-back position.

swipe informal ■ v. **1** hit or try to hit with a swinging blow. **2** steal. **3** pass (a swipe card) through an electronic reader. ■ n. a sweeping blow. ▸ an attack or criticism.
– DERIVATIVES **swiper** n.
– ORIGIN C18: perhaps a var. of **SWEEP**.

swipe card

swipe card ■ n. a plastic card bearing magnetically encoded information which is read when the card is slid through an electronic device.

swirl ■ v. move or cause to move in a twisting or spiralling pattern. ■ n. a swirling movement or pattern.
– DERIVATIVES **swirly** adj.
– ORIGIN Middle English: perhaps of Low German or Dutch origin.

swish ■ v. 1 move or cause to move with a hissing or rushing sound. 2 Basketball sink (a shot) without the ball touching the backboard or rim. ■ n. 1 a swishing sound or movement. 2 Basketball a swishing shot. ■ adj. Brit. informal impressively smart and fashionable.
– ORIGIN C18: imitative.

swishy ■ adj. 1 making a swishing sound or movement. 2 informal swish.

Swiss ■ adj. of or relating to Switzerland or its people. ■ n. (pl. same) a native or national of Switzerland, or a person of Swiss descent.
– ORIGIN C16: from French *Suisse*, from Middle High German *Swīz* 'Switzerland'.

Swiss cheese plant ■ n. a house plant with perforated leaves (supposedly resembling the holes in a Swiss cheese). [*Monstera deliciosa*.]

Swiss roll ■ n. a cake made from a sponge cake spread with a filling such as jam and rolled up.

switch ■ n. 1 a device for making and breaking an electrical connection. ▶ Computing a program variable which activates or deactivates a function. ▶ Computing a device which forwards data packets to an appropriate part of the network. 2 a change, especially a radical one. 3 a slender, flexible shoot cut from a tree. 4 a tress of hair used in hairdressing to supplement natural hair. ■ v. 1 change in position, direction, or focus. ▶ exchange. 2 (**switch something off/on**) turn an electrical device off (or on). 3 (**switch off**) informal cease to pay attention.
– DERIVATIVES **switchable** adj.
– ORIGIN C16: prob. from Low German.

switchback ■ n. 1 Brit. a road, railway, etc. with alternate sharp ascents and descents. ▶ a roller coaster. 2 N. Amer. a hairpin bend.

switchblade ■ n. chiefly N. Amer. another term for FLICK KNIFE.

switchboard ■ n. 1 an installation for the manual control of telephone connections. 2 an apparatus for varying connections between electric circuits.

switched-on ■ adj. informal aware of what is going on or up to date.

switcher ■ n. a device used to select or combine different video and audio signals.

switchgear ■ n. electrical switching equipment.

switch-hitter ■ n. Baseball an ambidextrous batter.
– DERIVATIVES **switch-hitting** adj.

swivel ■ n. a coupling between two parts enabling one to revolve without turning the other. ■ v. (**swivelled**, **swivelling**; US **swiveled**, **swiveling**) turn on or as if on a swivel.
– ORIGIN Middle English, from the base of Old English *swīfan* 'move (along a course), sweep'.

swivel chair ■ n. a chair able to be turned on its base to face in any direction.

swizzle stick ■ n. a stick used for frothing up or taking the fizz out of drinks.

swollen past participle of SWELL.

swoon ■ v. faint, especially from extreme emotion. ■ n. an occurrence of swooning.
– ORIGIN Middle English: as *swown* 'fainting', *aswoon* 'in a faint', both from Old English *geswōgen* 'overcome'.

swoop ■ v. 1 (especially of a bird) move rapidly downwards through the air. ▶ carry out a sudden raid. 2 informal seize with a sweeping motion. ■ n. an act of swooping.
– PHRASES **at** (or **in**) **one fell swoop** see FELL[4].
– ORIGIN C16: perhaps a var. of Old English *swāpan* 'sweep'.

swoosh /swuːʃ, swʊʃ/ ■ n. the sound produced by a sudden rush of air or liquid. ■ v. move with such a sound.
– ORIGIN C19: imitative.

swop ■ v.& n. variant spelling of SWAP.

sword ■ n. 1 a weapon with a long metal blade and a hilt with a handguard, used for thrusting or striking and often worn as part of ceremonial dress. ▶ (**the sword**) poetic/literary military power; violence. 2 (**swords**) one of the suits in a tarot pack.
– PHRASES **beat** (or **turn**) **swords into ploughshares** devote resources to peaceful rather than warlike ends. [with biblical allusion to Isaiah 2:4 and Micah 4:3.] **put to the sword** kill, especially in war.
– ORIGIN Old English, of Germanic origin.

sword-bearer ■ n. an official who carries a sword for a dignitary on formal occasions.

swordfish ■ n. (pl. same or **-fishes**) a large edible marine fish with a streamlined body and a long sword-like snout. [*Xiphias gladius*.]

sword of Damocles /ˈdaməkliːz/ ■ n. an impending danger.
– ORIGIN with ref. to *Damocles*, who flattered the Greek ruler Dionysius I so much that the king made him feast sitting under a sword suspended by a single hair.

sword of state ■ n. the sword carried in front of a sovereign on state occasions.

swordplay ■ n. the activity or skill of fencing with swords or foils.

swordsman ■ n. (pl. **-men**) a man who fights with a sword.
– DERIVATIVES **swordsmanship** n.

swordstick ■ n. a hollow walking stick containing a blade that can be used as a sword.

swordtail ■ n. a Central American freshwater fish popular in aquaria, the male of which has a tail with an elongated and brightly marked lower edge. [*Xiphophorus helleri*.]

swore past of SWEAR.

sworn past participle of SWEAR. ■ adj. 1 given under oath: *a sworn statement*. 2 determined to remain such: *sworn enemies*.

SWOT ■ abbrev. (in business) strengths, weaknesses, opportunities, threats.

swot ■ v. (**swotted**, **swotting**) (also **swot up**) informal study assiduously or intensively.
– ORIGIN C19: dialect var. of SWEAT.

swot week ■ n. S. African & Austral. (in some universities) a period when no lectures take place in order that students may prepare for exams.

swum past participle of SWIM.

swung past and past participle of SWING.

swung dash ■ n. a curving printed dash (~).

-sy ■ suffix forming diminutive nouns and adjectives such as *folksy*, *mopsy*, also pet names such as *Patsy*.

sybarite /ˈsɪbərʌɪt/ ■ n. a person who is self-indulgently fond of sensuous luxury.
– DERIVATIVES **sybaritic** adj. **sybaritism** n.
– ORIGIN C16 (orig. denoting an inhabitant of Sybaris, an ancient Greek city in southern Italy, noted for luxury): from Greek *Subarītēs*.

sycamore ■ n. 1 a large maple native to central and southern Europe. [*Acer pseudoplatanus*.] 2 (also **sycamore fig**) a Middle Eastern fig tree. [*Ficus sycomorus*.]
– ORIGIN Middle English: from Old French *sic(h)amor*, from Greek *sukomoros*, from *sukon* 'fig' + *moron* 'mulberry'.

sycophant /ˈsɪkəfant/ ■ n. a toady; a servile flatterer.
– DERIVATIVES **sycophancy** n. **sycophantic** adj. **sycophantically** adv.
– ORIGIN C16: from French *sycophante*, or from Greek *sukophantēs* 'informer', from *sukon* 'fig' + *phainein* 'to show', perhaps with ref. to making the insulting gesture of the 'fig' (sticking the thumb between two fingers) to informers.

sycosis /sʌɪˈkəʊsɪs/ ■ n. Medicine inflammation of facial hair follicles, caused by bacterial infection.
– ORIGIN C16: from Greek *sukōsis*, from *sukon* 'fig'.

Sydenham's chorea ■ n. a form of chorea chiefly affecting children, associated with rheumatic fever.

−ORIGIN C19: named after the C17 English physician Thomas *Sydenham*.

syenite /ˈsʌɪənʌɪt/ ■ n. Geology a coarse-grained grey igneous rock composed typically of alkali feldspar and hornblende.
−DERIVATIVES **syenitic** adj.
−ORIGIN C18: from French *syénite*, from Latin *Syenites (lapis)* '(stone) of *Syene*', Greek name of Aswan in Egypt.

syl- ■ prefix variant spelling of SYN- assimilated before *l* (as in *syllogism*).

syllabary /ˈsɪləb(ə)ri/ ■ n. (pl. **-ies**) a set of written characters representing syllables, serving the purpose of an alphabet.
−ORIGIN C19: from Latin *syllaba* 'syllable'.

syllabi plural form of SYLLABUS.

syllabic /sɪˈlabɪk/ ■ adj. of, relating to, or based on syllables. ▸ (of a consonant) constituting a whole syllable.
−DERIVATIVES **syllabically** adv. **syllabicity** n.

syllabification /sɪˌlabɪfɪˈkeɪʃ(ə)n/ (also **syllabication**) ■ n. the division of words into syllables.
−DERIVATIVES **syllabify** v. (**-ies**, **-ied**).

syllabize (also **-ise**) ■ v. divide into or articulate by syllables.

syllable /ˈsɪləb(ə)l/ ■ n. a unit of pronunciation having one vowel sound, with or without surrounding consonants, and forming all or part of a word. ■ v. pronounce clearly, syllable by syllable.
−DERIVATIVES **syllabled** adj.
−ORIGIN Middle English: from Old French *sillabe*, from Greek *sullabē*, from *sun-* 'together' + *lambanein* 'take'.

syllabub /ˈsɪləbʌb/ ■ n. a whipped cream dessert, typically flavoured with white wine or sherry.

syllabus /ˈsɪləbəs/ ■ n. (pl. **syllabuses** or **syllabi** /-bʌɪ/) the subjects in a course of study or teaching.
−ORIGIN C17: orig. a misreading of Latin *sittybas*, from Greek *sittuba* 'title slip, label'.

syllogism /ˈsɪləˌdʒɪz(ə)m/ ■ n. a form of reasoning in which a conclusion is drawn from two given or assumed propositions (premises); a common or middle term is present in the two premises but not in the conclusion, which may be invalid (e.g. *all dogs are animals; all animals have four legs; therefore all dogs have four legs*).
−DERIVATIVES **syllogistic** adj. **syllogistically** adv. **syllogize** (also **-ise**) v.
−ORIGIN Middle English: from Greek *sullogismos*, from *sullogizesthai*, from *sun-* 'with' + *logizesthai* 'to reason', from *logos* 'reasoning'.

sylph /sɪlf/ ■ n. 1 an imaginary spirit of the air. 2 a slender woman or girl.
−DERIVATIVES **sylphlike** adj.
−ORIGIN C17: perhaps from Latin *sylvestris* 'of the woods' + *nympha* 'nymph'.

sylvan (also **silvan**) ■ adj. chiefly poetic/literary consisting of or associated with woods; wooded. ▸ pleasantly rural or pastoral.
−ORIGIN C16: from French *sylvain* or Latin *Silvanus* 'woodland deity', from *silva* 'a wood'.

sylvatic /sɪlˈvatɪk/ ■ adj. Veterinary Medicine relating to or denoting forms of disease contracted by wild animals.
−ORIGIN 1930S: from Latin *silvaticus*, from *silva* 'wood'.

Sylvian fissure /ˈsɪlvɪən/ ■ n. Anatomy a large diagonal fissure which separates off the temporal lobe of the brain.
−ORIGIN C19: named after the C17 Flemish anatomist François de la Boë *Sylvius*.

sylvite /ˈsɪlvʌɪt/ ■ n. a colourless or white mineral consisting of potassium chloride.
−ORIGIN C19: from modern Latin (*sal digestivus*) *Sylvii*, the old name of this salt.

sym- ■ prefix variant spelling of SYN- assimilated before *b*, *m*, *p* (as in *symbiosis*, *symmetry*, *symphysis*).

symbiont /ˈsɪmbɪɒnt, -bʌɪ-/ ■ n. Biology an organism living in symbiosis with another.
−ORIGIN C19: from Greek *sumbiōn* 'living together', from *sumbioun* (see SYMBIOSIS).

symbiosis /ˌsɪmbɪˈəʊsɪs, -bʌɪ-/ ■ n. (pl. **symbioses** /-siːz/) Biology an interaction between two different organisms living in close physical association, especially to the advantage of both.
−DERIVATIVES **symbiotic** /-ˈɒtɪk/ adj. **symbiotically** adv.

−ORIGIN C19: from Greek *sumbiōsis* 'a living together', from *sumbioun* 'live together', from *sumbios* 'companion'.

symbol ■ n. 1 a thing that represents or stands for something else, especially a material object representing something abstract. 2 a mark or character used as a conventional representation of something, e.g. a letter standing for a chemical element or a character in musical notation.
−ORIGIN Middle English: from Latin *symbolum* 'symbol, Creed (as the mark of a Christian)', from Greek *sumbolon* 'mark, token', from *sun-* 'with' + *ballein* 'to throw'.

symbolic ■ adj. 1 serving as a symbol. 2 involving the use of symbols or symbolism.
−DERIVATIVES **symbolical** adj. **symbolically** adv.
−ORIGIN C17: from French *symbolique* or late Latin *symbolicus*, from Greek *sumbolikos*.

symbolic logic ■ n. the use of symbols to denote propositions, terms, and relations in order to assist reasoning.

symbolism ■ n. the use of symbols to represent ideas or qualities. ▸ symbolic meaning.
−DERIVATIVES **symbolist** n. & adj.

symbolize (also **-ise**) ■ v. be a symbol of. ▸ represent by means of symbols.
−DERIVATIVES **symbolization** (also **-isation**) n.

symbology ■ n. the study or use of symbols. ▸ symbols collectively.

symmetrical ■ adj. made up of exactly similar parts facing each other or around an axis; showing symmetry.
−DERIVATIVES **symmetric** adj. **symmetrically** adv.

symmetry /ˈsɪmɪtri/ ■ n. (pl. **-ies**) the quality of being made up of exactly similar parts facing each other or around an axis. ▸ correct or pleasing proportion of parts. ▸ similarity or exact correspondence. ▸ Physics & Mathematics the property of being unchanged by a given operation or process.
−DERIVATIVES **symmetrize** (also **-ise**) v.
−ORIGIN C16: from French *symétrie* or Latin *symmetria*, from Greek, from *sun-* 'with' + *metron* 'measure'.

sympathetic ■ adj. 1 feeling, showing, or expressing sympathy. ▸ showing approval of an idea or action. 2 likeable. ▸ designed in a sensitive or fitting way. 3 Physiology relating to or denoting the part of the autonomic nervous system supplying the internal organs, blood vessels, and glands, and balancing the action of the parasympathetic nerves. 4 of or denoting an effect which arises in response to a similar action elsewhere.
−DERIVATIVES **sympathetically** adv.

sympathetic magic ■ n. occult rituals using objects or actions to represent the event or person over which influence is sought.

sympathize (also **-ise**) ■ v. 1 feel or express sympathy. 2 agree with a sentiment or feeling.
−DERIVATIVES **sympathizer** (also **-iser**) n.

sympathomimetic /ˌsɪmpəθəʊmɪˈmɛtɪk, -mʌɪ-/ Medicine ■ adj. promoting the stimulation of sympathetic nerves. ■ n. a sympathomimetic drug.

sympathy ■ n. (pl. **-ies**) 1 feelings of pity and sorrow for someone else's misfortune. ▸ (**one's sympathies**) condolences. 2 understanding between people; common feeling. ▸ a favourable attitude. ▸ (**in sympathy**) relating harmoniously to something else; in keeping. ▸ the state or fact of responding in a way corresponding to an action elsewhere.
−ORIGIN C16: from Greek *sumpatheia*, from *sumpathēs*, from *sun-* 'with' + *pathos* 'feeling'.

sympatric /sɪmˈpatrɪk/ ■ adj. Biology (of animal or plant species or populations) occurring in the same or overlapping geographical areas. Compare with ALLOPATRIC.
−DERIVATIVES **sympatry** n.
−ORIGIN C20: from SYM- + Greek *patra* 'fatherland'.

sympetalous /sɪmˈpɛt(ə)ləs/ ■ adj. Botany having the petals united along their margins to form a tubular shape.

symphonic ■ adj. relating to or having the form or character of a symphony.
−DERIVATIVES **symphonically** adv.

symphonic poem

symphonic poem ■ n. another term for TONE POEM.
symphonist ■ n. a composer of symphonies.
symphony ■ n. (pl. **-ies**) an elaborate musical composition for full orchestra, typically in four movements with at least one in sonata form. ▶ chiefly historical an orchestral interlude in a large-scale vocal work. ▶ chiefly N. Amer. (especially in names) short for SYMPHONY ORCHESTRA.
– ORIGIN Middle English: from Old French *symphonie*, from Greek *sumphōnia*, from *sumphōnos* 'harmonious', from *sun-* 'together' + *phōnē* 'sound'.
symphony orchestra ■ n. a large classical orchestra, including string, wind, brass, and percussion instruments.
symphysis /ˈsɪmfɪsɪs/ ■ n. (pl. **symphyses** /-siːz/) Anatomy a place where two bones are immovably joined (e.g. the pubic bones in the pelvis) or completely fused (e.g. at the midline of the lower jaw).
– DERIVATIVES **symphyseal** (also **symphysial**) /-ˈfɪzɪəl/ adj.
– ORIGIN C16: from Greek *sumphusis*, from *sun-* 'together' + *phusis* 'growth'.
symposium /sɪmˈpəʊzɪəm/ ■ n. (pl. **symposia** /-zɪə/ or **symposiums**) a conference or meeting to discuss a particular academic or specialist subject. ▶ a collection of related papers by a number of contributors.
– ORIGIN C16: from Greek *sumposion*, from *sumpotēs* 'fellow drinker', from *sun-* 'together' + *potēs* 'drinker'.
symptom ■ n. Medicine a feature which indicates a condition of disease, in particular one apparent to the patient. Compare with SIGN. ▶ an indication of an undesirable situation.
– DERIVATIVES **symptomless** adj.
– ORIGIN Middle English *synthoma*, from Greek *sumptōma* 'chance, symptom', from *sumpiptein* 'happen'; later influenced by French *symptome*.
symptomatic ■ adj. acting as a symptom of something. ▶ Medicine exhibiting or involving symptoms.
– DERIVATIVES **symptomatically** adv.
symptomatology /ˌsɪm(p)təˈmɒtələdʒi/ ■ n. Medicine a set of symptoms.
syn- ■ prefix united; acting together: *synchrony*.
– ORIGIN from Greek *sun* 'with'.
synagogue /ˈsɪnəɡɒɡ/ ■ n. a building where a Jewish assembly or congregation meets for religious observance and instruction. ▶ such an assembly or congregation.
– DERIVATIVES **synagogal** adj. **synagogical** adj.
– ORIGIN Middle English: from Greek *sunagōgē* 'meeting', from *sun-* 'together' + *agein* 'bring'.
synapomorphy /sɪˈnapə(ʊ)ˌmɔːfi/ ■ n. (pl. **-ies**) Biology the possession by two organisms of a characteristic derived from one in an evolutionary ancestor.
– ORIGIN 1960s: from SYN- + APO- + Greek *morphē* 'form'.
synapse /ˈsaɪnaps, ˈsɪn-/ ■ n. a gap between two nerve cells, across which impulses pass by diffusion of a neurotransmitter.
– DERIVATIVES **synaptic** adj. **synaptically** adv.
– ORIGIN C19: from Greek *sunapsis*, from *sun-* 'together' + *hapsis* 'joining', from *haptein* 'to join'.
sync (also **synch**) informal ■ n. synchronization. ■ v. synchronize.
– PHRASES **in** (or **out of**) **sync** working well (or badly) together.
syncarpous /sɪnˈkɑːpəs/ ■ adj. Botany having the carpels united.
– ORIGIN C19: from SYN- + Greek *karpos* 'fruit'.
synchro /ˈsɪŋkrəʊ/ ■ n. **1** short for SYNCHROMESH. **2** synchronized or synchronization. **3** short for SYNCHRONIZED SWIMMING.
synchro- ■ comb. form synchronous: *synchrotron*.
synchromesh ■ n. a system of gear changing in which the driving and driven gearwheels are made to revolve at the same speed during engagement.
– ORIGIN 1920s: contraction of *synchronized mesh*.
synchronic /sɪŋˈkrɒnɪk/ ■ adj. concerned with something (especially a language) as it exists at one point in time. Often contrasted with DIACHRONIC.
– DERIVATIVES **synchronically** adv.
synchronicity /ˌsɪŋkrəˈnɪsɪti/ ■ n. **1** the simultaneous occurrence of events with no discernible causal connection. **2** the state of being synchronous or synchronic.
synchronism /ˈsɪŋkrənɪz(ə)m/ ■ n. another term for SYNCHRONY.
– DERIVATIVES **synchronistic** adj. **synchronistically** adv.
synchronize /ˈsɪŋkrənaɪz/ (also **-ise**) ■ v. cause to occur or operate at the same time or rate.
– DERIVATIVES **synchronization** (also **-isation**) n. **synchronizer** (also **-iser**) n.
synchronized swimming ■ n. a sport in which teams of swimmers perform coordinated or identical movements in time to music.
synchronous /ˈsɪŋkrənəs/ ■ adj. **1** existing or occurring at the same time. **2** another term for GEOSYNCHRONOUS.
– DERIVATIVES **synchronously** adv.
– ORIGIN C17: from late Latin *synchronus*, from Greek *sunkhronos*, from *sun-* 'together' + *khronos* 'time'.
synchronous motor ■ n. an electric motor having a speed exactly proportional to the current frequency.
synchrony /ˈsɪŋkrəni/ ■ n. **1** simultaneous action, development, or occurrence. **2** synchronic treatment or study.
synchrotron /ˈsɪŋkrə(ʊ)trɒn/ ■ n. Physics a cyclotron in which the magnetic field strength increases with the energy of the particles to keep their orbital radius constant.
synchrotron radiation ■ n. Physics polarized radiation emitted by a charged particle spinning in a magnetic field.
syncline /ˈsɪŋklaɪn/ ■ n. Geology a trough or fold of stratified rock in which the strata slope upwards from the axis. Compare with ANTICLINE.
– DERIVATIVES **synclinal** adj.
– ORIGIN C19: from SYN- + Greek *klinein* 'to lean'.
syncopate /ˈsɪŋkəpeɪt/ ■ v. [usu. as adj. **syncopated**] displace the beats or accents in (music or a rhythm) so that strong beats become weak and vice versa.
– DERIVATIVES **syncopation** n. **syncopator** n.
syncope /ˈsɪŋkəpi/ ■ n. **1** Medicine temporary loss of consciousness caused by low blood pressure. **2** Grammar the omission of sounds or letters from within a word, for example when *library* is pronounced /ˈlaɪbri/.
– DERIVATIVES **syncopal** adj.
– ORIGIN Middle English: from Greek *sunkopē*, from *sun-* 'together' + *koptein* 'strike, cut off'.
syncretism /ˈsɪŋkrɪtɪz(ə)m/ ■ n. **1** the amalgamation of different religions, cultures, or schools of thought. **2** Linguistics the merging of different inflectional varieties of a word during the development of a language.
– DERIVATIVES **syncretic** adj. **syncretist** n. & adj. **syncretistic** adj.
– ORIGIN C17: from Greek *sunkrētismos*, from *sunkrētizein* 'unite against a third party', from *sun-* 'together' + *krēs* 'Cretan' (orig. with ref. to ancient Cretan communities).
syncretize (also **-ise**) ■ v. attempt to amalgamate (differing religious beliefs, schools of thought, etc.).
– DERIVATIVES **syncretization** (also **-isation**) n.
syncytium /sɪnˈsɪtɪəm/ ■ n. (pl. **syncytia** /-tɪə/) Biology a single cell or cytoplasmic mass containing several nuclei.
– DERIVATIVES **syncytial** adj.
– ORIGIN C19: from SYN- + -CYTE.
syndactyl /sɪnˈdaktɪl/ ■ adj. Medicine & Zoology having digits wholly or partly united, either naturally (as in web-footed animals) or as a malformation.
– DERIVATIVES **syndactyly** n.
syndicalism ■ n. historical a movement for transferring the ownership and control of the means of production and distribution to workers' unions.
– DERIVATIVES **syndicalist** n. & adj.
– ORIGIN C20: from French *syndicalisme*, from *syndical*, from Greek *sundikos*, from *sun-* together + *dikē* 'justice'.
syndicate ■ n. /ˈsɪndɪkət/ a group of individuals or organizations combined to promote some common interest. ▶ an agency supplying material simultaneously to a number of news media. ■ v. /ˈsɪndɪkeɪt/ control or manage by a syndicate. ▶ publish or broadcast simultaneously in a number of media.
– DERIVATIVES **syndication** n.

– ORIGIN C17: from French *syndicat*, from medieval Latin *syndicatus*, from Greek *sundikos* (see **SYNDICALISM**).

syndrome ■ n. **1** a group of symptoms which consistently occur together. **2** a characteristic combination of opinions, emotions, or behaviour.
– DERIVATIVES **syndromic** adj.
– ORIGIN C16: from Greek *sundromē*, from *sun-* 'together' + *dramein* 'to run'.

synecdoche /sɪˈnɛkdəki/ ■ n. a figure of speech in which a part is made to represent the whole or vice versa, as in *South Africa lost by six wickets* (meaning 'the South African cricket team').
– DERIVATIVES **synecdochic** adj. **synecdochical** adj.
– ORIGIN Middle English: from Greek *sunekdokhē*, from *sun-* 'together' + *ekdekhesthai* 'take up'.

synecology /ˌsɪnɪˈkɒlədʒi/ ■ n. Biology the ecological study of whole plant or animal communities. Contrasted with **AUTECOLOGY**.
– DERIVATIVES **synecological** /-ˌiːkəˈlɒdʒɪk(ə)l, -ˌɛk-/ adj.

synergist ■ n. an agent that participates in synergy.
– DERIVATIVES **synergistic** adj. **synergistically** adv.

synergy /ˈsɪnədʒi/ (also **synergism**) ■ n. interaction or cooperation of two or more organizations, substances, or other agents to produce a combined effect greater than the sum of their separate effects.
– DERIVATIVES **synergetic** adj. **synergic** adj.
– ORIGIN C19: from Greek *sunergos* 'working together'.

syngamy /ˈsɪŋɡəmi/ ■ n. Biology the fusion of two cells in reproduction.
– ORIGIN 1904: from **SYN-** + Greek *gamos* 'marriage'.

syngas ■ n. a mixture of carbon monoxide and hydrogen used as a feedstock in making synthetic chemicals.
– ORIGIN 1970s: abbrev. of *synthesis gas*.

synod /ˈsɪnəd, -ɒd/ ■ n. **1** an assembly of the clergy (and sometimes also the laity) in a division of a Christian Church. **2** a Presbyterian ecclesiastical court above the presbyteries and subject to the General Assembly.
– DERIVATIVES **synodal** adj.
– ORIGIN Middle English: from Greek *sunodos* 'meeting', from *sun-* 'together' + *hodos* 'way'.

synodic /sɪˈnɒdɪk/ ■ adj. Astronomy relating to or involving a conjunction.
– ORIGIN C17: from Greek *sunodikos*, from *sunodos* (see **SYNOD**).

synodical ■ adj. Christian Church of, relating to, or constituted as a synod.

synonym /ˈsɪnənɪm/ ■ n. a word or phrase that means the same as another word or phrase in the same language, e.g. *shut* and *close*.
– DERIVATIVES **synonymic** adj. **synonymity** n. **synonymy** /sɪˈnɒnɪmi/ n.
– ORIGIN Middle English: from Greek *sunōnumon*, from *sunōnumos*, from *sun-* 'with' + *onoma* 'name'.

synonymous /sɪˈnɒnɪməs/ ■ adj. (of a word or phrase) having the same meaning as another word or phrase in the same language. ▸ closely associated with something: *his name was synonymous with victory*.
– DERIVATIVES **synonymously** adv. **synonymousness** n.

synopsis /sɪˈnɒpsɪs/ ■ n. (pl. **synopses** /-siːz/) a brief summary of something.
– DERIVATIVES **synopsize** (also **-ise**) v.
– ORIGIN C17: from Greek, from *sun-* 'together' + *opsis* 'seeing'.

synoptic ■ adj. **1** of, forming, or involving a synopsis or general view. **2** (**Synoptic**) relating to or denoting the Gospels of Matthew, Mark, and Luke, which describe events from a similar point of view, as contrasted with that of John.
– DERIVATIVES **synoptical** adj. **synoptically** adv.

synovial /saɪˈnəʊvɪəl, sɪ-/ ■ adj. relating to or denoting a type of joint which is surrounded by a thick flexible membrane containing a viscous fluid that lubricates the joint.
– ORIGIN C18: from modern Latin *synovia*, prob. formed arbitrarily by the C16 Swiss physician Paracelsus.

synovitis /ˌsaɪnə(ʊ)ˈvaɪtɪs, ˌsɪn-/ ■ n. Medicine inflammation of a synovial membrane.

syntagm /ˈsɪntam/ (also **syntagma** /sɪnˈtaɡmə/) ■ n. (pl. **syntagms**, **syntagmas**, or **syntagmata** /-mətə/) Linguistics a set of forms in a sequential relationship. Often contrasted with **PARADIGM**.
– DERIVATIVES **syntagmatic** /ˌsɪntaɡˈmatɪk/ adj. **syntagmatically** adv. **syntagmatics** pl. n.
– ORIGIN C17: from Greek *suntagma*, from *suntassein* 'arrange together'.

syntax /ˈsɪntaks/ ■ n. **1** the arrangement of words and phrases to create well-formed sentences. ▸ a set of rules for or an analysis of this. **2** the structure of statements in a computer language.
– DERIVATIVES **syntactic** adj. **syntactical** adj. **syntactically** adv.
– ORIGIN C16: from French *syntaxe*, or from Greek *suntaxis*, from *sun-* 'together' + *tassein* 'arrange'.

synth ■ n. informal short for **SYNTHESIZER**.
– DERIVATIVES **synthy** adj.

synthase /ˈsɪnθeɪz/ ■ n. Biochemistry an enzyme which brings about the linkage of two molecules.

synthesis /ˈsɪnθɪsɪs/ ■ n. (pl. **syntheses** /-siːz/) **1** the combination of components to form a connected whole. Often contrasted with **ANALYSIS**. **2** the production of chemical compounds by reaction from simpler materials. **3** Grammar the process of making compound and derivative words.
– DERIVATIVES **synthesist** n.
– ORIGIN C17: from Greek *sunthesis*, from *suntithenai* 'place together'.

synthesize /ˈsɪnθɪsaɪz/ (also **synthetize**, **-ise**) ■ v. **1** make by synthesis. ▸ combine into a coherent whole. **2** produce (sound) electronically.

synthesizer (also **-iser**) ■ n. an electronic musical instrument, typically operated by a keyboard, producing sounds by generating and combining signals of different frequencies.

synthetic /sɪnˈθɛtɪk/ ■ adj. **1** made by chemical synthesis, especially to imitate a natural product. ▸ not genuine; unnatural. **2** Logic having truth or falsity determinable by recourse to experience. Compare with **ANALYTIC**. **3** Linguistics (of a language) tending to use inflections rather than word order to express grammatical structure. Contrasted with **ANALYTIC**. ■ n. a synthetic substance, especially a textile fibre.
– DERIVATIVES **synthetical** adj. **synthetically** adv.
– ORIGIN C17: from French *synthétique*, from Greek *sunthetikos*, from *suntithenai* 'place together'.

syntype ■ n. Botany & Zoology each of a set of type specimens upon which the description and name of a new species is jointly based.

syphilis ■ n. a sexually transmitted bacterial disease, progressing if untreated from infection of the genitals via the skin and mucous membranes to the bones, muscles, and brain.
– DERIVATIVES **syphilitic** adj. & n.
– ORIGIN C18: from *Syphilis, sive Morbus Gallicus*, the title of a poem (1530), from the name of the character *Syphilus*, the supposed first sufferer of the disease.

syphon ■ n. & v. variant spelling of **SIPHON**.

Syrah /ˈsiːrə/ ■ n. another term for **SHIRAZ**.

syrette /sɪˈrɛt/ ■ n. Medicine, trademark a disposable syringe with a single dose of a drug.
– ORIGIN 1940s: from **SYRINGE** + **-ETTE**.

Syriac /ˈsɪrɪak/ ■ n. the language of ancient Syria, a western dialect of Aramaic.

Syrian /ˈsɪrɪən/ ■ n. a native or inhabitant of Syria. ■ adj. of or relating to Syria.

syringa ■ n. **1** (also **seringa**) S. African a tall tree bearing fragrant lilac flowers and yellow berries, native to Asia and Australasia. [*Melia azedarach*.] ▸ used in names of other trees, e.g. wild syringa. **2** another term for **MOCK ORANGE**.

syringe /sɪˈrɪn(d)ʒ, ˈsɪ-/ ■ n. a tube with a nozzle and piston or bulb for sucking in and ejecting liquid in a thin stream, often one fitted with a hollow needle for injecting or withdrawing fluids into or from the body. ■ v. (**syringing**) spray liquid into or over with a syringe.
– ORIGIN Middle English: from medieval Latin *syringa*, from *syrinx* (see **SYRINX**).

syrinx

syrinx /'sırıŋks/ ■ n. (pl. **syrinxes**) Ornithology the lower larynx or voice organ, especially in songbirds (in which it is well developed).
– ORIGIN C17: from Greek *surinx* 'pipe, channel'.

Syro- /'sʌɪrəʊ/ ■ comb. form Syrian; Syrian and ...: *Syro-Palestinian*.

syrphid /'sə:fɪd/ ■ n. Entomology a fly of the hoverfly family (Syrphidae).
– ORIGIN C19: from the genus name *Syrphus*, from Greek *surphos* 'gnat'.

syrup (US also **sirup**) ■ n. a thick sweet liquid made by dissolving sugar in boiling water. ▸ a thick sweet liquid containing medicine or used as a drink. ▸ a thick, sticky liquid obtained from sugar cane as part of the processing of sugar.
– ORIGIN Middle English: from Old French *sirop* or medieval Latin *siropus*, from Arabic *šarāb* 'beverage'.

syrupy (US also **sirupy**) ■ adj. **1** having the consistency or sweetness of syrup. **2** excessively sentimental.

sysadmin /sɪs'admɪn/ ■ n. informal term for SYSTEM ADMINISTRATOR.

system ■ n. **1** a complex whole; a set of things working together as a mechanism or interconnecting network. ▸ the human or animal body as a whole. **2** an organized scheme or method. ▸ orderliness; method. **3** the prevailing political or social order, especially when regarded as oppressive and intransigent. **4** Geology a major range of strata corresponding to a period in time.
– PHRASES **get something out of one's system** informal get rid of a preoccupation or anxiety.
– ORIGIN C17: from French *système* or late Latin *systema*, from Greek *sustēma*, from *sun-* 'with' + *histanai* 'set up'.

system administrator ■ n. a person who manages the operation of a computer system or particular electronic communication service.

systematic ■ adj. done or acting according to a fixed plan or system; methodical.
– DERIVATIVES **systematically** adv. **systematist** /'sɪstəmətɪst/ n.
– ORIGIN C18: from French *systématique*, from late Greek *sustēmatikos*, from *sustēma* (see SYSTEM).

systematic error ■ n. Statistics an error whose effect is not reduced when observations are averaged.

systematics ■ pl. n. [treated as sing.] the branch of biology concerned with classification and nomenclature; taxonomy.

systematic theology ■ n. a form of theology in which the aim is to arrange religious beliefs in a self-consistent whole.

systematize /'sɪstəmə,tʌɪz/ (also **-ise**) ■ v. arrange according to an organized system; make systematic.
– DERIVATIVES **systematization** (also **-isation**) n. **systematizer** (also **-iser**) n.

systemic /sɪ'stɛmɪk, -'sti:m-/ ■ adj. **1** of or relating to a system as a whole. **2** Physiology denoting the non-pulmonary part of the circulatory system. **3** (of an insecticide, fungicide, etc.) entering the plant via the roots or shoots and passing through the tissues. **4** Linguistics (of grammar) based on the conception of language as a network of systems determining options from which speakers make choices.
– DERIVATIVES **systemically** adv.

systemize (also **-ise**) ■ v. another term for SYSTEMATIZE.
– DERIVATIVES **systemization** (also **-isation**) n.

systems analyst ■ n. a person who analyses a complex process or operation in order to improve its efficiency, especially by applying a computer system.
– DERIVATIVES **systems analysis** n.

systole /'sɪst(ə)li/ ■ n. Physiology the phase of the heartbeat when the heart muscle contracts and pumps blood into the arteries. Often contrasted with DIASTOLE.
– DERIVATIVES **systolic** /-'stɒlɪk/ adj.
– ORIGIN C16: from Greek *sustolē*, from *sustellein* 'to contract'.

syzygy /'sɪzɪdʒi/ ■ n. (pl. **-ies**) **1** Astronomy conjunction or opposition, especially of the moon with the sun. **2** a pair of connected or corresponding things.
– ORIGIN C17: from Greek *suzugia*, from *suzugos* 'yoked, paired', from *sun-* 'with, together' + the stem of *zeugnunai* 'to yoke'.

Tt

T[1] (also **t**) ▪ n. (pl. **Ts** or **T's**) **1** the twentieth letter of the alphabet. **2** denoting the next after S in a set of items, categories, etc.
– PHRASES **to a T** informal exactly; to perfection.

T[2] ▪ abbrev. **1** tera- (10^{12}). **2** tesla. ▪ symb. **1** temperature. **2** Chemistry the hydrogen isotope tritium.

t ▪ abbrev. ton(s). ▪ symb. (*t*) Statistics a number characterizing the distribution of a sample taken from a population with a normal distribution (see **STUDENT'S T-TEST**).

Ta ▪ symb. the chemical element tantalum.

ta ▪ exclam. Brit. informal thank you.
– ORIGIN C18: a child's word.

TAB ▪ abbrev. S. African & Austral./NZ Totalizator Agency Board.

tab[1] ▪ n. **1** a small flap or strip of material attached to something, for holding, manipulation, identification, etc. **2** informal, chiefly N. Amer. a restaurant bill. **3** Aeronautics a hinged part of a control surface. ▪ v. (**tabbed**, **tabbing**) mark with a tab.
– PHRASES **keep tabs** (or **a tab**) **on** informal monitor the activities or development of. **pick up the tab** informal, chiefly N. Amer. pay for something.
– DERIVATIVES **tabbed** adj.
– ORIGIN Middle English: perhaps rel. to TAG[1].

tab[2] ▪ n. short for TABULATOR.

tab[3] ▪ n. informal a tablet, especially one containing an illicit drug.
– ORIGIN 1960s: abbrev.

tabard /'tabəd, -ɑːd/ ▪ n. a sleeveless jerkin consisting only of front and back pieces with a hole for the head.
– ORIGIN Middle English: from Old French *tabart*.

Tabasco /tə'baskəʊ/ ▪ n. trademark a pungent sauce made from capsicums.
– ORIGIN C19: named after the state of *Tabasco* in Mexico.

tabbouleh /tə'buːleɪ, 'tabuːleɪ/ ▪ n. a salad of cracked wheat mixed with finely chopped tomatoes, onions, parsley, etc.
– ORIGIN from Arabic *tabbūla*.

tabby ▪ n. (pl. **-ies**) **1** a grey or brownish cat mottled or streaked with dark stripes. **2** silk or other fabric with a watered pattern.
– ORIGIN C16 (denoting a striped silk taffeta): from French *tabis*, from Arabic *al-'Attābiyya*, the name of a part of Baghdad where it was manufactured.

tabernacle /'tabə,nak(ə)l/ ▪ n. **1** (in biblical use) a fixed or movable habitation, typically of light construction. ▸ a tent used as a sanctuary for the Ark of the Covenant by the Israelites during the Exodus. **2** a meeting place for Nonconformist or Mormon worship. **3** an ornamented receptacle or cabinet in which the reserved sacrament may be placed in Catholic churches. **4** a partly open socket on a sailing boat's deck into which a mast is fixed, with a pivot so that the mast can be lowered.
– DERIVATIVES **tabernacled** adj.
– ORIGIN Middle English: from Latin *tabernaculum* 'tent', diminutive of *taberna* 'hut, tavern'.

tabla /'tablə, 'tʌblə/ ▪ n. a pair of small hand drums fixed together, used in Indian music.
– ORIGIN from Persian and Urdu *tablah*, Hindi *tablā*, from Arabic *ṭabl* 'drum'.

tablature /'tablətʃə/ ▪ n. a form of musical notation indicating fingering rather than the pitch of notes, written on lines corresponding to e.g. the strings of a guitar.
– ORIGIN C16: from French, prob. from Italian *tavolatura*, from *tavolare* 'set to music'.

table ▪ n. **1** a piece of furniture with a flat top and one or more legs, providing a level surface for eating, writing, or working at. ▸ food provided in a restaurant or household. **2** a set of facts or figures systematically displayed, especially in columns. ▸ a league table. ▸ (**tables**) multiplication tables. **3** Architecture a flat, typically rectangular, vertical surface. ▸ a horizontal moulding, especially a cornice. ▸ a slab bearing an inscription. **4** a flat surface of a gem. ▸ a cut gem with two flat faces. **5** each half or quarter of a folding board for backgammon. ▪ v. **1** present formally for discussion or consideration at a meeting. **2** chiefly US postpone consideration of.
– PHRASES **bring something to the table** contribute something of value to a discussion, project, etc. **lay something on the table** make something known so that it can be discussed. **on the table** offered for discussion. **turn the tables** turn a position of disadvantage relative to someone else into one of advantage. **under the table 1** informal very drunk. **2** another term for *under the counter* (see COUNTER[1]).
– DERIVATIVES **tableful** n. (pl. **-fuls**).
– ORIGIN Old English *tabule* 'flat slab, inscribed tablet', from Latin *tabula* 'plank, tablet, list', reinforced in Middle English by Old French *table*.

tableau /'tabləʊ/ ▪ n. (pl. **tableaux** /-ləʊz/) a group of models or motionless figures representing a scene.
– ORIGIN C17: from French, diminutive of *table* (see TABLE).

tablecloth ▪ n. a cloth spread over a table, especially during meals.

table d'hôte /ˌtɑːbl(ə) 'dəʊt/ ▪ n. a restaurant meal offered at a fixed price and with few if any choices.
– ORIGIN C17: French, 'host's table'.

tableland ▪ n. a broad, high, level region; a plateau.

table manners ▪ pl. n. behaviour that is conventionally required while eating at table.

table mat ▪ n. a small mat used for protecting the surface of a table from hot dishes.

tablespoon ▪ n. a large spoon for serving food. ▸ (abbrev.: **tbsp**) the amount held by such a spoon, considered to be 15 millilitres when used as a measurement in cookery.
– DERIVATIVES **tablespoonful** n. (pl. **-fuls**).

tablet ▪ n. **1** a flat slab of stone, clay, or wood, used especially for an inscription. ▸ Architecture another term for TABLE (in sense 3). **2** a small disc or cylinder of a compressed solid substance, typically a medicine or drug; a pill. **3** a small flat piece of soap.
– ORIGIN Middle English: from Old French *tablete*, from a diminutive of Latin *tabula* (see TABLE).

table tennis ▪ n. an indoor game based on tennis, played with small bats and a small, hollow ball bounced on a table divided by a net.

tableware ▪ n. crockery, cutlery, and glassware used for serving and eating meals at a table.

table wine ▪ n. wine of moderate quality considered suitable for drinking with a meal.

tabloid ▪ n. a newspaper having pages half the size of those of the average broadsheet, typically popular in style and dominated by sensational stories.
– ORIGIN C19: from TABLET, orig. a proprietary term for a medicinal tablet; the current sense reflects the notion of 'concentrated, easily assimilable'.

taboo (also **tabu**) ▪ n. (pl. **taboos** or **tabus**) a social or religious custom placing prohibition or restriction on a particular thing or person. ▪ adj. prohibited or restricted by social custom. ▸ designated as sacred and prohibited. ▪ v. (**taboos**, **tabooed** or **tabus**, **tabued**) place under such prohibition.
– ORIGIN C18: from Tongan *tabu* 'set apart, forbidden'.

tabor /'teɪbə/ ▪ n. historical a small drum, especially one

tabouret

used simultaneously by the player of a simple pipe.
- ORIGIN Middle English: from Old French *tabour* 'drum'; perhaps rel. to Persian *tabīra* 'drum'.

tabouret /ˈtabərɛt, -reɪ/ (US also **taboret**) ■ n. a low stool or small table.
- ORIGIN C17: from French, 'stool', diminutive of *tabour* (see **TABOR**).

tabular /ˈtabjʊlə/ ■ adj. 1 (of data) consisting of or presented in columns or tables. 2 broad and flat like the top of a table. ▸ (of a crystal) relatively broad and thin, with two well-developed parallel faces.
- DERIVATIVES **tabularly** adv.
- ORIGIN C17: from Latin *tabularis*, from *tabula* (see **TABLE**).

tabula rasa /ˌtabjʊlə ˈrɑːzə/ ■ n. (pl. **tabulae rasae** /ˌtabjuli ˈrɑːziː/) an absence of preconceived ideas or predetermined goals; a clean slate.
- ORIGIN Latin, 'scraped tablet', i.e. a tablet with the writing erased.

tabulate /ˈtabjʊleɪt/ ■ v. arrange (data) in tabular form.
- DERIVATIVES **tabulation** n.

tabulator ■ n. a facility in a word-processing program, or a device on a typewriter, for advancing to a sequence of set positions in tabular work.

tac-au-tac /ˌtakəʊˈtak/ ■ n. Fencing a parry combined with a riposte.
- ORIGIN C20: French, 'clash for clash', from imitative *tac*.

tach /tak/ ■ n. informal short for **TACHOMETER**.

tachism /ˈtaʃɪz(ə)m/ (also **tachisme**) ■ n. a French style of painting originating in the 1940s, involving the use of dabs or splotches of colour.
- ORIGIN 1950s: from French *tachisme*, from *tache* 'a stain'.

tachistoscope /təˈkɪstəˌskəʊp/ ■ n. an instrument used for exposing objects to the eye for a very brief measured period of time.
- DERIVATIVES **tachistoscopic** adj.
- ORIGIN C19: from Greek *takhistos* 'swiftest' + **-SCOPE**.

tacho /ˈtakəʊ/ ■ n. (pl. **-os**) short for **TACHOGRAPH** or **TACHOMETER**.

tacho- ■ comb. form relating to speed: *tachograph*.
- ORIGIN from Greek *takhos* 'speed'.

tachograph ■ n. a tachometer used in commercial road vehicles to provide a record of engine speed over a period.

tachometer /taˈkɒmɪtə/ ■ n. an instrument which measures the working speed of an engine, typically in revolutions per minute.

tachycardia /ˌtakɪˈkɑːdɪə/ ■ n. an abnormally rapid heart rate.
- ORIGIN C19: from Greek, from *takhus* 'swift' + *kardia* 'heart'.

tachyon /ˈtakɪɒn/ ■ n. Physics a hypothetical particle that travels faster than light.

tacit /ˈtasɪt/ ■ adj. understood or implied without being stated.
- DERIVATIVES **tacitly** adv.
- ORIGIN C17: from Latin *tacitus* 'silent', from *tacere* 'be silent'.

taciturn /ˈtasɪtəːn/ ■ adj. reserved or uncommunicative in speech; saying little.
- DERIVATIVES **taciturnity** n. **taciturnly** adv.
- ORIGIN C18: from Latin *taciturnus*, from *tacitus* (see **TACIT**).

tack¹ ■ n. 1 a small, sharp broad-headed nail. ▸ N. Amer. a drawing pin. 2 a long stitch used to fasten fabrics together temporarily, prior to permanent sewing. 3 a method of dealing with a situation; a course of action. 4 Nautical an act of tacking. ▸ a sailing boat's course relative to the direction of the wind. 5 Nautical a rope for securing the corner of certain sails. ▸ the corner to which such a rope is fastened. 6 the quality of being sticky. ■ v. 1 fasten or fix with tacks or with temporary long stitches. 2 (**tack something on**) add or append something to something already existing. 3 Nautical (in sailing) change course by turning a boat's head into and through the wind. ▸ make a series of such changes of course while sailing.
- DERIVATIVES **tacker** n.
- ORIGIN Middle English: prob. rel. to Old French *tache* 'clasp, large nail'.

tack² ■ n. equipment used in horse riding, including the saddle and bridle.
- ORIGIN C18: contraction of **TACKLE**.

tack³ ■ n. informal cheap, shoddy, or tasteless material.
- ORIGIN 1980s: back-formation from **TACKY²**.

tackie ■ n. variant spelling of **TAKKIE**.

tackle ■ n. 1 the equipment required for a task or sport. 2 a mechanism consisting of ropes, pulley blocks, and hooks for lifting heavy objects. ▸ the running rigging and pulleys used to work a boat's sails. 3 (in sport) an act of tackling an opponent. 4 American Football a player who lines up next to the end along the line of scrimmage. ■ v. 1 make determined efforts to deal with (a problem or difficult task). ▸ initiate discussion with (someone) about a disputed or sensitive issue. 2 (in soccer, hockey, rugby, etc.) try to take the ball from (an opponent) by intercepting them.
- DERIVATIVES **tackler** n.
- ORIGIN Middle English: prob. from Middle Low German *takel*, from *taken* 'lay hold of'.

tackle block ■ n. a pulley over which a rope runs.

tackle fall ■ n. a rope for applying force to the blocks of a tackle.

tacky¹ ■ adj. (**-ier**, **-iest**) (of glue, paint, etc.) slightly sticky because not fully dry.
- DERIVATIVES **tackiness** n.

tacky² ■ adj. (**-ier**, **-iest**) informal showing poor taste and quality.
- DERIVATIVES **tackily** adv. **tackiness** n.
- ORIGIN C19 (denoting a horse of little value).

taco /ˈtakəʊ, ˈtɑːkəʊ/ ■ n. (pl. **-os**) a Mexican dish consisting of a folded or rolled tortilla filled with seasoned meat or beans.
- ORIGIN Mexican Spanish, from Spanish, 'plug, wad'.

taco chip ■ n. a fried fragment of a taco, spiced and eaten as a snack.

taconite /ˈtakənʌɪt/ ■ n. a low-grade iron ore consisting largely of chert.
- ORIGIN C20: from the name of the *Taconic* Range of mountains in the US.

tact ■ n. adroitness and sensitivity in dealing with others or with difficult issues.
- ORIGIN C17: from Latin *tactus* 'touch, sense of touch', from *tangere* 'to touch'.

tactful ■ adj. having or showing tact.
- DERIVATIVES **tactfully** adv. **tactfulness** n.

tactic ■ n. 1 an action or strategy carefully planned to achieve a specific end. 2 (**tactics**) the art of disposing armed forces in order of battle and of organizing operations, especially during contact with an enemy. Often contrasted with **STRATEGY**.
- DERIVATIVES **tactician** n.
- ORIGIN C18: from Greek *taktikē* (*tekhnē*) '(art) of tactics', from *taktikos*, from *taktos* 'ordered, arranged'.

tactical ■ adj. 1 done or planned to gain a specific military end. ▸ (of bombing or weapons) done or for use in immediate support of military or naval operations. Often contrasted with **STRATEGIC**. 2 planned in order to achieve an end beyond the immediate action. ▸ (of voting) aimed at preventing the strongest candidate from winning by supporting the next strongest, without regard to one's true political allegiance.
- DERIVATIVES **tactically** adv.

tacticity ■ n. Chemistry the stereochemical arrangement of the units in the main chain of a polymer.

tactile ■ adj. 1 of or connected with the sense of touch. ▸ perceptible or designed to be perceived by touch; tangible. 2 (of a person) given to touching others in a friendly or sympathetic way.
- DERIVATIVES **tactility** n.
- ORIGIN C17: from Latin *tactilis*, from *tangere* 'to touch'.

tactless ■ adj. having or showing a lack of tact.
- DERIVATIVES **tactlessly** adv. **tactlessness** n.

tad informal ■ adv. (**a tad**) to a minor extent; somewhat. ■ n. a small amount.
- ORIGIN C19 (denoting a small child): perhaps from **TADPOLE**.

ta-da /təˈdɑː/ ■ exclam. an imitation of a fanfare (used to indicate an impressive entrance or a dramatic announcement).
– ORIGIN C20: imitative.

Tadjik (also **Tadzhik**) ■ n. & adj. variant spelling of **TAJIK**.

tadpole ■ n. the tailed aquatic larva of an amphibian, breathing through gills and lacking legs until the later stages of its development.
– ORIGIN C15: from Old English *tāda* 'toad' + **POLL** (prob. because the tadpole seems to consist of a large head and a tail in its early development stage).

tae kwon do /ˌtaɪ kwɒn ˈdəʊ/ ■ n. a modern Korean martial art similar to karate.
– ORIGIN Korean, 'art of hand and foot fighting'.

tael /teɪl/ ■ n. 1 a weight used in China and the Far East, about 38 grams. 2 a former Chinese monetary unit.
– ORIGIN from Malay *tahil* 'weight'.

taffeta /ˈtafɪtə/ ■ n. a fine lustrous silk or similar synthetic fabric with a crisp texture.
– ORIGIN Middle English: from Old French *taffetas* or medieval Latin *taffata*, from Persian *tāftan* 'to shine'.

taffrail ■ n. a rail round a ship's stern.
– ORIGIN C19: alteration, by association with **RAIL**[1], of obsolete *tafferel* 'panel', from Dutch *tafereel*.

Taffy (also **Taff**) ■ n. (pl. **-ies**) Brit. informal, often offensive a Welshman.
– ORIGIN C17: representing a supposed Welsh pronunciation of the given name *Davy* or *David* (Welsh *Dafydd*).

taffy ■ n. (pl. **-ies**) N. Amer. a sweet similar to toffee.
– ORIGIN C19: earlier form of **TOFFEE**.

tag[1] ■ n. 1 a label providing identification or giving other information. ▸ an electronic device attached to someone or something for monitoring purposes. ▸ a nickname or popular description. ▸ US a vehicle licence plate. 2 a small piece or part that is attached to a main body. ▸ a ragged lock of wool on a sheep. ▸ the tip of an animal's tail when it is distinctively coloured. ▸ a loose or spare end of something; a leftover. ▸ a metal or plastic point at the end of a shoelace. 3 a frequently repeated quotation or stock phrase. ▸ Theatre a closing speech addressed to the audience. ▸ the refrain of a song. ▸ a phrase at the end of a piece of music. 4 Computing a character or set of characters appended to an item of data in order to identify it. ■ v. (**tagged**, **tagging**) 1 attach a label or tag to. 2 add to something as an afterthought. ▸ (**tag along**) accompany someone without invitation. ▸ Brit. informal follow (someone) closely. 3 shear away ragged locks of wool from (sheep).
– ORIGIN Middle English.

tag[2] ■ n. 1 a children's game in which one chases the rest, and anyone who is caught then becomes the pursuer. 2 Baseball the action of tagging a runner. ■ v. (**tagged**, **tagging**) 1 touch (someone being chased) in a game of tag. 2 Baseball put (a runner) out by touching with the ball or with the hand holding the ball.
– ORIGIN C18: perhaps a var. of obsolete *tig*, perhaps from the verb **TICK**[1].

Tagalog /təˈɡɑːlɒɡ/ ■ n. 1 a member of a people originally of central Luzon in the Philippine Islands. 2 the language of this people, the basis of the national language of the Philippines (Filipino).
– ORIGIN the name in Tagalog, from *tagá* 'native' + *ilog* 'river'.

tagetes /təˈdʒiːtiːz/ ■ n. a plant of a genus including some African and American marigolds. [Genus *Tagetes*.]
– ORIGIN from Latin *Tages*, the name of an Etruscan god.

tagine /təˈʒiːn, təˈdʒiːn/ ■ n. a North African stew of spiced meat and vegetables prepared by slow cooking in a shallow earthenware cooking dish with a tall, conical lid. ▸ the dish used for cooking tagines.
– ORIGIN Moroccan Arabic *ṭažin* from Arabic *ṭājin* 'frying pan'.

tagliatelle /ˌtaljəˈtɛleɪ, -li/ ■ pl. n. pasta in narrow ribbons.
– ORIGIN Italian, from *tagliare* 'to cut'.

tag line ■ n. informal, chiefly N. Amer. a catchphrase, slogan, or punchline.

tag sale ■ n. US a sale of miscellaneous second-hand items.

tag team ■ n. 1 a pair of wrestlers who fight as a team, taking the ring alternately. 2 informal, chiefly N. Amer. a pair of people working together.

tag wrestling ■ n. a form of wrestling involving tag teams.

tahini /tɑːˈhiːni/ (also **tahina** /tɑːˈhiːnə/) ■ n. a Middle Eastern paste or spread made from ground sesame seeds.
– ORIGIN from modern Greek *takhini*, from Arabic *ṭaḥana* 'to crush'.

Tahitian /tɑːˈhiːʃ(ə)n, -ˈhiːtɪən/ ■ n. 1 a native or national of Tahiti, or a person of Tahitian descent. 2 the Polynesian language of Tahiti. ■ adj. of or relating to Tahiti, its people, or their language.

tahr /tɑː/ (also **thar**) ■ n. a goat-like mammal found in Oman, southern India, and the Himalayas. [Genus *Hemitragus*: three species.]
– ORIGIN C19: a local word in Nepal.

t'ai chi ch'uan /ˌtaɪ tʃiː ˈtʃwɑːn/ (also **t'ai chi**) ■ n. 1 a Chinese martial art and system of callisthenics, consisting of sequences of very slow controlled movements. 2 (in Chinese philosophy) the ultimate source and limit of reality, from which spring yin and yang and all of creation.
– ORIGIN Chinese, 'great ultimate boxing'.

Taig /teɪɡ/ ■ n. informal, offensive (in Northern Ireland) a Protestant name for a Catholic.
– ORIGIN 1970s: var. of *Teague*, anglicized spelling of the Irish name *Tadhg*, a nickname for an Irishman.

taiga /ˈtaɪɡə/ ■ n. swampy coniferous forest of high northern latitudes, especially that between the tundra and steppes of Siberia.
– ORIGIN C19: from Russian *taĭga*, from Mongolian.

tail ■ n. 1 the hindmost part of an animal, especially when extended beyond the rest of the body, such as the flexible extension of the backbone in a vertebrate or the feathers at the hind end of a bird. 2 something extending downwards, outwards, or back like an animal's tail. ▸ the luminous trail of particles following a comet. ▸ the lower end of a pool or stream. ▸ the exposed end of a slate or tile in a roof. ▸ the final, more distant, or weaker part of something. ▸ Cricket the end of the batting order, with the weakest batsmen. 3 the rear part of an aircraft, with the tailplane and rudder. 4 (**tails**) the side of a coin without the image of a head on it (used when tossing a coin to determine a winner). 5 the lower or hanging part at the back of a shirt or coat. ▸ (**tails**) informal a tailcoat, or a man's formal evening suit with such a coat. 6 informal, chiefly N. Amer. a person's buttocks. ▸ informal women collectively regarded as a means of sexual gratification. 7 informal a person secretly following another to observe their movements. ■ v. 1 informal secretly follow and observe (someone). 2 (**tail off/away**) gradually diminish in amount, strength, or intensity. ▸ (**tail back**) (of traffic) become congested and form a tailback. 3 (**tail something in/into**) insert the end of a beam, stone, or brick into (a wall).
– PHRASES **on someone's tail** informal following someone closely. **with one's tail between one's legs** informal in a state of dejection or humiliation. **with one's tail up** informal in a confident or cheerful mood.
– DERIVATIVES **tailed** adj. **tailless** adj.
– ORIGIN Old English *tæġ(e)l*, from a Germanic base meaning 'hair, hairy tail'.

tailback ■ n. 1 a long queue of traffic extending back from a junction or obstruction. 2 American Football the offensive back stationed furthest from the line of scrimmage.

tailboard ■ n. Brit. a tailgate.

tail bone ■ n. less technical term for **COCCYX**.

tailcoat ■ n. a man's formal morning or evening coat, with a long skirt divided at the back into tails and cut away in front.

tail end ■ n. the last or hindmost part of something, in particular the batting order in cricket.
– DERIVATIVES **tail-ender** n. (Cricket).

tail-end Charlie ■ n. informal a crew member of a bomber aircraft who operates a gun from a compartment at the rear.

tail fin ■ n. **1** Zoology a fin at the posterior extremity of a fish's body, typically continuous with the tail. **2** a projecting vertical surface on the tail of an aircraft, housing the rudder. **3** an upswept projection on each rear corner of a motor car, popular in the 1950s.

tailgate ■ n. a hinged flap giving access to the back of a truck. ▶ the door at the back of an estate or hatchback car. ■ v. informal drive too closely behind (another vehicle).
– DERIVATIVES **tailgater** n.

tailing ■ n. **1** (**tailings**) the residue of something, especially ore. ▶ grain or flour of inferior quality. **2** the part of a beam or projecting brick or stone embedded in a wall.

tail light (also **tail lamp**) ■ n. a red light at the rear of a vehicle.

tailor ■ n. a person whose occupation is making clothes, especially men's outer garments for individual customers. ■ v. **1** (of a tailor) make (clothes) to fit individual customers. **2** (usu. **tailor something for/to**) make or adapt for a particular purpose or person.
– DERIVATIVES **tailoring** n.
– ORIGIN Middle English: from Anglo-Norman French *taillour* 'cutter', from late Latin *taliare* 'to cut'.

tailored ■ adj. (of clothes) smart, fitted, and well cut.

tailor-made ■ adj. **1** (of clothes) made by a tailor for a particular customer. **2** made or adapted for a particular purpose or person.

tailpiece ■ n. **1** the final or end part of something. ▶ the piece at the base of a stringed instrument to which the strings are attached. **2** a small decorative design at the foot of a page or the end of a chapter or book. ▶ a part added to the end of a piece of writing.

tailpipe ■ n. the rear section of the exhaust pipe of a motor vehicle.

tailplane ■ n. a horizontal aerofoil at the tail of an aircraft.

tail race ■ n. a fast-flowing stretch of a river or stream below a dam or watermill.

tailspin ■ n. **1** a spin by an aircraft. **2** a state of rapidly increasing chaos or panic. ■ v. (**-spinning**; past and past part. **-spun**) become out of control.

tailstock ■ n. the adjustable part of a lathe holding the fixed spindle.

tailwind ■ n. a wind blowing in the direction of travel of a vehicle or aircraft.

Taino /'taɪnəʊ/ ■ n. an extinct Caribbean language of the Arawakan group.
– ORIGIN from Taino *taino* 'noble, lord'.

taint ■ n. **1** a trace of a bad or undesirable quality or substance. ▶ a contaminating influence or effect. **2** an unpleasant smell. ■ v. **1** contaminate or pollute. ▶ affect with a bad or undesirable quality. **2** archaic (of food or water) become contaminated or polluted.
– DERIVATIVES **taintless** adj. (poetic/literary).
– ORIGIN Middle English: partly from Old French *teint* 'tinged', from Latin *tingere* 'to dye, tinge'; partly a shortening of archaic *attaint* 'infect (with a disease)'.

taipan[1] /'taɪpan/ ■ n. a foreigner who is head of a business in China.
– ORIGIN C19: from Chinese (Cantonese dialect) *daaihbāan*.

taipan[2] /'taɪpan/ ■ n. a large, brown, highly venomous Australian snake. [*Oxyuranus scutellatus*.]
– ORIGIN 1930s: from *dhayban*, the name in an extinct Aboriginal language.

Taiwanese /taɪwə'niːz/ ■ n. (pl. same) a native or inhabitant of Taiwan. ■ adj. of or relating to Taiwan.

Tajik /tɑːˈdʒiːk/ (also **Tadjik** or **Tadzhik**) ■ n. **1** a member of a mainly Muslim people inhabiting Tajikistan and parts of neighbouring countries. ▶ a native or national of the republic of Tajikistan. **2** (also **Tajiki** /tɑːˈdʒiːki/) the Iranian language of the Tajiks.
– ORIGIN from Persian *tājik* 'a Persian, someone who is neither an Arab nor a Turk'.

take ■ v. (past **took**; past part. **taken**) **1** lay hold of with one's hands; reach for and hold. ▶ consume as food, drink, medicine, or drugs. ▶ occupy (a place or position). ▶ buy, rent, or subscribe to. ▶ ascertain by measurement or observation. ▶ capture or gain possession of by force or military means. ▶ (of illness) suddenly strike or afflict. ▶ have sexual intercourse with. **2** remove from a place. ▶ subtract. **3** carry or bring with one; convey or guide. ▶ bring into a specified state. ▶ use as a route or a means of transport. **4** accept or receive. ▶ understand or accept as valid. ▶ acquire or assume (a position, state, or form). ▶ act on (an opportunity). ▶ experience or be affected by. ▶ regard, view, or deal with in a specified way. ▶ (**be taken by/with**) be attracted or charmed by. ▶ submit to, tolerate, or endure. ▶ (**take it**) assume. **5** make, undertake, or perform (an action or task). ▶ be taught or examined in (a subject). ▶ Brit. obtain (an academic degree) after fulfilling the required conditions. **6** require or use up (a specified amount of time). ▶ need or call for. ▶ hold; accommodate. ▶ wear or require (a particular size of garment). ▶ Grammar have or require as part of the appropriate construction. **7** (of a plant or seed) take root or begin to grow; germinate. ▶ (of an added substance) become successfully established. ■ n. **1** a scene or sequence of sound or vision photographed or recorded continuously at one time. ▶ a particular version of or approach to something: *his own whimsical take on life.* **2** an amount gained or acquired from one source or in one session. **3** Printing an amount of copy set up at one time or by one compositor.
– PHRASES **be on the take** informal take bribes. **be taken ill** become ill suddenly. **have what it takes** informal have the necessary qualities for success. **take something as read** Brit. assume something. **take five** informal, chiefly N. Amer. have a short break. **take someone in hand** undertake to control or reform someone. **take something in hand** start doing or dealing with a task. **take ill** (US **sick**) informal become ill suddenly. **take something ill** archaic resent something done or said. **take it on one** (or **oneself**) to do something decide to do something without asking for permission or advice. **take it out of** exhaust the strength of. **take that!** exclaimed when hitting someone or taking retributive action against them. **take one's time** not hurry.
– PHRASAL VERBS **take after** resemble (a parent or ancestor). **take against** Brit. begin to dislike (someone). **take something apart 1** dismantle something. **2** (**take someone/thing apart**) informal forcefully attack, criticize, or defeat someone or something. **take** (**away**) **from** detract from. **take something back 1** retract a statement. **2** return unsatisfactory goods to a shop. ▶ (of a shop) accept such goods. **3** Printing transfer text to the previous line. **take someone in** cheat or deceive someone. **take something in 1** make a garment tighter by altering its seams. **2** Nautical furl a sail. **3** encompass, understand, or absorb something. **4** casually visit or attend a place or event. **take off 1** (of an aircraft or bird) become airborne. ▶ (of an enterprise) become successful or popular. **2** (also **take oneself off**) depart hastily. **take someone off** informal mimic someone humorously. **take something off 1** remove clothing. **2** deduct part of an amount. **take on** Brit. informal become very upset, especially needlessly. **take someone on 1** engage an employee. **2** be willing or ready to meet an opponent. **take something on 1** undertake a task or responsibility. **2** acquire a particular meaning or quality. **take someone out** Bridge respond to a bid or double by one's partner by bidding a different suit. **take someone/thing out** informal kill, destroy, or disable. **take something out** obtain an official document or service. **take something out on** relieve frustration or anger by attacking or mistreating. **take something over 1** (also **take over**) assume control of or responsibility for something. **2** Printing transfer text to the next line. **take to 1** begin or fall into the habit of. **2** form a liking for. ▶ develop an ability for. **3** go to (a place) to escape danger. **take someone up 1** adopt someone as a protégé. **2** (usu. **take someone up on**) accept an offer or challenge from someone. **take something up 1** become interested or engaged in a pursuit. ▶ begin to hold or fulfil a position or post. ▶ accept an offer or challenge. **2** occupy time, space, or attention. **3** pursue a matter further. **take up with** begin to associate with (someone).
– DERIVATIVES **takable** (also **takeable**) adj. **taker** n.
– ORIGIN Old English *tacan* 'get, capture', from Old Norse *taka* 'grasp, lay hold of'.

takeaway ■ n. **1** a restaurant or shop selling cooked food to be eaten elsewhere. ▸ a meal or dish of such food. **2** Golf another term for **BACKSWING**.

take-home pay ■ n. the pay received by an employee after the deduction of tax and insurance.

take-off ■ n. **1** the action of becoming airborne. **2** an act of mimicking.

takeout ■ n. **1** chiefly N. Amer. a takeaway. **2** Bridge a bid (in a different suit) made in response to a bid or double by one's partner.

takeover ■ n. an act of assuming control of something, especially the buying-out of one company by another.

taking ■ n. **1** the action or process of taking. **2** (**takings**) the amount of money earned by a business from the sale of goods or services. ■ adj. dated captivating in manner; charming.
– PHRASES **for the taking** ready or available to take advantage of.
– DERIVATIVES **takingly** adv.

takkie /'taki/ (also **tackie** or **tekkie**) ■ n. S. African a flat soft shoe suitable for sports or casual wear; a running shoe.
– ORIGIN perhaps from *tacky* in the sense 'cheap, of poor quality'; the spelling reflects a perception that the word is of Afrikaans origin.

talapoin /'taləpɔɪn/ ■ n. **1** a Buddhist monk or priest. **2** a small West African monkey. [*Miopithecus talapoin*.]
– ORIGIN C16: from Portuguese *talapão*, from Mon *tala pói* 'lord of merit'.

talc ■ n. **1** talcum powder. **2** a soft mineral with a greasy feel, occurring as translucent masses or laminae and consisting of hydrated magnesium silicate. ■ v. (**talced**, **talcing**) powder or treat with talc.
– DERIVATIVES **talcose** adj. (Geology). **talcy** adj.

talcum powder ■ n. a preparation for the body and face consisting of the mineral talc in powdered form. ■ v. (**talcumed**, **talcuming**) powder with this substance.
– ORIGIN C16: from medieval Latin *talcum*, from Arabic *ṭalk*.

tale ■ n. a fictitious or true narrative or story, especially one that is imaginatively recounted. ▸ a lie.
– ORIGIN Old English *talu* 'telling, something told', of Germanic origin.

Taleban variant spelling of **TALIBAN**.

talebearer ■ n. dated a person who maliciously gossips or reveals secrets.
– DERIVATIVES **talebearing** n. & adj.

talent ■ n. **1** natural aptitude or skill. ▸ people possessing such aptitude or skill. ▸ informal people regarded as sexually attractive or as prospective sexual partners. **2** a former weight and unit of currency used by the ancient Romans and Greeks.
– DERIVATIVES **talentless** adj.
– ORIGIN Old English *talente*, *talentan* (as a unit of weight), from Latin *talentum* 'weight, sum of money', from Greek *talanton*.

talented ■ adj. having a natural aptitude or skill for something.

talent scout ■ n. a person whose job is searching for talented performers, especially in sport and entertainment.

tali plural form of **TALUS**[1].

Taliban /'talɪban/ (also **Taleban**) ■ n. a fundamentalist Muslim movement that ruled much of Afghanistan 1995–2001.
– ORIGIN from Persian *ṭālibān*, pl. of *ṭālib* 'student, seeker of knowledge', from Arabic.

talipes /'talɪpiːz/ ■ n. Medicine technical term for **CLUB FOOT**.
– ORIGIN C19: from Latin *talus* 'ankle' + *pes* 'foot'.

talisman /'talɪzmən/ ■ n. (pl. **talismans**) an object thought to have magic powers and to bring good luck.
– DERIVATIVES **talismanic** /-'manɪk/ adj.
– ORIGIN C17: from Arabic *ṭilsam*, apparently from an alteration of late Greek *telesma* 'completion, religious rite'.

talk ■ v. speak in order to give information or express ideas or feelings; converse or communicate by speech. ▸ have the power of speech. ▸ (**talk something over/through**) discuss something thoroughly. ▸ (**talk back**) reply defiantly or insolently. ▸ (**talk down to**) speak patronizingly or condescendingly to. ▸ (**talk someone round**) convince someone that they should adopt a particular point of view. ▸ (**talk someone into/out of**) persuade or dissuade someone to or from. ▸ (**talk something out**) Brit. (in Parliament) block the course of a bill by prolonging discussion to the time of adjournment. ▸ (**be talking**) informal be discussing in specified terms: *we're talking big money.* ▸ gossip. ■ n. **1** conversation; discussion. ▸ rumour, gossip, or speculation. ▸ (**the talk of**) a current subject of widespread gossip or speculation in. ▸ (**talks**) formal discussions or negotiations over a period. **2** an address or lecture.
– PHRASES **you can't** (or **can**) (US **shouldn't** or **should**) **talk** informal used to convey that a criticism made applies equally well to the person making it. **look** (or **hark**) **who's talking** another way of saying you can't talk. **now you're talking** informal expressing enthusiastic agreement or approval. **talk big** informal talk boastfully or over-confidently. **talk the hind leg off a donkey** see **DONKEY**. **talk nineteen to the dozen** see **DOZEN**.
– DERIVATIVES **talker** n.
– ORIGIN Middle English: from the Germanic base of **TALE** or **TELL**[1].

talkathon ■ n. informal a prolonged discussion or debate.
– ORIGIN 1930s (orig. US, denoting a debate artificially prolonged to prevent the progress of a bill): blend of **TALK** and **MARATHON**.

talkative ■ adj. fond of or given to talking.
– DERIVATIVES **talkatively** adv. **talkativeness** n.

talkback ■ n. **1** a system of two-way communication by loudspeaker. **2** another term for **PHONE-IN**.

talkfest ■ n. informal, chiefly N. Amer. a lengthy discussion or debate, especially as part of a television chat show.

talkie ■ n. informal a film with a soundtrack, as distinct from a silent film.

talking blues ■ pl. n. a style of blues music in which the lyrics are more or less spoken rather than sung.

talking book ■ n. a recorded reading of a book.

talking drum ■ n. each of a set of West African drums which are beaten to transmit a tonal language.

talking head ■ n. informal, chiefly derogatory a presenter or reporter on television who addresses the camera and is viewed in close-up.

talking point ■ n. a topic that invites discussion or argument.

talking shop (also **talk shop**) ■ n. Brit. a place or group regarded as a centre for unproductive talk rather than action.

talking-to ■ n. informal a sharp reprimand.

talk radio ■ n. chiefly N. Amer. a type of radio broadcast in which topical issues are discussed by the presenter and by listeners who phone in.

talk show ■ n. a chat show.

tall ■ adj. **1** of great or more than average height. ▸ measuring a specified distance from top to bottom. **2** fanciful and difficult to believe; unlikely: *a tall story*.
– PHRASES **a tall order** an unreasonable or difficult demand.
– DERIVATIVES **tallish** adj. **tallness** n.
– ORIGIN Middle English (in senses 'swift', also 'fine, handsome', and 'strong'): prob. from Old English *getæl* 'swift, prompt'.

tallboy ■ n. Brit. a tall chest of drawers in two sections, one standing on the other.

tallith /'talɪθ/ ■ n. a fringed shawl traditionally worn by Jewish men at prayer.
– ORIGIN from Rabbinical Hebrew *ṭallīt*, from biblical Hebrew *ṭillel* 'to cover'.

tallow ■ n. a hard fatty substance made from rendered animal fat, used in making candles and soap.
– DERIVATIVES **tallowy** adj.
– ORIGIN Middle English: perhaps from Middle Low German.

tall ship ■ n. a sailing ship with a high mast or masts.

tally

tally ■ n. (pl. **-ies**) **1** a current score or amount. ▸ a record of a score or amount. **2** a particular number taken as a group or unit to facilitate counting. ▸ a mark registering such a number. **3** (also **tally stick**) historical a piece of wood scored across with notches for the items of an account and then split into halves, each party keeping one. **4** an identifying label for a plant or tree. ■ v. (**-ies, -ied**) **1** agree or correspond. **2** calculate the total number of.
– ORIGIN Middle English: from Anglo-Norman French *tallie*, from Latin *talea* 'twig, cutting'.

tally-ho ■ exclam. a huntsman's cry to the hounds on sighting a fox. ■ v. (**-oes, -oed**) utter such a cry.
– ORIGIN C18: perhaps an alteration of French *taïaut*.

tallyman ■ n. (pl. **-men**) **1** Brit. a person who sells goods on credit, especially from door to door. **2** a person who keeps a score or record of something.

tally system ■ n. Brit. a system of selling goods on short-term credit or an instalment plan.

Talmud /ˈtalmʊd, -məd/ ■ n. the body of Jewish civil and ceremonial law and legend comprising the Mishnah and the Gemara.
– DERIVATIVES **Talmudic** adj. **Talmudical** adj. **Talmudist** n.
– ORIGIN from late Hebrew *talmūd* 'instruction', from Hebrew *lāmaḏ* 'learn'.

Talmud Torah ■ n. **1** the field of study concerned with the Jewish law. **2** a communal school where children are instructed in Judaism.

talon ■ n. **1** a claw, especially one belonging to a bird of prey. **2** the shoulder of a bolt against which the key presses to slide it in a lock. **3** (in various card games) the cards remaining undealt. **4** a printed form attached to a bearer bond that enables the holder to apply for a new sheet of coupons when the existing coupons have been used up. **5** Architecture an ogee moulding.
– DERIVATIVES **taloned** adj.
– ORIGIN Middle English: from Old French, 'heel', from Latin *talus* 'ankle bone, heel'.

talus[1] /ˈteɪləs/ ■ n. (pl. **tali** /-lʌɪ/) Anatomy the large bone in the ankle, which articulates with the tibia of the leg and the calcaneus and navicular bone of the foot.
– ORIGIN C16: from Latin, 'ankle, heel'.

talus[2] /ˈteɪləs/ ■ n. (pl. **taluses**) **1** a sloping mass of rock fragments at the foot of a cliff. **2** the sloping side of an earthwork, or of a wall that tapers to the top.
– ORIGIN C17: from French.

TAM ■ abbrev. television audience measurement.

tamagotchi /ˌtaməˈɡɒtʃi/ ■ n. trademark an electronic toy displaying a digital image of a creature, which has to be looked after by the 'owner' as if it were a pet.
– ORIGIN from Japanese.

tamale /təˈmɑːleɪ, -ˈmɑːli/ ■ n. a Mexican dish of seasoned meat and maize flour steamed or baked in maize husks.
– ORIGIN from Mexican Spanish *tamal*, pl. *tamales*, from Nahuatl *tamalli*.

tamari /təˈmɑːri/ ■ n. a variety of rich, naturally fermented soy sauce.
– ORIGIN from Japanese.

tamarillo /ˌtaməˈrɪləʊ/ ■ n. (pl. **-os**) the red egg-shaped fruit of a tropical South American plant (*Cyphomandra betaceae*).
– ORIGIN 1960s: an invented name, perhaps suggested by Spanish *tomatillo*, diminutive of *tomate* 'tomato'.

tamarin /ˈtam(ə)rɪn/ ■ n. a small forest-dwelling South American monkey of the marmoset family. [Genera *Saguinus* and *Leontopithecus*: several species.]
– ORIGIN C18: from French, from Carib.

tamarind /ˈtam(ə)rɪnd/ ■ n. **1** sticky brown acidic pulp from the pod of a tree of the pea family, used as a flavouring in Asian cookery. **2** the tropical African tree which yields these pods. [*Tamarindus indica*.]
– ORIGIN Middle English: from medieval Latin *tamarindus*, from Arabic *tamr hindī* 'Indian date'.

tamarisk /ˈtam(ə)rɪsk/ ■ n. a shrub or small tree with tiny scale-like leaves borne on slender branches. [Genus *Tamarix*: many species.]
– ORIGIN Middle English: from late Latin *tamariscus*, var. of Latin *tamarix*.

tamboti /tamˈbuːti, -ˈbʊəti/ ■ n. a deciduous southern African tree, with scented, durable wood and toxic latex. [*Spirostachys africana*.]
– ORIGIN C19: from isiXhosa and isiZulu *umthombothi* 'poison tree'.

tambour /ˈtambʊə/ ■ n. **1** historical a small drum. **2** a circular frame for holding fabric taut while it is being embroidered. **3** Architecture a wall of circular plan, such as one supporting a dome. ▸ each of the cylindrical stones forming the shaft of a column. ■ v. [often as adj. **tamboured**] decorate or embroider on a tambour.
– ORIGIN C15: from French *tambour* 'drum'; perhaps rel. to Persian *tabīra* 'drum'.

tambourine /ˌtambəˈriːn/ ■ n. a percussion instrument resembling a shallow drum with metal discs around the edge, played by being shaken or hit with the hand.
– DERIVATIVES **tambourinist** n.
– ORIGIN C16: from French *tambourin*, diminutive of TAMBOUR.

tame ■ adj. **1** (of an animal) not dangerous or frightened of people; domesticated. ▸ informal (of a person) willing to cooperate. **2** not exciting, adventurous, or controversial. ■ v. **1** domesticate (an animal). **2** make less powerful and easier to control.
– DERIVATIVES **tameable** (also **tamable**) adj. **tamely** adv. **tameness** n. **tamer** n.
– ORIGIN Old English, of Germanic origin.

tameletjie /ˌtaməˈlɛki/ (also **tamaletjie**) ■ n. S. African **1** a hard toffee, sometimes containing almonds or pine nuts. **2** mebos.
– ORIGIN Afrikaans, perhaps from Dutch *tabletje* 'tablet, slab'.

Tamil /ˈtamɪl/ ■ n. **1** a member of a people inhabiting parts of South India and Sri Lanka. **2** the Dravidian language of the Tamils.
– DERIVATIVES **Tamilian** adj. & n.
– ORIGIN the name in Tamil.

Tammany /ˈtaməni/ (also **Tammany Hall**) ■ n. N. Amer. a corrupt political organization or group.
– ORIGIN orig. the name of a powerful organization within the US Democratic Party that was widely associated with corruption and had headquarters at *Tammany* Hall, New York.

tam-o'-shanter /ˌtaməˈʃantə/ ■ n. a round Scottish cap with a bobble in the centre.
– ORIGIN C19: named after the hero of Robert Burns's poem *Tam o' Shanter* (1790).

tamoxifen /təˈmɒksɪfɛn/ ■ n. a synthetic drug used to treat breast cancer and infertility in women.
– ORIGIN 1970s: an arbitrary formation based on TRANS-, AMINE, OXY-[2], PHENOL, elements of the drug's chemical name.

tamp ■ v. **1** pack (a blast hole) full of clay or sand to concentrate the force of the explosion. **2** firmly ram or pack (a substance) down or into something.
– ORIGIN C19: prob. a back-formation from *tampin*, var. of TAMPION.

Tampax ■ n. (pl. same) trademark a sanitary tampon.
– ORIGIN 1930s: an arbitrary formation from TAMPON.

tamper ■ v. (**tamper with**) interfere with (something) without authority or so as to cause damage. ■ n. a machine or tool for tamping down earth or ballast.
– DERIVATIVES **tamperer** n.
– ORIGIN C16: alteration of the verb TEMPER.

tampion /ˈtampɪən/ ■ n. **1** a wooden stopper for the muzzle of a gun. **2** a plug for the top of an organ pipe.
– ORIGIN Middle English: from French *tampon* 'stopper'.

tampon ■ n. **1** a plug of soft material inserted into the vagina to absorb menstrual blood. **2** Medicine a plug of material used to stop a wound or block an opening in the body and absorb blood or secretions. ■ v. (**tamponed, tamponing**) plug with a tampon.
– ORIGIN C19: from French, var. of *tapon* 'plug, stopper', of Germanic origin.

tamponade /ˌtampəˈneɪd/ ■ n. Medicine **1** (also **cardiac tamponade**) compression of the heart by an accumulation of fluid in the pericardial sac. **2** the surgical use of a plug of absorbent material.

tan[1] ■ n. **1** a yellowish-brown colour. **2** a golden-brown shade of skin developed by pale-skinned people after

---

CONSONANTS   b but   d dog   f few   g get   h he   j yes   k cat   l leg   m man   n no   p pen   r red

exposure to the sun. **3** (also **tanbark**) bark of oak or other trees, bruised and used as a source of tannin for converting hides into leather. ▸ (also **spent tan**) such bark from which the tannin has been extracted, used for covering paths and in gardening. ■ v. **(tanned, tanning)** **1** [often as adj. **tanned**] give or acquire a tan after exposure to the sun. **2** convert (animal skin) into leather, especially by soaking in a liquid containing tannic acid. **3** informal, dated beat (someone) as a punishment. ■ adj. N. Amer. having a tan after exposure to the sun.
–DERIVATIVES **tannable** adj. **tannish** adj.
–ORIGIN Old English *tannian* 'convert into leather', prob. from medieval Latin *tannare*, perhaps of Celtic origin; reinforced in Middle English by Old French *tanner*.

tan² ■ abbrev. tangent.

tanager /ˈtanədʒə/ ■ n. a brightly coloured American songbird of the bunting family. [Subfamily Thraupinae: numerous species.]
–ORIGIN C17: from Tupi *tangará*, later refashioned on the genus name *Tanagra*.

tanbark /ˈtanbɑːk/ ■ n. see TAN¹ (sense 3).

tandem ■ n. **1** a bicycle with seats and pedals for two riders, one behind the other. **2** a carriage driven by two animals harnessed one in front of the other. **3** a group of two people or machines working together. ■ adv. one behind another.
–PHRASES **in tandem 1** alongside each other; together. **2** one behind another.
–ORIGIN C18: humorously from Latin, 'at length'.

tandoor /ˈtandʊə, tanˈdʊə/ ■ n. a clay oven of a type used originally in northern India and Pakistan.
–ORIGIN from Urdu *tandūr*, from Persian *tanūr*, from Arabic *tannūr* 'oven'.

tandoori /tanˈdʊəri/ ■ adj. denoting or relating to a style of Indian cooking based on the use of a tandoor.

tang¹ ■ n. **1** a strong taste, flavour, or smell. **2** the projection on the blade of a knife or other tool by which the blade is held firmly in the handle.
–ORIGIN Middle English: from Old Norse *tangi* 'point, tang of a knife'.

tang² ■ v. make a loud ringing or clanging sound.
–ORIGIN C16: imitative.

tanga /ˈtaŋɡə/ ■ n. chiefly Brit. a pair of briefs consisting of small panels connected by strings at the sides.
–ORIGIN C20: from Portuguese, of Bantu origin.

tangelo /ˈtan(d)ʒələʊ/ ■ n. (pl. -os) a hybrid of the tangerine and grapefruit.
–ORIGIN C20: blend of TANGERINE and POMELO.

tangent /ˈtan(d)ʒ(ə)nt/ ■ n. **1** a straight line or plane that touches a curve or curved surface at a point, but if extended does not cross it at that point. **2** Mathematics the trigonometric function that is equal to the ratio of the sides (other than the hypotenuse) opposite and adjacent to an angle in a right-angled triangle. **3** a completely different line of thought or action. ■ adj. (of a line or plane) touching, but not intersecting, a curve or curved surface.
–DERIVATIVES **tangency** n.
–ORIGIN C16: from Latin *tangere* 'touch'.

tangential /tanˈdʒɛnʃ(ə)l/ ■ adj. **1** of, relating to, or along a tangent. **2** having only a slight connection or relevance; peripheral. **3** diverging from a previous course; erratic.
–DERIVATIVES **tangentially** adv.

tangerine ■ n. **1** a small citrus fruit with a loose skin, especially one of a variety with deep orange-red skin. **2** the citrus tree which bears this fruit. [*Citrus reticulata*.] **3** a deep orange-red colour.
–ORIGIN C19: from *Tanger*, former name of *Tangier*, from where the fruit was exported.

tangible /ˈtan(d)ʒɪb(ə)l/ ■ adj. **1** perceptible by touch. **2** clear and definite; real. ■ n. a thing that is perceptible by touch.
–DERIVATIVES **tangibility** n. **tangibleness** n. **tangibly** adv.
–ORIGIN C16: from French, or from late Latin *tangibilis*, from Latin *tangere* 'to touch'.

tangle ■ v. **1** twist (strands) together into a confused mass. **2** (**tangle with**) informal become involved in a conflict with. ■ n. **1** a confused mass of something twisted together. **2** a confused or complicated state; a muddle. ▸ informal a fight, argument, or disagreement.

tantalite

–DERIVATIVES **tangly** adj.
–ORIGIN Middle English: prob. of Scandinavian origin and rel. to Swedish dialect *taggla* 'disarrange'.

tango ■ n. **1** (pl. -os) a ballroom dance originating in Buenos Aires, characterized by marked rhythms and postures and abrupt pauses. ▸ a piece of music in the style of this dance, typically in a slow, dotted duple rhythm. **2** a code word representing the letter T, used in radio communication. ■ v. (-oes, -oed) dance the tango.
–ORIGIN C19: from Latin American Spanish, perhaps of African origin.

tangram /ˈtangram/ ■ n. a Chinese geometrical puzzle consisting of a square cut into seven pieces which can be arranged to make various other shapes.
–ORIGIN C19.

tangy ■ adj. (-ier, -iest) having a strong, piquant flavour or smell.
–DERIVATIVES **tanginess** n.

tank ■ n. **1** a large receptacle or storage chamber, especially for liquid or gas. ▸ the container holding the fuel supply in a motor vehicle. **2** a receptacle with transparent sides in which to keep fish; an aquarium. **3** a heavy armoured fighting vehicle carrying guns and moving on a continuous articulated metal track. ■ v. **1** (**be/get tanked up**) informal drink heavily or become drunk. **2** (usu. **tank up**) fill the tank of a vehicle with fuel.
–DERIVATIVES **tankful** n. (pl. -fuls). **tankless** adj.
–ORIGIN C17: perhaps from Gujarati *tānkū* or Marathi *tānkē* 'underground cistern', prob. influenced by Portuguese *tangue* 'pond'.

tanka /ˈtɑːŋkə/ ■ n. (pl. **tankas**) a Tibetan religious painting on a scroll, hung as a banner in temples and carried in processions.
–ORIGIN from Tibetan *t'áṅ-ka* 'image, painting'.

tankage ■ n. **1** storage in a tank. **2** a fertilizer or animal feed obtained from the residue from tanks in which animal carcasses have been rendered.

tankard ■ n. a tall beer mug, typically made of silver or pewter, with a handle and sometimes a hinged lid.
–ORIGIN Middle English: perhaps rel. to Dutch *tanckaert*.

tank engine ■ n. a steam locomotive carrying fuel and water receptacles in its own frame, not in a tender.

tanker ■ n. a ship, road vehicle, or aircraft for carrying liquids, especially mineral oils, in bulk. ■ v. transport (a liquid) in a tanker.

tank farm ■ n. **1** a place where plants are grown in tanks of water without soil. **2** informal a site containing bulk oil or chemical storage tanks.

tank top ■ n. a close-fitting sleeveless top worn over a shirt or blouse.

tanner¹ ■ n. **1** a person employed to tan animal hides. **2** a lotion or cream designed to promote or simulate the development of a suntan.

tanner² ■ n. Brit. informal, historical a sixpence.
–ORIGIN C19.

tannery ■ n. (pl. -ies) a place where animal hides are tanned.

tannic acid ■ n. another term for TANNIN.
–DERIVATIVES **tannate** n.

tannie /ˈtʌni/ ■ n. S. African auntie.
–ORIGIN Afrikaans, diminutive of *tante*.

tannin ■ n. a yellowish or brownish bitter-tasting organic substance present in some galls, barks, etc.
–DERIVATIVES **tannic** adj.
–ORIGIN C19: from French *tanin*, from *tan* 'tanbark'.

tannoy Brit. ■ n. trademark a type of public address system. ■ v. transmit or announce over such a system.
–ORIGIN 1920s: contraction of *tantalum alloy*, which is used as a rectifier in the system.

tansy /ˈtanzi/ ■ n. a plant with yellow flat-topped button-like flower heads and aromatic leaves. [*Tanacetum vulgare* and related species.]
–ORIGIN Middle English: from Old French *tanesie*, prob. from medieval Latin *athanasia* 'immortality', from Greek.

tantalite /ˈtantəlʌɪt/ ■ n. a rare, dense black mineral

---
s sit   t top   v voice   w we   z zoo   ʃ she   ʒ decision   θ thin   ð this   ŋ ring   x loch   tʃ chip   dʒ jar

tantalize

consisting of a mixed oxide of iron, manganese, and tantalum, of which it is the principal source.
– ORIGIN C19: from TANTALUM.

tantalize (also **-ise**) ■ v. torment or tease with the sight or promise of something that is unobtainable or withheld.
– DERIVATIVES **tantalization** (also **-isation**) n. **tantalizer** (also **-iser**) n. **tantalizing** (also **-ising**) adj. **tantalizingly** (also **-isingly**) adv.
– ORIGIN C16: from *Tantalus* in Greek mythology, who was punished for his crimes by being provided with fruit and water which receded when he reached for them.

tantalum /ˈtantələm/ ■ n. the chemical element of atomic number 73, a hard silver-grey metal. (Symbol: **Ta**)
– DERIVATIVES **tantalic** adj.
– ORIGIN C19: from *Tantalus* (see TANTALIZE), with ref. to its frustrating insolubility in acids.

tantalus /ˈtantələs/ ■ n. Brit. a stand in which spirit decanters may be locked up though still visible.
– ORIGIN from *Tantalus* (see TANTALIZE).

tantamount ■ adj. (**tantamount to**) equivalent in seriousness to; virtually the same as.
– ORIGIN C17: from the earlier verb *tantamount* 'amount to as much', from Italian *tanto montare*.

tante /tɑːt, tɑːnt, ˈtantə/ ■ n. (among those of French, German, or Afrikaans origin) a respectful form of address for an older woman.
– ORIGIN French, Dutch *tante*, German *Tante* 'aunt'.

tant mieux /tɒ ˈmjəː/ ■ exclam. so much the better.
– ORIGIN from French.

tant pis /tɒ ˈpiː/ ■ exclam. so much the worse; too bad.
– ORIGIN from French.

tantra /ˈtantrə, ˈtʌntrə/ ■ n. 1 a Hindu or Buddhist mystical or magical text. 2 adherence to the doctrines or principles of the tantras, involving mantras, meditation, yoga, and ritual.
– DERIVATIVES **tantric** adj. **tantrism** n. **tantrist** n.
– ORIGIN Sanskrit, 'loom, groundwork, doctrine', from *tan* 'stretch'.

tantrum ■ n. an uncontrolled outburst of anger and frustration, typically in a young child.
– ORIGIN C18.

Tanzanian /ˌtanzəˈniːən/ ■ n. a native or inhabitant of Tanzania. ■ adj. of or relating to Tanzania.

tanzanite /ˈtanzənʌɪt/ ■ n. a blue gem variety of epidote.
– ORIGIN named after *Tanzania*, where it occurs.

Tao /taʊ, ˈtɑːʊ/ ■ n. (in Chinese philosophy) the absolute principle underlying the universe, combining within itself the principles of yin and yang and signifying the way, or code of behaviour, that is in harmony with the natural order.
– ORIGIN Chinese, '(right) way'.

Taoiseach /ˈtiːʃəx/ ■ n. the Prime Minister of the Irish Republic.
– ORIGIN Irish, 'chief, leader'.

Taoism /ˈtaʊɪz(ə)m, ˈtɑːʊ-/ ■ n. a Chinese philosophy based on the writings of Lao-Tzu (including the Tao-te-Ching), advocating humility and religious piety.
– DERIVATIVES **Taoist** n. & adj. **Taoistic** adj.

Tao-te-Ching /ˌtaʊtiːˈtʃɪŋ/ ■ n. the central Taoist text.
– ORIGIN Chinese, 'the Book of the Way and its Power'.

tap[1] ■ n. 1 a device by which a flow of liquid or gas from a pipe or container can be controlled. 2 an instrument for cutting a threaded hole in a material. 3 a device connected to a telephone for listening secretly to conversation. 4 (also **tapping**) an electrical connection made to some point between the end terminals of a transformer coil or other component. ■ v. (**tapped**, **tapping**) 1 draw liquid through the tap or spout of (a cask, barrel, etc.). 2 draw sap from (a tree) by cutting into it. 3 exploit or draw a supply from (a resource). ▸ informal obtain money or information from. 4 connect a device to (a telephone) so that conversation can be listened to secretly. 5 cut a thread in (something) to accept a screw.
– PHRASES **on tap** ready to be poured from a tap. ▸ informal freely available whenever needed.
– DERIVATIVES **tappable** adj.

– ORIGIN Old English *tæppa* 'stopper for a cask', *tæppian* 'provide (a cask) with a stopper', of Germanic origin.

tap[2] ■ v. (**tapped**, **tapping**) strike or knock with a quick light blow or blows. ▸ strike lightly and repeatedly against something else: *she was tapping her feet*. ■ n. 1 a quick light blow or the sound of such a blow. 2 tap dancing. ▸ a piece of metal attached to the toe and heel of a tap dancer's shoe to make a tapping sound. 3 (**taps**) [treated as sing. or pl.] US a bugle call for lights to be put out in army quarters. ▸ a similar call sounded at a military funeral. ▸ (in the Guide movement) a closing song sung at an evening camp fire or at the end of a meeting.
– DERIVATIVES **tapper** n.
– ORIGIN Middle English: from Old French *taper*, or of imitative origin.

tapas /ˈtapəs/ ■ pl. n. small Spanish savoury dishes, typically served with drinks at a bar.
– ORIGIN Spanish, 'cover, lid' (because the dishes were given free with the drink, served on a dish balanced on the glass).

tap dance ■ n. a dance performed wearing shoes fitted with metal taps, characterized by rhythmical tapping of the toes and heels. ■ v. (**tap-dance**) perform such a dance.
– DERIVATIVES **tap dancer** n. **tap-dancing** n.

tape ■ n. 1 light, flexible material in a narrow strip, used to hold, fasten, or mark off something. ▸ (also **adhesive tape**) a strip of paper or plastic coated with adhesive, used to stick things together. 2 long, narrow material with magnetic properties, used for recording sound, pictures, or computer data. ▸ a cassette or reel containing such material. 3 a strip of material stretched across the finishing line of a race, to be broken by the winner. 4 a tape measure. ■ v. 1 record (sound or pictures) on audio or video tape. 2 fasten, attach, or mark off with tape.
– ORIGIN Old English, perhaps rel. to Middle Low German *teppen* 'pluck, tear'.

tape deck ■ n. a piece of equipment for playing audio tapes, especially as part of a stereo system.

tape measure ■ n. a length of tape or thin flexible metal, marked at graded intervals for measuring.

tapenade /ˈtapənɑːd/ ■ n. a Provençal savoury paste or dip, made from black olives, capers, and anchovies.
– ORIGIN French, from Provençal.

taper ■ v. 1 diminish or reduce in thickness towards one end. 2 (usu. **taper off**) gradually lessen. ■ n. a slender candle. ▸ a wick coated with wax, used for conveying a flame.
– ORIGIN Old English, formed by alteration of *p-* to *t-*, from Latin *papyrus* (see PAPYRUS), the pith of which was used for candle wicks.

tape recorder ■ n. an apparatus for recording sounds on magnetic tape and afterwards reproducing them.
– DERIVATIVES **tape-record** v. **tape recording** n.

tape streamer ■ n. see STREAMER (sense 5).

tapestry ■ n. (pl. **-ies**) a piece of thick textile fabric with pictures or designs formed by weaving coloured weft threads or by embroidering on canvas.
– DERIVATIVES **tapestried** adj.
– ORIGIN Middle English: from Old French *tapisserie*, from *tapis* 'carpet, tapis'.

tapetum /təˈpiːtəm/ ■ n. Zoology a reflective layer of the choroid in the eyes of many animals, causing them to shine in the dark.
– ORIGIN C18: from Latin *tapete* 'carpet'.

tapeworm ■ n. a parasitic flatworm with a long ribbon-like body, the adult of which lives in the intestines. [Class Cestoda: many species.]

taphonomy /taˈfɒnəmi/ ■ n. the branch of palaeontology concerned with the processes of fossilization.
– DERIVATIVES **taphonomic** adj. **taphonomist** n.
– ORIGIN 1940s: from Greek *taphos* 'grave' + -NOMY.

tapioca /ˌtapɪˈəʊkə/ ■ n. a starchy substance in the form of hard white grains, obtained from cassava and used for puddings and other dishes.
– ORIGIN C18: from Tupi-Guarani *tipioca*, from *tipi* 'dregs' + *og, ok* 'squeeze out'.

tapir /ˈteɪpə, -ɪə/ ■ n. a hoofed mammal with a short flexible proboscis, native to tropical America and Malaysia. [Genus *Tapirus*: four species.]
– ORIGIN C18: from Tupi *tapyra*.

tapis /ˈtapiː/ ■ n. (pl. same) archaic a tapestry or richly decorated cloth, used as a hanging or a covering.
– ORIGIN French, from Old French *tapiz*, from Greek *tapētion*, diminutive of *tapēs* 'tapestry'.

tapotement /təˈpəʊtm(ə)nt/ ■ n. rapid and repeated striking of the body as a technique in massage.
– ORIGIN C19: French, from *tapoter* 'to tap'.

tappet /ˈtapɪt/ ■ n. a lever or projecting part on a machine which intermittently makes contact with a cam or other part so as to give or receive motion.
– ORIGIN C18: apparently a diminutive of TAP².

taproom ■ n. a room in which alcoholic drinks, especially beer, are available on tap.

taproot ■ n. a straight tapering root growing vertically downwards and forming the centre from which subsidiary rootlets spring.

tar¹ ■ n. a dark, thick flammable liquid distilled from wood or coal, used in road-making and for coating and preserving timber. ▸ a similar substance formed by burning tobacco or other material. ■ v. (**tarred, tarring**) [usu. as adj. **tarred**] cover with tar.
– PHRASES **beat** (or **whale**) **the tar out of** N. Amer. informal beat or thrash severely. **tar and feather** smear with tar and then cover with feathers as a punishment. **tar people with the same brush** consider specified people to have the same faults.
– ORIGIN Old English, of Germanic origin.

tar² ■ n. informal, dated a sailor.
– ORIGIN C17: perhaps an abbrev. of TARPAULIN.

taradiddle /ˈtarəˌdɪd(ə)l/ (also **tarradiddle**) ■ n. informal, chiefly Brit. **1** a petty lie. **2** pretentious nonsense.
– ORIGIN C18: perhaps rel. to DIDDLE.

taramasalata /ˌtarəməsəˈlɑːtə/ (also **tarama** /ˈtarəmə/) ■ n. a pinkish paste or dip made from the roe of certain fish, mixed with olive oil and seasoning.
– ORIGIN from modern Greek *taramas* 'roe' + *salata* 'salad'.

tarantella /ˌtar(ə)nˈtɛlə/ (also **tarantelle** /-ˈtɛl/) ■ n. a rapid whirling dance originating in southern Italy. ▸ a piece of music written in fast 6/8 time in the style of this dance.
– ORIGIN C18: Italian, from the name of the seaport *Taranto*; so named because it was thought to be a cure for tarantism, a psychological illness characterised by an impulse to dance.

tarantula /təˈrantjʊlə/ ■ n. **1** a very large hairy spider found chiefly in tropical and subtropical America. [Family Theraphosidae.] **2** a large black wolf spider of southern Europe. [*Lycosa tarentula*.]
– ORIGIN C16: from Old Italian *tarantola*, from the name of the seaport *Taranto* in southern Italy.

tar baby ■ n. informal a difficult problem which is only aggravated by attempts to solve it.
– ORIGIN with allusion to the doll smeared with tar as a trap for Brer Rabbit, in J. C. Harris's *Uncle Remus*.

tarboosh /tɑːˈbuːʃ/ ■ n. a man's cap similar to a fez, typically of red felt with a tassel at the top.
– ORIGIN C18: from Egyptian Arabic *ṭarbūš*, from Persian *sarpūš*, from *sar* 'head' + *pūš* 'cover'.

Tardigrada /ˌtɑːdɪˈɡreɪdə/ ■ pl. n. Zoology a small phylum that comprises the water bears.
– DERIVATIVES **tardigrade** /ˈtɑːdɪɡreɪd/ n.
– ORIGIN from Latin *tardigradus*, from *tardus* 'slow' + *gradi* 'to walk'.

tardive dyskinesia /ˌtɑːdɪv ˌdɪskɪˈniːzɪə/ ■ n. Medicine a neurological disorder characterized by involuntary movements of the face and jaw.
– ORIGIN 1960s: *tardive* from French *tardif, tardive* (see TARDY).

tardy ■ adj. (**-ier, -iest**) delaying or delayed beyond the right or expected time; late. ▸ slow in action or response; sluggish.
– DERIVATIVES **tardily** adv. **tardiness** n.
– ORIGIN C16: from French *tardif, -ive*, from Latin *tardus* 'slow'.

tare¹ /tɛː/ ■ n. **1** a vetch, especially the common vetch. **2** (**tares**) (in biblical use) a harmful weed resembling corn when young (Matthew 13:24–30).
– ORIGIN Middle English.

tare² /tɛː/ ■ n. an allowance made for the weight of the packaging in order to determine the net weight of goods. ▸ the weight of a vehicle without its fuel or load.
– ORIGIN Middle English: from French, 'deficiency, tare', from medieval Latin *tara*, from Arabic *ṭaraḥa* 'reject, deduct'.

targe /tɑːdʒ/ ■ n. archaic term for TARGET (in sense 3).
– ORIGIN Old English, of Germanic origin.

target ■ n. **1** a person, object, or place selected as the aim of an attack. ▸ a round or rectangular board marked with concentric circles, aimed at in archery or shooting. **2** an objective or result towards which efforts are directed: *a sales target*. **3** historical a small round shield or buckler. ▸ v. (**targeted, targeting**) select as an object of attention or attack. ▸ aim or direct (something).
– PHRASES **on** (or **off**) **target** succeeding (or not succeeding) in hitting or achieving the thing aimed at.
– DERIVATIVES **targetable** adj.
– ORIGIN Middle English: diminutive of TARGE.

target language ■ n. the language into which a text, document, or speech is translated.

tariff ■ n. **1** a tax or duty to be paid on a particular class of imports or exports. **2** a table of the fixed charges made by a business or professional person. **3** Law a scale of sentences and damages for crimes and injuries of different severities. ■ v. fix the price of (something) according to a tariff.
– ORIGIN C16: from Italian *tariffa*, from Arabic *'arrafa* 'notify'.

tarlatan /ˈtɑːlətən/ ■ n. a thin, open-weave muslin fabric, used for stiffening ball dresses.
– ORIGIN C18: from French *tarlatane*, prob. of Indian origin.

tarmac ■ n. (trademark in the UK) material used for surfacing roads or other outdoor areas, consisting of broken stone mixed with tar. ▸ a runway or other area surfaced with such material. ■ v. (**tarmacked, tarmacking**) surface with tarmac.
– ORIGIN C20: abbrev. of TARMACADAM.

tarmacadam /ˌtɑːməˈkadəm/ ■ n. another term for TARMAC.
– ORIGIN C19: from TAR¹ + MACADAM.

tarn ■ n. a small mountain lake.
– ORIGIN Middle English: from Old Norse *tjǫrn*.

tarnation ■ n. & exclam. chiefly N. Amer. used as a euphemism for 'damnation'.
– ORIGIN C18: alteration.

tarnish ■ v. **1** lose or cause to lose lustre, especially as a result of exposure to air or moisture. **2** make or become less valuable or respected. ■ n. dullness of colour; loss of brightness. ▸ a film or stain formed on an exposed surface of a mineral or metal.
– DERIVATIVES **tarnishable** adj.
– ORIGIN Middle English: from French *terniss-, ternir*, from *terne* 'dark, dull'.

taro /ˈtɑːrəʊ, ˈtarəʊ/ ■ n. a tropical Asian plant with edible starchy corms and fleshy leaves, grown as a staple in the Pacific. [*Colocasia esculenta*.]
– ORIGIN C18: of Polynesian origin.

tarot /ˈtarəʊ/ ■ n. playing cards, traditionally a pack of 78 with five suits, used for fortune telling.
– ORIGIN C16: from French, from Italian *tarocchi*.

tarp ■ n. informal, chiefly N. Amer. a tarpaulin sheet or cover.

tarpaulin /tɑːˈpɔːlɪn/ ■ n. heavy-duty waterproof cloth, originally of tarred canvas. ▸ a sheet or covering of this.
– ORIGIN C17: prob. from TAR¹ + PALL¹.

tar pit ■ n. a hollow in which natural tar accumulates by seepage.

tarpon /ˈtɑːpɒn/ ■ n. a large tropical marine fish of herring-like appearance. [*Tarpon atlanticus* (Atlantic) and *Megalops cyprinoides* (Indo-Pacific).]
– ORIGIN C17: prob. from Dutch *tarpoen*.

tarradiddle ■ n. variant spelling of TARADIDDLE.

tarragon /ˈtarəɡ(ə)n/ ■ n. a perennial plant of the daisy family, with narrow aromatic leaves that are used as a

culinary herb. [*Artemisia dracunculus*.]
–ORIGIN C16: representing medieval Latin *tragonia* and *tarchon*, perhaps from an Arabic alteration of Greek *drakōn* 'dragon'.

tarry[1] /ˈtɑːri/ ■ adj. (**-ier, -iest**) of, like, or covered with tar.
–DERIVATIVES **tarriness** n.

tarry[2] /ˈtari/ ■ v. (**-ies, -ied**) archaic stay longer than intended; delay leaving a place.
–ORIGIN Middle English.

tarsal /ˈtɑːs(ə)l/ Anatomy ■ adj. of or relating to the tarsus. ■ n. a bone of the tarsus.

tarsi plural form of TARSUS.

tarsier /ˈtɑːsɪə/ ■ n. a small tree-dwelling insectivorous primate with very large eyes, a long tufted tail, and very long hindlimbs, native to the islands of SE Asia. [Genus *Tarsius*.]
–ORIGIN C18: from French, from *tarse* 'tarsus', with ref. to the animal's long tarsal bones.

tarsus /ˈtɑːsəs/ ■ n. (pl. **tarsi** /-sʌɪ, -siː/) **1** Anatomy the group of small bones between the main part of the hindlimb and the metatarsus, forming the ankle and upper foot in humans. ▸ Zoology the shank of the leg of a bird or reptile. ▸ Zoology the foot or fifth leg joint of an insect or other arthropod, typically ending in a claw. **2** Anatomy a thin sheet of fibrous connective tissue supporting the edge of the eyelid.
–ORIGIN Middle English: from Greek *tarsos* 'flat of the foot, the eyelid'.

tart[1] ■ n. an open pastry case containing a sweet or savoury filling.
–DERIVATIVES **tartlet** n.
–ORIGIN Middle English: from Old French *tarte* or medieval Latin *tarta*.

tart[2] ■ n. informal, derogatory a prostitute or promiscuous woman. ■ v. (**tart oneself up**) informal, chiefly Brit. dress or make oneself up in order to look attractive. ▸ (**tart something up**) decorate or improve the appearance of something.
–DERIVATIVES **tartily** adv. **tartiness** n. **tarty** adj. (**-ier, -iest**).
–ORIGIN C19: prob. an abbrev. of SWEETHEART.

tart[3] ■ adj. **1** sharp or acid in taste. **2** (of a remark or tone of voice) cutting, bitter, or sarcastic.
–DERIVATIVES **tartly** adv. **tartness** n.
–ORIGIN Old English *teart* 'harsh, severe', of unknown origin.

tartan ■ n. a woollen cloth woven in one of several patterns of coloured checks and intersecting lines, especially of a design associated with a particular Scottish clan.
–ORIGIN C15: perhaps from Old French *tertaine*, denoting a kind of cloth.

Tartar /ˈtɑːtə/ ■ n. **1** historical a member of the combined forces of central Asian peoples, including Mongols and Turks. **2** (**tartar**) a harsh, fierce, or intractable person.
–ORIGIN from Old French *Tartare* or medieval Latin *Tartarus*, from TATAR.

tartar /ˈtɑːtə/ ■ n. **1** a hard calcified deposit that forms on the teeth and contributes to their decay. **2** a deposit of impure potassium hydrogen tartrate formed during the fermentation of wine.
–ORIGIN Middle English: from medieval Greek *tartaron*.

tartare /tɑːˈtɑː/ ■ adj. [postpos.] (of fish or meat) served raw, typically seasoned and shaped into small cakes.
–ORIGIN French, 'Tartar'.

tartar emetic ■ n. potassium antimony tartrate, a toxic compound used in dyeing and to treat protozoal disease in animals.

tartare sauce (also **tartar sauce**) ■ n. a cold sauce, typically eaten with fish, consisting of mayonnaise mixed with chopped onions, gherkins, and capers.

tartaric acid ■ n. Chemistry a crystalline organic acid which is present especially in unripe grapes and is used in baking powders and as a food additive.
–ORIGIN C18: from obsolete French *tartarique*, from medieval Latin *tartarum* (see TARTAR).

tarte Tatin /ˌtɑːt taˈtã/ ■ n. a type of upside-down apple tart consisting of pastry baked over slices of fruit in caramelized sugar, served fruit side up after cooking.
–ORIGIN French, from *tarte* 'tart' + *Tatin*, the surname of the sisters said to have created the dish.

tartrate /ˈtɑːtreɪt/ ■ n. Chemistry a salt or ester of tartaric acid.
–ORIGIN C18: from French, from *tartre* 'tartar'.

tartrazine /ˈtɑːtrəziːn/ ■ n. Chemistry a brilliant yellow synthetic dye derived from tartaric acid and used to colour food, drugs, and cosmetics.
–ORIGIN C19: from French *tartre* 'tartar'.

tartufo /tɑːˈtuːfəʊ/ ■ n. **1** an edible fungus, especially a truffle. **2** an Italian chocolate dessert of a creamy mousse-like consistency.
–ORIGIN Italian, 'truffle'.

Tarzan ■ n. a man of great agility and powerful physique.
–ORIGIN from the name of a fictitious character created by the American writer Edgar Rice Burroughs.

task ■ n. a piece of work. ■ v. **1** (usu. **be tasked with**) assign a particular task to. **2** make great demands on.
–PHRASES **take someone to task** reprimand or criticize someone.
–ORIGIN Middle English: from an Old Northern French var. of Old French *tasche*, from medieval Latin *tasca*, *taxa*, from Latin *taxare* (see TAX).

task force ■ n. an armed force organized for a special operation. ▸ a unit specially organized for a task.

taskmaster ■ n. a person who imposes an onerous workload on someone.

Tasmanian /tazˈmeɪnɪən/ ■ n. a native or inhabitant of the Australian state of Tasmania. ■ adj. of or relating to Tasmania.

Tasmanian devil ■ n. a heavily built aggressive marsupial with a large head, powerful jaws, and mainly black fur, found only in Tasmania. [*Sarcophilus harrisii*.]

Tasmanian wolf (also **Tasmanian tiger**) ■ n. a doglike carnivorous Tasmanian marsupial with striped hindquarters, probably extinct. [*Thylacinus cynocephalus*.]

tassel ■ n. **1** a tuft of hanging threads, knotted together at one end and used for decoration in soft furnishing and clothing. **2** the tufted head of some plants, especially a flower head with prominent stamens at the top of a maize stalk. ■ v. (**tasselled, tasselling**; US **tasseled, tasseling**) **1** provide with a tassel or tassels. **2** (of maize or other plants) form tassels.
–DERIVATIVES **tasselled** adj.
–ORIGIN Middle English: from Old French *tassel* 'clasp'.

Tassies ■ n. S. African informal Tassenberg (trademark), a popular red wine.

taste ■ n. **1** the sensation of flavour perceived in the mouth on contact with a substance. ▸ the faculty of perceiving this. **2** a small portion of food or drink taken as a sample. **3** a brief experience of something. **4** a person's liking for something. **5** the ability to discern what is of good quality or of a high aesthetic standard. ▸ conformity to a specified degree with generally held views on what is appropriate or offensive: *a joke in bad taste*. ■ v. **1** perceive or experience the flavour of. ▸ have a specified flavour. ▸ sample or test the flavour of. ▸ eat or drink a small portion of. **2** have a brief experience of.
–PHRASES **to taste** according to personal liking.
–DERIVATIVES **tasting** n.
–ORIGIN Middle English: from Old French *tast* (n.), *taster* (v.) 'touch, try, taste', perhaps from a blend of Latin *tangere* 'to touch' and *gustare* 'to taste'.

taste bud ■ n. any of the clusters of bulbous nerve endings on the tongue and in the lining of the mouth which provide the sense of taste.

tasteful ■ adj. showing good aesthetic judgement or appropriate behaviour.
–DERIVATIVES **tastefully** adv. **tastefulness** n.

tasteless ■ adj. **1** lacking flavour. **2** lacking in aesthetic judgement or constituting inappropriate behaviour.
–DERIVATIVES **tastelessly** adv. **tastelessness** n.

taster ■ n. **1** a person who tests food or drink by tasting it. ▸ a small cup for tasting wine. ▸ an instrument for extracting a small sample from within a cheese. **2** a sample or brief experience of something.

tasty ■ adj. (**-ier, -iest**) **1** (of food) having a pleasant,

distinct flavour. **2** informal, chiefly Brit. attractive; appealing.
– DERIVATIVES **tastily** adv. **tastiness** n.

tat[1] ■ n. Brit. informal tasteless or shoddy articles.
– ORIGIN C19: prob. a back-formation from TATTY.

tat[2] ■ v. (**tatted**, **tatting**) do tatting; make by tatting.
– ORIGIN C19: back-formation from TATTING.

tat[3] ■ n. (in phr. **tit for tat**) see TIT[3].

ta-ta ■ exclam. informal, chiefly Brit. goodbye.
– ORIGIN C19.

tatami /tə'tɑːmi/ ■ n. (pl. same or **tatamis**) a rush-covered straw mat forming a traditional Japanese floor covering.
– ORIGIN from Japanese.

Tatar /'tɑːtə/ ■ n. **1** a member of a Turkic people living in Tatarstan and various other parts of Russia and Ukraine. **2** the Turkic language of this people.
– ORIGIN the Turkic name of a Tartar tribe.

tater /'teɪtə/ ■ n. informal a potato.
– ORIGIN C18.

tatterdemalion /ˌtatədɪ'meɪljən/ ■ adj. tattered or dilapidated. ■ n. a person in tattered clothing.
– ORIGIN C17: from TATTERS or TATTERED.

tattered ■ adj. old and torn; in poor condition.
– ORIGIN Middle English: apparently from *tatter* 'scrap of cloth'; later treated as a past participle.

tatters ■ pl. n. irregularly torn pieces of cloth, paper, etc.
– PHRASES **in tatters** informal **1** torn; in shreds. **2** destroyed; ruined.
– ORIGIN Middle English: from Old Norse *tǫtrar* 'rags'.

tattersall /'tatəs(ə)l, -sɔːl/ ■ n. a woollen fabric with a pattern of coloured checks and intersecting lines, resembling a tartan.
– ORIGIN C19: named after *Tattersalls*, the firm of horse auctioneers, by association with the traditional design of horse blankets.

tattie ■ n. informal, chiefly Scottish a potato.
– ORIGIN C18.

tatting ■ n. **1** a kind of knotted lace made by hand with a small shuttle. **2** the process of making such lace.
– ORIGIN C19.

tattle ■ n. gossip; idle talk. ■ v. engage in tattle.
– DERIVATIVES **tattler** n.
– ORIGIN C15: from Middle Flemish *tatelen*, *tateren*, of imitative origin.

tattletale chiefly US ■ n. a telltale. ■ v. tell tales.

tattoo[1] ■ n. (pl. **tattoos**) **1** an evening drum or bugle signal recalling soldiers to their quarters. **2** a military display consisting of music, marching, and exercises. **3** a rhythmic tapping or drumming.
– ORIGIN C17 (orig. as *tap-too*) from Dutch *taptoe!* 'close the tap (of the cask)!'.

tattoo[2] ■ v. (**tattoos**, **tattooed**) mark with an indelible design by inserting pigment into punctures in the skin. ■ n. (pl. **tattoos**) a design made in such a way.
– DERIVATIVES **tattooer** n. **tattooist** n.
– ORIGIN C18: from Tahitian, Tongan, and Samoan *ta-tau* or Marquesan *ta-tu*.

tatty ■ adj. (**-ier**, **-iest**) informal worn and shabby; in poor condition.
– DERIVATIVES **tattily** adv. **tattiness** n.
– ORIGIN C16: apparently rel. to Old English *tættec* 'rag', of Germanic origin.

tau /tɔː, taʊ/ ■ n. **1** the nineteenth letter of the Greek alphabet (,), transliterated as 't'. **2** (also **tau particle**) Physics an unstable lepton with a charge of −1 and a mass roughly 3 500 times that of the electron.
– ORIGIN from Greek.

tau cross ■ n. a T-shaped cross.

taught past and past participle of TEACH.

taunt ■ n. a jeering or mocking remark made in order to wound or provoke. ■ v. provoke or wound with taunts.
– DERIVATIVES **taunter** n. **taunting** adj. **tauntingly** adv.
– ORIGIN C16: from French *tant pour tant* 'like for like, tit for tat', from *tant* 'so much', from Latin *tantus*.

taupe /təʊp/ ■ n. a grey tinged with brown.
– ORIGIN C20: from French, 'mole, moleskin', from Latin *talpa*.

taurine[1] /'tɔːriːn/ ■ n. Biochemistry a sulphur-containing amino acid important in the metabolism of fats.
– ORIGIN C19: from Greek *tauros* 'bull' (because it was orig. obtained from ox bile).

taurine[2] /'tɔːrʌɪn/ ■ adj. **1** of or like a bull. **2** of or relating to bullfighting.
– ORIGIN C17: from Latin *taurinus*, from *taurus* 'bull'.

Taurus /'tɔːrəs/ ■ n. **1** Astronomy a constellation (the Bull), said to represent a bull tamed by Jason (a hero of Greek mythology). **2** Astrology the second sign of the zodiac, which the sun enters about 21 April.
– DERIVATIVES **Taurean** /'tɔːriən, tɔː'riːən/ n. & adj.
– ORIGIN from Latin.

taut ■ adj. **1** stretched or pulled tight. ▸ (of muscles or nerves) tense. **2** (of writing, music, etc.) concise and controlled.
– DERIVATIVES **tauten** v. **tautly** adv. **tautness** n.
– ORIGIN Middle English *tought* 'distended', perhaps orig. a var. of TOUGH.

tauto- /'tɔːtəʊ/ ■ comb. form same: *tautology*.
– ORIGIN from Greek *tauto*, contraction of *to auto* 'the same'.

tautology /tɔː'tɒlədʒi/ ■ n. (pl. **-ies**) **1** the unnecessary repetition within a statement of the same thing in different words. **2** Logic a statement that is true by necessity or by virtue of its logical form.
– DERIVATIVES **tautological** adj. **tautologically** adv. **tautologist** n. **tautologize** (also **-ise**) v. **tautologous** adj.
– ORIGIN C16: from Greek, from *tautologos* 'repeating what has been said', from *tauto-* 'same' + *-logos* (see -LOGY).

tautomer /'tɔːtəmə/ ■ n. Chemistry each of two or more readily interconvertible isomers of a compound which exist together in equilibrium.
– DERIVATIVES **tautomeric** /-'mɛrɪk/ adj. **tautomerism** /-'tɒmərɪz(ə)m/ n.
– ORIGIN C20: blend of TAUTO- and ISOMER.

tavern ■ n. chiefly archaic or N. Amer. an inn or public house. ▸ S. African a licensed shebeen.
– DERIVATIVES **taverner** n.
– ORIGIN Middle English: from Old French *taverne*, from Latin *taberna* 'hut, tavern'.

taverna /tə'vɑːnə/ ■ n. a small Greek restaurant.
– ORIGIN modern Greek, from Latin *taberna* (see TAVERN).

taw /tɔː/ ■ n. a large marble. ▸ a game of marbles.
– ORIGIN C18.

tawdry ■ adj. (**-ier**, **-iest**) **1** showy but cheap and of poor quality. **2** sordid; sleazy.
– DERIVATIVES **tawdrily** adv. **tawdriness** n.
– ORIGIN C17: short for *tawdry lace*, a fine silk lace or ribbon, contraction of *St Audrey's lace*: *Audrey* was a later form of *Etheldrida*, patron saint of Ely in eastern England where tawdry laces, along with cheap imitations, were traditionally sold at a fair.

tawny ■ adj. (**-ier**, **-iest**) of an orange-brown or yellowish-brown colour. ■ n. this colour.
– DERIVATIVES **tawniness** n.
– ORIGIN Middle English: from Old French *tane*, from *tan* 'tanbark'.

tawny eagle ■ n. a mainly brown eagle native to many parts of SE Europe, Asia, and Africa. [*Aquila rapax*.]

tawny owl ■ n. a common Eurasian owl with either reddish-brown or grey plumage, and a familiar quavering hoot. [*Strix aluco*.]

tax ■ n. **1** a compulsory contribution to state revenue, levied by the government on personal income and business profits or added to the cost of some goods, services, and transactions. **2** a strain or heavy demand. ■ v. **1** impose a tax on. **2** make heavy demands on. **3** charge with a fault or wrongdoing. **4** Law examine and assess (the costs of a case).
– DERIVATIVES **taxable** adj. **taxer** n.
– ORIGIN Middle English: from Old French *taxer*, from Latin *taxare* 'to censure, charge, compute', perhaps from Greek *tassein* 'fix'.

taxa plural form of TAXON.

taxation ■ n. the levying of tax. ▸ money paid as tax.

tax avoidance ■ n. the arrangement of one's financial affairs to minimize tax liability within the law. Compare with TAX EVASION.

tax break ■ n. informal a tax concession or advantage allowed by government.

tax-deductible ■ adj. permitted to be deducted from taxable income.

tax evasion ■ n. the illegal non-payment or underpayment of tax. Compare with TAX AVOIDANCE.

tax exile ■ n. a person who chooses to live in a country or area with low rates of taxation to avoid paying high taxes.

tax haven ■ n. a country or independent area where taxes are levied at a low rate.

taxi ■ n. (pl. **taxis**) a motor vehicle licensed to transport passengers in return for payment of a fare. ▸ (in South Africa) a motor vehicle, typically a minibus, transporting passengers along a fixed route for a set fare but not operating to a timetable. ■ v. (**taxies, taxied, taxiing** or **taxying**) 1 (with reference to an aircraft) move or cause to move slowly along the ground before take-off or after landing. 2 travel in a taxi.
–ORIGIN C20: abbrev. of *taxicab* or *taximeter cab*.

taxicab ■ n. a taxi.

taxidermy /'taksɪˌdə:mi/ ■ n. the art of preparing, stuffing, and mounting the skins of animals so as to appear lifelike.
–DERIVATIVES **taxidermic** adj. **taxidermist** n.
–ORIGIN C19: from Greek *taxis* 'arrangement' + *derma* 'skin'.

taximeter ■ n. a device used in taxis that automatically records the distance travelled and the fare payable.

taxing ■ adj. physically or mentally demanding.

taxi rank (N. Amer. **taxi stand**) ■ n. a place where taxis park while waiting to be hired.

taxis /'taksɪs/ ■ n. (pl. **taxes** /'taksiːz/) 1 Biology a motion or orientation of a cell, organism, or part in response to an external stimulus. Compare with KINESIS. 2 Linguistics the systematic arrangement of linguistic units in linear sequence.
–ORIGIN C18: from Greek, 'arrangement', from *tassein* 'arrange'.

taxi war ■ n. S. African a violent conflict between taxi operators over the use of routes or taxi ranks.

taxiway ■ n. a route along which an aircraft taxies when moving to or from a runway.

taxman ■ n. (pl. **-men**) informal an inspector or collector of taxes.

taxol /'taksɒl/ ■ n. Medicine, trademark a compound, originally obtained from the bark of the Pacific yew tree, which inhibits the growth of certain cancers.
–ORIGIN 1970S: from Latin *taxus* 'yew'.

taxon /'taksɒn/ ■ n. (pl. **taxa** /'taksə/) Biology a taxonomic group of any rank.
–ORIGIN 1920S: back-formation from TAXONOMY.

taxonomy /tak'sɒnəmi/ ■ n. chiefly Biology the branch of science concerned with classification. ▸ a scheme of classification.
–DERIVATIVES **taxonomic** adj. **taxonomical** adj. **taxonomically** adv. **taxonomist** n.
–ORIGIN C19: coined in French from Greek *taxis* 'arrangement' + *-nomia* 'distribution'.

tax return ■ n. a form on which a taxpayer makes a statement of income and personal circumstances, used to assess liability for tax.

tax shelter ■ n. a financial arrangement made to avoid or minimize taxes.

tax year ■ n. a year as reckoned for taxation (in South Africa from 1 March).

Tay–Sachs disease /teɪˈsaks/ ■ n. an inherited metabolic disorder in which certain lipids accumulate in the brain, causing spasticity and death in childhood.
–ORIGIN C20: from the names of English ophthalmologist Warren *Tay* and American neurologist Bernard *Sachs*.

TB ■ abbrev. 1 (also **Tb**) terabyte(s). 2 tubercle bacillus; tuberculosis.

Tb ■ symb. the chemical element terbium.

t.b.a. ■ abbrev. to be announced.

T-bar ■ n. 1 a beam or bar shaped like the letter T. 2 a type of ski lift in the form of a series of inverted T-shaped bars for towing two skiers at a time uphill.

T-bone ■ n. a large choice piece of loin steak containing a T-shaped bone.

tbsp (also **tbs**) ■ abbrev. (pl. same or **tbsps**) tablespoonful.

Tc ■ symb. the chemical element technetium.

TCDD ■ abbrev. tetrachlorodibenzoparadioxin, fuller name of the chemical dioxin.

T-cell ■ n. another term for T-LYMPHOCYTE.

tchagra /'tʃagrə/ ■ n. an African shrike that feeds mainly on the ground, typically having a brown back and black eyestripe. [Genus *Tchagra*: several species.]
–ORIGIN perhaps imitative.

tchotchke /'tʃɒtʃkə/ ■ n. N. Amer. informal a trinket.
–ORIGIN 1960S: Yiddish.

TCP ■ n. trademark a germicidal solution containing various phenols and sodium salicylate.
–ORIGIN 1930S: abbrev. of *trichlorophenyl*, part of the chemical name of one of the ingredients.

TCP/IP ■ abbrev. Computing, trademark transmission control protocol/Internet protocol, used to govern the connection of computer systems to the Internet.

TD ■ abbrev. 1 technical drawing. 2 American Football touchdown.

Te ■ symb. the chemical element tellurium.

te ■ n. (in tonic sol-fa) the seventh note of a major scale. ▸ the note B in the fixed-doh system.
–ORIGIN C19: alteration of SI, adopted to avoid having two notes (*soh* and *si*) beginning with the same letter.

tea ■ n. 1 a hot drink made by infusing the dried, crushed leaves of the tea plant in boiling water. ▸ the dried leaves used to make tea. ▸ a similar drink made from the leaves, fruits, or flowers of other plants. 2 the evergreen shrub or small tree which produces these leaves, native to south and east Asia. [*Camellia sinensis*.] 3 chiefly Brit. a light afternoon meal consisting of sandwiches, cakes, etc., with tea to drink. ▸ S. African such a meal, taking place in the morning or afternoon. ▸ Brit. a cooked evening meal.
–ORIGIN C17: from Chinese (Min dialect) *te*, rel. to Mandarin *chá*.

tea bag ■ n. a small porous sachet containing tea leaves, on to which boiling water is poured in order to make tea.

tea ball ■ n. a hollow ball of perforated metal to hold tea leaves, over which boiling water is poured to make tea.

tea bread ■ n. a type of cake containing dried fruit that has been soaked in tea before baking.

tea break ■ n. a short rest period during the working day.

teacake ■ n. Brit. a light yeast-based sweet bun containing dried fruit, typically served toasted and buttered.

tea ceremony ■ n. an elaborate Japanese ritual of serving and drinking tea, as an expression of Zen Buddhist philosophy.

teach ■ v. (past and past part. **taught**) 1 impart knowledge to or instruct (someone) in how to do something, especially in a school or as part of a recognized programme. ▸ give instruction in (a subject or skill). ▸ cause to learn by example or experience. 2 advocate as a practice or principle.
–DERIVATIVES **teachability** n. **teachable** adj. **teaching** n.
–ORIGIN Old English *tǣcan* 'show, present, point out', of Germanic origin.

teacher ■ n. a person who teaches in a school.
–DERIVATIVES **teacherly** adj.

tea chest ■ n. a light metal-lined wooden box in which tea is transported.

teaching fellow ■ n. a university fellow who carries out teaching duties.

teaching hospital ■ n. a hospital affiliated to a medical school, in which medical students receive training.

tea cloth ■ n. a tea towel.

tea cosy ■ n. a thick or padded cover placed over a teapot to keep the tea hot.

teacup ■ n. a cup from which tea is drunk.
– DERIVATIVES **teacupful** n. (pl. **-fuls**).

tea dance ■ n. a dance held in the afternoon.

tea garden ■ n. a garden in which tea and other refreshments are served to the public.

teak ■ n. **1** hard durable wood used in shipbuilding and for making furniture. **2** the large deciduous tree native to India and SE Asia which yields this wood. [*Tectona grandis*.] ▶ used in names of other trees with similar wood, e.g. Zambezi teak.
– ORIGIN C17: from Portuguese *teca*, from Tamil and Malayalam *tēkku*.

teal ■ n. (pl. same or **teals**) **1** a small freshwater duck, typically with a blue-green speculum. [Genus *Anas*: several species.] **2** (also **teal blue**) a dark greenish-blue colour.
– ORIGIN Middle English.

tea lady ■ n. a woman employed to make and serve tea in a workplace.

tea light ■ n. a small, squat candle in a metal case, used for decoration or within a stand to keep food or drink warm.

team ■ n. [treated as sing. or pl.] **1** a group of players forming one side in a competitive game or sport. **2** two or more people working together. ▶ two or more animals, especially horses, in harness together to pull a vehicle. ■ v. **1** (**team up**) come together as a team to achieve a common goal. **2** (usu. **team something with**) match or coordinate one thing with (another). **3** harness (horses) together to pull a vehicle.
– ORIGIN Old English *tēam* 'team of draught animals', of Germanic origin.

teammate ■ n. a fellow member of a team.

team ministry ■ n. a group of clergy of incumbent status who minister jointly to several parishes under the leadership of a rector or vicar.

team player ■ n. a person who plays or works well as a member of a team.

team spirit ■ n. feelings of camaraderie among the members of a team.

teamster ■ n. **1** N. Amer. a truck driver. **2** a driver of a team of animals.

teamwork ■ n. the combined effective action of a group.

teapot ■ n. a pot with a handle, spout, and lid, in which tea is prepared.

tear[1] /tɛː/ ■ v. (past **tore**; past part. **torn**) **1** pull or rip apart or to pieces. ▶ rip a hole or split in. ▶ damage (a muscle or ligament) by overstretching it. ▶ (**tear something down**) demolish or destroy something. **2** disrupt and force apart (people). ▶ (**be torn**) be in a state of conflict and uncertainty between two opposing options or parties. **3** (**tear oneself away**) leave despite a strong desire to stay. **4** informal move very quickly and in a reckless or excited manner. **5** (**tear into**) attack verbally. ■ n. a hole or split caused by tearing.
– PHRASES **tear one's hair out** informal feel extreme desperation. **tear someone off a strip** (or **tear a strip off someone**) informal, chiefly Brit. rebuke someone angrily.
– DERIVATIVES **tearable** adj. **tearer** n.
– ORIGIN Old English *teran*, of Germanic origin.

tear[2] /tɪə/ ■ n. a drop of clear salty liquid secreted from glands in a person's eye when they are crying or when the eye is irritated.
– PHRASES **in tears** crying.
– DERIVATIVES **teary** adj.
– ORIGIN Old English *tēar*, of Germanic origin.

tearaway ■ n. Brit. a person who behaves in a wild or reckless manner.

teardrop ■ n. **1** a single tear. **2** [as modifier] shaped like a tear: *teardrop handles*.

tear duct ■ n. a passage through which tears pass from the lachrymal glands to the eye or from the eye to the nose.

tearful ■ adj. **1** crying or inclined to cry. **2** causing tears; sad.
– DERIVATIVES **tearfully** adv. **tearfulness** n.

tear gas ■ n. gas that causes severe irritation to the eyes, used in warfare and riot control. ■ v. (**tear-gas**) attack with tear gas.

tearing /ˈtɛːrɪŋ/ ■ adj. violent; extreme: *a tearing hurry*.

tear jerker ■ n. informal a story, film, or song that is calculated to evoke sadness or sympathy.
– DERIVATIVES **tear-jerking** adj.

tearless ■ adj. not crying.
– DERIVATIVES **tearlessly** adv. **tearlessness** n.

tea room ■ n. a small restaurant or café where tea and other light refreshments are served. ▶ S. African dated a café.

tea rose ■ n. a garden rose with flowers that are typically pale yellow with a pink tinge and have a delicate scent resembling that of tea. [Cultivars of the Chinese hybrid *Rosa × odorata*.]

tear sheet ■ n. a page that can be removed from a magazine, book, etc. for use separately.

tease ■ v. **1** playfully make fun of or attempt to provoke. ▶ tempt sexually. **2** gently pull or comb (tangled wool, hair, etc.) into separate strands. ▶ backcomb (hair) in order to make it appear fuller. **3** (**tease something out**) find something out by searching through a mass of information. ■ n. informal **1** an act of teasing. **2** a person who teases. ▶ a person who teases someone sexually with no intention of satisfying the desire aroused.
– DERIVATIVES **teasing** adj. & n. **teasingly** adv.
– ORIGIN Old English, of West Germanic origin.

teasel (also **teazle** or **teazel**) ■ n. **1** a tall prickly Eurasian plant with spiny purple flower heads. [Genus *Dipsacus*: several species.] **2** a dried head from a teasel, or a similar man-made device, used to raise a nap on woven cloth.
– ORIGIN Old English, of West Germanic origin.

teaser ■ n. **1** a person who teases others. **2** informal a tricky question or task. **3** a short introductory advertisement for a product, that stimulates interest by remaining cryptic.

tea set /ˈtiːsɛt/ ■ n. a set of crockery for serving tea.

teaspoon ■ n. a small spoon used for adding sugar to and stirring hot drinks or for eating some foods. ▶ (abbrev.: **tsp**) the amount held by such a spoon, considered to be 5 millilitres when used as a measurement in cookery.
– DERIVATIVES **teaspoonful** n. (pl. **-fuls**).

teat ■ n. **1** a nipple of the mammary gland of a female mammal. **2** a perforated plastic bulb by which an infant or young animal can suck milk from a bottle.
– ORIGIN Middle English: from Old French *tete*, prob. of Germanic origin.

tea towel ■ n. a cloth for drying washed crockery, cutlery, and glasses.

tea tree (also **ti tree**) ■ n. an Australasian flowering shrub or small tree with leaves that are sometimes used for tea. [Genera *Leptospermum* and *Melaleuca*: several species.]

tea tree oil ■ n. an essential oil with medicinal properties, extracted from the the tea tree, especially *Melaleuca alternifolia* and *Leptospermum scoparium*.

teazle (also **teazel**) ■ n. variant spelling of TEASEL.

tech (also **tec**) ■ n. informal **1** a technikon or technical college. **2** technology. **3** a technician.

techie /ˈtɛki/ (also **techy**) ■ n. (pl. **-ies**) informal a person who is an expert in technology, especially computing.

technetium /tɛkˈniːʃɪəm/ ■ n. the chemical element of atomic number 43, an artificially made radioactive metal. (Symbol: **Tc**)
– ORIGIN 1940s: from Greek *tekhnētos* 'artificial'.

technic /ˈtɛknɪk/ ■ n. **1** /also tɛkˈniːk/ chiefly US technique. **2** (**technics**) [treated as sing. or pl.] technical terms, details, and methods; technology.
– DERIVATIVES **technicist** n.
– ORIGIN C17: from Latin *technicus*, from Greek *tekhnikos*, from *tekhnē* 'art'.

technical ■ adj. **1** of or relating to a particular subject, art, or craft, or its techniques. ▶ requiring special knowledge to be understood. **2** of, involving, or concerned with applied and industrial sciences. ▶ relating to the operation of machines: *a technical fault*. **3** according to a strict application or interpretation of the law or rules. ■ n. chiefly N. Amer. a small truck with a machine gun mounted

technical college ■ n. a college of further education providing courses in applied sciences and other practical subjects.

technicality ■ n. (pl. **-ies**) **1** a small formal detail specified within a set of rules. **2** (**technicalities**) details of theory or practice within a particular field. **3** the use of technical terms or methods.

technical knockout ■ n. Boxing the ending of a fight by the referee on the grounds of a contestant's inability to continue, the opponent being declared the winner.

technician ■ n. **1** a person employed to look after technical equipment or do practical work in a laboratory. **2** an expert in the practical application of a science. ▸ a person skilled in the technique of an art or craft.

Technicolor ■ n. trademark **1** a process of colour cinematography using synchronized monochrome films, each of a different colour, to produce a colour print. **2** (**technicolor** or **technicolour**) informal vivid colour.
– DERIVATIVES **technicolored** (also **technicoloured**) adj.
– ORIGIN C20: blend of **TECHNICAL** and **COLOR**.

technikon ■ n. (in South Africa) an institution offering technical and vocational education at tertiary level.
– ORIGIN 1970s: from Greek *tekhnikos*, from *tekhnē* 'art, skill'.

technique ■ n. a way of carrying out a particular task, especially the execution of an artistic work or a scientific procedure. ▸ a procedure that is effective in achieving an aim.
– ORIGIN C19: from French, from Latin *technicus* (see **TECHNIC**).

techno ■ n. a style of fast, heavy electronic dance music, with few or no vocals.
– ORIGIN 1980s: abbrev. of *technological* (see **TECHNOLOGY**).

techno- ■ comb. form relating to technology or its use: *technophobe*.
– ORIGIN from Greek *tekhnē* 'art, craft'.

technobabble ■ n. informal incomprehensible technical jargon.

technocracy /tɛkˈnɒkrəsi/ ■ n. (pl. **-ies**) government by an elite of technical experts.
– DERIVATIVES **technocrat** n. **technocratic** adj. **technocratically** adv.

technology ■ n. (pl. **-ies**) the application of scientific knowledge for practical purposes. ▸ machinery and equipment based on such knowledge. ▸ the branch of knowledge concerned with applied sciences.
– DERIVATIVES **technological** adj. **technologically** adv. **technologist** n.
– ORIGIN C17: from Greek *tekhnologia* 'systematic treatment', from *tekhnē* 'art, craft' + *-logia* (see **-LOGY**).

technology transfer ■ n. the transfer of new technology from the originator to a secondary user.

technophile ■ n. a person who is enthusiastic about new technology.
– DERIVATIVES **technophilia** n. **technophilic** adj.

technophobe ■ n. a person who fears or dislikes new technology.
– DERIVATIVES **technophobia** n. **technophobic** adj.

technospeak ■ n. technobabble.

techy ■ n. variant spelling of **TECHIE**.

tectonic /tɛkˈtɒnɪk/ ■ adj. **1** Geology of or relating to the structure of the earth's crust and the large-scale processes which take place within it. **2** of or relating to building or construction.
– DERIVATIVES **tectonically** adv.
– ORIGIN C17: from Greek *tektonikos*, from *tektōn* 'carpenter, builder'.

tectonics ■ pl. n. [treated as sing. or pl.] Geology large-scale processes affecting the structure of the earth's crust.

tectonophysics /tɛkˌtɒnə(ʊ)ˈfɪzɪks/ ■ pl. n. [treated as sing.] the branch of geophysics concerned with the forces that cause movement and deformation in the earth's crust.
– ORIGIN 1950s: from **TECTONICS** + **PHYSICS**.

teddy ■ n. (pl. **-ies**) **1** (also **teddy bear**) a soft toy bear. **2** a woman's all-in-one undergarment.
– ORIGIN C20: from *Teddy*, familiar form of the given name *Theodore*: sense 1 alludes to the US President *Theodore* Roosevelt (1858–1919), an enthusiastic bear-hunter.

Teddy boy ■ n. Brit. (in the 1950s) a young man of a subculture characterized by a style of dress based on Edwardian fashion, hair slicked up in a quiff, and a liking for rock-and-roll music.
– ORIGIN from *Teddy*, familiar form of the given name *Edward* (with ref. to the style of dress).

Te Deum /tiː ˈdiːəm, teɪ ˈdeɪəm/ ■ n. a hymn beginning *Te Deum laudamus*, 'We praise Thee, O God', sung at matins or on special occasions such as a thanksgiving.
– ORIGIN from Latin.

tedious ■ adj. too long, slow, or dull.
– DERIVATIVES **tediously** adv. **tediousness** n.
– ORIGIN Middle English: from Old French *tedieus* or late Latin *taediosus*, from Latin *taedium* (see **TEDIUM**).

tedium ■ n. the state of being tedious.
– ORIGIN C17: from Latin *taedium*, from *taedere* 'be weary of'.

tee[1] ■ n. **1** a cleared space on a golf course, from which the ball is struck at the beginning of play for each hole. **2** a small peg with a concave head which is placed in the ground to support a golf ball before it is struck from a tee. **3** a mark aimed at in bowls, quoits, curling, and other similar games. ■ v. (**tees, teed, teeing**) Golf **1** (usu. **tee up**) place the ball on a tee ready to make the first stroke of the round or hole. **2** (**tee off**) begin a round or hole of golf by playing the ball from a tee.
– ORIGIN C17 (orig. Scots, as *teaz*).

tee[2] ■ n. informal, chiefly N. Amer. a T-shirt.

tee-hee ■ n. a titter or giggle. ■ v. (**tee-hees, tee-heed, tee-heeing**) titter or giggle.
– ORIGIN Middle English: imitative.

teem[1] ■ v. (**teem with**) be full of or swarming with.
– DERIVATIVES **teeming** adj.
– ORIGIN Old English *tēman*, *tīeman* 'give birth to, be or become pregnant': of Germanic origin.

teem[2] ■ v. (especially of rain) pour down; fall heavily.
– ORIGIN Middle English: from Old Norse *tœma* 'to empty', from *tómr* 'empty'.

teen informal ■ adj. of or relating to teenagers. ■ n. a teenager.

-teen ■ suffix forming the names of numerals from 13 to 19: *fourteen*.
– ORIGIN Old English, inflected form of **TEN**.

teenage ■ adj. denoting, relating to, or characteristic of a teenager or teenagers.
– DERIVATIVES **teenaged** adj.

teenager ■ n. a person aged between 13 and 19 years.

teens ■ pl. n. the years of a person's age from 13 to 19.
– ORIGIN C17: pl. of *teen*, independent usage of **-TEEN**.

teensy /ˈtiːnzi, -si/ ■ adj. (**-ier, -iest**) informal tiny.
– ORIGIN C19 (orig. US dialect): prob. an extension of **TEENY**.

teeny ■ adj. (**-ier, -iest**) informal tiny.
– ORIGIN C19: var. of **TINY**.

teeny-bopper ■ n. informal a young teenager who follows the latest fashions in clothes and pop music.
– DERIVATIVES **teeny-bop** adj.

teeny-weeny (also **teensy-weensy**) ■ adj. informal very tiny.

teepee ■ n. variant spelling of **TEPEE**.

tee shirt ■ n. variant spelling of **T-SHIRT**.

teeter ■ v. **1** move or balance unsteadily. **2** (often **teeter between**) waver between different courses.
– ORIGIN C19: var. of dialect *titter*, from Old Norse *titra* 'shake, shiver'.

teeter-totter N. Amer or dialect ■ n. a see-saw. ■ v. teeter; waver.
– ORIGIN C19: reduplication of **TEETER** or **TOTTER**.

teeth plural form of **TOOTH**.

teethe ■ v. cut one's milk teeth.
– DERIVATIVES **teething** n.
– ORIGIN Middle English: from **TEETH**.

teething ring ■ n. a small ring for an infant to bite on while teething.

teething troubles (also **teething problems**) ■ pl. n. short-term problems that occur in the early stages of a new project.

teetotal ■ adj. choosing or characterized by abstinence from alcohol.
– DERIVATIVES **teetotalism** n. **teetotaller** n.
– ORIGIN C19: emphatic extension of **TOTAL**, apparently first used by Richard Turner, a worker from Preston in north-west England, in a speech (1833) urging total abstinence from all alcohol.

teetotum /tiːˈtəʊtəm/ ■ n. a small spinning top spun with the fingers, especially one with four sides lettered to determine whether the spinner has won or lost.
– ORIGIN C18 (as *T totum*): from *T* (representing *totum*, inscribed on one side of the toy) + Latin *totum* 'the whole (stake)'.

teff /tɛf/ ■ n. an African cereal cultivated almost exclusively in Ethiopia, used mainly to make flour. [*Eragrostis tef*.]
– ORIGIN C18: from Amharic *ṭēf*.

tefillin /tɪˈfɪliːn/ ■ pl. n. collective term for Jewish phylacteries.
– ORIGIN from Aramaic *tĕpillīn* 'prayers'.

TEFL /ˈtɛf(ə)l/ ■ abbrev. teaching of English as a foreign language.

Teflon /ˈtɛflɒn/ ■ n. **1** trademark for **POLYTETRAFLUOROETHYLENE**. **2** [as modifier] (especially of a politician) having an undamaged reputation, in spite of scandal or misjudgement.
– ORIGIN 1940s: from **TETRA-** + **FLUORO-** + *-on* on the pattern of *nylon* and *rayon*.

Tejano /tɛˈhɑːnəʊ/ ■ n. (pl. **-os**) **1** a Mexican-American inhabitant of southern Texas. **2** a style of folk or popular music originating among the Tejanos, featuring accordion and guitar.
– ORIGIN American Spanish, alteration of *Texano* 'Texan'.

tekkie ■ n. variant spelling of **TAKKIE**.

tektite /ˈtɛktʌɪt/ ■ n. Geology a small black glassy object found in numbers over certain areas of the earth's surface, believed to have been formed as molten debris in meteorite impacts and scattered widely through the air.
– ORIGIN C20: coined in German from Greek *tēktos* 'molten'.

tel. (also **Tel.**) ■ abbrev. telephone.

telangiectasia /tɛˌlandʒɪɛkˈteɪzɪə/ (also **telangiectasis** /tɛˌlandʒɪˈɛktəsɪs/) ■ n. Medicine a condition characterized by dilatation of the capillaries, causing them to appear as small red or purple clusters on the skin or the surface of an organ.
– DERIVATIVES **telangiectatic** adj.
– ORIGIN C19: from Greek *telos* 'end' + *angeion* 'vessel' + *ektasis* 'dilatation'.

telco ■ n. (pl. **-os**) a telecommunications company.

tele- /ˈtɛli/ ■ comb. form **1** to or at a distance: *telekinesis*. ▸ used in names of instruments for operating over long distances: *telemeter*. **2** relating to television: *telecast*. **3** done by means of the telephone: *telemarketing*.
– ORIGIN from Greek *tēle-* 'far off'.

telebanking ■ n. a method of banking in which the customer conducts transactions by telephone.

telecast ■ n. a television broadcast. ■ v. (usu. **be telecast**) transmit by television.
– DERIVATIVES **telecaster** n.

telecentre ■ n. another term for **TELECOTTAGE**.

telecommunication ■ n. communication over a distance by cable, telegraph, telephone, or broadcasting. ▸ (**telecommunications**) [treated as sing.] the branch of technology concerned with this.

telecommute ■ v. work from home, communicating with a central workplace using equipment such as telephones, fax machines, and modems.
– DERIVATIVES **telecommuter** n. **telecommuting** n.

telecomputer ■ n. a device which combines the capabilities of a computer with those of a television and a telephone.
– DERIVATIVES **telecomputing** n.

telecoms (also **telecomms**) ■ pl. n. [treated as sing.] telecommunications.

teleconference ■ n. a conference with participants in different locations linked by telecommunication devices.
– DERIVATIVES **teleconferencing** n.

teleconverter ■ n. Photography a lens designed to be fitted in front of a standard lens to increase its effective focal length.

telecottage ■ n. a place, especially in a rural area, where computer equipment is available for communal use.

teledensity ■ n. the number of telephone main lines per 100 inhabitants in a country or region.

tele-evangelist ■ n. variant of **TELEVANGELIST**.

telefilm ■ n. a film made for or broadcast on television.

telegenic /ˌtɛlɪˈdʒɛnɪk/ ■ adj. having an appearance or manner that is attractive on television.
– ORIGIN 1930s (orig. US): from **TELE-** + **-GENIC**, on the pattern of *photogenic*.

telegram ■ n. a message sent by telegraph and delivered in written or printed form.

telegraph ■ n. a system or device for transmitting messages from a distance along a wire, especially one creating signals by making and breaking an electrical connection. ■ v. send (someone) a message by telegraph. ▸ send (a message) by telegraph.
– DERIVATIVES **telegrapher** /ˈtɛlɪˌɡrɑːfə, tɪˈlɛɡrəfə/ n. **telegraphist** /tɪˈlɛɡrəfɪst/ n. **telegraphy** /tɪˈlɛɡrəfi/ n.

telegraphese ■ n. informal the terse, abbreviated style of language used in telegrams.

telegraphic ■ adj. **1** of or by telegraphs or telegrams. **2** (of language) omitting inessential words; concise.
– DERIVATIVES **telegraphically** adv.

telegraph key ■ n. a button which is pressed to produce a signal when transmitting Morse code.

telegraph pole ■ n. a tall pole used to carry telegraph or telephone wires above the ground.

Telegu /ˈtɛlɪɡuː/ ■ n. variant spelling of **TELUGU**.

telekinesis /ˌtɛlɪkʌɪˈniːsɪs, -kɪˈniːsɪs/ ■ n. the supposed ability to move objects at a distance by mental power or other non-physical means.
– DERIVATIVES **telekinetic** adj.
– ORIGIN C19: from **TELE-** + Greek *kinēsis* 'motion'.

telemark Skiing ■ n. a turn with the outer ski advanced and the knee bent, performed on skis to which only the toe of each boot is fixed. ■ v. perform such a turn.
– ORIGIN C20: named after *Telemark*, a district in Norway, where it originated.

telemarketing ■ n. the marketing of goods or services by telephone calls to potential customers.
– DERIVATIVES **telemarketer** n.

telematics ■ pl. n. [treated as sing.] the branch of information technology which deals with the long-distance transmission of computerized information.
– DERIVATIVES **telematic** adj.
– ORIGIN 1970s: blend of **TELECOMMUNICATION** and **INFORMATICS**.

telemedicine ■ n. the remote diagnosis and treatment of patients by means of telecommunications technology.

telemessage ■ n. a message sent by telephone or telex and delivered in written form.

telemeter /ˈtɛlɪmiːtə, tɪˈlɛmɪtə/ ■ n. an apparatus for recording the readings of an instrument and transmitting them by radio. ■ v. transmit (readings) to a distant receiving set or station.
– DERIVATIVES **telemetric** adj. **telemetry** n.

teleology /ˌtɛlɪˈɒlədʒi, ˌtiːl-/ ■ n. (pl. **-ies**) **1** Philosophy the explanation of phenomena by the purpose they serve rather than by postulated causes. **2** Theology the doctrine of design and purpose in the material world.
– DERIVATIVES **teleologic** adj. **teleological** adj. **teleologically** adv. **teleologism** n. **teleologist** n.
– ORIGIN C18: from modern Latin *teleologia*, from Greek *telos* 'end' + *-logia* (see **-LOGY**).

teleost /ˈtɛlɪɒst, ˈtiːl-/ ■ n. Zoology a fish of a large group (division Teleostei) that comprises most bony fishes (apart from sturgeons, lungfishes, and some other kinds).
– ORIGIN C19: from Greek *teleos* 'complete' + *osteon* 'bone'.

telepathy

telepathy ■ n. the supposed communication of thoughts or ideas by means other than the known senses.
– DERIVATIVES **telepath** n. **telepathic** adj. **telepathically** adv. **telepathist** n. **telepathize** (also **-ise**) v.

telephone ■ n. 1 a system for transmitting voices over a distance using wire or radio, by converting acoustic vibrations to electrical signals. 2 an instrument used as part of such a system, typically including a handset with a transmitting microphone and a set of numbered buttons by which a connection can be made to another such instrument. ■ v. ring or speak to (someone) using the telephone. ▸ make a telephone call.
– DERIVATIVES **telephoner** n. **telephonic** adj. **telephonically** adv.

telephone box ■ n. a public booth or enclosure housing a payphone.

telephone directory ■ n. a book listing the names, addresses, and telephone numbers of the people in a particular area.

telephone exchange ■ n. a set of equipment that connects telephone lines during a call.

telephone number ■ n. a number assigned to a particular telephone and used in making connections to it.

telephonist ■ n. an operator of a telephone switchboard.

telephony /tɪˈlɛf(ə)ni/ ■ n. the working or use of telephones.

telephoto lens ■ n. (pl. **-os**) a lens with a longer focal length than standard, giving a narrow field of view and a magnified image.

teleport ■ n. a centre providing interconnections between different forms of telecommunications, especially one which links satellites to ground-based communications. ■ v. (especially in science fiction) transport or be transported across space and distance instantly.
– DERIVATIVES **teleportation** n.
– ORIGIN 1950s: back-formation from *teleportation* (1930s), from TELE- + a shortened form of *transportation*.

telepresence ■ n. the use of virtual reality technology, especially for remote control of machinery or for apparent participation in distant events.

teleprinter ■ n. a device for transmitting telegraph messages as they are keyed, and for printing messages received.

teleprompter ■ n. another term for AUTOCUE.

telescope ■ n. an optical instrument designed to make distant objects appear nearer, containing an arrangement of lenses, or of curved mirrors and lenses, by which rays of light are collected and focused and the resulting image magnified. ■ v. 1 (with reference to an object made of concentric tubular parts) slide or cause to slide into itself, so that it becomes smaller. 2 condense or conflate so as to occupy less space or time.
– DERIVATIVES **telescopic** adj. **telescopically** adv.

teleshopping ■ n. the ordering of goods by customers using a telephone or direct computer link.

teletex ■ n. trademark an enhanced version of telex.
– ORIGIN 1970s: prob. a blend of TELEX and TEXT.

teletext ■ n. a news and information service transmitted to televisions with appropriate receivers.

telethon ■ n. a very long television programme, typically one broadcast to raise money for a charity.
– ORIGIN 1940s (orig. US): from TELE- + *-thon* on the pattern of *marathon*.

teletype ■ n. trademark a kind of teleprinter. ▸ a message received and printed by a teleprinter. ■ v. send (a message) by means of a teleprinter.

teletypewriter ■ n. a teleprinter.

televangelist (also **tele-evangelist**) ■ n. chiefly N. Amer. an evangelical preacher who appears regularly on television.
– DERIVATIVES **televangelical** adj. **televangelism** n.

televise ■ v. record for or transmit by television.
– DERIVATIVES **televisable** adj. **televised** adj.
– ORIGIN 1920s: back-formation from TELEVISION.

television ■ n. 1 a system for converting visual images (usually with sound) into electrical signals, transmitting them by radio or other means, and displaying them electronically on a screen. 2 the activity, profession, or medium of broadcasting on television. 3 (also **television set**) a device with a screen for receiving television signals.

television tube ■ n. another term for PICTURE TUBE.

televisual ■ adj. relating to or suitable for television.
– DERIVATIVES **televisually** adv.

telework ■ v. another term for TELECOMMUTE.
– DERIVATIVES **teleworker** n.

telex ■ n. 1 an international system of telegraphy with printed messages transmitted and received by teleprinters using the public telecommunications network. 2 a device used for this. 3 a message sent by this system. ■ v. communicate with by telex. ▸ send (a message) by telex.
– ORIGIN 1930s: blend of TELEPRINTER and EXCHANGE.

Telkom /ˈtɛlkɒm/ ■ abbrev. (in South Africa) the parastatal telecommunications company.

tell¹ ■ v. (past and past part. **told**) 1 communicate information to. ▸ instruct (someone) to do something. ▸ relate (a story). ▸ reveal (information) in a non-verbal way: *the figures tell a different story*. ▸ divulge confidential information. ▸ (**tell on**) informal inform on. ▸ (**tell someone off**) informal reprimand someone. 2 determine correctly or with certainty. ▸ perceive (a distinction). 3 (often **tell on**) (of an experience or period of time) have a noticeable effect on someone. ▸ (of a particular factor) play a part in the success or otherwise of someone or something: *lack of fitness told against him*. 4 chiefly archaic count (the members of a group).
– PHRASES **tell tales** gossip about another person's secrets or faults. **tell the time** (or N. Amer. **tell time**) be able to ascertain the time from reading the face of a clock or watch. **tell someone where to get off** (or **where they get off**) informal angrily dismiss or rebuke someone. **there is no telling** conveying the impossibility of knowing what has happened or will happen. **you're telling me** informal emphasizing that one is already well aware of or in complete agreement with something.
– ORIGIN Old English *tellan* 'relate, count, estimate', of Germanic origin.

tell² ■ n. Archaeology (in the Middle East) a mound formed by the accumulated remains of ancient settlements.
– ORIGIN C19: from Arabic *tall* 'hillock'.

teller ■ n. 1 a person who deals with customers' transactions in a bank. 2 a person appointed to count votes. 3 a person who tells something.

telling ■ adj. having a striking or revealing effect; significant.
– DERIVATIVES **tellingly** adv.

telling-off ■ n. (pl. **tellings-off**) informal a reprimand.

telltale ■ adj. revealing or betraying something. ■ n. 1 a person who tells tales. 2 a device or object that automatically gives a visual indication of the state or presence of something.

telluric /tɛˈljʊərɪk/ ■ adj. 1 of the earth as a planet. 2 of the soil.
– ORIGIN C19: from Latin *tellus, tellur-* 'earth' + -IC.

telluric acid ■ n. Chemistry a crystalline acid made by oxidizing tellurium dioxide.
– DERIVATIVES **tellurate** n.

tellurium /tɛˈljʊərɪəm/ ■ n. the chemical element of atomic number 52, a brittle silvery-white semimetal resembling selenium. (Symbol: **Te**)
– DERIVATIVES **telluride** /ˈtɛljʊraɪd/ n.
– ORIGIN C19: from Latin *tellus, tellur-* 'earth'.

telly ■ n. (pl. **-ies**) informal term for TELEVISION.

telnet Computing ■ n. a network protocol or program that allows a user on one computer to log in to another computer that is part of the same network. ■ v. (**telnetted, telnetting**) informal log into a remote computer using a telnet program.
– ORIGIN 1970s: blend of TELECOMMUNICATION and NETWORK.

telomere /ˈtiːlə(ʊ)mɪə, ˈtɛl-/ ■ n. Genetics a compound structure at the end of a chromosome.
– DERIVATIVES **telomeric** adj.
– ORIGIN 1940s: from Greek *telos* 'end' + *meros* 'part'.

telophase /ˈtiːləʊfeɪz, ˈtɛl-/ ■ n. Biology the final stage of cell division, between anaphase and interphase, in which

the two daughter nuclei are formed.
– ORIGIN C19: from Greek *telos* 'end' + PHASE.

telos /ˈtɛlɒs/ ■ n. (pl. **teloi** /-lɔɪ/) chiefly Philosophy or poetic/literary an ultimate object or aim.
– ORIGIN Greek, 'end'.

telson /ˈtɛls(ə)n/ ■ n. Zoology the last segment in the abdomen in crustaceans, chelicerates, and embryonic insects.
– ORIGIN C19: from Greek, 'limit'.

Telugu /ˈtɛləɡuː/ (also **Telegu**) ■ n. (pl. same or **Telugus**) **1** a member of a people of SE India. **2** the Dravidian language of this people.
– ORIGIN from the name in Telugu, *teluṅgu*.

temblor /tɛmˈblɔː/ ■ n. US an earthquake.
– ORIGIN C19: from American Spanish.

Tembu ■ n. variant spelling of THEMBU.

temenos /ˈtɛmənɒs/ ■ n. (pl. **temenoi** /-nɔɪ/) Archaeology a sacred enclosure or precinct surrounding or adjacent to a temple.
– ORIGIN C19: from Greek, from the stem of *temnein* 'cut off'.

temerity /tɪˈmɛrɪti/ ■ n. excessive confidence or boldness.
– ORIGIN Middle English: from Latin *temeritas*, from *temere* 'rashly'.

Temne /ˈtɛmni/ ■ n. (pl. same or **Temnes**) **1** a member of a people of Sierra Leone. **2** the Niger–Congo language of this people, the main language of Sierra Leone.
– ORIGIN the name in Temne.

temp[1] informal ■ n. a temporary employee, typically an office worker who finds employment through an agency. ■ v. work as a temp.

temp[2] ■ abbrev. temperature.

tempeh /ˈtɛmpeɪ/ ■ n. an Indonesian dish consisting of deep-fried fermented soya beans.
– ORIGIN from Indonesian *tempe*.

temper ■ n. **1** a person's state of mind in terms of their being angry or calm. **2** a tendency to become angry easily. ▸ an angry state of mind. **3** the degree of hardness and elasticity in steel or other metal. ■ v. **1** improve the temper of (a metal) by reheating and then cooling it. **2** (often **be tempered with**) serve as a neutralizing or counterbalancing force to.
– PHRASES **keep** (or **lose**) **one's temper** retain (or fail to retain) composure or restraint when angry.
– ORIGIN Old English *temprian* 'bring into the required condition by mixing', from Latin *temperare* 'mingle, restrain'; the noun orig. denoted a proportionate mixture of elements, also the combination of the four bodily humours, formerly believed to be the basis of temperament.

tempera /ˈtɛmp(ə)rə/ ■ n. a method of painting with pigments dispersed in an emulsion miscible with water, typically egg yolk. ▸ emulsion used in tempera.
– ORIGIN C19: from Italian, in the phr. *pingere a tempera* 'paint in distemper'.

temperament ■ n. **1** a person's nature with regard to the effect it has on their behaviour. **2** the adjustment of intervals in tuning a piano or other musical instrument so as to fit the scale for use in different keys.
– ORIGIN Middle English: from Latin *temperamentum* 'correct mixture', from *temperare* 'mingle'; cf. TEMPER.

temperamental ■ adj. **1** relating to or caused by temperament. **2** liable to unreasonable changes of mood.
– DERIVATIVES **temperamentally** adv.

temperance ■ n. abstinence from alcoholic drink.
– ORIGIN Middle English: from Anglo-Norman French *temperaunce*, from Latin *temperantia* 'moderation', from *temperare* 'restrain'.

temperate ■ adj. **1** relating to or denoting a region or climate characterized by mild temperatures. **2** showing moderation or self-restraint.
– DERIVATIVES **temperately** adv. **temperateness** n.
– ORIGIN Middle English: from Latin *temperare* 'mingle, restrain'.

temperate zone ■ n. each of the two belts of latitude between the torrid zone and the northern and southern frigid zones.

temperature ■ n. **1** the degree or intensity of heat present in a substance or object. ▸ informal a body temperature above the normal: *he was running a temperature.* **2** the degree of excitement or tension present in a situation or discussion.
– ORIGIN Middle English: from French *température* or Latin *temperatura*, from *temperare* 'restrain'.

-tempered ■ comb. form having a specified temper or disposition: *ill-tempered.*
– DERIVATIVES **-temperedly** comb. form in corresponding adverbs. **-temperedness** comb. form in corresponding nouns.

tempest ■ n. a violent windy storm.
– PHRASES **a tempest in a teapot** North American term for a storm in a teacup (see STORM).
– ORIGIN Middle English: from Old French *tempeste*, from Latin *tempestas* 'season, weather, storm', from *tempus* 'time, season'.

tempestuous /tɛmˈpɛstjʊəs/ ■ adj. **1** very stormy. **2** characterized by strong and turbulent emotion.
– DERIVATIVES **tempestuously** adv. **tempestuousness** n.

tempi plural form of TEMPO.

Templar /ˈtɛmplə/ ■ n. historical a member of the Knights Templars, a powerful religious and military order.
– ORIGIN Middle English: from Old French *templier*, from medieval Latin *templarius*, from Latin *templum* (see TEMPLE[1]).

template /ˈtɛmplɪt, -pleɪt/ ■ n. **1** a shaped piece of rigid material used as a pattern for processes such as cutting out, shaping, or drilling. **2** something that serves as a model or example. ▸ Computing a preset format for a document or file. **3** a timber or plate used to distribute the weight in a wall or under a support.
– ORIGIN C17: prob. from TEMPLE[3].

temple[1] ■ n. a building devoted to the worship of a god or gods. ▸ N. Amer. a synagogue.
– ORIGIN Old English *templ*, reinforced in Middle English by Old French *temple*, both from Latin *templum* 'open or consecrated space'.

temple[2] ■ n. the flat part either side of the head between the forehead and the ear.
– ORIGIN Middle English: from Old French, from an alteration of Latin *tempora*, pl. of *tempus* 'temple of the head'.

temple[3] ■ n. a device in a loom for keeping the cloth taut.
– ORIGIN Middle English: from Old French, perhaps the same word as TEMPLE[2].

tempo ■ n. (pl. **tempos** or **tempi** /-piː/) **1** Music the speed at which a passage of music is played. **2** the pace of an activity or process.
– ORIGIN C17: from Italian, from Latin *tempus* 'time'.

temporal[1] /ˈtɛmp(ə)r(ə)l/ ■ adj. **1** of or relating to time. **2** relating to worldly affairs; secular.
– DERIVATIVES **temporally** adv.
– ORIGIN Middle English: from Old French *temporel* or Latin *temporalis*, from *tempus* 'time'.

temporal[2] /ˈtɛmp(ə)r(ə)l/ ■ adj. Anatomy of or situated in the temples of the head.

temporal bone ■ n. Anatomy either of a pair of bones which form part of the side of the skull on each side and enclose the middle and inner ear.

temporalis /ˌtɛmpəˈreɪlɪs/ ■ n. Anatomy a fan-shaped muscle which runs from the side of the skull to the back of the lower jaw.
– ORIGIN C17: from late Latin.

temporality ■ n. (pl. **-ies**) **1** the state of existing within or having some relationship with time. **2** (**temporalities**) the properties and revenues of a religious body or a member of the clergy.

temporal lobe ■ n. each of the paired lobes of the brain lying beneath the temples, including areas concerned with the understanding of speech.

temporal power ■ n. the power of a bishop or cleric, especially the Pope, in secular matters.

temporary ■ adj. lasting for only a limited period. ■ n. (pl. **-ies**) a person employed on a temporary basis.
– DERIVATIVES **temporarily** adv. **temporariness** n.
– ORIGIN C16: from Latin *temporarius*, from *tempus* 'time'.

temporize (also **-ise**) ▪ v. avoid making a decision or committing oneself in order to gain time.
– DERIVATIVES **temporization** (also **-isation**) n. **temporizer** (also **-iser**) n.
– ORIGIN C16: from French *temporiser* 'bide one's time'.

temporomandibular joint /ˌtempərəʊmanˈdɪbjʊlə/ ▪ n. Anatomy the hinge joint between the temporal bone and the lower jaw.

tempo rubato ▪ n. see RUBATO.

Tempranillo /ˌtemprəˈniːjəʊ, -ˈniːljəʊ/ ▪ n. a variety of wine grape grown in Spain, used to make Rioja wine.
– ORIGIN named after a village in northern Spain.

tempt ▪ v. **1** entice (someone) to do something against their better judgement. **2** attract; charm. **3** archaic risk provoking (a deity or abstract force).
– PHRASES **tempt fate** (or **providence**) do something that is risky or dangerous.
– DERIVATIVES **temptability** n. **temptable** adj. **tempting** adj. **temptingly** adv.
– ORIGIN Middle English: from Old French *tempter* 'to test', from Latin *temptare* 'handle, test, try'.

temptation ▪ n. the state or quality of being tempted; a desire to do something. ▸ a tempting thing.

tempter ▪ n. a person or thing that tempts. ▸ (**the Tempter**) the Devil.

temptress ▪ n. a woman who tempts, especially one who is sexually alluring.

tempura /ˈtempʊrə/ ▪ n. a Japanese dish of fish, shellfish, or vegetables, fried in batter.
– ORIGIN Japanese, prob. from Portuguese *tempêro* 'seasoning'.

ten ▪ cardinal number equivalent to the product of five and two; one more than nine; 10. (Roman numeral: **x** or **X**.)
– PHRASES **ten out of ten** denoting an excellent performance. **ten to one** very probably.
– DERIVATIVES **tenfold** adj. & adv.
– ORIGIN Old English, of Germanic origin.

tenable ▪ adj. **1** able to be maintained or defended against attack or objection. **2** (of an office, position, etc.) able to be held or used: *a scholarship tenable for three years*.
– DERIVATIVES **tenability** n.
– ORIGIN C16: from French, from *tenir* 'to hold'.

tenacious /tɪˈneɪʃəs/ ▪ adj. not readily relinquishing something; keeping a firm hold.
– DERIVATIVES **tenaciously** adv. **tenaciousness** n. **tenacity** /tɪˈnasɪti/ n.
– ORIGIN C17: from Latin *tenax*, *tenac-*, from *tenere* 'to hold'.

tenancy ▪ n. (pl. **-ies**) possession of land or property as a tenant.

tenant ▪ n. a person occupying rented land or property. ▸ Law a person holding real property by private ownership. ▪ v. (usu. **be tenanted**) occupy (property) as a tenant.
– DERIVATIVES **tenantless** adj.
– ORIGIN Middle English: from Old French, 'holding', from *tenir*, from Latin *tenere*.

tenant farmer ▪ n. a person who farms rented land.

tenantry ▪ n. **1** [treated as sing. or pl.] the tenants of an estate. **2** tenancy.

tench ▪ n. (pl. same) a European freshwater fish of the carp family, popular with anglers. [Genus *Tinca*.]
– ORIGIN Middle English: from Old French *tenche*, from late Latin *tinca*.

Ten Commandments ▪ pl. n. (in the Bible) the divine rules of conduct given by God to Moses on Mount Sinai, according to Exodus 20:1–17.

tend¹ ▪ v. **1** frequently behave in a particular way or have a certain characteristic: *written language tends to be formal*. ▸ (**tend to/towards**) be liable to possess (a particular characteristic). **2** go or move in a particular direction.
– ORIGIN Middle English: from Old French *tendre* 'stretch, tend', from Latin *tendere*.

tend² ▪ v. **1** care for or look after. ▸ archaic wait on as an attendant or servant. **2** US direct or manage.
– ORIGIN Middle English: shortening of ATTEND.

tendency ▪ n. (pl. **-ies**) **1** an inclination towards a particular characteristic or type of behaviour. **2** a group within a larger political party or movement.

tendentious /tɛnˈdɛnʃəs/ ▪ adj. calculated to promote a particular cause or point of view.
– DERIVATIVES **tendentiously** adv. **tendentiousness** n.
– ORIGIN C20: suggested by German *tendenziös*.

tender¹ ▪ adj. (**-er**, **-est**) **1** gentle and sympathetic. ▸ (**tender of**) archaic solicitous of. **2** (of food) easy to cut or chew. **3** (of a part of the body) sensitive. **4** young and vulnerable: *the tender age of five*. **5** requiring tact or careful handling. **6** Nautical (of a ship) leaning or inclined to roll in response to the wind.
– PHRASES **tender mercies** ironic attention or treatment not in the best interests of its recipients.
– DERIVATIVES **tenderly** adv. **tenderness** n.
– ORIGIN Middle English: from Old French *tendre*, from Latin *tener* 'tender, delicate'.

tender² ▪ v. **1** offer or present formally. ▸ make a formal written offer to carry out work, supply goods, etc. for a stated fixed price. **2** offer as payment. ▪ n. a tendered offer.
– PHRASES **put something out to tender** seek tenders to carry out work, supply goods, etc.
– DERIVATIVES **tenderer** n.
– ORIGIN C16: from Old French *tendre*, from Latin *tendere* (see TEND¹).

tender³ ▪ n. **1** a vehicle used by a fire service or the armed forces for carrying supplies or fulfilling a specified role. **2** a boat used to ferry people and supplies to and from a ship. **3** a truck closely coupled to a steam locomotive to carry fuel and water. **4** a person who looks after a machine, place, or other people.
– ORIGIN Middle English: from TEND² or shortening of *attender* (see ATTEND).

tenderfoot ▪ n. (pl. **tenderfoots** or **tenderfeet**) chiefly N. Amer. a newcomer or novice.

tender-hearted ▪ adj. having a kind, gentle, or sentimental nature.
– DERIVATIVES **tender-heartedness** n.

tenderize (also **-ise**) ▪ v. make (meat) more tender by beating or slow cooking.
– DERIVATIVES **tenderizer** (also **-iser**) n.

tenderloin ▪ n. **1** the tenderest part of a loin of beef, pork, etc., taken from under the short ribs in the hindquarters. ▸ US the undercut of a sirloin. **2** N. Amer. informal a district of a city where vice and corruption are prominent. [C19: orig. a term applied to a district of New York, seen as a 'choice' assignment by police because of the bribes offered there.]

tender-minded ▪ adj. sensitive.
– DERIVATIVES **tender-mindedness** n.

tendinitis /ˌtendɪˈnʌɪtəs/ (also **tendonitis** /ˌtendə-/) ▪ n. inflammation of a tendon.

tendon /ˈtendən/ ▪ n. a flexible but inelastic cord of strong fibrous tissue attaching a muscle to a bone. ▸ the hamstring of a quadruped.
– DERIVATIVES **tendinous** adj.
– ORIGIN Middle English: from French or medieval Latin *tendo(n-)*, translating Greek *tenōn* 'sinew', from *teinein* 'to stretch'.

tendresse /tɒˈdrɛs/ (also **tendre** /ˈtɒdr(ə)/) ▪ n. a feeling of fondness or love.
– ORIGIN from French.

tendril ▪ n. **1** a slender thread-like appendage of a climbing plant, which stretches out and twines round any suitable support. **2** a slender ringlet of hair.
– ORIGIN C16: prob. a diminutive of Old French *tendron* 'young shoot', from Latin *tener* 'tender'.

tendu leaf /teɪnˈduː/ ▪ n. the leaves of an ebony tree, gathered in India as a cheap tobacco substitute.
– ORIGIN Hindi *tendu*.

tenebrous /ˈtenɪbrəs/ ▪ adj. poetic/literary dark; shadowy.
– ORIGIN Middle English: from Latin *tenebrosus*, from *tenebrae* 'darkness'.

tenement /ˈtenəm(ə)nt/ ▪ n. **1** (especially in Scotland or the US) a separate residence within a house or block of

flats. ▸ (also **tenement house**) a house divided into several separate residences. **2** a piece of land held by an owner. ▸ Law any permanent property, e.g. lands or rents, held from a superior.
– ORIGIN Middle English: from medieval Latin *tenementum*, from *tenere* 'to hold'.

tenet /'tɛnɪt, 'tiːnɛt/ ■ n. a principle or belief.
– ORIGIN C16: from Latin, 'he holds', from *tenere*.

ten-gallon hat ■ n. a large, broad-brimmed hat, traditionally worn by cowboys.

tenner ■ n. informal Brit. a ten pound note. ▸ S. African a ten rand note.

tennis ■ n. a game in which two or four players strike a hollow rubber ball with rackets over a net stretched across a grass, clay or hard court. See also **REAL TENNIS**.
– ORIGIN Middle English *tenetz, tenes* 'real tennis', apparently from Old French *tenez* 'take, receive' (called by the server to an opponent), from *tenir*.

tennis elbow ■ n. inflammation of the tendons of the elbow (epicondylitis) caused by overuse of the forearm muscles.

tennis shoe ■ n. a light canvas or leather soft-soled shoe suitable for tennis or casual wear.

tenon ■ n. a projecting piece of wood made for insertion into a mortise in another piece. ■ v. (usu. **be tenoned**) join by means of a tenon. ▸ cut as a tenon.
– DERIVATIVES **tenoner** n.
– ORIGIN Middle English: from French, from *tenir* 'to hold', from Latin *tenere*.

tenon saw ■ n. a small saw with a strong brass or steel back for precise work.

tenor¹ ■ n. **1** a singing voice between baritone and alto or counter-tenor, the highest of the ordinary adult male range. **2** [as modifier] denoting an instrument of the second or third lowest pitch in its family. **3** (in full **tenor bell**) the largest and deepest bell of a ring or set.
– ORIGIN Middle English: from medieval Latin, from *tenere* 'to hold'; so named because the tenor part 'held' the melody.

tenor² ■ n. **1** the general meaning, sense, or content of something. **2** a prevailing character or direction: *the even tenor of life in the kitchen*. **3** Law the actual wording of a document. **4** Finance the time that must elapse before a bill of exchange or promissory note becomes due for payment.
– ORIGIN Middle English: from Old French *tenour*, from Latin *tenor* 'course, substance, import of a law', from *tenere* 'to hold'.

tenor clef ■ n. Music a clef placing middle C on the second-highest line of the stave, used chiefly for cello and bassoon music.

tenosynovitis /ˌtɛnəʊˌsaɪnə(ʊ)'vʌɪtɪs/ ■ n. Medicine inflammation and swelling of a tendon, especially in the wrist and typically caused by repetitive movement.
– ORIGIN C19: from Greek *tenōn* 'tendon' + **SYNOVITIS**.

tenotomy /təˈnɒtəmi/ ■ n. the surgical cutting of a tendon, especially as a remedy for club foot.
– ORIGIN C19: coined in French from Greek *tenōn* 'tendon' + *-tomia* (see **-TOMY**).

tenpin ■ n. a skittle used in tenpin bowling.

tenpin bowling ■ n. a game in which ten skittles are set up at the end of a track and bowled down with hard rubber or plastic balls.

tenrec /'tɛnrɛk/ ■ n. a small insectivorous mammal of Madagascar and the Comoro Islands. [Family Tenrecidae: many species.]
– ORIGIN C18: from French *tanrec*, from Malagasy *tàndraka*.

TENS ■ abbrev. transcutaneous electrical nerve stimulation, a technique designed to provide pain relief by applying electrodes to the skin.

tense¹ ■ adj. **1** (especially of a muscle) stretched tight or rigid. **2** (of a person) unable to relax. ▸ causing or showing anxiety and nervousness. **3** Phonetics (of a speech sound, especially a vowel) pronounced with the vocal muscles stretched tight. The opposite of **LAX**. ■ v. make or become tense.
– DERIVATIVES **tensely** adv. **tenseness** n. **tensity** n.
– ORIGIN C17: from Latin *tensus, tendere* 'stretch'.

tense² ■ n. Grammar a set of forms taken by a verb to indicate the time (and sometimes the continuance or completeness) of the action in relation to the time of the utterance.
– ORIGIN Middle English: from Old French *tens*, from Latin *tempus* 'time'.

tensile /'tɛnsʌɪl/ ■ adj. **1** of or relating to tension. **2** capable of being drawn out or stretched.
– DERIVATIVES **tensility** n.
– ORIGIN C17: from medieval Latin *tensilis*, from Latin *tendere* 'to stretch'.

tensile strength ■ n. the resistance of a material to breaking under tension. Compare with **COMPRESSIVE STRENGTH**.

tension ■ n. **1** the state of being tense. ▸ a strained state or condition resulting from forces acting in opposition to each other. **2** mental or emotional strain. ▸ a strained political or social state. **3** the degree of stitch tightness in knitting and machine sewing. **4** voltage of specified magnitude: *high tension*. ■ v. subject to tension.
– DERIVATIVES **tensional** adj. **tensionally** adv. **tensioner** n. **tensionless** adj.
– ORIGIN C16: from French, or from Latin *tensio(n-)*, from *tendere* 'stretch'.

tensive ■ adj. causing or expressing tension.

tensor /'tɛnsə, -sɔː/ ■ n. Anatomy a muscle that tightens or stretches a part of the body.
– ORIGIN C18: from Latin *tendere* 'to stretch'.

tent ■ n. a portable shelter made of cloth, supported by one or more poles and stretched tight by cords attached to pegs driven into the ground. ■ v. **1** cover with or as if with a tent. ▸ arrange in a tent-like shape. ▸ [as adj. **tented**] composed of or provided with tents. **2** live in a tent.
– ORIGIN Middle English: from Old French *tente*, from Latin *tendere* 'stretch'.

tentacle ■ n. **1** a long slender flexible appendage of an animal, used for grasping or moving about, or bearing sense organs. **2** a tendril or sensitive glandular hair on a plant. **3** an insidious spread of influence and control: *the Party's tentacles reached into every part of people's lives*.
– DERIVATIVES **tentacled** adj. **tentacular** adj. **tentaculate** adj.
– ORIGIN C18: from modern Latin *tentaculum*, from Latin *tentare, temptare* 'to feel, try'.

tentage ■ n. tents collectively.

tentative ■ adj. provisional. ▸ hesitant.
– DERIVATIVES **tentatively** adv. **tentativeness** n.
– ORIGIN C16: from medieval Latin *tentativus*, from *tentare*, var. of *temptare* 'handle, try'.

tent caterpillar ■ n. a moth caterpillar that lives gregariously inside a silken web in a tree.

tent dress ■ n. a full, loose-fitting dress having no waistline or darts.

tenter ■ n. a framework on which fabric can be held taut for drying or other treatment during manufacture.
– ORIGIN Middle English: from medieval Latin *tentorium*, from *tendere* 'stretch'.

tenterhook ■ n. historical a hook used to fasten cloth on a tenter.
– PHRASES **on tenterhooks** in a state of agitated suspense.

tenth ■ ordinal number constituting number ten in a sequence; 10th.
– DERIVATIVES **tenthly** adv.

tent stitch ■ n. a series of parallel diagonal stitches.

tenuity /tɪ'njuːɪti/ ■ n. lack of solidity or substance.
– ORIGIN Middle English: from Latin *tenuitas*, from *tenuis* 'thin'.

tenuous ■ adj. very weak or slight. ▸ very slender or fine.
– DERIVATIVES **tenuously** adv. **tenuousness** n.
– ORIGIN C16: from Latin *tenuis* 'thin'.

tenure /'tɛnjə/ ■ n. **1** the conditions under which land or buildings are held or occupied. **2** the holding of an office. ▸ the period of this. ■ v. give a permanent post to. ▸ [as adj. **tenured**] having or denoting such a post.
– PHRASES **security of tenure 1** the right of a tenant of property to occupy it after the lease expires (unless a court should order otherwise). **2** guaranteed permanent

employment after a probationary period.
– ORIGIN Middle English: from Old French, from *tenir* 'to hold', from Latin *tenere*.

tenure track ■ n. an employment structure whereby the holder of a post is guaranteed consideration for eventual tenure.

tenurial ■ adj. relating to the tenure of land.
– DERIVATIVES **tenurially** adv.

teosinte /ˌtiːəʊˈsɪnteɪ/ ■ n. a Mexican fodder grass believed to be a parent grass of maize. [*Zea mays* subsp. *mexicana*.]
– ORIGIN C19: from French *téosinté*, from Nahuatl *teocintli*, apparently from *teo:tl* 'god' + *cintli* 'dried ear of maize'.

tepal /ˈtɛp(ə)l, ˈtiːp(ə)l/ ■ n. Botany a petal or sepal in a flower in which there is no distinction between them.
– ORIGIN C19: from French *tépale*, blend of *pétale* 'petal' and *sépal* 'sepal'.

tepee /ˈtiːpiː/ (also **teepee** or **tipi**) ■ n. a conical tent made of skins or cloth on a frame of poles, used by American Indians of the Plains and Great Lakes regions.
– ORIGIN C18: from Sioux *tîpî* 'dwelling'.

tephra /ˈtɛfrə/ ■ n. Geology rock fragments and particles ejected by a volcanic eruption.
– ORIGIN 1940s: from Greek, 'ash, ashes'.

tephrochronology /ˌtɛfrə(ʊ)krəˈnɒlədʒi/ ■ n. Geology the dating of volcanic eruptions and other events by studying layers of tephra.
– DERIVATIVES **tephrochronological** adj.

tepid ■ adj. **1** lukewarm. **2** unenthusiastic.
– DERIVATIVES **tepidity** n. **tepidly** adv. **tepidness** n.
– ORIGIN Middle English: from Latin *tepidus*, from *tepere* 'be warm'.

tequila /tɛˈkiːlə/ ■ n. a Mexican liquor made from an agave.
– ORIGIN Mexican Spanish, named after the town of *Tequila* in Mexico.

tequila slammer ■ n. see **SLAMMER** (sense 2).

tequila sunrise ■ n. a cocktail of tequila, orange juice, and grenadine.

ter- ■ comb. form three; having three: *tercentenary*.
– ORIGIN from Latin *ter* 'thrice'.

tera- /ˈtɛrə/ ■ comb. form **1** denoting a factor of 10^{12}: *terawatt*. **2** Computing denoting a factor of 2^{40}: *terabyte*.
– ORIGIN from Greek *teras* 'monster'.

terabyte ■ n. Computing a unit of information equal to one million million (10^{12}) or (strictly) 2^{40} bytes.

teraflop ■ n. Computing a unit of computing speed equal to one million million floating-point operations per second.

terato- ■ comb. form relating to monsters or abnormal forms: *teratology*.
– ORIGIN from Greek *teras, terat-* 'monster'.

teratogen /tɛˈratədʒ(ə)n, ˈtɛrətədʒ(ə)n/ ■ n. an agent or factor causing malformation of an embryo.
– DERIVATIVES **teratogenesis** n. **teratogenic** adj. **tera-togenicity** n.

teratology /ˌtɛrəˈtɒlədʒi/ ■ n. Biology **1** the scientific study of congenital abnormalities and abnormal formations. **2** mythology relating to fantastic creatures and monsters.
– DERIVATIVES **teratological** /-lɒdʒɪk(ə)l/ adj.

teratoma /ˌtɛrəˈtəʊmə/ ■ n. (pl. **teratomas** or **teratomata** /-mətə/) Medicine a tumour composed of tissues not normally present at the site.

terawatt /ˈtɛrəwɒt/ ■ n. a unit of power equal to 10^{12} watts or a million megawatts.

terbium /ˈtəːbɪəm/ ■ n. the chemical element of atomic number 65, a silvery-white metal of the lanthanide series. (Symbol: **Tb**)
– ORIGIN C19: from *Ytterby* (see **YTTERBIUM**).

terce /təːs/ ■ n. a service forming part of the Divine Office of the Western Christian Church, traditionally said at the third hour of the day (9 a.m.).
– ORIGIN Middle English: from Old French, from Latin *tertius* 'third'.

tercentenary ■ n. (pl. **-ies**) a three-hundredth anniversary.
– DERIVATIVES **tercentennial** adj. & n.

tercet /ˈtəːsɪt/ ■ n. Prosody a set or group of three lines of verse rhyming together or connected by rhyme with an adjacent triplet.
– ORIGIN C16: from Italian *terzetto*, diminutive of *terzo* 'third', from Latin *tertius*.

teredo /təˈriːdəʊ/ ■ n. (pl. **-os**) Zoology a worm-like marine bivalve mollusc which bores into wood and can damage wooden structures. [*Teredo navalis* and related species.]
– ORIGIN Middle English: from Greek *terēdōn*; rel. to *teirein* 'rub hard, wear away'.

terephthalate /ˌtɛrəfˈθaleɪt/ ■ n. Chemistry a salt or ester of terephthalic acid.

terephthalic acid /ˌtɛrəfˈθalɪk/ ■ n. Chemistry a crystalline organic acid used in making polyester resins and other polymers.
– ORIGIN C19: blend of *terebic* 'of or from turpentine' and *phthalic acid*.

terete /təˈriːt/ ■ adj. chiefly Botany smooth and cylindrical or slightly tapering.
– ORIGIN C17: from Latin *teres, teret-* 'rounded off'.

tergum /ˈtəːɡəm/ ■ n. (pl. **terga**) Zoology a thickened dorsal plate on a body segment of an arthropod.
– ORIGIN C19: from Latin, 'back'.

-teria ■ suffix denoting self-service establishments: *washeteria*.
– ORIGIN on the pattern of (*cafe*)*teria*.

teriyaki /ˌtɛrɪˈjɑːki/ ■ n. a Japanese dish of fish or meat marinated in soy sauce and grilled. ▸ (also **teriyaki sauce**) a mixture of soy sauce, sake, and ginger, used in Japanese cookery as a marinade or glaze.
– ORIGIN from Japanese.

term ■ n. **1** a word or phrase used to describe a thing or to express a concept. ▸ (**terms**) a way of expressing oneself. ▸ Logic a word or words that may be the subject or predicate of a proposition. **2** a fixed or limited period for which something lasts or is intended to last. ▸ (also **full term**) the completion of a normal length of pregnancy. ▸ (also **term of years**) Law a tenancy of a fixed period. ▸ archaic a boundary or limit, especially of time. **3** each of the periods in the year during which instruction is given in a school, college, etc., or during which a law court holds sessions. **4** (**terms**) stipulated or agreed requirements. ▸ conditions with regard to payment. ▸ agreed conditions under which a dispute is settled. **5** Mathematics each of the quantities in a ratio, series, or mathematical expression. **6** Architecture a terminus. ■ v. call by a specified term.
– PHRASES **come to terms with** reconcile oneself to. **in terms of** (or **in ―― terms**) with regard to the aspect or subject specified. **the ―― term** a period that is a specified way into the future: *investments that pay dividends in the long term*. **on terms** in a state of friendship or equality. ▸ (in sport) level in score. **on ―― terms** on a specified footing. **terms of reference** the scope of an inquiry or discussion.
– DERIVATIVES **termly** adj. & adv.
– ORIGIN Middle English: from Old French *terme*, from Latin *terminus* 'end, boundary, limit'.

termagant /ˈtəːməɡ(ə)nt/ ■ n. a harsh-tempered or overbearing woman.
– ORIGIN Middle English: from Italian *Trivagante*, taken to be from Latin *tri-* 'three' + *vagant-* 'wandering', and to refer to the moon 'wandering' between heaven, earth, and hell.

terminable ■ adj. **1** able to be terminated. **2** coming to an end after a certain time.

terminal ■ adj. **1** of, forming, or situated at the end of something. ▸ of or forming a transport terminal. **2** (of a disease) predicted to lead to death. ▸ having or relating to a terminal disease. **3** informal extreme and irreversible. ■ n. **1** the end of a railway or other transport route, or a station at this point. ▸ a departure and arrival building for passengers at an airport. **2** a point of connection for closing an electric circuit. **3** a device at which a user enters data or commands for a computer and which displays the received output. **4** an installation where oil or gas is stored at the end of a pipeline or at a port. **5** (also **terminal figure**) Architecture a terminus. **6** Brit. a patient with a terminal illness.
– DERIVATIVES **terminally** adv.

– ORIGIN C19: from Latin *terminalis*, from *terminus* 'end, boundary'.

terminal velocity ■ n. Physics the constant speed that a freely falling object reaches when the resistance of the medium through which it is falling prevents further acceleration.

terminate ■ v. **1** bring to an end. ▸ end (a pregnancy) before term by artificial means. ▸ (of a train or bus service) end its journey. **2** (**terminate in**) have an end at (a specified place) or of (a specified form). **3** end the employment of. **4** euphemistic, chiefly N. Amer. assassinate.
– PHRASES **terminate someone with extreme prejudice** euphemistic, chiefly US murder someone.
– DERIVATIVES **termination** n. **terminational** adj.
– ORIGIN C16: from Latin *terminat-*, *terminare* 'to limit, end', from *terminus* 'end, boundary'.

terminator ■ n. **1** a person or thing that terminates. **2** Astronomy the dividing line between the light and dark part of a planetary body. **3** Biochemistry the region of a DNA molecule at which transcription ends.

termini plural form of TERMINUS.

terminological inexactitude ■ n. humorous a lie.
– ORIGIN first used by Winston Churchill in 1906.

terminology ■ n. (pl. **-ies**) the body of terms used in a subject of study, profession, etc.
– DERIVATIVES **terminological** adj. **terminologically** adv. **terminologist** n.
– ORIGIN C19: from German *Terminologie*, from medieval Latin *terminus* 'term'.

terminus ■ n. (pl. **termini** or **terminuses**) **1** a railway or bus terminal. ▸ an oil or gas terminal. **2** an end or extremity. **3** Architecture a figure of a human bust or animal ending in a square pillar from which it appears to spring, originally a boundary marker in ancient Rome.
– ORIGIN C16: from Latin, 'end, limit, boundary'.

terminus ad quem /ˌtəːmɪnəs ad ˈkwɛm/ ■ n. an end or finishing point. ▸ an aim or goal.
– ORIGIN Latin, 'end to which'.

terminus ante quem /ˌanti ˈkwɛm/ ■ n. the latest possible date.
– ORIGIN Latin, 'end before which'.

terminus post quem /pəʊst ˈkwɛm/ ■ n. the earliest possible date.
– ORIGIN Latin, 'end after which'.

termitarium /ˌtəːmʌɪˈtɛːrɪəm/ ■ n. (pl. **termitaria**) a colony of termites, typically within a mound of cemented earth.
– ORIGIN C19: from Latin *termes*, *termit-* 'termite'.

termitary /ˈtəːmɪtəri/ ■ n. (pl. **-ies**) a termitarium.

termite /ˈtəːmʌɪt/ ■ n. a small, pale soft-bodied social insect, typically making large nests of earth and feeding on wood. [Order Isoptera: many species.]
– ORIGIN C18: from late Latin *termes*, *termit-* 'woodworm', alteration of Latin *tarmes*.

term of years ■ n. see TERM (sense 2).

term paper ■ n. N. Amer. a long essay on a subject studied during a school or college term.

terms of trade ■ pl. n. Economics the ratio of an index of a country's export prices to an index of its import prices.

tern /təːn/ ■ n. a seabird related to the gulls, typically smaller and more slender, with long pointed wings and a forked tail. [*Sterna* and other genera: many species.]
– ORIGIN C17: of Scandinavian origin.

ternary /ˈtəːnəri/ ■ adj. composed of three parts.
▸ Mathematics using three as a base.
– ORIGIN Middle English: from Latin *ternarius*, from *terni* 'three at once'.

terne /təːn/ ■ n. a lead alloy containing about 20 per cent tin and often some antimony, used for plating steel.
– ORIGIN C19: prob. from French *terne* 'dull, tarnished'.

terotechnology /ˌtɛrə(ʊ)tɛkˈnɒlədʒi, ˌtɪərə(ʊ)-/ ■ n. chiefly Brit. the branch of technology and engineering concerned with the installation and maintenance of equipment.
– ORIGIN 1970s: from Greek *tērein* 'take care of' + TECHNOLOGY.

terpene /ˈtəːpiːn/ ■ n. Chemistry any of a large group of volatile unsaturated hydrocarbons with cyclic molecules, found in the essential oils of conifers and other plants.

– DERIVATIVES **terpenoid** n. & adj.
– ORIGIN C19: from German *Terpentin* 'turpentine'.

terpsichorean /ˌtəːpsɪkəˈriːən/ formal or humorous ■ adj. of or relating to dancing. ■ n. a dancer.
– ORIGIN C19: from *Terpsichore*, the ancient Greek and Roman Muse of dance.

terrace ■ n. **1** a patio. **2** each of a series of flat areas on a slope, used for cultivation. ▸ a flight of wide, shallow steps providing standing room for spectators in a stadium. ▸ Geology a natural horizontal shelf-like formation, such as a raised beach. **3** a row of houses built in one block in a uniform style. ■ v. make or form (sloping land) into terraces.
– DERIVATIVES **terracing** n.
– ORIGIN C16: from Old French, 'rubble, platform', from Latin *terra* 'earth'.

terraced ■ adj. **1** (of a house) forming part of a terrace. **2** (of land) having been formed into terraces.

terraced roof ■ n. a flat roof.

terracotta /ˌtɛrəˈkɒtə/ ■ n. **1** unglazed, typically brownish-red earthenware, used chiefly as an ornamental building material and in modelling. **2** a statuette or other object made of terracotta. **3** a strong brownish-red colour.
– ORIGIN C18: from Italian *terra cotta* 'baked earth'.

terra firma /ˈfəːmə/ ■ n. dry land; the ground.
– ORIGIN C17: from Latin, 'firm land'.

terraform ■ v. (especially in science fiction) transform (a planet) so as to resemble the earth.
– DERIVATIVES **terraformer** n.
– ORIGIN 1940s: from Latin *terra* 'earth' + FORM.

terrain /tɛˈreɪn/ ■ n. a stretch of land, especially with regard to its physical features.
– ORIGIN C18: from French, from a var. of Latin *terrenum*, from *terrenus* (see TERRENE).

terra incognita /ɪnˈkɒɡnɪtə, ˌɪnkɒɡˈniːtə/ ■ n. unknown territory.
– ORIGIN Latin, 'unknown land'.

terrane /tɛˈreɪn/ ■ n. Geology a geologically distinct region bounded by faults.
– ORIGIN C19: var. of TERRAIN.

terrapin ■ n. **1** a small freshwater turtle. [Order Chelonia: many species.] **2** (**Terrapin**) Brit. trademark a prefabricated one-storey building for temporary use.
– ORIGIN C17: of Algonquian origin.

terraqueous /tɛˈreɪkwɪəs/ ■ adj. consisting or formed of land and water.
– ORIGIN C17: from Latin *terra* 'land' + AQUEOUS.

terrarium /tɛˈrɛːrɪəm/ ■ n. (pl. **terrariums** or **terraria** /-rɪə/) **1** a vivarium for smaller land animals, e.g. reptiles or amphibians, typically in the form of a glass-fronted case. **2** a sealed transparent globe or similar container in which plants are grown.
– ORIGIN C19: from Latin *terra* 'earth', on the pattern of *aquarium*.

terra sigillata /ˌsɪdʒɪˈleɪtə/ ■ n. **1** astringent clay from Lemnos or Samos, formerly used as a medicine. **2** Samian ware.
– ORIGIN Middle English: from medieval Latin, 'sealed earth'.

terrazzo /tɛˈratsəʊ/ ■ n. flooring material consisting of chips of marble or granite set in concrete and polished smooth.
– ORIGIN C20: Italian, 'terrace'.

terrene /tɛˈriːn/ ■ adj. archaic **1** of or like earth. ▸ occurring on or inhabiting dry land. **2** worldly.
– ORIGIN Middle English: from Anglo-Norman French, from Latin *terrenus*, from *terra* 'earth'.

terrestrial /təˈrɛstrɪəl/ ■ adj. **1** of, on, or relating to the earth or dry land. ▸ (of an animal or plant) living on or in the ground. ▸ Astronomy (of a planet) resembling the earth. **2** denoting television broadcast other than by satellite. ■ n. an inhabitant of the earth.
– DERIVATIVES **terrestrially** adv.
– ORIGIN Middle English: from Latin *terrestris*, from *terra* 'earth'.

terrestrial globe ■ n. a spherical representation of the earth with a map on the surface.

terrestrial telescope ■ n. a telescope for observing terrestrial objects, giving an uninverted image.

terret /ˈtɛrɪt/ ■ n. each of the loops or rings on a horse's harness pad for the driving reins to pass through.
– ORIGIN C15: from Old French *touret*, diminutive of *tour* 'a turn'.

terre verte /tɛː ˈvɛːt/ ■ n. a greyish-green pigment made from the clay mineral glauconite, used for watercolours and tempera.
– ORIGIN C17: French, 'green earth'.

terrible ■ adj. **1** extremely bad, serious, or unpleasant. **2** troubled or guilty. **3** causing terror.
– DERIVATIVES **terribleness** n.
– ORIGIN Middle English: from Latin *terribilis*, from *terrere* 'frighten'.

terribly ■ adv. **1** extremely: *I'm terribly sorry.* **2** very badly.

terrier /ˈtɛrɪə/ ■ n. **1** a small dog of a breed originally used for turning out foxes and other animals from their earths. **2** a tenacious or eager person.
– ORIGIN Middle English: from Old French (*chien*) *terrier* 'earth (dog)', from medieval Latin *terrarius*, from Latin *terra* 'earth'.

terrific ■ adj. **1** of great size, amount, or intensity. ▸ informal excellent. **2** archaic causing terror.
– DERIVATIVES **terrifically** adv.
– ORIGIN C17: from Latin *terrificus*, from *terrere* 'frighten'.

terrify ■ v. (**-ies, -ied**) cause to feel terror.
– DERIVATIVES **terrifying** adj. **terrifyingly** adv.
– ORIGIN C16: from Latin *terrificare*, from *terrificus* (see **TERRIFIC**).

terrigenous /tɛˈrɪdʒɪnəs/ ■ adj. Geology denoting marine sediment eroded from the land.
– ORIGIN C17: from Latin *terrigenus*, from *terra* 'earth' + *-genus* 'born'.

terrine /təˈriːn/ ■ n. **1** a meat, fish, or vegetable mixture cooked or otherwise prepared in advance and allowed to cool or set in its container. **2** an oblong, typically earthenware, container for such a dish.
– ORIGIN C18: from French, 'large earthenware pot', from *terrin* 'earthen'.

territorial ■ adj. **1** of or relating to the ownership of land or sea. ▸ (of an animal) defending a territory. **2** of or relating to a territory or area. ▸ (**Territorial**) of or relating to a Territory. ■ n. (**Territorial**) (in the UK) a member of the Territorial Army.
– DERIVATIVES **territoriality** n. **territorially** adv.

Territorial Army ■ n. (in the UK) a volunteer force locally organized to provide a reserve of trained manpower for use in an emergency.

territorial waters ■ pl. n. the waters under the jurisdiction of a state, traditionally the part of the sea extending three miles from the shore.

territory ■ n. (pl. **-ies**) **1** an area under the jurisdiction of a ruler or state. **2** (**Territory**) (especially in the US, Canada, or Australia) an organized division of a country not having the full rights of a state. **3** Zoology an area defended by an animal against others of the same sex or species. **4** an area defended by a team or player in a game or sport. **5** an area in which one has certain rights or responsibilities. **6** an area of knowledge or experience. **7** land with a specified characteristic: *woodland territory*.
– ORIGIN Middle English: from Latin *territorium*, from *terra* 'land'.

terror ■ n. **1** extreme fear. ▸ the use of terror to intimidate people. ▸ a cause of terror. **2** (also **holy terror**) informal a person causing trouble or annoyance.
– ORIGIN Middle English: from Old French *terrour*, from Latin *terror*, from *terrere* 'frighten'.

terrorist ■ n. a person who uses violence and intimidation in the pursuit of political aims.
– DERIVATIVES **terrorism** n. **terroristic** adj. **terroristically** adv.

terrorize (also **-ise**) ■ v. create and maintain a feeling of terror in.
– DERIVATIVES **terrorization** (also **-isation**) n. **terrorizer** (also **-iser**) n.

terry ■ n. (pl. **-ies**) fabric with raised uncut loops of thread on both sides, used especially for towels.
– ORIGIN C18.

terse ■ adj. (**terser, tersest**) sparing in the use of words; abrupt.
– DERIVATIVES **tersely** adv. **terseness** n.
– ORIGIN C17 (orig. 'polished, trim', hence 'concise'): from Latin *tersus* 'wiped, polished'.

tertian /ˈtəːʃ(ə)n/ ■ adj. Medicine denoting a form of malaria causing a fever that recurs every second day.
– ORIGIN Middle English (*fever*) *terciane*, from Latin (*febris*) *tertiana*, from *tertius* 'third' (the fever recurring every third day by inclusive reckoning).

tertiary /ˈtəːʃ(ə)ri/ ■ adj. **1** third in order or level. ▸ relating to or denoting education at a level beyond that provided by schools. **2** relating to or denoting medical treatment provided at a specialist institution. **3** (**Tertiary**) Geology relating to or denoting the first period of the Cenozoic era (between the Cretaceous and Quaternary periods, about 65 to 1.64 million years ago). **4** Chemistry (of an organic compound) having its functional group on a carbon atom bonded to three other carbon atoms. ▸ Chemistry derived from ammonia by replacement of three hydrogen atoms by organic groups.
– ORIGIN C16: from Latin *tertiarius* 'of the third part or rank'.

tertiary industry ■ n. Economics the service industry of a country.

tervalent /təːˈveɪl(ə)nt/ ■ adj. Chemistry trivalent.

Terylene ■ n. trademark, chiefly Brit. a polyester fibre used to make light, crease-resistant clothing, bed linen, and sails.
– ORIGIN 1940s: formed by inversion of (*polyeth*)*ylene ter*(*ephthalate*).

terza rima /ˌtɛːtsə ˈriːmə/ ■ n. Prosody an arrangement of triplets, especially in iambic pentameter, that rhyme *aba bcb cdc* etc.
– ORIGIN Italian, 'third rhyme'.

TESL ■ abbrev. teaching of English as a second language.

tesla /ˈtɛslə, ˈtɛzlə/ (abbrev.: **T**) ■ n. Physics the SI unit of magnetic flux density.
– ORIGIN 1960s: named after the American electrical engineer Nikola *Tesla*.

Tesla coil ■ n. a form of induction coil producing high-frequency alternating currents.

TESOL /ˈtɛsɒl/ ■ abbrev. teaching of English to speakers of other languages.

tessellate /ˈtɛsəleɪt/ ■ v. **1** decorate (a floor) with mosaics. **2** Mathematics cover (a plane surface) by repeated use of a single shape, without gaps or overlapping.
– DERIVATIVES **tesselated** adj. **tesselation** n.
– ORIGIN C18: from late Latin *tessellare*, from *tessella*, diminutive of *tessera* (see **TESSERA**).

tessera /ˈtɛs(ə)rə/ ■ n. (pl. **tesserae** /-riː/) a small block of stone, tile, etc. used in a mosaic.
– DERIVATIVES **tesseral** adj.
– ORIGIN C17: from Greek, from *tesseres*, var. of *tessares* 'four'.

tessitura /ˌtɛsɪˈtjʊərə/ ■ n. Music the range within which most notes of a vocal part fall.
– ORIGIN Italian, 'texture'.

test[1] ■ n. **1** a procedure to establish the quality, performance, or reliability of something. ▸ a short examination of proficiency or knowledge. ▸ a difficult situation revealing the strength or quality of someone or something. ▸ an examination of part of the body or a body fluid for medical purposes. ▸ Chemistry a procedure employed to identify a substance or to reveal the presence or absence of a constituent within a substance. **2** a means of testing something. **3** short for **TEST MATCH**. **4** Metallurgy a movable hearth in a reverberatory furnace, used for separating gold or silver from lead. ■ v. subject to a test. ▸ produce a specified result in a medical test. ▸ Chemistry examine by means of a reagent. ▸ touch or taste before proceeding further.
– PHRASES **test the water** ascertain feelings or opinions before proceeding further.

– DERIVATIVES **testability** n. **testable** adj. **testee** n.
– ORIGIN Middle English (denoting a container used in assaying metals): from Latin *testu*, *testum* 'earthen pot', var. of *testa* 'jug, shell'.

test[2] ■ n. Zoology the shell or integument of some invertebrates and protozoans.
– ORIGIN C19: from Latin *testa* 'tile, jug, shell'.

testa ■ n. (pl. **testae** /-tiː/) Botany the protective outer covering of a seed.
– ORIGIN C18: from Latin, 'tile, shell'.

testaceous /tɛˈsteɪʃəs/ ■ adj. chiefly Entomology of a dull brick-red colour.
– ORIGIN C17: from Latin *testaceus*, from *testa* 'tile'.

testament ■ n. **1** a person's will. **2** evidence or proof of a fact, event, or quality. **3** (in biblical use) a covenant or dispensation. **4** (**Testament**) a division of the Bible. See also OLD TESTAMENT, NEW TESTAMENT. ▸ (**Testament**) a copy of the New Testament.
– ORIGIN Middle English: from Latin *testamentum* 'a will', from *testari* 'testify', in Christian Latin also translating Greek *diathēkē* 'covenant'.

testamentary ■ adj. of, relating to, or bequeathed or appointed through a will.

testate /ˈtɛsteɪt/ ■ adj. having made a valid will before one dies. ■ n. a person who dies testate.
– ORIGIN Middle English: from Latin *testatus* 'testified, witnessed', from *testari*, from *testis* 'a witness'.

testation ■ n. Law the disposal of property by will.

testator /tɛˈsteɪtə/ ■ n. Law. a person who has made a will or given a legacy.
– ORIGIN Middle English: from Anglo-Norman French *testatour*, from Latin *testator*, from *testari* 'testify'.

testatrix /tɛˈsteɪtrɪks/ ■ n. (pl. **testatrices** /-trɪsiːz/ or **testatrixes**) Law a female testator.
– ORIGIN C16: from late Latin, feminine of *testator* (see TESTATOR).

test bed ■ n. a piece of equipment for testing new machinery, especially aircraft engines.

test case ■ n. Law a case setting a precedent for other cases.

test drive ■ n. a drive taken in a motor vehicle that one is considering buying, in order to determine its qualities. ■ v. (**test-drive**) take (a vehicle) for a test drive.

tester[1] ■ n. **1** a person or device that tests. **2** a sample of a product allowing customers to try it before purchase.

tester[2] ■ n. a canopy over a four-poster bed.
– ORIGIN Middle English: from medieval Latin *testerium*, from a Romance word meaning 'head', from Latin *testa* 'tile'.

testes plural form of TESTIS.

test flight ■ n. a flight during which the performance of an aircraft or its equipment is tested.
– DERIVATIVES **test-fly** v.

testicle ■ n. either of the two oval organs that produce sperm in male mammals, enclosed in the scrotum behind the penis. Compare with TESTIS.
– DERIVATIVES **testicular** adj.
– ORIGIN Middle English: from Latin *testiculus*, diminutive of *testis* 'a witness' (i.e. to virility).

testify ■ v. (**-ies, -ied**) **1** give evidence as a witness in a law court. **2** serve as evidence or proof of something.
– DERIVATIVES **testifier** n.
– ORIGIN Middle English: from Latin *testificari*, from *testis* 'a witness'.

testimonial /ˌtɛstɪˈməʊnɪəl/ ■ n. a formal statement testifying to someone's character and qualifications. ▸ a public tribute to someone and to their achievements.

testimony ■ n. (pl. **-ies**) **1** a formal statement, especially one given in a court of law. **2** evidence or proof of something.
– ORIGIN Middle English: from Latin *testimonium*, from *testis* 'a witness'.

testing ground ■ n. an area or field of activity for the testing of a product or an idea.

testis /ˈtɛstɪs/ ■ n. (pl. **testes** /-tiːz/) Anatomy & Zoology an organ which produces sperm. Compare with TESTICLE.
– ORIGIN C18: from Latin (see TESTICLE).

1227

test match ■ n. an international cricket or rugby match played between teams representing two different countries.

testosterone /tɛˈstɒstərəʊn/ ■ n. a steroid hormone stimulating development of male secondary sexual characteristics.
– ORIGIN 1930s: from TESTIS + *sterone* (blend of STEROL and KETONE).

test pilot ■ n. a pilot who test-flies aircraft.

test tube ■ n. **1** a thin glass tube closed at one end, used to hold material for laboratory testing or experiments. **2** [as modifier] denoting things produced or processes performed in a laboratory.

test-tube baby ■ n. informal a baby conceived by in vitro fertilization.

testy ■ adj. irritable.
– DERIVATIVES **testily** adv. **testiness** n.
– ORIGIN Middle English: from Anglo-Norman French *testif*, from Old French *teste* 'head', from Latin *testa* 'shell'.

tetanus ■ n. **1** a bacterial disease causing rigidity and spasms of the voluntary muscles. **2** Physiology the prolonged contraction of a muscle caused by rapidly repeated stimuli.
– DERIVATIVES **tetanize** (also **-ise**) v. **tetanoid** adj.
– ORIGIN Middle English: from Greek *tetanos* 'muscular spasm', from *teinein* 'to stretch'.

tetany /ˈtɛt(ə)ni/ ■ n. Medicine a condition of intermittent muscular spasms, caused by parathyroid malfunction and consequent calcium deficiency.
– ORIGIN C19: from French *tétanie*, from Latin *tetanus* (see TETANUS).

tetchy (also **techy**) ■ adj. irritable.
– DERIVATIVES **tetchily** adv. **tetchiness** n.
– ORIGIN C16: prob. from a var. of Scots *tache* 'blotch, fault', from Old French *teche*.

tête-à-tête /ˌteɪtaˈteɪt, ˌteɪtɑːˈteɪt/ ■ n. (pl. same or **tête-à-têtes** pronunc. same) a private conversation between two people. ■ adj. & adv. involving or happening privately between two people.
– ORIGIN C17: French, 'head-to-head'.

tether ■ n. a rope or chain with which an animal is tied to restrict its movement. ■ v. tie with a tether.
– ORIGIN Middle English: from Old Norse *tjóthr*, from a Germanic base meaning 'fasten'.

tetra /ˈtɛtrə/ ■ n. a small brightly coloured tropical freshwater fish of the characin family, popular in aquaria. [*Paracheirodon innesi* (neon tetra, Amazonia), and other species.]
– ORIGIN C20: abbrev. of *Tetragonopterus* (former genus name), 'tetragonal-finned'.

tetra- (also **tetr-** before a vowel) ■ comb. form **1** four; having four: *tetragram*. **2** Chemistry (in names of compounds) containing four atoms or groups of a specified kind: *tetracycline*.
– ORIGIN from Greek, from *tettares* 'four'.

tetracycline /ˌtɛtrəˈsʌɪkliːn, -lɪn/ ■ n. Medicine any of a large group of antibiotics with a molecular structure containing four rings.
– ORIGIN 1950s: from TETRA- + CYCLIC.

tetrad /ˈtɛtrad/ ■ n. technical a group or set of four.
– ORIGIN C17: from Greek *tetras*, *tetrad-* 'four, a group of four'.

tetradactyl /ˌtɛtrəˈdaktɪl/ ■ adj. Zoology having four toes or fingers.
– DERIVATIVES **tetradactyly** n.

tetraethyl lead /ˌtɛtrəˈiːθʌɪl/ ■ n. Chemistry an oily organic compound of lead, used as an anti-knock agent in leaded petrol.

tetragonal /tɪˈtrag(ə)n(ə)l/ ■ adj. denoting a crystal system with three axes at right angles, two of them equal.
– DERIVATIVES **tetragonally** adv.
– ORIGIN C16: from Greek *tetragōnon*, from *tetragōnos* 'four-angled'.

tetrahedrite /ˌtɛtrəˈhiːdrʌɪt, -ˈhɛdrʌɪt/ ■ n. a grey mineral consisting of a sulphide of antimony, iron, and copper.

tetrahedron /ˌtɛtrəˈhiːdrən, -ˈhɛd-/ ■ n. (pl. **tetrahedra**

tetrahydrocannabinol

/-drə/ or **tetrahedrons**) a solid having four plane triangular faces.
– DERIVATIVES **tetrahedral** adj.
– ORIGIN C16: from late Greek *tetraedron*, from *tetraedros* 'four-sided'.

tetrahydrocannabinol /ˌtetrəˌhʌɪdrə(ʊ)'kanəbɪnɒl, -kə'nab-/ ■ n. Chemistry a crystalline compound that is the main active ingredient of cannabis.

tetralogy /tɪ'tralədʒi/ ■ n. (pl. **-ies**) **1** a group of four related literary or operatic works. **2** Medicine a set of four related symptoms occurring together.

tetramer /'tetrəmə/ ■ n. Chemistry a polymer comprising four monomer units.
– DERIVATIVES **tetrameric** adj.

tetramerous /tɪ'tram(ə)rəs/ ■ adj. Botany & Zoology having parts arranged in groups of four. ▶ consisting of four joints or parts.

tetrameter /tɪ'tramɪtə/ ■ n. Prosody a verse of four measures.
– ORIGIN C17: from late Latin *tetrametrus*, from Greek *tetrametros*, from *tetra-* 'four' + *metron* 'measure'.

tetraplegia /ˌtetrə'pliːdʒə/ ■ n. another term for QUADRIPLEGIA.
– DERIVATIVES **tetraplegic** adj. & n.

tetraploid /'tetrəplɔɪd/ Biology ■ adj. (of a cell or nucleus) containing four homologous sets of chromosomes. ▶ (of an organism) composed of such cells. ■ n. a tetraploid organism.
– DERIVATIVES **tetraploidy** n.

tetrapod ■ n. **1** Zoology an animal of a group (superclass Tetrapoda) which includes all vertebrates apart from fishes. **2** an object or structure with four feet, legs, or supports.
– ORIGIN C19: from modern Latin *tetrapodus*, from Greek *tetrapous* 'four-footed'.

tetrarch /'tetrɑːk/ ■ n. (in the Roman Empire) the governor of one of four divisions of a country or province. ▶ one of four joint rulers. ▶ archaic a subordinate ruler.
– DERIVATIVES **tetrarchy** n. (pl. **-ies**)
– ORIGIN Old English, from late Latin *tetrarcha*, from Greek *tetrarkhēs*, from *tetra-* 'four' + *arkhein* 'to rule'.

tetrastyle Architecture ■ n. a building or part of a building with four pillars. ■ adj. having four pillars.
– ORIGIN C18: from Greek *tetrastulos*, from *tetra-* 'four' + *stulos* 'column'.

tetrasyllable ■ n. a word having four syllables.
– DERIVATIVES **tetrasyllabic** adj.

tetrathlon /te'traθlɒn, -lən/ ■ n. a sporting contest in which participants compete in four events, typically riding, shooting, swimming, and running.
– ORIGIN 1950s: from TETRA- + Greek *athlon* 'contest', on the pattern of *pentathlon*.

tetratomic ■ adj. Chemistry consisting of four atoms.

tetravalent /ˌtetrə'veɪl(ə)nt/ ■ adj. Chemistry having a valency of four.

tetrode /'tetrəʊd/ ■ n. a thermionic valve with four electrodes.
– ORIGIN C20: from TETRA- + Greek *hodos* 'way'.

Teuton /'tjuːt(ə)n/ ■ n. a member of a people who lived in Jutland in the 4th century BC and fought the Romans in France in the 2nd century BC. ▶ often derogatory a German.
– ORIGIN from Latin *Teutones, Teutoni* (pl.), from an Indo-European root meaning 'people' or 'country'.

Teutonic /tjuː'tɒnɪk/ ■ adj. **1** of or relating to the Teutons. ▶ informal, often derogatory displaying characteristics popularly attributed to Germans. **2** archaic denoting the Germanic branch of the Indo-European language family. ■ n. archaic the language of the Teutons.
– DERIVATIVES **Teutonicism** n.

Tewa /'teɪwə/ ■ n. (pl. same or **Tewas**) **1** a member of a Pueblo Indian people of the Rio Grande area in the south-western US. **2** the Tanoan language of this people.
– ORIGIN from Tewa *téwa* 'moccasins'.

Texan ■ n. a native or inhabitant of the US state of Texas. ■ adj. of or relating to Texas.

Tex-Mex ■ adj. (especially of food and music) having a blend of Mexican and southern American features. ■ n. Tex-Mex music or food.
– ORIGIN 1940s: blend of *Texan* and *Mexican*.

text ■ n. **1** a written or printed work regarded in terms of content rather than form. ▶ the original words of an author or document. ▶ Computing data corresponding to a body of writing. **2** the main body of a book or other piece of writing, as distinct from appendices, illustrations, etc. **3** a written work chosen as a subject of study. ▶ a passage from the Bible or other religious work, especially as the subject of a sermon. **4** an SMS text message. ■ v. send an SMS text message (to).
– DERIVATIVES **textless** adj.
– ORIGIN Middle English: from Old Northern French *texte*, from Latin *textus* 'tissue, literary style' (in medieval Latin, 'Gospel'), from *texere* 'weave'.

textbook ■ n. a book used as a standard work for the study of a subject. ■ adj. conforming to an established standard.
– DERIVATIVES **textbookish** adj.

text editor ■ n. Computing a system or program allowing a user to edit text.

textile ■ n. a type of cloth or woven fabric. ▶ (**textiles**) the branch of industry involved in the manufacture of cloth. ■ adj. of or relating to fabric or weaving.
– ORIGIN C17: from Latin *textilis*, from *texere* 'weave'.

text message ■ n. an electronic communication sent and received via cellphone.
– DERIVATIVES **text messaging** n.

textual ■ adj. of or relating to a text or texts.
– DERIVATIVES **textually** adv.

textual criticism ■ n. the process of attempting to ascertain the original wording of a text.

textualist ■ n. a person adhering strictly to a text, especially that of the scriptures.
– DERIVATIVES **textualism** n.

textuality ■ n. **1** the quality or use of language characteristic of written works as opposed to spoken usage. **2** textualism.

texture ■ n. **1** the feel, appearance, or consistency of a surface or a substance. ▶ the character of a textile fabric as determined by its threads. **2** the quality created by the combination of elements in a work of music or literature. ■ v. [usu. as adj. **textured**] give a rough or raised texture to.
– DERIVATIVES **textural** adj. **texturally** adv. **textureless** adj.
– ORIGIN Middle English: from Latin *textura* 'weaving', from *texere* 'weave'.

textured vegetable protein ■ n. a protein obtained from soya beans and made to resemble minced meat.

texture mapping ■ n. Computing the application of patterns or images to three-dimensional graphics to enhance their realism.

texturize (also **-ise**) ■ v. impart a particular texture to. ▶ cut (hair) in such a way as to create extra fullness.

text wrap ■ n. (in word processing) a facility allowing text to surround embedded features such as pictures.

TFT ■ abbrev. Electronics thin-film transistor, used to make flat colour display screens.

TG ■ abbrev. transformational (or transformational-generative) grammar.

TGV ■ n. a French high-speed passenger train.
– ORIGIN abbrev. of French *train à grande vitesse*.

Th ■ symb. the chemical element thorium.

Th. ■ abbrev. Thursday.

-th¹ (also **-eth**) ■ suffix forming ordinal and fractional numbers from *four* onwards: *sixth*.
– ORIGIN Old English *-(o)tha, -(o)the*.

-th² ■ suffix forming nouns: **1** (from verbs) denoting an action or process: *growth*. **2** (from adjectives) denoting a state: *filth*.
– ORIGIN Old English *-thu, -tho, -th*.

-th³ ■ suffix variant spelling of -ETH² (as in *doth*).

Thai /tʌɪ/ ■ n. (pl. same or **Thais**) **1** a native or national of Thailand. ▶ a member of the largest ethnic group in Thailand. **2** the official language of Thailand. ■ adj. of or

relating to Thailand, its people, or their language.
– ORIGIN Thai, 'free'.

Thai stick ■ n. strong cannabis in leaf form, twisted into a tightly packed cylinder ready for smoking.

thalamus /'θaləməs/ ■ n. (pl. **thalami** /-mʌɪ, -miː/) Anatomy each of two masses of grey matter in the forebrain, relaying sensory information.
– DERIVATIVES **thalamic** /θə'lamɪk, 'θaləmɪk/ adj.
– ORIGIN C17: from Greek *thalamos*.

thalassotherapy /θəˌlasəʊ'θɛrəpi/ ■ n. the use of seawater in cosmetic and health treatment.
– ORIGIN C19: from Greek *thalassa* 'sea' + THERAPY.

thale cress /θeɪl/ ■ n. a small white-flowered plant of north temperate regions, commonly used in genetics experiments. [*Arabidopsis thaliana*.]
– ORIGIN C18: named after the German physician Johann Thal.

thali /'tɑːli/ ■ n. (pl. **thalis**) **1** a set meal at an Indian restaurant. **2** a metal plate on which Indian food is served.
– ORIGIN from Hindi *thālī*, from Sanskrit *sthālī*.

thalidomide /θə'lɪdəmʌɪd/ ■ n. a drug formerly used as a sedative, but found to cause fetal malformation when taken in early pregnancy.
– ORIGIN 1950s: from (ph)*thal*(ic acid) + (im)*ido* + (i)*mide*.

thalli plural form of THALLUS.

thallium /'θalɪəm/ ■ n. the chemical element of atomic number 81, a soft silvery-white metal whose compounds are very poisonous. (Symbol: **Tl**)
– ORIGIN C19: from Greek *thallos* 'green shoot', because of a green line in its spectrum.

thallophyte /'θalə(ʊ)fʌɪt/ ■ n. Botany a plant consisting of a thallus.
– ORIGIN C19: from *Thallophyta* (former taxon), from Greek *thallos* (see THALLUS) + -PHYTE.

thallus /'θaləs/ ■ n. (pl. **thalli** /-lʌɪ, -liː/) Botany a plant body not differentiated into stem, leaves, and roots and without a vascular system, typical of algae, fungi, lichens, and some liverworts.
– DERIVATIVES **thalloid** adj.
– ORIGIN C19: from Greek *thallos* 'green shoot'.

than ■ conj. & prep. **1** introducing the second element in a comparison. **2** used to introduce an exception or contrast. **3** used in expressions indicating one thing happening immediately after another.
– ORIGIN Old English *than(ne)*, *thon(ne)*, *thænne*, orig. the same word as THEN.

thanatology /ˌθanə'tɒlədʒi/ ■ n. the scientific study of death and practices associated with it.
– DERIVATIVES **thanatological** adj. **thanatologist** n.
– ORIGIN C19: from Greek *thanatos* 'death' + -LOGY.

Thanatos /'θanətɒs/ ■ n. (in Freudian theory) the death instinct. Often contrasted with EROS.
– ORIGIN from Greek *thanatos* 'death'.

thane /θeɪn/ ■ n. (in Anglo-Saxon England) a man granted land by the king or a military nobleman, ranking between a freeman and a hereditary noble. ▸ (in Scotland) a man who held land from a Scottish king and ranked with an earl's son.
– DERIVATIVES **thanedom** n.
– ORIGIN Old English *theg(e)n* 'servant, soldier', of Germanic origin.

thank ■ v. **1** express gratitude to. **2** ironic blame: *you have only yourself to thank.*
– PHRASES **I will thank you to do something** used to make a reproachful request. **thank goodness** (or **God** or **heavens**) an expression of relief. **thank one's lucky stars** feel grateful for one's good fortune.
– ORIGIN Old English, of Germanic origin.

thankful ■ adj. **1** pleased and relieved. **2** expressing gratitude.
– DERIVATIVES **thankfulness** n.

thankfully ■ adv. **1** in a thankful manner. **2** fortunately.

thankless ■ adj. **1** (of a job or task) unpleasant and unlikely to gain the appreciation of others. **2** (of a person) not showing or feeling gratitude.
– DERIVATIVES **thanklessly** adv. **thanklessness** n.

thank-offering ■ n. an offering made as an act of thanksgiving.

thanks ■ pl. n. an expression of gratitude. ▸ another way of saying THANK YOU.
– PHRASES **no thanks to** despite the unhelpfulness of. **thanks a million** informal thank you very much. **thanks to** due to.
– ORIGIN Old English *thancas*, pl. of *thanc* '(kindly) thought, gratitude', of Germanic origin.

thanksgiving ■ n. **1** the expression of gratitude, especially to God. **2** (**Thanksgiving** or **Thanksgiving Day**) (in North America) an annual national holiday marked by religious observances and a traditional meal, held in the US on the fourth Thursday in November, and in Canada usually on the second Monday in October.

thank you ■ exclam. a polite expression of gratitude. ■ n. an instance or means of expressing thanks.

thar /tɑː/ ■ n. variant of TAHR.

that ■ pron. & det. (pl. **those**) **1** used to identify a specific person or thing observed or heard by the speaker. ▸ referring to the more distant of two things near to the speaker. **2** referring to a specific thing previously mentioned or known. **3** used in singling out someone or something with a particular feature. **4** informal, chiefly Brit. expressing strong agreement with something just said: *'He's a fussy man.' 'He is that.'* **5** (pl. **that**) [as pron.] used instead of which, who, when, etc. to introduce a defining clause, especially one essential to identification. ■ adv. to such a degree. ▸ [with neg.] informal very: *he wasn't that far away.* ■ conj. **1** introducing a subordinate clause. **2** poetic/literary expressing a wish or regret.
– PHRASES **and all that** (or **and that**) informal and so on. **like that** informal instantly or effortlessly. **that is** (or **that is to say**) a formula introducing or following an explanation or further clarification. **that said** even so. **that's that** there is nothing more to do or say about the matter.
– ORIGIN Old English *thæt*, form of *se* 'the', of Germanic origin.

USAGE
When is it correct to use **that** and when should you use **which**? The general rule is that, when introducing a clause that defines or identifies something, it is acceptable to use either, as in *a book which aims to simplify scientific language* or *a book that aims to simplify scientific language*. However, **which** should always be used to introduce clauses giving additional information: *the book, which costs R295, has sold a million copies* not *the book, that costs R295, has sold a million copies*. See also **Relative clauses** in *Guide to Good English* p. SP 17.

thataway ■ adv. informal, chiefly N. Amer. that way.

thatch ■ n. **1** a roof covering of straw, reeds, or similar material. ▸ material used for such a covering. **2** informal the hair on a person's head. **3** dead stalks, moss, etc. on a lawn. ■ v. [often as adj. **thatched**] cover with thatch.
– DERIVATIVES **thatcher** n.
– ORIGIN Old English *theccan* 'cover', of Germanic origin.

Thatcherism ■ n. the political and economic policies advocated by the former UK Conservative Prime Minister Margaret Thatcher.
– DERIVATIVES **Thatcherite** n. & adj.

thaumatin /'θɔːmətɪn/ ■ n. a sweet-tasting protein isolated from a West African fruit, used as a sweetener in food.
– ORIGIN 1970s: *thaumat-* from *Thaumatococcus daniellii* (name of the plant from which the fruit is obtained).

thaumaturge /'θɔːmətəːdʒ/ ■ n. a worker of wonders or miracles.
– DERIVATIVES **thaumaturgic** adj. **thaumaturgical** adj. **thaumaturgist** n. **thaumaturgy** n.
– ORIGIN C18: from Greek *thaumatourgos*, from *thauma* 'marvel' + *-ergos* '-working'.

thaw ■ v. **1** (of ice, snow, or a frozen thing) become liquid or soft as a result of warming up. ▸ (**it thaws**), **it is thawing**, etc. the weather becomes warmer and causes snow and ice to melt. ▸ cause to thaw. **2** (of a part of the body) become warm enough to stop feeling numb. **3** make or become friendlier or more cordial. ■ n. **1** a period of

warmer weather that thaws ice and snow. **2** an increase in friendliness or cordiality.
– ORIGIN Old English, of West Germanic origin.

THC ■ abbrev. tetrahydrocannabinol.

the ■ det. **1** denoting one or more people or things already mentioned or assumed to be common knowledge; the definite article. ▸ used to refer to a person, place, or thing that is unique. ▸ (with a unit of time) the present. ▸ informal used instead of a possessive. ▸ used with a surname to refer to a family or married couple. **2** used to point forward to a following qualifying or defining clause or phrase. ▸ (chiefly with rulers and family members with the same name) used after a name to qualify it. **3** used to make a generalized reference rather than identifying a particular instance. **4** enough of. **5** (pronounced stressing 'the') used to indicate that someone or something is the best known or most important of that name or type. **6** used adverbially with comparatives to indicate how one amount or degree of something varies in relation to another. ▸ (usu. **all the** ——) used to emphasize the amount or degree to which something is affected.
– ORIGIN Old English *se, sēo, thæt,* superseded by forms from Northumbrian and North Mercian *thē,* of Germanic origin.

theatre (US **theater**) ■ n. **1** a building in which plays and other dramatic performances are given. **2** the writing and production of plays. **3** a play or other activity considered in terms of its dramatic quality. **4** (also **lecture theatre**) a room for lectures with seats in tiers. **5** an operating theatre. **6** the area in which something happens: *a new theatre of war has been opened up.* ▸ [as modifier] denoting weapons intermediate between tactical and strategic.
– ORIGIN Middle English: from Old French, or from Latin *theatrum,* from Greek *theatron,* from *theasthai* 'behold'.

Theatre of the Absurd ■ n. drama portraying the futility of human struggle in a senseless world.

theatric /θɪˈatrɪk/ ■ adj. theatrical. ■ n. (**theatrics**) theatricals.

theatrical ■ adj. **1** of, for, or relating to acting, actors, or the theatre. **2** excessively dramatic. ■ n. **1** a professional actor or actress. **2** (**theatricals**) theatrical performances or behaviour.
– DERIVATIVES **theatricalism** n. **theatricality** n. **theatricalization** (also **-isation**) n. **theatricalize** (also **-ise**) v. **theatrically** adv.

thebe /ˈtɛbə, ˈθeɪbeɪ/ ■ n. (pl. same) a monetary unit of Botswana, equal to one hundredth of a pula.
– ORIGIN Setswana, 'shield'.

theca /ˈθiːkə/ ■ n. (pl. **thecae** /-siː/) **1** Zoology a cup-like or tubular structure containing a coral polyp. **2** Botany each of the lobes of an anther, containing two pollen sacs.
– DERIVATIVES **thecate** adj.
– ORIGIN C17: from Greek *thēkē* 'case'.

thecodont /ˈθiːkədɒnt/ ■ n. Palaeontology a Triassic fossil reptile of a group ancestral to dinosaurs and other archosaurs.
– ORIGIN C19: from *Thecodontia,* from Greek *thēkē* 'case' + *odous, odont-* 'tooth' (because the teeth were fixed in sockets in the jaw).

thé dansant /ˌteɪ dɒˈsɒ̃/ ■ n. (pl. **thés dansants** pronunc. same) a tea dance.
– ORIGIN from French.

thee ■ pron. [second person sing.] archaic or dialect form of **you**, as the singular object of a verb or preposition.
– ORIGIN Old English *thē,* form of *thū* 'thou'.

theft ■ n. the action or crime of stealing.
– ORIGIN Old English, of Germanic origin.

their ■ possess. det. **1** belonging to or associated with the people or things previously mentioned or easily identified. **2** belonging to or associated with a person of unspecified sex (used in place of either 'he' or 'he or she'). **3** (**Their**) used in titles.
– ORIGIN Middle English: from Old Norse *their(r)a* 'of them', form of *sá.*

theirs ■ possess. pron. used to refer to something belonging to or associated with two or more people or things previously mentioned.
– ORIGIN Middle English: from **their** + **-s**.

theism /ˈθiːɪz(ə)m/ ■ n. belief in the existence of a god or gods, specifically of a creator who intervenes in the universe.
– DERIVATIVES **theist** n. **theistic** /-ˈɪstɪk/ adj.
– ORIGIN C17: from Greek *theos* 'god'.

them ■ pron. [third person pl.] **1** used as the object of a verb or preposition to refer to two or more people or things previously mentioned or easily identified. ▸ used after the verb 'to be' and after 'than' or 'as'. **2** referring to a person of unspecified sex (used in place of either 'he' or 'he or she'). ■ det. informal or dialect those.
– ORIGIN Middle English: from Old Norse *theim* 'to those, to them', form of *sá.*

thematic ■ adj. **1** having or relating to subjects or a particular subject. **2** Linguistics of or relating to the theme of an inflected word. ▸ (of a vowel) connecting the theme of a word to its inflections. ▸ (of a word) having a thematic vowel. ■ n. (**thematics**) [treated as sing. or pl.] a body of topics for study or discussion.
– DERIVATIVES **thematically** adv.
– ORIGIN C17: from Greek *thematikos,* from *thema* (see **THEME**).

thematize (also **-ise**) ■ v. **1** present or select as a theme. **2** Linguistics place (a word or phrase) at the start of a sentence to focus attention on it.
– DERIVATIVES **thematization** (also **-isation**) n.

Thembu /ˈtɛmbuː/ (also **Tembu**) ■ n. (pl. same or **Thembus**) a member of an isiXhosa-speaking people originating in present-day KwaZulu-Natal and now living in the Eastern Cape.
– ORIGIN from isiXhosa *umthembu.*

theme ■ n. **1** a subject or topic on which a person speaks, writes, or thinks. ▸ Linguistics the first major constituent of a clause, indicating the subject matter. Contrasted with **RHEME**. **2** Music a prominent or frequently recurring melody or group of notes in a composition. ▸ [as modifier] (of music) frequently recurring in or accompanying the beginning and end of a film, play, etc. **3** [as modifier] denoting a restaurant or pub in which the decor, food, and drink are intended to suggest a particular country, historical period, etc. **4** Linguistics the stem of a noun or verb. ■ v. [often as adj. **themed**] give a particular setting or ambience to.
– ORIGIN Middle English: from Latin *thema,* from Greek, 'proposition'; rel. to *tithenai* 'to set or place'.

theme park ■ n. an amusement park with a unifying setting or idea.

themself ■ pron. [third person sing.] informal used instead of 'himself' or 'herself' to refer to a person of unspecified sex.

USAGE
The standard reflexive form corresponding to **they** and **them** is **themselves**. The singular form **themself** has been used recently to correspond to the singular use of **they** when referring to a person of unspecified sex, as in *helping someone to help themself.* However, **themself** is not regarded as good English, and **themselves** should be used instead. For more details, see usage at **THEY**.

themselves ■ pron. [third person pl.] **1** used as the object of a verb or preposition to refer to a group of people or things previously mentioned as the subject of the clause. **2** [emphatic] used to emphasize a particular group of people or things mentioned. **3** used instead of 'himself' or 'herself' to refer to a person of unspecified sex.

then ■ adv. **1** at that time. **2** after that; next. ▸ also. **3** therefore.
– PHRASES **but then** (**again**) on the other hand. **then and there** immediately.
– ORIGIN Old English *thænne, thanne, thonne,* of Germanic origin.

thence (also **from thence**) ■ adv. formal **1** from a place or source previously mentioned. **2** as a consequence.
– ORIGIN Middle English *thennes,* from earlier *thenne,* from Old English *thanon,* of West Germanic origin.

thenceforth (also **from thenceforth**) ■ adv. archaic or poetic/literary from that time, place, or point onward.

thenceforward ■ adv. thenceforth.

theo- ■ comb. form relating to God or deities: *theocracy*.
– ORIGIN from Greek *theos* 'god'.

theocentric /ˌθiː(ə)ˈsɛntrɪk/ ■ adj. having God as a central focus.

theocracy /θɪˈɒkrəsi/ ■ n. (pl. **-ies**) a system of government in which priests rule in the name of God or a god.
– DERIVATIVES **theocrat** n. **theocratic** adj. **theocratically** adv.
– ORIGIN C17: from Greek *theokratia* (see **THEO-**, **-CRACY**).

theodicy /θɪˈɒdɪsi/ ■ n. (pl. **-ies**) the vindication of divine providence in view of the existence of evil.
– DERIVATIVES **theodicean** /-ˈsiːən/ adj.
– ORIGIN C18: from French *Théodicée*, the title of a work by Leibniz, from Greek *theos* 'god' + *dikē* 'justice'.

theodolite /θɪˈɒdəlʌɪt/ ■ n. a surveying instrument with a rotating telescope for measuring horizontal and vertical angles.
– DERIVATIVES **theodolitic** adj.
– ORIGIN C16: from modern Latin *theodelitus*.

theologian /θɪəˈləʊdʒɪən, -dʒ(ə)n/ ■ n. a person expert in or engaged in theology.

theology ■ n. (pl. **-ies**) the study of the nature of God and religious belief. ▸ religious beliefs and theory when systematically developed.
– DERIVATIVES **theological** adj. **theologically** adv. **theologist** n. **theologize** (also **-ise**) v.
– ORIGIN Middle English: from French *théologie*, from Latin *theologia*, from Greek, from *theos* 'god' + *-logia* (see **-LOGY**).

theorem /ˈθɪərəm/ ■ n. Physics & Mathematics a general proposition not self-evident but proved by a chain of reasoning. ▸ a rule in algebra or other branches of mathematics expressed by symbols or formulae.
– DERIVATIVES **theorematic** /-ˈmatɪk/ adj.
– ORIGIN C16: from French *théorème*, or from Greek *theōrēma* 'speculation, proposition'.

theoretical (also **theoretic**) ■ adj. concerned with or involving theory rather than its practical application. ▸ based on or calculated through theory.
– DERIVATIVES **theoretically** adv.

theoretician /ˌθɪərɪˈtɪʃ(ə)n/ ■ n. a person who develops or studies the theoretical framework of a subject.

theorist ■ n. a theoretician.

theorize (also **-ise**) ■ v. form a theory or theories about something. ▸ create a theoretical premise or framework for.
– DERIVATIVES **theorization** (also **-isation**) n. **theorizer** (also **-iser**) n.

theory ■ n. (pl. **-ies**) **1** a supposition or a system of ideas intended to explain something, especially one based on general principles independent of the thing to be explained. ▸ an idea accounting for or justifying something. **2** a set of principles on which an activity is based: *a theory of education*. ▸ Mathematics a collection of propositions illustrating the principles of a subject.
– PHRASES **in theory** in an ideal or hypothetical situation.
– ORIGIN C16: from Greek *theōria* 'contemplation, speculation'.

theosophy /θɪˈɒsəfi/ ■ n. any of a number of philosophies maintaining that a knowledge of God may be achieved through spiritual ecstasy, direct intuition, or special individual relations.
– DERIVATIVES **theosophic** adj. **theosophical** adj. **theosophically** adv. **theosophist** n.
– ORIGIN C17: from medieval Latin *theosophia*, from late Greek, from *theosophos* 'wise concerning God', from *theos* 'god' + *sophos* 'wise'.

therapeutic /ˌθɛrəˈpjuːtɪk/ ■ adj. of or relating to the healing of disease. ▸ having a good effect on the body or mind.
– DERIVATIVES **therapeutical** adj. **therapeutically** adv.
– ORIGIN C17: from Greek *therapeutikos*, from *therapeuein* 'minister to, treat medically'.

therapeutics ■ pl. n. [treated as sing.] the branch of medicine concerned with the treatment of disease and the action of remedial agents.

therapsid /θɛˈrapsɪd/ ■ n. Palaeontology a fossil reptile of a large group including the cynodonts, related to the ancestors of mammals.

– ORIGIN C20: from *Therapsida* (name of an order), from Greek *thēr* 'beast' + *hapsis* 'arch' (referring to the structure of the skull).

therapy ■ n. (pl. **-ies**) treatment intended to relieve or heal a disorder. ▸ short for **PSYCHOTHERAPY**.
– DERIVATIVES **therapist** n.
– ORIGIN C19: from Greek *therapeia* 'healing', from *therapeuein* 'minister to, treat medically'.

Theravada /ˌθɛrəˈvɑːdə/ (also **Theravada Buddhism**) ■ n. the more conservative of the two major traditions of Buddhism (the other being Mahayana).
– ORIGIN from Pali *theravāda* 'doctrine of the elders', from *thera* 'elder, old' + *vāda* 'speech, doctrine'.

there ■ adv. **1** in, at, or to that place or position. ▸ in that respect; on that issue. **2** used in attracting attention to someone or something. **3** (usu. **there is/are**) used to indicate the fact or existence of something. ■ exclam. **1** used to focus attention. **2** used to comfort someone.
– PHRASES **be there for** be available to provide support or comfort for. **have been there before** informal know all about a situation from experience. **here and there** in various places. **so there** informal used to express defiance. **there and then** immediately.
– ORIGIN Old English *thǣr*, *thēr* of Germanic origin.

thereabouts (also **thereabout**) ■ adv. **1** near that place. **2** used to indicate that a date or figure is approximate.

thereafter ■ adv. formal after that time.

thereat ■ adv. archaic or formal **1** at that place. **2** on account of or after that.

thereby ■ adv. by that means; as a result of that.

therefore ■ adv. for that reason; consequently.

therefrom ■ adv. archaic or formal from that or that place.

therein ■ adv. archaic or formal in that place, document, or respect.

thereinafter ■ adv. archaic or formal in a later part of that document.

thereinbefore ■ adv. archaic or formal in an earlier part of that document.

theremin /ˈθɛrəmɪn/ ■ n. an electronic musical instrument in which the tone is generated by two high-frequency oscillators and the pitch controlled by the movement of the performer's hand towards and away from the circuit.
– ORIGIN C20: named after its Russian inventor Lev Theremin.

thereof ■ adv. formal of the thing just mentioned; of that.

thereon ■ adv. formal on or following from the thing just mentioned.

there's ■ contr. **1** there is. **2** there has.

thereto ■ adv. archaic or formal to that or that place.

theretofore ■ adv. archaic or formal before that time.

thereunto ■ adv. archaic or formal to that.

thereupon ■ adv. formal immediately or shortly after that.

therewith ■ adv. archaic or formal **1** with or in the thing mentioned. **2** soon or immediately after that; forthwith.

therewithal ■ adv. archaic together with that; besides.

Theria /ˈθɪərɪə/ ■ pl. n. Zoology the marsupials and placental mammals.
– DERIVATIVES **therian** n. & adj.
– ORIGIN from Greek *thēria* 'wild animals'.

therm ■ n. a unit of heat equivalent to 1.055×10^8 joules.
– ORIGIN 1920s: from Greek *thermē* 'heat'.

thermal ■ adj. **1** of or relating to heat. ▸ another term for **GEOTHERMAL**. ▸ Physics relating to or denoting particles in thermodynamic equilibrium with their surroundings: *thermal neutrons*. **2** (of a garment) made of a fabric that provides good insulation to keep the body warm. ■ n. **1** an upward current of warm air, used by birds, gliders, and balloonists to gain height. **2** (**thermals**) thermal garments, especially underwear.
– DERIVATIVES **thermally** adv.
– ORIGIN C18: from Greek *thermē* 'heat'.

thermal capacity ■ n. the quantity of heat needed to raise the temperature of a body by one degree.

thermal efficiency ■ n. the efficiency of a heat engine measured by the ratio of the work done by it to the heat supplied to it.

thermal imaging ■ n. the technique of using the heat given off by an object to produce an image of it or locate it.
– DERIVATIVES **thermal imager** n.

thermal printer ■ n. a printer in which fine heated pins form characters on heat-sensitive paper.

thermal spring ■ n. a spring of naturally hot water.

thermic ■ adj. of or relating to heat.

thermionic ■ adj. relating to or denoting the emission of electrons from substances heated to very high temperatures.
– DERIVATIVES **thermionics** pl. n.

thermionic valve (US **thermionic tube**) ■ n. Electronics a vacuum tube giving a flow of thermionic electrons in one direction, used especially in the rectification of a current and in radio reception.

thermistor /ˈθəːmɪstə/ ■ n. an electrical resistor whose resistance is greatly reduced by heating, used for measurement and control.
– ORIGIN 1940s: contraction of *thermal resistor*.

thermite /ˈθəːmʌɪt/ (also **thermit** /-mɪt/) ■ n. a mixture of finely powdered aluminium and iron oxide that produces a very high temperature on combustion, used in welding and for incendiary bombs.
– ORIGIN C20: coined in German from THERMO-.

thermo- ■ comb. form relating to heat: *thermodynamics*.
– ORIGIN from Greek *thermos* 'hot', *thermē* 'heat'.

thermobaric /ˌθəːməʊˈbarɪk/ ■ adj. denoting a very large fuel-air bomb which ignites into a fireball when detonated, creating a powerful wave of pressure that sucks out oxygen from any confined spaces nearby.
– ORIGIN 1990s: from THERMO- + Greek *barus* 'heavy'.

thermochemistry ■ n. the branch of chemistry concerned with the quantities of heat evolved or absorbed during chemical reactions.
– DERIVATIVES **thermochemical** adj.

thermochromic /ˌθəːməʊˈkrəʊmɪk/ ■ adj. undergoing a reversible change of colour when heated or cooled.

thermocline /ˈθəːməʊklʌɪn/ ■ n. a temperature gradient in a lake or other body of water, separating layers at different temperatures.

thermocouple ■ n. a device for measuring or sensing a temperature difference, consisting of two wires of different metals connected at two points, between which a voltage is developed in proportion to any temperature difference.

thermodynamics ■ pl. n. [treated as sing.] the branch of science concerned with the relations between heat and other forms of energy involved in physical and chemical processes.
– DERIVATIVES **thermodynamic** adj. **thermodynamical** adj. **thermodynamically** adv. **thermodynamicist** n.

thermoelectric ■ adj. producing electricity by a difference of temperatures.
– DERIVATIVES **thermoelectrically** adv. **thermoelectricity** n.

thermogenesis /ˌθəːməʊˈdʒɛnɪsɪs/ ■ n. Physiology the production of bodily heat.
– DERIVATIVES **thermogenic** adj.

thermogram ■ n. a record made by a thermograph.

thermograph ■ n. an instrument that produces a record of the varying temperature or infrared radiation over an area or during a period of time.

thermography ■ n. 1 the production and use of thermograms, especially in medicine. 2 a printing technique in which a wet ink image is fused by heating with a resinous powder to produce a raised impression.
– DERIVATIVES **thermographic** adj.

thermohaline /ˌθəːməʊˈheɪlʌɪn, -ˈheɪliːn/ ■ adj. Oceanography relating to or denoting the circulation of seawater driven by temperature variations which cause changes in salinity and density.

thermolabile /ˌθəːməʊˈleɪbʌɪl, -bɪl/ ■ adj. chiefly Biochemistry readily destroyed or deactivated by heat.

thermoluminescence ■ n. the property of some ceramics and other materials of becoming luminescent when pretreated and heated, used as a means of dating ancient artefacts.
– DERIVATIVES **thermoluminescent** adj.

thermolysis /θəˈmɒlɪsɪs/ ■ n. Chemistry the breakdown of molecules by the action of heat.
– DERIVATIVES **thermolytic** adj.

thermometer ■ n. an instrument for measuring and indicating temperature, typically consisting of a graduated glass tube containing mercury or alcohol which expands when heated.
– DERIVATIVES **thermometric** adj. **thermometrical** adj. **thermometry** n.
– ORIGIN C17: from French *thermomètre* or modern Latin *thermometrum*, from THERMO- + *-metrum* 'measure'.

thermonuclear ■ adj. (chiefly with reference to weapons) using or denoting nuclear fusion reactions that occur at very high temperatures.

thermophile /ˈθəːməʊfʌɪl/ ■ n. Microbiology a bacterium or other micro-organism that grows best at higher than normal temperatures.
– DERIVATIVES **thermophilic** adj.

thermopile /ˈθəːməʊpʌɪl/ ■ n. a set of thermocouples arranged for measuring small quantities of radiant heat.

thermoplastic ■ adj. denoting substances (especially synthetic resins) which become plastic when heated. Often contrasted with THERMOSETTING.

thermoregulation ■ n. Physiology the regulation of bodily temperature.
– DERIVATIVES **thermoregulate** v. **thermoregulatory** adj.

Thermos ■ n. trademark a vacuum flask.
– ORIGIN C20: from Greek, 'hot'.

thermosetting (also **thermoset**) ■ adj. denoting substances (especially synthetic resins) which set permanently when heated. Often contrasted with THERMOPLASTIC.

thermosphere ■ n. the upper region of the atmosphere above the mesosphere.

thermostable ■ adj. chiefly Biochemistry not readily destroyed or deactivated by heat.

thermostat /ˈθəːməstat/ ■ n. a device that automatically regulates temperature or activates a device at a set temperature.
– DERIVATIVES **thermostatic** adj. **thermostatically** adv.

thermotropism /ˌθəːməʊˈtrəʊpɪz(ə)m/ ■ n. Biology the orientation of a plant or other organism in response to a source of heat.
– DERIVATIVES **thermotropic** adj.

theropod /ˈθɪərə(ʊ)pɒd/ ■ n. a dinosaur of a group including bipedal carnivores such as the carnosaurs and dromaeosaurs.
– ORIGIN 1930s: from *Theropoda* (pl.), from Greek *thēr* 'beast' + *pous, pod-* 'foot'.

thesaurus /θɪˈsɔːrəs/ ■ n. (pl. **thesauri** /-rʌɪ/ or **thesauruses**) a book that lists words in groups of synonyms and related concepts.
– ORIGIN C16: from Greek *thēsauros* 'storehouse, treasure'.

these plural form of THIS.

thesis /ˈθiːsɪs/ ■ n. (pl. **theses** /-siːz/) 1 a statement or theory that is put forward as a premise to be maintained or proved. 2 a long essay or dissertation involving personal research, written as part of a university degree. 3 /also ˈθɛsɪs/ Prosody an unstressed syllable or part of a metrical foot in Greek or Latin verse.
– ORIGIN Middle English: from Greek, 'placing, a proposition', from the root of *tithenai* 'to place'.

thespian /ˈθɛspɪən/ ■ adj. of or relating to drama and the theatre. ■ n. an actor or actress.
– ORIGIN C17: from the name of the Greek dramatic poet *Thespis* (6th century BC).

theta /ˈθiːtə/ ■ n. the eighth letter of the Greek alphabet (Θ, θ), transliterated as 'th'. ■ symb. 1 (θ) temperature. 2 (θ) a plane angle. 3 (θ) a polar coordinate. Often coupled with φ.
– ORIGIN from Greek.

theta rhythm ■ n. Physiology electrical activity observed in the brain under certain conditions, consisting of oscillations (theta waves) with a frequency of 4 to 7 hertz.

they ■ pron. [third person pl.] **1** used to refer to two or more people or things previously mentioned or easily identified. ▸ people in general. ▸ informal people in authority regarded collectively. **2** used to refer to a person of unspecified sex (in place of either 'he' or 'he or she').
– ORIGIN Middle English: from Old Norse *their*, pl. of *sá*.

> USAGE
> It is now widely held that the traditional use of **he** to refer to a person of either sex is outdated and sexist; the alternative, **he or she**, can be clumsy. It is now generally acceptable, therefore, to use **they** (with its counterparts **them**, **their**, and **themselves**) instead. This is especially the case where **they** follows an indefinite pronoun such as **anyone** or **someone** (*anyone can join if they are a resident*). In view of the growing acceptance of **they**, it is used in this dictionary in many cases where **he** would have been used formerly.

they'd ■ contr. **1** they had. **2** they would.
they'll ■ contr. **1** they shall. **2** they will.
they're ■ contr. they are.
they've ■ contr. they have.

thiamine /ˈθaɪəmiːn, -mɪn/ (also **thiamin**) ■ n. Biochemistry vitamin B₁, a compound found in unrefined cereals, beans, and liver, a deficiency of which causes beriberi.
– ORIGIN 1930s: from THIO- + AMINE.

thiazide /ˈθaɪəzaɪd/ ■ n. Medicine any of a class of sulphur-containing drugs that increase the excretion of sodium and chloride and are used as diuretics and to lower the blood pressure.
– ORIGIN 1950s: from elements of THIO- + AZINE + OXIDE.

thick ■ adj. **1** with opposite sides or surfaces relatively far apart. ▸ (of a garment or similar item) made of heavy material. **2** made up of a large number of things or people close together. ▸ (**thick with**) densely filled or covered with. ▸ (of the air or atmosphere) opaque, heavy, or dense: *thick fog*. **3** (of a liquid or a semi-liquid substance) relatively firm in consistency; not flowing freely. **4** informal of low intelligence; stupid. **5** (of a voice) not clear or distinct; hoarse or husky. ▸ (of an accent) very marked and difficult to understand. **6** informal having a very close, friendly relationship. ■ n. (**the thick**) the middle or the busiest part of something: *in the thick of battle*. ■ adv. in or with deep, dense, or heavy mass.
– PHRASES **be thick on the ground** see GROUND¹. **a bit thick** Brit. informal unfair or unreasonable. **give someone** (or **get**) **a thick ear** Brit. informal punish someone (or be punished) with a blow on the ear. **have a thick skin** see SKIN. **thick and fast** rapidly and in great numbers. (**as**) **thick as thieves** informal very close or friendly. (**as**) **thick as two (short) planks** (or **as a plank**) informal, chiefly Brit. very stupid. **the thick end of something** Brit. the greater part of something. **through thick and thin** under all circumstances, no matter how difficult.
– DERIVATIVES **thickish** adj. **thickly** adv.
– ORIGIN Old English, of Germanic origin.

thicken ■ v. make or become thick or thicker.
– PHRASES **the plot thickens** the situation is becoming more complicated and puzzling.
– DERIVATIVES **thickener** n.

thickening ■ n. **1** the process or result of becoming thicker. ▸ a thicker area of animal or plant tissue. **2** a substance added to a liquid to make it thicker.

thicket ■ n. a dense group of bushes or trees.
– ORIGIN Old English.

thick-knee ■ n. either of two species of plover-like birds with large yellow eyes and long yellowish legs. [*Burhinus capensis* (**spotted thick-knee**) and *B. vermiculatus* (**water thick-knee**).]

thickness ■ n. **1** the distance through an object, as distinct from width or height. ▸ a layer of material. ▸ a thicker part of something. **2** the state or quality of being thick. ■ v. plane or cut (wood) to a desired thickness.
– DERIVATIVES **thicknesser** n.

thickset ■ adj. (of a person or animal) heavily or solidly built; stocky.

thick-skulled (also **thick-witted**) ■ adj. dull and stupid.

thief ■ n. (pl. **thieves**) a person who steals another person's property.
– ORIGIN Old English, of Germanic origin.

thieve ■ v. be a thief; steal things.
– DERIVATIVES **thievery** n. **thieving** n. & adj. **thievish** adj. **thievishly** adv. **thievishness** n.
– ORIGIN Old English *thēofian*, from *thēof* 'thief'.

thigh ■ n. the part of the human leg between the hip and the knee. ▸ the corresponding part in other animals.
– DERIVATIVES **-thighed** adj.
– ORIGIN Old English, of Germanic origin.

thigh bone ■ n. the femur.

thigh-slapper ■ n. informal a very funny joke or anecdote.
– DERIVATIVES **thigh-slapping** adj.

thigmotropism /ˌθɪɡməˈ(ʊ)trəʊpɪz(ə)m/ ■ n. Biology the turning or bending of a plant or other organism in response to a touch stimulus.
– DERIVATIVES **thigmotropic** adj.
– ORIGIN C20: from Greek *thigma* 'touch' + TROPISM.

thimble ■ n. **1** a metal or plastic cap with a closed end, worn to protect the finger and push the needle in sewing. ▸ any short metal tube or ferrule. **2** Nautical a metal ring, concave on the outside, around which a loop of rope is spliced.
– ORIGIN Old English *thȳmel* 'finger-stall' (see THUMB).

thimbleful ■ n. (pl. **-fuls**) a small quantity of something.

thin ■ adj. (**thinner**, **thinnest**) **1** having opposite surfaces or sides close together. ▸ (of a garment or fabric) having become less thick as a result of wear. **2** having little flesh or fat on the body. **3** having few parts or members relative to the area covered or filled; sparse. ▸ not dense or heavy: *the thin cold air of the mountains*. **4** containing much liquid and not much solid substance. **5** (of a sound) faint and high-pitched. ▸ (of a smile) weak and forced. **6** too weak to justify a result or effect; inadequate: *the evidence is rather thin*. ■ adv. with little thickness or depth. ■ v. (**thinned**, **thinning**) **1** make or become less thick. **2** remove some plants from (a row or area) to allow the others more room to grow. **3** Golf hit (a ball) above its centre.
– PHRASES **have a thin time** Brit. informal have a miserable or uncomfortable time. **thin air** used to refer to the state of being invisible or non-existent. **the thin blue line** informal the police. **thin on the ground** see GROUND¹.
– DERIVATIVES **thinly** adv. **thinness** n. **thinnish** adj.
– ORIGIN Old English, of Germanic origin.

thine ■ possess. pron. archaic form of YOURS; the thing or things belonging to or associated with thee. ■ possess. det. form of THY used before a vowel.
– ORIGIN Old English *thīn*, of Germanic origin.

thing ■ n. **1** an object that one need not, cannot, or does not wish to give a specific name to. ▸ (**things**) personal belongings or clothing. **2** an inanimate material object, especially as distinct from a living sentient being. ▸ a living creature or plant. ▸ a person or animal in terms of one's feelings of pity, approval, etc.: *you lucky thing!* **3** an action, activity, concept, or thought. ▸ (**things**) unspecified circumstances or matters. **4** (**the thing**) informal what is needed or required. ▸ what is socially acceptable or fashionable. **5** (**one's thing**) informal one's special interest or concern.
– PHRASES **be on to a good thing** informal be in a situation that is pleasant, profitable, or easy. **be hearing** (or **seeing**) **things** imagine that one can hear (or see) something that is not in fact there. **a close** (or **near**) **thing** a narrow avoidance of something unpleasant. **do one's own thing** informal follow one's own inclinations regardless of others. **have a thing about** informal have a preoccupation or obsession with. **there is only one thing for it** there is only one possible course of action. (**now**) **there's a thing** informal used as an expression of surprise.
– ORIGIN Old English, of Germanic origin.

thingamabob /ˈθɪŋəməbɒb/ (also **thingumabob**, **thingamajig**, or **thingumajig** /ˈθɪŋəmədʒɪɡ/) ■ n. another term for THINGUMMY.

thingummy

thingummy /ˈθɪŋəmi/ (also **thingamy**) ■ n. (pl. **-ies**) informal a person or thing whose name one has forgotten, does not know, or does not wish to mention.
– ORIGIN C18: from THING.

thingy ■ n. (pl. **-ies**) another term for THINGUMMY.

think ■ v. (past and past part. **thought**) **1** have a particular opinion, belief, or idea about someone or something. **2** direct one's mind towards someone or something; use one's mind actively to form connected ideas. ▸ (**think of/about**) take into account or consideration. ▸ (**think of/about**) consider the possibility or advantages of. ▸ have a particular mental attitude or approach. ▸ (**think of**) have a particular opinion of. **3** call something to mind; remember. ■ n. informal an act of thinking.
– PHRASES **have (got) another think coming** informal used to express disagreement. **think aloud** express one's thoughts as they occur. **think better of** decide not to do (something) after reconsideration. **think big** see BIG. **think nothing** (or **little**) **of** consider (an activity others regard as odd, wrong, or difficult) as straightforward or normal. **think twice** consider a course of action carefully before embarking on it.
– PHRASAL VERBS **think back** recall a past event or time. **think on** dialect & N. Amer. think of or about. **think something out** (or **through**) consider something in all its aspects before taking action. **think something over** consider something carefully. **think something up** informal invent or devise something.
– DERIVATIVES **thinkable** adj. **thinker** n.
– ORIGIN Old English, of Germanic origin.

thinking ■ adj. using thought or rational judgement; intelligent. ■ n. a person's ideas or opinions. ▸ (**thinkings**) archaic thoughts; meditations.
– PHRASES **good thinking!** an expression of approval for an ingenious plan or observation. **put on one's thinking cap** informal meditate on a problem.

think tank ■ n. a body of experts providing advice and ideas on specific political or economic problems.
– DERIVATIVES **think-tanker** n.

thinner ■ n. a volatile solvent used to make paint or other solutions less viscous.

thinnings ■ pl. n. seedlings, trees, or fruit which have been thinned out to improve the growth of those remaining.

thio- ■ comb. form Chemistry denoting replacement of oxygen by sulphur in a compound: *thiosulphate*.
– ORIGIN from Greek *theion* 'sulphur'.

thiocyanate /ˌθaɪə(ʊ)ˈsaɪəneɪt/ ■ n. Chemistry a salt containing the anion SCN⁻.

thiol /ˈθaɪɒl/ ■ n. Chemistry an organic compound containing the group -SH, i.e. a sulphur-containing analogue of an alcohol.

thionyl /ˈθaɪənɪl/ ■ n. [as modifier] Chemistry of or denoting the divalent radical =SO.

thiopental ■ n. North American term for THIOPENTONE.

thiopentone /ˌθaɪə(ʊ)ˈpɛntəʊn/ ■ n. Medicine a sulphur-containing barbiturate drug used as a general anaesthetic and hypnotic, and (reputedly) as a truth drug.
– ORIGIN 1940s: from THIO- + a contraction of PENTOBARBITONE.

thiosulphate (US **thiosulfate**) ■ n. Chemistry a salt containing the anion $S_2O_3^{2-}$, i.e. a sulphate with one oxygen atom replaced by sulphur.

third ■ ordinal number **1** constituting number three in a sequence; 3rd. **2** (**a third/one third**) each of three equal parts into which something is or may be divided. **3** Music an interval spanning three consecutive notes in a diatonic scale, e.g. C to E (major third, equal to two tones) or A to C (minor third, equal to a tone and a semitone). ▸ Music the note which is higher by this interval than the tonic of a diatonic scale or root of a chord. **4** a place in the third grade in an examination, especially that for a degree.
– PHRASES **third time lucky** (or US **third time is the charm**) used to express the hope that one may succeed in the third attempt.
– DERIVATIVES **thirdly** adv.
– ORIGIN Old English, of Germanic origin.

third age ■ n. the period in life of active retirement, following middle age.
– DERIVATIVES **third ager** n.

third class ■ n. **1** a group of people or things considered together as the third best. **2** Brit. the third-highest division in the results of the examinations for a university degree. **3** chiefly historical the cheapest and least comfortable accommodation in a train or ship. ■ adj. & adv. of the third-best quality or in the third class.

third-degree ■ adj. **1** denoting burns of the most severe kind, affecting tissue below the skin. **2** Law, chiefly N. Amer. denoting the least serious category of a crime, especially murder. ■ n. (**the third degree**) long and harsh questioning to obtain information or a confession.

third estate ■ n. [treated as sing. or pl.] the third order or class in a country or society, comprising the common people. See also ESTATE (in sense 5).

third eye ■ n. **1** Hinduism & Buddhism the 'eye of insight' in the forehead of an image of a deity, especially the god Shiva. ▸ the faculty of intuitive insight or prescience. **2** informal term for PINEAL EYE.

third eyelid ■ n. informal term for NICTITATING MEMBRANE.

third force ■ n. **1** a political group or party acting as a check on conflict between two extreme or opposing groups. **2** S. African an unidentified group thought to have been involved in provoking internecine violence in order to disrupt the transition from apartheid to democracy. ▸ any similar group thought to be involved in provoking political or other unrest.

third man ■ n. Cricket a fielding position near the boundary behind the slips.

third party ■ n. a person or group besides the two primarily involved in a situation, especially in a dispute. ■ adj. **1** of or relating to a third party. **2** (of insurance) covering damage or injury suffered by a person other than the insured.

third person ■ n. **1** a third party. **2** see PERSON (sense 5).

third position ■ n. **1** Ballet a posture in which the turned-out feet are placed one in front of the other, so that the heel of the front foot fits into the hollow of the instep of the back foot. **2** Music a position of the left hand on the fingerboard of a stringed instrument nearer to the bridge than the second position.

third rail ■ n. an additional rail supplying electric current, used in some electric railway systems.

third-rate ■ adj. of inferior or very poor quality.
– DERIVATIVES **third-rater** n.

third reading ■ n. a third presentation of a bill to a legislative assembly.

third way ■ n. any option regarded as an alternative to two extremes, especially a political agenda which is centrist and consensus-based rather than left- or right-wing.

Third World ■ n. the developing countries of Asia, Africa, and Latin America.
– ORIGIN 1950s: translating *tiers monde*, first used to distinguish the developing countries from the capitalist and Communist blocs.

thirst ■ n. **1** a feeling of needing or wanting to drink. ▸ lack of the liquid needed to sustain life. **2** (**thirst for**) a strong desire for. ■ v. (**thirst for/after**) have a strong desire for.
– ORIGIN Old English, of Germanic origin.

thirsty ■ adj. (**-ier, -iest**) **1** feeling thirsty. ▸ (of land, plants, etc.) in need of water; dry or parched. ▸ (of an engine, plant, or crop) consuming a lot of fuel or water. **2** informal causing thirst: *modelling is thirsty work*.
– DERIVATIVES **thirstily** adv. **thirstiness** n.

thirteen ■ cardinal number equivalent to the sum of six and seven; one more than twelve, or seven less than twenty; 13. (Roman numeral: **xiii** or **XIII**.)
– DERIVATIVES **thirteenth** ordinal number
– ORIGIN Old English *thrēotīene*.

13th cheque (also **thirteenth cheque**) ■ n. S. African an annual pay bonus, equal to one month's salary.

thirty ■ cardinal number (pl. **-ies**) the number equivalent to the product of three and ten; ten less than forty; 30. (Roman numeral: **xxx** or **XXX**.)
– DERIVATIVES **thirtieth** ordinal number **thirtyfold** adj. & adv.
– ORIGIN Old English *thrītig*.

thirty-eight ■ n. a revolver of .38 calibre.

this ■ pron. & det. (pl. **these**) **1** used to identify a specific person or thing close at hand or being indicated or experienced. ▶ referring to the nearer of two things close to the speaker. **2** referring to a specific thing or situation just mentioned. **3** [as det.] used with periods of time related to the present. ■ adv. to the degree or extent indicated.
– PHRASES **this and that** (or **this, that, and the other**) informal various unspecified things. **this here** informal used to show emphasis.
– ORIGIN Old English, from *thes*, of West Germanic origin.

thistle ■ n. a widely distributed herbaceous plant of the daisy family, typically with a prickly stem and leaves and rounded heads of purple flowers. [*Carlina, Carduus*, and other genera.]
– DERIVATIVES **thistly** adj.
– ORIGIN Old English, of Germanic origin.

thistledown ■ n. the light fluffy down of thistle seeds, enabling them to be blown about in the wind.

thither /'ðɪðə/ ■ adv. archaic or poetic/literary to or towards that place.
– ORIGIN Old English *thider*, of Germanic origin.

thixotropy /θɪk'sɒtrəpi/ ■ n. Chemistry the property of becoming less viscous when subjected to an applied stress, such as being shaken or stirred.
– DERIVATIVES **thixotropic** adj.
– ORIGIN 1920s: from Greek *thixis* 'touching' + *tropē* 'turning'.

tho' (also **tho**) ■ conj. & adv. informal spelling of **THOUGH**.

tholeiite /'θəʊlɪʌɪt/ ■ n. Geology a silica-rich basaltic rock containing augite and pyroxene.
– DERIVATIVES **tholeiitic** /ˌθəʊlɪ'ɪtɪk/ adj.
– ORIGIN C19: from *Tholei*, the name of a village (now *Tholey*) in the Saarland, Germany.

Thomson's gazelle ■ n. a light brown gazelle with a dark band along the flanks, living in herds on the open plains of East Africa. [*Gazella thomsonii*.]
– ORIGIN C19: named after Joseph *Thomson* (1858–94), Scottish explorer.

thong ■ n. **1** a narrow strip of leather or other material, used especially as a fastening or as the lash of a whip. **2** a skimpy bathing garment or pair of panties like a G-string. **3** chiefly N. Amer. another term for **FLIP-FLOP** (in sense 1).
– DERIVATIVES **thonged** adj. **thongy** adj.
– ORIGIN Old English, of Germanic origin.

thoracic /θɔː'rasɪk/ ■ adj. Anatomy & Zoology of or relating to the thorax.

thorax /'θɔːraks/ ■ n. (pl. **thoraces** /'θɔːrəsiːz/ or **thoraxes**) Anatomy & Zoology the part of the body of a mammal between the neck and the abdomen, including the cavity enclosed by the ribs, breastbone, and dorsal vertebrae. ▶ Zoology the corresponding part of a bird, reptile, amphibian, or fish. ▶ Entomology the middle section of the body of an insect, between the head and the abdomen, bearing the legs and wings.
– ORIGIN Middle English: from Greek *thōrax*.

Thorazine /'θɔːrəziːn/ ■ n. trademark for **CHLORPROMAZINE**.
– ORIGIN 1950s: formed from elements of the systematic name.

thorium /'θɔːrɪəm/ ■ n. the chemical element of atomic number 90, a white radioactive metal of the actinide series. (Symbol: **Th**)
– ORIGIN C19: named after *Thor*, the Scandinavian god of thunder.

thorn ■ n. **1** a stiff, sharp-pointed woody projection on the stem or other part of a plant. **2** a thorny bush, shrub, or tree. ▶ (also **thorn tree**) (in southern Africa) an acacia tree, e.g. camel thorn. **3** an Old English and Icelandic runic letter, Þ or þ, representing the dental fricatives /ð/ and /θ/, eventually superseded by the digraph *th*.
– PHRASES **a thorn in someone's side** (or **flesh**) a source of continual annoyance or trouble.
– DERIVATIVES **thornless** adj.

Thousand Island dressing

– ORIGIN Old English, of Germanic origin.

thorn apple ■ n. a poisonous shrubby plant with large trumpet-shaped white flowers, toothed leaves, and a prickly fruit resembling that of a horse chestnut. [*Datura stramonium*.]

thornback ray ■ n. a prickly skinned ray which is often eaten as 'skate'. [*Raja clavata*.]

thornveld /'θɔːnfɛlt/ ■ n. S. African land on which thorny trees and bushes are the dominant vegetation.
– ORIGIN C19: blend of *thorn* + Afrikaans *veld* 'countryside'.

thorny ■ adj. (**-ier, -iest**) **1** having many thorns or thorn bushes. **2** causing distress, difficulty, or trouble.
– DERIVATIVES **thornily** adv. **thorniness** n.

thorough ■ adj. **1** complete with regard to every detail. ▶ performed with or showing great care and completeness. **2** absolute; utter (used for emphasis).
– DERIVATIVES **thoroughness** n.
– ORIGIN Old English *thuruh*, alteration of *thurh* 'through'.

thorough bass ■ n. Music basso continuo (see **CONTINUO**).

thoroughbred ■ adj. **1** of pure breed, especially of a breed of horse originating from English mares and Arab stallions. **2** informal of outstanding quality. ■ n. **1** a thoroughbred animal. **2** informal an outstanding or first-class person or thing.

thoroughfare ■ n. a road or path forming a route between two places.

thoroughgoing ■ adj. **1** involving or attending to every detail or aspect. **2** complete; absolute.

thoroughly /'θʌrəli/ ■ adv. **1** in a thorough manner. **2** very much; greatly.

those plural form of **THAT**.

thou[1] ■ pron. [second person sing.] archaic or dialect form of **YOU**, as the singular subject of a verb.
– ORIGIN Old English *thu*, of Germanic origin.

thou[2] ■ n. (pl. same or **thous**) informal a thousand.

though ■ conj. **1** despite the fact that; although. **2** however; but. ■ adv. however: *her first name was Rose, though no-one called her that.*
– ORIGIN Old English *thēah*, of Germanic origin; superseded in Middle English by forms from Old Norse *thó, thau*.

thought[1] ■ n. **1** an idea or opinion produced by thinking or occurring suddenly in the mind. ▶ (**one's thoughts**) one's mind or attention. ▶ an act of considering or remembering. **2** the action or process of thinking. ▶ careful consideration or attention. **3** the formation of opinions, especially as a philosophy or system of ideas, or the opinions so formed.
– PHRASES **a second thought** [with neg.] more than the slightest consideration. **a thought** dated to a small extent.
– ORIGIN Old English, of Germanic origin.

thought[2] past and past participle of **THINK**.

thought experiment ■ n. a mental assessment of the implications of a hypothesis.

thoughtful ■ adj. **1** absorbed in or involving thought. ▶ showing careful consideration or attention. **2** showing regard for other people.
– DERIVATIVES **thoughtfully** adv. **thoughtfulness** n.

thoughtless ■ adj. **1** not showing consideration for other people. **2** without consideration of the consequences.
– DERIVATIVES **thoughtlessly** adv. **thoughtlessness** n.

thought police ■ n. [treated as pl.] a group of people who aim to suppress ideas that deviate from the way of thinking that they believe to be correct.

thought transference ■ n. another term for **TELEPATHY**.

thousand ■ cardinal number (pl. **thousands** or (with numeral or quantifying word) same) **1** (**a/one thousand**) the number equivalent to the product of a hundred and ten; 1 000. (Roman numeral: **m** or **M**.) **2** (**thousands**) informal an unspecified large number.
– DERIVATIVES **thousandfold** adj. & adv. **thousandth** ordinal number.
– ORIGIN Old English, of Germanic origin.

Thousand Island dressing ■ n. a dressing for salad or

seafood consisting of mayonnaise with ketchup and chopped pickles.
– ORIGIN 1916: from the name of a large group of islands in the St Lawrence River between the US and Canada.

Thracian /ˈθreɪʃ(ə)n/ ■ n. a native or inhabitant of Thrace, an ancient country lying west of the Black Sea and north of the Aegean. ■ adj. of or relating to Thrace.

thrall /θrɔːl/ ■ n. the state of being in another's power.
– DERIVATIVES **thraldom** (also **thrálldom**) n.
– ORIGIN Old English *thrǽl* 'slave', from Old Norse *thrǽll*.

thrash (also **thresh**) ■ v. **1** beat repeatedly and violently with or as with a stick or whip. **2** move in a violent or uncontrolled way: *he lay thrashing around in pain*. **3** informal defeat heavily. **4** (**thrash something out**) discuss something frankly and thoroughly, especially to reach a decision. ■ n. **1** a violent or noisy movement of beating or thrashing. ▸ informal a fast and exciting motor race or other sporting event. **2** Brit. informal a party, especially a loud or lavish one. **3** (also **thrash metal**) a style of fast, loud, harsh-sounding rock music, combining elements of punk and heavy metal.
– DERIVATIVES **thrasher** n.
– ORIGIN Old English, var. of THRESH.

thread ■ n. **1** a long, thin strand of cotton, nylon, or other fibres used in sewing or weaving. **2** a long thin line or piece of something. **3** (also **screw thread**) a helical ridge on the outside of a screw, bolt, etc. or on the inside of a cylindrical hole, to allow two parts to be screwed together. **4** a theme or characteristic running throughout a situation or piece of writing. ▸ Computing a group of linked messages posted on the Internet that share a common subject or theme. ▸ Computing a programming structure or process formed by linking a number of separate elements or subroutines. **5** (**threads**) informal, chiefly N. Amer. clothes. ■ v. **1** pass a thread through (a needle). ▸ pass (a thread) through something and into the required position for use. ▸ put (beads or other objects) on a thread. **2** move or weave in and out of obstacles. **3** [usu. as adj. **threaded**] cut a screw thread in or on (a hole, screw, or other object).
– DERIVATIVES **threader** n. **thread-like** adj.
– ORIGIN Old English, of Germanic origin.

threadbare ■ adj. thin and tattered with age; worn out.

threadfin ■ n. an edible tropical marine fish with long streamers arising from its pectoral fins. [Family Polynemidae: several species.]

threadworm ■ n. a very slender parasitic nematode worm, especially a pinworm.

thready ■ adj. (**-ier**, **-iest**) **1** of, relating to, or resembling a thread. **2** (of a sound) thin and scarcely audible. ▸ Medicine (of a person's pulse) scarcely perceptible.

threat ■ n. **1** a statement of an intention to inflict injury, damage, or other hostile action as retribution. ▸ Law a menace of bodily harm, such as may restrain a person's freedom of action. **2** a person or thing likely to cause damage or danger. ▸ the possibility of trouble or danger.
– ORIGIN Old English *thrēat* 'oppression', of Germanic origin.

threaten ■ v. **1** make or express a threat to (someone) or to do (something). **2** put at risk; endanger. ▸ (of a situation or the weather) seem likely to produce an unwelcome result: *the air was raw and threatened rain*.
– DERIVATIVES **threatener** n. **threatening** adj. **threateningly** adv.

three ■ cardinal number equivalent to the sum of one and two; one more than two; 3. (Roman numeral: **iii** or **III**.)
– PHRASES **three parts** three out of four equal parts; three quarters.
– DERIVATIVES **threefold** adj. & adv.
– ORIGIN Old English *thrīe*, *thrīo*, *thrēo*, of Germanic origin.

three-colour process ■ n. Photography a means of reproducing natural colours by combining photographic images in the three primary colours.

three-dimensional ■ adj. having or appearing to have length, breadth, and depth.
– DERIVATIVES **three-dimensionality** n. **three-dimensionally** adv.

three-legged race ■ n. a race run by pairs of people, one member of each pair having their left leg tied to the right leg of the other.

three-line whip ■ n. a written notice, underlined three times to denote urgency, to members of a political party to attend a parliamentary vote.

threepence /ˈθrɛp(ə)ns, ˈθrʊ-, ˈθrʌ-/ ■ n. Brit. the sum of three pence, especially before decimalization (1971).

threepenny bit ■ n. Brit. historical a coin worth three old pence (1¼ p).

three-phase ■ adj. relating to or denoting an electricity supply using three separate alternating components with phases differing by a third of a period.

three-piece ■ adj. consisting of three matching items. ▸ (of a set of furniture) consisting of a sofa and two armchairs. ▸ (of a set of clothes) consisting of trousers or a skirt with a waistcoat and jacket. ■ n. **1** a set of three matching items. **2** a group consisting of three musicians.

three-pointer ■ n. Basketball a shot scored from outside the area of the court near the basket, which earns three points instead of two.

three-point landing ■ n. a landing of an aircraft on the two main wheels and the tailwheel or skid simultaneously.

three-point turn ■ n. a method of turning a vehicle round in a narrow space by moving forwards, backwards, and forwards again in a sequence of arcs.

three-quarter ■ adj. consisting of three quarters of something in terms of length, angle, time, etc. ■ n. **1** Rugby each of four players in a team positioned across the field behind the halfbacks. **2** (**the three-quarter**) a point in time forty-five minutes after any full hour of the clock. ■ adv. to a size or extent of three quarters.

three quarters ■ pl. n. three of the four equal parts into which something may be divided. ■ adv. to the extent of three quarters.

three-ring circus ■ n. a confused situation; a shambles.

threescore ■ cardinal number poetic/literary sixty.

three-wheeler ■ n. a vehicle with three wheels.

threnody /ˈθrɛnədi/ ■ n. (pl. **-ies**) a lament.
– ORIGIN C17: from Greek *thrēnōidia*, from *thrēnos* 'wailing' + *ōidē* 'song'.

thresh ■ v. **1** /θrɛʃ/ separate grain from (corn or related crops), typically with a flail or by the action of a revolving mechanism. **2** /θrɑʃ/ variant spelling of THRASH.
– DERIVATIVES **threshing** n.
– ORIGIN Old English, of Germanic origin.

thresher /ˈθrɛʃə/ ■ n. **1** a person or machine that threshes. **2** (also **thresher shark**) a shark with a long upper lobe to the tail, sometimes used in hunting to lash the water to guide its prey. [Genus *Alopias*.]

threshold /ˈθrɛʃəʊld, ˈθrɛʃˌhəʊld/ ■ n. **1** a strip of wood or stone forming the bottom of a doorway and crossed in entering a house or room. **2** a level or point at which something would start or cease to happen or come into effect. ▸ Physiology a limit below which a stimulus causes no reaction: *a low pain threshold*.
– ORIGIN Old English *therscold*, *threscold*; first element rel. to THRESH.

threw past of THROW.

thrice /θraɪs/ ■ adv. archaic or poetic/literary **1** three times. **2** extremely; very: *I was thrice blessed*.
– ORIGIN Middle English *thries*, from earlier *thrie*, from Old English *thrīga*.

thrift ■ n. **1** the quality of being careful and not wasteful with money and other resources. **2** a European plant which forms low-growing tufts of slender leaves with rounded pink flower heads, growing chiefly on sea cliffs and mountains. [*Armeria maritima*.]
– ORIGIN Middle English: from Old Norse, from *thrífa* 'grasp, get hold of'.

thriftless ■ adj. spending money in an extravagant and wasteful way.
– DERIVATIVES **thriftlessly** adv. **thriftlessness** n.

thrift shop (also **thrift store**) ■ n. a shop selling second-hand clothes and other household goods, typically to raise funds for a Church or charity.

thrifty ■ adj. (**-ier**, **-iest**) careful and prudent with money.
– DERIVATIVES **thriftily** adv. **thriftiness** n.

| VOWELS | a cat | ɑː arm | ɛ bed | ɛː hair | ə ago | əː her | ɪ sit | i cosy | iː see | ɒ hot | ɔː saw | ʌ run |

thrill ■ n. **1** a sudden feeling of excitement and pleasure. ▸ an experience that produces such a feeling. ▸ a wave or nervous tremor of emotion or sensation. **2** Medicine a vibratory movement or resonance heard through a stethoscope. ■ v. **1** have or cause to have a thrill. **2** (of an emotion or sensation) pass with a nervous tremor. ▸ quiver or tremble.
– PHRASES **thrills and spills** excitement and exhilaration.
– DERIVATIVES **thrilling** adj. **thrillingly** adv.
– ORIGIN Middle English (in the sense 'pierce'): alteration of dialect *thirl* 'pierce, bore'.

thriller ■ n. a novel, play, or film with an exciting plot, typically involving crime or espionage.

THRIP /θrɪp/ ■ abbrev. (in South Africa) Technology and Human Resources for Industry Programme.

thrips /θrɪps/ (also **thrip**) ■ n. (pl. same) a minute black insect which sucks plant sap, noted for swarming in warm still summer days. [Order Thysanoptera: many species.]
– ORIGIN C18: from Greek, 'woodworm'.

thrive ■ v. (past **thrived** or **throve**; past part. **thrived** or **thriven**) (of a child, animal, or plant) grow or develop well or vigorously. ▸ prosper; flourish.
– ORIGIN Middle English: from Old Norse *thrífask*, reflexive of *thrífa* 'grasp, get hold of'.

thro' ■ prep., adv., & adj. poetic/literary or informal spelling of **THROUGH**.

throat ■ n. **1** the passage which leads from the back of the mouth of a person or animal. ▸ the front part of the neck. **2** poetic/literary a voice of a person or a songbird. **3** Nautical the forward upper corner of a quadrilateral fore-and-aft sail.
– PHRASES **be at each other's throats** quarrel or fight. **force something down someone's throat** force something on a person's attention. **stick in one's throat** be unwelcome or unacceptable.
– DERIVATIVES **-throated** adj.
– ORIGIN Old English, of Germanic origin.

throatlatch (also **throatlash**) ■ n. a strap passing under a horse's throat to help keep the bridle in position.

throat microphone ■ n. a microphone attached to a speaker's throat and actuated by the larynx.

throaty ■ adj. (-ier, -iest) (of a voice or other sound) deep and husky.
– DERIVATIVES **throatily** adv. **throatiness** n.

throb ■ v. (**throbbed**, **throbbing**) **1** beat or sound with a strong, regular rhythm; pulsate steadily. **2** feel pain in a series of pulsations. ■ n. a strong, regular beat or sound.
– ORIGIN Middle English: prob. imitative.

throes /θrəʊz/ ■ pl. n. intense or violent pain and struggle.
– PHRASES **in the throes of** struggling in the midst of.
– ORIGIN Middle English *throwe* (sing.); perhaps rel. to Old English *thrēa*, *thrawu* 'calamity', influenced by *thrōwian* 'suffer'.

thrombi plural form of **THROMBUS**.

thrombin /ˈθrɒmbɪn/ ■ n. Biochemistry an enzyme in blood plasma which causes the clotting of blood by converting fibrinogen to fibrin.
– ORIGIN C19: from Greek *thrombos* 'blood clot'.

thrombo- ■ comb. form relating to the clotting of blood: *thromboembolism*.
– ORIGIN from Greek *thrombos* 'blood clot'.

thrombocyte /ˈθrɒmbə(ʊ)sʌɪt/ ■ n. another term for **PLATELET**.

thrombocytopenia /ˌθrɒmbə(ʊ)ˌsʌɪtəʊˈpiːnɪə/ ■ n. Medicine deficiency of platelets in the blood, leading to bleeding into the tissues, bruising, and slow blood clotting after injury.
– ORIGIN 1920s: from **THROMBOCYTE** + Greek *penia* 'poverty'.

thromboembolism /ˌθrɒmbəʊˈɛmbəlɪz(ə)m/ ■ n. Medicine obstruction of a blood vessel by a blood clot that has become dislodged from its original site.
– DERIVATIVES **thromboembolic** adj.

thrombolysis /θrɒmˈbɒlɪsɪs/ ■ n. Medicine the dissolution of a blood clot, especially as induced artificially by infusion of an enzyme into the blood.
– DERIVATIVES **thrombolytic** adj.

thrombose /θrɒmˈbəʊz, -s/ ■ v. affect with or be affected by thrombosis.

– ORIGIN C19: back-formation from **THROMBOSIS**.

thrombosis /θrɒmˈbəʊsɪs/ ■ n. (pl. **thromboses** /-siːz/) local coagulation or clotting of the blood in a part of the circulatory system.
– DERIVATIVES **thrombotic** adj.
– ORIGIN C18: from Greek *thrombōsis* 'curdling', from *thrombos* 'blood clot'.

thromboxane /θrɒmˈbɒkseɪn/ ■ n. Biochemistry a hormone released from blood platelets, which induces platelet aggregation and arterial constriction.

thrombus /ˈθrɒmbəs/ ■ n. (pl. **thrombi** /-bʌɪ/) a blood clot formed in situ within the vascular system of the body and impeding blood flow.
– ORIGIN C19: from Greek *thrombos* 'blood clot'.

throne ■ n. a ceremonial chair for a sovereign, bishop, or similar figure. ▸ (**the throne**) the power or rank of a sovereign: *the heir to the throne*. ■ v. poetic/literary place on a throne.
– ORIGIN Middle English: from Old French *trone*, from Greek *thronos* 'elevated seat'.

throng ■ n. a large, densely packed crowd. ■ v. flock or be present in great numbers.
– ORIGIN Old English (*ge*)*thrang* 'crowd, tumult', of Germanic origin.

throstle /ˈθrɒs(ə)l/ ■ n. Brit. old-fashioned term for **SONG THRUSH**.
– ORIGIN Old English, of Germanic origin.

throttle ■ n. a device controlling the flow of fuel or power to an engine. ■ v. **1** attack or kill by choking or strangling. **2** control (an engine or vehicle) with a throttle. ▸ (**throttle back/down**) reduce power by use of the throttle.
– DERIVATIVES **throttler** n.
– ORIGIN Middle English: perhaps from **THROAT**.

through ■ prep. & adv. **1** moving in one side and out of the other side of (an opening or location). ▸ so as to make a hole or passage in. ▸ [prep.] expressing the position or location of something beyond (an opening or an obstacle). ▸ expressing the extent of changing orientation. **2** continuing in time to or towards completion of. ▸ from beginning to end of (an experience or activity). **3** so as to inspect all or part of. **4** [prep.] N. Amer. up to and including (a particular point in a sequence): *from March 24 through May 7*. **5** by means of. **6** [adv.] so as to be connected by telephone. ■ adj. **1** (of public transport or a ticket) continuing or valid to the final destination. **2** (of traffic, roads, etc.) passing continuously from one side and out of the other side. **3** having successfully passed to the next stage of a competition. **4** informal, chiefly N. Amer. having finished an activity, relationship, etc.: *you and I are through*.
– PHRASES **through and through** thoroughly or completely.
– ORIGIN Old English, of Germanic origin.

throughout ■ prep. & adv. all the way through.

throughput ■ n. the amount of material or items passing through a system or process.

throve past of **THRIVE**.

throw ■ v. (past **threw**; past part. **thrown**) **1** propel with force through the air by a rapid movement of the arm and hand. ▸ send (one's opponent) to the ground in wrestling, judo, etc. ▸ (of a horse) unseat (its rider). ▸ Cricket bowl (the ball) with an illegitimate bent arm action. **2** move or put into place quickly, hurriedly, or roughly. **3** send suddenly into a particular position or condition: *he threw all her emotions into turmoil*. ▸ disconcert; confuse. **4** project, direct, or cast (light, an expression, etc.) in a particular direction. ▸ project (one's voice) so that it appears to come from somewhere else, as in ventriloquism. **5** form (ceramic ware) on a potter's wheel. ▸ turn (wood) on a lathe. ▸ twist (silk or other material) into yarn. **6** have (a fit or tantrum). **7** informal give or hold (a party). **8** informal lose (a race or contest) intentionally, especially in return for a bribe. **9** (of an animal) give birth to. ■ n. **1** an act of throwing. **2** a light cover for furniture. **3** Geology the extent of vertical displacement in a fault. **4** a machine or device by or on which an object is turned while being shaped. **5** the action or motion of a slide valve or of a crank, eccentric wheel, or cam. ▸ the extent of such motion.

throwaway

6 (**a throw**) informal a single turn, round, or item: *on-the-spot portraits at R25 a throw.*
– PHRASES **be thrown back on** be forced to rely on (something) because there is no alternative. **throw the bones** S. African make a prediction using divining bones. **throw good money after bad** incur further loss in a hopeless attempt to recoup a previous loss. **throw one's hand in** withdraw from a card game because one has a poor hand. ▶ withdraw; give up. **throw in the towel** (or **sponge**) (of boxers or their seconds) throw a towel (or sponge) into the ring as a token of defeat. ▶ admit defeat. **throw up one's hands** raise both hands in the air as an indication of one's exasperation.
– PHRASAL VERBS **throw something away** 1 discard something as useless or unwanted. ▶ waste or fail to make use of an opportunity or advantage. 2 (of an actor) deliver a line with deliberate underemphasis. **throw something in** 1 include something extra with something that is being sold or offered. 2 make a remark casually as an interjection in a conversation. **throw oneself into** start to do (something) with enthusiasm and vigour. **throw something off** 1 rid oneself of something. 2 write or utter something in an offhand manner. **throw something open** make something generally accessible. **throw someone out** 1 expel someone unceremoniously. 2 Cricket & Baseball put out an opponent by throwing the ball to the wicket or a base. **throw something out** 1 discard something as unwanted. 2 (of a court, legislature, or other body) dismiss or reject. 3 cause numbers or calculations to become inaccurate. **throw someone over** abandon or reject someone as a lover. **throw people together** bring people into contact, especially by chance. **throw something together** make or produce something hastily or without careful planning. **throw up** informal vomit. **throw something up** 1 abandon something. 2 produce something and bring it to notice.
– DERIVATIVES **throwable** adj. **thrower** n.
– ORIGIN Old English *thrāwan* 'to twist, turn', of West Germanic origin.

throwaway ▪ adj. 1 intended to be discarded after being used once or a few times. 2 (of a remark) expressed in a casual or understated way.

throwback ▪ n. a reversion to an earlier ancestral type or characteristic.

throw-in ▪ n. 1 Soccer & Rugby the act of throwing the ball from the sideline to restart play after the ball has gone into touch. 2 Rugby the act of putting the ball into a scrum.

thru ▪ prep., adv., & adj. chiefly US informal spelling of THROUGH.

thrum ▪ v. (**thrummed**, **thrumming**) make a continuous rhythmic humming sound. ▶ strum (the strings of a musical instrument) in a rhythmic way. ▪ n. a continuous rhythmic humming sound.
– ORIGIN C16: imitative.

thrush[1] ▪ n. a small or medium-sized songbird, typically with a brown back and spotted breast. [*Turdus* and other genera: many species.]
– ORIGIN Old English, of Germanic origin.

thrush[2] ▪ n. 1 infection of the mouth and throat by a yeast-like fungus (Genus *Candida*), causing whitish patches. ▶ infection of the female genitals with the same fungus. 2 a chronic condition affecting the frog of a horse's foot, causing the accumulation of a dark, foul-smelling substance.
– ORIGIN C17: sense 2 perhaps from dialect *frush*, perhaps from Old French *fourchette* 'frog of a horse's hoof'.

thrust ▪ v. (past and past part. **thrust**) 1 push suddenly or violently in the specified direction. 2 (of a thing) extend so as to project conspicuously. 3 (**thrust something on/upon**) impose something unwelcome on. ▪ n. 1 a sudden or violent lunge or attack. 2 the principal purpose or theme of a course of action or line of reasoning. 3 the propulsive force of a jet or rocket engine. 4 (also **thrust fault**) Geology a reverse fault of low angle, with older strata displaced horizontally over newer.
– ORIGIN Middle English: from Old Norse *thrýsta*; perhaps rel. to Latin *trudere* 'to thrust'.

thruster ▪ n. 1 a person or thing that thrusts. 2 a small rocket engine on a spacecraft, used to make alterations in its flight path or altitude. ▶ a secondary jet or propeller on a ship or offshore rig, used for accurate manoeuvring and maintenance of position. 3 a surfboard or sailboard capable of increased speed and manoeuvrability.

thrusting ▪ adj. 1 aggressively ambitious. 2 projecting in a conspicuous way.

thud ▪ n. a dull, leaden sound, such as that made by a heavy object falling to the ground. ▪ v. (**thudded**, **thudding**) move, fall, or strike something with a thud.
– DERIVATIVES **thudding** n. **thuddingly** adv.
– ORIGIN Middle English: prob. from Old English *thyddan* 'to thrust, push'.

thug ▪ n. a violent and uncouth man, especially a criminal.
– DERIVATIVES **thuggery** n. **thuggish** adj. **thuggishly** adv. **thuggishness** n.

> **HISTORY**
> **Thug** comes from the Hindi word *thag* 'swindler, thief', and beyond that goes back to ancient Sanskrit. The original Thugs were an organization of robbers and assassins in India, followers of the goddess Kali, who waylaid and strangled their victims in a ritually prescribed manner. The modern sense, denoting any violent man, was first recorded in 1839.

thuja /ˈθ(j)uːjə/ (also **thuya**) ▪ n. an evergreen coniferous tree of a genus that includes the western red cedar. [Genus *Thuja.*]
– ORIGIN from Greek *thuia*, denoting an African tree formerly in the genus.

thulium /ˈθ(j)uːlɪəm/ ▪ n. the chemical element of atomic number 69, a soft silvery-white metal of the lanthanide series. (Symbol: **Tm**)
– ORIGIN C19: from *Thule*, the name of a country identified by the ancients as the northernmost part of the world.

thumb ▪ n. the short, thick first digit of the hand, set lower and apart from the other four and opposable to them. ▪ v. 1 press, touch, or indicate with one's thumb. 2 turn over (pages) with or as if with one's thumb. ▶ [usu. as adj. **thumbed**] wear or soil (a book's pages) by repeated handling. 3 request or obtain (a lift) by signalling with one's thumb.
– PHRASES **hold thumbs** see HOLD. **suck something out of one's thumb** see SUCK. **thumb one's nose at** informal show disdain or contempt for. [with ref. to the gesture of putting one's thumb on one's nose and spreading the fingers.] **thumbs up** (or **down**) informal an indication of satisfaction or approval (or of rejection or failure). **under someone's thumb** completely under someone's influence or control.
– DERIVATIVES **thumbed** adj. **thumbless** adj.
– ORIGIN Old English *thūma*, of West Germanic origin.

thumb index ▪ n. a set of lettered indentations cut down the side of a book for easy reference.
– DERIVATIVES **thumb-indexed** adj.

thumbnail ▪ n. 1 the nail of the thumb. 2 [as modifier] brief or concise in description or representation.

thumb piano ▪ n. any of various musical instruments, mainly of African origin, made from strips of metal fastened to a resonator and played by plucking with the fingers and thumbs.

thumbscrew ▪ n. 1 an instrument of torture that crushes the thumbs. 2 a screw with a protruding winged or flattened head for turning with the thumb and forefinger.

thumbsuck S. African informal ▪ n. a guess or fabrication. ▶ [as modifier] denoting something made up or based on guesswork. ▪ v. guess or make up.

thumbtack ▪ n. North American term for DRAWING PIN.

thumbwheel ▪ n. a control device for electrical or mechanical equipment in the form of a wheel operated with the thumb.

thump ▪ v. 1 hit heavily, especially with the fist or a blunt implement. ▶ put down forcefully, noisily, or decisively. ▶ (of a person's heart or pulse) beat or pulsate strongly. 2 (**thump something out**) play a tune enthusiastically but heavy-handedly. 3 informal defeat heavily. ▪ n. a heavy dull blow or noise.
– DERIVATIVES **thumper** n.
– ORIGIN C16: imitative.

thumping ▪ adj. 1 pounding; throbbing. 2 informal impressively large: *a thumping 64 per cent majority.*

thunder ■ n. **1** a loud rumbling or crashing noise heard after a lightning flash due to the expansion of rapidly heated air. **2** a resounding loud deep noise. ■ v. **1** (**it thunders**), it is thundering, etc. thunder sounds. **2** move or cause to move heavily and forcefully. **3** speak loudly, angrily, and forcefully, especially to protest.
– DERIVATIVES **thunderer** n. **thundery** adj.
– ORIGIN Old English, of Germanic origin.

thunderbolt ■ n. a flash of lightning with a simultaneous crash of thunder. ▶ a supposed bolt or shaft believed to be the destructive agent in a lightning flash, especially as an attribute of a god such as Jupiter or Thor.

thunderclap ■ n. a crash of thunder.

thundercloud ■ n. a cumulus cloud with a towering or spreading top, charged with electricity and producing thunder and lightning.

thunderflash ■ n. a noisy but harmless pyrotechnic device used especially in military exercises.

thunderhead ■ n. a rounded, projecting head of a cumulus cloud, which portends a thunderstorm.

thundering ■ adj. **1** making a resounding, loud, deep noise. **2** informal extremely great, severe, or impressive: *a thundering bore*.
– DERIVATIVES **thunderingly** adv.

thunderous ■ adj. **1** of, relating to, or resembling thunder. **2** (of a person's expression or behaviour) very angry or menacing.
– DERIVATIVES **thunderously** adv. **thunderousness** n.

thunderstorm ■ n. a storm with thunder and lightning and typically also heavy rain or hail.

thunderstruck ■ adj. extremely surprised or shocked.

Thur. (also **Thurs.**) ■ abbrev. Thursday.

thurible /'θjʊərɪb(ə)l/ ■ n. a censer.
– ORIGIN Middle English: from Latin *thuribulum*, from *thus, thur-* 'incense'.

Thursday ■ n. the day of the week before Friday and following Wednesday. ■ adv. on Thursday. ▶ (**Thursdays**) on Thursdays; each Thursday.
– ORIGIN Old English *Thu(n)resdæg* 'day of thunder' (named after the Germanic thunder god Thor), translation of late Latin *Jovis dies* 'day of Jupiter'.

thus ■ adv. poetic/literary or formal **1** as a result or consequence of this; therefore. **2** in the manner now being indicated or exemplified; in this way. **3** to this point; so.
– ORIGIN Old English.

thuya ■ n. variant spelling of THUJA.

thwack ■ v. strike forcefully with a sharp blow. ■ n. a sharp blow.
– ORIGIN Middle English: imitative.

thwart /θwɔːt/ ■ v. prevent from succeeding in or accomplishing something. ■ n. a structural crosspiece forming a seat for a rower in a boat.
– ORIGIN Middle English *thwerte*, from *thwert* 'obstinate, adverse', from Old Norse, from *thverr* 'transverse'.

thy (also **thine** before a vowel) ■ possess. det. archaic or dialect form of YOUR.
– ORIGIN Middle English *thi* (orig. before words beginning with any consonant except *h*), reduced from *thin*, from Old English *thīn*.

thyme /taɪm/ ■ n. a low-growing aromatic plant of the mint family, used as a culinary herb. [*Thymus vulgaris* and related species.]
– DERIVATIVES **thymy** adj.
– ORIGIN Middle English: from Old French *thym*, from Greek *thumon*, from *thuein* 'burn, sacrifice'.

thymi plural form of THYMUS.

thymine /'θaɪmiːn/ ■ n. Biochemistry a compound which is one of the four constituent bases of nucleic acids.
– ORIGIN C19: from THYMUS.

thymus /'θaɪməs/ ■ n. (pl. **thymi** /-maɪ/) a lymphoid organ situated in the neck of vertebrates which produces T-lymphocytes for the immune system.
– ORIGIN C16: from Greek *thumos* 'excrescence, thymus gland'.

thyroid /'θaɪrɔɪd/ ■ n. **1** (also **thyroid gland**) a large ductless gland in the neck which secretes hormones regulating growth and development through the rate of metabolism. **2** (also **thyroid cartilage**) a large cartilage of the larynx, a projection of which forms the Adam's apple in humans.
– ORIGIN C18: from Greek (*khondros*) *thureoeidēs* 'shield-shaped (cartilage)', from *thureos* 'oblong shield'.

thyroid-stimulating hormone ■ n. another term for THYROTROPIN.

thyrotropin /ˌθaɪrə(ʊ)'trəʊpɪn/ (also **thyrotrophin** /-'trəʊfɪn/) ■ n. Biochemistry a hormone secreted by the pituitary gland which regulates the production of thyroid hormones.

thyroxine /θaɪ'rɒksiːn, -sɪn/ ■ n. Biochemistry the main hormone produced by the thyroid gland, acting to increase metabolic rate and so regulating growth and development.
– ORIGIN C20: from THYROID + OX-.

thyself ■ pron. [second person sing.] archaic or dialect form of YOURSELF, corresponding to the subject THOU[1].

Ti ■ symb. the chemical element titanium.

TIA ■ abbrev. Medicine transient ischaemic attack (a slight and temporary stroke).

Tia Maria /ˌtiːə mə'riːə/ ■ n. trademark a coffee-flavoured liqueur based on rum, made originally in the Caribbean.
– ORIGIN from Spanish *Tía María* 'Aunt Mary'.

tiara ■ n. a jewelled ornamental band worn on the front of a woman's hair. ▶ a high diadem encircled with three crowns and worn by a pope.
– ORIGIN C16: from Greek, partly via Italian.

Tibetan ■ n. **1** a native of Tibet or a person of Tibetan descent. **2** the language of Tibet. ■ adj. of or relating to Tibet, its people, or their language.

tibia /'tɪbɪə/ ■ n. (pl. **tibiae** /-biiː/) Anatomy the inner and typically larger of the two bones between the knee and the ankle, parallel with the fibula. ▶ Entomology the fourth segment of the leg of an insect, between the femur and the tarsus.
– DERIVATIVES **tibial** adj.
– ORIGIN Middle English: from Latin, 'shin bone'.

tic ■ n. a habitual spasmodic contraction of the muscles, most often in the face.
– ORIGIN C19: from French, from Italian *ticchio*.

tic douloureux /tɪk ˌduːlə'ruː, -'rɔː/ ■ n. another term for TRIGEMINAL NEURALGIA.
– ORIGIN C19: French, 'painful tic'.

tich /tɪtʃ/ ■ n. variant spelling of TITCH.

tick[1] ■ n. **1** a mark (✓) used to indicate that a textual item is correct or has been chosen or checked. **2** a regular short, sharp sound, especially that made every second by a clock or watch. ▶ Brit. informal a moment. **3** Stock Exchange the smallest amount by which the price of a security or future may fluctuate. ■ v. **1** mark with a tick. **2** make regular ticking sounds. **3** (**tick away/by/past**) (of time) pass inexorably. ▶ (**tick along**) proceed; progress. **4** (**tick over**) (of an engine) run slowly in neutral. **5** (**tick someone off**) Brit. informal reprimand or rebuke someone. **6** (**tick someone off**) informal, chiefly N. Amer. make someone angry.
– PHRASES **make someone tick** informal motivate someone.
– ORIGIN Middle English: prob. of Germanic origin.

tick[2] ■ n. a parasitic arachnid which attaches itself to the skin, from which it sucks blood. [Suborder Ixodida: many species.]
– ORIGIN Old English *ticia*, of Germanic origin.

tick[3] ■ n. (in phr. **on tick**) on credit.
– ORIGIN C17: short for TICKET in the phr. *on the ticket*, referring to a promise to pay.

tick bird ■ n. **1** S. African another term for CATTLE EGRET. **2** another term for OXPECKER.

tick-bite fever (in full **African tick-bite fever**) ■ n. a rickettsial fever affecting humans, caused by the bacterium *Rickettsia africae* and transmitted by ticks.

ticker ■ n. **1** Brit. informal a person's heart. **2** a telegraphic or electronic machine that prints out data on a strip of paper.

ticker tape ■ n. a paper strip on which messages are

ticket

printed by a ticker machine. ▸ [as modifier] denoting a parade or other event in which this or similar material is thrown from windows.

ticket ∎ n. **1** a piece of paper or card giving the holder a right to admission to a place or event or to travel on public transport. **2** a certificate or warrant, especially an official notice of a traffic offence. **3** a label attached to a retail product, giving its price, size, etc. **4** a list of candidates put forward by a party in an election. ▸ a set of principles or policies supported by a party in an election. **5** (**the ticket**) informal the desirable thing: *a holiday would be just the ticket.* **6** (**tickets**) S. African informal death or ruin; the end. ∎ v. (**ticketed**, **ticketing**) issue with a ticket.
– DERIVATIVES **ticketed** adj. **ticketless** adj.
– ORIGIN C16: shortening of obsolete French *étiquet*, from Old French *estiquet(te)*, from *estiquier* 'to fix'; cf. ETIQUETTE.

tickey /ˈtɪki/ ∎ n. (pl. **tickeys**) S. African a former silver coin worth three pence (2½ cents after decimalization), withdrawn from circulation in 1964.
– PHRASES **turn** (or **spin**) **on a tickey** make a very tight turn. **two bricks** (or **half a brick**) **and a tickey high** very small; very young.
– ORIGIN C19.

tickey box ∎ n. S. African informal a telephone box.

tick fever ∎ n. **1** any bacterial or rickettsial fever transmitted by the bite of a tick. **2** S. African another term for BABESIOSIS.

ticking ∎ n. a strong, durable material, typically striped, used to cover mattresses.
– ORIGIN C17: prob. from Middle Low German *tēke* or Middle Dutch *tike*, from Latin *theca* 'case'.

tickle ∎ v. **1** lightly touch in a way that causes itching or twitching and often laughter. ▸ catch (a trout) by lightly rubbing it so that it moves backwards into the hand. **2** be appealing or amusing to. ∎ n. an act of tickling or sensation of being tickled.
– PHRASES **be tickled pink** (or **to death**) informal be extremely amused or pleased. **tickle the ivories** informal play the piano.
– DERIVATIVES **tickler** n. **tickly** adj.
– ORIGIN Middle English: perhaps from TICK¹, or an alteration of Scots and dialect *kittle* 'to tickle'.

ticklish ∎ adj. **1** sensitive to being tickled. ▸ (of a cough) characterized by persistent irritation in the throat. **2** (of a situation or problem) difficult to deal with; sensitive.
– DERIVATIVES **ticklishly** adv. **ticklishness** n.

tick-tock ∎ n. the sound of a large clock ticking. ∎ v. make a tick-tock.
– ORIGIN C19: imitative; cf. TICK¹.

tic-tac-toe (also **tick-tack-toe**) ∎ n. North American term for NOUGHTS AND CROSSES.
– ORIGIN 1960s: imitative; from *tick-tack*, used earlier to denote games in which the pieces made clicking sounds.

tidal ∎ adj. relating to or affected by tides.
– DERIVATIVES **tidally** adv.

tidal basin ∎ n. a basin accessible or navigable only at high tide.

tidal bore ∎ n. a large wave or bore caused by the constriction of the spring tide as it enters a long, narrow, shallow inlet.

tidal wave ∎ n. **1** an exceptionally large ocean wave, especially one caused by an underwater earthquake or volcanic eruption. **2** a widespread or overwhelming manifestation of an emotion or phenomenon.

tidbit ∎ n. US spelling of TITBIT.

tiddler ∎ n. Brit. informal a small fish, especially a stickleback or minnow. ▸ a young or unusually small person or thing.
– ORIGIN C19: perhaps rel. to TIDDLY² or *tittlebat*, a childish form of *stickleback*.

tiddly¹ ∎ adj. (**-ier**, **-iest**) informal slightly drunk.
– ORIGIN C19 (as n. denoting an alcoholic drink): perhaps from slang *tiddlywink*, denoting an unlicensed public house.

tiddly² ∎ adj. (**-ier**, **-iest**) Brit. informal little; tiny.

– ORIGIN C19: var. of colloqial *tiddy*.

tiddlywink ∎ n. **1** (**tiddlywinks**) [treated as sing.] a game in which small plastic counters are flicked into a central receptacle, using a larger counter. **2** a counter used in such a game.
– ORIGIN C19 (orig. denoting an unlicensed public house, also a game of dominoes): perhaps rel. to TIDDLY¹.

tide ∎ n. **1** the alternate rising and falling of the sea due to the attraction of the moon and sun. **2** a powerful surge of feeling or trend of events: *a tide of euphoria.* ∎ v. (**tide someone over**) help someone through a difficult period, especially with financial assistance.
– DERIVATIVES **tideless** adj.
– ORIGIN Old English *tīd* 'time, period, era', of Germanic origin.

-tide ∎ comb. form poetic/literary denoting a specified time or season: *springtide.*

tideline ∎ n. a line left or reached by the sea on a shore at the highest point of a tide.

tidemark ∎ n. **1** a tideline. **2** a grimy mark left around a bath, bowl, etc. at the level reached by a liquid.

tide rip ∎ n. an area of rough water typically caused by opposing tides or by a rapid current passing over an uneven bottom.

tidewater ∎ n. water brought or affected by tides.

tideway ∎ n. a channel in which a tide runs, especially the tidal part of a river.

tidings ∎ pl. n. poetic/literary news; information.
– ORIGIN Old English *tīdung* 'announcement, piece of news', prob. from Old Norse *títhindi* 'news of events', from *títhr* 'occurring'.

tidy ∎ adj. (**-ier**, **-iest**) **1** arranged neatly and in order. ▸ inclined to keep things or one's appearance neat and in order. ▸ not messy; neat and controlled. **2** informal (of an amount, especially of money) considerable. ∎ n. (pl. **-ies**) **1** (also **tidy-up**) an act or spell of tidying. **2** a receptacle for holding small objects. ∎ v. (**-ies**, **-ied**) (often **tidy up**) make tidy. ▸ (**tidy something away**) put something away for the sake of tidiness.
– DERIVATIVES **tidily** adv. **tidiness** n.
– ORIGIN Middle English (orig. in sense 'timely, opportune'): from TIDE.

tie ∎ v. (**tying**) **1** attach or fasten with string, cord, etc. ▸ form into a knot or bow. ▸ (**tie someone up**) restrict someone's movement by binding their arms or legs or binding them to something. ▸ (**tie something up**) bring something to a satisfactory conclusion. **2** restrict; limit. ▸ (**tie someone down**) restrict someone to a particular situation or place. ▸ (usu. **be tied up**) informal occupy someone to the exclusion of other activity. ▸ (**tie something up**) invest or reserve capital so that it is not immediately available for use. **3** connect; link. ▸ (**tie in**) be or cause to be in harmony with something. ▸ hold together by a crosspiece or tie. **4** achieve the same score or ranking as another competitor. ∎ n. (pl. **-ies**) **1** a thing that ties. **2** a strip of material worn around the neck beneath a collar, tied in a knot at the front. **3** a rod or beam holding parts of a structure together. **4** a sports match between two or more players or teams in which the winners proceed to the next round of the competition: *a cup tie.* **5** a result in a game or match in which two or more competitors have tied. ▸ Cricket a game in which the scores are level and both sides have completed their innings. Compare with DRAW.
– DERIVATIVES **tieless** adj.
– ORIGIN Old English, of Germanic origin.

tie-back ∎ n. a decorative strip of fabric or cord used for holding an open curtain back from the window.

tie beam ∎ n. a horizontal beam connecting two rafters in a roof.

tie-break (also **tie-breaker**) ∎ n. a means of deciding a winner from competitors who have tied, in particular (in tennis) a game to decide the winner of a set when the score is six games all.

tie clip ∎ n. an ornamental clip for holding a tie in place.

tied ∎ adj. **1** (of a house) occupied subject to the tenant's working for its owner. ▸ Brit. (of a public house) owned and controlled by a brewery. **2** (of aid or an international loan) given subject to the condition that it should be spent on goods or services from the donor or lender.

| VOWELS | a cat | ɑː arm | ɛ bed | ɛː hair | ə ago | əː her | ɪ sit | i cosy | iː see | ɒ hot | ɔː saw | ʌ run |

tie-dye ▪ n. a method of producing textile patterns by tying parts of the fabric to shield it from the dye. ▪ v. dye by such a process.

tie-in ▪ n. a connection or association. ▶ a book, film, or other product produced to take commercial advantage of a related work in another medium.

tie line ▪ n. a transmission line connecting parts of a system, especially a telephone line connecting two private branch exchanges.

tiepin ▪ n. an ornamental pin for holding a tie in place.

tier ▪ n. **1** one of a series of rows or levels stacked one above the other. **2** a level or grade within a hierarchy.
– DERIVATIVES **tiered** adj.
– ORIGIN C15: from French *tire* 'sequence, order'.

tierce /tɪəs/ ▪ n. **1** another term for TERCE. **2** Fencing the third of eight parrying positions.
– ORIGIN Middle English: var. of TERCE.

tierced /tɪəst/ (also **tiercé** /'tjɔːseɪ/) ▪ adj. Heraldry divided into three equal parts of different tinctures.
– ORIGIN C18: orig. as *tiercé* 'divided into three parts', from French *tiercer*.

tiercel /'tɪəs(ə)l/ ▪ n. Falconry a male hawk, especially a peregrine or a goshawk. Compare with FALCON.
– ORIGIN Middle English: from Old French, from Latin *tertius* 'third', perhaps from the belief that the third egg of a clutch produced a male.

tie-up ▪ n. **1** a link or connection, especially one between commercial companies. **2** a place for mooring a boat.

TIFF ▪ abbrev. Computing tagged image file format.

tiff ▪ n. informal a quarrel.
– ORIGIN C18: prob. of dialect origin.

tiger ▪ n. **1** a very large solitary cat with a yellow-brown coat striped with black, native to the forests of Asia. [*Panthera tigris*.] **2** (also **tiger economy**) a dynamic economy, especially of one of the East Asian countries.
– DERIVATIVES **tigerish** adj. **tigerishly** adv.
– ORIGIN Middle English: from Old French *tigre*, from Latin *tigris*, from Greek.

Tiger balm ▪ n. trademark a mentholated ointment widely used in Eastern medicine for a variety of conditions.

tiger beetle ▪ n. a fast-running predatory beetle with spotted or striped wing cases. [Family Cicindelidae: many species.]

tiger fish ▪ n. (pl. same) a fierce predatory southern African freshwater fish, prized as a game fish. [*Hydrocynus vittatus*.]

tiger lily ▪ n. a tall Asian lily which has orange flowers spotted with black or purple. [*Lilium lancifolium*.]

tiger moth ▪ n. a stout moth which has boldly spotted and streaked wings and a hairy caterpillar. [Family Arctiidae.]

tiger prawn (also **tiger shrimp**) ▪ n. a large edible prawn marked with dark bands, found in the Indian and Pacific oceans. [*Penaeus monodon* and related species.]

tiger's eye (also **tiger eye**) ▪ n. a yellowish-brown semi-precious variety of quartz with a silky or chatoyant lustre.

tiger shark ▪ n. an aggressive shark of warm seas, with dark vertical stripes on the body. [*Galeocerdo cuvieri*.]

tiger's jaw (also **tiger jaw**) ▪ n. a small succulent South African plant with rosettes of toothed leaves resembling gaping jaws. [Genus *Faucaria*: several species.]

tiger snake ▪ n. **1** a yellowish snake with dark brown bands, found throughout Africa, the Near East, and parts of Europe (also known as cat snake). [Genus *Telescopus*: several species.] **2** a deadly Australian snake, typically marked with brown and yellow bands. [*Notechis scutatus*.]

tight ▪ adj. **1** fixed or fastened firmly; hard to move, undo, or open. ▶ (of clothes) close-fitting, especially uncomfortably so. ▶ (of a grip) very firm. ▶ well sealed against something such as water or air. **2** (of a rope, fabric, or surface) stretched so as to leave no slack. ▶ tense: *a tight smile*. **3** (of a form of control) strictly imposed. **4** (of a written work or form) concise. **5** (of an organization or group) disciplined and well coordinated. **6** (of an area or space) allowing little room for manoeuvre. ▶ (of money or time) limited; restricted. **7** secretive. **8** informal miserly. **9** informal drunk. ▪ adv. very firmly, closely, or tensely.

– PHRASES **a tight ship** a strictly controlled and disciplined organization or operation. **a tight corner** (or **spot** or **place**) a difficult situation.
– DERIVATIVES **tighten** v. **tightly** adv. **tightness** n.
– ORIGIN Middle English: prob. an alteration of *thight* 'firm, solid', later 'close-packed, dense', of Germanic origin.

tight-ass ▪ n. informal, chiefly N. Amer. an inhibited or repressed person.
– DERIVATIVES **tight-assed** adj.

tight end ▪ n. American Football an offensive end who lines up close to the tackle.

tight-fisted ▪ adj. informal not willing to spend or give much money; miserly.

tight head ▪ n. Rugby the prop forward supporting the hooker on the opposite side of the scrum from the loose head.

tight-knit (also **tightly knit**) ▪ adj. (of a group of people) bound together by strong relationships and common interests.

tight-lipped ▪ adj. with the lips firmly closed, especially as a sign of suppressed emotion or determined reticence.

tight money ▪ n. Finance money or finance that is available only at high rates of interest.

tightrope ▪ n. a rope or wire stretched high above the ground, on which acrobats perform balancing feats.

tights ▪ pl. n. a close-fitting garment made of a knitted yarn, covering the legs, hips, and bottom.

tightwad ▪ n. informal, chiefly N. Amer. a miserly person.

tigon /'tʌɪg(ə)n/ (also **tiglon** /'tʌɪɡlɒn, 'tɪɡ-/) ▪ n. the hybrid offspring of a male tiger and a lioness.

Tigre /'tiːɡreɪ/ ▪ n. a Semitic language spoken in Eritrea and adjoining parts of Sudan. Compare with TIGRINYA.
– ORIGIN the name in Tigre.

tigress ▪ n. a female tiger.

Tigrinya /tɪ'ɡriːnjə/ ▪ n. a Semitic language spoken in Tigray. Compare with TIGRE.
– ORIGIN the name in Tigrinya.

tik (also **tik-tik**) S. African ▪ n. methamphetamine. ▪ v. (**tikked**, **tikking**) informal use methamphetamine.
– DERIVATIVES **tikker** n.
– ORIGIN from Afrikaans *tik* 'click, tick', imitative of the sound emitted when smoked.

tike ▪ n. variant spelling of TYKE.

tikka /'tɪkə, 'tiːkə/ ▪ n. an Indian dish of small pieces of meat or vegetables marinated in a spice mixture.
– ORIGIN from Punjabi *ṭikkā*.

tilapia /tɪ'leɪpɪə, -'lɑːp-/ ▪ n. an African freshwater cichlid fish, introduced to many areas for food. [*Tilapia* and other genera: several species.]

tilde /'tɪldə/ ▪ n. an accent (~) placed over Spanish *n* when pronounced *ny* (as in *señor*) or Portuguese *a* or *o* when nasalized (as in *São Paulo*), or over a vowel in phonetic transcription, indicating nasalization. ▶ a similar symbol used in mathematics and logic to indicate negation, inversion, etc.
– ORIGIN C19: from Spanish, from Latin *titulus* (see TITLE).

tile /tʌɪl/ ▪ n. **1** a thin square or rectangular slab of baked clay, concrete, etc., used in overlapping rows for covering roofs. ▶ a similar slab of glazed pottery or other material for covering floors or walls. **2** a thin, flat piece used in Scrabble, mah-jong, and other games. ▪ v. **1** cover with tiles. **2** Computing arrange (two or more windows) on a computer screen so that they do not overlap.
– PHRASES **on the tiles** informal, chiefly Brit. having a lively night out.
– ORIGIN Old English *tigele*, from Latin *tegula*, from an Indo-European root meaning 'cover'.

tiler ▪ n. a person who lays tiles.

tiling ▪ n. **1** the action of laying tiles. ▶ a surface covered by tiles. **2** Computing a technique for tiling windows on a computer screen. **3** Mathematics a way of arranging identical plane shapes so that they completely cover an area without overlapping.

till[1] ▪ prep. & conj. less formal way of saying UNTIL.
– ORIGIN Old English *til*, of Germanic origin (not, as is commonly assumed, a shortened form of *until*).

till

till² ■ n. a cash register or drawer for money in a shop, bank, or restaurant.
– ORIGIN Middle English (in the sense 'drawer or compartment for valuables').

till³ ■ v. prepare and cultivate (land) for crops.
– DERIVATIVES **tillable** adj. **tillage** n.
– ORIGIN Old English *tilian* 'strive for, obtain by effort', of Germanic origin.

till⁴ ■ n. Geology boulder clay or other unstratified sediment deposited by melting glaciers or ice sheets.
– ORIGIN C17 (orig. Scots, denoting shale).

tiller¹ ■ n. a horizontal bar fitted to the head of a boat's rudder post and used for steering.
– ORIGIN Middle English: from Anglo-Norman French *telier* 'weaver's beam, stock of a crossbow', from medieval Latin *telarium*, from Latin *tela* 'web'.

tiller² ■ n. a lateral shoot from the base of the stem, especially in a grass or cereal. ■ v. develop tillers.
– DERIVATIVES **tillering** n.
– ORIGIN C17: apparently from Old English *telga* 'bough', of Germanic origin.

tiller³ ■ n. an implement or machine for breaking up soil; a plough or cultivator.

tilley lamp /'tɪli/ (also **tilly lamp**) ■ n. trademark a portable oil or paraffin lamp in which air pressure is used to supply the burner with fuel.
– ORIGIN 1930s: from the name of the manufacturers.

tillite /'tɪlʌɪt/ ■ n. Geology sedimentary rock composed of compacted glacial till.

tilt ■ v. 1 move or cause to move into a sloping position. ▶ move (a camera) in a vertical plane. 2 (**tilt at**) historical (in jousting) thrust at with a lance or other weapon. ▶ (**tilt with**) archaic engage in a contest with. ■ n. a tilting position or movement. ▶ an inclination or bias.
– PHRASES (**at**) **full tilt** with maximum speed or force. **tilt at windmills** attack imaginary enemies. [with allusion to the story of Don Quixote tilting at windmills, believing they were giants.]
– DERIVATIVES **tilter** n.
– ORIGIN Middle English: perhaps rel. to Old English *tealt* 'unsteady', or perhaps rel. to Norwegian *tylten* 'unsteady' and Swedish *tulta* 'totter'.

tilth ■ n. cultivation of land; tillage. ▶ the condition of tilled soil. ▶ prepared surface soil.
– ORIGIN Old English *tilth*, *tilthe*, from *tilian*.

timbale /tam'bɑːl/ ■ n. a dish of finely minced meat or fish cooked with other ingredients in a pastry shell or in a mould.
– ORIGIN French, 'drum'.

timber ■ n. wood prepared for use in building and carpentry. ▶ trees grown for such wood. ▶ a wooden beam or board used in building and shipbuilding. ■ exclam. used to warn that a tree is about to fall after being cut.
– DERIVATIVES **timbered** adj. **timbering** n.
– ORIGIN Old English in the sense 'a building', also 'building material', of Germanic origin.

timber-frame ■ adj. denoting a house or other structure having a wooden frame. ■ n. pre-prepared sections of wood used for building a house.
– DERIVATIVES **timber-framed** adj. **timber-framing** n.

timberline ■ n. chiefly N. Amer. another term for TREELINE.

timberman ■ n. (pl. -men) a person who works with timber.

timber wolf ■ n. a wolf of a large variety found mainly in northern North America, with grey brindled fur.

timbre /'tambə/ ■ n. the character or quality of a musical sound or voice as distinct from its pitch and intensity.
– ORIGIN C19: from French, from medieval Greek *timbanon*, from Greek *tumpanon* 'drum'.

timbrel /'tɪmbr(ə)l/ ■ n. archaic a tambourine or similar instrument.
– ORIGIN C16: perhaps a diminutive of obsolete *timbre*, in the same sense, from Old French (see TIMBRE).

time ■ n. 1 the indefinite continued progress of existence and events in the past, present, and future, regarded as a whole. 2 a point of time as measured in hours and minutes past midnight or noon. ▶ the favourable or appropriate moment to do something: *it was time to go*. ▶ (**a time**) an indefinite period: *he worked for a time as a gardener*. ▶ (also **times**) a more or less definite portion of time characterized by particular events or circumstances: *Victorian times*. ▶ (**one's time**) a period regarded as characteristic of a particular stage of one's life. ▶ the length of time taken to run a race or complete an activity. ▶ informal a prison sentence. ▶ an apprenticeship. 3 Brit. the moment at which the opening hours of a public house end. ▶ Baseball a moment at which play stops temporarily within a game. 4 time as allotted, available, or used: *a waste of time*. 5 the normal rate of pay for time spent working: *they are paid time and a half*. 6 an instance of something happening or being done: *the nurse came in four times a day*. 7 (**times**) (following a number) expressing multiplication. 8 the rhythmic pattern or tempo of a piece of music. ■ v. 1 arrange a time for. ▶ perform at a particular time. 2 measure the time taken by. 3 (**time something out**) Computing (of a computer or a program) cancel an operation automatically because a predefined interval of time has passed. 4 (**times**) informal multiply (a number).
– PHRASES **about time** conveying that something should have happened earlier. **all the time** at all times. ▶ very frequently or regularly. **at the same time** 1 simultaneously. 2 nevertheless. **at a time** separately in the specified groups or numbers: *he took the stairs two at a time*. **behind the times** not aware of or using the latest ideas or techniques. **for the time being** until some other arrangement is made. **have no time for** be unable or unwilling to spend time on. ▶ dislike or disapprove of. **in time 1** not late. 2 eventually. 3 in accordance with the appropriate musical rhythm or tempo. **keep good** (or **bad**) **time 1** (of a clock or watch) record time accurately (or inaccurately). 2 (of a person) be habitually punctual (or not punctual). **keep time** play or rhythmically accompany music in time. **on time** punctual; punctually. **pass the time of day** exchange greetings or casual remarks. **time immemorial** a point of time in the distant past beyond recall or knowledge. **the time of one's life** a period or occasion of exceptional enjoyment. **time out of mind** another way of saying time immemorial. **time will tell** the truth about something will be established in the future.
– ORIGIN Old English *tima*, of Germanic origin; rel. to TIDE.

time-and-motion study ■ n. a procedure in which the efficiency of an industrial or other operation is evaluated.

time bomb ■ n. a bomb designed to explode at a preset time.

time capsule ■ n. a container storing a selection of objects chosen as being typical of the present time, buried for discovery in the future.

time code ■ n. Electronics a coded signal on videotape or film giving information about such things as frame number or time of recording.

time constant ■ n. Physics a quantity (in units of time) expressing the speed of response of a device or system.

time frame ■ n. a specified period of time.

time-honoured ■ adj. (of a custom or tradition) respected or valued because it has existed for a long time.

timekeeper ■ n. 1 a person who records the amount of time taken by a process or activity. 2 a person regarded in terms of their punctuality. ▶ a watch or clock regarded in terms of its accuracy.
– DERIVATIVES **timekeeping** n.

time-lapse ■ adj. denoting the photographic technique of taking a sequence of frames at set intervals to record changes that take place slowly over time.

timeless ■ adj. not affected by the passage of time or changes in fashion.
– DERIVATIVES **timelessly** adv. **timelessness** n.

timeline ■ n. a line representing a set of data arranged in order of occurrence with equal time intervals between each value.

time lock ■ n. a lock fitted with a device that prevents it from being unlocked until a set time. ▶ a device built into a computer program to stop it operating after a certain time. ■ v. (**time-lock**) secure with a time lock.

CONSONANTS   b but   d dog   f few   g get   h he   j yes   k cat   l leg   m man   n no   p pen   r red

timely ■ adj. done or occurring at a favourable or appropriate time.
– DERIVATIVES **timeliness** n.

time machine ■ n. (in science fiction) a machine capable of time travel.

time off ■ n. time for rest or recreation away from one's usual work or studies.

timeous /'tAIməs/ ■ adj. chiefly S. African & Scottish in good time; sufficiently early.
– DERIVATIVES **timeously** adv.

time out ■ n. 1 chiefly N. Amer. time for rest or recreation. ▸ (**timeout**) a brief break from play in a game or sport. ▸ a brief period of time during which a misbehaving child is put on their own so as to regain control. 2 (**time-out**) Computing a cancellation or cessation that automatically occurs when a predefined interval of time has passed.

timepiece ■ n. an instrument for measuring time; a clock or watch.

timer ■ n. 1 an automatic mechanism for activating a device at a preset time. 2 a person or device that records the amount of time taken by a process or activity. 3 [in combination] indicating how many times someone has done something: *a first-timer*.

time-release ■ adj. denoting something that releases an active substance gradually.

timescale ■ n. the time allowed for or taken by a process or sequence of events.

time-server ■ n. 1 a person who changes their views to suit the prevailing circumstances or fashion. 2 a person who makes very little effort at work because they are waiting to leave or retire.
– DERIVATIVES **time-serving** adj.

timeshare ■ n. an arrangement whereby joint owners use a property as a holiday home at different specified times. ▸ a property owned in such a way.
– DERIVATIVES **time-sharing** n.

time sheet ■ n. a piece of paper for recording the number of hours worked.

time signature ■ n. Music an indication of rhythm following a clef, generally expressed as a fraction with the denominator defining the beat as a division of a semibreve and the numerator giving the number of beats in each bar.

times table ■ n. informal term for **MULTIPLICATION TABLE**.

time switch ■ n. a switch automatically activated at a preset time.

timetable ■ n. a list or plan of times at which events are scheduled to take place. ■ v. schedule to take place at a particular time.

time travel ■ n. (in science fiction) travel through time into the past or the future.
– DERIVATIVES **time traveller** n.

time trial ■ n. 1 (in various sports) a test of a competitor's individual speed over a set distance. 2 an exercise designed to test the time needed for a task or activity.

time warp ■ n. an imaginary distortion of space in relation to time whereby people or objects of one period can be moved to another.

time-worn ■ adj. impaired or made less striking as a result of age or long use.

timid ■ adj. (**-er**, **-est**) lacking in courage or confidence.
– DERIVATIVES **timidity** n. **timidly** adv. **timidness** n.
– ORIGIN C16: from Latin *timidus*, from *timere* 'to fear'.

timing ■ n. 1 the choice, judgement, or control of when something should be done. 2 a particular time when something happens. ▸ (in an internal-combustion engine) the times when the valves open and close, and the time of the ignition spark, in relation to the movement of the piston in the cylinder.

Timorese /ˌtiːmɔːˈriːz/ ■ n. (pl. same) a native or inhabitant of Timor, an island in the southern Malay Archipelago. ■ adj. of or relating to Timor.

timorous ■ adj. lacking in courage or confidence; nervous.
– DERIVATIVES **timorously** adv. **timorousness** n.
– ORIGIN Middle English: from Old French *temoreus*, from Latin *timor* 'fear', from *timere* 'to fear'.

1243

timpani /'tImpəni/ (also **tympani**) ■ pl. n. kettledrums.
– DERIVATIVES **timpanist** n.
– ORIGIN C19: from Italian, pl. of *timpano* 'kettledrum', from Latin *tympanum* (see **TYMPANUM**).

tin ■ n. 1 a silvery-white metal, the chemical element of atomic number 50. (Symbol: **Sn**) 2 a lidded airtight container made of tinplate or aluminium. ▸ a sealed container for preserving food, made of tinplate or aluminium; a can. ▸ an open metal container for baking food. ■ v. (**tinned**, **tinning**) 1 cover with a thin layer of tin. 2 [usu. as adj. **tinned**] preserve in a tin: *tinned fruit*.
– PHRASES **have a tin ear** informal be tone-deaf.
– DERIVATIVES **tinner** n. **tinware** n.
– ORIGIN Old English, of Germanic origin.

tincture /'tIŋ(k)tʃə/ ■ n. 1 a medicine made by dissolving a drug in alcohol. 2 a slight trace. 3 Heraldry any of the conventional colours used in coats of arms. ■ v. (**be tinctured**) be tinged, flavoured, or imbued with a slight trace.
– ORIGIN Middle English: from Latin *tinctura* 'dyeing', from *tingere* 'to dye or colour'.

tinder ■ n. dry, flammable material, such as wood or paper, used for lighting a fire.
– DERIVATIVES **tindery** adj.
– ORIGIN Old English, of Germanic origin.

tinderbox ■ n. historical a box containing tinder, flint, a steel, and other items for kindling fires.

tine /taIn/ ■ n. a prong or sharp point.
– DERIVATIVES **tined** adj.
– ORIGIN Old English, of Germanic origin.

tinea /'tIniə/ ■ n. technical term for **RINGWORM**.
– ORIGIN Middle English: from Latin, 'worm'.

tinfoil ■ n. foil made of aluminium or a similar metal, used especially for covering or wrapping food.

tinge ■ v. (**tinging** or **tingeing**) (often **be tinged**) 1 colour slightly. 2 have a slight influence on: *a visit tinged with sadness*. ■ n. a slight trace.
– ORIGIN C15: from Latin *tingere* 'to dip or colour'.

tin glaze ■ n. a glaze made white and opaque by the addition of tin oxide.
– DERIVATIVES **tin-glazed** adj.

tingle ■ n. a slight prickling or stinging sensation. ■ v. experience or cause to experience a tingle.
– DERIVATIVES **tingly** adj.
– ORIGIN Middle English: perhaps a var. of **TINKLE**.

tin god ■ n. a person, especially a minor official, who is pompous and self-important. ▸ an object of unjustified veneration or respect.

tin hat ■ n. informal, chiefly Brit. a soldier's steel helmet.

tinker ■ n. 1 an itinerant mender of pots, kettles, etc. 2 Brit., chiefly derogatory a gypsy or other person living in an itinerant community. 3 an act of tinkering with something. ■ v. (**tinker with**) attempt in a casual manner to repair or improve.
– PHRASES **not give a tinker's curse** (or **cuss** or **damn**) informal not care at all.
– DERIVATIVES **tinkerer** n.
– ORIGIN Middle English (first recorded in Anglo-Latin as a surname).

tinkle ■ v. 1 make or cause to make a light, clear ringing sound. 2 informal urinate. ■ n. 1 a tinkling sound. ▸ Brit. informal a telephone call. 2 informal an act of urinating.
– DERIVATIVES **tinkly** adj.
– ORIGIN Middle English: from obsolete *tink* 'to chink or clink', of imitative origin.

tinktinkie /ˌtIŋkˈtIŋki/ ■ n. S. African informal any small brown bird, especially a cisticola.
– ORIGIN Afrikaans: imitative.

tinnitus /tɪˈnaɪtəs, ˈtɪnɪtəs/ ■ n. Medicine ringing or buzzing in the ears.
– ORIGIN C19: from Latin, from *tinnire* 'to ring, tinkle', of imitative origin.

tinny ■ adj. 1 having a thin, metallic sound. 2 made of thin or poor-quality metal. 3 having an unpleasantly metallic taste.
– DERIVATIVES **tinnily** adv. **tinniness** n.

tinny

tin-opener

tin-opener ■ n. a tool for opening tins of food.

tinplate ■ n. sheet steel or iron coated with tin. ■ v. coat with tin.
– DERIVATIVES **tin-plated** adj.

tinpot ■ adj. informal (especially of a country or its leader) having or showing poor leadership or organization.

tinsel ■ n. **1** a form of decoration consisting of thin strips of shiny metal foil attached to a length of thread. **2** superficial attractiveness or glamour.
– DERIVATIVES **tinselled** adj. **tinselly** adj.
– ORIGIN Middle English: from Old French *estincele* 'spark', or *estinceler* 'to sparkle', from Latin *scintilla* 'a spark'.

Tinseltown ■ n. derogatory the superficially glamorous world of Hollywood and its film industry.

tinsmith ■ n. a person who makes or repairs articles of tin or tinplate.

tinsnips ■ pl. n. a pair of clippers for cutting sheet metal.

tin soldier ■ n. a toy soldier made of metal.

tint ■ n. **1** a shade or variety of colour. ▸ a trace of something. **2** the process or dye used in artificial colouring of the hair. **3** Printing an area of faint colour printed as a half-tone. ▸ a set of parallel engraved lines giving uniform shading. ■ v. colour slightly; tinge. ▸ dye (hair) with a tint.
– DERIVATIVES **tinter** n.
– ORIGIN C18: alteration of obsolete *tinct* 'to colour, tint', from Latin *tinctus* 'dyeing'.

Tinta Barocca ■ n. a variety of black grape originally from the Douro region of Portugal. ▸ a red wine made from this grape.

tintinnabulation /ˌtɪntɪnæbjʊˈleɪʃ(ə)n/ ■ n. a ringing or tinkling sound.
– ORIGIN C19: from Latin *tintinnabulum* 'tinkling bell'.

tin whistle ■ n. another term for PENNY WHISTLE.

tiny ■ adj. (**-ier**, **-iest**) very small. ■ n. (pl. **-ies**) informal a very young child.
– DERIVATIVES **tinily** adv. **tininess** n.
– ORIGIN C16: extension of obsolete *tine* 'small, diminutive'.

-tion ■ suffix forming nouns of action, condition, etc. such as *completion*.
– ORIGIN from Latin.

tip¹ ■ n. the pointed or rounded extremity of something slender or tapering. ▸ a small part fitted to the end of an object. ■ v. (**tipped**, **tipping**) **1** attach to or cover the tip of. **2** colour (something) at its tip or edge.
– PHRASES **on the tip of one's tongue** almost but not quite spoken or coming to mind.
– DERIVATIVES **tipped** adj.
– ORIGIN Middle English: from Old Norse *typpi* (n.), *typpa* (v.), *typptr* 'tipped'.

tip² ■ v. (**tipped**, **tipping**) **1** overbalance or cause to overbalance so as to fall or turn over. ▸ be or cause to be in a sloping position. **2** empty out (the contents of a container) by holding it at an angle. ▸ (**it tips down**), **it is tipping down**, etc. Brit. informal rain heavily. **3** strike or touch lightly. ▸ cause to move by a light strike or touch. **4** (**tip off**) Basketball put the ball in play by throwing it up between two opponents. ■ n. chiefly Brit. a place where rubbish is left. ▸ informal a dirty or untidy place.
– PHRASES **tip one's hand** N. Amer. informal reveal one's intentions inadvertently. **tip one's hat** raise or touch one's hat as a greeting or mark of respect.
– ORIGIN Middle English: perhaps of Scandinavian origin, influenced later by TIP¹ in the sense 'touch with a tip or point'.

tip³ ■ n. **1** a small sum of money given as a reward for services rendered. **2** a piece of practical advice. ▸ a prediction or piece of expert information about the likely winner of a race or contest. ■ v. (**tipped**, **tipping**) **1** give a tip to. **2** predict as likely to win or achieve something. **3** (**tip someone off**) informal give someone confidential information.
– PHRASES **tip someone the wink** Brit. informal secretly give someone confidential information.
– ORIGIN C17: prob. from TIP¹.

tip-and-run ■ n. an informal way of playing cricket in which the batsman must run after every hit.

tipi ■ n. variant spelling of TEEPEE.

tip-in ■ n. Basketball a score made by tipping a rebound into the basket.

tip-off ■ n. informal a piece of confidential information.

tipper ■ n. **1** a truck having a rear platform which can be raised at its front end, thus enabling a load to be discharged. **2** a person who regularly leaves a specified size of tip as a reward.

tippet ■ n. a woman's fur cape or woollen shawl.
– ORIGIN Middle English: prob. from an Anglo-Norman French derivative of TIP¹.

Tipp-Ex (also **Tippex**) ■ n. trademark a type of correction fluid. ■ v. delete with correction fluid.
– ORIGIN 1960s: from German, from *tippen* 'to type' and Latin *ex* 'out'.

tipping point ■ n. the point at which a slow gradual change accelerates and becomes irreversible, often with major consequences.

tipple ■ v. drink alcohol regularly. ■ n. informal an alcoholic drink.
– ORIGIN C15: back-formation from TIPPLER¹.

tippler¹ ■ n. a habitual drinker of alcohol.
– ORIGIN Middle English (denoting a retailer of alcoholic liquor).

tippler² ■ n. a revolving frame or cage in which a truck is inverted to discharge its load.
– ORIGIN C19: from dialect *tipple* 'tumble over'.

tippy-toe ■ v. informal, chiefly N. Amer. tiptoe.
– PHRASES **on tippy-toe** (or **tippy-toes**) on tiptoe.
– ORIGIN C19: alteration of TIPTOE.

tipster ■ n. a person who gives tips, especially about the likely winner of a race or contest.

tipsy ■ adj. (**-ier**, **-iest**) slightly drunk.
– DERIVATIVES **tipsily** adv. **tipsiness** n.
– ORIGIN C16: from the verb TIP².

tipsy tart ■ n. S. African a baked dessert made with nuts, dates, and a brandy sauce.

tiptoe ■ v. (**tiptoes**, **tiptoed**, **tiptoeing**) walk quietly and carefully with one's heels raised and one's weight on the balls of the feet.
– PHRASES **on tiptoe** (or **tiptoes**) with one's heels raised and one's weight on the balls of the feet.

tip-top ■ adj. of the very best; excellent. ■ n. **1** the highest part or point of excellence. **2** S. African & N. Amer. a line guide on a fishing rod.

Tiptronic ■ adj. trademark denoting an electronically-controlled car transmission system which permits the driver to select either automatic or manual gear shifts.

tip-up ■ adj. **1** denoting a seat that tips up vertically when unoccupied. **2** denoting the raisable rear platform of a tipper truck.

tirade /tʌɪˈreɪd, tɪ-/ ■ n. a long speech of angry criticism or accusation.
– ORIGIN C19: from French, 'long speech'.

tiramisu /ˌtɪrəmɪˈsuː/ ■ n. an Italian dessert consisting of layers of sponge cake soaked in coffee and brandy or liqueur, with powdered chocolate and mascarpone cheese.
– ORIGIN Italian, from the phr. *tira mi sù* 'pick me up'.

tire¹ ■ v. become or cause to become in need of rest or sleep. ▸ exhaust the patience or interest of. ▸ (**tire of**) become impatient or bored with.
– ORIGIN Old English *tēorian* (also in the sense 'fail, come to an end').

tire² ■ n. US spelling of TYRE.

tired ■ adj. **1** in need of sleep or rest; weary. **2** (of a thing) no longer fresh or in good condition. ▸ boring or uninteresting because overfamiliar: *tired clichés*. ▸ (**tired of**) bored or impatient with.
– PHRASES **tired and emotional** euphemistic drunk.
– DERIVATIVES **tiredly** adv. **tiredness** n.

tireless ■ adj. having or showing great effort or energy.
– DERIVATIVES **tirelessly** adv. **tirelessness** n.

tiresome ■ adj. causing one to feel bored or impatient.
– DERIVATIVES **tiresomely** adv. **tiresomeness** n.

tiro ■ n. variant spelling of TYRO.

'tis ■ contr. chiefly poetic/literary it is.

tisane /tɪˈzan/ ■ n. a herb tea.
– ORIGIN 1930s: from French.

Tishri /ˈtɪʃriː/ (also **Tisri** /ˈtɪzriː/) ■ n. (in the Jewish calendar) the first month of the civil and seventh of the religious year, usually coinciding with parts of September and October.
– ORIGIN from Hebrew *tišrī*.

tissue /ˈtɪʃuː, ˈtɪsjuː/ ■ n. **1** any of the distinct types of material of which animals or plants are made, consisting of specialized cells and their products. **2** tissue paper. ▸ a piece of absorbent paper, used especially as a disposable handkerchief. **3** fabric of a delicate gauzy texture. **4** a web-like structure or network: *a tissue of lies*.
– DERIVATIVES **tissuey** adj.
– ORIGIN Middle English: from Old French *tissu* 'woven', from *tistre*, from Latin *texere* 'to weave'.

tissue culture ■ n. Biology & Medicine the growth in an artificial medium of cells derived from living tissue. ▸ a cell culture of this kind.

tissue paper ■ n. very thin, soft paper.

tissue type ■ n. a class of tissues which are immunologically compatible with one another. ■ v. (**tissue-type**) determine the tissue type of.
– DERIVATIVES **tissue-typing** n.

tit¹ ■ n. a titmouse.
– ORIGIN C16: prob. of Scandinavian origin.

tit² ■ n. **1** vulgar slang a woman's breast. **2** informal, chiefly Brit. a foolish or ineffectual person. **3** military slang a push-button, especially one used to fire a gun or release a bomb.
– PHRASES **get on someone's tits** vulgar slang irritate someone intensely.
– ORIGIN Old English *tit* 'teat, nipple', of Germanic origin.

tit³ ■ n. (in phr. **tit for tat**) the infliction of an injury or insult in retaliation for one received.
– ORIGIN C16: var. of obsolete *tip for tap*.

Titan /ˈtaɪt(ə)n/ ■ n. **1** any of a family of giant gods in Greek mythology. **2** (**titan**) a person or thing of very great strength, intellect, or importance.

titanate /ˈtaɪtəneɪt/ ■ n. Chemistry a salt in which the anion contains both titanium and oxygen.

titanic¹ ■ adj. of exceptional strength, size, or power.
– DERIVATIVES **titanically** adv.
– ORIGIN from Greek *titanikos*, from *Titan* (see TITAN).

titanic² ■ adj. Chemistry of titanium with a valency of four; of titanium(IV). Compare with TITANOUS.
– ORIGIN C19: from TITANIUM.

titanium /tɪˈteɪnɪəm, tʌɪ-/ ■ n. the chemical element of atomic number 22, a hard silver-grey metal used in strong, light, corrosion-resistant alloys. (Symbol: **Ti**)
– ORIGIN C18: from TITAN, on the pattern of *uranium*.

titanium dioxide (also **titanium oxide**) ■ n. a white unreactive solid which occurs naturally as the mineral rutile and is used extensively as a white pigment. [TiO_2.]

titanous /ˈtaɪtənəs/ ■ adj. Chemistry of titanium with a lower valency, usually three. Compare with TITANIC².
– ORIGIN C19: from TITANIUM, on the pattern of *ferrous*.

titbit (N. Amer. **tidbit**) ■ n. **1** a small piece of tasty food. **2** a small and particularly interesting item of gossip or information.
– ORIGIN C17 (as *tyd bit, tid-bit*): from dialect *tid* 'tender' + BIT¹.

titch (also **tich**) ■ n. Brit. informal a small person.
– DERIVATIVES **titchy** adj. (**-ier, -iest**).
– ORIGIN 1930s: from *Little Tich*, stage name of Harry Relph, an English music-hall comedian of small stature, given the nickname because he resembled Arthur Orton, the unsuccessful claimant to the valuable Tichborne estate.

titer ■ n. US spelling of TITRE.

tithe /tʌɪð/ ■ n. one tenth of annual produce or earnings, formerly taken as a tax for the support of the Church and clergy. ■ v. subject to or pay as a tithe.
– ORIGIN Old English *tēotha* (adj. in the ordinal sense 'tenth').

titular

tithe barn ■ n. a barn built to hold produce made over as tithes.

tithing /ˈtʌɪðɪŋ/ ■ n. the practice of taking or paying a tithe.
– ORIGIN Old English *tēothung* (see TITHE).

Titian /ˈtɪʃ(ə)n/ ■ adj. (of hair) bright golden auburn.
– ORIGIN C19: from *Titian*, C16 Italian painter, by association with the bright auburn hair portrayed in many of his works.

titillate /ˈtɪtɪleɪt/ ■ v. **1** arouse to mild excitement or interest, especially through images or words. **2** archaic lightly touch; tickle.
– DERIVATIVES **titillating** adj. **titillatingly** adv. **titillation** n.
– ORIGIN C17 (*titillation* Middle English): from Latin *titillare* 'tickle'.

titivate /ˈtɪtɪveɪt/ ■ v. informal adorn or smarten up. ▸ (**titivate oneself**) adjust one's appearance.
– DERIVATIVES **titivation** n.
– ORIGIN C19 (in early use, also *tidivate*): perhaps from TIDY.

title ■ n. **1** the name of a book, musical composition, or other artistic work. ▸ a caption or credit in a film or broadcast. **2** a name that describes someone's position or job. **3** a word used before or instead of someone's name, indicating social or official rank, profession, or academic or marital status. **4** a descriptive or distinctive name that is earned or chosen: *the title of Best Restaurant of the Year*. **5** the position of being the champion of a major sports competition: *he won the world title*. **6** Law a right or claim to the ownership of property or to a rank or throne. ■ v. (usu. **be titled**) give a title to.
– DERIVATIVES **titled** adj.
– ORIGIN Old English *titul*, reinforced by Old French *title*, both from Latin *titulus* 'inscription, title'.

title deed ■ n. a legal document constituting evidence of a right, especially to ownership of property.

title music ■ n. music played during the credits at the beginning or end of a television programme or film.

title role ■ n. the part in a play or film from which the work's title is taken.

titmouse ■ n. (pl. **titmice**) a small songbird, typically foraging acrobatically among foliage and branches. [Many species, chiefly in the family Paridae.]
– ORIGIN Middle English: from TIT¹ + obsolete *mose* 'titmouse' (assimilated to MOUSE).

titrate /tʌɪˈtreɪt, tɪ-/ ■ v. **1** Chemistry ascertain the amount of a substance in (a solution) by measuring the volume of a standard reagent required to react with it. **2** Medicine continuously measure and adjust (a physiological function or drug dosage).
– DERIVATIVES **titratable** adj. **titration** n.
– ORIGIN C19: from French *titrer*, from *titre* in the sense 'fineness of alloyed gold or silver'.

titre /ˈtʌɪtə, ˈtiːtə/ (US **titer**) ■ n. **1** Chemistry the concentration of a solution as determined by titration. **2** Medicine the concentration of an antibody, determined by finding the highest dilution at which it is still active.
– ORIGIN C19: from French, from *titrer* (see TITRATE).

ti tree ■ n. variant spelling of TEA TREE.

titter ■ n. a short, half-suppressed laugh. ■ v. give a titter.
– DERIVATIVES **titterer** n. **tittering** n. & adj. **titteringly** adv.
– ORIGIN C17: imitative.

tittle ■ n. a tiny amount or part of something.
– ORIGIN Middle English: from Latin *titulus* (see TITLE), in medieval Latin, 'small stroke, accent'.

tittle-tattle ■ n. gossip. ■ v. engage in gossip.
– ORIGIN C16: reduplication of TATTLE.

tittup /ˈtɪtəp/ ■ v. (**tittuped, tittuping** or **tittupped, tittupping**) chiefly Brit. (in horse riding) proceed with jerky or exaggerated movements.
– ORIGIN C17 (as n.): perhaps imitative of hoof-beats.

titty (also **tittie**) ■ n. (pl. **-ies**) another term for TIT².

titular /ˈtɪtjʊlə/ ■ adj. **1** of or relating to a title. **2** holding or constituting a formal position or title without any real authority. ▸ (of a cleric) nominally appointed to serve a

tizzy

diocese, abbey, etc. no longer in existence (typically having real authority elsewhere).
– DERIVATIVES **titularly** adv.

tizzy (also **tizz**) ■ n. (pl. **-ies**) informal a state of nervous excitement or agitation.
– ORIGIN 1930s (orig. US).

tjaila /ˈtʃʌɪlə/ ■ n. & v. variant spelling of **SHAYILE**.

tjorrie /ˈtʃɒri/ (also **chorrie**) ■ n. S. African informal a jalopy.
– ORIGIN from Afrikaans *tjor* 'jalopy'.

T-junction ■ n. a junction in the shape of a 'T', especially a road junction at which one road joins another at right angles without crossing it.

TKO ■ abbrev. Boxing technical knockout.

Tl ■ symb. the chemical element thallium.

TLC ■ abbrev. **1** informal tender loving care. **2** S. African Transitional Local Council.

T-lymphocyte ■ n. Physiology a lymphocyte of a type produced or processed by the thymus gland and participating in the cell-mediated immune response. Compare with **B-LYMPHOCYTE**.
– ORIGIN 1970s: from *T* for *thymus*.

TM ■ abbrev. (trademark in the US) Transcendental Meditation.

Tm ■ symb. the chemical element thulium.

tmesis /ˈtmiːsɪs/ ■ n. (pl. **tmeses** /-siːz/) the separation of parts of a compound word by an intervening word (used informally for emphasis, e.g. *can't find it any-blooming-where*).
– ORIGIN C16: from Greek *tmēsis* 'cutting'.

TNT ■ abbrev. trinitrotoluene, a high explosive made by nitrating toluene.

to ■ prep. **1** expressing direction or position in relation to a particular location, point, or condition. ▸ (in telling the time) before (the hour specified). **2** identifying the person or thing affected. **3** identifying a particular relationship between one person or thing and another. ▸ indicating a rate of return on something: *ten miles to the gallon*. **4** indicating that two things are attached. **5** governing a phrase expressing someone's reaction to something: *to her astonishment, he smiled*. **6** used to introduce the second element in a comparison. **7** placed before a debit entry in accounting. ■ infinitive marker **1** used with the base form of a verb to indicate that the verb is in the infinitive. ▸ (**about to**) forming a future tense with reference to the immediate future. **2** used without a verb following when the missing verb is clearly understood: *she said she didn't want to*. ■ adv. so as to be closed or nearly closed.
– ORIGIN Old English, of West Germanic origin.

toad ■ n. **1** a tailless amphibian with a short stout body and short legs, typically having dry warty skin that can exude poison. [Many species, chiefly in the family Bufonidae.] **2** a detestable person.
– ORIGIN Old English.

toadfish ■ n. (pl. same or **-fishes**) a fish of warm seas with a wide head and large mouth, able to produce loud grunts. [Family Batrachoididae: several species.]

toad-in-the-hole ■ n. Brit. a dish consisting of sausages baked in batter.

toadstool ■ n. the spore-bearing fruiting body of a fungus, typically in the form of a rounded cap on a stalk, especially one that is inedible or poisonous.
– ORIGIN Middle English: a fanciful name.

toady ■ n. (pl. **-ies**) a person who behaves obsequiously towards others. ■ v. (**-ies**, **-ied**) act obsequiously.
– DERIVATIVES **toadyish** adj. **toadyism** n.
– ORIGIN C19: said to be a contraction of *toad-eater*, a charlatan's assistant who ate toads (regarded as poisonous) as a demonstration of the efficacy of the charlatan's remedy.

to and fro ■ adv. in a constant movement backwards and forwards or from side to side. ■ v. (**be toing and froing**) be moving to and fro. ▸ vacillate. ■ n. constant movement backwards and forwards. ▸ vacillation.
– DERIVATIVES **toing and froing** n.

toast¹ ■ n. **1** sliced bread browned on both sides by exposure to radiant heat. **2** an act or instance of raising glasses at a gathering and drinking together in honour of a person or thing. ▸ a person who is toasted or held in high regard. ■ v. **1** cook or brown by exposure to radiant heat. ▸ warm (oneself or part of one's body) beside a fire or other source or heat. **2** drink a toast to.
– PHRASES **be toast** informal, chiefly N. Amer. be finished, defunct, or dead. **have someone on toast** Brit. informal be in a position to deal with someone as one wishes.
– DERIVATIVES **toasted** adj. **toasty** adj. (**-ier**, **-iest**).

HISTORY
The verb **toast** entered Middle English meaning 'burn as the sun does, parch'; it came from Old French *toster* 'roast', from Latin *torrere* 'parch' (past participle *tostus*). The notion of drinking a *toast* goes back to the late 17th century, and originated in the practice of naming a lady whose health the company was requested to drink; the lady's name was supposed to flavour the drink like the pieces of spiced toast that were formerly added to wine.

toast² ■ v. (of a DJ) accompany a reggae backing track or music with improvised rhythmic speech.
– DERIVATIVES **toasting** n.
– ORIGIN C20: perhaps the same word as **TOAST¹**.

toaster ■ n. **1** an electrical device for making toast. **2** a DJ who toasts.

toastie ■ n. Brit. informal a toasted sandwich or snack.

toasting fork ■ n. a long-handled fork for making toast in front of a fire.

toastmaster (or **toastmistress**) ■ n. an official responsible for proposing toasts, introducing speakers, and making other formal announcements at a large social event.

tobacco ■ n. (pl. **-os**) **1** a preparation of the dried and fermented nicotine-rich leaves of an American plant, used for smoking or chewing. **2** the plant of the nightshade family yielding these leaves. [*Nicotiana tabacum*.]
– ORIGIN C16: from Spanish *tabaco*; perhaps from a Carib word denoting a tobacco pipe or from a Taino word for a primitive cigar, or from Arabic.

tobacco mosaic virus ■ n. a virus that causes mosaic disease in tobacco, much used in biochemical research.

tobacconist ■ n. a shopkeeper who sells cigarettes and tobacco.

tobacco plant ■ n. the plant which yields tobacco. See **TOBACCO** (sense 2). ▸ an ornamental plant related to this. [Genus *Nicotiana*.]

Tobagan /təˈbeɪɡən/ ■ n. a native or inhabitant of the Caribbean island of Tobago. ■ adj. of or relating to Tobago.

toboggan ■ n. a light, narrow vehicle, typically on runners, used for sliding downhill over snow or ice. ■ v. ride on a toboggan.
– DERIVATIVES **tobogganer** n. **tobogganing** n. **tobogganist** n.
– ORIGIN C19: from Canadian French *tabaganne*, from Micmac (an Algonquian language) *topaǧan* 'sled'.

toby jug ■ n. chiefly Brit. a beer jug or mug in the form of a stout old man wearing a three-cornered hat.
– ORIGIN C19: familiar form of the given name *Tobias*, and said to come from a poem (C18) about *Toby Philpot* (with a pun on *fill pot*), a soldier who liked to drink.

toccata /təˈkɑːtə/ ■ n. a musical composition for a keyboard instrument designed to exhibit the performer's touch and technique.
– ORIGIN C18: from Italian, from *toccare* 'to touch'.

tocopherol /tɒˈkɒfərɒl/ ■ n. Biochemistry vitamin E, any of a group of compounds found in wheatgerm oil, egg yolk, and leafy vegetables and important in the stabilization of cell membranes.
– ORIGIN 1930s: from Greek *tokos* 'offspring' + *pherein* 'to bear'.

tocsin /ˈtɒksɪn/ ■ n. archaic an alarm bell or signal.
– ORIGIN C16: from Old French *toquassen*, from Provençal *tocasenh*, from *tocar* 'to touch' + *senh* 'signal bell'.

tod ■ n. (in phr. **on one's tod**) Brit. informal on one's own.
– ORIGIN 1930s: from rhyming slang *Tod Sloan*, the name of an American jockey.

today ■ adv. on or in the course of this present day. ▸ at the present period of time; nowadays. ■ n. this present

day. ▸ the present period of time.
– PHRASES **today week** a week from today.
– ORIGIN Old English *tō dæg* 'on (this) day'; cf. **TOMORROW** and **TONIGHT**.

toddle ■ v. (of a young child) move with short unsteady steps while learning to walk. ▸ informal walk or go in a casual or leisurely way. ■ n. an act of toddling.
– ORIGIN C16.

toddler ■ n. a young child who is just beginning to walk.
– DERIVATIVES **toddlerhood** n.

toddy ■ n. (pl. **-ies**) **1** a drink made of spirits with hot water and sugar. **2** the sap of some kinds of palm, fermented to produce arrack.
– ORIGIN C17: from Marathi *tāḍī*, Hindi *tāṛī*, from Sanskrit *tāḍī* 'palmyra'.

to-do ■ n. informal a commotion or fuss.
– ORIGIN C16: from *to do* as in *much to do*, orig. meaning 'much needing to be done' but later interpreted as the adjective *much* and a noun; cf. **ADO**.

toe ■ n. **1** any of the five digits at the end of the human foot. ▸ any of the digits of the foot of a quadruped or bird. ▸ the part of an item of footwear that covers a person's toes. **2** the lower end, tip, or point of something. ▸ the tip of the head of a golf club. ■ v. (**toes**, **toed**, **toeing**) push, touch, or kick with one's toes. ▸ Golf strike (the ball) with the toe of the club.
– PHRASES **make someone's toes curl** informal bring about an extreme reaction of delight or disgust in someone. **on one's toes** ready and alert. **toe the line** comply with authority, especially unwillingly or under pressure. **turn up one's toes** informal die.
– DERIVATIVES **toed** adj. **toeless** adj.
– ORIGIN Old English, of Germanic origin.

toecap ■ n. a piece of steel or leather constituting or fitted over the front part of a boot or shoe.

toe clip ■ n. a clip on a bicycle pedal to prevent the foot from slipping.

toehold ■ n. **1** a small foothold. **2** a tentative position from which further progress may be made.

toe loop ■ n. Skating a jump in which the skater makes a full turn in the air, taking off from and landing on the outside edge of the same foot.

toenadering /ˈtuːnɑːdərɪŋ/ ■ n. S. African a closer association between people or groups, especially politically; a rapprochement.
– ORIGIN Afrikaans, from *toenader* 'approach, meet halfway'.

toenail ■ n. a nail on the upper surface of the tip of each toe.

toerag ■ n. Brit. informal a contemptible person.
– ORIGIN C19: orig. denoting a rag wrapped round the foot as a sock or, by extension, the wearer (such as a vagrant).

toe-tapping ■ adj. informal (of music) making one want to tap one's feet; lively.

toff ■ n. Brit. informal, derogatory a rich or upper-class person.
– ORIGIN C19: perhaps an alteration of **TUFT**, used to denote a gold tassel worn on the cap by titled undergraduates at Oxford and Cambridge universities.

toffee ■ n. a kind of firm or hard sweet which softens when sucked or chewed, made by boiling together sugar and butter.
– PHRASES **not be able to do something for toffee** Brit. informal be totally incompetent at doing something.
– ORIGIN C19: alteration of **TAFFY**.

toffee apple ■ n. an apple coated with a thin layer of toffee and fixed on a stick.

toffee-nosed ■ adj. informal, chiefly Brit. pretentiously superior; snobbish.
– DERIVATIVES **toffee nose** n.

tofu /ˈtəʊfuː/ ■ n. curd made from mashed soya beans, used chiefly in Asian and vegetarian cookery.
– ORIGIN from Japanese *tōfu*, from Chinese *dòufu*, from *dòu* 'beans' + *fŭ* 'rot, turn sour'.

tog¹ informal ■ n. (**togs**) clothes. ■ v. (**togged**, **togging**) (**be/get togged up/out**) be or get fully dressed for a particular occasion or activity.
– ORIGIN C18: an abbrev. of obsolete criminals' slang *togeman(s)* 'a light cloak', from French *toge* or Latin *toga* (see **TOGA**).

tog² ■ n. Brit. a unit of thermal resistance used to express the insulating properties of clothes and quilts.
– ORIGIN 1940s: from **TOG¹**, on the pattern of an earlier unit called the *clo* (first element of *clothes*).

toga /ˈtəʊɡə/ ■ n. a loose flowing outer garment worn by the citizens of ancient Rome, made of a single piece of cloth and covering the whole body apart from the right arm.
– ORIGIN Latin; rel. to *tegere* 'to cover'.

together ■ adv. **1** with or in proximity to another person or people. ▸ so as to touch or combine. ▸ in combination; collectively. ▸ into companionship or close association. ▸ (of two people) married or in a sexual relationship. ▸ so as to be united or in agreement. **2** at the same time. **3** without interruption. ■ adj. informal level-headed and well organized.
– PHRASES **together with** as well as.
– DERIVATIVES **togetherness** n.
– ORIGIN Old English *tōgædere*, based on the prep. **TO** + a West Germanic word rel. to **GATHER**.

toggle ■ n. **1** a narrow piece of wood or plastic attached to one side of a garment, pushed through a loop on the other side to act as a fastener. ▸ a pin or other crosspiece put through the eye of a rope or a link of a chain to keep it in place. ▸ (also **toggle bolt**) a kind of wall fastener for use on open-backed plasterboard, having a part that springs open or turns through 90° after it is inserted so as to prevent withdrawal. **2** Computing a key or command that is operated the same way but with opposite effect on successive occasions. ■ v. **1** Computing switch from one effect, feature, or state to another by using a toggle. **2** provide or fasten with a toggle or toggles.
– ORIGIN C18 (orig. in nautical use).

toggle switch ■ n. **1** an electric switch operated by means of a projecting lever that is moved up and down. **2** Computing another term for **TOGGLE**.

Togolese /ˌtəʊɡəˈliːz/ ■ n. (pl. same) a native or inhabitant of Togo, a country in West Africa. ■ adj. of or relating to Togo.

togt /tɒxt/ ■ adj. S. African, chiefly historical denoting or relating to casual employment or daily-paid labour.
– ORIGIN Afrikaans, from Dutch *tocht* 'expedition, journey'.

toil ■ v. work extremely hard or incessantly. ▸ move somewhere slowly and with difficulty. ■ n. exhausting work.
– DERIVATIVES **toiler** n.
– ORIGIN Middle English: from Anglo-Norman French *toiler* 'strive, dispute', *toil* 'confusion', from Latin *tudiculare* 'stir about', from *tudicula* 'machine for crushing olives'.

toile /twɑːl/ ■ n. **1** an early version of a finished garment made up in cheap material so that the design can be tested. **2** a translucent fabric. **3** short for **TOILE DE JOUY**.
– ORIGIN Middle English: from French *toile* 'cloth, web', from Latin *tela* 'web'.

toile de Jouy /də ˈʒwiː/ ■ n. a type of printed calico with a characteristic blue or red floral, figure, or landscape design on a light background.
– ORIGIN orig. made at *Jouy*-en-Josas, near Paris.

toilet ■ n. **1** a large bowl for urinating or defecating into, typically plumbed into a sewage system. **2** the process of washing oneself, dressing, and attending to one's appearance. ▸ [as modifier] denoting articles used in this process. ▸ v. (**toileted**, **toileting**) [usu. as noun **toileting**] assist or supervise (an infant or invalid) in using a toilet.

HISTORY
Toilet came from French *toilette* 'cloth, wrapper' and ultimately from Latin *tela* 'woven material, web'. In 16th-century English a **toilet** was originally a cloth for wrapping clothes, then a cloth cover for a dressing table, the articles used in dressing, and eventually the process of dressing and washing oneself. In the 19th century **toilet** came to denote a dressing room with washing facilities; from this the modern meaning of 'lavatory' arose in the early 20th century.

toilet bag ■ n. a waterproof bag for holding toothpaste, soap, etc. when travelling.

toilet paper ■ n. paper for wiping oneself clean after urination or defecation.

toiletries ■ pl. n. articles used in washing and taking care of one's body, such as soap and shampoo.

toilet set ■ n. a set of items used in arranging the hair, typically including a hairbrush, comb, and mirror.

toilette /twɑːˈlet/ ■ n. old-fashioned term for TOILET (in sense 2).
– ORIGIN C17: French (see TOILET).

toilet tissue ■ n. toilet paper.

toilet-train ■ v. teach (a young child) to use the toilet.

toilet water ■ n. a dilute form of perfume.

toils ■ pl. n. poetic/literary a situation regarded as a trap.
– ORIGIN C16 (denoting a net into which a hunted quarry is driven): pl. of *toil*, from Old French *toile* (see TOILE).

toilsome ■ adj. archaic or poetic/literary involving hard work.
– DERIVATIVES **toilsomely** adv. **toilsomeness** n.

toilworn ■ adj. poetic/literary exhausted by toil.

toise /tɔɪz/ ■ n. historical a former French unit of length, equal to about 1.95 metres.
– ORIGIN from French.

tokamak /ˈtəʊkəmak/ ■ n. Physics a toroidal (torus-shaped) apparatus for producing controlled fusion reactions in hot plasma.
– ORIGIN 1960s: Russian, from *toroidal'naya kameras magnitnym polem* 'toroidal chamber with magnetic field'.

Tokay /təʊˈkeɪ/ ■ n. a sweet aromatic wine, originally made near Tokaj in Hungary.

toke informal ■ n. a pull on a cigarette or pipe, typically one containing cannabis. ■ v. smoke cannabis or tobacco.
– DERIVATIVES **toker** n.
– ORIGIN 1950s.

token ■ n. **1** a thing serving to represent a fact, quality, feeling, etc. ▸ archaic a badge or favour worn to indicate allegiance to a person or party. ▸ archaic a word or object conferring authority on or serving to authenticate the speaker or holder. **2** a voucher that can be exchanged for goods or services. ▸ a metal or plastic disc used to operate a machine or in exchange for particular goods or services. **3** Linguistics an individual occurrence of a linguistic unit in speech or writing. Contrasted with TYPE. **4** Computing a sequence of bits passed between nodes in a fixed order and enabling a node to transmit information. ■ adj. **1** done for the sake of appearances or as a symbolic gesture. **2** chosen by way of tokenism to represent a particular group.
– PHRASES **by the same** (or **that** or **this**) **token** in the same way or for the same reason. **in token of** as a sign or symbol of.
– ORIGIN Old English, of Germanic origin.

tokenism ■ n. the practice of making only a perfunctory or symbolic effort to do a particular thing, especially by recruiting a small number of people from under-represented groups in order to give the appearance of sexual or racial equality within a workforce.
– DERIVATIVES **tokenistic** adj.

token ring ■ n. Computing a local area network in which a node can transmit only when in possession of a token, which is passed to each node in turn.

tokoloshe /ˈtɒkəlɒʃ, ˌtɒkəˈlɔːʃi/ (also **tikoloshe**) ■ n. (in southern African folklore) an evil imp or goblin, active mainly at night.
– ORIGIN from isiZulu *utokoloshe* or isiXhosa *uthikoloshe*, denoting a river-sprite.

toktokkie /ˌtɒkˈtɒki/ ■ n. S. African informal a brownish-black beetle, which makes a distinctive sound by tapping its abdomen on the ground. [Family Tenebrionidae.]
– ORIGIN Afrikaans, from Dutch *tokken* 'to tap'.

tolbooth ■ n. variant spelling of TOLLBOOTH.

told past and past participle of TELL[1].

tole /təʊl/ (also **tôle** /tɔːl/) ■ n. painted, enamelled, or lacquered tin plate used to make decorative domestic objects.
– ORIGIN 1940s: French *tôle* 'sheet iron'.

tolerable ■ adj. **1** able to be tolerated. **2** fairly good.
– DERIVATIVES **tolerability** n. **tolerably** adv.
– ORIGIN Middle English: from Latin *tolerabilis*, from *tolerare* (see TOLERATE).

tolerance ■ n. **1** the ability, willingness, or capacity to tolerate something. **2** an allowable amount of variation of a specified quantity, especially in the dimensions of a machine or part.
– ORIGIN Middle English: from Latin *tolerantia*, from *tolerare* (see TOLERATE).

tolerant ■ adj. **1** showing tolerance. **2** (of a plant, animal, or machine) able to endure specified conditions or treatment.
– DERIVATIVES **tolerantly** adv.

tolerate ■ v. **1** allow the existence or occurrence of (something that one dislikes or disagrees with) without interference. **2** endure (someone or something unpleasant) with forbearance. **3** be capable of continued exposure to (a drug, toxin, etc.) without adverse reaction.
– DERIVATIVES **toleration** n. **tolerator** n.
– ORIGIN C16 (*toleration* C15): from Latin *tolerare* 'endure'.

toll[1] /təʊl/ ■ n. **1** a charge payable to use a bridge or road. ▸ S. African & N. Amer. a charge for a long-distance telephone call. **2** the number of deaths or casualties arising from an accident, disaster, etc. **3** the cost or damage resulting from something. ■ v. [usu. as noun **tolling**] charge a toll for the use of (a bridge or road).
– PHRASES **take its toll** (or **take a heavy toll**) have an adverse effect.
– ORIGIN Old English, from medieval Latin *toloneum*, alteration of late Latin *teloneum*, from Greek *telōnion* 'toll house', from *telos* 'tax'.

toll[2] /təʊl/ ■ v. (with reference to a bell) sound or cause to sound with a slow, uniform succession of strokes. ▸ (of a bell) announce (the time, a service, or a person's death) in this way. ■ n. a single ring of a bell.
– ORIGIN Middle English: prob. a special use of dialect *toll* 'drag, pull'.

tollbooth (also **tolbooth**) ■ n. a roadside kiosk where tolls are paid.

toll gate ■ n. a barrier across a road where a toll must be paid to proceed further.

toll plaza ■ n. S. African & US a row of tollbooths on a toll road.

Toltec /ˈtɒltɛk/ ■ n. a member of an American Indian people that flourished in Mexico before the Aztecs.
– DERIVATIVES **Toltecan** adj.
– ORIGIN via Spanish from Nahuatl *toltecatl* 'a person from *Tula* (a town and former Toltec site in central Mexico)'.

toluene /ˈtɒljuiːn/ ■ n. Chemistry a colourless liquid hydrocarbon resembling benzene, present in coal tar and petroleum.
– ORIGIN C19: from *tolu*, denoting a fragrant South American balsam.

tom ■ n. the male of various animals, especially a domestic cat.
– ORIGIN Middle English (denoting an ordinary man): abbrev. of the given name *Thomas*.

Tom, Dick, and Harry (also **Tom, Dick, or Harry**) ■ n. ordinary people in general.

tomahawk /ˈtɒməhɔːk/ ■ n. a light axe formerly used as a tool or weapon by American Indians.
– ORIGIN C17: from a Virginia Algonquian language.

tomatillo /ˌtɒməˈtɪləʊ, -ˈtiːjəʊ, -ˈtiːljəʊ/ ■ n. (pl. **-os**) **1** an edible purple or yellow fruit used for sauces and preserves. **2** the Mexican plant which bears this fruit. [*Physalis philadelphica*.]
– ORIGIN C20: from Spanish, diminutive of *tomate* 'tomato'.

tomato ■ n. (pl. **-oes**) **1** a glossy red or yellow edible fruit, eaten as a vegetable or in salads. **2** the South American plant of the nightshade family which produces this fruit. [*Lycopersicon esculentum*.]
– DERIVATIVES **tomatoey** adj.
– ORIGIN C17: from French, Spanish, or Portuguese *tomate*, from Nahuatl *tomatl*.

tomb ■ n. **1** a burial place, especially a large underground vault. ▸ a monument to a dead person, erected over their

burial place. **2 (the tomb)** poetic/literary death.
– ORIGIN Middle English: from Old French *tombe*, from late Latin *tumba*, from Greek *tumbos*.

tombola /tɒmˈbəʊlə/ ■ n. a game, typically played at a fête or fair, in which tickets are drawn from a revolving drum to win prizes.
– ORIGIN C19: from French or Italian, from Italian *tombolare* 'turn a somersault'.

tombolo /ˈtɒmbələʊ/ ■ n. (pl. **-os**) a bar of sand or shingle joining an island to the mainland.
– ORIGIN C19: from Italian, 'sand dune'.

tomboy ■ n. a girl who enjoys rough, noisy activities traditionally associated with boys.
– DERIVATIVES **tomboyish** adj. **tomboyishness** n.

tombstone ■ n. a large, flat inscribed stone standing or laid over a grave.

tomcat ■ n. a male domestic cat.

tome ■ n. chiefly humorous a book, especially a large, scholarly one.
– ORIGIN C16: from French, from Greek *tomos* 'roll of papyrus, volume'.

tomentum /təˈmɛntəm/ ■ n. (pl. **tomenta** /-tə/) Botany a layer of matted woolly down on the surface of a plant.
– DERIVATIVES **tomentose** /təˈmɛntəʊs, ˈtəʊ-/ adj. **tomentous** adj.
– ORIGIN C17: from Latin, 'cushion stuffing'.

tomfoolery ■ n. foolish or silly behaviour.
– DERIVATIVES **tomfool** n. (dated).

Tommy ■ n. (pl. **-ies**) informal a British private soldier.
– ORIGIN C19: familiar form of the given name *Thomas*; from a use of the name *Thomas Atkins* in specimens of completed official forms in the British army.

tommy bar ■ n. a short bar used to turn a box spanner.

tommy gun ■ n. informal a type of sub-machine gun.
– ORIGIN 1920s: contraction of *Thompson gun*, named after John T. *Thompson*, the American army officer who conceived it.

tommyrot ■ n. informal, dated nonsense.

tomography /təˈmɒgrəfi/ ■ n. a technique for displaying a cross section through a human body or other solid object using X-rays or ultrasound.
– DERIVATIVES **tomogram** n. **tomographic** adj.
– ORIGIN 1930s: from Greek *tomos* 'slice, section' + -GRAPHY.

tomorrow ■ adv. **1** on the day after today. **2** in the near future. ■ n. **1** the day after today. **2** the near future.
– PHRASES **like there was no tomorrow** informal completely without restraint. **tomorrow week** a week from tomorrow.
– ORIGIN Middle English: from TO + MORROW; cf. TODAY and TONIGHT.

tomtit ■ n. a small, active titmouse or similar bird, especially (Brit.) the blue tit.

tom-tom ■ n. **1** a medium-sized cylindrical drum, of which one to three may be used in a drum kit. **2** a drum beaten with the hands, associated with North American Indian, African, or Eastern cultures.
– ORIGIN C17: from Hindi *ṭam ṭam*, Telugu *ṭamaṭama*, of imitative origin.

-tomy ■ comb. form cutting, especially as part of a surgical process: *episiotomy*.
– ORIGIN from Greek *-tomia* 'cutting'.

ton[1] /tʌn/ (abbrev.: **t**) ■ n. **1** (also **long ton**) a unit of weight equal to 2 240 lb avoirdupois (1 016.05 kg). **2** (also **short ton**) chiefly N. Amer. a unit of weight equal to 2 000 lb avoirdupois (907.18 kg). **3** short for METRIC TON. **4** (also **displacement ton**) a unit of measurement of a ship's weight representing the weight of water it displaces with the load line just immersed, equal to 2 240 lb or 35 cu. ft (0.99 cubic metres). **5** (also **freight ton**) a unit of weight or volume of sea cargo, equal to a metric ton (1 000 kg) or 40 cu. ft. (1.132 cubic metres). **6** (also **gross ton**) a unit of gross internal capacity, equal to 100 cu. ft (2.83 cubic metres).
▸ (also **net** or **register ton**) an equivalent unit of net internal capacity. **7** a unit of refrigerating power able to freeze 2 000 lb (907.19 kg) of water at 0°C in 24 hours. **8** a measure of capacity for various materials, especially 40 cu. ft (1.132 cubic metres) of wood. **9** informal a large number or amount. **10** informal, chiefly Brit. a hundred, in particular a speed of 100 mph (161 kmph), a score of 100 or more, or a sum of £100. ■ adv. (**tons**) informal much; a lot: *I feel tons better*.
– ORIGIN Middle English: var. of TUN, both spellings being used for the container and the weight.

ton[2] /tɒ̃/ ■ n. **1** fashionable style or distinction. **2 (the ton)**[treated as sing. or pl.] fashionable society.
– ORIGIN French, from Latin *tonus* (see TONE).

tonal /ˈtəʊn(ə)l/ ■ adj. **1** of or relating to tone. **2** of or relating to music written using conventional keys and harmony.
– DERIVATIVES **tonally** adv.

tonalite /ˈtɒn(ə)lʌɪt/ ■ n. Geology a coarse-grained igneous rock consisting chiefly of sodic plagioclase, quartz, and hornblende or other mafic minerals.
– ORIGIN C19: from *Tonale* Pass, northern Italy.

tonality ■ n. (pl. **-ies**) **1** the character of a piece of music as determined by the key in which it is played or the relations between the notes of a scale or key. **2** the use of conventional keys and harmony as the basis of musical composition. **3** the range of tones used in a picture.

tondo /ˈtɒndəʊ/ ■ n. (pl. **tondi** /-di/) a circular painting or relief.
– ORIGIN C19: from Italian, 'round object'.

tone ■ n. **1** a musical or vocal sound with reference to its pitch, quality, and strength. **2** a modulation of the voice expressing a feeling or mood. **3** general character: *trust her to lower the tone of the conversation*. **4** (also **whole tone**) a basic interval in classical Western music, equal to two semitones and separating, for example, the first and second notes of an ordinary scale; a major second. **5** the particular quality of brightness, deepness, or hue of a colour. ▸ the general effect of colour or of light and shade in a picture. **6** a musical note, warble, or other sound used as a signal on a telephone or answering machine. **7** Phonetics (in some languages, such as Chinese) a particular pitch pattern on a syllable used to make semantic distinctions. ▸ (in some languages, such as English) intonation on a word or phrase used to add functional meaning. **8** (also **muscle tone**) the normal level of firmness or slight contraction in a resting muscle. ■ v. **1** (often **tone something up**) give greater strength or firmness to (the body or a muscle). **2 (tone something down)** make something less harsh in sound or colour.
▸ make something less extreme or intense. **3 (tone with)** harmonize with in terms of colour.
– DERIVATIVES **-toned** adj. **toneless** adj. **tonelessly** adv.
– ORIGIN Middle English: from Old French *ton*, from Latin *tonus*, from Greek, from *teinein* 'to stretch'.

tone arm ■ n. the movable arm supporting the pickup of a record player.

tone-deaf ■ adj. unable to perceive differences of musical pitch accurately.
– DERIVATIVES **tone-deafness** n.

tone group (also **tone unit**) ■ n. Phonetics a group of words forming a distinctive unit in an utterance, containing a nucleus and optionally one or more other syllables before and after the nucleus.

toneme /ˈtəʊniːm/ ■ n. Phonetics a phoneme distinguished from another only by its tone.
– DERIVATIVES **tonemic** adj.
– ORIGIN 1920s: from TONE, on the pattern of *phoneme*.

tonepad ■ n. a device generating specific tones to control another device at the other end of a telephone line.

tone poem ■ n. a piece of orchestral music, typically in one movement, on a descriptive or rhapsodic theme.

toner ■ n. **1** an astringent liquid applied to the skin to reduce oiliness and improve its condition. **2** a device or exercise for toning a specified part of the body. **3** a black or coloured powder used in xerographic copying processes. **4** a chemical bath for changing the tone of a photographic print.

tong[1] ■ n. a Chinese association or secret society, frequently associated with organized crime.
– ORIGIN C19: from Chinese (Cantonese dialect) *t'òng* 'meeting place'.

tong[2] ■ v. curl (hair) using tongs.

Tonga /ˈtɒŋɡə/ ■ n. (pl. same or **Tongas**) **1** a member of any of three peoples of southern Africa, living mainly in Zambia, Malawi, and Mozambique. **2** any of the three different Bantu languages spoken by these peoples.
– ORIGIN the name in Tonga.

tonga /ˈtɒŋɡə/ ■ n. a light horse-drawn two-wheeled vehicle used in India.
– ORIGIN from Hindi *tā'ăgā*.

Tongan /ˈtɒŋən, ˈtɒŋ(ə)n/ ■ n. **1** a native or national of Tonga, an island group in the South Pacific. **2** the Polynesian language spoken in Tonga. ■ adj. of or relating to Tonga, its people, or their language.

tongs ■ pl. n. **1** a tool with two movable arms that are joined at one end, used for picking up and holding things. **2** short for **CURLING TONGS**.
– ORIGIN Old English, of Germanic origin.

tongue ■ n. **1** the fleshy muscular organ in the mouth, used for tasting, licking, swallowing, and (in humans) articulating speech. ▸ the tongue of an ox or lamb, as food. **2** a person's style or manner of speaking. **3** a particular language. **4** a strip of leather or fabric under the laces in a shoe, attached only at the front end. **5** the free-swinging metal piece inside a bell which strikes the bell to produce the sound. **6** a long, low promontory of land. **7** a projecting strip on a wooden board fitting into a groove on another. ■ v. (**tongues, tongued, tonguing**) lick or caress with the tongue.
– PHRASES **find** (or **lose**) **one's tongue** be able (or unable) to express oneself after a shock. **get one's tongue round** pronounce (words). **the gift of tongues** Christian Church the power of speaking in unknown languages, regarded as one of the gifts of the Holy Spirit (Acts 2). **give tongue 1** (of hounds) bark, especially on finding a scent. **2** express one's feelings or opinions freely. (**with**) **tongue in cheek** insincerely or ironically. **someone's tongue is hanging out** someone is very eager for something.
– DERIVATIVES **tongued** adj. **tongueless** adj.
– ORIGIN Old English, of Germanic origin.

tongue and groove ■ n. wooden planking in which adjacent boards are joined by means of interlocking ridges and hollows down their sides.
– DERIVATIVES **tongued-and-grooved** adj.

tongue-in-cheek ■ adj. & adv. with ironic or flippant intent.

tongue-lashing ■ n. a loud or severe scolding.

tongue-tied ■ adj. too shy or embarrassed to speak.

tongue-twister ■ n. a sequence of words, typically of an alliterative kind, that are difficult to pronounce quickly and correctly.
– DERIVATIVES **tongue-twisting** adj.

tonic ■ n. **1** a medicinal substance taken to give a feeling of vigour or well-being. **2** something with an invigorating effect. **3** short for **TONIC WATER**. **4** Music the first note in a scale which, in conventional harmony, provides the keynote of a piece of music. ■ adj. **1** Music relating to or denoting the first degree of a scale. **2** Phonetics denoting or relating to the syllable within a tone group that has greatest prominence. **3** Physiology relating to or restoring muscle tone. ▸ of or denoting continuous muscular contraction.
– DERIVATIVES **tonically** adv.
– ORIGIN C17: from French *tonique*, from Greek *tonikos* 'of or for stretching', from *tonos* (see **TONE**).

tonicity /tə(ʊ)ˈnɪsɪti/ ■ n. **1** muscle tone. **2** Linguistics the pattern of tones or stress in speech. **3** Biology osmotic pressure.

tonic sol-fa ■ n. a system of naming the notes of the scale used especially to teach singing, with doh as the keynote of all major keys and lah as the keynote of all minor keys. See **SOLMIZATION**.

tonic water ■ n. a carbonated soft drink with a bitter flavour, used as a mixer with gin or other spirits.

tonify /ˈtəʊnɪfʌɪ/ ■ v. (**-ies, -ied**) (of acupuncture or herbal medicine) increase the available energy of (a bodily part or system).
– DERIVATIVES **tonification** n.

tonight ■ adv. on the present or approaching evening or night. ■ n. the evening or night of the present day.
– ORIGIN Old English *tō niht*, from the preposition **TO** + **NIGHT**; cf. **TODAY** and **TOMORROW**.

tonka bean /ˈtɒŋkə/ ■ n. the black fragrant seed of a South American tree (*Dipteryx odorata*), used in perfumery and as flavouring.
– ORIGIN C18: *tonka*, a local word in Guyana.

ton-mile ■ n. one ton of goods carried one mile, as a unit of traffic.

tonnage ■ n. **1** weight in tons. **2** the size or carrying capacity of a ship measured in tons. ▸ shipping considered in terms of total carrying capacity.

tonne /tʌn/ ■ n. another term for **METRIC TON**.
– ORIGIN C19: from French; cf. **TON**.

tonneau /ˈtɒnəʊ/ ■ n. **1** the part of an open car occupied by the back seats. **2** (also **tonneau cover**) a protective cover for the seats in an open car or cabin cruiser when they are not in use.
– ORIGIN C18: French, 'cask, tun'.

tonometer /tə(ʊ)ˈnɒmɪtə/ ■ n. **1** a tuning fork or other instrument for measuring pitch. **2** an instrument for measuring pressure in an eyeball, blood vessel, etc.
– ORIGIN C18: from Greek *tonos* (see **TONE**) + -**METER**.

tonsil ■ n. either of two small masses of lymphoid tissue in the throat, one on each side of the root of the tongue.
– DERIVATIVES **tonsillar** adj.
– ORIGIN C16: from French *tonsilles* or Latin *tonsillae* (pl.).

tonsillectomy /ˌtɒnsɪˈlɛktəmi/ ■ n. (pl. **-ies**) a surgical operation to remove the tonsils.

tonsillitis ■ n. inflammation of the tonsils.

tonsorial /tɒnˈsɔːrɪəl/ ■ adj. formal or humorous of or relating to hairdressing.
– ORIGIN C19: from Latin *tonsorius*, from *tonsor* 'barber', from *tondere* 'shear, clip'.

tonsure /ˈtɒnsjə, ˈtɒnʃə/ ■ n. **1** a part of a monk's or priest's head left bare on top by shaving off the hair. **2** an act of shaving a monk's or priest's head in this way as a preparation for entering a religious order. ■ v. [often as adj. **tonsured**] give a tonsure to.
– ORIGIN Middle English: from Latin *tonsura*, from *tondere* 'shear, clip'.

tontine /tɒnˈtiːn, ˈtɒn-/ ■ n. an annuity shared by subscribers to a loan or common fund, the shares increasing as subscribers die until the last survivor enjoys the whole income.
– ORIGIN C18: from French, named after Lorenzo *Tonti*, a Neapolitan banker who started such a scheme to raise government loans in France.

ton-up ■ adj. informal, chiefly Brit. denoting a person achieving a speed of 100 mph or a score of 100 or more.

Tony ■ n. (pl. **Tonys**) (in the US) any of a number of awards given annually for outstanding achievement in the theatre in various categories.
– ORIGIN 1947: from the nickname of the American actress and director Antoinette Perry.

tony ■ adj. (**-ier, -iest**) N. Amer. informal fashionable, stylish, or high-class.
– ORIGIN C19: from **TONE**.

too ■ adv. **1** to a higher degree than is desirable, permissible, or possible. ▸ informal very. **2** in addition. ▸ more-over.
– PHRASES **none too** —— not very.
– ORIGIN Old English, stressed form of **TO**.

toodle-oo ■ exclam. informal, dated goodbye.
– ORIGIN C20: perhaps an alteration of French *à tout à l'heure* 'see you soon'.

took past of **TAKE**.

tool ■ n. **1** a device or implement, typically hand-held, used to carry out a particular function. **2** a thing used to help perform a job. **3** a person used by another. **4** a distinct design in the tooling of a book. ▸ a small stamp or roller used to make such a design. **5** vulgar slang a man's penis. ■ v. **1** (usu. **be tooled**) impress a design on (a leather book cover) with a heated tool. **2** equip or be equipped with tools for industrial production. **3** (**tool up**) or **be tooled up** Brit. informal be or become armed. **4** dress (stone) with a chisel.
– DERIVATIVES **tooler** n. **tooling** n.

– ORIGIN Old English, from a Germanic base meaning 'prepare'.

toolbar ■ n. Computing (in a program with a graphical user interface) a strip of icons used to perform certain functions.

toolmaker ■ n. a person who makes and maintains tools for use in a manufacturing process.
– DERIVATIVES **toolmaking** n.

toolset ■ n. Computing a set of software tools.

toon ■ n. informal a cartoon film or character.

toot ■ n. **1** a short, sharp sound made by a horn, trumpet, or similar instrument. **2** informal, chiefly N. Amer. a snort of a drug, especially cocaine. ▸ S. African informal a measure of an alcoholic drink. ■ v. **1** make or cause to make a toot. **2** informal, chiefly N. Amer. snort (cocaine).
– PHRASES **the whole toot** (or **tooty**) informal the whole number or quantity; everything.
– DERIVATIVES **tooter** n.
– ORIGIN C16: prob. from Middle Low German *tūten*.

tooth ■ n. (pl. **teeth**) **1** each of a set of hard, bony enamel-coated structures in the jaws, used for biting and chewing. **2** a similar projecting part, especially a cog on a gearwheel or a point on a saw or comb. **3** (**teeth**) genuine force or effectiveness: *the Charter would be fine if it had teeth.* **4** an appetite or liking for a particular thing.
– PHRASES **armed to the teeth** formidably armed. **fight tooth and nail** fight very fiercely. **get** (or **sink**) **one's teeth into** work energetically and productively on. **in the teeth of 1** directly against (the wind). **2** in spite of (opposition or difficulty).
– DERIVATIVES **toothed** adj. **tooth-like** adj.
– ORIGIN Old English *tōth* (pl. *tēth*), of Germanic origin.

toothache ■ n. pain in a tooth or teeth.

toothbrush ■ n. a small brush with a long handle, used for cleaning the teeth.

toothcomb ■ n. used with reference to a very thorough search: *the police went over the area with a fine toothcomb*.
– ORIGIN orig. from a misreading of the compound noun *fine-tooth comb*.

toothed whale ■ n. any of the large group of predatory whales with teeth, including sperm whales, killer whales, dolphins, porpoises, etc. [Suborder Odontoceti.]

tooth fairy ■ n. a fairy said to take children's milk teeth after they fall out and leave a coin under their pillow.

tooth glass (also **tooth mug**) ■ n. a glass for holding toothbrushes or dentures, or one used as a tumbler for mouthwash etc.

toothless ■ adj. **1** having no teeth. **2** lacking power or effectiveness.
– DERIVATIVES **toothlessly** adv. **toothlessness** n.

toothpaste ■ n. a paste used on a brush for cleaning the teeth.

toothpick ■ n. a short pointed piece of wood or plastic used for removing bits of food lodged between the teeth.

tooth powder ■ n. powder used for cleaning the teeth.

toothsome ■ adj. **1** (of food) temptingly tasty. **2** informal attractive; alluring.
– DERIVATIVES **toothsomely** adv. **toothsomeness** n.

toothy ■ adj. (**-ier**, **-iest**) having or showing numerous or prominent teeth.
– DERIVATIVES **toothily** adv.

tootle ■ v. **1** casually make a series of sounds on a horn, trumpet, etc. ▸ play (an instrument) or make (a sound or tune) in such a way. **2** informal go or travel in a leisurely way. ■ n. **1** an act or sound of tootling. **2** informal a leisurely journey.
– ORIGIN C19: from TOOT.

tootsie (also **tootsy**) ■ n. (pl. **-ies**) informal **1** a person's foot. **2** dated a young woman, especially one perceived as being sexually available.
– ORIGIN C19: humorous diminutive of FOOT.

top¹ ■ n. **1** the highest or uppermost point, part, or surface. ▸ the leaves, stems, and shoots of a plant, especially those of a vegetable grown for its root. **2** a thing or part placed on, fitted to, or covering the upper part of something. ▸ a platform at the head of a ship's mast. **3** a garment covering the upper part of the body. **4** (**the top**) the highest or most important rank, level, or position. ▸ the utmost degree: *she shouted at the top of her voice.* ▸ (**tops**) informal a particularly good person or thing. ▸ the high-frequency component of reproduced sound. **5** the end that is furthest from the speaker or a point of reference. **6** a bundle of long wool fibres prepared for spinning. **7** Physics one of six flavours of quark. ■ adj. **1** highest in position, rank, or degree. **2** furthest away from the speaker or a point of reference. ■ v. (**topped**, **topping**) **1** be more, better, or taller than. ▸ be at the highest place or rank in. **2** reach the top of (a hill, rise, etc.). **3** (usu. **be topped**) provide with a top or topping. ▸ complete (an outfit) with an upper garment, hat, or item of jewellery. **4** Golf mishit (the ball or a stroke) by hitting above the centre of the ball. ■ adv. (**tops**) informal at the most.
– PHRASES **at the top of one's game** informal at the height of one's powers. **from top to bottom** thoroughly. **from top to toe** all over. **get on top of** be more than (someone) can bear or cope with. **on top 1** on the highest point or surface. **2** in a leading or the dominant position. **3** in addition. **on top of 1** so as to cover. **2** in close proximity to. **3** in command or control of. **4** in addition to. **on top of the world** informal happy and elated. **over the top** informal **1** to an excessive or exaggerated degree. **2** chiefly historical over the parapet of a trench and into battle. **top and tail** remove the top and bottom of (a fruit or vegetable) while preparing it as food. **top dollar** informal a very high price. **the top of the tree** the highest level of a profession or career. **top ten** (or **twenty** etc.) the first ten (or twenty etc.) records in the pop music charts. **to top it all** as a culminating, typically unpleasant, event or action in a series.
– PHRASAL VERBS **top something off** (often **be topped off**) finish something in a memorable way. **top out** reach an upper limit. **top something out** put the highest structural feature on a building, typically as a ceremony to mark the building's completion. **top something up 1** add to a number or amount to bring it up to a certain level. **2** fill up a glass or other partly full container.
– DERIVATIVES **topmost** adj. **topped** adj.
– ORIGIN Old English *topp*, of Germanic origin.

top² (also **spinning top**) ■ n. a conical, spherical, or pear-shaped toy that may be set to spin.
– ORIGIN Old English.

topaz ■ n. **1** a precious stone, typically colourless, yellow, or pale blue, consisting of a fluorine-containing aluminium silicate. **2** a dark yellow colour.
– ORIGIN Middle English: from Old French *topace*, from Greek *topazos*.

top boot ■ n. chiefly historical a high boot with a broad band of a different material or colour at the top.

top brass ■ n. see BRASS (sense 4).

topcoat ■ n. **1** an overcoat. **2** an outer coat of paint.

top copy ■ n. the original copy of a letter or document of which carbon copies have been made.

top dog ■ n. informal a person who is successful or dominant in their field.

top-down ■ adj. **1** controlled from the highest level of government or management; hierarchical. **2** proceeding from the general to the particular.

top drawer ■ n. informal high social position or class. ■ adj. informal of the highest quality or social class.

top dressing ■ n. an application of manure or fertilizer to the surface layer of soil or a lawn.
– DERIVATIVES **top-dress** v.

tope¹ ■ v. archaic or poetic/literary drink alcohol to excess, especially habitually.
– DERIVATIVES **toper** n.
– ORIGIN C17: perhaps an alteration of obsolete *top* 'overbalance'.

tope² ■ n. a small greyish slender-bodied shark of inshore waters. [*Galeorhinus galeus* (E. Atlantic) and *G. australis* (Australia).]
– ORIGIN C17: perhaps of Cornish origin.

topee ■ n. variant spelling of TOPI¹.

top flight ■ n. the highest rank or level. ■ adj. of the highest rank or level.

top fruit ■ n. fruit grown on trees rather than bushes.

topgallant /tɒpˈgal(ə)nt, təˈgal-/ ■ n. 1 (also **topgallant mast**) the section of a square-rigged sailing ship's mast immediately above the topmast. 2 (also **topgallant sail**) a sail set on such a mast.

top hat ■ n. a man's formal hat with a high cylindrical crown.

top-heavy ■ adj. 1 disproportionately heavy at the top so as to be unstable. 2 (of an organization) having a disproportionately large number of senior executives.
– DERIVATIVES **top-heavily** adv. **top-heaviness** n.

Tophet /ˈtəʊfɪt/ ■ n. poetic/literary hell.
– ORIGIN Middle English: from Hebrew *tōpet*, the name of a place near Jerusalem used for idolatrous worship, including the sacrifice of children (see Jeremiah 19:6).

tophus /ˈtəʊfəs/ ■ n. (pl. **tophi** /-faɪ/) Medicine a deposit of crystalline uric acid at joints or in skin or cartilage, especially as a feature of gout.
– ORIGIN C17: from Latin, denoting loose porous stones of various kinds.

topi[1] /ˈtəʊpi/ (also **topee**) ■ n. (pl. **topis** or **topees**) 1 short for SOLA TOPI. 2 S. African a white embroidered skullcap worn by male Muslims.
– ORIGIN from Hindi *ṭopī* 'hat'.

topi[2] /ˈtəʊpi/ ■ n. (pl. same or **topis**) another term for TSESSEBE.
– ORIGIN C19: from Mende (a West African language).

topiary /ˈtəʊpɪəri/ ■ n. (pl. **-ies**) 1 the art or practice of clipping shrubs or trees into ornamental shapes. 2 shrubs or trees clipped in such a way.
– DERIVATIVES **topiarian** /-pɪˈɛːrɪən/ adj. **topiarist** n.
– ORIGIN C16: from French *topiaire*, from Latin *topiarius* 'ornamental gardener'.

topic ■ n. 1 a subject of a text, speech, conversation, etc. 2 Linguistics that part of a sentence about which something is said, typically the first major constituent.
– ORIGIN C15: from Latin *topica*, from Greek *ta topika* 'matters concerning commonplaces' (the title of a treatise by Aristotle).

topical ■ adj. 1 relating to or dealing with current affairs. 2 relating to a particular subject. 3 chiefly Medicine relating or applied directly to a part of the body.
– DERIVATIVES **topicality** n. **topically** adv.

topicalize (also **-ise**) ■ v. Linguistics make (a word, phrase, etc.) the topic of a sentence or discourse.
– DERIVATIVES **topicalization** (also **-isation**) n.

topknot ■ n. 1 a knot of hair arranged on the top of the head. 2 a decorative knot or bow of ribbon worn on the top of the head, popular in the 18th century. 3 a tuft or crest of hair or feathers on the head of an animal or bird.

topless ■ adj. having or leaving the breasts uncovered.
– DERIVATIVES **toplessness** n.

top-line ■ adj. of the highest quality or ranking.

topmast /ˈtɒpmɑːst, -məst/ ■ n. the second section of a square-rigged sailing ship's mast, immediately above the lower mast.

top-notch ■ adj. informal of the highest quality.
– DERIVATIVES **top-notcher** n.

topo /ˈtɒpəʊ/ ■ n. (pl. **-os**) informal a topographical map.

topocadastral /ˌtɒpəkəˈdastrəl/ ■ adj. (of a map) showing both topographical and cadastral features.

topography /təˈpɒɡrəfi/ ■ n. 1 the arrangement of the natural and artificial physical features of an area. ▸ a detailed description or representation on a map of such features. 2 Anatomy the arrangement or features of an organ.
– DERIVATIVES **topographer** n. **topographic** adj. **topographical** adj. **topographically** adv.
– ORIGIN Middle English: from Greek *topographia*, from *topos* 'place' + *-graphia* (see -GRAPHY).

topoi plural form of TOPOS.

topology /təˈpɒlədʒi/ ■ n. 1 Mathematics the study of geometrical properties and spatial relations which remain unaffected by smooth changes in shape or size of figures. 2 the way in which constituent parts are interrelated or arranged.
– DERIVATIVES **topological** adj. **topologically** adv. **topologist** n.
– ORIGIN C19: from Greek *topos* 'place' + -LOGY.

toponym /ˈtɒpənɪm/ ■ n. a place name, especially one derived from a topographical feature.
– DERIVATIVES **toponymic** adj. **toponymy** n.
– ORIGIN 1930s: from Greek *topos* 'place' + *onoma* 'a name'.

topos /ˈtɒpɒs/ ■ n. (pl. **topoi** /ˈtɒpɔɪ/) a traditional theme or formula in literature.
– ORIGIN 1940s: from Greek, 'place'.

toposcope /ˈtɒpəskəʊp/ ■ n. a circular dial or wall erected on a hilltop showing the direction and distance of designated features of the landscape.
– ORIGIN 1930s: from Greek *topos* 'place' + -SCOPE.

topper ■ n. 1 a person or thing that tops. 2 informal a top hat.

toppie[1] ■ n. S. African informal a middle-aged or elderly man. ▸ one's father.
– ORIGIN 1960s: perhaps from isiZulu *thopi* 'growing sparsely' (with ref. to thinning hair) or from Hindi *topi* 'hat'.

toppie[2] ■ n. S. African an African bulbul with a black or dark brown head and crest. [Genus *Pycnonotus*.]
– ORIGIN C19: shortening of TOPKNOT.

topping ■ n. a layer of food poured or spread over another food.

topple ■ v. overbalance or cause to overbalance and fall.
– ORIGIN C16: from TOP[1].

top rope Climbing ■ n. a rope lowered from above to the lead climber in a group, to give assistance at a difficult part of a climb. ■ v. (**top-rope**) climb (a route) using a top rope.

topsail /ˈtɒpseɪl, -s(ə)l/ ■ n. Nautical 1 a sail set on a ship's topmast. 2 a fore-and-aft sail set above the gaff.

top secret ■ adj. of the highest secrecy.

top shell ■ n. a marine mollusc having a low conical shell with a pearly interior. [Family Trochidae.]

topside ■ n. 1 the outer side of a round of beef. 2 the upper part of a ship's side, above the waterline. ■ adv. on or towards the upper decks of a ship.

top-slicing ■ n. 1 a method of assessing tax chargeable on a lump sum by averaging the sum out over the years it has accrued and charging accordingly. 2 the practice of setting aside a portion of a fund for a particular purpose before the remainder is distributed.

topsoil ■ n. the top layer of soil.

topspin ■ n. a fast forward spin given to a moving ball, often resulting in a curved path or a strong forward motion on rebounding.
– DERIVATIVES **topspinner** n.

topstitch ■ v. make a row of continuous decorative stitches on the right side of a garment or other article.

topsy-turvy ■ adj. & adv. 1 upside down. 2 in a state of confusion.
– DERIVATIVES **topsy-turvily** adv. **topsy-turviness** n.
– ORIGIN C16: a jingle apparently based on TOP[1] and obsolete *terve* 'overturn'.

toque /təʊk/ ■ n. 1 a woman's small hat, typically having a narrow, closely turned-up brim. 2 a tall white hat with a full pouched crown, worn by chefs.
– ORIGIN C16: from French.

tor /tɔː/ ■ n. a hill or rocky peak.
– ORIGIN Old English *torr*, perhaps of Celtic origin.

Torah /ˈtɔːrɑː, tɔːˈrɑː/ ■ n. (in Judaism) the law of God as revealed to Moses and recorded in the Pentateuch.
– ORIGIN from Hebrew *tōrāh* 'instruction, doctrine, law', from *yārāh* 'show, instruct'.

torc /tɔːk/ (also **torque**) ■ n. a neck ornament consisting of a band of twisted metal, worn especially by the ancient Gauls and Britons.
– ORIGIN C19: from French *torque*, from Latin *torques* (see TORCH).

torch ■ n. 1 a portable battery-powered electric lamp. 2 chiefly historical a portable means of illumination such as a

piece of wood soaked in tallow and ignited. **3** a valuable quality, principle, or cause, which needs to be protected and maintained: *the torch of freedom.* **4** chiefly N. Amer. a blowtorch. ■ v. informal set fire to.
– PHRASES **carry a torch for** suffer from unrequited love for. **put to the torch** (or **put a torch to**) destroy by burning.
– ORIGIN Middle English: from Old French *torche*, from Latin *torqua*, var. of *torques* 'necklace, wreath', from *torquere* 'to twist'.

torchère /tɔːˈʃɛː/ ■ n. a tall ornamental flat-topped stand for holding a candlestick.
– ORIGIN C20: French, from *torche* (see TORCH).

torchon /ˈtɔːʃ(ə)n/ (also **torchon lace**) ■ n. coarse bobbin lace with geometrical designs.
– ORIGIN C19: from French, 'duster, dishcloth'.

torch song ■ n. a sad or sentimental song of unrequited love.
– DERIVATIVES **torch singer** n.

tore past of TEAR[1].

toreador /ˈtɒrɪədɔː, ˌtɒrɪəˈdɔː/ ■ n. a bullfighter, especially one on horseback.
– ORIGIN Spanish, from *torear* 'fight bulls', from *toro* 'bull'.

torero /tɒˈrɛːrəʊ/ ■ n. (pl. **-os**) a bullfighter, especially one on foot.
– ORIGIN Spanish, from *toro* 'bull'.

tori plural form of TORUS.

torment ■ n. severe physical or mental suffering. ▶ a cause of torment. ■ v. **1** subject to torment. **2** annoy or tease unkindly.
– DERIVATIVES **tormented** adj. **tormentedly** adv. **tormenting** adj. **tormentingly** adv. **tormentor** n.
– ORIGIN Middle English: from Old French *torment* (n.), *tormenter* (v.), from Latin *tormentum* 'instrument of torture', from *torquere* 'to twist'.

tormentil /ˈtɔːm(ə)ntɪl/ ■ n. a low-growing Eurasian plant with bright yellow flowers. [*Potentilla erecta.*]
– ORIGIN Middle English: from French *tormentille*, from medieval Latin *tormentilla*.

torn past participle of TEAR[1].

tornado /tɔːˈneɪdəʊ/ ■ n. (pl. **-oes** or **-os**) a mobile, destructive vortex of violently winds having the appearance of a funnel-shaped cloud.
– DERIVATIVES **tornadic** /-ˈnadɪk/ adj.
– ORIGIN C16: perhaps an alteration of Spanish *tronada* 'thunderstorm', by association with Spanish *tornar* 'to turn'.

torpedo ■ n. (pl. **-oes**) **1** a cigar-shaped self-propelled underwater missile designed to be fired from a ship, submarine, or an aircraft and to explode on reaching a target. **2** US a railway fog signal. ■ v. (**-oes, -oed**) **1** attack with a torpedo or torpedoes. **2** ruin (a plan or project).
– DERIVATIVES **torpedo-like** adj.
– ORIGIN C16: from Latin, 'stiffness, numbness', by extension 'electric ray' (which gives a shock causing numbness).

torpedo boat ■ n. a small, fast, light warship armed with torpedoes.

torpedo tube ■ n. a tube in a submarine or other ship from which torpedoes are fired by the use of compressed air or an explosive charge.

torpid ■ adj. **1** mentally or physically inactive. **2** (of an animal) dormant, especially during hibernation.
– DERIVATIVES **torpidity** n. **torpidly** adv.
– ORIGIN Middle English: from Latin *torpidus*, from *torpere* 'be numb or sluggish'.

torpor ■ n. a state of mental or physical inactivity.

torque /tɔːk/ ■ n. **1** Mechanics a force that tends to cause rotation. **2** variant spelling of TORC. ■ v. apply torque to.
– DERIVATIVES **torquey** adj.
– ORIGIN C19: from Latin *torquere* 'to twist'.

torque converter ■ n. a device that transmits or multiplies torque generated by an engine.

torque wrench ■ n. a tool for setting and adjusting the tightness of nuts and bolts to a desired value.

torr /tɔː/ ■ n. (pl. same) a unit of pressure equivalent to 1 mm of mercury in a barometer and equal to 133.32 pascals.

tortoise

– ORIGIN 1940s: named after the C17 Italian mathematician and physicist Evangelista *Torricelli*.

torrent ■ n. **1** a strong and fast-moving stream of water or other liquid. **2** an overwhelmingly copious outpouring: *a torrent of abuse.*
– DERIVATIVES **torrential** adj. **torrentially** adv.
– ORIGIN C16: from Italian *torrente*, from Latin *torrent-* 'boiling, roaring', from *torrere* 'scorch'.

torrid ■ adj. **1** very hot and dry. **2** full of intense emotions arising from sexual love. **3** full of difficulty.
– DERIVATIVES **torridity** n. **torridly** adv.
– ORIGIN C16: from French *torride* or Latin *torridus*, from *torrere* 'parch, scorch'.

torrid zone ■ n. the hot central belt of the earth bounded by the tropics of Cancer and Capricorn.

torse /tɔːs/ ■ n. Heraldry a wreath.
– ORIGIN C16: from obsolete French, from Latin *torta*, from *torquere* 'twist'.

torsion /ˈtɔːʃ(ə)n/ ■ n. the action of twisting or the state of being twisted, especially of one end of an object relative to the other. ▶ the twisting of the cut end of an artery after surgery to impede bleeding.
– DERIVATIVES **torsional** adj. **torsionally** adv. **torsionless** adj.
– ORIGIN Middle English: from late Latin *torsio(n-)*, var. of *tortio(n-)* 'twisting, torture', from Latin *torquere* 'to twist'.

torsion balance ■ n. an instrument for measuring very weak forces by their effect upon a system of fine twisted wire.

torsion bar ■ n. a bar forming part of a vehicle suspension, twisting in response to the motion of the wheels and absorbing their vertical movement.

torsion pendulum ■ n. a pendulum that rotates rather than swings.

torsk /tɔːsk/ ■ n. a North Atlantic deep-water fish of the cod family. [*Brosme brosme.*]
– ORIGIN C18: from Norwegian, from Old Norse *thorskr*.

torso ■ n. (pl. **torsos** or US also **torsi**) **1** the trunk of the human body. **2** the trunk of a statue without, or considered independently of, the head and limbs. **3** an unfinished or mutilated thing, especially a work of art or literature.
– ORIGIN C18: from Italian, 'stalk, stump'.

tort ■ n. Law a wrongful act or an infringement of right (other than under contract) leading to legal liability.
– ORIGIN Middle English: from Old French, from medieval Latin *tortum* 'wrong, injustice', from *torquere* 'to twist'.

torte /ˈtɔːtə/ ■ n. (pl. **torten** /ˈtɔːt(ə)n/ or **tortes**) a sweet cake or tart.
– ORIGIN from German *Torte*, from late Latin *torta* 'round loaf, cake'.

tortelli /tɔːˈtɛli/ ■ pl. n. small pasta parcels stuffed with a cheese or vegetable mixture.
– ORIGIN Italian, pl. of *tortello* 'small cake, fritter'.

tortellini /ˌtɔːtəˈliːni/ ■ n. tortelli which have been rolled and formed into small rings.
– ORIGIN Italian, pl. of *tortellino*, diminutive of *tortello* 'small cake, fritter'.

torticollis /ˌtɔːtɪˈkɒlɪs/ ■ n. Medicine a condition in which the head becomes persistently turned to one side, often associated with painful muscle spasms.
– ORIGIN C19: from Latin *tortus* 'crooked, twisted' + *collum* 'neck'.

tortilla /tɔːˈtiːjə/ ■ n. **1** (in Mexican cookery) a thin, flat maize pancake, typically eaten with a savoury filling. **2** (in Spanish cookery) a thick omelette containing potato and other vegetables.
– ORIGIN Spanish, diminutive of *torta* 'cake'.

tortious /ˈtɔːʃəs/ ■ adj. Law constituting a tort; wrongful.
– DERIVATIVES **tortiously** adv.
– ORIGIN Middle English: from Anglo-Norman French *torcious*, from the stem of *torcion* 'extortion, violence', from late Latin *tortio(n-)* (see TORSION).

tortoise /ˈtɔːtəs, -tɔɪz/ ■ n. a slow-moving land reptile of warm climates, enclosed in a scaly or leathery domed shell

tortoiseshell

into which it can retract its head and legs. [Family Testudinidae: many species.]
– ORIGIN Middle English *tortu*, *tortuce*: from Old French *tortue*, from medieval Latin *tortuca*.

tortoiseshell ■ n. **1** the semi-transparent mottled yellow and brown shell of certain turtles, typically used to make jewellery or ornaments. ▸ a synthetic imitation of this. **2** a domestic cat with markings resembling tortoiseshell. **3** a common northern hemisphere butterfly with mottled orange, yellow, and black markings. [*Aglais*, *Nymphalis*, and other genera.]

tortrix /ˈtɔːtrɪks/ ■ n. (pl. **tortrices** /-trɪsiːz/) a small moth whose caterpillars live inside rolled leaves. [Family Tortricidae: many species.]
– DERIVATIVES **tortricid** n. & adj.
– ORIGIN C18: from Latin *tortor* 'twister'.

tortuous /ˈtɔːtʃʊəs, -jʊəs/ ■ adj. **1** full of twists and turns. **2** excessively lengthy and complex.
– DERIVATIVES **tortuosity** n. **tortuously** adv. **tortuousness** n.
– ORIGIN Middle English: from Latin *tortuosus*, from *tortus* 'twisting, a twist', from Latin *torquere* 'to twist'.

USAGE
The words **tortuous** and **torturous** have different core meanings. **Tortuous** means 'full of twists and turns' (*a tortuous route*), while **torturous** means 'characterized by pain or suffering' (*a torturous five days of fitness training*).

torture ■ n. **1** the action or practice of inflicting severe pain as a punishment or a forcible means of persuasion. **2** great suffering or anxiety. ■ v. subject to torture.
– DERIVATIVES **torturer** n.
– ORIGIN Middle English: from late Latin *tortura* 'twisting, torment', from Latin *torquere* 'to twist'.

torturous ■ adj. characterized by pain or suffering.
– DERIVATIVES **torturously** adv.
– ORIGIN C15: from Anglo-Norman French, from *torture* 'torture'.

torula /ˈtɒrʊlə, -(j)ʊlə/ ■ n. (pl. **torulae** /-liː/) a yeast used in medicine and as a food additive. [*Candida utilis*.]
– ORIGIN diminutive of Latin *torus* 'swelling, bolster'.

torus /ˈtɔːrəs/ ■ n. (pl. **tori** /-rʌɪ/ or **toruses**) **1** Geometry a surface or solid resembling a ring doughnut, formed by rotating a closed curve about a line which lies in the same plane but does not intersect it. **2** a ring-shaped object or chamber. **3** Architecture a large convex moulding, semicircular in cross section, especially as the lowest part of the base of a column.
– ORIGIN C16: from Latin *torus*, 'swelling, round moulding'.

Tory ■ n. (pl. **-ies**) **1** a member or supporter of the British Conservative Party. **2** a member of the English political party opposing the exclusion of James II from the succession and, later, of the British parliamentary party supporting the established religious and political order until the emergence of the Conservative Party in the 1830s. **3** US a colonist who supported the British side during the American Revolution.
– DERIVATIVES **Toryism** n.

HISTORY
Tory is probably derived from the Irish word *toraidhe* 'outlaw, highwayman', and was originally used of Irish peasants dispossessed by English settlers and living as robbers. It was extended to marauders in the Scottish Highlands, and then adopted in about 1679 as an abusive nickname for supporters of the future James II. After James's deposition **Tory** lost its negative connotations and was applied to members of the English, later British, parliamentary party which supported the established religious and political order and opposed the Whigs. This party became the Conservative Party in the 1830s.

tosh ■ n. Brit. informal rubbish; nonsense.
– ORIGIN C19.

toss ■ v. **1** throw lightly or casually. ▸ (of a horse) throw (a rider) off its back. ▸ throw (a coin) into the air so as to make a choice, based on which side of the coin faces uppermost when it lands. **2** move or cause to move from side to side or back and forth. ▸ jerk (one's head or hair) sharply backwards. ▸ shake or turn (food) in a liquid, so as to coat it lightly. **3** (**toss something off**) drink something rapidly or all at once. ▸ produce something rapidly or without thought or effort. ■ n. an act of tossing.
– PHRASES **give** (or **care**) **a toss** [usu. with neg.] informal care at all.
– ORIGIN C16.

tosser ■ n. Brit. vulgar slang a person who masturbates (used as a term of abuse).

tosspot ■ n. informal a habitual drinker (also used as a general term of abuse).

toss-up ■ n. informal **1** the tossing of a coin to make a choice. **2** a situation in which any of two or more outcomes or options is equally possible.

tostada /tɒˈstɑːdə/ (also **tostado** /tɒˈstɑːdəʊ/) ■ n. (pl. **tostadas** or **tostados**) a Mexican deep-fried maize pancake topped with a seasoned mixture of beans, mincemeat, and vegetables.
– ORIGIN Spanish, 'toasted', from *tostar*.

tot[1] ■ n. **1** a very young child. **2** a small drink of spirits.
– ORIGIN C18 (orig. dialect).

tot[2] ■ v. (**totted**, **totting**) (**tot something up**) **1** add up numbers or amounts. **2** accumulate something over time.
– ORIGIN C18: from archaic *tot* 'set of figures to be added up', abbrev. of TOTAL or of Latin *totum* 'the whole'.

tot[3] ■ v. (**totted**, **totting**) [usu. as noun **totting**] Brit. informal salvage saleable items from dustbins or rubbish heaps.
– DERIVATIVES **totter** n.
– ORIGIN C19: from slang *tot* 'bone'.

total ■ adj. **1** comprising the whole number or amount. **2** complete; absolute. ■ n. a total number or amount. ■ v. (**totalled**, **totalling**; US **totaled**, **totaling**) **1** amount in number to. ▸ find the total of. **2** informal destroy or kill.
– DERIVATIVES **totalization** (also **-isation**) n. **totalize** (also **-ise**) v. **totally** adv.
– ORIGIN Middle English: from medieval Latin *totalis*, from Latin *totus* 'whole'.

total eclipse ■ n. an eclipse in which the whole of the disc of the sun or moon is obscured.

total heat ■ n. another term for ENTHALPY.

total internal reflection ■ n. Physics the complete reflection of light (without refraction), occurring at an interface with a less dense medium when the angle of incidence exceeds the critical angle.

totalitarian /ˌtəʊtalɪˈtɛːrɪən, tə(ʊ)ˌtalɪ-/ ■ adj. of or relating to a centralized and dictatorial system of government requiring complete subservience to the state. ■ n. a person advocating such a system.
– DERIVATIVES **totalitarianism** n.

totality ■ n. **1** the whole of something. **2** Astronomy the moment or duration of total obscuration of the sun or moon during an eclipse.

totalizator (also **totalisator**) ■ n. **1** a device showing the number and amount of bets staked on a race, to facilitate the division of the total among those backing the winner. **2** another term for TOTE[1].

totalizer (also **-iser**) ■ n. another term for TOTALIZATOR.

Total Quality Management ■ n. a system of management based on the principle that every member of staff must be committed to maintaining high standards.

total war ■ n. a war which is unrestricted in terms of the weapons used, the territory or combatants involved, or the objectives pursued.

tote[1] ■ n. (**the tote**) informal a system of betting based on the use of the totalizator, in which dividends are calculated according to the amount staked rather than odds offered.

tote[2] ■ v. informal carry.
– DERIVATIVES **-toter** n.
– ORIGIN C17: prob. of dialect origin.

tote bag ■ n. a large bag for carrying a number of items.

totem /ˈtəʊtəm/ ■ n. a natural object or animal believed by a particular society to have spiritual significance and adopted by it as an emblem.
– DERIVATIVES **totemic** /-ˈtɛmɪk/ adj. **totemism** n. **totemist** n. **totemistic** adj.

– ORIGIN C18: from Ojibwa *nindoodem* 'my totem'.

totem pole ■ n. **1** a pole on which totems are hung or on which the images of totems are carved. **2** chiefly N. Amer. a hierarchy.

t'other /'tʌðə/ (also **tother**) ■ adj. & pron. dialect or humorous the other.
– ORIGIN Middle English *the tother*, wrong division of *thet other* 'the other'.

totter ■ v. **1** move in an unsteady way. **2** [usu. as adj. **tottering**] (of a building) shake or rock as if about to collapse. **3** be insecure or about to collapse. ■ n. a tottering gait.
– DERIVATIVES **tottery** adj.
– ORIGIN Middle English: from Middle Dutch *touteren* 'to swing'.

toucan /'tu:k(ə)n/ ■ n. a tropical American fruit-eating bird with a massive bill and typically brightly coloured plumage. [Genera *Ramphastos* and *Andigena*: several species.]
– ORIGIN C16: from Tupi *tucan*, imitative of its call.

touch ■ v. **1** come into or be in contact with. ▸ come or bring into mutual contact. ▸ bring one's hand or another part of one's body into contact with. ▸ strike (a ball) lightly in a specified direction. **2** harm or interfere with. ▸ take some of (a store, especially of money) for use. ▸ [usu. with neg.] consume (food or drink). **3** have an effect on. ▸ informal reach (a specified level or amount). ▸ [usu. with neg.] informal approach in excellence. **4** (often **be touched**) produce feelings of affection, gratitude, or sympathy in. **5** [with neg.] have any dealings with: *he took jobs that nobody else would touch*. **6** [as adj. **touched**] informal slightly mad. **7** (**touch someone for**) informal ask someone (for money) as a loan or gift. **8** (**touch something in**) chiefly Art lightly mark in details with a brush or pencil. ■ n. **1** an act of touching. ▸ a musician's manner of playing keys or strings or the manner in which an instrument's keys or strings respond to being played. ▸ a light stroke with a pen, pencil, etc. **2** the faculty of perception through physical contact, especially with the fingers. **3** a small amount. **4** a distinctive detail or feature. **5** a distinctive manner or method of dealing with something. **6** Rugby & Soccer the area beyond the sidelines, out of play. **7** S. African informal touch rugby. **8** Bell-ringing a series of changes shorter than a peal.
– PHRASES **in touch 1** in or into communication. **2** possessing up-to-date knowledge. **lose touch 1** cease to be in communication. **2** cease to be informed. **out of touch** lacking up-to-date knowledge or awareness. **to the touch** when touched. **touch bottom** be at the lowest or worst point. **touch of the sun 1** a slight attack of sunstroke. **2** some time spent in the sunlight.
– PHRASAL VERBS **touch at** (of a ship) call briefly at (a port). **touch down 1** Rugby touch the ground with the ball behind the opponents' goal line, scoring a try. **2** American Football score six points by being in possession of the ball behind the opponents' goal line. **3** (of an aircraft or spacecraft) land. **touch something off 1** cause something to ignite or explode by touching it with a match. ▸ cause something to happen suddenly. **2** (of a racehorse) defeat another horse in a race by a short margin. **touch on** (or **upon**) **1** deal briefly with (a subject). **2** come near to being. **touch someone up** Brit. informal caress someone without their consent for sexual pleasure. **touch something up** make small improvements to something.
– DERIVATIVES **touchable** adj.
– ORIGIN Middle English: the verb from Old French *tochier*, prob. from a Romance word; the noun orig. from Old French *touche*.

touch-and-go ■ adj. (of an outcome) possible but very uncertain.

touchback ■ n. American Football a ball downed behind one's own goal.

touchdown ■ n. **1** the moment at which an aircraft or part of a spacecraft touches down. **2** Rugby an act of touching down. **3** American Football a six-point score made by touching down.

touché /tu:'ʃeɪ/ ■ exclam. **1** (in fencing) used to acknowledge a hit by one's opponent. **2** used to acknowledge a good or clever point made at one's expense.
– ORIGIN French, 'touched', from *toucher*.

toucher ■ n. (in bowls) a wood that touches the jack.

touch football ■ n. a form of American football in which a ball-carrier is downed by touching instead of tackling.

touching ■ adj. arousing strong emotion; moving. ■ prep. concerning.
– DERIVATIVES **touchingly** adv. **touchingness** n.

touch-in-goal ■ n. Rugby the area at the corner of the field bounded by continuations of the touchline and the goal line.

touch judge ■ n. Rugby a linesman.

touchline ■ n. Rugby & Soccer the boundary line on each side of the field.

touch pad ■ n. a computer input device in the form of a small panel containing different touch-sensitive areas.

touchpaper ■ n. a strip of paper impregnated with nitre, for setting light to fireworks or gunpowder.

touch rugby ■ n. a form of rugby in which a ball-carrier is downed by touching instead of tackling.

touch screen ■ n. a display device which allows the user to interact with a computer by touching areas on the screen.

touchstone ■ n. **1** a piece of fine-grained dark schist or jasper formerly used for testing alloys of gold by observing the colour of the mark which they made on it. **2** a standard or criterion.

touch-tone ■ adj. denoting push-button telephones generating tones to dial rather than pulses.

touch-type ■ v. [often as noun **touch-typing**] type using all of one's fingers and without looking at the keys.
– DERIVATIVES **touch-typist** n.

touchy ■ adj. (**-ier**, **-iest**) **1** quick to take offence; oversensitive. **2** (of a situation or issue) requiring careful handling.
– DERIVATIVES **touchily** adv. **touchiness** n.
– ORIGIN C17: perhaps an alteration of TETCHY, influenced by TOUCH.

touchy-feely ■ adj. informal, often derogatory **1** openly expressing affection or other emotions, especially through physical contact. **2** characteristic of or relating to such behaviour.

tough ■ adj. **1** strong enough to withstand wear and tear. ▸ (of food, especially meat) difficult to cut or chew. **2** able to endure hardship, adversity, or pain. **3** strict and uncompromising. **4** involving considerable difficulty or hardship. **5** rough or violent. **6** used to express a lack of sympathy: *if you don't like it, tough*. ■ n. informal a rough and violent man.
– PHRASES **tough it out** informal endure a period of hardship or difficulty. **tough shit** (or **titty**) vulgar slang used to express a lack of sympathy.
– DERIVATIVES **toughish** adj. **toughly** adv. **toughness** n.
– ORIGIN Old English, of Germanic origin.

toughen ■ v. make or become tough.
– DERIVATIVES **toughener** n.

toughie ■ n. informal **1** a person who is tough and determined. **2** a difficult problem or question.

tough love ■ n. promotion of a person's welfare by enforcing certain constraints on them or requiring them to take responsibility for their actions.

tough-minded ■ adj. strong, realistic, and unsentimental.
– DERIVATIVES **tough-mindedness** n.

toupee /'tu:peɪ/ (also **toupet** /'tu:peɪ, 'tu:pɪt/) ■ n. a small wig or artificial hairpiece worn to cover a bald spot.
– ORIGIN C18: *toupee*, alteration of French *toupet* 'hair-tuft'.

tour ■ n. **1** a journey for pleasure in which several different places are visited. **2** a short trip to or through a place in order to view or inspect something. **3** a journey made by performers or a sports team, in which they perform or play in several different places. **4** (also **tour of duty**) a spell of duty on military or diplomatic service.
■ v. make a tour of. ▸ take (a performer, production, etc.) on tour.
– ORIGIN Middle English: from Old French, 'turn', from Greek *tornos* 'lathe'.

touraco ■ n. variant spelling of TURACO.

tour de force /ˌtʊə də ˈfɔːs/ ■ n. (pl. **tours de force** pronunc. same) a performance or achievement that has been accomplished with great skill.
– ORIGIN French, 'feat of strength'.

tour en l'air /ˌtʊə ɒ̃ leː/ ■ n. (pl. **tours en l'air** pronunc. same) Ballet a movement in which a dancer jumps straight upwards and completes at least one full revolution before landing.
– ORIGIN French, 'turn in the air'.

tourer ■ n. a car, caravan, or bicycle designed for touring.

Tourette's syndrome /tʊˈrets/ ■ n. Medicine a neurological disorder characterized by involuntary tics and vocalizations and often the compulsive utterance of obscenities.
– ORIGIN C19: named after the French neurologist Gilles de la Tourette.

touring car ■ n. a car with room for passengers and luggage.

tourism ■ n. the commercial organization and operation of holidays and visits to places of interest.

tourist ■ n. **1** a person who travels for pleasure. **2** a member of a touring sports team. ■ v. travel as a tourist.
– DERIVATIVES **touristic** adj. **touristically** adv.

tourist class ■ n. the cheapest accommodation or seating in a ship, aircraft, or hotel.

touristy ■ adj. informal, often derogatory relating to, appealing to, or visited by tourists.

tourmaline /ˈtʊəməlɪn, -liːn/ ■ n. a brittle grey or black mineral consisting of a boron aluminosilicate, with piezoelectric and polarizing properties, in its coloured forms used as a gem.
– ORIGIN C18: from French, from Sinhalese tōramalli 'carnelian'.

tournament ■ n. **1** a series of contests between a number of competitors, competing for an overall prize. **2** a medieval sporting event in which knights jousted with blunted weapons for a prize. **3** a modern event involving display of military techniques and exercises.
– ORIGIN Middle English: from Anglo-Norman French var. of Old French torneiement, from torneier (see TOURNEY).

tournedos /ˈtʊənədəʊ/ ■ n. (pl. same /-dəʊz/) a small round thick cut from a fillet of beef.
– ORIGIN French, from tourner 'to turn' + dos 'back'.

tourney /ˈtʊəni, ˈtɔːni/ ■ n. (pl. **-eys**) **1** a medieval joust. **2** a tournament.
– ORIGIN Middle English: from Old French tornei (n.), torneier (v.), from Latin tornus 'a turn'.

tourniquet /ˈtʊənɪkeɪ, ˈtɔː-/ ■ n. a device for stopping the flow of blood through an artery, typically by compressing a limb with a cord or tight bandage.
– ORIGIN C17: from French, prob. from Old French tournicle 'coat of mail', influenced by tourner 'to turn'.

tour operator ■ n. a travel agent specializing in package holidays.

tousle /ˈtaʊz(ə)l/ ■ v. (usu. as adj. **tousled**) make (something, especially a person's hair) untidy.
– ORIGIN Middle English: from dialect touse 'handle roughly', of Germanic origin.

tout[1] /taʊt/ ■ v. **1** attempt to sell (something), typically by a direct or persistent approach. **2** attempt to persuade people of the merits of. **3** Brit. sell (a ticket) for a popular event at a price higher than the official one. ■ n. **1** (also **ticket tout**) Brit. a person who buys up tickets for an event to resell them at a profit. **2** a person who touts.
– DERIVATIVES **touter** n.
– ORIGIN Middle English tute 'look out', of Germanic origin.

tout[2] /tuː/ ■ det. used before the name of a city to refer to its high society or people of importance: tout Washington.
– ORIGIN French, suggested by le tout Paris 'all (of) Paris'.

tout court /tuː ˈkʊə/ ■ adv. briefly; simply.
– ORIGIN French, 'very short'.

tout de suite /ˌtuː də ˈswiːt/ ■ adv. at once.
– ORIGIN French, 'quite in sequence'.

tovarish /tɒˈvɑːrɪʃ/ (also **tovarich**) ■ n. (in the former USSR) a comrade (often used as a form of address).
– ORIGIN from Russian tovarishch, from Turkic.

TOW ■ abbrev. tube-launched, optically guided, wire-guided (missile).

tow[1] ■ v. use a vehicle or boat to pull (another vehicle or boat) along. ■ n. an act of towing.
– PHRASES **in tow 1** (also **on tow**) being towed. **2** accompanying or following someone.
– DERIVATIVES **towable** adj. **towage** n.
– ORIGIN Old English togian 'draw, drag', of Germanic origin.

tow[2] ■ n. the coarse and broken part of flax or hemp prepared for spinning.
– ORIGIN Old English, of Germanic origin.

toward ■ prep. /təˈwɔːd, twɔːd, tɔːd/ variant of TOWARDS. ■ adj. /ˈtaʊəd/ archaic going on.
– ORIGIN Old English tōweard (see TO, -WARD).

towards /təˈwɔːdz, twɔːdz, tɔːdz/ (also **toward**) ■ prep. **1** in the direction of. **2** getting nearer to (a time or goal). **3** in relation to. **4** contributing to the cost of.
– ORIGIN Old English tōweardes (see TO, -WARD).

tow bar ■ n. a bar fitted to the back of a vehicle, used in towing a trailer or caravan.

tow-coloured ■ adj. (of hair) very light blonde.

towel ■ n. a piece of thick absorbent cloth or paper used for drying. ■ v. (**towelled, towelling**; US **toweled, toweling**) dry with a towel.
– ORIGIN Middle English: from Old French toaille, of Germanic origin.

towelling (US **toweling**) ■ n. thick absorbent cloth, typically cotton with uncut loops, used for towels and bathrobes.

tower ■ n. **1** a tall, narrow building, either free-standing or forming part of a building such as a church or castle. **2** a tall structure that houses machinery, operators, etc. **3** a tall structure used as a receptacle or for storage. ■ v. **1** rise to or reach a great height. **2** (of a bird) soar up to a great height, especially (of a falcon) so as to be able to swoop down on prey. **3** [as adj. **towering**] very important or influential. **4** [as adj. **towering**] very intense: a towering rage.
– DERIVATIVES **towered** adj. (chiefly poetic/literary).
– ORIGIN Old English torr, reinforced in Middle English by Old French tour, from Latin turris, from Greek.

tower block ■ n. a tall modern building containing numerous floors of offices or flats.

tow-headed ■ adj. having tow-coloured or untidy hair.
– DERIVATIVES **tow-head** n.

towline ■ n. a tow rope.

town ■ n. **1** a built-up area with a name, defined boundaries, and local government, that is larger than a village and generally smaller than a city. **2** the central part of a neighbourhood, with its business or shopping area. **3** densely populated areas, especially as contrasted with the country or suburbs. **4** the permanent residents of a university town. Often contrasted with GOWN.
– PHRASES **go to town** informal do something thoroughly or enthusiastically. **on the town** informal enjoying the nightlife of a city or town.
– ORIGIN Old English tūn 'enclosed piece of land, homestead, village', of Germanic origin.

town clerk ■ n. **1** N. Amer. a public official in charge of the records of a town. **2** the secretary and chief administrator of a municipality.

town council ■ n. the elected governing body in a municipality.
– DERIVATIVES **town councillor** n.

town crier ■ n. historical a person employed to make public announcements in the streets.

townee ■ n. variant spelling of TOWNIE.

town gas ■ n. chiefly historical coal gas.

town hall ■ n. a building used for the administration of local government.

town house ■ n. **1** a tall, narrow traditional terrace house, generally having three or more floors. ▶ a modern two- or three-storey house built as one of a row of similar houses. **2** an urban residence of a person owning another property in the country. **3** archaic a town hall.

VOWELS a cat ɑː arm ɛ bed eː hair ə ago əː her ɪ sit i cosy iː see ɒ hot ɔː saw ʌ run

townie (also **townee**) ▪ n. informal a person who lives in a town (used especially with reference to their supposed lack of familiarity with rural affairs).

town mayor ▪ n. the chairperson of a town council.

town planning ▪ n. the planning and control of the construction, growth, and development of a town or other urban area.
– DERIVATIVES **town planner** n.

townscape ▪ n. an urban landscape.

township ▪ n. 1 (in South Africa) a suburb or city of predominantly black occupation, formerly officially designated for black occupation by apartheid legislation. 2 N. Amer. a division of a county with some corporate powers. 3 Brit. historical a manor or parish as a territorial division. ▸ a small town or village forming part of a large parish. 4 Austral./NZ a small town.
– ORIGIN Old English *tūnscipe* 'the inhabitants of a village' (see TOWN, -SHIP).

township jive ▪ n. see JIVE (sense 2).

townsman (or **townswoman**) ▪ n. (pl. **-men** or **-women**) a person living in a particular town or city.

townspeople (also **townsfolk**) ▪ pl. n. the people living in a particular town or city.

towpath ▪ n. a path beside a river or canal, originally used as a pathway for horses towing barges.

towplane ▪ n. an aircraft that tows gliders.

tow rope ▪ n. a rope, cable, etc. used in towing.

toxaemia /tɒkˈsiːmɪə/ (US **toxemia**) ▪ n. Medicine 1 blood poisoning by toxins from a local bacterial infection. 2 (also **toxaemia of pregnancy**) pre-eclampsia.
– DERIVATIVES **toxaemic** adj.
– ORIGIN C19: from TOXI- + -AEMIA.

toxaphene /ˈtɒksəfiːn/ ▪ n. a synthetic amber waxy solid with an odour of chlorine and camphor, used as an insecticide.
– ORIGIN 1940s: from TOXIN + (*cam*)*phene*, a related terpene.

toxi- ▪ comb. form representing TOXIC or TOXIN.

toxic /ˈtɒksɪk/ ▪ adj. poisonous. ▸ of, relating to, or caused by poison. ▪ n. (**toxics**) poisonous substances.
– DERIVATIVES **toxically** adv. **toxicity** n.
– ORIGIN C17: from medieval Latin *toxicus* 'poisoned', from Latin *toxicum* 'poison'.

toxicant /ˈtɒksɪk(ə)nt/ ▪ n. a toxic substance introduced into the environment, e.g. a pesticide.
– ORIGIN C19: var. of INTOXICANT, differentiated in sense.

toxicology /ˌtɒksɪˈkɒlədʒi/ ▪ n. the branch of science concerned with the nature, effects, and detection of poisons.
– DERIVATIVES **toxicological** adj. **toxicologically** adv. **toxicologist** n.

toxic shock syndrome ▪ n. acute septicaemia in women, typically caused by bacterial infection from a retained tampon or IUD.

toxigenic /ˌtɒksɪˈdʒɛnɪk/ ▪ adj. (especially of a bacterium) producing a toxin or toxic effect.
– DERIVATIVES **toxigenicity** n.

toxin /ˈtɒksɪn/ ▪ n. a poison produced by a micro-organism or other organism and acting as an antigen in the body.
– ORIGIN C19: from TOXIC.

toxo- ▪ comb. form equivalent to TOXI-.

toxocara /ˌtɒksəˈkɑːrə/ ▪ n. a nematode worm which is a parasite of dogs, cats, and other animals and can be transmitted to humans. [Genus *Toxocara*.]
– DERIVATIVES **toxocariasis** n.
– ORIGIN from TOXO- + Greek *kara* 'head'.

toxoid ▪ n. Medicine a chemically modified toxin from a pathogenic micro-organism, which is no longer toxic but is still antigenic and can be used as a vaccine.

toxoplasmosis /ˌtɒksəʊplazˈməʊsɪs/ ▪ n. Medicine a disease caused by a parasitic protozoan, transmitted chiefly through undercooked meat, soil, or in cat faeces.
– ORIGIN 1930s: from *Toxoplasma* (genus name).

toy ▪ n. 1 an object for a child to play with, typically a model or miniature replica of something. ▸ a gadget or machine regarded as providing amusement for an adult. 2 [as modifier] denoting a diminutive breed or variety of dog. ▪ v. (**toy with**) 1 consider casually or indecisively. ▸ treat (someone) in a superficially amorous way. 2 move or handle absent-mindedly or nervously. ▸ eat or drink in an unenthusiastic or restrained way.
– PHRASES **throw** (**hurl**, **chuck**, etc.) **one's toys out of the cot** have a tantrum.
– DERIVATIVES **toylike** adj.
– ORIGIN Middle English (orig. denoting a funny story or remark).

toy boy ▪ n. informal a male lover who is much younger than his partner.

toyi-toyi /ˈtɔɪtɔɪ/ S. African ▪ n. (pl. **toyi-toyis**) a dance step characterized by high-stepping movements, typically performed at protest gatherings or marches. ▪ v. (**toyi-toyis**, **toyi-toyied**, **toyi-toying** or **toyi-toyiing**) perform such a dance.
– ORIGIN isiNdebele and Shona.

toytown ▪ adj. 1 resembling a model of a town in being seemingly in miniature. 2 having no real value or substance.

Tpr ▪ abbrev. Trooper.

TQM ▪ abbrev. Total Quality Management.

trabecula /trəˈbɛkjʊlə/ ▪ n. (pl. **trabeculae** /-liː/) Anatomy each of a series of partitions formed by bands or columns of connective tissue.
– DERIVATIVES **trabecular** adj. **trabeculate** /-lət/ adj.
– ORIGIN C19: from Latin, diminutive of *trabs* 'beam, timber'.

trace[1] ▪ v. 1 find by investigation. ▸ find or describe the origin or development of. 2 follow the course or position of with one's eye, mind, or finger. 3 copy (a drawing, map, or design) by drawing over its lines on a superimposed piece of transparent paper. ▸ draw (a pattern or line). 4 give an outline of. ▪ n. 1 a mark, object, or other indication of the existence or passing of something. ▸ a physical change in the brain associated with a memory. 2 a very small quantity. ▸ a barely discernible indication: *a trace of a smile.* 3 a line or pattern corresponding to something which is being recorded or measured. ▸ the projection or intersection of a curve on or with a plane. 4 a procedure to trace something, such as the place from which a telephone call was made.
– DERIVATIVES **traceability** n. **traceable** adj. **traceless** adj.
– ORIGIN Middle English: from Old French *trace* (n.), *tracier* (v.), from Latin *tractus* (see TRACT[1]).

trace[2] ▪ n. each of the two side straps, chains, or ropes by which a horse is attached to a vehicle that it is pulling.
– PHRASES **kick over the traces** become insubordinate or reckless.
– ORIGIN Middle English: from Old French *trais*, pl. of *trait* (see TRAIT).

trace element ▪ n. a chemical element present or required only in minute amounts.

trace fossil ▪ n. Geology a fossil of a footprint, trail, or other trace of an animal, rather than the animal itself.

tracer ▪ n. 1 a bullet or shell whose course is made visible by a trail of flames or smoke, used to assist in aiming. 2 a substance introduced into a system so that its subsequent distribution can be followed from its colour, radioactivity, or other distinctive property. 3 a device which transmits a signal and so can be located when attached to a moving vehicle or other object.

tracery ▪ n. (pl. **-ies**) 1 Architecture ornamental stone openwork, typically in the upper part of a Gothic window. 2 a delicate branching pattern.
– DERIVATIVES **traceried** adj.

trachea /trəˈkiːə, ˈtreɪkɪə/ ▪ n. (pl. **tracheae** /-kiːiː/ or **tracheas**) 1 Anatomy the membranous tube, reinforced by rings of cartilage, conveying air between the larynx and the bronchial tubes; the windpipe. 2 Entomology an air passage in the body of an insect. 3 Botany a duct or vessel in a plant.
– DERIVATIVES **tracheal** /ˈtreɪkɪəl/ adj. **tracheate** /ˈtreɪkɪeɪt/ adj.
– ORIGIN Middle English: from late Latin *trachia*, from Greek *trakheia* (*artēria*) 'rough (artery)'.

tracheo- /trəˈkiːəʊ, ˈtrakɪəʊ, ˈtreɪkɪəʊ/ ■ comb. form relating to the trachea: *tracheotomy*.

tracheotomy /ˌtrakɪˈɒtəmɪ/ (also **tracheostomy** /-ˈɒstəmɪ/) ■ n. (pl. **-ies**) Medicine an incision in the windpipe made to relieve an obstruction to breathing.

trachoma /trəˈkəʊmə/ ■ n. a contagious bacterial infection of the eye, causing inflamed granulation on the inner surface of the lids.
– DERIVATIVES **trachomatous** /-ˈkəʊmətəs, -ˈkɒmətəs/ adj.
– ORIGIN C17: from Greek *trakhōma* 'roughness'.

tracing ■ n. **1** a copy of a drawing, map, etc. made by tracing. **2** a faint or delicate mark or pattern. **3** another term for TRACE[1] (in sense 3).

track[1] ■ n. **1** a rough path or minor road. **2** a prepared course or circuit for racing. **3** a mark or line of marks left by a person, animal, or vehicle in passing. ▸ the course followed by someone or something. **4** a continuous line of rails on a railway. **5** a strip or rail along which something (e.g. a curtain) may be moved. **6** a continuous articulated metal band around the wheels of a heavy vehicle such as a tank, facilitating movement over rough or soft ground. **7** Electronics a continuous line of conductive material on a printed circuit board, connecting parts of a circuit. **8** a section of a record, compact disc, or cassette tape containing one song or piece of music. ▸ a lengthwise strip of magnetic tape containing one sequence of signals. ■ v. **1** follow the course or movements of. ▸ (**track someone/thing down**) find someone or something after a thorough or difficult search. ▸ follow a particular course. ▸ (of a film or television camera) move in relation to the subject being filmed. **2** (of wheels) run so that the back ones are exactly in the track of the front ones. **3** Electronics (of a tunable circuit or component) vary in frequency in the same way as another circuit or component. **4** (**track something up**) N. Amer. leave a trail of dirty footprints on a surface. ▸ (**track something in**) N. Amer. leave a trail of dirt, debris, or snow from one's feet.
– PHRASES **keep** (or **lose**) **track of** keep (or fail to keep) fully aware of or informed about. **make tracks** (**for**) informal leave (for a place). **off the track** departing from the right course of thinking or behaviour. **on the right** (or **wrong**) **track** following a course likely to result in success (or failure). **on track** following a course likely to achieve what is required. **stop** (or **be stopped**) **in one's tracks** informal be brought to a sudden and complete halt. **the wrong side of the tracks** informal a poor or less prestigious part of town.
– DERIVATIVES **trackage** n. (N. Amer.). **trackless** adj.
– ORIGIN C15: the noun from Old French *trac*, perhaps from Low German or Dutch *trek* 'draught, drawing'; the verb from French *traquer* or from the noun.

track[2] ■ v. tow (a canoe) along a waterway from the bank.
– ORIGIN C18: apparently from Dutch *trekken* 'to pull or travel'; the change of vowel was by association with TRACK[1].

trackball (also **tracker ball**) ■ n. a small ball set in a holder that can be rotated by hand to move a cursor on a computer screen.

trackbed ■ n. the foundation structure on which railway tracks are laid.

tracker ■ n. **1** a person who tracks. **2** an electronic tracking device.

track events ■ pl. n. athletic events that take place on a running track. Compare with FIELD EVENTS.

tracking ■ n. Electronics **1** the maintenance of a constant difference in frequency between connected circuits or components. **2** the formation of an electrically conducting path over the surface of an insulator.

tracking station ■ n. a place from which the movements of missiles, aircraft, or satellites are tracked.

tracklement ■ n. Brit. rare a savoury jelly, served with meat.
– ORIGIN 1950s.

track record ■ n. the past achievements or performance of a person, organization, or product.

track rod ■ n. a rod that connects the two front wheels of a motor vehicle and transmits the steering action from the steering column to the wheels.

track shoe ■ n. a running shoe.

tracksuit ■ n. a loose, warm outfit consisting of a sweatshirt and trousers, worn when exercising or as casual wear.

trackway ■ n. a path formed by the repeated treading of people or animals.

tract[1] ■ n. **1** a large area of land. **2** poetic/literary an indefinitely large extent. **3** a major passage in the body or other continuous elongated anatomical structure.
– ORIGIN Middle English: from Latin *tractus* 'drawing, draught', from *trahere* 'draw, pull'.

tract[2] ■ n. a short treatise in pamphlet form, typically on a religious subject.
– ORIGIN Middle English, an abbrev. of Latin *tractatus* (see TRACTATE).

tractable ■ adj. **1** easy to control or influence. **2** (of a situation or problem) easy to deal with.
– DERIVATIVES **tractability** n. **tractably** adv.
– ORIGIN C16: from Latin *tractabilis*, from *tractare* (see TRACTATE).

tractate /ˈtrakteɪt/ ■ n. formal a treatise.
– ORIGIN C15: from Latin *tractatus*, from *tractare* 'to handle'.

traction ■ n. **1** the action of pulling a thing along a surface. ▸ the motive power used for pulling, especially on a railway. **2** Medicine the application of a sustained pull on a limb or muscle, especially in order to maintain the position of a fractured bone or to correct a deformity. **3** the grip of a tyre on a road or a wheel on a rail.
– ORIGIN Middle English: from medieval Latin *tractio(n-)*, from Latin *trahere* 'draw, pull'.

traction engine ■ n. a steam or diesel-powered road vehicle used (especially formerly) for pulling very heavy loads.

tractive ■ adj. relating to or denoting power exerted in pulling, especially by a vehicle or other machine.

tractor ■ n. a powerful motor vehicle with large rear wheels, used chiefly on farms for hauling equipment and trailers.
– ORIGIN C18: from Latin, from *tract-*, *trahere* 'pull'.

tractor beam ■ n. (in science fiction) a beam of energy that can be used to move objects such as spaceships or hold them stationary.

trad informal ■ adj. (especially of music) traditional. ■ n. traditional jazz or folk music.

trade ■ n. **1** the buying and selling of goods and services. ▸ a business of a particular kind. **2** a job requiring manual skills and special training. ▸ (**the trade**) [treated as sing. or pl.] the people engaged in a particular area of business. **3** dated, chiefly derogatory the practice of making one's living in business, as opposed to in a profession or from unearned income. **4** a trade wind. **5** (in sport) a transfer; an exchange. ■ v. **1** buy and sell goods and services. ▸ buy or sell (a particular item or product). ▸ (especially of shares or currency) be bought and sold at a specified price. **2** exchange, typically as a commercial transaction. ▸ (**trade something in**) exchange a used article in part payment for another. ▸ (**trade something off**) exchange something of value, especially as part of a compromise. ▸ transfer (a player) to another club or team. **3** (**trade on**) take advantage of.
– DERIVATIVES **tradable** (or **tradeable**) adj. **trading** n.
– ORIGIN Middle English: from Middle Low German, 'track', of West Germanic origin.

trade book ■ n. a book published by a commercial publisher and intended for general readership.

trade deficit ■ n. the amount by which the cost of a country's imports exceeds the value of its exports.

trade discount ■ n. a discount on a retail price allowed or agreed between traders or to a retailer by a wholesaler.

traded option ■ n. an option on a stock exchange or futures exchange which can itself be bought and sold.

trade edition ■ n. an edition of a book intended for general sale rather than for book clubs or specialist suppliers.

trade gap ■ n. another term for TRADE DEFICIT.

trademark n. 1 a symbol, word, or words legally registered or established by use as representing a company or product. 2 a distinctive characteristic or object. ■ v. [usu. as adj. **trademarked**] provide with a trademark.

trade name n. 1 a name that has the status of a trademark. 2 a name by which something is known in a particular trade or profession.

trade-off n. a concession or benefit received in exchange for one given, especially as a compromise or part of a negotiation.

trade plates pl. n. Brit. temporary number plates used by car dealers or manufacturers on unlicensed cars.

trade price n. the price paid for goods by a retailer to a manufacturer or wholesaler.

trader n. 1 a person who trades goods, currency, or shares. 2 a merchant ship.

tradescantia /ˌtradɪˈskantɪə/ n. an American plant with triangular three-petalled flowers, often grown as a house plant. [Genus *Tradescantia*.]
– ORIGIN named in honour of the English botanist John Tradescant (1570–1638).

tradesman n. (pl. **-men**) a person engaged in trading or a trade, typically on a relatively small scale.

tradespeople pl. n. people engaged in trade.

trade surplus n. the amount by which the value of a country's exports exceeds the cost of its imports.

trade union (Brit. also **trades union**) n. an organized association of workers in a trade, group of trades, or profession, formed to protect and further their rights and interests.
– DERIVATIVES **trade unionism** n. **trade unionist** n.

trade-weighted adj. (especially of exchange rates) weighted according to the importance of the trade with the various countries involved.

trade wind n. a wind blowing steadily towards the equator from the north-east in the northern hemisphere or the south-east in the southern hemisphere, especially at sea.

HISTORY
Trade wind is first recorded from the mid 17th century, and comes from the obsolete phrase *blow trade* meaning 'blow steadily in the same direction'. **Trade** formerly meant 'course, direction' and 'track' before it acquired its modern meanings of 'an occupation' and 'buying and selling'. The importance of the trade winds to the transport of goods by sea misled 18th-century etymologists into connecting the word *trade* with 'commerce'.

trading estate n. Brit. a specially designed industrial and commercial area.

trading post n. a store or small settlement established for trading, typically in a remote place.

tradition n. 1 the transmission of customs or beliefs from generation to generation, or the fact of being so passed on. ▸ a long-established custom or belief passed on in this way. 2 an artistic or literary method or style established by an artist, writer, or movement, and subsequently followed by others.
– DERIVATIVES **traditionist** n. **traditionless** adj.
– ORIGIN Middle English: from Latin *traditio(n-)*, from *tradere* 'deliver, betray', from *trans-* 'across' + *dare* 'give'.

traditional adj. 1 of, relating to, or following tradition. 2 (of jazz) in the style of the early 20th century.
– DERIVATIVES **traditionally** adv.

traditional healer n. a healer who uses herbal remedies or divination to treat spiritual, psychological, and medical conditions.

traditional health practitioner n. formal term for TRADITIONAL HEALER.

traditionalism n. the upholding of tradition, especially so as to resist change.
– DERIVATIVES **traditionalist** n. & adj. **traditionalistic** adj.

traditional leader n. a king, chief, or tribal leader whose political authority is based on customary law.

traditional medicine n. remedies prepared from medicinal plants, especially as used by traditional healers.

traditional weapon n. S. African an assegai, stick, knobkerrie, or similar weapon customarily carried by African men on ceremonial occasions.

traduce /trəˈdjuːs/ ■ v. speak badly of or tell lies about.
– DERIVATIVES **traducement** n. **traducer** n.
– ORIGIN C16: from Latin *traducere* 'lead in front of others, expose to ridicule'.

traffic n. 1 vehicles moving on a public highway. 2 the movement of ships or aircraft. 3 the commercial transportation of goods or passengers. 4 the messages or signals transmitted through a communications system. 5 the action of trafficking. 6 archaic dealings or communication between people. ■ v. (**trafficked**, **trafficking**) deal or trade in something illegal.
– DERIVATIVES **trafficker** n.
– ORIGIN C16: from French *traffique*, Spanish *tráfico*, or Italian *traffico*.

traffic calming n. the deliberate slowing of traffic in residential areas, by building speed bumps or other obstructions.
– ORIGIN 1980s: translation of German *Verkehrsberuhigung*.

traffic circle n. chiefly S. African & N. Amer. a road junction at which traffic moves in one direction round a central island to reach one of the roads converging on it.

traffic island n. a small raised area in the middle of a road which provides a safe place for pedestrians to stand and marks a division between two streams of traffic.

traffic jam n. a line or lines of traffic at or virtually at a standstill.

traffic lights (also **traffic light** or **traffic signal**) pl. n. a set of automatically operated coloured lights for controlling traffic at road junctions, pedestrian crossings, and traffic circles.

traffic warden n. Brit. a uniformed official who locates and reports on infringements of parking regulations.

tragacanth /ˈtragəkanθ/ (also **gum tragacanth**) n. a white or reddish gum obtained from a plant (*Astragalus gummifer*), used in the food, textile, and pharmaceutical industries.
– ORIGIN C16: from French *tragacante*, from Greek *tragakantha* (name of the source plant, literally 'goat's thorn)'.

tragedian /trəˈdʒiːdɪən/ n. 1 (fem. **tragedienne** /trəˌdʒiːdɪˈɛn/) a tragic actor or actress. 2 a writer of tragedies.

tragedy n. (pl. **-ies**) 1 an event causing great suffering, destruction, and distress. 2 a serious play with an unhappy ending, especially one concerning the downfall of the protagonist.
– ORIGIN Middle English: from Old French *tragedie*, from Greek *tragōidia*, apparently from *tragos* 'goat' + *ōidē* 'song, ode'.

tragic adj. 1 extremely distressing or sad. ▸ suffering extreme distress or sadness. 2 of or relating to tragedy in a literary work.
– DERIVATIVES **tragical** adj. **tragically** adv.
– ORIGIN C16: from French *tragique*, from Greek *tragikos*, from *tragos* 'goat', associated with *tragōidia* (see **TRAGEDY**).

tragic flaw n. a fatal flaw leading to the downfall of a tragic hero or heroine.

tragic irony n. see IRONY[1].

tragicomedy /ˌtradʒɪˈkɒmɪdi/ n. (pl. **-ies**) a play or novel containing elements of both comedy and tragedy.
– DERIVATIVES **tragicomic** adj. **tragicomically** adv.
– ORIGIN C16: from French *tragicomédie* or Italian *tragicomedia*, from Latin, from *tragicus* (see **TRAGIC**) + *comoedia* (see **COMEDY**).

trail n. 1 a mark or a series of signs or objects left behind by the passage of someone or something. ▸ a track or scent used in following someone or hunting an animal. 2 a long thin part stretching behind or hanging down from something. 3 a beaten path through rough country. 4 a route planned or followed for a particular purpose: *the tourist trail*. ■ v. 1 draw or be drawn along behind. ▸ (of a plant) grow along the ground or so as to hang down.

trail bike

2 walk or move slowly or wearily. ▶ (of the voice or a speaker) fade gradually before stopping. ▶ be losing to an opponent in a game or contest. **3** follow the trail of. **4** advertise with a trailer.
– PHRASES **trail one's coat** deliberately provoke a quarrel or fight.
– ORIGIN Middle English: from Old French *traillier* 'to tow' or Middle Low German *treilen* 'haul (a boat)', from Latin *tragula* 'dragnet', from *trahere* 'to pull'.

trail bike ■ n. a light motorcycle for use in rough terrain.

trailblazer ■ n. **1** a person who makes a new track through wild country. **2** an innovator.
– DERIVATIVES **trailblazing** n. & adj.

trailer ■ n. **1** an unpowered vehicle towed by another. ▶ the rear section of an articulated truck. ▶ N. Amer. a caravan or mobile home. **2** an extract from a film or programme used for advance advertising. **3** a trailing plant. ■ v. **1** advertise with a trailer. **2** transport by trailer.

trailer park ■ n. N. Amer. **1** a caravan site. **2** [as modifier] US lacking refinement, taste, or quality: *a trailer-park floozy*.

trailer trash ■ n. US informal, derogatory poor, lower-class white people, typified as living in mobile homes.

trailer truck ■ n. US an articulated truck.

trailing edge ■ n. **1** the rear edge of a moving body, especially an aircraft wing or propeller blade. **2** Electronics the part of a pulse in which the amplitude diminishes.

trail mix ■ n. a mixture of dried fruit and nuts eaten as a snack food.

train ■ v. **1** teach (a person or animal) a particular skill or type of behaviour through regular practice and instruction. ▶ be taught in such a way. **2** make or become physically fit through a course of exercise and diet. **3** (**train something on**) point or aim something at. **4** cause (a plant) to grow in a particular direction or into a required shape. ■ n. **1** a series of railway carriages or wagons moved as a unit by a locomotive or by integral motors. **2** a number of vehicles or pack animals moving in a line. ▶ a retinue of attendants accompanying an important person. **3** a series of connected events, thoughts, etc. **4** a long piece of trailing material attached to the back of a formal dress or robe. **5** a series of gears or other connected parts in machinery.
– PHRASES **in train** in progress. **in someone/thing's train** following behind someone or something. **in** (or **out of**) **training** undergoing (or no longer undergoing) physical training for a sporting event. ▶ physically fit (or unfit) as a result of this.
– DERIVATIVES **trainability** n. **trainable** adj. **training** n. **trainload** n.
– ORIGIN Middle English: from Old French *train*, from *trahiner* (v.), from Latin *trahere* 'pull, draw'.

trainee ■ n. a person undergoing training for a particular job or profession.
– DERIVATIVES **traineeship** n.

trainer ■ n. **1** a person who trains people or animals. ▶ informal an aircraft or simulator used to train pilots. **2** British term for TAKKIE.

training college ■ n. a college providing education and training in specified skills, such as teaching.

training shoe ■ n. another term for TAKKIE.

trainspotter ■ n. chiefly Brit. **1** a person who collects locomotive numbers as a hobby. **2** often derogatory a person who obsessively studies the minutiae of any minority interest or specialized hobby.
– DERIVATIVES **trainspotting** n.

train surf ■ v. ride on the outside of a moving train (especially its roof) as an act of daring.
– DERIVATIVES **train surfer** n. **train surfing** n.

traipse /treɪps/ ■ v. walk or move wearily, reluctantly, or aimlessly. ■ n. a tedious or tiring walk.
– ORIGIN C16.

trait /treɪ, treɪt/ ■ n. a distinguishing quality or characteristic. ▶ a genetically determined characteristic.
– ORIGIN C16: from French, from Latin *tractus* (see TRACT¹).

traitor ■ n. a person who betrays their country, a cause, etc.

– DERIVATIVES **traitorous** adj. **traitorously** adv.
– ORIGIN Middle English: from Old French *traitour*, from Latin *traditor*, from *tradere* 'hand over'.

trajectory /trəˈdʒɛkt(ə)ri, ˈtradʒɪkt(ə)ri/ ■ n. (pl. **-ies**) **1** the path described by a projectile flying or an object moving under the action of given forces. **2** Geometry a curve or surface cutting a family of curves or surfaces at a constant angle.
– ORIGIN C17: from Latin *traject-*, *traicere* 'throw across'.

Trakehner /traˈkeɪnə/ ■ n. a saddle horse of a light breed first developed at the Trakehnen stud near Kaliningrad in Russia.
– ORIGIN C20: from German.

tram (also **tramcar**) ■ n. **1** a passenger vehicle powered by electricity conveyed by overhead cables, and running on rails laid in a public road. **2** historical a low four-wheeled cart or barrow used in coal mines.
– ORIGIN C16: from Middle Low German and Middle Dutch *trame* 'beam, barrow shaft'.

tramlines ■ n. **1** rails for a tramcar. **2** informal a pair of parallel lines at the sides of a tennis court or at the side or back of a badminton court.

trammel /ˈtram(ə)l/ ■ n. **1** (**trammels**) poetic/literary restrictions or impediments to freedom of action. **2** (also **trammel net**) a three-layered net, designed so that a pocket forms when fish attempt to swim through, thus trapping them. ■ v. (**trammelled, trammelling**; US **trammeled, trammeling**) constrain or impede.
– ORIGIN Middle English: from Old French *tramail*, from a medieval Latin var. of *trimaculum*, perhaps from Latin *tri-* 'three' + *macula* 'mesh'.

tramp ■ v. **1** walk heavily or noisily. **2** walk wearily or reluctantly over a long distance. ■ n. **1** an itinerant homeless person who lives by begging or doing casual work. **2** the sound of heavy steps. **3** a long walk. **4** a cargo vessel running between many different ports rather than sailing a fixed route. **5** informal, chiefly N. Amer. a promiscuous woman.
– DERIVATIVES **tramper** n. **trampish** adj.
– ORIGIN Middle English: prob. of Low German origin.

trample ■ v. **1** tread on and crush. **2** (**trample on/upon/over**) treat with contempt. ■ n. poetic/literary an act or sound of trampling.
– DERIVATIVES **trampler** n.
– ORIGIN Middle English: from TRAMP.

trampoline /ˈtrampəliːn/ ■ n. a strong fabric sheet connected by springs to a frame, used as a springboard and landing area in doing acrobatic or gymnastic exercises. ■ v. [usu. as noun **trampolining**] use a trampoline.
– DERIVATIVES **trampolinist** n.
– ORIGIN C18: from Italian *trampolino*, from *trampoli* 'stilts'.

tramway ■ n. a set of rails for a tram. ▶ a tram system.

trance /trɑːns/ ■ n. **1** a half-conscious state characterized by an absence of response to external stimuli, typically as induced by hypnosis or entered by a medium. **2** a state of abstraction. **3** (also **trance music**) a type of electronic dance music characterized by hypnotic rhythms. ■ v. poetic/literary put into a trance.
– DERIVATIVES **trance-like** adj.
– ORIGIN Middle English: from Old French *transir* 'depart, fall into a trance', from Latin *transire* 'go across'.

tranche /trɑːnʃ/ ■ n. a portion, especially of money.
– ORIGIN C15: from Old French, 'slice'.

trank ■ n. informal a tranquillizing drug.

tranny (also **trannie**) ■ n. (pl. **-ies**) informal **1** chiefly Brit. a transistor radio. **2** a photographic transparency. **3** N. Amer. the transmission in a motor vehicle. **4** a transvestite.

tranquil ■ adj. free from disturbance; calm.
– DERIVATIVES **tranquillity** (also **tranquility**) n. **tranquilly** adv.
– ORIGIN Middle English: from French *tranquille* or Latin *tranquillus*.

tranquillize (also **-ise**; US **tranquilize**) ■ v. [usu. as adj. **tranquillizing** (also **-ising**)] (of a drug) have a calming or sedative effect on. ▶ administer such a drug to.
– DERIVATIVES **tranquillizer** (also **-iser**) n.

trans- /trans, trɑːns, -nz/ ■ prefix **1** across; beyond: *transcontinental*. ▶ on or to the other side of: *transatlantic*. **2** through: *transonic*. ▶ into another state

or place: *translate*. ▶ transcending: *transpersonal*. **3** Chemistry (usu. *trans*-) denoting molecules in which two particular atoms or groups lie on opposite sides of a given plane, in particular denoting an isomer in which substituents at opposite ends of a carbon–carbon double bond are also on opposite sides of the bond: *trans-1,2-dichloroethene*.
– ORIGIN from Latin *trans* 'across'.

transaction ■ n. **1** an instance of buying or selling. ▶ the action of conducting business. **2** an exchange or interaction between people. **3** (**transactions**) published reports of proceedings at the meetings of a learned society. **4** an input message to a computer system dealt with as a single unit of work.
– DERIVATIVES **transact** v. **transactional** adj. **transactionally** adv. **transactor** n.
– ORIGIN Middle English: from late Latin *transactio(n-)*, from *transigere* 'drive through'.

transactional analysis ■ n. a system of popular psychology based on the idea that behaviour reflects an interchange between parental, adult, and childlike aspects of personality.

transalpine ■ adj. **1** of, relating to, or in the area beyond the Alps, especially as viewed from Italy. **2** crossing the Alps.
– ORIGIN C16: from Latin *transalpinus*, from *trans-* 'across' + *alpinus* (see ALPINE).

transatlantic ■ adj. **1** crossing the Atlantic. **2** concerning countries on both sides of the Atlantic, typically Britain and the US. **3** of, relating to, or situated on the other side of the Atlantic; Brit. American; N. Amer. British or European.

transaxle ■ n. an integral driving axle and differential gear in a motor vehicle.

transceiver ■ n. a combined radio transmitter and receiver.

transcend ■ v. **1** be or go beyond the range or limits of. **2** surpass.
– ORIGIN Middle English: from Old French *transcendre* or Latin *transcendere*, from *trans-* 'across' + *scandere* 'climb'.

transcendent ■ adj. transcending normal or physical human experience. ▶ (of God) existing apart from and not subject to the limitations of the material universe. Often contrasted with IMMANENT.
– DERIVATIVES **transcendence** n. **transcendently** adv.

transcendental ■ adj. **1** of or relating to a spiritual realm. ▶ relating to or denoting Transcendentalism. **2** Mathematics (of a quantity or function) not capable of being produced by the algebraical operations of addition, multiplication, and involution, or the inverse operations.
– DERIVATIVES **transcendentally** adv.

transcendentalism ■ n. **1** (**Transcendentalism**) a 19th-century idealistic philosophical and social movement influenced by romanticism, Platonism, and Kantian philosophy, which taught that divinity pervades all nature and humanity. **2** a system developed by Immanuel Kant, based on the idea that, in order to understand the nature of reality, one must first analyse the reasoning process which governs the nature of experience.
– DERIVATIVES **transcendentalist** n. & adj.

Transcendental Meditation ■ n. (trademark in the US) a technique for detaching oneself from anxiety and promoting harmony and self-realization by meditation and repetition of a mantra.

transcontinental ■ adj. crossing or extending across a continent or continents.
– DERIVATIVES **transcontinentally** adv.

transcribe ■ v. **1** put (thoughts, speech, or data) into written or printed form. **2** transliterate (foreign characters) or write or type out (shorthand, notes, etc.) into ordinary characters or full sentences. **3** arrange (a piece of music) for a different instrument, voice, etc. **4** Biochemistry synthesize (RNA) using a template of existing DNA (or vice versa), so that the genetic information is copied.
– DERIVATIVES **transcriber** n.
– ORIGIN C16: from Latin *transcribere*, from *trans-* 'across' + *scribere* 'write'.

transcript ■ n. **1** a written or printed version of material originally presented in another medium. **2** Biochemistry a length of RNA or DNA that has been transcribed.
– ORIGIN Middle English: from Old French *transcrit*, from Latin *transcriptum*, from *transcribere* (see TRANSCRIBE).

transcriptase /tran'skrɪpteɪz, trɑːn-/ ■ n. Biochemistry an enzyme which catalyses the formation of RNA from a DNA template, or (reverse transcriptase), the formation of DNA from an RNA template.

transcription ■ n. **1** a transcript. **2** the action or process of transcribing. **3** a piece of music transcribed for a different instrument, voice, etc. **4** a form in which a speech sound or a foreign character is represented.
– DERIVATIVES **transcriptional** adj. **transcriptionally** adv.

transcutaneous /ˌtranzkjuːˈteɪnɪəs, ˌtrɑːnz-, -nsˌ-/ ■ adj. existing, applied, or measured across the depth of the skin.

transdermal /ˌtranzˈdəːməl, trɑːnz, -nsˌ-/ ■ adj. relating to or denoting the application of a medicine or drug through the skin, especially by means of an adhesive patch.

transducer /tranzˈdjuːsə, trɑːnz-, -nsˌ-/ ■ n. a device that converts variations in a physical quantity, such as pressure or brightness, into an electrical signal, or vice versa.
– DERIVATIVES **transduce** v. **transduction** n.
– ORIGIN 1920s: from Latin *transducere* 'lead across'.

transect technical ■ v. cut across or make a transverse section in. ■ n. a straight line or narrow cross section along which observations or measurements are made.
– DERIVATIVES **transection** n.
– ORIGIN C17: from TRANS- + Latin *sect-*, *secare* 'divide by cutting'.

transept /ˈtransɛpt, ˈtrɑːn-/ ■ n. (in a cross-shaped church) either of the two parts forming the arms of the cross shape, projecting at right angles from the nave.
– ORIGIN C16: from modern Latin *transeptum* (see TRANS-, SEPTUM).

transexual ■ adj. & n. variant spelling of TRANSSEXUAL.

transfect /tranzˈfɛkt, trɑːnz-, -nsˌ-/ ■ v. Microbiology infect (a cell) with free nucleic acid. ▶ introduce (genetic material) in this way.
– DERIVATIVES **transfectant** n. **transfection** n.
– ORIGIN 1960s: from TRANS- + INFECT, or a blend of TRANSFER and INFECT.

transfer ■ v. (**transferred**, **transferring**) **1** move from one place to another. **2** move or cause to move to another department, occupation, etc. ▶ redirect (a telephone call) to a new line or extension. **3** change to another place, route, or means of transport during a journey. **4** make over the possession of (property, a right, or a responsibility) to another. **5** [usu. as adj. **transferred**] change (the sense of a word or phrase) by extension or metaphor. ■ n. **1** an act of transferring. **2** a small coloured picture or design on paper, which can be transferred to another surface by being pressed or heated.
– DERIVATIVES **transferability** n. **transferable** adj. **transferee** n. **transferor** n. (chiefly Law). **transferral** n.
– ORIGIN Middle English: from French *transférer* or Latin *transferre*, from *trans-* 'across' + *ferre* 'to bear'.

transference /ˈtransf(ə)r(ə)ns, ˈtrɑːns-, -nzˌ-/ ■ n. **1** the action of transferring or the process of being transferred. **2** Psychoanalysis the redirection of emotions originally felt in childhood.

transfer fee ■ n. a fee paid by one soccer or rugby club to another for the transfer of a player.

transfer payment ■ n. Economics a payment by a government not made in exchange for goods or services, such as a benefit payment or subsidy.

transferrin /transˈfɛrɪn, trɑːns-, -nzˌ-/ ■ n. Biochemistry a protein which transports iron in blood serum.
– ORIGIN 1940s: from TRANS- + Latin *ferrum* 'iron'.

transfer RNA ■ n. Biochemistry a folded form of RNA which transports amino acids from the cytoplasm of a cell to a ribosome.

transfiguration ■ n. **1** a complete transformation into a more beautiful or spiritual state. **2** (**the Transfiguration**) Christ's appearance in radiant glory to three of his disciples (Matthew 17:2 and Mark 9:2–3).

transfigure ■ v. (usu. **be transfigured**) transform into

transfix

something more beautiful or spiritual.
– ORIGIN Middle English: from Old French *transfigurer* or Latin *transfigurare*, from *trans-* 'across' + *figura* 'figure'.

transfix ■ v. **1** (usu. **be transfixed**) make motionless with horror, wonder, or astonishment. **2** pierce with a sharp implement or weapon.
– DERIVATIVES **transfixion** n.
– ORIGIN C16: from Latin *transfix-*, *transfigere* 'pierce through'.

transform ■ v. subject to or undergo transformation. ▸ change the voltage of (an electric current) by electromagnetic induction. ■ n. Mathematics & Linguistics the product of a transformation. ▸ a rule for making a transformation.
– DERIVATIVES **transformable** adj. **transformative** adj.
– ORIGIN Middle English: from Old French *transformer* or Latin *transformare* (see TRANS-, FORM).

transformation ■ n. **1** a marked change in nature, form, or appearance. ▸ (in South Africa) the post-apartheid process of social and political change to establish democracy and social equality. **2** Mathematics a process by which a figure is converted into another one of similar value. **3** Linguistics a process by which an element in the underlying logical deep structure of a sentence is converted to an element in the surface structure.
– DERIVATIVES **transformational** adj. **transformationally** adv.

transformational grammar ■ n. Linguistics grammar which describes a language in terms of transformations applied to an underlying deep structure in order to generate the surface structure of sentences which can actually occur.

transformer ■ n. a device for changing the voltage of an alternating current by electromagnetic induction.

transform fault ■ n. Geology a strike-slip fault occurring at the boundary between two plates of the earth's crust.

transfuse ■ v. **1** Medicine transfer (blood or its components) from one person or animal to another. ▸ inject (liquid) into a blood vessel to replace lost fluid. **2** permeate or infuse.
– DERIVATIVES **transfusion** n.
– ORIGIN Middle English: from Latin *transfus-*, *transfundere* 'pour from one container to another'.

transgender (also **transgendered**) ■ adj. transsexual.

transgenic /tranzˈdʒɛnɪk, trɑːnz-, -nsˈ-/ ■ adj. Biology containing genetic material into which DNA from a different organism has been artificially introduced.
– DERIVATIVES **transgenics** pl. n.
– ORIGIN 1980s: from TRANS- + GENE.

transglobal ■ adj. (of an expedition, enterprise, or network) moving or extending across or round the world.

transgress ■ v. **1** go beyond the limits set by (a moral principle, standard, law, etc.). **2** Geology (of the sea) spread over (an area of land).
– DERIVATIVES **transgression** n. **transgressive** adj. **transgressor** n.
– ORIGIN C15 (*transgression* Middle English): from Old French *transgresser* or Latin *transgress-*, *transgredi* 'step across'.

tranship ■ v. variant spelling of TRANS-SHIP.

transhumance /tranzˈhjuːməns, trɑːnz-, -nsˈ-/ ■ n. the action or practice of moving livestock seasonally from one grazing ground to another, typically to lowlands in winter and highlands in summer.
– DERIVATIVES **transhumant** adj.
– ORIGIN C20: from French, from *transhumer*, from Latin *trans-* 'across' + *humus* 'ground'.

transient /ˈtransɪənt, ˈtrɑːns-, -nzˈ-/ ■ adj. **1** lasting only for a short time. **2** staying or working in a place for a short time only. ■ n. **1** a transient person. **2** a momentary variation in current, voltage, or frequency.
– DERIVATIVES **transience** n. **transiency** n. **transiently** adv.
– ORIGIN C16: from Latin *transient-*, *transire* 'go across'.

transilluminate ■ v. pass strong light through (an organ or part of the body) in order to detect disease or abnormality.
– DERIVATIVES **transillumination** n.

transistor ■ n. **1** a semiconductor device with three connections, capable of amplification and rectification. **2** (also **transistor radio**) a portable radio using circuits containing transistors.
– DERIVATIVES **transistorization** (also -**isation**) n. **transistorize** (also -**ise**) v.
– ORIGIN 1940s: from TRANSFER + RESISTOR.

transit ■ n. **1** the carrying of people or things from one place to another. ▸ N. Amer. the conveyance of passengers on public transport. **2** an act of passing through or across a place. ▸ Astronomy the passage of a planet across the face of the sun, or of a moon across the face of a planet. ■ v. (**transited**, **transiting**) pass across or through.
– ORIGIN Middle English: from Latin *transitus*, from *transire* 'go across'.

transition ■ n. the process of changing from one state or condition to another. ▸ a period of such change.
– DERIVATIVES **transitional** adj. **transitionally** adv. **transitionary** adj.
– ORIGIN C16: from French, or from Latin *transitio(n-)*, from *transire* 'go across'.

transition metal (also **transition element**) ■ n. Chemistry any of the set of metallic elements occupying a central block in the periodic table, e.g. iron, manganese, chromium, and copper.

transitive /ˈtransɪtɪv, ˈtrɑːns-, -nz-/ ■ adj. **1** Grammar (of a verb or a sense or use of a verb) able to take a direct object (expressed or implied), e.g. *saw* in *he saw the donkey*. The opposite of INTRANSITIVE. **2** Logic & Mathematics (of a relation) such that, if it applies between successive members of a sequence, it must also apply between any two members taken in order.
– DERIVATIVES **transitively** adv. **transitiveness** n. **transitivity** n.
– ORIGIN C16: from late Latin *transitivus*, from *transit-* (see TRANSIT).

transitory /ˈtransɪt(ə)ri, ˈtrɑːns-, -nz-/ ■ adj. not permanent; short-lived.
– DERIVATIVES **transitorily** adv. **transitoriness** n.
– ORIGIN Middle English: from Old French *transitoire*, from Christian Latin *transitorius*, from *transit-* (see TRANSIT).

transit visa ■ n. a visa allowing its holder to pass through a country only, not to stay there.

Transkeian /tranˈskʌɪən/ ■ n. a native or inhabitant of the Transkei region of the Eastern Cape. ▸ an inhabitant of the former Transkei homeland. ■ adj. of or relating to the Transkei.

translate /transˈleɪt, trɑːns-, -nz-/ ■ v. **1** express the sense of (words or text) in another language. ▸ be expressed or be capable of being expressed in another language. **2** (**translate into**) or **translate something into** be converted or convert something into (another form or medium). ▸ Biology convert (a sequence of nucleotides in messenger RNA) to an amino-acid sequence during protein synthesis. **3** move from one place or condition to another. **4** Physics & Mathematics cause to undergo translation.
– DERIVATIVES **translatability** n. **translatable** adj.
– ORIGIN Middle English: from Latin *translat-*, *transferre* (see TRANSFER).

translation ■ n. **1** the action or process of translating. **2** a text or word that is translated. **3** formal or technical the process of moving something from one place to another. ▸ Physics & Mathematics movement of a body such that every point moves in the same direction and over the same distance, without any rotation, reflection, or change in size.
– DERIVATIVES **translational** adj. **translationally** adv.

translator ■ n. **1** a person who translates from one language into another. **2** a program that translates from one programming language into another.

transliterate ■ v. (usu. **be transliterated**) write or print (a letter or word) using the closest corresponding letters of a different alphabet or language.
– DERIVATIVES **transliteration** n. **transliterator** n.
– ORIGIN C19: from TRANS- + Latin *littera* 'letter'.

translocate ■ v. chiefly technical move from one place to another.
– DERIVATIVES **translocation** n.

translucent /transˈluːs(ə)nt, trɑːns-, -nz-/ ■ adj. allowing light to pass through partially; semi-transparent.

– DERIVATIVES **translucence** n. **translucency** n. **translucently** adv.
– ORIGIN C16: from Latin *translucent-*, *translucere* 'shine through'.

transmigrate ■ v. **1** (of the soul) pass into a different body after death. **2** rare migrate.
– DERIVATIVES **transmigration** n. **transmigrator** n. **transmigratory** adj.
– ORIGIN Middle English: from Latin *transmigrare* (see TRANS-, MIGRATE).

transmissible ■ adj. (especially of a disease, virus, etc.) able to be transmitted.
– DERIVATIVES **transmissibility** n.

transmission ■ n. **1** the action or process of transmitting or the state of being transmitted. **2** a programme or signal that is transmitted. **3** the mechanism by which power is transmitted from an engine to the axle in a motor vehicle.
– ORIGIN C17: from Latin *transmissio* (see TRANS-, MISSION).

transmission line ■ n. a conductor or conductors carrying electricity over large distances with minimum losses.

transmit ■ v. (**transmitted**, **transmitting**) **1** cause to pass on from one place or person to another. ▶ communicate (an idea or emotion). **2** broadcast or send out (an electrical signal or a radio or television programme). **3** allow (heat, light, etc.) to pass through a medium.
– DERIVATIVES **transmissive** adj. **transmissivity** n. (pl. **-ies**) (Physics). **transmittable** adj. **transmittal** n.
– ORIGIN Middle English: from Latin *transmittere*, from *trans-* 'across' + *mittere* 'send'.

transmittance ■ n. Physics the ratio of the light energy falling on a body to that transmitted through it.

transmitter ■ n. a device or installation used to generate and transmit electromagnetic waves carrying messages or signals, especially those of radio or television.

transmogrify /tranz'mɒgrɪfʌɪ, trɑːnz-, -ns-/ ■ v. (**-ies**, **-ied**) (usu. **be transmogrified**) chiefly humorous transform in a surprising or magical manner.
– DERIVATIVES **transmogrification** n.
– ORIGIN C17.

transmutation /tranzmjuː'teɪʃ(ə)n, trɑːnz-, -ns-/ ■ n. the action of transmuting or the state of being transmuted. ▶ the changing of one chemical element into another, either by a nuclear process or as a supposed operation in alchemy.
– DERIVATIVES **transmutational** adj. **transmutationist** n.

transmute /tranz'mjuːt, trɑːnz-, -ns-/ ■ v. change in form, nature, or substance. ▶ subject (an element) to transmutation.
– DERIVATIVES **transmutability** n. **transmutable** adj. **transmutative** adj. **transmuter** n.
– ORIGIN Middle English: from Latin *transmutare*, from *trans-* 'across' + *mutare* 'to change'.

transnational ■ adj. extending or operating across national boundaries. ■ n. a multinational company.
– DERIVATIVES **transnationalism** n. **transnationally** adv.

transoceanic ■ adj. **1** crossing an ocean. **2** coming from or situated beyond an ocean.

transom /'trans(ə)m/ ■ n. **1** the flat surface forming the stern of a boat. ▶ a horizontal beam reinforcing the stern of a boat. **2** a strengthening crossbar, in particular one set above a window or door. Compare with MULLION.
– PHRASES **over the transom** N. Amer. informal unsolicited.
– DERIVATIVES **transomed** adj.
– ORIGIN Middle English (earlier as *traversayn*): from Old French *traversin*, from *traverser* (see TRAVERSE).

transom window ■ n. a window set above the transom of a door or larger window.

transonic /tran'sɒnɪk, trɑːn-/ (also **trans-sonic**) ■ adj. denoting or relating to speeds close to that of sound.

trans-Pacific ■ adj. **1** crossing the Pacific. **2** of or relating to an area beyond the Pacific.

transparency ■ n. (pl. **-ies**) **1** the condition of being transparent. **2** a positive transparent photograph printed on plastic or glass, and viewed using a slide projector.

transparent /tran'spar(ə)nt, trɑːn-, -'spɛː-/ ■ adj. **1** allowing light to pass through so that objects behind can be distinctly seen. **2** obvious or evident. **3** Physics transmitting heat or other radiation without distortion. **4** Computing (of a process) functioning without the user being aware of its presence.
– DERIVATIVES **transparently** adv.
– ORIGIN Middle English: from Old French, from medieval Latin *transparere* 'shine through'.

transpersonal ■ adj. of, denoting, or dealing with states of consciousness beyond the limits of personal identity.

transpire ■ v. **1** (usu. **it transpires**) come to be known; prove to be so. **2** happen. **3** Botany (of a plant or leaf) give off water vapour through the stomata.
– DERIVATIVES **transpiration** n.
– ORIGIN Middle English: from French *transpirer* or medieval Latin *transpirare*, from Latin *trans-* 'through' + *spirare* 'breathe'.

transplant ■ v. /trans'plɑːnt, trɑːns-, -nz-/ **1** transfer to another place or situation. ▶ replant (a plant) in another place. **2** take (living tissue or an organ) and implant it in another part of the body or in another body.
■ n. /'transplɑːnt, 'trɑːns-, -nz-/ **1** an operation in which an organ or tissue is transplanted. **2** a person or thing that has been transplanted.
– DERIVATIVES **transplantable** /-'plɑːntəb(ə)l/ adj. **transplantation** /-'teɪʃ(ə)n/ n.
– ORIGIN Middle English: from late Latin *transplantare*, from Latin *trans-* 'across' + *plantare* 'to plant'.

transponder /tran'spɒndə, trɑːn-/ ■ n. a device for receiving a radio signal and automatically transmitting a different signal.
– ORIGIN 1940s: blend of TRANSMIT and RESPOND.

transport ■ v. **1** take or carry from one place to another by means of a vehicle, aircraft, or ship. ▶ historical send (a convict) to a penal colony. **2** (usu. **be transported**) overwhelm with a strong emotion, especially joy. ■ n. **1** a system or means of transporting. ▶ the action of transporting or the state of being transported. ▶ a large vehicle, ship, or aircraft for carrying troops or stores. **2** (**transports**) overwhelmingly strong emotions.
– DERIVATIVES **transportation** n.
– ORIGIN Middle English: from Old French *transporter* or Latin *transportare* 'carry across'.

transportable ■ adj. **1** able to be carried or moved. **2** historical (of an offender or an offence) punishable by transporting to a penal colony.
– DERIVATIVES **transportability** n.

transport café ■ n. British term for TRUCK STOP.

transporter ■ n. a large vehicle used to carry heavy objects, e.g. cars.

transpose ■ v. **1** cause to exchange places. **2** transfer to a different place or context. ▶ write or play (music) in a different key from the original. ■ n. Mathematics a matrix obtained from a given matrix by interchanging rows and columns.
– DERIVATIVES **transposable** adj. **transposal** n. **transposer** n. **transposition** n. **transpositional** adv.
– ORIGIN Middle English: from Old French *transposer*, from *trans-* 'across' + *poser* 'to place'.

transposon /trans'pəʊzɒn, trɑːns-, -nz-/ ■ n. Genetics a segment of bacterial DNA that can be translocated as a whole between chromosomal, phage, and plasmid DNA.
– ORIGIN 1970s: from *transposition*.

transputer /trans'pjuːtə, trɑːns-, -nz-/ ■ n. a microprocessor with integral memory designed for parallel processing.
– ORIGIN 1970s: blend of TRANSISTOR and COMPUTER.

transsexual (also **transexual**) ■ n. a person born with the physical characteristics of one sex who emotionally and psychologically feels that they belong to the opposite sex. ■ adj. of or relating to such a person.
– DERIVATIVES **transsexualism** n. **transsexuality** n.

trans-ship (also **tranship**) ■ v. (**-shipped**, **-shipping**) transfer (cargo) from one ship or other form of transport to another.
– DERIVATIVES **trans-shipment** n.

trans-sonic ■ adj. variant spelling of TRANSONIC.

transubstantiation ■ n. Christian Church the doctrine that the substance of the Eucharistic elements is converted into

transuranic

the body and blood of Christ at consecration, only the appearances of bread and wine still remaining. Compare with **CONSUBSTANTIATION**.

transuranic /ˌtrænsjʊˈrænɪk, ˌtrɑːns-, -nz-/ ■ adj. Chemistry (of an element) having a higher atomic number than uranium (92).

transversal /trænzˈvɜːs(ə)l, trɑːnz-, -ns-/ Geometry ■ adj. (of a line) cutting a system of lines. ■ n. a transversal line.
– DERIVATIVES **transversality** n. **transversally** adv.
– ORIGIN Middle English: from medieval Latin *transversalis*.

transverse /trænzˈvɜːs, trɑːnz-, -ns-/ ■ adj. situated or extending across something.
– DERIVATIVES **transversely** adv.
– ORIGIN Middle English: from Latin *transversus*, *transvertere* 'turn across'.

transverse flute ■ n. a flute which is held horizontally when played.

transverse wave ■ n. Physics a wave vibrating at right angles to the direction of propagation.

transvestite ■ n. a person, typically a man, who derives pleasure from dressing in clothes considered appropriate to the opposite sex.
– DERIVATIVES **transvestism** n. **transvestitism** n.
– ORIGIN 1920s: from German *Transvestit*, from Latin *trans-* 'across' + *vestire* 'clothe'.

Transylvanian /ˌtrænsɪlˈveɪnɪən/ ■ adj. of or relating to Transylvania, a large region of NW Romania.

trap ■ n. 1 a device or enclosure designed to catch and retain animals. 2 an unpleasant situation from which it is hard to escape. ▶ a trick betraying someone into acting contrary to their interests or intentions. 3 a container or device used to collect a specified thing. ▶ a curve in the waste pipe from a bath, basin, or toilet that is always full of liquid to prevent the upward passage of gases. 4 a bunker or other hollow on a golf course. 5 the compartment from which a greyhound is released at the start of a race. 6 a device for hurling an object such as a clay pigeon into the air to be shot at. 7 chiefly historical a light, two-wheeled carriage pulled by a horse or pony. 8 informal a person's mouth: *keep your trap shut!* 9 informal a percussion instrument in a jazz band. ■ v. (**trapped**, **trapping**) 1 catch (an animal) in a trap. 2 prevent from escaping. ▶ catch (something) somewhere so that it cannot be freed. 3 trick into doing something.
– DERIVATIVES **trap-like** adj.
– ORIGIN Old English *træppe*; rel. to Middle Dutch *trappe* and medieval Latin *trappa*.

trapdoor ■ n. 1 a hinged or removable panel in a floor, ceiling, or roof. 2 a feature of a computer program which allows surreptitious unauthorized access.

trapdoor spider ■ n. a spider which lives in a burrow with a hinged cover like a trapdoor. [Family Ctenizidae.]

trapeze ■ n. 1 (also **flying trapeze**) a horizontal bar hanging by two ropes and free to swing, used by acrobats in a circus. 2 Nautical a harness attached by a cable to a dinghy's mast, enabling a sailor to balance the boat by leaning out backwards over the windward side.
– ORIGIN C19: from French *trapèze*, from late Latin *trapezium* (see **TRAPEZIUM**).

trapezium /trəˈpiːzɪəm/ ■ n. (pl. **trapezia** /-zɪə/ or **trapeziums**) Geometry a quadrilateral with one pair of sides parallel. ▶ N. Amer. a quadrilateral with no sides parallel.
– ORIGIN C16: from Greek *trapezion*, from *trapeza* 'table'.

trapezius /trəˈpiːzɪəs/ ■ n. (pl. **trapezii** /-zɪaɪ/) Anatomy either of a pair of large triangular muscles extending over the back of the neck and shoulders and moving the head and shoulder blade.
– ORIGIN C18: from Greek *trapezion* 'trapezium' (because of the shape formed by the muscles).

trapezoid /ˈtrapɪzɔɪd, trəˈpiːzɔɪd/ ■ n. Geometry a quadrilateral with no sides parallel. ▶ N. Amer. a quadrilateral with one pair of sides parallel.
– DERIVATIVES **trapezoidal** adj.
– ORIGIN C18: from late Greek *trapezoeidēs*, from *trapeza* (see **TRAPEZIUM**).

trapper ■ n. a person who traps wild animals, especially for their fur.

trappings ■ pl. n. 1 the visible signs or objects associated with a particular situation or role: *I had the trappings of success.* 2 a horse's ornamental harness.
– ORIGIN Middle English: derivative of obsolete *trap* 'trappings'.

Trappist ■ adj. relating to or denoting a branch of the Cistercian order of monks noted for an austere rule including a vow of silence. ■ n. a member of this order.
– ORIGIN C19: from French *trappiste*, from *La Trappe* in Normandy, where the order was founded.

trap shooting ■ n. the sport of shooting at clay pigeons released from a spring trap.
– DERIVATIVES **trap shooter** n.

trash ■ n. chiefly N. Amer. 1 waste material; refuse. 2 worthless writing, art, etc. 3 a person or people regarded as being of very low social standing. ■ v. 1 informal, chiefly N. Amer. wreck or destroy. 2 informal, chiefly N. Amer. criticize severely. 3 [as adj. **trashed**] informal intoxicated with alcohol or drugs.
– DERIVATIVES **trashily** adv. **trashiness** n. **trashy** adj. (**-ier**, **-iest**).
– ORIGIN Middle English.

trash can ■ n. N. Amer. a dustbin.

trash talk informal US ■ n. insulting or boastful speech intended to demoralize, intimidate, or humiliate. ■ v. (**trash-talk**) use such speech.
– DERIVATIVES **trash talker** n.

trattoria /ˌtratəˈriːə/ ■ n. an Italian restaurant.
– ORIGIN from Italian.

trauma /ˈtrɔːmə, ˈtraʊmə/ ■ n. (pl. **traumas** or **traumata** /-mətə/) 1 a deeply distressing experience. 2 Medicine physical injury. 3 emotional shock following a stressful event.
– DERIVATIVES **traumatization** (also **-isation**) n. **traumatize** (also **-ise**) v.
– ORIGIN C17: from Greek, 'wound'.

traumatic /trɔːˈmatɪk, traʊ-/ ■ adj. 1 deeply disturbing or distressing: *a traumatic divorce.* 2 Medicine relating to or denoting physical injury.
– DERIVATIVES **traumatically** adv.

traumatism ■ n. chiefly technical a traumatic effect or condition.

travail /ˈtraveɪl/ poetic/literary ■ n. (also **travails**) painful or laborious effort. ▶ labour pains. ■ v. undergo such effort.
– ORIGIN Middle English: via Old French from medieval Latin *trepalium* 'instrument of torture', from Latin *tres* 'three' + *palus* 'stake'.

travel ■ v. (**travelled**, **travelling**; US also **traveled**, **traveling**) 1 make a journey. ▶ journey along (a road) or through (a region). 2 move or go. ▶ informal (especially of a vehicle) move quickly. 3 withstand a journey without impairment. ■ n. 1 the action of travelling. ▶ (**travels**) journeys, especially abroad. ▶ [as modifier] (of a device) sufficiently compact for use when travelling. 2 the range, rate, or mode of motion of a part of a machine.
– ORIGIN Middle English: var. of **TRAVAIL**.

travel agency (also **travel bureau**) ■ n. an agency that makes the necessary arrangements for travellers.
– DERIVATIVES **travel agent** n.

travelator /ˈtravəleɪtə/ (also **travolator**) ■ n. a moving walkway, typically at an airport.
– ORIGIN 1950s: from **TRAVEL**, suggested by **ESCALATOR**.

travelled /ˈtrav(ə)ld/ ■ adj. 1 having travelled to many places. 2 used by people travelling.

traveller (US also **traveler**) ■ n. 1 a person who is travelling or who often travels. 2 a gypsy. 3 (also **New Age traveller**) a person who holds New Age values and leads an itinerant and unconventional lifestyle. 4 Austral. an itinerant worker.

traveller's cheque ■ n. a cheque for a fixed amount that may be cashed or used in payment abroad after endorsement by the holder's signature.

traveller's joy ■ n. a tall scrambling wild clematis with small fragrant flowers and tufts of grey hairs around the seeds. [*Clematis brachiata* (southern Africa), *C. vitalba* (Eurasia), and related species.]

VOWELS　a cat　ɑː arm　ɛ bed　ɛː hair　ə ago　əː her　ɪ sit　i cosy　iː see　ɒ hot　ɔː saw　ʌ run

traveller's tale ■ n. a story about the unusual characteristics or customs of a foreign country, regarded as exaggerated or untrue.

travelling crane ■ n. a crane able to move on rails, especially along an overhead support.

travelling salesman ■ n. a representative of a firm who visits businesses to show samples and gain orders.

travelling scholarship ■ n. a scholarship given to enable the holder to travel for study or research.

travelling wave ■ n. Physics a wave in which the positions of maximum and minimum amplitude travel through the medium.

travelogue ■ n. a film, book, or illustrated lecture about a person's travels.
– ORIGIN C20: from TRAVEL, on the pattern of *monologue*.

travel-sick ■ adj. suffering from nausea caused by the motion of a moving vehicle, boat, or aircraft.
– DERIVATIVES **travel-sickness** n.

traverse /'travəs, trə'vɜːs/ ■ v. 1 travel or extend across or through. ▸ cross a rock face by means of a series of sideways movements from one practicable line of ascent or descent to another. ▸ ski diagonally across (a slope), losing only a little height. 2 move back and forth or sideways. ▸ turn (a large gun or other device on a pivot) to face a different direction. 3 Law deny (an allegation) in pleading. ■ n. 1 an act of traversing. 2 a part of a structure that extends or is fixed across something. 3 a mechanism enabling a large gun to be traversed. ▸ the sideways movement of a part in a machine. 4 a single line of survey, usually plotted from compass bearings and chained or paced distances between angular points.
– DERIVATIVES **traversable** adj. **traversal** n.
– ORIGIN Middle English: from Old French *traverser*, from late Latin *traversare*; noun from Old French *travers*, partly based on *traverser*.

travertine /'travətɪn/ ■ n. white or light-coloured calcareous rock deposited from mineral springs, used in building.
– ORIGIN C18: from Italian *travertino, tivertino*, from Latin *tiburtinus* 'of Tibur' (now Tivoli, near Rome).

travesty /'travɪsti/ ■ n. (pl. **-ies**) an absurd or grotesque misrepresentation. ■ v. (**-ies, -ied**) represent in such a way.
– ORIGIN C17: from French *travesti, travestir* 'disguise'.

travois /trə'vɔɪ/ ■ n. (pl. same /-'vɔɪz/) a V-shaped frame of poles pulled by a horse, formerly used by North American Indians to carry goods.
– ORIGIN C19: alteration of synonymous *travail*, from French.

travolator ■ n. variant spelling of TRAVELATOR.

trawl ■ v. 1 fish or catch with a trawl net or seine. 2 search thoroughly. ■ n. 1 an act of trawling. 2 (also **trawl net**) a large wide-mouthed fishing net dragged by a boat along the bottom of the sea or a lake. 3 (also **trawl line**) N. Amer. a long sea-fishing line along which are tied buoys supporting baited hooks on short lines.
– ORIGIN C16: prob. from Middle Dutch *traghelen* 'to drag'.

trawler ■ n. a fishing boat used for trawling.

tray ■ n. a flat, shallow container with a raised rim, typically used for carrying or holding things.
– DERIVATIVES **trayful** n. (pl. **-fuls**)
– ORIGIN Old English, from the Germanic base of TREE.

trayf /treɪf/ ■ adj. another term for TREIF.

TRC ■ abbrev. (in South Africa) Truth and Reconciliation Commission.

treacherous ■ adj. 1 guilty of or involving betrayal or deception. 2 (of ground, water, conditions, etc.) having hidden or unpredictable dangers.
– DERIVATIVES **treacherously** adv. **treacherousness** n. **treachery** n.
– ORIGIN Middle English: from Old French *trecherous*, from *trecheor* 'a cheat', from *trechier* 'to cheat'.

treacle ■ n. molasses. ▸ golden syrup.
– DERIVATIVES **treacly** adj.
– ORIGIN Middle English: from Old French *triacle*, from Greek *thēriakē* 'antidote against venom', from *thērion* 'wild beast'.

tread ■ v. (past **trod**; past part. **trodden** or **trod**) 1 walk in a specified way. ▸ walk on or along. 2 press down or crush with the feet. ■ n. 1 a manner or the sound of walking.

treat

2 (also **tread board**) the top surface of a step or stair. 3 the thick moulded part of a vehicle tyre that grips the road. ▸ the part of a wheel that touches the ground or rail. 4 the part of the sole of a shoe that rests on the ground.
– PHRASES **tread** (or **step**) **on someone's toes** offend someone by encroaching on their area of responsibility. **tread water 1** maintain an upright position in deep water by moving the feet with a walking movement and the hands with a downward circular motion. 2 fail to make progress.
– DERIVATIVES **treader** n.
– ORIGIN Old English, of West Germanic origin.

treadle /'trɛd(ə)l/ ■ n. a lever worked by the foot and imparting motion to a machine. ■ v. operate by a treadle.
– ORIGIN Old English *tredel* 'stair, step'.

treadmill ■ n. 1 a large wheel turned by the weight of people or animals treading on steps fitted into its inner surface, formerly used to drive machinery. 2 a device used for exercise consisting of a continuous moving belt on which to walk or run. 3 a job or situation that is tiring, boring, or unpleasant.

treadwheel ■ n. another term for TREADMILL (sense 1).

treason (also **high treason**) ■ n. the crime of betraying one's country, especially by attempting to kill or overthrow the sovereign or government.
– DERIVATIVES **treasonable** adj. **treasonably** adv. **treasonous** adj.
– ORIGIN Middle English: from Anglo-Norman French *treisoun*, from Latin *traditio(n-)*, from *tradere* 'hand over'.

treasure ■ n. 1 a quantity of precious metals, gems, or other valuable objects. ▸ a very valuable object. 2 informal a much loved or highly valued person. ■ v. 1 keep carefully (a valuable or valued item). 2 value highly.
– ORIGIN Middle English: from Old French *tresor*, from Greek *thēsauros* (see THESAURUS).

treasure hunt ■ n. a game in which players search for hidden objects by following a trail of clues.

treasurer ■ n. a person appointed to administer or manage the financial assets and liabilities of a society, company, etc. ▸ (also **Lord Treasurer**) Brit. historical the head of the Exchequer.
– DERIVATIVES **treasurership** n.

treasure trove ■ n. a hidden store of valuable or delightful things.
– ORIGIN Middle English: from Anglo-Norman French *tresor trové* 'found treasure'.

treasury ■ n. (pl. **-ies**) 1 the funds or revenue of a state, institution, or society. ▸ (**Treasury**) (in some countries) the government department responsible for the overall management of the economy. 2 a place where treasure is stored. 3 a collection of valuable or delightful things.
– ORIGIN Middle English: from Old French *tresorie* (see TREASURE).

Treasury bench ■ n. (in the UK) the front bench in the House of Commons occupied by the Prime Minister, the Chancellor of the Exchequer, and other members of the government.

Treasury bill ■ n. a short-dated government security, yielding no interest but issued at a discount on its redemption price.

Treasury note ■ n. US & historical a note issued by the Treasury for use as currency.

treat ■ v. 1 behave towards or deal with in a certain way. ▸ present or discuss (a subject). 2 give medical care or attention to. 3 apply a process or a substance to. 4 (**treat someone to**) provide someone with (food, drink, or entertainment) at one's expense. ▸ (**treat oneself**) do or have something very pleasurable. 5 (usu. **treat with**) negotiate terms. ■ n. 1 a surprise gift, event, etc. that gives great pleasure. 2 (**one's treat**) an act of treating someone to something.
– PHRASES ——— **a treat** informal doing something specified very well: ▸ (**look a treat**) look attractive. *their tactics worked a treat.*
– DERIVATIVES **treatable** adj. **treater** n.
– ORIGIN Middle English: from Old French *traitier*, from Latin *tractare* 'handle', from *trahere* 'draw, pull'.

treatise

treatise /ˈtriːtɪs, -ɪz/ ■ n. a written work dealing formally and systematically with a subject.
– ORIGIN Middle English: from Anglo-Norman French *tretis*, from Old French *traitier* (see TREAT).

treatment ■ n. 1 the process or manner of treating someone or something in a certain way. ▶ the presentation or discussion of a subject. 2 medical care for an illness or injury. 3 the use of a substance or process to preserve or give particular properties to something. 4 (**the full treatment**) informal used to indicate that something is done enthusiastically or vigorously.

treaty ■ n. (pl. **-ies**) a formally concluded and ratified agreement between states.
– ORIGIN Middle English: from Old French *traite*, from Latin *tractatus* (see TRACTATE).

treble[1] ■ adj. 1 consisting of three parts. 2 multiplied or occurring three times. ■ predet. three times as much or as many. ■ n. 1 Brit. three sporting victories or championships in the same season, event, etc. 2 a hit on the narrow ring enclosed by the two middle circles of a dartboard, scoring treble. 3 a thing which is three times larger than usual or is made up of three parts. ■ pron. an amount which is three times as large as usual. ■ v. make or become treble.
– ORIGIN Middle English: from Latin *triplus* (see TRIPLE).

treble[2] ■ n. 1 a high-pitched voice, especially a boy's singing voice. 2 [as modifier] denoting a relatively high-pitched member of a family of instruments. ▶ (also **treble bell**) the smallest and highest-pitched bell of a ring or set. 3 the high-frequency output of a radio or audio system, corresponding to the treble in music.
– ORIGIN Middle English: from TREBLE[1], because it was the highest part in a three-part contrapuntal composition.

treble clef ■ n. Music a clef placing G above middle C on the second-lowest line of the stave.

trebly ■ adj. (of sound, especially recorded music) having too much treble. ■ adv. three times as much.

trecento /treɪˈtʃɛntəʊ/ ■ n. (**the trecento**) the 14th century as a period of Italian art, architecture, or literature.
– ORIGIN Italian, '300', shortened from *milletrecento* '1300', used with ref. to the years 1300–99.

tree ■ n. 1 a woody perennial plant typically with a single stem or trunk growing to a considerable height and bearing lateral branches. 2 a wooden structure or part of a structure. 3 (also **tree diagram**) a diagram with a structure of branching connecting lines, representing different processes and relationships. ■ v. (**trees**, **treed**, **treeing**) 1 force (a hunted animal) to take refuge in a tree. 2 informal, chiefly US force into a difficult situation.
– PHRASES **out of one's tree** informal, chiefly N. Amer. crazy.
– DERIVATIVES **treeless** adj. **treelessness** n. **tree-like** adj.
– ORIGIN Old English, of Germanic origin.

tree fern ■ n. a large palm-like fern with a trunk-like stem. [*Cyathea*, *Dicksonia*, and other genera.]

tree frog ■ n. an arboreal frog that has long toes with adhesive disks and is typically small and brightly coloured. [Families Hylidae and Rhacophoridae: many species.]

tree fuchsia ■ n. an evergreen African shrub or tree with tubular orange-red flowers clustered characteristically on old wood. [*Halleria lucida*.]

tree heath ■ n. a white-flowered shrub of the heather family, with woody nodules that are used to make briar pipes. [*Erica arborea*.]

treehopper ■ n. a tree-dwelling jumping bug that lives chiefly in the tropics. [Family Membracidae: several species.]

tree house ■ n. a structure built in the branches of a tree for children to play in.

tree-hugger ■ n. informal, chiefly derogatory an environmental campaigner (used in reference to the practice of embracing a tree to prevent it from being felled).
– DERIVATIVES **tree-hugging** n.

treeline ■ n. 1 the altitude above which no trees grow on a mountain. 2 (in high northern (or southern) latitudes) the line north (or south) of which no trees grow.

treen ■ n. [treated as pl.] small domestic wooden objects, especially antiques.
– ORIGIN Old English *trēowen* 'wooden'.

tree of heaven ■ n. a tall, fast-growing Chinese tree, cultivated as an ornamental and shade tree. [*Ailanthus altissima*.]

tree of knowledge (also **tree of knowledge of good and evil**) ■ n. (in the Bible) the tree in the Garden of Eden bearing the forbidden fruit which Adam and Eve disobediently ate (Genesis 2:9, 3).

tree of life ■ n. 1 (**Tree of Life**) (in the Bible) a tree in the Garden of Eden whose fruit imparts eternal life (Genesis 3:22–24). 2 the thuja.

tree ring ■ n. each of a number of concentric rings in the cross section of a tree trunk, representing a single year's growth.

tree surgeon ■ n. a person who prunes and treats old or damaged trees in order to preserve them.
– DERIVATIVES **tree surgery** n.

tree toad ■ n. another term for TREE FROG.

tree tomato ■ n. another term for TAMARILLO.

tree wisteria (also **tree wistaria**) ■ n. a leguminous tree with drooping bunches of pale blue to violet flowers, native to southern Africa. [*Bolusanthus speciosus*.]

trefoil /ˈtrɛfɔɪl, ˈtriːfɔɪl/ ■ n. 1 a small plant with yellow flowers and three-lobed cloverlike leaves. [Genera *Trifolium* and *Lotus*: several species.] 2 an ornamental design of three rounded lobes like a clover leaf. 3 a thing having three parts, or a set of three.
– DERIVATIVES **trefoiled** adj.
– ORIGIN Middle English: from Anglo-Norman French *trifoil*, from Latin *trifolium*, from *tri-* 'three' + *folium* 'leaf'.

treif /treɪf/ (also **treifa** or **trayf**) ■ adj. (of food) not satisfying the requirements of Jewish law.
– ORIGIN C19: from Hebrew *ṭĕrēpāh* 'the flesh of an animal torn or mauled'.

trek ■ n. 1 a long or arduous journey, especially one made on foot. ▶ (**the Trek**) S. African short for GREAT TREK. ▶ S. African a stage of a journey. ▶ a migration of animals. 2 S. African short for TREK FISHING. ■ v. (**trekked**, **trekking**) go on a trek. ▶ historical, chiefly S. African migrate or journey by ox-wagon. ▶ (of wild animals) migrate.
– DERIVATIVES **trekker** n. **trekking** n.
– ORIGIN C19: from S. African Dutch *trek* (n.), *trekken* (v.) 'to pull, travel'.

trekboer /ˈtrɛkbʊə/ ■ n. S. African historical a nomadic Afrikaner farmer.
– ORIGIN C19: from TREK + Dutch *boer* 'farmer'.

trek fishing ■ n. S. African fishing by dropping a seine net from a boat and hauling it to shore from the beach.
– DERIVATIVES **trek fish** v. **trek fisherman** n. **trek fishery** n.

Trekkie ■ n. (pl. **-ies**) informal a fan of the US science-fiction television programme *Star Trek*.

trek net ■ n. & v. South African term for SEINE.
– DERIVATIVES **trek netter** n. **trek netting** n.

trellis ■ n. a framework of light wooden or metal bars used as a support for trees or creepers. ■ v. (**trellised**, **trellising**) [usu. as adj. **trellised**] provide or support with a trellis.
– ORIGIN Middle English: from Old French *trelis*, from Latin *trilix* 'three-ply', from *tri-* 'three' + *licium* 'warp thread'.

Trematoda /ˌtrɛməˈtəʊdə/ ■ pl. n. Zoology a class of flatworms that comprises those flukes that are internal parasites.
– DERIVATIVES **trematode** /ˈtrɛmətəʊd/ n.
– ORIGIN from Greek *trēmatōdēs* 'perforated', from *trēma* 'hole'.

tremble ■ v. shake involuntarily, typically as a result of anxiety, excitement, or frailty. ▶ be in a state of extreme apprehension. ▶ (of a thing) shake or quiver slightly. ■ n. a trembling feeling, movement, or sound.
– PHRASES **all of a tremble** informal extremely agitated or excited.
– DERIVATIVES **trembling** adj. **tremblingly** adv. **trembly** adj. (**-ier**, **-iest**) (informal).

– ORIGIN Middle English: from Old French *trembler*, from medieval Latin *tremulare*, from Latin *tremulus* (see TREMULOUS).

trembler ■ n. an automatic vibrator for making and breaking an electric circuit.

tremendous ■ adj. **1** very great in amount, scale, or intensity. ▸ archaic inspiring awe or dread. **2** informal extremely good or impressive; excellent.
– DERIVATIVES **tremendously** adv. **tremendousness** n.
– ORIGIN C17: from Latin *tremendus*, from *tremere* 'tremble'.

tremolite /'trɛm(ə)laɪt/ ■ n. a white to grey amphibole mineral which occurs widely in igneous rocks and is characteristic of metamorphosed dolomitic limestones.
– ORIGIN C18: from *Tremola* Valley, Switzerland.

tremolo ■ n. (pl. **-os**) a wavering effect in singing or playing some musical instruments.
– ORIGIN C18: from Italian.

tremor ■ n. **1** an involuntary quivering movement. ▸ (also **earth tremor**) a slight earthquake. **2** a sudden feeling of fear or excitement. ■ v. undergo a tremor or tremors.
– ORIGIN C17: from Latin *tremor*, from *tremere* 'to tremble'.

tremulous /'trɛmjʊləs/ ■ adj. shaking or quivering slightly. ▸ timid; nervous.
– DERIVATIVES **tremulously** adv. **tremulousness** n.
– ORIGIN C17: from Latin *tremulus*, from *tremere* 'to tremble'.

trench ■ n. **1** a long, narrow ditch. ▸ a ditch of this type dug by troops to provide shelter from enemy fire. **2** (also **ocean trench**) a long, narrow, deep depression in the ocean bed, typically running parallel to a plate boundary and marking a subduction zone. ■ v. dig a trench or trenches in. ▸ turn over the earth of (a field or garden) by digging a succession of adjoining ditches.
– ORIGIN Middle English: from Old French *trenche* (n.), *trenchier* (v.), from Latin *truncare* (see TRUNCATE).

trenchant /'trɛn(t)ʃ(ə)nt/ ■ adj. **1** vigorous or incisive in expression or style. **2** archaic or poetic/literary (of a weapon or tool) having a sharp edge.
– DERIVATIVES **trenchancy** n. **trenchantly** adv.
– ORIGIN Middle English: from Old French, 'cutting', from *trenchier* (see TRENCH).

trench coat ■ n. a loose belted, double-breasted raincoat in a military style.

trencher[1] ■ n. historical a wooden plate or platter.
– ORIGIN Middle English: from Anglo-Norman French *trenchour*, from Old French *trenchier* (see TRENCH).

trencher[2] ■ n. a machine or attachment used in digging trenches.

trencherman ■ n. (pl. **-men**) humorous a person who eats heartily or in a specified manner.

trench fever ■ n. a highly contagious rickettsial disease transmitted by lice, that infested soldiers in the trenches in the First World War.

trench foot ■ n. a painful condition of the feet caused by long immersion in cold water or mud and marked by blackening and death of surface tissue.

trench mortar ■ n. a light simple mortar designed to propel a bomb into enemy trenches.

trench warfare ■ n. a type of combat in which opposing troops fight from trenches facing each other.

trend ■ n. **1** a general direction in which something is developing or changing. **2** a fashion. ■ v. (especially of a geographical feature) bend or turn away in a specified direction.
– ORIGIN Old English *trendan* 'revolve, rotate', of Germanic origin.

trendify ■ v. informal, chiefly derogatory make fashionable.

trendsetter ■ n. a person who leads the way in fashion or ideas.
– DERIVATIVES **trendsetting** adj.

trendy informal ■ adj. (**-ier**, **-iest**) very fashionable or up to date. ■ n. (pl. **-ies**) a person of this type.
– DERIVATIVES **trendily** adv. **trendiness** n.

trepan /trɪ'pan/ ■ n. chiefly historical a trephine (crown saw) used by surgeons for perforating the skull. ■ v. (**tre-panned**, **trepanning**) perforate (a person's skull) with a trepan.

– DERIVATIVES **trepanation** /ˌtrɛpə'neɪʃ(ə)n/ n.
– ORIGIN Middle English: the noun from Greek *trupanon*, from *trupan* 'to bore', from *trupē* 'hole'; the verb from Old French *trepaner*.

trephine /trɪ'faɪn, -'fiːn/ ■ n. a crown saw used in surgery to remove a circle of tissue or bone. ■ v. operate on with a trephine.
– DERIVATIVES **trephination** /ˌtrɛfɪ'neɪʃ(ə)n/ n.
– ORIGIN C17: from Latin *tres fines* 'three ends', influenced by TREPAN.

trepidation ■ n. a feeling of fear or agitation about something that may happen.
– ORIGIN C15: from Latin *trepidatio(n-)*, from *trepidare* 'be agitated, tremble'.

treponeme /'trɛpəniːm/ (also **treponema** /-ə/) ■ n. a spirochaete bacterium of a genus (*Treponema*) including the causal agents of syphilis and yaws.
– DERIVATIVES **treponemal** adj.
– ORIGIN C20: from *Treponema*, from Greek *trepein* 'to turn' + *nēma* 'thread'.

trespass ■ v. **1** enter someone's land or property without their permission. ▸ (**trespass on**) make unfair claims on or take advantage of (something). **2** (**trespass against**) archaic or poetic/literary commit an offence against (a person or a set of rules). ■ n. **1** Law entry to a person's land or property without their permission. **2** archaic or poetic/literary a sin; an offence.
– DERIVATIVES **trespasser** n.
– ORIGIN Middle English: from Old French *trespasser* 'pass over, trespass', *trespas* 'passing across', from medieval Latin *transpassare* (see TRANS-, PASS[1]).

tress ■ n. a long lock of a woman's hair.
– DERIVATIVES **-tressed** adj.
– ORIGIN Middle English: from Old French *tresse*, perhaps from Greek *trikha* 'threefold'.

tressure /'trɛʃə, 'trɛs(j)ʊə/ ■ n. Heraldry a thin border inset from the edge of a shield, narrower than an orle and usually borne double.
– ORIGIN Middle English (denoting a band for the hair): from Old French *tressour* (see TRESS).

trestle ■ n. **1** a framework consisting of a horizontal beam supported by two pairs of sloping legs, used in pairs to support a flat surface such as a table top. **2** (also **trestlework**) an open braced framework used to support an elevated structure such as a bridge.
– ORIGIN Middle English: from Old French *trestel*, from Latin *transtrum* 'beam'.

trestle table ■ n. a table consisting of a board or boards laid on trestles.

trevally /trɪ'vali/ ■ n. (pl. **-ies**) a marine sporting fish of the Indo-Pacific. [*Caranx* and other genera: several species.]
– ORIGIN C19: prob. an alteration of *cavally* 'horse mackerel', from Spanish *caballo* 'horse'.

trews /truːz/ ■ pl. n. chiefly Brit. trousers. ▸ close-fitting tartan trousers worn by certain Scottish regiments.
– ORIGIN C16: from Irish *triús*, Scottish Gaelic *triubhas* (sing.).

tri- /traɪ/ ■ comb. form three; having three: *triathlon*. ▸ Chemistry (in names of compounds) containing three atoms or groups of a specified kind: *trichloroethane*.
– ORIGIN from Latin *tres*, Greek *treis* 'three'.

triable /'traɪəb(ə)l/ ■ adj. Law (of an offence or case) liable to a judicial trial.

triac /'traɪak/ ■ n. Electronics a three-electrode semiconductor device that will conduct in either direction when triggered by a positive or negative signal at the gate electrode.
– ORIGIN 1960s: from TRIODE + AC (short for *alternating current*).

triacetate /traɪ'asɪteɪt/ (also **cellulose triacetate**) ■ n. a form of cellulose acetate containing three acetate groups per glucose monomer, used as a basis for man-made fibres.

triad /'traɪad/ ■ n. **1** a group or set of three connected people or things. ▸ a chord of three musical notes, consisting of a given note with the third and fifth above it.

triage

2 a Chinese secret society involved in organized crime.
– DERIVATIVES **triadic** adj.
– ORIGIN C16: from French *triade*, or from Greek *trias*, *triad-*, from *treis* 'three'.

triage /ˈtrɑːʒ/ ■ n. **1** the action of sorting according to quality. **2** Medicine the assignment of degrees of urgency to wounds or illnesses to decide the order of treatment of a large number of patients.
– ORIGIN C18: from French, from *trier* 'separate out'.

trial ■ n. **1** a formal examination of evidence in order to decide guilt in a case of criminal or civil proceedings. **2** a test of performance, qualities, or suitability. ▸ a sports match to test the ability of players eligible for selection to a team. ▸ (**trials**) an event in which horses or dogs compete or perform. **3** something that tests a person's endurance or forbearance. ■ v. (**trialled**, **trialling**; US **trialed**, **trialing**) **1** test (something) to assess its suitability or performance. **2** (of a horse or dog) compete in trials.
– PHRASES **on trial 1** being tried in a court of law. **2** undergoing tests or scrutiny. **trial and error** the process of experimenting with various methods until one finds the most successful.
– ORIGIN Middle English: from Anglo-Norman French, or from medieval Latin *triallum*.

trial balance ■ n. a statement of all debits and credits in a double-entry account book, with any disagreement indicating an error.

trial balloon ■ n. a tentative measure taken or statement made to see how a new policy will be received.

trial court ■ n. a court of law where cases are first tried, as opposed to an appeal court.

trialist (Brit. also **triallist**) ■ n. **1** a person who participates in a sports trial or a trial of a new product. **2** chiefly S. African a person who is being, or has been, tried in court.

trialogue ■ n. a dialogue between three people.
– ORIGIN C16: from TRI- + DIALOGUE (the prefix *di-* misinterpreted as 'two').

trial run ■ n. a preliminary test of a new system or product.

triangle ■ n. **1** a plane figure with three straight sides and three angles. **2** something in the form of a triangle. **3** a musical instrument consisting of a steel rod bent into a triangle, sounded with a rod. **4** an emotional relationship involving a couple and a third person with whom one of them is involved.
– ORIGIN Middle English: from Old French *triangle* or Latin *triangulum*, from *triangulus* (see TRI-, ANGLE[1]).

triangle of forces ■ n. Physics a triangle whose sides represent in magnitude and direction three forces in equilibrium.

triangular ■ adj. shaped like a triangle. ▸ involving three people or parties. ▸ (of a pyramid) having a three-sided base.
– DERIVATIVES **triangularity** n. **triangularly** adv.

triangular number ■ n. any of the series of numbers (1, 3, 6, 10, 15, etc.) obtained by continued summation of the natural numbers 1, 2, 3, 4, 5, etc.

triangular trade ■ n. a multilateral system of trading in which a country pays for its imports from one country by its exports to another.

triangulate /trʌɪˈaŋɡjʊleɪt/ ■ v. **1** divide (an area) into triangles for surveying purposes. ▸ measure and map (an area) by the use of triangles with a known base length and base angles. ▸ determine (a height, distance, or location) in this way. **2** form into a triangle or triangles.

triangulation ■ n. **1** (in surveying) the tracing and measurement of a series or network of triangles in order to determine the distances and relative positions of points spread over a territory or region. **2** formation of or division into triangles.

triangulation point ■ n. another term for TRIG POINT.

Triassic /trʌɪˈasɪk/ ■ adj. Geology relating to or denoting the earliest period of the Mesozoic era (between the Permian and Jurassic periods, about 245 to 208 million years ago), a time when the first dinosaurs, ammonites, and primitive mammals appeared.

– ORIGIN C19: from late Latin *trias* (see TRIAD), because the strata are divisible into three groups.

triathlon /trʌɪˈaθlɒn, -lən/ ■ n. an athletic contest consisting of three different events, typically swimming, cycling, and long-distance running.
– DERIVATIVES **triathlete** n.
– ORIGIN 1970s: from TRI-, on the pattern of *decathlon*.

triatomic /ˌtrʌɪəˈtɒmɪk/ ■ adj. Chemistry consisting of three atoms.

triaxial /trʌɪˈaksɪəl/ ■ adj. having or relating to three axes, especially in mechanical or astronomical contexts.

triazine /ˈtrʌɪəziːn, trʌɪˈaziːn, -zɪn/ ■ n. Chemistry a compound whose molecule contains an unsaturated ring of three carbon and three nitrogen atoms.

tribal ■ adj. of or characteristic of a tribe or tribes. ▸ chiefly derogatory characterized by a tendency to form groups or by strong group loyalty. ■ n. (**tribals**) members of tribal communities, especially in the Indian subcontinent.
– DERIVATIVES **tribalism** n. **tribalist** n. **tribalistic** adj. **tribally** adv.

tribasic /trʌɪˈbeɪsɪk/ ■ adj. Chemistry (of an acid) having three replaceable hydrogen atoms.

tribe ■ n. **1** a social division in a traditional society consisting of linked families or communities with a common culture and dialect. ▸ derogatory a distinctive close-knit social or political group. ▸ (**tribes**) informal large numbers of people. **2** Biology a taxonomic category that ranks above genus and below family or subfamily.
– ORIGIN Middle English: from Old French *tribu* or Latin *tribus*; perhaps rel. to *tri-* 'three' and referring to the three divisions of the early people of Rome.

USAGE
In historical contexts, the word **tribe** is unexceptional (*the area was inhabited by Slavic tribes*). However, in contemporary contexts, used to refer to traditional societies today, use of the word can be problematic, associated, as it is, with past attitudes of white colonialists towards so-called primitive or uncivilized peoples. For this reason, it is generally preferable to use terms such as **community** or **people**.

tribesman (or **tribeswoman**) ■ n. (pl. **-men**, **-women**) a member of a tribe in a traditional society.

tribo- /ˈtrʌɪbəʊ, ˈtrɪbəʊ/ ■ comb. form relating to friction: *triboelectricity*.
– ORIGIN from Greek *tribos* 'rubbing'.

triboelectricity ■ n. electric charge generated by friction.

tribology /trʌɪˈbɒlədʒi/ ■ n. the branch of science and technology concerned with surfaces in relative motion, as in bearings.
– DERIVATIVES **tribological** adj. **tribologist** n.

tribulation /ˌtrɪbjʊˈleɪʃ(ə)n/ ■ n. a state of great trouble or suffering. ▸ a cause of this.
– ORIGIN Middle English: from eccles. Latin *tribulatio(n-)*, from Latin *tribulare* 'press, oppress', from *terere* 'rub'.

tribunal /trʌɪˈbjuːn(ə)l, trɪ-/ ■ n. **1** a body established to settle certain types of dispute. **2** a court of justice.
– ORIGIN Middle English: from Latin *tribunal* 'raised platform provided for magistrates' seats', from *tribunus* (see TRIBUNE[1]).

tribune[1] ■ n. **1** (also **tribune of the people**) an official in ancient Rome chosen by the plebeians to protect their interests. ▸ (also **military tribune**) a Roman legionary officer. **2** a popular leader; a champion of the people.
– DERIVATIVES **tribunate** n. **tribuneship** n.
– ORIGIN Middle English: from Latin *tribunus* 'head of a tribe', from *tribus* 'tribe'.

tribune[2] ■ n. **1** an apse in a basilica. **2** a dais, rostrum, or other raised area, especially in a church.
– ORIGIN C17: from Italian, from medieval Latin *tribuna*, alteration of Latin *tribunal* (see TRIBUNAL).

tributary /ˈtrɪbjʊt(ə)ri/ ■ n. (pl. **-ies**) **1** a river or stream flowing into a larger river or lake. **2** historical a person or state that pays tribute to another state or ruler.
– ORIGIN Middle English: from Latin *tributarius*, from *tributum* (see TRIBUTE).

tribute ■ n. **1** an act, statement, or gift that is intended to

show gratitude, respect, or admiration. ▶ something resulting from and indicating the worth of something else: *his victory was a tribute to his persistence.* **2** historical payment made periodically by one state or ruler to another, especially as a sign of dependence.
– ORIGIN Middle English: from Latin *tributum*, from *tribuere* 'assign' (orig. 'divide between tribes'), from *tribus* 'tribe'.

tricameral /trʌɪˈkam(ə)r(ə)l/ ■ adj. (in South Africa 1983–94) of or denoting the system whereby the legislature consisted of three ethnically-based houses.

trice /trʌɪs/ ■ n. (in phr. **in a trice**) in a moment; very quickly.
– ORIGIN Middle English *trice* 'a tug', figuratively 'an instant', from Middle Dutch *trīsen* 'pull sharply'.

tricentenary ■ n. (pl. **-ies**) another term for TERCENTENARY.
– DERIVATIVES **tricentennial** adj. & n.

triceps /ˈtrʌɪsɛps/ ■ n. (pl. same) Anatomy any of several muscles having three points of attachment at one end, particularly (also **triceps brachii** /ˈbreɪkɪʌɪ/) the large muscle at the back of the upper arm.
– ORIGIN C16: from Latin, 'three-headed', from *tri-* 'three' + *-ceps*, from *caput* 'head'.

triceratops /trʌɪˈsɛrətɒps/ ■ n. a large quadrupedal herbivorous dinosaur living at the end of the Cretaceous period, having a massive head with two large horns, a smaller horn on the beaked snout, and a bony frill above the neck.
– ORIGIN from Greek *trikeratos* 'three-horned' + *ōps* 'face'.

trichina /ˈtrɪkɪnə, trɪˈkʌɪnə/ ■ n. (pl. **trichinae** /-niː/) a parasitic nematode worm of humans and other mammals, the adults of which live in the small intestine. [Genus *Trichinella*.]
– ORIGIN C19: from Greek *trikhinos* 'of hair'.

trichinosis /ˌtrɪkɪˈnəʊsɪs/ ■ n. a disease caused by trichinae, typically from infected meat, characterized by digestive disturbance, fever, and muscular rigidity.

trichloroethane /ˌtrʌɪklɔːrəʊˈiːθeɪn, -klɒr-/ ■ n. Chemistry a colourless non-flammable volatile liquid, used as a solvent and cleaner.

trichlorophenol /ˌtrʌɪkloːrə(ʊ)ˈfiːnɒl, -klɒr-/ ■ n. Chemistry a synthetic crystalline compound used as an insecticide and preservative in the synthesis of pesticides.

tricho- /ˈtrɪkəʊ, ˈtrʌɪkəʊ/ ■ comb. form of or relating to hair: *trichology*.
– ORIGIN from Greek *thrix, trikhos* 'hair'.

trichology /trɪˈkɒlədʒi/ ■ n. the branch of medical and cosmetic study and practice concerned with the hair and scalp.
– DERIVATIVES **trichological** adj. **trichologist** n.

trichome /ˈtrʌɪkəʊm, ˈtrɪ-/ ■ n. Botany a small hair or other outgrowth from the epidermis of a plant, typically unicellular and glandular.
– ORIGIN C19: from Greek *trikhōma*, from *trikhoun* 'cover with hair'.

trichomonad /ˌtrɪkə(ʊ)ˈmɒnad/ ■ n. Zoology & Medicine a parasitic protozoan of an order (Trichomonadida) with four to six flagella, infesting the urogenital or digestive system.
– DERIVATIVES **trichomonal** adj.
– ORIGIN C19: from Greek *thrix, trikh-* 'hair' + *monas, monad-* 'unit'.

trichomoniasis /ˌtrɪkə(ʊ)məˈnʌɪəsɪs/ ■ n. Medicine infection with parasitic trichomonads.

Trichoptera /trʌɪˈkɒpt(ə)rə/ ■ pl. n. Entomology an order of insects that comprises the caddis flies.
– DERIVATIVES **trichopteran** n. & adj.
– ORIGIN from TRICHO- + *pteron* 'wing'.

trichotomy /trʌɪˈkɒtəmi, trɪ-/ ■ n. (pl. **-ies**) a division into three categories.
– DERIVATIVES **trichotomous** adj.
– ORIGIN C17: from Greek *trikha* 'threefold', on the pattern of *dichotomy*.

trichroic /trʌɪˈkrəʊɪk/ ■ adj. Crystallography (of a crystal) appearing with different colours when viewed along the three crystallographic directions.
– DERIVATIVES **trichroism** /ˈtrʌɪkrəʊɪz(ə)m/ n.

– ORIGIN C19: from Greek *trikhroos*, from *tri-* 'three' + *khrōs* 'colour'.

trichromatic /ˌtrʌɪkrəˈmatɪk/ ■ adj. **1** having or using three colours. **2** having normal colour vision, which is sensitive to all three primary colours.
– DERIVATIVES **trichromatism** n.

trick ■ n. **1** a cunning or skilful act or scheme intended to deceive or outwit someone. ▶ a mischievous practical joke. ▶ a skilful act performed for entertainment. ▶ an illusion: *a trick of the light.* ▶ [as modifier] intended to mystify or create an illusion: *a trick question.* ▶ [as modifier] chiefly N. Amer. liable to fail; defective: *a trick knee.* **2** (in bridge, whist, etc.) a sequence of cards forming a single round of play. **3** informal a prostitute's client. ■ v. **1** deceive or outwit with cunning or skill. ▶ (**trick someone into/out of**) deceive someone into doing or parting with. **2** (**trick someone out/up**) dress or decorate someone in an elaborate or showy way. **3** Heraldry sketch (a coat of arms) in outline, with the colours indicated by letters or signs.
– PHRASES **do the trick** informal achieve the required result. **how's tricks?** informal how are you? **trick or treat** chiefly N. Amer. a children's custom of calling at houses at Halloween with the threat of pranks if they are not given a small gift. **tricks of the trade** special ingenious techniques used in a profession or craft. **turn a trick** informal (of a prostitute) have a session with a client. **up to one's (old) tricks** informal misbehaving in a characteristic way.
– DERIVATIVES **tricker** n.
– ORIGIN Middle English: from an Old French var. of *triche*, from *trichier* 'deceive'.

trick cyclist ■ n. Brit. humorous a psychiatrist.

trickery ■ n. (pl. **-ies**) the practice of deception.

trickle ■ v. **1** (of a liquid) flow in a small stream. **2** (**trickle down**) (of wealth) gradually benefit the poorest as a result of the increasing wealth of the richest. **3** come or go slowly or gradually. ■ n. **1** a small flow of liquid. **2** a small group or number of people or things moving slowly.
– ORIGIN Middle English: imitative.

trickle charger ■ n. an electrical charger for batteries that works at a steady slow rate from the mains.

trickster ■ n. a person who cheats or deceives people.

tricksy ■ adj. (**-ier, -iest**) clever in an ingenious or deceptive way. ▶ (of a person) playful or mischievous.
– DERIVATIVES **tricksily** adv. **tricksiness** n.

tricky ■ adj. (**-ier, -iest**) **1** requiring care and skill because difficult or awkward. **2** deceitful, crafty, or skilful.
– DERIVATIVES **trickily** adv. **trickiness** n.

triclinic /trʌɪˈklɪnɪk/ ■ adj. denoting a crystal system with three unequal oblique axes.
– ORIGIN C19: from Greek TRI- + *-clinic*, on the pattern of *monoclinic*.

tricolour /ˈtrɪkələ, ˈtrʌɪkʌlə/ (US **tricolor**) ■ n. a flag with three bands or blocks of different colours, especially the French national flag. ■ adj. (also **tricoloured**) having three colours.

tricorne /ˈtrʌɪkɔːn/ (also **tricorn**) ■ adj. (of a hat) having a brim turned up on three sides. ■ n. a tricorne hat.
– ORIGIN C19: from French *tricorne* or Latin *tricornis*, from *tri-* 'three' + *cornu* 'horn'.

tricot /ˈtrɪkəʊ, ˈtriː-/ ■ n. a fine knitted fabric made of a natural or man-made fibre.
– ORIGIN C18: from French, 'knitting', from *tricoter* 'to knit'.

tricuspid /trʌɪˈkʌspɪd/ ■ adj. **1** denoting a tooth with three cusps or points. **2** relating to or denoting a valve formed of three triangular segments, particularly that between the right atrium and ventricle of the heart.
– ORIGIN C17: from TRI- + Latin *cuspis, cuspid-* 'cusp'.

tricycle ■ n. a vehicle similar to a bicycle, but having three wheels, two at the back and one at the front. ■ v. [often as noun **tricycling**] ride on a tricycle.
– DERIVATIVES **tricyclist** n.

tricyclic /trʌɪˈsʌɪklɪk/ ■ adj. Chemistry having three rings of atoms in its molecule. ■ n. Medicine any of a class of antidepressant drugs having molecules with three fused rings.

tridactyl /trʌɪˈdaktɪl/ ■ adj. Zoology having three toes or fingers.
– DERIVATIVES **tridactyly** n.
– ORIGIN C19: from TRI- + Greek *daktulos* 'finger'.

trident ■ n. a three-pronged spear, especially as an attribute of Poseidon (Neptune) or Britannia.
– ORIGIN Middle English: from Latin, from *tri-* 'three' + *dens, dent-* 'tooth'.

Tridentine /trɪˈdɛntʌɪn, trʌɪ-/ ■ adj. of or relating to the Council of Trent (1545–63), especially as the basis of Roman Catholic doctrine.
– ORIGIN from medieval Latin, from *Tridentum* 'Trent'.

Tridentine mass ■ n. the Latin Eucharistic liturgy used by the Roman Catholic Church from 1570 to 1964.

tridymite /ˈtrɪdɪmʌɪt/ ■ n. a high-temperature form of quartz found as thin hexagonal crystals in some igneous rocks and stony meteorites.
– ORIGIN C19: from German *Tridymit*, from Greek *tridumos* 'threefold', because it occurs in groups of three crystals.

tried past and past participle of TRY.

triene /ˈtrʌɪiːn/ ■ n. Chemistry an unsaturated hydrocarbon containing three double bonds between carbon atoms.

triennial /trʌɪˈɛnɪəl/ ■ adj. lasting for or recurring every three years.
– DERIVATIVES **triennially** adv.
– ORIGIN C16: from late Latin *triennis*, from *tri-* 'three' + *annus* 'year'.

triennium /trʌɪˈɛnɪəm/ ■ n. (pl. **triennia** /-nɪə/ or **trienniums**) a period of three years.
– ORIGIN C19: from Latin, from *tri-* 'three' + *annum* 'year'.

trier ■ n. 1 a person who always makes an effort, however unsuccessful they may be. 2 a person or body responsible for trying a judicial case.

trifacial nerves /trʌɪˈfeɪʃ(ə)l/ ■ pl. n. another term for TRIGEMINAL NERVES.

trifid /ˈtrʌɪfɪd/ ■ adj. chiefly Biology partly or wholly split into three divisions or lobes.
– ORIGIN C18: from Latin *trifidus*, from *tri-* 'three' + *fid-, findere* 'split, divide'.

trifle ■ n. 1 a thing of little value or importance. ▶ a small amount. 2 a cold dessert of sponge cake and fruit covered with layers of custard, jelly, and cream. ■ v. (**trifle with**) treat without seriousness or respect.
– DERIVATIVES **trifler** n.
– ORIGIN Middle English: noun from Old French *trufle*, form of *trufe* 'deceit'; verb from Old French *truffler* 'mock, deceive'.

trifling ■ adj. unimportant or trivial.
– DERIVATIVES **triflingly** adv.

trifocal ■ adj. (of a pair of glasses) having lenses with three parts with different focal lengths. ■ n. (**trifocals**) a pair of trifocal glasses.

trifoliate /trʌɪˈfəʊlɪət/ ■ adj. (of a compound leaf) having three leaflets.

triforium /trʌɪˈfɔːrɪəm/ ■ n. (pl. **triforia** /-rɪə/) a gallery or arcade above the arches of the nave, choir, and transepts of a church.
– ORIGIN C18: from Anglo-Latin.

triform ■ adj. technical composed of three parts.

trifurcate ■ v. /ˈtrʌɪfəkeɪt/ divide into three branches or forks. ■ adj. /-ˈfəːkət/ divided in this way.
– DERIVATIVES **trifurcation** n.
– ORIGIN C19: from Latin *trifurcus* 'three-forked', from *tri-* 'three' + *furca* 'fork'.

trig ■ n. informal trigonometry.

trigeminal nerves /trʌɪˈdʒɛmɪn(ə)l/ ■ pl. n. Anatomy the pair of large cranial nerves supplying the front part of the head.

trigeminal neuralgia ■ n. Medicine neuralgia involving one or more of the branches of the trigeminal nerves.

trigeminus /trʌɪˈdʒɛmɪnəs/ ■ n. (pl. **trigemini** /-nʌɪ/) Anatomy each of the trigeminal nerves.
– ORIGIN C19: from Latin, 'three born at the same birth', extended to mean 'threefold'.

trigger ■ n. 1 a device that releases a spring or catch and so sets off a mechanism, especially in order to fire a gun. 2 an event that causes something to happen. ■ v. 1 cause (a device) to function. 2 cause to happen or exist.
– DERIVATIVES **triggered** adj.
– ORIGIN C17: from dialect *tricker*, from Dutch *trekker*, from *trekken* 'to pull'.

trigger finger ■ n. 1 the forefinger of the right hand, used to pull the trigger of a gun. 2 Medicine a defect in a tendon causing a finger to jerk or snap straight when the hand is extended.

triggerfish ■ n. (pl. same or **-fishes**) a tropical marine fish with a large dorsal spine which can be erected and locked into place. [Family Balistidae: numerous species.]

trigger-happy ■ adj. apt to fire a gun or take other drastic action on the slightest provocation.

trigger point ■ n. 1 a circumstance or situation which causes an event to occur. 2 Physiology & Medicine a sensitive area of the body, stimulation or irritation of which causes a specific effect in another part.

triglyceride /trʌɪˈɡlɪsərʌɪd/ ■ n. Chemistry an ester formed from glycerol and three fatty acid groups, e.g. the main constituents of natural fats and oils.

triglyph /ˈtrʌɪɡlɪf/ ■ n. Architecture a tablet in a Doric frieze with three vertical grooves alternating with metopes.
– DERIVATIVES **triglyphic** adj.
– ORIGIN C16: from Greek *trigluphos*, from *tri-* 'three' + *gluphē* 'carving'.

trigonal /ˈtrɪɡ(ə)n(ə)l/ ■ adj. 1 triangular. ▶ chiefly Biology triangular in cross section. 2 denoting a crystal system with three equal axes separated by equal angles that are not right angles.
– DERIVATIVES **trigonally** adv.

trigonometry /ˌtrɪɡəˈnɒmɪtri/ ■ n. the branch of mathematics concerned with the relations of the sides and angles of triangles and with the relevant functions of any angles.
– DERIVATIVES **trigonometric** /-nəˈmɛtrɪk/ adj. **trigonometrical** adj.
– ORIGIN C17: from modern Latin *trigonometria*, from Greek *trigōnos* 'three-cornered' + -METRY.

trig point (S. African also **trig beacon**) ■ n. chiefly Brit. a reference point on high ground used in surveying, typically marked by a small pillar.

trigram /ˈtrʌɪɡram/ ■ n. 1 a trigraph. 2 each of the eight figures formed of three parallel lines that combine to form the sixty-four hexagrams of the I Ching.

trigraph /ˈtrʌɪɡrɑːf/ ■ n. a group of three letters representing one sound, for example German *sch-*.

trihedron /trʌɪˈhiːdrən, -ˈhɛdrən/ ■ n. (pl. **trihedra** /-drə/ or **trihedrons**) a solid figure having three sides or faces (in addition to the base or ends).
– DERIVATIVES **trihedral** adj. & n.
– ORIGIN C19 (*trihedral* C18): from TRI- + -HEDRON.

trike ■ n. informal 1 a tricycle. 2 a kind of microlight.

trilateral ■ adj. shared by or involving three parties. ▶ Geometry of, on, or with three sides. ■ n. a triangle.

trilby ■ n. (pl. **-ies**) chiefly Brit. a soft felt hat with a narrow brim and indented crown.
– DERIVATIVES **trilbied** adj.
– ORIGIN C19: from the name of George du Maurier's novel *Trilby* (1894), in the stage version of which such a hat was worn.

trilingual ■ adj. speaking three languages fluently. ▶ written or conducted in three languages.
– DERIVATIVES **trilingualism** n.

trilithon /trʌɪˈlɪθ(ə)n/ (also **trilith** /ˈtrʌɪlɪθ/) ■ n. Archaeology a megalithic structure consisting of two upright stones and a third across the top as a lintel.
– ORIGIN C18: from Greek, from *tri-* 'three' + *lithos* 'stone'.

trill ■ n. a quavering or vibratory sound, especially a rapid alternation of sung or played notes. ▶ the pronunciation of a consonant, especially *r*, with rapid vibration of the tongue against the hard or soft palate or the uvula. ■ v. produce a quavering or warbling sound; sing or pronounce with a trill.
– DERIVATIVES **triller** n.
– ORIGIN C17: from Italian *trillo* (n.), *trillare* (v.).

trillion ■ cardinal number (pl. **trillions** or (with numeral or

quantifying word) same) **1 (a/one trillion)** a million million (1 000 000 000 000 or 10¹²). **2 (trillions)** informal a very large number or amount.
– DERIVATIVES **trillionth** ordinal number.
– ORIGIN C17: from French, from *million*, by substitution of the prefix *tri-* 'three'.

trilobite /ˈtrʌɪlə(ʊ)bʌɪt, ˈtrɪ-/ ■ n. a fossil marine arthropod of the Palaeozoic era, with a segmented hindpart divided longitudinally into three lobes.
– ORIGIN C19: from *Trilobites*, from Greek *tri-* 'three' + *lobos* 'lobe'.

trilogy ■ n. (pl. **-ies**) a group of three related novels, plays, films, etc.

trim ■ v. (**trimmed**, **trimming**) **1** make (something) neat by cutting away irregular or unwanted parts. ▸ cut off (irregular or unwanted parts). ▸ reduce the size, amount, or number of. **2** decorate (something), especially along its edges. **3** adjust (a sail) to take advantage of the wind. ▸ adjust the balance of (a ship or aircraft), by rearranging its cargo or using its controls. ■ n. **1** additional decoration, especially along the edges. ▸ the upholstery or interior lining of a car. **2** an act of trimming. **3** the state of being in good order. **4** the degree to which an aircraft can be maintained at a constant altitude. **5** the way in which a ship floats in the water, especially in relation to the fore-and-aft line. ■ adj. (**trimmer**, **trimmest**) neat and smart; in good order.
– PHRASES **in trim 1** slim and fit. **2** Nautical in good order. **trim one's sails (to the wind)** make changes to suit one's new circumstances.
– DERIVATIVES **trimly** adv. **trimness** n.
– ORIGIN Old English *trymman*, *trymian* 'make firm, arrange'.

trimaran /ˈtrʌɪmərən/ ■ n. a yacht with three hulls in parallel.
– ORIGIN 1940s: from TRI- + CATAMARAN.

trimer /ˈtrʌɪmə/ ■ n. Chemistry a polymer comprising three monomer units.
– DERIVATIVES **trimeric** adj.

trimerous /ˈtrɪm(ə)rəs, ˈtrʌɪ-/ ■ adj. Botany & Zoology having parts arranged in groups of three. ▸ consisting of three joints or parts.

trimester /trʌɪˈmɛstə/ ■ n. **1** a period of three months, especially as a division of the duration of pregnancy. **2** each of the three terms in an academic year.
– DERIVATIVES **trimestral** adj. **trimestrial** adj.
– ORIGIN C19: from French *trimestre*, from Latin *trimestris*, from *tri-* 'three' + *mensis* 'month'.

trimeter /ˈtrɪmɪtə, ˈtrʌɪ-/ ■ n. Prosody a line of verse consisting of three metrical feet.
– DERIVATIVES **trimetric** adj.

trimmer ■ n. **1** a person or implement that trims. **2** (also **trimmer joist**) Architecture a crosspiece fixed between full-length joists to form part of the frame of an opening in a floor or roof. **3** a small capacitor or other component used to tune a circuit such as a radio set.

trimming ■ n. **1** (**trimmings**) small pieces trimmed off. **2** decoration, especially for clothing. ▸ (**the trimmings**) informal the traditional accompaniments to something.

trimpot ■ n. a small potentiometer used to make small adjustments to the value of resistance or voltage in an electronic circuit.

trim tab (also **trimming tab**) ■ n. Aeronautics an adjustable tab or aerofoil attached to a control surface, used to trim an aircraft in flight.

Trinidadian /ˌtrɪnɪˈdeɪdɪən, -ˈdadɪən/ ■ n. a native or inhabitant of the Caribbean island of Trinidad. ■ adj. of or relating to Trinidad.

Trinitarian /ˌtrɪnɪˈtɛːrɪən/ ■ adj. of or relating to belief in the doctrine of the Trinity. ■ n. a person who believes in the doctrine of the Trinity.
– DERIVATIVES **Trinitarianism** n.

trinitrotoluene /trʌɪˌnʌɪtrəʊˈtɒljuːiːn/ ■ n. fuller form of TNT.

trinity ■ n. (pl. **-ies**) **1** (**the Trinity** or **the Holy Trinity**) the three persons of the Christian Godhead; Father, Son, and Holy Spirit. **2** a group of three people or things.
– ORIGIN Middle English: from Old French *trinite*, from Latin *trinitas* 'triad', from *trinus* 'threefold'.

Trinity term ■ n. Brit. (in some universities) the term beginning after Easter.

trinket ■ n. a small ornament or item of jewellery that is of little value.
– DERIVATIVES **trinketry** n.
– ORIGIN C16.

trinomial /trʌɪˈnəʊmɪəl/ ■ adj. **1** (of an algebraic expression) consisting of three terms. **2** Biology (of a taxonomic name) consisting of three terms where the first is the name of the genus, the second that of the species, and the third that of the subspecies or variety. ■ n. a trinomial expression or taxonomic name.
– ORIGIN C17: from TRI-, on the pattern of *binomial*.

trio ■ n. (pl. **-os**) a set or group of three. ▸ a group of three musicians. ▸ a composition written for three musicians.
– ORIGIN C18: from Italian, from Latin *tres* 'three'.

triode /ˈtrʌɪəʊd/ ■ n. a thermionic valve having three electrodes. ▸ a semiconductor rectifier having three connections.
– ORIGIN C20: from TRI- + ELECTRODE.

trioxide ■ n. Chemistry an oxide containing three atoms of oxygen in its molecule or empirical formula.

trip ■ v. (**tripped**, **tripping**) **1** catch one's foot on something and stumble or fall. ▸ (**trip up**) make a mistake. **2** walk, run, or dance with quick light steps. **3** activate (a mechanism), especially by contact with a switch. ▸ (of part of an electric circuit) disconnect automatically as a safety measure. **4** Nautical release and raise (an anchor) from the seabed by means of a cable. ▸ turn (a yard or other object) from a horizontal to a vertical position for lowering. **5** informal experience hallucinations induced by taking a psychedelic drug, especially LSD. **6** go on a short journey. ■ n. **1** a journey or excursion, especially for pleasure. **2** an instance of tripping or falling. ▸ a mistake. **3** informal a hallucinatory experience caused by taking a psychedelic drug. ▸ an exciting or stimulating experience. ▸ a self-indulgent attitude or activity: *a power trip*. **4** a device that trips a mechanism, circuit, etc.
– PHRASES **trip the light fantastic** humorous dance. [from 'Trip it as you go On the light fantastic toe' (from the English poet John Milton's *L'Allegro*).]
– ORIGIN Middle English: from Old French *triper*, from Middle Dutch *trippen* 'to skip, hop'.

tripartite /trʌɪˈpɑːtʌɪt/ ■ adj. consisting of three parts. ▸ shared by or involving three parties.
– DERIVATIVES **tripartition** n.

tripe ■ n. **1** the first or second stomach of a cow or other ruminant used as food. **2** informal nonsense; rubbish.
– ORIGIN Middle English: from Old French.

trip hammer ■ n. a large, heavy pivoted hammer used in forging.

trip hop ■ n. a style of dance music combining elements of hip hop and dub reggae with softer sounds.

triphthong /ˈtrɪfθɒŋ/ ■ n. a union of three vowels (letters or sounds) pronounced in one syllable (as in *fire*). ▸ three written vowel characters representing the sound of a single vowel (as in b*eau*).
– DERIVATIVES **triphthongal** adj.
– ORIGIN C16: from French *triphtongue*.

triplane ■ n. an early type of aircraft with three pairs of wings, one above the other.

triple ■ adj. **1** consisting of or involving three parts, things, or people. **2** having three times the usual size, quality, or strength. ■ predet. three times as much or as many. ■ n. **1** a thing that is three times as large as usual or is made up of three parts. **2** (**triples**) Bell-ringing a system of change-ringing using seven bells, with three pairs changing places each time. **3** Baseball a hit which enables the batter to reach third base. ■ v. make or become three times as much or as many.
– DERIVATIVES **triply** adv.
– ORIGIN Middle English: from Latin *triplus*, from Greek *triplous*.

triple BEE ■ n. another term for BBBEE.

triple bond ■ n. Chemistry a chemical bond in which three pairs of electrons are shared between two atoms.

triple bottom line ■ n. a set of criteria used to evaluate

triple crown

a company's performance in terms of economic, environmental, and social practices. ▶ [as modifier] relating to or denoting compliance with these criteria: *triple bottom line businesses*.

triple crown ■ n. **1 (Triple Crown)** an award or honour for winning a group of three important events in a sport. **2** the papal tiara.

triple harp ■ n. a large harp without pedals, and with three rows of strings, the middle row providing sharps and flats.

triple jump ■ n. **1** an athletic event in which competitors attempt to jump as far as possible by performing a hop, a step, and a jump from a running start. **2** Skating a jump in which the skater makes three full turns while in the air. ■ v. **(triple-jump)** perform a triple jump.
–DERIVATIVES **triple jumper** n.

triple play ■ n. Baseball a defensive play in which three runners are put out.

triple point ■ n. Chemistry the temperature and pressure at which the solid, liquid, and vapour phases of a pure substance can coexist in equilibrium.

triple rhyme ■ n. a rhyme involving three syllables.

triplet ■ n. **1** one of three children or animals born at the same birth. **2** a set of three rhyming lines of verse. **3** technical a group of three similar things, e.g. lines in a spectrum.
–ORIGIN C17: from TRIPLE, on the pattern of *doublet*.

triplet code ■ n. Biology the genetic code in which a sequence of three nucleotides on a DNA or RNA molecule codes for a specific amino acid in protein synthesis.

triple time ■ n. musical time with three beats to the bar.

triple tonguing ■ n. Music a technique in which alternate movements of the tongue are made to facilitate rapid playing of a wind instrument.

triplex /ˈtrɪplɛks/ ■ n. **1 (Triplex)** Brit. trademark toughened or laminated safety glass, used especially for car windows. **2** N. Amer. a building divided into three self-contained residences. **3** Biochemistry a triple-stranded polynucleotide molecule. ■ v. **(be triplexed)** (of electrical equipment or systems) be provided or fitted in triplicate so as to ensure reliability.
–ORIGIN C17: from Latin, 'threefold', from *tri-* 'three' + *plicare* 'to fold'.

triplicate ■ adj. /ˈtrɪplɪkət/ existing in three copies or examples. ■ n. /ˈtrɪplɪkət/ archaic a thing which is part of a set of three copies or corresponding parts. ■ v. /ˈtrɪplɪkeɪt/ make three copies of. ▶ multiply by three.
–DERIVATIVES **triplication** /-ˈkeɪʃ(ə)n/ n. **triplicity** /trɪˈplɪsɪti/ n.
–ORIGIN Middle English: from Latin *triplicare* 'make three', from *triplex*, *triplic-* (see TRIPLEX).

triploid /ˈtrɪplɔɪd/ ■ adj. Genetics (of a cell or nucleus) containing three homologous sets of chromosomes.
–DERIVATIVES **triploidy** n.

tripmeter ■ n. a vehicle instrument that can be set to record the distance of individual journeys.

tripod /ˈtraɪpɒd/ ■ n. **1** a three-legged stand for supporting a camera or other apparatus. **2** archaic a stool, table, or cauldron resting on three legs.
–DERIVATIVES **tripodal** /ˈtrɪpəd(ə)l/ adj.
–ORIGIN C17: from Greek *tripod-*, from *tri-* 'three' + *pous*, *pod-* 'foot'.

tripos /ˈtraɪpɒs/ ■ n. the final honours examination for a BA degree at Cambridge University.
–ORIGIN C16: alteration of Latin *tripus* 'tripod', with ref. to the stool on which a designated graduate sat to deliver a satirical speech at the degree ceremony.

trippant /ˈtrɪp(ə)nt/ ■ adj. Heraldry (of a stag or deer) represented as walking.
–ORIGIN C17: from Old French, 'walking or springing lightly', from *tripper*.

tripper ■ n. informal, chiefly Brit. a person who goes on a pleasure trip or excursion.

tripple S. African ■ n. a horse's gait, between a walk and a trot. ■ v. move with such a gait.

–ORIGIN C19: from S. African Dutch *trippel(en)*, from Dutch *trippen* 'to skip, trip'.

trippy ■ adj. (**-ier**, **-iest**) informal resembling or inducing the hallucinatory effect produced by a psychedelic drug.

triptych /ˈtrɪptɪk/ ■ n. a picture or carving on three panels, typically hinged together vertically and used as an altarpiece. ▶ a set of three associated artistic, literary, or musical works.
–ORIGIN C18 (denoting a set of three writing tablets hinged or tied together): from TRI-, on the pattern of *diptych*.

tripwire ■ n. a wire that is stretched close to the ground and activates a trap, explosion, or alarm when disturbed.

triquetra /traɪˈkwɛtrə, -ˈkwiːtrə/ ■ n. (pl. **triquetrae** /-triː/) a symmetrical triangular ornament of three interlaced arcs used on metalwork and stone crosses.
–ORIGIN C16: from Latin, from *triquetrus* 'three-cornered'.

trireme /ˈtraɪriːm/ ■ n. an ancient Greek or Roman war galley with three banks of oars.
–ORIGIN from Latin *triremis*, from *tri-* 'three' + *remus* 'oar'.

trisect /traɪˈsɛkt/ ■ v. divide into three parts.
–DERIVATIVES **trisection** n. **trisector** n.
–ORIGIN C17: from TRI- + Latin *sect-*, *secare* 'divide, cut'.

trishaw /ˈtraɪʃɔː/ ■ n. a light three-wheeled vehicle with pedals, used in the Far East.
–ORIGIN 1940S: from TRI- + RICKSHAW.

triskaidekaphobia /ˌtrɪskaɪdɛkəˈfəʊbɪə/ ■ n. extreme superstition regarding the number thirteen.
–ORIGIN C20: from Greek *treiskaideka* 'thirteen' + -PHOBIA.

trismus /ˈtrɪzməs/ ■ n. Medicine spasm of the jaw muscles, causing the mouth to remain tightly closed, typically as a symptom of tetanus; lockjaw.
–ORIGIN C17: from Greek *trismos* 'a scream, grinding'.

trisomy /ˈtrɪsəmi/ ■ n. Medicine a condition in which an extra copy of a chromosome is present in the cell nuclei, causing developmental abnormalities.
–ORIGIN 1930S: from TRI- + -SOME[3].

trisomy-21 ■ n. Medicine the most common form of Down's syndrome, caused by an extra copy of chromosome number 21.

trisyllable /traɪˈsɪləb(ə)l/ ■ n. a word or metrical foot of three syllables.
–DERIVATIVES **trisyllabic** adj.

tritanopia /ˌtrɪtəˈnəʊpɪə/ ■ n. a rare form of colour blindness resulting from insensitivity to blue light, causing confusion of greens and blues. Compare with PROTANOPIA, DEUTERANOPIA.
–ORIGIN C20: from Greek *tritos* 'third' (referring to blue as the third colour in the spectrum) + AN-[1] + -OPIA.

trite ■ adj. (of a remark or idea) lacking originality or freshness; dull on account of overuse.
–DERIVATIVES **tritely** adv. **triteness** n.
–ORIGIN C16: from Latin *tritus*, from *terere* 'to rub'.

tritiated /ˈtrɪtɪeɪtɪd/ ■ adj. Chemistry denoting a compound in which the ordinary isotope of hydrogen has been replaced with tritium.
–DERIVATIVES **tritiation** n.

triticale /ˌtrɪtɪˈkeɪli/ ■ n. a hybrid cereal produced by crossing wheat and rye, grown as a fodder crop.
–ORIGIN 1950S: from a blend of the genus names *Triticum* 'wheat' and *Secale* 'rye'.

tritium /ˈtrɪtɪəm/ ■ n. Chemistry a radioactive isotope of hydrogen with a mass approximately three times that of the usual isotope. (Symbol: **T**)
–ORIGIN 1930S: from Greek *tritos* 'third'.

trito- /ˈtrɪtəʊ, ˈtraɪtəʊ/ ■ comb. form third.
–ORIGIN from Greek *tritos* 'third'.

triton ■ n. **1** Greek & Roman Mythology a minor sea god or merman represented as a man with a fish's tail and carrying a trident and shell-trumpet. **2** a marine mollusc with a tall spiral shell with a large aperture. [Genus *Charonia*.]

triturate /ˈtrɪtjʊreɪt/ ■ v. technical grind to a fine powder.
–DERIVATIVES **trituration** n. **triturator** n.
–ORIGIN C18: from Latin *triturat-* '(of corn) threshed', from *tritura* 'rubbing', from *terere*.

triumph ■ n. **1** a great victory or achievement. ▶ the state

of being victorious or successful. ▸ joy or satisfaction resulting from a success or victory. ▸ a highly successful example: *the arrest was a triumph of international co-operation.* **2** the processional entry of a victorious general into ancient Rome. ■ v. achieve a triumph.
▸ rejoice or exult at a triumph.
– DERIVATIVES **triumphal** adj.
– ORIGIN Middle English: from Old French *triumphe* (n.), from Latin *triump(h)us*, prob. from Greek *thriambos* 'hymn to Bacchus'.

triumphalism ■ n. excessive exultation over one's success or achievements.
– DERIVATIVES **triumphalist** adj. & n.

triumphant ■ adj. having won a battle or contest; victorious. ▸ jubilant after a victory or achievement.
– DERIVATIVES **triumphantly** adv.

triumvirate /trʌɪˈʌmvɪrət/ ■ n. a group of three powerful or notable people or things. ▸ (in ancient Rome) a group of three men holding power.

triune /ˈtrʌɪjuːn/ ■ adj. (especially with reference to the Trinity) consisting of three in one.
– DERIVATIVES **triunity** n. (pl. **-ies**).
– ORIGIN C17: from TRI- + Latin *unus* 'one'.

trivalent /trʌɪˈveɪl(ə)nt/ ■ adj. Chemistry having a valency of three.

trivet ■ n. an iron tripod placed over a fire for a cooking pot or kettle to stand on. ▸ an iron bracket designed to hook on to bars of a grate for a similar purpose.
– ORIGIN Middle English: from Latin *tripes*, *triped-* 'three-legged', from *tri-* 'three' + *pes* 'foot'.

trivia ■ pl. n. unimportant details or pieces of information.
– ORIGIN C20: from Latin *trivium* 'place where three roads meet', influenced by TRIVIAL.

trivial ■ adj. of little value or importance.
– DERIVATIVES **triviality** n. (pl. **-ies**). **trivially** adv.

HISTORY
Trivial entered Middle English from Latin *trivium* 'place where three roads meet', from *tri-* 'three' and *via* 'road, way'. A medieval **trivium** was an introductory course at a university involving the study of grammar, rhetoric, and logic. In the Middle Ages seven 'liberal arts' were recognized, of which the *trivium* contained the lower three and the *quadrivium* the upper four (the 'mathematical arts' of arithmetic, geometry, astronomy, and music). This association with elementary subjects led to **trivial** being used to mean 'of little value or importance' from the 16th century.

trivialize (also **-ise**) ■ v. make (something) seem less important or complex than it really is.
– DERIVATIVES **trivialization** (also **-isation**) n.

trivial name ■ n. **1** chiefly Chemistry a name that is in general use although not part of systematic nomenclature. **2** chiefly Zoology another term for SPECIFIC EPITHET.

-trix ■ suffix (pl. **-trices** /ˈtrɪsiːz, ˈtrʌɪsiːz/ or **-trixes**) (chiefly in legal terms) forming feminine agent nouns corresponding to masculine nouns ending in *-tor* (such as *executrix* corresponding to *executor*).
– ORIGIN from Latin.

tRNA ■ abbrev. Biology transfer RNA.

trocar /ˈtrəʊkɑː/ ■ n. a surgical instrument with a three-sided cutting point enclosed in a tube.
– ORIGIN C18: from French *trocart*, *trois-quarts*, from *trois* 'three' + *carre* 'side, face of an instrument'.

trochaic /trə(ʊ)ˈkeɪɪk/ Prosody ■ adj. consisting of or featuring trochees. ■ n. (**trochaics**) trochaic verse.

trochanter /trəˈkantə/ ■ n. **1** Anatomy any of a number of bony protuberances by which muscles are attached to the upper part of the thigh bone. **2** Entomology the small second segment of the leg of an insect, between the coxa and the femur.
– ORIGIN C17: from French, from Greek *trokhantēr*, from *trekhein* 'to run'.

trochee /ˈtrəʊkiː/ ■ n. Prosody a foot consisting of one long or stressed syllable followed by one short or unstressed syllable.
– ORIGIN C16: from Greek *trokhaios (pous)* 'running (foot)', from *trekhein* 'to run'.

trochlea /ˈtrɒklɪə/ ■ n. (pl. **trochleae** /-liː/) Anatomy a structure resembling or acting like a pulley, such as the groove at the lower end of the humerus forming part of the elbow joint.
– DERIVATIVES **trochlear** adj.
– ORIGIN C17: Latin, 'pulley'.

trochlear nerves ■ pl. n. Anatomy the pair of cranial nerves supplying the superior oblique muscle of the eyeballs.

trochoid /ˈtrəʊkɔɪd/ ■ adj. **1** Anatomy denoting a joint in which one element rotates on its own axis (e.g. the atlas vertebra). **2** Zoology (of a mollusc shell) conical with a flat base. ■ n. a trochoid joint.
– DERIVATIVES **trochoidal** adj.
– ORIGIN C18: from Greek *trokhoeidēs* 'wheel-like', from *trokhos* 'wheel'.

troctolite /ˈtrɒktə(ʊ)lʌɪt/ ■ n. Geology a form of gabbro typically having a spotted appearance likened to a trout's back.
– ORIGIN C19: from German *Troklotit*, from Greek *trōktēs*, a marine fish (taken to be 'trout').

trod past and past participle of TREAD.

trodden past participle of TREAD.

troepie /ˈtruːpi/ ■ n. variant spelling of TROOPIE.

troglodyte /ˈtrɒglədʌɪt/ ■ n. **1** a cave-dweller, especially a primitive or prehistoric one. **2** a person who is deliberately ignorant or old-fashioned.
– DERIVATIVES **troglodytic** /-ˈdɪtɪk/ adj. **troglodytism** n.
– ORIGIN C15: from Greek *trōglodutēs*, alteration of the name of an Ethiopian people, influenced by *trōglē* 'hole'.

trogon /ˈtrəʊgɒn/ ■ n. a brightly coloured bird of tropical forests. [Family Trogonidae: many species.]
– ORIGIN C18: from Greek *trōgōn*, from *trōgein* 'gnaw'.

troika /ˈtrɔɪkə/ ■ n. **1** a Russian vehicle pulled by a team of three horses abreast. ▸ a team of three horses for such a vehicle. **2** a group of three people working together, especially as administrators or managers.
– ORIGIN Russian, from *troe* 'set of three'.

troilism /ˈtrɔɪlɪz(ə)m/ ■ n. sexual activity involving three participants.
– ORIGIN 1950s: perhaps based on French *trois* 'three'.

Trojan ■ n. a native or inhabitant of ancient Troy in Asia Minor. ■ adj. of or relating to Troy.
– PHRASES **work like a Trojan** work extremely hard.

Trojan Horse ■ n. something intended to undermine or secretly overthrow an enemy or opponent. ▸ Computing a program designed to breach the security of a computer system while ostensibly performing some innocuous function.
– ORIGIN from the hollow wooden statue of a horse in which the ancient Greeks are said to have concealed themselves in order to enter Troy.

troll[1] /trəʊl, trɒl/ ■ n. (in folklore) an ugly cave-dwelling being depicted as either a giant or a dwarf.
– ORIGIN Middle English (in the sense 'witch'): from Old Norse and Swedish *troll*, Danish *trold*.

troll[2] /trəʊl, trɒl/ ■ v. **1** fish by trailing a baited line along behind a boat. ▸ search for something. **2** chiefly Brit. walk; stroll. **3** sing (something) in a happy and carefree way. **4** [usu. as noun **trolling**] Computing, informal send (an email message or Internet posting) intended to provoke a response by containing errors. ■ n. an act or instance of trolling. ▸ a line or bait used in such fishing.
– DERIVATIVES **troller** n.
– ORIGIN Middle English (in the sense 'stroll, roll'): cf. Old French *troller* 'wander in search of game' and Middle High German *trollen* 'stroll'.

trolley ■ n. (pl. **-eys**) **1** a large wheeled metal basket or frame used for transporting heavy or unwieldy items such as luggage or supermarket purchases. ▸ a small table on wheels or castors, used especially to convey food and drink. **2** (also **trolley wheel**) a wheel attached to a pole, used for collecting current from an overhead electric wire to drive a tram or bus. **3** short for TROLLEYBUS or TROLLEY CAR.
– PHRASES **off one's trolley** Brit. informal mad; insane.
– ORIGIN C19: of dialect origin, perhaps from TROLL[2].

trolleybus

trolleybus ■ n. a bus powered by electricity obtained from overhead wires by means of a trolley wheel.

trolley car ■ n. US a tram powered by electricity obtained from overhead wires by means of a trolley wheel.

trollop ■ n. dated or humorous a sexually disreputable or promiscuous woman.
– ORIGIN C17: perhaps rel. to archaic *trull* 'prostitute'.

trombone ■ n. a large brass wind instrument having an extendable slide with which different notes are made.
– DERIVATIVES **trombonist** n.
– ORIGIN C18: from Italian *tromba* 'trumpet'.

trommel /'trɒm(ə)l/ ■ n. 1 Mining a rotating cylindrical sieve or screen used for washing and sorting pieces of ore or coal. 2 S. African a metal trunk.
– ORIGIN C19: from German, 'drum'.

tromp ■ v. N. Amer. informal 1 trudge or tramp. 2 trample.
– ORIGIN C19: alteration of TRAMP.

trompe l'œil /ˌtrɒmp 'lɔɪ/ ■ n. (pl. **trompe l'œils** pronunc. same) visual illusion in art, especially as used to trick the eye into perceiving a painted detail as a three-dimensional object. ▸ a painting or design intended to create such an illusion.
– ORIGIN French, 'deceives the eye'.

-tron ■ suffix Physics 1 denoting a subatomic particle: *positron*. 2 denoting a particle accelerator: *cyclotron*. 3 denoting a thermionic valve: *ignitron*.
– ORIGIN from (*elec*)*tron*.

trona /'trəʊnə/ ■ n. a grey mineral consisting of hydrated sodium carbonate and bicarbonate, found as an evaporate.
– ORIGIN C18: from Swedish, from Arabic *naṭrūn* (see NATRON).

tronc /trɒŋk/ ■ n. (in a hotel or restaurant) a common fund into which tips and service charges are paid for distribution to the staff.
– ORIGIN 1920s: from French, 'collecting box'.

troop ■ n. 1 (**troops**) soldiers or armed forces. 2 a cavalry unit commanded by a captain. ▸ a unit of artillery and armoured formation. ▸ a group of three or more Scout patrols. 3 a group of people or animals of a particular kind. ■ v. (of a group of people) come or go together or in large numbers.
– PHRASES **troop the colour** Brit. perform the ceremony of parading a regiment's flag along ranks of soldiers.
– ORIGIN C16: from French *troupe*, back-formation from *troupeau*, diminutive of medieval Latin *troppus* 'flock', prob. of Germanic origin.

troop carrier ■ n. a large aircraft or armoured vehicle designed for transporting troops.

trooper ■ n. 1 a private soldier in a cavalry or armoured unit. 2 Austral./NZ & US a mounted police officer. ▸ US a state police officer.
– PHRASES **swear like a trooper** swear a great deal.

troopie /'truːpi/ (also **troepie**) ■ n. S. African informal a private soldier, especially during the time of conscription.

troopship ■ n. a ship for transporting troops.

trope /trəʊp/ ■ n. a figurative or metaphorical use of a word or expression.
– ORIGIN C16: via Latin from Greek *tropos* 'turn, way, trope', from *trepein* 'to turn'.

trophic /'trəʊfɪk, 'trɒfɪk/ ■ adj. 1 Ecology of or relating to feeding and nutrition. 2 (also **tropic**) Physiology (of a hormone or its effect) stimulating the activity of another endocrine gland.
– ORIGIN C19: from Greek *trophikos*, from *trophē* 'nourishment', from *trephein* 'nourish'.

-trophic ■ comb. form 1 relating to nutrition: *oligotrophic*. 2 relating to maintenance or regulation of a bodily organ or function, especially by a hormone: *gonadotrophic*.
– DERIVATIVES **-trophism** comb. form in corresponding nouns. **-trophy** comb. form in corresponding nouns.
– ORIGIN from Greek *trophikos*, from *trophē* 'nourishment'.

trophoblast /'trɒfə(ʊ)blast, 'trəʊf-/ ■ n. Embryology a layer of tissue on the outside of a mammalian blastula, supplying the embryo with nourishment and later forming the major part of the placenta.
– DERIVATIVES **trophoblastic** adj.

– ORIGIN from Greek *trophē* 'nourishment' + *blastos* 'germ, sprout'.

trophy ■ n. (pl. **-ies**) 1 a cup or other decorative object awarded as a prize for a victory or success. ▸ a souvenir of an achievement, especially a head of an animal taken when hunting. 2 (in ancient Greece or Rome) the weapons of a defeated army set up as a memorial of victory.
– ORIGIN C15: from French *trophée*, from Greek *tropaion*, from *tropē* 'a rout'.

trophy wife ■ n. informal, derogatory a young, attractive wife regarded as a status symbol for an older man.

tropic¹ /'trɒpɪk/ ■ n. 1 the parallel of latitude 23°26' north (**tropic of Cancer**) or south (**tropic of Capricorn**) of the equator. 2 (**the tropics**) the region between the tropics of Cancer and Capricorn. 3 Astronomy each of two corresponding circles on the celestial sphere where the sun appears to turn after reaching its greatest declination, marking the northern and southern limits of the ecliptic. ■ adj. tropical.
– ORIGIN Middle English: from Greek *tropikos*, from *tropē* 'turning', from *trepein* 'to turn'.

tropic² /'trɒpɪk/ ■ adj. 1 Biology relating to, consisting of, or exhibiting tropism. 2 Physiology variant spelling of TROPHIC.

-tropic ■ comb. form 1 turning towards: *heliotropic*. 2 affecting: *psychotropic*. 3 (especially in names of hormones) equivalent to -TROPHIC.
– ORIGIN from Greek *tropē* 'turn, turning'.

tropical ■ adj. of, typical of, or peculiar to the tropics. ▸ very hot and humid.
– DERIVATIVES **tropically** adv.

tropical storm (also **tropical cyclone**) ■ n. a localized, very intense low-pressure wind system, forming over tropical oceans and with winds of hurricane force.

tropical year ■ n. another term for SOLAR YEAR.

tropicbird ■ n. a tropical seabird with mainly white plumage and very long central tail feathers. [Genus *Phaethon*: three species.]

tropism /'trəʊpɪz(ə)m, 'trɒp-/ ■ n. Biology the turning of all or part of an organism in response to an external stimulus.
– ORIGIN C19: from Greek *tropos* 'turning'.

tropopause /'trɒpə(ʊ)pɔːz, 'trəʊp-/ ■ n. the interface between the troposphere and the stratosphere.
– ORIGIN C20: from Greek *tropos* 'turning' + PAUSE.

troposphere /'trɒpə(ʊ)sfɪə, 'trəʊp-/ ■ n. the lowest region of the atmosphere, extending from the earth's surface to a height of about 6–10 km (the lower boundary of the stratosphere).
– DERIVATIVES **tropospheric** adj.
– ORIGIN C20: from Greek *tropos* 'turning' + SPHERE.

Trot ■ n. informal, chiefly derogatory a Trotskyist or supporter of extreme left-wing views.

trot ■ v. (**trotted**, **trotting**) 1 (of a horse or other quadruped) proceed at a pace faster than a walk, lifting each diagonal pair of legs alternately. 2 (of a person) run at a moderate pace with short steps. ▸ informal go or walk briskly. 3 (**trot something out**) informal produce the same account that has been produced many times before. ■ n. 1 a trotting pace. ▸ an act or period of trotting. 2 (**the trots**) informal diarrhoea.
– PHRASES **on the trot** informal 1 Brit. in succession. 2 continually busy.
– ORIGIN Middle English: from Old French *trot* (n.), *troter* (v.), from medieval Latin *trottare*, of Germanic origin.

troth /trəʊθ, trɒθ/ ■ n. archaic or formal faith or loyalty when pledged in a solemn agreement or undertaking.
– PHRASES **pledge** (or **plight**) **one's troth** make a solemn pledge of commitment or loyalty, especially in marriage.
– ORIGIN Middle English: var. of TRUTH.

Trotskyism ■ n. the political or economic principles of the Russian revolutionary Leon Trotsky (1879–1940), especially the theory that socialism should be established throughout the world by continuing revolution.
– DERIVATIVES **Trotskyist** n. & adj. **Trotskyite** n. & adj. (derogatory).

trotter ■ n. 1 a horse bred or trained for the sport of trotting. 2 a pig's foot.

trotting ■ n. racing for trotting horses pulling a two-wheeled vehicle and driver.

troubadour /ˈtruːbədɔː/ ■ n. a French medieval lyric poet. ▶ a poet who writes verse to music.
– ORIGIN French, from Provençal *trobador*, from *trobar* 'invent, compose in verse'.

trouble ■ n. 1 difficulty or problems. ▶ malfunction; failure to work properly. ▶ effort or exertion. ▶ a cause of worry or inconvenience. ▶ (often in phr. **in trouble**) a situation in which one is liable to incur punishment or blame. 2 public unrest or disorder. ■ v. cause distress, pain, or inconvenience to. ▶ [as adj. **troubled**] showing or experiencing problems or anxiety. ▶ (**trouble about/over/with**) be distressed or anxious about. ▶ (**trouble to do something**) make the effort required to do something.
– PHRASES **ask for trouble** informal act in a way that is likely to incur problems or difficulties. **look for trouble** informal behave in a way that is likely to provoke an argument or fight. **trouble and strife** Brit. rhyming slang wife.
– ORIGIN Middle English: from Old French *truble* (n.), *trubler* (v.), from Latin *turbidus* (see TURBID).

troublemaker ■ n. a person who habitually causes trouble, especially by inciting others to defy those in authority.
– DERIVATIVES **troublemaking** n. & adj.

troubleshoot ■ v. [usu. as noun **troubleshooting**] analyse and solve problems for an organization. ▶ trace and correct faults in a mechanical or electronic system.
– DERIVATIVES **troubleshooter** n.

troublesome ■ adj. causing difficulty or annoyance.
– DERIVATIVES **troublesomely** adv. **troublesomeness** n.

trouble spot ■ n. a place where difficulties or conflict regularly occur.

troublous ■ adj. archaic or poetic/literary full of troubles.

trough ■ n. 1 a long, narrow open container for animals to eat or drink out of. ▶ a similar container, e.g. one for growing plants. 2 a channel used to convey a liquid. ▶ a long hollow in the earth's surface. 3 an elongated region of low barometric pressure. 4 a hollow between two wave crests in the sea. 5 a region around the minimum on a curve of variation of a quantity. ▶ a point of low activity or achievement.
– ORIGIN Old English *trog*, of Germanic origin.

trounce ■ v. defeat heavily in a contest. ▶ rebuke or punish severely.
– DERIVATIVES **trouncer** n.
– ORIGIN C16 (also in the sense 'afflict').

troupe ■ n. a group of dancers, actors, or other entertainers who tour to different venues.
– ORIGIN C19: from French, 'troop'.

trouper ■ n. 1 an actor or other entertainer, typically one with long experience. 2 a reliable and uncomplaining person.

trouser ■ n. [as modifier] relating to trousers.

trousers ■ pl. n. an outer garment covering the body from the waist to the ankles, with a separate part for each leg.
– PHRASES **catch someone with their trousers down** see catch someone with their pants down at PANTS. **wear the trousers** informal be the dominant partner in a relationship.
– DERIVATIVES **trousered** adj.
– ORIGIN C17: from archaic *trouse* (sing.) from Irish *triús* and Scottish Gaelic *triubhas* (see TREWS).

trouser suit ■ n. a pair of trousers and a matching jacket worn by women.

trousseau /ˈtruːsəʊ/ ■ n. (pl. **trousseaux** or **trousseaus** /-səʊz/) the clothes, linen, and other belongings collected by a bride for her marriage.
– ORIGIN C19: from French, diminutive of *trousse* 'bundle'.

trout ■ n. (pl. same or **trouts**) an edible fish of the salmon family, chiefly inhabiting fresh water. [*Salmo trutta* (brown trout, sea trout) and other species.] ■ v. [as noun **trouting**] fishing for trout.
– PHRASES **old trout** informal an annoying or bad-tempered old person, especially a woman.
– ORIGIN Old English *truht*, from late Latin *tructa*, from Greek *trōgein* 'gnaw'.

trove ■ n. a store of valuable or delightful things.
– ORIGIN C19: from TREASURE TROVE.

trow /trəʊ/ ■ v. archaic think or believe.
– ORIGIN Old English *trūwian*, *trēowian* 'to trust'; rel. to TRUCE.

1275

true

trowel ■ n. 1 a small hand-held tool with a flat, pointed blade, used to apply and spread mortar or plaster. 2 a small hand-held tool with a curved scoop for lifting plants or earth. ■ v. (**trowelled**, **trowelling**; US **troweled**, **troweling**) apply or spread with or as if with a trowel.
– ORIGIN Middle English: from Old French *truele*, from medieval Latin *truella*, from Latin *trulla* 'scoop'.

troy (also **troy weight**) ■ n. a system of weights used mainly for precious metals and gems, with a pound of 12 ounces or 5 760 grains. Compare with AVOIRDUPOIS.
– ORIGIN Middle English: from a weight used at the fair of *Troyes* in France.

truant ■ n. a pupil who stays away from school without leave or explanation. ■ adj. wandering; straying: *her truant husband*. ■ v. (also **play truant**) (of a pupil) stay away from school without leave or explanation.
– DERIVATIVES **truancy** n.
– ORIGIN Middle English (denoting a person begging through choice rather than necessity): from Old French, prob. of Celtic origin.

truce ■ n. an agreement between enemies to stop fighting for a certain time.
– ORIGIN Middle English *trewes*, from Old English *trēowa*, pl. of *trēow* 'belief, trust', of Germanic origin.

truck[1] ■ n. 1 a large road vehicle, used for carrying goods, materials, or troops. ▶ a railway vehicle for carrying freight. ▶ a low flat-topped trolley used for moving heavy items. 2 an undercarriage with four or six wheels pivoted beneath the end of a railway vehicle. ▶ each of two axle units on a skateboard, to which the wheels are attached. 3 a wooden disc at the top of a ship's mast or flagstaff, with holes for halyards to slide through. ■ v. chiefly N. Amer. 1 convey by truck. 2 informal go or proceed in a casual or leisurely way.
– DERIVATIVES **truckage** n. **truckload** n.
– ORIGIN Middle English: perhaps short for TRUCKLE in the sense 'wheel, pulley'.

truck[2] archaic ■ n. barter. ■ v. barter or exchange.
– PHRASES **have** (or **want**) **no truck with** avoid or wish to avoid dealings or association with.
– ORIGIN Middle English: prob. from Old French.

trucker ■ n. a long-distance truck driver.

truckle ■ n. a small barrel-shaped cheese, especially cheddar.
– ORIGIN Middle English (denoting a wheel or pulley): from Anglo-Norman French *trocle*, from Latin *trochlea* 'sheaf of a pulley'.

truckle bed ■ n. chiefly Brit. a low bed on wheels that can be stored under a larger bed.
– ORIGIN Middle English: from TRUCKLE in the sense 'wheel' + BED.

truck stop ■ n. a roadside café for drivers of haulage vehicles.

truculent /ˈtrʌkjʊl(ə)nt/ ■ adj. eager or quick to argue or fight; aggressively defiant.
– DERIVATIVES **truculence** n. **truculently** adv.
– ORIGIN C16: from Latin *truculentus*, from *trux*, *truc-* 'fierce'.

trudge ■ v. walk slowly and with heavy steps, typically because of exhaustion or harsh conditions. ■ n. a difficult or laborious walk.
– ORIGIN C16.

true ■ adj. (**truer**, **truest**) 1 in accordance with fact or reality. ▶ rightly or strictly so called; genuine. ▶ real or actual. 2 accurate or exact. ▶ (of a note) exactly in tune. ▶ (of a compass bearing) measured relative to true north. ▶ correctly positioned or aligned; upright or level. 3 loyal or faithful. ▶ (**true to**) accurately conforming to (a standard or expectation). ■ v. (**trues**, **trued**, **truing** or **trueing**) bring into the exact shape or position required.
– PHRASES **come true** actually happen or become the case. **out of** (**the**) **true** not in the correct or exact shape or alignment. **true to form** (or **type**) being or behaving as expected. **true to life** accurately representing real events or objects.
– DERIVATIVES **trueness** n.
– ORIGIN Old English *trēowe*, *trȳwe* 'steadfast, loyal'.

true-blue ■ adj. **1** extremely loyal or orthodox. **2** Brit. staunchly loyal to the Conservative Party. **3** real; genuine: *true-blue amateurs*.

true-born ■ adj. of a specified kind by birth; genuine.

true north ■ n. north according to the earth's axis, not magnetic north.

true rib ■ n. a rib which is attached directly to the breastbone.

truffle ■ n. **1** a strong-smelling underground fungus that resembles a rough-skinned potato, considered a culinary delicacy. [Families Tuberaceae and Terfeziaceae.] **2** a soft sweet made of a chocolate mixture, typically flavoured with rum and covered with cocoa. ■ v. [as noun **truffling**] hunting for truffles.
– ORIGIN C16: prob. from obsolete French *truffle*, perhaps from Latin *tuber* 'hump, swelling'.

truffled ■ adj. (of food) cooked, garnished, or stuffed with truffles.

trug ■ n. Brit. a shallow oblong basket made of strips of wood, traditionally used for carrying garden flowers and produce.
– ORIGIN Middle English: perhaps a dialect var. of TROUGH.

truism ■ n. **1** a statement that is obviously true and says nothing new or interesting. **2** Logic a proposition that states nothing beyond what is implied by any of its terms.
– DERIVATIVES **truistic** /-ˈɪstɪk/ adj.

truly ■ adv. **1** in a truthful way. **2** to the fullest degree; genuinely or properly. ▶ absolutely or completely. **3** in actual fact; really.
– PHRASES **yours truly** used as a formula for ending a letter. ▶ humorous used to refer to oneself.

trump¹ ■ n. **1** (in bridge, whist, etc.) a playing card of the suit chosen to rank above the others, which can win a trick where a card of a different suit has been led.
▶ (**trumps**) the suit having this rank in a particular hand.
▶ (in a tarot pack) any of a special suit of twenty-two cards depicting symbolic figures and scenes. **2** a valuable resource that may be used, especially as a surprise, to gain an advantage. ■ v. **1** play a trump on (a card of another suit). **2** beat by saying or doing something better.
3 (**trump something up**) invent a false accusation or excuse.
– PHRASES **come** (or **turn**) **up trumps** informal, chiefly Brit. have a better performance or outcome than expected.
▶ be especially generous or helpful.
– ORIGIN C16: alteration of TRIUMPH.

trump² ■ n. archaic a trumpet or a trumpet blast.
– ORIGIN Middle English: from Old French *trompe*, of Germanic origin; prob. imitative.

trumpery archaic ■ n. (pl. **-ies**) articles, practices, or beliefs of superficial appeal but little real value or worth. ■ adj. showy but worthless; delusive.
– ORIGIN Middle English: from Old French *tromperie*, from *tromper* 'deceive'.

trumpet ■ n. **1** a brass musical instrument with a flared bell and a bright, penetrating tone. **2** something shaped like a trumpet. **3** the loud cry of an elephant. ■ v. (**trumpeted**, **trumpeting**) **1** play a trumpet. **2** (of an elephant) make its characteristic loud cry. **3** proclaim widely or loudly.
– PHRASES **blow one's** (**own**) **trumpet** talk openly and boastfully about one's achievements.
– ORIGIN Middle English: from Old French *trompette*, diminutive of *trompe* (see TRUMP²).

trumpeter ■ n. **1** a person who plays a trumpet, especially a soldier who gives signals with a trumpet. **2** a pigeon of a domestic breed that makes a trumpet-like sound.

trumpet vine (also **trumpet creeper**) ■ n. a climbing shrub with orange or red trumpet-shaped flowers, cultivated as an ornamental. [*Campsis radicans* and *C. grandiflora*.]

truncate ■ v. /trʌnˈkeɪt, ˈtrʌn-/ [often as adj. **truncated**] shorten by cutting off the top or the end. ■ adj. /ˈtrʌŋkeɪt/ Botany & Zoology (of a leaf, feather, etc.) ending abruptly as if truncated.
– DERIVATIVES **truncation** n.

– ORIGIN C15 (*truncation* Middle English): from Latin *truncare* 'maim'.

truncheon /ˈtrʌn(t)ʃ(ə)n/ ■ n. chiefly Brit. a short thick stick carried as a weapon by a police officer.
– ORIGIN Middle English: from Old French *tronchon* 'stump', from Latin *truncus* 'trunk'.

trundle ■ v. move slowly and unevenly on or as if on wheels. ■ n. an act of trundling.
– ORIGIN C16: rel. to dialect *trendle*, *trindle* 'revolve'.

trundle bed ■ n. chiefly N. Amer. a truckle bed.

trunk ■ n. **1** the main woody stem of a tree as distinct from its branches and roots. ▶ the main part of an artery, nerve, or other structure from which smaller branches arise. **2** a person's or animal's body apart from the limbs and head. **3** the elongated, prehensile nose of an elephant. **4** a large box with a hinged lid for storing or transporting clothes and other articles. **5** N. Amer. the boot of a motor car. **6** [as modifier] of or relating to the main routes of a transport or communication network: *a trunk road*.
– DERIVATIVES **trunkful** n. (pl. **-fuls**). **trunkless** adj.
– ORIGIN Middle English: from Old French *tronc*, from Latin *truncus*.

trunk call ■ n. a long-distance telephone call made within the same country.

trunking ■ n. **1** a system of shafts or conduits for cables or ventilation. **2** the use or arrangement of trunk lines.

trunks ■ pl. n. men's shorts, worn especially for swimming or boxing.

trunnion /ˈtrʌnjən/ ■ n. a pin or pivot forming one of a pair on which something is supported.
– ORIGIN C17: from French *trognon* 'core, tree trunk'.

truss ■ n. **1** a framework of rafters, posts, and struts which supports a roof, bridge, or other structure. **2** a surgical appliance worn to support a hernia, typically a padded belt. **3** a large projection of stone or timber, typically one supporting a cornice. **4** a compact cluster of flowers or fruit growing on one stalk. ■ v. **1** tie up the wings and legs of (a chicken or other bird) before cooking. ▶ bind or tie up tightly. **2** [usu. as adj. **trussed**] support with a truss or trusses.
– ORIGIN Middle English: from Old French *trusse* (n.), *trusser* 'pack up, bind in', from late Latin *tors-, torquere* 'twist'.

trust ■ n. **1** firm belief in someone or something.
▶ acceptance of the truth of a statement without evidence or investigation. **2** the state of being responsible for someone or something: *a man in a position of trust*. **3** Law an arrangement whereby a person (a trustee) is made the nominal owner of property to be held or used for the benefit of one or more others. **4** a body of trustees. ▶ an organization or company managed by trustees. **5** (**Trust**) S. African historical relating to property purchased after 1936 by the South African Development Trust for the settlement of black people: *Trust land*. ■ v. **1** believe in the reliability, truth, ability, or strength of. ▶ (**trust someone with**) have the confidence to allow someone to have, use, or look after. ▶ (**trust someone/thing to**) commit someone or something to the safe keeping of.
▶ (**trust to**) place reliance on (luck, fate, etc.). **2** have confidence; hope (used as a polite formula): *I trust that you have enjoyed this book*.
– PHRASES **trust someone to —** it is characteristic or predictable for someone to act in the specified way.
– DERIVATIVES **trustable** adj. **trusted** adj. **truster** n. **trustful** adj. **trustfully** adv. **trustfulness** n.
– ORIGIN Middle English: from Old Norse *traust*, from *traustr* 'strong'; verb from Old Norse *treysta*.

Trustafarian /ˌtrʌstəˈfɛːrɪən/ ■ n. informal a rich young person who adopts an ethnic lifestyle and lives in a non-affluent urban area.
– ORIGIN 1990s: blend of TRUST FUND and RASTAFARIAN.

trust company ■ n. a company formed to act as a trustee or to deal with trusts.

trust deed ■ n. Law a deed of conveyance creating and setting out the conditions of a trust.

trustee ■ n. **1** Law an individual or member of a board given powers of administration of property in trust with a legal obligation to administer it solely for the purposes

specified. **2** a state made responsible for the government of an area by the United Nations.
– DERIVATIVES **trusteeship** n.

trustee in insolvency (also **trustee in bankruptcy**) ■ n. Law a person taking administrative responsibility for the financial affairs of a bankrupt.

trust fund ■ n. a fund consisting of assets belonging to a trust, held by the trustees for the beneficiaries.

trusting ■ adj. showing trust in or tending to trust others; not suspicious.
– DERIVATIVES **trustingly** adv.

trust territory ■ n. a territory under the trusteeship of the United Nations or of a state designated by them.

trustworthy ■ adj. able to be relied on as honest, truthful, or reliable.
– DERIVATIVES **trustworthily** adv. **trustworthiness** n.

trusty ■ adj. (-ier, -iest) archaic or humorous reliable or faithful: *their trusty steeds.* ■ n. (pl. -ies) a prisoner who is given special privileges or responsibilities in return for good behaviour.
– DERIVATIVES **trustily** adv. **trustiness** n.

truth ■ n. (pl. **truths** /truːðz, truːθs/) the quality or state of being true. ▸ (also **the truth**) that which is true as opposed to false. ▸ a fact or belief that is accepted as true.
– PHRASES **in truth** really; in fact. **to tell the truth** (or **truth to tell** or **if truth be told**) to be frank.
– ORIGIN Old English *trīewth*, *trēowth* 'faithfulness, constancy'.

truth commission ■ n. (**Truth Commission**, in full **Truth and Reconciliation Commission**) (in South Africa) a commission set up in 1995 to investigate human rights violations between 1960 and 1994. ▸ an official investigation by a committee into human rights violations occurring during a period of unrest. ▸ a committee established for this purpose.
– DERIVATIVES **truth commissioner** n.

truth condition ■ n. Logic the condition under which a given proposition is true. ▸ a statement of this condition, sometimes taken to be the meaning of the proposition.

truth drug ■ n. a drug supposedly able to induce a state in which a person answers questions truthfully.

truthful ■ adj. **1** telling or expressing the truth; honest. **2** (of a representation) true to life.
– DERIVATIVES **truthfully** adv. **truthfulness** n.

truth table ■ n. Logic **1** a diagram in rows showing how the truth or falsity of a proposition varies with that of its components. **2** Electronics a similar diagram of the outputs from all possible combinations of input.

truth value ■ n. Logic the attribute assigned to a proposition in respect of its truth or falsehood, which in classical logic has only two possible values (true or false).

try ■ v. (-ies, -ied) **1** make an attempt or effort to do something. ▸ (also **try something out**) test (something new or different) in order to see if it is suitable, effective, or pleasant. ▸ attempt to operate (a device), open (a door), contact (someone), etc.: *I tried the doors, but they were locked.* ▸ (**try something on**) put on an item of clothing to see if it fits or suits one. **2** make severe demands on: *Mary tried everyone's patience to the limit.* **3** subject (someone) to trial. ▸ investigate and decide (a case or issue) in a formal trial. ■ n. (pl. -ies) **1** an effort to accomplish something; an attempt. ▸ an act of testing something new or different. **2** Rugby an act of touching the ball down behind the opposing goal line, scoring points and entitling the scoring side to a kick at goal.
– PHRASES **tried and tested** (or **true**) having proved effective or reliable before. **try one's hand at** attempt to do for the first time. **try it on** Brit. informal deliberately test or attempt to deceive or seduce someone.
– ORIGIN Middle English: from Old French *trier* 'sift'.

trying ■ adj. difficult or annoying; hard to endure: *it had been a very trying day.*
– DERIVATIVES **tryingly** adv.

trypan blue ■ n. a diazo dye used as a biological stain.
– ORIGIN C20: *trypan* from **TRYPANOSOME**.

trypanosome /ˈtrɪp(ə)nəsəʊm, trɪˈpanə-/ ■ n. Medicine & Zoology a single-celled parasitic protozoan with a trailing flagellum, infesting the blood. [Genus *Trypanosoma*.]
– ORIGIN C20: from Greek *trupanon* 'borer' + -SOME³.

trypanosomiasis /ˌtrɪp(ə)nə(ʊ)-, trɪˌpanə(ʊ)sə(ʊ)ˈmʌɪəsɪs/ ■ n. Medicine a tropical disease caused by trypanosomes, especially sleeping sickness.

trypsin /ˈtrɪpsɪn/ ■ n. a digestive enzyme which breaks down proteins in the small intestine, secreted by the pancreas as trypsinogen.
– DERIVATIVES **tryptic** adj.
– ORIGIN C19: from Greek *tripsis* 'friction', from *tribein* 'to rub' (because it was first obtained by rubbing down the pancreas with glycerine).

trypsinogen /trɪpˈsɪnədʒ(ə)n/ ■ n. Biochemistry an inactive substance secreted by the pancreas, from which the digestive enzyme trypsin is formed.

tryptophan /ˈtrɪptəfan/ ■ n. Biochemistry an amino acid which is a constituent of most proteins and is an essential nutrient in the diet of vertebrates.
– ORIGIN C19: from *tryptic* 'relating to trypsin' + Greek *phainein* 'appear'.

trysail /ˈtrʌɪs(ə)l/ ■ n. a small strong fore-and-aft sail set on the mainmast or other mast of a sailing vessel in heavy weather.

tryst /trɪst/ poetic/literary ■ n. a private, romantic rendezvous between lovers. ■ v. keep or arrange a tryst.
– DERIVATIVES **tryster** n.
– ORIGIN Middle English: var. of obsolete *trist* 'an appointed place in hunting', from French *triste* or medieval Latin *trista*.

tsamma /ˈtsamə/ (also **tsamma melon**) ■ n. an edible wild watermelon with a greyish-green rind and pale yellow flesh. [*Citrullus lanatus*.]
– ORIGIN from Nama *tsamas* 'watermelon'.

tsar /zɑː, tsɑː/ (also **czar** or **tzar**) ■ n. **1** an emperor of Russia before 1917. **2** a person with great power in a particular area: *America's new drug tsar.*
– DERIVATIVES **tsardom** n. **tsarism** n. **tsarist** n. & adj.
– ORIGIN from Russian *tsar'*, representing Latin *Caesar*.

tsarevich /ˈzɑːrɪvɪtʃ, ˈtsɑː-, -ˈrjeɪ-/ (also **czarevich** or **tzarevich**) ■ n. historical the eldest son of a Russian tsar.
– ORIGIN Russian, 'son of a tsar'.

tsarina /zɑːˈriːnə, tsɑː-/ (also **czarina** or **tzarina**) ■ n. historical an empress of Russia before 1917.
– ORIGIN from German *Czarin*, *Zarin*, feminine of *Czar*, *Zar*.

tsessebe /ˈtsɛsəbi, tsɛˈseɪbi/ (also **tsessebi**) ■ n. a large antelope of sub-Saharan Africa, with a reddish coat and short curved horns. [*Damaliscus lunatus*.]
– ORIGIN C19: from Setswana.

tsetse /ˈtsɛtsi, ˈtɛtsi/ (also **tsetse fly**) ■ n. an African bloodsucking fly which transmits sleeping sickness and nagana. [Genus *Glossina*.]
– ORIGIN C19: from Setswana.

TSH ■ abbrev. thyroid-stimulating hormone.

T-shirt (also **tee shirt**) ■ n. a short-sleeved casual top, having the shape of a T when spread out flat.

Tshivenda /tʃɪˈvɛndə/ ■ n. the Bantu language of the Venda people.

tsk tsk /t(ə)sk t(ə)sk/ ■ exclam. expressing disapproval or annoyance.
– ORIGIN 1940s: imitative.

Tsonga /ˈtsɒŋɡə/ ■ n. (pl. same or **Tsongas**) **1** a member of a southern African people living in parts of South Africa, Zimbabwe, and Mozambique. **2** another term for **XITSONGA**.
– ORIGIN a local name, from either Xitsonga or isiZulu.

tsotsi /ˈtsɒtsi/ ■ n. (pl. **tsotsis**) S. African a black urban criminal.
– ORIGIN perhaps a Sesotho corruption of **ZOOT SUIT**, with ref. to the flashy clothes orig. associated with tsotsis.

Tsotsitaal /ˈtsɒtsɪtɑːl/ ■ n. S. African an Afrikaans-influenced township patois, which was originally a form of slang used by criminals, typically spoken in Gauteng.
– ORIGIN from **TSOTSI** + Afrikaans *taal* 'language'.

tsp ■ abbrev. (pl. same or **tsps**) teaspoonful.

T-square ■ n. a T-shaped instrument for drawing or testing right angles.

TSR ■ abbrev. Computing terminate and stay resident, denoting a type of program that remains in the memory of a microcomputer after it has finished running.

TSS ■ abbrev. toxic shock syndrome.

tsubo /ˈtsuːbəʊ/ ■ n. (pl. same or **-os**) (in complementary medicine) a point on the face or body to which pressure or other stimulation is applied during treatment.
– ORIGIN from Japanese.

tsunami /tsuːˈnɑːmi/ ■ n. (pl. same or **tsunamis**) a long high sea wave caused by an earthquake or other disturbance.
– ORIGIN C19: from Japanese, from *tsu* 'harbour' + *nami* 'wave'.

Tswana /ˈtswɑːnə/ (also **Motswana**) ■ n. (pl. same, **Tswanas**, or **Batswana**) 1 a member of a southern African people living in Botswana, South Africa, and neighbouring areas. 2 another term for SETSWANA.
– ORIGIN from Setswana *moTswana*, pl. *baTswana*.

TTL ■ abbrev. 1 Electronics transistor transistor logic, a widely used technology for making integrated circuits. 2 Photography (of a camera focusing system) through-the-lens.

Tu. ■ abbrev. Tuesday.

Tuareg /ˈtwɑːreɡ/ ■ n. (pl. same or **Tuaregs**) a member of a Berber people of the western and central Sahara.
– ORIGIN the name in Berber.

tub ■ n. 1 a low, wide, open container with a flat bottom used for holding liquids, growing plants, etc. ▸ a similar small plastic or cardboard container for food. ▸ informal a bath. ▸ Mining a container for conveying ore, coal, etc. 2 informal, derogatory a short, broad boat that handles awkwardly.
– DERIVATIVES **tubful** n. (pl. **-fuls**).
– ORIGIN Middle English: prob. rel. to Middle Low German, Middle Dutch *tubbe*.

tuba ■ n. a large brass wind instrument of bass pitch, with three to six valves and a broad bell facing upwards.
– ORIGIN C19: from Latin, 'trumpet'.

tubal ■ adj. of, relating to, or occurring in a tube, especially the Fallopian tubes: *tubal ligation*.

tubby ■ adj. (**-ier**, **-iest**) informal (of a person) short and rather fat.
– DERIVATIVES **tubbiness** n.

tube ■ n. 1 a long, hollow cylinder used for conveying or holding liquids or gases. ▸ a flexible metal or plastic container sealed at one end and having a cap at the other. ▸ material forming tubes; tubing. 2 Anatomy, Zoology, & Botany a hollow cylindrical organ or structure in an animal or plant. ▸ (**tubes**) informal a woman's Fallopian tubes. 3 (**the tube**) Brit. informal the underground railway system in London. ▸ a train running on this system. 4 a sealed container, typically of glass and either evacuated or filled with gas, containing two electrodes between which an electric current can be made to flow. 5 (**the tube**) N. Amer. informal television. 6 (in surfing) the hollow curve under the crest of a breaking wave. ■ v. 1 [usu. as adj. **tubed**] provide with a tube or tubes. 2 convey in a tube.
– PHRASES **go down the tube** (or **tubes**) informal be completely lost or wasted; fail utterly.
– DERIVATIVES **tubeless** adj.
– ORIGIN C17: from French *tube* or Latin *tubus*.

tubectomy ■ n. (pl. **-ies**) another term for SALPINGECTOMY.

tube foot ■ n. Zoology each of a large number of small flexible hollow appendages protruding from the body of an echinoderm, used either for locomotion or for collecting food.

tuber ■ n. 1 a much thickened underground part of a stem or rhizome, e.g. in the potato, serving as a food reserve and bearing buds from which new plants arise. ▸ a thickened fleshy root, e.g. of the dahlia. 2 Anatomy a rounded swelling or protuberant part.
– ORIGIN C17: from Latin, 'hump, swelling'.

tubercle /ˈtjuːbək(ə)l/ ■ n. 1 Anatomy, Zoology, & Botany a small rounded projection or protuberance, especially on a bone or on the surface of an animal or plant. 2 Medicine a small nodular lesion in the lungs or other tissues, characteristic of tuberculosis.
– DERIVATIVES **tuberculate** /-ˈbəːkjʊlət/ adj.
– ORIGIN C16: from Latin *tuberculum*, diminutive of *tuber* (see TUBER).

tubercle bacillus ■ n. the bacterium that causes tuberculosis. [*Mycobacterium tuberculosis*.]

tubercular /tjʊˈbəːkjʊlə/ ■ adj. 1 Medicine of, relating to, or affected with tuberculosis. 2 Biology & Medicine having or covered with tubercles. ■ n. a person with tuberculosis.

tuberculin /tjʊˈbəːkjʊlɪn/ ■ n. a sterile protein extract from cultures of tubercle bacillus, used to test for tuberculosis.
– ORIGIN C19: from Latin *tuberculum* (see TUBERCLE).

tuberculoid /tjʊˈbəːkjʊlɔɪd/ ■ adj. Medicine 1 resembling tuberculosis. 2 relating to or denoting the milder of the two principal forms of leprosy, marked by few, well-defined lesions similar to those of tuberculosis. Compare with LEPROMATOUS.

tuberculosis /tjʊˌbəːkjʊˈləʊsɪs/ ■ n. an infectious bacterial disease characterized by the growth of nodules (tubercles) in the tissues, especially the lungs.
– ORIGIN C19: from Latin *tuberculum* (see TUBERCLE).

tuberculous /tjʊˈbəːkjʊləs/ ■ adj. another term for TUBERCULAR.

tuberose /ˈtjuːbərəʊz/ ■ n. a Mexican plant with heavily scented white waxy flowers and a bulb-like base. [*Polianthes tuberosa*.] ■ adj. variant spelling of TUBEROUS.
– ORIGIN C17: from Latin *tuberosa*, from *tuberosus* 'with protuberances'.

tuberous /ˈtjuːb(ə)rəs/ (also **tuberose** /ˈtjuːb(ə)rəʊs/) ■ adj. 1 Botany resembling, forming, or having a tuber or tubers. 2 Medicine characterized by or affected by rounded swellings.
– DERIVATIVES **tuberosity** /-ˈrɒsɪti/ n.

tube worm ■ n. a fan worm or other marine worm which lives in a tube-like structure.

tubifex /ˈtjuːbɪfɛks/ ■ n. a small red annelid worm that lives in fresh water, partly buried in the mud. [Genus *Tubifex*.]
– ORIGIN from Latin *tubus* 'tube' + *-fex* from *facere* 'make'.

tubing ■ n. 1 a length or lengths of material in tubular form. 2 the leisure activity of riding on water or snow on a large inflated inner tube.

tub-thumping informal, derogatory ■ adj. expressing opinions in a loud and violent or dramatic manner. ■ n. the expression of opinions in such a way.
– DERIVATIVES **tub-thumper** n.

tubular ■ adj. 1 long, round, and hollow like a tube. ▸ made from a tube or tubes. 2 Medicine of or involving tubules or other tube-shaped structures. ■ n. short for TUBULAR TYRE.
– ORIGIN C17: from Latin *tubulus* 'small tube'.

tubular bells ■ pl. n. an orchestral instrument consisting of a row of vertically suspended metal tubes struck with a mallet.

tubular tyre ■ n. a completely enclosed tyre cemented on to the wheel rim, used on racing bicycles.

tubule /ˈtjuːbjuːl/ ■ n. 1 a minute tube, especially as an anatomical structure. 2 Anatomy each of the long, fine, convoluted tubules conveying urine from the glomeruli to the renal pelvis in the vertebrate kidney.
– ORIGIN C17: from Latin *tubulus*, diminutive of *tubus* 'tube'.

tubulin /ˈtjuːbjʊlɪn/ ■ n. Biochemistry a protein that is the main constituent of the microtubules of living cells.
– ORIGIN 1960s: from TUBULE.

TUC ■ abbrev. (in the UK) Trades Union Congress.

tuck ■ v. 1 push, fold, or turn under or between two surfaces or into a confined space. ▸ (**tuck something away**) store something in a secure place. ▸ (**tuck someone in/up**) settle someone in bed by pulling the edges of the bedclothes firmly under the mattress. 2 make a flattened, stitched fold in (a garment or material), to improve the fit or for decoration. 3 (**tuck in/into**) informal eat food heartily. ■ n. 1 a flattened, stitched fold in a garment or material. ▸ informal a surgical operation which involves removing a fold of flesh or fat. 2 Brit. informal food eaten by

children at school as a snack. **3** (also **tuck position**) (in diving, gymnastics, downhill skiing, etc.) a position with the knees bent and held close to the chest.
– DERIVATIVES **tucking** n.
– ORIGIN Old English *tūcian* 'punish, ill-treat', of West Germanic origin.

tucker informal ■ n. Austral./NZ food. ■ v. N. Amer. exhaust; wear out.

tuck shop ■ n. a small shop, especially in a school, selling sweets and snacks. ▸ S. African another term for SPAZA.

Tudor ■ adj. **1** of or relating to the English royal dynasty which held the throne from the accession of Henry VII in 1485 until the death of Elizabeth I in 1603. **2** of or denoting the prevalent architectural style of the Tudor period, characterized by half-timbering. ■ n. a member of this dynasty.

Tudor rose ■ n. a stylized figure of a rose used in architectural decoration in the Tudor period.

Tues. (also **Tue.**) ■ abbrev. Tuesday.

Tuesday ■ n. the day of the week before Wednesday and following Monday. ■ adv. on Tuesday. ▸ (**Tuesdays**) on Tuesdays; each Tuesday.
– ORIGIN Old English *Tiwesdæg*, named after the Germanic god *Tīw* (associated with Mars); translation of Latin *dies Marti* 'day of Mars'.

tufa /ˈtjuːfə/ ■ n. **1** a porous rock composed of calcium carbonate and formed by precipitation from water, e.g. around mineral springs. **2** another term for TUFF.
– DERIVATIVES **tufaceous** /-ˈfeɪʃəs/ adj.
– ORIGIN C18: from Italian, var. of *tufo* (see TUFF).

tuff /tʌf/ ■ n. a light, porous rock formed by consolidation of volcanic ash.
– DERIVATIVES **tuffaceous** /-ˈfeɪʃəs/ adj.
– ORIGIN C16: from Italian *tufo*, from late Latin *tofus*, Latin *tophus*, denoting loose porous stones.

tuffet ■ n. **1** a tuft or clump. **2** a footstool or low seat.
– ORIGIN C16: alteration of TUFT.

tuft ■ n. a bunch of threads, grass, or hair, held or growing together at the base. ▸ Anatomy a bunch of small blood vessels or other small anatomical structures. ■ v. **1** provide with a tuft or tufts. **2** strengthen (upholstery) by passing a cluster of threads through the material, so making depressions at regular intervals.
– DERIVATIVES **tufted** adj. **tufty** adj.
– ORIGIN Middle English: prob. from Old French *tofe*.

tufted duck ■ n. a Eurasian freshwater diving duck with a drooping crest, the male having mainly black and white plumage. [*Aythya fuligula*.]

tug ■ v. (**tugged**, **tugging**) **1** pull (something) hard or suddenly. **2** tow (a ship) by means of a tug or tugs. ■ n. **1** a hard or sudden pull. **2** (also **tugboat**) a small, powerful boat used for towing larger boats and ships, especially in harbour. ▸ an aircraft towing a glider.
– DERIVATIVES **tugger** n.
– ORIGIN Middle English: from the base of TOW¹.

tug of war ■ n. a contest in which two teams pull at opposite ends of a rope until one drags the other over a central line.

Tuinal /ˈtjuːɪnal, -nəl/ ■ n. trademark a sedative and hypnotic drug composed of two barbiturates.

tuition ■ n. teaching or instruction, especially of individuals or small groups. ▸ a fee charged for this.
– DERIVATIVES **tuitional** adj.
– ORIGIN Middle English: from Latin *tuitio(n-)*, from *tueri* 'to watch, guard'.

Tuks (also **Tukkies**) ■ n. S. African informal a nickname for the University of Pretoria.

tuk-tuk ■ n. a light, three-wheeled motorized vehicle, used chiefly in India and SE Asia.
– ORIGIN imitative.

tularaemia /ˌt(j)uːləˈriːmɪə/ (US **tularemia**) ■ n. a severe infectious disease of animals which is transmissible to humans, caused by a bacterium (*Pasteurella tularense*).
– DERIVATIVES **tularaemic** adj.
– ORIGIN 1920S: from *Tulare*, the county in California where it was first observed.

tulip ■ n. a bulbous spring-flowering plant of the lily family, with boldly coloured cup-shaped flowers. [Genus *Tulipa*: numerous complex hybrids.]
– ORIGIN C16: from French *tulipe*, from Persian *dulband* 'turban', from the shape of the expanded flower.

tulip tree ■ n. **1** a deciduous North American tree which has large distinctively lobed leaves and insignificant tulip-like flowers. [*Liriodendron tulipifera*.] **2** informal term for MAGNOLIA (in sense 1).

tulipwood ■ n. the ornamental wood of the tulip tree, or a similar wood from another tree.

tulle /tjuːl/ ■ n. a soft, fine net material, used for making veils and dresses.
– ORIGIN C19: from *Tulle*, a town in SW France.

tulp /tʊlp/ ■ n. S. African an African plant of the iris family, which is grown for its showy flowers but is toxic to livestock. [Genera *Homeria* and *Moraea*: several species.]
– ORIGIN C19: from S. African Dutch, from Dutch *tulp* 'tulip'.

tulsi /ˈtʊlsiː/ ■ n. a kind of basil which is cultivated by Hindus as a sacred plant. [*Ocimum sanctum*.]
– ORIGIN from Hindi *tūlsī*.

tum ■ n. informal a person's stomach or abdomen.

tumble ■ v. **1** fall suddenly, clumsily, or headlong. ▸ perform acrobatic feats, typically handsprings and somersaults. **2** decrease rapidly in amount or value. **3** dry in a tumbledryer. **4** rumple; disarrange. **5** informal have sexual intercourse with. **6** (**tumble to**) informal come to understand; realize: *he's tumbled to the fact that he was deceived*. **7** clean (castings, gemstones, etc.) in a tumbling barrel. ■ n. **1** an instance of tumbling. **2** an untidy or confused arrangement or state. **3** a handspring or other acrobatic feat.
– ORIGIN Middle English: from Middle Low German *tummelen*; cf. Old English *tumbian* 'to dance'; prob. influenced by Old French *tomber* 'to fall'.

tumbledown ■ adj. falling or fallen into ruin; dilapidated.

tumble-dryer ■ n. a machine that dries washed clothes by spinning them in hot air inside a rotating drum.
– DERIVATIVES **tumble-dry** v. (-**dries**, -**dried**).

tumbler ■ n. **1** a drinking glass with straight sides and no handle or stem. [formerly having a rounded bottom so as not to stand upright.] **2** an acrobat. **3** another term for TUMBLE-DRYER. **4** a pivoted piece in a lock that holds the bolt until lifted by a key. ▸ a notched pivoted plate in a gunlock. **5** an electrical switch worked by pushing a small sprung lever. **6** a tumbling barrel.

tumbleweed ■ n. N. Amer. & Austral./NZ a plant of arid regions which breaks off near the ground in late summer, forming light globular masses blown about by the wind. [Several species in the genera *Salsola* and *Amaranthus*.]

tumbling barrel ■ n. a revolving device containing an abrasive substance, in which castings, gemstones, or other hard objects can be cleaned by friction.

tumbril /ˈtʌmbr(ə)l, -brɪl/ (also **tumbrel**) ■ n. historical an open cart that tilted backwards to empty out its load, in particular one used to convey prisoners to the guillotine during the French Revolution.
– ORIGIN Middle English: from Old French *tomberel*, from *tomber* 'to fall'.

tumescent /tjuːˈmɛs(ə)nt/ ■ adj. swollen or becoming swollen.
– DERIVATIVES **tumescence** n. **tumescently** adv.
– ORIGIN C19: from Latin *tumescere* 'begin to swell', from *tumere* 'to swell'.

tumid /ˈtjuːmɪd/ ■ adj. (of a part of the body) swollen or bulging.
– DERIVATIVES **tumidity** n. **tumidly** adv.
– ORIGIN C16: from Latin *tumidus*, from *tumere* 'to swell'.

tummy ■ n. (pl. -**ies**) informal a person's stomach or abdomen.
– ORIGIN C19: child's pronunciation of STOMACH.

tummy button ■ n. informal a person's navel.

tumour (US **tumor**) ■ n. a swelling of a part of the body, generally without inflammation, caused by an abnormal growth of tissue, whether benign or malignant.
– DERIVATIVES **tumorous** adj.
– ORIGIN Middle English: from Latin *tumor*, from *tumere* 'to swell'.

tumult

tumult ■ n. **1** a loud, confused noise, as caused by a large mass of people. **2** confusion or disorder.
– ORIGIN Middle English: from Old French *tumulte* or Latin *tumultus*.

tumultuous /tjʊˈmʌltjʊəs/ ■ adj. **1** very loud or uproarious. **2** excited, confused, or disorderly.
– DERIVATIVES **tumultuously** adv. **tumultuousness** n.

tumulus /ˈtjuːmjʊləs/ ■ n. (pl. **tumuli** /-lʌɪ, -liː/) an ancient burial mound; a barrow.
– ORIGIN Middle English: from Latin; rel. to *tumere* 'swell'.

tun ■ n. a large beer or wine cask. ▸ a brewer's fermenting-vat.
– ORIGIN Old English *tunne*, from medieval Latin *tunna*, prob. of Gaulish origin.

tuna ■ n. (pl. same or **tunas**) a large and active predatory schooling fish of warm seas, extensively fished commercially. [*Thunnus* and other genera: several species.]
– ORIGIN C19: from Spanish *atún* 'tunny'.

tundish /ˈtʌndɪʃ/ ■ n. a broad open container or large funnel with one or more holes at the bottom, used especially in plumbing or metal-founding.

tundra /ˈtʌndrə/ ■ n. a vast, flat, treeless Arctic region in which the subsoil is permanently frozen.
– ORIGIN C16: from Lappish.

tune ■ n. a melody, especially one which characterizes a certain piece of music. ■ v. **1** adjust (a musical instrument) to the correct or uniform pitch. **2** adjust (a receiver circuit such as a radio or television) to the frequency of the required signal. ▸ (**tune in**) watch or listen to a television or radio broadcast. **3** adjust (an engine) or balance (mechanical parts) in order that they run smoothly and efficiently. **4** adjust or adapt to a particular purpose or situation. ▸ (**tune into**) become sensitive to. ▸ (**tune out**) informal stop listening or paying attention. **5** /tʃuːn/ S. African informal tell. ▸ tease; kid. ▸ (in phr. **tune someone grief**) annoy or provoke someone.
– PHRASES **in** (or **out of**) **tune 1** with correct (or incorrect) pitch or intonation. **2** (of a motor engine) properly (or poorly) adjusted. **3** in (or not in) agreement or harmony. **to the tune of** informal amounting to or involving: *he was in debt to the tune of forty thousand rand.*
– DERIVATIVES **tunable** (also **tuneable**) adj. **tuning** n.
– ORIGIN Middle English: alteration of TONE.

tuneful ■ adj. having a pleasing tune; melodious.
– DERIVATIVES **tunefully** adv. **tunefulness** n.

tuneless ■ adj. not pleasing to listen to; unmelodious.
– DERIVATIVES **tunelessly** adv. **tunelessness** n.

tuner ■ n. **1** a person who tunes musical instruments, especially pianos. **2** an electronic device used for tuning. **3** a separate unit for detecting and preamplifying a programme signal and supplying it to an audio amplifier.

tunesmith ■ n. informal a composer of popular music or songs.

tungstate /ˈtʌŋsteɪt/ ■ n. Chemistry a salt in which the anion contains both tungsten and oxygen.
– ORIGIN C19: from TUNGSTEN.

tungsten /ˈtʌŋst(ə)n/ ■ n. the chemical element of atomic number 74, a hard steel-grey metal with a very high melting point (3410°C), used to make electric light filaments. (Symbol: **W**)
– ORIGIN C18: from Swedish, from *tung* 'heavy' + *sten* 'stone'.

tungsten carbide ■ n. a very hard grey compound made by reaction of tungsten and carbon at high temperatures, used in making engineering dies, cutting and drilling tools, etc.

tunic ■ n. **1** a loose sleeveless garment reaching to the thigh or knees. ▸ a gymslip. **2** a close-fitting short coat worn as part of a uniform. **3** Biology & Anatomy an integument or membrane enclosing or lining an organ or part. ▸ Botany any of the concentric layers of a plant bulb, e.g. an onion.
– ORIGIN Old English, from Old French *tunique* or Latin *tunica*.

tunica /ˈtjuːnɪkə/ ■ n. (pl. **tunicae** /-kiː/) **1** Anatomy a membranous sheath enveloping or lining an organ. **2** Botany the outer layer of cells at the apex of a growing shoot.
– ORIGIN C17: from Latin, 'tunic'.

tunicate /ˈtjuːnɪkət, -keɪt/ ■ n. Zoology a marine invertebrate of a group which includes the sea squirts, with a rubbery or hard outer coat. [Subphylum Urochordata.] ■ adj. (also **tunicated**) Botany (of a plant bulb, e.g. an onion) having concentric layers.

tuning fork ■ n. a two-pronged steel device used for tuning instruments, which vibrates when struck to give a note of specific pitch.

tuning peg ■ n. any of the pegs in the neck of a stringed musical instrument, which can be turned to adjust the tension of the strings and so tune the instrument.

Tunisian /tjuːˈnɪzɪən/ ■ n. a native or inhabitant of Tunisia. ■ adj. of or relating to Tunisia.

tunnel ■ n. **1** an artificial underground passage, as built through a hill or under a building or by a burrowing animal. **2** an elongated polythene-covered frame under which plants are grown outdoors. ■ v. (**tunnelled**, **tunnelling**; US **tunneled**, **tunneling**) **1** dig or force a passage underground or through something. **2** Physics (of a particle) pass through a potential barrier.
– DERIVATIVES **tunneller** n.
– ORIGIN Middle English: from Old French *tonel*, diminutive of *tonne* 'cask'.

tunnel diode ■ n. Electronics a two-terminal semiconductor diode using tunnelling electrons to perform high-speed switching operations.

tunnel vision ■ n. **1** defective sight in which objects cannot be properly seen if not close to the centre of the field of view. **2** informal the tendency to focus exclusively on a single or limited objective or view.

tunny (also **tunny fish**) ■ n. (pl. same or **-ies**) a tuna, especially the bluefin.
– ORIGIN C16: from French *thon*, from Greek *thunnos*.

tup /tʌp/ chiefly Brit. ■ n. a ram. ■ v. (**tupped**, **tupping**) (of a ram) copulate with (a ewe).
– DERIVATIVES **tupping** n.
– ORIGIN Middle English.

Tupi /ˈtuːpi/ ■ n. (pl. same or **Tupis**) **1** a member of a group of American Indian peoples of the Amazon valley. **2** any of the languages of these peoples.
– DERIVATIVES **Tupian** adj.
– ORIGIN a local name.

Tupi-Guarani ■ n. a South American Indian language family whose principal members are Guarani and the Tupian languages.

tuple /ˈtjuːp(ə)l/ ■ n. Computing a data structure consisting of multiple parts. ▸ (in a relational database) an ordered set of data constituting a record.
– ORIGIN from -TUPLE.

tuppence ■ n. Brit. variant spelling of TWOPENCE.

tuppenny ■ adj. Brit. variant spelling of TWOPENNY.

Tupperware /ˈtʌpəwɛː/ ■ n. trademark a range of plastic containers used chiefly for storing food.
– ORIGIN 1950s: from *Tupper*, the name of the American manufacturer, + WARE[1].

turaco /ˈtʊərəkəʊ/ (also **touraco**) ■ n. (pl. **-os**) a fruit-eating African bird with brightly coloured plumage, a prominent crest, and a long tail. [*Tauraco* and other genera: several species.]
– ORIGIN C18: from French *touraco*, from a West African word.

turban ■ n. a man's headdress, consisting of a long length of material wound round a cap or the head, worn especially by Muslims and Sikhs.
– DERIVATIVES **turbaned** (also **turbanned**) adj.
– ORIGIN C16: from Turkish *tülbent*, from Persian *dulband*.

turbid /ˈtəːbɪd/ ■ adj. **1** (of a liquid) cloudy, opaque, or thick with suspended matter. **2** turbulent; confused.
– DERIVATIVES **turbidity** n. **turbidly** adv. **turbidness** n.
– ORIGIN Middle English: from Latin *turbidus*, from *turba* 'a crowd, a disturbance'.

turbidimeter /ˌtəːbɪˈdɪmɪtə/ ■ n. an instrument for measuring the turbidity of a liquid suspension.
– DERIVATIVES **turbidimetric** adj. **turbidimetry** n.

turbidite /ˈtəːbɪdʌɪt/ ■ n. Geology a sediment or rock deposited by a turbidity current.
– DERIVATIVES **turbiditic** adj.
– ORIGIN 1950s: from *turbidity* (see TURBID).

turbidity current ■ n. an underwater current flowing swiftly down owing to the weight of sediment it carries.

turbinal /ˈtəːbɪn(ə)l/ ■ n. Anatomy & Zoology each of three thin curved shelves of bone in the sides of the nasal cavity, covered in mucous membrane.
– ORIGIN C16: from Latin *turbo, turbin-* 'spinning top'.

turbinate /ˈtəːbɪnət/ ■ adj. chiefly Zoology (especially of a shell) shaped like a spinning top. ▸ Anatomy relating to or denoting the turbinals. ■ n. Anatomy another term for TURBINAL.
– ORIGIN C17: from Latin *turbinatus*, from *turbo* 'spinning top'.

turbine /ˈtəːbʌɪn, -ɪn/ ■ n. a machine for producing continuous power in which a wheel or rotor, typically fitted with vanes, is made to revolve by a fast-moving flow of water, steam, gas, air, or other fluid.
– ORIGIN C19: from French, from Latin *turbo, turbin-* 'spinning top, whirl'.

turbo /ˈtəːbəʊ/ ■ n. (pl. *-os*) short for TURBOCHARGER.

turbo- ■ comb. form having or driven by a turbine: *turboshaft.*

turbocharge ■ v. [usu. as adj. **turbocharged**] equip with a turbocharger.

turbocharger ■ n. a supercharger driven by a turbine powered by the engine's exhaust gases.

turbofan ■ n. a jet engine in which a turbine-driven fan provides additional thrust.

turbojet ■ n. a jet engine in which the jet gases also operate a turbine-driven compressor for compressing the air drawn into the engine.

turboprop ■ n. a jet engine in which a turbine is used to drive a propeller.

turboshaft ■ n. a gas turbine engine in which the turbine drives a shaft other than a propeller shaft.

turbot ■ n. (pl. same or **turbots**) a northern flatfish of inshore waters, which has large bony tubercles on the body and is prized as food. [*Scophthalmus maximus* (Europe) and other species.]
– ORIGIN Middle English: from Old French, of Scandinavian origin.

turbulent /ˈtəːbjʊl(ə)nt/ ■ adj. 1 disorderly or confused; not calm or controlled. 2 technical relating to or denoting irregular and disordered flow of fluids.
– DERIVATIVES **turbulence** n. **turbulently** adv.
– ORIGIN Middle English: from Latin *turbulentus* 'full of commotion', from *turba* 'crowd'.

Turcoman ■ n. variant spelling of TURKOMAN.

turd ■ n. vulgar slang 1 a lump of excrement. 2 an obnoxious or contemptible person.
– ORIGIN Old English, of Germanic origin.

tureen /tjʊˈriːn, tə-/ ■ n. a deep covered dish from which soup is served.
– ORIGIN C18: from French *terrine* (see TERRINE), from Old French *terrin* 'earthen', from Latin *terra* 'earth'.

turf ■ n. (pl. **turfs** or **turves**) 1 grass and the surface layer of earth held together by its roots. ▸ a piece of such grass and earth cut from the ground. 2 (also **black turf, turf soil**) S. African a heavy, clayey, but fertile black soil. 3 (**the turf**) horse racing or racecourses generally. 4 informal an area regarded as someone's territory; a sphere of influence or activity: *he did not like poachers on his turf.* ■ v. 1 informal force to leave somewhere: *they were turfed off the bus.* 2 cover with turf.
– DERIVATIVES **turfy** adj.
– ORIGIN Old English, of Germanic origin.

turf accountant ■ n. formal a bookmaker.

turgescent /təːˈdʒɛs(ə)nt/ ■ adj. chiefly technical becoming or seeming swollen or distended.
– DERIVATIVES **turgescence** n.
– ORIGIN C18: from Latin *turgescere* 'begin to swell', from *turgere* 'to swell'.

turgid /ˈtəːdʒɪd/ ■ adj. 1 swollen and distended or congested. 2 (of language or style) tediously pompous or bombastic.

– DERIVATIVES **turgidity** n. **turgidly** adv.
– ORIGIN C17: from Latin *turgidus*, from *turgere* 'to swell'.

turgor /ˈtəːɡə/ ■ n. chiefly Botany a state of turgidity and resulting rigidity of cells or tissues.
– ORIGIN C19: from late Latin, from *turgere* 'to swell'.

Turing machine ■ n. a mathematical model of a hypothetical computing machine which can use a predefined set of rules to determine a result from a set of input variables.
– ORIGIN named after the English mathematician Alan Turing (1912–54).

Turing test ■ n. a series of questions used as a test for intelligence in a computer.

Turk ■ n. 1 a native or national of Turkey, or a person of Turkish descent. 2 historical a member of any of the ancient peoples who spoke Turkic languages, including the Seljuks and Ottomans.
– ORIGIN Middle English: from Turkish *türk*.

Turkana /təːˈkɑːnə/ ■ n. (pl. same) 1 a member of an East African people living between Lake Turkana and the Nile. 2 the Nilotic language of the Turkana.
– ORIGIN a local name.

turkey ■ n. (pl. *-eys*) 1 a large mainly domesticated game bird native to North America, having a bald head and (in the male) red wattles. [*Meleagris gallopavo.*] 2 informal, chiefly N. Amer. something that is extremely unsuccessful, especially a play or film. 3 a stupid or inept person.
– PHRASES **talk turkey** N. Amer. informal discuss frankly and openly.
– ORIGIN C16: short for TURKEYCOCK or *turkeyhen*, orig. applied to the guineafowl (which was imported through Turkey), and then erroneously to the American bird.

turkeycock ■ n. a male turkey.

turkey oak ■ n. a southern European oak with a domed spreading crown and acorn cups with long outward-pointing scales. [*Quercus cerris.*]

Turkey red ■ n. a scarlet textile dye obtained from madder or alizarin.

turkey vulture (N. Amer. also **turkey buzzard**) ■ n. a common American vulture with black plumage and a bare red head. [*Cathartes aura.*]

Turkic /ˈtəːkɪk/ ■ adj. relating to or denoting a large group of Altaic languages of western and central Asia, including Turkish, Azerbaijani, and Tatar. ■ n. the Turkic languages collectively.

Turkish ■ n. the language of Turkey, a Turkic language written with the Roman alphabet. ■ adj. of or relating to Turkey or the Turks or their language.

Turkish bath ■ n. a cleansing or relaxing treatment that involves sitting in a room filled with very hot air or steam, followed by washing and massage. ▸ a building or room where such a treatment is available.

Turkish coffee ■ n. very strong black coffee served with the fine grounds in it.

Turkish delight ■ n. a sweet consisting of flavoured gelatin coated in icing sugar.

Turkish slipper ■ n. a soft heelless slipper with a turned-up toe.

Turkish Van ■ n. a cat of a long-haired breed, with a white body, auburn markings on the head and tail, and light orange eyes.
– ORIGIN 1960s: named after the town of *Van*, Turkey.

Turkmen /ˈtəːkmən/ ■ n. (pl. same or **Turkmens**) a member of a group of Turkic peoples inhabiting the region east of the Caspian Sea and south of the Aral Sea.
– ORIGIN from Persian *turkmān*, from Turkish *türkmen*; also influenced by Russian *turkmen*.

Turkoman /ˈtəːkə(ʊ)mən/ (also **Turcoman**) ■ n. (pl. **Turkomans**) 1 another term for TURKMEN. 2 a kind of large, soft, richly coloured rug made by the Turkmens.
– ORIGIN C17: from medieval Latin *Turcomannus*, from Persian *turkmān* (see TURKMEN).

Turk's head ■ n. an ornamental knot resembling a turban in shape, made in the end of a rope to form a stopper.

turmeric

turmeric /ˈtəːmərɪk/ ■ n. **1** a bright yellow aromatic powder obtained from the rhizome of a plant, used for flavouring and colouring in Asian cookery and formerly as a fabric dye. **2** the Asian plant of the ginger family from which this is obtained. [*Curcuma longa*.]
– ORIGIN Middle English: perhaps from French *terre mérite* 'deserving earth'.

turmoil ■ n. a state of great disturbance, confusion, or uncertainty.
– ORIGIN C16.

turn ■ v. **1** move or cause to move in a circular direction wholly or partly around an axis. ▶ move or cause to move into a different position, especially so as to face the opposite direction. ▶ change or cause to change direction. ▶ (of the tide) change from flood to ebb or vice versa. ▶ twist or sprain (an ankle). **2** change or cause to change in nature, state, form, or colour; make or become. ▶ (of leaves) change colour in the autumn. ▶ (with reference to milk) make or become sour. ▶ make or become nauseated: *the smell would turn the strongest stomach.* **3** (**turn to**) start doing or becoming involved with. ▶ go to for help or information. ▶ have recourse to: *he turned to drink and drugs for solace.* **4** shape on a lathe. **5** give a graceful or elegant form to. **6** make (a profit). ■ n. **1** an act of turning. ▶ a bend or curve in a road, path, river, etc. ▶ a place where a road meets or branches off another; a turning. ▶ Cricket deviation in the direction of the ball when bouncing off the pitch. ▶ one round in a coil of rope or other material. **2** a development or change in circumstances. ▶ a time when one period of time ends and another begins. ▶ (**the turn**) the beginning of the second nine holes of a round of golf. **3** an opportunity or obligation to do something that comes successively to each of a number of people. **4** a short walk or ride. **5** informal a shock. ▶ a brief feeling or experience of illness: *he's had another of his funny turns.* **6** the difference between the buying and selling price of stocks or other financial products. ▶ a profit made from such a difference. **7** a short performance, especially one of a number given by different performers.
– PHRASES **at every turn** on every occasion; continually. **by turns** alternately. **do someone a good** (or **bad**) **turn** do something that is helpful (or unhelpful) for someone. **in turn** in succession; one after the other. **on the turn** at a turning point; in a state of change. **out of turn** at a time when it is inappropriate or not one's turn. **take turns** (or **take it in turns**) (of two or more people) do something alternately or in succession. **to a turn** exactly the right degree: *beefburgers done to a turn.* **turn and turn about** chiefly Brit. one after another; in succession. **turn of mind** a particular way of thinking. **turn of speed** the ability to go fast when necessary. **turn something over in one's mind** think about or consider something thoroughly. **turn tail** informal turn round and run away.
– PHRASAL VERBS **turn against** (or **turn someone against**) become (or cause someone to become) hostile towards. **turn someone away** refuse admittance to someone. **turn someone/thing down 1** reject an offer of something or an application from someone. **2** (**turn something down**) adjust a control on an electrical device to reduce the volume, heat, etc. **turn in** informal go to bed in the evening. **turn someone/thing in** hand someone or something over to the authorities. **turn off** leave one road in order to join another. **turn someone off** informal cause someone to feel bored or repelled. **turn something off** stop the operation of something by means of a tap, switch, or button. **turn on 1** suddenly attack: *he turned on her with cold savagery.* **2** have as the main focus. **turn someone on** informal excite or stimulate someone, especially sexually. **turn something on** start the operation of something by means of a tap, switch, or button. **turn out 1** prove to be the case. **2** go somewhere in order to attend a meeting, vote, play in a game, etc. **turn someone out 1** eject or expel someone from a place. **2** Military call a guard from the guardroom. **3** (**be turned out**) be dressed in the manner specified. **turn something out 1** extinguish an electric light. **2** produce something. **3** empty something, especially one's pockets. **turn over 1** (of an engine) start or continue to run properly. **2** (of a business) have a turnover of. **turn someone/thing over** change or transfer custody or control of someone or something. **turn something round** (or **around**) reverse the previously poor performance of something. **turn up 1** be found, especially by chance. **2** put in an appearance; arrive. **turn something up 1** increase the volume or strength of sound, heat, etc. by turning a knob or switch on a device. **2** reveal or discover something. **3** shorten a garment by raising the hem.
– DERIVATIVES **turner** n.
– ORIGIN Old English, from Latin *tornare*, from *tornus* 'lathe', from Greek; prob. reinforced in Middle English by Old French *turner*.

turnaround (also **turnround**) ■ n. **1** an abrupt or unexpected change. **2** the process of completing or the time needed to complete a task.

turnbuckle ■ n. a coupling with internal screw threads used to connect two rods, lengths of boat's rigging, etc. lengthwise or to regulate their length or tension.

turncoat ■ n. a person who deserts one party or cause in order to join an opposing one.

Turner's syndrome ■ n. Medicine a genetic defect in which affected women have only one X chromosome, causing developmental abnormalities and infertility.
– ORIGIN 1940s: named after the American physician Henry Hubert *Turner*.

turnery ■ n. the action or skill of turning objects on a lathe. ▶ objects made on a lathe.

turning ■ n. **1** a place where a road branches off another. **2** the action or skill of using a lathe. ▶ (**turnings**) shavings resulting from turning an object on a lathe.

turning circle ■ n. the smallest circle in which a vehicle or vessel can turn without reversing.

turnip ■ n. **1** a round root with white or cream flesh which is eaten as a vegetable and also has edible leaves. **2** the European plant of the cabbage family which produces this root. [*Brassica rapa*.]
– DERIVATIVES **turnipy** adj.
– ORIGIN C16: first element of unknown origin + dialect *neep* 'turnip', from Old English, from Latin *napus*.

turnkey ■ n. (pl. **-eys**) archaic a jailer. ■ adj. of or involving a complete product or service ready for immediate use.

turn-off ■ n. **1** a junction at which a road branches off. **2** informal a person or thing causing one to feel bored or repelled.

turn-on ■ n. informal a person or thing that causes one to feel excited or sexually aroused.

turnout ■ n. the number of people attending or taking part in an event.

turnover ■ n. **1** the amount of money taken by a business in a particular period. **2** the rate at which employees leave a workforce and are replaced. ▶ the rate at which goods are sold and replaced in a shop. **3** a small pie made by folding a piece of pastry over on itself to enclose a filling. **4** (in a game) a loss of possession of the ball.

turnpike ■ n. historical a toll gate. ▶ a road on which a toll was collected. ▶ US a motorway on which a toll is charged.

turnround ■ n. another term for TURNAROUND.

turnstile ■ n. a mechanical gate consisting of revolving horizontal arms fixed to a vertical post, allowing only one person at a time to pass through.

turnstone ■ n. a small short-billed sandpiper noted for turning over stones to find small animals. [Genus *Arenaria*: two species.]

turntable ■ n. **1** a circular revolving plate supporting a gramophone record as it is played. **2** a circular revolving platform for turning a railway locomotive or other vehicle.

turn-up ■ n. Brit. **1** the end of a trouser leg folded upwards on the outside. **2** informal an unusual or unexpected event.

turpentine /ˈtəːp(ə)ntʌɪn/ ■ n. **1** (also **crude** or **gum turpentine**) an oleoresin secreted by certain pines and other trees and distilled to make rosin and oil of turpentine. **2** (also **oil of turpentine**) a volatile pungent oil distilled from this, used in mixing paints and varnishes and in liniment. ■ v. apply turpentine to.
– ORIGIN Middle English: from Old French *ter(e)bentine*, from Latin *ter(e)binthina (resina)* '(resin) of the terebinth'.

turpitude /ˈtəːpɪtjuːd/ ■ n. formal depravity; wickedness.
– ORIGIN C15: from French, or from Latin *turpitudo*, from *turpis* 'disgraceful, base'.

turps ▪ n. informal turpentine.
– ORIGIN C19: abbrev.

turquoise /ˈtəːkwɔɪz, -kwɑːz/ ▪ n. **1** a semi-precious stone, typically opaque and of a greenish-blue or sky-blue colour, consisting of a hydrated phosphate of copper and aluminium. **2** a greenish-blue colour like that of this stone.
– ORIGIN Middle English: from Old French *turqueise* 'Turkish (stone)'.

turret ▪ n. **1** a small tower at the corner of a building or wall, especially of a castle. **2** an armoured tower, typically one that revolves, for a gun and gunners in a ship, aircraft, fort, or tank. **3** a rotating holder for tools, especially on a lathe.
– DERIVATIVES **turreted** adj.
– ORIGIN Middle English: from Old French *tourete*, diminutive of *tour* 'tower'.

turret shell ▪ n. a mollusc with a long, slender, pointed spiral shell, typically brightly coloured and living in tropical seas. [*Turitella* and other genera.]

turtle ▪ n. **1** a marine or freshwater reptile with a bony or leathery shell and flippers or webbed toes. [Many species in the order Chelonia.] **2** Computing a directional cursor in a computer graphics system which can be instructed to move around a screen.
– PHRASES **turn turtle** (chiefly of a boat) turn upside down.
– ORIGIN C16: prob. an alteration of French *tortue* (see TORTOISE).

turtle dove ▪ n. a small dove with a soft purring call, noted for the apparent affection shown for its mate. [Genus *Streptopelia*: several species.]
– ORIGIN Middle English: *turtle* from Old English *turtla*, from Latin *turtur*, of imitative origin.

turtleneck ▪ n. a high, round, close-fitting neck on a knitted garment.

turves plural form of TURF.

Tuscan /ˈtʌskən/ ▪ adj. of or relating to Tuscany, its inhabitants, or the dialect of Italian spoken there. ▪ n. **1** a native or inhabitant of Tuscany. **2** the dialect of Italian spoken there.
– ORIGIN Middle English: from Latin *Tuscanus*, from *Tuscus* 'an Etruscan'.

tush¹ /tʌʃ/ ▪ exclam. archaic or humorous expressing disapproval, impatience, or dismissal.
– ORIGIN Middle English.

tush² /tʌʃ/ ▪ n. a long pointed tooth.
– ORIGIN Old English *tusc* (cf. TUSK).

tush³ /tʊʃ/ ▪ n. informal, chiefly N. Amer. a person's buttocks.
– ORIGIN 1960s: from Yiddish *tokhes*, from Hebrew *taḥaṯ* 'beneath'.

tusk ▪ n. a long, pointed tooth, especially one which protrudes from the closed mouth, as in the elephant, walrus, or wild boar.
– DERIVATIVES **tusked** adj.
– ORIGIN Old English *tux*, var. of *tusc*.

tusker ▪ n. an elephant or wild boar with well-developed tusks.

tusk shell ▪ n. a burrowing mollusc with a slender tusk-shaped shell which is open at both ends. [*Dentalium* and other genera, class Scaphopoda.]

tussie-mussie /ˈtʌsɪmʌsi/ ▪ n. (pl. **-ies**) a small bunch of flowers or aromatic herbs.
– ORIGIN Middle English.

tussive /ˈtʌsɪv/ ▪ adj. Medicine relating to coughing.
– ORIGIN C19: from Latin *tussis* 'a cough'.

tussle ▪ n. a vigorous struggle or scuffle. ▪ v. engage in a tussle.
– ORIGIN Middle English: perhaps a diminutive of dialect *touse* 'handle roughly'.

tussock /ˈtʌsək/ ▪ n. a dense clump or tuft of grass.
– DERIVATIVES **tussocky** adj.
– ORIGIN C16: perhaps an alteration of dialect *tusk* 'tuft'.

tussock grass ▪ n. a coarse grass which grows in tussocks. [*Nasella* and other genera.]

tussock moth ▪ n. a woodland moth whose adults and brightly coloured caterpillars both bear tufts of irritant hairs. [Family Lymantriidae: many species.]

tussore /ˈtʌsɔː, ˈtʌsə/ ▪ n. coarse silk from the larvae of the tussore moth and related species.
– ORIGIN C16: from Hindi *tasar*, from Sanskrit *tasara* 'shuttle'.

tussore moth ▪ n. a silk moth that is sometimes kept in India and China, with caterpillars that yield a strong but coarse brown silk. [*Antheraea mylitta*.]

tut ▪ exclam. & v. short for TUT-TUT.

tutee /tjuːˈtiː/ ▪ n. a student or pupil of a tutor.

tutelage /ˈtjuːtɪlɪdʒ/ ▪ n. **1** protection of or authority over someone or something; guardianship. **2** instruction; tuition.
– DERIVATIVES **tutelary** adj.
– ORIGIN C17: from Latin *tutela* 'keeping', from *tueri* 'watch'.

tutor ▪ n. **1** a private teacher, typically one who teaches a single pupil or a very small group. ▸ a university or college teacher responsible for assigned students. ▸ US an assistant lecturer in a college or university. **2** Brit. a book of instruction in a particular subject. ▪ v. act as a tutor to. ▸ work as a tutor.
– DERIVATIVES **tutorage** n. **tutorship** n.
– ORIGIN Middle English: from Old French *tutour* or Latin *tutor*, from *tueri* 'to watch, guard'.

tutorial ▪ n. a period of tuition given by a university or college tutor. ▸ an account or explanation of a subject, intended for private study. ▪ adj. of or relating to a tutor or a tutor's tuition.

Tutsi /ˈtʊtsi/ ▪ n. (pl. same or **Tutsis**) a member of a people forming a minority of the population of Rwanda and Burundi.
– ORIGIN a local name (cf. WATUSI).

tutti-frutti /ˌtʊtiˈfruːti/ ▪ n. (pl. **tutti-fruttis**) a type of ice cream or confectionery containing mixed fruits.
– ORIGIN Italian, 'all fruits'.

tut-tut (also **tut**) ▪ exclam. expressing disapproval or annoyance. ▪ v. (**tut-tutted**, **tut-tutting**) make such an exclamation.
– ORIGIN C16: natural utterance.

tutu /ˈtuːtuː/ ▪ n. a female ballet dancer's costume consisting of a bodice and an attached skirt incorporating numerous layers of fabric, this being either short and stiff and projecting horizontally from the waist (the classical tutu) or long, soft, and bell-shaped (the romantic tutu).
– ORIGIN C20: from French, child's alteration of *cucu*, informal diminutive of *cul* 'buttocks'.

Tuvaluan /ˌtuːvəˈluːən, tuːˈvɑːluən/ ▪ n. **1** a native or inhabitant of Tuvalu, a country made up of a number of islands in the SW Pacific. **2** the Austronesian language of Tuvalu. ▪ adj. of or relating to Tuvalu or its language.

tu-whit tu-whoo ▪ n. a stylized representation of the cry of the tawny owl.
– ORIGIN C16: imitative.

tux ▪ n. informal, chiefly N. Amer. a tuxedo.

tuxedo /tʌkˈsiːdəʊ/ ▪ n. (pl. **-os** or **-oes**) chiefly N. Amer. a man's dinner jacket. ▸ a formal evening suit including such a jacket.
– DERIVATIVES **tuxedoed** adj.
– ORIGIN C19: from *Tuxedo* Park, the site of a country club in New York.

tuyère /twiːˈjɛː, tuː-/ ▪ n. a nozzle through which air is forced into a smelter, furnace, or forge.
– ORIGIN C18: French, from *tuyau* 'pipe'.

TV ▪ abbrev. television.

TV dinner ▪ n. a prepared pre-packed meal that only requires heating before it is ready to eat.

TVP ▪ abbrev. trademark textured vegetable protein.

Twa /twɑː/ ▪ n. (pl. same or **Twas**) a member of a pygmy people inhabiting parts of Burundi, Rwanda, and the Democratic Republic of Congo.
– ORIGIN a local word meaning 'foreigner, outsider'.

twaddle ▪ n. informal trivial or foolish speech or writing.
– ORIGIN C18: alteration of earlier *twattle*.

twain ▪ cardinal number archaic term for TWO: *he split it in twain* | *never the twain shall meet*.
– ORIGIN Old English *twegen*, masculine of *twā* (see TWO).

twang

twang ▪ n. **1** a strong ringing sound such as that made by the plucked string of a musical instrument or a released bowstring. **2** a distinctive nasal pronunciation characteristic of the speech of an individual or region. ▪ v. **1** make or cause to make a twang. **2** utter with a twang.
– DERIVATIVES **twangy** adj.
– ORIGIN C16: imitative.

'twas ▪ contr. archaic or poetic/literary it was.

twat /twɒt, twæt/ ▪ n. vulgar slang **1** a woman's genitals. **2** a person regarded as stupid or obnoxious.
– ORIGIN C17.

tweak ▪ v. **1** twist or pull with a small but sharp movement. **2** informal improve by making fine adjustments. ▪ n. **1** an act of tweaking. **2** informal a fine adjustment.
– ORIGIN C17: prob. an alteration of dialect *twick* 'pull sharply'.

twee ▪ adj. (**tweer, tweest**) chiefly Brit. excessively or affectedly quaint, pretty, or sentimental.
– DERIVATIVES **tweely** adv.
– ORIGIN C20: representing a child's pronunciation of SWEET.

tweed ▪ n. a rough-surfaced woollen cloth, typically of mixed flecked colours, originally produced in Scotland. ▸ (**tweeds**) clothes made of tweed.
– ORIGIN C19: orig. a misreading of *tweel*, Scots form of TWILL, influenced by association with the river Tweed.

tweedy ▪ adj. (**-ier, -iest**) **1** made of tweed cloth. **2** informal of a robust conservative or rural character.
– DERIVATIVES **tweedily** adv. **tweediness** n.

'tween ▪ contr. archaic or poetic/literary between.

tweet (also **tweet tweet**) ▪ n. the chirp of a small or young bird. ▪ v. **1** make a chirping noise. **2** publish a message using the social networking service Twitter.
– ORIGIN C19: imitative.

tweeter ▪ n. a loudspeaker designed to reproduce high frequencies.

tweeze ▪ v. pluck or pull with or as if with tweezers.
– ORIGIN 1930s: back-formation from TWEEZERS.

tweezers ▪ pl. n. (also **a pair of tweezers**) a small instrument in the form of a pair of pincers for plucking out hairs and picking up small objects.
– ORIGIN C17: extended form of obsolete *tweeze* 'case of surgical instruments', shortening of *etweese*, from Old French, from *estuis* 'prison'.

twelfth /twelfθ/ ▪ ordinal number **1** constituting number twelve in a sequence; 12th. **2** (**a twelfth/one twelfth**) each of twelve equal parts into which something is or may be divided. **3** (**the** (**Glorious**) **Twelfth**) (in the UK) 12 August, the day on which the grouse-shooting season begins.
– DERIVATIVES **twelfthly** adv. **twelvefold** adj. & adv.

twelfth man ▪ n. Cricket a player acting as a reserve in a game.

Twelfth Night ▪ n. 6 January, the feast of the Epiphany. ▸ strictly, the evening of 5 January, formerly the twelfth and last day of Christmas festivities.

twelve ▪ cardinal number equivalent to the product of three and four; two more than ten; 12. (Roman numeral: **xii** or **XII**.)
– ORIGIN Old English *twelf(e)*, *from the base of* TWO + a second element (prob. expressing the sense 'left over'); of Germanic origin.

twelvemonth ▪ n. archaic a year.

twelve-note (also **twelve-tone**) ▪ adj. denoting a system of musical composition using the twelve chromatic notes of the octave on an equal basis without dependence on a key system, a technique central to serialism.

twelve-step ▪ adj. denoting or relating to a process of recovery from an addiction by following a twelve-stage programme, especially one devised or similar to that devised by Alcoholics Anonymous. ▪ v. [often as noun **twelve-stepping**] (of an addict) undergo such a programme.
– DERIVATIVES **twelve-stepper** n.

twenty ▪ cardinal number (pl. **-ies**) the number equivalent to the product of two and ten; ten less than thirty; 20.

(Roman numeral: **xx** or **XX**.)
– DERIVATIVES **twentieth** ordinal number . **twentyfold** adj. & adv.
– ORIGIN Old English *twentig*, from the base of TWO.

twenty-four-hour clock ▪ n. a method of measuring the time in hours from one to twenty-four, rather than from one to twelve.

24-7 (also **24/7**) ▪ adv. informal, chiefly N. Amer. twenty-four hours a day, seven days a week; all the time.

twenty-one ▪ n. the card game blackjack or pontoon.

twenty-twenty (also **20/20**) ▪ adj. denoting vision of normal acuity.
– ORIGIN with ref. to the fraction for normal visual acuity in eyesight tests.

'twere ▪ contr. archaic or poetic/literary it were.

twerp ▪ n. informal a silly or annoying person.
– ORIGIN C19.

Twi /twiː, tʃwiː/ ▪ n. (pl. same or **Twis**) **1** a member of an Akan-speaking people of Ghana. **2** another term for AKAN (the language).
– ORIGIN the name in Akan.

twice ▪ adv. **1** two times. **2** double in degree or quantity.
– ORIGIN Old English *twiges*, from the base of TWO.

twiddle ▪ v. play or fiddle with, typically in a purposeless or nervous way. ▸ archaic turn or move in a twirling way. ▪ n. **1** an act of twiddling. **2** a rapid or intricate series of musical notes.
– PHRASES **twiddle one's thumbs** be idle; have nothing to do.
– DERIVATIVES **twiddler** n. **twiddly** adj.
– ORIGIN C16: apparently imitative, combining *twirl* or *twist* with *fiddle*.

twig[1] ▪ n. a slender woody shoot growing from a branch or stem of a tree or shrub. ▸ Anatomy a small branch of a blood vessel or nerve.
– DERIVATIVES **twigged** adj. **twiggy** adj.
– ORIGIN Old English, of Germanic origin.

twig[2] ▪ v. (**twigged, twigging**) informal come to understand or realize something.
– ORIGIN C18.

twig snake ▪ n. a thin brown tree-dwelling venomous snake of southern and eastern Africa. [*Thelotornis capensis* and *T. kirtlandii*.]

twilight /ˈtwaɪlaɪt/ ▪ n. **1** the soft glowing light from the sky when the sun is below the horizon, caused by the reflection of the sun's rays from the atmosphere. **2** a period or state of obscurity or gradual decline.
– ORIGIN Middle English: from Old English *twi-* 'two' (prob. here used in sense 'half-') + LIGHT[1].

twilight sleep ▪ n. Medicine a state of partial narcosis or stupor without total loss of consciousness.

twilight zone ▪ n. **1** an area or state characterized by being indistinct, ambiguous, or intermediate, especially one showing decline. **2** the lowest level of the ocean to which light can penetrate.

twilit (also **twilighted**) ▪ adj. dimly illuminated by or as if by twilight.

twill ▪ n. a fabric so woven as to have a surface of diagonal parallel ridges.
– DERIVATIVES **twilled** adj.
– ORIGIN Middle English: from a var. of obsolete *twilly*, from Old English *twi-* 'two'.

'twill ▪ contr. archaic or poetic/literary it will.

twin ▪ n. **1** one of two children or animals born at the same birth. **2** something containing or consisting of two matching or corresponding parts. ▪ adj. **1** forming or being one of a twin. **2** forming a matching or closely connected pair. **3** (of a crystal) twinned. ▪ v. (**twinned, twinning**) **1** link; combine. ▸ link (a town or district) with another in a different country, for the purposes of cultural exchange. **2** [as adj. **twinned**] (of a crystal) that is a composite consisting of two (or more) parts which are reversed in orientation with respect to each other.
– DERIVATIVES **twinned** adj. **twinning** n.
– ORIGIN Old English *twinn* 'double', from *twi-* 'two'; rel. to Old Norse *tvinnr*.

twin bed ■ n. one of a pair of matching single beds in a room.
– DERIVATIVES **twin-bedded** adj.

twine ■ n. strong thread or string consisting of strands of hemp or cotton twisted together. ■ v. wind or cause to wind round something.
– ORIGIN Old English *twīn* 'thread, linen', from the Germanic base of *twi-* 'two' (with ref. to the number of strands).

twinge ■ n. **1** a sudden, sharp localized pain. **2** a brief, sharp pang of emotion. ■ v. (**twingeing** or **twinging**) (of a part of the body) suffer a twinge.
– ORIGIN Old English *twengan* 'pinch, wring', of Germanic origin.

twinkie ■ n. (pl. **-ies**) US trademark a small finger-shaped sponge cake with a white synthetic cream filling.
– ORIGIN C20: prob. rel. to TWINKLE.

twinkle ■ v. **1** (of a star or light) shine with a gleam that changes constantly from bright to faint. ▶ (of a person's eyes) sparkle, especially with amusement. **2** move lightly and rapidly. ■ n. a twinkling sparkle or gleam.
– PHRASES **in a twinkling (of an eye)** in an instant.
– DERIVATIVES **twinkler** n. **twinkly** adj.
– ORIGIN Old English, of Germanic origin.

twinkle-toed ■ adj. informal nimble and quick on one's feet.
– DERIVATIVES **twinkletoes** n.

twin-lens reflex ■ n. [as modifier] denoting a camera having two identical sets of lenses, either for taking stereoscopic pictures, or with one forming an image for viewing and the other an image to be photographed.

twin-screw ■ adj. (of a ship) having two propellers on separate shafts with opposite twists.

twinset ■ n. chiefly Brit. a woman's matching cardigan and jumper.

twin-tub ■ n. a type of washing machine having two top-loading drums, one for washing and the other for spin-drying.

twirl ■ v. spin quickly and lightly round. ■ n. an act of twirling. ▶ a spiralling or swirling shape.
– DERIVATIVES **twirler** n. **twirly** adj.
– ORIGIN C16: prob. an alteration (by association with WHIRL) of *tirl*, a var. of archaic *trill* 'twiddle, spin'.

twist ■ v. **1** form into a bent, curled, or distorted shape. ▶ turn or bend round or into a different direction. ▶ force or be forced out of the natural position by a twisting action: *he twisted his ankle playing tennis*. **2** rotate or cause to rotate around something that remains stationary; turn. ▶ move or cause to move around each other; interlace. ▶ take or have a winding course. **3** distort or misrepresent the meaning of. ▶ [as adj. **twisted**] (of a personality or behaviour) unpleasantly or unhealthily abnormal. **4** dance the twist. ■ n. **1** an act or instance of twisting. **2** a thing with a spiral shape. ▶ Brit. a paper packet with twisted ends. **3** force producing twisting; torque. ▶ forward motion combined with rotation about an axis. ▶ the rifling in the bore of a gun. **4** an unexpected, normally unwelcome, development of events. ▶ a new treatment or outlook: *she takes conventional subjects and gives them a twist*. **5** a fine strong thread consisting of twisted fibres. **6** a carpet with a tightly curled pile. **7** (**the twist**) a dance with a twisting movement of the body, popular in the 1960s.
– PHRASES **round the twist** informal crazy. **twist someone's arm** informal forcefully persuade someone to do something that they are reluctant to do. **twist in the wind** be left in a state of suspense or uncertainty.
– DERIVATIVES **twisty** adj.
– ORIGIN Old English, of Germanic origin; prob. from the base of TWIN.

twister ■ n. **1** Brit. informal a swindler; a dishonest person. **2** N. Amer. a tornado.

twit¹ ■ n. informal a silly or foolish person.
– DERIVATIVES **twittish** adj.
– ORIGIN 1930s (orig. dialect, in the sense 'tale-bearer'): perhaps from TWIT².

twit² ■ v. (**twitted**, **twitting**) informal tease, especially good-humouredly.
– ORIGIN Old English *ætwītan* 'reproach with', from *æt* 'at' + *witan* 'to blame'.

twitch ■ v. make or cause to make a short, sudden jerking movement. ■ n. **1** a twitching movement. **2** a pang: *he felt a twitch of annoyance*. **3** a small noose attached to a stick, which may be twisted around the upper lip or ear of a horse to subdue it during veterinary procedures.
– ORIGIN Middle English: of Germanic origin; rel. to Old English *twiccian* 'pull sharply'.

twitcher ■ n. informal a birdwatcher devoted to spotting rare birds.

twitchy ■ adj. (**-ier**, **-iest**) **1** informal nervous. **2** given to twitching.

twitter ■ v. **1** (of a bird) make a series of light tremulous sounds. **2** talk rapidly in a nervous or trivial way. ■ n. **1** a twittering sound. **2** trivial talk. **3** (**Twitter**) trademark a social networking service allowing users to view and publish short textual messages on the Internet.
– PHRASES **in** (or **of**) **a twitter** informal in a state of agitation or excitement.
– DERIVATIVES **twitterer** n. **twittery** adj.
– ORIGIN Middle English: imitative.

'twixt ■ contr. betwixt.

twizzle informal or dialect ■ v. spin or cause to spin around. ■ n. a twisting or spinning movement.
– ORIGIN C18: prob. imitative, influenced by TWIST.

two ■ cardinal number equivalent to the product of one and one; one less than three; 2. (Roman numeral: **ii** or **II**.)
– PHRASES **put two and two together** draw an obvious conclusion from what is known or evident. **that makes two of us** informal that is true of me also. **two by two** (or **two and two**) side by side in pairs. **two can play at that game** informal used to assert that one is equally capable of copying another's strategy, to their disadvantage. **two's company, three's a crowd** two people, especially lovers, should be left alone together.
– DERIVATIVES **twofold** adj. & adv.
– ORIGIN Old English *twā*, of Germanic origin.

two-bit ■ adj. N. Amer. informal insignificant, cheap, or worthless.

two-by-four ■ n. a length of wood with a rectangular cross section nominally two inches by four inches.

two-cycle ■ adj. another term for TWO-STROKE.

two-dimensional ■ adj. **1** having or appearing to have length and breadth but no depth. **2** lacking depth; superficial.
– DERIVATIVES **two-dimensionality** n. **two-dimensionally** adv.

two-faced ■ adj. insincere and deceitful.

two-fisted ■ adj. informal, chiefly N. Amer. tough, aggressive, or vigorous.

two-hander ■ n. a play for two actors.

two-horse ■ adj. (of a race or other contest) in which only two of the competitors or participants are likely winners.

twoness ■ n. the fact or state of being two; duality.

twopence /ˈtʌp(ə)ns/ (also **tuppence**) ■ n. Brit. **1** the sum of two pence, especially before decimalization (1971). **2** [with neg.] informal anything at all: *he didn't care twopence*.

twopenn'orth /tuːˈpɛnəθ/ ■ n. **1** an amount that is worth or costs twopence. **2** a paltry or insignificant amount.
– PHRASES **add** (or **put in**) **one's twopenn'orth** informal contribute one's opinion.

twopenny /ˈtʌp(ə)ni/ (also **tuppeny**) ■ adj. Brit. costing two pence, especially before decimalization (1971).

twopenny-halfpenny ■ adj. Brit. informal insignificant or worthless.

two-phase ■ adj. relating to or denoting an electricity supply using two separate alternating components with phases differing by half a period.

two-piece ■ adj. consisting of two matching items. ■ n. a two-piece suit.

two-step ■ n. a round dance with a sliding step in march or polka time.

two-stroke ■ adj. denoting an internal-combustion engine having its power cycle completed in one up-and-down movement of the piston.

two-time ■ v. informal be unfaithful to (a lover or spouse).
– DERIVATIVES **two-timer** n.

'twould ■ contr. archaic it would.

two-up two-down ■ n. Brit. informal a house with two reception rooms downstairs and two bedrooms upstairs.

two-way ■ adj. **1** involving movement or communication in opposite directions. **2** (of a switch) permitting a current to be switched on or off from either of two points.
– PHRASES **two-way street** a situation involving mutual or reciprocal action or obligation.

two-way mirror ■ n. a panel of glass that can be seen through from one side and is a mirror on the other.

two-wheeler ■ n. a bicycle or motorcycle.

-ty¹ ■ suffix forming nouns denoting quality or condition such as *beauty*.
– ORIGIN from Latin *-tas*, *-tat-*.

-ty² ■ suffix denoting specified groups of ten: *forty*.
– ORIGIN Old English *-tig*.

tycoon /tʌɪˈkuːn/ ■ n. a wealthy, powerful person in business or industry.
– ORIGIN C19: from Japanese *taikun* 'great lord'.

tying present participle of TIE.

tyke (also **tike**) ■ n. **1** informal a small child, especially a mischievous one. **2** a dog, especially a mongrel.
– ORIGIN Middle English: from Old Norse *tík* 'bitch'.

Tylenol /ˈθʌɪlənɒl/ ■ n. chiefly N. Amer. trademark for PARACETAMOL.

tympana plural form of TYMPANUM.

tympani ■ pl. n. variant spelling of TIMPANI.

tympanic /tɪmˈpanɪk/ ■ adj. **1** Anatomy of, relating to, or having a tympanum. **2** resembling or acting like a drumhead.

tympanum /ˈtɪmpənəm/ ■ n. (pl. **tympanums** or **tympana** /-nə/) **1** Anatomy & Zoology the membrane forming part of the organ of hearing, which vibrates in response to sound waves; the eardrum. **2** Architecture a vertical recessed triangular space forming the centre of a pediment, typically decorated. ▸ a similar space over a door between the lintel and the arch.
– ORIGIN C17: from Greek *tumpanon* 'drum'.

type ■ n. **1** a category of people or things having common characteristics. ▸ a person or thing considered as a representative of such a category. ▸ informal a person of a specified character or nature: *two sporty types in tracksuits*. ▸ Linguistics an abstract category or class of linguistic item or unit. Contrasted with TOKEN. **2** a person or thing symbolizing or exemplifying the defining characteristics of something. **3** printed characters or letters. ▸ a piece of metal with a raised letter or character on its upper surface, for use in letterpress printing. ▸ such pieces collectively. **4** Theology a foreshadowing in the Old Testament of a person or event of the Christian dispensation. ■ v. **1** write using a typewriter or computer. **2** Medicine determine the type to which (a person or their blood or tissue) belongs.
– DERIVATIVES **typing** n.
– ORIGIN C15: from French, or from Latin *typus*, from Greek *tupos* 'impression, figure, type'.

-type ■ suffix (forming adjectives) that is a certain type: *a champagne-type fizzy wine*.

Type A ■ n. a personality type characterized by ambition, impatience, and competitiveness, and thought to be susceptible to stress and heart disease.

type approval ■ n. official confirmation from a government or other body that a manufactured item meets required specifications.

Type B ■ n. a personality type characterized as easy-going and thought to have low susceptibility to stress.

typecast ■ v. (past and past part. **-cast**) (usu. **be typecast**) **1** cast (an actor or actress) repeatedly in the same type of role, as a result of the appropriateness of their appearance or previous success in such roles. **2** regard as fitting a stereotype.

typeface ■ n. Printing a particular design of type.

type founder ■ n. Printing a designer and maker of metal type.
– DERIVATIVES **type foundry** n.

type metal ■ n. Printing an alloy of lead, tin, and antimony, used for casting type.

typescript ■ n. a typed copy of a text.

typeset ■ v. (**-setting**; past and past part. **-set**) arrange or generate the type for (text to be printed).
– DERIVATIVES **typesetter** n. **typesetting** n.

type site ■ n. Archaeology a site where objects or materials regarded as typical of a particular period are found.

type specimen ■ n. Botany & Zoology the specimen, or each of a set of specimens, on which the description and name of a new species is based. See also HOLOTYPE, SYNTYPE.

typewriter ■ n. an electric, electronic, or manual machine with keys for producing print-like characters.
– DERIVATIVES **typewriting** n. **typewritten** adj.

typhoid (also **typhoid fever**) ■ n. an infectious bacterial fever with an eruption of red spots on the chest and abdomen and severe intestinal irritation.
– DERIVATIVES **typhoidal** adj.
– ORIGIN C19: from TYPHUS.

Typhoid Mary ■ n. (pl. **Typhoid Marys**) informal a transmitter of undesirable opinions or attitudes.
– ORIGIN the nickname of *Mary* Mallon (died 1938), an Irish-born cook who transmitted typhoid in the US.

typhoon /tʌɪˈfuːn/ ■ n. a tropical storm in the region of the Indian or western Pacific oceans.
– DERIVATIVES **typhonic** adj.
– ORIGIN C16: from Arabic *ṭūfān*; reinforced by Chinese dialect *tai fung* 'big wind'.

typhus /ˈtʌɪfəs/ ■ n. an infectious disease caused by rickettsiae, characterized by a purple rash, headaches, fever, and usually delirium.
– DERIVATIVES **typhous** adj.
– ORIGIN C17: from Greek *tuphos* 'smoke, stupor'.

typical ■ adj. **1** having the distinctive qualities of a particular type. ▸ characteristic of a particular person or thing. **2** symbolic: *the pit is typical of hell*.
– DERIVATIVES **typicality** /-ˈkalɪti/ n. **typically** adv.
– ORIGIN C17: from medieval Latin *typicalis*, from Greek *tupikos*, from *tupos* (see TYPE).

typify ■ v. (**-ies**, **-ied**) be typical of.
– DERIVATIVES **typification** n.

typist ■ n. a person skilled in typing, especially one who is employed for this purpose.

typo /ˈtʌɪpəʊ/ ■ n. (pl. **-os**) informal a typographical error.

typography /tʌɪˈpɒɡrəfi/ ■ n. **1** the art or process of setting and arranging types and printing from them. **2** the style and appearance of printed matter.
– DERIVATIVES **typographer** n. **typographic** adj. **typographical** adj. **typographically** adv.
– ORIGIN C17: from French *typographie* or modern Latin *typographia* (see TYPE, -GRAPHY).

typology ■ n. (pl. **-ies**) **1** a classification according to general type, especially in archaeology, psychology, or the social sciences. **2** the study and interpretation of types and symbols, originally especially in the Bible.
– DERIVATIVES **typological** /-əˈlɒdʒɪk(ə)l/ adj. **typologist** n.
– ORIGIN C19: from Greek *tupos* 'type' + -LOGY.

tyramine /ˈtʌɪrəmiːn/ ■ n. Biochemistry a compound in cheese and other foods which in some circumstances can cause high blood pressure.
– ORIGIN C20: from *tyr(osine)* + AMINE.

tyrannicide /tɪˈranɪsʌɪd, tʌɪ-/ ■ n. the killing of a tyrant. ▸ the killer of a tyrant.
– DERIVATIVES **tyrannicidal** adj.
– ORIGIN C17: from Latin *tyrannicida* 'killer of a tyrant'.

tyrannosaur /tɪˈranəsɔː, tʌɪ-/ (also **tyrannosaurus** /tɪˌranəˈsɔːrəs/) ■ n. a very large carnivorous dinosaur of the late Cretaceous period, with powerful jaws and small claw-like front legs.
– ORIGIN from Greek *turannos* 'tyrant' + *sauros* 'lizard'.

tyranny ■ n. (pl. **-ies**) **1** cruel and oppressive government or rule. ▸ a state under such rule. **2** cruel and arbitrary exercise of power or control.

– DERIVATIVES **tyrannical** adj. **tyrannically** adv. **tyrannize** (also **-ise**) v. **tyrannous** adj. **tyrannously** adv.
– ORIGIN Middle English: from Old French *tyrannie*, from Latin *turannus* (see **TYRANT**).

tyrant /ˈtʌɪr(ə)nt/ ■ n. **1** a cruel and oppressive ruler. **2** a person exercising power or control in a cruel and arbitrary way.
– ORIGIN Middle English: from Old French, via Latin from Greek *turannos*.

tyre (US **tire**) ■ n. **1** a rubber covering, typically inflated or surrounding an inflated inner tube, placed round a wheel to form a soft contact with the road. **2** a strengthening band of metal fitted around the rim of a wheel, especially of a railway vehicle.
– ORIGIN C15: perhaps a var. of archaic *tire*, shortening of **ATTIRE** (because the tyre was the 'clothing' of the wheel).

tyre gauge ■ n. a portable pressure gauge for measuring the air pressure in a tyre.

Tyrian /ˈtɪrɪən/ ■ n. a native or inhabitant of Tyre, an ancient Phoenician city and port on the Mediterranean (now a port in southern Lebanon). ■ adj. of or relating to Tyre.

Tyrian purple ■ n. see **PURPLE**.

tyro /ˈtʌɪrəʊ/ (also **tiro**) ■ n. (pl. **-os**) a beginner or novice.
– ORIGIN Middle English: from Latin *tiro*, medieval Latin *tyro* 'recruit'.

Tyrolean /ˌtɪrəˈliːən/ (also **Tyrolese** /ˌtɪrəˈliːz/) ■ n. a native or inhabitant of the Tyrol, an Alpine region of western Austria and northern Italy. ■ adj. of or relating to the Tyrol.

tyrosine /ˈtʌɪrəsiːn/ ■ n. Biochemistry an amino acid found in most proteins and important in the synthesis of some hormones.
– ORIGIN C19: from Greek *turos* 'cheese'.

tzar ■ n. variant spelling of **TSAR**.

tzarevich ■ n. variant spelling of **TSAREVICH**.

tzarina ■ n. variant spelling of **TSARINA**.

tzatziki /tsatˈsiːki/ ■ n. a Greek side dish of yogurt with cucumber, garlic, and often mint.
– ORIGIN from modern Greek.

tzedakah /tsɛˈdɒka/ ■ n. (among Jewish people) charitable giving, regarded as a moral obligation.
– ORIGIN from Hebrew *ṣĕḏāqāh* 'righteousness'.

tzigane /tsɪˈɡɑːn/ ■ n. (pl. same or **tziganes**) a Hungarian gypsy.
– ORIGIN C18: from Hungarian *c(z)igány*.

T-zone ■ n. the central part of a person's face, including the forehead, nose, and chin.
– ORIGIN *T* designating the shape of the area defined.

Uu

U[1] /juː/ (also **u**) ■ n. (pl. **Us** or **U's**) **1** the twenty-first letter of the alphabet. **2** denoting the next after T in a set of items, categories, etc.

U[2] /juː/ ■ symb. the chemical element uranium.

U[3] /juː/ ■ adj. informal, chiefly Brit. (of language or social behaviour) characteristic of or appropriate to the upper social classes.
– ORIGIN abbrev. of **UPPER CLASS**; coined in 1954 by Alan S. C. Ross, professor of linguistics, and popularized by Nancy Mitford's *Noblesse Oblige* (1956).

u ■ symb. [in combination] micro- (10⁻⁶). [substituted for MU.]

UAE ■ abbrev. United Arab Emirates.

UB40 ■ n. (in the UK) a card issued to a person registered as unemployed.

ubac /ˈjuːbak/ ■ n. Geography a mountain slope which receives little sunshine. Compare with **ADRET**.
– ORIGIN 1930s: from French, apparently from Latin *opacus* 'shady'.

U-bend ■ n. a section of a pipe, in particular of a waste pipe, shaped like a U.

uber- /ˈuːbə/ (also **über-**) ■ prefix denoting an outstanding or supreme example of a particular kind of person or thing: *an uberbabe.*
– ORIGIN German *über* 'over', on the pattern of *Übermensch*.

Übermensch /ˈuːbəˌmɛnʃ/ ■ n. the ideal superior man of the future who could rise above conventional Christian morality to create and impose his own values, originally described by Nietzsche in *Thus Spake Zarathustra* (1883–5).
– ORIGIN German, 'superhuman person'.

-ubility ■ suffix forming nouns from or corresponding to adjectives ending in *-uble* (such as *solubility* from *soluble*).

ubiquitin /juːˈbɪkwɪtɪn/ ■ n. Biochemistry a polypeptide found in living cells, involved in degrading defective and superfluous proteins.
– ORIGIN 1970s: from **UBIQUITOUS**.

ubiquitous /juːˈbɪkwɪtəs/ ■ adj. present, appearing, or found everywhere.
– DERIVATIVES **ubiquitously** adv. **ubiquitousness** n. **ubiquity** n.
– ORIGIN C19: from modern Latin *ubiquitas*, from Latin *ubique* 'everywhere'.

-uble ■ suffix (forming adjectives) able to: *voluble*. ► able to be: *soluble*.
– DERIVATIVES **-ubly** suffix forming corresponding adverbs.
– ORIGIN from Latin *-ubilis*.

U-boat ■ n. a German submarine of the First or Second World War.
– ORIGIN from German *U-boot*, abbrev. of *Unterseeboot* 'undersea boat'.

ubuntu /ʊˈbuntuː/ ■ n. S. African a spirit of fellowship, humanity, and compassion, especially as associated with African society.
– ORIGIN isiXhosa and isiZulu; 'humanity, goodness'.

u.c. ■ abbrev. upper case.

UCAS /ˈjuːkas/ ■ abbrev. (in the UK) Universities and Colleges Admissions Service.

UCT ■ abbrev. University of Cape Town.

UDA ■ abbrev. Ulster Defence Association (a Loyalist paramilitary organization).

udder ■ n. the mammary gland of female cattle, sheep, goats, horses, and related ungulates, hanging near the hind legs as a bag-like organ with two or more teats.
– DERIVATIVES **-uddered** adj.
– ORIGIN Old English *ūder*, of West Germanic origin.

UDF ■ abbrev. historical (in South Africa) United Democratic Front.

UDI ■ abbrev. unilateral declaration of independence.

UDM ■ abbrev. (in South Africa) United Democratic Movement.

udon /ˈuːdɒn/ ■ n. (in Japanese cookery) large noodles made from wheat flour.
– ORIGIN from Japanese.

UEFA /juːˈiːfə, -ˈeɪfə/ ■ abbrev. Union of European Football Associations.

UFO ■ n. (pl. **UFOs**) a mysterious object seen in the sky for which it is claimed no orthodox scientific explanation can be found, popularly said to be vehicles carrying extraterrestrials.
– DERIVATIVES **ufological** adj. **ufologist** n. **ufology** n.
– ORIGIN 1950s: acronym from *unidentified flying object*.

Ugandan /juːˈɡandən/ ■ n. a native or inhabitant of Uganda. ■ adj. of or relating to Uganda.

Ugaritic /juːɡəˈrɪtɪk/ ■ n. a pre-Phoenician Semitic language written in a distinctive cuneiform alphabet. ■ adj. of or relating to this language.

ugh ■ exclam. informal used to express disgust or horror.

Ugli fruit /ˈʌɡli/ ■ n. (pl. same) trademark a mottled green and yellow citrus fruit which is a hybrid of a grapefruit and tangerine.
– ORIGIN 1930s: *ugli*, alteration of **UGLY**.

ugly ■ adj. (**-ier**, **-iest**) **1** unpleasant or repulsive in appearance. **2** hostile or threatening; likely to involve unpleasantness. **3** S. African informal unkind; mean.
– DERIVATIVES **uglification** n. **uglify** v. **uglily** adv. **ugliness** n.
– ORIGIN Middle English: from Old Norse *uggligr* 'to be dreaded', from *ugga* 'to dread'.

ugly American ■ n. informal, chiefly US an American who behaves offensively when abroad.

ugly duckling ■ n. a person who turns out to be beautiful or talented against all expectations.
– ORIGIN from the title of one of Hans Christian Andersen's fairy tales, in which the 'ugly duckling' becomes a swan.

uh ■ exclam. used to represent a sound made to express hesitation or enquiry.

uhadi /ˈuːhɑːdi/ ■ n. a traditional Xhosa musical instrument consisting of a single-stringed bow with a resonating gourd.
– ORIGIN isiXhosa.

UHF ■ abbrev. ultra-high frequency.

uh-huh ■ exclam. used to express assent or as a non-committal response.
– ORIGIN 1920s: imitative.

uh-oh ■ exclam. used to express alarm or dismay.

UHT ■ abbrev. ultra heat treated (a process typically used to extend the shelf life of milk).

uh-uh ■ exclam. used to express a negative response.

UIF ■ abbrev. Unemployment Insurance Fund.

uillean pipes /ˈɪlɪn, ˈɪlən/ ■ pl. n. Irish bagpipes played using bellows worked by the elbow, and having three extra pipes on which chords can be played.
– ORIGIN C20: from Irish *píob uilleann* 'pipe of the elbow'.

uitlander /ˈeɪtlandə/ ■ n. S. African a foreigner or outsider.
– ORIGIN Afrikaans, 'outlander'.

ujamaa /ˌʊdʒaˈmɑː/ ■ n. (in Tanzania) a socialist system of self-help village cooperatives, established in the 1960s.
– ORIGIN Kiswahili, 'brotherhood'.

UK ■ abbrev. United Kingdom.

ukase /juːˈkeɪz/ ■ n. **1** (in tsarist Russia) a decree with the force of law. **2** an arbitrary or peremptory command.
– ORIGIN from Russian *ukaz* 'edict', from *ukazat* 'show, decree'.

Ukrainian ■ n. **1** a native or national of Ukraine, or a person of Ukrainian descent. **2** the Eastern Slavic language of Ukraine. ■ adj. of or relating to Ukraine, its people, or their language.

ukulele /ˌjuːkəˈleɪli/ ■ n. a small four-stringed guitar of Hawaiian origin.
– ORIGIN C19: from Hawaiian, 'jumping flea'.

ulama ■ n. variant spelling of ULEMA.

ulcer ■ n. an open sore on an external or internal surface of the body, caused by a break in the skin or mucous membrane which fails to heal.
– DERIVATIVES **ulcered** adj. **ulcerous** adj.
– ORIGIN Middle English: from Latin *ulcus, ulcer-*.

ulcerate ■ v. develop into or become affected by an ulcer.
– DERIVATIVES **ulceration** n. **ulcerative** adj.

-ule ■ suffix forming diminutive nouns such as *capsule*.
– ORIGIN from Latin *-ulus, -ula, -ulum*.

ulema /ˈuːləmə, ˈuːlɪmə, ˌuːləˈmɑː/ (also **ulama**) ■ n. **1** [treated as sing. or pl.] a body of Muslim scholars recognized as expert in Islamic sacred law and theology. **2** a member of such a body.
– ORIGIN from Arabic *'ulamā'*, pl. of *'ālim* 'learned', from *'alima* 'know'.

-ulent ■ suffix (forming adjectives) full of: *fraudulent*.
– DERIVATIVES **-ulence** suffix forming corresponding nouns.
– ORIGIN from Latin *-ulentus*.

ullage /ˈʌlɪdʒ/ ■ n. **1** the amount by which a container falls short of being full. **2** loss of liquid by evaporation or leakage.
– ORIGIN Middle English: from Anglo-Norman French *ulliage*, from Old French *euillier* 'fill up', from Latin *oculus* 'eye'.

ulna /ˈʌlnə/ ■ n. (pl. **ulnae** /-niː/ or **ulnas**) Anatomy & Zoology a bone of the forearm or forelimb, in humans the thinner and longer of the two.
– DERIVATIVES **ulnar** adj.
– ORIGIN Middle English (denoting the humerus): from Latin.

-ulous ■ suffix forming adjectives such as *incredulous*.
– ORIGIN from Latin *-ulosus, -ulus*.

Ulsterman (or **Ulsterwoman**) ■ n. (pl. **-men** or **-women**) a native or inhabitant of Northern Ireland or Ulster.

ult. ■ abbrev. **1** ultimate. **2** ultimo.

ulterior ■ adj. **1** other than what is obvious or admitted: *she had some ulterior motive in coming*. **2** beyond what is immediate or present.
– ORIGIN C17: from Latin, 'further, more distant'.

ultima plural form of ULTIMATUM.

ultimate ■ adj. **1** being or happening at the end of a process. **2** being the best or most extreme example of its kind: *the ultimate accolade*. **3** basic or fundamental. **4** Physics denoting the maximum possible strength of resistance beyond which an object breaks. ■ n. **1** (**the ultimate**) the best achievable or imaginable of its kind: *the ultimate in luxury*. **2** a final or fundamental fact or principle.
– DERIVATIVES **ultimacy** n. (pl. **-ies**). **ultimately** adv.
– ORIGIN C17: from late Latin *ultimatus*, from *ultimare* 'come to an end'.

ultima Thule ■ n. a distant unknown region; the extreme limit of travel and discovery.
– ORIGIN Latin, 'furthest Thule', a country to the north of Britain (prob. Norway), believed by ancient Greeks and Romans to be the northernmost part of the world.

ultimatum ■ n. (pl. **ultimatums** or **ultimata** /-tə/) a final demand or statement of terms, the rejection of which will result in retaliation or a breakdown in relations.
– ORIGIN C18: from Latin, from *ultimare* 'come to an end'.

ultimo /ˈʌltɪməʊ/ ■ adj. [postpos.] dated of last month.
– ORIGIN from Latin *ultimo mense* 'in the last month'.

ultra informal ■ n. an extremist. ■ adv. very.
– ORIGIN C19: an independent usage of ULTRA-, orig. as an abbrev. of French *ultra-royaliste*.

ultra- ■ prefix **1** beyond; on the other side of: *ultra-montane*. **2** extreme; to an extreme degree: *ultramicroscopic*.
– ORIGIN from Latin *ultra* 'beyond'.

ultracentrifuge ■ n. a very fast centrifuge used to precipitate or separate large biological molecules.
– DERIVATIVES **ultracentrifugation** n.

ultrafiltration ■ n. filtration using a medium fine enough to retain colloidal particles, viruses, or large molecules.

ultra-high frequency (abbrev.: **UHF**) ■ n. a radio frequency in the range 300 to 3 000 MHz.

ultramafic /ˌʌltrəˈmafɪk/ ■ adj. Geology relating to or denoting igneous rocks composed chiefly of mafic minerals.

ultramarine ■ n. a brilliant deep blue pigment originally obtained from lapis lazuli, and now made from powdered fired clay, sodium carbonate, sulphur, and resin.
– ORIGIN C16: from medieval Latin *ultramarinus* 'beyond the sea'; the name of the pigment is from obsolete Italian (*azzurro*) *oltramarino* '(azure) from overseas' (because the lapis lazuli was imported).

ultramicroscope ■ n. an optical microscope used to detect very small particles by observing light scattered from them.

ultramicroscopic ■ adj. too small to be seen by an ordinary optical microscope. ▸ of or relating to an ultra-microscope.

ultramontane /ˌʌltrəˈmɒnteɪn/ ■ adj. **1** advocating supreme papal authority in matters of faith and discipline. **2** situated on the other side of the Alps from the point of view of the speaker.
– DERIVATIVES **ultramontanism** n.
– ORIGIN C16: from medieval Latin *ultramontanus*, from Latin *ultra* 'beyond' + *mons* 'mountain'.

ultrasonic ■ adj. of or involving sound waves with a frequency above the upper limit of human hearing.
– DERIVATIVES **ultrasonically** adv.

ultrasonics ■ pl. n. **1** [treated as sing.] the science and application of ultrasonic waves. **2** [treated as sing. or pl.] ultrasound.

ultrasonography /ˌʌltrəsəˈnɒɡrəfi/ ■ n. Medicine a technique using echoes of ultrasound pulses to delineate objects or areas of different density in the body.
– DERIVATIVES **ultrasonographic** adj.

ultrasound ■ n. sound or other vibrations having an ultrasonic frequency, particularly as used in medical imaging.

ultrastructure ■ n. Biology fine structure that can only be seen with an electron microscope.

ultraviolet ■ n. electromagnetic radiation having a wavelength just shorter than that of violet light but longer than that of X-rays. ■ adj. of or denoting such radiation.

ultra vires /ˌʌltrə ˈvʌɪriːz, ˌʊltrə ˈviːreɪz/ ■ adj. & adv. Law beyond one's legal power or authority.
– ORIGIN Latin, 'beyond the powers'.

ululate /ˈjuːljʊleɪt, ˈʌl-/ ■ v. howl or wail, typically to express grief. ▸ (of women in some traditional societies) make a high wavering sound with the voice and tongue to express grief, joy, or respect.
– DERIVATIVES **ululant** adj. **ululation** n.
– ORIGIN C17: from Latin *ululat-, ululare* 'howl, shriek', of imitative origin.

um ■ exclam. expressing hesitation or a pause in speech.

-um ■ suffix variant spelling of -IUM (in sense 2).

umbel /ˈʌmb(ə)l/ ■ n. Botany a flower cluster in which stalks of nearly equal length spring from a common centre and form a flat or curved surface, characteristic of the parsley family.
– DERIVATIVES **umbellate** adj.
– ORIGIN C16: from obsolete French *umbelle* or Latin *umbella* 'sunshade'.

umber /ˈʌmbə/ ■ n. a natural pigment resembling but darker than ochre, normally dark yellowish-brown in

umbilical

colour (raw umber) or dark brown when roasted (burnt umber).
– ORIGIN C16: from French (*terre d')ombre* or Italian (*terra di) ombra* '(earth of) shadow'.

umbilical /ʌmˈbɪlɪk(ə)l, ˌʌmbɪˈlaɪk(ə)l/ ■ adj. **1** relating to or affecting the navel or umbilical cord. **2** extremely close; inseparable. **3** (of a pipe or cable) connecting someone or something to a source of essential supplies. ■ n. short for **UMBILICAL CORD**.
– DERIVATIVES **umbilically** adv.
– ORIGIN C16: from French *ombilical* or Latin *umbilicus* (see **UMBILICUS**).

umbilical cord ■ n. **1** a flexible cord-like structure containing blood vessels, attaching a fetus to the placenta during gestation. **2** a flexible cable, pipe, or other line carrying essential services or supplies.

umbilicate /ʌmˈbɪlɪkət/ ■ adj. Zoology & Botany having an umbilicus or central depression.

umbilicus /ʌmˈbɪlɪkəs, ˌʌmbɪˈlaɪkəs/ ■ n. (pl. **umbilici** /-saɪ/ or **umbiliuses**) **1** Anatomy the navel. **2** Zoology a central depression or hole in the whorl of some gastropod molluscs and many ammonites.
– ORIGIN C17: from Latin: rel. to Greek *omphalos*.

umbra /ˈʌmbrə/ ■ n. (pl. **umbras** or **umbrae** /-briː/) **1** the fully shaded inner region of a shadow cast by an opaque object, especially the area on the earth or moon experiencing totality in an eclipse. **2** Astronomy the dark central part of a sunspot.
– DERIVATIVES **umbral** adj.
– ORIGIN C16 (denoting a phantom or ghost): from Latin, 'shade'.

umbrage /ˈʌmbrɪdʒ/ ■ n. **1** offence or annoyance. **2** archaic shade or shadow, especially as cast by trees.
– DERIVATIVES **umbrageous** adj.

umbrella ■ n. **1** a device consisting of a circular fabric canopy on a folding metal frame supported by a central rod, used as protection against rain. **2** a protecting force or influence. ▸ a screen of fighter aircraft or anti-aircraft artillery. **3** [usu. as modifier] a thing that includes or contains many different parts: *an umbrella organization*.
– DERIVATIVES **umbrellaed** adj.
– ORIGIN C17: from Italian *ombrella*, diminutive of *ombra* 'shade'.

umbrella fund ■ n. an offshore investment fund which invests only in other investment funds.

umbrella pine ■ n. another term for **STONE PINE**. **2** a tall Japanese conifer with leaves growing in umbrella-like whorls. [*Sciadopitys verticillata*.]

umbrella thorn ■ n. a deciduous African acacia with a flattened crown, white flowers, and spirally twisted seed pods. [*Acacia tortilis*.] ▸ used in names of similar acacias.

umbrella tree ■ n. a plant with leaves or leaflets arranged in umbrella-like whorls. [*Schefflera actinophylla* (Australia) and *Magnolia tripetala* (N. America).]

Umbrian ■ n. a native or inhabitant of Umbria, a region of central Italy, especially in pre-Roman times. ■ adj. of or relating to Umbria, its people, or their languages.

umbriferous /ʌmˈbrɪf(ə)rəs/ ■ adj. poetic/literary providing shade.
– ORIGIN C17: from Latin *umbrifer*.

Umkhonto we Sizwe /ˌʊmˈkɒntəʊ wɛ ˈsɪzweɪ/ ■ n. S. African the armed wing of the African National Congress, now incorporated into the SANDF.
– ORIGIN isiXhosa, 'Spear of the Nation'.

umkhwetha /ʊmˈkwɛːtʌ/ ■ n. singular form of **ABAKHWETHA**.

umlaut /ˈʊmlaʊt/ Linguistics ■ n. **1** a mark (¨) used over a vowel, especially in German, to indicate a different vowel quality. **2** the process in Germanic languages by which the quality of a vowel was altered in certain phonetic contexts. ■ v. modify with an umlaut.
– ORIGIN C19: from German *Umlaut*, from *um* 'about' + *Laut* 'sound'.

umma /ˈʊmə/ (also **ummah**) ■ n. the whole community of Muslims bound together by ties of religion.
– ORIGIN Arabic, 'people, community'.

ump ■ n. informal an umpire.

umph ■ n. variant spelling of **OOMPH**.

umphokoqo /ʊmpɒˈkɔːkɔ, ʊmpɔːˈkɔːqɔ/ (also **mphokoqo**) ■ n. S. African crumbly porridge made of maize meal, often eaten with naturally curdled or fresh milk.
– ORIGIN from isiXhosa.

umpire ■ n. **1** (in certain sports) an official who watches a game or match closely to enforce the rules and arbitrate on matters arising from the play. **2** a person chosen to arbitrate between contending parties. ■ v. act as an umpire.
– DERIVATIVES **umpirage** n.
– ORIGIN Middle English (orig. as *noumpere*): from Old French *nonper* 'not equal'; the *n* was lost by wrong division of *a noumpere*.

umpteen ■ cardinal number informal indefinitely many.
– DERIVATIVES **umpteenth** ordinal number .
– ORIGIN C20: humorous formation based on -TEEN.

umrhubhe /ʊmˈxuːbi/ (also **umrhube**) ■ n. a traditional Xhosa mouth bow.
– ORIGIN from isiXhosa.

umvubo ■ n. S. African a dish of crumbly maize porridge and naturally curdled milk.
– ORIGIN from isiXhosa.

UN ■ abbrev. United Nations.

'un ■ contr. informal one.

un-[1] ■ prefix **1** (added to adjectives, participles, and their derivatives) denoting the absence of a quality or state; not: *uncharismatic*. ▸ the reverse of: *unselfish*. **2** (added to nouns) a lack of: *untruth*.
– ORIGIN Old English, of Germanic origin.

un-[2] ■ prefix added to verbs: **1** denoting the reversal or cancellation of an action or state: *unsettle*. **2** denoting deprivation, separation, or reduction to a lesser state: *unmask*. ▸ denoting release: *unhand*.
– ORIGIN Old English, of Germanic origin.

unabashed ■ adj. not embarrassed, disconcerted, or ashamed.
– DERIVATIVES **unabashedly** adv.

unabated ■ adj. without any reduction in intensity or strength.
– DERIVATIVES **unabatedly** adv.

unable ■ adj. lacking the skill, means, or opportunity to do something.

unabridged ■ adj. (of a text) not cut or shortened; complete.

unaccented ■ adj. having no accent, stress, or emphasis.

unacceptable ■ adj. not satisfactory or allowable.
– DERIVATIVES **unacceptability** n. **unacceptably** adv.

unaccompanied ■ adj. **1** having no companion or escort. **2** without instrumental accompaniment. **3** without something occurring at the same time.

unaccountable ■ adj. **1** unable to be explained. **2** not responsible for or required to justify consequences.
– DERIVATIVES **unaccountability** n. **unaccountably** adv.

unaccounted ■ adj. (**unaccounted for**) not taken into consideration or explained.

unaccustomed ■ adj. **1** not customary; unusual. **2** (**unaccustomed to**) not familiar with or used to.
– DERIVATIVES **unaccustomedly** adv.

unacknowledged ■ adj. **1** existing or having taken place but not accepted or admitted to. **2** deserving but not receiving recognition.

unacquainted ■ adj. **1** (**unacquainted with**) having no experience of or familiarity with. **2** not having met before.

unadjusted ■ adj. (especially of statistics) not adjusted or refined.

unadulterated ■ adj. **1** complete; utter. **2** having no inferior added substances.

unadventurous ■ adj. not offering, involving, or eager for new or stimulating things.
– DERIVATIVES **unadventurously** adv.

unadvisable ■ adj. another term for **INADVISABLE**.

unadvisedly ■ adv. in an unwise or rash manner.

unaesthetic ■ adj. **1** not visually pleasing. **2** not motivated by aesthetic principles.

unaffected ■ adj. **1** feeling or showing no effects. **2** sincere and genuine.
– DERIVATIVES **unaffectedly** adv. **unaffectedness** n.

unaffiliated ■ adj. not officially attached to or connected with an organization.

unaffordable ■ adj. too expensive to be afforded by the average person.

unafraid ■ adj. feeling no fear.

unaided ■ adj. needing or having no assistance.

unalienable ■ adj. another term for **INALIENABLE**.

unaligned ■ adj. **1** not placed or arranged in a straight line or in correct relative positions. **2** not allied with or supporting an organization or cause.

unalike ■ adj. differing from each other.

unalloyed ■ adj. **1** (of metal) not alloyed. **2** complete and unreserved.

unalterable ■ adj. not able to be changed.
– DERIVATIVES **unalterableness** n. **unalterably** adv.

unaltered ■ adj. remaining the same.

unambiguous ■ adj. without ambiguity.
– DERIVATIVES **unambiguity** n. **unambiguously** adv.

unambitious ■ adj. **1** not motivated by a strong desire to succeed. **2** not involving anything new, exciting, or demanding.
– DERIVATIVES **unambitiously** adv. **unambitiousness** n.

un-American ■ adj. **1** not in accordance with American characteristics. **2** US, chiefly historical contrary to the interests of the US and therefore treasonable.
– DERIVATIVES **un-Americanism** n.

unanalysable (US **unanalyzable**) ■ adj. not able to be explained or interpreted through methodical examination.

unaneled /ˌʌnəˈniːld/ ■ adj. archaic having died without receiving extreme unction.

unanimous /juːˈnanɪməs/ ■ adj. **1** fully in agreement. **2** (of an opinion, decision, or vote) held or carried by everyone involved.
– DERIVATIVES **unanimity** /ˌjuːnəˈnɪmɪti/ n. **unanimously** adv.
– ORIGIN C17: from Latin *unanimus*, from *unus* 'one' + *animus* 'mind'.

unannounced ■ adj. **1** not publicized. **2** without warning; unexpected.

unanswerable ■ adj. **1** unable to be answered. **2** unable to be refuted.
– DERIVATIVES **unanswerably** adv.

unanswered ■ adj. not answered or responded to.

unapologetic ■ adj. not acknowledging or expressing regret.
– DERIVATIVES **unapologetically** adv.

unappealable ■ adj. Law (of a case or ruling) not able to be referred to a higher court for review.

unappealing ■ adj. not inviting or attractive.
– DERIVATIVES **unappealingly** adv.

unappetizing (also **-ising**) ■ adj. not inviting or attractive.
– DERIVATIVES **unappetizingly** (also **-isingly**) adv.

unappreciated ■ adj. not fully understood, recognized, or valued.

unappreciative ■ adj. not fully understanding or recognizing something.

unapprehended ■ adj. **1** not perceived or understood. **2** not arrested.

unapproachable ■ adj. **1** not welcoming or friendly. **2** (of a place) remote and inaccessible.
– DERIVATIVES **unapproachability** n. **unapproachably** adv.

unapproved ■ adj. not officially accepted or sanctioned.

unarguable ■ adj. **1** not open to disagreement; certain. **2** not able to be argued.
– DERIVATIVES **unarguably** adv.

unarmed ■ adj. not equipped with or carrying weapons.

unary /ˈjuːnəri/ ■ adj. Mathematics consisting of or involving a single component or element.

unashamed ■ adj. feeling or showing no guilt or embarrassment.
– DERIVATIVES **unashamedly** adv. **unashamedness** n.

unasked ■ adj. **1** (of a question) not asked. **2** (often **unasked for**) not requested or sought.

unassailable ■ adj. unable to be attacked, questioned, or defeated.
– DERIVATIVES **unassailability** n. **unassailably** adv.

unassertive ■ adj. not having or showing a confident and forceful personality.
– DERIVATIVES **unassertively** adv. **unassertiveness** n.

unassisted ■ adj. not helped by anyone or anything.

unassociated ■ adj. not connected or associated.

unassuming ■ adj. not pretentious or arrogant.
– DERIVATIVES **unassumingly** adv. **unassumingness** n.

unattached ■ adj. **1** not working for or belonging to a particular organization. **2** without a spouse or established lover.

unattainable ■ adj. not able to be reached or achieved.
– DERIVATIVES **unattainableness** n. **unattainably** adv.

unattended ■ adj. **1** not dealt with. **2** not looked after.

unattractive ■ adj. not pleasing, appealing, or inviting.
– DERIVATIVES **unattractively** adv. **unattractiveness** n.

unattributed ■ adj. (of a quotation, story, or work of art) of unknown or unpublished provenance.
– DERIVATIVES **unattributable** adj. **unattributably** adv.

unauthorized (also **-ised**) ■ adj. not having official permission or approval.

unavailable ■ adj. **1** not at someone's disposal. **2** not free to do something.
– DERIVATIVES **unavailability** n.

unavailing ■ adj. achieving little or nothing.
– DERIVATIVES **unavailingly** adv.

unavoidable ■ adj. not able to be avoided or prevented; inevitable.
– DERIVATIVES **unavoidability** n. **unavoidably** adv.

unaware ■ adj. having no knowledge of a situation or fact. ■ adv. variant of **UNAWARES**.
– DERIVATIVES **unawareness** n.

unawares (also **unaware**) ■ adv. so as to surprise; unexpectedly.
– ORIGIN C16: from UNAWARE.

unbalance ■ v. **1** upset the balance of. **2** [often as adj. **unbalanced**] upset the mental equilibrium of; derange. **3** [as adj. **unbalanced**] treating aspects of something unequally; partial. ■ n. a lack of balance or stability.

unbanked ■ n. a person who does not have an account at a bank or other financial institution: *the rural unbanked*. ■ adj. of or relating to people who do not have a bank account: *unbanked households*.

unbearable ■ adj. not able to be endured or tolerated.
– DERIVATIVES **unbearableness** n. **unbearably** adv.

unbeatable ■ adj. **1** not able to be surpassed or defeated. **2** extremely good.

unbeaten ■ adj. not defeated or surpassed. ▸ Cricket (of a batsman) not out in his or her side's innings.

unbecoming ■ adj. **1** (especially of clothing) not flattering. **2** not fitting; unseemly.
– DERIVATIVES **unbecomingly** adv. **unbecomingness** n.

unbeknown (also **unbeknownst**) ■ adj. (**unbeknown to**) without the knowledge of.
– ORIGIN C17: from UN-¹ + archaic *beknown* 'known'.

unbelief ■ n. lack of religious belief.
– DERIVATIVES **unbeliever** n. **unbelieving** adj. **unbelievingly** adv.

unbelievable ■ adj. **1** unlikely to be true. **2** extraordinary.
– DERIVATIVES **unbelievability** n. **unbelievably** adv.

unbend ■ v. (past and past part. **unbent**) **1** straighten. **2** become less reserved, formal, or strict. **3** Nautical unfasten (sails) from yards and stays. ▸ untie (a rope) or cast (a cable) loose.

unbending ■ adj. austere and inflexible.
– DERIVATIVES **unbendingly** adv.

unbiased (also **unbiassed**) ■ adj. showing no prejudice; impartial.

unbidden ■ adj. **1** without having been invited. **2** arising without conscious effort.

unbleached ■ adj. (especially of paper, cloth, or flour) not bleached.

unblind ■ v. conduct (a test or experiment) in such a way that it is not blind.

unblock ■ v. **1** remove an obstruction from. **2** Bridge play in such a way that (a long suit) becomes established.

unblushing ■ adj. not feeling or showing embarrassment or shame.
– DERIVATIVES **unblushingly** adv.

unbolt ■ v. open by drawing back a bolt.

unborn ■ adj. (of a baby) not yet born.

unbound ■ adj. **1** not bound or restricted. **2** (of printed sheets) not bound together. ▶ (of a bound book) not provided with a permanent cover.

unbounded ■ adj. having no limits.
– DERIVATIVES **unboundedly** adv. **unboundedness** n.

unbowed ■ adj. not having submitted to pressure, demands, or accusations.

unbranded ■ adj. **1** (of a product) not bearing a brand name. **2** (of livestock) not branded with the owner's mark.

unbreachable ■ adj. not able to be breached or overcome.

unbreakable ■ adj. not liable to break or able to be broken.

unbreathable ■ adj. (of air) not fit or pleasant to breathe.

unbridgeable ■ adj. (of a gap or difference) not able to be bridged or made less significant.

unbridled ■ adj. uncontrolled; unconstrained.

unbroken ■ adj. **1** not broken; intact. **2** not interrupted. **3** not surpassed. **4** (of a horse) not broken in.
– DERIVATIVES **unbrokenly** adv. **unbrokenness** n.

unbuckle ■ v. unfasten the buckle of.

unbuild ■ v. [as adj. **unbuilt**] (of buildings or land) not yet built or built on.

unbundle ■ v. **1** market or charge for (items or services) separately rather than as part of a package. **2** split (a company or conglomerate) into its constituent businesses, especially prior to selling them off.
– DERIVATIVES **unbundler** n.

unburden ■ v. relieve of a burden. ▶ (**unburden oneself**) relieve oneself of anxiety or distress by confiding in someone.

unburnt (also **unburned**) ■ adj. **1** not damaged or destroyed by fire. **2** (especially of bricks) not exposed to heat in a kiln.

unbutton ■ v. **1** unfasten the buttons of. **2** informal relax and become less inhibited.

uncalled ■ adj. **1** not summoned or invited. **2** (**uncalled for**) undesirable and unnecessary.

uncanny ■ adj. (-ier, -iest) strange or mysterious.
– DERIVATIVES **uncannily** adv. **uncanniness** n.
– ORIGIN C16 (orig. Scots in the sense 'relating to the occult, malicious'): from UN-¹ + CANNY.

uncap ■ v. (**uncapped**, **uncapping**) **1** remove the cap from. **2** remove a limit from (a price, rate, etc.).

uncapped ■ adj. (of a player) never having been chosen as a member of a national sports team.

uncared ■ adj. (**uncared for**) not looked after properly.

uncaring ■ adj. **1** not displaying sympathy or concern for others. **2** not interested; unconcerned.
– DERIVATIVES **uncaringly** adv.

unceasing ■ adj. not ceasing; continuous.
– DERIVATIVES **unceasingly** adv.

unceremonious ■ adj. discourteous; abrupt.
– DERIVATIVES **unceremoniously** adv.

uncertain ■ adj. **1** not known, reliable, or definite. **2** not completely confident or sure.
– PHRASES **in no uncertain terms** clearly and forcefully.
– DERIVATIVES **uncertainly** adv. **uncertainty** n. (pl. **-ies**).

uncertainty principle ■ n. Physics the principle, stated by Werner Heisenberg, that the momentum and position of a particle cannot both be precisely determined at the same time.

unchallengeable ■ adj. not able to be disputed, opposed, or defeated.
– DERIVATIVES **unchallengeably** adv.

unchallenged ■ adj. **1** not disputed, opposed, or defeated. **2** not called on to prove one's identity.

unchallenging ■ adj. not presenting a challenge.

unchangeable ■ adj. not liable to variation or able to be altered.
– DERIVATIVES **unchangeability** n. **unchangeableness** n. **unchangeably** adv.

unchanged ■ adj. not changed; unaltered.

unchanging ■ adj. remaining the same.
– DERIVATIVES **unchangingly** adv.

uncharacteristic ■ adj. not typical of a particular person or thing.
– DERIVATIVES **uncharacteristically** adv.

uncharged ■ adj. **1** not accused of an offence under the law. **2** not carrying an electric charge. **3** not charged to a particular account.

uncharismatic ■ adj. lacking charisma.

uncharitable ■ adj. unkind or unsympathetic to others.
– DERIVATIVES **uncharitableness** n. **uncharitably** adv.

uncharted ■ adj. (of an area of land or sea) not mapped or surveyed.

unchaste ■ adj. relating to or engaging in sexual activity, especially of an illicit or extramarital nature.
– DERIVATIVES **unchastely** adv. **unchastity** n.

unchastened ■ adj. not chastened by a reproof or misfortune.

unchecked ■ adj. (of something undesirable) not controlled or restrained.

unchivalrous ■ adj. (of a man) discourteous, especially towards women.

unchristian ■ adj. not in accordance with the teachings of Christianity. ▶ ungenerous or unfair.
– DERIVATIVES **unchristianly** adv.

unchurched ■ adj. not belonging to or connected with a Church.

uncial /ˈʌnsɪəl, -ʃ(ə)l/ ■ adj. of or written in a majuscule script with rounded separated letters which is found in European manuscripts of the 4th–8th centuries and from which modern capital letters are derived. ■ n. an uncial letter, script, or manuscript.
– ORIGIN C17: from Latin, from *unciales litterae* 'uncial letters', from *uncia* 'inch'.

uncircumcised ■ adj. **1** (of a boy or man) not circumcised. **2** archaic irreligious or heathen.

uncivil ■ adj. discourteous; impolite.
– DERIVATIVES **uncivilly** adv.

uncivilized (also **-ised**) ■ adj. **1** not socially or culturally advanced. **2** impolite; bad-mannered.

unclad ■ adj. **1** unclothed; naked. **2** not provided with cladding.

unclaimed ■ adj. not having been claimed.

unclasp ■ v. **1** unfasten (a clasp or similar device). **2** release the grip of.

unclassifiable ■ adj. not able to be classified.

unclassified ■ adj. **1** not classified. **2** Brit. denoting a university degree without honours. ▶ (of a grade in an examination) denoting a fail.

uncle ■ n. the brother of one's father or mother or the husband of one's aunt. ▶ informal an unrelated adult male friend of a child.
– PHRASES **cry** (or **say**) **uncle** N. Amer. informal surrender or admit defeat.
– ORIGIN Middle English: from Old French *oncle*, from late Latin *aunculus*, alteration of Latin *avunculus* (see AVUNCULAR).

unclean ■ adj. **1** dirty. **2** immoral. **3** ritually impure and unfit for use or consumption. ▸ (in biblical use, of a spirit) evil.
– DERIVATIVES **uncleanness** n.

uncleanliness ■ n. the state of being dirty.

unclear ■ adj. **1** not easy to see, hear, or understand. **2** not obvious, definite, or certain.
– DERIVATIVES **unclearly** adv. **unclearness** n.

uncleared ■ adj. **1** (of a cheque) not having passed through a clearing house and been paid into the payee's account. **2** (of land) not cleared of vegetation.

unclench ■ v. release (a clenched part of the body).

Uncle Sam ■ n. a personification of the federal government or citizens of the US.
– ORIGIN C19: said to have arisen as a facetious expansion of the letters US.

Uncle Tom ■ n. derogatory, chiefly N. Amer. a black man considered to be excessively obedient or servile.
– ORIGIN 1920s: from the name of the hero of H. B. Stowe's *Uncle Tom's Cabin* (1852).

unclimbed ■ adj. (of a mountain or rock face) not previously climbed.
– DERIVATIVES **unclimbable** adj.

uncloak ■ v. poetic/literary uncover; reveal.

unclog ■ v. (**unclogged**, **unclogging**) remove accumulated matter from.

unclothed ■ adj. wearing no clothes; naked.

unclouded ■ adj. **1** (of the sky) not dark or overcast. **2** not troubled or spoiled by anything.

uncluttered ■ adj. not cluttered by too many objects or elements.

unco /ˈʌŋkə/ Scottish ■ adj. unusual or remarkable. ■ adv. remarkably; very.
– ORIGIN Middle English: alteration of UNCOUTH.

uncoil ■ v. straighten from a coiled or curled position.

uncoloured (US **uncolored**) ■ adj. **1** having no colour; neutral in colour. **2** not influenced, especially in a negative way.

uncombed ■ adj. (of a person's hair) not combed.

uncombined ■ adj. denoting a substance that is not chemically bound within a compound.

uncomely ■ adj. archaic or humorous (especially of a woman) not attractive. ▸ archaic not agreeable or suitable.

uncomfortable ■ adj. not physically comfortable. ▸ uneasy or awkward.
– DERIVATIVES **uncomfortableness** n. **uncomfortably** adv.

uncommercial ■ adj. not making, intended to make, or allowing a profit.

uncommon ■ adj. out of the ordinary; unusual. ▸ remarkably great: *an uncommon amount of noise*. ■ adv. archaic remarkably.
– DERIVATIVES **uncommonly** adv. **uncommonness** n.

uncommunicative ■ adj. unwilling to talk or impart information.
– DERIVATIVES **uncommunicatively** adv. **uncommunicativeness** n.

uncompetitive ■ adj. not competitive or marked by fair competition.
– DERIVATIVES **uncompetitively** adv. **uncompetitiveness** n.

uncomplaining ■ adj. not complaining; stoical.
– DERIVATIVES **uncomplainingly** adv.

uncomplicated ■ adj. simple or straightforward.
– DERIVATIVES **uncomplicatedly** adv. **uncomplicatedness** n.

uncomplimentary ■ adj. not complimentary; negative or insulting.

uncomprehending ■ adj. unable to comprehend something.
– DERIVATIVES **uncomprehendingly** adv.

uncompromising ■ adj. unwilling to make concessions; resolute. ▸ harsh or relentless.
– DERIVATIVES **uncompromisingly** adv. **uncompromisingness** n.

1293

uncontrolled

unconcealed ■ adj. (especially of an emotion) not concealed; obvious.

unconcern ■ n. a lack of worry or interest.

unconcerned ■ adj. showing or feeling a lack of worry or interest.
– DERIVATIVES **unconcernedly** adv.

unconditional ■ adj. not subject to any conditions.
– DERIVATIVES **unconditionality** n. **unconditionally** adv.

unconditioned ■ adj. **1** unconditional. **2** relating to or denoting instinctive reflexes or other behaviour not formed or influenced by conditioning or learning. **3** not subjected to a conditioning process.

unconfident ■ adj. not confident; hesitant.
– DERIVATIVES **unconfidently** adv.

unconfined ■ adj. **1** not confined to a limited space. **2** (of joy or excitement) very great.

unconfirmed ■ adj. not confirmed as to truth or validity.

unconformable ■ adj. Geology (of rock strata in contact) marking a discontinuity in the geological record, and typically not having the same direction of stratification.
– DERIVATIVES **uncomformably** adv.

unconformity ■ n. Geology a surface of contact between two groups of unconformable strata. ▸ the condition of being unconformable.

uncongenial ■ adj. **1** (of a person) not friendly or pleasant to be with. **2** unsuitable and therefore unlikely to promote success or well-being.

unconnected ■ adj. not joined together or to something else. ▸ not associated or linked in a sequence.
– DERIVATIVES **unconnectedly** adv. **unconnectedness** n.

unconquerable ■ adj. not conquerable: *unconquerable pride*.
– DERIVATIVES **unconquerably** adv. **unconquered** adj.

unconscionable /ʌnˈkɒnʃ(ə)nəb(ə)l/ ■ adj. not right or reasonable. ▸ unreasonably excessive: *they had to wait an unconscionable time*.
– DERIVATIVES **unconscionably** adv.
– ORIGIN C16: from UN-[1] + obsolete *conscionable*, from CONSCIENCE.

unconscious ■ adj. **1** not awake and aware of and responding to one's environment. **2** done or existing without one realizing. **3** (**unconscious of**) unaware of. ■ n. (**the unconscious**) the part of the mind which is inaccessible to the conscious mind but which affects behaviour and emotions.
– DERIVATIVES **unconsciously** adv. **unconsciousness** n.

unconsecrated ■ adj. not consecrated.

unconsidered ■ adj. **1** disregarded and unappreciated. **2** not thought about in advance; rash.

unconsolable ■ adj. inconsolable.
– DERIVATIVES **unconsolably** adv.

unconstitutional ■ adj. not in accordance with the political constitution or with procedural rules.
– DERIVATIVES **unconstitutionality** n. **unconstitutionally** adv.

unconstrained ■ adj. not restricted or limited.
– DERIVATIVES **unconstrainedly** adv.

unconsummated ■ adj. (of a marriage) not having been consummated.

uncontainable ■ adj. (especially of an emotion) very strong.

uncontaminated ■ adj. not contaminated.

uncontentious ■ adj. not contentious.

uncontested ■ adj. not contested.
– DERIVATIVES **uncontestedly** adv.

uncontrived ■ adj. not artificially created. ▸ not appearing artificial.

uncontrollable ■ adj. not controllable.
– DERIVATIVES **uncontrollableness** n. **uncontrollably** adv.

uncontrolled ■ adj. not controlled.
– DERIVATIVES **uncontrolledly** adv.

uncontroversial

uncontroversial ■ adj. not controversial; avoiding controversy.
– DERIVATIVES **uncontroversially** adv.

uncontroverted ■ adj. of which the truth or validity is not disputed.

unconventional ■ adj. not based on or conforming to what is generally done or believed.
– DERIVATIVES **unconventionality** n. **unconventionally** adv.

unconvinced ■ adj. not certain that something is true or can be relied on.

unconvincing ■ adj. failing to convince or impress.
– DERIVATIVES **unconvincingly** adv.

uncooked ■ adj. not cooked; raw.

uncool ■ adj. informal not fashionable or impressive.

uncooperative ■ adj. unwilling to help others or do what they ask.
– DERIVATIVES **uncooperatively** adv.

uncoordinated ■ adj. **1** badly organized. **2** (of a person or their movements) clumsy.

uncork ■ v. pull the cork out of.

uncorroborated ■ adj. not corroborated or confirmed by evidence.

uncountable ■ adj. too many to be counted.
– DERIVATIVES **uncountability** n. **uncountably** adv.

uncountable noun (also **uncount noun**) ■ n. another term for MASS NOUN.

uncounted ■ adj. not counted. ▸ very numerous.

uncouple ■ v. disconnect or become disconnected.

uncouth ■ adj. lacking good manners, refinement, or grace.
– DERIVATIVES **uncouthly** adv. **uncouthness** n.
– ORIGIN Old English *uncūth* 'unknown', from UN-¹ + *cūth*, from *cunnan* 'know, be able'.

uncover ■ v. remove a cover or covering from. ▸ discover (something previously secret or unknown).

uncritical ■ adj. not expressing criticism or using one's critical faculties.
– DERIVATIVES **uncritically** adv.

uncross ■ v. move (something) back from a crossed position.

uncrossed ■ adj. (of a cheque) not crossed.

uncrowded ■ adj. not crowded.

uncrowned ■ adj. not formally crowned as a monarch.

uncrushable ■ adj. (of a fabric) resistant to creasing.

UNCSTD ■ abbrev. United Nations Conference on Science and Technology for Development.

UNCTAD /ˈʌŋ(k)tad/ ■ abbrev. United Nations Conference on Trade and Development.

unction /ˈʌŋ(k)ʃ(ə)n/ ■ n. **1** formal the action of anointing someone with oil or ointment. ▸ short for EXTREME UNCTION. **2** an ointment. **3** a fervent manner of expression apparently arising from deep emotion, especially when assumed.
– ORIGIN Middle English: from Latin *unctio(n-)*, from *unguere* 'anoint'.

unctuous /ˈʌŋ(k)tjʊəs/ ■ adj. **1** excessively flattering or ingratiating. **2** having a greasy or soapy feel.
– DERIVATIVES **unctuously** adv. **unctuousness** n.
– ORIGIN Middle English: from medieval Latin *unctuosus*, from Latin *unctus* 'anointing', from *unguere* 'anoint'.

uncultivated ■ adj. **1** (of land) not used for growing crops. **2** (of a person) not highly educated.

uncultured ■ adj. not characterized by good taste, manners, or education.

uncured ■ adj. not preserved by salting, drying, or smoking.

uncurl ■ v. straighten from a curled position.

uncut ■ adj. not cut. ▸ (of a text, film, etc.) complete; unabridged. ▸ (of a stone, especially a diamond) not shaped by cutting. ▸ chiefly historical (of a book) with the edges of its pages not slit open or trimmed off. ▸ (of fabric) having its pile loops intact. ▸ (of alcohol or a drug) not diluted or adulterated.

undamaged ■ adj. not harmed or damaged.

undated ■ adj. not provided or marked with a date.

undaunted ■ adj. not intimidated or discouraged by difficulty, danger, or disappointment.
– DERIVATIVES **undauntedly** adv. **undauntedness** n.

undead ■ adj. (of a fictional being, especially a vampire) technically dead but still animate.

undeceive ■ v. tell (someone) that an idea or belief is mistaken.

undecidable ■ adj. not able to be firmly established or refuted. ▸ Logic (of a proposition or theorem) not able to be proved or disproved.
– DERIVATIVES **undecidability** n.

undecided ■ adj. not having made a decision; uncertain. ▸ not settled or resolved.
– DERIVATIVES **undecidedly** adv.

undecipherable ■ adj. (of speech or writing) not able to be read or understood.

undee /ˈʌndeɪ/ ■ adj. variant spelling of UNDY.

undefeated ■ adj. not defeated.

undefended ■ adj. not defended.

undefined ■ adj. not clear or defined.
– DERIVATIVES **undefinable** adj. **undefinably** adv.

undemanding ■ adj. (especially of a task) not demanding.

undemocratic ■ adj. not relating or according to democratic principles.
– DERIVATIVES **undemocratically** adv.

undemonstrative ■ adj. not tending to express feelings, especially of affection, openly.
– DERIVATIVES **undemonstratively** adv. **undemonstrativeness** n.

undeniable ■ adj. unable to be denied or disputed.
– DERIVATIVES **undeniably** adv.

under ■ prep. **1** extending or directly below. ▸ below or behind so as to cover or protect. ▸ planted with. **2** at a lower level, layer, or grade than. **3** expressing submission or subordination. ▸ as provided for by the rules of; in accordance with. ▸ used to express grouping or classification. **4** lower than (a specified amount, rate, or norm). **5** undergoing (a process). ■ adv. **1** extending or directly below something. **2** affected by an anaesthetic; unconscious.
– PHRASES **under way 1** (of a boat) moving through the water. **2** having started and making progress.
– DERIVATIVES **undermost** adj.
– ORIGIN Old English, of Germanic origin.

under- ■ prefix **1** below; beneath: *undercover*. ▸ lower in status; subordinate: *undersecretary*. **2** insufficiently; incompletely: *undernourished*.

underachieve ■ v. do less well than is expected.
– DERIVATIVES **underachievement** n. **underachiever** n.

under age ■ adj. too young to engage legally in a particular activity, especially drinking alcohol or having sex.

underarm ■ adj. & adv. (of a throw or stroke in sport) made with the arm or hand below shoulder level. ■ n. a person's armpit.

underbanked ■ n. a person who has a bank account but makes limited or no use of additional financial services and products. ■ adj. **1** inadequately provided with banking and financial services. **2** (of a person) having a bank account but making limited or no use of additional financial services and products offered by banks.

underbelly ■ n. (pl. **-ies**) **1** the soft underside or abdomen of an animal. **2** an area vulnerable to attack. **3** a hidden unpleasant or criminal part of society.

underbid ■ v. (**-bidding**; past and past part. **-bid**) **1** (in an auction) make a bid lower than another. **2** Bridge make a lower bid on (one's hand) than its strength warrants. ■ n. a bid that is lower than another or than is justified.
– DERIVATIVES **underbidder** n.

underbite ■ n. the projection of the lower teeth beyond the upper.

underbody ▪ n. (pl. **-ies**) the underside of a road vehicle, ship, or animal's body.

underbrush ▪ n. N. Amer. undergrowth in a forest.

undercapitalize (also **-ise**) ▪ v. provide (a company) with insufficient capital to achieve desired results.
– DERIVATIVES **undercapitalization** (also **-isation**) n.

undercarriage ▪ n. **1** a wheeled structure beneath an aircraft which supports the aircraft on the ground. **2** the supporting frame under the body of a vehicle.

undercharge ▪ v. charge (someone) a price or amount that is too low.

underclass ▪ n. the lowest social stratum in a country or community, consisting of the poor and unemployed.

undercliff ▪ n. a terrace or lower cliff formed by a landslip.

underclothes ▪ pl. n. clothes worn under others next to the skin.
– DERIVATIVES **underclothing** n.

undercoat ▪ n. **1** a layer of paint applied after the primer and before the topcoat. **2** an animal's underfur or down. ▪ v. apply a coat of undercoat to.

undercook ▪ v. [usu. as adj. **undercooked**] cook (something) insufficiently.

undercover ▪ adj. & adv. involving secret work for investigation or espionage: *an undercover operation*.

undercroft ▪ n. the crypt of a church.
– ORIGIN Middle English: from UNDER- + rare *croft* 'crypt', from Middle Dutch *crofte* 'cave', from Latin *crypta*.

undercurrent ▪ n. **1** a current of water below the surface and moving in a different direction from any surface current. **2** an underlying feeling or influence.

undercut ▪ v. (**-cutting**; past and past part. **-cut**) **1** offer goods or services at a lower price than (a competitor). **2** cut or wear away the part under (something, especially a cliff). ▸ weaken; undermine. ▸ cut away material to leave (a carved design) in relief. ▪ n. a space formed by the removal or absence of material from the lower part of something.

underdetermine ▪ v. account for (a theory or phenomenon) with less than the amount of evidence needed for proof or certainty.
– DERIVATIVES **underdetermination** n.

underdeveloped ▪ adj. not fully developed. ▸ (of a country or region) not advanced economically.
– DERIVATIVES **underdevelopment** n.

underdog ▪ n. a competitor thought to have little chance of winning a fight or contest. ▸ a person who has little status in society.

underdone ▪ adj. (of food) insufficiently cooked.

underdress ▪ v. (also **be underdressed**) dress too plainly or too informally for a particular occasion.

underemphasize (also **-ise**) ▪ v. place insufficient emphasis on.
– DERIVATIVES **underemphasis** n.

underemployed ▪ adj. not having sufficient or sufficiently demanding paid work.
– DERIVATIVES **underemployment** n.

underestimate ▪ v. estimate (something) to be smaller or less important than it really is. ▸ regard (someone) as less capable than they really are. ▪ n. an estimate that is too low.
– DERIVATIVES **underestimation** n.

underexpose ▪ v. Photography expose (film) for too short a time.
– DERIVATIVES **underexposure** n.

underfed ▪ adj. insufficiently fed or nourished.

underfelt ▪ n. felt laid under a carpet for protection or support.

underflow ▪ n. **1** an undercurrent. ▸ a horizontal flow of water through the ground. **2** Computing the generation of a number that is too small to be represented in the device meant to store it.

underfoot ▪ adv. **1** under one's feet; on the ground. **2** constantly present and in one's way.

underframe ▪ n. **1** the substructure of a motor vehicle or railway carriage. **2** the supporting frame of a chair seat or table top.

underfund ▪ v. provide with insufficient funding.
– DERIVATIVES **underfunding** n.

underfur ▪ n. an inner layer of short, fine fur or down underlying an animal's outer fur.

undergarment ▪ n. an article of underclothing.

undergird ▪ v. **1** secure or fasten from the underside, especially by a rope or chain passed underneath. **2** formal provide support or a firm basis for.

underglaze ▪ n. colour or decoration applied to pottery before the glaze is applied.

undergo ▪ v. (**-goes**; past **-went**; past part. **-gone**) experience or be subjected to (something unpleasant or arduous).
– ORIGIN Old English *undergān* 'undermine' (see UNDER-, GO[1]).

undergrad ▪ n. informal an undergraduate.

undergraduate ▪ n. a student at a university who has not yet taken a first degree.

underground ▪ adj. & adv. **1** beneath the surface of the ground. **2** in secrecy or hiding, especially as a result of carrying out subversive political activities. **3** seeking to explore alternative forms of lifestyle or artistic expression; radical and experimental. ▪ n. **1** Brit. an underground railway, especially the one in London. **2** a group or movement organized secretly to work against an existing regime. **3** a group or movement seeking to explore alternative forms of lifestyle or artistic expression.

undergrowth ▪ n. a dense growth of shrubs and other plants, especially under trees.

underhand (also **underhanded**) ▪ adj. **1** acting or done in a secret or dishonest way. **2** underarm.
– DERIVATIVES **underhandedly** adv.

underinsured ▪ adj. having inadequate insurance cover.
– DERIVATIVES **underinsurance** n.

underlay[1] ▪ v. (past and past part. **-laid**) place something under (something else), especially to support or raise it. ▪ n. material laid under a carpet for protection or support.

underlay[2] past tense of UNDERLIE.

underlever ▪ n. a lever behind the trigger guard on a rifle.

underlie ▪ v. (**-lying**; past **-lay**; past part. **-lain**) **1** lie or be situated under. **2** [often as adj. **underlying**] be the cause or basis of.

underline ▪ v. **1** draw a line under (a word or phrase) to give emphasis or indicate special type. **2** emphasize. ▪ n. a line drawn under a word or phrase.

underling ▪ n. chiefly derogatory a subordinate.

underlip ▪ n. the lower lip of a person or animal.

underlying present participle of UNDERLIE.

underman ▪ v. (**-manned**, **-manning**) fail to provide with enough workers or crew.

undermanager ▪ n. a manager who is subordinate to another manager.

undermentioned ▪ adj. mentioned at a later place in a book or document.

undermine ▪ v. **1** erode the base or foundation of (a rock formation). ▸ dig or excavate beneath (a building or fortification) so as to make it collapse. **2** damage or weaken, especially gradually or insidiously.
– DERIVATIVES **underminer** n.

underneath ▪ prep. & adv. **1** situated directly below. **2** so as to be concealed by. ▸ partly or wholly concealed by (a garment). ▪ n. the part or side facing towards the ground; the underside.
– ORIGIN Old English.

undernourished ▪ adj. having insufficient food for good health and condition.
– DERIVATIVES **undernourishment** n.

underpaid 1296

underpaid past and past participle of UNDERPAY.

underpants ■ pl. n. an undergarment, especially for men or boys, covering the lower part of the body and having two holes for the legs.

underpart ■ n. a lower part or portion. ▶ (**underparts**) the underside of an animal's body.

underpass ■ n. a road or pedestrian tunnel passing under another road or a railway.

underpay ■ v. (past and past part. **-paid**) pay too little to (someone) or for (something).
– DERIVATIVES **underpayment** n.

underperform ■ v. perform less well than expected.
– DERIVATIVES **underperformance** n.

underpin ■ v. (**-pinned**, **-pinning**) 1 support (a building or other structure) from below by laying a solid foundation or substituting stronger for weaker materials. 2 support, justify, or form the basis for.
– DERIVATIVES **underpinning** n.

underplant ■ v. plant or cultivate the ground around (a tall plant) with smaller plants.

underplay ■ v. 1 perform (a role or part) in a restrained way. 2 represent (something) as being less important than it really is.

underpopulated ■ adj. having an insufficient or very small population.
– DERIVATIVES **underpopulation** n.

underpowered ■ adj. lacking sufficient mechanical, electrical, or other power.

underprice ■ v. sell or offer at too low a price.

underprivileged ■ adj. not enjoying the same rights or standard of living as the majority of the population.

underproduce ■ v. 1 produce less of (a commodity) than is wanted or needed. 2 [often as adj. **underproduced**] record or produce (a song or film) in such a basic way that it appears rough or unfinished.
– DERIVATIVES **underproduction** n.

underrate ■ v. [often as adj. **underrated**] underestimate the extent, value, or importance of.

under-represent ■ v. provide with insufficient or inadequate representation.
– DERIVATIVES **under-representation** n.

under-resourced ■ adj. provided with insufficient resources.
– DERIVATIVES **under-resourcing** n.

undersaturated ■ adj. technical falling short of being saturated with a particular constituent.
– DERIVATIVES **undersaturation** n.

underscore ■ v. & n. another term for UNDERLINE.

undersea ■ adj. relating to or situated below the sea or the surface of the sea.

underseal ■ v. coat (the underpart of a motor vehicle) with waterproof material as protection against rust. ■ n. waterproof coating used in this way.

undersecretary ■ n. (pl. **-ies**) 1 (in the UK) a junior minister or senior civil servant. 2 (in the US) the principal assistant to a member of the cabinet.

undersell ■ v. (past and past part. **-sold**) 1 sell something at a lower price than (a competitor). 2 promote or rate (something) insufficiently.

underserved ■ adj. inadequately provided with a service or facility: *a medically underserved community*.

undersexed ■ adj. having unusually weak sexual desires.

undershirt ■ n. chiefly N. Amer. an undergarment worn under a shirt; a vest.

undershoot ■ v. (past and past part. **-shot**) 1 (of an aircraft) land short of (the runway). 2 fall short of (a point or target).

undershorts ■ pl. n. chiefly N. Amer. underpants.

undershot past and past participle of UNDERSHOOT. ■ adj. denoting a lower jaw which projects beyond the upper jaw.

underside ■ n. the bottom or lower side or surface of something.

undersigned formal ■ adj. appending one's signature to the document in question. ■ n. (**the undersigned**) the signatory or co-signatories to the document in question.

undersized (also **undersize**) ■ adj. of less than the usual size.

underskirt ■ n. a skirt worn under another; a petticoat.

underslung ■ adj. suspended from the underside of something.

undersold past and past participle of UNDERSELL.

undersow ■ v. (past part. **-sown**) sow (a later-growing crop) on land already seeded with another crop.

underspend ■ v. (past and past part. **-spent**) spend too little or less than has been planned. ■ n. an act of underspending.

understaff ■ v. provide (an organization) with too few members of staff to operate effectively.
– DERIVATIVES **understaffing** n.

understand ■ v. (past and past part. **-stood**) 1 perceive the intended meaning of (words, a language, or a speaker). ▶ perceive the significance, explanation, or cause of. ▶ interpret or view in a particular way. 2 infer from information received: *I understand you're at art school*. ▶ supply (a missing word, phrase, or idea) mentally. ▶ assume to be the case; take for granted.
– DERIVATIVES **understander** n.
– ORIGIN Old English *understandan* (see UNDER-, STAND).

understandable ■ adj. 1 able to be understood. 2 to be expected; natural, reasonable, or forgivable.
– DERIVATIVES **understandability** n. **understandably** adv.

understanding ■ n. 1 the ability to understand something; comprehension. ▶ the power of abstract thought; intellect. ▶ an individual's perception or judgement of a situation. 2 sympathetic awareness or tolerance. 3 an informal or unspoken agreement or arrangement. ■ adj. sympathetically aware of other people's feelings; tolerant and forgiving.
– DERIVATIVES **understandingly** adv.

understate ■ v. describe or represent (something) as being smaller or less significant than it really is.
– DERIVATIVES **understatement** n. **understater** n.

understated ■ adj. presented or expressed in a subtle and effective way.
– DERIVATIVES **understatedly** adv.

understeer ■ v. (of a motor vehicle) have a tendency to turn less sharply than is intended. ■ n. the tendency of a vehicle to turn in such a way.

understood past and past participle of UNDERSTAND.

understorey ■ n. (pl. **-eys**) Ecology a layer of vegetation beneath the main canopy of a forest.

understudy ■ n. (pl. **-ies**) an actor who learns another's role in order to be able to act in their absence. ■ v. (**-ies**, **-ied**) study (a role or actor) as an understudy.

undersubscribed ■ adj. 1 (of a course or event) having more places available than applications. 2 (of a share issue) having fewer applications for shares than there are shares available.

underswell ■ n. an undercurrent.

undertake ■ v. (past **-took**; past part. **-taken**) 1 commit oneself to and begin (an enterprise or responsibility); take on. 2 formally guarantee, pledge, or promise.

undertaker ■ n. a person whose business is preparing dead bodies for burial or cremation and making arrangements for funerals.

undertaking ■ n. 1 a formal pledge or promise to do something. ▶ a task that is taken on; an enterprise. 2 a company or business. 3 the management of funerals as a profession.

underthings ■ pl. n. underclothes.

undertone ■ n. 1 a subdued or muted tone of sound or colour. 2 an underlying quality or feeling.

undertook past participle of UNDERTAKE.

undertow ■ n. another term for UNDERCURRENT.

VOWELS **a** cat **ɑː** arm **ɛ** bed **ɛː** hair **ə** ago **əː** her **ɪ** sit **i** cosy **iː** see **ɒ** hot **ɔː** saw **ʌ** run

undertrick ■ n. Bridge a trick by which the declarer falls short of his or her contract.

underuse ■ v. /ˌʌndəˈjuːz/ [usu. as adj. **underused**] use (something) below the optimum level. ■ n. /ˌʌndəˈjuːs/ insufficient use.

underutilize (also **-ise**) ■ v. underuse.
– DERIVATIVES **underutilization** (also **-isation**) n.

undervalue ■ v. (**-values**, **-valued**, **-valuing**) [often as adj. **undervalued**] 1 rate insufficiently highly; fail to appreciate. 2 underestimate the financial value of.
– DERIVATIVES **undervaluation** n.

undervest ■ n. a vest worn as an undergarment.

underwater ■ adj. & adv. situated or occurring beneath the surface of the water.

underwear ■ n. clothing worn under other clothes next to the skin.

underweight ■ adj. 1 below a weight considered normal or desirable. 2 Finance having insufficient investment in a particular area. ■ v. apply too little weight to. ■ n. insufficient weight.

underwent past participle of UNDERGO.

underwhelm ■ v. humorous fail to impress or make a positive impact on.
– ORIGIN 1950s: suggested by OVERWHELM.

underwing ■ n. 1 the hindwing of an insect, especially when it is normally hidden by a forewing. 2 the underside of a bird's wing.

underwire ■ n. a semicircular wire support stitched under each cup of a bra.
– DERIVATIVES **underwired** adj.

underwood ■ n. small trees and shrubs growing beneath taller timber trees.

underwork ■ v. [usu. as adj. **underworked**] impose too little work on (someone).

underworld ■ n. 1 the world of criminals or of organized crime. 2 the mythical abode of the dead, imagined as being under the earth.

underwrite ■ v. (past **-wrote**; past part. **-written**) 1 sign and accept liability under (an insurance policy). ▶ accept (a liability or risk) in this way. 2 undertake to finance or otherwise support or guarantee. 3 engage to buy all the unsold shares in (an issue of new shares).
– DERIVATIVES **underwriter** n.

undescended ■ adj. Medicine (of a testicle) remaining in the abdomen instead of descending normally into the scrotum.

undeserved ■ adj. not warranted, merited, or earned.
– DERIVATIVES **undeservedly** adv.

undeserving ■ adj. not deserving or worthy of something positive, especially help or praise.
– DERIVATIVES **undeservingly** adv.

undesigned ■ adj. unintended.
– DERIVATIVES **undesignedly** adv.

undesirable ■ adj. not wanted or desirable because harmful, objectionable, or unpleasant. ■ n. a person considered to be objectionable in some way.
– DERIVATIVES **undesirability** n. **undesirableness** n. **undesirably** adv.

undesired ■ adj. (especially of an act or consequence) not wanted or desired.

undesirous ■ adj. (usu. **undesirous of**) formal not wanting or wishing something.

undetectable ■ adj. not able to be detected.
– DERIVATIVES **undetectability** n. **undetectably** adv.

undetected ■ adj. not detected or discovered.

undetermined ■ adj. not authoritatively decided or settled.

undeterred ■ adj. persevering despite setbacks.

undeveloped ■ adj. not having developed or been developed.

undeviating ■ adj. showing no deviation; constant and steady.
– DERIVATIVES **undeviatingly** adv.

undiagnosed ■ adj. not diagnosed or having been subject to diagnosis.

1297

undid past of UNDO.

undies ■ pl. n. informal articles of underwear.

undifferenced ■ adj. Heraldry (of arms) not made distinct by a mark of difference.

undifferentiated ■ adj. not different or differentiated.

undigested ■ adj. 1 (of food) not digested. 2 not having been properly understood or assimilated.

undignified ■ adj. appearing foolish and unseemly; lacking in dignity.

undiluted ■ adj. 1 (of a liquid) not diluted. 2 not moderated or weakened in any way.

undiminished ■ adj. not diminished, reduced, or lessened.

undiplomatic ■ adj. insensitive and tactless.
– DERIVATIVES **undiplomatically** adv.

undirected ■ adj. without a coherent plan or purpose.

undiscerning ■ adj. lacking judgement, insight, or taste.

undischarged ■ adj. (especially of a bankrupt) not discharged.

undisciplined ■ adj. lacking in discipline; uncontrolled in behaviour or manner.

undisclosed ■ adj. not revealed or made known.

undiscovered ■ adj. not discovered.

undiscriminating ■ adj. lacking good judgement or taste.

undiscussed ■ adj. not discussed.

undisguised ■ adj. (of a feeling) not disguised or concealed; open.
– DERIVATIVES **undisguisedly** adv.

undismayed ■ adj. not dismayed or discouraged by a setback.

undisputed ■ adj. not disputed or called in question; accepted.

undistinguishable ■ adj. indistinguishable.

undistinguished ■ adj. lacking distinction; unexceptional.

undistorted ■ adj. not distorted.

undistributed ■ adj. not distributed.

undisturbed ■ adj. not disturbed.

undivided ■ adj. 1 not divided, separated, or broken into parts. 2 devoted completely to one object: *my undivided attention.*

undo ■ v. (**undoes**; past **undid**; past part. **undone**) 1 unfasten, untie, or loosen. 2 cancel or reverse the effects or results of (a previous action or measure). 3 formal cause the downfall or ruin of.

undocumented ■ adj. 1 not recorded or proved by documents. 2 N. Amer. not having the appropriate legal document or licence.

undoing ■ n. a person's ruin or downfall. ▶ the cause of such ruin or downfall: *complacency was to be their undoing.*

undomesticated ■ adj. 1 (of an animal) not tamed. 2 not accustomed to domestic tasks.

undone ■ adj. 1 not tied or fastened. 2 not done or finished. 3 formal or humorous ruined by a disastrous setback.

undoubted ■ adj. not questioned or doubted by anyone.
– DERIVATIVES **undoubtable** adj. **undoubtably** adv. **undoubtedly** adv.

UNDP ■ abbrev. United Nations Development Programme.

undrained ■ adj. not emptied of water; not drained.

undramatic ■ adj. 1 lacking the qualities expected in drama. 2 unexciting.

undraped ■ adj. not covered with cloth or drapery. ▶ (of a model or subject in art) naked.

undreamed /ʌnˈdriːmd, -ˈdrɛmt/ (also **undreamt** /ʌnˈdrɛmt/) ■ adj. (**undreamed of**) not previously thought to be possible: *undreamed-of success.*

undress

undress ■ v. (also **get undressed**) take off one's clothes. ▸ take the clothes off (someone else). ■ n. **1** the state of being naked or only partially clothed. **2** Military ordinary clothing or uniform, as opposed to that worn on ceremonial occasions (full dress).

undressed ■ adj. **1** wearing no clothes; naked. **2** not treated, processed, or prepared for use. **3** (of food) not having a dressing.

undrinkable ■ adj. not fit to be drunk because of impurity or poor quality.

UNDRO ■ abbrev. United Nations Disaster Relief Office.

undue ■ adj. unwarranted or inappropriate because excessive or disproportionate.
– DERIVATIVES **unduly** adv.

undue influence ■ n. Law influence by which a person is induced to act otherwise than by their own free will or without adequate attention to the consequences.

undulant /'ʌndjul(ə)nt/ ■ adj. undulating.

undulant fever ■ n. brucellosis in humans.
– ORIGIN C19: so named because of the intermittent fever associated with the disease.

undulate /'ʌndjuleɪt/ ■ v. move with a smooth wave-like motion. ▸ [usu. as adj. **undulating**] have a wavy form or outline.
– DERIVATIVES **undulation** n. **undulatory** adj.
– ORIGIN C17: from late Latin *undulatus*, from Latin *unda* 'a wave'.

undutiful ■ adj. not respectful or obedient.
– DERIVATIVES **undutifully** adv. **undutifulness** n.

undy /'ʌndi/ (also **undee**) ■ adj. Heraldry another term for WAVY.

undyed ■ adj. (of fabric) not dyed; of its natural colour.

undying ■ adj. (especially of an emotion) lasting forever.
– DERIVATIVES **undyingly** adv.

unearned ■ adj. not earned or deserved.

unearned income ■ n. income from investments rather than from work.

unearned increment ■ n. an increase in the value of land or property without labour or expenditure on the part of the owner.

unearth ■ v. find in the ground by digging. ▸ discover by investigation or searching.

unearthly ■ adj. **1** unnatural or mysterious, especially in a disturbing way. **2** informal unreasonably early or inconvenient: *an unearthly hour*.
– DERIVATIVES **unearthliness** n.

unease ■ n. anxiety or discontent.

uneasy ■ adj. (**-ier**, **-iest**) causing or feeling anxiety; troubled or uncomfortable.
– DERIVATIVES **uneasily** adv. **uneasiness** n.

uneatable ■ adj. not fit to be eaten.

uneaten ■ adj. not eaten.

uneconomic ■ adj. not profitable or making efficient use of resources.

uneconomical ■ adj. wasteful of money or other resources; not economical.
– DERIVATIVES **uneconomically** adv.

unedifying ■ adj. distasteful; unpleasant: *the unedifying sight of two squabbling politicians*.
– DERIVATIVES **unedifyingly** adv.

unedited ■ adj. (of material for publication or broadcasting) not edited.

uneducated ■ adj. poorly educated.
– DERIVATIVES **uneducable** adj.

unelectable ■ adj. very likely to be defeated at an election.

unelected ■ adj. (of an official) not elected.

unembarrassed ■ adj. not feeling or showing embarrassment.

unembellished ■ adj. not embellished or decorated.

unemotional ■ adj. not having or showing strong feelings.
– DERIVATIVES **unemotionally** adv.

unemphatic ■ adj. not emphatic.
– DERIVATIVES **unemphatically** adv.

unemployable ■ adj. not able or likely to get paid employment because of a lack of skills or qualifications.
– DERIVATIVES **unemployability** n.

unemployed ■ adj. **1** without a paid job but available to work. **2** (of a thing) not in use.

unemployment ■ n. the state of being unemployed. ▸ the number or proportion of unemployed people.

unemployment benefit ■ n. payment made by the state or a trade union to an unemployed person.

unenclosed ■ adj. (especially of land) not enclosed.

unencumbered ■ adj. not having any burden or impediment. ▸ free of debt or other financial liability.

unending ■ adj. having or seeming to have no end. ▸ countless or continual: *unending demands*.
– DERIVATIVES **unendingly** adv. **unendingness** n.

unendowed ■ adj. not endowed, especially by donated funds.

unendurable ■ adj. not able to be tolerated or endured.
– DERIVATIVES **unendurably** adv.

unenforceable ■ adj. (especially of an obligation or law) impossible to enforce.

un-English ■ adj. not characteristic of English people or the English language.

unenlightened ■ adj. not enlightened in outlook.
– DERIVATIVES **unenlightening** adj. **unenlightenment** n.

unentangle ■ v. another term for DISENTANGLE.

unenterprising ■ adj. lacking initiative or entrepreneurial ability.

unenthusiastic ■ adj. not having or showing enthusiasm.
– DERIVATIVES **unenthusiastically** adv.

unenviable ■ adj. difficult, undesirable, or unpleasant.
– DERIVATIVES **unenviably** adv. **unenvied** adj.

UNEP ■ abbrev. United Nations Environment Programme.

unequal ■ adj. **1** not equal in quantity, size, or value. ▸ not fair, evenly balanced, or having equal advantage. **2** (usu. **unequal to**) not having the ability or resources to meet a challenge.
– DERIVATIVES **unequally** adv.

unequalled (US **unequaled**) ■ adj. superior to all others in performance or extent.

unequipped ■ adj. not equipped with the necessary items or skills.

unequivocal ■ adj. leaving no doubt; unambiguous.
– DERIVATIVES **unequivocally** adv. **unequivocalness** n.

unerring ■ adj. always right or accurate.
– DERIVATIVES **unerringly** adv. **unerringness** n.

unescapable ■ adj. unable to be avoided or denied.

UNESCO /juːˈnɛskəʊ/ ■ abbrev. United Nations Educational, Scientific, and Cultural Organization.

unescorted ■ adj. not escorted, especially for protection or security.

unessential ■ adj. inessential.

unethical ■ adj. not morally correct.
– DERIVATIVES **unethically** adv.

uneven ■ adj. **1** not level or smooth. **2** not regular, consistent, or equal. ▸ (of a contest) not equally balanced.
– DERIVATIVES **unevenly** adv. **unevenness** n.

uneven bars ■ pl. n. another term for ASYMMETRIC BARS.

uneventful ■ adj. not marked by interesting or exciting events.
– DERIVATIVES **uneventfully** adv. **uneventfulness** n.

unexamined ■ adj. not investigated or examined.

unexampled ■ adj. formal having no precedent or parallel.

unexceptionable ■ adj. not open to objection, but not particularly new or exciting.
– DERIVATIVES **unexceptionableness** n. **unexceptionably** adv.

unexceptional ■ adj. not out of the ordinary; usual.
– DERIVATIVES **unexceptionally** adv.

unexcitable ■ adj. not easily excited.
– DERIVATIVES **unexcitability** n.

unexciting ■ adj. not exciting; dull.

unexercised ■ adj. **1** not made use of or put into practice. **2** (of a person) not taking exercise; unfit.

unexpected ■ adj. not expected or regarded as likely to happen.
– DERIVATIVES **unexpectedly** adv. **unexpectedness** n.

unexpired ■ adj. (of an agreement or period of time) not yet having come to an end.

unexplained ■ adj. not made clear or accounted for.
– DERIVATIVES **unexplainable** adj. **unexplainably** adv.

unexploded ■ adj. (of a bomb or other explosive device) not having exploded.

unexploited ■ adj. (of resources) not used to maximum benefit.

unexplored ■ adj. not explored, investigated, or evaluated.

unexposed ■ adj. not exposed. ▸ (**unexposed to**) not introduced to or acquainted with.

unexpressed ■ adj. **1** (of a thought or feeling) not communicated or made known. **2** Genetics (of a gene) not appearing in a phenotype.

unexpurgated ■ adj. (of a text) complete and containing all the original material; not censored.

unfading ■ adj. not losing brightness, vitality, or strength.
– DERIVATIVES **unfadingly** adv.

unfailing ■ adj. **1** without error. **2** reliable or constant.
– DERIVATIVES **unfailingly** adv. **unfailingness** n.

unfair ■ adj. not based on or showing fairness; unjust. ▸ contrary to the rules of a game.
– DERIVATIVES **unfairly** adv. **unfairness** n.

unfaithful ■ adj. not faithful; disloyal. ▸ engaging in sexual relations with a person other than one's lover or spouse.
– DERIVATIVES **unfaithfully** adv. **unfaithfulness** n.

unfaltering ■ adj. not faltering; steady or resolute.
– DERIVATIVES **unfalteringly** adv.

unfamiliar ■ adj. **1** not known or recognized; uncharacteristic. **2** (**unfamiliar with**) not having knowledge or experience of.
– DERIVATIVES **unfamiliarity** n.

unfancied ■ adj. not considered likely to win.

unfashionable ■ adj. not fashionable or popular.
– DERIVATIVES **unfashionableness** n. **unfashionably** adv.

unfasten ■ v. open the fastening of; undo.

unfathomable ■ adj. **1** incapable of being fully explored or understood. **2** impossible to measure the depth or extent of.
– DERIVATIVES **unfathomableness** n. **unfathomably** adv. **unfathomed** adj.

unfavourable (US **unfavorable**) ■ adj. **1** expressing lack of approval or support. **2** adverse; inauspicious.
– DERIVATIVES **unfavourableness** n. **unfavourably** adv.

unfazed ■ adj. informal not disconcerted or perturbed.

unfeasible ■ adj. inconvenient or impractical.
– DERIVATIVES **unfeasibility** n. **unfeasibly** adv.

unfeeling ■ adj. **1** unsympathetic, harsh, or callous. **2** lacking physical sensation.
– DERIVATIVES **unfeelingly** adv. **unfeelingness** n.

unfeigned ■ adj. genuine; sincere.
– DERIVATIVES **unfeignedly** adv.

unfeminine ■ adj. lacking feminine qualities.
– DERIVATIVES **unfemininity** n.

unfenced ■ adj. not provided with fences.

unfermented ■ adj. not fermented.

unfertilized (also **-ised**) ■ adj. not fertilized.

unfetter ■ v. [usu. as adj. **unfettered**] release from restraint or inhibition.

unfilled ■ adj. not filled; vacant or empty.

unfiltered ■ adj. **1** not filtered. **2** not provided with a filter.

unfinished ■ adj. not finished; incomplete. ▸ not having been given an attractive surface appearance in manufacture.

unfit ■ adj. **1** unsuitable or inadequate for something. **2** not in good physical condition, especially through lack of regular exercise. ■ v. (**unfitted**, **unfitting**) archaic make unsuitable; disqualify.
– DERIVATIVES **unfitly** adv. **unfitness** n.

unfitted ■ adj. **1** unfit for something. **2** (of furniture, linen, etc.) not fitted.

unfitting ■ adj. unsuitable or unbecoming.
– DERIVATIVES **unfittingly** adv.

unfixed ■ adj. **1** unfastened; loose. **2** uncertain or variable.
– DERIVATIVES **unfix** v.

unflagging ■ adj. tireless; persistent.
– DERIVATIVES **unflaggingly** adv.

unflappable ■ adj. informal calm in a crisis.
– DERIVATIVES **unflappability** n. **unflappably** adv.

unflattering ■ adj. not flattering.
– DERIVATIVES **unflatteringly** adv.

unfledged ■ adj. not yet fledged. ▸ inexperienced; youthful.

unflinching ■ adj. not afraid or hesitant.
– DERIVATIVES **unflinchingly** adv.

unfocused (also **unfocussed**) ■ adj. **1** not focused; out of focus. **2** without a specific aim or direction.

unfold ■ v. **1** open or spread out from a folded position. **2** make or become revealed or disclosed.

unforced ■ adj. **1** produced naturally and without effort. **2** not compelled.
– DERIVATIVES **unforcedly** adv.

unforeseen ■ adj. not anticipated or predicted.
– DERIVATIVES **unforeseeable** adj.

unforgettable ■ adj. highly memorable.
– DERIVATIVES **unforgettably** adv.

unforgivable ■ adj. so bad as to be unable to be forgiven or excused.
– DERIVATIVES **unforgivably** adv.

unforgiven ■ adj. not forgiven.

unforgiving ■ adj. **1** not willing to forgive or excuse faults. **2** (of conditions) harsh; hostile.
– DERIVATIVES **unforgivingly** adv. **unforgivingness** n.

unformed ■ adj. **1** without a definite form. **2** not fully developed.

unforthcoming ■ adj. **1** not willing to divulge information. **2** not available when needed.

unfortunate ■ adj. **1** having bad fortune; unlucky. ▸ inauspicious. **2** regrettable or inappropriate. ■ n. a person who suffers bad fortune.
– DERIVATIVES **unfortunately** adv.

unfounded ■ adj. having no foundation or basis in fact.
– DERIVATIVES **unfoundedly** adv. **unfoundedness** n.

UNFPA ■ abbrev. United Nations Fund for Population Activities.

unfree ■ adj. deprived or devoid of liberty.
– DERIVATIVES **unfreedom** n.

unfreeze ■ v. (past **unfroze**; past part. **unfrozen**) **1** thaw. **2** remove restrictions on the use of (an asset).

unfrequented ■ adj. visited only rarely.

unfriended ■ adj. poetic/literary without friends.

unfriendly ■ adj. (**-ier**, **-iest**) not friendly.
– DERIVATIVES **unfriendliness** n.

unfrock ■ v. another term for DEFROCK.

unfroze past of UNFREEZE.

unfrozen past participle of UNFREEZE.

unfulfilled ■ adj. not fulfilled.
– DERIVATIVES **unfulfillable** adj. **unfulfilling** adj.

unfunded ■ adj. **1** not receiving funds; not having a fund. **2** (of a debt) repayable on demand; not funded.

unfunny ■ adj. (-ier, -iest) (especially of something intended to be funny) not amusing.
– DERIVATIVES **unfunnily** adv. **unfunniness** n.

unfurl ■ v. make or become spread out from a furled state.

unfurnished ■ adj. without furniture.

ungainly ■ adj. clumsy; awkward.
– DERIVATIVES **ungainliness** n.
– ORIGIN C17: from UN-¹ + obsolete *gainly* 'graceful', from Old Norse *gegn* 'straight'.

ungeared ■ adj. **1** not having gears. **2** (of a company) having no debt.

ungenerous ■ adj. not generous; mean.
– DERIVATIVES **ungenerously** adv. **ungenerousness** n.

ungentle ■ adj. not gentle; rough.
– DERIVATIVES **ungentleness** n. **ungently** adv.

ungentlemanly ■ adj. not appropriate to or behaving like a gentleman.
– DERIVATIVES **ungentlemanliness** n.

unget-at-able ■ adj. informal inaccessible.

ungiving ■ adj. **1** cold or stubborn towards other people. **2** not pliable; stiff.

unglazed ■ adj. not glazed.

unglued ■ adj. **1** not or no longer stuck. **2** informal confused and emotionally strained.

ungodly ■ adj. **1** irreligious or immoral. **2** informal unreasonably early or inconvenient.
– DERIVATIVES **ungodliness** n.

ungovernable ■ adj. impossible to control or govern.
– DERIVATIVES **ungovernability** n. **ungovernably** adv.

ungraceful ■ adj. lacking in grace; clumsy.
– DERIVATIVES **ungracefully** adv. **ungracefulness** n.

ungracious ■ adj. not gracious.
– DERIVATIVES **ungraciously** adv. **ungraciousness** n.

ungrammatical ■ adj. not conforming to grammatical rules.
– DERIVATIVES **ungrammaticality** n. (pl. **-ies**). **ungrammatically** adv. **ungrammaticalness** n.

ungrateful ■ adj. not feeling or showing gratitude.
– DERIVATIVES **ungratefully** adv. **ungratefulness** n.

ungrounded ■ adj. **1** groundless. **2** not electrically earthed. **3** (**ungrounded in**) not properly instructed or proficient in.

unguarded ■ adj. **1** without protection or a guard. **2** not well considered; careless.
– DERIVATIVES **unguardedly** adv. **unguardedness** n.

unguent /'ʌŋgwənt/ ■ n. a soft greasy or viscous substance used as ointment or for lubrication.
– ORIGIN Middle English: from Latin *unguentum*, from *unguere* 'anoint'.

ungulate /'ʌŋgjʊlət, -leɪt/ ■ n. Zoology a hoofed mammal. See ARTIODACTYLA, PERISSODACTYLA.
– ORIGIN C19: from late Latin *ungulatus*, from Latin *ungula* 'hoof'.

unhand ■ v. archaic or humorous release from one's grasp.

unhappy ■ adj. (-ier, -iest) not happy. ▶ unfortunate.
– DERIVATIVES **unhappily** adv. **unhappiness** n.

unharmed ■ adj. not harmed; uninjured.

unharness ■ v. remove a harness from.

unhatched ■ adj. not yet hatched.

UNHCR ■ abbrev. United Nations High Commissioner for Refugees.

unhealthful ■ adj. harmful to health.
– DERIVATIVES **unhealthfulness** n.

unhealthy ■ adj. (-ier, -iest) in poor health. ▶ not conducive to health.
– DERIVATIVES **unhealthily** adv. **unhealthiness** n.

unheard ■ adj. **1** not heard or listened to. **2** (**unheard of**) previously unknown.

unheated ■ adj. not heated.

unhedged ■ adj. **1** not bounded by a hedge. **2** not protected against loss by other dealings.

unheeded ■ adj. heard or noticed but disregarded.

unheeding ■ adj. not paying attention.
– DERIVATIVES **unheedingly** adv.

unhelpful ■ adj. not helpful.
– DERIVATIVES **unhelpfully** adv. **unhelpfulness** n.

unheralded ■ adj. not previously announced, expected, or recognized.

unhesitating ■ adj. without doubt or hesitation.
– DERIVATIVES **unhesitatingly** adv.

unhinge ■ v. **1** [usu. as adj. **unhinged**] make mentally unbalanced. ▶ throw into disorder. **2** take (a door) off its hinges.

unhistorical ■ adj. not in accordance with history or historical analysis.
– DERIVATIVES **unhistoric** adj. **unhistorically** adv.

unhitch ■ v. unhook or unfasten.

unholy ■ adj. (-ier, -iest) sinful; wicked. ▶ unnatural and potentially harmful: *an unholy alliance.* ▶ informal dreadful (used for emphasis).
– DERIVATIVES **unholiness** n.

unhook ■ v. unfasten or detach (something held by a hook).

unhoped ■ adj. (**unhoped for**) exceeding hope or expectation.

unhorse ■ v. drag or cause to fall from a horse.

unhoused ■ adj. having no accommodation or shelter.

unhung ■ adj. not hanging or hung.

unhurried ■ adj. moving, acting, or taking place without haste or urgency.
– DERIVATIVES **unhurriedly** adv.

unhurt ■ adj. not hurt or harmed.

unhygienic ■ adj. not hygienic.
– DERIVATIVES **unhygienically** adv.

unhyphenated ■ adj. not written with a hyphen.

uni ■ n. (pl. **unis**) informal university.

uni- ■ comb. form one; having or consisting of one: *unicycle.*
– ORIGIN from Latin *unus* 'one'.

Uniate /'juːnɪeɪt/ (also **Uniat**) ■ adj. of or denoting a Christian community in eastern Europe or the Near East acknowledging papal supremacy but with its own liturgy.
– ORIGIN C19: from Russian *uniat*, from *uniya*, from Latin *unio* (see UNION).

uniaxial /juːnɪ'aksɪəl/ ■ adj. having or relating to a single axis.
– DERIVATIVES **uniaxially** adv.

unicameral /juːnɪ'kam(ə)r(ə)l/ ■ adj. (of a legislative body) having a single legislative chamber.
– ORIGIN C19: from UNI- + Latin *camera* 'chamber'.

UNICEF /'juːnɪsɛf/ ■ abbrev. United Nations Children's (originally International Children's Emergency) Fund.

unicellular ■ adj. Biology consisting of a single cell.

unicity /juː'nɪsɪti/ ■ n. chiefly S. African a division of local government responsible for the centralized administration of a major city and its surrounding municipalities.

Unicode ■ n. Computing an international encoding standard for use with different languages and scripts, by which each letter, digit, or symbol is assigned a unique numeric value that applies across different platforms and programs.

unicorn ■ n. a mythical animal represented as a horse with a single straight horn projecting from its forehead.
– ORIGIN Middle English: from Latin *unicornis*, from *uni-* 'single' + *cornu* 'horn', translating Greek *monokerōs*.

unicorn fish ■ n. a fish with a horn-like projection on the head. [Genus *Naso* (Indo-Pacific).]

unicycle ■ n. a cycle with a single wheel, chiefly used by acrobats.
– DERIVATIVES **unicyclist** n.

unidentifiable ■ adj. unable to be identified.

unidentified ■ adj. not recognized or identified.

unidimensional ■ adj. having one dimension.

unidiomatic ▪ adj. not using or containing expressions natural to a native speaker of a language.

unidirectional ▪ adj. moving or operating in a single direction.
– DERIVATIVES **unidirectionality** n. **unidirectionally** adv.

UNIDO /juːˈniːdəʊ/ ▪ abbrev. United Nations Industrial Development Organization.

unification ▪ n. the process of being united.
– DERIVATIVES **unificatory** adj.

Unification Church ▪ n. an evangelical religious and political organization founded in 1954 in Korea by Sun Myung Moon.

unified field theory ▪ n. Physics a theory that describes two or more of the four interactions (electromagnetic, gravitational, weak, and strong) previously described by separate theories.

uniflow ▪ adj. involving flow in one direction, especially of steam or waste gases in an engine's cylinder.

uniform ▪ adj. not varying; the same in all cases and at all times. ▪ n. **1** the distinctive clothing worn by members of the same organization or body or by children attending certain schools. ▸ informal, chiefly N. Amer. a police officer wearing a uniform. **2** a code word representing the letter U, used in radio communication.
– DERIVATIVES **uniformed** adj. **uniformity** n. **uniformly** adv.
– ORIGIN C16: from French *uniforme* or Latin *uniformis* (see UNI-, FORM).

uniformitarianism ▪ n. Geology the theory that changes in the earth's crust during geological history have resulted from the action of continuous and uniform processes. Often contrasted with **CATASTROPHISM**.
– DERIVATIVES **uniformitarian** adj. & n.

unify /ˈjuːnɪfaɪ/ ▪ v. (-ies, -ied) make or become united or uniform.
– DERIVATIVES **unifier** n.
– ORIGIN C16: from French *unifier* or late Latin *unificare*.

unilateral ▪ adj. **1** performed by or affecting only one person, group, etc. **2** relating to or affecting only one side of an organ, the body, etc.
– DERIVATIVES **unilateralism** n. **unilateralist** n. & adj. **unilaterally** adv.

unilingual ▪ adj. another term for **MONOLINGUAL**.
– DERIVATIVES **unilingualism** n.

unilocular /juːnɪˈlɒkjʊlə/ ▪ adj. Botany & Zoology having only one loculus or cavity; single-chambered.

unimaginable ▪ adj. impossible to imagine or comprehend.
– DERIVATIVES **unimaginably** adv.

unimaginative ▪ adj. not using or displaying imagination; stolid and somewhat dull.
– DERIVATIVES **unimaginatively** adv. **unimaginativeness** n.

unimodal ▪ adj. having or involving one mode.

unimolecular ▪ adj. Chemistry consisting of or involving a single molecule.

unimpaired ▪ adj. not weakened or damaged.

unimpeachable ▪ adj. beyond reproach.
– DERIVATIVES **unimpeachably** adv.

unimpeded ▪ adj. not obstructed or hindered.

unimportant ▪ adj. lacking in importance.
– DERIVATIVES **unimportance** n.

unimpressed ▪ adj. not impressed.

unimpressive ▪ adj. not impressive.
– DERIVATIVES **unimpressively** adv. **unimpressiveness** n.

unimproved ▪ adj. not improved. ▸ (of land) not cleared or cultivated.

unincorporated ▪ adj. **1** not formed into a legal corporation. **2** not included as part of a whole.

uninflected ▪ adj. not varied by inflection.

uninfluenced ▪ adj. not influenced.

uninformative ▪ adj. not providing useful or interesting information.

uninformed ▪ adj. lacking awareness or understanding of the facts.

uninhabitable ▪ adj. unsuitable for living in.

uninhabited ▪ adj. without inhabitants.

uninhibited ▪ adj. expressing oneself or acting without restraint.
– DERIVATIVES **uninhibitedly** adv. **uninhibitedness** n.

uninitiated ▪ adj. without special knowledge or experience.

uninjured ▪ adj. not harmed or damaged.

uninspired ▪ adj. **1** unimaginative; dull. **2** not filled with excitement.

uninspiring ▪ adj. not producing excitement or interest.
– DERIVATIVES **uninspiringly** adv.

uninstall ▪ v. remove (an application or file) from a computer.
– DERIVATIVES **uninstaller** n.

uninsurable ▪ adj. not eligible for insurance cover.

uninsured ▪ adj. not covered by insurance.

unintelligent ▪ adj. lacking intelligence.
– DERIVATIVES **unintelligence** n. **unintelligently** adv.

unintelligible ▪ adj. impossible to understand.
– DERIVATIVES **unintelligibility** n. **unintelligibly** adv.

unintended ▪ adj. not planned or meant.

unintentional ▪ adj. not done on purpose.
– DERIVATIVES **unintentionally** adv.

uninterested ▪ adj. not interested or concerned.
– DERIVATIVES **uninterestedly** adv.

USAGE
On the meaning and use of **uninterested** and **disinterested**, see **DISINTERESTED**.

uninteresting ▪ adj. not interesting.
– DERIVATIVES **uninterestingly** adv. **uninterestingness** n.

uninterrupted ▪ adj. **1** continuous. **2** unobstructed.
– DERIVATIVES **uninterruptedly** adv.

uninterruptible ▪ adj. not able to be interrupted.

uninventive ▪ adj. not inventive.
– DERIVATIVES **uninventively** adv. **uninventiveness** n.

uninvited ▪ adj. arriving or acting without invitation.

uninviting ▪ adj. not attractive; unpleasant.
– DERIVATIVES **uninvitingly** adv.

uninvolved ▪ adj. not involved.

union ▪ n. **1** the action or fact of uniting or being united. ▸ a state of harmony or agreement. ▸ marriage; sexual coupling. **2** a club, society, or association formed by people with a common interest or purpose, especially a trade union. **3** (also **Union**) a political unit consisting of a number of provinces or states with the same central government. ▸ (**the Union**) the northern states of the US in the American Civil War. **4** Mathematics the set that comprises all the elements (and no others) contained in any of two or more given sets. **5** a joint or coupling for pipes. **6** a fabric made of different yarns, typically cotton and linen or silk.
– ORIGIN Middle English: from Old French, or from eccles. Latin *unio(n-)* 'unity', from Latin *unus* 'one'.

union catalogue ▪ n. a list of the combined holdings of several libraries.

Union flag ▪ n. another term for **UNION JACK**.

unionist ▪ n. **1** a member of a trade union. **2** (**Unionist**) a person in Northern Ireland in favour of union with Great Britain.
– DERIVATIVES **unionism** n. **unionistic** adj.

unionize (also **-ise**) ▪ v. become or cause to become members of a trade union.
– DERIVATIVES **unionization** (also **-isation**) n.

unionized (also **-ised**) ▪ adj. belonging to, or having workers belonging to, a trade union.

Union Jack ▪ n. the national flag of the United Kingdom, formed by combining the flags of St George, St Andrew, and St Patrick.

unipolar ■ adj. having or relating to a single pole or extremity. ▸ (of psychiatric illness) characterized by either depressive or manic episodes but not both. ▸ (of a nerve cell) having one axon. ▸ Electronics (of a transistor or other device) using either negative or positive charge carriers but not both.
– DERIVATIVES **unipolarity** /-'larɪti/ n.

unique ■ adj. being the only one of its kind; unlike anything else. ▸ (**unique to**) belonging or connected to (one particular person, group, or place). ▸ remarkable or unusual.
– DERIVATIVES **uniquely** adv. **uniqueness** n.
– ORIGIN C17: from Latin *unicus*, from *unus* 'one'.

unisex ■ adj. designed to be suitable for both sexes.

unisexual ■ adj. of one sex. ▸ Botany having either stamens or pistils but not both.
– DERIVATIVES **unisexuality** n. **unisexually** adv.

unison /'juːnɪs(ə)n/ ■ n. **1** simultaneous action or utterance. **2** Music a coincidence in pitch of sounds or notes. ■ adj. performed in unison.
– DERIVATIVES **unisonous** adj.
– ORIGIN Middle English: from Old French, or from late Latin *unisonus*, from Latin *uni-* 'one' + *sonus* 'sound'.

unit ■ n. **1** an individual thing or person regarded as single and complete; each of the individual components making up a larger whole. ▸ a device or part with a specified function. ▸ a self-contained or distinct section of a building or group of buildings. ▸ a subdivision of a larger military grouping. ▸ a self-contained part of an educational course. ▸ a single manufactured item. **2** a standard quantity in terms of which other quantities may be expressed. **3** one as a number or quantity.
– DERIVATIVES **unitize** (also **-ise**) v.
– ORIGIN C16: from Latin *unus*, prob. suggested by DIGIT.

unitard /'juːnɪtɑːd/ ■ n. a tight-fitting one-piece garment covering the whole body.
– ORIGIN 1960s: from UNI- + LEOTARD.

Unitarian /juːnɪ'tɛːrɪən/ Christian Church ■ adj. of or relating to belief in the unity of God and rejection of the doctrine of the Trinity. ■ n. a Christian holding this belief.
– DERIVATIVES **Unitarianism** n.
– ORIGIN C17: from modern Latin *unitarius*, from Latin *unitas* 'unity'.

unitary /'juːnɪt(ə)ri/ ■ adj. **1** single; uniform. ▸ of or denoting a system of government or organization in which the powers of constituent parts are vested in a central body. **2** of or relating to a unit or units.
– DERIVATIVES **unitarily** adv. **unitarist** n. **unitarity** /-'tarɪti/ n.

unit cell ■ n. Crystallography the smallest group of atoms from which an entire crystal can be built up by repetition.

unite ■ v. come or bring together for a common purpose or to form a whole.
– DERIVATIVES **united** adj. **unitedly** adv. **unitive** adj.
– ORIGIN Middle English: from Latin *unit-*, *unire* 'join together', from *unus* 'one'.

unitholder ■ n. a person with an investment in a unit trust.

unit trust ■ n. a trust managing a portfolio of stock exchange securities, in which small investors can buy units.

unity ■ n. (pl. **-ies**) **1** the state of being united or forming a whole. ▸ a thing forming a complex whole. **2** Mathematics the number one.
– ORIGIN Middle English: from Old French *unite*, from Latin *unitas*, from *unus* 'one'.

Univ. ■ abbrev. University.

univalent ■ adj. **1** /juː'veɪl(ə)nt/ Biology (of a chromosome) remaining unpaired during meiosis. **2** /juː'nɪ'veɪl(ə)nt/ Chemistry another term for MONOVALENT. ■ n. /juː'nɪvəl(ə)nt/ Biology a univalent chromosome.

univalve Zoology ■ adj. having one valve or shell. ■ n. a univalve mollusc; a gastropod.

universal ■ adj. of, affecting, or done by all people or things in the world or in a particular group; applicable to all cases. ▸ Logic denoting a proposition in which something is asserted of all of a class. Contrasted with PARTICULAR. ■ n. **1** Logic a universal proposition. **2** Philosophy a term or concept of general application. ▸ a nature or essence signified by a general term.
– DERIVATIVES **universality** n. **universally** adv.
– ORIGIN Middle English: from Old French, or from Latin *universalis*, from *universus* (see UNIVERSE).

universal donor ■ n. a person of blood group O, who can in theory donate blood to recipients of any ABO blood group.

universal indicator ■ n. Chemistry a mixture of dyes that changes colour gradually over a range of pH and is used to test for acids and alkalis.

universalism ■ n. **1** Christian Church the belief that all humankind will eventually be saved. **2** a concern for everyone without regard to national or sectional allegiances.
– DERIVATIVES **universalist** n. **universalistic** adj.

universalize (also **-ise**) ■ v. make universal.
– DERIVATIVES **universalizability** (also **-isability**) n. **universalization** (also **-isation**) n.

universal joint ■ n. a joint which can transmit rotary power by a shaft at any selected angle.

universal product code ■ n. a bar code.

universal suffrage ■ n. the right of all adults (with minor exceptions) to vote in political elections.

Universal Time ■ n. Greenwich Mean Time, as used internationally.

universe ■ n. **1** all existing matter and space considered as a whole; the cosmos. **2** a particular sphere of activity or experience.
– ORIGIN Middle English: from Old French *univers* or Latin *universum*, from *universus* 'combined into one, whole', from *uni-* 'one' + *versus* 'turned'.

university ■ n. (pl. **-ies**) a high-level educational institution in which students study for degrees and academic research is done.
– ORIGIN Middle English: from Old French *universite*, from Latin *universitas* 'the whole', in late Latin, 'guild', from *universus* (see UNIVERSE).

univocal /juː'nɪ'vəʊk(ə)l, juː'nɪvək(ə)l/ ■ adj. Philosophy having only one possible meaning; unambiguous.
– DERIVATIVES **univocality** n. **univocally** adv.

unjoined ■ adj. not joined together.

unjointed ■ adj. lacking a joint or joints; consisting of a single piece.

unjust ■ adj. not just; unfair.
– DERIVATIVES **unjustly** adv. **unjustness** n.

unjustifiable ■ adj. impossible to justify.
– DERIVATIVES **unjustifiably** adv.

unjustified ■ adj. not justified.

unkempt /ʌn'kɛm(p)t/ ■ adj. having an untidy or dishevelled appearance.
– DERIVATIVES **unkemptly** adv. **unkemptness** n.
– ORIGIN Middle English: from UN-[1] + *kempt* 'combed', from archaic *kemb*.

unkept ■ adj. **1** (of an undertaking) not honoured. **2** not tidy or cared for.

unkind ■ adj. inconsiderate and harsh.
– DERIVATIVES **unkindly** adv. **unkindness** n.

unkink ■ v. make or become straight.

unknowable ■ adj. not able to be known.
– DERIVATIVES **unknowability** n.

unknowing ■ adj. not knowing or aware.
– DERIVATIVES **unknowingly** adv. **unknowingness** n.

unknown ■ adj. not known or familiar. ■ n. an unknown person or thing. ▸ Mathematics an unknown quantity or variable.
– PHRASES **unknown to** without the knowledge of.
– DERIVATIVES **unknownness** n.

unknown quantity ■ n. a person or thing whose nature, value, or significance is not known or knowable.

Unknown Soldier (also **Unknown Warrior**) ■ n. an unidentified representative member of a country's armed forces killed in war, buried with special honours in a national memorial.

unlabelled (US **unlabeled**) ■ adj. without a label.

unlace ■ v. undo the laces of.

unladen ■ adj. not carrying a load.

unladylike ■ adj. not appropriate to or behaving like a lady.

unlaid[1] ■ adj. not laid.

unlaid[2] past and past participle of UNLAY.

unlamented ■ adj. not mourned or regretted.

unlash ■ v. unfasten (something securely tied down).

unlatch ■ v. unfasten the latch of.

unlawful ■ adj. not conforming to or permitted by the law or rules.
–DERIVATIVES **unlawfully** adv. **unlawfulness** n.

USAGE
On the difference between **unlawful** and **illegal**, see usage at ILLEGAL.

unlay ■ v. (past and past part. **unlaid**) Nautical untwist (a rope) into separate strands.

unleaded ■ adj. (especially of petrol) without added lead.

unlearn ■ v. (past and past part. **unlearned** or **unlearnt**) aim to discard (something learned) from one's memory.

unlearned[1] /ʌnˈlɜːnd, -ˈlɜːnɪd/ ■ adj. not well educated.
–DERIVATIVES **unlearnedly** adv.

unlearned[2] /ʌnˈlɜːnd/ (also **unlearnt** /-ˈlɜːnt/) ■ adj. not having been learned.

unleash ■ v. release from a leash or restraint.

unleavened ■ adj. made without yeast or other raising agent.

unless ■ conj. except when; if not.
–ORIGIN Middle English: from ON or IN (assimilated through lack of stress to UN-[1]) + LESS.

unlettered ■ adj. poorly educated or illiterate.

unlicensed ■ adj. not having an official licence.

unlike ■ prep. different from; not like. ▶ in contrast to. ▶ uncharacteristic of. ■ adj. dissimilar or different from each other.
–DERIVATIVES **unlikeness** n.
–ORIGIN Middle English: perhaps orig. an alteration of Old Norse *úlíkr*; cf. Old English *ungelīc*.

unlikely ■ adj. (-**ier**, -**iest**) not likely; improbable.
–DERIVATIVES **unlikelihood** n. **unlikeliness** n.

unlimited ■ adj. not limited or restricted; infinite.
–DERIVATIVES **unlimitedly** adv. **unlimitedness** n.

unlined[1] ■ adj. not marked with lines or wrinkles.

unlined[2] ■ adj. without a lining.

unlink ■ v. make no longer connected.

unlisted ■ adj. not included on a list, especially of stock exchange prices or telephone numbers.

unlit ■ adj. **1** not provided with lighting. **2** not having been lit.

unlivable ■ adj. **1** uninhabitable. **2** (of life) unbearable.

unlived-in ■ adj. not appearing to be inhabited or used.

unload ■ v. **1** remove a load from. ▶ remove (goods) from a vehicle, ship, etc. **2** informal get rid of (something unwanted). **3** remove (ammunition) from a gun or (film) from a camera.
–DERIVATIVES **unloader** n.

unlock ■ v. **1** undo the lock of (something) using a key. **2** make (something) available.

unlooked ■ adj. (**unlooked for**) unexpected; unforeseen.

unloose ■ v. undo; let free.

unloosen ■ v. another term for UNLOOSE.

unloved ■ adj. loved by no one.

1303

unlovely ■ adj. not attractive; ugly.
–DERIVATIVES **unloveliness** n.

unlucky ■ adj. (-**ier**, -**iest**) having, bringing, or resulting from bad luck.
–DERIVATIVES **unluckily** adv. **unluckiness** n.

unmade ■ adj. **1** (of a bed) not arranged tidily ready for sleeping in. **2** (of a road) without a hard, smooth surface.

unmake ■ v. (past and past part. **unmade**) reverse or undo the making of; annul or destroy.

unman ■ v. (**unmanned**, **unmanning**) poetic/literary deprive of manly qualities such as self-control or courage.

unmanageable ■ adj. difficult or impossible to manage or control.
–DERIVATIVES **unmanageableness** n. **unmanageably** adv.

unmanned ■ adj. not having or needing a crew or staff.

unmannerly ■ adj. not well mannered.
–DERIVATIVES **unmannerliness** n.

unmarked ■ adj. **1** not marked. **2** not noticed.

unmarried ■ adj. not married; single.

unmask ■ v. expose the true character of.
–DERIVATIVES **unmasker** n.

unmatched ■ adj. not matched or equalled.

unmeasurable ■ adj. not able to be measured objectively.
–DERIVATIVES **unmeasurably** adv.

unmeasured ■ adj. **1** not having been measured. **2** chiefly poetic/literary limitless.

unmelodious ■ adj. not melodious; discordant.
–DERIVATIVES **unmelodiously** adv.

unmentionable ■ adj. too embarrassing, offensive, or shocking to be spoken about. ■ n. chiefly humorous an unmentionable thing.
–DERIVATIVES **unmentionability** n. **unmentionableness** n. **unmentionably** adv.

unmerciful ■ adj. showing no mercy.
–DERIVATIVES **unmercifully** adv. **unmercifulness** n.

unmerited ■ adj. not deserved or merited.

unmetalled ■ adj. Brit. (of a road) not having a hard surface.

unmethodical ■ adj. not orderly and systematic.
–DERIVATIVES **unmethodically** adv.

unmetrical ■ adj. not composed in or using metre.

unmindful ■ adj. (**unmindful of**) not conscious or aware of.
–DERIVATIVES **unmindfully** adv. **unmindfulness** n.

unmissable ■ adj. that should not or cannot be missed.

unmistakable (also **unmistakeable**) ■ adj. not able to be mistaken for anything else.
–DERIVATIVES **unmistakability** n. **unmistakably** adv.

unmitigated ■ adj. absolute; unqualified.
–DERIVATIVES **unmitigatedly** adv.

unmixed ■ adj. not mixed.

unmoderated ■ adj. (of an Internet bulletin board or chat room) not monitored for inappropriate or offensive content.

unmoral ■ adj. not concerned with morality.
–DERIVATIVES **unmorality** n.

unmotivated ■ adj. **1** not motivated. **2** without apparent motive.

unmoved ■ adj. **1** not affected by emotion or excitement. **2** not changed in purpose or position.
–DERIVATIVES **unmovable** (also **unmoveable**) adj.

unmoving ■ adj. **1** not moving; still. **2** not stirring any emotion.

unmurmuring ■ adj. poetic/literary not complaining.
–DERIVATIVES **unmurmuringly** adv.

unmusical ■ adj. **1** not pleasing to the ear. **2** unskilled in or indifferent to music.
–DERIVATIVES **unmusicality** n. **unmusically** adv. **unmusicalness** n.

unmuzzle ■ v. 1 remove a muzzle from. 2 allow freedom of expression to.

unnameable (also **unnamable**) ■ adj. unmentionable.

unnatural ■ adj. 1 contrary to nature; abnormal. 2 affected; not spontaneous.
– DERIVATIVES **unnaturally** adv. **unnaturalness** n.

unnavigable ■ adj. not able to be sailed on by ships or boats.
– DERIVATIVES **unnavigability** n.

unnecessary ■ adj. not necessary; more than is necessary.
– DERIVATIVES **unnecessarily** adv. **unnecessariness** n.

unnerve ■ v. deprive of courage or confidence.
– DERIVATIVES **unnerving** adj. **unnervingly** adv.

unnoticeable ■ adj. not easily observed or noticed.
– DERIVATIVES **unnoticeably** adv.

unnoticed ■ adj. not noticed.

unnumbered ■ adj. 1 not assigned a number. 2 not counted; countless.

unoaked ■ adj. (of wine) not matured in an oak container.

unobliging ■ adj. not helpful or cooperative.

unobserved ■ adj. not observed; unseen.

unobstructed ■ adj. not obstructed.

unobtainable ■ adj. not able to be obtained.

unobtrusive ■ adj. not conspicuous or attracting attention.
– DERIVATIVES **unobtrusively** adv. **unobtrusiveness** n.

unoccupied ■ adj. not occupied.

unofficial ■ adj. not officially authorized or confirmed.
– DERIVATIVES **unofficially** adv.

unopened ■ adj. not opened.

unopposed ■ adj. not opposed; unchallenged.

unorganized (also **-ised**) ■ adj. 1 not organized. 2 not unionized.

unoriginal ■ adj. lacking originality; derivative.
– DERIVATIVES **unoriginality** n. **unoriginally** adv.

unorthodox ■ adj. contrary to what is usual, traditional, or accepted; not orthodox.
– DERIVATIVES **unorthodoxly** adv. **unorthodoxy** n.

unostentatious ■ adj. not ostentatious.
– DERIVATIVES **unostentatiously** adv. **unostentatiousness** n.

unowned ■ adj. 1 not having an owner. 2 not admitted to; unacknowledged.

unpack ■ v. 1 open and remove the contents of (a suitcase or container). ▸ remove from a packed container. 2 analyse into component elements. ▸ Computing convert (compressed data).
– DERIVATIVES **unpacker** n.

unpaid ■ adj. 1 (of a debt) not yet paid. 2 (of work or leave) undertaken without payment. ▸ (of a person) not receiving payment for work done.

unpaired ■ adj. 1 not arranged in pairs. 2 not forming one of a pair.

unpalatable ■ adj. 1 not pleasant to taste. 2 difficult to put up with or accept.
– DERIVATIVES **unpalatability** n. **unpalatably** adv.

unparalleled ■ adj. having no parallel or equal; exceptional.

unpardonable ■ adj. (of a fault or offence) unforgivable.
– DERIVATIVES **unpardonableness** n. **unpardonably** adv.

unparliamentary ■ adj. (especially of language) contrary to the rules or procedures of parliament.

unpasteurized (also **-ised**) ■ adj. not pasteurized.

unpatriotic ■ adj. not patriotic.
– DERIVATIVES **unpatriotically** adv.

unpaved ■ adj. lacking a metalled or paved surface.

unpeg ■ v. (**unpegged**, **unpegging**) 1 unfasten by the removal of pegs. 2 cease to maintain a fixed relationship between (a currency) and another currency.

unpeople ■ v. [usu. as adj. **unpeopled**] empty of people; depopulate.

unperson ■ n. (pl. **-persons**) a person whose name or existence is officially denied or ignored.

unperturbed ■ adj. not perturbed or concerned.
– DERIVATIVES **unperturbedly** adv.

unpick ■ v. 1 undo the sewing of (stitches or a garment). 2 carefully break down and analyse the different elements of (something), especially in order to find faults.

unpin ■ v. (**unpinned**, **unpinning**) unfasten or detach by removing a pin or pins.

unpitying ■ adj. not feeling or showing pity.
– DERIVATIVES **unpityingly** adv.

unplaceable ■ adj. not able to be placed or classified.

unplaced ■ adj. 1 not having or assigned to a specific place. 2 chiefly Horse Racing not one of the first three (sometimes four) to finish in a race.

unplanned ■ adj. not planned.

unplayable ■ adj. 1 not able to be played or played on. 2 (of music) too difficult or bad to perform.

unpleasant ■ adj. not pleasant; disagreeable.
– DERIVATIVES **unpleasantly** adv.

unpleasantness ■ n. 1 the state or quality of being unpleasant. 2 bad feeling or quarrelling between people.

unploughed (US **unplowed**) ■ adj. not having been ploughed.

unplug ■ v. (**unplugged**, **unplugging**) 1 disconnect (an electrical device) by removing its plug from a socket. 2 remove an obstacle or blockage from.

unplugged ■ adj. trademark (of pop or rock music) performed or recorded with acoustic rather than electrically amplified instruments.

unplumbed ■ adj. 1 not provided with plumbing. 2 not fully explored or understood.
– DERIVATIVES **unplumbable** adj.

unpolished ■ adj. 1 not having a polished surface. 2 (of a work) not polished.

unpolled ■ adj. 1 (of a voter) not having voted, or registered to vote, at an election. ▸ (of a vote) not cast at or registered for an election. 2 (of a person) not included in an opinion poll.

unpopular ■ adj. not liked or popular.
– DERIVATIVES **unpopularity** n.

unpopulated ■ adj. 1 without inhabitants. 2 (of a printed circuit board) having no components fitted.

unpowered ■ adj. having no fuel-burning source of power for propulsion.

unpractical ■ adj. another term for IMPRACTICAL (in sense 1).
– DERIVATIVES **unpracticality** n.

unpractised (US **unpracticed**) ■ adj. 1 not trained or experienced. 2 not often done before.

unprecedented /ʌnˈprɛsɪdɛntɪd/ ■ adj. never done or known before.
– DERIVATIVES **unprecedentedly** adv.

unpredictable ■ adj. not able to be predicted; changeable.
– DERIVATIVES **unpredictability** n. **unpredictably** adv.

unprejudiced ■ adj. without prejudice; unbiased.

unpremeditated ■ adj. not thought out or planned beforehand.
– DERIVATIVES **unpremeditatedly** adv.

unprepared ■ adj. 1 not ready or able to deal with something. 2 (of a thing) not made ready for use.
– DERIVATIVES **unpreparedness** n.

unprepossessing ■ adj. not attractive or appealing to the eye.

unpressurized (also **-ised**) ■ adj. (of a gas or its container) not having raised pressure that is produced or maintained artificially. ▸ (of an aircraft cabin) not having normal atmospheric pressure maintained at a high altitude.

unpretentious ■ adj. not pretentious; modest.
– DERIVATIVES **unpretentiously** adv. **unpretentiousness** n.

unprincipled ■ adj. not acting in accordance with moral principles.

unprintable ■ adj. (of words, comments, or thoughts) too offensive or shocking to be published.
– DERIVATIVES **unprintably** adv.

unproblematic ■ adj. not constituting or presenting a problem or difficulty.
– DERIVATIVES **unproblematical** adj. **unproblematically** adv.

unprocessed ■ adj. not processed.

unproductive ■ adj. **1** not producing or able to produce large amounts of goods, crops, etc. **2** not achieving much; not very useful.
– DERIVATIVES **unproductively** adv. **unproductiveness** n.

unprofessional ■ adj. below or contrary to the standards expected in a particular profession.
– DERIVATIVES **unprofessionalism** n. **unprofessionally** adv.

unprofitable ■ adj. not yielding a profit. ▶ not beneficial or useful.
– DERIVATIVES **unprofitability** n. **unprofitably** adv.

unpromising ■ adj. not giving hope of future success or good results.
– DERIVATIVES **unpromisingly** adv.

unprompted ■ adj. without being prompted.

unpronounceable ■ adj. too difficult to pronounce.
– DERIVATIVES **unpronounceably** adv.

unprotected ■ adj. **1** not protected or kept safe from harm. **2** (of sexual intercourse) performed without a condom.

unproven /ʌnˈpruːv(ə)n, -ˈprəʊ-/ (also **unproved** /-ˈpruːvd/) ■ adj. not demonstrated by evidence or argument as true or existing. ▶ not tried and tested.

unprovided ■ adj. not provided. ▶ (**unprovided for**) without sufficient money to cover the cost of living.

unprovoked ■ adj. (of an attack, crime, etc.) not directly provoked.

unpublished ■ adj. (of a work) not published. ▶ (of an author) having no writings published.
– DERIVATIVES **unpublishable** adj.

unpunished ■ adj. (of an offence or offender) not receiving any punishment or penalty.

unputdownable ■ adj. informal (of a book) so engrossing that one cannot stop reading it.

unqualified ■ adj. **1** not having the necessary qualifications or requirements. **2** without reservation or limitation; total: *an unqualified success.*
– DERIVATIVES **unqualifiedly** adv.

unquantifiable ■ adj. impossible to express or measure in terms of quantity.

unquenchable ■ adj. not able to be quenched.
– DERIVATIVES **unquenchably** adv.

unquestionable ■ adj. not able to be disputed or doubted.
– DERIVATIVES **unquestionability** n. **unquestionably** adv.

unquestioned ■ adj. **1** not disputed or doubted; certain. **2** accepted without question: *an unquestioned assumption.* **3** not subjected to questioning.
– DERIVATIVES **unquestioning** adj. **unquestioningly** adv.

unquiet ■ adj. restless; unable to be still. ▶ uneasy; anxious.
– DERIVATIVES **unquietly** adv. **unquietness** n.

unquote ■ v. (in phr. *quote —— unquote*) see QUOTE.

unquoted ■ adj. not quoted or listed on a stock exchange.

unrated ■ adj. not having received a rating.

unravel ■ v. (**unravelled**, **unravelling**; US **unraveled**, **unraveling**) **1** undo (twisted, knitted, or woven threads); unwind. ▶ become undone. **2** investigate and solve (a mystery or puzzle). **3** begin to fail or collapse.

unreachable ■ adj. unable to be reached or contacted.
– DERIVATIVES **unreachableness** n. **unreachably** adv.

unread ■ adj. not having been read.

unreadable ■ adj. **1** not clear enough to read; illegible. **2** too dull or difficult to be worth reading.
– DERIVATIVES **unreadability** n. **unreadably** adv.

unready ■ adj. **1** not ready or prepared. **2** archaic slow to act; hesitant.
– DERIVATIVES **unreadiness** n.

unreal ■ adj. **1** imaginary; not seeming real. **2** unrealistic. **3** informal incredible; amazing.
– DERIVATIVES **unreality** n. **unreally** adv.

unrealistic ■ adj. not realistic.
– DERIVATIVES **unrealistically** adv.

unrealized (also **-ised**) ■ adj. **1** not achieved or created. **2** not converted into money: *unrealized property assets.*

unreason ■ n. irrationality; lack of reasonable thought.

unreasonable ■ adj. **1** not guided by or based on good sense. **2** beyond the limits of acceptability.
– DERIVATIVES **unreasonableness** n. **unreasonably** adv.

unreasoning ■ adj. not guided by or based on reason; illogical.
– DERIVATIVES **unreasoned** adj. **unreasoningly** adv.

unreceptive ■ adj. not receptive.

unreciprocated ■ adj. not reciprocated; unrequited.

unreclaimed ■ adj. (especially of land) not reclaimed.

unrecognizable (also **-isable**) ■ adj. not able to be recognized.
– DERIVATIVES **unrecognizably** (also **-isably**) adv.

unrecognized (also **-ised**) ■ adj. **1** not identified from previous encounters or knowledge. **2** not acknowledged as valid; not officially recognized.

unreconciled ■ adj. not reconciled.

unreconstructed ■ adj. **1** not reconciled or converted to the current political theory or movement: *unreconstructed Communists.* **2** not rebuilt.

unrecorded ■ adj. not recorded.

unredeemed ■ adj. not redeemed.

unreel ■ v. **1** unwind. **2** (of a film) wind from one reel to another during projection.

unrefined ■ adj. **1** not processed to remove impurities. **2** not elegant or cultured.

unreflecting ■ adj. **1** not engaged in reflection or thought. **2** not reflecting light.
– DERIVATIVES **unreflectingly** adv. **unreflective** adj.

unregenerate /ˌʌnrɪˈdʒɛn(ə)rət/ ■ adj. not reforming or showing repentance; obstinately wrong or bad.
– DERIVATIVES **unregeneracy** n. **unregenerately** adv.

unregistered ■ adj. not officially recognized and recorded.

unregulated ■ adj. not controlled or supervised by regulations or laws.

unrehearsed ■ adj. not rehearsed.

unrelated ■ adj. not related.
– DERIVATIVES **unrelatedness** n.

unreleased ■ adj. (especially of a film or recording) not released.

unrelenting ■ adj. not yielding in strength, severity, or determination.
– DERIVATIVES **unrelentingly** adv. **unrelentingness** n.

unreliable ■ adj. not able to be relied upon.
– DERIVATIVES **unreliability** n. **unreliably** adv.

unrelieved ■ adj. **1** lacking variation or change; monotonous. **2** not provided with relief; not aided or assisted.
– DERIVATIVES **unrelievedly** adv.

unremarkable ■ adj. not particularly interesting or surprising.
– DERIVATIVES **unremarkably** adv.

unremarked ■ adj. not remarked upon; unnoticed.

unremitting ■ adj. never relaxing or slackening.
– DERIVATIVES **unremittingly** adv. **unremittingness** n.

unremunerative ■ adj. bringing little or no profit or income.
– DERIVATIVES **unremuneratively** adv.

unrepeatable ■ adj. **1** not able to be repeated. **2** too offensive or shocking to be said again.
– DERIVATIVES **unrepeatability** n.

unrepentant

unrepentant ▪ adj. showing no regret for one's wrong-doings.
– DERIVATIVES **unrepentantly** adv.

unreported ▪ adj. not reported.

unrepresentative ▪ adj. not typical of a class, group, or body of opinion.
– DERIVATIVES **unrepresentativeness** n.

unrequited ▪ adj. (of a feeling, especially love) not returned or rewarded.
– DERIVATIVES **unrequitedly** adv. **unrequitedness** n.

unreserved ▪ adj. **1** without reservations; complete. **2** frank and open. **3** not set apart or booked in advance.
– DERIVATIVES **unreservedly** adv.

unresolved ▪ adj. (of a problem, dispute, etc.) not resolved.
– DERIVATIVES **unresolvedly** /-vɪdli/ adv. **unresolvedness** n.

unresponsive ▪ adj. not responsive.
– DERIVATIVES **unresponsively** adv. **unresponsiveness** n.

unrest ▪ n. a state of rebellious dissatisfaction and agitation in a group of people: *civil unrest*. ▸ a state of uneasiness or disturbance.

unrestrained ▪ adj. not restrained or restricted.
– DERIVATIVES **unrestrainedly** adv. **unrestrainedness** n.

unrestricted ▪ adj. not limited or restricted.
– DERIVATIVES **unrestrictedly** adv.

unrewarding ▪ adj. not rewarding or satisfying.

unripe ▪ adj. not ripe.
– DERIVATIVES **unripeness** n.

unrivalled (US **unrivaled**) ▪ adj. surpassing all others.

unroll ▪ v. open or cause to open out from a rolled-up state.

unromantic ▪ adj. not romantic.
– DERIVATIVES **unromantically** adv.

unrope ▪ v. Climbing detach oneself from a rope.

unrounded ▪ adj. Phonetics (of a vowel) pronounced with the lips not rounded.

unruffled ▪ adj. not disordered or disturbed. ▸ (of a person) not agitated; calm.

unruly ▪ adj. (**-ier**, **-iest**) disorderly and disruptive; difficult to control.
– DERIVATIVES **unruliness** n.
– ORIGIN Middle English: from UN-¹ + archaic *ruly* 'disciplined; orderly', from RULE.

unsaddle ▪ v. remove the saddle from. ▸ dislodge from a saddle.

unsafe ▪ adj. not safe; dangerous.
– DERIVATIVES **unsafely** adv. **unsafeness** n.

unsafe sex ▪ n. sexual activity in which people do not take precautions to protect themselves against sexually transmitted diseases such as Aids.

unsaid past and past participle of UNSAY. ▪ adj. not said or uttered.

unsaleable (also **unsalable**) ▪ adj. not able to be sold.
– DERIVATIVES **unsaleability** n.

unsalted ▪ adj. not salted.

unsanitary ▪ adj. not sanitary.

unsatisfactory ▪ adj. unacceptable because poor or not good enough.
– DERIVATIVES **unsatisfactorily** adv. **unsatisfactoriness** n.

unsatisfied ▪ adj. not satisfied.

unsatisfying ▪ adj. not satisfying.
– DERIVATIVES **unsatisfyingly** adv.

unsaturated ▪ adj. Chemistry (of organic molecules) having carbon–carbon double or triple bonds and therefore not containing the greatest possible number of hydrogen atoms. ▸ denoting fats containing a high proportion of fatty acid molecules with double bonds.
– DERIVATIVES **unsaturation** n.

unsaved ▪ adj. not saved, in particular (in Christian use) not having had one's soul saved from damnation.

unsavoury (US **unsavory**) ▪ adj. **1** disagreeable to taste, smell, or look at. **2** objectionable; disreputable.
– DERIVATIVES **unsavourily** adv. **unsavouriness** n.

unsay ▪ v. (past and past part. **unsaid**) withdraw or retract (a statement).

unsayable ▪ adj. not able to be said, especially because considered too controversial or offensive.

unscarred ▪ adj. not scarred or damaged.

unscathed ▪ adj. without suffering any injury, damage, or harm.

unscented ▪ adj. not scented.

unscheduled ▪ adj. not scheduled.

unschooled ▪ adj. **1** lacking schooling or training. ▸ uncontrolled; undisciplined. **2** not affected; natural and spontaneous.

unscientific ▪ adj. **1** not in accordance with scientific principles or methodology. **2** lacking knowledge of or interest in science.
– DERIVATIVES **unscientifically** adv.

unscramble ▪ v. restore or convert to an intelligible or readable state.
– DERIVATIVES **unscrambler** n.

unscreened ▪ adj. **1** not subjected to screening. **2** not shown or broadcast. **3** not provided with a screen.

unscrew ▪ v. (with reference to a screw, lid, etc.) unfasten or be unfastened by twisting.

unscripted ▪ adj. said or delivered without a prepared script; impromptu.

unscrupulous ▪ adj. without moral scruples.
– DERIVATIVES **unscrupulously** adv. **unscrupulousness** n.

unseal ▪ v. remove or break the seal of.

unsealed ▪ adj. not sealed. ▸ (of a road) not surfaced with bitumen or a similar substance.

unseasonable ▪ adj. **1** (of weather) unusual for the time of year. **2** untimely; inopportune.
– DERIVATIVES **unseasonableness** n. **unseasonably** adv.

unseasonal ▪ adj. (especially of weather) unusual or inappropriate for the time of year.

unseasoned ▪ adj. **1** (of food) not flavoured with salt, pepper, or other spices. **2** (of timber) not treated or matured. **3** (of a person) inexperienced.

unseat ▪ v. **1** cause to fall from a saddle or seat. **2** remove from a position of power or authority.

unsecured ▪ adj. **1** (of a loan) made without an asset given as security. ▸ (of a creditor) having made such a loan. **2** not made secure or safe.

unseeded ▪ adj. (chiefly of a competitor in a sports tournament) not seeded.

unseeing ▪ adj. with one's eyes open but without noticing or seeing anything.
– DERIVATIVES **unseeingly** adv.

unseemly ▪ adj. **1** (of behaviour or actions) not proper or appropriate. **2** archaic unattractive.
– DERIVATIVES **unseemliness** n.

unseen ▪ adj. **1** not seen or noticed. **2** (of a passage for translation in an examination) not previously read or prepared.

unselfconscious ▪ adj. without self-consciousness; not shy or embarrassed.
– DERIVATIVES **unselfconsciously** adv. **unselfconsciousness** n.

unselfish ▪ adj. not selfish.
– DERIVATIVES **unselfishly** adv. **unselfishness** n.

unsentimental ▪ adj. not displaying or influenced by sentimental feelings.
– DERIVATIVES **unsentimentally** adv.

unserved ▪ adj. **1** not attended to or catered for. **2** (of a female animal) not mated with a male.

unserviceable ▪ adj. not in working order; unfit for use.
– DERIVATIVES **unserviceability** n.

unsettle ▪ v. cause to be anxious or uneasy; disturb.
– DERIVATIVES **unsettling** adj. **unsettlingly** adv.

unsettled ■ adj. 1 lacking stability; changeable or liable to change. ▶ agitated; uneasy. 2 not yet resolved. ▶ (of a bill) not yet paid. 3 (of an area) having no settlers or inhabitants.
– DERIVATIVES **unsettledness** n.

unsex ■ v. deprive of gender, sexuality, or the characteristic attributes of one or other sex.

unshackle ■ v. release from shackles or other restraints.

unshakeable (also **unshakable**) ■ adj. (of a belief, feeling, etc.) firm and unable to be changed or disputed.
– DERIVATIVES **unshakeability** n. **unshakeably** adv.

unshaken ■ adj. steadfast and unwavering.
– DERIVATIVES **unshakenly** adv.

unshaven ■ adj. not having shaved or been shaved.

unsheathe ■ v. draw or pull out (a knife or similar weapon) from a sheath.

unshed ■ adj. (of tears) welling in a person's eyes but not falling.

unshelled ■ adj. not extracted from its shell.

unship ■ v. (**unshipped**, **unshipping**) chiefly Nautical 1 remove (an oar, mast, or other object) from a fixed or regular position. 2 unload (a cargo) from a ship or boat.

unshockable ■ adj. impossible to shock.
– DERIVATIVES **unshockability** n.

unshorn ■ adj. (of hair or wool) not cut or shorn.

unsighted ■ adj. 1 lacking the power of sight. 2 (especially in sport) prevented from having a clear view. ▶ not seen.

unsightly ■ adj. unpleasant to look at; ugly.
– DERIVATIVES **unsightliness** n.

unsigned ■ adj. 1 not bearing a person's signature. ▶ not having signed a contract of employment. 2 Mathematics & Computing not having a plus or minus sign, or a bit representing this.

unsinkable ■ adj. (of a ship or boat) unable to be sunk.
– DERIVATIVES **unsinkability** n.

unskilful (also chiefly US **unskillful**) ■ adj. not having or showing skill.
– DERIVATIVES **unskilfully** adv. **unskilfulness** n.

unskilled ■ adj. not having or requiring special skill or training.

unsling ■ v. (past and past part. **unslung**) remove from a position of being slung or suspended.

unsmiling ■ adj. not smiling; serious or unfriendly.
– DERIVATIVES **unsmilingly** adv. **unsmilingness** n.

unsmoked ■ adj. 1 (of meat or fish) not cured by exposure to smoke. 2 (of tobacco or a cigarette) not having been smoked.

unsnap ■ v. (**unsnapped**, **unsnapping**) unfasten or open with a brisk movement and a sharp sound.

unsociable ■ adj. not making an effort to behave sociably. ▶ not conducive to friendly social relations.
– DERIVATIVES **unsociability** n. **unsociableness** n. **unsociably** adv.

unsocial ■ adj. 1 (of the hours of work of a job) falling outside the normal working day and thus socially inconvenient. 2 antisocial.
– DERIVATIVES **unsocially** adv.

unsold ■ adj. (of an item) not sold.

unsolicited ■ adj. not asked for; given or done voluntarily: *unsolicited junk mail*.

unsolved ■ adj. not solved.

unsophisticated ■ adj. 1 lacking refined worldly knowledge or tastes. 2 not complicated or highly developed; basic.
– DERIVATIVES **unsophisticatedly** adv. **unsophisticatedness** n. **unsophistication** n.

unsorted ■ adj. not sorted or arranged.

unsound ■ adj. 1 not safe or robust; in poor condition. ▶ injured, ill, or diseased. 2 not based on sound evidence or reasoning; unreliable or unacceptable. ▶ (of a person) not competent, reliable, or holding acceptable views.
– DERIVATIVES **unsoundly** adv. **unsoundness** n.

unsparing ■ adj. 1 merciless; severe. 2 given freely and generously.
– DERIVATIVES **unsparingly** adv. **unsparingness** n.

unspeakable ■ adj. not able to be expressed in words. ▶ too bad or horrific to express in words.
– DERIVATIVES **unspeakableness** n. **unspeakably** adv.

unspecialized (also **-ised**) ■ adj. not specialized.

unspecific ■ adj. not specific; vague.

unspecified ■ adj. not stated clearly or exactly.

unspectacular ■ adj. not spectacular; unremarkable.
– DERIVATIVES **unspectacularly** adv.

unspoilt (also **unspoiled**) ■ adj. not spoilt, in particular (of a place) not marred by development.

unspoken ■ adj. not expressed in speech; tacit.

unsporting ■ adj. not fair or sportsmanlike.
– DERIVATIVES **unsportingly** adv.

unsportsmanlike ■ adj. unsporting.

unsprung ■ adj. not provided with springs.

unstable ■ adj. 1 prone to change or collapse; not stable. 2 prone to psychiatric problems or sudden changes of mood.
– DERIVATIVES **unstableness** n. **unstably** adv.

unstained ■ adj. not stained.

unstated ■ adj. not stated or declared.

unsteady ■ adj. (**-ier**, **-iest**) 1 liable to fall or shake; not firm. 2 not uniform or regular.
– DERIVATIVES **unsteadily** adv. **unsteadiness** n.

unstep ■ v. (**unstepped**, **unstepping**) Nautical detach (a mast) from its step.

unstick ■ v. (past and past part. **unstuck**) cause to become no longer stuck together.
– PHRASES **come** (or **get**) **unstuck** informal fail.

unstinting ■ adj. given or giving without restraint; unsparing.
– DERIVATIVES **unstinted** adj. **unstintingly** adv.

unstop ■ v. (**unstopped**, **unstopping**) free from obstruction. ▶ remove the stopper from.

unstoppable ■ adj. impossible to stop or prevent.
– DERIVATIVES **unstoppability** n. **unstoppably** adv.

unstopper ■ v. remove the stopper from (a container).

unstressed ■ adj. 1 Phonetics (of a syllable) not pronounced with stress. 2 not subjected to stress.

unstring ■ v. (past and past part. **unstrung**) 1 [usu. as adj. **unstrung**] unnerve: *a mind unstrung by loneliness*. 2 remove or relax the string or strings of. 3 remove from a string.

unstructured ■ adj. without formal organization or structure.

unstuck past and past participle of UNSTICK.

unstudied ■ adj. not laboured or artificial; natural.
– DERIVATIVES **unstudiedly** adv.

unstuffy ■ adj. 1 friendly, informal, and approachable. 2 having fresh air or ventilation.

unsubscribe ■ v. remove one's name and address from an electronic mailing list.

unsubstantial ■ adj. having little or no solidity, reality, or factual basis.
– DERIVATIVES **unsubstantiality** n. **unsubstantially** adv.

unsubstantiated ■ adj. not supported or proven by evidence.

unsubtle ■ adj. not subtle; obvious; clumsy.

unsuccessful ■ adj. not successful.
– DERIVATIVES **unsuccessfully** adv. **unsuccessfulness** n.

unsuitable ■ adj. not fitting or appropriate.
– DERIVATIVES **unsuitability** n. **unsuitableness** n. **unsuitably** adv.

unsuited ■ adj. not right or appropriate.

unsullied ■ adj. not spoiled or made impure.

unsung ■ adj. not celebrated or praised: *unsung heroes of the industrial revolution*.

unsupervised ■ adj. not done or acting under supervision.

unsupportable ■ adj. insupportable.
– DERIVATIVES **unsupportably** adv.

unsupported ■ adj. **1** not supported. ▸ Computing (of a program, device, etc.) not having assistance for the user available from a manufacturer or system manager. **2** not borne out by evidence or facts.

unsure ■ adj. **1** lacking confidence. **2** not fixed or certain.
– DERIVATIVES **unsurely** adv. **unsureness** n.

unsurfaced ■ adj. (of a road or path) not provided with a durable upper layer.

unsurpassable ■ adj. not able to be surpassed.
– DERIVATIVES **unsurpassably** adv.

unsurpassed ■ adj. better or greater than any other.

unsurprising ■ adj. not unexpected and so not causing surprise.
– DERIVATIVES **unsurprisingly** adv.

unsuspected ■ adj. **1** not known or thought to exist; not imagined as possible. **2** not regarded with suspicion.
– DERIVATIVES **unsuspectedly** adv.

unsuspecting ■ adj. not aware of the presence of danger; feeling no suspicion.
– DERIVATIVES **unsuspectingly** adv.

unsustainable ■ adj. **1** not able to be sustained. ▸ Ecology upsetting the ecological balance by depleting natural resources. **2** not able to be upheld or defended.
– DERIVATIVES **unsustainably** adv.

unswayed ■ adj. not influenced or affected.

unsweetened ■ adj. (of food or drink) without added sugar or sweetener.

unswerving ■ adj. not changing or becoming weaker.
– DERIVATIVES **unswervingly** adv.

unsworn ■ adj. Law (of testimony or evidence) not given under oath.

unsymmetrical ■ adj. not symmetrical; asymmetrical.
– DERIVATIVES **unsymmetrically** adv.

unsympathetic ■ adj. **1** not sympathetic. ▸ not showing approval of an idea or action. **2** not likeable.
– DERIVATIVES **unsympathetically** adv.

unsystematic ■ adj. not done or acting according to a fixed plan or system; unmethodical.
– DERIVATIVES **unsystematically** adv.

untainted ■ adj. not contaminated, polluted, or tainted.

untameable (also **untamable**) ■ adj. not capable of being tamed or controlled.

untamed ■ adj. not tamed or controlled. ▸ (of land) wild or uncultivated: *the untamed wilderness*.

untangle ■ v. **1** free from tangles. **2** free from complications or confusion.

untanned ■ adj. **1** not converted into leather by tanning. **2** not tanned by exposure to the sun.

untapped ■ adj. (of a resource) not yet exploited or used.

untarnished ■ adj. **1** not tarnished. **2** not spoiled or ruined.

untasted ■ adj. (of food or drink) not sampled or tested for flavour.

untaught ■ adj. not having been taught or educated. ▸ not acquired by teaching; natural or spontaneous.

unteachable ■ adj. (of a pupil or skill) unable to be taught.

untempered ■ adj. **1** not moderated or lessened. **2** (of a material) not brought to the proper hardness or consistency.

untenable ■ adj. not able to be maintained or defended against attack or objection.
– DERIVATIVES **untenability** n. **untenably** adv.

untended ■ adj. not cared for or looked after; neglected.

Untermensch /ˈʊntəmɛn(t)ʃ/ ■ n. (pl. **Untermenschen** /-mɛn(t)ʃ(ə)n/) a person considered racially or socially inferior.
– ORIGIN German, 'underperson'.

untested ■ adj. not subjected to testing; unproven.
– DERIVATIVES **untestable** adj.

unthinkable ■ adj. too unlikely or undesirable to be considered a possibility.
– DERIVATIVES **unthinkability** n. **unthinkably** adv.

unthinking ■ adj. without proper consideration.
– DERIVATIVES **unthinkingly** adv. **unthinkingness** n.

unthought ■ adj. (**unthought of**) not imagined or dreamed of.

unthreatening ■ adj. not threatening.

untidy ■ adj. (**-ier**, **-iest**) not arranged tidily. ▸ (of a person) not inclined to be neat.
– DERIVATIVES **untidily** adv. **untidiness** n.

untie ■ v. (**untying**) undo or unfasten (something tied).

untied ■ adj. **1** not fastened or knotted. **2** (of an international loan or aid) given without special conditions.

until ■ prep. & conj. up to (the point in time or the event mentioned).
– ORIGIN Middle English: from Old Norse *und* 'as far as' + TILL[1] (the sense thus duplicated).

untimely ■ adj. happening or done at an unsuitable time; inappropriate. ▸ (of a death or end) happening too soon or sooner than normal.
– DERIVATIVES **untimeliness** n.

untiring ■ adj. continuing at the same rate without loss of vigour.
– DERIVATIVES **untiringly** adv.

untitled ■ adj. **1** (of a book or other work) having no title. **2** not having a title indicating high social or official rank.

unto ■ prep. **1** archaic term for TO. **2** archaic term for UNTIL.
– ORIGIN Middle English: from UNTIL, with TO replacing TILL[1] (in its northern dialect meaning 'to').

untold ■ adj. **1** too much or too many to be counted; indescribable: *thieves caused untold damage*. **2** not narrated or recounted.
– ORIGIN Old English *unteald* 'not counted' (see UN-[1], TOLD).

untouchable ■ adj. **1** not able to be touched or affected. **2** unable to be matched or rivalled. **3** of or belonging to the lowest-caste Hindu group or the people outside the caste system. ■ n. a member of the lowest-caste Hindu group, with whom contact is traditionally held to defile members of higher castes. See also SCHEDULED CASTE.
– DERIVATIVES **untouchability** n.

untouched ■ adj. **1** not handled, used, or tasted. ▸ (of a subject) not treated or discussed. **2** not affected, changed, or damaged in any way.

untoward ■ adj. unexpected and inappropriate or adverse.
– DERIVATIVES **untowardly** adv. **untowardness** n.

untraceable ■ adj. unable to be found or traced.
– DERIVATIVES **untraceably** adv.

untracked ■ adj. (of land) not previously traversed; without tracks.

untrained ■ adj. not having been trained.
– DERIVATIVES **untrainable** adj.

untrammelled (US also **untrammeled**) ■ adj. not restricted or hampered.

untransferable ■ adj. not able to be transferred to another place, occupation, or person.

untranslatable /ˌʌntransˈleɪtəb(ə)l, ˌʌntrɑːns-, -z-/ ■ adj. not able to be translated.
– DERIVATIVES **untranslatability** n.

untravelled (US also **untraveled**) ■ adj. **1** not having travelled much. **2** (of a road or region) not journeyed along or through.

untreatable ■ adj. for whom or which no medical care is available or possible.

untreated ■ adj. **1** not given treatment. **2** not treated by the use of a chemical, physical, or biological agent: *untreated sewage*.

untried ■ adj. **1** not yet tested; inexperienced. **2** Law (of an accused person) not yet subjected to a trial in court.

untrodden ■ adj. not having been walked on.

untroubled ■ adj. not troubled.

untrue ■ adj. **1** false or incorrect. **2** not faithful or loyal.

untrustworthy ■ adj. unable to be trusted.
– DERIVATIVES **untrustworthiness** n.

untruth ■ n. (pl. **untruths**) 1 a lie. 2 the quality of being false.

untruthful ■ adj. not truthful.
– DERIVATIVES **untruthfully** adv. **untruthfulness** n.

untuck ■ v. free from being tucked in or up.

untuned ■ adj. not tuned or in tune.

unturned ■ adj. not turned.

untutored ■ adj. not formally taught.

untwist ■ v. open or cause to open from a twisted position.

untying present participle of **UNTIE**.

untypical ■ adj. unusual.
– DERIVATIVES **untypically** adv.

unusable ■ adj. not fit to be used.

unused ■ adj. 1 not used. 2 (**unused to**) not accustomed to.

unusual ■ adj. 1 not habitually or commonly done or occurring. 2 remarkable; exceptional.
– DERIVATIVES **unusually** adv. **unusualness** n.

unutterable ■ adj. too great or awful to describe.
– DERIVATIVES **unutterably** adv.

unuttered ■ adj. not spoken or expressed.

unvalued ■ adj. not valued.

unvaried ■ adj. not varied.

unvarnished ■ adj. 1 not varnished. 2 plain and straightforward.

unvarying ■ adj. not varying.
– DERIVATIVES **unvaryingly** adv. **unvaryingness** n.

unveil ■ v. 1 remove a veil or covering from. 2 show or announce publicly for the first time.

unventilated ■ adj. not ventilated.

unverifiable ■ adj. unable to be verified.

unverified ■ adj. not verified.

unversed ■ adj. (**unversed in**) not versed in.

unviable ■ adj. not viable.
– DERIVATIVES **unviability** n.

unvisited ■ adj. not visited.

unvoiced ■ adj. 1 unuttered. 2 Phonetics (of a speech sound) uttered without vibration of the vocal cords.

unwaged ■ adj. unemployed or doing unpaid work. ▶ (of work) unpaid.

unwanted ■ adj. not wanted.

unwarrantable ■ adj. unjustifiable.
– DERIVATIVES **unwarrantably** adv.

unwarranted ■ adj. not warranted.

unwary ■ adj. not cautious.
– DERIVATIVES **unwarily** adv. **unwariness** n.

unwashed ■ adj. not washed.
– PHRASES **the (great) unwashed** derogatory the multitude of ordinary people.

unwatchable ■ adj. disturbing or uninteresting to watch.

unwatched ■ adj. not watched.

unwavering ■ adj. not wavering.
– DERIVATIVES **unwaveringly** adv.

unweaned ■ adj. not weaned.

unwearable ■ adj. not fit to be worn.

unwearied ■ adj. not wearied.
– DERIVATIVES **unweariedly** adv.

unwearying ■ adj. never tiring or slackening.
– DERIVATIVES **unwearyingly** adv.

unwed (also **unwedded**) ■ adj. not married.
– DERIVATIVES **unweddedness** n.

unweighted ■ adj. not weighted.

unwelcome ■ adj. not welcome.
– DERIVATIVES **unwelcomely** adv. **unwelcomeness** n.

unwelcoming ■ adj. inhospitable.

unwell ■ adj. ill.

unwept ■ adj. chiefly poetic/literary not mourned or lamented.

unwholesome ■ adj. not wholesome.
– DERIVATIVES **unwholesomely** adv. **unwholesomeness** n.

unwieldy ■ adj. (**-ier**, **-iest**) hard to move or manage because of its size, shape, or weight.
– DERIVATIVES **unwieldily** adv. **unwieldiness** n.
– ORIGIN Middle English: from UN-[1] + WIELDY (in the obsolete sense 'active').

unwilling ■ adj. not willing.
– DERIVATIVES **unwillingly** adv. **unwillingness** n.

unwind ■ v. (past and past part. **unwound**) 1 undo or be undone after winding or being wound. 2 relax.

unwinking ■ adj. (of a stare or light) unwavering.
– DERIVATIVES **unwinkingly** adv.

unwinnable ■ adj. not winnable.

unwisdom ■ n. folly.

unwise ■ adj. foolish.
– DERIVATIVES **unwisely** adv.
– ORIGIN Old English *unwis* (see UN-[1], WISE[1]).

unwished ■ adj. not wished for.

unwitting ■ adj. 1 not aware of the full facts: *an unwitting accomplice.* 2 unintentional.
– DERIVATIVES **unwittingly** adv. **unwittingness** n.
– ORIGIN Old English *unwitende* 'not knowing or realizing' (see UN-[1], WIT[2]).

unwomanly ■ adj. not womanly.
– DERIVATIVES **unwomanliness** n.

unwonted /ʌnˈwəʊntɪd/ ■ adj. unaccustomed or unusual.
– DERIVATIVES **unwontedly** adv. **unwontedness** n.

unwooded ■ adj. (of a wine) not stored in a wooden cask.

unworkable ■ adj. 1 impractical. 2 (of a material) not able to be worked.
– DERIVATIVES **unworkability** n.

unworked ■ adj. not cultivated, mined, or carved.

unworkmanlike ■ adj. badly done or made.

unworldly ■ adj. 1 having little awareness of the realities of life. 2 not seeming to belong to this world.
– DERIVATIVES **unworldliness** n.

unworn ■ adj. not worn.

unworried ■ adj. not worried.

unworthy ■ adj. (**-ier**, **-iest**) not worthy.
– DERIVATIVES **unworthily** adv. **unworthiness** n.

unwound past and past participle of **UNWIND**.

unwounded ■ adj. not wounded.

unwrap ■ v. (**unwrapped**, **unwrapping**) remove the wrapping from.

unwrinkled ■ adj. not wrinkled.

unwritten ■ adj. 1 not written. 2 (especially of a law) resting originally on custom or judicial decision rather than on statute.

unyielding ■ adj. not yielding.
– DERIVATIVES **unyieldingly** adv. **unyieldingness** n.

unyoke ■ v. release (animals) from a yoke.

unzip ■ v. (**unzipped**, **unzipping**) 1 unfasten the zip of. 2 Computing decompress (a compressed file).

up ■ adv. 1 towards a higher place or position. ▶ to or at a place perceived as higher: *a walk up to the shops.* ▶ (of the sun) visible in the sky. ▶ towards the north. 2 (often **up and about**) out of bed. 3 to the place where someone is. 4 at or to a higher level or value. ▶ winning by a specified margin. 5 into the desired or a proper condition. ▶ so as to be finished or closed. 6 into a happy mood. 7 in a publicly visible place. 8 (of sailing) against the current or the wind. 9 (**up with** ——) expressing support for a person or thing. ■ prep. 1 from a lower to a higher point of. 2 from one end to another of (a street or other area). 3 informal at or to (a place). ■ adj. 1 directed or moving towards a higher place or position. ▶ denoting trains travelling towards the main terminus. 2 (of the road) being repaired. 3 (of a jockey) in the saddle. 4 cheerful. 5 (of a computer system) working properly. 6 at an end. 7 Physics denoting a flavour of quark having a charge of +⅔. ■ n. informal a period of good fortune. ■ v. (**upped**, **upping**) 1 (**up and do something**) informal do something abruptly

or boldly. **2** increase (a level or amount). **3** lift up.
–PHRASES **it is all up with** informal it is the end or there is no hope for. **on the up and up** informal **1** Brit. steadily improving. **2** chiefly N. Amer. honest; sincere. **something is up** informal something unusual or undesirable is happening. **up against** close to or touching. ▸ informal confronted with. **up and doing** active. **up and down** in various places throughout. **up and running** functioning. **up before** appearing for a hearing in the presence of (a judge, magistrate, etc.). **up for 1** available for. **2** due or being considered for. **3** informal ready to take part in. **up hill and down dale** all over the place. **up on** well informed about. **up to 1** as far as. ▸ (also **up until**) until. **2** indicating a maximum amount. **3** [with neg. or in questions] good enough for. **4** capable of. **5** the duty or choice of. **6** informal occupied with. **up top** Brit. informal in the way of intelligence. **up yours** vulgar slang expressing contemptuous defiance or rejection. **what's up?** informal what is going on? ▸ what is the matter?
–ORIGIN Old English, of Germanic origin.

up- ▪ prefix **1** (added to verbs and their derivatives) upwards: *upturned*. ▸ to a more recent time: *update*. **2** (added to nouns) denoting motion up: *uphill*. **3** (added to nouns) higher: *upland*. ▸ increased: *uptempo*.

up-anchor ▪ v. (of a ship) weigh anchor.

up-and-coming ▪ adj. likely to become successful.
–DERIVATIVES **up-and-comer** n.

up-and-under ▪ n. Rugby a high kick allowing time for teammates to reach the point where the ball will come down.

Upanishad /uːˈpanɪʃad/ ▪ n. each of a series of Hindu sacred treatises written in Sanskrit and expounding the Vedas.
–ORIGIN from Sanskrit, 'sitting near (i.e. at the feet of a master)', from *upa* 'near' + *ni-ṣad* 'sit down'.

upbeat ▪ n. (in music) an unaccented beat preceding an accented beat. ▪ adj. informal cheerful; optimistic.

upbraid ▪ v. scold or reproach.
–ORIGIN Old English *upbrēdan* 'allege as a basis for censure', from BRAID in the obsolete sense 'brandish'.

upbringing ▪ n. the treatment and instruction received from one's parents throughout childhood.
–ORIGIN C15: from obsolete *upbring* 'to rear'.

upcast ▪ n. (also **upcast shaft**) a shaft through which air leaves a mine. ▪ v. (past and past part. **-cast**) cast upward.

upcoming ▪ adj. forthcoming.

upcountry ▪ adv. & adj. inland.

update ▪ v. /ʌpˈdeɪt/ **1** make more modern. **2** give the latest information to. ▪ n. /ˈʌpdeɪt/ an act of updating or an updated version.
–DERIVATIVES **updatable** adj. (Computing).

updo ▪ n. informal a women's hairstyle in which the hair is swept up and secured on top or at the back of the head.

updraught (US **updraft**) ▪ n. an upward current of air.

upend ▪ v. set or turn on its end or upside down.

upfield ▪ adv. **1** (in sport) in or to a position nearer to the opponents' end of a field. **2** Physics in a direction corresponding to increasing field strength.

upfront informal ▪ adv. (usu. **up front**) **1** at the front; in front. **2** (of a payment) in advance. ▪ adj. **1** bold and frank. **2** (of a payment) made in advance.

upgrade ▪ v. raise to a higher standard or rank. ▪ n. an act of upgrading or an upgraded version.
–PHRASES **on the upgrade** improving.
–DERIVATIVES **upgradeability** (also **upgradability**) n. **upgradeable** (also **upgradable**) adj.

upgrowth ▪ n. the process or result of growing upwards. ▸ an upward growth.

upheaval ▪ n. **1** a violent or sudden change or disruption. **2** an upward displacement of part of the earth's crust.

uphill ▪ adv. towards the top of a slope. ▪ adj. **1** sloping upwards. **2** difficult: *an uphill struggle*. ▪ n. an upward slope.

uphold ▪ v. (past and past part. **-held**) confirm or support.
▸ maintain (a custom or practice).
–DERIVATIVES **upholder** n.

upholster /ʌpˈhəʊlstə, -ˈhɒl-/ ▪ v. provide (furniture) with a soft, padded covering. ▸ cover the walls or furniture in (a room) with textiles.
–ORIGIN C19: back-formation from UPHOLSTERER.

upholsterer ▪ n. a person who upholsters furniture.
–ORIGIN C17: from the obsolete noun *upholster*, from UPHOLD in the obsolete sense 'keep in repair'.

upholstery ▪ n. **1** soft, padded textile used to upholster furniture. **2** the art or practice of upholstering.

upkeep ▪ n. the process of keeping something in good condition. ▸ the cost of this or of supporting a person.

upland ▪ n. (also **uplands**) an area of high or hilly land.

uplift ▪ v. **1** [usu. as adj. **uplifted**] raise. **2** (**be uplifted**) (of an island, mountain, etc.) be created by an upward movement of the earth's surface. **3** [usu. as adj. **uplifting**] elevate morally or spiritually. **4** improve the standard of living of an underdeveloped community through social or economic empowerment. ▪ n. **1** an act of uplifting. **2** support from a garment, especially for a woman's bust. **3** a morally or spiritually uplifting influence.
–DERIVATIVES **uplifter** n. **upliftment** n.

uplighter (also **uplight**) ▪ n. a lamp designed to throw light upwards.
–DERIVATIVES **uplighting** n.

uplink ▪ n. a communications link to a satellite. ▪ v. provide with or send by such a link.

upload Computing ▪ v. transfer (data) to a larger computer system. ▪ n. the action or process of uploading.

upmarket ▪ adj. & adv. towards or relating to the more expensive or affluent sector of the market.

upmost ▪ adj. uppermost.

upon ▪ prep. more formal term for ON.
–ORIGIN Middle English: from UP + ON, suggested by Old Norse *upp á*.

upper[1] ▪ adj. **1** situated above another part. ▸ higher in position or status. ▸ (often **Upper**) denoting a younger part of an archaeological or stratigraphic division. **2** situated on higher ground. **3** [in place names] situated to the north. ▪ n. the part of a boot or shoe above the sole.
–PHRASES **have** (or **gain**) **the upper hand** have (or gain) an advantage or control. **on one's uppers** informal extremely short of money. **the upper crust** informal the upper classes.
–ORIGIN Middle English.

upper[2] ▪ n. informal a stimulating drug, especially amphetamine.
–ORIGIN 1960s: from the verb UP.

upper case ▪ n. capital letters.
–ORIGIN referring orig. to two type cases positioned on an angled stand, the case containing the capital letters being higher.

upper chamber ▪ n. another term for UPPER HOUSE.

upper class ▪ n. [treated as sing. or pl.] the social group with the highest status, especially the aristocracy. ▪ adj. of, relating to, or characteristic of the upper class.

uppercut ▪ n. a punch delivered with an upwards motion and the arm bent.

upper house ▪ n. the higher house in a bicameral parliament or similar legislature. ▸ (**the Upper House**) (in the UK) the House of Lords.

uppermost ▪ adj. (also **upmost**) highest in place, rank, or importance. ▪ adv. at or to the uppermost position.

upper school ▪ n. **1** a secondary school for children aged from about fourteen upwards. **2** the section of a school comprising or catering for the older pupils.

uppish ▪ adj. informal arrogantly self-assertive.
–DERIVATIVES **uppishly** adv. **uppishness** n.

uppity ▪ adj. informal self-important.
–ORIGIN C19: a fanciful formation from UP.

upraise ▪ v. raise to a higher level.

uprate ▪ v. **1** increase the value of. **2** improve the performance of.

upright ■ adj. 1 vertical; erect. ▶ (of a piano) having vertical strings. 2 greater in height than breadth. 3 strictly honourable or honest. ■ adv. in or into an upright position. ■ n. a vertical post, structure, or line.
– DERIVATIVES **uprightly** adv. **uprightness** n.
– ORIGIN Old English, of Germanic origin.

uprising ■ n. an act of resistance or rebellion.

upriver ■ adv. & adj. towards or situated at a point nearer the source of a river.

uproar ■ n. a loud and impassioned noise or disturbance. ▶ a public expression of outrage.
– ORIGIN C16: from Middle Dutch *uproer*, from *op* 'up' + *roer* 'confusion'.

uproarious ■ adj. 1 characterized by or provoking loud noise or uproar. 2 very funny.
– DERIVATIVES **uproariously** adv. **uproariousness** n.

uproot ■ v. 1 pull (a plant, tree, etc.) out of the ground. 2 move (someone) from their home or a familiar location. 3 eradicate.

uprush ■ n. a sudden upward surge or flow.

UPS ■ abbrev. Computing uninterruptible power supply.

ups-a-daisy ■ exclam. variant spelling of UPSY-DAISY.

upscale ■ adj. & adv. chiefly N. Amer. upmarket.

upset ■ v. /ʌpˈsɛt/ (-**setting**; past and past part. **-set**) 1 make unhappy, disappointed, or worried. 2 knock over. 3 disrupt. ▶ disturb the digestion of (a person's stomach). 4 [often as noun **upsetting**] shorten and thicken the end or edge of (a metal bar, wheel rim, or other object). ■ n. /ˈʌpsɛt/ 1 a state of being upset. 2 an unexpected result or situation. ■ adj. 1 /ʌpˈsɛt/ unhappy, disappointed, or worried. 2 /ˈʌpsɛt/ (of a person's stomach) having disturbed digestion.
– DERIVATIVES **upsetter** n. **upsetting** adj. **upsettingly** adv.

upset price ■ n. a reserve price in an auction.

upshift ■ n. 1 a change to a higher gear. 2 an increase.

upshot ■ n. the eventual outcome or conclusion.

upside ■ n. 1 the positive aspect of something. 2 a rise in share prices.

upside down ■ adv. & adj. 1 with the upper part where the lower part should be. 2 in or into total disorder.
– ORIGIN Middle English: orig. *up so down*, perhaps in the sense 'up as if down'.

upside-down cake ■ n. a sponge cake baked over a layer of fruit in syrup and inverted for serving.

upsilon /ʌpˈsʌɪlən, juːp-, ˈʊpsɪlɒn, ˈjuːp-/ ■ n. the twentieth letter of the Greek alphabet (Υ, υ), transliterated as 'u' or (chiefly in English words derived through Latin) as 'y'.
– ORIGIN Greek, 'slender U', from *psilos* 'slender', referring to the need to distinguish upsilon from the diphthong *oi*: in late Greek the two had the same pronunciation.

upsize ■ v. chiefly N. Amer. increase or cause to increase in size or complexity.

upskill ■ v. [often as noun **upskilling**] teach (an employee) additional skills. ▶ (of an employee) learn additional skills.

upslope ■ n. an upward slope. ■ adv. & adj. at or towards a higher point on a slope.

upstage ■ adv. & adj. at or towards the back of a stage. ■ v. 1 divert attention from (someone) towards oneself. 2 (of an actor) move towards the back of a stage to make (another actor) face away from the audience.

upstairs ■ adv. on or to an upper floor. ■ adj. (also **upstair**) situated on an upper floor. ■ n. an upper floor.

upstand ■ n. an upright structure or object.

upstanding ■ adj. 1 respectable. 2 erect.

upstart ■ n. derogatory a person who has risen suddenly to prominence, especially one who behaves arrogantly.

upstate US ■ adj. & adv. of, in, or to a part of a state remote from its large cities, especially the northern part. ■ n. an upstate area.

upstream ■ adv. & adj. situated or moving in the direction opposite to that in which a stream or river flows.

upstroke ■ n. an upwards stroke.

upsurge ■ n. an increase.

upswept ■ adj. curved, sloping, or directed upwards. ▶ (of the hair) brushed upwards and off the face.

1311 **urban legend**

upswing ■ n. an upward trend.

upsy-daisy (also **ups-a-daisy**, **oops-a-daisy**) ■ exclam. expressing encouragement to a child who has fallen or is being lifted.
– ORIGIN C19: alteration of earlier *up-a-daisy*; cf. LACKADAISICAL.

uptake ■ n. the action of taking up or making use of something.
– PHRASES **be quick** (or **slow**) **on the uptake** informal be quick (or slow) to understand something.

uptempo ■ adj. & adv. Music played with a fast or increased tempo.

upthrow ■ v. (past **-threw**; past part. **-thrown**) Geology displace upwards.

upthrust ■ n. 1 Physics the upward force that a fluid exerts on a body floating in it. 2 Geology the upward movement of part of the earth's surface. ■ v. [usu. as adj. **upthrust**] thrust upwards.

uptick ■ n. a small increase.

uptight ■ adj. informal nervously tense or angry.

uptime ■ n. time during which a machine, especially a computer, is in operation.

up to date ■ adj. incorporating or aware of the latest developments and trends.

uptown ■ adj. & adv. of, in, or into the residential area of a town or city. ▶ [as adj.] of or characteristic of an affluent area or people. ■ n. an uptown area.

upturn ■ n. an improvement or upward trend. ■ v. [usu. as adj. **upturned**] turn upwards or upside down.

uPVC ■ abbrev. unplasticized polyvinyl chloride, a rigid form of PVC used for pipework and window frames.

upward ■ adv. (also **upwards**) towards a higher point or level. ■ adj. moving or leading towards a higher point or level.
– PHRASES **upwards** (or **upward**) **of** more than.
– DERIVATIVES **upwardly** adv.

upwarp ■ n. Geology a broad elevated area of the earth's surface.

upwelling ■ n. a rising up of seawater, magma, or other liquid. ■ adj. (especially of emotion) building up.

upwind /ʌpˈwɪnd/ ■ adv. & adj. into the wind.

ur- /ʊə/ ■ comb. form primitive; original; earliest: *urtext*.
– ORIGIN from German.

uracil /ˈjʊərəsɪl/ ■ n. Biochemistry a compound found in living tissue as a constituent base of RNA (and replaced by thymine in DNA).
– ORIGIN C19: from *ur*(ea) + *ac*(etic) + -IL.

uraemia /jʊˈriːmɪə/ (US **uremia**) ■ n. Medicine a raised level in the blood of urea and other nitrogenous waste compounds.
– DERIVATIVES **uraemic** adj.
– ORIGIN C19: from Greek *ouron* 'urine' + *haima* 'blood'.

uraninite /jʊˈranɪnʌɪt/ ■ n. a black, grey, or brown mineral consisting mainly of uranium dioxide.

uranium /jʊˈreɪnɪəm/ ■ n. the chemical element of atomic number 92, a grey dense radioactive metal used as a fuel in nuclear reactors. (Symbol: **U**)
– ORIGIN C18: from the name of the planet *Uranus*.

urban ■ adj. of or relating to a town or city.
– DERIVATIVES **urbanism** n. **urbanist** n. **urbanization** (also **-isation**) n. **urbanize** (also **-ise**) v.
– ORIGIN C17: from Latin *urbanus*, from *urbs* 'city'.

urbane /əːˈbeɪn/ ■ adj. (especially of a man) suave, courteous, and refined.
– DERIVATIVES **urbanely** adv.
– ORIGIN C16: from French *urbain* or Latin *urbanus* (see URBAN).

urbanite ■ n. informal a town or city dweller.

urbanity ■ n. 1 an urbane quality or manner. 2 urban life.

urban legend (also **urban myth**) ■ n. an entertaining story or piece of information of uncertain origin that is circulated as though true.

urban renewal ■ n. the redevelopment of slum areas in a large city.

urchin /'ɜːtʃɪn/ ■ n. **1** a mischievous child, especially a raggedly dressed one. **2** short for SEA URCHIN.
– ORIGIN Middle English *hirchon*, *urchon* 'hedgehog', from Old Northern French *herichon*, from Latin *hericius* 'hedgehog'.

Urdu /'ʊədu:, 'ɜː-/ ■ n. an Indic language closely related to Hindi.
– ORIGIN from Persian (*zabān-i-*)*urdū* '(language of the) camp' (because it developed as a lingua franca after the Muslim invasions between the occupying armies and the people of Delhi), *urdū* being from Turkic *ordu* (see HORDE).

-ure ■ suffix forming nouns: **1** denoting an action, process, or result: *closure*. **2** denoting an office or function: *judicature*. **3** denoting a collective: *legislature*.
– ORIGIN from Old French *-ure*, from Latin *-ura*.

urea /jʊˈriːə, 'jʊərɪə/ ■ n. Biochemistry a colourless crystalline compound which is the main nitrogenous breakdown product of protein metabolism in mammals and is excreted in urine.
– ORIGIN C19: from French *urée*, from Greek *ouron* 'urine'.

uremia ■ n. US spelling of URAEMIA.

ureter /jʊˈriːtə, 'jʊərɪtə/ ■ n. Anatomy & Zoology the duct by which urine passes from the kidney to the bladder or cloaca.
– DERIVATIVES **ureteral** adj. **ureteric** /jʊərɪˈtɛrɪk/ adj.
– ORIGIN C16: from French *uretère*, from Greek *ourētēr*, from *ourein* 'urinate'.

urethane /'jʊərɪθeɪn, jʊˈrɛθeɪn/ ■ n. **1** Chemistry ethyl carbamate, a synthetic crystalline compound used to make pesticides and fungicides. **2** short for POLYURETHANE.
– ORIGIN C19: from French *uréthane* (see UREA, ETHANE).

urethra /jʊˈriːθrə/ ■ n. Anatomy & Zoology the duct by which urine is conveyed out of the body, and which in male vertebrates also conveys semen.
– DERIVATIVES **urethral** adj.
– ORIGIN C17: from Greek *ourēthra*, from *ourein* 'urinate'.

urethritis /jʊərɪˈθraɪtɪs/ ■ n. Medicine inflammation of the urethra.

urge ■ v. encourage or entreat earnestly to do something. ▸ strongly recommend. ▸ encourage to move more quickly. ▸ (**urge someone on**) encourage someone to continue. ■ n. a strong desire or impulse.
– ORIGIN C16: from Latin *urgere* 'press, drive'.

urgent ■ adj. **1** requiring immediate action or attention. **2** earnest and insistent.
– DERIVATIVES **urgency** n. **urgently** adv.
– ORIGIN C15: from Latin *urgent-* 'pressing, driving', from *urgere* (see URGE).

-uria ■ comb. form in nouns denoting that a substance is present in the urine, especially in excess: *glycosuria*.
– ORIGIN from Greek *-ouria*, from *ouron* 'urine'.

uric acid ■ n. Biochemistry an almost insoluble nitrogenous compound which is the main excretory product of birds, reptiles, and insects.
– DERIVATIVES **urate** n.
– ORIGIN C19: from French *urique*, from *urine* (see URINE).

uridine /'jʊərɪdiːn/ ■ n. Biochemistry a nucleoside consisting of uracil combined with ribose.

urinal /jʊˈraɪn(ə)l, 'jʊərɪn(ə)l/ ■ n. a receptacle into which men may urinate, typically attached to the wall in a public toilet.

urinalysis /jʊərɪˈnalɪsɪs/ ■ n. (pl. **urinalyses** /-siːz/) Medicine analysis of urine by physical, chemical, and microscopical means.

urinary ■ adj. of or relating to urine. ▸ relating to or denoting the organs, structures, and ducts in which urine is produced and discharged.

urinate ■ v. discharge urine.
– DERIVATIVES **urination** n.
– ORIGIN C16: from medieval Latin *urinare* 'urinate'.

urine /'jʊərɪn, -raɪn/ ■ n. a pale yellowish fluid stored in the bladder and discharged through the urethra, consisting of excess water and substances removed from the blood by the kidneys.
– ORIGIN Middle English: from Latin *urina*.

URL ■ abbrev. Computing uniform (or universal) resource locator, the address of a World Wide Web page.

urn ■ n. **1** a tall, rounded vase with a stem and base, especially one for storing a cremated person's ashes. **2** a large metal container with a tap, in which water is heated for making tea or coffee. ▸ a container of this type in which tea or coffee is made and kept hot.
– ORIGIN Middle English: from Latin *urna*; rel. to *urceus* 'pitcher'.

uro-1 ■ comb. form of or relating to urine or the urinary organs: *urogenital*.
– ORIGIN from Greek *ouron* 'urine'.

uro-2 ■ comb. form Zoology relating to a tail or the caudal region: *urodele*.
– ORIGIN from Greek *oura* 'tail'.

Urochordata /jʊərə(ʊ)kɔːˈdeɪtə/ ■ pl. n. Zoology a subphylum of chordate animals comprising the tunicates.
– DERIVATIVES **urochordate** n. & adj.
– ORIGIN from URO-2 + CHORDATA.

Urodela /jʊərə(ʊ)ˈdiːlə/ ■ pl. n. Zoology an order of amphibians comprising the newts and salamanders.
– DERIVATIVES **urodele** /'jʊərə(ʊ)diːl/ n. & adj.
– ORIGIN from URO-2 'tail' + Greek *dēlos* 'evident'.

urogenital ■ adj. relating to or denoting both the urinary and genital organs.

urology /jʊˈrɒlədʒi/ ■ n. the branch of medicine concerned with the urinary system.
– DERIVATIVES **urologic** adj. **urological** adj. **urologist** n.

ursine /'ɜːsaɪn, -ɪn/ ■ adj. of, relating to, or resembling bears.
– ORIGIN C16: from Latin *ursinus*, from *ursus* 'bear'.

Ursuline /'ɜːsjʊlaɪn, -lɪn/ ■ n. a nun of an order founded in northern France in 1535 for nursing the sick and teaching girls. ■ adj. of or relating to this order.
– ORIGIN from St *Ursula*, the founder's patron saint.

urtext /'uːətɛkst/ ■ n. (pl. **urtexte** /-tə/) an original or the earliest version of a text.

urticaria /ɜːtɪˈkɛːrɪə/ ■ n. Medicine a rash of round, red weals on the skin which itch intensely, caused by an allergic reaction.
– ORIGIN C18: from Latin *urtica* 'nettle'.

Uruguayan /jʊərəˈgwaɪən/ ■ n. a native or inhabitant of Uruguay. ■ adj. of or relating to Uruguay.

US ■ abbrev. United States.

us ■ pron. [first person pl.] **1** used by a speaker to refer to himself or herself and one or more others as the object of a verb or preposition. ▸ used after the verb 'to be' and after 'than' or 'as'. ▸ informal to or for ourselves. **2** informal me.
– ORIGIN Old English, of Germanic origin.

USA ■ abbrev. **1** United States of America. **2** United States Army.

usable (also **useable**) ■ adj. able to be used.
– DERIVATIVES **usability** n.

USAF ■ abbrev. United States Air Force.

usage ■ n. **1** the action of using something or the fact of being used. **2** habitual or customary practice.

usance /'juːz(ə)ns/ ■ n. the time allowed for the payment of foreign bills of exchange.
– ORIGIN Middle English: from Old French, from the base of *user* 'to use'.

USB ■ abbrev. Computing universal serial bus.

USD ■ abbrev. United States dollar(s).

use ■ v. /juːz/ **1** take, hold, or deploy as a means of accomplishing or achieving something. ▸ (**use something up**) consume or expend the whole of something. ▸ informal take (an illegal drug). **2** treat in a particular way. ▸ exploit unfairly. **3** (**one could use**) informal one would like or benefit from. **4** /juːst/ (**used to**) did repeatedly or existed in the past. **5** /juːst/ (**be/get used to**) be or become familiar with through experience. ■ n. /juːs/ **1** the action of using or state of being used. ▸ the ability or power to

exercise or manipulate something: *he lost the use of his legs.* ▶ a purpose for or way in which something can be used. **2** value; advantage.
- PHRASES **have no use for** informal dislike or be impatient with. **make use of** benefit from. **use someone's name** cite someone as an authority or reference.
- ORIGIN Middle English: from Old French *us* (n.), *user* (v.), from Latin *usus*, *uti* 'to use'.

useable ■ adj. variant spelling of USABLE.

use-by date ■ n. the recommended date by which a perishable product should be used or consumed.

used /juːzd/ ■ adj. having already been used. ▶ second-hand.

useful ■ adj. **1** able to be used for a practical purpose or in several ways. **2** informal very able or competent.
- PHRASES **make oneself useful** do something that is of some value or benefit.
- DERIVATIVES **usefully** adv. **usefulness** n.

useful load ■ n. the load carried by an aircraft in addition to its own weight.

useless ■ adj. **1** serving no purpose. **2** informal having little ability or skill.
- DERIVATIVES **uselessly** adv. **uselessness** n.

Usenet ■ n. Computing an Internet service consisting of thousands of newsgroups.

user ■ n. **1** a person who uses or operates something. **2** a person who exploits others. **3** Law the continued use or enjoyment of a right.

user-friendly ■ adj. easy to use or understand.
- DERIVATIVES **user-friendliness** n.

usher ■ n. **1** a person who shows people to their seats in a theatre or cinema or at a wedding. **2** an official in a law court who swears in jurors and witnesses and keeps order. ■ v. show or guide somewhere.
- ORIGIN Middle English: from Anglo-Norman French *usser*, from medieval Latin *ustiarius*, from Latin *ostiarius*, from *ostium* 'door'.

usherette ■ n. a woman who shows people to their seats in a cinema or theatre.

USN ■ abbrev. United States Navy.

USS ■ abbrev. United States Ship.

USSR ■ abbrev. historical Union of Soviet Socialist Republics.

usual ■ adj. habitually or typically occurring or done. ■ n. (**the/one's usual**) informal the drink someone habitually prefers. ▶ the thing which is typically done or present.
- DERIVATIVES **usually** adv. **usualness** n.
- ORIGIN Middle English: from Old French, or from late Latin *usualis*, from *usus* (see USE).

usufruct /ˈjuːzjʊfrʌkt/ ■ n. Law the right to enjoy the use of another's property short of the destruction or waste of its substance.
- DERIVATIVES **usufructuary** adj. & n.
- ORIGIN C17: from medieval Latin *usufructus*, from Latin *usus (et) fructus* 'use (and) enjoyment'.

usurer /ˈjuːʒərə/ ■ n. a person who lends money at unreasonably high rates of interest.
- ORIGIN Middle English: from Old French *usure*, from Latin *usura* (see USURY).

usurious /juːˈʒʊərɪəs, juːˈzj-/ ■ adj. of or relating to usury.
- DERIVATIVES **usuriously** adv.

usurp /jʊˈzɜːp, jʊˈsɜːp/ ■ v. **1** take (a position of power) illegally or by force. ▶ supplant. **2** (**usurp on/upon**) archaic encroach or infringe upon.
- DERIVATIVES **usurpation** /ˌjuːzɜːˈpeɪʃ(ə)n, ˌjuːs-/ n. **usurper** n.
- ORIGIN Middle English: from Old French *usurper*, from Latin *usurpare* 'seize for use'.

usury /ˈjuːʒ(ə)ri/ ■ n. the practice of lending money at unreasonably high rates of interest. ▶ archaic interest at such rates.
- ORIGIN Middle English: from Anglo-Norman French *usurie*, or from medieval Latin *usuria*, from Latin *usura*, from *usus* (see USE).

UTC ■ abbrev. Universal Time Coordinated.

Utd ■ abbrev. United (in names of soccer teams).

ute /juːt/ ■ n. N. American & Austral./NZ informal a utility vehicle.

1313 **utter**

utensil ■ n. a tool or container, especially for household use.
- ORIGIN Middle English: from Old French *utensile*, from Latin *utensilis* 'usable', from *uti* (see USE).

uteri plural form of UTERUS.

uterine /ˈjuːtərɪn, -ʌɪn/ ■ adj. **1** of or relating to the uterus. **2** having the same mother but not the same father.
- ORIGIN Middle English: from UTERUS; sense 2 from late Latin *uterinus*.

uterus ■ n. (pl. **uteri** /-rʌɪ/) the womb.
- ORIGIN from Latin.

utile /ˈjuːtɪli/ ■ n. a large tropical African hardwood tree with wood used as a substitute for mahogany. [*Entandrophragma utile*.]
- ORIGIN 1950s: from Latin *utilis* 'useful'.

utilitarian /juːˌtɪlɪˈtɛːrɪən/ ■ adj. **1** useful or practical rather than attractive. **2** Philosophy of, relating to, or adhering to utilitarianism. ■ n. Philosophy an adherent of utilitarianism.

utilitarianism ■ n. the doctrine that actions are right if they are useful or for the benefit of a majority. ▶ the doctrine that the greatest happiness of the greatest number should be the guiding principle of conduct.

utility ■ n. (pl. **-ies**) **1** the state of being useful, profitable, or beneficial. ▶ (in game theory or economics) the value of that which is sought to be maximized in any situation involving a choice. **2** a public utility. **3** Computing a utility program. ■ adj. **1** useful, especially through having several functions. **2** functional rather than attractive.
- ORIGIN Middle English: from Old French *utilite*, from Latin *utilitas*, from *utilis* 'useful'.

utility knife ■ n. a Stanley knife.

utility pole ■ n. N. Amer. a telegraph pole.

utility program ■ n. Computing a program for carrying out a routine function.

utility room ■ n. a room with appliances for washing and other domestic work.

utility vehicle (also **utility truck**) ■ n. a truck having low sides and used for small loads.

utilize (also **-ise**) ■ v. make practical and effective use of.
- DERIVATIVES **utilizable** (also **-isable**) adj. **utilization** (also **-isation**) n. **utilizer** (also **-iser**) n.
- ORIGIN C19: from French *utiliser*, from Italian *utilizzare*, from Latin *utilis* 'useful'.

-ution ■ suffix (forming nouns) equivalent to -ATION (as in *solution*).
- ORIGIN from Latin *-utio(n-)*.

utmost ■ adj. most extreme; greatest. ■ n. (**the utmost**) the greatest or most extreme extent or amount.
- PHRASES **do one's utmost** do the most that one is able.
- ORIGIN Old English *ūt(e)mest* 'outermost'.

Utopia /juːˈtəʊpɪə/ ■ n. an imagined perfect place or state of things.
- ORIGIN the title of a book (1516) by Sir Thomas More, based on Greek *ou* 'not' + *topos* 'place'.

utopian ■ adj. idealistic. ■ n. an idealistic reformer.
- DERIVATIVES **utopianism** n.

utricle /ˈjuːtrɪk(ə)l/ ■ n. **1** Biology a small cell, sac, or bladder-like protuberance in an animal or plant. **2** (also **utriculus** /juːˈtrɪkjʊləs/) Anatomy the larger of the two fluid-filled sacs forming part of the labyrinth of the inner ear. Compare with SACCULE.
- DERIVATIVES **utricular** /juːˈtrɪkjʊlə/ adj.
- ORIGIN C18: from French *utricule* or Latin *utriculus*, diminutive of *uter* 'leather bag'.

utter[1] ■ adj. complete; absolute: *utter amazement.*
- DERIVATIVES **utterly** adv.
- ORIGIN Old English *ūtera*, *ūttra* 'outer', comparative of *ūt* 'out'.

utter[2] ■ v. **1** make (a sound) or say (something). **2** Law put (forged money) into circulation.
- DERIVATIVES **utterable** adj. **utterer** n.
- ORIGIN Middle English: from Middle Dutch *ūteren* 'speak, make known, give currency to (coins)'.

utterance

utterance ■ n. a word, statement, or sound uttered. ▸ the action of uttering. ▸ Linguistics an uninterrupted chain of speech or writing.

uttermost ■ adj. & n. another term for UTMOST.

U-turn ■ n. **1** the turning of a vehicle in a U-shaped course so as to face the opposite way. **2** a reversal of policy.

UV ■ abbrev. ultraviolet.

UVA ■ abbrev. ultraviolet radiation of relatively long wavelengths.

UVB ■ abbrev. ultraviolet radiation of relatively short wavelengths.

UVC ■ abbrev. ultraviolet radiation of very short wavelengths, which does not penetrate the earth's ozone layer.

uvea /ˈjuːvɪə/ ■ n. the pigmented layer of the eye, comprising the iris, choroid, and ciliary body.
– DERIVATIVES **uveal** adj. **uveitis** n.
– ORIGIN Middle English: from medieval Latin, from Latin *uva* 'grape'.

uvula /ˈjuːvjʊlə/ ■ n. (pl. **uvulae** /-liː/) Anatomy a fleshy extension at the back of the soft palate which hangs above the throat.
– ORIGIN Middle English: from late Latin, diminutive of Latin *uva* 'grape'.

uvular /ˈjuːvjʊlə/ ■ adj. **1** Phonetics articulated with the back of the tongue and the uvula, as *r* in French. **2** Anatomy of or relating to the uvula. ■ n. Phonetics a uvular consonant.

uxorial /ʌkˈsɔːrɪəl/ ■ adj. of or relating to a wife.
– ORIGIN C19: from Latin *uxor* 'wife'.

uxoricide /ʌkˈsɔːrɪsʌɪd/ ■ n. the killing of one's wife. ▸ a man who kills his wife.
– DERIVATIVES **uxoricidal** adj.
– ORIGIN C19: from Latin *uxor* 'wife' + -CIDE.

uxorious /ʌkˈsɔːrɪəs/ ■ adj. showing great or excessive fondness for one's wife.
– DERIVATIVES **uxoriously** adv. **uxoriousness** n.
– ORIGIN C16: from Latin *uxoriosus*, from *uxor* 'wife'.

Uzbek /ˈʊzbɛk, ˈʌz-/ ■ n. **1** a member of a Turkic people living mainly in Uzbekistan. ▸ a native or national of Uzbekistan. **2** the Turkic language of Uzbekistan.
– ORIGIN the name in Uzbek.

Uzi /ˈuːzi/ ■ n. a type of sub-machine gun.
– ORIGIN 1950s: from *Uziel* Gal, the Israeli army officer who designed it.

Vv

V¹ (also **v**) ▪ n. (pl. **Vs** or **V's**) **1** the twenty-second letter of the alphabet. **2** denoting the next after U in a set of items, categories, etc. **3** the Roman numeral for five. **4** [as modifier] denoting an internal-combustion engine with a number of cylinders arranged in two rows at an angle to each other.

V² ▪ abbrev. volt(s). ▪ symb. **1** the chemical element vanadium. **2** voltage or potential difference. **3** (in mathematical formulae) volume.

V-1 ▪ n. a small bomb powered by a simple jet engine, used by the Germans in the Second World War.
– ORIGIN abbrev. of German *Vergeltungswaffe* 'reprisal weapon'.

V-2 ▪ n. a rocket-powered flying bomb used by the Germans in the Second World War.
– ORIGIN see **V-1**.

v ▪ abbrev. **1** Grammar verb. **2** verse. **3** verso. **4** versus. **5** very. **6** (in textual references) vide. ▪ symb. velocity.

Vaalie /ˈvɑːli/ ▪ n. S. African humorous or derogatory a person from Gauteng (formerly part of the Transvaal).
– ORIGIN 1970s: from *Transvaal*, the name of a former region of South Africa north of the Vaal river.

vac ▪ n. informal a vacation.

vacancy ▪ n. (pl. **-ies**) **1** an unoccupied position or job. **2** an available room in a hotel, guest house, etc. **3** empty space. **4** lack of intelligence or understanding.

vacant ▪ adj. **1** not occupied; empty. ▶ (of a position) not filled. **2** showing no intelligence or interest.
– DERIVATIVES **vacantly** adv.
– ORIGIN Middle English: from Old French, or from Latin *vacare* 'remain empty'.

vacant possession ▪ n. ownership of a property on completion of a sale, any previous occupant having moved out.

vacate /veɪˈkeɪt, vəˈkeɪt/ ▪ v. **1** leave (a place). ▶ give up (a position or job). **2** Law cancel or annul (a judgement, contract, or charge).
– ORIGIN C17 (*vacation* Middle English): from Latin *vacare* 'leave empty'.

vacation ▪ n. **1** a holiday period between terms in universities and law courts. ▶ chiefly N. Amer. a holiday. **2** the action of vacating. ▪ v. chiefly N. Amer. take a holiday.
– DERIVATIVES **vacationer** n.

vaccinate /ˈvaksɪneɪt/ ▪ v. treat with a vaccine to produce immunity against a disease.
– DERIVATIVES **vaccination** n. **vaccinator** n.

vaccine /ˈvaksiːn, -ɪn/ ▪ n. Medicine an antigenic preparation used to stimulate the production of antibodies and provide immunity against a disease.
– ORIGIN C18: from Latin *vaccinus*, from *vacca* 'cow' (because of the early use of the cowpox virus against smallpox).

vaccinia /vakˈsɪnɪə/ ▪ n. Medicine cowpox or the virus causing it.
– ORIGIN C19: from Latin *vaccinus* (see **VACCINE**).

vacillate /ˈvasɪleɪt/ ▪ v. waver between different opinions or actions.
– DERIVATIVES **vacillation** n. **vacillator** n.
– ORIGIN C16: from Latin *vacillare* 'sway'.

vacua plural form of **VACUUM**.

vacuole /ˈvakjʊəl/ ▪ n. Biology a space or vesicle within the cytoplasm of a cell, enclosed by a membrane and typically containing fluid.
– DERIVATIVES **vacuolar** /ˈvakjʊələ/ adj. **vacuolation** n.
– ORIGIN C19: from French, diminutive of Latin *vacuus* 'empty'.

vacuous /ˈvakjʊəs/ ▪ adj. **1** showing a lack of thought or intelligence. **2** archaic empty.
– DERIVATIVES **vacuity** /vəˈkjuːɪti/ n. **vacuously** adv. **vacuousness** n.
– ORIGIN C17: from Latin *vacuus* 'empty'.

vacuum /ˈvakjʊəm/ ▪ n. (pl. **vacuums** or **vacua** /-jʊə/) **1** a space entirely devoid of matter. ▶ a space or container from which the air has been completely or partly removed. **2** a gap left by the loss or departure of someone or something important. **3** (pl. **vacuums**) informal a vacuum cleaner. ▪ v. informal clean with a vacuum cleaner.
– PHRASES **in a vacuum** in isolation from the normal context.
– ORIGIN C16: from Latin *vacuus* 'empty'.

vacuum brake ▪ n. a railway vehicle brake operated by changes in pressure in a pipe which is kept exhausted of air.

vacuum cleaner ▪ n. an electrical apparatus that collects dust from floors and other surfaces by means of suction.
– DERIVATIVES **vacuum-clean** v.

vacuum flask ▪ n. a container that keeps a substance hot or cold by means of a double wall enclosing a vacuum.

vacuum gauge ▪ n. a gauge for testing pressure after the production of a vacuum.

vacuum-pack ▪ v. seal (a product) in a pack or wrapping with the air removed. ▪ n. (**vacuum pack**) a pack of this kind.

vacuum tube ▪ n. a sealed glass tube containing a near-vacuum which allows the free passage of electric current.

vade mecum /ˌvɑːdi ˈmeɪkəm, ˌveɪdi ˈmiːkəm/ ▪ n. a handbook or guide kept constantly at hand.
– ORIGIN C17: modern Latin, 'go with me'.

vadose /ˈveɪdəʊs/ ▪ adj. relating to or denoting underground water in the zone above the water table. Compare with **PHREATIC**.
– ORIGIN C19: from Latin *vadosus*, from *vadum* 'shallow expanse of water'.

vagabond ▪ n. **1** a vagrant. **2** informal, dated a rogue. ▪ adj. having no settled home.
– DERIVATIVES **vagabondage** n.
– ORIGIN Middle English: from Old French, or from Latin *vagabundus*, from *vagari* 'wander'.

vagal ▪ adj. of or relating to the vagus nerve.

vagary /ˈveɪɡ(ə)ri/ ▪ n. (pl. **-ies**) an unexpected and inexplicable change.
– ORIGIN C16: from Latin *vagari* 'wander'.

vagi plural form of **VAGUS**.

vagina /vəˈdʒʌɪnə/ ▪ n. (pl. **vaginas** or **vaginae** /-niː/) the muscular tube leading from the vulva to the cervix in women and most female mammals.
– DERIVATIVES **vaginal** adj.
– ORIGIN C17: from Latin, 'sheath, scabbard'.

vaginismus /ˌvadʒɪˈnɪzməs/ ▪ n. painful spasmodic contraction of the vagina in response to physical contact or pressure, especially in sexual intercourse.
– ORIGIN C19: from Latin *vagina* (see **VAGINA**).

vaginitis /ˌvadʒɪˈnʌɪtɪs/ ▪ n. inflammation of the vagina.

vagrant /ˈveɪɡr(ə)nt/ ▪ n. **1** a person without a home or job. ▶ archaic a wanderer. **2** Ornithology a bird that has strayed from its usual range or migratory route. ▪ adj. of, relating to, or living like a vagrant; wandering. ▶ poetic/literary unpredictable or inconstant.
– DERIVATIVES **vagrancy** n. **vagrantly** adv.
– ORIGIN Middle English: from Anglo-Norman French *vagrant* 'wandering about', from *vagrer*.

vague ▪ adj. of uncertain or indefinite character or

---

s sit　　t top　　v voice　　w we　　z zoo　　ʃ she　　ʒ decision　　θ thin　　ð this　　ŋ ring　　x loch　　tʃ chip　　dʒ jar

meaning. ▸ imprecise in thought or expression.
– DERIVATIVES **vaguely** adv. **vagueness** n. **vaguish** adj.
– ORIGIN C16: from French, or from Latin *vagus* 'wandering, uncertain'.

vagus /'veɪgəs/ ■ n. (pl. **vagi** /-dʒaɪ, -gaɪ/) Anatomy each of the pair of cranial nerves supplying the heart, lungs, and other organs of the chest and abdomen.
– ORIGIN C19: from Latin (see **VAGUE**).

vain ■ adj. **1** having or showing an excessively high opinion of one's appearance or abilities. **2** useless. ▸ having no meaning or likelihood of fulfilment: *a vain boast.*
– PHRASES **in vain** without success. **take someone's name in vain** use someone's name in a way that shows a lack of respect.
– DERIVATIVES **vainly** adv.
– ORIGIN Middle English: from Latin *vanus* 'empty, without substance'.

vainglory ■ n. poetic/literary excessive vanity.
– DERIVATIVES **vainglorious** adj. **vaingloriously** adv. **vaingloriousness** n.
– ORIGIN Middle English: suggested by Old French *vaine gloire*, Latin *vana gloria*.

vair /vɛː/ ■ n. Heraldry fur represented by interlocking rows of blue and white shield-shaped or bell-shaped figures.
– ORIGIN Middle English: from Latin *varius* (see **VARIOUS**).

vairy /'vɛːri/ ■ adj. Heraldry resembling vair, typically in other colours.

valance /'val(ə)ns/ (also **valence**) ■ n. a length of decorative drapery attached to the canopy or frame of a bed to screen the structure or space beneath it. ▸ a sheet with a gathered border designed to hang down over the mattress and sides of a bed. ▸ a length of decorative drapery screening the curtain fittings above a window.
– DERIVATIVES **valanced** adj.
– ORIGIN Middle English: perhaps Anglo-Norman French, from a shortened form of Old French *avaler*.

vale /veɪl/ ■ n. poetic/literary (except in place names) a valley.
– PHRASES **vale of tears** poetic/literary the world as a scene of trouble or sorrow.
– ORIGIN Middle English: from Old French *val*, from Latin *vallis*.

valediction /ˌvalɪ'dɪkʃ(ə)n/ ■ n. the action of saying farewell. ▸ a farewell.
– ORIGIN C17: from Latin *vale* 'goodbye' + *dicere* 'to say', on the pattern of *benediction*.

valedictorian /ˌvalɪdɪk'tɔːrɪən/ ■ n. (in North America) a student who delivers the valedictory at a graduation ceremony.

valedictory /ˌvalɪ'dɪkt(ə)ri/ ■ adj. serving as a farewell. ■ n. (pl. **-ies**) a farewell address.

valence[1] /'veɪl(ə)ns/ ■ n. Chemistry another term for **VALENCY**.

valence[2] n. variant spelling of **VALANCE**.

valency /'veɪl(ə)nsi/ ■ n. (pl. **-ies**) Chemistry the combining power of an element, especially as measured by the number of hydrogen atoms it can displace or combine with.
– ORIGIN C17: from late Latin *valentia* 'power, competence'.

valentine ■ n. a card sent, often anonymously, on St Valentine's Day (14 February) to a person one loves or is attracted to. ▸ a person to whom one sends such a card.
– ORIGIN Middle English: from Old French *Valentin*, from Latin *Valentinus*, the name of two saints.

valerian /və'lɪərɪən/ ■ n. a European flowering plant, the root of which is used medicinally for its sedative properties. [*Valeriana officinalis*.]
– ORIGIN Middle English: from Old French *valeriane*, from medieval Latin *valeriana* (*herba*), from *Valerianus* 'of Valerius' (a personal name).

valet /'valɪt, 'valeɪ/ ■ n. **1** a man's personal male attendant, responsible for his clothes and appearance. ▸ a hotel employee performing such duties for guests. **2** a person employed to clean or park cars. ■ v. (**valeted, valeting**) **1** act as a valet to. ▸ work as a valet. **2** clean (a car).
– ORIGIN C15: from French; rel. to **VASSAL**.

valeta ■ n. variant spelling of **VELETA**.

valetudinarian /ˌvalɪtjuːdɪ'nɛːrɪən/ ■ n. a person who is unduly anxious about their health. ▸ a person in poor health. ■ adj. showing undue concern about one's health. ▸ in poor health.
– ORIGIN C18: from Latin *valetudinarius* 'in ill health'.

valetudinary /ˌvalɪ'tjuːdɪn(ə)ri/ ■ adj. & n. (pl. **-ies**) another term for **VALETUDINARIAN**.

valgus /'valgəs/ ■ n. Medicine a deformity involving oblique displacement of part of a limb away from the midline.
– ORIGIN C19: from Latin, 'knock-kneed'.

Valhalla /val'halə/ ■ n. (in Scandinavian mythology) a palace in which heroes killed in battle feasted for eternity.
– ORIGIN from Old Norse *Valhǫll*, from *valr* 'the slain' + *hǫll* 'hall'.

valiant ■ adj. showing courage or determination.
– DERIVATIVES **valiantly** adv.
– ORIGIN Middle English: from Old French *vailant*, from Latin *valere* 'be strong'.

valid ■ adj. **1** actually supporting the intended point or claim. **2** executed in compliance with the law. ▸ legally or officially acceptable.
– DERIVATIVES **validity** n. **validly** adv.
– ORIGIN C16: from French *valide* or Latin *validus* 'strong'.

validate ■ v. check or prove the validity of. ▸ confirm. ▸ make or declare legally valid.
– DERIVATIVES **validation** n.

valine /'veɪliːn/ ■ n. Biochemistry an amino acid which is an essential nutrient in the diet.
– ORIGIN C20: from *val*(*eric acid*).

valise /və'liːz/ ■ n. a small travelling bag or suitcase.
– ORIGIN C17: from French, from Italian *valigia*; cf. medieval Latin *valesia*.

Valium /'valɪəm/ ■ n. trademark for **DIAZEPAM**.
– ORIGIN 1960s.

Valkyrie /val'kɪəri, 'valkɪri/ ■ n. (in Scandinavian mythology) each of Odin's twelve handmaids who conducted slain warriors of their choice to Valhalla.
– ORIGIN from Old Norse *Valkyrja* 'chooser of the slain', from *valr* 'the slain' + *kyrja* 'chooser'.

valley ■ n. (pl. **-eys**) **1** a low area between hills or mountains, typically with a river or stream flowing through it. **2** Architecture an internal angle formed by the intersecting planes of a roof, or by the slope of a roof and a wall.
– ORIGIN Middle English: from Old French *valee*, from Latin *vallis*.

valor ■ n. US spelling of **VALOUR**.

valorize /'valəraɪz/ (also **-ise**) ■ v. give or ascribe value or validity to. ▸ artificially raise or fix the price or value of.
– DERIVATIVES **valorization** (also **-isation**) n.
– ORIGIN 1920s: back-formation from *valorization*, from French *valorisation*, from *valeur* 'value'.

valour (US **valor**) ■ n. courage in the face of danger, especially in battle.
– DERIVATIVES **valorous** adj.
– ORIGIN Middle English: from late Latin *valor*, from *valere* 'be strong'.

Valsalva manoeuvre /val'salvə/ ■ n. Medicine the action of attempting to exhale with the nostrils and mouth, or the glottis, closed, serving to increase pressure in the middle ear and the chest or equalize pressure in the ears.
– ORIGIN C19: named after the Italian anatomist Antonio M. Valsalva.

valuable ■ adj. worth a great deal of money. ▸ extremely useful or important. ■ n. (**valuables**) valuable things, especially small items of personal property.
– DERIVATIVES **valuably** adv.

valuation ■ n. an estimation of something's worth, especially one carried out by a professional valuer. ▸ the monetary worth estimated.
– DERIVATIVES **valuate** v.

value ■ n. **1** the regard that something is held to deserve; importance or worth. ▸ material or monetary worth. ▸ the worth of something compared to its price: *at R69.95 it's good value.* **2** (**values**) principles or standards of behaviour. **3** the numerical amount denoted by an algebraic term; a magnitude, quantity, or number. **4** Linguistics the meaning of a word or other linguistic unit.

▶ the sound represented by a letter or symbol. ■ v. (**values**, **valued**, **valuing**) **1** estimate the value of. **2** consider to be important or beneficial.
– DERIVATIVES **valueless** adj. **valuelessness** n. **valuer** n.
– ORIGIN Middle English: from Old French, from *valoir* 'be worth', from Latin *valere*.

value added ■ n. Economics the amount by which the value of an article is increased at each stage of its production, exclusive of initial costs. ■ adj. **1** (of goods) having added features for which the buyer is prepared to pay extra. **2** (of a company) offering specialized or extended services.

value added tax ■ n. a tax on the amount by which the value of an article has been increased at each stage of its production or distribution.

value judgement ■ n. an assessment of something as good or bad in terms of one's standards or priorities.

valve ■ n. **1** a device for controlling the passage of fluid through a pipe or duct, especially an automatic device allowing movement in one direction only. **2** a cylindrical mechanism to vary the effective length of the tube in a brass musical instrument. **3** Anatomy & Zoology a membranous fold in an organ or vessel which allows blood or other fluid to flow in one direction. **4** Zoology each of the halves of the hinged shell of a bivalve mollusc or brachiopod. **5** Botany each of the halves or sections into which a dry fruit dehisces.
– DERIVATIVES **valved** adj. **valveless** adj.
– ORIGIN Middle English (denoting a leaf of a folding or double door): from Latin *valva*.

valve gear ■ n. the mechanism that controls the opening and closing of the cylinder valves in a steam engine or internal-combustion engine.

valvular ■ adj. relating to, having, or acting as a valve or valves.

valvulitis /ˌvalvjʊˈlaɪtɪs/ ■ n. Medicine inflammation of the valves of the heart.

vamoose /vəˈmuːs/ ■ v. informal depart hurriedly.
– ORIGIN C19: from Spanish *vamos* 'let us go'.

vamp[1] ■ n. **1** the upper front part of a boot or shoe. **2** (in jazz and popular music) a short, simple introductory passage, usually repeated several times until otherwise instructed. ■ v. **1** repeat a short, simple passage of music. **2** (**vamp something up**) informal repair or improve something. **3** attach a new upper to (a boot or shoe).
– ORIGIN Middle English (denoting the foot of a stocking, later something patched or improvised): shortening of Old French *avantpie*, from *avant* 'before' + *pie* 'foot'.

vamp[2] informal ■ n. a woman who uses sexual attraction to exploit men. ■ v. blatantly set out to attract (a man).
– DERIVATIVES **vampish** adj. **vampishly** adv. **vampishness** n. **vampy** adj.
– ORIGIN C20: abbrev. of VAMPIRE.

vampire /ˈvampʌɪə/ ■ n. **1** (in folklore) a corpse supposed to leave its grave at night to drink the blood of the living. **2** a small bat that feeds on blood by piercing the skin with its incisor teeth, found mainly in tropical America. [*Desmodus rotundus* and other species.] **3** (also **vampire trap**) Theatre a small spring trapdoor used for sudden disappearances from a stage.
– DERIVATIVES **vampiric** /-ˈpɪrɪk/ adj. **vampirism** n.
– ORIGIN C18: from Hungarian *vampir*, perhaps from Turkish *uber* 'witch'.

van[1] ■ n. a covered motor vehicle used for transporting goods or people.
– ORIGIN C19: shortening of CARAVAN.

van[2] ■ n. (**the van**) **1** the foremost part of a company of people, especially the foremost division of an advancing military force. **2** the forefront.
– ORIGIN C17: abbrev. of VANGUARD.

van[3] ■ n. Brit. Tennis informal term for ADVANTAGE.

vanadate /ˈvanədeɪt/ ■ n. Chemistry a salt in which the anion contains both vanadium and oxygen.

vanadium /vəˈneɪdɪəm/ ■ n. the chemical element of atomic number 23, a hard grey metal used to make alloy steels. (Symbol: **V**)
– ORIGIN C19: from Old Norse *Vanadis* (a name of the Scandinavian goddess Freyja).

Van Allen belt ■ n. each of two regions of intense radiation partly surrounding the earth at heights of several thousand kilometres.
– ORIGIN C20: named after the American physicist J. A. *Van Allen*.

vandal ■ n. **1** a person who deliberately destroys or damages public or private property. **2** (**Vandal**) a member of a Germanic people that ravaged Gaul, Spain, Rome, and North Africa in the 4th–5th centuries.
– DERIVATIVES **vandalism** n. **vandalistic** adj.
– ORIGIN from Latin *Vandalus*, of Germanic origin.

vandalize (also **-ise**) ■ v. deliberately destroy or damage (property).
– DERIVATIVES **vandalization** (also **-isation**) n.

Van der Hum ■ n. a South African liqueur flavoured with tangerine peel, herbs, and spices.
– ORIGIN C19: perhaps a personal name.

van der Waals forces /ˌvan də ˈwɑːlz, ˈvɑːlz/ ■ pl. n. Chemistry weak, short-range electrostatic attractive forces between uncharged molecules, arising from the interaction of permanent or transient electric dipole moments.
– ORIGIN C19: named after the Dutch physicist Johannes *van der Waals*.

Vandyke /vanˈdʌɪk/ ■ n. (also **Vandyke beard**) a neat pointed beard.
– ORIGIN C18: named after the painter Sir Anthony *Van Dyck*, whose portraits frequently depict such styles.

Vandyke brown ■ n. a deep rich brown.

vane ■ n. **1** a broad blade attached to a rotating axis or wheel which pushes or is pushed by wind or water, forming part of a device such as a windmill, propeller, or turbine. ▶ a weathervane. **2** a projecting surface designed to guide the motion of a projectile, e.g. a feather on an arrow. **3** the flat part on either side of the shaft of a feather.
– DERIVATIVES **vaned** adj.
– ORIGIN Middle English: var. of obsolete *fane* 'banner', of Germanic origin.

vang /vaŋ/ ■ n. Nautical **1** each of two guy ropes running from the end of a gaff to the deck. **2** (also **boom vang**) a fitting used to pull a boat's boom down and help control the shape of the sail.
– ORIGIN C18: var. of obsolete *fang*, denoting a gripping device, from Old Norse *fang* 'grasp'.

vanguard ■ n. **1** the foremost part of an advancing army or naval force. **2** a group of people leading the way in new developments or ideas. ▶ a position at the forefront of developments or ideas.
– ORIGIN Middle English: shortening of Old French *avan(t)garde*, from *avant* 'before' + *garde* 'guard'.

vanilla ■ n. **1** a substance obtained from vanilla pods or produced artificially and used to flavour sweet foods or to impart a fragrant scent to cosmetic preparations. **2** a tropical climbing orchid with fragrant flowers and long pod-like fruit. [*Vanilla planifolia* and related species.] ■ adj. informal having no special or extra features.
– ORIGIN C17: from Spanish *vainilla* 'pod', diminutive of *vaina* 'sheath, pod', from Latin *vagina* 'sheath'.

vanish ■ v. **1** disappear suddenly and completely. ▶ gradually cease to exist. **2** Mathematics become zero.
– DERIVATIVES **vanishing** adj. **vanishingly** adv.
– ORIGIN Middle English: shortening of Old French *e(s)vaniss-*, *e(s)vanir*, from Latin *evanescere* 'die away'.

vanishing cream ■ n. a cream or ointment that leaves no visible trace when rubbed into the skin.

vanishing point ■ n. **1** the point at which receding parallel lines viewed in perspective appear to converge. **2** the point at which something that has been growing smaller or increasingly faint disappears altogether.

vanitas /ˈvanɪtaːs/ ■ n. a still-life painting of a 17th-century Dutch genre containing symbols of death or change as a reminder of their inevitability.
– ORIGIN Latin, 'vanity'.

Vanitory unit /ˈvanɪt(ə)ri/ ■ n. Brit. trademark a vanity unit.
– ORIGIN 1950s: *Vanitory* from VANITY.

vanity ■ n. (pl. **-ies**) **1** excessive pride in or admiration of one's own appearance or achievements. ▶ [as modifier]

vanity case

denoting a company publishing works at the author's expense. **2** the quality of being worthless or futile. **3** N. Amer. a dressing table.
– ORIGIN Middle English: from Old French *vanite*, from Latin *vanitas*, from *vanus* (see VAIN).

vanity case ■ n. a small case fitted with a mirror and compartments for make-up.

vanity mirror ■ n. a small mirror used for applying make-up, especially one fitted in a motor vehicle.

vanity plate ■ n. N. Amer. a vehicle licence plate bearing a distinctive or personalized combination of letters or numbers.

vanity table ■ n. a dressing table.

vanity unit ■ n. a unit consisting of a washbasin set into a flat top with cupboards beneath.

vanquish /ˈvaŋkwɪʃ/ ■ v. defeat thoroughly.
– DERIVATIVES **vanquishable** adj. **vanquisher** n.
– ORIGIN Middle English: from Old French *vencus*, *venquis* (past participle and past tense of *veintre*), from Latin *vincere* 'conquer'.

vantage /ˈvɑːntɪdʒ/ ■ n. (usu. **vantage point**) a place or position affording a good view.
– ORIGIN Middle English: from Anglo-Norman French, shortening of Old French *avantage* 'advantage'.

Vanuatuan /ˌvanuˈɑːtuːən/ ■ n. a native or inhabitant of Vanuatu, a country in the SW Pacific. ■ adj. of or relating to Vanuatu.

vapid /ˈvapɪd/ ■ adj. offering nothing that is stimulating or challenging.
– DERIVATIVES **vapidity** n. **vapidly** adv.
– ORIGIN C17 (orig. in sense 'lacking in flavour'): from Latin *vapidus*.

vapor ■ n. US spelling of VAPOUR.

vaporetto /ˌvapəˈrɛtəʊ/ ■ n. (pl. **vaporetti** /-ti/ or **vaporettos**) (in Venice) a canal boat for public transport.
– ORIGIN Italian, diminutive of *vapore* 'steam', from Latin *vapor*.

vaporize (also **-ise**) ■ v. convert or be converted into vapour.
– DERIVATIVES **vaporizable** (also **-isable**) adj. **vaporization** (also **-isation**) n.

vaporizer (also **-iser**) ■ n. a device that generates a vapour, especially for medicinal inhalation.

vapour (US **vapor**) ■ n. **1** a substance diffused or suspended in the air. ▶ Physics a gaseous substance that can be liquefied by pressure alone. Compare with GAS. **2** (**the vapours**) dated a sudden feeling of faintness or nervousness or a state of depression. ■ v. talk in a vacuous, boasting, or pompous way.
– DERIVATIVES **vaporous** adj. **vaporousness** n. **vapoury** adj.
– ORIGIN Middle English: from Old French, or from Latin *vapor* 'steam, heat'.

vapour density ■ n. Chemistry the density of a particular gas or vapour relative to that of hydrogen at the same pressure and temperature.

vapour pressure ■ n. Chemistry the pressure of a vapour in contact with its liquid or solid form.

vapour trail ■ n. a trail of condensed water from an aircraft or rocket at high altitude, seen as a white streak against the sky.

vapourware ■ n. Computing, informal software or hardware that has been advertised but is not yet available to buy.

VAR ■ abbrev. **1** value-added reseller. **2** value at risk.

var. ■ abbrev. variety.

varactor /vəˈraktə/ ■ n. a semiconductor diode with a capacitance dependent on the applied voltage.
– ORIGIN 1950s: from elements of *variable reactor*.

vari- ■ comb. form various: *variform*.
– ORIGIN from Latin *varius*.

variable ■ adj. **1** not consistent or having a fixed pattern; liable to vary. ▶ Mathematics (of a quantity) able to assume different numerical values. ▶ Biology (of a species) liable to deviate from the typical colour or form, or to occur in different colours or forms. **2** able to be changed or adapted. ▶ (of a gear) designed to give varying ratios or speeds. ■ n. a variable element, feature, fact, or quantity. ▶ Astronomy a star whose brightness changes (regularly or irregularly).
– DERIVATIVES **variability** n. **variableness** n. **variably** adv.

variance ■ n. **1** (usu. in phr. **at variance with**) the fact or quality of being different or inconsistent. ▶ the state of disagreeing or quarrelling. ▶ chiefly Law a discrepancy between two statements or documents. **2** Statistics a quantity equal to the square of the standard deviation.

variant ■ n. a form or version that varies from other forms of the same thing or from a standard.

variate /ˈvɛːrɪət/ ■ n. Statistics a quantity having a numerical value for each member of a group, especially one whose values occur according to a frequency distribution.

variation ■ n. **1** a change or slight difference in condition, amount, or level. ▶ (also **magnetic variation**) the angular difference between true north and magnetic north at a particular place. **2** a different or distinct form or version. ▶ Music a new but still recognizable version of a theme. ▶ Ballet a solo dance as part of a performance.
– DERIVATIVES **variational** adj.

variationist ■ n. Linguistics a person who studies variations in usage among different speakers of the same language.

varicella /ˌvarɪˈsɛlə/ ■ n. Medicine technical term for CHICKENPOX. ▶ (also **varicella zoster**) a herpesvirus that causes chickenpox and shingles; herpes zoster.
– ORIGIN C18: irregular diminutive of medieval Latin *variola* 'pustule'.

varicocele /ˈvarɪkə(ʊ)ˌsiːl/ ■ n. Medicine a mass of varicose veins in the spermatic cord.
– ORIGIN C18: from Latin *varix*, *varic-* 'dilated vein' + -CELE.

varicoloured /ˈvɛːrɪˌkʌləd/ (US **varicolored**) ■ adj. consisting of several different colours.

varicose /ˈvarɪkəʊs, -kəs, -z/ ■ adj. affected by a condition causing the swelling and tortuous lengthening of veins, most often in the legs.
– DERIVATIVES **varicosed** adj. **varicosity** n.
– ORIGIN Middle English: from Latin *varicosus*, from *varix* 'dilated vein'.

varied ■ adj. incorporating a number of different types or elements; showing variation or variety.
– DERIVATIVES **variedly** adv.

variegated /ˈvɛːrɪɡeɪtɪd, ˈvɛːrɪə-/ ■ adj. exhibiting different colours, especially as irregular patches or streaks.
– DERIVATIVES **variegation** /-ˈɡeɪʃ(ə)n/ n.
– ORIGIN C17: from Latin *variegare* 'make varied'.

varietal /vəˈrʌɪət(ə)l/ ■ adj. **1** (of a wine or grape) made from or belonging to a single specified variety of grape. **2** of, forming, or characteristic of a variety. ■ n. a varietal wine.
– DERIVATIVES **varietally** adv.

variety ■ n. (pl. **-ies**) **1** the quality or state of being different or diverse. **2** (**a variety of**) a number of things of the same general class that are distinct in character or quality. ▶ a thing which differs in some way from others of the same general class; a type. ▶ Biology a subspecies or cultivar. **3** a form of entertainment consisting of a series of different types of act, such as singing, dancing, and comedy.
– ORIGIN C15: from French *variété* or Latin *varietas*, from *varius* (see VARIOUS).

varifocal /ˌvɛːrɪˈfəʊk(ə)l/ ■ adj. denoting a lens that allows an infinite number of focusing distances for near, intermediate, and far vision. ■ n. (**varifocals**) varifocal glasses.

variform /ˈvɛːrɪfɔːm/ ■ adj. (of a group of things) differing from one another in form. ▶ (of a single thing or a mass) consisting of a variety of forms or things.

variometer /ˌvɛːrɪˈɒmɪtə/ ■ n. **1** a device for indicating an aircraft's rate of climb or descent. **2** a device whose total inductance can be varied. **3** an instrument for measuring variations in the earth's magnetic field.

variorum /ˌvɛːrɪˈɔːrəm/ ■ adj. (of an edition of an author's works) having notes by various editors or commentators. ▶ including variant readings from manuscripts or earlier editions. ■ n. a variorum edition.
– ORIGIN C18: from Latin *varius* 'diverse', from *editio cum notis variorum* 'edition with notes by various (commentators)'.

various ▪ adj. different from one another; of different kinds or sorts. ▸ having or showing different properties or qualities. ▪ det. & pron. more than one; individual and separate: *various people arrived late.*
– DERIVATIVES **variously** adv. **variousness** n.
– ORIGIN Middle English: from Latin *varius* 'changing, diverse'.

varistor /vɛːˈrɪstə, və-/ ▪ n. a semiconductor diode with resistance dependent on the applied voltage.
– ORIGIN 1930s: contraction of *varying resistor*.

varlet /ˈvɑːlɪt/ ▪ n. **1** archaic an unprincipled rogue. **2** historical an attendant or servant.
– DERIVATIVES **varletry** n.
– ORIGIN Middle English: from Old French, var. of *valet* (see VALET).

varmint /ˈvɑːmɪnt/ ▪ n. N. Amer. informal or dialect a troublesome or mischievous person or wild animal.
– ORIGIN C16: alteration of VERMIN.

varnish ▪ n. **1** a substance consisting of resin dissolved in a liquid, applied to wood to give a hard, clear, shiny surface when dry. **2** archaic an external or superficial appearance: *an outward varnish of civilization.* ▪ v. apply varnish to.
– DERIVATIVES **varnisher** n.
– ORIGIN Middle English: from Old French *vernis*, from medieval Latin *veronix* 'fragrant resin, sandarac' or medieval Greek *berenikē*, prob. from *Berenice*, a town in Cyrenaica.

varroa /ˈvarəʊə/ ▪ n. a microscopic mite which is a debilitating parasite of the honeybee. [*Varroa jacobsoni.*]
– ORIGIN 1970s: from the name of the Roman writer *Varro* (with ref. to his work on bee-keeping).

varsity ▪ n. (pl. **-ies**) Brit. dated or S. African university.
– ORIGIN C17: shortening of UNIVERSITY, reflecting an archaic pronunciation.

varve /vɑːv/ ▪ n. Geology a pair of thin layers of clay and silt of contrasting colour and texture which represent the deposit of a single year (summer and winter) in a lake.
– DERIVATIVES **varved** adj.
– ORIGIN C20; from Swedish *varv* 'layer'.

vary ▪ v. (**-ies, -ied**) **1** differ in size, degree, or nature from something else of the same general class. **2** change from one form or state to another. ▸ modify or change (something) to make it less uniform.
– DERIVATIVES **varying** adj. **varyingly** adv.
– ORIGIN Middle English: from Old French *varier* or Latin *variare*, from *varius* 'diverse'.

vas /vas/ ▪ n. (pl. **vasa** /ˈveɪsə/) Anatomy a vessel or duct.
– DERIVATIVES **vasal** /ˈveɪs(ə)l/ adj.
– ORIGIN C16: from Latin, 'vessel'.

vasbyt /ˈfasbeɪt/ S. African informal ▪ v. keep going in difficult circumstances; hang in. ▪ exclam. used to express encouragement.
– ORIGIN Afrikaans, 'bite hard', from *vas* 'firmly' + *byt* 'bite'.

vascular /ˈvaskjʊlə/ ▪ adj. relating to or denoting the system of vessels for carrying blood or (in plants) sap, water, and nutrients.
– DERIVATIVES **vascularity** /-ˈlarɪti/ n. **vascularization** (also **-isation**) n. **vascularize** (also **-ise**) v.
– ORIGIN C17: from Latin *vasculum*, diminutive of *vas* 'vessel'.

vascular bundle ▪ n. Botany a strand of conducting vessels in the stem or leaves of a plant, typically with phloem on the outside and xylem on the inside.

vascular plants ▪ pl. n. plants with vascular tissue, i.e. flowering plants, conifers, cycads, ferns, horsetails, and clubmosses.

vasculature /ˈvaskjʊlətʃə/ ▪ n. Anatomy the vascular system of a part of the body and its arrangement.

vasculitis /ˌvaskjʊˈlʌɪtɪs/ ▪ n. (pl. **vasculitides** /-ˈlʌɪtɪdiːz/) Medicine inflammation of a blood vessel or blood vessels.
– DERIVATIVES **vasculitic** /-ˈlɪtɪk/ adj.

vas deferens /ˈdɛfərɛnz/ ▪ n. (pl. **vasa deferentia** /ˌdɛfəˈrɛnʃɪə/) Anatomy the duct which conveys sperm from the testicle to the urethra.
– ORIGIN C16: from VAS + Latin *deferens* 'carrying away', from *deferre*.

vase ▪ n. a decorative container without handles, typically made of glass or china and used as an ornament or for displaying cut flowers.
– ORIGIN Middle English: from French, from Latin *vas* 'vessel'.

vasectomy /vəˈsɛktəmi/ ▪ n. (pl. **-ies**) the surgical cutting and sealing of part of each vas deferens, especially as a means of sterilization.
– DERIVATIVES **vasectomize** (also **-ise**) v.

vaseline /ˈvasɪliːn/ ▪ n. trademark a type of petroleum jelly used as an ointment and lubricant.
– ORIGIN C19: from German *Wasser* + Greek *elaion* 'oil'.

vaso- /ˈveɪzəʊ/ ▪ comb. form of or relating to a vessel or vessels, especially blood vessels: *vasoconstriction.*
– ORIGIN from Latin *vas* 'vessel'.

vasoactive ▪ adj. Physiology affecting the diameter of blood vessels (and hence blood pressure).

vasoconstriction ▪ n. the constriction of blood vessels, which increases blood pressure.
– DERIVATIVES **vasoconstrictive** adj. **vasoconstrictor** n.

vasodilation (also **vasodilatation** /-ˌdʌɪleɪˈteɪʃ(ə)n/) ▪ n. the dilatation of blood vessels, which decreases blood pressure.
– DERIVATIVES **vasodilator** n. **vasodilatory** adj.

vasomotor ▪ adj. causing or relating to the constriction or dilatation of blood vessels.

vasopressin /ˌveɪzəʊˈprɛsɪn/ ▪ n. Biochemistry a pituitary hormone which promotes water retention by the kidneys and increased blood pressure.

vasopressor /veɪzəʊˈprɛsə/ ▪ n. Medicine a drug or other agent which causes constriction of blood vessels.

vassal /ˈvas(ə)l/ ▪ n. **1** historical a holder of land by feudal tenure on conditions of homage and allegiance. **2** a person or country in a subordinate position to another.
– DERIVATIVES **vassalage** n.
– ORIGIN Middle English: from medieval Latin *vassallus* 'retainer', of Celtic origin.

vast ▪ adj. of very great extent or quantity; immense.
– DERIVATIVES **vastly** adv. **vastness** n.
– ORIGIN Middle English: from Latin *vastus* 'void, immense'.

VAT ▪ abbrev. value added tax.

vat ▪ n. a large tank or tub used to hold liquid. ▪ v. (**vatted, vatting**) place or treat in a vat.
– ORIGIN Middle English: dialect var. of obsolete *fat* 'container', of Germanic origin.

Vatican ▪ n. the palace and official residence of the Pope in Rome.

vaudeville /ˈvɔːdəvɪl, ˈvəʊd-/ ▪ n. **1** a type of entertainment popular in the early 20th century, featuring a mixture of musical and comedy acts. ▸ a stage play on a trivial theme with songs. **2** archaic a satirical or topical song.
– DERIVATIVES **vaudevillian** adj. & n.
– ORIGIN C18: from French, earlier *vau de ville* (or *vire*), apparently denoting songs composed by Olivier Basselin, a C15 fuller born in *Vau de Vire* in Normandy.

vault¹ /vɔːlt/ ▪ n. **1** a roof in the form of an arch or a series of arches, typical of churches and other large, formal buildings. **2** a large room or chamber used for storage, especially an underground one. ▸ a secure room in a bank in which valuables are stored. ▸ a chamber beneath a church or in a graveyard used for burials. **3** Anatomy the arched roof of a cavity, especially that of the skull. ▪ v. [usu. as adj. **vaulted**] provide with or form into an arched roof.
– ORIGIN Middle English: from Old French *voute*, from Latin *volvere* 'to roll'.

vault² /vɔːlt/ ▪ v. leap or spring while supporting or propelling oneself with the hands or a pole. ▪ n. an act of vaulting.
– DERIVATIVES **vaulter** n.
– ORIGIN C16: from Old French *volter* 'to turn (a horse), gambol'.

vaulting ▪ n. ornamental work in a vaulted roof or ceiling.

vaulting horse ■ n. a padded wooden block used for vaulting over by gymnasts and athletes.

vaunt /vɔːnt/ ■ v. [usu. as adj. **vaunted**] boast about or praise (something), especially excessively.
– DERIVATIVES **vaunting** adj. **vauntingly** adv.
– ORIGIN Middle English: the noun a shortening of obsolete *avaunt* 'boasting, a boast'; the verb from Old French *vanter*, from late Latin *vantare*, from Latin *vanus* 'vain, empty'.

VC ■ abbrev. **1** Vice-Chairman. **2** Vice-Chancellor. **3** Victoria Cross.

V-chip ■ n. a computer chip installed in a television receiver that can be programmed to block violent or sexually explicit material.

VCR ■ abbrev. video cassette recorder.

VD ■ abbrev. venereal disease.

VDU ■ abbrev. visual display unit.

veal ■ n. the flesh of a calf, used as food.
– ORIGIN Middle English: from Anglo-Norman French *ve(e)l*, from Latin *vitellus*, diminutive of *vitulus* 'calf'.

vector /'vɛktə/ ■ n. **1** Mathematics & Physics a quantity having direction as well as magnitude, especially as determining the position of one point in space relative to another. **2** an organism that transmits a particular disease or parasite from one animal or plant to another. ▶ Genetics a bacteriophage or plasmid which transfers genetic material into a cell. **3** a course to be taken by an aircraft. ■ v. direct (an aircraft in flight) to a desired point.
– DERIVATIVES **vectorial** /-'tɔːrɪəl/ adj. **vectorially** adv. **vectorization** (also **-isation**) n. **vectorize** (also **-ise**) v.
– ORIGIN C19: from Latin, 'carrier'.

vector product ■ n. Mathematics the product of two vectors which is itself a vector at right angles to both the original vectors and equal to the product of their magnitudes and the sine of the angle between them (written as **a** × **b**).

Veda /'veɪdə, 'viːdə/ ■ n. [treated as sing. or pl.] the most ancient Hindu scriptures, in particular the Rig Veda, Sama Veda, Yajur Veda, and Atharva Veda.
– ORIGIN Sanskrit, '(sacred) knowledge'.

Vedanta /vɪ'dɑːntə, -'da-, vɛ-/ ■ n. a Hindu philosophy based on the doctrine of the Upanishads, especially in its monistic form.
– DERIVATIVES **Vedantic** adj. **Vedantist** n.
– ORIGIN from Sanskrit *vedānta*, from *veda* (see **VEDA**) + *anta* 'end'.

VE day ■ n. the day (8 May) marking the Allied victory in Europe in 1945.
– ORIGIN abbrev. of *Victory in Europe*.

vedette /vɪ'dɛt/ ■ n. **1** historical a mounted sentry positioned beyond an army's outposts to observe the movements of the enemy. **2** informal, chiefly N. Amer. a star of the entertainment world.
– ORIGIN C17: from French, 'scout'.

Vedic /'veɪdɪk, 'viː-/ ■ adj. of or relating to the Veda or Vedas.

vee ■ n. something shaped like the letter V.

veejay ■ n. informal, chiefly N. Amer. a person who introduces and plays popular music videos.
– ORIGIN 1980s: representing a pronunciation of *VJ*, short for *video jockey*, on the pattern of *deejay*.

veer ■ v. **1** change direction suddenly. ▶ suddenly change in opinion, subject, etc. **2** (of the wind) change direction clockwise around the points of the compass. The opposite of **BACK**. ■ n. a sudden change of direction.
– ORIGIN C16: from French *virer*, perhaps from Latin *gyrare* (see **GYRATE**).

veg¹ /vɛdʒ/ ■ n. (pl. same) informal a vegetable or vegetables.

veg² /vɛdʒ/ ■ v. (**vegges, vegging, vegged**) (often **veg out**) informal relax to the point of complete inertia; vegetate.

vegan ■ n. a person who does not eat or use animal products.
– ORIGIN 1940s: from **VEGETARIAN**.

Vegeburger ■ n. trademark for **VEGGIE BURGER**.

Vegemite /'vɛdʒɪmʌɪt/ ■ n. Austral./NZ trademark a type of savoury spread made from concentrated yeast extract.
– ORIGIN 1920s: from **VEGETABLE**, on the pattern of *marmite*.

vegetable /'vɛdʒtəb(ə)l, 'vɛdʒɪtə-/ ■ n. **1** a plant or part of a plant used as food. **2** informal, derogatory a person who is incapable of normal mental or physical activity, especially through brain damage.
– ORIGIN Middle English (in the sense 'growing as a plant'): from Old French, or from late Latin *vegetabilis* 'animating', from Latin *vegetare* (see **VEGETATE**).

vegetable ivory ■ n. a hard white material obtained from the seeds of some species of palm tree.

vegetable oil ■ n. an oil derived from plants, e.g. olive oil or sunflower oil.

vegetal /'vɛdʒɪt(ə)l/ ■ adj. **1** formal of or relating to plants. **2** Biology denoting the pole or extremity of an embryo containing the less active cytoplasm. The opposite of **ANIMAL**.
– ORIGIN Middle English: from medieval Latin *vegetalis*, from Latin *vegetare* 'animate'.

vegetarian ■ n. a person who does not eat meat for moral, religious, or health reasons. ■ adj. eating or including no meat.
– DERIVATIVES **vegetarianism** n.

vegetate ■ v. live or spend a period of time in a dull, inactive, unchallenging way.
– ORIGIN C17 (*vegetative* Middle English): from Latin *vegetare* 'enliven'.

vegetated ■ adj. covered with vegetation or plant life.

vegetation ■ n. plants collectively, especially those found in a particular area or habitat.
– DERIVATIVES **vegetational** adj.

vegetative /'vɛdʒɪtətɪv, -teɪtɪv/ ■ adj. **1** Biology relating to or denoting reproduction or propagation achieved by asexual means, either naturally or artificially. **2** of or relating to vegetation or the growth of plants. **3** Medicine alive but comatose and without apparent brain activity or responsiveness.
– DERIVATIVES **vegetatively** adv. **vegetativeness** n.

veggie (also **vegie**) ■ n. & adj. informal another term for **VEGETARIAN** or **VEGETABLE**.

veggie burger (also trademark **Vegeburger**) ■ n. a savoury cake resembling a hamburger but made with vegetable protein or soya instead of meat.

vehement /'viːm(ə)nt/ ■ adj. showing strong feeling; forceful, passionate, or intense.
– DERIVATIVES **vehemence** n. **vehemently** adv.
– ORIGIN Middle English: from French *véhément* or Latin *vehement-* 'impetuous, violent', perhaps influenced by *vehere* 'carry'.

vehicle ■ n. **1** a thing used for transporting people or goods on land, e.g. a car, truck, or cart. **2** a means of expressing, embodying, or fulfilling something. ▶ a substance that facilitates the use of a drug, pigment, or other material mixed with it. ▶ a film, programme, song, etc., intended to display the leading performer to the best advantage.
– DERIVATIVES **vehicular** /vɪ'hɪkjʊlə/ adj.
– ORIGIN C17: from French *véhicule* or Latin *vehiculum*, from *vehere* 'carry'.

veil ■ n. **1** a piece of fine material worn to protect or conceal the face. ▶ a piece of fabric forming part of a nun's headdress, resting on the head and shoulders. **2** a thing that conceals, disguises, or obscures: *an eerie veil of mist*. **3** (in Jewish antiquity) the piece of precious cloth separating the sanctuary from the body of the Temple or the Tabernacle. ■ v. cover with or as though with a veil. ▶ [usu. as adj. **veiled**] partially conceal, disguise, or obscure: *a thinly veiled threat*.
– PHRASES **draw a veil over** avoid discussing or calling attention to (something embarrassing or unpleasant). **take the veil** become a nun.
– DERIVATIVES **veiling** n. **veilless** adj.
– ORIGIN Middle English: from Anglo-Norman French *veil(e)*, from Latin *vela*, pl. of *velum* (see **VELUM**).

vein ■ n. **1** any of the tubes forming part of the circulation system by which blood is conveyed from all parts of the body towards the heart. ▶ (in general use) a blood vessel. **2** (in plants) a slender rib running through a leaf, typically dividing or branching, and containing vascular tissue. ▶ (in

insects) a hollow rib forming part of the supporting framework of a wing. **3** a streak or stripe of a different colour in wood, marble, cheese, etc. ▸ a fracture in rock containing a deposit of minerals or ore. ▸ a source of a specified quality or other abstract resource: *a rich vein of satire.* **4** a distinctive quality, style, or tendency: *he closes his article in a humorous vein.*
– DERIVATIVES **veined** adj. **veining** n. **veinless** adj. **veinlet** n. **vein-like** adj. & adv. **veiny** adj. (**-ier, -iest**).
– ORIGIN Middle English: from Old French *veine*, from Latin *vena*.

veinous ▪ adj. having prominent or noticeable veins.

vela plural form of VELUM.

velamen /vɪˈleɪmən/ ▪ n. (pl. **velamina** /-mɪnə/) Botany an outer layer of empty cells in the aerial roots of epiphytic orchids and aroids.
– ORIGIN C19: from Latin, from *velare* 'to cover'.

velar /ˈviːlə/ ▪ adj. **1** of or relating to a veil or velum. **2** Phonetics (of a speech sound) pronounced with the back of the tongue near the soft palate, as in *k* and *g* in English. ▪ n. a velar sound.
– DERIVATIVES **velarization** /ˌviːlərʌɪˈzeɪʃ(ə)n/ (also **-isation**) n. **velarize** (also **-ise**) v.
– ORIGIN C18: from Latin *velaris*, from *velum* (see VELUM).

Velcro /ˈvɛlkrəʊ/ ▪ n. trademark a fastener consisting of two strips of thin plastic sheet, one covered with tiny loops and the other with tiny flexible hooks, which adhere when pressed together.
– DERIVATIVES **Velcroed** adj.
– ORIGIN 1960s: from French *velours croché* 'hooked velvet'.

veld /fɛlt, vɛlt/ (also **veldt**) ▪ n. open, uncultivated country or grassland in southern Africa.
– ORIGIN Afrikaans, from Dutch, 'field'.

veldskoen /ˈfɛltskʊn/ (S. African also **velskoen** /ˈfɛlskʊn/) ▪ n. (pl. **-skoens** or **-skoene**) a strong suede or leather shoe or boot.
– ORIGIN Afrikaans, 'field shoe', or from *vel* 'skin, hide' + *skoen* 'shoe'.

veleta /vəˈliːtə/ (also **valeta**) ▪ n. a ballroom dance in triple time, faster than a waltz and with partners side by side.
– ORIGIN C20: from Spanish, 'weathervane'.

veliger /ˈviːlɪdʒə/ ▪ n. Zoology the final larval stage of certain molluscs, having two ciliated flaps for swimming and feeding.
– ORIGIN C19: from VELUM + Latin *-ger* 'bearing'.

velleity /vɛˈliːɪti/ ▪ n. (pl. **-ies**) formal a wish or inclination not strong enough to lead to action.
– ORIGIN C17: from medieval Latin *velleitas*, from Latin *velle* 'to wish'.

vellie /ˈfɛli/ ▪ n. S. African informal a veldskoen.

vellum /ˈvɛləm/ ▪ n. fine parchment made originally from the skin of a calf.
– ORIGIN Middle English: from Old French *velin*, from *veel* (see VEAL).

velocimeter /ˌvɛləˈ(ʊ)sɪmɪtə/ ▪ n. an instrument for measuring velocity.
– DERIVATIVES **velocimetry** n.

velocipede /vɪˈlɒsɪpiːd/ ▪ n. historical an early form of bicycle propelled by working pedals on cranks fitted to the front axle.
– ORIGIN C19: from French *vélocipède*, from Latin *velox*, *veloc-* 'swift' + *pes*, *ped-* 'foot'.

velociraptor /vɪˌlɒsɪˈraptə/ ▪ n. a small dromaeosaurid dinosaur of the late Cretaceous period.
– ORIGIN from Latin *velox*, *veloc-* 'swift' + RAPTOR.

velocity /vɪˈlɒsɪti/ ▪ n. (pl. **-ies**) the speed of something in a given direction. ▸ (in general use) speed.
– ORIGIN Middle English: from French *vélocité* or Latin *velocitas*, from *velox* 'swift'.

velodrome /ˈvɛlədrəʊm/ ▪ n. a cycle-racing track with steeply banked curves.
– ORIGIN C19: from French *vélodrome*, from *vélo* 'bicycle' + *-drome*, denoting a place for running or racing, from Greek *dromos*, rel. to *dramein* 'to run'.

velour /vəˈlʊə/ (also **velours**) ▪ n. a plush woven fabric resembling velvet, chiefly used for soft furnishings and hats.
– ORIGIN C18: from French *velours* 'velvet'.

1321

velouté /vəˈluːteɪ/ ▪ n. a sauce made from a roux of butter and flour with chicken, veal, or pork stock.
– ORIGIN French, 'velvety'.

velum /ˈviːləm/ ▪ n. (pl. **vela** /-lə/) **1** Zoology a membrane, typically bordering a cavity, especially in certain molluscs, medusae, and other invertebrates. **2** Anatomy the soft palate.
– ORIGIN C18: from Latin, 'sail, curtain, covering, veil'.

velvet ▪ n. **1** a closely woven fabric of silk, cotton, or nylon with a thick short pile on one side. **2** soft downy skin that covers a deer's antler while it is growing.
– DERIVATIVES **velveted** adj. **velvety** adj.
– ORIGIN Middle English: from Old French *veluotte*, from *velu* 'velvety', from medieval Latin *villutus*, from Latin *villus* 'tuft, down'.

velvet ant ▪ n. a velvety-bodied hymenopterous insect whose larvae parasitize bees and wasps. [Family Mutillidae: numerous species.]

velveteen ▪ n. a cotton fabric with a pile resembling velvet.

velvet worm ▪ n. a tropical terrestrial invertebrate with a soft worm-like body and stumpy legs. [Phylum Onychophora.]

Ven. ▪ abbrev. Venerable (as the title of an archdeacon).

vena cava /ˌviːnə ˈkeɪvə/ ▪ n. (pl. **venae cavae** /-niː -viː/) each of two large veins carrying deoxygenated blood into the heart.
– ORIGIN C16: from Latin, 'hollow vein'.

venal /ˈviːn(ə)l/ ▪ adj. showing or motivated by susceptibility to bribery.
– DERIVATIVES **venality** n.
– ORIGIN C17: from Latin *venalis*, from *venum* 'thing for sale'.

venation /vɪˈneɪʃ(ə)n/ ▪ n. Biology the arrangement of veins in a leaf or in an insect's wing. ▸ the system of venous blood vessels in an animal.
– DERIVATIVES **venational** adj.
– ORIGIN C17: from Latin *vena* 'vein'.

vend ▪ v. **1** offer (small items) for sale, especially from a coin-operated machine. **2** Law or formal sell.
– DERIVATIVES **vendible** adj.
– ORIGIN C17 (*vendor* C16): from French *vendre* or Latin *vendere* 'sell'.

Venda /ˈvɛndə/ ▪ n. (pl. same or **Vendas**) **1** a member of a people living in the Limpopo province of South Africa and in southern Zimbabwe. **2** another term for TSHIVENDA.
– ORIGIN from the stem of Tshivenda *Muvenda* (in sense 1).

vendetta /vɛnˈdɛtə/ ▪ n. **1** a blood feud in which the family of a murdered person seeks vengeance on the murderer or the murderer's family. **2** a prolonged bitter quarrel with or campaign against someone.
– ORIGIN C19: from Italian, from Latin *vindicta* 'vengeance'.

vendeuse /vɒ̃ˈdəːz/ ▪ n. a saleswoman, especially one in a fashionable dress shop.
– ORIGIN from French.

vending machine ▪ n. a machine that dispenses small articles when a coin or token is inserted.

vendor (US also **vender**) ▪ n. **1** a person or company offering something for sale, especially a trader in the street. **2** Law the seller in a sale, especially of property.

veneer /vɪˈnɪə/ ▪ n. **1** a thin decorative covering of fine wood applied to a coarser wood or other material. ▸ a layer of wood used to make plywood. **2** an attractive appearance that covers or disguises true nature or feelings. ▪ v. [usu. as adj. **veneered**] cover with a veneer.
– DERIVATIVES **veneering** n.
– ORIGIN C18 (orig. as *fineer*): from German *furni(e)ren*, from Old French *fournir* 'furnish'.

venepuncture /ˈvɛnɪˌpʌŋ(k)tʃə, ˈviːnɪ-/ (also **venipuncture**) ▪ n. the puncture of a vein to withdraw a blood sample or for an intravenous injection.
– ORIGIN 1920s: from Latin *vena* 'vein' + PUNCTURE.

venerable

venerable ▪ adj. **1** accorded great respect because of age, wisdom, or character. **2** (in the Anglican Church) a title given to an archdeacon. **3** (in the Roman Catholic Church) a title given to a deceased person who has attained a

venerate

certain degree of sanctity but has not been fully beatified or canonized.
– DERIVATIVES **venerability** n. **venerableness** n. **venerably** adv.
– ORIGIN Middle English: from Old French, or from Latin *venerabilis*, from *venerari* (see VENERATE).

venerate /ˈvɛnəreɪt/ ■ v. regard with great respect.
– DERIVATIVES **veneration** n. **venerator** n.
– ORIGIN C17 (*veneration* Middle English): from Latin *venerari* 'adore, revere'.

venereal /vɪˈnɪərɪəl/ ■ adj. 1 of or relating to venereal disease. 2 formal of or relating to sexual desire or sexual intercourse.
– DERIVATIVES **venereally** adv.
– ORIGIN Middle English: from Latin *venereus*, from *venus*, *vener-* 'sexual love'.

venereal disease ■ n. a disease contracted by sexual intercourse with a person already infected.

venereology /vɪˌnɪərɪˈɒlədʒi/ ■ n. the branch of medicine concerned with venereal diseases.
– DERIVATIVES **venereological** adj. **venereologist** n.

venery /ˈvɛn(ə)ri/ ■ n. archaic sexual indulgence.
– ORIGIN Middle English: from medieval Latin *veneria*, from *venus* 'sexual love'.

venesection /ˌvɛnɪˈsɛkʃ(ə)n, ˈvɛnɪ-/ ■ n. another term for PHLEBOTOMY.
– ORIGIN C17: from medieval Latin *venae sectio(n-)* 'cutting of a vein'.

Venetian ■ adj. of or relating to Venice or its people. ■ n. a native or citizen of Venice.

venetian blind ■ n. a window blind consisting of horizontal slats which can be pivoted to control the amount of light that passes through.

Venetian red ■ n. a reddish-brown pigment consisting of ferric oxide.

Venezuelan /ˌvɛnɪˈzweɪlən/ ■ n. a native or inhabitant of Venezuela. ■ adj. of or relating to Venezuela.

vengeance /ˈvɛn(d)ʒ(ə)ns/ ■ n. punishment inflicted or retribution exacted for an injury or wrong.
– PHRASES **with a vengeance** with great intensity.
– ORIGIN Middle English: from Old French, from *venger* 'avenge'.

vengeful ■ adj. seeking to harm someone in return for a perceived injury.
– DERIVATIVES **vengefully** adv. **vengefulness** n.
– ORIGIN C16: from obsolete *venge* 'avenge' (see VENGEANCE).

venial /ˈviːnɪəl/ ■ adj. Christian Church denoting a sin that is not regarded as depriving the soul of divine grace. Often contrasted with MORTAL. ▸ (of a fault or offence) slight and pardonable.
– DERIVATIVES **veniality** /-ˈalɪti/ n. **venially** adv.
– ORIGIN Middle English: from late Latin *venialis*, from *venia* 'forgiveness'.

venipuncture ■ n. variant spelling of VENEPUNCTURE.

venison /ˈvɛnɪs(ə)n, ˈvɛnɪz(ə)n/ ■ n. meat from a deer or an antelope.
– ORIGIN Middle English: from Old French *veneso(u)n*, from Latin *venatio(n-)* 'hunting', from *venari* 'to hunt'.

Venn diagram ■ n. a diagram representing mathematical or logical sets as circles, common elements of the sets being represented by intersections of the circles.
– ORIGIN C20: named after the English logician John *Venn*.

venom ■ n. 1 poisonous fluid secreted by animals such as snakes and scorpions and typically injected into prey or aggressors by biting or stinging. 2 extreme malice, bitterness, or aggression.
– DERIVATIVES **venomed** adj.
– ORIGIN Middle English: from Old French *venim*, var. of *venin*, from Latin *venenum* 'poison'.

venomous /ˈvɛnəməs/ ■ adj. 1 secreting or capable of injecting venom. 2 very malicious, bitter, or aggressive.
– DERIVATIVES **venomously** adv. **venomousness** n.

venous /ˈviːnəs/ ■ adj. of or relating to a vein or the veins.
– DERIVATIVES **venosity** /vɪˈnɒsɪti/ n.

– ORIGIN C17: from Latin *venosus* 'having many veins', from *vena* 'vein'.

vent¹ ■ n. 1 an opening that allows air, gas, or liquid to pass out of or into a confined space. ▸ the opening of a volcano, through which lava and other materials are emitted. 2 (usu. in phr. **give vent to**) release or expression of a strong emotion, energy, etc. 3 the anus of a lower animal such as a fish, serving for both excretion and reproduction. ■ v. 1 give free expression to (a strong emotion). 2 discharge (air, gas, or liquid) through an outlet. ▸ provide with an outlet for air, gas, or liquid. ▸ permit air to enter (a beer cask).
– DERIVATIVES **vented** adj. **ventless** adj.
– ORIGIN Middle English: partly from French *vent* 'wind', from Latin *ventus*.

vent² ■ n. a slit in a garment, especially in the lower edge of the back of a coat through the seam.
– ORIGIN Middle English: alteration of dialect *fent*, from Old French *fente* 'slit', from Latin *findere* 'cleave'.

ventiduct /ˈvɛntɪdʌkt/ ■ n. Architecture an air passage, especially one for ventilation.
– ORIGIN C17: from Latin *ventus* 'wind' + *ductus* 'duct'.

ventifact /ˈvɛntɪfakt/ ■ n. Geology a stone shaped by the erosive action of wind-blown sand.
– ORIGIN C20: from Latin *ventus* 'wind' + *fact-*, *facere* 'make'.

ventilate ■ v. 1 cause air to enter and circulate freely in (a room or building). 2 discuss (an opinion or issue) in public. 3 Medicine subject to artificial respiration.
– DERIVATIVES **ventilation** n.
– ORIGIN Middle English: from Latin *ventilare* 'blow, winnow', from *ventus* 'wind'.

ventilator ■ n. 1 an appliance or aperture for ventilating a room or other space. 2 Medicine an appliance for artificial respiration; a respirator.
– DERIVATIVES **ventilatory** adj.

Ventolin /ˈvɛntəlɪn/ ■ n. trademark for SALBUTAMOL.
– ORIGIN 1960s: perhaps from VENTILATE.

ventouse /ˈvɛntuːs/ ■ n. Medicine a cup-shaped suction device applied to the baby's head to assist the birth.
– ORIGIN 1960s: from French, 'cupping-glass', from Latin *ventus* 'wind'.

ventral ■ adj. Anatomy,, Zoology, & Botany on or relating to the underside of an animal or plant; abdominal. Compare with DORSAL.
– DERIVATIVES **ventrally** adv.
– ORIGIN Middle English: from Latin *venter*, *ventr-* 'belly'.

ventral fin ■ n. Zoology another term for PELVIC FIN.

ventricle /ˈvɛntrɪk(ə)l/ ■ n. Anatomy 1 each of the two larger and lower cavities of the heart. 2 each of four connected fluid-filled cavities in the centre of the brain.
– DERIVATIVES **ventricular** /-ˈtrɪkjʊlə/ adj.
– ORIGIN Middle English: from Latin *ventriculus*, diminutive of *venter* 'belly'.

ventriloquist /vɛnˈtrɪləkwɪst/ ■ n. an entertainer who makes their voice seem to come from a dummy of a person or animal.
– DERIVATIVES **ventriloquial** /ˌvɛntrɪˈləʊkwɪəl/ adj. **ventriloquism** n. **ventriloquize** (also **-ise**) v. **ventriloquy** n.
– ORIGIN C17: from modern Latin *ventriloquium*, from Latin *venter* 'belly' + *loqui* 'speak'.

venture ■ n. a risky or daring journey or undertaking. ▸ a business enterprise involving considerable risk. ■ v. undertake a risky or daring journey or course of action. ▸ expose to the risk of loss.
– DERIVATIVES **venturer** n.
– ORIGIN Middle English: shortening of ADVENTURE.

venture capital ■ n. capital invested in a project in which there is a substantial element of risk.
– DERIVATIVES **venture capitalist** n.

Venture Scout ■ n. a member of the Scout Association aged between 16 and 20.

venturesome ■ adj. willing to take risks or embark on difficult or unusual courses of action.
– DERIVATIVES **venturesomeness** n.

venturi /vɛnˈtjʊəri/ ■ n. (pl. **venturis**) a short piece of narrow tube between wider sections for measuring flow rate or exerting suction.
– ORIGIN C19: named after the Italian physicist Giovanni B. Venturi.

venue /ˈvɛnjuː/ ■ n. the place where something happens, especially an event such as a concert or sports event.
– ORIGIN C16: from Old French, 'a coming', from *venir* 'come'.

venule /ˈvɛnjuːl/ ■ n. Anatomy a very small vein, especially one collecting blood from the capillaries.
– ORIGIN C19: from Latin *venula*, diminutive of *vena* 'vein'.

Venus flytrap ■ n. a small carnivorous bog plant with hinged leaves that spring shut on and digest insects which land on them. [*Dionaea muscipula*.]

Venusian /vɪˈnjuːzɪən/ ■ adj. of or relating to the planet Venus or its supposed inhabitants. ■ n. a hypothetical or fictional inhabitant of Venus.

veracious /vəˈreɪʃəs/ ■ adj. formal speaking or representing the truth.
– DERIVATIVES **veraciously** adv. **veraciousness** n.
– ORIGIN C17: from Latin *verax, verac-*, from *verus* 'true'.

veracity /vəˈrasɪti/ ■ n. conformity to facts; accuracy. ▸ habitual truthfulness.

veranda (also **verandah**) ■ n. a roofed platform along the outside of a house, level with the ground floor.
– DERIVATIVES **verandaed** adj.
– ORIGIN C18: from Hindi *varaṇḍā*, from Portuguese *varanda* 'railing, balustrade'.

verb ■ n. Grammar a word used to describe an action, state, or occurrence, and forming the main part of the predicate of a sentence, such as *hear, become,* or *happen*.
– DERIVATIVES **verbless** adj.
– ORIGIN Middle English: from Old French *verbe* or Latin *verbum* 'word, verb'.

verbal ■ adj. **1** relating to or in the form of words. **2** spoken rather than written; oral. ▸ informal tending to talk a lot. **3** Grammar relating to or derived from a verb. ■ n. **1** Grammar a word or words functioning as a verb. ▸ a verbal noun. **2** (also **verbals**) informal abuse; insults.
– DERIVATIVES **verbally** adv.

verbalism ■ n. **1** concentration on forms of expression rather than content. ▸ excessive or empty use of language. **2** a verbal expression.
– DERIVATIVES **verbalist** n. **verbalistic** adj.

verbalize (also **-ise**) ■ v. **1** express in words, especially by speaking aloud. **2** speak at length and with little real content. **3** make (a word, especially a noun) into a verb.
– DERIVATIVES **verbalization** (also **-isation**) n. **verbalizer** (also **-iser**) n.

verbal noun ■ n. Grammar a noun formed as an inflection of a verb and partly sharing its constructions, such as *smoking* in *smoking is forbidden*.

verbascum /vəˈbaskəm/ ■ n. a plant of a genus that comprises the mulleins. [Genus *Verbascum*.]
– ORIGIN from Latin, 'mullein'.

verbatim /vəːˈbeɪtɪm/ ■ adv. & adj. in exactly the same words as were used originally.
– ORIGIN C15: from medieval Latin, from Latin *verbum* 'word'.

verbena /vəˈbiːnə/ ■ n. a chiefly American ornamental plant with heads of bright showy flowers. [Genus *Verbena*.]
– ORIGIN from Latin, 'sacred bough', in medieval Latin 'vervain'.

verbiage /ˈvəːbɪɪdʒ/ ■ n. excessively lengthy or technical speech or writing.
– ORIGIN C18: from French, from obsolete *verbeier* 'to chatter'.

verbose /vəːˈbəʊs/ ■ adj. using or expressed in more words than are needed.
– DERIVATIVES **verbosely** adv. **verbosity** n.
– ORIGIN C17: from Latin *verbosus*, from *verbum* 'word'.

verboten /vəˈbəʊt(ə)n/ ■ adj. forbidden by an authority.
– ORIGIN from German.

verb phrase ■ n. Grammar the part of a sentence containing the verb and any direct or indirect object, but not the subject.

verdant /ˈvəːd(ə)nt/ ■ adj. green with grass or other lush vegetation.
– DERIVATIVES **verdancy** n. **verdantly** adv.
– ORIGIN C16: perhaps from Old French *verdeant*, from *verdoier* 'be green'.

Verdelho /vəːˈdɛljuː, -ljəʊ/ ■ n. (pl. **-os**) a white grape grown originally in Madeira. ▸ a medium Madeira made from this grape.
– ORIGIN from Portuguese.

verdict ■ n. **1** a decision on an issue of fact in a civil or criminal case or an inquest. **2** an opinion or judgement.
– ORIGIN Middle English: from Anglo-Norman French *verdit*, from Old French *veir* 'true' (from Latin *verus*) + *dit* (from Latin *dictum* 'saying').

verdigris /ˈvəːdɪgriː, -grɪːs/ ■ n. a bright bluish-green encrustation or patina formed on copper or brass by atmospheric oxidation.
– ORIGIN Middle English: from Old French *verte-gres*, earlier *vert de Grece* 'green of Greece'.

verdure /ˈvəːdjə, -jʊə/ ■ n. lush green vegetation.
– DERIVATIVES **verdured** adj. **verdurous** adj.
– ORIGIN Middle English: from Old French *verd* 'green'.

verge[1] ■ n. **1** an edge or border. ▸ a grass edging by the side of a road or path. ▸ Architecture an edge of tiles projecting over a gable. **2** an extreme limit beyond which something specified will happen: *I was on the verge of tears*. ■ v. (**verge on**) be very close or similar to.
– ORIGIN Middle English: from Latin *virga* 'rod'.

verge[2] ■ v. incline in a certain direction or towards a particular state.
– ORIGIN C17: from Latin *vergere* 'to bend, incline'.

vergence ■ n. **1** Physiology the simultaneous movement of the pupils of the eyes towards or away from one another during focusing. **2** Geology the direction in which a fold is inclined or overturned.
– ORIGIN 1980s: common element of *convergence* and *divergence*.

verger ■ n. **1** an official in a church who acts as a caretaker and attendant. **2** an officer who carries a rod before a bishop or dean as a symbol of office.
– ORIGIN Middle English: from Anglo-Norman French, from Latin *virga* 'staff, rod'.

Vergilian ■ adj. variant spelling of **VIRGILIAN**.

verglas /ˈvɛːglɑː/ ■ n. a thin coating of ice or frozen rain on an exposed surface.
– ORIGIN C19: French, from *verre* 'glass' + *glas* (now *glace*) 'ice'.

veridical /vɪˈrɪdɪk(ə)l/ ■ adj. formal truthful or coinciding with reality.
– DERIVATIVES **veridicality** n. **veridically** adv.
– ORIGIN C17: from Latin *veridicus*, from *verus* 'true' + *dicere* 'say'.

veriest ■ adj. archaic used to emphasize a description: *everyone but the veriest greenhorn knows by now*.
– ORIGIN superlative of **VERY**.

verification ■ n. the process of verifying. ▸ Philosophy the establishment by empirical means of the validity of a proposition. ▸ the process of ensuring that procedures laid down in weapons limitation agreements are followed.

verify /ˈvɛrɪfʌɪ/ ■ v. (**-ies, -ied**) **1** make sure or demonstrate that (something) is true, accurate, or justified. **2** Law swear to or support (a statement) by affidavit.
– DERIVATIVES **verifiable** adj. **verifiably** adv. **verifier** n.
– ORIGIN Middle English: from Old French *verifier*, from medieval Latin *verificare*, from *verus* 'true'.

verily ■ adv. archaic truly; certainly.
– ORIGIN Middle English: from **VERY**, suggested by Old French *verrai(e)ment*.

verisimilitude /ˌvɛrɪsɪˈmɪlɪtjuːd/ ■ n. the appearance of being true or real.
– DERIVATIVES **verisimilar** adj.
– ORIGIN C17: from Latin *verisimilitudo*, from *verisimilis* 'probable', from *verus* 'true' + *similis* 'like'.

verismo /vɛˈrɪzməʊ/ ■ n. realism in the arts (especially with reference to late 19th-century Italian opera).
– ORIGIN from Italian.

veritable ■ adj. genuine; actual; properly so called (used to qualify a metaphor): *a veritable price explosion.*
– DERIVATIVES **veritably** adv.
– ORIGIN Middle English: from Old French *verite* (see VERITY).

vérité /'vɛrɪteɪ/ ■ n. a genre of film and television emphasizing realism and naturalism.
– ORIGIN French, 'truth'.

verity ■ n. (pl. -ies) a true principle or belief, especially one of fundamental importance: *the eternal verities.* ▶ truth.
– ORIGIN Middle English: from Old French *verite*, from Latin *veritas*, from *verus* 'true'.

verjuice /'vəːdʒuːs/ ■ n. a sour juice obtained especially from crab apples or unripe grapes.
– ORIGIN Middle English: from Old French *vertjus*, from *vert* 'green' + *jus* 'juice'.

verkrampte /fɛˈkramptə/ ■ adj. S. African (also **verkramp** /fɛˈkramp/) conservative or reactionary. ■ n. a conservative or reactionary person.
– DERIVATIVES **verkramptheid** n.
– ORIGIN Afrikaans, 'narrow, cramped'.

verligte /fɛˈlɪxtə/ ■ adj. S. African (also **verlig**) progressive or enlightened. ■ n. a progressive or enlightened person.
– DERIVATIVES **verligtheid** n.
– ORIGIN Afrikaans, 'enlightened'.

vermeil /'vəːmeɪl, -mɪl/ ■ n. **1** gilded silver or bronze. **2** poetic/literary vermilion.
– ORIGIN Middle English: from Old French (see VERMILION).

vermi- ■ comb. form of or relating to a worm or worms, especially parasitic ones: *vermiform.*
– ORIGIN from Latin *vermis* 'worm'.

vermicelli /ˌvəːmɪˈtʃɛli, ˌvəːm-, -ˈsɛli/ ■ pl. n. **1** pasta made in long slender threads. **2** shreds of chocolate used to decorate cakes.
– ORIGIN Italian, pl. of *vermicello*, diminutive of *verme* 'worm'.

vermicide /'vəːmɪsʌɪd/ ■ n. a substance that is poisonous to worms.

vermiculated ■ adj. marked with sinuous or wavy lines.

vermiculite /vəˈmɪkjʊlʌɪt/ ■ n. a yellow or brown mineral found as an alteration product of mica and other minerals, used for insulation or as a moisture-retentive medium for growing plants.
– ORIGIN C19: from Latin *vermiculari* 'be full of worms' (because on expansion due to heat, it shoots out forms resembling small worms).

vermiculture /'vəːmɪkʌltʃə/ ■ n. the cultivation of earthworms, especially in order to use them to convert organic waste into fertilizer.

vermiform ■ adj. chiefly Zoology or Anatomy resembling or having the form of a worm.

vermifuge /'vəːmɪfjuːdʒ/ ■ n. Medicine an anthelmintic medicine.

vermilion /vəˈmɪljən/ (also **vermillion**) ■ n. a brilliant red colour.

> **HISTORY**
> **Vermilion**, from Old French *vermeillon*, derives from Latin *vermiculus*, meaning 'little worm'. This is a reference to a tiny grub-like Mediterranean insect now called the **kermes**: when crushed, the kermes yields a bright red dye. *Kermes* itself is originally an Arabic word, from which the colour terms **carmine** and **crimson** are derived.

vermin ■ n. [treated as pl.] **1** wild mammals and birds which are harmful to crops, farm animals, or game, or which carry disease. ▶ parasitic worms or insects. **2** very unpleasant and destructive people.
– DERIVATIVES **verminous** adj.
– ORIGIN Middle English: from Old French, from Latin *vermis* 'worm'.

vermouth /'vəːməθ, vəˈmuːθ/ ■ n. a red or white wine flavoured with aromatic herbs, chiefly drunk mixed with gin.
– ORIGIN from French *vermout*, from German *Wermut* 'wormwood'.

vernacular /vəˈnakjʊlə/ ■ n. the language or dialect spoken by the ordinary people of a country or region. ▶ informal the specialized terminology of a group or activity. ■ adj. **1** spoken as or using one's mother tongue rather than a second language. **2** (of architecture) concerned with domestic and functional rather than monumental buildings.
– DERIVATIVES **vernacularism** n. **vernacularity** n. **vernacularize** (also **-ise**) v. **vernacularly** adv.
– ORIGIN C17: from Latin *vernaculus* 'domestic, native'.

vernal /'vəːn(ə)l/ ■ adj. of, in, or appropriate to spring.
– DERIVATIVES **vernally** adv.
– ORIGIN C16: from Latin *vernalis*, from *vernus* 'of the spring', from *ver* 'spring'.

vernal equinox ■ n. the spring equinox.

vernalization (also **-isation**) ■ n. the cooling of seed during germination in order to accelerate flowering when it is planted.
– DERIVATIVES **vernalize** (also **-ise**) v.

vernation /vəːˈneɪʃ(ə)n/ ■ n. Botany the arrangement of bud scales or young leaves in a leaf bud before it opens. Compare with AESTIVATION.
– ORIGIN C18: from Latin *vernare* 'to grow (as in the spring)'.

vernier /'vəːnɪə/ ■ n. a small movable graduated scale for obtaining fractional parts of subdivisions on a fixed main scale of a barometer, sextant, or other measuring instrument.
– ORIGIN C18: named after Pierre *Vernier* (1580–1637), French mathematician.

vernissage /ˌvɛːnɪˈsɑːʒ/ ■ n. (pl. pronounced same) a private view of paintings before public exhibition.
– ORIGIN French, 'varnishing', orig. referring to the day prior to an exhibition when artists were allowed to retouch and varnish hung work.

vernix /'vəːnɪks/ ■ n. a greasy deposit covering the skin of a baby at birth.
– ORIGIN C16: from medieval Latin, var. of *veronix* (see VARNISH).

veronica ■ n. a herbaceous plant of north temperate regions, typically with upright stems bearing narrow pointed leaves and spikes of blue or purple flowers. [Genus *Veronica*: many species, including the speedwells.]
– ORIGIN C16: from medieval Latin, from the given name *Veronica*.

veronique /ˌvɛrəˈniːk/ ■ adj. [postpos.] denoting a dish, typically of fish or chicken, prepared or garnished with grapes.
– ORIGIN from the French given name *Véronique*.

Verreaux's eagle ■ n. a large African eagle, black with a white rump and characteristic white 'V' on its back. [*Aquila verreauxii.*]

verruca /vəˈruːkə/ ■ n. (pl. **verrucae** /-kiː, -siː/ or **verrucas**) a contagious wart on the sole of the foot. ▶ (in medical use) a wart of any kind.
– DERIVATIVES **verrucose** /ˈvɛrʊkəʊz, vəˈruː-/ adj. **verrucous** /ˈvɛrʊkəs, vəˈruː-/ adj.
– ORIGIN Middle English: from Latin.

versatile ■ adj. able to adapt or be adapted to many different functions or activities.
– DERIVATIVES **versatilely** adv. **versatility** n.
– ORIGIN C17: from French, or from Latin *versatilis*, from *versare* 'turn about, revolve'.

verse ■ n. **1** writing arranged with a metrical rhythm. **2** a group of lines that form a unit in a poem or song. **3** each of the short numbered divisions of a chapter in the Bible or other scripture.
– ORIGIN Old English *fers*, from Latin *versus* 'a turn of the plough, a furrow, a line of writing', from *vertere* 'to turn'; reinforced in Middle English by Old French *vers*.

versed ■ adj. (**versed in**) experienced or skilled in; knowledgeable about.
– ORIGIN C17: from French *versé* or Latin *versatus*, from *versari* 'be engaged in'.

versicoloured /'vəːsɪˌkʌləd/ (US **versicolored**) ■ adj. archaic **1** changing from one colour to another in different lights. **2** variegated.

−ORIGIN C18: from Latin *versicolor*, from *versus* 'turned' + *color* 'colour'.

versify ■ v. (**-ies, -ied**) turn into or express in verse.
−DERIVATIVES **versification** n. **versifier** n.

version ■ n. **1** a particular form of something differing in certain respects from an earlier form or from other forms of the same type of thing. ▶ an account of a matter from a particular person's point of view. **2** Medicine the manual turning of a fetus in the womb to make delivery easier.
−DERIVATIVES **versional** adj.
−ORIGIN Middle English (in the sense 'translation'): from French, or from medieval Latin *versio(n-)*, from Latin *vertere* 'to turn'.

vers libre /vɛː ˈliːbr(ə)/ ■ n. another term for FREE VERSE.
−ORIGIN from French.

verso /ˈvəːsəʊ/ ■ n. (pl. **-os**) **1** a left-hand page of an open book, or the back of a loose document. Contrasted with RECTO. **2** the reverse of something such as a coin or painting.
−ORIGIN C19: from Latin *verso (folio)* 'on the turned (leaf)'.

versus ■ prep. (especially in sporting and legal use) against. ▶ as opposed to; in contrast to.
−ORIGIN Middle English: from a medieval Latin use of Latin *versus* 'towards'.

vert /vəːt/ ■ n. Heraldry green.
−ORIGIN Middle English: via Old French from Latin *viridis* 'green'.

vertebra /ˈvəːtɪbrə/ ■ n. (pl. **vertebrae** /-breɪ, -briː/) each of the series of small bones forming the backbone.
−DERIVATIVES **vertebral** adj.
−ORIGIN C17: from Latin, from *vertere* 'to turn'.

vertebrate /ˈvəːtɪbrət/ ■ n. an animal of a large group (subphylum Vertebrata) distinguished by the possession of a backbone or spinal column, including mammals, birds, reptiles, amphibians, and fishes. Compare with INVERTEBRATE. ■ adj. of or relating to the vertebrates.
−ORIGIN C19: from Latin *vertebratus* 'jointed', from *vertebra* (see VERTEBRA).

vertex /ˈvəːtɛks/ ■ n. (pl. **vertices** /-tɪsiːz/ or **vertexes**) **1** the highest point; the top or apex. **2** Geometry each angular point of a polygon, polyhedron, or other figure. ▶ a meeting point of two lines that form an angle. **3** Anatomy the crown of the head.
−ORIGIN Middle English: from Latin, 'whirlpool, crown of a head, vertex', from *vertere* 'to turn'.

vertical ■ adj. **1** at right angles to a horizontal plane; having the top directly above the bottom. **2** Anatomy relating to the crown of the head. **3** involving or passing through all the different levels of a hierarchy or progression. ■ n. **1** a vertical line or plane. **2** an upright structure.
−DERIVATIVES **verticality** n. **verticalize** (also **-ise**) v. **vertically** adv.
−ORIGIN C16: from French, or from late Latin *verticalis*, from *vertex* (see VERTEX).

vertical angles ■ pl. n. Mathematics each of the pairs of opposite angles made by two intersecting lines.

vertical thinking ■ n. the solving of problems using conventional logical processes, as opposed to lateral thinking.

verticillium /ˌvəːtɪˈsɪlɪəm/ ■ n. a fungus causing wilt in plants. [Genus *Verticillium*.]
−ORIGIN from Latin *verticillus* 'whorl of a spindle'.

vertiginous /vəːˈtɪdʒɪnəs/ ■ adj. causing vertigo, especially by being extremely high or steep. ▶ relating to or affected by vertigo.
−DERIVATIVES **vertiginously** adv.

vertigo /ˈvəːtɪgəʊ/ ■ n. a sensation of whirling and loss of balance, caused by looking down from a great height or by disease affecting the inner ear or the vestibular nerve.
−ORIGIN Middle English: from Latin, 'whirling', from *vertere* 'to turn'.

vertisol /ˈvəːtɪsɒl/ ■ n. Soil Science a clayey soil with little organic matter, found in regions with distinct wet and dry seasons.
−ORIGIN 1960s: from VERTICAL + Latin *solum* 'soil'.

vertu ■ n. variant spelling of VIRTU.

vervain /ˈvəːveɪn/ ■ n. a herbaceous plant with small blue, white, or purple flowers, used in herbal medicine.

[*Verbena officinalis*.]
−ORIGIN Middle English: from Old French *verveine*, from Latin *verbena* (see VERBENA).

verve ■ n. vigour, spirit, and style.
−ORIGIN C17: from French, 'vigour', earlier 'form of expression'.

vervet monkey /ˈvəːvɪt/ ■ n. a common African monkey with greenish-brown upper parts and a black face. [*Cercopithecus aethiops*.]
−ORIGIN C19: from French.

Verwoerdian /fəˈvʊdɪən, fəˈwʊədɪən/ ■ adj. S. African relating to or influenced by the apartheid policies advocated by National Party Prime Minister H. F. Verwoerd (1901–1966).

very ■ adv. in a high degree. ▶ [with superlative or **own**] without qualification: *the very best quality*. ■ adj. **1** actual; precise: *his very words*. ▶ archaic real; genuine. **2** emphasizing an extreme point in time or space. **3** with no addition; mere.
−PHRASES **not very 1** in a low degree. **2** far from being. **very good** (or **well**) an expression of consent.
−ORIGIN Middle English: from Old French *verai*, from Latin *verus* 'true'.

Very light /ˈvɛri, ˈvɪəri/ ■ n. a flare fired into the air from a pistol for signalling or for temporary illumination.
−ORIGIN C20: named after the American naval officer Edward W. *Very*.

Very Reverend ■ adj. a title given to a dean in the Anglican Church.

Vesak /ˈvɛsak/ (also **Wesak** or **Vis*ā*kha**) ■ n. the most important Buddhist festival, commemorating the birth, enlightenment, and death of the Buddha.
−ORIGIN Sinhalese *vesak*, from Sanskrit *vaiśākha*, denoting the month April–May.

vesical /ˈvɛsɪk(ə)l, ˈviː-/ ■ adj. Anatomy & Medicine relating to or affecting the urinary bladder.
−ORIGIN C18: from Latin *vesica* 'bladder'.

vesicant /ˈvɛsɪkənt, ˈviː-/ ■ adj. tending to cause blistering. ■ n. an agent that causes blistering.
−ORIGIN Middle English: from late Latin *vesicare* 'form pustules', from *vesica* 'bladder'.

vesicate /ˈvɛsɪkeɪt, ˈviː-/ ■ v. chiefly Medicine blister.
−DERIVATIVES **vesication** n. **vesicatory** adj. & n.
−ORIGIN C17: from late Latin *vesicat-* 'having pustules', from *vesica* 'bladder'.

vesicle /ˈvɛsɪk(ə)l, ˈviː-/ ■ n. **1** Anatomy & Zoology a small fluid-filled sac or cyst within the body. ▶ Medicine a blister full of clear fluid. **2** Botany an air-filled swelling in a seaweed or other plant. **3** Geology a small cavity in volcanic rock, produced by gas bubbles.
−DERIVATIVES **vesicular** adj. **vesiculated** adj. **vesiculation** n.
−ORIGIN C16: from French *vésicule* or Latin *vesicula*, diminutive of *vesica* 'bladder'.

vespers ■ n. Christian Church a service of evening prayer.
−ORIGIN C15: from Old French *vespres* 'evensong', from Latin *vesperas*.

vespertine /ˈvɛspətʌɪn, -tɪn/ ■ adj. technical or poetic/literary of or relating to the evening.
−ORIGIN Middle English: from Latin *vespertinus*, from *vesper* 'evening'.

vessel ■ n. **1** a ship or large boat. **2** a hollow container used to hold liquid. **3** Anatomy & Zoology a duct or canal conveying blood or other fluid. ▶ Botany any of the tubular structures in the vascular system of a plant, serving to conduct water and nutrients from the root. **4** (chiefly in biblical use) a person regarded as embodying a particular quality: *she was inherently the weaker vessel*.
−ORIGIN Middle English: from Anglo-Norman French *vessel(e)*, from late Latin *vascellum*, diminutive of *vas* 'vessel'.

vest ■ n. **1** an undergarment worn on the upper part of the body, typically having no sleeves. **2** a similar garment worn for a particular purpose: *a bulletproof vest*. **3** N. Amer. & Austral. a waistcoat or sleeveless jacket. ■ v. **1** (**vest something in**) confer or bestow power, property, etc. on: *executive power is vested in the President*. ▶ (usu. **be**

vested with) give (someone) the legal right to power, property, etc. **2** put on vestments. ▸ poetic/literary dress.
– ORIGIN Middle English: verb from Old French *vestu* 'clothed', from *vestir*, from Latin *vestire*; noun from French *veste*, from Latin *vestis* 'garment'.

vesta ■ n. chiefly historical a short wooden or wax match.
– ORIGIN C19: from the name of *Vesta*, the Roman goddess of the hearth.

vestal ■ adj. **1** of or relating to the Roman goddess Vesta. **2** poetic/literary chaste; pure.

vestal virgin ■ n. (in ancient Rome) a virgin consecrated to the goddess Vesta and vowed to chastity.

vested interest ■ n. **1** Law an interest (usually in land or money held in trust) recognized as belonging to a particular person. **2** a personal stake in an undertaking or state of affairs, especially one with an expectation of financial gain.

vestibule /'vɛstɪbjuːl/ ■ n. **1** an antechamber or hall just inside the outer door of a building. **2** Anatomy a chamber or channel opening into another, especially in the inner ear.
– DERIVATIVES **vestibular** adj. (Anatomy). **vestibuled** adj.
– ORIGIN C17: from French, or from Latin *vestibulum* 'entrance court'.

vestibulocochlear nerves /vɛˌstɪbjʊləʊ'kɒkliə/ ■ pl. n. Anatomy the pair of cranial nerves transmitting impulses from the ears to the brain.

vestibulo-ocular reflex /vɛˌstɪbjʊləʊ'ɒkjʊlə/ ■ n. the reflex by which balance is maintained when the visual field is in motion.

vestige /'vɛstɪdʒ/ ■ n. a trace of something. ▸ the smallest amount.
– ORIGIN Middle English: from Latin *vestigium* 'footprint'.

vestigial /vɛ'stɪdʒɪəl, -dʒ(ə)l/ ■ adj. forming a very small remnant of something that was once greater or more noticeable.
– DERIVATIVES **vestigially** adv.

vestment ■ n. a chasuble or other robe worn by the clergy or choristers during services. ▸ archaic a garment, especially a ceremonial or official robe.
– ORIGIN Middle English: from Old French *vestiment*, from Latin *vestimentum*, from *vestire* (see VEST).

vestry ■ n. (pl. -ies) a room in or attached to a church, used as an office and for changing into ceremonial vestments. ▸ a meeting of parishioners, originally in a vestry, for the conduct of parochial business.
– DERIVATIVES **vestryman** n.
– ORIGIN Middle English: prob. from an Anglo-Norman French alteration of Old French *vestiarie*, from Latin *vestiarium*.

vesture ■ n. poetic/literary clothing.
– ORIGIN Middle English: from Old French, from Latin *vestire* 'clothe'.

vet[1] ■ n. a veterinary surgeon. ■ v. (**vetted**, **vetting**) make a careful and critical examination of (someone, especially of a person prior to employment).
– ORIGIN C19: abbrev. of VETERINARY or VETERINARIAN.

vet[2] ■ n. informal, chiefly N. Amer. a veteran.

vetch ■ n. a leguminous plant with purple, pink, or yellow flowers, some kinds of which are cultivated for silage or fodder. [*Vicia sativa* and other species.]
– ORIGIN Middle English: from Anglo-Norman French *veche*, from Latin *vicia*.

veteran ■ n. **1** a person who has had long experience in a particular field. **2** an ex-serviceman or -servicewoman.
– ORIGIN C16: from French *vétéran* or Latin *veteranus*, from *vetus* 'old'.

veteran car ■ n. an old style or model of car, specifically one made before 1919 or (strictly) before 1905. Compare with VINTAGE CAR.

Veterans Day ■ n. (in the US) the anniversary of the end of the First World War (11 November), honouring US veterans and victims of all wars.

veterinarian /ˌvɛt(ə)rɪ'nɛːrɪən/ ■ n. another term for VETERINARY SURGEON.

veterinary /'vɛt(ə)rɪn(ə)ri, 'vɛt(ə)nri/ ■ adj. of or relating to the diseases, injuries, and treatment of farm and domestic animals.
– ORIGIN C18: from Latin *veterinarius*, from *veterinae* 'cattle'.

veterinary surgeon ■ n. a person qualified to treat diseased or injured animals.

vetiver /'vɛtɪvə/ (also **vetivert**) ■ n. a fragrant extract or essential oil obtained from the root of an Indian grass (*Vetiveria zizanioides*), used in perfumery and aromatherapy.
– ORIGIN C19: from French *vétiver*, from Tamil *veṭṭivēr*, from *vēr* 'root'.

vetkoek /'fɛtkʊk/ ■ n. S. African a small cake made from deep-fried unsweetened dough.
– ORIGIN C19: Afrikaans, from *vet* 'fat' + *koek* 'cake'.

veto /'viːtəʊ/ ■ n. (pl. **-oes**) a constitutional right to reject a decision or proposal made by a law-making body. ▸ any prohibition. ■ v. (**-oes**, **-oed**) exercise a veto against. ▸ refuse to accept or allow.
– DERIVATIVES **vetoer** n.
– ORIGIN C17: from Latin, 'I forbid', used by Roman tribunes of the people when opposing measures of the Senate.

vex ■ v. cause to feel annoyed or worried.
– DERIVATIVES **vexation** n. **vexer** n. **vexing** adj. **vexingly** adv.
– ORIGIN Middle English: from Old French *vexer*, from Latin *vexare* 'shake, disturb'.

vexatious ■ adj. **1** causing annoyance or worry. **2** Law (of an action) brought without sufficient grounds for winning, purely to cause annoyance to the defendant.
– DERIVATIVES **vexatiously** adv. **vexatiousness** n.

vexed ■ adj. **1** difficult and much debated; problematic. **2** annoyed or worried.
– DERIVATIVES **vexedly** adv.

vexillology /ˌvɛksɪ'lɒlədʒi/ ■ n. the study of flags.
– DERIVATIVES **vexillological** adj. **vexillologist** n.
– ORIGIN 1950s: from Latin *vexillum* 'flag' + -LOGY.

VFR ■ abbrev. visual flight rules (used under conditions of good visibility).

VG ■ abbrev. **1** very good. **2** Vicar General.

VGA ■ abbrev. videographics array, a standard for defining colour display screens for computers.

vgc ■ abbrev. very good condition.

VHF ■ abbrev. very high frequency.

VHS ■ abbrev. trademark video home system (as used by domestic video recorders).

via ■ prep. travelling through (a place) en route to a destination. ▸ by way of; through. ▸ by means of.
– ORIGIN C18: from Latin *via* 'way, road'.

viable /'vʌɪəb(ə)l/ ■ adj. **1** capable of working successfully; feasible. **2** Botany (of a seed or spore) able to germinate. ▸ Medicine (of a fetus or unborn child) able to live after birth.
– DERIVATIVES **viability** n. **viably** adv.
– ORIGIN C19: from French, from *vie* 'life'.

viaduct ■ n. a long bridge-like structure, typically a series of arches, carrying a road or railway across a valley or other low ground.
– ORIGIN C19: from Latin *via* 'way', on the pattern of *aqueduct*.

Viagra /vʌɪ'agrə/ ■ n. trademark a synthetic compound used to enhance male potency.
– ORIGIN 1990s: apparently a blend of *virility* and the name *Niagara*.

vial /'vʌɪəl/ ■ n. a small container used especially for holding liquid medicines.
– ORIGIN Middle English: alteration of PHIAL.

via media /'miːdɪə, 'mɛdɪə/ ■ n. formal a middle way or compromise between extremes.
– ORIGIN from Latin.

viand /'vʌɪənd/ ■ n. archaic an item of food.
– ORIGIN Middle English: from Old French *viande* 'food', from an alteration of Latin *vivenda*, from *vivere* 'to live'.

via negativa /ˌneɡə'tiːvə/ ■ n. Theology a way of describing something by saying what it is not.
– ORIGIN Latin, 'negative path'.

viaticum /vʌɪ'atɪkəm/ ■ n. (pl. **viatica** /-kə/) **1** the Eucharist

as given to a person near or in danger of death. **2** archaic a supply of provisions or allowance of money for a journey.
– ORIGIN C16: from Latin *viaticus*, from *via* 'road'.

vibe ■ n. informal **1** the atmosphere or aura of a person or place as communicated to and felt by others. **2** (**vibes**) short for VIBRAPHONE.

vibist /ˈvʌɪbɪst/ ■ n. a musician who plays the vibraphone.

Vibracrete ■ n. S. African trademark precast concrete, typically used for boundary walls.

vibrant ■ adj. **1** full of energy and enthusiasm. ▶ (of colour or sound) bold and strong. **2** quivering; pulsating.
– DERIVATIVES **vibrancy** n. **vibrantly** adv.
– ORIGIN C17: from Latin *vibrant-* 'shaking to and fro', from *vibrare* (see VIBRATE).

vibraphone /ˈvʌɪbrəfəʊn/ ■ n. a musical percussion instrument with a double row of tuned metal bars, each above a tubular resonator containing a motor-driven rotating vane, giving a vibrato effect.
– DERIVATIVES **vibraphonist** n.
– ORIGIN 1920S: from VIBRATO + -PHONE.

vibrate ■ v. **1** move or cause to move with small movements rapidly to and fro. **2** (of a sound) resonate.
– DERIVATIVES **vibrating** adj.
– ORIGIN Middle English: from Latin *vibrare* 'move to and fro'.

vibration ■ n. **1** an instance of vibrating. ▶ Physics an oscillation of the parts of a fluid or an elastic solid whose equilibrium has been disturbed or of an electromagnetic wave. **2** (**vibrations**) informal a person's emotional state, the atmosphere of a place, or the associations of an object, as communicated to and felt by others.
– DERIVATIVES **vibrational** adj.

vibrato /vɪˈbrɑːtəʊ/ ■ n. Music a rapid, slight variation in pitch in singing or playing some musical instruments, producing a stronger or richer tone.
– ORIGIN C19: Italian, from *vibrare* 'vibrate'.

vibrator ■ n. a device that vibrates or causes vibration. ▶ a vibrating device used for massage or sexual stimulation.
– DERIVATIVES **vibratory** adj.

vibrio /ˈvɪbrɪəʊ, ˈvʌɪ-/ ■ n. (pl. **-os**) Medicine a water-borne bacterium of curved, rod-like shape, belonging to a group including the causative agent of cholera. [*Vibrio* and related genera.]
– ORIGIN from Latin *vibrare* 'vibrate'.

vibrissae /vʌɪˈbrɪsiː/ ■ pl. n. Zoology long stiff hairs growing around the mouth or elsewhere on the face of many mammals; whiskers.
– ORIGIN C17: from Latin, 'nostril hairs'.

viburnum /vɪˈbəːnəm, vʌɪ-/ ■ n. a shrub or small tree of temperate and warm regions, typically bearing flat or rounded clusters of small white flowers. [Genus *Viburnum*: many species.]
– ORIGIN from Latin, 'wayfaring tree'.

vicar ■ n. **1** (in the Church of England) an incumbent of a parish where tithes formerly passed to a chapter or religious house or layman. ▶ (in other Anglican Churches) a member of the clergy deputizing for another. ▶ (in the Roman Catholic Church) a representative or deputy of a bishop. ▶ (in the US Episcopal Church) a clergyman in charge of a chapel. **2** a cleric or choir member appointed to sing certain parts of a cathedral service.
– DERIVATIVES **vicarship** n.
– ORIGIN Middle English: from Old French *vicaire*, from Latin *vicarius* 'substitute', from *vic-* 'change, place'.

vicarage ■ n. the residence of a vicar. ▶ historical the benefice or living of a vicar.

vicar apostolic ■ n. **1** a Roman Catholic missionary. **2** a titular bishop.

vicar general ■ n. (pl. **vicars general**) an official serving as a deputy or representative of a bishop or archbishop.

vicariate /vɪˈkɛːrɪət, vʌɪ-/ ■ n. the office or authority of a vicar. ▶ a church or parish ministered to by a vicar.

vicarious /vɪˈkɛːrɪəs, vʌɪ-/ ■ adj. **1** experienced in the imagination through the feelings or actions of another person: *vicarious pleasure.* **2** acting or done for another.
– DERIVATIVES **vicariously** adv. **vicariousness** n.
– ORIGIN C17: from Latin *vicarius* (see VICAR).

vice[1] /vʌɪs/ ■ n. **1** immoral or wicked behaviour. ▶ criminal activities involving prostitution, pornography, or drugs. ▶ an immoral or wicked personal characteristic. ▶ a weakness of character; a bad habit. **2** (also **stable vice**) a bad or neurotic habit of stabled horses, typically arising as a result of boredom.
– DERIVATIVES **viceless** adj.
– ORIGIN Middle English: from Latin *vitium*.

vice[2] /vʌɪs/ (US **vise**) ■ n. a metal tool with movable jaws which are used to hold an object firmly in place while work is done on it.
– DERIVATIVES **vice-like** adj.
– ORIGIN Middle English: from Old French *vis*, from Latin *vitis* 'vine'.

vice- ■ comb. form next in rank to (typically denoting capacity to deputize for): *vice-president.*
– ORIGIN from Latin *vice* 'in place of'.

vice admiral ■ n. a high rank of naval officer, above rear admiral and below admiral.

vice chamberlain ■ n. a deputy chamberlain, especially (in the UK) the deputy of the Lord Chamberlain.

vice chancellor ■ n. a deputy chancellor, especially one of a university who discharges most of its administrative duties.

vice-president ■ n. an official or executive ranking below and deputizing for a president.
– DERIVATIVES **vice-presidency** n. (pl. **-ies**). **vice-presidential** adj.

viceregal ■ adj. of or relating to a viceroy.

vicereine /ˈvʌɪsreɪn/ ■ n. the wife of a viceroy, or a female viceroy.
– ORIGIN C19: French, from *vice-* 'in place of' + *reine* 'queen'.

viceroy /ˈvʌɪsrɔɪ/ ■ n. a ruler exercising authority in a colony on behalf of a sovereign.
– DERIVATIVES **viceroyal** adj. **viceroyship** n.
– ORIGIN C16: from archaic French, from *vice-* 'in place of' + *roi* 'king'.

viceroyalty ■ n. (pl. **-ies**) the office, position, or authority of a viceroy. ▶ a territory governed by a viceroy.

vice versa /ˌvʌɪs ˈvəːsə, ˌvʌɪsə/ ■ adv. with the main items in the preceding statement the other way round.
– ORIGIN C17: from Latin, 'in-turned position'.

vichyssoise /ˌviːʃɪˈswɑːz/ ■ n. a soup made with potatoes, leeks, and cream and typically served chilled.
– ORIGIN French of '*Vichy*', a town in central France.

vicinal /ˈvɪsɪn(ə)l, vɪˈsʌɪn(ə)l/ ■ adj. **1** neighbouring; adjacent. **2** Chemistry relating to or denoting substituents attached to adjacent atoms in a ring or chain.
– ORIGIN C17: from French, or from Latin *vicinalis*, from *vicinus* 'neighbour'.

vicinity ■ n. (pl. **-ies**) the area near or surrounding a particular place.
– ORIGIN C16: from Latin *vicinitas*, from *vicinus* 'neighbour'.

vicious ■ adj. cruel or violent. ▶ (of an animal) wild and dangerous.
– DERIVATIVES **viciously** adv. **viciousness** n.
– ORIGIN Middle English: from Old French *vicious* or Latin *vitiosus*, from *vitium* 'vice'.

vicious circle ■ n. a sequence of reciprocal cause and effect in which two or more elements intensify and aggravate each other, leading inexorably to a worsening of the situation.

vicissitude /vɪˈsɪsɪtjuːd, vʌɪ-/ ■ n. **1** a change of circumstances or fortune, typically for the worse. **2** poetic/literary alternation between opposite or contrasting things.
– DERIVATIVES **vicissitudinous** /-ˈtjuːdɪnəs/ adj.
– ORIGIN C17: from Latin *vicissitudo*, from *vicissim* 'by turns', from *vic-* 'turn, change'.

vicomte /ˈviːkɔ̃t, ˈviːkɒmt/ ■ n. (pl. pronounced same) a French nobleman corresponding in rank to a viscount.
– ORIGIN from French.

vicomtesse /ˌviːkɔ̃ˈtɛs, ˌviːkɒnˈtɛs/ ■ n. (pl. pronounced same) a French noblewoman corresponding in rank to a viscountess.
– ORIGIN from French.

victim ■ n. **1** a person harmed, injured, or killed as a result of a crime, accident, etc. **2** an animal or person killed as a religious sacrifice.
- PHRASES **fall victim to** be hurt, killed, or destroyed by.
- ORIGIN C15: from Latin *victima*.

victimize (also **-ise**) ■ v. single (someone) out for cruel or unjust treatment.
- DERIVATIVES **victimization** (also **-isation**) n. **victimizer** (also **-iser**)

victimless ■ adj. (of a crime) in which there is no injured party.

victimology ■ n. (pl. **-ies**) the study of the victims of crime and the psychological effects on them.

victor ■ n. **1** a person who defeats an enemy or opponent in a battle, game, or competition. **2** a code word representing the letter V, used in radio communication.
- ORIGIN Middle English: from Anglo-Norman French *victo(u)r* or Latin *victor*, from *vincere* 'conquer'.

Victoria lily ■ n. a tropical South American water lily which has gigantic floating leaves with raised sides. [Genus *Victoria*: two species.]

Victorian ■ adj. of or relating to the reign of Queen Victoria (1837–1901). ▶ of or relating to the attitudes and values associated with this period, especially those of prudishness and high moral tone. ■ n. a person who lived during the Victorian period.
- DERIVATIVES **Victorianism** n.

Victoriana ■ pl. n. articles, especially collectors' items, from the Victorian period.

Victoria plum ■ n. Brit. a plum of a large red dessert variety.

Victoria sandwich (also **Victoria sponge**) ■ n. Brit. a cake consisting of two layers of sponge with a jam filling.

victorious ■ adj. having won a victory; triumphant. ▶ of or characterized by victory.
- DERIVATIVES **victoriously** adv. **victoriousness** n.

victor ludorum /luːˈdɔːrəm/ ■ n. (fem. **victrix ludorum**, pl. **-trices** /-trɪsiːz/) the overall champion in a sports competition.
- ORIGIN Latin, 'victor of the games'.

victory ■ n. (pl. **-ies**) an act of defeating an enemy or opponent in a battle, game, or competition.
- ORIGIN Middle English: from Anglo-Norman French *victorie*, from Latin *victoria*.

victory roll ■ n. a roll performed by an aircraft as a sign of triumph, as after a successful mission.

victual /ˈvɪt(ə)l/ dated ■ n. (**victuals**) food or provisions. ■ v. (**victualled, victualling**; US **victualed, victualing**) **1** provide with food or other stores. **2** eat.
- ORIGIN Middle English: from Old French *vitaille*, from Latin *victualis*, from *victus* 'food'; the pronunciation still represents the early spelling *vittel*.

victualler /ˈvɪt(ə)lə/ (US **victualer**) ■ n. **1** Brit. a person who is licensed to sell alcoholic liquor. **2** dated a person providing or selling food or other provisions. ▶ a ship providing supplies for troops or other ships.

vicuña /vɪˈkjuːnjə, -kuː-, vɪˈkuːnə/ ■ n. **1** a wild relative of the llama, inhabiting mountainous regions of South America and valued for its fine silky wool. [*Vicugna vicugna*.] **2** cloth made from this wool.
- ORIGIN C17: from Spanish, from Quechua.

vid ■ n. informal short for VIDEO.

vide /ˈvɪdeɪ, ˈviː-, ˈvʌɪdi/ ■ v. see; consult (used as an instruction in a text to refer the reader elsewhere).
- ORIGIN Latin, 'see!', from *videre*.

videlicet /vɪˈdeliset, vʌɪ-, -ket/ ■ adv. more formal term for VIZ.
- ORIGIN Latin, from *videre* 'to see' + *licet* 'it is permissible'.

video ■ n. (pl. **-os**) the system of recording, reproducing, or broadcasting moving visual images on or from videotape. ▶ a film or other recording on videotape. ▶ a video cassette. ▶ a video recorder. ■ v. (**-oes, -oed**) film or make a video recording of.
- ORIGIN 1930s: from Latin *videre* 'to see', on the pattern of *audio*.

videoconference ■ n. an arrangement in which television sets linked to telephone lines are used to enable a group of people in different locations to communicate with each other in sound and vision.
- DERIVATIVES **videoconferencing** n.

videodisc ■ n. a CD-ROM or other disc used to store visual images.

video frequency ■ n. a frequency in the range used for video signals in television.

video game ■ n. a game played by electronically manipulating images produced by a computer program on a television screen or monitor.

videographics ■ pl. n. [also treated as sing.] visual images produced using computer technology.

videography ■ n. the process or art of making video films.
- DERIVATIVES **videographer** n.

video jockey ■ n. a person who introduces and plays music videos on television.

video-on-demand ■ n. a system in which viewers choose their own filmed entertainment, by means of a PC or interactive TV system.

videophile ■ n. an enthusiast for or devotee of video recordings or video technology.

videophone ■ n. a telephone device transmitting and receiving a visual image as well as sound.

VideoPlus ■ n. trademark a system for identifying broadcast television programmes by a numerical code which can be input into a video recorder in order to preset recording.

video recorder (also **video cassette recorder**) ■ n. a device which, when linked to a television set, can be used for recording on and playing videotapes.
- DERIVATIVES **video recording** n.

videotape ■ n. magnetic tape for recording and reproducing visual images and sound. ▶ a video cassette. ■ v. record on video.

vie /vʌɪ/ ■ v. (**vying**) compete eagerly with others in order to do or achieve something.
- ORIGIN C16: prob. a shortening of obsolete *envy*, from Latin *invitare* 'challenge'.

Vienna sausage ■ n. a small frankfurter made of pork, beef, or veal.

Viennese /vɪəˈniːz/ ■ n. a native or inhabitant of Vienna. ■ adj. of or relating to Vienna.

Viennese waltz ■ n. a waltz characterized by a slight anticipation of the second beat of the bar.

Vietcong /vjetˈkɒŋ/ ■ n. the Communist guerrilla force in Vietnam which fought the South Vietnamese government forces 1954–75 and opposed the South Vietnam and US forces in the Vietnam War.
- ORIGIN Vietnamese, 'Vietnamese Communist'.

Vietnamese ■ n. (pl. same) **1** a native or national of Vietnam, or a person of Vietnamese descent. **2** the language of Vietnam. ■ adj. of or relating to Vietnam, its people, or their language.

Vietnamese pot-bellied pig ■ n. a pig of a small, dark breed with short legs and a large stomach, sometimes kept as a pet.

view ■ n. **1** vision or sight, as from a particular position. ▶ a sight or prospect from a particular position, typically an appealing one. **2** a particular way of regarding something; an attitude or opinion. **3** an inspection of things for sale by prospective purchasers, especially of works of art. ■ v. **1** look at or inspect. ▶ inspect (a house or other property) with the prospect of buying or renting. ▶ watch on television. **2** regard in a particular light or with a particular attitude.
- PHRASES **in full view** clearly visible. **in view 1** visible. **2** in one's mind or as one's aim. **in view of** because or as a result of. **on view** being shown or exhibited to the public. **with a view to** with the hope or intention of.
- DERIVATIVES **viewable** adj. **viewing** n. **viewless** adj.
- ORIGIN Middle English: from Anglo-Norman French *vieue*, from *veoir* 'see', from Latin *videre*.

viewer ▪ n. **1** a person who views something. **2** a device for looking at film transparencies or similar photographic images.

viewership ▪ n. [treated as sing. or pl.] the audience for a particular television programme or channel.

viewfinder ▪ n. a device on a camera showing the field of view of the lens, used in framing and focusing the picture.

viewgraph ▪ n. a graph or other data produced as a transparency for projection on to a screen or for transmission during a teleconference.

viewpoint ▪ n. **1** a position affording a good view. **2** a point of view; an opinion.

viewport ▪ n. **1** a window in a spacecraft or in the conning tower of an oil rig. **2** Computing a framed area on a display screen for viewing information.

vigil /ˈvɪdʒɪl/ ▪ n. **1** a period of staying awake during the time usually spent asleep, especially to keep watch or pray. **2** (in the Christian Church) the eve of a festival or holy day as an occasion of religious observance. ▸ (**vigils**) nocturnal devotions.
– ORIGIN Middle English: from Latin *vigilia*, from *vigil* 'awake'.

vigilant ▪ adj. keeping careful watch for possible danger or difficulties.
– DERIVATIVES **vigilance** n. **vigilantly** adv.
– ORIGIN C15: from Latin *vigilant-*, *vigilare* 'keep awake'.

vigilante /ˌvɪdʒɪˈlænti/ ▪ n. a member of a self-appointed group of people who undertake law enforcement in their community without legal authority, typically because the legal agencies are thought to be inadequate.
– DERIVATIVES **vigilantism** n.
– ORIGIN C19: from Spanish, 'vigilant'.

vigneron /ˈviːnjərɒ̃/ ▪ n. a person who cultivates grapes for winemaking.
– ORIGIN French, from *vigne* 'vine'.

vignette /viːˈnjet, vɪ-/ ▪ n. **1** a brief evocative description, account, or episode. **2** a small illustration or portrait photograph which fades into its background without a definite border. ▸ a small ornamental design in a book or carving, typically based on foliage. ▪ v. portray in the style of a vignette. ▸ produce (a photograph) with softened or fading edges.
– ORIGIN Middle English (denoting a carved representation of a vine): from French, diminutive of *vigne* 'vine'.

vigor ▪ n. US spelling of VIGOUR.

vigorous ▪ adj. **1** strong, healthy, and full of energy. ▸ characterized by or involving physical strength, effort, or energy. **2** (of language) forceful.
– DERIVATIVES **vigorously** adv. **vigorousness** n.

vigour (US **vigor**) ▪ n. physical strength and good health. ▸ effort, energy, and enthusiasm. ▸ strong, healthy growth of a plant.
– ORIGIN Middle English: from Old French, from Latin *vigor*, from *vigere* 'be lively'.

Viking /ˈvaɪkɪŋ/ ▪ n. any of the Scandinavian seafaring pirates and traders who raided and settled in many parts of NW Europe in the 8th–11th centuries.
– ORIGIN from Old Norse *víkingr*, from *vík* 'creek' or Old English *wīc* 'camp, dwelling place'.

vile ▪ adj. **1** extremely unpleasant. **2** morally bad; wicked.
– DERIVATIVES **vilely** adv. **vileness** n.
– ORIGIN Middle English: from Latin *vilis* 'cheap, base'.

vilify /ˈvɪlɪfaɪ/ ▪ v. (**-ies**, **-ied**) speak or write about in an abusively disparaging manner.
– DERIVATIVES **vilification** /-fɪˈkeɪʃ(ə)n/ n. **vilifier** n.
– ORIGIN Middle English: from late Latin *vilificare*, from Latin *vilis* (see VILE).

villa ▪ n. **1** (especially in continental Europe) a large country residence in its own grounds. ▸ Brit. a detached or semi-detached house in a residential district. ▸ a rented holiday home abroad. **2** (in Roman times) a large country house, having an estate and consisting of buildings arranged around a courtyard.
– ORIGIN C17: from Italian, from Latin.

village ▪ n. a group of houses situated in a rural area, larger than a hamlet and smaller than a town. ▸ a self-contained district or community within a town or city: *the Olympic village*. ▸ N. Amer. a small municipality with limited corporate powers.

– DERIVATIVES **villager** n. **villagey** adj.
– ORIGIN Middle English: from Old French, from Latin *villa* 'country house'.

villain /ˈvɪlən/ ▪ n. a wicked person or a person guilty of a crime. ▸ (in a play or novel) a character whose evil actions or motives are important to the plot.
– DERIVATIVES **villainous** adj. **villainously** adv. **villainousness** n. **villainy** n.
– ORIGIN Middle English (in the sense 'a rustic'): from Old French *vilein*, from Latin *villa* (see VILLA).

villanelle /ˌvɪləˈnɛl/ ▪ n. a pastoral or lyrical poem of nineteen lines, with only two rhymes throughout, and some lines repeated.
– ORIGIN C19: from French, from Italian *villanello* 'rural'.

-ville ▪ comb. form informal used in fictitious place names with reference to a particular quality: *dullsville*.
– ORIGIN from French *ville* 'town'.

villein /ˈvɪlən, -eɪn/ ▪ n. (in medieval England) a feudal tenant entirely subject to a lord or manor to whom he paid dues and services in return for land.
– ORIGIN Middle English: var. of VILLAIN.

villeinage /ˈvɪlənɪdʒ, -leɪn-/ ▪ n. historical the tenure or status of a villein.

villi plural form of VILLUS.

villus /ˈvɪləs/ ▪ n. (pl. **villi** /-lʌɪ, -liː/) Anatomy any of numerous minute elongated projections set closely together on a surface, especially in the absorbent lining of the small intestine.
– DERIVATIVES **villous** adj.
– ORIGIN C18: from Latin, 'shaggy hair'.

vim ▪ n. informal energy; enthusiasm.
– ORIGIN C19 (orig. US): perhaps from Latin *vis* 'energy'.

VIN ▪ abbrev. vehicle identification number.

vinaceous /vʌɪˈneɪʃəs/ ▪ adj. of the colour of red wine.
– ORIGIN C17: from Latin *vinaceus*, from *vinum* 'wine'.

vinaigrette /ˌvɪnɪˈɡrɛt, ˌvɪneɪ-/ ▪ n. **1** salad dressing of oil, wine vinegar, and seasoning. **2** historical a small ornamental bottle for holding smelling salts.
– ORIGIN French, diminutive of *vinaigre* 'vinegar'.

vinca /ˈvɪŋkə/ ▪ n. another term for PERIWINKLE[1].
– ORIGIN 1930s: from *Vinca* (genus name), from late Latin *pervinca* (see PERIWINKLE[1]).

vincible /ˈvɪnsɪb(ə)l/ ▪ adj. poetic/literary able to be overcome or conquered.
– DERIVATIVES **vincibility** n.
– ORIGIN C16: from Latin *vincibilis*, from *vincere* 'to overcome'.

vindaloo /ˌvɪndəˈluː/ ▪ n. a very hot Indian curry made with meat or fish.
– ORIGIN prob. from Portuguese *vin d'alho* 'wine and garlic (sauce)', from *vinho* 'wine' + *alho* 'garlic'.

vindicate /ˈvɪndɪkeɪt/ ▪ v. clear of blame or suspicion; show to be right or justified.
– DERIVATIVES **vindicable** adj. **vindication** n. **vindicator** n. **vindicatory** adj.
– ORIGIN C16: from Latin *vindicare* 'claim, avenge'.

vindictive /vɪnˈdɪktɪv/ ▪ adj. having or showing a strong or unreasoning desire for revenge.
– DERIVATIVES **vindictively** adv. **vindictiveness** n.
– ORIGIN C17: from Latin *vindicta* 'vengeance'.

vine ▪ n. **1** a climbing or trailing woody-stemmed plant related to the grapevine. [*Vitis* and other genera.] ▸ used in names of climbing or trailing plants of other families, e.g. Russian vine. **2** the slender stem of a trailing or climbing plant.
– DERIVATIVES **viny** adj.
– ORIGIN Middle English: from Latin *vinea* 'vineyard, vine', from *vinum* 'wine'.

vine dresser ▪ n. a person who prunes, trains, and cultivates vines.

vinegar ▪ n. **1** a sour-tasting liquid containing acetic acid, obtained by fermenting dilute alcoholic liquids, typically wine, cider, or beer, and used as a condiment or for pickling. **2** sourness or peevishness of behaviour.
– DERIVATIVES **vinegarish** adj. **vinegary** adj.
– ORIGIN Middle English: from Old French *vyn egre*, from Latin *vinum* 'wine' + *acer* 'sour'.

vinery ■ n. (pl. **-ies**) a greenhouse for grapevines. ▶ a vineyard.

vine snake ■ n. another term for TWIG SNAKE.

vineyard ■ n. a plantation of grapevines, typically producing grapes used in winemaking.

vingt-et-un /ˌvãteɪˈɜːn/ ■ n. the card game pontoon or blackjack.
– ORIGIN French, 'twenty-one'.

vinho verde /ˌviːnəʊ ˈvɛːdi/ ■ n. a young Portuguese wine, not allowed to mature.
– ORIGIN Portuguese, 'green wine'.

vini- ■ comb. form of or relating to wine: *viniculture*.
– ORIGIN from Latin *vinum* 'wine'.

viniculture /ˈvɪnɪˌkʌltʃə/ ■ n. the cultivation of grapevines for winemaking.
– DERIVATIVES **vinicultural** adj. **viniculturist** n.

vinification /ˌvɪnɪfɪˈkeɪʃ(ə)n/ ■ n. the conversion of grape juice or other vegetable extract into wine by fermentation.
– DERIVATIVES **vinify** v. (**-ies, -ied**)

vining /ˈvaɪnɪŋ/ ■ n. the separation of leguminous crops from their vines and pods. ■ adj. (of a plant) having climbing or trailing woody stems like a vine.

vino /ˈviːnəʊ/ ■ n. (pl. **-os**) informal wine, especially that which is cheap or of inferior quality.
– ORIGIN Spanish and Italian, 'wine'.

vin ordinaire /vã ˌɔːdɪˈnɛː/ ■ n. (pl. **vins ordinaires**) cheap table wine for everyday use.
– ORIGIN French, 'ordinary wine'.

vinous /ˈvaɪnəs/ ■ adj. of, resembling, or associated with wine. ▶ of the reddish colour of wine.
– DERIVATIVES **vinosity** n. **vinously** adv.
– ORIGIN Middle English: from Latin *vinum* 'wine'.

vintage ■ n. 1 the year or place in which wine, especially wine of high quality, was produced. ▶ a wine of high quality made from the crop of a single identified district in a good year. ▶ the harvesting of grapes for wine-making. ▶ the grapes or wine of a particular season. 2 the time that something was produced. ■ adj. 1 relating to or denoting vintage wine. 2 denoting something from the past of high quality or which is the best of its type: *a vintage Sherlock Holmes adventure*.
– ORIGIN Middle English: alteration (influenced by VINTNER) of earlier *vendage*, from Old French *vendange*, from Latin *vindemia*, from *vinum* 'wine' + *demere* 'remove'.

vintage car ■ n. an old style or model of car, specifically one made between 1919 and 1930. Compare with VETERAN CAR.

vintager ■ n. a person who harvests grapes.

vintner /ˈvɪntnə/ ■ n. a wine merchant.
– ORIGIN Middle English: from Old French *vinetier*, from medieval Latin *vinetarius*, from Latin *vinetum* 'vineyard'.

vinyl /ˈvaɪn(ə)l/ ■ n. 1 synthetic resin or plastic based on polyvinyl chloride, used e.g. for wallpaper and emulsion paint and formerly for gramophone records. 2 /also ˈvaɪnʌɪl, -nɪl/ [as modifier] Chemistry of or denoting the unsaturated hydrocarbon radical -CH=CH$_2$, derived from ethylene: *vinyl chloride*.
– ORIGIN C19: from Latin *vinum* 'wine' (suggested by the relationship of ethylene to ethyl alcohol).

Viognier /vɪˈɒnjeɪ/ ■ n. a white wine grape grown chiefly in the northern Rhône area of France. ▶ a white wine made from the Viognier grape.

viol /ˈvaɪəl/ ■ n. a musical instrument of the Renaissance and baroque periods, typically six-stringed, held vertically and played with a bow.
– ORIGIN C15: from Old French *viele*, from Provençal *viola*.

viola[1] /vɪˈəʊlə/ ■ n. an instrument of the violin family, larger than the violin and tuned a fifth lower.
– ORIGIN C18: from Italian and Spanish.

viola[2] /ˈvaɪələ/ ■ n. a plant of a genus that includes the pansies and violets. [Genus *Viola*: many species.]
– ORIGIN from Latin, 'violet'.

viola da braccio /vɪˌəʊlə da ˈbratʃɪəʊ/ ■ n. an early musical instrument of the violin family (as distinct from a viol), specifically one corresponding to the modern viola.
– ORIGIN Italian, 'viol for the arm'.

viola da gamba /ˈgambə/ (also **viol da gamba**) ■ n. a viol, specifically a bass viol (corresponding to the modern cello).
– ORIGIN Italian, 'viol for the leg'.

violate ■ v. 1 break or fail to comply with (a rule or formal agreement). 2 treat with disrespect. 3 rape or sexually assault.
– DERIVATIVES **violable** adj. (rare). **violation** n. **violator** n.
– ORIGIN Middle English: from Latin *violare* 'treat violently'.

violence ■ n. behaviour involving physical force intended to hurt, damage, or kill. ▶ strength of emotion or an unpleasant or destructive natural force.

violent ■ adj. 1 using or involving violence. 2 very intense, forceful, or powerful.
– DERIVATIVES **violently** adv.
– ORIGIN Middle English: from Latin *violent-* 'vehement, violent'.

violet ■ n. 1 a small plant typically with purple, blue, or white five-petalled flowers. [Many species in the genus *Viola*, family Violaceae.] ▶ used in names of unrelated plants with similar flowers, e.g. African violet. 2 a bluish-purple colour seen at the end of the spectrum opposite red.
– ORIGIN Middle English: from Old French *violette*, diminutive of *viole*, from Latin *viola* 'violet'.

violin ■ n. a stringed musical instrument of treble pitch, having four strings and a body narrowed at the middle and with two f-shaped soundholes, played with a horsehair bow.
– DERIVATIVES **violinist** n.
– ORIGIN C16: from Italian *violino*, diminutive of *viola* (see VIOLA[1]).

violist ■ n. 1 /vɪˈəʊlɪst/ a viola player. 2 /ˈvaɪəlɪst/ a viol player.

violoncello /ˌvaɪələnˈtʃɛləʊ, ˌviːə-/ ■ n. formal term for CELLO.
– DERIVATIVES **violoncellist** n.
– ORIGIN C18: Italian, diminutive of *violone* (see VIOLONE).

violone /vɪəˈləʊneɪ, -ni/ ■ n. an early form of double bass, especially a large bass viol.
– ORIGIN Italian, from *viola* (see VIOLA[1]).

VIP ■ abbrev. 1 Biochemistry vasoactive intestinal polypeptide (or peptide), a substance which acts as a neurotransmitter. 2 very important person.

vipassana /vɪˈpasənə/ ■ n. (in Theravada Buddhism) meditation involving concentration on the body, or the insight which this provides.
– ORIGIN Pali, 'inward vision'.

viper /ˈvaɪpə/ ■ n. 1 a venomous snake with large hinged fangs. [Family Viperidae.] 2 a spiteful or treacherous person.
– DERIVATIVES **viperine** /-rʌɪn/ adj. **viperish** adj. **viperous** adj.
– ORIGIN C16: from French *vipère* or Latin *vipera*, from *vivus* 'alive' + *parere* 'bring forth' (with ref. to the former belief that vipers bore live young).

viper's bugloss ■ n. a bristly Eurasian plant of the borage family, with pink buds which open to blue flowers, formerly used in the treatment of snake bites. [*Echium vulgare*.]

viraemia /vaɪˈriːmɪə/ (also **viremia**) ■ n. Medicine the presence of viruses in the blood.
– DERIVATIVES **viraemic** adj.
– ORIGIN 1940s: from VIRUS + -AEMIA.

virago /vɪˈrɑːgəʊ, -ˈreɪgəʊ/ ■ n. (pl. **-os** or **-oes**) 1 a domineering, violent, or bad-tempered woman. 2 archaic a woman of masculine strength or spirit; a female warrior.
– ORIGIN Old English (the name given by Adam to Eve, following the Vulgate), from Latin, 'heroic woman, female warrior', from *vir* 'man'.

viral /ˈvaɪr(ə)l/ ■ adj. of the nature of, caused by, or relating to a virus or viruses.
– DERIVATIVES **virally** adv.

viral load ■ n. Medicine a measure of the number of viral particles present in an organism or environment, especially the number of HIV viruses in the bloodstream.

virement /ˈvaɪəm(ə)nt, ˈvɪəmɒ̃/ ■ n. Finance the process of

transferring items from one financial account to another.
– ORIGIN C20: from French, from *virer* 'to turn'.

viremia ■ n. variant spelling of **VIRAEMIA**.

Virgilian /vəˈdʒɪlɪən/ (also **Vergilian**) ■ adj. of, relating to, or in the style of the Roman poet Virgil (70–19 BC) or his works.

virgin ■ n. 1 a person, typically a woman, who has never had sexual intercourse. ▶ (**the Virgin**) the Virgin Mary. 2 a person who is naive or inexperienced in a particular context: *a political virgin*. ■ adj. 1 being, relating to, or appropriate for a virgin. 2 not yet used or exploited: *acres of virgin forest*. ▶ (of wool) not yet, or only once, spun or woven. ▶ (of olive oil) obtained from the first pressing of olives. ▶ (of metal) made from ore by smelting.
– ORIGIN Middle English: from Old French *virgine*, from Latin *virgo*.

virginal ■ adj. of, relating to, or appropriate for a virgin. ■ n. an early spinet with the strings parallel to the keyboard, popular in 16th- and 17th-century houses.
– DERIVATIVES **virginalist** n. **virginally** adv.
– ORIGIN Middle English: from Old French, or from Latin *virginalis*, from *virgo* 'young woman'; the instrument was perhaps so named because it was usually played by young women.

virgin birth ■ n. (**the Virgin Birth**) the doctrine of Christ's birth from a mother, Mary, who was a virgin.

Virginia ■ n. a type of tobacco grown and manufactured in Virginia.

Virginia creeper ■ n. a North American vine which is chiefly cultivated for its red autumn foliage. [*Parthenocissus quinquefolia* and other species.]

virginity ■ n. 1 the state of being a virgin. 2 the state of being innocent or inexperienced in a particular context.

Virgo /ˈvɜːɡəʊ/ ■ n. 1 Astronomy a large constellation (the Virgin), said to represent a maiden or goddess associated with the harvest. 2 Astrology the sixth sign of the zodiac, which the sun enters about 23 August.
– DERIVATIVES **Virgoan** n. & adj.
– ORIGIN from Latin.

virgo intacta /ˌvɜːɡəʊ ɪnˈtaktə/ ■ n. chiefly Law a girl or woman who has never had sexual intercourse, originally a virgin whose hymen is intact.
– ORIGIN Latin, 'untouched virgin'.

viridian /vɪˈrɪdɪən/ ■ n. a bluish-green pigment consisting of hydrated chromium hydroxide.
– ORIGIN C19: from Latin *viridis* 'green'.

virile ■ adj. (of a man) having strength, energy, and a strong sex drive. ▶ vigorous, strong, and manly.
– DERIVATIVES **virility** n.
– ORIGIN C15: from French *viril* or Latin *virilis*, from *vir* 'man'.

virilization /ˌvɪrɪlʌɪˈzeɪʃ(ə)n/ (also **-isation**) ■ n. Medicine the development in a female (or precociously in a boy) of male physical characteristics (such as body hair, deep voice, etc.), typically as a result of excess androgen production.
– DERIVATIVES **virilism** n.

viroid /ˈvʌɪrɔɪd/ ■ n. Microbiology an infectious entity affecting plants, smaller than a virus and consisting only of nucleic acid without a protein coat.

virology /vʌɪˈrɒlədʒi/ ■ n. the branch of science concerned with the study of viruses.
– DERIVATIVES **virological** adj. **virologically** adv. **virologist** n.

virtu /vɜːˈt(j)uː/ (also **vertu**) ■ n. curios or objets d'art collectively.
– PHRASES **article** (or **object**) **of virtu** an article that is interesting because of its antiquity, beauty, quality of workmanship, etc.
– ORIGIN C18: from Italian *virtù* 'virtue'; the var. *vertu* is an alteration, as if from French.

virtual /ˈvɜːtjʊəl/ ■ adj. 1 almost or nearly as described, but not completely or according to strict definition. 2 Computing not physically existing as such but made by software to appear to do so. 3 Optics relating to the points at which rays would meet if produced backwards: *a virtual image*. 4 Mechanics relating to or denoting infinitesimal displacements of a point in a system.
– DERIVATIVES **virtuality** /-jʊˈalɪti/ n.

– ORIGIN Middle English: from medieval Latin *virtualis*, from Latin *virtus* 'virtue'.

virtually ■ adv. nearly; almost.

virtual memory (also **virtual storage**) ■ n. Computing memory that appears to exist as main storage although most of it is supported by data held in secondary storage.

virtual reality ■ n. Computing the computer-generated simulation of a three-dimensional image or environment that can be interacted with in a seemingly real or physical way by using special electronic equipment.

virtue /ˈvɜːtjuː, -tʃuː/ ■ n. 1 behaviour showing high moral standards. ▶ a quality considered morally good or desirable. ▶ a good or useful quality of a thing. 2 archaic virginity or chastity.
– PHRASES **by** (or **in**) **virtue of** because or as a result of. **make a virtue of** derive benefit or advantage from submitting to (something unwelcome).
– DERIVATIVES **virtueless** adj.
– ORIGIN Middle English: from Old French *vertu*, from Latin *virtus* 'valour, merit, moral perfection', from *vir* 'man'.

virtuoso /ˌvɜːtjuˈəʊzəʊ, -səʊ/ ■ n. (pl. **virtuosi** /-si/ or **virtuosos**) a person highly skilled in music or another artistic pursuit.
– DERIVATIVES **virtuosic** adj. **virtuosity** n.
– ORIGIN C17: from Italian, 'learned, skilful'.

virtuous ■ adj. 1 having or showing high moral standards. 2 archaic (especially of a woman) chaste.
– DERIVATIVES **virtuously** adv. **virtuousness** n.

virtuous circle ■ n. a recurring cycle of events, the result of each one being to increase the beneficial effect of the next.

virulent /ˈvɪrʊl(ə)nt, ˈvɪrjʊ-/ ■ adj. 1 (of a disease or poison) extremely severe or harmful in its effects. ▶ (of a pathogen, especially a virus) highly infective. 2 bitterly hostile.
– DERIVATIVES **virulence** n. **virulently** adv.
– ORIGIN Middle English: from Latin *virulentus*, from *virus* (see **VIRUS**).

virus /ˈvʌɪrəs/ ■ n. 1 a submicroscopic infective particle, typically consisting of nucleic acid coated in protein, which is able to multiply within the cells of a host organism. ▶ informal an infection or disease caused by such an agent. 2 (also **computer virus**) a piece of code surreptitiously introduced into a system in order to corrupt it or destroy data.
– ORIGIN Middle English (denoting snake venom): from Latin, 'slimy liquid, poison'.

visa /ˈviːzə/ ■ n. an endorsement on a passport indicating that the holder is allowed to enter, leave, or stay for a specified period of time in a country.
– ORIGIN C19: from Latin *visa*, from *videre* 'to see'.

visage /ˈvɪzɪdʒ/ ■ n. poetic/literary a person's face, with reference to the form of the features. ▶ a person's facial expression.
– DERIVATIVES **visaged** adj.
– ORIGIN Middle English: via Old French from Latin *visus* 'sight', from *videre* 'to see'.

vis-à-vis /ˌviːzɑːˈviː/ ■ prep. 1 in relation to. 2 as compared with; as opposed to.
– ORIGIN C18: French, 'face to face', from Old French *vis* 'face'.

viscera /ˈvɪs(ə)rə/ ■ pl. n. (sing. **viscus**) the internal organs in the main cavities of the body, especially those in the abdomen, e.g. the intestines.
– ORIGIN C17: from Latin, pl. of *viscus*.

visceral ■ adj. 1 of or relating to the viscera. 2 relating to deep inward feelings rather than to the intellect.
– DERIVATIVES **viscerally** adv.

viscid /ˈvɪsɪd/ ■ adj. glutinous; sticky.
– DERIVATIVES **viscidity** n.
– ORIGIN C17: from late Latin *viscidus*, from Latin *viscum* 'birdlime'.

viscometer /vɪsˈkɒmɪtə/ ■ n. an instrument for measuring the viscosity of liquids.
– DERIVATIVES **viscometric** adj. **viscometry** n.

viscose

viscose /ˈvɪskəʊz, -kəʊs/ ■ n. **1** a viscous orange-brown solution obtained by treating cellulose with sodium hydroxide and carbon disulphide, used as the basis of manufacturing rayon and transparent cellulose film. **2** rayon fabric or fibre made from this.
– ORIGIN C19: from late Latin *viscosus*, from Latin *viscus* 'birdlime'.

viscosity /vɪˈskɒsɪti/ ■ n. (pl. **-ies**) the state of being viscous. ▶ a quantity expressing the magnitude of internal friction in a fluid, as measured by the force per unit area resisting uniform flow.

viscount /ˈvaɪkaʊnt/ ■ n. a British nobleman ranking above a baron and below an earl.
– DERIVATIVES **viscountcy** n.
– ORIGIN Middle English: from Old French *visconte*, from medieval Latin *vicecomes* (see VICE-, COUNT²).

viscountess /ˈvaɪkaʊntɪs/ ■ n. the wife or widow of a viscount, or a woman holding the rank of viscount in her own right.

viscous /ˈvɪskəs/ ■ adj. having a thick, sticky consistency between solid and liquid; having a high viscosity.
– DERIVATIVES **viscously** adv. **viscousness** n.
– ORIGIN Middle English: from Anglo-Norman French *viscous* or late Latin *viscosus*, from Latin *viscum* 'birdlime'.

viscus /ˈvɪskəs/ singular form of VISCERA.
– ORIGIN from Latin.

vise ■ n. US spelling of VICE².

visibility ■ n. the state of being able to see or be seen. ▶ the distance one can see as determined by light and weather conditions.

visible ■ adj. **1** able to be seen. ▶ Physics (of light) within the range of wavelengths to which the eye is sensitive. ▶ able to be perceived or noticed easily. ▶ in a position of public prominence. **2** of or relating to imports or exports of tangible commodities. ■ n. (**visibles**) visible imports or exports.
– DERIVATIVES **visibly** adv.
– ORIGIN Middle English: from Old French, or from Latin *visibilis*, from *videre* 'to see'.

Visigoth /ˈvɪzɪɡɒθ/ ■ n. a member of the branch of the Goths who invaded the Roman Empire between the 3rd and 5th centuries AD and ruled much of Spain until overthrown by the Moors in 711.
– DERIVATIVES **Visigothic** adj.
– ORIGIN from late Latin *Visigothus*, the first element possibly meaning 'west' (cf. OSTROGOTH).

vision ■ n. **1** the faculty or state of being able to see. **2** the ability to think about or plan the future with imagination or wisdom. ▶ a mental image of what the future will or could be like. **3** an experience of seeing something in a dream or trance, or as a supernatural apparition. ▶ a person or sight of unusual beauty. ■ v. imagine; envision.
– DERIVATIVES **visional** adj. **visionless** adj.
– ORIGIN Middle English: from Latin *visio(n-)*, from *videre* 'to see'.

visionary ■ adj. **1** thinking about or planning the future with imagination or wisdom. **2** of or relating to supernatural visions or visions in a dream or trance. ■ n. (pl. **-ies**) a visionary person.
– DERIVATIVES **visionariness** n.

visit ■ v. (**visited**, **visiting**) **1** go to see and spend some time with (someone) socially or as a guest. ▶ go to see and spend some time in (a place) as a tourist or guest. ▶ go to see for any specific purpose, such as to receive or give professional advice. **2** (usu. **be visited**) (with reference to something harmful or unpleasant) inflict or be inflicted on someone. ■ n. an act of visiting. ▶ a temporary stay at a place.
– DERIVATIVES **visitable** adj. **visiting** adj.
– ORIGIN Middle English: from Old French *visiter* or Latin *visitare* 'go to see'.

visitant ■ n. chiefly poetic/literary a supernatural being; an apparition.

visitation ■ n. **1** the appearance of a divine or supernatural being. **2** an official visit of inspection. **3** a divorced person's right to spend time with their children in the custody of a former spouse. **4** a disaster or difficulty regarded as a divine punishment. **5** (**the Visitation**) the visit of the Virgin Mary to Elizabeth related in Luke 1:39–56.

visiting card ■ n. a card bearing a person's name and address, sent or left in lieu of a formal visit.

visitor ■ n. **1** a person visiting a person or place, especially socially or as a tourist. **2** Ornithology a migratory bird present in a locality for only part of the year.

visitorial ■ adj. of or relating to an official visitor or visitation.

Visākha /vɪˈsɑːkə/ ■ n. variant of VESAK.

vis major ■ n. (pl. **vires majores**) Law unforeseeable circumstances that prevent someone from fulfilling a contract.
– ORIGIN Latin, 'superior strength'.

visor /ˈvaɪzə/ (also **vizor**) ■ n. **1** a movable part of a helmet that can be pulled down to cover the face. **2** a screen for protecting the eyes from unwanted light, especially one at the top of a vehicle windscreen. **3** N. Amer. a stiff peak at the front of a cap.
– DERIVATIVES **visored** adj.
– ORIGIN Middle English: from Anglo-Norman French *viser*, from Old French *vis* 'face', from Latin *visus* (see VISAGE).

vista ■ n. **1** a pleasing view, especially one seen through a long, narrow opening. **2** a mental view of an imagined future event or situation.
– ORIGIN C17: from Italian, 'view'.

visual /ˈvɪʒʊəl, -zj-/ ■ adj. of or relating to seeing or sight. ■ n. a picture, piece of film, or display used to illustrate or accompany something.
– DERIVATIVES **visuality** n. **visually** adv.
– ORIGIN Middle English: from late Latin *visualis*, from Latin *visus* 'sight', from *videre* 'to see'.

visual angle ■ n. Optics the angle formed at the eye by rays from the extremities of an object viewed.

visual display unit ■ n. Computing a device for displaying input signals as characters on a screen, typically incorporating a keyboard.

visualize (also **-ise**) ■ v. **1** form a mental image of; imagine. **2** make visible to the eye.
– DERIVATIVES **visualizable** (also **-isable**) adj. **visualization** (also **-isation**) n.

visual purple ■ n. a purplish-red light-sensitive pigment present in the retinas of humans and many other animal groups.

visuospatial /ˌvɪʒʊəʊˈspeɪʃ(ə)l, -zj-/ ■ adj. Psychology relating to or denoting the visual perception of the spatial relationships of objects.

vital ■ adj. **1** absolutely necessary; essential. ▶ indispensable to the continuance of life: *the vital organs*. **2** full of energy; lively. ■ n. (**vitals**) the body's important internal organs.
– DERIVATIVES **vitally** adv.
– ORIGIN Middle English: from Latin *vitalis*, from *vita* 'life'.

vital capacity ■ n. the greatest volume of air that can be expelled from the lungs after taking the deepest possible breath.

vital force ■ n. the energy or spirit which animates living creatures.

vitalism ■ n. chiefly Philosophy the theory that the origin and phenomena of life are dependent on a force or principle distinct from purely chemical or physical forces.
– DERIVATIVES **vitalist** n. & adj. **vitalistic** adj.

vitality ■ n. **1** the state of being strong and active; energy. **2** the power giving continuance of life, present in all living things.

vitalize /ˈvaɪt(ə)laɪz/ (also **-ise**) ■ v. give strength and energy to.
– DERIVATIVES **vitalization** (also **-isation**) n.

vital signs ■ pl. n. clinical measurements, specifically pulse rate, temperature, respiration rate, and blood pressure, that indicate the state of a patient's essential body functions.

vital statistics ■ pl. n. **1** quantitative data concerning the population, such as the number of births, marriages, and deaths. **2** informal the measurements of a woman's bust, waist, and hips.

vitamin /ˈvɪtəmɪn, ˈvʌɪt-/ ■ n. any of a group of organic compounds which are essential for normal growth and nutrition and are required in small quantities in the diet because they cannot be synthesized by the body.
– ORIGIN C20: from Latin *vita* 'life' + AMINE, because vitamins were orig. thought to contain an amino acid.

vitamin A ■ n. another term for RETINOL.

vitamin B ■ n. any of a group of substances essential for the working of certain enzymes in the body, including thiamine (vitamin B₁), riboflavin (vitamin B₂), pyridoxine (vitamin B₆), and cyanocobalamin (vitamin B₁₂).

vitamin C ■ n. another term for ASCORBIC ACID.

vitamin D ■ n. any of a group of compounds found in liver and fish oils, essential for the absorption of calcium and including calciferol (vitamin D₂) and cholecalciferol (vitamin D₃).

vitamin E ■ n. another term for TOCOPHEROL.

vitaminize (also **-ise**) ■ v. add vitamins to (food).

vitamin K ■ n. any of a group of compounds found mainly in green leaves and essential for the blood-clotting process, including phylloquinone (vitamin K₁) and menaquinone (vitamin K₂).

vitamin P ■ n. chiefly US the bioflavonoids, regarded collectively as a vitamin.

vitellin /vɪˈtɛlɪn, vʌɪ-/ ■ n. Biochemistry the chief protein constituent of egg yolk.
– ORIGIN C19: from Latin *vitellus* 'egg yolk'.

vitelline /vɪˈtɛlʌɪn, vʌɪ-, -lɪn/ ■ adj. Zoology of or relating to the yolk (or yolk sac) of an egg or embryo, or to yolk-producing organs.
– ORIGIN Middle English: from medieval Latin *vitellinus*, from Latin *vitellus* 'egg yolk'.

vitelline membrane ■ n. Embryology a transparent membrane surrounding and secreted by the fertilized ovum, preventing the entry of further spermatozoa.

vitiate /ˈvɪʃɪeɪt/ ■ v. formal spoil or impair the quality or efficiency of. ▸ destroy or impair the legal validity of.
– DERIVATIVES **vitiation** n. **vitiator** n.
– ORIGIN C16: from Latin *vitiat-*, *vitiare* 'impair'.

viticulture /ˈvɪtɪˌkʌltʃə/ ■ n. the cultivation of grapevines. ▸ the study of grape cultivation.
– DERIVATIVES **viticultural** adj. **viticulturist** n.
– ORIGIN C19: from Latin *vitis* 'vine' + CULTURE.

vitiligo /ˌvɪtɪˈlʌɪɡəʊ/ ■ n. Medicine a condition in which the pigment is lost from areas of the skin, causing whitish patches.
– ORIGIN C16: from Latin, denoting a skin disease.

vitreous /ˈvɪtrɪəs/ ■ adj. like glass in appearance or physical properties. ▸ (of a substance) derived from or containing glass.
– DERIVATIVES **vitreousness** n.
– ORIGIN Middle English: from Latin *vitreus*, from *vitrum* 'glass'.

vitreous humour ■ n. Anatomy the transparent jelly-like tissue filling the eyeball behind the lens.

vitrify /ˈvɪtrɪfʌɪ/ ■ v. (**-ies**, **-ied**) (often **be vitrified**) convert into glass or a glass-like substance, typically by exposure to heat.
– DERIVATIVES **vitrifiable** adj. **vitrification** /-fɪˈkeɪʃ(ə)n/ n.
– ORIGIN Middle English: from French *vitrifier* or based on Latin *vitrum* 'glass'.

vitriol /ˈvɪtrɪəl/ ■ n. 1 archaic or poetic/literary sulphuric acid. ▸ in names of metallic sulphates, e.g. blue vitriol (copper sulphate). 2 extreme bitterness or malice.
– DERIVATIVES **vitriolic** adj. **vitriolically** adv.
– ORIGIN Middle English: from Old French, or from medieval Latin *vitriolum*, from Latin *vitrum* 'glass'.

vittle ■ n. archaic variant spelling of VICTUAL.

vituperation ■ n. bitter and abusive language.

vituperative /vɪˈtjuːp(ə)rətɪv, vʌɪ-/ ■ adj. bitter and abusive.

viva¹ /ˈvʌɪvə/ ■ n. Brit. an oral examination, typically for an academic qualification.
– ORIGIN abbrev. of VIVA VOCE.

viva² /ˈviːvə/ ■ exclam. long live! (used to express acclaim or support).
– ORIGIN from Italian.

vivacious /vɪˈveɪʃəs, vʌɪ-/ ■ adj. (especially of a woman or child) attractively lively and animated.
– DERIVATIVES **vivaciously** adv. **vivaciousness** n. **vivacity** n.
– ORIGIN C17: from Latin *vivax*, *vivac-* 'lively, vigorous'.

vivarium /vʌɪˈvɛːrɪəm, vɪ-/ ■ n. (pl. **vivaria** /-rɪə/) an enclosure or structure used for keeping animals under semi-natural conditions for observation or study or as pets; an aquarium or terrarium.
– ORIGIN C17: from Latin, 'warren, fish pond'.

viva voce /ˌvʌɪvə ˈvəʊtʃeɪ, ˈvəʊtʃi/ ■ adj. (especially of an examination) oral rather than written. ■ adv. orally rather than in writing. ■ n. Brit. full form of VIVA¹.
– ORIGIN C16: from medieval Latin, 'with the living voice'.

viverrid /vɪˈvɛrɪd, vʌɪ-/ ■ n. Zoology a mammal of the civet family (Viverridae).
– ORIGIN C20: from Latin *viverra* 'ferret'.

vivid ■ adj. 1 producing powerful feelings or strong, clear images in the mind. 2 (of a colour) intensely deep or bright.
– DERIVATIVES **vividly** adv. **vividness** n.
– ORIGIN C17: from Latin *vividus*, from *vivere* 'to live'.

vivify /ˈvɪvɪfʌɪ/ ■ v. (**-ies**, **-ied**) enliven or animate.
– DERIVATIVES **vivification** /-fɪˈkeɪʃ(ə)n/ n.
– ORIGIN Middle English: from French *vivifier*, from late Latin *vivificare*, from Latin *vivus* 'living', from *vivere* 'to live'.

viviparous /vɪˈvɪp(ə)rəs, vʌɪ-/ ■ adj. 1 Zoology (of an animal) bringing forth live young which have developed inside the body of the parent. Compare with OVIPAROUS and OVOVIVIPAROUS. 2 Botany (of a plant) reproducing from buds which form plantlets while still attached to the parent plant, or from seeds which germinate within the fruit.
– DERIVATIVES **viviparity** /ˌvɪvɪˈparɪti/ n. **viviparously** adv.
– ORIGIN C17: from Latin *viviparus*, from *vivus* 'alive' + *-parus* 'bearing'.

vivisection ■ n. 1 the practice of performing operations on live animals for the purpose of experimentation or scientific research. 2 ruthlessly sharp and detailed criticism or analysis.
– DERIVATIVES **vivisect** v. **vivisectionist** n. & adj. **vivisector** n.
– ORIGIN C18: from Latin *vivus* 'living', on the pattern of *dissection*.

vixen ■ n. 1 a female fox. 2 a spiteful or quarrelsome woman.
– DERIVATIVES **vixenish** adj.
– ORIGIN Middle English *fixen*, perhaps from Old English *fyxen* 'of a fox'.

Viyella /vʌɪˈɛlə/ ■ n. trademark a fabric made from a twilled mixture of cotton and wool.
– ORIGIN C19: from *Via Gellia*, a valley in Derbyshire, in central England.

viz. ■ adv. namely; in other words (used to introduce a gloss or explanation).
– ORIGIN abbrev. of VIDELICET, *z* being a medieval Latin symbol for *-et*.

vizier /vɪˈzɪə, ˈvɪzɪə/ ■ n. historical a high official in some Muslim countries.
– ORIGIN C16: from Arabic *wazīr* 'caliph's chief counsellor'.

vizor ■ n. variant spelling of VISOR.

VJ ■ abbrev. video jockey.

VJ day ■ n. the day (15 August) in 1945 on which Japan ceased fighting in the Second World War, or the day (2 September) when Japan formally surrendered.
– ORIGIN *VJ*, abbrev. of *Victory over Japan*.

Vlakplaas /ˈflakplɑːs/ ■ n. [as modifier] S. African historical (under apartheid) denoting someone or something associated with the counter-insurgency unit of the South African Police.
– ORIGIN from the name of a farm outside Pretoria where the unit was based.

vlei /fleɪ/ ■ n. S. African a shallow natural pool of water or area of marshy ground.
– ORIGIN Afrikaans, from Dutch *vallei* 'valley'.

VLF ■ abbrev. very low frequency (denoting radio waves of frequency 3–30 kHz and wavelength 10–100 km).

vlog ■ n. a weblog presented in video form. ■ v. (**vlogs**, **vlogging**, **vlogged**) [usu. as noun **vlogging**] create a video recording to publish as part of a weblog.
– DERIVATIVES **vlogger** n.

VLSI ■ abbrev. Electronics very large-scale integration.

V-neck ■ n. a neckline having straight sides meeting at a point to form a V-shape.
– DERIVATIVES **V-necked** adj.

8vo ■ abbrev. octavo.

VOC ■ abbrev. historical *Vereenigde Oost-Indische Compagnie*, the Dutch name for the **DUTCH EAST INDIA COMPANY**.

vocabulary ■ n. (pl. **-ies**) **1** the body of words used in a particular language or in a particular sphere. ▶ the body of words known to an individual person. ▶ a list of difficult or foreign words with an explanation of their meanings. **2** a range of artistic or stylistic forms or techniques.
– ORIGIN C16: from medieval Latin *vocabularius*, from Latin *vocabulum* 'name, designation, noun', from *vocare* 'to call'.

vocal ■ adj. **1** of or relating to the human voice. ▶ Anatomy used in the production of speech sounds. **2** expressing opinions or feelings freely or loudly. **3** (of music) consisting of or incorporating singing. ■ n. **1** (also **vocals**) a musical performance involving singing. **2** a part of a piece of music that is sung.
– DERIVATIVES **vocality** n. **vocally** adv.
– ORIGIN Middle English: from Latin *vocalis*, from *vox* (see **VOICE**).

vocal cords (also **vocal folds**) ■ pl. n. folds of the membranous lining of the larynx which form a slit within the glottis and whose edges vibrate in the airstream to produce the voice.

USAGE
The correct term is **vocal cords**, not **vocal chords**.

vocalese /ˌvəʊkəˈliːz/ ■ n. a style of singing in which singers put words to jazz tunes or solos.

vocalic /vəˈkælɪk/ ■ adj. Phonetics of, relating to, or consisting of a vowel or vowels.

vocalist ■ n. a singer, especially in jazz or popular music.

vocalize /ˈvəʊk(ə)lʌɪz/ (also **-ise**) ■ v. **1** utter (a sound or word). ▶ express (something) with words. **2** Phonetics change (a consonant) to a semivowel or vowel.
– DERIVATIVES **vocalization** (also **-isation**) n. **vocalizer** (also **-iser**) n.

vocation /və(ʊ)ˈkeɪʃ(ə)n/ ■ n. **1** a strong feeling of suitability for a particular career or occupation. **2** a person's employment or main occupation, especially one requiring dedication. ▶ a trade or profession.
– ORIGIN Middle English: from Old French, or from Latin *vocatio(n-)*, from *vocare* 'to call'.

vocational ■ adj. of or relating to an occupation or employment. ▶ (of education or training) directed at a particular occupation and its skills.
– DERIVATIVES **vocationalism** n. **vocationalize** (also **-ise**) v. **vocationally** adv.

vocative /ˈvɒkətɪv/ Grammar ■ adj. relating to or denoting a case of nouns, pronouns, and adjectives used in addressing or invoking a person or thing. ■ n. a word in the vocative case.
– ORIGIN Middle English: from Old French *vocatif, -ive* or Latin *vocativus*, from *vocare* 'to call'.

vociferate /və(ʊ)ˈsɪfəreɪt/ ■ v. shout, complain, or argue loudly or vehemently.
– DERIVATIVES **vociferation** n.
– ORIGIN C16: from Latin *vociferari* 'exclaim'.

vociferous ■ adj. vehement or clamorous.
– DERIVATIVES **vociferously** adv. **vociferousness** n.

vocoder /ˈvəʊkəʊdə/ ■ n. a synthesizer that produces sounds from an analysis of speech input.
– ORIGIN 1930s: from **VOICE** + **CODE**.

VOD ■ abbrev. video-on-demand.

vodka /ˈvɒdkə/ ■ n. an alcoholic spirit of Russian origin made by distillation of rye, wheat, or potatoes.
– ORIGIN Russian, diminutive of *voda* 'water'.

vodun /ˈvəʊduːn/ ■ n. another term for **VOODOO**.
– ORIGIN Fon, 'fetish'.

voema ■ n. variant spelling of **VOOMA**.

voetsak /ˈfʊtsak/ (also **voetsek** /-sɛk/) ■ exclam. S. African used to drive away an animal, especially a dog, or (offensive) a person.
– ORIGIN C19: from S. African Dutch *voe(r)tsek*, from Dutch *voort seg ik* 'be off I say'.

voetstoots /ˈfʊtstʊəts, ˈfʊtstʊts/ (also **voetstoets**) ■ adv. S. African (indicating a condition of sale or purchase) as it stands; at the buyer's risk.
– ORIGIN 1930s: Afrikaans, from Dutch *met de voet te stoten* 'to push with the foot'.

vogue ■ n. (often in phr. **in/out of vogue**) the prevailing fashion or style at a particular time.
– DERIVATIVES **voguish** adj.
– ORIGIN C16: from French, from Italian *voga* 'rowing, fashion'.

voice ■ n. **1** the sound produced in a person's larynx and uttered through the mouth, as speech or song. ▶ the ability to speak or sing. ▶ vocal condition for singing or speaking: *the soprano is in good voice*. **2** the range of pitch or type of tone with which a person sings, such as soprano or tenor. ▶ a vocal part in a composition. **3** an opinion or attitude, or a means or agency by which it is expressed: *a dissenting voice*. **4** Phonetics sound uttered with resonance of the vocal cords (used in the pronunciation of vowels and certain consonants). **5** Grammar a form or set of forms of a verb showing the relation of the subject to the action. ■ v. **1** express in words. **2** [usu. as adj. **voiced**] Phonetics utter (a speech sound) with resonance of the vocal cords.
– DERIVATIVES **-voiced** adj.
– ORIGIN Middle English: from Old French *vois*, from Latin *vox, voc-*.

voice box ■ n. the larynx.

voiceless ■ adj. **1** lacking a voice; mute; speechless. **2** Phonetics (of a speech sound) uttered without resonance of the vocal cords.
– DERIVATIVES **voicelessly** adv. **voicelessness** n.

voicemail ■ n. a centralized electronic system which can store messages from telephone callers.

voice-over ■ n. a piece of narration in a film or broadcast not accompanied by an image of the speaker. ■ v. narrate (spoken material) in this way.

voiceprint ■ n. a visual record of speech, analysed with respect to frequency, duration, and amplitude.

void /vɔɪd/ ■ adj. **1** not valid or legally binding. **2** completely empty. ▶ (**void of**) free from; lacking. **3** (in bridge and whist) having been dealt no cards in a particular suit. ■ n. **1** a completely empty space. ▶ an unfilled space in a wall, building, or structure. **2** (in bridge and whist) a suit in which a player is dealt no cards. ■ v. **1** declare to be not valid or legally binding. **2** chiefly Medicine excrete (waste matter).
– DERIVATIVES **voidable** adj. **voidness** n.
– ORIGIN Middle English: from a dialect var. of Old French *vuide*; rel. to Latin *vacare* 'vacate'; the verb partly a shortening of **AVOID**, reinforced by Old French *voider*.

voidance ■ n. **1** the action or state of voiding or being voided. **2** chiefly Law an annulment of a contract.

voided ■ adj. Heraldry (of a bearing) having the central area cut away so as to show the field.

voila /vwʌˈlɑː/ ■ exclam. there it is; there you are.
– ORIGIN French *voilà*.

voile /vɔɪl, vwɑːl/ ■ n. a thin, semi-transparent fabric of cotton, wool, or silk.
– ORIGIN C19: French, 'veil'.

VOIP ■ abbrev. voice over Internet protocol, a technology for making telephone calls over the Internet in which speech sounds are converted into binary data.

vol. ■ abbrev. volume.

volant /ˈvəʊlənt/ ■ adj. Heraldry represented as flying.
– ORIGIN C16: from French, 'flying', from *voler* 'to fly'.

volar /ˈvəʊlə/ ■ adj. Anatomy relating to the palm of the hand or the sole of the foot.
– ORIGIN C19: from Latin *vola* 'hollow of hand or foot'.

volatile /ˈvɒlətʌɪl/ ■ adj. 1 (of a substance) easily evaporated at normal temperatures. 2 liable to change rapidly and unpredictably, especially for the worse. ▸ liable to display rapid changes of emotion. 3 (of a computer's memory) retaining data only as long as there is a power supply connected. ■ n. a volatile substance.
– DERIVATIVES **volatility** n. **volatilizable** (also **-isable**) adj. **volatilization** (also **-isation**) n. **volatilize** (also **-ise**) v.
– ORIGIN Middle English (in the senses 'creature that flies', 'birds'): from Old French *volatil* or Latin *volatilis*, from *volare* 'to fly'.

volatile oil ■ n. another term for ESSENTIAL OIL.

vol-au-vent /ˈvɒlə(ʊ)vɒ̃/ ■ n. a small round case of puff pastry filled with a savoury mixture.
– ORIGIN French, 'flight in the wind'.

volcanic ■ adj. 1 relating to or produced by a volcano or volcanoes. 2 (of a feeling or emotion) bursting out or liable to burst out violently.
– DERIVATIVES **volcanically** adv.

volcanic glass ■ n. another term for OBSIDIAN.

volcanicity ■ n. another term for VOLCANISM.

volcanism /ˈvɒlkənɪz(ə)m/ (also **vulcanism**) ■ n. Geology volcanic activity or phenomena.

volcano ■ n. (pl. **-oes** or **-os**) a mountain or hill having a crater or vent through which lava, rock fragments, hot vapour, and gas are or have been erupted from the earth's crust.
– ORIGIN C17: from Italian, from Latin *Volcanus* 'Vulcan', the Roman god of fire.

volcanology /ˌvɒlkəˈnɒlədʒi/ (also **vulcanology**) ■ n. the scientific study of volcanoes.
– DERIVATIVES **volcanological** adj. **volcanologist** n.

vole ■ n. a small mouse-like rodent with a rounded muzzle. [Subfamily Microtinae: numerous species.]
– ORIGIN C19 (orig. *vole-mouse*): from Norwegian *voll(mus)* 'field (mouse)'.

volition /vəˈlɪʃ(ə)n/ ■ n. (often in phr. **of one's own volition**) the faculty or power of using one's will.
– DERIVATIVES **volitional** adj. **volitionally** adv.
– ORIGIN C17: from French, or from medieval Latin *volitio(n-)*, from *volo* 'I wish'.

volk /fɒlk/ ■ n. (pl. **volke**) 1 S. African a nation or people, in particular the Afrikaner people. 2 the German people (with reference to Nazi ideology).
– ORIGIN from Dutch, Afrikaans, and German.

volley ■ n. (pl. **-eys**) 1 a number of bullets, arrows, or other projectiles discharged at one time. ▸ a series of utterances directed at someone in quick succession. 2 (in sport, especially tennis or soccer) a strike or kick of the ball made before it touches the ground. ■ v. (**-eys**, **-eyed**) 1 strike or kick (the ball) before it touches the ground. 2 utter or discharge in quick succession.
– DERIVATIVES **volleyer** n.
– ORIGIN C16: from French *volée*, from Latin *volare* 'to fly'.

volleyball ■ n. a game for two teams in which a large ball is hit by hand over a high net, the aim being to score points by making the ball reach the ground on the opponent's side of the court.

vols ■ abbrev. volumes.

volt /vəʊlt, vɒlt/ (abbrev.: **V**) ■ n. the SI unit of electromotive force, the difference of potential that would carry one ampere of current against one ohm resistance.
– ORIGIN C19: named after the Italian physicist Alessandro *Volta*.

voltage ■ n. an electromotive force or potential difference expressed in volts.

voltaic /vɒlˈteɪɪk/ ■ adj. of or relating to electricity produced by chemical action in a primary battery; galvanic.

volte /vɒlt, vəʊlt/ ■ n. Fencing a sudden quick movement to escape a thrust, especially a swing of the rear leg to turn the body sideways.
– ORIGIN C17: from French, from Italian *volta* 'a turn'.

1335

voluptuary

volte-face /vɒltˈfas, -ˈfɑːs/ ■ n. 1 an act of turning round so as to face in the opposite direction. 2 an abrupt and complete reversal of attitude, opinion, or position.
– ORIGIN C19: from French, from Italian *voltafaccia*, from Latin *volvere* 'to roll' + *facies* 'appearance, face'.

voltmeter ■ n. an instrument for measuring electric potential in volts.

voluble /ˈvɒljʊb(ə)l/ ■ adj. speaking or spoken incessantly and fluently.
– DERIVATIVES **volubility** n. **volubleness** n. **volubly** adv.
– ORIGIN Middle English: from French, or from Latin *volubilis*, from *volvere* 'to roll'.

volume ■ n. 1 a book forming part of a work or series. ▸ a single book or a bound collection of printed sheets. ▸ a consecutive sequence of issues of a periodical. 2 the amount of space occupied by a substance or object or enclosed within a container. ▸ the amount or quantity of something, especially when great. ▸ fullness or expansive thickness. 3 quantity or power of sound; degree of loudness.
– ORIGIN Middle English: from Old French *volum(e)*, from Latin *volumen* 'a roll', from *volvere* 'to roll'.

volumetric /ˌvɒljuˈmɛtrɪk/ ■ adj. of or relating to the measurement of volume.
– DERIVATIVES **volumetrically** adv.

voluminous /vəˈljuːmɪnəs/ ■ adj. 1 (of clothing or drapery) loose and ample. 2 (of writing) very lengthy and full.
– DERIVATIVES **voluminously** adv. **voluminousness** n.
– ORIGIN C17: partly from late Latin *voluminosus* 'having many coils', partly from Latin *volumen* (see VOLUME).

volumize (also **-ise**) ■ v. give volume or body to (hair).
– DERIVATIVES **volumizer** (also **-iser**) n.

voluntarism ■ n. 1 the principle of relying on voluntary action. 2 Philosophy the doctrine that the will is a fundamental or dominant factor in the individual or the universe.
– DERIVATIVES **voluntarist** n. & adj.

voluntary ■ adj. 1 done, given, or acting of one's own free will. ▸ Physiology under the conscious control of the brain. 2 working or done without payment. ▸ Law (of a conveyance or disposition) made without return in money or other consideration. ■ n. (pl. **-ies**) 1 an organ solo played before, during, or after a church service. ▸ historical a piece of music performed extempore or composed in a free style. 2 (in a competition) a special performance left to the performer's choice.
– DERIVATIVES **voluntarily** adv. **voluntariness** n.
– ORIGIN Middle English: from Old French *volontaire* or Latin *voluntarius*, from *voluntas* 'will'.

voluntaryism /ˈvɒlənt(ə)rɪˌɪz(ə)m/ ■ n. less common term for VOLUNTARISM (in sense 1).

voluntary school ■ n. (in the UK) a school which, though not established by the local education authority, is funded mainly (voluntary-aided), or entirely (voluntary-controlled) by it, and which typically encourages a particular set of religious beliefs.

voluntary sector ■ n. non-profit and community organizations considered collectively, especially those concerned with social development and welfare.

voluntary simplicity ■ n. a philosophy or way of life that rejects materialism, characterized by minimal consumption and environmental responsibility.

volunteer ■ n. 1 a person who freely offers to do something. ▸ a person who freely enrols for military service rather than being conscripted. 2 a person who works for an organization without being paid. 3 a plant that has not been deliberately planted. ■ v. 1 freely offer to do something. ▸ freely enrol for military service rather than being conscripted. ▸ commit (someone) to an undertaking without consulting them. 2 say or suggest something without being asked. 3 work for an organization without being paid.
– ORIGIN C16 (as n.): from French *volontaire* 'voluntary'.

volunteerism ■ n. the use or involvement of volunteer labour, especially in community services.

voluptuary /vəˈlʌptjʊəri/ ■ n. (pl. **-ies**) a person devoted to

voluptuous 1336

luxury and sensual pleasure. ■ adj. concerned with luxury and sensual pleasure.
–ORIGIN C17: from Latin volupt(u)arius, from voluptas 'pleasure'.

voluptuous /vəˈlʌptjʊəs/ ■ adj. **1** relating to or characterized by luxury or sensual pleasure. **2** (of a woman) curvaceous and sexually attractive.
–DERIVATIVES **voluptuously** adv. **voluptuousness** n.
–ORIGIN Middle English: from Old French voluptueux or Latin voluptuosus, from voluptas 'pleasure'.

volute /vəˈl(j)uːt/ ■ n. **1** Architecture a spiral scroll characteristic of Ionic capitals and also used in Corinthian and composite capitals. **2** a deep-water marine mollusc with a colourful thick spiral shell. [Voluta and other genera.]
–DERIVATIVES **voluted** adj.
–ORIGIN C16: from French, or from Latin voluta, from volvere 'to roll'.

volvox /ˈvɒlvɒks/ ■ n. Biology a green single-celled aquatic organism which forms minute free-swimming spherical colonies. [Genus Volvox.]
–ORIGIN Latin volvere 'to roll'.

volvulus /ˈvɒlvjʊləs/ ■ n. (pl. **volvuli** /ˈvɒlvjʊlʌɪ/, -liː/ or **volvuluses**) Medicine an obstruction caused by twisting of the stomach or intestine.
–ORIGIN C17: medieval Latin, from Latin volvere 'to roll'.

vomit ■ v. (**vomited**, **vomiting**) eject matter from the stomach through the mouth. ▸ emit in an uncontrolled stream or flow. ■ n. matter vomited from the stomach.
–DERIVATIVES **vomiter** n.
–ORIGIN Middle English: from Old French vomite (n.) or Latin vomitus, from vomere 'to vomit'.

voodoo ■ n. a black religious cult practised in the Caribbean and the southern US, combining elements of Roman Catholic ritual with traditional African rites and characterized by sorcery and spirit possession. ■ v. (**voodoos**, **voodooed**) affect by the practice of voodoo.
–DERIVATIVES **voodooism** n. **voodooist** n.
–ORIGIN C19: from Louisiana French, from Kwa vodũ.

vooma /ˈvuːmɑː/ (also **voema**, **woema**) ■ n. S. African informal speed or power; oomph.
–ORIGIN Afrikaans: imitative.

voorskot /ˈfʊəskɒt/ ■ n. S. African an advance payment made to a farmer for a crop, wool-clip, etc., calculated at a predetermined fixed price per kilogram.
–ORIGIN 1940S: Afrikaans, from voorskiet 'to advance (money)'.

Voortrekker /ˈfʊəˌtrɛkə/ ■ n. S. African **1** historical a member of a group of Dutch-speaking people who migrated from the Cape Colony in the 1830s. **2** a member of an Afrikaner youth movement similar to the Boy Scouts and Girl Guides.
–ORIGIN Afrikaans, from Dutch voor 'fore' + trekken 'to travel'.

voracious /vəˈreɪʃəs/ ■ adj. **1** wanting or devouring great quantities of food. **2** eagerly consuming something: voracious reading.
–DERIVATIVES **voraciously** adv. **voraciousness** n. **voracity** n.
–ORIGIN C17: from Latin vorax, vorac-, from vorare 'devour'.

-vorous /v(ə)rəs/ ■ comb. form feeding on a specified food: carnivorous.
–DERIVATIVES **-vora** /v(ə)rə/ comb. form in corresponding names of groups. **-vore** /vɔː/ comb. form in corresponding names of individuals within such groups.
–ORIGIN from Latin -vorus, from vorare 'devour'.

vortex /ˈvɔːtɛks/ ■ n. (pl. **vortexes** or **vortices** /-tɪsiːz/) a whirling mass, especially a whirlpool or whirlwind.
–DERIVATIVES **vortical** adj. **vorticity** /vɔːˈtɪsɪti/ n. **vorticose** adj. **vorticular** /vɔːˈtɪkjʊlə/ adj.
–ORIGIN C17: from Latin vortex, vortic- 'eddy', var. of VERTEX.

vorticella /ˌvɔːtɪˈsɛlə/ ■ n. Zoology a sedentary, single-celled aquatic animal with a contractile stalk and a bell-shaped body bearing a ring of cilia. [Genus Vorticella.]
–ORIGIN C18: diminutive of Latin vortex, vortic- 'eddy'.

Vorticism /ˈvɔːtɪsɪz(ə)m/ ■ n. a British artistic movement of 1914–15 influenced by cubism and futurism.
–DERIVATIVES **Vorticist** n. & adj.
–ORIGIN from Latin vortex, vortic- 'eddy'.

votary /ˈvəʊt(ə)ri/ ■ n. (pl. **-ies**) **1** a person who has made vows of dedication to religious service. **2** a devoted follower, adherent, or advocate.
–ORIGIN C16: from Latin vot-, vovere 'vow'.

vote ■ n. a formal indication of a choice between two or more candidates or courses of action, expressed typically through a ballot or a show of hands. ▸ an act of voting. ▸ (**the vote**) the right to indicate a choice in an election. ■ v. **1** give or register a vote. ▸ grant or confer by vote. **2** informal express a wish or suggestion.
–PHRASES **vote of (no) confidence** a vote showing that a majority continues to support (or no longer supports) the policy of a leader or governing body. **vote with one's feet** informal indicate an opinion by being present or absent or by some other course of action.
–DERIVATIVES **voteless** adj. **voter** n.
–ORIGIN Middle English: from Latin votum 'a vow, wish', from vovere 'to vow'.

voters' roll ■ n. an official list of the people in a district who are entitled to vote in an election.

votive ■ adj. offered or consecrated in fulfilment of a vow.
–ORIGIN C16: from Latin votivus, from votum (see VOTE).

vouch ■ v. (**vouch for**) assert or confirm the truth or accuracy of. ▸ confirm the identity or good character of.
–ORIGIN Middle English (in the sense 'summon (a person) to court to prove title to property'): from Old French voucher 'summon', from Latin vocare 'to call'.

voucher /ˈvaʊtʃə/ ■ n. a small printed piece of paper that entitles the holder to a discount, or that may be exchanged for goods or services. ▸ a receipt.

vouchsafe ■ v. give, grant, or disclose in a gracious or condescending manner.
–ORIGIN Middle English: orig. as the phr. vouch something safe on someone, i.e. 'warrant the secure conferment of'.

voussoir /ˈvuːswɑː/ ■ n. Architecture a wedge-shaped or tapered stone used to construct an arch.
–ORIGIN C18: via French from popular Latin volsorium, from Latin volvere 'to roll'.

Vouvray /ˈvuːvreɪ/ ■ n. dry white wine produced in the Vouvray district of the Loire Valley in France.

vow ■ n. a solemn promise. ▸ (**vows**) a set of such promises committing one to a prescribed role or course of action, especially marriage or a monastic career. ■ v. **1** solemnly promise to do something. **2** archaic dedicate to someone or something, especially a deity.
–ORIGIN Middle English: from Old French vou, from Latin votum (see VOTE); verb from Old French vouer.

vowel ■ n. a speech sound which is produced by comparatively open configuration of the vocal tract and which is capable of forming a syllable. ▸ a letter representing such a sound.
–DERIVATIVES **vowelled** (US **voweled**) adj. **vowelless** adj. **vowelly** adj.
–ORIGIN Middle English: from Old French vouel, from Latin vocalis (littera) 'vocal (letter)'.

vowelize (also **-ise**) ■ v. supply (something such as a Hebrew or shorthand text) with vowel points or signs representing vowels.

vowel point ■ n. each of a set of marks indicating vowels in writing phonetically explicit text in Semitic languages such as Hebrew and Arabic.

vox pop ■ n. informal popular opinion as represented by informal comments from members of the public.
–ORIGIN 1960S: abbrev. of VOX POPULI.

vox populi /ˈpɒpjuliː, -lʌɪ/ ■ n. the opinions or beliefs of the majority.
–ORIGIN C16: from Latin, 'the people's voice'.

voyage ■ n. a long journey involving travel by sea or in space. ■ v. go on a voyage. ▸ archaic sail over or along (a sea or river).
–DERIVATIVES **voyager** n.
–ORIGIN Middle English: from Old French voiage, from Latin viaticum 'provisions for a journey'.

voyeur /vwʌˈjəː, vɔɪ-/ ■ n. **1** a person who gains sexual pleasure from watching others when they are naked or

engaged in sexual activity. **2** a person who enjoys seeing the pain or distress of others.
– DERIVATIVES **voyeurism** n. **voyeuristic** adj. **voyeuristically** adv.
– ORIGIN C20: from French, from *voir* 'see'.

VP ▪ abbrev. Vice-President.

VPL ▪ abbrev. informal visible panty line.

VR ▪ abbrev. **1** Queen Victoria. [abbrev. of Latin *Victoria Regina*.] **2** variant reading. **3** virtual reality.

VRML ▪ abbrev. Computing virtual reality modelling language.

vroom informal ▪ v. (of a vehicle or its engine) make a roaring sound when travelling or running at high speed. ▪ n. the roaring sound of an engine or motor vehicle.
– ORIGIN 1960s: imitative.

vrot /frɒt/ ▪ adj. S. African informal rotten; very unpleasant. ▸ extremely drunk.
– ORIGIN 1910s: Afrikaans, from Dutch *verrotten* 'to rot'.

vs ▪ abbrev. versus.

V-sign ▪ n. **1** a sign resembling the letter V made with the first two fingers pointing up and the back of the hand facing outwards, used as a gesture of abuse or contempt. **2** a similar sign made with the palm of the hand facing outwards, used as a symbol or gesture of victory.

VSO ▪ abbrev. Voluntary Service Overseas.

VSOP ▪ abbrev. Very Special Old Pale, a kind of brandy.

VTOL ▪ abbrev. vertical take-off and landing.

VTR ▪ abbrev. videotape recorder.

vug /vʌg/ ▪ n. Geology a cavity in rock, lined with mineral crystals.
– DERIVATIVES **vuggy** adj. **vugular** adj.
– ORIGIN C19: from Cornish *vooga*.

Vulcanian /vʌlˈkeɪnɪən/ ▪ adj. Geology relating to or denoting a type of volcanic eruption marked by periodic explosive events.
– ORIGIN C20: from *Vulcano*, the name of a volcano in the Lipari Islands, Italy.

vulcanism /ˈvʌlkənɪz(ə)m/ ▪ n. variant spelling of VOLCANISM.

vulcanite /ˈvʌlkənʌɪt/ ▪ n. hard black vulcanized rubber.
– ORIGIN C19: from *Vulcan*, the Roman god of fire.

vulcanize /ˈvʌlkənʌɪz/ (also **-ise**) ▪ v. harden (rubber or rubber-like material) by treating it with sulphur at a high temperature.
– DERIVATIVES **vulcanization** (also **-isation**) n. **vulcanizer** (also **-iser**) n.

vulcanology ▪ n. variant spelling of VOLCANOLOGY.

vulgar ▪ adj. **1** lacking sophistication or good taste. ▸ making explicit reference to sex or bodily functions. **2** dated characteristic of or belonging to ordinary people.
– DERIVATIVES **vulgarity** n. (pl. **-ies**). **vulgarly** adv.
– ORIGIN Middle English: from Latin *vulgaris*, from *vulgus* 'common people'.

vulgar fraction ▪ n. another term for COMMON FRACTION.

vulgarian /vʌlˈgɛːrɪən/ ▪ n. an unrefined person, especially one with newly acquired power or wealth.

vulgarism ▪ n. a word or expression that is considered vulgar.

vulgarize (also **-ise**) ▪ v. **1** make less refined. **2** make commonplace or less subtle or complex.
– DERIVATIVES **vulgarization** (also **-isation**) n.

vulgar Latin ▪ n. informal Latin of classical times.

vulgar tongue ▪ n. the national or vernacular language of a people (especially as contrasted with Latin).

Vulgate /ˈvʌlgeɪt, -gət/ ▪ n. **1** the principal Latin version of the Bible, the official text for the Roman Catholic Church. **2** (**vulgate**) formal common or colloquial speech.
– ORIGIN from Latin *vulgata* (*editio(n-)*) '(edition) prepared for the public', from *vulgare*, from *vulgus* 'common people'.

vulnerable ▪ adj. **1** exposed to being attacked or harmed, either physically or emotionally. **2** Bridge (of a partnership) liable to higher penalties, either by convention or through having won one game in a series of successive games between the same people.
– DERIVATIVES **vulnerability** n. (pl. **-ies**). **vulnerableness** n. **vulnerably** adv.
– ORIGIN C17: from late Latin *vulnerabilis*, from Latin *vulnerare* 'to wound'.

vulpine /ˈvʌlpʌɪn/ ▪ adj. of, relating to, or reminiscent of a fox or foxes.
– ORIGIN C17: from Latin *vulpinus*, from *vulpes* 'fox'.

vulture /ˈvʌltʃə/ ▪ n. **1** a large bird of prey feeding chiefly on carrion, with the head and neck more or less bare of feathers. [Several species in the families Accipitridae (Old World) and Cathartidae (New World).] **2** a contemptible person who preys on or exploits others.
– DERIVATIVES **vulturine** /-rʌɪn/ adj. **vulturish** adj. **vulturous** adj.
– ORIGIN Middle English: from Anglo-Norman French *vultur*, from Latin *vulturius*.

vulva /ˈvʌlvə/ ▪ n. the female external genitals. ▸ Zoology the external opening of the vagina or reproductive tract in a female mammal or nematode.
– DERIVATIVES **vulval** adj. **vulvar** adj.
– ORIGIN Middle English: from Latin, 'womb'.

vulvitis /vʌlˈvʌɪtɪs/ ▪ n. Medicine inflammation of the vulva.

vuvuzela /vʊvʊˈzɛːlʌ/ ▪ n. S. African a long straight plastic horn, chiefly used by spectators at soccer matches.

vv. ▪ abbrev. **1** verses. **2** volumes.

vygie /ˈfeɪxi/ ▪ n. S. African a mesembryanthemum.
– ORIGIN 1920s: Afrikaans, 'little fig', abbrev. of S. African Dutch *vygebosch*, from Dutch *vijg* 'fig' + *bosch* 'bush'.

vying present participle of VIE.

W w

W¹ (also **w**) ■ n. (pl. **Ws** or **W's**) **1** the twenty-third letter of the alphabet. **2** denoting the next after V in a set of items, categories, etc.

W² ■ abbrev. **1** (in tables of sports results) games won. **2** watt(s). **3** West or Western. **4** Cricket (on scorecards) wicket(s). **5** women's (clothes size). ■ symb. the chemical element tungsten. [from modern Latin *wolframium*.]

w ■ abbrev. **1** weight. **2** Cricket (on scorecards) wide(s). **3** with.

waboom /'vɑːbʊ(ə)m/ ■ n. S. African a gnarled tree of the protea family with white globular flower heads and very hard reddish wood. [*Protea nitida*.]
– ORIGIN C18: from S. African Dutch, from *wa* 'wagon' + *boom* 'tree'.

wacke /'wakə/ ■ n. Geology a sandstone of which the mud matrix in which the grains are embedded amounts to between 15 and 75 per cent of the mass.
– ORIGIN C19: from German, from Middle High German *wacke* 'large stone'.

wacked ■ adj. variant spelling of **WHACKED**.

wacko (also **whacko**) informal, chiefly N. Amer. ■ adj. mad; insane. ■ n. (pl. **-os** or **-oes**) a crazy person.
– ORIGIN 1970s: from **WACKY** + **-O**.

wacky (also **whacky**) ■ adj. (**-ier, -iest**) informal funny or amusing in a slightly odd or peculiar way.
– DERIVATIVES **wackily** adv. **wackiness** n.
– ORIGIN C19: from **WHACK**.

wacky baccy ■ n. Brit. informal cannabis.

wad /wɒd/ ■ n. **1** a lump or bundle of a soft material, as used for padding, stuffing, or wiping. **2** a bundle of paper, banknotes, or documents. ▸ informal a large amount of something, especially money. ■ v. (**wadded, wadding**) [usu. as adj. **wadded**] **1** compress (a soft material) into a wad. **2** line, stuff, or stop with soft material.
– DERIVATIVES **wadding** n.
– ORIGIN C16: perhaps rel. to Dutch *watten*, French *ouate* 'padding, cotton wool'.

waddle ■ v. walk with short steps and a clumsy swaying motion. ■ n. a waddling gait.
– DERIVATIVES **waddler** n.
– ORIGIN C16: perhaps rel. to **WADE**.

wade ■ v. **1** walk through a liquid or viscous substance. **2** (**wade through**) read laboriously through (a long piece of writing). **3** (**wade in/into**) informal attack, intervene, or become involved in a vigorous or forceful way. ■ n. an act of wading.
– DERIVATIVES **wadable** (also **wadeable**) adj.
– ORIGIN Old English *wadan* 'move onward', also 'penetrate', from a Germanic word meaning 'go (through)'.

wader ■ n. **1** a sandpiper, plover, or other wading bird. **2** (**waders**) high waterproof boots, used by anglers.

wadi /'wɒdi, 'wɑːdi/ (also **wady**) ■ n. (pl. **wadis** or **wadies**) (in Arabic-speaking countries) a valley, ravine, or channel that is dry except in the rainy season.
– ORIGIN C17: from Arabic *wādī*.

wading pool ■ n. another term for **PADDLING POOL**.

wafer ■ n. **1** a very thin light, crisp sweet biscuit. **2** a thin disc of unleavened bread used in the Eucharist. **3** a disc of red paper stuck on a legal document as a seal. ▸ historical a small disc of dried paste formerly used for fastening letters or holding papers together. **4** Electronics a very thin slice of a semiconductor crystal used as the substrate for solid-state circuitry.
– DERIVATIVES **wafery** adj.
– ORIGIN Middle English: from an Anglo-Norman French var. of Old French *gaufre* (see **GOFFER**), from Middle Low German *wāfel* 'waffle'.

wafer-thin ■ adj. & adv. very thin or thinly.

Waffen SS /'vaf(ə)n/ ■ n. the combat units of the SS in Nazi Germany.
– ORIGIN German *Waffen* 'armed'.

waffle¹ informal ■ v. speak or write at length in a vague or trivial manner. ■ n. lengthy but vague or trivial talk or writing.
– DERIVATIVES **waffler** n. **waffly** adj.
– ORIGIN C17 (orig. in the sense 'yap, yelp'): from dialect *waff* 'yelp', of imitative origin.

waffle² ■ n. a small crisp batter cake, baked in a waffle iron and eaten hot with butter or syrup.
– ORIGIN C18: from Dutch *wafel*; cf. **WAFER** and **GOFFER**.

waffle iron ■ n. a utensil for baking waffles, consisting of two shallow metal pans hinged together.

waft /wɒft, wɑːft/ ■ v. pass easily or gently through the air. ■ n. a gentle movement of air. ▸ a scent carried in the air.
– ORIGIN C16 (in the sense 'escort (a ship)'): back-formation from obsolete *wafter* 'armed convoy vessel', from Low German, Dutch *wachten* 'to guard'.

wag¹ ■ v. (**wagged, wagging**) (especially with reference to an animal's tail) move rapidly to and fro. ■ n. a wagging movement.
– ORIGIN Middle English: from the Germanic base of Old English *wagian* 'to sway'.

wag² ■ n. informal a person who makes facetious jokes.
– ORIGIN C16 (denoting a young man or mischievous boy): prob. from obsolete *waghalter* 'person likely to be hanged'.

wage ■ n. (also **wages**) **1** a fixed regular payment for work, typically paid on a daily or weekly basis. ▸ (**wages**) Economics the part of total production that is the return to labour as earned income as distinct from the remuneration received by capital as unearned income. **2** the result or effect of doing something wrong or unwise: *the wages of sin*. ■ v. carry on (a war or campaign).
– DERIVATIVES **waged** adj.
– ORIGIN Middle English: from Anglo-Norman French and Old Northern French, of Germanic origin.

wager ■ n. & v. more formal term for **BET**.
– ORIGIN Middle English (also in the sense 'solemn pledge'): from Anglo-Norman French *wageure*, from *wager* 'to wage'.

wage slave ■ n. informal a person who is wholly dependent on income from employment.
– DERIVATIVES **wage slavery** n.

waggish ■ adj. informal humorous, playful, or facetious.
– DERIVATIVES **waggishly** adv. **waggishness** n.

waggle informal ■ v. move with short quick movements from side to side or up and down. ▸ swing (a golf club) loosely and to and fro over the ball before playing a shot. ■ n. an act of waggling.
– DERIVATIVES **waggler** n. **waggly** adj.
– ORIGIN C16: from **WAG¹**.

Wagnerian /vɑːɡˈnɪərɪən/ ■ adj. relating to the German composer Richard Wagner (1813–83). ■ n. an admirer or follower of Wagner.

Wagner tuba ■ n. a brass instrument combining features of the tuba and the French horn and first used in Wagner's *Der Ring des Nibelungen*.

wagon (also **waggon**) ■ n. **1** a vehicle, especially a horse-drawn one, for transporting goods. ▸ a covered vehicle, usually drawn by oxen, used by early settlers in South Africa. ▸ a light covered horse-drawn vehicle as used by early settlers in North America. ▸ chiefly N. Amer. a wheeled cart or hut used as a food stall. **2** a railway freight vehicle; a truck.

CONSONANTS **b** but **d** dog **f** few **g** get **h** he **j** yes **k** cat **l** leg **m** man **n** no **p** pen **r** red

- PHRASES **on the wagon** informal teetotal.
- DERIVATIVES **wagonload** n.
- ORIGIN C15: from Dutch *wagen*.

wagoner (also **waggoner**) ■ n. the driver of a wagon; a person who transports goods by wagon.

wagon-lit /ˌvagɔ̃ˈliː/ ■ n. (pl. **wagons-lits** pronunc. same) a sleeping car on a train in continental Europe.
- ORIGIN French, from *wagon* 'railway coach' + *lit* 'bed'.

wagon-roof (also **wagon-vault**) ■ n. another term for BARREL VAULT.

wagon train ■ n. historical a convoy or train of covered horse-drawn wagons, as used by pioneers or settlers in North America.

wagon tree ■ n. another term for WABOOM.

wagtail ■ n. a slender songbird with a long tail that is frequently wagged up and down. [*Motacilla capensis* (Cape Wagtail) and other species.]

Wahhabi /wəˈhɑːbi/ (also **Wahabi**) ■ n. (pl. **Wahhabis**) a member of a strictly orthodox Sunni Muslim sect, the predominant religious force in Saudi Arabia.
- DERIVATIVES **Wahhabism** n.
- ORIGIN named after the founder, Muhammad ibn Abd al-*Wahhab* (1703–92).

wahoo /wɑːˈhuː/ ■ n. a large predatory tropical marine fish of the mackerel family, prized as a game fish. [*Acanthocybium solanderi*.]
- ORIGIN C20.

wah-wah (also **wa-wa**) ■ n. a musical effect achieved on brass instruments by alternately applying and removing a mute and on an electric guitar by use of a pedal. ▸ a pedal for producing such an effect on an electric guitar.
- ORIGIN 1920s: imitative.

waif ■ n. a homeless and helpless person, especially a neglected or abandoned child. ▸ a person who appears thin or poorly nourished.
- DERIVATIVES **waifish** adj.
- ORIGIN Middle English (in *waif and stray*, denoting a piece of property found and, if unclaimed, falling to the lord of the manor): from an Anglo-Norman French var. of Old Northern French *gaif*, prob. of Scandinavian origin.

wail ■ n. a prolonged high-pitched cry of pain, grief, or anger. ▸ a sound resembling this. ■ v. 1 give or utter a wail. 2 poetic/literary manifest or feel deep sorrow for; lament.
- DERIVATIVES **wailer** n. **wailful** adj. (poetic/literary). **wailing** n. & adj. **wailingly** adv.
- ORIGIN Middle English: from Old Norse; rel. to WOE.

wain ■ n. archaic a wagon or cart.
- ORIGIN Old English *wæg(e)n*, of Germanic origin.

wainscot /ˈweɪnskɒt/ ■ n. an area of wooden panelling on the lower part of the walls of a room. ■ v. (**wainscoted**, **wainscoting** or **wainscotted**, **wainscotting**) line (a room or wall) with wooden panelling.
- DERIVATIVES **wainscoting** (also **wainscotting**) n.
- ORIGIN Middle English: from Middle Low German *wagenschot*, apparently from *wagen* 'wagon' + *schot*, prob. meaning 'partition'.

wainwright ■ n. historical a wagon-builder.

waist ■ n. 1 the part of the human body below the ribs and above the hips. 2 a narrow part in the middle of something, e.g. a violin, hourglass, etc. ▸ the middle part of a ship, between the forecastle and the quarterdeck.
- DERIVATIVES **waisted** adj. **waistless** adj.
- ORIGIN Middle English: apparently representing an Old English word from the Germanic root of WAX².

waistband ■ n. a strip of cloth encircling the waist, attached to a skirt or a pair of trousers.

waistcoat /ˈweɪs(t)kəʊt, ˈwɛskɪt/ ■ n. a close-fitting waist-length garment with no sleeves or collar and buttoning down the front, worn typically by men over a shirt and under a jacket.

waistline ■ n. the measurement around a person's body at the waist. ▸ the part of a garment that is shaped or constructed to fit at or near the waist.

wait ■ v. 1 stay where one is or delay action until a particular time or occurrence. ▸ be delayed or deferred. ▸ informal defer (a meal) until a person's arrival. ▸ [usu. as noun **waiting**] park a vehicle for a short time at the side of a road. 2 (**wait on/upon**) act as an attendant to. ▸ archaic

1339

walk

pay a respectful visit to. 3 act as a waiter or waitress. ■ n. a period of waiting.
- PHRASES **in wait** watching for an enemy or potential victim and preparing to attack them. **you wait** used to convey a threat, warning, or promise.
- ORIGIN Middle English: from Old Northern French *waitier*, of Germanic origin.

wait-a-bit ■ n. chiefly S. African an acacia or other tree with hooked thorns that catch clothing, including the buffalo thorn.
- ORIGIN C18: translation of Afrikaans *wag-'n-bietjie*.

waiter ■ n. 1 a man whose job is to serve customers at their tables in a restaurant. 2 a person who waits for a time, event, or opportunity. 3 a small tray; a salver.

waiting list (N. Amer. **wait list**) ■ n. a list of people waiting for something, especially housing or admission to a hospital or school.

waiting room ■ n. a room for people waiting to see a medical practitioner or to catch a bus or train.

waitress ■ n. a woman whose job is to serve customers at their tables in a restaurant.
- DERIVATIVES **waitressing** n.

waitron ■ n. a waiter or waitress.

waive ■ v. refrain from insisting on or applying (a right or claim).
- ORIGIN Middle English (orig. as a legal term relating to removal of the protection of the law): from an Anglo-Norman French var. of Old French *gaiver* 'allow to become a waif, abandon'.

waiver ■ n. an act or instance of waiving a right or claim. ▸ a document recording this.

Wakamba /waˈkambə/ plural form of KAMBA.

wakame /ˈwakameɪ/ ■ n. an edible brown seaweed used in Chinese and Japanese cookery. [*Undaria pinnatifida*.]
- ORIGIN from Japanese.

wake¹ ■ v. (past **woke**; past part. **woken**) (often **wake up**) emerge or cause to emerge from a state of sleep; stop sleeping. ▸ (**wake up to**) become alert to or aware of. ▸ cause to stir or come to life. ■ n. a watch or vigil held beside the body of someone who has died. ▸ (especially in Ireland) a party held after a funeral.
- DERIVATIVES **waker** n.
- ORIGIN Old English (recorded only in the past tense *wōc*), partly from *wacian* 'remain awake, hold a vigil', of Germanic origin.

wake² ■ n. a trail of disturbed water or air left by the passage of a ship or aircraft.
- PHRASES **in the wake of** following as a consequence or result.
- ORIGIN C15: prob. from Old Norse *vǫk, vaka* 'hole or opening in ice'.

wakeboarding ■ n. the sport of riding on a short, wide board resembling a surfboard while being towed behind a motor boat.
- DERIVATIVES **wakeboard** n.

wakeful ■ adj. unable or not needing to sleep. ▸ alert and vigilant.
- DERIVATIVES **wakefully** adv. **wakefulness** n.

waken ■ v. wake from sleep.
- ORIGIN Old English *wæcnan* 'be aroused', of Germanic origin.

Waldenses /wɒlˈdɛnsiːz/ ■ pl. n. a puritan religious sect originating in southern France.
- DERIVATIVES **Waldensian** adj. & n.
- ORIGIN named after the founder, Peter *Valdes* (d.1205).

Waldorf salad /ˈwɔːldɔːf/ ■ n. a salad made from apples, walnuts, celery, and mayonnaise.
- ORIGIN named after the *Waldorf*-Astoria Hotel in New York, where it was first served.

wale ■ n. 1 a ridge on a textured woven fabric such as corduroy. 2 a weal, especially as caused by being whipped or beaten.
- ORIGIN Old English *walu* 'stripe, weal'.

walk ■ v. 1 move at a regular and fairly slow pace by lifting and setting down each foot in turn. ▸ travel over (a route or area) on foot. ▸ (of a quadruped) proceed with the

walkabout

slowest gait, always having at least two feet on the ground at once. ▸ informal (of a thing) go missing or be stolen. ▸ Cricket (of a batsman) leave the field without waiting to be given out by the umpire. ▸ N. Amer. informal be released from suspicion or from a charge. **2** guide, accompany, or escort (someone) on foot. ▸ take (a dog) out for exercise. **3** Baseball reach first base automatically after not hitting at four balls pitched outside the strike zone. ■ n. **1** an excursion or act of travelling on foot. **2** an unhurried rate of movement on foot. ▸ the slowest gait of an animal. **3** a route for recreational walking.
–PHRASES **walking encyclopedia** (also **walking dictionary**) informal a person with an impressive knowledge of facts or words. **walk it** informal achieve a victory easily. **walk of life** the position within society that someone holds. **walk on eggshells** be extremely cautious about one's words or actions. **walk the talk** suit one's actions to one's words. **walk the wards** dated gain experience as a clinical medical student.
–PHRASAL VERBS **walk (all) over** informal treat in a thoughtless, disrespectful, and exploitative manner. ▸ defeat easily. **walk away** casually or irresponsibly abandon an involvement or responsibility. **walk off with** (or **away with**) informal **1** steal. **2** win. **walk out 1** depart suddenly or angrily. ▸ go on strike. **2** Brit. informal, dated go for walks in courtship.
–DERIVATIVES **walkable** adj.
–ORIGIN Old English *wealcan* 'roll, toss', also 'wander', of Germanic origin.

walkabout ■ n. **1** chiefly Brit. an informal stroll among a crowd conducted by an important visitor. **2** Austral. a journey on foot undertaken by an Australian Aboriginal in order to live in the traditional manner.
–PHRASES **go walkabout** go missing, especially as a result of theft.

walkathon ■ n. informal a long-distance walk organized as a fundraising event.
–ORIGIN 1930s: from WALK, on the pattern of *marathon*.

walker ■ n. **1** a person who walks. **2** short for BABY WALKER. **3** short for WALKING FRAME.

walkies ■ n. informal a spell of walking with a dog.
–PHRASES **go walkies** another way of saying go walkabout (see WALKABOUT).

walkie-talkie ■ n. **1** a portable two-way radio. **2** S. African informal (**walkie-talkies**) cooked chicken heads and feet.

walk-in ■ adj. (of a storage area) large enough to walk into.

walking frame ■ n. a frame used by disabled or infirm people for support while walking.

walking papers ■ pl. n. informal, chiefly N. Amer. notice of dismissal from a job.

walking stick ■ n. a stick with a curved handle used for support when walking.

walking wounded ■ pl. n. people who have been injured in a battle or major accident but who are still able to walk.

Walkman ■ n. (pl. **Walkmans** or **Walkmen**) trademark a type of personal stereo.

walk-on ■ adj. denoting or having a small non-speaking part in a play or film.

walkout ■ n. a sudden angry departure, especially as a protest or strike.

walkover ■ n. an easy victory.

walk-through ■ n. **1** an undemanding task or lacklustre performance. **2** a rough rehearsal of a play or film.

walk-up N. Amer. ■ adj. (of a building) allowing access to the upper floors by stairs only. ■ n. a building of this kind.

walkway ■ n. a raised passageway in a building, or a wide path in a park or garden.

wall ■ n. **1** a continuous vertical brick or stone structure that encloses or divides an area of land. ▸ a side of a building or room. **2** a protective or restrictive barrier likened to a wall: *a wall of silence*. **3** Soccer a line of defenders forming a barrier against a free kick taken near the penalty area. **4** Anatomy the membranous outer layer or lining of an organ or cavity. ■ v. enclose within walls.
▸ (**wall something up**) block or seal a place by building a wall. ▸ (**wall someone in/up**) confine someone in a restricted or sealed place.
–PHRASES **drive someone up the wall** informal make someone very irritated or angry. **go to the wall** informal (of a business) fail; go out of business. **hit the wall** (of an athlete) experience a sudden loss of energy in a long race. **off the wall** informal eccentric or unconventional. **wall-to-wall** informal (of a carpet) fitted to cover an entire floor. ▸ informal very numerous or plentiful.
–DERIVATIVES **walling** n.
–ORIGIN Old English, from Latin *vallum* 'rampart', from *vallus* 'stake'.

wallaby ■ n. (pl. **-ies**) an Australasian marsupial similar to but smaller than a kangaroo. [Numerous species in the family Macropodidae.]
–ORIGIN C19: from Dharuk (an extinct Aboriginal language) *walabi* or *waliba*.

Wallace's line ■ n. Zoology a hypothetical line marking the boundary between the Oriental and Australian zoogeographical regions.
–ORIGIN proposed by the English naturalist Alfred Russel *Wallace* (1823–1913).

wallah /ˈwɒlə/ ■ n. Indian or informal a person of a specified kind or having a specified role.
–ORIGIN from the Hindi suffix -*vālā* 'doer' (commonly interpreted in the sense 'fellow'), from Sanskrit *pālaka* 'keeper'.

wall bar ■ n. each of a set of parallel horizontal bars attached to the wall of a gymnasium, on which exercises are performed.

wallboard ■ n. a type of board made from wood pulp and plaster, used for covering walls and ceilings.

wallet ■ n. **1** a pocket-sized, flat, folding holder for money and plastic cards. **2** archaic a bag for holding provisions when travelling.
–ORIGIN Middle English: prob. via Anglo-Norman French from a Germanic word rel. to WELL².

wall eye ■ n. **1** an eye squinting outwards. **2** an eye with a streaked or opaque white iris.
–DERIVATIVES **wall-eyed** adj.
–ORIGIN C16: back-formation from earlier *wall-eyed*, from Old Norse *vagleygr*; rel. to Icelandic *vagl* 'film over the eye'.

wallflower ■ n. **1** a southern European plant with fragrant flowers that bloom in early spring. [*Cheiranthus cheiri*.] **2** informal a shy or excluded person at a dance or party, especially a girl without a partner.

Wall of Death ■ n. a fairground sideshow in which a motorcyclist rides around the inside walls of a vertical cylinder.

Walloon /wɒˈluːn/ ■ n. **1** a member of a people who speak a French dialect and live in southern and eastern Belgium and neighbouring parts of France. Compare with FLEMING. **2** the French dialect spoken by this people.
–ORIGIN from French *Wallon*, from medieval Latin *Wallo(n-)*, from the same Germanic origin as WELSH.

wallop informal ■ v. (**walloped**, **walloping**) **1** strike or hit very hard. ▸ heavily defeat (an opponent). **2** [as adj. **walloping**] strikingly large. ■ n. a heavy blow or punch.
–DERIVATIVES **walloping** n.
–ORIGIN Middle English: from Old Northern French *walop* (n.), *waloper* (v.), perhaps from a Germanic phr. meaning 'run well', from the bases of WELL¹ and LEAP.

wallow ■ v. **1** roll about or lie in mud or water. ▸ (of a boat or aircraft) roll from side to side. **2** (**wallow in**) indulge without restraint in (something pleasurable). ■ n. **1** an act of wallowing. **2** an area of mud or shallow water where mammals go to wallow.
–DERIVATIVES **wallower** n.
–ORIGIN Old English *walwian* 'roll about', of Germanic origin.

wall painting ■ n. a painting made directly on a wall, such as a fresco or mural.

wallpaper ■ n. **1** paper pasted in strips over the walls of a room to provide a decorative or textured surface. **2** something, especially music, providing a bland or unvaried background. **3** Computing an optional background pattern or picture on a screen. ■ v. apply wallpaper to (a wall or room).

wall plate ■ n. a timber laid horizontally in or on a wall as a support for a girder, rafter, or joist.

wally ■ n. (pl. **-ies**) Brit. informal a silly or inept person.
– ORIGIN 1960s: perhaps a shortened form of the given name *Walter*: the use possibly arose from an incident at a 1960s pop festival when a *Wally* became separated from his companions, his name being taken up as a chant by the crowd following numerous loudspeaker announcements.

walnut ■ n. **1** an edible wrinkled nut enclosed by a hard shell, produced inside a green fruit. **2** the tree which produces this nut, with compound leaves and valuable ornamental wood. [*Juglans regia* and related species.]
– ORIGIN Old English *walh-hnutu*, from a Germanic compound meaning 'foreign nut'.

walrus ■ n. a large gregarious marine mammal related to the eared seals, having two large downward-pointing tusks and found in the Arctic Ocean. [*Odobenus rosmarus*.]
– ORIGIN C18: prob. from Dutch *walrus*, perhaps by an inversion of elements (influenced by *walvis* 'whale-fish') of Old Norse *hrosshvalr* 'horse-whale'.

walrus moustache ■ n. a long, thick, drooping moustache.

waltz /wɔːl(t)s, wɒl-/ ■ n. a dance in triple time performed by a couple, who turn rhythmically round and round as they progress around the dance floor. ▸ a piece of music written for or in the style of this dance. ■ v. **1** dance a waltz. **2** move or act lightly, casually, or inconsiderately: *you can't just waltz in and expect to make a mark.*
– ORIGIN C18: from German *Walzer*, from *walzen* 'revolve'.

waltzer ■ n. **1** a person who dances the waltz. **2** a fairground ride in which cars spin round as they are carried round an undulating track.

WAN ■ abbrev. Computing wide area network.

wan /wɒn/ ■ adj. (of a person) pale and giving the impression of illness or exhaustion. ▸ (of light) pale; weak. ▸ (of a smile) weak; strained.
– DERIVATIVES **wanly** adv. **wanness** /ˈwɒnnɪs/ n.
– ORIGIN Old English *wann* 'dark, black'.

wand ■ n. **1** a stick or rod thought to have magic properties, used in casting spells or performing tricks. **2** a slender staff or rod, especially one held as a symbol of office. **3** (**wands**) one of the suits in some tarot packs, corresponding to batons in others. **4** a hand-held electronic device passed over a bar code to read the encoded data.
– ORIGIN Middle English: from Old Norse *vǫndr*, prob. of Germanic origin.

wander ■ v. walk or move in a leisurely, casual, or aimless way. ▸ move slowly away from a fixed point or place. ▸ move slowly through or over (a place or area). ■ n. an act or instance of wandering.
– DERIVATIVES **wanderer** n.
– ORIGIN Old English *wandrian*, of West Germanic origin; rel. to WEND and WIND².

wandering Jew ■ n. **1** a legendary person said to have been condemned by Christ to wander the earth until the second advent. **2** any of several species of trailing tradescantia. [*Tradescantia fluminensis* and other species.]

wanderlust ■ n. a strong desire to travel.
– ORIGIN C20: from German *Wanderlust*.

wane ■ v. **1** (of the moon) have a progressively smaller part of its visible surface illuminated, so that it appears to decrease in size. **2** decrease in vigour or extent; become weaker.
– PHRASES **on the wane** becoming weaker or less vigorous.
– ORIGIN Old English *wanian* 'lessen', of Germanic origin.

wangle informal ■ v. obtain (something desired) by persuading others to comply or by manipulating events. ■ n. an instance of obtaining something in such a way.
– DERIVATIVES **wangler** n.
– ORIGIN C19 (first recorded as printers' slang).

wank vulgar slang ■ v. masturbate. ■ n. an act of masturbating.
– ORIGIN 1940s.

Wankel engine /ˈwæŋk(ə)l, ˈvaŋ-/ ■ n. a rotary internal-combustion engine in which a curvilinear, triangular, eccentrically pivoted piston rotates in an elliptical chamber, forming three combustion spaces that vary in volume as it turns.
– ORIGIN 1960s: named after the German engineer Felix Wankel.

wanker ■ n. vulgar slang a stupid or contemptible person.

wanna ■ contr. informal want to; want a.

wannabe /ˈwɒnəbi/ ■ n. informal, derogatory a person who tries to be like someone else or to fit in with a particular group of people.

want ■ v. **1** have a desire to possess or do (something); wish for. ▸ wish to speak to (someone). ▸ desire (someone) sexually. **2** (**be wanted**) (of a suspected criminal) be sought by the police. **3** informal, chiefly Brit. (of a thing) require to be attended to: *the wheel wants greasing.* ▸ ought to, should, or need to do something. **4** (often **want for**) chiefly archaic lack or be short of something desirable or essential. ■ n. **1** chiefly archaic lack or deficiency. ▸ the state of being poor and in need of essentials; poverty. **2** a desire for something.
– ORIGIN Middle English: noun from Old Norse *vant*, *vanr* 'lacking'; verb from Old Norse *vanta* 'be lacking'.

wanting ■ adj. lacking in something required, necessary, or usual. ▸ informal deficient in intelligence.

wanton ■ adj. **1** (of a cruel or violent action) deliberate and unprovoked. **2** sexually immodest or promiscuous. **3** poetic/literary growing profusely; luxuriant. ▸ lively; playful. ■ n. archaic a sexually immodest or promiscuous woman.
– DERIVATIVES **wantonly** adv. **wantonness** n.
– ORIGIN Middle English *wantowen* 'rebellious, lacking discipline', from *wan-* 'badly' + Old English *togen* 'trained'.

WAP ■ abbrev. Computing Wireless Application Protocol, a standard through which portable devices such as cellphones may access an information network.

war ■ n. **1** a state of armed conflict between different nations, states, or armed groups. ▸ a state of competition, conflict, or hostility: *a price war.* ▸ a sustained campaign against something undesirable: *a war on drugs.* ■ v. (**warred**, **warring**) engage in a war.
– PHRASES **be in the wars** humorous (especially of a child) be hurt or injured. **war clouds** a threatening situation of instability in international relations.
– ORIGIN Old English *werre*, from an Anglo-Norman French var. of Old French *guerre*, from a Germanic base.

war baby ■ n. a child born in wartime, especially one fathered illegitimately by a serviceman.

warble ■ v. (of a bird) sing softly and with a succession of constantly changing notes. ▸ (of a person) sing in a trilling or quavering voice. ■ n. a warbling sound or utterance.
– ORIGIN Middle English: from Old Northern French *werble* (n.), *werbler* (v.), of Germanic origin.

warbler ■ n. **1** a small, active songbird, typically living in trees and bushes and having a warbling song. [Many species, chiefly in the families Sylviidae (Old World), Parulidae (N. America), and Acanthizidae (Australasia).] **2** informal a person who sings in a trilling or quavering voice.

war chest ■ n. a reserve of funds used for fighting a war.

war crime ■ n. an action carried out during the conduct of a war that violates accepted international rules of war.
– DERIVATIVES **war criminal** n.

war cry ■ n. a call made to rally soldiers for battle or to gather together participants in a campaign.

ward ■ n. **1** a room in a hospital, typically one allocated to a particular type of patient. **2** an administrative division of a city or town, typically represented by a councillor or councillors. **3** a child or young person under the care and control of a guardian appointed by their parents or a court. **4** any of the internal ridges or bars in a lock which prevent the turning of any key without corresponding grooves. ▸ the corresponding grooves in the bit of a key. **5** historical an area of ground enclosed by the encircling walls of a fortress or castle. ■ v. **1** (**ward someone/thing off**) prevent someone or something from harming or affecting one. **2** archaic guard; protect.
– DERIVATIVES **wardship** n.
– ORIGIN Old English *weard*, *weardian* 'keep safe, guard', of Germanic origin; reinforced in Middle English by Old Northern French *warde* (n.), *warder* (v.) 'guard'.

-ward (also **-wards**) ■ suffix **1** (usu. **-wards**) (forming adverbs) towards the specified place or direction: *homewards*. **2** (usu. **-ward**) (forming adjectives) turned or tending towards: *upward*.
– ORIGIN Old English, from a Germanic base meaning 'turn'.

war dance ■ n. a ceremonial dance performed before a battle or to celebrate victory.

warden ■ n. **1** a person responsible for the supervision of a particular place or procedure. **2** Brit. the head of certain schools, colleges, or other institutions. **3** chiefly N. Amer. a prison governor.
– DERIVATIVES **wardenship** n.
– ORIGIN Middle English: from Anglo-Norman French *wardein*, var. of Old French *guarden* 'guardian'.

warder ■ n. (fem. **wardress**) a prison guard.
– ORIGIN Middle English: from Anglo-Norman French *wardere*, from Old Northern French *warder* 'to guard'.

ward of court ■ n. a minor who is placed under the control or protection of a court, or of a court-appointed guardian.

wardrobe ■ n. **1** a large, tall cupboard in which clothes may be hung or stored. **2** a person's entire collection of clothes. **3** the costume department or costumes of a theatre or film company.
– ORIGIN Middle English (in the sense 'private chamber'): from Old Northern French *warderobe*, var. of Old French *garderobe* (see **GARDEROBE**).

wardroom ■ n. a commissioned officers' mess on board a warship.

-wards ■ suffix variant spelling of -**WARD**.

ware[1] /weː/ ■ n. **1** pottery, typically that of a specified type. ▶ manufactured articles of a specified type. **2** (**wares**) articles offered for sale.
– ORIGIN Old English *waru* 'commodities', of Germanic origin, perhaps the same word as Scots *ware* 'cautiousness', with the sense 'object of care'.

ware[2] /weː/ (also **'ware**) ■ v. beware (used as a warning cry).
– ORIGIN Old English *warian* 'be on one's guard', from a Germanic base meaning 'observe, take care'.

ware[3] /weː/ ■ adj. archaic aware.
– ORIGIN Old English *wær*, from the Germanic base of **WARE**[2].

-ware /weː/ ■ comb. form **1** denoting articles made of ceramic or used in cooking and serving food: *tableware*. **2** denoting a kind of software: *groupware*.

warehouse /'weːhaʊs/ ■ n. **1** a large building where raw materials or manufactured goods may be stored. **2** a large wholesale or retail store. ■ v. /also -haʊz/ store (goods) in a warehouse. ▶ place (imported goods) in a bonded warehouse pending the payment of import duty.
– DERIVATIVES **warehousing** n.

warehouse party ■ n. a large public party with dancing, typically organized without official permission.

warfare ■ n. engagement in or the state of war.

warfarin /'wɔːfərɪn/ ■ n. a water-soluble compound with anticoagulant properties, used as a rat poison and in the treatment of thrombosis.
– ORIGIN 1950s: from the initial letters of *Wisconsin Alumni Research Foundation* + -*arin*.

war game ■ n. **1** a military exercise carried out to test or improve tactical expertise. **2** a simulated military conflict carried out as a game or exercise in personal development. ■ v. (**war-game**) engage in war games.
– DERIVATIVES **war-gamer** n. **war gaming** n.

war grave ■ n. a grave of a member of the armed forces who has died on active service, especially one in a special cemetery.

warhead ■ n. the explosive head of a missile, torpedo, or similar weapon.

Warholian /wɔːˈhəʊlɪən/ ■ adj. of or relating to the work of the American artist Andy Warhol (*c*.1928–87).

warhorse ■ n. informal a veteran soldier, politician, sports player, etc. who has fought many campaigns or contests.

warlike ■ adj. **1** disposed towards or threatening war; hostile. **2** directed towards or prepared for war.

warlock ■ n. a man who practises witchcraft.
– ORIGIN Old English *wǣrloga* 'traitor, scoundrel, monster', also 'the Devil', from *wǣr* 'covenant' + an element rel. to *lēogan* 'belie, deny'.

warlord ■ n. a military commander, especially an aggressive regional commander with individual autonomy.

warm ■ adj. **1** of or at a fairly or comfortably high temperature. **2** (of clothes or coverings) made of a material that helps the body to retain heat. **3** having or showing enthusiasm, affection, or kindness. **4** (of a colour) containing red, yellow, or orange tones. **5** (of a scent or trail) fresh; strong. ▶ (in children's games) close to finding or guessing what is sought. ■ v. **1** make or become warm. **2** (**warm up**) or **down** prepare for (or recover from) strenuous physical exertion by doing gentle stretches and exercises. **3** (**warm up**) (of an engine or electrical appliance) reach a temperature high enough to allow it to operate efficiently. ▶ become livelier or more animated. **4** (**warm to/towards**) or N. Amer. **warm up to/towards** become more interested in or enthusiastic about. ▶ (**warm someone up**) or US **over** amuse or entertain an audience or crowd so as to make them more receptive to the main act. ■ n. **1** (**the warm**) a warm place or area. **2** an act of warming.
– DERIVATIVES **warmer** n. **warmish** adj. **warmly** adv. **warmness** n.
– ORIGIN Old English *wearm* (adj.), *werman*, *wearmian* (v.), of Germanic origin.

warmblood ■ n. a horse of a breed that is a cross between an Arab or similar breed and another breed of the draught or pony type.

warm-blooded ■ adj. **1** denoting animals (chiefly mammals and birds) which maintain a constant body temperature by their metabolism; homeothermic. **2** ardent; passionate.
– DERIVATIVES **warm-bloodedness** n.

warm-hearted ■ adj. sympathetic and kind.
– DERIVATIVES **warm-heartedly** adv. **warm-heartedness** n.

warming pan ■ n. historical a wide, flat brass pan on a long handle, filled with hot coals and used for warming a bed.

warmonger /'wɔːmʌŋɡə/ ■ n. a person who seeks to bring about or promote war.
– DERIVATIVES **warmongering** n. & adj.

warmth ■ n. **1** the quality, state, or sensation of being warm. **2** enthusiasm, affection, or kindness. **3** intensity of emotion.

warn ■ v. **1** inform of a possible danger, problem, etc. ▶ (**warn someone off**) order someone to keep away or to refrain from doing something. **2** give cautionary advice about actions or conduct to.
– DERIVATIVES **warner** n.
– ORIGIN Old English *war(e)nian*, *wearnian*, from a West Germanic base meaning 'be cautious'.

warning ■ n. **1** a statement or event that warns or serves as a cautionary example. **2** cautionary advice. **3** advance notice.
– DERIVATIVES **warningly** adv.

warning coloration ■ n. Zoology conspicuous colouring that warns a predator that an animal is unpalatable or poisonous.

warp ■ v. **1** become or cause to become bent or twisted out of shape, typically from the action of heat or damp. **2** make abnormal; distort. **3** (with reference to a ship) move or be moved along by hauling on a rope attached to a stationary object ashore. **4** arrange (yarn) so as to form the warp of a piece of cloth. **5** cover (land) with a deposit of alluvial soil by flooding. ■ n. **1** a distortion or twist in shape. **2** the lengthwise threads on a loom over and under which the weft threads are passed to make cloth. **3** a rope attached at one end to a fixed point and used for moving or mooring a ship. **4** archaic alluvial sediment.
– DERIVATIVES **warpage** n. **warper** n.
– ORIGIN Old English, of Germanic origin.

warpaint ■ n. **1** paint traditionally used to decorate the face and body before battle, especially by North American Indians. **2** informal elaborate or excessive make-up.

warpath ■ n. (in phr. **on the warpath**) in an angry and aggressive state.
– ORIGIN with ref. to American Indians heading towards a battle with an enemy.

war pension ■ n. a pension paid to someone who is disabled or bereaved by war.

warplane ■ n. an aircraft designed and equipped to engage in air combat or to drop bombs.

warrant ■ n. **1** an official authorization enabling the police or some other body to make an arrest, search premises, etc. **2** a document entitling the holder to receive goods, money, or services. **3** Finance a negotiable security allowing the holder to buy shares at a specified price at or before some future date. **4** justification or authority. ■ v. **1** justify or necessitate. **2** officially affirm or guarantee.
– PHRASES **I** (or **I'll**) **warrant** (**you**) dated no doubt.
– DERIVATIVES **warrantable** adj. **warrantableness** n. **warranter** n.
– ORIGIN Middle English (in the senses 'protector', 'safeguard', and 'protect from danger'): from vars of Old French *guarant* (n.), *guarantir* (v.), of Germanic origin.

warrant card ■ n. a document of authorization and identification carried by a police officer.

warrant officer ■ n. a rank of military officer below the commissioned officers and above the NCOs.

warranty ■ n. (pl. **-ies**) **1** a written guarantee, issued to the purchaser of an article by its manufacturer, promising to repair or replace it if necessary within a specified period. **2** an engagement by an insured party that certain statements are true or that certain conditions shall be fulfilled, the breach of it invalidating the policy.
– DERIVATIVES **warrantee** n. **warrantor** n.
– ORIGIN Middle English: from Anglo-Norman French *warantie*, var. of *garantie* (see **GUARANTY**).

warren ■ n. **1** (also **rabbit warren**) a network of interconnecting rabbit burrows. **2** a densely populated or labyrinthine building or district.
– ORIGIN Middle English: from an Anglo-Norman French var. of Old French *garenne* 'game park', of Gaulish origin.

warrior ■ n. (especially in former times) a brave or experienced soldier or fighter.
– ORIGIN Middle English: from Old Northern French *werreior*, var. of Old French *guerreior*, from *guerreier* 'make war', from *guerre* 'war'.

warship ■ n. a ship equipped with weapons and designed to take part in warfare at sea.

wart ■ n. **1** a small, hard, benign growth on the skin, caused by a virus. **2** any rounded excrescence on the skin of an animal or the surface of a plant.
– PHRASES **warts and all** informal including faults or unattractive qualities.
– DERIVATIVES **warty** adj.
– ORIGIN Old English, of Germanic origin.

warthog ■ n. an African wild pig with a large head, warty lumps on the face, and curved tusks. [*Phacochoerus aethiopicus.*]

wartime ■ n. a period during which a war is taking place.

war-torn ■ adj. (of a place) racked or devastated by war.

wary ■ adj. (**-ier**, **-iest**) cautious about possible dangers or problems.
– DERIVATIVES **warily** adv. **wariness** n.
– ORIGIN C15: from Old English *wær* 'aware'.

was first and third person singular past of **BE**.

wasabi /wəˈsɑːbi/ ■ n. a Japanese plant with a thick green root which tastes like strong horseradish and is used in cookery, especially in powder or paste form as an accompaniment to raw fish. [*Eutrema wasabi.*]
– ORIGIN C20: from Japanese.

wash ■ v. **1** clean with water and, typically, soap or detergent. ▸ remove (a stain or dirt) in this way. ▸ do one's laundry. **2** (of flowing water) carry or move in a particular direction. ▸ be carried by flowing water. ▸ sift metallic particles from (earth or gravel) by running water through it. **3** (**wash over**) occur all around without greatly affecting. **4** poetic/literary wet or moisten. **5** brush with a thin coat of dilute paint or ink. **6** [with neg.] informal seem convincing or genuine. ■ n. **1** an act of washing or an instance of being washed. ▸ a quantity of clothes needing to be or just having been washed. **2** the water or air disturbed by a moving boat or aircraft. ▸ the breaking of waves on a shore. **3** a medicinal or cleansing solution, especially one applied to the skin. **4** a thin coating of paint or metal. **5** silt or gravel carried by water and deposited as sediment.
– PHRASES **come out in the wash** informal be resolved eventually. **wash one's dirty linen** (or **laundry**) **in public** informal discuss one's personal affairs in public. **wash one's hands** euphemistic go to the toilet. **wash one's hands of** disclaim responsibility for. [orig. with biblical allusion to Matthew 27:24.]
– PHRASAL VERBS **wash something out 1** (usu. **be washed out**) cause an event to be postponed or cancelled because of rain. **2** (of a flood or downpour) make a breach in a road. **wash up 1** (also **wash something up**) clean crockery and cutlery after use. **2** N. Amer. clean one's hands and face.
– DERIVATIVES **washability** n. **washable** adj.
– ORIGIN Old English *wæscan* (v.), of Germanic origin.

washbag ■ n. Brit. a toilet bag.

washbasin ■ n. a basin, typically fixed to a wall or on a pedestal, used for washing one's hands and face.

washboard ■ n. **1** a board made of ridged wood or a sheet of corrugated zinc, against which clothes are scrubbed during washing. ▸ a similar board played as a percussion instrument by scraping. **2** N. Amer. a worn, uneven road surface. **3** [as modifier] denoting a man's stomach that is lean and has well-defined muscles.

washcloth ■ n. N. Amer. a facecloth.

washed out ■ adj. **1** faded by or as if by repeated washing. **2** pale and tired.

washed-up ■ adj. informal no longer effective or successful.

washer ■ n. **1** a person or device that washes. **2** a small flat ring fixed between two joining surfaces or between a nut and bolt to spread the pressure or act as a spacer.

washer-dryer ■ n. a washing machine with an inbuilt tumbledryer.

washerwoman ■ n. (pl. **-women**) a woman whose occupation is washing clothes.

washing ■ n. a quantity of clothes, bedlinen, etc. that is to be washed or has just been washed.

washing blue ■ n. another term for **BLUING** (in sense 1).

washing machine ■ n. a machine for washing clothes, bedlinen, etc.

washing powder ■ n. powdered detergent for washing laundry.

washing soda ■ n. sodium carbonate, used dissolved in water for washing and cleaning.

washing-up ■ n. crockery, cutlery, and other kitchen utensils that are to be washed.

washout ■ n. **1** informal a disappointing failure. **2** a breach in a road or railway track caused by flooding. **3** Geology a channel cut into a sedimentary deposit by rushing water and filled with younger material. **4** Medicine the removal of material from the body by washing with a fluid or by allowing it to be eliminated over a period.

washroom ■ n. N. Amer. a room with washing and toilet facilities.

washstand ■ n. chiefly historical a piece of furniture designed to hold a jug, bowl, or basin for washing one's hands and face.

wasn't ■ contr. was not.

Wasp ■ n. N. Amer. an upper- or middle-class American white Protestant, regarded as a member of the most powerful social group.
– DERIVATIVES **Waspish** adj.
– ORIGIN 1960s: from *white Anglo-Saxon Protestant*.

wasp ■ n. **1** a social insect with a narrow-waisted, typically black and yellow striped body, which carries a sting and builds elaborate nests from wood pulp. [*Vespula, Polistes,* and other genera.] **2** a hymenopterous insect of a large group resembling the social wasps in appearance and either solitary or parasitic in habits.
– ORIGIN Old English *wæfs, wæps, wæsp*, of West Germanic origin.

waspie

waspie ■ n. (pl. **-ies**) a woman's corset or belt designed to accentuate a slender waist.
– ORIGIN 1950s: diminutive of *wasp* from WASP WAIST.

waspish ■ adj. sharply irritable.
– DERIVATIVES **waspishly** adv. **waspishness** n.

wasp waist ■ n. a very narrow waist, especially one that is tightly corseted.
– DERIVATIVES **wasp-waisted** adj.

wassail /ˈwɒseɪl, ˈwɒs(ə)l, ˈwæ-/ archaic ■ n. **1** spiced ale or mulled wine drunk during celebrations for Twelfth Night and Christmas Eve. **2** lively festivities involving the drinking of much alcohol. ■ v. **1** make merry with much alcohol. **2** [usu. as noun **wassailing**] go from house to house at Christmas singing carols.
– DERIVATIVES **wassailer** n.
– ORIGIN Middle English *wæs hæil* 'be in (good) health!': from Old Norse *ves heill*.

wast /wɒst, wəst/ archaic or dialect second person singular past of BE.

wastage ■ n. **1** the action or process of wasting. ▶ an amount wasted. **2** (also **natural wastage**) the reduction in the size of a workforce as a result of voluntary resignation or retirement rather than enforced redundancy. ▶ the number of people leaving a job or further educational establishment before they have completed their training or education.

waste ■ v. **1** use carelessly, extravagantly, or to no purpose. **2** (usu. **be wasted on**) expend on an unappreciative recipient. **3** fail to make full or good use of. **4** (often **waste away**) become progressively weaker and more emaciated. **5** poetic/literary lay waste to. **6** N. Amer. informal kill or severely injure. **7** [as adj. **wasted**] informal under the influence of alcohol or illegal drugs. **8** poetic/literary (of time) pass away. ■ adj. **1** eliminated or discarded as no longer useful or required. **2** (of an area of land, typically an urban one) not used, cultivated, or built on. ■ n. **1** an act or instance of wasting. **2** unusable or unwanted material. **3** a large area of barren, typically uninhabited land.
– PHRASES **go to waste** be wasted. **lay waste to** (or **lay something** (**to**) **waste**) completely destroy. **waste of space** informal a person perceived as useless.
– ORIGIN Middle English: from Old Northern French *wast*(*e*) (n.), *waster* (v.), from Latin *vastus* 'unoccupied, uncultivated'.

waste-disposal unit (also **waste disposer**) ■ n. an electrically operated device fitted to the waste pipe of a kitchen sink for grinding up food waste.

wasteful ■ adj. using or expending something carelessly, extravagantly, or to no purpose.
– DERIVATIVES **wastefully** adv. **wastefulness** n.

wasteland ■ n. a barren or empty area of land.

waste pipe ■ n. a pipe carrying waste water, such as that from a sink or bath, to a drain.

waster ■ n. **1** a wasteful person or thing. **2** informal a person who does little or nothing of value.

wastrel /ˈweɪstr(ə)l/ ■ n. poetic/literary a wasteful or worthless person.
– ORIGIN C16 (denoting a strip of waste land): from WASTE + -REL.

watch ■ v. **1** look at attentively. ▶ keep under careful or protective observation. ▶ (**watch for**) look out for. **2** exercise care, caution, or restraint about. ▶ [usu. in imper.] (**watch out**) be careful. **3** maintain an interest in. ■ n. **1** a small timepiece worn typically on a strap on one's wrist. **2** an act or instance of watching. ▶ a period of vigil, typically during the night. **3** a fixed period of duty on a ship, usually lasting four hours. ▶ (also **port watch** or **starboard watch**) the officers and crew on duty during one such period. ▶ a shift worked by firefighters or police officers. **4** (also **night watch**) historical a watchman or group of watchmen who patrolled and guarded the streets of a town at night.
– PHRASES **be on the watch** be on the alert for danger or trouble. **keep watch** stay on the lookout for danger or trouble. **watch one's** (or **someone's**) **back** protect oneself (or someone else) against danger from an unexpected quarter. **the watches of the night** poetic/literary waking hours during the night.
– DERIVATIVES **watcher** n.
– ORIGIN Old English *wæcce* 'watchfulness', *wæccende* 'remaining awake'.

watchable ■ adj. moderately enjoyable to watch.
– DERIVATIVES **watchability** n.

watch chain ■ n. a metal chain securing a pocket watch.

watchdog ■ n. **1** a dog kept to guard private property. **2** a person or group that monitors the practices of companies providing a particular service or utility. ■ v. (-**dogged**, -**dogging**) maintain surveillance over.

watchfire ■ n. a fire maintained during the night as a signal or for the use of someone who is on watch.

watchful ■ adj. **1** alert and vigilant. **2** archaic wakeful.
– DERIVATIVES **watchfully** adv. **watchfulness** n.

watch glass ■ n. **1** a glass disc covering the dial of a watch. **2** a concave glass disc used in a laboratory to hold material for use in experiments.

watching brief ■ n. an interest in a proceeding in which one is not directly concerned.

watchmaker ■ n. a person who makes and repairs watches and clocks.
– DERIVATIVES **watchmaking** n.

watchman ■ n. (pl. **-men**) **1** a man employed to look after a building, especially at night. **2** historical a member of a night watch.

watchnight ■ n. a religious service held on New Year's Eve or Christmas Eve.

watch spring ■ n. a mainspring in a watch.

watchtower ■ n. a tower built to create an elevated observation point.

watchword ■ n. a word or phrase expressing a core aim or belief.

water ■ n. **1** the liquid which forms the seas, lakes, rivers, and rain and is the basis of the fluids of living organisms. [Chemical formula: H_2O.] ▶ (**the waters**) the water of a mineral spring as used medicinally. ▶ urine. ▶ (**waters**) amniotic fluid, especially as discharged shortly before birth. **2** (**the water**) a stretch of water, such as a river, sea, or lake. ▶ the surface of this. ▶ [as modifier] found in, on, or near the water. ▶ (**waters**) an area of sea regarded as under the jurisdiction of a particular country. **3** Finance capital stock which represents a book value greater than the true assets of a company. ■ v. **1** pour water over (a plant or an area of ground). ▶ give a drink of water to (an animal). ▶ take a fresh supply of water on board (a ship or steam train). **2** (of the eyes or mouth) produce tears or saliva. **3** dilute (a drink, typically an alcoholic one) with water. ▶ (**water something down**) make something less forceful or controversial by changing or leaving out certain details. **4** (of a river) flow through (an area). **5** Finance increase (a company's debt, or nominal capital) by the issue of new shares without a corresponding addition to assets.
– PHRASES **like water** in great quantities. **make water** (of a ship or boat) take in water through a leak. **of the first water 1** (of a diamond or pearl) of the greatest brilliance and transparency. **2** referring to a person or thing unsurpassed of their kind: *she was a bore of the first water*. **under water** submerged; flooded. **the water of life** whisky. **water on the brain** informal hydrocephalus. **water under the bridge** (or N. Amer. **water over the dam**) past events that are over and done with.
– DERIVATIVES **waterer** n. **waterless** adj.
– ORIGIN Old English *wæter* (n.), *wæterian* (v.), of Germanic origin.

water bailiff ■ n. **1** Brit. an official who enforces fishing laws. **2** chiefly S. African (in areas with no domestic water supply) a person appointed to collect payment for use of community water facilities.

water-based ■ adj. **1** (of a substance or solution) using or having water as a medium or main ingredient. **2** (of a sporting activity) carried out on water.

water bear ■ n. a minute animal with a short body and four pairs of stubby legs, living in fresh water. [Phylum Tardigrada.]

waterbed ■ n. a bed with a water-filled rubber or plastic mattress.

waterberry ■ n. an evergreen African tree which bears edible oblong purple berries. [*Syzygium cordatum*.]

waterbird ■ n. a bird that frequents water, especially one that habitually wades or swims in fresh water.

water birth ■ n. a birth in which the mother spends the final stages of labour in a birthing pool.

water biscuit ■ n. a thin, crisp unsweetened biscuit made from flour and water.

waterblommetjie /ˈvɑːtəblɒməki/ ■ n. S. African a southern African aquatic plant with edible flower clusters, popular as a vegetable. [*Aponogeton distachyos*.]
– ORIGIN Afrikaans, 'little water flower', from *water* 'water' + *blom* 'flower' + Afrikaans diminutive suffix *-ie*.

water bloom ■ n. another term for BLOOM (in sense 4).

water boatman ■ n. a flat-bodied aquatic bug with hind legs adapted as paddles for swimming. [Family Corixidae.]

water-borne ■ adj. 1 transported by water. 2 (of a disease) communicated or propagated by water.

waterbuck ■ n. a large African antelope occurring near rivers and lakes in the savannah. [*Kobus ellipsiprymnus*.]

water buffalo ■ n. a large black buffalo with heavy swept-back horns, used as a beast of burden throughout the tropics. [*Bubalus bubalus* (domesticated) and *B. arnee* (its wild ancestor).]

water butt ■ n. a large barrel used for catching and storing rainwater.

water cannon ■ n. a device that ejects a powerful jet of water, typically used to disperse a crowd.

water chestnut ■ n. 1 the crisp, white-fleshed tuber of a tropical aquatic sedge, used in oriental cookery. ▶ the sedge which yields this tuber. [*Eleocharis tuberosa*.] 2 (also **water caltrop**) an aquatic plant with small white flowers, producing an edible rounded seed with projecting horns. [*Trapa natans*.]

water clock ■ n. historical a clock that used the flow of water to measure time.

water closet ■ n. dated a flush toilet.

watercolour (US **watercolor**) ■ n. 1 artists' paint made with a water-soluble binder, and thinned with water rather than oil. 2 a picture painted with watercolours. 3 the art of painting with watercolours.
– DERIVATIVES **watercolourist** n.

water cooler ■ n. a dispenser of cooled drinking water, typically used in offices and other places of work.

watercourse ■ n. 1 a brook, stream, or artificially constructed water channel. 2 the bed along which this flows.

watercress ■ n. a cress which grows in running water and whose pungent leaves are used in salad. [*Nasturtium officinale*.]

water cure ■ n. chiefly historical a session of treatment by hydropathy.

water diviner ■ n. a person who searches for underground water by using a dowsing rod.

watered silk ■ n. silk that been treated in such a way as to give it a wavy lustrous finish.

waterfall ■ n. a cascade of water falling from a height, formed when a river or stream flows over a precipice or steep incline.

water flea ■ n. another term for DAPHNIA.

waterfowl ■ pl. n. ducks, geese, or other large aquatic birds, especially when regarded as game.

waterfront ■ n. a part of a town or city alongside a body of water.

water gas ■ n. a fuel gas consisting mainly of carbon monoxide and hydrogen, made by passing steam over incandescent coke.

water glass ■ n. a solution of sodium or potassium silicate which solidifies on exposure to air, used for preserving eggs and hardening artificial stone.

water hammer ■ n. a knocking noise in a water pipe that occurs when a tap is turned off briskly.

waterhole ■ n. a depression in which water collects, typically one at which animals drink.

water hyacinth ■ n. a free-floating tropical American water plant, widely introduced as an ornamental and in some places a serious weed of waterways. [*Eichhornia crassipes*.]

1345 **water-repellent**

water ice ■ n. a frozen dessert consisting of fruit juice or purée in a sugar syrup.

watering can ■ n. a portable water container with a long spout and a detachable perforated cap, used for watering plants.

watering hole ■ n. 1 a waterhole from which animals regularly drink. 2 informal a pub or bar.

watering place ■ n. 1 a place where fresh water can be obtained; a watering hole. 2 a spa or seaside resort.

water jacket ■ n. a casing containing water placed around something to protect it from extremes of temperature.
– DERIVATIVES **water-jacketed** adj.

water jump ■ n. a water-filled ditch or pool over which an athlete or horse must jump in a steeplechase or similar event.

water level ■ n. 1 the height reached by a body of water. 2 another term for WATER TABLE.

water lily ■ n. an ornamental aquatic plant with large round floating leaves and large, typically cup-shaped, floating flowers. [Family Nymphaeaceae: many species.]

waterline ■ n. 1 the level normally reached by the water on the side of a ship. 2 a line on a shore, riverbank, etc. marking the level reached by the sea or a river.

waterlogged ■ adj. saturated with or full of water.
– ORIGIN C18: from *waterlog* 'make (a ship) unmanageable by flooding', from WATER + LOG¹.

Waterloo /ˌwɔːtəˈluː/ ■ n. (usu. **meet one's Waterloo**) a decisive defeat or failure.
– ORIGIN *Waterloo*, a village in what is now Belgium, site of a battle in 1815 in which Napoleon was finally defeated.

water main ■ n. the main pipe in a water supply system.

waterman ■ n. (pl. **-men**) a boatman.

watermark ■ n. a faint design made in some paper during manufacture that is visible when held against the light and typically identifies the maker. ■ v. mark with such a design.

water meadow ■ n. a meadow that is periodically flooded by a stream or river.

water measurer ■ n. a long, thin aquatic bug which walks slowly on the surface film of water. [Genus *Hydrometra*: several species.]

watermelon ■ n. the large melon-like fruit of an African plant (*Citrullus lanatus*), with smooth green skin, red pulp, and watery juice.

watermill ■ n. a mill worked by a waterwheel.

water moccasin ■ n. another term for COTTONMOUTH.

water nymph ■ n. (in folklore and classical mythology) a nymph inhabiting or presiding over water, especially a naiad or nereid.

water of crystallization ■ n. Chemistry water molecules forming an essential part of the crystal structure of some compounds.

water pipe ■ n. a pipe for smoking tobacco, cannabis, etc., that draws the smoke along a tube through water to cool it.

water pistol ■ n. a toy pistol that shoots a jet of water.

waterplane ■ n. the horizontal plane which passes through a floating ship on a level with the waterline.

water polo ■ n. a seven-a-side game played by swimmers in a pool, with a ball like a football that is thrown into the opponents' net.

water power ■ n. power that is derived from the weight or motion of water, used as a force to drive machinery.
– DERIVATIVES **water-powered** adj.

waterproof ■ adj. impervious to water. ■ n. a waterproof garment. ■ v. make waterproof.
– DERIVATIVES **waterproofer** n. **waterproofness** n.

water rat ■ n. 1 a large semiaquatic rat-like rodent. [*Dasymys incomtus* (Africa) and other species.] 2 Brit. another term for WATER VOLE.

water-repellent ■ adj. having or denoting a finish or coating that is not easily penetrated by water.

water-resistant ■ adj. able to resist the penetration of water to some degree but not entirely.
– DERIVATIVES **water-resistance** n.

water scorpion ■ n. a predatory water bug with grasping forelegs. [Family Nepidae.]

watershed ■ n. **1** an area or ridge of land that separates waters flowing to different rivers, basins, or seas. **2** an event or period marking a turning point in a state of affairs.
– ORIGIN C19: from WATER + shed in the sense 'ridge of high ground' (rel. to SHED²), suggested by German *Wasserscheide*.

water shoot ■ n. a vigorous but unproductive shoot from the trunk, main branch, or root of a tree.

waterside ■ n. the area adjoining a sea, lake, or river.

waterski ■ n. (pl. **-skis**) each of a pair of skis enabling the wearer to skim the surface of the water when towed by a motor boat. ■ v. travel on waterskis.
– DERIVATIVES **waterskier** n.

water slide ■ n. a slide into a swimming pool, typically flowing with water and incorporating a number of twists and turns.

water softener ■ n. a device or substance that softens hard water by removing certain minerals.

water splash ■ n. a water-filled dip in a road.

water sports ■ pl. n. sports that are carried out on water, such as waterskiing and windsurfing.

waterspout ■ n. a rotating column of water and spray formed by a whirlwind occurring over the sea or other body of water.

water strider ■ n. a slender predatory bug which moves quickly across the surface film of water. [Family Gerridae.]

water table ■ n. the level below which the ground is saturated with water.

watertight ■ adj. **1** closely sealed, fastened, or fitted so as to prevent the passage of water. **2** (of an argument or account) unable to be disputed or questioned.

water torture ■ n. a form of torture in which the victim is exposed to the incessant dripping of water on the head or to the sound of dripping.

water tower ■ n. a tower supporting an elevated water tank, whose height creates the pressure required to distribute the water through a piped system.

water vole ■ n. a large semiaquatic vole which excavates burrows in the banks of rivers. [*Arvicola terrestris* (Europe) and other species.]

waterway ■ n. a river, canal, or other route for travel by water.

waterweed ■ n. vegetation growing in water, typically with inconspicuous flowers.

waterwheel ■ n. a large wheel driven by flowing water, used to work machinery or to raise water to a higher level.

water wings ■ pl. n. inflated floats fixed to the arms of someone learning to swim to give increased buoyancy.

waterworks ■ pl. n. **1** [treated as sing.] an establishment for managing a water supply. **2** informal the shedding of tears: *don't turn on the waterworks*. **3** euphemistic, humorous the urinary system.

watery ■ adj. **1** consisting of, containing, or resembling water. ▶ (of food or drink) thin or tasteless as a result of containing too much water. **2** weak; pale. **3** (of the sky) threatening rain.
– DERIVATIVES **wateriness** n.
– ORIGIN Old English *wæterig* (see WATER).

watsonia ■ n. a South African bulbous plant with sword-shaped leaves and spikes of brightly coloured tubular flowers. [Genus *Watsonia*.]
– ORIGIN C19: named after the Scottish naturalist William Watson (1715–87).

watt (abbrev.: **W**) ■ n. the SI unit of power, equivalent to one joule per second, corresponding to the rate of energy in an electric circuit where the potential difference is one volt and the current one ampere.
– ORIGIN C19: named after the Scottish engineer James Watt.

wattage ■ n. an amount of electrical power expressed in watts. ▶ the operating power of an electrical appliance expressed in watts.

watt-hour ■ n. a measure of electrical energy equivalent to a power consumption of one watt for one hour.

wattle¹ /ˈwɒt(ə)l/ ■ n. **1** a material for making fences, walls, etc., consisting of rods or stakes interlaced with twigs or branches. **2** any of several Australian acacias with pliant branches and cream, yellow, or golden flowers. [Genus *Acacia*: many species.] ■ v. make, enclose, or fill up with wattle.
– ORIGIN Old English *watul*.

wattle² /ˈwɒt(ə)l/ ■ n. a coloured fleshy lobe hanging from the head or neck of the turkey and some other birds.
– DERIVATIVES **wattled** adj.
– ORIGIN C16.

wattle and daub ■ n. a material formerly or traditionally used in building walls, consisting of wattle covered with mud or clay.

wattled crane ■ n. a large grey and white African crane with distinctive white wattles hanging from the base of the bill. [*Bugeranus carunculatus*.]

wattmeter ■ n. a meter for measuring electric power in watts.

Watusi /wəˈtuːsi/ (also **Watutsi** /wəˈtʊtsi/) ■ n. **1** [treated as pl.] the Tutsi people collectively (now dated in English use). **2** an energetic dance popular in the 1960s.
– ORIGIN a local name, from the pl. prefix *wa-* + TUTSI.

wave ■ v. **1** move one's hand to and fro in greeting or as a signal. ▶ move (one's hand or arm, or something held in one's hand) to and fro. ▶ (**wave someone/thing down**) wave one's hand to stop a driver or vehicle. **2** move to and fro with a swaying motion while remaining fixed to one point. **3** style (hair) so that it curls slightly. ▶ (of hair) grow with a slight curl. **4** (**wave something aside**) dismiss something as unnecessary or irrelevant. ■ n. **1** a ridge of water curling into an arched form and breaking on the shore or between two depressions in open water. ▶ (**the waves**) poetic/literary the sea. **2** a sudden occurrence of or increase in a specified phenomenon or emotion. **3** a gesture or signal made by waving one's hand. **4** a slightly curling lock of hair. ▶ a tendency to curl in a person's hair. **5** Physics a periodic disturbance of the particles of a substance which may be propagated without net movement of the particles, as in the passage of undulating motion or sound. ▶ a single curve in the course of this motion. ▶ a similar variation of an electromagnetic field in the propagation of light or other radiation.
– PHRASES **make waves** informal **1** create a significant impression. **2** cause trouble.
– DERIVATIVES **waveless** adj.
– ORIGIN Old English *wafian* (v.), from the Germanic base of WAVER; noun is an alteration of Middle English *wawe* '(sea) wave'.

waveband ■ n. a range of wavelengths between two given limits, used in radio transmission.

wave equation ■ n. Mathematics a differential equation expressing the properties of motion in waves.

waveform ■ n. Physics a curve showing the shape of a wave at a given time.

wavefront ■ n. Physics a surface containing points affected in the same way by a wave at a given time.

wave function ■ n. Physics a function that satisfies a wave equation and describes the properties of a wave.

waveguide ■ n. a metal tube or other device confining and conveying microwaves.

wavelength /ˈweɪvlɛŋθ, -lɛŋkθ/ ■ n. **1** Physics the distance between successive crests of a wave, especially as a distinctive feature of sound, light, radio waves, etc. **2** a person's way of thinking when communicated to another: *we weren't on the same wavelength*.

wavelet ■ n. a small wave.

wave mechanics ■ pl. n. [treated as sing.] Physics a method of analysis of the behaviour of atomic phenomena with particles represented by wave equations.

waver ■ v. **1** move quiveringly; flicker. **2** begin to weaken; falter. **3** be irresolute.

– DERIVATIVES **waverer** n. **wavering** n. & adj. **waveringly** adv. **wavery** adj.
– ORIGIN Middle English: from Old Norse *vafra* 'flicker', of Germanic origin.

wavetable ■ n. Computing a file or memory device containing data that represents a sound.

wave theory ■ n. Physics, historical the theory that light is propagated by a wave motion imparted to the ether by the molecular vibrations of the radiant body.

wave train ■ n. a group of waves of equal or similar wavelengths travelling in the same direction.

wavicle /ˈweɪvɪk(ə)l/ ■ n. Physics an entity having characteristic properties of both waves and particles.
– ORIGIN 1920s: blend of **WAVE** and **PARTICLE**.

wavy ■ adj. (**-ier**, **-iest**) having or consisting of a series of wave-like curves. ▶ Heraldry divided or edged with a line formed of alternating shallow curves.
– DERIVATIVES **wavily** adv. **waviness** n.

wa-wa ■ n. variant spelling of **WAH-WAH**.

wax[1] ■ n. beeswax. ▶ a white translucent material obtained by bleaching and purifying this, used to make candles and polishes. ▶ any similar viscous substance, especially a lipid or hydrocarbon. ■ v. polish or treat with wax. ▶ remove hair from (a part of the body) by applying wax and then peeling it off with the hairs.
– DERIVATIVES **waxer** n. **waxing** n.
– ORIGIN Old English *wæx*, *weax*, of Germanic origin.

wax[2] ■ v. 1 (of the moon) have a progressively larger part of its visible surface illuminated, so that it appears to increase in size. 2 poetic/literary become larger or stronger. 3 speak or write in the specified manner: *they waxed lyrical about the old days.*
– ORIGIN Old English *weaxan*, of Germanic origin.

waxberry ■ n. 1 an evergreen South African shrub with small wax-covered fruits, formerly used to make candles and polish. [*Myrica cordifolia*.] 2 a bayberry or other shrub with berries that have a waxy coating.

waxbill ■ n. a small finch-like songbird, typically brightly coloured and with a red bill that resembles sealing wax in colour. [Family Estrildidae: several species.]

waxcloth (also **waxed cloth**) ■ n. cloth that has been treated with wax or oil to make it waterproof.

waxed jacket ■ n. an outdoor jacket made of a waxed waterproof fabric.

waxed paper ■ n. paper treated with wax to make it waterproof or greaseproof.

waxen ■ adj. 1 having a smooth, pale, translucent surface like that of wax. 2 archaic or poetic/literary made of wax.

wax moth ■ n. a brownish moth whose larvae live damagingly in beehives, feeding on beeswax. [*Galleria mellonella* and other species.]

wax resist ■ n. a process similar to batik used in pottery and printing.

waxwork ■ n. a lifelike dummy modelled in wax. ▶ (**waxworks**) [treated as sing.] an exhibition of waxworks.

waxy ■ adj. (**-ier**, **-iest**) resembling wax in consistency or appearance.
– DERIVATIVES **waxily** adv. **waxiness** n.

way /weɪ/ ■ n. 1 a method, style, or manner of doing something. ▶ the typical manner in which someone behaves or in which something happens. 2 [in place names] a road, track, path, or street. ▶ a route or means taken in order to reach, enter, or leave a place. ▶ the route along which someone or something is travelling or would travel if unobstructed. ▶ a specified direction. ▶ (**one's way**) used with a verb and adverbial phrase to intensify the force of an action or to denote movement or progress. ▶ forward motion or momentum of a ship or boat through water. 3 the distance in space or time between two points. 4 informal a particular area or locality. 5 a particular aspect. 6 a specified condition or state. 7 (**ways**) parts into which something divides or is divided. ■ adv. informal at or to a considerable distance or extent (used before an adverb or preposition for emphasis). ▶ chiefly N. Amer. much. ▶ really (used for emphasis). [shortening of **AWAY**.]
– PHRASES **across** (Brit. also **over**) **the way** nearby, especially on the opposite side of the street. **by the way** incidentally. **by way of 1** via. **2** as a form of. **3** by means of. **come one's way** happen or become available to one. **get** (or **have**) **one's** (**own**) **way** get or do what one wants in spite of opposition. **give way 1** yield. **2** (of a support or structure) be unable to carry a load or withstand a force and collapse or break. **3** allow someone or something to be or go first. **4** (**give way to**) be replaced or superseded by. **go all** (or **the whole**) **way** informal have full sexual intercourse with someone. **go out of one's way** make a special effort to do something. **go one's own way** act independently or as one wishes, especially against contrary advice. **go one's way 1** (of events, circumstances, etc.) be favourable to one. **2** leave. **go someone's way** travel in the same direction as someone. **have it your** (**own**) **way** [in imper.] informal used to indicate grudging acceptance of something said or proposed, even though one is in disagreement with it. **have a way with** have a particular talent for dealing with or ability in. **have a way with one** have a charming and persuasive manner. **have one's way with** humorous have sexual intercourse with (someone) (typically implying that it is against their wishes). **in a way** (or **in some ways** or **in one way**) to a certain extent. **in someone/thing's** (**own**) **way** if regarded from a particular standpoint appropriate to that person or thing. **in no way** not at all. **keep** (or **stay**) **out of someone's way** avoid someone. **lead the way** go first along a route to show someone the way. ▶ be a pioneer. **look the other way** deliberately avoid seeing or noticing someone or something. **one way and another** taking most aspects or considerations into account. **one way or the other** (or **one way and another**) used to indicate that something is the case for any of various reasons. ▶ by some means. ▶ whichever of two given alternatives is the case. **on the** (or **its**) **way** about to arrive or happen. ▶ informal (of a child) conceived but not yet born. **on the** (or **one's**) **way out 1** informal going out of fashion or favour. **2** informal dying. **the other way round** (or **around**; Brit. also **about**) in the opposite position or direction. ▶ the opposite of what is expected or supposed. **out of the way 1** (of a place) remote. **2** dealt with or finished. ▶ (of a person) no longer an obstacle to someone's plans. **3** [usu. with neg.] unusual or exceptional. **way back** (also **way back when**) informal long ago. **the way of the Cross** the journey of Jesus to the place of his crucifixion. **the way of the world** the manner in which people typically behave or things typically happen. **ways and means** the methods and resources for achieving something. **way to go** N. Amer. informal used to express pleasure, approval, or excitement.
– ORIGIN Old English, of Germanic origin, from a base meaning 'move, carry'.

-way ■ suffix equivalent to **-WAYS**.

waybill ■ n. a list of passengers or goods being carried on a vehicle.

wayfarer ■ n. poetic/literary a person who travels on foot.
– DERIVATIVES **wayfaring** n.

waylay ■ v. (past and past part. **waylaid**) intercept in order to attack. ▶ intercept and detain with questions, conversation, etc.
– DERIVATIVES **waylayer** n.

way leave ■ n. a right of way granted by a landowner for payment and typically for purposes such as the erection of telegraph wires.

way-out ■ adj. informal unconventional or avant-garde.

waypoint ■ n. the computer-checked coordinates of each stage of a flight or sea journey. ▶ the GPS coordinates of a specific location on a route.

-ways ■ suffix forming adjectives and adverbs of direction or manner: *lengthways*. Compare with **-WISE**.

wayside ■ n. the edge of a road.
– PHRASES **fall by the wayside** fail to persist in an undertaking. [with biblical allusion to Luke 8:5.]

wayside pulpit ■ n. a board placed outside a place of worship, displaying a religious text or maxim.

way station ■ n. a stopping place on a journey.

wayward ■ adj. self-willed and unpredictable; perverse.
– DERIVATIVES **waywardly** adv. **waywardness** n.
– ORIGIN Middle English: shortening of obsolete *awayward* 'turned away'.

Wb ■ abbrev. weber(s).

WBA ■ abbrev. World Boxing Association.
WBC ■ abbrev. World Boxing Council.
WC ■ abbrev. water closet.
WCC ■ abbrev. World Council of Churches.

we ■ pron. [first person pl.] **1** used by a speaker to refer to himself or herself and one or more other people considered together or regarded as in the same category. ▸ people in general. **2** used in formal contexts for or by a royal person, or by a writer, to refer to himself or herself. **3** you (used condescendingly).
– ORIGIN Old English, of Germanic origin.

weak ■ adj. **1** lacking physical strength and energy. **2** liable to break or give way under pressure. ▸ not convincing or forceful. ▸ not secure, stable, or firmly established. ▸ (of prices or a market) having a downward tendency. **3** lacking power, influence, or ability. **4** lacking intensity. ▸ (of a liquid or solution) heavily diluted. ▸ (of features) not strongly marked. ▸ (of a syllable) unstressed. **5** Grammar denoting a class of verbs in Germanic languages that form the past tense and past participle by addition of a suffix (in English, typically *-ed*).
– PHRASES **the weaker sex** [treated as sing. or pl.] dated women regarded collectively. **weak at the knees** helpless with emotion.
– DERIVATIVES **weakish** adj.
– ORIGIN Old English *wāc* 'pliant, of little worth, not steadfast', reinforced in Middle English by Old Norse *veikr*, from a Germanic base meaning 'yield, give way'.

weaken ■ v. make or become weak.

weak ending ■ n. Prosody an unstressed syllable in a place at the end of a line of verse that normally receives a stress.

weak-kneed ■ adj. **1** weak and shaky from fear or excitement. **2** lacking in resolve or courage.

weakling ■ n. a weak person or animal.

weakly ■ adv. in a weak manner. ■ adj. (-ier, -iest) weak or sickly.
– DERIVATIVES **weakliness** n.

weakness ■ n. **1** the state or condition of being weak. **2** a disadvantage or fault. **3** a person or thing that one is unable to resist. ▸ (**weakness for**) a self-indulgent liking for.

weal¹ /wiːl/ ■ n. a red, swollen mark left on flesh by a blow or pressure. ▸ (also **wheal**) Medicine a temporarily raised and reddened area of skin, usually accompanied by itching. ■ v. mark with a weal.
– ORIGIN C19: var. of WALE, influenced by obsolete *wheal* 'suppurate'.

weal² /wiːl/ ■ n. formal that which is best for someone or something: *guardians of the public weal*.
– ORIGIN Old English *wela* 'wealth, well-being', of West Germanic origin.

wealth ■ n. **1** an abundance of valuable possessions or money. ▸ the state of being rich. **2** an abundance or profusion of something desirable.
– ORIGIN Middle English *welthe*, from WELL¹ or WEAL², on the pattern of *health*.

wealth tax ■ n. a tax levied on personal capital.

wealthy ■ adj. (-ier, -iest) having a great deal of money, resources, or assets; rich.
– DERIVATIVES **wealthily** adv.

wean ■ v. **1** accustom (an infant or other young mammal) to food other than its mother's milk. **2** (often **wean someone off**) make (someone) give up a habit or addiction. **3** (**be weaned on**) be strongly influenced by (something) from an early age.
– ORIGIN Old English, of Germanic origin.

weaner ■ n. a calf, lamb, or pig weaned during the current year.

weanling ■ n. a newly weaned animal.

weapon ■ n. **1** a thing designed or used for inflicting bodily harm or physical damage. **2** a means of gaining an advantage or defending oneself.
– DERIVATIVES **weaponed** adj. **weaponless** adj. **weaponry** n.
– ORIGIN Old English, of Germanic origin.

weapon of mass destruction ■ n. a nuclear, biological, or chemical weapon able to cause widespread devastation and loss of life.

weapons-grade ■ adj. denoting fissile material which is suitable for making nuclear weapons.

wear ■ v. (past **wore**; past part. **worn** /wɔːn/) **1** have on one's body or a part of one's body as clothing, decoration, or protection. **2** exhibit or present (a particular facial expression or appearance). **3** undergo or cause to undergo damage or destruction by friction or use. ▸ form (a hole, path, etc.) in this way. **4** withstand continued use to a specified degree: *the fabric wears well wash after wash*. **5** (**wear off**) lose effectiveness or intensity. **6** (**wear someone/thing down**) overcome someone or something by persistence. **7** (**wear someone/thing out**) exhaust someone or something. ▸ [as adj. **wearing**] mentally or physically tiring. **8** [usu. with neg.] informal tolerate or accept: *the environmental health people wouldn't wear it*. **9** (**wear on**) (of time) pass slowly or tediously. ■ n. **1** the action of wearing or the state of being worn. **2** clothing suitable for a particular purpose or of a particular type: *evening wear*. **3** damage sustained from continuous use. ▸ the capacity for withstanding such damage.
– PHRASES **wear thin** gradually dwindle or be used up.
– DERIVATIVES **wearability** n. **wearable** adj. **wearer** n. **wearingly** adv.
– ORIGIN Old English *werian*, of Germanic origin.

wearisome /ˈwɪərɪs(ə)m/ ■ adj. causing one to feel tired or bored; tiresome or tedious.
– DERIVATIVES **wearisomely** adv. **wearisomeness** n.

weary ■ adj. (-ier, -iest) **1** tired. ▸ causing tiredness. **2** (often **weary of**) reluctant to experience any more of. ■ v. (-ies, -ied) **1** make weary. **2** (**weary of**) grow tired of.
– DERIVATIVES **weariless** adj. **wearily** adv. **weariness** n. **wearying** adj. **wearyingly** adv.
– ORIGIN Old English, of West Germanic origin.

weasel ■ n. **1** a small slender carnivorous mammal of the northern hemisphere, with chestnut fur. [*Mustela nivalis* and other species.] ▸ used in names of other animals of the same family, e.g. African striped weasel (*Poecilogale albinucha*). **2** informal a deceitful or treacherous person. ■ v. (**weaselled**, **weaselling**; US **weaseled**, **weaseling**) **1** achieve through cunning or deceit. **2** behave or talk evasively.
– DERIVATIVES **weaselly** adj.
– ORIGIN Old English, of West Germanic origin.

weasel words ■ pl. n. statements that are intentionally ambiguous or misleading.

weather ■ n. **1** the state of the atmosphere at a place and time as regards temperature, wind, rain, etc. **2** [as modifier] windward. Contrasted with LEE. ■ v. **1** wear away or change in form or appearance by long exposure to the weather. ▸ (of rock or other material) be worn away or altered by such processes. **2** come safely through. **3** (in building) slope or bevel (a surface) to throw off rain. **4** Nautical (of a ship) get to the windward of (a cape). **5** [usu. as noun **weathering**] Falconry allow (a hawk) to spend a period perched in the open air.
– PHRASES **keep a weather eye on** be watchful for developments. **make heavy weather of** informal have unnecessary difficulty in dealing with (a task or problem). **under the weather** informal slightly unwell or depressed.
– ORIGIN Old English, of Germanic origin.

weather balloon ■ n. a balloon equipped with meteorological apparatus which is sent into the atmosphere to provide information about the weather.

weather-beaten ■ adj. damaged, worn, or tanned by exposure to the weather.

weatherboard ■ n. each of a series of horizontal boards nailed to outside walls with edges overlapping to keep out the rain. ■ v. fit with weatherboards.
– DERIVATIVES **weatherboarding** n.

weatherbound ■ adj. prevented by bad weather from travelling or proceeding with a course of action.

weathercock ■ n. a weathervane in the form of a cockerel. ■ v. (of a boat or aircraft) tend to turn to head into the wind.

weatherly ■ adj. Nautical (of a boat) able to sail close to the wind without drifting to leeward.

weatherman (or **weatherwoman**) ■ n. (pl. **-men** or **-women**) a person who broadcasts a description and forecast of weather conditions.

weather station ■ n. an observation post where weather conditions and meteorological data are observed and recorded.

weatherstrip ■ n. a strip of rubber, metal, or other material used to seal the edges of a door or window against rain and wind. ■ v. (**-stripped**, **-stripping**) apply such a strip to.
–DERIVATIVES **weatherstripping** n.

weathervane ■ n. a revolving pointer to show the direction of the wind, typically mounted on top of a building.

weave¹ ■ v. (past **wove**; past part. **woven** or **wove**) 1 form (fabric) by interlacing long threads passing in one direction with others at a right angle to them. ▸ [usu. as noun **weaving**] make fabric in this way, typically with a loom. 2 make (basketwork or a wreath) by interlacing rods or flowers. 3 (**weave something into**) make interconnected elements into (a story). ■ n. a particular style or manner in which fabric is woven.
–ORIGIN Old English *wefan*, of Germanic origin.

weave² ■ v. move from side to side to progress around obstructions.
–ORIGIN C16: prob. from Old Norse *veifa* 'to wave, brandish'.

weaver ■ n. 1 a person who weaves fabric. 2 (also **weaver bird**) a finch-like songbird of tropical Africa and Asia, related to the sparrows and building elaborately woven nests. [Family Ploceidae: numerous species.]

web ■ n. 1 a network of fine threads constructed by a spider from fluid secreted by its spinnerets, used to catch its prey. 2 a complex system of interconnected elements. ▸ (**the Web**) short for WORLD WIDE WEB. 3 a membrane between the toes of a swimming bird or other aquatic animal. 4 a thin flat part connecting thicker or more solid parts in machinery. 5 a roll of paper used in a continuous printing process. ■ v. (**webbed**, **webbing**) cover with or as if with a web.
–ORIGIN Old English *web(b)* 'woven fabric', of Germanic origin.

webbed ■ adj. 1 (of an animal's feet) having the toes connected by a web. ▸ *Medicine* (of fingers or toes) abnormally united by a fold of skin. 2 (of a band of material) made from webbing or similar fabric.

webbing ■ n. strong, closely woven fabric used chiefly for making straps and belts and for supporting the seats of upholstered chairs.

WebCam (also **webcam**) ■ n. trademark a digital camera connected to a computer, enabling the transmission of live or recorded visual images over the Internet. ■ v. (**webcammed**, **webcamming**) send or access images in this way.
–DERIVATIVES **webcamming** n. **webcammed** adj.

webcast ■ n. a live video broadcast of an event transmitted across the Internet.
–DERIVATIVES **webcasting** n.

Weber ■ n. trademark a type of three-legged portable braai, comprising a round enamelled metal bowl with a dome-shaped lid, in which food is cooked over charcoal.

weber /ˈveɪbə/ (abbrev.: **Wb**) ■ n. the SI unit of magnetic flux, sufficient to cause an electromotive force of one volt in a circuit of one turn when generated or removed in one second.
–ORIGIN C19: named after the German physicist Wilhelm Eduard *Weber*.

weblog ■ n. a personal website on which an individual records opinions, links to other sites, etc. on a regular basis.

webmaster ■ n. *Computing* a person who is responsible for a particular server on the World Wide Web.

web offset ■ n. offset printing on continuous paper fed from a reel.

web page ■ n. *Computing* a hypertext document accessible via the World Wide Web.

website ■ n. *Computing* a location connected to the Internet that maintains one or more web pages.

Wed. ■ abbrev. Wednesday.

wed ■ v. (**wedding**; past and past part. **wedded** or **wed**) 1 *formal or poetic/literary* marry. ▸ give or join in marriage. ▸ [as adj. **wedded**] of or concerning marriage. 2 combine (two desirable factors or qualities). 3 (**be wedded to**) be entirely devoted to (an activity, belief, etc.).
–ORIGIN Old English *weddian*, from the Germanic base of Scots *wed* 'a pledge'.

we'd ■ contr. 1 we had. 2 we should or we would.

wedding ■ n. a marriage ceremony, especially one including the associated celebrations.

wedding band ■ n. chiefly N. Amer. a wedding ring.

wedding breakfast ■ n. a celebratory meal eaten just after a wedding (at any time of day) by the couple and their guests.

wedding cake ■ n. 1 a rich iced cake, typically in two or more tiers, served at a wedding reception. 2 [as modifier] denoting a very ornate building.

wedding march ■ n. a piece of march music played at the entrance of the bride or the exit of the couple at a wedding.

wedding ring ■ n. a ring worn by a married person, given to them by their spouse at their wedding.

wedge ■ n. 1 a piece of wood, metal, etc. with a thick end that tapers to a thin edge, that is driven between two objects or parts of an object to secure or separate them. 2 a wedge-shaped thing or piece. ▸ a golf club with a low, angled face for maximum loft. 3 a shoe with a fairly high heel forming a solid block with the sole. ■ v. 1 fix in position using a wedge. 2 force into a narrow space.
–PHRASES **drive a wedge between** cause a breach between. **the thin end of the wedge** *informal* an action of little intrinsic importance that is likely to lead to more serious developments.
–ORIGIN Old English, of Germanic origin.

wedge-shaped ■ adj. 1 (of a solid object) tapering to a thin edge at one end. 2 (of a plane shape) V-shaped.

Wedgwood /ˈwedʒwʊd/ ■ n. 1 trademark ceramic ware made by the English potter Josiah *Wedgwood* (1730–95) and his successors, especially a kind of powder-blue stoneware with white embossed cameos. 2 a powder-blue colour characteristic of this stoneware.

wedlock ■ n. the state of being married.
–PHRASES **born in** (or **out of**) **wedlock** born of married (or unmarried) parents.
–ORIGIN Old English *wedlāc* 'marriage vow', from *wed* 'pledge' + the suffix *-lāc* (denoting action).

Wednesday ■ n. the day of the week before Thursday and following Tuesday. ■ adv. on Wednesday. ▸ (**Wednesdays**) on Wednesdays; each Wednesday.
–ORIGIN Old English *Wōdnesdæg*, named after the Germanic god *Odin*; translation of late Latin *Mercurii dies*.

Weds. ■ abbrev. Wednesday.

wee¹ ■ adj. (**weer**, **weest**) chiefly Scottish little.
–ORIGIN Middle English (orig. a noun use in Scots, usu. as *a little wee* 'a little bit'): from Old English *wēg(e)*.

wee² *informal* ■ n. an act of urinating. ▸ urine. ■ v. (**wees**, **weed**) urinate.
–ORIGIN 1930s: imitative.

weed ■ n. 1 a wild plant growing where it is not wanted and in competition with cultivated plants. 2 *informal* cannabis. ▸ (**the weed**) *informal* tobacco. 3 *informal* a weak or skinny person. ■ v. 1 remove weeds from. 2 (**weed something out**) remove inferior or unwanted items or members from something.
–DERIVATIVES **weeder** n. **weedless** adj.
–ORIGIN Old English *wēod* (n.), *wēodian* (v.).

Weed Eater ■ n. trademark a motorized grass trimmer with a rapidly rotating nylon cutting cord.

weedkiller ■ n. a substance used to destroy weeds.

weeds ■ pl. n. short for WIDOW'S WEEDS.

weedy ■ adj. (**-ier**, **-iest**) 1 containing or covered with many weeds. 2 *informal* thin and puny.
–DERIVATIVES **weediness** n.

week ■ n. 1 a period of seven days. ▸ the period of seven

weekday

days generally reckoned from and to midnight on Saturday night. ▸ (preceded by a specified day) a week after (that day). **2** the five days from Monday to Friday, or the time spent working during this period.
– ORIGIN Old English *wice*, of Germanic origin, from a base prob. meaning 'sequence, series'.

weekday ■ n. a day of the week other than Sunday or Saturday.

weekend ■ n. Saturday and Sunday. ■ v. informal spend a weekend somewhere.

weekly ■ adj. done, produced, or occurring once a week. ■ adv. once a week. ■ n. (pl. **-ies**) a newspaper or periodical issued every week.

ween ■ v. archaic think or suppose.
– ORIGIN Old English, of Germanic origin.

weenie ■ n. **1** informal a stupid or contemptible person. **2** another term for WIENER.

weeny ■ adj. (**-ier**, **-iest**) informal tiny.
– ORIGIN C18: from WEE[1], on the pattern of *tiny*; cf. TEENY.

weep ■ v. (past and past part. **wept**) **1** shed tears. ▸ archaic mourn for; shed tears over. **2** exude liquid. **3** [as adj. **weeping**] used in names of tree and shrub varieties with drooping branches, e.g. weeping cherry. ■ n. a fit or spell of shedding tears.
– DERIVATIVES **weeping** n. & adj. **weepingly** adv.
– ORIGIN Old English, of Germanic origin, prob. imitative.

weeper ■ n. **1** a person who weeps. **2** (**weepers**) historical mourning clothes, in particular a man's crape hatband or a widow's black crape veil and white cuffs.

weepie (also **weepy**) ■ n. (pl. **-ies**) informal a sentimental or emotional film, novel, or song.

weeping willow ■ n. a Eurasian willow with trailing branches and foliage reaching down to the ground. [*Salix × chrysocoma* and related species and hybrids.]

weepy ■ adj. (**-ier**, **-iest**) informal tearful; inclined to weep. ▸ sentimental. ■ n. variant spelling of WEEPIE.
– DERIVATIVES **weepily** adv. **weepiness** n.

weevil /ˈwiːv(ə)l, ˈwiːvɪl/ ■ n. a small beetle with an elongated snout, several kinds of which are pests of crops or stored foodstuffs. [Curculionidae and other families: many species.]
– DERIVATIVES **weevily** adj.
– ORIGIN Old English *wifel* 'beetle', from a Germanic base meaning 'move briskly'.

wee-wee informal ■ n. a child's word for urine. ■ v. urinate.
– ORIGIN 1930s: imitative.

w.e.f. ■ abbrev. with effect from.

weft ■ n. (in weaving) the crosswise threads that are passed over and under the warp threads on a loom to make cloth.
– ORIGIN Old English, of Germanic origin.

Wehrmacht /ˈvɛːrmɑːxt/ ■ n. the German armed forces from 1921 to 1945.
– ORIGIN German, 'defensive force'.

weigela /waɪˈdʒiːlə/ ■ n. an ornamental Asian flowering shrub with pink, red, or yellow flowers. [*Weigela florida* and related species.]
– ORIGIN C19: named after the German physician Christian E. *Weigel*.

weigh[1] ■ v. **1** find out how heavy (someone or something) is. ▸ have a specified weight. ▸ balance in the hands to assess the weight of. ▸ (**weigh something out**) measure and take out a portion of a particular weight. ▸ (**weigh someone down**) be heavy and cumbersome or oppressive to someone. ▸ (**weigh on**) be depressing or burdensome to. ▸ (**weigh in**) (of a boxer or jockey) be officially weighed before or after a contest. ▸ (**weigh out**) (of a jockey) be weighed before a race. **2** (often **weigh something up/ against**) assess the nature or importance of. ▸ (often **weigh against**) influence a decision or action. **3** (**weigh in**) informal make a forceful contribution to a competition or argument. ▸ (**weigh into**) join in or attack forcefully or enthusiastically.
– PHRASES **weigh anchor** Nautical take up the anchor when ready to sail.
– DERIVATIVES **weighable** adj. **weigher** n.

– ORIGIN Old English *wegan*, of Germanic origin.

weigh[2] ■ n. (in phr. **under weigh**) Nautical another way of saying under way (see UNDER).
– ORIGIN C18: from an erroneous association with *weigh anchor* (see WEIGH[1]).

weighbridge ■ n. a machine for weighing vehicles, set into the ground to be driven on to.

weigh-in ■ n. an official weighing, e.g. of boxers before a fight.

weight ■ n. **1** a body's relative mass or the quantity of matter contained by it, giving rise to a downward force; heaviness. ▸ Physics the force exerted on the mass of a body by a gravitational field. ▸ the quality of being heavy. ▸ a unit or system of units used for expressing how much something weighs. **2** a piece of metal known to weigh a definite amount and used on scales to determine how heavy something is. ▸ a heavy object, especially one being lifted or carried or used as a counterpoise in a mechanism. ▸ (**weights**) heavy blocks or discs used in weightlifting or weight training. **3** the surface density of cloth, used as a measure of its quality. **4** ability to influence decisions or actions. ▸ the importance attached to something. **5** a feeling of oppression or pressure: *a weight on one's mind*. ■ v. **1** hold (something) down by placing a heavy object on top of it. **2** attach importance or value to. ▸ plan or arrange so as to give someone or something an advantage. **3** assign a handicap weight to (a horse).
– PHRASES **be worth one's weight in gold** be exceedingly useful or helpful. **throw one's weight about** (or **around**) informal be unpleasantly self-assertive.
– ORIGIN Old English (*ge*)*wiht*, *of* Germanic origin; form influenced by WEIGH[1].

weighting ■ n. **1** allowance or adjustment made to take account of special circumstances or compensate for a distorting factor. **2** additional wages or salary paid to allow for a higher cost of living in a particular area.

weightless ■ adj. (of a body, especially in an orbiting spacecraft) not apparently acted on by gravity.
– DERIVATIVES **weightlessly** adv. **weightlessness** n.

weightlifting ■ n. the sport or activity of lifting barbells or other heavy weights.
– DERIVATIVES **weightlifter** n.

weight training ■ n. physical training that involves lifting weights.

weight-watcher ■ n. a person who is on a diet in order to lose weight.
– DERIVATIVES **weight-watching** n. & adj.

weighty ■ adj. (**-ier**, **-iest**) **1** weighing a great deal; heavy. **2** very serious and important. ▸ very influential.
– DERIVATIVES **weightily** adv. **weightiness** n.

Weimaraner /ˈvaɪməˌrɑːnə, ˈwaɪ-/ ■ n. a dog of a thin-coated, typically grey breed of pointer used as a gun dog.
– ORIGIN 1940s: from German, from *Weimar* in Germany, where the breed was developed.

weir ■ n. a low dam built across a river to raise the level of water upstream or regulate its flow.
– ORIGIN Old English *wer*, from *werian* 'dam up'.

weird ■ adj. **1** suggesting something supernatural; uncanny. ▸ informal very strange; bizarre. **2** archaic connected with fate. ■ n. archaic, chiefly Scottish a person's destiny. ■ v. (**weird someone out**) N. Amer. informal induce a sense of disbelief or alienation in someone.
– DERIVATIVES **weirdly** adv. **weirdness** n.

> **HISTORY**
> In Old English *weird*, then spelled *wyrd*, was a noun meaning 'destiny, fate', or, in the plural, 'the Fates' (the three goddesses supposed to determine the course of human life); it also meant 'an event or occurrence'. The adjective, first recorded in Middle English, meant 'having the power to control destiny', and was used especially in the phrase the Weird Sisters (originally meaning the Fates, later applied to the witches in Shakespeare's *Macbeth*. The modern sense 'uncanny, strange' did not develop until the early 19th century.

weirdo ■ n. (pl. **-os**) informal a strange or eccentric person.

welch /wɛltʃ/ ■ v. variant spelling of WELSH.

welcome ■ n. an instance or manner of greeting

someone. ■ exclam. a pleased or approving reaction. used to greet someone in a glad or friendly way. ■ v. **1** greet (someone arriving) in a glad, polite, or friendly way. **2** be glad to receive or hear of: *the decision was widely welcomed.* ■ adj. **1** (of a guest or new arrival) gladly received. **2** very pleasing because much needed or desired. **3** allowed or invited to do a specified thing: *you are welcome to join in.* ▸ (**welcome to**) used to indicate relief at relinquishing something to another: *you're welcome to it!*
– DERIVATIVES **welcomely** adv. **welcomeness** n. **welcomer** n. **welcoming** n. & adj. **welcomingly** adv.
– ORIGIN Old English *wilcuma* 'a person whose coming is pleasing', *wilcumian* (v.), from *wil-* 'desire, pleasure' + *cuman* 'come'; change to *wel-* influenced by Old French *bien venu* or Old Norse *velkominn*.

weld ■ v. **1** join together (metal parts) by heating the surfaces to the point of melting and pressing or hammering them together. ▸ forge (an article) by such means. **2** cause to combine and form a whole. ■ n. a welded joint.
– DERIVATIVES **weldability** n. **weldable** adj. **welder** n.
– ORIGIN C16: alteration of WELL² in the obsolete sense 'melt or weld (heated metal)'.

welfare ■ n. **1** the health, happiness, and fortunes of a person or group. **2** action or procedure designed to promote the basic physical and material well-being of people in need. ▸ financial support given for this purpose.
– ORIGIN Middle English: from WELL¹ + FARE.

welfare state ■ n. a system whereby the state undertakes to protect the health and well-being of its citizens, especially those in need, by means of grants, pensions, and other benefits.

welfarism ■ n. the principles or policies associated with a welfare state.
– DERIVATIVES **welfarist** n. & adj.

welkin /ˈwɛlkɪn/ ■ n. poetic/literary the sky or heaven.
– ORIGIN Old English *wolcen* 'cloud, sky', of West Germanic origin.

well¹ ■ adv. (**better**, **best**) **1** in a good or satisfactory way. ▸ in a condition of prosperity or comfort. ▸ archaic luckily; opportunely: *hail fellow, well met.* **2** in a thorough manner. ▸ to a great extent or degree; very much. ▸ Brit. informal very; extremely: *he was well out of order.* **3** very probably; in all likelihood. ▸ without difficulty. ▸ with good reason. ■ adj. (**better**, **best**) **1** in good health; free or recovered from illness. ▸ in a satisfactory state or position. **2** sensible; advisable. ■ exclam. used to express surprise, anger, resignation, etc., or when pausing in speech.
– PHRASES **as well 1** in addition; too. **2** (**as well**) or **just as well** with equal reason or an equally good result. ▸ sensible, appropriate, or desirable. **be well out of** Brit. informal be fortunate to be no longer involved in. **be well up on** (or **in**) know a great deal about. **leave** (or **let**) **well** (N. Amer. **enough**) **alone** refrain from interfering with or trying to improve something. **very well** used to express agreement or understanding. **well and truly** completely.
– DERIVATIVES **wellness** n.
– ORIGIN Old English *well(l)*, of Germanic origin.

USAGE
The adverb **well** is often used in combination with past participles to form adjectival compounds. The general stylistic principle for hyphenation is that if the adjectival compound is placed attributively (i.e. before the noun), it should be hyphenated (*a well-intentioned remark*) but that if it is placed predicatively (i.e. standing alone after the verb), it should not be hyphenated (*her remarks were well intentioned*). In this dictionary, the unhyphenated form is generally the only one given.

well² ■ n. **1** a shaft sunk into the ground to obtain water, oil, or gas. ▸ a depression made to hold liquid. **2** a plentiful source or supply: *a deep well of sympathy.* **3** an enclosed space in the middle of a building, giving room for stairs or a lift or allowing light or ventilation. **4** Physics a region of minimum potential. ■ v. (often **well up**) (of a liquid) rise up to the surface and spill or be about to spill. ▸ (of an emotion) arise and become more intense.
– ORIGIN Old English *wella*, of Germanic origin.

we'll ■ contr. we shall; we will.

well advised ■ adj. sensible; wise.

well worn

well appointed ■ adj. (of a building or room) having a high standard of equipment or furnishing.

well-being ■ n. the state of being comfortable, healthy, or happy.

well covered ■ adj. Brit. informal slightly plump.

well deck ■ n. an open space on the main deck of a ship, lying at a lower level between the forecastle and poop.

well disposed ■ adj. having a positive, sympathetic, or friendly attitude.

well done ■ adj. **1** carried out successfully or satisfactorily. **2** (of food) thoroughly cooked. ■ exclam. used to express congratulation or approval.

well earned ■ adj. fully merited or deserved.

well endowed ■ adj. having plentiful supplies of a resource. ▸ informal, humorous (of a man) having large genitals. ▸ informal, humorous (of a woman) large-breasted.

well favoured (US **well favored**) ■ adj. having special advantages, especially good looks.

well head ■ n. **1** the place where a spring comes out of the ground. **2** the structure over a well.

well-heeled ■ adj. informal wealthy.

well hung ■ adj. informal, humorous (of a man) having large genitals.

wellie ■ n. variant spelling of WELLY.

wellington (also **wellington boot**) ■ n. chiefly Brit. a knee-length waterproof rubber or plastic boot.
– ORIGIN C19: named after the British soldier and Prime Minister the 1st Duke of *Wellington*.

well knit ■ adj. (of a person) strongly and compactly built.

well known ■ adj. known widely or thoroughly.

well made ■ adj. **1** strongly or skilfully constructed. **2** (of a person) having a sturdy build.

well meaning (also **well meant**) ■ adj. having good intentions but not necessarily the desired effect.

well-nigh ■ adv. chiefly poetic/literary almost.

well off ■ adj. wealthy. ▸ in a favourable situation or circumstances.

well oiled ■ adj. **1** operating smoothly. **2** informal drunk.

well pleased ■ adj. highly gratified or satisfied.

well preserved ■ adj. (of an old person) showing little sign of ageing.

well rounded ■ adj. **1** having a pleasing curved shape. ▸ (of a person) plump. **2** having a mature personality and varied interests.

well set ■ adj. firmly established; solidly fixed or arranged. ▸ (also **well set-up**) (of a person) strongly built.

well spent ■ adj. (of money or time) usefully or profitably expended.

well spoken ■ adj. speaking in an educated and refined manner.

wellspring ■ n. poetic/literary term for WELL HEAD (in sense 1).

well thumbed ■ adj. (of a book) having been read often and bearing marks of frequent handling.

well-to-do ■ adj. wealthy; prosperous.

well travelled ■ adj. **1** (of a person) having travelled widely. **2** (of a route) much frequented by travellers.

well tried ■ adj. having been used often and therefore known to be reliable.

well trodden ■ adj. much frequented by travellers.

well turned ■ adj. **1** (of a phrase or compliment) elegantly expressed. **2** (of a woman's ankle or leg) attractively shaped.

well upholstered ■ adj. humorous (of a person) fat.

well-wisher ■ n. a person who desires happiness or success for another, or who expresses such a desire.

well worn ■ adj. showing the signs of extensive use or wear. ▸ (of a phrase or idea) used or repeated so often that it no longer has interest or significance.

welly (also **wellie**) ▪ n. (pl. **-ies**) informal **1** short for WELLINGTON. **2** Brit. power or vigour.

wels /wɛls, veIs/ ▪ n. a very large freshwater catfish found from central Europe to central Asia. [*Silurus glanis*.]
– ORIGIN C19: from German *Wels*.

Welsh ▪ n. the Celtic language of Wales. ▪ adj. of or relating to Wales, its people, or their language.
– DERIVATIVES **Welshman** n. **Welshness** n. **Welshwoman** n.
– ORIGIN Old English *Welisc, Wælisc*, from a Germanic word meaning 'foreigner', from Latin *Volcae*, the name of a Celtic people.

welsh (also **welch**) ▪ v. (**welsh on**) fail to honour (a debt or obligation).
– ORIGIN C19.

Welsh dresser ▪ n. a piece of wooden furniture with cupboards and drawers in the lower part and open shelves in the upper part.

Welsh harp ▪ n. another term for TRIPLE HARP.

Welsh onion ▪ n. an Asian onion that forms clusters of slender bulbs which resemble spring onions. [*Allium fistulosum.*]
– ORIGIN C18: *Welsh* from German *welsch* 'foreign'.

Welsh rarebit (also **Welsh rabbit**) ▪ n. another term for RAREBIT.

welt ▪ n. **1** a leather rim round the edge of the upper of a shoe, to which the sole is attached. ▸ a ribbed, reinforced, or decorative border of a garment or pocket. **2** a weal. ▪ v. provide with a welt.
– ORIGIN Middle English.

Weltanschauung /ˈvɛltˌanʃaʊʊŋ/ ▪ n. (pl. **Weltanschauungen** /-(ə)n/) a particular philosophy or view of life; a world view.
– ORIGIN German, from *Welt* 'world' + *Anschauung* 'perception'.

welter ▪ v. poetic/literary **1** move in a turbulent fashion. **2** lie steeped in blood. ▪ n. a large number of items in no order; a confused mass. ▸ a state of general disorder.
– ORIGIN Middle English: from Middle Dutch, Middle Low German *welteren*.

welterweight ▪ n. a weight in boxing and other sports intermediate between lightweight and middleweight.
– ORIGIN C19.

Weltschmerz /ˈvɛltˌʃmɛːts/ ▪ n. a feeling of melancholy and world-weariness.
– ORIGIN German, from *Welt* 'world' + *Schmerz* 'pain'.

welwitschia /wɛlˈwɪtʃɪə/ ▪ n. a desert plant with a long taproot and two large leathery leaves which lie flat on the ground, native to southern Africa. [*Welwitschia mirabilis*.]
– ORIGIN named after the Slovenian botanist Dr Friedrich *Welwitsch* (1806–72).

wen ▪ n. a boil or other swelling or growth on the skin, especially a sebaceous cyst.
– ORIGIN Old English *wen(n)*; cf. Low German *wehne* 'tumour, wart'.

wench /wɛn(t)ʃ/ ▪ n. **1** archaic or humorous a girl or young woman. **2** archaic a prostitute. ▪ v. archaic (of a man) consort with prostitutes.
– ORIGIN Middle English: abbrev. of obsolete *wenchel* 'child, servant, prostitute'.

wend ▪ v. (**wend one's way**) go slowly or by an indirect route.
– ORIGIN Old English *wendan* 'to turn, depart', of Germanic origin.

Wendy house ▪ n. **1** a toy house large enough for children to play in. **2** S. African a small prefabricated wooden building, used as living accommodation or as a storage shed.
– ORIGIN named after the house built around *Wendy* in J. M. Barrie's play *Peter Pan*.

Wensleydale /ˈwɛnzlɪdeɪl/ ▪ n. **1** a type of white cheese with a crumbly texture. **2** a sheep of a breed with long wool.
– ORIGIN named after *Wensleydale* in Yorkshire, England.

went past of GO[1].

wept past and past participle of WEEP.

were second person singular past, plural past, and past subjunctive of BE.

we're ▪ contr. we are.

weren't ▪ contr. were not.

werewolf /ˈwɛːwʊlf, ˈwɪə-, ˈwəː-/ ▪ n. (pl. **werewolves**) (in folklore) a person who periodically changes into a wolf, typically when there is a full moon.
– ORIGIN Old English *werewulf*; first element usu. identified with Old English *wer* 'man'.

wert /wəːt/ archaic second person singular past of BE.

Wesak /ˈvɛsak/ ▪ n. variant spelling of VESAK.

Wesleyan ▪ adj. relating to or denoting the teachings of the English preacher John Wesley (1703–91) or the main branch of the Methodist Church which he founded. ▪ n. a follower of Wesley or adherent of the main Methodist tradition.
– DERIVATIVES **Wesleyanism** n.

west ▪ n. (usu. **the west**) **1** the direction towards the point of the horizon where the sun sets at the equinoxes, on the left-hand side of a person facing north. **2** the west of a country, region, or town. ▸ (**the West**) Europe and North America seen in contrast to other civilizations. ▸ (**the West**) historical the non-Communist states of Europe and North America. ▪ adj. **1** lying towards, near, or facing the west. **2** (of a wind) blowing from the west. ▪ adv. to or towards the west.
– PHRASES **go west** Brit. informal be killed or lost.
– DERIVATIVES **westbound** adj. & adv.
– ORIGIN Old English, of Germanic origin.

westering ▪ adj. poetic/literary (especially of the sun) nearing the west.
– ORIGIN C17: from the literary verb *wester*, from WEST.

westerly ▪ adj. & adv. **1** in a westward position or direction. **2** (of a wind) blowing from the west. ▪ n. a wind blowing from the west. ▸ (**westerlies**) the belt of prevailing westerly winds in medium latitudes in the southern hemisphere.

western ▪ adj. **1** situated in, directed towards, or facing the west. **2** (usu. **Western**) living in, coming from, or characteristic of the west, in particular Europe and North America. ▪ n. a film or novel about cowboys in western North America.
– DERIVATIVES **westernmost** adj.

Western blot ▪ n. Biology an adaptation of the Southern blot procedure, used to identify specific amino-acid sequences in proteins.
– ORIGIN suggested by SOUTHERN BLOT.

Western Church ▪ n. the part of the Christian Church originating in the Western Roman Empire, including the Roman Catholic, Anglican, Lutheran, and Reformed Churches.

westerner ▪ n. a native or inhabitant of the west of a particular region or country.

westernize (also **-ise**) ▪ v. bring or come under the influence of the cultural, economic, or political systems of Europe and North America.
– DERIVATIVES **westernization** (also **-isation**) n.

Western saddle ▪ n. a saddle with a deep seat, high pommel and cantle, and broad stirrups.

western swing ▪ n. a style of country music influenced by jazz, popular in the 1930s.

West Germanic ▪ n. the western group of Germanic languages, comprising High and Low German, Dutch, Frisian, and English. ▪ adj. of or relating to West Germanic.

West Highland terrier ▪ n. a dog of a small, short-legged breed of terrier with a white coat and erect ears and tail.

West Indian ▪ n. a native or national of the West Indies, or a person of West Indian descent. ▪ adj. of or relating to the West Indies or its people.

westing ▪ n. **1** distance travelled or measured westward, especially at sea. **2** a figure or line representing westward distance on a map.

west-north-west ▪ n. the direction or compass point midway between west and north-west.

Westphalian /wɛstˈfeɪlɪən/ ■ n. a native or inhabitant of Westphalia, a former province of NW Germany. ■ adj. of or relating to Westphalia.

West Saxon ■ n. **1** a native or inhabitant of the Anglo-Saxon kingdom of Wessex. **2** the dialect of Old English used by the West Saxons.

west-south-west ■ n. the direction or compass point midway between west and south-west.

westward ■ adj. towards the west. ■ adv. (also **westwards**) in a westerly direction. ■ n. (**the westward**) a direction or region towards the west.
– DERIVATIVES **westwardly** adj. & adv.

wet ■ adj. (**wetter**, **wettest**) **1** covered or saturated with liquid. ▸ (of the weather) rainy. ▸ involving the use of water or liquid. **2** (of paint, ink, etc.) not yet having dried or hardened. **3** informal lacking forcefulness or strength of character; feeble. **4** informal (of an area) allowing the free sale of alcoholic drink. ■ v. (**wetting**; past and past part. **wet** or **wetted**) cover or touch with liquid. ▸ (especially of a baby or young child) urinate in or on. ▸ (**wet oneself**) urinate involuntarily. ■ n. **1** liquid that makes something damp. ▸ (**the wet**) rainy weather. **2** informal, chiefly Brit. a feeble person. **3** Brit. a Conservative politician (especially in the 1980s) with liberal tendencies.
– PHRASES **wet the baby's head** Brit. informal celebrate a baby's birth with a drink. **wet behind the ears** informal lacking experience; immature. **wet one's whistle** informal have a drink.
– DERIVATIVES **wetly** adv. **wetness** n. **wettable** adj. **wet-tish** adj.
– ORIGIN Old English *wǣt* (adj. and n.), *wǣtan* (v.); rel. to WATER.

wetback ■ n. US informal, derogatory a Mexican who is an illegal immigrant to the US.
– ORIGIN 1920s: so named from the practice of swimming the Rio Grande to reach the US.

wet bar ■ n. a bar or counter in the home for serving alcoholic drinks.

wet blanket ■ n. informal a person who spoils other people's enjoyment with their disapproving or unenthusiastic manner.

wet dream ■ n. an erotic dream that causes involuntary ejaculation of semen.

wet fish ■ n. fresh fish, as opposed to fish which has been frozen, cooked, or dried.

wet fly ■ n. an artificial fishing fly designed to sink below the surface of the water.

wether /ˈwɛðə/ ■ n. a castrated ram.
– ORIGIN Old English, of Germanic origin.

wetland ■ n. (also **wetlands**) swampy or marshy land.

wet lease ■ n. an arrangement for the hire of an aircraft with a flight crew and sometimes fuel.

wet look ■ n. a shiny appearance possessed by a clothing fabric or achieved by applying gel to the hair.

wet nurse ■ n. chiefly historical a woman employed to suckle another woman's child. ■ v. (**wet-nurse**) act as a wet nurse to. ▸ informal look after (someone) as though they were a helpless infant.

wet room ■ n. a bathroom in which the shower is open or set behind a single wall, its floor area being flush with the floor of the rest of the room.

wet rot ■ n. a brown fungus causing decay in moist timber. [*Coniophora puteana* and other species.]

wetsuit ■ n. a close-fitting rubber garment covering the entire body, worn for warmth in water sports or diving.

wetting agent ■ n. a chemical added to a liquid to reduce its surface tension and make it more effective in spreading over and penetrating surfaces.

wetware ■ n. human brain cells viewed as counterparts of computer systems.

we've ■ contr. we have.

w.f. ■ abbrev. Printing wrong fount.

WFTU ■ abbrev. World Federation of Trade Unions.

whack informal ■ v. **1** strike forcefully with a sharp blow. ▸ defeat heavily. ▸ place or insert roughly or carelessly. **2** N. Amer. murder. **3** (**whack off**) vulgar slang masturbate. ■ n. **1** a sharp or resounding blow. **2** a try or attempt. **3** a specified share of or contribution to something.
– PHRASES **out of whack** not working. **top** (or **full**) **whack** the maximum price or rate.
– DERIVATIVES **whacker** n.
– ORIGIN C18: imitative, or perhaps an alteration of THWACK.

whacked (also **whacked out** or **wacked**) ■ adj. informal **1** completely exhausted. **2** chiefly N. Amer. under the influence of drugs.

whacking ■ adj. informal very large.

whacko ■ adj. & n. (pl. **-os**) variant spelling of WACKO.

whacky ■ adj. variant spelling of WACKY.

whale ■ n. (pl. same or **whales**) a very large marine mammal with a horizontal tail fin and a blowhole on top of the head for breathing. [Order Cetacea.]
– PHRASES **a whale of a —** informal an exceedingly good example of something. **have a whale of a time** informal enjoy oneself very much.
– ORIGIN Old English, of Germanic origin.

whaleback ■ n. something shaped like a whale's back, especially an arched structure over the bow or stern part of a steamer's deck, or a large elongated hill.

whaleboat ■ n. a long manoeuvrable rowing boat with a bow at each end, formerly used in whaling.

whalebone ■ n. an elastic horny substance which grows in a series of thin parallel plates in the upper jaw of some whales and is used by them to strain plankton from the seawater; baleen. ▸ strips of this substance, formerly used as stays in corsets and dresses.

whale oil ■ n. oil obtained from the blubber of a whale, formerly used in oil lamps or for making soap.

whaler ■ n. **1** a whaling ship. ▸ a seaman engaged in whaling. **2** (usu. **whaler shark**) a large, slender-bodied shark of inshore waters. [*Carcharhinus brachyurus* and related species.]

whale shark ■ n. a very large tropical shark which feeds chiefly on plankton, the largest known fish. [*Rhincodon typus*.]

whaling ■ n. the practice or industry of hunting and killing whales for their oil, meat, or whalebone.

wham informal ■ exclam. used to express the sound of a forcible impact or the idea of a sudden and dramatic occurrence. ■ v. (**whammed**, **whamming**) strike something forcefully.

whammy ■ n. (pl. **-ies**) informal an event with a powerful and unpleasant effect; a blow.
– ORIGIN 1940s: from WHAM.

wharf /wɔːf/ ■ n. (pl. **wharves** or **wharfs**) a level quayside area to which a ship may be moored to load and unload.
– ORIGIN Old English, of Germanic origin.

wharfage ■ n. accommodation provided at a wharf for the loading, unloading, or storage of goods. ▸ payment made for such accommodation.

wharfie ■ n. Austral./NZ informal a dock labourer.

wharfinger /ˈwɔːfɪn(d)ʒə/ ■ n. an owner or keeper of a wharf.
– ORIGIN Middle English: from WHARFAGE.

wharves plural form of WHARF.

what ■ pron. & det. **1** asking for information specifying something. ▸ [as pron.] asking for repetition of something not heard or confirmation of something not understood. **2** [as pron.] the thing or things that. **3** whatever. **4** used to emphasize something surprising or remarkable. ■ interrog. adv. **1** to what extent? **2** informal, dated used for emphasis or to invite agreement: *poor show, what?*
– PHRASES **and** (or **or**) **what have you** informal and/or anything else similar. **and what not** informal and other similar things. **what about —?** **1** used when asking for information or an opinion. **2** used to make a suggestion. **what-d'you-call-it** (or **what's-its name**) informal a substitute for a name not recalled. **what for?** informal for what reason? **what if —? 1** what would result if —? **2** what does it matter if —? **what is more** and as an additional point; moreover. **what of —?** what is the

whatever

news concerning ——? **what of it?** why should that be considered significant? **what's-his** (or **-its**) **-name** another term for what-d'you-call-it. **what's what** informal what is useful or important. **what with** because of.
– ORIGIN Old English *hwæt*, of Germanic origin.

whatever ■ rel. pron. & det. used to emphasize a lack of restriction in referring to any thing, no matter what. ■ interrog. pron. used for emphasis instead of 'what' in questions. ■ adv. **1** [with neg.] at all; of any kind. **2** informal no matter what happens. ■ exclam. informal a response indicating a reluctance to discuss something, often implying indifference.

whatnot ■ n. informal **1** used to refer to an unidentified item or items having something in common with items already named. **2** a stand with shelves for small objects.

whatsit ■ n. informal a person or thing whose name one cannot recall, does not know, or does not wish to specify.

whatsoever ■ adv. [with neg.] at all. ■ det. & pron. archaic whatever.

what what ■ adv. S. African informal and so on; et cetera.

wheal ■ n. variant spelling of WEAL¹.

wheat ■ n. a cereal widely grown in temperate countries, the grain of which is ground to make flour for bread, pasta, etc. [*Triticum aestivum* and related species.]
– ORIGIN Old English *hwǣte* of Germanic origin.

wheatear ■ n. a songbird with black and grey, buff, or white plumage and a white rump. [Genus *Oenanthe*: several species.]
– ORIGIN C16: apparently from WHITE (assimilated to WHEAT) + ARSE (assimilated to EAR²).

wheaten ■ adj. made of wheat.

wheatgerm ■ n. a nutritious foodstuff of a dry floury consistency consisting of the extracted embryos of grains of wheat.

wheatgrass ■ n. another term for COUCH².

wheatmeal ■ n. flour made from wheat from which some of the bran and germ has been removed.

Wheatstone bridge ■ n. a device for measuring an unknown resistance by combining it in a circuit with known resistances and equalizing the potential at two points.
– ORIGIN C19: named after the English physicist Sir Charles Wheatstone.

whee ■ exclam. used to express delight or excitement.

wheedle ■ v. employ endearments or flattery to persuade someone to do something.
– DERIVATIVES **wheedler** n. **wheedling** adj. **wheedlingly** adv.
– ORIGIN C17: perhaps from German *wedeln* 'cringe, fawn'.

wheel ■ n. **1** a circular object that revolves on an axle, fixed below a vehicle to enable it to move over the ground or forming part of a machine. **2** something resembling a wheel or having a wheel as its essential part. ▶ a steering wheel. ▶ a device with a revolving disc or drum used in various games of chance. **3** (**wheels**) informal a car. **4** an instance of wheeling; a turn or rotation. ■ v. **1** push or pull (a vehicle with wheels). ▶ carry in or on a vehicle with wheels. ▶ (**wheel something in/on/out**) informal produce something that is unimpressive because it has been frequently seen or heard before. **2** fly or turn in a wide circle or curve. ▶ turn round quickly to face another way.
– PHRASES **on wheels 1** travelling by car or cycle. **2** Brit. informal smoothly. **wheel and deal** engage in commercial or political scheming, especially unscrupulously. **the wheel of Fortune** the wheel which the deity Fortune is fabled to turn as a symbol of random luck or change. **wheels within wheels** secret or indirect influences affecting a complex situation.
– DERIVATIVES **wheeled** adj. **wheelless** adj.
– ORIGIN Old English, of Germanic origin.

wheelbarrow ■ n. a small cart with a single wheel at the front and two supporting legs and two handles at the rear, used for carrying loads in building or gardening.

wheelbase ■ n. the distance between the front and rear axles of a vehicle.

wheelchair ■ n. a mobile wheeled chair for an invalid or disabled person.

wheel clamp ■ n. a device for immobilizing an unlawfully parked car. ■ v. (**wheel-clamp**) clamp (a car) with such a device.

wheeler ■ n. [in combination] a vehicle having a specified number of wheels.

wheeler-dealer (also **wheeler and dealer**) ■ n. a person who engages in commercial or political scheming.
– DERIVATIVES **wheeler-dealing** n.

wheelhouse ■ n. a shelter for the person at the wheel of a boat or ship.

wheelie ■ n. informal a trick or manoeuvre whereby a bicycle or motorcycle is ridden for a short distance with the front wheel raised off the ground.

wheelie bin (also **wheely bin**) ■ n. informal a large refuse bin set on wheels.

wheelspin ■ n. rotation of a vehicle's wheels without traction.

wheelwright ■ n. chiefly historical a person who makes or repairs wooden wheels.

wheesht /wiːʃt/ ■ exclam. variant of WHISHT.

wheeze ■ v. breathe with a whistling or rattling sound in the chest, as a result of obstruction in the air passages. ▶ (of a device) make an irregular rattling or spluttering sound. ■ n. **1** a sound of a person wheezing. **2** Brit. informal a clever or amusing scheme or trick.
– DERIVATIVES **wheezer** n. **wheezily** adv. **wheeziness** n. **wheezing** adj. **wheezingly** adv. **wheezy** adj.
– ORIGIN Middle English: prob. from Old Norse *hvæsa* 'to hiss'.

whelk ■ n. a predatory marine mollusc with a heavy pointed spiral shell. [Family Buccinidae.]
– ORIGIN Old English *wioloc*, *weoloc*.

whelm /wɛlm/ ■ v. archaic or poetic/literary engulf, submerge, or bury.
– ORIGIN Middle English: representing an Old English form parallel to *hwelfan* 'overturn (a vessel)'.

whelp ■ n. chiefly archaic **1** a puppy. ▶ a cub. **2** derogatory a boy or young man. ■ v. give birth to (a puppy).
– ORIGIN Old English, of Germanic origin.

when ■ interrog. adv. **1** at what time. ▶ how soon. **2** in what circumstances. ■ rel. adv. at which time or in which situation. ■ conj. **1** at or during the time that. ▶ at any time that; whenever. **2** after which; and just then. **3** in view of the fact that; considering that. **4** although; whereas.
– ORIGIN Old English *hwanne*, *hwenne*; of Germanic origin.

whence (also **from whence**) formal or archaic ■ interrog. adv. from what place or source. ■ rel. adv. from which; from where. ▶ to the place from which. ▶ as a consequence of which.
– ORIGIN Middle English *whennes*, from earlier *whenne*, from Old English *hwanon*; of Germanic origin.

> **USAGE**
> Strictly speaking, **whence** means 'from what place'. Thus, use of the preposition **from** is redundant and its use is considered incorrect by some. It is very common, though and has been used by reputable writers since the 14th century. It is now broadly accepted in standard English.

whencesoever ■ rel. adv. formal or archaic from whatever place or source.

whenever ■ conj. at whatever time; on whatever occasion. ▶ every time that. ■ interrog. adv. used for emphasis instead of 'when' in questions.

whensoever ■ conj. & adv. formal word for WHENEVER.

where ■ interrog. adv. in or to what place or position. ▶ in what direction or respect. ■ rel. adv. **1** at, in, or to which. **2** the place or situation in which. ▶ in or to a place or situation in which. ▶ in or to any place in which.
– ORIGIN Old English *hwǣr*, of Germanic origin.

whereabouts ■ interrog. adv. where or approximately where. ■ n. [treated as sing. or pl.] the place where someone or something is.

whereafter ■ rel. adv. formal after which.

whereas ■ conj. in contrast or comparison with the fact that. ▸ taking into consideration the fact that.

whereat ■ rel. adv. & conj. archaic or formal at which.

whereby ■ rel. adv. by which.

wherefore archaic ■ interrog. adv. for what reason. ■ rel. adv. & conj. as a result of which.

wherefrom ■ rel. adv. archaic from which or from where.

wherein ■ adv. formal **1** in which. **2** (in questions) in what place or respect.

whereof /wɛːˈrɒv/ ■ rel. adv. formal of what or which.

whereon ■ rel. adv. archaic on which.

wheresoever ■ adv. & conj. formal word for **WHEREVER**.

whereto /wɛːˈtuː/ ■ rel. adv. archaic or formal to which.

whereupon ■ conj. immediately after which.

wherever ■ rel. adv. in or to whatever place. ■ interrog. adv. used for emphasis instead of 'where' in questions. ■ conj. in every case when.

wherewith ■ rel. adv. formal or archaic with or by which.

wherewithal ■ n. the money or other resources needed for a particular purpose: *they lacked the wherewithal to pay.*

wherry /ˈwɛri/ ■ n. (pl. **-ies**) a light rowing boat used chiefly for carrying passengers. ▸ Brit. a large light barge.
–DERIVATIVES **wherryman** n. (pl. **-men**).
–ORIGIN Middle English.

whet /wɛt/ ■ v. (**whetted**, **whetting**) **1** sharpen the blade of (a tool or weapon). **2** excite or stimulate (someone's desire, interest, or appetite).
–ORIGIN Old English *hwettan*, of Germanic origin, based on an adjective meaning 'sharp'.

whether ■ conj. expressing a doubt or choice between alternatives. ▸ expressing an enquiry or investigation. ▸ indicating that a statement applies whichever of the alternatives mentioned is the case.
–PHRASES **whether or no 1** whether or not. **2** archaic in any case.
–ORIGIN Old English, of Germanic origin.

whetstone ■ n. a fine-grained stone used for sharpening cutting tools.

whew /hwjuː, fjuː/ ■ exclam. used to express surprise, relief, or a feeling of being very hot or tired.
–ORIGIN Middle English: imitative.

whey /weɪ/ ■ n. the watery part of milk that remains after the formation of curds.
–ORIGIN Old English, of Germanic origin.

whey-faced ■ adj. (of a person) pale, especially as a result of ill health, shock, or fear.

which ■ interrog. pron. & det. asking for information specifying one or more people or things from a definite set. ■ rel. pron. & det. used referring to something previously mentioned when introducing a clause giving further information.
–ORIGIN Old English *hwilc*, from the Germanic bases of **WHO** and **ALIKE**.

USAGE
On the differences between **which** and **that** in relative clauses, see usage at **THAT**.

whichever ■ rel. det. & pron. used to emphasize a lack of restriction in selecting one of a definite set of alternatives. ▸ regardless of which.

whicker ■ v. (of a horse) give a soft breathy whinny. ■ n. a sound of this type.
–ORIGIN C17: imitative.

whiff ■ n. **1** a smell that is smelt only briefly or faintly. ▸ informal an unpleasant smell. **2** a trace or hint of something bad or exciting: *a whiff of danger.* **3** a puff or breath of air or smoke. ■ v. get a brief or faint smell of. ▸ Brit. informal give off an unpleasant smell.
–DERIVATIVES **whiffy** adj. (**-ier**, **-iest**) (Brit. informal).
–ORIGIN C16: imitative.

whiffle ■ v. (of the wind) blow lightly in a specified direction. ▸ blow or move with a puff of air.
–ORIGIN C16: from **WHIFF**.

Whig ■ n. **1** a member of the British reforming party that sought the supremacy of Parliament, succeeded in the 19th century by the Liberal Party. **2** a supporter of the American Revolution. ▸ a member of a 19th-century American political party succeeded by the Republicans.
–DERIVATIVES **Whiggery** n. **Whiggish** adj. **Whiggism** n.
–ORIGIN prob. a shortening of Scots *whiggamore*, the nickname of C17 Scottish rebels, from *whig* 'to drive' + **MARE**[1].

while ■ n. **1** (**a while**) a period of time. ▸ for some time. **2** (**the while**) at the same time; meanwhile. ▸ poetic/literary during the time that. ■ conj. **1** at the same time as. **2** whereas (indicating a contrast). ▸ although. ■ rel. adv. during which. ■ v. (**while time away**) pass time in a leisurely manner.
–PHRASES **worth while** (or **worth one's while**) worth the time or effort spent.
–ORIGIN Old English *hwīl* 'period of time', of Germanic origin; the conjunction is an abbrev. of Old English *thā hwīle the* 'the while that'.

whiles ■ conj. archaic form of **WHILE**.
–ORIGIN Middle English: orig. in adverbs such as *somewhiles* 'formerly', *otherwhiles* 'at times'.

whilst ■ conj. & rel. adv. while.
–ORIGIN Middle English: from **WHILES** + *-t* as in **AGAINST**.

whim ■ n. a sudden desire or change of mind, especially one that is unusual or unexplained.
–ORIGIN C17.

whimbrel /ˈwɪmbr(ə)l/ ■ n. a small migratory curlew with a striped crown and a trilling call. [*Numenius phaeopus*.]
–ORIGIN C16: from **WHIMPER** or synonymous dialect *whimp* (imitative of the bird's call) + **-REL**.

whimper ■ v. make a series of low, feeble sounds expressive of fear, pain, or discontent. ■ n. a whimpering sound.
–DERIVATIVES **whimperer** n. **whimpering** n. **whimperingly** adv.
–ORIGIN C16: from dialect *whimp* 'to whimper', of imitative origin.

whimsical ■ adj. **1** playfully quaint or fanciful, especially in an appealing and amusing way. **2** acting or behaving in a capricious manner.
–DERIVATIVES **whimsicality** n. **whimsically** adv.

whimsy (also **whimsey**) ■ n. (pl. **-ies** or **-eys**) **1** playfully quaint or fanciful behaviour or humour. ▸ a thing that is fanciful or odd. **2** a whim.
–ORIGIN C17 (in the sense 'caprice').

whin[1] ■ n. chiefly N. English furze; gorse.
–ORIGIN Middle English: prob. of Scandinavian origin.

whin[2] (also **whinstone**) ■ n. hard, dark basaltic rock.
–ORIGIN Middle English.

whinchat /ˈwɪntʃat/ ■ n. a small Eurasian and North African songbird related to the stonechat, with a brown back and orange-buff underparts. [*Saxicola rubetra*.]
–ORIGIN C17: from **WHIN**[1] + **CHAT**[2].

whine ■ n. **1** a long, high-pitched complaining cry. ▸ a long, high-pitched unpleasant sound. **2** a feeble or petulant complaint. ■ v. **1** give or make a whine. **2** complain in a feeble or petulant way.
–DERIVATIVES **whiner** n. **whining** n. **whiningly** adv. **whiny** adj.
–ORIGIN Old English *hwīnan* 'whistle through the air'.

whinge informal ■ v. (**whingeing**) complain persistently and peevishly. ■ n. an act of whingeing.
–DERIVATIVES **whingeing** adj. **whingeingly** adv. **whinger** n. **whingy** adj.
–ORIGIN Old English, of Germanic origin.

whinny ■ n. (pl. **-ies**) a gentle, high-pitched neigh. ■ v. (**-ies**, **-ied**) (of a horse) make such a sound.
–ORIGIN Middle English: imitative.

whinstone ■ n. another term for **WHIN**[2].

whip ■ n. **1** a strip of leather or length of cord fastened to a handle, used for beating a person or urging on an animal. **2** an official of a political party appointed to maintain parliamentary discipline among its members, especially so as to ensure attendance and voting in debates. ▸ Brit. a written notice from such an official requesting attendance for voting. **3** a dessert made from cream or eggs beaten into a light fluffy mass. **4** a violent

whip aerial

striking or beating movement. **5** short for **WHIPPER-IN**. ▪v. (**whipped**, **whipping**) **1** beat with a whip. ▸ (of a flexible object or rain or wind) strike or beat violently. ▸ informal defeat heavily in a sporting contest. ▸ (**whip someone up**) deliberately excite or provoke someone. ▸ (**whip something up**) stimulate a particular feeling in someone. **2** move or take out fast or suddenly. ▸ (**whip something up**) make or prepare something, especially food, very quickly. **3** beat (cream, eggs, or other food) into a froth. **4** Brit. informal steal. **5** bind with spirally wound twine. ▸ sew or gather with overcast stitches.
– PHRASES **the whip hand** a position of power or control.
– DERIVATIVES **whip-like** adj. **whipper** n. **whipping** n.
– ORIGIN Middle English: prob. from Middle Low German and Middle Dutch *wippen* 'swing, leap, dance', from a Germanic base meaning 'move quickly'.

whip aerial (also **whip antenna**) ▪n. an aerial in the form of a long flexible wire or rod.

whipcord ▪n. **1** thin, tough, tightly twisted cord used for making the flexible end part of whips. **2** a closely woven ribbed worsted fabric, used for making garments such as jodhpurs.

whiplash ▪n. **1** the lashing action of a whip. ▸ the flexible part of a whip. **2** injury caused by a severe jerk to the head, typically in a motor accident. ▪v. jerk suddenly.

whipper-in ▪n. (pl. **whippers-in**) a huntsman's assistant who brings straying hounds back into the pack.

whippersnapper ▪n. informal a young and inexperienced person who is presumptuous or overconfident.
– ORIGIN C17: perhaps representing *whipsnapper*, expressing noise and unimportance.

whippet ▪n. a dog of a small slender breed originally produced as a cross between the greyhound and the terrier or spaniel, bred for racing.
– ORIGIN C17: partly from obsolete *whippet* 'move briskly'.

whipping boy ▪n. a person who is blamed or punished for the faults or incompetence of others.
– ORIGIN C17: orig. denoting a boy educated with a young prince and punished instead of him.

whipping post ▪n. historical a post to which offenders were tied to be whipped as a public punishment.

whippoorwill /ˈwɪpəwɪl/ ▪n. a North and Central American nightjar with a distinctive call. [*Caprimulgus vociferus*.]
– ORIGIN C18: imitative of its call.

whippy ▪adj. flexible; springy.
– DERIVATIVES **whippiness** n.

whip-round ▪n. informal a collection of contributions of money for a particular purpose.

whipsaw ▪n. a saw with a narrow blade and a handle at both ends, used typically by two people. ▪v. (past part. **-sawn** or **-sawed**) **1** cut with a whipsaw. **2** informal subject to two difficult situations or opposing pressures at the same time. **3** informal cheat or exploit.

whip scorpion ▪n. a scorpion-like arachnid with a long slender tail. [Order Uropygi.]

whip snake ▪n. a slender, fast-moving snake. [*Psammophis notostictus* (southern Africa), *Coluber viridiflavus* (Eurasia), and other species.]

whipworm ▪n. a parasitic nematode worm with a slender anterior part, especially one that infests the intestines of domestic animals. [Genus *Trichuris*.]

whir ▪n. & v. variant spelling of **WHIRR**.

whirl ▪v. move or cause to move rapidly round and round. ▸ move rapidly. ▸ (of the head or mind) seem to spin round. ▪n. **1** a rapid movement round and round. **2** frantic activity: *the mad social whirl*. **3** a sweet or biscuit with a spiral shape: *a hazelnut whirl*.
– PHRASES **give something a whirl** informal give something a try. **in a whirl** in a state of confusion.
– DERIVATIVES **whirler** n. **whirling** adj. **whirlingly** adv.
– ORIGIN Middle English: verb prob. from Old Norse *hvirfla* 'turn about'; noun partly from Middle Low German, Middle Dutch *werwel* 'spindle', or from Old Norse *hvirfill* 'circle', from a Germanic base meaning 'rotate'.

whirligig ▪n. **1** a toy that spins round, e.g. a top or

1356

windmill. **2** another term for **ROUNDABOUT** (in sense 2). **3** (also **whirligig beetle**) a small black water beetle which typically swims rapidly in circles on the surface. [Family Gyrinidae.]
– ORIGIN Middle English: from **WHIRL** + obsolete *gig* 'toy for whipping'.

whirlpool ▪n. **1** a quickly rotating mass of water in a river or sea into which objects may be drawn. **2** (also **whirlpool bath**) a heated pool in which hot aerated water is continuously circulated.

whirlwind ▪n. **1** a column of air moving rapidly round and round in a cylindrical or funnel shape. **2** a very energetic or tumultuous person or process: *a whirlwind of activity*. ▸ [as modifier] very rapid and unexpected: *a whirlwind romance*.
– PHRASES (**sow the wind and**) **reap the whirlwind** suffer serious consequences as a result of one's actions. [with biblical allusion to Hosea 8:7.]

whirlybird ▪n. informal, chiefly N. Amer. a helicopter.

whirr (also **whir**) ▪v. (**whirred**, **whirring**) (of something rapidly rotating or moving to and fro) make a low, continuous, regular sound. ▪n. a whirring sound.
– ORIGIN Middle English: prob. of Scandinavian origin; cf. **WHIRL**.

whisht /(h)wɪʃt/ (also **wheesht**) ▪exclam. chiefly Scottish & Irish hush!
– PHRASES **hold one's whisht** keep silent.
– ORIGIN natural exclam.: first recorded in English in C16.

whisk ▪v. **1** move or take suddenly, quickly, and lightly. **2** beat (a substance, especially cream or eggs) with a light, rapid movement. ▪n. **1** a utensil for whipping eggs or cream. **2** a bunch of grass, twigs, or bristles for flicking away dust or flies. **3** a brief, rapid action or movement.
– ORIGIN Middle English: of Scandinavian origin.

whisker ▪n. **1** a long projecting hair or bristle growing from the face or snout of an animal such as a cat.
▸ (**whiskers**) the hair growing on a man's face, especially on his cheeks. **2** (**a whisker**) informal a very small amount.
– PHRASES **have** (or **have grown**) **whiskers** informal (especially of a story) be very old.
– DERIVATIVES **whiskered** adj. **whiskery** adj.
– ORIGIN Middle English (orig. denoting a bundle of feathers, twigs, etc., used for whisking): from **WHISK**.

whisky ▪n. (pl. **-ies**) **1** (also Irish & US **whiskey**) a spirit distilled from malted grain, especially barley or rye. **2** (**whiskey**) a code word representing the letter W, used in radio communication.
– ORIGIN C18: abbrev. of obsolete *whiskybae*.

whisky mac ▪n. a drink consisting of whisky and ginger wine mixed in equal amounts.

whisky sour ▪n. a drink consisting of whisky mixed with lemon or lime juice.

whisper ▪v. speak very softly using one's breath rather than one's throat. ▸ poetic/literary rustle or murmur softly. ▸ (**be whispered**) be rumoured. ▪n. **1** a whispered word or phrase, or a whispering tone of voice. ▸ poetic/literary a soft rustling or murmuring sound. ▸ a rumour or piece of gossip. **2** a slight trace; a hint: *a whisper of interest*.
– DERIVATIVES **whisperer** n. **whispery** adj.
– ORIGIN Old English *hwisprian*, of Germanic origin.

whispering campaign ▪n. a systematic circulation of a rumour, especially in order to damage someone's reputation.

whispering gallery ▪n. a gallery or dome with acoustic properties such that a faint sound may be heard round its entire circumference.

whist /wɪst/ ▪n. a card game, usually for two pairs of players, in which points are scored according to the number of tricks won.
– ORIGIN C17: perhaps from **WHISK** (with ref. to whisking away the tricks).

whistle ▪n. **1** a clear, high-pitched sound made by forcing breath through a small hole between partly closed lips, or between one's teeth. ▸ any similar sound. **2** an instrument used to produce such a sound, especially for giving a signal. ▪v. **1** emit or produce a whistle.
▸ produce (a tune) in such a way. ▸ move rapidly through the air or a narrow opening with a whistling sound. **2** blow a whistle. **3** (**whistle for**) wish for or expect (something) in vain.

—PHRASES **blow the whistle on** informal bring (an illicit activity) to an end by informing on the person responsible. (**as**) **clean as a whistle** extremely clean or clear. **whistle something down the wind** let go or abandon something. **whistle in the dark** pretend to be unafraid.
—DERIVATIVES **whistler** n.
—ORIGIN Old English (*h*)*wistlian* (v.), (*h*)*wistle* (n.), of Germanic origin; imitative.

whistle-blower ■ n. informal a person who informs on someone engaged in an illicit activity.
—DERIVATIVES **whistle-blowing** n. & adj.

whistle-stop ■ adj. very fast and with only brief pauses: *a whistle-stop tour*.

Whit ■ n. short for WHITSUNTIDE.

whit ■ n. a very small part or amount.
—PHRASES **every whit** wholly. **not a whit** not at all.
—ORIGIN Middle English: an alteration of obsolete *wight* 'small amount'.

white ■ adj. **1** of the colour of milk or fresh snow, due to the reflection of all visible rays of light. ▶ very pale. ▶ (of coffee or tea) served with milk or cream. ▶ (of food such as bread or rice) light in colour through having been refined. **2** relating to or denoting a human group having light-coloured skin, especially of European ancestry. ▶ S. African historical reserved by law for those classified as white. **3** morally or spiritually pure. **4** (of wine) made from white grapes, or dark grapes with the skins removed, and having a yellowish colour. ■ n. **1** white colour or pigment. ▶ (also **whites**) white clothes or material. **2** (**White**) the player of the white pieces in chess or draughts. **3** the visible pale part of the eyeball around the iris. **4** the outer part (white when cooked) which surrounds the yolk of an egg; the albumen. **5** a member of a light-skinned people. **6** a white or cream butterfly. [*Pieris* and other genera, family Pieridae.] ■ v. (usu. **white something out**) turn (something) white. ▶ obliterate (a mistake) with white correction fluid.
—PHRASES **bleed someone/thing white** drain of wealth or resources. **whited sepulchre** poetic/literary a hypocrite. [with biblical allusion to Matthew 23:27.]
—DERIVATIVES **whiten** v. **whitener** n. **whiteness** n. **whitish** adj.
—ORIGIN Old English, of Germanic origin.

white ant ■ n. another term for TERMITE. ■ v. (**white-ant**) informal deliberately undermine (an organization, a person, an agreement, etc.).

white arsenic ■ n. arsenic trioxide, an extremely toxic soluble white solid.

whitebait ■ n. the small silvery-white young of herrings, sprats, and similar marine fish as food.

whitebeam ■ n. a European tree related to the rowan, with red berries and hairy oval leaves that are white underneath. [*Sorbus aria*.]

white belt ■ n. a white belt worn by a beginner in judo or karate.

whiteboard ■ n. a wipeable board with a white surface used for teaching or presentations.

white cell ■ n. less technical term for LEUCOCYTE.

white Christmas ■ n. a Christmas during which there is snow on the ground.

white-collar ■ adj. of or relating to the work done or people who work in an office or other professional environment.

white dwarf ■ n. Astronomy a small, very dense star that is typically the size of a planet.

white elephant ■ n. a possession that is useless or troublesome, especially one that is expensive to maintain or difficult to dispose of.
—ORIGIN from the story that the kings of Siam gave such animals to courtiers they disliked, in order to ruin the recipient by the great expense incurred in maintaining the animal.

white-eye ■ n. a small songbird with a ring of white feathers around the eye. [*Zosterops* and other genera.]

white feather ■ n. a white feather given to someone as a sign that they are considered a coward.
—ORIGIN C18: with ref. to a white feather in the tail of a game bird, being a mark of bad breeding.

whitefish ■ n. (pl. same or **-fishes**) **1** a mainly freshwater fish of the salmon family, widely used as food. [*Coregonus* and other genera: several species.] **2** a large South African barb, popular with anglers. [*Barbus andrewi*.]

white fish ■ n. fish with pale flesh, such as cod, plaice, and haddock.

white flag ■ n. a white flag or cloth used as a symbol of surrender, truce, or a desire to parley.

whitefly ■ n. (pl. same or **-flies**) a minute winged bug covered with powdery white wax, damaging plants by feeding on sap and coating them with honeydew. [Family Aleyrodidae: many species.]

white gold ■ n. a silver-coloured alloy of gold with nickel, platinum, or another metal.

white goods ■ pl. n. large domestic electrical goods such as refrigerators and washing machines. Compare with BROWN GOODS.

whitehead ■ n. informal a pale or white-topped pustule on the skin.

white heat ■ n. the temperature or state of something that is so hot that it emits white light.

white hope (also **great white hope**) ■ n. a person expected to bring much success to a team or organization.

white horses ■ pl. n. white-crested waves at sea.

white-hot ■ adj. so hot as to glow white.

white knight ■ n. a person or thing that comes to someone's aid. ▶ a person or company making an acceptable counter offer for a company facing a hostile takeover bid.

white-knuckle ■ adj. causing fear or nervous excitement: *a white-knuckle ride*.
—ORIGIN 1970s: with ref. to the effect caused by gripping tightly to steady oneself.

white-label ■ adj. denoting a musical recording for which the printed commercial label is not yet available, issued with a plain white label before general release for promotional purposes.

white lead ■ n. a white pigment consisting of a mixture of lead carbonate and lead hydroxide.

white lie ■ n. a harmless lie told to avoid hurting someone's feelings.

white light ■ n. apparently colourless light containing all the wavelengths of the visible spectrum at equal intensity (such as ordinary daylight).

white lightning ■ n. **1** N. Amer. illicit home-made whiskey, typically colourless and distilled from corn. **2** S. African another term for WITBLITS.

white lime ■ n. whitewash.

white list ■ n. informal a list of people or products viewed with approval.

white magic ■ n. magic used only for good purposes.

white matter ■ n. the paler tissue of the brain and spinal cord, consisting mainly of nerve fibres with their myelin sheaths.

white meat ■ n. pale meat such as poultry, veal, and rabbit.

white metal ■ n. a white or silvery alloy, especially a tin-based alloy used for the surfaces of bearings.

white mouse ■ n. an albino form of the house mouse.

white night ■ n. **1** a sleepless night. **2** a night when it is never properly dark, as in high latitudes in summer.

white noise ■ n. Physics noise containing many frequencies with equal intensities.

white-out ■ n. **1** a dense blizzard. ▶ a weather condition in which the features and horizon of snow-covered country are indistinguishable due to uniform light diffusion. **2** white correction fluid for covering typing mistakes.

White Paper ■ n. a government report giving information or proposals on an issue.

white pear ■ n. an evergreen tree, native to southern Africa, which bears black nuts with fleshy appendages. [*Apodytes dimidiata subsp. dimidiata*.] ▶ the hard wood of this tree, used for making furniture.

white pipe ■ n. S. African a mixture of cannabis, tobacco, and crushed Mandrax tablets.

white pointer ■ n. another term for GREAT WHITE SHARK.

white poplar ■ n. a poplar with lobed leaves that are white underneath and grey-green above. [*Populus alba*.]

white pudding ■ n. a kind of sausage made of oatmeal and suet.

white rose ■ n. Brit. the emblem of Yorkshire. ▸ historical the emblem of the Yorkists.

White Russian ■ n. 1 dated a Belorussian. 2 an opponent of the Bolsheviks during the Russian Civil War. 3 a cocktail made of vodka, coffee liqueur, and milk, served on ice. ■ adj. of or relating to White Russians.

white sauce ■ n. a sauce consisting of flour blended and cooked with butter and milk or stock.

white shark ■ n. see GREAT WHITE SHARK.

white slave ■ n. a woman tricked or forced into prostitution in a foreign country.
– DERIVATIVES **white slaver** n. **white slavery** n.

whites-only ■ adj. S. African historical (under apartheid) reserved for the use or participation of white people.

white spirit ■ n. a volatile colourless liquid distilled from petroleum, used as a paint thinner and solvent.

whitethroat ■ n. a migratory Eurasian and North African warbler with a grey head and white throat. [*Sylvia communis* and related species.]

white tie ■ n. a white bow tie worn by men as part of full evening dress. ▸ full evening dress.

white trash ■ n. N. Amer. derogatory poor white people, especially those living in the southern US.

whitewall ■ n. a tyre with a white stripe round the outside, or a white side wall.

whitewash ■ n. 1 a solution of lime and water or of whiting, size, and water, used for painting walls white. 2 a deliberate concealment of someone's mistakes or faults. 3 a victory by the same side in every game of a series. ■ v. 1 paint with whitewash. 2 conceal (mistakes or faults). 3 defeat with a whitewash.
– DERIVATIVES **whitewashed** adj.

white water ■ n. a fast shallow stretch of water in a river.

white wedding ■ n. a traditional wedding at which the bride wears a formal white dress.

white whale ■ n. another term for BELUGA (in sense 1).

white witch ■ n. a practitioner of witchcraft for altruistic purposes.

whitewood ■ n. light-coloured wood, especially when made up into furniture and ready for staining, varnishing, or painting.

whitework ■ n. embroidery worked in white thread on a white ground.

whitey ■ n. (pl. **-eys**) informal, derogatory a white person. ■ adj. with a whitish tinge.

whither archaic or poetic/literary ■ interrog. adv. to what place or state. ▸ what is the likely future of. ■ rel. adv. to which (with reference to a place). ▸ to whatever place.
– ORIGIN Old English *hwider*, from the Germanic base of WHICH.

whithersoever ■ rel. adv. archaic wherever.

whiting[1] ■ n. (pl. same) a slender-bodied marine fish with edible white flesh. [*Merlangius merlangus* and other species.]
– ORIGIN Middle English: from Middle Dutch *wijting*, from *wijt* 'white'.

whiting[2] ■ n. ground chalk used for purposes such as whitewashing and cleaning metal plate.

whitlow /ˈwɪtləʊ/ ■ n. an abscess in the soft tissue near a fingernail or toenail.
– ORIGIN Middle English: apparently from WHITE + FLAW in the sense 'crack', but perhaps rel. to Dutch *fijt* 'whitlow'.

Whitsun /ˈwɪts(ə)n/ ■ n. Whitsuntide.
– ORIGIN Middle English: from WHIT SUNDAY, reduced as if from *Whitsun Day*.

Whit Sunday ■ n. the seventh Sunday after Easter, a Christian festival commemorating the descent of the Holy Spirit at Pentecost (Acts 2).
– ORIGIN Old English *Hwita Sunnandæg*, 'white Sunday', prob. with ref. to the white robes of those newly baptized at Pentecost.

Whitsuntide /ˈwɪts(ə)ntaɪd/ ■ n. the weekend or week including Whit Sunday.

whittle ■ v. 1 carve (wood) by repeatedly cutting small slices from it. ▸ make by whittling. 2 (**whittle something away/down**) reduce something by degrees.
– ORIGIN C16: from dialect *whittle* 'knife'.

Whitworth ■ n. [as modifier] denoting a standard series of screw threads in imperial sizes.
– ORIGIN C19: from the name of the English engineer Sir Joseph *Whitworth*.

whiz-bang (also **whizz-bang**) ■ adj. informal impressively lively and fast-paced.

whizz (also **whiz**) ■ v. (**whizzed**, **whizzing**) 1 move quickly through the air with a whistling or whooshing sound. ▸ move or cause to move or go fast. ▸ (**whizz through**) do or deal with quickly. 2 informal urinate. ■ n. 1 a whizzing sound. 2 informal a fast movement or brief journey. 3 (also **wiz**) informal a person who is extremely clever at something. [C20: influenced by WIZARD.] 4 informal an act of urinating. 5 informal amphetamines.
– DERIVATIVES **whizzy** adj.
– ORIGIN C16: imitative.

whizz-kid (also **whiz-kid**) ■ n. informal a young person who is very successful or highly skilled.

WHO ■ abbrev. World Health Organization.

who ■ pron. 1 [interrog. pron.] what or which person or people. 2 [rel. pron.] introducing a clause giving further information about a person or people previously mentioned. ▸ archaic the person that; whoever.
– ORIGIN Old English *hwā*, of Germanic origin.

USAGE
According to formal grammar, **who** forms the subjective case, while **whom** forms the objective case and so should be used in object position in a sentence. In modern English there are many speakers who rarely use **whom** at all, employing **who** in all contexts; today this use is broadly accepted in standard English.

whoa /wəʊ/ (also **wo**) ■ exclam. used as a command to a horse to stop or slow down.
– ORIGIN Middle English: var. of HO.

who'd ■ contr. 1 who had. 2 who would.

whodunnit (US **whodunit**) ■ n. informal a story or play about a murder in which the identity of the murderer is not revealed until the end.
– ORIGIN 1930s: from *who done it?*, non-standard form of *who did it?*

whoever ■ rel. pron. the person or people who; any person who. ▸ regardless of who. ■ interrog. pron. used for emphasis instead of 'who' in questions.

whole ■ adj. 1 complete; entire. ▸ emphasizing a large extent or number: *a whole range of issues*. 2 in an unbroken or undamaged state. ▸ with no part removed. ■ n. 1 a thing that is complete in itself. 2 (**the whole**) all of something. ■ adv. informal emphasizing the novelty or distinctness of something: *a whole new meaning*.
– PHRASES **as a whole** in general. **in whole** entirely or fully. **on the whole** taking everything into account; in general. **the whole nine yards** informal, chiefly N. Amer. everything possible or available.
– DERIVATIVES **wholeness** n.
– ORIGIN Old English *hāl*, of Germanic origin.

whole cloth ■ n. cloth of the full size as manufactured, as distinguished from a piece cut off for a garment or other item.

wholefood ■ n. (also **wholefoods**) food that has been minimally processed and is free from additives.

wholehearted ■ adj. completely sincere and committed.
– DERIVATIVES **wholeheartedly** adv. **wholeheartedness** n.

whole-life ■ adj. relating to or denoting a life insurance policy that may be realized only on the death of the person insured.

wholemeal ■ adj. denoting flour or bread made from wholewheat, including the husk.

whole note ■ n. Music a semibreve.

whole number ■ n. a number without fractions; an integer.

wholesale ■ n. the selling of goods in large quantities to be retailed by others. ■ adv. **1** being sold in such a way. **2** on a large scale. ■ adj. done on a large scale; extensive. ■ v. sell (goods) wholesale.
–DERIVATIVES **wholesaler** n.
–ORIGIN Middle English: orig. as *by whole sale* 'in large quantities'.

wholescale ■ adj. another term for WHOLESALE.

wholesome ■ adj. conducive to or suggestive of good health and physical well-being. ▶ conducive to or promoting moral well-being.
–DERIVATIVES **wholesomely** adv. **wholesomeness** n.
–ORIGIN Middle English: prob. already in Old English (see WHOLE, -SOME¹).

whole tone ■ n. Music an interval of two semitones.

wholewheat ■ n. whole grains of wheat including the husk.

wholly /ˈhəʊlli, ˈhəʊli/ ■ adv. entirely; fully.
–ORIGIN Middle English: prob. already in Old English (see WHOLE, -LY²).

whom ■ pron. used instead of 'who' as the object of a verb or preposition.

USAGE
On the use of **who** and **whom**, see WHO.

whomever ■ pron. chiefly formal used instead of 'whoever' as the object of a verb or preposition.

whomso ■ pron. archaic used instead of 'whoso' as the object of a verb or preposition.

whomsoever ■ rel. pron. formal used instead of 'whosoever' as the object of a verb or preposition.

whoop /huːp, wuːp/ ■ n. **1** a loud cry of joy or excitement. **2** a long rasping indrawn breath. ■ v. give or make a whoop.
–PHRASES **whoop it up** informal enjoy oneself or celebrate unrestrainedly.
–ORIGIN Middle English: prob. imitative.

whoopee informal ■ exclam. /wʊˈpiː/ expressing wild excitement or joy. ■ n. /ˈwʊpi/ wild revelry.
–PHRASES **make whoopee 1** celebrate wildly. **2** have sexual intercourse.

whoopee cushion ■ n. a rubber cushion that makes a sound like the breaking of wind when someone sits on it.

whooper /ˈhuːpə, ˈw-/ ■ n. a large migratory swan with a black and yellow bill and a loud trumpeting call, breeding in northern Eurasia and Greenland. [*Cygnus cygnus*.]

whooping cough /ˈhuːpɪŋ/ ■ n. a contagious bacterial disease chiefly affecting children, characterized by convulsive coughs followed by a whoop.

whooping crane /ˈhuːpɪŋ, ˈw-/ ■ n. a large mainly white crane with a trumpeting call, breeding in central Canada and now endangered. [*Grus americana*.]

whoops (also **whoops-a-daisy**) ■ exclam. informal expressing mild dismay.
–ORIGIN 1920s: prob. an alteration of UPSY-DAISY.

whoosh /wʊʃ, wuːʃ/ (also **woosh**) ■ v. move or cause to move quickly or suddenly and with a rushing sound. ■ n. a whooshing movement. ■ exclam. used to express such a movement or sound.
–DERIVATIVES **whooshing** adj.
–ORIGIN C19: imitative.

whop /wɒp/ informal ■ v. (**whopped**, **whopping**) hit hard. ■ n. a heavy blow or its sound. ▶ the regular pulsing sound of a helicopter rotor.
–ORIGIN Middle English: var. of dialect *wap* 'strike'.

whopper ■ n. informal **1** a thing that is extremely large. **2** a gross or blatant lie.

whopping ■ adj. informal extremely large.

whore ■ n. derogatory a prostitute or promiscuous woman. ■ v. work as a prostitute. ▶ use the services of prostitutes. ▶ debase oneself by doing something for unworthy motives.

1359

wick

–DERIVATIVES **whoredom** n. **whoring** adj. & n. **whorish** adj.
–ORIGIN Old English *hōre*, of Germanic origin.

whorehouse ■ n. informal a brothel.

whoremonger (also **whoremaster**) ■ n. archaic a person who has dealings with prostitutes.

whoreson /ˈhɔːs(ə)n/ ■ n. archaic a despicable person.
–ORIGIN Middle English: from WHORE + SON, suggested by Anglo-Norman French *fiz a putain*.

whorl /wɔːl, wəːl/ ■ n. **1** Zoology each of the convolutions in the shell of a gastropod or ammonoid mollusc. **2** Botany a set of leaves, flowers, or branches springing from the stem at the same level and encircling it. ▶ Botany (in a flower) each of the sets of organs, especially the petals and sepals, arranged concentrically round the receptacle. **3** a complete circle in a fingerprint. ■ v. poetic/literary spiral or move in a twisted or convoluted fashion.
–DERIVATIVES **whorled** adj.
–ORIGIN Middle English (denoting a small flywheel): apparently a var. of WHIRL, influenced by Old English *wharve* 'whorl of a spindle'.

whortleberry /ˈwɔːt(ə)l,b(ə)ri, -ˈberi/ ■ n. a bilberry.
–ORIGIN C16: dialect var. of Middle English *hurtleberry*.

who's ■ contr. **1** who is. **2** who has.

USAGE
Do not confuse **who's** with **whose**. **Who's** is a contraction of 'who is' (*Who's that?*) or 'who has' (*Who's been eating the cheese?*). **Whose** means 'belonging to or associated with which person?' (*Whose turn is it?*) or 'of whom or which' (*the event, whose organisers are well-known*).

whose ■ interrog. possess. det.& pron. belonging to or associated with which person. ■ rel. possess. det. of whom or which.
–ORIGIN Old English *hwæs*, genitive of *hwā* 'who' and *hwæt* 'what'.

whosever ■ rel. pron. & det. belonging to or associated with whichever person; whoever's.

whoso ■ pron. archaic term for WHOEVER.
–ORIGIN Middle English: shortening Old English *swā hwā swā* 'so who so'.

whosoever ■ pron. formal term for WHOEVER.

who's who ■ n. a list or directory of facts about notable people.

whump /wʌmp, wʊmp/ ■ n. a dull thud. ■ v. make a whump. ▶ strike heavily.
–ORIGIN C19: imitative.

whup /wʌp/ ■ v. (**whupped**, **whupping**) informal, chiefly N. Amer. beat; thrash.
–ORIGIN C19: var. of WHIP.

why ■ interrog. adv. for what reason or purpose. ■ rel. adv. (with reference to a reason) on account of which; for which. ▶ the reason for which. ■ exclam. **1** expressing surprise or indignation. **2** used to add emphasis to a response. ■ n. (pl. **whys**) a reason or explanation.
–ORIGIN Old English *hwī*, *hwȳ* 'by what cause', instrumental case of *hwæt* 'what', of Germanic origin.

whydah /ˈwɪdə/ (also **whyda**) ■ n. **1** an African weaver bird, the male of which has a black back and a very long black tail used in display flight. [Genus *Vidua*: several species.] **2** another term for WIDOWBIRD.
–ORIGIN C18 (orig. *widow-bird*): alteration by association with *Whidah* (now Ouidah), a town in Benin.

wibble ■ v. informal another term for WOBBLE.
–DERIVATIVES **wibbly** adj.
–ORIGIN C19: independent usage of the first element of the reduplication *wibble-wobble*.

Wicca /ˈwɪkə/ ■ n. the religious cult of modern witchcraft.
–DERIVATIVES **Wiccan** adj. & n.
–ORIGIN Old English *wicca* 'witch'.

wick¹ ■ n. **1** a strip of porous material up which liquid fuel is drawn by capillary action to the flame in a candle, lamp, or lighter. **2** Medicine a gauze strip inserted in a

wound to drain it. ■ v. absorb or draw off (liquid) by capillary action.
- PHRASES **get on someone's wick** informal annoy someone.
- ORIGIN Old English *wēoce*, of West Germanic origin.

wick² ■ n. [in place names] a town, hamlet, or district.
- ORIGIN Old English *wīc* 'dwelling place', prob. from Latin *vicus* 'street, village'.

wicked ■ adj. (-er, -est) **1** evil or morally wrong. **2** playfully mischievous. **3** informal excellent; wonderful.
- DERIVATIVES **wickedly** adv. **wickedness** n.
- ORIGIN Middle English: prob. from Old English *wicca* 'witch'.

wicker ■ n. pliable twigs, typically of willow, plaited or woven to make items such as furniture and baskets.
- DERIVATIVES **wickerwork** n.
- ORIGIN Middle English: of Scandinavian origin; cf. Swedish *viker* 'willow'.

wicket ■ n. **1** Cricket each of the sets of three stumps with two bails across the top at either end of the pitch, defended by a batsman. ▶ the prepared strip of ground between these two sets of stumps. ▶ the dismissal of a batsman. **2** a small door or gate, especially one beside or in a larger one.
- PHRASES **at the wicket** Cricket **1** batting. **2** by the wicketkeeper. **a sticky wicket 1** Cricket a pitch that has been drying after rain and is difficult to bat on. **2** informal a tricky or awkward situation.
- ORIGIN Middle English: from Anglo-Norman French and Old Northern French *wiket*; usu. referred to the Germanic root of Old Norse *víkja* 'to turn, move'.

wicketkeeper ■ n. Cricket a fielder stationed close behind a batsman's wicket.
- DERIVATIVES **wicketkeeping** n.

widdershins /ˈwɪdəʃɪnz/ ■ adv. chiefly Scottish in a direction contrary to the sun's course (or anticlockwise), considered as unlucky.
- ORIGIN C16: from Middle Low German *weddersins*, from Middle High German *widersinnes*, from *wider* 'against' + *sin* 'direction'; the second element was associated with Scots *sin* 'sun'.

widdle informal ■ v. urinate. ■ n. an act of urinating. ▶ urine.
- ORIGIN 1950s: alteration of PIDDLE.

wide ■ adj. (**wider**, **widest**) **1** of great or more than average width. ▶ (after a measurement and in questions) from side to side. ▶ open to the full extent: *wide eyes*. **2** including a great variety of people or things. ▶ spread among a large number or over a large area: *wider share ownership*. ▶ [in combination] extending over the whole of: *industry-wide*. **3** at a considerable or specified distance from a point or mark. ▶ (especially in soccer) at or near the side of the field. ■ adv. **1** to the full extent. **2** far from a particular point or mark. ▶ (especially in soccer) at or near the side of the field. ■ n. (also **wide ball**) Cricket a ball that is judged to be too wide of the stumps for the batsman to play.
- PHRASES **wide awake** fully awake. **wide of the mark** a long way from an intended target. ▶ inaccurate. **wide open 1** (of a contest) of which the outcome is not predictable. **2** vulnerable to attack.
- DERIVATIVES **widely** adv. **wideness** n. **widish** adj.
- ORIGIN Old English *wīd* 'spacious, extensive', *wide* 'over a large area', of Germanic origin.

wide-angle ■ adj. (of a lens) having a short focal length and hence a field covering a wide angle.

wide area network ■ n. a computer network in which the computers connected may be far apart, generally having a radius of more than 1 km.

widebody ■ adj. (also **wide-bodied**) denoting a jet airliner with a wide fuselage. ■ n. (pl. -ies) a widebody aircraft.

wide boy ■ n. Brit. informal a man involved in petty criminal activities.

wide-eyed ■ adj. **1** having one's eyes wide open in amazement. **2** inexperienced; innocent.

widen ■ v. make or become wider.

wide receiver ■ n. American Football an offensive player positioned away from the line, used primarily as a pass receiver.

widescreen ■ adj. denoting a screen or a format used with a screen presenting a wide field of vision in relation to height.

widespread ■ adj. spread among a large number or over a large area.

widgeon ■ n. variant spelling of WIGEON.

widget /ˈwɪdʒɪt/ ■ n. informal a small gadget or mechanical device. ▶ Computing a component of a user interface with a particular function.
- ORIGIN 1930s (orig. US): perhaps an alteration of GADGET.

widow ■ n. **1** a woman who has lost her husband by death and has not married again. ▶ humorous a woman whose husband is often away participating in a specified sport or activity: *a golf widow*. **2** Printing a last word or short last line of a paragraph falling at the top of a page or column. ■ v. (**be widowed**) become a widow or widower.
- ORIGIN Old English *widewe*, from an Indo-European root meaning 'be empty'.

widowbird ■ n. **1** an African weaver bird, the male of which has mainly black plumage and typically a long tail used in leaping displays. [Genus *Euplectes*: several species.] **2** another term for WHYDAH.

widower ■ n. a man who has lost his wife by death and has not married again.

widowhood ■ n. the state or period of being a widow or widower.

widow's mite ■ n. a small monetary contribution from someone who is poor.
- ORIGIN with biblical allusion to Mark 12:43.

widow's peak ■ n. a V-shaped growth of hair towards the centre of the forehead.

widow's walk ■ n. N. Amer. a railed or balustraded platform built on a roof in early New England houses, providing an unimpeded view of the sea.
- ORIGIN 1930s: with ref. to its use as a viewpoint for return of a seafaring husband.

widow's weeds ■ pl. n. black clothes worn by a widow in mourning.
- ORIGIN C18: *weeds* (obsolete in the general sense 'garments') is from Old English *wǣd(e)*, of Germanic origin.

width /wɪtθ, wɪdθ/ ■ n. **1** the measurement or extent of something from side to side; the lesser of two or the least of three dimensions of a body. ▶ a piece of something at its full extent from side to side. **2** wide range or extent.
- ORIGIN C17: from WIDE + -TH², on the pattern of *breadth* (replacing *wideness*).

widthways (also **widthwise**) ■ adv. in a direction parallel with a thing's width.

wield ■ v. **1** hold and use (a weapon or tool). **2** have and be able to use (power or influence).
- DERIVATIVES **wielder** n.
- ORIGIN Old English *wealdan*, *wieldan* 'govern, subdue, direct', of Germanic origin.

wieldy ■ adj. (-ier, -iest) easily controlled or handled.
- ORIGIN C16: back-formation from UNWIELDY.

wiener /ˈwiːnə/ ■ n. (also informal **weenie**, **wienie** /ˈwiːni/) ■ n. N. Amer. a frankfurter or similar sausage.
- ORIGIN C20: abbrev. of German *Wienerwurst* 'Vienna sausage'.

Wiener schnitzel ■ n. a thin slice of veal that is breaded and fried.
- ORIGIN from German, 'Vienna cutlet'.

wife ■ n. (pl. **wives**) a married woman considered in relation to her husband. ▶ archaic or dialect a woman, especially an old or uneducated one.
- DERIVATIVES **wifehood** n. **wifeless** adj. **wifeliness** n. **wifely** adj.
- ORIGIN Old English *wīf* 'woman', of Germanic origin.

wife-swapping ■ n. informal the practice within a group of married couples of exchanging sexual partners on a casual basis.

Wi-Fi ■ abbrev. Wireless Fidelity, a group of technical standards enabling the transmission of data over wireless networks.

wig¹ ■ n. a covering for the head made of real or artificial hair.
– DERIVATIVES **wigged** adj. **wigless** adj.
– ORIGIN C17: shortening of PERIWIG.

wig² ■ v. (**wigged**, **wigging**) informal **1** Brit. dated rebuke severely. **2** (**wig out**) chiefly N. Amer. become deliriously excited.
– DERIVATIVES **wigging** n.
– ORIGIN C19: apparently from WIG¹, perhaps from BIGWIG and associated with a rebuke given by a person in authority.

wigeon /'wɪdʒ(ə)n/ (also **widgeon**) ■ n. a dabbling duck with mainly reddish-brown and grey plumage, the male having a whistling call. [Genus *Anas*: three species.]
– ORIGIN C16: perhaps of imitative origin and suggested by PIGEON¹.

wiggle ■ v. move or cause to move with short movements up and down or from side to side. ■ n. a wiggling movement.
– DERIVATIVES **wiggler** n. **wiggly** adj. (**-ier**, **-ist**).
– ORIGIN Middle English: from Middle Low German and Middle Dutch *wiggelen*.

wiggle room ■ n. informal capacity or scope for negotiation, especially in order to modify a previous statement or decision.

wiggy ■ adj. (**-ier**, **-iest**) informal, chiefly N. Amer. emotionally uncontrolled or weird.
– ORIGIN 1960s: from *wig out* (see WIG²).

wight ■ n. **1** archaic or dialect a person of a specified kind: *an unlucky wight*. **2** poetic/literary a spirit or ghost.
– ORIGIN Old English *wiht* 'thing, creature', of Germanic origin.

wigwam ■ n. a dome-shaped or conical dwelling made by fastening mats, skins, or bark over a framework of poles (as used formerly by some North American Indian peoples).
– ORIGIN C17: from Ojibwa *wigwaum*, Algonquian *wikiwam* 'their house'.

wiki /'wɪki, 'wiːkiː/ ■ n. a website or database developed collaboratively by a community of users, allowing any user to add and edit content.
– ORIGIN from *WikiWikiWeb* (1995), coined by the US programmer Ward Cunningham, from Hawaiian *wiki wiki* 'very quick', reduplication of *wiki* 'quick'.

wilco ■ exclam. expressing compliance or agreement (used in radio communication).
– ORIGIN 1940s (orig. in military use): abbrev. of *will comply*.

wild ■ adj. **1** (of animals or plants) living or growing in the natural environment; not domesticated or cultivated. ▸ (of people) not civilized; barbarous. ▸ (of scenery or a region) desolate-looking. **2** uncontrolled; unrestrained. ▸ haphazard: *a wild guess*. ▸ informal very enthusiastic or excited. ▸ informal very angry. ▸ (of looks, appearance, etc.) indicating distraction. ■ n. (**the wild**) a natural state or uncultivated or uninhabited region. ▸ (**the wilds**) a remote area.
– PHRASES **run wild** grow or behave without restraint or discipline. **wild and woolly** uncouth or rough.
– DERIVATIVES **wildish** adj. **wildly** adv. **wildness** n.
– ORIGIN Old English, of Germanic origin.

wild banana ■ n. S. African a banana-like tree native to southern Africa, widely grown as an ornamental. [*Strelitzia nicolai* and other species.]

wild card ■ n. **1** a playing card that can have any value, suit, colour, or other property in a game at the discretion of the player holding it. **2** a person or thing whose qualities are uncertain. **3** Computing a character that will match any character or sequence of characters in a search. **4** an opportunity to enter a sports competition without taking part in qualifying matches or being ranked at a particular level. ▸ a player or team given such an opportunity.

wildcat ■ n. **1** a small Eurasian and African cat, typically grey with black markings and a bushy tail, believed to be the ancestor of the domestic cat. [*Felis silvestris*.] ▸ a bobcat or other small felid. **2** a hot-tempered or ferocious person. **3** an exploratory oil well. ■ adj. **1** (of a strike) sudden and unofficial. **2** commercially unsound or risky. ■ v. US prospect for oil.
– DERIVATIVES **wildcatter** n.

1361

will

wild dagga ■ n. a southern African evergreen shrub which bears clusters of bright orange or white tubular flowers. [*Leonotis leonurus*.]

wild date palm ■ n. an African palm which bears small orange-brown fruits, cultivated as an ornamental. [*Phoenix reclinata*.]

wild dog ■ n. **1** any wild member of the dog family, e.g. a dingo or coyote. **2** (also **African wild dog**) a gregarious wild dog that has a dark coat with pale markings and a white-tipped tail, formerly found throughout sub-Saharan Africa. [*Lycaon pictus*.]

wild duck ■ n. another term for MALLARD.

wildebeest /'wɪldəbiːst, 'vɪ-/ ■ n. (pl. same or **wildebeests**) a large African antelope with a long head, a beard and mane, and a sloping back. [Genus *Connochaetes*: two species.]
– ORIGIN C19: from Afrikaans, 'wild beast'.

wilder /'wɪldə/ ■ v. archaic lead or drive astray. ▸ bewilder.
– ORIGIN C17: perhaps based on WILDERNESS.

wilderness ■ n. **1** an uncultivated, uninhabited, and inhospitable region. ▸ a neglected or abandoned area. ▸ (**wilderness area**) an area of land preserved in its natural state and protected from development. **2** a position of disfavour.
– PHRASES **a voice in the wilderness** an unheeded advocate of reform (see Matthew 3:3 etc.).
– ORIGIN Old English *wildēornes* 'land inhabited only by wild animals', from *wild dēor* 'wild deer'.

wild fig ■ n. a tree that is related to the cultivated fig, sometimes having a large spreading crown and grown as an ornamental and shade tree. [Genus *Ficus*: many species.]

wildfire ■ n. historical a highly flammable liquid used in warfare.
– PHRASES **spread like wildfire** spread with great speed.

wildfowl ■ pl. n. game birds, especially aquatic ones; waterfowl.

wild garlic ■ n. a bulbous southern African plant which bears mauve flowers on long stalks and smells of garlic when crushed, cultivated as an ornamental. [*Tulbaghia violacea* or *T. alliacea*.]

wild goose chase ■ n. a foolish and hopeless search for or pursuit of something unattainable.

wildlife ■ n. the native fauna (and sometimes flora) of a region.

wild oat ■ n. a grass which is related to the cultivated oat and is found as a weed of other cereals. [*Avena fatua*.]
– PHRASES **sow one's wild oats** see OAT.

wild olive ■ n. an evergreen tree that bears small purple-black berries. [*Olea europaea* subsp. *african*.] ▸ the hard wood of this tree, widely used for furniture and ornaments.

wild peach ■ n. an African evergreen tree that bears conspicuous red and black seeds, cultivated as an ornamental. [*Kiggelaria africana*.]

wild pitch ■ n. Baseball a pitch which is not hit by the batter and cannot be stopped by the catcher, enabling a base runner to advance.

wild plum ■ n. a southern African evergreen tree that bears edible red fruits, cultivated as an ornamental and shade tree. [*Harpephyllum caffrum*.]

wild rice ■ n. a tall aquatic American grass with edible grains, related to rice. [*Zizania aquatica*.]

wild silk ■ n. coarse silk produced by wild silkworms, especially tussore.

wild type ■ n. Genetics a strain, gene, or characteristic which prevails among individuals in natural conditions, as distinct from an atypical mutant type.

wile ■ n. a devious or cunning stratagem.
– ORIGIN Middle English: perhaps from an Old Norse word rel. to *vél* 'craft'.

wilful (also **willful**) ■ adj. **1** intentional; deliberate. **2** stubborn and determined.
– DERIVATIVES **wilfully** adv. **wilfulness** n.
– ORIGIN Middle English: from the noun WILL² + -FUL.

will¹ ■ modal v. (3rd sing. present **will**; past **would**)

will

will[1] 1 expressing the future tense. ▸ expressing a strong intention or assertion about the future. 2 expressing inevitable events. 3 expressing a request. ▸ expressing desire, consent, or willingness. 4 expressing facts about ability or capacity. 5 expressing habitual behaviour. 6 expressing probability or expectation about something in the present.
– ORIGIN Old English *wyllan*, of Germanic origin.

USAGE
On the difference in use between **will** and **shall**, see usage at **SHALL**.

will[2] ■ n. 1 the faculty by which a person decides on and initiates action. ▸ (also **will power**) control or restraint deliberately exerted. ▸ a desire or intention. 2 a legal document containing instructions for the disposition of one's money and property after one's death. ■ v. 1 chiefly formal or poetic/literary intend or desire to happen. ▸ bring about by the exercise of mental powers. 2 (**will something to**) bequeath something to. ▸ leave specified instructions in one's will.
– PHRASES **at will** at whatever time or in whatever way one pleases. **have a will of one's own** have a wilful character. **with the best will in the world** however good one's intentions. **with a will** energetically and resolutely.
– DERIVATIVES **-willed** adj. **willer** n.
– ORIGIN Old English *willa* (n.), *willian* (v.), of Germanic origin; rel. to WILL[1].

willful ■ adj. variant spelling of WILFUL.

Williams ■ n. a dessert pear of an early green variety.
– ORIGIN C19: named after its first distributor in England.

willie ■ n. variant spelling of WILLY.

willies ■ pl. n. (**the willies**) informal a strong feeling of nervous discomfort: *the room gave him the willies.*
– ORIGIN C19 (orig. US).

willie wagtail (also **willy wagtail**) ■ n. Brit. informal the pied wagtail.

willing ■ adj. ready, eager, or prepared to do something. ▸ given or done readily.
– DERIVATIVES **willingly** adv. **willingness** n.

will-o'-the-wisp ■ n. 1 a phosphorescent light seen hovering or floating at night on marshy ground, thought to result from the combustion of natural gases. 2 a person or thing that is difficult or impossible to reach or catch.
– ORIGIN C17: orig. as *Will with the wisp*, the sense of *wisp* being 'handful of (lighted) hay'.

willow ■ n. a tree or shrub of temperate climate which typically grows near water, has narrow leaves and pliant branches yielding osiers and wood, and bears catkins. [Genus *Salix*: many species.]
– ORIGIN Old English, of Germanic origin.

willow grouse ■ n. a northern-hemisphere bird of which the red grouse is a distinct subspecies. [*Lagopus lagopus*.]

willowherb ■ n. a plant with long narrow leaves and pink or pale purple flowers. [*Epilobium* and related genera: many species.]

willow pattern ■ n. a conventional design in pottery featuring a Chinese scene depicted in blue on white, typically including figures on a bridge, a willow tree, and birds.

willow warbler ■ n. a small migratory warbler with mainly drab plumage and a tuneful song. [*Phylloscopus trochilus* and related species.]

willowware ■ n. chiefly US pottery with a willow-pattern design.

willowy ■ adj. 1 bordered, shaded, or covered by willows. 2 (of a person) tall, slim, and lithe.

will power ■ n. see WILL[2] (sense 1).

willy (also **willie**) ■ n. (pl. **-ies**) informal a penis.
– ORIGIN C20: familiar form of the given name *William*.

willy-nilly ■ adv. 1 whether one likes it or not. 2 without direction or planning; haphazardly.
– ORIGIN C17: later spelling of *will I, nill I* 'I am willing, I am unwilling'.

willy wagtail ■ n. variant spelling of WILLIE WAGTAIL.

willy-willy ■ n. (pl. **-ies**) Austral. a whirlwind or dust storm.
– ORIGIN from Yindjibarndi (an Aboriginal language of western Australia).

Wilms' tumour /wɪlmz, vɪlmz/ ■ n. a malignant tumour of the kidney, of a type that occurs in young children.
– ORIGIN C20: named after the German surgeon Max *Wilms*.

wilt[1] ■ v. 1 (of a plant) become limp through loss of water, heat, or disease; droop. ▸ (of a person) lose one's energy or vigour. 2 leave (mown grass or a forage crop) in the open to dry partially before being collected for silage. ■ n. any of a number of fungal or bacterial diseases of plants characterized by wilting of the foliage.
– ORIGIN C17: perhaps an alteration of dialect *welk* 'lose freshness', of Low German origin.

wilt[2] archaic second person singular of WILL[1].

wily /ˈwaɪli/ ■ adj. (**-ier**, **-iest**) skilled at gaining an advantage, especially deceitfully.
– DERIVATIVES **wilily** adv. **wiliness** n.

wimmin ■ pl. n. non-standard spelling of 'women' adopted by some feminists to avoid the word ending *-men*.

WIMP[1] ■ n. Computing a set of software features and hardware devices designed to simplify or demystify computing operations for the user.
– ORIGIN 1980s: acronym from *windows, icons, mice, and pull-down menus* (or *pointers*).

WIMP[2] ■ n. Physics a hypothetical heavy subatomic particle postulated as a constituent of dark matter.
– ORIGIN 1980s: acronym from *weakly interacting massive particle*.

wimp informal ■ n. a weak and cowardly person. ■ v. (**wimp out**) withdraw from something in a cowardly way.
– DERIVATIVES **wimpish** adj. **wimpishly** adv. **wimpishness** n. **wimpy** adj.
– ORIGIN 1920s: perhaps from WHIMPER.

wimple ■ n. a cloth headdress covering the head, neck, and sides of the face, formerly worn by women and still by some nuns.
– DERIVATIVES **wimpled** adj.
– ORIGIN Old English, of Germanic origin.

win ■ v. (**winning**; past and past part. **won**) 1 be successful or victorious in (a contest or conflict). 2 acquire as a result of a contest, conflict, etc. ▸ gain (someone's attention, support, or love). ▸ (**win someone over**) gain the support or favour of someone. 3 (**win out/through**) manage to succeed or achieve something by effort. ▸ archaic manage to reach (a place) by effort. 4 obtain (ore) from a mine. ■ n. a victory, especially in a game or contest.
– PHRASES **win the day** be victorious. **win** (or **earn**) **one's spurs** historical gain a knighthood by an act of bravery. ▸ informal gain one's first distinction or honours.
– DERIVATIVES **winless** adj. **winnable** adj.
– ORIGIN Old English *winnan* 'strive, contend' also 'subdue and take possession of, acquire', of Germanic origin.

wince ■ v. give a slight involuntary grimace or flinch due to pain or distress. ■ n. an instance of wincing.
– DERIVATIVES **wincer** n. **wincing** adj. **wincingly** adv.
– ORIGIN Middle English: from an Anglo-Norman French var. of Old French *guenchir* 'turn aside'.

wincey ■ n. (pl. **-eys**) Brit. a strong, lightweight twilled fabric, typically made of wool with cotton or linen.
– ORIGIN C19: apparently an alteration of *linsey woolsey*, denoting a coarse fabric made of linen and wool.

winceyette /ˌwɪnsɪˈɛt/ ■ n. Brit. a lightweight napped flannelette, used especially for nightclothes.

winch ■ n. 1 a hauling or lifting device consisting of a rope or chain winding around a horizontal rotating drum, turned by a crank or by motor. 2 the crank of a wheel or axle. ■ v. hoist or haul with a winch.
– ORIGIN Old English *wince* 'reel, pulley', of Germanic origin.

Winchester /ˈwɪntʃɪstə/ (also **Winchester rifle**) ■ n. trademark a breech-loading side-action repeating rifle.
– ORIGIN named after the American rifle manufacturer Oliver F. *Winchester*.

wind[1] /wɪnd/ ■ n. 1 the perceptible natural movement of the air, especially in the form of a current blowing from a particular direction. ▸ the rush of air caused by a fast-moving body. 2 breath as needed in physical exertion, speech, playing an instrument, etc. 3 air swallowed while

---

CONSONANTS b but d dog f few g get h he j yes k cat l leg m man n no p pen r red

eating or gas generated in the stomach and intestines by digestion. **4** meaningless talk. **5** (also **winds**) [treated as sing. or pl.] wind or woodwind instruments forming a band or section of an orchestra. **6** a scent carried by the wind, indicating the proximity of an animal or person. ■ v. **1** cause to have difficulty breathing because of exertion or a blow to the stomach. **2** make (a baby) bring up wind after feeding by patting its back. **3** detect the scent of. **4** /waɪnd/ (past and past part. **winded** or **wound** /waʊnd/) poetic/literary sound (a bugle or call) by blowing.
– PHRASES **before the wind** Nautical with the wind blowing from astern. **get wind of** informal hear a rumour of. **off the wind** Nautical with the wind on the quarter. **on a wind** Nautical against a wind on either bow. **put** (or **have**) **the wind up** informal alarm or frighten (or be alarmed or frightened). **sail close to** (or **near**) **the wind 1** sail as nearly against the wind as is consistent with using its force. **2** informal verge on indecency, dishonesty, or disaster. **take the wind out of someone's sails** frustrate someone by anticipating an action or remark. **to the wind** (**s**) (or **the four winds**) in all directions.
– DERIVATIVES **windless** adj.
– ORIGIN Old English, of Germanic origin.

wind² /waɪnd/ ■ v. (past and past part. **wound** /waʊnd/) **1** move in or take a twisting or spiral course. **2** pass (something) around a thing or person so as to encircle or enfold them. ▸ (with reference to a length of something) twist or be twisted around itself or a core. **3** make (a clock or clockwork device) operate by turning a key or handle. ▸ turn (a key or handle) repeatedly. **4** move (an audio or video tape or a film) back or forwards to a desired point. ■ n. **1** a twist or turn in a course. **2** a single turn made when winding.
– PHRASAL VERBS **wind down 1** (of a clockwork mechanism) gradually lose power. **2** informal relax. **3** (also **wind something down**) draw or bring gradually to a close. **wind up** informal end up in a specified state, situation, or place. **wind someone up** informal tease or irritate someone. **wind something up 1** arrange the affairs of and dissolve a company. **2** gradually bring an activity to a conclusion. **3** informal increase the tension or power of something.
– ORIGIN Old English *windan* 'go rapidly, twine', of Germanic origin.

windage ■ n. the air resistance of a moving object or the force of the wind on a stationary object. ▸ the effect of the wind in deflecting a missile.

windbag ■ n. informal a person who talks a lot but says little of any value.
– DERIVATIVES **windbaggery** n.

windbound ■ adj. (of a ship) unable to sail because of extreme or contrary winds.

windbreak ■ n. a row of trees, wall, or screen providing shelter from the wind.

windbreaker ■ n. (trademark in the US) a wind-resistant jacket with a close-fitting neck, waistband, and cuffs.

windburn ■ n. reddening and soreness of the skin caused by prolonged exposure to the wind.
– DERIVATIVES **windburned** (also **windburnt**) adj.

windcheater ■ n. another term for WINDBREAKER.

wind chill ■ n. the cooling effect of wind on a surface.

wind chimes ■ pl. n. small decorative pieces of glass or metal suspended from a frame, typically hung near a door or window so as to tinkle in the draught.

winder /ˈwaɪndə/ ■ n. a device or mechanism for winding something, especially a watch, clock, or camera film.

windfall ■ n. **1** an apple or other fruit blown from a tree by the wind. **2** a piece of unexpected good fortune, especially a legacy.

windfall tax (also **windfall profits tax**) ■ n. a tax levied on an unexpectedly large profit, especially one regarded to be excessive or unfairly obtained.

wind farm ■ n. an area containing a group of energy-producing windmills or wind turbines.

windflower ■ n. an anemone.

wind gap ■ n. a valley cut through a ridge by a river which no longer flows through the valley.

wind gauge ■ n. an anemometer.

windhover ■ n. dialect a kestrel.

windshield

winding /ˈwaɪndɪŋ/ ■ n. **1** a twisting movement or course. **2** a thing that winds or is wound round something. ▸ a coil of conducting wire in an electric motor, generator, etc. ■ adj. having a twisting or spiral course.

winding sheet ■ n. a shroud.

wind instrument ■ n. a musical instrument in which sound is produced by the vibration of air. ▸ a woodwind instrument as distinct from a brass instrument.

windjammer ■ n. historical a merchant sailing ship.

windlass ■ n. a winch, especially one on a ship or in a harbour.
– ORIGIN Middle English: prob. an alteration of obsolete *windas*, from Old Norse *vindáss* 'winding pole'.

wind machine ■ n. **1** a machine used in the theatre or in film-making for producing a blast of air or imitating the sound of wind. **2** a wind-driven turbine.

windmill ■ n. **1** a building with sails or vanes that turn in the wind and generate power to grind corn into flour. ▸ a similar structure used to generate electricity or draw water. **2** a toy consisting of a stick with curved vanes attached that turn in the wind. ■ v. move (one's arms) in a manner suggestive of the sails of a windmill.

window ■ n. **1** an opening in a wall or roof, fitted with glass in a frame to admit light or air and allow people to see out. ▸ an opening through which customers are served in a bank, ticket office, etc. ▸ a space behind the window of a shop where goods are displayed. **2** a transparent panel in an envelope to show an address. **3** Computing a framed area on a display screen for viewing information. ▸ (**Windows**) [treated as sing.] trademark a GUI operating system for personal computers. **4** (**window on/into/to**) a means of observing and learning about. **5** an interval or opportunity for action. **6** Physics a range of electromagnetic wavelengths for which a medium (especially the atmosphere) is transparent.
– PHRASES **go out** (**of**) **the window** informal (of a plan or behaviour) be abandoned or cease to exist. **windows of the soul** the eyes.
– DERIVATIVES **windowed** adj. **windowless** adj.
– ORIGIN Middle English: from Old Norse *vindauga*, from *vindr* 'wind' + *auga* 'eye'.

window box ■ n. a long narrow box in which flowers and other plants are grown on an outside windowsill.

window dressing ■ n. **1** the arrangement of an attractive display in a shop window. **2** an adroit but superficial or misleading presentation of something.

window frame ■ n. a frame holding the glass of a window.

windowing ■ n. Computing the use of windows for the simultaneous display of more than one item on a screen.

window ledge ■ n. a window sill.

windowpane ■ n. a pane of glass in a window.

window seat ■ n. **1** a seat below a window, especially one in a bay or alcove. **2** a seat next to a window in an aircraft or train.

window-shop ■ v. look at the goods in shop windows, especially without intending to buy.
– DERIVATIVES **window-shopper** n.

window sill ■ n. a ledge or sill forming the bottom part of a window.

windpipe ■ n. the trachea.

wind rose ■ n. a diagram showing the relative frequency of wind directions at a place.

windrow ■ n. a long line of raked hay, corn sheaves, or peats drying in the wind.

windscreen ■ n. a glass screen at the front of a motor vehicle.

windscreen wiper ■ n. a device for keeping a windscreen clear of rain, typically with a rubber blade on an arm that moves in an arc.

wind shear ■ n. variation in wind velocity along a direction at right angles to the wind's direction, tending to exert a turning force.

windshield ■ n. chiefly N. Amer. a windscreen.

windsock

windsock ■ n. a light, flexible cylinder or cone mounted on a mast to show the direction and strength of the wind, especially at an airfield.

Windsor chair ■ n. a wooden dining chair with a semicircular back supported by upright rods.

Windsor knot ■ n. a large, loose triangular knot in a tie, produced by making extra turns when tying.

wind sprint ■ n. (in athletics) an exercise involving moving from a walk or slow run to a faster run and repeatedly reversing the process.

windstorm ■ n. a gale.

windsurfer ■ n. 1 a person who takes part in windsurfing. 2 (trademark in the US) a sailboard.

windsurfing ■ n. the sport of riding on water on a sailboard.
– DERIVATIVES **windsurf** v.

windswept ■ adj. exposed to strong winds. ▶ untidy after being exposed to the wind.

wind tunnel ■ n. a tunnel-like apparatus for producing an airstream past models of aircraft, buildings, etc., in order to investigate flow or the effect of wind on the full-size object.

wind-up ■ n. 1 Brit. informal an attempt to tease or irritate someone. 2 an act of concluding something. 3 Baseball the motions of a pitcher preparing to pitch the ball.

windward ■ adj. & adv. facing the wind or on the side facing the wind. Contrasted with LEEWARD. ■ n. the side from which the wind is blowing.

windy[1] /ˈwɪndi/ ■ adj. (-ier, -iest) 1 marked by or exposed to strong winds. 2 suffering from, marked by, or causing wind in the alimentary canal.
– DERIVATIVES **windily** adv. **windiness** n.

windy[2] /ˈwaɪndi/ ■ adj. (of a road or river) following a winding course.

windy dryer ■ n. S. African a cross-shaped frame linked by lengths of line, which is mounted on a pole and rotates in windy conditions, used for hanging clothes to dry outdoors.

wine ■ n. 1 an alcoholic drink made from fermented grape juice. ▶ a fermented alcoholic drink made from other fruits or plants. 2 short for WINE RED. ■ v. (**wine and dine someone**) entertain someone with drinks and a meal. ▶ take part in such entertainment.
– DERIVATIVES **winey** (also **winy**) adj.
– ORIGIN Old English *win*, of Germanic origin, based on Latin *vinum*.

wine bar ■ n. a bar or small restaurant where wine is the main drink available.

wine bottle ■ n. a glass bottle for wine, the standard size holding 75 cl.

wine box ■ n. a square carton of wine with a dispensing tap.

wine cellar ■ n. a cellar for storing wine. ▶ a stock of wine.

wine farm ■ n. chiefly S. African a farm on which grapes are grown and wine is produced.
– DERIVATIVES **wine farmer** n. **wine farming** n.

wine glass ■ n. a glass with a stem and foot, used for drinking wine.
– DERIVATIVES **wineglassful** n. (pl. **-fuls**).

winegrower ■ n. a grower of grapes for wine.

wine gum ■ n. a small coloured fruit-flavoured sweet made with gelatin.

wine list ■ n. a list of the wines available in a restaurant.

winemaker ■ n. a producer of wine.
– DERIVATIVES **winemaking** n.

wine of origin ■ n. S. African an official designation on a wine-bottle label indicating that the wine has been certified as coming from a recognized region or estate and is of a particular cultivar or vintage.

wine red ■ n. a dark red colour like that of red wine.

wine route ■ n. any circular tour in which wine farms are visited for the tasting and purchase of wine.

winery ■ n. (pl. **-ies**) an establishment where wine is made.

wineskin ■ n. an animal skin sewn up and used to hold wine.

wine tasting ■ n. judging the quality of wine by tasting it. ▶ an occasion for this.
– DERIVATIVES **wine taster** n.

wine vinegar ■ n. vinegar made from wine rather than malt.

wing ■ n. 1 a modified forelimb or other appendage enabling a bird, bat, insect, or other creature to fly. 2 a rigid horizontal structure projecting from both sides of an aircraft and supporting it in the air. ▶ (**wings**) a pilot's badge representing a pair of wings. 3 a raised part of the body of a vehicle above the wheel. 4 a part of a large building, especially one that projects from the main part. 5 Anatomy a lateral part or projection of an organ or structure. ▶ Botany a thin membranous appendage of a fruit or seed dispersed by the wind. 6 a group within an organization having particular views or a particular function. 7 (**the wings**) the sides of a theatre stage out of view of the audience. 8 the part of a soccer, rugby, or hockey field close to the sidelines. ▶ (also **wing forward**) an attacking player positioned near the sidelines. 9 a flank of a battle array. 10 an air force unit of several squadrons or groups. ■ v. 1 fly or move quickly, as if flying. ▶ archaic enable to fly or move rapidly. 2 shoot (a bird) in the wing, so as to prevent flight. ▶ wound superficially, especially in the arm or shoulder. 3 (**wing it**) informal speak or act without preparation.
– PHRASES **in the wings** ready for use or action at the appropriate time. **on the wing** (of a bird) in flight. **on a wing and a prayer** with only the slightest chance of success. **spread** (or **stretch** or **try**) **one's wings** extend one's activities and interests. **take wing** fly away. **under one's wing** in or into one's protective care.
– DERIVATIVES **winged** adj. **wingless** adj. **winglet** n. **wing-like** adj.
– ORIGIN Middle English: from Old Norse *vængir*, pl. of *vængr*; sense 3 of the verb was orig. theatrical slang meaning 'to play a role without properly knowing the text' (by relying on a prompter in the wings or by studying in the wings between scenes).

wing back ■ n. Soccer a player in a wide position on the field, taking part both in attack and defence.

wingbeat ■ n. one complete set of motions of a wing in flying.

wing case ■ n. each of a pair of modified toughened forewings covering the functional wings of a beetle or other insect.

wing chair ■ n. an armchair with side pieces projecting forwards from a high back.

wing collar ■ n. a high stiff shirt collar with turned-down corners.

wing commander ■ n. a rank of RAF officer, above squadron leader and below group captain.

wingding ■ n. informal, chiefly N. Amer. a lively event or party.
– ORIGIN 1920s (meaning 'spasm, seizure', especially one due to drug-taking).

winged words ■ pl. n. poetic/literary highly apposite or significant words.

winger ■ n. 1 an attacking player on the wing in soccer, hockey, etc. 2 [in combination] a member of a specified political wing: *a right-winger*.

wing forward ■ n. 1 see WING (sense 8). 2 another term for FLANKER.

wingman ■ n. (pl. **-men**) a pilot whose aircraft is positioned behind and outside the leading aircraft in a formation.

wing mirror ■ n. a rear-view mirror projecting from the side of a vehicle.

wing nut ■ n. a nut with a pair of projections for the fingers to turn it on a screw.

wingover ■ n. a manoeuvre in which an aircraft turns at the top of a steep climb and flies back along its original path.

wingspan (also **wingspread**) ■ n. the maximum extent across the wings of an aircraft, bird, etc., measured from tip to tip.

VOWELS a cat ɑː arm ɛ bed ɛː hair ə ago əː her ɪ sit i cosy iː see ɒ hot ɔː saw ʌ run

wingstroke ■ n. a wingbeat.

wing tip (also **wingtip shoe**) ■ n. N. Amer. a shoe with a toecap having a backward extending point and curving sides, resembling the shape of a wing.

wing walking ■ n. acrobatic stunts performed on the wings of an airborne aircraft.
– DERIVATIVES **wing walker** n.

wink ■ v. **1** close and open one eye quickly, typically as a signal of affection or greeting or to convey a message. **2** shine or flash intermittently. **3** (**wink at**) pretend not to notice (something bad). ■ n. an act of winking.
– PHRASES **as easy as winking** informal very easy or easily. **in the wink of an eye** (or **in a wink**) very quickly. **not sleep** (or **get**) **a wink** (or **not get a wink of sleep**) not sleep at all.
– ORIGIN Old English *wincian* 'close the eyes', of Germanic origin.

winkle ■ n. another term for PERIWINKLE². ■ v. (**winkle something out**) chiefly Brit. extract or obtain something with difficulty.
– ORIGIN C16: shortening of PERIWINKLE².

winkle-picker ■ n. informal a shoe with a long pointed toe, popular in the 1950s.

Winnebago /ˌwɪnəˈbeɪɡəʊ/ ■ n. (pl. **-os**) US trademark a motor vehicle with living accommodation for long-distance travelling or camping.
– ORIGIN Algonquian, 'person of the dirty water', referring to the muddy Fox River in Wisconsin.

winner /ˈwɪnə/ ■ n. a person or thing that wins. ▸ informal a successful or highly promising thing.

winning /ˈwɪnɪŋ/ ■ adj. **1** gaining, resulting in, or relating to victory. **2** attractive; endearing. ■ n. (**winnings**) money won, especially by gambling.
– DERIVATIVES **winningly** adv.

winningest ■ adj. informal, chiefly N. Amer. having achieved the most success.

winning post ■ n. a post marking the end of a race.

winnow ■ v. **1** blow air through (grain) in order to remove the chaff. ▸ remove (chaff) from grain. **2** examine in order to identify the most valuable or useful elements. ▸ identify (a valuable or useful element). **3** poetic/literary (of the wind) blow.
– DERIVATIVES **winnower** n.
– ORIGIN Old English *windwian*, from *wind* (see WIND¹).

wino ■ n. (pl. **-os**) informal a person who drinks excessive amounts of cheap wine or other alcohol.

winsome ■ adj. attractive or appealing.
– DERIVATIVES **winsomely** adv. **winsomeness** n.
– ORIGIN Old English *wynsum*, from *wyn* 'joy' + -SOME¹.

winter ■ n. **1** the coldest season of the year, after autumn and before spring. ▸ Astronomy the period from the winter solstice to the vernal equinox. **2** (**winters**) poetic/literary years. ■ adj. **1** (of fruit) ripening at the beginning of the winter season. **2** (of crops) sown in autumn. ■ v. **1** spend the winter in a particular place. **2** keep or feed (plants or cattle) during winter.
– ORIGIN Old English, of Germanic origin.

winter aconite ■ n. see ACONITE (sense 2).

winter garden ■ n. **1** a garden of plants, such as evergreens, that flourish in winter. **2** a conservatory in which flowers and other non-hardy plants are grown in winter.

wintergreen ■ n. **1** a low-growing plant of acid soils, with spikes of white bell-shaped flowers. [*Pyrola* and other genera.] **2** a creeping evergreen American shrub with spiny oil-producing leaves and waxy white flowers. [*Gaultheria procumbens*.] **3** (also **oil of wintergreen**) a pungent oil obtained from these plants or from the bark of a birch (*Betula lenta*), used medicinally and as a flavouring.
– ORIGIN C16: the plants so named because they remain green in winter.

winterize (also **-ise**) ■ v. (usu. **be winterized**) (also **-ised**) chiefly N. Amer. adapt or prepare for use in cold weather.
– DERIVATIVES **winterization** (also **-isation**) n.

Winter Olympics ■ pl. n. an international contest of winter sports held every four years at a two-year interval from the Olympic games.

winter school ■ n. a course of lectures held during school and university winter vacations.

winter sports ■ pl. n. sports performed on snow or ice.

winter squash ■ n. a squash of a variety with a hard rind, able to be stored.

wintersweet ■ n. a Chinese shrub which produces heavily scented yellow flowers in winter before the leaves appear. [*Chimonanthus praecox*.]

winter-tide ■ n. poetic/literary wintertime.

wintertime /ˈwɪntətʌɪm/ ■ n. the season or period of winter.

wintry (also **wintery**) ■ adj. (**-ier**, **-iest**) characteristic of winter, especially in being very cold or bleak.
– DERIVATIVES **wintrily** adv. **wintriness** n.

win-win ■ adj. of or denoting a situation in which each party benefits.

WIP ■ abbrev. work in progress.

wipe ■ v. **1** clean or dry by rubbing with a cloth or one's hand. ▸ remove (dirt or moisture) in this way. **2** spread (liquid) over a surface by rubbing. **3** (often **wipe something out**) remove or eliminate completely. ▸ erase (data) from a magnetic medium. **4** pass (a swipe card) over an electronic reader. ▸ pass (a light pen) over a bar code. ■ n. **1** an act of wiping. **2** an absorbent disposable cleaning cloth. **3** a cinematographic effect in which an existing picture seems to be wiped out by a new one.
– PHRASES **wipe the floor with** informal inflict a humiliating defeat on. **wipe the slate clean** make a fresh start.
– PHRASAL VERBS **wipe something off** subtract an amount from a value or debt. **wipe out** informal be capsized by a wave while surfing. ▸ fall over or off a vehicle. **wipe someone out 1** kill a large number of people. **2** ruin someone financially. **3** informal exhaust or intoxicate someone.
– DERIVATIVES **wipeable** adj.
– ORIGIN Old English, of Germanic origin.

wipe-out ■ n. informal **1** an instance of complete destruction. **2** a fall from a surfboard.

wiper ■ n. **1** a windscreen wiper. **2** an electrical contact which moves across a surface.

WIPO ■ abbrev. World Intellectual Property Organization.

wire ■ n. **1** metal drawn out into a thin flexible thread or rod. ▸ a length or quantity of wire used for fencing, to carry an electric current, etc. ▸ N. Amer. Horse Racing a wire stretched across and above the start and finish of a racecourse. **2** a concealed electronic listening device. **3** informal a telegram or cablegram. ■ v. **1** install electric circuits or wires in. **2** provide, fasten, or reinforce with wire. **3** informal, chiefly N. Amer. send a telegram or cablegram to. ▸ send (money) to (someone) by such means.
– PHRASES **by wire** by telegraph. **down to the wire** informal until the very last minute. **under the wire** N. Amer. informal just in time. **wire-to-wire** N. Amer. informal from start to finish.
– ORIGIN Old English *wīr*; of Germanic origin, prob. from the base of Latin *viere* 'plait, weave'.

wire brush ■ n. a brush with tough wire bristles for cleaning hard surfaces. ▸ a brush with wire strands, used on cymbals to produce a soft metallic sound. ■ v. (**wire-brush**) clean with a wire brush.

wired ■ adj. informal **1** making use of computers and information technology to transfer or receive information. **2** nervous, tense, or edgy. ▸ intoxicated by drugs or alcohol.

wire-draw ■ v. (past **-drew**; past part. **-drawn**) [often as noun **wire-drawing**] draw out (metal) into wire.

wire fraud ■ n. fraud involving the use of telecommunications or information technology.

wire gauge ■ n. a gauge for measuring the diameter of wire. ▸ any of a series of standard sizes of wire.

wire grass ■ n. grass with tough wiry stems.

wire-haired ■ adj. (especially of a dog breed) having wiry hair.

wireless ■ n. dated **1** (also **wireless set**) a radio receiving

wireline

set. **2** broadcasting or telegraphy using radio signals. ■ adj. lacking or not requiring wires.

wireline ■ n. **1** a telegraph or telephone wire. **2** (in the oil industry) a cable for lowering and raising tools and other equipment in a well shaft.

wireman ■ n. (pl. **-men**) an installer or repairer of electric wiring.

wirepuller ■ n. N. Amer. informal a politician or other person who exerts control or influence from behind the scenes.
– DERIVATIVES **wirepulling** n.

wire rope ■ n. a length of rope made from wires twisted together as strands.

wire service ■ n. a news agency that supplies syndicated news by teleprinter or other electronic means to newspapers, radio, and television stations.

wire stripper ■ n. a tool for removing the insulation from electric wires.

wiretapping ■ n. the practice of tapping a telephone line to monitor conversations secretly.
– DERIVATIVES **wiretap** n. & v. **wiretapper** n.

wire wheel ■ n. a wheel on a car, especially a sports car, having narrow metal spokes.

wire wool ■ n. another term for STEEL WOOL.

wireworm ■ n. the worm-like larva of a click beetle, which feeds on roots and can cause damage to crops.

wiring ■ n. **1** a system of wires providing electric circuits for a device or building. **2** informal the connections of the nervous system or brain, especially as determining behaviour.

wiry ■ adj. (**-ier**, **-iest**) **1** resembling wire in form and texture. **2** lean, tough, and sinewy.
– DERIVATIVES **wirily** adv. **wiriness** n.

wisdom ■ n. **1** the quality of being wise. **2** the body of knowledge and experience that develops within a specified society or period.
– PHRASES **in someone's wisdom** used ironically to suggest that an action is ill-judged: *in their wisdom they decided to dispense with him.*

wisdom tooth ■ n. each of the four hindmost molars in humans, which usually appear at about the age of twenty.

wise[1] ■ adj. **1** having or showing experience, knowledge, and good judgement. **2** (**wise to**) informal aware of, especially so as to know how to act. ■ v. (**wise up**) informal become alert or aware.
– PHRASES **be wise after the event** understand and assess something only after its implications have become obvious.
– DERIVATIVES **wisely** adv.
– ORIGIN Old English *wīs*, of Germanic origin; rel. to WIT[2].

wise[2] ■ n. archaic manner, way, or extent.
– PHRASES **in no wise** not at all.
– ORIGIN Old English *wīse*, of Germanic origin; rel. to WIT[2].

-wise ■ suffix **1** forming adjectives and adverbs of manner or respect such as *clockwise*. Compare with **-WAYS**. **2** informal with respect to: *price-wise*.

wiseacre /ˈwʌɪzeɪkə/ ■ n. a person with an affectation of wisdom or knowledge.
– ORIGIN C16: from Middle Dutch *wijsseggher* 'soothsayer', prob. from the Germanic base of WIT[2].

wisecrack informal ■ n. a witty remark or joke. ■ v. make a wisecrack.
– DERIVATIVES **wisecracker** n.

wise guy ■ n. informal a person who makes sarcastic or insolent remarks so as to demonstrate their cleverness.

wise man ■ n. a man versed in magic, witchcraft, or astrology.

wisent /ˈwiːz(ə)nt/ ■ n. the European bison. See BISON.
– ORIGIN C19: from German.

wise woman ■ n. chiefly historical a woman knowledgeable in herbal healing, magic charms, or other traditional lore.

wish ■ v. **1** desire something that cannot or probably will not happen. **2** want to do something. ▶ ask (someone) to do something or that (something) be done. **3** express a hope that (someone) has (happiness, success, etc.). ▶ (**wish something on**) [with neg.] hope that something unpleasant will happen to. ■ n. **1** a desire or hope, or an expression of this. ▶ (**wishes**) an expression of a hope for someone's happiness, success, or welfare. **2** a thing wished for.
– DERIVATIVES **-wisher** n.
– ORIGIN Old English *wȳscan*, of Germanic origin.

wishbone ■ n. **1** a forked bone (the furcula) between the neck and breast of a bird, especially one from a cooked bird which, when broken by two people, entitles the holder of the longer portion to make a wish. **2** a forked element in the suspension of a motor vehicle or aircraft, typically attached to a wheel at one end with the two arms hinged to the chassis. **3** Nautical a boom in two halves which curve outwards around a sail and meet aft of it.

wishful ■ adj. **1** having or expressing a wish for something to happen. **2** based on impractical wishes rather than facts: *wishful thinking*.
– DERIVATIVES **wishfully** adv. **wishfulness** n.

wish-fulfilment ■ n. the satisfying of wishes or desires in dreams or fantasies.

wishing well ■ n. a well into which one drops a coin and makes a wish.

wishy-washy ■ adj. **1** (of drink or soup) weak or thin. **2** feeble or insipid.
– ORIGIN C18: reduplication of archaic *washy* 'watery, insipid'.

wisp ■ n. **1** a small thin bunch, strand, or amount of something. **2** a small thin person.
– DERIVATIVES **wispily** adv. **wispiness** n. **wispy** adj. (**-ier**, **-iest**).
– ORIGIN Middle English.

wist past and past participle of WIT[2].

wisteria /wɪˈstɪərɪə/ (also **wistaria** /-ˈstɛːrɪə/) ■ n. a climbing shrub of east Asia and North America, with hanging clusters of pale bluish-lilac flowers. [Genus *Wisteria*: several species.]
– ORIGIN named after Caspar *Wistar* (or *Wister*) (1761–1818), American anatomist.

wistful ■ adj. having or showing a feeling of vague or regretful longing.
– DERIVATIVES **wistfully** adv. **wistfulness** n.
– ORIGIN C17: apparently from obsolete *wistly* 'intently', influenced by WISHFUL.

wit[1] ■ n. **1** (also **wits**) the capacity for inventive thought and quick understanding; keen intelligence. **2** a natural aptitude for using words and ideas in a quick and inventive way to create humour. **3** a person with this aptitude.
– PHRASES **be at one's wits' end** be completely at a loss as to what to do. **be frightened** (or **scared**) **out of one's wits** be extremely frightened. **gather** (or **collect**) **one's wits** allow oneself to think calmly and clearly in a demanding situation. **have** (or **keep**) **one's wits about one** be constantly alert. **live by one's wits** earn money by clever and sometimes dishonest means, having no regular employment.
– DERIVATIVES **-witted** adj.
– ORIGIN Old English *wit(t)*, *gewit(t)*, denoting the mind as the seat of consciousness, of Germanic origin; rel. to WIT[2].

wit[2] ■ v. (**wot**, **witting**; past and past part. **wist**) **1** archaic know. **2** (**to wit**) that is to say.
– ORIGIN Old English *witan*, of Germanic origin.

witblits /ˈvɪtblɪts/ (also **witblitz**) ■ n. S. African strong home-distilled liquor, usually colourless.
– ORIGIN Afrikaans, from *wit* 'white' + *blits* 'lightning'.

witch ■ n. **1** a woman thought to have evil magic powers. **2** a follower or practitioner of modern witchcraft. **3** informal an ugly or unpleasant old woman. **4** a fascinatingly attractive girl or woman. ■ v. **1** cast an evil spell on. **2** (of a girl or woman) enchant (a man).
– DERIVATIVES **witchlike** adj. **witchy** adj.
– ORIGIN Old English *wicca* (masculine), *wicce* (feminine), *wiccian* (v.).

witchcraft ■ n. the practice of magic, especially the use of spells and the invocation of evil spirits. See also WICCA.

witch doctor ■ n. (in some traditional societies) a person credited with powers of healing, divination, and protection against the magic of others.

witchery ■ n. **1** the practice of magic. **2** bewitching quality or power.

witches' broom ■ n. dense twiggy growth in a tree caused by infection with fungus (especially rusts), mites, or viruses.

witches' sabbath ■ n. see SABBATH (sense 2).

witchetty /'wɪtʃɪti/ (also **witchetty grub**) ■ n. (pl. **-ies**) a large whitish wood-eating larva of a beetle or moth, eaten as food by some Aboriginals.
– ORIGIN from Adnyamathanha (an Aboriginal language) *wityu* 'hooked stick (for extracting grubs)' + *varti* 'grub'.

witch hazel ■ n. **1** a shrub with fragrant yellow flowers. [*Hamamelis virginiana* (N. America) and other species.] **2** an astringent lotion made from the bark and leaves of this plant.
– ORIGIN C16: *witch*, var. of *wych* (see WYCH ELM).

witch-hunt ■ n. a campaign directed against a person or group holding views considered unorthodox or a threat to society.
– DERIVATIVES **witch-hunting** n.

witching hour ■ n. midnight, regarded as the time when witches are supposedly active.
– ORIGIN with allusion to *the witching time of night* from Shakespeare's *Hamlet* (III. ii. 377).

witchweed ■ n. a small parasitic plant which attaches itself to the roots of maize, sugar, and other plants. [Genus *Striga*.]

with ■ prep. **1** accompanied by. ▸ in the same direction as. **2** possessing; having. **3** indicating the instrument used to perform an action or the material used for a purpose. **4** in opposition to. **5** indicating the manner or attitude in which a person does something. **6** indicating responsibility. **7** in relation to. **8** employed by. ▸ using the services of. **9** affected by (a particular fact or condition). ▸ indicating the cause of an action or condition. **10** indicating separation or removal from something.
– PHRASES **away** (or **off** or **out** etc.) **with!** take or send away, out, etc. **be with someone** informal follow someone's meaning. **with it** informal **1** up to date or fashionable. **2** [usu. with neg.] alert and comprehending. **3** in addition. **with that** at that point.
– ORIGIN Old English, prob. a shortening of a Germanic preposition rel. to obsolete English *wither* 'adverse, opposite'.

withal /wɪˈðɔːl/ archaic ■ adv. **1** in addition. **2** nevertheless. ■ prep. with.
– ORIGIN Middle English: orig. as *with all*.

withdraw ■ v. (past **-drew**; past part. **-drawn**) **1** remove or take away. ▸ take (money) out of an account. **2** take back; discontinue or retract. **3** leave or cause to leave a place, especially a war zone. ▸ cease to participate in an activity or be a member of a team or organization. **4** depart to another place in search of quiet or privacy. ▸ retreat from social contact. **5** cease to take an addictive drug.
– DERIVATIVES **withdrawal** n.
– ORIGIN Middle English: from the prefix *with-* 'away' + DRAW.

withdrawing room ■ n. archaic term for DRAWING ROOM.

withdrawn past participle of WITHDRAW. ■ adj. unusually shy or reserved.

wither ■ v. **1** (of a plant) become dry and shrivelled. **2** become shrunken or wrinkled from age or disease. ▸ fall into decay or decline. **3** mortify with a scornful look or manner. ▸ [as adj. **withering**] scornful.
– DERIVATIVES **witheringly** adv.
– ORIGIN Middle English: apparently a var. of WEATHER.

withers ■ pl. n. the highest part of a horse's back, lying at the base of the neck above the shoulders.
– ORIGIN C16: apparently a reduced form of *widersome*, from obsolete *wither-* 'against' (as the part that resists the strain of the collar) + a second element of obscure origin.

withhold ■ v. (past and past part. **-held**) **1** refuse to give (something due to or desired by another). **2** suppress or restrain (an emotion or reaction).
– DERIVATIVES **withholder** n.
– ORIGIN Middle English: from the prefix *with-* 'away' + HOLD[1].

withholding tax ■ n. a tax levied by some countries on interest or dividends paid to a person resident outside that country.

within ■ prep. **1** inside. ▸ inside the range of. ▸ inside the bounds set by. **2** not further off than (a particular distance). **3** occurring inside (a particular period of time). ■ adv. **1** inside; indoors. **2** internally or inwardly.
– ORIGIN Old English *withinnan* 'on the inside'.

without ■ prep. **1** not accompanied by or having the use of. **2** in which the action mentioned does not happen. **3** archaic or poetic/literary outside. ■ adv. archaic or poetic/literary outside. ■ conj. archaic or dialect **1** without it being the case that. **2** unless.
– ORIGIN Old English *withūtan* 'on the outside'.

with-profits ■ adj. (of an insurance policy) allowing the holder to receive a share of the profits made by the company, typically in the form of a bonus.

withstand ■ v. (past and past part. **-stood**) **1** remain undamaged or unaffected by. **2** offer strong resistance or opposition to.
– DERIVATIVES **withstander** n.
– ORIGIN Old English *withstandan*, from the prefix *with-* 'against' + STAND.

withy /'wɪði/ ■ n. (pl. **withies**) **1** a tough flexible branch of an osier or other willow, used for tying, binding, or basketry. **2** another term for OSIER.
– ORIGIN Old English *wīthig*, of Germanic origin.

witless ■ adj. foolish; stupid.
– DERIVATIVES **witlessly** adv. **witlessness** n.

witness ■ n. **1** a person who sees an event take place. **2** a person giving sworn testimony to a court of law or the police. **3** a person who is present at the signing of a document and signs it themselves to confirm this. **4** evidence; proof. ▸ open profession of one's religious faith through words or actions. ■ v. **1** be a witness to. **2** be the place, period, etc. in which (a particular event) takes place. **3** (**witness to**) give or serve as evidence of. ▸ openly profess one's religious faith in.
– ORIGIN Old English.

witness box (also **witness stand**) ■ n. Law the place in a court where a witness stands to give evidence.

Wits /vɪts/ ■ abbrev. **1** University of the Witwatersrand. **2** Witwatersrand.

witter ■ v. (usu. **witter on**) informal, speak at length about trivial matters.
– ORIGIN C19: prob. imitative.

witticism ■ n. a witty remark.
– ORIGIN 1677: coined by John Dryden from *witty*, on the pattern of *criticism*.

witting ■ adj. **1** deliberate. **2** aware of the full facts.
– DERIVATIVES **wittingly** adv.
– ORIGIN Middle English: from WIT[2].

witty ■ adj. (**-ier**, **-iest**) showing or characterized by quick and inventive humour.
– DERIVATIVES **wittily** adv. **wittiness** n.

Witwatersrand /vɪtˈvɑːtəsrand, -rant/ ■ n. the area around Johannesburg, famous for its gold deposits.
– ORIGIN from Afrikaans *wit* 'white' + *watersrand* 'watershed'.

Wit Wolf /vɪt vɔlf/ ■ n. (pl. **Wit Wolwe**) S. African historical a member of the Wit Wolwe, a militant right-wing organization.
– ORIGIN Afrikaans, 'White Wolf'.

wives plural form of WIFE.

wiz ■ n. variant spelling of WHIZZ (in sense 3).

wizard ■ n. **1** a man who has magical powers, especially in legends and fairy tales. **2** a person who is very skilled in a particular field or activity.
– DERIVATIVES **wizardly** adj.
– ORIGIN Middle English (in the sense 'philosopher, sage'): from WISE[1].

wizardry ■ n. **1** the art or practice of magic. **2** great skill in a particular field or activity. ▸ the product of such skill: *hi-tech wizardry*.

wizened /ˈwɪz(ə)nd/ ▪ adj. shrivelled or wrinkled with age.
– ORIGIN C16: from archaic *wizen* 'shrivel', of Germanic origin.

wk ▪ abbrev. week.

WMD ▪ abbrev. weapon of mass destruction.

WML ▪ abbrev. Computing Wireless Mark-up Language.

WNW ▪ abbrev. west-north-west.

WO ▪ abbrev. Warrant Officer.

wo ▪ exclam. variant spelling of WHOA.

woad /wəʊd/ ▪ n. **1** a yellow-flowered plant whose leaves were formerly used to make blue dye. [*Isatis tinctoria*.] **2** the dye obtained from this plant, now superseded by synthetic products.
– ORIGIN Old English, of Germanic origin.

wobble ▪ v. move unsteadily from side to side. ► (of the voice) tremble. ► waver between different courses of action. ▪ n. a wobbling movement or sound.
– ORIGIN C17 (orig. as *wabble*): of Germanic origin.

wobble-board ▪ n. a platform mounted on a half sphere, used for exercising the ankles and improving balance.

wobbler ▪ n. **1** a person or thing that wobbles. **2** another term for WOBBLY.

wobbly ▪ adj. (-ier, -iest) **1** tending to wobble. ► weak and unsteady from illness, tiredness, or anxiety. **2** uncertain or insecure. ▪ n. informal a fit of temper or panic: *I drove off and threw a wobbly.*
– DERIVATIVES **wobbliness** n.

wodge ▪ n. informal a large piece or amount.
– ORIGIN C19: alteration of WEDGE.

woe ▪ n. poetic/literary **1** great sorrow or distress. **2** (**woes**) troubles.
– PHRASES **woe betide someone** (or **woe to someone**) humorous a person will be in trouble if they do a specified thing. **woe is me!** humorous an exclamation of sorrow or distress.
– ORIGIN natural exclamation of lament: recorded as *wā* in Old English and found in several Germanic languages.

woebegone /ˈwəʊbɪɡɒn/ ▪ adj. sad or miserable in appearance.
– ORIGIN Middle English: from WOE + *begone* 'surrounded', from obsolete *bego* 'go around, beset'.

woeful ▪ adj. **1** full of sorrow; miserable. **2** deplorable.
– DERIVATIVES **woefully** adv. **woefulness** n.

woema /ˈvʊmə/ ▪ n. variant spelling of VOOMA.

wog ▪ n. informal, offensive a person who is not white.
– ORIGIN 1920S.

wok ▪ n. a bowl-shaped frying pan used in Chinese cookery.
– ORIGIN Chinese (Cantonese dialect).

woke past of WAKE[1].

woken past participle of WAKE[1].

wold /wəʊld/ ▪ n. (especially in British place names) a piece of high, open, uncultivated land or moor.
– ORIGIN Old English *wald* 'wooded upland', of Germanic origin.

wolf ▪ n. (pl. **wolves**) **1** a carnivorous mammal which is the largest member of the dog family, living and hunting in packs. [*Canis lupus*.] ► used in names of similar or related mammals. **2** a rapacious or ferocious person. ► informal a man who habitually seduces women. ▪ v. (usu. **wolf something down**) devour (food) greedily.
– PHRASES **cry wolf** raise repeated false alarms, so that a real cry for help is ignored. **keep the wolf from the door** have enough money to avert hunger or destitution. **throw someone to the wolves** sacrifice someone so as to avert trouble for oneself. **a wolf in sheep's clothing** a person who appears friendly but is really hostile.
– DERIVATIVES **wolfish** adj. **wolfishly** adv. **wolf-like** adj.
– ORIGIN Old English, of Germanic origin.

wolfhound ▪ n. a dog of a large breed originally used to hunt wolves.

wolfram /ˈwʊlfrəm/ ▪ n. tungsten or its ore, especially as a commercial commodity.
– ORIGIN C18: from German, perhaps from *Wolf* 'wolf' + Middle High German *rām* 'soot', prob. orig. a pejorative miners' term referring to the ore's inferiority to tin.

wolframite ▪ n. a black or brown mineral consisting of a tungstate of iron and manganese.

wolfsbane /ˈwʊlfsbeɪn/ ▪ n. a northern European aconite with yellow or purple flowers. [*Aconitum lycoctonum* and related species.]

wolf spider ▪ n. a fast-moving ground spider which runs after and springs on its prey. [Family Lycosidae.]

wolf whistle ▪ n. a whistle with a rising and falling pitch, used to express sexual attraction or admiration. ▪ v. (**wolf-whistle**) whistle in such a way at.

wollastonite /ˈwɒləstənʌɪt/ ▪ n. a white or greyish mineral consisting of calcium silicate, used as a source of rock wool.
– ORIGIN C19: named after the English chemist William Hyde *Wollaston*.

Wolof /ˈwəʊlɒf/ ▪ n. (pl. same or **Wolofs**) **1** a member of a people living in Senegal and Gambia. **2** the Niger–Congo language of this people.
– ORIGIN the name in Wolof.

wolverine /ˈwʊlvəriːn/ ▪ n. a heavily built short-legged carnivorous mammal of northern tundra and forests. [*Gulo gulo*.]
– ORIGIN C16 (orig. as *wolvering*): from *wolv-*, pl. stem of WOLF.

wolves plural form of WOLF.

woman ▪ n. (pl. **women** /ˈwɪmɪn/) **1** an adult human female. **2** a female worker or employee. ► a female domestic help. **3** a wife or lover.
– PHRASES **the little woman** a condescending way of referring one's wife. **woman of letters** a female scholar or author. **woman of the streets** euphemistic, dated a prostitute. **woman to woman** in a direct and frank way between two women.
– DERIVATIVES **womanless** adj. **womanlike** adj. **womanliness** n. **womanly** adj.
– ORIGIN Old English *wīfmon, -man* (see WIFE, MAN).

-woman ▪ comb. form (pl. **-women** /-wɪmɪn/) **1** in nouns denoting a female of a specified nationality or origin: *Englishwoman*. **2** in nouns denoting a woman belonging to a specified group or having a specified occupation or role: *laywoman* | *oarswoman*.

womanhood ▪ n. **1** the state or condition of being a woman. **2** women considered collectively. **3** the qualities traditionally associated with women.

womanish ▪ adj. derogatory **1** suitable for or characteristic of a woman. **2** (of a man) effeminate.
– DERIVATIVES **womanishly** adv. **womanishness** n.

womanism ▪ n. (especially among black women) a form of feminism that acknowledges women's natural contribution to society.
– DERIVATIVES **womanist** n.

womanize (also **-ise**) ▪ v. [usu. as noun **womanizing** (also **-ising**)] (of a man) enter into numerous casual sexual relationships with women.
– DERIVATIVES **womanizer** (also **-iser**) n.

womankind ▪ n. women considered collectively.

womb ▪ n. the organ in the lower body of a woman or female mammal where offspring are conceived and in which they gestate before birth; the uterus.
– ORIGIN Old English, of Germanic origin.

wombat /ˈwɒmbat/ ▪ n. a burrowing plant-eating Australian marsupial which resembles a small bear with short legs. [*Vombatus ursinus* and other species.]
– ORIGIN C18: from Dharuk (an extinct Aboriginal language).

women plural form of WOMAN.

womenfolk ▪ pl. n. a group of women considered collectively.

Women's Day (also **National Women's Day**) ▪ n. S. African 9 August, a public holiday.

women's lib ▪ n. informal short for WOMEN'S LIBERATION.
– DERIVATIVES **women's libber** n.

women's liberation ▪ n. the liberation of women from inequalities and subservient status in relation to men, and from attitudes causing these (now generally replaced by the term *feminism*).

women's movement ■ n. a broad movement campaigning for women's liberation and rights.

women's rights ■ pl. n. rights that promote a position of legal and social equality of women with men.

women's studies ■ pl. n. [usu. treated as sing.] academic courses which focus on the roles, experiences, and achievements of women.

women's work ■ n. work traditionally undertaken by women, especially domestic tasks such as cooking and child rearing.

womyn /ˈwɪmɪn/ ■ pl. n. non-standard spelling of 'women' adopted by some feminists in order to avoid the word ending in -*men*.

won past and past participle of **WIN**.

wonder ■ n. **1** a feeling of surprise and admiration, caused by something beautiful, unexpected, or unfamiliar. **2** a person or thing that causes such a feeling. ▸ [as modifier] having remarkable properties or abilities. ■ v. **1** feel curious; desire to know. ▸ used to express a polite question or request. **2** feel doubt. **3** feel wonder.
– PHRASES **I shouldn't wonder** informal, chiefly Brit. I think it likely. **no** (or **little** or **small**) **wonder** it is not surprising. **nine days'** (or **seven-day** or **one-day**) **wonder** something that attracts great interest for a short while but is then forgotten. **wonders will never cease** often ironic an exclamation of surprise and pleasure. **work** (or **do**) **wonders** have a very beneficial effect.
– DERIVATIVES **wondering** adj. **wonderingly** adv.
– ORIGIN Old English *wundor* (n.), *wundrian* (v.), of Germanic origin.

wonderboom /ˈvɔndəbʊəm/ (in full **wonderboom fig**) ■ n. a wild fig native to southern Africa. [*Ficus salicifolia*.]
– ORIGIN C19: Afrikaans, from *wonder* 'marvel, wonder' + *boom* 'tree'.

wonderbox ■ n. S. African a wooden, cardboard or fabric box containing insulating material, into which hot, partially cooked food is placed to continue cooking.

wonderful ■ adj. extremely good, pleasant, or remarkable.
– DERIVATIVES **wonderfully** adv. **wonderfulness** n.

wonderland ■ n. a place full of wonderful things.

wonderlawn ■ n. S. African a creeping plant with small kidney-shaped leaves, cultivated as ground cover. [*Dichondra repens*.]

wonderment ■ n. a state of awed admiration or respect.

wonderstone ■ n. a soft massive blue-grey metamorphic rock of volcanic origin, used especially in the synthesis of industrial diamonds and for sculpture.

wondrous ■ adj. poetic/literary inspiring wonder. ■ adv. archaic wonderfully.
– DERIVATIVES **wondrously** adv. **wondrousness** n.
– ORIGIN C15: alteration of obsolete *wonders* (adj. and adv.), genitive of **WONDER**, on the pattern of *marvellous*.

wonga /ˈwɒŋɡə, ˈvɒŋɡə/ ■ n. Brit. informal money.
– ORIGIN C20: perhaps from Romany *wongar* 'coal', also 'money'.

wonk ■ n. informal, derogatory, chiefly N. Amer. a studious or hard-working person. ▸ (often **policy wonk**) a person who takes an excessive interest in minor details of political policy.
– ORIGIN 1920s.

wonky ■ adj. (-ier, -iest) informal **1** crooked; askew. **2** unsteady or faulty.
– DERIVATIVES **wonkily** adv. **wonkiness** n.
– ORIGIN C20: fanciful formation.

wont /wəʊnt/ ■ adj. archaic or poetic/literary accustomed: *he was wont to arise at 5.30.* ■ n. (**one's wont**) formal or humorous one's customary behaviour.
– ORIGIN Old English *gewunod*, from *wunian* 'dwell, be accustomed', of Germanic origin.

won't ■ contr. will not.

wonted /ˈwəʊntɪd/ ■ adj. archaic or poetic/literary usual.
– ORIGIN Middle English: from **WONT**.

wonton /ˈwɒntɒn/ ■ n. (in Chinese cookery) a small round dumpling with a savoury filling, typically served in soup.
– ORIGIN from Chinese (Cantonese dialect) *wān t'ān*.

woo ■ v. (**woos**, **wooed**) **1** try to gain the love of (a woman). **2** seek the support or custom of.
– DERIVATIVES **wooer** n.
– ORIGIN Old English *wōgian*, *āwōgian*.

wood ■ n. **1** the hard fibrous material forming the main substance of the trunk or branches of a tree or shrub, used for fuel or timber. ▸ (**the wood**) wooden barrels used for storing alcoholic drinks. ▸ a golf club with a wooden or other head that is relatively broad from face to back. ▸ another term for **BOWL**² (in sense 1). **2** (also **woods**) a small forest.
– PHRASES **be unable to see the wood** (or **the forest**) **for the trees** fail to grasp the main issue because of over-attention to details. **out of the wood** (or **woods**) [usu. with neg.] out of danger or difficulty. **touch** (or chiefly N. Amer. **knock on**) **wood** touch something wooden to ward off bad luck.
– DERIVATIVES **woodless** adj.
– ORIGIN Old English, of Germanic origin.

wood alcohol ■ n. crude methanol made by distillation from wood.

woodbine ■ n. the common honeysuckle.

woodblock ■ n. a block of wood from which woodcut prints are made.

woodchuck ■ n. a North American marmot with a heavy body and short legs. [*Marmota monax*.]
– ORIGIN C17: alteration (by association with **WOOD**) of an American Indian name.

woodcock ■ n. (pl. same) a long-billed woodland bird of the sandpiper family, with brown plumage. [*Scolopax rusticola* (Eurasia) and related species.]

woodcraft ■ n. chiefly N. Amer. **1** skill in woodwork. **2** knowledge of woodland, especially with reference to outdoor pursuits.

woodcut ■ n. a print of a type made from a design cut in relief in a block of wood, formerly used for book illustrations.

woodcutter ■ n. **1** a person who cuts down wood, especially for fuel. **2** a person who makes woodcuts.
– DERIVATIVES **woodcutting** n.

wooded ■ adj. (of land) covered with woods.

wooden ■ adj. **1** made of wood. ▸ like or characteristic of wood: *a dull wooden sound.* **2** stiff and awkward.
– DERIVATIVES **woodenly** adv. **woodenness** n.

wood engraving ■ n. **1** a print made from a finely detailed design cut into the end grain of a block of wood. **2** the technique of making such prints.
– DERIVATIVES **wood engraver** n.

wooden-head ■ n. informal a stupid person.
– DERIVATIVES **wooden-headed** adj. **wooden-headedness** n.

wooden spoon ■ n. chiefly Brit. a real or imaginary prize awarded to the person who is last in a race or competition.
– ORIGIN orig. a spoon given to the candidate coming last in the mathematical tripos at Cambridge University.

wood fibre ■ n. fibre obtained from wood and used especially in the manufacture of paper.

woodgrain ■ adj. denoting a surface or finish imitating the grain pattern of wood.

woodland ■ n. (also **woodlands**) land covered with trees.
– DERIVATIVES **woodlander** n.

woodlouse ■ n. (pl. **woodlice**) a small terrestrial crustacean with a greyish segmented body which it is able to roll into a ball. [*Oniscus* and other genera.]

woodman ■ n. (pl. -**men**) dated a forester or woodcutter.

wood nymph ■ n. (in folklore and classical mythology) a dryad or hamadryad.

woodpecker ■ n. a bird with a strong bill and a stiff tail, typically pecking at tree trunks to find insects and drumming on dead wood. [Family Picidae: many species.]

wood pigeon ■ n. a common large pigeon, mainly grey with white patches forming a ring round its neck. [*Columba palumbus*.]

wood pulp ■ n. wood fibre reduced chemically or mechanically to pulp and used in the manufacture of paper.

woodruff (also **sweet woodruff**) ■ n. a white-flowered plant with sweet-scented leaves used to flavour drinks and in perfumery. [*Galium odoratum*.]
– ORIGIN Old English *wudurofe*, from *wudu* 'wood' + an element of unknown meaning.

woodscrew ■ n. a tapering metal screw with a sharp point.

woodshed ■ n. a shed where firewood is stored.
– PHRASES **something nasty in the woodshed** Brit. informal a shocking or distasteful thing that has been kept secret. [from the novel *Cold Comfort Farm* by Stella Gibbons (1933).]

woodsman ■ n. (pl. **-men**) a forester, hunter, or woodcutter.

wood sorrel ■ n. a Eurasian woodland plant with clover-like leaves and pink or white flowers. [*Oxalis acetosella*.]

wood spirit ■ n. another term for WOOD ALCOHOL.

wood stain ■ n. a commercially produced substance for colouring wood.

woodsy ■ adj. of, relating to, or characteristic of wood or woodland.

woodturning ■ n. the activity of shaping wood with a lathe.
– DERIVATIVES **woodturner** n.

woodwasp ■ n. a large wasp-like sawfly with a long egg-laying tube which deposits its eggs in the trunks of trees. [Family Siricidae: several species.]

woodwind ■ n. [treated as sing. or pl.] wind instruments other than brass instruments forming a section of an orchestra, including flutes, oboes, clarinets, and bassoons.

wood wool ■ n. a mass of fine soft wood shavings, used as a packing material.

woodwork ■ n. **1** the wooden parts of a building or other structure. **2** the activity or skill of making things from wood.
– PHRASES **come out of the woodwork** (of an unpleasant person or thing) emerge from obscurity.
– DERIVATIVES **woodworker** n. **woodworking** n.

woodworm ■ n. **1** the wood-boring larva of the furniture beetle. **2** the damaged condition of wood resulting from infestation with this larva.

woody ■ adj. (**-ier**, **-iest**) **1** covered with trees. **2** made of, resembling, or suggestive of wood.
– DERIVATIVES **woodiness** n.

woodyard ■ n. a yard where wood is chopped or stored.

woof[1] /wʊf/ ■ n. the barking sound made by a dog. ■ v. bark.
– ORIGIN C19: imitative.

woof[2] /wuːf/ ■ n. another term for WEFT.
– ORIGIN Old English *ōwef*, a compound from the base of WEAVE[1]; Middle English *oof* later became *woof* by associated with WARP.

woofer /ˈwuːfə, ˈwʊfə/ ■ n. a loudspeaker designed to reproduce low frequencies.

wool ■ n. the fine soft curly or wavy hair forming the coat of a sheep, goat, or similar animal, especially when shorn and made into cloth or yarn. ▶ the soft underfur or down of some other mammals. ▶ a metal or mineral made into a mass of fine fibres: *lead wool*.
– PHRASES **pull the wool over someone's eyes** deceive someone.
– DERIVATIVES **wool-like** adj.
– ORIGIN Old English, of Germanic origin.

wool-gathering ■ n. indulgence in aimless thought.
– DERIVATIVES **wool-gather** v.

wool grower ■ n. a breeder of sheep for wool.

woollen (US **woolen**) ■ adj. made wholly or partly of wool. ■ n. (**woollens**) woollen garments.

woolly ■ adj. (**-ier**, **-iest**) **1** made of wool. ▶ (of an animal or plant) covered with wool or hair resembling wool. ▶ resembling wool in texture or appearance. **2** vague or confused: *woolly thinking*. **3** (of a sound) indistinct or distorted. ■ n. (pl. **-ies**) informal a woollen garment, especially a pullover.
– DERIVATIVES **woolliness** n.

woolly bear ■ n. **1** a hairy caterpillar of a tiger moth. **2** a hairy beetle larva.

woolshed ■ n. chiefly Austral./NZ a large shed for shearing and baling wool.

woomph /wʊmf, wʌmf/ ■ adv. & exclam. used to imitate a sound like that of a sudden blow or impact accompanied by an expulsion of air.

woosh ■ v., n., & exclam. variant spelling of WHOOSH.

woozy ■ adj. (**-ier**, **-iest**) informal unsteady, dizzy, or dazed.
– DERIVATIVES **woozily** adv. **wooziness** n.
– ORIGIN C19: of unknown origin.

wop ■ n. offensive an Italian or other southern European.
– ORIGIN C20 (orig. US): perhaps from Italian *guappo* 'bold, showy'.

Worcester /ˈwʊstə/ (also **Royal Worcester**) ■ n. trademark porcelain made at Worcester in England since 1751.

Worcester sauce (also **Worcestershire sauce**) ■ n. a pungent sauce containing soy sauce and vinegar, first made in Worcester, England.

word ■ n. **1** a single distinct meaningful element of speech or writing, used to form sentences with others. **2** a remark or statement. ▶ [with neg.] (**a word**) even the smallest amount of something spoken or written: *don't believe a word*. ▶ (**words**) angry talk. ▶ (**the word**) a command, slogan, or signal. **3** speech as distinct from action. **4** (**one's word**) a person's account of the truth, especially when it differs from that of another person. ▶ a promise or assurance. **5** (**words**) the text of a play, opera, or other performed piece. **6** news. **7** a basic unit of data in a computer, typically 16 or 32 bits long. ■ v. express in particular words.
– PHRASES **at a word** as soon as requested. **be as good as one's word** do what one has promised. **have a word** speak briefly to someone. **have a word in someone's ear** speak to someone privately and discreetly. **in other words** that is to say. **in so many words** [often with neg.] precisely in the way mentioned. **in a word** briefly. **a man** (or **woman**) **of his** (or **her**) **word** a person who keeps their promises. **on** (or **upon**) **my word** an exclamation of surprise or emphasis. **put words into someone's mouth 1** inaccurately report what someone has said. **2** prompt someone to say something inadvertently. **take someone at their word** interpret a person's words literally. **take the words out of someone's mouth** say what someone else was about to say. **take someone's word** (**for it**) believe what someone says or writes without checking for oneself. **too —— for words** informal extremely ——. **waste words** talk in vain. **the Word** (**of God**) **1** the Bible, or a part of it. **2** Jesus Christ (see LOGOS). **word for word** in exactly the same or, when translated, exactly equivalent words. **word of honour** a solemn promise. **word of mouth** spoken communication as a means of transmitting information. **the word on the street** informal a current rumour or piece of information. **a word to the wise** a hint or brief explanation given, that being all that is required.
– DERIVATIVES **wordage** n. **wordless** adj. **wordlessly** adv. **wordlessness** n.
– ORIGIN Old English, of Germanic origin.

word association ■ n. the spontaneous and unreflective production of other words in response to a given word, especially as a technique in psychiatric evaluation.

word blindness ■ n. less technical term for ALEXIA, or (less accurately) for DYSLEXIA.

wordbook ■ n. a study book containing lists of words and meanings or other related information.

word break (also **word division**) ■ n. Printing a point at which a word is split between two lines of text by means of a hyphen.

word class ■ n. a category of words of similar form or function; a part of speech.

wording ■ n. the words used to express something; the way in which something is expressed.

word-perfect ■ adj. (of an actor or speaker) knowing one's part or speech by heart.

wordplay ■ n. the witty exploitation of the meanings and ambiguities of words.

word processor ■ n. a purpose-built computer or program for storing, manipulating, and formatting text entered from a keyboard and providing a printout.
– DERIVATIVES **word-process** v. **word-processing** n.

wordsearch ■ n. a puzzle consisting of letters arranged in a grid, containing several hidden words written in any direction.

wordsmith ■ n. a skilled user of words.

wordy ■ adj. (**-ier, -iest**) using or expressed in too many words.
– DERIVATIVES **wordily** adv. **wordiness** n.

wore past of **WEAR**.

work ■ n. **1** activity involving mental or physical effort done in order to achieve a result. **2** such activity as a means of earning income. **3** a task or tasks to be undertaken. ▶ the materials for this. ▶ (**works**) Theology good or moral deeds. **4** a thing or things done or made; the result of an action. ▶ (**works**) the complete artistic production of a particular author, composer, or artist. **5** (**works**) [treated as sing.] a place where industrial or manufacturing processes are carried out. **6** (**works**) operations of building or repair. **7** (**works**) the mechanism of a clock or other machine. **8** Physics the exertion of force overcoming resistance or producing molecular change. **9** (**the works**) informal everything needed, desired, or expected. ■ v. (past and past part. **worked** or archaic **wrought**) **1** do work, especially as one's job. ▶ have a job. ▶ set to or keep at work. **2** (of a machine or system) function, especially properly or effectively. ▶ (with reference to a machine) be or cause to be in operation. **3** have the desired result. ▶ bring about. ▶ campaign. ▶ (**work on/upon**) exert influence on. **4** bring (a material or mixture) to a desired shape or consistency. ▶ (**work in**) produce articles or pictures using a particular material or medium. ▶ produce (an article or design) using a specified material or sewing stitch. ▶ cultivate (land) or extract materials from (a mine or quarry). **5** move or cause to move gradually or with difficulty into another position. ▶ (of a person's features) move violently or convulsively. **6** bring into a specified emotional state: *Harold had worked himself into a rage.* **7** Nautical make progress to windward, with repeated tacking.
– PHRASES **give someone the works** informal **1** tell someone everything. **2** treat someone harshly or violently. **have one's work cut out** be faced with a hard or lengthy task. **in the works** being planned, worked on, or produced. **work to rule** follow official working rules and hours exactly in order to reduce output and efficiency, especially as a form of industrial action. **work one's passage** pay for one's journey on a ship with work instead of money.
– PHRASAL VERBS **work something in** try to include something. **work something off 1** discharge a debt by working. **2** reduce or eliminate something by activity. **work out 1** be capable of being solved. **2** develop in a good or specified way. **3** engage in vigorous physical exercise. **work out at** be calculated at. **work someone out** understand someone's character. **work something out 1** solve something. **2** plan something in detail. **work someone over** informal beat someone up. **work up to** proceed gradually towards (something more advanced). **work someone up** (often **get worked up**) gradually bring someone, especially oneself, to a state of intense excitement, anger, or anxiety. **work something up 1** develop or improve something gradually. **2** develop by activity or effort.
– DERIVATIVES **workless** adj.
– ORIGIN Old English, of Germanic origin.

-work ■ comb. form **1** denoting things or parts made of a specified material or with specified tools: *silverwork*. **2** denoting a mechanism or structure of a specified kind: *clockwork*. **3** denoting ornamentation of a specified kind, or articles having such ornamentation: *knotwork*.

workable ■ adj. **1** able to be worked. **2** capable of producing the desired result.
– DERIVATIVES **workability** n. **workably** adv.

workaday ■ adj. not unusual or interesting; ordinary.

workaholic ■ n. informal a person who compulsively works excessively hard for unusually long hours.

– DERIVATIVES **workaholism** n.

workaround ■ n. Computing a method for overcoming a problem or limitation in a program or system.

workbench ■ n. a bench at which carpentry or other mechanical or practical work is done.

workbook ■ n. a student's book containing instruction and exercises relating to a particular subject.

work camp ■ n. a camp at which community work is done, especially by young volunteers.

worker ■ n. **1** a person who works. ▶ informal a person who works hard. **2** a neuter or undeveloped female bee, wasp, ant, etc., large numbers of which perform the basic work of a colony. **3** a person who achieves a specified thing: *a worker of miracles*.

Workers' Day ■ n. **1** May, celebrated in many countries as a public holiday in honour of workers, especially manual labourers.

work ethic ■ n. another term for **PROTESTANT ETHIC**.

work experience ■ n. short-term experience of employment, arranged for older pupils by schools.

workfare ■ n. a welfare system which requires some work or attendance for training from those receiving benefits.
– ORIGIN 1960s: from **WORK** + (*wel*)*fare*.

workforce ■ n. [treated as sing. or pl.] the people engaged in or available for work, either in an area or in a particular firm or industry.

work-harden ■ v. [often as noun **work-hardening**] Metallurgy toughen (a metal) as a result of cold-working.

workhorse ■ n. a person or machine that works hard and reliably over a long period.

workhouse ■ n. **1** historical (in the UK) a public institution in which the destitute of a parish received board and lodging in return for work. **2** US a prison in which petty offenders are expected to work.

working ■ adj. **1** having paid employment. ▶ engaged in manual labour. ▶ (of an animal) used in farming, hunting, or for guard duties. **2** functioning or able to function. ▶ (of parts of a machine) moving and causing a machine to operate. **3** good enough as the basis for work or argument and likely to be developed or improved later: *a working title*. ■ n. **1** a mine or a part of a mine from which minerals are being extracted. **2** (**workings**) the way in which a machine, organization, or system operates. ▶ the record of the successive calculations made in solving a mathematical problem. **3** a scheduled duty or trip performed by a locomotive, bus, etc.

working capital ■ n. Finance the capital of a business which is used in its day-to-day trading operations, calculated as the current assets minus the current liabilities.

working class ■ n. [treated as sing. or pl.] the social group consisting of people who are employed for wages, especially in manual or industrial work. ■ adj. of or relating to the working class.

working drawing ■ n. a scale drawing which serves as a guide for the construction or manufacture of something.

working girl ■ n. informal, euphemistic a prostitute.

working party (also **working group**) ■ n. a group appointed to study and report on a particular question and make recommendations.

workload ■ n. the amount of work to be done by someone or something.

workman ■ n. (pl. **-men**) **1** a man employed to do manual labour. **2** a person who works in a specified way.

workmanlike ■ adj. showing efficient competence.

workmanship ■ n. the degree of skill with which a product is made or a job done.

workmate ■ n. a person with whom one works; a colleague.

work of art ■ n. a creative product with strong imaginative or aesthetic appeal.

workout ■ n. a session of vigorous physical exercise.

workpeople ▪ pl. n. chiefly Brit. people in paid employment, especially in manual or industrial labour.

work permit ▪ n. an official document giving a foreigner permission to take a job in a country.

workpiece ▪ n. an object being worked on with a tool or machine.

workplace ▪ n. a place where people work, such as a factory or an office.

work rate ▪ n. the amount of energy that is expended in sport or physical exercise.

work release ▪ n. leave of absence from prison by day enabling a prisoner to continue in normal employment.

works council ▪ n. a group of employees representing a workforce in discussions with their employers.

worksheet ▪ n. 1 a paper listing questions or tasks for students. 2 a paper or table recording work done or in progress.

workshop ▪ n. 1 a room or building in which goods are manufactured or repaired. 2 a meeting at which a group engages in intensive discussion and activity on a particular subject or project. ▪ v. 1 present a workshop performance of (a dramatic work) so as to explore aspects of the production prior to formal staging. 2 explore (a subject) through intensive group discussion.

work-shy ▪ adj. disinclined to work.

workspace ▪ n. 1 an area rented or sold for commercial purposes. 2 Computing a memory storage facility for temporary use.

workstation ▪ n. 1 a desktop computer terminal, typically networked and more powerful than a personal computer. 2 an area where work of a particular nature is carried out, such as a location on an assembly line.

worktop ▪ n. a flat surface for working on, especially in a kitchen.

workweek ▪ n. the total number of hours or days worked in a week.

world ▪ n. 1 (**the world**) the earth with all its countries and peoples. ▸ all of the people on the earth. 2 a region or group of countries: *the English-speaking world*. 3 human and social interaction. ▸ (**one's world**) a person's life and activities. 4 all that belongs to a particular historical period or sphere of activity. 5 secular or material matters as opposed to spiritual ones. ▸ a stage of human life, either mortal or after death. 6 another planet like the earth.
– PHRASES **the best of both** (or **all possible**) **worlds** the benefits of widely differing situations, enjoyed at the same time. **bring someone into the world** give birth to or assist at the birth of someone. —— **in the world** used to express astonishment or disbelief in questions: *What in the world are they doing?* **man** (or **woman**) **of the world** a person who is experienced in the ways of sophisticated society. **not do something for the world** not do something whatever the inducement. **out of this world** informal extremely enjoyable or impressive. **think the world of** have a very high regard for. **the world and his wife** informal everybody. **the world, the flesh, and the devil** all forms of temptation to sin. **a** (or **the**) **world of** a very great deal of.
– ORIGIN Old English *w(e)oruld*, from a Germanic compound meaning 'age of man'.

world-beater ▪ n. a person or thing that is better than all others in its field.

world-class ▪ adj. of or among the best in the world.

World Cup ▪ n. a competition between teams from several countries in a sport, in particular an international soccer tournament held every four years.

world English ▪ n. the English language including all of its regional varieties, such as North American, Australian, and South African English.

world fair (also **world's fair**) ▪ n. an international exhibition of the industrial, scientific, technological, and artistic achievements of the participating nations.

world-famous ▪ adj. known throughout the world.

World Heritage Site ▪ n. a natural or man-made site or structure recognized as being of outstanding international importance and as deserving special protection.

worldly ▪ adj. (**-ier**, **-iest**) 1 of or concerned with material affairs rather than spiritual ones. 2 experienced and sophisticated.
– PHRASES **worldly goods** (or **possessions** or **wealth**) everything that someone owns.
– DERIVATIVES **worldliness** n.

worldly-wise ▪ adj. having sufficient experience not to be easily shocked or deceived.

world music ▪ n. music from the developing world incorporating traditional and/or popular elements.

world order ▪ n. a set of arrangements established internationally for preserving global political stability.

world power ▪ n. a country that has significant influence in international affairs.

world-ranking ▪ adj. among the best in the world.

world's fair ▪ n. variant form of WORLD FAIR.

world-shaking ▪ adj. very important; momentous.

world view ▪ n. a particular philosophy of life or conception of the world.

world war ▪ n. a war involving many large nations in all different parts of the world, especially the wars of 1914–18 and 1939–45.

world-weary ▪ adj. bored with or cynical about life.
– DERIVATIVES **world-weariness** n.

worldwide ▪ adj. extending or applicable throughout the world. ▪ adv. throughout the world.

World Wide Web ▪ n. Computing an extensive information system on the Internet providing facilities for documents to be connected to other documents by hypertext links.

worm ▪ n. 1 an earthworm or other creeping or burrowing invertebrate animal having a long slender soft body and no limbs. [Annelida, Nematoda (roundworms), Platyhelminthes (flatworms), and other phyla.] ▸ (**worms**) intestinal or other internal parasites. ▸ used in names of long slender insect larvae and other creatures, e.g. army worm, slow-worm. 2 a maggot regarded as eating dead bodies buried in the ground. 3 informal a weak or despicable person. 4 the threaded cylinder in a worm gear. 5 Computing a self-replicating program able to propagate itself across a network, typically having a detrimental effect. ▪ v. 1 move by crawling or wriggling. 2 (**worm one's way into**) insinuate one's way into. 3 (**worm something out of**) obtain information from by cunning persistence. 4 treat (an animal) with a preparation designed to expel parasitic worms.
– DERIVATIVES **worm-like** adj.
– ORIGIN Old English, of Germanic origin.

worm cast (also **worm casting**) ▪ n. a convoluted mass of soil, mud, or sand thrown up at the surface by a burrowing worm.

worm-eaten ▪ adj. (of wood) full of holes made by woodworm.

wormer ▪ n. a substance used to worm animals.

wormery ▪ n. (pl. **-ies**) a container in which worms are kept for study or bred, especially for fishing bait.

worm gear ▪ n. a mechanical arrangement consisting of a toothed wheel worked by a short revolving cylinder (worm) bearing a screw thread.

wormhole ▪ n. 1 a hole made by a burrowing insect larva or worm in wood, fruit, etc. 2 Physics a hypothetical connection between widely separated regions of space–time.

worm's-eye view ▪ n. a view as seen from below or from a humble position.

wormwood ▪ n. 1 a woody shrub with a bitter aromatic taste, used as an ingredient of vermouth and absinthe and in medicine. [*Artemisia absinthium* (Eurasia) and related species.] 2 bitterness or grief, or a source of this.
– ORIGIN Old English *wermōd*, associated with WORM and WOOD; cf. VERMOUTH.

wormy ▪ adj. (**-ier**, **-iest**) 1 full of worms; worm-eaten. 2 informal weak or despicable.
– DERIVATIVES **worminess** n.

worn past participle of WEAR. ■ adj. **1** suffering from wear. **2** very tired.

worn out ■ adj. **1** exhausted. **2** worn to the point of being no longer usable.

worrisome ■ adj. causing anxiety or concern.
– DERIVATIVES **worrisomely** adv.

worrit /ˈwʌrɪt/ ■ v. (**worrited**, **worriting**) & n. Brit. archaic another term for WORRY.
– ORIGIN C18: apparently an alteration of WORRY.

worry ■ v. (**-ies**, **-ied**) **1** feel or cause to feel troubled over actual or potential difficulties. ▸ [as adj. **worried**] expressing anxiety. **2** annoy or disturb. **3** (of a dog or other carnivorous animal) tear at or pull about with the teeth. ▸ (of a dog) chase and attack (livestock, especially sheep). **4** (**worry at**) pull at or fiddle with repeatedly. **5** (**worry something out**) discover or devise a solution by persistent thought. ■ n. (pl. **-ies**) the state of being worried. ▸ a source of anxiety.
– DERIVATIVES **worriedly** adv. **worrier** n. **worrying** adj. **worryingly** adv.

> **HISTORY**
> **Worry** comes from *wyrgan*, an Old English word of West Germanic origin, meaning 'strangle'. In *Middle English* it took on the meanings 'choke with a mouthful of food', 'seize by the throat and tear', and 'swallow greedily', and in the 16th century 'harass with repeated aggression'. This gave rise to 'annoy or disturb' in the late 17th century and 'cause anxiety to' in the early 19th century. The sense 'feel anxious or troubled' is not recorded until the end of the 19th century.

worry beads ■ pl. n. a string of beads that one fingers so as to calm oneself.

worrywart ■ n. informal a person who tends to worry unduly; a habitual worrier.

wors /vɔːs/ ■ n. S. African sausage, especially boerewors.
– ORIGIN Afrikaans, from Dutch *worst* 'sausage'.

worse ■ adj. **1** of poorer quality or lower standard. ▸ more serious, severe, or evil. **2** more ill or unhappy. ■ adv. **1** less well. **2** more seriously or severely. ■ n. a worse event or circumstance. ▸ (**the worse**) a worse condition.
– PHRASES **none the worse for** not adversely affected by. **or worse** or as an even worse unspecified alternative. **the worse for drink** rather drunk. **the worse for wear 1** worn. **2** feeling rather unwell, especially as a result of drinking too much alcohol. **worse off** less fortunate or prosperous.
– ORIGIN Old English *wyrsa*, *wiersa* (adj.), *wiers* (adv.), of Germanic origin.

worsen ■ v. make or become worse.

worship ■ n. **1** the feeling or expression of reverence and adoration for a deity. ▸ religious rites and ceremonies. **2** great admiration or devotion. **3** (**His/Your Worship**) a title of respect used chiefly to or of a magistrate or mayor. ■ v. (**worshipped**, **worshipping**; US also **worshiped**, **worshiping**) **1** show reverence and adoration for (a deity). **2** feel great admiration or devotion for.
– DERIVATIVES **worshipper** n.
– ORIGIN Old English *weorthscipe* 'worthiness, acknowledgement of worth' (see WORTH, -SHIP).

worshipful ■ adj. **1** feeling or showing reverence and admiration. **2** (**Worshipful**) Brit. a title given to justices of the peace and to certain old companies or their officers.
– DERIVATIVES **worshipfully** adv. **worshipfulness** n.

worst ■ adj. of the poorest quality or the lowest standard. ▸ most severe or serious. ■ adv. **1** most severely or seriously. **2** least well. ■ n. the worst event or circumstance. ▸ the worst part or stage of something. ■ v. (usu. **be worsted**) get the better of.
– PHRASES **at its** (or **someone's**) **worst** in the worst state possible. **at worst** (or **the worst**) in the worst possible case. **do one's worst** do as much damage as one can (often expressing defiance). **get** (or **have**) **the worst of it** suffer the most. **if the worst comes to the worst** if the most serious or difficult circumstances arise.
– ORIGIN Old English *wierresta*, *wyrresta* (adj.), *wierst*, *wyrst* (adv.), of Germanic origin.

worsted /ˈwʊstɪd/ ■ n. a fine smooth yarn spun from combed long-staple wool. ▸ fabric made from such yarn, having a close-textured surface with no nap.

WPC

– ORIGIN Middle English: from *Worstead*, the name of a parish in Norfolk, England.

wort /wɜːt/ ■ n. **1** [in combination] used in names of plants and herbs, especially those used formerly as food or medicinally, e.g. St John's wort. ▸ archaic such a plant or herb. **2** the sweet infusion of ground malt or other grain before fermentation, used to produce beer and distilled malt liquors.
– ORIGIN Old English, of Germanic origin.

worth ■ adj. **1** equivalent in value to the sum or item specified. ▸ having income or property amounting to a specified sum. **2** deserving to be treated or regarded in the way specified. ■ n. **1** the value or merit of someone or something. ▸ an amount of a commodity equivalent to a specified sum of money. **2** the amount that could be achieved or produced in a specified time.
– PHRASES **for all one is worth** informal as energetically or enthusiastically as one can. **for what it is worth** used when offering a suggestion or opinion without making a claim as to its validity.
– ORIGIN Old English *w(e)orth*, of Germanic origin.

worthless ■ adj. **1** having no real value or use. **2** having no good qualities.
– DERIVATIVES **worthlessly** adv. **worthlessness** n.

worthwhile ■ adj. worth the time, money, or effort spent.

worthy ■ adj. (**-ier**, **-iest**) **1** (often **worthy of**) deserving. ▸ good enough; suitable. **2** deserving effort, attention, or respect. **3** showing good intent but lacking in humour or imagination. ■ n. (pl. **-ies**) often humorous a person important in a particular sphere: *local worthies*.
– DERIVATIVES **worthily** adv. **worthiness** n.

-worthy ■ comb. form **1** deserving of a specified thing: *newsworthy*. **2** suitable for a specified thing: *roadworthy*.

wot second person singular present of WIT².

would ■ modal v. (3rd sing. present **would**) **1** past of WILL¹, in various senses. **2** (expressing the conditional mood) indicating the consequence of an imagined event. ▸ (**I would**) used to give advice. **3** expressing a desire. ▸ expressing consent. **4** expressing a polite request. **5** expressing a conjecture or opinion. **6** poetic/literary expressing a wish or regret.
– ORIGIN Old English *wolde*, past of *wyllan* (see WILL¹).

> **USAGE**
> On the differences in use between **would** and **should**, see usage at SHOULD.

would-be ■ adj. often derogatory desiring or aspiring to be a specified type of person.

wouldn't ■ contr. would not.

wouldst archaic second person singular of WOULD.

wound¹ /wuːnd/ ■ n. **1** an injury to living tissue caused by a cut, blow, or other impact. **2** an injury to a person's feelings or reputation. ■ v. inflict a wound on.
– DERIVATIVES **wounding** n. & adj. **woundingly** adv.
– ORIGIN Old English *wund* (n.), *wundian* (v.), of Germanic origin.

wound² past and past participle of WIND².

wove past of WEAVE¹.

woven past participle of WEAVE¹.

wove paper ■ n. paper made on a wire-gauze mesh so as to have a uniform unlined surface. Compare with LAID PAPER.
– ORIGIN Early C19: *wove*, var. of WOVEN.

wow¹ informal ■ exclam. (also **wowee**) expressing astonishment or admiration. ■ n. a sensational success. ■ v. impress and excite greatly.
– ORIGIN C16: natural exclamation; first recorded in Scots.

wow² ■ n. Electronics slow pitch fluctuation in sound reproduction, perceptible in long notes. Compare with FLUTTER (in sense 4).
– ORIGIN C20: imitative.

WP ■ abbrev. word processing or word processor.

w.p. ■ abbrev. weather permitting.

WPC ■ abbrev. (in the UK) woman police constable.

wpm ■ abbrev. words per minute (used after a number to indicate typing speed).

wrack[1] ■ v. variant spelling of RACK[1], RACK[4].

wrack[2] ■ n. a coarse brown seaweed which grows on the shoreline, often with air bladders providing buoyancy. [Several species belonging to *Fucus* and other genera.]
– ORIGIN C16: apparently from WRACK[4].

wrack[3] (also **rack**) ■ n. a mass of high, thick, fast-moving cloud.
– ORIGIN Middle English.

wrack[4] ■ n. archaic or dialect a shipwreck. ▶ wreckage.
– ORIGIN Middle English: from Middle Dutch *wrak*; rel. to WREAK and WRECK.

wraith /reɪθ/ ■ n. 1 a ghost or ghostly image of someone, especially one seen shortly before or after their death. 2 poetic/literary a wisp or faint trace.
– DERIVATIVES **wraith-like** adj.
– ORIGIN C16 (orig. Scots).

wrangle ■ n. a long and complicated dispute or argument. ■ v. 1 engage in a wrangle. 2 N. Amer. round up or take charge of (livestock).
– ORIGIN Middle English: cf. Low German *wrangeln*, from *wrangen* 'to struggle'.

wrangler ■ n. 1 a person in charge of horses or other livestock on a farm. ▶ a person who trains and takes care of animals on a film set. 2 a person engaging in a wrangle.

wrap ■ v. (**wrapped**, **wrapping**) 1 cover or enclose in paper or soft material. ▶ arrange (paper or soft material) round something, as a covering or for warmth or protection. ▶ place around so as to encircle. 2 Computing cause (a word or unit of text) to be carried over to a new line automatically. ▶ (of a word or unit of text) be carried over in such a way. 3 informal finish filming or recording. ■ n. 1 a loose outer garment or piece of material. ▶ (also **wrap-around**) [as modifier] (of a garment) worn wrapped round the body so that the edges overlap: *a wrap skirt*. 2 paper or material used for wrapping. 3 informal the end of a session of filming or recording. 4 a tortilla wrapped around a filling, eaten as a sandwich.
– PHRASES **under wraps** kept secret.
– PHRASAL VERBS **wrap up 1** (also **wrap someone up**) put on (or dress someone in) warm clothes. 2 Brit. informal be quiet; stop talking. 3 (**wrapped up**) engrossed or absorbed to the exclusion of other things. **wrap something up** 1 complete or conclude a meeting or other process. 2 win a game or competition.
– DERIVATIVES **wrapping** n.
– ORIGIN Middle English.

wrapper ■ n. 1 a piece of paper or other material used for wrapping something, especially something sold or for sale. ▶ the dust jacket of a book. 2 chiefly N. Amer. a tobacco leaf of superior quality enclosing a cigar.

wrasse /ras/ ■ n. (pl. same or **wrasses**) a marine fish with thick lips and strong teeth, typically brightly coloured. [Family Labridae: numerous species.]
– ORIGIN C17: from Cornish *wrah*; rel. to Welsh *gwrach* 'old woman'.

wrath /rɒθ, rɔːθ/ ■ n. extreme anger.
– ORIGIN Old English *wrǣththu*, from *wrāth* (see WROTH).

wrathful ■ adj. poetic/literary full of or characterized by intense anger.
– DERIVATIVES **wrathfully** adv. **wrathfulness** n.

wreak ■ v. 1 cause (a large amount of damage or harm). 2 inflict (vengeance). ▶ archaic avenge (a wronged person).
– DERIVATIVES **wreaker** n.
– ORIGIN Old English *wrecan* 'drive (out), avenge', of Germanic origin.

wreath ■ n. (pl. **wreaths** /riːðz, riːθs/) 1 an arrangement of flowers, leaves, or stems fastened in a ring and used for decoration or for laying on a grave. 2 a curl or ring of smoke or cloud.
– ORIGIN Old English *writha*, rel. to WRITHE.

wreathe /riːð/ ■ v. 1 (usu. **be wreathed**) envelop, surround, or encircle. ▶ poetic/literary twist or entwine round or over something. ▶ (of smoke) move with a curling motion. 2 form (flowers, leaves, etc.) into a wreath.

– ORIGIN C16: partly a back-formation from archaic *wrethen*, from WRITHE, reinforced by WREATH.

wreck ■ n. 1 the destruction of a ship at sea; a shipwreck. ▶ a ship destroyed in such a way. 2 a building, vehicle, etc. that has been destroyed or badly damaged. ▶ N. Amer. a road or rail crash. 3 a person whose physical or mental health or strength has failed: *an emotional wreck*. ■ v. 1 (usu. **be wrecked**) cause the destruction of (a ship) by sinking or breaking up. ▶ [as noun **wrecking**] chiefly historical the practice of destroying a ship in order to steal the cargo. 2 destroy or severely damage. ▶ spoil completely: *the eye injury wrecked his chances*. 3 [usu. as noun **wrecking**] chiefly N. Amer. engage in breaking up badly damaged vehicles or demolishing old buildings to obtain usable spares or scrap.
– ORIGIN Middle English: from Anglo-Norman French *wrec*, from the base of Old Norse *reka* 'to drive'.

wreckage ■ n. the remains of something that has been badly damaged or destroyed.

wrecked ■ adj. informal 1 exhausted. 2 drunk.

wrecker ■ n. 1 a person or thing that wrecks or destroys something. ▶ a person who breaks up damaged vehicles or demolishes old buildings to obtain usable spares or scrap. 2 N. Amer. a recovery vehicle.

wrecking ball ■ n. a heavy metal ball swung from a crane into a building to demolish it.

wren ■ n. a very small short-winged songbird with a cocked tail. [*Troglodytes troglodytes*.] ▶ any of numerous small songbirds of the same family (Troglodytidae) or of unrelated families.
– ORIGIN Old English, of Germanic origin.

wrench ■ n. 1 a sudden violent twist or pull. 2 a feeling of abrupt pain and distress caused by one's own or another's departure. 3 an adjustable tool like a spanner, used for gripping and turning nuts or bolts. 4 Mechanics a combination of a couple with a force along its axis. ■ v. 1 pull or twist suddenly and violently. ▶ injure (a part of the body) as a result of a sudden twisting movement. 2 turn or adjust with a wrench.
– ORIGIN Old English *wrencan* 'twist'.

wrest /rest/ ■ v. 1 forcibly pull from a person's grasp. ▶ take (power or control) after considerable effort or resistance. 2 archaic distort the meaning or interpretation of.
– ORIGIN Old English *wrǣstan* 'twist, tighten', of Germanic origin.

wrestle ■ v. 1 take part in a fight that involves close grappling with one's opponent, either as sport or in earnest. ▶ force into a particular position in such a way. ▶ extract or manipulate (an object) with difficulty and some physical effort. 2 struggle with a difficulty or problem. ■ n. 1 a wrestling bout or contest. 2 a hard struggle.
– DERIVATIVES **wrestler** n. **wrestling** n.
– ORIGIN Old English, from *wrǣstan* 'wrest'.

wretch ■ n. an unfortunate person. ▶ informal a contemptible person.
– ORIGIN Old English *wrecca* (also in the sense 'banished person'), of West Germanic origin.

wretched ■ n. (-**er**, -**est**) 1 in a very unhappy or unfortunate state; miserable. 2 used to express anger or annoyance: *she disliked the wretched man intensely*.
– DERIVATIVES **wretchedly** adv. **wretchedness** n.
– ORIGIN from WRETCH.

wriggle ■ v. 1 twist and turn with quick writhing movements. ▶ move with wriggling movements. 2 (**wriggle out of**) avoid by devious means. ■ n. a wriggling movement.
– DERIVATIVES **wriggler** n. **wriggly** adj.
– ORIGIN C15: from Middle Low German *wriggelen*, from *wriggen* 'twist, turn'.

wright ■ n. archaic (except in combination) a maker or builder: *playwright* | *shipwright*.
– ORIGIN Old English, of West Germanic origin.

wring ■ v. (past and past part. **wrung** /rʌŋ/) 1 squeeze and twist to force liquid from. ▶ extract (liquid) in this way. 2 break (an animal's neck) by twisting forcibly. ▶ squeeze (someone's hand) tightly. 3 (often **wring something from/out of**) obtain with difficulty or effort. 4 cause great

pain or distress to: *the letter wrung her heart.* ■ n. an act of wringing.
– PHRASES **wring one's hands** clasp and twist one's hands together as a gesture of distress or despair.
– ORIGIN Old English, of West Germanic origin.

wringer ■ n. a device for wringing water from wet clothes or other objects.

wringing ■ adj. extremely wet; soaked.

wrinkle ■ n. **1** a slight line or fold, especially in fabric or the skin of the face. **2** informal a clever innovation, or useful piece of information or advice. ■ v. [often as adj. **wrinkled**] make or become wrinkled.
– ORIGIN Middle English: possibly a back-formation from Old English *gewrinclod* 'sinuous'.

wrinkly ■ adj. (**-ier**, **-iest**) having many wrinkles. ■ n. (also **wrinklie**) (pl. **-ies**) informal, derogatory an old person.

wrist ■ n. **1** the joint connecting the hand with the forearm. ▸ the equivalent joint (the carpal joint) in the foreleg of a quadruped or the wing of a bird. **2** (also **wrist pin**) (in a machine) a stud projecting from a crank as an attachment for a connecting rod.
– ORIGIN Old English, of Germanic origin.

wristband ■ n. a band worn round the wrist, especially for identity purposes or as a sweatband.

wrist-drop ■ n. paralysis of the muscles which normally raise the hand at the wrist and extend the fingers.

wristlet ■ n. a band or bracelet worn on the wrist.

wristwatch ■ n. a watch worn on a strap round the wrist.

writ[1] ■ n. a form of written command in the name of a court or other legal authority to do or abstain from doing a specified act.
– ORIGIN Old English, from the Germanic base of WRITE.

writ[2] ■ v. archaic past participle of WRITE.
– PHRASES **writ large** in an obvious or exaggerated form.

write ■ v. (past **wrote**; past part. **written**) **1** mark (letters, words, or other symbols) on a surface, with a pen, pencil, or similar implement. ▸ have learnt and have the ability to do this: *he couldn't read or write.* ▸ fill out or complete in writing. ▸ (**write something up**) write a full or formal account of something. ▸ S. African & Canadian take (an exam or test). **2** write in a cursive hand, as opposed to printing individual letters. **3** write and send (a letter) to someone. ▸ chiefly N. Amer. write and send a letter to (someone). **4** compose (a text or work) in writing. ▸ compose (a musical work). **5** Computing enter (data) into a specified storage medium or location in store. **6** underwrite (an insurance policy).
– PHRASES **be written all over one's face** informal be obvious from one's expression. (**and**) **that's all she wrote** N. Amer. informal there is nothing more to be said.
– PHRASAL VERBS **write something down** reduce the nominal value of stock or goods. **write someone in** chiefly US (when voting) add the name of someone not on the original list of candidates and vote for them. **write something off** (**write someone/thing off**) dismiss someone or something as insignificant. **2** cancel the record of a bad debt; acknowledge the failure to recover an asset. **3** damage a vehicle so badly that it cannot be repaired or is not worth repairing.
– DERIVATIVES **writable** adj. (chiefly Computing).
– ORIGIN Old English *wrītan* 'score, form (letters) by carving, write', of Germanic origin.

write-back ■ n. Finance the process of restoring to profit a provision for bad or doubtful debts previously made against profits and no longer required.

write-down ■ n. Finance a reduction in the estimated or nominal value of an asset.

write-in ■ n. US a vote cast for an unlisted candidate by writing their name on a ballot paper.

write-off ■ n. **1** a vehicle, aircraft, etc. that is too badly damaged to be repaired. **2** a worthless or ineffectual person or thing. **3** Finance a cancellation from an account of a bad debt or worthless asset.

write-protect ■ v. Computing protect (a disk) from accidental writing or erasure.

writer ■ n. **1** a person who has written a particular text. ▸ a person who writes books or articles as a regular occupation. **2** Computing a device that writes data to a storage medium. **3** Brit. archaic a clerk, especially in the navy or in government offices.
– PHRASES **writer's block** the condition of being unable to think of what to write or how to proceed with writing. **writer's cramp** pain or stiffness in the hand caused by excessive writing.

writerly ■ adj. of or characteristic of a professional author. ▸ consciously literary.

write-up ■ n. a newspaper article giving the author's opinion of a recent event, performance, or product.

writhe /rʌɪð/ ■ v. twist or squirm in pain or as if in pain.
– ORIGIN Old English *wrīthan* 'make into coils, plait', of Germanic origin.

writing ■ n. **1** the activity or skill of writing. **2** written work, especially with regard to its style or quality. ▸ (**writings**) books or other written works. **3** a sequence of letters or symbols forming coherent words. ▸ handwriting.
– PHRASES **in writing** in written form. **the writing** (or N. Amer. **handwriting**) **is on the wall** there are clear signs that something unpleasant or unwelcome is going to happen.

writing paper ■ n. paper of good quality used for writing letters by hand.

writ of execution ■ n. Law a judicial order that a judgement be enforced.

written past participle of WRITE.

wrong ■ adj. **1** not correct or true. ▸ mistaken. **2** unjust, dishonest, or immoral. **3** in a bad or abnormal condition; amiss. ■ adv. in an unsuitable or undesirable manner or direction. ▸ with an incorrect result. ■ n. an unjust, dishonest, or immoral action. ■ v. act unjustly or dishonestly towards. ▸ mistakenly attribute bad motives to; misrepresent.
– PHRASES **get someone wrong** misunderstand someone, especially by falsely imputing malice. **get** (**hold of**) **the wrong end of the stick** misunderstand something. **in the wrong** responsible for a mistake or offence.
– DERIVATIVES **wronger** n. **wrongly** adv. **wrongness** n.
– ORIGIN Old English *wrang*, from Old Norse *rangr* 'awry, unjust'.

wrongdoing ■ n. illegal or dishonest behaviour.
– DERIVATIVES **wrongdoer** n.

wrong-foot ■ v. **1** (in a game) play so as to catch an opponent off balance. **2** place in a difficult or embarrassing situation by saying or doing something unexpected.

wrongful ■ adj. (of an act) not fair, just, or legal.
– DERIVATIVES **wrongfully** adv. **wrongfulness** n.

wrong-headed ■ adj. having or showing bad judgement; misguided.
– DERIVATIVES **wrong-headedly** adv. **wrong-headedness** n.

wrong side ■ n. the reverse side of something.
– PHRASES **on the wrong side of 1** out of favour with. **2** somewhat more than (a specified age). **wrong side out** inside out.

wrong'un ■ n. Brit. informal a person of bad character.
– ORIGIN C19: contraction of *wrong one*.

wrote past tense of WRITE.

wroth /rəʊθ, rɒθ/ ■ adj. archaic angry.
– ORIGIN Old English *wrāth*, of Germanic origin.

wrought /rɔːt/ ■ adj. **1** (of metals) beaten out or shaped by hammering. **2** [in combination] made or fashioned in the specified way: *well-wrought.* **3** (**wrought up**) upset and anxious.
– ORIGIN Middle English: archaic past and past participle of WORK.

wrought iron ■ n. a tough malleable form of iron suitable for forging or rolling rather than casting, obtained by puddling pig iron while molten.

wrung past and past participle of WRING.

wry /rʌɪ/ ■ adj. (**wryer**, **wryest** or **wrier**, **wriest**) **1** using or expressing dry, especially mocking, humour. **2** (of a person's face or features) twisted into an expression of

disgust, disappointment, or annoyance. **3** bending or twisted to one side.
— DERIVATIVES **wryly** adv. **wryness** n.
— ORIGIN C16: from Old English *wrigian* 'tend, incline', in Middle English 'deviate, swerve, contort'.

wryneck ■ n. a bird of the woodpecker family, with brown plumage and a habit of twisting its head backwards. [Genus *Jynx*.]

WSW ■ abbrev. west-south-west.

wt ■ abbrev. weight.

WTO ■ abbrev. World Trade Organization.

wunderkind /ˈvʊndəkɪnd/ ■ n. (pl. **wunderkinds** or **wunderkinder** /-kɪndə/) a person who achieves great success when relatively young.
— ORIGIN C19: from German, from *Wunder* 'wonder' + *Kind* 'child'.

Wurlitzer /ˈwɜːlɪtsə/ ■ n. trademark a large pipe organ or electric organ, especially one formerly used in cinemas.
— ORIGIN named after the American instrument-maker Rudolf *Wurlitzer* (1831–1914).

wurst /vɜːst, vʊəst, w-/ ■ n. German or Austrian sausage.
— ORIGIN from German *Wurst*.

wushu /wuːˈʃuː/ ■ n. the Chinese martial arts.
— ORIGIN from Chinese *wǔshù*, from *wǔ* 'military' + *shù* 'art'.

wuss /wʊs/ ■ n. informal a weak or ineffectual person.
— DERIVATIVES **wussy** n. (pl. **-ies**) & adj.
— ORIGIN 1980s.

WWF ■ abbrev. **1** World Wide Fund for Nature. **2** World Wrestling Federation.

WWI ■ abbrev. World War I.

WWII ■ abbrev. World War II.

WWW ■ abbrev. World Wide Web.

wych elm /wɪtʃ/ ■ n. a European elm with large rough leaves, chiefly growing in woodland or near flowing water. [*Ulmus glabra*.]
— ORIGIN C17: *wych*, used in names of trees with pliant branches, from Old English *wic(e)*, *apparently from a* Germanic root meaning 'bend'.

Wykehamist /ˈwɪkəmɪst/ ■ n. a past or present pupil of Winchester College in England.
— ORIGIN C18: from modern Latin *Wykehamista*, from the name of William of *Wykeham* (1324–1404), founder of the college.

WYSIWYG /ˈwɪziwɪɡ/ (also **wysiwyg**) ■ adj. Computing denoting the representation of text on-screen in a form exactly corresponding to its appearance on a printout.
— ORIGIN 1980s: acronym from *what you see is what you get*.

wyvern /ˈwaɪv(ə)n/ ■ n. Heraldry a winged two-legged dragon with a barbed tail.
— ORIGIN Middle English (denoting a viper): from Old French *wivre*, from Latin *vipera*.

Xx

X¹ (also **x**) ■ n. (pl. **Xs** or **X's**) **1** the twenty-fourth letter of the alphabet. **2** denoting the next after W in a set of items, categories, etc. **3** denoting an unknown or unspecified person or thing. **4** (usu. *x*) the first unknown quantity in an algebraic expression, usually the independent variable. ▸ denoting the principal or horizontal axis in a system of coordinates. **5** a cross-shaped written symbol, used: ▸ to indicate a position on a map. ▸ to indicate an incorrect answer. ▸ to symbolize a kiss. ▸ to indicate one's vote on a ballot paper. ▸ in place of the signature of a person who cannot write. **6** the Roman numeral for ten.

X² ■ symb. films classified as suitable for adults only (replaced in South Africa in 1996 by *X18*).

X³ ■ abbrev. informal the drug Ecstasy.

-x ■ suffix forming the plural of many nouns ending in -*u* taken from French: *tableaux*.
– ORIGIN from French.

Xanadu /'zanədu:/ ■ n. (pl. **Xanadus**) an imaginary wonderful place.
– ORIGIN alteration of *Shang-tu*, the name of an ancient city in SE Mongolia, as portrayed in Coleridge's poem *Kubla Khan* (1816).

Xanax /'zanaks/ ■ n. trademark for ALPRAZOLAM.

xanthine /'zanθi:n/ ■ n. Biochemistry a crystalline compound formed in the metabolic breakdown of nucleic acids and related to caffeine and other alkaloids.
– ORIGIN C19: from *xanthic*, from Greek *xanthos* 'yellow'.

xanthoma /zan'θəʊmə/ ■ n. (pl. **xanthomas** or **xanthomata** /-mətə/) Medicine an irregular yellow patch or nodule on the skin, caused by deposition of lipids.
– ORIGIN C19: from Greek *xanthos* 'yellow' + -OMA.

xanthophyll /'zanθə(ʊ)fɪl/ ■ n. Biochemistry a yellow or brown carotenoid plant pigment which causes the autumn colours of leaves.
– ORIGIN C19: from Greek *xanthos* 'yellow' + *phullon* 'leaf'.

X chromosome ■ n. Genetics (in humans and other mammals) a sex chromosome, two of which are normally present in female cells (designated XX) and only one in male cells (designated XY). Compare with Y CHROMOSOME.

xd ■ abbrev. ex dividend.

Xe ■ symb. the chemical element xenon.

Xenical /'zenɪk(ə)l/ ■ n. trademark a synthetic drug which blocks pancreatic enzymes involved in the digestion of fats, used to treat obesity.
– ORIGIN C20.

xeno- ■ comb. form **1** relating to a foreigner or foreigners: *xenophobia*. **2** other; different in origin: *xenograft*.
– ORIGIN from Greek *xenos* 'stranger, strange'.

xenobiotic /ˌzɛnə(ʊ)baɪˈɒtɪk/ ■ adj. relating to or denoting a substance that is foreign to the body or to an ecological system. ■ n. a substance of this kind.

xenocryst /'zɛnə(ʊ)krɪst/ ■ n. Geology a crystal in an igneous rock which is not derived from the original magma.
– ORIGIN C19: from XENO- + CRYSTAL.

xenograft ■ n. a tissue graft or organ transplant from a donor of a different species from the recipient.

xenolith /'zɛnə(ʊ)lɪθ/ ■ n. Geology a piece of rock within an igneous mass which is not derived from the original magma but has been introduced from elsewhere, especially the surrounding country rock.
– DERIVATIVES **xenolithic** adj.

xenon /'zɛnɒn, 'zi:-/ ■ n. the chemical element of atomic number 54, a member of the noble gas series, obtained by distillation of liquid air and used in some specialized electric lamps. (Symbol: **Xe**)
– ORIGIN C19: from Greek, from *xenos* 'strange'.

xenophobia ■ n. intense or irrational dislike or fear of people from other countries.
– DERIVATIVES **xenophobe** n. **xenophobic** adj.

Xenopus /'zɛnəpəs/ ■ n. another term for PLATANNA.
– ORIGIN C19: from XENO- + Greek *pous* 'foot'.

xenotransplantation ■ n. the process of grafting or transplanting organs or tissues between members of different species.
– DERIVATIVES **xenotransplant** n.

xeric /'zɪərɪk, 'zɛ-/ ■ adj. Ecology containing little moisture; very dry. Compare with HYDRIC and MESIC.
– ORIGIN 1920s: from Greek *xēros* 'dry'.

xeriscape /'zɪərɪskeɪp, 'zɛ-/ ■ n. a style of landscape design requiring little or no irrigation or other maintenance, used in arid regions.
– DERIVATIVES **xeriscaping** n.

xero- /'zɪərəʊ, 'zɛrəʊ/ ■ comb. form dry: *xerophyte*.
– ORIGIN from Greek *xēros* 'dry'.

xeroderma /ˌzɪərə(ʊ)'dəːmə, ˌzɛ-/ ■ n. any of various diseases characterized by extreme dryness of the skin, especially a mild form of ichthyosis.
– ORIGIN C19: from XERO- + Greek *derma* 'skin'.

xerography ■ n. a dry copying process in which powder adheres to parts of a surface remaining electrically charged after being exposed to light from an image of the document to be copied.
– DERIVATIVES **xerographic** adj. **xerographically** adv.

xeromorphic /ˌzɪərə'mɔːfɪk, ˌzɛ-/ ■ adj. Botany possessing features characteristic of a xerophilous plant.

xerophilous /zɪə'rɒfɪləs, zɛ-/ ■ adj. Botany & Zoology (of a plant or animal) adapted to a dry climate or habitat.
– DERIVATIVES **xerophile** n.

xerophthalmia /ˌzɪərɒf'θalmɪə, ˌzɛ-/ ■ n. Medicine abnormal dryness of the conjunctiva and cornea of the eye, typically associated with vitamin A deficiency.

xerophyte /'zɪərə(ʊ)faɪt, 'zɛ-/ ■ n. Botany a plant which needs very little water.
– DERIVATIVES **xerophytic** adj.

Xerox /'zɪərɒks, 'zɛ-/ ■ n. trademark a xerographic copying process. ▸ a copy made using such a process. ■ v. (**xerox**) copy (a document) by such a process.
– ORIGIN 1950s: an invented name, based on XEROGRAPHY.

x-height ■ n. the height of a lower-case x, considered characteristic of a given typeface or script.

Xhosa /'kɔːsə, 'ǁɔːsə/ ■ n. (pl. same or **Xhosas**) **1** a member of a South African people traditionally living in the Eastern Cape. **2** another term for ISIXHOSA.
– ORIGIN from isiXhosa *umXhosa*.

xi /ksaɪ, gzaɪ, saɪ, zaɪ/ ■ n. the fourteenth letter of the Greek alphabet (Ξ, ξ), transliterated as 'x'.
– ORIGIN from Greek.

xiphisternum /ˌzɪfɪ'stəːnəm/ ■ n. another term for XIPHOID PROCESS.
– ORIGIN C19: from Greek *xiphos* 'sword' + STERNUM.

xiphoid process /'zɪfɔɪd/ (also **xiphoid cartilage**) ■ n. Anatomy the cartilaginous section at the lower end of the sternum, not attached to any ribs.
– ORIGIN C18: from Greek *xiphoeidēs*, from *xiphos* 'sword'.

Xitsonga /ʃɪ'tsɒŋɡə/ ■ n. the Bantu language of the Tsonga people.

XL ■ abbrev. extra large (as a clothes size).

Xmas /'krɪsməs, 'ɛksməs/ ■ n. informal term for CHRISTMAS.
– ORIGIN *X* representing the initial chi of Greek *Khristos* 'Christ'.

XML ■ abbrev. Computing Extensible Mark-up Language, used chiefly on the Internet for data transfer and storage.

XOR ■ n. Electronics exclusive OR (a Boolean operator).

...d ■ adj. pornographic or indecent. ▶ (formerly) ...ing a film given an X classification.

X-ray ■ n. **1** an electromagnetic wave of very short wavelength (between ultraviolet and gamma rays), able to pass through many materials opaque to light. ▶ [as modifier] informal denoting an apparent or supposed faculty for seeing beyond an outward form: *X-ray eyes*. **2** a photograph or other image of the internal structure of an object, especially a part of the body, produced by passing X-rays through the object. **3** a code word representing the letter X, used in radio communication. ■ v. photograph or examine with X-rays.
– ORIGIN translation of German *X-Strahlen* (pl.), from *X-* (because, when discovered in 1895, the nature of the rays was unknown) + *Strahl* 'ray'.

X-ray astronomy ■ n. the branch of astronomy concerned with the detection and measurement of high-energy electromagnetic radiation emitted by celestial objects.

X-ray crystallography ■ n. the study of crystals and their structure by means of the diffraction of X-rays by the regularly spaced atoms of crystalline materials.

X-ray tube ■ n. Physics a device for generating X-rays by accelerating electrons to high energies and causing them to strike a metal target from which the X-rays are emitted.

xylem /ˈzʌɪləm/ ■ n. Botany the vascular tissue in plants which conducts water and dissolved nutrients upwards from the root and also helps to form the woody element in the stem.
– ORIGIN C19: from Greek *xulon* 'wood'.

xylene /ˈzʌɪliːn/ ■ n. Chemistry a volatile liquid hydrocarbon obtained by distilling wood, coal tar, or petroleum, used in fuels and solvents and in chemical synthesis.
– ORIGIN C19: from Greek *xulon* 'wood'.

xylo- /ˈzʌɪləʊ/ ■ comb. form of or relating to wood: *xylophone*.
– ORIGIN from Greek *xulon* 'wood'.

xylophagous /zʌɪˈlɒfəgəs/ ■ adj. Zoology feeding on or boring into wood.

xylophone ■ n. a musical instrument played by striking a row of wooden bars of graduated length with small beaters.
– DERIVATIVES **xylophonist** /zʌɪˈlɒfənɪst/ n.
– ORIGIN C19: from **XYLO-** + **-PHONE**.

xylose /ˈzʌɪləʊz, -s/ ■ n. Chemistry a sugar of the pentose class (with molecules containing five carbon atoms) which occurs widely in plants, especially as a component of hemicelluloses.

CONSONANTS   b but   d dog   f few   g get   h he   j yes   k cat   l leg   m man   n no   p pen   r red

Yy

Y¹ (also **y**) ■ n. (pl. **Ys** or **Y's**) **1** the twenty-fifth letter of the alphabet. **2** denoting the next after X in a set of items, categories, etc. **3** denoting an unknown or unspecified person or thing (coming second after 'x'). **4** (usu. *y*) the second unknown quantity in an algebraic expression, usually the dependent variable. ▶ denoting the secondary or vertical axis in a system of coordinates.

Y² ■ abbrev. yen. ■ symb. the chemical element yttrium.

y ■ abbrev. year(s).

-y¹ ■ suffix forming adjectives: **1** (from nouns and adjectives) full of; having the quality of: *messy*. ▶ with depreciatory reference: *boozy*. **2** (from verbs) inclined to; apt to: *sticky*.
– ORIGIN Old English *-ig*, of Germanic origin.

-y² (also **-ey** or **-ie**) ■ suffix forming diminutive nouns, pet names, etc.: *aunty*. ▶ forming verbs.
– ORIGIN Middle English: orig. Scots.

-y³ ■ suffix forming nouns: **1** denoting a state or quality: *jealousy*. **2** denoting an action or its result: *victory*.
– ORIGIN from French *-ie*, from Latin *-ia*, *-ium*, or Greek *-eia*, *-ia*.

yabber ■ v. informal chatter.
– ORIGIN prob. from Wuywurung (an Aboriginal language).

yabby (also **yabbie**) ■ n. (pl. **-ies**) Austral. a small freshwater crayfish. [*Charax destructor* and related species.]
– ORIGIN C19: from Wemba-wemba (an Aboriginal language).

YAC ■ abbrev. Biology yeast artificial chromosome.

yacht /jɒt/ ■ n. a medium-sized sailing boat equipped for cruising or racing. ▶ a powered boat equipped for cruising. ■ v. race or cruise in a yacht.
– DERIVATIVES **yachting** n.
– ORIGIN C16: from early modern Dutch *jaghte*, from *jaghtschip* 'fast pirate ship', from *jag(h)t* 'hunting' + *schip* 'ship'.

yachtie ■ n. informal a person who sails yachts.

yack ■ n. & v. variant spelling of YAK².

yackety-yak ■ n. & v. another term for YAK².
– ORIGIN 1950s: imitative.

Yagi antenna /'jɑːgi/ ■ n. a highly directional narrowband radio aerial made of several short rods mounted across an insulating support.
– ORIGIN 1940s: named after the Japanese engineer Hidetsugu *Yagi*.

yah¹ ■ exclam. **1** variant spelling of JA. **2** yes (used in representations of upper-class British speech).

yah² ■ exclam. expressing derision.
– ORIGIN C17: natural exclamation.

yahoo¹ /'jɑːhuː, jəˈhuː/ ■ n. informal a rude, coarse, or brutish person.
– ORIGIN C18: from the name of an imaginary race in Jonathan Swift's *Gulliver's Travels* (1726).

yahoo² /jɑːˈhuː, ja-/ ■ exclam. expressing great joy or excitement.
– ORIGIN C20: natural exclamation.

Yahweh /'jɑːweɪ/ (also **Yahveh** /-veɪ/) ■ n. a form of the Hebrew name of God used in the Bible.
– ORIGIN from Hebrew *YHWH* with added vowels; cf. JEHOVAH.

Yajur Veda /ˌjʌdʒʊə ˈveɪdə, -ˈviːdə/ ■ n. one of the four Vedas, used in the sacrificial ritual.
– ORIGIN from Sanskrit *yajus* 'sacrificial formula' and VEDA.

yak¹ ■ n. a large ox with shaggy hair, humped shoulders, and large horns, used in Tibet as a pack animal and for its milk, meat, and hide. [*Bos grunniens* (domesticated) and *B. mutus* (its wild ancestor).]
– ORIGIN C18: from Tibetan *gyag*.

yak² (also **yack**) informal ■ n. a trivial or unduly persistent conversation. ■ v. (**yakked**, **yakking**) talk at length about trivial or boring subjects.
– ORIGIN 1950s: imitative.

yakitori /ˌjakɪˈtɔːri/ ■ n. a Japanese dish of chicken pieces grilled on a skewer.
– ORIGIN Japanese, from *yaki* 'grilling, toasting' + *tori* 'bird'.

yakuza /jəˈkuːzə/ ■ n. (pl. same) (**the Yakuza**) a powerful Japanese criminal organization. ▶ a member of this organization; a Japanese gangster or racketeer.
– ORIGIN Japanese, from *ya* 'eight' + *ku* 'nine' + *za* 'three', referring to the worst hand in a gambling game.

Yale ■ n. trademark a type of lock with a latch bolt and a flat key with a serrated edge.
– ORIGIN C19: named after the American locksmith Linus *Yale* Jr.

yam ■ n. **1** the edible starchy tuber of a climbing plant, widely distributed in tropical and subtropical countries. **2** the plant which yields this tuber. [Genus *Dioscorea*: many species.] **3** N. Amer. a sweet potato.
– ORIGIN C16: from Portuguese *inhame* or obsolete Spanish *iñame*, prob. of West African origin.

yammer informal ■ n. loud and sustained noise. ■ v. **1** talk loudly and incessantly. **2** make a loud, incessant noise.
– DERIVATIVES **yammerer** n.
– ORIGIN Middle English: alteration of earlier *yomer*, from Old English *geōmrian* 'to lament'.

yang ■ n. (in Chinese philosophy) the active male principle of the universe, characterized as male and creative and associated with heaven, heat, and light. Contrasted with YIN.
– ORIGIN from Chinese *yáng* 'male genitals, sun, positive'.

Yank ■ n. informal **1** often derogatory an American. **2** US another term for YANKEE (in sense 2).

yank informal ■ v. pull with a jerk. ■ n. a sudden hard pull.
– ORIGIN C18 (Scots, in the sense 'sudden sharp blow').

Yankee ■ n. informal **1** often derogatory an American. **2** US an inhabitant of New England or one of the northern states. ▶ historical a Federal soldier in the Civil War. **3** (also **Yankee jib**) Nautical a large jib set forward of a staysail in light winds. **4** a code word representing the letter Y, used in radio communication.
– ORIGIN C18: recorded in the late 17th century as a nickname; perhaps from Dutch *Janke*, diminutive of *Jan* 'John'.

Yanomami /ˌjanəˈmɑːmi/ (also **Yanomamö** /-ˌmɑːməʊ/) ■ n. (pl. same) **1** a member of an American Indian people living in the forests of southern Venezuela and northern Brazil. **2** either of the two related languages of this people.
– ORIGIN the name in Yanomami, 'people'.

Yanqui /'jaŋki/ ■ n. variant spelling of YANKEE, as used in Latin American contexts.

yantra /'jantrə/ ■ n. a geometrical diagram, or any object, used as an aid to meditation in tantric worship.
– ORIGIN Sanskrit, 'device for holding'.

yap ■ v. (**yapped**, **yapping**) **1** give a sharp, shrill bark. **2** informal talk at length in an irritating manner. ■ n. a sharp, shrill bark.
– DERIVATIVES **yapper** n. **yappy** adj. (informal).
– ORIGIN C17: imitative.

yard¹ ■ n. **1** (abbrev.: **yd**) a unit of linear measure equal to 3 feet (0.9144 metre). ▶ a square or cubic yard, especially of sand or other building materials. **2** a cylindrical spar, tapering to each end, slung across a ship's mast for a sail to hang from.
– PHRASES **by the yard** in large numbers or quantities.
– ORIGIN Old English *gerd*, of West Germanic origin.

■ n. **1** a piece of uncultivated ground adjoining a ▭▭▭▭▭g, typically one enclosed by walls. ▸ an area of land used for a particular purpose or business: *a builder's yard.* **2** S. African & N. Amer. the garden of a house. **3** S. African a courtyard or similar area around which a number of rented makeshift dwellings are clustered. ■ v. **1** chiefly N. Amer. store or transport (wood) in or to a timber yard. **2** put (farm animals) into an enclosure.
– ORIGIN Old English *geard* 'building, home, region', from a Germanic base rel. to GARDEN and ORCHARD.

yardage ■ n. a distance or length measured in yards.

yardarm ■ n. the outer extremity of a ship's yard.

yardbird ■ n. US informal **1** a new military recruit, especially one assigned to menial tasks. **2** a convict.
– ORIGIN 1940s: perhaps suggested by JAILBIRD.

Yardie /ˈjɑːdi/ informal ■ n. **1** (among Jamaicans) a fellow Jamaican. **2** (in the UK) a member of a Jamaican or West Indian gang of criminals.
– ORIGIN 1980s: from Jamaican English, 'house, home'.

yardman ■ n. (pl. **-men**) **1** a person working in a railway or timber yard. **2** US a person who does various outdoor jobs.

yard of ale ■ n. Brit. the amount of beer (typically two to three pints) held by a narrow glass about a yard high.

yard sale ■ n. N. Amer. a sale of miscellaneous second-hand items held in the grounds of a private house.

yardstick ■ n. **1** a measuring rod a yard long. **2** a standard used for comparison.

yarmulke /ˈjɑːmʊlkə/ (also **yarmulka**) ■ n. a skullcap worn in public by Orthodox Jewish men or during prayer by other Jewish men.
– ORIGIN C20: from Yiddish *yarmolke*.

yarn ■ n. **1** spun thread used for knitting, weaving, or sewing. **2** informal a long or rambling story, especially one that is implausible. ▸ Austral./NZ a chat. ■ v. informal tell a yarn. ▸ Austral./NZ chat; talk.
– ORIGIN Old English, of Germanic origin.

yarrow ■ n. a plant with feathery leaves and heads of small white or pale pink aromatic flowers, used in herbal medicine. [*Achillea millefolium*.]
– ORIGIN Old English, of West Germanic origin.

yashmak /ˈjaʃmak/ ■ n. a veil concealing all of the face except the eyes, worn by some Muslim women in public.
– ORIGIN C19: from Turkish.

yatra /ˈjɑːtrɑː/ ■ n. Indian a procession or pilgrimage, especially one with a religious purpose.
– ORIGIN from Sanskrit *yātrā* 'journey', from *yā* 'go'.

yatter informal ■ v. talk incessantly; chatter. ■ n. incessant talk.
– ORIGIN C19: imitative.

yaw ■ v. (of a moving ship or aircraft) twist or oscillate about a vertical axis. ■ n. twisting or oscillation of a moving ship or aircraft about a vertical axis.
– ORIGIN C16.

yawl ■ n. **1** a two-masted fore-and-aft-rigged sailing boat with the mizzenmast stepped far aft so that the mizzen boom overhangs the stern. **2** historical a ship's jolly boat with four or six oars.
– ORIGIN C16: from Middle Low German *jolle* or Dutch *jol*.

yawn ■ v. **1** involuntarily open one's mouth wide and inhale deeply due to tiredness or boredom. **2** [usu. as adj. **yawning**] be wide open: *a yawning chasm*. ■ n. **1** an act of yawning. **2** informal a boring or tedious person, thing, or event.
– DERIVATIVES **yawningly** adv.
– ORIGIN Old English, of Germanic origin.

yawp ■ n. a harsh or hoarse cry or yelp. ■ v. shout or exclaim hoarsely.
– ORIGIN Middle English: imitative.

yaws ■ pl. n. [treated as sing.] a contagious tropical disease caused by a bacterium that enters skin abrasions and causes small crusted lesions which may develop into deep ulcers.
– ORIGIN C17: prob. from Carib *yaya*.

yay[1] /jeɪ/ ■ exclam. informal expressing triumph, approval, or encouragement.

yay[2] /jeɪ/ ■ adv. informal, chiefly N. Amer. (with measurements) so; to this extent: *I knew him when he was yay big.*
– ORIGIN 1960s: prob. a var. of YEA.

Yb ■ symb. the chemical element ytterbium.

Y chromosome ■ n. Genetics (in humans and other mammals) a sex chromosome which is normally present only in male cells, which are designated XY. Compare with X CHROMOSOME.

yclept /ɪˈklɛpt/ ■ adj. archaic or humorous by the name of.
– ORIGIN Old English *gecleopod*, from *cleopian* 'call', of Germanic origin.

yd ■ abbrev. yard (measure).

ye[1] ■ pron. [second person pl.] archaic or dialect plural form of THOU[1].
– ORIGIN Old English *gē*, of Germanic origin.

ye[2] ■ det. pseudo-archaic term for THE.

HISTORY
The modern use of *ye* has arisen from a misunderstanding. In Old English the sound *th-* was represented by a letter called the *thorn*, written þ. In medieval times this character came to be written identically with *y*, so that *the* could be written *ye*. This spelling was kept as a convenient abbreviation as late as the 19th century, but it was never pronounced as 'ye'.

yea archaic or formal ■ adv. yes. ■ n. an affirmative answer. ▸ (in the US Congress) an affirmative vote or voter.
– ORIGIN Old English, of Germanic origin.

yeah (also **yeh**) ■ exclam. & n. informal non-standard spelling of YES.

yean /jiːn/ ■ v. archaic (of a sheep or goat) give birth to (a lamb or kid).
– ORIGIN Middle English: perhaps representing an Old English verb rel. to *ēanian* 'to lamb'.

year /jɪə, jəː/ ■ n. **1** the time taken by the earth to make one revolution around the sun. **2** (also **calendar year** or **civil year**) the period of 365 days (or 366 days in leap years) starting from the first of January, used for reckoning time in ordinary affairs. ▸ a period of the same length as this starting at a different point. ▸ a similar period used for reckoning time according to other calendars. **3** (**one's years**) one's age or time of life. **4** (**years**) informal a very long time. **5** a set of students grouped together as being of roughly similar ages.
– PHRASES **in the year of grace** (or **Our Lord**) —— in the year —— AD. **a year and a day** the period specified in some legal matters to ensure the completion of a full year. **year in, year out** continuously or repeatedly over a period of years.
– ORIGIN Old English, of Germanic origin.

yearbook ■ n. an annual publication giving current information about and listing events of the previous year. ▸ N. Amer. an annual publication of the graduating class in a school or university, giving photographs of students and details of school activities in the previous year.

yearling ■ n. an animal of a year old, or in its second year. ▸ a racehorse in the calendar year after its year of foaling. ■ adj. **1** having lived or existed for a year. **2** Finance denoting a bond which is redeemable after one year.

yearly ■ adj. & adv. happening or produced once a year or every year.

yearn /jəːn/ ■ v. **1** have an intense feeling of loss and longing for something. **2** archaic be filled with compassion or warm feeling.
– DERIVATIVES **yearner** n. **yearning** n. **yearningly** adv.
– ORIGIN Old English *giernan*, from a Germanic base meaning 'eager'.

year-on-year ■ adj. (of figures, prices, etc.) as compared with the corresponding ones from a year earlier.

year-round ■ adj. happening or continuing throughout the year.

yeast ■ n. **1** a microscopic single-celled fungus capable of converting sugar into alcohol and carbon dioxide. [*Saccharomyces cerevisiae* (brewer's yeast) and related species.] ▸ a greyish-yellow preparation of this obtained chiefly from fermented beer, used as a fermenting agent,

to raise bread dough, and as a food supplement. **2** Biology any unicellular fungus that reproduces vegetatively by budding or fission, e.g. candida.
– ORIGIN Old English, of Germanic origin.

yeasty ■ adj. (-**ier**, -**iest**) **1** of, resembling, or containing yeast. **2** turbulent or restless.
– DERIVATIVES **yeastily** adv. **yeastiness** n.

yebo ■ exclam. S. African informal yes; used to show agreement or approval.
– ORIGIN isiZulu, 'yes'.

yeehaw (also **yeehah**) ■ exclam. N. Amer. an expression of enthusiasm or exuberance, typically associated with cowboys of the southern US.
– ORIGIN C20: natural exclamation.

yell ■ n. **1** a loud, sharp cry, especially of pain, surprise, or delight. **2** N. Amer. an organized rhythmic cheer, especially one used to support a sports team. ■ v. shout in a loud or piercing way.
– ORIGIN Old English, of Germanic origin.

yellow ■ adj. **1** of the colour between green and orange in the spectrum, a primary subtractive colour complementary to blue; coloured like ripe lemons or egg yolks. **2** offensive having a yellowish or olive skin (as used to describe Chinese or Japanese people). **3** denoting a warning of danger which is thought to be near but not actually imminent. **4** informal cowardly. **5** (of a book or newspaper) unscrupulously sensational. ■ n. **1** yellow colour or pigment. **2** used in names of yellow butterflies and moths, e.g. clouded yellow. ■ v. become a yellow colour, especially with age.
– PHRASES **the yellow peril** offensive the political or military threat regarded as being posed by the Chinese or by the peoples of SE Asia.
– DERIVATIVES **yellowed** adj. **yellowing** adj. **yellowish** adj. **yellowness** n. **yellowy** adj.
– ORIGIN Old English *geolu*, *geolo*, of West Germanic origin; rel. to GOLD.

yellow-belly ■ n. informal **1** a coward. **2** any of a number of animals with yellow underparts.
– DERIVATIVES **yellow-bellied** adj.

yellow bile ■ n. historical another term for CHOLER.

yellowcake ■ n. impure uranium oxide obtained during processing of uranium ore.
– ORIGIN 1950s: so named because it is obtained as a yellow precipitate.

yellow card ■ n. (especially in soccer) a yellow card shown by the referee to a player being cautioned. ■ v. (**yellow-card**) (of the referee) show a yellow card to.

yellow dog ■ n. N. Amer. informal a contemptible person or thing.

yellow fever ■ n. a tropical virus disease transmitted by mosquitoes, which affects the liver and kidneys, causing fever and jaundice, and is often fatal.

yellowfin ■ n. a widely distributed, commercially important tuna that has yellow anal and dorsal fins. [*Thunnus albacares*.]

yellowfish ■ n. a freshwater fish of the carp family, native to southern Africa and popular with anglers. [Genus *Barbus*: several species.]

yellow flag ■ n. **1** a ship's yellow or quarantine flag, used to indicate the presence or absence of disease aboard. **2** Motor Racing a yellow flag used to signal to drivers that there is a hazard ahead. **3** see FLAG[3].

yellowhammer ■ n. a common Eurasian bunting, the male of which has a yellow head, neck, and breast. [*Emberiza citrinella*.]
– ORIGIN C16: -*hammer* is perhaps from Old English *amore* (a kind of bird), perhaps conflated with *hama* 'feathers'.

yellow jersey ■ n. (in a cycling race involving stages) a yellow jersey worn each day by the rider who is ahead on time over the whole race, and presented to the rider with the shortest overall time at the finish of the race.

yellowlegs ■ n. a migratory sandpiper that resembles the greenshank but has yellowish legs, breeding in northern Canada. [Genus *Tringa*: two species.]

yellow metal ■ n. a form of brass containing about 60 parts copper and 40 parts zinc, with a little lead.

Yellow Pages ■ pl. n. trademark a telephone directory printed on yellow paper and listing businesses and other organizations according to the goods or services they offer.

yellow rice ■ n. S. African rice prepared with turmeric and raisins.

yellowtail ■ n. (pl. same or **yellowtails**) an amberjack or other marine fish with yellow on the tail.

yellowwood ■ n. a large evergreen forest tree native to southern Africa. [Genus *Podocarpus*: several species.] ▶ the hard yellow wood of this tree, used for furniture.

yelp ■ n. a short sharp cry, especially of pain or alarm. ■ v. utter a yelp or yelps.
– DERIVATIVES **yelper** n.
– ORIGIN Old English *g(i)elpan* (v.) 'to boast', later 'cry with a loud voice', from a Germanic imitative base.

Yemeni /ˈjɛməni/ ■ n. a native or inhabitant of Yemen. ■ adj. of or relating to Yemen.

Yemenite ■ n. another term for YEMENI. ▶ a Jew who was, or whose ancestors were, formerly resident in Yemen. ■ adj. of or relating to Yemeni Arabs or Jews.

yen[1] ■ n. (pl. same) the basic monetary unit of Japan.
– ORIGIN from Japanese *en* 'round'.

yen[2] informal ■ n. a longing or yearning. ■ v. (**yenned**, **yenning**) feel a longing or yearning.
– ORIGIN C19 (in the sense 'craving for a drug'): from Chinese *yǎn*.

yenta /ˈjɛntə/ ■ n. informal, chiefly N. Amer. a female gossip and busybody.
– ORIGIN 1920s: Yiddish, orig. a given name.

yeoman /ˈjəʊmən/ ■ n. (pl. -**men**) **1** historical a man holding a small landed estate; a freeholder. ▶ a person qualified for jury duties, electoral rights, etc. by virtue of possessing free land. **2** historical a servant in a royal or noble household, ranking between a sergeant and a groom or a squire and a page. **3** Brit. a member of the yeomanry force.
– PHRASES **yeoman service** efficient help.
– DERIVATIVES **yeomanly** adj.
– ORIGIN Middle English: prob. from YOUNG + MAN.

Yeoman of the Guard ■ n. a member of the British sovereign's bodyguard (now having only ceremonial duties).

yeomanry ■ n. [treated as sing. or pl.] historical a body of yeomen, or yeomen collectively. ▶ (in Britain) a volunteer cavalry force raised from the yeomanry (1794–1908).

Yeoman Warder ■ n. a warder at the Tower of London.

-**yer** ■ suffix variant spelling of -IER (as in *lawyer*).

yes ■ exclam. **1** used to give an affirmative response. **2** responding to someone addressing one or attracting one's attention. **3** questioning a remark. **4** expressing delight. ■ n. (pl. **yeses** or **yesses**) an affirmative answer, decision, or vote.
– ORIGIN Old English *gēse*, *gīse*, prob. from an unrecorded phr. meaning 'may it be so'.

yeshiva /jəˈʃiːvə/ ■ n. an Orthodox Jewish college or seminary.
– ORIGIN from Hebrew *yĕšībāh*.

yes-man ■ n. (pl. -**men**) informal a person who always agrees with their superiors.

yessir /ˈjɛsə, jɛsˈsəː/ ■ exclam. informal expressing assent, especially to a superior. ▶ N. Amer. expressing emphatic affirmation.
– ORIGIN C20: alteration of *yes sir*.

yester- ■ comb. form poetic/literary or archaic of yesterday: *yestereve*.
– ORIGIN Old English, of Germanic origin.

yesterday ■ adv. on the day before today. ▶ in the recent past. ■ n. the day before today. ▶ the recent past.
– ORIGIN Old English *giestran dæg*.

yesterday, today, and tomorrow ■ n. (pl. same) an evergreen shrub of the New World whose fragrant flowers change from deep purple to lavender to white, widely cultivated as an ornamental. [Genus *Brunfelsia*: several species.]

yesteryear ■ n. poetic/literary last year or the recent past.

yet ■ adv. **1** up until the present or a specified or implied

by now or then. ▶ [with neg.] as soon as the present or ...tified or implied time. ▶ from now into the future for a specified length of time. ▶ referring to something that will or may happen in the future: *I'll find her yet.* **2** still; even (emphasizing increase or repetition). **3** nevertheless; in spite of that. ■ conj. but at the same time; but nevertheless.
– PHRASES **nor yet** and also not.
– ORIGIN Old English *gīet(a)*.

yeti /ˈjeti/ ■ n. a large hairy manlike creature said to live in the highest part of the Himalayas.
– ORIGIN 1930s: from Tibetan *yeh-teh* 'little manlike animal'.

yew ■ n. a coniferous tree of the northern hemisphere with poisonous red berry-like fruit and dense, springy wood. [*Taxus baccata* and related species.]
– ORIGIN Old English, of Germanic origin.

Y-fronts ■ pl. n. trademark men's or boys' underpants with a branching seam at the front in the shape of an upside-down Y.

YHA ■ abbrev. Youth Hostels Association.

yho ■ exclam. variant spelling of YOH.

Yid ■ n. informal, offensive a Jew.
– ORIGIN C19: back-formation from YIDDISH.

Yiddish /ˈjɪdɪʃ/ ■ n. a language used by Jews in or from central and eastern Europe, originally a German dialect with words from Hebrew and several modern languages. ■ adj. of or relating to this language.
– DERIVATIVES **Yiddisher** n.
– ORIGIN C19: from Yiddish *yidish (daytsh)* 'Jewish (German)'.

yield ■ v. **1** produce or provide (a natural, agricultural, or industrial product). ▶ produce or deliver (a result or gain). ▶ generate (a specified financial return). **2** give way to demands or pressure; submit. ▶ relinquish possession of. ▶ concede (a point of dispute). ▶ give way to other traffic. **3** (of a mass or structure) give way under force or pressure. ■ n. an amount or result yielded.
– DERIVATIVES **yielder** n. **yielding** adj. **yieldingly** adv.
– ORIGIN Old English *g(i)eldan* 'pay, repay', of Germanic origin.

yield point ■ n. Physics the stress beyond which a material becomes plastic.

yield strength ■ n. Physics (in materials without a well-defined yield point) the stress at which a specific amount of plastic deformation is produced.

yikes ■ exclam. informal expressing shock and alarm, for humorous effect.
– ORIGIN 1970s: cf. YOICKS.

yin ■ n. (in Chinese philosophy) the passive female principle of the universe, characterized as female and sustaining and associated with earth, dark, and cold. Contrasted with YANG.
– ORIGIN from Chinese *yīn* 'feminine, moon, shade'.

yip /jɪp/ ■ n. a short, sharp cry or yelp, especially of excitement or delight. ■ v. (**yipped**, **yipping**) give a yip.
– ORIGIN C20 (orig. US): imitative.

yippee ■ exclam. expressing wild excitement or delight.
– ORIGIN natural exclamation: first recorded in American English in the 1920s.

yippie ■ n. (pl. **-ies**) a member of a group of young politically active hippies, originally in the US.
– ORIGIN 1960s: acronym from *Youth International Party* + the suffix *-ie*, suggested by HIPPY[1].

yips ■ pl. n. (**the yips**) informal extreme nervousness causing a golfer to miss easy putts.
– ORIGIN C20.

Yizkor /ˈjɪzkə/ ■ n. (pl. same or **Yizkors**) a memorial service held by Jews on certain holy days for deceased relatives or martyrs.
– ORIGIN from Hebrew *yizkōr* 'may (God) remember'.

Y2K ■ abbrev. year 2000 (with reference to the millennium bug).

-yl ■ suffix Chemistry forming names of radicals: *phenyl*.
– ORIGIN from Greek *hulē* 'wood, material'.

ylang-ylang /ˌiːlaŋˈiːlaŋ/ (also **ilang-ilang**) ■ n. **1** a sweet-scented essential oil obtained from the flowers of a tropical tree, used in perfumery and aromatherapy. **2** the yellow-flowered tree, native to Malaya and the Philippines, from which this oil is obtained. [*Cananga odorata*.]
– ORIGIN C19: from Tagalog *ilang-ilang*.

YMCA ■ abbrev. Young Men's Christian Association.

-yne ■ suffix Chemistry forming names of unsaturated compounds containing a triple bond: *ethyne*.
– ORIGIN alteration of -INE[4].

yo ■ exclam. informal **1** used to greet someone, attract their attention, or express excitement. **2** S. African variant spelling of YOH.
– ORIGIN natural exclamation: first recorded in Middle English.

yob ■ n. Brit. informal a rude and loutish young man.
– DERIVATIVES **yobbery** n. **yobbish** adj. **yobbishly** adv. **yobbishness** n. **yobby** adj.
– ORIGIN C19: back slang for BOY.

yobbo ■ n. (pl. **-os** or **-oes**) Brit. informal a yob.

yodel /ˈjəʊd(ə)l/ ■ v. (**yodelled**, **yodelling**; US **yodeled**, **yodeling**) practise a form of singing or calling marked by rapid alternation between the normal voice and falsetto. ■ n. a song or call delivered in such a way.
– DERIVATIVES **yodeller** n.
– ORIGIN C19: from German *jodeln*.

yoga ■ n. a Hindu spiritual and ascetic discipline, a part of which, including breath control, simple meditation, and the adoption of specific bodily postures, is widely practised for health and relaxation.
– DERIVATIVES **yogic** adj.
– ORIGIN Sanskrit, 'union'.

Yogalates /jəʊɡəˈlɑːtiːz/ (also trademark **Yogilates**) ■ n. a fitness routine that combines Pilates exercises with the postures and breathing techniques of yoga.
– ORIGIN 1990s: blend of YOGA and PILATES.

yogi ■ n. (pl. **yogis**) a person who is proficient in yoga.
– ORIGIN from Sanskrit *yogī*, from *yoga* (see YOGA).

yogic flying ■ n. a technique of Transcendental Meditation involving thrusting oneself off the ground while in the lotus position.

yogurt /ˈjɒɡət, ˈjəʊ-/ (also **yoghurt** or **yoghourt**) ■ n. a semi-solid sourish food prepared from milk fermented by added bacteria.
– ORIGIN C17: from Turkish *yoğurt*.

yoh (also **yho**, **yo**) ■ exclam. S. African informal expressing surprise, disbelief, shock, or admiration.

yo-ho ■ exclam. **1** dated used to attract attention. **2** (also **yo-ho-ho**) Nautical, archaic a seaman's chant used while hauling ropes.

yoicks /jɔɪks/ ■ exclam. used by fox-hunters to urge on the hounds.
– ORIGIN C18.

yoke ■ n. **1** a wooden crosspiece that is fastened over the necks of two animals and attached to a plough or cart that they pull in unison. ▶ (pl. same or **yokes**) a pair of yoked animals. ▶ something that represents a bond between two parties: *the yoke of marriage.* **2** a frame fitting over the neck and shoulders of a person, used for carrying pails or baskets. ▶ something that is regarded as oppressive or burdensome. **3** a part of a garment that fits over the shoulders and to which the main part of the garment is attached. **4** a crosspiece similar to a yoke, such as the crossbar of a rudder. ■ v. put a yoke on; couple or attach with or to a yoke.
– ORIGIN Old English, of Germanic origin.

yokel ■ n. an unsophisticated country person.
– ORIGIN C19: perhaps figuratively from dialect *yokel* 'green woodpecker'.

yolk /jəʊk/ ■ n. the yellow internal part of a bird's egg, which is rich in protein and fat and nourishes the developing embryo.
– DERIVATIVES **yolked** adj. **yolky** adj.
– ORIGIN Old English *geol(o)ca, from geolu* 'yellow'.

yolk sac ■ n. Zoology a membranous sac containing yolk attached to the embryos of reptiles and birds and the larvae of some fishes.

Yom Kippur /jɒm ˈkɪpə, kɪˈpʊə/ ■ n. the most solemn religious fast of the Jewish year, the last of the ten days of

penitence that begin with Rosh Hashana (the Jewish New Year).
– ORIGIN from Hebrew.

yomp Brit. informal ■ v. (of a soldier) march with heavy equipment over difficult terrain. ■ n. a march of such a kind.
– ORIGIN 1980s.

yon poetic/literary or dialect ■ det. & adv. yonder; that. ■ pron. yonder person or thing.
– ORIGIN Old English, of Germanic origin.

yonder archaic or dialect ■ adv. at some distance in the direction indicated; over there. ■ det. that or those (referring to something situated at a distance). ■ n. (**the yonder**) the far distance.
– ORIGIN Middle English: of Germanic origin.

yoni /ˈjəʊni/ ■ n. (pl. **yonis**) Hinduism the female organ, regarded as a symbol of divine procreative energy and conventionally represented by a circular stone.
– ORIGIN Sanskrit, 'source, womb, female genitals'.

yonks ■ pl. n. informal a very long time.
– ORIGIN 1960s: perhaps rel. to *donkey's years* (see DONKEY).

yoo-hoo ■ exclam. a call to attract attention.
– ORIGIN natural exclamation: first recorded in English in the 1920s.

yore ■ n. (in phr. **of yore**) poetic/literary of former times or long ago.
– ORIGIN Old English *geāra*, *geāre*.

york ■ v. Cricket (of a bowler) bowl out (a batsman) with a ball that pitches under the bat.
– ORIGIN C19: back-formation from YORKER.

yorker ■ n. Cricket a ball bowled so that it pitches immediately under the bat.
– ORIGIN prob. from *York*, suggesting its introduction by players of Yorkshire, an English county cricket team.

Yorkist ■ n. a follower of the House of York in the Wars of the Roses. ■ adj. of or relating to the House of York.

Yorkshire pudding ■ n. a baked batter pudding typically eaten with roast beef.

Yorkshire terrier ■ n. a dog of a small long-haired blue-grey and tan breed of terrier.

Yoruba /ˈjɒrʊbə/ ■ n. (pl. same or **Yorubas**) 1 a member of an African people of SW Nigeria and Benin. 2 the Kwa language of this people.
– ORIGIN the name in Yoruba.

you ■ pron. [second person sing. or pl.] 1 used to refer to the person or people that the speaker is addressing. ▸ used to refer to the person being addressed together with other people regarded in the same class. 2 used to refer to any person in general.
– PHRASES **you and yours** you together with your family and close friends.
– ORIGIN Old English *ēow*, accusative and dative of *gē* (see YE¹), of West Germanic origin.

you'd ■ contr. 1 you had. 2 you would.

you'll ■ contr. you will; you shall.

young ■ adj. (**-er**, **-est**) having lived or existed for only a short time; not far advanced in life. ▸ relating to, characteristic of, or consisting of young people. ■ n. [treated as pl.] young children or animals; offspring.
– DERIVATIVES **youngish** adj.
– ORIGIN Old English *g(e)ong*, *of* Germanic origin.

youngberry ■ n. (pl. **-ies**) a bramble of a variety which bears large edible reddish-black fruit, believed to be a hybrid of the dewberry.
– ORIGIN 1920s: named after the American horticulturalist B. M. *Young*.

young gun ■ n. informal an assertive and self-confident young man.

young lion ■ n. (in South Africa) a participant in the Soweto uprising of 1976, a protest by schoolchildren against the Bantu education system. ▸ a young political activist.

youngster ■ n. a child, young person, or young animal.

Young Turk ■ n. 1 a member of a revolutionary party in the Ottoman Empire in the late 19th and early 20th centuries. 2 a young person eager for radical change to the established order.

your /jɔː, jʊə/ ■ possess. det. 1 belonging to or associated with the person or people that the speaker is addressing. 2 belonging to or associated with any person in general. 3 (**Your**) used when addressing the holder of certain titles.
– ORIGIN Old English *ēower*, genitive of *gē* (see YE¹), of Germanic origin.

you're /jɔː, jə, jʊə/ ■ contr. you are.

yours ■ possess. pron. used to refer to something belonging to or associated with the person or people that the speaker is addressing.

yourself ■ pron. [second person sing.] (pl. **yourselves**) 1 used as the object of a verb or preposition when this is the same as the subject of the clause and the subject is the person or people being addressed. 2 [emphatic] you personally.

youse /juːz/ (also **yous**) ■ pron. dialect you (usually more than one person).

youth ■ n. (pl. **youths**) 1 the period between childhood and young adult age. ▸ the qualities of vigour, freshness, immaturity, etc. associated with being young. 2 [treated as sing. or pl.] young people. ▸ a young man.
– ORIGIN Old English *geoguth*, of Germanic origin; rel. to YOUNG.

youth club (also **youth centre**) ■ n. a place or organization providing leisure activities for young people.

Youth Day ■ n. S. African 16 June, a public holiday commemorating the Soweto uprising of 1976.

youthful ■ adj. young or seeming young. ▸ characteristic of young people.
– DERIVATIVES **youthfully** adv. **youthfulness** n.

youth hostel ■ n. a place providing cheap accommodation, aimed mainly at young people on holiday. ■ v. (**youth-hostel**) travel around, sleeping in youth hostels.
– DERIVATIVES **youth-hosteller** n.

you've ■ contr. you have.

yowl /jaʊl/ ■ n. a loud wailing cry of pain or distress. ■ v. make such a cry.
– ORIGIN Middle English: imitative.

yo-yo (trademark in the UK) ■ n. (pl. **-os**) 1 a toy consisting of a pair of joined discs with a deep groove between them in which string is attached and wound, which can be spun alternately downward and upward by its weight and momentum as the string unwinds and rewinds. ▸ a thing that repeatedly falls and rises again. 2 informal, chiefly N. Amer. a stupid, insane, or unpredictable person. ■ v. (**-oes**, **-oed**) move up and down repeatedly; fluctuate.
– ORIGIN 1915: prob. from a language of the Philippines.

yr ■ abbrev. 1 year or years. 2 younger. 3 your.

yrs ■ abbrev. 1 years. 2 yours (as a formula ending a letter).

ytterbium /ɪˈtɜːbɪəm/ ■ n. the chemical element of atomic number 70, a silvery-white metal of the lanthanide series. (Symbol: **Yb**)
– ORIGIN C19: from *Ytterby* in Sweden, where minerals containing several rare-earth elements were found.

yttrium /ˈɪtrɪəm/ ■ n. the chemical element of atomic number 39, a greyish-white metal resembling the rare-earth elements. (Symbol: **Y**)
– ORIGIN C19: from *Ytterby* (see YTTERBIUM).

yuan /juˈɑːn/ ■ n. (pl. same) the basic monetary unit of China.
– ORIGIN Chinese, 'round'; cf. YEN.

yucca /ˈjʌkə/ ■ n. a plant of the agave family with sword-like leaves and spikes of white bell-shaped flowers, native to warm regions of the US and Mexico. [Genus *Yucca*: many species.]
– ORIGIN C17: from Carib *yuca*.

yuck (also **yuk**) ■ exclam. informal used to express strong distaste or disgust.
– DERIVATIVES **yucky** (also **yukky**) adj.
– ORIGIN 1960s (orig. US): imitative.

Yugoslav /ˈjuːɡəˌslɑːv, ˌjuːɡə(ʊ)ˈslɑːv/ ■ n. a native or national of Yugoslavia, or a person of Yugoslav descent.
– DERIVATIVES **Yugoslavian** n. & adj.
– ORIGIN from Austrian German *Jugoslav*, from Serbo-Croat *jug* 'south' + SLAV.

yukata /jʊˈkata/ ■ n. (pl. same or **yukatas**) a light cotton kimono.
– ORIGIN Japanese, from *yu* 'hot water' (because orig. worn after a bath) + *kata(bira)* 'light kimono'.

Yule (also **Yuletide**) ■ n. archaic term for CHRISTMAS.
– ORIGIN Old English *gēol(a)*; *cf.* Old Norse *jól*, orig. applied to a heathen festival lasting twelve days.

yule log ■ n. a large log traditionally burnt in the hearth on Christmas Eve. ▸ a log-shaped chocolate cake eaten at Christmas.

yummy ■ adj. (**-ier**, **-iest**) informal delicious.

yum-yum ■ exclam. informal used to express pleasure at eating delicious food.
– ORIGIN C19: imitative.

yuppie (also **yuppy**) ■ n. (pl. **-ies**) informal, derogatory a well-paid young middle-class professional working in a city.
– DERIVATIVES **yuppiedom** n. **yuppification** n. **yuppify** v.
– ORIGIN 1980s: elaboration of the acronym from *young urban professional*.

yuppie flu ■ n. informal derogatory term for CHRONIC FATIGUE SYNDROME.

yurt /jʊət, jəːt/ ■ n. a circular tent of felt or skins used by nomads in Mongolia, Siberia, and Turkey.
– ORIGIN from Russian *yurta*, from Turkic *jurt*.

YWCA ■ abbrev. Young Women's Christian Association.

Zz

Z¹ /zɛd, US ziː/ (also **z**) ■ n. (pl. **Zs** or **Z's**) **1** the twenty-sixth letter of the alphabet. **2** denoting the next after Y in a set of items, categories, etc. **3** (usu. **z**) the third unknown quantity in an algebraic expression. ▸ denoting the third axis in a three-dimensional system of coordinates. **4** used in repeated form to represent buzzing or snoring.
–PHRASES **catch some Zs** informal, chiefly N. Amer. get some sleep.

Z² ■ abbrev. Zambia (international vehicle registration). ■ symb. Chemistry atomic number.

ZA ■ abbrev. South Africa (international vehicle registration).
–ORIGIN from Afrikaans *Zuid Afrika*.

zabaglione /ˌzabaˈljəʊni/ ■ n. an Italian dessert made of whipped egg yolks, sugar, and Marsala wine.
–ORIGIN from Italian.

Zairean /zʌˈɪərɪən/ (also **Zairian**) ■ n. former term for a native or inhabitant of the Democratic Republic of Congo (previously called Zaire). ■ adj. of or relating to the former Zaire.

zakat /zəˈkɑːt/ ■ n. obligatory payment made annually under Islamic law and used for charitable and religious purposes.
–ORIGIN from Arabic *zakā(t)* 'almsgiving'.

zama zama ■ n. S. African an illegal miner.
–ORIGIN C21: from isiZulu *zama* 'try, make an attempt'.

Zambian /ˈzambɪən/ ■ n. a native or inhabitant of Zambia. ■ adj. of or relating to Zambia.

Zantac /ˈzantak/ ■ n. trademark for **RANITIDINE**.
–ORIGIN C20: prob. from Z- + **ANTACID**.

ZANU (also **ZANU–PF**) ■ abbrev. Zimbabwe African National Union (Patriotic Front).

zany ■ adj. (**-ier**, **-iest**) amusingly unconventional and idiosyncratic. ■ n. **1** a zany person. **2** historical a comic performer partnering a clown, whom he imitated in an amusing way.
–DERIVATIVES **zanily** adv. **zaniness** n.
–ORIGIN C16: from French *zani* or Italian *zan(n)i*, Venetian form of *Gianni, Giovanni* 'John', stock name of the servants acting as clowns in the commedia dell'arte.

zap informal ■ v. (**zapped**, **zapping**) **1** destroy or obliterate. **2** move or propel suddenly and rapidly. ▸ use a remote control to change television channels, operate a video recorder, etc. ■ n. a sudden burst of energy or sound, or other sudden dramatic event.
–DERIVATIVES **zapper** n. **zappy** adj.
–ORIGIN 1920s (orig. US): imitative.

ZAPU /ˈzɑːpuː/ ■ abbrev. Zimbabwe African People's Union.

ZAR ■ abbrev. South African rand(s).

zarzuela /θɑːˈθweɪlə/ ■ n. a traditional Spanish form of musical comedy.
–ORIGIN Spanish, apparently from a place name.

zazen /zɑːˈzɛn/ ■ n. Zen meditation.
–ORIGIN Japanese, from *za* 'sitting' + *zen* (see **ZEN**).

ZCC ■ abbrev. S. African Zion Christian Church.

zeal /ziːl/ ■ n. great energy or enthusiasm for a cause or objective.
–ORIGIN Middle English: from Greek *zēlos*.

zealot /ˈzɛlət/ ■ n. **1** a fanatical and uncompromising follower of a religion or policy. **2** (**Zealot**) a member of an ancient Jewish sect aiming at a world Jewish theocracy and resisting the Romans until AD 70.
–DERIVATIVES **zealotry** n.
–ORIGIN C16: from Greek *zēlōtēs*, from *zēloun* 'be jealous', from *zēlos* (see **ZEAL**).

zealous /ˈzɛləs/ ■ adj. having or showing zeal.
–DERIVATIVES **zealously** adv. **zealousness** n.

zebra /ˈzɛbrə, ˈziːbrə/ ■ n. an African wild horse with black-and-white stripes and an erect mane. [*Equus burchellii* and other species.]
–ORIGIN C17: from Italian, Spanish, or Portuguese, orig. in the sense 'wild ass', perhaps from Latin *equiferus*, from *equus* 'horse' + *ferus* 'wild'.

zebra crossing ■ n. a pedestrian street crossing marked with broad white stripes.

zebra finch ■ n. a small Australian waxbill with a black and white striped face, popular as a cage bird. [*Poephila guttata*.]

zebra fish ■ n. a distinctively-coloured southern African sea bream with a silver-gold body and vertical black stripes. [*Diplodus cervinus*.]

zebu /ˈziːbuː/ ■ n. an ox of a humped breed originally domesticated in India.
–ORIGIN C18: from French *zébu*.

zeera ■ n. variant spelling of **JEERA**.

zein /ˈziːɪn/ ■ n. Biochemistry the principal protein of maize.
–ORIGIN C19: from *Zea* (genus name of maize).

zeitgeist /ˈzʌɪtɡʌɪst/ ■ n. the defining spirit or mood of a particular period of history.
–ORIGIN C19: from German *Zeitgeist*, from *Zeit* 'time' + *Geist* 'spirit'.

Zen ■ n. a Japanese school of Mahayana Buddhism emphasizing the value of meditation and intuition.
–ORIGIN Japanese, 'meditation', from Chinese *chán* 'quietude', from Sanskrit *dhyāna* 'meditation'.

zenana /zɪˈnɑːnə/ ■ n. (in India and Iran) the part of a house for the seclusion of women.
–ORIGIN from Persian and Urdu *zanānah*, from *zan* 'woman'.

Zend-Avesta ■ n. the Zoroastrian sacred writings, comprising the Avesta (the text) and the Zend (the commentary).
–ORIGIN *Zend* from Persian *zand* 'interpretation'.

Zener diode /ˈziːnə/ ■ n. Electronics a semiconductor diode in which at a critical reverse voltage a large reverse current can flow.
–ORIGIN 1950s: named after the American physicist Clarence M. *Zener*.

zenith /ˈzɛnɪθ/ ■ n. **1** the point in the sky directly overhead. The opposite of **NADIR**. **2** the highest point in the sky reached by a given celestial object. **3** the time at which something is most powerful or successful.
–DERIVATIVES **zenithal** adj.
–ORIGIN Middle English: from Old French or medieval Latin *cenit*, from Arabic *samt (ar-ra's)* 'path (over the head)'.

zeolite /ˈziːəlʌɪt/ ■ n. any of a large group of minerals consisting of hydrated aluminosilicates, used as cation exchangers and molecular sieves.
–DERIVATIVES **zeolitic** /-ˈlɪtɪk/ adj.
–ORIGIN C18: from Swedish and German *zeolit*, from Greek *zein* 'to boil' + **-LITE** (from their characteristic swelling when heated).

zephyr /ˈzɛfə/ ■ n. poetic/literary a soft gentle breeze.
–ORIGIN Old English *zefferus*, denoting a personification of the west wind, from Greek *zephuros*.

Zeppelin /ˈzɛp(ə)lɪn/ ■ n. historical a large German dirigible airship of the early 20th century.
–ORIGIN named after Ferdinand, Count von *Zeppelin*, German airship pioneer.

zero /ˈzɪərəʊ/ ■ cardinal number (pl. **-os**) the figure 0; nought; nothing. ▸ a temperature of 0°C (32°F), marking the freezing point of water. ▸ informal a worthless or insignificant person. ■ v. (**-oes**, **-oed**) **1** adjust (an

...ment) to zero. **2** set the sights of (a gun) for firing. ► (**zero in on**) take aim at or focus attention on.
– ORIGIN C17: from French *zéro* or Italian *zero*, from Arabic *ṣifr* 'cipher'.

zero-based ■ adj. Finance (of budgeting) in which items are costed anew rather than related to previous figures.

zero-coupon bond ■ n. a bond issued at a deep discount but paying no interest.

zero hour ■ n. the time at which a military or other operation is set to begin.

zero-sum ■ adj. denoting a game or situation in which whatever is gained by one side is lost by the other.

zero tolerance ■ n. strict enforcement of the law regarding any form of anti-social behaviour.

zest ■ n. **1** great enthusiasm and energy. ► excitement or piquancy. **2** the outer coloured part of the peel of citrus fruit, used as flavouring.
– DERIVATIVES **zestful** adj. **zestfully** adv. **zestfulness** n. **zesty** adj.
– ORIGIN C15: from French *zeste* 'orange or lemon peel'.

zester ■ n. a kitchen utensil for scraping or peeling zest from citrus fruit.

zeta /'ziːtə/ ■ n. the sixth letter of the Greek alphabet (Z, ζ), transliterated as 'z'.
– ORIGIN from Greek.

zhoozh /ʒʊʒ, ʒuːʒ/ (also **zhoosh**, **zhuzh**) informal ■ v. (**zhoozh someone/thing up**) make more stylish or attractive. ■ adj. stylish; fashionable; chic.
– ORIGIN 1970s: Polari, prob. imitative.

zidovudine /zɪ'dɒvjʊdiːn, -'dəʊ-/ ■ n. Medicine an antiviral drug used to slow the growth of HIV infection in the body.
– ORIGIN 1980s: alteration of **AZIDOTHYMIDINE**.

ZIF socket ■ n. a socket for electronic devices that is designed not to damage them during insertion.
– ORIGIN C20: acronym from *zero insertion force*.

ziggurat /'zɪɡʊrat/ ■ n. (in ancient Mesopotamia) a rectangular stepped tower.
– ORIGIN from Akkadian *ziqqurratu*.

zigzag ■ n. a line or course having abrupt alternate right and left turns. ► a turn on such a course. ■ adj. & adv. veering to right and left alternately. ■ v. (**zigzagged, zigzagging**) take a zigzag course.
– ORIGIN C18: from French, from German *Zickzack*, first applied to fortifications.

zilch /zɪltʃ/ informal, chiefly N. Amer. ■ pron. nothing. ■ det. not any; no.
– ORIGIN 1960s: perhaps from a Mr *Zilch*, a character in the 1930s magazine *Ballyhoo*.

zillion ■ cardinal number informal an extremely large number of people or things.
– DERIVATIVES **zillionaire** n. **zillionth** ordinal number.
– ORIGIN 1940s: from Z (perhaps as a symbol of an unknown quantity) + **MILLION**.

Zimbabwean /zɪm'bɑːbwɪən, -weɪən/ ■ n. a native or inhabitant of Zimbabwe. ■ adj. of or relating to Zimbabwe.

Zimbo informal ■ n. (pl. **-os**) a Zimbabwean. ■ adj. Zimbabwean.

Zimmer /'zɪmə/ (also **Zimmer frame**) ■ n. trademark a kind of walking frame.
– ORIGIN 1950s: from *Zimmer* Orthopaedic Limited, the name of the manufacturer.

zinc ■ n. the chemical element of atomic number 30, a silvery-white metal which is a constituent of brass and is used for galvanizing iron and steel. (Symbol: **Zn**) ► ■ v. /zɪŋ(k)t/ (**zinced**) coat with zinc.
– ORIGIN C17: from German *Zink*.

zinc blende ■ n. another term for **SPHALERITE**.

zinc ointment ■ n. ointment containing zinc oxide, used for various skin conditions.

zinc white ■ n. a white pigment consisting of zinc oxide.

'zine ■ n. informal a magazine, especially a fanzine.

Zinfandel /'zɪnfəndɛl/ ■ n. a variety of wine grape grown chiefly in California. ► a red or blush wine made from this grape.
– ORIGIN C19.

zing informal ■ n. energy, enthusiasm, or liveliness. ■ v. move swiftly.
– DERIVATIVES **zingy** adj.
– ORIGIN C20: imitative.

zinnia /'zɪnɪə/ ■ n. an American plant of the daisy family, cultivated for its bright showy flowers. [Genus *Zinnia*.]
– ORIGIN named after the C18 German physician and botanist Johann G. *Zinn*.

Zion /'zʌɪən/ (also **Sion**) ■ n. **1** the hill of Jerusalem on which the city of David was built. ► the Jewish people or religion. **2** (in Christian thought) the heavenly city or kingdom of heaven. **3** a land to which people in exile hope to return, especially (among Jews) Israel or (among Rastafarians) Africa.
– ORIGIN Old English, from eccles. Latin *Sion*, from Hebrew *ṣīyōn*.

Zion Christian Church ■ n. the largest indigenous church in South Africa, which combines a form of Pentecostalism with traditional African customs.

Zionism¹ /'zʌɪənɪz(ə)m/ ■ n. a movement for the development and protection of a Jewish nation in Israel.
– DERIVATIVES **Zionist** n. & adj.

Zionism² ■ n. S. African the beliefs and practices of the Zion Christian Church.
– DERIVATIVES **Zionist** n. & adj.

zip ■ n. **1** a fastener consisting of two flexible strips of metal or plastic with interlocking projections closed or opened by pulling a slide along them. **2** informal energy; vigour. ■ pron. N. Amer. informal nothing at all. ■ v. (**zipped, zipping**) **1** fasten with a zip. **2** informal move or propel at high speed. **3** Computing compress (a file) so that it takes up less space.
– ORIGIN C19: imitative.

zip code (also **ZIP code**) ■ n. US a postal code consisting of five or nine digits.
– ORIGIN 1960s: acronym from *zone improvement plan*.

zipless ■ adj. informal (of a sexual encounter) brief, uncomplicated, and passionate.
– ORIGIN 1970s: coined by the US author Erica Jong.

ziplock (also trademark **Ziploc**) ■ adj. denoting a plastic bag with strips along the opening that can be pressed together to reseal it.

zipper chiefly N. Amer. ■ n. a zip fastener. ■ v. fasten with a zipper.

zippy ■ adj. (**-ier, -iest**) informal bright, fresh, or lively. ► speedy.
– DERIVATIVES **zippily** adv. **zippiness** n.

zip-up ■ adj. fastened with a zip.

zircon /'zəːkɒn/ ■ n. a mineral consisting of zirconium silicate, typically brown but sometimes in translucent forms of gem quality.
– ORIGIN C18: from German *Zirkon*.

zirconia /zəː'kəʊnɪə/ ■ n. zirconium dioxide, a white solid used in ceramic glazes and refractory coatings. [ZrO_2.]
– ORIGIN C18: from **ZIRCON**.

zirconium /zəː'kəʊnɪəm/ ■ n. the chemical element of atomic number 40, a hard silver-grey metal. (Symbol: **Zr**)
– ORIGIN from **ZIRCON**.

zit ■ n. informal, chiefly N. Amer. a spot on the skin.
– ORIGIN 1960s.

zither /'zɪðə/ ■ n. a musical instrument consisting of a flat wooden soundbox with numerous strings stretched across it, placed horizontally and played with the fingers and a plectrum.
– DERIVATIVES **zitherist** n.
– ORIGIN C19: from German, from Latin *cithara* (see **CITTERN**).

zloty /'zlɒti/ ■ n. (pl. same, **zlotys** or **zloties**) the basic monetary unit of Poland.
– ORIGIN Polish, 'golden'.

Zn ■ symb. the chemical element zinc.

zodiac /'zəʊdɪak/ ■ n. a belt of the heavens within about 8° of the ecliptic, including all apparent positions of the sun, moon, and planets and divided by astrologers into twelve equal divisions or signs.

– DERIVATIVES **zodiacal** /zə(ʊ)'dʌɪək(ə)l/ adj.
– ORIGIN Middle English: from Old French *zodiaque*, from Greek *zōidiakos*, from *zōidion* 'sculptured animal figure', diminutive of *zōion* 'animal'.

zodiacal light ■ n. Astronomy a faint elongated cone of light sometimes seen in the night sky, extending from the horizon along the ecliptic.

zoetrope /'zəʊɪtrəʊp/ ■ n. a cylinder with a series of pictures on the inner surface that, when viewed through slits with the cylinder rotating, give an impression of continuous motion.
– ORIGIN C19: from Greek *zōē* 'life' + *-tropos* 'turning'.

Zohar /'zəʊhɑː/ ■ n. the chief text of the Jewish Kabbalah, presented as an allegorical or mystical interpretation of the Pentateuch.
– ORIGIN from Hebrew *zōhar* 'light, splendour'.

zol ■ n. informal a cannabis cigarette. ▸ S. African cannabis.
– ORIGIN 1940s.

zombie ■ n. 1 a corpse supposedly revived by witchcraft, especially in certain African and Caribbean religions. 2 informal a lifeless, apathetic, or completely unresponsive person. 3 a computer controlled by a hacker without the owner's knowledge, which is made to send large quantities of data to a website, making it inaccessible to other users.
– DERIVATIVES **zombification** n. **zombify** v. [-ies, -ied]
– ORIGIN C19: of West African origin; cf. Kikongo *zumbi* 'fetish'.

zona pellucida /ˌzəʊnə pɪˈluːsɪdə/ ■ n. (pl. **zonae pellucidae** /ˌzəʊniː pɪˈluːsɪdiː/) Anatomy & Zoology the thick transparent membrane surrounding a mammalian ovum before implantation.
– ORIGIN C19: from Latin, 'pellucid girdle'.

zonation /zəʊˈneɪʃ(ə)n/ ■ n. distribution in or division into distinct zones.

zone ■ n. 1 an area distinguished on the basis of a particular characteristic, use, restriction, etc. ▸ (also **time zone**) a range of longitudes where a common standard time is used. 2 chiefly Botany & Zoology an encircling band or stripe of distinctive colour, texture, etc. ■ v. divide into or assign to zones.
– DERIVATIVES **zonal** adj. **zonally** adv.
– ORIGIN Middle English: from French, or from Latin *zona* 'girdle', from Greek *zōnē*.

zoned ■ adj. divided into zones.

zone plate ■ n. a glass plate marked out into concentric rings alternately transparent and opaque, used like a lens to focus light.

zone refining ■ n. a method of purifying a crystalline solid by causing a narrow molten zone to travel slowly along a rod to one end, at which impurities become concentrated.

zone therapy ■ n. a system of alternative medicine in which different parts of the feet or hands are associated with different parts of the body.

zonk ■ v. informal 1 hit or strike heavily. 2 (usu. **zonk out**) fall suddenly and heavily asleep.
– ORIGIN 1940s: imitative.

zonked ■ adj. informal under the influence of drugs or alcohol.

zoo ■ n. an establishment which keeps wild animals for study, conservation, or display to the public.
– ORIGIN C19: abbrev. of **ZOOLOGICAL GARDEN**, orig. applied specifically to that of Regent's Park, London.

zoo- ■ comb. form of animals; relating to animal life: *zoogeography*.
– ORIGIN from Greek *zōion* 'animal'.

zoogeography /ˌzuːə(ʊ)dʒɪˈɒɡrəfi, ˌzəʊ(ʊ)-, ˌzuːˈdʒɪ-/ ■ n. the branch of zoology concerned with the geographical distribution of animals.
– DERIVATIVES **zoogeographer** n. **zoogeographic** adj. **zoogeographical** adj. **zoogeographically** adv.

zooid /'zuːɔɪd, 'zəʊ-, 'zuːɪd/ ■ n. Zoology an animal arising from another by budding or division, especially each of the individuals which make up a colonial organism.
– DERIVATIVES **zooidal** /zuːˈɔɪd(ə)l, zəʊ-, 'zuːɪd(ə)l/ adj.
– ORIGIN C19: from **ZOO-** + **-OID**.

zookeeper ■ n. an animal attendant employed in a zoo.

zoological garden ■ n. dated a zoo.

zoology /zuːˈɒlədʒi, zəʊ-/ ■ n. the scientific study of the behaviour, structure, physiology, classification, and distribution of animals. ▸ the animal life of a particular region or geological period.
– DERIVATIVES **zoological** adj. **zoologically** adv. **zoologist** n.

zoom ■ v. 1 (especially of a car or aircraft) move or travel very quickly. 2 (of a camera) change smoothly from a long shot to a close-up or vice versa. ■ n. the action of a camera zooming. ▸ short for **ZOOM LENS**.
– ORIGIN C19: imitative.

zoom lens ■ n. a lens allowing a camera to zoom by varying the focal length.

zoomorphic /ˌzuːə(ʊ)ˈmɔːfɪk, ˌzəʊə(ʊ)-, zuːˈmɔːfɪk/ ■ adj. having or representing animal forms or gods of animal form.
– DERIVATIVES **zoomorphism** n.
– ORIGIN C19: from **ZOO-** + Greek *morphē* 'form'.

zoonosis /ˌzuːəˈnəʊsɪs, ˌzəʊə-/ ■ n. (pl. **zoonoses** /-siːz/) Medicine any disease which can be transmitted to humans from animals.
– DERIVATIVES **zoonotic** adj.
– ORIGIN C19: from **ZOO-** + Greek *nosos* 'disease'.

zoophyte /'zuːəfʌɪt, 'zəʊə-, 'zuːfʌɪt/ ■ n. Zoology, dated a plant-like animal, especially a coral, sea anemone, sponge, or sea lily.

zooplankton /ˌzuːə(ʊ)ˈplaŋ(k)t(ə)n, ˌzəʊə(ʊ)-, 'zuːplaŋ(k)t(ə)n/ ■ n. Biology plankton consisting of small animals.

zoospore /'zuːəspɔː, 'zəʊə-, 'zuːspɔː/ ■ n. Biology a spore of certain algae, fungi, etc., capable of swimming by means of a flagellum.

zoot suit ■ n. a man's suit characterized by a long loose jacket with padded shoulders and high-waisted tapering trousers, popular in the 1940s.
– ORIGIN 1940s: rhyming formation on **SUIT**.

zorbing /'zɔːbɪŋ/ ■ n. a sport in which a participant is secured inside an inner capsule in a large, transparent ball which is then rolled along the ground or down hills.
– ORIGIN 1990s: invented word from *zorb* (the name of the ball used in this activity).

zori /'zɔːri, 'zɒri/ ■ n. (pl. **zoris**) a traditional Japanese flip-flop, originally with a straw sole.
– ORIGIN from Japanese.

zorilla /zɒˈrɪlə/ ■ n. a skunk-like black and white carnivorous mammal inhabiting arid regions of southern Africa. [*Ictonyx striatus*.]
– ORIGIN C18: from Spanish *zorrilla*, diminutive of *zorro* 'fox'.

Zoroastrianism /ˌzɒrəʊˈastrɪəˌnɪz(ə)m/ ■ n. a monotheistic pre-Islamic religion of ancient Persia founded by the prophet Zoroaster (Zarathustra) in the 6th century BC.
– DERIVATIVES **Zoroastrian** adj. & n.

Zouave /zuːˈɑːv, zwɑːv/ ■ n. 1 a member of a French light-infantry corps, originally formed of Algerians and long retaining an oriental uniform. 2 (**zouaves**) women's trousers with wide tops, tapering to a narrow ankle.
– ORIGIN C19: from French, from Kabyle (a Berber dialect) *Zouaoua*, the name of a tribe.

zouk /zuːk/ ■ n. an exuberant style of popular music combining Caribbean and Western elements.
– ORIGIN 1970s: Guadeloupian Creole, 'to party'.

zounds /zaʊndz/ ■ exclam. archaic or humorous expressing surprise or indignation.
– ORIGIN C16: contraction from (*God*)*'s wounds*.

Zozo hut (also **zozo**) ■ n. S. African a prefabricated building used for accommodation, classrooms, storage, etc.
– ORIGIN *Zozo*: 1970s, from the name of the company supplying such buildings, which was named after a monkey in children's stories by H. A. Rey.

Zr ■ symb. the chemical element zirconium.

zucchetto /tsʊˈkɛtəʊ/ ■ n. (pl. **-os**) a Roman Catholic cleric's skullcap: black for a priest, purple for a bishop, red for a cardinal, and white for the Pope.
– ORIGIN C19: from Italian *zucchetta*, diminutive of *zucca* 'gourd, head'.

...ini /zʊˈkiːni/ ■ n. (pl. same or **zucchinis**) a baby [marrow.]
— [ORIGIN] Italian, pl. of *zucchino*, diminutive of *zucca* 'gourd'.

zugzwang /ˈzʌɡzwaŋ, ˈzuːg-/ ■ n. Chess a situation in which the obligation to make a move is a serious disadvantage.
— ORIGIN C20: from German *Zug* 'move' + *Zwang* 'compulsion'.

Zulu /ˈzuːluː/ ■ n. **1** a member of a South African people living mainly in KwaZulu-Natal. **2** another term for ISIZULU. **3** a code word representing the letter Z, used in radio communication.
— ORIGIN from isiZulu *umZulu*.

Zulu love letter ■ n. S. African a beaded square or rectangle with symbolic designs, traditionally worn by Zulu women as a brooch or necklace during courtship or marriage.

Zuma year ■ n. S. African informal a year of mandatory community service that recent medical graduates must complete before registering to practise.
— ORIGIN named after the former South African Health Minister, Nkosazana Dlamini *Zuma* who introduced the scheme in 1997.

Zuni /ˈzuːni/ (also **Zuñi**) ■ n. (pl. same or **Zunis**) **1** a member of a Pueblo Indian people of western New Mexico. **2** the language of this people.

ZW ■ abbrev. Zimbabwe (international vehicle registration).

zwitterion /ˈzwɪtərʌɪən, ˈtsvɪ-/ ■ n. Chemistry an ion having separate positively and negatively charged groups.
— DERIVATIVES **zwitterionic** adj.
— ORIGIN C20: from German, from *Zwitter* 'a hybrid' + *Ion* 'ion'.

zydeco /ˈzʌɪdɪkəʊ/ ■ n. a kind of black American dance music originally from southern Louisiana, typically featuring accordion and guitar.
— ORIGIN 1960s: Louisiana Creole, possibly from French *les haricots* in a dance-tune title.

zygo- ■ comb. form relating to joining or pairing: *zygodactyl*.
— ORIGIN from Greek *zugon* 'yoke'.

zygodactyl /ˌzʌɪɡə(ʊ)ˈdaktɪl, zɪɡ-/ ■ adj. Ornithology having two toes pointing forward and two backward.
— DERIVATIVES **zygodactyly** n.

zygoma /zʌɪˈɡəʊmə, zɪɡ-/ ■ n. (pl. **zygomata** /-tə/) Anatomy the bony arch of the cheek formed by connection of the zygomatic and temporal bones.
— DERIVATIVES **zygomatic** adj.
— ORIGIN C17: from Greek *zugōma*, from *zugon* 'yoke'.

zygomatic bone ■ n. Anatomy the bone forming the prominent part of the cheek and the outer side of the eye socket.

zygomorphic /ˌzʌɪɡə(ʊ)ˈmɔːfɪk, ˌzɪɡ-/ ■ adj. Botany (of a flower) bilaterally symmetrical, as in a snapdragon. Compare with ACTINOMORPHIC.
— DERIVATIVES **zygomorphy** n.

Zygoptera /zʌɪˈɡɒptərə/ ■ pl. n. Entomology a suborder of insects which comprises the damselflies.
— DERIVATIVES **zygopteran** n. & adj.
— ORIGIN from Greek *zugon* 'yoke' + *pteron* 'wing'.

zygote /ˈzʌɪɡəʊt/ ■ n. Biology a cell resulting from the fusion of two gametes.
— DERIVATIVES **zygotic** /-ˈɡɒtɪk/ adj.
— ORIGIN C19: from Greek *zugōtos* 'yoked', from *zugoun* 'to yoke'.

zymase /ˈzʌɪmeɪz/ ■ n. Biochemistry a mixture of enzymes obtained from yeast which promote alcoholic fermentation.
— ORIGIN C19: from French, from Greek *zumē* 'leaven'.

zymogen /ˈzʌɪmə(ʊ)dʒ(ə)n/ ■ n. Biochemistry an inactive substance which is converted into an enzyme when activated by another enzyme.

zymurgy /ˈzʌɪmɜːdʒi/ ■ n. the study or practice of fermentation in brewing, winemaking, or distilling.
— ORIGIN C19: from Greek *zumē* 'leaven', on the pattern of *metallurgy*.